California

CIVIL PRACTICE
STATUTES AND RULES
Annotated

2014

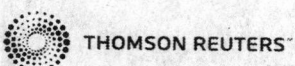
THOMSON REUTERS

Mat# 41250826

ISBN: 978–0–314–66844–8

SCOPE AND CONTENTS

Legislation

Includes all laws through c. 800 of the 2013 portion of the 2013–2014 Regular Session, the end of the 2013–2014 First Extraordinary Session, and Res. c. 123 (S.C.A.3), subject to approval at the June 3, 2014 election.

Court Rules

This pamphlet contains court rules pertaining to civil matters only. For all court rules, please see West's California Rules of Court State Pamphlet. For criminal statutes and rules, see West's California Penal Code Desktop Pamphlet and West's California Penal and Evidence Codes Desktop Volume.

The court rules incorporated in this pamphlet reflect all amendments available through October 25, 2013.

Annotative Material

This pamphlet contains cross references to other sections of the code; references to Witkin, Rutter, and Miller & Starr publications, and Judicial Council Forms; Law Revision Commission Comments; and a California Jury Instructions Table.

Presentation of Changes

Additions or changes in statutes affected by 2013 legislation are indicated by underlining; deletions are indicated by asterisks. In court rules, additions or changes are indicated by underlining; deletions are indicated by strikethroughs.

Repealed and Reserved Provisions

Repealed and reserved statutes and court rules are omitted.

Effective Dates of Legislation

All California legislative enactments in 2013 are effective January 1, 2014, unless indicated otherwise.

Veto Messages

Codified legislation which is subject to a governor's veto is followed by an italicized note indicating that fact. For the text of the message, please consult the Historical and Statutory Notes for the provision in *West's Annotated California Codes* or the material pertaining to the legislation affecting the provision in *West's California Legislative Service*.

ADDITIONAL INFORMATION OR RESEARCH ASSISTANCE

For additional information or research assistance call the West reference attorneys at 1-800-REF-ATTY (1-800-733-2889). Contact West's editorial department directly with your questions and suggestions by e-mail at west.editor@thomson.com.

*

ABBREVIATIONS

Admin Proc	Administrative Proceedings (Witkin California Procedure)
Agency	Agency and Employment (Witkin Summary of California Law)
Attack	Attack on Judgment in Trial Court (Witkin California Procedure)
Attys	Attorneys (Witkin California Procedure)
Com Prop	Commercial Property (Witkin Summary of California Law)
Const Law	Constitutional Law (Witkin Summary of California Law)
Corp	Corporations (Witkin Summary of California Law)
Enf Judgm	Enforcement of Judgment (Witkin California Procedure)
H & W	Husband and Wife (Witkin Summary of California Law)
Judgm	Judgment (Witkin California Procedure)
Jurisd	Jurisdiction (Witkin California Procedure)
Neg Inst	Negotiable Instruments (Witkin Summary of California Law)
Partn	Partnership (Witkin Summary of California Law)
P & C	Parent and Child (Witkin Summary of California Law)
Pers Prop	Personal Property (Witkin Summary of California Law)
Plead	Pleading (Witkin California Procedure)
Prov Rem	Provisional Remedies (Witkin California Procedure)
PWT	Proceedings Without Trial (Witkin California Procedure)
Real Prop	Real Property (Witkin Summary of California Law)
Sec Trans–PP	Secured Transactions in Personal Property (Witkin Summary of California Law)
Sec Trans–Real P	Secured Transactions in Real Property (Witkin Summary of California Law)
Tax	Taxation (Witkin Summary of California Law)
Wills	Wills and Probate (Witkin Summary of California Law)
Witkin, Procedure (4th ed)	Witkin California Procedure (4th ed)
Witkin, Summary (10th ed)	Witkin Summary of California Law (10th ed)
Work Comp	Workers' Compensation (Witkin Summary of California Law)
Writs	Extraordinary Writs (Witkin California Procedure)

THOMSON REUTERS PROVIEW™

This title is one of many now available on your tablet as an eBook.

Take your research mobile. Powered by the Thomson Reuters ProView™ app, our eBooks deliver the same trusted content as your print resources, but in a compact, on-the-go format.

ProView eBooks are designed for the way you work. You can add your own notes and highlights to the text, and all of your annotations will transfer electronically to every new edition of your eBook.

You can also instantly verify primary authority with built-in links to WestlawNext® and KeyCite®, so you can be confident that you're accessing the most current and accurate information.

To find out more about ProView eBooks and available discounts, call 1-800-344-5009.

TABLE OF SECTIONS AFFECTED

This table indicates sections affected by 2013 legislation

Civil Practice Statutes and Rules

TABLE OF SECTIONS AFFECTED

TABLE OF SECTIONS AFFECTED

CIVIL CODE

Sec.	Effect	Chap.	Sec.
6716	Added	605	21
6718	Added	605	21
6720	Added	605	21
6722	Added	605	21
prec. § 6750 Div. 4 Pt. 5.3 ch. 6	Added	605	21
prec. § 6750 Div. 4 Pt. 5.3 ch. 6 art. 1	Added	605	21
6750	Added	605	21
6752	Added	605	21
prec. § 6756 Div. 4 Pt. 5.3 ch. 6 art. 2	Added	605	21
6756	Added	605	21
prec. § 6758 Div. 4 Pt. 5.3 ch. 6 art. 3	Added	605	21
6758	Added	605	21
prec. § 6760 Div. 4 Pt. 5.3 ch. 6 art. 4	Added	605	21
6760	Added	605	21
prec. § 6800 Div. 4 Pt. 5.3 ch. 7	Added	605	21
prec. § 6800 Div. 4 Pt. 5.3 ch. 7 art. 1	Added	605	21
6800	Added	605	21
6804	Added	605	21
prec. § 6808 Div. 4 Pt. 5.3 ch. 7 art. 2	Added	605	21
6808	Added	605	21
6810	Added	605	21
6812	Added	605	21
6814	Added	605	21
6816	Added	605	21
6818	Added	605	21
6819	Added	605	21
prec. § 6820 Div. 4 Pt. 5.3 ch. 7 art. 3	Added	605	21
6820	Added	605	21
6822	Added	605	21
6824	Added	605	21
6826	Added	605	21
6828	Added	605	21
prec. § 6840 Div. 4 Pt. 5.3 ch. 8	Added	605	21
6840	Added	605	21
prec. § 6850 Div. 4 Pt. 5.3 ch. 9	Added	605	21
prec. § 6850 Div. 4 Pt. 5.3 ch. 9 art. 1	Added	605	21
6850	Added	605	21
6854	Added	605	21
prec. § 6856 Div. 4 Pt. 5.3 ch. 9 art. 2	Added	605	21
6856	Added	605	21
6858	Added	605	21
6860	Added	605	21

CIVIL CODE

Sec.	Effect	Chap.	Sec.
prec. § 6870 Div. 4 Pt. 5.3 ch. 10	Added	605	21
6870	Added	605	21
6874	Added	605	21
6876	Added	605	21

CODE OF CIVIL PROCEDURE

Sec.	Effect	Chap.	Sec.
86	Amended	605	22
116.232	Amended	31	1
116.540	Amended	605	23
116.940	Amended	76	21
129	Amended	53	1
425.50	Amended	76	22
481.207	Amended	531	2
481.220	Amended	531	3
527.6	Amended	158	1
	Added	158	2
580b	Amended	65	2
580d	Amended	65	3
581.5	Added	64	3
583.161	Amended	40	1
680.340	Amended	531	4
680.350	Amended	531	5
681.035	Added	15	1
683.140	Amended	176	1
684.115	Amended	76	23
687.010	Amended	156	1
697.530	Amended	531	6
699.510	Amended	176	2
700.010	Amended	64	4
703.120	Repealed	15	2
706.103	Amended	64	5
706.104	Amended	64	6
706.108	Amended	64	7
706.122	Amended	64	8
1161.3	Amended	130	3
1218	Amended	352	56
1277	Amended	651	1
	Added	651	2
1278	Amended	651	3
	Added	651	4
1282.4	Amended	76	24
1513.5	Amended	362	1
1530	Amended	362	2
1540	Amended	128	1
1856	Amended	81	1
1986.1	Amended	519	1
2030.300	Amended	18	1
2031.310	Amended	18	2
2033.290	Amended	18	3

EVIDENCE CODE

Sec.	Effect	Chap.	Sec.
452.5	Amended	150	1
912	Amended	123	1
prec. § 965 Div. 8 ch. 4 art. 3.5	Added	123	2
965	Added	123	2
966	Added	123	2
967	Added	123	2

TABLE OF SECTIONS AFFECTED

TABLE OF CONTENTS

CIVIL CODE

TABLE OF CONTENTS—CIVIL CODE

TABLE OF CONTENTS—CIVIL CODE

DIVISION 3. OBLIGATIONS

TABLE OF CONTENTS—CIVIL CODE

TABLE OF CONTENTS—CIVIL CODE

TABLE OF CONTENTS—CIVIL CODE

CODE OF CIVIL PROCEDURE

TABLE OF CONTENTS—CODE OF CIVIL PROCEDURE

PART 1. OF COURTS OF JUSTICE

TABLE OF CONTENTS—CODE OF CIVIL PROCEDURE

TABLE OF CONTENTS—CODE OF CIVIL PROCEDURE

TABLE OF CONTENTS—CODE OF CIVIL PROCEDURE

TABLE OF CONTENTS—CODE OF CIVIL PROCEDURE

TABLE OF CONTENTS—CODE OF CIVIL PROCEDURE

PART 4. MISCELLANEOUS PROVISIONS

EVIDENCE CODE

BUSINESS AND PROFESSIONS CODE

GOVERNMENT CODE

TITLE 1. GENERAL

TABLE OF CONTENTS—GOVERNMENT CODE

TITLE 2. GOVERNMENT OF THE STATE OF CALIFORNIA

TITLE 3. GOVERNMENT OF COUNTIES

TITLE 8. THE ORGANIZATION AND GOVERNMENT OF COURTS

RULES OF THE STATE BAR OF CALIFORNIA

CALIFORNIA RULES OF PROFESSIONAL CONDUCT

RULES OF COURT

TITLE 1. RULES APPLICABLE TO ALL COURTS

TITLE 2. TRIAL COURT RULES

TABLE OF CONTENTS—COURT RULES

TITLE 4. CRIMINAL RULES

TABLE OF CONTENTS—COURT RULES

TITLE 7. PROBATE RULES

TITLE 8. APPELLATE RULES

TABLE OF CONTENTS—COURT RULES

TITLE 9. RULES ON LAW PRACTICE, ATTORNEYS, AND JUDGES

TITLE 10. JUDICIAL ADMINISTRATION RULES

STANDARDS OF JUDICIAL ADMINISTRATION

ETHICS STANDARDS FOR NEUTRAL ARBITRATORS IN CONTRACTUAL ARBITRATION

(Page 3029)

APPENDIX TO CALIFORNIA RULES OF COURT

CALIFORNIA COURTS OF APPEAL

CALIFORNIA JURY INSTRUCTIONS
(Page 3073)

FEDERAL RULES/EVIDENCE CODE CONVERSION TABLE
(Page 3079)

INDEX
(Page I–1)

CIVIL CODE

TITLE OF THE ACT

Section

§ 1. Title and Divisions of Code

TITLE AND DIVISIONS OF THIS ACT. This Act shall be known as The Civil Code of the State of California, and is in Four Divisions, as follows:

I.—The First Relating to Persons.

II.—The Second to Property.

III.—The Third to Obligations.

IV.—The Fourth Contains General Provisions Relating to the Three Preceding Divisions. *(Enacted in 1872.)*

Research References

Rutter, Cal. Practice Guide: Personal Injury Ch. 3-F, F. MICRA Provisions Affecting Damages.

15 NO. 4 Miller & Starr, California Real Estate Newsalert 7, Deeds.

16 NO. 4 Miller & Starr, California Real Estate Newsalert 1, Premises and Landowner Liability: the Supreme Court Continues Its Expansion of Potential Liability for Personal Injuries.

16 NO. 4 Miller & Starr, California Real Estate Newsalert 19, Subdivisions.

19 NO. 1 Miller & Starr, California Real Estate Newsalert 1, The Perata Foreclosure Bill (SB 1137): New Rights for Defaulting Borrowers and Tenants; New Complications for Foreclosing Lenders.

4 Witkin Cal. Proc. 5th Pleading § 543, (S 543) Other Actions Distinguished.

6 Witkin Cal. Proc. 5th Proceedings Without Trial § 273, Compensatory Damage Claim Not Dispositive of Cause of Action.

12 Witkin, California Summary 10th Real Property § 526, (S 526) Changes in Short-Term Leases.

1 Witkin Cal. Summ. 10th Contracts § 321, (S 321) No Confidential Relationship.

13 Witkin, California Summary 10th Personal Property § 124, (S 124) in General.

11 Witkin, California Summary 10th Community Property § 52, in General.

11 Witkin, California Summary 10th Husband and Wife § 48, (S 48) Confidential Marriage.

6 Witkin, California Summary 10th Torts § 1031, Financial Injury.

6 Witkin, California Summary 10th Torts § 1103, (S 1103) in General.

13 Witkin, California Summary 10th Equity § 52, (S 52) Option to Pay is Insufficient.

PRELIMINARY PROVISIONS

Section

§ 2. Effective date of Code

WHEN THIS CODE TAKES EFFECT. This Code takes effect at twelve o'clock noon, on the first day of January, eighteen hundred and seventy-three. *(Enacted in 1872.)*

Research References

Rutter, Cal. Practice Guide: Real Prop. Transactions Ch. 2-C, C. Broker's Relationship and Obligations to Principal and Third Parties.

Rutter, Cal. Practice Guide: Real Prop. Transactions Ch. 4-E, E. Drafting the Purchase and Sale Agreement-Terms and Conditions.

20 NO. 4 Miller & Starr, California Real Estate Newsalert 6, Deeds of Trust.

1 Witkin Cal. Summ. 10th Contracts § 759, (S 759) Discharge by Performance.

13 Witkin, California Summary 10th Personal Property § 124, (S 124) in General.

5 Witkin, California Summary 10th Torts § 145, (S 145) Related Immunities.

§ 3. Code provisions not retroactive

NOT RETROACTIVE. No part of it is retroactive, unless expressly so declared. *(Enacted in 1872.)*

Research References

Rutter, Cal. Practice Guide: Civil Appeals & Writs Ch. 8-D, D. Limits on Assertion of Issues on Appeal.

4 Witkin, California Summary 10th Sales § 277, (S 277) Prohibited Terms and Acts.

5 Witkin, California Summary 10th Torts § 729, Abduction of Child.

6 Witkin, California Summary 10th Torts § 997, Miscellaneous Professionals.

7 Witkin, California Summary 10th Constitutional Law § 634, Initiative Measure.

§ 4. Strict construction rule inapplicable; liberal construction

RULES OF CONSTRUCTION. The rule of the common law, that statutes in derogation thereof are to be strictly construed, has no application to this Code. The Code establishes the law of this State respecting the subjects to which it relates, and its provisions are to be liberally construed with a view to effect its objects and to promote justice. *(Enacted in 1872.)*

Research References

Rutter, Cal. Practice Guide: Real Prop. Transactions Ch. 4-D, D. Selecting the Form of Written Agreement.
13 Witkin, California Summary 10th Personal Property § 242, Towing and Storage Lien.
6 Witkin, California Summary 10th Torts § 1260, (S 1260) Statutory Development.
4 Witkin, California Summary 10th Secured Transactions in Personal Property § 200, Consumer Transactions.

§ 5. Continuation of similar existing law or common law

PROVISIONS SIMILAR TO EXISTING LAWS, HOW CONSTRUED. The provisions of this Code, so far as they are substantially the same as existing statutes or the common law, must be construed as continuations thereof, and not as new enactments. *(Enacted in 1872.)*

§ 6. Effect on prior proceedings or rights

ACTIONS, ETC., NOT AFFECTED. No action or proceeding commenced before this Code takes effect, and no right accrued, is affected by its provisions. *(Enacted in 1872.)*

Research References

13 Witkin, California Summary 10th Personal Property § 124, (S 124) in General.
4 Witkin, California Summary 10th Sales § 51, Nature and Effect.
11 Witkin, California Summary 10th Husband and Wife § 371, (S 371) Civil Remedies.

§ 7. Holidays

Holidays within the meaning of this code are every Sunday and such other days as are specified or provided for as holidays in the Government Code of the State of California. *(Enacted in 1872. Amended by Code Am.1880, c. 50, p. 9, § 1; Stats.1889, c. 44, p. 47, § 1; Stats.1893, c. 158, p. 186, § 1; Stats.1897, c. 18, p. 14, § 1; Stats.1907, c. 293, p. 565, § 1; Stats.1907, Ex.Sess., c. 5, p. 5, § 1; Stats.1909, c. 30, p. 23, § 1; Stats.1911, c. 320, p. 520, § 1; Stats.1925, c. 92, p. 224, § 1; Stats.1955, c. 165, p. 613, § 1.)*

Research References

Miller and Starr California Real Estate § 6:24, Timeliness of Performance.
Miller and Starr California Real Estate § 11:68, Constructive Notice of Interests Barred by the Statute of Limitations--"Ancient Documents" and the Marketable Record Title Act.
14 NO. 2 Miller & Starr, California Real Estate Newsalert 14, Landlord and Tenant.
1 Witkin Cal. Summ. 10th Contracts § 764, Time Specified and Extensions.
1 Witkin Cal. Summ. 10th Contracts § 897, (S 897) Attorneys' Fees.
13 Witkin, California Summary 10th Personal Property § 124, (S 124) in General.

§ 7.1. Optional bank holidays

Optional bank holidays within the meaning of Section 9 are:

(a) Any closing of a bank because of an extraordinary situation, as that term is defined in the Bank Extraordinary Situation Closing Act (Chapter 20 (commencing with Section 3600) of Division 1 of the Financial Code).

(b) Every Saturday.

(c) Every Sunday.

(d) January 1st.

(e) The third Monday in January, known as "Dr. Martin Luther King, Jr. Day."

(f) February 12, known as "Lincoln Day."

(g) The third Monday in February.

(h) The last Monday in May.

(i) July 4th.

(j) The first Monday in September.

(k) September 9th, known as "Admission Day."

(l) The second Monday in October, known as "Columbus Day."

(m) November 11th, known as "Veteran's Day."

(n) December 25th.

(o) Good Friday from 12 noon until closing.

(p) The Thursday in November appointed as "Thanksgiving Day."

(q) Any Monday following any Sunday on which January 1st, February 12th, July 4th, September 9th, November 11th, or December 25th falls.

(r) Any Friday preceding any Saturday on which July 4th, September 9th, or December 25th falls. *(Added by Stats.1994, c. 668 (S.B.1405), § 1.)*

Research References

Miller and Starr California Real Estate § 10:185, Recording and Mailing.
Miller and Starr California Real Estate § 10:186, Reinstatement--In General.
1 Witkin Cal. Summ. 10th Contracts § 764, Time Specified and Extensions.

§ 9. Business days; optional bank holidays not business days; acts to be performed on optional bank holidays

All other days than those mentioned in Section 7 are business days for all purposes; provided, that as to any act appointed by law or contract, or in any other way, to be performed by, at, or through any bank organized under the laws of or doing business in this state, any optional bank holiday as defined in Section 7.1 is not a business day; and provided, that any act appointed by law or contract, or in any other way, to be performed on any day which is an optional bank holiday as defined in Section 7.1, by, at, or through any bank or branch or office thereof, whether acting in its own behalf or in any other capacity whatsoever, may be performed on that optional bank holiday if the bank or branch or office by, at, or through which the act is to be performed is open for the transaction of business on that optional bank holiday, or, at the option of the person obligated to perform the act, it may be performed on the next succeeding business day. *(Enacted in 1872. Amended by Stats.1905, c. 17, p. 11, § 2; Stats.1939, c. 414, p. 1748, § 1; Stats.1955, c. 198, p. 670, § 1; Stats.1955, c. 599, p. 1091, § 1; Stats.1973, c. 285, p. 694, § 1; Stats.1979, c. 159, p. 357, § 1; Stats.1981, c. 67, § 1, eff. June 16, 1981; Stats.1982, c. 1203, p. 4383, § 1, eff. Sept. 22, 1982; Stats.1985, c. 147, § 1, eff. July 8, 1985; Stats.1994, c. 668 (S.B.1405), § 2.)*

Research References

Miller and Starr California Real Estate § 27:81, Owner's Remedies for Late Performance--Liquidated Damages.
1 Witkin Cal. Summ. 10th Contracts § 764, Time Specified and Extensions.

§ 10. Time; computation

COMPUTATION OF TIME. The time in which any act provided by law is to be done is computed by excluding the first day and including the last, unless the last day is a holiday, and then it is also excluded. *(Enacted in 1872.)*

Research References

Rutter, Cal. Practice Guide: Real Prop. Transactions Ch. 4-A, A. Property to be Sold.
Miller and Starr California Real Estate § 28:56, Statute of Limitations; Time to File a Complaint.

1 Witkin Cal. Summ. 10th Contracts § 764, Time Specified and Extensions.

§ 11. Holidays; certain acts performable on next business day

CERTAIN ACTS NOT TO BE DONE ON HOLIDAYS. Whenever any act of a secular nature, other than a work of necessity or mercy, is appointed by law or contract to be performed upon a particular day, which day falls upon a holiday, it may be performed upon the next business day, with the same effect as if it had been performed upon the day appointed. *(Enacted in 1872.)*

Research References

Rutter, Cal. Practice Guide: Real Prop. Transactions Ch. 4-E, E. Drafting the Purchase and Sale Agreement-Terms and Conditions.
Miller and Starr California Real Estate § 2:9, Mode and Manner of Exercise.
Miller and Starr California Real Estate § 6:24, Timeliness of Performance.
Miller and Starr California Real Estate § 1:163, Conditions Concurrent--Performance; Requirements for an Effective Tender.
1 Witkin Cal. Summ. 10th Contracts § 764, Time Specified and Extensions.

§ 12. Joint authority construed

JOINT AUTHORITY CONSTRUED. Words giving a joint authority to three or more public officers or other persons are construed as giving such authority to a majority of them, unless it is otherwise expressed in the Act giving the authority. *(Enacted in 1872.)*

Research References

13 Witkin, California Summary 10th Personal Property § 39, (S 39) Other Statutes Dealing With Unclaimed Property.

§ 13. Words and phrases; construction

WORDS AND PHRASES, HOW CONSTRUED. Words and phrases are construed according to the context and the approved usage of the language; but technical words and phrases, and such others as may have acquired a peculiar and appropriate meaning in law, or are defined in the succeeding section, are to be construed according to such peculiar and appropriate meaning or definition. *(Enacted in 1872.)*

Research References

1 Witkin Cal. Summ. 10th Contracts § 1021, (S 1021) Exception: Performing Defendant's Duty.

§ 14. Words and phrases; construction; tense; gender; number

Words used in this code in the present tense include the future as well as the present; words used in the masculine gender include the feminine and neuter; the singular number includes the plural, and the plural the singular; the word person includes a corporation as well as a natural person; county includes city and county; writing includes printing and typewriting; oath includes affirmation or declaration; and every mode of oral statement, under oath or affirmation, is embraced by the term "testify," and every written one in the term "depose"; signature or subscription includes mark, when the person cannot write, his name being written near it, by a person who writes his own name as a witness; provided, that when a signature is by mark it must in order that the same may be acknowledged or may serve as the signature to any sworn statement be witnessed by two persons who must subscribe their own names as witnesses thereto. The following words have in this code the signification attached to them in this section, unless otherwise apparent from the context:

1. The word "property" includes property real and personal;

2. The words "real property" are coextensive with lands, tenements, and hereditaments;

3. The words "personal property" include money, goods, chattels, things in action, and evidences of debt;

4. The word "month" means a calendar month, unless otherwise expressed;

5. The word "will" includes codicil;

6. The word "section" whenever hereinafter employed refers to a section of this code, unless some other code or statute is expressly mentioned. *(Enacted in 1872. Amended by Code Am.1873–74, c. 612, p. 181, § 1; Stats.1903, c. 281, p. 407, § 1.)*

Research References

Rutter, Cal. Practice Guide: Real Prop. Transactions Ch. 4-A, A. Property to be Sold.
Miller and Starr California Real Estate § 19:2, Lease as Personal Property or Real Property.
Miller and Starr California Real Estate § 8:29, Requirements of Grantor's Signature.
Miller and Starr California Real Estate § 11:26, Form and Content of the Certificate of Acknowledgement.
Miller and Starr California Real Estate § 10:184, Execution of the Notice of Default.
19 NO. 2 Miller & Starr, California Real Estate Newsalert 14, Easements.
13 Witkin, California Summary 10th Personal Property § 90, Test of Mobility.
9 Witkin, California Summary 10th Corporations § 1, (S 1) Nature of Corporation.
5 Witkin, California Summary 10th Torts § 155, Proceedings of Professional Society or Committee.

§ 17. Certified mail; compliance with mailing provisions

Wherever any notice or other communication is required by this code to be mailed by registered mail, the mailing of such notice or other communication by certified mail shall be deemed to be a sufficient compliance with the requirements of law. *(Added by Stats.1959, c. 426, p. 2364, § 1.)*

Research References

Miller and Starr California Real Estate § 15:36, Use Requirements--Permission by the Property Owner; Posted or Recorded Notice.
Miller and Starr California Real Estate § 16:13, When Possession is "Hostile and Adverse".
Miller and Starr California Real Estate § 17:37, Generally; Definitions.

§ 18. Notice; actual and constructive

NOTICE, ACTUAL AND CONSTRUCTIVE. Notice is:

1. Actual—which consists in express information of a fact; or,

2. Constructive—which is imputed by law. *(Enacted in 1872.)*

Research References

Rutter, Cal. Practice Guide: Civ. Pro. Before Trial Ch. 5-G, G. Relief from Default.
Rutter, Cal. Practice Guide: Enforcing Judgments/Debts Ch. 6C-6, Priority Rules.
Miller and Starr California Real Estate § 11:59, What Constitutes Actual Notice.
19 NO. 5 Miller & Starr, California Real Estate Newsalert 1, Moving Up in a Down Market: Rediscovering Equitable Subrogation.
8 Witkin Cal. Proc. 5th Attack Judgment Trial Court § 212, (S 212) Strict Construction.

§ 19. Constructive notice

Every person who has actual notice of circumstances sufficient to put a prudent man upon inquiry as to a particular fact, has constructive notice of the fact itself in all cases in which, by prosecuting such inquiry, he might have learned such fact. *(Enacted in 1872. Amended by Code Am.1873–74, c. 612, p. 182, § 3.)*

Research References

Rutter, Cal. Practice Guide: Real Prop. Transactions Ch. 4-E, E. Drafting the Purchase and Sale Agreement-Terms and Conditions.

Miller and Starr California Real Estate § 1:150, Reliance by Injured Party--Effect of Buyer's Inspection of the Property.

Miller and Starr California Real Estate § 11:81, Notice Implied from Circumstances Which Require Investigation.

3 Witkin Cal. Proc. 5th Actions § 623, Conversion by Original Wrongful Act.

§ 20. Repeal or abrogation of prior laws; effect

EFFECT OF REPEAL. No statute, law, or rule is continued in force because it is consistent with the provisions of this Code on the same subject; but in all cases provided for by this Code, all statutes, laws, and rules heretofore in force in this State, whether consistent or not with the provisions of this Code, unless expressly continued in force by it, are repealed or abrogated.

This repeal or abrogation does not revive any former law heretofore repealed, nor does it affect any right already existing or accrued, or any action or proceeding already taken, except as in this Code provided. *(Enacted in 1872.)*

§ 21. Citation of act adopting Code

THIS ACT, HOW CITED. This Act, whenever cited, enumerated, referred to, or amended, may be designated simply as "The Civil Code," adding, when necessary, the number of the section. *(Enacted in 1872.)*

DEFINITIONS AND SOURCES OF LAW

Section
22.   Law defined.
22.1.   Supreme power; expression of will.
22.2.   Common law of England; rule of decision.

§ 22. Law defined

Law is a solemn expression of the will of the supreme power of the State. *(Added by Stats.1951, c. 655, p. 1833, § 1.)*

Research References

Miller and Starr California Real Estate § 28:84, Recovery of Attorney's Fees.

§ 22.1. Supreme power; expression of will

The will of the supreme power is expressed:

(a) By the Constitution.

(b) By statutes. *(Added by Stats.1951, c. 655, p. 1833, § 1.)*

§ 22.2. Common law of England; rule of decision

The common law of England, so far as it is not repugnant to or inconsistent with the Constitution of the United States, or the Constitution or laws of this State, is the rule of decision in all the courts of this State. *(Added by Stats.1951, c. 655, p. 1833, § 1.)*

Research References

9 Witkin Cal. Proc. 5th Appeal § 484, (S 484) Distinction: Common Law as Rule of Decision.

9 Witkin Cal. Proc. 5th Appeal § 813, (S 813) in General.

6 Witkin, California Summary 10th Torts § 1678, Former Rule Denying Recovery.

13 Witkin, California Summary 10th Trusts § 24, (S 24) Role of Common Law.

EFFECT OF THE 1872 CODES

Section
23.   Time of passage of 1872 Codes.
23.1.   Inconsistent statutes of 1872 session to prevail over 1872 Codes.
23.2.   Construction of 1872 Codes.
23.3.   Conflicting provisions of titles of 1872 Codes.
23.4.   Conflicting provisions of chapters of 1872 Codes.
23.5.   Conflicting provisions of articles of 1872 Codes.
23.6.   Conflicting provisions of sections of 1872 Codes.

§ 23. Time of passage of 1872 Codes

With relation to the laws passed at the 1872 Session of the Legislature, the Political Code, Civil Code, Code of Civil Procedure, and Penal Code, shall be construed as though each had been passed on the first day of the session. *(Added by Stats.1951, c. 655, p. 1833, § 2.)*

Research References

Miller and Starr California Real Estate § 28:84, Recovery of Attorney's Fees.

§ 23.1. Inconsistent statutes of 1872 session to prevail over 1872 Codes

The provisions of any law passed at the 1872 Session of the Legislature which contravene or are inconsistent with the provisions of any of the four codes passed at the 1872 Session prevail. *(Added by Stats.1951, c. 655, p. 1833, § 2.)*

§ 23.2. Construction of 1872 Codes

With relation to each other, the provisions of the four codes shall be construed as though all such codes had been passed at the same moment of time and were parts of the same statute. *(Added by Stats.1951, c. 655, p. 1833, § 2.)*

§ 23.3. Conflicting provisions of titles of 1872 Codes

If the provisions of any title conflict with or contravene the provisions of another title, the provisions of each title shall prevail as to all matters and questions arising out of the subject matter of the title. *(Added by Stats.1951, c. 655, p. 1833, § 2.)*

§ 23.4. Conflicting provisions of chapters of 1872 Codes

If the provisions of any chapter conflict with or contravene the provisions of another chapter of the same title, the provisions of each chapter shall prevail as to all matters and questions arising out of the subject matter of the chapter. *(Added by Stats.1951, c. 655, p. 1833, § 2.)*

§ 23.5. Conflicting provisions of articles of 1872 Codes

If the provisions of any article conflict with or contravene the provisions of another article of the same chapter, the provisions of each article shall prevail as to all matters and questions arising out of the subject matter of the article. *(Added by Stats.1951, c. 655, p. 1833, § 2.)*

§ 23.6. Conflicting provisions of sections of 1872 Codes

If conflicting provisions are found in different sections of the same chapter or article, the provisions of the sections last in numerical order shall prevail, unless such construction is inconsistent with the meaning of the chapter or article. *(Added by Stats.1951, c. 655, p. 1833, § 2.)*

Division 1
PERSONS

Part 1

PERSONS WITH UNSOUND MIND

Law Revision Commission Comments

Part 1 (commencing with Section 25) of Division 1 is replaced by a new Part 1 (commencing with Civil Code Section 38) (persons of unsound mind), by Civil Code Section 43.1 (child conceived but not yet born), by Code of Civil Procedure Section 340.4 (statute of limitations on pre-birth injury), and by Division 11 (commencing with Section 6500) of the Family Code (minors). [23 Cal.L.Rev.Comm. Reports 1 (1993)].

§ 38. Person without understanding; contract; necessaries; liability

A person entirely without understanding has no power to make a contract of any kind, but the person is liable for the reasonable value of things furnished to the person necessary for the support of the person or the person's family. *(Added by Stats.1992, c. 163 (A.B.2641), § 3, operative Jan. 1, 1994.)*

Law Revision Commission Comments

Section 38 restates former Civil Code Section 38 without substantive change. [22 Cal.L.Rev.Comm. Reports 1 (1992)].

Research References

Rutter, Cal. Practice Guide: Real Prop. Transactions Ch. 4-C, C. Parties to the Purchase Agreement.
Rutter, Cal. Practice Guide: Real Prop. Transactions Ch. 11-A, A. Factors Affecting Choice of Remedies.
Miller and Starr California Real Estate § 1:14, Mental Incapacity; in General--Persons "Entirely Without Understanding".
Miller and Starr California Real Estate § 8:23, Mental Incapacity to Convey.
3 Witkin Cal. Proc. 5th Actions § 701, Effect of Judicial Determination.
1 Witkin Cal. Summ. 10th Contracts § 50, (S 50) in General.
1 Witkin Cal. Summ. 10th Contracts § 52, Insanity Without Adjudication.
1 Witkin Cal. Summ. 10th Contracts § 1021, (S 1021) Exception: Performing Defendant's Duty.
4 Witkin, California Summary 10th Sales § 233, Illustrations.

14 Witkin, California Summary 10th Wills and Probate § 953, (S 953) in General.

§ 39. Conveyance or contract; rescission; rebuttable presumption

(a) A conveyance or other contract of a person of unsound mind, but not entirely without understanding, made before the incapacity of the person has been judicially determined, is subject to rescission, as provided in Chapter 2 (commencing with Section 1688) of Title 5 of Part 2 of Division 3.

(b) A rebuttable presumption affecting the burden of proof that a person is of unsound mind shall exist for purposes of this section if the person is substantially unable to manage his or her own financial resources or resist fraud or undue influence. Substantial inability may not be proved solely by isolated incidents of negligence or improvidence. *(Added by Stats.1992, c. 163 (A.B.2641), § 3, operative Jan. 1, 1994. Amended by Stats.1995, c. 842 (S.B.730), § 1.)*

Law Revision Commission Comments

Section 39 restates former Civil Code Section 39 without substantive change. [22 Cal.L.Rev.Comm. Reports 1 (1992)].

Research References

Rutter, Cal. Practice Guide: A.D.R. Ch. 5-D, D. Defenses to Enforcement.
Rutter, Cal. Practice Guide: Real Prop. Transactions Ch. 4-C, C. Parties to the Purchase Agreement.
Rutter, Cal. Practice Guide: Real Prop. Transactions Ch. 11-A, A. Factors Affecting Choice of Remedies.
Miller and Starr California Real Estate § 1:15, Mental Incapacity; in General--Persons Failing to "Fully Understand".
Miller and Starr California Real Estate § 8:23, Mental Incapacity to Convey.
1 Witkin Cal. Summ. 10th Contracts § 50, (S 50) in General.
1 Witkin Cal. Summ. 10th Contracts § 55, (S 55) Voidable Contracts.
1 Witkin Cal. Summ. 10th Contracts § 57, Manic Depressive Psychosis.
1 Witkin Cal. Summ. 10th Contracts § 935, (S 935) Grounds for Rescission.
4 Witkin, California Summary 10th Sales § 233, Illustrations.
11 Witkin, California Summary 10th Husband and Wife § 161, (S 161) Insanity.
14 Witkin, California Summary 10th Wills and Probate § 953, (S 953) in General.

§ 40. Judicial determination of incapacity; powers; conservatorship

(a) Subject to Section 1871 of the Probate Code, and subject to Part 1 (commencing with Section 5000) of Division 5 of the Welfare and Institutions Code, after his or her incapacity has been judicially determined a person of unsound mind can make no conveyance or other contract, nor delegate any power or waive any right, until his or her restoration to capacity.

(b) Subject to Sections 1873 to 1876, inclusive, of the Probate Code, the establishment of a conservatorship under Division 4 (commencing with Section 1400) of the Probate Code is a judicial determination of the incapacity of the conservatee for the purposes of this section. *(Added by Stats.1992, c. 163 (A.B.2641), § 3, operative Jan. 1, 1994.)*

Law Revision Commission Comments

Section 40 continues former Civil Code Section 40 without substantive change. [22 Cal.L.Rev.Comm. Reports 1 (1992)].

Research References

Rutter, Cal. Practice Guide: Real Prop. Transactions Ch. 4-C, C. Parties to the Purchase Agreement.

Rutter, Cal. Practice Guide: Real Prop. Transactions Ch. 11-A, A. Factors Affecting Choice of Remedies.

Miller and Starr California Real Estate § 1:13, Mental Incapacity; in General--Unsound Mind; Adjudicated Situations.

Miller and Starr California Real Estate § 8:23, Mental Incapacity to Convey.

Miller and Starr California Real Estate § 34:113, Grounds for Cancellation.

1 Witkin Cal. Summ. 10th Contracts § 50, (S 50) in General.

1 Witkin Cal. Summ. 10th Contracts § 53, (S 53) in General.

1 Witkin Cal. Summ. 10th Contracts § 54, (S 54) Conservatee.

1 Witkin Cal. Summ. 10th Contracts § 55, (S 55) Voidable Contracts.

4 Witkin, California Summary 10th Sales § 233, Illustrations.

14 Witkin, California Summary 10th Wills and Probate § 953, (S 953) in General.

14 Witkin, California Summary 10th Wills and Probate § 954, (S 954) Limited or Temporary Conservatee.

§ 41.   Civil liability; exemplary damages

A person of unsound mind, of whatever degree, is civilly liable for a wrong done by the person, but is not liable in exemplary damages unless at the time of the act the person was capable of knowing that the act was wrongful. *(Added by Stats.1992, c. 163 (A.B.2641), § 3, operative Jan. 1, 1994.)*

Law Revision Commission Comments

Section 41 continues former Civil Code Section 41 without substantive change, insofar as former Section 41 related to a person of unsound mind. [22 Cal.L.Rev.Comm. Reports 1 (1992)].

Research References

Miller and Starr California Real Estate § 1:15, Mental Incapacity; in General--Persons Failing to "Fully Understand".

Miller and Starr California Real Estate § 16:38, Life Tenant and Remainderman.

5 Witkin, California Summary 10th Torts § 26, (S 26) Mentally Disabled Persons.

6 Witkin, California Summary 10th Torts § 1353, (S 1353) Medicine.

6 Witkin, California Summary 10th Torts § 1580, in General.

Part 2

PERSONAL RIGHTS

§ 43. General personal rights

Besides the personal rights mentioned or recognized in the Government Code, every person has, subject to the qualifications and restrictions provided by law, the right of protection from bodily restraint or harm, from personal insult, from defamation, and from injury to his personal relations. *(Enacted in 1872. Amended by Stats.1953, c. 604, p. 1849, § 1.)*

Research References

California Practice Guide: Employment Litigation Ch. 10-E, E. Harasser's Individual Liability.
12 Witkin, California Summary 10th Real Property § 599, Other Acts and Powers of Entity Are Not Affected.
5 Witkin, California Summary 10th Torts § 1, (S 1) Definitions and Distinctions.

§ 43.1. Unborn child deemed existing person

A child conceived, but not yet born, is deemed an existing person, so far as necessary for the child's interests in the event of the child's subsequent birth. *(Added by Stats.1992, c. 163 (A.B.2641), § 4, operative Jan. 1, 1994.)*

Law Revision Commission Comments

Section 43.1 continues the first part of former Civil Code Section 29 without substantive change. See also Code Civ.Proc. § 340.4 (statute of limitations for injury before birth). [22 Cal.L.Rev.Comm.Reports 1 (1992)].

Research References

Miller and Starr California Real Estate § 8:27, Capacity of the Grantee.
3 Witkin Cal. Proc. 5th Actions § 443, Limitation in Statute Creating Right.
3 Witkin Cal. Proc. 5th Actions § 459, (S 459) Period Shortened.
3 Witkin Cal. Proc. 5th Actions § 553, (S 553) Scope of Statute.
3 Witkin Cal. Proc. 5th Actions § 589, (S 589) Prenatal Injuries.

5 Witkin, California Summary 10th Torts § 728, (S 728) Injury to Unborn Child.
6 Witkin, California Summary 10th Torts § 1393, Child of Presumed Parent.
14 Witkin, California Summary 10th Wills and Probate § 87, Afterborn Heirs.
14 Witkin, California Summary 10th Wills and Probate § 232, Time When Class is Ascertained.
2 Witkin Cal. Summ. 10th Workers' Compensation § 65, Fetal Injury in Workplace.

§ 43.3. Breastfeeding; location

Notwithstanding any other provision of law, a mother may breastfeed her child in any location, public or private, except the private home or residence of another, where the mother and the child are otherwise authorized to be present. *(Added by Stats.1997, c. 59 (A.B.157), § 1.)*

§ 43.4. Fraudulent promise to marry or cohabit not actionable

A fraudulent promise to marry or to cohabit after marriage does not give rise to a cause of action for damages. *(Added by Stats.1959, c. 381, p. 2306, § 1.)*

Research References

3 Witkin Cal. Proc. 5th Actions § 167, (S 167) False Promise in Unenforceable Contract.
5 Witkin, California Summary 10th Torts § 785, Promise Inducing Marriage: Damages.
5 Witkin, California Summary 10th Torts § 786, Promise to Support.

§ 43.5. Wrongs not actionable

No cause of action arises for:

(a) Alienation of affection.

(b) Criminal conversation.

(c) Seduction of a person over the age of legal consent.

(d) Breach of promise of marriage. *(Added by Stats.1939, c. 128, p. 1245, § 2.)*

Research References

3 Witkin Cal. Proc. 5th Actions § 166, (S 166) Analysis and Criticism.
3 Witkin Cal. Proc. 5th Actions § 167, (S 167) False Promise in Unenforceable Contract.
11 Witkin, California Summary 10th Community Property § 272, Nature of Theory.
5 Witkin, California Summary 10th Torts § 441, in General.
5 Witkin, California Summary 10th Torts § 442, Warrant Defective on Face.
5 Witkin, California Summary 10th Torts § 443, Arrest of Wrong Person.
5 Witkin, California Summary 10th Torts § 723, (S 723) Types of Actions.
5 Witkin, California Summary 10th Torts § 724, (S 724) Distinction: Professional Negligence.
5 Witkin, California Summary 10th Torts § 784, Promise Inducing Transfer: Restitution.
5 Witkin, California Summary 10th Torts § 786, Promise to Support.
5 Witkin, California Summary 10th Torts § 790, (S 790) Representation of Sterility.
6 Witkin, California Summary 10th Torts § 1046, in General.
6 Witkin, California Summary 10th Torts § 1047, Duty Provable, But Not Established.

§ 43.55. Arrest under warrant regular on face not actionable

(a) There shall be no liability on the part of, and no cause of action shall arise against, any peace officer who makes an arrest pursuant to a warrant of arrest regular upon its face if the peace officer in making the arrest acts without malice and in the reasonable belief that the person arrested is the one referred to in the warrant.

(b) As used in this section, a "warrant of arrest regular upon its face" includes both of the following:

(1) A paper arrest warrant that has been issued pursuant to a judicial order.

(2) A judicial order that is entered into an automated warrant system by law enforcement or court personnel authorized to make those entries at or near the time the judicial order is made. *(Formerly § 43.5(a), added by Stats.1945, c. 1117, p. 2126, § 1. Renumbered § 43.55 and amended by Stats.1986, c. 248, § 15. Amended by Stats.2005, c. 706 (A.B.1742), § 2.)*

Research References

5 Witkin, California Summary 10th Torts § 161, Reliance on Court Process or Order.

5 Witkin, California Summary 10th Torts § 348, Nature of Immunities and Defenses.

5 Witkin, California Summary 10th Torts § 441, in General.

5 Witkin, California Summary 10th Torts § 442, Warrant Defective on Face.

5 Witkin, California Summary 10th Torts § 443, Arrest of Wrong Person.

§ 43.56. Foster parents; alienation of child's affection

No cause of action arises against a foster parent for alienation of affection of a foster child. *(Formerly § 43.55, added by Stats.1986, c. 1330, § 2, eff. Sept. 29, 1986. Amended by Stats.1988, c. 195, § 1, eff. June 16, 1988. Renumbered § 43.56 and amended by Stats.1990, c. 216 (S.B.2510), § 5.)*

§ 43.6. Immunity from liability; actions against parents on childbirth claims; defenses and damages in third party actions

(a) No cause of action arises against a parent of a child based upon the claim that the child should not have been conceived or, if conceived, should not have been allowed to have been born alive.

(b) The failure or refusal of a parent to prevent the live birth of his or her child shall not be a defense in any action against a third party, nor shall the failure or refusal be considered in awarding damages in any such action.

(c) As used in this section "conceived" means the fertilization of a human ovum by a human sperm. *(Added by Stats.1981, c. 331, § 1.)*

Research References

6 Witkin, California Summary 10th Torts § 981, (S 981) No Cause of Action Against Parent.

6 Witkin, California Summary 10th Torts § 982, (S 982) Recovery Limited to Special Damages.

§ 43.7. Immunity from liability; mental health professional quality assurance committees; professional societies, members or staff; peer review or insurance underwriting committees; hospital governing board

(a) There shall be no monetary liability on the part of, and no cause of action for damages shall arise against, any member of a duly appointed mental health professional quality assurance committee that is established in compliance with Section 14725 of the Welfare and Institutions Code, for any act or proceeding undertaken or performed within the scope of the functions of the committee which is formed to review and evaluate the adequacy, appropriateness, or effectiveness of the care and treatment planned for, or provided to, mental health patients in order to improve quality of care by mental health professionals if the committee member acts without malice, has made a reasonable effort to obtain the facts of the matter as to which he or she acts, and acts in reasonable belief that the action taken by him or her is warranted by the facts known to him or her after the reasonable effort to obtain facts.

(b) There shall be no monetary liability on the part of, and no cause of action for damages shall arise against, any professional society, any member of a duly appointed committee of a medical specialty society, or any member of a duly appointed committee of a state or local professional society, or duly appointed member of a committee of a professional staff of a licensed hospital (provided the professional staff operates pursuant to written bylaws that have been approved by the governing board of the hospital), for any act or proceeding undertaken or performed within the scope of the functions of the committee which is formed to maintain the professional standards of the society established by its bylaws, or any member of any peer review committee whose purpose is to review the quality of medical, dental, dietetic, chiropractic, optometric, acupuncture, psychotherapy, or veterinary services rendered by physicians and surgeons, dentists, dental hygienists, podiatrists, registered dietitians, chiropractors, optometrists, acupuncturists, veterinarians, marriage and family therapists, professional clinical counselors, or psychologists, which committee is composed chiefly of physicians and surgeons, dentists, dental hygienists, podiatrists, registered dietitians, chiropractors, optometrists, acupuncturists, veterinarians, marriage and family therapists, professional clinical counselors, or psychologists for any act or proceeding undertaken or performed in reviewing the quality of medical, dental, dietetic, chiropractic, optometric, acupuncture, psychotherapy, or veterinary services rendered by physicians and surgeons, dentists, dental hygienists, podiatrists, registered dietitians, chiropractors, optometrists, acupuncturists, veterinarians, marriage and family therapists, professional clinical counselors, or psychologists or any member of the governing board of a hospital in reviewing the quality of medical services rendered by members of the staff if the professional society, committee, or board member acts without malice, has made a reasonable effort to obtain the facts of the matter as to which he, she, or it acts, and acts in reasonable belief that the action taken by him, her, or it is warranted by the facts known to him, her, or it after the reasonable effort to obtain facts. "Professional society" includes legal, medical, psychological, dental, dental hygiene, dietetic, accounting, optometric, acupuncture, podiatric, pharmaceutic, chiropractic, physical therapist, veterinary, licensed marriage and family therapy, licensed clinical social work, licensed professional clinical counselor, and engineering organizations having as members at least 25 percent of the eligible persons or licentiates in the geographic area served by the particular society. However, if the society has fewer than 100 members, it shall have as members at least a majority of the eligible persons or licentiates in the geographic area served by the particular society.

"Medical specialty society" means an organization having as members at least 25 percent of the eligible physicians and surgeons within a given professionally recognized medical specialty in the geographic area served by the particular society.

(c) This section does not affect the official immunity of an officer or employee of a public corporation.

(d) There shall be no monetary liability on the part of, and no cause of action for damages shall arise against, any physician and surgeon, podiatrist, or chiropractor who is a member of an underwriting committee of an interindemnity or reciprocal or interinsurance exchange or mutual company for any act or proceeding undertaken or performed in evaluating physicians and surgeons, podiatrists, or chiropractors for the writing of professional liability insurance, or any act or proceeding undertaken or performed in evaluating physicians and surgeons for the writing of an interindemnity, reciprocal, or interinsurance contract as specified in Section 1280.7 of the Insurance Code, if the evaluating physician and surgeon, podiatrist, or chiropractor acts without malice, has made a reasonable effort to obtain the facts of the matter as to which he or she acts, and acts in reasonable belief that the action taken by him or her is warranted by the facts known to him or her after the reasonable effort to obtain the facts.

(e) This section shall not be construed to confer immunity from liability on any quality assurance committee established in compliance with Section 14725 of the Welfare and Institutions Code or hospital. In any case in which, but for the enactment of the preceding provisions of this section, a cause of action would arise against a quality assurance committee established in compliance with Section 14725 of the Welfare and Institutions Code or hospital, the cause of action shall exist as if the preceding provisions of this section had not been enacted. *(Added by Stats.1961, c. 623, p. 1780, § 1. Amended by Stats.1963, c. 806, p. 1836, § 1; Stats.1969, c. 264, p. 616, § 1; Stats.1973, c. 191, p. 493, § 1; Stats.1976, c. 532, p. 1287, § 1; Stats.1977, c. 241, p. 1085, § 1; Stats.1977, c. 934, p. 2858, § 1; Stats.1978, c. 268, p. 555, § 1; Stats.1978, c. 503, p. 1647, § 1; Stats.1980, c. 454, § 1, operative Jan. 1, 1990; Stats.1982, c. 234, p. 765, § 2, eff. June 2, 1982; Stats.1982, c. 705, p. 2862, § 1; Stats.1983, c. 289, § 1; Stats.1983, c. 297, § 1; Stats.1983, c. 1081, § 1.8; Stats.1984, c. 515, § 1; Stats.1984, c. 1012, § 1; Stats.1986, c. 669, § 2; Stats.1987, c. 1169, § 2, operative Jan. 1, 1990; Stats.1994, c. 815 (S.B.1279), § 1; Stats.2002, c. 1013 (S.B.2026), § 72; Stats.2010, c. 82 (A.B.1730), § 1; Stats.2011, c. 381 (S.B.146), § 14; Stats.2012, c. 34 (S.B.1009), § 3, eff. June 27, 2012, operative July 1, 2012.)*

Research References

5 Witkin, California Summary 10th Torts § 155, Proceedings of Professional Society or Committee.
6 Witkin, California Summary 10th Torts § 1064, (S 1064) Distinction: Medical Proctor.

§ 43.8. Immunity from liability for communication on evaluation of practitioner of healing or veterinary arts

(a) In addition to the privilege afforded by Section 47, there shall be no monetary liability on the part of, and no cause of action for damages shall arise against, any person on account of the communication of information in the possession of that person to any hospital, hospital medical staff, veterinary hospital staff, professional society, medical, dental, podiatric, psychology, marriage and family therapy, professional clinical counselor, or veterinary school, professional licensing board or division, committee or panel of a licensing board, the Senior Assistant Attorney General of the Health Quality Enforcement Section appointed under Section 12529 of the Government Code, peer review committee, quality assurance committees established in compliance with Sections 4070 and 5624 of the Welfare and Institutions Code, or underwriting committee described in Section 43.7 when the communication is intended to aid in the evaluation of the qualifications, fitness, character, or insurability of a practitioner of the healing or veterinary arts.

(b) The immunities afforded by this section and by Section 43.7 shall not affect the availability of any absolute privilege that may be afforded by Section 47.

(c) Nothing in this section is intended in any way to affect the California Supreme Court's decision in Hassan v. Mercy American River Hospital (2003) 31 Cal.4th 709, holding that subdivision (a) provides a qualified privilege. *(Added by Stats.1974, c. 1086, p. 2313, § 1. Amended by Stats.1975, 2nd Ex.Sess., c. 1, p. 3968, § 24.4; Stats.1976, c. 532, p. 1287, § 2; Stats.1977, c. 934, p. 2859, § 2; Stats.1982, c. 234, p. 767, § 3, eff. June 2, 1982; Stats.1982, c. 705, p. 2863, § 2; Stats.1983, c. 1081, § 2; Stats.1984, c. 515, § 4; Stats.1983, c. 1081, § 2, operative Jan. 1, 1990; Stats.1990, c. 1597 (S.B.2375), § 30; Stats.2002, c. 664 (A.B.3034), § 31; Stats.2007, c. 36 (S.B.822), § 1; Stats.2008, c. 23 (A.B.164), § 1; Stats.2011, c. 381 (S.B.146), § 15.)*

Research References

Rutter, Cal. Practice Guide: Civ. Pro. Before Trial Ch. 8C-3, "Not Privileged".

5 Witkin, California Summary 10th Torts § 155, Proceedings of Professional Society or Committee.
5 Witkin, California Summary 10th Torts § 581, Scope of Privilege.
5 Witkin, California Summary 10th Torts § 594, in General.

§ 43.9. Immunity from liability; health care providers; unsolicited referrals from tests by multiphasic screening unit; notice

(a) There shall be no liability on the part of, and no cause of action shall accrue against, any health care provider for professional negligence on account of the receipt by such provider of an unsolicited referral, arising from a test performed by a multiphasic screening unit, for any act or omission, including the failure to examine, treat, or refer for examination or treatment any person concerning whom an unsolicited referral has been received. The immunity from liability granted by this subdivision shall only apply where a health provider meets the obligations established in subdivision (c).

(b) Every multiphasic screening unit shall notify each person it tests that the person should contact the health provider to whom the test results are sent within 10 days and that the health provider may not be obligated to interpret the results or provide further care. The multiphasic screening unit shall include the words "PATIENT TEST RESULTS" on the envelope of any test results sent to a health care provider, and shall include the address of the person tested in the test result material sent to the health care provider.

Nothing contained in this section shall relieve any health care provider from liability, if any, when at the time of receipt of the unsolicited referral there exists a provider-patient relationship, or a contract for health care services, or following receipt of such unsolicited referral there is established or reestablished a provider-patient relationship.

(c) A health care provider who receives unsolicited test results from a multiphasic screening unit shall receive immunity from liability pursuant to subdivision (a) only if the provider who receives such test results and does not wish to evaluate them, or evaluates them and takes no further action, either notifies the multiphasic screening unit of that fact or returns the test results within 21 days. If the health care provider reviews the test results and determines that they indicate a substantial risk of serious illness or death the provider shall make a reasonable effort to notify the person tested of the presumptive finding within 14 days after the provider has received the test results.

(d) For the purposes of this section:

(1) "Health care provider" means any person licensed or certified pursuant to Division 2 (commencing with Section 500) of the Business and Professions Code, or licensed pursuant to the Osteopathic Initiative Act or the Chiropractic Initiative Act, or licensed pursuant to Chapter 2.5 (commencing with Section 1440) of Division 2 of the Health and Safety Code, and any clinic, health dispensary, or health facility licensed pursuant to Division 2 (commencing with Section 1200) of the Health and Safety Code. "Health care provider" also includes the legal representatives of a health care provider.

(2) "Professional negligence" means an action for personal injury or wrongful death proximately caused by a health care provider's negligent act or omission to act in the rendering of professional services, provided that such services are within the scope of services for which the health care provider is licensed and are not within any restriction imposed by the licensing agency or any licensed hospital.

(3) "Unsolicited referral" means any written report regarding the health, physical or mental condition of any person which was forwarded or delivered to a health care provider without prior request by such provider.

(4) A "multiphasic screening unit" means a facility which does not prescribe or treat patients but performs diagnostic testing only. *(Added by Stats.1978, c. 1296, p. 4249, § 1. Amended by Stats.1980, c. 676, § 38.)*

Research References

5 Witkin, California Summary 10th Torts § 156, Referrals of Patients or Clients.

§ 43.91. Immunity from liability; members of professional society of persons licensed under the Real Estate Law; peer review committees

(a) There shall be no monetary liability on the part of, and no cause of action shall arise against, any member of a duly appointed committee of a professional society which comprises a substantial percentage of the persons licensed pursuant to Part 1 (commencing with Section 10000) of Division 4 of the Business and Professions Code and situated in the geographic area served by the particular society, for any act or proceeding undertaken or performed within the scope of the functions of any such committee which is formed to maintain the professional standards of the society established by its bylaws, if such member acts without malice, has made a reasonable effort to obtain the facts of the matter as to which he acts, and acts in reasonable belief that the action taken by him is warranted by the facts known to him after such reasonable effort to obtain facts.

(b) There shall be no monetary liability on the part of, and no cause of action for damages shall arise against, any person on account of the communication of information in the possession of such person to any committee specified in subdivision (a) when such communication is intended to aid in the evaluation of the qualifications, fitness or character of a member or applicant for membership in any such professional society, and does not represent as true any matter not reasonably believed to be true.

(c) The immunities afforded by this section shall not affect the availability of any absolute privilege which may be afforded by Section 47.

(d) This section shall not be construed to confer immunity from liability on any professional society. In any case in which, but for the enactment of this section, a cause of action would arise against a professional society, such cause of action shall exist as if this section had not been enacted. *(Added by Stats.1980, c. 492, § 1.)*

Research References

5 Witkin, California Summary 10th Torts § 155, Proceedings of Professional Society or Committee.

§ 43.92. Psychotherapists; duty to protect from violent behavior of patient; immunity from monetary liability; interpretation of section

(a) There shall be no monetary liability on the part of, and no cause of action shall arise against, any person who is a psychotherapist as defined in Section 1010 of the Evidence Code in failing to protect from a patient's threatened violent behavior or failing to predict and protect from a patient's violent behavior except if the patient has communicated to the psychotherapist a serious threat of physical violence against a reasonably identifiable victim or victims.

(b) There shall be no monetary liability on the part of, and no cause of action shall arise against, a psychotherapist who, under the limited circumstances specified in subdivision (a), discharges his or her duty to protect by making reasonable efforts to communicate the threat to the victim or victims and to a law enforcement agency.

(c) It is the intent of the Legislature that the amendments made by the act [1] adding this subdivision only change the name

of the duty referenced in this section from a duty to warn and protect to a duty to protect. Nothing in this section shall be construed to be a substantive change, and any duty of a psychotherapist shall not be modified as a result of changing the wording in this section.

(d) It is the intent of the Legislature that a court interpret this section, as amended by the act [1] adding this subdivision, in a manner consistent with the interpretation of this section as it read prior to January 1, 2013. *(Added by Stats.1985, c. 737, § 1. Amended by Stats.2006, c. 136 (A.B.733), § 1; Stats.2012, c. 149 (S.B.1134), § 1.)*

  [1] Stats.2012, c. 149 (S.B.1134).

Research References

Rutter, Cal. Practice Guide: Civil Trials & Evidence Ch. 8C-H, H. Opinion Evidence.
Rutter, Cal. Practice Guide: Civil Trials & Evidence Ch. 8E-A, A. Privileges.
Rutter, Cal. Practice Guide: Personal Injury Ch. 3-F, F. MICRA Provisions Affecting Damages.
11 Witkin, California Summary 10th Husband and Wife § 10A, (New)-Ex Parte Communications With Mediator or Evaluator.
6 Witkin, California Summary 10th Torts § 1051, Statutory Limitation.

§ 43.93. Psychotherapists; patient's cause of action for sexual contact; definitions

(a) For the purposes of this section the following definitions are applicable:

(1) "Psychotherapy" means the professional treatment, assessment, or counseling of a mental or emotional illness, symptom, or condition.

(2) "Psychotherapist" means a physician and surgeon specializing in the practice of psychiatry, a psychologist, a psychological assistant, a marriage and family therapist, a registered marriage and family therapist intern or trainee, an educational psychologist, an associate clinical social worker, a licensed clinical social worker, a professional clinical counselor, or a registered clinical counselor intern or trainee.

(3) "Sexual contact" means the touching of an intimate part of another person. "Intimate part" and "touching" have the same meanings as defined in subdivisions (f) and (d), respectively, of Section 243.4 of the Penal Code. For the purposes of this section, sexual contact includes sexual intercourse, sodomy, and oral copulation.

(4) "Therapeutic relationship" exists during the time the patient or client is rendered professional service by the psychotherapist.

(5) "Therapeutic deception" means a representation by a psychotherapist that sexual contact with the psychotherapist is consistent with or part of the patient's or former patient's treatment.

(b) A cause of action against a psychotherapist for sexual contact exists for a patient or former patient for injury caused by sexual contact with the psychotherapist, if the sexual contact occurred under any of the following conditions:

(1) During the period the patient was receiving psychotherapy from the psychotherapist.

(2) Within two years following termination of therapy.

(3) By means of therapeutic deception.

(c) The patient or former patient may recover damages from a psychotherapist who is found liable for sexual contact. It is not a defense to the action that sexual contact with a patient occurred outside a therapy or treatment session or that it occurred off the premises regularly used by the psychotherapist for therapy or treatment sessions. No cause of action shall exist between spouses within a marriage.

(d) In an action for sexual contact, evidence of the plaintiff's sexual history is not subject to discovery and is not admissible as evidence except in either of the following situations:

(1) The plaintiff claims damage to sexual functioning.

(2) The defendant requests a hearing prior to conducting discovery and makes an offer of proof of the relevancy of the history, and the court finds that the history is relevant and the probative value of the history outweighs its prejudicial effect.

The court shall allow the discovery or introduction as evidence only of specific information or examples of the plaintiff's conduct that are determined by the court to be relevant. The court's order shall detail the information or conduct that is subject to discovery. *(Added by Stats.1987, c. 1474, § 1. Amended by Stats.1992, c. 890 (S.B.1394), § 5; Stats.1993, c. 589 (A.B.2211), § 19; Stats.2002, c. 1013 (S.B.2026), § 73; Stats.2011, c. 381 (S.B.146), § 16.)*

Research References

Rutter, Cal. Practice Guide: Civ. Pro. Before Trial Ch. 8B-1, Leave of Court Generally Not Required.
Rutter, Cal. Practice Guide: Personal Injury Ch. 3-F, F. MICRA Provisions Affecting Damages.
Rutter, Cal. Practice Guide: Personal Injury Ch. 6-A, A. Scope of Discovery and Limitations.
Rutter, Cal. Practice Guide: Personal Injury Ch. 9-F, F. Examination of Witnesses.
5 Witkin, California Summary 10th Torts § 382, Statutory Actions.
5 Witkin, California Summary 10th Torts § 416, Consent Fraudulently Obtained.
6 Witkin, California Summary 10th Torts § 1046, in General.

§ 43.95. Immunity of professional society for referral services or telephone information library; duty to disclose disciplinary actions

(a) There shall be no monetary liability on the part of, and no cause of action for damages shall arise against, any professional society or any nonprofit corporation authorized by a professional society to operate a referral service, or their agents, employees, or members, for referring any member of the public to any professional member of the society or service, or for acts of negligence or conduct constituting unprofessional conduct committed by a professional to whom a member of the public was referred, so long as any of the foregoing persons or entities has acted without malice, and the referral was made at no cost added to the initial referral fee as part of a public service referral system organized under the auspices of the professional society. Further, there shall be no monetary liability on the part of, and no cause of action for damages shall arise against, any professional society for providing a telephone information library available for use by the general public without charge, nor against any nonprofit corporation authorized by a professional society for providing a telephone information library available for use by the general public without charge. "Professional society" includes legal, psychological, architectural, medical, dental, dietetic, accounting, optometric, podiatric, pharmaceutic, chiropractic, veterinary, licensed marriage and family therapy, licensed clinical social work, professional clinical counselor, and engineering organizations having as members at least 25 percent of the eligible persons or licentiates in the geographic area served by the particular society. However, if the society has less than 100 members, it shall have as members at least a majority of the eligible persons or licentiates in the geographic area served by the particular society. " Professional society" also includes organizations with referral services that have been authorized by the State Bar of California and operated in accordance with its Minimum Standards for a Lawyer Referral Service in California,

and organizations that have been established to provide free assistance or representation to needy patients or clients.

(b) This section shall not apply whenever the professional society, while making a referral to a professional member of the society, fails to disclose the nature of any disciplinary action of which it has actual knowledge taken by a state licensing agency against that professional member. However, there shall be no duty to disclose a disciplinary action in either of the following cases:

(1) Where a disciplinary proceeding results in no disciplinary action being taken against the professional to whom a member of the public was referred.

(2) Where a period of three years has elapsed since the professional to whom a member of the public was referred has satisfied any terms, conditions, or sanctions imposed upon the professional as disciplinary action; except that if the professional is an attorney, there shall be no time limit on the duty to disclose. *(Added by Stats.1987, c. 727, § 4, operative July 1, 1993. Amended by Stats.1988, c. 312, § 2, operative July 1, 1993; Stats.2002, c. 1013 (S.B.2026), § 74; Stats.2011, c. 381 (S.B.146), § 17.)*

Research References

1 Witkin Cal. Proc. 5th Attorneys § 11, in General.
5 Witkin, California Summary 10th Torts § 156, Referrals of Patients or Clients.

§ 43.96. Information to be provided to a complainant; immunity

(a) Any medical or podiatric society, health facility licensed or certified under Division 2 (commencing with Section 1200) of the Health and Safety Code, state agency as defined in Section 11000 of the Government Code, or local government agency that receives written complaints related to the professional competence or professional conduct of a physician and surgeon or doctor of podiatric medicine from the public shall inform the complainant that the Medical Board of California or the California Board of Podiatric Medicine, as the case may be, is the only authority in the state that may take disciplinary action against the license of the named licensee, and shall provide to the complainant the address and toll-free telephone number of the applicable state board.

(b) The immunity provided in Section 2318 of the Business and Professions Code and in Section 47 shall apply to complaints and information made or provided to a board pursuant to this section. *(Added by Stats.1993, c. 1267 (S.B.916), § 48. Amended by Stats.1994, c. 1206 (S.B.1775), § 26; Stats.1995, c. 708 (S.B.609), § 12.)*

Research References

5 Witkin, California Summary 10th Torts § 155, Proceedings of Professional Society or Committee.

§ 43.97. Medical staff or membership privilege denial or restriction; immunity from liability; unreported or intentional injury exceptions

There shall be no monetary liability on the part of, and no cause of action for damages, other than economic or pecuniary damages, shall arise against, a hospital for any action taken upon the recommendation of its medical staff, or against any other person or organization for any action taken, or restriction imposed, which is required to be reported pursuant to Section 805 of the Business and Professions Code, if that action or restriction is reported in accordance with Section 805 of the Business and Professions Code. This section shall not apply to an action knowingly and intentionally taken for the purpose of injuring a person affected by the action or infringing upon a person's rights. *(Added by Stats.1981, c. 926, § 1. Amended by Stats.1986, c. 1274, § 5; Stats.2006, c. 538 (S.B.1852), § 36.)*

§ 43.98. Communications by consultants to Director of Department of Managed Health Care; health care services; monetary liability

(a) There shall be no monetary liability on the part of, and no cause of action shall arise against, any consultant on account of any communication by that consultant to the Director of the Department of Managed Health Care or any other officer, employee, agent, contractor, or consultant of the Department of Managed Health Care, when that communication is for the purpose of determining whether health care services have been or are being arranged or provided in accordance with the Knox–Keene Health Care Service Plan Act of 1975 (Chapter 2.2 (commencing with Section 1340) of Division 2 of the Health and Safety Code) and any regulation adopted thereunder and the consultant does all of the following:

(1) Acts without malice.

(2) Makes a reasonable effort to obtain the facts of the matter communicated.

(3) Acts with a reasonable belief that the communication is warranted by the facts actually known to the consultant after a reasonable effort to obtain the facts.

(4) Acts pursuant to a contract entered into on or after January 1, 1998, between the Commissioner of Corporations and a state licensing board or committee, including, but not limited to, the Medical Board of California, or pursuant to a contract entered into on or after January 1, 1998, with the Commissioner of Corporations pursuant to Section 1397.6 of the Health and Safety Code.

(5) Acts pursuant to a contract entered into on or after July 1, 2000, between the Director of the Department of Managed Health Care and a state licensing board or committee, including, but not limited to, the Medical Board of California, or pursuant to a contract entered into on or after July 1, 1999, with the Director of the Department of Managed Health Care pursuant to Section 1397.6 of the Health and Safety Code.

(b) The immunities afforded by this section shall not affect the availability of any other privilege or immunity which may be afforded under this part. Nothing in this section shall be construed to alter the laws regarding the confidentiality of medical records. *(Added by Stats.1997, c. 139 (A.B.564), § 1. Amended by Stats.1999, c. 525 (A.B.78), § 4; Stats.2000, c. 857 (A.B.2903), § 3.)*

Research References

Rutter, Cal. Practice Guide: Insurance Litigation Ch. 6E–D, D. Managed Care Plans.
5 Witkin, California Summary 10th Torts § 152, Reports Respecting Health Care Plans and Facilities.

§ 43.99. Immunity from monetary liability; building and other inspectors; independent quality review of plans, specifications or work on residential buildings under the State Housing Law; exceptions

(a) There shall be no monetary liability on the part of, and no cause of action for damages shall arise against, any person or other legal entity that is under contract with an applicant for a residential building permit to provide independent quality review of the plans and specifications provided with the application in order to determine compliance with all applicable requirements imposed pursuant to the State Housing Law (Part 1.5 (commencing with Section 17910) of Division 13 of the Health and Safety Code), or any rules or regulations adopted pursuant to that law, or under contract with that applicant to provide independent quality review of the work of improvement to determine compliance with these plans and specifications, if the person or other legal entity meets the requirements of this section and one of the following applies:

(1) The person, or a person employed by any other legal entity, performing the work as described in this subdivision, has completed not less than five years of verifiable experience in the appropriate field and has obtained certification as a building inspector, combination inspector, or combination dwelling inspector from the International Conference of Building Officials (ICBO) and has successfully passed the technical written examination promulgated by ICBO for those certification categories.

(2) The person, or a person employed by any other legal entity, performing the work as described in this subdivision, has completed not less than five years of verifiable experience in the appropriate field and is a registered professional engineer, licensed general contractor, or a licensed architect rendering independent quality review of the work of improvement or plan examination services within the scope of his or her registration or licensure.

(3) The immunity provided under this section does not apply to any action initiated by the applicant who retained the qualified person.

(4) A "qualified person" for purposes of this section means a person holding a valid certification as one of those inspectors.

(b) Except for qualified persons, this section shall not relieve from, excuse, or lessen in any manner, the responsibility or liability of any person, company, contractor, builder, developer, architect, engineer, designer, or other individual or entity who develops, improves, owns, operates, or manages any residential building for any damages to persons or property caused by construction or design defects. The fact that an inspection by a qualified person has taken place may not be introduced as evidence in a construction defect action, including any reports or other items generated by the qualified person. This subdivision shall not apply in any action initiated by the applicant who retained the qualified person.

(c) Nothing in this section, as it relates to construction inspectors or plans examiners, shall be construed to alter the requirements for licensure, or the jurisdiction, authority, or scope of practice, of architects pursuant to Chapter 3 (commencing with Section 5500) of Division 3 of the Business and Professions Code, professional engineers pursuant to Chapter 7 (commencing with Section 6700) of Division 3 of the Business and Professions Code, or general contractors pursuant to Chapter 9 (commencing with Section 7000) of Division 3 of the Business and Professions Code.

(d) Nothing in this section shall be construed to alter the immunity of employees of the Department of Housing and Community Development under the Government Claims Act (Division 3.6 (commencing with Section 810) of Title 1 of the Government Code) when acting pursuant to Section 17965 of the Health and Safety Code.

(e) The qualifying person shall engage in no other construction, design, planning, supervision, or activities of any kind on the work of improvement, nor provide quality review services for any other party on the work of improvement.

(f) The qualifying person, or other legal entity, shall maintain professional errors and omissions insurance coverage in an amount not less than two million dollars ($2,000,000).

(g) The immunity provided by subdivision (a) does not inure to the benefit of the qualified person for damages caused to the applicant solely by the negligence or willful misconduct of the qualified person resulting from the provision of services under the contract with the applicant. *(Added by Stats.2002, c. 722 (S.B.800), § 2. Amended by Stats.2012, c. 759 (A.B.2690), § 1.)*

Subdivision (d) of Section 43.99 is amended to more accurately refer to the content of Division 3.6 (commencing with Section 810) of Title 1 of the Government Code. See City of Stockton v. Superior Court, 42 Cal. 4th 730, 734, 741–42, 171 P.3d 20, 68 Cal. Rptr. 3d 295 (2007); see also Gov't Code § 810 (stating that Division 3.6 of Title 1 of the Government Code may be referred to as "Government Claims Act"). [41 Cal.L.Rev.Comm. Reports 285 (2011)].

Research References
Miller and Starr California Real Estate § 29:2, Statutory Liability Under "SB800" for Residential Units Sold New After January 1, 2003.
Miller and Starr California Real Estate § 29:46, Independent Inspector's Immunities.
13 NO. 3 Miller & Starr, California Real Estate Newsalert 1, Change to Spare: The New California Construction Warranty and Defects Law Under SB 800.
5 Witkin, California Summary 10th Torts § 160, Independent Quality Review for Residential Construction.
6 Witkin, California Summary 10th Torts § 1163, (S 1163) Scope of Legislation.

§ 44. Defamation

Defamation is effected by either of the following:

(a) Libel.

(b) Slander. *(Enacted in 1872. Amended by Stats.1980, c. 676, § 39.)*

Research References
California Practice Guide: Employment Litigation Ch. 5-D, D. Defamation.
Rutter, Cal. Practice Guide: Enforcing Judgments/Debts Ch. 2-C, C. Tort Liability.
5 Witkin, California Summary 10th Torts § 529, Nature of Tort.

§ 45. Libel

LIBEL, WHAT. Libel is a false and unprivileged publication by writing, printing, picture, effigy, or other fixed representation to the eye, which exposes any person to hatred, contempt, ridicule, or obloquy, or which causes him to be shunned or avoided, or which has a tendency to injure him in his occupation. *(Enacted in 1872.)*

Research References
Rutter, Cal. Practice Guide: Civil Appeals & Writs Form 7:D, Petition for Writ of Supersedeas or Other Stay Order.
Rutter, Cal. Practice Guide: Civil Trials & Evidence Ch. 17-E, E. Attorney Fees as Costs.
Rutter, Cal. Practice Guide: Civil Trials & Evidence Ch. 8D-B, B. Hearsay vs. Nonhearsay.
California Practice Guide: Employment Litigation Ch. 5-D, D. Defamation.
Rutter, Cal. Practice Guide: Enforcing Judgments/Debts Ch. 2-C, C. Tort Liability.
5 Witkin Cal. Proc. 5th Pleading § 738, (S 738) Pleading of Falsity is Not Required.
5 Witkin, California Summary 10th Torts § 529, Nature of Tort.
5 Witkin, California Summary 10th Torts § 530, Libel and Slander Distinguished.
5 Witkin, California Summary 10th Torts § 539, Statutory Definition.
5 Witkin, California Summary 10th Torts § 542, Charges of Criminal Conduct.
5 Witkin, California Summary 10th Torts § 551, (S 551) Statutory Definition.
5 Witkin, California Summary 10th Torts § 675, Special Damages Requirement.

§ 45a. Libel on its face; other actionable defamatory language

A libel which is defamatory of the plaintiff without the necessity of explanatory matter, such as an inducement, innuendo or other extrinsic fact, is said to be a libel on its face. Defamatory language not libelous on its face is not actionable unless the plaintiff alleges and proves that he has suffered special damage as a proximate result thereof. Special damage is defined in Section 48a of this code. *(Added by Stats.1945, c. 1489, p. 2762, § 1.)*

Research References
Rutter, Cal. Practice Guide: Civil Appeals & Writs Form 7:D, Petition for Writ of Supersedeas or Other Stay Order.
Rutter, Cal. Practice Guide: Enforcing Judgments/Debts Ch. 2-C, C. Tort Liability.
5 Witkin Cal. Proc. 5th Pleading § 735, (S 735) Elements of Cause of Action.
5 Witkin, California Summary 10th Torts § 541, California Doctrine of Libel Per Se.
5 Witkin, California Summary 10th Torts § 675, Special Damages Requirement.

§ 46. Slander, false and unprivileged publications which constitute

Slander is a false and unprivileged publication, orally uttered, and also communications by radio or any mechanical or other means which:

1. Charges any person with crime, or with having been indicted, convicted, or punished for crime;

2. Imputes in him the present existence of an infectious, contagious, or loathsome disease;

3. Tends directly to injure him in respect to his office, profession, trade or business, either by imputing to him general disqualification in those respects which the office or other occupation peculiarly requires, or by imputing something with reference to his office, profession, trade, or business that has a natural tendency to lessen its profits;

4. Imputes to him impotence or a want of chastity; or

5. Which, by natural consequence, causes actual damage. *(Enacted in 1872. Amended by Stats.1945, c. 1489, p. 2762, § 2.)*

Research References
Rutter, Cal. Practice Guide: Civil Appeals & Writs Form 7:D, Petition for Writ of Supersedeas or Other Stay Order.
Rutter, Cal. Practice Guide: Civil Trials & Evidence Ch. 17-E, E. Attorney Fees as Costs.
Rutter, Cal. Practice Guide: Civil Trials & Evidence Ch. 8D-B, B. Hearsay vs. Nonhearsay.
California Practice Guide: Employment Litigation Ch. 5-D, D. Defamation.
Rutter, Cal. Practice Guide: Enforcing Judgments/Debts Ch. 2-C, C. Tort Liability.
5 Witkin Cal. Proc. 5th Pleading § 738, (S 738) Pleading of Falsity is Not Required.
5 Witkin, California Summary 10th Torts § 529, Nature of Tort.
5 Witkin, California Summary 10th Torts § 530, Libel and Slander Distinguished.
5 Witkin, California Summary 10th Torts § 551, (S 551) Statutory Definition.
5 Witkin, California Summary 10th Torts § 552, (S 552) Slander Per Se.
5 Witkin, California Summary 10th Torts § 553, (S 553) Injury to Business or Professional Reputation.

§ 47. Privileged publication or broadcast

A privileged publication or broadcast is one made:

(a) In the proper discharge of an official duty.

(b) In any (1) legislative proceeding, (2) judicial proceeding, (3) in any other official proceeding authorized by law, or (4) in the initiation or course of any other proceeding authorized by law and reviewable pursuant to Chapter 2 (commencing with Section 1084) of Title 1 of Part 3 of the Code of Civil Procedure, except as follows:

(1) An allegation or averment contained in any pleading or affidavit filed in an action for marital dissolution or legal

separation made of or concerning a person by or against whom no affirmative relief is prayed in the action shall not be a privileged publication or broadcast as to the person making the allegation or averment within the meaning of this section unless the pleading is verified or affidavit sworn to, and is made without malice, by one having reasonable and probable cause for believing the truth of the allegation or averment and unless the allegation or averment is material and relevant to the issues in the action.

(2) This subdivision does not make privileged any communication made in furtherance of an act of intentional destruction or alteration of physical evidence undertaken for the purpose of depriving a party to litigation of the use of that evidence, whether or not the content of the communication is the subject of a subsequent publication or broadcast which is privileged pursuant to this section. As used in this paragraph, "physical evidence" means evidence specified in Section 250 of the Evidence Code or evidence that is property of any type specified in Chapter 14 (commencing with Section 2031.010) of Title 4 of Part 4 of the Code of Civil Procedure.

(3) This subdivision does not make privileged any communication made in a judicial proceeding knowingly concealing the existence of an insurance policy or policies.

(4) A recorded lis pendens is not a privileged publication unless it identifies an action previously filed with a court of competent jurisdiction which affects the title or right of possession of real property, as authorized or required by law.

(c) In a communication, without malice, to a person interested therein, (1) by one who is also interested, or (2) by one who stands in such a relation to the person interested as to afford a reasonable ground for supposing the motive for the communication to be innocent, or (3) who is requested by the person interested to give the information. This subdivision applies to and includes a communication concerning the job performance or qualifications of an applicant for employment, based upon credible evidence, made without malice, by a current or former employer of the applicant to, and upon request of, one whom the employer reasonably believes is a prospective employer of the applicant. This subdivision authorizes a current or former employer, or the employer's agent, to answer whether or not the employer would rehire a current or former employee. This subdivision shall not apply to a communication concerning the speech or activities of an applicant for employment if the speech or activities are constitutionally protected, or otherwise protected by Section 527.3 of the Code of Civil Procedure or any other provision of law.

(d)(1) By a fair and true report in, or a communication to, a public journal, of (A) a judicial, (B) legislative, or (C) other public official proceeding, or (D) of anything said in the course thereof, or (E) of a verified charge or complaint made by any person to a public official, upon which complaint a warrant has been issued.

(2) Nothing in paragraph (1) shall make privileged any communication to a public journal that does any of the following:

(A) Violates Rule 5–120 of the State Bar Rules of Professional Conduct.

(B) Breaches a court order.

(C) Violates any requirement of confidentiality imposed by law.

(e) By a fair and true report of (1) the proceedings of a public meeting, if the meeting was lawfully convened for a lawful purpose and open to the public, or (2) the publication of the matter complained of was for the public benefit. *(Enacted in 1872. Amended by Code Am.1873–74, c. 612, p. 184, § 11; Stats.1895, c. 163, p. 167, § 1; Stats.1927, c. 866, p. 1881, § 1;*

Stats.1945, c. 1489, p. 2763, § 3; Stats.1979, c. 184, p. 403, § 1; Stats.1990, c. 1491 (A.B.3765), § 1; Stats.1991, c. 432 (A.B.529), § 1; Stats.1992, c. 615 (S.B.1804), § 1; Stats.1994, c. 364 (A.B.2778), § 1; Stats.1994, c. 700 (S.B.1457), § 2.5; Stats.1996, c. 1055 (S.B.1540), § 2; Stats.2002, c. 1029 (A.B.2868), § 1, eff. Sept. 28, 2002; Stats.2004, c. 182 (A.B.3081), § 4, operative July 1, 2005.)

Law Revision Commission Comments

Subdivision (b) of Section 47 is amended to reflect nonsubstantive reorganization of the rules governing civil discovery. [33 Cal.L.Rev. Comm. Reports 977 (2004)].

Research References

Rutter, Cal. Practice Guide: A.D.R. Ch. 2-E, E. Conducting Negotiations.

Rutter, Cal. Practice Guide: A.D.R. Ch. 5-H, H. Conduct of Arbitration Proceedings.

Rutter, Cal. Practice Guide: Civ. Pro. Before Trial Ch. 1-C, C. Prelawsuit Notices, Claims and Demands.

Rutter, Cal. Practice Guide: Civ. Pro. Before Trial Ch. 4-F, F. Procedures for Challenging Service of Summons.

Rutter, Cal. Practice Guide: Civ. Pro. Before Trial Ch. 8E-6, Subpoena to Nonparty Deponent or Business Records Custodian.

Rutter, Cal. Practice Guide: Civ. Pro. Before Trial Ch. 7(II)-D, D. Activities Protected by Anti-SLAPP Statute.

Rutter, Cal. Practice Guide: Civ. Pro. Before Trial Ch. 7(II)-F, F. Procedure.

Rutter, Cal. Practice Guide: Civ. Pro. Before Trial Ch. 12(II)-H, H. Professional Responsibility Considerations Re Settlements.

Rutter, Cal. Practice Guide: Civil Trials & Evidence Ch. 1-O, O. Addressing the Media.

Rutter, Cal. Practice Guide: Civil Trials & Evidence Ch. 8E-A, A. Privileges.

California Practice Guide: Employment Litigation Ch. 5-D, D. Defamation.

California Practice Guide: Employment Litigation Ch. 5-K, K. Invasion of Privacy.

California Practice Guide: Employment Litigation Ch. 5-L, L. Other Statutory Claims.

California Practice Guide: Employment Litigation Ch. 5-M, M. Liability of Supervisors or Coworkers Individually.

California Practice Guide: Employment Litigation Ch. 10-E, E. Harasser's Individual Liability.

California Practice Guide: Employment Litigation Ch. 18-C, C. Contractual Arbitration.

Rutter, Cal. Practice Guide: Enforcing Judgments/Debts Ch. 2-B, B. Statutory Liability and Procedures.

Rutter, Cal. Practice Guide: Enforcing Judgments/Debts Ch. 2-C, C. Tort Liability.

Rutter, Cal. Practice Guide: Enforcing Judgments/Debts Ch. 4-A, A. Attachment.

Rutter, Cal. Practice Guide: Family Law Ch. 6-A, A. Child Support.

Rutter, Cal. Practice Guide: Family Law Ch. 7-B, B. Contested Custody Proceedings, Generally.

Rutter, Cal. Practice Guide: Insurance Litigation Ch. 11-C, C. Fraud.

Rutter, Cal. Practice Guide: Insurance Litigation Ch. 11-J, J. Other Torts Not Necessarily Related to Insurer "Bad Faith".

Rutter, Cal. Practice Guide: Insurance Litigation Ch. 15-A, A. Actions Against Insurers.

Rutter, Cal. Practice Guide: Insurance Litigation Ch. 12A-E, E. Persons Who May be Sued for Tortious Breach of Implied Covenant (Proper Defendants).

Rutter, Cal. Practice Guide: Insurance Litigation Ch. 12C-D, D. Application-Matters Held "Unreasonable".

Rutter, Cal. Practice Guide: Insurance Litigation Ch. 12D-L, L. Statutory Privileges.

Rutter, Cal. Practice Guide: Insurance Litigation Ch. 12D-L, Outline L.

Rutter, Cal. Practice Guide: Personal Injury Ch. 3-C, C. Specific Items of Compensatory Damages.

Rutter, Cal. Practice Guide: Personal Injury Ch. 4-C, C. Effective Settlement Negotiations.

Rutter, Cal. Practice Guide: Personal Injury Ch. 4-G, G. Concluding and Enforcing Settlement.

Rutter, Cal. Practice Guide: Personal Injury Ch. 6-A, A. Scope of Discovery and Limitations.

Rutter, Cal. Practice Guide: Personal Injury Ch. 6-B, B. Overview of Selected Discovery Procedures.

Rutter, Cal. Practice Guide: Personal Injury Ch. 6-A, Outline a.

Rutter, Cal. Practice Guide: Personal Injury Gen. Matls., Highlights.

Rutter, Cal. Practice Guide: Real Prop. Transactions Ch. 6-I, I. Real Property Foreclosures and Antideficiency Laws.

Rutter, Cal. Practice Guide: Real Prop. Transactions Ch. 11-I, I. Lis Pendens.

Rutter, Cal. Practice Guide: Real Prop. Transactions Gen. Matls., Highlights.

Rutter, Cal. Practice Guide: Prof. Responsibility Ch. 2-D, D. In-Person Solicitation for Profit.

Rutter, Cal. Practice Guide: Prof. Responsibility Ch. 2-J, J. Other Statutes Regulating Lawyer Advertising and Solicitation.

Rutter, Cal. Practice Guide: Prof. Responsibility Ch. 5-K, K. Fee Recovery/Enforcing Fee Agreements.

Rutter, Cal. Practice Guide: Prof. Responsibility Ch. 6-D, D. Professional Liability.

Rutter, Cal. Practice Guide: Prof. Responsibility Ch. 8-D, D. Restrictions on Speech and Behavior Outside Courtroom.

Rutter, Cal. Practice Guide: Prof. Responsibility Ch. 11-E, E. Receiving Complaints of Attorney Misconduct.

Rutter, Cal. Practice Guide: Prof. Responsibility Ch. 8-D, Outline D.

Miller and Starr California Real Estate § 11:6, Instruments Subject to Recording--List of Recordable Documents.

Miller and Starr California Real Estate § 4:41, Disciplinary Process--Complaint, Investigation and Accusation.

Miller and Starr California Real Estate § 11:46, Privileged Publication.

Miller and Starr California Real Estate § 11:48, Pecuniary Loss.

Miller and Starr California Real Estate § 11:65, Recorded Documents that Do Not Give Constructive Notice--Documents Not Specifically Stated to Impart Constructive Notice by Statute or Which Are Specifically Stated Not to Impart Constructive...

Miller and Starr California Real Estate § 29:48, Home Inspector's Duties.

Miller and Starr California Real Estate § 29:76, Systems for Resolving Defective Construction Disputes.

Miller and Starr California Real Estate § 35:50, Defenses to Petition to Compel Arbitration--In General.

Miller and Starr California Real Estate § 7:224, Liability of Insurer for Erroneously Including an Invalid Exception.

Miller and Starr California Real Estate § 7:225, Contract Liability to Third Persons on the Policy.

Miller and Starr California Real Estate § 10:185, Recording and Mailing.

Miller and Starr California Real Estate § 10:199, Publication, Mailing, and Recording the Notice.

Miller and Starr California Real Estate § 11:148, Nature and Effect of a Lis Pendens.

Miller and Starr California Real Estate § 11:149, Procedural and Formal Requirements for a Lis Pendens.

Miller and Starr California Real Estate § 11:150, Actions in Which a Lis Pendens May or Must be Recorded.

Miller and Starr California Real Estate § 11:153, Expungement of a Lis Pendens--Policy.

Miller and Starr California Real Estate § 19:188, Notice Required by Statute.

Miller and Starr California Real Estate § 19:241, Anti-SLAPP Lawsuits in the Context of Landlord-Tenant Disputes.

Miller and Starr California Real Estate § 25A:15, Procedures for Preparing an Environmental Impact Report.

Miller and Starr California Real Estate § 25B:93, Foreclosure of Lien by Sale; Redemption Rights.

Miller and Starr California Real Estate § 34:146, "Anti-SLAPP" Litigation.

14 NO. 1 Miller & Starr, California Real Estate Newsalert 13, Recording and Priorities.

15 NO. 2 Miller & Starr, California Real Estate Newsalert 1, SLAPP Happy: An Analysis of California's Anti-SLAPP (Strategic Lawsuits Against Public Participation) Statute.

15 NO. 3 Miller & Starr, California Real Estate Newsalert 11, Landlord and Tenant.

15 NO. 5 Miller & Starr, California Real Estate Newsalert 12, Landlord and Tenant.

18 NO. 5 Miller & Starr, California Real Estate Newsalert 17, Landlord and Tenant.

18 NO. 3 Miller & Starr, California Real Estate Newsalert 18, Landlord and Tenant.

18 NO. 2 Miller & Starr, California Real Estate Newsalert 19, Landlord and Tenant.

18 NO. 4 Miller & Starr, California Real Estate Newsalert 26, CEQA.

19 NO. 2 Miller & Starr, California Real Estate Newsalert 1, Anti-SLAPP Motions in Real Estate Litigation: an Update.

19 NO. 6 Miller & Starr, California Real Estate Newsalert 3, Alternative Dispute Resolution.

19 NO. 3 Miller & Starr, California Real Estate Newsalert 24, Remedies.

19 NO. 4 Miller & Starr, California Real Estate Newsalert 34, Deeds of Trust.

20 NO. 1 Miller & Starr, California Real Estate Newsalert 16, Landlord and Tenant.

20 NO. 5 Miller & Starr, California Real Estate Newsalert 16, Judicial Remedies.

20 NO. 5 Miller & Starr, California Real Estate Newsalert 17, Landlord and Tenant.

20 NO. 4 Miller & Starr, California Real Estate Newsalert 40, Recording and Priorities.

22 NO. 3 Miller & Starr, California Real Estate Newsalert 19, Recording and Priorities.

3 Witkin Cal. Proc. 5th Actions § 371, (S 371) Nature and Purpose.

3 Witkin Cal. Proc. 5th Actions § 557, (S 557) Conspiracy: Postponed Accrual.

1 Witkin Cal. Proc. 5th Attorneys § 571, in General.

7 Witkin Cal. Proc. 5th Judgment § 197, (S 197) in General.

5 Witkin Cal. Proc. 5th Pleading § 1019, (S 1019) in General.

5 Witkin Cal. Proc. 5th Pleading § 1022, in General.

5 Witkin Cal. Proc. 5th Pleading § 1023, Illustrations.

5 Witkin Cal. Proc. 5th Pleading § 1030, (S 1030) Illegal Speech.

5 Witkin Cal. Proc. 5th Pleading § 1037, (S 1037) Plaintiff's Inability to Meet Burden as Matter of Law.

5 Witkin Cal. Proc. 5th Pleading § 1101, Justification or Privilege.

7 Witkin Cal. Proc. 5th Trial § 65, (S 65) Remedies of Sanctioned Attorney.

2 Witkin, California Summary 10th Insurance § 246, (S 246) Conduct of Litigation.

2 Witkin, California Summary 10th Insurance § 251, Traditional Tort Actions.

12 Witkin, California Summary 10th Real Property § 574, (S 574) Single Family Dwellings, New Construction, and Vacancy Controls.

11 Witkin, California Summary 10th Community Property § 248, Tort Action for Concealment.

4 Witkin, California Summary 10th Security Transactions in Real Property § 144, in General.

5 Witkin, California Summary 10th Torts § 21, (S 21) Tort Recovery Precluded by Public Policy: Perjury or False Defense.

5 Witkin, California Summary 10th Torts § 155, Proceedings of Professional Society or Committee.

5 Witkin, California Summary 10th Torts § 186, Statutory Privileged Communications.

5 Witkin, California Summary 10th Torts § 455, Privilege.

5 Witkin, California Summary 10th Torts § 458, Collectors' Tactics.

5 Witkin, California Summary 10th Torts § 470, Other Torts Distinguished.

5 Witkin, California Summary 10th Torts § 473, No Defense of Absolute Privilege.

5 Witkin, California Summary 10th Torts § 488, (S 488) Action or Special Proceeding.

5 Witkin, California Summary 10th Torts § 495, (S 495) Contractual Arbitration.

5 Witkin, California Summary 10th Torts § 501, (S 501) Dismissal Reflecting on Merits.

5 Witkin, California Summary 10th Torts § 508, (S 508) Some, But Not All, Claims or Amounts Supported by Probable Cause.

5 Witkin, California Summary 10th Torts § 528, (S 528) Defense of Absolute Privilege.

5 Witkin, California Summary 10th Torts § 548, Political Cartoons.

5 Witkin, California Summary 10th Torts § 562, Statutory Framework.

5 Witkin, California Summary 10th Torts § 563, Scope of Privilege.

5 Witkin, California Summary 10th Torts § 564, in General.

5 Witkin, California Summary 10th Torts § 565, High Ranking Officials.

5 Witkin, California Summary 10th Torts § 566, Lower Ranking Officials.

5 Witkin, California Summary 10th Torts § 567, in General.

5 Witkin, California Summary 10th Torts § 569, Relevancy Limitation.

5 Witkin, California Summary 10th Torts § 571, Steps Before and After Trial.

§ 47.5. Peace officers; defamation action against person filing false complaint alleging misconduct, criminal conduct, or incompetence

Notwithstanding Section 47, a peace officer may bring an action for defamation against an individual who has filed a complaint with that officer's employing agency alleging misconduct, criminal conduct, or incompetence, if that complaint is false, the complaint was made with knowledge that it was false and that it was made with spite, hatred, or ill will. Knowledge that the complaint was false may be proved by a showing that the complainant had no reasonable grounds to believe the statement was true and that the complainant exhibited a reckless disregard for ascertaining the truth. *(Added by Stats.1982, c. 1588, p. 6272, § 1.)*

Validity

This section was held unconstitutional on its face, as violative of the right to free speech, in the decision of

Walker v. Kiousis (App. 4 Dist. 2001) 114 Cal.Rptr.2d 69, 93 Cal.App.4th 1432.

Research References

§ 48. Privileged publication or broadcast; malice not inferred

In the case provided for in subdivision (c) of Section 47, malice is not inferred from the communication. *(Enacted in 1872. Amended by Stats.1895, c. 163, p. 168, § 2; Stats.1945, c. 1489, p. 2763, § 4; Stats.2003, c. 62 (S.B.600), § 11.)*

Research References

§ 48a. Libel in newspaper; slander by radio broadcast

1. In any action for damages for the publication of a libel in a newspaper, or of a slander by radio broadcast, plaintiff shall recover no more than special damages unless a correction be demanded and be not published or broadcast, as hereinafter provided. Plaintiff shall serve upon the publisher, at the place of publication or broadcaster at the place of broadcast, a written notice specifying the statements claimed to be libelous and demanding that the same be corrected. Said notice and demand must be served within 20 days after knowledge of the publication or broadcast of the statements claimed to be libelous.

2. If a correction be demanded within said period and be not published or broadcast in substantially as conspicuous a manner in said newspaper or on said broadcasting station as were the statements claimed to be libelous, in a regular issue thereof published or broadcast within three weeks after such service, plaintiff, if he pleads and proves such notice, demand and failure to correct, and if his cause of action be maintained, may recover general, special and exemplary damages; provided that no exemplary damages may be recovered unless the plaintiff shall prove that defendant made the publication or broadcast with actual malice and then only in the discretion of the court or jury, and actual malice shall not be inferred or presumed from the publication or broadcast.

3. A correction published or broadcast in substantially as conspicuous a manner in said newspaper or on said broadcasting station as the statements claimed in the complaint to be libelous, prior to receipt of a demand therefor, shall be of the same force and effect as though such correction had been published or broadcast within three weeks after a demand therefor.

4. As used herein, the terms "general damages," "special damages," "exemplary damages" and "actual malice," are defined as follows:

(a) "General damages" are damages for loss of reputation, shame, mortification and hurt feelings;

(b) "Special damages" are all damages which plaintiff alleges and proves that he has suffered in respect to his property, business, trade, profession or occupation, including such amounts of money as the plaintiff alleges and proves he has expended as a result of the alleged libel, and no other;

(c) "Exemplary damages" are damages which may in the discretion of the court or jury be recovered in addition to general and special damages for the sake of example and by way of punishing a defendant who has made the publication or broadcast with actual malice;

(d) "Actual malice" is that state of mind arising from hatred or ill will toward the plaintiff; provided, however, that such a state of mind occasioned by a good faith belief on the part of the defendant in the truth of the libelous publication or broadcast at the time it is published or broadcast shall not constitute actual malice. *(Added by Stats.1931, c. 1018, p. 2034, § 1. Amended by Stats.1945, c. 1489, p. 2763, § 5.)*

Research References

Rutter, Cal. Practice Guide: Civil Appeals & Writs Form 7:D, Petition for Writ of Supersedeas or Other Stay Order.
Rutter, Cal. Practice Guide: Civ. Pro. Before Trial Ch. 1-C, C. Prelawsuit Notices, Claims and Demands.
Rutter, Cal. Practice Guide: Enforcing Judgments/Debts Ch. 2-C, C. Tort Liability.
3 Witkin Cal. Proc. 5th Actions § 204, (S 204) Demand.
9 Witkin Cal. Proc. 5th Appeal § 537, Case Poorly Considered.
5 Witkin Cal. Proc. 5th Pleading § 737, (S 737) Defamation in Newspaper or Broadcast.
5 Witkin Cal. Proc. 5th Pleading § 942, Defamation.
5 Witkin, California Summary 10th Torts § 571, Steps Before and After Trial.
5 Witkin, California Summary 10th Torts § 581, Scope of Privilege.
5 Witkin, California Summary 10th Torts § 629, (S 629) Background and Scope of Statute.
5 Witkin, California Summary 10th Torts § 630, Necessity.
5 Witkin, California Summary 10th Torts § 631, Persons Served.
5 Witkin, California Summary 10th Torts § 633, (S 633) Retraction.
5 Witkin, California Summary 10th Torts § 634, Publisher and Author.
5 Witkin, California Summary 10th Torts § 636, Slander.
5 Witkin, California Summary 10th Torts § 637, Publication in Magazines.
5 Witkin, California Summary 10th Torts § 673, Nature of Wrong.
5 Witkin, California Summary 10th Torts § 675, Special Damages Requirement.
6 Witkin, California Summary 10th Torts § 1651, (S 1651) Scope of Personal Injury.
6 Witkin, California Summary 10th Torts § 1701, General Damages.
6 Witkin, California Summary 10th Torts § 1702, Special Damages.

§ 48.5. Defamation by radio; non-liability of owner, licensee or operator of broadcasting station or network

(1) The owner, licensee or operator of a visual or sound radio broadcasting station or network of stations, and the agents or employees of any such owner, licensee or operator, shall not be liable for any damages for any defamatory statement or matter published or uttered in or as a part of a visual or sound radio broadcast by one other than such owner, licensee or operator, or agent or employee thereof, if it shall be alleged and proved by such owner, licensee or operator, or agent or employee thereof, that such owner, licensee or operator, or such agent or employee, has exercised due care to prevent the publication or utterance of such statement or matter in such broadcast.

(2) If any defamatory statement or matter is published or uttered in or as a part of a broadcast over the facilities of a network of visual or sound radio broadcasting stations, the owner, licensee or operator of any such station, or network of stations, and the agents or employees thereof, other than the owner, licensee or operator of the station, or network of stations, originating such broadcast, and the agents or employees thereof, shall in no event be liable for any damages for any such defamatory statement or matter.

(3) In no event, however, shall any owner, licensee or operator of such station or network of stations, or the agents or employees thereof, be liable for any damages for any defamatory statement or matter published or uttered, by one other than such owner, licensee or operator, or agent or employee thereof, in or as a part of a visual or sound radio broadcast by or on behalf of any candidate for public office, which broadcast cannot be censored by reason of the provisions of federal statute or regulation of the Federal Communications Commission.

(4) As used in this Part 2, the terms "radio," "radio broadcast," and "broadcast," are defined to include both visual and sound radio broadcasting.

(5) Nothing in this section contained shall deprive any such owner, licensee or operator, or the agent or employee thereof, of

any rights under any other section of this Part 2. *(Added by Stats.1949, c. 1258, p. 2213, § 1.)*

Research References

Rutter, Cal. Practice Guide: Civil Appeals & Writs Form 7:D, Petition for Writ of Supersedeas or Other Stay Order.
5 Witkin, California Summary 10th Torts § 530, Libel and Slander Distinguished.
5 Witkin, California Summary 10th Torts § 628, (S 628) Radio or Television Broadcaster.
5 Witkin, California Summary 10th Torts § 629, (S 629) Background and Scope of Statute.

§ 48.7. Child abuse; prohibition against libel or slander action while charges pending; tolling of limitations; pleadings; demurrer; attorney fees and costs

(a) No person charged by indictment, information, or other accusatory pleading of child abuse may bring a civil libel or slander action against the minor, the parent or guardian of the minor, or any witness, based upon any statements made by the minor, parent or guardian, or witness which are reasonably believed to be in furtherance of the prosecution of the criminal charges while the charges are pending before a trial court. The charges are not pending within the meaning of this section after dismissal, after pronouncement of judgment, or during an appeal from a judgment.

Any applicable statute of limitations shall be tolled during the period that such charges are pending before a trial court.

(b) Whenever any complaint for libel or slander is filed which is subject to the provisions of this section, no responsive pleading shall be required to be filed until 30 days after the end of the period set forth in subdivision (a).

(c) Every complaint for libel or slander based on a statement that the plaintiff committed an act of child abuse shall state that the complaint is not barred by subdivision (a). A failure to include that statement shall be grounds for a demurrer.

(d) Whenever a demurrer against a complaint for libel or slander is sustained on the basis that the complaint was filed in violation of this section, attorney's fees and costs shall be awarded to the prevailing party.

(e) Whenever a prosecutor is informed by a minor, parent, guardian, or witness that a complaint against one of those persons has been filed which may be subject to the provisions of this section, the prosecutor shall provide that person with a copy of this section.

(f) As used in this section, child abuse has the meaning set forth in Section 11165 of the Penal Code. *(Added by Stats.1981, c. 253, § 1.)*

Research References

3 Witkin Cal. Proc. 5th Actions § 721, in General.
5 Witkin Cal. Proc. 5th Pleading § 736, (S 736) Effect of Privilege.
5 Witkin, California Summary 10th Torts § 145, (S 145) Related Immunities.
5 Witkin, California Summary 10th Torts § 591, (S 591) in General.

§ 48.8. Communications to school personnel regarding threats to commit violence on the school grounds involving deadly or dangerous weapons; liability for defamation

(a) A communication by any person to a school principal, or a communication by a student attending the school to the student's teacher or to a school counselor or school nurse and any report of that communication to the school principal, stating that a specific student or other specified person has made a threat to commit violence or potential violence on the school grounds involving the use of a firearm or other deadly or dangerous weapon, is a communication on a matter of public concern and is subject to liability in defamation only upon a showing by clear and convincing evidence that the communication or report was made with knowledge of its falsity or with reckless disregard for the truth or falsity of the communication. Where punitive damages are alleged, the provisions of Section 3294 shall also apply.

(b) As used in this section, "school" means a public or private school providing instruction in kindergarten or grades 1 to 12, inclusive. *(Added by Stats.2001, c. 570 (A.B.1717), § 1.)*

Research References

5 Witkin, California Summary 10th Torts § 164, Report Regarding Threat of Violence on School Grounds.
5 Witkin, California Summary 10th Torts § 591, (S 591) in General.

§ 48.9. Anonymous witness program; immunity

(a) An organization which sponsors or conducts an anonymous witness program, and its employees and agents, shall not be liable in a civil action for damages resulting from its receipt of information regarding possible criminal activity or from dissemination of that information to a law enforcement agency.

(b) The immunity provided by this section shall apply to any civil action for damages, including, but not limited to, a defamation action or an action for damages resulting from retaliation against a person who provided information.

(c) The immunity provided by this section shall not apply in any of the following instances:

(1) The information was disseminated with actual knowledge that it was false.

(2) The name of the provider of the information was disseminated without that person's authorization and the dissemination was not required by law.

(3) The name of the provider of information was obtained and the provider was not informed by the organization that the disclosure of his or her name may be required by law.

(d) As used in this section, an "anonymous witness program" means a program whereby information relating to alleged criminal activity is received from persons, whose names are not released without their authorization unless required by law, and disseminated to law enforcement agencies. *(Added by Stats. 1983, c. 495, § 1.)*

Research References

5 Witkin, California Summary 10th Torts § 163, Disclosure by Anonymous Witness Program.
5 Witkin, California Summary 10th Torts § 591, (S 591) in General.

§ 49. Personal relations, acts forbidden by

The rights of personal relations forbid:

(a) The abduction or enticement of a child from a parent, or from a guardian entitled to its custody;

(b) The seduction of a person under the age of legal consent;

(c) Any injury to a servant which affects his ability to serve his master, other than seduction, abduction or criminal conversation. *(Enacted in 1872. Amended by Stats.1905, c. 70, p. 68, § 1; Stats.1939, c. 128, p. 1245, § 1; Stats.1939, c. 1103, p. 3037, § 5.)*

Research References

Rutter, Cal. Practice Guide: Family Law Ch. 7-G, G. Removal of Child from Jurisdiction; Wrongful Taking or Withholding of Child.
Rutter, Cal. Practice Guide: Personal Injury Ch. 3-B, B. Potential Claimants in a Personal Injury Case.
Rutter, Cal. Practice Guide: Personal Injury Ch. 3-G, G. Independent Damages Claims.
3 Witkin Cal. Proc. 5th Actions § 5, Remedy for Every Wrong.
9 Witkin Cal. Proc. 5th Appeal § 537, Case Poorly Considered.

5 Witkin, California Summary 10th Torts § 143, Subsequent Concealment of Victim.
5 Witkin, California Summary 10th Torts § 192, Comparative Impairment Analysis.
5 Witkin, California Summary 10th Torts § 723, (S 723) Types of Actions.
5 Witkin, California Summary 10th Torts § 729, Abduction of Child.
5 Witkin, California Summary 10th Torts § 755, Interference With Employment Relation.
3 Witkin, California Summary 10th Agency and Employment § 162, (S 162) Torts.

§ 50. Force, right to use

Any necessary force may be used to protect from wrongful injury the person or property of oneself, or of a wife, husband, child, parent, or other relative, or member of one's family, or of a ward, servant, master, or guest. *(Enacted in 1872. Amended by Code Am.1873–74, c. 612, p. 184, § 12.)*

Research References

Miller and Starr California Real Estate § 22:61, Liability for Wrongful or Criminal Conduct of Third Persons--Commercial Landlord's Liability for Criminal Conduct.
Miller and Starr California Real Estate § 22:73, Liability to Trespassers.
5 Witkin, California Summary 10th Torts § 417, (S 417) Nature and Scope of Privilege.
5 Witkin, California Summary 10th Torts § 419, (S 419) Use of Reasonable Force.
6 Witkin, California Summary 10th Torts § 1099, Person Committing Serious Felony.
6 Witkin, California Summary 10th Torts § 1141, No Duty to Comply With Criminal's Demand.

§ 51. Unruh Civil Rights Act; equal rights; business establishments; violation

(a) This section shall be known, and may be cited, as the Unruh Civil Rights Act.

(b) All persons within the jurisdiction of this state are free and equal, and no matter what their sex, race, color, religion, ancestry, national origin, disability, medical condition, genetic information, marital status, or sexual orientation are entitled to the full and equal accommodations, advantages, facilities, privileges, or services in all business establishments of every kind whatsoever.

(c) This section shall not be construed to confer any right or privilege on a person that is conditioned or limited by law or that is applicable alike to persons of every sex, color, race, religion, ancestry, national origin, disability, medical condition, marital status, or sexual orientation or to persons regardless of their genetic information.

(d) Nothing in this section shall be construed to require any construction, alteration, repair, structural or otherwise, or modification of any sort whatsoever, beyond that construction, alteration, repair, or modification that is otherwise required by other provisions of law, to any new or existing establishment, facility, building, improvement, or any other structure, nor shall anything in this section be construed to augment, restrict, or alter in any way the authority of the State Architect to require construction, alteration, repair, or modifications that the State Architect otherwise possesses pursuant to other laws.

(e) For purposes of this section:

(1) "Disability" means any mental or physical disability as defined in Sections 12926 and 12926.1 of the Government Code.

(2)(A) "Genetic information" means, with respect to any individual, information about any of the following:

(i) The individual's genetic tests.

(ii) The genetic tests of family members of the individual.

(iii) The manifestation of a disease or disorder in family members of the individual.

(B) "Genetic information" includes any request for, or receipt of, genetic services, or participation in clinical research that includes genetic services, by an individual or any family member of the individual.

(C) "Genetic information" does not include information about the sex or age of any individual.

(3) "Medical condition" has the same meaning as defined in subdivision (h) of Section 12926 of the Government Code.

(4) "Religion" includes all aspects of religious belief, observance, and practice.

(5) "Sex" includes, but is not limited to, pregnancy, childbirth, or medical conditions related to pregnancy or childbirth. "Sex" also includes, but is not limited to, a person's gender. "Gender" means sex, and includes a person's gender identity and gender expression. "Gender expression" means a person's gender-related appearance and behavior whether or not stereotypically associated with the person's assigned sex at birth.

(6) "Sex, race, color, religion, ancestry, national origin, disability, medical condition, genetic information, marital status, or sexual orientation" includes a perception that the person has any particular characteristic or characteristics within the listed categories or that the person is associated with a person who has, or is perceived to have, any particular characteristic or characteristics within the listed categories.

(7) "Sexual orientation" has the same meaning as defined in subdivision (r) of Section 12926 of the Government Code.

(f) A violation of the right of any individual under the federal Americans with Disabilities Act of 1990 (P.L. 101–336 [1]) shall also constitute a violation of this section. *(Added by Stats.1905, c. 413, p. 553, § 1. Amended by Stats.1919, c. 210, p. 309, § 1; Stats.1923, c. 235, p. 485, § 1; Stats.1959, c. 1866, p. 4424, § 1; Stats.1961, c. 1187, p. 2920, § 1; Stats.1974, c. 1193, p. 2568, § 1; Stats.1987, c. 159, § 1; Stats.1992, c. 913 (A.B.1077), § 3; Stats.1998, c. 195 (A.B.2702), § 1; Stats.2000, c. 1049 (A.B.2222), § 2; Stats.2005, c. 420 (A.B.1400), § 3; Stats.2011, c. 261 (S.B.559), § 3; Stats.2011, c. 719 (A.B.887), § 1.5.)*

[1] For public law sections classified to U.S.C.A., see U.S.C.A. Tables.

Research References

Rutter, Cal. Practice Guide: A.D.R. Ch. 5-D, D. Defenses to Enforcement.

Rutter, Cal. Practice Guide: A.D.R. Ch. 5-E, E. Claims Subject to Arbitration (Arbitrability).

Rutter, Cal. Practice Guide: A.D.R. Ch. 3B-C, C. Statutorily-Mandated ADR.

Rutter, Cal. Practice Guide: Civil Appeals & Writs Ch. 9-D, D. Procedural Rules.

Rutter, Cal. Practice Guide: Civil Appeals & Writs Ch. 13-B, B. Petition for Review Procedures.

Rutter, Cal. Practice Guide: Civil Appeals & Writs Ch. 13-C, C. Briefs on the Merits After Grant of Review.

Rutter, Cal. Practice Guide: Civ. Pro. Before Trial Ch. 9(I)-D, D. Hearing.

Rutter, Cal. Practice Guide: Civ. Pro. Before Trial Ch. 12(II)-E, E. Motion to Determine "Good Faith" of "Piecemeal" Settlement (CCP § 877.6).

Rutter, Cal. Practice Guide: Civil Trials & Evidence Ch. 1-K, K. Continuance Motions.

Rutter, Cal. Practice Guide: Civil Trials & Evidence Ch. 12-D, D. Other Motions During Trial.

California Practice Guide: Employment Litigation Ch. 5-L, L. Other Statutory Claims.

California Practice Guide: Employment Litigation Ch. 7-A, A. Title VII and the California Fair Employment and Housing Act.

California Practice Guide: Employment Litigation Ch. 7-G, G. Unruh Civil Rights Act.

California Practice Guide: Employment Litigation Ch. 9-A, A. Americans With Disabilities Act (Ada).

Rutter, Cal. Practice Guide: Insurance Litigation Ch. 2-B, B. Insurance Applications.

Rutter, Cal. Practice Guide: Insurance Litigation Ch. 11-K, K. Statutory Liability.

Rutter, Cal. Practice Guide: Insurance Litigation Ch. 15-C, C. Arbitration/Appraisal/Mediation.

Rutter, Cal. Practice Guide: Insurance Litigation Ch. 6E-D, D. Managed Care Plans.

Rutter, Cal. Practice Guide: Landlord-Tenant Gen. Matls, Highlights.

Rutter, Cal. Practice Guide: Personal Injury Ch. 4-D, D. Techniques Where Settlement Not Forthcoming.

Rutter, Cal. Practice Guide: Personal Injury Ch. 5-B, B. When to Sue-Statute of Limitations.

Rutter, Cal. Practice Guide: Personal Injury Ch. 9-A, A. Assignment to Trial.

Rutter, Cal. Practice Guide: Real Prop. Transactions Ch. 2-C, C. Broker's Relationship and Obligations to Principal and Third Parties.

Miller and Starr California Real Estate § 20:1, Applicable Legislation.

Miller and Starr California Real Estate § 20:2, The Unruh Civil Rights Act--Coverage.

Miller and Starr California Real Estate § 20:3, The Unruh Civil Rights Act--"Business Establishment".

Miller and Starr California Real Estate § 20:4, The Unruh Civil Rights Act--Sale or Rental of Real Property.

Miller and Starr California Real Estate § 20:5, The Unruh Civil Rights Act--Age Discrimination.

Miller and Starr California Real Estate § 20:7, The Unruh Civil Rights Act--Disability Discrimination.

Miller and Starr California Real Estate § 20:9, The Unruh Civil Rights Act--Marital Status; Sexual Orientation.

Miller and Starr California Real Estate § 4:38, Grounds for Discipline--In General.

Miller and Starr California Real Estate § 8:57, Conveyance in Violation of Public Policy or Statute.

Miller and Starr California Real Estate § 20:21, California Fair Employment and Housing Act--Enforcement of the Act.

Miller and Starr California Real Estate § 20:28, Americans With Disabilities Act.

Miller and Starr California Real Estate § 20:29, Discrimination by a Real Estate Broker.

Miller and Starr California Real Estate § 22:75, Injuries to Additional Unique Plaintiff Categories.

Miller and Starr California Real Estate § 24:32, Defenses to Enforcement--Public Policy or Discrimination.

Miller and Starr California Real Estate § 24:34, Defenses to Enforcement--Mandatory Deletion of Certain Discriminatory Restrictions.

Miller and Starr California Real Estate § 24:40, Amendment to Restrictions--Deletion of Discriminatory Covenants.

Miller and Starr California Real Estate § 27:56, Home Improvement Contracts--Contracts for Installment Payments, Cash Discounts, or Finance Charges.

Miller and Starr California Real Estate § 35:70, Disqualification of the Arbitrator.

Miller and Starr California Real Estate § 25B:66, Restrictions on Alienation.

Miller and Starr California Real Estate § 25B:77, Restrictions on Occupancy of a Living Unit.

Miller and Starr California Real Estate § 20:7.10, The Unruh Civil Rights Act--Genetic Information Discrimination.

Miller and Starr California Real Estate § 36:1.10, Loan Applications.

15 NO. 3 Miller & Starr, California Real Estate Newsalert 1, We're Not in Kansas Anymore: Disability Discrimination Case Reaches New Frontiers.

16 NO. 4 Miller & Starr, California Real Estate Newsalert 10, Discrimination.

16 NO. 5 Miller & Starr, California Real Estate Newsalert 26, State Board of Equalization Issues Comprehensive Summary and Qs and As for Transfers of Base Year Values of Principal Residences.

17 NO. 2 Miller & Starr, California Real Estate Newsalert 1, The "Big Daddy" of Civil Rights Acts (Unruh Act) Nears Fifty.

19 NO. 2 Miller & Starr, California Real Estate Newsalert 13, Discrimination.

19 NO. 1 Miller & Starr, California Real Estate Newsalert 19, Landowners' Liability.

20 NO. 1 Miller & Starr, California Real Estate Newsalert 9, Discrimination.

21 NO. 6 Miller & Starr, California Real Estate Newsalert 10, Discrimination.

21 NO. 3 Miller & Starr, California Real Estate Newsalert 12, Discrimination.

21 NO. 4 Miller & Starr, California Real Estate Newsalert 13, Discrimination.

3 Witkin Cal. Proc. 5th Actions § 558, (S 558) Civil Rights Violations.

3 Witkin Cal. Proc. 5th Actions § 664, (S 664) in General.

9 Witkin Cal. Proc. 5th Administrative Proceedings § 188, (S 188) Department of Fair Employment and Housing.

2 Witkin Cal. Proc. 5th Courts § 32, (S 32) Accommodation of Persons With Disabilities.

7 Witkin Cal. Proc. 5th Judgment § 223, (S 223) Civil Rights Actions.

4 Witkin Cal. Proc. 5th Pleading § 155, in General.

4 Witkin Cal. Proc. 5th Pleading § 285, Benefits of Class Action Not Substantial.

5 Witkin Cal. Proc. 5th Pleading § 908, in General.

6 Witkin Cal. Proc. 5th Proceedings Without Trial § 515, (S 515) Illustrations.

2 Witkin, California Summary 10th Insurance § 6, (S 6) Governing Law.

12 Witkin, California Summary 10th Real Property § 116, Age.

12 Witkin, California Summary 10th Real Property § 201, (S 201) California Statute.

12 Witkin, California Summary 10th Real Property § 683, Discrimination Against Children.

6 Witkin, California Summary 10th Torts § 1131, Assault Involving Firearms.

7 Witkin, California Summary 10th Constitutional Law § 389, Exclusion of Women from Membership.

7 Witkin, California Summary 10th Constitutional Law § 526, Religious Discrimination Against Advertisers.

8 Witkin, California Summary 10th Constitutional Law § 891, Insurance.

8 Witkin, California Summary 10th Constitutional Law § 892, Public Programs and Activities.

8 Witkin, California Summary 10th Constitutional Law § 895, Hate Crimes, Intimidation, and Threats of Violence.

8 Witkin, California Summary 10th Constitutional Law § 897, Other Discrimination Statutes.

8 Witkin, California Summary 10th Constitutional Law § 898, in General.

8 Witkin, California Summary 10th Constitutional Law § 899, Business Establishments.

8 Witkin, California Summary 10th Constitutional Law § 903, (S 903) Cult Awareness Network.

8 Witkin, California Summary 10th Constitutional Law § 904, (S 904) Boy Scouts.

8 Witkin, California Summary 10th Constitutional Law § 905, (S 905) in General.

8 Witkin, California Summary 10th Constitutional Law § 906, (S 906) Business Discrimination.

8 Witkin, California Summary 10th Constitutional Law § 908, (S 908) Housing Discrimination.

8 Witkin, California Summary 10th Constitutional Law § 910, (S 910) Classification Based on Marital Status.

8 Witkin, California Summary 10th Constitutional Law § 912, (S 912) Economic Criteria.

8 Witkin, California Summary 10th Constitutional Law § 914, Enforcement.

8 Witkin, California Summary 10th Constitutional Law § 915, Nature and Purpose of Act.

8 Witkin, California Summary 10th Constitutional Law § 941, (S 941) Other Prohibited Discrimination.

8 Witkin, California Summary 10th Constitutional Law § 945, (S 945) in General.

8 Witkin, California Summary 10th Constitutional Law § 957, in General.

8 Witkin, California Summary 10th Constitutional Law § 908A, (S 908A) (New)-Marital Status Discrimination.

8 Witkin, California Summary 10th Constitutional Law § 908B, (S 908B) (New)-Sexual Orientation Discrimination.

13 Witkin, California Summary 10th Equity § 121, Rental Car Company Practices.

§ 51.1. Mandatory service on State Solicitor General of each party's brief or petition and brief in causes of action based on violation of civil rights statutes

If a violation of Section 51, 51.5, 51.7, 51.9, or 52.1 is alleged or the application or construction of any of these sections is in issue in any proceeding in the Supreme Court of California, a state court of appeal, or the appellate division of a superior court, each party shall serve a copy of the party's brief or petition and brief, on the State Solicitor General at the Office of the Attorney General. No brief may be accepted for filing unless the proof of service shows service on the State Solicitor General. Any party failing to comply with this requirement shall be given a reasonable opportunity to cure the failure before the court imposes any sanction and, in that instance, the court shall allow the Attorney General reasonable additional time to file a brief in the matter. *(Added by Stats.2002, c. 244 (A.B.2524), § 1.)*

Research References

Rutter, Cal. Practice Guide: Civil Appeals & Writs Ch. 9-D, D. Procedural Rules.

Rutter, Cal. Practice Guide: Civil Appeals & Writs Ch. 13-B, B. Petition for Review Procedures.

Rutter, Cal. Practice Guide: Civil Appeals & Writs Ch. 13-C, C. Briefs on the Merits After Grant of Review.

Rutter, Cal. Practice Guide: Civil Appeals & Writs Ch. 15-E, E. Procedures on Writ Review.

17 NO. 2 Miller & Starr, California Real Estate Newsalert 1, The "Big Daddy" of Civil Rights Acts (Unruh Act) Nears Fifty.

9 Witkin Cal. Proc. 5th Appeal § 717, (S 717) Service and Filing.

§ 51.2. Age discrimination in sale or rental of housing prohibited; housing designed to meet physical and social needs of senior citizens; exceptions; intent; age preferences in federally approved housing programs

(a) Section 51 shall be construed to prohibit a business establishment from discriminating in the sale or rental of housing based upon age. Where accommodations are designed to meet the physical and social needs of senior citizens, a business establishment may establish and preserve that housing for senior citizens, pursuant to Section 51.3, except housing as to which Section 51.3 is preempted by the prohibition in the federal Fair Housing Amendments Act of 1988 (Public Law 100–430) [1] and implementing regulations against discrimination on the basis of familial status. For accommodations constructed before February 8, 1982, that meet all the criteria for senior citizen housing specified in Section 51.3, a business establishment may establish and preserve that housing development for senior citizens without the housing development being designed to meet physical and social needs of senior citizens.

(b) This section is intended to clarify the holdings in Marina Point, Ltd. v. Wolfson (1982) 30 Cal.3d 72 and O'Connor v. Village Green Owners Association (1983) 33 Cal.3d 790.

(c) This section shall not apply to the County of Riverside.

(d) A housing development for senior citizens constructed on or after January 1, 2001, shall be presumed to be designed to meet the physical and social needs of senior citizens if it includes all of the following elements:

(1) Entryways, walkways, and hallways in the common areas of the development, and doorways and paths of access to and within the housing units, shall be as wide as required by current laws applicable to new multifamily housing construction for provision of access to persons using a standard-width wheelchair.

(2) Walkways and hallways in the common areas of the development shall be equipped with standard height railings or grab bars to assist persons who have difficulty with walking.

(3) Walkways and hallways in the common areas shall have lighting conditions which are of sufficient brightness to assist persons who have difficulty seeing.

(4) Access to all common areas and housing units within the development shall be provided without use of stairs, either by means of an elevator or sloped walking ramps.

(5) The development shall be designed to encourage social contact by providing at least one common room and at least some common open space.

(6) Refuse collection shall be provided in a manner that requires a minimum of physical exertion by residents.

(7) The development shall comply with all other applicable requirements for access and design imposed by law, including, but not limited to, the Fair Housing Act (42 U.S.C. Sec. 3601 et seq.), the Americans with Disabilities Act (42 U.S.C. Sec. 12101 et seq.), and the regulations promulgated at Title 24 of the California Code of Regulations that relate to access for persons with disabilities or handicaps. Nothing in this section shall be construed to limit or reduce any right or obligation applicable under those laws.

(e) Selection preferences based on age, imposed in connection with a federally approved housing program, do not constitute age discrimination in housing. *(Added by Stats.1984, c. 787, § 1. Amended by Stats.1989, c. 501, § 1; Stats.1993, c. 830 (S.B.137), § 1, eff. Oct. 6, 1993; Stats.1996, c. 1147 (S.B.2097), § 2; Stats.1999, c. 324 (S.B.382), § 1; Stats.2000, c. 1004 (S.B.2011), § 2; Stats.2002, c. 726 (A.B.2787), § 2; Stats.2010, c. 524 (S.B.1252), § 2.)*

1 Public law sections classified to U.S.C.A., see U.S.C.A. Tables.

Research References

Miller and Starr California Real Estate § 20:2, The Unruh Civil Rights Act--Coverage.
Miller and Starr California Real Estate § 20:5, The Unruh Civil Rights Act--Age Discrimination.
Miller and Starr California Real Estate § 24:32, Defenses to Enforcement--Public Policy or Discrimination.
Miller and Starr California Real Estate § 25B:79, Age Restrictions on Occupancy.
17 NO. 2 Miller & Starr, California Real Estate Newsalert 1, The "Big Daddy" of Civil Rights Acts (Unruh Act) Nears Fifty.
21 NO. 4 Miller & Starr, California Real Estate Newsalert 13, Discrimination.
8 Witkin, California Summary 10th Constitutional Law § 908, (S 908) Housing Discrimination.

§ 51.3. Housing; age limitations; necessity for senior citizen housing

(a) The Legislature finds and declares that this section is essential to establish and preserve specially designed accessible housing for senior citizens. There are senior citizens who need special living environments and services, and find that there is an inadequate supply of this type of housing in the state.

(b) For the purposes of this section, the following definitions apply:

(1) "Qualifying resident" or "senior citizen" means a person 62 years of age or older, or 55 years of age or older in a senior citizen housing development.

(2) "Qualified permanent resident" means a person who meets both of the following requirements:

(A) Was residing with the qualifying resident or senior citizen prior to the death, hospitalization, or other prolonged absence of, or the dissolution of marriage with, the qualifying resident or senior citizen.

(B) Was 45 years of age or older, or was a spouse, cohabitant, or person providing primary physical or economic support to the qualifying resident or senior citizen.

(3) "Qualified permanent resident" also means a disabled person or person with a disabling illness or injury who is a child or grandchild of the senior citizen or a qualified permanent resident as defined in paragraph (2) who needs to live with the senior citizen or qualified permanent resident because of the disabling condition, illness, or injury. For purposes of this

section, "disabled" means a person who has a disability as defined in subdivision (b) of Section 54. A "disabling injury or illness" means an illness or injury which results in a condition meeting the definition of disability set forth in subdivision (b) of Section 54.

(A) For any person who is a qualified permanent resident under this paragraph whose disabling condition ends, the owner, board of directors, or other governing body may require the formerly disabled resident to cease residing in the development upon receipt of six months' written notice; provided, however, that the owner, board of directors, or other governing body may allow the person to remain a resident for up to one year after the disabling condition ends.

(B) The owner, board of directors, or other governing body of the senior citizen housing development may take action to prohibit or terminate occupancy by a person who is a qualified permanent resident under this paragraph if the owner, board of directors, or other governing body finds, based on credible and objective evidence, that the person is likely to pose a significant threat to the health or safety of others that cannot be ameliorated by means of a reasonable accommodation; provided, however, that the action to prohibit or terminate the occupancy may be taken only after doing both of the following:

(i) Providing reasonable notice to and an opportunity to be heard for the disabled person whose occupancy is being challenged, and reasonable notice to the coresident parent or grandparent of that person.

(ii) Giving due consideration to the relevant, credible, and objective information provided in the hearing. The evidence shall be taken and held in a confidential manner, pursuant to a closed session, by the owner, board of directors, or other governing body in order to preserve the privacy of the affected persons.

The affected persons shall be entitled to have present at the hearing an attorney or any other person authorized by them to speak on their behalf or to assist them in the matter.

(4) "Senior citizen housing development" means a residential development developed, substantially rehabilitated, or substantially renovated for, senior citizens that has at least 35 dwelling units. Any senior citizen housing development which is required to obtain a public report under Section 11010 of the Business and Professions Code and which submits its application for a public report after July 1, 2001, shall be required to have been issued a public report as a senior citizen housing development under Section 11010.05 of the Business and Professions Code. No housing development constructed prior to January 1, 1985, shall fail to qualify as a senior citizen housing development because it was not originally developed or put to use for occupancy by senior citizens.

(5) "Dwelling unit" or "housing" means any residential accommodation other than a mobilehome.

(6) "Cohabitant" refers to persons who live together as husband and wife, or persons who are domestic partners within the meaning of Section 297 of the Family Code.

(7) "Permitted health care resident" means a person hired to provide live-in, long-term, or terminal health care to a qualifying resident, or a family member of the qualifying resident providing that care. For the purposes of this section, the care provided by a permitted health care resident must be substantial in nature and must provide either assistance with necessary daily activities or medical treatment, or both.

A permitted health care resident shall be entitled to continue his or her occupancy, residency, or use of the dwelling unit as a permitted resident in the absence of the senior citizen from the dwelling unit only if both of the following are applicable:

(A) The senior citizen became absent from the dwelling due to hospitalization or other necessary medical treatment and expects to return to his or her residence within 90 days from the date the absence began.

(B) The absent senior citizen or an authorized person acting for the senior citizen submits a written request to the owner, board of directors, or governing board stating that the senior citizen desires that the permitted health care resident be allowed to remain in order to be present when the senior citizen returns to reside in the development.

Upon written request by the senior citizen or an authorized person acting for the senior citizen, the owner, board of directors, or governing board shall have the discretion to allow a permitted health care resident to remain for a time period longer than 90 days from the date that the senior citizen's absence began, if it appears that the senior citizen will return within a period of time not to exceed an additional 90 days.

(c) The covenants, conditions, and restrictions and other documents or written policy shall set forth the limitations on occupancy, residency, or use on the basis of age. Any such limitation shall not be more exclusive than to require that one person in residence in each dwelling unit may be required to be a senior citizen and that each other resident in the same dwelling unit may be required to be a qualified permanent resident, a permitted health care resident, or a person under 55 years of age whose occupancy is permitted under subdivision (h) of this section or under subdivision (b) of Section 51.4. That limitation may be less exclusive, but shall at least require that the persons commencing any occupancy of a dwelling unit include a senior citizen who intends to reside in the unit as his or her primary residence on a permanent basis. The application of the rules set forth in this subdivision regarding limitations on occupancy may result in less than all of the dwellings being actually occupied by a senior citizen.

(d) The covenants, conditions, and restrictions or other documents or written policy shall permit temporary residency, as a guest of a senior citizen or qualified permanent resident, by a person of less than 55 years of age for periods of time, not less than 60 days in any year, that are specified in the covenants, conditions, and restrictions or other documents or written policy.

(e) Upon the death or dissolution of marriage, or upon hospitalization, or other prolonged absence of the qualifying resident, any qualified permanent resident shall be entitled to continue his or her occupancy, residency, or use of the dwelling unit as a permitted resident. This subdivision shall not apply to a permitted health care resident.

(f) The condominium, stock cooperative, limited-equity housing cooperative, planned development, or multiple-family residential rental property shall have been developed for, and initially been put to use as, housing for senior citizens, or shall have been substantially rehabilitated or renovated for, and immediately afterward put to use as, housing for senior citizens, as provided in this section; provided, however, that no housing development constructed prior to January 1, 1985, shall fail to qualify as a senior citizen housing development because it was not originally developed for or originally put to use for occupancy by senior citizens.

(g) The covenants, conditions, and restrictions or other documents or written policies applicable to any condominium, stock cooperative, limited-equity housing cooperative, planned development, or multiple-family residential property that contained age restrictions on January 1, 1984, shall be enforceable only to the extent permitted by this section, notwithstanding lower age restrictions contained in those documents or policies.

(h) Any person who has the right to reside in, occupy, or use the housing or an unimproved lot subject to this section on January 1, 1985, shall not be deprived of the right to continue that residency, occupancy, or use as the result of the enactment of this section.

(i) The covenants, conditions, and restrictions or other documents or written policy of the senior citizen housing development shall permit the occupancy of a dwelling unit by a permitted health care resident during any period that the person is actually providing live-in, long-term, or hospice health care to a qualifying resident for compensation. For purposes of this subdivision, the term "for compensation" shall include provisions of lodging and food in exchange for care.

(j) Notwithstanding any other provision of this section, this section shall not apply to the County of Riverside. *(Added by Stats.1984, c. 1333, § 1. Amended by Stats.1985, c. 1505, § 2; Stats.1989, c. 190, § 1; Stats.1994, c. 464 (S.B.1560), § 1; Stats.1995, c. 147 (S.B.332), § 1; Stats.1996, c. 1147 (S.B.2097), § 3; Stats.1999, c. 324 (S.B.382), § 2; Stats.2000, c. 1004 (S.B.2011), § 3.)*

Research References

Rutter, Cal. Practice Guide: Real Prop. Transactions Ch. 4-A, A. Property to be Sold.

Miller and Starr California Real Estate § 20:2, The Unruh Civil Rights Act--Coverage.

Miller and Starr California Real Estate § 20:5, The Unruh Civil Rights Act--Age Discrimination.

Miller and Starr California Real Estate § 24:32, Defenses to Enforcement--Public Policy or Discrimination.

Miller and Starr California Real Estate § 25C:8, Subdivisions Requiring a Public Report; Common Interest Developments.

Miller and Starr California Real Estate § 25B:79, Age Restrictions on Occupancy.

Miller and Starr California Real Estate § 25C:43, Phased Subdivisions, Master-Planned Communities, and Other Long-Term Projects.

12 Witkin, California Summary 10th Real Property § 116, Age.

8 Witkin, California Summary 10th Constitutional Law § 908, (S 908) Housing Discrimination.

§ 51.4.   Exemption from special design requirement

(a) The Legislature finds and declares that the requirements for senior housing under Sections 51.2 and 51.3 are more stringent than the requirements for that housing under the federal Fair Housing Amendments Act of 1988 (P.L. 100–430) in recognition of the acute shortage of housing for families with children in California. The Legislature further finds and declares that the special design requirements for senior housing under Sections 51.2 and 51.3 may pose a hardship to some housing developments that were constructed before the decision in Marina Point, Ltd. v. Wolfson (1982) 30 Cal.3d 721. The Legislature further finds and declares that the requirement for specially designed accommodations in senior housing under Sections 51.2 and 51.3 provides important benefits to senior citizens and also ensures that housing exempt from the prohibition of age discrimination is carefully tailored to meet the compelling societal interest in providing senior housing.

(b) Any person who resided in, occupied, or used, prior to January 1, 1990, a dwelling in a senior citizen housing development that relied on the exemption to the special design requirement provided by this section prior to January 1, 2001, shall not be deprived of the right to continue that residency, occupancy, or use as the result of the changes made to this section by the enactment of Chapter 1004 of the Statutes of 2000.

(c) This section shall not apply to the County of Riverside. *(Added by Stats.1989, c. 501, § 2. Amended by Stats.1991, c. 59 (A.B.125), § 1, eff. June 17, 1991; Stats.1996, c. 1147 (S.B.2097), § 4; Stats.2000, c. 1004 (S.B.2011), § 4; Stats.2006, c. 538 (S.B.1852), § 37.)*

Research References

Miller and Starr California Real Estate § 20:2, The Unruh Civil Rights Act--Coverage.
Miller and Starr California Real Estate § 20:5, The Unruh Civil Rights Act--Age Discrimination.
Miller and Starr California Real Estate § 24:32, Defenses to Enforcement--Public Policy or Discrimination.
Miller and Starr California Real Estate § 25B:79, Age Restrictions on Occupancy.
8 Witkin, California Summary 10th Constitutional Law § 908, (S 908) Housing Discrimination.

§ 51.5. Discrimination, boycott, blacklist, etc.; business establishments; equal rights

(a) No business establishment of any kind whatsoever shall discriminate against, boycott or blacklist, or refuse to buy from, contract with, sell to, or trade with any person in this state on account of any characteristic listed or defined in subdivision (b) or (e) of Section 51, or of the person's partners, members, stockholders, directors, officers, managers, superintendents, agents, employees, business associates, suppliers, or customers, because the person is perceived to have one or more of those characteristics, or because the person is associated with a person who has, or is perceived to have, any of those characteristics.

(b) As used in this section, "person" includes any person, firm, association, organization, partnership, business trust, corporation, limited liability company, or company.

(c) This section shall not be construed to require any construction, alteration, repair, structural or otherwise, or modification of any sort whatsoever, beyond that construction, alteration, repair, or modification that is otherwise required by other provisions of law, to any new or existing establishment, facility, building, improvement, or any other structure, nor shall this section be construed to augment, restrict, or alter in any way the authority of the State Architect to require construction, alteration, repair, or modifications that the State Architect otherwise possesses pursuant to other laws. *(Added by Stats.1976, c. 366, p. 1013, § 1. Amended by Stats.1987, c. 159, § 2; Stats.1992, c. 913 (A.B.1077), § 3.2; Stats.1994, c. 1010 (S.B.2053), § 28; Stats. 1998, c. 195 (A.B.2702), § 2; Stats.1999, c. 591 (A.B.1670), § 2; Stats.2000, c. 1049 (A.B.2222), § 3; Stats.2005, c. 420 (A.B.1400), § 4.)*

Research References

Miller and Starr California Real Estate § 20:2, The Unruh Civil Rights Act--Coverage.
Miller and Starr California Real Estate § 20:7, The Unruh Civil Rights Act--Disability Discrimination.
16 NO. 4 Miller & Starr, California Real Estate Newsalert 10, Discrimination.
16 NO. 5 Miller & Starr, California Real Estate Newsalert 26, State Board of Equalization Issues Comprehensive Summary and Qs and As for Transfers of Base Year Values of Principal Residences.
21 NO. 6 Miller & Starr, California Real Estate Newsalert 10, Discrimination.
7 Witkin Cal. Proc. 5th Judgment § 223, (S 223) Civil Rights Actions.
4 Witkin Cal. Proc. 5th Pleading § 155, in General.
4 Witkin Cal. Proc. 5th Pleading § 285, Benefits of Class Action Not Substantial.
7 Witkin, California Summary 10th Constitutional Law § 526, Religious Discrimination Against Advertisers.
8 Witkin, California Summary 10th Constitutional Law § 899, Business Establishments.
8 Witkin, California Summary 10th Constitutional Law § 906, (S 906) Business Discrimination.
8 Witkin, California Summary 10th Constitutional Law § 914, Enforcement.
8 Witkin, California Summary 10th Constitutional Law § 941, (S 941) Other Prohibited Discrimination.

8 Witkin, California Summary 10th Constitutional Law § 957, in General.

§ 51.6. Gender Tax Repeal Act of 1995

(a) This section shall be known, and may be cited, as the Gender Tax Repeal Act of 1995.

(b) No business establishment of any kind whatsoever may discriminate, with respect to the price charged for services of similar or like kind, against a person because of the person's gender.

(c) Nothing in subdivision (b) prohibits price differences based specifically upon the amount of time, difficulty, or cost of providing the services.

(d) Except as provided in subdivision (f), the remedies for a violation of this section are the remedies provided in subdivision (a) of Section 52. However, an action under this section is independent of any other remedy or procedure that may be available to an aggrieved party.

(e) This act does not alter or affect the provisions of the Health and Safety Code, the Insurance Code, or other laws that govern health care service plan or insurer underwriting or rating practices.

(f)(1) The following business establishments shall clearly and conspicuously disclose to the customer in writing the pricing for each standard service provided:

(A) Tailors or businesses providing aftermarket clothing alterations.

(B) Barbers or hair salons.

(C) Dry cleaners and laundries providing services to individuals.

(2) The price list shall be posted in an area conspicuous to customers. Posted price lists shall be in no less than 14–point boldface type and clearly and completely display pricing for every standard service offered by the business under paragraph (1).

(3) The business establishment shall provide the customer with a complete written price list upon request.

(4) The business establishment shall display in a conspicuous place at least one clearly visible sign, printed in no less than 24–point boldface type, which reads: "CALIFORNIA LAW PROHIBITS ANY BUSINESS ESTABLISHMENT FROM DISCRIMINATING, WITH RESPECT TO THE PRICE CHARGED FOR SERVICES OF SIMILAR OR LIKE KIND, AGAINST A PERSON BECAUSE OF THE PERSON'S GENDER. A COMPLETE PRICE LIST IS AVAILABLE UPON REQUEST."

(5) A business establishment that fails to correct a violation of this subdivision within 30 days of receiving written notice of the violation is liable for a civil penalty of one thousand dollars ($1,000).

(6) For the purposes of this subdivision, "standard service" means the 15 most frequently requested services provided by the business. *(Added by Stats.1995, c. 866 (A.B.1100), § 1. Amended by Stats.2001, c. 312 (A.B.1088), § 1.)*

Research References

Miller and Starr California Real Estate § 20:8, The Unruh Civil Rights Act--Gender Discrimination.
7 Witkin Cal. Proc. 5th Judgment § 223, (S 223) Civil Rights Actions.
4 Witkin Cal. Proc. 5th Pleading § 155, in General.
4 Witkin Cal. Proc. 5th Pleading § 285, Benefits of Class Action Not Substantial.
8 Witkin, California Summary 10th Constitutional Law § 905, (S 905) in General.

8 Witkin, California Summary 10th Constitutional Law § 914, Enforcement.

§ 51.7. Freedom from violence or intimidation

(a) All persons within the jurisdiction of this state have the right to be free from any violence, or intimidation by threat of violence, committed against their persons or property because of political affiliation, or on account of any characteristic listed or defined in subdivision (b) or (e) of Section 51, or position in a labor dispute, or because another person perceives them to have one or more of those characteristics. The identification in this subdivision of particular bases of discrimination is illustrative rather than restrictive.

(b) This section does not apply to statements concerning positions in a labor dispute which are made during otherwise lawful labor picketing. *(Added by Stats.1976, c. 1293, p. 5778, § 2. Amended by Stats.1984, c. 1437, § 1; Stats.1985, c. 497, § 1; Stats.1987, c. 1277, § 2; Stats.1994, c. 407 (S.B.1595), § 1; Stats.2005, c. 420 (A.B.1400), § 5.)*

Research References

Rutter, Cal. Practice Guide: A.D.R. Ch. 5-E, E. Claims Subject to Arbitration (Arbitrability).

Rutter, Cal. Practice Guide: A.D.R. Ch. 5-H, H. Conduct of Arbitration Proceedings.

Rutter, Cal. Practice Guide: A.D.R. Ch. 5-I, I. Arbitrator's Award.

California Practice Guide: Employment Litigation Ch. 5-L, L. Other Statutory Claims.

California Practice Guide: Employment Litigation Ch. 7-G, G. Unruh Civil Rights Act.

California Practice Guide: Employment Litigation Ch. 10-A, A. Sources of Law Prohibiting Harassment.

California Practice Guide: Employment Litigation Ch. 16-A, A. Failure to Exhaust Administrative Remedies.

California Practice Guide: Employment Litigation Ch. 17-C, C. Extracontractual Compensatory Damages (Tort and Statutory).

California Practice Guide: Employment Litigation Ch. 7-G, Outline G.

California Practice Guide: Employment Litigation Ch. 10-A, Outline a.

Rutter, Cal. Practice Guide: Personal Injury Ch. 5-B, B. When to Sue-Statute of Limitations.

Miller and Starr California Real Estate § 20:2, The Unruh Civil Rights Act--Coverage.

Miller and Starr California Real Estate § 20:9, The Unruh Civil Rights Act--Marital Status; Sexual Orientation.

Miller and Starr California Real Estate § 20:11, The Unruh Civil Rights Act--Violations and Enforcement.

Miller and Starr California Real Estate § 20:21, California Fair Employment and Housing Act--Enforcement of the Act.

Miller and Starr California Real Estate § 35:84, Ancillary Remedies.

Miller and Starr California Real Estate § 19:132, Landlord's Liability to Persons Injured on the Premises.

16 NO. 4 Miller & Starr, California Real Estate Newsalert 10, Discrimination.

16 NO. 5 Miller & Starr, California Real Estate Newsalert 26, State Board of Equalization Issues Comprehensive Summary and Qs and As for Transfers of Base Year Values of Principal Residences.

17 NO. 2 Miller & Starr, California Real Estate Newsalert 1, The "Big Daddy" of Civil Rights Acts (Unruh Act) Nears Fifty.

21 NO. 3 Miller & Starr, California Real Estate Newsalert 12, Discrimination.

3 Witkin Cal. Proc. 5th Actions § 483, (S 483) Three Years.

9 Witkin Cal. Proc. 5th Administrative Proceedings § 188, (S 188) Department of Fair Employment and Housing.

4 Witkin Cal. Proc. 5th Pleading § 155, in General.

5 Witkin, California Summary 10th Torts § 303, (S 303) Discriminatory Allocation of Protective Services During Riot.

8 Witkin, California Summary 10th Constitutional Law § 895, Hate Crimes, Intimidation, and Threats of Violence.

8 Witkin, California Summary 10th Constitutional Law § 898, in General.

8 Witkin, California Summary 10th Constitutional Law § 914, Enforcement.

8 Witkin, California Summary 10th Constitutional Law § 915, Nature and Purpose of Act.

8 Witkin, California Summary 10th Constitutional Law § 941, (S 941) Other Prohibited Discrimination.

8 Witkin, California Summary 10th Constitutional Law § 945, (S 945) in General.

8 Witkin, California Summary 10th Constitutional Law § 949, Accusation, Hearing, and Decision.

8 Witkin, California Summary 10th Constitutional Law § 950, Damages and Penalties.

§ 51.8. Discrimination; franchises

(a) No franchisor shall discriminate in the granting of franchises solely on account of any characteristic listed or defined in subdivision (b) or (e) of Section 51 of the franchisee and the composition of a neighborhood or geographic area reflecting any characteristic listed or defined in subdivision (b) or (e) of Section 51 in which the franchise is located. Nothing in this section shall be interpreted to prohibit a franchisor from granting a franchise to prospective franchisees as part of a program or programs to make franchises available to persons lacking the capital, training, business experience, or other qualifications ordinarily required of franchisees, or any other affirmative action program adopted by the franchisor.

(b) Nothing in this section shall be construed to require any construction, alteration, repair, structural or otherwise, or modification of any sort whatsoever, beyond that construction, alteration, repair, or modification that is otherwise required by other provisions of law, to any new or existing establishment, facility, building, improvement, or any other structure, nor shall anything in this section be construed to augment, restrict, or alter in any way the authority of the State Architect to require construction, alteration, repair, or modifications that the State Architect otherwise possesses pursuant to other laws. *(Added by Stats.1980, c. 1303, § 1. Amended by Stats.1987, c. 159, § 3; Stats.1992, c. 913 (A.B.1077), § 3.4; Stats.1998, c. 195 (A.B. 2702), § 3; Stats.2005, c. 420 (A.B.1400), § 6.)*

Research References

Miller and Starr California Real Estate § 20:2, The Unruh Civil Rights Act--Coverage.

Miller and Starr California Real Estate § 20:7, The Unruh Civil Rights Act--Disability Discrimination.

16 NO. 4 Miller & Starr, California Real Estate Newsalert 10, Discrimination.

16 NO. 5 Miller & Starr, California Real Estate Newsalert 26, State Board of Equalization Issues Comprehensive Summary and Qs and As for Transfers of Base Year Values of Principal Residences.

12 Witkin, California Summary 10th Real Property § 202, (S 202) Expanded Scope of Rule.

8 Witkin, California Summary 10th Constitutional Law § 897, Other Discrimination Statutes.

8 Witkin, California Summary 10th Constitutional Law § 957, in General.

§ 51.9. Sexual harassment; business, service and professional relationships

(a) A person is liable in a cause of action for sexual harassment under this section when the plaintiff proves all of the following elements:

(1) There is a business, service, or professional relationship between the plaintiff and defendant. Such a relationship may exist between a plaintiff and a person, including, but not limited to, any of the following persons:

(A) Physician, psychotherapist, or dentist. For purposes of this section, "psychotherapist" has the same meaning as set forth in paragraph (1) of subdivision (c) of Section 728 of the Business and Professions Code.

(B) Attorney, holder of a master's degree in social work, real estate agent, real estate appraiser, accountant, banker, trust officer, financial planner loan officer, collection service, building contractor, or escrow loan officer.

(C) Executor, trustee, or administrator.

(D) Landlord or property manager.

(E) Teacher.

(F) A relationship that is substantially similar to any of the above.

(2) The defendant has made sexual advances, solicitations, sexual requests, demands for sexual compliance by the plaintiff, or engaged in other verbal, visual, or physical conduct of a sexual nature or of a hostile nature based on gender, that were unwelcome and pervasive or severe.

(3) There is an inability by the plaintiff to easily terminate the relationship.

(4) The plaintiff has suffered or will suffer economic loss or disadvantage or personal injury, including, but not limited to, emotional distress or the violation of a statutory or constitutional right, as a result of the conduct described in paragraph (2).

(b) In an action pursuant to this section, damages shall be awarded as provided by subdivision (b) of Section 52.

(c) Nothing in this section shall be construed to limit application of any other remedies or rights provided under the law.

(d) The definition of sexual harassment and the standards for determining liability set forth in this section shall be limited to determining liability only with regard to a cause of action brought under this section. *(Added by Stats.1994, c. 710 (S.B.612), § 2. Amended by Stats.1996, c. 150 (S.B.195), § 1; Stats.1999, c. 964 (A.B.519), § 1.)*

Research References

California Practice Guide: Employment Litigation Ch. 5-K, K. Invasion of Privacy.
California Practice Guide: Employment Litigation Ch. 10-A, A. Sources of Law Prohibiting Harassment.
California Practice Guide: Employment Litigation Ch. 10-A, Outline a.
Rutter, Cal. Practice Guide: Prof. Responsibility Ch. 1-G, G. Prohibition Against Discriminatory Practices.
Miller and Starr California Real Estate § 20:8, The Unruh Civil Rights Act--Gender Discrimination.
21 NO. 3 Miller & Starr, California Real Estate Newsalert 12, Discrimination.
3 Witkin Cal. Proc. 5th Actions § 558, (S 558) Civil Rights Violations.
3 Witkin Cal. Proc. 5th Actions § 664, (S 664) in General.
4 Witkin Cal. Proc. 5th Pleading § 155, in General.
3 Witkin, California Summary 10th Agency and Employment § 139, (S 139) Nature and Effect.
8 Witkin, California Summary 10th Constitutional Law § 896, Sexual Harassment in Business and Professional Relationships.

§ 51.10. Age discrimination in sale or rental of housing prohibited; construction of Unruh Civil Rights Act; senior housing; intent; age preferences in federally approved housing programs; application of section

(a) Section 51 shall be construed to prohibit a business establishment from discriminating in the sale or rental of housing based upon age. A business establishment may establish and preserve housing for senior citizens, pursuant to Section 51.11, except housing as to which Section 51.11 is preempted by the prohibition in the federal Fair Housing Amendments Act of 1988 (Public Law 100–430)[1] and implementing regulations against discrimination on the basis of familial status.

(b) This section is intended to clarify the holdings in Marina Point, Ltd. v. Wolfson (1982) 30 Cal.3d 721, and O'Connor v. Village Green Owners Association (1983) 33 Cal.3d 790.

(c) Selection preferences based on age, imposed in connection with a federally approved housing program, do not constitute age discrimination in housing.

(d) This section shall only apply to the County of Riverside. *(Added by Stats.1996, c. 1147 (S.B.2097), § 5. Amended by Stats.2004, c. 183 (A.B.3082), § 23; Stats.2010, c. 524 (S.B.1252), § 3.)*

[1] Public law sections classified to U.S.C.A., see U.S.C.A. Tables.

Research References

21 NO. 4 Miller & Starr, California Real Estate Newsalert 13, Discrimination.
8 Witkin, California Summary 10th Constitutional Law § 908, (S 908) Housing Discrimination.

§ 51.11. Riverside County; establishment or preservation of senior housing; legislative findings and declarations; definitions; requirements; qualification of development; application of section

(a) The Legislature finds and declares that this section is essential to establish and preserve housing for senior citizens. There are senior citizens who need special living environments, and find that there is an inadequate supply of this type of housing in the state.

(b) For the purposes of this section, the following definitions apply:

(1) "Qualifying resident" or "senior citizen" means a person 62 years of age or older, or 55 years of age or older in a senior citizen housing development.

(2) "Qualified permanent resident" means a person who meets both of the following requirements:

(A) Was residing with the qualifying resident or senior citizen prior to the death, hospitalization, or other prolonged absence of, or the dissolution of marriage with, the qualifying resident or senior citizen.

(B) Was 45 years of age or older, or was a spouse, cohabitant, or person providing primary physical or economic support to the qualifying resident or senior citizen.

(3) "Qualified permanent resident" also means a disabled person or person with a disabling illness or injury who is a child or grandchild of the senior citizen or a qualified permanent resident as defined in paragraph (2) who needs to live with the senior citizen or qualified permanent resident because of the disabling condition, illness, or injury. For purposes of this section, "disabled" means a person who has a disability as defined in subdivision (b) of Section 54. A "disabling injury or illness" means an illness or injury which results in a condition meeting the definition of disability set forth in subdivision (b) of Section 54.

(A) For any person who is a qualified permanent resident under paragraph (3) whose disabling condition ends, the owner, board of directors, or other governing body may require the formerly disabled resident to cease residing in the development upon receipt of six months' written notice; provided, however, that the owner, board of directors, or other governing body may allow the person to remain a resident for up to one year, after the disabling condition ends.

(B) The owner, board of directors, or other governing body of the senior citizen housing development may take action to prohibit or terminate occupancy by a person who is a qualified permanent resident under paragraph (3) if the owner, board of directors, or other governing body finds, based on credible and objective evidence, that the person is likely to pose a significant threat to the health or safety of others that cannot be ameliorated by means of a reasonable accommodation; provided, however, that action to prohibit or terminate the occupancy may be taken only after doing both of the following:

(i) Providing reasonable notice to and an opportunity to be heard for the disabled person whose occupancy is being challenged, and reasonable notice to the coresident parent or grandparent of that person.

(ii) Giving due consideration to the relevant, credible, and objective information provided in that hearing. The evidence shall be taken and held in a confidential manner, pursuant to a closed session, by the owner, board of directors, or other governing body in order to preserve the privacy of the affected persons.

The affected persons shall be entitled to have present at the hearing an attorney or any other person authorized by them to speak on their behalf or to assist them in the matter.

(4) "Senior citizen housing development" means a residential development developed with more than 20 units as a senior community by its developer and zoned as a senior community by a local governmental entity, or characterized as a senior community in its governing documents, as these are defined in Section 4150, or qualified as a senior community under the federal Fair Housing Amendments Act of 1988 [1], as amended. Any senior citizen housing development which is required to obtain a public report under Section 11010 of the Business and Professions Code and which submits its application for a public report after July 1, 2001, shall be required to have been issued a public report as a senior citizen housing development under Section 11010.05 of the Business and Professions Code.

(5) "Dwelling unit" or "housing" means any residential accommodation other than a mobilehome.

(6) "Cohabitant" refers to persons who live together as husband and wife, or persons who are domestic partners within the meaning of Section 297 of the Family Code.

(7) "Permitted health care resident" means a person hired to provide live-in, long-term, or terminal health care to a qualifying resident, or a family member of the qualifying resident providing that care. For the purposes of this section, the care provided by a permitted health care resident must be substantial in nature and must provide either assistance with necessary daily activities or medical treatment, or both.

A permitted health care resident shall be entitled to continue his or her occupancy, residency, or use of the dwelling unit as a permitted resident in the absence of the senior citizen from the dwelling unit only if both of the following are applicable:

(A) The senior citizen became absent from the dwelling due to hospitalization or other necessary medical treatment and expects to return to his or her residence within 90 days from the date the absence began.

(B) The absent senior citizen or an authorized person acting for the senior citizen submits a written request to the owner, board of directors, or governing board stating that the senior citizen desires that the permitted health care resident be allowed to remain in order to be present when the senior citizen returns to reside in the development.

Upon written request by the senior citizen or an authorized person acting for the senior citizen, the owner, board of directors, or governing board shall have the discretion to allow a permitted health care resident to remain for a time period longer than 90 days from the date that the senior citizen's absence began, if it appears that the senior citizen will return within a period of time not to exceed an additional 90 days.

(c) The covenants, conditions, and restrictions and other documents or written policy shall set forth the limitations on occupancy, residency, or use on the basis of age. Any limitation shall not be more exclusive than to require that one person in residence in each dwelling unit may be required to be a senior citizen and that each other resident in the same dwelling unit may be required to be a qualified permanent resident, a permitted health care resident, or a person under 55 years of age whose occupancy is permitted under subdivision (g) of this section or subdivision (b) of Section 51.12. That limitation may be less exclusive, but shall at least require that the persons commencing any occupancy of a dwelling unit include a senior citizen who intends to reside in the unit as his or her primary residence on a permanent basis. The application of the rules set forth in this subdivision regarding limitations on occupancy may result in less than all of the dwellings being actually occupied by a senior citizen.

(d) The covenants, conditions, and restrictions or other documents or written policy shall permit temporary residency, as a guest of a senior citizen or qualified permanent resident, by a person of less than 55 years of age for periods of time, not more than 60 days in any year, that are specified in the covenants, conditions, and restrictions or other documents or written policy.

(e) Upon the death or dissolution of marriage, or upon hospitalization, or other prolonged absence of the qualifying resident, any qualified permanent resident shall be entitled to continue his or her occupancy, residency, or use of the dwelling unit as a permitted resident. This subdivision shall not apply to a permitted health care resident.

(f) The covenants, conditions, and restrictions or other documents or written policies applicable to any condominium, stock cooperative, limited-equity housing cooperative, planned development, or multiple-family residential property that contained age restrictions on January 1, 1984, shall be enforceable only to the extent permitted by this section, notwithstanding lower age restrictions contained in those documents or policies.

(g) Any person who has the right to reside in, occupy, or use the housing or an unimproved lot subject to this section on or after January 1, 1985, shall not be deprived of the right to continue that residency, occupancy, or use as the result of the enactment of this section by Chapter 1147 of the Statutes of 1996.

(h) A housing development may qualify as a senior citizen housing development under this section even though, as of January 1, 1997, it does not meet the definition of a senior citizen housing development specified in subdivision (b), if the development complies with that definition for every unit that becomes occupied after January 1, 1997, and if the development was once within that definition, and then became noncompliant with the definition as the result of any one of the following:

(1) The development was ordered by a court or a local, state, or federal enforcement agency to allow persons other than qualifying residents, qualified permanent residents, or permitted health care residents to reside in the development.

(2) The development received a notice of a pending or proposed action in, or by, a court, or a local, state, or federal enforcement agency, which action could have resulted in the development being ordered by a court or a state or federal enforcement agency to allow persons other than qualifying residents, qualified permanent residents, or permitted health care residents to reside in the development.

(3) The development agreed to allow persons other than qualifying residents, qualified permanent residents, or permitted health care residents to reside in the development by entering into a stipulation, conciliation agreement, or settlement agreement with a local, state, or federal enforcement agency or with a private party who had filed, or indicated an intent to file, a complaint against the development with a local, state, or federal enforcement agency, or file an action in a court.

(4) The development allowed persons other than qualifying residents, qualified permanent residents, or permitted health care residents to reside in the development on the advice of counsel in order to prevent the possibility of an action being filed

by a private party or by a local, state, or federal enforcement agency.

(i) The covenants, conditions, and restrictions or other documents or written policy of the senior citizen housing development shall permit the occupancy of a dwelling unit by a permitted health care resident during any period that the person is actually providing live-in, long-term, or hospice health care to a qualifying resident for compensation.

(j) This section shall only apply to the County of Riverside. *(Added by Stats.1996, c. 1147 (S.B.2097), § 6. Amended by Stats.1999, c. 324 (S.B.382), § 3; Stats.2000, c. 1004 (S.B.2011), § 5; Stats.2012, c. 181 (A.B.806), § 19, operative Jan. 1, 2014.)*

[1] See Short Title note under 42 U.S.C.A. § 3601 for classification of the Act to the Code.

Law Revision Commission Comments

Subdivision (b)(4) of Section 51.11 is amended to correct a cross-reference to former Section 1351(j).

Subdivision (c) is amended to make a stylistic revision. [40 Cal.L.Rev. Comm. Reports 235 (2010)].

Research References

Miller and Starr California Real Estate § 20:2, The Unruh Civil Rights Act--Coverage.
Miller and Starr California Real Estate § 20:5, The Unruh Civil Rights Act--Age Discrimination.
8 Witkin, California Summary 10th Constitutional Law § 908, (S 908) Housing Discrimination.

§ 51.12. Riverside County; senior housing; legislative findings and declarations; right of residency, occupancy, or use; application of section

(a) The Legislature finds and declares that the requirements for senior housing under Sections 51.10 and 51.11 are more stringent than the requirements for that housing under the federal Fair Housing Amendments Act of 1988 (Public Law 100–430).[1]

(b) Any person who resided in, occupied, or used, prior to January 1, 1990, a dwelling in a senior citizen housing development which relied on the exemption to the special design requirement provided by Section 51.4 as that section read prior to January 1, 2001, shall not be deprived of the right to continue that residency, or occupancy, or use as the result of the changes made to this section by the enactment of Senate Bill 1382 or Senate Bill 2011 at the 1999–2000 Regular Session of the Legislature.

(c) This section shall only apply to the County of Riverside. *(Added by Stats.1996, c. 1147 (S.B.2097), § 7. Amended by Stats.2000, c. 1004 (S.B.2011), § 6.)*

[1] See Short Title note under 42 U.S.C.A. § 3601 for classification of the Act to the Code.

Research References

Miller and Starr California Real Estate § 20:2, The Unruh Civil Rights Act--Coverage.
Miller and Starr California Real Estate § 20:5, The Unruh Civil Rights Act--Age Discrimination.

§ 51.13. Discounts or other benefits conferred on consumers who have suffered loss or reduction of employment or wages

Any discount or other benefit offered to or conferred on a consumer or prospective consumer by a business because the consumer or prospective consumer has suffered the loss or reduction of employment or reduction of wages shall not be considered an arbitrary discrimination in violation of Section 51. *(Added by Stats.2009, c. 641 (S.B.367), § 1, eff. Nov. 2, 2009.)*

Research References

Miller and Starr California Real Estate § 20:2, The Unruh Civil Rights Act--Coverage.
8 Witkin, California Summary 10th Constitutional Law § 898, in General.

§ 52. Denial of civil rights or discrimination; damages; civil action by people or person aggrieved; intervention; unlawful practice complaint

(a) Whoever denies, aids or incites a denial, or makes any discrimination or distinction contrary to Section 51, 51.5, or 51.6, is liable for each and every offense for the actual damages, and any amount that may be determined by a jury, or a court sitting without a jury, up to a maximum of three times the amount of actual damage but in no case less than four thousand dollars ($4,000), and any attorney's fees that may be determined by the court in addition thereto, suffered by any person denied the rights provided in Section 51, 51.5, or 51.6.

(b) Whoever denies the right provided by Section 51.7 or 51.9, or aids, incites, or conspires in that denial, is liable for each and every offense for the actual damages suffered by any person denied that right and, in addition, the following:

(1) An amount to be determined by a jury, or a court sitting without a jury, for exemplary damages.

(2) A civil penalty of twenty-five thousand dollars ($25,000) to be awarded to the person denied the right provided by Section 51.7 in any action brought by the person denied the right, or by the Attorney General, a district attorney, or a city attorney. An action for that penalty brought pursuant to Section 51.7 shall be commenced within three years of the alleged practice.

(3) Attorney's fees as may be determined by the court.

(c) Whenever there is reasonable cause to believe that any person or group of persons is engaged in conduct of resistance to the full enjoyment of any of the rights described in this section, and that conduct is of that nature and is intended to deny the full exercise of those rights, the Attorney General, any district attorney or city attorney, or any person aggrieved by the conduct may bring a civil action in the appropriate court by filing with it a complaint. The complaint shall contain the following:

(1) The signature of the officer, or, in his or her absence, the individual acting on behalf of the officer, or the signature of the person aggrieved.

(2) The facts pertaining to the conduct.

(3) A request for preventive relief, including an application for a permanent or temporary injunction, restraining order, or other order against the person or persons responsible for the conduct, as the complainant deems necessary to ensure the full enjoyment of the rights described in this section.

(d) Whenever an action has been commenced in any court seeking relief from the denial of equal protection of the laws under the Fourteenth Amendment to the Constitution of the United States on account of race, color, religion, sex, national origin, or disability, the Attorney General or any district attorney or city attorney for or in the name of the people of the State of California may intervene in the action upon timely application if the Attorney General or any district attorney or city attorney certifies that the case is of general public importance. In that action, the people of the State of California shall be entitled to the same relief as if it had instituted the action.

(e) Actions brought pursuant to this section are independent of any other actions, remedies, or procedures that may be available to an aggrieved party pursuant to any other law.

(f) Any person claiming to be aggrieved by an alleged unlawful practice in violation of Section 51 or 51.7 may also file a verified complaint with the Department of Fair Employment and Housing pursuant to Section 12948 of the Government Code.

(g) This section does not require any construction, alteration, repair, structural or otherwise, or modification of any sort whatsoever, beyond that construction, alteration, repair, or modification that is otherwise required by other provisions of law, to any new or existing establishment, facility, building, improvement, or any other structure, nor does this section augment, restrict, or alter in any way the authority of the State Architect to require construction, alteration, repair, or modifications that the State Architect otherwise possesses pursuant to other laws.

(h) For the purposes of this section, "actual damages" means special and general damages. This subdivision is declaratory of existing law. *(Added by Stats.1905, c. 413, p. 553, § 2. Amended by Stats.1919, c. 210, p. 309, § 2; Stats.1923, c. 235, p. 485, § 2; Stats.1959, c. 1866, p. 4424, § 2; Stats.1974, c. 1193, p. 2568, § 2; Stats.1976, c. 366, p. 1013, § 2; Stats.1976, c. 1293, p. 5778, § 2.5; Stats.1978, c. 1212, p. 3927, § 1; Stats.1981, c. 521, § 1, eff. Sept. 16, 1981; Stats.1986, c. 244, § 1; Stats.1987, c. 159, § 4; Stats.1989, c. 459, § 1; Stats.1991, c. 607 (S.B.98), § 2; Stats. 1991, c. 839 (A.B.1169), § 2; Stats.1992, c. 913 (A.B.1077), § 3.6; Stats.1994, c. 535 (S.B.1288), § 1; Stats.1998, c. 195 (A.B.2702), § 4; Stats.1999, c; 964 (A.B.519), § 2; Stats.2000, c. 98 (A.B. 2719), § 2; Stats.2001, c. 261 (A.B.587), § 1; Stats.2005, c. 123 (A.B.378), § 1.)*

Research References

Rutter, Cal. Practice Guide: A.D.R. Ch. 5-E, E. Claims Subject to Arbitration (Arbitrability).

Rutter, Cal. Practice Guide: Civil Trials & Evidence Ch. 17-D, D. Costs.

Rutter, Cal. Practice Guide: Civil Trials & Evidence Ch. 17-E, E. Attorney Fees as Costs.

California Practice Guide: Employment Litigation Ch. 5-L, L. Other Statutory Claims.

California Practice Guide: Employment Litigation Ch. 7-G, G. Unruh Civil Rights Act.

Rutter, Cal. Practice Guide: Insurance Litigation Ch. 11-K, K. Statutory Liability.

Rutter, Cal. Practice Guide: Landlord-Tenant Gen. Matls, Highlights.

Rutter, Cal. Practice Guide: Personal Injury Ch. 3-A, A. Introduction.

Rutter, Cal. Practice Guide: Personal Injury Ch. 3-E, E. Punitive Damages.

Rutter, Cal. Practice Guide: Personal Injury Ch. 5-B, B. When to Sue-Statute of Limitations.

Rutter, Cal. Practice Guide: Personal Injury Ch. 5-B, Outline B.

Miller and Starr California Real Estate § 20:7, The Unruh Civil Rights Act--Disability Discrimination.

Miller and Starr California Real Estate § 20:11, The Unruh Civil Rights Act--Violations and Enforcement.

Miller and Starr California Real Estate § 20:29, Discrimination by a Real Estate Broker.

Miller and Starr California Real Estate § 34:99, Punitive Damages--Judicial Review.

20 NO. 1 Miller & Starr, California Real Estate Newsalert 9, Discrimination.

3 Witkin Cal. Proc. 5th Actions § 483, (S 483) Three Years.

2 Witkin Cal. Proc. 5th Courts § 282, (S 282) Particular Actions.

7 Witkin Cal. Proc. 5th Judgment § 95, (S 95) Prevailing Party in Specified Actions.

7 Witkin Cal. Proc. 5th Judgment § 223, (S 223) Civil Rights Actions.

4 Witkin Cal. Proc. 5th Pleading § 155, in General.

4 Witkin Cal. Proc. 5th Pleading § 215, Special Statutes.

5 Witkin, California Summary 10th Torts § 303, (S 303) Discriminatory Allocation of Protective Services During Riot.

6 Witkin, California Summary 10th Torts § 1570, Treble Damages.

8 Witkin, California Summary 10th Constitutional Law § 895, Hate Crimes, Intimidation, and Threats of Violence.

8 Witkin, California Summary 10th Constitutional Law § 896, Sexual Harassment in Business and Professional Relationships.

8 Witkin, California Summary 10th Constitutional Law § 897, Other Discrimination Statutes.

8 Witkin, California Summary 10th Constitutional Law § 898, in General.

8 Witkin, California Summary 10th Constitutional Law § 906, (S 906) Business Discrimination.

8 Witkin, California Summary 10th Constitutional Law § 907, (S 907) Racial Discrimination.

8 Witkin, California Summary 10th Constitutional Law § 910, (S 910) Classification Based on Marital Status.

8 Witkin, California Summary 10th Constitutional Law § 914, Enforcement.

8 Witkin, California Summary 10th Constitutional Law § 957, in General.

8 Witkin, California Summary 10th Constitutional Law § 959, Enforcement.

§ 52.1. Civil actions for protection of rights; damages, injunctive and other equitable relief; violations of orders

(a) If a person or persons, whether or not acting under color of law, interferes by threats, intimidation, or coercion, or attempts to interfere by threats, intimidation, or coercion, with the exercise or enjoyment by any individual or individuals of rights secured by the Constitution or laws of the United States, or of the rights secured by the Constitution or laws of this state, the Attorney General, or any district attorney or city attorney may bring a civil action for injunctive and other appropriate equitable relief in the name of the people of the State of California, in order to protect the peaceable exercise or enjoyment of the right or rights secured. An action brought by the Attorney General, any district attorney, or any city attorney may also seek a civil penalty of twenty-five thousand dollars ($25,-000). If this civil penalty is requested, it shall be assessed individually against each person who is determined to have violated this section and the penalty shall be awarded to each individual whose rights under this section are determined to have been violated.

(b) Any individual whose exercise or enjoyment of rights secured by the Constitution or laws of the United States, or of rights secured by the Constitution or laws of this state, has been interfered with, or attempted to be interfered with, as described in subdivision (a), may institute and prosecute in his or her own name and on his or her own behalf a civil action for damages, including, but not limited to, damages under Section 52, injunctive relief, and other appropriate equitable relief to protect the peaceable exercise or enjoyment of the right or rights secured.

(c) An action brought pursuant to subdivision (a) or (b) may be filed either in the superior court for the county in which the conduct complained of occurred or in the superior court for the county in which a person whose conduct complained of resides or has his or her place of business. An action brought by the Attorney General pursuant to subdivision (a) also may be filed in the superior court for any county wherein the Attorney General has an office, and in that case, the jurisdiction of the court shall extend throughout the state.

(d) If a court issues a temporary restraining order or a preliminary or permanent injunction in an action brought pursuant to subdivision (a) or (b), ordering a defendant to refrain from conduct or activities, the order issued shall include the following statement: VIOLATION OF THIS ORDER IS A CRIME PUNISHABLE UNDER SECTION 422.77 OF THE PENAL CODE.

(e) The court shall order the plaintiff or the attorney for the plaintiff to deliver, or the clerk of the court to mail, two copies of any order, extension, modification, or termination thereof granted pursuant to this section, by the close of the business day on which the order, extension, modification, or termination was granted, to each local law enforcement agency having jurisdiction over the residence of the plaintiff and any other locations where the court determines that acts of violence against the plaintiff are likely to occur. Those local law enforcement agencies shall be designated by the plaintiff or the attorney for the plaintiff. Each appropriate law enforcement agency receiving any order, extension, or modification of any order issued pursuant to this section

Civil

shall serve forthwith one copy thereof upon the defendant. Each appropriate law enforcement agency shall provide to any law enforcement officer responding to the scene of reported violence, information as to the existence of, terms, and current status of, any order issued pursuant to this section.

(f) A court shall not have jurisdiction to issue an order or injunction under this section, if that order or injunction would be prohibited under Section 527.3 of the Code of Civil Procedure.

(g) An action brought pursuant to this section is independent of any other action, remedy, or procedure that may be available to an aggrieved individual under any other provision of law, including, but not limited to, an action, remedy, or procedure brought pursuant to Section 51.7.

(h) In addition to any damages, injunction, or other equitable relief awarded in an action brought pursuant to subdivision (b), the court may award the petitioner or plaintiff reasonable attorney's fees.

(i) A violation of an order described in subdivision (d) may be punished either by prosecution under Section 422.77 of the Penal Code, or by a proceeding for contempt brought pursuant to Title 5 (commencing with Section 1209) of Part 3 of the Code of Civil Procedure. However, in any proceeding pursuant to the Code of Civil Procedure, if it is determined that the person proceeded against is guilty of the contempt charged, in addition to any other relief, a fine may be imposed not exceeding one thousand dollars ($1,000), or the person may be ordered imprisoned in a county jail not exceeding six months, or the court may order both the imprisonment and fine.

(j) Speech alone is not sufficient to support an action brought pursuant to subdivision (a) or (b), except upon a showing that the speech itself threatens violence against a specific person or group of persons; and the person or group of persons against whom the threat is directed reasonably fears that, because of the speech, violence will be committed against them or their property and that the person threatening violence had the apparent ability to carry out the threat.

(k) No order issued in any proceeding brought pursuant to subdivision (a) or (b) shall restrict the content of any person's speech. An order restricting the time, place, or manner of any person's speech shall do so only to the extent reasonably necessary to protect the peaceable exercise or enjoyment of constitutional or statutory rights, consistent with the constitutional rights of the person sought to be enjoined. *(Added by Stats.1987, c. 1277, § 3. Amended by Stats.1990, c. 392 (A.B. 2683), § 1; Stats.1991, c. 607 (S.B.98), § 3; Stats.2000, c. 98 (A.B.2719), § 3; Stats.2001, c. 261 (A.B.587), § 2; Stats.2002, c. 784 (S.B.1316), § 11; Stats.2004, c. 700 (S.B.1234), § 1.)*

Law Revision Commission Comments

Subdivision (e) of Section 52.1 is amended to reflect elimination of the county clerk's role as ex officio clerk of the superior court. See former Gov't Code § 26800 (county clerk acting as clerk of superior court). The powers, duties, and responsibilities formerly exercised by the county clerk as ex officio clerk of the court are delegated to the court administrative or executive officer, and the county clerk is relieved of those powers, duties, and responsibilities. See Gov't Code §§ 69840 (powers, duties, and responsibilities of clerk of court and deputy clerk of court), 71620 (trial court personnel). [32 Cal.L.Rev.Comm. Reports 65 (2002)].

Research References

Rutter, Cal. Practice Guide: A.D.R. Ch. 5-H, H. Conduct of Arbitration Proceedings.
Rutter, Cal. Practice Guide: A.D.R. Ch. 5-I, I. Arbitrator's Award.
California Practice Guide: Employment Litigation Ch. 5-L, L. Other Statutory Claims.
California Practice Guide: Employment Litigation Ch. 7-G, G. Unruh Civil Rights Act.

California Practice Guide: Employment Litigation Ch. 10-A, A. Sources of Law Prohibiting Harassment.
California Practice Guide: Employment Litigation Ch. 7-G, Outline G.
California Practice Guide: Employment Litigation Ch. 10-A, Outline a.
Rutter, Cal. Practice Guide: Personal Injury Ch. 3-E, E. Punitive Damages.
Rutter, Cal. Practice Guide: Personal Injury Ch. 3-G, G. Independent Damages Claims.
Rutter, Cal. Practice Guide: Real Prop. Transactions Ch. 2-C, C. Broker's Relationship and Obligations to Principal and Third Parties.
Miller and Starr California Real Estate § 20:11, The Unruh Civil Rights Act--Violations and Enforcement.
Miller and Starr California Real Estate § 35:84, Ancillary Remedies.
3 Witkin Cal. Proc. 5th Actions § 558, (S 558) Civil Rights Violations.
3 Witkin Cal. Proc. 5th Actions § 664, (S 664) in General.
7 Witkin Cal. Proc. 5th Judgment § 95, (S 95) Prevailing Party in Specified Actions.
7 Witkin Cal. Proc. 5th Judgment § 235, (S 235) Statutory Authorization.
5 Witkin, California Summary 10th Torts § 368, (S 368) Institution or Prosecution of Judicial or Administrative Proceeding.
8 Witkin, California Summary 10th Constitutional Law § 895, Hate Crimes, Intimidation, and Threats of Violence.
8 Witkin, California Summary 10th Constitutional Law § 898, in General.

§ 52.2.   Court of competent jurisdiction; defined; actions

An action pursuant to Section 52 or 54.3 may be brought in any court of competent jurisdiction. A "court of competent jurisdiction" shall include small claims court if the amount of the damages sought in the action does not exceed the jurisdictional limits stated in Sections 116.220 and 116.221 of the Code of Civil Procedure. *(Added by Stats.1998, c. 195 (A.B.2702), § 5. Amended by Stats.2006, c. 167 (A.B.2618), § 1.)*

Research References

Rutter, Cal. Practice Guide: Civ. Pro. Before Trial Ch. 3-A, A. Subject Matter Jurisdiction (Competency).
Miller and Starr California Real Estate § 20:11, The Unruh Civil Rights Act--Violations and Enforcement.
17 NO. 4 Miller & Starr, California Real Estate Newsalert 2, Statutory Update:.
17 NO. 6 Miller & Starr, California Real Estate Newsalert 20, Table of Statutes (Newsalert Vol 17).
2 Witkin Cal. Proc. 5th Courts § 282, (S 282) Particular Actions.
8 Witkin, California Summary 10th Constitutional Law § 914, Enforcement.
8 Witkin, California Summary 10th Constitutional Law § 959, Enforcement.

§ 52.3.   Law enforcement officers;   prohibitions against conduct depriving persons of Constitutional rights, privileges, or immunities;   civil actions

(a) No governmental authority, or agent of a governmental authority, or person acting on behalf of a governmental authority, shall engage in a pattern or practice of conduct by law enforcement officers that deprives any person of rights, privileges, or immunities secured or protected by the Constitution or laws of the United States or by the Constitution or laws of California.

(b) The Attorney General may bring a civil action in the name of the people to obtain appropriate equitable and declaratory relief to eliminate the pattern or practice of conduct specified in subdivision (a), whenever the Attorney General has reasonable cause to believe that a violation of subdivision (a) has occurred. *(Added by Stats.2000, c. 622 (A.B.2484), § 1.)*

Research References

8 Witkin, California Summary 10th Constitutional Law § 897, Other Discrimination Statutes.

§ 52.4.   Civil action for damages arising from gender violence

(a) Any person who has been subjected to gender violence may bring a civil action for damages against any responsible party. The plaintiff may seek actual damages, compensatory damages, punitive damages, injunctive relief, any combination of those, or any other appropriate relief. A prevailing plaintiff may also be awarded attorney's fees and costs.

(b) An action brought pursuant to this section shall be commenced within three years of the act, or if the victim was a minor when the act occurred, within eight years after the date the plaintiff attains the age of majority or within three years after the date the plaintiff discovers or reasonably should have discovered the psychological injury or illness occurring after the age of majority that was caused by the act, whichever date occurs later.

(c) For purposes of this section, "gender violence," is a form of sex discrimination and means any of the following:

(1) One or more acts that would constitute a criminal offense under state law that has as an element the use, attempted use, or threatened use of physical force against the person or property of another, committed at least in part based on the gender of the victim, whether or not those acts have resulted in criminal complaints, charges, prosecution, or conviction.

(2) A physical intrusion or physical invasion of a sexual nature under coercive conditions, whether or not those acts have resulted in criminal complaints, charges, prosecution, or conviction.

(d) Notwithstanding any other laws that may establish the liability of an employer for the acts of an employee, this section does not establish any civil liability of a person because of his or her status as an employer, unless the employer personally committed an act of gender violence. *(Added by Stats.2002, c. 842 (A.B.1928), § 2.)*

Research References

Rutter, Cal. Practice Guide: Civ. Pro. Before Trial Ch. 9(II)-A, A. Injunctions.
California Practice Guide: Employment Litigation Ch. 10-A, A. Sources of Law Prohibiting Harassment.
California Practice Guide: Employment Litigation Ch. 10-A, Outline a.
3 Witkin Cal. Proc. 5th Actions § 483, (S 483) Three Years.
3 Witkin Cal. Proc. 5th Actions § 487, (S 487) Eight Years.
3 Witkin Cal. Proc. 5th Actions § 593, (S 593) Statutory Rule.
11 Witkin, California Summary 10th Husband and Wife § 371, (S 371) Civil Remedies.
5 Witkin, California Summary 10th Torts § 468, Gender-Related Violence.
8 Witkin, California Summary 10th Constitutional Law § 897, Other Discrimination Statutes.

§ 52.5. Civil action for damages to victims of human trafficking

(a) A victim of human trafficking, as defined in Section 236.1 of the Penal Code, may bring a civil action for actual damages, compensatory damages, punitive damages, injunctive relief, any combination of those, or any other appropriate relief. A prevailing plaintiff may also be awarded attorney's fees and costs.

(b) In addition to the remedies specified herein, in any action under subdivision (a), the plaintiff may be awarded up to three times his or her actual damages or ten thousand dollars ($10,000), whichever is greater. In addition, punitive damages may also be awarded upon proof of the defendant's malice, oppression, fraud, or duress in committing the act of human trafficking.

(c) An action brought pursuant to this section shall be commenced within five years of the date on which the trafficking victim was freed from the trafficking situation, or if the victim was a minor when the act of human trafficking against the victim occurred, within eight years after the date the plaintiff attains the age of majority.

(d) If a person entitled to sue is under a disability at the time the cause of action accrues, so that it is impossible or impracticable for him or her to bring an action, then the time of the disability is not part of the time limited for the commencement of the action. Disability will toll the running of the statute of limitation for this action.

(1) Disability includes being a minor, insanity, imprisonment, or other incapacity or incompetence.

(2) The statute of limitations shall not run against an incompetent or minor plaintiff simply because a guardian ad litem has been appointed. A guardian ad litem's failure to bring a plaintiff's action within the applicable limitation period will not prejudice the plaintiff's right to do so after his or her disability ceases.

(3) A defendant is estopped to assert a defense of the statute of limitations when the expiration of the statute is due to conduct by the defendant inducing the plaintiff to delay the filing of the action, or due to threats made by the defendant causing duress upon the plaintiff.

(4) The suspension of the statute of limitations due to disability, lack of knowledge, or estoppel applies to all other related claims arising out of the trafficking situation.

(5) The running of the statute of limitations is postponed during the pendency of any criminal proceedings against the victim.

(e) The running of the statute of limitations may be suspended where a person entitled to sue could not have reasonably discovered the cause of action due to circumstances resulting from the trafficking situation, such as psychological trauma, cultural and linguistic isolation, and the inability to access services.

(f) A prevailing plaintiff may also be awarded reasonable attorney's fees and litigation costs including, but not limited to, expert witness fees and expenses as part of the costs.

(g) Any restitution paid by the defendant to the victim shall be credited against any judgment, award, or settlement obtained pursuant to this section. Any judgment, award, or settlement obtained pursuant to an action under this section shall be subject to the provisions of Section 13963 of the Government Code.

(h) Any civil action filed under this section shall be stayed during the pendency of any criminal action arising out of the same occurrence in which the claimant is the victim. As used in this section, a "criminal action" includes investigation and prosecution, and is pending until a final adjudication in the trial court, or dismissal. *(Added by Stats.2005, c. 240 (A.B.22), § 2.)*

Research References

5 Witkin, California Summary 10th Torts § 468A, (New)-Human Trafficking.

§ 52.6. Notice to be posted at specified businesses and establishments; slavery and human trafficking; location of posting; contents; languages; model notice; civil penalties

(a) Each of the following businesses and other establishments shall, upon the availability of the model notice described in subdivision (d), post a notice that complies with the requirements of this section in a conspicuous place near the public entrance of the establishment or in another conspicuous location in clear view of the public and employees where similar notices are customarily posted:

(1) On-sale general public premises licensees under the Alcoholic Beverage Control Act (Division 9 (commencing with Section 23000) of the Business and Professions Code).

(2) Adult or sexually oriented businesses, as defined in subdivision (a) of Section 318.5 of the Penal Code.

(3) Primary airports, as defined in Section 47102(16) of Title 49 of the United States Code.

(4) Intercity passenger rail or light rail stations.

(5) Bus stations.

(6) Truck stops. For purposes of this section, "truck stop" means a privately owned and operated facility that provides food, fuel, shower or other sanitary facilities, and lawful overnight truck parking.

(7) Emergency rooms within general acute care hospitals.

(8) Urgent care centers.

(9) Farm labor contractors, as defined in subdivision (b) of Section 1682 of the Labor Code.

(10) Privately operated job recruitment centers.

(11) Roadside rest areas.

(12) Businesses or establishments that offer massage or bodywork services for compensation and are not described in paragraph (1) of subdivision (b) of Section 4612 of the Business and Professions Code.

(b) The notice to be posted pursuant to subdivision (a) shall be at least eight and one-half inches by 11 inches in size, written in a 16–point font, and shall state the following:

"If you or someone you know is being forced to engage in any activity and cannot leave—whether it is commercial sex, housework, farm work, construction, factory, retail, or restaurant work, or any other activity—call the National Human Trafficking Resource Center at 1–888–373–7888 or the California Coalition to Abolish Slavery and Trafficking (CAST) at 1–888–KEY–2–FRE(EDOM) or 1–888–539–2373 to access help and services.

Victims of slavery and human trafficking are protected under United States and California law.

The hotlines are:
· Available 24 hours a day, 7 days a week.
· Toll-free.
· Operated by nonprofit, nongovernmental organizations.
· Anonymous and confidential.
· Accessible in more than 160 languages.
· Able to provide help, referral to services, training, and general information."

(c) The notice to be posted pursuant to subdivision (a) shall be printed in English, Spanish, and in one other language that is the most widely spoken language in the county where the establishment is located and for which translation is mandated by the federal Voting Rights Act (42 U.S.C. Sec. 1973 et seq.), as applicable. This section does not require a business or other establishment in a county where a language other than English or Spanish is the most widely spoken language to print the notice in more than one language in addition to English and Spanish.

(d) On or before April 1, 2013, the Department of Justice shall develop a model notice that complies with the requirements of this section and make the model notice available for download on the department's Internet Web site.

(e) A business or establishment that fails to comply with the requirements of this section is liable for a civil penalty of five hundred dollars ($500) for a first offense and one thousand dollars ($1,000) for each subsequent offense. A government entity identified in Section 17204 of the Business and Professions Code may bring an action to impose a civil penalty pursuant to

this subdivision against a business or establishment if a local or state agency with authority to regulate that business or establishment has satisfied both of the following:

(1) Provided the business or establishment with reasonable notice of noncompliance, which informs the business or establishment that it is subject to a civil penalty if it does not correct the violation within 30 days from the date the notice is sent to the business or establishment.

(2) Verified that the violation was not corrected within the 30–day period described in paragraph (1). *(Added by Stats.2012, c. 515 (S.B.1193), § 1.)*

§ 52.7. Subcutaneous implanting of identification device; penalties; limitations; restitution; liberal construction; independent action; existing law; definitions

(a) Except as provided in subdivision (g), a person shall not require, coerce, or compel any other individual to undergo the subcutaneous implanting of an identification device.

(b)(1) Any person who violates subdivision (a) may be assessed an initial civil penalty of no more than ten thousand dollars ($10,000), and no more than one thousand dollars ($1,000) for each day the violation continues until the deficiency is corrected. That civil penalty may be assessed and recovered in a civil action brought in any court of competent jurisdiction. The court may also grant a prevailing plaintiff reasonable attorney's fees and litigation costs, including, but not limited to, expert witness fees and expenses as part of the costs.

(2) A person who is implanted with a subcutaneous identification device in violation of subdivision (a) may bring a civil action for actual damages, compensatory damages, punitive damages, injunctive relief, any combination of those, or any other appropriate relief.

(3) Additionally, punitive damages may also be awarded upon proof of the defendant's malice, oppression, fraud, or duress in requiring, coercing, or compelling the plaintiff to undergo the subcutaneous implanting of an identification device.

(c)(1) An action brought pursuant to this section shall be commenced within three years of the date upon which the identification device was implanted.

(2) If the victim was a dependent adult or minor when the implantation occurred, actions brought pursuant to this section shall be commenced within three years after the date the plaintiff, or his or her guardian or parent, discovered or reasonably should have discovered the implant, or within eight years after the plaintiff attains the age of majority, whichever date occurs later.

(3) The statute of limitations shall not run against a dependent adult or minor plaintiff simply because a guardian ad litem has been appointed. A guardian ad litem's failure to bring a plaintiff's action within the applicable limitation period will not prejudice the plaintiff's right to do so.

(4) A defendant is estopped to assert a defense of the statute of limitations when the expiration of the statute is due to conduct by the defendant inducing the plaintiff to delay the filing of the action, or due to threats made by the defendant causing duress upon the plaintiff.

(d) Any restitution paid by the defendant to the victim shall be credited against any judgment, award, or settlement obtained pursuant to this section. Any judgment, award, or settlement obtained pursuant to an action under this section shall be subject to the provisions of Section 13963 of the Government Code.

(e) The provisions of this section shall be liberally construed so as to protect privacy and bodily integrity.

(f) Actions brought pursuant to this section are independent of any other actions, remedies, or procedures that may be available to an aggrieved party pursuant to any other law.

(g) This section shall not in any way modify existing statutory or case law regarding the rights of parents or guardians, the rights of children or minors, or the rights of dependent adults.

(h) For purposes of this section:

(1) "Identification device" means any item, application, or product that is passively or actively capable of transmitting personal information, including, but not limited to, devices using radio frequency technology.

(2) "Person" means an individual, business association, partnership, limited partnership, corporation, limited liability company, trust, estate, cooperative association, or other entity.

(3) "Personal information" includes any of the following data elements to the extent they are used alone or in conjunction with any other information used to identify an individual:

(A) First or last name.

(B) Address.

(C) Telephone number.

(D) E-mail, Internet Protocol, or Web site address.

(E) Date of birth.

(F) Driver's license number or California identification card number.

(G) Any unique personal identifier number contained or encoded on a driver's license or identification card issued pursuant to Section 13000 of the Vehicle Code.

(H) Bank, credit card, or other financial institution account number.

(I) Any unique personal identifier contained or encoded on a health insurance, health benefit, or benefit card or record issued in conjunction with any government-supported aid program.

(J) Religion.

(K) Ethnicity or nationality.

(L) Photograph.

(M) Fingerprint or other biometric identifier.

(N) Social security number.

(O) Any unique personal identifier.

(4) "Require, coerce, or compel" includes physical violence, threat, intimidation, retaliation, the conditioning of any private or public benefit or care on consent to implantation, including employment, promotion, or other employment benefit, or by any means that causes a reasonable person of ordinary susceptibilities to acquiesce to implantation when he or she otherwise would not.

(5) "Subcutaneous" means existing, performed, or introduced under or on the skin. *(Added by Stats.2007, c. 538 (S.B.362), § 1.)*

Research References

3 Witkin Cal. Proc. 5th Actions § 483, (S 483) Three Years.
3 Witkin Cal. Proc. 5th Actions § 487, (S 487) Eight Years.
5 Witkin, California Summary 10th Torts § 468B, (New)-Implantation of Identification Device.

§ 53. Restrictions upon transfer or use of realty because of sex, race, color, religion, ancestry, national origin, or disability

(a) Every provision in a written instrument relating to real property that purports to forbid or restrict the conveyance, encumbrance, leasing, or mortgaging of that real property to any person because of any characteristic listed or defined in subdivision (b) or (e) of Section 51 is void, and every restriction or prohibition as to the use or occupation of real property because of any characteristic listed or defined in subdivision (b) or (e) of Section 51 is void.

(b) Every restriction or prohibition, whether by way of covenant, condition upon use or occupation, or upon transfer of title to real property, which restriction or prohibition directly or indirectly limits the acquisition, use or occupation of that property because of any characteristic listed or defined in subdivision (b) or (e) of Section 51 is void.

(c) In any action to declare that a restriction or prohibition specified in subdivision (a) or (b) is void, the court shall take judicial notice of the recorded instrument or instruments containing the prohibitions or restrictions in the same manner that it takes judicial notice of the matters listed in Section 452 of the Evidence Code. *(Added by Stats.1961, c. 1877, p. 3976, § 1. Amended by Stats.1965, c. 299, p. 1356, § 6, operative Jan. 1, 1967; Stats.1974, c. 1193, p. 2568, § 3; Stats.1987, c. 159, § 5; Stats.1992, c. 913 (A.B.1077), § 3.8; Stats.2005, c. 420 (A.B. 1400), § 7.)*

Law Revision Commission Comments

This revision of Section 53 provides, in effect, that the court may take judicial notice of the matter specified in subdivision (c) and is required to take judicial notice of such matter upon request if the party making the request supplies the court with sufficient information. See EVIDENCE CODE §§ 452 and 453 and the *Comments* thereto.

Research References

Miller and Starr California Real Estate § 20:2, The Unruh Civil Rights Act--Coverage.
Miller and Starr California Real Estate § 24:1, Types of Enforceable Restrictions.
Miller and Starr California Real Estate § 8:57, Conveyance in Violation of Public Policy or Statute.
Miller and Starr California Real Estate § 9:40, Restraints Based on Transferee's Membership in Protected Class.
Miller and Starr California Real Estate § 20:29, Discrimination by a Real Estate Broker.
Miller and Starr California Real Estate § 24:32, Defenses to Enforcement--Public Policy or Discrimination.
Miller and Starr California Real Estate § 24:40, Amendment to Restrictions--Deletion of Discriminatory Covenants.
16 NO. 4 Miller & Starr, California Real Estate Newsalert 10, Discrimination.
16 NO. 5 Miller & Starr, California Real Estate Newsalert 26, State Board of Equalization Issues Comprehensive Summary and Qs and As for Transfers of Base Year Values of Principal Residences.
17 NO. 2 Miller & Starr, California Real Estate Newsalert 1, The "Big Daddy" of Civil Rights Acts (Unruh Act) Nears Fifty.
19 NO. 5 Miller & Starr, California Real Estate Newsalert 14, Discrimination.
4 Witkin Cal. Proc. 5th Pleading § 287, in General.
12 Witkin, California Summary 10th Real Property § 116, Age.
12 Witkin, California Summary 10th Real Property § 201, (S 201) California Statute.
12 Witkin, California Summary 10th Real Property § 202, (S 202) Expanded Scope of Rule.
12 Witkin, California Summary 10th Real Property § 341, (S 341) Expiration.
12 Witkin, California Summary 10th Real Property § 442, in General.
8 Witkin, California Summary 10th Constitutional Law § 897, Other Discrimination Statutes.
8 Witkin, California Summary 10th Constitutional Law § 898, in General.
8 Witkin, California Summary 10th Constitutional Law § 957, in General.

Part 2.5

BLIND AND OTHER PHYSICALLY DISABLED PERSONS

§ 54. Right to streets, highways, and other public places; disability

(a) Individuals with disabilities or medical conditions have the same right as the general public to the full and free use of the streets, highways, sidewalks, walkways, public buildings, medical facilities, including hospitals, clinics, and physicians' offices, public facilities, and other public places.

(b) For purposes of this section:

(1) "Disability" means any mental or physical disability as defined in Section 12926 of the Government Code.

(2) "Medical condition" has the same meaning as defined in subdivision (h) of Section 12926 of the Government Code.

(c) A violation of the right of an individual under the Americans with Disabilities Act of 1990 (Public Law 101–336) also constitutes a violation of this section. *(Added by Stats.1968, c. 461, p. 1024, § 1. Amended by Stats.1992, c. 913 (A.B.1077), § 4; Stats.1994, c. 1257 (S.B.1240), § 1; Stats.1996, c. 498 (S.B.1687), § 1; Stats.2000, c. 1049 (A.B.2222), § 4.)*

Research References

Rutter, Cal. Practice Guide: A.D.R. Ch. 3B-C, C. Statutorily-Mandated ADR.

Rutter, Cal. Practice Guide: Civil Trials & Evidence Ch. 17-E, E. Attorney Fees as Costs.

Miller and Starr California Real Estate § 20:7, The Unruh Civil Rights Act--Disability Discrimination.

Miller and Starr California Real Estate § 20:28, Americans With Disabilities Act.

Miller and Starr California Real Estate § 20:29, Discrimination by a Real Estate Broker.

Miller and Starr California Real Estate § 22:75, Injuries to Additional Unique Plaintiff Categories.

18 NO. 1 Miller & Starr, California Real Estate Newsalert 19, Landowners' Liability.

19 NO. 2 Miller & Starr, California Real Estate Newsalert 13, Discrimination.

19 NO. 1 Miller & Starr, California Real Estate Newsalert 19, Landowners' Liability.

4 Witkin Cal. Proc. 5th Pleading § 287, in General.

8 Witkin, California Summary 10th Constitutional Law § 941, (S 941) Other Prohibited Discrimination.

8 Witkin, California Summary 10th Constitutional Law § 957, in General.

8 Witkin, California Summary 10th Constitutional Law § 958, Physical Access.

8 Witkin, California Summary 10th Constitutional Law § 959, Enforcement.

§ 54.1. Access to public conveyances, places of public accommodation, amusement or resort, and housing accommodations

(a)(1) Individuals with disabilities shall be entitled to full and equal access, as other members of the general public, to accommodations, advantages, facilities, medical facilities, including hospitals, clinics, and physicians' offices, and privileges of all common carriers, airplanes, motor vehicles, railroad trains, motorbuses, streetcars, boats, or any other public conveyances or modes of transportation (whether private, public, franchised, licensed, contracted, or otherwise provided), telephone facilities, adoption agencies, private schools, hotels, lodging places, places of public accommodation, amusement, or resort, and other places to which the general public is invited, subject only to the conditions and limitations established by law, or state or federal regulation, and applicable alike to all persons.

(2) As used in this section, "telephone facilities" means tariff items and other equipment and services that have been approved by the Public Utilities Commission to be used by individuals with disabilities in a manner feasible and compatible with the existing telephone network provided by the telephone companies.

(3) "Full and equal access," for purposes of this section in its application to transportation, means access that meets the standards of Titles II and III of the Americans with Disabilities Act of 1990 (Public Law 101–336) [1] and federal regulations adopted pursuant thereto, except that, if the laws of this state prescribe higher standards, it shall mean access that meets those higher standards.

(b)(1) Individuals with disabilities shall be entitled to full and equal access, as other members of the general public, to all housing accommodations offered for rent, lease, or compensation in this state, subject to the conditions and limitations established by law, or state or federal regulation, and applicable alike to all persons.

(2) "Housing accommodations" means any real property, or portion thereof, that is used or occupied, or is intended, arranged, or designed to be used or occupied, as the home, residence, or sleeping place of one or more human beings, but shall not include any accommodations included within subdivision (a) or any single-family residence the occupants of which rent, lease, or furnish for compensation not more than one room therein.

(3)(A) Any person renting, leasing, or otherwise providing real property for compensation shall not refuse to permit an individual with a disability, at that person's expense, to make reasonable modifications of the existing rented premises if the modifications are necessary to afford the person full enjoyment of the premises. However, any modifications under this paragraph may be conditioned on the disabled tenant entering into an agreement to restore the interior of the premises to the condition existing prior to the modifications. No additional security may be required on account of an election to make modifications to the rented premises under this paragraph, but the lessor and tenant may negotiate, as part of the agreement to restore the premises, a provision requiring the disabled tenant to pay an amount into an escrow account, not to exceed a reasonable estimate of the cost of restoring the premises.

(B) Any person renting, leasing, or otherwise providing real property for compensation shall not refuse to make reasonable accommodations in rules, policies, practices, or services, when those accommodations may be necessary to afford individuals with a disability equal opportunity to use and enjoy the premises.

(4) Nothing in this subdivision shall require any person renting, leasing, or providing for compensation real property to modify his or her property in any way or provide a higher degree of care for an individual with a disability than for an individual who is not disabled.

(5) Except as provided in paragraph (6), nothing in this part shall require any person renting, leasing, or providing for compensation real property, if that person refuses to accept tenants who have dogs, to accept as a tenant an individual with a disability who has a dog.

(6)(A) It shall be deemed a denial of equal access to housing accommodations within the meaning of this subdivision for any person, firm, or corporation to refuse to lease or rent housing accommodations to an individual who is blind or visually impaired on the basis that the individual uses the services of a guide dog, an individual who is deaf or hearing impaired on the basis that the individual uses the services of a signal dog, or to an individual with any other disability on the basis that the individual uses the services of a service dog, or to refuse to permit such an individual who is blind or visually impaired to keep a guide dog, an individual who is deaf or hearing impaired to keep a signal dog, or an individual with any other disability to keep a service dog on the premises.

(B) Except in the normal performance of duty as a mobility or signal aid, nothing contained in this paragraph shall be construed to prevent the owner of a housing accommodation from establishing terms in a lease or rental agreement that reasonably regulate the presence of guide dogs, signal dogs, or service dogs on the premises of a housing accommodation, nor shall this paragraph be construed to relieve a tenant from any liability otherwise imposed by law for real and personal property damages caused by such a dog when proof of the same exists.

(C)(i) As used in this subdivision, "guide dog" means any guide dog that was trained by a person licensed under Chapter 9.5 (commencing with Section 7200) of Division 3 of the Business and Professions Code or as defined in the regulations implementing Title III of the Americans with Disabilities Act of 1990 (Public Law 101–336).

(ii) As used in this subdivision, "signal dog" means any dog trained to alert an individual who is deaf or hearing impaired to intruders or sounds.

(iii) As used in this subdivision, "service dog" means any dog individually trained to the requirements of the individual with a disability, including, but not limited to, minimal protection work, rescue work, pulling a wheelchair, or fetching dropped items.

(7) It shall be deemed a denial of equal access to housing accommodations within the meaning of this subdivision for any person, firm, or corporation to refuse to lease or rent housing accommodations to an individual who is blind or visually impaired, an individual who is deaf or hearing impaired, or other individual with a disability on the basis that the individual with a disability is partially or wholly dependent upon the income of his or her spouse, if the spouse is a party to the lease or rental agreement. Nothing in this subdivision, however, shall prohibit a lessor or landlord from considering the aggregate financial status of an individual with a disability and his or her spouse.

(c) Visually impaired or blind persons and persons licensed to train guide dogs for individuals who are visually impaired or blind pursuant to Chapter 9.5 (commencing with Section 7200) of Division 3 of the Business and Professions Code or guide dogs as defined in the regulations implementing Title III of the Americans with Disabilities Act of 1990 (Public Law 101–336), and persons who are deaf or hearing impaired and persons authorized to train signal dogs for individuals who are deaf or hearing impaired, and other individuals with a disability and persons authorized to train service dogs for individuals with a disability, may take dogs, for the purpose of training them as guide dogs, signal dogs, or service dogs in any of the places specified in subdivisions (a) and (b). These persons shall ensure that the dog is on a leash and tagged as a guide dog, signal dog, or service dog by identification tag issued by the county clerk, animal control department, or other agency, as authorized by Chapter 3.5 (commencing with Section 30850) of Division 14 of the Food and Agricultural Code. In addition, the person shall be liable for any provable damage done to the premises or facilities by his or her dog.

(d) A violation of the right of an individual under the Americans with Disabilities Act of 1990 (Public Law 101–336) also constitutes a violation of this section, and nothing in this section shall be construed to limit the access of any person in violation of that act.

(e) Nothing in this section shall preclude the requirement of the showing of a license plate or disabled placard when required by enforcement units enforcing disabled persons parking violations pursuant to Sections 22507.8 and 22511.8 of the Vehicle Code. *(Added by Stats.1968, c. 461, p. 1092, § 1. Amended by Stats.1969, c. 832, p. 1664, § 1; Stats.1972, c. 819, p. 1465, § 1; Stats.1974, c. 108, p. 223, § 1; Stats.1976, c. 971, p. 2269, § 1; Stats.1976, c. 972, p. 2272, § 1.5; Stats.1977, c. 700, p. 2256, § 1; Stats.1978, c. 380, p. 1128, § 12; Stats.1979, c. 293, p. 1092, § 1; Stats.1980, c. 773, § 1; Stats.1988, c. 1595, § 2; Stats.1992, c. 913 (A.B.1077), § 5; Stats.1993, c. 1149 (A.B.1419), § 4; Stats.1993, c. 1214 (A.B.551), § 1.5; Stats.1994, c. 1257 (S.B.1240), § 2; Stats.1996, c. 498 (S.B.1687), § 1.5.)*

1 42 U.S.C.A. § 12101 et seq.

Research References

Rutter, Cal. Practice Guide: A.D.R. Ch. 3B-C, C. Statutorily-Mandated ADR.

Rutter, Cal. Practice Guide: Civ. Pro. Before Trial Ch. 5-B, B. Entry of Default.

Rutter, Cal. Practice Guide: Civil Trials & Evidence Ch. 17-E, E. Attorney Fees as Costs.

Miller and Starr California Real Estate § 20:2, The Unruh Civil Rights Act--Coverage.

Miller and Starr California Real Estate § 20:7, The Unruh Civil Rights Act--Disability Discrimination.

Miller and Starr California Real Estate § 19:77, Nature of and Obligation to Pay Rent.

Miller and Starr California Real Estate § 25B:66, Restrictions on Alienation.

14 NO. 2 Miller & Starr, California Real Estate Newsalert 8, Discrimination.

15 NO. 2 Miller & Starr, California Real Estate Newsalert 6, Discrimination.

18 NO. 1 Miller & Starr, California Real Estate Newsalert 19, Landowners' Liability.

20 NO. 6 Miller & Starr, California Real Estate Newsalert 8, Discrimination.

6 Witkin Cal. Proc. 5th Proceedings Without Trial § 154, (S 154) Notice of Damages.

8 Witkin, California Summary 10th Constitutional Law § 941, (S 941) Other Prohibited Discrimination.

8 Witkin, California Summary 10th Constitutional Law § 957, in General.

8 Witkin, California Summary 10th Constitutional Law § 958, Physical Access.

8 Witkin, California Summary 10th Constitutional Law § 959, Enforcement.

§ 54.2. Guide, signal or service dogs; right to accompany individuals with a disability and trainers; damages

(a) Every individual with a disability has the right to be accompanied by a guide dog, signal dog, or service dog, especially trained for the purpose, in any of the places specified in Section 54.1 without being required to pay an extra charge or security deposit for the guide dog, signal dog, or service dog. However, the individual shall be liable for any damage done to the premises or facilities by his or her dog.

(b) Individuals who are blind or otherwise visually impaired and persons licensed to train guide dogs for individuals who are blind or visually impaired pursuant to Chapter 9.5 (commencing with Section 7200) of Division 3 of the Business and Professions Code or as defined in regulations implementing Title III of the Americans with Disabilities Act of 1990 (Public Law 101–336),[1] and individuals who are deaf or hearing impaired and persons authorized to train signal dogs for individuals who are deaf or hearing impaired, and individuals with a disability and persons who are authorized to train service dogs for the individuals with a disability may take dogs, for the purpose of training them as guide dogs, signal dogs, or service dogs in any of the places specified in Section 54.1 without being required to pay an extra charge or security deposit for the guide dog, signal dog, or service dog. However, the person shall be liable for any damage done to the premises or facilities by his or her dog. These persons shall ensure the dog is on a leash and tagged as a guide dog, signal dog, or service dog by an identification tag issued by the county clerk, animal control department, or other agency, as authorized by Chapter 3.5 (commencing with Section 30850) of Title 14 of the Food and Agricultural Code.

A violation of the right of an individual under the Americans with Disabilities Act of 1990 (Public Law 101–336) also constitutes a violation of this section, and nothing in this section shall be construed to limit the access of any person in violation of that act.

(c) As used in this section, the terms "guide dog," "signal dog," and "service dog" have the same meanings as specified in Section 54.1.

(d) Nothing in this section precludes the requirement of the showing of a license plate or disabled placard when required by enforcement units enforcing disabled persons parking violations pursuant to Sections 22507.8 and 22511.8 of the Vehicle Code. *(Added by Stats.1968, c. 461, p. 1092, § 1. Amended by Stats.1972, c. 819, p. 1466, § 2; Stats.1979, c. 293, p. 1092, § 2; Stats.1980, c. 773, § 2; Stats.1988, c. 1595, § 3; Stats.1992, c. 913 (A.B.1077), § 6; Stats.1994, c. 1257 (S.B.1240), § 3; Stats.1996, c. 498 (S.B.1687), § 2.)*

1 42 U.S.C.A. § 12101 et seq.

Research References

Miller and Starr California Real Estate § 20:7, The Unruh Civil Rights Act--Disability Discrimination.

8 Witkin, California Summary 10th Constitutional Law § 941, (S 941) Other Prohibited Discrimination.

8 Witkin, California Summary 10th Constitutional Law § 957, in General.

8 Witkin, California Summary 10th Constitutional Law § 959, Enforcement.

§ 54.25. Peace officer or firefighter assigned to canine unit; handler of search and rescue dog; duty away from home jurisdiction; discrimination; civil fine

(a)(1) A peace officer or firefighter assigned to a canine unit or the handler of a search and rescue dog assigned to duty away from his or her home jurisdiction because of a declared federal, state, or local emergency, or an official mutual aid request or training, and in the course and scope of his or her duties shall not be denied service based on the presence of the dog or discriminated against in hotels, lodging establishments, eating establishments, or public transportation by being required to pay an extra charge or security deposit for the dog. However, the peace officer's law enforcement agency, the firefighter's fire agency, or the handler of a search and rescue dog shall be liable for any damages to the premises or facilities caused by the dog.

(2) Any person, firm, association, or corporation, or the agent of any person, firm, association, or corporation that prevents a peace officer or a firefighter assigned to a canine unit and his or her dog or the handler of a search and rescue dog and his or her dog from exercising, or interferes in the exercise of, the rights specified in this section is subject to a civil fine not exceeding one thousand dollars ($1,000).

(b) For purposes of this section, the following definitions apply:

(1) "Declared emergency" is any emergency declared by the President of the United States, the Governor of a state, or local authorities.

(2) "Handler of a search and rescue dog" means a person in possession of a dog that is in training to become registered and approved as a search and rescue dog, or that is currently registered and approved for tasks, including, but not limited to, locating missing persons, discovering controlled substances, explosives, or cadavers, or locating victims in collapsed structures, and assisting with peace officer on-command searches for suspects and victims at crime scenes.

(3) "Peace officer's or firefighter's dog" means a dog owned by a public law enforcement agency or fire department and under the control of a peace officer or firefighter assigned to a canine unit that has been trained in matters, including, but not limited to, discovering controlled substances, explosives, cadavers, victims in collapsed structures, and peace officer on-command searches for suspects and victims at crime scenes.

(4) "Search and rescue dog" means a dog that is officially affiliated with, or sponsored by, a governmental agency and that has been trained and approved as a search and rescue dog, or that is currently registered and approved for search and rescue work with a search and rescue team affiliated with the California Emergency Management Agency. The term also includes a dog that is in training to become registered and approved for that work.

(c) Nothing in this section is intended to affect any civil remedies available for a violation of this section.

(d) This section is intended to provide accessibility without discrimination to a peace officer or firefighter with a peace officer's or firefighter's dog or a handler of a search and rescue dog with a search and rescue dog in hotels, lodging places, eating establishments, and public transportation.

(e) Nothing in this section is intended to prevent the removal of the search and rescue dog in the event the search and rescue dog creates an excessive disturbance to the quiet enjoyment of the property. In the event of an excessive disturbance, the peace officer, firefighter, or handler of the search and rescue dog shall be given a minimum of one warning notice of the excessive disturbance and an opportunity to correct the disturbance. The mere presence of the dog within the hotel, lodging establishment, food establishment, or public transportation shall not be considered an excessive disturbance. *(Added by Stats.2008, c. 226 (A.B.2131), § 1. Amended by Stats.2010, c. 92 (A.B.2243), § 1.)*

Research References

8 Witkin, California Summary 10th Constitutional Law § 905, (S 905) in General.

§ 54.3. Violations; liability

(a) Any person or persons, firm or corporation who denies or interferes with admittance to or enjoyment of the public facilities as specified in Sections 54 and 54.1 or otherwise interferes with the rights of an individual with a disability under Sections 54, 54.1 and 54.2 is liable for each offense for the actual damages and any amount as may be determined by a jury, or the court sitting without a jury, up to a maximum of three times the amount of actual damages but in no case less than one thousand dollars ($1,000), and attorney's fees as may be determined by the court in addition thereto, suffered by any person denied any of the rights provided in Sections 54, 54.1, and 54.2. "Interfere," for purposes of this section, includes, but is not limited to, preventing or causing the prevention of a guide dog, signal dog, or service dog from carrying out its functions in assisting a disabled person.

(b) Any person who claims to be aggrieved by an alleged unlawful practice in violation of Section 54, 54.1, or 54.2 may also file a verified complaint with the Department of Fair Employment and Housing pursuant to Section 12948 of the Government Code. The remedies in this section are nonexclusive and are in addition to any other remedy provided by law, including, but not limited to, any action for injunctive or other equitable relief available to the aggrieved party or brought in the name of the people of this state or of the United States.

(c) A person may not be held liable for damages pursuant to both this section and Section 52 for the same act or failure to act. *(Added by Stats.1968, c. 461, p. 1092, § 1. Amended by Stats.1976, c. 971, p. 2270, § 2; Stats.1976, c. 972, p. 2274, § 2.5; Stats.1977, c. 881, p. 2650, § 1; Stats.1981, c. 395, § 1; Stats. 1992, c. 913 (A.B.1077), § 7; Stats.1994, c. 1257 (S.B.1240), § 4; Stats.1996, c. 498 (S.B.1687), § 2.3.)*

Research References

Miller and Starr California Real Estate § 20:7, The Unruh Civil Rights Act--Disability Discrimination.
Miller and Starr California Real Estate § 22:75, Injuries to Additional Unique Plaintiff Categories.
19 NO. 1 Miller & Starr, California Real Estate Newsalert 19, Landowners' Liability.
20 NO. 1 Miller & Starr, California Real Estate Newsalert 9, Discrimination.
20 NO. 2 Miller & Starr, California Real Estate Newsalert 13, Discrimination.
2 Witkin Cal. Proc. 5th Courts § 282, (S 282) Particular Actions.
7 Witkin Cal. Proc. 5th Judgment § 223, (S 223) Civil Rights Actions.
8 Witkin, California Summary 10th Constitutional Law § 914, Enforcement.
8 Witkin, California Summary 10th Constitutional Law § 958, Physical Access.
8 Witkin, California Summary 10th Constitutional Law § 959, Enforcement.

§ 54.4. Blind or visually impaired pedestrian; failure to carry cane or use guide dog

A blind or otherwise visually impaired pedestrian shall have all of the rights and privileges conferred by law upon other persons in any of the places, accommodations, or conveyances specified in Sections 54 and 54.1, notwithstanding the fact that the person is not carrying a predominantly white cane (with or without a red tip), or using a guide dog. The failure of a blind or otherwise visually impaired person to carry such a cane or to use such a guide dog shall not constitute negligence per se. *(Added by Stats.1968, c. 461, p. 1092, § 1. Amended by Stats.1994, c. 1257 (S.B.1240), § 5.)*

§ 54.5. White cane safety day; proclamation

Each year, the Governor shall publicly proclaim October 15 as White Cane Safety Day. He or she shall issue a proclamation in which:

(a) Comments shall be made upon the significance of this chapter.

(b) Citizens of the state are called upon to observe the provisions of this chapter and to take precautions necessary to the safety of disabled persons.

(c) Citizens of the state are reminded of the policies with respect to disabled persons declared in this chapter and he urges the citizens to cooperate in giving effect to them.

(d) Emphasis shall be made on the need of the citizenry to be aware of the presence of disabled persons in the community and to keep safe and functional for the disabled the streets, highways, sidewalks, walkways, public buildings, public facilities, other public places, places of public accommodation, amusement and resort, and other places to which the public is invited, and to offer assistance to disabled persons upon appropriate occasions.

(e) It is the policy of this state to encourage and enable disabled persons to participate fully in the social and economic life of the state and to engage in remunerative employment. *(Added by Stats.1968, c. 461, p. 1092, § 1. Amended by Stats.1994, c. 1257 (S.B.1240), § 6.)*

§ 54.6. Visually impaired

As used in this part, "visually impaired" includes blindness and means having central visual acuity not to exceed $20/200$ in the better eye, with corrected lenses, as measured by the Snellen test, or visual acuity greater than $20/200$, but with a limitation in the field of vision such that the widest diameter of the visual field subtends an angle not greater than 20 degrees. *(Added by Stats.1968, c. 461, p. 1092, § 1. Amended by Stats.1994, c. 1257 (S.B.1240), § 7; Stats.2006, c. 538 (S.B.1852), § 38.)*

§ 54.7. Zoos or wild animal parks; facilities for guide, service or signal dogs accompanying individuals with a disability

(a) Notwithstanding any other provision of law, the provisions of this part shall not be construed to require zoos or wild animal parks to allow guide dogs, signal dogs, or service dogs to accompany individuals with a disability in areas of the zoo or park where zoo or park animals are not separated from members of the public by a physical barrier. As used in this section, "physical barrier" does not include an automobile or other conveyance.

(b) Any zoo or wild animal park that does not permit guide dogs, signal dogs, or service dogs to accompany individuals with a disability therein shall maintain, free of charge, adequate kennel facilities for the use of guide dogs, signal dogs, or service dogs belonging to these persons. These facilities shall be of a character commensurate with the anticipated daily attendance of individuals with a disability. The facilities shall be in an area not accessible to the general public, shall be equipped with water and utensils for the consumption thereof, and shall otherwise be safe, clean, and comfortable.

(c) Any zoo or wild animal park that does not permit guide dogs to accompany blind or visually impaired persons therein shall provide free transportation to blind or visually impaired persons on any mode of transportation provided for members of the public.

Each zoo or wild animal park that does not permit service dogs to accompany individuals with a disability shall provide free transportation to individuals with a disability on any mode of transportation provided for a member of the public in cases where the person uses a wheelchair and it is readily apparent that the person is unable to maintain complete or independent mobility without the aid of the service dog.

(d) Any zoo or wild animal park that does not permit guide dogs to accompany blind or otherwise visually impaired persons therein shall provide sighted escorts for blind or otherwise visually impaired persons if they are unaccompanied by a sighted person.

(e) As used in this section, "wild animal park" means any entity open to the public on a regular basis, licensed by the United States Department of Agriculture under the Animal Welfare Act as an exhibit, and operating for the primary purposes of conserving, propagating, and exhibiting wild and exotic animals, and any marine, mammal, or aquatic park open to the general public. *(Added by Stats.1979, c. 525, p. 1718, § 1. Amended by Stats.1988, c. 1595, § 4; Stats.1994, c. 1257 (S.B. 1240), § 8.)*

Research References

8 Witkin, California Summary 10th Constitutional Law § 957, in General.

§ 54.8. Hearing impaired persons; assistive listening systems in civil or criminal proceedings; notice of need; availability; use in proceedings

(a) In any civil or criminal proceeding, including, but not limited to, traffic, small claims court, family court proceedings and services, and juvenile court proceedings, in any court-ordered or court-provided alternative dispute resolution, including mediation and arbitration, or in any administrative hearing of a public agency, where a party, witness, attorney, judicial employee, judge, juror, or other participant who is hearing impaired, the individual who is hearing impaired, upon his or her request, shall be provided with a functioning assistive listening system or a computer-aided transcription system. Any individual requiring this equipment shall give advance notice of his or her need to the appropriate court or agency at the time the hearing is set or not later than five days before the hearing.

(b) Assistive listening systems include, but are not limited to, special devices which transmit amplified speech by means of audio-induction loops, radio frequency systems (AM or FM), or infrared transmission. Personal receivers, headphones, and neck loops shall be available upon request by individuals who are hearing impaired.

(c) If a computer-aided transcription system is requested, sufficient display terminals shall be provided to allow the individual who is hearing impaired to read the real-time transcript of the proceeding without difficulty.

(d) A sign shall be posted in a prominent place indicating the availability of, and how to request, an assistive listening system and a computer-aided transcription system. Notice of the availability of the systems shall be posted with notice of trials.

(e) Each superior court shall have at least one portable assistive listening system for use in any court facility within the county. When not in use, the system shall be stored in a location determined by the court.

(f) The Judicial Council shall develop and approve official forms for notice of the availability of assistive listening systems and computer-aided transcription systems for individuals who are hearing impaired. The Judicial Council shall also develop and maintain a system to record utilization by the courts of these assistive listening systems and computer-aided transcription systems.

(g) If the individual who is hearing impaired is a juror, the jury deliberation room shall be equipped with an assistive listening system or a computer-aided transcription system upon the request of the juror.

(h) A court reporter may be present in the jury deliberating room during a jury deliberation if the services of a court reporter for the purpose of operating a computer-aided transcription system are required for a juror who is hearing impaired.

(i) In any of the proceedings referred to in subdivision (a), or in any administrative hearing of a public agency, in which the individual who is hearing impaired is a party, witness, attorney, judicial employee, judge, juror, or other participant, and has requested use of an assistive listening system or computer-aided transcription system, the proceedings shall not commence until the system is in place and functioning.

(j) As used in this section, "individual who is hearing impaired" means an individual with a hearing loss, who, with sufficient amplification or a computer-aided transcription system, is able to fully participate in the proceeding.

(k) In no case shall this section be construed to prescribe a lesser standard of accessibility or usability than that provided by Title II of the Americans with Disabilities Act of 1990 (Public Law 101–336) and federal regulations adopted pursuant to that act. *(Added by Stats.1989, c. 1002, § 1. Amended by Stats.1992, c. 913 (A.B.1077), § 8; Stats.1993, c. 1214 (A.B.551), § 2; Stats.2001, c. 824 (A.B.1700), § 1.)*

Research References

Rutter, Cal. Practice Guide: Civil Trials & Evidence Ch. 5-A, A. Obtaining Prospective Jurors.
8 Witkin, California Summary 10th Constitutional Law § 957, in General.

§ 54.9. Touch-screen self-service check-in devices at hotels or facilities providing passenger transportation services; manufacturers and distributors to offer devices containing necessary technology

(a) On and after January 1, 2009, a manufacturer or distributor of touch-screen devices used for the purpose of self-service check-in at a hotel or at a facility providing passenger transportation services shall offer for availability touch-screen self-service check-in devices that contain the necessary technology.

(b) For purposes of this section, "necessary technology" means technology that enables a person with a visual impairment to do the following:

(1) Enter any personal information necessary to process a transaction in a manner that ensures the same degree of personal privacy afforded to those without visual impairments.

(2) Use the device independently and without the assistance of others in the same manner afforded to those without visual impairments.

(c) For purposes of this section, "hotel" means any hotel, motel, bed and breakfast inn, or other similar transient lodging establishment, but it does not include any residential hotel as defined in Section 50519 of the Health and Safety Code.

(d) This section shall not be construed to preclude or limit any other existing right or remedy as it pertains to self-service check-in devices and accessibility. *(Added by Stats.2006, c. 546 (A.B.768), § 2.)*

§ 55. Violations; injunction; action by person actually or potentially aggrieved

Any person who is aggrieved or potentially aggrieved by a violation of Section 54 or 54.1 of this code, Chapter 7 (commencing with Section 4450) of Division 5 of Title 1 of the Government Code, or Part 5.5 (commencing with Section 19955) of Division 13 of the Health and Safety Code may bring an action to enjoin the violation. The prevailing party in the action shall be entitled to recover reasonable attorney's fees. *(Added by Stats.1974, c. 1443, p. 3150, § 1.)*

Research References

Rutter, Cal. Practice Guide: A.D.R. Ch. 3B-C, C. Statutorily-Mandated ADR.
Rutter, Cal. Practice Guide: Civil Trials & Evidence Ch. 17-E, E. Attorney Fees as Costs.
Miller and Starr California Real Estate § 20:7, The Unruh Civil Rights Act--Disability Discrimination.
Miller and Starr California Real Estate § 20:28, Americans With Disabilities Act.
19 NO. 1 Miller & Starr, California Real Estate Newsalert 10, Discrimination.
19 NO. 4 Miller & Starr, California Real Estate Newsalert 36, Discrimination.
20 NO. 5 Miller & Starr, California Real Estate Newsalert 11, Discrimination.
21 NO. 1 Miller & Starr, California Real Estate Newsalert 11, Discrimination.
7 Witkin Cal. Proc. 5th Judgment § 223, (S 223) Civil Rights Actions.
7 Witkin Cal. Proc. 5th Judgment § 265, (S 265) Relief Obtained Without Judgment.
8 Witkin, California Summary 10th Constitutional Law § 959, Enforcement.

§ 55.1. Violations; injunctions; district or city attorney, attorney general

In addition to any remedies available under the federal Americans with Disabilities Act of 1990, Public Law 101-336 (42 U.S.C. Sec. 12102), or other provisions of law, the district attorney, the city attorney, the Department of Rehabilitation acting through the Attorney General, or the Attorney General may bring an action to enjoin any violation of Section 54 or 54.1. *(Added by Stats.1976, c. 869, p. 1979, § 1. Amended by Stats.1994, c. 1257 (S.B.1240), § 9.)*

Research References

7 Witkin Cal. Proc. 5th Judgment § 95, (S 95) Prevailing Party in Specified Actions.
8 Witkin, California Summary 10th Constitutional Law § 959, Enforcement.

§ 55.2. Mandatory service on State Solicitor General of each party's brief or petition and brief in causes of action based on violation of civil rights statutes

If a violation of Section 54, 54.1, 54.2, or 54.3 is alleged or the application or construction of any of these sections is in issue in any proceeding in the Supreme Court of California, a state court of appeal, or the appellate division of a superior court, each party shall serve a copy of the party's brief or petition and brief, on the State Solicitor General at the Office of the Attorney General. No brief may be accepted for filing unless the proof of service shows service on the State Solicitor General. Any party failing to comply with this requirement shall be given a reasonable opportunity to cure the failure before the court imposes any sanction and, in that instance, the court shall allow the Attorney General reasonable additional time to file a brief in the matter. *(Added by Stats.2002, c. 244 (A.B.2524), § 2.)*

Research References

Rutter, Cal. Practice Guide: Civil Appeals & Writs Ch. 9-D, D. Procedural Rules.

Rutter, Cal. Practice Guide: Civil Appeals & Writs Ch. 13-B, B. Petition for Review Procedures.
Rutter, Cal. Practice Guide: Civil Appeals & Writs Ch. 13-C, C. Briefs on the Merits After Grant of Review.
Rutter, Cal. Practice Guide: Civil Appeals & Writs Ch. 15-E, E. Procedures on Writ Review.
9 Witkin Cal. Proc. 5th Appeal § 717, (S 717) Service and Filing.

§ 55.3. Written advisory to accompany demand letter or complaint; contents

(a) For purposes of this section, the following shall apply:

(1) "Complaint" means a civil complaint that is filed or is to be filed with a court and is sent to or served upon a defendant on the basis of one or more construction-related accessibility claims, as defined in this section.

(2) "Construction-related accessibility claim" means any claim of a violation of any construction-related accessibility standard, as defined by paragraph (6) of subdivision (a) of Section 55.52, with respect to a place of public accommodation. "Construction-related accessibility claim" does not include a claim of interference with housing within the meaning of paragraph (2) of subdivision (b) of Section 54.1, or any claim of interference caused by something other than the construction- related accessibility condition of the property, including, but not limited to, the conduct of any person.

(3) "Demand for money" means a prelitigation written document or oral statement that is provided or issued to a building owner or tenant, or the owner's or tenant's agent or employee, that does all of the following:

(A) Alleges that the site is in violation of one or more construction-related accessibility standards, as defined in paragraph (6) of subdivision (a) of Section 55.52, or alleges one or more construction-related accessibility claims, as defined in paragraph (2).

(B) Contains or makes a request or demand for money or an offer or agreement to accept money.

(C) Is provided or issued whether or not the attorney intends to file a complaint, or eventually files a complaint, in state or federal court.

(4) "Demand letter" means a prelitigation written document that is provided to a building owner or tenant, or the owner's or tenant's agent or employee, that alleges the site is in violation of one or more construction-related accessibility standards, as defined in paragraph (6) of subdivision (a) of Section 55.52, or alleges one or more construction-related accessibility claims, as defined in paragraph (2), and is provided whether or not the attorney intends to file a complaint, or eventually files a complaint, in state or federal court.

(b) An attorney shall provide a written advisory on the form described in subdivision (c), or, until that form is available, on a separate page or pages that are clearly distinguishable from the demand letter or complaint, with each demand letter or complaint sent to or served upon a defendant or potential defendant. The advisory shall not be required in subsequent communications following the initial demand letter or initial complaint unless a new construction-related accessibility claim is asserted in the subsequent demand letter or amended complaint. The advisory shall state as follows:

STATE LAW REQUIRES THAT YOU GET THIS IMPORTANT ADVISORY INFORMATION FOR BUILDING OWNERS AND TENANTS

This information is available in English, Spanish, Chinese, Vietnamese, and Korean through the Judicial Council of California. Persons with visual impairments can get assistance in viewing this form through the Judicial Council Internet Web site at www.courts.ca.gov.

California law requires that you receive this information because the demand letter or court complaint you received with this document claims that your building or property does not comply with one or more existing construction-related accessibility laws or regulations protecting the civil rights of persons with disabilities to access public places.

YOU HAVE IMPORTANT LEGAL OBLIGATIONS. Compliance with disability access laws is a serious and significant responsibility that applies to all California building owners and tenants with buildings open for business to the public. You may obtain information about your legal obligations and how to comply with disability access laws through the Division of the State Architect at www.dgs.ca.gov. Information is also available from the California Commission on Disability Access at www.ccda.ca.gov/guide.htm.

YOU HAVE IMPORTANT LEGAL RIGHTS. The allegations made in the accompanying demand letter or court complaint do not mean that you are required to pay any money unless and until a court finds you liable. Moreover, RECEIPT OF A DEMAND LETTER OR COURT COMPLAINT AND THIS ADVISORY DOES NOT NECESSARILY MEAN YOU WILL BE FOUND LIABLE FOR ANYTHING. You will have the right if you are later sued to fully present your explanation why you believe you have not in fact violated disability access laws or have corrected the violation or violations giving rise to the claim.

You have the right to seek assistance or advice about this demand letter or court complaint from any person of your choice. If you have insurance, you may also wish to contact your insurance provider. Your best interest may be served by seeking legal advice or representation from an attorney, but you may also represent yourself and file the necessary court papers to protect your interests if you are served with a court complaint. If you have hired an attorney to represent you, you should immediately notify your attorney.

If a court complaint has been served on you, you will get a separate advisory notice with the complaint advising you of special options and procedures available to you under certain conditions.

ADDITIONAL THINGS YOU SHOULD KNOW: If the document accompanying this notice is a demand letter from a lawyer and not a formal court complaint, the lawyer is generally required by law to also provide a copy of it to the State Bar of California, until January 1, 2016, in order that the State Bar may determine whether the demand letter complies with legal requirements, INCLUDING THAT THE DEMAND LETTER MAY NOT MAKE A REQUEST OR DEMAND FOR MONEY OR AN OFFER OR AGREEMENT TO ACCEPT MONEY. Any demand letter or court complaint must list the lawyer's State Bar license number on the document.

You are encouraged, but are not required, to provide the State Bar with a copy of the demand letter so the State Bar is aware that you received this demand letter and may determine whether it is in compliance with specified legal requirements. A copy of the letter can be sent to the State Bar by facsimile transmission to 1–415–538–2171, or by mail to the State Bar of California, 180 Howard Street, San Francisco, CA, 94105, Attention: Professional Competence.

(c) On or before July 1, 2013, the Judicial Council shall update the form that may be used by attorneys to comply with the requirements of subdivision (b). The form shall be in substantially the same format and include all of the text set forth in subdivision (b). The form shall be available in English, Spanish, Chinese, Vietnamese, and Korean, and shall include a statement that the form is available in additional languages, and the Judicial Council Internet Web site address where the different versions of the form may be located. The form shall include Internet Web site information for the Division of the State Architect and the California Commission on Disability Access.

(d) Subdivision (b) shall apply only to a demand letter or complaint made by an attorney. Nothing in this section is intended to affect the right to file a civil complaint under any other law or regulation protecting the physical access rights of persons with disabilities. Additionally, nothing in this section requires a party to provide or send a demand letter to another party before proceeding against that party with a civil complaint.

(e) This section shall not apply to any action brought by the Attorney General, or by any district attorney, city attorney, or county counsel. *(Added by Stats.2008, c. 549 (S.B.1608), § 2. Amended by Stats.2011, c. 419 (S.B.384), § 2; Stats.2012, c. 162 (S.B.1171), § 9; Stats.2012, c. 383 (S.B.1186), § 3, eff. Sept. 19, 2012.)*

Contingent Operation

Operation of this section is contingent upon availability of funding under the terms of Stats.2008, c. 549 (S.B.1608) § 12.

Research References

Rutter, Cal. Practice Guide: A.D.R. App. A, Selected Statutes Providing for ADR.

Rutter, Cal. Practice Guide: A.D.R. Ch. 3B-C, C. Statutorily-Mandated ADR.

Rutter, Cal. Practice Guide: A.D.R. Gen. Matls., Highlights.

Rutter, Cal. Practice Guide: Civ. Pro. Before Trial Ch. 1-C, C. Prelawsuit Notices, Claims and Demands.

Rutter, Cal. Practice Guide: Civ. Pro. Before Trial Ch. 6-B, B. Complaints.

Rutter, Cal. Practice Guide: Prof. Responsibility Ch. 11-A, A. Grounds for Discipline.

Miller and Starr California Real Estate § 22:75.10, Construction-Related Accessibility Claims.

19 NO. 4 Miller & Starr, California Real Estate Newsalert 12, Discrimination.

1 Witkin Cal. Proc. 5th Attorneys § 480, Statutory Framework.

§ 55.31. Demand letter alleging construction-related accessibility claim; inclusion of statement of facts; inclusion of prelitigation settlement negotiation offer; prohibition on inclusion of request or demand for money or offer or agreement to accept money; prohibition on issuance of demand for money; violation; application

(a) Commencing January 1, 2013, a demand letter alleging a construction-related accessibility claim, as defined in subdivision (a) of Section 55.3, shall state facts sufficient to allow a reasonable person to identify the basis of the violation or violations supporting the claim, including all of the following:

(1) A plain language explanation of the specific access barrier or barriers the individual encountered, or by which the individual alleges he or she was deterred, with sufficient information about the location of the barrier to enable a reasonable person to identify the access barrier.

(2) The way in which the barrier encountered interfered with the individual's full and equal use or access, or in which it deterred the individual, on each particular occasion.

(3) The date or dates of each particular occasion on which the individual encountered the specific access barrier, or on which he or she was deterred.

(b) A demand letter may offer prelitigation settlement negotiations, but shall not include a request or demand for money or an offer or agreement to accept money.

(1) With respect to potential monetary damages for an alleged construction-related accessibility claim or claims, a demand letter shall not state any specific potential monetary liability for any asserted claim or claims, and may only state: "The property owner or tenant, or both, may be civilly liable for actual and statutory damages for a violation of a construction-related accessibility requirement."

(2) Notwithstanding any other law, a demand letter meeting the requirements of this section shall be deemed to satisfy the requirements for prelitigation notice of a potential claim when prelitigation notice is required by statute or common law for an award of attorney's fees.

(3) This subdivision and subdivision (a) do not apply to a demand for money, which is governed by subdivision (c).

(c) An attorney, or a person acting at the direction of an attorney, shall not issue a demand for money as defined in subdivision (a) of Section 55.3. This subdivision does not apply to a demand letter as defined in subdivision (a) of Section 55.3.

(d)(1) A violation of subdivision (b) or (c) constitutes cause for the imposition of discipline of an attorney. Subdivisions (b) and (c) do not prohibit an attorney from presenting a settlement figure or specification of damages in response to a request from the building owner or tenant, or the owner's or tenant's authorized agent or employee, following a demand letter provided pursuant to Section 55.3.

(2) Any liability for a violation of subdivision (c) is as provided in paragraph (1) of this subdivision. A violation of subdivision (c) does not create a new cause of action.

(e) Subdivision (c) does not prohibit any prelitigation settlement discussion of liability for damages and attorney's fees that occurs after a written or oral agreement is reached between the parties for the repair or correction of the alleged violation or violations of a construction-related accessibility standard.

(f) Subdivision (c) shall not apply to a claim involving physical injury and resulting special damages, but a demand for money relating to that claim that is sent shall otherwise comply with the requirements of subdivision (a) and Section 55.32.

(g) Nothing in this section shall apply to a demand or statement of alleged damages made in a prelitigation claim presented to a governmental entity as required by state or federal law, including, but not limited to, claims made under Part 3 (commencing with Section 900) of Division 3.6 of the Government Code.

(h) If subdivision (c) is not operative or becomes inoperative for any reason, the requirements of subdivision (a) and Section 55.32 shall apply to any written demand for money. (*Added by Stats.2012, c. 383 (S.B.1186), § 4, eff. Sept. 19, 2012.*)

§ 55.32. Demand letter or complaint; duties of attorney; violation; report by State Bar; review and report by California Commission on Disability Access; application

Section operative until Jan. 1, 2016. See, also, section operative Jan. 1, 2016.

(a) An attorney who provides a demand letter, as defined in subdivision (a) of Section 55.3, shall do all of the following:

(1) Include the attorney's State Bar license number in the demand letter.

(2) Contemporaneously with providing the demand letter, send a copy of the demand letter to the State Bar of California by facsimile transmission at 1–415–538–2171, or by mail to 180 Howard Street, San Francisco, CA, 94105, Attention: Professional Competence.

(3) Within five business days of providing the demand letter, send a copy of the demand letter to the California Commission on Disability Access.

(b) An attorney who sends or serves a complaint, as defined in subdivision (a) of Section 55.3, shall send a copy of the complaint to the California Commission on Disability Access within five business days of sending or serving the complaint.

(c) A violation of paragraph (2) or (3) of subdivision (a) or subdivision (b) shall constitute cause for the imposition of discipline of an attorney where a copy of the complaint or demand letter is not sent to the California Commission on Disability Access within five business days, or a copy of the demand letter is not sent to the State Bar within five business days. In the event the State Bar receives information indicating that an attorney has failed to send a copy of the complaint or demand letter to the California Commission on Disability Access within five business days, the State Bar shall investigate to determine whether paragraph (3) of subdivision (a) or subdivision (b) has been violated.

(d) Notwithstanding subdivisions (a) and (b), an attorney is not required to send to the State Bar of California or the California Commission on Disability Access a copy of any subsequent demand letter or amended complaint in the same dispute following the initial demand letter or complaint, unless that subsequent demand letter or amended complaint alleges a new construction-related accessibility claim.

(e) A demand letter or complaint sent to the California Commission on Disability Access shall be for the informational purposes of Section 8299.08 of the Government Code. A demand letter received by the State Bar from either the sender or recipient of the demand letter shall be reviewed by the State Bar to determine whether subdivision (b) or (c) of Section 55.31 has been violated.

(f)(1) Commencing July 31, 2013, and annually each July 31 thereafter, the State Bar shall report to the Legislature and the Chairs of the Senate and Assembly Committees on Judiciary, both of the following with respect to demand letters received by the State Bar:

(A) The number of investigations opened to date on a suspected violation of subdivision (b) or (c) of Section 55.31.

(B) Whether any disciplinary action resulted from the investigation, and the results of that disciplinary action.

(2) A report to be submitted pursuant to this subdivision shall be submitted in compliance with Section 9795 of the Government Code.

(g) The California Commission on Disability Access shall review and report on the demand letters and complaints it receives as provided in Section 8299.08 of the Government Code.

(h) Paragraphs (2) and (3) of subdivision (a) and subdivision (b) shall not apply to a demand letter or complaint sent or filed by an attorney employed or retained by a qualified legal services project or a qualified support center, as defined in Section 6213 of the Business and Professions Code, when acting within the scope of employment in asserting a construction-related accessibility claim. The Legislature finds and declares that qualified legal services projects and support centers are extensively regulated by the State Bar of California, and that there is no evidence of any abusive use of demand letters or complaints by these organizations. The Legislature further finds that, in light of the evidence of the extraordinarily small number of construction-related accessibility cases brought by regulated legal services programs, and given the resources of those programs, exempting regulated legal services programs from the requirements of this section to report to the California Commission on Disability

Civil

Access will not affect the purpose of the reporting to, and tabulation by, the commission of all other construction-related accessibility claims.

(i) This section shall become operative on January 1, 2013.

(j) This section shall remain in effect only until January 1, 2016, and as of that date is repealed, unless a later enacted statute, that is enacted before January 1, 2016, deletes or extends that date. *(Added by Stats.2012, c. 383 (S.B.1186), § 5, eff. Sept. 19, 2012, operative Jan. 1, 2013.)*

Repeal

For repeal of this section, see its terms.

§ 55.32. Demand letter or complaint; duties of attorney; violation; report by State Bar; review and report by California Commission on Disability Access; effect of expiration of ground for discipline; application

Section operative Jan. 1, 2016. See, also, section operative until Jan. 1, 2016.

(a) An attorney who provides a demand letter, as defined in subdivision (a) of Section 55.3, shall do all of the following:

(1) Include the attorney's State Bar license number in the demand letter.

(2) Within five business days of providing the demand letter, send a copy of the demand letter to the California Commission on Disability Access.

(b) An attorney who sends or serves a complaint, as defined in subdivision (a) of Section 55.3, shall send a copy of the complaint to the California Commission on Disability Access within five business days of sending or serving the complaint.

(c) A violation of paragraph (2) of subdivision (a) or subdivision (b) shall constitute cause for the imposition of discipline of an attorney if a copy of the demand letter or complaint is not sent to the California Commission on Disability Access within five business days. In the event the State Bar receives information indicating that an attorney has failed to send a copy of the demand letter or complaint to the California Commission on Disability Access within five business days, the State Bar shall investigate to determine whether paragraph (2) of subdivision (a) or subdivision (b) has been violated.

(d) Notwithstanding subdivisions (a) and (b), an attorney is not required to send to the California Commission on Disability Access a copy of any subsequent demand letter or amended complaint in the same dispute following the initial demand letter or complaint, unless that subsequent demand letter or amended complaint alleges a new construction-related accessibility claim.

(e) A demand letter sent to the California Commission on Disability Access shall be for the informational purposes of Section 8299.08 of the Government Code. A demand letter received by the State Bar from the recipient of the demand letter shall be reviewed by the State Bar to determine whether subdivision (b) or (c) of Section 55.31 has been violated.

(f)(1) Notwithstanding Section 10231.5 of the Government Code, on or before July 31, 2016, and annually thereafter, the State Bar shall report to the Legislature and the Chairs of the Senate and Assembly Judiciary Committees, both of the following with respect to demand letters received by the State Bar:

(A) The number of investigations opened to date on a suspected violation of subdivision (b) or (c) of Section 55.31.

(B) Whether any disciplinary action resulted from the investigation, and the results of that disciplinary action.

(2) A report to be submitted pursuant to this subdivision shall be submitted in compliance with Section 9795 of the Government Code.

(g) The California Commission on Disability Access shall review and report on the demand letters and complaints it receives as provided in Section 8299.08 of the Government Code.

(h) The expiration of any ground for discipline of an attorney shall not affect the imposition of discipline for any act prior to the expiration. An act or omission that constituted cause for imposition of discipline of an attorney when committed or omitted prior to January 1, 2016, shall continue to constitute cause for the imposition of discipline of that attorney on and after January 1, 2016.

(i) Paragraph (2) of subdivision (a) and subdivision (b) shall not apply to a demand letter or complaint sent or filed by an attorney employed or retained by a qualified legal services project or a qualified support center, as defined in Section 6213 of the Business and Professions Code, when acting within the scope of employment in asserting a construction-related accessibility claim. The Legislature finds and declares that qualified legal services projects and support centers are extensively regulated by the State Bar of California, and that there is no evidence of any abusive use of demand letters or complaints by these organizations. The Legislature further finds that, in light of the evidence of the extraordinarily small number of construction-related accessibility cases brought by regulated legal services programs, and given the resources of those programs, exempting regulated legal services programs from the requirements of this section to report to the California Commission on Disability Access will not affect the purpose of the reporting to, and tabulation by, the commission of all other construction-related accessibility claims.

(j) This section shall become operative on January 1, 2016. *(Added by Stats.2012, c. 383 (S.B.1186), § 6, eff. Sept. 19, 2012, operative Jan. 1, 2016.)*

Part 2.52

CONSTRUCTION–RELATED ACCESSIBILITY STANDARDS COMPLIANCE

Contingent Operation

Operation of this Part is contingent upon availability of funding under the terms of Stats.2008, c. 549 (S.B.1608) § 12.

§ 55.51. Short title; application

This part shall be known, and may be cited, as the Construction–Related Accessibility Standards Compliance Act. Notwithstanding any other provision of law, the provisions of this part shall apply to any construction-related accessibility claim, as defined in this part, including, but not limited to, any claim brought under Section 51, 54, 54.1, or 55. *(Added by Stats.2008, c. 549 (S.B.1608), § 3.)*

Contingent Operation

Operation of this Part is contingent upon availability of funding under the terms of Stats.2008, c. 549 (S.B.1608) § 12.

Research References

Rutter, Cal. Practice Guide: Civ. Pro. Before Trial Ch. 12(I)-B, B. Case Management ("Fast Track") System.
Miller and Starr California Real Estate § 22:75.10, Construction-Related Accessibility Claims.
19 NO. 4 Miller & Starr, California Real Estate Newsalert 12, Discrimination.
8 Witkin, California Summary 10th Constitutional Law § 958, Physical Access.

§ 55.52. Definitions

(a) For purposes of this part, the following definitions apply:

(1) "Construction-related accessibility claim" means any civil claim in a civil action with respect to a place of public accommodation, including, but not limited to, a claim brought under Section 51, 54, 54.1, or 55, based wholly or in part on an alleged violation of any construction-related accessibility standard, as defined in paragraph (6).

(2) "Application for stay and early evaluation conference" means an application to be filed with the court that meets the requirements of subdivision (c) of Section 55.54.

(3) "Certified access specialist" or "CASp" means any person who has been certified pursuant to Section 4459.5 of the Government Code.

(4) "Meets applicable standards" means the site was inspected by a CASp and determined to meet all applicable construction-related accessibility standards pursuant to paragraph (1) of subdivision (a) of Section 55.53. A site that is "CASp inspected" on or before the effective date of the amendments made to this section by Senate Bill 1186 of the 2011–12 Regular Session of the Legislature means that the site "meets applicable standards."

(5) "Inspected by a CASp" means the site was inspected by a CASp and is pending a determination by the CASp that the site meets applicable construction-related accessibility standards pursuant to paragraph (2) of subdivision (a) of Section 55.53. A site that is "CASp determination pending" on or before the effective date of the amendments made to this section by Senate Bill 1186 of the 2011–12 Regular Session of the Legislature means that the site was "inspected by a CASp."

(6) "Construction-related accessibility standard" means a provision, standard, or regulation under state or federal law requiring compliance with standards for making new construction and existing facilities accessible to persons with disabilities, including, but not limited to, any provision, standard, or regulation set forth in Section 51, 54, 54.1, or 55 of this code, Section 19955.5 of the Health and Safety Code, the California Building Standards Code (Title 24 of the California Code of Regulations), the federal Americans with Disabilities Act of 1990 (Public Law 101–336; 42 U.S.C. Sec. 12101 et seq.), and the federal Americans with Disabilities Act Accessibility Guidelines (Appendix A to Part 36 of Title 28 of the Code of Federal Regulations).

(7) "Place of public accommodation" has the same meaning as "public accommodation," as set forth in Section 12181(7) of Title 42 of the United States Code and the federal regulations adopted pursuant to that section.

(8) "Qualified defendant" means a defendant in an action that includes a construction-related accessibility claim that is asserted against a place of public accommodation that met the requirements of "meets applicable standards" or "inspected by a CASp" prior to the date the defendant was served with the summons and complaint in that action. To be a qualified defendant, the defendant is not required to have been the party who hired any CASp, so long as the basis of the alleged liability of the defendant is a construction-related accessibility claim. To determine whether a defendant is a qualified defendant, the court need not make a finding that the place of public accommodation complies with all applicable construction-related accessibility standards as a matter of law. The court need only determine that the place of public accommodation has a status of "meets applicable standards" or "inspected by a CASp."

(9) "Site" means a place of public accommodation.

(b) Unless otherwise indicated, terms used in this part relating to civil procedure have the same meanings that those terms have in the Code of Civil Procedure. *(Added by Stats.2008, c. 549 (S.B.1608), § 3. Amended by Stats.2012, c. 383 (S.B.1186), § 7, eff. Sept. 19, 2012.)*

Contingent Operation

Operation of this Part is contingent upon availability of funding under the terms of Stats.2008, c. 549 (S.B.1608) § 12.

Research References

Rutter, Cal. Practice Guide: A.D.R. Ch. 3B-C, C. Statutorily-Mandated ADR.
Rutter, Cal. Practice Guide: Civ. Pro. Before Trial Ch. 1-C, C. Prelawsuit Notices, Claims and Demands.
Rutter, Cal. Practice Guide: Civ. Pro. Before Trial Ch. 6-B, B. Complaints.
19 NO. 4 Miller & Starr, California Real Estate Newsalert 12, Discrimination.

§ 55.53. Certified access specialists (CASp); post-inspection compliance requirements; conflicting regulations or standards; post-inspection notice to owner or tenant of public accommodation; inspection certificate

(a) For purposes of this part, a certified access specialist shall, upon completion of the inspection of a site, comply with the following:

(1) For a meets applicable standards site, if the CASp determines the site meets all applicable construction-related accessibility standards, the CASp shall provide a written inspection report to the requesting party that includes both of the following:

(A) An identification and description of the inspected structures and areas of the site.

(B) A signed and dated statement that includes both of the following:

(i) A statement that, in the opinion of the CASp, the inspected structures and areas of the site meet construction-related accessibility standards. The statement shall clearly indicate whether the determination of the CASp includes an assessment of readily achievable barrier removal.

(ii) If corrections were made as a result of the CASp inspection, an itemized list of all corrections and dates of completion.

(2) For an inspected by a CASp site, if the CASp determines that corrections are needed to the site in order for the site to meet all applicable construction-related accessibility standards, the CASp shall provide a signed and dated written inspection report to the requesting party that includes all of the following:

(A) An identification and description of the inspected structures and areas of the site.

(B) A statement that, in the opinion of the CASp, the inspected structures and areas of the site need correction to meet construction-related accessibility standards. This statement shall clearly indicate whether the determination of the CASp includes an assessment of readily achievable barrier removal.

(C) An identification and description of the structures or areas of the site that need correction and the correction needed.

(D) A schedule of completion for each of the corrections within a reasonable timeframe.

(b) For purposes of this section, in determining whether the site meets applicable construction-related accessibility standards when there is a conflict or difference between a state and federal provision, standard, or regulation, the state provision, standard, or regulation shall apply unless the federal provision, standard, or regulation is more protective of accessibility rights.

(c) Every CASp who conducts an inspection of a place of public accommodation shall, upon completing the inspection of the site, provide the building owner or tenant who requested the inspection with the following notice, which the State Architect shall make available as a form on the State Architect's Internet Web site:

NOTICE TO PRIVATE PROPERTY OWNER/TENANT:

YOU ARE ADVISED TO KEEP IN YOUR RECORDS ANY WRITTEN INSPECTION REPORT AND ANY OTHER DOCUMENTATION CONCERNING YOUR PROPERTY SITE THAT IS GIVEN TO YOU BY A CERTIFIED ACCESS SPECIALIST.

IF YOU BECOME A DEFENDANT IN A LAWSUIT THAT INCLUDES A CLAIM CONCERNING A SITE INSPECTED BY A CERTIFIED ACCESS SPECIALIST, YOU MAY BE ENTITLED TO A COURT STAY (AN ORDER TEMPORARILY STOPPING ANY LAWSUIT) OF THE CLAIM AND AN EARLY EVALUATION CONFERENCE.

IN ORDER TO REQUEST THE STAY AND EARLY EVALUATION CONFERENCE, YOU WILL NEED TO VERIFY THAT A CERTIFIED ACCESS SPECIALIST HAS INSPECTED THE SITE THAT IS THE SUBJECT OF THE CLAIM. YOU WILL ALSO BE REQUIRED TO PROVIDE THE COURT AND THE PLAINTIFF WITH THE COPY OF A WRITTEN INSPECTION REPORT BY THE CERTIFIED ACCESS SPECIALIST, AS SET FORTH IN CIVIL CODE SECTION 55.54. THE APPLICATION FORM AND INFORMATION ON HOW TO REQUEST A STAY AND EARLY EVALUATION CONFERENCE MAY BE OBTAINED AT www.courts.ca.gov/selfhelp-start.htm.

YOU ARE ENTITLED TO REQUEST, FROM A CERTIFIED ACCESS SPECIALIST WHO HAS CONDUCTED AN INSPECTION OF YOUR PROPERTY, A WRITTEN INSPECTION REPORT AND OTHER DOCUMENTATION AS SET FORTH IN CIVIL CODE SECTION 55.53. YOU ARE ALSO ENTITLED TO REQUEST THE ISSUANCE OF A DISABILITY ACCESS INSPECTION CERTIFICATE, WHICH YOU MAY POST ON YOUR PROPERTY.

(d)(1) Commencing July 1, 2010, a local agency shall employ or retain at least one building inspector who is a certified access specialist. The certified access specialist shall provide consultation to the local agency, permit applicants, and members of the public on compliance with state construction-related accessibility standards with respect to inspections of a place of public accommodation that relate to permitting, plan checks, or new construction, including, but not limited to, inspections relating to tenant improvements that may impact access. If a local agency employs or retains two or more certified access specialists to comply with this subdivision, at least one-half of the certified

access specialists shall be building inspectors who are certified access specialists.

(2) Commencing January 1, 2014, a local agency shall employ or retain a sufficient number of building inspectors who are certified access specialists to conduct permitting and plan check services to review for compliance with state construction-related accessibility standards by a place of public accommodation with respect to new construction, including, but not limited to, projects relating to tenant improvements that may impact access. If a local agency employs or retains two or more certified access specialists to comply with this subdivision, at least one-half of the certified access specialists shall be building inspectors who are certified access specialists.

(3) If a permit applicant or member of the public requests consultation from a certified access specialist, the local agency may charge an amount limited to a reasonable hourly rate, an estimate of which shall be provided upon request in advance of the consultation. A local government may additionally charge or increase permitting, plan check, or inspection fees to the extent necessary to offset the costs of complying with this subdivision. Any revenues generated from an hourly or other charge or fee increase under this subdivision shall be used solely to offset the costs incurred to comply with this subdivision. A CASp inspection pursuant to subdivision (a) by a building inspector who is a certified access specialist shall be treated equally for legal and evidentiary purposes as an inspection conducted by a private CASp. Nothing in this subdivision shall preclude permit applicants or any other person with a legal interest in the property from retaining a private CASp at any time.

(e)(1) Every CASp who completes an inspection of a place of public accommodation shall, upon a determination that the site meets applicable standards pursuant to paragraph (1) of subdivision (a) or is inspected by a CASp pursuant to paragraph (2) of subdivision (a), provide the building owner or tenant requesting the inspection with a numbered disability access inspection certificate indicating that the site has undergone inspection by a certified access specialist. The disability access inspection certificate shall be dated and signed by the CASp inspector, and shall contain the inspector's name and license number. Upon issuance of a certificate, the CASp shall record the issuance of the numbered certificate, the name and address of the recipient, and the type of report issued pursuant to subdivision (a) in a record book the CASp shall maintain for that purpose.

(2) Beginning March 1, 2009, the State Architect shall make available for purchase by any local building department or CASp sequentially numbered disability access inspection certificates that are printed with a watermark or other feature to deter forgery and that comply with the information requirements specified in subdivision (a).

(3) The disability access inspection certificate may be posted on the premises of the place of public accommodation, unless, following the date of inspection, the inspected site has been modified or construction has commenced to modify the inspected site in a way that may impact compliance with construction-related accessibility standards.

(f) Nothing in this section or any other law is intended to require a property owner or tenant to hire a CASp. A property owner's or tenant's election not to hire a CASp shall not be admissible to prove that person's lack of intent to comply with the law. *(Added by Stats.2008, c. 549 (S.B.1608), § 3. Amended by Stats.2012, c. 383 (S.B.1186), § 8, eff. Sept. 19, 2012.)*

Contingent Operation

Operation of this Part is contingent upon availability of funding under the terms of Stats.2008, c. 549 (S.B.1608) § 12.

Research References

Rutter, Cal. Practice Guide: A.D.R. Ch. 3B-C, C. Statutorily-Mandated ADR.

Rutter, Cal. Practice Guide: Civ. Pro. Before Trial Ch. 1-C, C. Prelawsuit Notices, Claims and Demands.

Rutter, Cal. Practice Guide: Civ. Pro. Before Trial Ch. 6-B, B. Complaints.

Miller and Starr California Real Estate § 22:75.10, Construction-Related Accessibility Claims.

19 NO. 4 Miller & Starr, California Real Estate Newsalert 12, Discrimination.

8 Witkin, California Summary 10th Constitutional Law § 958, Physical Access.

§ 55.54. Service of summons and complaint in construction-related accessibility claim action; simultaneous service of specified notice and application for early evaluation conference; actions following service; construction and application of provisions

(a)(1) An attorney who causes a summons and complaint to be served in an action that includes a construction-related accessibility claim, including, but not limited to, a claim brought under Section 51, 54, 54.1, or 55, shall, at the same time, cause to be served a copy of the application form specified in subdivision (c) and a copy of the following notice, including, until January 1, 2013, the bracketed text, to the defendant on separate papers that shall be served with the summons and complaint:

ADVISORY NOTICE TO DEFENDANT

YOU MAY BE ENTITLED TO ASK FOR A COURT STAY (AN ORDER TEMPORARILY STOPPING ANY LAWSUIT) AND EARLY EVALUATION CONFERENCE IN THIS LAWSUIT AND MAY BE ASSESSED REDUCED STATUTORY DAMAGES IF YOU MEET CERTAIN CONDITIONS.

If the construction-related accessibility claim pertains to a site that has a Certified Access Specialist (CASp) inspection report for that site, or to a site where new construction or improvement was approved after January 1, 2008, by the local building permit and inspection process, you may make an immediate request for a court stay and early evaluation conference in the construction-related accessibility claim by filing the attached application form with the court. You may be entitled to the court stay and early evaluation conference regarding the accessibility claim only if ALL of the statements in the application form applicable to you are true.

FURTHER, if you are a defendant described above (with a CASp inspection report or with new construction after January 1, 2008), and, to the best of your knowledge, there have been no modifications or alterations completed or commenced since the CASp report or building department approval of the new construction or improvement that impacted compliance with construction-related accessibility standards with respect to the plaintiff's claim, your liability for minimum statutory damages may be reduced to $1,000 for each offense, unless the violation was intentional, and if all construction-related accessibility violations giving rise to the claim are corrected within 60 days of being served with this complaint.

IN ADDITION, if your business is a small business that, over the previous three years, or the existence of the business if less than three years, employs 25 or fewer employees on average over that time period and meets specified gross receipts criteria, you may also be entitled to the court stay and early evaluation conference and your minimum statutory damages for each claim may be reduced to $2,000 for each offense, unless the violation was intentional, and if all the alleged construction-related accessibility violations are corrected within 30 days of being served with the complaint.

If you plan to correct the violations giving rise to the claim, you should take pictures and measurements or similar action to document the condition of the physical barrier asserted to be the basis for a violation before undertaking any corrective action in case a court needs to see the condition of a barrier before it was corrected.

The court will schedule the conference to be held within 70 days after you file the attached application form.

[If you are not a defendant with a CASp inspection report, until a form is adopted by the Judicial Council, you may use the attached form if you modify the form and supplement it with your declaration stating any one of the following:

(1) Until January 1, 2018, that the site's new construction or improvement on or after January 1, 2008, and before January 1, 2016, was approved pursuant to the local building permit and inspection process; that, to the best of your knowledge, there have been no modifications or alterations completed or commenced since the building department approval that impacted compliance with construction-related accessibility standards with respect to the plaintiff's claim; and that all violations giving rise to the claim have been corrected, or will be corrected within 60 days of the complaint being served.

(2) That the site's new construction or improvement passed inspection by a local building department inspector who is a certified access specialist; that, to the best of your knowledge, there have been no modifications or alterations completed or commenced since that inspection approval that impacted compliance with construction-related accessibility standards with respect to the plaintiff's claim; and that all violations giving rise to the claim have been corrected, or will be corrected within 60 days of the complaint being served.

(3) That your business is a small business with 25 or fewer employees and meets the gross receipts criteria set out in Section 55.56 of the Civil Code, and that all violations giving rise to the claim have been corrected, or will be corrected within 30 days of being served with the complaint.]

The court will also issue an immediate stay of the proceedings unless the plaintiff has obtained a temporary restraining order in the construction-related accessibility claim. You may obtain a copy of the application form, filing instructions, and additional information about the stay and early evaluation conference through the Judicial Council Internet Web site at www.courts.ca.gov/selfhelp-start.htm.

You may file the application after you are served with a summons and complaint, but no later than your first court pleading or appearance in this case, which is due within 30 days after you receive the summons and complaint. If you do not file the application, you will still need to file your reply to the lawsuit within 30 days after you receive the summons and complaint to contest it. You may obtain more information about how to represent yourself and how to file a reply without hiring an attorney at www.courts.ca.gov/selfhelp-start.htm.

You may file the application without the assistance of an attorney, but it may be in your best interest to immediately seek the assistance of an attorney experienced in disability access laws when you receive a summons and complaint. You may make an offer to settle the case, and it may be in your interest to put that offer in writing so that it may be considered under Section 55.55 of the Civil Code.

(2) An attorney who files a Notice of Substitution of Counsel to appear as counsel for a plaintiff who, acting in propria persona, had previously filed a complaint in an action that

includes a construction-related accessibility claim, including, but not limited to, a claim brought under Section 51, 54, 54.1, or 55, shall, at the same time, cause to be served a copy of the application form specified in subdivision (c) and a copy of the notice specified in paragraph (1) upon the defendant on separate pages that shall be attached to the Notice of Substitution of Counsel.

(b)(1) Notwithstanding any other law, upon being served with a summons and complaint asserting a construction-related accessibility claim, including, but not limited to, a claim brought under Section 51, 54, 54.1, or 55, a qualified defendant, or other defendant as defined in paragraph (2), may file a request for a court stay and early evaluation conference in the proceedings of that claim prior to or simultaneous with that defendant's responsive pleading or other initial appearance in the action that includes the claim. If that defendant filed a timely request for stay and early evaluation conference before a responsive pleading was due, the period for filing a responsive pleading shall be tolled until the stay is lifted. Any responsive pleading filed simultaneously with a request for stay and early evaluation conference may be amended without prejudice, and the period for filing that amendment shall be tolled until the stay is lifted.

(2) This subdivision shall also apply to a defendant if any of the following apply:

(A) Until January 1, 2018, the site's new construction or improvement on or after January 1, 2008, and before January 1, 2016, was approved pursuant to the local building permit and inspection process, and the defendant declares with the application that, to the best of the defendant's knowledge, there have been no modifications or alterations completed or commenced since that approval that impacted compliance with construction-related accessibility standards with respect to the plaintiff's claim, and that all violations have been corrected, or will be corrected within 60 days of being served with the complaint.

(B) The site's new construction or improvement was approved by a local public building department inspector who is a certified access specialist, and the defendant declares with the application that, to the best of the defendant's knowledge, there have been no modifications or alterations completed or commenced since that approval that impacted compliance with construction-related accessibility standards with respect to the plaintiff's claim, and that all violations have been corrected, or will be corrected within 60 days of being served with the complaint.

(C) The defendant is a small business described in subdivision (f) of Section 55.56, and the defendant declares with the application that all violations have been corrected, or will be corrected within 30 days of being served with the complaint.

(3) Notwithstanding any other law, if the plaintiff had acted in propria persona in filing a complaint that includes a construction-related accessibility claim, including, but not limited to, a claim brought under Section 51, 54, 54.1, or 55, a qualified defendant, or a defendant described by paragraph (2), who is served with a Notice of Substitution of Counsel shall have 30 days to file an application for a stay and an early evaluation conference. The application may be filed prior to or after the defendant's filing of a responsive pleading or other initial appearance in the action that includes the claim, except that an application may not be filed in a claim in which an early evaluation conference or settlement conference has already been held on the claim.

(c)(1) An application for an early evaluation conference and stay by a qualified defendant shall include a signed declaration that states both of the following:

(A) The site identified in the complaint has been CASp-inspected or meets applicable standards, or is CASp determination pending or has been inspected by a CASp, and if the site is

CASp-inspected or meets applicable standards, there have been no modifications completed or commenced since the date of inspection that may impact compliance with construction-related accessibility standards to the best of the defendant's knowledge.

(B) An inspection report pertaining to the site has been issued by a CASp. The inspection report shall be provided to the court and the plaintiff at least 15 days prior to the court date set for the early evaluation conference.

(2) An application for an early evaluation conference and stay by a defendant described by subparagraph (A) of paragraph (2) of subdivision (b), which may be filed until January 1, 2018, shall include a signed declaration that states all of the following:

(A) The site's new construction or improvement was approved pursuant to the local building permit and inspection process on or after January 1, 2008, and before January 1, 2016.

(B) To the best of the defendant's knowledge there have been no modifications or alterations completed or commenced since that approval that impacted compliance with construction-related accessibility standards with respect to the plaintiff's claim.

(C) All construction-related violations giving rise to the claim have been corrected, or will be corrected within 60 days of the complaint being served upon the defendant.

(3) An application for an early evaluation conference and stay by a defendant described in subparagraph (B) of paragraph (2) of subdivision (b) shall include a signed declaration that states all of the following:

(A) The site's new construction or improvement was approved by a local building department inspector who is a certified access specialist.

(B) To the best of the defendant's knowledge there have been no modifications or alterations completed or commenced since that approval that impacted compliance with construction-related accessibility standards with respect to the plaintiff's claim.

(C) All construction related violations giving rise to the claim have been corrected, or will be corrected within 60 days of the complaint being served upon the defendant.

(4) An application for an early evaluation conference and stay by a defendant described by subparagraph (C) of paragraph (2) of subdivision (b) shall include the materials listed in paragraphs (5) and (6) of this subdivision, and shall include a signed declaration that states both of the following:

(A) The defendant is a small business that employs 25 or fewer employees and meets the gross receipts eligibility criteria provided in paragraph (2) of subdivision (f) of Section 55.56.

(B) All construction-related violations giving rise to the claim have been corrected, or will be corrected within 30 days of the complaint being served upon the defendant.

(5) An application for an early evaluation conference and stay by a small business defendant under paragraph (4) shall include evidence showing correction of all violations within 30 days of the service of the complaint and served upon the plaintiff with the reply unless the application is filed prior to completion of the corrections. In that event, the evidence shall be provided to the court and served upon the plaintiff within 10 days of the court order as provided in paragraph (4) of subdivision (d). This paragraph shall not be construed to extend the permissible time under subdivision (f) of Section 55.56 to make the corrections.

(6) An application for an early evaluation conference and stay by a small business defendant under paragraph (4) shall also include both of the following, which shall be confidential

documents filed only with the court and not served upon or available to the plaintiff:

(A) Proof of the defendant's number of employees, as shown by wage report forms filed with the Employment Development Department.

(B) Proof of the defendant's average gross receipts for the previous three years, or for the existence of the business if less than three years, as shown by a federal or state tax document.

(7) The following provisional request and notice forms may be used and filed by a qualified defendant until forms are adopted by the Judicial Council for those purposes pursuant to subdivision (*l*):

ATTORNEY OR PARTY WITHOUT ATTORNEY (Name, State Bar number if attorney, and address):	FOR COURT USE ONLY
TELEPHONE NO.: FAX NO. (Optional):	
E-MAIL ADDRESS (Optional):	
ATTORNEY FOR (Name):	

SUPERIOR COURT OF CALIFORNIA, COUNTY OF _____	
STREET ADDRESS:	
MAILING ADDRESS:	
CITY AND ZIP CODE:	
BRANCH NAME:	

PLAINTIFF:	
DEFENDANT:	

DEFENDANT'S APPLICATION FOR STAY AND EARLY EVALUATION CONFERENCE PURSUANT TO CIVIL CODE SECTION 55.54 (CONSTRUCTION-RELATED ACCESSIBILITY CLAIM)	CASE NUMBER:

(Information about this application and the filing instructions may be obtained at http:// www.courtinfo.ca.gov/selfhelp/.)

1. Defendant (name) _____ requests a stay of proceedings and early evaluation conference pursuant to Civil Code Section 55.54.

2. The complaint in this case alleges a construction-related accessibility claim as defined under Civil Code Section 55.52(a)(1).

3. The claim concerns a site that (check the box if the statement is true):
    a. _____ Has been inspected by a Certified Access Specialist (CASp) and determined to be CASp inspected or CASp determination pending and, if CASp inspected, there have been no modifications completed or commenced since the date of inspection that may impact compliance with construction-related accessibility standards to the best of defendant's knowledge; and
    b. _____ An inspection report by a Certified Access Specialist (CASp) relating to the site has been issued.
    (Both (a) and (b) must be met for the court to order a Stay and Early Evaluation Conference.)

4. I am requesting the court to:
    a. Stay the proceedings relating to the construction-related accessibility claim.
    b. Schedule an Early Evaluation Conference.
    c. Order Defendant to file a confidential copy of the Certified Access Specialist (CASp) report with the court and serve a copy of the report on the Plaintiff at least fifteen (15) days before the Early Evaluation Conference date.
    d. Order Plaintiff to file the statement required by Civil Code Section 55.54(d)(6)(A)–(D) with the court and serve a copy of the statement on the Defendant at least fifteen (15) days before the date of the Early Evaluation Conference.

I declare under penalty of perjury under the laws of the State of California that the foregoing is true and correct.

Date:

_____   _____
(TYPE OR PRINT NAME OF DECLARANT)   (SIGNATURE OF DECLARANT)

_____
(TITLE OF DECLARANT)

DEFENDANT'S APPLICATION FOR EARLY EVALUATION CONFERENCE AND STAY OF PROCEEDINGS
(Construction-related Accessibility Claim)   Provisional Form

ATTORNEY OR PARTY WITHOUT ATTORNEY (Name, State Bar number if attorney, and address):	FOR COURT USE ONLY
TELEPHONE NO.: FAX NO. (Optional): E-MAIL ADDRESS (Optional): ATTORNEY FOR (Name):	
SUPERIOR COURT OF CALIFORNIA, COUNTY OF _____ STREET ADDRESS: MAILING ADDRESS: CITY AND ZIP CODE: BRANCH NAME:	
PLAINTIFF: DEFENDANT:	
NOTICE OF STAY OR PROCEEDINGS AND EARLY EVALUATION CONFERENCE (CONSTRUCTION-RELATED ACCESSIBILITY CLAIM)	CASE NUMBER:

Stay of Proceedings

For a period of 90 days from the date of the filing of this court notice, unless otherwise ordered by the court, the parties are stayed from taking any further action relating to the construction-related accessibility claim or claims in this case.

This stay does not apply to any construction-related accessibility claim in which the plaintiff has obtained temporary injunctive relief which is still in place.

Notice of Early Evaluation Conference

1. This action includes a construction-related accessibility claim under Civil Code Section 55.52(a)(1) or other provision of law.

2. A defendant has requested an early evaluation conference and a stay of proceedings under Civil Code Section 55.54.

3. The early evaluation conference is scheduled as follows:

    a. Date: Time: Dept.   Room:

    b. The conference will be held at .... the court address shown above, or .... at:

4. The plaintiff and defendant shall attend with any other person needed for settlement of the case unless, with court approval, a party's disability requires the party's participation by a telephone appearance or other alternate means or through the personal appearance of an authorized representative.

5. The defendant that requested the conference and stay of proceedings must file with the court and serve on all parties a copy of the CASp report for the site that is the subject of the construction-related accessibility claim at least fifteen (15) days before the date set for the early evaluation conference. The CASp report is confidential and only available as set forth below and in Civil Code Section 55.54(d)(1).

6. The CASp report shall be marked "CONFIDENTIAL" and may be disclosed only to counsel, the parties to the action, the parties' attorneys, those individuals employed or retained by the attorneys to assist in the litigation, and insurance representatives or others involved in the evaluation and settlement of the case.

7. The plaintiff shall file with the court and serve on all parties at least fifteen (15) days before the date set for the early evaluation conference a statement of, to the extent known, all of the following:
    a. An itemized list of specific issues on the subject premises that are the basis of the claimed construction-related accessibility violations in the plaintiff's complaint;
    b. The amount of damages claimed;
    c. The amount of attorney's fees and costs incurred to date, if any, that are being claimed; and
    d. Any demand for settlement of the case in its entirety.

8. A copy of this Notice and Order and the Defendant's Application shall be served on the plaintiff or plaintiff's attorney by hand delivering it or mailing it to the address listed on the complaint on the same date that the court issues this Notice and Order of Stay of Proceedings and Early Evaluation Conference.

Date: _____   Clerk, by _____, Deputy

More information about this Notice and Order and the defendant's application, and instructions to assist plaintiff and defendants in complying with this Notice and Order, may be obtained at http://www.courtinfo.ca.gov/selfhelp/.)

Requests for Accommodation

Assistive listening systems, computer-assisted real-time captioning, or sign language interpreter services are available if you ask at least 5 days before the date on which you are to appear. Contact the clerk's office or go to www.courtinfo.ca.gov/forms for Request for Accommodations by Persons with Disabilities and Order (form MC-410). (Civil Code Section 54.8)

Proof of Service

(Required from Defendant Filing Application for Stay and Early Evaluation Conference)

I served a copy of the defendant's Application For Stay and Early Evaluation Conference Pursuant To Civil Code Section 55.54 and the court Notice and Order of Stay of Proceedings and Early Evaluation Conference (check one):

_____ On the Plaintiff's attorney.

_____ On the Plaintiff who is not represented by an attorney.

By hand delivering it or mailing it to the address listed on the complaint on the day the court issued this Notice and Order of Stay of Proceedings and Early Evaluation Conference.

I declare under penalty of perjury of the laws of the State of California that the foregoing is true and correct.

Dated: _____

Type or Print Name _____   Signature _____

Address of named person _____

NOTICE OF STAY OF PROCEEDINGS AND EARLY EVALUATION CONFERENCE
(Construction-related Accessibility Claim)   Provisional Form

---

(8) The provisional forms and any replacement Judicial Council forms shall include the defendant's declaration of proof of service of the application, the notice of the court's order, and the court's order pursuant to subdivision (d).

(d) Upon the filing of an application for stay and early evaluation conference by a qualified defendant, or a defendant described by paragraph (2) of subdivision (b), the court shall immediately issue an order that does all of the following:

(1) Grants a 90–day stay of the proceedings with respect to the construction-related accessibility claim, unless the plaintiff has obtained temporary injunctive relief that is still in place for the construction-related accessibility claim.

(2) Schedules a mandatory early evaluation conference for a date as soon as possible from the date of the order, but in no event later than 70 days after issuance of the order, and in no event earlier than 50 days after the filing of the request.

(3) Directs the parties, and any other person whose authority is required to negotiate and enter into settlement, to appear in person at the time set for the conference. Appearance by counsel shall not satisfy the requirement that the parties or those with negotiation and settlement authority personally appear, provided, however, that the court may allow a party who is unable to attend in person due to his or her disability to

participate in the hearing by telephone or other alternative means or through a representative authorized to settle the case.

(4)(A) Directs the qualified defendant to file with the court and serve on the plaintiff a copy of any relevant CASp inspection report at least 15 days before the date of the conference. The CASp inspection report is confidential and is available only as set forth in paragraph (5) of this subdivision and in paragraph (4) of subdivision (e).

(B) Directs a defendant described by subparagraph (A) or (B) of paragraph (2) of subdivision (b) who has filed a declaration stating that the violation or violations have been corrected, or will be corrected within 60 days of service of the complaint to file with the court and serve on the plaintiff evidence showing correction of the violation or violations within 10 calendar days after the completion of the corrections.

(C) Directs a defendant described by subparagraph (C) of paragraph (2) of subdivision (b) who has filed a declaration stating that the violation or violations have been corrected, or will be corrected within 30 days of service of the complaint to file with the court and serve on the plaintiff within 10 days after issuance of the court order evidence of correction of the violation or violations, if that evidence showing correction was not filed previously with the application and served on the plaintiff.

(5) Directs the parties that the CASp inspection report may be disclosed only to the court, the parties to the action, the parties' attorneys, those individuals employed or retained by the attorneys to assist in the litigation, and insurance representatives or others involved in the evaluation and settlement of the case.

(6) Directs the plaintiff to file with the court and serve on the defendant at least 15 days before the date of the conference a statement that includes, to the extent reasonably known, for use solely for the purpose of the early evaluation conference, all of the following:

(A) An itemized list of specific conditions on the subject premises that are the basis of the claimed violations of construction-related accessibility standards in the plaintiff's complaint.

(B) The amount of damages claimed.

(C) The amount of attorney's fees and costs incurred to date, if any, that are being claimed.

(D) Any demand for settlement of the case in its entirety.

(e)(1) A party failing to comply with any court order may be subject to court sanction at the court's discretion.

(2)(A) The court shall lift the stay when the defendant has failed to file and serve the CASp inspection report prior to the early evaluation conference and has failed also to produce the report at the time of the early evaluation conference, unless the defendant shows good cause for that failure.

(B) The court shall lift the stay when a defendant described by paragraph (2) of subdivision (b) has failed to file and serve the evidence showing correction of the violation or violations as required by law.

(3) The court may lift the stay at the conclusion of the early evaluation conference upon a showing of good cause by the plaintiff. Good cause may include the defendant's failure to make reasonably timely progress toward completion of corrections noted by a CASp.

(4) The CASp inspection report filed and served pursuant to subdivision (d) shall remain confidential throughout the stay and shall continue to be confidential until the conclusion of the claim, whether by dismissal, settlement, or final judgment, unless there is a showing of good cause by any party. Good cause may include the defendant's failure to make reasonably timely progress toward completion of corrections noted by a CASp.

The confidentiality of the inspection report shall terminate upon the conclusion of the claim, unless the owner of the report obtains a court order pursuant to the California Rules of Court to seal the record.

(f) All discussions at the early evaluation conference shall be subject to Section 1152 of the Evidence Code. It is the intent of the Legislature that the purpose of the evaluation conference shall include, but not be limited to, evaluation of all of the following, as applicable:

(1) Whether the defendant is entitled to the 90–day stay for some or all of the identified issues in the case, as a qualified defendant.

(2) The current condition of the site and the status of any plan of corrections, including whether the qualified defendant has corrected or is willing to correct the alleged violations, and the timeline for doing so.

(3) Whether subdivision (f) of Section 55.56 may be applicable to the case, and whether all violations giving rise to the claim have been corrected within the specified time periods.

(4) Whether the case, including any claim for damages or injunctive relief, can be settled in whole or in part.

(5) Whether the parties should share other information that may facilitate early evaluation and resolution of the dispute.

(g) Nothing in this section precludes any party from making an offer to compromise pursuant to Section 998 of the Code of Civil Procedure.

(h) For a claim involving a qualified defendant, as provided in paragraph (1) of subdivision (b), the court may schedule additional conferences and may extend the 90–day stay for good cause shown, but not to exceed one additional 90–day extension.

(i) Early evaluation conferences shall be conducted by a superior court judge or commissioner, or a court early evaluation conference officer. A commissioner shall not be qualified to conduct early evaluation conferences pursuant to this subdivision unless he or she has received training regarding disability access requirements imposed by the federal Americans with Disabilities Act of 1990 (Public Law 101–336; 42 U.S.C. Sec. 12101 et seq.), state laws that govern access to public facilities, and federal and state regulations adopted pursuant to those laws. For purposes of this subdivision, a "court early evaluation conference officer" means an attorney employed by the court who has received training regarding disability access requirements imposed by the federal Americans with Disabilities Act of 1990, state laws that govern access to public facilities, and federal and state regulations adopted pursuant to those laws. Attorneys serving in this capacity may also be utilized by the court for other purposes not related to these proceedings.

(j) Nothing in this part shall be deemed to make any inspection report, opinion, statement, or other finding or conclusion of a CASp binding on the court, or to abrogate in any manner the ultimate authority of the court to make all appropriate findings of fact and law. The CASp inspection report and any opinion, statement, finding, or conclusion therein shall be given the weight the trier of fact finds that it deserves.

(k) Nothing in this part shall be construed to invalidate or limit any California construction-related accessibility standard that provides greater or equal protection for the rights of individuals with disabilities than is afforded by the federal Americans with Disabilities Act (Public Law 101–336; 42 U.S.C. Sec. 12101 et seq.) and the federal regulations adopted pursuant to that act.

(l)(1) The Judicial Council shall, by January 1, 2013, prepare and post on its Internet Web site instructions and a form for use by a qualified defendant, or other defendant described by paragraph (2) of subdivision (b), to file an application for stay and early evaluation conference as provided in subdivisions (b) and (c), a form for the court's notice of stay and early evaluation conference, and any other forms appropriate to implement the provisions relating to early evaluation conferences. Until those forms are adopted, the Judicial Council shall post on its Internet Web site the provisional forms set forth in subdivision (c).

(2) Until the adoption of the forms as provided in paragraph (1), the provisional application form may be used by a defendant described by paragraph (2) of subdivision (b).

(3) In lieu of the provisions specified in number 3 of page 1 of the application form set forth in paragraph (7) of subdivision (c), the application shall include one of the following declarations of the defendant as to the basis for the application, as follows:

(A) That all of the following apply to a defendant described by subparagraph (A) of paragraph (2) of subdivision (b):

(i) The site's new construction or improvement was approved pursuant to the local building permit and inspection process on or after January 1, 2008, and before January 1, 2016.

(ii) To the best of the defendant's knowledge there have been no modifications or alterations completed or commenced since that approval that impacted compliance with construction-related accessibility standards with respect to the plaintiff's claim.

(iii) All the violations giving rise to the claim have been corrected, or will be corrected within 60 days of the complaint being served.

(B) That all of the following apply to a defendant described by subparagraph (B) of paragraph (2) of subdivision (b):

(i) The site's new construction or improvement was approved by a local public building department inspector who is a certified access specialist.

(ii) To the best of the defendant's knowledge there have been no modifications or alterations completed or commenced since that approval that impacted compliance with construction-related accessibility standards with respect to the plaintiff's claim.

(iii) All the violations giving rise to the claim have been corrected, or will be corrected within 60 days of the complaint being served.

(C) That both of the following apply to a defendant described by subparagraph (C) of paragraph (2) of subdivision (b):

(i) The defendant is a small business described in paragraph (2) of subdivision (f) of Section 55.56.

(ii) The violation or violations giving rise to the claim have been corrected, or will be corrected within 30 days of the complaint being served.

(4) In lieu of the provision specified in number 4(c) of page 1 of the application form set forth in paragraph (7) of subdivision (c), the application shall include a request that the court order the defendant to do either of the following:

(A) For a defendant who has filed a declaration stating that all violations have been corrected, or will be corrected within 60 days of service of the complaint, file with the court and serve on the plaintiff evidence showing correction of the violation or violations within 10 calendar days of the completion of the corrections.

(B) For a defendant who is a small business that has filed a declaration stating that all the violations have been corrected, or will be corrected within 30 days of the service of the complaint, file with the court and serve on the plaintiff evidence showing correction of the violation or violations within 10 calendar days after issuance of the court order, if that evidence showing

correction was not filed previously with the application and served on the plaintiff.

(5) The Judicial Council shall also prepare and post on its Internet Web site instructions and cover pages to assist plaintiffs and defendants, respectively, to comply with their filing responsibilities under subdivision (d). The cover pages shall also provide for the party's declaration of proof of service of the pertinent document served under the court order.

(m) The stay provisions shall not apply to any construction-related accessibility claim in which the plaintiff has been granted temporary injunctive relief that remains in place.

(n) This section shall not apply to any action brought by the Attorney General, or by any district attorney, city attorney, or county counsel.

(o) The amendments to this section made by Senate Bill 1186 of the 2011–12 Regular Session of the Legislature shall apply only to claims filed on or after the operative date of that act. Nothing in this part is intended to affect any complaint filed before that date.

(p) Nothing in this part is intended to affect existing law regarding class action requirements. *(Added by Stats.2008, c. 549 (S.B.1608), § 3. Amended by Stats.2009, c. 569 (S.B.209), § 1; Stats.2012, c. 383 (S.B.1186), § 9, eff. Sept. 19, 2012.)*

Contingent Operation

Operation of this Part is contingent upon availability of funding under the terms of Stats.2008, c. 549 (S.B.1608) § 12.

Research References

Rutter, Cal. Practice Guide: A.D.R. App. A, Selected Statutes Providing for ADR.

Rutter, Cal. Practice Guide: A.D.R. Ch. 3B-C, C. Statutorily-Mandated ADR.

Rutter, Cal. Practice Guide: A.D.R. Gen. Matls., Highlights.

Rutter, Cal. Practice Guide: Civ. Pro. Before Trial Ch. 1-C, C. Prelawsuit Notices, Claims and Demands.

Rutter, Cal. Practice Guide: Civ. Pro. Before Trial Ch. 6-B, B. Complaints.

Rutter, Cal. Practice Guide: Civ. Pro. Before Trial Ch. 12(I)-B, B. Case Management ("Fast Track") System.

Miller and Starr California Real Estate § 20:7, The Unruh Civil Rights Act--Disability Discrimination.

Miller and Starr California Real Estate § 22:75.10, Construction-Related Accessibility Claims.

19 NO. 4 Miller & Starr, California Real Estate Newsalert 12, Discrimination.

8 Witkin, California Summary 10th Constitutional Law § 958, Physical Access.

§ 55.545. Mandatory evaluation conference; application; actions following application; construction and application of provisions

(a) A defendant who does not qualify for an early evaluation conference pursuant Section 55.54, or who forgoes the provisions of Section 55.54, may request a mandatory evaluation conference. A plaintiff may, if the defendant does not make the request with the filing of the responsive pleadings, request a mandatory evaluation conference by filing an application within 15 days of the defendant's filing of responsive pleadings.

(b) Upon being served with a summons and complaint asserting a construction-related accessibility claim, including, but not limited to, a claim brought under Section 51, 54, 54.1, or 55, a defendant may file an application for a mandatory evaluation conference in the proceedings of that claim simultaneous with the defendant's responsive pleading or other initial appearance in the action that includes the claim. Until the application form for the mandatory evaluation conference is developed by the Judicial Council and posted on its Internet Web site pursuant to subdivision (j), a defendant may request the calendaring of the mandatory evaluation conference in a separate application filed with the defendant's responsive pleadings.

(c) Upon the filing of a request or application for a mandatory evaluation conference by a defendant or plaintiff, the court shall schedule a mandatory evaluation conference for a date as soon as possible from the date of the request or application, but in no event later than 180 days after the date of request or application, or earlier than 120 days after the filing of the request or application. Upon mutual stipulation for an extension of the conference date, the mandatory evaluation conference may be extended for up to 30 days. The court's notice of conference shall also do all of the following:

(1) Direct the parties, and any other person whose authority is required to negotiate and enter into settlement, to appear in person at the time set for the conference. Appearance by counsel shall not satisfy the requirement that the parties, or those with negotiation and settlement authority, personally appear. However, the court may allow a party who is unable to attend in person due to his or her disability to participate in the hearing by telephone or other alternative means, or through a representative authorized to settle the case.

(2) Direct the plaintiff to file with the court and serve on the defendant, at least 30 days before the date of mandatory evaluation conference, a statement that includes, to the extent reasonably known, for use solely for the purpose of the mandatory evaluation conference, all of the following:

(A) An itemized list of specific conditions on the site that are the basis of the claimed violations of construction-related accessibility standards in the plaintiff's complaint.

(B) The amount of damages claimed.

(C) The amount of attorney's fees and costs incurred to date, if any, that are being claimed.

(D) Any demand for settlement of the case in its entirety.

(3) Direct the defendant to file with the court and serve on the plaintiff, at least 30 days before the date of the mandatory evaluation conference, a statement of the defendant detailing any remedial action or remedial correction plan undertaken, or to be undertaken, by the defendant to correct the alleged violations.

(d) A party failing to comply with any court order is subject to court sanction at the court's discretion.

(e) All discussions at the mandatory evaluation conference shall be subject to Section 1152 of the Evidence Code. It is the intent of the Legislature that the purpose of the evaluation conference shall include, but not be limited to, evaluation of all of the following:

(1) The current condition of the site and the status of any plan of correction, including whether the defendant has corrected, or is willing to correct, the alleged violations, and the timeline for doing so.

(2) Whether the case, including any claim for damages or injunctive relief, can be settled in whole or in part.

(3) Whether the parties should share other information that may facilitate evaluation and resolution of the dispute.

(f) Nothing in this section precludes any party from making an offer to compromise pursuant to Section 998 of the Code of Civil Procedure.

(g) The court may schedule additional conferences.

(h) Mandatory evaluation conferences shall be conducted by a superior court judge or commissioner, or by a court early evaluation conference officer as provided in subdivision (i) of Section 55.54.

(i) If an inspection report by a certified access specialist is offered by the defendant, the provisions of Section 55.54 relating to the use and confidentiality of that report shall apply.

(j)(1) The Judicial Council shall prepare and post on its Internet Web site instructions and a form for a party to use to file an application for a mandatory evaluation conference and a form for the court's notice of the mandatory evaluation conference. Until those forms are adopted, a party and the court may use an ad hoc form that complies with the requirements of this section.

(2) The Judicial Council shall also prepare and post on its Internet Web site instructions and cover pages to assist plaintiffs and defendants, respectively, to comply with their filing responsibilities under subdivision (c).

(k) The mandatory evaluation conference may, at the court's discretion, be scheduled or combined with the case management conference within the time period specified in subdivision (c).

(l) This section shall not apply to any action brought by the Attorney General, or by any district attorney, city attorney, or county counsel.

(m) This section shall apply only to claims filed on or after January 1, 2013. Nothing in this section is intended to affect any complaint filed before that date. *(Added by Stats.2012, c. 383 (S.B.1186), § 10, eff. Sept. 19, 2012.)*

Contingent Operation

Operation of this Part is contingent upon availability of funding under the terms of Stats.2008, c. 549 (S.B.1608) § 12.

Research References

Rutter, Cal. Practice Guide: A.D.R. Ch. 3B-C, C. Statutorily-Mandated ADR.

Part 2.53

ATTORNEY'S FEES AND STATUTORY DAMAGES IN CONSTRUCTION–RELATED ACCESSIBILITY STANDARDS CLAIMS

Section

Contingent Operation

Operation of this Part is contingent upon availability of funding under the terms of Stats.2008, c. 549 (S.B.1608) § 12.

§ 55.55. Attorney's fees and costs; additional factors to consider

Notwithstanding subdivision (f) of Section 55.54, in determining an award of reasonable attorney's fees and recoverable costs with respect to any construction-related accessibility claim, the court may consider, along with other relevant information, written settlement offers made and rejected by the parties. Nothing in this section affects or modifies the inadmissibility of evidence regarding offers of compromise pursuant to Section 1152 of the Evidence Code, including, but not limited to, inadmissibility to prove injury or damage. *(Added by Stats.2008, c. 549 (S.B.1608), § 4.)*

Contingent Operation

Operation of this Part is contingent upon availability of funding under the terms of Stats.2008, c. 549 (S.B.1608) § 12.

Research References

Miller and Starr California Real Estate § 20:7, The Unruh Civil Rights Act--Disability Discrimination.
Miller and Starr California Real Estate § 22:75.10, Construction-Related Accessibility Claims.
19 NO. 4 Miller & Starr, California Real Estate Newsalert 12, Discrimination.

§ 55.56. Grounds for award of statutory damages

(a) Statutory damages under either subdivision (a) of Section 52 or subdivision (a) of Section 54.3 may be recovered in a construction-related accessibility claim against a place of public accommodation only if a violation or violations of one or more construction-related accessibility standards denied the plaintiff full and equal access to the place of public accommodation on a particular occasion.

(b) A plaintiff is denied full and equal access only if the plaintiff personally encountered the violation on a particular occasion, or the plaintiff was deterred from accessing a place of public accommodation on a particular occasion.

(c) A violation personally encountered by a plaintiff may be sufficient to cause a denial of full and equal access if the plaintiff experienced difficulty, discomfort, or embarrassment because of the violation.

(d) A plaintiff demonstrates that he or she was deterred from accessing a place of public accommodation on a particular occasion only if both of the following apply:

(1) The plaintiff had actual knowledge of a violation or violations that prevented or reasonably dissuaded the plaintiff from accessing a place of public accommodation that the plaintiff intended to use on a particular occasion.

(2) The violation or violations would have actually denied the plaintiff full and equal access if the plaintiff had accessed the place of public accommodation on that particular occasion.

(e) Statutory damages may be assessed pursuant to subdivision (a) based on each particular occasion that the plaintiff was denied full and equal access, and not upon the number of violations of construction-related accessibility standards identified at the place of public accommodation where the denial of full and equal access occurred. If the place of public accommodation consists of distinct facilities that offer distinct services, statutory damages may be assessed based on each denial of full and equal access to the distinct facility, and not upon the number of violations of construction-related accessibility standards identified at the place of public accommodation where the denial of full and equal access occurred.

(f)(1) Notwithstanding any other law, a defendant's liability for statutory damages in a construction-related accessibility claim against a place of public accommodation is reduced to a minimum of one thousand dollars ($1,000) for each offense if the defendant demonstrates that it has corrected all construction-related violations that are the basis of a claim within 60 days of being served with the complaint, and the defendant demonstrates any of the following:

(A) The structure or area of the alleged violation was determined to be "CASp-inspected" or "meets applicable standards" and, to the best of the defendant's knowledge, there were no modifications or alterations that impacted compliance with construction-related accessibility standards with respect to the plaintiff's claim that were completed or commenced between the date of that determination and the particular occasion on which the plaintiff was allegedly denied full and equal access.

(B) The structure or area of the alleged violation was the subject of an inspection report indicating "CASp determination pending" or "Inspected by a CASp," and the defendant has either implemented reasonable measures to correct the alleged violation * * * before the particular occasion on which the plaintiff was allegedly denied full and equal access, or the defendant was in the process of correcting the alleged violation within a reasonable time and manner * * * before the particular occasion on which the plaintiff was allegedly denied full and equal access.

(C) For a claim alleging a construction-related accessibility violation filed before January 1, 2018, the structure or area of the alleged violation was a new construction or an improvement that was approved by, and passed inspection by, the local building department permit and inspection process on or after January 1, 2008, and before January 1, 2016, and, to the best of the defendant's knowledge, there were no modifications or alterations that impacted compliance with respect to the plaintiff's claim that were completed or commenced between the completion date of the new construction or improvement and the particular occasion on which the plaintiff was allegedly denied full and equal access.

(D) The structure or area of the alleged violation was new construction or an improvement that was approved by, and passed inspection by, a local building department official who is a certified access specialist, and, to the best of the defendant's knowledge, there were no modifications or alterations that affected compliance with respect to the plaintiff's claim that were completed or commenced between the completion date of the new construction or improvement and the particular occasion on which the plaintiff was allegedly denied full and equal access.

(2) Notwithstanding any other law, a defendant's liability for statutory damages in a construction-related accessibility claim against a place of public accommodation is reduced to a minimum of two thousand dollars ($2,000) for each offense if the defendant demonstrates both of the following:

(A) The defendant has corrected all construction-related violations that are the basis of a claim within 30 days of being served with the complaint.

(B) The defendant is a small business that has employed 25 or fewer employees on average over the past three years, or for the years it has been in existence if less than three years, as evidenced by wage report forms filed with the Economic Development Department, and has average annual gross receipts of less than three million five hundred thousand dollars ($3,500,000) over the previous three years, or for the years it has been in existence if less than three years, as evidenced by federal or state income tax returns. The average annual gross receipts dollar amount shall be adjusted biannually by the Department of General Services for changes in the California Consumer Price Index for All Urban Consumers, as compiled by the Department of Industrial Relations. The Department of General Services shall post that adjusted amount on its Internet Web site.

(3) This subdivision shall not be applicable to intentional violations.

(4) Nothing in this subdivision affects the awarding of actual damages, or affects the awarding of treble actual damages.

(5) This subdivision shall apply only to claims filed on or after the effective date of Senate Bill 1186 of the 2011–12 Regular Session of the Legislature. Nothing in this subdivision is intended to affect a complaint filed before that date.

(g) This section does not alter the applicable law for the awarding of injunctive or other equitable relief for a violation or violations of one or more construction-related accessibility standards, nor alter any legal obligation of a party to mitigate damages.

(h) In assessing liability under subdivision (d), in an action alleging multiple claims for the same construction-related accessibility violation on different particular occasions, the court shall consider the reasonableness of the plaintiff's conduct in light of the plaintiff's obligation, if any, to mitigate damages. *(Added by Stats.2008, c. 549 (S.B.1608), § 4. Amended by Stats.2012, c. 383 (S.B.1186), § 11, eff. Sept. 19, 2012; Stats.2013, c. 76 (A.B.383), § 9.)*

Contingent Operation

Operation of this Part is contingent upon availability of funding under the terms of Stats.2008, c. 549 (S.B.1608) § 12.

Research References

Miller and Starr California Real Estate § 22:75.10, Construction-Related Accessibility Claims.
19 NO. 4 Miller & Starr, California Real Estate Newsalert 12, Discrimination.
8 Witkin, California Summary 10th Constitutional Law § 914, Enforcement.
8 Witkin, California Summary 10th Constitutional Law § 959, Enforcement.

§ 55.57. Application of Part

(a) This part shall apply only to claims filed on or after January 1, 2009. Nothing in this part is intended to affect litigation filed before that date, and no inference shall be drawn from provisions contained in this part concerning the state of the law as it existed prior to January 1, 2009.

(b) Nothing in this part is intended to affect existing law regarding class action requirements. *(Added by Stats.2008, c. 549 (S.B.1608), § 4.)*

Contingent Operation

Operation of this Part is contingent upon availability of funding under the terms of Stats.2008, c. 549 (S.B.1608) § 12.

Research References

Miller and Starr California Real Estate § 22:75.10, Construction-Related Accessibility Claims.
19 NO. 4 Miller & Starr, California Real Estate Newsalert 12, Discrimination.

Part 2.6

CONFIDENTIALITY OF MEDICAL INFORMATION

CHAPTER 1. DEFINITIONS

§ 56. Short title

This part may be cited as the Confidentiality of Medical Information Act. *(Added by Stats.1981, c. 782, § 2.)*

Research References

California Practice Guide: Employment Litigation Ch. 5-K, K. Invasion of Privacy.
California Practice Guide: Employment Litigation Ch. 12-B, B. Family and Medical Leave Act (FMLA)/California Family Rights Act (CFRA).
5 Witkin, California Summary 10th Torts § 572, Quasi-Judicial Proceedings.
5 Witkin, California Summary 10th Torts § 591, (S 591) in General.
5 Witkin, California Summary 10th Torts § 666, (S 666) in General.
5 Witkin, California Summary 10th Torts § 669, (S 669) Failure to Protect Security of Personal Information.
7 Witkin, California Summary 10th Constitutional Law § 580, (S 580) in General.
7 Witkin, California Summary 10th Constitutional Law § 605, (S 605) Medical Records and Information.

§ 56.05. Definitions

For purposes of this part:

(a) "Authorization" means permission granted in accordance with Section 56.11 or 56.21 for the disclosure of medical information.

(b) "Authorized recipient" means any person who is authorized to receive medical information pursuant to Section 56.10 or 56.20.

(c) "Confidential communications request" means a request by a subscriber or enrollee that health care service plan communications containing medical information be communicated to him or her at a specific mail or email address or specific telephone number, as designated by the subscriber or enrollee.

(d) "Contractor" means any person or entity that is a medical group, independent practice association, pharmaceutical benefits manager, or a medical service organization and is not a health care service plan or provider of health care. "Contractor" does not include insurance institutions as defined in subdivision (k) of Section 791.02 of the Insurance Code or pharmaceutical benefits managers licensed pursuant to the Knox–Keene Health Care Service Plan Act of 1975 (Chapter 2.2 (commencing with Section 1340) of Division 2 of the Health and Safety Code).

(e) "Endanger" means that the subscriber or enrollee fears that disclosure of his or her medical information could subject the subscriber or enrollee to harassment or abuse.

(f) "Enrollee" has the same meaning as that term is defined in Section 1345 of the Health and Safety Code.

(g) "Health care service plan" means any entity regulated pursuant to the Knox–Keene Health Care Service Plan Act of 1975 (Chapter 2.2 (commencing with Section 1340) of Division 2 of the Health and Safety Code).

(h) "Licensed health care professional" means any person licensed or certified pursuant to Division 2 (commencing with Section 500) of the Business and Professions Code, the Osteopathic Initiative Act or the Chiropractic Initiative Act, or Division 2.5 (commencing with Section 1797) of the Health and Safety Code.

(i) "Marketing" means to make a communication about a product or service that encourages recipients of the communication to purchase or use the product or service.

"Marketing" does not include any of the following:

(1) Communications made orally or in writing for which the communicator does not receive direct or indirect remuneration, including, but not limited to, gifts, fees, payments, subsidies, or other economic benefits, from a third party for making the communication.

(2) Communications made to current enrollees solely for the purpose of describing a provider's participation in an existing health care provider network or health plan network of a Knox–Keene licensed health plan to which the enrollees already subscribe; communications made to current enrollees solely for the purpose of describing if, and the extent to which, a product or service, or payment for a product or service, is provided by a provider, contractor, or plan or included in a plan of benefits of a Knox–Keene licensed health plan to which the enrollees already subscribe; or communications made to plan enrollees describing the availability of more cost-effective pharmaceuticals.

(3) Communications that are tailored to the circumstances of a particular individual to educate or advise the individual about treatment options, and otherwise maintain the individual's adherence to a prescribed course of medical treatment, as provided in Section 1399.901 of the Health and Safety Code, for a chronic and seriously debilitating or life-threatening condition as defined in subdivisions (d) and (e) of Section 1367.21 of the Health and Safety Code, if the health care provider, contractor, or health plan receives direct or indirect remuneration, including, but not limited to, gifts, fees, payments, subsidies, or other economic benefits, from a third party for making the communication, if all of the following apply:

(A) The individual receiving the communication is notified in the communication in typeface no smaller than 14–point type of the fact that the provider, contractor, or health plan has been remunerated and the source of the remuneration.

(B) The individual is provided the opportunity to opt out of receiving future remunerated communications.

(C) The communication contains instructions in typeface no smaller than 14–point type describing how the individual can opt out of receiving further communications by calling a toll-free number of the health care provider, contractor, or health plan making the remunerated communications. No further communication may be made to an individual who has opted out after 30 calendar days from the date the individual makes the opt out request.

(j) "Medical information" means any individually identifiable information, in electronic or physical form, in possession of or derived from a provider of health care, health care service plan, pharmaceutical company, or contractor regarding a patient's medical history, mental or physical condition, or treatment. "Individually identifiable" means that the medical information includes or contains any element of personal identifying information sufficient to allow identification of the individual, such as the patient's name, address, electronic mail address, telephone number, or social security number, or other information that, alone or in combination with other publicly available information, reveals the individual's identity.

(k) "Patient" means any natural person, whether or not still living, who received health care services from a provider of health care and to whom medical information pertains.

(l) "Pharmaceutical company" means any company or business, or an agent or representative thereof, that manufactures, sells, or distributes pharmaceuticals, medications, or prescription drugs. "Pharmaceutical company" does not include a pharmaceutical benefits manager, as included in subdivision (c), or a provider of health care.

(m) "Provider of health care" means any person licensed or certified pursuant to Division 2 (commencing with Section 500) of the Business and Professions Code; any person licensed pursuant to the Osteopathic Initiative Act or the Chiropractic Initiative Act; any person certified pursuant to Division 2.5 (commencing with Section 1797) of the Health and Safety Code; any clinic, health dispensary, or health facility licensed pursuant to Division 2 (commencing with Section 1200) of the Health and Safety Code. "Provider of health care" does not include insurance institutions as defined in subdivision (k) of Section 791.02 of the Insurance Code.

(n) "Sensitive services" means all health care services described in Sections 6924, 6925, 6926, 6927, 6928, and 6929 of the Family Code, and Sections 121020 and 124260 of the Health and Safety Code, obtained by a patient at or above the minimum age specified for consenting to the service specified in the section.

(o) "Subscriber" has the same meaning as that term is defined in Section 1345 of the Health and Safety Code. *(Added by Stats.1981, c. 782, § 2. Amended by Stats.1984, c. 1391, § 3; Stats.1999, c. 526 (S.B.19), § 1; Stats.2000, c. 1067 (S.B.2094), § 1; Stats.2002, c. 853 (A.B.2191), § 1; Stats.2003, c. 562 (A.B.715), § 1; Stats.2013, c. 444 (S.B.138), § 2.)*

Research References

California Practice Guide: Employment Litigation Ch. 5-K, K. Invasion of Privacy.

10 Witkin, California Summary 10th Parent and Child § 150, Confidentiality of Information.

2 Witkin Cal. Summ. 10th Workers' Compensation § 158, Nondisclosure of Medical Information.

§ 56.06. Business organized for the purpose of maintaining medical information in order to supply information to individual or health care provider for specified purposes; business offering hardware or software designed to make medical information available to individuals or health care providers; confidentiality; penalties

(a) Any business organized for the purpose of maintaining medical information, as defined in subdivision (g) of Section 56.05, in order to make the information available to an individual or to a provider of health care at the request of the individual or a provider of health care, for purposes of allowing the individual to manage his or her information, or for the diagnosis and treatment of the individual, shall be deemed to be a provider of health care subject to the requirements of this part. However, nothing in this section shall be construed to make a business specified in this subdivision a provider of health care for purposes of any law other than this part, including laws that specifically incorporate by reference the definitions of this part.

(b) Any business that offers software or hardware to consumers, including a mobile application or other related device that is designed to maintain medical information, as defined in subdivision (g) of Section 56.05, in order to make the information available to an individual or a provider of health care at the request of the individual or a provider of health care, for purposes of allowing the individual to manage his or her information, or for the diagnosis, treatment, or management of a medical condition of the individual, shall be deemed to be a provider of health care subject to the requirements of this part. However, nothing in this section shall be construed to make a business specified in this subdivision a provider of health care for purposes of any law other than this part, including laws that specifically incorporate by reference the definitions of this part.

(c) Any business described in subdivision (a) or (b) shall maintain the same standards of confidentiality required of a provider of health care with respect to medical information disclosed to the business.

(d) Any business described in subdivision (a) or (b) shall be subject to the penalties for improper use and disclosure of medical information prescribed in this part. *(Added by Stats. 1993, c. 1004 (A.B.336), § 1. Amended by Stats.2007, c. 699 (A.B.1298), § 1; Stats.2013, c. 296 (A.B.658), § 1.)*

§ 56.07. Medical profile, summary, or information provided; patient's written request; application

(a) Except as provided in subdivision (c), upon the patient's written request, any corporation described in Section 56.06, or any other entity that compiles or maintains medical information for any reason, shall provide the patient, at no charge, with a copy of any medical profile, summary, or information maintained by the corporation or entity with respect to the patient.

(b) A request by a patient pursuant to this section shall not be deemed to be an authorization by the patient for the release or disclosure of any information to any person or entity other than the patient.

(c) This section shall not apply to any patient records that are subject to inspection by the patient pursuant to Section 123110 of the Health and Safety Code and shall not be deemed to limit the right of a health care provider to charge a fee for the preparation of a summary of patient records as provided in Section 123130 of the Health and Safety Code. This section shall not apply to a health care service plan licensed pursuant to Chapter 2.2 (commencing with Section 1340) of Division 2 of the Health and Safety Code or a disability insurer licensed pursuant to the Insurance Code. This section shall not apply to medical information compiled or maintained by a fire and casualty insurer or its retained counsel in the regular course of investigating or litigating a claim under a policy of insurance that it has written. For the purposes of this section, a fire and casualty insurer is an insurer writing policies that may be sold by a fire and casualty licensee pursuant to Section 1625 of the Insurance Code. *(Added by Stats.2000, c. 1066 (S.B.1903), § 1.)*

CHAPTER 2. DISCLOSURE OF MEDICAL INFORMATION BY PROVIDERS

§ 56.10. Authorization; compelled disclosure; other permitted disclosures

(a) A provider of health care, health care service plan, or contractor shall not disclose medical information regarding a patient of the provider of health care or an enrollee or subscriber of a health care service plan without first obtaining an authorization, except as provided in subdivision (b) or (c).

(b) A provider of health care, a health care service plan, or a contractor shall disclose medical information if the disclosure is compelled by any of the following:

(1) By a court pursuant to an order of that court.

(2) By a board, commission, or administrative agency for purposes of adjudication pursuant to its lawful authority.

(3) By a party to a proceeding before a court or administrative agency pursuant to a subpoena, subpoena duces tecum, notice to appear served pursuant to Section 1987 of the Code of Civil Procedure, or any provision authorizing discovery in a proceeding before a court or administrative agency.

(4) By a board, commission, or administrative agency pursuant to an investigative subpoena issued under Article 2 (commencing with Section 11180) of Chapter 2 of Part 1 of Division 3 of Title 2 of the Government Code.

(5) By an arbitrator or arbitration panel, when arbitration is lawfully requested by either party, pursuant to a subpoena duces tecum issued under Section 1282.6 of the Code of Civil Procedure, or another provision authorizing discovery in a proceeding before an arbitrator or arbitration panel.

(6) By a search warrant lawfully issued to a governmental law enforcement agency.

(7) By the patient or the patient's representative pursuant to Chapter 1 (commencing with Section 123100) of Part 1 of Division 106 of the Health and Safety Code.

(8) By a coroner, when requested in the course of an investigation by the coroner's office for the purpose of identifying the decedent or locating next of kin, or when investigating deaths that may involve public health concerns, organ or tissue donation, child abuse, elder abuse, suicides, poisonings, accidents, sudden infant deaths, suspicious deaths, unknown deaths, or criminal deaths, or upon notification of, or investigation of, imminent deaths that may involve organ or tissue donation pursuant to Section 7151.15 of the Health and Safety Code, or when otherwise authorized by the decedent's representative. Medical information requested by the coroner under this paragraph shall be limited to information regarding the patient who

is the decedent and who is the subject of the investigation or who is the prospective donor and shall be disclosed to the coroner without delay upon request.

(9) When otherwise specifically required by law.

(c) A provider of health care or a health care service plan may disclose medical information as follows:

(1) The information may be disclosed to providers of health care, health care service plans, contractors, or other health care professionals or facilities for purposes of diagnosis or treatment of the patient. This includes, in an emergency situation, the communication of patient information by radio transmission or other means between emergency medical personnel at the scene of an emergency, or in an emergency medical transport vehicle, and emergency medical personnel at a health facility licensed pursuant to Chapter 2 (commencing with Section 1250) of Division 2 of the Health and Safety Code.

(2) The information may be disclosed to an insurer, employer, health care service plan, hospital service plan, employee benefit plan, governmental authority, contractor, or * * * other person or entity responsible for paying for health care services rendered to the patient, to the extent necessary to allow responsibility for payment to be determined and payment to be made. If (A) the patient is, by reason of a comatose or other disabling medical condition, unable to consent to the disclosure of medical information and (B) no other arrangements have been made to pay for the health care services being rendered to the patient, the information may be disclosed to a governmental authority to the extent necessary to determine the patient's eligibility for, and to obtain, payment under a governmental program for health care services provided to the patient. The information may also be disclosed to another provider of health care or health care service plan as necessary to assist the other provider or health care service plan in obtaining payment for health care services rendered by that provider of health care or health care service plan to the patient.

(3) The information may be disclosed to a person or entity that provides billing, claims management, medical data processing, or other administrative services for providers of health care or health care service plans or for any of the persons or entities specified in paragraph (2). However, information so disclosed shall not be further disclosed by the recipient in a way that would violate this part.

(4) The information may be disclosed to organized committees and agents of professional societies or of medical staffs of licensed hospitals, licensed health care service plans, professional standards review organizations, independent medical review organizations and their selected reviewers, utilization and quality control peer review organizations as established by Congress in Public Law 97–248 in 1982, contractors, or persons or organizations insuring, responsible for, or defending professional liability that a provider may incur, if the committees, agents, health care service plans, organizations, reviewers, contractors, or persons are engaged in reviewing the competence or qualifications of health care professionals or in reviewing health care services with respect to medical necessity, level of care, quality of care, or justification of charges.

(5) The information in the possession of a provider of health care or health care service plan may be reviewed by a private or public body responsible for licensing or accrediting the provider of health care or health care service plan. However, no patient-identifying medical information may be removed from the premises except as expressly permitted or required elsewhere by law, nor shall that information be further disclosed by the recipient in a way that would violate this part.

(6) The information may be disclosed to the county coroner in the course of an investigation by the coroner's office when requested for all purposes not included in paragraph (8) of subdivision (b).

(7) The information may be disclosed to public agencies, clinical investigators, including investigators conducting epidemiologic studies, health care research organizations, and accredited public or private nonprofit educational or health care institutions for bona fide research purposes. However, no information so disclosed shall be further disclosed by the recipient in a way that would disclose the identity of a patient or violate this part.

(8) A provider of health care or health care service plan that has created medical information as a result of employment-related health care services to an employee conducted at the specific prior written request and expense of the employer may disclose to the employee's employer that part of the information that:

(A) Is relevant in a lawsuit, arbitration, grievance, or other claim or challenge to which the employer and the employee are parties and in which the patient has placed in issue his or her medical history, mental or physical condition, or treatment, provided that information may only be used or disclosed in connection with that proceeding.

(B) Describes functional limitations of the patient that may entitle the patient to leave from work for medical reasons or limit the patient's fitness to perform his or her present employment, provided that no statement of medical cause is included in the information disclosed.

(9) Unless the provider of health care or a health care service plan is notified in writing of an agreement by the sponsor, insurer, or administrator to the contrary, the information may be disclosed to a sponsor, insurer, or administrator of a group or individual insured or uninsured plan or policy that the patient seeks coverage by or benefits from, if the information was created by the provider of health care or health care service plan as the result of services conducted at the specific prior written request and expense of the sponsor, insurer, or administrator for the purpose of evaluating the application for coverage or benefits.

(10) The information may be disclosed to a health care service plan by providers of health care that contract with the health care service plan and may be transferred among providers of health care that contract with the health care service plan, for the purpose of administering the health care service plan. Medical information shall not otherwise be disclosed by a health care service plan except in accordance with this part.

(11) This part does not prevent the disclosure by a provider of health care or a health care service plan to an insurance institution, agent, or support organization, subject to Article 6.6 (commencing with Section 791) of Chapter 1 of Part 2 of Division 1 of the Insurance Code, of medical information if the insurance institution, agent, or support organization has complied with all of the requirements for obtaining the information pursuant to Article 6.6 (commencing with Section 791) of Chapter 1 of Part 2 of Division 1 of the Insurance Code.

(12) The information relevant to the patient's condition, care, and treatment provided may be disclosed to a probate court investigator in the course of an investigation required or authorized in a conservatorship proceeding under the Guardianship–Conservatorship Law as defined in Section 1400 of the Probate Code, or to a probate court investigator, probation officer, or domestic relations investigator engaged in determining the need for an initial guardianship or continuation of an existing guardianship.

(13) The information may be disclosed to an organ procurement organization or a tissue bank processing the tissue of a decedent for transplantation into the body of another person, but only with respect to the donating decedent, for the purpose

of aiding the transplant. For the purpose of this paragraph, "tissue bank" and "tissue" have the same meanings as defined in Section 1635 of the Health and Safety Code.

(14) The information may be disclosed when the disclosure is otherwise specifically authorized by law, including, but not limited to, the voluntary reporting, either directly or indirectly, to the federal Food and Drug Administration of adverse events related to drug products or medical device problems, or to disclosures made pursuant to subdivisions (b) and (c) of Section 11167 of the Penal Code by a person making a report pursuant to Sections 11165.9 and 11166 of the Penal Code, provided that those disclosures concern a report made by that person.

(15) Basic information, including the patient's name, city of residence, age, sex, and general condition, may be disclosed to a state-recognized or federally recognized disaster relief organization for the purpose of responding to disaster welfare inquiries.

(16) The information may be disclosed to a third party for purposes of encoding, encrypting, or otherwise anonymizing data. However, no information so disclosed shall be further disclosed by the recipient in a way that would violate this part, including the unauthorized manipulation of coded or encrypted medical information that reveals individually identifiable medical information.

(17) For purposes of disease management programs and services as defined in Section 1399.901 of the Health and Safety Code, information may be disclosed as follows: (A) to an entity contracting with a health care service plan or the health care service plan's contractors to monitor or administer care of enrollees for a covered benefit, if the disease management services and care are authorized by a treating physician, or (B) to a disease management organization, as defined in Section 1399.900 of the Health and Safety Code, that complies fully with the physician authorization requirements of Section 1399.902 of the Health and Safety Code, if the health care service plan or its contractor provides or has provided a description of the disease management services to a treating physician or to the health care service plan's or contractor's network of physicians. This paragraph does not require physician authorization for the care or treatment of the adherents of a well-recognized church or religious denomination who depend solely upon prayer or spiritual means for healing in the practice of the religion of that church or denomination.

(18) The information may be disclosed, as permitted by state and federal law or regulation, to a local health department for the purpose of preventing or controlling disease, injury, or disability, including, but not limited to, the reporting of disease, injury, vital events, including, but not limited to, birth or death, and the conduct of public health surveillance, public health investigations, and public health interventions, as authorized or required by state or federal law or regulation.

(19) The information may be disclosed, consistent with applicable law and standards of ethical conduct, by a psychotherapist, as defined in Section 1010 of the Evidence Code, if the psychotherapist, in good faith, believes the disclosure is necessary to prevent or lessen a serious and imminent threat to the health or safety of a reasonably foreseeable victim or victims, and the disclosure is made to a person or persons reasonably able to prevent or lessen the threat, including the target of the threat.

(20) The information may be disclosed as described in Section 56.103.

(21)(A) The information may be disclosed to an employee welfare benefit plan, as defined under Section 3(1) of the Employee Retirement Income Security Act of 1974 (29 U.S.C. Sec. 1002(1)), which is formed under Section 302(c)(5) of the Taft–Hartley Act (29 U.S.C. Sec. 186(c)(5)), to the extent that the employee welfare benefit plan provides medical care, and

may also be disclosed to an entity contracting with the employee welfare benefit plan for billing, claims management, medical data processing, or other administrative services related to the provision of medical care to persons enrolled in the employee welfare benefit plan for health care coverage, if all of the following conditions are met:

(i) The disclosure is for the purpose of determining eligibility, coordinating benefits, or allowing the employee welfare benefit plan * * * or the contracting entity * * * to advocate on the behalf of a patient or enrollee with a provider, a health care service plan, or a state or federal regulatory agency.

(ii) The request for the information is accompanied by a written authorization for the release of the information submitted in a manner consistent with subdivision (a) and Section 56.11.

(iii) The disclosure is authorized by and made in a manner consistent with the Health Insurance Portability and Accountability Act of 1996 (Public Law 104–191).

(iv) Any information disclosed is not further used or disclosed by the recipient in any way that would directly or indirectly violate this part or the restrictions imposed by Part 164 of Title 45 of the Code of Federal Regulations, including the manipulation of the information in any way that might reveal individually identifiable medical information.

(B) For purposes of this paragraph, Section 1374.8 of the Health and Safety Code shall not apply.

(22) Information may be disclosed pursuant to subdivision (a) of Section 15633.5 of the Welfare and Institutions Code by a person required to make a report pursuant to Section 15630 of the Welfare and Institutions Code, provided that the disclosure under subdivision (a) of Section 15633.5 concerns a report made by that person. Covered entities, as they are defined in Section 160.103 of Title 45 of the Code of Federal Regulations, shall comply with the requirements of the Health Insurance Portability and Accountability Act (HIPAA) privacy rule pursuant to subsection (c) of Section 164.512 of Title 45 of the Code of Federal Regulations if the disclosure is not for the purpose of public health surveillance, investigation, intervention, or reporting an injury or death.

(d) Except to the extent expressly authorized by a patient, enrollee, or subscriber, or as provided by subdivisions (b) and (c), a provider of health care, health care service plan, contractor, or corporation and its subsidiaries and affiliates shall not intentionally share, sell, use for marketing, or otherwise use medical information for a purpose not necessary to provide health care services to the patient.

(e) Except to the extent expressly authorized by a patient or enrollee or subscriber or as provided by subdivisions (b) and (c), a contractor or corporation and its subsidiaries and affiliates shall not further disclose medical information regarding a patient of the provider of health care or an enrollee or subscriber of a health care service plan or insurer or self-insured employer received under this section to a person or entity that is not engaged in providing direct health care services to the patient or his or her provider of health care or health care service plan or insurer or self-insured employer. *(Added by Stats.2000, c. 1068 (A.B.1836), § 1.16, operative Jan. 1, 2003. Amended by Stats. 2002, c. 123 (A.B.1958), § 1, operative Jan. 1, 2003; Stats.2003, c. 562 (A.B.715), § 2; Stats.2006, c. 874 (S.B.1430), § 2; Stats. 2007, c. 506 (A.B.1178), § 1; Stats.2007, c. 552 (A.B.1687), § 2; Stats.2007, c. 553 (A.B.1727), § 1.9; Stats.2008, c. 179 (S.B.1498), § 27; Stats.2009, c. 493 (A.B.952), § 1; Stats.2010, c. 540 (A.B.2028), § 1; Stats.2013, c. 341 (A.B.1297), § 1.)*

Research References

Rutter, Cal. Practice Guide: Civ. Pro. Before Trial Ch. 1-B, B. Prelawsuit Investigations, Research and Analysis.

Rutter, Cal. Practice Guide: Civ. Pro. Before Trial Ch. 8C-5, Privacy Protection.

Rutter, Cal. Practice Guide: Civil Trials & Evidence Ch. 8E-A, A. Privileges.

California Practice Guide: Employment Litigation Ch. 1-A, A. Background.

California Practice Guide: Employment Litigation Ch. 19-F, F. Discovery.

Rutter, Cal. Practice Guide: Personal Injury Ch. 1-D, D. General Concerns and Advice to Client Upon Accepting Employment; Execution of Necessary Authorizations.

Rutter, Cal. Practice Guide: Personal Injury Ch. 6-A, A. Scope of Discovery and Limitations.

Rutter, Cal. Practice Guide: Personal Injury Ch. 6-B, B. Overview of Selected Discovery Procedures.

Rutter, Cal. Practice Guide: Personal Injury Ch. 9-G, G. Expert Witnesses.

7 Witkin, California Summary 10th Constitutional Law § 580, (S 580) in General.

§ 56.1007. Disclosure of medical information to specified persons involved with patient's care or health care payments; disclosure of medical information for other purposes

(a) A provider of health care, health care service plan, or contractor may, in accordance with subdivision (c) or (d), disclose to a family member, other relative, domestic partner, or a close personal friend of the patient, or any other person identified by the patient, the medical information directly relevant to that person's involvement with the patient's care or payment related to the patient's health care.

(b) A provider of health care, health care service plan, or contractor may use or disclose medical information to notify, or assist in the notification of, including identifying or locating, a family member, a personal representative of the patient, a domestic partner, or another person responsible for the care of the patient of the patient's location, general condition, or death. Any use or disclosure of medical information for those notification purposes shall be in accordance with the provisions of subdivision (c), (d), or (e), as applicable.

(c)(1) Except as provided in paragraph (2), if the patient is present for, or otherwise available prior to, a use or disclosure permitted by subdivision (a) or (b) and has the capacity to make health care decisions, the provider of health care, health care service plan, or contractor may use or disclose the medical information if it does any of the following:

(A) Obtains the patient's agreement.

(B) Provides the patient with the opportunity to object to the disclosure, and the patient does not express an objection.

(C) Reasonably infers from the circumstances, based on the exercise of professional judgment, that the patient does not object to the disclosure.

(2) A provider of health care who is a psychotherapist, as defined in Section 1010 of the Evidence Code, may use or disclose medical information pursuant to this subdivision only if the psychotherapist complies with subparagraph (A) or (B) of paragraph (1).

(d) If the patient is not present, or the opportunity to agree or object to the use or disclosure cannot practicably be provided because of the patient's incapacity or an emergency circumstance, the provider of health care, health care service plan, or contractor may, in the exercise of professional judgment, determine whether the disclosure is in the best interests of the patient and, if so, disclose only the medical information that is directly relevant to the person's involvement with the patient's health care. A provider of health care, health care service plan, or contractor may use professional judgment and its experience with common practice to make reasonable inferences of the patient's best interest in allowing a person to act on behalf of the patient to pick up filled prescriptions, medical supplies, X-rays, or other similar forms of medical information.

(e) A provider of health care, health care service plan, or contractor may use or disclose medical information to a public or private entity authorized by law or by its charter to assist in disaster relief efforts, for the purpose of coordinating with those entities the uses or disclosures permitted by subdivision (b). The requirements in subdivisions (c) and (d) apply to those uses and disclosures to the extent that the provider of health care, health care service plan, or contractor, in the exercise of professional judgment, determines that the requirements do not interfere with the ability to respond to the emergency circumstances.

(f) Nothing in this section shall be construed to interfere with or limit the access authority of Protection and Advocacy, Inc., the Office of Patients' Rights, or any county patients' rights advocates to access medical information pursuant to any state or federal law. *(Added by Stats.2006, c. 833 (A.B.3013), § 1.)*

§ 56.101. Medical information; confidentiality; negligence; protection and preservation; patient access

(a) Every provider of health care, health care service plan, pharmaceutical company, or contractor who creates, maintains, preserves, stores, abandons, destroys, or disposes of medical information shall do so in a manner that preserves the confidentiality of the information contained therein. Any provider of health care, health care service plan, pharmaceutical company, or contractor who negligently creates, maintains, preserves, stores, abandons, destroys, or disposes of medical information shall be subject to the remedies and penalties provided under subdivisions (b) and (c) of Section 56.36.

(b)(1) An electronic health record system or electronic medical record system shall do the following:

(A) Protect and preserve the integrity of electronic medical information.

(B) Automatically record and preserve any change or deletion of any electronically stored medical information. The record of any change or deletion shall include the identity of the person who accessed and changed the medical information, the date and time the medical information was accessed, and the change that was made to the medical information.

(2) A patient's right to access or receive a copy of his or her electronic medical records upon request shall be consistent with applicable state and federal laws governing patient access to, and the use and disclosures of, medical information.

(c) This section shall apply to an "electronic medical record" or "electronic health record" that meets the definition of "electronic health record," as that term is defined in Section 17921(5) of Title 42 of the United States Code. *(Added by Stats.1999, c. 526 (S.B.19), § 3. Amended by Stats.2000, c. 1067 (S.B.2094), § 4; Stats.2002, c. 853 (A.B.2191), § 2; Stats.2011, c. 714 (S.B.850), § 1.)*

§ 56.102. Disclosure of medical information by pharmaceutical company; authorizations, releases, consents, or waivers; exceptions

(a) A pharmaceutical company may not require a patient, as a condition of receiving pharmaceuticals, medications, or prescription drugs, to sign an authorization, release, consent, or waiver that would permit the disclosure of medical information that otherwise may not be disclosed under Section 56.10 or any other provision of law, unless the disclosure is for one of the following purposes:

(1) Enrollment of the patient in a patient assistance program or prescription drug discount program.

(2) Enrollment of the patient in a clinical research project.

(3) Prioritization of distribution to the patient of a prescription medicine in limited supply in the United States.

(4) Response to an inquiry from the patient communicated in writing, by telephone, or by electronic mail.

(b) Except as provided in subdivision (a) or Section 56.10, a pharmaceutical company may not disclose medical information provided to it without first obtaining a valid authorization from the patient. *(Added by Stats.2002, c. 853 (A.B.2191), § 3.)*

§ 56.103. Disclosure of a minor's medical information; mental health condition

(a) A provider of health care may disclose medical information to a county social worker, a probation officer, or any other person who is legally authorized to have custody or care of a minor for the purpose of coordinating health care services and medical treatment provided to the minor.

(b) For purposes of this section, health care services and medical treatment includes one or more providers of health care providing, coordinating, or managing health care and related services, including, but not limited to, a provider of health care coordinating health care with a third party, consultation between providers of health care and medical treatment relating to a minor, or a provider of health care referring a minor for health care services to another provider of health care.

(c) For purposes of this section, a county social worker, a probation officer, or any other person who is legally authorized to have custody or care of a minor shall be considered a third party who may receive any of the following:

(1) Medical information described in Sections 56.05 and 56.10.

(2) Protected health information described in Section 160.103 of Title 45 of the Code of Federal Regulations.

(d) Medical information disclosed to a county social worker, probation officer, or any other person who is legally authorized to have custody or care of a minor shall not be further disclosed by the recipient unless the disclosure is for the purpose of coordinating health care services and medical treatment of the minor and the disclosure is authorized by law. Medical information disclosed pursuant to this section may not be admitted into evidence in any criminal or delinquency proceeding against the minor. Nothing in this subdivision shall prohibit identical evidence from being admissible in a criminal proceeding if that evidence is derived solely from lawful means other than this section and is permitted by law.

(e)(1) Notwithstanding Section 56.104, if a provider of health care determines that the disclosure of medical information concerning the diagnosis and treatment of a mental health condition of a minor is reasonably necessary for the purpose of assisting in coordinating the treatment and care of the minor, that information may be disclosed to a county social worker, probation officer, or any other person who is legally authorized to have custody or care of the minor. The information shall not be further disclosed by the recipient unless the disclosure is for the purpose of coordinating mental health services and treatment of the minor and the disclosure is authorized by law.

(2) As used in this subdivision, "medical information" does not include psychotherapy notes as defined in Section 164.501 of Title 45 of the Code of Federal Regulations.

(f) The disclosure of information pursuant to this section is not intended to limit the disclosure of information when that disclosure is otherwise required by law.

(g) For purposes of this section, "minor" means a minor taken into temporary custody or as to who a petition has been filed with the court, or who has been adjudged to be a dependent child or ward of the juvenile court pursuant to Section 300 or 601 of the Welfare and Institutions Code.

(h)(1) Except as described in paragraph (1) of subdivision (e), nothing in this section shall be construed to limit or otherwise affect existing privacy protections provided for in state or federal law.

(2) Nothing in this section shall be construed to expand the authority of a social worker, probation officer, or custodial caregiver beyond the authority provided under existing law to a parent or a patient representative regarding access to medical information. *(Added by Stats.2007, c. 552 (A.B.1687), § 3. Amended by Stats.2008, c. 699 (S.B.1241), § 1; Stats.2008, c. 700 (A.B.2352), § 1.)*

§ 56.104. Patient's participation in outpatient treatment with psychotherapist; request for information; application of section

(a) Notwithstanding subdivision (c) of Section 56.10, except as provided in subdivision (e), no provider of health care, health care service plan, or contractor may release medical information to persons or entities who have requested that information and who are authorized by law to receive that information pursuant to subdivision (c) of Section 56.10, if the requested information specifically relates to the patient's participation in outpatient treatment with a psychotherapist, unless the person or entity requesting that information submits to the patient pursuant to subdivision (b) and to the provider of health care, health care service plan, or contractor a written request, signed by the person requesting the information or an authorized agent of the entity requesting the information, that includes all of the following:

(1) The specific information relating to a patient's participation in outpatient treatment with a psychotherapist being requested and its specific intended use or uses.

(2) The length of time during which the information will be kept before being destroyed or disposed of. A person or entity may extend that timeframe, provided that the person or entity notifies the provider, plan, or contractor of the extension. Any notification of an extension shall include the specific reason for the extension, the intended use or uses of the information during the extended time, and the expected date of the destruction of the information.

(3) A statement that the information will not be used for any purpose other than its intended use.

(4) A statement that the person or entity requesting the information will destroy the information and all copies in the person's or entity's possession or control, will cause it to be destroyed, or will return the information and all copies of it before or immediately after the length of time specified in paragraph (2) has expired.

(b) The person or entity requesting the information shall submit a copy of the written request required by this section to the patient within 30 days of receipt of the information requested, unless the patient has signed a written waiver in the form of a letter signed and submitted by the patient to the provider of health care or health care service plan waiving notification.

(c) For purposes of this section, "psychotherapist" means a person who is both a "psychotherapist" as defined in Section 1010 of the Evidence Code and a "provider of health care" as defined in * * * Section 56.05.

(d) This section does not apply to the disclosure or use of medical information by a law enforcement agency or a regulatory agency when required for an investigation of unlawful activity or for licensing, certification, or regulatory purposes, unless the disclosure is otherwise prohibited by law.

(e) This section shall not apply to any of the following:

(1) Information authorized to be disclosed pursuant to paragraph (1) of subdivision (c) of Section 56.10.

(2) Information requested from a psychotherapist by law enforcement or by the target of the threat subsequent to a disclosure by that psychotherapist authorized by paragraph (19) of subdivision (c) of Section 56.10, in which the additional information is clearly necessary to prevent the serious and imminent threat disclosed under that paragraph.

(3) Information disclosed by a psychotherapist pursuant to paragraphs (14) and (22) of subdivision (c) of Section 56.10 and requested by an agency investigating the abuse reported pursuant to those paragraphs.

(f) Nothing in this section shall be construed to grant any additional authority to a provider of health care, health care service plan, or contractor to disclose information to a person or entity without the patient's consent. *(Added by Stats.1999, c. 527 (A.B.416), § 3. Amended by Stats.2004, c. 463 (S.B.598), § 1; Stats.2009, c. 464 (A.B.681), § 1; Stats.2010, c. 540 (A.B.2028), § 2; Stats.2013, c. 444 (S.B.138), § 3.)*

Research References

Rutter, Cal. Practice Guide: Civil Trials & Evidence Ch. 8E-A, A. Privileges.

§ 56.105. Professional negligence actions; settlement or compromise; authorization to disclose medical records to persons or organizations defending professional liability

Whenever, prior to the service of a complaint upon a defendant in any action arising out of the professional negligence of a person holding a valid physician's and surgeon's certificate issued pursuant to Chapter 5 (commencing with Section 2000) of Division 2 of the Business and Professions Code, or a person holding a valid license as a marriage and family therapist issued pursuant to Chapter 13 (commencing with Section 4980) of Division 2 of the Business and Professions Code, a demand for settlement or offer to compromise is made on a patient's behalf, the demand or offer shall be accompanied by an authorization to disclose medical information to persons or organizations insuring, responsible for, or defending professional liability that the certificate holder may incur. The authorization shall be in accordance with Section 56.11 and shall authorize disclosure of that information that is necessary to investigate issues of liability and extent of potential damages in evaluating the merits of the demand for settlement or offer to compromise.

Notice of any request for medical information made pursuant to an authorization as provided by this section shall be given to the patient or the patient's legal representative. The notice shall describe the inclusive subject matter and dates of the materials requested and shall also authorize the patient or the patient's legal representative to receive, upon request, copies of the information at his or her expense.

Nothing in this section shall be construed to waive or limit any applicable privileges set forth in the Evidence Code except for the disclosure of medical information subject to the patient's authorization. Nothing in this section shall be construed as authorizing a representative of any person from whom settlement has been demanded to communicate in violation of the physician-patient privilege with a treating physician, or to communicate in violation of the psychotherapist-patient privilege with a treating licensed marriage and family therapist, except for the medical information request.

The requirements of this section are independent of the requirements of Section 364 of the Code of Civil Procedure. *(Added by Stats.1985, c. 484, § 1. Amended by Stats.2013, c. 58 (S.B.282), § 1.)*

Research References

Rutter, Cal. Practice Guide: Civ. Pro. Before Trial Ch. 1-C, C. Prelawsuit Notices, Claims and Demands.

Rutter, Cal. Practice Guide: Personal Injury Ch. 1-D, D. General Concerns and Advice to Client Upon Accepting Employment; Execution of Necessary Authorizations.

Rutter, Cal. Practice Guide: Personal Injury Ch. 4-A, A. General Considerations.

§ 56.106. Disclosure of minor's mental health records; minor removed from custody of parent or guardian

(a) Notwithstanding Section 3025 of the Family Code, paragraph (2) of subdivision (c) of Section 56.11, or any other provision of law, a psychotherapist who knows that a minor has been removed from the custody of his or her parent or guardian pursuant to Article 6 (commencing with Section 300) to Article 10 (commencing with Section 360), inclusive, of Chapter 2 of Part 1 of Division 2 of the Welfare and Institutions Code shall not release the mental health records of the minor patient and shall not disclose mental health information about that minor patient based upon an authorization to release those records signed by the minor's parent or guardian. This restriction shall not apply if the juvenile court has issued an order authorizing the parent or guardian to sign an authorization for the release of the mental health records or the information about the minor patient after finding that such an order would not be detrimental to the minor patient.

(b) For purposes of this section, the following definitions apply:

(1) "Mental health records" means mental health records as defined by subdivision (b) of Section 123105 of the Health and Safety Code.

(2) "Psychotherapist" means a provider of health care as defined in Section 1010 of the Evidence Code.

(c) When the juvenile court has issued an order authorizing the parent or guardian to sign an authorization for the release of the mental health records or information about that minor patient under the circumstances described in subdivision (a), the parent or guardian seeking the release of the minor's records or information about the minor shall present a copy of the court order to the psychotherapist before any records or information may be released pursuant to the signed authorization.

(d) Nothing in this section shall be construed to prevent or limit a psychotherapist's authority under subdivision (a) of Section 123115 of the Health and Safety Code to deny a parent's or guardian's written request to inspect or obtain copies of the minor patient's mental health records, notwithstanding the fact that the juvenile court has issued an order authorizing the parent or guardian to sign an authorization for the release of the mental health records or information about that minor patient. Liability for a psychotherapist's decision not to release the mental health records of the minor patient or not to disclose information about the minor patient pursuant to the authority of subdivision (a) of Section 123115 of the Health and Safety Code shall be governed by that section.

(e) Nothing in this section shall be construed to impose upon a psychotherapist a duty to inquire or investigate whether a child has been removed from the physical custody of his or her parent or guardian pursuant to Article 6 (commencing with Section 300) to Article 10 (commencing with Section 360), inclusive, of

Chapter 2 of Part 1 of Division 2 of the Welfare and Institutions Code when a parent or guardian presents the minor's psychotherapist with an authorization to release information or the mental health records regarding the minor patient. *(Added by Stats.2012, c. 657 (S.B.1407), § 1.)*

§ 56.107. Health care service plans; steps to protect medical information

(a) Notwithstanding any other law, and to the extent permitted by federal law, a health care service plan shall take the following steps to protect the confidentiality of a subscriber's or enrollee's medical information on and after January 1, 2015:

(1) A health care service plan shall permit subscribers and enrollees to request, and shall accommodate requests for, communication in the form and format requested by the individual, if it is readily producible in the requested form and format, or at alternative locations, if the subscriber or enrollee clearly states either that the communication discloses medical information or provider name and address relating to receipt of sensitive services or that disclosure of all or part of the medical information or provider name and address could endanger the subscriber or enrollee.

(2) A health care service plan may require the subscriber or enrollee to make a request for a confidential communication described in paragraph (1), in writing or by electronic transmission.

(3) A health care service plan may require that a confidential communications request contain a statement that the request pertains to either medical information related to the receipt of sensitive services or that disclosure of all or part of the medical information could endanger the subscriber or enrollee. The health care service plan shall not require an explanation as to the basis for a subscriber's or enrollee's statement that disclosure could endanger the subscriber or enrollee.

(4) The confidential communication request shall be valid until the subscriber or enrollee submits a revocation of the request or a new confidential communication request is submitted.

(5) For the purposes of this section, a confidential communications request shall be implemented by the health care service plan within seven calendar days of receipt of an electronic transmission or telephonic request or within 14 calendar days of receipt by first-class mail. The health care service plan shall acknowledge receipt of the confidential communications request and advise the subscriber or enrollee of the status of implementation of the request if a subscriber or enrollee contacts the health care service plan.

(b) Notwithstanding subdivision (a), the provider of health care may make arrangements with the subscriber or enrollee for the payment of benefit cost sharing and communicate that arrangement with the health care service plan.

(c) A health care service plan shall not condition enrollment or coverage on the waiver of rights provided in this section. *(Added by Stats.2013, c. 444 (S.B.138), § 4.)*

§ 56.11. Authorization; form and contents

Any person or entity that wishes to obtain medical information pursuant to subdivision (a) of Section 56.10, other than a person or entity authorized to receive medical information pursuant to subdivision (b) or (c) of Section 56.10, except as provided in paragraph (21) of subdivision (c) of Section 56.10, shall obtain a valid authorization for the release of this information.

An authorization for the release of medical information by a provider of health care, health care service plan, pharmaceutical company, or contractor shall be valid if it:

(a) Is handwritten by the person who signs it or is in a typeface no smaller than 14–point type.

(b) Is clearly separate from any other language present on the same page and is executed by a signature which serves no other purpose than to execute the authorization.

(c) Is signed and dated by one of the following:

(1) The patient. A patient who is a minor may only sign an authorization for the release of medical information obtained by a provider of health care, health care service plan, pharmaceutical company, or contractor in the course of furnishing services to which the minor could lawfully have consented under Part 1 (commencing with Section 25) or Part 2.7 (commencing with Section 60).

(2) The legal representative of the patient, if the patient is a minor or an incompetent. However, authorization may not be given under this subdivision for the disclosure of medical information obtained by the provider of health care, health care service plan, pharmaceutical company, or contractor in the course of furnishing services to which a minor patient could lawfully have consented under Part 1 (commencing with Section 25) or Part 2.7 (commencing with Section 60).

(3) The spouse of the patient or the person financially responsible for the patient, where the medical information is being sought for the sole purpose of processing an application for health insurance or for enrollment in a nonprofit hospital plan, a health care service plan, or an employee benefit plan, and where the patient is to be an enrolled spouse or dependent under the policy or plan.

(4) The beneficiary or personal representative of a deceased patient.

(d) States the specific uses and limitations on the types of medical information to be disclosed.

(e) States the name or functions of the provider of health care, health care service plan, pharmaceutical company, or contractor that may disclose the medical information.

(f) States the name or functions of the persons or entities authorized to receive the medical information.

(g) States the specific uses and limitations on the use of the medical information by the persons or entities authorized to receive the medical information.

(h) States a specific date after which the provider of health care, health care service plan, pharmaceutical company, or contractor is no longer authorized to disclose the medical information.

(i) Advises the person signing the authorization of the right to receive a copy of the authorization. *(Added by Stats.1981, c. 782, § 2. Amended by Stats.1999, c. 526 (S.B.19), § 4; Stats.2000, c. 1066 (S.B.1903), § 3; Stats.2002, c. 853 (A.B.2191), § 4; Stats. 2003, c. 562 (A.B.715), § 3; Stats.2009, c. 493 (A.B.952), § 2.)*

Research References

Rutter, Cal. Practice Guide: Personal Injury Ch. 1-D, D. General Concerns and Advice to Client Upon Accepting Employment; Execution of Necessary Authorizations.

§ 56.12. Copy of authorization to patient or signatory on demand

Upon demand by the patient or the person who signed an authorization, a provider of health care, health care service plan, pharmaceutical company, or contractor possessing the authorization shall furnish a true copy thereof. *(Added by Stats.1981, c. 782, § 2. Amended by Stats.1999, c. 526 (S.B.19), § 5; Stats. 2002, c. 853 (A.B.2191), § 5.)*

§ 56.13. Further disclosure by recipient of medical information

A recipient of medical information pursuant to an authorization as provided by this chapter or pursuant to the provisions of subdivision (c) of Section 56.10 may not further disclose that medical information except in accordance with a new authorization that meets the requirements of Section 56.11, or as specifically required or permitted by other provisions of this chapter or by law. *(Added by Stats.1981, c. 782, § 2.)*

§ 56.14. Communication of limitations of authorization to recipient of medical information

A provider of health care, health care service plan, or contractor that discloses medical information pursuant to the authorizations required by this chapter shall communicate to the person or entity to which it discloses the medical information any limitations in the authorization regarding the use of the medical information. No provider of health care, health care service plan, or contractor that has attempted in good faith to comply with this provision shall be liable for any unauthorized use of the medical information by the person or entity to which the provider, plan, or contractor disclosed the medical information. *(Added by Stats.1981, c. 782, § 2. Amended by Stats.1999, c. 526 (S.B.19), § 6.)*

§ 56.15. Cancellation or modification of authorization; written notice

Nothing in this part shall be construed to prevent a person who could sign the authorization pursuant to subdivision (c) of Section 56.11 from cancelling or modifying an authorization. However, the cancellation or modification shall be effective only after the provider of health care actually receives written notice of the cancellation or modification. *(Added by Stats.1981, c. 782, § 2.)*

§ 56.16. Release of limited information on specific patient; written request by patient to prohibit

For disclosures not addressed by Section 56.1007, unless there is a specific written request by the patient to the contrary, nothing in this part shall be construed to prevent a general acute care hospital, as defined in subdivision (a) of Section 1250 of the Health and Safety Code, upon an inquiry concerning a specific patient, from releasing at its discretion any of the following information: the patient's name, address, age, and sex; a general description of the reason for treatment (whether an injury, a burn, poisoning, or some unrelated condition); the general nature of the injury, burn, poisoning, or other condition; the general condition of the patient; and any information that is not medical information as defined in * * * Section 56.05. *(Added by Stats.1981, c. 782, § 2. Amended by Stats.2006, c. 833 (A.B.3013), § 2; Stats.2013, c. 76 (A.B.383), § 10; Stats.2013, c. 444 (S.B.138), § 5.)*

Research References

California Practice Guide: Employment Litigation Ch. 5-K, K. Invasion of Privacy.

Rutter, Cal. Practice Guide: Personal Injury Ch. 1-D, D. General Concerns and Advice to Client Upon Accepting Employment; Execution of Necessary Authorizations.

CHAPTER 2.5. DISCLOSURE OF GENETIC TEST RESULTS BY A HEALTH CARE SERVICE PLAN

§ 56.17. Genetic test results; unlawful disclosure; written authorization; penalties

(a) This section shall apply to the disclosure of genetic test results contained in an applicant's or enrollee's medical records by a health care service plan.

(b) Any person who negligently discloses results of a test for a genetic characteristic to any third party in a manner that identifies or provides identifying characteristics of the person to whom the test results apply, except pursuant to a written authorization as described in subdivision (g), shall be assessed a civil penalty in an amount not to exceed one thousand dollars ($1,000) plus court costs, as determined by the court, which penalty and costs shall be paid to the subject of the test.

(c) Any person who willfully discloses the results of a test for a genetic characteristic to any third party in a manner that identifies or provides identifying characteristics of the person to whom the test results apply, except pursuant to a written authorization as described in subdivision (g), shall be assessed a civil penalty in an amount not less than one thousand dollars ($1,000) and no more than five thousand dollars ($5,000) plus court costs, as determined by the court, which penalty and costs shall be paid to the subject of the test.

(d) Any person who willfully or negligently discloses the results of a test for a genetic characteristic to a third party in a manner that identifies or provides identifying characteristics of the person to whom the test results apply, except pursuant to a written authorization as described in subdivision (g), that results in economic, bodily, or emotional harm to the subject of the test, is guilty of a misdemeanor punishable by a fine not to exceed ten thousand dollars ($10,000).

(e) In addition to the penalties listed in subdivisions (b) and (c), any person who commits any act described in subdivision (b) or (c) shall be liable to the subject for all actual damages, including damages for economic, bodily, or emotional harm which is proximately caused by the act.

(f) Each disclosure made in violation of this section is a separate and actionable offense.

(g) The applicant's "written authorization," as used in this section, shall satisfy the following requirements:

(1) Is written in plain language and is in a typeface no smaller than 14–point type.

(2) Is dated and signed by the individual or a person authorized to act on behalf of the individual.

(3) Specifies the types of persons authorized to disclose information about the individual.

(4) Specifies the nature of the information authorized to be disclosed.

(5) States the name or functions of the persons or entities authorized to receive the information.

(6) Specifies the purposes for which the information is collected.

(7) Specifies the length of time the authorization shall remain valid.

(8) Advises the person signing the authorization of the right to receive a copy of the authorization. Written authorization is required for each separate disclosure of the test results.

(h) This section shall not apply to disclosures required by the Department of Health Services necessary to monitor compliance with Chapter 1 (commencing with Section 124975) of Part 5 of Division 106 of the Health and Safety Code, nor to disclosures required by the Department of Managed Care necessary to administer and enforce compliance with Section 1374.7 of the Health and Safety Code.

(i) For purposes of this section, "genetic characteristic" has the same meaning as that set forth in subdivision (d) of Section 1374.7 of the Health and Safety Code. *(Added by Stats.1995, c. 695 (S.B.1020), § 1. Amended by Stats.1996, c. 1023 (S.B.1497), § 25, eff. Sept. 29, 1996; Stats.1996, c. 532 (S.B.1740), § 1; Stats.1999, c. 311 (S.B.1185), § 1; Stats.1999, c. 525 (A.B.78), § 5; Stats.2000, c. 857 (A.B.2903), § 4; Stats.2000, c. 941 (S.B.1364), § 1; Stats.2003, c. 562 (A.B.715), § 4.)*

Research References

7 Witkin, California Summary 10th Constitutional Law § 605, (S 605) Medical Records and Information.

CHAPTER 3. USE AND DISCLOSURE OF MEDICAL INFORMATION BY EMPLOYERS

Section
56.20. Confidentiality; prohibition of discrimination due to refusal to sign authorization; prohibition of disclosure; exceptions.
56.21. Authorization for disclosure by employer.
56.22. Copy of authorization to patient or signatory.
56.23. Communication of limitations of authorization to person to whom disclosure made.
56.24. Cancellation or modification of authorization.
56.245. Further disclosure by recipient of medical information.

§ 56.20. Confidentiality; prohibition of discrimination due to refusal to sign authorization; prohibition of disclosure; exceptions

(a) Each employer who receives medical information shall establish appropriate procedures to ensure the confidentiality and protection from unauthorized use and disclosure of that information. These procedures may include, but are not limited to, instruction regarding confidentiality of employees and agents handling files containing medical information, and security systems restricting access to files containing medical information.

(b) No employee shall be discriminated against in terms or conditions of employment due to that employee's refusal to sign an authorization under this part. However, nothing in this section shall prohibit an employer from taking such action as is necessary in the absence of medical information due to an employee's refusal to sign an authorization under this part.

(c) No employer shall use, disclose, or knowingly permit its employees or agents to use or disclose medical information which the employer possesses pertaining to its employees without the patient having first signed an authorization under Section 56.11 or Section 56.21 permitting such use or disclosure, except as follows:

(1) The information may be disclosed if the disclosure is compelled by judicial or administrative process or by any other specific provision of law.

(2) That part of the information which is relevant in a lawsuit, arbitration, grievance, or other claim or challenge to which the employer and employee are parties and in which the patient has placed in issue his or her medical history, mental or physical condition, or treatment may be used or disclosed in connection with that proceeding.

(3) The information may be used only for the purpose of administering and maintaining employee benefit plans, including health care plans and plans providing short-term and long-term disability income, workers' compensation and for determining eligibility for paid and unpaid leave from work for medical reasons.

(4) The information may be disclosed to a provider of health care or other health care professional or facility to aid the diagnosis or treatment of the patient, where the patient or other person specified in subdivision (c) of Section 56.21 is unable to authorize the disclosure.

(d) If an employer agrees in writing with one or more of its employees or maintains a written policy which provides that particular types of medical information shall not be used or disclosed by the employer in particular ways, the employer shall obtain an authorization for such uses or disclosures even if an authorization would not otherwise be required by subdivision (c). *(Added by Stats.1981, c. 782, § 2.)*

Research References

California Practice Guide: Employment Litigation Ch. 5-K, K. Invasion of Privacy.
California Practice Guide: Employment Litigation Ch. 12-B, B. Family and Medical Leave Act (FMLA)/California Family Rights Act (CFRA).

§ 56.21. Authorization for disclosure by employer

An authorization for an employer to disclose medical information shall be valid if it complies with all of the following:

(a) Is handwritten by the person who signs it or is in a typeface no smaller than 14–point type.

(b) Is clearly separate from any other language present on the same page and is executed by a signature that serves no purpose other than to execute the authorization.

(c) Is signed and dated by one of the following:

(1) The patient, except that a patient who is a minor may only sign an authorization for the disclosure of medical information obtained by a provider of health care in the course of furnishing services to which the minor could lawfully have consented under Part 1 (commencing with Section 25) or Part 2.7 (commencing with Section 60) of Division 1.

(2) The legal representative of the patient, if the patient is a minor or incompetent. However, authorization may not be given under this subdivision for the disclosure of medical information that pertains to a competent minor and that was created by a provider of health care in the course of furnishing services to which a minor patient could lawfully have consented under Part 1 (commencing with Section 25) or Part 2.7 (commencing with Section 60) of Division 1.

(3) The beneficiary or personal representative of a deceased patient.

(d) States the limitations, if any, on the types of medical information to be disclosed.

(e) States the name or functions of the employer or person authorized to disclose the medical information.

(f) States the names or functions of the persons or entities authorized to receive the medical information.

(g) States the limitations, if any, on the use of the medical information by the persons or entities authorized to receive the medical information.

(h) States a specific date after which the employer is no longer authorized to disclose the medical information.

(i) Advises the person who signed the authorization of the right to receive a copy of the authorization. *(Added by Stats.1981, c. 782, § 2. Amended by Stats.2003, c. 562 (A.B.715), § 5; Stats.2006, c. 538 (S.B.1852), § 39.)*

§ 56.22. Copy of authorization to patient or signatory

Upon demand by the patient or the person who signed an authorization, an employer possessing the authorization shall furnish a true copy thereof. *(Added by Stats.1981, c. 782, § 2.)*

§ 56.23. Communication of limitations of authorization to person to whom disclosure made

An employer that discloses medical information pursuant to an authorization required by this chapter shall communicate to the person or entity to which it discloses the medical information any limitations in the authorization regarding the use of the medical information. No employer that has attempted in good faith to comply with this provision shall be liable for any unauthorized use of the medical information by the person or entity to which the employer disclosed the medical information. *(Added by Stats.1981, c. 782, § 2.)*

§ 56.24. Cancellation or modification of authorization

Nothing in this part shall be construed to prevent a person who could sign the authorization pursuant to subdivision (c) of Section 56.21 from cancelling or modifying an authorization. However, the cancellation or modification shall be effective only after the employer actually receives written notice of the cancellation or modification. *(Added by Stats.1981, c. 782, § 2.)*

§ 56.245. Further disclosure by recipient of medical information

A recipient of medical information pursuant to an authorization as provided by this chapter may not further disclose such medical information unless in accordance with a new authorization that meets the requirements of Section 56.21, or as specifically required or permitted by other provisions of this chapter or by law. *(Added by Stats.1981, c. 782, § 2.)*

CHAPTER 4. RELATIONSHIP OF CHAPTERS 2 AND 3

Section
56.25. Disclosure by employer who is provider of health care.

§ 56.25. Disclosure by employer who is provider of health care

(a) An employer that is a provider of health care shall not be deemed to have violated Section 56.20 by disclosing, in accordance with Chapter 2 (commencing with Section 56.10), medical information possessed in connection with providing health care services to the provider's patients.

(b) An employer shall not be deemed to have violated Section 56.20 because a provider of health care that is an employee or agent of the employer uses or discloses, in accordance with Chapter 2 (commencing with Section 56.10), medical information possessed by the provider in connection with providing health care services to the provider's patients.

(c) A provider of health care that is an employer shall not be deemed to have violated Section 56.10 by disclosing, in accordance with Chapter 3 (commencing with Section 56.20), medical information possessed in connection with employing the provider's employees. Information maintained by a provider of health care in connection with employing the provider's employees shall not be deemed to be medical information for purposes of Chapter 3 (commencing with Section 56.20), unless it would be deemed medical information if received or maintained by an employer that is not a provider of health care. *(Added by Stats.1981, c. 782, § 2.)*

CHAPTER 5. USE AND DISCLOSURE OF MEDICAL AND OTHER INFORMATION BY THIRD PARTY ADMINISTRATORS AND OTHERS

Section
56.26. Prohibition; exceptions; inapplicability of section.
56.265. Annuity contracts; disclosure of individually identifiable information concerning health, medical or genetic history; prohibition.

§ 56.26. Prohibition; exceptions; inapplicability of section

(a) No person or entity engaged in the business of furnishing administrative services to programs that provide payment for health care services shall knowingly use, disclose, or permit its employees or agents to use or disclose medical information possessed in connection with performing administrative functions for a program, except as reasonably necessary in connection with the administration or maintenance of the program, or as required by law, or with an authorization.

(b) An authorization required by this section shall be in the same form as described in Section 56.21, except that "third party administrator" shall be substituted for "employer" wherever it appears in Section 56.21.

(c) This section shall not apply to any person or entity that is subject to the Insurance Information Privacy Act or to Chapter 2 (commencing with Section 56.10) or Chapter 3 (commencing with Section 56.20). *(Added by Stats.1981, c. 782, § 2. Amended by Stats.2004, c. 183 (A.B.3082), § 24.)*

§ 56.265. Annuity contracts; disclosure of individually identifiable information concerning health, medical or genetic history; prohibition

A person or entity that underwrites or sells annuity contracts or contracts insuring, guaranteeing, or indemnifying against loss, harm, damage, illness, disability, or death, and any affiliate of that person or entity, shall not disclose individually identifiable information concerning the health of, or the medical or genetic history of, a customer, to any affiliated or nonaffiliated depository institution, or to any other affiliated or nonaffiliated third party for use with regard to the granting of credit. *(Added by Stats.2000, c. 278 (A.B.2797), § 2.)*

CHAPTER 6. RELATIONSHIP TO EXISTING LAW

Section
56.27. Employer that is insurance institution, agent or support organization; disclosure not in violation of § 56.20.
56.28. Patient's right to access.
56.29. Information Practices Act of 1977; applicability.
56.30. Exemptions from limitations of this part.
56.31. Disclosure or use of medical information under subdivision (f) of Section 56.30; HIV infection or exposure; employment incident.

§ 56.27. Employer that is insurance institution, agent or support organization; disclosure not in violation of § 56.20

An employer that is an insurance institution, insurance agent, or insurance support organization subject to the Insurance Information and Privacy Protection Act, Article 6.6 (commencing with Section 791) of Part 2 of Division 1 of the Insurance Code, shall not be deemed to have violated Section 56.20 by disclosing medical information gathered in connection with an insurance transaction in accordance with that act. *(Added by Stats.1981, c. 782, § 2.)*

§ 56.28. Patient's right to access

Nothing in this part shall be deemed to affect existing laws relating to a patient's right of access to his or her own medical information, or relating to disclosures made pursuant to Section 1158 of the Evidence Code, or relating to privileges established under the Evidence Code. *(Added by Stats.1981, c. 782, § 2.)*

§ 56.29. Information Practices Act of 1977; applicability

(a) Nothing in Chapter 1 (commencing with Section 1798) of Title 1.8 of Part 4 of Division 3 shall be construed to permit the acquisition or disclosure of medical information regarding a patient without an authorization, where the authorization is required by this part.

(b) The disclosure of medical information regarding a patient which is subject to subdivision (b) of Section 1798.24 shall be made only with an authorization which complies with the provisions of this part. Such disclosure may be made only within the time limits specified in subdivision (b) of Section 1798.24.

(c) Where the acquisition or disclosure of medical information regarding a patient is prohibited or limited by any provision of Chapter 1 (commencing with Section 1798) of Title 1.8 of Part 4 of Division 3, the prohibition or limit shall be applicable in addition to the requirements of this part. *(Added by Stats.1981, c. 782, § 2.)*

§ 56.30. Exemptions from limitations of this part

The disclosure and use of the following medical information shall not be subject to the limitations of this part:

(a) (Mental health and developmental disabilities) Information and records obtained in the course of providing services under Division 4 (commencing with Section 4000), Division 4.1 (commencing with Section 4400), Division 4.5 (commencing with Section 4500), Division 5 (commencing with Section 5000), Division 6 (commencing with Section 6000), or Division 7 (commencing with Section 7100) of the Welfare and Institutions Code.

(b) (Public social services) Information and records that are subject to Sections 10850, 14124.1, and 14124.2 of the Welfare and Institutions Code.

(c) (State health services, communicable diseases, developmental disabilities) Information and records maintained pursuant to former Chapter 2 (commencing with Section 200) of Part 1 of Division 1 of the Health and Safety Code and pursuant to the Communicable Disease Prevention and Control Act (subdivision (a) of Section 27 of the Health and Safety Code).

(d) (Licensing and statistics) Information and records maintained pursuant to Division 2 (commencing with Section 1200) and Part 1 (commencing with Section 102100) of Division 102 of the Health and Safety Code; pursuant to Chapter 3 (commencing with Section 1200) of Division 2 of the Business and Professions Code; and pursuant to Section 8608, 8817, or 8909 of the Family Code.

(e) (Medical survey, workers' safety) Information and records acquired and maintained or disclosed pursuant to Sections 1380 and 1382 of the Health and Safety Code and pursuant to Division 5 (commencing with Section 6300) of the Labor Code.

(f) (Industrial accidents) Information and records acquired, maintained, or disclosed pursuant to Division 1 (commencing with Section 50), Division 4 (commencing with Section 3200), Division 4.5 (commencing with Section 6100), and Division 4.7 (commencing with Section 6200) of the Labor Code.

(g) (Law enforcement) Information and records maintained by a health facility which are sought by a law enforcement agency under Chapter 3.5 (commencing with Section 1543) of Title 12 of Part 2 of the Penal Code.

(h) (Investigations of employment accident or illness) Information and records sought as part of an investigation of an on-the-job accident or illness pursuant to Division 5 (commencing with Section 6300) of the Labor Code or pursuant to Section 105200 of the Health and Safety Code.

(i) (Alcohol or drug abuse) Information and records subject to the federal alcohol and drug abuse regulations (Part 2 (commencing with Section 2.1) of Subchapter A of Chapter 1 of Title 42 of the Code of Federal Regulations) or to Section 11977 of the Health and Safety Code dealing with narcotic and drug abuse.

(j) (Patient discharge data) Nothing in this part shall be construed to limit, expand, or otherwise affect the authority of the California Health Facilities Commission to collect patient discharge information from health facilities.

(k) Medical information and records disclosed to, and their use by, the Insurance Commissioner, the Director of the Department of Managed Health Care, the Division of Industrial Accidents, the Workers' Compensation Appeals Board, the Department of Insurance, or the Department of Managed Health Care.

(*l*) Medical information and records related to services provided on and after January 1, 2006, disclosed to, and their use by, the Managed Risk Medical Insurance Board to the same extent that those records are required to be provided to the board related to services provided on and after July 1, 2009, to comply with Section 403 of the federal Children's Health Insurance Program Reauthorization Act of 2009 (Public Law 111–3)[1], applying subdivision (c) of Section 1932 of the federal Social Security Act[2]. *(Added by Stats.1981, c. 782, § 2. Amended by Stats.1990, c. 1363 (A.B.3532), § 1, operative July 1, 1991; Stats.1992, c. 163 (A.B.2641), § 5, operative Jan. 1, 1994; Stats. 1993, c. 1004 (A.B.336), § 2; Stats.1996, c. 1023 (S.B.1497), § 26, eff. Sept. 29, 1996; Stats.1999, c. 526 (S.B.19), § 7; Stats.2000, c. 1067 (S.B.2094), § 3; Stats.2010, c. 717 (S.B.853), § 1, eff. Oct. 19, 2010.)*

1 Public law sections classified to U.S.C.A., see U.S.C.A. Tables.

2 42 U.S.C.A. § 1396u-2.

Law Revision Commission Comments

Subdivision (d) of Section 56.30 is amended to substitute references to the Family Code provisions that replaced the former Civil Code provisions. [22 Cal.L.Rev.Comm.Reports 1 (1992)].

§ 56.31. Disclosure or use of medical information under subdivision (f) of Section 56.30; HIV infection or exposure; employment incident

Notwithstanding any other provision of law, nothing in subdivision (f) of Section 56.30 shall permit the disclosure or use of medical information regarding whether a patient is infected with or exposed to the human immunodeficiency virus without the prior authorization from the patient unless the patient is an injured worker claiming to be infected with or exposed to the human immunodeficiency virus through an exposure incident arising out of and in the course of employment. *(Added by Stats.1999, c. 766 (A.B.435), § 1.)*

CHAPTER 7. VIOLATIONS

§ 56.35. Compensatory and punitive damages; attorneys' fees and costs

In addition to any other remedies available at law, a patient whose medical information has been used or disclosed in violation of Section 56.10 or 56.104 or 56.20 or subdivision (a) of Section 56.26 and who has sustained economic loss or personal injury therefrom may recover compensatory damages, punitive damages not to exceed three thousand dollars ($3,000), attorneys' fees not to exceed one thousand dollars ($1,000), and the costs of litigation. *(Added by Stats.1981, c. 782, § 2. Amended by Stats.1999, c. 527 (A.B.416), § 4.)*

Research References

California Practice Guide: Employment Litigation Ch. 5-K, K. Invasion of Privacy.

§ 56.36. Misdemeanors; violations; remedies

(a) Any violation of the provisions of this part that results in economic loss or personal injury to a patient is punishable as a misdemeanor.

(b) In addition to any other remedies available at law, any individual may bring an action against any person or entity who has negligently released confidential information or records concerning him or her in violation of this part, for either or both of the following:

(1) Except as provided in subdivision (e), nominal damages of one thousand dollars ($1,000). In order to recover under this paragraph, it shall not be necessary that the plaintiff suffered or was threatened with actual damages.

(2) The amount of actual damages, if any, sustained by the patient.

(c)(1) In addition, any person or entity that negligently discloses medical information in violation of the provisions of this part shall also be liable, irrespective of the amount of damages suffered by the patient as a result of that violation, for an administrative fine or civil penalty not to exceed two thousand five hundred dollars ($2,500) per violation.

(2)(A) Any person or entity, other than a licensed health care professional, who knowingly and willfully obtains, discloses, or uses medical information in violation of this part shall be liable for an administrative fine or civil penalty not to exceed twenty-five thousand dollars ($25,000) per violation.

(B) Any licensed health care professional, who knowingly and willfully obtains, discloses, or uses medical information in violation of this part shall be liable on a first violation, for an administrative fine or civil penalty not to exceed two thousand five hundred dollars ($2,500) per violation, or on a second violation for an administrative fine or civil penalty not to exceed ten thousand dollars ($10,000) per violation, or on a third and subsequent violation for an administrative fine or civil penalty not to exceed twenty-five thousand dollars ($25,000) per violation. Nothing in this subdivision shall be construed to limit the liability of a health care service plan, a contractor, or a provider of health care that is not a licensed health care professional for any violation of this part.

(3)(A) Any person or entity, other than a licensed health care professional, who knowingly or willfully obtains or uses medical information in violation of this part for the purpose of financial gain shall be liable for an administrative fine or civil penalty not to exceed two hundred fifty thousand dollars ($250,000) per violation and shall also be subject to disgorgement of any proceeds or other consideration obtained as a result of the violation.

(B) Any licensed health care professional, who knowingly and willfully obtains, discloses, or uses medical information in violation of this part for financial gain shall be liable on a first violation, for an administrative fine or civil penalty not to exceed five thousand dollars ($5,000) per violation, or on a second violation for an administrative fine or civil penalty not to exceed twenty-five thousand dollars ($25,000) per violation, or on a third and subsequent violation for an administrative fine or civil penalty not to exceed two hundred fifty thousand dollars ($250,000) per violation and shall also be subject to disgorgement of any proceeds or other consideration obtained as a result of the violation. Nothing in this subdivision shall be construed to limit the liability of a health care service plan, a contractor, or a provider of health care that is not a licensed health care professional for any violation of this part.

(4) Nothing in this subdivision shall be construed as authorizing an administrative fine or civil penalty under both paragraphs (2) and (3) for the same violation.

(5) Any person or entity who is not permitted to receive medical information pursuant to this part and who knowingly and willfully obtains, discloses, or uses medical information without written authorization from the patient shall be liable for a civil penalty not to exceed two hundred fifty thousand dollars ($250,000) per violation.

(d) In assessing the amount of an administrative fine or civil penalty pursuant to subdivision (c), the Office of Health Information Integrity, licensing agency, or certifying board or court shall consider any one or more of the relevant circumstances presented by any of the parties to the case including, but not limited to, the following:

(1) Whether the defendant has made a reasonable, good faith attempt to comply with this part.

(2) The nature and seriousness of the misconduct.

(3) The harm to the patient, enrollee, or subscriber.

(4) The number of violations.

(5) The persistence of the misconduct.

(6) The length of time over which the misconduct occurred.

(7) The willfulness of the defendant's misconduct.

(8) The defendant's assets, liabilities, and net worth.

(e)(1) In an action brought by an individual pursuant to subdivision (b) on or after January 1, 2013, in which the defendant establishes the affirmative defense in paragraph (2), the court shall award any actual damages and reasonable attorney's fees and costs, but may not award nominal damages for a violation of this part.

(2) The defendant is entitled to an affirmative defense if all of the following are established, subject to the equitable considerations in paragraph (3):

(A) The defendant is a covered entity or business associate, as defined in Section 160.103 of Title 45 of the Code of Federal Regulations, in effect as of January 1, 2012.

(B) The defendant has complied with any obligations to notify all persons entitled to receive notice regarding the release of the information or records.

(C) The release of confidential information or records was solely to another covered entity or business associate.

(D) The release of confidential information or records was not an incident of medical identity theft. For purposes of this subparagraph, "medical identity theft" means the use of an individual's personal information, as defined in Section 1798.80, without the individual's knowledge or consent, to obtain medical goods or services, or to submit false claims for medical services.

(E) The defendant took appropriate preventive actions to protect the confidential information or records against release consistent with the defendant's obligations under this part or other applicable state law and the Health Insurance Portability and Accountability Act of 1996 (Public Law 104–191) (HIPAA) and all HIPAA Administrative Simplification Regulations in effect on January 1, 2012, contained in Parts 160, 162, and 164 of Title 45 of the Code of Federal Regulations and Part 2 of Title 42 of the Code of Federal Regulations, including, but not limited to:

(i) Developing and implementing security policies and procedures.

(ii) Designating a security official who is responsible for developing and implementing its security policies and procedures, including educating and training the workforce.

(iii) Encrypting the information or records, and protecting against the release or use of the encryption key and passwords, or transmitting the information or records in a manner designed to provide equal or greater protections against improper disclosures.

(F) The defendant took reasonable and appropriate corrective action after the release of the confidential information or records, and the covered entity or business associate that received the confidential information or records destroyed or returned the confidential information or records in the most expedient time possible and without unreasonable delay, consistent with any measures necessary to determine the scope of the breach and restore the reasonable integrity of the data system. A court may consider this subparagraph to be established if the defendant shows in detail that the covered entity or business associate could not destroy or return the confidential information or records because of the technology utilized.

(G) The covered entity or business associate that received the confidential information or records, or any of its agents, independent contractors, or employees, regardless of the scope of the employee's employment, did not retain, use, or release the information or records.

(H) After the release of the confidential information or records, the defendant took reasonable and appropriate action to prevent a future similar release of confidential information or records.

(I) The defendant has not previously established an affirmative defense pursuant to this subdivision, or the court determines, in its discretion, that application of the affirmative defense is compelling and consistent with the purposes of this section to promote reasonable conduct in light of all the facts.

(3)(A) In determining whether the affirmative defense may be established pursuant to paragraph (2), the court shall consider the equity of the situation, including, but not limited to, (i) whether the defendant has previously violated this part, regardless of whether an action has previously been brought, and (ii) the nature of the prior violation.

(B) To the extent the court allows discovery to determine whether there has been any other violation of this part that the court will consider in balancing the equities, the defendant shall not provide any medical information, as defined in Section 56.05. The court, in its discretion, may enter a protective order prohibiting the further use of any personal information, as defined in Section 1798.80, about the individual whose medical information may have been disclosed in a prior violation.

(4) In an action under this subdivision in which the defendant establishes the affirmative defense pursuant to paragraph (2), a plaintiff shall be entitled to recover reasonable attorney's fees and costs without regard to an award of actual or nominal damages or the imposition of administrative fines or civil penalties.

(5) In an action brought by an individual pursuant to subdivision (b) on or after January 1, 2013, in which the defendant establishes the affirmative defense pursuant to paragraph (2), a

defendant shall not be liable for more than one judgment on the merits under this subdivision for releases of confidential information or records arising out of the same event, transaction, or occurrence.

(f)(1) The civil penalty pursuant to subdivision (c) shall be assessed and recovered in a civil action brought in the name of the people of the State of California in any court of competent jurisdiction by any of the following:

(A) The Attorney General.

(B) Any district attorney.

(C) Any county counsel authorized by agreement with the district attorney in actions involving violation of a county ordinance.

(D) Any city attorney of a city.

(E) Any city attorney of a city and county having a population in excess of 750,000, with the consent of the district attorney.

(F) A city prosecutor in any city having a full-time city prosecutor or, with the consent of the district attorney, by a city attorney in any city and county.

(G) The Director of the Office of Health Information Integrity may recommend that any person described in subparagraphs (A) to (F), inclusive, bring a civil action under this section.

(2) If the action is brought by the Attorney General, one-half of the penalty collected shall be paid to the treasurer of the county in which the judgment was entered, and one-half to the General Fund. If the action is brought by a district attorney or county counsel, the penalty collected shall be paid to the treasurer of the county in which the judgment was entered. Except as provided in paragraph (3), if the action is brought by a city attorney or city prosecutor, one-half of the penalty collected shall be paid to the treasurer of the city in which the judgment was entered and one-half to the county in which the judgment was entered.

(3) If the action is brought by a city attorney of a city and county, the entire amount of the penalty collected shall be paid to the treasurer of the city and county in which the judgment was entered.

(4) Nothing in this section shall be construed as authorizing both an administrative fine and civil penalty for the same violation.

(5) Imposition of a fine or penalty provided for in this section shall not preclude imposition of any other sanctions or remedies authorized by law.

(6) Administrative fines or penalties issued pursuant to Section 1280.15 of the Health and Safety Code shall offset any other administrative fine or civil penalty imposed under this section for the same violation.

(g) For purposes of this section, "knowing" and "willful" shall have the same meanings as in Section 7 of the Penal Code.

(h) No person who discloses protected medical information in accordance with the provisions of this part shall be subject to the penalty provisions of this part. *(Added by Stats.1981, c. 782, § 2. Amended by Stats.1999, c. 526 (S.B.19), § 8; Stats.2008, c. 602 (A.B.211), § 1; Stats.2012, c. 437 (A.B.439), § 1.)*

§ 56.37. Authorization, release, consent, or waiver; enforceability

(a) No provider of health care, health care service plan, or contractor may require a patient, as a condition of receiving health care services, to sign an authorization, release, consent, or waiver that would permit the disclosure of medical information that otherwise may not be disclosed under Section 56.10 or any other provision of law. However, a health care service plan or disability insurer may require relevant enrollee or subscriber medical information as a condition of the medical underwriting process, provided that Sections 1374.7 and 1389.1 of the Health and Safety Code are strictly observed.

(b) Any waiver by a patient of the provisions of this part, except as authorized by Section 56.11 or 56.21 or subdivision (b) of Section 56.26, shall be deemed contrary to public policy and shall be unenforceable. *(Added by Stats.1981, c. 782, § 2. Amended by Stats.1999, c. 526 (S.B.19), § 9.)*

Part 2.7

MEDICAL CLAIMS DATA ERROR CORRECTION

§ 57. Receipt of health care claims data; compliance with requirements for error correction required; definitions

(a) A qualified entity, as defined in Section 1395kk(e)(2) of Title 42 of the United States Code, that receives claims data from a health care service plan or health insurer shall comply with the requirements governing provider and supplier requests for error correction established under Section 401.717 of Title 42 of the Code of Federal Regulations for all claims data received, including data from sources other than Medicare.

(b) For purposes of this section, the following definitions apply:

(1) "Provider" means a hospital, a skilled nursing facility, a comprehensive outpatient rehabilitation facility, a home health agency, a hospice, a clinic, or a rehabilitation agency.

(2) "Supplier" means a physician and surgeon or other health care practitioner, or an entity that furnishes health care services other than a provider. *(Added by Stats.2012, c. 869 (S.B.1196), § 1.)*

Part 2.9

CALIFORNIA FAIR DEALERSHIP LAW

Section
80. Citation.
81. Definitions.
82. Liberal construction; purposes and policies.
83. Refusal to grant dealership; prohibited grounds.
84. Termination, cancellation, or refusal to renew dealership agreement; prohibited grounds.
85. Refusal to make or consent to assignment, sale, transfer, or bequest of dealership; prohibited grounds.
86. Attorney's fees; costs.

§ 80. Citation

This part may be cited as the California Fair Dealership Law. *(Added by Stats.1980, c. 914, § 1.)*

Research References

8 Witkin, California Summary 10th Constitutional Law § 897, Other Discrimination Statutes.

§ 81. Definitions

As used in this part:

(a) "Person" means a natural person, partnership, joint venture, corporation, limited liability company, or other entity.

(b) "Dealership" means a contract or agreement, either express or implied, whether oral or written, between two or more persons, by which a person is granted the right to sell or distribute goods or services, or to use a trade name, trademark, service mark, logotype, or advertising or other commercial symbol, in which there is a community of interest in the business of offering, selling, or distributing goods or services at wholesale, or at retail, by lease, agreement, or otherwise.

(c) "Grantor" means a person who sells, leases, or otherwise transfers a dealership.

(d) "Community of interest" means a continuing financial interest between the grantor and grantee in either the operation of the dealership or the marketing of goods or services.

(e) "Dealer" means a person who is a grantee of a dealership situated in this state.

(f) "Grant" means a sale, lease, or transfer of any kind. *(Added by Stats.1980, c. 914, § 1. Amended by Stats.1994, c. 1010 (S.B.2053), § 29.)*

Research References

8 Witkin, California Summary 10th Constitutional Law § 897, Other Discrimination Statutes.

§ 82. Liberal construction; purposes and policies

This part shall be liberally construed and applied to promote its underlying purposes and policies, which are as follows:

(a) The prohibition of discrimination based upon any characteristic listed or defined in subdivision (b) or (e) of Section 51 in the granting, sale, transfer, bequest, termination, and nonrenewal of dealerships.

(b) The requirements of this part shall not be varied by contract or agreement and any portion of a contract or agreement purporting to do so is void and unenforceable. *(Added by Stats.1980, c. 914, § 1. Amended by Stats.2007, c. 568 (A.B.14), § 10.)*

§ 83. Refusal to grant dealership; prohibited grounds

On or after January 1, 1981, no grantor, directly or indirectly, shall refuse to grant a dealership to any person because of any characteristic listed or defined in subdivision (b) or (e) of Section 51. *(Added by Stats.1980, c. 914, § 1. Amended by Stats.2007, c. 568 (A.B.14), § 11.)*

§ 84. Termination, cancellation, or refusal to renew dealership agreement; prohibited grounds

On or after January 1, 1981, no grantor, directly or indirectly, may terminate, cancel, or refuse to renew a dealership agreement with a dealer because of any characteristic listed or defined in subdivision (b) or (e) of Section 51. *(Added by Stats.1980, c. 914, § 1. Amended by Stats.2007, c. 568 (A.B.14), § 12.)*

§ 85. Refusal to make or consent to assignment, sale, transfer, or bequest of dealership; prohibited grounds

On or after January 1, 1981, no grantor or dealer, directly or indirectly, shall refuse to make or to consent to an assignment, sale, transfer, or bequest of a dealership to any person, or to the intestate succession to the dealership by any person, because of any characteristic listed or defined in subdivision (b) or (e) of Section 51. This section shall not be construed to create any right in a dealer to assign, sell, transfer, or bequeath a dealership where the right did not exist prior to January 1, 1981. *(Added by Stats.1980, c. 914, § 1. Amended by Stats.2007, c. 568 (A.B.14), § 13.)*

§ 86. Attorney's fees; costs

The prevailing party in any action based on a violation of the provisions of this part shall be entitled to recover reasonable attorney's fees and taxable court costs. *(Added by Stats.1980, c. 914, § 1.)*

Division 2
PROPERTY

Part 1

PROPERTY IN GENERAL

Title 1

NATURE OF PROPERTY

§ 654. Ownership; property defined

PROPERTY, WHAT. The ownership of a thing is the right of one or more persons to possess and use it to the exclusion of others. In this Code, the thing of which there may be ownership is called property. *(Enacted in 1872.)*

Research References

Miller and Starr California Real Estate § 17:1, in General; Definitions.
Miller and Starr California Real Estate § 17:2, Property as "Bundle of Rights".
Miller and Starr California Real Estate § 24:6, Covenants Burdening Land for the Benefit of Other Land--Creation After the 1968-1969 Amendments.
Miller and Starr California Real Estate § 11:101, Effect of Foreclosure on Rights of Tenants in Possession.
12 Witkin, California Summary 10th Real Property § 127, (S 127) in General.
13 Witkin, California Summary 10th Personal Property § 1, General Meaning.

§ 655. Things subject to ownership

IN WHAT PROPERTY MAY EXIST. There may be ownership of all inanimate things which are capable of appropriation or of manual delivery; of all domestic animals; of all obligations; of such products of labor or skill as the composition of an author, the good will of a business, trade marks and signs, and of rights created or granted by statute. *(Enacted in 1872.)*

Research References

Miller and Starr California Real Estate § 17:1, in General; Definitions.
13 Witkin, California Summary 10th Personal Property § 1, General Meaning.

13 Witkin, California Summary 10th Equity § 79, (S 79) Statutory Protection.

§ 656. Ownership of wild animals

WILD ANIMALS. Animals wild by nature are the subjects of ownership, while living, only when on the land of the person claiming them, or when tamed, or taken and held in possession, or disabled and immediately pursued. *(Enacted in 1872.)*

Research References

13 Witkin, California Summary 10th Personal Property § 21, (S 21) Wild Animals and Fish.

§ 657. Classification of property

REAL AND PERSONAL. Property is either:

1. Real or immovable; or,

2. Personal or movable. *(Enacted in 1872.)*

Research References

Rutter, Cal. Practice Guide: Real Prop. Transactions Ch. 4-A, A. Property to be Sold.
Miller and Starr California Real Estate § 17:1, in General; Definitions.
Miller and Starr California Real Estate § 10:38, What is Assignable; Procedure.
Miller and Starr California Real Estate § 17:37, Generally; Definitions.

§ 658. Real property defined

Real or immovable property consists of:

1. Land;

2. That which is affixed to land;

3. That which is incidental or appurtenant to land;

4. That which is immovable by law; except that for the purposes of sale, emblements, industrial growing crops and things attached to or forming part of the land, which are agreed to be severed before sale or under the contract of sale, shall be treated as goods and be governed by the provisions of the title of this code regulating the sales of goods. *(Enacted in 1872. Amended by Stats.1931, c. 1070, p. 2259, § 4.)*

Research References

Rutter, Cal. Practice Guide: Real Prop. Transactions Ch. 4-A, A. Property to be Sold.
Miller and Starr California Real Estate § 17:6, in General; Personal Property Secured Transactions.
Miller and Starr California Real Estate § 17:19, Constructive Severance.
Miller and Starr California Real Estate § 17:30, Things Growing, Generally.
Miller and Starr California Real Estate § 17:31, Timber.
Miller and Starr California Real Estate § 17:32, Crops.
Miller and Starr California Real Estate § 17:37, Generally; Definitions.
13 Witkin, California Summary 10th Personal Property § 90, Test of Mobility.
13 Witkin, California Summary 10th Personal Property § 92, Growing Crops and Trees.
13 Witkin, California Summary 10th Personal Property § 93, Standing Timber.
13 Witkin, California Summary 10th Personal Property § 97, (S 97) Agreement and Constructive Severance.

4 Witkin, California Summary 10th Sales § 26, (S 26) Goods to be Severed.

§ 659. Land defined

Land is the material of the earth, whatever may be the ingredients of which it is composed, whether soil, rock, or other substance, and includes free or occupied space for an indefinite distance upwards as well as downwards, subject to limitations upon the use of airspace imposed, and rights in the use of airspace granted, by law. *(Enacted in 1872. Amended by Stats.1963, c. 860, p. 2096, § 5.)*

Research References

Rutter, Cal. Practice Guide: Real Prop. Transactions Ch. 4-A, A. Property to be Sold.
Miller and Starr California Real Estate § 14:2, in General; Nature and Extent.
Miller and Starr California Real Estate § 24:6, Covenants Burdening Land for the Benefit of Other Land--Creation After the 1968-1969 Amendments.
Miller and Starr California Real Estate § 8:60, Appurtenances Pass With Conveyance.
Miller and Starr California Real Estate § 17:21, Minerals--In General.
Miller and Starr California Real Estate § 17:28, Airspace.
12 Witkin, California Summary 10th Real Property § 3, Definitions.
12 Witkin, California Summary 10th Real Property § 403, (S 403) Hostile or Adverse Use.
13 Witkin, California Summary 10th Personal Property § 90, Test of Mobility.

§ 660. Fixtures defined

A thing is deemed to be affixed to land when it is attached to it by roots, as in the case of trees, vines, or shrubs; or imbedded in it, as in the case of walls; or permanently resting upon it, as in the case of buildings; or permanently attached to what is thus permanent, as by means of cement, plaster, nails, bolts, or screws; except that for the purposes of sale, emblements, industrial growing crops and things attached to or forming part of the land, which are agreed to be severed before sale or under the contract of sale, shall be treated as goods and be governed by the provisions of the title of this code regulating the sales of goods. *(Enacted in 1872. Amended by Stats.1931, c. 1070, p. 2259, § 5.)*

Research References

Rutter, Cal. Practice Guide: Real Prop. Transactions Ch. 4-A, A. Property to be Sold.
Rutter, Cal. Practice Guide: Real Prop. Transactions Ch. 6-H, H. Security for Promissory Note.
Miller and Starr California Real Estate § 17:6, in General; Personal Property Secured Transactions.
Miller and Starr California Real Estate § 17:19, Constructive Severance.
Miller and Starr California Real Estate § 17:30, Things Growing, Generally.
Miller and Starr California Real Estate § 17:31, Timber.
Miller and Starr California Real Estate § 17:32, Crops.
Miller and Starr California Real Estate § 17:37, Generally; Definitions.
Miller and Starr California Real Estate § 17:38, Tests for Determining Whether an Item is a Fixture.
Miller and Starr California Real Estate § 17:40, Tests for Determining Whether an Item is a Fixture--Means of Annexation; Difficulty of Removal.
Miller and Starr California Real Estate § 17:68, Buildings, Mobilehomes, and Boats.
Miller and Starr California Real Estate § 27:16, Defining "Public Works" Projects Under the Prevailing Wage Law.
Miller and Starr California Real Estate § 30A:32, Crops, Trees and Vegetation.
20 NO. 4 Miller & Starr, California Real Estate Newsalert 1, Contractor Beware: the Fine Line Between "Public Works" and "Private Projects" Under California's Prevailing Wage Law.
13 Witkin, California Summary 10th Personal Property § 92, Growing Crops and Trees.

13 Witkin, California Summary 10th Personal Property § 93, Standing Timber.
13 Witkin, California Summary 10th Personal Property § 94, (S 94) Nature of Doctrine and Tests.
13 Witkin, California Summary 10th Personal Property § 97, (S 97) Agreement and Constructive Severance.
4 Witkin, California Summary 10th Sales § 26, (S 26) Goods to be Severed.
4 Witkin, California Summary 10th Security Transactions in Real Property § 67, Subsequent Mortgage.

§ 662. Appurtenances to land

APPURTENANCES. A thing is deemed to be incidental or appurtenant to land when it is by right used with the land for its benefit, as in the case of a way, or watercourse, or of a passage for light, air, or heat from or across the land of another. *(Enacted in 1872.)*

Research References

Rutter, Cal. Practice Guide: Real Prop. Transactions Ch. 4-A, A. Property to be Sold.
Miller and Starr California Real Estate § 15:6, Appurtenant Easements; Conveyance or Encumbrance of the Dominant Tenement.
Miller and Starr California Real Estate § 15:8, Determination as Appurtenant Easement or Easement in Gross.
Miller and Starr California Real Estate § 8:60, Appurtenances Pass With Conveyance.
Miller and Starr California Real Estate § 15:10, Easements for Light, Air, or View.
Miller and Starr California Real Estate § 17:25, Water Rights.
Miller and Starr California Real Estate § 24:24, Nature of the Right to Enforce Restrictions; Appurtenant to Benefited Property.
13 Witkin, California Summary 10th Personal Property § 90, Test of Mobility.

§ 663. Personal property defined

PERSONAL PROPERTY. Every kind of property that is not real is personal. *(Enacted in 1872.)*

Research References

Rutter, Cal. Practice Guide: Real Prop. Transactions Ch. 4-A, A. Property to be Sold.
Miller and Starr California Real Estate § 10:38, What is Assignable; Procedure.
13 Witkin, California Summary 10th Personal Property § 90, Test of Mobility.

Title 2

OWNERSHIP

CHAPTER 1. OWNERS

§ 669. Ownership

OWNER. All property has an owner, whether that owner is the State, and the property public, or the owner an individual, and the property private. The State may also hold property as a private proprietor. *(Enacted in 1872.)*

Research References

Rutter, Cal. Practice Guide: Real Prop. Transactions Ch. 4-A, A. Property to be Sold.

Miller and Starr California Real Estate § 17:26, Water Rights--Regulation of Water Rights.

13 Witkin, California Summary 10th Personal Property § 27, (S 27) in General.

§ 670. State property

The State is the owner of all land below tide water, and below ordinary high-water mark, bordering upon tide water within the State; of all land below the water of a navigable lake or stream; of all property lawfully appropriated by it to its own use; of all property dedicated to the State; and of all property of which there is no other owner. *(Enacted in 1872. Amended by Code Am.1873–74, c. 612, p. 217, § 99.)*

Research References

Miller and Starr California Real Estate § 8:67, Water as Property Boundary--Where Adjacent to Tidewaters.

Miller and Starr California Real Estate § 8:68, Water as Property Boundary--Where Adjacent to Nontidal Waters.

Miller and Starr California Real Estate § 17:26, Water Rights--Regulation of Water Rights.

Miller and Starr California Real Estate § 26:35, Special Statutory Dedication Procedures.

21 NO. 5 Miller & Starr, California Real Estate Newsalert 9, Deeds.

13 Witkin, California Summary 10th Personal Property § 27, (S 27) in General.

§ 671. Persons authorized to own property

Any person, whether citizen or alien, may take, hold, and dispose of property, real or personal, within this State. *(Enacted in 1872. Amended by Code Am.1873–74, c. 612, p. 218, § 100.)*

Research References

Miller and Starr California Real Estate § 17:2, Property as "Bundle of Rights".

12 Witkin, California Summary 10th Real Property § 206, (S 206) Capacity to Acquire and Transfer Land.

CHAPTER 2. MODIFICATION OF OWNERSHIP

ARTICLE 1. INTERESTS IN PROPERTY

§ 678. Absolute or qualified ownership

Ownership, absolute or qualified. The ownership of property is either:

1. Absolute; or,

2. Qualified. *(Enacted in 1872.)*

Research References

Miller and Starr California Real Estate § 9:2, Classification, Generally.

13 Witkin, California Summary 10th Personal Property § 27, (S 27) in General.

§ 679. Absolute ownership defined

When absolute. The ownership of property is absolute when a single person has the absolute dominion over it, and may use it or dispose of it according to his pleasure, subject only to general laws. *(Enacted in 1872.)*

Research References

Rutter, Cal. Practice Guide: Real Prop. Transactions Ch. 4-C, C. Parties to the Purchase Agreement.

Miller and Starr California Real Estate § 9:2, Classification, Generally.

Miller and Starr California Real Estate § 17:2, Property as "Bundle of Rights".

Miller and Starr California Real Estate § 11:101, Effect of Foreclosure on Rights of Tenants in Possession.

13 Witkin, California Summary 10th Personal Property § 27, (S 27) in General.

§ 680. Qualified ownership defined

When qualified. The ownership of property is qualified:

1. When it is shared with one or more persons;

2. When the time of enjoyment is deferred or limited;

3. When the use is restricted. *(Enacted in 1872.)*

Research References

Rutter, Cal. Practice Guide: Real Prop. Transactions Ch. 4-C, C. Parties to the Purchase Agreement.

Miller and Starr California Real Estate § 9:2, Classification, Generally.

13 Witkin, California Summary 10th Personal Property § 27, (S 27) in General.

§ 681. Several ownership defined

Several ownership, what. The ownership of property by a single person is designated as a sole or several ownership. *(Enacted in 1872.)*

Research References

Rutter, Cal. Practice Guide: Real Prop. Transactions Ch. 4-C, C. Parties to the Purchase Agreement.

Miller and Starr California Real Estate § 9:2, Classification, Generally.

Miller and Starr California Real Estate § 12:1, Cotenancies Defined.

Miller and Starr California Real Estate § 12:23, Characteristics; Creation--Right of Survivorship.

13 Witkin, California Summary 10th Personal Property § 27, (S 27) in General.

§ 682. Ownership by several persons; types

OWNERSHIP OF SEVERAL PERSONS. The ownership of property by several persons is either:

1. Of joint interests;
2. Of partnership interests;
3. Of interests in common;
4. Of community interest of husband and wife. *(Enacted in 1872.)*

Research References

Rutter, Cal. Practice Guide: Real Prop. Transactions Ch. 4-C, C. Parties to the Purchase Agreement.
Rutter, Cal. Practice Guide: Real Prop. Transactions Ch. 12-A, A. General Considerations.
Miller and Starr California Real Estate § 9:2, Classification, Generally.
Miller and Starr California Real Estate § 12:1, Cotenancies Defined.
Miller and Starr California Real Estate § 12:40, Basic Rules for Determining Character of Property; Definitions.
12 Witkin, California Summary 10th Real Property § 32, (S 32) in General.
13 Witkin, California Summary 10th Personal Property § 27, (S 27) in General.
13 Witkin, California Summary 10th Personal Property § 35, (S 35) Coownership of Automobile.

§ 682.1. Community property of husband and wife; subject to express declaration in transfer documents; application and operation of section

(a) Community property of a husband and wife, when expressly declared in the transfer document to be community property with right of survivorship, and which may be accepted in writing on the face of the document by a statement signed or initialed by the grantees, shall, upon the death of one of the spouses, pass to the survivor, without administration, pursuant to the terms of the instrument, subject to the same procedures, as property held in joint tenancy. Prior to the death of either spouse, the right of survivorship may be terminated pursuant to the same procedures by which a joint tenancy may be severed. Part I (commencing with Section 5000) of Division 5 of the Probate Code and Chapter 2 (commencing with Section 13540), Chapter 3 (commencing with Section 13550) and Chapter 3.5 (commencing with Section 13560) of Part 2 of Division 8 of the Probate Code apply to this property.

(b) This section does not apply to a joint account in a financial institution to which Part 2 (commencing with Section 5100) of Division 5 of the Probate Code applies.

(c) This section shall become operative on July 1, 2001, and shall apply to instruments created on or after that date. *(Added by Stats.2000, c. 645 (A.B.2913), § 1, operative July 1, 2001.)*

Research References

California Real Estate Forms (Miller & Starr) § 1:133, Grant Deed.
California Real Estate Forms (Miller & Starr) § 1:134, Interspousal Grant Deed.
California Real Estate Forms (Miller & Starr) § 1:135, Quitclaim Deed.
Rutter, Cal. Practice Guide: Real Prop. Transactions Ch. 4-C, C. Parties to the Purchase Agreement.
Rutter, Cal. Practice Guide: Real Prop. Transactions Ch. 12-A, A. General Considerations.
Rutter, Cal. Practice Guide: Real Prop. Transactions Ch. 13(I)-B, B. Basis of Acquired Property.
Miller and Starr California Real Estate § 8:39, Community Property; Voidable Transfers.
Miller and Starr California Real Estate § 12:22, Characteristics; Creation.
Miller and Starr California Real Estate § 12:23, Characteristics; Creation--Right of Survivorship.

Miller and Starr California Real Estate § 12:38, Determination as Community or Separate Property, in General.
Miller and Starr California Real Estate § 12:40, Basic Rules for Determining Character of Property; Definitions.
Miller and Starr California Real Estate § 12:42, Basic Rules for Determining Character of Property; Definitions--Presumption from Joint Title.
Miller and Starr California Real Estate § 12:61, Disposition on Death of a Spouse.
17 NO. 3 Miller & Starr, California Real Estate Newsalert 1, Always a Bridesmaid? Unveiling California's Domestic Partner Laws, Including Their Impact on Real Property.
11 Witkin, California Summary 10th Community Property § 157, (S 157) Conversion to Community Property With Right of Survivorship.
11 Witkin, California Summary 10th Community Property § 251, (S 251) Disposition of Community Property.
14 Witkin, California Summary 10th Wills and Probate § 76, Surviving Spouse's Share in Community and Quasi-Community Property.
14 Witkin, California Summary 10th Wills and Probate § 103, Testamentary Disposition of Property.
14 Witkin, California Summary 10th Wills and Probate § 266, (S 266) Community Property With Right of Survivorship.
14 Witkin, California Summary 10th Wills and Probate § 319, Joint Tenancy With Former Spouse.

§ 683. Joint tenancy; definition; method of creation

(a) A joint interest is one owned by two or more persons in equal shares, by a title created by a single will or transfer, when expressly declared in the will or transfer to be a joint tenancy, or by transfer from a sole owner to himself or herself and others, or from tenants in common or joint tenants to themselves or some of them, or to themselves or any of them and others, or from a husband and wife, when holding title as community property or otherwise to themselves or to themselves and others or to one of them and to another or others, when expressly declared in the transfer to be a joint tenancy, or when granted or devised to executors or trustees as joint tenants. A joint tenancy in personal property may be created by a written transfer, instrument, or agreement.

(b) Provisions of this section do not apply to a joint account in a financial institution if Part 2 (commencing with Section 5100) of Division 5 of the Probate Code applies to such account. *(Enacted in 1872. Amended by Stats.1929, c. 93, p. 172, § 1; Stats.1931, c. 1051, p. 2205, § 1; Stats.1935, c. 234, p. 912, § 1; Stats.1955, c. 178, p. 645, § 1; Stats.1983, c. 92, § 1, operative July 1, 1984; Stats.1989, c. 397, § 1, operative July 1, 1990; Stats.1990, c. 79 (A.B.759), § 1, operative July 1, 1991.)*

Law Revision Commission Comments

Section 683 is amended to add subdivision (b) to make clear that this section does not apply to a joint account in a credit union or an industrial loan company to which the newly enacted provisions of the Probate Code (Sections 5100–5407) apply. [16 Cal.L.Rev. Comm.Reports 129 (1982); 83 S.J. 3245].

Subdivision (c) of Section 683 is deleted to reflect the expansion of the California Multiple-Party Accounts Law to include banks, savings and loan associations, and other like organizations. See Prob.Code § 5128 ("financial institution" defined). Banks are now governed by subdivision (b). [20 Cal.L.Rev.Comm.Reports 145 (1990)].

Subdivision (b) of Section 683 is amended to correct a cross-reference. This is a technical, nonsubstantive change. [20 Cal.L.Rev.Comm.Reports 1001 (1990)].

Research References

Rutter, Cal. Practice Guide: Real Prop. Transactions Ch. 4-C, C. Parties to the Purchase Agreement.
Rutter, Cal. Practice Guide: Real Prop. Transactions Ch. 12-A, A. General Considerations.
Miller and Starr California Real Estate § 9:2, Classification, Generally.
Miller and Starr California Real Estate § 1:65, Provisions Applicable to Real Estate Transactions.
Miller and Starr California Real Estate § 12:22, Characteristics; Creation.

Miller and Starr California Real Estate § 12:24, Common Law and Statutory Requisites of Creation.

Miller and Starr California Real Estate § 12:25, Common Law and Statutory Requisites of Creation--Unities of Time and Title.

12 Witkin, California Summary 10th Real Property § 33, (S 33) in General.

12 Witkin, California Summary 10th Real Property § 35, Creation of Joint Tenancy.

12 Witkin, California Summary 10th Real Property § 36, (S 36) Equitable Interest.

12 Witkin, California Summary 10th Real Property § 51, (S 51) Lease.

1 Witkin Cal. Summ. 10th Contracts § 343, California Codes.

1 Witkin Cal. Summ. 10th Contracts § 400, (S 400) Miscellaneous Provisions.

13 Witkin, California Summary 10th Personal Property § 30, (S 30) Nature of Joint Tenancy.

13 Witkin, California Summary 10th Personal Property § 33, (S 33) Proceeds of Joint Tenancy Property.

§ 683.1. Joint tenancy; safe-deposit box

No contract or other arrangement made after the effective date of this section between any person, firm, or corporation engaged in the business of renting safe-deposit boxes and the renter or renters of a safe-deposit box, shall create a joint tenancy in or otherwise establish ownership in any of the contents of such safe-deposit box. Any such contract or other arrangement purporting so to do shall be to such extent void and of no effect. *(Added by Stats.1949, c. 1597, p. 2845, § 1.)*

Research References

13 Witkin, California Summary 10th Personal Property § 34, Safe Deposit Boxes.

§ 683.2. Joint tenancy; severance; right of survivorship; applicable law

(a) Subject to the limitations and requirements of this section, in addition to any other means by which a joint tenancy may be severed, a joint tenant may sever a joint tenancy in real property as to the joint tenant's interest without the joinder or consent of the other joint tenants by any of the following means:

(1) Execution and delivery of a deed that conveys legal title to the joint tenant's interest to a third person, whether or not pursuant to an agreement that requires the third person to reconvey legal title to the joint tenant.

(2) Execution of a written instrument that evidences the intent to sever the joint tenancy, including a deed that names the joint tenant as transferee, or of a written declaration that, as to the interest of the joint tenant, the joint tenancy is severed.

(b) Nothing in this section authorizes severance of a joint tenancy contrary to a written agreement of the joint tenants, but a severance contrary to a written agreement does not defeat the rights of a purchaser or encumbrancer for value in good faith and without knowledge of the written agreement.

(c) Severance of a joint tenancy of record by deed, written declaration, or other written instrument pursuant to subdivision (a) is not effective to terminate the right of survivorship of the other joint tenants as to the severing joint tenant's interest unless one of the following requirements is satisfied:

(1) Before the death of the severing joint tenant, the deed, written declaration, or other written instrument effecting the severance is recorded in the county where the real property is located.

(2) The deed, written declaration, or other written instrument effecting the severance is executed and acknowledged before a notary public by the severing joint tenant not earlier than three days before the death of that joint tenant and is recorded in the county where the real property is located not later than seven days after the death of the severing joint tenant.

(d) Nothing in subdivision (c) limits the manner or effect of:

(1) A written instrument executed by all the joint tenants that severs the joint tenancy.

(2) A severance made by or pursuant to a written agreement of all the joint tenants.

(3) A deed from a joint tenant to another joint tenant.

(e) Subdivisions (a) and (b) apply to all joint tenancies in real property, whether the joint tenancy was created before, on, or after January 1, 1985, except that in the case of the death of a joint tenant before January 1, 1985, the validity of a severance under subdivisions (a) and (b) is determined by the law in effect at the time of death. Subdivisions (c) and (d) do not apply to or affect a severance made before January 1, 1986, of a joint tenancy. *(Added by Stats.1984, c. 519, § 1. Amended by Stats.1985, c. 157, § 1.)*

Research References

Rutter, Cal. Practice Guide: Real Prop. Transactions Ch. 4-C, C. Parties to the Purchase Agreement.

Rutter, Cal. Practice Guide: Real Prop. Transactions Ch. 12-A, A. General Considerations.

Rutter, Cal. Practice Guide: Real Prop. Transactions Ch. 12-B, B. Agreements Regarding Co-Ownership Rights and Obligations.

Miller and Starr California Real Estate § 8:15, Requirements.

Miller and Starr California Real Estate § 12:29, Methods and Effect of Termination--Termination by Conveyance.

Miller and Starr California Real Estate § 12:30, Methods and Effect of Termination--Termination by Agreement, Declaration, or an Action for Partition.

12 Witkin, California Summary 10th Real Property § 58, (S 58) Joint Tenant's Conveyance to Self.

12 Witkin, California Summary 10th Real Property § 60, Nature and Purpose of Statute.

12 Witkin, California Summary 10th Real Property § 61, Methods of Severance.

12 Witkin, California Summary 10th Real Property § 62, Recordation.

12 Witkin, California Summary 10th Real Property § 63, Severance Under Statute is Not Transfer of Property.

§ 684. Partnership interest defined

PARTNERSHIP INTEREST, WHAT. A partnership interest is one owned by several persons, in partnership, for partnership purposes. *(Enacted in 1872.)*

Research References

Rutter, Cal. Practice Guide: Real Prop. Transactions Ch. 4-C, C. Parties to the Purchase Agreement.

Rutter, Cal. Practice Guide: Real Prop. Transactions Ch. 12-A, A. General Considerations.

Miller and Starr California Real Estate § 9:2, Classification, Generally.

§ 685. Interest in common defined

INTEREST IN COMMON, WHAT. An interest in common is one owned by several persons, not in joint ownership or partnership. *(Enacted in 1872.)*

Research References

Rutter, Cal. Practice Guide: Real Prop. Transactions Ch. 4-C, C. Parties to the Purchase Agreement.

Rutter, Cal. Practice Guide: Real Prop. Transactions Ch. 12-A, A. General Considerations.

Miller and Starr California Real Estate § 9:2, Classification, Generally.

Miller and Starr California Real Estate § 12:33, Definition.

Miller and Starr California Real Estate § 12:35, Creation and Characteristics.

12 Witkin, California Summary 10th Real Property § 39, in General.

§ 686. Interest in common; interests excluded

WHAT INTERESTS ARE IN COMMON. Every interest created in favor of several persons in their own right is an interest in common, unless acquired by them in partnership, for partnership purposes, or unless declared in its creation to be a joint interest, as provided in Section 683, or unless acquired as community property. *(Enacted in 1872.)*

Research References

Rutter, Cal. Practice Guide: Real Prop. Transactions Ch. 4-C, C. Parties to the Purchase Agreement.
Rutter, Cal. Practice Guide: Real Prop. Transactions Ch. 12-A, A. General Considerations.
Miller and Starr California Real Estate § 12:33, Definition.
12 Witkin, California Summary 10th Real Property § 35, Creation of Joint Tenancy.
12 Witkin, California Summary 10th Real Property § 39, in General.
12 Witkin, California Summary 10th Real Property § 40, Failure of Joint Tenancy.
13 Witkin, California Summary 10th Personal Property § 27, (S 27) in General.

§ 687.   Community property defined

Community property is property that is community property under Part 2 (commencing with Section 760) of Division 4 of the Family Code. *(Enacted in 1872.   Amended by Stats.1992, c. 163 (A.B.2641), § 6, operative Jan. 1, 1994.)*

Law Revision Commission Comments

Section 687 is amended to adopt the definition of community property provided by Section 65 of the Family Code. Part 2 (commencing with Section 760) of Division 4 of the Family Code contains detailed rules that determine whether property is community or separate property.   [22 Cal.L.Rev.Comm.Reports 1 (1992)].

Research References

Rutter, Cal. Practice Guide: Real Prop. Transactions Ch. 12-A, A. General Considerations.
Miller and Starr California Real Estate § 12:36, Origin; Requirement of Marriage; Domestic Partnerships.

§ 688.   Interests as to time

INTERESTS AS TO TIME.   In respect to the time of enjoyment, an interest in property is either:

1.   Present or future; and,

2.   Perpetual or limited.   *(Enacted in 1872.)*

Research References

Miller and Starr California Real Estate § 9:2, Classification, Generally.

§ 689.   Present interest defined

PRESENT INTEREST, WHAT.   A present interest entitles the owner to the immediate possession of the property. *(Enacted in 1872.)*

Research References

Miller and Starr California Real Estate § 9:2, Classification, Generally.
12 Witkin, California Summary 10th Real Property § 127, (S 127) in General.

§ 690.   Future interest defined

FUTURE INTEREST, WHAT.   A future interest entitles the owner to the possession of the property only at a future period. *(Enacted in 1872.)*

Research References

Miller and Starr California Real Estate § 9:2, Classification, Generally.
Miller and Starr California Real Estate § 9:25, Definitions.
Miller and Starr California Real Estate § 9:26, Reversions.

12 Witkin, California Summary 10th Real Property § 127, (S 127) in General.

§ 691.   Perpetual interest defined

PERPETUAL INTEREST, WHAT.   A perpetual interest has a duration equal to that of the property.   *(Enacted in 1872.)*

Research References

Miller and Starr California Real Estate § 9:2, Classification, Generally.
12 Witkin, California Summary 10th Real Property § 16, in General.

§ 692.   Limited interest defined

LIMITED INTEREST, WHAT.   A limited interest has a duration less than that of the property.   *(Enacted in 1872.)*

Research References

Miller and Starr California Real Estate § 9:2, Classification, Generally.

§ 696.   Future interests; alternative

TWO OR MORE FUTURE INTERESTS.   Two or more future interests may be created to take effect in the alternative, so that if the first in order fails to vest, the next in succession shall be substituted for it, and take effect accordingly.   *(Enacted in 1872.)*

§ 697.   Future interests; improbability of contingency; validity

CERTAIN FUTURE INTERESTS NOT TO BE VOID.   A future interest is not void merely because of the improbability of the contingency on which it is limited to take effect.   *(Enacted in 1872.)*

§ 698.   Future interests; posthumous children

POSTHUMOUS CHILDREN.   When a future interest is limited to successors, heirs, issue, or children, posthumous children are entitled to take in the same manner as if living at the death of their parent. *(Enacted in 1872.)*

Research References

Miller and Starr California Real Estate § 11:101, Effect of Foreclosure on Rights of Tenants in Possession.
12 Witkin, California Summary 10th Real Property § 135, (S 135) Remainder Vested Subject to Open.
14 Witkin, California Summary 10th Wills and Probate § 232, Time When Class is Ascertained.

§ 699.   Future interests; transfer of title

QUALITIES OF EXPECTANT ESTATES.   Future interests pass by succession, will, and transfer, in the same manner as present interests. *(Enacted in 1872.)*

Research References

Miller and Starr California Real Estate § 8:58, in General; Transferable Property Interests.
Miller and Starr California Real Estate § 9:25, Definitions.
Miller and Starr California Real Estate § 9:30, Remainders--Vested or Contingent Nature.
12 Witkin, California Summary 10th Real Property § 169, (S 169) Transferability of Future Interests.

§ 700.   Future interests; possibilities

SAME.   A mere possibility, such as the expectancy of an heir apparent, is not to be deemed an interest of any kind. *(Enacted in 1872.)*

Research References

Miller and Starr California Real Estate § 9:25, Definitions.

§ 701.   Real property; classification of interests

INTERESTS IN REAL PROPERTY.   In respect to real or immovable property, the interests mentioned in this Chapter are denominated estates, and are specially named and classified in Part II of this Division. *(Enacted in 1872.)*

Research References

Miller and Starr California Real Estate § 9:1, "Estate" Defined.
Miller and Starr California Real Estate § 19:2, Lease as Personal Property or Real Property.
12 Witkin, California Summary 10th Real Property § 9, (S 9) Nature of Estates in Real Property.

§ 702. Personal property; classification of interests

SAME. The names and classification of interests in real property have only such application to interests in personal property as is in this Division of the Code expressly provided. *(Enacted in 1872.)*

Research References

Miller and Starr California Real Estate § 9:1, "Estate" Defined.

§ 703. Future interests; recognition

WHAT FUTURE INTERESTS ARE RECOGNIZED. No future interest in property is recognized by the law, except such as is defined in this Division of the Code. *(Enacted in 1872.)*

Research References

Miller and Starr California Real Estate § 9:2, Classification, Generally.
12 Witkin, California Summary 10th Real Property § 127, (S 127) in General.

ARTICLE 2. CONDITIONS OF OWNERSHIP

Section
707. Time of enjoyment of property.
708. Condition precedent or subsequent.
709. Conditions precedent; validity.
710. Conditions in restraint of marriage.
711. Conditions in restraint of alienation.
711.5. Housing purchase or rehabilitation loans by state or local entity directly or indirectly; assumptions; denial; acceleration of principal; change in interest.
712. Conditions restraining right to display sign advertising property for sale, lease or exchange.
713. Local regulations; signs advertising property for sale, lease or exchange.
714. Unenforceability of deeds, contracts or instruments prohibiting or restricting installation or use of solar energy system.
714.1. Solar energy systems; common interest developments; approval; maintenance; indemnification or reimbursement.
714.5. Structures constructed in offsite facility or factory and moved or transported in sections or modules to real property; prohibition of sale, lease, rental or use of real property; management documents.

§ 707. Time of enjoyment of property

FIXING THE TIME OF ENJOYMENT. The time when the enjoyment of property is to begin or end may be determined by computation, or be made to depend on events. In the latter case, the enjoyment is said to be upon condition. *(Enacted in 1872.)*

Research References

Miller and Starr California Real Estate § 24:1, Types of Enforceable Restrictions.

§ 708. Condition precedent or subsequent

CONDITIONS. Conditions are precedent or subsequent. The former fix the beginning, the latter the ending, of the right. *(Enacted in 1872.)*

Research References

Miller and Starr California Real Estate § 24:1, Types of Enforceable Restrictions.

§ 709. Conditions precedent; validity

CERTAIN CONDITIONS PRECEDENT VOID. If a condition precedent requires the performance of an act wrong of itself, the instrument containing it is so far void, and the right cannot exist. If it requires the performance of an act not wrong of itself, but otherwise unlawful, the instrument takes effect and the condition is void. *(Enacted in 1872.)*

Research References

Miller and Starr California Real Estate § 28:95, General Conditions of the Bond.

§ 710. Conditions in restraint of marriage

Conditions imposing restraints upon marriage, except upon the marriage of a minor, are void; but this does not affect limitations where the intent was not to forbid marriage, but only to give the use until marriage. *(Enacted in 1872. Amended by Code Am.1873–74, c. 612, p. 218, § 101.)*

Research References

12 Witkin, California Summary 10th Real Property § 197, Void Condition Against Marriage.
12 Witkin, California Summary 10th Real Property § 198, Valid Limitation Until Marriage.

§ 711. Conditions in restraint of alienation

CONDITIONS RESTRAINING ALIENATION VOID. Conditions restraining alienation, when repugnant to the interest created, are void. *(Enacted in 1872.)*

Research References

Rutter, Cal. Practice Guide: Real Prop. Transactions Ch. 7-B, B. Sale of Ground Lease Tenant's Interest-Preliminary Concerns Re Assignment and Subletting.
Miller and Starr California Real Estate § 2:16, Sale or Assignment.
Miller and Starr California Real Estate § 20:6, The Unruh Civil Rights Act--Age Discrimination in Mobilehome Parks.
Miller and Starr California Real Estate § 24:7, Environmental Covenants, Development Agreements, and Other Statutory Agreements that May Run With the Land.
Miller and Starr California Real Estate § 9:37, Conditions and Covenants Restraining Alienability--In General.
Miller and Starr California Real Estate § 9:38, Conditions and Covenants Restraining Alienability--Specific Types of Restraints.
Miller and Starr California Real Estate § 9:39, Restraints on Use or Occupancy.
Miller and Starr California Real Estate § 19:73, Requirement of Landlord's Consent; Condition to a Transfer--Duty of Landlord to Act "Reasonably".
Miller and Starr California Real Estate § 31:30, Restrictions on Occupancy.
19 NO. 6 Miller & Starr, California Real Estate Newsalert 1, Enforceable Resale Restrictions: Keeping the Doors Open for Long-Term Affordable Housing.
2 Witkin Cal. Proc. 5th Jurisdiction § 294, Decisions Applying General Principle.
12 Witkin, California Summary 10th Real Property § 120, Transfer Rights.
12 Witkin, California Summary 10th Real Property § 190, Rule Against Restraints.
12 Witkin, California Summary 10th Real Property § 192, Types of Invalid Restraints.
12 Witkin, California Summary 10th Real Property § 193, Partial Restraints.
12 Witkin, California Summary 10th Real Property § 196, (S 196) Other Reasonable Restraints.
12 Witkin, California Summary 10th Real Property § 552, (S 552) Adoption of Minority Rule.

12 Witkin, California Summary 10th Real Property § 555, (S 555) Authorized Restrictions on Right.

12 Witkin, California Summary 10th Real Property § 556, (S 556) Illustration of Permissible Restraint on Right.

§ 711.5. Housing purchase or rehabilitation loans by state or local entity directly or indirectly; assumptions; denial; acceleration of principal; change in interest

(a) Notwithstanding the provisions of Sections 711 and 1916.5, a state or local public entity directly or indirectly providing housing purchase or rehabilitation loans shall have the authority to deny assumptions, or require the denial of assumptions, by a subsequent ineligible purchaser or transferee of the prior borrower of the obligation of any such loan made for the purpose of rehabilitating or providing affordable housing. If such a subsequent purchaser or transferee does not meet such an entity's eligibility requirements, that entity may accelerate or may require the acceleration of the principal balance of the loan to be all due and payable upon the sale or transfer of the property.

(b) As a condition of authorizing assumption of a loan pursuant to this section, the entity may recast the repayment schedule for the remainder of the term of the loan by increasing the interest to the current market rate at the time of assumption, or to such lower rate of interest as is the maximum allowed by an entity that provided any insurance or other assistance which results in an assumption being permitted. Any additional increment of interest produced by increasing the rate of interest upon a loan pursuant to this subdivision shall be transmitted or forwarded to the entity for deposit in the specified fund from which the loan was made, or, if no such fund exists, or the public entity has directed otherwise, then to the general fund of such entity.

(c) The state or local public entity providing assistance as specified in this section may implement appropriate measures to assure compliance with this section. (Added by Stats.1979, c. 971, p. 3330, § 1, eff. Sept. 22, 1979.)

Research References

Miller and Starr California Real Estate § 9:38, Conditions and Covenants Restraining Alienability--Specific Types of Restraints.

Miller and Starr California Real Estate § 10:108, Enforceability of the "Due-On-Sale" Clause (The Garn Act).

19 NO. 6 Miller & Starr, California Real Estate Newsalert 1, Enforceable Resale Restrictions: Keeping the Doors Open for Long-Term Affordable Housing.

§ 712. Conditions restraining right to display sign advertising property for sale, lease or exchange

(a) Every provision contained in or otherwise affecting a grant of a fee interest in, or purchase money security instrument upon, real property in this state heretofore or hereafter made, which purports to prohibit or restrict the right of the property owner or his or her agent to display or have displayed on the real property, or on real property owned by others with their consent, or both, signs which are reasonably located, in plain view of the public, are of reasonable dimensions and design, and do not adversely affect public safety, including traffic safety, and which advertise the property for sale, lease, or exchange, or advertise directions to the property, by the property owner or his or her agent is void as an unreasonable restraint upon the power of alienation.

(b) This section shall operate retrospectively, as well as prospectively, to the full extent that it may constitutionally operate retrospectively.

(c) A sign that conforms to the ordinance adopted in conformity with Section 713 shall be deemed to be of reasonable dimension and design pursuant to this section. (Added by Stats.1965, c. 1591, p. 3684, § 1. Amended by Stats.1975, c. 147,

p. 281, § 1; Stats.1983, c. 51, § 1; Stats.1990, c. 1282 (A.B.2949), § 1; Stats.1992, c. 773 (S.B.1474), § 2; Stats.1993, c. 589 (A.B.2211), § 20.)

Research References

Rutter, Cal. Practice Guide: Real Prop. Transactions Ch. 2-E, E. Listing Agreements.

Miller and Starr California Real Estate § 9:41, Restraints on Signs Advertising Property for Sale or Lease.

Miller and Starr California Real Estate § 25B:94, Amendment of the Governing Documents.

18 NO. 5 Miller & Starr, California Real Estate Newsalert 4, Common Interest Developments.

12 Witkin, California Summary 10th Real Property § 203, Restriction Against for Sale Sign on Property.

§ 713. Local regulations; signs advertising property for sale, lease or exchange

(a) Notwithstanding any provision of any ordinance, an owner of real property or his or her agent may display or have displayed on the owner's real property, and on real property owned by others with their consent, signs which are reasonably located, in plain view of the public, are of reasonable dimensions and design, and do not adversely affect public safety, including traffic safety, as determined by the city, county, or city and county, advertising the following:

(1) That the property is for sale, lease, or exchange by the owner or his or her agent.

(2) Directions to the property.

(3) The owner's or agent's name.

(4) The owner's or agent's address and telephone number.

(b) Nothing in this section limits any authority which a person or local governmental entity may have to limit or regulate the display or placement of a sign on a private or public right-of-way. (Added by Stats.1975, c. 147, p. 281, § 2. Amended by Stats.1983, c. 51, § 2; Stats.1990, c. 1282 (A.B.2949), § 2; Stats.1992, c. 773 (S.B.1474), § 3.)

Research References

Rutter, Cal. Practice Guide: Real Prop. Transactions Ch. 2-E, E. Listing Agreements.

Miller and Starr California Real Estate § 9:41, Restraints on Signs Advertising Property for Sale or Lease.

12 Witkin, California Summary 10th Real Property § 203, Restriction Against for Sale Sign on Property.

§ 714. Unenforceability of deeds, contracts or instruments prohibiting or restricting installation or use of solar energy system

(a) Any covenant, restriction, or condition contained in any deed, contract, security instrument, or other instrument affecting the transfer or sale of, or any interest in, real property, and any provision of a governing document, as defined in Section 4150 or 6552, that effectively prohibits or restricts the installation or use of a solar energy system is void and unenforceable.

(b) This section does not apply to provisions that impose reasonable restrictions on solar energy systems. However, it is the policy of the state to promote and encourage the use of solar energy systems and to remove obstacles thereto. Accordingly, reasonable restrictions on a solar energy system are those restrictions that do not significantly increase the cost of the system or significantly decrease its efficiency or specified performance, or that allow for an alternative system of comparable cost, efficiency, and energy conservation benefits.

(c)(1) A solar energy system shall meet applicable health and safety standards and requirements imposed by state and local permitting authorities.

(2) A solar energy system for heating water shall be certified by the Solar Rating Certification Corporation (SRCC) or other nationally recognized certification agencies. SRCC is a nonprofit third party supported by the United States Department of Energy. The certification shall be for the entire solar energy system and installation.

(3) A solar energy system for producing electricity shall also meet all applicable safety and performance standards established by the National Electrical Code, the Institute of Electrical and Electronics Engineers, and accredited testing laboratories such as Underwriters Laboratories and, where applicable, rules of the Public Utilities Commission regarding safety and reliability.

(d) For the purposes of this section:

(1)(A) For solar domestic water heating systems or solar swimming pool heating systems that comply with state and federal law, "significantly" means an amount exceeding 20 percent of the cost of the system or decreasing the efficiency of the solar energy system by an amount exceeding 20 percent, as originally specified and proposed.

(B) For photovoltaic systems that comply with state and federal law, "significantly" means an amount not to exceed two thousand dollars ($2,000) over the system cost as originally specified and proposed, or a decrease in system efficiency of an amount exceeding 20 percent as originally specified and proposed.

(2) "Solar energy system" has the same meaning as defined in paragraphs (1) and (2) of subdivision (a) of Section 801.5.

(e)(1) Whenever approval is required for the installation or use of a solar energy system, the application for approval shall be processed and approved by the appropriate approving entity in the same manner as an application for approval of an architectural modification to the property, and shall not be willfully avoided or delayed.

(2) For an approving entity that is * * * an association, as defined in Section 4080 or 6528, and that is not a public entity, both of the following shall apply:

(A) The approval or denial of an application shall be in writing.

(B) If an application is not denied in writing within 60 days from the date of receipt of the application, the application shall be deemed approved, unless that delay is the result of a reasonable request for additional information.

(f) Any entity, other than a public entity, that willfully violates this section shall be liable to the applicant or other party for actual damages occasioned thereby, and shall pay a civil penalty to the applicant or other party in an amount not to exceed one thousand dollars ($1,000).

(g) In any action to enforce compliance with this section, the prevailing party shall be awarded reasonable attorney's fees.

(h)(1) A public entity that fails to comply with this section may not receive funds from a state-sponsored grant or loan program for solar energy. A public entity shall certify its compliance with the requirements of this section when applying for funds from a state-sponsored grant or loan program.

(2) A local public entity may not exempt residents in its jurisdiction from the requirements of this section. *(Added by Stats.1978, c. 1154, p. 3542, § 3. Amended by Stats.1990, c. 1517 (A.B.3689), § 2, operative July 1, 1991; Stats.1992, c. 1222 (A.B.3554), § 1; Stats.1994, c. 382 (S.B.1553), § 1; Stats.1995, c. 91 (S.B.975), § 16; Stats.2002, c. 570 (S.B.1534), § 1; Stats.2003, c. 290 (A.B.1407), § 1; Stats.2004, c. 789 (A.B.2473), § 2; Stats.2008, c. 40 (A.B.1892), § 1; Stats.2008, c. 539 (A.B.2180), § 2; Stats.2012, c. 181 (A.B.806), § 20, operative Jan. 1, 2014; Stats.2013, c. 605 (S.B.752), § 8.)*

Law Revision Commission Comments

Section 714 is amended to correct cross-references to former Section 1351(a), (j). [40 Cal.L.Rev.Comm. Reports 235 (2010)].

Subdivision (a) of Section 714 is amended to add a cross-reference to Section 6552, reflecting the enactment of the Commercial and Industrial Common Interest Development Act (Civ. Code §§ 6500–6876).

Paragraph (2) of subdivision (e) is amended to add a cross-reference to Section 6528, and to make a conforming terminological change, for the same reason. [42 Cal.L.Rev.Comm. Reports 1 (2012)].

Research References

Miller and Starr California Real Estate § 9:39, Restraints on Use or Occupancy.
Miller and Starr California Real Estate § 14:38, Rights to Protection and Siting of Solar Energy Facilities.
Miller and Starr California Real Estate § 15:11, Solar Easements.
Miller and Starr California Real Estate § 22:12, Obstruction of Light and Air.
Miller and Starr California Real Estate § 24:16, Creation--Common Interest Developments.
Miller and Starr California Real Estate § 24:22, Types of Enforceable Restrictions--Solar Shade and Energy Systems.
Miller and Starr California Real Estate § 25B:75, Restrictions on Solar Energy Systems.
15 NO. 4 Miller & Starr, California Real Estate Newsalert 6, Covenants.
19 NO. 3 Miller & Starr, California Real Estate Newsalert 1, The Solar Shade Control Act- from Trees Versus Solar to Trees and Solar?
19 NO. 4 Miller & Starr, California Real Estate Newsalert 6, Common Interest Developments.
20 NO. 5 Miller & Starr, California Real Estate Newsalert 8, Covenants.
22 NO. 3 Miller & Starr, California Real Estate Newsalert 4, Common Interest Developments.
12 Witkin, California Summary 10th Real Property § 118, Improvements and Modifications.
12 Witkin, California Summary 10th Real Property § 385, Solar Easement.
12 Witkin, California Summary 10th Real Property § 444, No Prohibition of Solar Energy Systems.

§ 714.1. Solar energy systems; common interest developments; approval; maintenance; indemnification or reimbursement

Notwithstanding Section 714, any association, as defined in Section 4080 or 6528, may impose reasonable provisions which:

(a) Restrict the installation of solar energy systems installed in common areas, as defined in Section 4095 or 6532, to those systems approved by the association.

(b) Require the owner of a separate interest, as defined in Section 4185 or 6564, to obtain the approval of the association for the installation of a solar energy system in a separate interest owned by another.

(c) Provide for the maintenance, repair, or replacement of roofs or other building components.

(d) Require installers of solar energy systems to indemnify or reimburse the association or its members for loss or damage caused by the installation, maintenance, or use of the solar energy system. *(Added by Stats.1992, c. 1222 (A.B.3554), § 2. Amended by Stats.2012, c. 181 (A.B.806), § 21, operative Jan. 1, 2014; Stats.2013, c. 605 (S.B.752), § 9.)*

Law Revision Commission Comments

Section 714.1 is amended to correct cross-references to former Section 1351(a), (b), (l). [40 Cal.L.Rev.Comm. Reports 235 (2010)].

Section 714.1 is amended to add cross-references to Sections 6528, 6532, and 6534, reflecting the enactment of the Commercial and Industrial Common Interest Development Act (Civ. Code §§ 6500–6876). [42 Cal.L.Rev.Comm. Reports 1 (2012)].

Research References

Miller and Starr California Real Estate § 9:39, Restraints on Use or Occupancy.

Miller and Starr California Real Estate § 14:38, Rights to Protection and Siting of Solar Energy Facilities.

Miller and Starr California Real Estate § 15:11, Solar Easements.

Miller and Starr California Real Estate § 24:22, Types of Enforceable Restrictions--Solar Shade and Energy Systems.

Miller and Starr California Real Estate § 25B:75, Restrictions on Solar Energy Systems.

19 NO. 3 Miller & Starr, California Real Estate Newsalert 1, The Solar Shade Control Act- from Trees Versus Solar to Trees and Solar?

12 Witkin, California Summary 10th Real Property § 118, Improvements and Modifications.

12 Witkin, California Summary 10th Real Property § 444, No Prohibition of Solar Energy Systems.

§ 714.5. Structures constructed in offsite facility or factory and moved or transported in sections or modules to real property; prohibition of sale, lease, rental or use of real property; management documents

The covenants, conditions, and restrictions or other management documents shall not prohibit the sale, lease, rent, or use of real property on the basis that the structure intended for occupancy on the real property is constructed in an offsite facility or factory, and subsequently moved or transported in sections or modules to the real property. Nothing herein shall preclude the governing instruments from being uniformly applied to all structures subject to the covenants, conditions, and restrictions or other management documents.

This section shall apply to covenants, conditions, and restrictions or other management documents adopted on and after the effective date of this section. *(Added by Stats.1987, c. 1339, § 1.)*

Research References

Miller and Starr California Real Estate § 24:22, Types of Enforceable Restrictions--Solar Shade and Energy Systems.

Miller and Starr California Real Estate § 24:32, Defenses to Enforcement--Public Policy or Discrimination.

Miller and Starr California Real Estate § 25B:66, Restrictions on Alienation.

ARTICLE 3. DURATION OF LEASES

Section

715. Execution of certain leases; commencement in possession within 30 years.

717. Leases of agricultural land; duration.

718. Leases; town or city lots; municipal property; tidelands and submerged lands.

718f. Leases; production of minerals, oil, gas or other hydrocarbons; duration.

719. Leases; city property; maximum term; conditions.

§ 715. Execution of certain leases; commencement in possession within 30 years

A lease to commence at a time certain or upon the happening of a future event becomes invalid if its term does not actually commence in possession within 30 years after its execution. *(Added by Stats.1991, c. 156 (A.B.1577), § 3.)*

Law Revision Commission Comments

Former Section 715 is generally superseded by the Uniform Statutory Rule Against Perpetuities in Probate Code Sections 21200–21225. See Prob.Code § 21225(e) (interests held by charities and government that are excluded from rule). [20 Cal.L.Rev.Comm.Reports 2501 (1990)].

Section 715 is a new provision that places a 30–year limit on leases that might have been voidable future interests under the rule against perpetuities provided in former Civil Code Section 715.2. [20 Cal.L.Rev.Comm.Reports 2501 (1990)].

Research References

Rutter, Cal. Practice Guide: Real Prop. Transactions Ch. 7-A, A. Nature and Characteristics of Ground Lease.

Miller and Starr California Real Estate § 9:35, Rule Against Perpetuities--Transfers and Interests Subject to the Rule.

Miller and Starr California Real Estate § 19:34, Contract Term Provided in the Lease--Commencement Upon Completion of Improvements.

12 Witkin, California Summary 10th Real Property § 173, Constitution and Early Statutes.

12 Witkin, California Summary 10th Real Property § 189, Other Limitations on Excluded Transactions.

12 Witkin, California Summary 10th Real Property § 525, Statutory Restrictions.

§ 717. Leases of agricultural land; duration

No lease or grant of land for agricultural or horticultural purposes for a longer period than 51 years, in which shall be reserved any rent or service of any kind, shall be valid. *(Enacted in 1872. Amended by Stats.1895, c. 82, p. 75, § 1; Stats.1909, c. 662, p. 1000, § 1; Stats.1915, c. 176, p. 349, § 1; Stats.1963, c. 1906, p. 3897, § 1.)*

Research References

California Real Estate Forms (Miller & Starr) § 2:27, Ground Lease.

Rutter, Cal. Practice Guide: Real Prop. Transactions Ch. 7-A, A. Nature and Characteristics of Ground Lease.

Miller and Starr California Real Estate § 19:2, Lease as Personal Property or Real Property.

Miller and Starr California Real Estate § 19:33, Contract Term Provided in the Lease.

12 Witkin, California Summary 10th Real Property § 525, Statutory Restrictions.

§ 718. Leases; town or city lots; municipal property; tidelands and submerged lands

No lease or grant of any town or city lot, which reserves any rent or service of any kind, and which provides for a leasing or granting period in excess of 99 years, shall be valid. The property owned by, or that held by, or under the management and control of, any municipality, or any department or board thereof, may be leased for a period not to exceed 55 years. The property of any municipality not acquired for park purposes may, for the purpose of producing, or effecting the production of minerals, oil, gas or other hydrocarbon substances, be leased for a period not to exceed 35 years. Any tidelands or submerged lands, granted to any city by the State of California, may be leased for a period not to exceed 66 years unless the grant from the state of the use thereof provides specifically the term for which said lands may be leased. Tidelands and submerged lands owned or controlled by any city, together with the wharves, docks, piers and other structures or improvements thereon, and so much of the uplands abutting thereon as, in the judgment of the city council, or other governing body, of said city, may be necessary for the proper development and use of its waterfront and harbor facilities, may be leased for a period not to exceed 66 years. Said tidelands, submerged lands and uplands may be so leased only for industrial uses, the improvement and development of any harbor, or harbors, of said city, the construction and maintenance of wharves, docks, piers or bulkhead piers, or any other public use or purpose consistent with the requirements of commerce or navigation at, or in, any such harbor or harbors. *(Enacted in 1872. Amended by Stats.1903, c. 210, p. 247, § 1; Stats.1911, c. 708, p. 1391, § 1; Stats.1915, c. 176, p. 349, § 2; Stats.1917, c. 572, p. 798, § 1; Stats.1927, c. 689, p. 1173, § 1; Stats.1929, c. 170, p. 322, § 1; Stats.1935, c. 695, p. 1893, § 1; Stats.1941, c. 492, p. 1800, § 1; Stats.1961, c. 2010, p. 4220, § 1; Stats.1967, c. 228, p. 1359, § 1.)*

Research References

California Real Estate Forms (Miller & Starr) § , Ground Lease.

Rutter, Cal. Practice Guide: Real Prop. Transactions Ch. 7-A, A. Nature and Characteristics of Ground Lease.

Miller and Starr California Real Estate § 8:38, Conveyance by a Public Entity.

Miller and Starr California Real Estate § 19:25, Capacity of the Parties--Lease of Property Owned by the State, County, or City.

Miller and Starr California Real Estate § 19:33, Contract Term Provided in the Lease.

Miller and Starr California Real Estate § 19:40, Successive Extensions or Renewals.

22 NO. 6 Miller & Starr, California Real Estate Newsalert 18, Landlord and Tenant.

12 Witkin, California Summary 10th Real Property § 189, Other Limitations on Excluded Transactions.

12 Witkin, California Summary 10th Real Property § 525, Statutory Restrictions.

§ 718f. Leases; production of minerals, oil, gas or other hydrocarbons; duration

A lease of land for the purpose of effecting the production of minerals, oil, gas, or other hydrocarbon substances from other lands may be made for a period certain or determinable by any future event prescribed by the parties but no such lease shall be enforceable after 99 years from the commencement of the term thereof. *(Added by Stats.1953, c. 1344, p. 2904, § 1.)*

Research References

California Real Estate Forms (Miller & Starr) § 2:27, Ground Lease.

Rutter, Cal. Practice Guide: Real Prop. Transactions Ch. 7-A, A. Nature and Characteristics of Ground Lease.

Miller and Starr California Real Estate § 17:24, Minerals--Oil and Gas Leases.

Miller and Starr California Real Estate § 19:33, Contract Term Provided in the Lease.

12 Witkin, California Summary 10th Real Property § 525, Statutory Restrictions.

12 Witkin, California Summary 10th Real Property § 792, (S 792) Ordinary Lease Distinguished.

§ 719. Leases; city property; maximum term; conditions

Notwithstanding the 55-year limitation imposed by Section 718, property owned by, or held by, or under the management and control of, any city, or any department or board thereof, may be leased for a period which exceeds 55 years but does not exceed 99 years, if all of the following conditions are met:

(a) The lease shall be subject to periodic review by the city and shall take into consideration the then current market conditions. The local legislative body may, prior to final execution of the lease, establish the lease provisions which will periodically be reviewed, and determine when those provisions are to be reviewed.

(b) Any lease entered into by any city pursuant to this section shall be authorized by an ordinance adopted by the legislative body. The ordinance shall be subject to referendum in the manner prescribed by law for ordinances of cities.

(c) Prior to adopting an ordinance authorizing a lease, the legislative body shall hold a public hearing. Notice of the time and place of the hearing shall be published pursuant to Section 6066 of the Government Code, in one or more newspapers of general circulation within the city and shall be mailed to any person requesting special notice, to any present tenant of the public property, and to all owners of land adjoining the property.

(d) Any lease shall be awarded to the bidder which, in the determination of the legislative body, offers the greatest economic return to the city, after competitive bidding conducted in the manner determined by the legislative body. Notice inviting bids shall be published pursuant to Section 6066 in one or more newspapers of general circulation within the city.

(e) The provisions of subdivisions (b), (c), and (d) of this section do not apply to any charter city, which may utilize a procedure as specified by charter or adopted by ordinance in accordance with its charter.

(f) This section shall not apply to leases of property acquired for park purposes; to leases for the purpose of producing mineral, oil, gas, or other hydrocarbon substances; nor to leases of tidelands or submerged lands or improvements thereon. *(Added by Stats.1983, c. 720, § 1.)*

Research References

Rutter, Cal. Practice Guide: Real Prop. Transactions Ch. 7-A, A. Nature and Characteristics of Ground Lease.

Miller and Starr California Real Estate § 19:2, Lease as Personal Property or Real Property.

Miller and Starr California Real Estate § 8:38, Conveyance by a Public Entity.

Miller and Starr California Real Estate § 19:25, Capacity of the Parties--Lease of Property Owned by the State, County, or City.

Miller and Starr California Real Estate § 19:33, Contract Term Provided in the Lease.

12 Witkin, California Summary 10th Real Property § 525, Statutory Restrictions.

ARTICLE 4. ACCUMULATIONS

Section

722. Dispositions of income of property; governing rules.

723. Accumulations; validity.

724. Accumulation of income of property; time limit; exception.

725. Accumulations; income of property; directions beyond limit.

726. Accumulations; destitute beneficiaries.

§ 722. Dispositions of income of property; governing rules

Dispositions of the income of property to accrue and to be received at any time subsequent to the execution of the instrument creating such disposition are governed by the rules relating to future interests. *(Enacted in 1872. Amended by Stats.1991, c. 156 (A.B.1577), § 12.)*

Law Revision Commission Comments

Section 722 is amended to reflect relocation of statutes concerning perpetuities to the Probate Code. See Prob.Code §§ 21200–21231 (superseding former Civil Code §§ 715–716.5). [20 Cal.L.Rev.Comm.Reports 2501 (1990)].

Research References

Miller and Starr California Real Estate § 9:35, Rule Against Perpetuities--Transfers and Interests Subject to the Rule.

§ 723. Accumulations; validity

Accumulations, when void. All directions for the accumulation of the income of property, except such as are allowed by this Title, are void. *(Enacted in 1872.)*

Research References

13 Witkin, California Summary 10th Trusts § 23, Other Provisions Governing Trusts.

13 Witkin, California Summary 10th Trusts § 37, (S 37) Rule Against Accumulations.

§ 724. Accumulation of income of property; time limit; exception

(a) An accumulation of the income of property may be directed by any will, trust or transfer in writing sufficient to pass the property or create the trust out of which the fund is to arise, for the benefit of one or more persons, objects or purposes, but may not extend beyond the time permitted for the vesting of future interests.

(b) Notwithstanding subdivision (a), the income arising from real or personal property held in a trust forming part of a profit-sharing plan of an employer for the exclusive benefit of its employees or their beneficiaries or forming part of a retirement plan formed primarily for the purpose of providing benefits for employees on or after retirement may be permitted to accumulate until the fund is sufficient, in the opinion of the trustee or trustees, to accomplish the purposes of the trust. *(Enacted in 1872. Amended by Stats.1929, c. 143, p. 276, § 1; Stats.1959, c. 470, p. 2405, § 4; Stats.1991, c. 156 (A.B.1577), § 13.)*

Law Revision Commission Comments

Section 724 is amended to reflect the revision and relocation of the statutes concerning perpetuities to the Probate Code. See Prob. Code §§ 21200–21231 (superseding former Civil Code §§ 715–716.5). Subdivision (b) restates the last clause of former Section 715.3 relating to accumulations without substantive change. [20 Cal.L.Rev.Comm.Reports 2501 (1990)].

Research References

Miller and Starr California Real Estate § 9:35, Rule Against Perpetuities--Transfers and Interests Subject to the Rule.
13 Witkin, California Summary 10th Trusts § 37, (S 37) Rule Against Accumulations.

§ 725. Accumulations; income of property; directions beyond limit

If the direction for an accumulation of the income of property is for a longer term than is limited in the last section, the direction only, whether separable or not from the other provisions of the instrument, is void as respects the time beyond the limit prescribed in said last section, and no other part of such instrument is affected by the void portion of such direction. *(Enacted in 1872. Amended by Stats.1929, c. 143, p. 276, § 2.)*

Research References

22 NO. 3 Miller & Starr, California Real Estate Newsalert 1, Show Me Your Papers: Sales and Assignments of Secured Real Estate Loans and the California Foreclosure Process.
13 Witkin, California Summary 10th Trusts § 37, (S 37) Rule Against Accumulations.

§ 726. Accumulations; destitute beneficiaries

When one or more persons for whose benefit an accumulation of income has been directed is or are destitute of other sufficient means of support or education, the proper court, upon application, may direct a suitable sum to be applied thereto out of the fund directed to be accumulated for the benefit of such person or persons. *(Enacted in 1872. Amended by Stats.1929, c. 143, p. 276, § 3.)*

Research References

Miller and Starr California Real Estate § 33:39, Secured Creditor Actions--Inspection for Hazardous Substances.
Miller and Starr California Real Estate § 34:57, Buyer's Default; Seller's Remedies.
13 Witkin, California Summary 10th Trusts § 37, (S 37) Rule Against Accumulations.
13 Witkin, California Summary 10th Trusts § 210, Changed Circumstances.

CHAPTER 2.6. LEGAL ESTATES PRINCIPAL AND INCOME LAW

§ 731. Short title

This chapter may be cited as the Legal Estates Principal and Income Law. *(Added by Stats.1968, c. 193, p. 482, § 1, eff. May 28, 1968, operative July 1, 1968.)*

Research References

Miller and Starr California Real Estate § 9:33, The Legal Estates Principal and Income Law.
Miller and Starr California Real Estate § 13:62, Property Eligible for the Probate Homestead.
Miller and Starr California Real Estate § 22:11, Indecent or Offensive Acts--Adult Entertainment; First Amendment Protection.
Miller and Starr California Real Estate § 22:28, Actions by Public Entities.
21 NO. 4 Miller & Starr, California Real Estate Newsalert 15, Landowners' Liability.
12 Witkin, California Summary 10th Real Property § 170, (S 170) Principal and Income Law.
13 Witkin, California Summary 10th Trusts § 167, (S 167) Adoption of Revised Act.
14 Witkin, California Summary 10th Wills and Probate § 772, (S 772) Liability of Property.

§ 731.01. Effect on personal income tax and bank and corporation tax

Nothing in this chapter shall affect the provisions of the Personal Income Tax Law and the Bank and Corporation Tax Law. *(Added by Stats.1968, c. 193, p. 482, § 1, eff. May 28, 1968, operative July 1, 1968.)*

§ 731.02. Applicability to transactions by which principal established without interposition of a trust

This chapter shall apply to all transactions by which a principal was established without the interposition of a trust on or after September 13, 1941, or is hereafter so established. Transactions by which a principal is held in trust are governed by Chapter 3 (commencing with Section 16300) of Part 4 of Division 9 of the Probate Code. *(Added by Stats.1968, c. 193, p. 482, § 1, eff. May 28, 1968, operative July 1, 1968. Amended by Stats.1986, c. 820, § 3, operative July 1, 1987.)*

Law Revision Commission Comments

Section 731.02 is amended to correct a cross-reference to the Revised Uniform Principal and Income Act. [18 Cal.L.Rev.Comm. Reports 501 (1986)].

Research References

Miller and Starr California Real Estate § 9:33, The Legal Estates Principal and Income Law.

12 Witkin, California Summary 10th Real Property § 170, (S 170)
    Principal and Income Law.

§ 731.03. Definitions

(a) "Principal" as used in this chapter means any realty or personalty which has been so set aside or limited by the owner thereof or a person thereto legally empowered that it and any substitutions for it are eventually to be conveyed, delivered, or paid to a person, while the return therefrom or use thereof or any part of such return or use is in the meantime to be taken or received by or held for accumulation for the same or another person;

(b) "Income" as used in this chapter means the return derived from principal;

(c) "Tenant" as used in this chapter means the person to whom income is presently or currently payable, or for whom it is accumulated or who is entitled to the beneficial use of the principal presently and for a time prior to its distribution;

(d) "Remainderman" as used in this chapter means the person ultimately entitled to the principal, whether named or designated by the terms of the transaction by which the principal was established or determined by operation of law. *(Added by Stats.1968, c. 193, p. 482, § 1, eff. May 28, 1968, operative July 1, 1968.)*

Research References

Miller and Starr California Real Estate § 9:33, The Legal Estates
    Principal and Income Law.

§ 731.04. Law governing ascertainment of income and principal and apportionment of receipts and expenses; exception

This chapter shall govern the ascertainment of income and principal and the apportionment of receipts and expenses between tenants and remaindermen in all cases where a principal has been established without the interposition of a trust, except that in the establishment of the principal, provision may be made touching all matters covered by this chapter, and the person establishing the principal may himself direct the manner of ascertainment of income and principal and the apportionment of receipts and expenses or grant discretion to the tenant or other person to do so, and such provision and direction, where not otherwise contrary to law shall control notwithstanding this chapter. The exercise by the tenant or other designated person, of such discretionary power if in good faith and according to his best judgment, shall be conclusive, irrespective of whether it may be in accordance with the determination which the court having jurisdiction would have made. *(Added by Stats.1968, c. 193, p. 482, § 1, eff. May 28, 1968, operative July 1, 1968.)*

Research References

Miller and Starr California Real Estate § 9:33, The Legal Estates
    Principal and Income Law.
12 Witkin, California Summary 10th Real Property § 170, (S 170)
    Principal and Income Law.

§ 731.05. Principal and income

(a) All receipts of money or other property paid or delivered as rent of realty or hire of personalty, or interest on money loaned, or interest on or the rental or use value of property wrongfully withheld or tortiously damaged or otherwise in return for the use of principal, shall be deemed income unless otherwise expressly provided in this chapter. Dividends on corporate shares, payable in stock or otherwise, shall be deemed income except as provided in Section 731.07.

(b) All receipts of money or other property paid or delivered as the consideration for the sale or other transfer, not a leasing or letting, of property forming a part of principal, or as a repayment of loans, or in liquidation of the assets of a corporation, or as the proceeds of property taken on eminent domain proceedings where separate awards to tenant and remainderman are not made, or as proceeds of insurance upon property forming a part of the principal except where such insurance has been issued for the benefit of either tenant or remainderman alone, or otherwise as a refund or replacement or change in form of principal, shall be deemed principal unless otherwise expressly provided in this chapter. Any profit or loss resulting upon any change in form of principal shall inure to or fall upon principal, except in the case of property referred to and defined by Section 731.14, in which case the provisions of Section 731.14 shall govern.

(c) All income, after payment of expenses properly chargeable to it, shall be paid and delivered to the tenant or retained by him if already in his possession or held for accumulation where legally so directed by the terms of the transaction by which the principal was established; while the principal shall be held for ultimate distribution as determined by the terms of the transaction by which it was established or by law, except in the case of property referred to and defined by Section 731.14, in which case the provisions of Section 731.14 shall govern. *(Added by Stats.1968, c. 193, p. 483, § 1, eff. May 28, 1968, operative July 1, 1968.)*

§ 731.06. Death of tenant; payments already made; income received after termination of right to income

Whenever a tenant's right to income shall cease by death, or in any other manner, all payments theretofore actually paid to the tenant shall belong to the tenant or to his personal representative; all income actually received after such termination shall be paid to the person next entitled to income by the terms of the transaction by which the principal was established. *(Added by Stats.1968, c. 193, p. 483, § 1, eff. May 28, 1968, operative July 1, 1968.)*

Research References

Miller and Starr California Real Estate § 9:33, The Legal Estates
    Principal and Income Law.
12 Witkin, California Summary 10th Real Property § 170, (S 170)
    Principal and Income Law.

§ 731.07. Interests in corporations and distribution of corporate assets

(a) All dividends on shares of a corporation forming a part of the principal which are payable

(1) In shares of the declaring corporation of the same kind and rank as the shares on which such dividend is paid; and

(2) In shares of the declaring corporation of a different kind or rank to the extent that they represent a capitalization of surplus not derived from earnings, shall be deemed principal.

Subject to the provisions of this section, all dividends, other than those awarded to principal under (1) and (2) above, including ordinary and extraordinary dividends and dividends payable in shares or other securities or obligations of corporations other than the declaring corporation, shall be deemed income.

Where the tenant shall have the option of receiving a dividend either in cash or in the shares of the declaring corporation, it shall be considered as a cash dividend and deemed income, irrespective of the choice made by the tenant except as provided in subdivision (f) of this section.

(b) All rights to subscribe to the shares or other securities or obligations of a corporation accruing on account of the ownership of shares or other securities in such corporation, and the proceeds of any sale of such rights, shall be deemed principal. All rights to subscribe to the shares or other securities or obligations of a corporation accruing on account of the ownership of shares or other securities in another corporation, and the proceeds of any sale of such rights shall be deemed income.

(c) Where the assets of a corporation are liquidated, amounts paid upon corporate shares as cash dividends declared before such liquidation occurred or as arrears of preferred or guaranteed dividends shall be deemed income; all other amounts paid upon corporate shares on disbursement of the corporate assets to the stockholders shall be deemed principal. All disbursements of corporate assets to the stockholders, whenever made, which are designated by the corporation as a return of capital or division of corporate property shall be deemed principal.

(d) Where a corporation succeeds another by merger, consolidation, or reorganization or otherwise acquires its assets, and the corporate shares of the succeeding corporation are issued to the shareholders of the original corporation in like proportion to, or in substitution for, their shares of the original corporation, the two corporations shall be considered a single corporation in applying the provisions of this section. But, two corporations shall not be considered a single corporation under this section merely because one owns corporate shares of or otherwise controls or directs the other.

(e) In applying this section the date when a dividend accrues to the person who is entitled to it shall be held to be the date specified by the corporation as the one on which the stockholders entitled thereto are determined, or in default thereof the date of declaration of the dividend.

(f) Distributions made from ordinary income by a regulated investment company or by a trust qualifying and electing to be taxed under federal law as a real estate investment trust are income. All other distributions made by the company or trust, including distributions from capital gains, depreciation, or depletion, whether in the form of cash or an option to take new stock or cash or an option to purchase additional shares, are principal.

(g) The tenant may rely upon the statement of the paying corporation as to whether dividends are paid from profits or earnings or are a return of capital or division of corporate property, and as to any other fact, relevant under any provision of this chapter, concerning the source or character of dividends or disbursements of corporate assets. *(Added by Stats.1968, c. 193, p. 484, § 1, eff. May 28, 1968, operative July 1, 1968.)*

Research References

12 Witkin, California Summary 10th Real Property § 170, (S 170) Principal and Income Law.

§ 731.08. Bonds or other obligations for payment of money

Where any part of the principal consists of bonds or other obligations for the payment of money, they shall be deemed principal at their inventory value as fixed by the appraiser or appraisers regularly appointed by the court, or, in default thereof, at their market value at the time the principal was established, or at their cost where purchased later, regardless of their par or maturity value; and upon their respective maturities or upon their sale or other disposition any loss or gain realized thereon shall fall upon or inure to the principal, except in the case of property referred to and defined by Section 731.14, in which case the provisions of Section 731.14 shall govern. Where any part of the principal consists of a bond or other obligation for the payment of money, bearing no stated interest but redeemable at maturity or a future time at an amount in excess of the amount in consideration of which it was issued, such accretion, as when realized, shall inure to income. *(Added by Stats.1968, c. 193, p. 485, § 1, eff. May 28, 1968, operative July 1, 1968.)*

Research References

12 Witkin, California Summary 10th Real Property § 170, (S 170) Principal and Income Law.

§ 731.09. Use of principal in continuation of business

(a) Whenever a tenant is authorized by the terms of the transaction by which the principal was established or by law, to use any part of the principal in the continuance of a business which the original owner of the property comprising the principal had been carrying on, the net profits of such business attributable to such principal shall be deemed income.

(b) Where such business consists of buying and selling property, the net profits for any period shall be ascertained by deducting from the gross returns during, and the inventory value of the property at the end of, such period, the expenses during, and the inventory value of the property at the beginning of, such period.

(c) Where such business does not consist of buying and selling property, the net income shall be computed in accordance with the customary practice of such business, but not in such way as to decrease the principal.

(d) Any increase in the value of the principal used in such business shall be deemed principal, and all losses in any one calendar year, after the income from such business for that year has been exhausted, shall fall upon principal. *(Added by Stats.1968, c. 193, p. 485, § 1, eff. May 28, 1968, operative July 1, 1968.)*

Research References

12 Witkin, California Summary 10th Real Property § 170, (S 170) Principal and Income Law.

§ 731.10. Animals used in business or held as part of principal

Where any part of the principal consists of animals employed in business, the provisions of Section 731.09 shall apply; and in other cases where the animals are held as a part of the principal partly or wholly because of the offspring or increase which they are expected to produce, all offspring or increase shall be deemed principal to the extent necessary to maintain the original number of such animals and the remainder shall be deemed income; and in all other cases such offspring or increase shall be deemed income. *(Added by Stats.1968, c. 193, p. 486, § 1, eff. May 28, 1968, operative July 1, 1968.)*

Research References

12 Witkin, California Summary 10th Real Property § 170, (S 170) Principal and Income Law.

§ 731.11. Timber, mineral, oil or gas, or other natural resources lands

(a) Where any part of the principal consists of property in lands from which may be taken timber, minerals, oils, gas, or other natural resources, and the tenant in possession is not under a duty to change the form of the investment of the principal, or (the duty to change the form of the investment being absent) is authorized by law or by the terms of the transaction by which the principal was established, to lease or otherwise develop such natural resources, and no provision is made for the disposition of the net proceeds thereof after the payment of expenses and carrying charges on such property, such proceeds shall be deemed income, whether received as rent or bonus on a lease or as a consideration, by way of royalties or otherwise for the permanent severance of such natural resources from the lands. A duty to change the form of the investment shall be negatived, and authority to develop such natural resources shall be deemed to exist (not excluding other cases where appropriate intent is manifested) where: (1) the resources or the right to exploit them is specifically devised or granted, or (2) where development or exploitation of the resources had begun prior to the transaction by which the principal was established, or (3) where by the terms of that transaction a general authority to lease or otherwise develop is conferred, or (4) where the lands are directed to be retained. The fact that such property received upon creation of the principal does not fall within the category of investments which the tenant or a trustee would be authorized to make under the law or the terms of the particular instrument by which the principal is established, nor the conferring of a mere authority, as distinguished from a direction, to sell such property, shall not be deemed to evidence an intent that the form of the investment shall be changed.

(b) Where any part of the principal consists of property in lands containing such natural resources, and the conditions under which the proceeds thereof become income shall not exist, then in the absence of the expression of contrary intent in the terms of the transaction by which the principal was established, all such proceeds from such resources, not in excess of 5 percent per annum of the inventory value of such resources as fixed by the appraiser or appraisers regularly appointed by the court, or in default thereof their fair market value at the time the principal was established, or their cost if acquired later, shall be deemed income and the remainder principal.

(c) Nothing in this section shall be construed to abrogate or extend any right which may otherwise have accrued by law to a tenant to develop or work such natural resources for his own benefit. (Added by Stats.1968, c. 193, p. 486, § 1, eff. May 28, 1968, operative July 1, 1968.)

Research References

12 Witkin, California Summary 10th Real Property § 170, (S 170) Principal and Income Law.

§ 731.12. Property subject to depletion

Where any part of the principal consists of property subject to depletion, such as leaseholds, patents, copyrights, and royalty rights, and the tenant in possession is not under a duty to change the form of the investment of the principal, the full amount of rents, royalties, or income from the property shall be income to the tenant; but where the tenant is under a duty to change the form of the investment, either at once or as soon as a reasonable price, not representing an undue sacrifice of value, may be obtained, then the rents, royalties or income from such property not in excess of 5 percent per annum of its inventory value as fixed by the appraiser or appraisers regularly appointed by the court, or in default thereof its market value at the time the principal was established or at its cost where purchased later, shall be deemed income and the remainder principal. (Added by Stats.1968, c. 193, p. 487, § 1, eff. May 28, 1968, operative July 1, 1968.)

Research References

12 Witkin, California Summary 10th Real Property § 170, (S 170) Principal and Income Law.

§ 731.13. Delay in change of investment

(a) Where any part of a principal in the possession of a tenant consists of realty or personalty which for more than a year and until disposed of as hereinafter stated has not produced an average net income of at least 1 percent per annum of its inventory value as fixed by the appraiser or appraisers regularly appointed by the court, or in default thereof its market value at the time the principal was established or of its cost where purchased or otherwise acquired later, and the tenant is under a duty to change the form of the investment as soon as a reasonable price, not representing an undue sacrifice of value, may be obtained and such change is delayed, but is made before

the principal is finally distributed, then the tenant shall be entitled to share in the net proceeds received from the property as delayed income to the extent hereinafter stated.

(b) Such income shall be the difference between the net proceeds received from the property and the amount which, had it been placed at simple interest at the rate of 5 percent per annum for the period during which the change was delayed, would have produced the net proceeds at the time of change, but in no event shall such income be more than the amount by which the net proceeds exceed the inventory value of the property as fixed by the appraiser or appraisers regularly appointed by the court, or in default thereof its market value at the time the principal was established or its cost where purchased later. The net proceeds shall consist of the gross proceeds received from the property less any expenses incurred in disposing of it and less all carrying charges which have been paid out of principal during the period while it has been unproductive.

(c) The change shall be taken to have been delayed from the time when the duty to make it first arose, which shall be presumed in the absence of evidence to the contrary, to be one year after the tenant first received the property if then unproductive, otherwise one year after it became unproductive.

(d) If the tenant has received any income from the property or has had any beneficial use thereof during the period while the change has been delayed, his share of the delayed income shall be reduced by the amount of such income received or the value of the use had.

(e) As between successive tenants, or a tenant and a remainderman, delayed income shall be apportioned in the same manner as provided for income by Section 731.06. (Added by Stats.1968, c. 193, p. 487, § 1, eff. May 28, 1968, operative July 1, 1968.)

Research References

12 Witkin, California Summary 10th Real Property § 170, (S 170) Principal and Income Law.

§ 731.14. Obligations for payment of money

(a) Where any part of the principal in possession of the tenant consists of an obligation for the payment of money secured by a mortgage or other hypothecation of real or personal property, and by reason of the enforcement of such obligation or by agreement in lieu of enforcement the tenant acquires any property, real or personal, of whatsoever kind, including a money judgment, such property shall be treated as a single substituted asset, and thereafter all income therefrom, expenses incident thereto and proceeds received upon sale, satisfaction, or transfer thereof, not a leasing or letting, excepting gain or profit on such sale, satisfaction or transfer, shall be apportioned in the same manner as provided by this chapter for property of like character acquired by purchase or held as a part of the estate at the time the principal was established.

Gain or profit realized on sale, satisfaction, or transfer, not a leasing or a letting, of property referred to in this section shall be credited to the income in an amount up to, but not exceeding, the accrued unpaid interest on the original obligation secured by such property as of the date of its acquisition by enforcement of the obligation or agreement in lieu thereof, and the balance shall be credited to principal. Such credit to income on account of accrued interest shall be in addition to any and all other credits due income by the terms of any other section of this chapter. Should any portion of such credit to income on account of accrued interest be in a form other than cash, then, and in that event, the full amount of such credit to income shall be paid first out of any sums received from the conversion of such asset into cash whether by payment, sale, or transfer before any sums so received shall be paid to principal.

As between successive tenants or a tenant and a remainderman, all sums paid hereunder on account of accrued interest shall be apportioned in the same manner as provided for income by Section 731.06.

The cost price of the property shall be the unpaid balance of the principal sum of the debt secured by such property, plus all sums whenever paid on any of the following items:

(1) All costs, charges, and expenses incident to the acquisition of such property;

(2) All taxes, bonds, and assessments, or any of them, which were payable at the date of the acquisition of such property by the tenant, excepting, however, interest accruing thereon from the date of the acquisition of such property by the tenant; and all such sums shall be a charge against the principal.

(b) Upon the sale, surrender, or other disposition of a bond, debenture, note, or other evidence of an indebtedness, voluntarily created, or of a certificate of deposit evidencing the deposit of any such instrument with a protective or reorganization committee, or of stock or other security received through participation in the enforcement of such obligation or the foreclosure of the security therefor, upon which bond or other obligation there is overdue unpaid interest which accrued after the establishment of the principal, the proceeds realized upon such sale, surrender, or other disposition, after repayment (1) of expenses incurred in connection therewith and (2) of any sums paid to protect or preserve such security, shall be divided pro rata between income and principal, computing interest at the rate specified in such obligation. The amount allocable to income shall in no case exceed the interest accrued and unpaid on the original obligation up to the time of such sale or other disposition or, where another security has been received in lieu of the original obligation, the income which would have accrued on the latter up to such time, less income received from the original or the substituted security. The terms sale, surrender, or other disposition, as above used, shall include compromise, settlement, accord and satisfaction, and similar arrangements. *(Added by Stats.1968, c. 193, p. 488, § 1, eff. May 28, 1968, operative July 1, 1968.)*

Research References

18 NO. 2 Miller & Starr, California Real Estate Newsalert 1, The Marketable Record Title Act- Is Private Foreclosure Barred Ten Years After Maturity, or Not?
12 Witkin, California Summary 10th Real Property § 170, (S 170) Principal and Income Law.

§ 731.15. Expenses

(a) All ordinary expenses incurred in connection with the principal or with its administration and management, including regularly recurring taxes assessed against any portion of the principal, water rates, premiums on insurance taken upon the estates of both tenant and remainderman, interest on mortgages on the principal, ordinary repairs, compensation of assistants and court costs on regular accountings, except attorneys' fees shall be paid out of income. But such expenses where incurred in disposing of, or as carrying charges on, unproductive property as defined in Section 731.13, shall be paid out of principal, subject to the provisions of subdivision (b) of Section 731.13. Attorneys' fees for ordinary or current services shall be paid one-half out of income; one-half out of principal or in such other proportion as the court may direct.

(b) Attorneys' fees and other costs incurred in maintaining or defending any action to protect the property or assure the title thereof, unless due to the fault or cause of the tenant, costs of, or assessments for, improvements to property forming part of the principal, brokers' commissions, title charges, and other costs incurred in connection with purchasing, selling, or leasing property, or investing or reinvesting principal, and all other

expenses, except as specified in subdivision (a) of this section, shall be paid out of principal. Any tax levied by any authority, federal, state, or foreign, upon profit or gain defined under the terms of subdivision (b) of Section 731.05 shall be paid out of principal, notwithstanding such tax may be denominated a tax upon income by the taxing authority. *(Added by Stats.1968, c. 193, p. 489, § 1, eff. May 28, 1968, operative July 1, 1968.)*

Research References

Miller and Starr California Real Estate § 9:33, The Legal Estates Principal and Income Law.
12 Witkin, California Summary 10th Real Property § 170, (S 170) Principal and Income Law.

CHAPTER 3. RIGHTS OF OWNERS

§ 732. Products and accessions of property

INCREASE OF PROPERTY. The owner of a thing owns also all its products and accessions. *(Enacted in 1872.)*

Research References

Miller and Starr California Real Estate § 17:38, Tests for Determining Whether an Item is a Fixture.

§ 733. Future interests; income of property

IN CERTAIN CASES, WHO ENTITLED TO INCOME OF PROPERTY. When, in consequence of a valid limitation of a future interest, there is a suspension of the power of alienation or of the ownership during the continuation of which the income is undisposed of, and no valid direction for its accumulation is given, such income belongs to the persons presumptively entitled to the next eventual interest. *(Enacted in 1872.)*

Research References

Miller and Starr California Real Estate § 9:33, The Legal Estates Principal and Income Law.
12 Witkin, California Summary 10th Real Property § 139, (S 139) Acceleration.
6 Witkin, California Summary 10th Torts § 1734, Wilful and Malicious Trespass: Treble Damages.

CHAPTER 4. TERMINATION OF OWNERSHIP

§ 739. Defeat of future interests; birth of posthumous child

FUTURE INTERESTS, WHEN DEFEATED. A future interest, depending on the contingency of the death of any person without successors, heirs, issue, or children, is defeated by the birth of a posthumous child of such person, capable of taking by succession. *(Enacted in 1872.)*

Research References

14 Witkin, California Summary 10th Wills and Probate § 232, Time When Class is Ascertained.

§ 740. Defeat of future interests; condition provided; adjudication

SAME. A future interest may be defeated in any manner or by any act or means which the party creating such interest provided for or authorized in the creation thereof; nor is a future interest, thus liable to be defeated, to be on that ground adjudged void in its creation. *(Enacted in 1872.)*

Research References

Miller and Starr California Real Estate § 9:30, Remainders--Vested or Contingent Nature.
Miller and Starr California Real Estate § 9:31, Remainders--Termination; Court Proceedings.
13 Witkin, California Summary 10th Trusts § 213, (S 213) Termination by Operation of Law.

§ 741. Future interests; alienation or loss of precedent interest

FUTURE INTERESTS, WHEN NOT DEFEATED. No future interest can be defeated or barred by any alienation or other act of the owner of the intermediate or precedent interest, nor by any destruction of such precedent interest by forfeiture, surrender, merger, or otherwise, except as provided by the next section, or where a forfeiture is imposed by statute as a penalty for the violation thereof. *(Enacted in 1872.)*

Research References

Miller and Starr California Real Estate § 16:6, Nature of Possession Required--Possession by a Tenant.
Miller and Starr California Real Estate § 9:21, Rights and Powers.
Miller and Starr California Real Estate § 9:31, Remainders--Termination; Court Proceedings.
Miller and Starr California Real Estate § 9:32, Remainders--Rights of Remainder Holders.
Miller and Starr California Real Estate § 15:35, Use Requirements--Hostile, Adverse, and Under Claim of Right.
12 Witkin, California Summary 10th Real Property § 127, (S 127) in General.
12 Witkin, California Summary 10th Real Property § 138, (S 138) Doctrine of Destructibility Abolished.
12 Witkin, California Summary 10th Real Property § 143, (S 143) Against Life Tenant.
12 Witkin, California Summary 10th Real Property § 403, (S 403) Hostile or Adverse Use.

§ 742. Future interests; premature determination of precedent interest

SAME. No future interest, valid in its creation, is defeated by the determination of the precedent interest before the happening of the contingency on which the future interest is limited to take effect; but should such contingency afterwards happen, the future interest takes effect in the same manner and to the same extent as if the precedent interest had continued to the same period. *(Enacted in 1872.)*

Research References

Miller and Starr California Real Estate § 9:21, Rights and Powers.
Miller and Starr California Real Estate § 9:31, Remainders--Termination; Court Proceedings.
12 Witkin, California Summary 10th Real Property § 138, (S 138) Doctrine of Destructibility Abolished.

Title 3

GENERAL DEFINITIONS

Section
748. Income of property defined.
749. Time of creation of limitation, condition, or interest.

§ 748. Income of property defined

INCOME, WHAT. The income of property, as the term is used in this Part of the Code, includes the rents and profits of real property, the interest of money, dividends upon stock, and other produce of personal property. *(Enacted in 1872.)*

§ 749. Time of creation of limitation, condition, or interest

TIME OF CREATION, WHAT. The delivery of the grant, where a limitation, condition, or future interest is created by grant, and the death of the testator, where it is created by will, is to be deemed the time of the creation of the limitation, condition, or interest, within the meaning of this Part of the Code. *(Enacted in 1872.)*

Research References

Miller and Starr California Real Estate § 9:20, Creation.
Miller and Starr California Real Estate § 9:29, Remainders and Executory Interests (Powers of Termination).

Part 2

REAL OR IMMOVABLE PROPERTY

Title 1

GENERAL PROVISIONS

Section
755. Real estate; law governing.

§ 755. Real estate; law governing

Real property within this State is governed by the law of this State, except where the title is in the United States. *(Enacted in 1872. Amended by Code Am.1873–74, c. 612, p. 218, § 102.)*

Research References

Miller and Starr California Real Estate § 17:4, Jurisdiction.

Title 2

ESTATES IN REAL PROPERTY

CHAPTER 1. ESTATES IN GENERAL

Section
761. Estates in real property; kinds.
762. Estate in fee simple defined.

Section

763. Estates tail abolished; fee simple and fee simple absolute.
764. Fee tails as contingent remainders.
765. Freeholds; chattels real; chattel interests.
766. Estate for life of third person; freehold.
767. Future estate; permissible limitation.
768. Reversion defined.
769. Remainder defined.
773. Authorized future estates and limitations.
778. Remainders; conditional limitation.
779. Heirs of life tenant; taking as purchasers.
780. Remainders; construction of intent.
781. Power of appointment; effect.
782. Discriminatory restrictions in deeds; invalidity; familial status.
782.5. Discriminatory restrictions in deeds or other title-related instruments; deemed revised to omit restrictions; familial status.
783. "Condominium" defined.
783.1. Stock cooperatives; separate and correlative interests.
784. Restriction defined.

§ 761. Estates in real property; kinds

ENUMERATION OF ESTATES. Estates in real property, in respect to the duration of their enjoyment, are either:

1. Estates of inheritance or perpetual estates;
2. Estates for life;
3. Estates for years; or,
4. Estates at will. *(Enacted in 1872.)*

Research References

Rutter, Cal. Practice Guide: Enforcing Judgments/Debts Ch. 6A-11, Property Subject to Enforcement Procedures.
Rutter, Cal. Practice Guide: Real Prop. Transactions Ch. 4-B, B. Interests to be Conveyed.
Miller and Starr California Real Estate § 9:1, "Estate" Defined.
Miller and Starr California Real Estate § 9:2, Classification, Generally.
Miller and Starr California Real Estate § 19:2, Lease as Personal Property or Real Property.
Miller and Starr California Real Estate § 9:29, Remainders and Executory Interests (Powers of Termination).
Miller and Starr California Real Estate § 11:192, Personal Property and Fixtures; General Rules of Priority.
12 Witkin, California Summary 10th Real Property § 16, in General.

§ 762. Estate in fee simple defined

Every estate of inheritance is a fee, and every such estate, when not defeasible or conditional, is a fee simple or an absolute fee. *(Enacted in 1872. Amended by Code Am.1873–74, c. 612, p. 218, § 103.)*

Research References

Rutter, Cal. Practice Guide: Real Prop. Transactions Ch. 4-B, B. Interests to be Conveyed.
Miller and Starr California Real Estate § 9:3, Fee Simple Absolute.
Miller and Starr California Real Estate § 9:29, Remainders and Executory Interests (Powers of Termination).
Miller and Starr California Real Estate § 11:101, Effect of Foreclosure on Rights of Tenants in Possession.
12 Witkin, California Summary 10th Real Property § 16, in General.

§ 763. Estates tail abolished; fee simple and fee simple absolute

CONDITIONAL FEES AND ESTATES TAIL ABOLISHED. Estates tail are abolished, and every estate which would be at common law adjudged to be a fee tail is a fee simple; and if no valid remainder is limited thereon, is a fee simple absolute. *(Enacted in 1872.)*

Research References

Miller and Starr California Real Estate § 9:3, Fee Simple Absolute.
Miller and Starr California Real Estate § 9:20, Creation.
12 Witkin, California Summary 10th Real Property § 16, in General.
12 Witkin, California Summary 10th Real Property § 22, (S 22) by Deed.

§ 764. Fee tails as contingent remainders

CERTAIN REMAINDERS VALID. Where a remainder in fee is limited upon any estate, which would by the common law be adjudged a fee tail, such remainder is valid as a contingent limitation upon a fee, and vests in possession on the death of the first taker, without issue living at the time of his death. *(Enacted in 1872.)*

Research References

Miller and Starr California Real Estate § 9:17, Estate Subject to Executory Limitation.
Miller and Starr California Real Estate § 9:20, Creation.

§ 765. Freeholds; chattels real; chattel interests

Estates of inheritance and for life are called estates of freehold; estates for years are chattels real; and estates at will are chattel interests, but are not subject to enforcement of a money judgment. *(Enacted in 1872. Amended by Stats.1982, c. 497, p. 2135, § 2, operative July 1, 1983.)*

Law Revision Commission Comments

Section 765 is amended to conform to the terminology of Title 9 (commencing with Section 680.010) of Part 2 of the Code of Civil Procedure (Enforcement of Judgments Law) (15 Cal.L.Rev.Comm. Reports 2001).

Research References

Rutter, Cal. Practice Guide: Enforcing Judgments/Debts Ch. 6A-11, Property Subject to Enforcement Procedures.
Rutter, Cal. Practice Guide: Real Prop. Transactions Ch. 4-B, B. Interests to be Conveyed.
Miller and Starr California Real Estate § 9:2, Classification, Generally.
Miller and Starr California Real Estate § 19:2, Lease as Personal Property or Real Property.
Miller and Starr California Real Estate § 9:19, Definitions.
Miller and Starr California Real Estate § 9:29, Remainders and Executory Interests (Powers of Termination).
8 Witkin Cal. Proc. 5th Enforcement of Judgment § 60, (S 60) in General.
12 Witkin, California Summary 10th Real Property § 10, (S 10) Classification of Estates.
12 Witkin, California Summary 10th Real Property § 504, Nature of Estate.

§ 766. Estate for life of third person; freehold

An estate during the life of a third person, whether limited to heirs or otherwise, is a freehold. *(Enacted in 1872. Amended by Code Am.1873–74, c. 612, p. 218, § 104.)*

Research References

Rutter, Cal. Practice Guide: Real Prop. Transactions Ch. 4-B, B. Interests to be Conveyed.
Miller and Starr California Real Estate § 9:19, Definitions.
Miller and Starr California Real Estate § 9:29, Remainders and Executory Interests (Powers of Termination).
12 Witkin, California Summary 10th Real Property § 10, (S 10) Classification of Estates.

§ 767. Future estate; permissible limitation

FUTURE ESTATES, WHAT. A future estate may be limited by the act of the party to commence in possession at a future day, either without the intervention of a precedent estate, or on the termination, by lapse of time or otherwise, of a precedent estate created at the same time. *(Enacted in 1872.)*

Research References

Rutter, Cal. Practice Guide: Real Prop. Transactions Ch. 4-B, B. Interests to be Conveyed.
12 Witkin, California Summary 10th Real Property § 132, Executory Interests.

§ 768. Reversion defined

REVERSIONS. A reversion is the residue of an estate left by operation of law in the grantor or his successors, or in the successors of a testator, commencing in possession on the determination of a particular estate granted or devised. *(Enacted in 1872.)*

Research References

Miller and Starr California Real Estate § 9:26, Reversions.
12 Witkin, California Summary 10th Real Property § 128, Reversion.

§ 769. Remainder defined

REMAINDERS. When a future estate, other than a reversion, is dependent on a precedent estate, it may be called a remainder, and may be created and transferred by that name. *(Enacted in 1872.)*

Research References

Miller and Starr California Real Estate § 9:29, Remainders and Executory Interests (Powers of Termination).
12 Witkin, California Summary 10th Real Property § 131, Nature of Remainder.
12 Witkin, California Summary 10th Real Property § 132, Executory Interests.

§ 773. Authorized future estates and limitations

Subject to the rules of this title, and of Part 1 of this division, a freehold estate, as well as a chattel real, may be created to commence at a future day; an estate for life may be created in a term of years, and a remainder limited thereon; a remainder of a freehold or chattel real, either contingent or vested, may be created, expectant on the determination of a term of years; and a fee may be limited on a fee, upon a contingency, which, if it should occur, must happen within the period prescribed by the statutory rule against perpetuities in Article 2 (commencing with Section 21205) of Chapter 1 of Part 2 of Division 11 of the Probate Code. *(Enacted in 1872. Amended by Stats.1951, c. 1463, p. 3443, § 6; Stats.1991, c. 156 (A.B.1577), § 14.)*

Law Revision Commission Comments

Section 773 is amended to refer incorporate the new statutory rule against perpetuities which supersedes the rule provided by former Section 715.2. See Prob. Code §§ 21200–21231 (statutory rule against perpetuities). [20 Cal.L.Rev.Comm.Reports 2501 (1990)].

Research References

Miller and Starr California Real Estate § 9:17, Estate Subject to Executory Limitation.
Miller and Starr California Real Estate § 9:19, Definitions.
Miller and Starr California Real Estate § 9:29, Remainders and Executory Interests (Powers of Termination).
Miller and Starr California Real Estate § 9:34, Rule Against Perpetuities--In General.
12 Witkin, California Summary 10th Real Property § 132, Executory Interests.
12 Witkin, California Summary 10th Real Property § 173, Constitution and Early Statutes.

§ 778. Remainders; conditional limitation

REMAINDER UPON A CONTINGENCY. A remainder may be limited on a contingency which, in case it should happen, will operate to abridge or determine the precedent estate; and every such remainder is to be deemed a conditional limitation. *(Enacted in 1872.)*

Research References

Miller and Starr California Real Estate § 9:17, Estate Subject to Executory Limitation.
Miller and Starr California Real Estate § 9:29, Remainders and Executory Interests (Powers of Termination).
12 Witkin, California Summary 10th Real Property § 132, Executory Interests.

§ 779. Heirs of life tenant; taking as purchasers

HEIRS OF A TENANT FOR LIFE, WHEN TO TAKE AS PURCHASERS. When a remainder is limited to the heirs, or heirs of the body, of a person to whom a life estate in the same property is given, the persons who, on the termination of the life estate, are the successors or heirs of the body of the owner for life, are entitled to take by virtue of the remainder so limited to them, and not as mere successors of the owner for life. *(Enacted in 1872.)*

Research References

Miller and Starr California Real Estate § 9:20, Creation.
12 Witkin, California Summary 10th Real Property § 11, (S 11) Rule in Shelley's Case Abolished.
12 Witkin, California Summary 10th Real Property § 22, (S 22) by Deed.

§ 780. Remainders; construction of intent

CONSTRUCTION OF CERTAIN REMAINDERS. When a remainder on an estate for life or for years is not limited on a contingency defeating or avoiding such precedent estate, it is to be deemed intended to take effect only on the death of the first taker, or the expiration, by lapse of time, of such term of years. *(Enacted in 1872.)*

Research References

Rutter, Cal. Practice Guide: Real Prop. Transactions Ch. 4-B, B. Interests to be Conveyed.
Miller and Starr California Real Estate § 9:29, Remainders and Executory Interests (Powers of Termination).
12 Witkin, California Summary 10th Real Property § 139, (S 139) Acceleration.

§ 781. Power of appointment; effect

EFFECT OF POWER OF APPOINTMENT. A general or special power of appointment does not prevent the vesting of a future estate limited to take effect in case such power is not executed. *(Enacted in 1872.)*

Research References

Miller and Starr California Real Estate § 9:30, Remainders--Vested or Contingent Nature.
12 Witkin, California Summary 10th Real Property § 136, (S 136) Remainder Vested Subject to Complete Defeasance.
13 Witkin, California Summary 10th Trusts § 213, (S 213) Termination by Operation of Law.

§ 782. Discriminatory restrictions in deeds; invalidity; familial status

(a) Any provision in any deed of real property in California, whether executed before or after the effective date of this section, that purports to restrict the right of any persons to sell, lease, rent, use, or occupy the property to persons having any characteristic listed in subdivision (a) or (d) of Section 12955 of the Government Code, as those bases are defined in Sections 12926, 12926.1, subdivision (m) and paragraph (1) of subdivision (p) of Section 12955 and Section 12955.2 of the Government Code, by providing for payment of a penalty, forfeiture, reverter, or otherwise, is void.

(b) Notwithstanding subdivision (a), with respect to familial status, subdivision (a) shall not be construed to apply to housing for older persons, as defined in Section 12955.9 of the Government Code. With respect to familial status, nothing in subdivision (a) shall be construed to affect Sections 51.2, 51.3, 51.4,

51.10, 51.11, and 799.5 of this code, relating to housing for senior citizens. Subdivision (d) of Section 51, Section 4760, and Section 6714 of this code, and subdivisions (n), (o), and (p) of Section 12955 of the Government Code shall apply to subdivision (a). *(Added by Stats.1961, c. 1078, p. 2540, § 1. Amended by Stats.1965, c. 283, p. 1283, § 2; Stats.2006, c. 578 (A.B.2800), § 4; Stats.2012, c. 181 (A.B.806), § 22, operative Jan. 1, 2014; Stats.2013, c. 605 (S.B.752), § 10.)*

Law Revision Commission Comments

Section 782 is amended to correct a cross-reference to former Section 1360. [40 Cal.L.Rev.Comm. Reports 235 (2010)].

Section 782 is amended to add a cross-reference to Section 6714, reflecting the enactment of the Commercial and Industrial Common Interest Development Act (Civ. Code §§ 6500–6876). [42 Cal.L.Rev. Comm. Reports 1 (2012)].

Research References

Miller and Starr California Real Estate § 8:57, Conveyance in Violation of Public Policy or Statute.
Miller and Starr California Real Estate § 9:40, Restraints Based on Transferee's Membership in Protected Class.
Miller and Starr California Real Estate § 20:16, California Fair Employment and Housing Act--Disability Discrimination.
Miller and Starr California Real Estate § 20:29, Discrimination by a Real Estate Broker.
Miller and Starr California Real Estate § 24:32, Defenses to Enforcement--Public Policy or Discrimination.
17 NO. 4 Miller & Starr, California Real Estate Newsalert 2, Statutory Update:.
17 NO. 6 Miller & Starr, California Real Estate Newsalert 20, Table of Statutes (Newsalert Vol 17).
12 Witkin, California Summary 10th Real Property § 192, Types of Invalid Restraints.
12 Witkin, California Summary 10th Real Property § 201, (S 201) California Statute.
12 Witkin, California Summary 10th Real Property § 442, in General.
8 Witkin, California Summary 10th Constitutional Law § 897, Other Discrimination Statutes.

§ 782.5. Discriminatory restrictions in deeds or other title-related instruments; deemed revised to omit restrictions; familial status

(a) Any deed or other written instrument that relates to title to real property, or any written covenant, condition, or restriction annexed or made a part of, by reference or otherwise, any deed or instrument that relates to title to real property, which contains any provision that purports to forbid, restrict, or condition the right of any person or persons to sell, buy, lease, rent, use, or occupy the property on account of any basis listed in subdivision (a) or (d) of Section 12955 of the Government Code, as those bases are defined in Sections 12926, 12926.1, subdivision (m) and paragraph (1) of subdivision (p) of Section 12955, and Section 12955.2 of the Government Code, with respect to any person or persons, shall be deemed to be revised to omit that provision.

(b) Notwithstanding subdivision (a), with respect to familial status, subdivision (a) shall not be construed to apply to housing for older persons, as defined in Section 12955.9 of the Government Code. With respect to familial status, nothing in subdivision (a) shall be construed to affect Sections 51.2, 51.3, 51.4, 51.10, 51.11, and 799.5 of this code, relating to housing for senior citizens. Subdivision (d) of Section 51, Section 4760, and Section 6714 of this code, and subdivisions (n), (o), and (p) of Section 12955 of the Government Code shall apply to subdivision (a).

(c) This section shall not be construed to limit or expand the powers of a court to reform a deed or other written instrument. *(Added by Stats.1987, c. 500, § 1. Amended by Stats.2006, c. 578*

(A.B.2800), § 5; Stats.2012, c. 181 (A.B.806), § 23, operative Jan. 1, 2014; Stats.2013, c. 605 (S.B.752), § 11.)

Law Revision Commission Comments

Subdivision (a) of Section 782.5 is amended to make stylistic revisions.
Subdivision (b) is amended to correct a cross-reference to former Section 1360. [40 Cal.L.Rev.Comm. Reports 235 (2010)].
Subdivision (b) of Section 782.5 is amended to add a cross-reference to Section 6714, reflecting the enactment of the Commercial and Industrial Common Interest Development Act (Civ. Code §§ 6500–6876). [42 Cal.L.Rev.Comm. Reports 1 (2012)].

Research References

Miller and Starr California Real Estate § 8:57, Conveyance in Violation of Public Policy or Statute.
Miller and Starr California Real Estate § 9:40, Restraints Based on Transferee's Membership in Protected Class.
Miller and Starr California Real Estate § 20:16, California Fair Employment and Housing Act--Disability Discrimination.
Miller and Starr California Real Estate § 24:32, Defenses to Enforcement--Public Policy or Discrimination.
17 NO. 4 Miller & Starr, California Real Estate Newsalert 2, Statutory Update:.
17 NO. 6 Miller & Starr, California Real Estate Newsalert 20, Table of Statutes (Newsalert Vol 17).
12 Witkin, California Summary 10th Real Property § 201, (S 201) California Statute.
1 Witkin Cal. Summ. 10th Contracts § 276, (S 276) Nature of Remedy.

§ 783. "Condominium" defined

A condominium is an estate in real property described in Section 4125 or 6542. A condominium may, with respect to the duration of its enjoyment, be either (1) an estate of inheritance or perpetual estate, (2) an estate for life, (3) an estate for years, such as a leasehold or a subleasehold, or (4) any combination of the foregoing. *(Added by Stats.1985, c. 874, § 9. Amended by Stats.2012, c. 181 (A.B.806), § 24, operative Jan. 1, 2014; Stats. 2013, c. 605 (S.B.752), § 12.)*

Law Revision Commission Comments

Section 783 is amended to correct a cross-reference to former Section 1351(f). [40 Cal.L.Rev.Comm. Reports 235 (2010)].
Section 783 is amended to add a cross-reference to Section 6542, reflecting the enactment of the Commercial and Industrial Common Interest Development Act (Civ. Code §§ 6500–6876). [42 Cal.L.Rev. Comm. Reports 1 (2012)].

Research References

Rutter, Cal. Practice Guide: Enforcing Judgments/Debts Ch. 6E-6, "Homestead" Exemption.
Rutter, Cal. Practice Guide: Real Prop. Transactions Ch. 2-C, C. Broker's Relationship and Obligations to Principal and Third Parties.
Rutter, Cal. Practice Guide: Real Prop. Transactions Ch. 4-A, A. Property to be Sold.
Rutter, Cal. Practice Guide: Real Prop. Transactions Ch. 4-E, E. Drafting the Purchase and Sale Agreement-Terms and Conditions.
Miller and Starr California Real Estate § 9:1, "Estate" Defined.
Miller and Starr California Real Estate § 8:60, Appurtenances Pass With Conveyance.
Miller and Starr California Real Estate § 13:17, Types of Property that Qualify.
Miller and Starr California Real Estate § 13:22, Residency, Ownership and Use.
Miller and Starr California Real Estate § 25B:5, Condominiums--Definition and Description.
Miller and Starr California Real Estate § 25C:8, Subdivisions Requiring a Public Report; Common Interest Developments.
Miller and Starr California Real Estate § 7:118, List of CLTA Adopted Endorsements--Definition and Description CLTA Adopted Endorsements.
8 Witkin Cal. Proc. 5th Enforcement of Judgment § 216, (S 216) in General.
12 Witkin, California Summary 10th Real Property § 86, (S 86) Other Statutes.

12 Witkin, California Summary 10th Real Property § 89, (S 89) Condominium, Condominium Plan, and Condominium Project.

12 Witkin, California Summary 10th Real Property § 474, Scope of Inspection.

§ 783.1. Stock cooperatives; separate and correlative interests

In a stock cooperative, as defined in Section 4190 or 6566, both the separate interest, as defined in paragraph (4) of subdivision (a) of Section 4185 or in paragraph (3) of subdivision (a) of Section 6564, and the correlative interest in the stock cooperative corporation, however designated, are interests in real property. *(Added by Stats.1985, c. 874, § 10. Amended by Stats.2012, c. 181 (A.B.806), § 25, operative Jan. 1, 2014; Stats. 2013, c. 605 (S.B.752), § 13.)*

Law Revision Commission Comments

Section 783.1 is amended to correct cross-references to former Section 1351(l)(4), (m). [40 Cal.L.Rev.Comm. Reports 235 (2010)].

Section 783.1 is amended to add cross-references to Sections 6564(a)(4) and 6566, reflecting the enactment of the Commercial and Industrial Common Interest Development Act (Civ. Code §§ 6500–6876). [42 Cal.L.Rev.Comm. Reports 1 (2012)].

Research References

Rutter, Cal. Practice Guide: Real Prop. Transactions Ch. 4-A, A. Property to be Sold.

Miller and Starr California Real Estate § 25B:8, Stock Cooperatives.

12 Witkin, California Summary 10th Real Property § 86, (S 86) Other Statutes.

12 Witkin, California Summary 10th Real Property § 91, (S 91) Stock Cooperative.

§ 784. Restriction defined

"Restriction," when used in a statute that incorporates this section by reference, means a limitation on, or provision affecting, the use of real property in a deed, declaration, or other instrument, whether in the form of a covenant, equitable servitude, condition subsequent, negative easement, or other form of restriction. *(Added by Stats.1998, c. 14 (A.B.707), § 1.)*

Law Revision Commission Comments

Section 784 provides a definition of "restriction" for application in Code of Civil Procedure Section 336 (statute of limitations). The reference to "declaration" includes a declaration of restrictions in a common interest development intended to be enforceable as equitable servitudes. See Section 1353(a). [28 Cal.L.Rev.Comm. Reports App. 4 (1998)].

Research References

Rutter, Cal. Practice Guide: Real Prop. Transactions Ch. 4-A, A. Property to be Sold.

Miller and Starr California Real Estate § 15:9, Affirmative and Negative Easements.

Miller and Starr California Real Estate § 24:1, Types of Enforceable Restrictions.

Miller and Starr California Real Estate § 24:29, Rights of Enforcement-- Statute of Limitations.

Miller and Starr California Real Estate § 25B:2, Definitions of Terms Used in This Chapter.

Miller and Starr California Real Estate § 25B:107, Enforcement of the Restrictions--Statute of Limitations.

18 NO. 5 Miller & Starr, California Real Estate Newsalert 4, Common Interest Developments.

3 Witkin Cal. Proc. 5th Actions § 485, (S 485) Five Years.

CHAPTER 2. TERMINATION OF ESTATES

§ 789. Termination of tenancy or other estate at will; written notice to tenant

A tenancy or other estate at will, however created, may be terminated by the landlord's giving notice in writing to the tenant, in the manner prescribed by Section 1162 of the Code of Civil Procedure, to remove from the premises within a period of not less than 30 days, to be specified in the notice. *(Enacted in 1872. Amended by Stats.1911, c. 44, p. 61, § 1; Stats.2002, c. 664 (A.B.3034), § 32.)*

Research References

Rutter, Cal. Practice Guide: Real Prop. Transactions Ch. 4-B, B. Interests to be Conveyed.

Miller and Starr California Real Estate § 19:31, Tenancy at Will.

Miller and Starr California Real Estate § 19:188, Notice Required by Statute.

Miller and Starr California Real Estate § 19:192, Timing and Service of a Notice of Termination.

5 Witkin Cal. Proc. 5th Pleading § 643, Lessee Holding Over.

12 Witkin, California Summary 10th Real Property § 679, Tenancy at Will.

§ 789.3. Utility services; prevention of access to property; removal of doors, windows or personalty; intent to terminate occupancy; liability of landlord; injunctive relief

(a) A landlord shall not with intent to terminate the occupancy under any lease or other tenancy or estate at will, however created, of property used by a tenant as his residence willfully cause, directly or indirectly, the interruption or termination of any utility service furnished the tenant, including, but not limited to, water, heat, light, electricity, gas, telephone, elevator, or refrigeration, whether or not the utility service is under the control of the landlord.

(b) In addition, a landlord shall not, with intent to terminate the occupancy under any lease or other tenancy or estate at will, however created, of property used by a tenant as his or her residence, willfully:

(1) Prevent the tenant from gaining reasonable access to the property by changing the locks or using a bootlock or by any other similar method or device;

(2) Remove outside doors or windows; or

(3) Remove from the premises the tenant's personal property, the furnishings, or any other items without the prior written consent of the tenant, except when done pursuant to the procedure set forth in Chapter 5 (commencing with Section 1980) of Title 5 of Part 4 of Division 3.

Nothing in this subdivision shall be construed to prevent the lawful eviction of a tenant by appropriate legal authorities, nor shall anything in this subdivision apply to occupancies defined by subdivision (b) of Section 1940.

(c) Any landlord who violates this section shall be liable to the tenant in a civil action for all of the following:

(1) Actual damages of the tenant.

(2) An amount not to exceed one hundred dollars ($100) for each day or part thereof the landlord remains in violation of this section. In determining the amount of such award, the court shall consider proof of such matters as justice may require; however, in no event shall less than two hundred fifty dollars ($250) be awarded for each separate cause of action. Subse-

quent or repeated violations, which are not committed contemporaneously with the initial violation, shall be treated as separate causes of action and shall be subject to a separate award of damages.

(d) In any action under subdivision (c) the court shall award reasonable attorney's fees to the prevailing party. In any such action the tenant may seek appropriate injunctive relief to prevent continuing or further violation of the provisions of this section during the pendency of the action. The remedy provided by this section is not exclusive and shall not preclude the tenant from pursuing any other remedy which the tenant may have under any other provision of law. *(Added by Stats.1971, c. 1275, p. 2494, § 1. Amended by Stats.1979, c. 333, p. 1191, § 1.)*

Research References

Miller and Starr California Real Estate § 31:32, Termination of Tenancies--Mobilehomes.

Miller and Starr California Real Estate § 34:82, Amount of Fees; Allocation.

Miller and Starr California Real Estate § 34:99, Punitive Damages--Judicial Review.

Miller and Starr California Real Estate § 19:157, Covenant of Quiet Enjoyment and Possession--Wrongful Actual or Constructive Eviction.

Miller and Starr California Real Estate § 19:158, Covenant of Quiet Enjoyment and Possession--Termination of Utilities.

Miller and Starr California Real Estate § 19:162, Elements of the Offense--Forcible Entry.

Miller and Starr California Real Estate § 19:181, Insolvency or Bankruptcy of the Tenant--A Lease May be Assumed or Rejected.

19 NO. 5 Miller & Starr, California Real Estate Newsalert 22, Landlord and Tenant.

12 Witkin, California Summary 10th Real Property § 614, Original Statute.

12 Witkin, California Summary 10th Real Property § 615, Expanded Statute.

6 Witkin, California Summary 10th Torts § 1569, Nature and Validity of Penalties.

§ 790. Right of re-entry or possession

EFFECT OF NOTICE. After such notice has been served, and the period specified by such notice has expired, but not before, the landlord may reenter, or proceed according to law to recover possession. *(Enacted in 1872.)*

Research References

Miller and Starr California Real Estate § 19:188, Notice Required by Statute.

12 Witkin, California Summary 10th Real Property § 679, Tenancy at Will.

§ 791. Re-entry, how effected

Whenever the right of re-entry is given to a grantor or a lessor in any grant or lease or otherwise, such reentry may be made at any time after the right has accrued, upon three days' notice, as provided in sections 1161 and 1162, Code of Civil Procedure; provided, however, that the said three days' notice shall not be required in cases where the hiring of real property is for a term not specified by the parties and where such hiring was terminated under and in accordance with the provisions of section 1946 of the Civil Code. *(Enacted in 1872. Amended by Stats.1931, c. 1033, p. 2180, § 1.)*

Research References

Miller and Starr California Real Estate § 19:33, Contract Term Provided in the Lease.

Miller and Starr California Real Estate § 19:188, Notice Required by Statute.

Miller and Starr California Real Estate § 19:201, Landlord's Alternative Remedies for Tenant's Breach; When Notice is Required.

Miller and Starr California Real Estate § 19:202, Form and Contents of the Notice; Curable and Noncurable Breaches.

12 Witkin, California Summary 10th Real Property § 668, Construction of Forfeiture Clause.

12 Witkin, California Summary 10th Real Property § 721, (S 721) Where No Notice is Necessary.

§ 792. Summary proceedings for possession

SUMMARY PROCEEDINGS IN CERTAIN CASES PROVIDED FOR. Summary proceedings for obtaining possession of real property forcibly entered, or forcibly and unlawfully detained, are provided for in Sections 1159 to 1175, both inclusive, of the Code of Civil Procedure. *(Enacted in 1872.)*

Research References

12 Witkin, California Summary 10th Real Property § 703, (S 703) Nature of Remedy.

§ 793. Possessory action, when maintainable

An action for the possession of real property leased or granted, with a right of re-entry, may be maintained at any time, after the right to re-enter has accrued, without the notice prescribed in section seven hundred and ninety-one. *(Enacted in 1872. Amended by Stats.1905, c. 438, p. 599, § 1.)*

Research References

12 Witkin, California Summary 10th Real Property § 702, (S 702) Ejectment.

CHAPTER 2.5.   MOBILEHOME RESIDENCY LAW

ARTICLE 1.   GENERAL

§ 798.   Citation of chapter

This chapter shall be known and may be cited as the "Mobilehome Residency Law." *(Added by Stats.1978, c. 1035, p. 3194, § 4. Amended by Stats.1992, c. 958 (S.B.1655), § 1, eff. Sept. 28, 1992.)*

Research References

Rutter, Cal. Practice Guide: Civil Appeals & Writs Ch. 14-B, B. Recovery of Appellate Costs and Attorney Fees.

Rutter, Cal. Practice Guide: Civ. Pro. Before Trial Ch. 11-A, A. Voluntary Dismissals.

Rutter, Cal. Practice Guide: Civil Trials & Evidence Ch. 17-E, E. Attorney Fees as Costs.

Rutter, Cal. Practice Guide: Landlord-Tenant Form 11:A, Sample Mobilehome Park Rental Agreement.

Rutter, Cal. Practice Guide: Personal Injury Ch. 3-E, E. Punitive Damages.

Rutter, Cal. Practice Guide: Real Prop. Transactions Ch. 4-A, A. Property to be Sold.

Miller and Starr California Real Estate § 31:1, Definitions.

Miller and Starr California Real Estate § 31:2, Regulation.

Miller and Starr California Real Estate § 19:92, Property Subject to Control; Exceptions and Exemptions--Application to Mobilehome Parks.

Miller and Starr California Real Estate § 31:16, Basis for Special Relationship Involving Mobilehome Tenancies.

Miller and Starr California Real Estate § 31:17, Distinction When Park Owned by Residents.

Miller and Starr California Real Estate § 31:25, Park Management.

Miller and Starr California Real Estate § 31:32, Termination of Tenancies--Mobilehomes.

14 NO. 2 Miller & Starr, California Real Estate Newsalert 17, Mobilehomes.

12 Witkin, California Summary 10th Real Property § 503, Statutory Framework.

12 Witkin, California Summary 10th Real Property § 715, Tenant's Remedies.

12 Witkin, California Summary 10th Real Property § 761, (S 761) Governing Law.

§ 798.1. Application of definitions

Unless the provisions or context otherwise requires, the following definitions shall govern the construction of this chapter. *(Added by Stats.1978, c. 1031, p. 3178, § 1.)*

Research References

12 Witkin, California Summary 10th Real Property § 762, (S 762) Definitions.

§ 798.2. Management

"Management" means the owner of a mobilehome park or an agent or representative authorized to act on his behalf in connection with matters relating to a tenancy in the park. *(Added by Stats.1978, c. 1031, p. 3178, § 1.)*

Research References

Miller and Starr California Real Estate § 31:7, Management.

Miller and Starr California Real Estate § 31:25, Park Management.

12 Witkin, California Summary 10th Real Property § 762, (S 762) Definitions.

§ 798.3. Mobilehome

(a) "Mobilehome" is a structure designed for human habitation and for being moved on a street or highway under permit pursuant to Section 35790 of the Vehicle Code. Mobilehome includes a manufactured home, as defined in Section 18007 of the Health and Safety Code, and a mobilehome, as defined in Section 18008 of the Health and Safety Code, but, except as provided in subdivision (b), does not include a recreational vehicle, as defined in Section 799.29 of this code and Section 18010 of the Health and Safety Code or a commercial coach as defined in Section 18001.8 of the Health and Safety Code.

(b) "Mobilehome," for purposes of this chapter, other than Section 798.73, also includes trailers and other recreational vehicles of all types defined in Section 18010 of the Health and

Safety Code, other than motor homes, truck campers, and camping trailers, which are used for human habitation if the occupancy criteria of either paragraph (1) or (2), as follows, are met:

(1) The trailer or other recreational vehicle occupies a mobilehome site in the park, on November 15, 1992, under a rental agreement with a term of one month or longer, and the trailer or other recreational vehicle occupied a mobilehome site in the park prior to January 1, 1991.

(2) The trailer or other recreational vehicle occupies a mobilehome site in the park for nine or more continuous months commencing on or after November 15, 1992.

"Mobilehome" does not include a trailer or other recreational vehicle located in a recreational vehicle park subject to Chapter 2.6 (commencing with Section 799.20). *(Added by Stats.1978, c. 1033, p. 3187, § 2. Amended by Stats.1980, c. 502, § 1; Stats.1982, c. 419, p. 1770, § 1; Stats.1983, c. 1124, § 1, operative July 1, 1984; Stats.1992, c. 958 (S.B.1655), § 2, eff. Sept. 28, 1992; Stats.1993, c. 666 (A.B.503), § 1; Stats.2005, c. 595 (S.B.253), § 1.)*

Research References

Miller and Starr California Real Estate § 31:1, Definitions.

Miller and Starr California Real Estate § 31:16, Basis for Special Relationship Involving Mobilehome Tenancies.

16 NO. 4 Miller & Starr, California Real Estate Newsalert 15, Mobilehomes.

16 NO. 5 Miller & Starr, California Real Estate Newsalert 26, State Board of Equalization Issues Comprehensive Summary and Qs and As for Transfers of Base Year Values of Principal Residences.

12 Witkin, California Summary 10th Real Property § 762, (S 762) Definitions.

§ 798.4. Mobilehome park

"Mobilehome park" is an area of land where two or more mobilehome sites are rented, or held out for rent, to accommodate mobilehomes used for human habitation. *(Added by Stats.1978, c. 1031, p. 3178, § 1.)*

Research References

Rutter, Cal. Practice Guide: Real Prop. Transactions Ch. 4-A, A. Property to be Sold.

12 Witkin, California Summary 10th Real Property § 762, (S 762) Definitions.

§ 798.6. Park

"Park" is a manufactured housing community as defined in Section 18210.7 of the Health and Safety Code, or a mobilehome park. *(Formerly § 798.5, added by Stats.1978, c. 1031, p. 3178, § 1. Renumbered § 798.6 and amended by Stats.1980, c. 502, § 5. Amended by Stats.1993, c. 858 (A.B.2177), § 1; Stats.2007, c. 596 (A.B.382), § 1.)*

Research References

12 Witkin, California Summary 10th Real Property § 762, (S 762) Definitions.

§ 798.7. New construction

"New Construction" means any newly constructed spaces initially held out for rent after January 1, 1990. *(Added by Stats.1989, c. 412, § 1.)*

Research References

Miller and Starr California Real Estate § 31:27, Effect of Rent Control Ordinance.

Miller and Starr California Real Estate § 31:29, Duties Regarding Common Areas.

12 Witkin, California Summary 10th Real Property § 768, New Construction.

§ 798.8. Rental agreement

"Rental agreement" is an agreement between the management and the homeowner establishing the terms and conditions
of a park tenancy. A lease is a rental agreement. *(Formerly
§ 798.6, added by Stats.1978, c. 1031, p. 3178, § 1. Renumbered
§ 798.8 and amended by Stats.1980, c. 502, § 6. Amended by
Stats.1982, c. 1397, p. 5319, § 1.)*

Research References

Miller and Starr California Real Estate § 31:38, Rental or Leasing of
Mobilehomes.
12 Witkin, California Summary 10th Real Property § 762, (S 762)
Definitions.

§ 798.9. Homeowner

"Homeowner" is a person who has a tenancy in a mobilehome
park under a rental agreement. *(Added by Stats.1978, c. 1031, p.
3178, § 1. Amended by Stats.1982, c. 1397, p. 5320, § 2.)*

Research References

12 Witkin, California Summary 10th Real Property § 762, (S 762)
Definitions.

§ 798.10. Change of use

"Change of use" means a use of the park for a purpose other
than the rental, or the holding out for rent, of two or more
mobilehome sites to accommodate mobilehomes used for human
habitation, and does not mean the adoption, amendment, or
repeal of a park rule or regulation. A change of use may affect
an entire park or any portion thereof. "Change of use"
includes, but is not limited to, a change of the park or any
portion thereof to a condominium, stock cooperative, planned
unit development, or any form of ownership wherein spaces
within the park are to be sold. *(Added by Stats.1979, c. 945, p.
3266, § 1. Amended by Stats.1980, c. 137, § 1.)*

Research References

Miller and Starr California Real Estate § 31:32, Termination of Tenan-
cies--Mobilehomes.
12 Witkin, California Summary 10th Real Property § 762, (S 762)
Definitions.

§ 798.11. Resident

"Resident" is a homeowner or other person who lawfully
occupies a mobilehome. *(Formerly § 798.7, added by Stats.1978,
c. 1031, p. 3178, § 1. Renumbered § 748.10 and amended by
Stats.1980, c. 502, § 7. Renumbered § 798.11 and amended by
Stats.1981, c. 714, § 50. Amended by Stats.1982, c. 1397, p. 5320,
§ 3.)*

Research References

12 Witkin, California Summary 10th Real Property § 762, (S 762)
Definitions.

§ 798.12. Tenancy

"Tenancy" is the right of a homeowner to the use of a site
within a mobilehome park on which to locate, maintain, and
occupy a mobilehome, site improvements, and accessory structures for human habitation, including the use of the services and
facilities of the park. *(Formerly § 798.8, added by Stats.1978, c.
1031, p. 3178, § 1. Amended by Stats.1978, c. 1033, p. 3187, § 3.
Renumbered § 798.12 and amended by Stats.1980, c. 502, § 8.
Amended by Stats.1982, c. 1397, p. 5320, § 4.)*

Research References

Miller and Starr California Real Estate § 31:25, Park Management.

12 Witkin, California Summary 10th Real Property § 762, (S 762)
Definitions.

§ 798.13. State employee housing

(a) This chapter does not apply to any area owned, operated,
or maintained by the state for the purpose of providing employee
housing or space for a mobilehome owned or occupied by an
employee of the state.

(b) Notwithstanding subdivision (a), a state employer shall
provide the occupant of a privately owned mobilehome that is
situated in an employee housing area owned, operated, or
maintained by the state, and that is occupied by a state employee
by agreement with his or her state employer and subject to the
terms and conditions of that state employment, with a minimum
of 60–days' notice prior to terminating the tenancy for any
reason. *(Added by Stats.2000, c. 471 (A.B.2008), § 1.)*

§ 798.14. Notices; personal delivery or by mail

(a) Unless otherwise provided, all notices required by this
chapter shall be either delivered personally to the homeowner or
deposited in the United States mail, postage prepaid, addressed
to the homeowner at his or her site within the mobilehome park.

(b) All notices required by this chapter to be delivered prior
to February 1 of each year may be combined in one notice that
contains all the information required by the sections under which
the notices are given. *(Added by Stats.1988, c. 301, § 1.
Amended by Stats.2012, c. 478 (A.B.2150), § 1.)*

Research References

Miller and Starr California Real Estate § 31:16, Basis for Special
Relationship Involving Mobilehome Tenancies.
Miller and Starr California Real Estate § 31:25, Park Management.
Miller and Starr California Real Estate § 31:33, Required Notice for
Termination.
12 Witkin, California Summary 10th Real Property § 776, (S 776) Notices
and Disclosures.

ARTICLE 2.   RENTAL AGREEMENT

§ 798.15. Writing; required contents; repair of sudden or unforeseeable breakdown or deterioration of improvements; required notice

The rental agreement shall be in writing and shall contain, in
addition to the provisions otherwise required by law to be
included, all of the following:

(a) The term of the tenancy and the rent therefor.

(b) The rules and regulations of the park.

(c) A copy of the text of this chapter shall be provided as an exhibit and shall be incorporated into the rental agreement by reference. Management shall do one of the following prior to February 1 of each year, if a significant change was made in this chapter by legislation enacted in the prior year:

(1) Provide all homeowners with a copy of this chapter.

(2) Provide written notice to all homeowners that there has been a change to this chapter and that they may obtain one copy of this chapter from management at no charge. Management shall provide a copy within a reasonable time, not to exceed seven days, upon request.

(d) A provision specifying that (1) it is the responsibility of the management to provide and maintain physical improvements in the common facilities in good working order and condition and (2) with respect to a sudden or unforeseeable breakdown or deterioration of these improvements, the management shall have a reasonable period of time to repair the sudden or unforeseeable breakdown or deterioration and bring the improvements into good working order and condition after management knows or should have known of the breakdown or deterioration. For purposes of this subdivision, a reasonable period of time to repair a sudden or unforeseeable breakdown or deterioration shall be as soon as possible in situations affecting a health or safety condition, and shall not exceed 30 days in any other case except where exigent circumstances justify a delay.

(e) A description of the physical improvements to be provided the homeowner during his or her tenancy.

(f) A provision listing those services which will be provided at the time the rental agreement is executed and will continue to be offered for the term of tenancy and the fees, if any, to be charged for those services.

(g) A provision stating that management may charge a reasonable fee for services relating to the maintenance of the land and premises upon which a mobilehome is situated in the event the homeowner fails to maintain the land or premises in accordance with the rules and regulations of the park after written notification to the homeowner and the failure of the homeowner to comply within 14 days. The written notice shall state the specific condition to be corrected and an estimate of the charges to be imposed by management if the services are performed by management or its agent.

(h) All other provisions governing the tenancy.

(i) A copy of the following notice. Management shall also, prior to February 1 of each year, provide a copy of the following notice to all homeowners:

IMPORTANT NOTICE TO ALL MANUFACTURED HOME/MOBILEHOME OWNERS: CALIFORNIA LAW REQUIRES THAT YOU BE MADE AWARE OF THE FOLLOWING:

The Mobilehome Residency Law (MRL), found in Section 798 et seq. of the Civil Code, establishes the rights and responsibilities of homeowners and park management. The MRL is deemed a part of the terms of any park rental agreement or lease. This notice is intended to provide you with a general awareness of selected parts of the MRL. It does not serve as a legal explanation or interpretation. For authoritative information, you must read and understand the laws. These laws change from time to time. In any year in which the law has changed, you may obtain one copy of the full text of the law from management at no charge. This notice is required by Civil Code Section 798.15(i) and the information provided may not be current.

Homeowners and park management have certain rights and responsibilities under the MRL. These include, but are not limited to:

1. Management must give a homeowner written notice of any increase in his or her rent at least 90 days before the date of the increase. (Civil Code Section 798.30)

2. No rental or sales agreement may contain a provision by which a purchaser or a homeowner waives any of his or her rights under the MRL. (Civil Code Sections 798.19, 798.77)

3. Management may not terminate or refuse to renew a homeowner's tenancy except for one or more of the authorized reasons set forth in the MRL. (Civil Code Sections 798.55, 798.56)

4. A homeowner must give written notice to the management of not less than 60 days before vacating his or her tenancy. (Civil Code Section 798.59)

5. Homeowners, residents, and their guests must comply with the rental agreement or lease, including the reasonable rules and regulations of the park and all applicable local ordinances and state laws and regulations relating to mobilehomes. Failure to comply could be grounds for eviction from the park. (Civil Code Section 798.56)

6. Homeowners must pay rent, utility charges, and reasonable incidental service charges in a timely manner. Failure to comply could be grounds for eviction from the park. (Civil Code Section 798.56)

7. Homeowners have a right to peacefully assemble and freely communicate with respect to mobilehome living and for social or educational purposes. Homeowners have a right to meet in the park, at reasonable hours and in a reasonable manner, for any lawful purpose. Homeowners may not be charged a cleaning deposit in order to use the park clubhouse for meetings of resident organizations or for other lawful purposes, such as to hear from political candidates, so long as a homeowner of the park is hosting the meeting and all park residents are allowed to attend. Homeowners may not be required to obtain liability insurance in order to use common facilities unless alcohol is served. (Civil Code Sections 798.50, 798.51)

8. If a home complies with certain standards, the homeowner is entitled to sell it in place in the park. Management may require certain upgrades. Management may not require a homeowner to sell his or her home to the park, may not charge a transfer or selling fee, and may not require a homeowner to use a broker or dealer approved by the park. A homeowner has a right to advertise his or her home for sale. Management may deny approval of a buyer, but only for certain reasons listed in the law. (Civil Code Sections 798.70–798.74)

9. Management has the right to enter the space upon which a mobilehome is situated for maintenance of utilities, trees, and driveways; for inspection and maintenance of the space in accordance with the rules and regulations of the park when the homeowner or resident fails to maintain the space; and for protection and maintenance of the mobilehome park at any reasonable time, but not in a manner or at a time that would interfere with the resident's quiet enjoyment of his or her home. (Civil Code Section 798.26)

10. A homeowner may not make any improvements or alterations to his or her space or home without following the rules and regulations of the park and all applicable local ordinances and state laws and regulations, which may include obtaining a permit to construct, and, if required by park rules or the rental agreement, without prior written approval of management. Failure to

comply could be grounds for eviction from the park. (Civil Code Section 798.56)

(Added by Stats.1978, c. 1031, p. 3178, § 1. Amended by Stats.1978, c. 1033, p. 3186, § 4; Stats.1980, c. 137, § 2; Stats.1981, c. 667, § 1; Stats.1982, c. 1397, p. 5320, § 5; Stats.1983, c. 519, § 1; Stats.1987, c. 126, § 1; Stats.1993, c. 666 (A.B.503), § 2; Stats.2010, c. 90 (A.B.2120), § 1; Stats.2012, c. 478 (A.B.2150), § 2.)

Research References

Rutter, Cal. Practice Guide: Landlord-Tenant Form 11:A, Sample Mobilehome Park Rental Agreement.

Miller and Starr California Real Estate § 31:7, Management.

Miller and Starr California Real Estate § 31:26, Requirement of Written Rental Agreement.

Miller and Starr California Real Estate § 31:28, Required Notices and Disclosure Forms to Tenants.

Miller and Starr California Real Estate § 31:29, Duties Regarding Common Areas.

19 NO. 3 Miller & Starr, California Real Estate Newsalert 20, Landlord and Tenant.

21 NO. 4 Miller & Starr, California Real Estate Newsalert 16, Mobilehomes.

12 Witkin, California Summary 10th Real Property § 764, (S 764) Required and Optional Provisions.

§ 798.16. Inclusion of other provisions; return of executed copy

(a) The rental agreement may include other provisions permitted by law, but need not include specific language contained in state or local laws not a part of this chapter.

(b) Management shall return an executed copy of the rental agreement to the homeowner within 15 business days after management has received the rental agreement signed by the homeowner. *(Added by Stats.1978, c. 1031, p. 3178, § 1. Amended by Stats.1978, c. 1033, p. 3188, § 5; Stats.1981, c. 667, § 2; Stats.2004, c. 302 (A.B.2351), § 1.)*

Research References

Miller and Starr California Real Estate § 31:26, Requirement of Written Rental Agreement.

15 NO. 4 Miller & Starr, California Real Estate Newsalert 14, Mobilehomes.

12 Witkin, California Summary 10th Real Property § 764, (S 764) Required and Optional Provisions.

§ 798.17. Exemption from local rent control measures; right to inspect agreement

(a)(1) Rental agreements meeting the criteria of subdivision (b) shall be exempt from any ordinance, rule, regulation, or initiative measure adopted by any local governmental entity which establishes a maximum amount that a landlord may charge a tenant for rent. The terms of a rental agreement meeting the criteria of subdivision (b) shall prevail over conflicting provisions of an ordinance, rule, regulation, or initiative measure limiting or restricting rents in mobilehome parks, only during the term of the rental agreement or one or more uninterrupted, continuous extensions thereof. If the rental agreement is not extended and no new rental agreement in excess of 12 months' duration is entered into, then the last rental rate charged for the space under the previous rental agreement shall be the base rent for purposes of applicable provisions of law concerning rent regulation, if any.

(2) In the first sentence of the first paragraph of a rental agreement entered into on or after January 1, 1993, pursuant to this section, there shall be set forth a provision in at least 12–point boldface type if the rental agreement is printed, or in capital letters if the rental agreement is typed, giving notice to the homeowner that the rental agreement will be exempt from any ordinance, rule, regulation, or initiative measure adopted by

any local governmental entity which establishes a maximum amount that a landlord may charge a tenant for rent.

(b) Rental agreements subject to this section shall meet all of the following criteria:

(1) The rental agreement shall be in excess of 12 months' duration.

(2) The rental agreement shall be entered into between the management and a homeowner for the personal and actual residence of the homeowner.

(3) The homeowner shall have at least 30 days from the date the rental agreement is first offered to the homeowner to accept or reject the rental agreement.

(4) The homeowner who signs a rental agreement pursuant to this section may void the rental agreement by notifying management in writing within 72 hours of returning the signed rental agreement to management. This paragraph shall only apply if management provides the homeowner a copy of the signed rental agreement at the time the homeowner returns the signed rental agreement.

(5) The homeowner who signs a rental agreement pursuant to this section may void the agreement within 72 hours of receiving an executed copy of the rental agreement pursuant to Section 798.16. This paragraph shall only apply if management does not provide the homeowner with a copy of the signed rental agreement at the time the homeowner returns the signed rental agreement.

(c) If, pursuant to paragraph (3) or (4) of subdivision (b), the homeowner rejects the offered rental agreement or rescinds a signed rental agreement, the homeowner shall be entitled to instead accept, pursuant to Section 798.18, a rental agreement for a term of 12 months or less from the date the offered rental agreement was to have begun. In the event the homeowner elects to have a rental agreement for a term of 12 months or less, including a month-to-month rental agreement, the rental agreement shall contain the same rental charges, terms, and conditions as the rental agreement offered pursuant to subdivision (b), during the first 12 months, except for options, if any, contained in the offered rental agreement to extend or renew the rental agreement.

(d) Nothing in subdivision (c) shall be construed to prohibit the management from offering gifts of value, other than rental rate reductions, to homeowners who execute a rental agreement pursuant to this section.

(e) With respect to any space in a mobilehome park that is exempt under subdivision (a) from any ordinance, rule, regulation, or initiative measure adopted by any local governmental entity that establishes a maximum amount that a landlord may charge a homeowner for rent, and notwithstanding any ordinance, rule, regulation, or initiative measure, a mobilehome park shall not be assessed any fee or other exaction for a park space that is exempt under subdivision (a) imposed pursuant to any ordinance, rule, regulation, or initiative measure. No other fee or other exaction shall be imposed for a park space that is exempt under subdivision (a) for the purpose of defraying the cost of administration thereof.

(f) At the time the rental agreement is first offered to the homeowner, the management shall provide written notice to the homeowner of the homeowner's right (1) to have at least 30 days to inspect the rental agreement, and (2) to void the rental agreement by notifying management in writing within 72 hours of receipt of an executed copy of the rental agreement. The failure of the management to provide the written notice shall make the rental agreement voidable at the homeowner's option upon the homeowner's discovery of the failure. The receipt of any written notice provided pursuant to this subdivision shall be acknowledged in writing by the homeowner.

(g) No rental agreement subject to subdivision (a) that is first entered into on or after January 1, 1993, shall have a provision which authorizes automatic extension or renewal of, or automatically extends or renews, the rental agreement for a period beyond the initial stated term at the sole option of either the management or the homeowner.

(h) This section does not apply to or supersede other provisions of this part or other state law. *(Added by Stats.1985, c. 1084, § 1. Amended by Stats.1986, c. 1416, § 1; Stats.1990, c. 1013 (S.B.2010), § 1; Stats.1990, c. 1046 (S.B.2009), § 2; Stats. 1991, c. 24 (S.B.132), § 1, eff. May 7, 1991, operative May 10, 1991; Stats.1991, c. 170 (S.B.360), § 1; Stats.1992, c. 427 (A.B.3355), § 11; Stats.1992, c. 289 (S.B.1454), § 1; Stats.1993, c. 9 (S.B.6), § 1, eff. April 29, 1993; Stats.2012, c. 477 (A.B.1938), § 1.)*

Research References

Rutter, Cal. Practice Guide: Landlord-Tenant Form 11:A, Sample Mobilehome Park Rental Agreement.

Miller and Starr California Real Estate § 19:92, Property Subject to Control; Exceptions and Exemptions--Application to Mobilehome Parks.

Miller and Starr California Real Estate § 31:23, Mobilehome Residency Law.

Miller and Starr California Real Estate § 31:27, Effect of Rent Control Ordinance.

12 Witkin, California Summary 10th Real Property § 766, (S 766) Term.

12 Witkin, California Summary 10th Real Property § 767, Long-Term Agreements.

12 Witkin, California Summary 10th Real Property § 768, New Construction.

12 Witkin, California Summary 10th Real Property § 769, Space that is Not Principal Residence.

12 Witkin, California Summary 10th Real Property § 777, Homeowner Meetings.

§ 798.18. Term; comparable monthly charges for one year as for month-to-month tenancy; automatic extension or renewal

(a) A homeowner shall be offered a rental agreement for (1) a term of 12 months, or (2) a lesser period as the homeowner may request, or (3) a longer period as mutually agreed upon by both the homeowner and management.

(b) No rental agreement shall contain any terms or conditions with respect to charges for rent, utilities, or incidental reasonable service charges that would be different during the first 12 months of the rental agreement from the corresponding terms or conditions that would be offered to the homeowners on a month-to-month basis.

(c) No rental agreement for a term of 12 months or less shall include any provision which authorizes automatic extension or renewal of, or automatically extends or renews, the rental agreement beyond the initial term for a term longer than 12 months at the sole option of either the management or the homeowner. *(Added by Stats.1978, c. 1031, p. 3178, § 1. Amended by Stats.1978, c. 1032, p. 3186, § 2; Stats.1978, c. 1033, p. 3188, § 7.5; Stats.1980, c. 206, § 1; Stats.1981, c. 667, § 4; Stats.1982, c. 1397, p. 5320, § 6; Stats.1992, c. 289 (S.B.1454), § 2.)*

Research References

Miller and Starr California Real Estate § 19:92, Property Subject to Control; Exceptions and Exemptions--Application to Mobilehome Parks.

Miller and Starr California Real Estate § 31:26, Requirement of Written Rental Agreement.

12 Witkin, California Summary 10th Real Property § 766, (S 766) Term.

§ 798.19. Waiver of rights; public policy

No rental agreement for a mobilehome shall contain a provision by which the homeowner waives his or her rights under the provisions of Articles 1 to 8, inclusive, of this chapter. Any such waiver shall be deemed contrary to public policy and void. *(Added by Stats.1978, c. 1031, p. 3178, § 1. Amended by Stats.1978, c. 1033, p. 3188, § 8; Stats.1982, c. 1397, p. 5320, § 7.)*

Research References

Miller and Starr California Real Estate § 31:26, Requirement of Written Rental Agreement.

12 Witkin, California Summary 10th Real Property § 765, (S 765) Invalid Provisions.

§ 798.19.5. Sale of mobilehome; right of first refusal to management

A rental agreement entered into or renewed on and after January 1, 2006, shall not include a clause, rule, regulation, or any other provision that grants to management the right of first refusal to purchase a homeowner's mobilehome that is in the park and offered for sale to a third party pursuant to Article 7 (commencing with Section 798.70). This section does not preclude a separate agreement for separate consideration granting the park owner or management a right of first refusal to purchase the homeowner's mobilehome that is in the park and offered for sale. *(Added by Stats.2005, c. 35 (S.B.237), § 1.)*

Research References

Miller and Starr California Real Estate § 31:26, Requirement of Written Rental Agreement.

16 NO. 4 Miller & Starr, California Real Estate Newsalert 15, Mobilehomes.

16 NO. 5 Miller & Starr, California Real Estate Newsalert 26, State Board of Equalization Issues Comprehensive Summary and Qs and As for Transfers of Base Year Values of Principal Residences.

12 Witkin, California Summary 10th Real Property § 765, (S 765) Invalid Provisions.

§ 798.20. Private club membership not to be denied on discriminatory basis; familial status

(a) Membership in any private club or organization that is a condition for tenancy in a park shall not be denied on any basis listed in subdivision (a) or (d) of Section 12955 of the Government Code, as those bases are defined in Sections 12926, 12926.1, subdivision (m) and paragraph (1) of subdivision (p) of Section 12955, and Section 12955.2 of the Government Code.

(b) Notwithstanding subdivision (a), with respect to familial status, subdivision (a) shall not be construed to apply to housing for older persons, as defined in Section 12955.9 of the Government Code. With respect to familial status, nothing in subdivision (a) shall be construed to affect Sections 51.2, 51.3, 51.4, 51.10, 51.11, and 799.5, relating to housing for senior citizens. Subdivision (d) of Section 51 and Section 4760 of this code and subdivisions (n), (o), and (p) of Section 12955 of the Government Code shall apply to subdivision (a). *(Added by Stats.1978, c. 1031, p. 3178, § 1. Amended by Stats.2006, c. 578 (A.B.2800), § 6; Stats.2012, c. 181 (A.B.806), § 26, operative Jan. 1, 2014.)*

Law Revision Commission Comments

Section 798.20 is amended to correct a cross-reference to former Section 1360. [40 Cal.L.Rev.Comm. Reports 235 (2010)].

Research References

Miller and Starr California Real Estate § 20:29, Discrimination by a Real Estate Broker.

Miller and Starr California Real Estate § 31:30, Restrictions on Occupancy.

17 NO. 4 Miller & Starr, California Real Estate Newsalert 2, Statutory Update:.

17 NO. 6 Miller & Starr, California Real Estate Newsalert 20, Table of Statutes (Newsalert Vol 17).

12 Witkin, California Summary 10th Real Property § 765, (S 765) Invalid Provisions.

8 Witkin, California Summary 10th Constitutional Law § 897, Other Discrimination Statutes.

§ 798.21. Rent control measures; space not used as principal residence; exemptions

(a) Notwithstanding Section 798.17, if a mobilehome space within a mobilehome park is not the principal residence of the homeowner and the homeowner has not rented the mobilehome to another party, it shall be exempt from any ordinance, rule, regulation, or initiative measure adopted by any city, county, or city and county, which establishes a maximum amount that the landlord may charge a tenant for rent.

(b) Nothing in this section is intended to require any homeowner to disclose information concerning his or her personal finances. Nothing in this section shall be construed to authorize management to gain access to any records which would otherwise be confidential or privileged.

(c) For purposes of this section, a mobilehome shall be deemed to be the principal residence of the homeowner, unless a review of state or county records demonstrates that the homeowner is receiving a homeowner's exemption for another property or mobilehome in this state, or unless a review of public records reasonably demonstrates that the principal residence of the homeowner is out of state.

(d) Before modifying the rent or other terms of tenancy as a result of a review of records, as described in subdivision (c), the management shall notify the homeowner, in writing, of the proposed changes and provide the homeowner with a copy of the documents upon which management relied.

(e) The homeowner shall have 90 days from the date the notice described in subdivision (d) is mailed to review and respond to the notice. Management may not modify the rent or other terms of tenancy prior to the expiration of the 90–day period or prior to responding, in writing, to information provided by the homeowner. Management may not modify the rent or other terms of tenancy if the homeowner provides documentation reasonably establishing that the information provided by management is incorrect or that the homeowner is not the same person identified in the documents. However, nothing in this subdivision shall be construed to authorize the homeowner to change the homeowner's exemption status of the other property or mobilehome owned by the homeowner.

(f) This section does not apply under any of the following conditions:

(1) The homeowner is unable to rent or lease the mobilehome because the owner or management of the mobilehome park in which the mobilehome is located does not permit, or the rental agreement limits or prohibits, the assignment of the mobilehome or the subletting of the park space.

(2) The mobilehome is being actively held available for sale by the homeowner, or pursuant to a listing agreement with a real estate broker licensed pursuant to Chapter 3 (commencing with Section 10130) of Part 1 of Division 4 of the Business and Professions Code, or a mobilehome dealer, as defined in Section 18002.6 of the Health and Safety Code. A homeowner, real estate broker, or mobilehome dealer attempting to sell a mobilehome shall actively market and advertise the mobilehome for sale in good faith to bona fide purchasers for value in order to remain exempt pursuant to this subdivision.

(3) The legal owner has taken possession or ownership, or both, of the mobilehome from a registered owner through either a surrender of ownership interest by the registered owner or a foreclosure proceeding. *(Added by Stats.1996, c. 392 (S.B.1181), § 1. Amended by Stats.2003, c. 132 (A.B.1173), § 1.)*

Research References

Rutter, Cal. Practice Guide: Landlord-Tenant Gen. Matls, Highlights.

Miller and Starr California Real Estate § 19:92, Property Subject to Control; Exceptions and Exemptions--Application to Mobilehome Parks.

Miller and Starr California Real Estate § 31:27, Effect of Rent Control Ordinance.

14 NO. 4 Miller & Starr, California Real Estate Newsalert 10, Landlord and Tenant.

14 NO. 4 Miller & Starr, California Real Estate Newsalert 13, Mobilehomes.

23 NO. 1 Miller & Starr, California Real Estate Newsalert 19, Mobilehomes.

12 Witkin, California Summary 10th Real Property § 769, Space that is Not Principal Residence.

§ 798.22. Recreational vehicles in mobilehome parks; designated areas

(a) In any new mobilehome park that is developed after January 1, 1982, mobilehome spaces shall not be rented for the accommodation of recreational vehicles as defined by Section 799.29 unless the mobilehome park has a specifically designated area within the park for recreational vehicles, which is separate and apart from the area designated for mobilehomes. Recreational vehicles may be located only in the specifically designated area.

(b) Any new mobilehome park that is developed after January 1, 1982, is not subject to the provisions of this section until 75 percent of the spaces have been rented for the first time. *(Added by Stats.1982, c. 1146, p. 4122, § 1. Amended by Stats.1993, c. 666 (A.B.503), § 3.)*

Research References

Miller and Starr California Real Estate § 31:8, Enforcement Responsibilities.

12 Witkin, California Summary 10th Real Property § 765, (S 765) Invalid Provisions.

ARTICLE 3. RULES AND REGULATIONS

§ 798.23. Park owners and employees; compliance; exceptions

(a) The owner of the park, and any person employed by the park, shall be subject to, and comply with, all park rules and regulations, to the same extent as residents and their guests.

(b) Subdivision (a) of this section does not apply to either of the following:

(1) Any rule or regulation that governs the age of any resident or guest.

(2) Acts of a park owner or park employee which are undertaken to fulfill a park owner's maintenance, management, and business operation responsibilities. *(Added by Stats.1993, c. 520 (A.B.217), § 1. Amended by Stats.1994, c. 340 (S.B.1510), § 1; Stats.2002, c. 672 (S.B.1410), § 1.)*

Research References

Miller and Starr California Real Estate § 31:31, Adoption and Enforcement of Rules.

12 Witkin, California Summary 10th Real Property § 775, (S 775) Rules and Regulations.

§ 798.23.5. Rental of homeowner's primary residence, or sublet of space; conditions

(a)(1) Management shall permit a homeowner to rent his or her home that serves as the homeowner's primary residence or sublet his or her space, under the circumstances described in paragraph (2) and subject to the requirements of this section.

(2) A homeowner shall be permitted to rent or sublet pursuant to paragraph (1) if a medical emergency or medical treatment requires the homeowner to be absent from his or her home and this is confirmed in writing by an attending physician.

(b) The following provisions shall apply to a rental or sublease pursuant to this section:

(1) The minimum term of the rental or sublease shall be six months, unless the management approves a shorter term, but no greater than 12 months, unless management approves a longer term.

(2) The management may require approval of a prospective renter or sublessee, subject to the process and restrictions provided by subdivision (a) of Section 798.74 for prospective purchasers of mobilehomes. A prospective sublessee shall comply with any rule or regulation limiting residency based on age requirements, pursuant to Section 798.76. The management may charge a prospective sublessee a credit screening fee for the actual cost of any personal reference check or consumer credit report that is provided by a consumer credit reporting agency, as defined in Section 1785.3, if the management or his or her agent requires that personal reference check or consumer credit report.

(3) The renter or sublessee shall comply with all rules and regulations of the park. The failure of a renter or sublessee to comply with the rules and regulations of the park may result in the termination of the homeowner's tenancy in the mobilehome park, in accordance with Section 798.56. A homeowner's tenancy may not be terminated under this paragraph if the homeowner completes an action for unlawful detainer or executes a judgment for possession, pursuant to Chapter 4 (commencing with Section 1159) of Title 3 of Part 3 of the Code of Civil Procedure within 60 days of the homeowner receiving notice of termination of tenancy.

(4) The homeowner shall remain liable for the mobilehome park rent and other park charges.

(5) The management may require the homeowner to reside in the mobilehome park for a term of one year before management permits the renting or subletting of a mobilehome or mobilehome space.

(6) Notwithstanding subdivision (a) of Section 798.39, if a security deposit has been refunded to the homeowner pursuant to subdivision (b) or (c) of Section 798.39, the management may require the homeowner to resubmit a security deposit in an amount or value not to exceed two months' rent in addition to the first month's rent. Management may retain this security deposit for the duration of the term of the rental or sublease.

(7) The homeowner shall keep his or her current address and telephone number on file with the management during the term of rental or sublease. If applicable, the homeowner may provide the name, address, and telephone number of his or her legal representative.

(c) A homeowner may not charge a renter or sublessee more than an amount necessary to cover the cost of space rent, utilities, and scheduled loan payments on the mobilehome, if any. *(Added by Stats.2002, c. 672 (S.B.1410), § 2. Amended by Stats.2011, c. 296 (A.B.1023), § 32.)*

Research References

Miller and Starr California Real Estate § 31:30, Restrictions on Occupancy.

13 NO. 4 Miller & Starr, California Real Estate Newsalert 15, Mobilehomes.

12 Witkin, California Summary 10th Real Property § 775, (S 775) Rules and Regulations.

12 Witkin, California Summary 10th Real Property § 783, (S 783) Renting or Subletting in Medical Emergency.

§ 798.24. Common area facilities

Each common area facility shall be open or available to residents at all reasonable hours and the hours of the common area facility shall be posted at the facility. *(Added by Stats.1983, c. 503, § 1. Amended by Stats.1994, c. 380 (S.B.1508), § 1; Stats.2001, c. 83 (A.B.1202), § 1.)*

Research References

Miller and Starr California Real Estate § 31:29, Duties Regarding Common Areas.

12 Witkin, California Summary 10th Real Property § 774, (S 774) Maintenance of Premises.

§ 798.25. Amendments to park rules and regulations; written notice; meeting with homeowners

(a) Except as provided in subdivision (d), when the management proposes an amendment to the park's rules and regulations, the management shall meet and consult with the homeowners in the park, their representatives, or both, after written notice has been given to all the homeowners in the park 10 days or more before the meeting. The notice shall set forth the proposed amendment to the park's rules and regulations and shall state the date, time, and location of the meeting.

(b) Except as provided in subdivision (d) following the meeting and consultation with the homeowners, the noticed amendment to the park's rules and regulations may be implemented, as to any homeowner, with the consent of that homeowner, or without the homeowner's consent upon written notice of not less than six months, except for regulations applicable to recreational facilities, which may be amended without homeowner consent upon written notice of not less than 60 days.

(c) Written notice to a homeowner whose tenancy commences within the required period of notice of a proposed amendment to the park's rules and regulations under subdivision (b) or (d) shall constitute compliance with this section where the written notice is given before the inception of the tenancy.

(d) When the management proposes an amendment to the park's rules and regulations mandated by a change in the law, including, but not limited to, a change in a statute, ordinance, or governmental regulation, the management may implement the amendment to the park's rules and regulations, as to any homeowner, with the consent of that homeowner or without the homeowner's consent upon written notice of not less than 60 days. For purposes of this subdivision, the management shall specify in the notice the citation to the statute, ordinance, or regulation, including the section number, that necessitates the proposed amendment to the park's rules and regulations.

(e) Any amendment to the park's rules and regulations that creates a new fee payable by the homeowner and that has not been expressly agreed upon by the homeowner and management in the written rental agreement or lease, shall be void and unenforceable. *(Added by Stats.1978, c. 1033, p. 3186, § 10. Amended by Stats.1982, c. 1397, p. 5321, § 8; Stats.1983, c. 519, § 2; Stats.1993, c. 102 (A.B.285), § 1; Stats.1999, c. 323 (S.B.351), § 1; Stats.2004, c. 622 (S.B.1176), § 1; Stats.2005, c. 22 (S.B.1108), § 11.)*

Research References

Rutter, Cal. Practice Guide: Landlord-Tenant Gen. Matls, Highlights.
Miller and Starr California Real Estate § 31:18, Rent, Fees, and Services.
Miller and Starr California Real Estate § 31:31, Adoption and Enforcement of Rules.
15 NO. 4 Miller & Starr, California Real Estate Newsalert 14, Mobilehomes.
20 NO. 4 Miller & Starr, California Real Estate Newsalert 38, Mobilehomes.
12 Witkin, California Summary 10th Real Property § 775, (S 775) Rules and Regulations.
12 Witkin, California Summary 10th Real Property § 777, Homeowner Meetings.
12 Witkin, California Summary 10th Real Property § 782, (S 782) Sale Following Death of Mobilehome Owner.

§ 798.25.5. Void and unenforceable rules or regulations

Any rule or regulation of a mobilehome park that (a) is unilaterally adopted by the management, (b) is implemented without the consent of the homeowners, and (c) by its terms purports to deny homeowners their right to a trial by jury or which would mandate binding arbitration of any dispute between the management and homeowners shall be void and unenforceable. *(Added by Stats.1993, c. 889 (A.B.1012), § 1.)*

Research References

Miller and Starr California Real Estate § 31:31, Adoption and Enforcement of Rules.

§ 798.26. Right of entry by ownership or management; consent; revocation

(a) Except as provided in subdivision (b), the ownership or management of a park shall have no right of entry to a mobilehome or enclosed accessory structure without the prior written consent of the resident. The consent may be revoked in writing by the resident at any time. The ownership or management shall have a right of entry upon the land upon which a mobilehome is situated for maintenance of utilities, trees, and driveways, for maintenance of the premises in accordance with the rules and regulations of the park when the homeowner or resident fails to so maintain the premises, and protection of the mobilehome park at any reasonable time, but not in a manner or at a time that would interfere with the resident's quiet enjoyment.

(b) The ownership or management of a park may enter a mobilehome or enclosed accessory structure without the prior written consent of the resident in case of an emergency or when the resident has abandoned the mobilehome or accessory structure. *(Formerly § 789.16, added by Stats.1978, c. 396, p. 1252, § 1. Renumbered § 798.26 and amended by Stats.1978, c. 1033, p. 3188, § 10.5. Amended by Stats.1981, c. 667, § 5; Stats.1982, c. 1397, p. 5321, § 9; Stats.1983, c. 519, § 3; Stats.2000, c. 423 (A.B.862), § 1; Stats.2004, c. 302 (A.B.2351), § 2; Stats.2008, c. 115 (S.B.1234), § 1.)*

Research References

Miller and Starr California Real Estate § 31:24, When Park Owned by Mobilehome Owners.
Miller and Starr California Real Estate § 31:29, Duties Regarding Common Areas.
12 Witkin, California Summary 10th Real Property § 774, (S 774) Maintenance of Premises.

§ 798.27. Written notice of nature of zoning permit and duration of lease to homeowners and prospective homeowners

(a) The management shall give written notice to all homeowners and prospective homeowners concerning the following matters: (1) the nature of the zoning or use permit under which the mobilehome park operates. If the mobilehome park is operating pursuant to a permit subject to a renewal or expiration date, the relevant information and dates shall be included in the notice. (2) The duration of any lease of the mobilehome park, or any portion thereof, in which the management is a lessee.

(b) If a change occurs concerning the zoning or use permit under which the park operates or a lease in which the management is a lessee, all homeowners shall be given written notice within 30 days of that change. Notification regarding the change of use of the park, or any portion thereof, shall be governed by subdivision (g) of Section 798.56. A prospective homeowner shall be notified prior to the inception of the tenancy. *(Added by Stats.1980, c. 864, § 1. Amended by Stats.1981, c. 667, § 6; Stats.1982, c. 1397, p. 5321, § 10; Stats.1991, c. 190 (A.B.600), § 1.)*

Research References

Miller and Starr California Real Estate § 31:28, Required Notices and Disclosure Forms to Tenants.
12 Witkin, California Summary 10th Real Property § 776, (S 776) Notices and Disclosures.

§ 798.28. Disclosure of mobilehome park owner

The management of a mobilehome park shall disclose, in writing, the name, business address, and business telephone number of the mobilehome park owner upon the request of a homeowner. *(Added by Stats.1981, c. 505, § 1. Amended by Stats.1982, c. 1397, p. 5322, § 11; Stats.1991, c. 62 (A.B.577), § 1.)*

Research References

Miller and Starr California Real Estate § 31:7, Management.
Miller and Starr California Real Estate § 31:25, Park Management.
12 Witkin, California Summary 10th Real Property § 776, (S 776) Notices and Disclosures.

§ 798.28.5. Motor vehicles; removal from park; notice of intent to remove

(a) Except as otherwise provided in this section, the management may cause the removal, pursuant to Section 22658 of the Vehicle Code, of a vehicle other than a mobilehome that is parked in the park when there is displayed a sign at each entrance to the park as provided in paragraph (1) of subdivision (a) of Section 22658 of the Vehicle Code.

(b)(1) Management may not cause the removal of a vehicle from a homeowner's or resident's driveway or a homeowner's or resident's designated parking space except if management has first posted on the windshield of the vehicle a notice stating management's intent to remove the vehicle in seven days and stating the specific park rule that the vehicle has violated that justifies its removal. After the expiration of seven days following the posting of the notice, management may remove a vehicle that remains in violation of a rule for which notice has been posted upon the vehicle. If a vehicle rule violation is corrected within seven days after the rule violation notice is posted on the vehicle, the vehicle may not be removed. If a vehicle upon which a rule violation notice has been posted is removed from the park by a homeowner or resident and subsequently is returned to the park still in violation of the rule stated in the notice, management is not required to post any additional notice on the vehicle, and the vehicle may be removed after the expiration of the seven-day period following the original notice posting.

(2) If a vehicle poses a significant danger to the health or safety of a park resident or guest, or if a homeowner or resident requests to have a vehicle removed from his or her driveway or designated parking space, the requirements of paragraph (1) do not apply, and management may remove the vehicle pursuant to Section 22658 of the Vehicle Code. *(Formerly § 798.285, added by Stats.1993, c. 32 (S.B.209), § 1. Renumbered § 798.28.5 and amended by Stats.2004, c. 302 (A.B.2351), § 3.)*

Research References

Miller and Starr California Real Estate § 31:29, Duties Regarding Common Areas.
12 Witkin, California Summary 10th Real Property § 774, (S 774) Maintenance of Premises.

§ 798.29.   Ombudsman signs

The management shall post a mobilehome ombudsman sign provided by the Department of Housing and Community Development, as required by Section 18253.5 of the Health and Safety Code. *(Added by Stats.1988, c. 333, § 1. Amended by Stats. 1996, c. 402 (S.B.1594), § 1.)*

Research References

Miller and Starr California Real Estate § 31:7, Management.
12 Witkin, California Summary 10th Real Property § 763, (S 763) Mobilehome Ombudsman.

§ 798.29.6.   Installation of accommodations for the disabled

The management shall not prohibit a homeowner or resident from installing accommodations for the disabled on the home or the site, lot, or space on which the mobilehome is located, including, but not limited to, ramps or handrails on the outside of the home, as long as the installation of those facilities complies with code, as determined by an enforcement agency, and those facilities are installed pursuant to a permit, if required for the installation, issued by the enforcement agency. The management may require that the accommodations installed pursuant to this section be removed by the current homeowner at the time the mobilehome is removed from the park or pursuant to a written agreement between the current homeowner and the management prior to the completion of the resale of the mobilehome in place in the park. This section is not exclusive and shall not be construed to condition, affect, or supersede any other provision of law or regulation relating to accessibility or accommodations for the disabled. *(Added by Stats.2008, c. 170 (S.B.1107), § 1.)*

Research References

Miller and Starr California Real Estate § 31:18, Rent, Fees, and Services.
19 NO. 4 Miller & Starr, California Real Estate Newsalert 22, Mobile-homes.
12 Witkin, California Summary 10th Real Property § 775, (S 775) Rules and Regulations.

ARTICLE 3.5.   FEES AND CHARGES

§ 798.30.   Notice of rent increase

The management shall give a homeowner written notice of any increase in his or her rent at least 90 days before the date of the increase. *(Added by Stats.1978, c. 1031, p. 3178, § 1. Amended by Stats.1982, c. 1397, p. 5322, § 12; Stats.1993, c. 448 (A.B.870), § 1.)*

Research References

Miller and Starr California Real Estate § 31:21, Rent Increases.
12 Witkin, California Summary 10th Real Property § 772, (S 772) Method of Charging Proper Fees.

§ 798.31.   Authorized fees

A homeowner shall not be charged a fee for other than rent, utilities, and incidental reasonable charges for services actually rendered.

A homeowner shall not be charged a fee for obtaining a lease on a mobilehome lot for (1) a term of 12 months, or (2) a lesser period as the homeowner may request. A fee may be charged for a lease of more than one year if the fee is mutually agreed upon by both the homeowner and management. *(Added by Stats.1978, c. 1031, p. 3178, § 1. Amended by Stats.1982, c. 1397, p. 5322, § 13; Stats.1984, c. 624, § 1.)*

Research References

Miller and Starr California Real Estate § 31:18, Rent, Fees, and Services.
15 NO. 5 Miller & Starr, California Real Estate Newsalert 16, Mobile-homes.
17 NO. 4 Miller & Starr, California Real Estate Newsalert 15, Mobile-homes.
12 Witkin, California Summary 10th Real Property § 771, (S 771) Improper Fees and Charges.
12 Witkin, California Summary 10th Real Property § 772, (S 772) Method of Charging Proper Fees.

§ 798.32.   Charge for unlisted services; notice; expiration date of fees

(a) A homeowner shall not be charged a fee for services actually rendered which are not listed in the rental agreement unless he or she has been given written notice thereof by the management, at least 60 days before imposition of the charge.

(b) Those fees and charges specified in subdivision (a) shall be separately stated on any monthly or other periodic billing to the homeowner. If the fee or charge has a limited duration or is amortized for a specified period, the expiration date shall be stated on the initial notice and each subsequent billing to the homeowner while the fee or charge is billed to the homeowner. *(Added by Stats.1978, c. 1031, p. 3178, § 1. Amended by Stats.1982, c. 1397, p. 5322, § 14; Stats.1992, c. 338 (S.B.1365), § 1.)*

Research References

Miller and Starr California Real Estate § 31:18, Rent, Fees, and Services.
12 Witkin, California Summary 10th Real Property § 771, (S 771) Improper Fees and Charges.

§ 798.33. Pets

(a) No lease agreement entered into, modified, or renewed on or after January 1, 2001, shall prohibit a homeowner from keeping at least one pet within the park, subject to reasonable rules and regulations of the park. This section may not be construed to affect any other rights provided by law to a homeowner to keep a pet within the park.

(b) A homeowner shall not be charged a fee for keeping a pet in the park unless the management actually provides special facilities or services for pets. If special pet facilities are maintained by the management, the fee charged shall reasonably relate to the cost of maintenance of the facilities or services and the number of pets kept in the park.

(c) For purposes of this section, "pet" means any domesticated bird, cat, dog, aquatic animal kept within an aquarium, or other animal as agreed to between the management and the homeowner. *(Added by Stats.1978, c. 1031, p. 3178, § 1. Amended by Stats.1978, c. 1033, p. 3189, § 11; Stats.1982, c. 1397, p. 5322, § 15; Stats.1989, c. 42, § 1; Stats.2000, c. 551 (A.B.860), § 1.)*

Research References

Miller and Starr California Real Estate § 31:18, Rent, Fees, and Services.
15 NO. 3 Miller & Starr, California Real Estate Newsalert 1, We're Not in Kansas Anymore: Disability Discrimination Case Reaches New Frontiers.
12 Witkin, California Summary 10th Real Property § 765, (S 765) Invalid Provisions.
12 Witkin, California Summary 10th Real Property § 771, (S 771) Improper Fees and Charges.

§ 798.34. Guests and live-in health and supportive care providers

(a) A homeowner shall not be charged a fee for a guest who does not stay with him or her for more than a total of 20 consecutive days or a total of 30 days in a calendar year. A person who is a guest, as described in this subdivision, shall not be required to register with the management.

(b) A homeowner who is living alone and who wishes to share his or her mobilehome with one person may do so, and a fee shall not be imposed by management for that person. The person shall be considered a guest of the homeowner and any agreement between the homeowner and the person shall not change the terms and conditions of the rental agreement between management and the homeowner. The guest shall comply with the provisions of the rules and regulations of the mobilehome park.

(c) A homeowner may share his or her mobilehome with any person over 18 years of age if that person is providing live-in health care or live-in supportive care to the homeowner pursuant to a written treatment plan prepared by the homeowner's physician. A fee shall not be charged by management for that person. That person shall have no rights of tenancy in the park, and any agreement between the homeowner and the person shall not change the terms and conditions of the rental agreement between management and the homeowner. That person shall comply with the rules and regulations of the mobilehome park.

(d) A senior homeowner who resides in a mobilehome park that has implemented rules or regulations limiting residency based on age requirements for housing for older persons, pursuant to Section 798.76, may share his or her mobilehome with any person over 18 years of age if this person is a parent, sibling, child, or grandchild of the senior homeowner and requires live-in health care, live-in supportive care, or supervision pursuant to a written treatment plan prepared by a physician and surgeon. Management may not charge a fee for this person. Any agreement between the senior homeowner and this person shall not change the terms and conditions of the rental agreement between management and the senior homeowner. Unless otherwise agreed upon, park management shall not be required to manage, supervise, or provide for this person's care during his or her stay in the mobilehome park. This person shall have no rights of tenancy in the park, but shall comply with the rules and regulations of the mobilehome park. A violation of the mobilehome park rules and regulations by this person shall be deemed a violation of the rules and regulations by the homeowner pursuant to subdivision (d) of Section 798.56. As used in this subdivision, "senior homeowner" means a homeowner who is 55 years of age or older. *(Added by Stats.1978, c. 1031, p. 3178, § 1. Amended by Stats.1981, c. 240, § 1; Stats.1982, c. 1397, p. 5322, § 16; Stats.1983, c. 128, § 1; Stats.1990, c. 881 (S.B.2547), § 1; Stats.1992, c. 337 (S.B.1314), § 1; Stats.1996, c. 157 (S.B.1624), § 1; Stats.2008, c. 170 (S.B.1107), § 2.)*

Research References

Miller and Starr California Real Estate § 20:6, The Unruh Civil Rights Act--Age Discrimination in Mobilehome Parks.
Miller and Starr California Real Estate § 31:18, Rent, Fees, and Services.
19 NO. 4 Miller & Starr, California Real Estate Newsalert 22, Mobilehomes.
12 Witkin, California Summary 10th Real Property § 771, (S 771) Improper Fees and Charges.

§ 798.35. Number of immediate family members

A homeowner shall not be charged a fee based on the number of members in his or her immediate family. As used in this section, the "immediate family" shall be limited to the homeowner, his or her spouse, their parents, their children, and their grandchildren under 18 years of age. *(Added by Stats.1978, c. 1031, p. 3178, § 1. Amended by Stats.1980, c. 845, § 1; Stats.1982, c. 1397, p. 5322, § 17; Stats.1995, c. 24 (A.B.283), § 1.)*

Research References

Miller and Starr California Real Estate § 31:18, Rent, Fees, and Services.
12 Witkin, California Summary 10th Real Property § 771, (S 771) Improper Fees and Charges.

§ 798.36. Rule enforcement; removal of personal property; notice; costs; sale or auction of property

(a) A homeowner shall not be charged a fee for the enforcement of any of the rules and regulations of the park, except a reasonable fee may be charged by management for the maintenance or cleanup, as described in subdivision (b), of the land and premises upon which the mobilehome is situated in the event the homeowner fails to do so in accordance with the rules and regulations of the park after written notification to the homeowner and the failure of the homeowner to comply within 14 days. The written notice shall state the specific condition to be corrected and an estimate of the charges to be imposed by management if the services are performed by management or its agent.

(b)(1) If management determines, in good faith, that the removal of a homeowner's or resident's personal property from the land and premises upon which the mobilehome is situated is necessary to bring the premises into compliance with the reasonable rules and regulations of the park or the provisions of the Mobilehome Parks Act (Part 2.1 (commencing with Section 18200) of Division 13 of the Health and Safety Code) or Title 25 of the California Code of Regulations, management may remove the property to a reasonably secure storage facility. Management shall provide written notice of at least 14 days of its intent to remove the personal property, including a description of the property to be removed. The notice shall include the rule, regulation, or code justifying the removal and shall provide an estimate of the charges to be imposed by management. The property to be removed shall not include the mobilehome or its appurtenances or accessory structures.

(2) The homeowner or resident shall be responsible for reimbursing to management the actual, reasonable costs, if any, of removing and storing the property. These costs incurred by management in correcting the rules violation associated with the removal and storage of the property, are deemed reasonable incidental service charges and may be collected pursuant to subdivision (e) of Section 798.56 if a notice of nonpayment of the removal and storage fees, as described in paragraph (3), is personally served on the homeowner.

(3) Within seven days from the date the property is removed to a storage area, management shall provide the homeowner or resident a written notice that includes an inventory of the property removed, the location where the property may be claimed, and notice that the cost of removal and storage shall be paid by the resident or homeowner. If, within 60 days, the homeowner or resident does not claim the property, the property shall be deemed to be abandoned, and management may dispose of the property in any manner. The homeowner's or resident's liability for storage charges shall not exceed 60 days. If the homeowner or resident claims the property, but has not reimbursed management for storage costs, management may bill those costs in a monthly statement which shall constitute notice of nonpayment, and the costs shall become the obligation of the homeowner or resident. If a resident or homeowner communicates in writing his or her intent to abandon the property before 60 days has expired, management may dispose of the property immediately and no further storage charges shall accrue.

(4) If management elects to dispose of the property by way of sale or auction, and the funds received from the sale or auction exceed the amount owed to management, management shall refund the difference to the homeowner or resident within 15 days from the date of management's receipt of the funds from the sale or auction. The refund shall be delivered to the homeowner or resident by first-class mail postage prepaid to his or her address in the park, or by personal delivery, and shall include an accounting specifying the costs of removal and storage of the property incurred by management in correcting the rules violation and the amount of proceeds realized from any sale or auction. If a sale or auction of the property yields less than the costs incurred by management, the homeowner or resident shall be responsible for the difference, and this amount shall be deemed a reasonable incidental service charge and may be collected pursuant to subdivision (e) of Section 798.56 if a notice of nonpayment of the removal and storage fees, as described in paragraph (3), is personally served on the homeowner. If management elects to proceed under this section, it may not also terminate the tenancy pursuant to subdivision (d) of Section 798.56 based upon the specific violations relied upon to proceed under this section. In any proceeding under this section, management shall bear the burden of proof that enforcement was undertaken in a nondiscriminatory, nonselective fashion. *(Added by Stats.1978, c. 1031, p. 3178, § 1. Amended by Stats.1982, c. 1397, p. 5322, § 18; Stats.1983, c. 519, § 4; Stats.2005, c. 24 (S.B.125), § 1.)*

Research References

Miller and Starr California Real Estate § 31:18, Rent, Fees, and Services.
16 NO. 4 Miller & Starr, California Real Estate Newsalert 15, Mobilehomes.

16 NO. 5 Miller & Starr, California Real Estate Newsalert 26, State Board of Equalization Issues Comprehensive Summary and Qs and As for Transfers of Base Year Values of Principal Residences.
12 Witkin, California Summary 10th Real Property § 771, (S 771) Improper Fees and Charges.

§ 798.37. Entry, installation or hookup fees; landscaping and maintenance charges

A homeowner may not be charged a fee for the entry, installation, hookup, or landscaping as a condition of tenancy except for an actual fee or cost imposed by a local governmental ordinance or requirement directly related to the occupancy of the specific site upon which the mobilehome is located and not incurred as a portion of the development of the mobilehome park as a whole. However, reasonable landscaping and maintenance requirements may be included in the park rules and regulations. The management may not require a homeowner or prospective homeowner to purchase, rent, or lease goods or services for landscaping, remodeling, or maintenance from any person, company, or corporation. *(Added by Stats.1978, c. 1031, p. 3178, § 1. Amended by Stats.1980, c. 845, § 2; Stats.1982, c. 1397, p. 5322, § 19; Stats.1983, c. 519, § 5; Stats.2004, c. 302 (A.B.2351), § 4.)*

Research References

Miller and Starr California Real Estate § 31:18, Rent, Fees, and Services.
Miller and Starr California Real Estate § 31:22, Utility Services.
15 NO. 4 Miller & Starr, California Real Estate Newsalert 14, Mobilehomes.
12 Witkin, California Summary 10th Real Property § 771, (S 771) Improper Fees and Charges.

§ 798.37.5. Trimming, pruning, or removal of trees; responsibility of mobilehome park management

(a) With respect to trees on rental spaces in a mobilehome park, park management shall be solely responsible for the trimming, pruning, or removal of any tree, and the costs thereof, upon written notice by a homeowner or a determination by park management that the tree poses a specific hazard or health and safety violation. In the case of a dispute over that assertion, the park management or a homeowner may request an inspection by the Department of Housing and Community Development or a local agency responsible for the enforcement of the Mobilehome Parks Act (Part 2.1 (commencing with Section 18200) of Division 3 of the Health and Safety Code) in order to determine whether a violation of that act exists.

(b) With respect to trees in the common areas of a mobilehome park, park management shall be solely responsible for the trimming, pruning, or removal of any tree, and the costs thereof.

(c) Park management shall be solely responsible for the maintenance, repair, replacement, paving, sealing, and the expenses related to the maintenance of all driveways installed by park management including, but not limited to, repair of root damage to driveways and foundation systems and removal. Homeowners shall be responsible for the maintenance, repair, replacement, paving, sealing, and the expenses related to the maintenance of a homeowner installed driveway. A homeowner may be charged for the cost of any damage to the driveway caused by an act of the homeowner or a breach of the homeowner's responsibilities under the rules and regulations so long as those rules and regulations are not inconsistent with the provisions of this section.

(d) No homeowner may plant a tree within the mobilehome park without first obtaining written permission from the management.

(e) This section shall not apply to alter the terms of any rental agreement in effect prior to January 1, 2001, between the park management and the homeowner regarding the responsibility for the maintenance of trees and driveways within the mobilehome park, except that upon any renewal or extension, the rental agreement shall be subject to this section. This section is not intended to abrogate the content of any existing rental agreement or other written agreements regarding trees or driveways that are in effect prior to January 1, 2001.

(f) This section shall only apply to rental agreements entered into, renewed, or extended on or after January 1, 2001.

(g) Any mobilehome park rule or regulation shall be in compliance with this section. *(Added by Stats.2000, c. 423 (A.B.862), § 2.)*

Research References

Miller and Starr California Real Estate § 31:7, Management.
12 Witkin, California Summary 10th Real Property § 774, (S 774) Maintenance of Premises.

§ 798.38. Lien or security interest by mutual agreement; exception

The management shall not acquire a lien or security interest, other than an interest arising by reason of process issued to enforce a judgment of any court, in a mobilehome located in the park unless it is mutually agreed upon by both the homeowner and management. Any billing and payment upon the obligation shall be kept separate from current rent. *(Formerly § 798.40, added by Stats.1986, c. 390, § 1. Renumbered § 798.38 and amended by Stats.2009, c. 558 (S.B.111), § 5.)*

Research References

Miller and Starr California Real Estate § 31:22, Utility Services.
Miller and Starr California Real Estate § 31:37, Tax and Possessory Liens.
15 NO. 4 Miller & Starr, California Real Estate Newsalert 14, Mobilehomes.

§ 798.39. Security deposit; amount; refund; application

(a) The management may only demand a security deposit on or before initial occupancy and the security deposit may not be in an amount or value in excess of an amount equal to two months' rent that is charged at the inception of the occupancy, in addition to any rent for the first month. In no event shall additional security deposits be demanded of a homeowner following the initial occupancy.

(b) As to all security deposits collected on or after January 1, 1989, after the homeowner has promptly paid to the management, within five days of the date the amount is due, all of the rent, utilities, and reasonable service charges for any 12-consecutive-month period subsequent to the collection of the security deposit by the management, or upon resale of the mobilehome, whichever occurs earlier, the management shall, upon the receipt of a written request from the homeowner, refund to the homeowner the amount of the security deposit within 30 days following the end of the 12-consecutive-month period of the prompt payment or the date of the resale of the mobilehome.

(c) As to all security deposits collected prior to January 1, 1989, upon the extension or renewal of the rental agreement or lease between the homeowner and the management, and upon the receipt of a written request from the homeowner, if the homeowner has promptly paid to the management, within five days of the date the amount is due, all of the rent, utilities, and reasonable service charges for the 12–consecutive–month period preceding the receipt of the written request, the management shall refund to the homeowner the amount of the security deposit within 60 days.

(d) As to all security deposits collected prior to January 1, 1989, and not disbursed pursuant to subdivision (c), in the event that the mobilehome park is sold or transferred to any other party or entity, the selling park owner shall deposit in escrow an amount equal to all security deposits that the park owner holds. The seller's escrow instructions shall direct that, upon close of escrow, the security deposits therein that were held by the selling park owner (including the period in escrow) for 12 months or more, shall be disbursed to the persons who paid the deposits to the selling park owner and promptly paid, within five days of the date the amount is due, all rent, utilities, and reasonable service charges for the 12–month period preceding the close of escrow.

(e) Any and all security deposits in escrow that were held by the selling park owner that are not required to be disbursed pursuant to subdivision (b), (c), or (d) shall be disbursed to the successors in interest to the selling or transferring park owner, who shall have the same obligations of the park's management and ownership specified in this section with respect to security deposits. The disbursal may be made in escrow by a debit against the selling park owner and a credit to the successors in interest to the selling park owner.

(f) The management shall not be required to place any security deposit collected in an interest-bearing account or to provide a homeowner with any interest on the security deposit collected.

(g) Nothing in this section shall affect the validity of title to real property transferred in violation of this section. *(Added by Stats.1988, c. 59, § 1. Amended by Stats.1994, c. 119 (S.B.1386), § 1; Stats.2001, c. 151 (A.B.210), § 1.)*

Research References

Miller and Starr California Real Estate § 31:20, Security Deposits.
12 Witkin, California Summary 10th Real Property § 773, (S 773) Security Deposits.
12 Witkin, California Summary 10th Real Property § 783, (S 783) Renting or Subletting in Medical Emergency.

§ 798.39.5. Prohibition of charge, fee or increase of rent to reflect cost to management of violations of chapter

(a)(1) The management shall not charge or impose upon a homeowner any fee or increase in rent which reflects the cost to the management of any fine, forfeiture, penalty, money damages, or fee assessed or awarded by a court of law or an enforcement agency against the management for a violation of this chapter or Part 2.1 (commencing with Section 18200) of Division 13 of the Health and Safety Code, including any attorney's fees and costs incurred by the management in connection therewith.

(2) This section shall not apply to violations for which the registered owner of the mobilehome is initially responsible pursuant to subdivision (b) of Section 18420 of the Health and Safety Code.

(b) A court shall consider the remoteness in time of the assessment or award against the management of any fine, forfeiture, penalty, money damages, or fee in determining whether the homeowner has met the burden of proof that the fee or increase in rent is in violation of this section.

(c) Any provision in a rental agreement entered into, renewed, or modified on or after January 1, 1995, that permits a fee or increase in rent that reflects the cost to the management of any money damages awarded against the management for a violation of this chapter shall be void. *(Formerly § 798.42, added by Stats.1990, c. 1374 (S.B.2446), § 1. Amended by Stats.1994, c. 1254 (A.B.3566), § 1. Renumbered § 798.39.5 and amended by Stats.2009, c. 558 (S.B.111), § 6. Amended by Stats.2012, c. 477 (A.B.1938), § 2.)*

Research References

Miller and Starr California Real Estate § 31:18, Rent, Fees, and Services.

ARTICLE 4.   UTILITIES

§ 798.40.   Utility meter service; billing; rate schedule

(a) Where the management provides both master-meter and submeter service of utilities to a homeowner, for each billing period the cost of the charges for the period shall be separately stated along with the opening and closing readings for his or her meter. The management shall post, in a conspicuous place, the * * * specific current residential utility rate schedule as published by the serving utility or the Internet Web site address of the specific current residential utility rate schedule. If the management elects to post the Internet Web site address where the schedule may be accessed, the management shall also: (1) provide a copy of the specific current residential utility rate schedule, upon request, at no cost; and (2) state in the posting that a homeowner may request a copy of the rate schedule from management.

(b) If a third-party billing agent or company prepares utility billing for the park, the management shall disclose on each resident's billing, the name, address, and telephone number of the billing agent or company. *(Formerly § 798.38, added by Stats.1978, c. 1031, p. 3178, § 1. Amended by Stats.1981, c. 714, § 51; Stats.1982, c. 1397, p. 5322, § 20; Stats.2004, c. 728 (S.B.1163), § 1. Renumbered § 798.40 and amended by Stats. 2009, c. 558 (S.B.111), § 3. Amended by Stats.2013, c. 201 (S.B.196), § 1.)*

Research References

Miller and Starr California Real Estate § 31:22, Utility Services.

Miller and Starr California Real Estate § 31:37, Tax and Possessory Liens.

12 Witkin, California Summary 10th Real Property § 771, (S 771) Improper Fees and Charges.

§ 798.41.   Utility service fees; separate billing; application; expiration date of fees

(a) Where a rental agreement, including a rental agreement specified in Section 798.17, does not specifically provide otherwise, the park management may elect to bill a homeowner separately for utility service fees and charges assessed by the utility for services provided to or for spaces in the park. Any separately billed utility fees and charges shall not be deemed to be included in the rent charged for those spaces under the rental agreement, and shall not be deemed to be rent or a rent increase for purposes of any ordinance, rule, regulation, or initiative measure adopted or enforced by any local governmental entity which establishes a maximum amount that a landlord may charge a tenant for rent, provided that at the time of the initial separate billing of any utility fees and charges the rent chargeable under the rental agreement or the base rent chargeable under the terms of a local rent control provision is simultaneously reduced by an amount equal to the fees and charges separately billed. The amount of this reduction shall be equal to the average amount charged to the park management for that utility service for that space during the 12 months immediately preceding notice of the commencement of the separate billing for that utility service.

Utility services to which this section applies are natural gas or liquid propane gas, electricity, water, cable television, garbage or refuse service, and sewer service.

(b) This section does not apply to rental agreements entered into prior to January 1, 1991, until extended or renewed on or after that date.

(c) Nothing in this section shall require rental agreements to provide for separate billing to homeowners of fees and charges specified in subdivision (a).

(d) Those fees and charges specified in subdivision (a) shall be separately stated on any monthly or other periodic billing to the homeowner. If the fee or charge has a limited duration or is amortized for a specified period, the expiration date shall be stated on the initial notice and each subsequent billing to the homeowner while the fee or charge is billed to the homeowner. *(Added by Stats.1990, c. 1013 (S.B.2010), § 2. Amended by Stats.1992, c. 160 (S.B.1658), § 1; Stats.1992, c. 338 (S.B.1365), § 2.)*

Research References

Miller and Starr California Real Estate § 19:92, Property Subject to Control; Exceptions and Exemptions--Application to Mobilehome Parks.

Miller and Starr California Real Estate § 31:22, Utility Services.

12 Witkin, California Summary 10th Real Property § 772, (S 772) Method of Charging Proper Fees.

6 Witkin, California Summary 10th Torts § 1571, Recovery of Both Penalty and Punitive Damages.

§ 798.42.   Interruption in utility service within mobilehome park; written advance notice by ownership or management; liability

The management shall provide, by posting notice on the mobilehomes of all affected homeowners and residents, at least 72 hours' written advance notice of an interruption in utility service of more than two hours for the maintenance, repair, or replacement of facilities of utility systems over which the management has control within the park, provided that the interruption is not due to an emergency. The management shall be liable only for actual damages sustained by a homeowner or resident for violation of this section.

"Emergency," for purposes of this section, means the interruption of utility service resulting from an accident or act of nature, or cessation of service caused by other than the management's regular or planned maintenance, repair, or replacement of utility facilities. *(Formerly § 798.29.5, added by Stats.1992, c. 317 (S.B.1389), § 1. Renumbered § 798.42 and amended by Stats. 2009, c. 558 (S.B.111), § 1.)*

Research References

Miller and Starr California Real Estate § 31:18, Rent, Fees, and Services.
Miller and Starr California Real Estate § 31:22, Utility Services.

12 Witkin, California Summary 10th Real Property § 771, (S 771) Improper Fees and Charges.

§ 798.43. Homeowner's meter measuring utility service to common areas; disclosure prior to tenancy

(a) Except as provided in subdivision (b), whenever a homeowner is responsible for payment of gas, water, or electric utility service, management shall disclose to the homeowner any condition by which a gas, water, or electric meter on the homeowner's site measures gas, water, or electric service for common area facilities or equipment, including lighting, provided that management has knowledge of the condition.

Management shall disclose this information prior to the inception of the tenancy or upon discovery and shall complete either of the following:

(1) Enter into a mutual written agreement with the homeowner for compensation by management for the cost of the portion of the service measured by the homeowner's meter for the common area facilities or equipment to the extent that this cost accrues on or after January 1, 1991.

(2) Discontinue using the meter on the homeowner's site for the utility service to the common area facilities and equipment.

(b) On and after January 1, 1994, if the electric meter on the homeowner's site measures electricity for lighting mandated by Section 18602 of the Health and Safety Code and this lighting provides lighting for the homeowner's site, management shall be required to comply with subdivision (a). *(Formerly § 798.41, added by Stats.1990, c. 380 (A.B.3259), § 1. Renumbered § 798.43 and amended by Stats.1991, c. 1091 (A.B.1487), § 15. Amended by Stats.1993, c. 147 (A.B.1140), § 1.)*

Research References

Miller and Starr California Real Estate § 31:22, Utility Services.

§ 798.43.1. California Alternate Rates for Energy (CARE) program; assistance to low-income persons for utility costs; duties of management of master-meter parks; notice; application processes and procedures; discount notice on billing statements

(a) The management of a master-meter park shall give written notice to homeowners and residents on or before February 1 of each year in their utility billing statements about assistance to low-income persons for utility costs available under the California Alternate Rates for Energy (CARE) program, established pursuant to Section 739.1 of the Public Utilities Code. The notice shall include CARE information available to master-meter customers from their serving utility, to include, at a minimum: (1) the fact that CARE offers a discount on monthly gas or electric bills for qualifying low-income residents; and (2) the telephone number of the serving utility which provides CARE information and applications. The park shall also post the notice in a conspicuous place in the clubhouse, or if there is no clubhouse, in a conspicuous public place in the park.

(b) The management of a master-meter park may accept and help process CARE program applications from homeowners and residents in the park, fill in the necessary account or other park information required by the serving utility to process the applications, and send the applications to the serving utility. The management shall not deny a homeowner or resident who chooses to submit a CARE application to the utility himself or herself any park information, including a utility account number, the serving utility requires to process a homeowner or resident CARE program application.

(c) The management of a master-meter park shall pass through the full amount of the CARE program discount in monthly utility billings to homeowners and residents who have qualified for the CARE rate schedule, as defined in the serving utility's applicable rate schedule. The management shall notice the discount on the billing statement of any homeowner or resident who has qualified for the CARE rate schedule as either the itemized amount of the discount or a notation on the statement that the homeowner or resident is receiving the CARE discount on the electric bill, the gas bill, or both the electric and gas bills.

(d) "Master-meter park" as used in this section means "master-meter customer" as used in Section 739.5 of the Public Utilities Code. *(Added by Stats.2001, c. 437 (S.B.920), § 1.)*

Research References

Miller and Starr California Real Estate § 31:22, Utility Services.

§ 798.44. Mobilehome park owners or residents; sale of liquified petroleum gas; limit on price that can be charged

(a) The management of a park that does not permit mobilehome owners or park residents to purchase liquefied petroleum gas for use in the mobilehome park from someone other than the mobilehome park management shall not sell liquefied petroleum gas to mobilehome owners and residents within the park at a cost which exceeds 110 percent of the actual price paid by the management of the park for liquefied petroleum gas.

(b) The management of a park shall post in a visible location the actual price paid by management for liquefied petroleum gas sold pursuant to subdivision (a).

(c) This section shall apply only to mobilehome parks regulated under the Mobilehome Residency Law. This section shall not apply to recreational vehicle parks, as defined in Section 18215 of the Health and Safety Code, which exclusively serve recreational vehicles, as defined in Section 18010 of the Health and Safety Code.

(d) Nothing in this section is intended to abrogate any rights a mobilehome park owner may have under Section 798.31 of the Civil Code.

(e) In addition to a mobilehome park described in subdivision (a), the requirements of subdivisions (a) and (b) shall apply to a mobilehome park where requirements of federal, state, or local law or regulation, including, but not limited to, requirements for setbacks between mobilehomes, prohibit homeowners or residents from installing their own liquefied petroleum gas supply tanks, notwithstanding that the management of the mobilehome park permits mobilehome owners and park residents to buy their own liquefied petroleum gas. *(Added by Stats.1999, c. 326 (S.B.476), § 2. Amended by Stats.2000, c. 232 (S.B.1612), § 1; Stats.2009, c. 558 (S.B.111), § 7.)*

Research References

Miller and Starr California Real Estate § 31:22, Utility Services.

ARTICLE 4.5. RENT CONTROL

Section

§ 798.45. New construction; rent control exemption

Notwithstanding Section 798.17, "new construction" as defined in Section 798.7, shall be exempt from any ordinance, rule, regulation, or initiative measure adopted by any city, county, or city and county, which establishes a maximum amount that a landlord may charge a tenant for rent. *(Added by Stats.1989, c. 412, § 2.)*

Research References

Miller and Starr California Real Estate § 31:27, Effect of Rent Control Ordinance.
12 Witkin, California Summary 10th Real Property § 768, New Construction.

§ 798.49. Separate charges for certain fees, assessments, or other costs; exceptions

(a) Except as provided in subdivision (d), the local agency of any city, including a charter city, county, or city and county, which administers an ordinance, rule, regulation, or initiative measure that establishes a maximum amount that management may charge a tenant for rent shall permit the management to separately charge a homeowner for any of the following:

(1) The amount of any fee, assessment or other charge first imposed by a city, including a charter city, a county, a city and county, the state, or the federal government on or after January 1, 1995, upon the space rented by the homeowner.

(2) The amount of any increase on or after January 1, 1995, in an existing fee, assessment or other charge imposed by any governmental entity upon the space rented by the homeowner.

(3) The amount of any fee, assessment or other charge upon the space first imposed or increased on or after January 1, 1993, pursuant to any state or locally mandated program relating to housing contained in the Health and Safety Code.

(b) If management has charged the homeowner for a fee, assessment, or other charge specified in subdivision (a) that was increased or first imposed on or after January 1, 1993, and the fee, assessment, or other charge is decreased or eliminated thereafter, the charge to the homeowner shall be decreased or eliminated accordingly.

(c) The amount of the fee, assessment or other charges authorized by subdivision (a) shall be separately stated on any billing to the homeowner. Any change in the amount of the fee, assessment, or other charges that are separately billed pursuant to subdivision (a) shall be considered when determining any rental adjustment under the local ordinance.

(d) This section shall not apply to any of the following:

(1) Those fees, assessments, or charges imposed pursuant to the Mobilehome Parks Act (Part 2.1 (commencing with Section 18200) of Division 13 of the Health and Safety Code), unless specifically authorized by Section 18502 of the Health and Safety Code.

(2) Those costs that are imposed on management by a court pursuant to Section 798.39.5.

(3) Any fee or other exaction imposed upon management for the specific purpose of defraying the cost of administration of any ordinance, rule, regulation, or initiative measure that establishes a maximum amount that management may charge a tenant for rent.

(4) Any tax imposed upon the property by a city, including a charter city, county, or city and county.

(e) Those fees and charges specified in subdivision (a) shall be separately stated on any monthly or other periodic billing to the homeowner. If the fee or charge has a limited duration or is amortized for a specified period, the expiration date shall be stated on the initial notice and each subsequent billing to the homeowner while the fee or charge is billed to the homeowner. *(Added by Stats.1992, c. 338 (S.B.1365), § 3. Amended by Stats.1994, c. 340 (S.B.1510), § 2; Stats.2012, c. 770 (A.B.2697), § 1.)*

Research References

Miller and Starr California Real Estate § 19:92, Property Subject to Control; Exceptions and Exemptions--Application to Mobilehome Parks.
Miller and Starr California Real Estate § 31:18, Rent, Fees, and Services.
15 NO. 5 Miller & Starr, California Real Estate Newsalert 12, Landlord and Tenant.
15 NO. 5 Miller & Starr, California Real Estate Newsalert 16, Mobilehomes.
17 NO. 4 Miller & Starr, California Real Estate Newsalert 15, Mobilehomes.
12 Witkin, California Summary 10th Real Property § 772, (S 772) Method of Charging Proper Fees.

ARTICLE 5. HOMEOWNER COMMUNICATIONS AND MEETINGS

Section

§ 798.50. Legislative intent

It is the intent of the Legislature in enacting this article to ensure that homeowners and residents of mobilehome parks have the right to peacefully assemble and freely communicate with one another and with others with respect to mobilehome living or for social or educational purposes. *(Added by Stats. 1989, c. 198, § 2.)*

Research References

12 Witkin, California Summary 10th Real Property § 777, Homeowner Meetings.

§ 798.51. Homeowner meetings; invitations to public officials to speak; canvassing and petitioning of homeowners; use of park recreation hall or clubhouse; liability insurance; vehicle parking

(a) No provision contained in any mobilehome park rental agreement, rule, or regulation shall deny or prohibit the right of any homeowner or resident in the park to do any of the following:

(1) Peacefully assemble or meet in the park, at reasonable hours and in a reasonable manner, for any lawful purpose. Meetings may be held in the park community or recreation hall or clubhouse when the facility is not otherwise in use, and, with the consent of the homeowner, in any mobilehome within the park.

(2) Invite public officials, candidates for public office, or representatives of mobilehome owner organizations to meet with homeowners and residents and speak upon matters of public interest, in accordance with Section 798.50.

(3) Canvass and petition homeowners and residents for non-commercial purposes relating to mobilehome living, election to public office, or the initiative, referendum, or recall processes, at reasonable hours and in a reasonable manner, including the distribution or circulation of information.

(b) A homeowner or resident may not be charged a cleaning deposit in order to use the park recreation hall or clubhouse for meetings of resident organizations for any of the purposes stated in Section 798.50 and this section, whether or not guests or visitors from outside the park are invited to attend the meeting, if a homeowner or resident of the park is hosting the meeting and all homeowners or residents of the park are allowed to attend.

(c) A homeowner or resident may not be required to obtain liability insurance in order to use common area facilities for the purposes specified in this section and Section 798.50. However, if alcoholic beverages are to be served at any meeting or private function, a liability insurance binder may be required by the park ownership or management. The ownership or management of a mobilehome park may prohibit the consumption of alcoholic beverages in the park common area facilities if the terms of the rental agreement or the rules and regulations of the park prohibit it.

(d) A homeowner, organization, or group of homeowners using a recreation hall or clubhouse pursuant to this section shall be required to adhere to any limitations or restrictions regarding vehicle parking or maximum occupancy for the clubhouse or recreation hall.

(e) A homeowner or resident may not be prohibited from displaying a political campaign sign relating to a candidate for election to public office or to the initiative, referendum, or recall process in the window or on the side of a manufactured home or mobilehome, or within the site on which the home is located or installed. The size of the face of a political sign may not exceed six square feet, and the sign may not be displayed in excess of a period of time from 90 days prior to an election to 15 days following the election, unless a local ordinance within the jurisdiction where the mobilehome park is located imposes a more restrictive period of time for the display of such a sign. *(Added by Stats.1989, c. 198, § 2. Amended by Stats.2001, c. 83 (A.B.1202), § 2; Stats.2003, c. 249 (S.B.116), § 1.)*

Research References

Miller and Starr California Real Estate § 31:29, Duties Regarding Common Areas.
14 NO. 4 Miller & Starr, California Real Estate Newsalert 13, Mobilehomes.
12 Witkin, California Summary 10th Real Property § 775, (S 775) Rules and Regulations.
12 Witkin, California Summary 10th Real Property § 777, Homeowner Meetings.

§ 798.52. Civil action; abridgment of rights

Any homeowner or resident who is prevented by management from exercising the rights provided for in Section 798.51 may bring an action in a court of law to enjoin enforcement of any rule, regulation, or other policy which unreasonably deprives a homeowner or resident of those rights. *(Added by Stats.1989, c. 198, § 2.)*

Research References

12 Witkin, California Summary 10th Real Property § 775, (S 775) Rules and Regulations.
12 Witkin, California Summary 10th Real Property § 777, Homeowner Meetings.

ARTICLE 5.5. HOMEOWNERS MEETINGS WITH MANAGEMENT

Section
798.53. Meetings and consultation by management with homeowners; notice.

§ 798.53. Meetings and consultation by management with homeowners; notice

The management shall meet and consult with the homeowners, upon written request, within 30 days of the request, either individually, collectively, or with representatives of a group of homeowners who have signed a request to be so represented on the following matters:

(a) Resident concerns regarding existing park rules that are not subject to Section 798.25.

(b) Standards for maintenance of physical improvements in the park.

(c) Addition, alteration, or deletion of service, equipment, or physical improvements.

(d) Rental agreements offered pursuant to Section 798.17.

Any collective meeting shall be conducted only after notice thereof has been given to all the requesting homeowners 10 days or more before the meeting. *(Added by Stats.1989, c. 198, § 3. Amended by Stats.1994, c. 340 (S.B.1510), § 3.)*

Research References

Miller and Starr California Real Estate § 31:29, Duties Regarding Common Areas.
12 Witkin, California Summary 10th Real Property § 777, Homeowner Meetings.

ARTICLE 6. TERMINATION OF TENANCY

Section
798.55. Protection from actual or constructive eviction; termination or refusal to renew; grounds; notice; title search costs; residents remaining after notice; waiver.
798.56. Authorized reasons for termination.
798.56a. Notice by legal owner and junior lienholders to management of course of action after receipt of notice to terminate; failure to provide responsive notice.
798.57. Statement of reasons in notice.
798.58. Termination to make site available for buyer or renter of mobilehome from park owner or owner's agent; prohibitions.
798.59. Notice by homeowner; time.
798.60. Application of other laws.
798.61. Abandoned mobilehomes; definition; determination; notice; petition for declaration of abandonment; hearing; judgment; redemption; inventory; notice of intent to sell; storage costs; public sale; accounting; title.

§ 798.55. Protection from actual or constructive eviction; termination or refusal to renew; grounds; notice; title search costs; residents remaining after notice; waiver

(a) The Legislature finds and declares that, because of the high cost of moving mobilehomes, the potential for damage resulting therefrom, the requirements relating to the installation of mobilehomes, and the cost of landscaping or lot preparation, it is necessary that the owners of mobilehomes occupied within mobilehome parks be provided with the unique protection from actual or constructive eviction afforded by the provisions of this chapter.

(b)(1) The management may not terminate or refuse to renew a tenancy, except for a reason specified in this article and upon the giving of written notice to the homeowner, in the manner prescribed by Section 1162 of the Code of Civil Procedure, to sell or remove, at the homeowner's election, the mobilehome from the park within a period of not less than 60 days, which period shall be specified in the notice. A copy of this notice shall be sent to the legal owner, as defined in Section 18005.8 of the Health and Safety Code, each junior lienholder, as defined in Section 18005.3 of the Health and Safety Code, and the registered owner of the mobilehome, if other than the homeowner, by United States mail within 10 days after notice to the homeowner. The copy may be sent by regular mail or by certified or registered mail with return receipt requested, at the option of the management.

(2) The homeowner shall pay past due rent and utilities upon the sale of a mobilehome pursuant to paragraph (1).

(c) If the homeowner has not paid the rent due within three days after notice to the homeowner, and if the first notice was not sent by certified or registered mail with return receipt requested, a copy of the notice shall again be sent to the legal owner, each junior lienholder, and the registered owner, if other than the homeowner, by certified or registered mail with return receipt requested within 10 days after notice to the homeowner. Copies of the notice shall be addressed to the legal owner, each junior lienholder, and the registered owner at their addresses, as set forth in the registration card specified in Section 18091.5 of the Health and Safety Code.

(d) If management obtains a court judgment against a homeowner or resident, the cost incurred by management in obtaining a title search for the purpose of complying with the notice requirements of this section shall be recoverable as a cost of suit.

(e) The resident of a mobilehome that remains in the mobilehome park after service of the notice to sell or remove the mobilehome shall continue to be subject to this chapter and the rules and regulations of the park, including rules regarding maintenance of the space.

(f) No lawful act by the management to enforce this chapter or the rules and regulations of the park may be deemed or construed to waive or otherwise affect the notice to remove the mobilehome. *(Added by Stats.1978, c. 1031, p. 3178, § 1. Amended by Stats.1978, c. 1033, p. 3189, § 13; Stats.1979, c. 493, p. 1661, § 1; Stats.1980, c. 1149, § 4; Stats.1982, c. 1397, p. 5323, § 24; Stats.1983, c. 519, § 7; Stats.1983, c. 1124, § 2, operative July 1, 1984; Stats.1992, c. 835 (A.B.2715), § 1; Stats.1993, c. 666 (A.B.503), § 4; Stats.1998, c. 542 (S.B.2095), § 1; Stats.2003, c. 561 (A.B.682), § 1; Stats.2005, c. 24 (S.B.125), § 2.)*

Research References

Miller and Starr California Real Estate § 31:32, Termination of Tenancies--Mobilehomes.

Miller and Starr California Real Estate § 31:33, Required Notice for Termination.

Miller and Starr California Real Estate § 31:43, Sale of a Mobilehome by a Tenant.

14 NO. 4 Miller & Starr, California Real Estate Newsalert 13, Mobilehomes.

16 NO. 4 Miller & Starr, California Real Estate Newsalert 15, Mobilehomes.

16 NO. 5 Miller & Starr, California Real Estate Newsalert 26, State Board of Equalization Issues Comprehensive Summary and Qs and As for Transfers of Base Year Values of Principal Residences.

12 Witkin, California Summary 10th Real Property § 775, (S 775) Rules and Regulations.

12 Witkin, California Summary 10th Real Property § 779, (S 779) Repair or Removal of Home.

12 Witkin, California Summary 10th Real Property § 784, (S 784) in General.

12 Witkin, California Summary 10th Real Property § 785, (S 785) Notice of Termination.

12 Witkin, California Summary 10th Real Property § 789, Actions and Penalties.

§ 798.56. Authorized reasons for termination

A tenancy shall be terminated by the management only for one or more of the following reasons:

(a) Failure of the homeowner or resident to comply with a local ordinance or state law or regulation relating to mobilehomes within a reasonable time after the homeowner receives a notice of noncompliance from the appropriate governmental agency.

(b) Conduct by the homeowner or resident, upon the park premises, that constitutes a substantial annoyance to other homeowners or residents.

(c)(1) Conviction of the homeowner or resident for prostitution, for a violation of subdivision (d) of Section 243, paragraph (2) of subdivision (a), or subdivision (b), of Section 245, Section 288, or Section 451, of the Penal Code, or a felony controlled substance offense, if the act resulting in the conviction was committed anywhere on the premises of the mobilehome park, including, but not limited to, within the homeowner's mobilehome.

(2) However the tenancy may not be terminated for the reason specified in this subdivision if the person convicted of the offense has permanently vacated, and does not subsequently reoccupy, the mobilehome.

(d) Failure of the homeowner or resident to comply with a reasonable rule or regulation of the park that is part of the rental agreement or any amendment thereto.

No act or omission of the homeowner or resident shall constitute a failure to comply with a reasonable rule or regulation unless and until the management has given the homeowner written notice of the alleged rule or regulation violation and the homeowner or resident has failed to adhere to the rule or regulation within seven days. However, if a homeowner has been given a written notice of an alleged violation of the same rule or regulation on three or more occasions within a 12–month period after the homeowner or resident has violated that rule or regulation, no written notice shall be required for a subsequent violation of the same rule or regulation.

Nothing in this subdivision shall relieve the management from its obligation to demonstrate that a rule or regulation has in fact been violated.

(e)(1) Nonpayment of rent, utility charges, or reasonable incidental service charges; provided that the amount due has been unpaid for a period of at least five days from its due date, and provided that the homeowner shall be given a three-day written notice subsequent to that five-day period to pay the amount due or to vacate the tenancy. For purposes of this subdivision, the five-day period does not include the date the payment is due. The three-day written notice shall be given to the homeowner in the manner prescribed by Section 1162 of the Code of Civil Procedure. A copy of this notice shall be sent to the persons or entities specified in subdivision (b) of Section 798.55 within 10 days after notice is delivered to the homeowner. If the homeowner cures the default, the notice need not be sent. The notice may be given at the same time as the 60 days' notice required for termination of the tenancy. A three-day notice given pursuant to this subdivision shall contain the following provisions printed in at least 12–point boldface type at the top of the notice, with the appropriate number written in the blank:

"Warning: This notice is the (insert number) three-day notice for nonpayment of rent, utility charges, or other reasonable incidental services that has been served upon you in the last 12 months. Pursuant to Civil Code Section 798.56 (e)(5), if you have been given a three-day notice to either pay rent, utility charges, or other reasonable incidental services or to vacate your tenancy on three or more occasions within a 12–month period, management is not required to give you a further three-day period to pay rent or vacate the tenancy before your tenancy can be terminated."

(2) Payment by the homeowner prior to the expiration of the three-day notice period shall cure a default under this subdivision. If the homeowner does not pay prior to the expiration of the three-day notice period, the homeowner shall remain liable for all payments due up until the time the tenancy is vacated.

(3) Payment by the legal owner, as defined in Section 18005.8 of the Health and Safety Code, any junior lienholder, as defined in Section 18005.3 of the Health and Safety Code, or the registered owner, as defined in Section 18009.5 of the Health and Safety Code, if other than the homeowner, on behalf of the homeowner prior to the expiration of 30 calendar days following the mailing of the notice to the legal owner, each junior lienholder, and the registered owner provided in subdivision (b) of Section 798.55, shall cure a default under this subdivision with respect to that payment.

(4) Cure of a default of rent, utility charges, or reasonable incidental service charges by the legal owner, any junior lienholder, or the registered owner, if other than the homeowner, as provided by this subdivision, may not be exercised more than twice during a 12–month period.

(5) If a homeowner has been given a three-day notice to pay the amount due or to vacate the tenancy on three or more occasions within the preceding 12–month period and each notice includes the provisions specified in paragraph (1), no written three-day notice shall be required in the case of a subsequent nonpayment of rent, utility charges, or reasonable incidental service charges.

In that event, the management shall give written notice to the homeowner in the manner prescribed by Section 1162 of the Code of Civil Procedure to remove the mobilehome from the park within a period of not less than 60 days, which period shall be specified in the notice. A copy of this notice shall be sent to the legal owner, each junior lienholder, and the registered owner of the mobilehome, if other than the homeowner, as specified in paragraph (b) of Section 798.55, by certified or registered mail, return receipt requested, within 10 days after notice is sent to the homeowner.

(6) When a copy of the 60 days' notice described in paragraph (5) is sent to the legal owner, each junior lienholder, and the registered owner of the mobilehome, if other than the homeowner, the default may be cured by any of them on behalf of the homeowner prior to the expiration of 30 calendar days following the mailing of the notice, if all of the following conditions exist:

(A) A copy of a three-day notice sent pursuant to subdivision (b) of Section 798.55 to a homeowner for the nonpayment of rent, utility charges, or reasonable incidental service charges was not sent to the legal owner, junior lienholder, or registered owner, of the mobilehome, if other than the homeowner, during the preceding 12–month period.

(B) The legal owner, junior lienholder, or registered owner of the mobilehome, if other than the homeowner, has not previously cured a default of the homeowner during the preceding 12–month period.

(C) The legal owner, junior lienholder or registered owner, if other than the homeowner, is not a financial institution or mobilehome dealer.

If the default is cured by the legal owner, junior lienholder, or registered owner within the 30–day period, the notice to remove the mobilehome from the park described in paragraph (5) shall be rescinded.

(f) Condemnation of the park.

(g) Change of use of the park or any portion thereof, provided:

(1) The management gives the homeowners at least 15 days' written notice that the management will be appearing before a local governmental board, commission, or body to request permits for a change of use of the mobilehome park.

(2) After all required permits requesting a change of use have been approved by the local governmental board, commission, or body, the management shall give the homeowners six months' or more written notice of termination of tenancy.

If the change of use requires no local governmental permits, then notice shall be given 12 months or more prior to the management's determination that a change of use will occur. The management in the notice shall disclose and describe in detail the nature of the change of use.

(3) The management gives each proposed homeowner written notice thereof prior to the inception of his or her tenancy that the management is requesting a change of use before local governmental bodies or that a change of use request has been granted.

(4) The notice requirements for termination of tenancy set forth in Sections 798.56 and 798.57 shall be followed if the proposed change actually occurs.

(5) A notice of a proposed change of use given prior to January 1, 1980, that conforms to the requirements in effect at that time shall be valid. The requirements for a notice of a proposed change of use imposed by this subdivision shall be governed by the law in effect at the time the notice was given.

(h) The report required pursuant to subdivisions (b) and (i) of Section 65863.7 of the Government Code shall be given to the homeowners or residents at the same time that notice is required pursuant to subdivision (g) of this section.

(i) For purposes of this section, "financial institution" means a state or national bank, state or federal savings and loan association or credit union, or similar organization, and mobilehome dealer as defined in Section 18002.6 of the Health and Safety Code or any other organization that, as part of its usual course of business, originates, owns, or provides loan servicing for loans secured by a mobilehome. *(Added by Stats.1978, c. 1031, p. 3178, § 1. Amended by Stats.1978, c. 1033, p. 3189, § 14; Stats.1979, c. 945, p. 3266, § 2; Stats.1979, c. 1185, p. 4268, § 1.5; Stats.1980, c. 1149, § 5; Stats.1981, c. 714, § 52; Stats. 1981, c. 458, § 1; Stats.1982, c. 777, p. 3030, § 1; Stats.1982, c. 1397, p. 5325, § 25.5; Stats.1983, c. 519, § 8; Stats.1983, c. 1124, § 3, operative July 1, 1984; Stats.1987, c. 55, § 1; Stats.1987, c. 883, § 2; Stats.1988, c. 171, § 1; Stats.1988, c. 301, § 2.5; Stats.1990, c. 42 (A.B.1209), § 1; Stats.1990, c. 1357 (A.B.4156), § 1.5; Stats.1998, c. 427 (A.B.1888), § 1; Stats.2003, c. 85 (A.B.805), § 1; Stats.2003, c. 388 (A.B.767), § 1.5.)*

Research References

Miller and Starr California Real Estate § 31:18, Rent, Fees, and Services.
Miller and Starr California Real Estate § 31:32, Termination of Tenancies--Mobilehomes.
Miller and Starr California Real Estate § 31:33, Required Notice for Termination.
Miller and Starr California Real Estate § 19:156, Covenant of Quiet Enjoyment and Possession.
14 NO. 4 Miller & Starr, California Real Estate Newsalert 13, Mobilehomes.
12 Witkin, California Summary 10th Real Property § 599, Other Acts and Powers of Entity Are Not Affected.
12 Witkin, California Summary 10th Real Property § 775, (S 775) Rules and Regulations.
12 Witkin, California Summary 10th Real Property § 783, (S 783) Renting or Subletting in Medical Emergency.
12 Witkin, California Summary 10th Real Property § 786, (S 786) Grounds for Termination.

§ 798.56a. Notice by legal owner and junior lienholders to management of course of action after receipt of notice to terminate; failure to provide responsive notice

(a) Within 60 days after receipt of, or no later than 65 days after the mailing of, the notice of termination of tenancy pursuant to any reason provided in Section 798.56, the legal owner, if any, and each junior lienholder, if any, shall notify the management in writing of at least one of the following:

(1) Its offer to sell the obligation secured by the mobilehome to the management for the amount specified in its written offer. In that event, the management shall have 15 days following receipt of the offer to accept or reject the offer in writing. If the offer is rejected, the person or entity that made the offer shall have 10 days in which to exercise one of the other options contained in this section and shall notify management in writing of its choice.

(2) Its intention to foreclose on its security interest in the mobilehome.

(3) Its request that the management pursue the termination of tenancy against the homeowner and its offer to reimburse management for the reasonable attorney's fees and court costs incurred by the management in that action. If this request and offer are made, the legal owner, if any, or junior lienholder, if any, shall reimburse the management the amount of reasonable attorney's fees and court costs, as agreed upon by the management and the legal owner or junior lienholder, incurred by the management in an action to terminate the homeowner's tenancy, on or before the earlier of (A) the 60th calendar day following receipt of written notice from the management of the aggregate amount of those reasonable attorney's fees and costs or (B) the date the mobilehome is resold.

(b) A legal owner, if any, or junior lienholder, if any, may sell the mobilehome within the park to a third party and keep the mobilehome on the site within the mobilehome park until it is resold only if all of the following requirements are met:

(1) The legal owner, if any, or junior lienholder, if any, notifies management in writing of the intention to exercise either option described in paragraph (2) or (3) of subdivision (a) within 60 days following receipt of, or no later than 65 days after the mailing of, the notice of termination of tenancy and satisfies all of the responsibilities and liabilities of the homeowner owing to the management for the 90 days preceding the mailing of the notice of termination of tenancy and then continues to satisfy these responsibilities and liabilities as they accrue from the date of the mailing of that notice until the date the mobilehome is resold.

(2) Within 60 days following receipt of, or no later than 65 days after the mailing of, the notice of termination of tenancy, the legal owner or junior lienholder commences all repairs and necessary corrective actions so that the mobilehome complies with park rules and regulations in existence at the time the notice of termination of tenancy was given as well as the health and safety standards specified in Sections 18550, 18552, and 18605 of the Health and Safety Code, and completes these repairs and corrective actions within 90 calendar days of that notice, or before the date that the mobilehome is sold, whichever is earlier.

(3) The legal owner, if any, or junior lienholder, if any, complies with the requirements of Article 7 (commencing with Section 798.70) as it relates to the transfer of the mobilehome to a third party.

(c) For purposes of subdivision (b), the "homeowner's responsibilities and liabilities" means all rents, utilities, reasonable maintenance charges of the mobilehome and its premises, and reasonable maintenance of the mobilehome and its premises pursuant to existing park rules and regulations.

(d) If the homeowner files for bankruptcy, the periods set forth in this section are tolled until the mobilehome is released from bankruptcy.

(e) Notwithstanding any other provision of law, including, but not limited to, Section 18099.5 of the Health and Safety Code, if neither the legal owner nor a junior lienholder notifies the management of its decision pursuant to subdivision (a) within the period allowed, or performs as agreed within 30 days, or if a registered owner of a mobilehome, that is not encumbered by a lien held by a legal owner or a junior lienholder, fails to comply with a notice of termination and is either legally evicted or vacates the premises, the management may either remove the mobilehome from the premises and place it in storage or store it on its site. In this case, notwithstanding any other provision of law, the management shall have a warehouse lien in accordance with Section 7209 of the Commercial Code against the mobilehome for the costs of dismantling and moving, if appropriate, as well as storage, that shall be superior to all other liens, except the lien provided for in Section 18116.1 of the Health and Safety Code, and may enforce the lien pursuant to Section 7210 of the Commercial Code either after the date of judgment in an unlawful detainer action or after the date the mobilehome is physically vacated by the resident, whichever occurs earlier. Upon completion of any sale to enforce the warehouse lien in accordance with Section 7210 of the Commercial Code, the management shall provide the purchaser at the sale with evidence of the sale, as shall be specified by the Department of Housing and Community Development, that shall, upon proper request by the purchaser of the mobilehome, register title to the mobilehome to this purchaser, whether or not there existed a legal owner or junior lienholder on this title to the mobilehome.

(f) All written notices required by this section shall be sent to the other party by certified or registered mail with return receipt requested.

(g) Satisfaction, pursuant to this section, of the homeowner's accrued or accruing responsibilities and liabilities shall not cure the default of the homeowner. *(Added by Stats.1990, c. 1357 (A.B.4156), § 2. Amended by Stats.1992, c. 88 (A.B.2548), § 1; Stats.1992, c. 835 (A.B.2715), § 2; Stats.1996, c. 95 (A.B.2781), § 1; Stats.1998, c. 542 (S.B.2095), § 2; Stats.2010, c. 610 (A.B.2762), § 1.6.)*

Research References

Miller and Starr California Real Estate § 31:34, Notice to and Rights of Legal Owner and Junior Lienors.
12 Witkin, California Summary 10th Real Property § 788, (S 788) Rights of Legal Owners and Junior Lienholders.

§ 798.57. Statement of reasons in notice

The management shall set forth in a notice of termination, the reason relied upon for the termination with specific facts to permit determination of the date, place, witnesses, and circumstances concerning that reason. Neither reference to the section number or a subdivision thereof, nor a recital of the language of this article will constitute compliance with this section. *(Added by Stats.1978, c. 1031, p. 3178, § 1.)*

Research References

Miller and Starr California Real Estate § 31:33, Required Notice for Termination.

§ 798.58. Termination to make site available for buyer or renter of mobilehome from park owner or owner's agent; prohibitions

Tenancy may only be terminated for reasons contained in Section 798.56, and a tenancy may not be terminated for the purpose of making a homeowner's site available for a person who purchased or proposes to purchase, or rents or proposes to rent, a mobilehome from the owner of the park or the owner's agent. *(Added by Stats.1978, c. 1031, p. 3178, § 1. Amended by Stats.1982, c. 1397, p. 5326, § 26; Stats.2002, c. 672 (S.B.1410), § 3.)*

Research References

Miller and Starr California Real Estate § 31:32, Termination of Tenan-
    cies--Mobilehomes.
12 Witkin, California Summary 10th Real Property § 786, (S 786)
    Grounds for Termination.

§ 798.59. Notice by homeowner; time

A homeowner shall give written notice to the management of
not less than 60 days before vacating his or her tenancy. *(Added
by Stats.1978, c. 1031, p. 3178, § 1. Amended by Stats.1982, c.
1397, p. 5326, § 27.)*

Research References

Miller and Starr California Real Estate § 31:33, Required Notice for
    Termination.
12 Witkin, California Summary 10th Real Property § 779, (S 779) Repair
    or Removal of Home.
12 Witkin, California Summary 10th Real Property § 784, (S 784) in
    General.

§ 798.60. Application of other laws

The provisions of this article shall not affect any rights or
proceedings set forth in Chapter 4 (commencing with Section
1159) of Title 3 of Part 3 of the Code of Civil Procedure except
as otherwise provided herein. *(Added by Stats.1978, c. 1031, p.
3178, § 1. Amended by Stats.1978, c. 1033, p. 3190, § 15.)*

Research References

Miller and Starr California Real Estate § 31:16, Basis for Special
    Relationship Involving Mobilehome Tenancies.
Miller and Starr California Real Estate § 31:32, Termination of Tenan-
    cies--Mobilehomes.
12 Witkin, California Summary 10th Real Property § 784, (S 784) in
    General.

§ 798.61. Abandoned mobilehomes; definition; determina-
tion; notice; petition for declaration of abandonment;
hearing; judgment; redemption; inventory; notice of intent to sell; storage costs; public sale; accounting; title

(a)(1) As used in this section, "abandoned mobilehome"
means a mobilehome about which all of the following are true:

(A) It is located in a mobilehome park on a site for which no
rent has been paid to the management for the preceding 60 days.

(B) It is unoccupied.

(C) A reasonable person would believe it to be abandoned.

(2) For purposes of this section:

(A) "Mobilehome" shall include a trailer coach, as defined in
Section 635 of the Vehicle Code, or a recreational vehicle, as
defined in Section 18010 of the Health and Safety Code, if the
trailer coach or recreational vehicle also satisfies the requirements of paragraph (1), including being located on any site
within a mobilehome park, even if the site is in a separate
designated section pursuant to Section 18215 of the Health and
Safety Code.

(B) "Abandoned mobilehome" shall include a mobilehome
that is uninhabitable because of its total or partial destruction
that cannot be rehabilitated, if the mobilehome also satisfies the
requirements of paragraph (1).

(b) After determining a mobilehome in a mobilehome park to
be an abandoned mobilehome, the management shall post a
notice of belief of abandonment on the mobilehome for not less
than 30 days, and shall deposit copies of the notice in the United
States mail, postage prepaid, addressed to the homeowner at the
last known address and to any known registered owner, if
different from the homeowner, and to any known holder of a
security interest in the abandoned mobilehome. This notice
shall be mailed by registered or certified mail with a return
receipt requested.

(c) Thirty or more days following posting pursuant to subdivision (b), the management may file a petition in the superior
court in the county in which the mobilehome park is located, for
a judicial declaration of abandonment of the mobilehome. A
proceeding under this subdivision is a limited civil case. Copies
of the petition shall be served upon the homeowner, any known
registered owner, and any known person having a lien or security
interest of record in the mobilehome by posting a copy on the
mobilehome and mailing copies to those persons at their last
known addresses by registered or certified mail with a return
receipt requested in the United States mail, postage prepaid.

(d)(1) Hearing on the petition shall be given precedence over
other matters on the court's calendar.

(2) If, at the hearing, the petitioner shows by a preponderance
of the evidence that the criteria for an abandoned mobilehome
has been satisfied and no party establishes an interest therein at
the hearing, the court shall enter a judgment of abandonment,
determine the amount of charges to which the petitioner is
entitled, and award attorney's fees and costs to the petitioner.
For purposes of this subdivision, an interest in the mobilehome
shall be established by evidence of a right to possession of the
mobilehome or a security or ownership interest in the mobilehome.

(3) A default may be entered by the court clerk upon request
of the petitioner, and a default judgment shall be thereupon
entered, if no responsive pleading is filed within 15 days after
service of the petition by mail.

(e)(1) Within 10 days following a judgment of abandonment,
the management shall enter the abandoned mobilehome and
complete an inventory of the contents and submit the inventory
to the court.

(2) During this period the management shall post and mail
notice of intent to sell the abandoned mobilehome and its
contents under this section, and announcing the date of sale, in
the same manner as provided for the notice of determination of
abandonment under subdivision (b).

(3) At any time prior to the sale of a mobilehome under this
section, any person having a right to possession of the mobilehome may recover and remove it from the premises upon
payment to the management of all rent or other charges due,
including reasonable costs of storage and other costs awarded by
the court. Upon receipt of this payment and removal of the
mobilehome from the premises pursuant to this paragraph, the
management shall immediately file an acknowledgment of satisfaction of judgment pursuant to Section 724.030 of the Code of
Civil Procedure.

(f) Following the judgment of abandonment, but not less than
10 days following the notice of sale specified in subdivision (e),
the management may conduct a public sale of the abandoned
mobilehome and its contents. The management may bid at the
sale and shall have the right to offset its bids to the extent of the
total amount due it under this section. The proceeds of the sale
shall be retained by the management, but any unclaimed amount
thus retained over and above the amount to which the management is entitled under this section shall be deemed abandoned
property and shall be paid into the treasury of the county in
which the sale took place within 30 days of the date of the sale.
The former homeowner or any other owner may claim any or all
of that unclaimed amount within one year from the date of
payment to the county by making application to the county
treasurer or other official designated by the county. If the
county pays any or all of that unclaimed amount to a claimant,
neither the county nor any officer or employee of the county is
liable to any other claimant as to the amount paid.

(g) Within 30 days of the date of the sale, the management shall submit to the court an accounting of the moneys received from the sale and the disposition of the money and the items contained in the inventory submitted to the court pursuant to subdivision (e).

(h) The management shall provide the purchaser at the sale with a copy of the judgment of abandonment and evidence of the sale, as shall be specified by the State Department of Housing and Community Development or the Department of Motor Vehicles, which shall register title in the abandoned mobilehome to the purchaser upon presentation thereof. The sale shall pass title to the purchaser free of any prior interest, including any security interest or lien, except the lien provided for in Section 18116.1 of the Health and Safety Code, in the abandoned mobilehome. *(Added by Stats.1986, c. 1153, § 1. Amended by Stats.1988, c. 301, § 3; Stats.1991, c. 564 (A.B.743), § 1; Stats.1995, c. 446 (S.B.69), § 1; Stats.1998, c. 931 (S.B.2139), § 12, eff. Sept. 28, 1998; Stats.2003, c. 449 (A.B.1712), § 2.)*

Law Revision Commission Comments

Section 798.61 is amended to accommodate unification of the municipal and superior courts in a county. Cal. Const. art. VI, § 5(e). In a county in which there is no municipal court, the relevant geographical unit is the county rather than judicial district. *Cf.* Code Civ. Proc. § 38 & Comment ("judicial district" defined). The section is also amended to reflect elimination of the justice court. Cal. Const. art. VI, §§ 1, 5(b).

A limited civil case is within the original jurisdiction of the municipal court or of the superior court in a county in which there is no municipal court. Cal. Const. art. VI, 10 (superior court jurisdiction); Code Civ. Proc. §§ 85, 85.1 (limited civil cases). See also Code Civ. Proc. §§ 91, 904.2, 1085 (trial procedures and writ and appellate jurisdiction for limited civil cases). [28 Cal.L.Rev.Comm. Reports 51 (1998)].

Research References

Rutter, Cal. Practice Guide: Civ. Pro. Before Trial Ch. 3-A, A. Subject Matter Jurisdiction (Competency).

Rutter, Cal. Practice Guide: Civ. Pro. Before Trial Ch. 12(I)-C, C. Claims for Trial Setting Preference.

Miller and Starr California Real Estate § 31:46, Sale of an Abandoned Mobilehome by the Park Owner.

2 Witkin Cal. Proc. 5th Courts § 244, (S 244) Forcible Entry and Unlawful Detainer.

5 Witkin Cal. Proc. 5th Pleading § 856, (S 856) Special Kind of Declaratory Relief.

12 Witkin, California Summary 10th Real Property § 787, (S 787) Abandoned Mobilehome.

ARTICLE 7. TRANSFER OF MOBILEHOME OR MOBILEHOME PARK

§ 798.70. Advertising

A homeowner, an heir, joint tenant, or personal representative of the estate who gains ownership of a mobilehome in the mobilehome park through the death of the owner of the mobilehome who was a homeowner at the time of his or her death, or the agent of any such person, may advertise the sale or exchange of his or her mobilehome, or, if not prohibited by the terms of an agreement with the management, may advertise the rental of his or her mobilehome, by displaying a sign in the window of the mobilehome, or by a sign posted on the side of the mobilehome facing the street, or by a sign in front of the mobilehome facing the street, stating that the mobilehome is for sale or exchange or, if not prohibited, for rent by the owner of the mobilehome or his or her agent. Any such person also may display a sign conforming to these requirements indicating that the mobilehome is on display for an "open house," unless the park rules prohibit the display of an open house sign. The sign shall state the name, address, and telephone number of the owner of the mobilehome or his or her agent and the sign face shall not exceed 24 inches in width and 36 inches in height. Signs posted in front of a mobilehome pursuant to this section may be of an H-frame or A-frame design with the sign face perpendicular to, but not extending into, the street. Homeowners may attach to the sign or their mobilehome tubes or holders for leaflets which provide information on the mobilehome for sale, exchange, or rent. *(Added by Stats.1978, c. 1031, p. 3178, § 1. Amended by Stats.1978, c. 1033, p. 3190, § 17; Stats.1982, c. 1397, p. 5327, § 28; Stats.1986, c. 174, § 1; Stats.1989, c. 745, § 1; Stats.1993, c. 329 (S.B.293), § 1.)*

Research References

Miller and Starr California Real Estate § 9:41, Restraints on Signs Advertising Property for Sale or Lease.

Miller and Starr California Real Estate § 31:44, Restrictions of On-Site Advertising.

12 Witkin, California Summary 10th Real Property § 765, (S 765) Invalid Provisions.

12 Witkin, California Summary 10th Real Property § 778, (S 778) Listing for Sale.

12 Witkin, California Summary 10th Real Property § 781, (S 781) Purchaser's Acceptance of Rental Agreement.

12 Witkin, California Summary 10th Real Property § 782, (S 782) Sale Following Death of Mobilehome Owner.

12 Witkin, California Summary 10th Real Property § 788, (S 788) Rights of Legal Owners and Junior Lienholders.

§ 798.71. Showing or listing for sale a manufactured home or mobilehome by management

(a)(1) The management may not show or list for sale a manufactured home or mobilehome without first obtaining the owner's written authorization. The authorization shall specify the terms and conditions regarding the showing or listing.

(2) Management may require that a homeowner advise management in writing that his or her manufactured home or mobilehome is for sale. If management requires that a homeowner advise management in writing that his or her manufactured home or mobilehome is for sale, failure to comply with this requirement does not invalidate a transfer.

(b) The management shall prohibit neither the listing nor the sale of a manufactured home or mobilehome within the park by the homeowner, an heir, joint tenant, or personal representative of the estate who gains ownership of a manufactured home or mobilehome in the mobilehome park through the death of the owner of the manufactured home or mobilehome who was a homeowner at the time of his or her death, or the agent of any such person other than the management.

(c) The management shall not require the selling homeowner, or an heir, joint tenant, or personal representative of the estate who gains ownership of a manufactured home or mobilehome in the mobilehome park through the death of the owner of the manufactured home or mobilehome who was a homeowner at the time of his or her death, to authorize the management or any other specified broker, dealer, or person to act as the agent in the sale of a manufactured home or mobilehome as a condition of resale of the home in the park or of management's approval of the buyer or prospective homeowner for residency in the park.

(d) The management shall not require a homeowner, who is replacing a mobilehome or manufactured home on a space in the park, in which he or she resides, to use a specific broker, dealer, or other person as an agent in the purchase of or installation of the replacement home.

(e) Nothing in this section shall be construed as affecting the provisions of the Health and Safety Code governing the licensing of manufactured home or mobilehome salespersons or dealers. *(Added by Stats.1978, c. 1031, p. 3178, § 1. Amended by Stats.1982, c. 1346, p. 5031, § 1; Stats.1983, c. 1076, § 1; Stats.1988, c. 498, § 1; Stats.1989, c. 745, § 2; Stats.2003, c. 767 (A.B.1287), § 1; Stats.2004, c. 567 (S.B.1090), § 1; Stats.2009, c. 66 (S.B.804), § 1.)*

Research References

Miller and Starr California Real Estate § 6:3, Who Can Serve as an Escrow Holder.
Miller and Starr California Real Estate § 31:43, Sale of a Mobilehome by a Tenant.
Miller and Starr California Real Estate § 31:44, Restrictions of On-Site Advertising.
15 NO. 4 Miller & Starr, California Real Estate Newsalert 14, Mobilehomes.
20 NO. 4 Miller & Starr, California Real Estate Newsalert 16, Mobilehomes.
12 Witkin, California Summary 10th Real Property § 778, (S 778) Listing for Sale.

§ 798.72. Transfer or selling fees; request for service; purchase fees; performance of service

(a) The management shall not charge a homeowner, an heir, joint tenant, or personal representative of the estate who gains ownership of a mobilehome in the mobilehome park through the death of the owner of the mobilehome who was a homeowner at the time of his or her death, or the agent of any such person a transfer or selling fee as a condition of a sale of his mobilehome within a park unless the management performs a service in the sale. The management shall not perform any such service in connection with the sale unless so requested, in writing, by the homeowner, an heir, joint tenant, or personal representative of the estate who gains ownership of a mobilehome in the mobilehome park through the death of the owner of the

mobilehome who was a homeowner at the time of his or her death, or the agent of any such person.

(b) The management shall not charge a prospective homeowner or his or her agent, upon purchase of a mobilehome, a fee as a condition of approval for residency in a park unless the management performs a specific service in the sale. The management shall not impose a fee, other than for a credit check in accordance with subdivision (b) of Section 798.74, for an interview of a prospective homeowner. *(Added by Stats.1978, c. 1031, p. 3178, § 1. Amended by Stats.1982, c. 1397, p. 5327, § 29; Stats.1988, c. 498, § 2; Stats.1989, c. 745, § 3.)*

Research References

Miller and Starr California Real Estate § 31:43, Sale of a Mobilehome by a Tenant.
12 Witkin, California Summary 10th Real Property § 778, (S 778) Listing for Sale.

§ 798.73. Removal upon sale to third party; conditions; notice

The management shall not require the removal of a mobilehome from the park in the event of the sale of the mobilehome to a third party during the term of the homeowner's rental agreement or in the 60 days following the initial notice required by paragraph (1) of subdivision (b) of Section 798.55. However, in the event of a sale to a third party, in order to upgrade the quality of the park, the management may require that a mobilehome be removed from the park where:

(a) It is not a "mobilehome" within the meaning of Section 798.3.

(b) It is more than 20 years old, or more than 25 years old if manufactured after September 15, 1971, and is 20 feet wide or more, and the mobilehome does not comply with the health and safety standards provided in Sections 18550, 18552, and 18605 of the Health and Safety Code and the regulations established thereunder, as determined following an inspection by the appropriate enforcement agency, as defined in Section 18207 of the Health and Safety Code.

(c) The mobilehome is more than 17 years old, or more than 25 years old if manufactured after September 15, 1971, and is less than 20 feet wide, and the mobilehome does not comply with the construction and safety standards under Sections 18550, 18552, and 18605 of the Health and Safety Code and the regulations established thereunder, as determined following an inspection by the appropriate enforcement agency, as defined in Section 18207 of the Health and Safety Code.

(d) It is in a significantly rundown condition or in disrepair, as determined by the general condition of the mobilehome and its acceptability to the health and safety of the occupants and to the public, exclusive of its age. The management shall use reasonable discretion in determining the general condition of the mobilehome and its accessory structures. The management shall bear the burden of demonstrating that the mobilehome is in a significantly rundown condition or in disrepair. The management of the park may not require repairs or improvements to the park space or property owned by the management, except for damage caused by the actions or negligence of the homeowner or an agent of the homeowner.

(e) The management shall not require a mobilehome to be removed from the park, pursuant to this section, unless the management has provided to the homeowner notice particularly specifying the condition that permits the removal of the mobilehome. *(Added by Stats.1978, c. 1034, p. 3194, § 2. Amended by Stats.1982, c. 1392, p. 5306, § 1; Stats.1982, c. 1397, p. 5327, § 30.5; Stats.1991, c. 576 (A.B.932), § 1; Stats.1994, c. 729 (A.B.3203), § 1; Stats.1997, c. 367 (A.B.672), § 1; Stats.2003, c.*

561 (A.B.682), § 2; Stats.2007, c. 549 (A.B.446), § 1; Stats.2008, c. 179 (S.B.1498), § 28.)

Research References

Miller and Starr California Real Estate § 31:43, Sale of a Mobilehome by a Tenant.

14 NO. 4 Miller & Starr, California Real Estate Newsalert 13, Mobilehomes.

18 NO. 4 Miller & Starr, California Real Estate Newsalert 20, Mobilehomes.

18 NO. 4 Miller & Starr, California Real Estate Newsalert 45, Table of Statutes (Newsalert Vol 18).

12 Witkin, California Summary 10th Real Property § 779, (S 779) Repair or Removal of Home.

§ 798.73.5. Sales or transfer of mobilehomes remaining in park; repairs or improvements; conditions; written summary or repairs

(a) In the case of a sale or transfer of a mobilehome that will remain in the park, the management may only require repairs or improvements to the mobilehome, its appurtenances, or an accessory structure that meet all of the following conditions:

(1) Except as provided by Section 798.83, the repair or improvement is to the mobilehome, its appurtenances, or an accessory structure that is not owned and installed by the management.

(2) The repair or improvement is based upon or is required by a local ordinance or state statute or regulation relating to mobilehomes, or a rule or regulation of the mobilehome park that implements or enforces a local ordinance or a state statute or regulation relating to mobilehomes.

(3) The repair or improvement relates to the exterior of the mobilehome, its appurtenances, or an accessory structure that is not owned and installed by the management.

(b) The management, in the case of sale or transfer of a mobilehome that will remain in the park, shall provide a homeowner with a written summary of repairs or improvements that management requires to the mobilehome, its appurtenances, or an accessory structure that is not owned and installed by the management no later than 10 business days following the receipt of a request for this information, as part of the notice required by Section 798.59. This summary shall include specific references to park rules and regulations, local ordinances, and state statutes and regulations relating to mobilehomes upon which the request for repair or improvement is based.

(c) The provisions of this section enacted at the 1999–2000 Regular Session of the Legislature are declarative of existing law as they pertain to allowing park management to enforce park rules and regulations; these provisions specifically limit repairs and improvements that can be required of a homeowner by park management at the time of sale or transfer to the same repairs and improvements that can be required during any other time of a residency. *(Added by Stats.2000, c. 554 (A.B.2239), § 1.)*

Research References

12 Witkin, California Summary 10th Real Property § 779, (S 779) Repair or Removal of Home.

§ 798.74. Prior approval of purchaser; grounds for withholding; financial information; notice of acceptance or rejection; interview; fee; credit or refund

(a) The management may require the right of prior approval of a purchaser of a mobilehome that will remain in the park and that the selling homeowner or his or her agent give notice of the sale to the management before the close of the sale. Approval cannot be withheld if the purchaser has the financial ability to pay the rent and charges of the park unless the management reasonably determines that, based on the purchaser's prior tenancies, he or she will not comply with the rules and regulations of the park. In determining whether the purchaser has the financial ability to pay the rent and charges of the park, the management shall not require the purchaser to submit copies of any personal income tax returns in order to obtain approval for residency in the park. However, management may require the purchaser to document the amount and source of his or her gross monthly income or means of financial support.

Upon request of any prospective homeowner who proposes to purchase a mobilehome that will remain in the park, management shall inform that person of the information management will require in order to determine if the person will be acceptable as a homeowner in the park.

Within 15 business days of receiving all of the information requested from the prospective homeowner, the management shall notify the seller and the prospective homeowner, in writing, of either acceptance or rejection of the application, and the reason if rejected. During this 15-day period the prospective homeowner shall comply with the management's request, if any, for a personal interview. If the approval of a prospective homeowner is withheld for any reason other than those stated in this article, the management or owner may be held liable for all damages proximately resulting therefrom.

(b) If the management collects a fee or charge from a prospective purchaser of a mobilehome in order to obtain a financial report or credit rating, the full amount of the fee or charge shall be credited toward payment of the first month's rent for that mobilehome purchaser. If, for whatever reason, the prospective purchaser is rejected by the management, the management shall refund to the prospective purchaser the full amount of that fee or charge within 30 days from the date of rejection. If the prospective purchaser is approved by the management, but, for whatever reason, the prospective purchaser elects not to purchase the mobilehome, the management may retain the fee, or a portion thereof, to defray its administrative costs under this section. *(Added by Stats.1978, c. 541, p. 1703, § 2; Stats.1978, c. 1031, p. 3178, § 18. Amended by Stats.1982, c. 1397, p. 5328, § 31; Stats.1985, c. 76, § 1; Stats.1987, c. 830, § 1; Stats.1988, c. 522, § 1; Stats.1990, c. 645 (S.B.2340), § 1.)*

Research References

Rutter, Cal. Practice Guide: Landlord-Tenant Form 11:A, Sample Mobilehome Park Rental Agreement.

Miller and Starr California Real Estate § 31:43, Sale of a Mobilehome by a Tenant.

12 Witkin, California Summary 10th Real Property § 778, (S 778) Listing for Sale.

12 Witkin, California Summary 10th Real Property § 780, (S 780) Management's Prior Approval of Purchaser.

12 Witkin, California Summary 10th Real Property § 783, (S 783) Renting or Subletting in Medical Emergency.

§ 798.74.4. Disclosure requirements

The transfer or sale of a manufactured home or mobilehome in a mobilehome park is subject to the transfer disclosure requirements and provisions set forth in Article 1.5 (commencing with Section 1102) of Chapter 2 of Title 4 of Part 4 of the Civil Code. The requirements include, but are not limited to, the use of the Manufactured Home and Mobilehome Transfer Disclosure Statement set forth in Section 1102.6d of the Civil Code. *(Added by Stats.2003, c. 249 (S.B.116), § 2.)*

Research References

Rutter, Cal. Practice Guide: Real Prop. Transactions Ch. 2-C, C. Broker's Relationship and Obligations to Principal and Third Parties.

Rutter, Cal. Practice Guide: Real Prop. Transactions Ch. 4-A, A. Property to be Sold.

Miller and Starr California Real Estate § 31:43, Sale of a Mobilehome by a Tenant.

Miller and Starr California Real Estate § 31:47, Authority of Real Estate Brokers.

14 NO. 4 Miller & Starr, California Real Estate Newsalert 13, Mobilehomes.

12 Witkin, California Summary 10th Real Property § 480, (S 480) Included Transfers.

3 Witkin, California Summary 10th Agency and Employment § 66, (S 66) Legislative Response.

§ 798.74.5. Information for prospective homeowners within a mobilehome park

(a) Within two business days of receiving a request from a prospective homeowner for an application for residency for a specific space within a mobilehome park, if the management has been advised that the mobilehome occupying that space is for sale, the management shall give the prospective homeowner a separate document in at least 12–point type entitled "INFORMATION FOR PROSPECTIVE HOMEOWNERS," which includes the following statements:

"As a prospective homeowner you are being provided with certain information you should know prior to applying for tenancy in a mobilehome park. This is not meant to be a complete list of information.

Owning a home in a mobilehome park incorporates the dual role of " homeowner" (the owner of the home) and park resident or tenant (also called a "homeowner" in the Mobilehome Residency Law). As a homeowner under the Mobilehome Residency Law, you will be responsible for paying the amount necessary to rent the space for your home, in addition to other fees and charges described below. You must also follow certain rules and regulations to reside in the park.

If you are approved for tenancy, and your tenancy commences within the next 30 days, your beginning monthly rent will be $____ (must be completed by the management) for space number ____ (must be completed by the management). Additional information regarding future rent or fee increases may also be provided.

In addition to the monthly rent, you will be obligated to pay to the park the following additional fees and charges listed below. Other fees or charges may apply depending upon your specific requests. Metered utility charges are based on use.

_____

(Management shall describe the fee or charge and a good faith estimate of each fee or charge.)

Some spaces are governed by an ordinance, rule, regulation, or initiative measure that limits or restricts rents in mobilehome parks. These laws are commonly known as "rent control." Prospective purchasers who do not occupy the mobilehome as their principal residence may be subject to rent levels which are not governed by these laws. (Civil Code Section 798.21) Long-term leases specify rent increases during the term of the lease. By signing a rental agreement or lease for a term of more than one year, you may be removing your rental space from a local rent control ordinance during the term, or any extension, of the lease if a local rent control ordinance is in effect for the area in which the space is located.

A fully executed lease or rental agreement, or a statement signed by the park's management and by you stating that you and the management have agreed to the terms and conditions of a rental agreement, is required to complete the sale or escrow process of the home. You have no rights to tenancy without a properly executed lease or agreement or that statement. (Civil Code Section 798.75)

If the management collects a fee or charge from you in order to obtain a financial report or credit rating, the full amount of the fee or charge will be either credited toward your first month's rent or, if you are rejected for any reason, refunded to you. However, if you are approved by management, but, for whatever reason, you elect not to purchase the mobilehome, the management may retain the fee to defray its administrative costs. (Civil Code Section 798.74)

We encourage you to request from management a copy of the lease or rental agreement, the park's rules and regulations, and a copy of the Mobilehome Residency Law. Upon request, park management will provide you a copy of each document. We urge you to read these documents before making the decision that you want to become a mobilehome park resident.

Dated: _____

Signature of Park Manager: _____

Acknowledge Receipt by Prospective Homeowner: _____ "

(b) Management shall provide a prospective homeowner, upon his or her request, with a copy of the rules and regulations of the park and with a copy of this chapter. *(Added by Stats.2003, c. 767 (A.B.1287), § 2, operative Oct. 1, 2004. Amended by Stats.2012, c. 337 (A.B.317), § 1.)*

Research References

Miller and Starr California Real Estate § 31:28, Required Notices and Disclosure Forms to Tenants.

Miller and Starr California Real Estate § 31:43, Sale of a Mobilehome by a Tenant.

14 NO. 4 Miller & Starr, California Real Estate Newsalert 13, Mobilehomes.

§ 798.75. Sale or transfer of mobilehome to remain in park; required documents; unlawful occupant

(a) An escrow, sale, or transfer agreement involving a mobilehome located in a park at the time of the sale, where the mobilehome is to remain in the park, shall contain a copy of either a fully executed rental agreement or a statement signed by the park's management and the prospective homeowner that the parties have agreed to the terms and conditions of a rental agreement.

(b) In the event the purchaser fails to execute the rental agreement, the purchaser shall not have any rights of tenancy.

(c) In the event that an occupant of a mobilehome has no rights of tenancy and is not otherwise entitled to occupy the mobilehome pursuant to this chapter, the occupant is considered an unlawful occupant if, after a demand is made for the surrender of the mobilehome park site, for a period of five days, the occupant refuses to surrender the site to the mobilehome park management. In the event the unlawful occupant fails to comply with the demand, the unlawful occupant shall be subject to the proceedings set forth in Chapter 4 (commencing with Section 1159) of Title 3 of Part 3 of the Code of Civil Procedure.

(d) The occupant of the mobilehome shall not be considered an unlawful occupant and shall not be subject to the provisions of subdivision (c) if all of the following conditions are present:

(1) The occupant is the registered owner of the mobilehome.

(2) The management has determined that the occupant has the financial ability to pay the rent and charges of the park; will comply with the rules and regulations of the park, based on the occupant's prior tenancies; and will comply with this article.

(3) The management failed or refused to offer the occupant a rental agreement. *(Added by Stats.1978, c. 1031, p. 3178, § 1. Amended by Stats.1981, c. 667, § 8; Stats.1983, c. 519, § 9; Stats.1987, c. 323, § 1; Stats.1989, c. 119, § 1; Stats.1990, c. 645 (S.B.2340), § 2.)*

Research References

Miller and Starr California Real Estate § 31:43, Sale of a Mobilehome by a Tenant.

Miller and Starr California Real Estate § 31:57, Escrow Requirements. 12 Witkin, California Summary 10th Real Property § 781, (S 781) Purchaser's Acceptance of Rental Agreement.

§ 798.75.5. Mobilehome park rental agreement disclosure form; homeowner provided copy

(a) The management shall provide a prospective homeowner with a completed written disclosure form concerning the park described in subdivision (b) at least three days prior to execution of a rental agreement or statement signed by the park management and the prospective homeowner that the parties have agreed to the terms and conditions of the rental agreement. The management shall update the information on the disclosure form annually, or, in the event of a material change in the condition of the mobilehome park, at the time of the material change in that condition.

(b) The written disclosure form shall read as follows:

Mobilehome Park Rental Agreement Disclosure Form

THIS DISCLOSURE STATEMENT CONCERNS THE MOBILEHOME PARK KNOWN AS

_____ LOCATED AT _____
park name   park address

IN THE CITY OF _____ COUNTY OF _____

STATE OF CALIFORNIA.

THIS STATEMENT IS A DISCLOSURE OF THE CONDITION OF THE PARK AND PARK COMMON AREAS AS OF _____ IN COMPLIANCE WITH SECTION 798.75.5 OF THE CIVIL CODE.
date

IT IS NOT A WARRANTY OF ANY KIND BY THE MOBILEHOME PARK OWNER OR PARK MANAGEMENT AND IS NOT A SUBSTITUTE FOR ANY INSPECTION BY THE PROSPECTIVE HOMEOWNER/LESSEE OF THE SPACE TO BE RENTED OR LEASED OR OF THE PARK, INCLUDING ALL COMMON AREAS REFERENCED IN THIS STATEMENT. THIS STATEMENT DOES NOT CREATE ANY NEW DUTY OR NEW LIABILITY ON THE PART OF THE MOBILEHOME PARK OWNER OR MOBILEHOME PARK MANAGEMENT OR AFFECT ANY DUTIES THAT MAY HAVE EXISTED PRIOR TO THE ENACTMENT OF SECTION 798.75.5 OF THE CIVIL CODE, OTHER THAN THE DUTY TO DISCLOSE THE INFORMATION REQUIRED BY THE STATEMENT.

Are you (the mobilehome park owner/mobilehome park manager) aware of any of the following:

A. Park or common area facilities	B. Does the park contain this facility?		C. Is the facility in operation?		D. Does the facility have any known substantial defects?		E. Are there any uncorrected park citations or notices of abatement relating to the facilities issued by a public agency?		F. Is there any substantial, uncorrected damage to the facility from fire, flood, earthquake, or landslides?		G. Are there any pending lawsuits by or against the park affecting the facilities or alleging defects in the facilities?		H. Is there any encroachment, easement, non-conforming use, or violation of setback requirements regarding this park common area facility?	
	Yes	No	Yes	No	Yes	No	Yes	No	Yes	No	Yes	No	Yes	No
Clubhouse														
Walkways														
Streets, roads, and access														
Electric utility system														
Water utility system														
Gas utility system														
Common area lighting system														
Septic or sewer system														
Playground														
RV storage														
Parking areas														
Swimming pool														
Spa pool														
Laundry														
Other common area facilities*														

*If there are other important park or common area facilities, please specify (attach additional sheets if necessary):
_____
_____

If any item in C is checked "no", or any item in D, E, F, G, or H is checked "yes", please explain (attach additional sheets if necessary): _____

The mobilehome park owner/park manager states that the information herein has been delivered to the prospective homeowner/lessee a minimum of three days prior to execution of a rental agreement and is true and correct to the best of the park owner/park manager's knowledge as of the date signed by the park owner/manager.

Park Owner/Manager: _____ By: _____ Date: _____
                              print name   signature

I/WE ACKNOWLEDGE RECEIPT OF A COMPLETED COPY OF THE PARK OWNER/MANAGER STATEMENT.

Prospective Homeowner
Lessee _____ Park Owner/Manager _____
Date: _____   Title

Prospective Homeowner
Lessee _____ Park Owner/Manager _____
Date: _____   Title

(Added by Stats.1999, c. 517 (S.B.534), § 1.)

Research References

Miller and Starr California Real Estate § 31:28, Required Notices and Disclosure Forms to Tenants.
Miller and Starr California Real Estate § 31:57, Escrow Requirements.
12 Witkin, California Summary 10th Real Property § 781, (S 781) Purchaser's Acceptance of Rental Agreement.

§ 798.76. Regulations limiting residency based on age requirements for housing for older persons; compliance with federal act

The management may require that a prospective purchaser comply with any rule or regulation limiting residency based on age requirements for housing for older persons, provided that the rule or regulation complies with the federal Fair Housing Act, as amended by Public Law 104–76, and implementing regulations. *(Added by Stats.1978, c. 1031, p. 3178, § 1. Amended by Stats.1992, c. 182 (S.B.1234), § 1.5; Stats.1992, c. 666 (A.B.3453), § 1; Stats.1993, c. 1277 (A.B.2244), § 1; Stats. 1996, c. 61 (S.B.1585), § 1, eff. June 10, 1996.)*

Research References

Miller and Starr California Real Estate § 20:6, The Unruh Civil Rights Act--Age Discrimination in Mobilehome Parks.
Miller and Starr California Real Estate § 31:18, Rent, Fees, and Services.
Miller and Starr California Real Estate § 31:30, Restrictions on Occupancy.
Miller and Starr California Real Estate § 31:43, Sale of a Mobilehome by a Tenant.
Miller and Starr California Real Estate § 25B:79, Age Restrictions on Occupancy.
12 Witkin, California Summary 10th Real Property § 781, (S 781) Purchaser's Acceptance of Rental Agreement.
12 Witkin, California Summary 10th Real Property § 783, (S 783) Renting or Subletting in Medical Emergency.
8 Witkin, California Summary 10th Constitutional Law § 908, (S 908) Housing Discrimination.

§ 798.77. Waiver of rights; public policy

No rental or sale agreement shall contain a provision by which the purchaser or homeowner waives his or her rights under this chapter. Any such waiver shall be deemed contrary to public policy and shall be void and unenforceable. *(Added by Stats. 1978, c. 1031, p. 3178, § 1. Amended by Stats.1978, c. 1033, p. 3191, § 19; Stats.1982, c. 1397, p. 5328, § 32; Stats.1983, c. 519, § 10.)*

Research References

Miller and Starr California Real Estate § 31:43, Sale of a Mobilehome by a Tenant.
12 Witkin, California Summary 10th Real Property § 781, (S 781) Purchaser's Acceptance of Rental Agreement.

§ 798.78. Rights of heir, joint tenant or personal representative of the estate

(a) An heir, joint tenant, or personal representative of the estate who gains ownership of a mobilehome in the mobilehome park through the death of the owner of the mobilehome who was a homeowner at the time of his or her death shall have the right to sell the mobilehome to a third party in accordance with the provisions of this article, but only if all the homeowner's responsibilities and liabilities to the management regarding rent, utilities, and reasonable maintenance of the mobilehome and its premises which have arisen since the death of the homeowner have been satisfied as they have accrued pursuant to the rental agreement in effect at the time of the death of the homeowner up until the date the mobilehome is resold.

(b) In the event that the heir, joint tenant, or personal representative of the estate does not satisfy the requirements of subdivision (a) with respect to the satisfaction of the homeowner's responsibilities and liabilities to the management which accrue pursuant to the rental agreement in effect at the time of the death of the homeowner, the management shall have the right to require the removal of the mobilehome from the park.

(c) Prior to the sale of a mobilehome by an heir, joint tenant, or personal representative of the estate, that individual may replace the existing mobilehome with another mobilehome, either new or used, or repair the existing mobilehome so that the mobilehome to be sold complies with health and safety standards provided in Sections 18550, 18552, and 18605 of the Health and Safety Code, and the regulations established thereunder. In the event the mobilehome is to be replaced, the replacement mobilehome shall also meet current standards of the park as contained in the park's most recent written requirements issued to prospective homeowners.

(d) In the event the heir, joint tenant, or personal representative of the estate desires to establish a tenancy in the park, that individual shall comply with those provisions of this article which identify the requirements for a prospective purchaser of a mobilehome that remains in the park. *(Added by Stats.1979, c. 198, p. 437, § 1. Amended by Stats.1982, c. 477, p. 2079, § 1; Stats.1982, c. 1397, p. 5328, § 32.5; Stats.1989, c. 745, § 4.)*

Research References

Miller and Starr California Real Estate § 22:16, Successors in Interest.
Miller and Starr California Real Estate § 31:43, Sale of a Mobilehome by a Tenant.
20 NO. 3 Miller & Starr, California Real Estate Newsalert 22, Mobilehomes.
20 NO. 4 Miller & Starr, California Real Estate Newsalert 38, Mobilehomes.
12 Witkin, California Summary 10th Real Property § 782, (S 782) Sale Following Death of Mobilehome Owner.

§ 798.79. Right of legal owner or junior lienholder to sell mobilehome within park

(a) Any legal owner or junior lienholder who forecloses on his or her security interest in a mobilehome located in a mobilehome park shall have the right to sell the mobilehome within the park to a third party in accordance with this article, but only if all of the homeowner's responsibilities and liabilities to the management regarding rent, utilities, and reasonable maintenance of a mobilehome and its premises are satisfied by the foreclosing creditor as they accrue through the date the mobilehome is resold.

(b) In the event the legal owner or junior lienholder has received from the management a copy of the notice of termination of tenancy for nonpayment of rent or other charges, the foreclosing creditor's right to sell the mobilehome within the park to a third party shall also be governed by Section 798.56a. *(Added by Stats.1979, c. 1185, p. 4629, § 2. Amended by Stats.1982, c. 477, p. 2079, § 2; Stats.1982, c. 1397, p. 5328, § 33.5; Stats.1983, c. 1124, § 4, operative July 1, 1984; Stats.1990, c. 1357 (A.B.4156), § 3; Stats.1991, c. 190 (A.B.600), § 2.)*

Research References

Miller and Starr California Real Estate § 31:43, Sale of a Mobilehome by a Tenant.
12 Witkin, California Summary 10th Real Property § 782, (S 782) Sale Following Death of Mobilehome Owner.

§ 798.80. Offer to sell park or entry into listing agreement for sale of park; notice by owner to officers of resident organization

(a) Not less than 30 days nor more than one year prior to an owner of a mobilehome park entering into a written listing agreement with a licensed real estate broker, as defined in Article 1 (commencing with Section 10130) of Chapter 3 of Part 1 of Division 4 of the Business and Professions Code, for the sale of the park, or offering to sell the park to any party, the owner shall provide written notice of his or her intention to sell the mobilehome park by first-class mail or by personal delivery to the president, secretary, and treasurer of any resident organization formed by homeowners in the mobilehome park as a nonprofit corporation, pursuant to Section 23701v of the Revenue and Taxation Code, stock cooperative corporation, or other entity for purposes of converting the mobilehome park to condominium or stock cooperative ownership interests and for purchasing the mobilehome park from the management of the mobilehome park. An offer to sell a park shall not be construed

as an offer under this subdivision unless it is initiated by the park owner or agent.

(b) An owner of a mobilehome park shall not be required to comply with subdivision (a) unless the following conditions are met:

(1) The resident organization has first furnished the park owner or park manager a written notice of the name and address of the president, secretary, and treasurer of the resident organization to whom the notice of sale shall be given.

(2) The resident organization has first notified the park owner or manager in writing that the park residents are interested in purchasing the park. The initial notice by the resident organization shall be made prior to a written listing or offer to sell the park by the park owner, and the resident organization shall give subsequent notice once each year thereafter that the park residents are interested in purchasing the park.

(3) The resident organization has furnished the park owner or park manager a written notice, within five days, of any change in the name or address of the officers of the resident organization to whom the notice of sale shall be given.

(c) Nothing in this section affects the validity of title to real property transferred in violation of this section, although a violation shall subject the seller to civil action pursuant to Article 8 (commencing with Section 798.84) by homeowner residents of the park or the resident organization.

(d) Nothing in this section affects the ability of a licensed real estate broker, as defined in Article 1 (commencing with Section 10130) of Chapter 3 of Part 1 of Division 4 of the Business and Professions Code, to collect a commission pursuant to an executed contract between the broker and the mobilehome park owner.

(e) Subdivision (a) does not apply to any of the following:

(1) Any sale or other transfer by a park owner who is a natural person to any relation specified in Section 6401 or 6402 of the Probate Code.

(2) Any transfer by gift, devise, or operation of law.

(3) Any transfer by a corporation to an affiliate. As used in this paragraph, "affiliate" means any shareholder of the transferring corporation, any corporation or entity owned or controlled, directly or indirectly, by the transferring corporation, or any other corporation or entity controlled, directly or indirectly, by any shareholder of the transferring corporation.

(4) Any transfer by a partnership to any of its partners.

(5) Any conveyance resulting from the judicial or nonjudicial foreclosure of a mortgage or deed of trust encumbering a mobilehome park or any deed given in lieu of such a foreclosure.

(6) Any sale or transfer between or among joint tenants or tenants in common owning a mobilehome park.

(7) The purchase of a mobilehome park by a governmental entity under its powers of eminent domain. *(Added by Stats. 1986, c. 648, § 2. Amended by Stats.1990, c. 421 (A.B.2944), § 1; Stats.1994, c. 219 (S.B.1280), § 1.)*

Research References

Rutter, Cal. Practice Guide: Landlord-Tenant Form 11:A, Sample Mobilehome Park Rental Agreement.
Rutter, Cal. Practice Guide: Real Prop. Transactions Ch. 4-A, A. Property to be Sold.
Miller and Starr California Real Estate § 31:45, Sale of Mobilehome Park by the Owner.

12 Witkin, California Summary 10th Real Property § 780, (S 780) Management's Prior Approval of Purchaser.

§ 798.81. Listing; sales agent; restrictions by management prohibited

The management (1) shall not prohibit the listing or sale of a used mobilehome within the park by the homeowner, an heir, joint tenant, or personal representative of the estate who gains ownership of a mobilehome in the mobilehome park through the death of the owner of the mobilehome who was a homeowner at the time of his or her death, or the agent of any such person other than the management, (2) nor require the selling homeowner to authorize the management to act as the agent in the sale of a mobilehome as a condition of approval of the buyer or prospective homeowner for residency in the park. *(Added by Stats.1988, c. 1033, § 1. Amended by Stats.1989, c. 745, § 5.)*

Research References

Miller and Starr California Real Estate § 31:43, Sale of a Mobilehome by a Tenant.
12 Witkin, California Summary 10th Real Property § 778, (S 778) Listing for Sale.

§ 798.82. School facilities fee; written disclosure; time

The management, at the time of an application for residency, shall disclose in writing to any person who proposes to purchase or install a manufactured home or mobilehome on a space, on which the construction of the pad or foundation system commenced after September 1, 1986, and no other manufactured home or mobilehome was previously located, installed, or occupied, that the manufactured home or mobilehome may be subject to a school facilities fee under Sections 53080 and 53080.4 of, and Chapter 4.9 (commencing with Section 65995) of Division 1 of Title 7 of, the Government Code. *(Added by Stats.1994, c. 983 (S.B.1461), § 1.)*

Research References

Miller and Starr California Real Estate § 31:18, Rent, Fees, and Services.

§ 798.83. Mobilehomes remaining in park; required repairs and improvements

In the case of a sale or transfer of a mobilehome that will remain in the park, the management of the park shall not require repairs or improvements to the park space or property owned by the management, except for damage caused by the actions or negligence of the homeowner or an agent of the homeowner. *(Added by Stats.1997, c. 367 (A.B.672), § 2.)*

Research References

12 Witkin, California Summary 10th Real Property § 779, (S 779) Repair or Removal of Home.

ARTICLE 8.   ACTIONS, PROCEEDINGS, AND PENALTIES

Section
798.84. Failure to maintain common facilities or reduction of service; notice of impending action; requisites.
798.85. Attorney's fees and costs.
798.86. Willful violation by management; additional penalty; punitive damages.
798.87. Public nuisances; remedy by civil action or abatement; parties.
798.88. Violation of reasonable rule or regulation of mobilehome park; injunction; temporary restraining order.

Section
798.88. Violation of reasonable rule or regulation of mobilehome park; injunction; temporary restraining order.

§ 798.84. Failure to maintain common facilities or reduction of service; notice of impending action; requisites

(a) No action based upon the management's alleged failure to maintain the physical improvements in the common facilities in good working order or condition or alleged reduction of service may be commenced by a homeowner unless the management has been given at least 30 days' prior notice of the intention to commence the action.

(b) The notice shall be in writing, signed by the homeowner or homeowners making the allegations, and shall notify the management of the basis of the claim, the specific allegations, and the remedies requested. A notice by one homeowner shall be deemed to be sufficient notice of the specific allegation to the management of the park by all of the homeowners in the park.

(c) The notice may be served in the manner prescribed in Chapter 5 (commencing with Section 1010) of Title 14 of Part 2 of the Code of Civil Procedure.

(d) For purposes of this section, management shall be deemed to be notified of an alleged failure to maintain the physical improvements in the common facilities in good working order or condition or of an alleged reduction of services upon substantial compliance by the homeowner or homeowners with the provisions of subdivisions (b) and (c), or when management has been notified of the alleged failure to maintain or the alleged reduction of services by a state or local agency.

(e) If the notice is served within 30 days of the expiration of the applicable statute of limitations, the time for the commencement of the action shall be extended 30 days from the service of the notice.

(f) This section does not apply to actions for personal injury or wrongful death. *(Added by Stats.1988, c. 1592, § 1.)*

Research References

Miller and Starr California Real Estate § 31:7, Management.
Miller and Starr California Real Estate § 31:29, Duties Regarding Common Areas.
Miller and Starr California Real Estate § 31:36, Notice of Litigation by a Tenant; Attorney's Fees; Penalties.
12 Witkin, California Summary 10th Real Property § 789, Actions and Penalties.

§ 798.85. Attorney's fees and costs

In any action arising out of the provisions of this chapter the prevailing party shall be entitled to reasonable attorney's fees and costs. A party shall be deemed a prevailing party for the purposes of this section if the judgment is rendered in his or her favor or where the litigation is dismissed in his or her favor prior to or during the trial, unless the parties otherwise agree in the settlement or compromise. *(Added by Stats.1978, c. 1031, p. 3178, § 1. Amended by Stats.1978, c. 1033, p. 3191, § 21; Stats.1983, c. 519, § 11.)*

Research References

Rutter, Cal. Practice Guide: Civ. Pro. Before Trial Ch. 11-A, A. Voluntary Dismissals.
Rutter, Cal. Practice Guide: Civil Trials & Evidence Ch. 17-E, E. Attorney Fees as Costs.
Rutter, Cal. Practice Guide: Enforcing Judgments/Debts Ch. 3-C, C. Prelawsuit Considerations.
Rutter, Cal. Practice Guide: Real Prop. Transactions Ch. 11-C, C. Seller's Remedies Upon Buyer's Breach-Damages and Specific Performance.
Rutter, Cal. Practice Guide: Prof. Responsibility Ch. 2-D, D. In-Person Solicitation for Profit.

Miller and Starr California Real Estate § 31:36, Notice of Litigation by a Tenant; Attorney's Fees; Penalties.

17 NO. 5 Miller & Starr, California Real Estate Newsalert 14, Mobilehomes.

7 Witkin Cal. Proc. 5th Judgment § 201, (S 201) Distinction: Fees Incurred in Defending Noncontract Claims.

7 Witkin Cal. Proc. 5th Judgment § 230, (S 230) Actions Involving Real Property or Environmental Issues.

12 Witkin, California Summary 10th Real Property § 739, (S 739) Costs and Attorneys' Fees.

12 Witkin, California Summary 10th Real Property § 789, Actions and Penalties.

§ 798.86. Willful violation by management; additional penalty; punitive damages

(a) If a homeowner or former homeowner of a park is the prevailing party in a civil action, including a small claims court action, against the management to enforce his or her rights under this chapter, the homeowner, in addition to damages afforded by law, may, in the discretion of the court, be awarded an amount not to exceed two thousand dollars ($2,000) for each willful violation of this chapter by the management.

(b) A homeowner or former homeowner of a park who is the prevailing party in a civil action against management to enforce his or her rights under this chapter may be awarded either punitive damages pursuant to Section 3294 of the Civil Code or the statutory penalty provided by subdivision (a). *(Added by Stats.1978, c. 1031, p. 3178, § 1. Amended by Stats.1978, c. 1033, p. 3191, § 22; Stats.1982, c. 1397, p. 5329, § 34; Stats.1983, c. 519, § 12; Stats.1997, c. 141 (A.B.591), § 1; Stats.2003, c. 98 (A.B.693), § 1.)*

Research References

Rutter, Cal. Practice Guide: Personal Injury Ch. 3-E, E. Punitive Damages.

Miller and Starr California Real Estate § 31:9, Abatement of Nuisances.

Miller and Starr California Real Estate § 31:29, Duties Regarding Common Areas.

Miller and Starr California Real Estate § 31:36, Notice of Litigation by a Tenant; Attorney's Fees; Penalties.

14 NO. 4 Miller & Starr, California Real Estate Newsalert 13, Mobilehomes.

15 NO. 5 Miller & Starr, California Real Estate Newsalert 16, Mobilehomes.

12 Witkin, California Summary 10th Real Property § 789, Actions and Penalties.

§ 798.87. Public nuisances; remedy by civil action or abatement; parties

(a) The substantial failure of the management to provide and maintain physical improvements in the common facilities in good working order and condition shall be deemed a public nuisance. Notwithstanding Section 3491, this nuisance may only be remedied by a civil action or abatement.

(b) The substantial violation of a mobilehome park rule shall be deemed a public nuisance. Notwithstanding Section 3491, this nuisance may only be remedied by a civil action or abatement.

(c) A civil action pursuant to this section may be brought by a park resident, the park management, or in the name of the people of the State of California, by any of the following:

(1) The district attorney or the county counsel of the jurisdiction in which the park, or the greater portion of the park, is located.

(2) The city attorney or city prosecutor if the park is located within the jurisdiction of the city.

(3) The Attorney General. *(Added by Stats.1982, c. 1392, p. 5306, § 2. Amended by Stats.1983, c. 187, § 1; Stats.1990, c. 1374 (S.B.2446), § 2; Stats.2002, c. 141 (A.B.2382), § 1.)*

Research References

Miller and Starr California Real Estate § 31:7, Management.

Miller and Starr California Real Estate § 31:9, Abatement of Nuisances.

Miller and Starr California Real Estate § 31:17, Distinction When Park Owned by Residents.

Miller and Starr California Real Estate § 31:32, Termination of Tenancies--Mobilehomes.

13 NO. 4 Miller & Starr, California Real Estate Newsalert 15, Mobilehomes.

12 Witkin, California Summary 10th Real Property § 789, Actions and Penalties.

§ 798.88. Violation of reasonable rule or regulation of mobilehome park; injunction; temporary restraining order

Section operative until Jan. 1, 2016. See, also, section operative Jan. 1, 2016.

(a) In addition to any right under Article 6 (commencing with Section 798.55) to terminate the tenancy of a homeowner, any person in violation of a reasonable rule or regulation of a mobilehome park may be enjoined from the violation as provided in this section.

(b) A petition for an order enjoining a continuing or recurring violation of any reasonable rule or regulation of a mobilehome park may be filed by the management thereof within the limited jurisdiction of the superior court of the county in which the mobilehome park is located. At the time of filing the petition, the petitioner may obtain a temporary restraining order in accordance with subdivision (a) of Section 527 of the Code of Civil Procedure. A temporary order restraining the violation may be granted, with notice, upon the petitioner's affidavit showing to the satisfaction of the court reasonable proof of a continuing or recurring violation of a rule or regulation of the mobilehome park by the named homeowner or resident and that great or irreparable harm would result to the management or other homeowners or residents of the park from continuance or recurrence of the violation.

(c) A temporary restraining order granted pursuant to this subdivision shall be personally served upon the respondent homeowner or resident with the petition for injunction and notice of hearing thereon. The restraining order shall remain in effect for a period not to exceed 15 days, except as modified or sooner terminated by the court.

(d) Within 15 days of filing the petition for an injunction, a hearing shall be held thereon. If the court, by clear and convincing evidence, finds the existence of a continuing or recurring violation of a reasonable rule or regulation of the mobilehome park, the court shall issue an injunction prohibiting the violation. The duration of the injunction shall not exceed three years.

(e) However, not more than three months prior to the expiration of an injunction issued pursuant to this section, the management of the mobilehome park may petition under this section for a new injunction where there has been recurring or continuous violation of the injunction or there is a threat of future violation of the mobilehome park's rules upon termination of the injunction.

(f) Nothing shall preclude a party to an action under this section from appearing through legal counsel or in propria persona.

(g) The remedy provided by this section is nonexclusive and nothing in this section shall be construed to preclude or limit any rights the management of a mobilehome park may have to terminate a tenancy.

(h) This section shall remain in effect only until January 1, 2016, and as of that date is repealed, unless a later enacted statute, that is enacted before January 1, 2016, deletes or extends that date. *(Added by Stats.1991, c. 270 (S.B.459), § 1. Amended by Stats.2012, c. 99 (A.B.2272), § 1.)*

Repeal

For repeal of this section, see its terms.

Research References

Miller and Starr California Real Estate § 31:31, Adoption and Enforcement of Rules.
12 Witkin, California Summary 10th Real Property § 775, (S 775) Rules and Regulations.
12 Witkin, California Summary 10th Real Property § 789, Actions and Penalties.

§ 798.88. Violation of reasonable rule or regulation of mobilehome park; injunction; temporary restraining order

Section operative Jan. 1, 2016. See, also, section operative until Jan. 1, 2016.

(a) In addition to any right under Article 6 (commencing with Section 798.55) to terminate the tenancy of a homeowner, any person in violation of a reasonable rule or regulation of a mobilehome park may be enjoined from the violation as provided in this section.

(b) A petition for an order enjoining a continuing or recurring violation of any reasonable rule or regulation of a mobilehome park may be filed by the management thereof with the superior court for the county in which the mobilehome park is located. At the time of filing the petition, the petitioner may obtain a temporary restraining order in accordance with subdivision (a) of Section 527 of the Code of Civil Procedure. A temporary order restraining the violation may be granted, with notice, upon the petitioner's affidavit showing to the satisfaction of the court reasonable proof of a continuing or recurring violation of a rule or regulation of the mobilehome park by the named homeowner or resident and that great or irreparable harm would result to the management or other homeowners or residents of the park from continuance or recurrence of the violation.

(c) A temporary restraining order granted pursuant to this subdivision shall be personally served upon the respondent homeowner or resident with the petition for injunction and notice of hearing thereon. The restraining order shall remain in effect for a period not to exceed 15 days, except as modified or sooner terminated by the court.

(d) Within 15 days of filing the petition for an injunction, a hearing shall be held thereon. If the court, by clear and convincing evidence, finds the existence of a continuing or recurring violation of a reasonable rule or regulation of the mobilehome park, the court shall issue an injunction prohibiting the violation. The duration of the injunction shall not exceed three years.

(e) However, not more than three months prior to the expiration of an injunction issued pursuant to this section, the management of the mobilehome park may petition under this section for a new injunction where there has been recurring or continuous violation of the injunction or there is a threat of future violation of the mobilehome park's rules upon termination of the injunction.

(f) Nothing shall preclude a party to an action under this section from appearing through legal counsel or in propria persona.

(g) The remedy provided by this section is nonexclusive and nothing in this section shall be construed to preclude or limit any rights the management of a mobilehome park may have to terminate a tenancy.

(h) This section shall become operative on January 1, 2016. *(Added by Stats.2012, c. 99 (A.B.2272), § 2, operative Jan. 1, 2016.)*

Research References

Miller and Starr California Real Estate § 31:31, Adoption and Enforcement of Rules.
12 Witkin, California Summary 10th Real Property § 775, (S 775) Rules and Regulations.
12 Witkin, California Summary 10th Real Property § 789, Actions and Penalties.

ARTICLE 9. SUBDIVISIONS, COOPERATIVES, AND CONDOMINIUMS

§ 799. Definitions

As used in this article:

(a) "Ownership or management" means the ownership or management of a subdivision, cooperative, or condominium for mobilehomes, or of a resident-owned mobilehome park.

(b) "Resident" means a person who maintains a residence in a subdivision, cooperative, or condominium for mobilehomes, or a resident-owned mobilehome park.

(c) "Resident–owned mobilehome park" means any entity other than a subdivision, cooperative, or condominium for mobilehomes, through which the residents have an ownership interest in the mobilehome park. *(Added by Stats.1978, c. 1031, p. 3178, § 1. Amended by Stats.1979, c. 198, p. 437, § 2; Stats.1996, c. 61 (S.B.1585), § 2, eff. June 10, 1996; Stats.1997, c. 72 (S.B.484), § 1.)*

Research References

Miller and Starr California Real Estate § 31:17, Distinction When Park Owned by Residents.
Miller and Starr California Real Estate § 31:24, When Park Owned by Mobilehome Owners.
Miller and Starr California Real Estate § 31:32, Termination of Tenancies--Mobilehomes.

12 Witkin, California Summary 10th Real Property § 761, (S 761) Governing Law.

§ 799.1.   Application of article

(a) Except as provided in subdivision (b), this article shall govern the rights of a resident who has an ownership interest in the subdivision, cooperative, or condominium for mobilehomes, or a resident-owned mobilehome park in which his or her mobilehome is located or installed. In a subdivision, cooperative, or condominium for mobilehomes, or a resident-owned mobilehome park, Article 1 (commencing with Section 798) to Article 8 (commencing with Section 798.84), inclusive, shall apply only to a resident who does not have an ownership interest in the subdivision, cooperative, or condominium for mobilehomes, or the resident-owned mobilehome park, in which his or her mobilehome is located or installed.

(b) Notwithstanding subdivision (a), in a mobilehome park owned and operated by a nonprofit mutual benefit corporation, established pursuant to Section 11010.8 of the Business and Professions Code, whose members consist of park residents where there is no recorded subdivision declaration or condominium plan, Article 1 (commencing with Section 798) to Article 8 (commencing with Section 798.84), inclusive, shall govern the rights of members who are residents that rent their space from the corporation. *(Added by Stats.1995, c. 103 (S.B.110), § 2. Amended by Stats.1996, c. 61 (S.B.1585), § 3, eff. June 10, 1996; Stats.1997, c. 72 (S.B.484), § 2; Stats.2010, c. 175 (S.B.1047), § 1; Stats.2011, c. 296 (A.B.1023), § 33; Stats.2012, c. 492 (S.B.1421), § 1, eff. Sept. 23, 2012.)*

§ 799.1.5.   Advertising; sale, exchange or rental of mobilehome; display of signs

A homeowner or resident, or an heir, joint tenant, or personal representative of the estate who gains ownership of a mobilehome through the death of the resident of the mobilehome who was a resident at the time of his or her death, or the agent of any of those persons, may advertise the sale or exchange of his or her mobilehome or, if not prohibited by the terms of an agreement with the management or ownership, may advertise the rental of his or her mobilehome by displaying a sign in the window of the mobilehome, or by a sign posted on the side of the mobilehome facing the street, or by a sign in front of the mobilehome facing the street, stating that the mobilehome is for sale or exchange or, if not prohibited, for rent by the owner of the mobilehome or his or her agent. Any such person also may display a sign conforming to these requirements indicating that the mobilehome is on display for an "open house," unless the park rules prohibit the display of an open house sign. The sign shall state the name, address, and telephone number of the owner of the mobilehome or his or her agent. The sign face may not exceed 24 inches in width and 36 inches in height. Signs posted in front of a mobilehome pursuant to this section may be of an H-frame or A-frame design with the sign face perpendicular to, but not extending into, the street. A homeowner or resident, or an heir, joint tenant, or personal representative of the estate who gains ownership of a mobilehome through the death of the resident of the mobilehome who was a resident at the time of his or her death, or the agent of any of those persons, may attach to the sign or their mobilehome tubes or holders for leaflets that provide information on the mobilehome for sale, exchange, or rent. *(Formerly § 799.1, added by Stats.1978, c. 1031, p. 3178, § 1. Amended by Stats.1978, c. 1033, p. 3191, § 23; Stats.1979, c. 198, p. 437, § 3; Stats.1983, c. 519, § 13. Renumbered § 799.1.5 and amended by Stats.1995, c. 103 (S.B.110), § 1. Amended by Stats.2004, c. 302 (A.B.2351), § 5; Stats.2005, c. 22 (S.B.1108), § 12.)*

Research References

Miller and Starr California Real Estate § 9:41, Restraints on Signs Advertising Property for Sale or Lease.
Miller and Starr California Real Estate § 31:24, When Park Owned by Mobilehome Owners.

§ 799.2.   Listing or showing mobilehome by ownership or management; written authorization

The ownership or management shall not show or list for sale a mobilehome owned by a resident without first obtaining the resident's written authorization. The authorization shall specify the terms and conditions regarding the showing or listing.

Nothing contained in this section shall be construed to affect the provisions of the Health and Safety Code governing the licensing of mobilehome salesmen. *(Added by Stats.1978, c. 1031, p. 3178, § 1. Amended by Stats.1979, c. 198, p. 437, § 4; Stats.1983, c. 519, § 14.)*

Research References

Miller and Starr California Real Estate § 31:24, When Park Owned by Mobilehome Owners.

§ 799.2.5.   Right of entry to mobilehome by ownership or management; prior written consent; revocation of consent; emergency

(a) Except as provided in subdivision (b), the ownership or management shall have no right of entry to a mobilehome without the prior written consent of the resident. The consent may be revoked in writing by the resident at any time. The ownership or management shall have a right of entry upon the land upon which a mobilehome is situated for maintenance of utilities, trees, and driveways, for maintenance of the premises in accordance with the rules and regulations of the subdivision, cooperative, or condominium for mobilehomes, or resident-owned mobilehome park when the homeowner or resident fails to so maintain the premises, and protection of the subdivision, cooperative, or condominium for mobilehomes, or resident-owned mobilehome park at any reasonable time, but not in a manner or at a time that would interfere with the resident's quiet enjoyment.

(b) The ownership or management may enter a mobilehome without the prior written consent of the resident in case of an emergency or when the resident has abandoned the mobilehome. *(Added by Stats.2004, c. 302 (A.B.2351), § 6. Amended by Stats.2006, c. 538 (S.B.1852), § 40.)*

Research References

Miller and Starr California Real Estate § 31:24, When Park Owned by Mobilehome Owners.
Miller and Starr California Real Estate § 31:29, Duties Regarding Common Areas.
15 NO. 4 Miller & Starr, California Real Estate Newsalert 14, Mobilehomes.
12 Witkin, California Summary 10th Real Property § 774, (S 774) Maintenance of Premises.

§ 799.3.   Sale to third party; prohibition against required removal

The ownership or management shall not require the removal of a mobilehome from a subdivision, cooperative, or condominium for mobilehomes, or resident-owned mobilehome park in the event of its sale to a third party. *(Added by Stats.1978, c. 1031, p. 3178, § 1. Amended by Stats.1978, c. 1033, p. 3191, § 24; Stats.1979, c. 198, p. 437, § 5; Stats.1996, c. 61 (S.B.1585), § 4, eff. June 10, 1996; Stats.1997, c. 72 (S.B.484), § 3.)*

Research References

Miller and Starr California Real Estate § 31:24, When Park Owned by Mobilehome Owners.

Miller and Starr California Real Estate § 31:32, Termination of Tenancies--Mobilehomes.

§ 799.4. Prior approval of purchaser; grounds for withholding

The ownership or management may require the right to prior approval of the purchaser of a mobilehome that will remain in the subdivision, cooperative, or condominium for mobilehomes, or resident-owned mobilehome park and that the selling resident, or his or her agent give notice of the sale to the ownership or management before the close of the sale. Approval cannot be withheld if the purchaser has the financial ability to pay the fees and charges of the subdivision, cooperative, or condominium for mobilehomes, or resident-owned mobilehome park unless the ownership or management reasonably determines that, based on the purchaser's prior residences, he or she will not comply with the rules and regulations of the subdivision, cooperative, or condominium for mobilehomes, or resident-owned mobilehome park. *(Added by Stats.1978, c. 1031, p. 3178, § 1. Amended by Stats.1979, c. 198, p. 437, § 6; Stats.1983, c. 519, § 15; Stats.1996, c. 61 (S.B.1585), § 5, eff. June 10, 1996; Stats.1997, c. 72 (S.B.484), § 4.)*

Research References

Miller and Starr California Real Estate § 31:24, When Park Owned by Mobilehome Owners.

§ 799.5. Purchaser; compliance with residency based on age requirements for housing for older persons regulations; compliance with federal act

The ownership or management may require that a purchaser of a mobilehome that will remain in the subdivision, cooperative, or condominium for mobilehomes, or resident-owned mobilehome park comply with any rule or regulation limiting residency based on age requirements for housing for older persons, provided that the rule or regulation complies with the provisions of the federal Fair Housing Act, as amended by Public Law 104–76, and implementing regulations. *(Added by Stats.1978, c. 1031, p. 3178, § 1. Amended by Stats.1993, c. 1277 (A.B.2244), § 2; Stats.1996, c. 61 (S.B.1585), § 6, eff. June 10, 1996; Stats.1997, c. 72 (S.B.484), § 5.)*

Research References

Miller and Starr California Real Estate § 20:6, The Unruh Civil Rights Act--Age Discrimination in Mobilehome Parks.
Miller and Starr California Real Estate § 24:32, Defenses to Enforcement--Public Policy or Discrimination.
Miller and Starr California Real Estate § 31:24, When Park Owned by Mobilehome Owners.
Miller and Starr California Real Estate § 31:30, Restrictions on Occupancy.

§ 799.6. Waiver of rights; public policy

No agreement shall contain any provision by which the purchaser waives his or her rights under the provisions of this article. Any such waiver shall be deemed contrary to public policy and void and unenforceable. *(Formerly § 799.8, added by Stats.1978, c. 1031, p. 3178, § 1. Renumbered § 799.6 and amended by Stats.1978, c. 1033, p. 3192, § 27. Amended by Stats.1983, c. 519, § 16.)*

§ 799.7. Interruption in utility service; written advance notice; liability; emergency

The ownership or management shall provide, by posting notice on the mobilehomes of all affected homeowners and residents, at least 72 hours' written advance notice of an interruption in utility service of more than two hours for the maintenance, repair, or replacement of facilities of utility systems over which the management has control within the subdivision, cooperative, or condominium for mobilehomes, or resident-owned mobilehome park, if the interruption is not due to an emergency. The ownership or management shall be liable only for actual damages sustained by a homeowner or resident for violation of this section.

"Emergency," for purposes of this section, means the interruption of utility service resulting from an accident or act of nature, or cessation of service caused by other than the management's regular or planned maintenance, repair, or replacement of utility facilities. *(Added by Stats.1992, c. 317 (S.B.1389), § 2. Amended by Stats.1996, c. 61 (S.B.1585), § 7, eff. June 10, 1996; Stats.1997, c. 72 (S.B.484), § 6.)*

Research References

Miller and Starr California Real Estate § 31:24, When Park Owned by Mobilehome Owners.
12 Witkin, California Summary 10th Real Property § 615, Expanded Statute.

§ 799.8. School facilities fee; written disclosure; time

The management, at the time of an application for residency, shall disclose in writing to any person who proposes to purchase or install a manufactured home or mobilehome on a space or lot, on which the construction of the pad or foundation system commenced after September 1, 1986, and no other manufactured home or mobilehome was previously located, installed, or occupied, that the manufactured home or mobilehome may be subject to a school facilities fee under Sections 53080 and 53080.4 of, and Chapter 4.9 (commencing with Section 65995) of Division 1 of Title 7 of, the Government Code. *(Added by Stats.1994, c. 983 (S.B.1461), § 2.)*

Research References

Miller and Starr California Real Estate § 31:18, Rent, Fees, and Services.
Miller and Starr California Real Estate § 31:24, When Park Owned by Mobilehome Owners.

§ 799.9. Homeowner sharing mobilehome with others; live-in health care, live-in support care or supervision; relatives requiring care

(a) A homeowner may share his or her mobilehome with any person 18 years of age or older if that person is providing live-in health care, live-in supportive care, or supervision to the homeowner pursuant to a written treatment plan prepared by a physician and surgeon. A fee shall not be charged by management for that person. That person shall have no rights of tenancy in, and shall comply with the rules and regulations of, the subdivision, cooperative, or condominium for mobilehomes, or resident-owned mobilehome park.

(b) A senior homeowner who resides in a subdivision, cooperative, or condominium for mobilehomes, or a resident-owned mobilehome park, that has implemented rules or regulations limiting residency based on age requirements for housing for older persons, pursuant to Section 799.5, may share his or her mobilehome with any person 18 years of age or older if this person is a parent, sibling, child, or grandchild of the senior homeowner and requires live-in health care, live-in supportive care, or supervision pursuant to a written treatment plan prepared by a physician and surgeon. A fee shall not be charged by management for that person. Unless otherwise agreed upon, the management shall not be required to manage, supervise, or provide for this person's care during his or her stay in the subdivision, cooperative, or condominium for mobilehomes, or resident-owned mobilehome park. That person shall have no rights of tenancy in, and shall comply with the rules and regulations of, the subdivision, cooperative, or condominium for mobilehomes, or resident-owned mobilehome park. As used in this subdivision, "senior homeowner" means a homeowner or resident who is 55 years of age or older. *(Added by Stats.1997, c.*

72 (S.B.484), § 7. Amended by Stats.2008, c. 170 (S.B.1107), § 3.)

Research References

Miller and Starr California Real Estate § 20:6, The Unruh Civil Rights Act--Age Discrimination in Mobilehome Parks.

Miller and Starr California Real Estate § 31:17, Distinction When Park Owned by Residents.

Miller and Starr California Real Estate § 31:24, When Park Owned by Mobilehome Owners.

19 NO. 4 Miller & Starr, California Real Estate Newsalert 22, Mobilehomes.

§ 799.10. Political campaign signs; right to display; restrictions

A resident may not be prohibited from displaying a political campaign sign relating to a candidate for election to public office or to the initiative, referendum, or recall process in the window or on the side of a manufactured home or mobilehome, or within the site on which the home is located or installed. The size of the face of a political sign may not exceed six square feet, and the sign may not be displayed in excess of a period of time from 90 days prior to an election to 15 days following the election, unless a local ordinance within the jurisdiction where the manufactured home or mobilehome subject to this article is located imposes a more restrictive period of time for the display of such a sign. In the event of a conflict between the provisions of this section and the provisions of Part 5 (commencing with Section 4000) of Division 4, relating to the size and display of political campaign signs, the provisions of this section shall prevail. (Added by Stats.2003, c. 249 (S.B.116), § 3. Amended by Stats.2012, c. 181 (A.B.806), § 27, operative Jan. 1, 2014.)

Law Revision Commission Comments

Section 799.10 is amended to correct a cross-reference to former Civil Code Sections 1350–1378. [40 Cal.L.Rev.Comm. Reports 235 (2010)].

Research References

Miller and Starr California Real Estate § 31:29, Duties Regarding Common Areas.

14 NO. 4 Miller & Starr, California Real Estate Newsalert 13, Mobilehomes.

12 Witkin, California Summary 10th Real Property § 775, (S 775) Rules and Regulations.

§ 799.11. Installation of accommodations for the disabled

The ownership or management shall not prohibit a homeowner or resident from installing accommodations for the disabled on the home or the site, lot, or space on which the mobilehome is located, including, but not limited to, ramps or handrails on the outside of the home, as long as the installation of those facilities complies with code, as determined by an enforcement agency, and those facilities are installed pursuant to a permit, if required for the installation, issued by the enforcement agency. The management may require that the accommodations installed pursuant to this section be removed by the current homeowner at the time the mobilehome is removed from the park or pursuant to a written agreement between the current homeowner and the management prior to the completion of the resale of the mobilehome in place in the park. This section is not exclusive and shall not be construed to condition, affect, or supersede any other provision of law or regulation relating to accessibility or accommodation for the disabled. (Added by Stats.2008, c. 170 (S.B.1107), § 4.)

Research References

19 NO. 4 Miller & Starr, California Real Estate Newsalert 22, Mobilehomes.

12 Witkin, California Summary 10th Real Property § 775, (S 775) Rules and Regulations.

CHAPTER 2.6. RECREATIONAL VEHICLE PARK OCCUPANCY LAW

ARTICLE 1. DEFINITIONS

§ 799.20. Short title

This chapter shall be known and may be cited as the Recreational Vehicle Park Occupancy Law. (Added by Stats. 1992, c. 310 (A.B.3074), § 2.)

Research References

Miller and Starr California Real Estate § 31:35, Recreational Vehicles.

12 Witkin, California Summary 10th Real Property § 761, (S 761) Governing Law.

12 Witkin, California Summary 10th Real Property § 762, (S 762) Definitions.

§ 799.21. Definitions; construction of chapter

Unless the provisions or context otherwise require, the following definitions shall govern the construction of this chapter. (Added by Stats.1992, c. 310 (A.B.3074), § 2.)

§ 799.22. Defaulting occupant

"Defaulting occupant" means an occupant who fails to pay for his or her occupancy in a park or who fails to comply with reasonable written rules and regulations of the park given to the occupant upon registration. (Added by Stats.1992, c. 310 (A.B. 3074), § 2.)

§ 799.23. Defaulting resident

"Defaulting resident" means a resident who fails to pay for his or her occupancy in a park, fails to comply with reasonable written rules and regulations of the park given to the resident upon registration or during the term of his or her occupancy in the park, or who violates any of the provisions contained in Article 5 (commencing with Section 799.70). (Added by Stats. 1992, c. 310 (A.B.3074), § 2.)

§ 799.24. Defaulting tenant

"Defaulting tenant" means a tenant who fails to pay for his or her occupancy in a park or fails to comply with reasonable written rules and regulations of the park given to the person upon registration or during the term of his or her occupancy in the park. *(Added by Stats.1992, c. 310 (A.B.3074), § 2.)*

§ 799.25. Guest

"Guest" means a person who is lawfully occupying a recreational vehicle located in a park but who is not an occupant, tenant, or resident. An occupant, tenant, or resident shall be responsible for the actions of his or her guests. *(Added by Stats.1992, c. 310 (A.B.3074), § 2.)*

§ 799.26. Management

"Management" means the owner of a recreational vehicle park or an agent or representative authorized to act on his or her behalf in connection with matters relating to the park. *(Added by Stats.1992, c. 310 (A.B.3074), § 2.)*

§ 799.27. Occupancy and occupy

"Occupancy" and "occupy" refer to the use of a recreational vehicle park lot by an occupant, tenant, or resident. *(Added by Stats.1992, c. 310 (A.B.3074), § 2.)*

Research References

Miller and Starr California Real Estate § 31:35, Recreational Vehicles.

§ 799.28. Occupant

"Occupant" means the owner or operator of a recreational vehicle who has occupied a lot in a park for 30 days or less. *(Added by Stats.1992, c. 310 (A.B.3074), § 2.)*

Research References

Miller and Starr California Real Estate § 31:35, Recreational Vehicles.

§ 799.29. Recreational vehicle

"Recreational vehicle" has the same meaning as defined in Section 18010 of the Health and Safety Code. *(Added by Stats.1992, c. 310 (A.B.3074), § 2.)*

Research References

12 Witkin, California Summary 10th Real Property § 762, (S 762) Definitions.
12 Witkin, California Summary 10th Real Property § 765, (S 765) Invalid Provisions.

§ 799.30. Recreational vehicle park or park

"Recreational vehicle park" or "park" has the same meaning as defined in Section 18862.39 of the Health and Safety Code. *(Added by Stats.1992, c. 310 (A.B.3074), § 2. Amended by Stats.2004, c. 530 (A.B.1964), § 1.)*

Research References

12 Witkin, California Summary 10th Real Property § 761, (S 761) Governing Law.

§ 799.31. Resident

"Resident" means a tenant who has occupied a lot in a park for nine months or more. *(Added by Stats.1992, c. 310 (A.B. 3074), § 2.)*

Research References

Miller and Starr California Real Estate § 31:35, Recreational Vehicles.

§ 799.32. Tenant

"Tenant" means the owner or operator of a recreational vehicle who has occupied a lot in a park for more than 30 consecutive days. *(Added by Stats.1992, c. 310 (A.B.3074), § 2.)*

ARTICLE 2. GENERAL PROVISIONS

§ 799.40. Cumulative and additional rights

The rights created by this chapter shall be cumulative and in addition to any other legal rights the management of a park may have against a defaulting occupant, tenant, or resident, or that an occupant, tenant, or resident may have against the management of a park. *(Added by Stats.1992, c. 310 (A.B.3074), § 2.)*

§ 799.41. Application to mobilehomes

Nothing in this chapter shall apply to a mobilehome as defined in Section 18008 of the Health and Safety Code or to a manufactured home as defined in Section 18007 of the Health and Safety Code. *(Added by Stats.1992, c. 310 (A.B.3074), § 2.)*

Research References

12 Witkin, California Summary 10th Real Property § 761, (S 761) Governing Law.

§ 799.42. Occupant registration or tenant rental agreements; waiver of rights

No occupant registration agreement or tenant rental agreement shall contain a provision by which the occupant or tenant waives his or her rights under the provisions of this chapter, and any waiver of these rights shall be deemed contrary to public policy and void. *(Added by Stats.1992, c. 310 (A.B.3074), § 2.)*

§ 799.43. Registration agreements; form and contents

The registration agreement between a park and an occupant thereof shall be in writing and shall contain, in addition to the provisions otherwise required by law to be included, the term of the occupancy and the rent therefor, the fees, if any, to be charged for services which will be provided by the park, and a statement of the grounds for which a defaulting occupant's recreational vehicle may be removed as specified in Section 799.22 without a judicial hearing after the service of a 72-hour notice pursuant to this chapter and the telephone number of the local traffic law enforcement agency. *(Added by Stats.1992, c. 310 (A.B.3074), § 2.)*

Research References

Miller and Starr California Real Estate § 31:35, Recreational Vehicles.

§ 799.44. Rules and regulations; copy given at registration

At the time of registration, an occupant shall be given a copy of the rules and regulations of the park. *(Added by Stats.1992, c. 310 (A.B.3074), § 2.)*

Research References
Miller and Starr California Real Estate § 31:35, Recreational Vehicles.

§ 799.45. Offer of rental agreement

The management may offer a rental agreement to an occupant of the park who intends to remain in the park for a period in excess of 30 consecutive days. *(Added by Stats.1992, c. 310 (A.B.3074), § 2.)*

§ 799.46. Removal of recreational vehicle; display of warning signs

At the entry to a recreational vehicle park, or within the separate designated section for recreational vehicles within a mobilehome park, there shall be displayed in plain view on the property a sign indicating that the recreational vehicle may be removed from the premises for the reasons specified in Sections 799.22 and 1866 and containing the telephone number of the local traffic law enforcement agency. Nothing in this section shall prevent management from additionally displaying the sign in other locations within the park. *(Added by Stats.1992, c. 310 (A.B.3074), § 2. Amended by Stats.2004, c. 530 (A.B.1964), § 2.)*

Research References
Miller and Starr California Real Estate § 31:35, Recreational Vehicles.

ARTICLE 3. DEFAULTING OCCUPANTS

§ 799.55. Removal of recreational vehicle; notice; correction of payment deficiency

Except as provided in subdivision (b) of Section 1866, as a prerequisite to the right of management to have a defaulting occupant's recreational vehicle removed from the lot which is the subject of the registration agreement between the park and the occupant pursuant to Section 799.57, the management shall serve a 72–hour written notice as prescribed in Section 799.56. A defaulting occupant may correct his or her payment deficiency within the 72–hour period during normal business hours. *(Added by Stats.1992, c. 310 (A.B.3074), § 2. Amended by Stats.2004, c. 530 (A.B.1964), § 3.)*

Research References
Miller and Starr California Real Estate § 31:32, Termination of Tenancies--Mobilehomes.
Miller and Starr California Real Estate § 31:35, Recreational Vehicles.

§ 799.56. Service of notice on defaulting occupant; incapacitated occupants or nonmotorized vehicles; date to quit

(a) The 72-hour written notice shall be served by delivering a copy to the defaulting occupant personally or to a person of suitable age and discretion who is occupying the recreational vehicle located on the lot. In the latter event, a copy of the notice shall also be affixed in a conspicuous place on the recreational vehicle and shall be sent through the mail addressed to the occupant at the place where the property is located and, if available, any other address which the occupant has provided to management in the registration agreement. Delivery of the 72-hour notice to a defaulting occupant who is incapable of removing the occupant's recreational vehicle from the park because of a physical incapacity shall not be sufficient to satisfy the requirements of this section.

(b) In the event that the defaulting occupant is incapable of removing the occupant's recreational vehicle from the park because of a physical incapacity or because the recreational vehicle is not motorized and cannot be moved by the occupant's vehicle, the default shall be cured within 72 hours, but the date to quit shall be no less than seven days after service of the notice.

(c) The management shall also serve a copy of the notice to the city police if the park is located in a city, or, if the park is located in an unincorporated area, to the county sheriff. *(Added by Stats.1992, c. 310 (A.B.3074), § 2.)*

Research References
Miller and Starr California Real Estate § 31:35, Recreational Vehicles.

§ 799.57. Authority of management to remove recreational vehicle; statement in notice

The written 72-hour notice shall state that if the defaulting occupant does not remove the recreational vehicle from the premises of the park within 72 hours after receipt of the notice, the management has authority pursuant to Section 799.58 to have the recreational vehicle removed from the lot to the nearest secured storage facility. *(Added by Stats.1992, c. 310 (A.B.3074), § 2.)*

§ 799.58. Removal of persons from recreational vehicle; removal of vehicle; voidance of notice

Subsequent to serving a copy of the notice specified in this article to the city police or county sheriff, whichever is appropriate, and after the expiration of 72 hours following service of the notice on the defaulting occupant, the police or sheriff, shall remove or cause to be removed any person in the recreational vehicle. The management may then remove or cause the removal of a defaulting occupant's recreational vehicle parked on the premises of the park to the nearest secured storage facility. The notice shall be void seven days after the date of service of the notice. *(Added by Stats.1992, c. 310 (A.B.3074), § 2.)*

Research References
Miller and Starr California Real Estate § 31:35, Recreational Vehicles.

§ 799.59. Standard of care in removing vehicles

When the management removes or causes the removal of a defaulting occupant's recreational vehicle, the management and the individual or entity that removes the recreational vehicle shall exercise reasonable and ordinary care in removing the recreational vehicle to the storage area. *(Added by Stats.1992, c. 310 (A.B.3074), § 2.)*

Research References
Miller and Starr California Real Estate § 31:35, Recreational Vehicles.

ARTICLE 4. DEFAULTING TENANTS

§ 799.65. Termination of tenancy for nonpayment of rent, utilities, or service charges; notice; liability of tenant

The management may terminate the tenancy of a defaulting tenant for nonpayment of rent, utilities, or reasonable incidental service charges, provided the amount due shall have been unpaid for a period of five days from its due date, and provided the tenant has been given a three-day written notice subsequent to that five-day period to pay the total amount due or to vacate the park. For purposes of this section, the five-day period does not include the date the payment is due. The three-day notice shall be given to the tenant in the manner prescribed by Section 1162 of the Code of Civil Procedure. Any payment of the total charges due, prior to the expiration of the three-day period, shall cure any default of the tenant. In the event the tenant does not pay prior to the expiration of the three-day notice period, the tenant shall remain liable for all payments due up until the time the tenancy is vacated. *(Added by Stats.1992, c. 310 (A.B.3074), § 2.)*

Research References

Miller and Starr California Real Estate § 31:35, Recreational Vehicles.

§ 799.66. Termination or refusal to renew right of occupancy for other than nonpayment of rent or other charges

The management may terminate or refuse to renew the right of occupancy of a tenant for other than nonpayment of rent or other charges upon the giving of a written notice to the tenant in the manner prescribed by Section 1162 of the Code of Civil Procedure to remove the recreational vehicle from the park. The notice need not state the cause for termination but shall provide not less than 30 days' notice of termination of the tenancy. *(Added by Stats.1992, c. 310 (A.B.3074), § 2. Amended by Stats.1994, c. 167 (S.B.1349), § 1.)*

Research References

Miller and Starr California Real Estate § 31:35, Recreational Vehicles.

§ 799.67. Evictions

Evictions pursuant to this article shall be subject to the requirements set forth in Chapter 4 (commencing with Section 1159) of Title 3 of Part 3 of the Code of Civil Procedure, except as otherwise provided in this article. *(Added by Stats.1992, c. 310 (A.B.3074), § 2.)*

ARTICLE 5. DEFAULTING RESIDENTS

Section
799.70. Notice of termination; reasons for termination.
799.71. Evictions.

§ 799.70. Notice of termination; reasons for termination

The management may terminate or refuse to renew the right of occupancy of a defaulting resident upon the giving of a written notice to the defaulting resident in the manner prescribed by Section 1162 of the Code of Civil Procedure to remove the recreational vehicle from the park. This notice shall provide not less than 60 days' notice of termination of the right of occupancy and shall specify one of the following reasons for the termination of the right of occupancy:

(a) Nonpayment of rent, utilities, or reasonable incidental service charges; provided, that the amount due has been unpaid for a period of five days from its due date, and provided that the resident shall be given a three-day written notice subsequent to that five-day period to pay the total amount due or to vacate the park. For purposes of this subdivision, the five-day period does not include the date the payment is due. The three-day notice shall be given to the resident in the manner prescribed by

Section 1162 of the Code of Civil Procedure. The three-day notice may be given at the same time as the 60-day notice required for termination of the right of occupancy; provided, however, that any payment of the total charges due, prior to the expiration of the three-day period, shall cure any default of the resident. In the event the resident does not pay prior to the expiration of the three-day notice period, the resident shall remain liable for all payments due up until the time the tenancy is vacated.

(b) Failure of the resident to comply with a local ordinance or state law or regulation relating to the recreational vehicle park or recreational vehicles within a reasonable time after the resident or the management receives a notice of noncompliance from the appropriate governmental agency and the resident has been provided with a copy of that notice.

(c) Conduct by the resident or guest, upon the park premises, which constitutes a substantial annoyance to other occupants, tenants, or residents.

(d) Conviction of the resident of prostitution, or a felony controlled substance offense, if the act resulting in the conviction was committed anywhere on the premises of the park, including, but not limited to, within the resident's recreational vehicle.

However, the right of occupancy may not be terminated for the reason specified in this subdivision if the person convicted of the offense has permanently vacated, and does not subsequently reoccupy, the recreational vehicle.

(e) Failure of the resident or a guest to comply with a rule or regulation of the park which is part of the rental agreement or any amendment thereto.

No act or omission of the resident or guest shall constitute a failure to comply with a rule or regulation unless the resident has been notified in writing of the violation and has failed to correct the violation within seven days of the issuance of the written notification.

(f) Condemnation of the park.

(g) Change of use of the park or any portion thereof. *(Added by Stats.1992, c. 310 (A.B.3074), § 2.)*

Research References

Miller and Starr California Real Estate § 31:35, Recreational Vehicles.

§ 799.71. Evictions

Evictions pursuant to this article shall be subject to the requirements set forth in Chapter 4 (commencing with Section 1159) of Title 3 of Part 3 of the Code of Civil Procedure, except as otherwise provided in this article. *(Added by Stats.1992, c. 310 (A.B.3074), § 2.)*

Research References

Miller and Starr California Real Estate § 31:35, Recreational Vehicles.

ARTICLE 6. LIENS FOR RECREATIONAL VEHICLES AND ABANDONED POSSESSIONS

Section
799.75. Liens; disposition of abandoned possessions.

§ 799.75. Liens; disposition of abandoned possessions

The management shall have a lien upon the recreational vehicle and the contents therein for the proper charges due from a defaulting occupant, tenant, or resident. Such a lien shall be identical to that authorized by Section 1861, and shall be enforced as provided by Sections 1861 to 1861.28, inclusive. Disposition of any possessions abandoned by an occupant, tenant, or resident at a park shall be performed pursuant to

Chapter 5 (commencing with Section 1980) of Title 5 of Part 4 of Division 3. *(Added by Stats.1992, c. 310 (A.B.3074), § 2.)*

ARTICLE 7. ACTIONS AND PROCEEDINGS

Section
799.78.   Attorney's fees and costs.
799.79.   Willful violation by management; additional penalty.

§ 799.78. Attorney's fees and costs

In any action arising out of the provisions of this chapter, the prevailing party shall be entitled to reasonable attorney's fees and costs. A party shall be deemed a prevailing party for the purposes of this section if the judgment is rendered in his or her favor or where the litigation is dismissed in his or her favor prior to or during the trial, unless the parties otherwise agree in the settlement or compromise. *(Added by Stats.1992, c. 310 (A.B. 3074), § 2.)*

§ 799.79. Willful violation by management; additional penalty

In the event that an occupant, tenant, or resident or a former occupant, tenant, or resident is the prevailing party in a civil action against the management to enforce his or her rights under this chapter, the occupant, tenant, or resident, in addition to damages afforded by law, may, in the discretion of the court, be awarded an amount not to exceed five hundred dollars ($500) for each willful violation of any provision of this chapter by the management. *(Added by Stats.1992, c. 310 (A.B.3074), § 2.)*

CHAPTER 2.7. FLOATING HOME RESIDENCY LAW

ARTICLE 1. GENERAL PROVISIONS

§ 800.   Short title

This chapter shall be known and may be cited as the Floating Home Residency Law. *(Added by Stats.1990, c. 1505 (A.B.3139), § 1.)*

§ 800.1.   Construction of chapter

Unless the provisions or context otherwise requires, the following definitions shall govern the construction of this chapter. *(Added by Stats.1990, c. 1505 (A.B.3139), § 1.)*

§ 800.2.   Management

"Management" means the owner of a floating home marina or an agent or representative authorized to act on his or her behalf in connection with matters relating to a tenancy in the floating home marina. *(Added by Stats.1990, c. 1505 (A.B.3139), § 1.)*

§ 800.3.   Floating home

"Floating home" has the same meaning as defined in subdivision (d) of Section 18075.55 of the Health and Safety Code. *(Added by Stats.1990, c. 1505 (A.B.3139), § 1.)*

§ 800.4.   Floating home marina

"Floating home marina" means an area where five or more floating home berths are rented, or held out for rent, to accommodate floating homes, but does not include a marina where 10 percent or fewer of the berths are leased or held out to lease to floating homes nor a marina or harbor (a) which is managed by a nonprofit organization, the property, assets, and profits of which may not inure to any individual or group of individuals, but only to another nonprofit organization; (b) the rules and regulations of which are set by majority vote of the berthholders thereof; and (c) which contains berths for fewer than 25 floating homes. *(Added by Stats.1990, c. 1505 (A.B. 3139), § 1. Amended by Stats.1991, c. 942 (A.B.628), § 1.)*

§ 800.5.   Rental agreement

"Rental agreement" means an agreement between the management and the homeowner establishing the terms and conditions of a tenancy. A lease is a rental agreement. *(Added by Stats.1990, c. 1505 (A.B.3139), § 1.)*

§ 800.6.   Homeowner

"Homeowner" means a person who owns or resides in a floating home which is in a floating home marina pursuant to a rental agreement with management. *(Added by Stats.1990, c. 1505 (A.B.3139), § 1.)*

§ 800.7.   Change of use

"Change of use" means a use of the floating home marina for a purpose other than the rental, or the holding out for rent, of five or more floating home berths, and does not mean the adoption, amendment, or repeal of a floating home marina rule or regulation. A change of use may affect an entire floating home marina or any portion thereof. "Change of use" includes, but is not limited to, a change of the floating home marina or any portion thereof to a condominium, stock cooperative, or any form of ownership wherein spaces within the floating home marina are to be sold. *(Added by Stats.1990, c. 1505 (A.B.3139), § 1.)*

§ 800.8. Resident

"Resident" means a homeowner or other person who lawfully occupies a floating home. *(Added by Stats.1990, c. 1505 (A.B.3139), § 1.)*

§ 800.9. Tenancy

"Tenancy" means the right of a homeowner to the use of a berth within a floating home marina on which to locate, maintain, and occupy a floating home, and accessory structures or vessels, including the use of the services and facilities of the floating home marina. *(Added by Stats.1990, c. 1505 (A.B.3139), § 1.)*

ARTICLE 2. RENTAL AGREEMENT

Section
800.20. Copies of notices; availability.
800.21. Written rental agreement; contents.
800.22. Inclusion of other provisions permitted by law.
800.23. Agreements offered to homeowners; contents.
800.24. Waiver of rights prohibited.
800.25. Private club membership not to be denied on discriminatory basis; familial status.
800.26. Copies of chapter; notice of availability.

§ 800.20. Copies of notices; availability

Unless otherwise provided, the management shall make available to floating homeowners, upon request, copies of all notices required by this article and Article 3 (commencing with Section 800.30). *(Added by Stats.1990, c. 1505 (A.B.3139), § 1.)*

Research References

Miller and Starr California Real Estate § 31:4, Floating Home Residency Law.

§ 800.21. Written rental agreement; contents

The rental agreement shall be in writing and shall contain, in addition to the provisions otherwise required by law to be included, all of the following:

(a) The term of the tenancy and the rent therefor.

(b) The rules and regulations of the floating home marina.

(c) A reference to this chapter and a statement that a copy of it is available from the marina upon request.

(d) A provision specifying that it is the responsibility of the management to provide and maintain physical improvements in the common facilities in good working order and condition.

(e) A description of the physical improvements to be provided the homeowner during his or her tenancy.

(f) A provision listing those services which will be provided at the time the rental agreement is executed and will continue to be offered for the term of tenancy and the fees, if any, to be charged for those services.

(g) All other provisions governing the tenancy. *(Added by Stats.1990, c. 1505 (A.B.3139), § 1.)*

§ 800.22. Inclusion of other provisions permitted by law

The rental agreement may include other provisions permitted by law, but need not include specific language contained in state or local laws not a part of this chapter. *(Added by Stats.1990, c. 1505 (A.B.3139), § 1.)*

§ 800.23. Agreements offered to homeowners; contents

(a) A homeowner shall be offered a rental agreement for (1) a term of 12 months, (2) a lesser period as mutually agreed upon by both the homeowner and the management, (3) a longer period as mutually agreed upon by both the homeowner and the management, or (4) a longer period as necessary to secure financing from a conventional lending institution.

(b) Rental agreements for a prescribed term shall not contain any terms or conditions with respect to charges for rent, utilities, or incidental reasonable service charges that would be different during the first 12 months of the agreement from the corresponding terms or conditions that would be offered to the homeowner or homeowners on a month-to-month basis. *(Added by Stats.1990, c. 1505 (A.B.3139), § 1.)*

§ 800.24. Waiver of rights prohibited

No rental agreement for a floating home berth shall contain a provision by which the homeowner waives his or her rights under any of the provisions of this chapter. Any waiver of these rights shall be deemed contrary to public policy and void. *(Added by Stats.1990, c. 1505 (A.B.3139), § 1.)*

§ 800.25. Private club membership not to be denied on discriminatory basis; familial status

(a) Membership in any private club or organization that is a condition for tenancy in a floating home marina shall not be denied on any basis listed in subdivision (a) or (d) of Section 12955 of the Government Code, as those bases are defined in Sections 12926, 12926.1, subdivision (m) and paragraph (1) of subdivision (p) of Section 12955, and Section 12955.2 of the Government Code.

(b) Notwithstanding subdivision (a), with respect to familial status, subdivision (a) shall not be construed to apply to housing for older persons, as defined in Section 12955.9 of the Government Code. With respect to familial status, nothing in subdivision (a) shall be construed to affect Sections 51.2, 51.3, 51.4, 51.10, 51.11, and 799.5, relating to housing for senior citizens. Subdivision (d) of Section 51 and Section 4760 of this code and subdivisions (n), (o), and (p) of Section 12955 of the Government Code shall apply to subdivision (a). *(Added by Stats.1990, c. 1505 (A.B.3139), § 1. Amended by Stats.2006, c. 578 (A.B. 2800), § 7; Stats.2012, c. 181 (A.B.806), § 28, operative Jan. 1, 2014.)*

Law Revision Commission Comments

Section 800.25 is amended to correct a cross-reference to former Section 1360. [40 Cal.L.Rev.Comm. Reports 235 (2010)].

Research References

Miller and Starr California Real Estate § 20:29, Discrimination by a Real Estate Broker.
17 NO. 4 Miller & Starr, California Real Estate Newsalert 2, Statutory Update:.
17 NO. 6 Miller & Starr, California Real Estate Newsalert 20, Table of Statutes (Newsalert Vol 17).

§ 800.26. Copies of chapter; notice of availability

On or before March 12, 1991, the management shall notify all floating homeowners, in writing, that a copy of the Floating Home Residency Law is available to them, upon request, from the management. *(Added by Stats.1990, c. 1505 (A.B.3139), § 1.)*

ARTICLE 3.   RULES AND REGULATIONS

Section
800.30.   Common area facilities; hours.
800.31.   Amendment of rules or regulations; written notice.
800.32.   Right of entry; written consent required; exceptions.
800.33.   Zoning or use permits; duration of lease where management lessee; written notice to home-owners.
800.34.   Name and address of floating home marina owner; disclosure.
800.35.   Entry in floating home by management of floating home marina; prior written consent; exceptions.
800.36.   Abandonment of floating home not owned by marina; notice of belief of abandonment; delivery or mail; form; proof of nonabandonment.
800.37.   Abandonment of floating home owned by marina.

§ 800.30.   Common area facilities; hours

Each common area facility shall be open or available to residents at all reasonable hours, and the hours of the common area facility shall be posted at the facility. *(Added by Stats.1990, c. 1505 (A.B.3139), § 1.)*

§ 800.31.   Amendment of rules or regulations; written notice

A rule or regulation of the floating home marina may be amended at any time with the consent of a homeowner, or without his or her consent upon written notice to him or her of not less than six months. Written notice to a new homeowner, whose tenancy commences within the required period of notice, of a proposed amendment shall constitute compliance with this section where the written notice is given to him or her before the inception of his or her tenancy. *(Added by Stats.1990, c. 1505 (A.B.3139), § 1.)*

§ 800.32.   Right of entry; written consent required; exceptions

(a) Except as provided in subdivision (b), and notwithstanding any other provision of law to the contrary, the ownership or management of a floating home marina, cooperative, or condominium for floating homes shall have no right of entry to a floating home without the prior written consent of the resident. This consent may be revoked in writing by the resident at any time. The ownership or management shall have a right of entry into the berth in which a floating home is situated for correction of what management determines to be a hazardous condition at any time, or for maintenance of utilities, docks, and common areas at any reasonable time, but not in a manner or at a time which would interfere with the resident's quiet enjoyment.

(b) The ownership or management of a floating home marina, cooperative, or condominium may enter a floating home without the prior written consent of the resident in case of an emergency or when the resident has abandoned the floating home. *(Added by Stats.1990, c. 1505 (A.B.3139), § 1.)*

§ 800.33.   Zoning or use permits; duration of lease where management lessee; written notice to homeowners

(a) The management shall give written notice to all home-owners and prospective homeowners concerning the following matters: (1) the nature of the zoning or use permit under which the floating home marina operates, (2) if the floating home marina is operating pursuant to a permit subject to a renewal or expiration date, the relevant information and dates shall be included in the notice, and (3) the duration of any lease of the floating home marina, or any portion thereof, in which the management is a lessee.

(b) If a change occurs concerning the zoning or use permit under which the floating home marina operates, a change occurs to the lease under which the management is a lessee and that change could affect the homeowner, including the termination of the lease, litigation occurs regarding termination of the lease, or expiration of a use permit occurs, all homeowners shall be given written notice at least 30 days prior to the effective date of the change. Notification regarding the change of use of the floating home marina, or any portion thereof, shall be governed by subdivision (f) of Section 800.71. A prospective homeowner shall be notified prior to the inception of the tenancy. *(Added by Stats.1990, c. 1505 (A.B.3139), § 1.)*

§ 800.34.   Name and address of floating home marina owner; disclosure

The management of a floating home marina shall disclose, in writing, the name and address of the floating home marina owner upon the request of a homeowner. *(Added by Stats.1990, c. 1505 (A.B.3139), § 1.)*

§ 800.35.   Entry in floating home by management of floating home marina; prior written consent; exceptions

(a) The management of a floating home marina may enter a floating home, which is owned by the marina, only upon the prior written consent of the renter, except:

(1) In case of an emergency.

(2) Upon reasonable notice and during regular business hours, to make necessary or agreed repairs.

(3) When the homeowner has abandoned the premises.

(4) Pursuant to court order.

(b) The management of a floating home marina may enter a floating home, not owned by the marina, only upon prior written consent, except:

(1) In case of an emergency.

(2) When the homeowner has abandoned the premises.

(3) Pursuant to a court order. *(Added by Stats.1991, c. 942 (A.B.628), § 2.)*

§ 800.36.   Abandonment of floating home not owned by marina; notice of belief of abandonment; delivery or mail; form; proof of nonabandonment

(a) A floating home not owned by a floating home marina shall be deemed abandoned by the homeowner, and the lease shall terminate, if the floating home marina gives written notice of its belief of abandonment as provided in this section and the homeowner fails to give the marina written notice, prior to the date of termination specified in the marina's notice, stating that he or she does not intend to abandon the floating home and stating an address at which the homeowner may be served by certified mail in any action for unlawful detainer of the marina.

(b) The marina may give a notice of belief of abandonment to the homeowner pursuant to this section only where the rent on the marina has been due and unpaid for at least 45 consecutive days and the marina management reasonably believes that the homeowner has abandoned the floating home. The date of termination of the lease shall be specified in the marina's notice and shall be not less than 15 days after the notice is served personally or, if mailed, not less than 18 days after the notice is deposited in the mail.

(c) The marina's notice of belief of abandonment shall be personally delivered to the homeowner or sent by first-class mail, postage prepaid, to the homeowner at his or her last known address and, if there is reason to believe that the notice sent to that address will not be received by the homeowner, also to such other address, if any, known to the marina where the homeowner may reasonably be expected to receive the notice.

(d) The notice of belief of abandonment shall be in substantially the following form:

Notice of Belief of Abandonment

To:

_____

(Name of homeowner)

_____

(Address of homeowner)

This notice is given pursuant to Section 800.36 of the Civil Code concerning the floating home marina leased by you at _____ (state location of the property by address or other sufficient description). The rent on this marina has been due and unpaid for 45 consecutive days and the marina believes that you have abandoned the floating home.

The floating home will be deemed abandoned within the meaning of Section 1951.2 of the Civil Code and your lease will terminate on _____ (here insert a date not less than 15 days after this notice is served personally or, if mailed, not less than 18 days after this notice is deposited in the mail) unless before that date the undersigned receives at the address indicated below a written notice from you stating both of the following:

(1) Your intent not to abandon the floating home.

(2) An address at which you may be served by certified mail in any action for unlawful detainer of the floating home marina.

You are required to pay the rent due and unpaid on this marina as required by the lease, and your failure to do so can lead to a court proceeding against you.

Dated: _____

_____

(Signature of marina manager/owner)

_____

(Type or print name of marina manager/owner)

_____

(Address to which the homeowner is to send notice)

(e) The floating home shall not be deemed to be abandoned pursuant to this section if the homeowner proves any of the following:

(1) At the time the notice of belief of abandonment was given, the rent was not due and unpaid for 45 consecutive days.

(2) At the time the notice of belief of abandonment was given, it was not reasonable for the marina to believe that the homeowner had abandoned the floating home. The fact that the marina management knew that the homeowner left personal property on the floating home does not, of itself, justify a finding that the marina management did not reasonably believe that the homeowner had abandoned the floating home.

(3) Prior to the date specified in the marina's notice, the homeowner gave written notice to the lessor stating his or her intent not to abandon the floating home and stating an address at which he or she may be served by certified mail in any action for unlawful detainer of the marina.

(4) During the period commencing 45 days before the time the notice of belief of abandonment was given and ending on the date the lease would have terminated pursuant to the notice, the homeowner paid to the marina all or a portion of the rent due and unpaid.

(f) Nothing in this section precludes the marina or the homeowner from otherwise proving that the floating home has been abandoned by the homeowner within the meaning of Section 1951.2.

(g) Nothing in this section precludes the marina from serving a notice requiring the homeowner to pay rent or quit as provided in Section 800.71 at any time permitted by that section, or affects the time and manner of giving any other notice required or permitted by law. The giving of the notice provided by this section does not satisfy the requirements of Sections 1161 and 1162 of the Code of Civil Procedure. *(Added by Stats.1991, c. 942 (A.B.628), § 3.)*

Research References

Rutter, Cal. Practice Guide: Landlord-Tenant Form 13:A, Notice of Belief of Abandonment of Floating Home (CC § 800.36(D)).

§ 800.37. Abandonment of floating home owned by marina

A floating home which is owned by a floating home marina shall be deemed abandoned according to the procedures and requirements of Section 1951.3. *(Added by Stats.1991, c. 942 (A.B.628), § 4.)*

ARTICLE 4. FEES AND CHARGES

Section

§ 800.40. Increase in rent; advance written notice

The management shall give a homeowner written notice of any increase in his or her rent at least 30 days before the date of the increase, and the reason for the increase, including the basis for any calculation used in determining the amount of the increase. *(Added by Stats.1990, c. 1505 (A.B.3139), § 1. Amended by Stats.1991, c. 942 (A.B.628), § 5.)*

§ 800.41. Prohibited fees; fees for rental agreements in excess of one year

A homeowner shall not be charged a fee for other than rent, utilities, and incidental reasonable charges for services actually rendered.

A homeowner shall not be charged a fee for obtaining a rental agreement on a floating home berth for (1) a term of 12 months, or (2) a lesser period as mutually agreed upon by both the homeowner and the management. A fee may be charged for a rental agreement of more than one year if the fee is mutually agreed upon by both the homeowner and management. *(Added by Stats.1990, c. 1505 (A.B.3139), § 1.)*

§ 800.42. Fees for rendered services not listed in rental agreement; written notice

A homeowner shall not be charged a fee for services actually rendered which are not listed in the rental agreement unless he or she has been given written notice thereof by the management, at least 60 days before imposition of the charge. *(Added by Stats.1990, c. 1505 (A.B.3139), § 1.)*

§ 800.43.   Fees for keeping pets;   special pet facilities

A homeowner shall not be charged a fee for keeping a pet in the floating home marina unless the management actually provides special facilities or services for pets. If special pet facilities are maintained by the management, the fee charged shall reasonably relate to the cost of maintenance of the facilities or services and the number of pets kept in the floating home marina. *(Added by Stats.1990, c. 1505 (A.B.3139), § 1.)*

§ 800.44.   Fees for guests

(a) A homeowner shall not be charged a fee for a guest who does not stay with him or her for more than a total of 20 consecutive days or a total of 30 days in a calendar year. Such a guest shall not be required to register with the management.

(b) A homeowner who is living alone and who wishes to share his or her floating home with one person may do so, and a fee shall not be imposed by management for that person. The person shall be considered a guest of the homeowner and any agreement between the homeowner and the person shall not change the terms and conditions of the rental agreement between management and the homeowner. The guest shall comply with the provisions of the rules and regulations of the floating home marina. *(Added by Stats.1990, c. 1505 (A.B.3139), § 1.)*

§ 800.45.   Fee based on number of immediate family members

A homeowner shall not be charged a fee based on the number of members in his or her immediate family. As used in this section, the "immediate family" includes the homeowner and his or her spouse, their parents, and their children. *(Added by Stats.1990, c. 1505 (A.B.3139), § 1.)*

§ 800.46.   Fees for enforcement of rules and regulations

A homeowner shall not be charged a fee for the enforcement of any of the rules and regulations of the floating home marina. *(Added by Stats.1990, c. 1505 (A.B.3139), § 1.)*

§ 800.47.   Entry, installation, hookup, or landscaping fees

Unless the homeowner specifically requests the service in writing from the management, a homeowner shall not be charged a fee for the entry, installation, hookup, or landscaping as a condition of tenancy except for an actual fee or cost imposed by a local governmental ordinance or requirement directly related to the occupancy of the specific berth where the floating home is located and not incurred as a portion of the development of the floating home marina as a whole. However, reasonable landscaping and maintenance requirements may be included in the floating home marina rules and regulations. The management shall not require a homeowner or prospective homeowner to purchase, rent, or lease goods or services for landscaping from any person, company, or corporation. *(Added by Stats.1990, c. 1505 (A.B.3139), § 1.)*

§ 800.48.   Master meter and submeter utility services;   separate billing;   posting of rates schedule

Where the management provides both master meter and submeter service of utilities to a homeowner, for each billing period the cost of the charges for the period shall be separately stated along with the opening and closing readings for his or her meter. The management shall post in a conspicuous place, the prevailing residential utilities rate schedule as published by the serving utility. *(Added by Stats.1990, c. 1505 (A.B.3139), § 1.)*

§ 800.49.   Security deposits;   amount;   refund;   transfer of management's interests;   interest;   application of section

(a) The management may only demand a security deposit on or before initial occupancy and the security deposit may not be in an amount or value in excess of an amount equal to two months' rent that is charged at the inception of the tenancy, in addition to any rent for the first month. In no event shall additional security deposits be demanded of a homeowner following initial occupancy.

(b) After the homeowner has promptly paid to the management within five days of the date the amount is due, all of the rent, utilities, and reasonable service charges for any 12-consecutive-month period subsequent to the collection of the security deposit by the management, or upon resale of the floating home, whichever occurs earlier, the management shall, upon the receipt of a written request from the homeowner, refund to the homeowner the amount of the security deposit within 30 days following the end of the 12-consecutive-month period of prompt payment or the date of the resale of the floating home.

(c) In the event that the interest in the floating home marina is transferred to any other party or entity, the successor in interest shall have the same obligations of management contained in this section with respect to the security deposit.

(d) The management shall not be required to place any security deposit collected in an interest-bearing account or to provide a homeowner with any interest on the security deposit collected.

(e) This section applies to all security deposits collected on or after January 1, 1991. *(Added by Stats.1990, c. 1505 (A.B.3139), § 1. Amended by Stats.1991, c. 942 (A.B.628), § 6.)*

§ 800.50.   Liens or security interests

The management shall not acquire a lien or security interest, other than an interest arising by reason of process issued to enforce a judgment of any court, in a floating home located in the floating home marina unless it is mutually agreed upon by both the homeowner and management. Any billing and payment upon the obligation shall be kept separate from current rent. *(Added by Stats.1990, c. 1505 (A.B.3139), § 1.)*

ARTICLE 5.   HOMEOWNER MEETINGS

§ 800.60.   Homeowner or resident meetings

The management shall permit meetings by homeowners or residents of a floating home in the marina, or any or all of them, relating to floating home living or social or educational purposes, including forums for or speeches of public officials or candidates for public office, to be held in any community facility if the meeting is held at reasonable hours and when the facility is not otherwise in use. The management's private office is not to be considered a community facility unless so designated by the management. *(Added by Stats.1990, c. 1505 (A.B.3139), § 1.)*

§ 800.61.   Management meetings with homeowners;   collective meetings

The management shall meet and consult with the homeowners, upon written request, within 30 days of the request, either individually, collectively, or with representatives of a group of homeowners who have signed a request to be so represented on the following matters:

(a) Amendments to floating home marina rules and regulations.

(b) Standards for maintenance or physical improvements in the floating home marina.

(c) Addition, alteration, or deletion of services, equipment or physical improvements.

(d) Rental agreements offered pursuant to Article 2 (commencing with Section 800.20).

Any collective meeting shall be conducted only after notice thereof has been given to all the requesting homeowners 10 days or more before the meeting. *(Added by Stats.1990, c. 1505 (A.B.3139), § 1.)*

ARTICLE 6. TERMINATION OF TENANCY

Section
800.70. Legislative findings and declarations; termination or refusal to renew tenancy; notice.
800.71. Termination of tenancy; permitted reasons.
800.72. Notice of termination; contents.
800.73. Termination to make home available for purchaser prohibited.
800.74. Vacation of tenancy; written notice.
800.75. Effect of article on rights relating to summary proceedings for obtaining possession of real property.

§ 800.70. Legislative findings and declarations; termination or refusal to renew tenancy; notice

(a) The Legislature finds and declares that, because of the high cost of moving floating homes, the potential for damage resulting therefrom, the requirements relating to the installation of floating homes, and current government policy limiting the availability of floating home berths, it is necessary that the owners of floating homes within floating home marinas be provided with the unique protection from actual or constructive eviction afforded by the provisions of this chapter.

(b) The management shall not terminate or refuse to renew a tenancy, except for a reason specified in this article and upon the giving of written notice to the homeowner in the manner prescribed by Section 1162 of the Code of Civil Procedure, to remove the floating home from the floating home marina within a period of not less than 60 days, which period shall be specified in the notice. A copy of this notice shall be sent to the legal owner, as defined in Section 18005.8 of the Health and Safety Code, each junior lienholder, as defined in Section 18005.3 of the Health and Safety Code, and the registered owner of the floating home, if other than the homeowner, by United States mail within 10 days after notice to the homeowner, addressed to the legal owner, each junior lienholder, and the registered owner at their addresses, as set forth in the registration card specified in Section 18091.5 of the Health and Safety Code. *(Added by Stats.1990, c. 1505 (A.B.3139), § 1.)*

§ 800.71. Termination of tenancy; permitted reasons

A tenancy shall be terminated by the management only for one or more of the following reasons:

(a) Failure of the homeowner or resident to comply with a local ordinance or state law or regulation relating to floating homes within a reasonable time after the homeowner receives a notice of noncompliance from the appropriate governmental agency.

(b) Conduct by the homeowner or resident, upon the floating home marina premises, which constitutes a substantial annoyance to other homeowners or residents.

(c) Failure of the homeowner or resident to comply with a reasonable rule or regulation of the floating home marina as set forth in the rental agreement or any amendment thereto. The management may not impose unreasonable restrictions on the right of the homeowner to sublet his or her floating home.

No act or omission of the homeowner or resident shall constitute a failure to comply with a reasonable rule or regulation unless and until the management has given the homeowner written notice of the alleged rule or regulation violation and the homeowner or resident has failed to adhere to the rule or regulation within seven days. However, if a homeowner has been given a written notice of an alleged violation of the same rule or regulation on three or more occasions within a 12-month period after the homeowner or resident has violated that rule or regulation, no written notice shall be required for a subsequent violation of the same rule or regulation.

Nothing in this subdivision shall relieve the management from its obligation to demonstrate that a rule or regulation has in fact been violated.

(d) (1) Nonpayment of rent, utility charges, or reasonable incidental service charges; if the amount due has been unpaid for a period of at least five days from its due date, and provided, that the homeowner shall be given a three-day written notice subsequent to that five-day period to pay the amount due or to vacate the tenancy. The three-day written notice shall be given to the homeowner in the manner prescribed by Section 1162 of the Code of Civil Procedure. The notice may be given at the same time as the 60 days' notice required for termination of the tenancy.

Payment by the homeowner prior to the expiration of the three-day notice period shall cure a default under this subdivision.

(2) However, if a homeowner has been given a three-day notice to pay the amount due or to vacate the tenancy on three or more occasions within the preceding 12-month period, no written three-day notice shall be required for a subsequent nonpayment of rent, utility charges, or reasonable incidental service charges.

(3) Payment by the legal owner, any junior lienholder, or the registered owner, if other than the homeowner, on behalf of the homeowner prior to the expiration of 30 calendar days following the mailing of the notice to the legal owner, each junior lienholder, and the registered owner provided in subdivision (b) of Section 800.70, shall cure a default under this subdivision with respect to that payment.

(4) The homeowner shall remain liable for all payments due up until the time the tenancy is vacated.

(5) Cure of a default of rent, utility charges, or reasonable incidental service charges by the legal owner, any junior lienholder, or the registered owner, if other than the homeowner, as provided by this subdivision, may not be exercised more than twice during a 12-month period.

(e) Condemnation of the floating home marina.

(f) Change of use of the floating home marina or any portion thereof, provided:

(1) The management gives the homeowners at least 60 days' written notice that the management will be appearing before a local governmental board, commission, or body to request permits for a change of use of the floating home marina.

(2) After all required permits requesting a change of use have been approved by the local governmental board, commission, or body, the management shall give the homeowners six months' or more written notice of termination of tenancy.

If the change of use requires no local governmental permits, then notice shall be given 12 months or more prior to the management's determination that a change of use will occur. The management in the notice shall disclose and describe in detail the nature of the change of use.

(3) The management gives each proposed homeowner written notice thereof prior to the inception of his or her tenancy that the management is requesting a change of use before local governmental bodies or that a change of use request has been granted.

(4) The notice requirements for termination of tenancy set forth in this section and Section 800.72 shall be followed if the proposed change actually occurs.

(5) The requirements for a notice of a proposed change of use imposed by this subdivision shall be governed by the law in effect at the time the notice was given. *(Added by Stats.1990, c. 1505 (A.B.3139), § 1.)*

§ 800.72. Notice of termination; contents

The management shall set forth in a notice of termination the reason relied upon for the termination with specific facts to permit determination of the date, place, witnesses, and circumstances concerning that reason. Neither reference to the section number or a subdivision thereof nor a recital of the language of this article constitutes compliance with this section. *(Added by Stats.1990, c. 1505 (A.B.3139), § 1.)*

§ 800.73. Termination to make home available for purchaser prohibited

No tenancy shall be terminated for the purpose of making a homeowner's berth available for a person who purchases a floating home from the owner of the floating home marina or his or her agent. *(Added by Stats.1990, c. 1505 (A.B.3139), § 1.)*

§ 800.74. Vacation of tenancy; written notice

A homeowner shall give written notice to the management of not less than 60 days before vacating his or her tenancy. *(Added by Stats.1990, c. 1505 (A.B.3139), § 1.)*

§ 800.75. Effect of article on rights relating to summary proceedings for obtaining possession of real property

The provisions of this article shall not affect any rights or proceedings set forth in Chapter 4 (commencing with Section 1159) of Title 3 of Part 3 of the Code of Civil Procedure except as otherwise provided in those sections. *(Added by Stats.1990, c. 1505 (A.B.3139), § 1.)*

Research References

Miller and Starr California Real Estate § 31:4, Floating Home Residency Law.

ARTICLE 7. TRANSFER OF A FLOATING HOME

§ 800.80. Advertisement of sale or rental by owner; sign

A homeowner or his or her agent may advertise the sale or exchange of his or her floating home, or, if not prohibited by the terms of an agreement with the management, may advertise the rental of his or her floating home, by displaying a sign in the window of the floating home, or by a sign posted on the side of the floating home facing the dock or water or both, stating that the floating home is for sale or exchange or, if not prohibited, for rent by the owner of the floating home or his or her agent. The sign shall state the name, address, and telephone number of the owner of the floating home or his or her agent and may be at least 24 inches in width and 18 inches in height. *(Added by Stats.1990, c. 1505 (A.B.3139), § 1.)*

Research References

Miller and Starr California Real Estate § 31:4, Floating Home Residency Law.

§ 800.82. Showing or listing for sale by management; authorization

(a) The management shall not show or list for sale a floating home without first obtaining the owner's written authorization. The authorization shall specify the terms and conditions regarding the showing or listing.

(b) The management shall prohibit neither the listing nor the sale of a floating home within the floating home marina by the homeowner, or an agent of the homeowner to authorize the management to act as the agent in the sale of a floating home as a condition of management's approval of buyer or prospective homeowner for residency in the floating home marina. *(Added by Stats.1990, c. 1505 (A.B.3139), § 1.)*

§ 800.83. Transfer or selling fees; condition of approval for residency fees

(a) The management shall not charge a homeowner, or his or her agent a transfer or selling fee as a condition of a sale of his or her floating home within a floating home marina unless the management performs a service in the sale. The management shall not perform any such service in connection with the sale unless so requested in writing, by the homeowner or his or her agent.

(b) The management shall not charge a prospective homeowner or his or her agent, upon purchase of a floating home, a fee as a condition of approval for residency in a floating home marina unless the management performs a specific service in the sale. The management shall not impose a fee, other than for a credit check in accordance with subdivision (b) of Section 800.85, for an interview of a prospective homeowner. *(Added by Stats.1990, c. 1505 (A.B.3139), § 1.)*

§ 800.84. Removal of home upon sale prohibited as term of rental agreement

The management shall not require the removal of a floating home from the floating home marina in the event of its sale to a third party during the term of the homeowner's rental agreement. *(Added by Stats.1990, c. 1505 (A.B.3139), § 1.)*

§ 800.85. Right of prior approval; fees for obtaining financial reports

(a) The management may require the right of prior approval of a purchaser of a floating home that will remain in the floating home marina and that the selling homeowner or his or her agent give notice of the sale to the management before the close of the sale. Approval cannot be withheld if the purchaser has the financial ability to pay the rent and charges of the floating home marina unless the management reasonably determines that, based on the purchaser's prior tenancies, he or she will not comply with the rules and regulations of the floating home marina. In determining whether the purchaser has the financial ability to pay the rent and charges of the floating home marina, the management shall not require the purchaser to submit copies of any personal income tax returns in order to obtain approval for residency in the floating home marina. However, management may require the purchaser to document the amount and source of his or her gross monthly income or means of financial support. If the ownership or management rejects a purchaser as a prospective homeowner, the ownership or management shall inform the selling homeowner in writing of its reasons for the rejection. If the approval of a purchaser is withheld for any reason other than those stated in this article, the management or owner may be held liable for all damages proximately resulting therefrom.

(b) If the management collects a fee or charge from a prospective purchaser of a floating home in order to obtain a financial report or credit rating, the full amount of the fee or charge shall be credited toward payment of the first month's rent for that floating home purchaser. If, for whatever reason, the prospective purchaser is rejected by the management, the management shall refund to the prospective purchaser the full amount of that fee or charge within 30 days from the date of rejection. If the prospective purchaser is approved by the management, but, for whatever reason, the prospective purchaser elects not to purchase the floating home, the management may retain the fee, or a portion thereof, to defray its administrative costs under this section. *(Added by Stats.1990, c. 1505 (A.B.3139), § 1.)*

§ 800.86. Escrow, sale or transfer agreement for home to remain in marina; rental agreement signed by purchaser; unlawful occupant

(a) An escrow, sale, or transfer agreement involving a floating home located in the floating home marina at the time of sale, where the floating home is to remain in the floating home marina, shall contain a provision signed by the purchaser stating that by his or her signature he or she has agreed to the terms of a rental agreement. A copy of a fully executed rental agreement signed by both the purchaser and floating home marina management will satisfy the requirements of this section.

(b) In the event the purchaser fails to execute the rental agreement, the purchaser shall not have any rights of tenancy.

(c) In the event that an occupant of a floating home has no rights of tenancy and is not otherwise entitled to occupy the floating home pursuant to this chapter, the occupant shall be considered an unlawful occupant if, after a demand is made for the surrender of the floating home marina berth, for a period of five days, the occupant has refused to surrender the berth to the floating home marina management. In the event the unlawful occupant fails to comply with the demand, the unlawful occupant shall be subject to the proceedings set forth in Chapter 4 (commencing with Section 1159) of Title 3 of Part 3 of the Code of Civil Procedure.

(d) The occupant of the floating home shall not be considered an unlawful occupant and shall not be subject to the provisions of subdivision (c) if all of the following conditions exist:

(1) The occupant is the registered owner of the floating home.

(2) The management has determined that the occupant has the financial ability to pay the rent and charges of the floating home marina, will comply with the rules and regulations of the

floating home marina, based on the occupant's prior tenancies, and will comply with this article.

(3) The management failed or refused to offer the occupant a rental agreement. *(Added by Stats.1990, c. 1505 (A.B.3139), § 1.)*

§ 800.87. Waiver of rights under article prohibited

No rental or sale agreement shall contain a provision by which the purchaser or homeowner waives his or her rights under this article. Any waiver thereof shall be deemed contrary to public policy and shall be void and unenforceable. *(Added by Stats. 1990, c. 1505 (A.B.3139), § 1.)*

§ 800.88. Heirs or joint tenants gaining ownership through death of owner; rights to sell

An heir or joint tenant who gains ownership of a floating home in the floating home marina through the death of the owner of the floating home who is a homeowner shall have the right to sell the floating home to a third party in accordance with this article, but only if all the homeowner's responsibilities and liabilities to the management regarding rent, utilities, and reasonable maintenance of the floating home and its premises which have arisen after the transfer of ownership to the heir or joint tenant have been satisfied up until the date the floating home is resold. *(Added by Stats.1990, c. 1505 (A.B.3139), § 1. Amended by Stats.1991, c. 942 (A.B.628), § 7.)*

§ 800.89. Legal owners or junior lienholders foreclosing on security interests; rights to sell

Any legal owner or junior lienholder who forecloses on his or her security interest in a floating home located in a floating home marina shall have the right to sell the floating home within the floating home marina to a third party in accordance with the provisions of this article, but only if all the homeowner's responsibilities and liabilities to the management regarding rent, utilities, and reasonable maintenance of a floating home and it's premises are satisfied by the foreclosing creditor through the date the floating home is resold. *(Added by Stats.1990, c. 1505 (A.B.3139), § 1.)*

§ 800.90. Prohibited acts by management

The management (1) shall not prohibit the listing or sale of a used floating home within the floating home marina by the homeowner, or an agent of the homeowner other than the management, (2) nor require the selling homeowner to authorize the management to act as the agent in the sale of a floating home as a condition of approval of the buyer or prospective homeowner for residency in the floating home marina. *(Added by Stats.1990, c. 1505 (A.B.3139), § 1.)*

§ 800.91. Actions for management's alleged failure to maintain physical improvements in common facilities or services; notice

(a) No action based upon the management's alleged failure to maintain the physical improvements in the common facilities in good working order or condition or alleged reduction of service may be commenced by a homeowner unless the management has been given at least 30 days' prior notice of the intention to commence the action.

(b) The notice shall be in writing, signed by the homeowner or homeowners making the allegations, and shall notify the management of the basis of the claim, the specific allegations, and the remedies requested. A notice by one homeowner shall be deemed to be sufficient notice of the specific allegation to the management of the floating home marina by all of the homeowners in the floating home marina.

(c) The notice may be served in the manner prescribed in Chapter 5 (commencing with Section 1010) of Title 14 of Part 2 of the Code of Civil Procedure.

(d) For purposes of this section, management shall be deemed to be notified of an alleged failure to maintain the physical improvements in the common facilities in good working order or condition or of an alleged reduction of services upon substantial compliance by the homeowner or homeowners with the provisions of subdivisions (b) and (c), or when management has been notified of the alleged failure to maintain or the alleged reduction of services by a state or local agency.

(e) If the notice is served within 30 days of the expiration of the applicable statute of limitations, the time for the commencement of the action shall be extended 30 days from the service of the notice.

(f) This section does not apply to actions for personal injury or wrongful death. *(Added by Stats.1990, c. 1505 (A.B.3139), § 1.)*

ARTICLE 8.   TRANSFER OF A FLOATING HOME MARINA

Section
800.100.   Entry into written listing agreement; notice; conditions; application of section.

§ 800.100.   Entry into written listing agreement; notice; conditions; application of section

(a) When the owner of a floating home marina enters into a written listing agreement with a licensed real estate broker, as defined in Article 1 (commencing with Section 10130) of Chapter 2 of Part 1 of Division 4 of the Business and Professions Code, for the sale of the marina or offers to sell the marina to any party, the owner shall provide written notice by first-class mail or by personal delivery to the president, secretary, and treasurer of the resident organization, not less than 30 days but no more than one year prior to entering into any written listing agreement for the sale of the marina, or making any offer to sell the marina to any party. An offer to sell a marina shall not be construed as an offer under this subdivision unless it is initiated by the marina owner or his or her agent.

(b) An owner of a floating home marina is not required to comply with subdivision (a) unless the following conditions are met:

(1) The resident organization has first furnished the marina owner or marina manager a written notice of the name and address of the president, secretary, and treasurer of the resident organization to whom the notice of sale shall be given.

(2) The resident organization has first notified the marina owner or manager in writing that the marina residents are interested in purchasing the marina. The initial notice by the resident organization shall be made prior to a written listing or offer to sell the marina by the marina owner, and the resident organization shall give subsequent notice once each year thereafter that the marina residents are interested in purchasing the marina.

(3) The resident organization has furnished the marina owner or marina manager a written notice, within five days, of any change in the name or address of the officers of the resident organization to whom the notice of sale shall be given.

(c) Nothing in this section affects the validity of title to real property transferred in violation of this section, although a violation shall subject the seller to civil action pursuant to Article 9 (commencing with Section 800.200) by homeowner residents of the marina or by the resident organization.

(d) Nothing in this section affects the ability of a licensed real estate broker to collect a commission pursuant to an executed contract between the broker and the floating home marina owner.

(e) This section does not apply to any of the following:

(1) Any sale or other transfer by a marina owner who is a natural person to any relation specified in Section 6401 or 6402 of the Probate Code.

(2) Any transfer by gift, devise, or operation of law.

(3) Any transfer by a corporation to an affiliate. As used in this paragraph, "affiliate" means any shareholder of the transferring corporation, any corporation or entity owned or controlled, directly or indirectly, by the transferring corporation, or any other corporation or entity controlled, directly or indirectly, by any shareholder of the transferring corporation.

(4) Any transfer by a partnership to any of its partners.

(5) Any conveyance resulting from the judicial or nonjudicial foreclosure of a mortgage or deed of trust encumbering a floating home marina or any deed given in lieu of such a foreclosure.

(6) Any sale or transfer between or among joint tenants or tenants in common owning a floating home marina.

(7) The purchase of a floating home marina by a governmental entity under its powers of eminent domain. *(Added by Stats.1990, c. 1505 (A.B.3139), § 1.   Amended by Stats.1991, c. 942 (A.B.628), § 8; Stats.2004, c. 183 (A.B.3082), § 25.)*

Research References

Miller and Starr California Real Estate § 31:4, Floating Home Residency Law.

ARTICLE 9.   ACTIONS, PROCEEDINGS, AND PENALTIES

Section
800.200.   Attorney's fees and costs for prevailing party; awards for willful violations.
800.201.   Violations deemed public nuisances; remedy.

§ 800.200.   Attorney's fees and costs for prevailing party; awards for willful violations

In any action arising out of the provisions of this chapter the prevailing party shall be entitled to reasonable attorney's fees and costs. A party shall be deemed a prevailing party for the purposes of this section if the judgment is rendered in his or her favor or where the litigation is dismissed in his or her favor prior to or during the trial, unless the parties otherwise agree in the settlement or compromise.

In the event a homeowner or former homeowner of a floating home marina is the prevailing party in a civil action against the management to enforce his or her rights under the provisions of this chapter, the homeowner, in addition to damages afforded by law, may, in the discretion of the court, be awarded an amount not to exceed five hundred dollars ($500) for each willful violation of those provisions by the management. *(Added by Stats.1990, c. 1505 (A.B.3139), § 1.)*

§ 800.201.   Violations deemed public nuisances; remedy

(a) The substantial failure of the management to provide and maintain physical improvements in the common facilities in good working order and condition shall be deemed a public nuisance. Notwithstanding the provisions of Section 3491, such a nuisance only may be remedied by a civil action or abatement.

(b) The substantial violation of a floating home marina rule shall be deemed a public nuisance. Notwithstanding the provisions of Section 3491, such a nuisance only may be remedied by a civil action or abatement. *(Added by Stats.1990, c. 1505 (A.B. 3139), § 1.)*

ARTICLE 10. COOPERATIVES AND CONDOMINIUMS

§ 800.300. Definitions

As used in this article:

(a) "Ownership or management" means the ownership or management of a cooperative or condominium for floating homes.

(b) "Resident" means a person who maintains a residence in a cooperative or condominium for floating homes. *(Added by Stats.1990, c. 1505 (A.B.3139), § 1.)*

§ 800.301. Advertisement of sale or rental of home; sign

A resident may advertise the sale or exchange of his or her floating home or, if not prohibited by the terms of an agreement with the management or ownership, may advertise the rental of his or her floating home by displaying a sign in the window of his or her floating home stating that the floating home is for sale or exchange or, if not prohibited, for rent by the owner of the floating home or his or her agent. The sign shall state the name, address, and telephone number of the owner of the floating home or his or her agent, and shall be 24 inches in width and 18 inches in length. *(Added by Stats.1990, c. 1505 (A.B.3139), § 1. Amended by Stats.1991, c. 942 (A.B.628), § 9.)*

§ 800.302. Showing or listing for sale by owner or management; resident's written authorization

The ownership or management shall not show or list for sale a floating home owned by a resident without first obtaining the resident's written authorization. The authorization shall specify the terms and conditions regarding the showing or listing. *(Added by Stats.1990, c. 1505 (A.B.3139), § 1. Amended by Stats.1991, c. 942 (A.B.628), § 10.)*

§ 800.303. Removal from cooperative or condominium upon sale to third party prohibited

The ownership or management shall not require the removal of a floating home from a cooperative or condominium in the event of its sale to a third party. *(Added by Stats.1990, c. 1505 (A.B.3139), § 1.)*

§ 800.304. Right of prior approval

The ownership or management may require the right to prior approval of the purchaser of a floating home that will remain in the cooperative or condominium for floating homes and that the selling resident or his or her agent give notice of the sale to the ownership or management before the close of the sale. Approval cannot be withheld if the purchaser has the financial ability to pay the fees and charges of the cooperative or condominium unless the ownership or management reasonably determines that, based on the purchaser's prior residences, he or she will not comply with the rules and regulations of the cooperative or condominium. *(Added by Stats.1990, c. 1505 (A.B.3139), § 1.)*

§ 800.305. Waiver of rights under article prohibited

No agreement shall contain any provision by which the purchaser waives his or her rights under this article. Any waiver thereof shall be deemed contrary to public policy and void and unenforceable. *(Added by Stats.1990, c. 1505 (A.B.3139), § 1.)*

§ 800.306. Application of chapter

This chapter applies only to the relationship between the management and the homeowners and residents of floating home marinas. Nothing in this chapter affects residential use of tide and submerged lands, including the public trust doctrine or any legislative grant of tide and submerged lands to a public entity, or the administration of these lands by the State Lands Commission or a legislative grantee. In addition, this chapter does not supplant, lessen, modify, or otherwise affect past or future regulation of floating homes or floating home marinas by the San Francisco Bay Conservation and Development Commission pursuant to the McAteer-Petris Act. *(Added by Stats.1990, c. 1505 (A.B.3139), § 1.)*

CHAPTER 3.   SERVITUDES

§ 801. Easements; servitudes attached to land

The following land burdens, or servitudes upon land, may be attached to other land as incidents or appurtenances, and are then called easements:

1.   The right of pasture;

2.   The right of fishing;

3.   The right of taking game;

4.   The right-of-way;

5.   The right of taking water, wood, minerals, and other things;

6.   The right of transacting business upon land;

7.   The right of conducting lawful sports upon land;

8.   The right of receiving air, light, or heat from or over, or discharging the same upon or over land;

9.   The right of receiving water from or discharging the same upon land;

10.   The right of flooding land;

11.   The right of having water flow without diminution or disturbance of any kind;

12.   The right of using a wall as a party wall;

13. The right of receiving more than natural support from adjacent land or things affixed thereto;

14. The right of having the whole of a division fence maintained by a coterminous owner;

15. The right of having public conveyances stopped, or of stopping the same on land;

16. The right of a seat in church;

17. The right of burial;

18. The right of receiving sunlight upon or over land as specified in Section 801.5. *(Enacted in 1872. Amended by Stats.1978, c. 1154, p. 3542, § 4.)*

Research References

Rutter, Cal. Practice Guide: Real Prop. Transactions Ch. 4-B, B. Interests to be Conveyed.

Miller and Starr California Real Estate § 15:1, Easement Defined; Profits Distinguished.

Miller and Starr California Real Estate § 15:6, Appurtenant Easements; Conveyance or Encumbrance of the Dominant Tenement.

Miller and Starr California Real Estate § 24:1, Types of Enforceable Restrictions.

Miller and Starr California Real Estate § 8:60, Appurtenances Pass With Conveyance.

Miller and Starr California Real Estate § 14:19, Lateral Support-- Common Law Rule.

Miller and Starr California Real Estate § 14:29, Definition; Creation.

Miller and Starr California Real Estate § 14:30, Rights and Duties of the Parties.

Miller and Starr California Real Estate § 14:35, Right to Protection of Views and Sunlight; in General.

Miller and Starr California Real Estate § 14:38, Rights to Protection and Siting of Solar Energy Facilities.

Miller and Starr California Real Estate § 15:10, Easements for Light, Air, or View.

Miller and Starr California Real Estate § 15:11, Solar Easements.

18 NO. 1 Miller & Starr, California Real Estate Newsalert 12, Easements.

12 Witkin, California Summary 10th Real Property § 383, Appurtenant and in Gross.

12 Witkin, California Summary 10th Real Property § 384, Typical Easements.

12 Witkin, California Summary 10th Real Property § 385, Solar Easement.

12 Witkin, California Summary 10th Real Property § 387, Profits.

12 Witkin, California Summary 10th Real Property § 406, Recorded Covenant.

§ 801.5. Solar easement and solar energy system defined; minimum description in instrument

(a) The right of receiving sunlight as specified in subdivision 18 of Section 801 shall be referred to as a solar easement. "Solar easement" means the right of receiving sunlight across real property of another for any solar energy system.

As used in this section, "solar energy system" means either of the following:

(1) Any solar collector or other solar energy device whose primary purpose is to provide for the collection, storage, and distribution of solar energy for space heating, space cooling, electric generation, or water heating.

(2) Any structural design feature of a building, whose primary purpose is to provide for the collection, storage, and distribution of solar energy for electricity generation, space heating or cooling, or for water heating.

(b) Any instrument creating a solar easement shall include, at a minimum, all of the following:

(1) A description of the dimensions of the easement expressed in measurable terms, such as vertical or horizontal angles measured in degrees, or the hours of the day on specified dates during which direct sunlight to a specified surface of a solar collector, device, or structural design feature may not be obstructed, or a combination of these descriptions.

(2) The restrictions placed upon vegetation, structures, and other objects that would impair or obstruct the passage of sunlight through the easement.

(3) The terms or conditions, if any, under which the easement may be revised or terminated. *(Added by Stats.1978, c. 1154, p. 3543, § 5.   Amended by Stats.2000, c. 537 (S.B.1345), § 2.)*

Research References

Miller and Starr California Real Estate § 15:6, Appurtenant Easements; Conveyance or Encumbrance of the Dominant Tenement.

Miller and Starr California Real Estate § 14:38, Rights to Protection and Siting of Solar Energy Facilities.

Miller and Starr California Real Estate § 15:11, Solar Easements.

Miller and Starr California Real Estate § 22:12, Obstruction of Light and Air.

19 NO. 3 Miller & Starr, California Real Estate Newsalert 1, The Solar Shade Control Act- from Trees Versus Solar to Trees and Solar?

12 Witkin, California Summary 10th Real Property § 384, Typical Easements.

12 Witkin, California Summary 10th Real Property § 385, Solar Easement.

12 Witkin, California Summary 10th Real Property § 444, No Prohibition of Solar Energy Systems.

§ 801.7. Extent of railroad right-of-way; railroad corporation defined

(a) When a right-of-way is granted pursuant to Section 801 or 802 to a railroad corporation whose primary business is the transportation of passengers, the grant shall include, but not be limited to, a right-of-way for the location, construction, and maintenance of the railroad corporation's necessary works and for every necessary adjunct thereto.

(b) A "railroad corporation" shall have the same definition as provided in Section 230 of the Public Utilities Code. *(Added by Stats.1982, c. 1553, p. 6061, § 1.)*

§ 802. Servitudes unattached

The following land burdens, or servitudes upon land, may be granted and held, though not attached to land:

One—The right to pasture, and of fishing and taking game.

Two—The right of a seat in church.

Three—The right of burial.

Four—The right of taking rents and tolls.

Five—The right of way.

Six—The right of taking water, wood, minerals, or other things. *(Enacted in 1872.   Amended by Code Am.1873–74, c. 612, p. 219, § 108.)*

Research References

Rutter, Cal. Practice Guide: Real Prop. Transactions Ch. 4-B, B. Interests to be Conveyed.

Miller and Starr California Real Estate § 15:1, Easement Defined; Profits Distinguished.

Miller and Starr California Real Estate § 15:6, Appurtenant Easements; Conveyance or Encumbrance of the Dominant Tenement.

Miller and Starr California Real Estate § 15:7, Easement in Gross.

Miller and Starr California Real Estate § 24:1, Types of Enforceable Restrictions.

Miller and Starr California Real Estate § 8:60, Appurtenances Pass With Conveyance.

Miller and Starr California Real Estate § 14:19, Lateral Support-- Common Law Rule.

12 Witkin, California Summary 10th Real Property § 383, Appurtenant and in Gross.

12 Witkin, California Summary 10th Real Property § 384, Typical Easements.

12 Witkin, California Summary 10th Real Property § 387, Profits.

12 Witkin, California Summary 10th Real Property § 420, (S 420) Transferability and Succession.

§ 803. Dominant and servient tenements

DESIGNATION OF ESTATES. The land to which an easement is attached is called the dominant tenement; the land upon which a burden or servitude is laid is called the servient tenement. *(Enacted in 1872.)*

Research References

Rutter, Cal. Practice Guide: Real Prop. Transactions Ch. 4-B, B. Interests to be Conveyed.

Miller and Starr California Real Estate § 15:6, Appurtenant Easements; Conveyance or Encumbrance of the Dominant Tenement.

Miller and Starr California Real Estate § 15:7, Easement in Gross.

12 Witkin, California Summary 10th Real Property § 383, Appurtenant and in Gross.

§ 804. Persons who may create servitudes

BY WHOM GRANTABLE. A servitude can be created only by one who has a vested estate in the servient tenement. *(Enacted in 1872.)*

Research References

Miller and Starr California Real Estate § 24:1, Types of Enforceable Restrictions.

Miller and Starr California Real Estate § 15:10, Easements for Light, Air, or View.

§ 805. Persons who cannot hold servitudes

BY WHOM HELD. A servitude thereon cannot be held by the owner of the servient tenement. *(Enacted in 1872.)*

Research References

Rutter, Cal. Practice Guide: Real Prop. Transactions Ch. 4-B, B. Interests to be Conveyed.

Miller and Starr California Real Estate § 15:5, Definition and Nature of an Easement.

Miller and Starr California Real Estate § 24:1, Types of Enforceable Restrictions.

Miller and Starr California Real Estate § 15:75, Merger.

Miller and Starr California Real Estate § 25:46, Streets, Roads, Easements, and Transit Facilities.

16 NO. 1 Miller & Starr, California Real Estate Newsalert 14, Easements.

12 Witkin, California Summary 10th Real Property § 388, (S 388) in General.

12 Witkin, California Summary 10th Real Property § 421, Release or Merger.

§ 806. Extent of servitude; determination

EXTENT OF SERVITUDES. The extent of a servitude is determined by the terms of the grant, or the nature of the enjoyment by which it was acquired. *(Enacted in 1872.)*

Research References

Miller and Starr California Real Estate § 15:53, Location of Easements by Prescription or Implied Dedication.

Miller and Starr California Real Estate § 15:54, Extent of Permitted Use; Rules of General Application.

Miller and Starr California Real Estate § 15:56, Use of Express Easements.

Miller and Starr California Real Estate § 15:58, Use of Prescriptive Easements.

12 Witkin, California Summary 10th Real Property § 388, (S 388) in General.

12 Witkin, California Summary 10th Real Property § 414, Implied Grant.

§ 807. Partition of dominant tenement; apportionment of servitude

APPORTIONING EASEMENTS. In case of partition of the dominant tenement the burden must be apportioned according to the division of the dominant tenement, but not in such a way as to increase the burden upon the servient tenement. *(Enacted in 1872.)*

Research References

Miller and Starr California Real Estate § 12:16, Right of Partition--Partition by a Physical Division of the Property.

Miller and Starr California Real Estate § 15:55, Increased or Changed Use.

Miller and Starr California Real Estate § 15:60, Use by Other Persons, or for Additional Property; Subdivision of the Dominant Tenement.

12 Witkin, California Summary 10th Real Property § 78, (S 78) Division of Property.

§ 808. Owner of future estate in dominant tenement; use of easement

RIGHTS OF OWNER OF FUTURE ESTATE. The owner of a future estate in a dominant tenement may use easements attached thereto for the purpose of viewing waste, demanding rent, or removing an obstruction to the enjoyment of such easements, although such tenement is occupied by a tenant. *(Enacted in 1872.)*

Research References

Miller and Starr California Real Estate § 15:66, Easement Owners.

12 Witkin, California Summary 10th Real Property § 144, (S 144) Against Third Parties.

12 Witkin, California Summary 10th Real Property § 382, Definition and Distinctions.

§ 809. Enforcement of easement; parties plaintiff

ACTIONS BY OWNER AND OCCUPANT OF DOMINANT TENEMENT. The owner of any estate in a dominant tenement, or the occupant of such tenement, may maintain an action for the enforcement of an easement attached thereto. *(Enacted in 1872.)*

Research References

Miller and Starr California Real Estate § 15:72, Remedies for Interference With the Use of an Easement.

12 Witkin, California Summary 10th Real Property § 144, (S 144) Against Third Parties.

12 Witkin, California Summary 10th Real Property § 382, Definition and Distinctions.

§ 810. Owner of servient tenement; possessory action

ACTIONS BY OWNER OF SERVIENT TENEMENT. The owner in fee of a servient tenement may maintain an action for the possession of the land, against any one unlawfully possessed thereof, though a servitude exists thereon in favor of the public. *(Enacted in 1872.)*

Research References

Miller and Starr California Real Estate § 15:64, Servient Tenement Owners.

12 Witkin, California Summary 10th Real Property § 412, Right to Use Property.

§ 811. Extinguishment of servitude

HOW EXTINGUISHED. A servitude is extinguished:

1. By the vesting of the right to the servitude and the right to the servient tenement in the same person;

2. By the destruction of the servient tenement;

3. By the performance of any act upon either tenement, by the owner of the servitude, or with his assent, which is incompatible with its nature or exercise; or,

4. When the servitude was acquired by enjoyment, by disuse thereof by the owner of the servitude for the period prescribed for acquiring title by enjoyment. *(Enacted in 1872.)*

Research References

Rutter, Cal. Practice Guide: Real Prop. Transactions Ch. 4-B, B. Interests to be Conveyed.
Miller and Starr California Real Estate § 15:73, Methods of Termination.
Miller and Starr California Real Estate § 15:75, Merger.
Miller and Starr California Real Estate § 15:76, Destruction of the Servient Tenement.
Miller and Starr California Real Estate § 15:77, Incompatible Acts by the Easement Owner.
Miller and Starr California Real Estate § 15:78, Nonuse.
Miller and Starr California Real Estate § 15:79, Abandonment of Private Easements.
Miller and Starr California Real Estate § 15:80, Abandonment of Public Easements.
Miller and Starr California Real Estate § 24:11, Creation--Creation by Recorded Declaration.
16 NO. 1 Miller & Starr, California Real Estate Newsalert 14, Easements.
19 NO. 2 Miller & Starr, California Real Estate Newsalert 14, Easements.
12 Witkin, California Summary 10th Real Property § 388, (S 388) in General.
12 Witkin, California Summary 10th Real Property § 421, Release or Merger.
12 Witkin, California Summary 10th Real Property § 424, Nonuse.
12 Witkin, California Summary 10th Real Property § 426, Incompatible Act of Easement's Owner.
12 Witkin, California Summary 10th Real Property § 427, (S 427) Involuntary Destruction.

§ 813. Consent to use of land; recordation of notice; revocation

The holder of record title to land may record in the office of the recorder of any county in which any part of the land is situated, a description of said land and a notice reading substantially as follows: "The right of the public or any person to make any use whatsoever of the above described land or any portion thereof (other than any use expressly allowed by a written or recorded map, agreement, deed or dedication) is by permission, and subject to control, of owner: Section 813, Civil Code."

The recorded notice is conclusive evidence that subsequent use of the land during the time such notice is in effect by the public or any user for any purpose (other than any use expressly allowed by a written or recorded map, agreement, deed or dedication) is permissive and with consent in any judicial proceeding involving the issue as to whether all or any portion of such land has been dedicated to public use or whether any user has a prescriptive right in such land or any portion thereof. The notice may be revoked by the holder of record title by recording a notice of revocation in the office of the recorder wherein the notice is recorded. After recording a notice pursuant to this section, and prior to any revocation thereof, the owner shall not prevent any public use appropriate thereto by physical obstruction, notice or otherwise.

In the event of use by other than the general public, any such notices, to be effective, shall also be served by registered mail on the user.

The recording of a notice pursuant to this section shall not be deemed to affect rights vested at the time of recording.

The permission for public use of real property provided for in such a recorded notice may be conditioned upon reasonable restrictions on the time, place, and manner of such public use, and no use in violation of such restrictions shall be considered public use for purposes of a finding of implied dedication. *(Added by Stats.1963, c. 735, p. 1749, § 1. Amended by Stats.1971, c. 941, p. 1845, § 1.)*

Research References

Miller and Starr California Real Estate § 11:6, Instruments Subject to Recording--List of Recordable Documents.
Miller and Starr California Real Estate § 26:4, Requirement of Offer by the Owner.
Miller and Starr California Real Estate § 15:31, Public or Private Easement by Prescription.
Miller and Starr California Real Estate § 15:36, Use Requirements--Permission by the Property Owner; Posted or Recorded Notice.
Miller and Starr California Real Estate § 16:13, When Possession is "Hostile and Adverse".
Miller and Starr California Real Estate § 22:70, Exception to Exemption; Entry by Invitation or for Consideration.
Miller and Starr California Real Estate § 26:11, Offer Implied from Public Use--In General.
Miller and Starr California Real Estate § 26:12, Offer Implied from Public Use--Nature and Extent of Public Use Required.
Miller and Starr California Real Estate § 26:18, Offer Implied from Public Use--Procedures to Prevent an Implied Dedication by Public Use.
12 Witkin, California Summary 10th Real Property § 250, (S 250) Statutory Limitations.
12 Witkin, California Summary 10th Real Property § 404, (S 404) Permissive Use.
12 Witkin, California Summary 10th Real Property § 429, (S 429) Revocable Licenses.

CHAPTER 4.   CONSERVATION EASEMENTS

§ 815.   Legislative findings and declaration

The Legislature finds and declares that the preservation of land in its natural, scenic, agricultural, historical, forested, or open-space condition is among the most important environmental assets of California. The Legislature further finds and declares it to be the public policy and in the public interest of this state to encourage the voluntary conveyance of conservation easements to qualified nonprofit organizations. *(Added by Stats.1979, c. 179, p. 398, § 1.)*

Research References

Rutter, Cal. Practice Guide: Real Prop. Transactions Ch. 4-B, B. Interests to be Conveyed.
Miller and Starr California Real Estate § 15:7, Easement in Gross.
21 NO. 4 Miller & Starr, California Real Estate Newsalert 39, Subdivisions, Land Use Planning, and Approvals.
12 Witkin, California Summary 10th Real Property § 337, (S 337) Enactment of Marketable Record Title Statute.
12 Witkin, California Summary 10th Real Property § 386, Conservation Easement.
12 Witkin, California Summary 10th Real Property § 881, Open Space.

§ 815.1.   Conservation easement

For the purposes of this chapter, "conservation easement" means any limitation in a deed, will, or other instrument in the form of an easement, restriction, covenant, or condition, which is or has been executed by or on behalf of the owner of the land subject to such easement and is binding upon successive owners of such land, and the purpose of which is to retain land predominantly in its natural, scenic, historical, agricultural, forested, or open-space condition. *(Added by Stats.1979, c. 179, p. 398, § 1.)*

Research References

Rutter, Cal. Practice Guide: Real Prop. Transactions Ch. 4-B, B. Interests to be Conveyed.
Miller and Starr California Real Estate § 15:12, Public Trust, Navigation and Conservation Easements.
12 Witkin, California Summary 10th Real Property § 386, Conservation Easement.

§ 815.2. Nature

(a) A conservation easement is an interest in real property voluntarily created and freely transferable in whole or in part for the purposes stated in Section 815.1 by any lawful method for the transfer of interests in real property in this state.

(b) A conservation easement shall be perpetual in duration.

(c) A conservation easement shall not be deemed personal in nature and shall constitute an interest in real property notwithstanding the fact that it may be negative in character.

(d) The particular characteristics of a conservation easement shall be those granted or specified in the instrument creating or transferring the easement. *(Added by Stats.1979, c. 179, p. 398, § 1.)*

Research References

Rutter, Cal. Practice Guide: Real Prop. Transactions Ch. 4-B, B. Interests to be Conveyed.
Miller and Starr California Real Estate § 15:12, Public Trust, Navigation and Conservation Easements.
12 Witkin, California Summary 10th Real Property § 386, Conservation Easement.

§ 815.3. Entities authorized to acquire and hold conservation easements

Only the following entities or organizations may acquire and hold conservation easements:

(a) A tax-exempt nonprofit organization qualified under Section 501(c) (3) of the Internal Revenue Code [1] and qualified to do business in this state which has as its primary purpose the preservation, protection, or enhancement of land in its natural, scenic, historical, agricultural, forested, or open-space condition or use.

(b) The state or any city, county, city and county, district, or other state or local governmental entity, if otherwise authorized to acquire and hold title to real property and if the conservation easement is voluntarily conveyed. No local governmental entity may condition the issuance of an entitlement for use on the applicant's granting of a conservation easement pursuant to this chapter.

(c) A federally recognized California Native American tribe or a nonfederally recognized California Native American tribe that is on the contact list maintained by the Native American Heritage Commission to protect a California Native American prehistoric, archaeological, cultural, spiritual, or ceremonial place, if the conservation easement is voluntarily conveyed. *(Added by Stats.1979, c. 179, p. 398, § 1. Amended by Stats.1981, c. 478, § 1; Stats.2004, c. 905 (S.B.18), § 2.)*

[1] 26 U.S.C.A. § 501(c)(3).

Research References

Rutter, Cal. Practice Guide: Real Prop. Transactions Ch. 4-B, B. Interests to be Conveyed.
Miller and Starr California Real Estate § 25:2, Legal Basis for Land Use Regulation.
Miller and Starr California Real Estate § 15:12, Public Trust, Navigation and Conservation Easements.

Miller and Starr California Real Estate § 25:38, Permitted Conditions for Approval.
21 NO. 4 Miller & Starr, California Real Estate Newsalert 39, Subdivisions, Land Use Planning, and Approvals.
12 Witkin, California Summary 10th Real Property § 386, Conservation Easement.
8 Witkin, California Summary 10th Constitutional Law § 1047, in General.

§ 815.4. Reservation of interests in grantor

All interests not transferred and conveyed by the instrument creating the easement shall remain in the grantor of the easement, including the right to engage in all uses of the land not affected by the easement nor prohibited by the easement or by law. *(Added by Stats.1979, c. 179, p. 398, § 1.)*

Research References

Miller and Starr California Real Estate § 15:12, Public Trust, Navigation and Conservation Easements.
12 Witkin, California Summary 10th Real Property § 386, Conservation Easement.

§ 815.5. Recordation

Instruments creating, assigning, or otherwise transferring conservation easements shall be recorded in the office of the county recorder of the county where the land is situated, in whole or in part, and such instruments shall be subject in all respects to the recording laws. *(Added by Stats.1979, c. 179, p. 398, § 1.)*

Research References

Miller and Starr California Real Estate § 11:6, Instruments Subject to Recording--List of Recordable Documents.
Miller and Starr California Real Estate § 15:12, Public Trust, Navigation and Conservation Easements.
12 Witkin, California Summary 10th Real Property § 386, Conservation Easement.

§ 815.7. Enforcement of easement; injunctive relief; damages; costs

(a) No conservation easement shall be unenforceable by reason of lack of privity of contract or lack of benefit to particular land or because not expressed in the instrument creating it as running with the land.

(b) Actual or threatened injury to or impairment of a conservation easement or actual or threatened violation of its terms may be prohibited or restrained, or the interest intended for protection by such easement may be enforced, by injunctive relief granted by any court of competent jurisdiction in a proceeding initiated by the grantor or by the owner of the easement.

(c) In addition to the remedy of injunctive relief, the holder of a conservation easement shall be entitled to recover money damages for any injury to such easement or to the interest being protected thereby or for the violation of the terms of such easement. In assessing such damages there may be taken into account, in addition to the cost of restoration and other usual rules of the law of damages, the loss of scenic, aesthetic, or environmental value to the real property subject to the easement.

(d) The court may award to the prevailing party in any action authorized by this section the costs of litigation, including reasonable attorney's fees. *(Added by Stats.1979, c. 179, p. 398, § 1.)*

Research References

Miller and Starr California Real Estate § 15:12, Public Trust, Navigation and Conservation Easements.

12 Witkin, California Summary 10th Real Property § 386, Conservation Easement.

§ 815.9. Political subdivisions; authority to hold comparable easements

Nothing in this chapter shall be construed to impair or conflict with the operation of any law or statute conferring upon any political subdivision the right or power to hold interests in land comparable to conservation easements, including, but not limited to, Chapter 12 (commencing with Section 6950) of Division 7 of Title 1 of, Chapter 6.5 (commencing with Section 51050), Chapter 6.6 (commencing with Section 51070) and Chapter 7 (commencing with Section 51200) of Part 1 of Division 1 of Title 5 of, and Article 10.5 (commencing with Section 65560) of Chapter 3 of Title 7 of, the Government Code, and Article 1.5 (commencing with Section 421) of Chapter 3 of Part 2 of Division 1 of the Revenue and Taxation Code. *(Added by Stats.1979, c. 179, p. 398, § 1.)*

Research References

Miller and Starr California Real Estate § 15:12, Public Trust, Navigation and Conservation Easements.
12 Witkin, California Summary 10th Real Property § 386, Conservation Easement.

§ 815.10. Enforceable restrictions for purposes of assessment of land

A conservation easement granted pursuant to this chapter constitutes an enforceable restriction, for purposes of Section 402.1 of the Revenue and Taxation Code. *(Added by Stats.1984, c. 777, § 1.)*

Research References

Miller and Starr California Real Estate § 15:7, Easement in Gross.
12 Witkin, California Summary 10th Real Property § 386, Conservation Easement.

§ 816. Liberal construction of chapter

The provisions of this chapter shall be liberally construed in order to effectuate the policy and purpose of Section 815. *(Added by Stats.1979 c. 179, p. 398, § 1)*

Research References

Miller and Starr California Real Estate § 15:7, Easement in Gross.
12 Witkin, California Summary 10th Real Property § 386, Conservation Easement.

CHAPTER 5. HOUSING COOPERATIVES AND HOUSING COOPERATIVE TRUSTS

§ 817. Limited-equity housing cooperative; workforce housing cooperative trust; requirements; purchase and sale of stock or membership interest; application of corporate equity; amendment of bylaws and articles of incorporation

"Limited-equity housing cooperative" or a "workforce housing cooperative trust" means a corporation organized on a cooperative basis that, in addition to complying with Section 817.1 as may be applicable, meets all of the following requirements:

(a) The corporation is any of the following:

(1) Organized as a nonprofit public benefit corporation pursuant to Part 2 (commencing with Section 5110) of Division 2 of Title 1 of the Corporations Code.

(2) Holds title to real property as the beneficiary of a trust providing for distribution for public or charitable purposes upon termination of the trust.

(3) Holds title to real property subject to conditions that will result in reversion to a public or charitable entity upon dissolution of the corporation.

(4) Holds a leasehold interest, of at least 20 years' duration, conditioned on the corporation's continued qualification under this section, and provides for reversion to a public entity or charitable corporation.

(b)(1) The articles of incorporation or bylaws require the purchase and sale of the stock or membership interest of resident owners who cease to be permanent residents, at no more than a transfer value determined as provided in the articles or bylaws, and that shall not exceed the aggregate of the following:

(A) The consideration paid for the membership or shares by the first occupant of the unit involved, as shown on the books of the corporation.

(B) The value, as determined by the board of directors of the corporation, of any improvements installed at the expense of the member or a prior member with the prior approval of the board of directors.

(C) Accumulated simple interest, an inflation allowance at a rate that may be based on a cost-of-living index, an income index, or market-interest index, or compound interest if specified in the articles of incorporation or bylaws. For newly formed corporations, accumulated simple interest shall apply. Any increment pursuant to this paragraph shall not exceed a 10–percent annual increase on the consideration paid for the membership or share by the first occupant of the unit involved.

(2)(A) Except as provided in subparagraph (B), for purposes of a return of transfer value, both of the following are prohibited:

(i) A board of directors returning transfer value, either full or partial, to a member while he or she still remains a member.

(ii) An existing member accepting the return of his or her transfer value, either full or partial.

(B) A board of directors may return to an existing member and the existing member may accept return of his or her transfer value in the event that the member moves within the cooperative from a category of unit initially valued at a higher price to a different category of unit valued at a lower price.

(c) The articles of incorporation or bylaws require the board of directors to sell the stock or membership interest purchased as provided in subdivision (b) to new member-occupants or resident shareholders at a price that does not exceed the "transfer value" paid for the unit.

(d) The "corporate equity," that is defined as the excess of the current fair market value of the corporation's real property over the sum of the current transfer values of all shares or membership interests, reduced by the principal balance of outstanding encumbrances upon the corporate real property as a whole, shall be applied as follows:

(1) So long as any such encumbrance remains outstanding, the corporate equity shall not be used for distribution to members, but only for the following purposes, and only to the extent authorized by the board, subject to the provisions and limitations of the articles of incorporation and bylaws:

(A) For the benefit of the corporation or the improvement of the real property.

(B) For expansion of the corporation by acquisition of additional real property.

(C) For public benefit or charitable purposes.

(2) Upon sale of the property, dissolution of the corporation, or occurrence of a condition requiring termination of the trust or reversion of title to the real property, the corporate equity is required by the articles, bylaws, or trust or title conditions to be paid out, or title to the property transferred, subject to outstanding encumbrances and liens, for the transfer value of membership interests or shares, for use for a public or charitable purpose.

(e) Amendment of the bylaws and articles of incorporation requires the affirmative vote of at least two-thirds of the resident-owner members or shareholders. *(Added by Stats.2009, c. 520 (A.B.1246), § 2.)*

Research References

Miller and Starr California Real Estate § 25C:8, Subdivisions Requiring a Public Report; Common Interest Developments.

12 Witkin, California Summary 10th Real Property § 91, (S 91) Stock Cooperative.

§ 817.1. Workforce housing cooperative trust; additional requirements; operation at multiple locations; creation

(a) A "workforce housing cooperative trust" is an entity organized pursuant to this section that complies with Section 817 and with all of the following:

(1) Allows the governing board to be composed of two classes of board members. One class is elected by the residents, and one class is appointed by sponsor organizations, including employer and employee organizations, chambers of commerce, government entities, unions, religious organizations, nonprofit organizations, cooperative organizations, and other forms of organizations. Resident members shall elect a majority of the board members. However, sponsor organizations may appoint up to one less than a majority of the board members. The numerical composition and class of the sponsor and resident board members shall be set in the articles of incorporation and in the bylaws.

(2) Requires the charter board of a workforce housing cooperative trust to be composed of only sponsor board members, to remain in place for one year after the first resident occupancy. One year after the first resident occupancy, the resident members shall elect a single board member. Three years after the first resident occupancy, resident members shall elect a majority of the board members.

(3) Prohibits the removal of the appointees of sponsor organizations, except for cause.

(4) Allows for the issuance of separate classes of shares to sponsor organizations or support organizations. These shares shall be denominated as "workforce housing shares" and shall receive a rate of return of no more than 10 percent simple interest pursuant to subparagraph (C) of paragraph (1) of subdivision (b) of Section 817.

(5) Requires, in order to amend the bylaws or articles of incorporation of a workforce housing cooperative trust, the affirmative vote of at least a majority of the resident-owner members or shareholders and a majority of each class of board members. The rights of the sponsor board members or the sponsors shall not be changed without the affirmative vote of two-thirds of the sponsor board members.

(b) A workforce housing cooperative trust shall be entitled to operate at multiple locations in order to sponsor limited-equity housing cooperatives. A workforce housing cooperative trust may either own or lease land for the purpose of developing limited-equity housing cooperatives.

(c) A workforce housing cooperative trust may be created when at least 51 percent of the occupied units in a multifamily property that is in foreclosure support efforts to buy the building or property. *(Added by Stats.2009, c. 520 (A.B.1246), § 2.)*

Research References

Miller and Starr California Real Estate § 25C:8, Subdivisions Requiring a Public Report; Common Interest Developments.

§ 817.2. Dissolution of limited-equity housing cooperative or workforce housing cooperative trust; procedure

The procedure for the dissolution of a limited-equity housing cooperative or workforce housing cooperative trust that receives or has received a public subsidy shall be as follows:

(a) The city, or the county for any unincorporated area, in which the limited-equity housing cooperative or workforce housing cooperative trust is located, shall hold a public hearing. The cooperative or trust shall pay for all costs associated with the public hearing.

(b) The city or county shall provide notice to all interested parties. The notice shall be given at least 120 days prior to the date of the hearing. The city or county shall obtain a list of all other limited-equity housing cooperatives and cooperative development organizations in the state from the California Center for Cooperative Development, if the list exists, and provide notice to all of the entities on the list in an effort to create a merger with an existing limited-equity housing cooperative or workforce housing cooperative trust. The notice shall be mailed first class, postage prepaid, in the United States mail.

(c) If the dissolving limited-equity housing cooperative or workforce housing cooperative trust merges with an existing cooperative or trust, to the extent possible, the merger shall be with the geographically closest cooperative or trust.

(d) If the dissolving limited-equity housing cooperative or workforce housing cooperative trust does not merge with an existing cooperative or trust, both of the following shall occur:

(1) Upon completion of the public hearing required pursuant to subdivision (a), the city or county shall adopt a resolution approving of the dissolution and make a finding that the dissolution plan meets the requirements of state and federal law, meets the donative intent standards of the United States Internal Revenue Service, and is free of private inurement, which includes, but is not limited to, a prohibition on any member receiving any payment in excess of the transfer value to which he or she is entitled pursuant to subdivision (b) of Section 817.

(2) The city or county shall forward all of the information and written testimony from the hearing to the Office of the Attorney General for the Attorney General to consider as part of his or her ruling on the dissolution. *(Added by Stats.2009, c. 520 (A.B.1246), § 2.)*

§ 817.3. Sponsor organizations; legal standing of member

Each entity named as a sponsor organization of a workforce housing cooperative trust formed pursuant to Section 817 shall have the legal standing of a member unless it revokes, in writing, its sponsorship. *(Added by Stats.2009, c. 520 (A.B.1246), § 2.)*

§ 817.4. Attorney's fees and costs; prohibited use of corporate funds

(a) In any action instituted on or after January 1, 2010, against a board of directors and its members based upon a breach of corporate or fiduciary duties or a failure to comply with the requirements of this chapter, a prevailing plaintiff may recover reasonable attorney's fees and costs.

(b) If an organization formed under this chapter uses public funds, it shall not use any corporate funds to avoid compliance with this chapter or to pursue dissolution if the intent or outcome is for some or all of the members to receive any payment in excess of the transfer value to which he or she is entitled pursuant to subdivision (b) of Section 817. *(Added by Stats.2009, c. 520 (A.B.1246), § 2.)*

Title 3

RIGHTS AND OBLIGATIONS OF OWNERS

CHAPTER 1. RIGHTS OF OWNERS

ARTICLE 1. INCIDENTS OF OWNERSHIP

§ 818. Life tenant; rights; restriction

RIGHTS OF TENANT FOR LIFE. The owner of a life estate may use the land in the same manner as the owner of a fee simple, except that he must do no act to the injury of the inheritance. *(Enacted in 1872.)*

Research References

Miller and Starr California Real Estate § 9:21, Rights and Powers.
Miller and Starr California Real Estate § 9:22, Duties and Liabilities; Waste.
12 Witkin, California Summary 10th Real Property § 24, (S 24) Possession, Use, and Actions.
12 Witkin, California Summary 10th Real Property § 31, (S 31) Waste and Permissible Use.
12 Witkin, California Summary 10th Real Property § 371, (S 371) What Constitutes Waste.

§ 819. Tenant for years or at will; rights

RIGHTS OF TENANT FOR YEARS, ETC. A tenant for years or at will, unless he is a wrong-doer by holding over, may occupy the buildings, take the annual products of the soil, work mines and quarries open at the commencement of his tenancy. *(Enacted in 1872.)*

Research References

Miller and Starr California Real Estate § 17:36, Crops--Lease of the Realty.

§ 820. Tenant for years or at will; limitation on rights

SAME. A tenant for years or at will has no other rights to the property than such as are given to him by the agreement or instrument by which his tenancy is acquired, or by the last section. *(Enacted in 1872.)*

Research References

Miller and Starr California Real Estate § 15:25, Lease of Part of Property.
Miller and Starr California Real Estate § 19:27, Description of the Premises--Appurtenances; Implied Easements.

§ 821. Grantees of rents and reversions; rights

RIGHTS OF GRANTEES OF RENTS AND REVERSION. A person to whom any real property is transferred or devised, upon which rent has been reserved, or to whom any such rent is transferred, is entitled to the same remedies for recovery of rent, for non-performance of any of the terms of the lease, or for any waste or cause of forfeiture, as his grantor or devisor might have had. *(Enacted in 1872.)*

Research References

Miller and Starr California Real Estate § 12:7, Waste by a Cotenant.
Miller and Starr California Real Estate § 2:19, Right to Possession; Waste.
Miller and Starr California Real Estate § 10:57, Trustor's Remedies for Injuries to the Property Caused by Third Persons.
Miller and Starr California Real Estate § 19:59, Transfer of the Reversion.
Miller and Starr California Real Estate § 19:83, Persons Entitled to Receive Rent.
Miller and Starr California Real Estate § 10:220, Possession and Rents After Trustee's Sale.
Miller and Starr California Real Estate § 19:220, Parties.

§ 822. Lessor; remedies against assignee of lessee

Whatever remedies the lessor of any real property has against his immediate lessee for the breach of any agreement in the lease, or for recovery of the possession, he has against the assignees of the lessee, for any cause of action accruing while they are such assignees, except where the assignment is made by way of security for a loan, and is not accompanied by possession of the premises. *(Enacted in 1872. Amended by Code Am.1873–74, c. 612, p. 219, § 109; Stats.1905, c. 439, p. 599, § 1.)*

Research References

Miller and Starr California Real Estate § 19:63, Liability of the Parties; Tenant-Assignor Liability to the Landlord--Assignee Rights and Liabilities Vis-à-Vis the Landlord.
12 Witkin, California Summary 10th Real Property § 537, Right to Assign or Sublease.

§ 823. Lessee and assigns; remedies against lessor and assigns

RIGHTS OF LESSEES AND THEIR ASSIGNEES, ETC. Whatever remedies the lessee of any real property may have against his immediate lessor, for the breach of any agreement in the lease, he may have against the assigns of the lessor, and the assigns of the lessee may have against the lessor and his assigns, except upon covenants against incumbrances[1] or relating to the title or possession of the premises. *(Enacted in 1872.)*

---

[1] So in chaptered bill.

Research References

Rutter, Cal. Practice Guide: Real Prop. Transactions Ch. 4-E, E. Drafting the Purchase and Sale Agreement-Terms and Conditions.

Miller and Starr California Real Estate § 19:59, Transfer of the Reversion.

Miller and Starr California Real Estate § 19:63, Liability of the Parties; Tenant-Assignor Liability to the Landlord--Assignee Rights and Liabilities Vis-à-Vis the Landlord.

12 Witkin, California Summary 10th Real Property § 537, Right to Assign or Sublease.

§ 824. Lease for life; recovery of rent

REMEDY ON LEASES FOR LIFE. Rent due upon a lease for life may be recovered in the same manner as upon a lease for years. *(Enacted in 1872.)*

Research References

Miller and Starr California Real Estate § 9:21, Rights and Powers.

Miller and Starr California Real Estate § 19:77, Nature of and Obligation to Pay Rent.

§ 825. Rent dependent upon life; recovery

RENT DEPENDENT ON LIFE. Rent dependent on the life of a person may be recovered after as well as before his death. *(Enacted in 1872.)*

Research References

Miller and Starr California Real Estate § 9:21, Rights and Powers.

Miller and Starr California Real Estate § 19:77, Nature of and Obligation to Pay Rent.

§ 826. Remaindermen and reversioners; remedies for injuries to inheritance

REMEDY OF REVERSIONERS, ETC. A person having an estate in fee, in remainder or reversion, may maintain an action for any injury done to the inheritance, notwithstanding an intervening estate for life or years, and although, after its commission, his estate is transferred, and he has no interest in the property at the commencement of the action. *(Enacted in 1872.)*

Research References

Miller and Starr California Real Estate § 16:6, Nature of Possession Required--Possession by a Tenant.

Miller and Starr California Real Estate § 9:22, Duties and Liabilities; Waste.

Miller and Starr California Real Estate § 9:32, Remainders--Rights of Remainder Holders.

Miller and Starr California Real Estate § 15:35, Use Requirements--Hostile, Adverse, and Under Claim of Right.

12 Witkin, California Summary 10th Real Property § 31, (S 31) Waste and Permissible Use.

12 Witkin, California Summary 10th Real Property § 143, (S 143) Against Life Tenant.

12 Witkin, California Summary 10th Real Property § 144, (S 144) Against Third Parties.

12 Witkin, California Summary 10th Real Property § 372, (S 372) Trespass Distinguished.

12 Witkin, California Summary 10th Real Property § 403, (S 403) Hostile or Adverse Use.

§ 827. Leases; term less than a month; change in terms; notice

(a) Except as provided in subdivision (b), in all leases of lands or tenements, or of any interest therein, from week to week, month to month, or other period less than a month, the landlord may, upon giving notice in writing to the tenant, in the manner prescribed by Section 1162 of the Code of Civil Procedure, change the terms of the lease to take effect, as to tenancies for less than one month, upon the expiration of a period at least as long as the term of the hiring itself, and, as to tenancies from month to month, to take effect at the expiration of not less than 30 days, but if that change takes effect within a rental term, the rent accruing from the first day of the term to the date of that change shall be computed at the rental rate obtained immediately prior to that change; provided, however, that it shall be competent for the parties to provide by an agreement in writing that a notice changing the terms thereof may be given at any time not less than seven days before the expiration of a term, to be effective upon the expiration of the term.

The notice, when served upon the tenant, shall in and of itself operate and be effectual to create and establish, as a part of the lease, the terms, rents, and conditions specified in the notice, if the tenant shall continue to hold the premises after the notice takes effect.

(b)(1) In all leases of a residential dwelling, or of any interest therein, from week to week, month to month, or other period less than a month, the landlord may increase the rent provided in the lease or rental agreement, upon giving written notice to the tenant, as follows, by either of the following procedures:

(A) By delivering a copy to the tenant personally.

(B) By serving a copy by mail under the procedures prescribed in Section 1013 of the Code of Civil Procedure.

(2) If the proposed rent increase for that tenant is 10 percent or less of the rental amount charged to that tenant at any time during the 12 months prior to the effective date of the increase, either in and of itself or when combined with any other rent increases for the 12 months prior to the effective date of the increase, the notice shall be delivered at least 30 days prior to the effective date of the increase, and subject to Section 1013 of the Code of Civil Procedure if served by mail.

(3) For an increase in rent greater than the amount described in paragraph (2), the minimum notice period required pursuant to that paragraph shall be increased by an additional 30 days, and subject to Section 1013 of the Code of Civil Procedure if served by mail. This paragraph does not apply to an increase in rent caused by a change in a tenant's income or family composition as determined by a recertification required by statute or regulation.

(c) If a state or federal statute, state or federal regulation, recorded regulatory agreement, or contract provides for a longer period of notice regarding a rent increase than that provided in subdivision (a) or (b), the personal service or mailing of the notice shall be in accordance with the longer period. *(Added by Code Am.1873–74, c. 612, p. 220, § 110. Amended by Stats.1907, c. 39, p. 58, § 1; Stats.1929, c. 138, p. 256, § 1; Stats.1937, c. 356, p. 774, § 1; Stats.1939, c. 1013, p. 2799, § 1; Stats.1947, c. 676, p. 1708, § 1; Stats.2000, c. 680 (S.B.1745), § 2; Stats.2001, c. 593 (A.B.1160), § 1, eff. Oct. 9, 2001; Stats.2002, c. 664 (A.B.3034), § 33; Stats.2004, c. 568 (S.B.1145), § 1.)*

Research References

California Real Estate Forms (Miller & Starr) § 2:19, Retail Lease–Power Shopping Center.

Rutter, Cal. Practice Guide: Landlord-Tenant Form 2:A, Residential Rental Agreement.

Miller and Starr California Real Estate § 19:55, Requirements for Modification of Lease Terms.

Miller and Starr California Real Estate § 19:82, Modification of the Rent.

Miller and Starr California Real Estate § 19:91, Property Subject to Control; Exceptions and Exemptions--State Exemption of Specified Residential Rental Properties.

Miller and Starr California Real Estate § 19:114, Use of the Common Areas.

15 NO. 4 Miller & Starr, California Real Estate Newsalert 12, Landlord and Tenant.

22 NO. 4 Miller & Starr, California Real Estate Newsalert 15, Landlord and Tenant.

12 Witkin, California Summary 10th Real Property § 526, (S 526) Changes in Short-Term Leases.

12 Witkin, California Summary 10th Real Property § 569, (S 569) Form and Determination of Payment.

12 Witkin, California Summary 10th Real Property § 573, (S 573) in General.

ARTICLE 2.   BOUNDARIES

Section

§ 829.   Owner in fee; rights

RIGHTS OF OWNER.   The owner of land in fee has the right to the surface and to everything permanently situated beneath or above it.   *(Enacted in 1872.)*

Research References

Rutter, Cal. Practice Guide: Real Prop. Transactions Ch. 4-A, A. Property to be Sold.

Miller and Starr California Real Estate § 14:2, in General; Nature and Extent.

Miller and Starr California Real Estate § 8:60, Appurtenances Pass With Conveyance.

Miller and Starr California Real Estate § 17:28, Airspace.

12 Witkin, California Summary 10th Real Property § 17, Fee Simple Absolute.

§ 830.   Water as boundary

Except where the grant under which the land is held indicates a different intent, the owner of the upland, when it borders on tide water, takes to ordinary high-water mark; when it borders upon a navigable lake or stream, where there is no tide, the owner takes to the edge of the lake or stream, at low-water mark; when it borders upon any other water, the owner takes to the middle of the lake or stream.   *(Enacted in 1872.   Amended by Code Am.1873–74, c. 612, p. 220, § 111.)*

Research References

Miller and Starr California Real Estate § 8:66, Water as Property Boundary--In General.

Miller and Starr California Real Estate § 8:67, Water as Property Boundary--Where Adjacent to Tidewaters.

Miller and Starr California Real Estate § 8:68, Water as Property Boundary--Where Adjacent to Nontidal Waters.

Miller and Starr California Real Estate § 15:12, Public Trust, Navigation and Conservation Easements.

12 Witkin, California Summary 10th Real Property § 275, (S 275) General Rule.

12 Witkin, California Summary 10th Real Property § 276, (S 276) Land Subject to Public Trust.

§ 831.   Way as boundary

BOUNDARIES BY WAYS.   An owner of land bounded by a road or street is presumed to own to the center of the way, but the contrary may be shown.   *(Enacted in 1872.)*

Research References

Rutter, Cal. Practice Guide: Real Prop. Transactions Ch. 4-B, B. Interests to be Conveyed.

Miller and Starr California Real Estate § 8:65, Road, Street or Highway as Property Boundary.

Miller and Starr California Real Estate § 15:45, Estoppel; Executed Oral Conveyance; Irrevocable License.

Miller and Starr California Real Estate § 15:81, Abandonment of Public Easements--Effect on the Rights of Abutting Property Owners.

Miller and Starr California Real Estate § 26:31, Fee or Easement.

16 NO. 1 Miller & Starr, California Real Estate Newsalert 2, Dedication.

12 Witkin, California Summary 10th Real Property § 272, Presumption of Ownership to Center Line.

12 Witkin, California Summary 10th Real Property § 273, (S 273) General Rule.

12 Witkin, California Summary 10th Real Property § 274, (S 274) Distinctions.

12 Witkin, California Summary 10th Real Property § 360, (S 360) Distinctions.

§ 832.   Lateral and subjacent support; excavations; degree of care; damages; protection of other structures

Each coterminous owner is entitled to the lateral and subjacent support which his land receives from the adjoining land, subject to the right of the owner of the adjoining land to make proper and usual excavations on the same for purposes of construction or improvement, under the following conditions:

1.   Any owner of land or his lessee intending to make or to permit an excavation shall give reasonable notice to the owner or owners of adjoining lands and of buildings or other structures, stating the depth to which such excavation is intended to be made, and when the excavating will begin.

2.   In making any excavation, ordinary care and skill shall be used, and reasonable precautions taken to sustain the adjoining land as such, without regard to any building or other structure which may be thereon, and there shall be no liability for damage done to any such building or other structure by reason of the excavation, except as otherwise provided or allowed by law.

3.   If at any time it appears that the excavation is to be of a greater depth than are the walls or foundations of any adjoining building or other structure, and is to be so close as to endanger the building or other structure in any way, then the owner of the building or other structure must be allowed at least 30 days, if he so desires, in which to take measures to protect the same from any damage, or in which to extend the foundations thereof, and he must be given for the same purposes reasonable license to enter on the land on which the excavation is to be or is being made.

4.   If the excavation is intended to be or is deeper than the standard depth of foundations, which depth is defined to be a depth of nine feet below the adjacent curb level, at the point where the joint property line intersects the curb and if on the land of the coterminous owner there is any building or other structure the wall or foundation of which goes to standard depth or deeper then the owner of the land on which the excavation is being made shall, if given the necessary license to enter on the adjoining land, protect the said adjoining land and any such building or other structure thereon without cost to the owner thereof, from any damage by reason of the excavation, and shall be liable to the owner of such property for any such damage, excepting only for minor settlement cracks in buildings or other structures.   *(Enacted in 1872.   Amended by Code Am.1873–74, c. 612, p. 221, § 112; Stats.1931, c. 776, p. 1616, § 1; Stats.1968, c. 835, p. 1606, § 1.)*

Research References

Rutter, Cal. Practice Guide: Real Prop. Transactions Ch. 4-A, A. Property to be Sold.

Miller and Starr California Real Estate § 14:18, Subjacent Support.

Miller and Starr California Real Estate § 14:19, Lateral Support--Common Law Rule.

Miller and Starr California Real Estate § 14:20, Lateral Support--Statutory Modifications of the Common Law Rule.

Miller and Starr California Real Estate § 14:21, Lateral Support--Notice to Adjacent Owners.

Miller and Starr California Real Estate § 14:22, Lateral Support--Depth of an Excavation.

Miller and Starr California Real Estate § 14:23, Lateral Support--Limitations on Excavator's Liability for Negligence.

Miller and Starr California Real Estate § 14:24, Lateral Support--Liability of Nonowner Excavators.

Miller and Starr California Real Estate § 14:26, Damages.

13 NO. 6 Miller & Starr, California Real Estate Newsalert 8, Inverse Condemnation.

12 Witkin, California Summary 10th Real Property § 377, (S 377) Support for Land.

12 Witkin, California Summary 10th Real Property § 378, in General.

12 Witkin, California Summary 10th Real Property § 379, Deep Excavations.

12 Witkin, California Summary 10th Real Property § 380, Excavator's Protective Efforts.

12 Witkin, California Summary 10th Real Property § 381, (S 381) Subjacent Support.

6 Witkin, California Summary 10th Torts § 1414, (S 1414) Theory of Ultrahazardous Activity.

6 Witkin, California Summary 10th Torts § 1426, Excavation and Earth Moving.

8 Witkin, California Summary 10th Constitutional Law § 1134, Compensation Without Tort Liability.

§ 833. Trees; trunks upon land of one owner; ownership

TREES WHOSE TRUNKS ARE WHOLLY ON LAND OF ONE. Trees whose trunks stand wholly upon the land of one owner belong exclusively to him, although their roots grow into the land of another. *(Enacted in 1872.)*

Research References

Miller and Starr California Real Estate § 14:8, Ownership of Trees; Overhanging Branches and Roots.

§ 834. Line trees; common ownership

LINE TREES. Trees whose trunks stand partly on the land of two or more coterminous owners, belong to them in common. *(Enacted in 1872.)*

Research References

Miller and Starr California Real Estate § 14:8, Ownership of Trees; Overhanging Branches and Roots.

Miller and Starr California Real Estate § 14:12, Trees Located on Common Boundary.

23 NO. 2 Miller & Starr, California Real Estate Newsalert 3, Adjoining Landowners.

12 Witkin, California Summary 10th Real Property § 374, in General.

CHAPTER 2. OBLIGATIONS OF OWNERS

§ 840. Tenant for life; duties

DUTIES OF TENANT FOR LIFE. The owner of a life estate must keep the buildings and fences in repair from ordinary waste, and must pay the taxes and other annual charges, and a just proportion of extraordinary assessments benefiting the whole inheritance. *(Enacted in 1872.)*

Research References

Miller and Starr California Real Estate § 9:22, Duties and Liabilities; Waste.

Miller and Starr California Real Estate § 9:23, Taxes, Assessments, and Liens.

Miller and Starr California Real Estate § 14:29, Definition; Creation.

12 Witkin, California Summary 10th Real Property § 30, (S 30) in General.

12 Witkin, California Summary 10th Real Property § 31, (S 31) Waste and Permissible Use.

§ 841. Maintenance of boundaries, monuments, and fences; responsibilities of adjoining landowners; definitions

(a) Adjoining landowners shall share equally in the responsibility for maintaining the boundaries and monuments between them.

(b)(1) Adjoining landowners are presumed to share an equal benefit from any fence dividing their properties and, unless otherwise agreed to by the parties in a written agreement, shall be presumed to be equally responsible for the reasonable costs of construction, maintenance, or necessary replacement of the fence.

(2) Where a landowner intends to incur costs for a fence described in paragraph (1), the landowner shall give 30 days' prior written notice to each affected adjoining landowner. The notice shall include notification of the presumption of equal responsibility for the reasonable costs of construction, maintenance, or necessary replacement of the fence. The notice shall include a description of the nature of the problem facing the shared fence, the proposed solution for addressing the problem, the estimated construction or maintenance costs involved to address the problem, the proposed cost sharing approach, and the proposed timeline for getting the problem addressed.

(3) The presumption in paragraph (1) may be overcome by a preponderance of the evidence demonstrating that imposing equal responsibility for the reasonable costs of construction, maintenance, or necessary replacement of the fence would be unjust. In determining whether equal responsibility for the reasonable costs would be unjust, the court shall consider all of the following:

(A) Whether the financial burden to one landowner is substantially disproportionate to the benefit conferred upon that landowner by the fence in question.

(B) Whether the cost of the fence would exceed the difference in the value of the real property before and after its installation.

(C) Whether the financial burden to one landowner would impose an undue financial hardship given that party's financial circumstances as demonstrated by reasonable proof.

(D) The reasonableness of a particular construction or maintenance project, including all of the following:

(i) The extent to which the costs of the project appear to be unnecessary or excessive.

(ii) The extent to which the costs of the project appear to be the result of the landowner's personal aesthetic, architectural, or other preferences.

(E) Any other equitable factors appropriate under the circumstances.

(4) Where a party rebuts the presumption in paragraph (1) by a preponderance of the evidence, the court shall, in its discretion, consistent with the party's circumstances, order either a contribution of less than an equal share for the costs of construction, maintenance, or necessary replacement of the fence, or order no contribution.

(c) For the purposes of this section, the following terms have the following meanings:

(1) "Landowner" means a private person or entity that lawfully holds any possessory interest in real property, and does not include a city, county, city and county, district, public corporation, or other political subdivision, public body, or public agency.

(2) "Adjoining" means contiguous to or in contact with. *(Added by Stats.2013, c. 86 (A.B.1404), § 3.)*

§ 841.4. Spite fences

Any fence or other structure in the nature of a fence unnecessarily exceeding 10 feet in height maliciously erected or maintained for the purpose of annoying the owner or occupant of adjoining property is a private nuisance. Any owner or occupant of adjoining property injured either in his comfort or the enjoyment of his estate by such nuisance may enforce the remedies against its continuance prescribed in Title 3, Part 3, Division 4 of this code.[1] *(Added by Stats.1953, c. 37, p. 674, § 2.)*

[1] Section 3501 et seq.

Research References

Miller and Starr California Real Estate § 14:34, Spite Fences.
Miller and Starr California Real Estate § 22:13, Spite Fences.
21 NO. 6 Miller & Starr, California Real Estate Newsalert 16, Landowners' Liability.
12 Witkin, California Summary 10th Real Property § 373, (S 373) in General.
13 Witkin, California Summary 10th Equity § 140, Other Conditions or Activities.

§ 843. Concurrent ownership; ouster; procedure; damages

(a) If real property is owned concurrently by two or more persons, a tenant out of possession may establish an ouster from possession by a tenant in possession in the manner provided in this section. This section does not apply to the extent the tenant out of possession is not entitled to possession or an alternative remedy is provided under the terms of an agreement between the cotenants or the instrument creating the cotenancy or another written instrument that indicates the possessory rights or remedies of the cotenants. This section supplements and does not limit any other means by which an ouster may be established.

(b) A tenant out of possession may serve on a tenant in possession a written demand for concurrent possession of the property. The written demand shall make specific reference to this section and to the time within which concurrent possession must be offered under this section. Service of the written demand shall be made in the same manner as service of summons in a civil action. An ouster is established 60 days after service is complete if, within that time, the tenant in possession does not offer and provide unconditional concurrent possession of the property to the tenant out of possession.

(c) A claim for damages for an ouster established pursuant to this section may be asserted by an independent action or in an action for possession or partition of the property or another appropriate action or proceeding, subject to any applicable statute of limitation.

(d) Nothing in this section precludes the cotenants, at any time before or after a demand is served, from seeking partition of the property or from making an agreement as to the right of possession among the cotenants, the payment of reasonable rental value in lieu of possession, or any other terms that may be appropriate. *(Added by Stats.1984, c. 241, § 1.)*

Law Revision Commission Comments

Section 843 provides a procedure by which a tenant out of possession of property may establish an ouster and recover damages, without the need to show that the tenant in possession has forcibly excluded or prevented use of the property by the tenant out of possession. *Cf.* Brunscher v. Reagh, 164 Cal.App.2d 174, 330 P.2d 396 (1958); De Harlan v. Harlan, 74 Cal.App.2d 555, 168 P.2d 985 (1946) (forcible exclusion or prevention of use). One cotenant ousted by another is entitled to recover damages resulting from the ouster, which ordinarily amounts to a proportionate share of the value of the use and occupation of the land from the time of the ouster. Zaslow v. Kroenert, 29 Cal.2d 541, 176 P.2d 1 (1946). Nothing in this section changes the general law governing damages, defenses, and offsets in the case of an ouster. Establishment of an ouster under this section may also mark the beginning of the period required for the tenant in possession to establish title by adverse possession against the tenant out of possession. It should be noted that the provisions of this section are inapplicable to the extent the possessory rights and remedies of the cotenants are governed by a cotenancy agreement or other applicable instrument. [17 Cal.L.Rev.Comm. Reports 1023 (1984)].

Research References

Miller and Starr California Real Estate § 12:5, Ouster.
12 Witkin, California Summary 10th Real Property § 42, Law Revision Commission Recommendation.
12 Witkin, California Summary 10th Real Property § 43, Statutory Procedure.
12 Witkin, California Summary 10th Real Property § 44, Conduct of Cotenant in Possession.

§ 845. Easements; maintenance; failure to pay owner's share of costs; snow removal

(a) The owner of any easement in the nature of a private right-of-way, or of any land to which any such easement is attached, shall maintain it in repair.

(b) If the easement is owned by more than one person, or is attached to parcels of land under different ownership, the cost of maintaining it in repair shall be shared by each owner of the easement or the owners of the parcels of land, as the case may be, pursuant to the terms of any agreement entered into by the parties for that purpose. In the absence of an agreement, the cost shall be shared proportionately to the use made of the easement by each owner.

(c) If any owner refuses to perform, or fails after demand in writing to pay the owner's proportion of the cost, an action to recover that owner's share of the cost, or for specific performance or contribution, may be brought by the other owners, either jointly or severally. The action may be brought before, during, or after performance of the maintenance work, as follows:

(1) The action may be brought in small claims court if the amount claimed to be due as the owner's proportion of the cost does not exceed the jurisdictional limit of the small claims court. A small claims judgment shall not affect apportionment of any future costs that are not requested in the small claims action.

(2) Except as provided in paragraph (1), the action shall be filed in superior court and, notwithstanding Section 1141.13 of the Code of Civil Procedure, the action shall be subject to judicial arbitration pursuant to Chapter 2.5 of Title 3 of Part 3 (commencing with Section 1141.10) of the Code of Civil Procedure. A superior court judgment shall not affect apportionment of any future costs that are not requested in the action, unless otherwise provided in the judgment.

(3) In the absence of an agreement addressing the maintenance of the easement, any action for specific performance or contribution shall be brought in a court in the county in which the easement is located.

(4) Nothing in this section precludes the use of any available alternative dispute resolution program to resolve actions regarding the maintenance of easements in the small claims court or the superior court.

(d) In the event that snow removal is not required under subdivision (a), or under any independent contractual or statutory duty, an agreement entered into pursuant to subdivision (b) to maintain the easement in repair shall be construed to include snow removal within the maintenance obligations of the agreement if all of the following exist:

(1) Snow removal is not expressly precluded by the terms of the agreement.

(2) Snow removal is necessary to provide access to the properties served by the easement.

(3) Snow removal is approved in advance by the property owners or their elected representatives in the same manner as provided by the agreement for repairs to the easement.

(e) This section does not apply to rights-of-way held or used by railroad common carriers subject to the jurisdiction of the Public Utilities Commission. *(Added by Stats.1939, c. 755, p. 2285, § 1. Amended by Stats.1985, c. 985, § 1; Stats.1993, c. 196 (S.B.370), § 1; Stats.2012, c. 244 (A.B.1927), § 1.)*

Research References

Rutter, Cal. Practice Guide: A.D.R. App. A, Selected Statutes Providing for ADR.
Rutter, Cal. Practice Guide: A.D.R. Ch. 5-A, A. General Considerations.
Miller and Starr California Real Estate § 15:67, Maintenance and Repair.
Miller and Starr California Real Estate § 25C:7, Subdivisions Requiring a Public Report; Standard Subdivisions.
Miller and Starr California Real Estate § 35:23, Public Policy in Favor of Arbitration.
Miller and Starr California Real Estate § 25C:29, Vehicular Access, Water, and Other Utilities.
12 Witkin, California Summary 10th Real Property § 47, Contribution.
12 Witkin, California Summary 10th Real Property § 418, in General.
12 Witkin, California Summary 10th Real Property § 419, Jointly Owned Easement.

§ 846. Permission to enter for recreational purposes

An owner of any estate or any other interest in real property, whether possessory or nonpossessory, owes no duty of care to keep the premises safe for entry or use by others for any recreational purpose or to give any warning of hazardous conditions, uses of, structures, or activities on such premises to persons entering for such purpose, except as provided in this section.

A "recreational purpose," as used in this section, includes such activities as fishing, hunting, camping, water sports, hiking, spelunking, sport parachuting, riding, including animal riding, snowmobiling, and all other types of vehicular riding, rock collecting, sightseeing, picnicking, nature study, nature contacting, recreational gardening, gleaning, hang gliding, winter sports, and viewing or enjoying historical, archaeological, scenic, natural, or scientific sites.

An owner of any estate or any other interest in real property, whether possessory or nonpossessory, who gives permission to another for entry or use for the above purpose upon the premises does not thereby (a) extend any assurance that the premises are safe for such purpose, or (b) constitute the person to whom permission has been granted the legal status of an invitee or licensee to whom a duty of care is owed, or (c) assume responsibility for or incur liability for any injury to person or property caused by any act of such person to whom permission has been granted except as provided in this section.

This section does not limit the liability which otherwise exists (a) for willful or malicious failure to guard or warn against a dangerous condition, use, structure or activity; or (b) for injury suffered in any case where permission to enter for the above purpose was granted for a consideration other than the consideration, if any, paid to said landowner by the state, or where consideration has been received from others for the same purpose; or (c) to any persons who are expressly invited rather than merely permitted to come upon the premises by the landowner.

Nothing in this section creates a duty of care or ground of liability for injury to person or property. *(Added by Stats.1963, c. 1759, p. 3511, § 1. Amended by Stats.1970, c. 807, p. 1530, § 1; Stats.1971, c. 1028, p. 1975, § 1; Stats.1972, c. 1200, p. 2322, § 1; Stats.1976, c. 1303, p. 5859, § 1; Stats.1978, c. 86, p. 221, § 1; Stats.1979, c. 150, p. 347, § 1; Stats.1980, c. 408, § 1; Stats.1988, c. 129, § 1.)*

Research References

Rutter, Cal. Practice Guide: Civil Appeals & Writs Form 5:D, Motion to Augment the Record.
Miller and Starr California Real Estate § 15:4, Lease Distinguished.
Miller and Starr California Real Estate § 15:36, Use Requirements--Permission by the Property Owner; Posted or Recorded Notice.
Miller and Starr California Real Estate § 22:66, Recreational Users of Property: Exemption from Liability.
Miller and Starr California Real Estate § 22:67, Recreational Activities Which Qualify for the Exemption.
Miller and Starr California Real Estate § 22:68, Property Which Qualifies for the Exemption.
Miller and Starr California Real Estate § 22:69, Persons Entitled to the Exemption.
Miller and Starr California Real Estate § 22:70, Exception to Exemption; Entry by Invitation or for Consideration.
Miller and Starr California Real Estate § 22:71, Exception to Exemption; Willful or Malicious Acts of the Owner.
Miller and Starr California Real Estate § 29:26, Negligence Liability to Third Persons.
16 NO. 3 Miller & Starr, California Real Estate Newsalert 12, Landowners' Liability.
17 NO. 4 Miller & Starr, California Real Estate Newsalert 13, Landowners' Liability.
19 NO. 6 Miller & Starr, California Real Estate Newsalert 16, Landowners' Liability.
19 NO. 5 Miller & Starr, California Real Estate Newsalert 23, Landowners' Liability.
21 NO. 1 Miller & Starr, California Real Estate Newsalert 19, Landowners' Liability.
12 Witkin, California Summary 10th Real Property § 3, Definitions.
12 Witkin, California Summary 10th Real Property § 919, Navigable Waters.
5 Witkin, California Summary 10th Torts § 275, in General.
5 Witkin, California Summary 10th Torts § 277, Nature of Activity.
6 Witkin, California Summary 10th Torts § 870, (S 870) Wilful Misconduct.
6 Witkin, California Summary 10th Torts § 1087, (S 1087) Instructions.
6 Witkin, California Summary 10th Torts § 1103, (S 1103) in General.
6 Witkin, California Summary 10th Torts § 1104, (S 1104) Constitutionality of Statute.
6 Witkin, California Summary 10th Torts § 1106, Playing on Machinery.
6 Witkin, California Summary 10th Torts § 1107, in General.
6 Witkin, California Summary 10th Torts § 1108, Suitability Requirement Abrogated.
6 Witkin, California Summary 10th Torts § 1109, (S 1109) Owner of Estate or Interest in Real Property.
6 Witkin, California Summary 10th Torts § 1110, (S 1110) Exception for Public Property.
6 Witkin, California Summary 10th Torts § 1111, (S 1111) Liability for Wilful Misconduct.

§ 846.1. Public entry for recreational purposes; injury or damage; owner or public entity as defendant; claim for reasonable attorney's fees

(a) Except as provided in subdivision (c), an owner of any estate or interest in real property, whether possessory or nonpossessory, who gives permission to the public for entry on or use of the real property pursuant to an agreement with a public or nonprofit agency for purposes of recreational trail use, and is a defendant in a civil action brought by, or on behalf of, a person who is allegedly injured or allegedly suffers damages on the real property, may present a claim to the California Victim Compensation and Government Claims Board for reasonable attorney's fees incurred in this civil action if any of the following occurs:

(1) The court has dismissed the civil action upon a demurrer or motion for summary judgment made by the owner or upon its own motion for lack of prosecution.

(2) The action was dismissed by the plaintiff without any payment from the owner.

(3) The owner prevails in the civil action.

(b) Except as provided in subdivision (c), a public entity, as defined in Section 831.5 of the Government Code, that gives permission to the public for entry on or use of real property for a recreational purpose, as defined in Section 846, and is a defendant in a civil action brought by, or on behalf of, a person who is allegedly injured or allegedly suffers damages on the real property, may present a claim to the California Victim Compensation and Government Claims Board for reasonable attorney's fees incurred in this civil action if any of the following occurs:

(1) The court has dismissed the civil action upon a demurrer or motion for summary judgment made by this public entity or upon its own motion for lack of prosecution.

(2) The action was dismissed by the plaintiff without any payment from the public entity.

(3) The public entity prevails in the civil action.

(c) An owner of any estate or interest in real property, whether possessory or nonpossessory, or a public entity, as defined in Section 831.5 of the Government Code, that gives permission to the public for entry on, or use of, the real property for a recreational purpose, as defined in Section 846, pursuant to an agreement with a public or nonprofit agency, and is a defendant in a civil action brought by, or on behalf of, a person who seeks to restrict, prevent, or delay public use of that property, may present a claim to the California Victim Compensation and Government Claims Board for reasonable attorney's fees incurred in the civil action if any of the following occurs:

(1) The court has dismissed the civil action upon a demurrer or motion for summary judgment made by the owner or public entity or upon its own motion for lack of prosecution.

(2) The action was dismissed by the plaintiff without any payment from the owner or public entity.

(3) The owner or public entity prevails in the civil action.

(d) The California Victim Compensation and Government Claims Board shall allow the claim if the requirements of this section are met. The claim shall be paid from an appropriation to be made for that purpose. Reasonable attorney's fees, for purposes of this section, may not exceed an hourly rate greater than the rate charged by the Attorney General at the time the award is made, and may not exceed an aggregate amount of twenty-five thousand dollars ($25,000). This subdivision shall not apply if a public entity has provided for the defense of this civil action pursuant to Section 995 of the Government Code. This subdivision shall also not apply if an owner or public entity has been provided a legal defense by the state pursuant to any contract or other legal obligation.

(e) The total of claims allowed by the board pursuant to this section shall not exceed two hundred thousand dollars ($200,-000) per fiscal year. *(Added by Stats.1996, c. 932 (A.B.2291), § 1. Amended by Stats.1999, c. 775 (S.B.243), § 1; Stats.2006, c. 538 (S.B.1852), § 41.)*

Research References

Miller and Starr California Real Estate § 22:66, Recreational Users of Property: Exemption from Liability.
Miller and Starr California Real Estate § 22:72, Recreational or Hazardous Activities on Certain Public Property.
7 Witkin Cal. Proc. 5th Judgment § 234, in General.
5 Witkin, California Summary 10th Torts § 275, in General.
6 Witkin, California Summary 10th Torts § 1103, (S 1103) in General.

§ 846.2. Invitees on land to glean food for charitable purposes; liability; limited immunity

No cause of action shall arise against the owner, tenant, or lessee of land or premises for injuries to any person who has been expressly invited on that land or premises to glean agricultural or farm products for charitable purposes, unless that person's injuries were caused by the gross negligence or willful and wanton misconduct of the owner, tenant, or lessee. The immunity provided by this section does not apply if the owner, tenant, or lessee received any consideration for permitting the gleaning activity. *(Added by Stats.1988, c. 1062, § 1.)*

Research References

Miller and Starr California Real Estate § 22:67, Recreational Activities Which Qualify for the Exemption.
6 Witkin, California Summary 10th Torts § 1112, No Liability to Gleaners of Agricultural Products.

§ 846.5. Surveyors; right of entry; use of boundary evidence and performance of surveys; freeways

(a) The right of entry upon or to real property to investigate and utilize boundary evidence, and to perform surveys, is a right of persons legally authorized to practice land surveying and it shall be the responsibility of the owner or tenant who owns or controls property to provide reasonable access without undue delay. The right of entry is not contingent upon the provision of prior notice to the owner or tenant. However, the owner or tenant shall be notified of the proposed time of entry where practicable.

(b) The requirements of subdivision (a) do not apply to monuments within access-controlled portions of freeways.

(c) When required for a property survey, monuments within a freeway right-of-way shall be referenced to usable points outside the access control line by the agency having jurisdiction over the freeway when requested in writing by the registered civil engineer or licensed land surveyor who is to perform the property survey. The work shall be done within a reasonable time period by the agency in direct cooperation with the engineer or surveyor and at no charge to him. *(Added by Stats.1973, c. 435, p. 903, § 1. Amended by Stats.1982, c. 427, p. 1781, § 1.)*

Research References

5 Witkin, California Summary 10th Torts § 697, Other Privileged Entries.

§ 847. Immunity from liability; injuries or death occurring on property during or after the commission of certain felonies

(a) An owner, including, but not limited to, a public entity, as defined in Section 811.2 of the Government Code, of any estate or any other interest in real property, whether possessory or nonpossessory, shall not be liable to any person for any injury or death that occurs upon that property during the course of or after the commission of any of the felonies set forth in subdivision (b) by the injured or deceased person.

(b) The felonies to which the provisions of this section apply are the following: (1) Murder or voluntary manslaughter; (2) mayhem; (3) rape; (4) sodomy by force, violence, duress, menace, or threat of great bodily harm; (5) oral copulation by force, violence, duress, menace, or threat of great bodily harm;

(6) lewd acts on a child under the age of 14 years; (7) any felony punishable by death or imprisonment in the state prison for life; (8) any other felony in which the defendant inflicts great bodily injury on any person, other than an accomplice, or any felony in which the defendant uses a firearm; (9) attempted murder; (10) assault with intent to commit rape or robbery; (11) assault with a deadly weapon or instrument on a peace officer; (12) assault by a life prisoner on a noninmate; (13) assault with a deadly weapon by an inmate; (14) arson; (15) exploding a destructive device or any explosive with intent to injure; (16) exploding a destructive device or any explosive causing great bodily injury; (17) exploding a destructive device or any explosive with intent to murder; (18) burglary; (19) robbery; (20) kidnapping; (21) taking of a hostage by an inmate of a state prison; (22) any felony in which the defendant personally used a dangerous or deadly weapon; (23) selling, furnishing, administering, or providing heroin, cocaine, or phencyclidine (PCP) to a minor; (24) grand theft as defined in Sections 487 and 487a of the Penal Code; and (25) any attempt to commit a crime listed in this subdivision other than an assault.

(c) The limitation on liability conferred by this section arises at the moment the injured or deceased person commences the felony or attempted felony and extends to the moment the injured or deceased person is no longer upon the property.

(d) The limitation on liability conferred by this section applies only when the injured or deceased person's conduct in furtherance of the commission of a felony specified in subdivision (b) proximately or legally causes the injury or death.

(e) The limitation on liability conferred by this section arises only upon the charge of a felony listed in subdivision (b) and the subsequent conviction of that felony or a lesser included felony or misdemeanor arising from a charge of a felony listed in subdivision (b). During the pendency of any such criminal action, a civil action alleging this liability shall be abated and the statute of limitations on the civil cause of action shall be tolled.

(f) This section does not limit the liability of an owner or an owner's agent which otherwise exists for willful, wanton, or criminal conduct, or for willful or malicious failure to guard or warn against a dangerous condition, use, structure, or activity.

(g) The limitation on liability provided by this section shall be in addition to any other available defense. *(Added by Stats.1985, c. 1541, § 1.)*

Research References

Miller and Starr California Real Estate § 22:59, Liability for Wrongful or Criminal Conduct of Third Persons.
Miller and Starr California Real Estate § 22:73, Liability to Trespassers.
6 Witkin, California Summary 10th Torts § 1099, Person Committing Serious Felony.
6 Witkin, California Summary 10th Torts § 1657, (S 1657) in General.

§ 848. Mineral rights owners; notice of entry on real property to exercise rights; timing; contents; injunctions

(a) Except as provided in subdivision (c), the owner of mineral rights, as defined by Section 883.110, in real property shall give a written notice prior to the first entry to the owner of the real property who is listed as the assessee on the current local assessment roll or to the owner's representative, or to the lessee of the real property if different from the mineral rights owner, and to any public utility that has a recorded interest in the real property if there is to be excavation of the utility interest, under the following circumstances:

(1) If the mineral rights owner or its agent intends to enter real property for the purpose of undertaking non-surface-disrupting activities such as surveying, water and mineral testing, and removal of debris and equipment not involving use of an articulated vehicle on the real property, the owner or agent shall provide a minimum of five days' notice. Reasonable attempts shall be made to deliver the notice by acknowledged personal delivery, but if that cannot occur, the notice shall be delivered by registered letter and be received a minimum of five days prior to the entrance on the property. The notice shall specify all of the following:

(A) Date of entry.

(B) Estimated length of time the property will be occupied.

(C) General nature of the work.

(2) If the mineral rights owner or its agent intends to enter real property for the purpose of excavation or other surface-disrupting activities such as drilling new wells, constructing structures, bringing articulated vehicles or excavation equipment on the real property, or reclamation of the real property after the surface has been disturbed, the owner or agent shall provide a minimum of 30 days' notice. The notice shall specify both of the following:

(A) The extent and location of the prospecting, mining, or extraction operation.

(B) The approximate time or times of entry and exit upon the real property.

(3) If a mineral rights owner's entry to the real property ceases for a period of one year or more, any further entry by the mineral rights owner for the purpose of surface-disturbing activities pursuant to paragraph (2) shall require written notice pursuant to this subdivision.

(b)(1) If a mineral rights owner has been authorized by the Division of Oil, Gas, and Geothermal Resources to drill a relief well or to take other immediate actions in response to an emergency situation, or if the division or its agent is drilling a relief well or taking other immediate actions in response to an emergency situation, the notice provisions under paragraph (2) of subdivision (a) shall be waived.

(2) For purposes of this subdivision, an "emergency" means immediate action is necessary to protect life, health, property, or natural resources.

(c) The notice specified in subdivision (a) shall not be required if the owner of the real property or assessee has a current, already negotiated surface use, access use, or similar agreement with the mineral rights owner, lessee, agent, or operator.

(d) If the mineral rights owner has not complied with the notice requirement specified in subdivision (a), the owner of the real property listed on the current assessment roll or any public utility which has a recorded interest in the real property may request a court to enjoin the prospecting, mining, or extracting operation until the mineral rights owner has complied. The absence of a known owner on the assessment roll or any public utility which has a recorded interest in the real property relieves the mineral rights owner of the obligation to give the written notice to the owner or public utility.

(e) For purposes of this section, an "acknowledged personal delivery" means that the written notice is personally delivered to the owner, the owner's representative, or lessee, and the owner, the owner's representative, or lessee acknowledges, in writing, receipt of the notice. *(Added by Stats.1988, c. 535, § 1. Amended by Stats.2012, c. 542 (A.B.1966), § 1.)*

Research References

Miller and Starr California Real Estate § 17:21, Minerals--In General.

12 Witkin, California Summary 10th Real Property § 17, Fee Simple Absolute.

CHAPTER 3. ENVIRONMENTAL RESPONSIBILITY ACCEPTANCE ACT

§ 850. Construction of chapter; definitions

The definitions set forth in Section 25260 of the Health and Safety Code govern the construction of this chapter. In addition, the following definitions apply for purposes of this chapter only:

(a) "Actual awareness" means actual knowledge of a fact pertaining to an obligation under this chapter, including actual knowledge of a release exceeding the notification threshold. Only actual awareness possessed by those employees or representatives of an owner of a site who are responsible for monitoring, responding to or otherwise addressing the release shall be attributable to the owner. Only actual awareness possessed by those employees or representatives of a potentially responsible party who are responsible for monitoring, responding to, or otherwise addressing, the release shall be attributable to the potentially responsible party.

(b) "Commitment statement" means a written statement executed by the notice recipient which recites expressly the language specified in Section 854.

(c) "Mediation" means an informal process in which the disputing parties select a neutral third party to assist them in reaching a negotiated settlement in which the neutral third party has no power to impose a solution on the parties, but rather has the power only to assist the parties in shaping solutions to meet their interests and objectives.

(d) "Negative response" means a written response by the recipient of a notice of potential liability indicating that the recipient will not undertake any response action, or a deemed negative response pursuant to subdivision (c) of Section 851 in the event of the recipient's failure to respond.

(e) "Neutral third party" means an experienced professional, such as an attorney, engineer, environmentalist, hydrologist, or retired judge, who has served as a mediator.

(f) "Notice of potential liability" means a notice, sent by the owner of the site, stating that a release that exceeds the notification threshold has occurred at the site and that the owner believes that the recipient of the notice is a responsible party with respect to the release. The notice of potential liability shall describe the location of the site and the nature of the release.

(g) "Notice recipient" means any one of the following:

(1) A person who receives a notice of potential liability pursuant to subdivision (a) of Section 851.

(2) A person who provides a release report pursuant to subdivision (b) of Section 851.

(3) A person who offers a commitment statement to the owner of a site pursuant to subdivision (c) of Section 851.

(h) "Notification threshold" means any release of such a magnitude that:

(1) The release is the subject of a response action which has been ordered by, or is being performed by, an oversight agency; or

(2) The release is impeding the ability of the owner of the site to sell, lease, or otherwise use the site.

(i) "Operation and maintenance" means any activity as defined in subdivision (a) of Section 25318.5 of the Health and Safety Code.

(j) "Oversight agency" means any agency, as defined in subdivision (c) of Section 25260 of the Health and Safety Code, that has jurisdiction over a response action performed in connection with a release that is the subject of a notice of potential liability. Subject to any other limitation imposed by law, an oversight agency retains full discretion as to when it exercises jurisdiction over a site.

(k) "Reasonable steps," as used in subdivision (a) of Section 851, means the least expensive means available to ascertain the potentially responsible parties. If the owner cannot otherwise identify any apparent, potentially responsible parties, then "reasonable steps" includes:

(1) Conducting a title search; and

(2) Reviewing all environmental reports in the owner's possession of which the owner has actual awareness pertaining to the site.

(l) "Release" means the release, as defined in Sections 25320 and 25321 of the Health and Safety Code, of a hazardous material or hazardous materials.

(m) "Release report" means a notice sent by a responsible party to the owner of the site stating that a release has occurred on the site which is likely to exceed the notification threshold. The release report shall describe the location of the site and the nature of the release.

(n) "Remedial action" means any action as defined in Section 25322 of the Health and Safety Code.

(o) "Removal action" means any action as defined in subdivision (a) of Section 25323 of the Health and Safety Code.

(p) "Response action" means any removal actions, including, but not limited to, site investigations and remedial actions, including, but not limited to, operation and maintenance measures.

(q) "Responsible party" means any person who is liable under state or local law for taking action in response to a release.

(r) "Site" means any parcel of commercial, industrial, or agricultural real property where a hazardous materials release has occurred.

(s) "Written action" means any official action by any oversight agency where the oversight agency has expressly exercised its cleanup authority in writing, pursuant to the oversight agency's procedures, directing a response action at the site. *(Added by Stats.1997, c. 873 (S.B.1081), § 1.)*

Research References

Rutter, Cal. Practice Guide: Landlord-Tenant Form 2:B, Standard Shopping Center Lease.
Rutter, Cal. Practice Guide: Real Prop. Transactions Ch. 5-B, B. Governing Legislation.

Rutter, Cal. Practice Guide: Real Prop. Transactions Ch. 5-C, C. Liability Under CERCLA and California Superfund.

Miller and Starr California Real Estate § 23:28, Special Statute: Private Resolution of Disputes Regarding Responsibility for Cleanup of Contamination.

12 Witkin, California Summary 10th Real Property § 907, Other California Statutes.

§ 851. Owner with actual awareness of release; notice of potential liability; release report; commitment statement; response; duty to mitigate; application of common law; application of chapter

(a) An owner of a site who has actual awareness of a release exceeding the notification threshold shall take all reasonable steps as defined in subdivision (j) of Section 850 to expeditiously identify the potentially responsible parties. The owner shall, as soon as reasonably possible after obtaining actual awareness of the potentially responsible parties, send a notice of potential liability to the identified potentially responsible parties and the agency, as defined in subdivision (c) of Section 25260 of the Health and Safety Code, that the owner believes to be the appropriate oversight agency. For any release exceeding the notification threshold of which the owner has actual awareness that occurred prior to, but within three years of, the effective date of this section, the notice shall be given on or before December 31, 1998.

(b) A potentially responsible party who has actual awareness of a release which is likely to exceed the notification threshold shall as soon as reasonably possible after obtaining actual awareness of the release provide the owner of the site where the release occurred with a release report. For any release exceeding the notification threshold of which the potentially responsible party has actual awareness that occurred prior to, but within three years of, the effective date of this section, the release report shall be given on or before December 31, 1998. A potentially responsible party may issue, at the potentially responsible party's option, a commitment statement to the owner of the site within 120 days of the potentially responsible party's issuance of a release report. The fact that a release report is issued shall not constitute an admission of liability and may not be admitted as evidence against a potentially responsible party in any litigation.

(c) When a notice of potential liability is issued, a notice recipient shall respond to the owner, in writing, and by certified mail, return receipt requested, within 120 days from the date that the notice of potential liability was mailed. The notice recipient's response shall be either a commitment statement or a negative response. The notice recipient's failure to submit the written response within the 120–day period, or failure to strictly comply with the form of the written response, as provided in Section 854, shall be deemed a negative response. The owner may agree in writing to extend the period during which the notice recipient may respond to the notice of potential liability. An extension of up to 120 days shall be provided if the notice recipient commits to do a site investigation, the results of which shall be provided to the owner and the oversight agency.

(d)(1) The common law duty to mitigate damages shall apply to any failure of the owner of a site to give a timely notice of potential liability when the owner is required to give this notice pursuant to this chapter. Where an owner fails to mitigate damages by not giving a timely notice of potential liability, the owner's damage claim shall be reduced in accordance with common law principles by the amount that the potentially responsible party proves would have likely been mitigated had a timely notice of potential liability been given.

(2) Common law principles shall apply to the failure of the potentially responsible party to issue a timely release report. Where a potentially responsible party fails to give a timely release report, the potentially responsible party, in accordance with common law principles, shall be responsible to the owner of the site, for damages that the owner proves are likely caused by such failure to provide a release report.

(3) Any party who argues the applicability of this subdivision carries the burden of proof in that regard.

(4) Nothing in this section is intended to create a new cause of action or defense beyond that which already exists under common law.

(5) Subdivisions (a) and (b), and paragraphs (1) and (2) of this subdivision, shall not apply when the party to whom a notice of potential liability or release report is owed already possesses actual awareness of the information required to be transmitted in such notice of potential liability or release report.

(e)(1) Except as provided in paragraph (2), the requirements of this chapter shall not apply to a site listed pursuant to Section 25356 of the Health and Safety Code for response action pursuant to Chapter 6.8 (commencing with Section 25300) of Division 20 of the Health and Safety Code or to a site where an oversight agency has issued an order or entered into an enforceable agreement pursuant to any authority, including, but not limited to, an order or enforceable agreement entered into by a local agency, the Department of Toxic Substance Control, the State Water Resources Control Board, or a regional water quality control board pursuant to Chapter 6.5 (commencing with Section 25100), Chapter 6.7 (commencing with Section 25280), Chapter 6.75 (commencing with Section 25299.10), Chapter 6.8 (commencing with Section 25300), Chapter 6.85 (commencing with Section 25396), or Chapter 6.11 (commencing with Section 25404) of Division 20 of the Health and Safety Code, or pursuant to Division 7 (commencing with Section 13000) of the Water Code.

(2) The requirements of this chapter shall apply if either of the following applies:

(A) The order or enforceable agreement is issued or entered into after the owner accepts a commitment statement.

(B) The Department of Toxic Substance Control, State Water Resources Control Board, or regional water quality control board that issued the order or entered into an enforceable agreement consents in writing to the applicability of this chapter to the site.

(f) It is the intent of the Legislature for this chapter to resolve disputes between, and affect the rights of, private parties only. Nothing in this chapter shall affect the authority of the Department of Toxic Substance Control, the State Water Resources Control Board, a regional water quality control board, or any other oversight agency.

(g) Notwithstanding any other provision of this chapter, any time prior to accepting a commitment statement, the owner may provide the notice to the notice recipient that the provisions of subdivision (c), paragraph (2) of subdivision (e), and Sections 852 and 854, shall not apply to the site, in which case the provisions of subdivision (c), paragraph (2) of subdivision (e), and Sections 852 and 854 shall not apply to the site and the owner and notice recipient shall be entitled to pursue all other legal remedies and defenses authorized by law. *(Added by Stats.1997, c. 873 (S.B.1081), § 1.)*

Research References

Rutter, Cal. Practice Guide: A.D.R. App. A, Selected Statutes Providing for ADR.

Rutter, Cal. Practice Guide: Real Prop. Transactions Ch. 5-C, C. Liability Under CERCLA and California Superfund.

Miller and Starr California Real Estate § 23:28, Special Statute: Private Resolution of Disputes Regarding Responsibility for Cleanup of Contamination.

12 Witkin, California Summary 10th Real Property § 907, Other California Statutes.

§ 852. Commitment statement; acceptance or rejection; mediation; effect of accepted commitment statement; construction of chapter; actions; statute of limitations

(a) Within 45 days after issuance of the commitment statement, the owner may transmit to the notice recipient by certified mail, return receipt requested, an executed copy of the commitment statement, indicating its acceptance. If the owner does not execute the commitment statement, the commitment statement shall be deemed to have been rejected upon expiration of the 45–day period. A notice recipient has no obligation with respect to the provisions of a rejected commitment statement.

(b)(1) Except as otherwise provided in this chapter, or unless the owner or the notice recipient has elected not to proceed with the mediation, if the owner rejects the commitment statement, the owner and notice recipient shall participate in a mediation process prior to the commencement of any litigation which pertains to a release covered by the commitment statement. The mediation process shall be supervised by a neutral third party mutually agreed upon by the owner and the notice recipient in order to mediate a mutually agreeable settlement between the owner and notice recipient of all issues related to the release.

(2) Either the notice recipient or the owner may elect not to proceed further with the mediation process at any time prior to completion of those proceedings.

(3) To the extent a mutually agreeable settlement is reached which allocates the liability and assigns the rights and obligations of the owner and notice recipient in a manner different from or inconsistent with this chapter, the settlement shall supersede the terms of this chapter pursuant to subdivision (f) of Section 853. If a settlement of all issues cannot be reached within 90 days after the owner's rejection of the commitment statement, the neutral third party shall declare the mediation process unsuccessful and terminate the process. The owner and notice recipient may mutually agree to extend the mediation process but shall communicate any such extension in writing to the neutral third party. If the party issuing the commitment statement fails, for any reason, to participate in the mediation within 90 days of the rejection of the commitment statement, the owner may proceed with litigation.

(4) After the termination of an unsuccessful mediation process, the parties shall be free to litigate or otherwise resolve their respective claims. The parties may mutually agree to the terms of the commitment statement at any time after the termination of an unsuccessful mediation process, in which case this chapter shall govern the rights and obligations of the parties.

(5) Any applicable statute of limitations shall be tolled for 90 days following issuance of a notice of potential liability, a release report, or a commitment statement.

(6) Any applicable statute of limitations shall be tolled from the time the owner rejects a commitment statement until the termination of the mediation process. If mediation is not commenced within 90 days after the owner's rejection of the commitment statement, the tolling of the statute of limitations shall terminate unless otherwise agreed to by the parties.

(7) Unless the owner and notice recipient agree otherwise, the fees and costs of the neutral third party shall be borne equally by the notice recipient and the owner.

(c) Upon taking effect, the commitment statement shall have all of the following results:

(1) The commitment statement shall constitute a binding promise that the notice recipient will undertake any response action as required by an oversight agency through a written action, directed to the owner or notice recipient, in connection with the release that is the subject of the notice of potential liability or release report. The commitment statement shall not create any obligations with respect to releases occurring after the commitment statement is signed, or with respect to any other release that is not the subject of the notice of potential liability.

(2) The commitment statement shall constitute a binding promise that the owner shall provide reasonable site access to the notice recipient to take any action that is reasonably necessary or appropriate to conduct a response action. This grant of access shall not affect the rights of the owner if the notice recipient's activities onsite result in physical damage to the site which the notice recipient fails to repair within a reasonable period after completion of all onsite activities. Unless otherwise ordered by the oversight agency, the notice recipient shall take all reasonable steps to avoid interfering with the owner's use of the site.

(3) Except for civil actions seeking damages for personal injury or wrongful death, once a commitment statement has been accepted, the court shall stay any action brought by the owner of the site against the notice recipient that issued the commitment statement, including, but not limited to, actions in trespass, nuisance, negligence, and strict liability, which arise from or relate to a release for which a commitment statement has been issued. The stay shall be effective for a period of not more than two years from the date of acceptance of the commitment statement, but only so long as the site response action is proceeding to the satisfaction of an oversight agency. The stay shall not apply to any civil action that is based on fraud, failure to disclose, or misrepresentation related to any transaction between the owner of the site and the notice recipient, to any civil action for breach of the commitment statement, or to any civil action which is unrelated to the release. The owner and notice recipient may elect to extend the period of the stay by written agreement.

(4) In an action by an owner who has accepted a commitment statement against the notice recipient who issued the commitment statement, and which arises from or relates to a release for which a commitment statement has been issued, only the following damages shall be recoverable to the extent otherwise authorized by law:

(A) Damages for personal injuries or wrongful death caused by the release.

(B) Damages for breach of a commitment statement.

(C) Damages from the failure of a prospective purchaser to perform under a sales contract because of the release, where such failure to perform occurs prior to the issuance of the commitment statement.

(D) Damages for the lost use of the property prior to the issuance of a commitment statement caused by the release.

(E) Recovery of costs of investigating and responding to the release where such costs are incurred prior to the issuance of the commitment statement.

(F) Remedies for any breach of a preexisting contract entered into prior to the acceptance of a commitment statement.

(G) Damages for lost rents and any other damages recoverable under law associated with lost use of the site caused by any notice recipient during site response action activities.

(5) An owner may obtain rescission of a commitment statement if a notice recipient repudiates its obligations under the commitment statement, in which case Sections 852 and 854 shall no longer apply to the site.

(6) The notice recipient and owner shall copy each other with respect to all correspondence and proposed workplans to and from the oversight agency that relate to the site.

(d) Nothing in this chapter shall affect the authority of an oversight agency under the law to bring an administrative, criminal, or civil action against either a notice recipient or the owner, nor does it compel any action on the part of the oversight agency.

(e) At any time after the commitment statement is accepted, either the owner or the notice recipient may file an action against the other for material breach of rights and obligations associated with the commitment statement. Subject to the stay provided for in paragraph (3) of subdivision (c), the parties may litigate these claims in the same action as any other claims they may have in connection with the release that is the subject of the commitment statement.

(f) Whenever a notice recipient issues a commitment statement, the following notice shall be provided in 14 point boldface type if printed or in boldface capital letters if typed:

"THIS FORM WAS DEVELOPED AS PART OF A PROCESS ENACTED BY THE CALIFORNIA LEGISLATURE TO PROVIDE OWNERS OF PROPERTY AND POTENTIALLY RESPONSIBLE PARTIES AN ALTERNATIVE TO LITIGATING DISPUTES OVER CONTAMINATION. IT IS YOUR OPTION AS TO WHETHER YOU SIGN THIS FORM OR OTHERWISE PARTICIPATE IN THIS PROCESS. IF YOU CHOOSE NOT TO PARTICIPATE IN THE PROCESS, YOU SHOULD NOTIFY THE PARTY WHO SENT YOU THIS FORM. THIS FORM INVOLVES A TRADEOFF WHEREBY EACH PARTY ACQUIRES AND RELINQUISHES CERTAIN RIGHTS. UNDER THIS FORM, THE PROPERTY OWNER GETS THE ASSURANCE THAT THE POTENTIALLY RESPONSIBLE PARTY IS OBLIGATED TO PERFORM INVESTIGATORY AND CLEANUP ACTIONS IN THE EVENT THAT GOVERNMENT AUTHORITIES ELECT TO REQUIRE THESE ACTIONS. ON THE OTHER HAND, THE PROPERTY OWNER FOREGOES CERTAIN CLAIMS ASSOCIATED WITH RESIDUAL CONTAMINATION THAT GOVERNMENTAL AUTHORITIES ALLOW TO REMAIN IN PLACE ON THE PROPERTY. IF YOU ELECT NOT TO SIGN THIS FORM, THE PROCESS DEVELOPED BY THE LEGISLATURE CONTEMPLATES THAT YOU WILL ATTEMPT TO MEDIATE ANY DISPUTES REGARDING THE CONTAMINATION. HOWEVER, MEDIATION IS NEITHER MANDATORY NOR BINDING. IF YOU HAVE QUESTIONS ABOUT THE PROCESS, YOU MAY WISH TO CONSULT AN ATTORNEY."

(g) Any applicable statute of limitations shall be tolled for two and one-half years from the date of acceptance of the commitment statement. If at the end of two years from the date of acceptance of the commitment statement an oversight agency has not issued a written action directed to the owner or notice recipient, the owner has 60 days in which he or she may terminate the commitment statement; and, in this event, it shall have no further force or effect. In the event the owner terminates the commitment statement, subdivision (c) shall no longer apply to the site and shall no longer govern the rights and obligations of the owner or notice recipient. *(Added by Stats. 1997, c. 873 (S.B.1081), § 1.)*

Research References

Rutter, Cal. Practice Guide: A.D.R. App. A, Selected Statutes Providing for ADR.
Rutter, Cal. Practice Guide: Real Prop. Transactions Ch. 5-C, C. Liability Under CERCLA and California Superfund.
Miller and Starr California Real Estate § 23:28, Special Statute: Private Resolution of Disputes Regarding Responsibility for Cleanup of Contamination.

12 Witkin, California Summary 10th Real Property § 907, Other California Statutes.

§ 853. Commitment statements; admissions; admissibility; construction of chapter; actions; contract rights; application of chapter

(a) Neither the failure to issue a commitment statement nor its issuance shall be construed as an admission that the recipient of the notice of potential liability is liable under any federal, state, or local law, including common law, for the release that the party agrees to investigate or respond. Neither the failure to issue a commitment statement nor the contents of the commitment statement shall be admissible evidence in any proceeding, as defined in Section 901 of the Evidence Code, except that the contents of the commitment statement shall be admissible evidence in an action to enforce the commitment statement to the extent that such contents would be admissible under other applicable law.

(b) Nothing in this chapter shall subject a notice recipient to any damages, fines, or penalties for a failure to make a written response, either positive or negative, to a notice of potential liability.

(c) Nothing in this chapter shall subject the owner of a site to any damages, fines, or penalties for a failure to send a notice of potential liability pursuant to Section 851. Failure by the owner of a site to send a notice of potential liability of a release in a timely fashion shall not be deemed to create any liability for the owner under a theory of negligence per se.

(d) Nothing in this chapter imposes an affirmative duty on the owner of a site, or any potentially responsible party, to discover, or determine the nature or extent of, a hazardous materials release at the site. This chapter does not affect such an affirmative duty to the extent it is imposed by any other law.

(e) Subject to the defenses specified in Section 101(35) and 107(b) of the federal Comprehensive Environmental Response, Compensation, and Liability Act of 1980, as amended (42 U.S.C. Secs. 9601(35) and 9607(b)), a cause of action is hereby established whereby a notice recipient may recover from any responsible party any reasonable response costs for conducting a response action as may be approved or overseen by an oversight agency or as incurred pursuant to a commitment statement. Liability among responsible parties shall be allocated based upon the equitable factors specified in subdivision (c) of Section 25356.3 of the Health and Safety Code. No third-party beneficiary rights are created by a commitment statement, except as provided in subdivision (b) of Section 854. This cause of action applies to costs incurred prior to enactment of this subdivision. However, no recovery may be obtained under this subdivision for costs incurred more than three years prior to the filing of litigation to recover those costs. The cause of action established pursuant to this subdivision shall not apply against a current or former owner of a site unless that owner operated a business that caused a release being addressed by a response action at the site and the costs incurred by the notice recipient were in response to a release caused by the owner.

(f) Nothing in this chapter shall affect or limit the rights of an owner under preexisting contract. Nothing in this chapter shall affect or limit the right of a notice recipient and owner to agree to an allocation of liability or to an assignment of rights and obligations that is different from or inconsistent with this chapter. Such agreements shall supersede the terms of this chapter.

(g) Nothing in this chapter shall make a notice recipient a responsible party, beyond the obligations the notice recipient undertakes pursuant to this chapter.

(h) Nothing in this chapter shall apply to causes of action for wrongful death or personal injury. However, the pleading of a cause of action for wrongful death or personal injury shall not affect the applicability of this chapter to other causes of action in the same civil action. *(Added by Stats.1997, c. 873 (S.B.1081), § 1.)*

Research References

Rutter, Cal. Practice Guide: Real Prop. Transactions Ch. 5-C, C. Liability Under CERCLA and California Superfund.

Miller and Starr California Real Estate § 23:28, Special Statute: Private Resolution of Disputes Regarding Responsibility for Cleanup of Contamination.

§ 854. Form of commitment statement

A commitment statement shall be executed in substantially the following form:

COUNTY OF _____
STATE OF
CALIFORNIA

NOTICE OF ASSUMPTION OF GOVERNMENT IMPOSED SITE INVESTIGATION AND/OR REMEDIAL ACTION ORDERS ("COMMITMENT STATEMENT")

(a) The undersigned notice recipient is aware of, or has received a notice of potential liability pursuant to, Section 851 of the Civil Code ("notice of potential liability") in connection with a release of hazardous materials at a parcel of property ("site") having the following legal description: (Insert description here)

(b) The undersigned notice recipient and the undersigned owner of the site and the owner's successors, heirs, and assigns agree, upon the proper and timely execution and delivery of this commitment statement, to abide by the requirements of Chapter 3 (commencing with Section 850) of Title 3 of Part 2 of Division 2 in connection with the release that is the subject of the notice of potential liability.

(c) The undersigned notice recipient hereby commits to undertake any response action as required by an oversight agency through a written action, directed to the owner or notice recipient, in connection with the release that is the subject of the notice of potential liability or release report. This commitment runs with the land and binds, in addition to the current owner of the site, all of the owner's successors in interest, including current and future lenders having a security interest in the site.

(d) The owner of the site and the owner's successors, heirs, and assigns agree, upon the proper and timely execution and delivery of this commitment statement, to all of the following:

(1) The undersigned notice recipient or the party's designee shall be allowed such access to the site as may be required to perform its obligations under this commitment statement, provided that the undersigned notice recipient shall be liable for any physical damage it causes in conducting a response action, which the notice recipient fails to repair within a reasonable period after completion of all onsite activities.

(2) The parties, their successors, heirs, and assigns shall provide each other with copies of any communication or correspondence with an oversight agency in connection with the release of hazardous materials at the site.

(3) Provided that the undersigned notice recipient performs all of its obligations under this commitment statement, and except as otherwise provided in subdivisions (c) and (e) of Section 852 of the Civil Code, no claim for damages, accruing after the acceptance of the commitment statement, shall be brought against the undersigned notice recipient by the owner of the site or by the owner's successors, heirs, and assigns.

(e) The contents of this commitment statement shall be inadmissible evidence in any proceeding, as defined in Section 901 of the Evidence Code, except in an action to enforce this commitment statement to the extent that such contents would be admissible under other applicable law. This commitment statement may be enforced fully by the owner of the site and all parties identified in paragraph (b). There are no third-party beneficiary rights created by this commitment statement.

(f) The owner of the site shall provide a copy of this commitment statement to any prospective purchaser or lessee of the site until this commitment statement is terminated or until all response actions have been completed in accordance with the commitment statement.

(g) If the owner transfers the site, the owner shall notify the undersigned parties to this commitment statement, by mail, within 14 business days of the property transfer.

(h) As provided by law, this commitment statement shall become effective if the owner executes this commitment statement within 45 days from the date of issuance, in which case its terms shall go into effect upon receipt of that acceptance by the issuer of this commitment statement. If the owner rejects this commitment statement, the rejection shall be subject to the mediation provisions of subdivision (b) of Section 852.

(i) If at the end of two years from the date of acceptance of this commitment statement, an oversight agency has not issued a written action directed to the owner or notice recipient, the owner has 60 days in which he or she may terminate the commitment statement; and, in this event, it shall have no further force or effect.

_____ _____
Notice recipient   Date
(Notice recipient's name,
address, and telephone number)
(Notarial affidavit)

_____ _____
Owner   Date
(Owner's name, address,
and telephone number)
(Notarial affidavit)

(Added by Stats.1997, c. 873 (S.B.1081), § 1.)

Research References

Rutter, Cal. Practice Guide: Real Prop. Transactions Ch. 5-C, C. Liability Under CERCLA and California Superfund.

Miller and Starr California Real Estate § 23:28, Special Statute: Private Resolution of Disputes Regarding Responsibility for Cleanup of Contamination.

§ 855. Effective date of § 851 notification requirements

The notification requirements of Section 851 shall not become effective until 180 days after the effective date of this chapter. *(Added by Stats.1997, c. 873 (S.B.1081), § 1.)*

Title 5

MARKETABLE RECORD TITLE

CHAPTER 1. GENERAL PROVISIONS

ARTICLE 1. CONSTRUCTION

Section
880.020. Legislative declaration and purpose.
880.030. Construction not to limit or affect equitable principles or recording statutes.

§ 880.020. Legislative declaration and purpose

(a) The Legislature declares as public policy that:

(1) Real property is a basic resource of the people of the state and should be made freely alienable and marketable to the extent practicable in order to enable and encourage full use and development of the real property, including both surface and subsurface interests.

(2) Interests in real property and defects in titles created at remote times, whether or not of record, often constitute unreasonable restraints on alienation and marketability of real property because the interests are no longer valid or have been abandoned or have otherwise become obsolete.

(3) Such interests and defects produce litigation to clear and quiet titles, cause delays in real property title transactions, and hinder marketability of real property.

(4) Real property title transactions should be possible with economy and expediency. The status and security of recorded real property titles should be determinable to the extent practicable from an examination of recent records only.

(b) It is the purpose of the Legislature in enacting this title to simplify and facilitate real property title transactions in furtherance of public policy by enabling persons to rely on record title to the extent provided in this title, with respect to the property interests specified in this title, subject only to the limitations expressly provided in this title and notwithstanding any provision or implication to the contrary in any other statute or in the common law. This title shall be liberally construed to effect the legislative purpose. *(Added by Stats.1982, c. 1268, p. 4671, § 1. Amended by Stats.2011, c. 46 (S.B.284), § 1.)*

Law Revision Commission Comments

Subdivision (a) of Section 880.020 is drawn from North Carolina marketable title legislation, N.C. Gen. Stat. § 47B–1 (1976; Supp. 1981). The declaration of public policy is intended to demonstrate the significance of the state interest served by this title and the importance of the retroactive application of the law to the effectuation of that interest. See In re Marriage of Bouquet, 16 Cal.3d 583, 592, 546 P.2d 1371, 1376, 128 Cal.Rptr. 427, 432 (1976) (upholding changes in the community property laws as retroactively applied).

A statute may require recordation of previously executed instruments or of extensions of time if a reasonable time is allowed for recordation. See discussion in 1 A. Bowman, Ogden's Revised California Real Property Law § 10.4, at 415–16 (1974). The burden on holders of old interests of recording a notice of intent to preserve or an extension of time is outweighed by the public good of more secure land transactions. See, e.g., Wichelman v. Messner, 250 Minn. 88, 121, 83 N.W.2d 800, 825 (1957) (upholding Minnesota marketable title legislation):

. . . [A] number of marketable title acts have been passed by various states. Such limiting statutes are considered vital to all who are engaged in or concerned with the conveyance of real property. They proceed upon the theory that the economic advantages of being able to pass uncluttered title to land far outweigh any value which the outdated restrictions may have for the person in whose favor they operate. These statutes reflect the appraisal of state legislatures of the "actual economic significance of these interests weighed against the inconvenience and expense caused by

their continued existence for unlimited periods without regard to altered circumstances." . . . They must be construed in the light of the public good in terms of more secure land transactions which outweighs the burden and risk imposed upon owners of old outstanding rights to record their interests.

Subdivision (b) is drawn from Section 9 of the Model Marketable Title Act. If the application of a particular statute or common law rule conflicts with the provisions of this title, this title governs. (16 Cal.L.Rev. Comm. Reports 401).

Subdivision (b) of Section 880.020 is amended to correct a typographical error. [39 Cal.L.Rev.Comm. Reports 99 (2009)].

Research References

California Real Estate Forms (Miller & Starr) § 1:19, Agreement for Purchase and Sale of Realty–Build-To-Suit.

California Real Estate Forms (Miller & Starr) § 1:23, Purchase and Sale Agreement–Residential Project.

California Real Estate Forms (Miller & Starr) § 1:25, Purchase and Sale Agreement–Multi-Tenant Residential Property (With Lease-Back).

Rutter, Cal. Practice Guide: Real Prop. Transactions Ch. 3-F, F. Alternatives to Endorsements.

Miller and Starr California Real Estate § 9:4, Fee Simple Defeasible--In General.

Miller and Starr California Real Estate § 11:68, Constructive Notice of Interests Barred by the Statute of Limitations--"Ancient Documents" and the Marketable Record Title Act.

Miller and Starr California Real Estate § 15:82, Abandonment by Nonuse for 20 Years.

Miller and Starr California Real Estate § 10:130, Ancient Mortgages; Debt Secured by a Mortgage.

Miller and Starr California Real Estate § 10:132, Ancient Mortgages; Debt Secured by a Deed of Trust.

Miller and Starr California Real Estate § 11:117, Option Contracts.

Miller and Starr California Real Estate § 11:119, Executory and Installment Contracts--Expiration of the Recorded Memorandum.

12 Witkin, California Summary 10th Real Property § 337, (S 337) Enactment of Marketable Record Title Statute.

11 Witkin, California Summary 10th Husband and Wife § 5, Generally Applicable Procedures.

4 Witkin, California Summary 10th Security Transactions in Real Property § 121, Mortgage.

4 Witkin, California Summary 10th Security Transactions in Real Property § 122, Deed of Trust.

§ 880.030. Construction not to limit or affect equitable principles or recording statutes

Nothing in this title shall be construed to:

(a) Limit application of the principles of waiver and estoppel, laches, and other equitable principles.

(b) Affect the operation of any statute governing the effect of recording or failure to record, except as specifically provided in this title. *(Added by Stats.1982, c. 1268, p. 4672, § 1.)*

Law Revision Commission Comments

Subdivision (a) of Section 880.030 is new; notwithstanding the maximum record duration or period of enforceability of interests in property pursuant to this title, the owner of an interest may waive or be estopped from asserting the interest within the prescribed time, or other equitable defenses may apply. Subdivision (b) is drawn from Section 7 of the Model Marketable Title Act. (16 Cal.L.Rev.Comm. Reports 401).

Research References

Rutter, Cal. Practice Guide: Real Prop. Transactions Ch. 3-F, F. Alternatives to Endorsements.

Miller and Starr California Real Estate § 11:68, Constructive Notice of Interests Barred by the Statute of Limitations--"Ancient Documents" and the Marketable Record Title Act.

Miller and Starr California Real Estate § 10:130, Ancient Mortgages; Debt Secured by a Mortgage.

Miller and Starr California Real Estate § 10:132, Ancient Mortgages; Debt Secured by a Deed of Trust.

Miller and Starr California Real Estate § 11:117, Option Contracts.

12 Witkin, California Summary 10th Real Property § 337, (S 337) Enactment of Marketable Record Title Statute.

ARTICLE 2.   APPLICATION OF TITLE

§ 880.240.   Interests not subject to expiration pursuant to title

The following interests are not subject to expiration or expiration of record pursuant to this title:

(a) The interest of a person in possession (including use or occupancy) of real property and the interest of a person under whom a person in possession claims, to the extent the possession would have been revealed by reasonable inspection or inquiry.

(b) An interest of the United States or pursuant to federal law in real property that is not subjected by federal law to the recording requirements of the state and that has not terminated under federal law.

(c) An interest of the state or a local public entity in real property.

(d) A conservation easement pursuant to Chapter 4 (commencing with Section 815) of Title 2.   *(Added by Stats.1982, c. 1268, p. 4672, § 1.)*

Law Revision Commission Comments

Subdivision (a) of Section 880.240 is drawn from Section 3–306(2) of the Uniform Simplification of Land Transfers Act (1977). Subdivision (a) makes clear that if a person in possession claims under another person, whether by lease, license or otherwise, the interest of the other person does not expire.

Subdivision (b) is drawn from Section 6 of the Model Marketable Title Act and Section 3–306(4) of the Uniform Act. The Comment to the Model Act states, "The exception as to claims of the United States would probably exist whether stated in the statute or not."

Subdivision (c) is comparable to provisions in a number of jurisdictions that have enacted marketable record title legislation. The interest of a public entity is not subject to fractionalization and the current address of the public entity is always known.

Subdivision (d) recognizes that a conservation easement may be created that is perpetual in duration. Section 815.2. (16 Cal.L.Rev.Comm. Reports 401).

Research References

Miller and Starr California Real Estate § 9:10, Expiration of the Power of Termination--In General.
Miller and Starr California Real Estate § 11:68, Constructive Notice of Interests Barred by the Statute of Limitations--"Ancient Documents" and the Marketable Record Title Act.
Miller and Starr California Real Estate § 10:130, Ancient Mortgages; Debt Secured by a Mortgage.
Miller and Starr California Real Estate § 10:132, Ancient Mortgages; Debt Secured by a Deed of Trust.
Miller and Starr California Real Estate § 11:117, Option Contracts.
Miller and Starr California Real Estate § 11:119, Executory and Installment Contracts--Expiration of the Recorded Memorandum.
12 Witkin, California Summary 10th Real Property § 337, (S 337) Enactment of Marketable Record Title Statute.
12 Witkin, California Summary 10th Real Property § 346, (S 346) Statutory Provisions.

§ 880.250.   Absolute nature of times prescribed; extending time; revival of interests

(a) The times prescribed in this title for expiration or expiration of record of an interest in real property or for enforcement, for bringing an action, or for doing any other required act are absolute and apply notwithstanding any disability or lack of knowledge of any person or any provisions for tolling a statute of limitation and notwithstanding any longer time applicable pursuant to any statute of limitation.

(b) Nothing in this title extends the period for enforcement, for bringing an action, or for doing any other required act, or revives an interest in real property that expires and is unenforceable, pursuant to any applicable statute of limitation.   *(Added by Stats.1982, c. 1268, p. 4672, § 1.)*

Law Revision Commission Comments

Subdivision (a) of Section 880.250 makes clear that there can be no off-record waivers, extensions, or tolling of the expiration time for, or enforceability of, an interest in real property pursuant to this title. While off-record waivers, extensions, or tolling (including partial payments in the case of a mortgage or deed of trust) may be effective for purposes of general statutes of limitation, they cannot extend the duration or enforceability of an interest past the times prescribed in this title. Whether a recorded waiver, extension, or tolling is effective depends upon the statute governing the particular interest. Compare Section 882.020 (waiver or extension of time for enforcement of mortgage or deed of trust) with Section 885.030 (no waiver or extension of time for expiration of power of termination).

Subdivision (b) is drawn from Section 7 of the Model Marketable Title Act and Section 3–308 of the Uniform Simplification of Land Transfers Act (1977). (16 Cal.L.Rev.Comm. Reports 401).

Research References

Miller and Starr California Real Estate § 9:5, Fee Simple Defeasible--Determinable Fee With Possibility of Reverter.
Miller and Starr California Real Estate § 11:68, Constructive Notice of Interests Barred by the Statute of Limitations--"Ancient Documents" and the Marketable Record Title Act.
Miller and Starr California Real Estate § 10:130, Ancient Mortgages; Debt Secured by a Mortgage.
Miller and Starr California Real Estate § 10:132, Ancient Mortgages; Debt Secured by a Deed of Trust.
Miller and Starr California Real Estate § 11:117, Option Contracts.
12 Witkin, California Summary 10th Real Property § 337, (S 337) Enactment of Marketable Record Title Statute.

§ 880.260.   Action or proceeding tolling expiration or expiration of record

An interest in real property, as specified in this title, does not expire or expire of record and is not unenforceable pursuant to this title at the time prescribed in this title if within the time an action is commenced to enforce, establish, clear title to, or otherwise affect the interest and a notice of the pendency of the action is recorded as provided by law. For the purpose of this section, action includes special proceeding and arbitration proceeding.   *(Added by Stats.1982, c. 1268, p. 4673, § 1.)*

Law Revision Commission Comments

Section 880.260 makes clear that there is no expiration of an interest in real property by operation of law pursuant to this title if a lis pendens is recorded before expiration. This is a specific application of the general provisions governing the effect of a lis pendens. See Code Civ.Proc. § 409. (16 Cal.L.Rev.Comm. Reports 401).

Research References

Rutter, Cal. Practice Guide: Real Prop. Transactions Ch. 3-F, F. Alternatives to Endorsements.
Miller and Starr California Real Estate § 9:10, Expiration of the Power of Termination--In General.
Miller and Starr California Real Estate § 11:68, Constructive Notice of Interests Barred by the Statute of Limitations--"Ancient Documents" and the Marketable Record Title Act.
Miller and Starr California Real Estate § 10:130, Ancient Mortgages; Debt Secured by a Mortgage.
Miller and Starr California Real Estate § 10:132, Ancient Mortgages; Debt Secured by a Deed of Trust.
Miller and Starr California Real Estate § 11:117, Option Contracts.

16 NO. 6 Miller & Starr, California Real Estate Newsalert 6, Deeds of Trust.
12 Witkin, California Summary 10th Real Property § 337, (S 337) Enactment of Marketable Record Title Statute.

ARTICLE 3.   PRESERVATION OF INTERESTS

Section
880.310.   Recordation of notice of intent.
880.320.   Persons entitled to record notice of intent.
880.330.   Requisites of notice of intent.
880.340.   Form of notice of intent.
880.350.   County of recording notice of intent.
880.360.   Slandering title; recording notice of intent.
880.370.   Extension of time for recordation of notice.

§ 880.310.   Recordation of notice of intent

(a) If the time within which an interest in real property expires pursuant to this title depends upon recordation of a notice of intent to preserve the interest, a person may preserve the person's interest from expiration by recording a notice of intent to preserve the interest before the interest expires pursuant to this title. Recordation of a notice of intent to preserve an interest in real property after the interest has expired pursuant to this title does not preserve the interest.

(b) Recordation of a notice of intent to preserve an interest in real property does not preclude a court from determining that an interest has been abandoned or is otherwise unenforceable pursuant to other law, whether before or after the notice of intent to preserve the interest is recorded, and does not validate or make enforceable a claim or interest that is otherwise invalid or unenforceable. Recordation of a notice of intent to preserve an interest in real property creates a presumption affecting the burden of proof that the person who claims the interest has not abandoned and does not intend to abandon the interest. *(Added by Stats.1982, c. 1268, p. 4673, § 1.)*

Law Revision Commission Comments

Subdivision (a) of Section 880.310 is drawn from Sections 2(d) and 4(a) of the Model Marketable Title Act and Sections 3–303(3) and 3–305 of the Uniform Simplification of Land Transfers Act (1977). Subdivision (a) imposes no limit on the number of times a notice of intent to preserve may be recorded; so long as the interest has not expired at the time of recordation, preservation of an interest in perpetuity is possible. If a person owns a part interest in real property, the notice of intent preserves only the part interest owned by the person for whom the notice is recorded. If a person owns an interest in real property that is one of several related interests in real property, the notice of intent preserves only the interest owned by the person for whom the notice is recorded and not the related interests of other persons. However, a person may record an interest on behalf of other owners of the interest, if so authorized by the others. See Section 880.320 (who may record notice).

Subdivision (b) is drawn from Section 3–309 of the Uniform Act, with the addition of language to make clear that a notice of intent to preserve does not affect the validity of any interest in real property under law apart from this title but that the notice creates a presumption against abandonment. [16 Cal.L.Rev.Comm. Reports 401].

Research References

Rutter, Cal. Practice Guide: Real Prop. Transactions Ch. 3-F, F. Alternatives to Endorsements.
Miller and Starr California Real Estate § 11:6, Instruments Subject to Recording--List of Recordable Documents.
Miller and Starr California Real Estate § 11:68, Constructive Notice of Interests Barred by the Statute of Limitations--"Ancient Documents" and the Marketable Record Title Act.
Miller and Starr California Real Estate § 10:130, Ancient Mortgages; Debt Secured by a Mortgage.
Miller and Starr California Real Estate § 10:132, Ancient Mortgages; Debt Secured by a Deed of Trust.
Miller and Starr California Real Estate § 11:117, Option Contracts.

12 Witkin, California Summary 10th Real Property § 349, Recordation of Notice.
4 Witkin, California Summary 10th Security Transactions in Real Property § 121, Mortgage.

§ 880.320.   Persons entitled to record notice of intent

A notice of intent to preserve an interest in real property may be recorded by any of the following persons:

(a) A person who claims the interest.

(b) Another person acting on behalf of a claimant if the person is authorized to act on behalf of the claimant or if the claimant is one of a class whose identity cannot be established or is uncertain at the time of recording the notice of intent to preserve the interest. *(Added by Stats.1982, c. 1268, p. 4673, § 1.)*

Law Revision Commission Comments

Section 880.320 is drawn from the third sentence of Section 4(a) of the Model Marketable Title Act and Section 3–305 of the Uniform Simplification of Land Transfers Act (1977). (16 Cal.L.Rev.Comm. Reports 401).

Research References

Miller and Starr California Real Estate § 11:68, Constructive Notice of Interests Barred by the Statute of Limitations--"Ancient Documents" and the Marketable Record Title Act.
Miller and Starr California Real Estate § 10:132, Ancient Mortgages; Debt Secured by a Deed of Trust.
12 Witkin, California Summary 10th Real Property § 349, Recordation of Notice.

§ 880.330.   Requisites of notice of intent

Subject to all statutory requirements for recorded documents:

(a) A notice of intent to preserve an interest in real property shall be in writing and signed and verified by or on behalf of the claimant. If the notice is made on behalf of a claimant, the notice shall include a statement of the authority of the person making the notice.

(b) The notice shall contain all of the following information:

(1) The name and mailing address of the claimant. If the notice is made by or on behalf of more than one claimant the notice shall contain the name and mailing address of each claimant.

(2) A statement of the character of interest claimed. The statement shall include a reference by record location to the recorded document that creates or evidences the interest in the claimant.

(3) A legal description of the real property in which the interest is claimed. The description may be the same as that contained in the recorded document that creates or evidences the interest in the claimant. *(Added by Stats.1982, c. 1268, p. 4673, § 1.)*

Law Revision Commission Comments

Section 880.330 is drawn from portions of Sections 4(a) and (5) of the Model Marketable Title Act and from Sections 2–302(b) and 2–308(b) of the Uniform Simplification of Land Transfers Act (1977). Under subdivision (b), if the interest is a restriction that affects the use or enjoyment of more than one parcel of real property that was created by a recorded document containing a general description of all of the parcels, the legal description required may be the same as the general description. The introductory portion of Section 880.330 makes clear that all other statutory requirements must be complied with. See, e.g., Section 1170 (recorded document must be duly acknowledged or proved and certified) (16 Cal.L.Rev.Comm. Reports 401).

Research References

Miller and Starr California Real Estate § 11:68, Constructive Notice of Interests Barred by the Statute of Limitations--"Ancient Documents" and the Marketable Record Title Act.

Miller and Starr California Real Estate § 10:130, Ancient Mortgages;
   Debt Secured by a Mortgage.
12 Witkin, California Summary 10th Real Property § 346, (S 346)
   Statutory Provisions.
12 Witkin, California Summary 10th Real Property § 348, (S 348)
   Statutory Provisions.
12 Witkin, California Summary 10th Real Property § 350, Content and
   Form of Notice.

§ 880.340. Form of notice of intent

Subject to all statutory requirements for recorded documents,
a notice of intent to preserve an interest in real property shall be
in substantially the following form:

RECORDING INFORMATION

Recording requested by: FOR USE OF COUNTY RE-
                                 CORDER

After recording return to:

                                 Indexing instructions.
                                 This notice must be indexed
                                    as follows:
                                 Grantor and grantee index-
                                    each claimant is a grantor.

NOTICE OF INTENT TO PRESERVE INTEREST

This notice is intended to preserve an interest in real property
from extinguishment pursuant to Title 5 (commencing with
Section 880.020) of Part 2 of Division 2 of the Civil Code
(Marketable Record Title).

Claimant   Name:
                Mailing address: (must be given for each
                   claimant)

Interest   Character (e.g., power of termination): Rec-
                   ord location of document creating or evi-
                   dencing interest in claimant:

Real Property   Legal description (may be same as in record-
                   ed document creating or evidencing interest
                   in claimant):

I assert under penalty of perjury that this notice is not recorded
for the purpose of slandering title to real property and I am
informed and believe that the information contained in this
notice is true. If this notice is made on behalf of a claimant, I
assert under penalty of perjury that I am authorized to act on
behalf of the claimant.

Signed: _____ Date: _____
           (claimant)

       _____
       (person acting on be-
       half of claimant)

Certificate of acknowledgment required.

*(Added by Stats.1982, c. 1268, p. 4674, § 1. Amended by
Stats.2012, c. 94 (A.B.1642), § 1.)*

Law Revision Commission Comments

Section 880.340 incorporates the requirements of Section 880.330
(contents of notice). The introductory portion of Section 880.340 makes
clear that all other statutory requirements must be complied with. See,
e.g., Gov't Code § 27351.6 (printed forms) (16 Cal.L.Rev.Comm. Reports
401).

Research References

Miller and Starr California Real Estate § 11:68, Constructive Notice of
   Interests Barred by the Statute of Limitations--"Ancient Documents"
   and the Marketable Record Title Act.
Miller and Starr California Real Estate § 10:130, Ancient Mortgages;
   Debt Secured by a Mortgage.
Miller and Starr California Real Estate § 10:132, Ancient Mortgages;
   Debt Secured by a Deed of Trust.
12 Witkin, California Summary 10th Real Property § 346, (S 346)
   Statutory Provisions.
12 Witkin, California Summary 10th Real Property § 348, (S 348)
   Statutory Provisions.
12 Witkin, California Summary 10th Real Property § 350, Content and
   Form of Notice.

§ 880.350. County of recording notice of intent

(a) A notice of intent to preserve an interest in real property
shall be recorded in the county in which the real property is
situated.

(b) The county recorder shall index a notice of intent to
preserve an interest in real property in the index of grantors and
grantees. The index entry shall be for the grantor, and for the
purpose of this index, the claimant under the notice shall be
deemed to be the grantor. If a notice of intent to preserve is
recorded by or on behalf of more than one claimant, each
claimant shall be deemed to be a grantor and a separate index
entry shall be made for each claimant. *(Added by Stats.1982, c.
1268, p. 4675, § 1.)*

Law Revision Commission Comments

Section 880.350 is drawn from a portion of Section 5 of the Model
Marketable Title Act. The manner of recording the notice is prescribed
in Government Code Section 27322 and the fee for recording is prescribed
in Government Code Section 27361 et seq. (16 Cal.L.Rev.Comm.
Reports 401).

Research References

Miller and Starr California Real Estate § 11:6, Instruments Subject to
   Recording--List of Recordable Documents.
Miller and Starr California Real Estate § 11:68, Constructive Notice of
   Interests Barred by the Statute of Limitations--"Ancient Documents"
   and the Marketable Record Title Act.
Miller and Starr California Real Estate § 10:130, Ancient Mortgages;
   Debt Secured by a Mortgage.
Miller and Starr California Real Estate § 10:132, Ancient Mortgages;
   Debt Secured by a Deed of Trust.
12 Witkin, California Summary 10th Real Property § 349, Recordation of
   Notice.

§ 880.360. Slandering title; recording notice of intent

A person shall not record a notice of intent to preserve an
interest in real property for the purpose of slandering title to the
real property. If the court in an action or proceeding to
establish or quiet title determines that a person recorded a
notice of intent to preserve an interest for the purpose of
slandering title, the court shall award against the person the cost
of the action or proceeding, including a reasonable attorney's
fee, and the damages caused by the recording. *(Added by
Stats.1982, c. 1268, p. 4675, § 1.)*

Law Revision Commission Comments

Section 880.360 is comparable to provisions in a number of jurisdictions
that have enacted marketable record title legislation, and makes clear that
recordation of a notice of intent to preserve an interest under this title is
not privileged. Section 880.360 does not affect the elements of the cause
of action for slander of title and codifies the measure of recovery for
slander of title, with the addition of reasonable attorney's fees. See 4 B.
Witkin, Summary of California Law Torts § 328 (8th ed. 1974). (16
Cal.L.Rev.Comm. Reports 401).

Research References

Miller and Starr California Real Estate § 11:68, Constructive Notice of Interests Barred by the Statute of Limitations--"Ancient Documents" and the Marketable Record Title Act.

Miller and Starr California Real Estate § 10:130, Ancient Mortgages; Debt Secured by a Mortgage.

Miller and Starr California Real Estate § 10:132, Ancient Mortgages; Debt Secured by a Deed of Trust.

12 Witkin, California Summary 10th Real Property § 351, Slander of Title by Recording.

§ 880.370.   Extension of time for recordation of notice

If the period prescribed by statute during which a notice of intent to preserve an interest in real property must be recorded expires before, on, or within five years after the operative date of the statute, the period is extended until five years after the operative date of the statute. *(Added by Stats.1982, c. 1268, p. 4675, § 1.)*

Law Revision Commission Comments

Section 880.370 is drawn from Section 10 of the Model Marketable Title Act and Section 7–101(d) of the Uniform Simplification of Land Transfers Act (1977) (two years) (16 Cal.L.Rev.Comm. Reports 401).

Research References

Miller and Starr California Real Estate § 9:10, Expiration of the Power of Termination--In General.

Miller and Starr California Real Estate § 11:68, Constructive Notice of Interests Barred by the Statute of Limitations--"Ancient Documents" and the Marketable Record Title Act.

Miller and Starr California Real Estate § 15:82, Abandonment by Nonuse for 20 Years.

Miller and Starr California Real Estate § 11:117, Option Contracts.

12 Witkin, California Summary 10th Real Property § 14, Interest Passing.

12 Witkin, California Summary 10th Real Property § 343, (S 343) Operative Date of Provisions.

12 Witkin, California Summary 10th Real Property § 349, Recordation of Notice.

CHAPTER 2.   ANCIENT MORTGAGES AND DEEDS OF TRUST

§ 882.020.   Expiration date; lien of security interest of record; power of sale deemed exercised

(a) Unless the lien of a mortgage, deed of trust, or other instrument that creates a security interest of record in real property to secure a debt or other obligation has earlier expired pursuant to Section 2911, the lien expires at, and is not enforceable by action for foreclosure commenced, power of sale exercised, or any other means asserted after, the later of the following times:

(1) If the final maturity date or the last date fixed for payment of the debt or performance of the obligation is ascertainable from the recorded evidence of indebtedness, 10 years after that date.

(2) If the final maturity date or the last date fixed for payment of the debt or performance of the obligation is not ascertainable from the recorded evidence of indebtedness, or if there is no final maturity date or last date fixed for payment of the debt or performance of the obligation, 60 years after the date the instrument that created the security interest was recorded.

(3) If a notice of intent to preserve the security interest is recorded within the time prescribed in paragraph (1) or (2), 10 years after the date the notice is recorded.

(b) For the purpose of this section, a power of sale is deemed to be exercised upon recordation of the deed executed pursuant to the power of sale.

(c) The times prescribed in this section may be extended in the same manner and to the same extent as a waiver made pursuant to Section 360.5 of the Code of Civil Procedure, except that an instrument is effective to extend the prescribed times only if it is recorded before expiration of the prescribed times. *(Added by Stats.1982, c. 1268, p. 4676, § 1. Amended by Stats.2006, c. 575 (A.B.2624), § 1.)*

Research References

California Real Estate Forms (Miller & Starr) § 3:8, Deed of Trust, Security Agreement, and Fixture Filing With Assignment of Rents and Agreements.

California Real Estate Forms (Miller & Starr) § 3:14, Construction Deed of Trust, Security Agreement, and Fixture Filing With Assignment of Rents and Agreements.

Rutter, Cal. Practice Guide: Real Prop. Transactions Ch. 3-F, F. Alternatives to Endorsements.

Miller and Starr California Real Estate § 11:6, Instruments Subject to Recording--List of Recordable Documents.

Miller and Starr California Real Estate § 11:68, Constructive Notice of Interests Barred by the Statute of Limitations--"Ancient Documents" and the Marketable Record Title Act.

Miller and Starr California Real Estate § 10:130, Ancient Mortgages; Debt Secured by a Mortgage.

Miller and Starr California Real Estate § 10:132, Ancient Mortgages; Debt Secured by a Deed of Trust.

13 NO. 5 Miller & Starr, California Real Estate Newsalert 5, Deeds of Trust.

16 NO. 6 Miller & Starr, California Real Estate Newsalert 6, Deeds of Trust.

16 NO. 3 Miller & Starr, California Real Estate Newsalert 13, Recording and Priorities.

16 NO. 4 Miller & Starr, California Real Estate Newsalert 26, Deeds of Trust.

17 NO. 4 Miller & Starr, California Real Estate Newsalert 2, Statutory Update:.

17 NO. 6 Miller & Starr, California Real Estate Newsalert 20, Table of Statutes (Newsalert Vol 17).

18 NO. 2 Miller & Starr, California Real Estate Newsalert 1, The Marketable Record Title Act- Is Private Foreclosure Barred Ten Years After Maturity, or Not?

20 NO. 3 Miller & Starr, California Real Estate Newsalert 10, Deeds of Trust.

21 NO. 4 Miller & Starr, California Real Estate Newsalert 25, Deeds of Trust.

3 Witkin Cal. Proc. 5th Actions § 430, (S 430) Types of Limitation Statutes.

12 Witkin, California Summary 10th Real Property § 338, Ancient Mortgages and Deeds of Trust.

4 Witkin, California Summary 10th Security Transactions in Real Property § 121, Mortgage.

4 Witkin, California Summary 10th Security Transactions in Real Property § 122, Deed of Trust.

§ 882.030.   Effect of expiration of lien of security interest

Expiration of the lien of a mortgage, deed of trust, or other security interest pursuant to this chapter or any other statute renders the lien unenforceable by any means commenced or asserted thereafter and is equivalent for all purposes to a certificate of satisfaction, reconveyance, release, or other discharge of the security interest, and execution and recording of a certificate of satisfaction, reconveyance, release, or other discharge is not necessary to terminate or evidence the termination of the security interest. Nothing in this section precludes execution and recording at any time of a certificate of satisfaction, reconveyance, release, or other discharge. *(Added by Stats.1982, c. 1268, p. 4676, § 1.)*

Research References

Rutter, Cal. Practice Guide: Real Prop. Transactions Ch. 3-F, F. Alternatives to Endorsements.

Miller and Starr California Real Estate § 11:68, Constructive Notice of Interests Barred by the Statute of Limitations--"Ancient Documents" and the Marketable Record Title Act.

Miller and Starr California Real Estate § 10:130, Ancient Mortgages; Debt Secured by a Mortgage.

Miller and Starr California Real Estate § 10:132, Ancient Mortgages; Debt Secured by a Deed of Trust.

16 NO. 4 Miller & Starr, California Real Estate Newsalert 26, Deeds of Trust.

18 NO. 2 Miller & Starr, California Real Estate Newsalert 1, The Marketable Record Title Act- Is Private Foreclosure Barred Ten Years After Maturity, or Not?

12 Witkin, California Summary 10th Real Property § 338, Ancient Mortgages and Deeds of Trust.

4 Witkin, California Summary 10th Security Transactions in Real Property § 122, Deed of Trust.

§ 882.040. Application of chapter

(a) Subject to Section 880.370 (grace period for recording notice) and except as otherwise provided in this section, this chapter applies on the operative date to all mortgages, deeds of trust, and other instruments that create a security interest in real property to secure a debt or other obligation, whether executed or recorded before, on, or after the operative date.

(b) This chapter shall not cause the lien of a mortgage, deed of trust, or other security interest in real property to expire or become unenforceable before the passage of five years after the operative date of this chapter. *(Added by Stats.1982, c. 1268, p. 4676, § 1.)*

Research References

Miller and Starr California Real Estate § 10:130, Ancient Mortgages; Debt Secured by a Mortgage.

Miller and Starr California Real Estate § 10:132, Ancient Mortgages; Debt Secured by a Deed of Trust.

12 Witkin, California Summary 10th Real Property § 338, Ancient Mortgages and Deeds of Trust.

4 Witkin, California Summary 10th Security Transactions in Real Property § 121, Mortgage.

CHAPTER 3.   MINERAL RIGHTS

ARTICLE 1.   GENERAL PROVISIONS

§ 883.110.   Mineral right defined

As used in this chapter, "mineral right" means an interest in minerals, regardless of character, whether fugacious or nonfugacious, organic or inorganic, that is created by grant or reservation, regardless of form, whether a fee or lesser interest, mineral, royalty, or leasehold, absolute or fractional, corporeal or incorporeal, and includes express or implied appurtenant surface rights. *(Added by Stats.1984, c. 240, § 2.)*

Law Revision Commission Comments

Section 883.110 defines mineral rights broadly to include a fee interest as well as any lesser interest and to include oil and gas as well as in-place minerals such as ores, metals, and coal. *Cf.* In re Waltz, 197 Cal. 263, 240 P. 19 (1925) (characterizing mineral rights). Section 883.110 also makes clear that for the purposes of this chapter, surface rights appurtenant to a mineral interest are included within the meaning of "mineral right." *Cf.* Callahan v. Martin, 3 Cal.2d 110, 43 P.2d 788 (1935) (grant of minerals includes implied right of entry to extract them). [17 Cal.L.Rev.Comm.Reports 957 (1984)].

Research References

Miller and Starr California Real Estate § 11:68, Constructive Notice of Interests Barred by the Statute of Limitations--"Ancient Documents" and the Marketable Record Title Act.

Miller and Starr California Real Estate § 17:21, Minerals--In General.

12 Witkin, California Summary 10th Real Property § 17, Fee Simple Absolute.

12 Witkin, California Summary 10th Real Property § 189, Other Limitations on Excluded Transactions.

12 Witkin, California Summary 10th Real Property § 346, (S 346) Statutory Provisions.

12 Witkin, California Summary 10th Real Property § 793, (S 793) Abandonment of Interest.

§ 883.120.   Application of chapter; mineral rights reserved to United States; mineral rights not subject to expiration

(a) This chapter does not apply to a mineral right reserved to the United States (whether in a patent, pursuant to federal law, or otherwise) or to an oil or gas lease, mining claim, or other mineral right of a person entitled pursuant thereto, to the extent provided in Section 880.240.

(b) This chapter does not apply to a mineral right of the state or a local public entity, or of any other person, to the extent provided in Section 880.240. *(Added by Stats.1984, c. 240, § 2.)*

Law Revision Commission Comments

Section 883.120 is a specific application of Section 880.240 (interest of United States and other interests not subject to expiration), and is included for purposes of cross-referencing. [17 Cal.L.Rev.Comm.Reports 957 (1984)].

Research References

Miller and Starr California Real Estate § 17:21, Minerals--In General.

12 Witkin, California Summary 10th Real Property § 346, (S 346) Statutory Provisions.

§ 883.130.   Abandoned mineral rights

Nothing in this chapter limits or affects the common law governing abandonment of a mineral right or any other procedure provided by statute for clearing an abandoned mineral right from title to real property. *(Added by Stats.1984, c. 240, § 2.)*

Law Revision Commission Comments

Section 883.130 makes clear that although this chapter includes a statute by which a dormant mineral right may be terminated (see Sections 883.210–883.270), this chapter is not intended to limit the common law of abandonment of mineral rights. See, e.g., Gerhard v. Stephens, 68 Cal.2d 864, 442 P.2d 692, 69 Cal.Rptr. 612 (1968) (mineral right in oil and gas subject to abandonment). Thus, for example, nothing in this article affects the common law determination of abandonment of an oil or gas lease. See, e.g., Banks v. Calstar Petroleum Co., 82 Cal.App.2d 789, 187 P.2d 127 (1947); Berry v. Kelly, 90 Cal.App.2d 486, 203 P.2d 80 (1949). Nor is this chapter the exclusive means by which title to property may be cleared of an abandoned mineral right. See, e.g., Code Civ.Proc. §§ 760.010–764.070 (quiet title). [17 Cal.L.Rev.Comm.Reports 957 (1984)].

Research References

Miller and Starr California Real Estate § 17:21, Minerals--In General.

12 Witkin, California Summary 10th Real Property § 346, (S 346) Statutory Provisions.

§ 883.140. Mineral right lease; expiration or abandonment; quitclaim deed

(a) As used in this section:

(1) "Lessee" includes an assignee or other successor in interest of the lessee.

(2) "Lessor" includes a successor in interest or heir or grantee of the lessor.

(b) If the term of a mineral right lease has expired or a mineral right lease has been abandoned by the lessee, the lessee shall, within 30 days after demand therefor by the lessor, execute, acknowledge, and deliver, or cause to be recorded, a deed quitclaiming all interest in and to the mineral rights covered by the lease. If the expiration or abandonment covers less than the entire interest of the lessee, the lessee shall execute, acknowledge, and deliver an appropriate instrument or notice of surrender or termination that covers the interest that has expired or been abandoned.

(c) If the lessee fails to comply with the requirements of this section, the lessee is liable for all damages sustained by the lessor as a result of the failure, including, but not limited to, court costs and reasonable attorney's fees in an action to clear title to the lessor's interest. The lessee shall also forfeit to the lessor the sum of one hundred fifty dollars ($150).

(d) Nothing in this section makes a quitclaim deed or other instrument or notice of surrender or termination, or a demand therefor, a condition precedent to an action to clear title to the lessor's interest. *(Added by Stats.1984, c. 240, § 2.)*

Law Revision Commission Comments

Section 883.140 continues the substance of former Section 794. *Cf.* Section 886.020 and Comment thereto (release of contract for sale of real property). [17 Cal.L.Rev.Comm.Reports 957 (1984)].

Research References

Miller and Starr California Real Estate § 17:21, Minerals--In General.
12 Witkin, California Summary 10th Real Property § 346, (S 346) Statutory Provisions.

ARTICLE 2. TERMINATION OF DORMANT MINERAL RIGHT

Section
883.210. Action to terminate dormant mineral right.
883.220. Dormant rights; conditions.
883.230. Notice of intent to preserve mineral right; effect.
883.240. Actions; place; procedure.
883.250. Late notice of intent to preserve mineral right; condition of dismissal of action.
883.260. Termination under article; effect.
883.270. Application of article.

§ 883.210. Action to terminate dormant mineral right

The owner of real property subject to a mineral right may bring an action to terminate the mineral right pursuant to this article if the mineral right is dormant. *(Added by Stats.1984, c. 240, § 2.)*

Law Revision Commission Comments

Section 883.210 authorizes termination of dormant mineral rights, subject to the limitations and conditions in this article. This is consistent with public policy to enable and encourage full use and development of real property, including both surface and subsurface interests. Section 880.020 (declaration of policy and purposes). Section 883.210 is also consistent with the common law rule that mineral rights in oil and gas are

subject to abandonment, and applies to mineral rights in other substances as well. See Sections 883.110 ("mineral right" defined) and 883.130 (law governing abandonment not affected) and Comments thereto; *cf.* Section 883.140 (clearing record of expired or abandoned mineral right lease). This article supplements common law principles of abandonment by providing a separate and independent basis for terminating a dormant mineral right. [17 Cal.L.Rev.Comm.Reports 957 (1984)].

Research References

Miller and Starr California Real Estate § 11:68, Constructive Notice of Interests Barred by the Statute of Limitations--"Ancient Documents" and the Marketable Record Title Act.
12 Witkin, California Summary 10th Real Property § 346, (S 346) Statutory Provisions.

§ 883.220. Dormant rights; conditions

For the purpose of this article, a mineral right is dormant if all of the following conditions are satisfied for a period of 20 years immediately preceding commencement of the action to terminate the mineral right:

(a) There is no production of the minerals and no exploration, drilling, mining, development, or other operations that affect the minerals, whether on or below the surface of the real property or on other property, whether or not unitized or pooled with the real property.

(b) No separate property tax assessment is made of the mineral right or, if made, no taxes are paid on the assessment.

(c) No instrument creating, reserving, transferring, or otherwise evidencing the mineral right is recorded. *(Added by Stats.1984, c. 240, § 2.)*

Law Revision Commission Comments

Section 883.220 defines dormancy for the purpose of this article; it does not affect the common law of abandonment. See Section 883.130 (law governing abandonment not affected). The 20-year period prescribed in Section 883.220 is consistent with the 20-year period prescribed by statute for termination of a right of entry or occupation of surface lands under an oil or gas lease. Code Civ.Proc. §§ 772.010–772.060. The 20-year period can be extended indefinitely by recordation of a notice of intent to preserve the mineral right. Section 883.230 (preservation of mineral right). [17 Cal.L.Rev.Comm.Reports 957 (1984)].

Research References

Miller and Starr California Real Estate § 11:68, Constructive Notice of Interests Barred by the Statute of Limitations--"Ancient Documents" and the Marketable Record Title Act.
Miller and Starr California Real Estate § 17:21, Minerals--In General.
12 Witkin, California Summary 10th Real Property § 346, (S 346) Statutory Provisions.

§ 883.230. Notice of intent to preserve mineral right; effect

(a) An owner of a mineral right may at any time record a notice of intent to preserve the mineral right.

(b) In lieu of the statement of the character of the interest claimed and the record location of the documents creating or evidencing the mineral rights claimed as otherwise required by paragraph (2) of subdivision (b) of Section 880.330 and in lieu of the legal description of the real property in which the interest is claimed as otherwise required by paragraph (3) of subdivision (b) of Section 880.330 and notwithstanding the provisions of Section 880.340 or any other provision in this title, a notice of intent to preserve a mineral right may refer generally and without specificity to any or all mineral rights claimed by claimant in any real property situated in the county.

(c) A mineral right is not dormant for the purpose of this article if:

(1) A notice of intent to preserve the mineral right is recorded within 20 years immediately preceding commencement of the action to terminate the mineral right.

(2) A notice of intent to preserve the mineral right is recorded pursuant to Section 883.250 after commencement of the action to terminate the mineral right. *(Added by Stats.1984, c. 240, § 2.)*

Law Revision Commission Comments

Section 883.230 makes recording a notice of intent to preserve a mineral right conclusive evidence of non-dormancy for purposes of this article. Recording a notice of intent to preserve also creates a presumption affecting the burden of proof that the claimant has not abandoned the mineral right for purposes of a determination of abandonment pursuant to common law. Section 880.310 (notice of intent to preserve interest). [17 Cal.L.Rev.Comm.Reports 957 (1984)].

Research References

Miller and Starr California Real Estate § 11:6, Instruments Subject to Recording--List of Recordable Documents.
Miller and Starr California Real Estate § 11:68, Constructive Notice of Interests Barred by the Statute of Limitations--"Ancient Documents" and the Marketable Record Title Act.
Miller and Starr California Real Estate § 17:21, Minerals--In General.
Miller and Starr California Real Estate § 25:26, Preparation and Filing of Parcel Maps.
12 Witkin, California Summary 10th Real Property § 346, (S 346) Statutory Provisions.

§ 883.240. Actions; place; procedure

(a) An action to terminate a mineral right pursuant to this article shall be brought in the superior court of the county in which the real property subject to the mineral right is located.

(b) The action shall be brought in the same manner and shall be subject to the same procedure as an action to quiet title pursuant to Chapter 4 (commencing with Section 760.010) of Title 10 of Part 2 of the Code of Civil Procedure, to the extent applicable. *(Added by Stats.1984, c. 240, § 2.)*

Law Revision Commission Comments

Section 883.240 incorporates, insofar as applicable, the general quiet title procedures for an action to terminate a dormant mineral right pursuant to this article. See Code Civ.Proc. §§ 760.010–764.070. [17 Cal.L.Rev.Comm.Reports 957 (1984)].

Research References

Miller and Starr California Real Estate § 17:21, Minerals--In General.
12 Witkin, California Summary 10th Real Property § 346, (S 346) Statutory Provisions.

§ 883.250. Late notice of intent to preserve mineral right; condition of dismissal of action

In an action to terminate a mineral right pursuant to this article, the court shall permit the owner of the mineral right to record a late notice of intent to preserve the mineral right as a condition of dismissal of the action, upon payment into court for the benefit of the owner of the real property the litigation expenses attributable to the mineral right or portion thereof as to which the notice is recorded. As used in this section, the term "litigation expenses" means recoverable costs and expenses reasonably and necessarily incurred in preparation for the action, including a reasonable attorney's fee. *(Added by Stats.1984, c. 240, § 2.)*

Research References

Miller and Starr California Real Estate § 11:68, Constructive Notice of Interests Barred by the Statute of Limitations--"Ancient Documents" and the Marketable Record Title Act.
Miller and Starr California Real Estate § 17:21, Minerals--In General.

12 Witkin, California Summary 10th Real Property § 346, (S 346) Statutory Provisions.

§ 883.260. Termination under article; effect

A mineral right terminated pursuant to this article is unenforceable and is deemed to have expired. A court order terminating a mineral right pursuant to this article is equivalent for all purposes to a conveyance of the mineral right to the owner of the real property. *(Added by Stats.1984, c. 240, § 2.)*

Law Revision Commission Comments

Section 883.260 makes clear that termination of a dormant mineral right has the effect of a reconveyance to the surface owner. See also Section 883.240 (court procedure) and Code Civ.Proc. §§ 764.010–764.070 (effect of quiet title judgment). [17 Cal.L.Rev.Comm.Reports 957 (1984)].

Research References

Miller and Starr California Real Estate § 17:21, Minerals--In General.
12 Witkin, California Summary 10th Real Property § 346, (S 346) Statutory Provisions.

§ 883.270. Application of article

Subject to Section 880.370 (grace period for recording notice), this article applies to all mineral rights, whether executed or recorded before, on, or after January 1, 1985. *(Added by Stats.1984, c. 240, § 2.)*

Law Revision Commission Comments

Section 883.270 makes clear the legislative intent to apply this article to mineral interests existing on the date this article becomes operative (January 1, 1985). Section 880.370 provides a five-year grace period for recording a notice of intent to preserve a mineral interest that would be subject to termination pursuant to this article before, on, or within five years after the operative date of this article. See Sections 883.230 (preservation of mineral right) and 880.370 (grace period for recording notice) and Comments thereto. [17 Cal.L.Rev.Comm.Reports 957 (1984)].

Research References

Miller and Starr California Real Estate § 11:68, Constructive Notice of Interests Barred by the Statute of Limitations--"Ancient Documents" and the Marketable Record Title Act.
Miller and Starr California Real Estate § 17:21, Minerals--In General.
12 Witkin, California Summary 10th Real Property § 346, (S 346) Statutory Provisions.

CHAPTER 4. UNEXERCISED OPTIONS

§ 884.010. Expiration date; recorded instrument

If a recorded instrument creates or gives constructive notice of an option to purchase real property, the option expires of record if no conveyance, contract, or other instrument that gives notice of exercise or extends the option is recorded within the following times:

(a) If the expiration date of the option is ascertainable from the recorded instrument, six months after that expiration date.

(b) If the expiration date of the option is not ascertainable from the recorded instrument or the recorded instrument indicates that the option provides no expiration date, six months after the date the instrument that creates or gives constructive notice of the option is recorded.

(c) This section shall become operative on January 1, 2013. *(Added by Stats.2011, c. 46 (S.B.284), § 3, operative Jan. 1, 2013.)*

Research References

California Real Estate Forms (Miller & Starr) § 1:13, Right of First Refusal Agreement.

California Real Estate Forms (Miller & Starr) § 1:14, Right of First Offer Agreement.

California Real Estate Forms (Miller & Starr) § 1:15, Option Agreement–Long Form.

California Real Estate Forms (Miller & Starr) § 1:24, Combination Purchase and Option Agreement–Residential Lots Being Acquired from a Bankrupt Seller.

California Real Estate Forms (Miller & Starr) § 1:56, Memorandum of Right of First Refusal.

California Real Estate Forms (Miller & Starr) § 1:57, Memorandum of Right of First Offer.

California Real Estate Forms (Miller & Starr) § 1:58, Memorandum of Option.

California Real Estate Forms (Miller & Starr) § 1:59, Memorandum of Exercise of Option.

California Real Estate Forms (Miller & Starr) § 2:40, Memorandum of Lease and Right of First Refusal, Right of First Offer, or Option to Purchase Property.

California Real Estate Forms (Miller & Starr) § 2:66, Residential Lease With Purchase Option.

Rutter, Cal. Practice Guide: Real Prop. Transactions Ch. 3-F, F. Alternatives to Endorsements.

Rutter, Cal. Practice Guide: Real Prop. Transactions Ch. 8-A, A. Overview.

Rutter, Cal. Practice Guide: Real Prop. Transactions Ch. 8-B, B. Options to Purchase.

Rutter, Cal. Practice Guide: Real Prop. Transactions Ch. 8-D, D. Preemptive Purchase Rights-Rights of First Refusal and Rights of First Offer.

Rutter, Cal. Practice Guide: Real Prop. Transactions Gen. Matls., Highlights.

Miller and Starr California Real Estate § 11:6, Instruments Subject to Recording--List of Recordable Documents.

Miller and Starr California Real Estate § 5:65, Authority of Representative Regarding Leases, Options, and Financing.

Miller and Starr California Real Estate § 11:68, Constructive Notice of Interests Barred by the Statute of Limitations--"Ancient Documents" and the Marketable Record Title Act.

Miller and Starr California Real Estate § 11:117, Option Contracts.

22 NO. 4 Miller & Starr, California Real Estate Newsalert 18, Recording and Priorities.

12 Witkin, California Summary 10th Real Property § 189, Other Limitations on Excluded Transactions.

12 Witkin, California Summary 10th Real Property § 325, Effect of Proper Recordation.

12 Witkin, California Summary 10th Real Property § 339, Unexercised Options.

14 Witkin, California Summary 10th Wills and Probate § 497, Authority to Grant Option.

§ 884.020. Effect of expiration of record

Upon the expiration of record of an option to purchase real property, the recorded instrument that creates or gives constructive notice of the option ceases to be notice to any person or to put any person on inquiry with respect to the exercise or existence of the option or of any contract, conveyance, or other writing that may have been executed pursuant to the option. *(Added by Stats.1982, c. 1268, p. 4677, § 1.)*

Law Revision Commission Comments

Section 884.020 continues the substance of a portion of former Section 1213.5. An option that has expired of record does not affect third persons but may still affect the parties to the option. See Section 884.010 (expiration of record) and Comment thereto. [16 Cal.L.Rev.Comm. Reports 401]

Research References

Rutter, Cal. Practice Guide: Real Prop. Transactions Ch. 3-F, F. Alternatives to Endorsements.

Rutter, Cal. Practice Guide: Real Prop. Transactions Ch. 8-A, A. Overview.

Rutter, Cal. Practice Guide: Real Prop. Transactions Ch. 8-B, B. Options to Purchase.

Rutter, Cal. Practice Guide: Real Prop. Transactions Ch. 8-D, D. Preemptive Purchase Rights-Rights of First Refusal and Rights of First Offer.

Miller and Starr California Real Estate § 11:6, Instruments Subject to Recording--List of Recordable Documents.

Miller and Starr California Real Estate § 11:68, Constructive Notice of Interests Barred by the Statute of Limitations--"Ancient Documents" and the Marketable Record Title Act.

Miller and Starr California Real Estate § 11:117, Option Contracts.

Miller and Starr California Real Estate § 11:119, Executory and Installment Contracts--Expiration of the Recorded Memorandum.

12 Witkin, California Summary 10th Real Property § 339, Unexercised Options.

§ 884.030. Application of chapter

(a) Except as otherwise provided in this section, this chapter applies on the operative date to all recorded instruments that create or give constructive notice of options to purchase real property, whether executed or recorded before, on, or after the operative date.

(b) This chapter shall not cause an option that expires according to its terms within one year before, on, or within one year after the operative date of this chapter to expire of record until one year after the operative date.

(c) This chapter shall not cause an option that provides no expiration date and that is recorded before the operative date of this chapter to expire of record until five years after the operative date of this chapter.

(d) Nothing in this chapter affects a recorded instrument that has ceased to be notice to any person or put any person on inquiry with respect to the exercise or existence of an option pursuant to former Section 1213.5 before the operative date of this chapter. *(Added by Stats.1982, c. 1268, p. 4677, § 1.)*

Law Revision Commission Comments

Subdivision (a) of Section 884.030 continues the effect of former Section 1213.5 to govern all options now in existence or hereafter created. Subdivision (b) is intended to protect fixed term option holders who may have relied on the one-year expiration period formerly provided in Section 1213.5. Subdivision (c) is intended to protect indefinite term option holders before the operative date of this statute from expiration until an adequate time after the operative date, during which time an exercise or extension of the option may be recorded. Subdivision (d) makes clear that this chapter does not revive options that have expired pursuant to prior law (16 Cal.L.Rev.Comm. Reports 401).

Research References

Miller and Starr California Real Estate § 11:6, Instruments Subject to Recording--List of Recordable Documents.

Miller and Starr California Real Estate § 5:65, Authority of Representative Regarding Leases, Options, and Financing.

12 Witkin, California Summary 10th Real Property § 339, Unexercised Options.

CHAPTER 5. POWERS OF TERMINATION

Section
885.070. Operative date; application of chapter; prior breach of restriction on fee simple estate.

§ 885.010. Definitions

(a) As used in this chapter:

(1) "Power of termination" means the power to terminate a fee simple estate in real property to enforce a restriction in the form of a condition subsequent to which the fee simple estate is subject, whether the power is characterized in the instrument that creates or evidences it as a power of termination, right of entry or reentry, right of possession or repossession, reserved power of revocation, or otherwise, and includes a possibility of reverter that is deemed to be and is enforceable as a power of termination pursuant to Section 885.020.

(2) "Power of termination" includes the power created in a transferee to terminate a fee simple estate in real property to enforce a restriction on the use of the real property in the form of a limitation or condition subsequent to which the fee simple estate is subject, whether the power is characterized in the instrument that creates or evidences it as an executory interest, executory limitation, or otherwise, and includes the interest known at common law as an executory interest preceded by a fee simple determinable.

(b) A power of termination is an interest in the real property.

(c) For the purpose of applying this chapter to other statutes relating to powers of termination, the terms "right of reentry," "right of repossession for breach of condition subsequent," and comparable terms used in the other statutes mean "power of termination" as defined in this section. *(Added by Stats.1982, c. 1268, p. 4677, § 1. Amended by Stats.1991, c. 156 (A.B.1577), § 15.)*

Law Revision Commission Comments

Section 885.010 redefines the right of entry as a power of termination, the more descriptive and technically accurate of the two terms. See, e.g., Parry v. Berkeley Hall School Foundation, 10 Cal.2d 422, 74 P.2d 55 (1937). Places in the code where old terminology is used include Sections 791 and 793 ("right of re-entry") and 1046 ("right of reentry, or of repossession for breach of condition subsequent").

Despite redefinition, the power of termination is an interest in property and is subject to provisions governing property interests. See, e.g., Section 699 (future interests pass by succession, will, and transfer). A power of termination is transferable whether it would be classified at common law as a right of entry or possibility of reverter. See Section 1046. This resolves uncertainty in the case law. See, e.g., Johnston v. City of Los Angeles, 176 Cal. 479, 168 P. 1047 (1917) and Victoria Hospital Assn. v. All Persons, 169 Cal. 455, 147 P. 124 (1915). (16 Cal.L.Rev.Comm. Reports 401).

Section 885.010 is amended to include an executory limitation on a fee simple within the scope of this chapter. The language of subdivision (a)(2) extends the definition of "power of termination" to include an executory interest created in a transferee of real property. For the purpose of this chapter, the inclusion of such executory interests extends the traditional use of the term "power of termination" beyond rights of entry and related interests that were retained by the grantor. The traditional description of an executory interest preceded by a fee simple determinable in subdivision (a)(2) makes the coverage of this provision complete. The fee simple determinable is abolished in Section 885.020. See Comment to Section 885.020.

Executory interests are also subject to the limitations provided in the statutory rule against perpetuities. See Prob.Code §§ 21202 (application of statutory rule), 21205 (90-year wait-and-see period). Thus, an executory interest that becomes invalid under the statutory rule against perpetuities may not be renewed under this chapter. Similarly, if an executory interest terminates under this chapter, it is fully terminated and does not continue for purposes of the statutory rule against perpetuities. See Section 885.060 (effect of expiration of power of termination). [21 Cal.L.Rev.Comm.Reports 53 (1991)].

§ 885.015. Application of chapter; power of termination

This chapter does not apply to any of the following:

(a) A power of termination conditioned upon the continued production or removal of oil or gas or other minerals.

(b) A power of termination as to separately owned improvements or fixtures conditioned upon the continued leasehold or possessory interest in the underlying land. *(Added by Stats.1982, c. 1268, p. 4678, § 1. Amended by Stats.1991, c. 156 (A.B.1577), § 16.)*

§ 885.020. Fees simple determinable and possibilities of reverter abolished

Fees simple determinable and possibilities of reverter are abolished. Every estate that would be at common law a fee simple determinable is deemed to be a fee simple subject to a restriction in the form of a condition subsequent. Every interest that would be at common law a possibility of reverter is deemed to be and is enforceable as a power of termination. *(Added by Stats.1982, c. 1268, p. 4678, § 1.)*

Law Revision Commission Comments

Section 885.020 abolishes the estate known at common law as the fee simple determinable and the interest known at common law as the possibility of reverter. Cf. Section 763 (estates tail abolished). Ky.Rev.Stats. § 381.218 (Baldwin 1979) (fee simple determinable and possibility of reverter abolished). These interests were recognized late in California jurisprudence and added little to California land law. See Dabney v. Edwards, 5 Cal.2d 1, 53 P.2d 962 (1935) (recognizing fee simple determinable and possibility of reverter). Section 885.020 applies to existing estates and interests as well as to those created after its enactment. See Section 885.070 (transitional provisions). Section 885.020 does not affect determinable life estates or determinable terms for years; it applies only to fee simple estates. See

Section 885.010 ("power of termination" defined). (16 Cal.L.Rev.Comm. Reports 401).

Research References

Rutter, Cal. Practice Guide: Real Prop. Transactions Ch. 3-F, F. Alternatives to Endorsements.

Miller and Starr California Real Estate § 9:4, Fee Simple Defeasible--In General.

Miller and Starr California Real Estate § 9:5, Fee Simple Defeasible--Determinable Fee With Possibility of Reverter.

Miller and Starr California Real Estate § 9:17, Estate Subject to Executory Limitation.

Miller and Starr California Real Estate § 9:27, Possibility of Reverter.

Miller and Starr California Real Estate § 9:28, Right of Re-Entry (Power of Termination).

12 Witkin, California Summary 10th Real Property § 16, in General.

12 Witkin, California Summary 10th Real Property § 129, (S 129) Terminology.

12 Witkin, California Summary 10th Real Property § 340, (S 340) Definitions.

§ 885.030. Expiration dates; recorded instruments; contrary provisions

(a) A power of termination of record expires at the later of the following times:

(1) Thirty years after the date the instrument reserving, transferring, or otherwise evidencing the power of termination is recorded.

(2) Thirty years after the date a notice of intent to preserve the power of termination is recorded, if the notice is recorded within the time prescribed in paragraph (1).

(3) Thirty years after the date an instrument reserving, transferring, or otherwise evidencing the power of termination or a notice of intent to preserve the power of termination is recorded, if the instrument or notice is recorded within 30 years after the date such an instrument or notice was last recorded.

(b) This section applies notwithstanding any provision to the contrary in the instrument reserving, transferring, or otherwise evidencing the power of termination or in another recorded document unless the instrument or other recorded document provides an earlier expiration date. *(Added by Stats.1982, c. 1268, p. 4678, § 1.)*

Law Revision Commission Comments

Section 885.030 provides for expiration of a power of termination after 30 years, notwithstanding a longer or indefinite period provided in the instrument reserving the power. The expiration period supplements the rule against perpetuities. The rule against perpetuities does not apply to reversionary powers of termination. See Strong v. Shatto, 45 Cal.App. 29, 187 P. 159 (1919); Prob.Code § 21225(g) (exclusion from statutory rule against perpetuities). Executory interests remain subject to the limitations provided in the statutory rule against perpetuities. See Comment to Section 885.010; Prob.Code §§ 21202 (application of statutory rule), 21205 (90-year wait-and-see period).

The expiration period runs from the date of recording rather than the date of creation of the power of termination because the primary purpose of Section 885.030 is to clear record title. The expiration period can be extended for up to 30 years at a time by recordation of a notice of intent to preserve the power of termination. See Section 880.310 (notice of intent to preserve interest). Recordation of a notice of intent to preserve the power of termination does not enable enforcement of a power that has expired because it has become obsolete due to changed conditions or otherwise. See Sections 880.310 (notice of intent to preserve interest), 885.040 (obsolete power of termination), & Comments.

For the effect of expiration of a power of termination pursuant to this section, see Section 885.060 (effect of expiration). This section does not affect conservation easements pursuant to Sections 815–816. See Section 880.240 (interests excepted from title) & Comment. See also Section 885.015 (exceptions from chapter) & Comment. [21 Cal.L.Rev.Comm. Reports 53 (1991)].

Research References

Rutter, Cal. Practice Guide: Real Prop. Transactions Ch. 3-F, F. Alternatives to Endorsements.

Miller and Starr California Real Estate § 11:6, Instruments Subject to Recording--List of Recordable Documents.

Miller and Starr California Real Estate § 26:5, Express Grant--In General.

Miller and Starr California Real Estate § 9:10, Expiration of the Power of Termination--In General.

Miller and Starr California Real Estate § 9:11, Expiration of the Power of Termination--Statute of Limitations.

Miller and Starr California Real Estate § 9:27, Possibility of Reverter.

Miller and Starr California Real Estate § 9:29, Remainders and Executory Interests (Powers of Termination).

Miller and Starr California Real Estate § 11:68, Constructive Notice of Interests Barred by the Statute of Limitations--"Ancient Documents" and the Marketable Record Title Act.

12 Witkin, California Summary 10th Real Property § 341, (S 341) Expiration.

§ 885.040. Obsolete powers; expiration; grants to public entities, etc.

(a) If a power of termination becomes obsolete, the power expires.

(b) As used in this section, a power of termination is obsolete if any of the following circumstances applies:

(1) The restriction to which the fee simple estate is subject is of no actual and substantial benefit to the holder of the power.

(2) Enforcement of the power would not effectuate the purpose of the restriction to which the fee simple estate is subject.

(3) It would be otherwise inequitable to enforce the power because of changed conditions or circumstances.

(c) No power of termination shall expire under this section during the life of the grantor if it arises from a grant by a natural person without consideration to a public entity or to a society, corporation, institution, or association exempt by the laws of this state from taxation. *(Added by Stats.1982, c. 1268, p. 4678, § 1.)*

Research References

Rutter, Cal. Practice Guide: Real Prop. Transactions Ch. 3-F, F. Alternatives to Endorsements.

Miller and Starr California Real Estate § 9:12, Defenses to Enforcement--Equitable Relief.

Miller and Starr California Real Estate § 9:15, Defenses to Enforcement--Change of Conditions.

Miller and Starr California Real Estate § 9:29, Remainders and Executory Interests (Powers of Termination).

Miller and Starr California Real Estate § 11:68, Constructive Notice of Interests Barred by the Statute of Limitations--"Ancient Documents" and the Marketable Record Title Act.

12 Witkin, California Summary 10th Real Property § 341, (S 341) Expiration.

§ 885.050. Exercise of power; notice or civil action; record

A power of termination shall be exercised only by notice or by civil action and, if the power of termination is of record, the exercise shall be of record. The notice shall be given, and any civil action shall be commenced, within five years after breach of the restriction to which the fee simple estate is subject, or such longer period as may be agreed to by the parties by a waiver or extension recorded before expiration of that period. *(Added by Stats.1982, c. 1268, p. 4678, § 1.)*

Law Revision Commission Comments

Section 885.050 provides that even if a power of termination is phrased in terms of a right of entry, the power may be exercised only by notice or by civil action. This is consistent with Sections 791 (notice) and 793 (action for possession). See also Jordan v. Talbot, 55 Cal.2d 597, 361 P.2d 20, 12 Cal.Rptr. 488 (1961) (right of entry in lease).

Section 885.050 makes clear that the statutory limitation period applicable to a power of termination is five years. Cf. Code Civ.Proc. §§ 319–320 (five years). Former law was not clear. Compare, e.g., 3 B. Witkin, Summary of California Law Real Property § 188, at 1926 (8th ed. 1973) (enforcement within a "reasonable time") and Lincoln v. Narom Development Co., 10 Cal.App.3d 619, 89 Cal.Rptr. 128 (1970) (statute of limitation not applicable) with 2 A. Bowman, Ogden's Revised California Real Property Law § 23.32 (1975) (five years pursuant to Code of Civil Procedure Section 320).

Although Section 885.050 prescribes the limitation period for exercise of a power of termination to enforce breach of a restriction, it does not otherwise affect the existence or continued vitality of the power of termination as to other breaches. Nor does Section 885.050 preclude earlier termination of a power of termination through waiver or estoppel. See Section 880.030(a) (application of waiver and estoppel). See, e.g., Santa Monica v. Jones, 104 Cal.App.2d 463, 232 P.2d 55 (1951) (waiver); Wedum-Aldahl Co. v. Miller, 18 Cal.App.2d 745, 64 P.2d 762 (1937) (waiver or estoppel); Hanna v. Rodeo Vallejo Ferry Co., 89 Cal.App. 462, 265 P. 287 (1928) (waiver or estoppel) (16 Cal.L.Rev.Comm. Reports 401).

Research References

Miller and Starr California Real Estate § 9:6, Fee Simple Defeasible--Fee Simple on Condition Subsequent.
Miller and Starr California Real Estate § 9:11, Expiration of the Power of Termination--Statute of Limitations.
Miller and Starr California Real Estate § 9:27, Possibility of Reverter.
Miller and Starr California Real Estate § 9:28, Right of Re-Entry (Power of Termination).
Miller and Starr California Real Estate § 9:35, Rule Against Perpetuities--Transfers and Interests Subject to the Rule.
12 Witkin, California Summary 10th Real Property § 20, (S 20) Breach, Termination, and Waiver.
12 Witkin, California Summary 10th Real Property § 342, (S 342) Exercise.

§ 885.060. Effect of expiration of power; application to equitable servitude; construction of law

(a) Expiration of a power of termination pursuant to this chapter makes the power unenforceable and is equivalent for all purposes to a termination of the power of record and a quitclaim of the power to the owner of the fee simple estate, and execution and recording of a termination and quitclaim is not necessary to terminate or evidence the termination of the power.

(b) Expiration of a power of termination pursuant to this chapter terminates the restriction to which the fee simple estate is subject and makes the restriction unenforceable by any other means, including, but not limited to, injunction and damages.

(c) However, subdivision (b) does not apply to a restriction for which a power of termination has expired under this chapter if the restriction is also an equitable servitude alternatively enforceable by injunction. Such an equitable servitude shall remain enforceable by injunction and any other available remedies, but shall not be enforceable by a power of termination. This subdivision does not constitute a change in, but is declaratory of, the existing law. However, nothing in this subdivision shall be construed to make enforceable any restriction prohibited or made unenforceable by other provisions of law, including Section 53. *(Added by Stats.1982, c. 1268, p. 4679, § 1. Amended by Stats.1990, c. 1114 (A.B.3220), § 1.)*

Law Revision Commission Comments

Section 885.060 provides for the clearing of record title to real property by operation of law after a power of termination has expired under Section 885.030 (expiration of power of termination). Title can be cleared by judicial decree prior to the time prescribed in Section 885.030 in case of an obsolete power of termination. See Section 885.040 (obsolete power of termination); Hess v. Country Club Park, 213 Cal. 613, 2 P.2d 782 (1931) (16 Cal.L.Rev.Comm. Reports 401).

Research References

Rutter, Cal. Practice Guide: Real Prop. Transactions Ch. 3-F, F. Alternatives to Endorsements.
Miller and Starr California Real Estate § 9:6, Fee Simple Defeasible--Fee Simple on Condition Subsequent.
Miller and Starr California Real Estate § 9:8, Fee Simple Defeasible--Power of Termination (Right of Re-Entry); Enforcement.
Miller and Starr California Real Estate § 26:5, Express Grant--In General.
Miller and Starr California Real Estate § 9:11, Expiration of the Power of Termination--Statute of Limitations.
Miller and Starr California Real Estate § 9:27, Possibility of Reverter.
Miller and Starr California Real Estate § 9:28, Right of Re-Entry (Power of Termination).
Miller and Starr California Real Estate § 11:68, Constructive Notice of Interests Barred by the Statute of Limitations--"Ancient Documents" and the Marketable Record Title Act.
Miller and Starr California Real Estate § 24:41, Expiration; Termination.
12 Witkin, California Summary 10th Real Property § 341, (S 341) Expiration.

§ 885.070. Operative date; application of chapter; prior breach of restriction on fee simple estate

(a) Subject to Section 880.370 (grace period for recording notice) and except as otherwise provided in this section, this chapter applies on the operative date to all powers of termination, whether executed or recorded before, on, or after the operative date.

(b) If breach of the restriction to which the fee simple estate is subject occurred before the operative date of this chapter and the power of termination is not exercised before the operative date of this chapter, the power of termination shall be exercised, or in the case of a power of termination of record, exercised of record, within the earlier of the following times:

(1) The time that would be applicable pursuant to the law in effect immediately prior to the operative date of this chapter.

(2) Five years after the operative date of this chapter.

(c) As used in this section, "operative date" means the operative date of this chapter as enacted or, with respect to any amendment of a section of this chapter, the operative date of the amendment. *(Added by Stats.1982, c. 1268, p. 4679, § 1. Amended by Stats.1991, c. 156 (A.B.1577), § 17.)*

Law Revision Commission Comments

Subdivision (a) of Section 885.070 makes clear the legislative intent to apply this chapter immediately to existing powers of termination. Section 880.370 provides a five-year grace period for recording a notice of intent to preserve a power of termination that expires by operation of this chapter before, on, or within five years after the operative date of this chapter.

Subdivision (b) provides a five-year grace period to enable enforcement of powers of termination that would be barred upon enactment of this chapter by the absolute limitation period for enforcement provided by Section 885.050 (time for exercise of power) and a shorter grace period for enforcement of powers of termination that would be barred within five years after enactment of this chapter (16 Cal.L.Rev.Comm. Reports 401).

Subdivision (c) is added to Section 885.070 to clarify the application of this section to executory interests included within the scope of this chapter by the amendment of Section 885.010. The effect is the same as the effect on powers of termination when this chapter was enacted. See 1982 Cal.Stat. ch. 1268, § 1. [21 Cal.L.Rev.Comm.Reports 53 (1991)].

Research References

Miller and Starr California Real Estate § 9:5, Fee Simple Defeasible--Determinable Fee With Possibility of Reverter.
Miller and Starr California Real Estate § 9:10, Expiration of the Power of Termination--In General.

12 Witkin, California Summary 10th Real Property § 343, (S 343) Operative Date of Provisions.

CHAPTER 6. UNPERFORMED CONTRACTS FOR SALE OF REAL PROPERTY

Section

886.010. Definitions.
886.020. Demand; release of unperformed contract; action to clear title.
886.030. Expiration date; recorded extension; waiver.
886.040. Effect of expiration of recorded contract.
886.050. Application of chapter; limitation on expiration of recorded contracts.

§ 886.010.   Definitions

As used in this chapter:

(a) "Contract for sale of real property" means an agreement wherein one party agrees to convey title to real property to another party upon the satisfaction of specified conditions set forth in the contract and which requires conveyance of title within one year from the date of formation of the contract, whether designated in the agreement a "contract for sale of real property," "land sale contract," "deposit receipt," "agreement for sale," "agreement to convey," or otherwise.

(b) "Recorded contract for sale of real property" includes the entire terms of a contract for sale of real property that is recorded in its entirety or is evidenced by a recorded memorandum or short form of the contract. *(Added by Stats.1982, c. 1268, p. 4679, § 1.)*

Law Revision Commission Comments

Section 886.010 is drawn from Sections 2985 and 2985.51 and Business and Professions Code Section 10029 (real property sales contracts), but applies only to contracts of a type not covered by the other sections (contracts to be performed within one year). The section also applies to agreements to convey that are dependent on performance of conditions other than payment of money. Real property sales contracts (not to be performed within one year), popularly called installment land contracts (not to be performed within one year. (16 Cal.L.Rev.Comm. Reports 401).

Research References

Miller and Starr California Real Estate § 11:68, Constructive Notice of Interests Barred by the Statute of Limitations--"Ancient Documents" and the Marketable Record Title Act.
Miller and Starr California Real Estate § 11:119, Executory and Install-ment Contracts--Expiration of the Recorded Memorandum.
12 Witkin, California Summary 10th Real Property § 344, Unperformed Contracts for Sale of Real Property.

§ 886.020.   Demand; release of unperformed contract; action to clear title

If the party to whom title to real property is to be conveyed pursuant to a recorded contract for the sale of real property fails to satisfy the specified conditions set forth in the contract and does not seek performance of the contract or restitution of amounts paid under the contract, the party shall, upon demand therefor made after the operative date of this chapter, execute a release of the contract, duly acknowledged for record, to the party who agreed to convey title. Willful violation of this section by the party to whom title is to be conveyed without good cause makes the party liable for the damages the party who agreed to convey title sustains by reason of the violation, including but not limited to court costs and reasonable attorney's fees in an action to clear title to the real property. Nothing in this section makes a release or a demand therefor a condition precedent to an action to clear title to the real property. *(Added by Stats.1982, c. 1268, p. 4679, § 1.)*

Law Revision Commission Comments

Section 886.020 is new. Cf. Section 2941 (reconveyance upon termi-nation of a mortgage or deed of trust); Section 1109 (reconveyance of estate on condition that is defeated by nonperformance). Section 886.020 is intended to enhance marketability of title clouded by an unperformed real property sales contract without the need to quiet title or await the lapse of the five-year period provided in Section 886.030 (expiration of record of unperformed contract for sale of real property). (16 Cal.L.Rev. Comm. Reports 401).

Research References

Miller and Starr California Real Estate § 11:119, Executory and Install-ment Contracts--Expiration of the Recorded Memorandum.
12 Witkin, California Summary 10th Real Property § 344, Unperformed Contracts for Sale of Real Property.

§ 886.030.   Expiration date; recorded extension; waiver

(a) Except as otherwise provided in this section, a recorded contract for sale of real property expires of record at the later of the following times:

(1) Five years after the date for conveyance of title provided in the contract or, if no date for conveyance of title is provided in the contract, five years after the last date provided in the contract for satisfaction of the specified conditions set forth in the contract.

(2) If there is a recorded extension of the contract within the time prescribed in paragraph (1), five years after the date for conveyance of title provided in the extension or, if no date for conveyance of title is provided in the extension, five years after the last date provided in the extension for satisfaction of the specified conditions set forth in the contract.

(b) The time prescribed in this section may be waived or extended only by an instrument that is recorded before expira-tion of the prescribed times. *(Added by Stats.1982, c. 1268, p. 4680, § 1.)*

Law Revision Commission Comments

Section 886.030 prescribes the maximum duration of a contract for sale of real property of record for purposes of marketability. The maximum duration does not affect the rights and obligations of the parties to the contract but only the effect of the recorded notice of the contract on third parties. See Section 886.040 (effect of expiration). Section 886.030 operates to clear record title of the contract after the time prescribed even though the general statute of limitation to enforce the contract may not have run due to tolling, possession by the purchaser, or for some other cause. The section does not extend the time provided by the general statute of limitation that applies to enforcement of a real property sales contract. See Code Civ.Proc. § 337(1) (four-year limitation period). The cloud on title of an unperformed real property sales contract, whether or not barred by the general statute of limitation, may be removed by judicial action or may be removed by operation of law after passage of the time prescribed in this section. See Section 886.040 (effect of expiration).

Subdivision (a) adopts the five-year period of the Model Act Limiting Encumbrances Arising from Recorded Land Contracts (Simes & Taylor 1960). The effect of subdivision (a) is to prescribe a maximum life for a real property sales contract based exclusively on the record for marketabil-ity of title purposes.

Subdivision (b) provides that a waiver or extension of the expiration date of a real property sales contract must be recorded to be effective. This accomplishes the purpose of enabling a determination of marketabili-ty based on the record alone. [16 Cal.L.Rev.Comm. Reports 401]

Research References

Rutter, Cal. Practice Guide: Real Prop. Transactions Ch. 3-F, F. Alternatives to Endorsements.
Miller and Starr California Real Estate § 11:68, Constructive Notice of Interests Barred by the Statute of Limitations--"Ancient Documents" and the Marketable Record Title Act.
Miller and Starr California Real Estate § 11:119, Executory and Install-ment Contracts--Expiration of the Recorded Memorandum.

12 Witkin, California Summary 10th Real Property § 344, Unperformed Contracts for Sale of Real Property.

§ 886.040. Effect of expiration of recorded contract

Upon the expiration of record of a recorded contract for sale of real property pursuant to this chapter, the contract has no effect, and does not constitute an encumbrance or cloud, on the title to the real property as against a person other than a party to the contract. *(Added by Stats.1982, c. 1268, p. 4680, § 1.)*

Law Revision Commission Comments

Section 886.040 is drawn from the Model Act Limiting Encumbrances Arising from Recorded Land Contracts (Simes & Taylor 1960). A contract for sale of real property that has expired of record does not affect third persons but may still affect the parties to the contract. See Section 886.030 (expiration of record of contract for sale of real property) and Comment thereto. In addition, expiration of record does not affect the interest of a person in possession of the real property. Section 880.240 (interests excepted from title). (16 Cal.L.Rev.Comm. Reports 401).

Research References

Miller and Starr California Real Estate § 11:68, Constructive Notice of Interests Barred by the Statute of Limitations--"Ancient Documents" and the Marketable Record Title Act.
Miller and Starr California Real Estate § 11:119, Executory and Installment Contracts--Expiration of the Recorded Memorandum.
12 Witkin, California Summary 10th Real Property § 344, Unperformed Contracts for Sale of Real Property.

§ 886.050. Application of chapter; limitation on expiration of recorded contracts

(a) Except as otherwise provided in this section, this chapter applies on the operative date to all recorded contracts for sale of real property, whether recorded before, on, or after the operative date.

(b) This chapter shall not cause a recorded contract for sale of real property to expire of record before the passage of two years after the operative date of this chapter. *(Added by Stats.1982, c. 1268, p. 4680, § 1.)*

Law Revision Commission Comments

Section 886.050 makes clear the legislative intent to apply this chapter immediately to existing contracts for sale of real property. It provides a two-year grace period to enable enforcement of contracts that would expire upon enactment of this chapter and a shorter grace period for enforcement of contracts that would expire within two years after enactment of this chapter. The two-year grace period does not operate as an extension of the statute of limitation itself. See Code Civ.Proc. §§ 337(1) (statute of limitation). Notwithstanding the grace period for expiration, a person required to execute a release of the contract pursuant to Section 886.020 (release of unperformed contract for sale of real property) has an immediate duty to do so upon request therefor upon the operative date of this chapter. (16 Cal.L.Rev.Comm. Reports 401).

Research References

12 Witkin, California Summary 10th Real Property § 344, Unperformed Contracts for Sale of Real Property.

CHAPTER 7. ABANDONED EASEMENTS

§ 887.010. Definition of "easement"

As used in this chapter, "easement" means a burden or servitude upon land, whether or not attached to other land as an incident or appurtenance, that allows the holder of the burden or servitude to do acts upon the land. *(Added by Stats.1985, c. 157, § 2.)*

Law Revision Commission Comments

Section 887.010 provides a special definition of an easement for the purposes of this chapter. This chapter applies to affirmative easements, whether appurtenant or in gross. Contrast Sections 801 and 803 ("easement" is an appurtenant servitude). Negative easements are not governed by this chapter. [18 Cal.L.Rev.Comm. Reports 257 (1985)].

Research References

Rutter, Cal. Practice Guide: Real Prop. Transactions Ch. 3-F, F. Alternatives to Endorsements.
Miller and Starr California Real Estate § 15:5, Definition and Nature of an Easement.
Miller and Starr California Real Estate § 11:68, Constructive Notice of Interests Barred by the Statute of Limitations--"Ancient Documents" and the Marketable Record Title Act.
Miller and Starr California Real Estate § 15:82, Abandonment by Nonuse for 20 Years.
12 Witkin, California Summary 10th Real Property § 189, Other Limitations on Excluded Transactions.
12 Witkin, California Summary 10th Real Property § 348, (S 348) Statutory Provisions.
12 Witkin, California Summary 10th Real Property § 422, (S 422) Private Easement.

§ 887.020. Application of chapter

This chapter does not apply to an easement that is part of a unified or reciprocal system for the mutual benefit of multiple parties. *(Added by Stats.1985, c. 157, § 2.)*

Law Revision Commission Comments

Section 887.020 is intended to exclude planned developments and their sets of interrelated easements and servitudes from the scope of this chapter. Thus condominium covenants, conditions, and restrictions would not be covered, nor would reciprocal easement agreements.

Easements held by public entities and conservation easements are not subject to expiration pursuant to this section. See Section 880.240 (interests excepted from title); Section 887.080 (abandoned easement deemed to have expired). [18 Cal.L.Rev.Comm. Reports 257 (1985)].

Research References

Miller and Starr California Real Estate § 11:68, Constructive Notice of Interests Barred by the Statute of Limitations--"Ancient Documents" and the Marketable Record Title Act.
Miller and Starr California Real Estate § 15:79, Abandonment of Private Easements.
Miller and Starr California Real Estate § 15:82, Abandonment by Nonuse for 20 Years.
12 Witkin, California Summary 10th Real Property § 348, (S 348) Statutory Provisions.

§ 887.030. Common law

This chapter supplements and does not limit or otherwise affect the common law governing abandonment of an easement or any other procedure provided by statute or otherwise for clearing an abandoned easement from title to real property. *(Added by Stats.1985, c. 157, § 2.)*

Law Revision Commission Comments

Section 887.030 makes clear that although this chapter prescribes a standard for determining that an easement has been abandoned, it is not intended to limit the common law of abandonment of easements. See discussion in 3 B. Witkin, Summary of California Law *Real Property* §§ 374–376 (8th ed. 1973); 1 A. Bowman, Ogden's Revised California Real Property Law §§ 13.49–13.50 (1974); 3 H. Miller & M. Starr,

Current Law of California Real Estate §§ 18:64–18:66 (rev.1977). [18 Cal.L.Rev.Comm. Reports 257 (1985)].

Research References

Miller and Starr California Real Estate § 11:68, Constructive Notice of Interests Barred by the Statute of Limitations--"Ancient Documents" and the Marketable Record Title Act.

Miller and Starr California Real Estate § 15:79, Abandonment of Private Easements.

Miller and Starr California Real Estate § 15:82, Abandonment by Nonuse for 20 Years.

12 Witkin, California Summary 10th Real Property § 348, (S 348) Statutory Provisions.

§ 887.040. Bringing action; venue; procedure

(a) The owner of real property subject to an easement may bring an action to establish the abandonment of the easement and to clear record title of the easement.

(b) The action shall be brought in the superior court of the county in which the real property subject to the easement is located.

(c) The action shall be brought in the same manner and shall be subject to the same procedure as an action to quiet title pursuant to Chapter 4 (commencing with Section 760.010) of Title 10 of Part 2 of the Code of Civil Procedure, to the extent applicable. *(Added by Stats.1985, c. 157, § 2.)*

Law Revision Commission Comments

Subdivision (a) of Section 887.040 authorizes an action to establish abandonment of an easement, subject to the limitations and conditions in this chapter. This is consistent with public policy to enable and encourage full use and development of real property. Section 880.020 (declaration of policy and purposes). This is also consistent with the common law rule that easements are subject to abandonment. See Section 887.030 and Comment thereto (common law of abandonment not affected). This chapter supplements common law principles of abandonment by providing a separate and independent basis for determining abandonment of an easement.

Subdivisions (b) and (c) incorporate, insofar as applicable, the general quiet title procedures for an action pursuant to this chapter. See Code Civ.Proc. §§ 760.010–764.070. [18 Cal.L.Rev.Comm. Reports 257 (1985)].

Research References

Rutter, Cal. Practice Guide: Real Prop. Transactions Ch. 3-F, F. Alternatives to Endorsements.

Miller and Starr California Real Estate § 15:79, Abandonment of Private Easements.

Miller and Starr California Real Estate § 15:82, Abandonment by Nonuse for 20 Years.

12 Witkin, California Summary 10th Real Property § 348, (S 348) Statutory Provisions.

§ 887.050. Conditions necessary

(a) For purposes of this chapter, an easement is abandoned if all of the following conditions are satisfied for a period of 20 years immediately preceding commencement of the action to establish abandonment of the easement:

(1) The easement is not used at any time.

(2) No separate property tax assessment is made of the easement or, if made, no taxes are paid on the assessment.

(3) No instrument creating, reserving, transferring, or otherwise evidencing the easement is recorded.

(b) This section applies notwithstanding any provision to the contrary in the instrument creating, reserving, transferring, or otherwise evidencing the easement or in another recorded document, unless the instrument or other document provides an earlier expiration date. *(Added by Stats.1985, c. 157, § 2.)*

Law Revision Commission Comments

Section 887.050 provides for expiration of an unused easement after 20 years, notwithstanding a longer or an indefinite period provided in the instrument creating the easement. This reverses prior law that an easement obtained by grant cannot be lost by mere nonuse. See, *e.g.*, discussion in 3 B. Witkin, Summary of California Law *Real Property* § 376 (8th ed. 1973); 1 A. Bowman, Ogden's Revised California Real Property Law § 13.49 (1974); 3 H. Miller & M. Starr, Current Law of California Real Estate § 18:66 (rev. 1977).

The expiration period can be extended for up to 20 years at a time by recordation of a notice of intent to preserve the easement before the easement expires. See Section 887.060 (preservation of easement). Recordation of a notice of intent to preserve the easement does not necessarily preclude abandonment of the easement pursuant to general principles governing abandonment for nonuse upon a showing of intent to abandon. See Section 880.310 (notice of intent to preserve interest); see also discussion in 3 B. Witkin, Summary of California Law *Real Property* § 374 (8th ed. 1973); 1 A. Bowman, Ogden's Revised California Real Property Law § 13.50 (1974); and 3 H. Miller & M. Starr, Current Law of California Real Estate § 18:64 (rev.1977).

For purposes of subdivision (a)(3), in the case of an appurtenant easement, a transfer of the dominant tenement without reference to the easement does not start the 20–year period running anew, even though such a transfer may be effective to convey the easement. Sections 1084, 1104. [18 Cal.L.Rev.Comm. Reports 257 (1985)].

Research References

Rutter, Cal. Practice Guide: Real Prop. Transactions Ch. 3-F, F. Alternatives to Endorsements.

Miller and Starr California Real Estate § 11:68, Constructive Notice of Interests Barred by the Statute of Limitations--"Ancient Documents" and the Marketable Record Title Act.

Miller and Starr California Real Estate § 15:79, Abandonment of Private Easements.

Miller and Starr California Real Estate § 15:82, Abandonment by Nonuse for 20 Years.

12 Witkin, California Summary 10th Real Property § 348, (S 348) Statutory Provisions.

12 Witkin, California Summary 10th Real Property § 424, Nonuse.

§ 887.060. Notice of intent to preserve easement; recording

(a) The owner of an easement may at any time record a notice of intent to preserve the easement.

(b) In lieu of the statement of the character of the interest claimed and the record location of the documents creating or evidencing the easement claimed, as otherwise required by paragraph (2) of subdivision (b) of Section 880.330, and in lieu of the legal description of the real property in which the interest is claimed, as otherwise required by paragraph (3) of subdivision (b) of Section 880.330, and notwithstanding the provisions of Section 880.340, or any other provision in this title, a notice of intent to preserve an easement may refer generally and without specificity to any or all easements claimed by the claimant in any real property situated in the county.

(c) An easement is not abandoned for purposes of this chapter if either of the following occurs:

(1) A notice of intent to preserve the easement is recorded within 20 years immediately preceding commencement of the action to establish the abandonment of the easement.

(2) A notice of intent to preserve the easement is recorded pursuant to Section 887.070 after commencement of the action to establish the abandonment of the easement and before judgment is entered in the action. *(Added by Stats.1985, c. 157, § 2.)*

Law Revision Commission Comments

Section 887.060 makes recording a notice of intent to preserve an easement conclusive evidence of non-abandonment for purposes of this chapter. Recording a notice of intent to preserve also creates a presumption affecting the burden of proof that the claimant has not abandoned the easement for purposes of a determination of abandonment pursuant to common law. Section 880.310 (notice of intent to preserve interest). [18 Cal.L.Rev.Comm. Reports 257 (1985)].

Research References

Rutter, Cal. Practice Guide: Real Prop. Transactions Ch. 3-F, F. Alternatives to Endorsements.
Miller and Starr California Real Estate § 11:68, Constructive Notice of Interests Barred by the Statute of Limitations--"Ancient Documents" and the Marketable Record Title Act.
Miller and Starr California Real Estate § 15:79, Abandonment of Private Easements.
Miller and Starr California Real Estate § 15:82, Abandonment by Nonuse for 20 Years.
12 Witkin, California Summary 10th Real Property § 348, (S 348) Statutory Provisions.

§ 887.070.   Late notice of intent to preserve easement; recording; litigation expenses

In an action to establish the abandonment of an easement pursuant to this chapter, the court shall permit the owner of the easement to record a late notice of intent to preserve the easement as a condition of dismissal of the action, upon payment into court for the benefit of the owner of the real property the litigation expenses attributable to the easement or portion thereof as to which the notice is recorded. As used in this section, the term "litigation expenses" means recoverable costs and expenses reasonably and necessarily incurred in preparation for the action, including a reasonable attorney's fee. *(Added by Stats.1985, c. 157, § 2.)*

Law Revision Commission Comments

Section 887.070 enables the owner of an easement to preserve the easement, after commencement of an action to establish its abandonment and clear title, by filing a late notice of intent to preserve the interest. This authority is conditioned upon payment of the property owner's litigation expenses. Litigation expenses include disbursements made for title reports and other disbursements made in preparation for the litigation as well as court costs and attorneys fees incurred in connection with the litigation. [18 Cal.L.Rev.Comm. Reports 257 (1985)].

Research References

Rutter, Cal. Practice Guide: Real Prop. Transactions Ch. 3-F, F. Alternatives to Endorsements.
Miller and Starr California Real Estate § 11:68, Constructive Notice of Interests Barred by the Statute of Limitations--"Ancient Documents" and the Marketable Record Title Act.
Miller and Starr California Real Estate § 15:79, Abandonment of Private Easements.
Miller and Starr California Real Estate § 15:82, Abandonment by Nonuse for 20 Years.
16 NO. 5 Miller & Starr, California Real Estate Newsalert 9, Easements.
12 Witkin, California Summary 10th Real Property § 348, (S 348) Statutory Provisions.

§ 887.080.   Court order; enforceability

An abandoned easement is unenforceable and is deemed to have expired. A court order establishing abandonment of an easement pursuant to this chapter is equivalent for all purposes to a conveyance of the easement to the owner of the real property. *(Added by Stats.1985, c. 157, § 2.)*

Law Revision Commission Comments

Section 887.080 makes clear that establishment of abandonment of an easement has the effect of a reconveyance to the owner of the land. See also Section 887.040 (action authorized) and Code Civ.Proc. §§ 764.010–764.070 (effect of quiet title judgment). [18 Cal.L.Rev.Comm. Reports 257 (1985)].

Research References

Miller and Starr California Real Estate § 15:79, Abandonment of Private Easements.

Miller and Starr California Real Estate § 15:82, Abandonment by Nonuse for 20 Years.
12 Witkin, California Summary 10th Real Property § 348, (S 348) Statutory Provisions.

§ 887.090.   Application of chapter; exceptions

Subject to Sections 880.370 (grace period for recording notice) and 887.020, this chapter applies to all easements, whether executed or recorded before, on, or after January 1, 1986. *(Added by Stats.1985, c. 157, § 2.)*

Law Revision Commission Comments

Section 887.090 makes clear the legislative intent to apply this chapter to easements existing on the date this chapter becomes operative (January 1, 1986). Section 880.370 provides a five-year grace period for recording a notice of intent to preserve an easement that would be subject to termination pursuant to this chapter before, on, or within five years after the operative date of this chapter. See Sections 887.060 (preservation of easement) and 880.370 (grace period for recording notice) and Comments thereto. [18 Cal.L.Rev.Comm. Reports 257 (1985)].

Research References

Miller and Starr California Real Estate § 9:34, Rule Against Perpetuities--In General.
Miller and Starr California Real Estate § 11:68, Constructive Notice of Interests Barred by the Statute of Limitations--"Ancient Documents" and the Marketable Record Title Act.
Miller and Starr California Real Estate § 15:82, Abandonment by Nonuse for 20 Years.
12 Witkin, California Summary 10th Real Property § 348, (S 348) Statutory Provisions.

Title 6

RENT SKIMMING

Section
890.   Definitions.
891.   Civil rights and remedies; invalidity of waiver; applicability of statutes.
892.   Criminal penalties; prior convictions; limitations; other remedies or penalties.
893.   Affirmative defense; burden of producing evidence, burden of proof.
894.   Severability.

§ 890.   Definitions

(a)(1) "Rent skimming" means using revenue received from the rental of a parcel of residential real property at any time during the first year period after acquiring that property without first applying the revenue or an equivalent amount to the payments due on all mortgages and deeds of trust encumbering that property.

(2) For purposes of this section, "rent skimming" also means receiving revenue from the rental of a parcel of residential real property where the person receiving that revenue, without the consent of the owner or owner's agent, asserted possession or ownership of the residential property, whether under a false claim of title, by trespass, or any other unauthorized means, rented the property to another, and collected rents from the other person for the rental of the property. This paragraph does not apply to any tenant, subtenant, lessee, sublessee, or assignee, nor to any other hirer having a lawful occupancy interest in the residential dwelling.

(b) "Multiple acts of rent skimming" means knowingly and willfully rent skimming with respect to each of five or more parcels of residential real property acquired within any two-year period.

(c) "Person" means any natural person, any form of business organization, its officers and directors, and any natural person who authorizes rent skimming or who, being in a position of control, fails to prevent another from rent skimming. *(Added by Stats.1986, c. 838, § 1. Amended by Stats.1998, c. 193 (A.B.583), § 1.)*

Research References

California Real Estate Forms (Miller & Starr) § 3:8, Deed of Trust, Security Agreement, and Fixture Filing With Assignment of Rents and Agreements.
California Real Estate Forms (Miller & Starr) § 3:9, Assignment of Lessor's Interest in Leases and Seller's Interest in Contracts for Sale.
California Real Estate Forms (Miller & Starr) § 3:14, Construction Deed of Trust, Security Agreement, and Fixture Filing With Assignment of Rents and Agreements.
California Real Estate Forms (Miller & Starr) § 3:22, Assignment of Leases and Rents–Conduit Loans.
Miller and Starr California Real Estate § 10:62, Rent Skimming.
Miller and Starr California Real Estate § 16:26, Capacity; Quiet Title Action by an Adverse Possessor.
Miller and Starr California Real Estate § 19:84, Persons Entitled to Receive Rent--Rent Skimming.
4 Witkin, California Summary 10th Security Transactions in Real Property § 96, Rent Skimming.
7 Witkin, California Summary 10th Constitutional Law § 201, Economic Oppression.

§ 891. Civil rights and remedies; invalidity of waiver; applicability of statutes

(a) A seller of an interest in residential real property who received a promissory note or other evidence of indebtedness for all or a portion of its purchase price secured by a lien on the property may bring an action against any person who has engaged in rent skimming with respect to that property. A seller who prevails in the action shall recover all actual damages and reasonable attorney's fees and costs. The court may award any appropriate equitable relief. The court shall award exemplary damages of not less than three times the actual damages if the defendant has engaged in multiple acts of rent skimming and may award exemplary damages in other cases.

(b) A seller of an interest in residential real property who reacquires the interest from a person who has engaged in rent skimming with respect to that property, or a law enforcement agency, may request the court for an order declaring that the reacquired interest is not encumbered by any lien that is or has the effect of a judgment lien against the person who engaged in rent skimming if the lien is not related to any improvement of the property and does not represent security for loan proceeds made by a bona fide lien holder without knowledge of facts constituting a violation of this title. The motion or application shall be made with at least 30 days' advance written notice to all persons who may be affected by the order, including lienholders, and shall be granted unless the interests of justice would not be served by such an order.

(c) A mortgagee or beneficiary under a deed of trust encumbering residential real property may bring an action against a person who has engaged in rent skimming with respect to that property as one of multiple acts of rent skimming, whether or not the person has become contractually bound by an obligation secured by the mortgage or deed of trust. The mortgagee or beneficiary who prevails in the action shall recover actual damages to the extent of the amount of the rent collected on the encumbered property and attorney's fees and costs. The court also may order any appropriate equitable relief and may award exemplary damages.

(d) A tenant of residential real property may bring an action against a person who has engaged in rent skimming with respect to that property for the recovery of actual damages, including any security, as defined in Section 1950.5, and moving expenses if the property is sold at a foreclosure sale and the tenant was required to move. A prevailing plaintiff in such an action shall be awarded reasonable attorney's fees and costs. The court also may award exemplary damages; it shall award exemplary damages of at least three times the amount of actual damages if the payments due under any deed of trust or mortgage were two or more months delinquent at the time the tenant rented the premises or if the defendant has engaged in multiple acts of rent skimming.

(e) The rights and remedies provided in this section are in addition to any other rights and remedies provided by law.

(f) Rent skimming is unlawful, and any waiver of the provisions of this section are void and unenforceable as contrary to public policy.

(g) Sections 580a, 580b, 580d, and 726 of the Code of Civil Procedure do not apply to any action brought under this title. *(Added by Stats.1986, c. 838, § 1.)*

Research References

Miller and Starr California Real Estate § 10:62, Rent Skimming.
Miller and Starr California Real Estate § 19:84, Persons Entitled to Receive Rent--Rent Skimming.
4 Witkin, California Summary 10th Security Transactions in Real Property § 96, Rent Skimming.

§ 892. Criminal penalties; prior convictions; limitations; other remedies or penalties

(a) Any person who engages in multiple acts of rent skimming is subject to criminal prosecution. Each act of rent skimming comprising the multiple acts of rent skimming shall be separately alleged. A person found guilty of five acts shall be punished by imprisonment pursuant to subdivision (h) of Section 1170 of the Penal Code or by imprisonment in a county jail for not more than one year, by a fine of not more than ten thousand dollars ($10,000), or by both that fine and imprisonment. A person found guilty of additional acts shall be separately punished for each additional act by imprisonment pursuant to subdivision (h) of Section 1170 of the Penal Code or by imprisonment in a county jail for not more than one year, by a fine of not more than ten thousand dollars ($10,000), or by both that fine and imprisonment.

(b) If a defendant has been once previously convicted of a violation of subdivision (a), any subsequent knowing and willful act of rent skimming shall be punishable by imprisonment pursuant to subdivision (h) of Section 1170 of the Penal Code or by imprisonment in a county jail for not more than one year, or by a fine of not more than ten thousand dollars ($10,000), or by both that fine and imprisonment.

(c) A prosecution for a violation of this section shall be commenced within three years after the date of the acquisition of the last parcel of property that was the subject of the conduct for which the defendant is prosecuted.

(d) The penalties under this section are in addition to any other remedies or penalties provided by law for the conduct proscribed by this section. *(Added by Stats.1986, c. 838, § 1. Amended by Stats.2011, c. 15 (A.B.109), § 31, eff. April 4, 2011, operative Oct. 1, 2011.)*

Research References

Miller and Starr California Real Estate § 10:62, Rent Skimming.
Miller and Starr California Real Estate § 16:26, Capacity; Quiet Title Action by an Adverse Possessor.
Miller and Starr California Real Estate § 19:84, Persons Entitled to Receive Rent--Rent Skimming.

4 Witkin, California Summary 10th Security Transactions in Real Property § 96, Rent Skimming.

§ 893. Affirmative defense; burden of producing evidence, burden of proof

(a) It is an affirmative defense for a natural person who is a defendant in a civil action brought under Section 891, or a criminal action brought under Section 892, if all of the following occurred:

(1) The defendant used the rental revenue due but not paid to holders of mortgages or deeds of trust to make payments to any of the following:

(A) Health care providers, as defined in paragraph (2) of subdivision (c) of Section 6146 of the Business and Professions Code, for the unforeseen and necessary medical treatment of the defendant or his or her spouse, parents, or children.

(B) Licensed contractors or material suppliers to correct the violation of any statute, ordinance, or regulation relating to the habitability of the premises.

(2) The defendant made the payments within 30 days of receiving the rental revenue.

(3) The defendant had no other source of funds from which to make the payments.

(b) The defendant has the burden of producing evidence of each element of the defense specified in subdivision (a) in a criminal action under Section 892 and the burden of proof of each element of the defense in a civil action under Section 891. *(Added by Stats.1986, c. 838, § 1.)*

Research References

Miller and Starr California Real Estate § 10:62, Rent Skimming.
Miller and Starr California Real Estate § 19:84, Persons Entitled to Receive Rent--Rent Skimming.
4 Witkin, California Summary 10th Security Transactions in Real Property § 96, Rent Skimming.

§ 894. Severability

If any provision of this title or the application thereof to any person or circumstances is held to be unconstitutional, the remainder of the title and the application of its provisions to other persons and circumstances shall not be affected thereby. *(Added by Stats.1986, c. 838, § 1.)*

Title 7

REQUIREMENTS FOR ACTIONS FOR CONSTRUCTION DEFECTS

CHAPTER 1. DEFINITIONS

§ 895. Definitions

(a) "Structure" means any residential dwelling, other building, or improvement located upon a lot or within a common area.

(b) "Designed moisture barrier" means an installed moisture barrier specified in the plans and specifications, contract documents, or manufacturer's recommendations.

(c) "Actual moisture barrier" means any component or material, actually installed, that serves to any degree as a barrier against moisture, whether or not intended as a barrier against moisture.

(d) "Unintended water" means water that passes beyond, around, or through a component or the material that is designed to prevent that passage.

(e) "Close of escrow" means the date of the close of escrow between the builder and the original homeowner. With respect to claims by an association, as defined in Section 4080, "close of escrow" means the date of substantial completion, as defined in Section 337.15 of the Code of Civil Procedure, or the date the builder relinquishes control over the association's ability to decide whether to initiate a claim under this title, whichever is later.

(f) "Claimant" or "homeowner" includes the individual owners of single-family homes, individual unit owners of attached dwellings and, in the case of a common interest development, any association as defined in Section 4080. *(Added by Stats. 2002, c. 722 (S.B.800), § 3. Amended by Stats.2012, c. 181 (A.B.806), § 29, operative Jan. 1, 2014.)*

Law Revision Commission Comments

Subdivision (c) of Section 895 is amended to make a stylistic revision. Subdivisions (e) and (f) are amended to correct cross-references to former Section 1351(a). [40 Cal.L.Rev.Comm. Reports 235 (2010)].

Research References

Rutter, Cal. Practice Guide: A.D.R. App. A, Selected Statutes Providing for ADR.
Rutter, Cal. Practice Guide: A.D.R. Ch. 5-D, D. Defenses to Enforcement.
Rutter, Cal. Practice Guide: A.D.R. Ch. 3B-C, C. Statutorily-Mandated ADR.
Rutter, Cal. Practice Guide: Insurance Litigation Ch. 7E-A, A. General Considerations.
Miller and Starr California Real Estate § 29:2, Statutory Liability Under "SB800" for Residential Units Sold New After January 1, 2003.
Miller and Starr California Real Estate § 29:8, Contractor's Statutory Liability as to Residences Sold New After January 1, 2003.
Miller and Starr California Real Estate § 29:9, General Principles Concerning Owner's Damages.
Miller and Starr California Real Estate § 27:46, Indemnity Provisions; Wrap-Up Insurance.
Miller and Starr California Real Estate § 27:53, Builder Obligations for Residences Sold New After January 1, 2003 ("SB 800").
Miller and Starr California Real Estate § 29:10, Measure of Owner's Damages for Defective Construction.
Miller and Starr California Real Estate § 29:17, Express and Implied Indemnity.
Miller and Starr California Real Estate § 29:18, Subcontractor's Liability.
Miller and Starr California Real Estate § 29:19, Liability of Material Suppliers and Manufacturers.
Miller and Starr California Real Estate § 29:21, "Developer" Defined; Theories of Liability.
Miller and Starr California Real Estate § 29:30, Measure of Damages Applicable to Developers.
Miller and Starr California Real Estate § 29:46, Independent Inspector's Immunities.
Miller and Starr California Real Estate § 29:62, Procedures and Limitations Applicable to Residences First Sold New After January 1, 2003.
Miller and Starr California Real Estate § 29:63, Breach of Contract.
Miller and Starr California Real Estate § 29:69, When Statutes Commence to Run.
Miller and Starr California Real Estate § 29:70, Tolling and Extension.
Miller and Starr California Real Estate § 29:76, Systems for Resolving Defective Construction Disputes.
Miller and Starr California Real Estate § 25B:108, Homeowner's Actions.

13 NO. 3 Miller & Starr, California Real Estate Newsalert 1, Change to Spare: The New California Construction Warranty and Defects Law Under SB 800.

13 NO. 6 Miller & Starr, California Real Estate Newsalert 1, Using Basura to Make Construction Defect Claims Arbitrable, or Woodside to Send Them to a Referee.

13 NO. 4 Miller & Starr, California Real Estate Newsalert 4, Construction Defects.

14 NO. 2 Miller & Starr, California Real Estate Newsalert 1, "The Outer Limit": The California Supreme Court Reigns in the 10-Year Statute of Repose for Construction Defects.

14 NO. 5 Miller & Starr, California Real Estate Newsalert 8, Defective Construction.

19 NO. 2 Miller & Starr, California Real Estate Newsalert 4, Alternative Dispute Resolution.

19 NO. 2 Miller & Starr, California Real Estate Newsalert 6, Common Interest Developments.

21 NO. 5 Miller & Starr, California Real Estate Newsalert 1. Watch Your Step-If Its S.B. 800 Alternative Prelitigation Procedures Are Not Enforceable, a Builder Cannot Compel a Home Purchaser to Comply With the Statutory S.B. 800 Prelitigation...

21 NO. 1 Miller & Starr, California Real Estate Newsalert 1, is an Arbitration Provision in Recorded CC&RS Ever Enforceable by the Developer?

21 NO. 5 Miller & Starr, California Real Estate Newsalert 11, Defective Construction.

3 Witkin Cal. Proc. 5th Actions § 226, Actions on Construction Defects.

3 Witkin Cal. Proc. 5th Actions § 607, (S 607) Distinctions.

3 Witkin Cal. Proc. 5th Actions § 616, Action by Homeowner for Defects in Original Construction of Residence.

3 Witkin Cal. Proc. 5th Actions § 617, Defects in Construction of Residential Real Property: Ten Years.

3 Witkin Cal. Proc. 5th Actions § 760, (S 760) General Rule of Tolling.

12 Witkin, California Summary 10th Real Property § 463, (S 463) Sellers of New Construction.

6 Witkin, California Summary 10th Torts § 1162, (S 1162) in General.

6 Witkin, California Summary 10th Torts § 1163, (S 1163) Scope of Legislation.

6 Witkin, California Summary 10th Torts § 1164, (S 1164) Actionable Defects.

6 Witkin, California Summary 10th Torts § 1165, (S 1165) Right to Repair and Other Prelitigation Requirements.

6 Witkin, California Summary 10th Torts § 1166, (S 1166) Action and Relief.

6 Witkin, California Summary 10th Torts § 1167, (S 1167) Liability of Contractors, Suppliers, Product Manufacturers, and Design Professionals.

6 Witkin, California Summary 10th Torts § 1501, Seller.

6 Witkin, California Summary 10th Torts § 1502, Manufacturer or Supplier of Component Part.

6 Witkin, California Summary 10th Torts § 1504, (S 1504) Developer of Planned Development Project.

6 Witkin, California Summary 10th Torts § 1505, (S 1505) Subcontractor.

CHAPTER 2. ACTIONABLE DEFECTS

Section

896. Building standards for original construction intended to be sold as an individual dwelling unit.

897. Function or component of a structure; scope of standards within chapter.

§ 896. Building standards for original construction intended to be sold as an individual dwelling unit

In any action seeking recovery of damages arising out of, or related to deficiencies in, the residential construction, design, specifications, surveying, planning, supervision, testing, or observation of construction, a builder, and to the extent set forth in Chapter 4 (commencing with Section 910), a general contractor, subcontractor, material supplier, individual product manufacturer, or design professional, shall, except as specifically set forth in this title, be liable for, and the claimant's claims or causes of action shall be limited to violation of, the following standards, except as specifically set forth in this title. This title applies to original construction intended to be sold as an individual dwelling unit. As to condominium conversions, this title does not apply to or does not supersede any other statutory or common law.

(a) With respect to water issues:

(1) A door shall not allow unintended water to pass beyond, around, or through the door or its designed or actual moisture barriers, if any.

(2) Windows, patio doors, deck doors, and their systems shall not allow water to pass beyond, around, or through the window, patio door, or deck door or its designed or actual moisture barriers, including, without limitation, internal barriers within the systems themselves. For purposes of this paragraph, "systems" include, without limitation, windows, window assemblies, framing, substrate, flashings, and trim, if any.

(3) Windows, patio doors, deck doors, and their systems shall not allow excessive condensation to enter the structure and cause damage to another component. For purposes of this paragraph, "systems" include, without limitation, windows, window assemblies, framing, substrate, flashings, and trim, if any.

(4) Roofs, roofing systems, chimney caps, and ventilation components shall not allow water to enter the structure or to pass beyond, around, or through the designed or actual moisture barriers, including, without limitation, internal barriers located within the systems themselves. For purposes of this paragraph, "systems" include, without limitation, framing, substrate, and sheathing, if any.

(5) Decks, deck systems, balconies, balcony systems, exterior stairs, and stair systems shall not allow water to pass into the adjacent structure. For purposes of this paragraph, "systems" include, without limitation, framing, substrate, flashing, and sheathing, if any.

(6) Decks, deck systems, balconies, balcony systems, exterior stairs, and stair systems shall not allow unintended water to pass within the systems themselves and cause damage to the systems. For purposes of this paragraph, "systems" include, without limitation, framing, substrate, flashing, and sheathing, if any.

(7) Foundation systems and slabs shall not allow water or vapor to enter into the structure so as to cause damage to another building component.

(8) Foundation systems and slabs shall not allow water or vapor to enter into the structure so as to limit the installation of the type of flooring materials typically used for the particular application.

(9) Hardscape, including paths and patios, irrigation systems, landscaping systems, and drainage systems, that are installed as part of the original construction, shall not be installed in such a way as to cause water or soil erosion to enter into or come in contact with the structure so as to cause damage to another building component.

(10) Stucco, exterior siding, exterior walls, including, without limitation, exterior framing, and other exterior wall finishes and fixtures and the systems of those components and fixtures, including, but not limited to, pot shelves, horizontal surfaces, columns, and plant-ons, shall be installed in such a way so as not to allow unintended water to pass into the structure or to pass beyond, around, or through the designed or actual moisture barriers of the system, including any internal barriers located within the system itself. For purposes of this paragraph, "systems" include, without limitation, framing, substrate, flashings, trim, wall assemblies, and internal wall cavities, if any.

(11) Stucco, exterior siding, and exterior walls shall not allow excessive condensation to enter the structure and cause damage to another component. For purposes of this paragraph, "sys-

tems" include, without limitation, framing, substrate, flashings, trim, wall assemblies, and internal wall cavities, if any.

(12) Retaining and site walls and their associated drainage systems shall not allow unintended water to pass beyond, around, or through its designed or actual moisture barriers including, without limitation, any internal barriers, so as to cause damage. This standard does not apply to those portions of any wall or drainage system that are designed to have water flow beyond, around, or through them.

(13) Retaining walls and site walls, and their associated drainage systems, shall only allow water to flow beyond, around, or through the areas designated by design.

(14) The lines and components of the plumbing system, sewer system, and utility systems shall not leak.

(15) Plumbing lines, sewer lines, and utility lines shall not corrode so as to impede the useful life of the systems.

(16) Sewer systems shall be installed in such a way as to allow the designated amount of sewage to flow through the system.

(17) Showers, baths, and related waterproofing systems shall not leak water into the interior of walls, flooring systems, or the interior of other components.

(18) The waterproofing system behind or under ceramic tile and tile countertops shall not allow water into the interior of walls, flooring systems, or other components so as to cause damage. Ceramic tile systems shall be designed and installed so as to deflect intended water to the waterproofing system.

(b) With respect to structural issues:

(1) Foundations, load bearing components, and slabs, shall not contain significant cracks or significant vertical displacement.

(2) Foundations, load bearing components, and slabs shall not cause the structure, in whole or in part, to be structurally unsafe.

(3) Foundations, load bearing components, and slabs, and underlying soils shall be constructed so as to materially comply with the design criteria set by applicable government building codes, regulations, and ordinances for chemical deterioration or corrosion resistance in effect at the time of original construction.

(4) A structure shall be constructed so as to materially comply with the design criteria for earthquake and wind load resistance, as set forth in the applicable government building codes, regulations, and ordinances in effect at the time of original construction.

(c) With respect to soil issues:

(1) Soils and engineered retaining walls shall not cause, in whole or in part, damage to the structure built upon the soil or engineered retaining wall.

(2) Soils and engineered retaining walls shall not cause, in whole or in part, the structure to be structurally unsafe.

(3) Soils shall not cause, in whole or in part, the land upon which no structure is built to become unusable for the purpose represented at the time of original sale by the builder or for the purpose for which that land is commonly used.

(d) With respect to fire protection issues:

(1) A structure shall be constructed so as to materially comply with the design criteria of the applicable government building codes, regulations, and ordinances for fire protection of the occupants in effect at the time of the original construction.

(2) Fireplaces, chimneys, chimney structures, and chimney termination caps shall be constructed and installed in such a way so as not to cause an unreasonable risk of fire outside the fireplace enclosure or chimney.

(3) Electrical and mechanical systems shall be constructed and installed in such a way so as not to cause an unreasonable risk of fire.

(e) With respect to plumbing and sewer issues:

Plumbing and sewer systems shall be installed to operate properly and shall not materially impair the use of the structure by its inhabitants. However, no action may be brought for a violation of this subdivision more than four years after close of escrow.

(f) With respect to electrical system issues:

Electrical systems shall operate properly and shall not materially impair the use of the structure by its inhabitants. However, no action shall be brought pursuant to this subdivision more than four years from close of escrow.

(g) With respect to issues regarding other areas of construction:

(1) Exterior pathways, driveways, hardscape, sidewalls, sidewalks, and patios installed by the original builder shall not contain cracks that display significant vertical displacement or that are excessive. However, no action shall be brought upon a violation of this paragraph more than four years from close of escrow.

(2) Stucco, exterior siding, and other exterior wall finishes and fixtures, including, but not limited to, pot shelves, horizontal surfaces, columns, and plant-ons, shall not contain significant cracks or separations.

(3)(A) To the extent not otherwise covered by these standards, manufactured products, including, but not limited to, windows, doors, roofs, plumbing products and fixtures, fireplaces, electrical fixtures, HVAC units, countertops, cabinets, paint, and appliances shall be installed so as not to interfere with the products' useful life, if any.

(B) For purposes of this paragraph, "useful life" means a representation of how long a product is warranted or represented, through its limited warranty or any written representations, to last by its manufacturer, including recommended or required maintenance. If there is no representation by a manufacturer, a builder shall install manufactured products so as not to interfere with the product's utility.

(C) For purposes of this paragraph, "manufactured product" means a product that is completely manufactured offsite.

(D) If no useful life representation is made, or if the representation is less than one year, the period shall be no less than one year. If a manufactured product is damaged as a result of a violation of these standards, damage to the product is a recoverable element of damages. This subparagraph does not limit recovery if there has been damage to another building component caused by a manufactured product during the manufactured product's useful life.

(E) This title does not apply in any action seeking recovery solely for a defect in a manufactured product located within or adjacent to a structure.

(4) Heating shall be installed so as to be capable of maintaining a room temperature of 70 degrees Fahrenheit at a point three feet above the floor in any living space if the heating was installed pursuant to a building permit application submitted prior to January 1, 2008, or capable of maintaining a room temperature of 68 degrees Fahrenheit at a point three feet above the floor and two feet from exterior walls in all habitable rooms at the design temperature if the heating was installed pursuant to a building permit application submitted on or before January 1, 2008.

(5) Living space air-conditioning, if any, shall be provided in a manner consistent with the size and efficiency design criteria

specified in Title 24 of the California Code of Regulations or its successor.

(6) Attached structures shall be constructed to comply with interunit noise transmission standards set by the applicable government building codes, ordinances, or regulations in effect at the time of the original construction. If there is no applicable code, ordinance, or regulation, this paragraph does not apply. However, no action shall be brought pursuant to this paragraph more than one year from the original occupancy of the adjacent unit.

(7) Irrigation systems and drainage shall operate properly so as not to damage landscaping or other external improvements. However, no action shall be brought pursuant to this paragraph more than one year from close of escrow.

(8) Untreated wood posts shall not be installed in contact with soil so as to cause unreasonable decay to the wood based upon the finish grade at the time of original construction. However, no action shall be brought pursuant to this paragraph more than two years from close of escrow.

(9) Untreated steel fences and adjacent components shall be installed so as to prevent unreasonable corrosion. However, no action shall be brought pursuant to this paragraph more than four years from close of escrow.

(10) Paint and stains shall be applied in such a manner so as not to cause deterioration of the building surfaces for the length of time specified by the paint or stain manufacturers' representations, if any. However, no action shall be brought pursuant to this paragraph more than five years from close of escrow.

(11) Roofing materials shall be installed so as to avoid materials falling from the roof.

(12) The landscaping systems shall be installed in such a manner so as to survive for not less than one year. However, no action shall be brought pursuant to this paragraph more than two years from close of escrow.

(13) Ceramic tile and tile backing shall be installed in such a manner that the tile does not detach.

(14) Dryer ducts shall be installed and terminated pursuant to manufacturer installation requirements. However, no action shall be brought pursuant to this paragraph more than two years from close of escrow.

(15) Structures shall be constructed in such a manner so as not to impair the occupants' safety because they contain public health hazards as determined by a duly authorized public health official, health agency, or governmental entity having jurisdiction. This paragraph does not limit recovery for any damages caused by a violation of any other paragraph of this section on the grounds that the damages do not constitute a health hazard. (Added by Stats.2002, c. 722 (S.B.800), § 3. Amended by Stats.2003, c. 762 (A.B.903), § 1; Stats.2006, c. 567 (A.B.2303), § 2; Stats.2012, c. 770 (A.B.2697), § 2.)

Research References

Rutter, Cal. Practice Guide: A.D.R. Ch. 3B-C, C. Statutorily-Mandated ADR.
Rutter, Cal. Practice Guide: Civ. Pro. Before Trial Ch. 1-C, C. Prelawsuit Notices, Claims and Demands.
Rutter, Cal. Practice Guide: Insurance Litigation Ch. 7E-A, A. General Considerations.
Rutter, Cal. Practice Guide: Insurance Litigation Ch. 7E-B, B. Commercial General Liability (CGL) Policies.
Miller and Starr California Real Estate § 29:2, Statutory Liability Under "SB800" for Residential Units Sold New After January 1, 2003.
Miller and Starr California Real Estate § 27:53, Builder Obligations for Residences Sold New After January 1, 2003 ("SB 800").
Miller and Starr California Real Estate § 29:10, Measure of Owner's Damages for Defective Construction.

Miller and Starr California Real Estate § 29:17, Express and Implied Indemnity.
Miller and Starr California Real Estate § 29:19, Liability of Material Suppliers and Manufacturers.
Miller and Starr California Real Estate § 29:61, Certificates of Merit.
Miller and Starr California Real Estate § 29:62, Procedures and Limitations Applicable to Residences First Sold New After January 1, 2003.
Miller and Starr California Real Estate § 29:64, Negligence.
Miller and Starr California Real Estate § 29:69, When Statutes Commence to Run.
Miller and Starr California Real Estate § 29:72, Limitations Period for Patent Defects.
Miller and Starr California Real Estate § 29:74, Actions Within and Outside the 10-Year Statute.
13 NO. 3 Miller & Starr, California Real Estate Newsalert 1, Change to Spare: The New California Construction Warranty and Defects Law Under SB 800.
19 NO. 4 Miller & Starr, California Real Estate Newsalert 35, Defective Construction.
21 NO. 5 Miller & Starr, California Real Estate Newsalert 1. Watch Your Step-If Its S.B. 800 Alternative Prelitigation Procedures Are Not Enforceable, a Builder Cannot Compel a Home Purchaser to Comply With the Statutory S.B. 800 Prelitigation...
3 Witkin Cal. Proc. 5th Actions § 617, Defects in Construction of Residential Real Property: Ten Years.
4 Witkin, California Summary 10th Sales § 51, Nature and Effect.
5 Witkin, California Summary 10th Torts § 121, (S 121) Void Clauses.
6 Witkin, California Summary 10th Torts § 1163, (S 1163) Scope of Legislation.
6 Witkin, California Summary 10th Torts § 1164, (S 1164) Actionable Defects.
6 Witkin, California Summary 10th Torts § 1167, (S 1167) Liability of Contractors, Suppliers, Product Manufacturers, and Design Professionals.

§ 897. Function or component of a structure; scope of standards within chapter

The standards set forth in this chapter are intended to address every function or component of a structure. To the extent that a function or component of a structure is not addressed by these standards, it shall be actionable if it causes damage. (Added by Stats.2002, c. 722 (S.B.800), § 3.)

Research References

Rutter, Cal. Practice Guide: A.D.R. Ch. 3B-C, C. Statutorily-Mandated ADR.
Miller and Starr California Real Estate § 29:2, Statutory Liability Under "SB800" for Residential Units Sold New After January 1, 2003.
Miller and Starr California Real Estate § 29:17, Express and Implied Indemnity.
13 NO. 3 Miller & Starr, California Real Estate Newsalert 1, Change to Spare: The New California Construction Warranty and Defects Law Under SB 800.
5 Witkin, California Summary 10th Torts § 121, (S 121) Void Clauses.
6 Witkin, California Summary 10th Torts § 1164, (S 1164) Actionable Defects.

CHAPTER 3. OBLIGATIONS

Section
907. Homeowner maintenance obligations, schedules and practices.

§ 900. Fit and finish; limited warranty; scope

As to fit and finish items, a builder shall provide a homebuyer with a minimum one-year express written limited warranty covering the fit and finish of the following building components. Except as otherwise provided by the standards specified in Chapter 2 (commencing with Section 896), this warranty shall cover the fit and finish of cabinets, mirrors, flooring, interior and exterior walls, countertops, paint finishes, and trim, but shall not apply to damage to those components caused by defects in other components governed by the other provisions of this title. Any fit and finish matters covered by this warranty are not subject to the provisions of this title. If a builder fails to provide the express warranty required by this section, the warranty for these items shall be for a period of one year. *(Added by Stats.2002, c. 722 (S.B.800), § 3.)*

Research References

Miller and Starr California Real Estate § 29:2, Statutory Liability Under "SB800" for Residential Units Sold New After January 1, 2003.
Miller and Starr California Real Estate § 27:53, Builder Obligations for Residences Sold New After January 1, 2003 ("SB 800").
13 NO. 3 Miller & Starr, California Real Estate Newsalert 1, Change to Spare: The New California Construction Warranty and Defects Law Under SB 800.
14 NO. 2 Miller & Starr, California Real Estate Newsalert 1, "The Outer Limit": The California Supreme Court Reigns in the 10-Year Statute of Repose for Construction Defects.
21 NO. 5 Miller & Starr, California Real Estate Newsalert 1. Watch Your Step-If Its S.B. 800 Alternative Prelitigation Procedures Are Not Enforceable, a Builder Cannot Compel a Home Purchaser to Comply With the Statutory S.B. 800 Prelitigation...
6 Witkin, California Summary 10th Torts § 1164, (S 1164) Actionable Defects.

§ 901. Enhanced protection agreement; length of time; minimum standards

A builder may, but is not required to, offer greater protection or protection for longer time periods in its express contract with the homeowner than that set forth in Chapter 2 (commencing with Section 896). A builder may not limit the application of Chapter 2 (commencing with Section 896) or lower its protection through the express contract with the homeowner. This type of express contract constitutes an "enhanced protection agreement." *(Added by Stats.2002, c. 722 (S.B.800), § 3.)*

Research References

Miller and Starr California Real Estate § 29:2, Statutory Liability Under "SB800" for Residential Units Sold New After January 1, 2003.
Miller and Starr California Real Estate § 27:53, Builder Obligations for Residences Sold New After January 1, 2003 ("SB 800").
13 NO. 3 Miller & Starr, California Real Estate Newsalert 1, Change to Spare: The New California Construction Warranty and Defects Law Under SB 800.
6 Witkin, California Summary 10th Torts § 1164, (S 1164) Actionable Defects.

§ 902. Enhanced protection agreement; determination of enforceability

If a builder offers an enhanced protection agreement, the builder may choose to be subject to its own express contractual provisions in place of the provisions set forth in Chapter 2 (commencing with Section 896). If an enhanced protection agreement is in place, Chapter 2 (commencing with Section 896) no longer applies other than to set forth minimum provisions by which to judge the enforceability of the particular provisions of the enhanced protection agreement. *(Added by Stats.2002, c. 722 (S.B.800), § 3.)*

Research References

6 Witkin, California Summary 10th Torts § 1164, (S 1164) Actionable Defects.

§ 903. Enhanced protection agreement; time to elect agreement; standards where provisions are unenforceable

If a builder offers an enhanced protection agreement in place of the provisions set forth in Chapter 2 (commencing with Section 896), the election to do so shall be made in writing with the homeowner no later than the close of escrow. The builder shall provide the homeowner with a complete copy of Chapter 2 (commencing with Section 896) and advise the homeowner that the builder has elected not to be subject to its provisions. If any provision of an enhanced protection agreement is later found to be unenforceable as not meeting the minimum standards of Chapter 2 (commencing with Section 896), a builder may use this chapter in lieu of those provisions found to be unenforceable. *(Added by Stats.2002, c. 722 (S.B.800), § 3.)*

Research References

Miller and Starr California Real Estate § 29:2, Statutory Liability Under "SB800" for Residential Units Sold New After January 1, 2003.
Miller and Starr California Real Estate § 27:53, Builder Obligations for Residences Sold New After January 1, 2003 ("SB 800").
13 NO. 3 Miller & Starr, California Real Estate Newsalert 1, Change to Spare: The New California Construction Warranty and Defects Law Under SB 800.
6 Witkin, California Summary 10th Torts § 1164, (S 1164) Actionable Defects.

§ 904. Enhanced protection agreement; disputed terms; notice of claim against builder

If a builder has elected to use an enhanced protection agreement, and a homeowner disputes that the particular provision or time periods of the enhanced protection agreement are not greater than, or equal to, the provisions of Chapter 2 (commencing with Section 896) as they apply to the particular deficiency alleged by the homeowner, the homeowner may seek to enforce the application of the standards set forth in this chapter as to those claimed deficiencies. If a homeowner seeks to enforce a particular standard in lieu of a provision of the enhanced protection agreement, the homeowner shall give the builder written notice of that intent at the time the homeowner files a notice of claim pursuant to Chapter 4 (commencing with Section 910). *(Added by Stats.2002, c. 722 (S.B.800), § 3.)*

Research References

6 Witkin, California Summary 10th Torts § 1164, (S 1164) Actionable Defects.

§ 905. Enhanced protection agreement; binding determination of applicable building standards; waiver; privity with nonoriginal homeowners

If a homeowner seeks to enforce Chapter 2 (commencing with Section 896), in lieu of the enhanced protection agreement in a subsequent litigation or other legal action, the builder shall have the right to have the matter bifurcated, and to have an immediately binding determination of his or her responsive pleading within 60 days after the filing of that pleading, but in no event after the commencement of discovery, as to the application of either Chapter 2 (commencing with Section 896) or the enhanced protection agreement as to the deficiencies claimed by the homeowner. If the builder fails to seek that determination in the timeframe specified, the builder waives the right to do so and the standards set forth in this title shall apply. As to any nonoriginal homeowner, that homeowner shall be deemed in privity for purposes of an enhanced protection agreement only to the extent that the builder has recorded the enhanced protection agreement on title or provided actual notice to the nonoriginal homeowner of the enhanced protection agreement. If the enhanced protection agreement is not recorded on title or no actual notice has been provided, the standards set forth in this title apply to any nonoriginal homeowners' claims. *(Added by Stats.2002, c. 722 (S.B.800), § 3.)*

Research References

Miller and Starr California Real Estate § 29:2, Statutory Liability Under "SB800" for Residential Units Sold New After January 1, 2003.

13 NO. 3 Miller & Starr, California Real Estate Newsalert 1, Change to Spare: The New California Construction Warranty and Defects Law Under SB 800.

6 Witkin, California Summary 10th Torts § 1164, (S 1164) Actionable Defects.

§ 906. Prelitigation procedures; governing law

A builder's election to use an enhanced protection agreement addresses only the issues set forth in Chapter 2 (commencing with Section 896) and does not constitute an election to use or not use the provisions of Chapter 4 (commencing with Section 910). The decision to use or not use Chapter 4 (commencing with Section 910) is governed by the provisions of that chapter. *(Added by Stats.2002, c. 722 (S.B.800), § 3.)*

Research References

Miller and Starr California Real Estate § 29:2, Statutory Liability Under "SB800" for Residential Units Sold New After January 1, 2003.

13 NO. 3 Miller & Starr, California Real Estate Newsalert 1, Change to Spare: The New California Construction Warranty and Defects Law Under SB 800.

§ 907. Homeowner maintenance obligations, schedules and practices

A homeowner is obligated to follow all reasonable maintenance obligations and schedules communicated in writing to the homeowner by the builder and product manufacturers, as well as commonly accepted maintenance practices. A failure by a homeowner to follow these obligations, schedules, and practices may subject the homeowner to the affirmative defenses contained in Section 944. *(Added by Stats.2002, c. 722 (S.B.800), § 3.)*

Research References

Miller and Starr California Real Estate § 29:2, Statutory Liability Under "SB800" for Residential Units Sold New After January 1, 2003.

13 NO. 3 Miller & Starr, California Real Estate Newsalert 1, Change to Spare: The New California Construction Warranty and Defects Law Under SB 800.

CHAPTER 4. PRELITIGATION PROCEDURE

§ 910. Written notice of claim

Prior to filing an action against any party alleged to have contributed to a violation of the standards set forth in Chapter 2 (commencing with Section 896), the claimant shall initiate the following prelitigation procedures:

(a) The claimant or his or her legal representative shall provide written notice via certified mail, overnight mail, or personal delivery to the builder, in the manner prescribed in this section, of the claimant's claim that the construction of his or her residence violates any of the standards set forth in Chapter 2 (commencing with Section 896). That notice shall provide the claimant's name, address, and preferred method of contact, and shall state that the claimant alleges a violation pursuant to this part against the builder, and shall describe the claim in reasonable detail sufficient to determine the nature and location, to the extent known, of the claimed violation. In the case of a group of homeowners or an association, the notice may identify the claimants solely by address or other description sufficient to apprise the builder of the locations of the subject residences. That document shall have the same force and effect as a notice of commencement of a legal proceeding.

(b) The notice requirements of this section do not preclude a homeowner from seeking redress through any applicable normal customer service procedure as set forth in any contractual, warranty, or other builder-generated document; and, if a homeowner seeks to do so, that request shall not satisfy the notice requirements of this section. *(Added by Stats.2002, c. 722 (S.B.800), § 3.)*

Research References

Rutter, Cal. Practice Guide: A.D.R. Ch. 3B-C, C. Statutorily-Mandated ADR.

Rutter, Cal. Practice Guide: Civ. Pro. Before Trial Ch. 1-C, C. Prelawsuit Notices, Claims and Demands.

Rutter, Cal. Practice Guide: Civ. Pro. Before Trial Ch. 1-E, E. Prelawsuit ADR Requirement.

Miller and Starr California Real Estate § 29:2, Statutory Liability Under "SB800" for Residential Units Sold New After January 1, 2003.

Miller and Starr California Real Estate § 29:17, Express and Implied Indemnity.

Miller and Starr California Real Estate § 29:71, Special Maximum Periods; Latent and Patent Defects.

Miller and Starr California Real Estate § 29:76, Systems for Resolving Defective Construction Disputes.

13 NO. 3 Miller & Starr, California Real Estate Newsalert 1, Change to Spare: The New California Construction Warranty and Defects Law Under SB 800.

20 NO. 2 Miller & Starr, California Real Estate Newsalert 12, Defective Construction.

21 NO. 5 Miller & Starr, California Real Estate Newsalert 1. Watch Your Step-If Its S.B. 800 Alternative Prelitigation Procedures Are Not Enforceable, a Builder Cannot Compel a Home Purchaser to Comply With the Statutory S.B. 800 Prelitigation...

22 NO. 4 Miller & Starr, California Real Estate Newsalert 30, Defective Construction.

23 NO. 3 Miller & Starr, California Real Estate Newsalert 8, Defective Construction.

3 Witkin Cal. Proc. 5th Actions § 226, Actions on Construction Defects.

3 Witkin Cal. Proc. 5th Actions § 617, Defects in Construction of Residential Real Property: Ten Years.

3 Witkin Cal. Proc. 5th Actions § 760, (S 760) General Rule of Tolling.

6 Witkin, California Summary 10th Torts § 1165, (S 1165) Right to Repair and Other Prelitigation Requirements.

6 Witkin, California Summary 10th Torts § 1167, (S 1167) Liability of Contractors, Suppliers, Product Manufacturers, and Design Professionals.

§ 911. "Builder" defined

(a) For purposes of this title, except as provided in subdivision (b), "builder" means any entity or individual, including, but not limited to a builder, developer, general contractor, contractor, or original seller, who, at the time of sale, was also in the business of selling residential units to the public for the property that is the subject of the homeowner's claim or was in the business of building, developing, or constructing residential units for public purchase for the property that is the subject of the homeowner's claim.

(b) For the purposes of this title, "builder" does not include any entity or individual whose involvement with a residential unit that is the subject of the homeowner's claim is limited to his or her capacity as general contractor or contractor and who is not a partner, member of, subsidiary of, or otherwise similarly affiliated with the builder. For purposes of this title, these nonaffiliated general contractors and nonaffiliated contractors shall be treated the same as subcontractors, material suppliers, individual product manufacturers, and design professionals. *(Added by Stats.2002, c. 722 (S.B.800), § 3. Amended by Stats.2003, c. 762 (A.B.903), § 2.)*

Research References

Rutter, Cal. Practice Guide: A.D.R. Ch. 3B-C, C. Statutorily-Mandated ADR.

Rutter, Cal. Practice Guide: Civ. Pro. Before Trial Ch. 1-C, C. Prelawsuit Notices, Claims and Demands.

Rutter, Cal. Practice Guide: Insurance Litigation Ch. 7E-A, A. General Considerations.

Miller and Starr California Real Estate § 29:2, Statutory Liability Under "SB800" for Residential Units Sold New After January 1, 2003.

Miller and Starr California Real Estate § 27:46, Indemnity Provisions; Wrap-Up Insurance.

Miller and Starr California Real Estate § 29:11, Owner's Insurance Coverage.

Miller and Starr California Real Estate § 29:17, Express and Implied Indemnity.

Miller and Starr California Real Estate § 29:21, "Developer" Defined; Theories of Liability.

3 Witkin Cal. Proc. 5th Actions § 226, Actions on Construction Defects.

6 Witkin, California Summary 10th Torts § 1163, (S 1163) Scope of Legislation.

§ 912. Document disclosure by builder; designated agent to accept claims and act on builder's behalf; notice to homeowners and purchasers

A builder shall do all of the following:

(a) Within 30 days of a written request by a homeowner or his or her legal representative, the builder shall provide copies of all relevant plans, specifications, mass or rough grading plans, final soils reports, <u>Bureau</u> of Real Estate public reports, and available engineering calculations, that pertain to a homeowner's residence specifically or as part of a larger development tract. The request shall be honored if it states that it is made relative to structural, fire safety, or soils provisions of this title. However, a builder is not obligated to provide a copying service, and reasonable copying costs shall be borne by the requesting party. A builder may require that the documents be copied onsite by the requesting party, except that the homeowner may, at his or her option, use his or her own copying service, which may include an offsite copy facility that is bonded and insured. If a builder can show that the builder maintained the documents, but that they later became unavailable due to loss or destruction that was not the fault of the builder, the builder may be excused from the requirements of this subdivision, in which case the builder shall act with reasonable diligence to assist the homeowner in obtaining those documents from any applicable government authority or from the source that generated the document. However, in that case, the time limits specified by this section do not apply.

(b) At the expense of the homeowner, who may opt to use an offsite copy facility that is bonded and insured, the builder shall provide to the homeowner or his or her legal representative copies of all maintenance and preventative maintenance recommendations that pertain to his or her residence within 30 days of service of a written request for those documents. Those documents shall also be provided to the homeowner in conjunction with the initial sale of the residence.

(c) At the expense of the homeowner, who may opt to use an offsite copy facility that is bonded and insured, a builder shall provide to the homeowner or his or her legal representative copies of all manufactured products maintenance, preventive maintenance, and limited warranty information within 30 days of a written request for those documents. These documents shall also be provided to the homeowner in conjunction with the initial sale of the residence.

(d) At the expense of the homeowner, who may opt to use an offsite copy facility that is bonded and insured, a builder shall provide to the homeowner or his or her legal representative copies of all of the builder's limited contractual warranties in accordance with this part in effect at the time of the original sale of the residence within 30 days of a written request for those documents. Those documents shall also be provided to the homeowner in conjunction with the initial sale of the residence.

(e) A builder shall maintain the name and address of an agent for notice pursuant to this chapter with the Secretary of State or, alternatively, elect to use a third party for that notice if the builder has notified the homeowner in writing of the third party's name and address, to whom claims and requests for information under this section may be mailed. The name and address of the agent for notice or third party shall be included with the original sales documentation and shall be initialed and acknowledged by the purchaser and the builder's sales representative.

This subdivision applies to instances in which a builder contracts with a third party to accept claims and act on the builder's behalf. A builder shall give actual notice to the homeowner that the builder has made such an election, and shall include the name and address of the third party.

(f) A builder shall record on title a notice of the existence of these procedures and a notice that these procedures impact the legal rights of the homeowner. This information shall also be included with the original sales documentation and shall be initialed and acknowledged by the purchaser and the builder's sales representative.

(g) A builder shall provide, with the original sales documentation, a written copy of this title, which shall be initialed and acknowledged by the purchaser and the builder's sales representative.

(h) As to any documents provided in conjunction with the original sale, the builder shall instruct the original purchaser to provide those documents to any subsequent purchaser.

(i) Any builder who fails to comply with any of these requirements within the time specified is not entitled to the protection of this chapter, and the homeowner is released from the requirements of this chapter and may proceed with the filing of an action, in which case the remaining chapters of this part shall continue to apply to the action. *(Added by Stats.2002, c. 722 (S.B.800), § 3. Amended by Stats.2003, c. 762 (A.B.903), § 3; Stats.2013, c. 352 (A.B.1317), § 50, eff. Sept. 26, 2013, operative July 1, 2013.)*

Research References

Rutter, Cal. Practice Guide: A.D.R. Ch. 3B-C, C. Statutorily-Mandated ADR.
Rutter, Cal. Practice Guide: Civ. Pro. Before Trial Ch. 1-C, C. Prelawsuit Notices, Claims and Demands.
Miller and Starr California Real Estate § 29:2, Statutory Liability Under "SB800" for Residential Units Sold New After January 1, 2003.
Miller and Starr California Real Estate § 27:53, Builder Obligations for Residences Sold New After January 1, 2003 ("SB 800").
Miller and Starr California Real Estate § 29:19, Liability of Material Suppliers and Manufacturers.
13 NO. 3 Miller & Starr, California Real Estate Newsalert 1, Change to Spare: The New California Construction Warranty and Defects Law Under SB 800.
20 NO. 2 Miller & Starr, California Real Estate Newsalert 12, Defective Construction.
21 NO. 5 Miller & Starr, California Real Estate Newsalert 1. Watch Your Step-If Its S.B. 800 Alternative Prelitigation Procedures Are Not Enforceable, a Builder Cannot Compel a Home Purchaser to Comply With the Statutory S.B. 800 Prelitigation...
22 NO. 4 Miller & Starr, California Real Estate Newsalert 30, Defective Construction.
23 NO. 3 Miller & Starr, California Real Estate Newsalert 8, Defective Construction.
12 Witkin, California Summary 10th Real Property § 463, (S 463) Sellers of New Construction.
6 Witkin, California Summary 10th Torts § 1165, (S 1165) Right to Repair and Other Prelitigation Requirements.

§ 913. Written acknowledgement of claim; time to respond; contents

A builder or his or her representative shall acknowledge, in writing, receipt of the notice of the claim within 14 days after receipt of the notice of the claim. If the notice of the claim is served by the claimant's legal representative, or if the builder receives a written representation letter from a homeowner's attorney, the builder shall include the attorney in all subsequent substantive communications, including, without limitation, all written communications occurring pursuant to this chapter, and all substantive and procedural communications, including all written communications, following the commencement of any subsequent complaint or other legal action, except that if the builder has retained or involved legal counsel to assist the builder in this process, all communications by the builder's

counsel shall only be with the claimant's legal representative, if any. *(Added by Stats.2002, c. 722 (S.B.800), § 3.)*

Research References

Rutter, Cal. Practice Guide: A.D.R. Ch. 3B-C, C. Statutorily-Mandated ADR.
Rutter, Cal. Practice Guide: Civ. Pro. Before Trial Ch. 1-C, C. Prelawsuit Notices, Claims and Demands.
Miller and Starr California Real Estate § 29:2, Statutory Liability Under "SB800" for Residential Units Sold New After January 1, 2003.
13 NO. 3 Miller & Starr, California Real Estate Newsalert 1, Change to Spare: The New California Construction Warranty and Defects Law Under SB 800.
21 NO. 5 Miller & Starr, California Real Estate Newsalert 1. Watch Your Step-If Its S.B. 800 Alternative Prelitigation Procedures Are Not Enforceable, a Builder Cannot Compel a Home Purchaser to Comply With the Statutory S.B. 800 Prelitigation...
6 Witkin, California Summary 10th Torts § 1165, (S 1165) Right to Repair and Other Prelitigation Requirements.

§ 914. Election to pursue other nonadversarial contractual procedures; affect of Title 7 upon exiting statutory or decisional law

(a) This chapter establishes a nonadversarial procedure, including the remedies available under this chapter which, if the procedure does not resolve the dispute between the parties, may result in a subsequent action to enforce the other chapters of this title. A builder may attempt to commence nonadversarial contractual provisions other than the nonadversarial procedures and remedies set forth in this chapter, but may not, in addition to its own nonadversarial contractual provisions, require adherence to the nonadversarial procedures and remedies set forth in this chapter, regardless of whether the builder's own alternative nonadversarial contractual provisions are successful in resolving the dispute or ultimately deemed enforceable.

At the time the sales agreement is executed, the builder shall notify the homeowner whether the builder intends to engage in the nonadversarial procedure of this section or attempt to enforce alternative nonadversarial contractual provisions. If the builder elects to use alternative nonadversarial contractual provisions in lieu of this chapter, the election is binding, regardless of whether the builder's alternative nonadversarial contractual provisions are successful in resolving the ultimate dispute or are ultimately deemed enforceable.

(b) Nothing in this title is intended to affect existing statutory or decisional law pertaining to the applicability, viability, or enforceability of alternative dispute resolution methods, alternative remedies, or contractual arbitration, judicial reference, or similar procedures requiring a binding resolution to enforce the other chapters of this title or any other disputes between homeowners and builders. Nothing in this title is intended to affect the applicability, viability, or enforceability, if any, of contractual arbitration or judicial reference after a nonadversarial procedure or provision has been completed. *(Added by Stats.2002, c. 722 (S.B.800), § 3.)*

Research References

Rutter, Cal. Practice Guide: A.D.R. Ch. 3B-C, C. Statutorily-Mandated ADR.
Rutter, Cal. Practice Guide: Civ. Pro. Before Trial Ch. 1-C, C. Prelawsuit Notices, Claims and Demands.
Miller and Starr California Real Estate § 29:2, Statutory Liability Under "SB800" for Residential Units Sold New After January 1, 2003.
13 NO. 3 Miller & Starr, California Real Estate Newsalert 1, Change to Spare: The New California Construction Warranty and Defects Law Under SB 800.
21 NO. 5 Miller & Starr, California Real Estate Newsalert 1. Watch Your Step-If Its S.B. 800 Alternative Prelitigation Procedures Are Not Enforceable, a Builder Cannot Compel a Home Purchaser to Comply With the Statutory S.B. 800 Prelitigation...

22 NO. 4 Miller & Starr, California Real Estate Newsalert 30, Defective Construction.

6 Witkin, California Summary 10th Torts § 1165, (S 1165) Right to Repair and Other Prelitigation Requirements.

§ 915. Application of prelitigation provisions upon certain failures to act by builder

If a builder fails to acknowledge receipt of the notice of a claim within the time specified, elects not to go through the process set forth in this chapter, or fails to request an inspection within the time specified, or at the conclusion or cessation of an alternative nonadversarial proceeding, this chapter does not apply and the homeowner is released from the requirements of this chapter and may proceed with the filing of an action. However, the standards set forth in the other chapters of this title shall continue to apply to the action. *(Added by Stats.2002, c. 722 (S.B.800), § 3.)*

Research References

Rutter, Cal. Practice Guide: Civ. Pro. Before Trial Ch. 1-C, C. Prelawsuit Notices, Claims and Demands.

21 NO. 5 Miller & Starr, California Real Estate Newsalert 1. Watch Your Step-If Its S.B. 800 Alternative Prelitigation Procedures Are Not Enforceable, a Builder Cannot Compel a Home Purchaser to Comply With the Statutory S.B. 800 Prelitigation...

§ 916. Builder election to inspect

(a) If a builder elects to inspect the claimed unmet standards, the builder shall complete the initial inspection and testing within 14 days after acknowledgment of receipt of the notice of the claim, at a mutually convenient date and time. If the homeowner has retained legal representation, the inspection shall be scheduled with the legal representative's office at a mutually convenient date and time, unless the legal representative is unavailable during the relevant time periods. All costs of builder inspection and testing, including any damage caused by the builder inspection, shall be borne by the builder. The builder shall also provide written proof that the builder has liability insurance to cover any damages or injuries occurring during inspection and testing. The builder shall restore the property to its pretesting condition within 48 hours of the testing. The builder shall, upon request, allow the inspections to be observed and electronically recorded, video recorded, or photographed by the claimant or his or her legal representative.

(b) Nothing that occurs during a builder's or claimant's inspection or testing may be used or introduced as evidence to support a spoliation defense by any potential party in any subsequent litigation.

(c) If a builder deems a second inspection or testing reasonably necessary, and specifies the reasons therefor in writing within three days following the initial inspection, the builder may conduct a second inspection or testing. A second inspection or testing shall be completed within 40 days of the initial inspection or testing. All requirements concerning the initial inspection or testing shall also apply to the second inspection or testing.

(d) If the builder fails to inspect or test the property within the time specified, the claimant is released from the requirements of this section and may proceed with the filing of an action. However, the standards set forth in the other chapters of this title shall continue to apply to the action.

(e) If a builder intends to hold a subcontractor, design professional, individual product manufacturer, or material supplier, including an insurance carrier, warranty company, or service company, responsible for its contribution to the unmet standard, the builder shall provide notice to that person or entity sufficiently in advance to allow them to attend the initial, or if requested, second inspection of any alleged unmet standard and to participate in the repair process. The claimant and his or her

legal representative, if any, shall be advised in a reasonable time prior to the inspection as to the identity of all persons or entities invited to attend. This subdivision does not apply to the builder's insurance company. Except with respect to any claims involving a repair actually conducted under this chapter, nothing in this subdivision shall be construed to relieve a subcontractor, design professional, individual product manufacturer, or material supplier of any liability under an action brought by a claimant. *(Added by Stats.2002, c. 722 (S.B.800), § 3. Amended by Stats.2003, c. 762 (A.B.903), § 4; Stats.2009, c. 88 (A.B.176), § 12.)*

Law Revision Commission Comments

Subdivision (a) of Section 916 is amended to reflect advances in recording technology and for consistency of terminology. For a similar reform, see 2002 Cal. Stat. ch. 1068 (replacing numerous references to "audiotape" in Civil Discovery Act with either "audio technology," "audio recording," or "audio record," as context required). [37 Cal. L. Revision Comm'n Reports 211 (2007)].

Research References

Rutter, Cal. Practice Guide: A.D.R. Ch. 3B-C, C. Statutorily-Mandated ADR.

Rutter, Cal. Practice Guide: Civ. Pro. Before Trial Ch. 1-C, C. Prelawsuit Notices, Claims and Demands.

Miller and Starr California Real Estate § 29:2, Statutory Liability Under "SB800" for Residential Units Sold New After January 1, 2003.

13 NO. 3 Miller & Starr, California Real Estate Newsalert 1, Change to Spare: The New California Construction Warranty and Defects Law Under SB 800.

21 NO. 5 Miller & Starr, California Real Estate Newsalert 1. Watch Your Step-If Its S.B. 800 Alternative Prelitigation Procedures Are Not Enforceable, a Builder Cannot Compel a Home Purchaser to Comply With the Statutory S.B. 800 Prelitigation...

6 Witkin, California Summary 10th Torts § 1165, (S 1165) Right to Repair and Other Prelitigation Requirements.

§ 917. Written offer to repair

Within 30 days of the initial or, if requested, second inspection or testing, the builder may offer in writing to repair the violation. The offer to repair shall also compensate the homeowner for all applicable damages recoverable under Section 944, within the timeframe for the repair set forth in this chapter. Any such offer shall be accompanied by a detailed, specific, step-by-step statement identifying the particular violation that is being repaired, explaining the nature, scope, and location of the repair, and setting a reasonable completion date for the repair. The offer shall also include the names, addresses, telephone numbers, and license numbers of the contractors whom the builder intends to have perform the repair. Those contractors shall be fully insured for, and shall be responsible for, all damages or injuries that they may cause to occur during the repair, and evidence of that insurance shall be provided to the homeowner upon request. Upon written request by the homeowner or his or her legal representative, and within the timeframes set forth in this chapter, the builder shall also provide any available technical documentation, including, without limitation, plans and specifications, pertaining to the claimed violation within the particular home or development tract. The offer shall also advise the homeowner in writing of his or her right to request up to three additional contractors from which to select to do the repair pursuant to this chapter. *(Added by Stats.2002, c. 722 (S.B.800), § 3.)*

Research References

Rutter, Cal. Practice Guide: A.D.R. Ch. 3B-C, C. Statutorily-Mandated ADR.

Rutter, Cal. Practice Guide: Civ. Pro. Before Trial Ch. 1-C, C. Prelawsuit Notices, Claims and Demands.

Miller and Starr California Real Estate § 29:2, Statutory Liability Under "SB800" for Residential Units Sold New After January 1, 2003.

13 NO. 3 Miller & Starr, California Real Estate Newsalert 1, Change to Spare: The New California Construction Warranty and Defects Law Under SB 800.
21 NO. 5 Miller & Starr, California Real Estate Newsalert 1. Watch Your Step-If Its S.B. 800 Alternative Prelitigation Procedures Are Not Enforceable, a Builder Cannot Compel a Home Purchaser to Comply With the Statutory S.B. 800 Prelitigation...
6 Witkin, California Summary 10th Torts § 1165, (S 1165) Right to Repair and Other Prelitigation Requirements.

§ 918. Homeowner response to repair offer

Upon receipt of the offer to repair, the homeowner shall have 30 days to authorize the builder to proceed with the repair. The homeowner may alternatively request, at the homeowner's sole option and discretion, that the builder provide the names, addresses, telephone numbers, and license numbers for up to three alternative contractors who are not owned or financially controlled by the builder and who regularly conduct business in the county where the structure is located. If the homeowner so elects, the builder is entitled to an additional noninvasive inspection, to occur at a mutually convenient date and time within 20 days of the election, so as to permit the other proposed contractors to review the proposed site of the repair. Within 35 days after the request of the homeowner for alternative contractors, the builder shall present the homeowner with a choice of contractors. Within 20 days after that presentation, the homeowner shall authorize the builder or one of the alternative contractors to perform the repair. *(Added by Stats.2002, c. 722 (S.B.800), § 3.)*

Research References

Rutter, Cal. Practice Guide: A.D.R. Ch. 3B-C, C. Statutorily-Mandated ADR.
Rutter, Cal. Practice Guide: Civ. Pro. Before Trial Ch. 1-C, C. Prelawsuit Notices, Claims and Demands.
Miller and Starr California Real Estate § 29:2, Statutory Liability Under "SB800" for Residential Units Sold New After January 1, 2003.
21 NO. 5 Miller & Starr, California Real Estate Newsalert 1. Watch Your Step-If Its S.B. 800 Alternative Prelitigation Procedures Are Not Enforceable, a Builder Cannot Compel a Home Purchaser to Comply With the Statutory S.B. 800 Prelitigation...
6 Witkin, California Summary 10th Torts § 1165, (S 1165) Right to Repair and Other Prelitigation Requirements.

§ 919. Mediation by mutual agreement; unresolved disputes; repairs

The offer to repair shall also be accompanied by an offer to mediate the dispute if the homeowner so chooses. The mediation shall be limited to a four-hour mediation, except as otherwise mutually agreed before a nonaffiliated mediator selected and paid for by the builder. At the homeowner's sole option, the homeowner may agree to split the cost of the mediator, and if he or she does so, the mediator shall be selected jointly. The mediator shall have sufficient availability such that the mediation occurs within 15 days after the request to mediate is received and occurs at a mutually convenient location within the county where the action is pending. If a builder has made an offer to repair a violation, and the mediation has failed to resolve the dispute, the homeowner shall allow the repair to be performed either by the builder, its contractor, or the selected contractor. *(Added by Stats.2002, c. 722 (S.B.800), § 3.)*

Research References

Rutter, Cal. Practice Guide: A.D.R. Ch. 3B-C, C. Statutorily-Mandated ADR.
Rutter, Cal. Practice Guide: A.D.R. Gen. Matls., Highlights.
Rutter, Cal. Practice Guide: Civ. Pro. Before Trial Ch. 1-C, C. Prelawsuit Notices, Claims and Demands.
Miller and Starr California Real Estate § 29:2, Statutory Liability Under "SB800" for Residential Units Sold New After January 1, 2003.

Miller and Starr California Real Estate § 35:15, Statutory Provisions for Mediations (And Arbitration) of Real Property Disputes.
Miller and Starr California Real Estate § 25B:113, Arbitration or Other Resolution of Disputes With the Subdivider.
13 NO. 3 Miller & Starr, California Real Estate Newsalert 1, Change to Spare: The New California Construction Warranty and Defects Law Under SB 800.
21 NO. 5 Miller & Starr, California Real Estate Newsalert 1. Watch Your Step-If Its S.B. 800 Alternative Prelitigation Procedures Are Not Enforceable, a Builder Cannot Compel a Home Purchaser to Comply With the Statutory S.B. 800 Prelitigation...
6 Witkin, California Summary 10th Torts § 1165, (S 1165) Right to Repair and Other Prelitigation Requirements.

§ 920. Claimant right to file action

If the builder fails to make an offer to repair or otherwise strictly comply with this chapter within the times specified, the claimant is released from the requirements of this chapter and may proceed with the filing of an action. If the contractor performing the repair does not complete the repair in the time or manner specified, the claimant may file an action. If this occurs, the standards set forth in the other chapters of this part shall continue to apply to the action. *(Added by Stats.2002, c. 722 (S.B.800), § 3.)*

Research References

Rutter, Cal. Practice Guide: A.D.R. Ch. 3B-C, C. Statutorily-Mandated ADR.
Miller and Starr California Real Estate § 29:2, Statutory Liability Under "SB800" for Residential Units Sold New After January 1, 2003.
13 NO. 3 Miller & Starr, California Real Estate Newsalert 1, Change to Spare: The New California Construction Warranty and Defects Law Under SB 800.
6 Witkin, California Summary 10th Torts § 1166, (S 1166) Action and Relief.

§ 921. Repair work; time and date scheduled; completion date

(a) In the event that a resolution under this chapter involves a repair by the builder, the builder shall make an appointment with the claimant, make all appropriate arrangements to effectuate a repair of the claimed unmet standards, and compensate the homeowner for all damages resulting therefrom free of charge to the claimant. The repair shall be scheduled through the claimant's legal representative, if any, unless he or she is unavailable during the relevant time periods. The repair shall be commenced on a mutually convenient date within 14 days of acceptance or, if an alternative contractor is selected by the homeowner, within 14 days of the selection, or, if a mediation occurs, within seven days of the mediation, or within five days after a permit is obtained if one is required. The builder shall act with reasonable diligence in obtaining any such permit.

(b) The builder shall ensure that work done on the repairs is done with the utmost diligence, and that the repairs are completed as soon as reasonably possible, subject to the nature of the repair or some unforeseen event not caused by the builder or the contractor performing the repair. Every effort shall be made to complete the repair within 120 days. *(Added by Stats.2002, c. 722 (S.B.800), § 3.)*

Research References

Rutter, Cal. Practice Guide: A.D.R. Ch. 3B-C, C. Statutorily-Mandated ADR.
6 Witkin, California Summary 10th Torts § 1165, (S 1165) Right to Repair and Other Prelitigation Requirements.

§ 922. Electronic recordation, video recordation, or photographs during repair work

The builder shall, upon request, allow the repair to be observed and electronically recorded, video recorded, or photographed by the claimant or his or her legal representative.

Nothing that occurs during the repair process may be used or introduced as evidence to support a spoliation defense by any potential party in any subsequent litigation. *(Added by Stats. 2002, c. 722 (S.B.800), § 3. Amended by Stats.2009, c. 88 (A.B.176), § 13.)*

Law Revision Commission Comments

Section 922 is amended to reflect advances in recording technology and for consistency of terminology. For a similar reform, see 2002 Cal. Stat. ch. 1068 (replacing numerous references to "audiotape" in Civil Discovery Act with either "audio technology," "audio recording," or "audio record," as context required). [37 Cal. L. Revision Comm'n Reports 211 (2007)].

§ 923. Documentation relating to repair work; requests for copies

The builder shall provide the homeowner or his or her legal representative, upon request, with copies of all correspondence, photographs, and other materials pertaining or relating in any manner to the repairs. *(Added by Stats.2002, c. 722 (S.B.800), § 3.)*

Research References

Rutter, Cal. Practice Guide: Civ. Pro. Before Trial Ch. 1-C, C. Prelawsuit Notices, Claims and Demands.

§ 924. Partial repair of claims; statement of reasons

If the builder elects to repair some, but not all of, the claimed unmet standards, the builder shall, at the same time it makes its offer, set forth with particularity in writing the reasons, and the support for those reasons, for not repairing all claimed unmet standards. *(Added by Stats.2002, c. 722 (S.B.800), § 3.)*

Research References

Rutter, Cal. Practice Guide: Civ. Pro. Before Trial Ch. 1-C, C. Prelawsuit Notices, Claims and Demands.
21 NO. 5 Miller & Starr, California Real Estate Newsalert 1. Watch Your Step-If Its S.B. 800 Alternative Prelitigation Procedures Are Not Enforceable, a Builder Cannot Compel a Home Purchaser to Comply With the Statutory S.B. 800 Prelitigation...

§ 925. Failure to repair within time allowed

If the builder fails to complete the repair within the time specified in the repair plan, the claimant is released from the requirements of this chapter and may proceed with the filing of an action. If this occurs, the standards set forth in the other chapters of this title shall continue to apply to the action. *(Added by Stats.2002, c. 722 (S.B.800), § 3.)*

Research References

Rutter, Cal. Practice Guide: Civ. Pro. Before Trial Ch. 1-C, C. Prelawsuit Notices, Claims and Demands.
Miller and Starr California Real Estate § 29:2, Statutory Liability Under "SB800" for Residential Units Sold New After January 1, 2003.
13 NO. 3 Miller & Starr, California Real Estate Newsalert 1, Change to Spare: The New California Construction Warranty and Defects Law Under SB 800.
6 Witkin, California Summary 10th Torts § 1166, (S 1166) Action and Relief.

§ 926. Release or waiver in exchange for repair work

The builder may not obtain a release or waiver of any kind in exchange for the repair work mandated by this chapter. At the conclusion of the repair, the claimant may proceed with filing an action for violation of the applicable standard or for a claim of inadequate repair, or both, including all applicable damages available under Section 944. *(Added by Stats.2002, c. 722 (S.B.800), § 3.)*

Research References

Rutter, Cal. Practice Guide: Civ. Pro. Before Trial Ch. 1-C, C. Prelawsuit Notices, Claims and Demands.
Miller and Starr California Real Estate § 29:2, Statutory Liability Under "SB800" for Residential Units Sold New After January 1, 2003.
13 NO. 3 Miller & Starr, California Real Estate Newsalert 1, Change to Spare: The New California Construction Warranty and Defects Law Under SB 800.
21 NO. 5 Miller & Starr, California Real Estate Newsalert 1. Watch Your Step-If Its S.B. 800 Alternative Prelitigation Procedures Are Not Enforceable, a Builder Cannot Compel a Home Purchaser to Comply With the Statutory S.B. 800 Prelitigation...
6 Witkin, California Summary 10th Torts § 1165, (S 1165) Right to Repair and Other Prelitigation Requirements.

§ 927. Claims for violation of statutory process or inadequate repair; limitation of action; extension of time

If the applicable statute of limitations has otherwise run during this process, the time period for filing a complaint or other legal remedies for violation of any provision of this title, or for a claim of inadequate repair, is extended from the time of the original claim by the claimant to 100 days after the repair is completed, whether or not the particular violation is the one being repaired. If the builder fails to acknowledge the claim within the time specified, elects not to go through this statutory process, or fails to request an inspection within the time specified, the time period for filing a complaint or other legal remedies for violation of any provision of this title is extended from the time of the original claim by the claimant to 45 days after the time for responding to the notice of claim has expired. If the builder elects to attempt to enforce its own nonadversarial procedure in lieu of the procedure set forth in this chapter, the time period for filing a complaint or other legal remedies for violation of any provision of this part is extended from the time of the original claim by the claimant to 100 days after either the completion of the builder's alternative nonadversarial procedure, or 100 days after the builder's alternative nonadversarial procedure is deemed unenforceable, whichever is later. *(Added by Stats.2002, c. 722 (S.B.800), § 3.)*

Research References

Rutter, Cal. Practice Guide: Civ. Pro. Before Trial Ch. 1-C, C. Prelawsuit Notices, Claims and Demands.
Miller and Starr California Real Estate § 29:2, Statutory Liability Under "SB800" for Residential Units Sold New After January 1, 2003.
Miller and Starr California Real Estate § 29:62, Procedures and Limitations Applicable to Residences First Sold New After January 1, 2003.
Miller and Starr California Real Estate § 29:70, Tolling and Extension.
Miller and Starr California Real Estate § 29:72, Limitations Period for Patent Defects.
13 NO. 3 Miller & Starr, California Real Estate Newsalert 1, Change to Spare: The New California Construction Warranty and Defects Law Under SB 800.
14 NO. 2 Miller & Starr, California Real Estate Newsalert 1, "The Outer Limit": The California Supreme Court Reigns in the 10-Year Statute of Repose for Construction Defects.
21 NO. 5 Miller & Starr, California Real Estate Newsalert 1. Watch Your Step-If Its S.B. 800 Alternative Prelitigation Procedures Are Not Enforceable, a Builder Cannot Compel a Home Purchaser to Comply With the Statutory S.B. 800 Prelitigation...
3 Witkin Cal. Proc. 5th Actions § 617, Defects in Construction of Residential Real Property: Ten Years.
3 Witkin Cal. Proc. 5th Actions § 760, (S 760) General Rule of Tolling.

§ 928. Mediation after repair completion

If the builder has invoked this chapter and completed a repair, prior to filing an action, if there has been no previous mediation between the parties, the homeowner or his or her legal representative shall request mediation in writing. The mediation shall be limited to four hours, except as otherwise mutually agreed before a nonaffiliated mediator selected and paid for by the builder. At the homeowner's sole option, the homeowner may agree to split the cost of the mediator and if he or she does so, the mediator shall be selected jointly. The mediator shall have sufficient availability such that the mediation will occur within 15 days after the request for mediation is received and shall occur at a mutually convenient location within the county where the action is pending. In the event that a mediation is used at this point, any applicable statutes of limitations shall be tolled from the date of the request to mediate until the next court day after the mediation is completed, or the 100–day period, whichever is later. *(Added by Stats.2002, c. 722 (S.B.800), § 3.)*

Research References

Rutter, Cal. Practice Guide: A.D.R. Ch. 3B-C, C. Statutorily-Mandated ADR.
Miller and Starr California Real Estate § 29:2, Statutory Liability Under "SB800" for Residential Units Sold New After January 1, 2003.
Miller and Starr California Real Estate § 35:15, Statutory Provisions for Mediations (And Arbitration) of Real Property Disputes.
Miller and Starr California Real Estate § 25B:113, Arbitration or Other Resolution of Disputes With the Subdivider.
13 NO. 3 Miller & Starr, California Real Estate Newsalert 1, Change to Spare: The New California Construction Warranty and Defects Law Under SB 800.
3 Witkin Cal. Proc. 5th Actions § 617, Defects in Construction of Residential Real Property: Ten Years.
6 Witkin, California Summary 10th Torts § 1165, (S 1165) Right to Repair and Other Prelitigation Requirements.

§ 929. Cash offer in lieu of repair; release

(a) Nothing in this chapter prohibits the builder from making only a cash offer and no repair. In this situation, the homeowner is free to accept the offer, or he or she may reject the offer and proceed with the filing of an action. If the latter occurs, the standards of the other chapters of this title shall continue to apply to the action.

(b) The builder may obtain a reasonable release in exchange for the cash payment. The builder may negotiate the terms and conditions of any reasonable release in terms of scope and consideration in conjunction with a cash payment under this chapter. *(Added by Stats.2002, c. 722 (S.B.800), § 3.)*

Research References

Rutter, Cal. Practice Guide: Civ. Pro. Before Trial Ch. 1-C, C. Prelawsuit Notices, Claims and Demands.
Miller and Starr California Real Estate § 29:2, Statutory Liability Under "SB800" for Residential Units Sold New After January 1, 2003.
13 NO. 3 Miller & Starr, California Real Estate Newsalert 1, Change to Spare: The New California Construction Warranty and Defects Law Under SB 800.
6 Witkin, California Summary 10th Torts § 1165, (S 1165) Right to Repair and Other Prelitigation Requirements.

§ 930. Failure to act within mandated timeframes and other requirements; right to file action; motion to stay proceedings

(a) The time periods and all other requirements in this chapter are to be strictly construed, and, unless extended by the mutual agreement of the parties in accordance with this chapter, shall govern the rights and obligations under this title. If a builder fails to act in accordance with this section within the timeframes mandated, unless extended by the mutual agreement of the parties as evidenced by a postclaim written confirmation by the affected homeowner demonstrating that he or she has knowingly and voluntarily extended the statutory timeframe, the claimant may proceed with filing an action. If this occurs, the standards of the other chapters of this title shall continue to apply to the action.

(b) If the claimant does not conform with the requirements of this chapter, the builder may bring a motion to stay any subsequent court action or other proceeding until the require-

ments of this chapter have been satisfied. The court, in its discretion, may award the prevailing party on such a motion, his or her attorney's fees and costs in bringing or opposing the motion. *(Added by Stats.2002, c. 722 (S.B.800), § 3.)*

Research References

Miller and Starr California Real Estate § 29:2, Statutory Liability Under "SB800" for Residential Units Sold New After January 1, 2003.
13 NO. 3 Miller & Starr, California Real Estate Newsalert 1, Change to Spare: The New California Construction Warranty and Defects Law Under SB 800.

§ 931. Causes of action or damages exceeding scope of actionable defects; applicability of standards

If a claim combines causes of action or damages not covered by this part, including, without limitation, personal injuries, class actions, other statutory remedies, or fraud-based claims, the claimed unmet standards shall be administered according to this part, although evidence of the property in its unrepaired condition may be introduced to support the respective elements of any such cause of action. As to any fraud-based claim, if the fact that the property has been repaired under this chapter is deemed admissible, the trier of fact shall be informed that the repair was not voluntarily accepted by the homeowner. As to any class action claims that address solely the incorporation of a defective component into a residence, the named and unnamed class members need not comply with this chapter. *(Added by Stats.2002, c. 722 (S.B.800), § 3.)*

Research References

Rutter, Cal. Practice Guide: A.D.R. Ch. 5-D, D. Defenses to Enforcement.
Miller and Starr California Real Estate § 29:2, Statutory Liability Under "SB800" for Residential Units Sold New After January 1, 2003.
13 NO. 3 Miller & Starr, California Real Estate Newsalert 1, Change to Spare: The New California Construction Warranty and Defects Law Under SB 800.
19 NO. 2 Miller & Starr, California Real Estate Newsalert 4, Alternative Dispute Resolution.
6 Witkin, California Summary 10th Torts § 1165, (S 1165) Right to Repair and Other Prelitigation Requirements.

§ 932. Subsequently discovered claims of unmet standards

Subsequently discovered claims of unmet standards shall be administered separately under this chapter, unless otherwise agreed to by the parties. However, in the case of a detached single family residence, in the same home, if the subsequently discovered claim is for a violation of the same standard as that which has already been initiated by the same claimant and the subject of a currently pending action, the claimant need not reinitiate the process as to the same standard. In the case of an attached project, if the subsequently discovered claim is for a violation of the same standard for a connected component system in the same building as has already been initiated by the same claimant, and the subject of a currently pending action, the claimant need not reinitiate this process as to that standard. *(Added by Stats.2002, c. 722 (S.B.800), § 3.)*

Research References

Miller and Starr California Real Estate § 29:2, Statutory Liability Under "SB800" for Residential Units Sold New After January 1, 2003.
13 NO. 3 Miller & Starr, California Real Estate Newsalert 1, Change to Spare: The New California Construction Warranty and Defects Law Under SB 800.

§ 933. Evidence of repair efforts

If any enforcement of these standards is commenced, the fact that a repair effort was made may be introduced to the trier of fact. However, the claimant may use the condition of the property prior to the repair as the basis for contending that the repair work was inappropriate, inadequate, or incomplete, or that the violation still exists. The claimant need not show that the repair work resulted in further damage nor that damage has continued to occur as a result of the violation. *(Added by Stats.2002, c. 722 (S.B.800), § 3.)*

Research References

Miller and Starr California Real Estate § 29:2, Statutory Liability Under "SB800" for Residential Units Sold New After January 1, 2003.

13 NO. 3 Miller & Starr, California Real Estate Newsalert 1, Change to Spare: The New California Construction Warranty and Defects Law Under SB 800.

§ 934. Evidence of conduct during enforcement process

Evidence of both parties' conduct during this process may be introduced during a subsequent enforcement action, if any, with the exception of any mediation. Any repair efforts undertaken by the builder, shall not be considered settlement communications or offers of settlement and are not inadmissible in evidence on such a basis. *(Added by Stats.2002, c. 722 (S.B.800), § 3.)*

Research References

Miller and Starr California Real Estate § 29:2, Statutory Liability Under "SB800" for Residential Units Sold New After January 1, 2003.

13 NO. 3 Miller & Starr, California Real Estate Newsalert 1, Change to Spare: The New California Construction Warranty and Defects Law Under SB 800.

§ 935. Construction of chapter with similar provisions

To the extent that provisions of this chapter are enforced and those provisions are substantially similar to provisions in Section 6000, but an action is subsequently commenced under Section 6000, the parties are excused from performing the substantially similar requirements under Section 6000. *(Added by Stats.2002, c. 722 (S.B.800), § 3. Amended by Stats.2012, c. 181 (A.B.806), § 30, operative Jan. 1, 2014.)*

Law Revision Commission Comments

Section 935 is amended to correct cross-references to former Section 1375. [40 Cal.L.Rev.Comm. Reports 235 (2010)].

Research References

Rutter, Cal. Practice Guide: A.D.R. Ch. 3B-C, C. Statutorily-Mandated ADR.

Rutter, Cal. Practice Guide: Civ. Pro. Before Trial Ch. 1-C, C. Prelawsuit Notices, Claims and Demands.

Rutter, Cal. Practice Guide: Civ. Pro. Before Trial Ch. 1-E, E. Prelawsuit ADR Requirement.

Miller and Starr California Real Estate § 25B:108, Homeowner's Actions.

Miller and Starr California Real Estate § 25B:111, Conditions Precedent to an Action for Construction Defects.

§ 936. Parties subject to application of title; determination; defenses available; joint and several liability; strict liability

Each and every provision of the other chapters of this title apply to general contractors, subcontractors, material suppliers, individual product manufacturers, and design professionals to the extent that the general contractors, subcontractors, material suppliers, individual product manufacturers, and design professionals caused, in whole or in part, a violation of a particular standard as the result of a negligent act or omission or a breach of contract. In addition to the affirmative defenses set forth in Section 945.5, a general contractor, subcontractor, material supplier, design professional, individual product manufacturer, or other entity may also offer common law and contractual defenses as applicable to any claimed violation of a standard. All actions by a claimant or builder to enforce an express contract, or any provision thereof, against a general contractor, subcontractor, material supplier, individual product manufactur-

er, or design professional is preserved. Nothing in this title modifies the law pertaining to joint and several liability for builders, general contractors, subcontractors, material suppliers, individual product manufacturer, and design professionals that contribute to any specific violation of this title. However, the negligence standard in this section does not apply to any general contractor, subcontractor, material supplier, individual product manufacturer, or design professional with respect to claims for which strict liability would apply. *(Added by Stats.2002, c. 722 (S.B.800), § 3. Amended by Stats.2003, c. 762 (A.B.903), § 5.)*

Research References

Rutter, Cal. Practice Guide: Civ. Pro. Before Trial Ch. 1-C, C. Prelawsuit Notices, Claims and Demands.

Miller and Starr California Real Estate § 29:2, Statutory Liability Under "SB800" for Residential Units Sold New After January 1, 2003.

Miller and Starr California Real Estate § 27:53, Builder Obligations for Residences Sold New After January 1, 2003 ("SB 800").

Miller and Starr California Real Estate § 29:18, Subcontractor's Liability.

Miller and Starr California Real Estate § 29:61, Certificates of Merit.

13 NO. 3 Miller & Starr, California Real Estate Newsalert 1, Change to Spare: The New California Construction Warranty and Defects Law Under SB 800.

6 Witkin, California Summary 10th Torts § 1164, (S 1164) Actionable Defects.

6 Witkin, California Summary 10th Torts § 1167, (S 1167) Liability of Contractors, Suppliers, Product Manufacturers, and Design Professionals.

6 Witkin, California Summary 10th Torts § 1502, Manufacturer or Supplier of Component Part.

6 Witkin, California Summary 10th Torts § 1505, (S 1505) Subcontractor.

§ 937. Construction with professional negligence actions

Nothing in this title shall be interpreted to eliminate or abrogate the requirement to comply with Section 411.35 of the Code of Civil Procedure or to affect the liability of design professionals, including architects and architectural firms, for claims and damages not covered by this title. *(Added by Stats.2002, c. 722 (S.B.800), § 3.)*

Research References

Miller and Starr California Real Estate § 29:61, Certificates of Merit.

§ 938. Application of Title 7 to certain residences

This title applies only to new residential units where the purchase agreement with the buyer was signed by the seller on or after January 1, 2003. *(Added by Stats.2002, c. 722 (S.B.800), § 3. Amended by Stats.2003, c. 762 (A.B.903), § 6.)*

Research References

Rutter, Cal. Practice Guide: Civ. Pro. Before Trial Ch. 1-C, C. Prelawsuit Notices, Claims and Demands.

Miller and Starr California Real Estate § 29:2, Statutory Liability Under "SB800" for Residential Units Sold New After January 1, 2003.

Miller and Starr California Real Estate § 29:76, Systems for Resolving Defective Construction Disputes.

13 NO. 3 Miller & Starr, California Real Estate Newsalert 1, Change to Spare: The New California Construction Warranty and Defects Law Under SB 800.

21 NO. 5 Miller & Starr, California Real Estate Newsalert 1. Watch Your Step-If Its S.B. 800 Alternative Prelitigation Procedures Are Not Enforceable, a Builder Cannot Compel a Home Purchaser to Comply With the Statutory S.B. 800 Prelitigation...

22 NO. 4 Miller & Starr, California Real Estate Newsalert 30, Defective Construction.

6 Witkin, California Summary 10th Torts § 1163, (S 1163) Scope of Legislation.

CHAPTER 5. PROCEDURE

Section
941.   Limitation of action; tolling.

§ 941. Limitation of action; tolling

(a) Except as specifically set forth in this title, no action may be brought to recover under this title more than 10 years after substantial completion of the improvement but not later than the date of recordation of a valid notice of completion.

(b) As used in this section, "action" includes an action for indemnity brought against a person arising out of that person's performance or furnishing of services or materials referred to in this title, except that a cross-complaint for indemnity may be filed pursuant to subdivision (b) of Section 428.10 of the Code of Civil Procedure in an action which has been brought within the time period set forth in subdivision (a).

(c) The limitation prescribed by this section may not be asserted by way of defense by any person in actual possession or the control, as owner, tenant or otherwise, of such an improvement, at the time any deficiency in the improvement constitutes the proximate cause for which it is proposed to make a claim or bring an action.

(d) Sections 337.15 and 337.1 of the Code of Civil Procedure do not apply to actions under this title.

(e) Existing statutory and decisional law regarding tolling of the statute of limitations shall apply to the time periods for filing an action or making a claim under this title, except that repairs made pursuant to Chapter 4 (commencing with Section 910), with the exception of the tolling provision contained in Section 927, do not extend the period for filing an action, or restart the time limitations contained in subdivision (a) or (b) of Section 7091 of the Business and Professions Code. If a builder arranges for a contractor to perform a repair pursuant to Chapter 4 (commencing with Section 910), as to the builder the time period for calculating the statute of limitation in subdivision (a) or (b) of Section 7091 of the Business and Professions Code shall pertain to the substantial completion of the original construction and not to the date of repairs under this title. The time limitations established by this title do not apply to any action by a claimant for a contract or express contractual provision. Causes of action and damages to which this chapter does not apply are not limited by this section. *(Added by Stats.2002, c. 722 (S.B.800), § 3. Amended by Stats.2003, c. 62 (S.B.600), § 12; Stats.2003, c. 762 (A.B.903), § 7.)*

Research References

Miller and Starr California Real Estate § 29:2, Statutory Liability Under "SB800" for Residential Units Sold New After January 1, 2003.
Miller and Starr California Real Estate § 29:62, Procedures and Limitations Applicable to Residences First Sold New After January 1, 2003.
Miller and Starr California Real Estate § 29:63, Breach of Contract.
Miller and Starr California Real Estate § 29:64, Negligence.
Miller and Starr California Real Estate § 29:70, Tolling and Extension.
Miller and Starr California Real Estate § 29:72, Limitations Period for Patent Defects.
Miller and Starr California Real Estate § 29:73, Maximum 10-Year Period.
Miller and Starr California Real Estate § 29:74, Actions Within and Outside the 10-Year Statute.
13 NO. 3 Miller & Starr, California Real Estate Newsalert 1, Change to Spare: The New California Construction Warranty and Defects Law Under SB 800.
3 Witkin Cal. Proc. 5th Actions § 484, (S 484) Four Years.
3 Witkin Cal. Proc. 5th Actions § 488, (S 488) Ten Years.
3 Witkin Cal. Proc. 5th Actions § 607, (S 607) Distinctions.
3 Witkin Cal. Proc. 5th Actions § 616, Action by Homeowner for Defects in Original Construction of Residence.
3 Witkin Cal. Proc. 5th Actions § 617, Defects in Construction of Residential Real Property: Ten Years.
3 Witkin Cal. Proc. 5th Actions § 760, (S 760) General Rule of Tolling.
6 Witkin, California Summary 10th Torts § 1166, (S 1166) Action and Relief.
6 Witkin, California Summary 10th Torts § 1167, (S 1167) Liability of Contractors, Suppliers, Product Manufacturers, and Design Professionals.

§ 942. Sufficiency of claim for violation of Chapter 2 standards

In order to make a claim for violation of the standards set forth in Chapter 2 (commencing with Section 896), a homeowner need only demonstrate, in accordance with the applicable evidentiary standard, that the home does not meet the applicable standard, subject to the affirmative defenses set forth in Section 945.5. No further showing of causation or damages is required to meet the burden of proof regarding a violation of a standard set forth in Chapter 2 (commencing with Section 896), provided that the violation arises out of, pertains to, or is related to, the original construction. *(Added by Stats.2003, c. 762 (A.B.903), § 9.)*

Research References

Rutter, Cal. Practice Guide: Insurance Litigation Ch. 7E-B, B. Commercial General Liability (CGL) Policies.
Miller and Starr California Real Estate § 29:2, Statutory Liability Under "SB800" for Residential Units Sold New After January 1, 2003.
Miller and Starr California Real Estate § 29:9, General Principles Concerning Owner's Damages.
13 NO. 3 Miller & Starr, California Real Estate Newsalert 1, Change to Spare: The New California Construction Warranty and Defects Law Under SB 800.
14 NO. 4 Miller & Starr, California Real Estate Newsalert 4, Defective Construction.
21 NO. 5 Miller & Starr, California Real Estate Newsalert 1. Watch Your Step-If Its S.B. 800 Alternative Prelitigation Procedures Are Not Enforceable, a Builder Cannot Compel a Home Purchaser to Comply With the Statutory S.B. 800 Prelitigation...
6 Witkin, California Summary 10th Torts § 1166, (S 1166) Action and Relief.
6 Witkin, California Summary 10th Torts § 1167, (S 1167) Liability of Contractors, Suppliers, Product Manufacturers, and Design Professionals.

§ 943. Exclusiveness of title; exceptions

(a) Except as provided in this title, no other cause of action for a claim covered by this title or for damages recoverable under Section 944 is allowed. In addition to the rights under this title, this title does not apply to any action by a claimant to enforce a contract or express contractual provision, or any action for fraud, personal injury, or violation of a statute. Damages awarded for the items set forth in Section 944 in such other cause of action shall be reduced by the amounts recovered pursuant to Section 944 for violation of the standards set forth in this title.

(b) As to any claims involving a detached single-family home, the homeowner's right to the reasonable value of repairing any nonconformity is limited to the repair costs, or the diminution in current value of the home caused by the nonconformity, whichever is less, subject to the personal use exception as developed under common law. *(Formerly § 942, added by Stats.2002, c. 722 (S.B.800), § 3. Renumbered § 943 and amended by Stats.2003, c. 762 (A.B.903), § 8.)*

Research References

Rutter, Cal. Practice Guide: A.D.R. Ch. 5-D, D. Defenses to Enforcement.
Miller and Starr California Real Estate § 29:2, Statutory Liability Under "SB800" for Residential Units Sold New After January 1, 2003.

Miller and Starr California Real Estate § 29:64, Negligence.

19 NO. 2 Miller & Starr, California Real Estate Newsalert 4, Alternative Dispute Resolution.

6 Witkin, California Summary 10th Torts § 1163, (S 1163) Scope of Legislation.

6 Witkin, California Summary 10th Torts § 1166, (S 1166) Action and Relief.

§ 944. Damages; determination of amount

If a claim for damages is made under this title, the homeowner is only entitled to damages for the reasonable value of repairing any violation of the standards set forth in this title, the reasonable cost of repairing any damages caused by the repair efforts, the reasonable cost of repairing and rectifying any damages resulting from the failure of the home to meet the standards, the reasonable cost of removing and replacing any improper repair by the builder, reasonable relocation and storage expenses, lost business income if the home was used as a principal place of a business licensed to be operated from the home, reasonable investigative costs for each established violation, and all other costs or fees recoverable by contract or statute. *(Added by Stats.2002, c. 722 (S.B.800), § 3.)*

Research References

Miller and Starr California Real Estate § 29:2, Statutory Liability Under "SB800" for Residential Units Sold New After January 1, 2003.

Miller and Starr California Real Estate § 29:9, General Principles Concerning Owner's Damages.

Miller and Starr California Real Estate § 29:10, Measure of Owner's Damages for Defective Construction.

Miller and Starr California Real Estate § 29:64, Negligence.

13 NO. 3 Miller & Starr, California Real Estate Newsalert 1, Change to Spare: The New California Construction Warranty and Defects Law Under SB 800.

21 NO. 5 Miller & Starr, California Real Estate Newsalert 1. Watch Your Step-If Its S.B. 800 Alternative Prelitigation Procedures Are Not Enforceable, a Builder Cannot Compel a Home Purchaser to Comply With the Statutory S.B. 800 Prelitigation...

6 Witkin, California Summary 10th Torts § 1166, (S 1166) Action and Relief.

6 Witkin, California Summary 10th Torts § 1167, (S 1167) Liability of Contractors, Suppliers, Product Manufacturers, and Design Professionals.

§ 945. Binding effect upon original purchasers and their successors-in-interest

The provisions, standards, rights, and obligations set forth in this title are binding upon all original purchasers and their successors-in-interest. For purposes of this title, associations and others having the rights set forth in Sections 4810 and 4815 shall be considered to be original purchasers and shall have standing to enforce the provisions, standards, rights, and obligations set forth in this title. *(Added by Stats.2002, c. 722 (S.B.800), § 3. Amended by Stats.2005, c. 37 (S.B.853), § 1; Stats.2012, c. 181 (A.B.806), § 31, operative Jan. 1, 2014.)*

Law Revision Commission Comments

Section 945 is amended to correct the cross-reference to former Code of Civil Procedure Section 383. This is a nonsubstantive change. The substance of former Code of Civil Procedure Section 383 is continued in Sections 1368.3 and 1368.4. See 2004 Cal. Stat. ch. 754, §§ 4, 7; *Alternative Dispute Resolution in Common Interest Developments*, 33 Cal. L. Revision Comm'n Reports 689 (2003).

Section 945 is amended to correct cross-references to former Sections 1368.3 and 1368.4. [40 Cal.L.Rev.Comm. Reports 235 (2010)].

Research References

Miller and Starr California Real Estate § 29:2, Statutory Liability Under "SB800" for Residential Units Sold New After January 1, 2003.

13 NO. 3 Miller & Starr, California Real Estate Newsalert 1, Change to Spare: The New California Construction Warranty and Defects Law Under SB 800.

14 NO. 1 Miller & Starr, California Real Estate Newsalert 14, Subdivisions.

16 NO. 4 Miller & Starr, California Real Estate Newsalert 19, Subdivisions.

16 NO. 5 Miller & Starr, California Real Estate Newsalert 26, State Board of Equalization Issues Comprehensive Summary and Qs and As for Transfers of Base Year Values of Principal Residences.

21 NO. 5 Miller & Starr, California Real Estate Newsalert 1. Watch Your Step-If Its S.B. 800 Alternative Prelitigation Procedures Are Not Enforceable, a Builder Cannot Compel a Home Purchaser to Comply With the Statutory S.B. 800 Prelitigation...

6 Witkin, California Summary 10th Torts § 1163, (S 1163) Scope of Legislation.

§ 945.5. Affirmative defenses

A builder, general contractor, subcontractor, material supplier, individual product manufacturer, or design professional, under the principles of comparative fault pertaining to affirmative defenses, may be excused, in whole or in part, from any obligation, damage, loss, or liability if the builder, general contractor, subcontractor, material supplier, individual product manufacturer, or design professional, can demonstrate any of the following affirmative defenses in response to a claimed violation:

(a) To the extent it is caused by an unforeseen act of nature which caused the structure not to meet the standard. For purposes of this section an "unforeseen act of nature" means a weather condition, earthquake, or manmade event such as war, terrorism, or vandalism, in excess of the design criteria expressed by the applicable building codes, regulations, and ordinances in effect at the time of original construction.

(b) To the extent it is caused by a homeowner's unreasonable failure to minimize or prevent those damages in a timely manner, including the failure of the homeowner to allow reasonable and timely access for inspections and repairs under this title. This includes the failure to give timely notice to the builder after discovery of a violation, but does not include damages due to the untimely or inadequate response of a builder to the homeowner's claim.

(c) To the extent it is caused by the homeowner or his or her agent, employee, general contractor, subcontractor, independent contractor, or consultant by virtue of their failure to follow the builder's or manufacturer's recommendations, or commonly accepted homeowner maintenance obligations. In order to rely upon this defense as it relates to a builder's recommended maintenance schedule, the builder shall show that the homeowner had written notice of these schedules and recommendations and that the recommendations and schedules were reasonable at the time they were issued.

(d) To the extent it is caused by the homeowner or his or her agent's or an independent third party's alterations, ordinary wear and tear, misuse, abuse, or neglect, or by the structure's use for something other than its intended purpose.

(e) To the extent that the time period for filing actions bars the claimed violation.

(f) As to a particular violation for which the builder has obtained a valid release.

(g) To the extent that the builder's repair was successful in correcting the particular violation of the applicable standard.

(h) As to any causes of action to which this statute does not apply, all applicable affirmative defenses are preserved. *(Added by Stats.2002, c. 722 (S.B.800), § 3. Amended by Stats.2003, c. 762 (A.B.903), § 10.)*

Research References

Rutter, Cal. Practice Guide: A.D.R. Ch. 5-D, D. Defenses to Enforcement.

Miller and Starr California Real Estate § 29:2, Statutory Liability Under "SB800" for Residential Units Sold New After January 1, 2003.

Miller and Starr California Real Estate § 29:8, Contractor's Statutory Liability as to Residences Sold New After January 1, 2003.

Miller and Starr California Real Estate § 29:9, General Principles Concerning Owner's Damages.

Miller and Starr California Real Estate § 27:46, Indemnity Provisions; Wrap-Up Insurance.

Miller and Starr California Real Estate § 27:53, Builder Obligations for Residences Sold New After January 1, 2003 ("SB 800").

Miller and Starr California Real Estate § 29:10, Measure of Owner's Damages for Defective Construction.

Miller and Starr California Real Estate § 29:17, Express and Implied Indemnity.

Miller and Starr California Real Estate § 29:18, Subcontractor's Liability.

Miller and Starr California Real Estate § 29:19, Liability of Material Suppliers and Manufacturers.

Miller and Starr California Real Estate § 29:21, "Developer" Defined; Theories of Liability.

Miller and Starr California Real Estate § 29:30, Measure of Damages Applicable to Developers.

Miller and Starr California Real Estate § 29:46, Independent Inspector's Immunities.

Miller and Starr California Real Estate § 29:62, Procedures and Limitations Applicable to Residences First Sold New After January 1, 2003.

Miller and Starr California Real Estate § 29:70, Tolling and Extension.

Miller and Starr California Real Estate § 29:76, Systems for Resolving Defective Construction Disputes.

13 NO. 3 Miller & Starr, California Real Estate Newsalert 1, Change to Spare: The New California Construction Warranty and Defects Law Under SB 800.

13 NO. 6 Miller & Starr, California Real Estate Newsalert 1, Using Basura to Make Construction Defect Claims Arbitrable, or Woodside to Send Them to a Referee.

13 NO. 4 Miller & Starr, California Real Estate Newsalert 4, Construction Defects.

19 NO. 2 Miller & Starr, California Real Estate Newsalert 4, Alternative Dispute Resolution.

19 NO. 2 Miller & Starr, California Real Estate Newsalert 6, Common Interest Developments.

19 NO. 4 Miller & Starr, California Real Estate Newsalert 35, Defective Construction.

21 NO. 5 Miller & Starr, California Real Estate Newsalert 1. Watch Your Step-If Its S.B. 800 Alternative Prelitigation Procedures Are Not Enforceable, a Builder Cannot Compel a Home Purchaser to Comply With the Statutory S.B. 800 Prelitigation...

21 NO. 5 Miller & Starr, California Real Estate Newsalert 11, Defective Construction.

6 Witkin, California Summary 10th Torts § 1166, (S 1166) Action and Relief.

6 Witkin, California Summary 10th Torts § 1167, (S 1167) Liability of Contractors, Suppliers, Product Manufacturers, and Design Professionals.

Part 3

PERSONAL OR MOVABLE PROPERTY

Title 1

PERSONAL PROPERTY IN GENERAL

Section
946. Personal property; law of domicile.

§ 946. Personal property; law of domicile

If there is no law to the contrary, in the place where personal property is situated, it is deemed to follow the person of its owner, and is governed by the law of his domicile. *(Enacted in*

1872. *Repealed by Code Am.1873–74, c. 612, p. 223, § 123. Reenacted by Code Am.1875–76, c. 167, p. 78, § 1.)*

Research References

Miller and Starr California Real Estate § 17:4, Jurisdiction.
14 Witkin, California Summary 10th Wills and Probate § 53, in General.

Title 2

PARTICULAR KINDS OF PERSONAL PROPERTY

CHAPTER 1. THINGS IN ACTION

ARTICLE 1. TRANSFER OF THINGS IN ACTION

Section
953.   Thing in action defined.
954.   Transfer of things in action.
954.5. Perfection of transfer of right represented by judgment.
955.   Nonnegotiable instruments; transfer; notice.
955.1. Payment intangibles; assignments; priorities; notice to obligor.

§ 953. Thing in action defined

A thing in action is a right to recover money or other personal property by a judicial proceeding. *(Enacted in 1872. Amended by Code Am.1873–74, c. 612, p. 223, § 125.)*

Research References

22 NO. 3 Miller & Starr, California Real Estate Newsalert 1, Show Me Your Papers: Sales and Assignments of Secured Real Estate Loans and the California Foreclosure Process.

1 Witkin Cal. Summ. 10th Contracts § 720, (S 720) in General.

13 Witkin, California Summary 10th Personal Property § 136, Chose Not Evidenced by Writing.

§ 954. Transfer of things in action

A thing in action, arising out of the violation of a right of property, or out of an obligation, may be transferred by the owner. *(Enacted in 1872. Amended by Stats.1990, c. 79 (A.B.759), § 2, operative July 1, 1991.)*

Law Revision Commission Comments

The second sentence of Section 954 is deleted because it is unnecessary and is an inadequate statement of the applicable law. The substantive rules concerning passage of causes of action are stated elsewhere. See, e.g., Code Civ.Proc. § 353; Prob.Code §§ 573, 7000–7001. This amendment is not a substantive change. [20 Cal.L.Rev.Comm.Reports 1001 (1990)].

Research References

Rutter, Cal. Practice Guide: Enforcing Judgments/Debts Ch. 6G-11, Enforcement of Judgment by Assignees.

Rutter, Cal. Practice Guide: Insurance Litigation Ch. 13-B, B. Extracontractual Compensatory Damages.

Miller and Starr California Real Estate § 17:2, Property as "Bundle of Rights".

Miller and Starr California Real Estate § 1:124, Definitions; Burden of Proof.

Miller and Starr California Real Estate § 11:42, Property Interests Protected.

Miller and Starr California Real Estate § 12:57, Management and Control--Restriction on Gifts of Community Property.

Miller and Starr California Real Estate § 25B:102, Enforcement of the Restrictions--Enforcement by a Member.

19 NO. 6 Miller & Starr, California Real Estate Newsalert 7, Common Interest Developments.

22 NO. 3 Miller & Starr, California Real Estate Newsalert 1, Show Me Your Papers: Sales and Assignments of Secured Real Estate Loans and the California Foreclosure Process.

3 Witkin Cal. Proc. 5th Actions § 13, Former Law: Survivable Claims.

4 Witkin Cal. Proc. 5th Pleading § 127, (S 127) Assignment of Beneficial Interest.

1 Witkin Cal. Summ. 10th Contracts § 720, (S 720) in General.

1 Witkin Cal. Summ. 10th Contracts § 721, (S 721) Distinctions.

5 Witkin, California Summary 10th Torts § 23, (S 23) Survival of Tort Liability.

§ 954.5. Perfection of transfer of right represented by judgment

(a) Subject to subdivisions (b) and (c), a transfer of a right represented by a judgment excluded from coverage of Division 9 of the Commercial Code by paragraph (9) of subdivision (d) of Section 9109 of the Commercial Code shall be deemed perfected as against third persons upon there being executed and delivered to the transferee an assignment thereof in writing.

(b) As between bona fide assignees of the same right for value without notice, the assignee who first becomes an assignee of record, by filing an acknowledgment of assignment of judgment with the court as provided in Section 673 of the Code of Civil Procedure or otherwise becoming an assignee of record, has priority.

(c) The filing of an acknowledgment of assignment of the judgment with the court under Section 673 of the Code of Civil Procedure is not, of itself, notice to the judgment debtor so as to invalidate any payments made by the judgment debtor that would otherwise be applied to the satisfaction of the judgment. *(Added by Stats.1982, c. 497, p. 2135, § 4, operative July 1, 1983. Amended by Stats.1999, c. 991 (S.B.45), § 1.8, operative July 1, 2001.)*

Law Revision Commission Comments

Section 954.5 continues the substance of a former portion of Section 955.1, but Section 954.5 changes prior law concerning the priorities of conflicting bona fide assignees of the same judgment for value without notice; such an assignee who first files an acknowledgment of assignment of judgment under Code of Civil Procedure Section 673 (or otherwise becomes an assignee of record) obtains a priority over other assignees of the same judgment. Under prior law formerly found in Section 955.1, the good faith, for value, without notice, assignee who first gave notice of the assignment in writing to the judgment debtor had priority. Nothing in Section 954.5 requires the filing of an acknowledgment of assignment of judgment with the court in order to accomplish the transfer of the interest in the judgment; the section merely covers the priorities between conflicting bona fide assignees of the same right for value and without notice and protects the judgment debtor who pays the judgment creditor without notice of the assignment. (15 Cal.L.Rev.Comm. Reports 2001).

Research References

Rutter, Cal. Practice Guide: Enforcing Judgments/Debts Ch. 6G-11, Enforcement of Judgment by Assignees.

8 Witkin Cal. Proc. 5th Enforcement of Judgment § 24, Enforcement by Assignee.

§ 955. Nonnegotiable instruments; transfer; notice

A transfer other than one intended to create a security interest (paragraph (1) or (3) of subdivision (a) of Section 9109 of the Commercial Code) of a nonnegotiable instrument which is otherwise negotiable within Division 3 of the Commercial Code but which is not payable to order or to bearer and a sale of accounts, chattel paper, payment intangibles, or promissory notes as part of a sale of the business out of which they arose (paragraph (4) of subdivision (d) of Section 9109 of the Commercial Code) shall be deemed perfected against third persons when such property rights have been endorsed or assigned in writing and in the case of such instruments or chattel paper delivered to the transferee, whether or not notice of such transfer or sale has been given to the obligor; but such endorsement, assignment, or delivery is not, of itself, notice to the obligor so as to invalidate any payments made by the obligor to the transferor. *(Added by Stats.1941, c. 1025, p. 2655, § 1. Amended by Stats.1953, c. 1242, p. 2806, § 2; Stats.1963, c. 819, p. 1997, § 3, eff. Jan. 1, 1965; Stats.1982, c. 497, p. 2135, § 5, operative July 1, 1983; Stats.1999, c. 991 (S.B.45), § 2, operative July 1, 2001.)*

Law Revision Commission Comments

Section 955 is amended to delete the reference to "contract rights" since that term is no longer used in the Commercial Code and to make other technical changes (15 Cal.L.Rev.Comm. Reports 2001).

Research References

22 NO. 3 Miller & Starr, California Real Estate Newsalert 1, Show Me Your Papers: Sales and Assignments of Secured Real Estate Loans and the California Foreclosure Process.

§ 955.1. Payment intangibles; assignments; priorities; notice to obligor

(a) Except as provided in Sections 954.5 and 955 and subject to subdivisions (b) and (c), a transfer other than one intended to create a security interest (paragraph (1) or (3) of subdivision (a) of Section 9109 of the Commercial Code) of any payment intangible (Section 9102 of the Commercial Code) and any transfer of accounts, chattel paper, payment intangibles, or promissory notes excluded from the coverage of Division 9 of the Commercial Code by paragraph (4) of subdivision (d) of Section 9109 of the Commercial Code shall be deemed perfected as against third persons upon there being executed and delivered to the transferee an assignment thereof in writing.

(b) As between bona fide assignees of the same right for value without notice, the assignee first giving notice thereof to the obligor in writing has priority.

(c) The assignment is not, of itself, notice to the obligor so as to invalidate any payments made by the obligor to the transferor.

(d) This section does not apply to transfers or assignments of transition property, as defined in Section 840 of the Public Utilities Code, or to transfers or assignments of recovery property, as defined in Section 848 of the Public Utilities Code. *(Added by Stats.1953, c. 1242, p. 2806, § 3. Amended by Stats.1955, c. 741, p. 1238, § 1; Stats.1963, c. 819, p. 1997, § 4, eff. Jan. 1, 1965; Stats.1982, c. 497, p. 2136, § 6, operative July 1, 1983; Stats.1996, c. 854 (A.B.1890), § 2, eff. Sept. 24, 1996; Stats.1999, c. 991 (S.B.45), § 3, operative July 1, 2001; Stats.2004, c. 46 (S.B.772), § 2, eff. June 7, 2004.)*

Law Revision Commission Comments

Section 955.1 is amended to delete the reference to "contract rights," since that term is no longer used in the Commercial Code. The reference to a "right represented by a judgment" is deleted because this provision is superseded by Section 954.5. The other changes are not substantive. (15 Cal.L.Rev.Comm. Reports 2001).

Research References

Rutter, Cal. Practice Guide: Enforcing Judgments/Debts Ch. 6G-5, Assignment Order.

Rutter, Cal. Practice Guide: Enforcing Judgments/Debts Ch. 6G-7, Charging Orders Against Debtor Partnership/LLC Interests.

Miller and Starr California Real Estate § 10:38, What is Assignable; Procedure.

Miller and Starr California Real Estate § 10:39, Rights of the Parties.

8 Witkin Cal. Proc. 5th Enforcement of Judgment § 24, Enforcement by
    Assignee.
8 Witkin Cal. Proc. 5th Enforcement of Judgment § 306, (S 306) Effect of
    Assignment.
1 Witkin Cal. Summ. 10th Contracts § 738, in General.

CHAPTER 3.   PRODUCTS OF THE MIND

§ 980.   Ownership; works not fixed in tangible medium; sound recordings; inventions or designs

(a)(1) The author of any original work of authorship that is not fixed in any tangible medium of expression has an exclusive ownership in the representation or expression thereof as against all persons except one who orginally [1] and independently creates the same or similar work. A work shall be considered not fixed when it is not embodied in a tangible medium of expression or when its embodiment in a tangible medium of expression is not sufficiently permanent or stable to permit it to be perceived, reproduced, or otherwise communicated for a period of more than transitory duration, either directly or with the aid of a machine or device.

(2) The author of an original work of authorship consisting of a sound recording initially fixed prior to February 15, 1972, has an exclusive ownership therein until February 15, 2047, as against all persons except one who independently makes or duplicates another sound recording that does not directly or indirectly recapture the actual sounds fixed in such prior sound recording, but consists entirely of an independent fixation of other sounds, even though such sounds imitate or simulate the sounds contained in the prior sound recording.

(b) The inventor or proprietor of any invention or design, with or without delineation, or other graphical representation, has an exclusive ownership therein, and in the representation or expression thereof, which continues so long as the invention or design and the representations or expressions thereof made by him remain in his possession. *(Enacted in 1872. Amended by Stats.1947, c. 1107, p. 2546, § 1; Stats.1949, c. 921, p. 1686, § 1; Stats.1982, c. 574, p. 2533, § 2.)*

1 So in chaptered copy.

Research References

Miller and Starr California Real Estate § 17:1, in General; Definitions.
Miller and Starr California Real Estate § 27:111, Ownership and Copy-
    right of Plans and Specifications.
21 NO. 2 Miller & Starr, California Real Estate Newsalert 1, Who Owns
    the Plans? Owners, Architects and Engineers, and the Federal Law of
    Copyright.
13 Witkin, California Summary 10th Personal Property § 46, Former Law.

13 Witkin, California Summary 10th Personal Property § 47, Revised
    Statutes.
13 Witkin, California Summary 10th Personal Property § 69, No Property
    Right.
13 Witkin, California Summary 10th Personal Property § 74, (S 74)
    Common Law Right During Possession.
5 Witkin, California Summary 10th Torts § 722, Literary Infringement or
    Plagiarism.

§ 981.   Joint ownership; works not fixed in tangible medium; inventions or designs

(a) Unless otherwise agreed, an original work of authorship not fixed in any tangible medium of expression and in the creation of which several persons are jointly concerned, is owned by them in equal proportion.

(b) Unless otherwise agreed, an invention or design in the production of which several persons are jointly concerned is owned by them as follows:

(1) If the invention or design is single, in equal proportions.

(2) If it is not single, in proportion to the contribution of each. *(Enacted in 1872. Amended by Stats.1947, c. 1107, p. 2546, § 2; Stats.1949, c. 921, p. 1686, § 2; Stats.1982, c. 574, p. 2533, § 3.)*

Research References

Miller and Starr California Real Estate § 27:111, Ownership and Copy-
    right of Plans and Specifications.
13 Witkin, California Summary 10th Personal Property § 30, (S 30)
    Nature of Joint Tenancy.
13 Witkin, California Summary 10th Personal Property § 47, Revised
    Statutes.
13 Witkin, California Summary 10th Personal Property § 74, (S 74)
    Common Law Right During Possession.

§ 982.   Transfers of ownership; right of reproduction

(a) The owner of any rights in any original works of authorship not fixed in any tangible medium of expression may transfer the ownership therein.

(b) The owner of any invention or design, or of any representation or expression thereof, may transfer his or her proprietary interest in it.

(c) Notwithstanding any other provision in this section, whenever a work of fine art is transferred, whether by sale or on commission or otherwise, by or on behalf of the artist who created it, or that artist's heir, legatee, or personal representative, the right of reproduction thereof is reserved to such artist or such heir, legatee, or personal representative until it passes into the public domain by act or operation of law, unless that right is expressly transferred by a document in writing in which reference is made to the specific right of reproduction, signed by the owner of the rights conveyed or that person's duly authorized agent. If the transfer is pursuant to an employment relationship, the right of reproduction is transferred to the employer, unless it is expressly reserved in writing. If the transfer is pursuant to a legacy or inheritance, the right of reproduction is transferred to the legatee or heir, unless it is expressly reserved by will or codicil. Nothing contained herein, however, shall be construed to prohibit the fair use of such work of fine art.

(d) As used in subdivision (c):

(1) "Fine art" means any work of visual art, including but not limited to, a drawing, painting, sculpture, mosaic, or photograph, a work of calligraphy, work of graphic art (including an etching, lithograph, offset print, silk screen, or a work of graphic art of like nature), crafts (including crafts in clay, textile, fiber, wood, metal, plastic, and like materials), or mixed media (including a collage, assemblage, or any combination of the foregoing art media).

(2) "Artist" means the creator of a work of fine art.

(3) "Right of reproduction", at the present state of commerce and technology shall be interpreted as including, but shall not be limited to, the following: reproduction of works of fine art as prints suitable for framing; facsimile casts of sculpture; reproductions used for greeting cards; reproductions in general books and magazines not devoted primarily to art, and in newspapers in other than art or news sections, when such reproductions in books, magazines, and newspapers are used for purposes similar to those of material for which the publishers customarily pay; art films; television, except from stations operated for educational purposes, or on programs for educational purposes from all stations; and reproductions used in any form of advertising, including magazines, calendars, newspapers, posters, billboards, films or television.

(e) The amendments to this section made at the 1975–76 Regular Session shall only apply to transfers made on or after January 1, 1976. *(Enacted in 1872. Amended by Stats.1947, c. 1107, p. 2546, § 3; Stats.1949, c. 921, p. 1686, § 3; Stats.1975, c. 952, p. 2128, § 1; Stats.1982, c. 574, p. 2533, § 4.)*

Research References

Miller and Starr California Real Estate § 27:111, Ownership and Copyright of Plans and Specifications.
13 Witkin, California Summary 10th Personal Property § 47, Revised Statutes.
13 Witkin, California Summary 10th Personal Property § 48, Reproduction Rights in Fine Arts.
13 Witkin, California Summary 10th Personal Property § 74, (S 74) Common Law Right During Possession.

§ 983. Inventions or designs; effect of making public

If the owner of any invention or design intentionally makes it public, a copy or reproduction may be made public by any person, without responsiblily [1] to the owner, so far as the law of this state is concerned. *(Enacted in 1872. Amended by Stats. 1947, c. 1107, p. 2546, § 4; Stats.1949, c. 921, p. 1686, § 4; Stats.1982, c. 574, p. 2534, § 5.)*

[1] So in chaptered copy.

Research References

Miller and Starr California Real Estate § 27:111, Ownership and Copyright of Plans and Specifications.
13 Witkin, California Summary 10th Personal Property § 47, Revised Statutes.
13 Witkin, California Summary 10th Personal Property § 74, (S 74) Common Law Right During Possession.

§ 984. Inventions or designs; rights of subsequent or original producers

If the owner of an invention or design does not make it public, any other person subsequently and originally producing the same thing has the same right therein as the prior inventor, which is exclusive to the same extent against all persons except the prior inventor, or those claiming under him. *(Added by Stats.1949, c. 921, p. 1687, § 5.)*

§ 985. Private writings; ownership; publication

PRIVATE WRITINGS. Letters and other private communications in writing belong to the person to whom they are addressed and delivered; but they cannot be published against the will of the writer, except by authority of law. *(Enacted in 1872.)*

§ 986. Work of fine art; sale; payment of percentage to artist or deposit for Arts Council; failure to pay; action for damages; exemptions

(a) Whenever a work of fine art is sold and the seller resides in California or the sale takes place in California, the seller or the seller's agent shall pay to the artist of such work of fine art or to such artist's agent 5 percent of the amount of such sale. The right of the artist to receive an amount equal to 5 percent of the amount of such sale may be waived only by a contract in writing providing for an amount in excess of 5 percent of the amount of such sale. An artist may assign the right to collect the royalty payment provided by this section to another individual or entity. However, the assignment shall not have the effect of creating a waiver prohibited by this subdivision.

(1) When a work of fine art is sold at an auction or by a gallery, dealer, broker, museum, or other person acting as the agent for the seller the agent shall withhold 5 percent of the amount of the sale, locate the artist and pay the artist.

(2) If the seller or agent is unable to locate and pay the artist within 90 days, an amount equal to 5 percent of the amount of the sale shall be tranferred [1] to the Arts Council.

(3) If a seller or the seller's agent fails to pay an artist the amount equal to 5 percent of the sale of a work of fine art by the artist or fails to transfer such amount to the Arts Council, the artist may bring an action for damages within three years after the date of sale or one year after the discovery of the sale, whichever is longer. The prevailing party in any action brought under this paragraph shall be entitled to reasonable attorney fees, in an amount as determined by the court.

(4) Moneys received by the council pursuant to this section shall be deposited in an account in the Special Deposit Fund in the State Treasury.

(5) The Arts Council shall attempt to locate any artist for whom money is received pursuant to this section. If the council is unable to locate the artist and the artist does not file a written claim for the money received by the council within seven years of the date of sale of the work of fine art, the right of the artist terminates and such money shall be transferred to the council for use in acquiring fine art pursuant to the Art in Public Buildings program set forth in Chapter 2.1 (commencing with Section 15813) of Part 10b of Division 3 of Title 2, of the Government Code.

(6) Any amounts of money held by any seller or agent for the payment of artists pursuant to this section shall be exempt from enforcement of a money judgment by the creditors of the seller or agent.

(7) Upon the death of an artist, the rights and duties created under this section shall inure to his or her heirs, legatees, or personal representative, until the 20th anniversary of the death of the artist. The provisions of this paragraph shall be applicable only with respect to an artist who dies after January 1, 1983.

(b) Subdivision (a) shall not apply to any of the following:

(1) To the initial sale of a work of fine art where legal title to such work at the time of such initial sale is vested in the artist thereof.

(2) To the resale of a work of fine art for a gross sales price of less than one thousand dollars ($1,000).

(3) Except as provided in paragraph (7) of subdivision (a), to a resale after the death of such artist.

(4) To the resale of the work of fine art for a gross sales price less than the purchase price paid by the seller.

(5) To a transfer of a work of fine art which is exchanged for one or more works of fine art or for a combination of cash, other property, and one or more works of fine art where the fair market value of the property exchanged is less than one thousand dollars ($1,000).

(6) To the resale of a work of fine art by an art dealer to a purchaser within 10 years of the initial sale of the work of fine art by the artist to an art dealer, provided all intervening resales are between art dealers.

(7) To a sale of a work of stained glass artistry where the work has been permanently attached to real property and is sold as part of the sale of the real property to which it is attached.

(c) For purposes of this section, the following terms have the following meanings:

(1) "Artist" means the person who creates a work of fine art and who, at the time of resale, is a citizen of the United States, or a resident of the state who has resided in the state for a minimum of two years.

(2) "Fine art" means an original painting, sculpture, or drawing, or an original work of art in glass.

(3) "Art dealer" means a person who is actively and principally engaged in or conducting the business of selling works of fine art for which business such person validly holds a sales tax permit.

(d) This section shall become operative on January 1, 1977, and shall apply to works of fine art created before and after its operative date.

(e) If any provision of this section or the application thereof to any person or circumstance is held invalid for any reason, such invalidity shall not affect any other provisions or applications of this section which can be effected, without the invalid provision or application, and to this end the provisions of this section are severable.

(f) The amendments to this section enacted during the 1981–82 Regular Session of the Legislature shall apply to transfers of works of fine art, when created before or after January 1, 1983, that occur on or after that date. *(Added by Stats.1976, c. 1228, p. 5542, § 1.¹ Amended by Stats.1982, c. 497, p. 2136, § 7, operative July 1, 1983; Stats.1982, c. 1609, p. 6433, § 1.5.)*

¹ So in chaptered copy.

Validity

For validity of this section, see Estate of Graham v. Sotheby's Inc., C.D.Cal.2012, 860 F.Supp.2d 1117, 103 U.S.P.Q.2d 1142.

Research References

Rutter, Cal. Practice Guide: Enforcing Judgments/Debts Ch. 6A-11, Property Subject to Enforcement Procedures.
8 Witkin Cal. Proc. 5th Enforcement of Judgment § 60, (S 60) in General.
13 Witkin, California Summary 10th Personal Property § 49, Fine Arts Resale Royalties Act.

§ 987. Preservation of works of art

(a) The Legislature hereby finds and declares that the physical alteration or destruction of fine art, which is an expression of the artist's personality, is detrimental to the artist's reputation, and artists therefore have an interest in protecting their works of fine art against any alteration or destruction; and that there is also a public interest in preserving the integrity of cultural and artistic creations.

(b) As used in this section:

(1) "Artist" means the individual or individuals who create a work of fine art.

(2) "Fine art" means an original painting, sculpture, or drawing, or an original work of art in glass, of recognized quality, but shall not include work prepared under contract for commercial use by its purchaser.

(3) "Person" means an individual, partnership, corporation, limited liability company, association or other group, however organized.

(4) "Frame" means to prepare, or cause to be prepared, a work of fine art for display in a manner customarily considered to be appropriate for a work of fine art in the particular medium.

(5) "Restore" means to return, or cause to be returned, a deteriorated or damaged work of fine art as nearly as is feasible to its original state or condition, in accordance with prevailing standards.

(6) "Conserve" means to preserve, or cause to be preserved, a work of fine art by retarding or preventing deterioration or damage through appropriate treatment in accordance with prevailing standards in order to maintain the structural integrity to the fullest extent possible in an unchanging state.

(7) "Commercial use" means fine art created under a work-for-hire arrangement for use in advertising, magazines, newspapers, or other print and electronic media.

(c)(1) No person, except an artist who owns and possesses a work of fine art which the artist has created, shall intentionally commit, or authorize the intentional commission of, any physical defacement, mutilation, alteration, or destruction of a work of fine art.

(2) In addition to the prohibitions contained in paragraph (1), no person who frames, conserves, or restores a work of fine art shall commit, or authorize the commission of, any physical defacement, mutilation, alteration, or destruction of a work of fine art by any act constituting gross negligence. For purposes of this section, the term "gross negligence" shall mean the exercise of so slight a degree of care as to justify the belief that there was an indifference to the particular work of fine art.

(d) The artist shall retain at all times the right to claim authorship, or, for a just and valid reason, to disclaim authorship of his or her work of fine art.

(e) To effectuate the rights created by this section, the artist may commence an action to recover or obtain any of the following:

(1) Injunctive relief.

(2) Actual damages.

(3) Punitive damages. In the event that punitive damages are awarded, the court shall, in its discretion, select an organization or organizations engaged in charitable or educational activities involving the fine arts in California to receive any punitive damages.

(4) Reasonable attorneys' and expert witness fees.

(5) Any other relief which the court deems proper.

(f) In determining whether a work of fine art is of recognized quality, the trier of fact shall rely on the opinions of artists, art dealers, collectors of fine art, curators of art museums, and other persons involved with the creation or marketing of fine art.

(g) The rights and duties created under this section:

(1) Shall, with respect to the artist, or if any artist is deceased, his or her heir, beneficiary, devisee, or personal representative, exist until the 50th anniversary of the death of the artist.

(2) Shall exist in addition to any other rights and duties which may now or in the future be applicable.

(3) Except as provided in paragraph (1) of subdivision (h), may not be waived except by an instrument in writing expressly so providing which is signed by the artist.

(h)(1) If a work of fine art cannot be removed from a building without substantial physical defacement, mutilation, alteration, or destruction of the work, the rights and duties created under this section, unless expressly reserved by an instrument in writing signed by the owner of the building, containing a legal description of the property and properly recorded, shall be deemed waived. The instrument, if properly recorded, shall be binding on subsequent owners of the building.

(2) If the owner of a building wishes to remove a work of fine art which is a part of the building but which can be removed from

the building without substantial harm to the fine art, and in the course of or after removal, the owner intends to cause or allow the fine art to suffer physical defacement, mutilation, alteration, or destruction, the rights and duties created under this section shall apply unless the owner has diligently attempted without success to notify the artist, or, if the artist is deceased, his or her heir, beneficiary, devisee, or personal representative, in writing of his or her intended action affecting the work of fine art, or unless he or she did provide notice and that person failed within 90 days either to remove the work or to pay for its removal. If the work is removed at the expense of the artist, his or her heir, beneficiary, devisee, or personal representative, title to the fine art shall pass to that person.

(3) If a work of fine art can be removed from a building scheduled for demolition without substantial physical deface-ment, mutilation, alteration, or destruction of the work, and the owner of the building has notified the owner of the work of fine art of the scheduled demolition or the owner of the building is the owner of the work of fine art, and the owner of the work of fine art elects not to remove the work of fine art, the rights and duties created under this section shall apply, unless the owner of the building has diligently attempted without success to notify the artist, or, if the artist is deceased, his or her heir, beneficiary, devisee, or personal representative, in writing of the intended action affecting the work of fine art, or unless he or she did provide notice and that person failed within 90 days either to remove the work or to pay for its removal. If the work is removed at the expense of the artist, his or her heir, beneficiary, devisee, or personal representative, title to the fine art shall pass to that person.

(4) Nothing in this subdivision shall affect the rights of authorship created in subdivision (d) of this section.

(i) No action may be maintained to enforce any liability under this section unless brought within three years of the act complained of or one year after discovery of the act, whichever is longer.

(j) This section shall become operative on January 1, 1980, and shall apply to claims based on proscribed acts occurring on or after that date to works of fine art whenever created.

(k) If any provision of this section or the application thereof to any person or circumstance is held invalid for any reason, the invalidity shall not affect any other provisions or applications of this section which can be effected without the invalid provision or application, and to this end the provisions of this section are severable. *(Added by Stats.1979, c. 409, p. 1501, § 1. Amended by Stats.1982, c. 1517, p. 5882, § 1; Stats.1982, c. 1609, p. 6437, § 2.5; Stats.1989, c. 482, § 1; Stats.1994, c. 1010 (S.B.2053), § 30.)*

Research References

Miller and Starr California Real Estate § 27:111, Ownership and Copy-right of Plans and Specifications.
13 Witkin, California Summary 10th Personal Property § 50, (S 50) Purpose and Nature of Act.
13 Witkin, California Summary 10th Personal Property § 51, (S 51) Prohibition of Alteration.
13 Witkin, California Summary 10th Personal Property § 52, (S 52) Rights of Artist.
13 Witkin, California Summary 10th Personal Property § 53, (S 53) Removal of Work from Building.
13 Witkin, California Summary 10th Personal Property § 54, (S 54) Remedies of Artist.
13 Witkin, California Summary 10th Personal Property § 55, Preservation of Integrity of Fine Art.
13 Witkin, California Summary 10th Personal Property § 61, (S 61) Visual Artists Rights Act.

§ 988. Ownership of physical work of art; reservation upon conveyance of other ownership rights; resolution of ambiguity

(a) For the purpose of this section:

(1) The term "artist" means the creator of a work of art.

(2) The term "work of art" means any work of visual or graphic art of any media including, but not limited to, a painting, print, drawing, sculpture, craft, photograph, or film.

(b) Whenever an exclusive or nonexclusive conveyance of any right to reproduce, prepare derivative works based on, distribute copies of, publicly perform, or publicly display a work of art is made by or on behalf of the artist who created it or the owner at the time of the conveyance, ownership of the physical work of art shall remain with and be reserved to the artist or owner, as the case may be, unless such right of ownership is expressly transferred by an instrument, note, memorandum, or other writing, signed by the artist, the owner, or their duly authorized agent.

(c) Whenever an exclusive or nonexclusive conveyance of any right to reproduce, prepare derivative works based on, distribute copies of, publicly perform, or publicly display a work of art is made by or on behalf of the artist who created it or the owner at the time of the conveyance, any ambiguity with respect to the nature or extent of the rights conveyed shall be resolved in favor of the reservation of rights by the artist or owner, unless in any given case the federal copyright law provides to the contrary. *(Added by Stats.1982, c. 1319, p. 4873, § 1.)*

Research References

13 Witkin, California Summary 10th Personal Property § 47, Revised Statutes.

§ 989. Preservation of cultural and artistic creations

(a) The Legislature hereby finds and declares that there is a public interest in preserving the integrity of cultural and artistic creations.

(b) As used in this section:

(1) "Fine art" means an original painting, sculpture, or drawing, or an original work of art in glass, of recognized quality, and of substantial public interest.

(2) "Organization" means a public or private not-for-profit entity or association, in existence at least three years at the time an action is filed pursuant to this section, a major purpose of which is to stage, display, or otherwise present works of art to the public or to promote the interests of the arts or artists.

(3) "Cost of removal" includes reasonable costs, if any, for the repair of damage to the real property caused by the removal of the work of fine art.

(c) An organization acting in the public interest may com-mence an action for injunctive relief to preserve or restore the integrity of a work of fine art from acts prohibited by subdivision (c) of Section 987.

(d) In determining whether a work of fine art is of recognized quality and of substantial public interest the trier of fact shall rely on the opinions of those described in subdivision (f) of Section 987.

(e)(1) If a work of fine art cannot be removed from real property without substantial physical defacement, mutilation, alteration, or destruction of such work, no action to preserve the integrity of the work of fine art may be brought under this section. However, if an organization offers some evidence giving rise to a reasonable likelihood that a work of art can be removed from the real property without substantial physical defacement, mutilation, alteration, or destruction of the work, and is prepared to pay the cost of removal of the work, it may bring a legal action for a determination of this issue. In that action the organization shall be entitled to injunctive relief to preserve the integrity of the work of fine art, but shall also have the burden of proof. The action shall commence within 30 days after filing. No action may be brought under this paragraph if the organization's interest in preserving the work of art is in conflict with an instrument described in paragraph (1) of subdivision (h) of Section 987.

(2) If the owner of the real property wishes to remove a work of fine art which is part of the real property, but which can be removed from the real property without substantial harm to such fine art, and in the course of or after removal, the owner intends to cause or allow the fine art to suffer physical defacement, mutilation, alteration, or destruction the owner shall do the following:

(A) If the artist or artist's heir, legatee, or personal representative fails to take action to remove the work of fine art after the notice provided by paragraph (2) of subdivision (h) of Section 987, the owner shall provide 30 days' notice of his or her intended action affecting the work of art. The written notice shall be a display advertisement in a newspaper of general circulation in the area where the fine art is located. The notice required by this paragraph may run concurrently with the notice required by subdivision (h) of Section 987.

(i) If within the 30-day period an organization agrees to remove the work of fine art and pay the cost of removal of the work, the payment and removal shall occur within 90 days of the first day of the 30-day notice.

(ii) If the work is removed at the expense of an organization, title to the fine art shall pass to that organization.

(B) If an organization does not agree to remove the work of fine art within the 30-day period or fails to remove and pay the cost of removal of the work of fine art within the 90-day period the owner may take the intended action affecting the work of fine art.

(f) To effectuate the rights created by this section, the court may do the following:

(1) Award reasonable attorney's and expert witness fees to the prevailing party, in an amount as determined by the court.

(2) Require the organization to post a bond in a reasonable amount as determined by the court.

(g) No action may be maintained under this section unless brought within three years of the act complained of or one year after discovery of such act, whichever is longer.

(h) This section shall become operative on January 1, 1983, and shall apply to claims based on acts occurring on or after that date to works of fine art, whenever created.

(i) If any provision of this section or the application thereof to any person or circumstances is held invalid, such invalidity shall not affect other provisions or applications of this section which can be given effect without the invalid provision or application, and to this end the provisions of this section are severable. *(Added by Stats.1982, c. 1517, p. 5888, § 4.)*

Research References

Miller and Starr California Real Estate § 17:1, in General; Definitions.

13 Witkin, California Summary 10th Personal Property § 55, Preservation of Integrity of Fine Art.

CHAPTER 4. OTHER KINDS OF PERSONAL PROPERTY

§ 994. Instruments of title, ownership

TITLE DEEDS. Instruments essential to the title of real property, and which are not kept in a public office as a record, pursuant to law, belong to the person in whom, for the time being, such title may be vested, and pass with the title. *(Enacted in 1872.)*

Research References

Miller and Starr California Real Estate § 11:2, Enforceability of Unrecorded Instruments.

§ 996. Fur bearing animals raised in captivity; ownership; protection of law

Whenever fur bearing animals, which are by their nature known as wild animals, have been brought into, or born in, restraint or captivity upon any farm or ranch for the purpose of cultivating or pelting their furs, such animals, together with their offspring or increase, shall be the subjects of ownership, lien, and all kinds of absolute and other property rights, the same as purely domestic animals, in whatever situation, location, or condition such fur bearing animals may thereafter come or be, and regardless of their remaining in or escaping from such restraint or captivity. Such fur bearing animals shall receive the same protection of law, and in the same way and to the same extent shall be the subject of trespass or larceny as other personal property and shall be considered and classified as domestic animals for the purpose of and within the meaning of any statute or law relating generally to domestic animals, other than dogs and cats or other pets, or relating to farming, to animal husbandry, or to the encouragement of agriculture, unless any such statute or law is impossible of application to such fur bearing animals. *(Added by Stats.1941, c. 404, p. 1689, § 1.)*

Research References

13 Witkin, California Summary 10th Personal Property § 21, (S 21) Wild Animals and Fish.

§ 997. Porcelain painting and stained glass artistry

In this state, for any purpose, porcelain painting and stained glass artistry shall be considered a fine art and not a craft. *(Added by Stats.1979, c. 202, p. 446, § 1. Amended by Stats.1982, c. 1609, p. 6439, § 3.)*

Research References

13 Witkin, California Summary 10th Personal Property § 48, Reproduction Rights in Fine Arts.

13 Witkin, California Summary 10th Personal Property § 49, Fine Arts Resale Royalties Act.

§ 998. Electronic data processing or telecommunications goods and services; vendor transactions with private schools

Any private vendor of electronic data processing equipment or telecommunications goods and services may sell or lease equipment, goods, or services to a private school for the same price and on similar terms as the vendor sells or leases the equipment, goods, or services to a public school or school district. *(Added by Stats.1988, c. 858, § 1.)*

Part 4

ACQUISITION OF PROPERTY

Title 1

MODES IN WHICH PROPERTY MAY BE ACQUIRED

§ 1000. Acquisition of property

PROPERTY, HOW ACQUIRED. Property is acquired by:

1. Occupancy;

2. Accession;

3. Transfer;

4. Will; or,

5. Succession. *(Enacted in 1872.)*

Research References

Miller and Starr California Real Estate § 16:1, "Adverse Possession" Defined; Necessary Facts to Prove.
Miller and Starr California Real Estate § 17:2, Property as "Bundle of Rights".
Miller and Starr California Real Estate § 16:26, Capacity; Quiet Title Action by an Adverse Possessor.
Miller and Starr California Real Estate § 17:38, Tests for Determining Whether an Item is a Fixture.
Miller and Starr California Real Estate § 19:84, Persons Entitled to Receive Rent--Rent Skimming.
13 Witkin, California Summary 10th Personal Property § 27, (S 27) in General.

§ 1001. Appurtenant easement; acquisition by eminent domain by private property owner to provide utility service

(a) As used in this section, "utility service" means water, gas, electric, drainage, sewer, or telephone service.

(b) Any owner of real property may acquire by eminent domain an appurtenant easement to provide utility service to the owner's property.

(c) In lieu of the requirements of Section 1240.030 of the Code of Civil Procedure, the power of eminent domain may be exercised to acquire an appurtenant easement under this section only if all of the following are established:

(1) There is a great necessity for the taking.

(2) The location of the easement affords the most reasonable service to the property to which it is appurtenant, consistent with the least damage to the burdened property.

(3) The hardship to the owner of the appurtenant property, if the taking is not permitted, clearly outweighs any hardship to the owner of the burdened property. *(Added by Stats.1976, c. 994, p. 2362, § 1.)*

Law Revision Commission Comments

Section 1001 and Section 1238 of the Code of Civil Procedure to which it refers are superseded by Code of Civil Procedure Sections 1240.010 (public use limitation) and 1240.020 (statutory delegation of condemnation authority required) and by specific statements of the condemnation authority of particular persons for particular public uses which are found in the various codes. See Comment to Code Civ.Proc. § 1240.020 and the Comment to former Code Civ.Proc. § 1238.

Section 1001 is added to provide the right of eminent domain to private persons for the limited [purpose] of . . . making utility connections. . . . This restores authority found under former Section 1001 (repealed Cal.Stats.1975, Ch. 1240, § 1). . . . The exercise of eminent domain authority under Section 1001 is subject to consent of the appropriate local public entities under Code of Civil Procedure Sections 1245.310–1245.390 to the same extent as quasi-public condemnors. See Code Civ.Proc. § 1245.325.

Condemnation under this section must comply with the provisions of the Eminent Domain Law. See Code Civ.Proc. § 1230.020 (law governing exercise of eminent domain power). Under the Eminent Domain Law, there must be "public necessity" for the acquisition (Code Civ.Proc. § 1240.030), and any necessary interest in property may be acquired (Code Civ.Proc. § 1240.110); under Section 1001, however, there must be "great necessity" for the acquisition and only an easement may be acquired. See also *Linggi v. Garovotti*, 45 Cal.2d 20, 286 P.2d 15 (1955) (condemnation by private person for sewer connection a public use, but a "stronger showing" of necessity required than if plaintiff were a public or quasi-public entity). It should be noted that the condemnor must pay compensation for the easement taken and for damage to the property from which it is taken. See Code Civ.Proc. §§ 1263.010–1263.620.

Research References

Miller and Starr California Real Estate § 15:44, Condemnation.
Miller and Starr California Real Estate § 25:42, Construction of Public Improvements.
Miller and Starr California Real Estate § 30A:6, Public Agencies and Other Entities With the Power of Eminent Domain.
8 Witkin, California Summary 10th Constitutional Law § 1112, (S 1112) Nature of Power.
8 Witkin, California Summary 10th Constitutional Law § 1117, Private Person.
8 Witkin, California Summary 10th Constitutional Law § 1178, Private Person's Utility Easement.
8 Witkin, California Summary 10th Constitutional Law § 1203, (S 1203) Consent to Proceeding by Quasi-Public Entity.

§ 1002. Temporary right to enter adjacent or nearby property; exercise of eminent domain by private property owner to repair or reconstruct land or improvements

(a) Subject to the provisions of Article 3 (commencing with Section 1245.310) of Chapter 4 of Title 7 of Part 3 of the Code of Civil Procedure, the power of eminent domain may be exercised by an owner of real property to acquire a temporary right to enter upon adjacent or nearby property to repair or reconstruct land or improvements, if all of the following conditions are established or met:

(1) There is a necessity to do the repair or reconstruction work and there is a great necessity to enter upon the adjacent or nearby property to do the repair or reconstruction work because (A) the repair or reconstruction work cannot be done safely without entry, or the cost of performing the repair or reconstruction work without entry would be substantially higher; and (B) the property without repair or reconstruction adversely affects the surrounding community.

(2) The right to enter upon the adjacent or nearby land will be exercised in a manner which provides the least damage to the property and the least inconvenience or annoyance to the

occupants or owners thereof consistent with satisfactory completion of the repair or reconstruction work.

(3) The hardship to the person seeking to exercise the power of eminent domain, if that power is not exercised, clearly outweighs any hardship to the owner or occupant of the adjacent or nearby property.

(b) No entry shall be made upon the property to be condemned until an eminent domain proceeding has been commenced and then only after a court order permitting entry is issued or after judgment is entered for the plaintiff.

A deposit of security, in the form of cash or a bond, shall be made to the court in an amount the court determines is necessary to permit the owner of the adjacent or nearby property to restore the property to the condition it was in prior to the entry, if the person exercising the power of eminent domain does not do so within a reasonable period of time as determined by the court.

(c) The court may order the person acquiring the temporary right to enter the land of another, pursuant to this section, to pay the owner of the land subject to that temporary right a reasonable amount of rent for the use of the land.

(d) "Adjacent" or "nearby" for purposes of this section shall mean land contiguous with the property needing repair or reconstruction, or land through which the party granted temporary access must pass to reach adjacent land.

(e) The provisions of this section shall not apply to the temporary entry upon lands used primarily for the commercial production of agricultural commodities and forest products. *(Added by Stats.1982, c. 1239, p. 4564, § 1.)*

Research References

Miller and Starr California Real Estate § 14:22, Lateral Support--Depth of an Excavation.
Miller and Starr California Real Estate § 25:42, Construction of Public Improvements.
Miller and Starr California Real Estate § 30A:6, Public Agencies and Other Entities With the Power of Eminent Domain.
8 Witkin, California Summary 10th Constitutional Law § 1117, Private Person.
8 Witkin, California Summary 10th Constitutional Law § 1179, Private Person's Repair Easement.
8 Witkin, California Summary 10th Constitutional Law § 1203, (S 1203) Consent to Proceeding by Quasi-Public Entity.

Title 2

OCCUPANCY

Section
1006. Title by occupancy; extent.
1007. Title by prescription; adverse possession; exemption of public property.
1008. Title by prescription; permissive use.
1009. Legislative findings.

§ 1006.   Title by occupancy; extent

Occupancy for any period confers a title sufficient against all except the state and those who have title by prescription, accession, transfer, will, or succession; but the title conferred by occupancy is not a sufficient interest in real property to enable the occupant or the occupant's privies to commence or maintain an action to quiet title, unless the occupancy has ripened into title by prescription. *(Enacted in 1872. Amended by Stats.1915, c. 554, p. 933, § 1; Stats.1980, c. 44, § 1.)*

Law Revision Commission Comments

Section 1006 is amended to reflect the relocation of the quiet title provisions and to make nonsubstantive drafting improvements.

Research References

Miller and Starr California Real Estate § 16:1, "Adverse Possession" Defined; Necessary Facts to Prove.
Miller and Starr California Real Estate § 16:26, Capacity; Quiet Title Action by an Adverse Possessor.
Miller and Starr California Real Estate § 16:43, Political Entities and Public Agencies--Property Held in a Governmental Capacity.
Miller and Starr California Real Estate § 19:232, Recovery of Possession; Writ of Possession.
Miller and Starr California Real Estate § 34:104, Who Can Bring the Action.
12 Witkin, California Summary 10th Real Property § 208, (S 208) Possession as Evidence of Title.

§ 1007.   Title by prescription; adverse possession; exemption of public property

Occupancy for the period prescribed by the Code of Civil Procedure as sufficient to bar any action for the recovery of the property confers a title thereto, denominated a title by prescription, which is sufficient against all, but no possession by any person, firm or corporation no matter how long continued of any land, water, water right, easement, or other property whatsoever dedicated to a public use by a public utility, or dedicated to or owned by the state or any public entity, shall ever ripen into any title, interest or right against the owner thereof. *(Enacted in 1872. Amended by Stats.1935, c. 519, p. 1592, § 1; Stats.1968, c. 1112, p. 2125, § 1.)*

Research References

Miller and Starr California Real Estate § 16:1, "Adverse Possession" Defined; Necessary Facts to Prove.
Miller and Starr California Real Estate § 15:29, Elements and Requirements.
Miller and Starr California Real Estate § 15:38, Prescriptive Period.
Miller and Starr California Real Estate § 16:17, in General; Statutory Period.
Miller and Starr California Real Estate § 16:43, Political Entities and Public Agencies--Property Held in a Governmental Capacity.
Miller and Starr California Real Estate § 16:44, Political Entities and Public Agencies--Property Held in a Proprietary Capacity.
Miller and Starr California Real Estate § 16:45, Property Owned by a Public Utility.
Miller and Starr California Real Estate § 17:25, Water Rights.
3 Witkin Cal. Proc. 5th Actions § 489, Express Statutory Provisions.
12 Witkin, California Summary 10th Real Property § 212, (S 212) in General.
12 Witkin, California Summary 10th Real Property § 213, Public Property.
12 Witkin, California Summary 10th Real Property § 214, Property Dedicated to Public Use.
12 Witkin, California Summary 10th Real Property § 401, (S 401) Elements of Prescriptive Right.
12 Witkin, California Summary 10th Real Property § 405, (S 405) No Duty to Compensate Owner of Property.
12 Witkin, California Summary 10th Real Property § 949, Nature of Prescriptive Right.
13 Witkin, California Summary 10th Personal Property § 123, Adverse Possession.

§ 1008.   Title by prescription; permissive use

No use by any person or persons, no matter how long continued, of any land, shall ever ripen into an easement by prescription, if the owner of such property posts at each entrance to the property or at intervals of not more than 200 feet along the boundary a sign reading substantially as follows: "Right to pass by permission, and subject to control, of owner: Section 1008, Civil Code." *(Added by Stats.1965, c. 926, p. 2540, § 1.)*

Research References

Rutter, Cal. Practice Guide: Real Prop. Transactions Ch. 4-B, B. Interests to be Conveyed.

Miller and Starr California Real Estate § 26:4, Requirement of Offer by the Owner.

Miller and Starr California Real Estate § 15:31, Public or Private Easement by Prescription.

Miller and Starr California Real Estate § 15:36, Use Requirements-- Permission by the Property Owner; Posted or Recorded Notice.

Miller and Starr California Real Estate § 16:13, When Possession is "Hostile and Adverse".

Miller and Starr California Real Estate § 22:70, Exception to Exemption; Entry by Invitation or for Consideration.

Miller and Starr California Real Estate § 26:18, Offer Implied from Public Use--Procedures to Prevent an Implied Dedication by Public Use.

16 NO. 6 Miller & Starr, California Real Estate Newsalert 8, Easements.

12 Witkin, California Summary 10th Real Property § 250, (S 250) Statutory Limitations.

12 Witkin, California Summary 10th Real Property § 404, (S 404) Permissive Use.

§ 1009. Legislative findings

(a) The Legislature finds that:

(1) It is in the best interests of the state to encourage owners of private real property to continue to make their lands available for public recreational use to supplement opportunities available on tax-supported publicly owned facilities.

(2) Owners of private real property are confronted with the threat of loss of rights in their property if they allow or continue to allow members of the public to use, enjoy or pass over their property for recreational purposes.

(3) The stability and marketability of record titles is clouded by such public use, thereby compelling the owner to exclude the public from his property.

(b) Regardless of whether or not a private owner of real property has recorded a notice of consent to use of any particular property pursuant to Section 813 of the Civil Code or has posted signs on such property pursuant to Section 1008 of the Civil Code, except as otherwise provided in subdivision (d), no use of such property by the public after the effective date of this section shall ever ripen to confer upon the public or any governmental body or unit a vested right to continue to make such use permanently, in the absence of an express written irrevocable offer of dedication of such property to such use, made by the owner thereof in the manner prescribed in subdivision (c) of this section, which has been accepted by the county, city, or other public body to which the offer of dedication was made, in the manner set forth in subdivision (c).

(c) In addition to any procedure authorized by law and not prohibited by this section, an irrevocable offer of dedication may be made in the manner prescribed in Section 7050 of the Government Code to any county, city, or other public body, and may be accepted or terminated, in the manner prescribed in that section, by the county board of supervisors in the case of an offer of dedication to a county, by the city council in the case of an offer of dedication to a city, or by the governing board of any other public body in the case of an offer of dedication to such body.

(d) Where a governmental entity is using private lands by an expenditure of public funds on visible improvements on or across such lands or on the cleaning or maintenance related to the public use of such lands in such a manner so that the owner knows or should know that the public is making such use of his land, such use, including any public use reasonably related to the purposes of such improvement, in the absence of either express permission by the owner to continue such use or the taking by the owner of reasonable steps to enjoin, remove or prohibit such use, shall after five years ripen to confer upon the governmental entity a vested right to continue such use.

(e) Subdivision (b) shall not apply to any coastal property which lies within 1,000 yards inland of the mean high tide line of the Pacific Ocean, and harbors, estuaries, bays and inlets thereof, but not including any property lying inland of the Carquinez Straits bridge, or between the mean high tide line and the nearest public road or highway, whichever distance is less.

(f) No use, subsequent to the effective date of this section, by the public of property described in subdivision (e) shall constitute evidence or be admissible as evidence that the public or any governmental body or unit has any right in such property by implied dedication if the owner does any of the following actions:

(1) Posts signs, as provided in Section 1008, and renews the same, if they are removed, at least once a year, or publishes annually, pursuant to Section 6066 of the Government Code, in a newspaper of general circulation in the county or counties in which the land is located, a statement describing the property and reading substantially as follows: "Right to pass by permission and subject to control of owner: Section 1008, Civil Code."

(2) Records a notice as provided in Section 813.

(3) Enters into a written agreement with any federal, state, or local agency providing for the public use of such land.

After taking any of the actions set forth in paragraph (1), (2), or (3), and during the time such action is effective, the owner shall not prevent any public use which is appropriate under the permission granted pursuant to such paragraphs by physical obstruction, notice, or otherwise.

(g) The permission for public use of real property referred to in subdivision (f) may be conditioned upon reasonable restrictions on the time, place, and manner of such public use, and no use in violation of such restrictions shall be considered public use for purposes of a finding of implied dedication. (*Added by Stats.1971, c. 941, p. 1846, § 2.*)

Research References

Miller and Starr California Real Estate § 11:6, Instruments Subject to Recording--List of Recordable Documents.

Miller and Starr California Real Estate § 26:3, Common-Law Dedication Defined.

Miller and Starr California Real Estate § 26:4, Requirement of Offer by the Owner.

Miller and Starr California Real Estate § 15:31, Public or Private Easement by Prescription.

Miller and Starr California Real Estate § 25:60, Offers for Dedication to Public Use.

Miller and Starr California Real Estate § 26:11, Offer Implied from Public Use--In General.

Miller and Starr California Real Estate § 26:12, Offer Implied from Public Use--Nature and Extent of Public Use Required.

Miller and Starr California Real Estate § 26:13, Offer Implied from Public Use--Land Adjacent to Water.

Miller and Starr California Real Estate § 26:14, Offer Implied from Public Use--Relation to the Conduct of the Owner.

Miller and Starr California Real Estate § 26:15, Offer Implied from Public Use--Period of Use.

Miller and Starr California Real Estate § 26:16, Offer Implied from Public Use--Adverse Possession or Prescription Compared.

Miller and Starr California Real Estate § 26:17, Offer Implied from Public Use--Use by a Public Agency.

Miller and Starr California Real Estate § 26:18, Offer Implied from Public Use--Procedures to Prevent an Implied Dedication by Public Use.

Miller and Starr California Real Estate § 26:22, Acceptance by Public Use.

14 NO. 5 Miller & Starr, California Real Estate Newsalert 7, Dedication.

12 Witkin, California Summary 10th Real Property § 250, (S 250) Statutory Limitations.

Title 3

ACCESSION

CHAPTER 1.   ACCESSION TO REAL PROPERTY

§ 1013.   Fixtures; affixing without agreement to remove

When a person affixes his property to the land of another, without an agreement permitting him to remove it, the thing affixed, except as otherwise provided in this chapter, belongs to the owner of the land, unless he chooses to require the former to remove it or the former elects to exercise the right of removal provided for in Section 1013.5 of this chapter. *(Enacted in 1872. Amended by Code Am.1873–74, c. 612, p. 224, § 128; Stats.1953, c. 1175, p. 2674, § 1.)*

Research References

Miller and Starr California Real Estate § 2:19, Right to Possession; Waste.
Miller and Starr California Real Estate § 17:38, Tests for Determining Whether an Item is a Fixture.
Miller and Starr California Real Estate § 17:47, Parties to Contract of Sale.
Miller and Starr California Real Estate § 17:49, Licensees.
Miller and Starr California Real Estate § 17:50, Trespassers.
Miller and Starr California Real Estate § 17:51, Landlords and Tenants.
12 Witkin, California Summary 10th Real Property § 684, (S 684) in Absence of Covenant.
13 Witkin, California Summary 10th Personal Property § 97, (S 97) Agreement and Constructive Severance.
13 Witkin, California Summary 10th Personal Property § 98, Nature of Statute.
13 Witkin, California Summary 10th Personal Property § 99, Fixtures Installed by Tenant.

§ 1013.5.   Fixtures; removal

(a) **Right of removal; payment of damages.** When any person, acting in good faith and erroneously believing because of a mistake either of law or fact that he has a right to do so, affixes improvements to the land of another, such person, or his successor in interest, shall have the right to remove such improvements upon payment, as their interests shall appear, to the owner of the land, and any other person having any interest therein who acquired such interest for value after the commencement of the work of improvement and in reliance thereon, of all their damages proximately resulting from the affixing and removal of such improvements.

(b) **Parties; lis pendens; costs and attorney's fee.** In any action brought to enforce such right the owner of the land and encumbrancers of record shall be named as defendants, a notice of pendency of action shall be recorded before trial, and the owner of the land shall recover his costs of suit and a reasonable attorney's fee to be fixed by the court.

(c) **Interlocutory judgment.** If it appears to the court that the total amount of damages cannot readily be ascertained prior to the removal of the improvements, or that it is otherwise in the interests of justice, the court may order an interlocutory judgment authorizing the removal of the improvements upon condition precedent that the plaintiff pay into court the estimated total damages, as found by the court or as stipulated.

(d) **Consent of lienholder.** If the court finds that the holder of any lien upon the property acquired his lien in good faith and for value after the commencement of the work of improvement and in reliance thereon, or that as a result of the making or affixing of the improvements there is any lien against the property under Article XX, Section 15, of the Constitution of this State, judgment authorizing removal, final or interlocutory, shall not be given unless the holder of each such lien shall have consented to the removal of the improvements. Such consent shall be in writing and shall be filed with the court.

(e) **Nature of right created.** The right created by this section is a right to remove improvements from land which may be exercised at the option of one who, acting in good faith and erroneously believing because of a mistake either of law or fact that he has a right to do so, affixes such improvements to the land of another. This section shall not be construed to affect or qualify the law as it existed prior to the 1953 amendment of this section with regard to the circumstances under which a court of equity will refuse to compel removal of an encroachment. *(Added by Stats.1953, c. 1175, p. 2674, § 2. Amended by Stats.1955, c. 73, p. 514, § 1.)*

Research References

Miller and Starr California Real Estate § 14:3, Interests Protected.
Miller and Starr California Real Estate § 17:43, Where Improver Does Not Believe He or She Owns the Improved Property.
Miller and Starr California Real Estate § 17:44, Where Improver Believes He or She Owns the Improved Property.
Miller and Starr California Real Estate § 17:48, Optionees.
Miller and Starr California Real Estate § 17:49, Licensees.
Miller and Starr California Real Estate § 17:50, Trespassers.
Miller and Starr California Real Estate § 11:150, Actions in Which a Lis Pendens May or Must be Recorded.
14 NO. 5 Miller & Starr, California Real Estate Newsalert 13, Fixtures.
3 Witkin Cal. Proc. 5th Actions § 381, (S 381) Specific Mandatory Statutes.
7 Witkin Cal. Proc. 5th Judgment § 21, Statutory Types.
7 Witkin Cal. Proc. 5th Judgment § 87, (S 87) Distinctions.
7 Witkin Cal. Proc. 5th Judgment § 158, (S 158) Other Types of Fee Awards.
4 Witkin Cal. Proc. 5th Pleading § 193, (S 193) Joinder Required by Special Statutes.
12 Witkin, California Summary 10th Real Property § 461, Equitable Lien and Lis Pendens.
12 Witkin, California Summary 10th Real Property § 462, (S 462) Other Relief.
12 Witkin, California Summary 10th Real Property § 684, (S 684) in Absence of Covenant.
13 Witkin, California Summary 10th Personal Property § 94, (S 94) Nature of Doctrine and Tests.
13 Witkin, California Summary 10th Personal Property § 98, Nature of Statute.
13 Witkin, California Summary 10th Personal Property § 99, Fixtures Installed by Tenant.
13 Witkin, California Summary 10th Personal Property § 100, Fixtures Installed by Buyer.
13 Witkin, California Summary 10th Personal Property § 102, Fixtures Installed by Grantor or Mortgagor.

4 Witkin, California Summary 10th Security Transactions in Real Property § 67, Subsequent Mortgage.

§ 1014. Alluvion

ALLUVION. Where, from natural causes, land forms by imperceptible degrees upon the bank of a river or stream, navigable or not navigable, either by accumulation of material or by the recession of the stream, such land belongs to the owner of the bank, subject to any existing right of way over the bank. *(Enacted in 1872.)*

Research References

Miller and Starr California Real Estate § 8:69, Water as Property Boundary--Effect of Erosion, Accretion, and Reliction.
12 Witkin, California Summary 10th Real Property § 236, (S 236) in General.
12 Witkin, California Summary 10th Real Property § 238, (S 238) State's Right.

§ 1015. Avulsion

SUDDEN REMOVAL OF BANK. If a river or stream, navigable or not navigable, carries away, by sudden violence, a considerable and distinguishable part of a bank, and bears it to the opposite bank, or to another part of the same bank, the owner of the part carried away may reclaim it within a year after the owner of the land to which it has been united takes possession thereof. *(Enacted in 1872.)*

Research References

Miller and Starr California Real Estate § 8:70, Water as Property Boundary--Effect of Avulsion, Earth Movement and Subsidence.
12 Witkin, California Summary 10th Real Property § 237, (S 237) Avulsion.

§ 1016. Islands; navigable streams state ownership

ISLANDS, IN NAVIGABLE STREAMS. Islands and accumulations of land, formed in the beds of streams which are navigable, belong to the State, if there is no title or prescription to the contrary. *(Enacted in 1872.)*

Research References

Miller and Starr California Real Estate § 8:69, Water as Property Boundary--Effect of Erosion, Accretion, and Reliction.
12 Witkin, California Summary 10th Real Property § 238, (S 238) State's Right.

§ 1017. Islands; non-navigable streams

IN UNNAVIGABLE STREAMS. An island, or an accumulation of land, formed in a stream which is not navigable, belongs to the owner of the shore on that side where the island or accumulation is formed; or, if not formed on one side only, to the owners of the shore on the two sides, divided by an imaginary line drawn through the middle of the river. *(Enacted in 1872.)*

Research References

Miller and Starr California Real Estate § 8:69, Water as Property Boundary--Effect of Erosion, Accretion, and Reliction.
12 Witkin, California Summary 10th Real Property § 236, (S 236) in General.

§ 1018. Islands; division of stream

ISLANDS FORMED BY DIVISION OF STREAM. If a stream, navigable or not navigable, in forming itself a new arm, divides itself and surrounds land belonging to the owner of the shore, and thereby forms an island, the island belongs to such owner. *(Enacted in 1872.)*

Research References

Miller and Starr California Real Estate § 8:69, Water as Property Boundary--Effect of Erosion, Accretion, and Reliction.

12 Witkin, California Summary 10th Real Property § 236, (S 236) in General.

§ 1019. Tenants; removal of fixtures

A tenant may remove from the demised premises, any time during the continuance of his term, anything affixed thereto for purposes of trade, manufacture, ornament, or domestic use, if the removal can be effected without injury to the premises, unless the thing has, by the manner in which it is affixed, become an integral part of the premises. *(Added by Code Am.1873–74, c. 612, p. 224, § 129.)*

Research References

Miller and Starr California Real Estate § 17:38, Tests for Determining Whether an Item is a Fixture.
Miller and Starr California Real Estate § 17:52, Landlords and Tenants--Trade Fixture Doctrine.
Miller and Starr California Real Estate § 17:54, Landlords and Tenants--Termination of Right of Removal.
Miller and Starr California Real Estate § 17:66, Commercial Property Fixtures.
12 Witkin, California Summary 10th Real Property § 684, (S 684) in Absence of Covenant.
13 Witkin, California Summary 10th Personal Property § 99, Fixtures Installed by Tenant.

CHAPTER 2. ACCESSION TO PERSONAL PROPERTY

Section
1025. Single thing formed from several things; owner of principal part.
1026. Principal part; separation of lessor but more valuable part.
1027. Principal part; value; bulk.
1028. Ownership of thing made by uniting materials and workmanship.
1029. Ownership of thing made of inseparable materials.
1030. Ownership of thing made from materials of several owners.
1031. Ownership of thing made by willful trespasser.
1032. Election between thing and value.
1033. Damages for wrongful use of materials.

§ 1025. Single thing formed from several things; owner of principal part

ACCESSION BY UNITING SEVERAL THINGS. When things belonging to different owners have been united so as to form a single thing, and cannot be separated without injury, the whole belongs to the owner of the thing which forms the principal part; who must, however, reimburse the value of the residue to the other owner, or surrender the whole to him. *(Enacted in 1872.)*

Research References

Miller and Starr California Real Estate § 17:38, Tests for Determining Whether an Item is a Fixture.
13 Witkin, California Summary 10th Personal Property § 121, (S 121) Accession.

§ 1026. Principal part; separation of lessor but more valuable part

PRINCIPAL PART, WHAT. That part is to be deemed the principal to which the other has been united only for the use, ornament, or completion of the former, unless the latter is the more valuable, and has been united without the knowledge of its owner, who may, in the latter case, require it to be separated and returned to him, although some injury should result to the thing to which it has been united. *(Enacted in 1872.)*

Research References

13 Witkin, California Summary 10th Personal Property § 121, (S 121) Accession.

§ 1027. Principal part; value; bulk

SAME. If neither part can be considered the principal, within the rule prescribed by the last section, the more valuable, or, if the values are nearly equal, the more considerable in bulk, is to be deemed the principal part. *(Enacted in 1872.)*

Research References

13 Witkin, California Summary 10th Personal Property § 121, (S 121) Accession.

§ 1028. Ownership of thing made by uniting materials and workmanship

UNITING MATERIALS AND WORKMANSHIP. If one makes a thing from materials belonging to another, the latter may claim the thing on reimbursing the value of the workmanship, unless the value of the workmanship exceeds the value of the materials, in which case the thing belongs to the maker, on reimbursing the value of the materials. *(Enacted in 1872.)*

Research References

13 Witkin, California Summary 10th Personal Property § 121, (S 121) Accession.

§ 1029. Ownership of thing made of inseparable materials

INSEPARABLE MATERIALS. Where one has made use of materials which in part belong to him and in part to another, in order to form a thing of a new description, without having destroyed any of the materials, but in such a way that they cannot be separated without inconvenience, the thing formed is common to both proprietors; in proportion, as respects the one, of the materials belonging to him, and as respects the other, of the materials belonging to him and the price of his workmanship. *(Enacted in 1872.)*

§ 1030. Ownership of thing made from materials of several owners

MATERIALS OF SEVERAL OWNERS. When a thing has been formed by the admixture of several materials of different owners, and neither can be considered the principal substance, an owner without whose consent the admixture was made may require a separation, if the materials can be separated without inconvenience. If they cannot be thus separated, the owners acquire the thing in common, in proportion to the quantity, quality, and value of their materials; but if the materials of one were far superior to those of the others, both in quantity and value, he may claim the thing on reimbursing to the others the value of their materials. *(Enacted in 1872.)*

§ 1031. Ownership of thing made by willful trespasser

WILLFUL TRESPASSERS. The foregoing sections of this Article are not applicable to cases in which one willfully uses the materials of another without his consent; but, in such cases, the product belongs to the owner of the material, if its identity can be traced. *(Enacted in 1872.)*

Research References

13 Witkin, California Summary 10th Personal Property § 121, (S 121) Accession.

§ 1032. Election between thing and value

OWNER MAY ELECT BETWEEN THE THING AND ITS VALUE. In all cases where one whose material has been used without his knowledge, in order to form a product of a different description, can claim an interest in such product, he has an option to demand either restitution of his material in kind, in the same quantity, weight, measure, and quality, or the value thereof; or where he is entitled to the product, the value thereof in place of the product. *(Enacted in 1872.)*

Research References

13 Witkin, California Summary 10th Personal Property § 121, (S 121) Accession.

§ 1033. Damages for wrongful use of materials

WRONGDOER LIABLE IN DAMAGES. One who wrongfully employs materials belonging to another is liable to him in damages, as well as under the foregoing provisions of this Chapter. *(Enacted in 1872.)*

Research References

13 Witkin, California Summary 10th Personal Property § 121, (S 121) Accession.

Title 4

TRANSFER

CHAPTER 1. TRANSFERS IN GENERAL

ARTICLE 1. DEFINITION OF TRANSFER

§ 1039. Transfer defined

TRANSFER, WHAT. Transfer is an act of the parties, or of the law, by which the title to property is conveyed from one living person to another. *(Enacted in 1872.)*

Research References

Miller and Starr California Real Estate § 2:7, Option Contracts--Definition and Requirements.
Miller and Starr California Real Estate § 8:1, Definitions and Terminology.
Miller and Starr California Real Estate § 8:15, Requirements.
Miller and Starr California Real Estate § 8:27, Capacity of the Grantee.
1 Witkin Cal. Summ. 10th Contracts § 707, Nature of Assignment.

§ 1040. Voluntary transfer defined

VOLUNTARY TRANSFER. A voluntary transfer is an executed contract, subject to all rules of law concerning contracts in general; except that a consideration is not necessary to its validity. *(Enacted in 1872.)*

Research References

Miller and Starr California Real Estate § 8:2, Rules of Interpretation; Extrinsic Evidence.
20 NO. 2 Miller & Starr, California Real Estate Newsalert 8, Contracts.
12 Witkin, California Summary 10th Real Property § 262, Consideration.

ARTICLE 2.   WHAT MAY BE TRANSFERRED

Section
1044.   Property subject to transfer.
1045.   Possibility; transferability.
1046.   Right of re-entry or repossession; transferability.
1047.   Real estate in adverse possession; transfer of title.

§ 1044.   Property subject to transfer

WHAT MAY BE TRANSFERRED.   Property of any kind may be transferred, except as otherwise provided by this Article.   *(Enacted in 1872.)*

Research References

California Real Estate Forms (Miller & Starr) § 1:14, Right of First Offer Agreement.
California Real Estate Forms (Miller & Starr) § 1:15, Option Agreement–Long Form.
California Real Estate Forms (Miller & Starr) § 1:16, Option Agreement–Short Form.
California Real Estate Forms (Miller & Starr) § 1:24, Combination Purchase and Option Agreement–Residential Lots Being Acquired from a Bankrupt Seller.
California Real Estate Forms (Miller & Starr) § 2:52, Option to Lease.
California Real Estate Forms (Miller & Starr) § 2:66, Residential Lease With Purchase Option.
Rutter, Cal. Practice Guide: Insurance Litigation Ch. 13-B, B. Extracontractual Compensatory Damages.
Miller and Starr California Real Estate § 15:7, Easement in Gross.
Miller and Starr California Real Estate § 17:2, Property as "Bundle of Rights".
Miller and Starr California Real Estate § 8:58, in General; Transferable Property Interests.
Miller and Starr California Real Estate § 9:30, Remainders--Vested or Contingent Nature.
Miller and Starr California Real Estate § 19:69, Application of a Covenant or Condition Against Transfer.
22 NO. 3 Miller & Starr, California Real Estate Newsalert 1, Show Me Your Papers: Sales and Assignments of Secured Real Estate Loans and the California Foreclosure Process.
12 Witkin, California Summary 10th Real Property § 420, (S 420) Transferability and Succession.

§ 1045.   Possibility; transferability

POSSIBILITY.   A mere possibility, not coupled with an interest, cannot be transferred.   *(Enacted in 1872.)*

Research References

Miller and Starr California Real Estate § 8:58, in General; Transferable Property Interests.
Miller and Starr California Real Estate § 9:25, Definitions.
1 Witkin Cal. Summ. 10th Contracts § 722, (S 722) Expectancies.

§ 1046.   Right of re-entry or repossession; transferability

RIGHT OF RE-ENTRY CAN BE TRANSFERRED.   A right of re-entry, or of repossession for breach of condition subsequent, can be transferred.   *(Enacted in 1872.)*

Research References

Miller and Starr California Real Estate § 9:6, Fee Simple Defeasible--Fee Simple on Condition Subsequent.
Miller and Starr California Real Estate § 9:8, Fee Simple Defeasible--Power of Termination (Right of Re-Entry); Enforcement.
Miller and Starr California Real Estate § 8:58, in General; Transferable Property Interests.
Miller and Starr California Real Estate § 9:25, Definitions.

12 Witkin, California Summary 10th Real Property § 169, (S 169) Transferability of Future Interests.
1 Witkin Cal. Summ. 10th Contracts § 720, (S 720) in General.

§ 1047.   Real estate in adverse possession;   transfer of title

OWNER OUSTED OF POSSESSION MAY TRANSFER.   Any person claiming title to real property in the adverse possession of another may transfer it with the same effect as if in actual possession.   *(Enacted in 1872.)*

Research References

Miller and Starr California Real Estate § 16:1, "Adverse Possession" Defined; Necessary Facts to Prove.

ARTICLE 3.   MODE OF TRANSFER

Section
1052.   Oral transfers;   when permissible.
1053.   Grant defined.
1054.   Necessity of delivery.
1055.   Presumption as to date of delivery.
1056.   Delivery necessarily absolute.
1057.   Delivery in escrow.
1057.3.   Release of escrow funds;   failure to comply;   liability.
1057.5.   Escrow agents;   prohibited acts;   conflicts of interest.
1057.6.   Escrow transactions;   disclosure statement;   title insurance.
1057.7.   Escrow instructions;   statement of license or authority.
1058.   Redelivery or cancellation of grant;   effect.
1058.5.   Nonacceptance of recorded deed;   rescission of invalidated trustee's deed;   notice;   recordation;   effect.
1059.   Constructive delivery of grant.

§ 1052.   Oral transfers;   when permissible

WHEN ORAL.   A transfer may be made without writing, in every case in which a writing is not expressly required by statute.   *(Enacted in 1872.)*

Research References

Miller and Starr California Real Estate § 17:5, Transfer and Recording.
Miller and Starr California Real Estate § 8:58, in General; Transferable Property Interests.
22 NO. 3 Miller & Starr, California Real Estate Newsalert 1, Show Me Your Papers: Sales and Assignments of Secured Real Estate Loans and the California Foreclosure Process.
1 Witkin Cal. Summ. 10th Contracts § 709, Requisites of Assignment.

§ 1053.   Grant defined

A transfer in writing is called a grant, or conveyance, or bill of sale.   The term "grant," in this and the next two Articles, includes all these instruments, unless it is specially applied to real property.   *(Enacted in 1872.   Amended by Code Am.1873–74, c. 612, p. 225, § 130.)*

Research References

Miller and Starr California Real Estate § 6:1, Definition of an Escrow.
Miller and Starr California Real Estate § 8:1, Definitions and Terminology.
Miller and Starr California Real Estate § 8:58, in General; Transferable Property Interests.
20 NO. 5 Miller & Starr, California Real Estate Newsalert 20, Mechanics' Liens.
22 NO. 3 Miller & Starr, California Real Estate Newsalert 1, Show Me Your Papers: Sales and Assignments of Secured Real Estate Loans and the California Foreclosure Process.

12 Witkin, California Summary 10th Real Property § 256, (S 256) Nature of Grant.

§ 1054. Necessity of delivery

DELIVERY NECESSARY. A grant takes effect, so as to vest the interest intended to be transferred, only upon its delivery by the grantor. *(Enacted in 1872.)*

Research References

Miller and Starr California Real Estate § 8:41, "Delivery" Defined.
Miller and Starr California Real Estate § 11:71, Defects in the Record Title Enforceable Against a Bona Fide Purchaser--Lack of Delivery of Prior Instrument.
Miller and Starr California Real Estate § 19:20, Lease as a Contract and Conveyance--Form, Execution, Delivery, and Recordation.
20 NO. 2 Miller & Starr, California Real Estate Newsalert 8, Contracts.
22 NO. 3 Miller & Starr, California Real Estate Newsalert 1, Show Me Your Papers: Sales and Assignments of Secured Real Estate Loans and the California Foreclosure Process.
12 Witkin, California Summary 10th Real Property § 291, in General.

§ 1055. Presumption as to date of delivery

DATE. A grant duly executed is presumed to have been delivered at its date. *(Enacted in 1872.)*

Research References

Miller and Starr California Real Estate § 8:3, Requirements; Form and Content.
Miller and Starr California Real Estate § 8:42, Presumptions and Proof--Generally.
12 Witkin, California Summary 10th Real Property § 295, (S 295) Presumptions and Inferences.

§ 1056. Delivery necessarily absolute

DELIVERY TO GRANTEE IS NECESSARILY ABSOLUTE. A grant cannot be delivered to the grantee conditionally. Delivery to him, or to his agent as such, is necessarily absolute, and the instrument takes effect thereupon, discharged of any condition on which the delivery was made. *(Enacted in 1872.)*

Research References

Miller and Starr California Real Estate § 6:1, Definition of an Escrow.
Miller and Starr California Real Estate § 6:3, Who Can Serve as an Escrow Holder.
Miller and Starr California Real Estate § 6:30, Requirement of a Contract.
Miller and Starr California Real Estate § 8:46, Conditional Delivery to the Grantee.
Miller and Starr California Real Estate § 19:20, Lease as a Contract and Conveyance--Form, Execution, Delivery, and Recordation.
22 NO. 3 Miller & Starr, California Real Estate Newsalert 1, Show Me Your Papers: Sales and Assignments of Secured Real Estate Loans and the California Foreclosure Process.
12 Witkin, California Summary 10th Real Property § 297, (S 297) No Delivery.
12 Witkin, California Summary 10th Real Property § 298, (S 298) Unconditional Delivery.

§ 1057. Delivery in escrow

DELIVERY IN ESCROW. A grant may be deposited by the grantor with a third person, to be delivered on performance of a condition, and, on delivery by the depositary, it will take effect. While in the possession of the third person, and subject to condition, it is called an escrow. *(Enacted in 1872.)*

Research References

Rutter, Cal. Practice Guide: Real Prop. Transactions Ch. 4-F, F. Use of an Escrow.
Miller and Starr California Real Estate § 6:1, Definition of an Escrow.
21 NO. 3 Miller & Starr, California Real Estate Newsalert 1, to Do or Not to Do-Whose Instructions to Follow in Closing an Escrow.

12 Witkin, California Summary 10th Real Property § 301, (S 301) Nature of Escrow.
12 Witkin, California Summary 10th Real Property § 310, Liability for Refusal to Effect Release of Funds.

§ 1057.3. Release of escrow funds; failure to comply; liability

(a) It shall be the obligation of a buyer and seller who enter into a contract to purchase and sell real property to ensure that all funds deposited into an escrow account are returned to the person who deposited the funds or who is otherwise entitled to the funds under the contract, if the purchase of the property is not completed by the date set forth in the contract for the close of escrow or any duly executed extension thereof.

(b) Any buyer or seller who fails to execute any document required by the escrow holder to release funds on deposit in an escrow account as provided in subdivision (a) within 30 days following a written demand for the return of funds deposited in escrow by the other party shall be liable to the person making the deposit for all of the following:

(1) The amount of the funds deposited in escrow not held in good faith to resolve a good faith dispute.

(2) Damages of treble the amount of the funds deposited in escrow not held to resolve a good faith dispute, but liability under this paragraph shall not be less than one hundred dollars ($100) or more than one thousand dollars ($1,000).

(3) Reasonable attorney's fees incurred in any action to enforce this section.

(c) Notwithstanding subdivision (b), there shall be no cause of action under this section, and no party to a contract to purchase and sell real property shall be liable, for failure to return funds deposited in an escrow account by a buyer or seller, if the funds are withheld in order to resolve a good faith dispute between a buyer and seller. A party who is denied the return of the funds deposited in escrow is entitled to damages under this section only upon proving that there was no good faith dispute as to the right to the funds on deposit.

(d) Upon the filing of a cause of action pursuant to this section, the escrow holder shall deposit the sum in dispute, less any cancellation fee and charges incurred, with the court in which the action is filed and be discharged of further responsibility for the funds.

(e) Neither any document required by the escrow holder to release funds deposited in an escrow account nor the acceptance of funds released from escrow, by any principal to the escrow transaction, shall be deemed a cancellation or termination of the underlying contract to purchase and sell real property, unless the cancellation is specifically stated therein. If the escrow instructions constitute the only contract between the buyer and seller, no document required by the escrow holder to release funds deposited in an escrow account shall abrogate a cause of action for breach of a contractual obligation to purchase or sell real property, unless the cancellation is specifically stated therein.

(f) For purposes of this section:

(1) "Close of escrow" means the date, specified event, or performance of prescribed condition upon which the escrow agent is to deliver the subject of the escrow to the person specified in the buyer's instructions to the escrow agent.

(2) "Good faith dispute" means a dispute in which the trier of fact finds that the party refusing to return the deposited funds had a reasonable belief of his or her legal entitlement to withhold the deposited funds. The existence of a "good faith dispute" shall be determined by the trier of fact.

(3) "Property" means real property containing one to four residential units at least one of which at the time the escrow is created is to be occupied by the buyer. The buyer's statement as

to his or her intention to occupy one of the units is conclusive for the purposes of this section.

(g) Nothing in this section restricts the ability of an escrow holder to file an interpleader action in the event of a dispute as to the proper distribution of funds deposited in an escrow account. *(Added by Stats.1990, c. 13 (A.B.546), § 1.)*

Research References

California Real Estate Forms (Miller & Starr) § 1:94, California Residential Purchase Agreement and Joint Escrow Instructions.
California Real Estate Forms (Miller & Starr) § 1:113, Cancellation of Contract, Release or Deposit and Joint Escrow Instructions.
Rutter, Cal. Practice Guide: Real Prop. Transactions Ch. 4-F, F. Use of an Escrow.
Miller and Starr California Real Estate § 6:14, Agency--Duty to Hold Contents of Escrow Until Conditions Are Satisfied.
Miller and Starr California Real Estate § 6:16, Funds Held in Trust; Restrictions on Disbursement.
Miller and Starr California Real Estate § 6:26, Return of Deposit.
12 Witkin, California Summary 10th Real Property § 310, Liability for Refusal to Effect Release of Funds.

§ 1057.5. Escrow agents; prohibited acts; conflicts of interest

Except for the normal compensation of his own employees, no person acting as an escrow agent whether required to be licensed as such or not, shall pay over to any other person any commission, fee, or other consideration as compensation for referring, soliciting, handling, or servicing escrow customers or accounts.

No escrow agent shall enter into any arrangement, either of his own making or of a subsidiary nature, or through any other person having a dual capacity, or through any person having a direct or indirect interest in the escrow, or other device, permitting any fee, commission, or compensation which is contingent upon the performance of any act, condition, or instruction set forth in an escrow, to be drawn or paid, either in whole or in part, or in kind or its equivalent, prior to the actual closing and completion of the escrow.

The provisions of this section shall not be deemed to supersede, negate, or modify any of the provisions of Section 12404 of the Insurance Code. *(Added by Stats.1967, c. 678, p. 2047, § 1.)*

Research References

12 Witkin, California Summary 10th Real Property § 302, (S 302) Escrow Agents.

§ 1057.6. Escrow transactions; disclosure statement; title insurance

In an escrow transaction for the purchase or simultaneous exchange of real property, where a policy of title insurance will not be issued to the buyer or to the parties to the exchange, the following notice shall be provided in a separate document to the buyer or parties exchanging real property, which shall be signed and acknowledged by them:

"IMPORTANT: IN A PURCHASE OR EXCHANGE OF REAL PROPERTY, IT MAY BE ADVISABLE TO OBTAIN TITLE INSURANCE IN CONNECTION WITH THE CLOSE OF ESCROW SINCE THERE MAY BE PRIOR RECORDED LIENS AND ENCUMBRANCES WHICH AFFECT YOUR INTEREST IN THE PROPERTY BEING ACQUIRED. A NEW POLICY OF TITLE INSURANCE SHOULD BE OBTAINED IN ORDER TO ENSURE YOUR INTEREST IN THE PROPERTY THAT YOU ARE ACQUIRING." *(Added by Stats.1992, c. 194 (S.B.1738), § 1.)*

Research References

California Real Estate Forms (Miller & Starr) § 1:78, Sellers Mandatory Disclosure Statement.
Rutter, Cal. Practice Guide: Real Prop. Transactions Ch. 4-E, E. Drafting the Purchase and Sale Agreement-Terms and Conditions.
Rutter, Cal. Practice Guide: Real Prop. Transactions Ch. 4-F, F. Use of an Escrow.
Miller and Starr California Real Estate § 7:4, Title Insurance Definitions.
Miller and Starr California Real Estate § 3:42, Specific Disclosures Required by Statute.
Miller and Starr California Real Estate § 6:13, Agency--Duty to Disclose.
12 Witkin, California Summary 10th Real Property § 352, (S 352) Nature and Distinctions.

§ 1057.7. Escrow instructions; statement of license or authority

All written escrow instructions executed by a buyer or seller, whether prepared by a person subject to Division 6 (commencing with Section 17000) of the Financial Code, or by a person exempt from that division under Section 17006 of the Financial Code, shall contain a statement in not less than 10-point type which shall include the license name and the name of the department issuing the license or authority under which the person is operating. This section shall not apply to supplemental escrow instructions or modifications to escrow instructions.

This section shall become operative on July 1, 1993. *(Added by Stats.1992, c. 861 (A.B.2583), § 2, operative July 1, 1993.)*

Research References

Rutter, Cal. Practice Guide: Real Prop. Transactions Ch. 4-F, F. Use of an Escrow.
Miller and Starr California Real Estate § 6:6, Other Escrow Holder Regulations.
Miller and Starr California Real Estate § 4:32, Broker as an Escrow Agent.

§ 1058. Redelivery or cancellation of grant; effect

SURRENDERING OR CANCELING GRANT DOES NOT RECONVEY. Redelivering a grant of real property to the grantor, or canceling it, does not operate to retransfer the title. *(Enacted in 1872.)*

Research References

Miller and Starr California Real Estate § 6:14, Agency--Duty to Hold Contents of Escrow Until Conditions Are Satisfied.
Miller and Starr California Real Estate § 6:34, Effect of a Premature Return to the Depositor.
Miller and Starr California Real Estate § 8:41, "Delivery" Defined.
12 Witkin, California Summary 10th Real Property § 291, in General.

§ 1058.5. Nonacceptance of recorded deed; rescission of invalidated trustee's deed; notice; recordation; effect

(a) A notice of nonacceptance of a recorded deed executed by a holder of a security interest, which notice identifies the security interest, contains a legal description of the property, properly identifies the parties to the deed, the date of recordation of the deed, the county in which the project is located, and the county assessor's parcel number of the real property referenced in the deed, may be recorded in the office of the county recorder where the real property is located.

(b) Where a trustee's deed is invalidated by a pending bankruptcy or otherwise, recordation of a notice of rescission of the trustee's deed, which notice properly identifies the deed of trust, the identification numbers used by the recorder or the books and pages at which the trustee's deed and deed of trust are recorded, the names of all trustors and beneficiaries, the location of the property subject to the deed of trust, and the reason for rescission, shall restore the condition of record title to the real property described in the trustee's deed and the existence and priority of all lienholders to the status quo prior to the recordation of the trustee's deed upon sale. Only the trustee or beneficiary who caused the trustee's deed to be recorded, or his or her successor in interest, may record a notice of rescission. *(Added by Stats.1993, c. 724 (A.B.1196), § 1. Amended by Stats.1997, c. 74 (S.B.665), § 1.)*

Research References

Rutter, Cal. Practice Guide: Real Prop. Transactions Ch. 6-I, I. Real Property Foreclosures and Antideficiency Laws.
Miller and Starr California Real Estate § 10:43, Deed in Lieu of Foreclosure.
Miller and Starr California Real Estate § 10:149, Effect of Foreclosure Sale Before or After a Bankruptcy Petition.
Miller and Starr California Real Estate § 10:206, When the Sale Becomes Final; Reformation.
4 Witkin, California Summary 10th Security Transactions in Real Property § 167, Notice of Rescission.

§ 1059. Constructive delivery of grant

CONSTRUCTIVE DELIVERY. Though a grant be not actually delivered into the possession of the grantee, it is yet to be deemed constructively delivered in the following cases:

1. Where the instrument is, by the agreement of the parties at the time of execution, understood to be delivered, and under such circumstances that the grantee is entitled to immediate delivery; or,

2. Where it is delivered to a stranger for the benefit of the grantee, and his assent is shown, or may be presumed. *(Enacted in 1872.)*

Research References

Miller and Starr California Real Estate § 6:36, Application of the "Relation Back" Rule.
Miller and Starr California Real Estate § 8:41, "Delivery" Defined.
Miller and Starr California Real Estate § 8:47, Conditional Delivery to a Third Person--In General.
Miller and Starr California Real Estate § 8:48, Conditional Delivery to a Third Person--With Intent to Vest Title on Death.
Miller and Starr California Real Estate § 11:132, Relation to Prior Interests--In General.
12 Witkin, California Summary 10th Real Property § 291, in General.
12 Witkin, California Summary 10th Real Property § 315, Exceptions.

ARTICLE 4. INTERPRETATION OF GRANTS

Section
1066. Interpretation.
1067. Limitations in grant.
1068. Recitals.
1069. Interpretation in favor of grantee; exception.
1070. Irreconcilable parts.
1072. Words of inheritance or succession.

§ 1066. Interpretation

GRANTS, HOW INTERPRETED. Grants are to be interpreted in like manner with contracts in general, except so far as is otherwise provided in this Article. *(Enacted in 1872.)*

Research References

Rutter, Cal. Practice Guide: Real Prop. Transactions Ch. 4-B, B. Interests to be Conveyed.
Miller and Starr California Real Estate § 8:2, Rules of Interpretation; Extrinsic Evidence.
Miller and Starr California Real Estate § 9:8, Fee Simple Defeasible--Power of Termination (Right of Re-Entry); Enforcement.
Miller and Starr California Real Estate § 15:16, Rules of Construction.
22 NO. 3 Miller & Starr, California Real Estate Newsalert 1, Show Me Your Papers: Sales and Assignments of Secured Real Estate Loans and the California Foreclosure Process.

12 Witkin, California Summary 10th Real Property § 13, Contract Rules Apply.

§ 1067. Limitations in grant

LIMITATIONS, HOW CONTROLLED. A clear and distinct limitation in a grant is not controlled by other words less clear and distinct. *(Enacted in 1872.)*

Research References

Miller and Starr California Real Estate § 8:2, Rules of Interpretation; Extrinsic Evidence.

§ 1068. Recitals

RECITALS, WHEN RESORTED TO. If the operative words of a grant are doubtful, recourse may be had to its recitals to assist the construction. *(Enacted in 1872.)*

Research References

Miller and Starr California Real Estate § 8:2, Rules of Interpretation; Extrinsic Evidence.

§ 1069. Interpretation in favor of grantee; exception

INTERPRETATION AGAINST GRANTOR. A grant is to be interpreted in favor of the grantee, except that a reservation in any grant, and every grant by a public officer or body, as such, to a private party, is to be interpreted in favor of the grantor. *(Enacted in 1872.)*

Research References

Rutter, Cal. Practice Guide: Real Prop. Transactions Ch. 4-B, B. Interests to be Conveyed.
Miller and Starr California Real Estate § 8:2, Rules of Interpretation; Extrinsic Evidence.
Miller and Starr California Real Estate § 9:9, Interpretation to Avoid Forfeiture.
Miller and Starr California Real Estate § 8:62, Description of the Property--Rules of Construction; Ambiguities, Conflicting Calls, Monuments and Surveys.
Miller and Starr California Real Estate § 15:16, Rules of Construction.
Miller and Starr California Real Estate § 15:17, Rules of Construction--Right-Of-Way as Easement or Fee Simple.
Miller and Starr California Real Estate § 15:18, Rules of Construction--"Reservation" of an Easement, or "Exception" of a Fee Simple.
Miller and Starr California Real Estate § 15:24, Sale of Property or Division of Title--Implied Reservation to the Grantor.
Miller and Starr California Real Estate § 17:22, Minerals--Geothermal Resources.
17 NO. 2 Miller & Starr, California Real Estate Newsalert 10, Easements.
21 NO. 5 Miller & Starr, California Real Estate Newsalert 7, Contracts.
12 Witkin, California Summary 10th Real Property § 13, Contract Rules Apply.
12 Witkin, California Summary 10th Real Property § 390, (S 390) Instruments Construed as Grants of Fee.
12 Witkin, California Summary 10th Real Property § 407, (S 407) in General.

§ 1070. Irreconcilable parts

IRRECONCILABLE PROVISIONS. If several parts of a grant are absolutely irreconcilable, the former part prevails. *(Enacted in 1872.)*

Research References

Miller and Starr California Real Estate § 8:2, Rules of Interpretation; Extrinsic Evidence.
Miller and Starr California Real Estate § 15:17, Rules of Construction--Right-Of-Way as Easement or Fee Simple.

Miller and Starr California Real Estate § 10:181, Notice of Default--In General.

§ 1072. Words of inheritance or succession

WORDS OF INHERITANCE UNNECESSARY. Words of inheritance or succession are not requisite to transfer a fee in real property. *(Enacted in 1872.)*

Research References

Rutter, Cal. Practice Guide: Real Prop. Transactions Ch. 4-B, B. Interests to be Conveyed.
Miller and Starr California Real Estate § 9:3, Fee Simple Absolute.
Miller and Starr California Real Estate § 15:16, Rules of Construction.
12 Witkin, California Summary 10th Real Property § 14, Interest Passing.

ARTICLE 5.   EFFECT OF TRANSFER

Section
1084.   Incidents.
1085.   Person not a party to grant; acquisition of interest or benefit.

§ 1084.   Incidents

INCIDENTS. The transfer of a thing transfers also all its incidents, unless expressly excepted; but the transfer of an incident to a thing does not transfer the thing itself. *(Enacted in 1872.)*

Research References

Rutter, Cal. Practice Guide: Enforcing Judgments/Debts Ch. 3-A, A. Evaluating the Claim.
Miller and Starr California Real Estate § 15:6, Appurtenant Easements; Conveyance or Encumbrance of the Dominant Tenement.
Miller and Starr California Real Estate § 8:60, Appurtenances Pass With Conveyance.
Miller and Starr California Real Estate § 10:18, Personal Property Located on the Realty.
Miller and Starr California Real Estate § 10:38, What is Assignable; Procedure.
Miller and Starr California Real Estate § 15:20, Sale of Property or Division of Title.
Miller and Starr California Real Estate § 15:24, Sale of Property or Division of Title--Implied Reservation to the Grantor.
Miller and Starr California Real Estate § 17:37, Generally; Definitions.
Miller and Starr California Real Estate § 17:46, Parties to Conveyance.
Miller and Starr California Real Estate § 10:263, Definitions; Guarantor, Surety.
Miller and Starr California Real Estate § 11:194, Priority Between a Deed of Trust and a Security Interest in Fixtures.
22 NO. 3 Miller & Starr, California Real Estate Newsalert 1, Show Me Your Papers: Sales and Assignments of Secured Real Estate Loans and the California Foreclosure Process.
23 NO. 1 Miller & Starr, California Real Estate Newsalert 14, Judicial Remedies.
1 Witkin Cal. Summ. 10th Contracts § 734, (S 734) Incidental Rights Pass With Assignment.

§ 1085.   Person not a party to grant; acquisition of interest or benefit

GRANT MAY INURE TO BENEFIT OF STRANGER. A present interest, and the benefit of a condition or covenant respecting property, may be taken by any natural person under a grant, although not named a party thereto. *(Enacted in 1872.)*

Research References

Miller and Starr California Real Estate § 8:26, Identification of the Grantee.
Miller and Starr California Real Estate § 8:58, in General; Transferable Property Interests.
Miller and Starr California Real Estate § 15:18, Rules of Construction-- "Reservation" of an Easement, or "Exception" of a Fee Simple.

22 NO. 3 Miller & Starr, California Real Estate Newsalert 1, Show Me Your Papers: Sales and Assignments of Secured Real Estate Loans and the California Foreclosure Process.
9 Witkin Cal. Proc. 5th Administrative Proceedings § 147, (S 147) Rulemaking by Private Organizations.

ARTICLE 6.   AGENCY LISTINGS FOR THE TRANSFER OF CERTAIN PROPERTY

Section
1086.   Definitions.
1087.   Multiple listing services; compensation of selling agent.
1088.   Placement of listing; responsibility for accuracy.
1089.   Compensation agreement; open listing.
1089.5. Personal representative contracts; application of article.
1090.   Listing agent as selling agent.

§ 1086.   Definitions

As used in this article, the following terms have the meanings stated in this section:

(a) "Property" means real property or a mobilehome, as defined in Section 18008 of the Health and Safety Code.

(b) "Sell" and "sale" include lease and exchange.

(c) "Buyer" includes a lessee in case of a lease and the party with whom property is exchanged in case of an exchange.

(d) An "agent" is one authorized by law to act in that capacity for that type of property, and is licensed as a real estate broker under Chapter 3 (commencing with Section 10130) of Part 1 of Division 4 of the Business and Professions Code or is a licensee, as defined in Section 18006 of the Health and Safety Code.

(e) An "appraiser" is one licensed or certified under Part 3 (commencing with Section 11300) of Division 4 of the Business and Professions Code.

(f) A "listing" is a written contract between an owner of property and an agent by which the agent has been authorized to sell the property or to find or obtain a buyer.

A listing may be any of the following:

(1) An "exclusive right to sell listing" is a listing whereby the owner grants to an agent, for a specified period of time, the exclusive right to sell or to find or obtain a buyer for the property, and the agent is entitled to the agreed compensation if during that period of time the property is sold, no matter who effected the sale, or the listing agent receives and presents to the owner any enforceable offer from a ready, able, and willing buyer on terms authorized by the listing or accepted by the owner. The exclusive right to sell listing may provide for compensation of the listing agent if the property is sold within a specified period after termination of the listing to anyone with whom the agent has had negotiations before that termination.

(2) An "exclusive agency listing" is the same as an "exclusive right to sell listing," except that the owner reserves the right to sell directly but not through any other agent and, in that event, without obligation to pay compensation to the agent.

(3) An "open listing" is a listing which grants no exclusive rights or priorities to the listing agent, and a commission is payable to the agent only if the agent procures and presents to the owner an enforceable offer from a ready, able, and willing buyer on the terms authorized by the listing or accepted by the owner, before the property is otherwise sold either through another agent or by the owner directly and before the listing expires by its terms or is revoked.

(g) A "listing agent" is one who has obtained a listing of property of the kind in respect of which he or she is authorized by law to act as an agent for compensation.

(h) A "selling agent" is an agent participant in a multiple listing service who acts in cooperation with a listing agent and who sells, or finds and obtains a buyer for, the property.

(i) "Sold" includes leased and exchanged. A property is sold when a legally binding commitment to sell the property comes into existence. *(Added by Stats.1982, c. 547, p. 2486, § 1. Amended by Stats.1988, c. 113, § 3, eff. May 25, 1988, operative July 1, 1988; Stats.1993, c. 331 (S.B.914), § 3.)*

Law Revision Commission Comments

Paragraph (4) of subdivision (e) of Section 1086 is superseded by Civil Code Section 1089.5 (application of article). [19 Cal.L.Rev.Comm.Reports 1033 (1987)].

Research References

California Real Estate Forms (Miller & Starr) § 1:1, Overview of a Commercial Real Estate Purchase and Sale Transaction.
California Real Estate Forms (Miller & Starr) § 1:2, Overview of a Residential Real Estate Purchase and Sale Transaction.
California Real Estate Forms (Miller & Starr) § 1:85, Cooperating Broker Compensation Agreement.
California Real Estate Forms (Miller & Starr) § 1:88, Buyer Nonagency Agreement.
Rutter, Cal. Practice Guide: A.D.R. Ch. 5-D, D. Defenses to Enforcement.
Rutter, Cal. Practice Guide: Real Prop. Transactions Ch. 2-D, D. Broker Compensation.
Rutter, Cal. Practice Guide: Real Prop. Transactions Ch. 2-E, E. Listing Agreements.
Miller and Starr California Real Estate § 3:11, Disclosure of Agency Relationships.
Miller and Starr California Real Estate § 3:41, Agent's Duty to Disclose; in General--Disclosures by Transfer Disclosure Statement.
Miller and Starr California Real Estate § 3:44, Negligence Liability--Duty to Inspect Property Being Sold.
Miller and Starr California Real Estate § 4:28, Listings.
Miller and Starr California Real Estate § 5:19, Construing a Listing Agreement--In General.
Miller and Starr California Real Estate § 5:24, Multiple Listing Services; Access and Regulations.
Miller and Starr California Real Estate § 5:25, Definitions and Overview of Types of Listing Agreements--In General.
Miller and Starr California Real Estate § 5:27, The "Open" Listing.
Miller and Starr California Real Estate § 5:28, The "Exclusive-Agency" Listing.
Miller and Starr California Real Estate § 5:29, The "Exclusive Right-To-Sell" Listing.
Miller and Starr California Real Estate § 5:32, The "Multiple Listing" Agreement.
Miller and Starr California Real Estate § 5:34, The Buyer's "Listing".
Miller and Starr California Real Estate § 5:56, Recovery of Compensation by a Salesperson.
1 Witkin Cal. Summ. 10th Contracts § 607, Realtors Multiple Listing Service.

§ 1087. Multiple listing services; compensation of selling agent

A multiple listing service is a facility of cooperation of agents and appraisers, operating through an intermediary which does not itself act as an agent or appraiser, through which agents establish express or implied legal relationships with respect to listed properties, or which may be used by agents and appraisers, pursuant to the rules of the service, to prepare market evaluations and appraisals of real property. If an open listing is placed in the multiple listing service, the total compensation that the owner is to pay shall go to the selling agent who procures an enforceable offer from a ready, able, and willing buyer on the terms accepted by the owner. An open listing need specify no compensation to the selling agent, but may state that the

compensation is to be negotiated between the selling agent and the owner. *(Added by Stats.1982, c. 547, p. 2487, § 1. Amended by Stats.1993, c. 331 (S.B.914), § 4.)*

Research References

Rutter, Cal. Practice Guide: Real Prop. Transactions Ch. 2-C, C. Broker's Relationship and Obligations to Principal and Third Parties.
Rutter, Cal. Practice Guide: Real Prop. Transactions Ch. 2-D, D. Broker Compensation.
Rutter, Cal. Practice Guide: Real Prop. Transactions Ch. 2-E, E. Listing Agreements.
Miller and Starr California Real Estate § 5:24, Multiple Listing Services; Access and Regulations.
Miller and Starr California Real Estate § 5:25, Definitions and Overview of Types of Listing Agreements--In General.
Miller and Starr California Real Estate § 5:27, The "Open" Listing.
Miller and Starr California Real Estate § 5:32, The "Multiple Listing" Agreement.

§ 1088. Placement of listing; responsibility for accuracy

A listing may not be placed in a multiple listing service unless authorized or directed by the owner in the listing.

If an agent or appraiser places a listing or other information in the multiple listing service, that agent or appraiser shall be responsible for the truth of all representations and statements made by the agent or appraiser of which that agent or appraiser had knowledge or reasonably should have had knowledge to anyone injured by their falseness or inaccuracy. *(Added by Stats.1982, c. 547, p. 2487, § 1. Amended by Stats.1993, c. 331 (S.B.914), § 5.)*

Research References

Rutter, Cal. Practice Guide: Real Prop. Transactions Ch. 2-C, C. Broker's Relationship and Obligations to Principal and Third Parties.
Rutter, Cal. Practice Guide: Real Prop. Transactions Ch. 2-E, E. Listing Agreements.
Miller and Starr California Real Estate § 3:26, Duty to Exercise Skill, Care, and Diligence; Negligence Liability.
Miller and Starr California Real Estate § 3:37, Fraud; Negligent Misrepresentation.
Miller and Starr California Real Estate § 3:45, Duty Owed to Third Persons.
Miller and Starr California Real Estate § 4:98, Appraiser's Liability.
Miller and Starr California Real Estate § 5:32, The "Multiple Listing" Agreement.

§ 1089. Compensation agreement; open listing

An open listing may contain an agreement by the owner to pay the listing agent compensation in any amount, at any time, and for any services, other than for selling the property or procuring or finding a buyer, as the agreement may specify. *(Added by Stats.1982, c. 547, p. 2487, § 1.)*

Research References

Miller and Starr California Real Estate § 5:27, The "Open" Listing.

§ 1089.5. Personal representative contracts; application of article

Subject to the limitations, conditions, and requirements of Chapter 18 (commencing with Section 10000) of Part 5 of Division 7 of the Probate Code, this article applies to property defined in Section 1086 that is covered by a contract described in Section 10150 of the Probate Code. *(Added by Stats.1988, c. 113, § 4, eff. May 25, 1988, operative July 1, 1988.)*

Law Revision Commission Comments

Section 1089.5 is added to make clear that Sections 1086–1090 of the Civil Code apply to the placing of a listing under Section 10150 of the Probate Code in a multiple listing service, except that the Civil Code sections are subject to the limitations, conditions, and requirements of the

Probate Code provisions relating to sales of property in a decedent's estate. [19 Cal.L.Rev.Comm.Reports 1033 (1987)].

§ 1090. Listing agent as selling agent

Nothing in this article shall preclude a listing agent from also being the selling agent. *(Added by Stats.1982, c. 547, p. 2487, § 1.)*

Research References

Miller and Starr California Real Estate § 3:12, Dual Agency.
Miller and Starr California Real Estate § 19:232, Recovery of Possession; Writ of Possession.

ARTICLE 7. UNLAWFUL INFLUENCE OF APPRAISERS

Section
1090.5. Valuation of real estate; improper influence; violation.

§ 1090.5. Valuation of real estate; improper influence; violation

(a) No person with an interest in a real estate transaction involving a valuation shall improperly influence or attempt to improperly influence the development, reporting, result, or review of that valuation, through coercion, extortion, bribery, intimidation, compensation, or instruction. For purposes of this section, a valuation is defined as an estimate of the value of real property in written or electronic form, other than one produced solely by an automated valuation model or system. Prohibited acts include, but are not limited to, the following:

(1) Seeking to influence a person who prepares a valuation to report a minimum or maximum value for the property being valued. Such influence may include, but is not limited to:

(A) Requesting that a person provide a preliminary estimate or opinion of value prior to entering into a contract with that person for valuation services.

(B) Conditioning whether to hire a person based on an expectation of the value conclusion likely to be returned by that person.

(C) Conditioning the amount of a person's compensation on the value conclusion returned by that person.

(D) Providing to a person an anticipated, estimated, encouraged, or desired valuation prior to their completion of a valuation.

(2) Withholding or threatening to withhold timely payment to a person or entity that prepares a valuation, or provides valuation management functions, because that person or entity does not return a value at or above a certain amount.

(3) Implying to a person who prepares a valuation that current or future retention of that person depends on the amount at which the person estimates the value of real property.

(4) Excluding a person who prepares a valuation from consideration for future engagement because the person reports a value that does not meet or exceed a predetermined threshold.

(5) Conditioning the compensation paid to a person who prepares a valuation on consummation of the real estate transaction for which the valuation is prepared.

(6) Requesting the payment of compensation to achieve higher priority in the assignment of valuation business.

(b) Subdivision (a) does not prohibit a person with an interest in a real estate transaction from doing any of the following:

(1) Asking a person who performs a valuation to do any of the following:

(A) Consider additional, appropriate property information, including information about comparable properties.

(B) Provide further detail, substantiation, or explanation for the person's value conclusion.

(C) Correct errors in a valuation report.

(2) Obtaining multiple valuations, for purposes of selecting the most reliable valuation.

(3) Withholding compensation due to breach of contract or substandard performance of services.

(4) Providing a copy of the sales contract in connection with a purchase transaction.

(c) If a person who violates this section is licensed or registered under any state licensing or registration law and the violation occurs within the course and scope of the person's duties as a licensee or registrant, the violation shall be deemed a violation of that law.

(d) Nothing in this section shall be construed to authorize communications that are otherwise prohibited under existing law. *(Added by Stats.2007, c. 291 (S.B.223), § 2, eff. Oct. 5, 2007. Amended by Stats.2009, c. 173 (S.B.237), § 21; Stats.2011, c. 716 (S.B.6), § 5.)*

Research References

Rutter, Cal. Practice Guide: Real Prop. Transactions Ch. 6-L, L. Real Estate Appraisals.
Rutter, Cal. Practice Guide: Real Prop. Transactions Gen. Matls., Highlights.
Miller and Starr California Real Estate § 4:38, Grounds for Discipline--In General.
Miller and Starr California Real Estate § 4:99, Improper Influencing of an Appraiser.
Miller and Starr California Real Estate § 36:14, Liability for Negligent Appraisal.
18 NO. 4 Miller & Starr, California Real Estate Newsalert 22, Regulation of the Real Estate Industry.
18 NO. 4 Miller & Starr, California Real Estate Newsalert 45, Table of Statutes (Newsalert Vol 18).
20 NO. 4 Miller & Starr, California Real Estate Newsalert 18, Regulation of the Real Estate Industry.
22 NO. 4 Miller & Starr, California Real Estate Newsalert 19, Regulation of Real Estate and Mortgage Professionals.
12 Witkin, California Summary 10th Real Property § 500, (S 500) Conduct of Appraisal Practice.

CHAPTER 2. TRANSFER OF REAL PROPERTY

ARTICLE 1. MODE OF TRANSFER

§ 1091. Method of transfer

REQUISITES FOR TRANSFER OF CERTAIN ESTATES. An estate in real property, other than an estate at will or for a term not exceeding one year, can be transferred only by operation of law, or by an instrument in writing, subscribed by the party disposing of the same, or by his agent thereunto authorized by writing. *(Enacted in 1872.)*

Research References

California Real Estate Forms (Miller & Starr) § 1:133, Grant Deed.
Rutter, Cal. Practice Guide: Real Prop. Transactions Ch. 4-A, A. Property to be Sold.
Rutter, Cal. Practice Guide: Real Prop. Transactions Ch. 4-B, B. Interests to be Conveyed.
Rutter, Cal. Practice Guide: Real Prop. Transactions Ch. 4-C, C. Parties to the Purchase Agreement.
Rutter, Cal. Practice Guide: Real Prop. Transactions Ch. 4-D, D. Selecting the Form of Written Agreement.
Rutter, Cal. Practice Guide: Real Prop. Transactions Ch. 7-C, C. Representing the Purchasing Tenant.
Miller and Starr California Real Estate § 5:8, Transactions Included in the Statute of Frauds.
Miller and Starr California Real Estate § 8:1, Definitions and Terminology.
Miller and Starr California Real Estate § 8:2, Rules of Interpretation; Extrinsic Evidence.
Miller and Starr California Real Estate § 8:3, Requirements; Form and Content.
Miller and Starr California Real Estate § 1:65, Provisions Applicable to Real Estate Transactions.
Miller and Starr California Real Estate § 1:67, Agreement that Will Not be Performed Within One Year from the Date it is Made--Oral Leases.
Miller and Starr California Real Estate § 1:69, Contract for the Sale, Gift, or Financing of Real Property.
Miller and Starr California Real Estate § 1:81, Written Authority Required; the Equal Dignities Rule.
Miller and Starr California Real Estate § 10:5, Form and Interpretation.
Miller and Starr California Real Estate § 11:6, Instruments Subject to Recording--List of Recordable Documents.
Miller and Starr California Real Estate § 17:5, Transfer and Recording.
Miller and Starr California Real Estate § 5:16, Exception: Estoppel to Raise Statute of Frauds as a Defense.
Miller and Starr California Real Estate § 8:28, Insertion of Name After Execution by the Grantor.
Miller and Starr California Real Estate § 8:29, Requirements of Grantor's Signature.
Miller and Starr California Real Estate § 8:30, Execution by an Agent or Attorney-In-Fact.
Miller and Starr California Real Estate § 8:39, Community Property; Voidable Transfers.
Miller and Starr California Real Estate § 8:58, in General; Transferable Property Interests.
Miller and Starr California Real Estate § 8:61, Description of the Property--In General; Effect of Deficient or Ambiguous Descriptions.
Miller and Starr California Real Estate § 11:12, Required Form and Contents--Signature of the Property Owner.
Miller and Starr California Real Estate § 17:21, Minerals--In General.
Miller and Starr California Real Estate § 17:23, Minerals--Oil and Gas.
Miller and Starr California Real Estate § 19:21, Lease as a Contract and Conveyance--Application of the Statute of Frauds/Translation of Leases Into Other Languages.

Miller and Starr California Real Estate § 19:61, Requirements for a Valid Assignment.
20 NO. 5 Miller & Starr, California Real Estate Newsalert 20, Mechanics' Liens.
22 NO. 3 Miller & Starr, California Real Estate Newsalert 1, Show Me Your Papers: Sales and Assignments of Secured Real Estate Loans and the California Foreclosure Process.
12 Witkin, California Summary 10th Real Property § 268, Writing and Subscription.
12 Witkin, California Summary 10th Real Property § 520, Execution and Delivery.
1 Witkin Cal. Summ. 10th Contracts § 385, Scope of Statute.
1 Witkin Cal. Summ. 10th Contracts § 388, (S 388) Equal Dignities Rule.
1 Witkin Cal. Summ. 10th Contracts § 389, Agent Acting Mechanically.

§ 1092. Grant; form

A grant of an estate in real property may be made in substance as follows:

"I, A B, grant to C D all that real property situated in (insert name of county) County, State of California, bounded (or described) as follows: (here insert property description, or if the land sought to be conveyed has a descriptive name, it may be described by the name, as for instance, 'The Norris Ranch.')

Witness my hand this (insert day) day of (insert month), 20____.

AB"

(Enacted in 1872. Amended by Stats.1999, c. 608 (A.B.1342), § 4.)

Research References

California Real Estate Forms (Miller & Starr) § 1:133, Grant Deed.
Miller and Starr California Real Estate § 8:3, Requirements; Form and Content.
Miller and Starr California Real Estate § 8:61, Description of the Property--In General; Effect of Deficient or Ambiguous Descriptions.
Miller and Starr California Real Estate § 11:161, Ad Valorem Tax Liens--Sale of the Property.
12 Witkin, California Summary 10th Real Property § 271, Methods of Description.

§ 1093. Consolidation of separate and distinct legal descriptions into single instrument of conveyance or security document; effect on separate nature of property

Absent the express written statement of the grantor contained therein, the consolidation of separate and distinct legal descriptions of real property contained in one or more deeds, mortgages, patents, deeds of trust, contracts of sale, or other instruments of conveyance or security documents, into a subsequent single deed, mortgage, patent, deed of trust, contract of sale, or other instrument of conveyance or security document (whether by means of an individual listing of the legal descriptions in a subsequent single instrument of conveyance or security document, or by means of a consolidated legal description comprised of more than one previously separate and distinct legal description), does not operate in any manner to alter or affect the separate and distinct nature of the real property so described in the subsequent single instrument of conveyance or security document containing either the listing of or the consolidated legal description of the parcels so conveyed or secured thereby.

This section does not constitute a change in, but is declaratory of, the existing law. *(Added by Stats.1985, c. 911, § 1.)*

Research References

Miller and Starr California Real Estate § 8:75, Consolidation of Descriptions; Non-Merger of Multiple Parcels in a Single Deed.
Miller and Starr California Real Estate § 25:13, Application to Land Divisions Prior to the Effective Date of the Act.
Miller and Starr California Real Estate § 25:14, Merger of Contiguous Parcels.

12 Witkin, California Summary 10th Real Property § 256, (S 256) Nature of Grant.

§ 1095. Attorney in fact; execution of instruments

ATTORNEY IN FACT, HOW MUST EXECUTE FOR PRINCIPAL. When an attorney in fact executes an instrument transferring an estate in real property, he must subscribe the name of his principal to it, and his own name as attorney in fact. *(Enacted in 1872.)*

Research References

Miller and Starr California Real Estate § 8:30, Execution by an Agent or Attorney-In-Fact.
12 Witkin, California Summary 10th Real Property § 268, Writing and Subscription.
14 Witkin, California Summary 10th Wills and Probate § 835, (S 835) Nature and Scope of Instrument.

§ 1096. Conveyance after change of name; procedure

Any person in whom the title of real estate is vested, who shall afterwards, from any cause, have his or her name changed, must, in any conveyance of said real estate so held, set forth the name in which he or she derived title to said real estate. Any conveyance, though recorded as provided by law, which does not comply with the foregoing provision shall not impart constructive notice of the contents thereof to subsequent purchasers and encumbrancers, but such conveyance is valid as between the parties thereto and those who have notice thereof. *(Added by Stats.1905, c. 443, p. 602, § 1. Amended by Stats.1947, c. 1314, p. 2852, § 1.)*

Research References

Miller and Starr California Real Estate § 8:17, Assumed or Fictitious Names of the Grantor.
Miller and Starr California Real Estate § 8:20, Correction of Identity by Deed.
Miller and Starr California Real Estate § 11:36, Transfer After Change of Name.
12 Witkin, California Summary 10th Real Property § 264, Conveyance in Different Name.

§ 1097. Exercise of option or completion of contract for sale of single family residential property; fee of vendor or lessor

No vendor or lessor of a single family residential property shall contract for or exact any fee in excess of ten dollars ($10) for the act of signing and delivering a document in connection with the transfer, cancellation or reconveyance of any title or instrument at the time the buyer or lessee exercises an option to buy, or completes performance of the contract for the sale of, the property.

The provisions of this section shall apply prospectively only. *(Added by Stats.1965, c. 352, p. 1458, § 1.)*

Research References

Miller and Starr California Real Estate § 2:9, Mode and Manner of Exercise.
Miller and Starr California Real Estate § 10:5, Form and Interpretation.
Miller and Starr California Real Estate § 2:13, Sale or Encumbrance.
Miller and Starr California Real Estate § 9:42, Transfer Fees.
Miller and Starr California Real Estate § 19:135, Exercise of the Option.
Miller and Starr California Real Estate § 25C:36, Required Provisions of the Purchase Agreement.
4 Witkin, California Summary 10th Security Transactions in Real Property § 24, (S 24) in General.

§ 1098. "Transfer fee" defined

A "transfer fee" is any fee payment requirement imposed within a covenant, restriction, or condition contained in any deed, contract, security instrument, or other document affecting the transfer or sale of, or any interest in, real property that requires a fee be paid upon transfer of the real property. A transfer fee does not include any of the following:

(a) Fees or taxes imposed by a governmental entity.

(b) Fees pursuant to mechanics' liens.

(c) Fees pursuant to court-ordered transfers, payments, or judgments.

(d) Fees pursuant to property agreements in connection with a legal separation or dissolution of marriage.

(e) Fees, charges, or payments in connection with the administration of estates or trusts pursuant to Division 7 (commencing with Section 7000), Division 8 (commencing with Section 13000), or Division 9 (commencing with Section 15000) of the Probate Code.

(f) Fees, charges, or payments imposed by lenders or purchasers of loans, as these entities are described in subdivision (c) of Section 10232 of the Business and Professions Code.

(g) Assessments, charges, penalties, or fees authorized by the Davis–Stirling Common Interest Development Act (Part 5 (commencing with Section 4000) of Division 4) or by the Commercial and Industrial Common Interest Development Act (Part 5.3 (commencing with Section 6500) of Division 4).

(h) Fees, charges, or payments for failing to comply with, or for transferring the real property prior to satisfying, an obligation to construct residential improvements on the real property.

(i) Any fee reflected in a document recorded against the property on or before December 31, 2007, that is separate from any covenants, conditions, and restrictions, and that substantially complies with subdivision (a) of Section 1098.5 by providing a prospective transferee notice of the following:

(1) Payment of a transfer fee is required.

(2) The amount or method of calculation of the fee.

(3) The date or circumstances under which the transfer fee payment requirement expires, if any.

(4) The entity to which the fee will be paid.

(5) The general purposes for which the fee will be used. *(Added by Stats.2007, c. 689 (A.B.980), § 1. Amended by Stats.2012, c. 181 (A.B.806), § 32, operative Jan. 1, 2014; Stats. 2013, c. 605 (S.B.752), § 14.)*

Law Revision Commission Comments

Section 1098 is amended to correct a cross-reference to former Sections 1350–1378. [40 Cal.L.Rev.Comm. Reports 235 (2010)].

Subdivision (g) of Section 1098 is amended to add a cross-reference to Part 5.3 (commencing with Section 6500) of Division 4, reflecting the enactment of the Commercial and Industrial Common Interest Development Act (Civ. Code §§ 6500–6876). [42 Cal.L.Rev.Comm. Reports 1 (2012)].

Research References

Rutter, Cal. Practice Guide: Real Prop. Transactions Ch. 4-E, E. Drafting the Purchase and Sale Agreement-Terms and Conditions.
Miller and Starr California Real Estate § 9:42, Transfer Fees.
Miller and Starr California Real Estate § 24:25, Rights of Enforcement--Generally.
Miller and Starr California Real Estate § 24:32, Defenses to Enforcement--Public Policy or Discrimination.
Miller and Starr California Real Estate § 25C:36, Required Provisions of the Purchase Agreement.
18 NO. 4 Miller & Starr, California Real Estate Newsalert 21, Recording and Priorities.
18 NO. 4 Miller & Starr, California Real Estate Newsalert 45, Table of Statutes (Newsalert Vol 18).

12 Witkin, California Summary 10th Real Property § 491B, (S 491B) (New)-Notice of Transfer Fee.

§ 1098.5. Transfer fee documentation; requirements

(a) For transfer fees, as defined in Section 1098, imposed prior to January 1, 2008, the receiver of the fee, as a condition of payment of the fee on or after January 1, 2009, shall record, on or before December 31, 2008, against the real property in the office of the county recorder for the county in which the real property is located a separate document that meets all of the following requirements:

(1) The title of the document shall be "Payment of Transfer Fee Required" in at least 14–point boldface type.

(2) The document shall include all of the following information:

(A) The names of all current owners of the real property subject to the transfer fee, and the legal description and assessor's parcel number for the affected real property.

(B) The amount, if the fee is a flat amount, or the percentage of the sales price constituting the cost of the fee.

(C) If the real property is residential property, actual dollar-cost examples of the fee for a home priced at two hundred fifty thousand dollars ($250,000), five hundred thousand dollars ($500,000), and seven hundred fifty thousand dollars ($750,000).

(D) The date or circumstances under which the transfer fee payment requirement expires, if any.

(E) The purpose for which the funds from the fee will be used.

(F) The entity to which funds from the fee will be paid and specific contact information regarding where the funds are to be sent.

(G) The signature of the authorized representative of the entity to which funds from the fee will be paid.

(b) When a transfer fee, as defined in Section 1098, is imposed upon real property on or after January 1, 2008, the person or entity imposing the transfer fee, as a condition of payment of the fee, shall record in the office of the county recorder for the county in which the real property is located, concurrently with the instrument creating the transfer fee requirement, a separate document that meets all of the following requirements:

(1) The title of the document shall be "Payment of Transfer Fee Required" in at least 14–point boldface type.

(2) The document shall include all of the following information:

(A) The names of all current owners of the real property subject to the transfer fee, and the legal description and assessor's parcel number for the affected real property.

(B) The amount, if the fee is a flat amount, or the percentage of the sales price constituting the cost of the fee.

(C) If the real property is residential property, actual dollar-cost examples of the fee for a home priced at two hundred fifty thousand dollars ($250,000), five hundred thousand dollars ($500,000), and seven hundred fifty thousand dollars ($750,000).

(D) The date or circumstances under which the transfer fee payment requirement expires, if any.

(E) The purpose for which the funds from the fee will be used.

(F) The entity to which funds from the fee will be paid and specific contact information regarding where the funds are to be sent.

(G) The signature of the authorized representative of the entity to which funds from the fee will be paid.

(c) The recorder shall only be responsible for examining that the document required by subdivision (a) or (b) contains the information required by subparagraphs (A), (F), and (G) of paragraph (2) of subdivision (a) or (b). The recorder shall index the document under the names of the persons and entities identified in subparagraphs (A) and (F) of paragraph (2) of subdivision (a) or (b). The recorder shall not examine any other information contained in the document required by subdivision (a) or (b). *(Added by Stats.2007, c. 689 (A.B.980), § 2.)*

Research References

Rutter, Cal. Practice Guide: Real Prop. Transactions Ch. 4-E, E. Drafting the Purchase and Sale Agreement-Terms and Conditions.
Miller and Starr California Real Estate § 9:42, Transfer Fees.
Miller and Starr California Real Estate § 24:25, Rights of Enforcement--Generally.
Miller and Starr California Real Estate § 24:32, Defenses to Enforcement--Public Policy or Discrimination.
Miller and Starr California Real Estate § 25C:36, Required Provisions of the Purchase Agreement.
18 NO. 4 Miller & Starr, California Real Estate Newsalert 21, Recording and Priorities.
18 NO. 4 Miller & Starr, California Real Estate Newsalert 45, Table of Statutes (Newsalert Vol 18).

§ 1099. Delivery to transferee of structural pest control inspection report and certification

(a) As soon as practical before transfer of title of any real property or the execution of a real property sales contract as defined in Section 2985, the transferor, fee owner, or his agent, shall deliver to the transferee a copy of a structural pest control inspection report prepared pursuant to Section 8516 of the Business and Professions Code upon which any certification in accordance with Section 8519 of the Business and Professions Code may be made, provided that certification or preparation of a report is a condition of the contract effecting that transfer, or is a requirement imposed as a condition of financing such transfer.

(b) If a notice of work completed as contemplated by Section 8518 of the Business and Professions Code, indicating action by a structural pest control licensee in response to an inspection report delivered or to be delivered under provisions of subdivision (a), or a certification pursuant to Section 8519 of the Business and Professions Code, has been received by a transferor or his agent before transfer of title or execution of a real property sales contract as defined in Section 2985, it shall be furnished to the transferee as soon as practical before transfer of title or the execution of such real property sales contract.

(c) Delivery to a transferee as used in this section means delivery in person or by mail to the transferee himself or any person authorized to act for him in the transaction or to such additional transferees who have requested such delivery from the transferor or his agent in writing. For the purposes of this section, delivery to either husband or wife shall be deemed delivery to a transferee, unless the contract affecting the transfer states otherwise.

(d) No transfer of title of real property shall be invalidated solely because of the failure of any person to comply with the provisions of this section unless such failure is an act or omission which would be a valid ground for rescission of such transfer in the absence of this section. *(Added by Stats.1974, c. 649, p. 1512, § 2, operative July 1, 1975.)*

Research References

Rutter, Cal. Practice Guide: Real Prop. Transactions Ch. 2-C, C. Broker's Relationship and Obligations to Principal and Third Parties.
Rutter, Cal. Practice Guide: Real Prop. Transactions Ch. 4-E, E. Drafting the Purchase and Sale Agreement-Terms and Conditions.

Miller and Starr California Real Estate § 3:42, Specific Disclosures Required by Statute.

Miller and Starr California Real Estate § 1:144, Duty of Seller of Real Property to Disclose--Statutory Duty of Disclosure.

Miller and Starr California Real Estate § 1:160, Duty to Make Good-Faith Attempt to Satisfy a Condition--Condition Based on Approval or Satisfaction.

Miller and Starr California Real Estate § 29:55, Inspection and Report.

12 Witkin, California Summary 10th Real Property § 471, (S 471) Types of Disclosures.

1 Witkin Cal. Summ. 10th Contracts § 780, (S 780) Vendor and Purchaser.

3 Witkin, California Summary 10th Agency and Employment § 63, in General.

ARTICLE 1.4. INSTALLATION OF WATER USE EFFICIENCY IMPROVEMENTS

Section

§ 1101.1. Legislative findings and declarations regarding water supply

The Legislature finds and declares all of the following:

(a) Adequate water supply reliability for all uses is essential to the future economic and environmental health of California.

(b) Environmentally sound strategies to meet future water supply and wastewater treatment needs are key to protecting and restoring aquatic resources in California.

(c) There is a pressing need to address water supply reliability issues raised by growing urban areas.

(d) Economic analysis by urban water agencies has identified urban water conservation as a cost-effective approach to addressing water supply needs.

(e) There are many water conservation practices that produce significant energy and other resource savings that should be encouraged as a matter of state policy.

(f) Since the 1991 signing of the "Memorandum of Understanding Regarding Urban Water Conservation in California," many urban water and wastewater treatment agencies have gained valuable experience that can be applied to produce significant statewide savings of water, energy, and associated infrastructure costs. This experience indicates a need to regularly revise and update water conservation methodologies and practices.

(g) To address these concerns, it is the intent of the Legislature to require that residential and commercial real property built and available for use or occupancy on or before January 1, 1994, be equipped with water-conserving plumbing fixtures.

(h) It is further the intent of the Legislature that retail water suppliers are encouraged to provide incentives, financing mechanisms, and funding to assist property owners with these retrofit obligations. *(Added by Stats.2009, c. 587 (S.B.407), § 1.)*

§ 1101.2. Application of article to specified properties

Except as provided in Section 1101.7, this article shall apply to residential and commercial real property built and available for use on or before January 1, 1994. *(Added by Stats.2009, c. 587 (S.B.407), § 1.)*

Research References

Miller and Starr California Real Estate § 3:41, Agent's Duty to Disclose; in General--Disclosures by Transfer Disclosure Statement.

Miller and Starr California Real Estate § 1:145, Duty of Seller of Real Property to Disclose--Transfer Disclosure Statement in Residential Sales.

20 NO. 4 Miller & Starr, California Real Estate Newsalert 5, Contracts.

§ 1101.3. Definitions

For the purposes of this article:

(a) "Commercial real property" means any real property that is improved with, or consisting of, a building that is intended for commercial use, including hotels and motels, that is not a single-family residential real property or a multifamily residential real property.

(b) "Multifamily residential real property" means any real property that is improved with, or consisting of, a building containing more than one unit that is intended for human habitation, or any mixed residential-commercial buildings or portions thereof that are intended for human habitation. Multi-family residential real property includes residential hotels but does not include hotels and motels that are not residential hotels.

(c) "Noncompliant plumbing fixture" means any of the following:

(1) Any toilet manufactured to use more than 1.6 gallons of water per flush.

(2) Any urinal manufactured to use more than one gallon of water per flush.

(3) Any showerhead manufactured to have a flow capacity of more than 2.5 gallons of water per minute.

(4) Any interior faucet that emits more than 2.2 gallons of water per minute.

(d) "Single-family residential real property" means any real property that is improved with, or consisting of, a building containing not more than one unit that is intended for human habitation.

(e) "Water-conserving plumbing fixture" means any fixture that is in compliance with current building standards applicable to a newly constructed real property of the same type.

(f) "Sale or transfer" means the sale or transfer of an entire real property estate or the fee interest in that real property estate and does not include the sale or transfer of a partial interest, including a leasehold. *(Added by Stats.2009, c. 587 (S.B.407), § 1.)*

Research References

20 NO. 4 Miller & Starr, California Real Estate Newsalert 5, Contracts.

§ 1101.4. Single-family residential real property; non-compliant plumbing fixtures; replacement with water-conserving plumbing fixtures

(a) On and after January 1, 2014, for all building alterations or improvements to single-family residential real property, as a condition for issuance of a certificate of final completion and occupancy or final permit approval by the local building department, the permit applicant shall replace all noncompliant plumbing fixtures with water-conserving plumbing fixtures.

(b) On or before January 1, 2017, noncompliant plumbing fixtures in any single-family residential real property shall be replaced by the property owner with water-conserving plumbing fixtures.

(c) On and after January 1, 2017, a seller or transferor of single-family residential real property shall disclose in writing to the prospective purchaser or transferee the requirements of subdivision (b) and whether the real property includes any noncompliant plumbing fixtures. *(Added by Stats.2009, c. 587 (S.B.407), § 1.)*

Research References

Miller and Starr California Real Estate § 1:144, Duty of Seller of Real Property to Disclose--Statutory Duty of Disclosure.
20 NO. 4 Miller & Starr, California Real Estate Newsalert 5, Contracts.
22 NO. 4 Miller & Starr, California Real Estate Newsalert 9, Contracts.

§ 1101.5. Multifamily residential real property and commercial real property; noncompliant plumbing fixtures; replacement with water-conserving plumbing fixtures

(a) On or before January 1, 2019, all noncompliant plumbing fixtures in any multifamily residential real property and in any commercial real property shall be replaced with water-conserving plumbing fixtures.

(b) An owner or the owner's agent may enter the owner's property for the purpose of installing, repairing, testing, and maintaining water-conserving plumbing fixtures required by this section, consistent with notice requirements of Section 1954.

(c) On and after January 1, 2019, the water-conserving plumbing fixtures required by this section shall be operating at the manufacturer's rated water consumption at the time that the tenant takes possession. A tenant shall be responsible for notifying the owner or owner's agent if the tenant becomes aware that a water-conserving plumbing fixture within his or her unit is not operating at the manufacturer's rated water consumption. The owner or owner's agent shall correct an inoperability in a water-conserving plumbing fixture upon notice by the tenant or if detected by the owner or the owner's agent.

(d)(1) On and after January 1, 2014, all noncompliant plumbing fixtures in any multifamily residential real property and any commercial * * * real property shall be replaced with water-conserving plumbing fixtures in the following circumstances:

(A) For building additions in which the sum of concurrent building permits by the same permit applicant would increase the floor area of the space in a building by more than 10 percent, the building permit applicant shall replace all noncompliant plumbing fixtures in the building.

(B) For building alterations or improvements in which the total construction cost estimated in the building permit is greater than one hundred fifty thousand dollars ($150,000), the building permit applicant shall replace all noncompliant plumbing fixtures that service the specific area of the improvement.

(C) Notwithstanding subparagraph (A) or (B), for any alterations or improvements to a room in a building that require a building permit and that room contains any noncompliant plumbing fixtures, the building permit applicant shall replace all noncompliant plumbing fixtures in that room.

(2) Replacement of all noncompliant plumbing fixtures with water-conserving plumbing fixtures, as described in paragraph (1), shall be a condition for issuance of a certificate of final completion and occupancy or final permit approval by the local building department.

(e) On and after January 1, 2019, a seller or transferor of multifamily residential real property or of commercial real property shall disclose to the prospective purchaser or transferee, in writing, the requirements of subdivision (a) and whether the property includes any noncompliant plumbing fixtures. This disclosure may be included in other transactional documents. *(Added by Stats.2009, c. 587 (S.B.407), § 1. Amended by Stats.2013, c. 183 (S.B.745), § 1.)*

Research References

Miller and Starr California Real Estate § 1:144, Duty of Seller of Real Property to Disclose--Statutory Duty of Disclosure.
20 NO. 4 Miller & Starr, California Real Estate Newsalert 5, Contracts.
22 NO. 4 Miller & Starr, California Real Estate Newsalert 9, Contracts.

§ 1101.6. Demolition permit; one-year postponement of article requirements

The duty of an owner or building permit applicant to comply with the requirements of this article shall be postponed for one year from the date of issuance of a demolition permit for the building. If the building is demolished within the one-year postponement, the requirements of this article shall not apply. If the building is not demolished after the expiration of one year, the provisions of this article shall apply, subject to appeal to the local building department, even though the demolition permit is still in effect or a new demolition permit has been issued. *(Added by Stats.2009, c. 587 (S.B.407), § 1.)*

§ 1101.7. Excluded properties

This article shall not apply to any of the following:

(a) Registered historical sites.

(b) Real property for which a licensed plumber certifies that, due to the age or configuration of the property or its plumbing, installation of water-conserving plumbing fixtures is not technically feasible.

(c) A building for which water service is permanently disconnected. *(Added by Stats.2009, c. 587 (S.B.407), § 1.)*

Research References

20 NO. 4 Miller & Starr, California Real Estate Newsalert 5, Contracts.

§ 1101.8. Local ordinances or policies

A city, county, or city and county, or a retail water supplier may do either of the following:

(a) Enact local ordinances or establish policies that promote compliance with this article.

(b) Enact local ordinances or establish policies that will result in a greater amount of water savings than those provided for in this article. *(Added by Stats.2009, c. 587 (S.B.407), § 1.)*

Research References

20 NO. 4 Miller & Starr, California Real Estate Newsalert 5, Contracts.

§ 1101.9. Noncompliant plumbing fixture retrofit ordinances; exemption from article requirements

Any city, county, or city and county that has adopted an ordinance requiring retrofit of noncompliant plumbing fixtures prior to July 1, 2009, shall be exempt from the requirements of this article so long as the ordinance remains in effect. *(Added by Stats.2009, c. 587 (S.B.407), § 1.)*

Research References

20 NO. 4 Miller & Starr, California Real Estate Newsalert 5, Contracts.

ARTICLE 1.5. DISCLOSURES UPON TRANSFER OF RESIDENTIAL PROPERTY

§ 1102. Application of article; waiver of requirements

(a) Except as provided in Section 1102.2, this article applies to any transfer by sale, exchange, installment land sale contract, as defined in Section 2985, lease with an option to purchase, any other option to purchase, or ground lease coupled with improvements, of real property or residential stock cooperative, improved with or consisting of not less than one nor more than four dwelling units.

(b) Except as provided in Section 1102.2, this article shall apply to a resale transaction entered into on or after January 1, 2000, for a manufactured home, as defined in Section 18007 of the Health and Safety Code, or a mobilehome, as defined in Section 18008 of the Health and Safety Code, which manufactured home or mobilehome is classified as personal property and intended for use as a residence.

(c) Any waiver of the requirements of this article is void as against public policy. *(Added by Stats.1985, c. 1574, § 2, operative Jan. 1, 1987. Amended by Stats.1986, c. 460, § 1; Stats.1994, c. 817 (S.B.1377), § 1; Stats.1995, c. 335 (A.B.530), § 1; Stats.1996, c. 677 (S.B.1704), § 1; Stats.1997, c. 71 (S.B. 384), § 1, eff. July 14, 1997; Stats.1998, c. 693 (S.B.1988), § 1; Stats.1999, c. 517 (S.B.534), § 2.)*

Research References

California Real Estate Forms (Miller & Starr) § 1:5, Non-Residential Statutory Disclosure Checklist.

California Real Estate Forms (Miller & Starr) § 1:94, California Residential Purchase Agreement and Joint Escrow Instructions.

California Real Estate Forms (Miller & Starr) § 1:115, Real Estate Transfer Disclosure Statement.

California Real Estate Forms (Miller & Starr) § 1:131, Seller Property Questionnaire.

Rutter, Cal. Practice Guide: Real Prop. Transactions Ch. 2-C, C. Broker's Relationship and Obligations to Principal and Third Parties.

Rutter, Cal. Practice Guide: Real Prop. Transactions Ch. 2-E, E. Listing Agreements.

Rutter, Cal. Practice Guide: Real Prop. Transactions Ch. 4-A, A. Property to be Sold.

Rutter, Cal. Practice Guide: Real Prop. Transactions Ch. 4-E, E. Drafting the Purchase and Sale Agreement-Terms and Conditions.

Rutter, Cal. Practice Guide: Real Prop. Transactions Ch. 11-B, B. Determining Breach.

Rutter, Cal. Practice Guide: Real Prop. Transactions Ch. 11-C, C. Seller's Remedies Upon Buyer's Breach-Damages and Specific Performance.

Rutter, Cal. Practice Guide: Real Prop. Transactions Ch. 11-E, E. Damages for Fraud.

Rutter, Cal. Practice Guide: Real Prop. Transactions Ch. 2-C Outline, Outline C.

Miller and Starr California Real Estate § 3:40, Agent's Duty to Disclose; in General--Statutory Duty to Disclose.

Miller and Starr California Real Estate § 3:41, Agent's Duty to Disclose; in General--Disclosures by Transfer Disclosure Statement.

Miller and Starr California Real Estate § 3:44, Negligence Liability--Duty to Inspect Property Being Sold.

Miller and Starr California Real Estate § 3:46, Statute of Limitations.

Miller and Starr California Real Estate § 1:142, Duty of Seller of Real Property to Disclose--Disclosure Duty on Sale of Nonresidential Property.

Miller and Starr California Real Estate § 1:144, Duty of Seller of Real Property to Disclose--Statutory Duty of Disclosure.

Miller and Starr California Real Estate § 1:145, Duty of Seller of Real Property to Disclose--Transfer Disclosure Statement in Residential Sales.

Miller and Starr California Real Estate § 31:43, Sale of a Mobilehome by a Tenant.

Miller and Starr California Real Estate § 31:47, Authority of Real Estate Brokers.

Miller and Starr California Real Estate § 25B:91, Collection of Assessments.

Miller and Starr California Real Estate § 25C:19, Additional Information for a Common-Interest Project.

Miller and Starr California Real Estate § 25C:36, Required Provisions of the Purchase Agreement.

Miller and Starr California Real Estate § 25C:39, Duty to Disclose Material Facts to a Buyer.

14 NO. 1 Miller & Starr, California Real Estate Newsalert 3, Contracts.

15 NO. 6 Miller & Starr, California Real Estate Newsalert 1, Refuse to Mediate and (Under Some Contracts) Wave Goodbye to Your Attorney's Fees.

16 NO. 4 Miller & Starr, California Real Estate Newsalert 1, Premises and Landowner Liability: the Supreme Court Continues Its Expansion of Potential Liability for Personal Injuries.

18 NO. 1 Miller & Starr, California Real Estate Newsalert 1, Disclosures in California Residential Real Property Sales.

3 Witkin Cal. Proc. 5th Actions § 482, (S 482) Two Years.

12 Witkin, California Summary 10th Real Property § 471, (S 471) Types of Disclosures.

12 Witkin, California Summary 10th Real Property § 475, Disclosure of Information in Booklets.

12 Witkin, California Summary 10th Real Property § 476, Statute of Limitations.

12 Witkin, California Summary 10th Real Property § 479, (S 479) Nature of Requirement.

12 Witkin, California Summary 10th Real Property § 480, (S 480) Included Transfers.

12 Witkin, California Summary 10th Real Property § 481, (S 481) Excluded Transfers.

12 Witkin, California Summary 10th Real Property § 482, (S 482) No Waiver of Disclosure Requirements.

12 Witkin, California Summary 10th Real Property § 483, (S 483) Content and Intended Use.

12 Witkin, California Summary 10th Real Property § 485, (S 485) Delivery of Statement.

12 Witkin, California Summary 10th Real Property § 487, (S 487) Natural Hazard Disclosure Statement.

12 Witkin, California Summary 10th Real Property § 488, (S 488) Homeowner's Guide to Earthquake Safety.

12 Witkin, California Summary 10th Real Property § 490, (S 490) Manufactured Home Statement.

12 Witkin, California Summary 10th Real Property § 491, (S 491) Continuing Lien Securing Facilities Tax or Bonds.

12 Witkin, California Summary 10th Real Property § 492, (S 492) Location of Sex Offenders.

12 Witkin, California Summary 10th Real Property § 493, (S 493) Military, Industrial, and Airport Influences.

12 Witkin, California Summary 10th Real Property § 494, (S 494) in General.

12 Witkin, California Summary 10th Real Property § 495, (S 495) Sanctions for Noncompliance.

12 Witkin, California Summary 10th Real Property § 496, (S 496) Regulation of Inspectors.

12 Witkin, California Summary 10th Real Property § 761, (S 761) Governing Law.

12 Witkin, California Summary 10th Real Property § 491A, (S 491A) (New)-Notice of Supplemental Tax Bill.

4 Witkin, California Summary 10th Security Transactions in Real Property § 165, (S 165) Grounds.

5 Witkin, California Summary 10th Torts § 797, Real Estate Transactions.

3 Witkin, California Summary 10th Agency and Employment § 63, in General.

3 Witkin, California Summary 10th Agency and Employment § 66, (S 66) Legislative Response.

§ 1102.1. Legislative intent

(a) In enacting Chapter 817 of the Statutes of 1994, it was the intent of the Legislature to clarify and facilitate the use of the real estate disclosure statement, as specified in Section 1102.6. The Legislature intended the statement to be used by transferors making disclosures required under this article and by agents making disclosures required by Section 2079 on the agent's portion of the real estate disclosure statement, in transfers subject to this article. In transfers not subject to this article, agents may make required disclosures in a separate writing. The Legislature did not intend to affect the existing obligations of the parties to a real estate contract, or their agents, to disclose any fact materially affecting the value and desirability of the property, including, but not limited to, the physical conditions of the property and previously received reports of physical inspections noted on the disclosure form set forth in Section 1102.6 or 1102.6a, and that nothing in this article shall be construed to change the duty of a real estate broker or salesperson pursuant to Section 2079.

It is also the intent of the Legislature that the delivery of a real estate transfer disclosure statement may not be waived in an "as is" sale, as held in Loughrin v. Superior Court (1993) 15 Cal. App. 4th 1188.

(b) In enacting Chapter 677 of the Statutes of 1996, it was the intent of the Legislature to clarify and facilitate the use of the manufactured home and mobilehome transfer disclosure statement applicable to the resale of a manufactured home or mobilehome pursuant to subdivision (b) of Section 1102. The Legislature intended the statements to be used by transferors making disclosures required under this article and by agents making disclosures required by Section 2079 on the agent's portion of the disclosure statement and as required by Section 18046 of the Health and Safety Code on the dealer's portion of the manufactured home and mobilehome transfer disclosure statement, in transfers subject to this article. In transfers not subject to this article, agents may make required disclosures in a separate writing. The Legislature did not intend to affect the existing obligations of the parties to a real estate contract, or their agents, to disclose any fact materially affecting the value and desirability of the property, including, but not limited to, the physical conditions of the property and previously received reports of physical inspections noted on the disclosure form set forth in Section 1102.6 or 1102.6a or to affect the existing obligations of the parties to a manufactured home or mobilehome purchase contract, and nothing in this article shall be construed to change the duty of a real estate broker or salesperson pursuant to Section 2079 or the duty of a manufactured home or mobilehome dealer or salesperson pursuant to Section 18046 of the Health and Safety Code.

It is also the intent of the Legislature that the delivery of a mobilehome transfer disclosure statement may not be waived in an "as is" sale.

(c) It is the intent of the Legislature that manufactured home and mobilehome dealers and salespersons and real estate brokers and salespersons use the form provided pursuant to Section 1102.6d. It is also the intent of the Legislature for sellers of manufactured homes or mobilehomes who are neither manufactured home dealers or salespersons nor real estate brokers or salespersons to use the Manufactured Home/Mobilehome Transfer Disclosure Statement contained in Section 1102.6d. (Added by Stats.1995, c. 335 (A.B.530), § 2. Amended by Stats.1996, c. 240 (A.B.2383), § 1; Stats.1999, c. 517 (S.B.534), § 3.)

Research References

California Real Estate Forms (Miller & Starr) § 1:5, Non-Residential Statutory Disclosure Checklist.

Rutter, Cal. Practice Guide: Real Prop. Transactions Ch. 2-C, C. Broker's Relationship and Obligations to Principal and Third Parties.

Rutter, Cal. Practice Guide: Real Prop. Transactions Ch. 4-E, E. Drafting the Purchase and Sale Agreement-Terms and Conditions.

Miller and Starr California Real Estate § 3:39, Agent's Duty to Disclose; in General--Common Law Duty to Disclose Material Facts.

Miller and Starr California Real Estate § 3:41, Agent's Duty to Disclose; in General--Disclosures by Transfer Disclosure Statement.

Miller and Starr California Real Estate § 3:44, Negligence Liability--Duty to Inspect Property Being Sold.

Miller and Starr California Real Estate § 1:143, Duty of Seller of Real Property to Disclose--Materiality of Facts to be Disclosed.

Miller and Starr California Real Estate § 1:144, Duty of Seller of Real Property to Disclose--Statutory Duty of Disclosure.

Miller and Starr California Real Estate § 1:145, Duty of Seller of Real Property to Disclose--Transfer Disclosure Statement in Residential Sales.

Miller and Starr California Real Estate § 31:43, Sale of a Mobilehome by a Tenant.

18 NO. 1 Miller & Starr, California Real Estate Newsalert 1, Disclosures in California Residential Real Property Sales.

12 Witkin, California Summary 10th Real Property § 482, (S 482) No Waiver of Disclosure Requirements.

12 Witkin, California Summary 10th Real Property § 483, (S 483) Content and Intended Use.

12 Witkin, California Summary 10th Real Property § 490, (S 490) Manufactured Home Statement.

4 Witkin, California Summary 10th Security Transactions in Real Property § 165, (S 165) Grounds.

§ 1102.2. Nonapplication of article

This article does not apply to the following:

(a) Transfers which are required to be preceded by the furnishing to a prospective transferee of a copy of a public report pursuant to Section 11018.1 of the Business and Professions Code and transfers which can be made without a public report pursuant to Section 11010.4 of the Business and Professions Code.

(b) Transfers pursuant to court order, including, but not limited to, transfers ordered by a probate court in the administration of an estate, transfers pursuant to a writ of execution, transfers by any foreclosure sale, transfers by a trustee in bankruptcy, transfers by eminent domain, and transfers resulting from a decree for specific performance.

(c) Transfers to a mortgagee by a mortgagor or successor in interest who is in default, transfers to a beneficiary of a deed of trust by a trustor or successor in interest who is in default, transfers by any foreclosure sale after default, transfers by any foreclosure sale after default in an obligation secured by a mortgage, transfers by a sale under a power of sale or any foreclosure sale under a decree of foreclosure after default in an obligation secured by a deed of trust or secured by any other instrument containing a power of sale, transfers by a mortgagee or a beneficiary under a deed of trust who has acquired the real property at a sale conducted pursuant to a power of sale under a mortgage or deed of trust or a sale pursuant to a decree of foreclosure or has acquired the real property by a deed in lieu of foreclosure, transfers to the legal owner or lienholder of a manufactured home or mobilehome by a registered owner or successor in interest who is in default, or transfers by reason of any foreclosure of a security interest in a manufactured home or mobilehome.

(d) Transfers by a fiduciary in the course of the administration of a decedent's estate, guardianship, conservatorship, or trust. This exemption shall not apply to a transfer if the trustee is a natural person who is sole trustee of a revocable trust and he or she is a former owner of the property or an occupant in possession of the property within the preceding year.

(e) Transfers from one coowner to one or more other coowners.

(f) Transfers made to a spouse, or to a person or persons in the lineal line of consanguinity of one or more of the transferors.

(g) Transfers between spouses resulting from a judgment of dissolution of marriage or of legal separation or from a property settlement agreement incidental to that judgment.

(h) Transfers by the Controller in the course of administering Chapter 7 (commencing with Section 1500) of Title 10 of Part 3 of the Code of Civil Procedure.

(i) Transfers under Chapter 7 (commencing with Section 3691) or Chapter 8 (commencing with Section 3771) of Part 6 of Division 1 of the Revenue and Taxation Code.

(j) Transfers or exchanges to or from any governmental entity. *(Formerly § 1102.1, added by Stats.1985, c. 1574, § 2, operative Jan. 1, 1987. Amended by Stats.1986, c. 460, § 2; Stats.1992, c. 163 (A.B.2641), § 7, operative Jan. 1, 1994. Renumbered § 1102.2 and amended by Stats.1995, c. 335 (A.B.530), § 3. Amended by Stats.1999, c. 119 (A.B.594), § 1; Stats.1999, c. 517 (S.B.534), § 4.5; Stats.2000, c. 135 (A.B.2539), § 11.)*

Law Revision Commission Comments

Subdivision (g) of Section 1102.1 is amended to substitute "judgment" for "decree" to conform to the terminology of the Family Code. [22 Cal.L.Rev.Comm.Reports 1 (1992)].

Research References

California Real Estate Forms (Miller & Starr) § 1:94, California Residential Purchase Agreement and Joint Escrow Instructions.
Rutter, Cal. Practice Guide: Real Prop. Transactions Ch. 2-C, C. Broker's Relationship and Obligations to Principal and Third Parties.
Rutter, Cal. Practice Guide: Real Prop. Transactions Ch. 4-E, E. Drafting the Purchase and Sale Agreement-Terms and Conditions.
Miller and Starr California Real Estate § 3:39, Agent's Duty to Disclose; in General--Common Law Duty to Disclose Material Facts.
Miller and Starr California Real Estate § 3:41, Agent's Duty to Disclose; in General--Disclosures by Transfer Disclosure Statement.
Miller and Starr California Real Estate § 3:44, Negligence Liability--Duty to Inspect Property Being Sold.
Miller and Starr California Real Estate § 1:144, Duty of Seller of Real Property to Disclose--Statutory Duty of Disclosure.
Miller and Starr California Real Estate § 1:145, Duty of Seller of Real Property to Disclose--Transfer Disclosure Statement in Residential Sales.
Miller and Starr California Real Estate § 28:39, When Notice of Completion Recorded.
Miller and Starr California Real Estate § 31:43, Sale of a Mobilehome by a Tenant.
Miller and Starr California Real Estate § 36:11, Fraud.
Miller and Starr California Real Estate § 25C:39, Duty to Disclose Material Facts to a Buyer.
18 NO. 1 Miller & Starr, California Real Estate Newsalert 1, Disclosures in California Residential Real Property Sales.
12 Witkin, California Summary 10th Real Property § 120, Transfer Rights.
12 Witkin, California Summary 10th Real Property § 481, (S 481) Excluded Transfers.
12 Witkin, California Summary 10th Real Property § 487, (S 487) Natural Hazard Disclosure Statement.
12 Witkin, California Summary 10th Real Property § 761, (S 761) Governing Law.
4 Witkin, California Summary 10th Security Transactions in Real Property § 165, (S 165) Grounds.

§ 1102.3. Delivery of required written statement from transferor to prospective transferee; indication of compliance with article; disclosures delivered after offer to purchase; time to terminate

The transferor of any real property subject to this article shall deliver to the prospective transferee the written statement required by this article, as follows:

(a) In the case of a sale, as soon as practicable before transfer of title.

(b) In the case of transfer by a real property sales contract, as defined in Section 2985, or by a lease together with an option to purchase, or a ground lease coupled with improvements, as soon as practicable before execution of the contract. For the purpose of this subdivision, "execution" means the making or acceptance of an offer.

With respect to any transfer subject to subdivision (a) or (b), the transferor shall indicate compliance with this article either on the receipt for deposit, the real property sales contract, the lease, or any addendum attached thereto or on a separate document.

If any disclosure, or any material amendment of any disclosure, required to be made by this article, is delivered after the execution of an offer to purchase, the transferee shall have three days after delivery in person or five days after delivery by deposit in the mail, to terminate his or her offer by delivery of a written notice of termination to the transferor or the transferor's agent. *(Formerly § 1102.2, added by Stats.1985, c. 1574, § 2, operative Jan. 1, 1987. Amended by Stats.1986, c. 460, § 3. Renumbered § 1102.3 and amended by Stats.1995, c. 335 (A.B.530), § 4.)*

Research References

California Real Estate Forms (Miller & Starr) § 1:94, California Residential Purchase Agreement and Joint Escrow Instructions.

Rutter, Cal. Practice Guide: Real Prop. Transactions Ch. 2-C, C. Broker's Relationship and Obligations to Principal and Third Parties.

Rutter, Cal. Practice Guide: Real Prop. Transactions Ch. 4-E, E. Drafting the Purchase and Sale Agreement-Terms and Conditions.

Miller and Starr California Real Estate § 3:41, Agent's Duty to Disclose; in General--Disclosures by Transfer Disclosure Statement.

Miller and Starr California Real Estate § 1:144, Duty of Seller of Real Property to Disclose--Statutory Duty of Disclosure.

Miller and Starr California Real Estate § 1:145, Duty of Seller of Real Property to Disclose--Transfer Disclosure Statement in Residential Sales.

18 NO. 1 Miller & Starr, California Real Estate Newsalert 1, Disclosures in California Residential Real Property Sales.

12 Witkin, California Summary 10th Real Property § 483, (S 483) Content and Intended Use.

12 Witkin, California Summary 10th Real Property § 485, (S 485) Delivery of Statement.

12 Witkin, California Summary 10th Real Property § 487, (S 487) Natural Hazard Disclosure Statement.

§ 1102.3a. Manufactured home or mobilehome; delivery of statement by transferor; termination of offer

(a) The transferor of any manufactured home or mobilehome subject to this article shall deliver to the prospective transferee the written statement required by this article, as follows:

(1) In the case of a sale, or a lease with an option to purchase, of a manufactured home or mobilehome, involving an agent, as defined in Section 18046 of the Health and Safety Code, as soon as practicable, but no later than the close of escrow for the purchase of the manufactured home or mobilehome.

(2) In the case of a sale, or lease with an option to purchase, of a manufactured home or mobilehome, not involving an agent, as defined in Section 18046 of the Health and Safety Code, at the time of execution of any document by the prospective transferee with the transferor for the purchase of the manufactured home or mobilehome.

(b) With respect to any transfer subject to this section, the transferor shall indicate compliance with this article either on the transfer disclosure statement, any addendum thereto, or on a separate document.

(c) If any disclosure, or any material amendment of any disclosure, required to be made pursuant to subdivision (b) of Section 1102, is delivered after the execution of an offer to purchase, the transferee shall have three days after delivery in person or five days after delivery by deposit in the mail, to terminate his or her offer by delivery of a written notice of termination to the transferor. (Added by Stats.1999, c. 517 (S.B.534), § 5.)

Research References

Rutter, Cal. Practice Guide: Real Prop. Transactions Ch. 4-E, E. Drafting the Purchase and Sale Agreement-Terms and Conditions.

12 Witkin, California Summary 10th Real Property § 490, (S 490) Manufactured Home Statement.

§ 1102.4. Errors, inaccuracies, or omissions of information delivered; liability of transferor; delivery of information by public agency; delivery of reports or opinions prepared by experts

(a) Neither the transferor nor any listing or selling agent shall be liable for any error, inaccuracy, or omission of any information delivered pursuant to this article if the error, inaccuracy, or omission was not within the personal knowledge of the transferor or that listing or selling agent, was based on information timely provided by public agencies or by other persons providing information as specified in subdivision (c) that is required to be disclosed pursuant to this article, and ordinary care was exercised in obtaining and transmitting it.

(b) The delivery of any information required to be disclosed by this article to a prospective transferee by a public agency or other person providing information required to be disclosed pursuant to this article shall be deemed to comply with the requirements of this article and shall relieve the transferor or any listing or selling agent of any further duty under this article with respect to that item of information.

(c) The delivery of a report or opinion prepared by a licensed engineer, land surveyor, geologist, structural pest control operator, contractor, or other expert, dealing with matters within the scope of the professional's license or expertise, shall be sufficient compliance for application of the exemption provided by subdivision (a) if the information is provided to the prospective transferee pursuant to a request therefor, whether written or oral. In responding to such a request, an expert may indicate, in writing, an understanding that the information provided will be used in fulfilling the requirements of Section 1102.6 and, if so, shall indicate the required disclosures, or parts thereof, to which the information being furnished is applicable. Where such a statement is furnished, the expert shall not be responsible for any items of information, or parts thereof, other than those expressly set forth in the statement. (Added by Stats.1985, c. 1574, § 2, operative Jan. 1, 1987. Amended by Stats.1986, c. 460, § 4.)

Research References

Rutter, Cal. Practice Guide: Real Prop. Transactions Ch. 4-E, E. Drafting the Purchase and Sale Agreement-Terms and Conditions.

Miller and Starr California Real Estate § 3:41, Agent's Duty to Disclose; in General--Disclosures by Transfer Disclosure Statement.

Miller and Starr California Real Estate § 3:42, Specific Disclosures Required by Statute.

Miller and Starr California Real Estate § 3:44, Negligence Liability--Duty to Inspect Property Being Sold.

Miller and Starr California Real Estate § 1:144, Duty of Seller of Real Property to Disclose--Statutory Duty of Disclosure.

Miller and Starr California Real Estate § 1:145, Duty of Seller of Real Property to Disclose--Transfer Disclosure Statement in Residential Sales.

12 Witkin, California Summary 10th Real Property § 494, (S 494) in General.

§ 1102.5. Information subsequently rendered inaccurate; required information unknown or not available

If information disclosed in accordance with this article is subsequently rendered inaccurate as a result of any act, occurrence, or agreement subsequent to the delivery of the required disclosures, the inaccuracy resulting therefrom does not constitute a violation of this article. If at the time the disclosures are required to be made, an item of information required to be disclosed is unknown or not available to the transferor, and the transferor or his or her agent has made a reasonable effort to ascertain it, the transferor may use an approximation of the information, provided the approximation is clearly identified as such, is reasonable, is based on the best information available to the transferor or his or her agent, and is not used for the purpose of circumventing or evading this article. (Added by Stats.1985, c. 1574, § 2, operative Jan. 1, 1987.)

Research References

Rutter, Cal. Practice Guide: Real Prop. Transactions Ch. 4-E, E. Drafting the Purchase and Sale Agreement-Terms and Conditions.

Miller and Starr California Real Estate § 3:41, Agent's Duty to Disclose; in General--Disclosures by Transfer Disclosure Statement.

Miller and Starr California Real Estate § 1:140, Duty of Seller of Real Property to Disclose.

Miller and Starr California Real Estate § 1:145, Duty of Seller of Real Property to Disclose--Transfer Disclosure Statement in Residential Sales.

12 Witkin, California Summary 10th Real Property § 494, (S 494) in General.

§ 1102.6. Disclosure form

Section operative until July 1, 2014. See, also, section operative July 1, 2014.

The disclosures required by this article pertaining to the property proposed to be transferred are set forth in, and shall be made on a copy of, the following disclosure form:

REAL ESTATE TRANSFER DISCLOSURE STATEMENT

THIS DISCLOSURE STATEMENT CONCERNS THE REAL PROPERTY SITUATED IN THE CITY OF _____, COUNTY OF _____, STATE OF CALIFORNIA, DESCRIBED AS _____. THIS STATEMENT IS A DISCLOSURE OF THE CONDITION OF THE ABOVE DESCRIBED PROPERTY IN COMPLIANCE WITH SECTION 1102 OF THE CIVIL CODE AS OF _____, 20___. IT IS NOT A WARRANTY OF ANY KIND BY THE SELLER(S) OR ANY AGENT(S) REPRESENTING ANY PRINCIPAL(S) IN THIS TRANSACTION, AND IS NOT A SUBSTITUTE FOR ANY INSPECTIONS OR WARRANTIES THE PRINCIPAL(S) MAY WISH TO OBTAIN.

I

COORDINATION WITH OTHER DISCLOSURE FORMS

This Real Estate Transfer Disclosure Statement is made pursuant to Section 1102 of the Civil Code. Other statutes require disclosures, depending upon the details of the particular real estate transaction (for example: special study zone and purchase money liens on residential property).

Substituted Disclosures: The following disclosures and other disclosures required by law, including the Natural Hazard Disclosure Report/Statement that may include airport annoyances, earthquake, fire, flood, or special assessment information, have or will be made in connection with this real estate transfer, and are intended to satisfy the disclosure obligations on this form, where the subject matter is the same:

☐   Inspection reports completed pursuant to the contract of sale or receipt for deposit.

☐   Additional inspection reports or disclosures:

_____

_____

_____

II

SELLER'S INFORMATION

The Seller discloses the following information with the knowledge that even though this is not a warranty, prospective Buyers may rely on this information in deciding whether and on what terms to purchase the subject property. Seller hereby authorizes any agent(s) representing any principal(s) in this transaction to provide a copy of this statement to any person or entity in connection with any actual or anticipated sale of the property.

THE FOLLOWING ARE REPRESENTATIONS MADE BY THE SELLER(S) AND ARE NOT THE REPRESENTATIONS OF THE AGENT(S), IF ANY. THIS INFORMATION IS A DISCLOSURE AND IS NOT INTENDED TO BE PART OF ANY CONTRACT BETWEEN THE BUYER AND SELLER:

Seller ___ is ___ is not occupying the property.

A.   The subject property has the items checked below (read across):*

____Range	____Oven	____Microwave
____Dishwasher	____Trash Compactor	____Garbage Disposal
____Washer/Dryer Hookups		____Rain Gutters
____Burglar Alarms	____Carbon Monoxide	____Fire Alarm
____TV Antenna	Device(s)	____Intercom
____Central Heating	____Satellite Dish	____Evaporator Cooler(s)
____Wall/Window Air Cndtng.	____Central Air Cndtng.	____Public Sewer System
____Septic Tank	____Sprinklers	____Water Softener
____Patio/Decking	____Sump Pump	____Gazebo
____Sauna	____Built-in Barbecue	
____Hot Tub ____Locking		
Safety Cover		____Spa ____Locking
____Security Gate(s)	____Pool ____Child	Safety Cover
	Resistant Barrier	____Number Remote
	____Automatic Garage	Controls

Garage: ___Attached	___Door Opener(s)	___Carport
Pool/Spa Heater: ___Gas	___Not Attached	___Electric
Water Heater: ___Gas	___Solar	___ Private Utility or Other _____
	___Well	___Water-conserving plumbing fixtures
Water Supply: ___City	___Bottled	
Gas Supply: ___Utility	___Window Security	
___Window Screens	Bars ___Quick-Release Mechanism on Bedroom Windows	

Exhaust Fan(s) in _____ 220 Volt Wiring in _____ Fireplace(s) in _____
Gas Starter _____ Roof(s): Type: _____ Age: _____ (approx.)
Other: _____
Are there, to the best of your (Seller's) knowledge, any of the above that are not in operating condition? ___
Yes ___ No. If yes, then describe.
(Attach additional sheets if necessary): _____
_____
_____
_____

B. Are you (Seller) aware of any significant defects/malfunctions in any of the following?
___Yes ___No. If yes, check appropriate space(s) below.
___Interior Walls ___Ceilings ___Floors ___Exterior Walls ___Insulation ___Roof(s) ___Windows ___Doors ___Foundation ___Slab(s) ___Driveways ___Sidewalks ___Walls/Fences ___Electrical Systems ___Plumbing/ Sewers/Septics ___Other
Structural Components (Describe:_____)
If any of the above is checked, explain. (Attach additional sheets if necessary):_____
_____
_____
_____

* Installation of a listed appliance, device, or amenity is not a precondition of sale or transfer of the dwelling. The carbon monoxide device, garage door opener, or child-resistant pool barrier may not be in compliance with the safety standards relating to, respectively, carbon monoxide device standards of Chapter 8 (commencing with Section 13260) of Part 2 of Division 12 of, automatic reversing device standards of Chapter 12.5 (commencing with Section 19890) of Part 3 of Division 13 of, or the pool safety standards of Article 2.5 (commencing with Section 115920) of Chapter 5 of Part 10 of Division 104 of, the Health and Safety Code. Window security bars may not have quick-release mechanisms in compliance with the 1995 edition of the California Building Standards Code. Section 1101.4 of the Civil Code requires all single-family residences built on or before January 1, 1994, to be equipped with water-conserving plumbing fixtures after January 1, 2017. Additionally, on and after January 1, 2014, a single-family residence built on or before January 1, 1994, that is altered or improved is required to be equipped with water-conserving plumbing fixtures as a condition of final approval. Fixtures in this dwelling may not comply with Section 1101.4 of the Civil Code.

C. Are you (Seller) aware of any of the following:

1. Substances, materials, or products which may be an environmental hazard such as, but not limited to, asbestos, formaldehyde, radon gas, lead-based paint, mold, fuel or chemical storage tanks, and contaminated soil or water on the subject property ___Yes ___No
2. Features of the property shared in common with adjoining landowners, such as walls, fences, and driveways, whose use or responsibility for maintenance may have an effect on the subject property . . . . ___Yes ___No
3. Any encroachments, easements or similar matters that may affect your interest in the subject property . . . . ___Yes ___No
4. Room additions, structural modifications, or other alterations or repairs made without necessary permits . . . . ___Yes ___No
5. Room additions, structural modifications, or other alterations or repairs not in compliance with building codes . . . . ___Yes ___No
6. Fill (compacted or otherwise) on the property or any portion thereof . . . . ___Yes ___No
7. Any settling from any cause, or slippage, sliding, or other soil problems . . . . ___Yes ___No
8. Flooding, drainage or grading problems . . . . ___Yes ___No
9. Major damage to the property or any of the structures from fire, earthquake, floods, or landslides . . . . ___Yes ___No
10. Any zoning violations, nonconforming uses, violations of "setback" requirements ___Yes ___No
11. Neighborhood noise problems or other nuisances . . . . ___Yes ___No
12. CC&Rs or other deed restrictions or obligations . . . . ___Yes ___No
13. Homeowners' Association which has any authority over the subject property . . . . ___Yes ___No
14. Any "common area" (facilities such as pools, tennis courts, walkways, or other areas co-owned in undivided interest with others) . . . . ___Yes ___No
15. Any notices of abatement or citations against the property . . . . ___Yes ___No
16. Any lawsuits by or against the Seller threatening to or affecting this real property, including any lawsuits alleging a defect or deficiency in this real property or

"common areas" (facilities such as pools, tennis courts, walkways, or other areas co-owned in undivided interest with others) . . . . ___Yes ___No

If the answer to any of these is yes, explain. (Attach additional sheets if necessary.):

_____

D. 1. The Seller certifies that the property, as of the close of escrow, will be in compliance with Section 13113.8 of the Health and Safety Code by having operable smoke detectors(s) which are approved, listed, and installed in accordance with the State Fire Marshal's regulations and applicable local standards.

2. The Seller certifies that the property, as of the close of escrow, will be in compliance with Section 19211 of the Health and Safety Code by having the water heater tank(s) braced, anchored, or strapped in place in accordance with applicable law.

Seller certifies that the information herein is true and correct to the best of the Seller's knowledge as of the date signed by the Seller.

Seller _____   Date _____
Seller _____   Date _____

III

AGENT'S INSPECTION DISCLOSURE

(To be completed only if the Seller is represented by an agent in this transaction.)

THE UNDERSIGNED, BASED ON THE ABOVE INQUIRY OF THE SELLER(S) AS TO THE CONDITION OF THE PROPERTY AND BASED ON A REASONABLY COMPETENT AND DILIGENT VISUAL INSPECTION OF THE ACCESSIBLE AREAS OF THE PROPERTY IN CONJUNCTION WITH THAT INQUIRY, STATES THE FOLLOWING:

☐ Agent notes no items for disclosure.

☐ Agent notes the following items:

_____
_____
_____

Agent (Broker
Representing Seller) _____ By _____ Date_____
        (Please Print)   (Associate Licensee
                                   orBroker Signature)

IV

AGENT'S INSPECTION DISCLOSURE

(To be completed only if the agent who has obtained the offer is other than the agent above.)

THE UNDERSIGNED, BASED ON THE REASONABLY COMPETENT AND DILIGENT VISUAL INSPECTION OF THE ACCESSIBLE AREAS OF THE PROPERTY, STATES THE FOLLOWING:

☐ Agent notes no items for disclosure.

☑ Agent notes the following items:

_____
_____
_____

Agent (Broker
Obtaining the Offer) _____ By _____ Date_____
        (Please Print)   (Associate Licensee
                                   orBroker Signature)

V

BUYER(S) AND SELLER(S) MAY WISH TO OBTAIN PROFESSIONAL ADVICE AND/OR INSPEC-
TIONS OF THE PROPERTY AND TO PROVIDE FOR APPROPRIATE PROVISIONS IN A
CONTRACT BETWEEN BUYER(S) AND SELLER(S) WITH RESPECT TO ANY ADVICE/INSPEC-
TIONS/ DEFECTS.

I/WE ACKNOWLEDGE RECEIPT OF A COPY OF THIS STATEMENT.

Seller _____ Date _____   Buyer _____ Date _____
Seller _____ Date _____   Buyer _____ Date _____

Agent (Broker
Representing Seller) _____ By _____ Date_____
                        (Please Print)   (Associate Licensee
                                              or Broker Signature)

Agent (Broker
Obtaining the Offer) _____ By _____ Date_____
                        (Please Print)   (Associate Licensee
                                              or Broker Signature)

SECTION 1102.3 OF THE CIVIL CODE PROVIDES A BUYER WITH THE RIGHT TO RESCIND A
PURCHASE CONTRACT FOR AT LEAST THREE DAYS AFTER THE DELIVERY OF THIS
DISCLOSURE IF DELIVERY OCCURS AFTER THE SIGNING OF AN OFFER TO PURCHASE. IF
YOU WISH TO RESCIND THE CONTRACT, YOU MUST ACT WITHIN THE PRESCRIBED
PERIOD.

A REAL ESTATE BROKER IS QUALIFIED TO ADVISE ON REAL ESTATE.IF YOU DESIRE
LEGAL ADVICE, CONSULT YOUR ATTORNEY.

(Added by Stats.1985, c. 1574, § 2, operative Jan. 1, 1987. Amended by Stats.1986, c. 460, § 5; Stats.1989, c. 171, § 1; Stats.1990, c. 1336 (A.B.3600), § 2, operative July 1, 1991; Stats.1994, c. 817 (S.B.1377), § 2; Stats.1996, c. 240 (A.B.2383), § 2; Stats.1996, c. 925 (A.B.3305), § 1; Stats.1996, c. 926 (A.B.3026), § 1.5, operative July 1, 1997; Stats.2001, c. 584 (S.B.732), § 1; Stats.2002, c. 664 (A.B.3034), § 35; Stats.2002, c. 496 (A.B.2776), § 3, operative Jan. 1, 2004; Stats.2003, c. 62 (S.B.600), § 13; Stats.2010, c. 19 (S.B.183), § 1; Stats.2011, c. 61 (S.B.837), § 1.)

§ 1102.6. Disclosure form

Section operative July 1, 2014. See, also, section operative until July 1, 2014.

(a) The disclosures required by this article pertaining to the property proposed to be transferred are set forth in, and shall be made on a copy of, the following disclosure form:

REAL ESTATE TRANSFER DISCLOSURE STATEMENT

THIS DISCLOSURE STATEMENT CONCERNS THE REAL PROPERTY SITUATED IN THE CITY
OF _____, COUNTY OF _____, STATE OF CALIFORNIA, DESCRIBED AS
_____. THIS STATEMENT IS A DIS-
CLOSURE OF THE CONDITION OF THE ABOVE DESCRIBED PROPERTY IN COMPLIANCE
WITH SECTION 1102 OF THE CIVIL CODE AS OF _____, 20 _____. IT IS NOT A
WARRANTY OF ANY KIND BY THE SELLER(S) OR ANY AGENT(S) REPRESENTING ANY
PRINCIPAL(S) IN THIS TRANSACTION, AND IS NOT A SUBSTITUTE FOR ANY INSPECTIONS
OR WARRANTIES THE PRINCIPAL(S) MAY WISH TO OBTAIN.

I

COORDINATION WITH OTHER DISCLOSURE FORMS

This Real Estate Transfer Disclosure Statement is made pursuant to Section 1102 of the Civil Code. Other statutes require disclosures, depending upon the details of the particular real estate transaction (for example: special study zone and purchase-money liens on residential property).
Substituted Disclosures: The following disclosures and other disclosures required by law, including the Natural Hazard Disclosure Report/Statement that may include airport annoyances, earthquake, fire, flood, or special assessment information, have or will be made in connection with this real estate transfer, and are intended to satisfy the disclosure obligations on this form, where the subject matter is the same:

☐ Inspection reports completed pursuant to the contract of sale or receipt for deposit.

☐ Additional inspection reports or disclosures:

_____

II

SELLER'S INFORMATION

The Seller discloses the following information with the knowledge that even though this is not a warranty, prospective Buyers may rely on this information in deciding whether and on what terms to purchase the subject property. Seller hereby authorizes any agent(s) representing any principal(s) in this transaction to provide a copy of this statement to any person or entity in connection with any actual or anticipated sale of the property.

THE FOLLOWING ARE REPRESENTATIONS MADE BY THE SELLER(S) AND ARE NOT THE REPRESENTATIONS OF THE AGENT(S), IF ANY. THIS INFORMATION IS A DISCLOSURE AND IS NOT INTENDED TO BE PART OF ANY CONTRACT BETWEEN THE BUYER AND SELLER:

Seller __is __is not occupying the property.

A. The subject property has the items checked below (read across):*

__ Range	__ Oven	__ Microwave
__ Dishwasher	__ Trash Compactor	__ Garbage Disposal
__ Washer/Dryer Hookups		__ Rain Gutters
__ Burglar Alarms	__ Carbon Monoxide	__ Fire Alarm
__ TV Antenna	Device(s)	__ Intercom
__ Central Heating	__ Satellite Dish	__ Evaporator Cooler(s)
__ Wall/Window Air Cndtng.	__ Central Air Cndtng.	__ Public Sewer System
__ Septic Tank	__ Sprinklers	__ Water Softener
__ Patio/Decking	__ Sump Pump	__ Gazebo
__ Sauna	__ Built-in Barbecue	

__ Hot Tub__Locking
   Safety Cover

__ Security Gate(s)

       __ Pool__Child
       Resistant Barrier
       __ Automatic Garage

                                    __ Spa__Locking
                                      Safety Cover

Garage:__Attached
Pool/Spa Heater:__Gas
Water Heater:__Gas

       Door Opener(s)
       __ Not Attached
       __ Solar

                                    __ Number Remote
                                    Controls
                                    __ Carport
                                    __ Electric
                                    __ Private Utility or
                                    Other_____

Water Supply: __City
Gas Supply: __Utility
__Window Screens

       __ Well
       __ Bottled
       __ Window Security
       Bars__Quick–Release Mech-
       anism on Bedroom Windows

                                    __ Water-conserving
                                    plumbing fixtures

Exhaust Fan(s) in _____ 220 Volt Wiring in _____ Fireplace(s) in _____
Gas Starter _____ Roof(s): Type: _____ Age: _____ (approx.)
Other: _____
Are there, to the best of your (Seller's) knowledge, any of the above that are not in operating condition?
__Yes __No. If yes, then describe.
(Attach additional sheets if necessary): _____
_____
_____

B. Are you (Seller) aware of any significant defects/malfunctions in any of the following?
__Yes __No. If yes, check appropriate space(s) below.
__Interior Walls __Ceilings __Floors __Exterior Walls __Insulation __Roof(s)
__Windows __Doors __Foundation __Slab(s) __Driveways __Sidewalks
__Walls/Fences __Electrical Systems __Plumbing/ Sewers/Septics __Other
Structural Components (Describe: _____
_____)

If any of the above is checked, explain. (Attach additional sheets if necessary): _____
_____
_____

---

* Installation of a listed appliance, device, or amenity is not a precondition of sale or transfer of the dwelling. The carbon monoxide device, garage door opener, or child-resistant pool barrier may not be in compliance with the safety standards relating to, respectively, carbon monoxide device standards of Chapter 8 (commencing with Section 13260) of Part 2 of Division 12 of, automatic reversing device standards of Chapter 12.5 (commencing with Section 19890) of Part 3 of Division 13 of, or the pool safety standards of Article 2.5 (commencing with Section 115920) of Chapter 5 of Part 10 of Division 104 of, the Health and Safety Code. Window security bars may not have quick-release mechanisms in compliance with the 1995 edition of the California Building Standards Code. Section 1101.4 of the Civil Code requires all single-family residences built on or before January 1, 1994, to be equipped with water-conserving plumbing fixtures after January 1, 2017. Additionally, on and after January 1, 2014, a single-family residence built on or before January 1, 1994, that is altered or improved is required to be equipped with water-conserving plumbing fixtures as a condition of final approval. Fixtures in this dwelling may not comply with Section 1101.4 of the Civil Code.

C.   Are you (Seller) aware of any of the following: ....
1. Substances, materials, or products which may be an environmental hazard such as, but not limited to, asbestos, formaldehyde, radon gas, lead-based paint, mold, fuel or chemical storage tanks, and contaminated soil or water on the subject property
.... ___Yes ___No
2. Features of the property shared in common with adjoining landowners, such as walls, fences, and driveways, whose use or responsibility for maintenance may have an effect on the subject property .... ___Yes ___No
3. Any encroachments, easements or similar matters that may affect your interest in the subject property .... ___Yes ___No
4. Room additions, structural modifications, or other alterations or repairs made without necessary permits .... ___Yes ___No
5. Room additions, structural modifications, or other alterations or repairs not in compliance with building codes .... ___Yes ___No
6. Fill (compacted or otherwise) on the property or any portion thereof ...... ___Yes ___No
7. Any settling from any cause, or slippage, sliding, or other soil problems ... ___Yes ___No
8. Flooding, drainage or grading problems .... ___Yes ___No
9. Major damage to the property or any of the structures from fire, earthquake, floods, or landslides .... ___Yes ___No
10. Any zoning violations, nonconforming uses, violations of "setback" requirements
.... ___Yes ___No
11. Neighborhood noise problems or other nuisances .... ___Yes ___No
12. CC&Rs or other deed restrictions or obligations .... ___Yes ___No
13. Homeowners' Association which has any authority over the subject property
.... ___Yes ___No
14. Any "common area" (facilities such as pools, tennis courts, walkways, or other areas co-owned in undivided interest with others) .... ___Yes ___No
15. Any notices of abatement or citations against the property .... ___Yes ___No
16. Any lawsuits by or against the Seller threatening to or affecting this real property, claims for damages by the seller pursuant to Section 910 or 914 threatening to or affecting this real property, claims for breach of warranty pursuant to Section 900 threatening to or affecting this real property, or claims for breach of an enhanced protection agreement pursuant to Section 903 threatening to or affecting this real property, including any lawsuits or claims for damages pursuant to Section 910 or 914 alleging a defect or deficiency in this real property or "common areas" (facilities such as pools, tennis courts, walkways, or other areas co-owned in undivided interest with others) .... ___Yes ___No

If the answer to any of these is yes, explain. (Attach additional sheets if necessary.): _____
_____

D. 1. The Seller certifies that the property, as of the close of escrow, will be in compliance with Section 13113.8 of the Health and Safety Code by having operable smoke detectors(s) which are approved, listed, and installed in accordance with the State Fire Marshal's regulations and applicable local standards.
    2. The Seller certifies that the property, as of the close of escrow, will be in compliance with Section 19211 of the Health and Safety Code by having the water heater tank(s) braced, anchored, or strapped in place in accordance with applicable law.

Seller certifies that the information herein is true and correct to the best of the Seller's knowledge as of the date signed by the Seller.

Seller _____ Date _____
Seller _____ Date _____

III

AGENT'S INSPECTION DISCLOSURE

(To be completed only if the Seller is represented by an agent in this transaction.)

THE UNDERSIGNED, BASED ON THE ABOVE INQUIRY OF THE SELLER(S) AS TO THE CONDITION OF THE PROPERTY AND BASED ON A REASONABLY COMPETENT AND DILIGENT VISUAL INSPECTION OF THE ACCESSIBLE AREAS OF THE PROPERTY IN CONJUNCTION WITH THAT INQUIRY, STATES THE FOLLOWING:

☐   Agent notes no items for disclosure.

☐   Agent notes the following items:

_____
_____
_____

Agent (Broker
Representing Seller) _____ By _____ Date _____
            (Please Print)   (Associate Licensee
                                          or Broker Signature)

IV

AGENT'S INSPECTION DISCLOSURE

(To be completed only if the agent who has obtained the offer is other than the agent above.)

THE UNDERSIGNED, BASED ON A REASONABLY COMPETENT AND DILIGENT VISUAL INSPECTION OF THE ACCESSIBLE AREAS OF THE PROPERTY, STATES THE FOLLOWING:

☐   Agent notes no items for disclosure.

☐   Agent notes the following items:

_____
_____
_____

Agent (Broker
Obtaining the Offer) _____ By _____ Date _____
            (Please Print)   (Associate Licensee
                                          or Broker Signature)

V

BUYER(S) AND SELLER(S) MAY WISH TO OBTAIN PROFESSIONAL ADVICE AND/ OR INSPECTIONS OF THE PROPERTY AND TO PROVIDE FOR APPROPRIATE PROVISIONS IN A CONTRACT BETWEEN BUYER(S) AND SELLER(S) WITH RESPECT TO ANY ADVICE/ INSPECTIONS/DEFECTS.

I/WE ACKNOWLEDGE RECEIPT OF A COPY OF THIS STATEMENT.

Seller _____ Date _____   Buyer _____ Date _____
Seller _____ Date _____   Buyer _____ Date _____

Agent (Broker
Representing Seller) _____ By _____ Date _____
            (Please Print)   (Associate Licensee
                                          or Broker Signature)

Agent (Broker
Obtaining the Offer) _____ By _____ Date _____
            (Please Print)   (Associate Licensee
                                          or Broker Signature)

SECTION 1102.3 OF THE CIVIL CODE PROVIDES A BUYER WITH THE RIGHT TO RESCIND A PURCHASE CONTRACT FOR AT LEAST THREE DAYS AFTER THE DELIVERY OF THIS DISCLOSURE IF DELIVERY OCCURS AFTER THE SIGNING OF AN OFFER TO PURCHASE. IF

YOU WISH TO RESCIND THE CONTRACT, YOU MUST ACT WITHIN THE PRESCRIBED PERIOD.

A REAL ESTATE BROKER IS QUALIFIED TO ADVISE ON REAL ESTATE. IF YOU DESIRE LEGAL ADVICE, CONSULT YOUR ATTORNEY.

(b) The amendments to this section by the act [1] adding this subdivision shall become operative on July 1, 2014. *(Added by Stats.1985, c. 1574, § 2, operative Jan. 1, 1987. Amended by Stats.1986, c. 460, § 5; Stats.1989, c. 171, § 1; Stats.1990, c. 1336 (A.B.3600), § 2, operative July 1, 1991; Stats.1994, c. 817 (S.B.1377), § 2; Stats.1996, c. 240 (A.B.2383), § 2; Stats.1996, c. 925 (A.B.3305), § 1; Stats.1996, c. 926 (A.B.3026), § 1.5, operative July 1, 1997; Stats.2001, c. 584 (S.B.732), § 1; Stats.2002, c. 664 (A.B.3034), § 35; Stats.2002, c. 496 (A.B.2776), § 3, operative Jan. 1, 2004; Stats.2003, c. 62 (S.B.600), § 13; Stats.2010, c. 19 (S.B.183), § 1; Stats.2011, c. 61 (S.B.837), § 1; Stats.2013, c. 431 (S.B.652), § 1, operative July 1, 2014.)*

[1] Stats.2013, c. 431 (S.B.652).

Research References

California Real Estate Forms (Miller & Starr) § 1:5, Non-Residential Statutory Disclosure Checklist.

California Real Estate Forms (Miller & Starr) § 1:94, California Residential Purchase Agreement and Joint Escrow Instructions.

Rutter, Cal. Practice Guide: Insurance Litigation Ch. 6H-B, B. Types of Policies and Services Provided by Title Insurers.

Rutter, Cal. Practice Guide: Real Prop. Transactions Ch. 2-C, C. Broker's Relationship and Obligations to Principal and Third Parties.

Rutter, Cal. Practice Guide: Real Prop. Transactions Ch. 3-C, C. Types of Title Insurance Policies.

Rutter, Cal. Practice Guide: Real Prop. Transactions Ch. 4-E, E. Drafting the Purchase and Sale Agreement-Terms and Conditions.

Rutter, Cal. Practice Guide: Real Prop. Transactions Ch. 11-E, E. Damages for Fraud.

Rutter, Cal. Practice Guide: Real Prop. Transactions Gen. Matls., Highlights.

Miller and Starr California Real Estate § 3:41, Agent's Duty to Disclose; in General--Disclosures by Transfer Disclosure Statement.

Miller and Starr California Real Estate § 3:42, Specific Disclosures Required by Statute.

Miller and Starr California Real Estate § 3:44, Negligence Liability--Duty to Inspect Property Being Sold.

Miller and Starr California Real Estate § 1:144, Duty of Seller of Real Property to Disclose--Statutory Duty of Disclosure.

Miller and Starr California Real Estate § 1:145, Duty of Seller of Real Property to Disclose--Transfer Disclosure Statement in Residential Sales.

Miller and Starr California Real Estate § 23:19, Duty of Owner to Disclose Presence of Hazardous Substances to Buyer, Tenant, or Employees.

Miller and Starr California Real Estate § 19:117, Landlord's Statutory Duty of Maintenance.

Miller and Starr California Real Estate § 25B:62, Duty to Disclose Defects to Unit Purchasers.

13 NO. 3 Miller & Starr, California Real Estate Newsalert 2, Update on the Toxic Mold Protection Act.

13 NO. 4 Miller & Starr, California Real Estate Newsalert 18, Subdivisions.

19 NO. 6 Miller & Starr, California Real Estate Newsalert 1, Enforceable Resale Restrictions: Keeping the Doors Open for Long-Term Affordable Housing.

19 NO. 5 Miller & Starr, California Real Estate Newsalert 9, Contracts.

21 NO. 4 Miller & Starr, California Real Estate Newsalert 8, Contracts.

22 NO. 4 Miller & Starr, California Real Estate Newsalert 9, Contracts.

12 Witkin, California Summary 10th Real Property § 482, (S 482) No Waiver of Disclosure Requirements.

12 Witkin, California Summary 10th Real Property § 483, (S 483) Content and Intended Use.

12 Witkin, California Summary 10th Real Property § 484, (S 484) Environmental Hazards.

12 Witkin, California Summary 10th Real Property § 489, (S 489) Local Option Statement.

12 Witkin, California Summary 10th Real Property § 490, (S 490) Manufactured Home Statement.

12 Witkin, California Summary 10th Real Property § 494, (S 494) in General.

12 Witkin, California Summary 10th Real Property § 491B, (S 491B) (New)-Notice of Transfer Fee.

3 Witkin, California Summary 10th Agency and Employment § 63, in General.

3 Witkin, California Summary 10th Agency and Employment § 66, (S 66) Legislative Response.

§ 1102.6a. Disclosure form

(a) On and after July 1, 1990, any city or county may elect to require disclosures on the form set forth in subdivision (b) in addition to those disclosures required by Section 1102.6. However, this section does not affect or limit the authority of a city or county to require disclosures on a different disclosure form in connection with transactions subject to this article pursuant to an ordinance adopted prior to July 1, 1990. An ordinance like this adopted prior to July 1, 1990, may be amended thereafter to revise the disclosure requirements of the ordinance, in the discretion of the city council or county board of supervisors.

(b) Disclosures required pursuant to this section pertaining to the property proposed to be transferred, shall be set forth in, and shall be made on a copy of, the following disclosure form:

LOCAL OPTION

REAL ESTATE TRANSFER DISCLOSURE STATEMENT

THIS DISCLOSURE STATEMENT CONCERNS THE REAL PROPERTY SITUATED IN THE CITY OF _____, COUNTY OF _____, STATE OF CALIFORNIA, DESCRIBED AS _____. THIS STATEMENT IS A DISCLOSURE OF THE CONDITION OF THE ABOVE–DESCRIBED PROPERTY IN COMPLIANCE WITH ORDINANCE NO. _____ OF THE _____ CITY OR COUNTY CODE AS OF _____, 20 ___. IT IS NOT A WARRANTY OF ANY KIND BY THE SELLER(S) OR ANY AGENT(S) REPRESENTING ANY PRINCIPAL(S) IN THIS TRANSACTION, AND IS NOT A SUBSTITUTE FOR ANY INSPECTIONS OR WARRANTIES THE PRINCIPAL(S) MAY WISH TO OBTAIN.

I

SELLER'S INFORMATION

The Seller discloses the following information with the knowledge that even though this is not a warranty, prospective Buyers may rely on this information in deciding whether and on what terms to purchase the subject property. Seller hereby authorizes any agent(s) representing any principal(s) in this transaction to provide a copy of this statement to any person or entity in connection with any actual or anticipated sale of the property.

THE FOLLOWING ARE REPRESENTATIONS MADE BY THE SELLER(S) AS REQUIRED BY THE CITY OR COUNTY OF _____, AND ARE NOT THE REPRESENTATIONS OF THE AGENT(S), IF ANY. THIS INFORMATION IS A DISCLOSURE AND IS NOT INTENDED TO BE PART OF ANY CONTRACT BETWEEN THE BUYER AND SELLER.

1. _____
   _____
   _____

2. _____
   _____
   _____

(Example: Adjacent land is zoned for timber production which may be subject to harvest.)

Seller certifies that the information herein is true and correct to the best of the Seller's knowledge as of the date signed by the Seller.

Seller _____   Date _____
Seller _____   Date _____

                                II

BUYER(S) AND SELLER(S) MAY WISH TO OBTAIN PROFESSIONAL ADVICE AND/ OR INSPECTIONS OF THE PROPERTY AND TO PROVIDE FOR APPROPRIATE PROVISIONS IN A CONTRACT BETWEEN BUYER AND SELLER(S) WITH RESPECT TO ANY ADVICE INSPECTIONS/DEFECTS.

I/WE ACKNOWLEDGE RECEIPT OF A COPY OF THIS STATEMENT.

Seller _____ Date _____   Buyer _____ Date _____
Seller _____ Date _____   Buyer _____ Date _____

Agent (Broker Representing Seller) _____   By _____ Date _____
                                                  (Associate Licensee or
                                                  Broker–Signature)

Agent (Broker Obtaining the Offer) _____   By _____ Date _____
                                                  (Associate Licensee or
                                                  Broker–Signature)

A REAL ESTATE BROKER IS QUALIFIED TO ADVISE ON REAL ESTATE. IF YOU DESIRE LEGAL ADVICE, CONSULT YOUR ATTORNEY.

(c) This section does not preclude the use of addenda to the form specified in subdivision (b) to facilitate the required disclosures. This section does not preclude a city or county from using the disclosure form specified in subdivision (b) for a purpose other than that specified in this section.

(d)(1) On and after January 1, 2005, if a city or county adopts a different or additional disclosure form pursuant to this section regarding the proximity or effects of an airport, the statement in that form shall contain, at a minimum, the information in the statement "Notice of Airport in Vicinity" found in Section 11010 of the Business and Professions Code, or Section 1103.4 or 4255.

(2) On and after January 1, 2006, if a city or county does not adopt a different or additional disclosure form pursuant to this section, then the provision of an "airport influence area" disclosure pursuant to Section 11010 of the Business and Professions Code, or Section 1103.4 or 4255, or if there is not a current airport influence map, a written disclosure of an airport

within two statute miles, shall be deemed to satisfy any city or county requirements for the disclosure of airports in connection with transfers of real property. (Added by Stats.1989, c. 171, § 2. Amended by Stats.2004, c. 66 (A.B.920), § 1; Stats.2012, c. 181 (A.B.806), § 33, operative Jan. 1, 2014.)

Law Revision Commission Comments

Subdivision (a) of Section 1102.6a is amended to make stylistic revisions.

Subdivision (d) is amended to correct cross-references to the airport disclosure provisions of former Section 1353. [40 Cal.L.Rev.Comm. Reports 235 (2010)].

§ 1102.6b. Disclosure to prospective purchaser of continuing lien securing special tax levy, fixed lien assessments, or contractual assessment program; satisfaction of disclosure notice requirements

(a) This section applies to all transfers of real property for which all of the following apply:

(1) The transfer is subject to this article.

(2) The property being transferred is subject to a continuing lien securing the levy of special taxes pursuant to the Mello–Roos Community Facilities Act (Chapter 2.5 (commencing with Section 53311) of Part 1 of Division 2 of Title 5 of the Government Code), to a fixed lien assessment collected in installments to secure bonds issued pursuant to the Improvement Bond Act of 1915 (Division 10 (commencing with Section 8500) of the Streets and Highways Code), or to a contractual assessment program authorized pursuant to Chapter 29 (commencing with Section 5898.10) of Part 3 of Division 7 of the Streets and Highway Code.

(3) A notice is not required pursuant to Section 53341.5 of the Government Code.

(b) In addition to any other disclosure required pursuant to this article, the seller of any real property subject to this section shall make a good faith effort to obtain a disclosure notice concerning the special tax as provided for in Section 53340.2 of the Government Code, or a disclosure notice concerning an assessment installment as provided in Section 53754 of the Government Code, from each local agency that levies a special tax pursuant to the Mello–Roos Community Facilities Act, or that collects assessment installments to secure bonds issued pursuant to the Improvement Bond Act of 1915 (Division 10 (commencing with Section 8500) of the Streets and Highways Code), or a disclosure notice concerning the contractual assessment as provided in Section 5898.24 of the Streets and Highways Code, on the property being transferred, and shall deliver that notice or those notices to the prospective purchaser, as long as the notices are made available by the local agency.

(c)(1) The seller of real property subject to this section may satisfy the disclosure notice requirements in regard to the bonds issued pursuant to the Improvement Bond Act of 1915 (Division 10 (commencing with Section 8500) of the Streets and Highways Code) by delivering a disclosure notice that is substantially equivalent and obtained from another source, until December 31, 2004.

(2) The seller of real property subject to this section may satisfy the disclosure notice requirements in regard to the assessments collected under the contractual assessment program authorized pursuant to Chapter 29 (commencing with Section 5898.10) of Part 3 of Division 7 of the Streets and Highway Code by delivering a disclosure notice that is substantially equivalent and obtained from another source.

(3) For the purposes of this section, a substantially equivalent disclosure notice includes, but is not limited to, a copy of the most recent year's property tax bill or an itemization of current assessment amounts applicable to the property.

(d)(1) Notwithstanding subdivision (c), at any time after the effective date of this section, the seller of real property subject to this section may satisfy the disclosure notice requirements of this section by delivering a disclosure notice obtained from a nongovernmental source that satisfies the requirements of paragraph (2).

(2) A notice provided by a private entity other than a designated office, department, or bureau of the levying entity may be modified as needed to clearly and accurately describe a special tax pursuant to the Mello–Roos Community Facilities Act levied against the property or to clearly and accurately consolidate information about two or more districts that levy or are authorized to levy a special tax pursuant to the Mello–Roos Community Facilities Act against the property, and shall include the name of the Mello–Roos entity levying taxes against the property, the annual tax due for the Mello–Roos entity for the current tax year, the maximum tax that may be levied against the property in any year, the percentage by which the maximum tax

for the Mello–Roos entity may increase per year, and the date until the tax may be levied against the property for the Mello–Roos entity and a contact telephone number, if available, for further information about the Mello–Roos entity. A notice provided by a private entity other than a designated office, department, or bureau of the levying entity may be modified as needed to clearly and accurately describe special assessments and bonds pursuant to the Improvement Bond Act of 1915 levied against the property, or to clearly and accurately consolidate information about two or more districts that levy or are authorized to levy special assessments and bonds pursuant to the Improvement Bond Act of 1915 against the property, and shall include the name of the special assessments and bonds issued pursuant to the Improvement Bond Act of 1915, the current annual tax on the property for the special assessments and bonds issued pursuant to the Improvement Bond Act of 1915 and a contact telephone number, if available, for further information about the special assessments and bonds issued pursuant to the Improvement Bond Act of 1915.

(3) This section does not change the ability to make disclosures pursuant to Section 1102.4 of the Civil Code.

(e) If a disclosure received pursuant to subdivision (b), (c), or (d) has been delivered to the transferee, a seller or his or her agent is not required to provide additional information concerning, and information in the disclosure shall be deemed to satisfy the responsibility of the seller or his or her agent to inform the transferee regarding the special tax or assessment installments and the district. Notwithstanding subdivision (b), (c), or (d), nothing in this section imposes a duty to discover a special tax or assessment installments or the existence of any levying district not actually known to the agents. *(Added by Stats.1992, c. 772 (S.B.1464), § 1.3, operative July 1, 1993. Amended by Stats.2001, c. 673 (S.B.1122), § 1; Stats.2002, c. 770 (S.B.1879), § 1, eff. Sept. 21, 2002; Stats.2002, c. 771 (A.B.337), § 1; Stats.2003, c. 62 (S.B.600), § 14; Stats.2009, c. 444 (A.B.474), § 1.)*

Research References

California Real Estate Forms (Miller & Starr) § 1:94, California Residential Purchase Agreement and Joint Escrow Instructions.

Rutter, Cal. Practice Guide: Real Prop. Transactions Ch. 2-C, C. Broker's Relationship and Obligations to Principal and Third Parties.

Miller and Starr California Real Estate § 3:42, Specific Disclosures Required by Statute.

Miller and Starr California Real Estate § 1:144, Duty of Seller of Real Property to Disclose--Statutory Duty of Disclosure.

13 NO. 4 Miller & Starr, California Real Estate Newsalert 6, Contracts/Agency.

20 NO. 4 Miller & Starr, California Real Estate Newsalert 5, Contracts.

12 Witkin, California Summary 10th Real Property § 491, (S 491) Continuing Lien Securing Facilities Tax or Bonds.

12 Witkin, California Summary 10th Real Property § 495, (S 495) Sanctions for Noncompliance.

12 Witkin, California Summary 10th Real Property § 491A, (S 491A) (New)-Notice of Supplemental Tax Bill.

§ 1102.6c. Seller's notice of supplemental property tax bill; requirements

(a) In addition to any other disclosure required pursuant to this article, it shall be the sole responsibility of the seller of any real property subject to this article, or his or her agent, to deliver to the prospective purchaser a disclosure notice that includes both of the following:

(1) A notice, in at least 12–point type or a contrasting color, as follows:

"California property tax law requires the Assessor to revalue real property at the time the ownership of the property changes. Because of this law, you may receive one or two supplemental tax bills, depending on when your loan closes.

The supplemental tax bills are not mailed to your lender. If you have arranged for your property tax payments to be paid through an impound account, the supplemental tax bills will not be paid by your lender. It is your responsibility to pay these supplemental bills directly to the Tax Collector.

If you have any question concerning this matter, please call your local Tax Collector's Office."

(2) A title, in at least 14–point type or a contrasting color, that reads as follows: "Notice of Your 'Supplemental' Property Tax Bill."

(b) The disclosure notice requirements of this section may be satisfied by delivering a disclosure notice pursuant to Section 1102.6b that satisfies the requirements of subdivision (a). *(Added by Stats.2005, c. 392 (A.B.459), § 2.)*

Research References

Rutter, Cal. Practice Guide: Real Prop. Transactions Ch. 2-C, C. Broker's Relationship and Obligations to Principal and Third Parties.
Miller and Starr California Real Estate § 3:44, Negligence Liability--Duty to Inspect Property Being Sold.
Miller and Starr California Real Estate § 1:144, Duty of Seller of Real Property to Disclose--Statutory Duty of Disclosure.
Miller and Starr California Real Estate § 25C:17, Notice of Intention; Requirements.
Miller and Starr California Real Estate § 25C:39, Duty to Disclose Material Facts to a Buyer.
16 NO. 4 Miller & Starr, California Real Estate Newsalert 5, Contracts.
16 NO. 5 Miller & Starr, California Real Estate Newsalert 26, State Board of Equalization Issues Comprehensive Summary and Qs and As for Transfers of Base Year Values of Principal Residences.
18 NO. 1 Miller & Starr, California Real Estate Newsalert 1, Disclosures in California Residential Real Property Sales.
12 Witkin, California Summary 10th Real Property § 491A, (S 491A) (New)-Notice of Supplemental Tax Bill.

§ 1102.6d. Manufactured home and mobilehome transfer disclosure statement

Except for manufactured homes and mobilehomes located in a common interest development governed by Part 5 (commencing with Section 4000) of Division 4, the disclosures applicable to the resale of a manufactured home or mobilehome pursuant to subdivision (b) of Section 1102 are set forth in, and shall be made on a copy of, the following disclosure form:

MANUFACTURED HOME AND MOBILEHOME: TRANSFER DISCLOSURE STATEMENT

THIS DISCLOSURE STATEMENT CONCERNS THE MANUFACTURED HOME OR MOBILEHOME (HEREAFTER REFERRED TO AS "HOME") LOCATED AT _____ IN THE CITY OF _____, COUNTY OF _____, STATE OF CALIFORNIA, DESCRIBED AS

YEAR MAKE   SERIAL #(s) HCD DECAL # or Equivalent
THIS STATEMENT IS A DISCLOSURE OF THE CONDITION OF THE ABOVE-DESCRIBED HOME IN COMPLIANCE WITH SUBDIVISION (b) OF SECTION 1102 OF THE CIVIL CODE AND SECTIONS 18025 AND 18046 OF THE HEALTH AND SAFETY CODE AS OF _____

DATE

IT IS NOT A WARRANTY OF ANY KIND BY THE LAWFUL OWNER OF THE MANUFACTURED HOME OR MOBILEHOME WHO OFFERS THE HOME FOR SALE (HEREAFTER THE SELLER), OR ANY AGENT(S) REPRESENTING ANY PRINCIPAL(S) IN THIS TRANS-

ACTION, AND IS NOT A SUBSTITUTE FOR ANY INSPECTIONS OR WARRANTIES THE PRINCIPAL(S) MAY WISH TO OBTAIN, AN "AGENT" MEANS ANY DEALER OR SALESPERSON LICENSED PURSUANT TO PART 2 (COMMENCING WITH SECTION 18000) OF THE HEALTH AND SAFETY CODE, OR A REAL ESTATE BROKER OR SALESPERSON LICENSED PURSUANT TO DIVISION 4 (COMMENCING WITH SECTION 10000) OF DIVISION 13 OF THE BUSINESS AND PROFESSIONS CODE.

I

COORDINATION WITH OTHER DISCLOSURE & INFORMATION

This Manufactured Home and Mobilehome Transfer Disclosure Statement is made pursuant to Article 1.5 (commencing with Section 1102) of Chapter 2 of Title 4 of Part 4 of Division 2 of the Civil Code. Other statutes require disclosures, or other information may be important to the prospective buyer, depending upon the details of the particular transaction (including, but not limited to, the condition of the park in which the manufactured home or mobilehome will be located; disclosures required or information provided by the Mobilehome Residency Law. Section 798 of the Civil Code et seq.; the mobilehome park rental agreement or lease: the mobilehome park rules and regulations; and park and lot inspection reports, if any, completed by the state or a local enforcement agency). Substituted Disclosures: The following disclosures have or will be made in connection with this transfer, and are intended to satisfy the disclosure obligations of this form, where the subject matter is the same:

☐ Home inspection reports completed pursuant to the contract of sale or receipt for deposit.

☐ Additional inspection reports or disclosures: _____

II

SELLER'S INFORMATION

The Seller discloses the following information with the knowledge that even though this is not a warranty, prospective buyers may rely on this information in deciding whether, and on what terms, to purchase the subject Home. Seller hereby authorizes any agent(s), as defined in Section 18046 of the Health and Safety Code, representing any principal(s) in this transaction to provide a copy of this statement to any person or entity in connection with any actual or anticipated sale of the Home.

THE FOLLOWING ARE REPRESENTATIONS MADE BY THE SELLER(S) AND ARE NOT THE REPRESENTATIONS OF THE AGENT(S), IF ANY, AS DEFINED IN SECTION 18046 OF THE HEALTH AND SAFETY CODE. THIS INFORMATION IS A DISCLOSURE AND IS NOT INTENDED TO BE PART OF ANY CONTRACT BETWEEN THE BUYER AND THE SELLER.

Seller __ is __ is not occupying the Home.

A. The subject Home includes the items checked below which are being sold with the Home (read across):*

___ Range   ___ Oven   ___ Microwave
___ Dishwasher   ___ Trash Compactor ___ Garbage Disposal
___ Burglar Alarm   ___ Fire Alarm

___ TV Antenna

___ Central Heating

___ Evaporative Cooler(s)

___ Porch Decking

___ Private Sauna

___ Private Hot Tub

___ Solar/Spa Heater

___ Electric Water Heater

___ Carport Awning

___ Automatic Garage Door Opener(s)

___ Window Secure Bars

___ Earthquake Resistant Bracing System

___ Carbon Monoxide Device(s)

___ Satellite Dish

___ Central Air Cndtng.

___ Sump Pump

___ Porch Awning

___ Private Spa

___ Hot Tub Locking Cvr

___ Gas Water Heater

___ Attached Garage

___ Remote Controls

___ Bedroom Window Quick Release Mechanism

___ Washer/Dryer Hookups

___ Intercom

___ Wall/Window Air Cndtng.

___ Water Softener

___ Gazebo

___ Spa Locking Safety Cvr

___ Gas/Spa Heater

___ Solar Water Heater

___ Bottled Propane

___ Detached Garage

___ Window Screens

___ Rain Gutters

Exhaust Fan(s) in _____

Fireplace(s) in _____

Roof(s) and type(s) _____
Other _____

___ Porch Awning, ___ Carport Awning, ___ Other Awnings, ___ Skirting,
___ Home Foundation or Support System,
___ Other Structural Components (Describe: _____)

220 Volt Wiring in _____

Gas Starter(s) _____

Roof age (Approximate) _____

If any of the above is checked, explain. (Attach additional sheets if necessary): _____
_____
_____

* Installation of a listed appliance, device, or amenity is not a precondition of sale or transfer of the home. The carbon monoxide device, garage door opener, or child-resistant pool barrier may not be in compliance with the safety standards relating to, respectively, carbon monoxide device standards of Chapter 8 (commencing with Section 13260) of Part 2 of Division 12 of, automatic reversing device standards of Chapter 12.5 (commencing with Section 19890) of Part 3 of Division 13 of, or the pool safety standards of Article 2.5 (commencing with Section 115920) of Chapter 5 of Part 10 of Division 104 of the Health and Safety Code. Window security bars may not have quick-release mechanisms in compliance with the 1995 edition of the California Building Standards Code.

Are there, to the best of your (Seller's) knowledge, any of the above that are not in operating condition? ___ Yes ___ No. If yes, then describe. (Attach additional sheets if necessary):
_____
_____

B. Are you (the Seller) aware of any significant defects/malfunctions in any of the following in connection with the Home?

___ Yes ___ No If yes, check appropriate space(s) below:

___ Interior Walls, ___ Ceilings, ___ Floors, ___ Exterior Walls, ___ Insulation,
___ Roof(s), ___ Windows, ___ Doors, ___ Home Electrical Systems, ___ Plumbing,
___ Porch or Deck, ___ Porch Steps & Railings, ___ Other Steps & Railings,

C. Are you (the Seller) aware of any of the following:

1. Substances, materials, or products which may be an environmental hazard, such as, but not limited to, asbestos, formaldehyde, radon gas, lead-based paint, or chemical storage tanks on the subject home interior or exterior ....   ___ Yes   ___ No

2. Room additions, structural modifications, or other alterations or repairs made without necessary permits .....   ___ Yes   ___ No

3. Room additions, structural modifications, or other alterations or repairs not in compliance with applicable codes .   ___ Yes   ___ No

4. Any settling from slippage, sliding or problems with leveling of the home or the foundation or support system ...   ___ Yes   ___ No

5. Drainage or grading problems with the home, space or lot ....   ___ Yes   ___ No

6. Damage to the home or accessory structures being sold with the home from fire, flood, earthquake, or landslides .   ___ Yes   ___ No

7. Any notices of abatement or citations against the home or accessory structures being sold with the home ....   ___ Yes   ___ No

8. Any lawsuits by or against the seller threatening to or affecting the home or the accessory structures being sold with the home, including any lawsuits alleging any defect or deficiency in the home or accessories sold with the home .....   ___ Yes   ___ No

9. Neighborhood noise problems or other nuisances ....   ___ Yes   ___ No

10. Any encroachment, easement, nonconforming use or violation of setback requirements with the home, accessory structures being sold with the home, or space ....   ___ Yes   ___ No

If the answer to any of these is yes, explain. (Attach additional sheets if necessary.): _____
_____
_____

D. 1. The Seller certifies that the home, as of the close of escrow, will be in compliance with Section 13113.8 of the Health and Safety Code by having operable smoke detectors(s) which are approved, listed, and installed in accordance with the State Fire Marshal's regulations and applicable local standards.

2. The Seller certifies that the home, as of the close of escrow, will be in compliance Section 19211 of the Health and Safety Code by having the water heater tank(s) braced, anchored, or strapped in place in accordance with applicable law.

Seller certifies that the information herein is true and correct to the best of the Seller's knowledge as of the date signed by the Seller.

Seller _____ Date _____
Seller _____ Date _____

III

AGENT'S INSPECTION DISCLOSURE

(To be completed only if the Seller is represented by an Agent in this transaction)

THE UNDERSIGNED, BASED ON THE ABOVE INQUIRY OF THE SELLER(S) AS TO THE CONDITION OF THE HOME AND BASED ON A REASONABLY COMPETENT AND DILIGENT VISUAL INSPECTION OF THE ACCESSIBLE AREAS OF THE HOME IN CONJUNCTION WITH THAT INQUIRY, STATES THE FOLLOWING:

☐ Agent notes no items for disclosure.
☐ Agent notes the following items:

_____
_____
_____

Agent
Representing Seller _____ By _____ Date _____
                          (Please Print)   (Signature)

IV

AGENT'S INSPECTION DISCLOSURE

(To be completed only if the Agent who has obtained the offer is other than the Agent above.)

THE UNDERSIGNED, BASED ON A REASONABLY COMPETENT AND DILIGENT VISUAL INSPECTION OF THE ACCESSIBLE AREAS OF THE HOME, STATES THE FOLLOWING:

☐ Agent notes no items for disclosure.
☐ Agent notes the following items:

_____
_____
_____

Agent
Representing Buyer _____ By _____ Date _____
                          (Please Print)   (Signature)

V

BUYER(S) AND SELLER(S) MAY WISH TO OBTAIN PROFESSIONAL ADVICE AND/ OR INSPECTIONS OF THE HOME AND TO PROVIDE FOR APPROPRIATE PROVISIONS IN A CONTRACT BETWEEN THE BUYER(S) AND SELLER(S) WITH RESPECT TO ANY ADVICE/ INSPECTIONS/DEFECTS.

I/WE ACKNOWLEDGE RECEIPT OF A COPY OF THIS STATEMENT.

Seller _____ Date _____ Buyer _____ Date _____
Seller _____ Date _____ Buyer _____ Date _____

Agent
Representing Seller _____ By _____ Date _____
                          (Please Print)   (Signature)

Agent
Representing Buyer _____ By _____ Date _____
                          (Please Print)   (Signature)

VI

SECTION 1102.3a OF THE CIVIL CODE PROVIDES A PROSPECTIVE BUYER WITH THE RIGHT TO RESCIND THE PURCHASE OF THE MANUFACTURED HOME OR MOBILEHOME FOR AT LEAST THREE DAYS AFTER DELIVERY OF THIS DISCLOSURE. IF DELIVERY OCCURS

AFTER THE SIGNING OF AN OFFER TO PURCHASE. IF YOU WISH TO RESCIND THE CONTRACT, YOU MUST ACT WITHIN THE PRESCRIBED PERIOD.

A MANUFACTURED HOME OR MOBILEHOME DEALER OR A REAL ESTATE BROKER IS QUALIFIED TO PROVIDE ADVICE ON THE SALE OF A MANUFACTURED HOME OR MOBILEHOME. IF YOU DESIRE LEGAL ADVICE, CONSULT YOUR ATTORNEY.

(Added by Stats.1999, c. 517 (S.B.534), § 6. Amended by Stats.2010, c. 19 (S.B.183), § 2; Stats.2012, c. 181 (A.B.806), § 34, operative Jan. 1, 2014.)

Law Revision Commission Comments

Section 1102.6d is amended to correct a cross-reference to former Sections 1350–1378. [40 Cal.L.Rev.Comm. Reports 235 (2010)].

§ 1102.6e. Transfer fee disclosure statement; requirements

If a property being transferred on or after January 1, 2008, is subject to a transfer fee, as defined in Section 1098, the transferor shall provide, at the same time as the transfer disclosure statement required pursuant to Section 1102.6 is provided, an additional disclosure statement containing all of the following:

(a) Notice that payment of a transfer fee is required upon transfer of the property.

(b) The amount of the fee required for the asking price of the real property and a description of how the fee is calculated.

(c) Notice that the final amount of the fee may be different if the fee is based upon a percentage of the final sale price.

(d) The entity to which funds from the fee will be paid.

(e) The purposes for which funds from the fee will be used.

(f) The date or circumstances under which the obligation to pay the transfer fee expires, if any. *(Added by Stats.2007, c. 689 (A.B.980), § 3.)*

Research References

Rutter, Cal. Practice Guide: Real Prop. Transactions Ch. 4-E, E. Drafting the Purchase and Sale Agreement-Terms and Conditions.
Miller and Starr California Real Estate § 24:25, Rights of Enforcement-- Generally.
Miller and Starr California Real Estate § 24:32, Defenses to Enforce-ment--Public Policy or Discrimination.
18 NO. 4 Miller & Starr, California Real Estate Newsalert 21, Recording and Priorities.
18 NO. 4 Miller & Starr, California Real Estate Newsalert 45, Table of Statutes (Newsalert Vol 18).
12 Witkin, California Summary 10th Real Property § 491B, (S 491B) (New)-Notice of Transfer Fee.

§ 1102.7. Good faith required

Each disclosure required by this article and each act which may be performed in making the disclosure, shall be made in good faith. For purposes of this article, "good faith" means honesty in fact in the conduct of the transaction. *(Added by Stats.1985, c. 1574, § 2, operative Jan. 1, 1987.)*

Research References

Rutter, Cal. Practice Guide: Real Prop. Transactions Ch. 4-E, E. Drafting the Purchase and Sale Agreement-Terms and Conditions.
Miller and Starr California Real Estate § 3:41, Agent's Duty to Disclose; in General--Disclosures by Transfer Disclosure Statement.
Miller and Starr California Real Estate § 3:44, Negligence Liability--Duty to Inspect Property Being Sold.
Miller and Starr California Real Estate § 1:145, Duty of Seller of Real Property to Disclose--Transfer Disclosure Statement in Residential Sales.
18 NO. 1 Miller & Starr, California Real Estate Newsalert 1, Disclosures in California Residential Real Property Sales.

12 Witkin, California Summary 10th Real Property § 494, (S 494) in General.

§ 1102.8. Specification of items for disclosure not limitation on other disclosure obligations

The specification of items for disclosure in this article does not limit or abridge any obligation for disclosure created by any other provision of law or which may exist in order to avoid fraud, misrepresentation, or deceit in the transfer transaction. *(Added by Stats.1985, c. 1574, § 2, operative Jan. 1, 1987.)*

Research References

Rutter, Cal. Practice Guide: Real Prop. Transactions Ch. 2-C, C. Broker's Relationship and Obligations to Principal and Third Parties.
Rutter, Cal. Practice Guide: Real Prop. Transactions Ch. 4-E, E. Drafting the Purchase and Sale Agreement-Terms and Conditions.
Miller and Starr California Real Estate § 3:26, Duty to Exercise Skill, Care, and Diligence; Negligence Liability.
Miller and Starr California Real Estate § 3:27, Duty to Disclose-- Generally.
Miller and Starr California Real Estate § 3:41, Agent's Duty to Disclose; in General--Disclosures by Transfer Disclosure Statement.
Miller and Starr California Real Estate § 3:44, Negligence Liability--Duty to Inspect Property Being Sold.
Miller and Starr California Real Estate § 1:140, Duty of Seller of Real Property to Disclose.
Miller and Starr California Real Estate § 1:144, Duty of Seller of Real Property to Disclose--Statutory Duty of Disclosure.
Miller and Starr California Real Estate § 1:145, Duty of Seller of Real Property to Disclose--Transfer Disclosure Statement in Residential Sales.
Miller and Starr California Real Estate § 10:209, Liability for the Defective Condition of the Property.
18 NO. 1 Miller & Starr, California Real Estate Newsalert 1, Disclosures in California Residential Real Property Sales.
12 Witkin, California Summary 10th Real Property § 494, (S 494) in General.

§ 1102.9. Amendment of disclosures

Any disclosure made pursuant to this article may be amended in writing by the transferor or his or her agent, but the amendment shall be subject to Section 1102.3 or 1102.3a. *(Added by Stats.1985, c. 1574, § 2, operative Jan. 1, 1987. Amended by Stats.1996, c. 240 (A.B.2383), § 3; Stats.1999, c. 517 (S.B.534), § 7.)*

Research References

Rutter, Cal. Practice Guide: Real Prop. Transactions Ch. 4-E, E. Drafting the Purchase and Sale Agreement-Terms and Conditions.
Miller and Starr California Real Estate § 3:41, Agent's Duty to Disclose; in General--Disclosures by Transfer Disclosure Statement.
Miller and Starr California Real Estate § 1:145, Duty of Seller of Real Property to Disclose--Transfer Disclosure Statement in Residential Sales.
12 Witkin, California Summary 10th Real Property § 485, (S 485) Delivery of Statement.
12 Witkin, California Summary 10th Real Property § 490, (S 490) Manufactured Home Statement.

§ 1102.10. Delivery of disclosures; personal delivery or mail

Delivery of disclosures required by this article shall be by personal delivery to the tranferee [1] or by mail to the prospective transferee. For the purposes of this article, delivery to the spouse of a transferee shall be deemed delivery to the transferee, unless provided otherwise by contract. *(Added by Stats.1985, c. 1574, § 2, operative Jan. 1, 1987.)*

¹ So in chaptered copy.

Research References

Rutter, Cal. Practice Guide: Real Prop. Transactions Ch. 4-E, E. Drafting the Purchase and Sale Agreement-Terms and Conditions.
Miller and Starr California Real Estate § 3:41, Agent's Duty to Disclose; in General--Disclosures by Transfer Disclosure Statement.
Miller and Starr California Real Estate § 1:145, Duty of Seller of Real Property to Disclose--Transfer Disclosure Statement in Residential Sales.
12 Witkin, California Summary 10th Real Property § 485, (S 485) Delivery of Statement.

§ 1102.11. Escrow agent not deemed agent for purposes of disclosure; exception

Any person or entity, other than a real estate licensee licensed pursuant to Part 1 (commencing with Section 10000) of Division 4 of the Business and Professions Code, acting in the capacity of an escrow agent for the transfer of real property subject to this article shall not be deemed the agent of the transferor or transferee for purposes of the disclosure requirements of this article, unless the person or entity is empowered to so act by an express written agreement to that effect. The extent of such an agency shall be governed by the written agreement. *(Added by Stats.1985, c. 1574, § 2, operative Jan. 1, 1987.)*

Research References

Miller and Starr California Real Estate § 3:41, Agent's Duty to Disclose; in General--Disclosures by Transfer Disclosure Statement.
Miller and Starr California Real Estate § 1:145, Duty of Seller of Real Property to Disclose--Transfer Disclosure Statement in Residential Sales.
12 Witkin, California Summary 10th Real Property § 485, (S 485) Delivery of Statement.

§ 1102.12. Licensed real estate brokers as agents in transaction; delivery of disclosure; advising transferee of rights to disclosure; record

(a) If more than one licensed real estate broker is acting as an agent in a transaction subject to this article, the broker who has obtained the offer made by the transferee shall, except as otherwise provided in this article, deliver the disclosure required by this article to the transferee, unless the transferor has given other written instructions for delivery.

(b) If a licensed real estate broker responsible for delivering the disclosures under this section cannot obtain the disclosure document required and does not have written assurance from the transferee that the disclosure has been received, the broker shall advise the transferee in writing of his or her rights to the disclosure. A licensed real estate broker responsible for delivering disclosures under this section shall maintain a record of the action taken to effect compliance in accordance with Section 10148 of the Business and Professions Code. *(Added by Stats.1985, c. 1574, § 2, operative Jan. 1, 1987. Amended by Stats.1986, c. 460, § 6.)*

Research References

Rutter, Cal. Practice Guide: Real Prop. Transactions Ch. 2-C, C. Broker's Relationship and Obligations to Principal and Third Parties.
Miller and Starr California Real Estate § 3:41, Agent's Duty to Disclose; in General--Disclosures by Transfer Disclosure Statement.
Miller and Starr California Real Estate § 4:27, Duty to Disclose--Inspection and Disclosure for Residential Transactions.
Miller and Starr California Real Estate § 1:145, Duty of Seller of Real Property to Disclose--Transfer Disclosure Statement in Residential Sales.

12 Witkin, California Summary 10th Real Property § 485, (S 485) Delivery of Statement.

§ 1102.13. Failure to comply with article; transfer not invalidated; damages

No transfer subject to this article shall be invalidated solely because of the failure of any person to comply with any provision of this article. However, any person who willfully or negligently violates or fails to perform any duty prescribed by any provision of this article shall be liable in the amount of actual damages suffered by a transferee. *(Added by Stats.1985, c. 1574, § 2, operative Jan. 1, 1987.)*

Research References

Rutter, Cal. Practice Guide: Real Prop. Transactions Ch. 2-C, C. Broker's Relationship and Obligations to Principal and Third Parties.
Rutter, Cal. Practice Guide: Real Prop. Transactions Ch. 4-E, E. Drafting the Purchase and Sale Agreement-Terms and Conditions.
Rutter, Cal. Practice Guide: Real Prop. Transactions Ch. 11-E, E. Damages for Fraud.
Rutter, Cal. Practice Guide: Real Prop. Transactions Ch. 11-E Outline, Outline E.
Miller and Starr California Real Estate § 3:26, Duty to Exercise Skill, Care, and Diligence; Negligence Liability.
Miller and Starr California Real Estate § 3:41, Agent's Duty to Disclose; in General--Disclosures by Transfer Disclosure Statement.
Miller and Starr California Real Estate § 3:42, Specific Disclosures Required by Statute.
Miller and Starr California Real Estate § 1:144, Duty of Seller of Real Property to Disclose--Statutory Duty of Disclosure.
Miller and Starr California Real Estate § 1:145, Duty of Seller of Real Property to Disclose--Transfer Disclosure Statement in Residential Sales.
14 NO. 1 Miller & Starr, California Real Estate Newsalert 3, Contracts.
12 Witkin, California Summary 10th Real Property § 495, (S 495) Sanctions for Noncompliance.
6 Witkin, California Summary 10th Torts § 1714, Elements of Damage.

§ 1102.14. Definitions

(a) As used in this article, "listing agent" means listing agent as defined in subdivision (f) of Section 1086.

(b) As used in this article, "selling agent" means selling agent as defined in subdivision (g) of Section 1086, exclusive of the requirement that the agent be a participant in a multiple listing service as defined in Section 1087. *(Added by Stats.1986, c. 460, § 7.)*

Research References

California Real Estate Forms (Miller & Starr) § 1:88, Buyer Nonagency Agreement.
Miller and Starr California Real Estate § 3:41, Agent's Duty to Disclose; in General--Disclosures by Transfer Disclosure Statement.
Miller and Starr California Real Estate § 3:44, Negligence Liability--Duty to Inspect Property Being Sold.
12 Witkin, California Summary 10th Real Property § 494, (S 494) in General.

§ 1102.15. Former federal or state ordnance locations; definition

The seller of residential real property subject to this article who has actual knowledge of any former federal or state ordnance locations within the neighborhood area shall give written notice of that knowledge as soon as practicable before transfer of title.

For purposes of this section, "former federal or state ordnance locations" means an area identified by an agency or instrumentality of the federal or state government as an area once used for military training purposes which may contain potentially explosive munitions. "Neighborhood area" means within one mile of the residential real property.

The disclosure required by this section does not limit or abridge any obligation for disclosure created by any other law or that may exist in order to avoid fraud, misrepresentation, or deceit in the transfer transaction. *(Added by Stats.1989, c. 294, § 1.)*

Research References

California Real Estate Forms (Miller & Starr) § 1:94, California Residential Purchase Agreement and Joint Escrow Instructions.
California Real Estate Forms (Miller & Starr) § 1:118, Supplemental Statutory and Contractual Disclosures.
Rutter, Cal. Practice Guide: Real Prop. Transactions Ch. 2-C, C. Broker's Relationship and Obligations to Principal and Third Parties.
Miller and Starr California Real Estate § 3:44, Negligence Liability--Duty to Inspect Property Being Sold.
Miller and Starr California Real Estate § 1:144, Duty of Seller of Real Property to Disclose--Statutory Duty of Disclosure.
12 Witkin, California Summary 10th Real Property § 493, (S 493) Military, Industrial, and Airport Influences.

§ 1102.155. Water-conserving plumbing fixture requirement; noncompliant plumbing fixtures

Section operative Jan. 1, 2017.

(a)(1) The seller of residential real property subject to this article shall disclose, in writing, that Section 1101.4 of the Civil Code requires that California single-family residences be equipped with water-conserving plumbing fixtures on or before January 1, 2017, and shall disclose whether the property includes any noncompliant plumbing fixtures.

(2) The seller shall affirm that this representation is that of the seller and not a representation of any agent, and that this disclosure is not intended to be part of any contract between the buyer and the seller. The seller shall further affirm that this disclosure is not a warranty of any kind by the seller or any agent representing any principal in the transaction and is not a substitute for any inspections that or warranties any principal may wish to obtain.

(b) This section shall become operative on January 1, 2017. *(Added by Stats.2009, c. 587 (S.B.407), § 2, operative Jan. 1, 2017.)*

Research References

Miller and Starr California Real Estate § 1:144, Duty of Seller of Real Property to Disclose--Statutory Duty of Disclosure.
20 NO. 4 Miller & Starr, California Real Estate Newsalert 5, Contracts.
22 NO. 4 Miller & Starr, California Real Estate Newsalert 9, Contracts.

§ 1102.16. Window security bars and safety release mechanism; disclosure

The disclosure of the existence of any window security bars and any safety release mechanism on those window security bars shall be made pursuant to Section 1102.6 or 1102.6a of the Civil Code. *(Added by Stats.1996, c. 926 (A.B.3026), § 2, operative July 1, 1997. Amended by Stats.2004, c. 183 (A.B.3082), § 26.)*

Research References

Rutter, Cal. Practice Guide: Real Prop. Transactions Ch. 2-C, C. Broker's Relationship and Obligations to Principal and Third Parties.
Miller and Starr California Real Estate § 1:145, Duty of Seller of Real Property to Disclose--Transfer Disclosure Statement in Residential Sales.

§ 1102.17. Sellers of residential real property; written notice of knowledge of property with respect to industrial use

The seller of residential real property subject to this article who has actual knowledge that the property is adjacent to, or zoned to allow, an industrial use described in Section 731a of the Code of Civil Procedure, or affected by a nuisance created by such a use, shall give written notice of that knowledge as soon as practicable before transfer of title. *(Added by Stats.1999, c. 876 (A.B.248), § 2. Amended by Stats.2004, c. 66 (A.B.920), § 2.)*

Research References

California Real Estate Forms (Miller & Starr) § 1:5, Non-Residential Statutory Disclosure Checklist.
California Real Estate Forms (Miller & Starr) § 1:94, California Residential Purchase Agreement and Joint Escrow Instructions.
California Real Estate Forms (Miller & Starr) § 1:118, Supplemental Statutory and Contractual Disclosures.
Rutter, Cal. Practice Guide: Real Prop. Transactions Ch. 2-C, C. Broker's Relationship and Obligations to Principal and Third Parties.
Miller and Starr California Real Estate § 3:41, Agent's Duty to Disclose; in General--Disclosures by Transfer Disclosure Statement.
Miller and Starr California Real Estate § 3:44, Negligence Liability--Duty to Inspect Property Being Sold.
Miller and Starr California Real Estate § 1:144, Duty of Seller of Real Property to Disclose--Statutory Duty of Disclosure.
Miller and Starr California Real Estate § 1:145, Duty of Seller of Real Property to Disclose--Transfer Disclosure Statement in Residential Sales.
15 NO. 4 Miller & Starr, California Real Estate Newsalert 5, Contracts.
18 NO. 1 Miller & Starr, California Real Estate Newsalert 1, Disclosures in California Residential Real Property Sales.
12 Witkin, California Summary 10th Real Property § 493, (S 493) Military, Industrial, and Airport Influences.

ARTICLE 1.7. DISCLOSURE OF NATURAL AND ENVIRONMENTAL HAZARDS, RIGHT-TO-FARM, AND OTHER DISCLOSURES UPON TRANSFER OF RESIDENTIAL PROPERTY

§ 1103. Application of article; transfer by sale, exchange, installment land sale contract, lease with option to purchase of real property

(a) Except as provided in Section 1103.1, this article applies to the transfer by sale, exchange, installment land sale contract, as defined in Section 2985, lease with an option to purchase, any other option to purchase, or ground lease coupled with improvements, of any real property described in subdivision (c), or residential stock cooperative, improved with or consisting of not less than one nor more than four dwelling units.

(b) Except as provided in Section 1103.1, this article shall apply to a resale transaction entered into on or after January 1, 2000, for a manufactured home, as defined in Section 18007 of the Health and Safety Code, that is classified as personal property intended for use as a residence, or a mobilehome, as defined in Section 18008 of the Health and Safety Code, that is classified as personal property intended for use as a residence, if the real property on which the manufactured home or mobilehome is located is real property described in subdivision (c).

(c) This article shall apply to the transactions described in subdivisions (a) and (b) only if the transferor or his or her agent is required by one or more of the following to disclose the property's location within a hazard zone:

(1) A person who is acting as an agent for a transferor of real property that is located within a special flood hazard area (any type Zone "A" or "V") designated by the Federal Emergency Management Agency, or the transferor if he or she is acting without an agent, shall disclose to any prospective transferee the fact that the property is located within a special flood hazard area if either:

(A) The transferor, or the transferor's agent, has actual knowledge that the property is within a special flood hazard area.

(B) The local jurisdiction has compiled a list, by parcel, of properties that are within the special flood hazard area and a notice has been posted at the offices of the county recorder, county assessor, and county planning agency that identifies the location of the parcel list.

(2) A person who is acting as an agent for a transferor of real property that is located within an area of potential flooding designated pursuant to Section 8589.5 of the Government Code, or the transferor if he or she is acting without an agent, shall disclose to any prospective transferee the fact that the property is located within an area of potential flooding if either:

(A) The transferor, or the transferor's agent, has actual knowledge that the property is within an inundation area.

(B) The local jurisdiction has compiled a list, by parcel, of properties that are within the inundation area and a notice has been posted at the offices of the county recorder, county assessor, and county planning agency that identifies the location of the parcel list.

(3) A transferor of real property that is located within a very high fire hazard severity zone, designated pursuant to Section 51178 of the Government Code, shall disclose to any prospective transferee the fact that the property is located within a very high fire hazard severity zone and is subject to the requirements of Section 51182 of the Government Code if either:

(A) The transferor, or the transferor's agent, has actual knowledge that the property is within a very high fire hazard severity zone.

(B) A map that includes the property has been provided to the local agency pursuant to Section 51178 of the Government Code and a notice has been posted at the offices of the county recorder, county assessor, and county planning agency that identifies the location of the map and any information regarding changes to the map received by the local agency.

(4) A person who is acting as an agent for a transferor of real property that is located within an earthquake fault zone, designated pursuant to Section 2622 of the Public Resources Code, or the transferor if he or she is acting without an agent, shall disclose to any prospective transferee the fact that the property is located within a delineated earthquake fault zone if either:

(A) The transferor, or the transferor's agent, has actual knowledge that the property is within a delineated earthquake fault zone.

(B) A map that includes the property has been provided to the city or county pursuant to Section 2622 of the Public Resources Code and a notice has been posted at the offices of the county recorder, county assessor, and county planning agency that identifies the location of the map and any information regarding changes to the map received by the county.

(5) A person who is acting as an agent for a transferor of real property that is located within a seismic hazard zone, designated pursuant to Section 2696 of the Public Resources Code, or the transferor if he or she is acting without an agent, shall disclose to any prospective transferee the fact that the property is located within a seismic hazard zone if either:

(A) The transferor, or the transferor's agent, has actual knowledge that the property is within a seismic hazard zone.

(B) A map that includes the property has been provided to the city or county pursuant to Section 2696 of the Public Resources Code and a notice has been posted at the offices of the county recorder, county assessor, and county planning agency that identifies the location of the map and any information regarding changes to the map received by the county.

(6) A transferor of real property that is located within a state responsibility area determined by the board, pursuant to Section 4125 of the Public Resources Code, shall disclose to any prospective transferee the fact that the property is located within a wildland area that may contain substantial forest fire risks and hazards and is subject to the requirements of Section 4291 if either:

(A) The transferor, or the transferor's agent, has actual knowledge that the property is within a wildland fire zone.

(B) A map that includes the property has been provided to the city or county pursuant to Section 4125 of the Public Resources Code and a notice has been posted at the offices of the county recorder, county assessor, and county planning agency that identifies the location of the map and any information regarding changes to the map received by the county.

(d) Any waiver of the requirements of this article is void as against public policy. *(Added by Stats.1999, c. 876 (A.B.248), § 3. Amended by Stats.2000, c. 135 (A.B.2539), § 12; Stats. 2003–2004, 1st Ex.Sess., c. 8 (S.B.25), § 1, eff. May 5, 2003; Stats.2003, c. 741 (S.B.1049), § 2; Stats.2004, c. 183 (A.B.3082), § 27.)*

Research References

California Real Estate Forms (Miller & Starr) § 1:94, California Residential Purchase Agreement and Joint Escrow Instructions.

California Real Estate Forms (Miller & Starr) § 1:116, Natural Hazard Disclosure Statement.

Rutter, Cal. Practice Guide: Real Prop. Transactions Ch. 2-C, C. Broker's Relationship and Obligations to Principal and Third Parties.

Rutter, Cal. Practice Guide: Real Prop. Transactions Ch. 4-E, E. Drafting the Purchase and Sale Agreement-Terms and Conditions.

Miller and Starr California Real Estate § 1:144, Duty of Seller of Real Property to Disclose--Statutory Duty of Disclosure.

Miller and Starr California Real Estate § 25C:18, Information Required for a Standard Subdivision.

Miller and Starr California Real Estate § 25C:39, Duty to Disclose Material Facts to a Buyer.

Miller and Starr California Real Estate § 3:44.10, Disclosures for Properties Located in Natural Hazards Areas.

19 NO. 4 Miller & Starr, California Real Estate Newsalert 27, Subdivision Offerings, Sales, and Leasing.

12 Witkin, California Summary 10th Real Property § 486, (S 486) Types of Hazards.

12 Witkin, California Summary 10th Real Property § 487, (S 487) Natural Hazard Disclosure Statement.

3 Witkin, California Summary 10th Agency and Employment § 63, in General.

3 Witkin, California Summary 10th Agency and Employment § 66, (S 66) Legislative Response.

§ 1103.1. Application of article; exclusions

(a) This article does not apply to the following transfers:

(1) Transfers pursuant to court order, including, but not limited to, transfers ordered by a probate court in administration of an estate, transfers pursuant to a writ of execution, transfers by any foreclosure sale, transfers by a trustee in bankruptcy, transfers by eminent domain, and transfers resulting from a decree for specific performance.

(2) Transfers to a mortgagee by a mortgagor or successor in interest who is in default, transfers to a beneficiary of a deed of trust by a trustor or successor in interest who is in default, transfers by any foreclosure sale after default, transfers by any foreclosure sale after default in an obligation secured by a mortgage, transfers by a sale under a power of sale or any foreclosure sale under a decree of foreclosure after default in an obligation secured by a deed of trust or secured by any other instrument containing a power of sale, or transfers by a mortgagee or a beneficiary under a deed of trust who has acquired the real property at a sale conducted pursuant to a power of sale under a mortgage or deed of trust or a sale pursuant to a decree of foreclosure or has acquired the real property by a deed in lieu of foreclosure.

(3) Transfers by a fiduciary in the course of the administration of a decedent's estate, guardianship, conservatorship, or trust.

(4) Transfers from one coowner to one or more other coowners.

(5) Transfers made to a spouse, or to a person or persons in the lineal line of consanguinity of one or more of the transferors.

(6) Transfers between spouses resulting from a judgment of dissolution of marriage or of legal separation of the parties or from a property settlement agreement incidental to that judgment.

(7) Transfers by the Controller in the course of administering Chapter 7 (commencing with Section 1500) of Title 10 of Part 3 of the Code of Civil Procedure.

(8) Transfers under Chapter 7 (commencing with Section 3691) or Chapter 8 (commencing with Section 3771) of Part 6 of Division 1 of the Revenue and Taxation Code.

(9) Transfers or exchanges to or from any governmental entity.

(b) Transfers not subject to this article may be subject to other disclosure requirements, including those under Sections 8589.3, 8589.4, and 51183.5 of the Government Code and Sections 2621.9, 2694, and 4136 of the Public Resources Code. In transfers not subject to this article, agents may make required disclosures in a separate writing. *(Added by Stats.1999, c. 876 (A.B.248), § 3.)*

Research References

California Real Estate Forms (Miller & Starr) § 1:94, California Residential Purchase Agreement and Joint Escrow Instructions.

Rutter, Cal. Practice Guide: Real Prop. Transactions Ch. 2-C, C. Broker's Relationship and Obligations to Principal and Third Parties.

Rutter, Cal. Practice Guide: Real Prop. Transactions Ch. 4-E, E. Drafting the Purchase and Sale Agreement-Terms and Conditions.

Miller and Starr California Real Estate § 1:144, Duty of Seller of Real Property to Disclose--Statutory Duty of Disclosure.

Miller and Starr California Real Estate § 3:44.10, Disclosures for Properties Located in Natural Hazards Areas.

12 Witkin, California Summary 10th Real Property § 487, (S 487) Natural Hazard Disclosure Statement.

§ 1103.2. Natural Hazard Disclosure Statement

(a) The disclosures required by this article are set forth in, and shall be made on a copy of, the following Natural Hazard Disclosure Statement:

II

NATURAL HAZARD DISCLOSURE STATEMENT

This statement applies to the following property: _____

The transferor and his or her agent(s) or a third–party consultant disclose the following information with the knowledge that even though this is not a warranty, prospective transferees may rely on this information in deciding whether and on what terms to purchase the subject property. Transferor hereby authorizes any agent(s) representing any principal(s) in this action to provide a copy of this statement to any person or entity in connection with any actual or anticipated sale of the property.

The following are representations made by the transferor and his or her agent(s) based on their knowledge and maps drawn by the state and federal governments. This information is a disclosure and is not intended to be part of any contract between the transferee and transferor.

THIS REAL PROPERTY LIES WITHIN THE FOLLOWING HAZARDOUS AREA(S):

A SPECIAL FLOOD HAZARD AREA (Any type Zone "A" or "V") designated by the Federal Emergency Management Agency.

Yes _____ No _____   Do not know and
                             information not
                             available from local
                             jurisdiction _____

AN AREA OF POTENTIAL FLOODING shown on a dam failure inundation map pursuant to Section 8589.5 of the Government Code.

Yes _____ No _____   Do not know and
                             information not
                             available from local
                             jurisdiction

A VERY HIGH FIRE HAZARD SEVERITY ZONE pursuant to Section 51178 or 51179 of the Government Code. The owner of this property is subject to the maintenance requirements of Section 51182 of the Government Code.

Yes _____ No _____

A WILDLAND AREA THAT MAY CONTAIN SUBSTANTIAL FOREST FIRE RISKS AND HAZARDS pursuant to Section 4125 of the Public Resources Code. The owner of this property is subject to the maintenance requirements of Section 4291 of the Public Resources Code. Additionally, it is not the state's responsibility to provide fire protection services to any building or structure located within the wildlands unless the Department of Forestry and Fire Protection has entered into a cooperative agreement with a local agency for those purposes pursuant to Section 4142 of the Public Resources Code.

Yes _____   No _____

AN EARTHQUAKE FAULT ZONE pursuant to Section 2622 of the Public Resources Code.

Yes _____   No _____

A SEISMIC HAZARD ZONE pursuant to Section 2696 of the Public Resources Code.

Yes (Landslide Zone) ___   Yes (Liquefaction Zone) ___
No _____   Map not yet released by
                           state ___

THESE HAZARDS MAY LIMIT YOUR ABILITY TO DEVELOP THE REAL PROPERTY, TO OBTAIN INSURANCE, OR TO RECEIVE ASSISTANCE AFTER A DISASTER.

THE MAPS ON WHICH THESE DISCLOSURES ARE BASED ESTIMATE WHERE NATURAL HAZARDS EXIST. THEY ARE NOT DEFINITIVE INDICATORS OF WHETHER OR NOT A PROPERTY WILL BE AFFECTED BY A NATURAL DISASTER. TRANSFEREE(S) AND TRANSFEROR(S) MAY WISH TO OBTAIN PROFESSIONAL ADVICE REGARDING THOSE HAZARDS AND OTHER HAZARDS THAT MAY AFFECT THE PROPERTY.

Signature of Transferor(s) _____ Date _____
Signature of Transferor(s) _____ Date _____

Agent(s) _____ Date _____
Agent(s) _____ Date _____

Check only one of the following:

☐ Transferor(s) and their agent(s) represent that the information herein is true and correct to the best of their knowledge as of the date signed by the transferor(s) and agent(s).

☐ Transferor(s) and their agent(s) acknowledge that they have exercised good faith in the selection of a third-party report provider as required in Civil Code Section 1103.7, and that the representations made in this Natural Hazard Disclosure Statement are based upon information provided by the independent third-party disclosure provider as a substituted disclosure pursuant to Civil Code Section 1103.4. Neither transferor(s) nor their agent(s) (1) has independently verified the information contained in this statement and report or (2) is personally aware of any errors or inaccuracies in the information contained on the statement. This statement was prepared by the provider below:

Third-Party
Disclosure Provider(s) _____ Date _____

Transferee represents that he or she has read and understands this document. Pursuant to Civil Code Section 1103.8, the representations made in this Natural Hazard Disclosure Statement do not constitute all of the transferor's or agent's disclosure obligations in this transaction.

Signature of Transferee(s) _____ Date _____
Signature of Transferee(s) _____ Date _____

(b) If an earthquake fault zone, seismic hazard zone, very high fire hazard severity zone, or wildland fire area map or accompanying information is not of sufficient accuracy or scale that a reasonable person can determine if the subject real property is included in a natural hazard area, the transferor or transferor's agent shall mark "Yes" on the Natural Hazard Disclosure Statement. The transferor or transferor's agent may mark "No" on the Natural Hazard Disclosure Statement if he or she attaches a report prepared pursuant to subdivision (c) of Section 1103.4 that verifies the property is not in the hazard zone. Nothing in this subdivision is intended to limit or abridge any existing duty of the transferor or the transferor's agents to exercise reasonable care in making a determination under this subdivision.

(c) If the Federal Emergency Management Agency has issued a Letter of Map Revision confirming that a property is no longer within a special flood hazard area, then the transferor or transferor's agent may mark "No" on the Natural Hazard Disclosure Statement, even if the map has not yet been updated. The transferor or transferor's agent shall attach a copy of the Letter of Map Revision to the disclosure statement.

(d) If the Federal Emergency Management Agency has issued a Letter of Map Revision confirming that a property is within a special flood hazard area and the location of the letter has been posted pursuant to subdivision (g) of Section 8589.3 of the Government Code, then the transferor or transferor's agent shall mark "Yes" on the Natural Hazard Disclosure Statement, even if the map has not yet been updated. The transferor or transferor's agent shall attach a copy of the Letter of Map Revision to the disclosure statement.

(e) The disclosure required pursuant to this article may be provided by the transferor and the transferor's agent in the Local Option Real Estate Disclosure Statement described in Section 1102.6a, provided that the Local Option Real Estate Disclosure Statement includes substantially the same information and substantially the same warnings that are required by this section.

(f)(1) The legal effect of a consultant's report delivered to satisfy the exemption provided by Section 1103.4 is not changed when it is accompanied by a Natural Hazard Disclosure Statement.

(2) A consultant's report shall always be accompanied by a completed and signed Natural Hazard Disclosure Statement.

(3) In a disclosure statement required by this section, an agent and third-party provider may cause his or her name to be preprinted in lieu of an original signature in the portions of the form reserved for signatures. The use of a preprinted name shall not change the legal effect of the acknowledgment.

(g) The disclosure required by this article is only a disclosure between the transferor, the transferor's agents, and the transferee, and shall not be used by any other party, including, but not limited to, insurance companies, lenders, or governmental agencies, for any purpose.

(h) In any transaction in which a transferor has accepted, prior to June 1, 1998, an offer to purchase, the transferor, or his or her agent, shall be deemed to have complied with the requirement of subdivision (a) if the transferor or agent delivers to the prospective transferee a statement that includes substantially the same information and warning as the Natural Hazard Disclosure Statement. *(Added by Stats.1999, c. 876 (A.B.248), § 3. Amended by Stats.2003–2004, 1st Ex.Sess., c. 8 (S.B.25), § 2, eff. May 5, 2003; Stats.2003, c. 741 (S.B.1049), § 3; Stats.2004, c. 66 (A.B.920), § 3.)*

Research References

Rutter, Cal. Practice Guide: Real Prop. Transactions Ch. 2-C, C. Broker's Relationship and Obligations to Principal and Third Parties.

Rutter, Cal. Practice Guide: Real Prop. Transactions Ch. 4-E, E. Drafting the Purchase and Sale Agreement-Terms and Conditions.

Miller and Starr California Real Estate § 1:144, Duty of Seller of Real Property to Disclose--Statutory Duty of Disclosure.

Miller and Starr California Real Estate § 1:145, Duty of Seller of Real Property to Disclose--Transfer Disclosure Statement in Residential Sales.

Miller and Starr California Real Estate § 3:44.10, Disclosures for Properties Located in Natural Hazards Areas.

15 NO. 4 Miller & Starr, California Real Estate Newsalert 5, Contracts.

12 Witkin, California Summary 10th Real Property § 486, (S 486) Types of Hazards.

12 Witkin, California Summary 10th Real Property § 487, (S 487) Natural Hazard Disclosure Statement.

§ 1103.3. Transferor's delivery of written statement to prospective transferee

(a) The transferor of any real property subject to this article shall deliver to the prospective transferee the written statement required by this article, as follows:

(1) In the case of a sale, as soon as practicable before transfer of title.

(2) In the case of transfer by a real property sales contract, as defined in Section 2985, or by a lease together with an option to purchase, or a ground lease coupled with improvements, as soon as practicable before execution of the contract. For the purpose of this subdivision, "execution" means the making or acceptance of an offer.

(b) The transferor shall indicate compliance with this article either on the receipt for deposit, the real property sales contract, the lease, any addendum attached thereto, or on a separate document.

(c) If any disclosure, or any material amendment of any disclosure, required to be made pursuant to this article is delivered after the execution of an offer to purchase, the transferee shall have three days after delivery in person or five days after delivery by deposit in the mail to terminate his or her offer by delivery of a written notice of termination to the transferor or the transferor's agent. *(Added by Stats.1999, c. 876 (A.B.248), § 3.)*

Research References

Rutter, Cal. Practice Guide: Real Prop. Transactions Ch. 2-C, C. Broker's Relationship and Obligations to Principal and Third Parties.

Rutter, Cal. Practice Guide: Real Prop. Transactions Ch. 4-E, E. Drafting the Purchase and Sale Agreement-Terms and Conditions.

12 Witkin, California Summary 10th Real Property § 487, (S 487) Natural Hazard Disclosure Statement.

§ 1103.4. Errors, inaccuracies, or omissions in any information delivered under article; liability; notice of airport in vicinity; notice of San Francisco Bay Conservation and Development Commission; notice of right to farm; notice of mining operations

(a) Neither the transferor nor any listing or selling agent shall be liable for any error, inaccuracy, or omission of any information delivered pursuant to this article if the error, inaccuracy, or omission was not within the personal knowledge of the transferor or the listing or selling agent, and was based on information timely provided by public agencies or by other persons providing information as specified in subdivision (c) that is required to be disclosed pursuant to this article, and ordinary care was exercised in obtaining and transmitting the information.

(b) The delivery of any information required to be disclosed by this article to a prospective transferee by a public agency or other person providing information required to be disclosed pursuant to this article shall be deemed to comply with the requirements of this article and shall relieve the transferor or any listing or selling agent of any further duty under this article with respect to that item of information.

(c) The delivery of a report or opinion prepared by a licensed engineer, land surveyor, geologist, or expert in natural hazard discovery dealing with matters within the scope of the professional's license or expertise shall be sufficient compliance for application of the exemption provided by subdivision (a) if the information is provided to the prospective transferee pursuant to a request therefor, whether written or oral. In responding to that request, an expert may indicate, in writing, an understanding that the information provided will be used in fulfilling the requirements of Section 1103.2 and, if so, shall indicate the required disclosures, or parts thereof, to which the information being furnished is applicable. Where that statement is furnished, the expert shall not be responsible for any items of information, or parts thereof, other than those expressly set forth in the statement.

(1) In responding to the request, the expert shall determine whether the property is within an airport influence area as defined in subdivision (b) of Section 11010 of the Business and Professions Code. If the property is within an airport influence area, the report shall contain the following statement:

NOTICE OF AIRPORT IN VICINITY

This property is presently located in the vicinity of an airport, within what is known as an airport influence area. For that reason, the property may be subject to some of the annoyances or inconveniences associated with proximity to airport operations (for example: noise, vibration, or odors). Individual sensitivities to those annoyances can vary from person to person. You may wish to consider what airport annoyances, if any, are associated with the property before you complete your purchase and determine whether they are acceptable to you.

(2) In responding to the request, the expert shall determine whether the property is within the jurisdiction of the San Francisco Bay Conservation and Development Commission, as defined in Section 66620 of the Government Code. If the property is within the commission's jurisdiction, the report shall contain the following notice:

NOTICE OF SAN FRANCISCO BAY CONSERVATION AND DEVELOPMENT COMMISSION JURISDICTION

This property is located within the jurisdiction of the San Francisco Bay Conservation and Development Commission. Use and development of property within the commission's jurisdiction may be subject to special regulations, restrictions, and permit requirements. You may wish to investigate and determine whether they are acceptable to you and your intended use of the property before you complete your transaction.

(3) In responding to the request, the expert shall determine whether the property is presently located within one mile of a parcel of real property designated as "Prime Farmland," "Farmland of Statewide Importance," "Unique Farmland," "Farmland of Local Importance," or "Grazing Land" on the most current "Important Farmland Map" issued by the California Department of Conservation, Division of Land Resource Protection, utilizing solely the county-level GIS map data, if any, available on the Farmland Mapping and Monitoring Program Web site. If the residential property is within one mile of a designated farmland area, the report shall contain the following notice:

NOTICE OF RIGHT TO FARM

This property is located within one mile of a farm or ranch land designated on the current county-level GIS "Important Farmland Map," issued by the California Department of Conservation, Division of Land Resource Protection. Accordingly, the property may be subject to inconveniences or discomforts resulting from agricultural operations that are a normal and necessary aspect of living in a community with a strong rural character and a healthy agricultural sector. Customary agricultural practices in farm operations may include, but are not limited to, noise, odors, dust, light, insects, the operation of pumps and machinery, the storage and disposal of manure, bee pollination, and the ground or aerial application of fertilizers, pesticides, and herbicides. These agricultural practices may occur at any time during the 24–hour day. Individual sensitivities to those practices can vary from person to person. You may wish to consider the impacts of such agricultural practices before you complete your purchase. Please be advised that you may be barred from obtaining legal remedies against agricultural practices conducted in a manner consistent with proper and accepted customs and standards pursuant to Section 3482.5 of the Civil Code or any pertinent local ordinance.

(4) In responding to the request, the expert shall determine, utilizing map coordinate data made available by the Office of Mine Reclamation, whether the property is presently located within one mile of a mine operation for which map coordinate data has been reported to the director pursuant to Section 2207 of the Public Resources Code. If the expert determines, from the available map coordinate data, that the residential property is located within one mile of a mine operation, the report shall contain the following notice:

NOTICE OF MINING OPERATIONS:

This property is located within one mile of a mine operation for which the mine owner or operator has reported mine location data to the Department of Conservation pursuant to Section 2207 of the Public Resources Code. Accordingly, the property may be subject to inconveniences resulting from mining operations. You may wish to consider the impacts of these practices before you complete your transaction. *(Added by Stats.1999, c. 876 (A.B.248), § 3. Amended by Stats.2002, c. 496 (A.B.2776), § 4, operative Jan. 1, 2004; Stats.2004, c. 618 (S.B.1568), § 2; Stats.2008, c. 686 (A.B.2881), § 3; Stats.2011, c. 253 (S.B.110), § 1.)*

Research References

California Real Estate Forms (Miller & Starr) § 1:94, California Residential Purchase Agreement and Joint Escrow Instructions.
Rutter, Cal. Practice Guide: Real Prop. Transactions Ch. 2-C, C. Broker's Relationship and Obligations to Principal and Third Parties.
Rutter, Cal. Practice Guide: Real Prop. Transactions Gen. Matls., Highlights.
Miller and Starr California Real Estate § 1:144, Duty of Seller of Real Property to Disclose--Statutory Duty of Disclosure.
Miller and Starr California Real Estate § 3:44.10, Disclosures for Properties Located in Natural Hazards Areas.
13 NO. 4 Miller & Starr, California Real Estate Newsalert 18, Subdivisions.
19 NO. 4 Miller & Starr, California Real Estate Newsalert 27, Subdivision Offerings, Sales, and Leasing.
12 Witkin, California Summary 10th Real Property § 486, (S 486) Types of Hazards.
12 Witkin, California Summary 10th Real Property § 487, (S 487) Natural Hazard Disclosure Statement.
12 Witkin, California Summary 10th Real Property § 493, (S 493) Military, Industrial, and Airport Influences.
12 Witkin, California Summary 10th Real Property § 494, (S 494) in General.

§ 1103.5. Transferor's relief from duty regarding items of information

(a) After a transferor and his or her agent comply with Section 1103.2, they shall be relieved of further duty under this article with respect to those items of information. The transferor and his or her agent shall not be required to provide notice to

the transferee if the information provided subsequently becomes inaccurate as a result of any governmental action, map revision, changed information, or other act or occurrence, unless the transferor or agent has actual knowledge that the information has become inaccurate.

(b) If information disclosed in accordance with this article is subsequently rendered inaccurate as a result of any governmental action, map revision, changed information, or other act or occurrence subsequent to the delivery of the required disclosures, the inaccuracy resulting therefrom does not constitute a violation of this article. *(Added by Stats.1999, c. 876 (A.B.248), § 3.)*

Research References

California Real Estate Forms (Miller & Starr) § 1:94, California Residential Purchase Agreement and Joint Escrow Instructions.
Rutter, Cal. Practice Guide: Real Prop. Transactions Ch. 2-C, C. Broker's Relationship and Obligations to Principal and Third Parties.
Miller and Starr California Real Estate § 1:144, Duty of Seller of Real Property to Disclose--Statutory Duty of Disclosure.
Miller and Starr California Real Estate § 3:44.10, Disclosures for Properties Located in Natural Hazards Areas.
12 Witkin, California Summary 10th Real Property § 494, (S 494) in General.

§ 1103.7. Acts of disclosure made in good faith

Each disclosure required by this article and each act that may be performed in making the disclosure shall be made in good faith. For purposes of this article, "good faith" means honesty in fact in the conduct of the transaction. *(Added by Stats.1999, c. 876 (A.B.248), § 3.)*

Research References

Rutter, Cal. Practice Guide: Real Prop. Transactions Ch. 2-C, C. Broker's Relationship and Obligations to Principal and Third Parties.
Miller and Starr California Real Estate § 1:144, Duty of Seller of Real Property to Disclose--Statutory Duty of Disclosure.
Miller and Starr California Real Estate § 3:44.10, Disclosures for Properties Located in Natural Hazards Areas.

§ 1103.8. Obligations for disclosure created under other laws

(a) The specification of items for disclosure in this article does not limit or abridge any obligation for disclosure created by any other provision of law or that may exist in order to avoid fraud, misrepresentation, or deceit in the transfer transaction. The legislature does not intend to affect the existing obligations of the parties to a real estate contract, or their agents, to disclose any fact materially affecting the value and desirability of the property, including, but not limited to, the physical condition of the property and previously received reports of physical inspection noted on the disclosure form provided pursuant to Section 1102.6 or 1102.6a.

(b) Nothing in this article shall be construed to change the duty of a real estate broker or salesperson pursuant to Section 2079. *(Added by Stats.1999, c. 876 (A.B.248), § 3.)*

Research References

Rutter, Cal. Practice Guide: Real Prop. Transactions Ch. 2-C, C. Broker's Relationship and Obligations to Principal and Third Parties.
Rutter, Cal. Practice Guide: Real Prop. Transactions Ch. 4-E, E. Drafting the Purchase and Sale Agreement-Terms and Conditions.
Miller and Starr California Real Estate § 3:44, Negligence Liability--Duty to Inspect Property Being Sold.
Miller and Starr California Real Estate § 1:144, Duty of Seller of Real Property to Disclose--Statutory Duty of Disclosure.

12 Witkin, California Summary 10th Real Property § 494, (S 494) in General.

§ 1103.9. Amendments to disclosures

Any disclosure made pursuant to this article may be amended in writing by the transferor or his or her agent, but the amendment shall be subject to Section 1103.3. *(Added by Stats.1999, c. 876 (A.B.248), § 3.)*

Research References

Rutter, Cal. Practice Guide: Real Prop. Transactions Ch. 2-C, C. Broker's Relationship and Obligations to Principal and Third Parties.

Miller and Starr California Real Estate § 1:144, Duty of Seller of Real Property to Disclose--Statutory Duty of Disclosure.

§ 1103.10. Delivery of disclosures; personal delivery by mail

Delivery of disclosures required by this article shall be by personal delivery to the transferee or by mail to the prospective transferee. For the purposes of this article, delivery to the spouse of a transferee shall be deemed delivery to the transferee, unless provided otherwise by contract. *(Added by Stats.1999, c. 876 (A.B.248), § 3.)*

Research References

Rutter, Cal. Practice Guide: Real Prop. Transactions Ch. 2-C, C. Broker's Relationship and Obligations to Principal and Third Parties.

Miller and Starr California Real Estate § 1:144, Duty of Seller of Real Property to Disclose--Statutory Duty of Disclosure.

§ 1103.11. Escrow agents for transfer of real property; not agent of transferor or transferee

Any person or entity, other than a real estate licensee licensed pursuant to Part 1 (commencing with Section 10000) of Division 4 of the Business and Professions Code, acting in the capacity of an escrow agent for the transfer of real property subject to this article shall not be deemed the agent of the transferor or transferee for purposes of the disclosure requirements of this article, unless the person or entity is empowered to so act by an express written agreement to that effect. The extent of that agency shall be governed by the written agreement. *(Added by Stats.1999, c. 876 (A.B.248), § 3.)*

Research References

Rutter, Cal. Practice Guide: Real Prop. Transactions Ch. 2-C, C. Broker's Relationship and Obligations to Principal and Third Parties.

Miller and Starr California Real Estate § 1:144, Duty of Seller of Real Property to Disclose--Statutory Duty of Disclosure.

Miller and Starr California Real Estate § 3:44.10, Disclosures for Properties Located in Natural Hazards Areas.

12 Witkin, California Summary 10th Real Property § 487, (S 487) Natural Hazard Disclosure Statement.

§ 1103.12. Licensed real estate broker obtaining offer from transferee; duty of delivery

(a) If more than one licensed real estate broker is acting as an agent in a transaction subject to this article, the broker who has obtained the offer made by the transferee shall, except as otherwise provided in this article, deliver the disclosure required by this article to the transferee, unless the transferor has given other written instructions for delivery.

(b) If a licensed real estate broker responsible for delivering the disclosures under this section cannot obtain the disclosure document required and does not have written assurance from the transferee that the disclosure has been received, the broker shall advise the transferee in writing of his or her rights to the disclosure. A licensed real estate broker responsible for delivering disclosures under this section shall maintain a record of the action taken to effect compliance in accordance with Section

10148 of the Business and Professions Code. *(Added by Stats.1999, c. 876 (A.B.248), § 3.)*

Research References

Rutter, Cal. Practice Guide: Real Prop. Transactions Ch. 2-C, C. Broker's Relationship and Obligations to Principal and Third Parties.

Miller and Starr California Real Estate § 1:144, Duty of Seller of Real Property to Disclose--Statutory Duty of Disclosure.

Miller and Starr California Real Estate § 3:44.10, Disclosures for Properties Located in Natural Hazards Areas.

12 Witkin, California Summary 10th Real Property § 487, (S 487) Natural Hazard Disclosure Statement.

§ 1103.13. Invalidation of transfer; effect of noncompliance with article

No transfer subject to this article shall be invalidated solely because of the failure of any person to comply with any provision of this article. However, any person who willfully or negligently violates or fails to perform any duty prescribed by any provision of this article shall be liable in the amount of actual damages suffered by a transferee. *(Added by Stats.1999, c. 876 (A.B.248), § 3.)*

Research References

Rutter, Cal. Practice Guide: Real Prop. Transactions Ch. 2-C, C. Broker's Relationship and Obligations to Principal and Third Parties.

Miller and Starr California Real Estate § 1:144, Duty of Seller of Real Property to Disclose--Statutory Duty of Disclosure.

Miller and Starr California Real Estate § 3:44.10, Disclosures for Properties Located in Natural Hazards Areas.

12 Witkin, California Summary 10th Real Property § 495, (S 495) Sanctions for Noncompliance.

§ 1103.14. Definitions

(a) As used in this article, "listing agent" means listing agent as defined in subdivision (f) of Section 1086.

(b) As used in this article, "selling agent" means selling agent as defined in subdivision (g) of Section 1086, exclusive of the requirement that the agent be a participant in a multiple listing service as defined in Section 1087. *(Added by Stats.1999, c. 876 (A.B.248), § 3.)*

Research References

Miller and Starr California Real Estate § 1:144, Duty of Seller of Real Property to Disclose--Statutory Duty of Disclosure.

Miller and Starr California Real Estate § 25C:39, Duty to Disclose Material Facts to a Buyer.

12 Witkin, California Summary 10th Real Property § 487, (S 487) Natural Hazard Disclosure Statement.

ARTICLE 1.8. BUYER'S CHOICE ACT

Repeal

For repeal of this article, see Civil Code § 1103.23.

§ 1103.20. Short title

This article shall be known, and may be cited, as the Buyer's Choice Act. *(Added by Stats.2009, c. 264 (A.B.957), § 1, eff. Oct. 11, 2009.)*

Repeal

For repeal of this article, see Civil Code § 1103.23.

Research References

Rutter, Cal. Practice Guide: Real Prop. Transactions Ch. 3-B, B. Title Companies.

Rutter, Cal. Practice Guide: Real Prop. Transactions Ch. 6-I, I. Real Property Foreclosures and Antideficiency Laws.

20 NO. 4 Miller & Starr, California Real Estate Newsalert 18, Regulation of the Real Estate Industry.

§ 1103.21. Legislative findings and declarations; sales of foreclosed properties

(a) The Legislature finds and declares:

(1) Sales of foreclosed properties have become a dominant portion of homes on the resale real estate market.

(2) The recent troubled real estate market has resulted in a concentration of the majority of homes available for resale within the hands of foreclosing lenders and has dramatically changed the market dynamics affecting ordinary home buyers.

(3) Preserving the fair negotiability of contract terms is an important policy goal to be preserved in real estate transactions.

(4) The potential for unfairness occasioned by the resale of large numbers of foreclosed homes on the market requires that protections against abuses be made effective immediately.

(5) The federal Real Estate Settlement Procedures Act (RESPA) creates general rules for fair negotiation of settlement services, prohibits kickbacks and specifically prohibits a seller in a federally related transaction from requiring a buyer to purchase title insurance from a particular insurer.

(6) California law does not specifically prohibit a seller from imposing, as a condition of sale of a foreclosed home, the purchase of title insurance or escrow services from a particular insurer or provider.

(7) Therefore it is necessary to add this act to California law to provide to a home buyer protection that follows the RESPA model and applies to, and prevents, the conditioning of a sale of a foreclosed home on the buyer's purchase of title insurance from a particular insurer or title company and/or the buyer's purchase of escrow services from a particular provider.

(b) It is the intent of the Legislature that, for the purpose of this act, the sale of a residential real property is deemed to include the receipt of an offer to purchase that residential real property. *(Added by Stats.2009, c. 264 (A.B.957), § 1, eff. Oct. 11, 2009.)*

Repeal

For repeal of this article, see Civil Code § 1103.23.

Research References

Miller and Starr California Real Estate § 6:3, Who Can Serve as an Escrow Holder.

Miller and Starr California Real Estate § 10:208, Purchaser's Title.

Miller and Starr California Real Estate § 10:231, Sheriff's Deed; Purchaser's Title.

§ 1103.22. Seller of residential real properties; requiring purchase of title insurance or escrow service from particular insurer or agent prohibited; violations

(a) A seller of residential real property improved by four or fewer dwelling units shall not require directly or indirectly, as a condition of selling the property, that title insurance covering the property or escrow service provided in connection with the sale of the property be purchased by the buyer from a particular title insurer or escrow agent. This section does not prohibit a buyer from agreeing to accept the services of a title insurer or an escrow agent recommended by the seller if written notice of the right to make an independent selection of those services is first provided by the seller to the buyer.

(b) For purposes of this section:

(1) [1]Escrow service" means service provided by a person licensed pursuant to Division 6 (commencing with Section 17000) of the Financial Code, or exempt from licensing pursuant to Section 17006 of the Financial Code.

(2) "Seller" means a mortgagee or beneficiary under a deed of trust who acquired title to residential real property improved by four or fewer dwelling units at a foreclosure sale, including a trustee, agent, officer, or other employee of any such mortgagee or beneficiary.

(3) "Title insurance" means insurance offered by an insurer admitted in this state to transact title insurance pursuant to Chapter 1 (commencing with Section 12340) of Part 6 of the Insurance Code.

(c) A seller who violates this section shall be liable to a buyer in an amount equal to three times all charges made for the title insurance or escrow service. In addition, any person who violates this section shall be deemed to have violated his or her license law and shall be subject to discipline by his or her licensing entity.

(d) A transaction subject to this section shall not be invalidated solely because of the failure of any person to comply with any provision of this act. *(Added by Stats.2009, c. 264 (A.B.957), § 1, eff. Oct. 11, 2009.)*

[1] So in enrolled bill.

Repeal

For repeal of this article, see Civil Code § 1103.23.

Research References

Rutter, Cal. Practice Guide: Real Prop. Transactions Ch. 3-B, B. Title Companies.

Rutter, Cal. Practice Guide: Real Prop. Transactions Ch. 6-I, I. Real Property Foreclosures and Antideficiency Laws.

Miller and Starr California Real Estate § 6:3, Who Can Serve as an Escrow Holder.

Miller and Starr California Real Estate § 10:208, Purchaser's Title.

Miller and Starr California Real Estate § 10:231, Sheriff's Deed; Purchaser's Title.

20 NO. 4 Miller & Starr, California Real Estate Newsalert 18, Regulation of the Real Estate Industry.

§ 1103.23. Duration of article

This article shall remain in effect only until January 1, 2015, and as of that date is repealed, unless a later enacted statute, that is enacted before January 1, 2015, deletes or extends that date. *(Added by Stats.2009, c. 264 (A.B.957), § 1, eff. Oct. 11, 2009.)*

Research References

Miller and Starr California Real Estate § 6:3, Who Can Serve as an Escrow Holder.

Miller and Starr California Real Estate § 10:208, Purchaser's Title.

Miller and Starr California Real Estate § 10:231, Sheriff's Deed; Purchaser's Title.

ARTICLE 2. EFFECT OF TRANSFER

§ 1104. Easements passing with property

WHAT EASEMENTS PASS WITH PROPERTY. A transfer of real property passes all easements attached thereto, and creates in favor thereof an easement to use other real property of the person whose estate is transferred in the same manner and to the same extent as such property was obviously and permanently used by the person whose estate is transferred, for the benefit thereof, at the time when the transfer was agreed upon or completed. *(Enacted in 1872.)*

Research References

Rutter, Cal. Practice Guide: Real Prop. Transactions Ch. 4-B, B. Interests to be Conveyed.

Miller and Starr California Real Estate § 15:6, Appurtenant Easements; Conveyance or Encumbrance of the Dominant Tenement.

Miller and Starr California Real Estate § 15:20, Sale of Property or Division of Title.

Miller and Starr California Real Estate § 15:22, Sale of Property or Division of Title--Existing Known Use.

Miller and Starr California Real Estate § 15:24, Sale of Property or Division of Title--Implied Reservation to the Grantor.

Miller and Starr California Real Estate § 15:51, Location of Implied Easements.

Miller and Starr California Real Estate § 26:35, Special Statutory Dedication Procedures.

15 NO. 2 Miller & Starr, California Real Estate Newsalert 7, Easements.

19 NO. 2 Miller & Starr, California Real Estate Newsalert 14, Easements.

22 NO. 1 Miller & Starr, California Real Estate Newsalert 14, Easements.

12 Witkin, California Summary 10th Real Property § 392, (S 392) Kinds of Transfers.

12 Witkin, California Summary 10th Real Property § 393, Obvious and Permanent Use.

12 Witkin, California Summary 10th Real Property § 397, Implied Reservation.

12 Witkin, California Summary 10th Real Property § 406, Recorded Covenant.

12 Witkin, California Summary 10th Real Property § 420, (S 420) Transferability and Succession.

§ 1105. Fee simple title; presumption

WHEN FEE SIMPLE TITLE IS PRESUMED TO PASS. A fee simple title is presumed to be intended to pass by a grant of real property, unless it appears from the grant that a lesser estate was intended. *(Enacted in 1872.)*

Research References

California Real Estate Forms (Miller & Starr) § 1:133, Grant Deed.

California Real Estate Forms (Miller & Starr) § 1:134, Interspousal Grant Deed.

California Real Estate Forms (Miller & Starr) § 1:135, Quitclaim Deed.

Rutter, Cal. Practice Guide: Real Prop. Transactions Ch. 4-B, B. Interests to be Conveyed.

Miller and Starr California Real Estate § 8:2, Rules of Interpretation; Extrinsic Evidence.

Miller and Starr California Real Estate § 9:3, Fee Simple Absolute.

Miller and Starr California Real Estate § 8:59, Property Interest Transferred; Presumptions.

Miller and Starr California Real Estate § 10:26, Evidence of the Parties' Intentions.

Miller and Starr California Real Estate § 15:17, Rules of Construction--Right-Of-Way as Easement or Fee Simple.

Miller and Starr California Real Estate § 15:24, Sale of Property or Division of Title--Implied Reservation to the Grantor.

Miller and Starr California Real Estate § 24:11, Creation--Creation by Recorded Declaration.

Miller and Starr California Real Estate § 26:31, Fee or Easement.

16 NO. 1 Miller & Starr, California Real Estate Newsalert 2, Dedication.

12 Witkin, California Summary 10th Real Property § 14, Interest Passing.

12 Witkin, California Summary 10th Real Property § 256, (S 256) Nature of Grant.

12 Witkin, California Summary 10th Real Property § 390, (S 390) Instruments Construed as Grants of Fee.

§ 1106. Subsequently acquired title; passage by operation of law

SUBSEQUENTLY ACQUIRED TITLE PASSES BY OPERATION OF LAW. Where a person purports by proper instrument to grant real property in fee simple, and subsequently acquires any title, or claim of title thereto, the same passes by operation of law to the grantee, or his successors. *(Enacted in 1872.)*

Research References

Miller and Starr California Real Estate § 8:1, Definitions and Terminology.

Miller and Starr California Real Estate § 8:58, in General; Transferable Property Interests.

Miller and Starr California Real Estate § 8:72, Transfer of Property Previously Conveyed.

Miller and Starr California Real Estate § 8:73, After-Acquired Title.

Miller and Starr California Real Estate § 10:19, "After-Acquired" Title.

Miller and Starr California Real Estate § 19:56, Landlord's Reversion.

Miller and Starr California Real Estate § 11:100, Priority of the Purchaser's Title from a Foreclosure Sale.

12 Witkin, California Summary 10th Real Property § 334, in General.

4 Witkin, California Summary 10th Security Transactions in Real Property § 34, What Property Can be Mortgaged.

13 Witkin, California Summary 10th Equity § 193, (S 193) Distinctions.

§ 1107. Conclusiveness of grant; exception

GRANT, HOW FAR CONCLUSIVE ON PURCHASERS. Every grant of an estate in real property is conclusive against the grantor, also against every one subsequently claiming under him, except a purchaser or incumbrancer who in good faith and for a valuable consideration acquires a title or lien by an instrument that is first duly recorded. *(Enacted in 1872.)*

Research References

Miller and Starr California Real Estate § 11:1, Rules Governing Priorities; Relation to Notice and Recording.

Miller and Starr California Real Estate § 11:3, Effect of Recording Statutes on Priority.

Miller and Starr California Real Estate § 11:50, Definitions; Rules of Priority.

Miller and Starr California Real Estate § 11:59, What Constitutes Actual Notice.

Miller and Starr California Real Estate § 11:101, Effect of Foreclosure on Rights of Tenants in Possession.

Miller and Starr California Real Estate § 11:152, Effect of Lis Pendens on Prior Interests.

22 NO. 3 Miller & Starr, California Real Estate Newsalert 1, Show Me Your Papers: Sales and Assignments of Secured Real Estate Loans and the California Foreclosure Process.

6 Witkin Cal. Proc. 5th Provisional Remedies § 179, Securities.

6 Witkin Cal. Proc. 5th Provisional Remedies § 186, (S 186) Other Rules of Priority.

§ 1108. Estate for life or years; purported transfer of greater estate than that owned

CONVEYANCES BY OWNER FOR LIFE OR FOR YEARS. A grant made by the owner of an estate for life or years, purporting to transfer a greater estate than that he could lawfully transfer, does not work a forfeiture of his estate, but passes to the grantee all the estate which the grantor could lawfully transfer. *(Enacted in 1872.)*

Research References

Miller and Starr California Real Estate § 8:1, Definitions and Terminology.
Miller and Starr California Real Estate § 24:6, Covenants Burdening Land for the Benefit of Other Land--Creation After the 1968-1969 Amendments.
Miller and Starr California Real Estate § 9:21, Rights and Powers.

§ 1109. Defeated grant upon condition subsequent; reconveyance

GRANT MADE ON CONDITION SUBSEQUENT. Where a grant is made upon condition subsequent, and is subsequently defeated by the non-performance of the condition, the person otherwise entitled to hold under the grant must reconvey the property to the grantor or his successors, by grant, duly acknowledged for record. *(Enacted in 1872.)*

Research References

Miller and Starr California Real Estate § 9:8, Fee Simple Defeasible--Power of Termination (Right of Re-Entry); Enforcement.
Miller and Starr California Real Estate § 24:1, Types of Enforceable Restrictions.

§ 1110. Grant on condition precedent; performance of condition; effect

An instrument purporting to be a grant of real property, to take effect upon condition precedent, passes the estate upon the performance of the condition. *(Enacted in 1872. Amended by Code Am.1873-74, c. 612, p. 225, § 132.)*

Research References

Miller and Starr California Real Estate § 8:46, Conditional Delivery to the Grantee.
Miller and Starr California Real Estate § 9:18, Estate Subject to Condition Precedent.

§ 1111. Grants of rents, reversions and remainders

GRANT OF RENTS, REVERSIONS, AND REMAINDERS. Grants of rents or of reversions or of remainders are good and effectual without attornments of the tenants; but no tenant who, before notice of the grant, shall have paid rent to the grantor, must suffer any damage thereby. *(Enacted in 1872.)*

Research References

Miller and Starr California Real Estate § 19:58, Estoppel of Tenant to Deny Landlord's Title--Effect of Attornment of the Tenant to a Stranger.
Miller and Starr California Real Estate § 19:59, Transfer of the Reversion.
Miller and Starr California Real Estate § 19:83, Persons Entitled to Receive Rent.
Miller and Starr California Real Estate § 11:101, Effect of Foreclosure on Rights of Tenants in Possession.
12 Witkin, California Summary 10th Real Property § 506, Lessor's Transfer and Tenant's Attornment.

§ 1112. Grant of land bounded by highway

A transfer of land, bounded by a highway, passes the title of the person whose estate is transferred to the soil of the highway in front to the center thereof, unless a different intent appears from the grant. *(Enacted in 1872. Amended by Code Am.1873-74, c. 612, p. 225, § 133.)*

Research References

Rutter, Cal. Practice Guide: Real Prop. Transactions Ch. 4-B, B. Interests to be Conveyed.
Miller and Starr California Real Estate § 8:65, Road, Street or Highway as Property Boundary.
Miller and Starr California Real Estate § 15:45, Estoppel; Executed Oral Conveyance; Irrevocable License.
Miller and Starr California Real Estate § 15:81, Abandonment of Public Easements--Effect on the Rights of Abutting Property Owners.
Miller and Starr California Real Estate § 26:31, Fee or Easement.
16 NO. 1 Miller & Starr, California Real Estate Newsalert 2, Dedication.
12 Witkin, California Summary 10th Real Property § 272, Presumption of Ownership to Center Line.
12 Witkin, California Summary 10th Real Property § 273, (S 273) General Rule.
12 Witkin, California Summary 10th Real Property § 274, (S 274) Distinctions.

§ 1113. Grant; implied covenants

IMPLIED COVENANTS. From the use of the word "grant" in any conveyance by which an estate of inheritance or fee simple is to be passed, the following covenants, and none other, on the part of the grantor for himself and his heirs to the grantee, his heirs, and assigns, are implied, unless restrained by express terms contained in such conveyance:

1. That previous to the time of the execution of such conveyance, the grantor has not conveyed the same estate, or any right, title, or interest therein, to any person other than the grantee;

2. That such estate is at the time of the execution of such conveyance free from encumbrances done, made, or suffered by the grantor, or any person claiming under him.

Such covenants may be sued upon in the same manner as if they had been expressly inserted in the conveyance. *(Enacted in 1872.)*

Research References

California Real Estate Forms (Miller & Starr) § 1:133, Grant Deed.
California Real Estate Forms (Miller & Starr) § 1:134, Interspousal Grant Deed.
California Real Estate Forms (Miller & Starr) § 1:135, Quitclaim Deed.
Rutter, Cal. Practice Guide: Real Prop. Transactions Ch. 4-A, A. Property to be Sold.
Rutter, Cal. Practice Guide: Real Prop. Transactions Ch. 4-E, E. Drafting the Purchase and Sale Agreement-Terms and Conditions.
Rutter, Cal. Practice Guide: Real Prop. Transactions Ch. 11-D, D. Buyer's Remedies Upon Seller's Breach-Damages and Specific Performance.
Miller and Starr California Real Estate § 8:6, Implied Covenants--Generally.
Miller and Starr California Real Estate § 8:7, Implied Covenants--Personal Nature.
Miller and Starr California Real Estate § 8:8, Condition of Title at the Time of the Conveyance.
Miller and Starr California Real Estate § 8:9, Effect of Grantee's Knowledge of the Condition of Title.
Miller and Starr California Real Estate § 8:10, Grantor's Liability.
Miller and Starr California Real Estate § 8:11, Grantee's Remedies.
Miller and Starr California Real Estate § 1:140, Duty of Seller of Real Property to Disclose.
Miller and Starr California Real Estate § 24:11, Creation--Creation by Recorded Declaration.
12 Witkin, California Summary 10th Real Property § 257, (S 257) Implied Covenants.
1 Witkin Cal. Summ. 10th Contracts § 237, Act Restriction.

§ 1114. Incumbrances defined

The term "incumbrances" includes taxes, assessments, and all liens upon real property. *(Enacted in 1872. Amended by Code Am.1873-74, c. 612, p. 225, § 134.)*

Research References

Rutter, Cal. Practice Guide: Insurance Litigation Ch. 6H-B, B. Types of Policies and Services Provided by Title Insurers.

Rutter, Cal. Practice Guide: Real Prop. Transactions Ch. 3-C, C. Types of Title Insurance Policies.

Miller and Starr California Real Estate § 8:6, Implied Covenants-- Generally.

Miller and Starr California Real Estate § 2:21, Taxes.

Miller and Starr California Real Estate § 2:23, Liens and Encumbrances.

Miller and Starr California Real Estate § 7:48, Indemnity for Defects, Liens, and Encumbrances.

12 Witkin, California Summary 10th Real Property § 360, (S 360) Distinctions.

§ 1115. Lineal and collateral warranties abolished; covenants; effect upon heirs and devisees

LINEAL AND COLLATERAL WARRANTIES ABOLISHED. Lineal and collateral warranties, with all their incidents, are abolished; but the heirs and devisees of every person who has made any covenant or agreement in reference to the title of, in, or to any real property, are answerable upon such covenant or agreement to the extent of the land descended or devised to them, in the cases and in the manner prescribed by law. *(Enacted in 1872.)*

Research References

Miller and Starr California Real Estate § 8:7, Implied Covenants-- Personal Nature.

Miller and Starr California Real Estate § 1:124, Definitions; Burden of Proof.

Miller and Starr California Real Estate § 25B:101, Enforcement of the Restrictions.

§ 1133. Property subject to blanket encumbrance but exempt from compliance with § 11013.2; notice to prospective purchaser or lessee; civil and criminal liability

(a) If a lot, parcel, or unit of a subdivision is subject to a blanket encumbrance, as defined in Section 11013 of the Business and Professions Code, but is exempt from a requirement of compliance with Section 11013.2 of the Business and Professions Code, the subdivider, his or her agent, or representative, shall not sell, or lease for a term exceeding five years, the lot, parcel, or unit, nor cause it to be sold, or leased for a term exceeding five years, until the prospective purchaser or lessee of the lot, parcel, or unit has been furnished with and has signed a true copy of the following notice:

> BUYER/LESSEE IS AWARE OF THE FACT THAT THE LOT, PARCEL, OR UNIT WHICH HE OR SHE IS PROPOSING TO PURCHASE OR LEASE IS SUBJECT TO A DEED OF TRUST, MORTGAGE, OR OTHER LIEN KNOWN AS A "BLANKET ENCUMBRANCE."
>
> IF BUYER/LESSEE PURCHASES OR LEASES THIS LOT, PARCEL, OR UNIT, HE OR SHE COULD LOSE THAT INTEREST THROUGH FORECLOSURE OF THE BLANKET ENCUMBRANCE OR OTHER LEGAL PROCESS EVEN THOUGH BUYER/LESSEE IS NOT DELINQUENT IN HIS OR HER PAYMENTS OR OTHER OBLIGATIONS UNDER THE MORTGAGE, DEED OF TRUST, OR LEASE.

———————————————————

Date   Signature of Buyer or Lessee

(b) "Subdivision," as used in subdivision (a), means improved or unimproved land that is divided or proposed to be divided for the purpose of sale, lease, or financing, whether immediate or future, into two or more lots, parcels, or units and includes a condominium project, as defined in Section 4125 or 6542, a

community apartment project, as defined in Section 4105, a stock cooperative, as defined in Section 4190 or 6566, and a limited equity housing cooperative, as defined in Section 4190.

(c) The failure of the buyer or lessee to sign the notice shall not invalidate any grant, conveyance, lease, or encumbrance.

(d) Any person or entity who willfully violates the provisions of this section shall be liable to the purchaser of a lot or unit which is subject to the provisions of this section for actual damages, and, in addition thereto, shall be guilty of a public offense punishable by a fine in an amount not to exceed five hundred dollars ($500). In an action to enforce the liability or fine, the prevailing party shall be awarded reasonable attorney's fees. *(Added by Stats.1982, c. 148, § 3, eff. April 5, 1982. Amended by Stats.1985, c. 874, § 12; Stats.2012, c. 181 (A.B.806), § 35, operative Jan. 1, 2014; Stats.2013, c. 605 (S.B.752), § 15.)*

Law Revision Commission Comments

Subdivision (b) of Section 1133 is amended to correct cross-references to former Section 1351(d), (f), (m).

Subdivision (d) is amended to make a stylistic revision. [40 Cal.L.Rev. Comm. Reports 235 (2010)].

Subdivision (b) of Section 1133 is amended to add cross-references to Sections 6542 and 6566, reflecting the enactment of the Commercial and Industrial Common Interest Development Act (Civ. Code §§ 6500–6876). [42 Cal.L.Rev.Comm. Reports 1 (2012)].

Research References

Miller and Starr California Real Estate § 8:8, Condition of Title at the Time of the Conveyance.

Miller and Starr California Real Estate § 25C:11, Projects Not Requiring a Notice of Intention or Public Report.

Miller and Starr California Real Estate § 25C:12, Requirements for Exempt Subdivisions.

Miller and Starr California Real Estate § 25C:35, Lots or Units Subject to a Blanket Encumbrance.

22 NO. 1 Miller & Starr, California Real Estate Newsalert 14, Easements.

12 Witkin, California Summary 10th Real Property § 820, (S 820) by Real Estate Commissioner.

§ 1134. Statement of defects or disclaimer; termination of purchase agreement; definitions

(a) As soon as practicable before transfer of title for the first sale of a unit in a residential condominium, community apartment project, or stock cooperative which was converted from an existing dwelling to a condominium project, community apartment project, or stock cooperative, the owner or subdivider, or agent of the owner or subdivider, shall deliver to a prospective buyer a written statement listing all substantial defects or malfunctions in the major systems in the unit and common areas of the premises, or a written statement disclaiming knowledge of any such substantial defects or malfunctions. The disclaimer may be delivered only after the owner or subdivider has inspected the unit and the common areas and has not discovered a substantial defect or malfunction which a reasonable inspection would have disclosed.

(b) If any disclosure required to be made by this section is delivered after the execution of an agreement to purchase, the buyer shall have three days after delivery in person or five days after delivery by deposit in the mail, to terminate his or her agreement by delivery of written notice of that termination to the owner, subdivider, or agent. Any disclosure delivered after the execution of an agreement to purchase shall contain a statement describing the buyer's right, method and time to rescind as prescribed by this subdivision.

(c) For the purposes of this section:

(1) "Major systems" includes, but is not limited to, the roof, walls, floors, heating, air conditioning, plumbing, electrical

systems or components of a similar or comparable nature, and recreational facilities.

(2) Delivery to a prospective buyer of the written statement required by this section shall be deemed effected when delivered personally or by mail to the prospective buyer or to an agent thereof, or to a spouse unless the agreement provides to the contrary. Delivery shall also be made to additional prospective buyers who have made a request therefor in writing.

(3) "Prospective buyer" includes any person who makes an offer to purchase a unit in the condominium, community apartment project, or stock cooperative.

(d) Any person who willfully fails to carry out the requirements of this section shall be liable in the amount of actual damages suffered by the buyer.

(e) Nothing in this section shall preclude the injured party from pursuing any remedy available under any other provision of law.

(f) No transfer of title to a unit subject to the provisions of this chapter shall be invalid solely because of the failure of any person to comply with the requirements of this section.

(g) The written statement required by this section shall not abridge or limit any other obligation of disclosure created by any other provision of law or which is or may be required to avoid fraud, deceit, or misrepresentation in the transaction. *(Added by Stats.1981, c. 811, § 1, operative July 1, 1982.)*

Research References

Rutter, Cal. Practice Guide: Real Prop. Transactions Ch. 2-C, C. Broker's Relationship and Obligations to Principal and Third Parties.
Miller and Starr California Real Estate § 3:42, Specific Disclosures Required by Statute.
Miller and Starr California Real Estate § 1:144, Duty of Seller of Real Property to Disclose--Statutory Duty of Disclosure.
Miller and Starr California Real Estate § 36:11, Fraud.
Miller and Starr California Real Estate § 25B:91, Collection of Assessments.
Miller and Starr California Real Estate § 25C:40, Notice to Buyer of Property Converted to a Common Interest Subdivision; Right to Rescind.
12 Witkin, California Summary 10th Real Property § 86, (S 86) Other Statutes.
12 Witkin, California Summary 10th Real Property § 471, (S 471) Types of Disclosures.
12 Witkin, California Summary 10th Real Property § 687, (S 687) State Requirements.

CHAPTER 3. TRANSFER OF PERSONAL PROPERTY

ARTICLE 1. MODE OF TRANSFER

§ 1135. Ship; method of transfer

An interest in a ship can be transferred only by operation of law, or by written instrument, subscribed by the person making the transfer, or by his agent. *(Enacted in 1872. Amended by Stats.1931, c. 1070, p. 2259, § 6.)*

Research References

1 Witkin Cal. Summ. 10th Contracts § 343, California Codes.

§ 1140. Dies, molds and forms; transfer of rights and title to molder by operation of law; notice; disposition by molder; rights under patent, copyright and unfair competition laws

(a) For purposes of this section:

(1) The term "customer" means any individual or entity who causes or caused a molder to fabricate, cast, or otherwise make a die, mold, or form.

(2) The term "molder" means any individual or entity, including, but not limited to, a tool or die maker, who fabricates, casts, or otherwise makes a die, mold, or form.

(3) For purposes of this section, the term "within three years following the last prior use" shall be construed to include any period following the last prior use of a die, mold, or form regardless of whether or not that period precedes the effective date of this section.

(b) In the absence of any agreement to the contrary, the customer shall have all rights and title to any die, mold, or form in the possession of the molder.

(c) If a customer does not claim possession from a molder of a die, mold, or form within three years following the last prior use thereof, all rights and title to any die, mold, or form may be transferred by operation of law to the molder for the purpose of destroying or otherwise disposing of such die, mold, or form, consistent with this section.

(d) If a molder chooses to have all rights and title to any die, mold, or form transferred to the molder by operation of law, the molder shall send written notice by registered mail to the chief executive officer of the customer or, if the customer is not a business entity, to the customer himself or herself at the customer's last known address indicating that the molder intends to terminate the customer's rights and title by having all such rights and title transferred to the molder by operation of law pursuant to this section.

(e) If a customer does not respond in person or by mail to claim possession of the particular die, mold, or form within 120 days following the date the notice was sent, or does not make other contractual arrangements with the molder for storage thereof, all rights and title of the customer shall transfer by operation of law to the molder. Thereafter, the molder may destroy or otherwise dispose of the particular mold, tool, or die as the molder's own property without any risk of liability to the customer, except that this section shall not be construed in any manner to affect any right of the customer, under federal patent or copyright law or any state or federal law pertaining to unfair competition. *(Added by Stats.1979, c. 180, p. 400, § 1. Amended by Stats.1981, c. 290, § 1.)*

Research References

13 Witkin, California Summary 10th Personal Property § 39, (S 39) Other Statutes Dealing With Unclaimed Property.

ARTICLE 3. GIFTS

§ 1146. Gift defined

GIFTS DEFINED. A gift is a transfer of personal property, made voluntarily, and without consideration. *(Enacted in 1872.)*

Research References

13 Witkin, California Summary 10th Personal Property § 124, (S 124) in General.

11 Witkin, California Summary 10th Community Property § 52, in General.

§ 1147.   Verbal gift; requisites

GIFT, HOW MADE.   A verbal gift is not valid, unless the means of obtaining possession and control of the thing are given, nor, if it is capable of delivery, unless there is an actual or symbolical delivery of the thing to the donee.   *(Enacted in 1872.)*

Research References

13 Witkin, California Summary 10th Personal Property § 136, Chose Not Evidenced by Writing.

§ 1148.   Revocability

A gift, other than a gift in view of impending death, cannot be revoked by the giver.   *(Enacted in 1872. Amended by Stats.1991, c. 1055 (S.B.271), § 2.)*

Law Revision Commission Comments

Section 1148 is amended to refer to a gift in view of "impending" death, consistent with Probate Code Sections 5701–5705. [20 Cal.L.Rev.Comm.Reports 2869 (1990)].

Research References

13 Witkin, California Summary 10th Personal Property § 124, (S 124) in General.

13 Witkin, California Summary 10th Personal Property § 151, Rescission for Mistake or Fraud.

CHAPTER 4.   RECORDING TRANSFERS

ARTICLE 2.   MODE OF RECORDING

§ 1169.   Place of recordation

IN WHAT OFFICE.   Instruments entitled to be recorded must be recorded by the County Recorder of the county in which the real property affected thereby is situated.   *(Enacted in 1872.)*

Research References

California Real Estate Forms (Miller & Starr) § 1:13, Right of First Refusal Agreement.

California Real Estate Forms (Miller & Starr) § 1:56, Memorandum of Right of First Refusal.

California Real Estate Forms (Miller & Starr) § 1:57, Memorandum of Right of First Offer.

California Real Estate Forms (Miller & Starr) § 1:58, Memorandum of Option.

California Real Estate Forms (Miller & Starr) § 1:59, Memorandum of Exercise of Option.

California Real Estate Forms (Miller & Starr) § 2:40, Memorandum of Lease and Right of First Refusal, Right of First Offer, or Option to Purchase Property.

California Real Estate Forms (Miller & Starr) § 2:50, Lease Termination Agreement.

California Real Estate Forms (Miller & Starr) § 2:51, Surrender of Leasehold.

California Real Estate Forms (Miller & Starr) § 2:56, Subordination, Nondisturbance, and Attornment Agreement.

California Real Estate Forms (Miller & Starr) § 2:94, Notarial Acknowledgment.

California Real Estate Forms (Miller & Starr) § 3:55, Subordination, Nondisturbance, and Attornment Agreement.

California Real Estate Forms (Miller & Starr) § 3:56, Subordination Agreement (Deed of Trust to Deed of Trust).

California Real Estate Forms (Miller & Starr) § 3:69, Note and Deed of Trust Assumption Agreement.

California Real Estate Forms (Miller & Starr) § 3:72, Consent, Assignment and Assumption Agreement and First Amendment to Loan Documents.

California Real Estate Forms (Miller & Starr) § 1:133, Grant Deed.

California Real Estate Forms (Miller & Starr) § 1:134, Interspousal Grant Deed.

California Real Estate Forms (Miller & Starr) § 3:72.50, Amendment to Promissory Note and Deed of Trust–Extending Maturity Date.

Rutter, Cal. Practice Guide: Real Prop. Transactions Ch. 6-H, H. Security for Promissory Note.

Rutter, Cal. Practice Guide: Real Prop. Transactions Ch. 12-B, B. Agreements Regarding Co-Ownership Rights and Obligations.

Miller and Starr California Real Estate § 11:6, Instruments Subject to Recording--List of Recordable Documents.

Miller and Starr California Real Estate § 11:16, Place of Recording.

12 Witkin, California Summary 10th Real Property § 319, General Requirements.

14 Witkin, California Summary 10th Wills and Probate § 846, Formalities of Execution.

§ 1170.   Time instrument deemed recorded

An instrument is deemed to be recorded when, being duly acknowledged or proved and certified, it is deposited in the Recorder's office, with the proper officer, for record.   *(Enacted in 1872. Amended by Code Am.1873–74, c. 612, p. 226, § 138.)*

Research References

Rutter, Cal. Practice Guide: Enforcing Judgments/Debts Ch. 6K-1, Acknowledgment of Full Satisfaction of Judgment.

Miller and Starr California Real Estate § 11:11, Required Form and Contents--Digital Recording Systems.

Miller and Starr California Real Estate § 11:21, When Recording is Complete--To be Legally Effective.

Miller and Starr California Real Estate § 11:22, When Recording is Complete--For Constructive Notice.

Miller and Starr California Real Estate § 11:23, Purpose and Effect; Required for Recordation.

Miller and Starr California Real Estate § 13:33, Recordation.

16 NO. 2 Miller & Starr, California Real Estate Newsalert 7, Deeds of Trust.

22 NO. 3 Miller & Starr, California Real Estate Newsalert 19, Recording and Priorities.

12 Witkin, California Summary 10th Real Property § 323, (S 323) Necessity of Actual Copying.

§ 1171.   Grants and mortgages; separate sets of books

BOOKS OF RECORD.   Grants, absolute in terms, are to be recorded in one set of books, and mortgages in another. *(Enacted in 1872.)*

Research References

Miller and Starr California Real Estate § 11:11, Required Form and Contents--Digital Recording Systems.

§ 1172.   Recorder; duties

The duties of county recorders, in respect to recording instruments, are prescribed by the Government Code.   *(Enacted in 1872. Amended by Stats.1959, c. 593, p. 2564, § 1.)*

§ 1173. Vessels; mode of recording

TRANSFER OF VESSELS. The mode of recording transfers of ships registered under the laws of the United States is regulated by Acts of Congress. *(Enacted in 1872.)*

ARTICLE 3. PROOF AND ACKNOWLEDGMENT OF INSTRUMENTS

§ 1180. Persons before whom proof or acknowledgment may be made

The proof or acknowledgment of an instrument may be made at any place within this state before a justice, retired justice, or clerk of the Supreme Court, a justice, retired justice, or clerk of any court of appeal or judge or retired judge of a superior court, or the Secretary of the Senate or Chief Clerk of the Assembly. *(Enacted in 1872. Amended by Code Am.1880, c. 39, p. 2, § 1; Stats.1953, c. 457, p. 1701, § 1; Stats.1967, c. 17, p. 826, § 3; Stats.1986, c. 1417, § 1; Stats.1999, c. 20 (S.B.301), § 1.)*

Research References

Rutter, Cal. Practice Guide: Enforcing Judgments/Debts Ch. 6K-1, Acknowledgment of Full Satisfaction of Judgment.
Rutter, Cal. Practice Guide: Real Prop. Transactions Ch. 11-I, I. Lis Pendens.
Miller and Starr California Real Estate § 11:24, Qualifying Officers.
12 Witkin, California Summary 10th Real Property § 288, (S 288) in General.

§ 1181. Notaries public; officers before whom proof or acknowledgment may be made

The proof or acknowledgment of an instrument may be made before a notary public at any place within this state, or within the county or city and county in this state in which the officer specified below was elected or appointed, before either:

(a) A clerk of a superior court.

(b) A county clerk.

(c) A court commissioner.

(d) A retired judge of a municipal or justice court.

(e) A district attorney.

(f) A clerk of a board of supervisors.

(g) A city clerk.

(h) A county counsel.

(i) A city attorney.

(j) Secretary of the Senate.

(k) Chief Clerk of the Assembly. *(Enacted in 1872. Amended by Code Am.1880, c. 39, p. 2, § 2; Stats.1891, c. 150, p. 214, § 1; Stats.1911, c. 247, p. 429, § 1; Stats.1941, c. 1096, p. 2789, § 1; Stats.1945, c. 240, p. 705, § 2; Stats.1951, c. 1676, p. 3861, § 3; Stats.1953, c. 457, p. 1701, § 2; Stats.1959, c. 1162, p. 2352, § 1; Stats.1961, c. 49, p. 988, § 1; Stats.1963, c. 200, p. 938, § 1; Stats.1968, c. 576, p. 1244, § 1; Stats.1971, c. 27, p. 38, § 1; Stats.1981, c. 390, § 1; Stats.1986, c. 1417, § 2; Stats.1992, c. 876 (A.B.3296), § 3; Stats.1998, c. 931 (S.B.2139), § 13, eff. Sept. 28, 1998; Stats.1999, c. 20 (S.B.301), § 2; Stats.2002, c. 784 (S.B. 1316), § 12.)*

Law Revision Commission Comments

Subdivision (a) of Section 1181 is amended to reflect elimination of the justice court. Cal. Const. art. VI, §§ 1, 5(b). The reference to a retired judge of a justice court is maintained in subdivision (d) to enable retired judges of justice courts to continue to take proofs or acknowledgments of instruments. [28 Cal.L.Rev.Comm. Reports 51 (1998)].

Subdivisions (a) and (d) of Section 1181 are amended to reflect unification of the municipal and superior courts pursuant to Article VI, Section 5(e), of the California Constitution. [32 Cal.L.Rev.Comm. Reports 68 (2002)].

Research References

Rutter, Cal. Practice Guide: Civ. Pro. Before Trial Ch. 9(I)-J, J. Motion to Expunge Lis Pendens.
Rutter, Cal. Practice Guide: Real Prop. Transactions Ch. 11-I, I. Lis Pendens.
Miller and Starr California Real Estate § 11:24, Qualifying Officers.
2 Witkin Cal. Proc. 5th Courts § 344, (S 344) Statutory Duties.
12 Witkin, California Summary 10th Real Property § 288, (S 288) in General.
12 Witkin, California Summary 10th Real Property § 289, (S 289) Appointment and Authority of Notaries.

§ 1182. Proof or acknowledgment of instrument; out of state

The proof or acknowledgment of an instrument may be made without this state, but within the United States, and within the jurisdiction of the officer, before any of the following:

(1) A justice, judge, or clerk of any court of record of the United States.

(2) A justice, judge, or clerk of any court of record of any state.

(3) A commissioner appointed by the Governor or Secretary of State for that purpose.

(4) A notary public.

(5) Any other officer of the state where the acknowledgment is made authorized by its laws to take such proof or acknowledgment. *(Enacted in 1872. Amended by Stats.1971, c. 1611, p. 3469, § 1.)*

Research References

Miller and Starr California Real Estate § 11:24, Qualifying Officers.

12 Witkin, California Summary 10th Real Property § 288, (S 288) in General.

§ 1183. Officers outside country

The proof or acknowledgment of an instrument may be made without the United States, before any of the following:

(a) A minister, commissioner, or chargè d'affaires of the United States, resident and accredited in the country where the proof or acknowledgment is made.

(b) A consul, vice consul, or consular agent of the United States, resident in the country where the proof or acknowledgment is made.

(c) A judge of a court of record of the country where the proof or acknowledgment is made.

(d) Commissioners appointed by the Governor or Secretary of State for that purpose.

(e) A notary public.

If the proof or acknowledgment is made before a notary public, the signature of the notary public shall be proved or acknowledged (1) before a judge of a court of record of the country where the proof or acknowledgment is made, or (2) by any American diplomatic officer, consul general, consul, vice consul, or consular agent, or (3) by an apostille (certification) affixed to the instrument pursuant to the terms of The Hague Convention Abolishing the Requirement of Legalization for Foreign Public Documents. *(Enacted in 1872. Amended by Code Am.1873–74, c. 612, p. 227, § 139; Stats.1939, c. 249, p. 1505, § 1; Stats.1943, c. 28, p. 156, § 1; Stats.1963, c. 144, p. 816, § 1; Stats.1971, c. 1611, p. 3469, § 2; Stats.1982, c. 520, § 13; Stats.1984, c. 1017, § 1.)*

Research References

Rutter, Cal. Practice Guide: Enforcing Judgments/Debts Ch. 6B-11, Release of Real Property Judgment Lien.
Miller and Starr California Real Estate § 11:24, Qualifying Officers.
12 Witkin, California Summary 10th Real Property § 288, (S 288) in General.
10 Witkin, California Summary 10th Parent and Child § 96, Agreement and Order.

§ 1183.5. Notarial acts

Any officer on active duty or performing inactive-duty training in the armed forces having the general powers of a notary public pursuant to Section 936 or 1044a of Title 10 of the United States Code (Public Law 90-632 and 101-510) and any successor statutes may perform all notarial acts for any person serving in the armed forces of the United States, wherever he or she may be, or for any spouse of a person serving in the armed forces, wherever he or she may be, or for any person eligible for legal assistance under laws and regulations of the United States, wherever he or she may be, for any person serving with, employed by, or accompanying such armed forces outside the United States and outside the Canal Zone, Puerto Rico, Guam and the Virgin Islands, and any person subject to the Uniform Code of Military Justice outside of the United States.

Any instrument acknowledged by any such officer or any oath or affirmation made before such officer shall not be rendered invalid by the failure to state therein the place of execution or acknowledgment. No seal or authentication of the officer's certificate of acknowledgment or of any jurat signed by him or her shall be required but the officer taking the acknowledgment shall endorse thereon or attach thereto a certificate substantially in a form authorized by the laws of this state or in the following form:

On this the _____ day of _____, 19___, before me _____, the undersigned officer, personally appeared _____ known to me (or satisfactorily proven) to be (a)

serving in the armed forces of the United States, (b) a spouse of a person serving in the armed forces of the United States, or (c) a person serving with, employed by, or accompanying the armed forces of the United States outside the United States and outside the Canal Zone, Puerto Rico, Guam, and the Virgin Islands, and to be the person whose name is subscribed to the within instrument and acknowledged that he or she executed the same. And the undersigned does further certify that he or she is at the date of this certificate a commissioned officer of the armed forces of the United States having the general powers of a notary public under the provisions of Section 936 or 1044a of Title 10 of the United States Code (Public Law 90-632 and 101-510).

_____
Signature of officer, rank, branch of service and capacity in which signed.

To any affidavit subscribed and sworn to before such officer there shall be attached a jurat substantially in the following form:

Subscribed and sworn to before me on this _____ day of _____, 19___.

_____
Signature of officer, rank, branch of service and capacity in which signed.

The recitals contained in any such certificate or jurat shall be prima facie evidence of the truth thereof, and any certificate of acknowledgment, oath or affirmation purporting to have been made by any commissioned officer of the Army, Air Force, Navy, Marine Corps or Coast Guard shall, notwithstanding the omission of any specific recitals therein, constitute presumptive evidence of the existence of the facts necessary to authorize such acknowledgment, oath or affirmation to be taken by the certifying officer pursuant to this section. *(Added by Stats.1943, c. 28, p. 156, § 2. Amended by Stats.1943, c. 365, p. 1600, § 1; Stats.1945, c. 106, p. 414, § 1; Stats.1947, c. 10, p. 483, § 1; Stats.1949, c. 1186, p. 2106, § 2; Stats.1951, c. 386, p. 1185, § 1; Stats.1953, c. 603, p. 1848, § 1; Stats.1957, c. 898, p. 2109, § 1; Stats.1974, c. 91, p. 186, § 1; Stats.1992, c. 77 (S.B.208), § 1; Stats.1994, c. 587 (A.B.3600), § 1.)*

Research References

Miller and Starr California Real Estate § 11:24, Qualifying Officers.
Miller and Starr California Real Estate § 11:26, Form and Content of the Certificate of Acknowledgement.
12 Witkin, California Summary 10th Real Property § 288, (S 288) in General.
10 Witkin, California Summary 10th Parent and Child § 96, Agreement and Order.

§ 1184. Proof or acknowledgment of instruments; deputies

When any of the officers mentioned in Sections 1180, 1181, 1182, and 1183 are authorized by law to appoint a deputy, the acknowledgment or proof may be taken by such deputy, in the name of his principal. *(Enacted in 1872. Amended by Stats. 1953, c. 457, p. 1701, § 3.)*

Research References

Miller and Starr California Real Estate § 11:24, Qualifying Officers.

12 Witkin, California Summary 10th Real Property § 288, (S 288) in General.

§ 1185. Acknowledgments; requisites; civil penalties

(a) The acknowledgment of an instrument shall not be taken unless the officer taking it has satisfactory evidence that the person making the acknowledgment is the individual who is described in and who executed the instrument.

(b) For purposes of this section, "satisfactory evidence" means the absence of information, evidence, or other circumstances that would lead a reasonable person to believe that the person making the acknowledgment is not the individual he or she claims to be and any one of the following:

(1)(A) The oath or affirmation of a credible witness personally known to the officer, whose identity is proven to the officer upon presentation of a document satisfying the requirements of paragraph (3) or (4), that the person making the acknowledgment is personally known to the witness and that each of the following are true:

(i) The person making the acknowledgment is the person named in the document.

(ii) The person making the acknowledgment is personally known to the witness.

(iii) That it is the reasonable belief of the witness that the circumstances of the person making the acknowledgment are such that it would be very difficult or impossible for that person to obtain another form of identification.

(iv) The person making the acknowledgment does not possess any of the identification documents named in paragraphs (3) and (4).

(v) The witness does not have a financial interest in the document being acknowledged and is not named in the document.

(B) A notary public who violates this section by failing to obtain the satisfactory evidence required by subparagraph (A) shall be subject to a civil penalty not exceeding ten thousand dollars ($10,000). An action to impose this civil penalty may be brought by the Secretary of State in an administrative proceeding or a public prosecutor in superior court, and shall be enforced as a civil judgment. A public prosecutor shall inform the secretary of any civil penalty imposed under this subparagraph.

(2) The oath or affirmation under penalty of perjury of two credible witnesses, whose identities are proven to the officer upon the presentation of a document satisfying the requirements of paragraph (3) or (4), that each statement in paragraph (1) is true.

(3) Reasonable reliance on the presentation to the officer of any one of the following, if the document is current or has been issued within five years:

(A) An identification card or driver's license issued by the Department of Motor Vehicles.

(B) A passport issued by the Department of State of the United States.

(C) An inmate identification card issued by the Department of Corrections and Rehabilitation, if the inmate is in custody in prison.

(4) Reasonable reliance on the presentation of any one of the following, provided that a document specified in subparagraphs (A) to (E), inclusive, shall either be current or have been issued within five years and shall contain a photograph and description of the person named on it, shall be signed by the person, shall bear a serial or other identifying number, and, in the event that the document is a passport, shall have been stamped by the United States Citizenship and Immigration Services of the Department of Homeland Security:

(A) A passport issued by a foreign government.

(B) A driver's license issued by a state other than California or by a Canadian or Mexican public agency authorized to issue driver's licenses.

(C) An identification card issued by a state other than California.

(D) An identification card issued by any branch of the Armed Forces of the United States.

* * *

(E) An employee identification card issued by an agency or office of the State of California, or by an agency or office of a city, county, or city and county in this state.

* * *

(c) An officer who has taken an acknowledgment pursuant to this section shall be presumed to have operated in accordance with the provisions of law.

(d) A party who files an action for damages based on the failure of the officer to establish the proper identity of the person making the acknowledgment shall have the burden of proof in establishing the negligence or misconduct of the officer.

(e) A person convicted of perjury under this section shall forfeit any financial interest in the document. *(Enacted in 1872. Amended by Stats.1905, c. 445, p. 603, § 2; Stats.1982, c. 197, § 1, eff. May 12, 1982; Stats.1987, c. 307, § 1; Stats.1988, c. 842, § 1; Stats.1993, c. 1044 (A.B.1090), § 1; Stats.2007, c. 399 (A.B.886), § 1; Stats.2008, c. 179 (S.B.1498), § 29; Stats.2008, c. 67 (A.B.2452), § 1; Stats.2010, c. 328 (S.B.1330), § 28; Stats.2013, c. 159 (A.B.625), § 2.)*

Research References

Rutter, Cal. Practice Guide: Civil Trials & Evidence Ch. 8C-B, B. Writings.
Miller and Starr California Real Estate § 11:23, Purpose and Effect; Required for Recordation.
Miller and Starr California Real Estate § 11:26, Form and Content of the Certificate of Acknowledgement.
Miller and Starr California Real Estate § 11:27, Failure to Make Proper Identification.
Miller and Starr California Real Estate § 11:29, Liability of the Notary-- In General.
12 Witkin, California Summary 10th Real Property § 285, (S 285) Knowledge of Officer.

§ 1188. Certificate of acknowledgment

An officer taking the acknowledgment of an instrument shall endorse thereon or attach thereto a certificate * * * pursuant to Section 1189. *(Enacted in 1872. Amended by Code Am.1873–74, c. 612, p. 227, § 140; Stats.1990, c. 1070 (S.B.2251), § 1; Stats.2013, c. 78 (A.B.464), § 1.)*

Research References

Miller and Starr California Real Estate § 11:26, Form and Content of the Certificate of Acknowledgement.

§ 1189. Certificate of acknowledgment; form; sufficiency of out of state acknowledgment; force and effect of acknowledgment under prior laws; civil penalties

(a)(1) Any certificate of acknowledgment taken within this state shall be in the following form:

State of California)
County of _____)

On _____

before me, (here insert name and title of the officer), personally appeared _____ who proved to me on the basis of satisfactory evidence to be the person(s) whose name(s) is/are subscribed to the within instrument and acknowledged to me that he/she/they executed the same in his/her/their authorized capacity(ies), and that by his/her/their signature(s) on the instrument the person(s), or the entity upon behalf of which the person(s) acted, executed the instrument.

I certify under PENALTY OF PERJURY under the laws of the State of California that the foregoing paragraph is true and correct.

WITNESS my hand and official seal.

Signature _____ (Seal)

(2) A notary public who willfully states as true any material fact that he or she knows to be false shall be subject to a civil penalty not exceeding ten thousand dollars ($10,000). An action to impose a civil penalty under this subdivision may be brought by the Secretary of State in an administrative proceeding or any public prosecutor in superior court, and shall be enforced as a civil judgment. A public prosecutor shall inform the secretary of any civil penalty imposed under this section.

(b) Any certificate of acknowledgment taken in another place shall be sufficient in this state if it is taken in accordance with the laws of the place where the acknowledgment is made.

(c) On documents to be filed in another state or jurisdiction of the United States, a California notary public may complete any acknowledgment form as may be required in that other state or jurisdiction on a document, provided the form does not require the notary to determine or certify that the signer holds a particular representative capacity or to make other determinations and certifications not allowed by California law.

(d) An acknowledgment provided prior to January 1, 1993, and conforming to applicable provisions of former Sections 1189, 1190, 1190a, 1190.1, 1191, and 1192, as repealed by Chapter 335 of the Statutes of 1990, shall have the same force and effect as if those sections had not been repealed. *(Added by Stats.1990, c. 335 (A.B.2581), § 2. Amended by Stats.1990, c. 1070 (S.B.2251), § 2; Stats.1991, c. 157 (A.B.1750), § 1; Stats.1996, c. 97 (A.B.3304), § 1; Stats.2005, c. 295 (A.B.361), § 1; Stats.2007, c. 399 (A.B.886), § 2.)*

Research References

California Real Estate Forms (Miller & Starr) § 1:13, Right of First Refusal Agreement.
California Real Estate Forms (Miller & Starr) § 1:56, Memorandum of Right of First Refusal.
California Real Estate Forms (Miller & Starr) § 1:57, Memorandum of Right of First Offer.
California Real Estate Forms (Miller & Starr) § 1:58, Memorandum of Option.
California Real Estate Forms (Miller & Starr) § 1:59, Memorandum of Exercise of Option.
California Real Estate Forms (Miller & Starr) § 2:39, Memorandum of Lease.
California Real Estate Forms (Miller & Starr) § 2:40, Memorandum of Lease and Right of First Refusal, Right of First Offer, or Option to Purchase Property.
California Real Estate Forms (Miller & Starr) § 2:50, Lease Termination Agreement.
California Real Estate Forms (Miller & Starr) § 2:51, Surrender of Leasehold.

California Real Estate Forms (Miller & Starr) § 2:56, Subordination, Nondisturbance, and Attornment Agreement.
California Real Estate Forms (Miller & Starr) § 2:94, Notarial Acknowledgment
California Real Estate Forms (Miller & Starr) § 3:55, Subordination, Nondisturbance, and Attornment Agreement.
California Real Estate Forms (Miller & Starr) § 3:56, Subordination Agreement (Deed of Trust to Deed of Trust).
California Real Estate Forms (Miller & Starr) § 3:69, Note and Deed of Trust Assumption Agreement.
California Real Estate Forms (Miller & Starr) § 3:72, Consent, Assignment and Assumption Agreement and First Amendment to Loan Documents.
California Real Estate Forms (Miller & Starr) § 1:133, Grant Deed.
California Real Estate Forms (Miller & Starr) § 1:134, Interspousal Grant Deed.
California Real Estate Forms (Miller & Starr) § 3:72.50, Amendment to Promissory Note and Deed of Trust–Extending Maturity Date.
Miller and Starr California Real Estate § 11:23, Purpose and Effect; Required for Recordation.
Miller and Starr California Real Estate § 11:26, Form and Content of the Certificate of Acknowledgement.
Miller and Starr California Real Estate § 11:27, Failure to Make Proper Identification.
Miller and Starr California Real Estate § 11:29, Liability of the Notary-- In General.
12 Witkin, California Summary 10th Real Property § 284, (S 284) Form of Acknowledgment.

§ 1190. Certificate of acknowledgment as prima facie evidence; duly authorized person

The certificate of acknowledgment of an instrument executed on behalf of an incorporated or unincorporated entity by a duly authorized person in the form specified in Section 1189 shall be prima facie evidence that the instrument is the duly authorized act of the entity named in the instrument and shall be conclusive evidence thereof in favor of any good faith purchaser, lessee, or encumbrancer. "Duly authorized person," with respect to a domestic or foreign corporation, includes the president, vice president, secretary, and assistant secretary of the corporation. *(Added by Stats.1990, c. 1070 (S.B.2251), § 3.)*

Research References

Miller and Starr California Real Estate § 11:12, Required Form and Contents--Signature of the Property Owner.
Miller and Starr California Real Estate § 11:23, Purpose and Effect; Required for Recordation.
Miller and Starr California Real Estate § 11:26, Form and Content of the Certificate of Acknowledgement.
Miller and Starr California Real Estate § 11:27, Failure to Make Proper Identification.
12 Witkin, California Summary 10th Real Property § 284, (S 284) Form of Acknowledgment.

§ 1193. Certificate of acknowledgment; authentication

OFFICERS MUST AFFIX THEIR SIGNATURES. Officers taking and certifying acknowledgments or proof of instruments for record, must authenticate their certificates by affixing thereto their signatures, followed by the names of their offices; also, their seals of office, if by the laws of the State or country where the acknowledgment or proof is taken, or by authority of which they are acting, they are required to have official seals. *(Enacted in 1872.)*

Research References

Miller and Starr California Real Estate § 11:26, Form and Content of the Certificate of Acknowledgement.
12 Witkin, California Summary 10th Real Property § 284, (S 284) Form of Acknowledgment.

§ 1195. Proof of execution; methods; certificate form

(a) Proof of the execution of an instrument, when not acknowledged, may be made by any of the following:

(1) By the party executing it, or either of them.

(2) By a subscribing witness.

(3) By other witnesses, in cases mentioned in Section 1198.

(b)(1) Proof of the execution of a power of attorney, grant deed, mortgage, deed of trust, quitclaim deed, security agreement, or any instrument affecting real property is not permitted pursuant to Section 27287 of the Government Code, though proof of the execution of a trustee's deed or deed of reconveyance is permitted.

(2) Proof of the execution for any instrument requiring a notary public to obtain a thumbprint from the party signing the document in the notary public's journal is not permitted.

(c) Any certificate for proof of execution taken within this state shall be in the following form* * *:

State of California

              ss.

County of _____

On ___ (date), before me, * * *___ (name and title of officer), personally appeared ___ (name of subscribing witness), proved to me to be the person whose name is subscribed to the within instrument, as a witness thereto, on the oath of ___ (name of credible witness), a credible witness who is known to me and provided a satisfactory identifying document. (name of subscribing witness), being by me duly sworn, said that he/she was present and saw/heard ___ (name[s] of principal[s]), the same person(s) described in and whose name(s) is/are subscribed to the within or attached instrument in his/her/their authorized capacity(ies) as (a) party(ies) thereto, execute or acknowledge executing the same, and that said affiant subscribed his/her name to the within or attached instrument as a witness at the request of ___ (name[s] of principal[s]).

WITNESS my hand and official seal.

Signature_____ (* * *Seal)

(Enacted in 1872. Amended by Stats.1997, c. 319 (S.B.618), § 1; Stats.2011, c. 296 (A.B.1023), § 34; Stats.2011, c. 269 (A.B.75), § 3; Stats.2012, c. 202 (A.B.2326), § 1; Stats.2013, c. 76 (A.B.383), § 11; Stats.2013, c. 78 (A.B.464), § 2.)

Research References

Miller and Starr California Real Estate § 8:29, Requirements of Grantor's Signature.
Miller and Starr California Real Estate § 11:23, Purpose and Effect; Required for Recordation.
Miller and Starr California Real Estate § 11:26, Form and Content of the Certificate of Acknowledgement.
Miller and Starr California Real Estate § 11:27, Failure to Make Proper Identification.
22 NO. 4 Miller & Starr, California Real Estate Newsalert 18, Recording and Priorities.

§ 1196. Subscribing witness; proof

A witness shall be proved to be a subscribing witness by the oath of a credible witness who provides the officer with any document satisfying the requirements of paragraph (3) or (4) of subdivision (b) of Section 1185. *(Enacted in 1872. Amended by Stats.1982, c. 197, § 7, eff. May 12, 1982; Stats.2008, c. 67 (A.B.2452), § 2.)*

§ 1197. Subscribing witness; items to be proved

WITNESS MUST PROVE, WHAT. The subscribing witness must prove that the person whose name is subscribed to the instrument as a party is the person described in it, and that such person executed it, and that the witness subscribed his name thereto as a witness. *(Enacted in 1872.)*

§ 1198. Proof of handwriting; when authorized

HANDWRITING MAY BE PROVED, WHEN. The execution of an instrument may be established by proof of the handwriting of the party and of a subscribing witness, if there is one, in the following cases:

1. When the parties and all the subscribing witnesses are dead; or,

2. When the parties and all the subscribing witnesses are non-residents of the State; or,

3. When the place of their residence is unknown to the party desiring the proof, and cannot be ascertained by the exercise of due diligence; or,

4. When the subscribing witness conceals himself, or cannot be found by the officer by the exercise of due diligence in attempting to serve the subpoena or attachment; or,

5. In case of the continued failure or refusal of the witness to testify, for the space of one hour, after his appearance. *(Enacted in 1872.)*

Research References

Miller and Starr California Real Estate § 11:23, Purpose and Effect; Required for Recordation.
Miller and Starr California Real Estate § 11:26, Form and Content of the Certificate of Acknowledgement.

§ 1199. Proof of handwriting; scope

The evidence taken under the preceding section must satisfactorily prove to the officer the following facts:

One. The existence of one or more of the conditions mentioned therein; and,

Two. That the witness testifying knew the person whose name purports to be subscribed to the instrument as a party, and is well acquainted with his signature, and that it is genuine; and,

Three. That the witness testifying personally knew the person who subscribed the instrument as a witness, and is well acquainted with his signature, and that it is genuine; and,

Four. The place of residence of the witness. *(Enacted in 1872. Amended by Code Am.1873–74, c. 612, p. 227, § 141.)*

Research References

Miller and Starr California Real Estate § 11:23, Purpose and Effect; Required for Recordation.
Miller and Starr California Real Estate § 11:26, Form and Content of the Certificate of Acknowledgement.

§ 1200. Proof of execution; certificate; contents

CERTIFICATE OF PROOF. An officer taking proof of the execution of any instrument must, in his certificate indorsed thereon or attached thereto, set forth all the matters required by law to be done or known by him, or proved before him on the proceeding, together with the names of all the witnesses examined before him, their places of residence respectively, and the substance of their testimony. *(Enacted in 1872.)*

§ 1201. Authority of officers taking proof

OFFICERS AUTHORIZED TO DO CERTAIN THINGS. Officers authorized to take the proof of instruments are authorized in such proceedings:

1. To administer oaths or affirmations, as prescribed in Section 2093, Code of Civil Procedure;

2. To employ and swear interpreters;

3. To issue subpoena, as prescribed in Section 1986, Code of Civil Procedure;

4. To punish for contempt, as prescribed in Sections 1991, 1993, 1994, Code of Civil Procedure.

The civil damages and forfeiture to the party aggrieved are prescribed in Section 1992, Code of Civil Procedure. *(Enacted in 1872.)*

§ 1202. Defective certificate; action for correction

When the acknowledgment or proof of the execution of an instrument is properly made, but defectively certified, any party interested may have an action in the superior court to obtain a judgment correcting the certificate. *(Enacted in 1872. Amended by Stats.1905, c. 445, p. 604, § 4.)*

Research References

Miller and Starr California Real Estate § 11:12, Required Form and Contents--Signature of the Property Owner.
Miller and Starr California Real Estate § 11:23, Purpose and Effect; Required for Recordation.
5 Witkin Cal. Proc. 5th Pleading § 806, (S 806) Nature of Action.

§ 1203. Action for judgment proving instrument

Any person interested under an instrument entitled to be proved for record, may institute an action in the superior court against the proper parties to obtain a judgment proving such instrument. *(Enacted in 1872. Amended by Stats.1905, c. 445, p. 604, § 5.)*

Research References

Miller and Starr California Real Estate § 11:12, Required Form and Contents--Signature of the Property Owner.
Miller and Starr California Real Estate § 11:23, Purpose and Effect; Required for Recordation.
5 Witkin Cal. Proc. 5th Pleading § 856, (S 856) Special Kind of Declaratory Relief.

§ 1204. Judgment proving instrument; effect

EFFECT OF JUDGMENT IN SUCH ACTION. A certified copy of the judgment in a proceeding instituted under either of the two preceding sections, showing the proof of the instrument, and attached thereto, entitles such instrument to record, with like effect as if acknowledged. *(Enacted in 1872.)*

Research References

Miller and Starr California Real Estate § 11:23, Purpose and Effect; Required for Recordation.
5 Witkin Cal. Proc. 5th Pleading § 806, (S 806) Nature of Action.

§ 1205. Conveyances prior to code; law governing

CONVEYANCES HERETOFORE MADE TO BE GOVERNED BY THEN EXIST-ING LAWS. The legality of the execution, acknowledgment, proof, form, or record of any conveyance or other instrument made before this Code goes into effect, executed, acknowledged, proved, or recorded is not affected by anything contained in this Chapter, but depends for its validity and legality upon the laws in force when the act was performed. *(Enacted in 1872.)*

§ 1206. Conveyances prior to code; evidence; recording

RECORDING, AND AS EVIDENCE, TO BE GOVERNED BY THEN EXISTING LAWS. All conveyances of real property made before this Code goes into effect, and acknowledged or proved according to the laws in force at the time of such making and acknowledgment or proof, have the same force as evidence, and may be recorded in the same manner and with the like effect, as conveyances executed and acknowledged in pursuance of this Chapter. *(Enacted in 1872.)*

§ 1207. Defectively executed instruments; validity

Any instrument affecting the title to real property, one year after the same has been copied into the proper book of record,

kept in the office of any county recorder, imparts notice of its contents to subsequent purchasers and encumbrancers, notwithstanding any defect, omission, or informality in the execution of the instrument, or in the certificate of acknowledgment thereof, or the absence of any such certificate; but nothing herein affects the rights of purchasers or encumbrancers previous to the taking effect of this act. Duly certified copies of the record of any such instrument may be read in evidence with like effect as copies of an instrument duly acknowledged and recorded; provided, when such copying in the proper book of record occurred within five years prior to the trial of the action, it is first shown that the original instrument was genuine. *(Added by Code Am.1983–74, c. 612, p. 228, § 142. Amended by Stats.1897, c. 74, p. 64, § 1; Stats.1903, c. 97, p. 108, § 1; Stats.1909, c. 54, p. 45, § 1; Stats.1913, c. 71, p. 75, § 1; Stats.1915, c. 626, p. 1211, § 1; Stats.1919, c. 163, p. 244, § 1; Stats.1921, c. 97, p. 94, § 1; Stats.1927, c. 489, p. 828, § 1.)*

Research References

Miller and Starr California Real Estate § 11:8, Evidentiary Effect of Recording.
Miller and Starr California Real Estate § 8:53, Altered Deed.
Miller and Starr California Real Estate § 11:23, Purpose and Effect; Required for Recordation.
Miller and Starr California Real Estate § 11:25, Effect of a Notary's Interest in the Transaction.
Miller and Starr California Real Estate § 11:26, Form and Content of the Certificate of Acknowledgement.
Miller and Starr California Real Estate § 11:60, Recordation as Constructive Notice.
Miller and Starr California Real Estate § 11:70, Defects in the Record Title Enforceable Against a Bona Fide Purchaser--In General.
Miller and Starr California Real Estate § 11:72, Defects in the Record Title Enforceable Against a Bona Fide Purchaser--Alteration of Instrument Before Recording.
Miller and Starr California Real Estate § 13:32, Execution and Acknowledgment.
Miller and Starr California Real Estate § 11:118, Executory and Installment Contracts--In General.
12 Witkin, California Summary 10th Real Property § 284, (S 284) Form of Acknowledgment.

ARTICLE 4. EFFECT OF RECORDING, OR THE WANT THEREOF

§ 1213. Record of conveyances; constructive notice; recording certified copies; effect

Every conveyance of real property or an estate for years therein acknowledged or proved and certified and recorded as prescribed by law from the time it is filed with the recorder for record is constructive notice of the contents thereof to subsequent purchasers and mortgagees; and a certified copy of such a recorded conveyance may be recorded in any other county and when so recorded the record thereof shall have the same force and effect as though it was of the original conveyance and where the original conveyance has been recorded in any county wherein the property therein mentioned is not situated a certified copy of the recorded conveyance may be recorded in the county where such property is situated with the same force and effect as if the original conveyance had been recorded in that county. *(Enacted in 1872. Amended by Stats.1897, c. 68, p. 59, § 1; Stats.1909, c. 179, p. 278, § 1; Stats.1989, c. 698, § 1.)*

Research References

Rutter, Cal. Practice Guide: Real Prop. Transactions Ch. 4-D, D. Selecting the Form of Written Agreement.

Rutter, Cal. Practice Guide: Real Prop. Transactions Ch. 8-B, B. Options to Purchase.

Miller and Starr California Real Estate § 8:1, Definitions and Terminology.

Miller and Starr California Real Estate § 11:1, Rules Governing Priorities; Relation to Notice and Recording.

Miller and Starr California Real Estate § 11:3, Effect of Recording Statutes on Priority.

Miller and Starr California Real Estate § 11:4, Instruments Subject to Recording--Requirements.

Miller and Starr California Real Estate § 11:6, Instruments Subject to Recording--List of Recordable Documents.

Miller and Starr California Real Estate § 19:2, Lease as Personal Property or Real Property.

Miller and Starr California Real Estate § 24:7, Environmental Covenants, Development Agreements, and Other Statutory Agreements that May Run With the Land.

Miller and Starr California Real Estate § 10:16, Property Interests that Are Lienable.

Miller and Starr California Real Estate § 11:16, Place of Recording.

Miller and Starr California Real Estate § 11:22, When Recording is Complete--For Constructive Notice.

Miller and Starr California Real Estate § 11:23, Purpose and Effect; Required for Recordation.

Miller and Starr California Real Estate § 11:60, Recordation as Constructive Notice.

Miller and Starr California Real Estate § 11:64, Recorded Documents that Do Not Give Constructive Notice--Documents Not Affecting Title to Real Property and Not Otherwise Authorized for Recordation.

Miller and Starr California Real Estate § 11:65, Recorded Documents that Do Not Give Constructive Notice--Documents Not Specifically Stated to Impart Constructive Notice by Statute or Which Are Specifically Stated Not to Impart Constructive...

Miller and Starr California Real Estate § 11:66, Recorded Documents that Do Not Give Constructive Notice--Documents Not Affecting Real Property.

Miller and Starr California Real Estate § 11:99, General Rules of Lien Priority.

Miller and Starr California Real Estate § 19:20, Lease as a Contract and Conveyance--Form, Execution, Delivery, and Recordation.

Miller and Starr California Real Estate § 19:61, Requirements for a Valid Assignment.

Miller and Starr California Real Estate § 24:11, Creation--Creation by Recorded Declaration.

Miller and Starr California Real Estate § 28:37, Claim of Lien--Necessity, Purpose, and Effect.

Miller and Starr California Real Estate § 10:152, Court's Authority to Modify Rights of Secured Lender.

Miller and Starr California Real Estate § 11:150, Actions in Which a Lis Pendens May or Must be Recorded.

Miller and Starr California Real Estate § 11:192, Personal Property and Fixtures; General Rules of Priority.

Miller and Starr California Real Estate § 11:194, Priority Between a Deed of Trust and a Security Interest in Fixtures.

19 NO. 6 Miller & Starr, California Real Estate Newsalert 1, Enforceable Resale Restrictions: Keeping the Doors Open for Long-Term Affordable Housing.

19 NO. 5 Miller & Starr, California Real Estate Newsalert 10, Covenants, Conditions, and Restrictions.

20 NO. 4 Miller & Starr, California Real Estate Newsalert 26, Deeds of Trust.

8 Witkin Cal. Proc. 5th Enforcement of Judgment § 70, Abstract of Judgment.

4 Witkin Cal. Proc. 5th Pleading § 481, (S 481) Actual Ignorance.

12 Witkin, California Summary 10th Real Property § 323, (S 323) Necessity of Actual Copying.

4 Witkin, California Summary 10th Security Transactions in Real Property § 49, (S 49) Effect of Recordation.

§ 1214. Prior recording of subsequent conveyances, mortgages, judgments

Every conveyance of real property or an estate for years therein, other than a lease for a term not exceeding one year, is void as against any subsequent purchaser or mortgagee of the same property, or any part thereof, in good faith and for a valuable consideration, whose conveyance is first duly recorded, and as against any judgment affecting the title, unless the conveyance shall have been duly recorded prior to the record of notice of action. *(Enacted in 1872. Amended by Stats.1895, c. 48, p. 50, § 1; Stats.1989, c. 698, § 2.)*

Research References

Rutter, Cal. Practice Guide: Enforcing Judgments/Debts Ch. 6G-5, Assignment Order.

Rutter, Cal. Practice Guide: Real Prop. Transactions Ch. 7-C, C. Representing the Purchasing Tenant.

Rutter, Cal. Practice Guide: Real Prop. Transactions Ch. 8-B, B. Options to Purchase.

Miller and Starr California Real Estate § 8:1, Definitions and Terminology.

Miller and Starr California Real Estate § 11:1, Rules Governing Priorities; Relation to Notice and Recording.

Miller and Starr California Real Estate § 11:2, Enforceability of Unrecorded Instruments.

Miller and Starr California Real Estate § 11:3, Effect of Recording Statutes on Priority.

Miller and Starr California Real Estate § 11:4, Instruments Subject to Recording--Requirements.

Miller and Starr California Real Estate § 11:6, Instruments Subject to Recording--List of Recordable Documents.

Miller and Starr California Real Estate § 19:2, Lease as Personal Property or Real Property.

Miller and Starr California Real Estate § 10:16, Property Interests that Are Lienable.

Miller and Starr California Real Estate § 11:16, Place of Recording.

Miller and Starr California Real Estate § 11:22, When Recording is Complete--For Constructive Notice.

Miller and Starr California Real Estate § 11:35, Transfer of Interest Before Title Recorded; Conveyance After Death of Record Owner.

Miller and Starr California Real Estate § 11:39, Conveyance by Bankrupt or by Trustee in Bankruptcy Whose Credentials Are Unrecorded.

Miller and Starr California Real Estate § 11:50, Definitions; Rules of Priority.

Miller and Starr California Real Estate § 11:59, What Constitutes Actual Notice.

Miller and Starr California Real Estate § 11:60, Recordation as Constructive Notice.

Miller and Starr California Real Estate § 11:64, Recorded Documents that Do Not Give Constructive Notice--Documents Not Affecting Title to Real Property and Not Otherwise Authorized for Recordation.

Miller and Starr California Real Estate § 11:66, Recorded Documents that Do Not Give Constructive Notice--Documents Not Affecting Real Property.

Miller and Starr California Real Estate § 11:90, Possession by a Tenant as Notice of the Tenant's Interest.

Miller and Starr California Real Estate § 11:93, Notice of Rights Acquired by Adverse Possession or Prescription.

Miller and Starr California Real Estate § 15:70, Enforcement of an Easement Against a Bona Fide Purchaser of the Servient Tenement.

Miller and Starr California Real Estate § 19:20, Lease as a Contract and Conveyance--Form, Execution, Delivery, and Recordation.

Miller and Starr California Real Estate § 19:61, Requirements for a Valid Assignment.

Miller and Starr California Real Estate § 10:150, Effect of the Automatic Stay.

Miller and Starr California Real Estate § 11:101, Effect of Foreclosure on Rights of Tenants in Possession.

Miller and Starr California Real Estate § 11:127, Relation to Prior Interests.

Miller and Starr California Real Estate § 11:147, Priority of Judgments and Pending Litigation; in General.

Miller and Starr California Real Estate § 11:148, Nature and Effect of a Lis Pendens.

Miller and Starr California Real Estate § 11:149, Procedural and Formal Requirements for a Lis Pendens.

Miller and Starr California Real Estate § 11:150, Actions in Which a Lis Pendens May or Must be Recorded.

Miller and Starr California Real Estate § 11:151, Effect of Recorded Lis Pendens on Subsequent Interests.

Miller and Starr California Real Estate § 11:152, Effect of Lis Pendens on Prior Interests.

Miller and Starr California Real Estate § 11:192, Personal Property and Fixtures; General Rules of Priority.

19 NO. 2 Miller & Starr, California Real Estate Newsalert 22, Recording and Priorities.

22 NO. 3 Miller & Starr, California Real Estate Newsalert 1, Show Me Your Papers: Sales and Assignments of Secured Real Estate Loans and the California Foreclosure Process.

8 Witkin Cal. Proc. 5th Enforcement of Judgment § 306, (S 306) Effect of Assignment.

12 Witkin, California Summary 10th Real Property § 327, (S 327) Rule of Prior Recordation.

12 Witkin, California Summary 10th Real Property § 328, What Constitutes Bona Fide Purchase.

12 Witkin, California Summary 10th Real Property § 329, Bona Fide Encumbrancer.

12 Witkin, California Summary 10th Real Property § 333, (S 333) Judgment Creditor in Action Affecting Title.

4 Witkin, California Summary 10th Security Transactions in Real Property § 49, (S 49) Effect of Recordation.

13 Witkin, California Summary 10th Trusts § 251, Title.

§ 1215. Conveyance defined

CONVEYANCE DEFINED. The term "conveyance," as used in Sections 1213 and 1214, embraces every instrument in writing by which any estate or interest in real property is created, aliened, mortgaged, or incumbered, or by which the title to any real property may be affected, except wills. *(Enacted in 1872.)*

Research References

Rutter, Cal. Practice Guide: Real Prop. Transactions Ch. 4-A, A. Property to be Sold.

Rutter, Cal. Practice Guide: Real Prop. Transactions Ch. 8-B, B. Options to Purchase.

Miller and Starr California Real Estate § 8:1, Definitions and Terminology.

Miller and Starr California Real Estate § 10:7, Execution and Delivery.

Miller and Starr California Real Estate § 11:1, Rules Governing Priorities; Relation to Notice and Recording.

Miller and Starr California Real Estate § 11:4, Instruments Subject to Recording--Requirements.

Miller and Starr California Real Estate § 11:6, Instruments Subject to Recording--List of Recordable Documents.

Miller and Starr California Real Estate § 11:23, Purpose and Effect; Required for Recordation.

Miller and Starr California Real Estate § 11:60, Recordation as Constructive Notice.

Miller and Starr California Real Estate § 11:64, Recorded Documents that Do Not Give Constructive Notice--Documents Not Affecting Title to Real Property and Not Otherwise Authorized for Recordation.

Miller and Starr California Real Estate § 11:65. Recorded Documents that Do Not Give Constructive Notice--Documents Not Specifically Stated to Impart Constructive Notice by Statute or Which Are Specifically Stated Not to Impart Constructive...

Miller and Starr California Real Estate § 11:93, Notice of Rights Acquired by Adverse Possession or Prescription.

Miller and Starr California Real Estate § 11:99, General Rules of Lien Priority.

Miller and Starr California Real Estate § 24:11, Creation--Creation by Recorded Declaration.

Miller and Starr California Real Estate § 28:37, Claim of Lien--Necessity, Purpose, and Effect.

Miller and Starr California Real Estate § 10:152, Court's Authority to Modify Rights of Secured Lender.

Miller and Starr California Real Estate § 11:192, Personal Property and Fixtures; General Rules of Priority.

Miller and Starr California Real Estate § 11:194, Priority Between a Deed of Trust and a Security Interest in Fixtures.

15 NO. 1 Miller & Starr, California Real Estate Newsalert 2, Recording and Priorities.

19 NO. 6 Miller & Starr, California Real Estate Newsalert 1, Enforceable Resale Restrictions: Keeping the Doors Open for Long-Term Affordable Housing.

22 NO. 3 Miller & Starr, California Real Estate Newsalert 1, Show Me Your Papers: Sales and Assignments of Secured Real Estate Loans and the California Foreclosure Process.

12 Witkin, California Summary 10th Real Property § 329, Bona Fide Encumbrancer.

§ 1216. Power of attorney, revocation

No power contained in an instrument to convey or execute instruments affecting real property which has been recorded is revoked by any act of the party by whom it was executed, unless the instrument containing such revocation is also acknowledged or proved, certified and recorded, in the same office in which the instrument containing the power was recorded. *(Enacted in 1872. Amended by Stats.1970, c. 323, p. 717, § 1.)*

Research References

Rutter, Cal. Practice Guide: Real Prop. Transactions Ch. 4-C, C. Parties to the Purchase Agreement.

Miller and Starr California Real Estate § 1:91, Nonstatutory Form of Agent's Written Authority.

Miller and Starr California Real Estate § 1:92, Statutory Provisions for Powers of Attorney.

Miller and Starr California Real Estate § 10:7, Execution and Delivery.

Miller and Starr California Real Estate § 11:2, Enforceability of Unrecorded Instruments.

Miller and Starr California Real Estate § 11:6, Instruments Subject to Recording--List of Recordable Documents.

Miller and Starr California Real Estate § 8:30, Execution by an Agent or Attorney-In-Fact.

Miller and Starr California Real Estate § 8:31, Scope of Agent's Authority; Power of Attorney.

Miller and Starr California Real Estate § 11:23, Purpose and Effect; Required for Recordation.

3 Witkin, California Summary 10th Agency and Employment § 215, (S 215) Revocation, Death, or Incapacity of Principal.

3 Witkin, California Summary 10th Agency and Employment § 216, (S 216) Methods of Giving Notice.

14 Witkin, California Summary 10th Wills and Probate § 835, (S 835) Nature and Scope of Instrument.

§ 1217. Unrecorded instrument; validity between parties

UNRECORDED INSTRUMENT VALID BETWEEN THE PARTIES. An unrecorded instrument is valid as between the parties thereto and those who have notice thereof. *(Enacted in 1872.)*

Research References

Rutter, Cal. Practice Guide: Real Prop. Transactions Ch. 6-H, H. Security for Promissory Note.

Miller and Starr California Real Estate § 10:7, Execution and Delivery.

Miller and Starr California Real Estate § 11:1, Rules Governing Priorities; Relation to Notice and Recording.

Miller and Starr California Real Estate § 11:2, Enforceability of Unrecorded Instruments.

Miller and Starr California Real Estate § 11:50, Definitions; Rules of Priority.

Miller and Starr California Real Estate § 11:59, What Constitutes Actual Notice.

Miller and Starr California Real Estate § 19:20, Lease as a Contract and Conveyance--Form, Execution, Delivery, and Recordation.

Miller and Starr California Real Estate § 11:184, Priority of Federal Tax Liens--Relation to Liens of Deeds of Trust and Mortgages.

16 NO. 3 Miller & Starr, California Real Estate Newsalert 13, Recording and Priorities.

20 NO. 5 Miller & Starr, California Real Estate Newsalert 20, Mechanics' Liens.

22 NO. 3 Miller & Starr, California Real Estate Newsalert 1, Show Me Your Papers: Sales and Assignments of Secured Real Estate Loans and the California Foreclosure Process.

12 Witkin, California Summary 10th Real Property § 254, (S 254) Requisites of Deed.

12 Witkin, California Summary 10th Real Property § 327, (S 327) Rule of Prior Recordation.

§ 1218. Recording certified copies of instrument or certified copy of record; effect

A certified copy of an instrument affecting the title to real property, once recorded, or a certified copy of the record of such instrument may be recorded in any other county, and, when so recorded, the record thereof has the same force and effect as though it was of the original instrument. *(Added by Stats.1905, c. 446, p. 604, § 1. Amended by Stats.1913, c. 191, p. 335, § 1.)*

Research References

Rutter, Cal. Practice Guide: Real Prop. Transactions Ch. 12-A, A. General Considerations.

Miller and Starr California Real Estate § 11:16, Place of Recording.

§ 1219. Oil and gas leases; manner of recording and giving constructive notice; fictitious oil and gas leases

Oil and gas leases may be acknowledged or proved, certified and recorded in like manner and with like effect, as grants of real property. However, an oil and gas lease may be recorded and constructive notice of the same and the contents of that lease given in the following manner:

Any person may record in the office of county recorder of any county fictitious oil and gas leases. Those fictitious oil and gas leases need not be acknowledged, or proved, or certified, to be recorded or entitled to record. Oil and gas leases shall have noted upon the face thereof that they are fictitious. The county recorder shall index and record fictitious oil and gas leases in the same manner as other oil and gas leases are recorded, and shall note on all indices and records of the same that they are fictitious. Thereafter, any of the provisions of any recorded fictitious oil and gas lease may be included for any and all purposes in any oil and gas lease by reference therein to those provisions, without setting the same forth in full, if the fictitious oil and gas lease is of record in the county in which the oil and gas lease adopting or including by reference any of the provisions of the lease is recorded. The reference shall contain a statement, as to each county in which the oil and gas lease containing such a reference is recorded, of the date the fictitious oil and gas lease was recorded, the county recorder's office in which it is recorded, and the book or volume and the first page of the records or the recorder's instrument number in the recorder's office in which the fictitious oil and gas lease was recorded, and a statement by paragraph numbers or any other method that will definitely identify the same, of the specific provisions of any fictitious oil and gas lease that are being adopted and included therein. The recording of any oil and gas lease which has included any provisions by reference shall operate as constructive notice of the whole including the terms, as a part of the written contents of any oil and gas lease, of any provisions so included by reference as though the same were written in full therein. The parties bound or to be bound by provisions so adopted and included by reference shall be bound thereby in the same manner and with like effect for all purposes as though the provisions had been and were set forth in full in the oil and gas lease. *(Added by Stats.1955, c. 1541, p. 2824, § 1. Amended by Stats.2009, c. 54 (S.B.544), § 4.)*

Research References

Miller and Starr California Real Estate § 11:6, Instruments Subject to Recording--List of Recordable Documents.

Miller and Starr California Real Estate § 15:1, Easement Defined; Profits Distinguished.

Miller and Starr California Real Estate § 11:12, Required Form and Contents--Signature of the Property Owner.

Miller and Starr California Real Estate § 17:21, Minerals--In General.

Miller and Starr California Real Estate § 17:23, Minerals--Oil and Gas.

Miller and Starr California Real Estate § 17:24, Minerals--Oil and Gas Leases.

12 Witkin, California Summary 10th Real Property § 283, Nature of Requirement.

12 Witkin, California Summary 10th Real Property § 794, (S 794) Special Problems.

§ 1220. Standing timber or trees; recordation of instruments

Contracts for the purchase or sale of standing timber or trees, for severance or otherwise, and all instruments in writing by which any estate or interest in, or right to cut, standing timber or trees is created, aliened, mortgaged or encumbered or by which the title to any standing timber or trees may be affected, may be acknowledged or proved, certified and recorded in like manner and with like effect, as grants of real property, and all statutory provisions relating to the recordation or nonrecordation of conveyances of real property and to the effect thereof shall apply to such contracts and instruments with like effect.

Any such contracts for purchase and sale or instruments in writing affecting the title to standing timber or trees, executed and delivered before the effective date of the amendment of this section at the 1959 Regular Session of the Legislature but unrecorded before such date, shall become subject to all statutory provisions relating to the recordation or nonrecordation of conveyances of real property and to the effect thereof one year from said effective date. *(Added by Stats.1957, c. 1937, p. 3467, § 1. Amended by Stats.1959, c. 1795, p. 4276, § 1.)*

Research References

Miller and Starr California Real Estate § 11:3, Effect of Recording Statutes on Priority.

Miller and Starr California Real Estate § 11:6, Instruments Subject to Recording--List of Recordable Documents.

Miller and Starr California Real Estate § 11:66, Recorded Documents that Do Not Give Constructive Notice--Documents Not Affecting Real Property.

Miller and Starr California Real Estate § 17:31, Timber.

Miller and Starr California Real Estate § 11:199, Priority Between Deeds of Trust and Security Interests in Timber.

12 Witkin, California Summary 10th Real Property § 318, (S 318) Unusual Instruments.

CHAPTER 5. UNLAWFUL TRANSFERS

Section

1227. Instruments made with intent to defraud; invalidity as to bona fide purchasers or incumbrancers.

1228. Instruments made with intent to defraud; subsequent purchasers or incumbrancers with notice, effect.

1229. Power to revoke; execution by subsequent grant or charge.

1230. Power to revoke; when deemed executed.

1231. Other provisions concerning unlawful transfers.

§ 1227. Instruments made with intent to defraud; invalidity as to bona fide purchasers or incumbrancers

CERTAIN INSTRUMENTS VOID AGAINST PURCHASERS, ETC. Every instrument, other than a will, affecting an estate in real property, including every charge upon real property, or upon its rents or profits, made with intent to defraud prior or subsequent purchasers thereof, or incumbrancers thereon, is void as against every purchaser or incumbrancer, for value, of the same property, or the rents or profits thereof. *(Enacted in 1872.)*

Research References

Miller and Starr California Real Estate § 10:7, Execution and Delivery.
Miller and Starr California Real Estate § 8:54, Fraud.
Miller and Starr California Real Estate § 11:73, Defects in the Record Title Enforceable Against a Bona Fide Purchaser--Fraud on Obtaining an Instrument.
Miller and Starr California Real Estate § 11:99, General Rules of Lien Priority.
Miller and Starr California Real Estate § 11:124, Relation to Prior Interests.
Miller and Starr California Real Estate § 11:127, Relation to Prior Interests.
Miller and Starr California Real Estate § 1:58.10, Sufficiency of Consideration Under Uniform Fraudulent Conveyance Act.
8 Witkin Cal. Proc. 5th Enforcement of Judgment § 506, (S 506) Unlawful Transfers of Real Property.

§ 1228. Instruments made with intent to defraud; subsequent purchasers or incumbrancers with notice, effect

NOT VOID AGAINST PURCHASER HAVING NOTICE, UNLESS FRAUD IS MUTUAL. No instrument is to be avoided under the last section, in favor of a subsequent purchaser or incumbrancer having notice thereof at the time his purchase was made, or his lien acquired, unless the person in whose favor the instrument was made was privy to the fraud intended. *(Enacted in 1872.)*

Research References

Miller and Starr California Real Estate § 10:7, Execution and Delivery.
Miller and Starr California Real Estate § 8:54, Fraud.
Miller and Starr California Real Estate § 11:73, Defects in the Record Title Enforceable Against a Bona Fide Purchaser--Fraud on Obtaining an Instrument.
Miller and Starr California Real Estate § 11:99, General Rules of Lien Priority.
8 Witkin Cal. Proc. 5th Enforcement of Judgment § 506, (S 506) Unlawful Transfers of Real Property.

§ 1229. Power to revoke; execution by subsequent grant or charge

POWER TO REVOKE, WHEN DEEMED EXECUTED. Where a power to revoke or modify an instrument affecting the title to, or the enjoyment of, an estate in real property, is reserved to the grantor, or given to any other person, a subsequent grant of, or charge upon, the estate, by the person having the power of revocation, in favor of a purchaser or incumbrancer for value, operates as a revocation of the original instrument, to the extent of the power, in favor of such purchaser or incumbrancer. *(Enacted in 1872.)*

Research References

Miller and Starr California Real Estate § 9:10, Expiration of the Power of Termination--In General.
8 Witkin Cal. Proc. 5th Enforcement of Judgment § 506, (S 506) Unlawful Transfers of Real Property.
12 Witkin, California Summary 10th Real Property § 146, (S 146) Statutory Development.

§ 1230. Power to revoke; when deemed executed

SAME. Where a person having a power of revocation, within the provisions of the last section, is not entitled to execute it until after the time at which he makes such a grant or charge as is described in that section, the power is deemed to be executed as soon as he is entitled to execute it. *(Enacted in 1872.)*

Research References

Miller and Starr California Real Estate § 9:8, Fee Simple Defeasible-- Power of Termination (Right of Re-Entry); Enforcement.

8 Witkin Cal. Proc. 5th Enforcement of Judgment § 506, (S 506) Unlawful Transfers of Real Property.

§ 1231. Other provisions concerning unlawful transfers

OTHER PROVISIONS. Other provisions concerning unlawful transfers are contained in Part II, Division Fourth, of this Code,[1] concerning the Special Relations of Debtor and Creditor. *(Enacted in 1872.)*

[1] Section 3429 et seq.

Research References

Miller and Starr California Real Estate § 1:58.10, Sufficiency of Consideration Under Uniform Fraudulent Conveyance Act.

Title 8

WATER RIGHTS

Section
1410a.   Waters flowing out of state; use.
1414.   Appropriation of waters; priority.
1415.   Appropriation of waters; notice; contents; posting; recordation.
1416.   Appropriation of waters; construction of works; dams; county or municipal works.
1417.   Appropriation of waters; completion defined.
1418.   Appropriation of waters; right of use, relation back to time of notice.
1419.   Appropriation of waters; forfeiture.
1420.   Appropriation of waters; rights of existing claimants.
1421.   Book for recording notices.
1422.   Appropriation of waters; time to commence works on public reservations.

§ 1410a. Waters flowing out of state; use

The entire flow of water in any natural stream which carries water from the State of California into any other state is subject to use in the State of California, under the laws of the State of California, and the right may be, so far as not already acquired by use in the State of California, acquired and held under the laws of the State of California. The rights to the use of such water held under the laws of the State of California, shall be prior and superior to any rights to the waters of such streams held under the laws of any other state. *(Added by Stats.1913, c. 88, p. 93, § 1.)*

Research References

Miller and Starr California Real Estate § 17:26, Water Rights--Regulation of Water Rights.

§ 1414. Appropriation of waters; priority

FIRST IN TIME, FIRST IN RIGHT. As between appropriators, the one first in time is the first in right. *(Enacted in 1872.)*

Research References

Miller and Starr California Real Estate § 17:25, Water Rights.
Miller and Starr California Real Estate § 17:27, Water Rights--Priority of Water Rights.

§ 1415. Appropriation of waters; notice; contents; posting; recordation

A person desiring to appropriate water must post a notice, in writing, in a conspicuous place at the point of intended diversion, stating therein:

1.   That he claims the water there flowing to the extent of (giving the number) inches, measured under a four-inch pressure;

2. The purposes for which he claims it, and the place of intended use;

3. The means by which he intends to divert it, and the size of the flume, ditch, pipe, or aqueduct in which he intends to divert it.

A copy of the notice must, within ten days after it is posted, be recorded in the office of the recorder of the county in which it is posted. After filing such copy for record, the place of intended diversion or the place of intended use or the means by which it is intended to divert the water, may be changed by the person posting said notice or his assigns, if others are not injured by such change. This provision applies to notices already filed as well as to notices hereafter filed. *(Enacted in 1872. Amended by Stats.1903, c. 262, p. 361, § 1.)*

Research References

Miller and Starr California Real Estate § 17:25, Water Rights.

§ 1416. Appropriation of waters; construction of works; dams; county or municipal works

Within sixty days after the notice is posted, the claimant must commence the excavation or construction of the works in which he intends to divert the water, or the survey, road or trail building, necessarily incident thereto, and must prosecute the work diligently and uninterruptedly to completion, unless temporarily interrupted by snows or rain; provided, that if the erection of a dam has been recommended by the California débris [1] commission at or near the place where it is intended to divert the water, the claimant shall have sixty days after the completion of such dam in which to commence the excavation or construction of the works in which he intends to divert the water; provided, that whenever any city and county, or any incorporated city or town within this state makes, or has made, or acquires, or has acquired any appropriation of any of the waters of this state in accordance with the provisions of section 1415 of this code, it shall not be necessary for such city and county, city or town to commence the work for development of more of the water so claimed than is actually necessary for the immediate needs of such city and county, city or town and it shall be held to be a sufficient compliance with the requirements of this chapter, to the full amount of water stated in the notice posted and recorded, for such city and county, city or town to within sixty days make the necessary surveys, or within six months to authorize the issuance of municipal bonds, for the construction of the necessary works designed to supply such city and county, city or town with the water required for immediate use. Any appropriation heretofore made by any such city and county, city or town in connection with which surveys were at any time made, or an issue of bonds authorized for the construction of any portion of the works necessary for a diversion of any part of the water appropriated, is hereby confirmed to the full amount of water stated in the original notice or notices. *(Enacted in 1872. Amended by Stats.1895, c. 74, p. 70, § 1; Stats.1903, c. 272, p. 396, § 1; Stats.1907, c. 429, p. 780, § 1; Stats.1911, c. 730, p. 1419, § 1.)*

[1] So in chaptered bill.

Research References

Miller and Starr California Real Estate § 17:25, Water Rights.

§ 1417. Appropriation of waters; completion defined

COMPLETION DEFINED. By "completion" is meant conducting the waters to the place of intended use. *(Enacted in 1872.)*

Research References

Miller and Starr California Real Estate § 17:25, Water Rights.

§ 1418. Appropriation of waters; right of use, relation back to time of notice

DOCTRINE OF RELATION APPLIED. By a compliance with the above rules the claimant's right to the use of the water relates back to the time the notice was posted. *(Enacted in 1872.)*

Research References

Miller and Starr California Real Estate § 17:25, Water Rights.

§ 1419. Appropriation of waters; forfeiture

FORFEITURE. A failure to comply with such rules deprives the claimants of the right to the use of the water as against a subsequent claimant who complies therewith. *(Enacted in 1872.)*

Research References

Miller and Starr California Real Estate § 17:25, Water Rights.

§ 1420. Appropriation of waters; rights of existing claimants

RIGHTS OF PRESENT CLAIMANT. Persons who have heretofore claimed the right to water, and who have not constructed works in which to divert it, and who have not diverted nor applied it to some useful purpose, must, after this Title takes effect, and within twenty days thereafter, proceed as in this Title provided, or their right ceases. *(Enacted in 1872.)*

§ 1421. Book for recording notices

RECORDER TO KEEP BOOK IN WHICH TO RECORD NOTICES. The Recorder of each county must keep a book, in which he must record the notices provided for in this Title. *(Enacted in 1872.)*

Research References

Miller and Starr California Real Estate § 17:25, Water Rights.

§ 1422. Appropriation of waters; time to commence works on public reservations

If the place of intended diversion or any part of the route of intended conveyance of water so claimed, be within, and a part of, any national park, forest reservation, or other public reservation, and be so shown in the notice of appropriation of said water, then the claimant shall have sixty days, after the grant of authority to occupy and use such park or reservation for such intended purpose, within which to commence the excavation or construction of said works; provided that within sixty days after the posting of said notice of appropriation, as provided in section 1415 of the Civil Code, the claimant shall in good faith commence (and thereafter diligently and continuously, except when temporarily interrupted by snow or rain, prosecute to completion) such surveys and other work as under the regulations governing such park or reservations, may be required as preliminary to, or for use with, an application for such authority; and provided also that the claimant shall in good faith on completion of said survey and preliminary work, apply to the officer, board, or body, having charge of such park or reservation, for such authority, and shall thereafter, prosecute said application with reasonable diligence. *(Added by Stats.1903, c. 272, p. 397, § 2.)*

Research References

Miller and Starr California Real Estate § 17:25, Water Rights.

Division 3

OBLIGATIONS

Part 1

OBLIGATIONS IN GENERAL

Title 1

DEFINITION OF OBLIGATIONS

§ 1427. Obligation defined

OBLIGATION, WHAT. An obligation is a legal duty, by which a person is bound to do or not to do a certain thing. *(Enacted in 1872.)*

Research References

Miller and Starr California Real Estate § 1:1, Nature of Real Estate Contracts.
22 NO. 3 Miller & Starr, California Real Estate Newsalert 1, Show Me Your Papers: Sales and Assignments of Secured Real Estate Loans and the California Foreclosure Process.
1 Witkin Cal. Summ. 10th Contracts § 1, Contract.

§ 1428. Creation and enforcement

An obligation arises either from:

One—The contract of the parties; or,

Two—The operation of law. An obligation arising from operation of law may be enforced in the manner provided by law, or by civil action or proceeding. *(Enacted in 1872. Amended by Code Am.1873–74, c. 612, p. 239, § 181½.)*

Research References

Miller and Starr California Real Estate § 1:1, Nature of Real Estate Contracts.
22 NO. 3 Miller & Starr, California Real Estate Newsalert 1, Show Me Your Papers: Sales and Assignments of Secured Real Estate Loans and the California Foreclosure Process.
3 Witkin Cal. Proc. 5th Actions § 3, Statutory Declarations.
3 Witkin Cal. Proc. 5th Actions § 4, Obligation May be Enforced.
3 Witkin Cal. Proc. 5th Actions § 5, Remedy for Every Wrong.
1 Witkin Cal. Summ. 10th Contracts § 1, Contract.

Title 2

INTERPRETATION OF OBLIGATIONS

CHAPTER 1. GENERAL RULES OF INTERPRETATION

§ 1429. General rules of interpretation

GENERAL RULES. The rules which govern the interpretation of contracts are prescribed by Part II of this Division.[1] Other obligations are interpreted by the same rules by which statutes of a similar nature are interpreted. *(Enacted in 1872.)*

[1] Section 1549 et seq.

Research References

Miller and Starr California Real Estate § 1:112, Accord and Satisfaction-- Acceptance of Satisfaction by a Creditor.

CHAPTER 2. JOINT OR SEVERAL OBLIGATIONS

§ 1430. Classification of obligations

OBLIGATIONS, JOINT OR SEVERAL, ETC. An obligation imposed upon several persons, or a right created in favor of several persons, may be:

1. Joint;

2. Several; or,

3. Joint and several. *(Enacted in 1872.)*

Research References

1 Witkin Cal. Summ. 10th Contracts § 108, (S 108) in General.
1 Witkin Cal. Summ. 10th Contracts § 114, (S 114) Joint and Several Rights.

§ 1431. Joint liability

An obligation imposed upon several persons, or a right created in favor of several persons, is presumed to be joint, and not several, except as provided in Section 1431.2, and except in the special cases mentioned in the title on the interpretation of contracts. This presumption, in the case of a right, can be overcome only by express words to the contrary. *(Enacted in 1872. Amended by § 2 of Initiative Measure, approved by the People, June 3, 1986.)*

Research References

California Real Estate Forms (Miller & Starr) § 3:37, Continuing Guaranty.

California Real Estate Forms (Miller & Starr) § 3:38, Completion Guaranty.

Rutter, Cal. Practice Guide: Civ. Pro. Before Trial Ch. 1-B, B. Prelawsuit Investigations, Research and Analysis.

Rutter, Cal. Practice Guide: Personal Injury Ch. 1-A, A. Initial Client Interview.

Rutter, Cal. Practice Guide: Real Prop. Transactions Ch. 4-E, E. Drafting the Purchase and Sale Agreement-Terms and Conditions.

Miller and Starr California Real Estate § 22:56, Negligence of an Independent Contractor; Overview; History.

Miller and Starr California Real Estate § 29:77, Shared Liability When Wrongdoer is Insolvent or Otherwise Unavailable.

3 Witkin Cal. Proc. 5th Actions § 177, Contributing Tortfeasors and Respondeat Superior.

12 Witkin, California Summary 10th Real Property § 106, Property Damage.

1 Witkin Cal. Summ. 10th Contracts § 108, (S 108) in General.

1 Witkin Cal. Summ. 10th Contracts § 114, (S 114) Joint and Several Rights.

5 Witkin, California Summary 10th Torts § 52, (S 52) Nature, Purpose, and Validity.

5 Witkin, California Summary 10th Torts § 57, Between Tortfeasors Subject and Not Subject to Liability.

5 Witkin, California Summary 10th Torts § 235, Periodic Payment of Judgment.

§ 1431.1. Findings and declaration of purpose

The People of the State of California find and declare as follows:

a) The legal doctrine of joint and several liability, also known as "the deep pocket rule", has resulted in a system of inequity and injustice that has threatened financial bankruptcy of local governments, other public agencies, private individuals and businesses and has resulted in higher prices for goods and services to the public and in higher taxes to the taxpayers.

b) Some governmental and private defendants are perceived to have substantial financial resources or insurance coverage and have thus been included in lawsuits even though there was little or no basis for finding them at fault. Under joint and several liability, if they are found to share even a fraction of the fault, they often are held financially liable for all the damage. The People—taxpayers and consumers alike—ultimately pay for these lawsuits in the form of higher taxes, higher prices and higher insurance premiums.

c) Local governments have been forced to curtail some essential police, fire and other protections because of the soaring costs of lawsuits and insurance premiums.

Therefore, the People of the State of California declare that to remedy these inequities, defendants in tort actions shall be held financially liable in closer proportion to their degree of fault. To treat them differently is unfair and inequitable.

The People of the State of California further declare that reforms in the liability laws in tort actions are necessary and proper to avoid catastrophic economic consequences for state and local governmental bodies as well as private individuals and businesses. *(Added by § 3 of Initiative Measure, approved by the People, June 3, 1986.)*

Research References

Rutter, Cal. Practice Guide: Civ. Pro. Before Trial Ch. 12(II)-E, E. Motion to Determine "Good Faith" of "Piecemeal" Settlement (CCP § 877.6).

Rutter, Cal. Practice Guide: Insurance Litigation Ch. 12B-B, B. Bad Faith Refusal to Settle.

7 Witkin Cal. Proc. 5th Judgment § 41, Noneconomic Damages.

5 Witkin, California Summary 10th Torts § 52, (S 52) Nature, Purpose, and Validity.

§ 1431.2. Several liability for non-economic damages

(a) In any action for personal injury, property damage, or wrongful death, based upon principles of comparative fault, the liability of each defendant for non-economic damages shall be several only and shall not be joint. Each defendant shall be liable only for the amount of non-economic damages allocated to that defendant in direct proportion to that defendant's percentage of fault, and a separate judgment shall be rendered against that defendant for that amount.

(b)(1) For purposes of this section, the term "economic damages" means objectively verifiable monetary losses including medical expenses, loss of earnings, burial costs, loss of use of property, costs of repair or replacement, costs of obtaining substitute domestic services, loss of employment and loss of business or employment opportunities.

(2) For the purposes of this section, the term "non-economic damages" means subjective, non-monetary losses including, but not limited to, pain, suffering, inconvenience, mental suffering, emotional distress, loss of society and companionship, loss of consortium, injury to reputation and humiliation. *(Added by § 4 of Initiative Measure, approved by the People, June 3, 1986.)*

Research References

Rutter, Cal. Practice Guide: Civil Appeals & Writs Ch. 8-C, C. Standards of Appellate Review.

Rutter, Cal. Practice Guide: Civ. Pro. Before Trial Ch. 1-B, B. Prelawsuit Investigations, Research and Analysis.

Rutter, Cal. Practice Guide: Civ. Pro. Before Trial Ch. 12(II)-E, E. Motion to Determine "Good Faith" of "Piecemeal" Settlement (CCP § 877.6).

Rutter, Cal. Practice Guide: Civil Trials & Evidence Ch. 13-B, B. Proper vs. Improper Closing Argument.

Rutter, Cal. Practice Guide: Civil Trials & Evidence Ch. 13-D, D. Preparing for Closing Argument.

Rutter, Cal. Practice Guide: Civil Trials & Evidence Ch. 17-A, A. Verdicts.

Rutter, Cal. Practice Guide: Civil Trials & Evidence Ch. 17-C, C. Entry of Judgment.

Rutter, Cal. Practice Guide: Civil Trials & Evidence Ch. 17-D, D. Costs.

Rutter, Cal. Practice Guide: Insurance Litigation Ch. 8-B, B. Contribution Between Insurers.

Rutter, Cal. Practice Guide: Personal Injury Ch. 1-A, A. Initial Client Interview.

Rutter, Cal. Practice Guide: Personal Injury Ch. 1-B, B. Initial Evaluation of Case: Decision to Accept or Reject Employment or Undertake Further Evaluation of Claim.

Rutter, Cal. Practice Guide: Personal Injury Ch. 1-D, D. General Concerns and Advice to Client Upon Accepting Employment; Execution of Necessary Authorizations.

Rutter, Cal. Practice Guide: Personal Injury Ch. 3-A, A. Introduction.

Rutter, Cal. Practice Guide: Personal Injury Ch. 3-B, B. Potential Claimants in a Personal Injury Case.

Rutter, Cal. Practice Guide: Personal Injury Ch. 3-C, C. Specific Items of Compensatory Damages.

Rutter, Cal. Practice Guide: Personal Injury Ch. 3-D, D. Mitigating Factors in Reduction of Damages.

Rutter, Cal. Practice Guide: Personal Injury Ch. 3-F, F. MICRA Provisions Affecting Damages.

Rutter, Cal. Practice Guide: Personal Injury Ch. 3-G, G. Independent Damages Claims.

Rutter, Cal. Practice Guide: Personal Injury Ch. 4-A, A. General Considerations.

Rutter, Cal. Practice Guide: Personal Injury Ch. 4-B, B. Determining Settlement Value.

Rutter, Cal. Practice Guide: Personal Injury Ch. 4-D, D. Techniques Where Settlement Not Forthcoming.

Rutter, Cal. Practice Guide: Personal Injury Ch. 5-C, C. Selected Issues Affecting Parties.

Rutter, Cal. Practice Guide: Personal Injury Ch. 5-E, E. Selected Pleading Issues.

Rutter, Cal. Practice Guide: Personal Injury Ch. 6-A, A. Scope of Discovery and Limitations.

Rutter, Cal. Practice Guide: Personal Injury Ch. 8-B, B. After Trial Date Set (Three to Four Months Before Trial).

Rutter, Cal. Practice Guide: Personal Injury Ch. 9-M, M. Verdicts and Judgment.

Rutter, Cal. Practice Guide: Personal Injury Ch. 10-A, A. Motion for New Trial.

Rutter, Cal. Practice Guide: Prof. Responsibility Ch. 6-D, D. Professional Liability.

Miller and Starr California Real Estate § 22:56, Negligence of an Independent Contractor; Overview; History.

Miller and Starr California Real Estate § 29:10, Measure of Owner's Damages for Defective Construction.

Miller and Starr California Real Estate § 29:30, Measure of Damages Applicable to Developers.

19 NO. 6 Miller & Starr, California Real Estate Newsalert 16, Landowners' Liability.

21 NO. 1 Miller & Starr, California Real Estate Newsalert 19, Landowners' Liability.

3 Witkin Cal. Proc. 5th Actions § 177, Contributing Tortfeasors and Respondeat Superior.

7 Witkin Cal. Proc. 5th Judgment § 41, Noneconomic Damages.

6 Witkin Cal. Proc. 5th Proceedings Without Trial § 88, Offer by Multiple Defendants.

11 Witkin, California Summary 10th Community Property § 43, (S 43) Spouse's Negligence as Concurring Cause.

11 Witkin, California Summary 10th Community Property § 186, Interspousal Injuries.

5 Witkin, California Summary 10th Torts § 52, (S 52) Nature, Purpose, and Validity.

5 Witkin, California Summary 10th Torts § 53, (S 53) Several Liability for Noneconomic Damages.

5 Witkin, California Summary 10th Torts § 54, Basic Rule.

5 Witkin, California Summary 10th Torts § 56, Between Original and Successive Tortfeasors.

5 Witkin, California Summary 10th Torts § 57, Between Tortfeasors Subject and Not Subject to Liability.

5 Witkin, California Summary 10th Torts § 58, Between Settling and Nonsettling Tortfeasors.

5 Witkin, California Summary 10th Torts § 61, in General.

5 Witkin, California Summary 10th Torts § 62, Claims Involving Both Negligent and Intentional Torts.

5 Witkin, California Summary 10th Torts § 82, Condition that Settling Tortfeasor Participate in Trial.

5 Witkin, California Summary 10th Torts § 99, Noneconomic Damages Under Proposition 51.

6 Witkin, California Summary 10th Torts § 1720, Market Value.

9 Witkin, California Summary 10th Partnership § 9, (S 9) Nature and Distinctions.

§ 1431.3.　Law of immunity

Nothing contained in this measure is intended, in any way, to alter the law of immunity. *(Added by § 5 of Initiative Measure, approved by the People, June 3, 1986.)*

Research References

5 Witkin, California Summary 10th Torts § 52, (S 52) Nature, Purpose, and Validity.

§ 1431.4.　Amendment or repeal of measure

This measure may be amended or repealed by either of the procedures set forth in this section. If any portion of subsection (a) is declared invalid, then subsection (b) shall be the exclusive means of amending or repealing this measure.

(a) This measure may be amended to further its purposes by statute, passed in each house by rollcall vote entered in the journal, two-thirds of the membership concurring and signed by the Governor, if at least 20 days prior to passage in each house the bill in its final form has been delivered to the Secretary of State for distribution to the news media.

(b) This measure may be amended or repealed by a statute that becomes effective only when approved by the electors.

(Added by § 6 of Initiative Measure, approved by the People, June 3, 1986.)

Research References

7 Witkin Cal. Proc. 5th Judgment § 41, Noneconomic Damages.

5 Witkin, California Summary 10th Torts § 52, (S 52) Nature, Purpose, and Validity.

§ 1431.5.　Severability

If any provision of this measure, or the application of any such provision to any person or circumstances, shall be held invalid, the remainder of this measure to the extent it can be given effect, or the application of such provision to persons or circumstances other than those as to which it is held invalid, shall not be affected thereby, and to this end the provisions of this measure are severable. *(Added by § 7 of Initiative Measure, approved by the People, June 3, 1986.)*

Research References

Rutter, Cal. Practice Guide: Civ. Pro. Before Trial Ch. 12(II)-E, E. Motion to Determine "Good Faith" of "Piecemeal" Settlement (CCP § 877.6).

Rutter, Cal. Practice Guide: Insurance Litigation Ch. 12B-B, B. Bad Faith Refusal to Settle.

Rutter, Cal. Practice Guide: Prof. Responsibility Ch. 6-D, D. Professional Liability.

§ 1432.　Contribution among joint obligors

Except as provided in Section 877 of the Code of Civil Procedure, a party to a joint, or joint and several obligation, who satisfies more than his share of the claim against all, may require a proportionate contribution from all the parties joined with him. *(Enacted in 1872. Amended by Stats.1987, c. 677, § 1.)*

Research References

Rutter, Cal. Practice Guide: Civil Appeals & Writs Ch. 2-D, D. Standing to Appeal.

Rutter, Cal. Practice Guide: Enforcing Judgments/Debts Ch. 3-A, A. Evaluating the Claim.

Rutter, Cal. Practice Guide: Enforcing Judgments/Debts Ch. 6G-11, Enforcement of Judgment by Assignees.

Rutter, Cal. Practice Guide: Insurance Litigation Ch. 8-B, B. Contribution Between Insurers.

Miller and Starr California Real Estate § 10:263, Definitions; Guarantor, Surety.

9 Witkin Cal. Proc. 5th Appeal § 40, Judgment Affecting Other Parties.

2 Witkin, California Summary 10th Insurance § 4, (S 4) Insurer's Rights of Subrogation, Contribution, and Indemnity.

1 Witkin Cal. Summ. 10th Contracts § 113, Contribution.

13 Witkin, California Summary 10th Equity § 179, (S 179) Nature of Doctrine.

CHAPTER 3.　CONDITIONAL OBLIGATIONS

Section

§ 1434.　Conditional obligation defined

OBLIGATION, WHEN CONDITIONAL. An obligation is conditional, when the rights or duties of any party thereto depend upon the occurrence of an uncertain event. *(Enacted in 1872.)*

§ 1435. Kinds of conditions

CONDITIONS, KINDS OF. Conditions may be precedent, concurrent, or subsequent. *(Enacted in 1872.)*

§ 1436. Condition precedent defined

CONDITIONS PRECEDENT. A condition precedent is one which is to be performed before some right dependent thereon accrues, or some act dependent thereon is performed. *(Enacted in 1872.)*

§ 1437. Condition concurrent defined

CONDITIONS CONCURRENT. Conditions concurrent are those which are mutually dependent, and are to be performed at the same time. *(Enacted in 1872.)*

§ 1438. Condition subsequent defined

CONDITION SUBSEQUENT. A condition subsequent is one referring to a future event, upon the happening of which the obligation becomes no longer binding upon the other party, if he chooses to avail himself of the condition. *(Enacted in 1872.)*

§ 1439. Performance; necessity

PERFORMANCE, ETC. OF CONDITIONS, WHEN ESSENTIAL. Before any party to an obligation can require another party to perform any act under it, he must fulfill all conditions precedent thereto imposed upon himself; and must be able and offer to fulfill all conditions concurrent so imposed upon him on the like fulfillment by the other party, except as provided by the next section. *(Enacted in 1872.)*

§ 1440. Performance; excuse

WHEN PERFORMANCE, ETC., EXCUSED. If a party to an obligation gives notice to another, before the latter is in default, that he will not perform the same upon his part, and does not retract such notice before the time at which performance upon his part is due, such other party is entitled to enforce the obligation without previously performing or offering to perform any conditions upon his part in favor of the former party. *(Enacted in 1872.)*

§ 1441. Impossible or unlawful conditions

IMPOSSIBLE OR UNLAWFUL CONDITIONS VOID. A condition in a contract, the fulfillment of which is impossible or unlawful, within the meaning of the Article on the Object of Contracts, or which is repugnant to the nature of the interest created by the contract, is void. *(Enacted in 1872.)*

§ 1442. Forfeiture; strict construction

CONDITIONS INVOLVING FORFEITURE, HOW CONSTRUED. A condition involving a forfeiture must be strictly interpreted against the party for whose benefit it is created. *(Enacted in 1872.)*

Rutter, Cal. Practice Guide: Real Prop. Transactions Ch. 4-E, E. Drafting the Purchase and Sale Agreement-Terms and Conditions.

Miller and Starr California Real Estate § 9:9, Interpretation to Avoid Forfeiture.

Miller and Starr California Real Estate § 24:1, Types of Enforceable Restrictions.

Miller and Starr California Real Estate § 34:2, What Constitutes a Breach of Contract.

Miller and Starr California Real Estate § 1:156, Nature of a Condition.

Miller and Starr California Real Estate § 10:71, Payment or Performance of the Secured Obligation.

Miller and Starr California Real Estate § 19:48, Covenants and Conditions Distinguished.

Miller and Starr California Real Estate § 19:69, Application of a Covenant or Condition Against Transfer.

Miller and Starr California Real Estate § 19:111, Specification or Restriction of Use.

Miller and Starr California Real Estate § 19:200, Termination for Cause or Default.

18 NO. 6 Miller & Starr, California Real Estate Newsalert 8, Deeds of Trust.

12 Witkin, California Summary 10th Real Property § 19, (S 19) Construction to Avoid Forfeiture.

1 Witkin Cal. Summ. 10th Contracts § 826, (S 826) Construction to Avoid.

CHAPTER 4. ALTERNATIVE OBLIGATIONS

Section

§ 1448. Right of selection

WHO HAS THE RIGHT OF SELECTION. If an obligation requires the performance of one of two acts, in the alternative, the party required to perform has the right of selection, unless it is otherwise provided by the terms of the obligation. *(Enacted in 1872.)*

Research References

Miller and Starr California Real Estate § 1:59, Rules of Contract Interpretation.

Miller and Starr California Real Estate § 34:2, What Constitutes a Breach of Contract.

Miller and Starr California Real Estate § 10:74, Partial Performance.

§ 1449. Loss of right

RIGHT OF SELECTION, HOW LOST. If the party having the right of selection between alternative acts does not give notice of his selection to the other party within the time, if any, fixed by the obligation for that purpose, or, if none is so fixed, before the time at which the obligation ought to be performed, the right of selection passes to the other party. *(Enacted in 1872.)*

Research References

Miller and Starr California Real Estate § 1:59, Rules of Contract Interpretation.

Miller and Starr California Real Estate § 34:2, What Constitutes a Breach of Contract.

Miller and Starr California Real Estate § 10:74, Partial Performance.

§ 1450. Indivisibility of alternatives

ALTERNATIVES INDIVISIBLE. The party having the right of selection between alternative acts must select one of them in its entirety, and cannot select part of one and part of another without the consent of the other party. *(Enacted in 1872.)*

Research References

Miller and Starr California Real Estate § 1:59, Rules of Contract Interpretation.

Miller and Starr California Real Estate § 34:2, What Constitutes a Breach of Contract.

Miller and Starr California Real Estate § 10:74, Partial Performance.

§ 1451. Nullity of one or more alternatives

NULLITY OF ONE OR MORE OF ALTERNATIVE OBLIGATIONS. If one of the alternative acts required by an obligation is such as the law will not enforce, or becomes unlawful, or impossible of performance, the obligation is to be interpreted as though the other stood alone. *(Enacted in 1872.)*

Research References

Miller and Starr California Real Estate § 1:59, Rules of Contract Interpretation.

Miller and Starr California Real Estate § 34:2, What Constitutes a Breach of Contract.

Miller and Starr California Real Estate § 10:74, Partial Performance.

1 Witkin Cal. Summ. 10th Contracts § 834, (S 834) Discharge of Duty.

Title 3

TRANSFER OF OBLIGATIONS

Section

§ 1457. Burden of obligation; consent

BURDEN OF OBLIGATION NOT TRANSFERABLE. The burden of an obligation may be transferred with the consent of the party entitled to its benefit, but not otherwise, except as provided by Section 1466. *(Enacted in 1872.)*

Research References

Rutter, Cal. Practice Guide: Insurance Litigation Ch. 1-A, A. Insurance-In General.

Rutter, Cal. Practice Guide: Insurance Litigation Ch. 8-D, D. Reinsurance.

Rutter, Cal. Practice Guide: Insurance Litigation Ch. 11-K, K. Statutory Liability.

Rutter, Cal. Practice Guide: Real Prop. Transactions Ch. 4-A, A. Property to be Sold.

Rutter, Cal. Practice Guide: Real Prop. Transactions Ch. 4-E, E. Drafting the Purchase and Sale Agreement-Terms and Conditions.

Miller and Starr California Real Estate § 1:22, Assignment of Contracts.

Miller and Starr California Real Estate § 2:16, Sale or Assignment.

Miller and Starr California Real Estate § 24:1, Types of Enforceable Restrictions.
Miller and Starr California Real Estate § 24:5, Covenants Burdening Land for the Benefit of Other Land--Effect of the 1968-1969 Amendments on Pre-Existing Covenants.
Miller and Starr California Real Estate § 10:37, Trustor as a Surety.
Miller and Starr California Real Estate § 19:62, Liability of the Parties; Tenant-Assignor Liability to the Landlord.
1 Witkin Cal. Summ. 10th Contracts § 730, (S 730) Liability to Promisee.
13 Witkin, California Summary 10th Equity § 112, Insurance Practices.

§ 1458. Right arising from obligation

RIGHTS ARISING OUT OF OBLIGATION TRANSFERABLE. A right arising out of an obligation is the property of the person to whom it is due, and may be transferred as such. *(Enacted in 1872.)*

Research References

Rutter, Cal. Practice Guide: Real Prop. Transactions Ch. 4-E, E. Drafting the Purchase and Sale Agreement-Terms and Conditions.
Miller and Starr California Real Estate § 17:2, Property as "Bundle of Rights".
22 NO. 3 Miller & Starr, California Real Estate Newsalert 1, Show Me Your Papers: Sales and Assignments of Secured Real Estate Loans and the California Foreclosure Process.
1 Witkin Cal. Summ. 10th Contracts § 720, (S 720) in General.

§ 1459. Non-negotiable instruments; indorsement

NON-NEGOTIABLE INSTRUMENTS MAY BE TRANSFERRED. A non-negotiable written contract for the payment of money or personal property may be transferred by indorsement, in like manner with negotiable instruments. Such indorsement shall transfer all the rights of the assignor under the instrument to the assignee, subject to all equities and defenses existing in favor of the maker at the time of the indorsement. *(Enacted in 1872.)*

Research References

Miller and Starr California Real Estate § 1:22, Assignment of Contracts.
Miller and Starr California Real Estate § 24:1, Types of Enforceable Restrictions.
22 NO. 3 Miller & Starr, California Real Estate Newsalert 1, Show Me Your Papers: Sales and Assignments of Secured Real Estate Loans and the California Foreclosure Process.
22 NO. 1 Miller & Starr, California Real Estate Newsalert 25, Usury.
1 Witkin Cal. Summ. 10th Contracts § 735, in General.

§ 1460. Covenants running with land defined

COVENANTS RUNNING WITH LAND, WHAT. Certain covenants, contained in grants of estates in real property, are appurtenant to such estates, and pass with them, so as to bind the assigns of the covenantor and to vest in the assigns of the covenantee, in the same manner as if they had personally entered into them. Such covenants are said to run with the land. *(Enacted in 1872.)*

Research References

Rutter, Cal. Practice Guide: Real Prop. Transactions Ch. 4-A, A. Property to be Sold.
Miller and Starr California Real Estate § 24:1, Types of Enforceable Restrictions.
Miller and Starr California Real Estate § 24:2, Definition and Explanation of Covenants that "Run With the Land".
Miller and Starr California Real Estate § 24:4, Covenants Burdening Land for the Benefit of Other Land--Prior to the 1968 and 1969 Amendments to Civil Code § 4168.
Miller and Starr California Real Estate § 24:5, Covenants Burdening Land for the Benefit of Other Land--Effect of the 1968-1969 Amendments on Pre-Existing Covenants.
Miller and Starr California Real Estate § 19:54, Enforcement of Covenants by and Against Successors.
Miller and Starr California Real Estate § 19:59, Transfer of the Reversion.
Miller and Starr California Real Estate § 24:24, Nature of the Right to Enforce Restrictions; Appurtenant to Benefited Property.

12 Witkin, California Summary 10th Real Property § 433, Running Covenant.

§ 1461. Covenants running with land

WHAT COVENANTS RUN WITH LAND. The only covenants which run with the land are those specified in this Title, and those which are incidental thereto. *(Enacted in 1872.)*

Research References

Rutter, Cal. Practice Guide: Real Prop. Transactions Ch. 4-A, A. Property to be Sold.
Miller and Starr California Real Estate § 24:1, Types of Enforceable Restrictions.
Miller and Starr California Real Estate § 24:2, Definition and Explanation of Covenants that "Run With the Land".
Miller and Starr California Real Estate § 24:3, Covenants for the Benefit of Land Conveyed.
Miller and Starr California Real Estate § 24:4, Covenants Burdening Land for the Benefit of Other Land--Prior to the 1968 and 1969 Amendments to Civil Code § 4168.
Miller and Starr California Real Estate § 24:5, Covenants Burdening Land for the Benefit of Other Land--Effect of the 1968-1969 Amendments on Pre-Existing Covenants.
12 Witkin, California Summary 10th Real Property § 433, Running Covenant.

§ 1462. Covenants running with land; direct benefit of existing property

SAME. Every covenant contained in a grant of an estate in real property, which is made for the direct benefit of the property, or some part of it then in existence, runs with the land. *(Enacted in 1872.)*

Research References

Rutter, Cal. Practice Guide: Real Prop. Transactions Ch. 4-A, A. Property to be Sold.
Miller and Starr California Real Estate § 8:7, Implied Covenants--Personal Nature.
Miller and Starr California Real Estate § 24:2, Definition and Explanation of Covenants that "Run With the Land".
Miller and Starr California Real Estate § 24:3, Covenants for the Benefit of Land Conveyed.
Miller and Starr California Real Estate § 24:4, Covenants Burdening Land for the Benefit of Other Land--Prior to the 1968 and 1969 Amendments to Civil Code § 4168.
Miller and Starr California Real Estate § 19:54, Enforcement of Covenants by and Against Successors.
Miller and Starr California Real Estate § 10:122, Enforcement; Executed Contracts.
21 NO. 1 Miller & Starr, California Real Estate Newsalert 1, is an Arbitration Provision in Recorded CC&RS Ever Enforceable by the Developer?
12 Witkin, California Summary 10th Real Property § 438, Abrogation of Privity Requirement.

§ 1463. Covenants running with land; direct benefit of existing property; list

SAME. The last section includes covenants "of warranty," "for quiet enjoyment," or for further assurance on the part of a grantor, and covenants for the payment of rent, or of taxes or assessments upon the land, on the part of a grantee. *(Enacted in 1872.)*

Research References

Miller and Starr California Real Estate § 24:3, Covenants for the Benefit of Land Conveyed.
Miller and Starr California Real Estate § 19:54, Enforcement of Covenants by and Against Successors.

12 Witkin, California Summary 10th Real Property § 438, Abrogation of Privity Requirement.

§ 1465. Covenants running with land; persons bound

WHO ARE BOUND BY COVENANTS. A covenant running with the land binds those only who acquire the whole estate of the covenantor in some part of the property. *(Enacted in 1872.)*

Research References

Rutter, Cal. Practice Guide: Real Prop. Transactions Ch. 4-A, A. Property to be Sold.

Miller and Starr California Real Estate § 8:7, Implied Covenants--Personal Nature.

Miller and Starr California Real Estate § 24:2, Definition and Explanation of Covenants that "Run With the Land".

Miller and Starr California Real Estate § 24:6, Covenants Burdening Land for the Benefit of Other Land--Creation After the 1968-1969 Amendments.

Miller and Starr California Real Estate § 19:54, Enforcement of Covenants by and Against Successors.

Miller and Starr California Real Estate § 24:28, Rights of Enforcement--Apportionment of Burdens and Benefits.

12 Witkin, California Summary 10th Real Property § 436, Succession to Interest of Original Party.

12 Witkin, California Summary 10th Real Property § 439, Present Law.

§ 1466. Covenants running with land; persons not bound

WHO ARE NOT. No one, merely by reason of having acquired an estate subject to a covenant running with the land, is liable for a breach of the covenant before he acquired the estate, or after he has parted with it or ceased to enjoy its benefits. *(Enacted in 1872.)*

Research References

Rutter, Cal. Practice Guide: Real Prop. Transactions Ch. 4-A, A. Property to be Sold.

Miller and Starr California Real Estate § 24:2, Definition and Explanation of Covenants that "Run With the Land".

Miller and Starr California Real Estate § 24:6, Covenants Burdening Land for the Benefit of Other Land--Creation After the 1968-1969 Amendments.

Miller and Starr California Real Estate § 24:7, Environmental Covenants, Development Agreements, and Other Statutory Agreements that May Run With the Land.

Miller and Starr California Real Estate § 19:54, Enforcement of Covenants by and Against Successors.

Miller and Starr California Real Estate § 23:21, Recorded Notice Concerning Hazardous Waste Property or Border-Zone Property.

Miller and Starr California Real Estate § 24:24, Nature of the Right to Enforce Restrictions; Appurtenant to Benefited Property.

Miller and Starr California Real Estate § 24:27, Rights of Enforcement--Successor Liability.

Miller and Starr California Real Estate § 24:28, Rights of Enforcement--Apportionment of Burdens and Benefits.

Miller and Starr California Real Estate § 25B:13, Contents of Governing Documents for the Management of a Common Interest Subdivision.

Miller and Starr California Real Estate § 25B:91, Collection of Assessments.

19 NO. 2 Miller & Starr, California Real Estate Newsalert 18, Landlord and Tenant.

12 Witkin, California Summary 10th Real Property § 433, Running Covenant.

12 Witkin, California Summary 10th Real Property § 439, Present Law.

§ 1467. Covenants running with land; apportionment

APPORTIONMENT OF COVENANTS. Where several persons, holding by several titles, are subject to the burden or entitled to the benefit of a covenant running with the land, it must be apportioned among them according to the value of the property subject to it held by them respectively, if such value can be ascertained, and if not, then according to their respective interests in point of quantity. *(Enacted in 1872.)*

Research References

Miller and Starr California Real Estate § 24:1, Types of Enforceable Restrictions.

Miller and Starr California Real Estate § 24:2, Definition and Explanation of Covenants that "Run With the Land".

Miller and Starr California Real Estate § 24:4, Covenants Burdening Land for the Benefit of Other Land--Prior to the 1968 and 1969 Amendments to Civil Code § 4168.

Miller and Starr California Real Estate § 11:14, Required Form and Contents--Property Description.

Miller and Starr California Real Estate § 19:54, Enforcement of Covenants by and Against Successors.

Miller and Starr California Real Estate § 24:28, Rights of Enforcement--Apportionment of Burdens and Benefits.

12 Witkin, California Summary 10th Real Property § 436, Succession to Interest of Original Party.

12 Witkin, California Summary 10th Real Property § 439, Present Law.

§ 1468. Covenants running with land of both covenantor and covenantee; successive owners

Each covenant, made by an owner of land with the owner of other land or made by a grantor of land with the grantee of land conveyed, or made by the grantee of land conveyed with the grantor thereof, to do or refrain from doing some act on his own land, which doing or refraining is expressed to be for the benefit of the land of the covenantee, runs with both the land owned by or granted to the covenantor and the land owned by or granted to the covenantee and shall, except as provided by Section 1466, or as specifically provided in the instrument creating such covenant, and notwithstanding the provisions of Section 1465, benefit or be binding upon each successive owner, during his ownership, of any portion of such land affected thereby and upon each person having any interest therein derived through any owner thereof where all of the following requirements are met:

(a) The land of the covenantor which is to be affected by such covenants, and the land of covenantee to be benefited, are particularly described in the instrument containing such covenants;

(b) Such successive owners of the land are in such instrument expressed to be bound thereby for the benefit of the land owned by, granted by, or granted to the covenantee;

(c) Each such act relates to the use, repair, maintenance or improvement of, or payment of taxes and assessments on, such land or some part thereof, or if the land owned by or granted to each consists of undivided interests in the same parcel or parcels, the suspension of the right of partition or sale in lieu of partition for a period which is reasonable in relation to the purpose of the covenant;

(d) The instrument containing such covenants is recorded in the office of the recorder of each county in which such land or some part thereof is situated.

Where several persons are subject to the burden of any such covenant, it shall be apportioned among them pursuant to Section 1467, except that where only a portion of such land is so affected thereby, such apportionment shall be only among the several owners of such portion. This section shall apply to the mortgagee, trustee or beneficiary of a mortgage or deed of trust upon such land or any part thereof while but only while he, in such capacity, is in possession thereof. *(Added by Stats.1905, c. 450, p. 610, § 1. Amended by Stats.1968, c. 680, p. 1377, § 1; Stats.1969, c. 245, p. 594, § 1; Stats.1973, c. 474, p. 948, § 1, eff. Sept. 11, 1973.)*

Research References

Rutter, Cal. Practice Guide: Real Prop. Transactions Ch. 4-A, A. Property to be Sold.

Miller and Starr California Real Estate § 11:6, Instruments Subject to Recording--List of Recordable Documents.

Miller and Starr California Real Estate § 24:1, Types of Enforceable Restrictions.

Miller and Starr California Real Estate § 24:2, Definition and Explanation of Covenants that "Run With the Land".

Miller and Starr California Real Estate § 24:3, Covenants for the Benefit of Land Conveyed.

Miller and Starr California Real Estate § 24:4, Covenants Burdening Land for the Benefit of Other Land--Prior to the 1968 and 1969 Amendments to Civil Code § 4168.

Miller and Starr California Real Estate § 24:5, Covenants Burdening Land for the Benefit of Other Land--Effect of the 1968-1969 Amendments on Pre-Existing Covenants.

Miller and Starr California Real Estate § 24:6, Covenants Burdening Land for the Benefit of Other Land--Creation After the 1968-1969 Amendments.

Miller and Starr California Real Estate § 24:7, Environmental Covenants, Development Agreements, and Other Statutory Agreements that May Run With the Land.

Miller and Starr California Real Estate § 24:9, Creation--Generally.

Miller and Starr California Real Estate § 11:14, Required Form and Contents--Property Description.

Miller and Starr California Real Estate § 11:34, "Chain of Title" Defined; Effect of a Recorded Document Not in the Chain of Title.

Miller and Starr California Real Estate § 12:21, Right of Partition--Defenses to Partition; Waiver or Estoppel.

Miller and Starr California Real Estate § 23:21, Recorded Notice Concerning Hazardous Waste Property or Border-Zone Property.

Miller and Starr California Real Estate § 24:16, Creation--Common Interest Developments.

Miller and Starr California Real Estate § 24:17, Rules of Construction; Evidence.

Miller and Starr California Real Estate § 24:25, Rights of Enforcement--Generally.

Miller and Starr California Real Estate § 24:28, Rights of Enforcement--Apportionment of Burdens and Benefits.

Miller and Starr California Real Estate § 24:31, Defenses to Enforcement--Change of Conditions.

Miller and Starr California Real Estate § 10:122, Enforcement; Executed Contracts.

Miller and Starr California Real Estate § 25B:103, Enforcement of the Restrictions--Enforcement by the Subdivider or a Public Entity.

Miller and Starr California Real Estate § 25B:113, Arbitration or Other Resolution of Disputes With the Subdivider.

19 NO. 5 Miller & Starr, California Real Estate Newsalert 10, Covenants, Conditions, and Restrictions.

21 NO. 1 Miller & Starr, California Real Estate Newsalert 1, is an Arbitration Provision in Recorded CC&RS Ever Enforceable by the Developer?

21 NO. 5 Miller & Starr, California Real Estate Newsalert 6, Construction Law and Contracting.

12 Witkin, California Summary 10th Real Property § 434, Intention that Covenant Run.

12 Witkin, California Summary 10th Real Property § 435, Relation to Land.

12 Witkin, California Summary 10th Real Property § 436, Succession to Interest of Original Party.

12 Witkin, California Summary 10th Real Property § 438, Abrogation of Privity Requirement.

12 Witkin, California Summary 10th Real Property § 439, Present Law.

12 Witkin, California Summary 10th Real Property § 440, California Law.

§ 1469. Lessor's affirmative covenants as to contiguous land; successive owners

Each covenant made by the lessor in a lease of real property to do any act or acts on other real property which is owned by the lessor and is contiguous (except for intervening public streets, alleys or sidewalks) to the real property demised to the lessee shall, except as provided by Section 1466, be binding upon each successive owner, during his ownership, of any portion of such contiguous real property affected thereby where all of the following requirements are met:

(a) Such contiguous real property is particularly described in the lease;

(b) Such successive owners are in the lease expressed to be bound thereby for the benefit of the demised real property;

(c) Each such act relates to the use, repair, maintenance or improvement of, or payment of taxes and assessments on, such contiguous real property or some part thereof;

(d) The lease is recorded in the same manner as grants of real property, in the office of the recorder of each county in which such contiguous real property or some part thereof is situate. Such lease shall include the description of any such contiguous land described in any unrecorded instrument, the contents of which unrecorded instrument are incorporated by reference in such recorded lease.

Where several persons are subject to the burden of any such covenant, it shall be apportioned among them pursuant to Section 1467, except that where only a portion of such contiguous real property is so affected thereby, such apportionment shall be only among the several owners of such portion. This section shall apply to the mortgagee, trustee or beneficiary of a mortgage or deed of trust upon such contiguous real property or any part thereof while but only while he, in such capacity, is in possession thereof. *(Added by Stats.1953, c. 652, p. 1903, § 1. Amended by Stats.1965, c. 1502, p. 3527, § 1.)*

Research References

Miller and Starr California Real Estate § 11:6, Instruments Subject to Recording--List of Recordable Documents.

Miller and Starr California Real Estate § 24:2, Definition and Explanation of Covenants that "Run With the Land".

Miller and Starr California Real Estate § 24:4, Covenants Burdening Land for the Benefit of Other Land--Prior to the 1968 and 1969 Amendments to Civil Code § 4168.

Miller and Starr California Real Estate § 24:6, Covenants Burdening Land for the Benefit of Other Land--Creation After the 1968-1969 Amendments.

Miller and Starr California Real Estate § 11:14, Required Form and Contents--Property Description.

Miller and Starr California Real Estate § 11:34, "Chain of Title" Defined; Effect of a Recorded Document Not in the Chain of Title.

Miller and Starr California Real Estate § 19:52, Implied Covenants--Landlord's Covenant Not to Compete.

Miller and Starr California Real Estate § 19:54, Enforcement of Covenants by and Against Successors.

Miller and Starr California Real Estate § 24:28, Rights of Enforcement--Apportionment of Burdens and Benefits.

Miller and Starr California Real Estate § 7:152, When Property Insured is a Leasehold Estate (CLTA Forms 104.6, 107.5, 119, 119.1, 119.2, 119.3, 119.4, 119.5, 119.6, 124.2, 124.3).

22 NO. 3 Miller & Starr, California Real Estate Newsalert 1, Show Me Your Papers: Sales and Assignments of Secured Real Estate Loans and the California Foreclosure Process.

12 Witkin, California Summary 10th Real Property § 431, Nature of Covenant.

12 Witkin, California Summary 10th Real Property § 434, Intention that Covenant Run.

12 Witkin, California Summary 10th Real Property § 439, Present Law.

12 Witkin, California Summary 10th Real Property § 660, Nature and Validity.

§ 1470. Lessor's negative covenants as to contiguous land; successive owners

Each covenant made by the lessor in a lease of real property not to use or permit to be used contrary to the terms of such lease any other real property which is owned by the lessor and is contiguous (except for intervening public streets, alleys or sidewalks) to the real property demised to the lessee shall, except as provided by Section 1466, be binding upon each successive owner, during his ownership, of any portion of such contiguous real property affected thereby and upon each person having any interest therein derived through any owner thereof where all of the following requirements are met:

(a) Such contiguous real property is particularly described in the lease;

(b) Such successive owners and persons having any such interest are in the lease expressed to be bound thereby for the benefit of the demised real property;

(c) The lease is recorded in the same manner as grants of real property, in the office of the recorder of each county in which such contiguous real property or some part thereof is situate. Such lease shall include therein the description of any such contiguous land described in any unrecorded instrument, the contents of which unrecorded instrument are incorporated by reference in such recorded lease.

Where several persons are subject to the burden of any such covenant, it shall be apportioned among them pursuant to Section 1467, except that where only a portion of such contiguous real property is so affected thereby, such apportionment shall be only among the several owners of, and persons having any such interest in, such portion. This section shall apply to the mortgagee, trustee or beneficiary of a mortgage or deed of trust upon such contiguous real property or any part thereof while and only while he, in such capacity, is in possession thereof. *(Added by Stats.1953, c. 652, p. 1904, § 2. Amended by Stats.1963, c. 2054, p. 4297, § 1.)*

Research References

Rutter, Cal. Practice Guide: Real Prop. Transactions Ch. 4-A, A. Property to be Sold.
Miller and Starr California Real Estate § 11:6, Instruments Subject to Recording--List of Recordable Documents.
Miller and Starr California Real Estate § 24:2, Definition and Explanation of Covenants that "Run With the Land".
Miller and Starr California Real Estate § 24:4, Covenants Burdening Land for the Benefit of Other Land--Prior to the 1968 and 1969 Amendments to Civil Code § 4168.
Miller and Starr California Real Estate § 24:6, Covenants Burdening Land for the Benefit of Other Land--Creation After the 1968-1969 Amendments.
Miller and Starr California Real Estate § 11:14, Required Form and Contents--Property Description.
Miller and Starr California Real Estate § 11:34, "Chain of Title" Defined; Effect of a Recorded Document Not in the Chain of Title.
Miller and Starr California Real Estate § 19:52, Implied Covenants--Landlord's Covenant Not to Compete.
Miller and Starr California Real Estate § 19:54, Enforcement of Covenants by and Against Successors.
Miller and Starr California Real Estate § 24:28, Rights of Enforcement--Apportionment of Burdens and Benefits.
Miller and Starr California Real Estate § 7:152, When Property Insured is a Leasehold Estate (CLTA Forms 104.6, 107.5, 119, 119.1, 119.2, 119.3, 119.4, 119.5, 119.6, 124.2, 124.3).
12 Witkin, California Summary 10th Real Property § 431, Nature of Covenant.
12 Witkin, California Summary 10th Real Property § 434, Intention that Covenant Run.
12 Witkin, California Summary 10th Real Property § 439, Present Law.
12 Witkin, California Summary 10th Real Property § 660, Nature and Validity.

§ 1471. Covenants to do or refrain from doing; persons bound; successive owners; requirements; apportionment of burden; certified copies to California Environmental Protection Agency

(a) Notwithstanding Section 1468 or any other provision of law, a covenant made by an owner of land or by the grantee of land to do or refrain from doing some act on his or her own land, which doing or refraining is expressed to be for the benefit of the covenantee, regardless of whether or not it is for the benefit of land owned by the covenantee, shall run with the land owned by or granted to the covenantor if all the following requirements are met:

(1) The land of the covenantor that is to be affected by the covenant is particularly described in the instrument containing the covenant.

(2) The successive owners of the land are expressed to be bound thereby for the benefit of the covenantee in the instrument containing the covenant.

(3) Each act that the owner or grantee will do or refrain from doing relates to the use of land and each act is reasonably necessary to protect present or future human health or safety or the environment as a result of the presence on the land of hazardous materials, as defined in Section 25260 of the Health and Safety Code.

(4) The instrument containing the covenant is recorded in the office of the recorder of each county in which the land or some portion thereof is situated and the instrument includes in its title the words: "Environmental Restriction."

(b) Except as provided by Section 1466 or as specifically provided in the instrument creating a covenant made pursuant to this section, the covenant shall be binding upon each successive owner, during his or her ownership, of any portion of the land affected thereby and upon each person having any interest therein derived through any owner thereof.

(c) If several persons are subject to the burden of a covenant recorded pursuant to this section, it shall be apportioned among them pursuant to Section 1467, except if only a portion of the land is so affected thereby, the apportionment shall be only among the several owners of that portion.

(d) This section shall apply to the mortgagee, trustee, or beneficiary of a mortgage or deed of trust upon the land or any part thereof while, but only while, he or she, in that capacity, is in possession thereof.

(e)(1) If an instrument containing a covenant is recorded pursuant to paragraph (4) of subdivision (a) as an "Environmental Restriction," in accordance with this section, the office of the recorder of the county may send a certified copy of the instrument to the California Environmental Protection Agency, for posting on its Web site, for informational purposes only, pursuant to Section 57012 of the Health and Safety Code, unless the instrument indicates that it is required by a board or department specified in paragraphs (1) to (3), inclusive, of subdivision (d) of Section 57012 of the Health and Safety Code.

(2) Notwithstanding any provision of law, the office of the recorder of the county and any of its employees shall not be subject to any liability under any state law or in any action for damages if the office of the recorder does not send a certified copy of the instrument pursuant to paragraph (1).

(f) The office of the recorder of the county may assess a reasonable fee, as determined by resolution of its governing body, to cover the costs of taking the action authorized by subdivision (e). *(Added by Stats.1995, c. 188 (A.B.1120), § 1. Amended by Stats.2002, c. 592 (A.B.2436), § 1.)*

Research References

Rutter, Cal. Practice Guide: Real Prop. Transactions Ch. 4-A, A. Property to be Sold.
Rutter, Cal. Practice Guide: Real Prop. Transactions Ch. 5-E, E. Addressing Environmental Hazards Liability Concerns of Real Property Buyers and Sellers.
Miller and Starr California Real Estate § 11:6, Instruments Subject to Recording--List of Recordable Documents.
Miller and Starr California Real Estate § 24:1, Types of Enforceable Restrictions.
Miller and Starr California Real Estate § 24:2, Definition and Explanation of Covenants that "Run With the Land".
Miller and Starr California Real Estate § 24:7, Environmental Covenants, Development Agreements, and Other Statutory Agreements that May Run With the Land.

Miller and Starr California Real Estate § 1:144, Duty of Seller of Real Property to Disclose--Statutory Duty of Disclosure.

Miller and Starr California Real Estate § 19:54, Enforcement of Covenants by and Against Successors.

Miller and Starr California Real Estate § 23:21, Recorded Notice Concerning Hazardous Waste Property or Border-Zone Property.

Miller and Starr California Real Estate § 24:28, Rights of Enforcement--Apportionment of Burdens and Benefits.

13 NO. 4 Miller & Starr, California Real Estate Newsalert 12, Hazardous Substances.

Title 4

EXTINCTION OF OBLIGATIONS

CHAPTER 1. PERFORMANCE

§ 1473. Performance

OBLIGATION EXTINGUISHED BY PERFORMANCE. Full performance of an obligation, by the party whose duty it is to perform it, or by any other person on his behalf, and with his assent, if accepted by the creditor, extinguishes it. *(Enacted in 1872.)*

Research References

Miller and Starr California Real Estate § 34:2, What Constitutes a Breach of Contract.

Miller and Starr California Real Estate § 10:71, Payment or Performance of the Secured Obligation.

Miller and Starr California Real Estate § 10:73, Performance by a Third Person.

22 NO. 3 Miller & Starr, California Real Estate Newsalert 1, Show Me Your Papers: Sales and Assignments of Secured Real Estate Loans and the California Foreclosure Process.

1 Witkin Cal. Summ. 10th Contracts § 759, (S 759) Discharge by Performance.

§ 1474. Performance by one of several joint obligors

PERFORMANCE BY ONE OF SEVERAL JOINT DEBTORS. Performance of an obligation, by one of several persons who are jointly liable under it, extinguishes the liability of all. *(Enacted in 1872.)*

Research References

Miller and Starr California Real Estate § 34:2, What Constitutes a Breach of Contract.

Miller and Starr California Real Estate § 10:73, Performance by a Third Person.

1 Witkin Cal. Summ. 10th Contracts § 111, Performance and Discharge.

§ 1475. Performance to one of joint obligees; exception

PERFORMANCE TO ONE OF JOINT CREDITORS. An obligation in favor of several persons is extinguished by performance rendered to any of them, except in the case of a deposit made by owners in common, or in joint ownership, which is regulated by the Title on Deposit. *(Enacted in 1872.)*

Research References

Miller and Starr California Real Estate § 34:2, What Constitutes a Breach of Contract.

Miller and Starr California Real Estate § 10:71, Payment or Performance of the Secured Obligation.

22 NO. 3 Miller & Starr, California Real Estate Newsalert 1, Show Me Your Papers: Sales and Assignments of Secured Real Estate Loans and the California Foreclosure Process.

1 Witkin Cal. Summ. 10th Contracts § 114, (S 114) Joint and Several Rights.

§ 1476. Performance in manner directed by creditors

EFFECT OF DIRECTIONS BY CREDITORS. If a creditor, or any one of two or more joint creditors, at any time directs the debtor to perform his obligation in a particular manner, the obligation is extinguished by performance in that manner, even though the creditor does not receive the benefit of such performance. *(Enacted in 1872.)*

Research References

Rutter, Cal. Practice Guide: Enforcing Judgments/Debts Ch. 3-B, B. Collection Without Suit.

Rutter, Cal. Practice Guide: Enforcing Judgments/Debts Gen. Matls., Highlights.

Miller and Starr California Real Estate § 34:2, What Constitutes a Breach of Contract.

Miller and Starr California Real Estate § 10:71, Payment or Performance of the Secured Obligation.

Miller and Starr California Real Estate § 10:72, Payment by Check.

1 Witkin Cal. Summ. 10th Contracts § 768, (S 768) Conditional Payment by Mailing Check.

§ 1477. Partial performance; effect

PARTIAL PERFORMANCE. A partial performance of an indivisible obligation extinguishes a corresponding proportion thereof, if the benefit of such performance is voluntarily retained by the creditor, but not otherwise. If such partial performance is of such a nature that the creditor cannot avoid retaining it without injuring his own property, his retention thereof is not presumed to be voluntary. *(Enacted in 1872.)*

Research References

Miller and Starr California Real Estate § 34:2, What Constitutes a Breach of Contract.

Miller and Starr California Real Estate § 1:102, Modification of Written Agreement by Subsequent Oral Agreement--Modification of a Written Agreement by Subsequent Executory Oral Agreement: Part Performance.

Miller and Starr California Real Estate § 10:74, Partial Performance.

Miller and Starr California Real Estate § 19:82, Modification of the Rent.

1 Witkin Cal. Summ. 10th Contracts § 759, (S 759) Discharge by Performance.

§ 1478. Payment defined

PAYMENT, WHAT. Performance of an obligation for the delivery of money only, is called payment. *(Enacted in 1872.)*

Research References

Miller and Starr California Real Estate § 34:2, What Constitutes a Breach of Contract.

Miller and Starr California Real Estate § 10:71, Payment or Performance of the Secured Obligation.

Miller and Starr California Real Estate § 10:72, Payment by Check.

22 NO. 3 Miller & Starr, California Real Estate Newsalert 1, Show Me Your Papers: Sales and Assignments of Secured Real Estate Loans and the California Foreclosure Process.

§ 1479. Act of performance applicable to two or more obligations; application to specific obligation

Where a debtor, under several obligations to another, does an act, by way of performance, in whole or in part, which is equally applicable to two or more of such obligations, such performance must be applied as follows:

One—If, at the time of performance, the intention or desire of the debtor that such performance should be applied to the extinction of any particular obligation, be manifested to the creditor, it must be so applied.

Two—If no such application be then made, the creditor, within a reasonable time after such performance, may apply it toward the extinction of any obligation, performance of which was due to him from the debtor at the time of such performance; except that if similar obligations were due to him both individually and as a trustee, he must, unless otherwise directed by the debtor, apply the performance to the extinction of all such obligations in equal proportion; and an application once made by the creditor cannot be rescinded without the consent of [the] debtor.

Three—If neither party makes such application within the time prescribed herein, the performance must be applied to the extinction of obligations in the following order; and, if there be more than one obligation of a particular class, to the extinction of all in that class, ratably:

1. Of interest due at the time of the performance.

2. Of principal due at that time.

3. Of the obligation earliest in date of maturity.

4. Of an obligation not secured by a lien or collateral undertaking.

5. Of an obligation secured by a lien or collateral undertaking. *(Enacted in 1872. Amended by Code 1873–74, c. 612, p. 239, § 182.)*

Research References

Rutter, Cal. Practice Guide: Real Prop. Transactions Ch. 6-F, F. Promissory Note.
Miller and Starr California Real Estate § 10:75, Application and Allocation of Payments.
Miller and Starr California Real Estate § 27:94, Joint Checks.
Miller and Starr California Real Estate § 10:269, Limitation of Liability.
3 Witkin Cal. Proc. 5th Actions § 57, (S 57) Limitation on Substantive Right.
1 Witkin Cal. Summ. 10th Contracts § 765, Specification by Parties.
1 Witkin Cal. Summ. 10th Contracts § 766, Statutory Rules.

CHAPTER 2. OFFER OF PERFORMANCE

§ 1485. Extinction of obligation

OBLIGATION EXTINGUISHED BY OFFER OF PERFORMANCE. An obligation is extinguished by an offer of performance, made in conformity to the rules herein prescribed, and with intent to extinguish the obligation. *(Enacted in 1872.)*

Research References

Rutter, Cal. Practice Guide: Enforcing Judgments/Debts Ch. 6A-5, Amount Recoverable Under Judgment.
Rutter, Cal. Practice Guide: Insurance Litigation Ch. 15-B, B. Actions by Insurers.
Miller and Starr California Real Estate § 1:163, Conditions Concurrent-- Performance; Requirements for an Effective Tender.
Miller and Starr California Real Estate § 10:188, Method of Reinstatement.
22 NO. 1 Miller & Starr, California Real Estate Newsalert 11, Deeds of Trust.
1 Witkin Cal. Summ. 10th Contracts § 769, Offer of Performance.

§ 1486. Partial performance

OFFER OF PARTIAL PERFORMANCE. An offer of partial performance is of no effect. *(Enacted in 1872.)*

Research References

Miller and Starr California Real Estate § 1:163, Conditions Concurrent-- Performance; Requirements for an Effective Tender.
Miller and Starr California Real Estate § 10:188, Method of Reinstatement.
1 Witkin Cal. Summ. 10th Contracts § 771, Requisites of Tender.

§ 1487. Person required to make offer

BY WHOM TO BE MADE. An offer of performance must be made by the debtor, or by some person on his behalf and with his assent. *(Enacted in 1872.)*

Research References

1 Witkin Cal. Summ. 10th Contracts § 771, Requisites of Tender.

§ 1488. Procedure in making offer

An offer of performance must be made to the creditor, or to any one of two or more joint creditors, or to a person authorized by one or more of them to receive or collect what is due under the obligation, if such creditor or authorized person is present at the place where the offer may be made; and if not, wherever the creditor may be found. *(Enacted in 1872. Amended by Code Am.1873–74, c. 612, p. 240, § 183.)*

Research References

22 NO. 3 Miller & Starr, California Real Estate Newsalert 1, Show Me Your Papers: Sales and Assignments of Secured Real Estate Loans and the California Foreclosure Process.
1 Witkin Cal. Summ. 10th Contracts § 114, (S 114) Joint and Several Rights.
1 Witkin Cal. Summ. 10th Contracts § 761, (S 761) Place of Performance.
1 Witkin Cal. Summ. 10th Contracts § 771, Requisites of Tender.

§ 1489. Place of offer

WHERE OFFER MAY BE MADE. In the absence of an express provision to the contrary, an offer of performance may be made, at the option of the debtor:

1. At any place appointed by the creditor; or,

2. Wherever the person to whom the offer ought to be made can be found; or,

3.   If such person cannot, with reasonable diligence, be found within this State, and within a reasonable distance from his residence or place of business, or if he evades the debtor, then at his residence or place of business, if the same can, with reasonable diligence, be found within the State; or,

4.   If this cannot be done, then at any place within this State. *(Enacted in 1872.)*

Research References

22 NO. 3 Miller & Starr, California Real Estate Newsalert 1, Show Me Your Papers: Sales and Assignments of Secured Real Estate Loans and the California Foreclosure Process.
3 Witkin Cal. Proc. 5th Actions § 842, Promise Must be Express.
3 Witkin Cal. Proc. 5th Actions § 856, No Place Specified.
1 Witkin Cal. Summ. 10th Contracts § 761, (S 761) Place of Performance.
1 Witkin Cal. Summ. 10th Contracts § 771, Requisites of Tender.

§ 1490. Time of offer

WHEN OFFER MUST BE MADE.   Where an obligation fixes a time for its performance, an offer of performance must be made at that time, within reasonable hours, and not before nor afterwards. *(Enacted in 1872.)*

Research References

Miller and Starr California Real Estate § 1:163, Conditions Concurrent--Performance; Requirements for an Effective Tender.
Miller and Starr California Real Estate § 10:95, Trustor's Right of Prepayment; "Locked-In" Loans.
1 Witkin Cal. Summ. 10th Contracts § 771, Requisites of Tender.

§ 1491. Time of offer; performance time not fixed

SAME.   Where an obligation does not fix the time for its performance, an offer of performance may be made at any time before the debtor, upon a reasonable demand, has refused to perform. *(Enacted in 1872.)*

Research References

Miller and Starr California Real Estate § 1:163, Conditions Concurrent--Performance; Requirements for an Effective Tender.
1 Witkin Cal. Summ. 10th Contracts § 771, Requisites of Tender.

§ 1492. Offer of compensation for delay

COMPENSATION AFTER DELAY IN PERFORMANCE.   Where delay in performance is capable of exact and entire compensation, and time has not been expressly declared to be of the essence of the obligation, an offer of performance, accompanied with an offer of such compensation, may be made at any time after it is due, but without prejudice to any rights acquired by the creditor, or by any other person, in the meantime. *(Enacted in 1872.)*

Research References

Miller and Starr California Real Estate § 2:24, Time of the Essence; Waiver.
Miller and Starr California Real Estate § 9:12, Defenses to Enforcement--Equitable Relief.
Miller and Starr California Real Estate § 1:161, Conditions Concurrent.
Miller and Starr California Real Estate § 1:162, Conditions Concurrent--Performance; When "Time is of the Essence" in a Contract.
Miller and Starr California Real Estate § 1:163, Conditions Concurrent--Performance; Requirements for an Effective Tender.
1 Witkin Cal. Summ. 10th Contracts § 815, (S 815) Delay in Performance.

§ 1493. Good faith

OFFER TO BE MADE IN GOOD FAITH.   An offer of performance must be made in good faith, and in such manner as is most likely, under the circumstances, to benefit the creditor. *(Enacted in 1872.)*

Research References

Miller and Starr California Real Estate § 1:163, Conditions Concurrent--Performance; Requirements for an Effective Tender.
Miller and Starr California Real Estate § 10:188, Method of Reinstatement.
1 Witkin Cal. Summ. 10th Contracts § 771, Requisites of Tender.

§ 1494. Conditions

CONDITIONAL OFFER.   An offer of performance must be free from any conditions which the creditor is not bound, on his part, to perform. *(Enacted in 1872.)*

Research References

Rutter, Cal. Practice Guide: Enforcing Judgments/Debts Ch. 6A-5, Amount Recoverable Under Judgment.
Miller and Starr California Real Estate § 1:163, Conditions Concurrent--Performance; Requirements for an Effective Tender.
Miller and Starr California Real Estate § 34:34, When Interest Commences to Accrue and Cessation.
Miller and Starr California Real Estate § 10:188, Method of Reinstatement.
1 Witkin Cal. Summ. 10th Contracts § 771, Requisites of Tender.

§ 1495. Ability and willingness to perform

ABILITY AND WILLINGNESS ESSENTIAL.   An offer of performance is of no effect if the person making it is not able and willing to perform according to the offer. *(Enacted in 1872.)*

Research References

Miller and Starr California Real Estate § 1:163, Conditions Concurrent--Performance; Requirements for an Effective Tender.
Miller and Starr California Real Estate § 34:34, When Interest Commences to Accrue and Cessation.
Miller and Starr California Real Estate § 10:188, Method of Reinstatement.
Miller and Starr California Real Estate § 10:212, Requirement of Tender.
1 Witkin Cal. Summ. 10th Contracts § 771, Requisites of Tender.
1 Witkin Cal. Summ. 10th Contracts § 772, in General.

§ 1496. Production of thing to be delivered

PRODUCTION OF THING TO BE DELIVERED NOT NECESSARY.   The thing to be delivered, if any, need not in any case be actually produced, upon an offer of performance, unless the offer is accepted. *(Enacted in 1872.)*

Research References

1 Witkin Cal. Summ. 10th Contracts § 771, Requisites of Tender.

§ 1497. Separation of thing offered

THING OFFERED TO BE KEPT SEPARATE.   A thing, when offered by way of performance, must not be mixed with other things from which it cannot be separated immediately and without difficulty. *(Enacted in 1872.)*

§ 1498. Offer dependent upon performance of conditions

PERFORMANCE OF CONDITION PRECEDENT.   When a debtor is entitled to the performance of a condition precedent to, or concurrent with, performance on his part, he may make his offer to depend upon the due performance of such condition. *(Enacted in 1872.)*

Research References

Rutter, Cal. Practice Guide: Real Prop. Transactions Ch. 11-B, B. Determining Breach.
Miller and Starr California Real Estate § 1:163, Conditions Concurrent--Performance; Requirements for an Effective Tender.
Miller and Starr California Real Estate § 34:34, When Interest Commences to Accrue and Cessation.
Miller and Starr California Real Estate § 10:188, Method of Reinstatement.
1 Witkin Cal. Summ. 10th Contracts § 771, Requisites of Tender.

1 Witkin Cal. Summ. 10th Contracts § 792, (S 792) Conditions Concurrent.

§ 1499. Receipt for property delivered in performance

WRITTEN RECEIPTS. A debtor has a right to require from his creditor a written receipt for any property delivered in performance of his obligation. *(Enacted in 1872.)*

§ 1500. Offer of payment; deposit; notice

An obligation for the payment of money is extinguished by a due offer of payment, if the amount is immediately deposited in the name of the creditor, with some bank or savings and loan association within this state, of good repute, and notice thereof is given to the creditor. *(Enacted in 1872. Amended by Stats.1981, c. 632, § 1, eff. Sept. 23, 1981.)*

Research References

Rutter, Cal. Practice Guide: Enforcing Judgments/Debts Ch. 3-B, B. Collection Without Suit.
Rutter, Cal. Practice Guide: Insurance Litigation Ch. 15-B, B. Actions by Insurers.
Miller and Starr California Real Estate § 10:71, Payment or Performance of the Secured Obligation.
Miller and Starr California Real Estate § 34:34, When Interest Commences to Accrue and Cessation.
Miller and Starr California Real Estate § 10:188, Method of Reinstatement.
Miller and Starr California Real Estate § 10:197, Mode of Redemption.
Miller and Starr California Real Estate § 19:214, Nature of the Remedy.
1 Witkin Cal. Summ. 10th Contracts § 775, (S 775) Deposit in Bank Distinguished.
4 Witkin, California Summary 10th Security Transactions in Real Property § 219, (S 219) Payment or Tender.

§ 1501. Time for objection to mode of offer

OBJECTIONS TO MODE OF OFFER. All objections to the mode of an offer of performance, which the creditor has an opportunity to state at the time to the person making the offer, and which could be then obviated by him, are waived by the creditor, if not then stated. *(Enacted in 1872.)*

Research References

Miller and Starr California Real Estate § 2:9, Mode and Manner of Exercise.
Miller and Starr California Real Estate § 1:100, Modification of Written Agreement by Subsequent Oral Agreement.
Miller and Starr California Real Estate § 1:163, Conditions Concurrent-- Performance; Requirements for an Effective Tender.
16 NO. 4 Miller & Starr, California Real Estate Newsalert 26, Deeds of Trust.
1 Witkin Cal. Summ. 10th Contracts § 772, in General.
1 Witkin Cal. Summ. 10th Contracts § 773, Timely Correction of Mistake.

§ 1502. Title to thing offered in performance

TITLE TO THING OFFERED. The title to a thing duly offered in performance of an obligation passes to the creditor, if the debtor at the time signifies his intention to that effect. *(Enacted in 1872.)*

§ 1503. Deposit of thing offered

CUSTODY OF THING OFFERED. The person offering a thing, other than money, by way of performance, must, if he means to treat it as belonging to the creditor, retain it as a depositary for hire, until the creditor accepts it, or until he has given reasonable notice to the creditor that he will retain it no longer, and, if with reasonable diligence he can find a suitable depositary therefor, until he has deposited it with such person. *(Enacted in 1872.)*

§ 1504. Effect of offer on interest and incidents of obligation

EFFECT OF OFFER ON ACCESSORIES OF OBLIGATION. An offer of payment or other performance, duly made, though the title to the thing offered be not transferred to the creditor, stops the running of interest on the obligation, and has the same effect upon all its incidents as a performance thereof. *(Enacted in 1872.)*

Research References

Rutter, Cal. Practice Guide: Enforcing Judgments/Debts Ch. 3-B, B. Collection Without Suit.
Miller and Starr California Real Estate § 34:34, When Interest Commences to Accrue and Cessation.
Miller and Starr California Real Estate § 10:188, Method of Reinstatement.
Miller and Starr California Real Estate § 19:214, Nature of the Remedy.
22 NO. 3 Miller & Starr, California Real Estate Newsalert 1, Show Me Your Papers: Sales and Assignments of Secured Real Estate Loans and the California Foreclosure Process.
1 Witkin Cal. Summ. 10th Contracts § 770, Effect on Incidents of Obligation.

§ 1505. Refusal of thing offered; retention

CREDITOR'S RETENTION OF THING WHICH HE REFUSES TO ACCEPT. If anything is given to a creditor by way of performance, which he refuses to accept as such, he is not bound to return it without demand; but if he retains it, he is a gratuitous depositary thereof. *(Enacted in 1872.)*

Research References

Miller and Starr California Real Estate § 1:112, Accord and Satisfaction-- Acceptance of Satisfaction by a Creditor.
1 Witkin Cal. Summ. 10th Contracts § 957, Retention of Check Without Cashing.

CHAPTER 3. PREVENTION OF PERFORMANCE OR OFFER

Section
1511. Causes excusing performance.
1512. Performance prevented by creditor.
1514. Performance prevented by cause excusing performance.
1515. Refusal to accept performance before offer.

§ 1511. Causes excusing performance

The want of performance of an obligation, or of an offer of performance, in whole or in part, or any delay therein, is excused by the following causes, to the extent to which they operate:

1. When such performance or offer is prevented or delayed by the act of the creditor, or by the operation of law, even though there may have been a stipulation that this shall not be an excuse; however, the parties may expressly require in a contract that the party relying on the provisions of this paragraph give written notice to the other party or parties, within a reasonable time after the occurrence of the event excusing performance, of an intention to claim an extension of time or of an intention to bring suit or of any other similar or related intent, provided the requirement of such notice is reasonable and just;

2. When it is prevented or delayed by an irresistible, superhuman cause, or by the act of public enemies of this state or of the United States, unless the parties have expressly agreed to the contrary; or,

3. When the debtor is induced not to make it, by any act of the creditor intended or naturally tending to have that effect, done at or before the time at which such performance or offer may be made, and not rescinded before that time. *(Enacted in 1872. Amended by Stats.1965, c. 1730, p. 3888, § 1.)*

Research References

California Real Estate Forms (Miller & Starr) § 4:4, Construction Contract–Cost Plus a Fixed Fee With a Guaranteed Maximum Price.

California Real Estate Forms (Miller & Starr) § 4:5, Construction Agreement–Cost Plus a Percentage Fee With a Guaranteed Maximum Price.

California Real Estate Forms (Miller & Starr) § 4:6, Construction Contract–Fixed Price–Commercial Project.

California Real Estate Forms (Miller & Starr) § 4:7, Construction Contract–Turnkey Industrial Project (Lump-Sum).

California Real Estate Forms (Miller & Starr) § 4:11, Construction Contract0–Construction Manager Representing Owner's Interests.

California Real Estate Forms (Miller & Starr) § 4:15, Development Agreement.

California Real Estate Forms (Miller & Starr) § 4:21, Environmental Surveying–General Conditions.

California Real Estate Forms (Miller & Starr) § 4:14.50, Construction Agreement–Cost Plus a Percentage Fee With a Control Estimate.

Rutter, Cal. Practice Guide: Real Prop. Transactions Ch. 11-B, B. Determining Breach.

Miller and Starr California Real Estate § 1:163, Conditions Concurrent--Performance; Requirements for an Effective Tender.

Miller and Starr California Real Estate § 1:166, Excuse or Waiver of Conditions.

Miller and Starr California Real Estate § 27:72, Waiver of Strict Compliance.

Miller and Starr California Real Estate § 27:75, Construction Delay--Owner Caused Delay.

Miller and Starr California Real Estate § 27:81, Owner's Remedies for Late Performance--Liquidated Damages.

Miller and Starr California Real Estate § 27:85, Contractor's Remedies--"No Damages for Delay" Clauses.

Miller and Starr California Real Estate § 27:117, Wrongful Termination by the Owner; Remedies.

Miller and Starr California Real Estate § 27:120, Impossibility of Performance.

22 NO. 3 Miller & Starr, California Real Estate Newsalert 5, Construction Law and Contracting.

3 Witkin Cal. Proc. 5th Actions § 230, (S 230) Other Actions.

1 Witkin Cal. Summ. 10th Contracts § 774, (S 774) Excuse of Tender Where Useless.

1 Witkin Cal. Summ. 10th Contracts § 828, Nature of Excuse and California Statutes.

1 Witkin Cal. Summ. 10th Contracts § 831, (S 831) Promisor's Duty Discharged.

1 Witkin Cal. Summ. 10th Contracts § 836, Provision Requiring Notice of Intent.

1 Witkin Cal. Summ. 10th Contracts § 837, Contract Provision to Shift Risk.

1 Witkin Cal. Summ. 10th Contracts § 839, Operation of Law.

1 Witkin Cal. Summ. 10th Contracts § 840, Act of Public Enemy and War.

1 Witkin Cal. Summ. 10th Contracts § 851, (S 851) Prevention of Other Party's Performance.

§ 1512. Performance prevented by creditor

If the performance of an obligation be prevented by the creditor, the debtor is entitled to all the benefits which he would have obtained if it had been performed by both parties. *(Enacted in 1872. Amended by Code Am.1873–74, c. 612, p. 240, § 184.)*

Research References

Miller and Starr California Real Estate § 1:166, Excuse or Waiver of Conditions.

Miller and Starr California Real Estate § 27:83, Contractor's Remedies--Damages, Rescission.

Miller and Starr California Real Estate § 27:117, Wrongful Termination by the Owner; Remedies.

§ 1514. Performance prevented by cause excusing performance

SAME. If performance of an obligation is prevented by any cause excusing performance, other than the act of the creditor, the debtor is entitled to a ratable proportion of the consideration to which he would have been entitled upon full performance, according to the benefit which the creditor receives from the actual performance. *(Enacted in 1872.)*

Research References

Miller and Starr California Real Estate § 27:117, Wrongful Termination by the Owner; Remedies.

§ 1515. Refusal to accept performance before offer

EFFECT OF REFUSAL TO ACCEPT PERFORMANCE BEFORE OFFER. A refusal by a creditor to accept performance, made before an offer thereof, is equivalent to an offer and refusal, unless, before performance is actually due, he gives notice to the debtor of his willingness to accept it. *(Enacted in 1872.)*

Research References

Miller and Starr California Real Estate § 1:163, Conditions Concurrent--Performance; Requirements for an Effective Tender.

1 Witkin Cal. Summ. 10th Contracts § 774, (S 774) Excuse of Tender Where Useless.

CHAPTER 4. ACCORD AND SATISFACTION

Section

1521. Accord defined.
1522. Accord; necessity of execution.
1523. Satisfaction defined.
1524. Satisfaction; part performance.
1525. Part payment of disputed sum.
1526. Check or draft tendered in full discharge of claim; acceptance; protest; composition or extension agreement between debtor and creditors; release of claim.

§ 1521. Accord defined

An accord is an agreement to accept, in extinction of an obligation, something different from or less than that to which the person agreeing to accept is entitled. *(Enacted in 1872. Amended by Code Am.1873–74, c. 612, p. 240, § 186.)*

Research References

Rutter, Cal. Practice Guide: Enforcing Judgments/Debts Ch. 3-B, B. Collection Without Suit.

Miller and Starr California Real Estate § 1:109, Accord and Satisfaction--General Requirements.

Miller and Starr California Real Estate § 1:113, Accord and Satisfaction--Consideration; Necessity for a Dispute or Unliquidated Claim.

1 Witkin Cal. Summ. 10th Contracts § 950, Nature of Accord and Satisfaction.

1 Witkin Cal. Summ. 10th Contracts § 959, Rule and Theory.

§ 1522. Accord; necessity of execution

EFFECT OF ACCORD. Though the parties to an accord are bound to execute it, yet it does not extinguish the obligation until it is fully executed. *(Enacted in 1872.)*

Research References

Miller and Starr California Real Estate § 1:109, Accord and Satisfaction--General Requirements.

1 Witkin Cal. Summ. 10th Contracts § 951, Effect of Accord.

1 Witkin Cal. Summ. 10th Contracts § 959, Rule and Theory.

§ 1523. Satisfaction defined

SATISFACTION, WHAT. Acceptance, by the creditor, of the consideration of an accord extinguishes the obligation, and is called satisfaction. *(Enacted in 1872.)*

Research References

Rutter, Cal. Practice Guide: Enforcing Judgments/Debts Ch. 3-B, B. Collection Without Suit.

Miller and Starr California Real Estate § 1:109, Accord and Satisfaction--General Requirements.

1 Witkin Cal. Summ. 10th Contracts § 950, Nature of Accord and Satisfaction.

1 Witkin Cal. Summ. 10th Contracts § 959, Rule and Theory.

§ 1524. Satisfaction; part performance

Part performance of an obligation, either before or after a breach thereof, when expressly accepted by the creditor in writing, in satisfaction, or rendered in pursuance of an agreement in writing for that purpose, though without any new consideration, extinguishes the obligation. *(Enacted in 1872. Amended by Code Am.1873–74, c. 612, p. 241, § 187.)*

Research References

Miller and Starr California Real Estate § 1:102, Modification of Written Agreement by Subsequent Oral Agreement--Modification of a Written Agreement by Subsequent Executory Oral Agreement: Part Performance.
Miller and Starr California Real Estate § 1:112, Accord and Satisfaction--Acceptance of Satisfaction by a Creditor.
Miller and Starr California Real Estate § 1:113, Accord and Satisfaction--Consideration; Necessity for a Dispute or Unliquidated Claim.
Miller and Starr California Real Estate § 19:82, Modification of the Rent.
1 Witkin Cal. Summ. 10th Contracts § 343, California Codes.
1 Witkin Cal. Summ. 10th Contracts § 959, Rule and Theory.
1 Witkin Cal. Summ. 10th Contracts § 960, Check Containing Written Release.

§ 1525. Part payment of disputed sum

It is the public policy of this State, in the best interests of the taxpayer and of the litigant, to encourage fair dealing and to promote justice by reducing litigated matters to the lowest level of jurisdiction.

In case of a dispute over total money due on a contract and it is conceded by the parties that part of the money is due, the debtor may pay, without condition, the amount conceded to be due, leaving to the other party all remedies to which he might otherwise be entitled as to any balance claimed.

If any conditions are attached to the payment, this section shall not be deemed to have limited the remedies available to the other party under other provisions of law on the original amount claimed. *(Added by Stats.1963, c. 1495, p. 3074, § 1.)*

Research References

Miller and Starr California Real Estate § 1:102, Modification of Written Agreement by Subsequent Oral Agreement--Modification of a Written Agreement by Subsequent Executory Oral Agreement: Part Performance.
Miller and Starr California Real Estate § 34:34, When Interest Commences to Accrue and Cessation.
Miller and Starr California Real Estate § 7:216, Duty to Investigate and Pay Claims of the Insured.
Miller and Starr California Real Estate § 27:105, Payment as Waiver by Owner or by Contractor.
2 Witkin Cal. Proc. 5th Jurisdiction § 22, (S 22) in General.
1 Witkin Cal. Summ. 10th Contracts § 759, (S 759) Discharge by Performance.

§ 1526. Check or draft tendered in full discharge of claim; acceptance; protest; composition or extension agreement between debtor and creditors; release of claim

(a) Where a claim is disputed or unliquidated and a check or draft is tendered by the debtor in settlement thereof in full discharge of the claim, and the words "payment in full" or other words of similar meaning are notated on the check or draft, the acceptance of the check or draft does not constitute an accord and satisfaction if the creditor protests against accepting the tender in full payment by striking out or otherwise deleting that notation or if the acceptance of the check or draft was inadvertent or without knowledge of the notation.

(b) Notwithstanding subdivision (a), the acceptance of a check or draft constitutes an accord and satisfaction if a check or draft is tendered pursuant to a composition or extension agreement between a debtor and its creditors, and pursuant to that composition or extension agreement, all creditors of the same class are accorded similar treatment, and the creditor receives the check or draft with knowledge of the restriction.

A creditor shall be conclusively presumed to have knowledge of the restriction if a creditor either:

(1) Has, previous to the receipt of the check or draft, executed a written consent to the composition or extension agreement.

(2) Has been given, not less than 15 days nor more than 90 days prior to receipt of the check or draft, notice, in writing, that a check or draft will be tendered with a restrictive endorsement and that acceptance and cashing of the check or draft will constitute an accord and satisfaction.

(c) Notwithstanding subdivision (a), the acceptance of a check or draft by a creditor constitutes an accord and satisfaction when the check or draft is issued pursuant to or in conjunction with a release of a claim.

(d) For the purposes of paragraph (2) of subdivision (b), mailing the notice by first-class mail, postage prepaid, addressed to the address shown for the creditor on the debtor's books or such other address as the creditor may designate in writing constitutes notice. *(Added by Stats.1987, c. 1268, § 1.)*

Validity

This section was held to be superceded, as to discharge of an unliquidated claim or a claim subject to a bona fide dispute by tendering a negotiable instrument as full satisfaction of the claim, by Commercial Code § 3311, in the decision of Woolridge v. J.F.L. Electric, Inc., 2002, 117 Cal.Rptr.2d 771, 96 Cal.App.4th Supp. 52.

Research References

Rutter, Cal. Practice Guide: Enforcing Judgments/Debts Ch. 3-B, B. Collection Without Suit.
Rutter, Cal. Practice Guide: Personal Injury Ch. 4-G, G. Concluding and Enforcing Settlement.
Miller and Starr California Real Estate § 1:112, Accord and Satisfaction--Acceptance of Satisfaction by a Creditor.
Miller and Starr California Real Estate § 1:113, Accord and Satisfaction--Consideration; Necessity for a Dispute or Unliquidated Claim.
Miller and Starr California Real Estate § 10:75, Application and Allocation of Payments.
Miller and Starr California Real Estate § 27:96, Partial Payment; Accord and Satisfaction.
1 Witkin Cal. Summ. 10th Contracts § 952, (S 952) in General.
4 Witkin, California Summary 10th Negotiable Instruments § 19, (S 19) to Resolve Dispute.

CHAPTER 5. NOVATION

Section
1530. Novation defined.
1531. Methods.
1532. Applicability of contract rules.
1533. Rescission.

§ 1530. Novation defined

NOVATION, WHAT. Novation is the substitution of a new obligation for an existing one. *(Enacted in 1872.)*

Research References

Rutter, Cal. Practice Guide: Civil Trials & Evidence Ch. 8E-G, G. Parol Evidence Rule.
Rutter, Cal. Practice Guide: Real Prop. Transactions Ch. 7-D, D. Representing the Selling Tenant.
Miller and Starr California Real Estate § 1:106, Novation; Definition and Requirements.
Miller and Starr California Real Estate § 1:107, Modification and Novation Compared.

18 NO. 4 Miller & Starr, California Real Estate Newsalert 10, Escheat.
1 Witkin Cal. Summ. 10th Contracts § 961, (S 961) Nature and Effect.

§ 1531. Methods

MODES OF NOVATION. Novation is made:

1. By the substitution of a new obligation between the same parties, with intent to extinguish the old obligation;

2. By the substitution of a new debtor in place of the old one, with intent to release the latter; or,

3. By the substitution of a new creditor in place of the old one, with intent to transfer the rights of the latter to the former. *(Enacted in 1872.)*

Research References

Rutter, Cal. Practice Guide: Real Prop. Transactions Ch. 7-D, D. Representing the Selling Tenant.
Miller and Starr California Real Estate § 1:106, Novation; Definition and Requirements.
Miller and Starr California Real Estate § 19:55, Requirements for Modification of Lease Terms.
18 NO. 4 Miller & Starr, California Real Estate Newsalert 10, Escheat.
1 Witkin Cal. Summ. 10th Contracts § 961, (S 961) Nature and Effect.

§ 1532. Applicability of contract rules

NOVATION A CONTRACT. Novation is made by contract, and is subject to all the rules concerning contracts in general. *(Enacted in 1872.)*

Research References

Rutter, Cal. Practice Guide: Civil Trials & Evidence Ch. 8E-G, G. Parol Evidence Rule.
Miller and Starr California Real Estate § 1:106, Novation; Definition and Requirements.
Miller and Starr California Real Estate § 1:107, Modification and Novation Compared.
18 NO. 4 Miller & Starr, California Real Estate Newsalert 10, Escheat.
1 Witkin Cal. Summ. 10th Contracts § 961, (S 961) Nature and Effect.
1 Witkin Cal. Summ. 10th Contracts § 962, in General.

§ 1533. Rescission

When the obligation of a third person, or an order upon such person is accepted in satisfaction, the creditor may rescind such acceptance if the debtor prevents such person from complying with the order, or from fulfilling the obligation; or if, at the time the obligation or order is received, such person is insolvent, and this fact is unknown to the creditor, or if, before the creditor can with reasonable diligence present the order to the person upon whom it is given, he becomes insolvent. *(Enacted in 1872. Amended by Code Am.1873–74, c. 612, p. 241, § 188.)*

Research References

Miller and Starr California Real Estate § 1:107, Modification and Novation Compared.
1 Witkin Cal. Summ. 10th Contracts § 935, (S 935) Grounds for Rescission.
1 Witkin Cal. Summ. 10th Contracts § 961, (S 961) Nature and Effect.

CHAPTER 6. RELEASE

§ 1541. Extinction of obligations

OBLIGATION EXTINGUISHED BY RELEASE. An obligation is extinguished by a release therefrom given to the debtor by the creditor, upon a new consideration, or in writing, with or without new consideration. *(Enacted in 1872.)*

Research References

California Practice Guide: Employment Litigation Ch. 16-K, K. Settlements and Releases.
Rutter, Cal. Practice Guide: Insurance Litigation Ch. 12D-I, I. Settlement and Release.
Rutter, Cal. Practice Guide: Personal Injury Ch. 4-G, G. Concluding and Enforcing Settlement.
Miller and Starr California Real Estate § 1:99, Modification of a Contract; Executed Oral Agreement--Consideration Required for a Modification of a Written Agreement.
Miller and Starr California Real Estate § 1:105, Mutual Rescission--Release Compared to Rescission or Novation.
Miller and Starr California Real Estate § 1:113, Accord and Satisfaction--Consideration; Necessity for a Dispute or Unliquidated Claim.
1 Witkin Cal. Summ. 10th Contracts § 946, (S 946) Validity and Effect.
1 Witkin Cal. Summ. 10th Contracts § 959, Rule and Theory.
1 Witkin Cal. Summ. 10th Contracts § 960, Check Containing Written Release.

§ 1542. General release; extent

A general release does not extend to claims which the creditor does not know or suspect to exist in his or her favor at the time of executing the release, which if known by him or her must have materially affected his or her settlement with the debtor. *(Enacted in 1872. Amended by Code Am.1873–74, c. 612, p. 241, § 189; Stats.2004, c. 183 (A.B.3082), § 28.)*

Research References

California Real Estate Forms (Miller & Starr) § 1:15, Option Agreement–Long Form.
California Real Estate Forms (Miller & Starr) § 1:28, Purchase and Sale Agreement–Hotel.
California Real Estate Forms (Miller & Starr) § 1:29, Purchase and Sale Agreement–Seller Oriented With Seller Financing.
California Real Estate Forms (Miller & Starr) § 1:34, Installment Land Sale Contract With Power of Sale.
California Real Estate Forms (Miller & Starr) § 2:26, Triple Net Lease–Industrial Build-To-Suit Lease.
California Real Estate Forms (Miller & Starr) § 2:50, Lease Termination Agreement.
California Real Estate Forms (Miller & Starr) § 2:51, Surrender of Leasehold.
California Real Estate Forms (Miller & Starr) § 3:67, Deed in Lieu of Foreclosure–Release (Exhibit B to Transfer Agreement).
California Real Estate Forms (Miller & Starr) § 3:69, Note and Deed of Trust Assumption Agreement.
California Real Estate Forms (Miller & Starr) § 1:145, Seller's Covenants, Warranties, and Representations–Office Building or Other Structure (Seller-Oriented).
Rutter, Cal. Practice Guide: Civil Trials & Evidence Ch. 8E-G, G. Parol Evidence Rule.
California Practice Guide: Employment Litigation Ch. 16-K, K. Settlements and Releases.
California Practice Guide: Employment Litigation Form 8:A, Settlement and Release for Use When Litigation Pending.
California Practice Guide: Employment Litigation Form 8:B, Release for Use Where No Litigation Pending.
California Practice Guide: Employment Litigation Form 8:C, Settlement and Release for Group Termination Programs.
California Practice Guide: Employment Litigation Form 16:A, Settlement and Release.
California Practice Guide: Employment Litigation Ch. 16-K, Outline K.
Rutter, Cal. Practice Guide: Enforcing Judgments/Debts Form 4:O, Defendant's Release of Wrongful Attachment Claims.
Rutter, Cal. Practice Guide: Family Law Form 9:D, Marital Settlement Agreement.
Rutter, Cal. Practice Guide: Fed.Civ.Pro. Before Trial Form 15:C, Release Agreement.

Rutter, Cal. Practice Guide: Insurance Litigation Ch. 12D-I, I. Settlement and Release.

Rutter, Cal. Practice Guide: Insurance Litigation Form 15:C, Settlement Agreement.

Rutter, Cal. Practice Guide: Landlord-Tenant Form 2:B, Standard Shopping Center Lease.

Rutter, Cal. Practice Guide: Personal Injury Ch. 4-G, G. Concluding and Enforcing Settlement.

Rutter, Cal. Practice Guide: Personal Injury Form 4:J, Sample Release Agreement.

Rutter, Cal. Practice Guide: Real Prop. Transactions Ch. 5-E, E. Addressing Environmental Hazards Liability Concerns of Real Property Buyers and Sellers.

Rutter, Cal. Practice Guide: Prof. Responsibility Ch. 4-E, E. Conflicts Based on Lawyer's Personal Interests or Relationships.

Rutter, Cal. Practice Guide: Prof. Responsibility Ch. 5-F, F. Formalizing Fee Agreements.

Rutter, Cal. Practice Guide: Prof. Responsibility Ch. 5-J, J. Fee Disputes With Existing Clients.

Rutter, Cal. Practice Guide: Prof. Responsibility Ch. 6-F, F. Waiver/Settlement of Malpractice Claim.

Rutter, Cal. Practice Guide: Prof. Responsibility Ch. 5-F, Outline F.

Miller and Starr California Real Estate § 27:51, Modification and Alteration of Construction Contracts.

Miller and Starr California Real Estate § 10:143, Home Equity Sales Contracts Involving the Sale or Conveyance of Residential Property in Foreclosure.

Miller and Starr California Real Estate § 10:144, Remedies for Violation.

Miller and Starr California Real Estate § 27:105, Payment as Waiver by Owner or by Contractor.

20 NO. 1 Miller & Starr, California Real Estate Newsalert 8, Deeds of Trust.

1 Witkin Cal. Summ. 10th Contracts § 680, Other Rights.

1 Witkin Cal. Summ. 10th Contracts § 947, Statutory Prohibition.

1 Witkin Cal. Summ. 10th Contracts § 948, Routine Waiver Invalid.

2 Witkin Cal. Summ. 10th Workers' Compensation § 365, Claims Outside Workers' Compensation Law.

§ 1542.1. Defense of health care providers by Attorney General or other legal counsel provided by state; scope of release

Notwithstanding Section 1542, a provider of health care, as defined in Section 56.05, or its officers, employees, agents, or subcontractors, shall release the state and its officers, employees, and agents, from any claim arising from the defense of the provider of health care by the Attorney General, or other legal counsel provided by the state pursuant to Section 12511.5 of the Government Code. *(Added by Stats.1995, c. 749 (A.B.1177), § 2, eff. Oct. 10, 1995.)*

§ 1543. One or more joint debtors

A release of one of two or more joint debtors does not extinguish the obligations of any of the others, unless they are mere guarantors; nor does it affect their right to contribution from him or her, except as provided in Section 877 of the Code of Civil Procedure. *(Enacted in 1872. Amended by Stats.1987, c. 677, § 1.5.)*

Research References

1 Witkin Cal. Summ. 10th Contracts § 111, Performance and Discharge.

Part 2

CONTRACTS

Title 1

NATURE OF A CONTRACT

CHAPTER 1. DEFINITION

§ 1549. Contract defined

CONTRACT, WHAT. A contract is an agreement to do or not to do a certain thing. *(Enacted in 1872.)*

Research References

Rutter, Cal. Practice Guide: Real Prop. Transactions Ch. 8-B, B. Options to Purchase.

Miller and Starr California Real Estate § 1:1, Nature of Real Estate Contracts.

Miller and Starr California Real Estate § 2:9, Mode and Manner of Exercise.

1 Witkin Cal. Summ. 10th Contracts § 1, Contract.

§ 1550. Essential elements

ESSENTIAL ELEMENTS OF CONTRACT. It is essential to the existence of a contract that there should be:

1. Parties capable of contracting;

2. Their consent;

3. A lawful object; and,

4. A sufficient cause or consideration. *(Enacted in 1872.)*

Research References

California Real Estate Forms (Miller & Starr) § 1:8, Letter of Intent–Nonbinding.

California Real Estate Forms (Miller & Starr) § 1:9, Letter of Intent–Binding.

California Real Estate Forms (Miller & Starr) § 1:15, Option Agreement–Long Form.

California Real Estate Forms (Miller & Starr) § 1:21, Purchase and Sale Agreement–Commercial Property Subject to Tenant Leases.

California Real Estate Forms (Miller & Starr) § 1:22, Agreement of Purchase and Sale–Multi-Property.

California Real Estate Forms (Miller & Starr) § 1:24, Combination Purchase and Option Agreement–Residential Lots Being Acquired from a Bankrupt Seller.

California Real Estate Forms (Miller & Starr) § 1:30, Planned Development Deposit Receipt and Agreement of Sale.

California Real Estate Forms (Miller & Starr) § 1:31, Condominium Deposit Receipt and Agreement of Sale.

California Real Estate Forms (Miller & Starr) § 2:66, Residential Lease With Purchase Option.

Rutter, Cal. Practice Guide: A.D.R. Ch. 5-A, A. General Considerations.

Rutter, Cal. Practice Guide: Real Prop. Transactions Ch. 4-C, C. Parties to the Purchase Agreement.

Rutter, Cal. Practice Guide: Real Prop. Transactions Ch. 8-B, B. Options to Purchase.

Rutter, Cal. Practice Guide: Real Prop. Transactions Ch. 11-A, A. Factors Affecting Choice of Remedies.

Miller and Starr California Real Estate § 1:8, Required Elements for Creation; Mutual Assent.

Miller and Starr California Real Estate § 2:9, Mode and Manner of Exercise.

Miller and Starr California Real Estate § 1:51, Necessity for Consideration.

Miller and Starr California Real Estate § 8:57, Conveyance in Violation of Public Policy or Statute.

Miller and Starr California Real Estate § 1:114, Free and Real Consent Required.

Miller and Starr California Real Estate § 28:97, Measure of Surety's Liability.

21 NO. 2 Miller & Starr, California Real Estate Newsalert 2, Alternative Dispute Resolution.

2 Witkin, California Summary 10th Insurance § 47, (S 47) Validity.

1 Witkin Cal. Summ. 10th Contracts § 116, (S 116) in General.

1 Witkin Cal. Summ. 10th Contracts § 202, (S 202) Requirement of Consideration.

1 Witkin Cal. Summ. 10th Contracts § 420, (S 420) Illegal Object.

11 Witkin, California Summary 10th Husband and Wife § 59, (S 59) Fault Theory Eliminated for Dissolution.

CHAPTER 2.   PARTIES

Section

§ 1556.   Persons capable of contracting

WHO MAY CONTRACT.   All persons are capable of contracting, except minors, persons of unsound mind, and persons deprived of civil rights.   *(Enacted in 1872.)*

Research References

Rutter, Cal. Practice Guide: A.D.R. Ch. 5-D, D. Defenses to Enforcement.

Rutter, Cal. Practice Guide: Real Prop. Transactions Ch. 4-C, C. Parties to the Purchase Agreement.

Rutter, Cal. Practice Guide: Real Prop. Transactions Ch. 11-A, A. Factors Affecting Choice of Remedies.

1 Witkin Cal. Summ. 10th Contracts § 25, General Rule.

1 Witkin Cal. Summ. 10th Contracts § 58, Persons Deprived of Civil Rights.

§ 1557.   Capacity of minors and persons of unsound mind

(a) The capacity of a minor to contract is governed by Division 11 (commencing with Section 6500) of the Family Code.

(b) The capacity of a person of unsound mind to contract is governed by Part 1 (commencing with Section 38) of Division 1. *(Added by Stats.1992, c. 163 (A.B.2641), § 9, operative Jan. 1, 1994.)*

Law Revision Commission Comments

Section 1557 restates former Section 1557 without substantive change. [22 Cal.L.Rev.Comm.Reports 1 (1992)].

Research References

Rutter, Cal. Practice Guide: Real Prop. Transactions Ch. 4-C, C. Parties to the Purchase Agreement.

Rutter, Cal. Practice Guide: Real Prop. Transactions Ch. 11-A, A. Factors Affecting Choice of Remedies.

§ 1558.   Identification of parties; necessity

IDENTIFICATION OF PARTIES NECESSARY.   It is essential to the validity of a contract, not only that the parties should exist, but that it should be possible to identify them.   *(Enacted in 1872.)*

Research References

Rutter, Cal. Practice Guide: Real Prop. Transactions Ch. 4-C, C. Parties to the Purchase Agreement.

Rutter, Cal. Practice Guide: Real Prop. Transactions Ch. 11-A, A. Factors Affecting Choice of Remedies.

§ 1559.   Enforcement by third party beneficiary

WHEN CONTRACT FOR BENEFIT OF THIRD PERSON MAY BE ENFORCED. A contract, made expressly for the benefit of a third person, may be enforced by him at any time before the parties thereto rescind it.   *(Enacted in 1872.)*

Research References

Rutter, Cal. Practice Guide: Civ. Pro. Before Trial Ch. 2-A, A. Standing to Sue-"Real Party in Interest" Requirement.

Rutter, Cal. Practice Guide: Civ. Pro. Before Trial Ch. 3-B, B. Jurisdiction Over Parties-Personal Jurisdiction.

Rutter, Cal. Practice Guide: Fed.Civ.Pro. Before Trial Ch. 7-A, A. "Real Party in Interest" Requirement.

Rutter, Cal. Practice Guide: Insurance Litigation Ch. 3-C, C. Anatomy of Insurance Policy.

Rutter, Cal. Practice Guide: Insurance Litigation Ch. 8-D, D. Reinsurance.

Rutter, Cal. Practice Guide: Real Prop. Transactions Ch. 4-E, E. Drafting the Purchase and Sale Agreement-Terms and Conditions.

Rutter, Cal. Practice Guide: Real Prop. Transactions Ch. 11-G, G. Rescission.

Miller and Starr California Real Estate § 24:4, Covenants Burdening Land for the Benefit of Other Land--Prior to the 1968 and 1969 Amendments to Civil Code § 4168.

Miller and Starr California Real Estate § 5:62, Third-Party Beneficiary of the Sales Contract.

Miller and Starr California Real Estate § 6:18, Liability to Third Persons.

Miller and Starr California Real Estate § 1:108, Assignment and Novation Compared.

Miller and Starr California Real Estate § 29:18, Subcontractor's Liability.

Miller and Starr California Real Estate § 34:17, When Specific Performance is Available; Prerequisites.

Miller and Starr California Real Estate § 25B:110, Actions for Construction Defects.

18 NO. 3 Miller & Starr, California Real Estate Newsalert 11, Defective Construction.

19 NO. 5 Miller & Starr, California Real Estate Newsalert 22, Landlord and Tenant.

4 Witkin Cal. Proc. 5th Pleading § 143, Action by Third-Party Beneficiary.

2 Witkin, California Summary 10th Insurance § 70, Third-Party Beneficiaries.

2 Witkin, California Summary 10th Insurance § 304, Exception: Suit as Third-Party Beneficiary Under Traditional Contract Principles.

1 Witkin Cal. Summ. 10th Contracts § 685, (S 685) Nature of Right.

1 Witkin Cal. Summ. 10th Contracts § 686, Creditor and Donee Beneficiaries.

1 Witkin Cal. Summ. 10th Contracts § 701, Illustrations.

1 Witkin Cal. Summ. 10th Contracts § 740, Liability of Assignee.

CHAPTER 3.   CONSENT

Section

Section

§ 1565. Essentials of consent

ESSENTIALS OF CONSENT. The consent of the parties to a contract must be:

1. Free;

2. Mutual; and,

3. Communicated by each to the other. *(Enacted in 1872.)*

Research References

Rutter, Cal. Practice Guide: Real Prop. Transactions Ch. 11-A, A. Factors Affecting Choice of Remedies.
Miller and Starr California Real Estate § 1:8, Required Elements for Creation; Mutual Assent.
Miller and Starr California Real Estate § 1:114, Free and Real Consent Required.
Miller and Starr California Real Estate § 34:83, General Principles; Election of Remedies.
18 NO. 4 Miller & Starr, California Real Estate Newsalert 10, Escheat.
1 Witkin Cal. Summ. 10th Contracts § 116, (S 116) in General.
1 Witkin Cal. Summ. 10th Contracts § 187, Necessity of Communication.

§ 1566. Consent not free; rescission

CONSENT, WHEN VOIDABLE. A consent which is not free is nevertheless not absolutely void, but may be rescinded by the parties, in the manner prescribed by the Chapter on Rescission. *(Enacted in 1872.)*

Research References

Rutter, Cal. Practice Guide: A.D.R. Ch. 5-D, D. Defenses to Enforcement.
Rutter, Cal. Practice Guide: Real Prop. Transactions Ch. 11-A, A. Factors Affecting Choice of Remedies.
Miller and Starr California Real Estate § 1:114, Free and Real Consent Required.
Miller and Starr California Real Estate § 34:83, General Principles; Election of Remedies.
1 Witkin Cal. Summ. 10th Contracts § 285, (S 285) in General.
1 Witkin Cal. Summ. 10th Contracts § 299, Fraud in Inception.
1 Witkin Cal. Summ. 10th Contracts § 935, (S 935) Grounds for Rescission.

§ 1567. Reality or freedom of consent; causes for defeating

APPARENT CONSENT, WHEN NOT FREE. An apparent consent is not real or free when obtained through:

1. Duress;

2. Menace;

3. Fraud;

4. Undue influence; or,

5. Mistake. *(Enacted in 1872.)*

Research References

Rutter, Cal. Practice Guide: Personal Injury Ch. 3-D, D. Mitigating Factors in Reduction of Damages.
Miller and Starr California Real Estate § 1:114, Free and Real Consent Required.
Miller and Starr California Real Estate § 34:83, General Principles; Election of Remedies.

§ 1568. Consent obtained by cause defeating reality or freedom

WHEN DEEMED TO HAVE BEEN OBTAINED BY FRAUD, ETC. Consent is deemed to have been obtained through one of the causes mentioned in the last section only when it would not have been given had such cause not existed. *(Enacted in 1872.)*

Research References

Miller and Starr California Real Estate § 1:114, Free and Real Consent Required.
Miller and Starr California Real Estate § 1:120, Material Versus Collateral Fact.
Miller and Starr California Real Estate § 1:148, Reliance by Injured Party.
Miller and Starr California Real Estate § 34:83, General Principles; Election of Remedies.
1 Witkin Cal. Summ. 10th Contracts § 260, General Principle.

§ 1569. Duress

DURESS, WHAT. Duress consists in:

1. Unlawful confinement of the person of the party, or of the husband or wife of such party, or of an ancestor, descendant, or adopted child of such party, husband, or wife;

2. Unlawful detention of the property of any such person; or,

3. Confinement of such person, lawful in form, but fraudulently obtained, or fraudulently made unjustly harrassing [1] or oppressive. *(Enacted in 1872.)*

[1] So in chaptered bill.

Research References

Rutter, Cal. Practice Guide: Personal Injury Ch. 3-D, D. Mitigating Factors in Reduction of Damages.
Miller and Starr California Real Estate § 34:5, Economic Duress as Basis for Rescission.
Miller and Starr California Real Estate § 34:113, Grounds for Cancellation.
8 Witkin Cal. Proc. 5th Attack Judgment Trial Court § 235, (S 235) Judgment Obtained by Duress.
1 Witkin Cal. Summ. 10th Contracts § 309, (S 309) Nature and Kinds of Duress.

§ 1570. Menace

MENACE, WHAT. Menace consists in a threat:

1. Of such duress as is specified in Subdivisions 1 and 3 of the last section;

2. Of unlawful and violent injury to the person or property of any such person as is specified in the last section; or,

3. Of injury to the character of any such person. *(Enacted in 1872.)*

Research References

Miller and Starr California Real Estate § 34:5, Economic Duress as Basis for Rescission.
1 Witkin Cal. Summ. 10th Contracts § 309, (S 309) Nature and Kinds of Duress.
1 Witkin Cal. Summ. 10th Contracts § 311, in General.

§ 1571. Kinds of fraud

FRAUD, ACTUAL OR CONSTRUCTIVE. Fraud is either actual or constructive. *(Enacted in 1872.)*

§ 1572. Actual fraud

ACTUAL FRAUD, WHAT. Actual fraud, within the meaning of this Chapter, consists in any of the following acts, committed by a party to the contract, or with his connivance, with intent to deceive another party thereto, or to induce him to enter into the contract:

1. The suggestion, as a fact, of that which is not true, by one who does not believe it to be true;

2. The positive assertion, in a manner not warranted by the information of the person making it, of that which is not true, though he believes it to be true;

3. The suppression of that which is true, by one having knowledge or belief of the fact;

4. A promise made without any intention of performing it; or,

5. Any other act fitted to deceive. *(Enacted in 1872.)*

§ 1573. Constructive fraud

CONSTRUCTIVE FRAUD. Constructive fraud consists:

1. In any breach of duty which, without an actually fraudulent intent, gains an advantage to the person in fault, or any one claiming under him, by misleading another to his prejudice, or to the prejudice of any one claiming under him; or,

2. In any such act or omission as the law specially declares to be fraudulent, without respect to actual fraud. *(Enacted in 1872.)*

§ 1574. Actual fraud; question of fact

ACTUAL FRAUD A QUESTION OF FACT. Actual fraud is always a question of fact. *(Enacted in 1872.)*

1 Witkin Cal. Summ. 10th Contracts § 286, Elements: Traditional Listing.

§ 1575. Undue influence

UNDUE INFLUENCE, WHAT. Undue influence consists:

1. In the use, by one in whom a confidence is reposed by another, or who holds a real or apparent authority over him, of such confidence or authority for the purpose of obtaining an unfair advantage over him;

2. In taking an unfair advantage of another's weakness of mind; or,

3. In taking a grossly oppressive and unfair advantage of another's necessities or distress. *(Enacted in 1872.)*

Research References

California Practice Guide: Employment Litigation Ch. 16-K, K. Settlements and Releases.
Miller and Starr California Real Estate § 8:55, Undue Influence.
Miller and Starr California Real Estate § 34:113, Grounds for Cancellation.
4 Witkin Cal. Proc. 5th Pleading § 549, Cases Not Involving Confidential Relationship.
1 Witkin Cal. Summ. 10th Contracts § 57, Manic Depressive Psychosis.
1 Witkin Cal. Summ. 10th Contracts § 316, (S 316) Nature and Types.
1 Witkin Cal. Summ. 10th Contracts § 321, (S 321) No Confidential Relationship.

§ 1576. Kinds of mistake

MISTAKE, WHAT. Mistake may be either of fact or law. *(Enacted in 1872.)*

Research References

Rutter, Cal. Practice Guide: Personal Injury Ch. 4-D, D. Techniques Where Settlement Not Forthcoming.
Rutter, Cal. Practice Guide: Real Prop. Transactions Ch. 11-G, G. Rescission.
Miller and Starr California Real Estate § 1:115, Types of Mistake.

§ 1577. Mistake of fact

MISTAKE OF FACT. Mistake of fact is a mistake, not caused by the neglect of a legal duty on the part of the person making the mistake, and consisting in:

1. An unconscious ignorance or forgetfulness of a fact past or present, material to the contract; or,

2. Belief in the present existence of a thing material to the contract, which does not exist, or in the past existence of such a thing, which has not existed. *(Enacted in 1872.)*

Research References

Rutter, Cal. Practice Guide: Insurance Litigation Ch. 5-E, E. Reformation.
Rutter, Cal. Practice Guide: Real Prop. Transactions Ch. 11-F, F. Reformation.
Rutter, Cal. Practice Guide: Real Prop. Transactions Ch. 11-G, G. Rescission.
Miller and Starr California Real Estate § 1:115, Types of Mistake.
Miller and Starr California Real Estate § 1:119, Negligence as a Bar to Relief.
Miller and Starr California Real Estate § 1:123, Remedies for Mistake.
Miller and Starr California Real Estate § 27:36, Relief from a Mistake in Bid--Private Contracts.
Miller and Starr California Real Estate § 34:11, Nature of the Remedy; Requirement of a Prior Agreement.
18 NO. 3 Miller & Starr, California Real Estate Newsalert 21, Remedies.
1 Witkin Cal. Summ. 10th Contracts § 260, General Principle.
1 Witkin Cal. Summ. 10th Contracts § 262, in General.
1 Witkin Cal. Summ. 10th Contracts § 269, Relief Denied.
1 Witkin Cal. Summ. 10th Contracts § 270, Excusable Neglect.

1 Witkin Cal. Summ. 10th Contracts § 282, Effect of Plaintiff's Negligence.

§ 1578. Mistake of law

MISTAKE OF LAW. Mistake of law constitutes a mistake, within the meaning of this Article, only when it arises from:

1. A misapprehension of the law by all parties, all supposing that they knew and understood it, and all making substantially the same mistake as to the law; or,

2. A misapprehension of the law by one party, of which the others are aware at the time of contracting, but which they do not rectify. *(Enacted in 1872.)*

Research References

Rutter, Cal. Practice Guide: Real Prop. Transactions Ch. 11-G, G. Rescission.
Miller and Starr California Real Estate § 1:122, Mistake of Law.
1 Witkin Cal. Summ. 10th Contracts § 272, (S 272) in General.
1 Witkin Cal. Summ. 10th Contracts § 274, Unilateral Mistake.
14 Witkin, California Summary 10th Wills and Probate § 724, (S 724) Order.

§ 1579. Mistake of foreign law

MISTAKE OF FOREIGN LAWS. Mistake of foreign laws is a mistake of fact. *(Enacted in 1872.)*

Research References

Rutter, Cal. Practice Guide: Real Prop. Transactions Ch. 11-A, A. Factors Affecting Choice of Remedies.
Miller and Starr California Real Estate § 1:122, Mistake of Law.
Miller and Starr California Real Estate § 1:136, Misrepresentation of Law as a Representation of Fact.
1 Witkin Cal. Summ. 10th Contracts § 272, (S 272) in General.

§ 1580. Mutuality of consent

MUTUALITY OF CONSENT. Consent is not mutual, unless the parties all agree upon the same thing in the same sense. But in certain cases defined by the Chapter on Interpretation, they are to be deemed so to agree without regard to the fact. *(Enacted in 1872.)*

Research References

Rutter, Cal. Practice Guide: Real Prop. Transactions Ch. 11-A, A. Factors Affecting Choice of Remedies.
Miller and Starr California Real Estate § 1:8, Required Elements for Creation; Mutual Assent.
Miller and Starr California Real Estate § 1:116, Mistake that Precludes Formation of a Contract.

§ 1581. Communication; consent

COMMUNICATION OF CONSENT. Consent can be communicated with effect, only by some act or omission of the party contracting, by which he intends to communicate it, or which necessarily tends to such communication. *(Enacted in 1872.)*

Research References

Miller and Starr California Real Estate § 1:32, Termination by Revocation by the Offeror.
1 Witkin Cal. Summ. 10th Contracts § 160, (S 160) When Revocation Becomes Effective.
1 Witkin Cal. Summ. 10th Contracts § 187, Necessity of Communication.

§ 1582. Communication; acceptance of proposal

MODE OF COMMUNICATING ACCEPTANCE OF PROPOSAL. If a proposal prescribes any conditions concerning the communication of its acceptance, the proposer is not bound unless they are conformed to; but in other cases any reasonable and usual mode may be adopted. *(Enacted in 1872.)*

Research References

Rutter, Cal. Practice Guide: Real Prop. Transactions Ch. 8-B, B. Options to Purchase.
Miller and Starr California Real Estate § 2:9, Mode and Manner of Exercise.
Miller and Starr California Real Estate § 1:39, When Acceptance is Effective.
Miller and Starr California Real Estate § 19:135, Exercise of the Option.
1 Witkin Cal. Summ. 10th Contracts § 160, (S 160) When Revocation Becomes Effective.
1 Witkin Cal. Summ. 10th Contracts § 189, (S 189) Prescribed Manner or Reasonable Manner.
1 Witkin Cal. Summ. 10th Contracts § 191, in General.

§ 1583. Communication; completion

WHEN COMMUNICATION DEEMED COMPLETE. Consent is deemed to be fully communicated between the parties as soon as the party accepting a proposal has put his acceptance in the course of transmission to the proposer, in conformity to the last section. *(Enacted in 1872.)*

Research References

Miller and Starr California Real Estate § 2:9, Mode and Manner of Exercise.
Miller and Starr California Real Estate § 1:32, Termination by Revocation by the Offeror.
Miller and Starr California Real Estate § 1:39, When Acceptance is Effective.
1 Witkin Cal. Summ. 10th Contracts § 160, (S 160) When Revocation Becomes Effective.
1 Witkin Cal. Summ. 10th Contracts § 177, (S 177) Effective on Deposit in Mail.
1 Witkin Cal. Summ. 10th Contracts § 189, (S 189) Prescribed Manner or Reasonable Manner.
1 Witkin Cal. Summ. 10th Contracts § 191, in General.

§ 1584. Acceptance of proposal; performing conditions or acceptance of consideration

ACCEPTANCE BY PERFORMANCE OF CONDITIONS. Performance of the conditions of a proposal, or the acceptance of the consideration offered with a proposal, is an acceptance of the proposal. *(Enacted in 1872.)*

Research References

Miller and Starr California Real Estate § 1:41, Silence as Acceptance of Bilateral Contract.
1 Witkin Cal. Summ. 10th Contracts § 195, Conduct as Acceptance.
1 Witkin Cal. Summ. 10th Contracts § 199, Notification to Offeror.

§ 1584.5. Voluntary and unsolicited sending of goods, wares, merchandise or services; receipt deemed unconditional gift; action to enjoin billing

No person, firm, partnership, association, or corporation, or agent or employee thereof, shall, in any manner, or by any means, offer for sale goods, wares, merchandise, or services, where the offer includes the voluntary and unsolicited sending or providing of goods, wares, merchandise, or services not actually ordered or requested by the recipient, either orally or in writing. The receipt of any goods, wares, merchandise, or services shall for all purposes be deemed an unconditional gift to the recipient who may use or dispose of the goods, wares, merchandise, or services in any manner he or she sees fit without any obligation on his or her part to the sender or provider.

If, after any receipt deemed to be an unconditional gift under this section, the sender or provider continues to send bill statements or requests for payment with respect to the gift, an action may be brought by the recipient to enjoin the conduct, in which action there may also be awarded reasonable attorney's fees and costs to the prevailing party.

For the purposes of this section and limited to merchandise or services offered for sale through the mails, the "voluntary and unsolicited sending or providing of goods, wares, merchandise, or services not actually ordered or requested by the recipient, either orally or in writing," includes any merchandise or services selected by the company and offered to the consumer which will be mailed to him or her for sale or on approval or provided to him or her unless he or she exercises an option to reject the offer of sale or receipt on approval. Merchandise or services selected by the seller and offered for sale on a periodic basis must be affirmatively ordered by a statement or card signed by the consumer as to each periodic offer of merchandise or services. This paragraph shall not apply to any of the following:

(a) Contractual plans or arrangements complying with this subdivision under which the seller periodically provides the consumer with a form or announcement card which the consumer may use to instruct the seller not to ship the offered merchandise. Any instructions not to ship merchandise included on the form or card shall be printed in type as large as all other instructions and terms stated on the form or card. The form or card shall specify a date by which it shall be mailed by the consumer (the "mailing date") or received by the seller (the "return date") to prevent shipment of the offered merchandise. The seller shall mail the form or card either at least 25 days prior to the return date or at least 20 days prior to the mailing date, or provide a mailing date of at least 10 days after receipt by the consumer, except that whichever system the seller chooses for mailing the form or card, the system must be calculated to afford the consumer at least 10 days in which to mail his or her form or card. The form or card shall be preaddressed to the seller so that it may serve as a postal reply card or, alternatively, the form or card shall be accompanied by a return envelope addressed to seller. Upon the membership contract or application form or on the same page and immediately adjacent to the contract or form, and in clear and conspicuous language, there shall be disclosed the material terms of the plan or arrangement including all of the following:

(1) That aspect of the plan under which the subscriber must notify the seller, in the manner provided for by the seller, if he or she does not wish to purchase or receive the selection.

(2) Any obligation assumed by the subscriber to purchase a minimum quantity of merchandise.

(3) The right of a contract-complete subscriber to cancel his or her membership at any time.

(4) Whether billing charges will include an amount for postage and handling.

(b) Other contractual plans or arrangements not covered under subdivision (a), such as continuity plans, subscription arrangements, standing order arrangements, supplements and series arrangements under which the seller periodically ships merchandise to a consumer who has consented in advance to receive the merchandise on a periodic basis. *(Added by Stats. 1969, c. 400, p. 931, § 1. Amended by Stats.1971, c. 1623, p. 3494, § 1, operative July 1, 1972; Stats.1973, c. 916, p. 1697, § 1, operative Jan. 1, 1975; Stats.1985, c. 80, § 1.)*

Research References

1 Witkin Cal. Summ. 10th Contracts § 196, Exception: Unsolicited Merchandise or Services.
13 Witkin, California Summary 10th Personal Property § 124, (S 124) in General.
4 Witkin, California Summary 10th Sales § 395, (S 395) Unsolicited Sending of Merchandise or Services.

§ 1584.6. Membership in organization making retail sales to members; notification of termination; receipt of unordered goods, wares or merchandise deemed unconditional gift

If a person is a member of an organization which makes retail sales of any goods, wares, or merchandise to its members, and the person notifies the organization of his termination of membership by certified mail, return receipt requested, any unordered goods, wares, or merchandise which are sent to the person after 30 days following execution of the return receipt for the certified letter by the organization, shall for all purposes be deemed unconditional gifts to the person, who may use or dispose of the goods, wares, or merchandise in any manner he sees fit without any obligation on his part to the organization.

If the termination of a person's membership in such organization breaches any agreement with the organization, nothing in this section shall relieve the person from liability for damages to which he might be otherwise subjected to pursuant to law, but he shall not be subject to any damages with respect to any goods, wares, or merchandise which are deemed unconditional gifts to him under this section.

If after any receipt deemed to be an unconditional gift under this section, the sender continues to send bill statements or requests for payment with respect thereto, an action may be brought by the recipient to enjoin such conduct, in which action there may also be awarded reasonable attorneys' fees and costs to the prevailing party. *(Added by Stats.1969, c. 400, p. 931, § 2.)*

Research References

1 Witkin Cal. Summ. 10th Contracts § 196, Exception: Unsolicited Merchandise or Services.
13 Witkin, California Summary 10th Personal Property § 124, (S 124) in General.

§ 1585. Acceptance of proposal; absolute acceptance; qualified acceptance

ACCEPTANCE MUST BE ABSOLUTE. An acceptance must be absolute and unqualified, or must include in itself an acceptance of that character which the proposer can separate from the rest, and which will conclude the person accepting. A qualified acceptance is a new proposal. *(Enacted in 1872.)*

Research References

Rutter, Cal. Practice Guide: Personal Injury Ch. 4-D, D. Techniques Where Settlement Not Forthcoming.
Rutter, Cal. Practice Guide: Real Prop. Transactions Ch. 4-D, D. Selecting the Form of Written Agreement.
Rutter, Cal. Practice Guide: Real Prop. Transactions Ch. 8-B, B. Options to Purchase.
Rutter, Cal. Practice Guide: Real Prop. Transactions Ch. 11-A, A. Factors Affecting Choice of Remedies.
Miller and Starr California Real Estate § 1:42, Communication of Acceptance; Unilateral Contract.
Miller and Starr California Real Estate § 1:43, Effect of New Term or Condition in the "Acceptance".
Miller and Starr California Real Estate § 1:44, Effect of Offeree's Expression of Condition Implied in the Offer.
Miller and Starr California Real Estate § 1:49, Effect of a Counteroffer.
1 Witkin Cal. Summ. 10th Contracts § 183, General Rule.
1 Witkin Cal. Summ. 10th Contracts § 185, in General.

§ 1586. Revocation of proposal; time

REVOCATION OF PROPOSAL. A proposal may be revoked at any time before its acceptance is communicated to the proposer, but not afterwards. *(Enacted in 1872.)*

Research References

Rutter, Cal. Practice Guide: A.D.R. Ch. 5-D, D. Defenses to Enforcement.
Miller and Starr California Real Estate § 1:32, Termination by Revocation by the Offeror.
Miller and Starr California Real Estate § 27:23, Procurement of Private Works Contracts.

1 Witkin Cal. Summ. 10th Contracts § 164, (S 164) General Rule of Revocability.

§ 1587. Revocation of proposal; method

REVOCATION, HOW MADE. A proposal is revoked:

1. By the communication of notice of revocation by the proposer to the other party, in the manner prescribed by Sections 1581 and 1583, before his acceptance has been communicated to the former;

2. By the lapse of the time prescribed in such proposal for its acceptance, or if no time is so prescribed, the lapse of a reasonable time without communication of the acceptance;

3. By the failure of the acceptor to fulfill a condition precedent to acceptance; or,

4. By the death or insanity of the proposer. *(Enacted in 1872.)*

Research References

California Real Estate Forms (Miller & Starr) § 1:23, Purchase and Sale Agreement–Residential Project.
California Real Estate Forms (Miller & Starr) § 1:33, Real Estate Purchase Contract and Receipt for Deposit–Income Property.
Rutter, Cal. Practice Guide: Real Prop. Transactions Ch. 8-B, B. Options to Purchase.
Miller and Starr California Real Estate § 1:28, Termination of an Offer.
Miller and Starr California Real Estate § 1:29, Termination by the Lapse of Time.
Miller and Starr California Real Estate § 1:30, Termination by the Death or Insanity of the Offeror or Offeree.
Miller and Starr California Real Estate § 1:32, Termination by Revocation by the Offeror.
1 Witkin Cal. Summ. 10th Contracts § 157, Lapse of Prescribed or Reasonable Time.
1 Witkin Cal. Summ. 10th Contracts § 158, Death or Incapacity of Offeror or Offeree.
1 Witkin Cal. Summ. 10th Contracts § 159, (S 159) In General.
1 Witkin Cal. Summ. 10th Contracts § 160, (S 160) When Revocation Becomes Effective.

§ 1588. Ratification of voidable contract

RATIFICATION OF CONTRACT, VOID FOR WANT OF CONSENT. A contract which is voidable solely for want of due consent, may be ratified by a subsequent consent. *(Enacted in 1872.)*

Research References

Rutter, Cal. Practice Guide: Real Prop. Transactions Ch. 11-A, A. Factors Affecting Choice of Remedies.
17 NO. 4 Miller & Starr, California Real Estate Newsalert 18, Subdivisions.

§ 1589. Consent by acceptance of benefits

ASSUMPTION OF OBLIGATION BY ACCEPTANCE OF BENEFITS. A voluntary acceptance of the benefit of a transaction is equivalent to a consent to all the obligations arising from it, so far as the facts are known, or ought to be known, to the person accepting. *(Enacted in 1872.)*

Research References

Rutter, Cal. Practice Guide: A.D.R. Ch. 5-F, F. Arbitration by and Against Nonsignatories.
Rutter, Cal. Practice Guide: Real Prop. Transactions Ch. 4-E, E. Drafting the Purchase and Sale Agreement-Terms and Conditions.
Rutter, Cal. Practice Guide: Real Prop. Transactions Ch. 11-A, A. Factors Affecting Choice of Remedies.
Miller and Starr California Real Estate § 1:41, Silence as Acceptance of Bilateral Contract.
Miller and Starr California Real Estate § 11:77, Notice to Partners and Corporate Officers.
Miller and Starr California Real Estate § 19:63, Liability of the Parties; Tenant-Assignor Liability to the Landlord--Assignee Rights and Liabilities Vis-à-Vis the Landlord.

1 Witkin Cal. Summ. 10th Contracts § 195, Conduct as Acceptance.

1 Witkin Cal. Summ. 10th Contracts § 740, Liability of Assignee.

§ 1590. Gifts in contemplation of marriage; recovery

Where either party to a contemplated marriage in this State makes a gift of money or property to the other on the basis or assumption that the marriage will take place, in the event that the donee refuses to enter into the marriage as contemplated or that it is given up by mutual consent, the donor may recover such gift or such part of its value as may, under all of the circumstances of the case, be found by a court or jury to be just. *(Added by Stats.1939, c. 128, p. 1245, § 3.)*

Research References

13 Witkin, California Summary 10th Personal Property § 154, Revocation of Gift in Contemplation of Marriage.

CHAPTER 4. OBJECT OF A CONTRACT

Section

§ 1595. Object defined

OBJECT, WHAT. The object of a contract is the thing which it is agreed, on the part of the party receiving the consideration, to do or not to do. *(Enacted in 1872.)*

§ 1596. Object; elements

REQUISITES OF OBJECT. The object of a contract must be lawful when the contract is made, and possible and ascertainable by the time the contract is to be performed. *(Enacted in 1872.)*

Research References

Rutter, Cal. Practice Guide: Real Prop. Transactions Ch. 11-A, A. Factors Affecting Choice of Remedies.

Miller and Starr California Real Estate § 1:9, Lawful Object.

Miller and Starr California Real Estate § 28:95, General Conditions of the Bond.

1 Witkin Cal. Summ. 10th Contracts § 828, Nature of Excuse and California Statutes.

§ 1597. Impossibility defined

IMPOSSIBILITY, WHAT. Everything is deemed possible except that which is impossible in the nature of things. *(Enacted in 1872.)*

Research References

1 Witkin Cal. Summ. 10th Contracts § 830, Subjective and Objective Impossibility.

1 Witkin Cal. Summ. 10th Contracts § 841, Destruction or Nonexistence of Subject Matter.

§ 1598. Object unlawful, impossible or unascertainable

WHEN CONTRACT WHOLLY VOID. Where a contract has but a single object, and such object is unlawful, whether in whole or in part, or wholly impossible of performance, or so vaguely expressed as to be wholly unascertainable, the entire contract is void. *(Enacted in 1872.)*

Research References

Rutter, Cal. Practice Guide: A.D.R. Ch. 5-D, D. Defenses to Enforcement.

California Practice Guide: Employment Litigation Ch. 18-C, C. Contractual Arbitration.

Rutter, Cal. Practice Guide: Real Prop. Transactions Ch. 11-A, A. Factors Affecting Choice of Remedies.

Miller and Starr California Real Estate § 34:4, Grounds for Rescission.

Miller and Starr California Real Estate § 34:8, Effect of Rescission.

Miller and Starr California Real Estate § 8:57, Conveyance in Violation of Public Policy or Statute.

19 NO. 3 Miller & Starr, California Real Estate Newsalert 20, Landlord and Tenant.

1 Witkin Cal. Summ. 10th Contracts § 420, (S 420) Illegal Object.

§ 1599. One of several objects unlawful; effect

WHEN CONTRACT PARTIALLY VOID. Where a contract has several distinct objects, of which one at least is lawful, and one at least is unlawful, in whole or in part, the contract is void as to the latter and valid as to the rest. *(Enacted in 1872.)*

Research References

Rutter, Cal. Practice Guide: A.D.R. Ch. 5-D, D. Defenses to Enforcement.

California Practice Guide: Employment Litigation Ch. 4-A, A. Employment Presumed at Will.

California Practice Guide: Employment Litigation Ch. 18-C, C. Contractual Arbitration.

Rutter, Cal. Practice Guide: Real Prop. Transactions Ch. 2-D, D. Broker Compensation.

Rutter, Cal. Practice Guide: Real Prop. Transactions Ch. 11-A, A. Factors Affecting Choice of Remedies.

Rutter, Cal. Practice Guide: Prof. Responsibility Ch. 5-D, D. Ethical Limitations on Attorney Fees.

Rutter, Cal. Practice Guide: Prof. Responsibility Ch. 5-K, K. Fee Recovery/Enforcing Fee Agreements.

Miller and Starr California Real Estate § 1:9, Lawful Object.

19 NO. 3 Miller & Starr, California Real Estate Newsalert 20, Landlord and Tenant.

20 NO. 6 Miller & Starr, California Real Estate Newsalert 2, Broker's Compensation.

1 Witkin Cal. Summ. 10th Contracts § 330, (S 330) Commercial Code and California Statute.

1 Witkin Cal. Summ. 10th Contracts § 421, General Principles.

CHAPTER 5. CONSIDERATION

Section

§ 1605. Good consideration defined

GOOD CONSIDERATION, WHAT. Any benefit conferred, or agreed to be conferred, upon the promisor, by any other person, to which the promisor is not lawfully entitled, or any prejudice suffered, or agreed to be suffered, by such person, other than such as he is at the time of consent lawfully bound to suffer, as an inducement to the promisor, is a good consideration for a promise. *(Enacted in 1872.)*

Research References

Rutter, Cal. Practice Guide: Real Prop. Transactions Ch. 8-B, B. Options to Purchase.

Rutter, Cal. Practice Guide: Real Prop. Transactions Ch. 11-A, A. Factors Affecting Choice of Remedies.

Miller and Starr California Real Estate § 1:51, Necessity for Consideration.

Miller and Starr California Real Estate § 1:53, "Consideration" Defined.

Miller and Starr California Real Estate § 1:54, The Consideration Must be "Bargained For".

Miller and Starr California Real Estate § 1:55, Performance of a Legal Obligation.

Miller and Starr California Real Estate § 1:56, What Constitutes Sufficient Consideration to Support an Action for Damages.

Miller and Starr California Real Estate § 27:51, Modification and Alteration of Construction Contracts.

20 NO. 6 Miller & Starr, California Real Estate Newsalert 1, Are "Free Look" Provisions in Real Estate Purchase Contracts Still Viable?: An Analysis of Steiner v. Thexton*.

20 NO. 5 Miller & Starr, California Real Estate Newsalert 7, Contracts.

1 Witkin Cal. Summ. 10th Contracts § 203, (S 203) Benefit or Detriment.

1 Witkin Cal. Summ. 10th Contracts § 205, (S 205) Value and Adequacy.

1 Witkin Cal. Summ. 10th Contracts § 218, Duty Owed to Other Contracting Party.

§ 1606. Good consideration; legal or moral obligation

HOW FAR LEGAL OR MORAL OBLIGATION IS A GOOD CONSIDERATION. An existing legal obligation resting upon the promisor, or a moral obligation originating in some benefit conferred upon the promisor, or prejudice suffered by the promisee, is also a good consideration for a promise, to an extent corresponding with the extent of the obligation, but no further or otherwise. *(Enacted in 1872.)*

Research References

Miller and Starr California Real Estate § 1:53, "Consideration" Defined.

Miller and Starr California Real Estate § 11:53, Requirement and Adequacy of Consideration--In General.

1 Witkin Cal. Summ. 10th Contracts § 222, Traditional Rule.

1 Witkin Cal. Summ. 10th Contracts § 223, (S 223) in General.

§ 1607. Lawfulness of consideration

CONSIDERATION LAWFUL. The consideration of a contract must be lawful within the meaning of Section 1667. *(Enacted in 1872.)*

Research References

Rutter, Cal. Practice Guide: Prof. Responsibility Ch. 5-D, D. Ethical Limitations on Attorney Fees.

Miller and Starr California Real Estate § 8:57, Conveyance in Violation of Public Policy or Statute.

2 Witkin, California Summary 10th Insurance § 47, (S 47) Validity.

1 Witkin Cal. Summ. 10th Contracts § 216, (S 216) in General.

1 Witkin Cal. Summ. 10th Contracts § 419, (S 419) Illegal Consideration.

§ 1608. Illegal consideration; effect

EFFECT OF ITS ILLEGALITY. If any part of a single consideration for one or more objects, or of several considerations for a single object, is unlawful, the entire contract is void. *(Enacted in 1872.)*

Research References

Rutter, Cal. Practice Guide: Real Prop. Transactions Ch. 11-A, A. Factors Affecting Choice of Remedies.

Miller and Starr California Real Estate § 1:6, Void and Voidable Contracts.

Miller and Starr California Real Estate § 1:9, Lawful Object.

Miller and Starr California Real Estate § 34:4, Grounds for Rescission.

Miller and Starr California Real Estate § 34:8, Effect of Rescission.

Miller and Starr California Real Estate § 8:57, Conveyance in Violation of Public Policy or Statute.

17 NO. 5 Miller & Starr, California Real Estate Newsalert 5, Contracts.

1 Witkin Cal. Summ. 10th Contracts § 419, (S 419) Illegal Consideration.

1 Witkin Cal. Summ. 10th Contracts § 422, Liberal Rule of Severability.

§ 1609. Executed and executory consideration

CONSIDERATION EXECUTED OR EXECUTORY. A consideration may be executed or executory, in whole or in part. In so far as it is executory, it is subject to the provisions of Chapter IV [1] of this Title. *(Enacted in 1872.)*

[1] So in chaptered bill.

§ 1610. Executory consideration; specification of amount or means of ascertainment

EXECUTORY CONSIDERATION. When a consideration is executory, it is not indispensable that the contract should specify its amount or the means of ascertaining it. It may be left to the decision of a third person, or regulated by any specified standard. *(Enacted in 1872.)*

§ 1611. Ascertainment of consideration

HOW ASCERTAINED. When a contract does not determine the amount of the consideration, nor the method by which it is to be ascertained, or when it leaves the amount thereof to the discretion of an interested party, the consideration must be so much money as the object of the contract is reasonably worth. *(Enacted in 1872.)*

Research References

Miller and Starr California Real Estate § 1:3, Express and Implied Contracts.

Miller and Starr California Real Estate § 27:87, Quantum Meruit Recovery.

Miller and Starr California Real Estate § 35:38, Issues Subject to Arbitration--Examples.

§ 1612. Contract providing impossible method of ascertainment; invalidity

Where a contract provides an exclusive method by which its consideration is to be ascertained, which method is on its face impossible of execution, the entire contract is void; but this section shall not apply to the cases provided for in sections 1729 and 1730 of this code. *(Enacted in 1872. Amended by Stats. 1931, c. 1070, p. 2259, § 7.)*

Research References

1 Witkin Cal. Summ. 10th Contracts § 420, (S 420) Illegal Object.

§ 1613. Contract providing apparently possible method of ascertainment

Where a contract provides an exclusive method by which its consideration is to be ascertained, which method appears possible on its face, but in fact is, or becomes, impossible of execution, such provision only is void; but this section shall not apply to the cases provided for in sections 1729 and 1730 of this code. *(Enacted in 1872. Amended by Stats.1931, c. 1070, p. 2260, § 8.)*

Research References

1 Witkin Cal. Summ. 10th Contracts § 420, (S 420) Illegal Object.

§ 1614. Written instrument; presumption of consideration

WRITTEN INSTRUMENT PRESUMPTIVE EVIDENCE OF CONSIDERATION. A written instrument is presumptive evidence of a consideration. *(Enacted in 1872.)*

Research References

Rutter, Cal. Practice Guide: Civil Trials & Evidence Ch. 8G-C, C. Presumptions.

Rutter, Cal. Practice Guide: Civil Trials & Evidence Ch. 8G-D, D. Burdens and Standards of Proof.

Rutter, Cal. Practice Guide: Real Prop. Transactions Ch. 8-B, B. Options to Purchase.

Rutter, Cal. Practice Guide: Real Prop. Transactions Ch. 11-A, A. Factors Affecting Choice of Remedies.

Miller and Starr California Real Estate § 1:53, "Consideration" Defined.

Miller and Starr California Real Estate § 1:99, Modification of a Contract; Executed Oral Agreement--Consideration Required for a Modification of a Written Agreement.

Miller and Starr California Real Estate § 11:53, Requirement and Adequacy of Consideration--In General.

Miller and Starr California Real Estate § 10:263, Definitions; Guarantor, Surety.

4 Witkin Cal. Proc. 5th Pleading § 521, Consideration Need Not be Pleaded.

1 Witkin Cal. Summ. 10th Contracts § 206, (S 206) Presumption of Consideration.

§ 1615. Want of consideration; burden of proof

BURDEN OF PROOF TO INVALIDATE SUFFICIENT CONSIDERATION. The burden of showing a want of consideration sufficient to support an instrument lies with the party seeking to invalidate or avoid it. *(Enacted in 1872.)*

Research References

Rutter, Cal. Practice Guide: Enforcing Judgments/Debts Ch. 3-A, A. Evaluating the Claim.

Rutter, Cal. Practice Guide: Real Prop. Transactions Ch. 8-B, B. Options to Purchase.

Rutter, Cal. Practice Guide: Real Prop. Transactions Ch. 11-A, A. Factors Affecting Choice of Remedies.

Miller and Starr California Real Estate § 1:53, "Consideration" Defined.

Title 2

MANNER OF CREATING CONTRACTS

§ 1619. Express or implied contracts

A contract is either express or implied. *(Enacted in 1872.)*

Research References

Miller and Starr California Real Estate § 1:3, Express and Implied Contracts.

§ 1620. Express contract defined

An express contract is one, the terms of which are stated in words. *(Enacted in 1872.)*

Research References

California Practice Guide: Employment Litigation Ch. 4-B, B. Agreements Limiting At-Will Termination.

Miller and Starr California Real Estate § 1:3, Express and Implied Contracts.

1 Witkin Cal. Summ. 10th Contracts § 102, (S 102) Express and Implied in Fact Contracts.

3 Witkin, California Summary 10th Agency and Employment § 230, (S 230) Enforceability of Express Contract.

§ 1621. Implied contract defined

An implied contract is one, the existence and terms of which are manifested by conduct. *(Enacted in 1872.)*

Research References

California Practice Guide: Employment Litigation Ch. 4-B, B. Agreements Limiting At-Will Termination.

Miller and Starr California Real Estate § 1:3, Express and Implied Contracts.

1 Witkin Cal. Summ. 10th Contracts § 102, (S 102) Express and Implied in Fact Contracts.

3 Witkin, California Summary 10th Agency and Employment § 232, (S 232) Totality of Circumstances Test.

§ 1622. Oral contracts; authorization

All contracts may be oral, except such as are specially required by statute to be in writing. *(Enacted in 1872.)*

Research References

Miller and Starr California Real Estate § 1:98, Modification of a Contract; Executed Oral Agreement.

Miller and Starr California Real Estate § 4:57, Persons and Transactions Requiring a Real Estate License.

§ 1623. Statute of frauds; enforcement of contract oral by reason of fraud

Where a contract, which is required by law to be in writing, is prevented from being put into writing by the fraud of a party thereto, any other party who is by such fraud led to believe that it is in writing, and acts upon such belief to his prejudice, may enforce it against the fraudulent party. *(Enacted in 1872.)*

Research References

Miller and Starr California Real Estate § 1:77, Waiver--Exception: Fraud and Other Torts.

Miller and Starr California Real Estate § 5:17, Exception: Fraud and Other Torts.

Miller and Starr California Real Estate § 19:21, Lease as a Contract and Conveyance--Application of the Statute of Frauds/Translation of Leases Into Other Languages.

§ 1624. Statute of frauds

(a) The following contracts are invalid, unless they, or some note or memorandum thereof, are in writing and subscribed by the party to be charged or by the party's agent:

(1) An agreement that by its terms is not to be performed within a year from the making thereof.

(2) A special promise to answer for the debt, default, or miscarriage of another, except in the cases provided for in Section 2794.

(3) An agreement for the leasing for a longer period than one year, or for the sale of real property, or of an interest therein; such an agreement, if made by an agent of the party sought to be charged, is invalid, unless the authority of the agent is in writing, subscribed by the party sought to be charged.

(4) An agreement authorizing or employing an agent, broker, or any other person to purchase or sell real estate, or to lease real estate for a longer period than one year, or to procure, introduce, or find a purchaser or seller of real estate or a lessee or lessor of real estate where the lease is for a longer period than one year, for compensation or a commission.

(5) An agreement that by its terms is not to be performed during the lifetime of the promisor.

(6) An agreement by a purchaser of real property to pay an indebtedness secured by a mortgage or deed of trust upon the property purchased, unless assumption of the indebtedness by the purchaser is specifically provided for in the conveyance of the property.

(7) A contract, promise, undertaking, or commitment to loan money or to grant or extend credit, in an amount greater than one hundred thousand dollars ($100,000), not primarily for personal, family, or household purposes, made by a person engaged in the business of lending or arranging for the lending of money or extending credit. For purposes of this section, a contract, promise, undertaking or commitment to loan money secured solely by residential property consisting of one to four dwelling units shall be deemed to be for personal, family, or household purposes.

(b) Notwithstanding paragraph (1) of subdivision (a):

(1) An agreement or contract that is valid in other respects and is otherwise enforceable is not invalid for lack of a note, memorandum, or other writing and is enforceable by way of action or defense, provided that the agreement or contract is a qualified financial contract as defined in paragraph (2) and (A) there is, as provided in paragraph (3), sufficient evidence to indicate that a contract has been made or (B) the parties thereto by means of a prior or subsequent written contract, have agreed to be bound by the terms of the qualified financial contract from the time they reached agreement (by telephone, by exchange of electronic messages, or otherwise) on those terms.

(2) For purposes of this subdivision, a "qualified financial contract" means an agreement as to which each party thereto is other than a natural person and that is any of the following:

(A) For the purchase and sale of foreign exchange, foreign currency, bullion, coin or precious metals on a forward, spot, next-day value or other basis.

(B) A contract (other than a contract for the purchase of a commodity for future delivery on, or subject to the rules of, a contract market or board of trade) for the purchase, sale, or transfer of any commodity or any similar good, article, service, right, or interest that is presently or in the future becomes the subject of a dealing in the forward contract trade, or any product or byproduct thereof, with a maturity date more than two days after the date the contract is entered into.

(C) For the purchase and sale of currency, or interbank deposits denominated in United States dollars.

(D) For a currency option, currency swap, or cross-currency rate swap.

(E) For a commodity swap or a commodity option (other than an option contract traded on, or subject to the rules of a contract market or board of trade).

(F) For a rate swap, basis swap, forward rate transaction, or an interest rate option.

(G) For a security-index swap or option, or a security or securities price swap or option.

(H) An agreement that involves any other similar transaction relating to a price or index (including, without limitation, any transaction or agreement involving any combination of the foregoing, any cap, floor, collar, or similar transaction with respect to a rate, commodity price, commodity index, security or securities price, security index, other price index, or loan price).

(I) An option with respect to any of the foregoing.

(3) There is sufficient evidence that a contract has been made in any of the following circumstances:

(A) There is evidence of an electronic communication (including, without limitation, the recording of a telephone call or the tangible written text produced by computer retrieval), admissible in evidence under the laws of this state, sufficient to indicate that in the communication a contract was made between the parties.

(B) A confirmation in writing sufficient to indicate that a contract has been made between the parties and sufficient against the sender is received by the party against whom enforcement is sought no later than the fifth business day after the contract is made (or any other period of time that the parties may agree in writing) and the sender does not receive, on or before the third business day after receipt (or the other period of time that the parties may agree in writing), written objection to a material term of the confirmation. For purposes of this subparagraph, a confirmation or an objection thereto is received at the time there has been an actual receipt by an individual responsible for the transaction or, if earlier, at the time there has been constructive receipt, which is the time actual receipt by that individual would have occurred if the receiving party, as an organization, had exercised reasonable diligence. For the purposes of this subparagraph, a "business day" is a day on which both parties are open and transacting business of the kind involved in that qualified financial contract that is the subject of confirmation.

(C) The party against whom enforcement is sought admits in its pleading, testimony, or otherwise in court that a contract was made.

(D) There is a note, memorandum, or other writing sufficient to indicate that a contract has been made, signed by the party against whom enforcement is sought or by its authorized agent or broker.

For purposes of this paragraph, evidence of an electronic communication indicating the making in that communication of a contract, or a confirmation, admission, note, memorandum, or writing is not insufficient because it omits or incorrectly states one or more material terms agreed upon, as long as the evidence provides a reasonable basis for concluding that a contract was made.

(4) For purposes of this subdivision, the tangible written text produced by telex, telefacsimile, computer retrieval, or other process by which electronic signals are transmitted by telephone or otherwise shall constitute a writing, and any symbol executed or adopted by a party with the present intention to authenticate a writing shall constitute a signing. The confirmation and notice of objection referred to in subparagraph (B) of paragraph (3) may be communicated by means of telex, telefacsimile, computer, or other similar process by which electronic signals are transmitted by telephone or otherwise, provided that a party claiming to have communicated in that manner shall, unless the parties have otherwise agreed in writing, have the burden of

establishing actual or constructive receipt by the other party as set forth in subparagraph (B) of paragraph (3).

(c) This section does not apply to leases subject to Division 10 (commencing with Section 10101) of the Commercial Code. *(Enacted in 1872. Amended by Code Am.1873–74, c. 612, p. 241, § 190; Code Am.1877–78, c. 165, p. 86, § 1; Stats.1905, c. 451, p. 610, § 1; Stats.1931, c. 1070, p. 2260, § 9; Stats.1937, c. 316, p. 695, § 2; Stats.1963, c. 814, p. 1843, § 1; Stats.1967, c. 52, p. 953, § 1; Stats.1983, c. 842, § 6, operative Jan. 1, 1985; Stats.1985, c. 1315, § 1; Stats.1988, c. 1096, § 1; Stats.1988, c. 1368, § 1.5, operative Jan. 1, 1990; Stats.1998, c. 78 (S.B.1865), § 1.)*

Law Revision Commission Comments

Section 1624 is amended to delete the last portion of subdivision 6 (agreement to devise or bequeath property or to make any provision by will) which is superseded by Probate Code Section 150. [16 Cal.L.Rev.Comm.Reports 2301 (1982)].

Research References

Rutter, Cal. Practice Guide: Civil Trials & Evidence Ch. 8E-G, G. Parol Evidence Rule.

California Practice Guide: Employment Litigation Ch. 4-B, B. Agreements Limiting At-Will Termination.

California Practice Guide: Employment Litigation Ch. 16-K, K. Settlements and Releases.

Rutter, Cal. Practice Guide: Enforcing Judgments/Debts Ch. 3-A, A. Evaluating the Claim.

Rutter, Cal. Practice Guide: Personal Injury Ch. 4-G, G. Concluding and Enforcing Settlement.

Rutter, Cal. Practice Guide: Real Prop. Transactions Ch. 2-A, A. Preliminary Considerations.

Rutter, Cal. Practice Guide: Real Prop. Transactions Ch. 2-C, C. Broker's Relationship and Obligations to Principal and Third Parties.

Rutter, Cal. Practice Guide: Real Prop. Transactions Ch. 2-D, D. Broker Compensation.

Rutter, Cal. Practice Guide: Real Prop. Transactions Ch. 4-A, A. Property to be Sold.

Rutter, Cal. Practice Guide: Real Prop. Transactions Ch. 4-C, C. Parties to the Purchase Agreement.

Rutter, Cal. Practice Guide: Real Prop. Transactions Ch. 4-D, D. Selecting the Form of Written Agreement.

Rutter, Cal. Practice Guide: Real Prop. Transactions Ch. 6-C, C. Loan Applications and Loan Commitments.

Rutter, Cal. Practice Guide: Real Prop. Transactions Ch. 6-G, G. Assuming Existing Financing or Purchasing Subject to Existing Financing.

Rutter, Cal. Practice Guide: Real Prop. Transactions Ch. 7-C, C. Representing the Purchasing Tenant.

Rutter, Cal. Practice Guide: Real Prop. Transactions Ch. 8-B, B. Options to Purchase.

Rutter, Cal. Practice Guide: Real Prop. Transactions Ch. 10-C, C. Property Management Agreement.

Rutter, Cal. Practice Guide: Real Prop. Transactions Ch. 11-A, A. Factors Affecting Choice of Remedies.

Miller and Starr California Real Estate § 5:6, Application of the Statute of Frauds--In General.

Miller and Starr California Real Estate § 5:7, Application of the Statute of Frauds--In General--Application to Compensation Agreement of a Finder or Middleman.

Miller and Starr California Real Estate § 5:8, Transactions Included in the Statute of Frauds.

Miller and Starr California Real Estate § 8:2, Rules of Interpretation; Extrinsic Evidence.

Miller and Starr California Real Estate § 1:22, Assignment of Contracts.

Miller and Starr California Real Estate § 1:65, Provisions Applicable to Real Estate Transactions.

Miller and Starr California Real Estate § 1:66, Agreement that Will Not be Performed Within One Year from the Date it is Made.

Miller and Starr California Real Estate § 1:67, Agreement that Will Not be Performed Within One Year from the Date it is Made--Oral Leases.

Miller and Starr California Real Estate § 1:68, Agreement to Answer for the Debt of Another; Buyer's Agreement to Pay Seller's Obligations.

Miller and Starr California Real Estate § 1:69, Contract for the Sale, Gift, or Financing of Real Property.

Miller and Starr California Real Estate § 1:72, Effect When Statute of Frauds Not Satisfied.

Miller and Starr California Real Estate § 1:76, Waiver--Exception: Estoppel to Assert the Statute of Frauds.

Miller and Starr California Real Estate § 1:78, Signature Required.

Miller and Starr California Real Estate § 1:81, Written Authority Required; the Equal Dignities Rule.

Miller and Starr California Real Estate § 19:2, Lease as Personal Property or Real Property.

Miller and Starr California Real Estate § 24:4, Covenants Burdening Land for the Benefit of Other Land--Prior to the 1968 and 1969 Amendments to Civil Code § 4168.

Miller and Starr California Real Estate § 24:6, Covenants Burdening Land for the Benefit of Other Land--Creation After the 1968-1969 Amendments.

Miller and Starr California Real Estate § 36:3, Requirement that Commitment be in Writing.

Miller and Starr California Real Estate § 4:57, Persons and Transactions Requiring a Real Estate License.

Miller and Starr California Real Estate § 5:10, Form of the Memorandum--Signature of the Principal.

Miller and Starr California Real Estate § 5:13, Exception: Agreement Between Brokers to Share a Commission.

Miller and Starr California Real Estate § 5:14, Exception: Agreement by Broker to Pay Finder's Fee.

Miller and Starr California Real Estate § 5:16, Exception: Estoppel to Raise Statute of Frauds as a Defense.

Miller and Starr California Real Estate § 5:17, Exception: Fraud and Other Torts.

Miller and Starr California Real Estate § 5:18, Broker Agreements and Listings Defined.

Miller and Starr California Real Estate § 5:21, Property Management Employment Agreements.

Miller and Starr California Real Estate § 5:22, Loan Brokerage and Servicing Agreements.

Miller and Starr California Real Estate § 5:34, The Buyer's "Listing".

Miller and Starr California Real Estate § 6:30, Requirement of a Contract.

Miller and Starr California Real Estate § 8:28, Insertion of Name After Execution by the Grantor.

Miller and Starr California Real Estate § 8:30, Execution by an Agent or Attorney-In-Fact.

Miller and Starr California Real Estate § 8:39, Community Property; Voidable Transfers.

Miller and Starr California Real Estate § 1:106, Novation; Definition and Requirements.

Miller and Starr California Real Estate § 10:36, Grantee "Assumes".

Miller and Starr California Real Estate § 10:90, Extension and Renewal.

Miller and Starr California Real Estate § 17:24, Minerals--Oil and Gas Leases.

Miller and Starr California Real Estate § 19:14, Requisites and Validity.

Miller and Starr California Real Estate § 19:19, Lease as a Contract and Conveyance.

Miller and Starr California Real Estate § 19:21, Lease as a Contract and Conveyance--Application of the Statute of Frauds/Translation of Leases Into Other Languages.

Miller and Starr California Real Estate § 19:61, Requirements for a Valid Assignment.

Miller and Starr California Real Estate § 24:39, Amendment to Restrictions--Generally.

Miller and Starr California Real Estate § 28:30, Result of a Failure to Draft and Serve the Notice Properly.

Miller and Starr California Real Estate § 28:94, General Form of the Bond.

Miller and Starr California Real Estate § 10:123, Nature of Foreclosure; Termination of Redemption.

15 NO. 6 Miller & Starr, California Real Estate Newsalert 1, Refuse to Mediate and (Under Some Contracts) Wave Goodbye to Your Attorney's Fees.

17 NO. 6 Miller & Starr, California Real Estate Newsalert 4, Contracts.

18 NO. 3 Miller & Starr, California Real Estate Newsalert 6, Contracts.

19 NO. 6 Miller & Starr, California Real Estate Newsalert 1, Enforceable Resale Restrictions: Keeping the Doors Open for Long-Term Affordable Housing.

19 NO. 3 Miller & Starr, California Real Estate Newsalert 11, Deeds of Trust.

20 NO. 2 Miller & Starr, California Real Estate Newsalert 8, Contracts.

22 NO. 2 Miller & Starr, California Real Estate Newsalert 1, Did Someone Say Estoppel?-Courts Show Greater Acceptance of Applying Equitable Principles to Enforce Oral Forbearance Agreements.

22 NO. 2 Miller & Starr, California Real Estate Newsalert 9, Deeds of Trust.

22 NO. 3 Miller & Starr, California Real Estate Newsalert 13, Holding Title.

5 Witkin, Cal. Proc. 5th Pleading § 1072, Statute of Frauds.

12 Witkin, California Summary 10th Real Property § 520, Execution and Delivery.

1 Witkin Cal. Summ. 10th Contracts § 343, California Codes.

1 Witkin Cal. Summ. 10th Contracts § 344, Defense Waived If Not Asserted.

1 Witkin Cal. Summ. 10th Contracts § 354, (S 354) California Cases.

1 Witkin Cal. Summ. 10th Contracts § 359, (S 359) Who is Party to be Charged.

1 Witkin Cal. Summ. 10th Contracts § 363, in General.

1 Witkin Cal. Summ. 10th Contracts § 364, Commencement and Computation of Period.

1 Witkin Cal. Summ. 10th Contracts § 371, (S 371) Contract Not to be Performed During Lifetime.

1 Witkin Cal. Summ. 10th Contracts § 372, (S 372) Scope of Statute.

1 Witkin Cal. Summ. 10th Contracts § 383, (S 383) Qualified Financial Contract.

1 Witkin Cal. Summ. 10th Contracts § 385, Scope of Statute.

1 Witkin Cal. Summ. 10th Contracts § 388, (S 388) Equal Dignities Rule.

1 Witkin Cal. Summ. 10th Contracts § 391, Liability of Principal to Agent.

1 Witkin Cal. Summ. 10th Contracts § 392, (S 392) Nature and Effect of Statute.

1 Witkin Cal. Summ. 10th Contracts § 393, Oral Agreement to Lease.

1 Witkin Cal. Summ. 10th Contracts § 395, Oral Finders Agreement.

1 Witkin Cal. Summ. 10th Contracts § 397, (S 397) Distinctions.

1 Witkin Cal. Summ. 10th Contracts § 398, (S 398) Contract to Loan Money or Extend Credit.

1 Witkin Cal. Summ. 10th Contracts § 399, (S 399) Marital and Premarital Agreements.

1 Witkin Cal. Summ. 10th Contracts § 400, (S 400) Miscellaneous Provisions.

1 Witkin Cal. Summ. 10th Contracts § 414, Real Estate Broker's Authorization.

1 Witkin Cal. Summ. 10th Contracts § 417, (S 417) Qualified Financial Contract.

1 Witkin Cal. Summ. 10th Contracts § 418, (S 418) Personal Property Leases.

4 Witkin, California Summary 10th Security Transactions in Real Property § 108, (S 108) Manner and Requisites of Assumption.

5 Witkin, California Summary 10th Torts § 788, Representations Concerning Credit.

3 Witkin, California Summary 10th Agency and Employment § 75, (S 75) in General.

3 Witkin, California Summary 10th Agency and Employment § 233, in General.

14 Witkin, California Summary 10th Wills and Probate § 326, (S 326) Contracts Concerning Will or Succession.

§ 1624.5. Written contract; sale of personal property exceeding $5000; exceptions

(a) Except in the cases described in subdivision (b), a contract for the sale of personal property is not enforceable by way of action or defense beyond five thousand dollars ($5,000) in amount or value of remedy unless there is some record, as defined in subdivision (m) of Section 1633.2, but solely to the extent permitted by applicable law, that indicates that a contract for sale has been made between the parties at a defined or stated price, reasonably identifies the subject matter, and is signed, including by way of electronic signature, as defined in subdivision (h) of Section 1633.2, but solely to the extent permitted by applicable law, by the party against whom enforcement is sought or by his or her authorized agent.

(b) Subdivision (a) does not apply to contracts governed by the Commercial Code, including contracts for the sale of goods (Section 2201 of the Commercial Code), contracts for the sale of securities (Section 8113 of the Commercial Code), and security agreements (Sections 9201 and 9203 of the Commercial Code).

(c) Subdivision (a) does not apply to a qualified financial contract as that term is defined in paragraph (2) of subdivision (b) of Section 1624 if either of the following exists:

(1) There is, as provided in paragraph (3) of subdivision (b) of Section 1624, sufficient evidence to indicate that a contract has been made.

(2) The parties thereto, by means of a prior or subsequent written contract, have agreed to be bound by the terms of the qualified financial contract from the time they reach agreement (by telephone, by exchange of electronic messages, or otherwise) on those terms. *(Added by Stats.2006, c. 254 (S.B.1481), § 1.)*

Research References

1 Witkin Cal. Summ. 10th Contracts § 384, (S 384) Sale of Chose in Action of $5,000 Value.

4 Witkin, California Summary 10th Sales § 32, Statute of Frauds.

§ 1625. Written contracts; effect on negotiations or stipulations

The execution of a contract in writing, whether the law requires it to be written or not, supersedes all the negotiations or stipulations concerning its matter which preceded or accompanied the execution of the instrument. *(Enacted in 1872. Amended by Stats.1905, c. 451, p. 611, § 2.)*

Research References

Rutter, Cal. Practice Guide: Civil Trials & Evidence Ch. 8E-G, G. Parol Evidence Rule.

Miller and Starr California Real Estate § 1:60, Parol Evidence; Extrinsic Evidence Rules.

Miller and Starr California Real Estate § 1:106, Novation; Definition and Requirements.

Miller and Starr California Real Estate § 19:55, Requirements for Modification of Lease Terms.

21 NO. 4 Miller & Starr, California Real Estate Newsalert 23, Contracts.

22 NO. 3 Miller & Starr, California Real Estate Newsalert 6, Contracts.

2 Witkin, California Summary 10th Insurance § 30, Oral Contracts.

§ 1626. Written contracts; effective upon delivery

A contract in writing takes effect upon its delivery to the party in whose favor it is made, or to his agent. *(Enacted in 1872.)*

Research References

2 Witkin, California Summary 10th Insurance § 45, in General.

§ 1627. Written contracts; law governing

The provisions of the Chapter on Transfers in General, concerning the delivery of grants, absolute and conditional, apply to all written contracts. *(Enacted in 1872.)*

Research References

Miller and Starr California Real Estate § 19:20, Lease as a Contract and Conveyance--Form, Execution, Delivery, and Recordation.

§ 1628. Seals; method of affixing

A corporate or official seal may be affixed to an instrument by a mere impression upon the paper or other material on which such instrument is written. *(Enacted in 1872.)*

§ 1629. Sealed and unsealed instruments; distinctions abolished

All distinctions between sealed and unsealed instruments are abolished. *(Enacted in 1872.)*

Research References

Miller and Starr California Real Estate § 1:7, Sealed and Unsealed Contracts.

Miller and Starr California Real Estate § 8:3, Requirements; Form and Content.

12 Witkin, California Summary 10th Real Property § 254, (S 254) Requisites of Deed.

1 Witkin Cal. Summ. 10th Contracts § 3, in General.

§ 1630. Bailment contracts with automobile parking lots; requirements

Except as provided in Section 1630.5, a printed contract of bailment providing for the parking or storage of a motor vehicle shall not be binding, either in whole or in part, on the vehicle owner or on the person who leaves the vehicle with another, unless the contract conforms to the following:

(a) "This contract limits our liability—read it" is printed at the top in capital letters of 10-point type or larger.

(b) All the provisions of the contract are printed legibly in eight-point type or larger.

(c) Acceptance of benefits under a contract included within the provisions of this section shall not be construed a waiver of this section, and it shall be unlawful to issue such a contract on condition that provisions of this section are waived.

A copy of the contract printed in large type, in an area at least 17 by 22 inches, shall be posted in a conspicuous place at each entrance of the parking lot.

Nothing in this section shall be construed to prohibit the enactment of city ordinances on this subject that are not less restrictive, and such enactments are expressly authorized. *(Added by Stats.1957, c. 1472, p. 2794, § 1. Amended by Stats.1970, c. 1277, p. 2311, § 1.)*

Research References

1 Witkin Cal. Summ. 10th Contracts § 123, (S 123) in General.

1 Witkin Cal. Summ. 10th Contracts § 684, Miscellaneous Substantive Rights.

13 Witkin, California Summary 10th Personal Property § 176, (S 176) Under Commercial Code.

13 Witkin, California Summary 10th Personal Property § 186, Invalid Disclaimer of Liability.

§ 1630.5. Automobile parking lots; liability for theft

The provisions of any contract of bailment for the parking or storage of a motor vehicle shall not exempt the bailee from liability, either in whole or in part, for the theft of any motor vehicle, when such motor vehicle is parked or stored with such bailee, and the keys are required by such bailee to be left in the parked or stored vehicle. *(Added by Stats.1970, c. 1277, p. 2311, § 2.)*

Research References

1 Witkin Cal. Summ. 10th Contracts § 663, (S 663) Automobiles.

§ 1631. Sale of mining machinery; bill of sale; record; contents

Every person in this State who sells machinery used or to be used for mining purposes shall, at the time of sale, give to the buyer a bill of sale for the machinery. The seller shall keep a written record of the sale, giving the date thereof, describing the machinery, and showing the name and address of the buyer, and the buyer, if in this State, shall keep a record of his purchase, giving the name and address of the seller, describing the machinery, and showing the date of the purchase. *(Added by Stats.1959, c. 222, p. 2130, § 1.)*

§ 1632. Translation of contracts negotiated in language other than English; necessity; exceptions

(a) The Legislature hereby finds and declares all of the following:

(1) This section was enacted in 1976 to increase consumer information and protections for the state's sizeable and growing Spanish-speaking population.

(2) Since 1976, the state's population has become increasingly diverse and the number of Californians who speak languages other than English as their primary language at home has increased dramatically.

(3) According to data from the United States Census of 2000, of the more than 12 million Californians who speak a language other than English in the home, approximately 4.3 million speak an Asian dialect or another language other than Spanish. The top five languages other than English most widely spoken by Californians in their homes are Spanish, Chinese, Tagalog, Vietnamese, and Korean. Together, these languages are spoken by approximately 83 percent of all Californians who speak a language other than English in their homes.

(b) Any person engaged in a trade or business who negotiates primarily in Spanish, Chinese, Tagalog, Vietnamese, or Korean, orally or in writing, in the course of entering into any of the following, shall deliver to the other party to the contract or agreement and prior to the execution thereof, a translation of the contract or agreement in the language in which the contract or agreement was negotiated, which includes a translation of every term and condition in that contract or agreement:

(1) A contract or agreement subject to the provisions of Title 2 (commencing with Section 1801) of, and Chapter 2b (commencing with Section 2981) and Chapter 2d (commencing with Section 2985.7) of Title 14 of, Part 4 of Division 3.

(2) A loan or extension of credit secured other than by real property, or unsecured, for use primarily for personal, family or household purposes.

(3) A lease, sublease, rental contract or agreement, or other term of tenancy contract or agreement, for a period of longer than one month, covering a dwelling, an apartment, or mobile-home, or other dwelling unit normally occupied as a residence.

(4) Notwithstanding paragraph (2), a loan or extension of credit for use primarily for personal, family or household purposes where the loan or extension of credit is subject to the provisions of Article 7 (commencing with Section 10240) of Chapter 3 of Part 1 of Division 4 of the Business and Professions Code, or Division 7 (commencing with Section 18000), or Division 9 (commencing with Section 22000) of the Financial Code.

(5) Notwithstanding paragraph (2), a reverse mortgage as described in Chapter 8 (commencing with Section 1923) of Title 4 of Part 4 of Division 3.

(6) A contract or agreement, containing a statement of fees or charges, entered into for the purpose of obtaining legal services, when the person who is engaged in business is currently licensed to practice law pursuant to Chapter 4 (commencing with Section 6000) of Division 3 of the Business and Professions Code.

(7) A foreclosure consulting contract subject to Article 1.5 (commencing with Section 2945) of Chapter 2 of Title 14 of Part 4 of Division 3.

(c) Notwithstanding subdivision (b), for a loan subject to this part and to Article 7 (commencing with Section 10240) of Chapter 3 of Part 1 of Division 4 of the Business and Professions Code, the delivery of a translation of the statement to the borrower required by Section 10240 of the Business and Professions Code in any of the languages specified in subdivision (b) in which the contract or agreement was negotiated, is in compliance with subdivision (b).

(d) At the time and place where a lease, sublease, or rental contract or agreement described in subdivision (b) is executed, notice in any of the languages specified in subdivision (b) in which the contract or agreement was negotiated shall be provided to the lessee or tenant.

(e) Provision by a supervised financial organization of a translation of the disclosures required by Regulation M or Regulation Z, and, if applicable, Division 7 (commencing with Section 18000) or Division 9 (commencing with Section 22000) of the Financial Code in any of the languages specified in subdivision (b) in which the contract or agreement was negotiated, prior to the execution of the contract or agreement, shall also be deemed in compliance with the requirements of subdivision (b) with regard to the original contract or agreement.

(1) "Regulation M" and "Regulation Z" mean any rule, regulation, or interpretation promulgated by the Board of Governors of the Federal Reserve System and any interpretation or approval issued by an official or employee duly authorized by the board to issue interpretations or approvals dealing with, respectively, consumer leasing or consumer lending, pursuant to the Federal Truth in Lending Act, as amended (15 U.S.C. Sec. 1601 et seq.).

(2) As used in this section, "supervised financial organization" means a bank, savings association as defined in Section 5102 of the Financial Code, credit union, or holding company, affiliate, or subsidiary thereof, or any person subject to Article 7 (commencing with Section 10240) of Chapter 3 of Part 1 of Division 4 of the Business and Professions Code, or Division 7 (commencing with Section 18000) or Division 9 (commencing with Section 22000) of the Financial Code.

(f) At the time and place where a contract or agreement described in paragraph (1) or (2) of subdivision (b) is executed, a notice in any of the languages specified in subdivision (b) in which the contract or agreement was negotiated shall be conspicuously displayed to the effect that the person described in subdivision (b) is required to provide a contract or agreement in the language in which the contract or agreement was negotiated, or a translation of the disclosures required by law in the language in which the contract or agreement was negotiated, as the case may be. If a person described in subdivision (b) does business at more than one location or branch, the requirements of this section shall apply only with respect to the location or branch at which the language in which the contract or agreement was negotiated is used.

(g) The term "contract" or "agreement," as used in this section, means the document creating the rights and obligations of the parties and includes any subsequent document making substantial changes in the rights and obligations of the parties. The term "contract" or "agreement" does not include any subsequent documents authorized or contemplated by the original document such as periodic statements, sales slips or invoices representing purchases made pursuant to a credit card agreement, a retail installment contract or account or other revolving sales or loan account, memoranda of purchases in an add-on sale, or refinancing of a purchase as provided by, or pursuant to, the original document.

The term "contract" or "agreement" does not include a home improvement contract as defined in Sections 7151.2 and 7159 of the Business and Professions Code, nor does it include plans, specifications, description of work to be done and materials to be used, or collateral security taken or to be taken for the retail buyer's obligation contained in a contract for the installation of goods by a contractor licensed pursuant to Chapter 9 (commencing with Section 7000) of Division 3 of the Business and Professions Code, if the home improvement contract or installation contract is otherwise a part of a contract described in subdivision (b).

Matters ordinarily incorporated by reference in contracts or agreements as described in paragraph (3) of subdivision (b), including, but not limited to, rules and regulations governing a tenancy and inventories of furnishings to be provided by the person described in subdivision (b), are not included in the term "contract" or "agreement."

(h) This section does not apply to any person engaged in a trade or business who negotiates primarily in a language other than English, as described by subdivision (b), if the party with whom he or she is negotiating is a buyer of goods or services, or receives a loan or extension of credit, or enters an agreement obligating himself or herself as a tenant, lessee, or sublessee, or similarly obligates himself or herself by contract or lease, and the party negotiates the terms of the contract, lease, or other obligation through his or her own interpreter.

As used in this subdivision, "his or her own interpreter" means a person, not a minor, able to speak fluently and read with full understanding both the English language and any of the languages specified in subdivision (b) in which the contract or agreement was negotiated, and who is not employed by, or whose service is made available through, the person engaged in the trade or business.

(i) Notwithstanding subdivision (b), a translation may retain the following elements of the executed English-language contract or agreement without translation: names and titles of individuals and other persons, addresses, brand names, trade names, trademarks, registered service marks, full or abbreviated designations of the make and model of goods or services, alphanumeric codes, numerals, dollar amounts expressed in numerals, dates, and individual words or expressions having no generally accepted non-English translation. It is permissible, but not required, that this translation be signed.

(j) The terms of the contract or agreement which is executed in the English language shall determine the rights and obligations of the parties. However, the translation of the contract or the disclosures required by subdivision (e) in any of the languages specified in subdivision (b) in which the contract or agreement was negotiated shall be admissible in evidence only to show that no contract was entered into because of a substantial difference in the material terms and conditions of the contract and the translation.

(k) Upon a failure to comply with the provisions of this section, the person aggrieved may rescind the contract or agreement in the manner provided by this chapter. When the contract for a consumer credit sale or consumer lease which has been sold and assigned to a financial institution is rescinded pursuant to this subdivision, the consumer shall make restitution to and have restitution made by the person with whom he or she made the contract, and shall give notice of rescission to the assignee. Notwithstanding that the contract was assigned without recourse, the assignment shall be deemed rescinded and the assignor shall promptly repurchase the contract from the assignee. *(Added by Stats.1974, c. 1446, p. 3156, § 1. Amended by Stats.1975, c. 892, p. 1972, § 1; Stats.1976, c. 312, p. 624, § 1, eff. July 2, 1976, operative July 1, 1976; Stats.1981, c. 724, p. 2833, § 3; Stats.1988, c. 1531, § 1; Stats.2001, c. 306 (A.B.446), § 35; Stats.2002, c. 664 (A.B.3034), § 38; Stats.2003, c. 330 (A.B.309), § 1, operative July 1, 2004; Stats.2003, c. 589 (S.B.146), § 1; Stats.2003, c. 589 (S.B.146), § 1.5, operative July 1, 2004; Stats. 2006, c. 202 (S.B.1609), § 1; Stats.2008, c. 278 (A.B.180), § 1, operative July 1, 2009.)*

Research References

Rutter, Cal. Practice Guide: Real Prop. Transactions Ch. 1-C, C. Attorney Fees and Costs Agreements.

Rutter, Cal. Practice Guide: Real Prop. Transactions Ch. 2-B, B. Licensing and Regulatory Requirements.

Rutter, Cal. Practice Guide: Real Prop. Transactions Ch. 6-B, B. Sources and Kinds of Financing.

Rutter, Cal. Practice Guide: Real Prop. Transactions Ch. 6-I, I. Real Property Foreclosures and Antideficiency Laws.
Rutter, Cal. Practice Guide: Prof. Responsibility Ch. 5-F, F. Formalizing Fee Agreements.
Miller and Starr California Real Estate § 10:7, Execution and Delivery.
Miller and Starr California Real Estate § 4:58, Requirements in Making or Arranging a Loan--In General.
Miller and Starr California Real Estate § 4:61, Requirements in Making or Arranging a Loan--Mortgage Loan Disclosure Statement to Borrower.
Miller and Starr California Real Estate § 19:20, Lease as a Contract and Conveyance--Form, Execution, Delivery, and Recordation.
Miller and Starr California Real Estate § 19:21, Lease as a Contract and Conveyance--Application of the Statute of Frauds/Translation of Leases Into Other Languages.
Miller and Starr California Real Estate § 36:21, Disclosure Requirements.
Miller and Starr California Real Estate § 36:23, Remedies and Penalties.
Miller and Starr California Real Estate § 36:1.30, Loans Negotiated in Languages Other Than English.
Miller and Starr California Real Estate § 19:59.10, Termination of Residential Tenancy Following Foreclosure of Landlord's Interest.
Miller and Starr California Real Estate § 10:145.10, Regulation of Compensation and Advance Fees for Residential Loan Modifications and Forbearances (Which May Include "Short Sales" and Refinancings).
14 NO. 4 Miller & Starr, California Real Estate Newsalert 10, Landlord and Tenant.
19 NO. 1 Miller & Starr, California Real Estate Newsalert 1, The Perata Foreclosure Bill (SB 1137): New Rights for Defaulting Borrowers and Tenants; New Complications for Foreclosing Lenders.
19 NO. 4 Miller & Starr, California Real Estate Newsalert 10, Deeds of Trust.
20 NO. 4 Miller & Starr, California Real Estate Newsalert 6, Deeds of Trust.
1 Witkin Cal. Proc. 5th Attorneys § 154, Formal Contract.
12 Witkin, California Summary 10th Real Property § 519, Form.
1 Witkin Cal. Summ. 10th Contracts § 124, (S 124) of Translation.
4 Witkin, California Summary 10th Sales § 252, in General.
4 Witkin, California Summary 10th Security Transactions in Real Property § 23, Reverse Mortgage.
4 Witkin, California Summary 10th Security Transactions in Real Property § 37, (S 37) Aspects Regulated.
4 Witkin, California Summary 10th Security Transactions in Real Property § 151, Posting, Publication, and Recording.
4 Witkin, California Summary 10th Security Transactions in Real Property § 229, (S 229) Rights of Owner and Obligations of Consultant.

§ 1632.5. Supervised financial organizations negotiating primarily in Spanish, Chinese, Tagalog, Vietnamese, or Korean; contracts for loans or extensions of credit secured by residential real property; delivery in foreign language prior to execution; version executed in English to govern rights and responsibilities; exceptions

(a) A supervised financial organization that negotiates primarily in Spanish, Chinese, Tagalog, Vietnamese, or Korean, whether orally or in writing, in the course of entering into a contract or agreement for a loan or extension of credit secured by residential real property, shall deliver to the other party to that contract or agreement prior to the execution of the contract or agreement the form described in subdivision (i) for that language.

(b) For purposes of this section:

(1) "Contract" or "agreement" shall have the same meaning as defined in subdivision (g) of Section 1632.

(2) "Supervised financial organization" means a bank, savings association, as defined in Section 5102 of the Financial Code, credit union, or holding company, affiliate, or subsidiary thereof, or any person subject to Division 7 (commencing with Section 18000), Division 9 (commencing with Section 22000), or Division 20 (commencing with Section 50000) of the Financial Code.

(c)(1) With respect to a contract or agreement for a loan or extension of credit secured by residential real property as described in subdivision (a), a supervised financial organization that complies with this section shall be deemed in compliance with Section 1632.

(2) A supervised financial organization that complies with Section 1632, with respect to a contract or agreement for a loan or extension of credit secured by residential real property as described in subdivision (a), shall be deemed in compliance with this section.

(d) The supervised financial organization shall provide the form described in subdivision (i) to the borrower no later than three business days after receipt of the written application, and if any of the loan terms summarized materially change after provision of the translated form but prior to consummation of the loan, the supervised financial organization shall provide an updated version of the translated form prior to consummation of the loan.

(e)(1) This section does not apply to a supervised financial organization that negotiates primarily in a language other than English, as described by subdivision (a), if the party with whom the supervised financial organization is negotiating, negotiates the terms of the contract through his or her own interpreter.

(2) For purposes of this subdivision, "his or her own interpreter" means a person, not a minor, able to speak fluently and read with full understanding both the English language and one of the languages specified in subdivision (a) that is the language in which the contract was negotiated, who is not employed by, and whose services are not made available through, the person engaged in the trade or business.

(f) Notwithstanding subdivision (a), a translated form may retain any of the following elements of the executed English language contract or agreement without translation:

(1) Names and titles of individuals and other persons.

(2) Addresses, brand names, trade names, trademarks, or registered service marks.

(3) Full or abbreviated designations of the make and model of goods or services.

(4) Alphanumeric codes.

(5) Individual words or expressions having no generally accepted non–English translation.

(g) The terms of the contract or agreement which is executed in the English language shall determine the rights and obligations of the parties. However, the translation of the form described in subdivision (i) and required by subdivision (a) shall be admissible in evidence only to show that no contract or agreement was entered into because of a substantial difference in the material terms and conditions of the contract or agreement and the prior translated form provided to the borrower.

(h)(1) A licensing agency may, by order, after appropriate notice and opportunity for hearing, levy administrative penalties against a supervised financial organization that violates any provision of this section, and the supervised financial organization may be liable for administrative penalties, up to the amounts of two thousand five hundred dollars ($2,500) for the first violation, five thousand dollars ($5,000) for the second violation, and ten thousand dollars ($10,000) for each subsequent violation. Except for licensing agencies exempt from the provisions of the Administrative Procedure Act, any hearing shall be held in accordance with the Administrative Procedure Act (Chapter 5 (commencing with Section 11500) of Part 1 of Division 3 of Title 2 of the Government Code), and the licensing agency shall have all the powers granted under that act.

(2) A licensing agency may exercise any and all authority and powers available to it under any other provisions of law to administer and enforce this section, including, but not limited to, investigating and examining the licensed person's books and records, and charging and collecting the reasonable costs for these activities. The licensing agency shall not charge a licensed person twice for the same service. Any civil, criminal, and administrative authority and remedies available to the licensing agency pursuant to its licensing law may be sought and employed in any combination deemed advisable by the licensing agency to enforce the provisions of this section.

(3) Any supervised financial organization that violates any provision of this section shall be deemed to have violated its licensing law.

(4) Nothing in this section shall be construed to impair or impede the Attorney General from bringing an action to enforce this division.

(i) The Department of Corporations and the Department of Financial Institutions shall create a form to be made available in each of the languages set forth in subdivision (a) for use by a supervised financial organization to summarize the terms of a mortgage loan pursuant to subdivision (a). In creating the form, the Department of Corporations and the Department of Financial Institutions may use as guidance the United States Department of Housing and Urban Development's Good Faith Estimate disclosure form.

(j) This section shall not apply to federally chartered banks, credit unions, savings banks, or thrifts.

(k) Except as otherwise provided in subdivision (h), this section shall not be construed to create or enhance any claim, right of action, or civil liability that did not previously exist under state law, or limit any claim, right of action, or civil liability that otherwise exists under state law.

(*l*) An action against a supervised financial organization for a violation of this section may only be brought by a licensing agency or by the Attorney General.

(m) This section shall become operative beginning on July 1, 2010, or 90 days following the issuance of a form by both the Department of Corporations and the Department of Financial Institutions pursuant to subdivision (i), whichever occurs later. *(Added by Stats.2009, c. 274 (A.B.1160), § 1, operative Sept. 26, 2010.)*

Research References

Miller and Starr California Real Estate § 10:7, Execution and Delivery.
Miller and Starr California Real Estate § 4:58, Requirements in Making or Arranging a Loan--In General.
Miller and Starr California Real Estate § 36:1.30, Loans Negotiated in Languages Other Than English.
20 NO. 4 Miller & Starr, California Real Estate Newsalert 6, Deeds of Trust.
1 Witkin Cal. Summ. 10th Contracts § 124, (S 124) of Translation.
4 Witkin, California Summary 10th Security Transactions in Real Property § 37, (S 37) Aspects Regulated.

§ 1633. Electronically transmitted application to enter into brokerage agreement

(a) Notwithstanding any other provision of law, an application by a prospective customer to enter into a brokerage agreement with a broker-dealer, which application is transmitted electronically and is accompanied by the prospective customer's electronic signature or digital signature as described in subdivisions (d), (e), (f), and (g), shall be deemed, upon acceptance by the broker-dealer, to be a fully executed, valid, enforceable, and irrevocable written contract, unless grounds exist which would render any other contract invalid, unenforceable, or revocable.

(b) Nothing in this section abrogates or limits any existing law that would otherwise apply to contracts governed by this section, or any theory of liability or any remedy otherwise available at law.

(c) "Broker–dealer," for purposes of this section, means any broker-dealer licensed pursuant to Part 3 (commencing with Section 25200) of Division 1 of Title 4 of the Corporations Code or exempted from licensing pursuant thereto.

(d) "Electronic" means relating to technology having electrical, digital, magnetic, wireless, optical, electromagnetic, or similar capabilities.

(e) "Electronic record" means a record created, generated, sent, communicated, received, or stored electronically.

(f) "Electronic signature" means an electronic sound, symbol, or process attached to or logically associated with an electronic record and executed or adopted by a person with the intent to sign the electronic record.

(g) "Digital signature," for the purposes of this section, means an electronic identifier, created by a computer, that is intended by the party using it to have the same force and effect as the use of a manual signature. The use of a digital signature shall have the same force or effect as a manual signature if it embodies all of the following attributes:

(1) It is unique to the person using it.

(2) It is capable of verification.

(3) It is under the sole control of the person using it.

(4) It is linked to data in a manner that if the data is changed, the digital signature is invalidated.

(h) The use of an electronic signature or digital signature shall have the same force or effect as a manual signature.

(i) The application that is transmitted electronically pursuant to subdivision (a) shall comply with all applicable federal and state securities laws and regulations relating to disclosures to prospective customers. Unless those laws and regulations currently require disclosures to be displayed or printed in bold, to be of specific type or print size, and to be placed prominently at specified locations within the application, the disclosures shall be displayed prominently and printed in capital letters, in bold type and displayed or printed immediately above the signature line. Disclosures shall be written in plain English. The full text of the disclosures shall be contained in the application as required by this subdivision.

(j) Whenever a disclosure to a prospective customer is required under federal or state law or regulation to be confirmed as having been made, the application that is transmitted electronically pursuant to subdivision (a) shall provide a means by which the prospective customer shall confirm that he or she has read the disclosure. *(Added by Stats.1999, c. 213 (S.B.1124), § 1, eff. July 28, 1999.)*

Title 2.5

ELECTRONIC TRANSACTIONS

§ 1633.1. Short title

This title may be cited as the Uniform Electronic Transactions Act. *(Added by Stats.1999, c. 428 (S.B.820), § 1.)*

Research References

Miller and Starr California Real Estate § 5:9, Form of the Memorandum.
Miller and Starr California Real Estate § 1:39, When Acceptance is Effective.
Miller and Starr California Real Estate § 1:60, Parol Evidence; Extrinsic Evidence Rules.
Miller and Starr California Real Estate § 1:79, Form of the Memorandum.
4 Witkin Cal. Proc. 5th Pleading § 21, (S 21) Nature of Filing Process.
2 Witkin, California Summary 10th Insurance § 73A, (S 73A) (New)-Electronic Transactions.
1 Witkin Cal. Summ. 10th Contracts § 11, Uniform Act.
4 Witkin, California Summary 10th Sales § 353, (S 353) Electronic Commerce.

§ 1633.2. Definitions

In this title the following terms have the following definitions:

(a) "Agreement" means the bargain of the parties in fact, as found in their language or inferred from other circumstances and from rules, regulations, and procedures given the effect of agreements under laws otherwise applicable to a particular transaction.

(b) "Automated transaction" means a transaction conducted or performed, in whole or in part, by electronic means or electronic records, in which the acts or records of one or both parties are not reviewed by an individual in the ordinary course in forming a contract, performing under an existing contract, or fulfilling an obligation required by the transaction.

(c) "Computer program" means a set of statements or instructions to be used directly or indirectly in an information processing system in order to bring about a certain result.

(d) "Contract" means the total legal obligation resulting from the parties' agreement as affected by this title and other applicable law.

(e) "Electronic" means relating to technology having electrical, digital, magnetic, wireless, optical, electromagnetic, or similar capabilities.

(f) "Electronic agent" means a computer program or an electronic or other automated means used independently to initiate an action or respond to electronic records or performances in whole or in part, without review by an individual.

(g) "Electronic record" means a record created, generated, sent, communicated, received, or stored by electronic means.

(h) "Electronic signature" means an electronic sound, symbol, or process attached to or logically associated with an electronic record and executed or adopted by a person with the intent to sign the electronic record.

(i) "Governmental agency" means an executive, legislative, or judicial agency, department, board, commission, authority, institution, or instrumentality of the federal government or of a state or of a county, municipality, or other political subdivision of a state.

(j) "Information" means data, text, images, sounds, codes, computer programs, software, data bases, or the like.

(k) "Information processing system" means an electronic system for creating, generating, sending, receiving, storing, displaying, or processing information.

(*l*) "Person" means an individual, corporation, business trust, estate, trust, partnership, limited liability company, association, joint venture, governmental agency, public corporation, or any other legal or commercial entity.

(m) "Record" means information that is inscribed on a tangible medium or that is stored in an electronic or other medium and is retrievable in perceivable form.

(n) "Security procedure" means a procedure employed for the purpose of verifying that an electronic signature, record, or performance is that of a specific person or for detecting changes or errors in the information in an electronic record. The term includes a procedure that requires the use of algorithms or other codes, identifying words or numbers, encryption, or callback or other acknowledgment procedures.

(*o*) "Transaction" means an action or set of actions occurring between two or more persons relating to the conduct of business, commercial, or governmental affairs. *(Added by Stats.1999, c. 428 (S.B.820), § 1.)*

Research References

Rutter, Cal. Practice Guide: Civil Trials & Evidence Ch. 8E-A, A. Privileges.
Miller and Starr California Real Estate § 5:9, Form of the Memorandum.
Miller and Starr California Real Estate § 1:79, Form of the Memorandum.
1 Witkin Cal. Summ. 10th Contracts § 13, Definitions.

§ 1633.3. Application of title

Section operative until Jan. 1, 2019. See, also, section operative Jan. 1, 2019.

(a) Except as otherwise provided in subdivisions (b) and (c), this title applies to electronic records and electronic signatures relating to a transaction.

(b) This title does not apply to transactions subject to the following laws:

(1) A law governing the creation and execution of wills, codicils, or testamentary trusts.

(2) Division 1 (commencing with Section 1101) of the Uniform Commercial Code, except Sections * * * 1206 and 1306.

(3) Divisions 3 (commencing with Section 3101), 4 (commencing with Section 4101), 5 (commencing with Section 5101), 8 (commencing with Section 8101), 9 (commencing with Section 9101), and 11 (commencing with Section 11101) of the Uniform Commercial Code.

(4) A law that requires that specifically identifiable text or disclosures in a record or a portion of a record be separately signed, including initialed, from the record. However, this paragraph does not apply to Section 1677 or 1678 of this code or Section 1298 of the Code of Civil Procedure.

(c) This title does not apply to any specific transaction described in Section 17511.5 of the Business and Professions Code, Section 56.11, 56.17, 798.14, 1133, or 1134 of, Section 1689.6, 1689.7, or 1689.13 of, Chapter 2.5 (commencing with Section 1695) of Title 5 of Part 2 of Division 3 of, Section 1720, 1785.15, 1789.14, 1789.16, * * * or 1793.23 of, Chapter 1 (commencing with Section 1801) of Title 2 of Part 4 of Division 3 of, Section 1861.24, 1862.5, 1917.712, 1917.713, 1950.5, 1950.6, 1983, 2924b, 2924c, 2924f, 2924i, 2924j, 2924.3, or 2937 of, Article 1.5 (commencing with Section 2945) of Chapter 2 of Title 14 of Part 4 of Division 3 of, Section 2954.5 or 2963 of, Chapter 2b (commencing with Section 2981) or 2d (commencing with Section 2985.7) of Title 14 of Part 4 of Division 3 of, Section 3071.5 of, * * * Part 5 (commencing with Section 4000) of Division 4 of, * * * or Part 5.3 (commencing with Section 6500) of Division 4 of this code, subdivision (b) of Section 18608 or Section 22328 of the Financial Code, Section 1358.15, 1365, 1368.01, 1368.1, 1371, or 18035.5 of the Health and Safety Code, Section 662, paragraph (2) of subdivision (a) of Section 663, 664, 667.5, 673, 677, paragraph (2) of subdivision (a) of Section 678, subdivisions (a) and (b) of Section 678.1, Section 786, * * * 10113.7, 10127.7, 10127.9, 10127.10, 10192.18, 10199.44, 10199.46, 10235.16, 10235.40, 10509.4, 10509.7, 11624.09, or 11624.1 of the Insurance Code, Section 779.1, 10010.1, or 16482 of the Public Utilities Code, or Section 9975 or 11738 of the Vehicle Code. An electronic record may not be substituted for any notice that is required to be sent pursuant to Section 1162 of the Code of Civil Procedure. Nothing in this subdivision shall be construed to prohibit the recordation of any document with a county recorder by electronic means.

(d) This title applies to an electronic record or electronic signature otherwise excluded from the application of this title under subdivision (b) when used for a transaction subject to a law other than those specified in subdivision (b).

(e) A transaction subject to this title is also subject to other applicable substantive law.

(f) The exclusion of a transaction from the application of this title under subdivision (b) or (c) shall be construed only to exclude the transaction from the application of this title, but shall not be construed to prohibit the transaction from being conducted by electronic means if the transaction may be conducted by electronic means under any other applicable law.

(g) This section shall remain in effect only until January 1, 2019, and as of that date is repealed, unless a later enacted statute, that is enacted before January 1, 2019, deletes or extends that date. *(Added by Stats.1999, c. 428 (S.B.820), § 1. Amended by Stats.2009, c. 433 (A.B.328), § 1; Stats.2012, c. 181 (A.B.806), § 36, operative Jan. 1, 2014; Stats.2013, c. 369 (S.B.251), § 1; Stats.2013, c. 605 (S.B.752), § 16.5.)*

Repeal

For repeal of this section, see its terms.

Law Revision Commission Comments

Section 1633.3 is amended to correct a cross-reference to former Sections 1350–1376. It also adds a reference to former Section 1378. [40 Cal.L.Rev.Comm. Reports 235 (2010)].

Subdivision (c) of Section 1633.3 is amended to add a cross-reference to Part 5.3 (commencing with Section 6500) of Division 4, reflecting the enactment of the Commercial and Industrial Common Interest Development Act (Civ. Code §§ 6500–6876). [42 Cal.L.Rev.Comm. Reports 1 (2012)].

Research References

Miller and Starr California Real Estate § 1:39, When Acceptance is Effective.

Miller and Starr California Real Estate § 1:79, Form of the Memorandum.

2 Witkin, California Summary 10th Insurance § 73A, (S 73A) (New)-Electronic Transactions.

12 Witkin, California Summary 10th Real Property § 680, Periodic Tenancy.

12 Witkin, California Summary 10th Real Property § 727, (S 727) Methods of Service.

1 Witkin Cal. Summ. 10th Contracts § 11, Uniform Act.

1 Witkin Cal. Summ. 10th Contracts § 14, Applicability.

§ 1633.3. Application of title

Section operative Jan. 1, 2019. See, also, section operative until Jan. 1, 2019.

(a) Except as otherwise provided in subdivisions (b) and (c), this title applies to electronic records and electronic signatures relating to a transaction.

(b) This title does not apply to transactions subject to the following laws:

(1) A law governing the creation and execution of wills, codicils, or testamentary trusts.

(2) Division 1 (commencing with Section 1101) of the Uniform Commercial Code, except Sections 1206 and 1306.

(3) Divisions 3 (commencing with Section 3101), 4 (commencing with Section 4101), 5 (commencing with Section 5101), 8 (commencing with Section 8101), 9 (commencing with Section 9101), and 11 (commencing with Section 11101) of the Uniform Commercial Code.

(4) A law that requires that specifically identifiable text or disclosures in a record or a portion of a record be separately signed, including initialed, from the record. However, this paragraph does not apply to Section 1677 or 1678 of this code or Section 1298 of the Code of Civil Procedure.

(c) This title does not apply to any specific transaction described in Section 17511.5 of the Business and Professions Code, Section 56.11, 56.17, 798.14, 1133, or 1134 of, Section 1689.6, 1689.7, or 1689.13 of, Chapter 2.5 (commencing with Section 1695) of Title 5 of Part 2 of Division 3 of, Section 1720, 1785.15, 1789.14, 1789.16, or 1793.23 of, Chapter 1 (commencing with Section 1801) of Title 2 of Part 4 of Division 3 of, Section 1861.24, 1862.5, 1917.712, 1917.713, 1950.5, 1950.6, 1983, 2924b, 2924c, 2924f, 2924i, 2924j, 2924.3, or 2937 of, Article 1.5 (commencing with Section 2945) of Chapter 2 of Title 14 of Part 4 of Division 3 of, Section 2954.5 or 2963 of, Chapter 2b (commencing with Section 2981) or 2d (commencing with Section 2985.7) of Title 14 of Part 4 of Division 3 of, Section 3071.5 of Part 5 (commencing with Section 4000) of Division 4 of, or Part 5.3 (commencing with Section 6500) of Division 4 of this code, subdivision (b) of Section 18608 or Section 22328 of the Financial Code, Section 1358.15, 1365, 1368.01, 1368.1, 1371, or 18035.5 of the Health and Safety Code, Section 662, 663, 664, 667.5, 673, 677, 678, 678.1, 786, 10086, 10113.7, 10127.7, 10127.9, 10127.10, 10192.18, 10199.44, 10199.46, 10235.16, 10235.40, 10509.4, 10509.7, 11624.09, or 11624.1 of the Insurance Code, Section 779.1, 10010.1, or 16482 of the Public Utilities Code, or Section 9975 or 11738 of the Vehicle Code. An electronic record may not be substituted for any notice that is required to be sent pursuant to Section 1162 of the Code of Civil Procedure. Nothing in this subdivision shall be construed to prohibit the recordation of any document with a county recorder by electronic means.

(d) This title applies to an electronic record or electronic signature otherwise excluded from the application of this title under subdivision (b) when used for a transaction subject to a law other than those specified in subdivision (b).

(e) A transaction subject to this title is also subject to other applicable substantive law.

(f) The exclusion of a transaction from the application of this title under subdivision (b) or (c) shall be construed only to exclude the transaction from the application of this title, but shall not be construed to prohibit the transaction from being conducted by electronic means if the transaction may be conducted by electronic means under any other applicable law.

(g) This section shall become operative on January 1, 2019. *(Added by Stats.2013, c. 369 (S.B.251), § 3, operative Jan. 1, 2019.)*

§ 1633.4. Further application of title

This title applies to any electronic record or electronic signature created, generated, sent, communicated, received, or stored on or after January 1, 2000. *(Added by Stats.1999, c. 428 (S.B.820), § 1.)*

Research References

1 Witkin Cal. Summ. 10th Contracts § 11, Uniform Act.

§ 1633.5. Record or signature requirement; agreement to transact electronically

(a) This title does not require a record or signature to be created, generated, sent, communicated, received, stored, or otherwise processed or used by electronic means or in electronic form.

(b) This title applies only to a transaction between parties each of which has agreed to conduct the transaction by electronic means. Whether the parties agree to conduct a transaction by electronic means is determined from the context and surrounding circumstances, including the parties' conduct. Except for a separate and optional agreement the primary purpose of which is to authorize a transaction to be conducted by electronic means, an agreement to conduct a transaction by electronic means may not be contained in a standard form contract that is not an electronic record. An agreement in such a standard form contract may not be conditioned upon an agreement to conduct transactions by electronic means. An agreement to conduct a transaction by electronic means may not be inferred solely from the fact that a party has used electronic means to pay an account or register a purchase or warranty. This subdivision may not be varied by agreement.

(c) A party that agrees to conduct a transaction by electronic means may refuse to conduct other transactions by electronic means. If a seller sells goods or services by both electronic and nonelectronic means and a buyer purchases the goods or services by conducting the transaction by electronic means, the buyer may refuse to conduct further transactions regarding the goods or services by electronic means. This subdivision may not be varied by agreement.

(d) Except as otherwise provided in this title, the effect of any of its provisions may be varied by agreement. The presence in certain provisions of this title of the words "unless otherwise agreed," or words of similar import, does not imply that the effect of other provisions may not be varied by agreement. *(Added by Stats.1999, c. 428 (S.B.820), § 1.)*

Research References

Miller and Starr California Real Estate § 5:9, Form of the Memorandum.
Miller and Starr California Real Estate § 1:79, Form of the Memorandum.
Miller and Starr California Real Estate § 5:10, Form of the Memorandum--Signature of the Principal.
1 Witkin Cal. Summ. 10th Contracts § 18, Agreement to Transact Electronically.

§ 1633.6. Construction and application of title

This title shall be construed and applied according to all of the following:

(1) To facilitate electronic transactions consistent with other applicable law.

(2) To be consistent with reasonable practices concerning electronic transactions and with the continued expansion of those practices.

(3) To effectuate its general purpose to make uniform the law with respect to the subject of this title among states enacting it. *(Added by Stats.1999, c. 428 (S.B.820), § 1.)*

Research References

1 Witkin Cal. Summ. 10th Contracts § 12, Construction.

§ 1633.7. Legal effect or enforceability of electronic record, signature, or contract

(a) A record or signature may not be denied legal effect or enforceability solely because it is in electronic form.

(b) A contract may not be denied legal effect or enforceability solely because an electronic record was used in its formation.

(c) If a law requires a record to be in writing, an electronic record satisfies the law.

(d) If a law requires a signature, an electronic signature satisfies the law. *(Added by Stats.1999, c. 428 (S.B.820), § 1.)*

Research References

Rutter, Cal. Practice Guide: Real Prop. Transactions Ch. 4-D, D. Selecting the Form of Written Agreement.
Miller and Starr California Real Estate § 5:9, Form of the Memorandum.
Miller and Starr California Real Estate § 1:79, Form of the Memorandum.
Miller and Starr California Real Estate § 5:10, Form of the Memorandum--Signature of the Principal.
1 Witkin Cal. Summ. 10th Contracts § 19, Legal Effect or Enforceability of Electronic Record, Signature, or Contract.

§ 1633.8. Requirement to provide, send, or deliver information in writing; electronic satisfaction

(a) If parties have agreed to conduct a transaction by electronic means and a law requires a person to provide, send, or deliver information in writing to another person, that requirement is satisfied if the information is provided, sent, or delivered, as the case may be, in an electronic record capable of retention by the recipient at the time of receipt. An electronic record is not capable of retention by the recipient if the sender or its information processing system inhibits the ability of the recipient to print or store the electronic record.

(b) If a law other than this title requires a record to be posted or displayed in a certain manner, to be sent, communicated, or transmitted by a specified method, or to contain information that is formatted in a certain manner, all of the following rules apply:

(1) The record shall be posted or displayed in the manner specified in the other law.

(2) Except as otherwise provided in paragraph (2) of subdivision (d), the record shall be sent, communicated, or transmitted by the method specified in the other law.

(3) The record shall contain the information formatted in the manner specified in the other law.

(c) If a sender inhibits the ability of a recipient to store or print an electronic record, the electronic record is not enforceable against the recipient.

(d) The requirements of this section may not be varied by agreement, except as follows:

(1) To the extent a law other than this title requires information to be provided, sent, or delivered in writing but permits that requirement to be varied by agreement, the requirement under subdivision (a) that the information be in the form of an electronic record capable of retention may also be varied by agreement.

(2) A requirement under a law other than this title to send, communicate, or transmit a record by first-class mail may be varied by agreement to the extent permitted by the other law. *(Added by Stats.1999, c. 428 (S.B.820), § 1.)*

Research References

Miller and Starr California Real Estate § 1:39, When Acceptance is Effective.
Miller and Starr California Real Estate § 1:79, Form of the Memorandum.
1 Witkin Cal. Summ. 10th Contracts § 21, Requirement of Writing.

§ 1633.9. Attribution of electronic record or signature

(a) An electronic record or electronic signature is attributable to a person if it was the act of the person. The act of the person may be shown in any manner, including a showing of the efficacy of any security procedure applied to determine the person to which the electronic record or electronic signature was attributable.

(b) The effect of an electronic record or electronic signature attributed to a person under subdivision (a) is determined from the context and surrounding circumstances at the time of its creation, execution, or adoption, including the parties' agreement, if any, and otherwise as provided by law. *(Added by Stats.1999, c. 428 (S.B.820), § 1.)*

Research References

Miller and Starr California Real Estate § 1:79, Form of the Memorandum.
1 Witkin Cal. Summ. 10th Contracts § 15, Attribution of Electronic Record or Signature.

§ 1633.10. Change or error in electronic record; rules

If a change or error in an electronic record occurs in a transmission between parties to a transaction, the following rules apply:

(1) If the parties have agreed to use a security procedure to detect changes or errors and one party has conformed to the procedure, but the other party has not, and the nonconforming party would have detected the change or error had that party also conformed, the conforming party may avoid the effect of the changed or erroneous electronic record.

(2) In an automated transaction involving an individual, the individual may avoid the effect of an electronic record that resulted from an error made by the individual in dealing with the electronic agent of another person if the electronic agent did not provide an opportunity for the prevention or correction of the error and, at the time the individual learns of the error, all of the following conditions are met:

(i) The individual promptly notifies the other person of the error and that the individual did not intend to be bound by the electronic record received by the other person.

(ii) The individual takes reasonable steps, including steps that conform to the other person's reasonable instructions, to return to the other person or, if instructed by the other person, to destroy the consideration received, if any, as a result of the erroneous electronic record.

(iii) The individual has not used or received any benefit or value from the consideration, if any, received from the other person.

(3) If neither paragraph (1) nor (2) applies, the change or error has the effect provided by other law, including the law of mistake, and the parties' contract, if any.

(4) Paragraphs (2) and (3) may not be varied by agreement. *(Added by Stats.1999, c. 428 (S.B.820), § 1.)*

Research References

Miller and Starr California Real Estate § 1:79, Form of the Memorandum.

1 Witkin Cal. Summ. 10th Contracts § 16, Change or Error in Electronic Record.

§ 1633.11. Notarization and signature under penalty of perjury requirements

(a) If a law requires that a signature be notarized, the requirement is satisfied with respect to an electronic signature if an electronic record includes, in addition to the electronic signature to be notarized, the electronic signature of a notary public together with all other information required to be included in a notarization by other applicable law.

(b) In a transaction, if a law requires that a statement be signed under penalty of perjury, the requirement is satisfied with respect to an electronic signature, if an electronic record includes, in addition to the electronic signature, all of the information as to which the declaration pertains together with a declaration under penalty of perjury by the person who submits the electronic signature that the information is true and correct. *(Added by Stats.1999, c. 428 (S.B.820), § 1.)*

Research References

Miller and Starr California Real Estate § 1:79, Form of the Memorandum.
1 Witkin Cal. Summ. 10th Contracts § 22, Requirement of Notarization and Signature Under Penalty of Perjury.

§ 1633.12. Retaining records; electronic satisfaction

(a) If a law requires that a record be retained, the requirement is satisfied by retaining an electronic record of the information in the record, if the electronic record reflects accurately the information set forth in the record at the time it was first generated in its final form as an electronic record or otherwise, and the electronic record remains accessible for later reference.

(b) A requirement to retain a record in accordance with subdivision (a) does not apply to any information the sole purpose of which is to enable the record to be sent, communicated, or received.

(c) A person may satisfy subdivision (a) by using the services of another person if the requirements of subdivision (a) are satisfied.

(d) If a law requires a record to be retained in its original form, or provides consequences if the record is not retained in its original form, that law is satisfied by an electronic record retained in accordance with subdivision (a).

(e) If a law requires retention of a check, that requirement is satisfied by retention of an electronic record of the information on the front and back of the check in accordance with subdivision (a).

(f) A record retained as an electronic record in accordance with subdivision (a) satisfies a law requiring a person to retain a record for evidentiary, audit, or like purposes, unless a law enacted after the effective date of this title specifically prohibits the use of an electronic record for a specified purpose.

(g) This section does not preclude a governmental agency from specifying additional requirements for the retention of a record subject to the agency's jurisdiction. *(Added by Stats.1999, c. 428 (S.B.820), § 1.)*

Research References

Miller and Starr California Real Estate § 1:79, Form of the Memorandum.

1 Witkin Cal. Summ. 10th Contracts § 23, Requirement to Retain Records.

§ 1633.13. Evidence in electronic form; admissibility

In a proceeding, evidence of a record or signature may not be excluded solely because it is in electronic form. *(Added by Stats.1999, c. 428 (S.B.820), § 1.)*

Research References

Miller and Starr California Real Estate § 1:79, Form of the Memorandum.

1 Witkin Cal. Summ. 10th Contracts § 11, Uniform Act.

§ 1633.14. Automated transaction rules

(a) In an automated transaction, the following rules apply:

(1) A contract may be formed by the interaction of electronic agents of the parties, even if no individual was aware of or reviewed the electronic agents' actions or the resulting terms and agreements.

(2) A contract may be formed by the interaction of an electronic agent and an individual, acting on the individual's own behalf or for another person, including by an interaction in which the individual performs actions that the individual is free to refuse to perform and which the individual knows or has reason to know will cause the electronic agent to complete the transaction or performance.

(b) The terms of the contract are determined by the substantive law applicable to it. *(Added by Stats.1999, c. 428 (S.B.820), § 1.)*

Research References

1 Witkin Cal. Summ. 10th Contracts § 20, Automated Transactions.

§ 1633.15. Sending and receiving records; timing

(a) Unless the sender and the recipient agree to a different method of sending that is reasonable under the circumstances, an electronic record is sent when the information is addressed properly or otherwise directed properly to the recipient and either (1) enters an information processing system outside the control of the sender or of a person that sent the electronic record on behalf of the sender, or (2) enters a region of an information processing system that is under the control of the recipient.

(b) Unless the sender and the recipient agree to a different method of receiving that is reasonable under the circumstances, an electronic record is received when the electronic record enters an information processing system that the recipient has designated or uses for the purpose of receiving electronic records or information of the type sent, in a form capable of being processed by that system, and from which the recipient is able to retrieve the electronic record.

(c) Subdivision (b) applies even if the place the information processing system is located is different from the place the electronic record is deemed to be received under subdivision (d).

(d) Unless otherwise expressly provided in the electronic record or agreed between the sender and the recipient, an electronic record is deemed to be sent from the sender's place of business and to be received at the recipient's place of business or, if the recipient is an individual acting on his or her own behalf, at the recipient's place of residence. For purposes of this subdivision, the following rules apply:

(1) If the sender or recipient has more than one place of business, the place of business of that person is the place having the closest relationship to the underlying transaction.

(2) If the sender or the recipient does not have a place of business, the place of business is the sender's or recipient's residence, as the case may be.

(e) An electronic record is received under subdivision (b) even if no individual is aware of its receipt.

(f) Receipt of an electronic acknowledgment from an information processing system described in subdivision (b) establishes that a record was received but, by itself, does not establish that the content sent corresponds to the content received.

(g) If a person is aware that an electronic record purportedly sent under subdivision (a), or purportedly received under subdivision (b), was not actually sent or received, the legal effect of the sending or receipt is determined by other applicable law. Except to the extent permitted by the other law, this subdivision may not be varied by agreement. *(Added by Stats.1999, c. 428 (S.B.820), § 1.)*

Research References

Miller and Starr California Real Estate § 1:79, Form of the Memorandum.

2 Witkin, California Summary 10th Insurance § 73A, (S 73A) (New)- Electronic Transactions.

1 Witkin Cal. Summ. 10th Contracts § 17, Sending and Receiving Records.

§ 1633.16. Notice of right to cancel

If a law other than this title requires that a notice of the right to cancel be provided or sent, an electronic record may not substitute for a writing under that other law unless, in addition to satisfying the requirements of that other law and this title, the notice of cancellation may be returned by electronic means. This section may not be varied by agreement. *(Added by Stats.1999, c. 428 (S.B.820), § 1.)*

Research References

Miller and Starr California Real Estate § 1:79, Form of the Memorandum.

1 Witkin Cal. Summ. 10th Contracts § 24, (S 24) Notice of Right to Cancel.

§ 1633.17. Regulation of electronic signature

No state agency, board, or commission may require, prohibit, or regulate the use of an electronic signature in a transaction in which the agency, board, or commission is not a party unless a law other than this title expressly authorizes the requirement, prohibition, or regulation. *(Added by Stats.1999, c. 428 (S.B. 820), § 1.)*

Research References

Miller and Starr California Real Estate § 5:9, Form of the Memorandum.
Miller and Starr California Real Estate § 1:79, Form of the Memorandum.

1 Witkin Cal. Summ. 10th Contracts § 11, Uniform Act.

Title 3

INTERPRETATION OF CONTRACTS

§ 1635.   Public and private contracts; uniformity of interpretation

All contracts, whether public or private, are to be interpreted by the same rules, except as otherwise provided by this Code. *(Enacted in 1872.)*

Research References

Miller and Starr California Real Estate § 19:47, Rules of Interpretation.

2 Witkin, California Summary 10th Insurance § 48, Governing Rules and Principles.

1 Witkin Cal. Summ. 10th Contracts § 741, (S 741) Nature of Interpretation.

1 Witkin Cal. Summ. 10th Contracts § 742, (S 742) General Application of Rules.

§ 1636.   Mutual intention to be given effect

A contract must be so interpreted as to give effect to the mutual intention of the parties as it existed at the time of contracting, so far as the same is ascertainable and lawful. *(Enacted in 1872.)*

Research References

Rutter, Cal. Practice Guide: Civil Trials & Evidence Ch. 8C-K, K. Stipulations.

Rutter, Cal. Practice Guide: Civil Trials & Evidence Ch. 8E-G, G. Parol Evidence Rule.

California Practice Guide: Employment Litigation Ch. 3-B, B. Liability Insurance-General Considerations.

Rutter, Cal. Practice Guide: Insurance Litigation Ch. 4-B, B. "Plain Meaning" vs. Ambiguity.

Rutter, Cal. Practice Guide: Insurance Litigation Ch. 4-C, C. Rules for Resolving Ambiguity.

Rutter, Cal. Practice Guide: Real Prop. Transactions Ch. 4-B, B. Interests to be Conveyed.

Rutter, Cal. Practice Guide: Real Prop. Transactions Ch. 4-E, E. Drafting the Purchase and Sale Agreement-Terms and Conditions.

Miller and Starr California Real Estate § 8:2, Rules of Interpretation; Extrinsic Evidence.

Miller and Starr California Real Estate § 1:59, Rules of Contract Interpretation.

Miller and Starr California Real Estate § 15:16, Rules of Construction.

Miller and Starr California Real Estate § 15:56, Use of Express Easements.

Miller and Starr California Real Estate § 24:17, Rules of Construction; Evidence.

19 NO. 5 Miller & Starr, California Real Estate Newsalert 9, Contracts.

19 NO. 1 Miller & Starr, California Real Estate Newsalert 11, Easements.

20 NO. 6 Miller & Starr, California Real Estate Newsalert 10, Escrows.

2 Witkin, California Summary 10th Insurance § 48, Governing Rules and Principles.

1 Witkin Cal. Summ. 10th Contracts § 744, (S 744) Intention of Parties: Objective Test.

§ 1637.   Ascertainment of intention

For the purpose of ascertaining the intention of the parties to a contract, if otherwise doubtful, the rules given in this Chapter are to be applied. *(Enacted in 1872.)*

Research References

1 Witkin Cal. Summ. 10th Contracts § 741, (S 741) Nature of Interpretation.

§ 1638.   Ascertainment of intention; language

The language of a contract is to govern its interpretation, if the language is clear and explicit, and does not involve an absurdity. *(Enacted in 1872.)*

Research References

Rutter, Cal. Practice Guide: Civil Trials & Evidence Ch. 8E-G, G. Parol Evidence Rule.

California Practice Guide: Employment Litigation Ch. 3-B, B. Liability Insurance-General Considerations.

Rutter, Cal. Practice Guide: Insurance Litigation Ch. 4-B, B. "Plain Meaning" vs. Ambiguity.

Miller and Starr California Real Estate § 1:59, Rules of Contract Interpretation.

Miller and Starr California Real Estate § 1:60, Parol Evidence; Extrinsic Evidence Rules.

Miller and Starr California Real Estate § 6:21, Duty of a Party to Comply With Instructions.

Miller and Starr California Real Estate § 7:35, Clear and Ambiguous Language.

23 NO. 3 Miller & Starr, California Real Estate Newsalert 7, Covenants, Equitable Servitudes, and Other Restrictions.

2 Witkin, California Summary 10th Insurance § 55, in General.

1 Witkin Cal. Summ. 10th Contracts § 741, (S 741) Nature of Interpretation.

4 Witkin, California Summary 10th Sales § 205, Illustrations: Personal Injury and Property Damage.

§ 1639.   Ascertainment of intention; written contracts

When a contract is reduced to writing, the intention of the parties is to be ascertained from the writing alone, if possible; subject, however, to the other provisions of this Title. *(Enacted in 1872.)*

Research References

Rutter, Cal. Practice Guide: Civil Trials & Evidence Ch. 8E-G, G. Parol Evidence Rule.

California Practice Guide: Employment Litigation Ch. 3-B, B. Liability Insurance-General Considerations.

Rutter, Cal. Practice Guide: Real Prop. Transactions Ch. 2-E, E. Listing Agreements.

Rutter, Cal. Practice Guide: Real Prop. Transactions Ch. 3-A, A. Nature of Title Insurance.

Rutter, Cal. Practice Guide: Real Prop. Transactions Ch. 4-A, A. Property to be Sold.

Miller and Starr California Real Estate § 8:2, Rules of Interpretation; Extrinsic Evidence.

Miller and Starr California Real Estate § 1:59, Rules of Contract Interpretation.

Miller and Starr California Real Estate § 7:38, Coverage Analysis.

2 Witkin, California Summary 10th Insurance § 55, in General.

1 Witkin Cal. Summ. 10th Contracts § 741, (S 741) Nature of Interpretation.

§ 1640. Writing disregarded; unexpressed intention

When, through fraud, mistake, or accident, a written contract fails to express the real intention of the parties, such intention is to be regarded, and the erroneous parts of the writing disregarded. *(Enacted in 1872.)*

Research References

Miller and Starr California Real Estate § 34:11, Nature of the Remedy; Requirement of a Prior Agreement.

§ 1641. Whole contract, effect to be given

The whole of a contract is to be taken together, so as to give effect to every part, if reasonably practicable, each clause helping to interpret the other. *(Enacted in 1872.)*

Research References

Rutter, Cal. Practice Guide: Insurance Litigation Ch. 4-B, B. "Plain Meaning" vs. Ambiguity.
Miller and Starr California Real Estate § 1:59, Rules of Contract Interpretation.
Miller and Starr California Real Estate § 7:37, General Rules of Construction.
Miller and Starr California Real Estate § 19:47, Rules of Interpretation.
14 NO. 5 Miller & Starr, California Real Estate Newsalert 16, Landlord and Tenant.
1 Witkin Cal. Summ. 10th Contracts § 746, Single Writing.

§ 1642. Several contracts as parts of one transaction

Several contracts relating to the same matters, between the same parties, and made as parts of substantially one transaction, are to be taken together. *(Enacted in 1872.)*

Research References

Rutter, Cal. Practice Guide: Real Prop. Transactions Ch. 4-F, F. Use of an Escrow.
Rutter, Cal. Practice Guide: Real Prop. Transactions Ch. 11-A, A. Factors Affecting Choice of Remedies.
Miller and Starr California Real Estate § 2:6, Escrow Instructions as a Contract.
Miller and Starr California Real Estate § 1:59, Rules of Contract Interpretation.
Miller and Starr California Real Estate § 1:79, Form of the Memorandum.
Miller and Starr California Real Estate § 10:5, Form and Interpretation.
Miller and Starr California Real Estate § 6:30, Requirement of a Contract.
Miller and Starr California Real Estate § 34:69, Effect of Two or More Contracts in One Transaction.
Miller and Starr California Real Estate § 35:25, Written Agreement Required.
1 Witkin Cal. Summ. 10th Contracts § 747, Several Writings.

§ 1643. Interpretation in favor of contract

A contract must receive such an interpretation as will make it lawful, operative, definite, reasonable, and capable of being carried into effect, if it can be done without violating the intention of the parties. *(Enacted in 1872.)*

Research References

Rutter, Cal. Practice Guide: Real Prop. Transactions Ch. 7-C, C. Representing the Purchasing Tenant.
Miller and Starr California Real Estate § 1:59, Rules of Contract Interpretation.
Miller and Starr California Real Estate § 19:47, Rules of Interpretation.
Miller and Starr California Real Estate § 34:17, When Specific Performance is Available; Prerequisites.
Miller and Starr California Real Estate § 11:210, Executory Seller Subordination Agreements--Specific Performance of Contract When New Lien Not to Secure a Construction Loan.

1 Witkin Cal. Summ. 10th Contracts § 750, General Rule.

§ 1644. Sense of words

The words of a contract are to be understood in their ordinary and popular sense, rather than according to their strict legal meaning; unless used by the parties in a technical sense, or unless a special meaning is given to them by usage, in which case the latter must be followed. *(Enacted in 1872.)*

Research References

California Practice Guide: Employment Litigation Ch. 3-B, B. Liability Insurance-General Considerations.
Rutter, Cal. Practice Guide: Insurance Litigation Ch. 3-C, C. Anatomy of Insurance Policy.
Rutter, Cal. Practice Guide: Insurance Litigation Ch. 4-B, B. "Plain Meaning" vs. Ambiguity.
Miller and Starr California Real Estate § 1:59, Rules of Contract Interpretation.
Miller and Starr California Real Estate § 1:60, Parol Evidence; Extrinsic Evidence Rules.
Miller and Starr California Real Estate § 5:20, Construing a Listing Agreement--Principles of Interpretation.
Miller and Starr California Real Estate § 7:35, Clear and Ambiguous Language.
Miller and Starr California Real Estate § 23:75, General Rules of Interpretation of Insurance Policies.
Miller and Starr California Real Estate § 11:201, Subordination Agreements; in General.
14 NO. 1 Miller & Starr, California Real Estate Newsalert 5, Defective Construction.
16 NO. 4 Miller & Starr, California Real Estate Newsalert 28, Estates; Restraints; Perpetuities.
2 Witkin, California Summary 10th Insurance § 56, Lay Interpretation Governs.
2 Witkin, California Summary 10th Insurance § 93, "Damages.".
1 Witkin Cal. Summ. 10th Contracts § 745, (S 745) Ordinary Words and Technical Language.

§ 1645. Sense of words; technical words

Technical words are to be interpreted as usually understood by persons in the profession or business to which they relate, unless clearly used in a different sense. *(Enacted in 1872.)*

Research References

Rutter, Cal. Practice Guide: Insurance Litigation Ch. 3-C, C. Anatomy of Insurance Policy.
Rutter, Cal. Practice Guide: Insurance Litigation Ch. 4-B, B. "Plain Meaning" vs. Ambiguity.
Miller and Starr California Real Estate § 1:59, Rules of Contract Interpretation.
Miller and Starr California Real Estate § 1:60, Parol Evidence; Extrinsic Evidence Rules.
Miller and Starr California Real Estate § 5:20, Construing a Listing Agreement--Principles of Interpretation.
2 Witkin, California Summary 10th Insurance § 53, Reference to Drafting History, Interpretive Materials, and Advertising.
1 Witkin Cal. Summ. 10th Contracts § 745, (S 745) Ordinary Words and Technical Language.

§ 1646. Law and usage of place

A contract is to be interpreted according to the law and usage of the place where it is to be performed; or, if it does not indicate a place of performance, according to the law and usage of the place where it is made. *(Enacted in 1872.)*

Research References

California Practice Guide: Employment Litigation Ch. 19-A, A. Plaintiff's Forum Selection.
Rutter, Cal. Practice Guide: Insurance Litigation Ch. 4-B, B. "Plain Meaning" vs. Ambiguity.
Rutter, Cal. Practice Guide: Insurance Litigation Ch. 15-D, D. Filing Considerations.

Rutter, Cal. Practice Guide: Real Prop. Transactions Ch. 4-E, E. Drafting the Purchase and Sale Agreement-Terms and Conditions.

2 Witkin, California Summary 10th Insurance § 25, (S 25) in General.

1 Witkin Cal. Summ. 10th Contracts § 70, (S 70) Statute of Limitations.

1 Witkin Cal. Summ. 10th Contracts § 90, (S 90) California Cases and Statutes.

§ 1646.5. Law governing rights and duties of parties; agreement; exceptions; application

Notwithstanding Section 1646, the parties to any contract, agreement, or undertaking, contingent or otherwise, relating to a transaction involving in the aggregate not less than two hundred fifty thousand dollars ($250,000), including a transaction otherwise covered by subdivision (a) of Section 1301 of the Commercial Code, may agree that the law of this state shall govern their rights and duties in whole or in part, whether or not the contract, agreement, or undertaking or transaction bears a reasonable relation to this state. This section does not apply to any contract, agreement, or undertaking (a) for labor or personal services, (b) relating to any transaction primarily for personal, family, or household purposes, or (c) to the extent provided to the contrary in subdivision (c) of Section 1301 of the Commercial Code.

This section applies to contracts, agreements, and undertakings entered into before, on, or after its effective date; it shall be fully retroactive. Contracts, agreements, and undertakings selecting California law entered into before the effective date of this section shall be valid, enforceable, and effective as if this section had been in effect on the date they were entered into; and actions and proceedings commencing in a court of this state before the effective date of this section may be maintained as if this section were in effect on the date they were commenced. *(Added by Stats.1992, c. 615 (S.B.1804), § 2. Amended by Stats.2006, c. 254 (S.B.1481), § 1.5.)*

Research References

Rutter, Cal. Practice Guide: Civ. Pro. Before Trial Ch. 3-B, B. Jurisdiction Over Parties-Personal Jurisdiction.

Rutter, Cal. Practice Guide: Insurance Litigation Ch. 15-D, D. Filing Considerations.

Miller and Starr California Real Estate § 21:41, Conflict of Laws.

2 Witkin Cal. Proc. 5th Jurisdiction § 392, Effect of Choice of Law Provision.

1 Witkin Cal. Summ. 10th Contracts § 68, (S 68) Distinction: Contracts Involving Transaction of $250,000 or Over.

§ 1647. Circumstances

A contract may be explained by reference to the circumstances under which it was made, and the matter to which it relates. *(Enacted in 1872.)*

Research References

Rutter, Cal. Practice Guide: Civil Trials & Evidence Ch. 8E-G, G. Parol Evidence Rule.

Miller and Starr California Real Estate § 1:60, Parol Evidence; Extrinsic Evidence Rules.

Miller and Starr California Real Estate § 15:16, Rules of Construction.

1 Witkin Cal. Summ. 10th Contracts § 748, (S 748) Surrounding Circumstances.

§ 1648. Restriction to object

However broad may be the terms of a contract, it extends only to those things concerning which it appears that the parties intended to contract. *(Enacted in 1872.)*

Research References

Rutter, Cal. Practice Guide: A.D.R. Ch. 5-E, E. Claims Subject to Arbitration (Arbitrability).

Miller and Starr California Real Estate § 1:60, Parol Evidence; Extrinsic Evidence Rules.

1 Witkin Cal. Summ. 10th Contracts § 754, (S 754) Inconsistency Between Parts of Contract.

§ 1649. Ambiguity or uncertainty; promise

If the terms of a promise are in any respect ambiguous or uncertain, it must be interpreted in the sense in which the promisor believed, at the time of making it, that the promisee understood it. *(Enacted in 1872.)*

Research References

California Practice Guide: Employment Litigation Ch. 3-B, B. Liability Insurance-General Considerations.

Rutter, Cal. Practice Guide: Insurance Litigation Ch. 4-C, C. Rules for Resolving Ambiguity.

Miller and Starr California Real Estate § 1:59, Rules of Contract Interpretation.

Miller and Starr California Real Estate § 6:21, Duty of a Party to Comply With Instructions.

Miller and Starr California Real Estate § 7:36, Ambiguity.

2 Witkin, California Summary 10th Insurance § 60, in General.

1 Witkin Cal. Summ. 10th Contracts § 744, (S 744) Intention of Parties: Objective Test.

§ 1650. Particular clauses; general intent

Particular clauses of a contract are subordinate to its general intent. *(Enacted in 1872.)*

Research References

1 Witkin Cal. Summ. 10th Contracts § 754, (S 754) Inconsistency Between Parts of Contract.

§ 1651. Printed forms; insertions under special directions; written parts

Where a contract is partly written and partly printed, or where part of it is written or printed under the special directions of the parties, and with a special view to their intention, and the remainder is copied from a form originally prepared without special reference to the particular parties and the particular contract in question, the written parts control the printed parts, and the parts which are purely original control those which are copied from a form. And if the two are absolutely repugnant, the latter must be so far disregarded. *(Enacted in 1872.)*

Research References

Rutter, Cal. Practice Guide: Insurance Litigation Ch. 3-B, B. Policy Forms; Standard vs. Nonstandard Forms.

Rutter, Cal. Practice Guide: Insurance Litigation Ch. 4-B, B. "Plain Meaning" vs. Ambiguity.

Miller and Starr California Real Estate § 1:59, Rules of Contract Interpretation.

Miller and Starr California Real Estate § 6:30, Requirement of a Contract.

Miller and Starr California Real Estate § 27:50, Rules of Contract Interpretation.

1 Witkin Cal. Summ. 10th Contracts § 754, (S 754) Inconsistency Between Parts of Contract.

§ 1652. Reconcilement of repugnancies

Repugnancy in a contract must be reconciled, if possible, by such an interpretation as will give some effect to the repugnant clauses, subordinate to the general intent and purpose of the whole contract. *(Enacted in 1872.)*

Research References

Miller and Starr California Real Estate § 1:59, Rules of Contract Interpretation.

Miller and Starr California Real Estate § 6:30, Requirement of a Contract.

1 Witkin Cal. Summ. 10th Contracts § 754, (S 754) Inconsistency Between Parts of Contract.

4 Witkin, California Summary 10th Sales § 205, Illustrations: Personal Injury and Property Damage.

§ 1653. Inconsistent words

Words in a contract which are wholly inconsistent with its nature, or with the main intention of the parties, are to be rejected. *(Enacted in 1872.)*

Research References

Miller and Starr California Real Estate § 1:59, Rules of Contract Interpretation.
2 Witkin, California Summary 10th Insurance § 64, (S 64) in General.
1 Witkin Cal. Summ. 10th Contracts § 754, (S 754) Inconsistency Between Parts of Contract.

§ 1654. Uncertainty; interpretation against person causing

In cases of uncertainty not removed by the preceding rules, the language of a contract should be interpreted most strongly against the party who caused the uncertainty to exist. *(Enacted in 1872. Amended by Stats.1982, c. 1120, p. 4045, § 1.)*

Research References

California Real Estate Forms (Miller & Starr) § 2:19, Retail Lease–Power Shopping Center.
California Real Estate Forms (Miller & Starr) § 5:47, Terms and Conditions (Miscellaneous Provisions) Subparagraph 1.3.7.13 (Addition).
California Real Estate Forms (Miller & Starr) § 5:198, Subcontract (With Progress Payments).
Rutter, Cal. Practice Guide: A.D.R. Ch. 5-E, E. Claims Subject to Arbitration (Arbitrability).
California Practice Guide: Employment Litigation Ch. 3-B, B. Liability Insurance-General Considerations.
Rutter, Cal. Practice Guide: Family Law Ch. 6-B, B. Spousal Support.
Rutter, Cal. Practice Guide: Insurance Litigation Ch. 4-C, C. Rules for Resolving Ambiguity.
Rutter, Cal. Practice Guide: Personal Injury Ch. 1-C, C. Formation of Attorney-Client Relationship: the Employment Agreement.
Rutter, Cal. Practice Guide: Personal Injury Ch. 3-D, D. Mitigating Factors in Reduction of Damages.
Rutter, Cal. Practice Guide: Real Prop. Transactions Ch. 1-C, C. Attorney Fees and Costs Agreements.
Rutter, Cal. Practice Guide: Real Prop. Transactions Ch. 2-E, E. Listing Agreements.
Rutter, Cal. Practice Guide: Real Prop. Transactions Ch. 4-E, E. Drafting the Purchase and Sale Agreement-Terms and Conditions.
Rutter, Cal. Practice Guide: Real Prop. Transactions Ch. 4-F, F. Use of an Escrow.
Rutter, Cal. Practice Guide: Real Prop. Transactions Ch. 7-C, C. Representing the Purchasing Tenant.
Rutter, Cal. Practice Guide: Prof. Responsibility Ch. 5-K, K. Fee Recovery/Enforcing Fee Agreements.
Miller and Starr California Real Estate § 2:2, Deposit Receipt as a Contract of Sale.
Miller and Starr California Real Estate § 1:60, Parol Evidence; Extrinsic Evidence Rules.
Miller and Starr California Real Estate § 7:36, Ambiguity.
Miller and Starr California Real Estate § 15:16, Rules of Construction.
Miller and Starr California Real Estate § 19:47, Rules of Interpretation.
Miller and Starr California Real Estate § 27:43, Contract Terms--Public Works Contracts.
Miller and Starr California Real Estate § 27:50, Rules of Contract Interpretation.
Miller and Starr California Real Estate § 35:29, Interpretation of Arbitration Agreements.
14 NO. 5 Miller & Starr, California Real Estate Newsalert 16, Landlord and Tenant.
19 NO. 1 Miller & Starr, California Real Estate Newsalert 18, Landlord and Tenant.
22 NO. 3 Miller & Starr, California Real Estate Newsalert 6, Contracts.
1 Witkin Cal. Summ. 10th Contracts § 757, (S 757) Interpretation Against Party Causing Uncertainty.

4 Witkin, California Summary 10th Sales § 205, Illustrations: Personal Injury and Property Damage.

§ 1655. Implied stipulations

Stipulations which are necessary to make a contract reasonable, or conformable to usage, are implied, in respect to matters concerning which the contract manifests no contrary intention. *(Enacted in 1872.)*

Research References

Miller and Starr California Real Estate § 28:96, Interpretation of the Bond.
1 Witkin Cal. Summ. 10th Contracts § 751, Rejecting or Supplying Words.
1 Witkin Cal. Summ. 10th Contracts § 755, in General.
1 Witkin Cal. Summ. 10th Contracts § 794, (S 794) Nature and Purpose.
1 Witkin Cal. Summ. 10th Contracts § 796, (S 796) Liberal Test.

§ 1656. Implied incidents

All things that in law or usage are considered as incidental to a contract, or as necessary to carry it into effect, are implied therefrom, unless some of them are expressly mentioned therein, when all other things of the same class are deemed to be excluded. *(Enacted in 1872.)*

Research References

Rutter, Cal. Practice Guide: Insurance Litigation Ch. 4-C, C. Rules for Resolving Ambiguity.
Rutter, Cal. Practice Guide: Real Prop. Transactions Ch. 4-E, E. Drafting the Purchase and Sale Agreement-Terms and Conditions.
1 Witkin Cal. Summ. 10th Contracts § 794, (S 794) Nature and Purpose.

§ 1656.1. Sales tax reimbursement to retailer; addition to sales price; rebuttable presumptions; schedule

(a) Whether a retailer may add sales tax reimbursement to the sales price of the tangible personal property sold at retail to a purchaser depends solely upon the terms of the agreement of sale. It shall be presumed that the parties agreed to the addition of sales tax reimbursement to the sales price of tangible personal property sold at retail to a purchaser if:

(1) The agreement of sale expressly provides for such addition of sales tax reimbursement;

(2) Sales tax reimbursement is shown on the sales check or other proof of sale; or

(3) The retailer posts in his or her premises in a location visible to purchasers, or includes on a price tag or in an advertisement or other printed material directed to purchasers, a notice to the effect that reimbursement for sales tax will be added to the sales price of all items or certain items, whichever is applicable.

(b) It shall be presumed that the property, the gross receipts from the sale of which is subject to the sales tax, is sold at a price which includes tax reimbursement if the retailer posts in his or her premises, or includes on a price tag or in an advertisement (whichever is applicable) one of the following notices:

(1) "All prices of taxable items include sales tax reimbursement computed to the nearest mill."

(2) "The price of this item includes sales tax reimbursement computed to the nearest mill."

(c)(1) The State Board of Equalization shall prepare and make available for inspection and duplication or reproduction a sales tax reimbursement schedule which shall be identical with the following tables up to the amounts specified therein:

4¾ percent

Price	Tax
.01– .10	.00
.11– .31	.01

Price	Tax
.32– .52	.02
.53– .73	.03
.74– .94	.04
.95–1.15	.05

5 percent

Price	Tax
.01– .09	.00
.10– .29	.01
.30– .49	.02
.50– .69	.03
.70– .89	.04
.90–1.09	.05

5¼ percent

Price	Tax
.01– .09	.00
.10– .28	.01
.29– .47	.02
.48– .66	.03
.67– .85	.04
.86–1.04	.05

5½ percent

Price	Tax
.01– .09	.00
.10– .27	.01
.28– .45	.02
.46– .63	.03
.64– .81	.04
.82– .99	.05
1.00–1.18	.06

5¾ percent

Price	Tax
.01– .08	.00
.09– .26	.01
.27– .43	.02
.44– .60	.03
.61– .78	.04
.79– .95	.05
.96–1.13	.06

6 percent

Price	Tax
.01– .08	.00
.09– .24	.01
.25– .41	.02
.42– .58	.03
.59– .74	.04
.75– .91	.05
.92–1.08	.06

6¼ percent

Price	Tax
.01– .07	.00
.08– .23	.01
.24– .39	.02
.40– .55	.03
.56– .71	.04
.72– .87	.05
.88–1.03	.06

6½ percent

Price	Tax
.01– .07	.00
.08– .23	.01
.24– .38	.02

Price	Tax
.39– .53	.03
.54– .69	.04
.70– .84	.05
.85– .99	.06
1.00–1.15	.07

6¾ percent

Price	Tax
.01– .07	.00
.08– .22	.01
.23– .37	.02
.38– .51	.03
.52– .66	.04
.67– .81	.05
.82– .96	.06
.97–1.11	.07

7 percent

Price	Tax
.01– .07	.00
.08– .21	.01
.22– .35	.02
.36– .49	.03
.50– .64	.04
.65– .78	.05
.79– .92	.06
.93–1.07	.07

7¼ percent

Price	Tax
.01– .06	.00
.07– .20	.01
.21– .34	.02
.35– .48	.03
.49– .62	.04
.63– .75	.05
.76– .89	.06
.90–1.03	.07

7½ percent

Price	Tax
.01– .06	.00
.07– .19	.01
.20– .33	.02
.34– .46	.03
.47– .59	.04
.60– .73	.05
.74– .86	.06
.87– .99	.07
1.00–1.13	.08

(2) Reimbursement on sales prices in excess of those shown in the schedules may be computed by applying the applicable tax rate to the sales price, rounded off to the nearest cent by eliminating any fraction less than one-half cent and increasing any fraction of one-half cent or over to the next higher cent.

(3) If sales tax reimbursement is added to the sales price of tangible personal property sold at retail, the retailer shall use a schedule provided by the board, or a schedule approved by the board.

(d) The presumptions created by this section are rebuttable presumptions. *(Added by Stats.1978, c. 1211, p. 3915, § 1. Amended by Stats.1985, c. 20, § 1, eff. March 29, 1985, operative April 1, 1985; Stats.1990, c. 1528 (S.B.2196), § 1.)*

9 Witkin, California Summary 10th Taxation § 344, Privilege Tax on Retailer.

9 Witkin, California Summary 10th Taxation § 346, Gross Receipts.

9 Witkin, California Summary 10th Taxation § 369, Enforcement and Collection.

§ 1657. Performance; time

If no time is specified for the performance of an act required to be performed, a reasonable time is allowed. If the act is in its nature capable of being done instantly—as, for example, if it consists in the payment of money only—it must be performed immediately upon the thing to be done being exactly ascertained. *(Enacted in 1872.)*

Research References

Rutter, Cal. Practice Guide: Real Prop. Transactions Ch. 4-E, E. Drafting the Purchase and Sale Agreement-Terms and Conditions.

Rutter, Cal. Practice Guide: Real Prop. Transactions Ch. 8-B, B. Options to Purchase.

Rutter, Cal. Practice Guide: Real Prop. Transactions Ch. 11-B, B. Determining Breach.

Miller and Starr California Real Estate § 1:26, Performance; Terms of Sale.

Miller and Starr California Real Estate § 1:34, Exception to Right to Revoke; Partial Performance of the Act of Acceptance of a Unilateral Contract.

Miller and Starr California Real Estate § 6:24, Timeliness of Performance.

Miller and Starr California Real Estate § 1:161, Conditions Concurrent.

Miller and Starr California Real Estate § 10:88, Maturity of the Secured Obligation.

Miller and Starr California Real Estate § 17:43, Where Improver Does Not Believe He or She Owns the Improved Property.

Miller and Starr California Real Estate § 27:70, Contractual Completion Date; "Reasonable Time" Rule.

14 NO. 3 Miller & Starr, California Real Estate Newsalert 5, Contracts.

18 NO. 2 Miller & Starr, California Real Estate Newsalert 7, Contracts.

19 NO. 4 Miller & Starr, California Real Estate Newsalert 1, California Supreme Court Reduces Terms Required to Specifically Enforce a Real Property Sales Contract to Three P's: Parties, Price, and Property Description.

19 NO. 4 Miller & Starr, California Real Estate Newsalert 32, Contracts.

1 Witkin Cal. Summ. 10th Contracts § 116, (S 116) in General.

1 Witkin Cal. Summ. 10th Contracts § 760, (S 760) Demand of Performance.

1 Witkin Cal. Summ. 10th Contracts § 762, Reasonable Time.

1 Witkin Cal. Summ. 10th Contracts § 763, Payment of Money.

§ 1659. Joint and several promise; presumption; promisors benefiting from consideration

Where all the parties who unite in a promise receive some benefit from the consideration, whether past or present, their promise is presumed to be joint and several. *(Enacted in 1872.)*

Research References

Rutter, Cal. Practice Guide: Real Prop. Transactions Ch. 4-E, E. Drafting the Purchase and Sale Agreement-Terms and Conditions.

Miller and Starr California Real Estate § 1:59, Rules of Contract Interpretation.

1 Witkin Cal. Summ. 10th Contracts § 109, (S 109) Joint and Several Obligation.

1 Witkin Cal. Summ. 10th Contracts § 110, (S 110) Several Obligation.

§ 1660. Joint and several promise; presumption; several persons executing promise in singular number

A promise, made in the singular number, but executed by several persons, is presumed to be joint and several. *(Enacted in 1872.)*

Research References

Rutter, Cal. Practice Guide: Real Prop. Transactions Ch. 4-E, E. Drafting the Purchase and Sale Agreement-Terms and Conditions.

Miller and Starr California Real Estate § 1:59, Rules of Contract Interpretation.

1 Witkin Cal. Summ. 10th Contracts § 109, (S 109) Joint and Several Obligation.

§ 1661. Executed and executory contracts defined

An executed contract is one, the object of which is fully performed. All others are executory. *(Enacted in 1872.)*

Research References

Miller and Starr California Real Estate § 1:5, Executed and Executory Contracts.

Miller and Starr California Real Estate § 1:51, Necessity for Consideration.

Miller and Starr California Real Estate § 1:101, Modification of Written Agreement by Subsequent Oral Agreement--Modification by Executed Oral Agreement.

1 Witkin Cal. Summ. 10th Contracts § 101, Executory and Executed.

§ 1662. Uniform Vendor and Purchaser Risk Act

Any contract hereafter made in this State for the purchase and sale of real property shall be interpreted as including an agreement that the parties shall have the following rights and duties, unless the contract expressly provides otherwise:

(a) If, when neither the legal title nor the possession of the subject matter of the contract has been transferred, all or a material part thereof is destroyed without fault of the purchaser or is taken by eminent domain, the vendor cannot enforce the contract, and the purchaser is entitled to recover any portion of the price that he has paid;

(b) If, when either the legal title or the possession of the subject matter of the contract has been transferred, all or any part thereof is destroyed without fault of the vendor or is taken by eminent domain, the purchaser is not thereby relieved from a duty to pay the price, nor is he entitled to recover any portion thereof that he has paid.

This section shall be so interpreted and construed as to effectuate its general purpose to make uniform the law of those states which enact it.

This section may be cited as the Uniform Vendor and Purchaser Risk Act. *(Added by Stats.1947, c. 497, p. 1486, § 1.)*

Research References

California Real Estate Forms (Miller & Starr) § 1:17, Purchase and Sale Agreement–Unimproved Real Property–With Escrow Instructions.

California Real Estate Forms (Miller & Starr) § 1:18, Purchase and Sale Agreement–Raw Land.

California Real Estate Forms (Miller & Starr) § 1:19, Agreement for Purchase and Sale of Realty–Build-To-Suit.

California Real Estate Forms (Miller & Starr) § 1:20, Purchase and Sale Agreement–Small Commercial Properties Subject to Tenant Leases.

California Real Estate Forms (Miller & Starr) § 1:22, Agreement of Purchase and Sale–Multi-Property.

California Real Estate Forms (Miller & Starr) § 1:26, Purchase and Sale Agreement–Seller-Oriented Short Form.

California Real Estate Forms (Miller & Starr) § 1:27, Purchase and Sale Agreement–Multitenant Residential Property.

California Real Estate Forms (Miller & Starr) § 1:28, Purchase and Sale Agreement–Hotel.

California Real Estate Forms (Miller & Starr) § 1:29, Purchase and Sale Agreement–Seller Oriented With Seller Financing.

California Real Estate Forms (Miller & Starr) § 1:32, Hotel Purchase and Sale Agreement With Escrow Instructions.

California Real Estate Forms (Miller & Starr) § 1:33, Real Estate Purchase Contract and Receipt for Deposit–Income Property.

California Real Estate Forms (Miller & Starr) § 1:94, California Residential Purchase Agreement and Joint Escrow Instructions.

Rutter, Cal. Practice Guide: Insurance Litigation Ch. 6B-A, A. "Insurable Interest" Requirement.

Rutter, Cal. Practice Guide: Real Prop. Transactions Ch. 4-E, E. Drafting the Purchase and Sale Agreement-Terms and Conditions.

Rutter, Cal. Practice Guide: Real Prop. Transactions Ch. 8-B, B. Options to Purchase.
Miller and Starr California Real Estate § 2:25, Risk of Loss.
Miller and Starr California Real Estate § 6:37, Risk of Loss of the Property; Proration.
Miller and Starr California Real Estate § 19:47, Rules of Interpretation.
Miller and Starr California Real Estate § 30A:30, Fixtures, Equipment, and Improvements.
12 Witkin, California Summary 10th Real Property § 2, Uniform Laws and Model Acts.
12 Witkin, California Summary 10th Real Property § 311, Grantor's Title During Escrow.
13 Witkin, California Summary 10th Equity § 175, (S 175) Risk of Loss.

§ 1663. Introduction of the euro as a medium of payment

(a) As used in this section, the following terms shall have the following meanings:

(1) "Euro" means the currency of participating member states of the European Union that adopt a single currency in accordance with the Treaty on European Union signed February 7, 1992, as amended from time to time.

(2) "Introduction of the euro" includes, but is not limited to, the implementation from time to time of economic and monetary union in member states of the European Union in accordance with the Treaty on European Union signed February 7, 1992, as amended from time to time.

(3) "ECU" or "European Currency Unit" means the currency basket that is from time to time used as the unit of account of the European community, as defined in European Council Regulation No. 3320/94.

(b) If a subject or medium of payment of a contract, security, or instrument is the ECU or a currency that has been substituted or replaced by the euro, the euro shall be a commercially reasonable substitute and substantial equivalent that may be either tendered or used in determining the value of the ECU or currency, in each case at the conversion rate specified in, and otherwise calculated in accordance with, the regulations adopted by the Council of the European Union.

(c) The introduction of the euro, the tendering of euros in connection with any obligation in compliance with subdivision (b), the determining of the value of any obligation in compliance with subdivision (b), or the calculating or determining of the subject or medium of payment of a contract, security, or instrument with reference to an interest rate or other basis that has been substituted or replaced due to the introduction of the euro and that is a commercially reasonable substitute and substantial equivalent, shall neither have the effect of discharging or excusing performance under any contract, security, or instrument, nor give a party the right unilaterally to alter or terminate any contract, security, or instrument.

(d) This section shall be subject to any agreements between parties with specific reference to, or agreement regarding, the introduction of the euro.

(e) Notwithstanding the Commercial Code or any other law of this state, this section shall apply to all contracts, securities, and instruments, including contracts with respect to commercial transactions, and shall not be deemed to be displaced by any other law of this state.

(f) In the event of other currency changes, the provisions of this section with respect to the euro shall not be interpreted as creating any negative inference or negative presumption regarding the validity or enforceability of contracts, securities, or instruments denominated in whole or part in those other currencies. *(Added by Stats.1998, c. 62 (A.B.185), § 1, eff. June 4, 1998.)*

Research References

1 Witkin Cal. Summ. 10th Contracts § 758, (S 758) Contracts Containing Medium of Payment in European Currency.
4 Witkin, California Summary 10th Negotiable Instruments § 10, General Definition.

Title 4

UNLAWFUL CONTRACTS

§ 1667. Unlawfulness defined

That is not lawful which is:

1. Contrary to an express provision of law;

2. Contrary to the policy of express law, though not expressly prohibited; or,

3. Otherwise contrary to good morals. *(Enacted in 1872.)*

Research References

Rutter, Cal. Practice Guide: Real Prop. Transactions Ch. 11-A, A. Factors Affecting Choice of Remedies.
Rutter, Cal. Practice Guide: Prof. Responsibility Ch. 5-D, D. Ethical Limitations on Attorney Fees.
Miller and Starr California Real Estate § 1:9, Lawful Object.
22 NO. 2 Miller & Starr, California Real Estate Newsalert 11, Easements.
2 Witkin, California Summary 10th Insurance § 47, (S 47) Validity.
1 Witkin Cal. Summ. 10th Contracts § 426, Loan to Gambler.
1 Witkin Cal. Summ. 10th Contracts § 451, (S 451) in General.
1 Witkin Cal. Summ. 10th Contracts § 672, (S 672) Meaning of Term "Negligent" in C.C. 1668.
11 Witkin, California Summary 10th Community Property § 32, Agreements Violating Public Policy.
11 Witkin, California Summary 10th Husband and Wife § 59, (S 59) Fault Theory Eliminated for Dissolution.

§ 1668. Contracts contrary to policy of law

All contracts which have for their object, directly or indirectly, to exempt anyone from responsibility for his own fraud, or willful injury to the person or property of another, or violation of law, whether willful or negligent, are against the policy of the law. *(Enacted in 1872.)*

Research References

California Practice Guide: Employment Litigation Ch. 5-A, A. Wrongful Discharge in Violation of Public Policy (Tameny Claims).
California Practice Guide: Employment Litigation Ch. 5-D, D. Defamation.
California Practice Guide: Employment Litigation Ch. 16-K, K. Settlements and Releases.
Rutter, Cal. Practice Guide: Insurance Litigation Ch. 7A-G, G. Intentional Acts Limitation.

Rutter, Cal. Practice Guide: Insurance Litigation Ch. 12B-B, B. Bad Faith Refusal to Settle.

Rutter, Cal. Practice Guide: Personal Injury Ch. 3-D, D. Mitigating Factors in Reduction of Damages.

Rutter, Cal. Practice Guide: Real Prop. Transactions Ch. 11-E, E. Damages for Fraud.

Miller and Starr California Real Estate § 1:153, Contractual Provision Against Fraud Liability.

Miller and Starr California Real Estate § 1:155, Liability Insurance Does Not Cover Fraud or Contract Liability.

Miller and Starr California Real Estate § 22:60, Liability for Wrongful or Criminal Conduct of Third Persons--Residential Landlord's Liability for Criminal Conduct.

Miller and Starr California Real Estate § 22:61, Liability for Wrongful or Criminal Conduct of Third Persons--Commercial Landlord's Liability for Criminal Conduct.

Miller and Starr California Real Estate § 29:17, Express and Implied Indemnity.

Miller and Starr California Real Estate § 34:83, General Principles; Election of Remedies.

Miller and Starr California Real Estate § 35:24, Federal Arbitration Act.

Miller and Starr California Real Estate § 35:29, Interpretation of Arbitration Agreements.

Miller and Starr California Real Estate § 35:38, Issues Subject to Arbitration--Examples.

Miller and Starr California Real Estate § 34:100, Punitive Damages--Insurance Coverage.

16 NO. 1 Miller & Starr, California Real Estate Newsalert 6, Commercial Arbitration.

16 NO. 4 Miller & Starr, California Real Estate Newsalert 21, Commercial Arbitration.

17 NO. 3 Miller & Starr, California Real Estate Newsalert 2, Commercial Arbitration.

17 NO. 5 Miller & Starr, California Real Estate Newsalert 5, Contracts.

18 NO. 5 Miller & Starr, California Real Estate Newsalert 17, Landlord and Tenant.

2 Witkin, California Summary 10th Insurance § 100, in General.

2 Witkin, California Summary 10th Insurance § 226, in General.

2 Witkin, California Summary 10th Insurance § 324, in General.

1 Witkin Cal. Summ. 10th Contracts § 304, (S 304) Representations Made by Party.

1 Witkin Cal. Summ. 10th Contracts § 422, Liberal Rule of Severability.

1 Witkin Cal. Summ. 10th Contracts § 660, California Code.

1 Witkin Cal. Summ. 10th Contracts § 662, (S 662) Medicine.

1 Witkin Cal. Summ. 10th Contracts § 663, (S 663) Automobiles.

1 Witkin Cal. Summ. 10th Contracts § 664, (S 664) Employment.

1 Witkin Cal. Summ. 10th Contracts § 665, (S 665) Other Areas.

1 Witkin Cal. Summ. 10th Contracts § 666, (S 666) Statutory Prohibitions.

1 Witkin Cal. Summ. 10th Contracts § 671, (S 671) Valid Despite C.C. 1668.

1 Witkin Cal. Summ. 10th Contracts § 672, (S 672) Meaning of Term "Negligent" in C.C. 1668.

1 Witkin Cal. Summ. 10th Contracts § 675, (S 675) "Sole Remedy" Provision in Employment Contract.

1 Witkin Cal. Summ. 10th Contracts § 671A, (S 671A) (New)-Distinction: "Any Negligent Act" Does Not Include Gross Negligence.

4 Witkin, California Summary 10th Sales § 94, Where Warranty is Fraudulent.

5 Witkin, California Summary 10th Torts § 231, Insurance Coverage.

5 Witkin, California Summary 10th Torts § 767, (S 767) Governing Statutes.

5 Witkin, California Summary 10th Torts § 812, (S 812) in General.

13 Witkin, California Summary 10th Equity § 123, Other Practices.

§ 1669. Restraint of marriage

Every contract in restraint of the marriage of any person, other than a minor, is void. *(Added by Stats.1977, c. 198, p. 718, § 1, operative July 1, 1978.)*

Law Revision Commission Comments

Section 1669 continues without change former Section 1676. [13 Cal.L.Rev.Comm. Reports 1735 (1976)].

Research References

1 Witkin Cal. Summ. 10th Contracts § 619, Contract Restraining Marriage.

§ 1669.5. Minor victim of unlawful sex act; payment of money or other consideration; application; district attorney enforcement; deposit to State Children's Trust Fund

(a) Any contract for the payment of money or other consideration to a minor who has been alleged to be the victim of an unlawful sex act, or to his or her legal representative, by the alleged perpetrator of that unlawful sex act, or his or her legal representative, entered into on or after the time of the alleged unlawful sex act, and providing for any payments to be made more than one year after the date of the execution of the contract, is void as contrary to public policy. A district attorney may bring an action or intervene in any action to enjoin enforcement of any contract which is in violation of this section.

(b) This section does not apply after the date of the final judgment in a criminal case against the alleged perpetrator for the unlawful sex act described in subdivision (a).

(c) This section does not apply to a contract for the payment of money or other consideration made from a nonrevocable trust established for the benefit of the minor if the alleged perpetrator has no direct or indirect access to, or control over, the trust.

(d) This section does not apply to an alleged perpetrator of an unlawful sex act against a minor to the extent he or she agrees to pay, or is required by court order to pay, child support for that minor upon a dissolution or legal separation.

(e) For purposes of this section, "unlawful sex act," means a felony sex offense committed against a minor.

(f) Notwithstanding subdivision (a), any contract declared void as contrary to public policy under this section may still be enforced by a district attorney against the payor, and the proceeds thereof shall be deposited in the State Children's Trust Fund pursuant to Section 18969 of the Welfare and Institutions Code. *(Added by Stats.1993–94, 1st Ex.Sess., c. 54 (S.B.35), § 1, eff. Nov. 30, 1994.)*

Research References

1 Witkin Cal. Summ. 10th Contracts § 641, (S 641) Contract to Pay Child Sex Victim.

§ 1669.7. Contract for consideration for providing information obtained as a result of witnessing a crime; validity; civil actions

A contract for the payment of money or other consideration in violation of Section 132.5 of the Penal Code is void as contrary to public policy. The Attorney General or the district attorney of the county in which a violation of Section 132.5 of the Penal Code occurs may bring a civil action, or intervene in any civil action, to enjoin the enforcement of a contract that violates that section. *(Added by Stats.1994, c. 869 (S.B.1999), § 1.)*

Research References

1 Witkin Cal. Summ. 10th Contracts § 636, (S 636) Contracts Involving Evidence.

§ 1670. Construction contract with public agency; disputes; resolution

Any dispute arising from a construction contract with a public agency, which contract contains a provision that one party to the contract or one party's agent or employee shall decide any disputes arising under that contract, shall be resolved by submitting the dispute to independent arbitration, if mutually agreeable, otherwise by litigation in a court of competent jurisdiction. *(Added by Stats.1978, c. 1374, p. 4556, § 1.)*

Research References

California Real Estate Forms (Miller & Starr) § 3:7, Promissory Note.

California Real Estate Forms (Miller & Starr) § 3:13, Promissory Note Secured by Construction Deed of Trust.

California Real Estate Forms (Miller & Starr) § 3:20, Promissory Note–Conduit Loan.

Rutter, Cal. Practice Guide: A.D.R. Ch. 5-D, D. Defenses to Enforcement.

Miller and Starr California Real Estate § 19:79, Accelerated Payment.

Miller and Starr California Real Estate § 27:112, Supervisorial Authority.

1 Witkin Cal. Proc. 5th Attorneys § 282, (S 282) Conditions for Rescission.

1 Witkin Cal. Summ. 10th Contracts § 503, (S 503) in General.

1 Witkin Cal. Summ. 10th Contracts § 533, (S 533) Nature and Purpose of Revision.

1 Witkin Cal. Summ. 10th Contracts § 537, (S 537) Prepayment Fee Contingent on Late Interest Payments.

1 Witkin Cal. Summ. 10th Contracts § 540, (S 540) in General.

1 Witkin Cal. Summ. 10th Contracts § 995, (S 995) California Law.

§ 1670.5. Unconscionable contract or clause of contract; finding as matter of law; remedies

(a) If the court as a matter of law finds the contract or any clause of the contract to have been unconscionable at the time it was made the court may refuse to enforce the contract, or it may enforce the remainder of the contract without the unconscionable clause, or it may so limit the application of any unconscionable clause as to avoid any unconscionable result.

(b) When it is claimed or appears to the court that the contract or any clause thereof may be unconscionable the parties shall be afforded a reasonable opportunity to present evidence as to its commercial setting, purpose, and effect to aid the court in making the determination. *(Added by Stats.1979, c. 819, p. 2827, § 3, eff. Sept. 19, 1979.)*

Research References

Rutter, Cal. Practice Guide: A.D.R. Ch. 5-D, D. Defenses to Enforcement.

Rutter, Cal. Practice Guide: Civ. Pro. Before Trial Ch. 14-A, A. General Considerations.

California Practice Guide: Employment Litigation Ch. 18-C, C. Contractual Arbitration.

Rutter, Cal. Practice Guide: Enforcing Judgments/Debts Ch. 3-C, C. Prelawsuit Considerations.

Rutter, Cal. Practice Guide: Insurance Litigation Ch. 4-E, E. Unconscionability.

Rutter, Cal. Practice Guide: Insurance Litigation Ch. 15-C, C. Arbitration/Appraisal/Mediation.

Rutter, Cal. Practice Guide: Personal Injury Ch. 3-D, D. Mitigating Factors in Reduction of Damages.

Rutter, Cal. Practice Guide: Real Prop. Transactions Ch. 7-B, B. Sale of Ground Lease Tenant's Interest-Preliminary Concerns Re Assignment and Subletting.

Rutter, Cal. Practice Guide: Real Prop. Transactions Ch. 11-A, A. Factors Affecting Choice of Remedies.

Rutter, Cal. Practice Guide: Prof. Responsibility Ch. 5-D, D. Ethical Limitations on Attorney Fees.

Miller and Starr California Real Estate § 1:64, Unconscionability as a Defense to Enforcement.

Miller and Starr California Real Estate § 21:33, Who is Liable for Usury Penalties--Exemptions.

Miller and Starr California Real Estate § 35:24, Federal Arbitration Act.

Miller and Starr California Real Estate § 35:53, Unconscionability.

Miller and Starr California Real Estate § 10:142, Protection Against "Unconscionable Advantage" of the Property Owner in Foreclosure.

14 NO. 3 Miller & Starr, California Real Estate Newsalert 1, Court of Appeal Finds Title Insurance Arbitration Provision Enforceable, Without Reaching "Unconscionability" Analysis.

6 Witkin Cal. Proc. 5th Proceedings Without Trial § 518, Discrimination Claims.

6 Witkin Cal. Proc. 5th Proceedings Without Trial § 538, (S 538) Unconscionable Contract or Term.

1 Witkin Cal. Summ. 10th Contracts § 322, (S 322) Alternate Approaches.

1 Witkin Cal. Summ. 10th Contracts § 330, (S 330) Commercial Code and California Statute.

1 Witkin Cal. Summ. 10th Contracts § 332, (S 332) in General.

1 Witkin Cal. Summ. 10th Contracts § 339, Bank Depositor's Signature Card.

1 Witkin Cal. Summ. 10th Contracts § 341, Employment Contract Terminating Commissions.

1 Witkin Cal. Summ. 10th Contracts § 541, (S 541) Fees Against Credit Card Customers.

1 Witkin Cal. Summ. 10th Contracts § 827, (S 827) Excuse of Condition or Equitable Relief.

4 Witkin, California Summary 10th Sales § 7, (S 7) Adoption in California.

4 Witkin, California Summary 10th Sales § 91, Strict Construction.

4 Witkin, California Summary 10th Sales § 207, (S 207) Agreement Limiting Consequential Damages.

4 Witkin, California Summary 10th Sales § 296, (S 296) Consumers Legal Remedies Act.

13 Witkin, California Summary 10th Equity § 40, Unconscionable Contract.

§ 1670.6. Telemarketing sales; unlawful contracts

A contract with a consumer located in California for the purchase of a good or service that is made in connection with a telephone solicitation made in or from outside of California and is primarily for personal, family, or household use, is unlawful if, with respect to that telephone solicitation, the telemarketer is in violation of Section 310.4(a)(6)(i) of, or has not complied with Section 310.5(a)(5) of, the Federal Trade Commission's Telemarketing Sales Rule (16 C.F.R. Part 310), as published in the Federal Register, Volume 68, Number 19, on January 29, 2003. This section shall apply only to those entities subject to, and does not apply to any transaction exempted under Section 310.6 of, the Telemarketing Sales Rule (16 C.F.R. Part 310), as published in the Federal Register, Volume 68, Number 19, on January 29, 2003. *(Added by Stats.2003, c. 77 (A.B.88), § 1.)*

Research References

4 Witkin, California Summary 10th Sales § 390, (S 390) Telephone Sellers.

§ 1670.7. Provision deducting from wages for cost of emigrating and transporting; void

Any provision of a contract that purports to allow a deduction from a person's wages for the cost of emigrating and transporting that person to the United States is void as against public policy. *(Added by Stats.2008, c. 258 (A.B.1278), § 1. Amended by Stats.2009, c. 35 (S.B.174), § 2.)*

Research References

1 Witkin Cal. Summ. 10th Contracts § 658A, (S 658A) (New)-Contracts for Bringing Person to United States.

Title 4.5

LIQUIDATED DAMAGES

CHAPTER 1. GENERAL PROVISIONS

§ 1671. Validity; standards for determination; applicability of section

(a) This section does not apply in any case where another statute expressly applicable to the contract prescribes the rules or standard for determining the validity of a provision in the contract liquidating the damages for the breach of the contract.

(b) Except as provided in subdivision (c), a provision in a contract liquidating the damages for the breach of the contract is valid unless the party seeking to invalidate the provision establishes that the provision was unreasonable under the circumstances existing at the time the contract was made.

(c) The validity of a liquidated damages provision shall be determined under subdivision (d) and not under subdivision (b) where the liquidated damages are sought to be recovered from either:

(1) A party to a contract for the retail purchase, or rental, by such party of personal property or services, primarily for the party's personal, family, or household purposes; or

(2) A party to a lease of real property for use as a dwelling by the party or those dependent upon the party for support.

(d) In the cases described in subdivision (c), a provision in a contract liquidating damages for the breach of the contract is void except that the parties to such a contract may agree therein upon an amount which shall be presumed to be the amount of damage sustained by a breach thereof, when, from the nature of the case, it would be impracticable or extremely difficult to fix the actual damage. *(Enacted in 1872. Amended by Stats.1977, c. 198, p. 718, § 5, operative July 1, 1978.)*

Law Revision Commission Comments

Section 1671 is amended to provide in subdivision (b) a new general rule favoring the enforcement of liquidated damages provisions except against a consumer in a consumer case. In a consumer case, the prior law under former Sections 1670 and 1671, continued in subdivision (d), still applies.

Subdivision (a). Subdivision (a) makes clear that Section 1671 does not affect other statutes that govern liquidation of damages for breach of certain types of contracts. E.g. Civil Code §§ 1675–1681 (default on contact to purchase real property); Com. Code § 2718 (sales transactions under the Commercial Code). For provisions relating to late payment charges and liquidated damages for late completion, see, e.g., Bus. & Prof. Code § 10242.5 (certain real estate loans); Civil Code §§ 1803.6 (retail installment sales), 2954.4 (loan on single-family, owner-occupied dwelling), 2982 (automobile sales finance); Educ. Code §§ 90226 (construction contracts for state university and colleges), 92050 (construction contracts for University of California); Fin. Code §§ 14852 (credit unions), 18249, 18250, 18631 (industrial loan companies), 22480(a) (5) (personal property brokers); Govt. Code §§ 14376 (state public works contracts), 53069.85 (contracts with cities, counties, and districts), 54348 (penalty for nonpayment of local agency charges); Pub.Res. Code § 6224 (penalty for nonpayment to State Lands Commission); Sts. & Hwys. Code §§ 5254.5 (liquidated damages under Improvement Act of 1911), 6442 (penalty for nonpayment under Improvement Act of 1911), 10503.1 (liquidated damages under Municipal Improvement Act of 1913). These other statutes—not Section 1671—govern the situations to which they apply. Of course, where there are exceptions to the coverage of some provision governing liquidated damages in certain types of contracts, Section 1671 does apply. E.g., Fin. Code §§ 18191 (exception to Sections 18249 and 18250), 22053 (exception to Section 22480). Note that Section 1676, which provides a rule governing liquidated damages for the buyer's default on a contract for the sale of nonresidential real property, incorporates subdivision (b) of Section 1671.

It should be noted that Section 1671(a) makes Section 1671 not applicable where the validity of the liquidated damages provision is governed by federal law or a regulation adopted pursuant thereto. For example, the Federal Home Loan Bank Board has issued a regulation which prescribes the maximum late payment charge that may be made with respect to home loans made after July 31, 1976, by federally chartered savings and loan associations. 41 Fed.Reg. 18,287 (1976) (to be codified in 12 C.F.R. § 545.6–11).

Subdivision (b). Subdivision (b) provides that a reasonable liquidated damages provision is valid, but subdivision (d) rather than subdivision (b) applies where liquidated damages are sought to be recovered from the consumer in a consumer case. See subdivision (c).

In the cases where subdivision (b) applies, the burden of proof on the issue of reasonableness is on the party seeking to invalidate the liquidated damages provision. The subdivision limits the circumstances that may be taken into account in the determination of reasonableness to those in existence "at the time the contract was made." The validity of the liquidated damages provision depends upon its reasonableness at the time the contract was made and not as it appears in retrospect. Accordingly, the amount of damages actually suffered has no bearing on the validity of the liquidated damages provision. For a contrary rule, see Com. Code § 2718 (damages may be liquidated at an amount which is reasonable in the light of "anticipated or actual harm") and Civil Code § 1675(e) (2) (subsequent sale as bearing on reasonableness of provision liquidating damages to seller in case of default by buyer of residential property).

Unlike subdivision (d), subdivision (b) gives the parties considerable leeway in determining the damages for breach. All the circumstances existing at the time of the making of the contract are considered, including the relationship that the damages provided in the contract bear to the range of harm that reasonably could be anticipated at the time of the making of the contract. Other relevant considerations in the determination of whether the amount of liquidated damages is so high or so low as to be unreasonable include, but are not limited to, such matters as the relative equality of the bargaining power of the parties, whether the parties were represented by lawyers at the time the contract was made, the anticipation of the parties that proof of actual damages would be costly or inconvenient, the difficulty of proving causation and foreseeability, and whether the liquidated damages provision is included in a form contract.

Subdivision (c). Subdivision (c) makes the prior law under former Sections 1670 and 1671, continued in subdivision (d), applicable where liquidated damages are sought to be recovered from the consumer in a contract for the retail purchase, or rental, of personal property or services, primarily for personal, family, or household purposes, or for the lease of real property to be used as a dwelling by the party or persons dependent on the party for support. Of course, where the party seeking to avoid the liquidated damages provision is the nonconsumer party, subdivision (b) is applicable.

Subdivision (d). Subdivision (d) continues without substantive change the requirements of former Sections 1670 and 1671. The revision made in the former language of these sections is not intended to alter the substance of those sections as interpreted by the courts. For a discussion of the former law continued in subdivision (d), see Sweet, Liquidated Damages in California, 60 Cal.L.Rev. 84 (1972), reprinted in 11 Cal.L. Revision Comm'n Reports at 1229 (1973).

Deposits. Instead of promising to pay a fixed sum as liquidated damages in case of a breach, a party to a contract may provide a deposit as security for the performance of his contractual obligations. If the parties provide that the deposit shall be liquidated damages for a breach of the contract, the question whether the deposit may be retained in case of a breach is determined in accordance with the standard provided in subdivision (b) or subdivision (d), whichever applies. See also Sections 1675–1681 (real property purchase contract). On the other hand, if the parties do not intend that the deposit shall constitute liquidated damages in the event of a breach, the deposit is merely a fund to secure the payment of actual damages if any are determined. See, e.g., Civil Code § 1950.5 (payment or deposit to secure performance of rental agreement). Compare Civil Code § 1951.5 (liquidation of damages authorized in real property lease). [13 Cal.L.Rev.Comm. Reports 1735 (1976)].

Research References

California Real Estate Forms (Miller & Starr) § 3:7, Promissory Note.
California Real Estate Forms (Miller & Starr) § 4:5, Construction Agreement–Cost Plus a Percentage Fee With a Guaranteed Maximum Price.
California Real Estate Forms (Miller & Starr) § 4:6, Construction Contract–Fixed Price–Commercial Project.
California Real Estate Forms (Miller & Starr) § 1:17, Purchase and Sale Agreement–Unimproved Real Property–With Escrow Instructions.
California Real Estate Forms (Miller & Starr) § 1:24, Combination Purchase and Option Agreement–Residential Lots Being Acquired from a Bankrupt Seller.
California Real Estate Forms (Miller & Starr) § 1:29, Purchase and Sale Agreement–Seller Oriented With Seller Financing.

California Real Estate Forms (Miller & Starr) § 2:16, Office Lease–Multistory Office Building.

California Real Estate Forms (Miller & Starr) § 2:17, Office Lease–Mixed Use Building.

California Real Estate Forms (Miller & Starr) § 2:18, Office Lease–Office/Warehouse Building With Four or Fewer Tenants.

California Real Estate Forms (Miller & Starr) § 2:19, Retail Lease—Power Shopping Center.

California Real Estate Forms (Miller & Starr) § 2:20, Retail Lease—Shopping Center With for Profit Parking Garage.

California Real Estate Forms (Miller & Starr) § 2:22, Retail Lease—Regional Shopping Center.

California Real Estate Forms (Miller & Starr) § 2:23, Retail Lease—Small Strip-Shopping Center.

California Real Estate Forms (Miller & Starr) § 2:24, Retail Lease—Restaurant.

California Real Estate Forms (Miller & Starr) § 2:25, Industrial Lease.

California Real Estate Forms (Miller & Starr) § 2:26, Triple Net Lease—Industrial Build-To-Suit Lease.

California Real Estate Forms (Miller & Starr) § 2:28, Triple Net Lease—Stand-Alone Building.

California Real Estate Forms (Miller & Starr) § 2:29, Parking Garage Lease.

California Real Estate Forms (Miller & Starr) § 2:32, Gross Lease—Small Commercial Property.

California Real Estate Forms (Miller & Starr) § 2:62, Standard Industrial/Commercial Multi-Tenant Lease—Net.

California Real Estate Forms (Miller & Starr) § 2:63, Standard Industrial/Commercial Multi-Tenant Lease—Gross.

California Real Estate Forms (Miller & Starr) § 2:65, Residential Lease.

California Real Estate Forms (Miller & Starr) § 2:66, Residential Lease With Purchase Option.

California Real Estate Forms (Miller & Starr) § 3:13, Promissory Note Secured by Construction Deed of Trust.

California Real Estate Forms (Miller & Starr) § 3:20, Promissory Note—Conduit Loan.

California Real Estate Forms (Miller & Starr) § 3:57, Loan Purchase and Sale Agreement.

California Real Estate Forms (Miller & Starr) § 1:166, Liquidated Damages.

Rutter, Cal. Practice Guide: Civil Trials & Evidence Ch. 8G-C, C. Presumptions.

California Practice Guide: Employment Litigation Ch. 17-B, B. Contract Damages.

California Practice Guide: Employment Litigation Ch. 18-A, A. Settlement Considerations.

California Practice Guide: Employment Litigation Form 8:A, Settlement and Release for Use When Litigation Pending.

California Practice Guide: Employment Litigation Form 16:A, Settlement and Release.

Rutter, Cal. Practice Guide: Enforcing Judgments/Debts Ch. 2-B, B. Statutory Liability and Procedures.

Rutter, Cal. Practice Guide: Enforcing Judgments/Debts Ch. 3-C, C. Prelawsuit Considerations.

Rutter, Cal. Practice Guide: Landlord-Tenant Form 2:B, Standard Shopping Center Lease.

Rutter, Cal. Practice Guide: Real Prop. Transactions Ch. 4-E, E. Drafting the Purchase and Sale Agreement-Terms and Conditions.

Rutter, Cal. Practice Guide: Real Prop. Transactions Ch. 6-F, F. Promissory Note.

Rutter, Cal. Practice Guide: Real Prop. Transactions Form 4:H, (Attorney-Drafted) Purchase and Sale Agreement and Joint Escrow Instructions.

Miller and Starr California Real Estate § 5:60, Broker's Share of the Retained ("Forfeited") Deposit or Liquidated Damages.

Miller and Starr California Real Estate § 10:80, Late Charges.

Miller and Starr California Real Estate § 19:78, Time and Place of Payment; Late Charges.

Miller and Starr California Real Estate § 19:79, Accelerated Payment.

Miller and Starr California Real Estate § 27:81, Owner's Remedies for Late Performance--Liquidated Damages.

Miller and Starr California Real Estate § 34:37, Liquidated Damages--Generally.

Miller and Starr California Real Estate § 34:38, Liquidated Damages--In Real Property Marketing Contracts.

Miller and Starr California Real Estate § 34:60, Buyer's Right to Restitution.

Miller and Starr California Real Estate § 35:83, Authority of the Arbitrators; Issues and Remedies.

Miller and Starr California Real Estate § 10:100, Validity of Prepayment Penalties.

Miller and Starr California Real Estate § 10:101, Reasonableness of Amount.

Miller and Starr California Real Estate § 19:211, Landlord's Recovery of Liquidated Damages and Equitable Relief.

Miller and Starr California Real Estate § 25C:36, Required Provisions of the Purchase Agreement.

13 NO. 6 Miller & Starr, California Real Estate Newsalert 9, Landlord and Tenant.

15 NO. 2 Miller & Starr, California Real Estate Newsalert 9, Landlord and Tenant.

19 NO. 6 Miller & Starr, California Real Estate Newsalert 15, Landlord and Tenant.

19 NO. 5 Miller & Starr, California Real Estate Newsalert 21, Judicial Remedies.

1 Witkin Cal. Proc. 5th Attorneys § 282, (S 282) Conditions for Rescission.

12 Witkin, California Summary 10th Real Property § 701, Liquidated Damages.

1 Witkin Cal. Summ. 10th Contracts § 330, (S 330) Commercial Code and California Statute.

1 Witkin Cal. Summ. 10th Contracts § 503, (S 503) in General.

1 Witkin Cal. Summ. 10th Contracts § 505, (S 505) Late-Charge Interest.

1 Witkin Cal. Summ. 10th Contracts § 506, (S 506) Rule and Test.

1 Witkin Cal. Summ. 10th Contracts § 531, Recovery Without Actual Damages Suffered.

1 Witkin Cal. Summ. 10th Contracts § 533, (S 533) Nature and Purpose of Revision.

1 Witkin Cal. Summ. 10th Contracts § 534, (S 534) Organization and Scope of Law.

1 Witkin Cal. Summ. 10th Contracts § 535, (S 535) General Rule of Validity.

1 Witkin Cal. Summ. 10th Contracts § 536, (S 536) Deposits.

1 Witkin Cal. Summ. 10th Contracts § 537, (S 537) Prepayment Fee Contingent on Late Interest Payments.

1 Witkin Cal. Summ. 10th Contracts § 538, (S 538) Service Installations.

1 Witkin Cal. Summ. 10th Contracts § 540, (S 540) in General.

1 Witkin Cal. Summ. 10th Contracts § 541, (S 541) Fees Against Credit Card Customers.

1 Witkin Cal. Summ. 10th Contracts § 542, (S 542) Agreement to Pay Collection Costs.

1 Witkin Cal. Summ. 10th Contracts § 543, Lease of Dwelling.

1 Witkin Cal. Summ. 10th Contracts § 544, (S 544) Scope of Chapter.

1 Witkin Cal. Summ. 10th Contracts § 545, (S 545) Residential Property: in General.

1 Witkin Cal. Summ. 10th Contracts § 546, (S 546) Residential Property: Proof.

1 Witkin Cal. Summ. 10th Contracts § 548, (S 548) Other Real Property.

1 Witkin Cal. Summ. 10th Contracts § 549, Public Works Construction Contracts.

4 Witkin, California Summary 10th Sales § 212, Liquidated Damages.

13 Witkin, California Summary 10th Equity § 118, Employment Practices.

CHAPTER 2. DEFAULT ON REAL PROPERTY PURCHASE CONTRACT

Section

§ 1675. Residential property; failure of buyer to complete the purchase; validity of contract provisions; newly constructed attached condominium units

Section operative until July 1, 2014. See,
also, section operative July 1, 2014.

(a) As used in this section, "residential property" means real property primarily consisting of a dwelling that meets both of the following requirements:

(1) The dwelling contains not more than four residential units.

(2) At the time the contract to purchase and sell the property is made, the buyer intends to occupy the dwelling or one of its units as his or her residence.

(b) A provision in a contract to purchase and sell residential property that provides that all or any part of a payment made by the buyer shall constitute liquidated damages to the seller upon the buyer's failure to complete the purchase of the property is valid to the extent that payment in the form of cash or check, including a postdated check, is actually made if the provision satisfies the requirements of Sections 1677 and 1678 and either subdivision (c) or (d) of this section.

(c) If the amount actually paid pursuant to the liquidated damages provision does not exceed 3 percent of the purchase price, the provision is valid to the extent that payment is actually made unless the buyer establishes that the amount is unreasonable as liquidated damages.

(d) If the amount actually paid pursuant to the liquidated damages provision exceeds 3 percent of the purchase price, the provision is invalid unless the party seeking to uphold the provision establishes that the amount actually paid is reasonable as liquidated damages.

(e) For the purposes of subdivisions (c) and (d), the reasonableness of an amount actually paid as liquidated damages shall be determined by taking into account both of the following:

(1) The circumstances existing at the time the contract was made.

(2) The price and other terms and circumstances of any subsequent sale or contract to sell and purchase the same property if the sale or contract is made within six months of the buyer's default.

(f)(1) Notwithstanding either subdivision (c) or (d), for the initial sale of newly constructed attached condominium units, as defined pursuant to Section 783, that involves the sale of an attached residential condominium unit located within a structure of 10 or more residential condominium units and the amount actually paid to the seller pursuant to the liquidated damages provision exceeds 3 percent of the purchase price of the residential unit in the transaction, both of the following shall occur in the event of a buyer's default:

(A) The seller shall perform an accounting of its costs and revenues related to and fairly allocable to the construction and sale of the residential unit within 60 calendar days after the final close of escrow of the sale of the unit within the structure.

(B) The accounting shall include any and all costs and revenues related to the construction and sale of the residential property and any delay caused by the buyer's default. The seller shall make reasonable efforts to mitigate any damages arising from the default. The seller shall refund to the buyer any amounts previously retained as liquidated damages in excess of the greater of either 3 percent of the originally agreed-upon purchase price of the residential property or the amount of the seller's losses resulting from the buyer's default, as calculated by the accounting.

(2) The refund shall be sent to the buyer's last known address within 90 days after the final close of escrow of the sale or lease of all the residential condominium units within the structure.

(3) If the amount retained by the seller after the accounting does not exceed 3 percent of the purchase price, the amount is valid unless the buyer establishes that the amount is unreasonable as liquidated damages pursuant to subdivision (e).

(4) Subdivision (d) shall not apply to any dispute regarding the reasonableness of any amount retained as liquidated damages pursuant to this subdivision.

(5) Notwithstanding the time periods regarding the performance of the accounting set forth in paragraph (1), if a new qualified buyer has entered into a contract to purchase the residential property in question, the seller shall perform the accounting within 60 calendar days after a new qualified buyer has entered into a contract to purchase.

(6) As used in this subdivision, "structure" means either of the following:

(A) Improvements constructed on a common foundation.

(B) Improvements constructed by the same owner that must be constructed concurrently due to the design characteristics of the improvements or physical characteristics of the property on which the improvements are located.

(7) As used in this subdivision, "new qualified buyer" means a buyer who either:

(A) Has been issued a loan commitment, which satisfies the purchase agreement loan contingency requirement, by an institutional lender to obtain a loan for an amount equal to the purchase price less any downpayment possessed by the buyer.

(B) Has contracted to pay a purchase price that is greater than or equal to the purchase price to be paid by the original buyer.

(g)(1)(A) Notwithstanding subdivision (c), (d), or (f), for the initial sale of newly constructed attached condominium units, as defined pursuant to Section 783, that involves the sale of an attached residential condominium unit described in subparagraph (B), and the amount actually paid to the seller pursuant to the liquidated damages provision exceeds 6 percent of the purchase price of the residential unit in the transaction, both of the following shall occur in the event of a buyer's default:

(i) The seller shall perform an accounting of its costs and revenues related to and fairly allocable to the construction and sale of the residential unit within 60 calendar days after the final close of escrow of the sale of the unit within the structure.

(ii) The accounting shall include any and all costs and revenues related to the construction and sale of the residential property and any delay caused by the buyer's default. The seller shall make reasonable efforts to mitigate any damages arising from the default. The seller shall refund to the buyer any amounts previously retained as liquidated damages in excess of the greater of either 6 percent of the originally agreed-upon purchase price of the residential property or the amount of the seller's losses resulting from the buyer's default, as calculated by the accounting.

(B) This subdivision applies to an attached residential condominium unit for which both of the following are true:

(i) The unit is located within a structure of 20 or more residential condominium units, standing over eight stories high, that is high-density infill development, as defined in paragraph (10) of subdivision (a) of Section 21159.24 of the Public Resources Code, and that is located in a city, county, or city and county with a population density of 1,900 residents per square mile or greater, as evidenced by the 2000 United States census.

(ii) The purchase price of the unit was more than one million dollars ($1,000,000).

(2) The refund shall be sent to the buyer's last known address within 90 days after the final close of escrow of the sale or lease of all the residential condominium units within the structure.

(3) If the amount retained by the seller after the accounting does not exceed 6 percent of the purchase price, the amount is valid unless the buyer establishes that the amount is unreasonable as liquidated damages pursuant to subdivision (e).

(4) Subdivision (d) shall not apply to any dispute regarding the reasonableness of any amount retained as liquidated damages pursuant to this subdivision.

(5) Notwithstanding the time periods regarding the performance of the accounting set forth in paragraph (1), if a new qualified buyer has entered into a contract to purchase the residential property in question, the seller shall perform the accounting within 60 calendar days after a new qualified buyer has entered into a contract to purchase.

(6) As used in this subdivision, "structure" means either of the following:

(A) Improvements constructed on a common foundation.

(B) Improvements constructed by the same owner that must be constructed concurrently due to the design characteristics of the improvements or physical characteristics of the property on which the improvements are located.

(7) As used in this subdivision, "new qualified buyer" means a buyer who either:

(A) Has been issued a loan commitment, which satisfies the purchase agreement loan contingency requirement, by an institutional lender to obtain a loan for an amount equal to the purchase price less any downpayment possessed by the buyer.

(B) Has contracted to pay a purchase price that is greater than or equal to the purchase price to be paid by the original buyer.

(8) Commencing on July 1, 2010, and annually on each July 1 thereafter, the dollar amount of the minimum purchase price specified in paragraph (1) shall be adjusted. The Real Estate Commissioner shall determine the amount of the adjustment based on the change in the median price of a single family home in California, as determined by the most recent data available from the Federal Housing Finance Board. Upon determining the amount of the adjustment, the Real Estate Commissioner shall publish the current dollar amount of the minimum purchase price on the Internet Web site of the Bureau of Real Estate.

(9) Prior to the execution of a contract for sale of a residential condominium unit subject to this subdivision, the seller shall provide to the buyer the following notice, in at least 12–point type:

"Important Notice Regarding Your Deposit: Under California law, in a contract for the initial sale of a newly constructed attached condominium unit in a building over eight stories tall, containing 20 or more residential units, and located in a high-density infill development in a city, county, or city and county with 1,900 residents or more per square mile, where the price is more than one million dollars ($1,000,000), as adjusted by the Bureau of Real Estate, liquidated damages of 6 percent of the purchase price are presumed valid if the buyer defaults, unless the buyer establishes that the amount is unreasonable."

If the seller fails to provide this notice to the buyer prior to the execution of the contract, the amount of any liquidated damages shall be subject to subdivisions (c) and (d).

(h) This section shall become inoperative on July 1, 2014, and, as of January 1, 2015, is repealed, unless a later enacted statute, that becomes operative on or before January 1, 2015, deletes or extends the dates on which it becomes inoperative and is repealed. *(Added by Stats.1977, c. 198, p. 719, § 7, operative July 1, 1978. Amended by Stats.2003, c. 434 (A.B.728), § 3; Stats. 2008, c. 665 (A.B.2020), § 1; Stats.2009, c. 140 (A.B.1164), § 25; Stats.2013, c. 352 (A.B.1317), § 51, eff. Sept. 26, 2013, operative July 1, 2013.)*

Inoperative Date and Repeal

For inoperative date and repeal of this section, see its terms.

Law Revision Commission Comments

Section 1675 governs the validity of a provision that all or any part of a payment made by the buyer shall constitute liquidated damages for the buyer's default in a contract to purchase and sell residential property as defined in subdivision (a). The section is an exception to the general provisions of Section 1671. It should be noted that there are additional requirements concerning the form and execution of the liquidated damages provision: The liquidated damages provision is valid only if it is separately signed or initialed by the parties as required by Sections 1677 and 1678 and, if the contract is printed, the provision satisfies the type size requirements of Section 1677. Section 1675 does not apply to real property sales contracts as defined in Section 2985. See Section 1681.

Under Section 1675, a provision liquidating the damages if the buyer defaults is valid only to the extent that the buyer has actually paid in the form of cash or a check (including a postdated check) the amount of liquidated damages. Hence, if the liquidated damages provision specifies liquidated damages for the buyer's default in an amount greater than the amount actually paid by the buyer, the provision is valid only to the extent of the amount actually paid; the seller may not enforce the greater amount specified in the provision. Where the amount paid is greater than the amount specified as liquidated damages, only the amount so specified may be retained as liquidated damages for the buyer's default. Section 1675 recognizes that generally the buyer of residential housing, including the buyer who does not read the contract or does not understand it, expects to lose the "earnest money" deposit if the purchase of the property is not completed.

Subdivisions (c) and (d) are designed to protect the buyer of residential housing from forfeiting an unreasonably large amount as liquidated damages for the failure to complete the purchase of the property. If the amount paid is not in excess of three percent, the buyer has the burden of establishing that the amount is unreasonable in order to invalidate the liquidated damages provision. If the amount paid exceeds three percent of the purchase price, the party seeking to uphold the provision (generally the seller) has the burden of establishing that such amount was reasonable. Under subdivision (d), a buyer may seek to uphold a liquidated damages provision where the amount paid is three percent or more of the purchase price in order to limit the buyer's liability where the seller may be able to show higher actual damages in the absence of a valid provision.

Subdivision (e) provides the standard for determining the reasonableness of an amount paid as liquidated damages. Reasonableness is to be judged at the time the contract was made, but the court is also required to consider the price, terms, and other circumstances of a sale or contract for the sale of the property within six months after the buyer's default. The circumstances to be considered by the court in determining reasonableness include, but are not limited to, items such as the cost of taxes, interest, and insurance during the period after the original contract to purchase the property was made and any additional broker fees which are a result of the buyer's default. As to the interpretation of "under the circumstances existing at the time the contract was made," see the discussion in the Comment to Section 1671.

Section 1675 does not apply to contract provisions concerning anything other than liquidated damages for the buyer's failure to purchase the property. See Section 1679. Section 1675 does not, for example, apply to a provision liquidating the damages if the seller fails to perform. Nor does the section affect the seller's right to obtain specific performance. See Section 1680.

Where a liquidated damages provision is valid under this section, the limitations of Section 3307 (damages for breach of agreement to purchase real estate) do not apply. [13 Cal.L.Rev.Comm. Reports 1735 (1976)].

Research References

California Real Estate Forms (Miller & Starr) § 1:30, Planned Development Deposit Receipt and Agreement of Sale.

California Real Estate Forms (Miller & Starr) § 1:31, Condominium Deposit Receipt and Agreement of Sale.

California Real Estate Forms (Miller & Starr) § 1:33, Real Estate Purchase Contract and Receipt for Deposit—Income Property.

California Real Estate Forms (Miller & Starr) § 1:94, California Residential Purchase Agreement and Joint Escrow Instructions.

Rutter, Cal. Practice Guide: Real Prop. Transactions Ch. 4-E, E. Drafting the Purchase and Sale Agreement-Terms and Conditions.

Miller and Starr California Real Estate § 34:37, Liquidated Damages--Generally.

Miller and Starr California Real Estate § 34:38, Liquidated Damages--In Real Property Marketing Contracts.

Miller and Starr California Real Estate § 10:236, Policy Objectives; the "Standard" Transaction.

Miller and Starr California Real Estate § 25C:34, Restrictions on the Receipt and Disbursement of the Buyer's Funds; When No Blanket Encumbrance.

Miller and Starr California Real Estate § 25C:36, Required Provisions of the Purchase Agreement.

Miller and Starr California Real Estate § 25C:70, Regulation of Sales Contracts and Other Marketing Materials; Required Delivery of Documents.

13 NO. 6 Miller & Starr, California Real Estate Newsalert 13, Remedies - Breach of Contract.

14 NO. 4 Miller & Starr, California Real Estate Newsalert 16, Remedies.

14 NO. 4 Miller & Starr, California Real Estate Newsalert 17, Subdivisions.

19 NO. 4 Miller & Starr, California Real Estate Newsalert 27, Subdivision Offerings, Sales, and Leasing.

20 NO. 5 Miller & Starr, California Real Estate Newsalert 16, Judicial Remedies.

1 Witkin Cal. Summ. 10th Contracts § 534, (S 534) Organization and Scope of Law.

1 Witkin Cal. Summ. 10th Contracts § 535, (S 535) General Rule of Validity.

1 Witkin Cal. Summ. 10th Contracts § 536, (S 536) Deposits.

1 Witkin Cal. Summ. 10th Contracts § 544, (S 544) Scope of Chapter.

1 Witkin Cal. Summ. 10th Contracts § 545, (S 545) Residential Property: in General.

1 Witkin Cal. Summ. 10th Contracts § 546, (S 546) Residential Property: Proof.

1 Witkin Cal. Summ. 10th Contracts § 547, (S 547) Condominiums.

1 Witkin Cal. Summ. 10th Contracts § 548, (S 548) Other Real Property.

1 Witkin Cal. Summ. 10th Contracts § 901, (S 901) Measure of Damages.

§ 1675. Residential property; failure of buyer to complete the purchase; validity of contract provisions; newly constructed attached condominium units

Section operative July 1, 2014. See, also, section operative until July 1, 2014.

(a) As used in this section, "residential property" means real property primarily consisting of a dwelling that meets both of the following requirements:

(1) The dwelling contains not more than four residential units.

(2) At the time the contract to purchase and sell the property is made, the buyer intends to occupy the dwelling or one of its units as his or her residence.

(b) A provision in a contract to purchase and sell residential property that provides that all or any part of a payment made by the buyer shall constitute liquidated damages to the seller upon the buyer's failure to complete the purchase of the property is valid to the extent that payment in the form of cash or check, including a postdated check, is actually made if the provision satisfies the requirements of Sections 1677 and 1678 and either subdivision (c) or (d) of this section.

(c) If the amount actually paid pursuant to the liquidated damages provision does not exceed 3 percent of the purchase price, the provision is valid to the extent that payment is actually made unless the buyer establishes that the amount is unreasonable as liquidated damages.

(d) If the amount actually paid pursuant to the liquidated damages provision exceeds 3 percent of the purchase price, the provision is invalid unless the party seeking to uphold the provision establishes that the amount actually paid is reasonable as liquidated damages.

(e) For the purposes of subdivisions (c) and (d), the reasonableness of an amount actually paid as liquidated damages shall be determined by taking into account both of the following:

(1) The circumstances existing at the time the contract was made.

(2) The price and other terms and circumstances of any subsequent sale or contract to sell and purchase the same property if the sale or contract is made within six months of the buyer's default.

(f)(1) Notwithstanding either subdivision (c) or (d), for the initial sale of newly constructed attached condominium units, as defined pursuant to Section 783, that involves the sale of an attached residential condominium unit located within a structure of 10 or more residential condominium units and the amount actually paid to the seller pursuant to the liquidated damages provision exceeds 3 percent of the purchase price of the residential unit in the transaction both of the following shall occur in the event of a buyer's default:

(A) The seller shall perform an accounting of its costs and revenues related to and fairly allocable to the construction and sale of the residential unit within 60 calendar days after the final close of escrow of the sale of the unit within the structure.

(B) The accounting shall include any and all costs and revenues related to the construction and sale of the residential property and any delay caused by the buyer's default. The seller shall make reasonable efforts to mitigate any damages arising from the default. The seller shall refund to the buyer any amounts previously retained as liquidated damages in excess of the greater of either 3 percent of the originally agreed-upon purchase price of the residential property or the amount of the seller's losses resulting from the buyer's default, as calculated by the accounting.

(2) The refund shall be sent to the buyer's last known address within 90 days after the final close of escrow of the sale or lease of all the residential condominium units within the structure.

(3) If the amount retained by the seller after the accounting does not exceed 3 percent of the purchase price, the amount is valid unless the buyer establishes that the amount is unreasonable as liquidated damages pursuant to subdivision (e).

(4) Subdivision (d) shall not apply to any dispute regarding the reasonableness of any amount retained as liquidated damages pursuant to this subdivision.

(5) Notwithstanding the time periods regarding the performance of the accounting set forth in paragraph (1), if a new qualified buyer has entered into a contract to purchase the residential property in question, the seller shall perform the accounting within 60 calendar days after a new qualified buyer has entered into a contract to purchase.

(6) As used in this subdivision, "structure" means either of the following:

(A) Improvements constructed on a common foundation.

(B) Improvements constructed by the same owner that must be constructed concurrently due to the design characteristics of the improvements or physical characteristics of the property on which the improvements are located.

(7) As used in this subdivision, "new qualified buyer" means a buyer who either:

(A) Has been issued a loan commitment, which satisfies the purchase agreement loan contingency requirement, by an institutional lender to obtain a loan for an amount equal to the purchase price less any downpayment possessed by the buyer.

(B) Has contracted to pay a purchase price that is greater than or equal to the purchase price to be paid by the original buyer.

(g) This section shall become operative on July 1, 2014. *(Added by Stats.2008, c. 665 (A.B.2020), § 2, operative July 1, 2014.)*

§ 1676. General validity of contract provisions

Except as provided in Section 1675, a provision in a contract to purchase and sell real property liquidating the damages to the seller if the buyer fails to complete the purchase of the property is valid if it satisfies the requirements of Section 1677 and the requirements of subdivision (b) of Section 1671. *(Added by Stats.1977, c. 198, p. 719, § 7, operative July 1, 1978.)*

Law Revision Commission Comments

Section 1676 applies the standard of subdivision (b) of Section 1671 to a liquidated damages provision for the buyer's default in a contract to purchase and sell real property other than residential property as defined in subdivision (a) of Section 1675. See Comment to Section 1671. Hence, if the applicable requirements of Section 1677 are satisfied, the liquidated damages provision is valid unless the buyer establishes that the provision was unreasonable under the circumstances existing at the time the contract was made. See the discussion in the Comment to Section 1671 for an interpretation of this standard.

The liquidated damages provision is not valid unless it is separately signed or initialed by the parties and, if the contract is printed, the provision satisfies certain type size requirements. See Section 1677.

Section 1676 does not apply to contract provisions concerning anything other than liquidated damages for the buyer's failure to purchase the property. See Section 1679. Section 1676 does not, for example, apply to a provision liquidation damages if the seller fails to perform. Nor does the section affect the seller's right to obtain specific performance. See Section 1680. Section 1676 does not apply to real property sales contracts as defined in Section 2985. See Section 1681.

Where a liquidated damages provision is valid under this section, the limitations of Section 3307 (damages for breach of agreement to purchase real estate) do not apply. [13 Cal.L.Rev.Comm. Reports 1735 (1976)].

Research References

California Real Estate Forms (Miller & Starr) § 1:17, Purchase and Sale Agreement—Unimproved Real Property—With Escrow Instructions.
California Real Estate Forms (Miller & Starr) § 1:29, Purchase and Sale Agreement—Seller Oriented With Seller Financing.
California Real Estate Forms (Miller & Starr) § 1:166, Liquidated Damages.
Rutter, Cal. Practice Guide: Real Prop. Transactions Ch. 4-E, E. Drafting the Purchase and Sale Agreement-Terms and Conditions.
Miller and Starr California Real Estate § 34:38, Liquidated Damages--In Real Property Marketing Contracts.
Miller and Starr California Real Estate § 25C:70, Regulation of Sales Contracts and Other Marketing Materials; Required Delivery of Documents.
1 Witkin Cal. Summ. 10th Contracts § 544, (S 544) Scope of Chapter.
1 Witkin Cal. Summ. 10th Contracts § 548, (S 548) Other Real Property.
1 Witkin Cal. Summ. 10th Contracts § 901, (S 901) Measure of Damages.

§ 1677. Requirements; validity of contract provisions

A provision in a contract to purchase and sell real property liquidating the damages to the seller if the buyer fails to complete the purchase of the property is invalid unless:

(a) The provision is separately signed or initialed by each party to the contract; and

(b) If the provision is included in a printed contract, it is set out either in at least 10-point bold type or in contrasting red print in at least eight-point bold type. *(Added by Stats.1977, c. 198, p. 719, § 7, operative July 1, 1978.)*

Law Revision Commission Comments

Section 1677 establishes formal requirements for execution of a provision liquidating the damages if the buyer defaults in his agreement to purchase real property. The provision is invalid unless separately signed or initialed by each party to the contract. This requirement is adapted from the Real Estate Purchase Contract and Receipt for Deposit, approved in form only for use in "simple transactions" by the California Real Estate Association and the State Bar of California. The requirement is extended to all contracts providing for the forfeiture of payments as liquidated damages to the seller if the buyer fails to complete the purchase. This will make it more likely that the parties will appreciate the consequences of this important provision. See also Section 1678 (separate signing or initialing for subsequent payments in the case of residential property). The requirement of a separate signing or initialing provided by this section does not apply to anything other than liquidated damages for the buyer's failure to purchase the property.

Section 1677 also establishes minimum type size for a provision in a printed contract to purchase and sell real property liquidating the damages to the seller if the buyer fails to purchase the property. The type size requirements are designed to provide further assurance that the parties will be aware of the consequences of the liquidated damages provision. The provision for contrasting red print in at least eight-point bold type is taken from Section 2984.1 of the Civil Code (contract provision regarding insurance coverage in conditional sales contract). The alternative provision, requiring at least 10-point bold type, is comparable to that found in various other recently enacted statutes. E.g., Civil Code §§ 1803.2 and 1803.7 (retail installment contracts), 1916.5 (variable interest provision), 2984.3 (buyer's acknowledgment of delivery of copy of conditional sale contract) [13 Cal.L.Rev.Comm. Reports 1735 (1976)].

Research References

California Real Estate Forms (Miller & Starr) § 1:8, Letter of Intent—Nonbinding.
California Real Estate Forms (Miller & Starr) § 1:9, Letter of Intent—Binding.
California Real Estate Forms (Miller & Starr) § 1:17, Purchase and Sale Agreement—Unimproved Real Property—With Escrow Instructions.
California Real Estate Forms (Miller & Starr) § 1:18, Purchase and Sale Agreement—Raw Land.
California Real Estate Forms (Miller & Starr) § 1:20, Purchase and Sale Agreement—Small Commercial Properties Subject to Tenant Leases.
California Real Estate Forms (Miller & Starr) § 1:21, Purchase and Sale Agreement—Commercial Property Subject to Tenant Leases.
California Real Estate Forms (Miller & Starr) § 1:22, Agreement of Purchase and Sale—Multi-Property
California Real Estate Forms (Miller & Starr) § 1:23, Purchase and Sale Agreemen—Residential Project.
California Real Estate Forms (Miller & Starr) § 1:24, Combination Purchase and Option Agreement—Residential Lots Being Acquired from a Bankrupt Seller.
California Real Estate Forms (Miller & Starr) § 1:26, Purchase and Sale Agreement—Seller-Oriented Short Form.
California Real Estate Forms (Miller & Starr) § 1:27, Purchase and Sale Agreement—Multitenant Residential Property.
California Real Estate Forms (Miller & Starr) § 1:28, Purchase and Sale Agreement—Hotel.
California Real Estate Forms (Miller & Starr) § 1:29, Purchase and Sale Agreement—Seller Oriented With Seller Financing.
California Real Estate Forms (Miller & Starr) § 1:30, Planned Development Deposit Receipt and Agreement of Sale.
California Real Estate Forms (Miller & Starr) § 1:31, Condominium Deposit Receipt and Agreement of Sale.
California Real Estate Forms (Miller & Starr) § 1:32, Hotel Purchase and Sale Agreement With Escrow Instructions.
California Real Estate Forms (Miller & Starr) § 1:33, Real Estate Purchase Contract and Receipt for Deposit—Income Property.
California Real Estate Forms (Miller & Starr) § 1:76, Standard Offer, Agreement and Escrow Instructions for Purchase of Real Estate.
California Real Estate Forms (Miller & Starr) § 1:94, California Residential Purchase Agreement and Joint Escrow Instructions.
California Real Estate Forms (Miller & Starr) § 1:166, Liquidated Damages.
Rutter, Cal. Practice Guide: Real Prop. Transactions Ch. 4-E, E. Drafting the Purchase and Sale Agreement-Terms and Conditions.

Miller and Starr California Real Estate § 34:38, Liquidated Damages--In Real Property Marketing Contracts.

Miller and Starr California Real Estate § 25C:34, Restrictions on the Receipt and Disbursement of the Buyer's Funds; When No Blanket Encumbrance.

Miller and Starr California Real Estate § 25C:70, Regulation of Sales Contracts and Other Marketing Materials; Required Delivery of Documents.

1 Witkin Cal. Summ. 10th Contracts § 14, Applicability.

1 Witkin Cal. Summ. 10th Contracts § 545, (S 545) Residential Property: in General.

1 Witkin Cal. Summ. 10th Contracts § 548, (S 548) Other Real Property.

§ 1678. Multiple payments; liquidated damages under § 1675; requirements

If more than one payment made by the buyer is to constitute liquidated damages under Section 1675, the amount of any payment after the first payment is valid as liquidated damages only if (1) the total of all such payments satisfies the requirements of Section 1675 and (2) a separate liquidated damages provision satisfying the requirements of Section 1677 is separately signed or initialed by each party to the contract for each such subsequent payment. *(Added by Stats.1977, c. 198, p. 719, § 7, operative July 1, 1978.)*

Law Revision Commission Comments

Section 1678 is included to protect the buyer of residential property by requiring a separately signed or initialed agreement whenever any payment made after the first payment is to be liquidated damages if the buyer fails to purchase real property. The section recognizes that frequently a deposit is made at the time the agreement to sell and to purchase the property is made and a second payment is made at the time the escrow is opened. The payment made at the time the escrow is opened (or at some other time) can be retained by the seller as liquidated damages only if there is a valid agreement so providing and there is a separate signing or initialing for the subsequent payment. The standard provided by Section 1675 is applied to the total of all payments—the first and any subsequent payments—designated as liquidated damages by the contract. [13 Cal.L.Rev.Comm. Reports 1735 (1976)].

Research References

California Real Estate Forms (Miller & Starr) § 1:94, California Residential Purchase Agreement and Joint Escrow Instructions.

Rutter, Cal. Practice Guide: Real Prop. Transactions Ch. 4-E, E. Drafting the Purchase and Sale Agreement-Terms and Conditions.

Miller and Starr California Real Estate § 34:38, Liquidated Damages--In Real Property Marketing Contracts.

Miller and Starr California Real Estate § 25C:34, Restrictions on the Receipt and Disbursement of the Buyer's Funds; When No Blanket Encumbrance.

Miller and Starr California Real Estate § 25C:70, Regulation of Sales Contracts and Other Marketing Materials; Required Delivery of Documents.

1 Witkin Cal. Summ. 10th Contracts § 14, Applicability.

1 Witkin Cal. Summ. 10th Contracts § 545, (S 545) Residential Property: in General.

§ 1679. Applicability of chapter; specified provisions

This chapter applies only to a provision for liquidated damages to the seller if the buyer fails to complete the purchase of real property. The validity of any other provision for liquidated damages in a contract to purchase and sell real property shall be determined under Section 1671. *(Added by Stats.1977, c. 198, p. 719, § 7, operative July 1, 1978.)*

Law Revision Commission Comments

Section 1679 makes clear that this chapter does not apply to contract provisions concerning anything other than liquidated damages for the buyer's failure to purchase the property. The chapter does not apply, for example, to a provision liquidating the damages if the seller fails to perform. Such damages are covered by Section 1671. Nor does the chapter affect the seller's right to obtain specific performance. See Section 1680. [13 Cal.L.Rev.Comm. Reports 1735 (1976)].

Research References

Rutter, Cal. Practice Guide: Real Prop. Transactions Ch. 4-E, E. Drafting the Purchase and Sale Agreement-Terms and Conditions.

Miller and Starr California Real Estate § 34:38, Liquidated Damages--In Real Property Marketing Contracts.

1 Witkin Cal. Summ. 10th Contracts § 544, (S 544) Scope of Chapter.

1 Witkin Cal. Summ. 10th Contracts § 545, (S 545) Residential Property: in General.

§ 1680. Specific performance; applicability of chapter

Nothing in this chapter affects any right a party to a contract for the purchase and sale of real property may have to obtain specific performance. *(Added by Stats.1977, c. 198, p. 719, § 7, operative July 1, 1978.)*

Law Revision Commission Comments

Section 1680 makes clear that this chapter does not affect the rule under existing California law that the right of the seller to obtain specific performance of a contract for the purchase of real property is not affected by the inclusion in the contract of a provision liquidating the damages to the seller if the buyer defaults on his agreement to purchase the property. See Section 3389, People v. Ocean Shore R.R., 90 Cal.App.2d 464, 203 P.2d 579 (1949), and other cases interpreting Section 3389. [13 Cal. L.Rev.Comm. Reports 1735 (1976)].

Research References

Rutter, Cal. Practice Guide: Real Prop. Transactions Ch. 11-C, C. Seller's Remedies Upon Buyer's Breach-Damages and Specific Performance.

Miller and Starr California Real Estate § 5:60, Broker's Share of the Retained ("Forfeited") Deposit or Liquidated Damages.

Miller and Starr California Real Estate § 34:38, Liquidated Damages--In Real Property Marketing Contracts.

1 Witkin Cal. Summ. 10th Contracts § 544, (S 544) Scope of Chapter.

§ 1681. Real property sales contracts; applicability of chapter

This chapter does not apply to real property sales contracts as defined in Section 2985. *(Added by Stats.1977, c. 198, p. 719, § 7, operative July 1, 1978.)*

Law Revision Commission Comments

Section 1681 makes clear that this chapter does not apply to real property sales contracts as defined in Section 2985 (commonly called installment land contracts). No change is made in the law that governs the extent to which payments made pursuant to such contracts may be forfeited upon the buyer's default. [13 Cal.L.Rev.Comm. Reports 1735 (1976)].

Research References

Rutter, Cal. Practice Guide: Real Prop. Transactions Ch. 4-E, E. Drafting the Purchase and Sale Agreement-Terms and Conditions.

Miller and Starr California Real Estate § 34:38, Liquidated Damages--In Real Property Marketing Contracts.

Miller and Starr California Real Estate § 34:60, Buyer's Right to Restitution.

1 Witkin Cal. Summ. 10th Contracts § 544, (S 544) Scope of Chapter.

Title 5

EXTINCTION OF CONTRACTS

CHAPTER 1.   CONTRACTS, HOW EXTINGUISHED

Section
1682.   Contract, extinguishment.

§ 1682.   Contract, extinguishment

A contract may be extinguished in like manner with any other obligation, and also in the manner prescribed by this Title. *(Enacted in 1872.)*

CHAPTER 2.   RESCISSION

Section

1688.	Extinguishment.
1689.	Grounds.
1689.2.	Endless chain scheme.
1689.3.	Dental services; contracts directly with office or plan; right to compensation.
1689.5.	Definitions.
1689.6.	Right to cancel home solicitation contracts or offers; "personal emergency response unit" defined.
1689.7.	Home solicitation contract or offer for purchase of personal emergency response unit; required statements relating to cancellation.
1689.8.	Liens on real property; home solicitation contracts; offers for home improvement goods or services; retail installment sales.
1689.9.	Goods affixed to realty; effect of subsequent sale or encumbrance of realty.
1689.10.	Tender by seller to buyer of payments or goods traded in; retention of and lien on goods delivered.
1689.11.	Tender by buyer to seller of goods delivered by seller pursuant to contract or offer.
1689.12.	Waiver or confession of judgment of provisions; voidness.
1689.13.	Conditions making §§ 1689.5, 1689.6, 1689.7, 1689.10, 1689.12 and 1689.14 not apply to a contract.
1689.14.	Repairs or restoration of residential premises damaged by a disaster.
1689.15.	Right of contractor to commence work on a service and repair project; necessary conditions; right of cancellation.
1689.20.	Seminar sales solicitation contracts or offers; cancellation rights and procedures.
1689.21.	Seminar sales contracts; notice of cancellation; language and contents; copy to buyer.
1689.22.	Seller's tender of payments or evidence of indebtedness upon cancellation; buyer's rights in goods delivered by seller.
1689.23.	Buyer's tender of goods upon cancellation; duty of care; compensation of seller for services.
1689.24.	Definitions.
1690.	Stipulations against right; effect.
1691.	Procedure.
1692.	Relief based on rescission.
1693.	Effect upon relief of delay in notice of rescission or in restoration of benefits.

§ 1688.   Extinguishment

A contract is extinguished by its rescission. *(Enacted in 1872.)*

Research References

Rutter, Cal. Practice Guide: A.D.R. Ch. 5-D, D. Defenses to Enforcement.
Rutter, Cal. Practice Guide: Insurance Litigation Ch. 5-F, F. Rescission by Insurer.

Rutter, Cal. Practice Guide: Insurance Litigation Ch. 15-B, B. Actions by Insurers.
Rutter, Cal. Practice Guide: Real Prop. Transactions Ch. 11-G, G. Rescission.
Miller and Starr California Real Estate § 34:4, Grounds for Rescission.
Miller and Starr California Real Estate § 34:8, Effect of Rescission.
Miller and Starr California Real Estate § 1:103, Mutual Rescission.
Miller and Starr California Real Estate § 1:104, Mutual Rescission-- Unilateral Rescission; Types of Mutual Rescission.
4 Witkin Cal. Proc. 5th Pleading § 541, (S 541) Nature of Action.
1 Witkin Cal. Summ. 10th Contracts § 926, (S 926) Rescission Distinguished.

§ 1689.   Grounds

(a) A contract may be rescinded if all the parties thereto consent.

(b) A party to a contract may rescind the contract in the following cases:

(1) If the consent of the party rescinding, or of any party jointly contracting with him, was given by mistake, or obtained through duress, menace, fraud, or undue influence, exercised by or with the connivance of the party as to whom he rescinds, or of any other party to the contract jointly interested with such party.

(2) If the consideration for the obligation of the rescinding party fails, in whole or in part, through the fault of the party as to whom he rescinds.

(3) If the consideration for the obligation of the rescinding party becomes entirely void from any cause.

(4) If the consideration for the obligation of the rescinding party, before it is rendered to him, fails in a material respect from any cause.

(5) If the contract is unlawful for causes which do not appear in its terms or conditions, and the parties are not equally at fault.

(6) If the public interest will be prejudiced by permitting the contract to stand.

(7) Under the circumstances provided for in Sections 39, 1533, 1566, 1785[1], 1789[2], 1930 and 2314 of this code, Section 2470 of the Corporations Code[3], Sections 331, 338, 359, 447, 1904 and 2030 of the Insurance Code or any other statute providing for rescission. *(Enacted in 1872. Amended by Stats. 1931, c. 1070, p. 2260, § 10; Stats.1961, c. 589, p. 1733, § 1.)*

[1] Repealed. See, now, Commercial Code § 2610.

[2] Former section repealed. See, now, Commercial Code §§ 2106, 2507, 2601, 2607, 2608, 2711, 2714, 2715, 2717.

[3] Repealed. See, now, Commercial Code §§ 8301, 8315.

Research References

Rutter, Cal. Practice Guide: A.D.R. Ch. 5-D, D. Defenses to Enforcement.
Rutter, Cal. Practice Guide: Civil Trials & Evidence Ch. 2-C, C. Cases in Which Jury Trial May be Demanded.
Rutter, Cal. Practice Guide: Insurance Litigation Ch. 5-F, F. Rescission by Insurer.
Rutter, Cal. Practice Guide: Insurance Litigation Ch. 5-G, G. Rescission by Insured.
Rutter, Cal. Practice Guide: Insurance Litigation Ch. 5-H, H. Mutual Rescission.
Rutter, Cal. Practice Guide: Real Prop. Transactions Ch. 11-A, A. Factors Affecting Choice of Remedies.
Rutter, Cal. Practice Guide: Real Prop. Transactions Ch. 11-G, G. Rescission.
Miller and Starr California Real Estate § 3:11, Disclosure of Agency Relationships.
Miller and Starr California Real Estate § 34:1, Available Remedies.
Miller and Starr California Real Estate § 34:4, Grounds for Rescission.
Miller and Starr California Real Estate § 5:53, Termination of the Listing; Owner's Right to Revoke.
Miller and Starr California Real Estate § 8:56, Failure of Consideration.
Miller and Starr California Real Estate § 1:103, Mutual Rescission.

Miller and Starr California Real Estate § 1:104, Mutual Rescission--Unilateral Rescission; Types of Mutual Rescission.

Miller and Starr California Real Estate § 1:118, Unilateral Mistake.

Miller and Starr California Real Estate § 1:123, Remedies for Mistake.

Miller and Starr California Real Estate § 1:127, Innocent Misrepresentation.

Miller and Starr California Real Estate § 23:19, Duty of Owner to Disclose Presence of Hazardous Substances to Buyer, Tenant, or Employees.

Miller and Starr California Real Estate § 28:97, Measure of Surety's Liability.

Miller and Starr California Real Estate § 34:83, General Principles; Election of Remedies.

15 NO. 6 Miller & Starr, California Real Estate Newsalert 1, Refuse to Mediate and (Under Some Contracts) Wave Goodbye to Your Attorney's Fees.

3 Witkin Cal. Proc. 5th Actions § 206, (S 206) Notice of Rescission.

6 Witkin Cal. Proc. 5th Proceedings Without Trial § 542, Fraud Directed to Arbitration Provision.

2 Witkin, California Summary 10th Insurance § 224, (S 224) Right to Rescind.

1 Witkin Cal. Summ. 10th Contracts § 262, in General.

1 Witkin Cal. Summ. 10th Contracts § 276, (S 276) Nature of Remedy.

1 Witkin Cal. Summ. 10th Contracts § 285, (S 285) in General.

1 Witkin Cal. Summ. 10th Contracts § 307, Ground for Rescission.

1 Witkin Cal. Summ. 10th Contracts § 685, (S 685) Nature of Right.

1 Witkin Cal. Summ. 10th Contracts § 704, in General.

1 Witkin Cal. Summ. 10th Contracts § 813, Theory of Constructive Condition.

1 Witkin Cal. Summ. 10th Contracts § 927, (S 927) Mutual Consent.

1 Witkin Cal. Summ. 10th Contracts § 930, Equitable Action Abolished.

1 Witkin Cal. Summ. 10th Contracts § 933, Executed Contract.

1 Witkin Cal. Summ. 10th Contracts § 935, (S 935) Grounds for Rescission.

§ 1689.2. Endless chain scheme

A participant in an endless chain scheme, as defined in Section 327 of the Penal Code, may rescind the contract upon which the scheme is based, and may recover all consideration paid pursuant to the scheme, less any amounts paid or consideration provided to the participant pursuant to the scheme. In addition, the court may, upon motion, award reasonable attorney's fees to a prevailing plaintiff. *(Added by Stats.1989, c. 436, § 1.)*

Research References

1 Witkin Cal. Summ. 10th Contracts § 633, Endless Chain Scheme.

§ 1689.3. Dental services; contracts directly with office or plan; right to compensation

Any patient who contracts directly with a dental office or plan for services may rescind the contract or plan until midnight of the third business day after the day on which the patient signs the contract or plan. If services have been provided to the patient, the dental office shall be entitled to compensation for those services. *(Added by Stats.1991, c. 596 (A.B.1283), § 2.)*

Research References

4 Witkin, California Summary 10th Sales § 350, (S 350) Dental Services.

§ 1689.5. Definitions

As used in Sections 1689.6 to 1689.11, inclusive, and in Section 1689.14:

(a) "Home solicitation contract or offer" means any contract, whether single or multiple, or any offer which is subject to approval, for the sale, lease, or rental of goods or services or both, made at other than appropriate trade premises in an amount of twenty-five dollars ($25) or more, including any interest or service charges. "Home solicitation contract" does not include any contract under which the buyer has the right to rescind pursuant to Title 1, Chapter 2, Section 125 of the Federal Consumer Credit Protection Act (P.L. 90–321) and the regulations promulgated pursuant thereto.

(b) "Appropriate trade premises," means premises where either the owner or seller normally carries on a business, or where goods are normally offered or exposed for sale in the course of a business carried on at those premises.

(c) "Goods" means tangible chattels bought for use primarily for personal, family, or household purposes, including certificates or coupons exchangeable for these goods, and including goods that, at the time of the sale or subsequently, are to be so affixed to real property as to become a part of the real property whether or not severable therefrom, but does not include any vehicle required to be registered under the Vehicle Code, nor any goods sold with this vehicle if sold under a contract governed by Section 2982, and does not include any mobilehome, as defined in Section 18008 of the Health and Safety Code, nor any goods sold with this mobilehome if either are sold under a contract subject to Section 18036.5 of the Health and Safety Code.

(d) "Services" means work, labor and services, including, but not limited to, services furnished in connection with the repair, restoration, alteration, or improvement of residential premises, or services furnished in connection with the sale or repair of goods as defined in Section 1802.1, and courses of instruction, regardless of the purpose for which they are taken, but does not include the services of attorneys, real estate brokers and salesmen, securities dealers or investment counselors, physicians, optometrists, or dentists, nor financial services offered by banks, savings institutions, credit unions, industrial loan companies, personal property brokers, consumer finance lenders, or commercial finance lenders, organized pursuant to state or federal law, that are not connected with the sale of goods or services, as defined herein, nor the sale of insurance that is not connected with the sale of goods or services as defined herein, nor services in connection with the sale or installation of mobilehomes or of goods sold with a mobilehome if either are sold or installed under a contract subject to Section 18036.5 of the Health and Safety Code, nor services for which the tariffs, rates, charges, costs, or expenses, including in each instance the time sale price, is required by law to be filed with and approved by the federal government or any official, department, division, commission, or agency of the United States or of the state.

(e) "Business day" means any calendar day except Sunday, or the following business holidays: New Year's Day, Washington's Birthday, Memorial Day, Independence Day, Labor Day, Columbus Day, Veterans' Day, Thanksgiving Day, and Christmas Day.

(f) This section shall become operative on January 1, 2006. *(Added by Stats.1971, c. 375, p. 739, § 1. Amended by Stats.1972, c. 1415, p. 3078, § 2; Stats.1973, c. 554, p. 1076, § 1; Stats.1981, c. 975, p. 3721, § 1.5; Stats.1985, c. 660, § 1; Stats.1986, c. 1229, § 2; Stats.1988, c. 1104, § 1; Stats.1993–94, 1st Ex.Sess., c. 51 (A.B.57), § 1; Stats.2004, c. 566 (S.B.30), § 15, operative July 1, 2005; Stats.2005, c. 48 (S.B.1113), § 23, eff. July 18, 2005, operative Jan. 1, 2006.)*

Operative Effect

Stats.2005, c. 48 (S.B.1113), was enacted and immediately effective on July 18, 2005. Section 22 of that act explicitly amended § 1689.5 as amended by § 1 of Stats.1993–94, c. 51. Section 23 of c. 48 explicitly amended § 1689.5 as amended by § 15 of Stats.2004, c. 566 (S.B.30). Chapter 566 became operative on July 1, 2005, by terms of § 21 of that act. The § 22 text, repealed by its terms on Jan. 1, 2006, undid the changes made by c. 566. The § 23 text, operative by its terms on Jan. 1, 2006, reapplied those changes. Section 31 of c. 48 repealed Stats.2004, c. 566, § 21. The general effective date for 2004 regular session laws is Jan. 1, 2005.

Research References

Rutter, Cal. Practice Guide: Real Prop. Transactions Ch. 6-I, I. Real Property Foreclosures and Antideficiency Laws.

Miller and Starr California Real Estate § 27:54, Home Solicitation Contracts.

Miller and Starr California Real Estate § 25C:66, Regulation of Time-Shares; in General.

16 NO. 4 Miller & Starr, California Real Estate Newsalert 4, Construction Contracts.

16 NO. 5 Miller & Starr, California Real Estate Newsalert 26, State Board of Equalization Issues Comprehensive Summary and Qs and As for Transfers of Base Year Values of Principal Residences.

4 Witkin, California Summary 10th Sales § 290, (S 290) Nature and Scope of Statute.

4 Witkin, California Summary 10th Sales § 329, Buyer's Right to Cancel.

4 Witkin, California Summary 10th Sales § 390, (S 390) Telephone Sellers.

4 Witkin, California Summary 10th Sales § 397, (S 397) Water Treatment Contracts.

§ 1689.6. Right to cancel home solicitation contracts or offers; "personal emergency response unit" defined

(a)(1) Except for a contract written pursuant to Section 7151.2 or 7159.10 of the Business and Professions Code, in addition to any other right to revoke an offer, the buyer has the right to cancel a home solicitation contract or offer until midnight of the third business day after the day on which the buyer signs an agreement or offer to purchase which complies with Section 1689.7.

(2) In addition to any other right to revoke an offer, the buyer has the right to cancel a home solicitation contract written pursuant to Section 7151.2 of the Business and Professions Code until midnight of the third business day after the buyer receives a signed and dated copy of the contract or offer to purchase that complies with Section 1689.7 of this code.

(3)(A) In addition to any other right to revoke an offer, the buyer has the right to cancel a home solicitation contract or offer to purchase written pursuant to Section 7159.10 of the Business and Professions Code, until the buyer receives a signed and dated copy of a service and repair contract that complies with the contract requirements specified in Section 7159.10 of the Business and Professions Code and the work commences.

(B) For any contract written pursuant to Section 7159.10 of the Business and Professions Code, or otherwise presented to the buyer as a service and repair contract, unless all of the conforming requirements listed under subdivision (a) of that section are met, the requirements set forth under Section 7159 of the Business and Professions Code shall be applicable, regardless of the aggregate contract price, including the right to cancel as set forth under this section.

(b) In addition to any other right to revoke an offer, any buyer has the right to cancel a home solicitation contract or offer for the purchase of a personal emergency response unit until midnight of the seventh business day after the day on which the buyer signs an agreement or offer to purchase which complies with Section 1689.7. This subdivision shall not apply to a personal emergency response unit installed with, and as part of, a home security alarm system subject to the Alarm Company Act (Chapter 11.6 (commencing with Section 7590) of Division 3 of the Business and Professions Code) which has two or more stationary protective devices used to enunciate an intrusion or fire and is installed by an alarm company operator operating under a current license issued pursuant to the Alarm Company Act, which shall instead be subject to subdivision (a).

(c) In addition to any other right to revoke an offer, a buyer has the right to cancel a home solicitation contract or offer for the repair or restoration of residential premises damaged by a disaster that was not void pursuant to Section 1689.14, until midnight of the seventh business day after the buyer signs and dates the contract unless the provisions of Section 1689.15 are applicable.

(d) Cancellation occurs when the buyer gives written notice of cancellation to the seller at the address specified in the agreement or offer.

(e) Notice of cancellation, if given by mail, is effective when deposited in the mail properly addressed with postage prepaid.

(f) Notice of cancellation given by the buyer need not take the particular form as provided with the contract or offer to purchase and, however expressed, is effective if it indicates the intention of the buyer not to be bound by the home solicitation contract or offer.

(g) "Personal emergency response unit," for purposes of this section, means an in-home radio transmitter device or two-way radio device generally, but not exclusively, worn on a neckchain, wrist strap, or clipped to clothing, and connected to a telephone line through which a monitoring station is alerted of an emergency and emergency assistance is summoned. *(Added by Stats.1971, c. 375, p. 740, § 2. Amended by Stats.1973, c. 554, p. 1077, § 2; Stats.1991, c. 394 (A.B.585), § 1; Stats.1992, c. 145 (A.B.2378), § 1; Stats.1993–94, 1st Ex.Sess., c. 51 (A.B.57), § 2; Stats.2004, c. 566 (S.B.30), § 16, operative July 1, 2005; Stats. 2005, c. 48 (S.B.1113), § 25, eff. July 18, 2005, operative Jan. 1, 2006; Stats.2005, c. 385 (A.B.316), § 11.)*

Operative Effect

Stats.2005, c. 48 (S.B.1113), was enacted and immediately effective on July 18, 2005. Section 24 of that act explicitly amended § 1689.6 as amended by § 1 of Stats.1993–94, c. 51. Section 25 of c. 48 explicitly amended § 1689.6 as amended by § 15 of Stats.2004, c. 566 (S.B.30). Chapter 566 became operative on July 1, 2005, by terms of § 21 of that act. The § 24 text, repealed by its terms on Jan. 1, 2006, undid the changes made by c. 566. The § 25 text, operative by its terms on Jan. 1, 2006, reapplied those changes. Section 31 of c. 48 repealed Stats.2004, c. 566, § 21. The general effective date for 2004 regular session laws is Jan. 1, 2005.

Research References

Miller and Starr California Real Estate § 27:54, Home Solicitation Contracts.

16 NO. 4 Miller & Starr, California Real Estate Newsalert 4, Construction Contracts.

16 NO. 5 Miller & Starr, California Real Estate Newsalert 26, State Board of Equalization Issues Comprehensive Summary and Qs and As for Transfers of Base Year Values of Principal Residences.

4 Witkin, California Summary 10th Sales § 329, Buyer's Right to Cancel.

§ 1689.7. Home solicitation contract or offer for purchase of personal emergency response unit; required statements relating to cancellation

(a)(1) Except for contracts written pursuant to Sections 7151.2 and 7159.10 of the Business and Professions Code, in a home solicitation contract or offer, the buyer's agreement or offer to purchase shall be written in the same language, e.g., Spanish, as principally used in the oral sales presentation, shall be dated, shall be signed by the buyer, and except as provided in paragraph (2), shall contain in immediate proximity to the space reserved for his or her signature, a conspicuous statement in a size equal to at least 10–point boldface type, as follows: "You, the buyer, may cancel this transaction at any time prior to midnight of the third business day after the date of this transaction. See the attached notice of cancellation form for an explanation of this right."

(2) The statement required pursuant to this subdivision for a home solicitation contract or offer for the purchase of a personal emergency response unit, as defined in Section 1689.6, that is not

installed with and as part of a home security alarm system subject to the Alarm Company Act (Chapter 11.6 (commencing with Section 7590) of Division 3 of the Business and Professions Code) that has two or more stationary protective devices used to enunciate an intrusion or fire and is installed by an alarm company operator operating under a current license issued pursuant to the Alarm Company Act, is as follows: "You, the buyer, may cancel this transaction at any time prior to midnight of the seventh business day after the date of this transaction. See the attached notice of cancellation form for an explanation of this right."

(3) Except for contracts written pursuant to Sections 7151.2 and 7159.10 of the Business and Professions Code, the statement required pursuant to this subdivision for the repair or restoration of residential premises damaged by a disaster pursuant to subdivision (c) of Section 1689.6 is as follows: "You, the buyer, may cancel this transaction at any time prior to midnight of the seventh business day after the date of this transaction. See the attached notice of cancellation form for an explanation of this right."

(4) A home solicitation contract written pursuant to Section 7151.2 of the Business and Professions Code shall be written in the same language, e.g., Spanish, as principally used in the oral sales presentation. The contract, or an attachment to the contract that is subject to Section 7159 of the Business and Professions Code shall include in immediate proximity to the space reserved for his or her signature, the following statement in a size equal to at least 12–point boldface type, which shall be dated and signed by the buyer:

"Three–Day Right to Cancel

You, the buyer, have the right to cancel this contract within three business days. You may cancel by e-mailing, mailing, faxing, or delivering a written notice to the contractor at the contractor's place of business by midnight of the third business day after you received a signed and dated copy of the contract that includes this notice. Include your name, your address, and the date you received the signed copy of the contract and this notice.

If you cancel, the contractor must return to you anything you paid within 10 days of receiving the notice of cancellation. For your part, you must make available to the contractor at your residence, in substantially as good condition as you received it, any goods delivered to you under this contract or sale. Or, you may, if you wish, comply with the contractor's instructions on how to return the goods at the contractor's expense and risk. If you do make the goods available to the contractor and the contractor does not pick them up within 20 days of the date of your notice of cancellation, you may keep them without any further obligation. If you fail to make the goods available to the contractor, or if you agree to return the goods to the contractor and fail to do so, then you remain liable for performance of all obligations under the contract."

(b) The agreement or offer to purchase shall contain on the first page, in a type size no smaller than that generally used in the body of the document, the following: (1) the name and address of the seller to which the notice is to be mailed, and (2) the date the buyer signed the agreement or offer to purchase.

(c) Except for contracts written pursuant to Sections 7151.2 and 7159.10 of the Business and Professions Code, or except as provided in subdivision (d), the agreement or offer to purchase shall be accompanied by a completed form in duplicate, captioned "Notice of Cancellation" which shall be attached to the agreement or offer to purchase and be easily detachable, and which shall contain in type of at least 10–point the following statement written in the same language, e.g., Spanish, as used in the contract:

"Notice of Cancellation"
/enter date of transaction/

———————————————
(Date)

"You may cancel this transaction, without any penalty or obligation, within three business days from the above date.

If you cancel, any property traded in, any payments made by you under the contract or sale, and any negotiable instrument executed by you will be returned within 10 days following receipt by the seller of your cancellation notice, and any security interest arising out of the transaction will be canceled.

If you cancel, you must make available to the seller at your residence, in substantially as good condition as when received, any goods delivered to you under this contract or sale, or you may, if you wish, comply with the instructions of the seller regarding the return shipment of the goods at the seller's expense and risk.

If you do make the goods available to the seller and the seller does not pick them up within 20 days of the date of your notice of cancellation, you may retain or dispose of the goods without any further obligation. If you fail to make the goods available to the seller, or if you agree to return the goods to the seller and fail to do so, then you remain liable for performance of all obligations under the contract."

To cancel this transaction, mail or deliver a signed and dated copy of this cancellation notice, or any other written notice, or send a telegram
to ——————————————————,
/name of seller/

at ——————————————————
/address of seller's place of business/

not later than midnight of ———————————.
(Date)

I hereby cancel this transaction. ——————————
(Date)

———————————————
(Buyer's signature)

(d) Any agreement or offer to purchase a personal emergency response unit, as defined in Section 1689.6, which is not installed with and as part of a home security alarm system subject to the Alarm Company Act which has two or more stationary protective devices used to enunciate an intrusion or fire and is installed by an alarm company operator operating under a current license issued pursuant to the Alarm Company Act, shall be subject to the requirements of subdivision (c), and shall be accompanied by the "Notice of Cancellation" required by subdivision (c), except that the first paragraph of that notice shall be deleted and replaced with the following paragraph:

You may cancel this transaction, without any penalty or obligation, within seven business days from the above date.

(e) A home solicitation contract written pursuant to Section 7151.2 of the Business and Professions Code for the repair or restoration of residential premises damaged by a disaster that is subject to subdivision (c) of Section 1689.6, shall be written in the same language, e.g., Spanish, as principally used in the oral sales presentation. The contract, or an attachment to the contract that is subject to Section 7159 of the Business and Professions Code shall include, in immediate proximity to the space reserved for his or her signature, the following statement in a size equal to at least 12–point boldface type, which shall be signed and dated by the buyer:

"Seven–Day Right to Cancel

You, the buyer, have the right to cancel this contract within seven business days. You may cancel by e-mailing, mailing, faxing, or delivering a written notice to the contractor at the contractor's place of business by midnight of the seventh business day after you received a signed and dated copy of the contract that includes this notice. Include your name, your address, and the date you received the signed copy of the contract and this notice.

If you cancel, the contractor must return to you anything you paid within 10 days of receiving the notice of cancellation. For your part, you must make available to the contractor at your residence, in substantially as good condition as you received it, any goods delivered to you under this contract or sale. Or, you may, if you wish, comply with the contractor's instructions on how to return the goods at the contractor's expense and risk. If you do make the goods available to the contractor and the contractor does not pick them up within 20 days of the date of your notice of cancellation, you may keep them without any further obligation. If you fail to make the goods available to the contractor, or if you agree to return the goods to the contractor and fail to do so, then you remain liable for performance of all obligations under the contract."

(f) The seller shall provide the buyer with a copy of the contract or offer to purchase and the attached notice of cancellation, and shall inform the buyer orally of his or her right to cancel and the requirement that cancellation be in writing, at the time the home solicitation contract or offer is executed.

(g) Until the seller has complied with this section the buyer may cancel the home solicitation contract or offer.

(h) "Contract or sale" as used in subdivision (c) means "home solicitation contract or offer" as defined by Section 1689.5. *(Added by Stats.1971, c. 375, p. 741, § 3. Amended by Stats.1973, c. 554, p. 1078, § 3; Stats.1974, c. 175, p. 348, § 1, eff. April 17, 1974; Stats.1991, c. 394 (A.B.585), § 2; Stats.1992, c. 145 (A.B.2378), § 2; Stats.1993, c. 589 (A.B.2211), § 22; Stats.1993–94, 1st Ex.Sess., c. 51 (A.B.57), § 3; Stats.2004, c. 566 (S.B.30), § 17, operative July 1, 2005; Stats.2005, c. 48 (S.B.1113), § 27, eff. July 1, 2005, operative Jan. 1, 2006; Stats.2005, c. 385 (A.B.316), § 12.)*

Operative Effect

Stats.2005, c. 48 (S.B.1113), was enacted and immediately effective on July 18, 2005. Section 26 of that act explicitly amended § 1689.7 as amended by § 3 of Stats.1993–94, c. 51. Section 27 of c. 48 explicitly amended § 1689.7 as amended by § 17 of Stats.2004, c. 566 (S.B.30). Chapter 566 became operative on July 1, 2005, by terms of § 21 of that act. The § 26 text, repealed by its terms on Jan. 1, 2006, undid the changes made by c. 566. The § 27 text, operative by its terms on Jan. 1, 2006, reapplied those changes. Section 31 of c. 48 repealed Stats.2004, c. 566, § 21. The general effective date for 2004 regular session laws is Jan. 1, 2005.

Research References

Miller and Starr California Real Estate § 27:54, Home Solicitation Contracts.
15 NO. 3 Miller & Starr, California Real Estate Newsalert 3, Construction Contracts.
16 NO. 4 Miller & Starr, California Real Estate Newsalert 4, Construction Contracts.

16 NO. 5 Miller & Starr, California Real Estate Newsalert 26, State Board of Equalization Issues Comprehensive Summary and Qs and As for Transfers of Base Year Values of Principal Residences.
1 Witkin Cal. Summ. 10th Contracts § 123, (S 123) in General.
4 Witkin, California Summary 10th Sales § 329, Buyer's Right to Cancel.

§ 1689.8. Liens on real property; home solicitation contracts; offers for home improvement goods or services; retail installment sales

(a) Every home solicitation contract or offer for home improvement goods or services which provides for a lien on real property is subject to the provisions of Chapter 1 (commencing with Section 1801) of Title 2 of Part 4 of Division 3.

(b) For purposes of this section, "home improvement goods or services" means goods and services, as defined in Section 1689.5, which are bought in connection with the improvement of real property. Such home improvement goods and services include, but are not limited to, burglar alarms, carpeting, texture coating, fencing, air conditioning or heating equipment, and termite extermination. Home improvement goods include goods which, at the time of sale or subsequently, are to be so affixed to real property as to become a part of real property whether or not severable therefrom. *(Added by Stats.1979, c. 1012, p. 3439, § 6.)*

Research References

4 Witkin, California Summary 10th Sales § 290, (S 290) Nature and Scope of Statute.

§ 1689.9. Goods affixed to realty; effect of subsequent sale or encumbrance of realty

Where the goods sold under any home solicitation contract are so affixed to real property as to become a part thereof, whether or not severable therefrom, the buyer shall not have the right to cancel as provided in Section 1689.6 or Section 1689.7 if, subsequent to his signing such contract, he has sold or encumbered such real property to a bona fide purchaser or encumbrancer who was not a party to such sale of goods or to any loan agreement in connection therewith. *(Added by Stats.1971, c. 375, p. 741, § 5.)*

Research References

Miller and Starr California Real Estate § 27:54, Home Solicitation Contracts.
4 Witkin, California Summary 10th Sales § 329, Buyer's Right to Cancel.

§ 1689.10. Tender by seller to buyer of payments or goods traded in; retention of and lien on goods delivered

(a) Except as provided in Sections 1689.6 to 1689.11, inclusive, within 10 days after a home solicitation contract or offer has been canceled, the seller must tender to the buyer any payments made by the buyer and any note or other evidence of indebtedness.

(b) If the downpayment includes goods traded in, the goods must be tendered in substantially as good condition as when received.

(c) Until the seller has complied with the obligations imposed by Sections 1689.7 to 1689.11, inclusive, the buyer may retain possession of goods delivered to him by the seller and has a lien on the goods for any recovery to which he is entitled. *(Added by Stats.1971, c. 375, p. 742, § 6. Amended by Stats.1973, c. 554, p. 1079, § 5.)*

Research References

Miller and Starr California Real Estate § 27:54, Home Solicitation Contracts.

18 NO. 2 Miller & Starr, California Real Estate Newsalert 1, The Marketable Record Title Act- Is Private Foreclosure Barred Ten Years After Maturity, or Not?

4 Witkin, California Summary 10th Sales § 329, Buyer's Right to Cancel.

§ 1689.11. Tender by buyer to seller of goods delivered by seller pursuant to contract or offer

(a) Except as provided in subdivision (c) of Section 1689.10, within 20 days after a home solicitation contract or offer has been canceled, the buyer, upon demand, must tender to the seller any goods delivered by the seller pursuant to the sale or offer, but he is not obligated to tender at any place other than his own address. If the seller fails to demand possession of goods within 20 days after cancellation, the goods become the property of the buyer without obligation to pay for them.

(b) The buyer has a duty to take reasonable care of the goods in his possession both prior to cancellation and during the 20-day period following. During the 20-day period after cancellation, except for the buyer's duty of care, the goods are at the seller's risk.

(c) If the seller has performed any services pursuant to a home solicitation contract or offer prior to its cancellation, the seller is entitled to no compensation. If the seller's services result in the alteration of property of the buyer, the seller shall restore the property to substantially as good condition as it was at the time the services were rendered. *(Added by Stats.1971, c. 375, p. 742, § 7. Amended by Stats.1973, c. 554, p. 1079, § 6.)*

Research References

Miller and Starr California Real Estate § 27:54, Home Solicitation Contracts.

4 Witkin, California Summary 10th Sales § 329, Buyer's Right to Cancel.

§ 1689.12. Waiver or confession of judgment of provisions; voidness

Any waiver or confession of judgment of the provisions of Sections 1689.5 to 1689.11, inclusive, shall be deemed contrary to public policy and shall be void and unenforceable. *(Added by Stats.1971, c. 375, p. 743, § 8. Amended by Stats.1973, c. 554, p. 1080, § 7.)*

Research References

Miller and Starr California Real Estate § 27:54, Home Solicitation Contracts.

4 Witkin, California Summary 10th Sales § 329, Buyer's Right to Cancel.

§ 1689.13. Conditions making §§ 1689.5, 1689.6, 1689.7, 1689.10, 1689.12 and 1689.14 not apply to a contract

Sections 1689.5, 1689.6, 1689.7, 1689.10, 1689.12, and 1689.14 do not apply to a contract that meets all of the following requirements:

(a) The contract is initiated by the buyer or his or her agent or insurance representative.

(b) The contract is executed in connection with making of emergency or immediately necessary repairs that are necessary for the immediate protection of persons or real or personal property.

(c) The buyer gives the seller a separate statement that is dated and signed that describes the situation that requires immediate remedy, and expressly acknowledges and waives the right to cancel the sale within three or seven business days, whichever applies.

(d) This section shall become operative on January 1, 2006. *(Added by Stats.2004, c. 566 (S.B.30), § 19, operative July 1, 2005. Amended by Stats.2005, c. 48 (S.B.1113), § 29, eff. July 18, 2005, operative Jan. 1, 2006.)*

Research References

Miller and Starr California Real Estate § 27:54, Home Solicitation Contracts.

15 NO. 4 Miller & Starr, California Real Estate Newsalert 4, Construction Contracts.

16 NO. 4 Miller & Starr, California Real Estate Newsalert 4, Construction Contracts.

16 NO. 5 Miller & Starr, California Real Estate Newsalert 26, State Board of Equalization Issues Comprehensive Summary and Qs and As for Transfers of Base Year Values of Principal Residences.

4 Witkin, California Summary 10th Sales § 329, Buyer's Right to Cancel.

§ 1689.14. Repairs or restoration of residential premises damaged by a disaster

(a) Any home solicitation contract or offer for the repair or restoration of residential premises signed by the buyer on or after the date on which a disaster causes damage to the residential premises, but not later than midnight of the seventh business day after this date, shall be void, unless the buyer or his or her agent or insurance representative solicited the contract or offer at the appropriate trade premises of the seller. Any contract covered by this subdivision shall not be void if solicited by the buyer or his or her agent or insurance representative regardless of where the contract is made. For purposes of this section, buyer solicitation includes a telephone call from the buyer to the appropriate trade premises of the seller whether or not the call is in response to a prior home solicitation.

(b) As used in this section and Section 1689.6, "disaster" means an earthquake, flood, fire, hurricane, riot, storm, tidal wave, or other similar sudden or catastrophic occurrence for which a state of emergency has been declared by the President of the United States or the Governor or for which a local emergency has been declared by the executive officer or governing body of any city, county, or city and county. *(Added by Stats.1993–94, 1st Ex.Sess., c. 51 (A.B.57), § 5. Amended by Stats.1995, c. 123 (A.B.1610), § 1, eff. July 18, 1995.)*

Research References

Miller and Starr California Real Estate § 27:57, Contracts for Repair Due to a Natural Disaster.

Miller and Starr California Real Estate § 25C:66, Regulation of Time-Shares; in General.

4 Witkin, California Summary 10th Sales § 329, Buyer's Right to Cancel.

§ 1689.15. Right of contractor to commence work on a service and repair project; necessary conditions; right of cancellation

Notwithstanding any other provision of law, a contractor who is duly licensed pursuant to Chapter 9 (commencing with Section 7000) of Division 3 of the Business and Professions Code may commence work on a service and repair project as soon as the buyer receives a signed and dated copy of a service and repair contract that meets all of the contract requirements specified in Section 7159.10 of the Business and Professions Code. The buyer retains any right of cancellation applicable to home solicitations under Sections 1689.5 to 1689.14, inclusive, until such time as the buyer receives a signed and dated copy of a service and repair contract that meets all of the contract requirements specified in Section 7159.10 of the Business and Professions Code and the licensee in fact commences that project, at which time any cancellation rights provided in Sections 1689.5 to 1689.14, inclusive, are extinguished by operation of law. *(Added by Stats.2004, c. 566 (S.B.30), § 20, operative July 1, 2005. Amended by Stats.2005, c. 48 (S.B.1113), § 30, eff. July 18, 2005, operative Jan. 1, 2006; Stats.2005, c. 385 (A.B.316), § 13.)*

Operative Effect

Stats.2005, c. 48 (S.B.1113), was enacted and immediately effective on July 18, 2005. Stats.2004, c. 566 (S.B.30), became operative on July 1, 2005, by terms of § 21 of that act. Section 31 of c. 48 repealed Stats.2004, c. 566, § 21. The general effective date for 2004 regular session laws is Jan. 1, 2005.

Research References

16 NO. 4 Miller & Starr, California Real Estate Newsalert 4, Construction Contracts.
16 NO. 5 Miller & Starr, California Real Estate Newsalert 26, State Board of Equalization Issues Comprehensive Summary and Qs and As for Transfers of Base Year Values of Principal Residences.

§ 1689.20. Seminar sales solicitation contracts or offers; cancellation rights and procedures

(a) In addition to any other right to revoke an offer, the buyer has the right to cancel a seminar sales solicitation contract or offer until midnight of the third "business day" after the day on which the buyer signs an agreement or offer to purchase which complies with Section 1689.21.

(b) Cancellation occurs when the buyer gives written notice of cancellation to the seller at the address specified in the agreement or offer.

(c) Notice of cancellation, if given by mail, is effective when deposited in the mail properly addressed with postage prepaid.

(d) Notice of cancellation given by the buyer need not take the particular form as provided with the contract or offer to purchase and, however expressed, is effective if it indicates the intention of the buyer not to be bound by the seminar sales solicitation contract or offer. *(Added by Stats.1989, c. 724, § 1.)*

Research References

Miller and Starr California Real Estate § 27:58, Seminar Sales Contracts.
Miller and Starr California Real Estate § 25C:66, Regulation of Time-Shares; in General.
4 Witkin, California Summary 10th Sales § 383, (S 383) Seminar Sales Solicitation Contracts.

§ 1689.21. Seminar sales contracts; notice of cancellation; language and contents; copy to buyer

(a) In a seminar sales solicitation contract or offer, the buyer's agreement or offer to purchase shall be written in the same language, e.g., Spanish, as principally used in the oral sales presentation, shall be dated, signed by the buyer, and shall contain in immediate proximity to the space reserved for his or her signature, a conspicuous statement in a size equal to at least 10-point bold type, as follows: "You, the buyer, may cancel this transaction at any time prior to midnight of the third business day after the date of this transaction. See the attached notice of cancellation form for an explanation of this right."

(b) The agreement or offer to purchase shall contain on the first page, in a type size no smaller than that generally used in the body of the document, each of the following:

(1) The name and address of the seller to which the notice is to be mailed.

(2) The date the buyer signed the agreement or offer to purchase.

(c) The agreement or offer to purchase shall be accompanied by a completed form in duplicate, captioned "Notice of Cancellation," which shall be attached to the agreement or offer to purchase and be easily detachable, and which shall contain in type of at least 10-point, the following statement written in the same language, e.g., Spanish, as used in the contract:

"Notice of Cancellation"

/enter date of transaction/

_____

      (Date)

You may cancel this transaction, without any penalty or obligation, within three business days from the above date.

If you cancel, any property traded in, any payments made by you under the contract or sale, and any negotiable instrument executed by you will be returned within 10 days following receipt by the seller of your cancellation notice, and any security interest arising out of the transaction will be canceled.

If you cancel, you must make available to the seller at your residence, in substantially as good condition as when received, any goods delivered to you under this contract or sale, or you may, if you wish, comply with the instructions of the seller regarding the return shipment of the goods at the seller's expense and risk.

If you do make the goods available to the seller and the seller does not pick them up within 20 days of the date of your notice of cancellation, you may retain or dispose of the goods without any further obligation. If you fail to make the goods available to the seller, or if you agree to return the goods to the seller and fail to do so, then you remain liable for performance of all obligations under the contract.

To cancel this transaction, mail or deliver a signed and dated copy of this cancellation notice, or any other written notice, or send a telegram to

_____ at _____
/name of seller/   /Address of sellers place of business/
not later than midnight of _____

                      (Date)

I hereby cancel this transaction _____

                      (Date)

_____

(Buyer's signature)

(d) The seller shall provide the buyer with a copy of the contract or offer to purchase and the attached notice of cancellation, and shall inform the buyer orally of his or her right to cancel at the time the seminar sales solicitation contract or offer is executed.

(e) Until the seller has complied with this section, the buyer may cancel the seminar sales solicitation contract or offer.

(f) "Contract or sale" as used in subdivision (c), means "seminar sales solicitation contract or offer" as defined by Section 1689.24. *(Added by Stats.1989, c. 724, § 2.)*

Research References

Miller and Starr California Real Estate § 27:58, Seminar Sales Contracts.
4 Witkin, California Summary 10th Sales § 383, (S 383) Seminar Sales Solicitation Contracts.

§ 1689.22. Seller's tender of payments or evidence of indebtedness upon cancellation; buyer's rights in goods delivered by seller

(a) Except as provided in Sections 1689.20 and 1689.21, within 10 days after a seminar sales solicitation contract or offer has been cancelled, the seller must tender to the buyer any payments made by the buyer and any note or other evidence of indebtedness.

(b) If the downpayment includes goods traded in, the goods must be tendered in substantially as good condition as when received.

(c) Until the seller has complied with the obligations imposed by Sections 1689.20 and 1689.21, the buyer may retain possession of goods delivered to him or her by the seller and has a lien on the goods for any recovery to which he or she is entitled. *(Added by Stats.1989, c. 724, § 3.)*

Research References

18 NO. 2 Miller & Starr, California Real Estate Newsalert 1, The Marketable Record Title Act- Is Private Foreclosure Barred Ten Years After Maturity, or Not?

4 Witkin, California Summary 10th Sales § 383, (S 383) Seminar Sales Solicitation Contracts.

§ 1689.23. Buyer's tender of goods upon cancellation; duty of care; compensation of seller for services

(a) Except as provided in subdivision (c) of Section 1689.22, within 20 days after a seminar sales solicitation contract or offer has been canceled, the buyer, upon demand, must tender to the seller any goods delivered by the seller pursuant to the sale or offer, but he or she is not obligated to tender at any place other than his or her own address. If the seller fails to demand possession of goods within 20 days after cancellation, the goods become the property of the buyer without obligation to pay for them.

(b) The buyer has a duty to take reasonable care of the goods in his or her possession, both prior to cancellation and during the 20-day period following. During the 20-day period after cancellation, except for the buyer's duty of care, the goods are at the seller's risk.

(c) If the seller has performed any services pursuant to a seminar sales solicitation contract or offer prior to its cancellation, the seller is entitled to no compensation. If the seller's services result in the alteration of property of the buyer, the seller shall restore the property to substantially as good condition as it was at the time the services were rendered. *(Added by Stats.1989, c. 724, § 4.)*

Research References

4 Witkin, California Summary 10th Sales § 383, (S 383) Seminar Sales Solicitation Contracts.

§ 1689.24. Definitions

As used in Sections 1689.20 to 1689.23, inclusive:

(a) "Seminar sales solicitation contract or offer" means any contract, whether single or multiple, or any offer which is subject to approval, for the sale, lease, or rental of goods or services or both, made using selling techniques in a seminar setting in an amount of twenty-five dollars ($25) or more, including any interest or service charges. "Seminar sales solicitation contract" does not include any contract under which the buyer has the right to rescind pursuant to Title 1, Chapter 2, Section 125 of the Federal Consumer Credit Protection Act (P.L. 90–321) [1] and the regulations promulgated pursuant thereto or any contract which contains a written and dated statement signed by the prospective buyer stating that the negotiation between the parties was initiated by the prospective buyer.

(b) "Seminar setting" means premises other than the residence of the buyer.

(c) "Goods" means tangible chattels bought for use primarily for personal, family, or household purposes, including certificates or coupons exchangeable for these goods, and including goods which, at the time of the sale or subsequently, are to be so affixed to real property as to become a part of the real property whether or not severable therefrom, but does not include any vehicle required to be registered under the Vehicle Code, nor any goods sold with a vehicle if sold under a contract governed by Section 2982, and does not include any mobilehome, as defined in Section 18008 of the Health and Safety Code, nor any goods sold with a mobilehome if either are sold under a contract subject to Section 18036.5 of the Health and Safety Code.

(d) "Services" means work, labor and services, including, but not limited to, services furnished in connection with the repair, alteration, or improvement of residential premises, or services furnished in connection with the sale or repair of goods as defined in Section 1802.1, and courses of instruction, regardless of the purpose for which they are taken, but does not include the services of attorneys, real estate brokers and salesmen, securities dealers or investment counselors, physicians, optometrists, or dentists, nor financial services offered by banks, savings institutions, credit unions, industrial loan companies, personal property brokers, consumer finance lenders, or commercial finance lenders, organized pursuant to state or federal law, which are not connected with the sale of goods or services, as defined herein, nor the sale of insurance which is not connected with the sale of goods or services as defined herein, nor services in connection with the sale or installation of mobilehomes or of goods sold with a mobilehome if either are sold or installed under a contract subject to Section 18036.5 of the Health and Safety Code, nor services for which the tariffs, rates, charges, costs, or expenses, including in each instance the time sale price, is required by law to be filed with and approved by the federal government or any official, department, division, commission, or agency of the United States or of the State of California.

(e) "Business day" means any calendar day except Sunday, or the following business holidays: New Year's Day, Washington's Birthday, Memorial Day, Independence Day, Labor Day, Columbus Day, Veterans' Day, Thanksgiving Day, and Christmas Day. *(Added by Stats.1989, c. 724, § 5.)*

[1] 15 U.S.C.A. § 1635.

Research References

Miller and Starr California Real Estate § 27:58, Seminar Sales Contracts.
Miller and Starr California Real Estate § 25C:66, Regulation of Time-Shares; in General.
4 Witkin, California Summary 10th Sales § 383, (S 383) Seminar Sales Solicitation Contracts.

§ 1690. Stipulations against right; effect

A stipulation that errors of description shall not avoid a contract, or shall be the subject of compensation, or both, does not take away the right of rescission for fraud, nor for mistake, where such mistake is in a matter essential to the inducement of the contract, and is not capable of exact and entire compensation. *(Enacted in 1872.)*

Research References

Rutter, Cal. Practice Guide: Real Prop. Transactions Ch. 11-G, G. Rescission.

§ 1691. Procedure

Subject to Section 1693, to effect a rescission a party to the contract must, promptly upon discovering the facts which entitle him to rescind if he is free from duress, menace, undue influence or disability and is aware of his right to rescind:

(a) Give notice of rescission to the party as to whom he rescinds; and

(b) Restore to the other party everything of value which he has received from him under the contract or offer to restore the same upon condition that the other party do likewise, unless the latter is unable or positively refuses to do so.

When notice of rescission has not otherwise been given or an offer to restore the benefits received under the contract has not otherwise been made, the service of a pleading in an action or proceeding that seeks relief based on rescission shall be deemed to be such notice or offer or both. *(Enacted in 1872. Amended by Stats.1961, c. 589, p. 1734, § 2.)*

Research References

Rutter, Cal. Practice Guide: Civ. Pro. Before Trial Ch. 1-C, C. Prelawsuit Notices, Claims and Demands.

Rutter, Cal. Practice Guide: Civil Trials & Evidence Ch. 2-C, C. Cases in Which Jury Trial May be Demanded.

California Practice Guide: Employment Litigation Ch. 8-B, B. California Fair Employment and Housing Act.

Rutter, Cal. Practice Guide: Insurance Litigation Ch. 1-F, F. Regulation of Insurance Companies.

Rutter, Cal. Practice Guide: Insurance Litigation Ch. 5-F, F. Rescission by Insurer.

Rutter, Cal. Practice Guide: Insurance Litigation Ch. 15-B, B. Actions by Insurers.

Rutter, Cal. Practice Guide: Real Prop. Transactions Ch. 11-G, G. Rescission.

Miller and Starr California Real Estate § 34:6, Requirement of Prompt Notice of Rescission.

Miller and Starr California Real Estate § 34:7, Waiver of the Right to Rescind.

Miller and Starr California Real Estate § 5:53, Termination of the Listing; Owner's Right to Revoke.

Miller and Starr California Real Estate § 10:142, Protection Against "Unconscionable Advantage" of the Property Owner in Foreclosure.

3 Witkin Cal. Proc. 5th Actions § 130, (S 130) Legal Action for Restitution.

3 Witkin Cal. Proc. 5th Actions § 206, (S 206) Notice of Rescission.

4 Witkin Cal. Proc. 5th Pleading § 542, (S 542) Elements of Cause of Action.

2 Witkin, California Summary 10th Insurance § 230, (S 230) Exercise of Right.

2 Witkin, California Summary 10th Insurance § 251, Traditional Tort Actions.

1 Witkin Cal. Summ. 10th Contracts § 930, Equitable Action Abolished.

1 Witkin Cal. Summ. 10th Contracts § 940, Notice of Rescission.

1 Witkin Cal. Summ. 10th Contracts § 941, Offer to Restore Consideration.

1 Witkin Cal. Summ. 10th Contracts § 942, (S 942) in General.

1 Witkin Cal. Summ. 10th Contracts § 944, Pleading as Notice or Offer.

1 Witkin Cal. Summ. 10th Contracts § 945, Delay in Notice or Offer.

5 Witkin, California Summary 10th Torts § 828, (S 828) Affirmance and Damages.

§ 1692. Relief based on rescission

When a contract has been rescinded in whole or in part, any party to the contract may seek relief based upon such rescission by (a) bringing an action to recover any money or thing owing to him by any other party to the contract as a consequence of such rescission or for any other relief to which he may be entitled under the circumstances or (b) asserting such rescission by way of defense or cross-complaint.

If in an action or proceeding a party seeks relief based upon rescission and the court determines that the contract has not been rescinded, the court may grant any party to the action any other relief to which he may be entitled under the circumstances.

A claim for damages is not inconsistent with a claim for relief based upon rescission. The aggrieved party shall be awarded complete relief, including restitution of benefits, if any, conferred by him as a result of the transaction and any consequential damages to which he is entitled; but such relief shall not include duplicate or inconsistent items of recovery.

If in an action or proceeding a party seeks relief based upon rescission, the court may require the party to whom such relief is granted to make any compensation to the other which justice may require and may otherwise in its judgment adjust the equities between the parties. *(Added by Stats.1961, c. 589, p. 1734, § 3. Amended by Stats.1971, c. 244, p. 373, § 1, operative July 1, 1972.)*

Law Revision Commission Comments

The amendment of Section 1692 merely deletes the reference to a "counterclaim." Counterclaims have been abolished; claims that formerly were asserted as counterclaims are now asserted as cross-complaints. See Code of Civil Procedure Section 428.80. [10 Cal.L.Rev.Comm.Reports 501 (1970)].

Research References

Rutter, Cal. Practice Guide: Insurance Litigation Ch. 5-F, F. Rescission by Insurer.

Rutter, Cal. Practice Guide: Real Prop. Transactions Ch. 11-A, A. Factors Affecting Choice of Remedies.

Rutter, Cal. Practice Guide: Real Prop. Transactions Ch. 11-G, G. Rescission.

Miller and Starr California Real Estate § 34:3, Election of Remedies.

Miller and Starr California Real Estate § 34:4, Grounds for Rescission.

Miller and Starr California Real Estate § 34:9, "Reimbursement" or "Consequential Damages".

Miller and Starr California Real Estate § 7:73, Losses Resulting from the Fraud of the Insured.

Miller and Starr California Real Estate § 32:15, Election of Remedies.

Miller and Starr California Real Estate § 34:39, Damages for Pain and Suffering.

17 NO. 1 Miller & Starr, California Real Estate Newsalert 15, Remedies.

20 NO. 5 Miller & Starr, California Real Estate Newsalert 16, Judicial Remedies.

3 Witkin Cal. Proc. 5th Actions § 182, (S 182) Distinction: Restitution and Damages.

3 Witkin Cal. Proc. 5th Actions § 183, Manifestation Without Suit.

7 Witkin Cal. Proc. 5th Judgment § 27, Restitution.

4 Witkin Cal. Proc. 5th Pleading § 541, (S 541) Nature of Action.

1 Witkin Cal. Summ. 10th Contracts § 317, (S 317) Effect of Undue Influence.

1 Witkin Cal. Summ. 10th Contracts § 854, Binding Election.

1 Witkin Cal. Summ. 10th Contracts § 936, (S 936) in General.

1 Witkin Cal. Summ. 10th Contracts § 938, Conditions of Rescission Relief.

1 Witkin Cal. Summ. 10th Contracts § 943, (S 943) Specific Restitution Without Prior Offer.

§ 1693. Effect upon relief of delay in notice of rescission or in restoration of benefits

When relief based upon rescission is claimed in an action or proceeding, such relief shall not be denied because of delay in giving notice of rescission unless such delay has been substantially prejudicial to the other party.

A party who has received benefits by reason of a contract that is subject to rescission and who in an action or proceeding seeks relief based upon rescission shall not be denied relief because of a delay in restoring or in tendering restoration of such benefits before judgment unless such delay has been substantially prejudicial to the other party; but the court may make a tender of restoration a condition of its judgment. *(Added by Stats.1961, c. 589, p. 1735, § 4.)*

Research References

Rutter, Cal. Practice Guide: Insurance Litigation Ch. 15-A, A. Actions Against Insurers.

Rutter, Cal. Practice Guide: Real Prop. Transactions Ch. 11-G, G. Rescission.

Miller and Starr California Real Estate § 34:7, Waiver of the Right to Rescind.

3 Witkin Cal. Proc. 5th Actions § 206, (S 206) Notice of Rescission.

2 Witkin, California Summary 10th Insurance § 251, Traditional Tort Actions.

1 Witkin Cal. Summ. 10th Contracts § 943, (S 943) Specific Restitution Without Prior Offer.

1 Witkin Cal. Summ. 10th Contracts § 945, Delay in Notice or Offer.

5 Witkin, California Summary 10th Torts § 828, (S 828) Affirmance and Damages.

CHAPTER 2.1. DATING SERVICE CONTRACTS

Section

§ 1694. Dating service contract; definition

As used in this chapter, a dating service contract is any contract with any organization that offers dating, matrimonial, or social referral services by any of the following means:

(a) An exchange of names, telephone numbers, addresses, and statistics.

(b) A photograph or video selection process.

(c) Personal introductions provided by the organization at its place of business.

(d) A social environment provided by the organization intended primarily as an alternative to other singles' bars or club-type environments. *(Added by Stats.1989, c. 138, § 1.)*

Research References

Rutter, Cal. Practice Guide: A.D.R. Ch. 5-D, D. Defenses to Enforcement.

4 Witkin, California Summary 10th Sales § 348, (S 348) Dating Service Contracts.

§ 1694.1. Cancellation; notice; refund

(a) In addition to any other right to revoke an offer, the buyer has the right to cancel a dating service contract or offer, until midnight of the third business day after the day on which the buyer signs an agreement or offer to purchase those services.

(b) Cancellation occurs when the buyer gives written notice of cancellation by mail, telegram, or delivery to the seller at the address specified in the agreement or offer.

(c) Notice of cancellation, if given by mail, is effective when deposited in the mail properly addressed with postage prepaid.

(d) Notice of cancellation given by the buyer need not take the particular form as provided in the contract or offer to purchase and, however expressed, is effective if it indicates the intention of the buyer not to be bound by the dating service contract.

(e) All moneys paid pursuant to any contract for dating services shall be refunded within 10 days of receipt of the notice of cancellation.

(f) The buyer may notify the dating service of his or her intent to cancel the contract within the three-day period specified in this section and stop the processing of a credit card voucher or check by telephone notification to the dating service. However, this does not negate the obligation of the buyer to cancel the contract by mail, telegram, or delivery as required pursuant to this section. *(Added by Stats.1989, c. 138, § 1. Amended by Stats.1993, c. 359 (A.B.1323), § 1.)*

Research References

4 Witkin, California Summary 10th Sales § 348, (S 348) Dating Service Contracts.

§ 1694.2. Contract form and content

(a) A dating service contract shall be in writing. A copy of the contract shall be provided to the buyer at the time he or she signs the contract.

(b) Every dating service contract shall contain on its face, and in close proximity to the space reserved for the signature of the buyer, a conspicuous statement in a size equal to at least 10-point boldface type, as follows:

"You, the buyer, may cancel this agreement, without any penalty or obligation, at any time prior to midnight of the original contract seller's third business day following the date of this contract, excluding Sundays and holidays. To cancel this agreement, mail or deliver a signed and dated notice, or send a telegram which states that you, the buyer, are canceling this agreement, or words of similar effect. This notice shall be sent to:

_____

(Name of the business that sold you the contract)
_____ .''

(Address of the business that sold you the contract)

(c) The dating service contract shall contain on the first page, in a type size no smaller than that generally used in the body of the document, the name and address of the dating service operator to which the notice of cancellation is to be mailed; and the date the buyer signed the contract.

(d) No dating service contract shall require payments or financing by the buyer over a period in excess of two years from the date the contract is entered into, nor shall the term of any such contract be measured by the life of the buyer. However, the services to be rendered to the buyer under the contract may extend over a period beginning within six months and ending within three years of the date the contract is entered into.

(e) If a dating service contract is not in compliance with this chapter, the buyer may, at any time, cancel the contract. *(Added by Stats.1989, c. 138, § 1. Amended by Stats.1993, c. 359 (A.B.1323), § 2.)*

Research References

4 Witkin, California Summary 10th Sales § 348, (S 348) Dating Service Contracts.

§ 1694.3. Death, disability, or relocation

Every dating service contract shall contain language providing that:

(a) If by reason of death or disability the buyer is unable to receive all services for which the buyer has contracted, the buyer and the buyer's estate may elect to be relieved of the obligation to make payments for services other than those received before death or the onset of disability, except as provided in paragraph (3).

(1) If the buyer has prepaid any amount for services, so much of the amount prepaid that is allocable to services that the buyer has not received shall be promptly refunded to the buyer or his or her representative.

(2) "Disability" means a condition which precludes the buyer from physically using the services specified in the contract during the term of disability and the condition is verified in writing by a physician designated and remunerated by the buyer. The written verification of the physician shall be presented to the seller.

(3) If the physician determines that the duration of the disability will be less than six months, the seller may extend the term of the contract for a period of six months at no additional charge to the buyer in lieu of cancellation.

(b) If the buyer relocates his or her primary residence further than 50 miles from the dating service office and is unable to transfer the contract to a comparable facility, the buyer may elect to be relieved of the obligation to make payment for services other than those received prior to that relocation, and if the buyer has prepaid any amount for dating services, so much of the amount prepaid that is allocable to services that the buyer has not received shall be promptly refunded to the buyer. A buyer who elects to be relieved of further obligation pursuant to this subdivision may be charged a predetermined fee not to exceed one hundred dollars ($100) or, if more than half the life of the contract has expired, a predetermined fee not to exceed fifty dollars ($50). *(Added by Stats.1989, c. 138, § 1.)*

Research References

4 Witkin, California Summary 10th Sales § 348, (S 348) Dating Service Contracts.

§ 1694.4. Noncompliance with chapter; fraud; civil action; installment contracts; refund; waiver

(a) Any contract for dating services which does not comply with this chapter is void and unenforceable.

(b) Any contract for dating services entered into under willful and fraudulent or misleading information or advertisements of the seller is void and unenforceable.

(c) Any buyer injured by a violation of this chapter may bring an action for the recovery of damages in a court of competent jurisdiction. Judgment may be entered for three times the amount at which the actual damages are assessed. Reasonable attorney fees may be awarded to the prevailing party.

(d) Notwithstanding the provisions of any contract to the contrary, whenever the contract price is payable in installments and the buyer is relieved from making further payments or entitled to a refund under this chapter, the buyer shall be entitled to receive a refund or refund credit of that portion of the cash price as is allocable to the services not actually received by the buyer. The refund of any finance charge shall be computed according to the "sum of the balance method," also known as the "Rule of 78."

(e) Any waiver by the buyer of this chapter is void and unenforceable. *(Added by Stats.1989, c. 138, § 1.)*

Research References

4 Witkin, California Summary 10th Sales § 348, (S 348) Dating Service Contracts.

CHAPTER 2.2.   WEIGHT LOSS CONTRACTS

Section
1694.5.   Weight loss contract; definition.
1694.6.   Cancellation; notice; refund.
1694.7.   Contract form and content.
1694.8.   Death, disability, or relocation.
1694.9.   Noncompliance with chapter; fraud; civil action; installment contracts; waiver.

§ 1694.5.   Weight loss contract; definition

(a) As used in this chapter, a weight loss contract is a contract with any weight loss program or center that offers any of the following:

(1) Instruction, counseling, supervision, or assistance in weight reduction, body shaping, diet, and eating habits, by persons who are not licensed health care professionals.

(2) Use of facilities of a weight loss center for any of the purposes specified in paragraph (1).

(3) Membership in any group, club, association, or organization formed for any of the purposes specified in paragraph (1).

(4) Prepackaged, or premeasured "diet foods" provided by the weight loss program or center.

(b) This chapter does not apply to any contract for health studio services as defined in Section 1812.81. *(Added by Stats.1989, c. 138, § 2.)*

Research References

4 Witkin, California Summary 10th Sales § 398, (S 398) Weight Loss Contracts.

§ 1694.6.   Cancellation; notice; refund

(a) In addition to any other right to revoke an offer, the buyer has the right to cancel a weight loss contract or offer until midnight of the third business day after the day on which the buyer signs an agreement or offer to purchase those services.

(b) Cancellation occurs when the buyer gives written notice of cancellation by mail, telegram, or delivery to the seller at the address specified in the agreement or offer.

(c) Notice of cancellation, if given by mail, is effective when deposited in the mail properly addressed with postage prepaid.

(d) Notice of cancellation given by the buyer need not take the particular form as provided in the contract or offer to purchase and, however expressed, is effective if it indicates the intention of the buyer not to be bound by the weight loss contract.

(e) All moneys paid pursuant to any weight loss contract shall be refunded within 10 days of receipt of the notice of cancellation.

(f) The buyer may notify the weight loss program of his or her intent to cancel the contract within the three-day period specified in this section and stop the processing of a credit card voucher or check by telephone notification to the weight loss program. However, this does not negate the obligation of the buyer to cancel the contract by mail, telegram, or delivery as required pursuant to this section. *(Added by Stats.1989, c. 138, § 2. Amended by Stats.1993, c. 359 (A.B.1323), § 3.)*

Research References

4 Witkin, California Summary 10th Sales § 398, (S 398) Weight Loss Contracts.

§ 1694.7.   Contract form and content

(a) A weight loss contract shall be in writing. A copy of the contract shall be provided to the buyer at the time he or she signs the contract.

(b) Every weight loss contract shall contain on its face, and in close proximity to the space reserved for the signature of the buyer, a conspicuous statement in a size equal to at least 10-point boldface type, as follows:

"You, the buyer, may cancel this agreement, without any penalty or obligation, at any time prior to midnight of the original contract seller's third business day following the date of this contract, excluding Sundays and holidays. To cancel this agreement, mail or deliver a signed and dated notice, or send a telegram which states that you, the buyer, are canceling this agreement, or words of similar effect. This notice shall be sent to:

_____
(Name of the business that sold you the contract)
_____."
(Address of the business that sold you the contract)

(c) The weight loss contract shall contain on the first page, in a type size no smaller than that generally used in the body of the document, the name and address of the weight loss program operator to which the notice of cancellation is to be mailed; and the date the buyer signed the contract.

(d) No weight loss contract shall require payments or financing by the buyer over a period in excess of two years from the date the contract is entered into, nor shall the term of any such contract be measured by the life of the buyer. The services to be rendered to the buyer under the contract shall not extend for more than three years after the date the contract is entered into.

(e) If a weight loss contract is not in compliance with this chapter, the buyer may, at any time, cancel the contract. *(Added by Stats.1989, c. 138, § 2. Amended by Stats.1993, c. 359 (A.B.1323), § 4.)*

Research References

4 Witkin, California Summary 10th Sales § 398, (S 398) Weight Loss Contracts.

§ 1694.8. Death, disability, or relocation

Every weight loss contract shall contain language providing that:

(a) If by reason of death or disability the buyer is unable to receive all services for which the buyer has contracted, the buyer and the buyer's estate may elect to be relieved of the obligation to make payments for services other than those received before death or the onset of disability, except as provided in paragraph (3).

(1) If the buyer has prepaid any amount for services, so much of the amount prepaid that is allocable to services that the buyer has not received shall be promptly refunded to the buyer or his or her representative.

(2) "Disability" means a condition which precludes the buyer from physically using the services specified in the contract during the term of disability and the condition is verified in writing by a physician designated and remunerated by the buyer. The written verification of the physician shall be presented to the seller.

(3) If the physician determines that the duration of the disability will be less than six months, the seller may extend the term of the contract for a period of six months at no additional charge to the buyer in lieu of cancellation.

(b) If the buyer relocates his or her primary residence further than 50 miles from the weight loss center and is unable to transfer the contract to a comparable facility, the buyer may elect to be relieved of the obligation to make payment for services other than those received prior to that relocation, and if the buyer has prepaid any amount for weight loss services, so much of the amount prepaid that is allocable to services that the buyer has not received shall be promptly refunded to the buyer. A buyer who elects to be relieved of further obligation pursuant to this subdivision may be charged a predetermined fee not to exceed one hundred dollars ($100) or, if more than half the life of the contract has expired, a predetermined fee not to exceed fifty dollars ($50). *(Added by Stats.1989, c. 138, § 2.)*

Research References

4 Witkin, California Summary 10th Sales § 398, (S 398) Weight Loss Contracts.

§ 1694.9. Noncompliance with chapter; fraud; civil action; installment contracts; waiver

(a) Any contract for weight loss services which does not comply with this chapter is void and unenforceable.

(b) Any contract for weight loss services entered into under willful and fraudulent or misleading information or advertisements of the seller is void and unenforceable.

(c) Any buyer injured by a violation of this chapter may bring an action for the recovery of damages in a court of competent jurisdiction. Judgment may be entered for three times the

amount at which the actual damages are assessed if the violation is willful. Reasonable attorney fees may be awarded to the prevailing party.

(d) Notwithstanding the provisions of any contract to the contrary, whenever the contract price is payable in installments and the buyer is relieved from making further payments or entitled to a refund under this chapter, the buyer shall be entitled to receive a refund or refund credit of that portion of the cash price as is allocable to the services not actually received by the buyer. The refund of any finance charge shall be computed according to the "sum of the balance method," also known as the "Rule of 78."

(e) Any waiver by the buyer of this chapter is void and unenforceable. *(Added by Stats.1989, c. 138, § 2.)*

Research References

4 Witkin, California Summary 10th Sales § 398, (S 398) Weight Loss Contracts.

CHAPTER 2.5. HOME EQUITY SALES CONTRACTS

§ 1695. Legislative findings and declarations

(a) The Legislature finds and declares that homeowners whose residences are in foreclosure have been subjected to fraud, deception, and unfair dealing by home equity purchasers. The recent rapid escalation of home values, particularly in the urban areas, has resulted in a significant increase in home equities which are usually the greatest financial asset held by the homeowners of this state. During the time period between the commencement of foreclosure proceedings and the scheduled foreclosure sale date, homeowners in financial distress, especially the poor, elderly, and financially unsophisticated, are vulnerable to the importunities of equity purchasers who induce homeowners to sell their homes for a small fraction of their fair market values through the use of schemes which often involve oral and written misrepresentations, deceit, intimidation, and other unreasonable commercial practices.

(b) The Legislature declares that it is the express policy of the state to preserve and guard the precious asset of home equity, and the social as well as the economic value of homeownership.

(c) The Legislature further finds that equity purchasers have a significant impact upon the economy and well-being of this state and its local communities, and therefore the provisions of this chapter are necessary to promote the public welfare.

(d) The intent and purposes of this chapter are the following:

(1) To provide each homeowner with information necessary to make an informed and intelligent decision regarding the sale of his or her home to an equity purchaser; to require that the sales agreement be expressed in writing; to safeguard the public against deceit and financial hardship; to insure, foster, and encourage fair dealing in the sale and purchase of homes in foreclosure; to prohibit representations that tend to mislead; to prohibit or restrict unfair contract terms; to afford homeowners a reasonable and meaningful opportunity to rescind sales to equity purchasers; and to preserve and protect home equities for the homeowners of this state.

(2) This chapter shall be liberally construed to effectuate this intent and to achieve these purposes. *(Added by Stats.1979, c. 1029, p. 3536, § 1.)*

Research References

Rutter, Cal. Practice Guide: Real Prop. Transactions Ch. 4-D, D. Selecting the Form of Written Agreement.
Rutter, Cal. Practice Guide: Real Prop. Transactions Ch. 4-E, E. Drafting the Purchase and Sale Agreement-Terms and Conditions.
Rutter, Cal. Practice Guide: Real Prop. Transactions Ch. 6-I, I. Real Property Foreclosures and Antideficiency Laws.
Miller and Starr California Real Estate § 3:42, Specific Disclosures Required by Statute.
Miller and Starr California Real Estate § 10:141, Sale or Refinance of Residential Real Property in Foreclosure--In General.
Miller and Starr California Real Estate § 10:142, Protection Against "Unconscionable Advantage" of the Property Owner in Foreclosure.
Miller and Starr California Real Estate § 10:143, Home Equity Sales Contracts Involving the Sale or Conveyance of Residential Property in Foreclosure.
20 NO. 1 Miller & Starr, California Real Estate Newsalert 8, Deeds of Trust.
21 NO. 5 Miller & Starr, California Real Estate Newsalert 10, Deeds of Trust.
9 Witkin, California Summary 10th Corporations § 9, Nature of Doctrine.
4 Witkin, California Summary 10th Security Transactions in Real Property § 222, (S 222) Nature and Purpose of Legislation.
4 Witkin, California Summary 10th Security Transactions in Real Property § 223, (S 223) Definitions.
4 Witkin, California Summary 10th Security Transactions in Real Property § 224, (S 224) Rights of Seller and Obligations of Purchaser.
4 Witkin, California Summary 10th Security Transactions in Real Property § 225, (S 225) Purchaser's Representative.

§ 1695.1. Definitions

The following definitions apply to this chapter:

(a) "Equity purchaser" means any person who acquires title to any residence in foreclosure, except a person who acquires such title as follows:

(1) For the purpose of using such property as a personal residence.

(2) By a deed in lieu of foreclosure of any voluntary lien or encumbrance of record.

(3) By a deed from a trustee acting under the power of sale contained in a deed of trust or mortgage at a foreclosure sale

conducted pursuant to Article 1 (commencing with Section 2920) of Chapter 2 of Title 14 of Part 4 of Division 3.

(4) At any sale of property authorized by statute.

(5) By order or judgment of any court.

(6) From a spouse, blood relative, or blood relative of a spouse.

(b) "Residence in foreclosure" and "residential real property in foreclosure" means residential real property consisting of one-to four-family dwelling units, one of which the owner occupies as his or her principal place of residence, and against which there is an outstanding notice of default, recorded pursuant to Article 1 (commencing with Section 2920) of Chapter 2 of Title 14 of Part 4 of Division 3.

(c) "Equity seller" means any seller of a residence in foreclosure.

(d) "Business day" means any calendar day except Sunday, or the following business holidays: New Year's Day, Washington's Birthday, Memorial Day, Independence Day, Labor Day, Columbus Day, Veterans' Day, Thanksgiving Day, and Christmas Day.

(e) "Contract" means any offer or any contract, agreement, or arrangement, or any term thereof, between an equity purchaser and equity seller incident to the sale of a residence in foreclosure.

(f) "Property owner" means the record title owner of the residential real property in foreclosure at the time the notice of default was recorded. *(Added by Stats.1979, c. 1029, p. 3536, § 1. Amended by Stats.1980, c. 423, p. 835, § 4, eff. July 11, 1980.)*

Research References

Rutter, Cal. Practice Guide: Real Prop. Transactions Ch. 4-D, D. Selecting the Form of Written Agreement.
Rutter, Cal. Practice Guide: Real Prop. Transactions Ch. 6-I, I. Real Property Foreclosures and Antideficiency Laws.
Miller and Starr California Real Estate § 10:142, Protection Against "Unconscionable Advantage" of the Property Owner in Foreclosure.
Miller and Starr California Real Estate § 10:143, Home Equity Sales Contracts Involving the Sale or Conveyance of Residential Property in Foreclosure.
Miller and Starr California Real Estate § 10:236, Policy Objectives; the "Standard" Transaction.
19 NO. 4 Miller & Starr, California Real Estate Newsalert 34, Deeds of Trust.
21 NO. 5 Miller & Starr, California Real Estate Newsalert 10, Deeds of Trust.
4 Witkin, California Summary 10th Security Transactions in Real Property § 223, (S 223) Definitions.

§ 1695.2. Written contract; size of type; language; signature and date

Every contract shall be written in letters of a size equal to 10-point bold type, in the same language principally used by the equity purchaser and equity seller to negotiate the sale of the residence in foreclosure and shall be fully completed and signed and dated by the equity seller and equity purchaser prior to the execution of any instrument of conveyance of the residence in foreclosure. *(Added by Stats.1979, c. 1029, p. 3536, § 1.)*

Research References

Rutter, Cal. Practice Guide: Real Prop. Transactions Ch. 4-D, D. Selecting the Form of Written Agreement.
Rutter, Cal. Practice Guide: Real Prop. Transactions Ch. 6-I, I. Real Property Foreclosures and Antideficiency Laws.
Miller and Starr California Real Estate § 10:143, Home Equity Sales Contracts Involving the Sale or Conveyance of Residential Property in Foreclosure.

4 Witkin, California Summary 10th Security Transactions in Real Property § 224, (S 224) Rights of Seller and Obligations of Purchaser.

§ 1695.3. Contents; survival of contract

Every contract shall contain the entire agreement of the parties and shall include the following terms:

(a) The name, business address, and the telephone number of the equity purchaser.

(b) The address of the residence in foreclosure.

(c) The total consideration to be given by the equity purchaser in connection with or incident to the sale.

(d) A complete description of the terms of payment or other consideration including, but not limited to, any services of any nature which the equity purchaser represents he will perform for the equity seller before or after the sale.

(e) The time at which possession is to be transferred to the equity purchaser.

(f) The terms of any rental agreement.

(g) A notice of cancellation as provided in subdivision (b) of Section 1695.5.

(h) The following notice in at least 14-point boldface type, if the contract is printed or in capital letters if the contract is typed, and completed with the name of the equity purchaser, immediately above the statement required by Section 1695.5(a):

"NOTICE REQUIRED BY CALIFORNIA LAW

Until your right to cancel this contract has ended,

_____
(Name)
or anyone working for_____
(Name)

CANNOT ask you to sign or have you sign any deed or any other document."

The contract required by this section shall survive delivery of any instrument of conveyance of the residence in foreclosure, and shall have no effect on persons other than the parties to the contract. *(Added by Stats.1979, c. 1029, p. 3536, § 1. Amended by Stats.1980, c. 423, p. 835, § 5, eff. July 11, 1980.)*

Research References

Rutter, Cal. Practice Guide: Real Prop. Transactions Ch. 4-D, D. Selecting the Form of Written Agreement.
Rutter, Cal. Practice Guide: Real Prop. Transactions Ch. 6-I, I. Real Property Foreclosures and Antideficiency Laws.
Miller and Starr California Real Estate § 10:143, Home Equity Sales Contracts Involving the Sale or Conveyance of Residential Property in Foreclosure.
Miller and Starr California Real Estate § 10:144, Remedies for Violation.
4 Witkin, California Summary 10th Security Transactions in Real Property § 224, (S 224) Rights of Seller and Obligations of Purchaser.

§ 1695.4. Right of cancellation; time and manner of exercise

(a) In addition to any other right of rescission, the equity seller has the right to cancel any contract with an equity purchaser until midnight of the fifth business day following the day on which the equity seller signs a contract that complies with this chapter or until 8 a.m. on the day scheduled for the sale of the property pursuant to a power of sale conferred in a deed of trust, whichever occurs first.

(b) Cancellation occurs when the equity seller personally delivers written notice of cancellation to the address specified in the contract or sends a telegram indicating cancellation to that address.

(c) A notice of cancellation given by the equity seller need not take the particular form as provided with the contract and,

however expressed, is effective if it indicates the intention of the equity seller not to be bound by the contract. *(Added by Stats.1979, c. 1029, p. 3536, § 1. Amended by Stats.1997, c. 50 (A.B.669), § 1.)*

Research References

Rutter, Cal. Practice Guide: Real Prop. Transactions Ch. 4-D, D. Selecting the Form of Written Agreement.
Rutter, Cal. Practice Guide: Real Prop. Transactions Ch. 6-I, I. Real Property Foreclosures and Antideficiency Laws.
Miller and Starr California Real Estate § 10:144, Remedies for Violation.
4 Witkin, California Summary 10th Security Transactions in Real Property § 224, (S 224) Rights of Seller and Obligations of Purchaser.

§ 1695.5. Right of cancellation; notice of right; form

(a) The contract shall contain in immediate proximity to the space reserved for the equity seller's signature a conspicuous statement in a size equal to at least 12–point bold type, if the contract is printed or in capital letters if the contract is typed, as follows:

"You may cancel this contract for the sale of your house without any penalty or obligation at any time before

_____
(Date and time of day)
See the attached notice of cancellation form for an explanation of this right."
The equity purchaser shall accurately enter the date and time of day on which the rescission right ends.

(b) The contract shall be accompanied by a completed form in duplicate, captioned "notice of cancellation" in a size equal to 12–point bold type, if the contract is printed or in capital letters if the contract is typed, followed by a space in which the equity purchaser shall enter the date on which the equity seller executes any contract. This form shall be attached to the contract, shall be easily detachable, and shall contain in type of at least 10–point, if the contract is printed or in capital letters if the contract is typed, the following statement written in the same language as used in the contract:

"NOTICE OF CANCELLATION

_____
(Enter date contract signed)

You may cancel this contract for the sale of your house, without any penalty or obligation, at any time before

_____
(Enter date and time of day)
To cancel this transaction, personally deliver a signed and dated copy of this cancellation notice, or send a telegram to _____
(Name of purchaser)
at _____
(Street address of purchaser's place of business)
NOT LATER THAN _____.
(Enter date and time of day)
I hereby cancel this transaction _____.
(Date)
_____ ,,
(Seller's signature)

(c) The equity purchaser shall provide the equity seller with a copy of the contract and the attached notice of cancellation.

(d) Until the equity purchaser has complied with this section, the equity seller may cancel the contract. *(Added by Stats.1979, c. 1029, p. 3536, § 1. Amended by Stats.1980, c. 423, p. 836, § 6, eff. July 11, 1980; Stats.1997, c. 50 (A.B.669), § 2.)*

Research References

Rutter, Cal. Practice Guide: Real Prop. Transactions Ch. 4-D, D. Selecting the Form of Written Agreement.

Rutter, Cal. Practice Guide: Real Prop. Transactions Ch. 6-I, I. Real Property Foreclosures and Antideficiency Laws.

Miller and Starr California Real Estate § 10:143, Home Equity Sales Contracts Involving the Sale or Conveyance of Residential Property in Foreclosure.

Miller and Starr California Real Estate § 10:144, Remedies for Violation.

20 NO. 1 Miller & Starr, California Real Estate Newsalert 8, Deeds of Trust.

4 Witkin, California Summary 10th Security Transactions in Real Property § 224, (S 224) Rights of Seller and Obligations of Purchaser.

§ 1695.6. Contract requirements; responsibility of equity purchaser; prohibited transactions; bona fide purchasers and encumbrancers; cancellation; return of original documents; untrue or misleading statements; encumbrances

(a) The contract as required by Sections 1695.2, 1695.3, and 1695.5, shall be provided and completed in conformity with those sections by the equity purchaser.

(b) Until the time within which the equity seller may cancel the transaction has fully elapsed, the equity purchaser shall not do any of the following:

(1) Accept from any equity seller an execution of, or induce any equity seller to execute, any instrument of conveyance of any interest in the residence in foreclosure.

(2) Record with the county recorder any document, including, but not limited to, any instrument of conveyance, signed by the equity seller.

(3) Transfer or encumber or purport to transfer or encumber any interest in the residence in foreclosure to any third party, provided no grant of any interest or encumbrance shall be defeated or affected as against a bona fide purchaser or encumbrancer for value and without notice of a violation of this chapter, and knowledge on the part of any such person or entity that the property was "residential real property in foreclosure" shall not constitute notice of a violation of this chapter. This section shall not be deemed to abrogate any duty of inquiry which exists as to rights or interests of persons in possession of the residential real property in foreclosure.

(4) Pay the equity seller any consideration.

(c) Within 10 days following receipt of a notice of cancellation given in accordance with Sections 1695.4 and 1695.5, the equity purchaser shall return without condition any original contract and any other documents signed by the equity seller.

(d) An equity purchaser shall make no untrue or misleading statements regarding the value of the residence in foreclosure, the amount of proceeds the equity seller will receive after a foreclosure sale, any contract term, the equity seller's rights or obligations incident to or arising out of the sale transaction, the nature of any document which the equity purchaser induces the equity seller to sign, or any other untrue or misleading statement concerning the sale of the residence in foreclosure to the equity purchaser.

(e) Whenever any equity purchaser purports to hold title as a result of any transaction in which the equity seller grants the residence in foreclosure by any instrument which purports to be an absolute conveyance and reserves or is given by the equity purchaser an option to repurchase such residence, the equity purchaser shall not cause any encumbrance or encumbrances to be placed on such property or grant any interest in such property to any other person without the written consent of the equity seller. Nothing in this subdivision shall preclude the application of paragraph (3) of subdivision (b). *(Added by Stats.1979, c. 1029, p. 3536, § 1. Amended by Stats.1980, c. 423, p. 837, § 7, eff. July 11, 1980; Stats.1997, c. 50 (A.B.669), § 3.)*

Research References

Rutter, Cal. Practice Guide: Real Prop. Transactions Ch. 4-D, D. Selecting the Form of Written Agreement.

Rutter, Cal. Practice Guide: Real Prop. Transactions Ch. 6-I, I. Real Property Foreclosures and Antideficiency Laws.

Miller and Starr California Real Estate § 10:143, Home Equity Sales Contracts Involving the Sale or Conveyance of Residential Property in Foreclosure.

Miller and Starr California Real Estate § 10:144, Remedies for Violation.

4 Witkin, California Summary 10th Security Transactions in Real Property § 224, (S 224) Rights of Seller and Obligations of Purchaser.

4 Witkin, California Summary 10th Security Transactions in Real Property § 226, (S 226) Penalties and Seller's Remedies.

§ 1695.7. Actions by equity seller for recovery of damages or other equitable relief against equity purchaser for violation of enumerated sections

An equity seller may bring an action for the recovery of damages or other equitable relief against an equity purchaser for a violation of any subdivision of Section 1695.6 or Section 1695.13. The equity seller shall recover actual damages plus reasonable attorneys' fees and costs. In addition, the court may award exemplary damages or equitable relief, or both, if the court deems such award proper, but in any event shall award exemplary damages in an amount not less than three times the equity seller's actual damages for any violation of paragraph (3) of subdivision (b) of Section 1695.6 or Section 1695.13; or the court may award a civil penalty of up to two thousand five hundred dollars ($2,500), but it may not award both exemplary damages and a civil penalty. Any action brought pursuant to this section shall be commenced within four years after the date of the alleged violation. *(Added by Stats.1979, c. 1029, p. 3536, § 1. Amended by Stats.1980, c. 423, p. 838, § 8, eff. July 11, 1980; Stats.2003, c. 74 (S.B.455), § 1.)*

Research References

Rutter, Cal. Practice Guide: Real Prop. Transactions Ch. 4-D, D. Selecting the Form of Written Agreement.

Rutter, Cal. Practice Guide: Real Prop. Transactions Ch. 6-I, I. Real Property Foreclosures and Antideficiency Laws.

Miller and Starr California Real Estate § 10:144, Remedies for Violation.

14 NO. 4 Miller & Starr, California Real Estate Newsalert 3, Deeds of Trust.

21 NO. 5 Miller & Starr, California Real Estate Newsalert 10, Deeds of Trust.

7 Witkin Cal. Proc. 5th Judgment § 230, (S 230) Actions Involving Real Property or Environmental Issues.

4 Witkin, California Summary 10th Security Transactions in Real Property § 226, (S 226) Penalties and Seller's Remedies.

§ 1695.8. Violations by equity purchaser; criminal penalties

Any equity purchaser who violates any subdivision of Section 1695.6 or who engages in any practice which would operate as a fraud or deceit upon an equity seller shall, upon conviction, be punished by a fine of not more than twenty-five thousand dollars ($25,000), by imprisonment in the county jail for not more than one year, or pursuant to subdivision (h) of Section 1170 of the Penal Code, or by both that fine and imprisonment for each violation. *(Added by Stats.1979, c. 1029, p. 3536, § 1. Amended by Stats.1985, c. 270, § 1; Stats.2003, c. 74 (S.B.455), § 2; Stats.2011, c. 15 (A.B.109), § 32, eff. April 4, 2011, operative Oct. 1, 2011.)*

Research References

Rutter, Cal. Practice Guide: Real Prop. Transactions Ch. 4-D, D. Selecting the Form of Written Agreement.

Rutter, Cal. Practice Guide: Real Prop. Transactions Ch. 6-I, I. Real Property Foreclosures and Antideficiency Laws.

Miller and Starr California Real Estate § 10:144, Remedies for Violation.

14 NO. 4 Miller & Starr, California Real Estate Newsalert 3, Deeds of Trust.

20 NO. 1 Miller & Starr, California Real Estate Newsalert 8, Deeds of Trust.
4 Witkin, California Summary 10th Security Transactions in Real Property § 226, (S 226) Penalties and Seller's Remedies.

§ 1695.9. Nonexclusivity of chapter

The provisions of this chapter are not exclusive and are in addition to any other requirements, rights, remedies, and penalties provided by law. *(Added by Stats.1979, c. 1029, p. 3536, § 1.)*

Research References

Rutter, Cal. Practice Guide: Real Prop. Transactions Ch. 4-D, D. Selecting the Form of Written Agreement.
Miller and Starr California Real Estate § 10:142, Protection Against "Unconscionable Advantage" of the Property Owner in Foreclosure.
4 Witkin, California Summary 10th Security Transactions in Real Property § 226, (S 226) Penalties and Seller's Remedies.

§ 1695.10. Waiver

Any waiver of the provisions of this chapter shall be void and unenforceable as contrary to the public policy. *(Added by Stats.1979, c. 1029, p. 3536, § 1.)*

Research References

Rutter, Cal. Practice Guide: Real Prop. Transactions Ch. 4-D, D. Selecting the Form of Written Agreement.
Miller and Starr California Real Estate § 10:143, Home Equity Sales Contracts Involving the Sale or Conveyance of Residential Property in Foreclosure.
4 Witkin, California Summary 10th Security Transactions in Real Property § 222, (S 222) Nature and Purpose of Legislation.

§ 1695.11. Severability

If any provision of this chapter, or if any application thereof to any person or circumstance is held unconstitutional, the remainder of this chapter and the application of its provisions to other persons and circumstances shall not be affected thereby. *(Added by Stats.1979, c. 1029, p. 3536, § 1.)*

§ 1695.12. Absolute conveyance with repurchase option deemed loan transaction; rights of bona fide purchasers or encumbrancers

In any transaction in which an equity seller purports to grant a residence in foreclosure to an equity purchaser by any instrument which appears to be an absolute conveyance and reserves to himself or herself or is given by the equity purchaser an option to repurchase, such transaction shall create a presumption affecting the burden of proof, which may be overcome by clear and convincing evidence to the contrary that the transaction is a loan transaction, and the purported absolute conveyance is a mortgage; however, such presumption shall not apply to a bona fide purchaser or encumbrancer for value without notice of a violation of this chapter, and knowledge on the part of any such person or entity that the property was "residential real property in foreclosure" shall not constitute notice of a violation of this chapter. This section shall not be deemed to abrogate any duty of inquiry which exists as to rights or interests of persons in possession of the residential real property in foreclosure. *(Added by Stats.1979, c. 1029, p. 3536, § 1. Amended by Stats.1980, c. 423, p. 838, § 9, eff. July 11, 1980.)*

Research References

Miller and Starr California Real Estate § 10:143, Home Equity Sales Contracts Involving the Sale or Conveyance of Residential Property in Foreclosure.

4 Witkin, California Summary 10th Security Transactions in Real Property § 224, (S 224) Rights of Seller and Obligations of Purchaser.

§ 1695.13. Prohibited acts

It is unlawful for any person to initiate, enter into, negotiate, or consummate any transaction involving residential real property in foreclosure, as defined in Section 1695.1, if such person, by the terms of such transaction, takes unconscionable advantage of the property owner in foreclosure. *(Added by Stats.1980, c. 423, p. 839, § 10, eff. July 11, 1980.)*

Research References

Miller and Starr California Real Estate § 4:13, Activities Not Requiring a Real Estate License.
Miller and Starr California Real Estate § 4:83, Residential Mortgage Lenders or Servicers; Licensing and Regulation by Department of Corporations.
Miller and Starr California Real Estate § 10:142, Protection Against "Unconscionable Advantage" of the Property Owner in Foreclosure.
Miller and Starr California Real Estate § 10:144, Remedies for Violation.
4 Witkin, California Summary 10th Security Transactions in Real Property § 224, (S 224) Rights of Seller and Obligations of Purchaser.
4 Witkin, California Summary 10th Security Transactions in Real Property § 226, (S 226) Penalties and Seller's Remedies.

§ 1695.14. Rescission

(a) In any transaction involving residential real property in foreclosure, as defined in Section 1695.1, which is in violation of Section 1695.13 is voidable and the transaction may be rescinded by the property owner within two years of the date of the recordation of the conveyance of the residential real property in foreclosure.

(b) Such rescission shall be effected by giving written notice as provided in Section 1691 to the equity purchaser and his successor in interest, if the successor is not a bona fide purchaser or encumbrancer for value as set forth in subdivision (c), and by recording such notice with the county recorder of the county in which the property is located, within two years of the date of the recordation of the conveyance to the equity purchaser. The notice of rescission shall contain the names of the property owner and the name of the equity purchaser in addition to any successor in interest holding record title to the real property and shall particularly describe such real property. The equity purchaser and his successor in interest if the successor is not a bona fide purchaser or encumbrancer for value as set forth in subdivision (c), shall have 20 days after the delivery of the notice in which to reconvey title to the property free and clear of encumbrances created subsequent to the rescinded transaction. Upon failure to reconvey title within such time, the rescinding party may bring an action to enforce the rescission and for cancellation of the deed.

(c) The provisions of this section shall not affect the interest of a bona fide purchaser or encumbrancer for value if such purchase or encumbrance occurred prior to the recordation of the notice of rescission pursuant to subdivision (b). Knowledge that the property was residential real property in foreclosure shall not impair the status of such persons or entities as bona fide purchasers or encumbrancers for value. This subdivision shall not be deemed to abrogate any duty of inquiry which exists as to rights or interests of persons in possession of the residential real property in foreclosure.

(d) In any action brought to enforce a rescission pursuant to this section, the prevailing party shall be entitled to costs and reasonable attorneys fees.

(e) The remedies provided by this section shall be in addition to any other remedies provided by law. *(Added by Stats.1980, c. 423, p. 839, § 11, eff. July 11, 1980.)*

Research References

Miller and Starr California Real Estate § 10:142, Protection Against "Unconscionable Advantage" of the Property Owner in Foreclosure.
4 Witkin, California Summary 10th Security Transactions in Real Property § 226, (S 226) Penalties and Seller's Remedies.

§ 1695.15. Liability of equity purchaser for statements or acts committed by representative

(a) An equity purchaser is liable for all damages resulting from any statement made or act committed by the equity purchaser's representative in any manner connected with the equity purchaser's acquisition of a residence in foreclosure, receipt of any consideration or property from or on behalf of the equity seller, or the performance of any act prohibited by this chapter.

(b) "Representative" for the purposes of this section means a person who in any manner solicits, induces, or causes any property owner to transfer title or solicits any member of the property owner's family or household to induce or cause any property owner to transfer title to the residence in foreclosure to the equity purchaser. *(Added by Stats.1990, c. 1537 (S.B.2641), § 1.)*

Research References

Rutter, Cal. Practice Guide: Real Prop. Transactions Ch. 4-D, D. Selecting the Form of Written Agreement.
Miller and Starr California Real Estate § 10:143, Home Equity Sales Contracts Involving the Sale or Conveyance of Residential Property in Foreclosure.
4 Witkin, California Summary 10th Security Transactions in Real Property § 225, (S 225) Purchaser's Representative.
4 Witkin, California Summary 10th Security Transactions in Real Property § 226, (S 226) Penalties and Seller's Remedies.

§ 1695.16. Limitation of liability under section 1695.15; voiding provision or contract; arbitration

(a) Any provision of a contract which attempts or purports to limit the liability of the equity purchaser under Section 1695.15 shall be void and shall at the option of the equity seller render the equity purchase contract void. The equity purchaser shall be liable to the equity seller for all damages proximately caused by that provision. Any provision in a contract which attempts or purports to require arbitration of any dispute arising under this chapter shall be void at the option of the equity seller only upon grounds as exist for the revocation of any contract.

(b) This section shall apply to any contract entered into on or after January 1, 1991. *(Added by Stats.1990, c. 1537 (S.B.2641), § 2.)*

Research References

Rutter, Cal. Practice Guide: Real Prop. Transactions Ch. 4-D, D. Selecting the Form of Written Agreement.
Miller and Starr California Real Estate § 10:143, Home Equity Sales Contracts Involving the Sale or Conveyance of Residential Property in Foreclosure.
4 Witkin, California Summary 10th Security Transactions in Real Property § 224, (S 224) Rights of Seller and Obligations of Purchaser.
4 Witkin, California Summary 10th Security Transactions in Real Property § 225, (S 225) Purchaser's Representative.

§ 1695.17. Representative of equity purchaser; statements to be provided to seller; remedies

(a) Any representative, as defined in subdivision (b) of Section 1695.15, deemed to be the agent or employee, or both the agent and the employee of the equity purchaser shall be required to provide both of the following:

(1) Written proof to the equity seller that the representative has a valid current California Real Estate Sales License and that the representative is bonded by an admitted surety insurer in an amount equal to twice the fair market value of the real property which is the subject of the contract.

(2) A statement in writing, under penalty of perjury, that the representative has a valid current California Real Estate Sales License, is bonded by an admitted surety insurer in an amount equal to at least twice the value of the real property which is the subject of the contract and has complied with paragraph (1). The written statement required by this paragraph shall be provided to all parties to the contract prior to the transfer of any interest in the real property which is the subject of the contract.

(b) The failure to comply with subdivision (a) shall at the option of the equity seller render the equity purchase contract void and the equity purchaser shall be liable to the equity seller for all damages proximately caused by the failure to comply. *(Added by Stats.1990, c. 1537 (S.B.2641), § 3.)*

Validity

This section was held unconstitutional as a violation of the void-for-vagueness doctrine of the due process clause in the decision of Schweitzer v. Westminster Investments (App. 4 Dist. 2007) 69 Cal.Rptr.3d 472, 157 Cal.App.4th 1195, review denied.

Research References

Rutter, Cal. Practice Guide: Real Prop. Transactions Ch. 4-D, D. Selecting the Form of Written Agreement.
Miller and Starr California Real Estate § 10:143, Home Equity Sales Contracts Involving the Sale or Conveyance of Residential Property in Foreclosure.
4 Witkin, California Summary 10th Security Transactions in Real Property § 225, (S 225) Purchaser's Representative.
4 Witkin, California Summary 10th Security Transactions in Real Property § 226, (S 226) Penalties and Seller's Remedies.

CHAPTER 3. MODIFICATION AND CANCELLATION

§ 1697. Oral contract

A contract not in writing may be modified in any respect by consent of the parties, in writing, without a new consideration, and is extinguished thereby to the extent of the modification. *(Enacted in 1872. Amended by Code Am.1873–74, c. 612, p. 242, § 192; Stats.1976, c. 109, p. 170, § 2.)*

Law Revision Commission Comments

Section 1697 is amended to substitute "modified" for "altered" and "modification" for "new alteration" to conform with the terminology used in new Section 1698. [13 Cal.L.Rev.Comm. Reports 301, 2129 (1975)].

Research References

Miller and Starr California Real Estate § 1:81, Written Authority Required; the Equal Dignities Rule.
Miller and Starr California Real Estate § 1:98, Modification of a Contract; Executed Oral Agreement.
1 Witkin Cal. Summ. 10th Contracts § 964, (S 964) in General.
1 Witkin Cal. Summ. 10th Contracts § 966, Purpose of Revision.

1 Witkin Cal. Summ. 10th Contracts § 967, Modification of Contract Not in Writing.

§ 1698. Written contract; oral agreement; rules of law

(a) A contract in writing may be modified by a contract in writing.

(b) A contract in writing may be modified by an oral agreement to the extent that the oral agreement is executed by the parties.

(c) Unless the contract otherwise expressly provides, a contract in writing may be modified by an oral agreement supported by new consideration. The statute of frauds (Section 1624) is required to be satisfied if the contract as modified is within its provisions.

(d) Nothing in this section precludes in an appropriate case the application of rules of law concerning estoppel, oral novation and substitution of a new agreement, rescission of a written contract by an oral agreement, waiver of a provision of a written contract, or oral independent collateral contracts. *(Added by Stats.1976, c. 109, p. 171, § 4.)*

Law Revision Commission Comments

Section 1698 states rules concerning modification of a written contract. Subdivisions (a) and (b) continue the substance of former Section 1698. Subdivision (c) is derived from subdivisions (2) and (3) of Commercial Code Section 2209. The rules provided by subdivisions (b) and (c) merely describe cases where proof of an oral modification is permitted; these rules do not, however, affect in any way the burden of the party claiming that there was an oral modification to produce sufficient evidence to persuade the trier of fact that the parties actually did make an oral modification of the contract.

Subdivision (c) retains the requirement of the rule in D. L. Godbey & Sons Construction Co. v. Deane, 39 Cal.2d 429, 246 P.2d 946 (1952), that the oral modification be supported by new consideration. Compare Com. Code § 2209(1) (new consideration not required). However, the requirement in Godbey that the party seeking enforcement of the oral modification must have executed his part of the agreement is not continued.

Subdivision (c) makes clear that the Statute of Frauds, Section 1624, must be satisfied where the contract as modified is within its provisions. However, the contract is not "within" the provisions of the Statute of Frauds where the contract as modified does not fall into a category described in Section 1624 or where a doctrine such as part performance takes the contract as modified out of the statute. See 1 B. Witkin, Summary of California Law, Contracts §§ 214–260, at 192–226 (8th ed. 1973).

The introductory clause of subdivision (c) recognizes that the parties may prevent enforcement of executory oral modifications by providing in the written contract that it may only be modified in writing. See Com. Code § 2209(2) for a comparable requirement. Such a provision would not apply to an oral modification valid under subdivision (b). Also, the principles described in subdivision (d) may be applied to permit oral modification although the written contract expressly provides that modifications must be in writing. See MacIsaac & Menke Co. v. Cardox Corp., 193 Cal.App.2d 661, 14 Cal.Rptr. 523 (1961); 1st Olympic Corp. v. Hawryluk, 185 Cal.App.2d 832, 8 Cal.Rptr. 728 (1960); Frank T. Hickey, Inc. v. Los Angeles Jewish Community Council, 128 Cal.App.2d 676, 276 P.2d 52 (1955).

Subdivision (d) makes clear that Section 1698 does not affect related principles of law. See Wade v. Markwell & Co., 118 Cal.App.2d 410, 420–421, 258 P.2d 497, 502–503 (1953) (estoppel); Pearsall v. Henry, 153 Cal. 314, 95 P. 159 (1908) (oral novation and substitution of a new agreement); Treadwell v. Nickel, 194 Cal. 243, 258–259, 228 P. 25, 32 (1924) (rescission of a written contract by an oral agreement); Bardeen v. Commander Oil Co., 40 Cal.App.2d 341, 104 P.2d 875 (1940) (waiver of a provision of a written contract); Lacy Mfg. Co. v. Gold Crown Mining Co., 52 Cal.App.2d 568, 577–578, 126 P.2d 644, 649–650 (1942) (oral independent collateral contract). [13 Cal.L.Rev.Comm. Reports 301, 2129 (1975)].

Research References

Rutter, Cal. Practice Guide: Civil Trials & Evidence Ch. 8E-G, G. Parol Evidence Rule.

California Practice Guide: Employment Litigation Ch. 4-B, B. Agreements Limiting At-Will Termination.

Rutter, Cal. Practice Guide: Family Law Ch. 17-B, B. Spousal Support.

Rutter, Cal. Practice Guide: Real Prop. Transactions Ch. 2-D, D. Broker Compensation.

Rutter, Cal. Practice Guide: Real Prop. Transactions Ch. 4-D, D. Selecting the Form of Written Agreement.

Miller and Starr California Real Estate § 5:6, Application of the Statute of Frauds--In General.

Miller and Starr California Real Estate § 1:51, Necessity for Consideration.

Miller and Starr California Real Estate § 1:52, Exception; Promissory Estoppel.

Miller and Starr California Real Estate § 1:60, Parol Evidence; Extrinsic Evidence Rules.

Miller and Starr California Real Estate § 1:65, Provisions Applicable to Real Estate Transactions.

Miller and Starr California Real Estate § 1:81, Written Authority Required; the Equal Dignities Rule.

Miller and Starr California Real Estate § 1:98, Modification of a Contract; Executed Oral Agreement.

Miller and Starr California Real Estate § 1:99, Modification of a Contract; Executed Oral Agreement--Consideration Required for a Modification of a Written Agreement.

Miller and Starr California Real Estate § 5:26, Definitions and Overview of Types of Listing Agreements--Construction of a Particular Listing.

Miller and Starr California Real Estate § 1:100, Modification of Written Agreement by Subsequent Oral Agreement.

Miller and Starr California Real Estate § 1:101, Modification of Written Agreement by Subsequent Oral Agreement--Modification by Executed Oral Agreement.

Miller and Starr California Real Estate § 1:102, Modification of Written Agreement by Subsequent Oral Agreement--Modification of a Written Agreement by Subsequent Executory Oral Agreement: Part Performance.

Miller and Starr California Real Estate § 1:104, Mutual Rescission--Unilateral Rescission; Types of Mutual Rescission.

Miller and Starr California Real Estate § 10:90, Extension and Renewal.

Miller and Starr California Real Estate § 19:55, Requirements for Modification of Lease Terms.

Miller and Starr California Real Estate § 19:61, Requirements for a Valid Assignment.

Miller and Starr California Real Estate § 27:51, Modification and Alteration of Construction Contracts.

Miller and Starr California Real Estate § 27:66, Changes in the Work--Exceptions to the Prior Written Consent Requirement.

Miller and Starr California Real Estate § 10:123, Nature of Foreclosure; Termination of Redemption.

Miller and Starr California Real Estate § 10:201, Postponement of the Sale.

19 NO. 3 Miller & Starr, California Real Estate Newsalert 11, Deeds of Trust.

22 NO. 2 Miller & Starr, California Real Estate Newsalert 1, Did Someone Say Estoppel?-Courts Show Greater Acceptance of Applying Equitable Principles to Enforce Oral Forbearance Agreements.

1 Witkin Cal. Summ. 10th Contracts § 343, California Codes.

1 Witkin Cal. Summ. 10th Contracts § 400, (S 400) Miscellaneous Provisions.

1 Witkin Cal. Summ. 10th Contracts § 965, (S 965) Former Law on Oral Modification.

1 Witkin Cal. Summ. 10th Contracts § 966, Purpose of Revision.

1 Witkin Cal. Summ. 10th Contracts § 968, Modification of Written Contract.

1 Witkin Cal. Summ. 10th Contracts § 969, Other Rules Unaffected.

4 Witkin, California Summary 10th Sales § 40, Modification and Waiver.

3 Witkin, California Summary 10th Agency and Employment § 234, Parol Evidence Rule and Express Terms Doctrine.

§ 1699. Written contract; extinction by destruction or cancellation

The destruction or cancellation of a written contract, or of the signature of the parties liable thereon, with intent to extinguish the obligation thereof, extinguishes it as to all the parties consenting to the act. *(Enacted in 1872.)*

Research References

Miller and Starr California Real Estate § 1:103, Mutual Rescission.
Miller and Starr California Real Estate § 34:112, Cancellation of Instruments: Nature of the Remedy.

§ 1700. Written contract; extinction by destruction, cancellation or material alteration by beneficiary

The intentional destruction, cancellation, or material alteration of a written contract, by a party entitled to any benefit under it, or with his consent, extinguishes all the executory obligations of the contract in his favor, against parties who do not consent to the act. *(Enacted in 1872.)*

Research References

Miller and Starr California Real Estate § 1:97, Alteration of a Written Contract.
Miller and Starr California Real Estate § 8:53, Altered Deed.
Miller and Starr California Real Estate § 11:72, Defects in the Record Title Enforceable Against a Bona Fide Purchaser--Alteration of Instrument Before Recording.
1 Witkin Cal. Summ. 10th Contracts § 970, Obligations Discharged.

§ 1701. Destruction or alteration of duplicate

Where a contract is executed in duplicate, an alteration or destruction of one copy, while the other exists, is not within the provisions of the last section. *(Enacted in 1872.)*

Research References

Miller and Starr California Real Estate § 1:97, Alteration of a Written Contract.

Part 3

OBLIGATIONS IMPOSED BY LAW

Section

1708.	Injuring person or property of another, or infringing upon any of his or her rights.
1708.5.	Sexual battery; damages; equitable relief.
1708.6.	Liability for tort of domestic violence.
1708.7.	Stalking; tort action; damages and equitable remedies.
1708.8.	Physical or constructive invasion of privacy; damages and equitable remedies; employee-employer relationships; defenses.
1709.	Deceit; damages.
1710.	Deceit defined.
1710.1.	Removal of manufacturer's distinguishing number or identification mark from mechanical or electrical devices or appliances; liability.
1710.2.	Occupant of property afflicted with or who died from AIDS; failure to disclose to transferee; no cause of action; state preemption of AIDS disclosure.
1711.	Deceit to defraud public or particular class.
1712.	Restoration of thing wrongfully acquired; exceptions.
1713.	Restoration of thing wrongfully acquired; demand.
1714.	Responsibility for willful acts and negligence; furnishing alcoholic beverages; legislative intent; liability of social hosts; liability of parents, guardians, or adults who furnish alcoholic beverages to minors.
1714.01.	Domestic partners; negligent infliction of emotional distress; damages.
1714.1.	Liability of parents and guardians for willful misconduct of minor.

Section

1714.2.	Cardiopulmonary resuscitation; emergency care; immunity from civil liability.
1714.21.	Defibrillators; CPR; immunity from civil liability.
1714.22.	Opioid antagonist; prescription and dispensing permitted by authorized licensed health care providers to persons at risk of opioid-related overdose or persons in position to assist person at risk; standing distribution orders; overdose prevention and treatment training; immunity from liability.
1714.23.	Administration of epinephrine auto-injector; liability for civil damages; requirements for immunity.
1714.25.	Donations by food facilities to nonprofit charitable organizations; immunity.
1714.26.	Vision screenings and eyeglasses provided by nonprofit charitable organizations and licensed optometrists, ophthalmologists, or trained volunteers working with such organizations; limitation of liability; exceptions.
1714.3.	Liability of parent or guardian for injury to person or property caused by discharge of firearm by minor under 18.
1714.4.	Knowingly assisting child support obligor escape, evade, or avoid paying court-ordered or court-approved child support; application to financial institutions.
1714.41.	Knowingly assisting a child support obligor to escape, evade, or avoid paying child support; included actions.
1714.43.	Retailers to disclose efforts to eradicate slavery and human trafficking from direct supply chain for tangible goods; definitions; posting on Internet Website; contents; injunctive relief for violation.
1714.45.	Products liability; consumer products known by consumers to be inherently unsafe.
1714.5.	Defense shelters or other necessary facility for emergency purposes.
1714.55.	Retail or wholesale telecommunications service provider of 9–1–1 service; liability for civil claim, damage, or loss; definitions.
1714.6.	Compliance with military orders or regulations under Emergency Services Act; suspension of civil and criminal liability.
1714.7.	Injury while getting on, riding on, or getting off, moving locomotive or railroad car without authority; exemption of owner or operator from liability; exception.
1714.8.	Health care providers; professional negligence or malpractice; exemption from liability; definition.
1714.9.	Responsibility for willful acts or want of ordinary care causing injury to peace officers, firefighters or emergency service personnel; circumstances; comparative fault; subrogation; exception.
1714.10.	Attorney client civil conspiracy; proof and court determination prior to pleading; defense; limitations; appeal.
1714.11.	Donation of fire protection apparatus or equipment; immunity from liability for damage or injury resulting from use; conditions.
1715.	Other obligations.
1716.	Solicitations for orders; notice or disclaimer; penalties.
1717.	Action on contract; award of attorney's fees and costs; prevailing party; deposit of amounts in insured, interest-bearing account; damages not based on contract.
1717.5.	Action on contract based on book account; award of attorney's fees for the prevailing party; effect of written agreement; scope of application.

§ 1708. Injuring person or property of another, or infringing upon any of his or her rights

Every person is bound, without contract, to abstain from injuring the person or property of another, or infringing upon any of his or her rights. *(Enacted in 1872. Amended by Stats.2002, c. 664 (A.B.3034), § 38.5.)*

Research References

Miller and Starr California Real Estate § 36:1, Applicable Theories of Liability.

Miller and Starr California Real Estate § 36:6, Liability to the Borrower for Negligent Disbursement of Loan Funds.

Miller and Starr California Real Estate § 29:32, Liability to Third Persons.

Miller and Starr California Real Estate § 29:53, Negligence, Fraud, and Fiduciary Liabilities.

5 Witkin, California Summary 10th Torts § 1, (S 1) Definitions and Distinctions.

5 Witkin, California Summary 10th Torts § 17, State Constitution.

5 Witkin, California Summary 10th Torts § 729, Abduction of Child.

3 Witkin, California Summary 10th Agency and Employment § 565, No Tort Damages for Illegal Strike.

§ 1708.5. Sexual battery; damages; equitable relief

(a) A person commits a sexual battery who does any of the following:

(1) Acts with the intent to cause a harmful or offensive contact with an intimate part of another, and a sexually offensive contact with that person directly or indirectly results.

(2) Acts with the intent to cause a harmful or offensive contact with another by use of his or her intimate part, and a sexually offensive contact with that person directly or indirectly results.

(3) Acts to cause an imminent apprehension of the conduct described in paragraph (1) or (2), and a sexually offensive contact with that person directly or indirectly results.

(b) A person who commits a sexual battery upon another is liable to that person for damages, including, but not limited to, general damages, special damages, and punitive damages.

(c) The court in an action pursuant to this section may award equitable relief, including, but not limited to, an injunction, costs, and any other relief the court deems proper.

(d) For the purposes of this section "intimate part" means the sexual organ, anus, groin, or buttocks of any person, or the breast of a female.

(e) The rights and remedies provided in this section are in addition to any other rights and remedies provided by law.

(f) For purposes of this section "offensive contact" means contact that offends a reasonable sense of personal dignity. *(Added by Stats.1990, c. 1531 (S.B.2336), § 1.)*

Research References

Rutter, Cal. Practice Guide: Civ. Pro. Before Trial Ch. 9(II)-A, A. Injunctions.

Rutter, Cal. Practice Guide: Personal Injury Ch. 3-C, C. Specific Items of Compensatory Damages.

Rutter, Cal. Practice Guide: Personal Injury Ch. 3-E, E. Punitive Damages.

11 Witkin, California Summary 10th Husband and Wife § 371, (S 371) Civil Remedies.

5 Witkin, California Summary 10th Torts § 382, Statutory Actions.

§ 1708.6. Liability for tort of domestic violence

(a) A person is liable for the tort of domestic violence if the plaintiff proves both of the following elements:

(1) The infliction of injury upon the plaintiff resulting from abuse, as defined in subdivision (a) of Section 13700 of the Penal Code.

(2) The abuse was committed by the defendant, a person having a relationship with the plaintiff as defined in subdivision (b) of Section 13700 of the Penal Code.

(b) A person who commits an act of domestic violence upon another is liable to that person for damages, including, but not limited to, general damages, special damages, and punitive damages pursuant to Section 3294.

(c) The court, in an action pursuant to this section, may grant to a prevailing plaintiff equitable relief, an injunction, costs, and any other relief that the court deems proper, including reasonable attorney's fees.

(d) The rights and remedies provided in this section are in addition to any other rights and remedies provided by law.

(e) The time for commencement of an action under this section is governed by Section 340.15 of the Code of Civil Procedure. *(Added by Stats.2002, c. 193 (A.B.1933), § 2.)*

Research References

Rutter, Cal. Practice Guide: Civ. Pro. Before Trial Ch. 9(II)-A, A. Injunctions.

11 Witkin, California Summary 10th Husband and Wife § 371, (S 371) Civil Remedies.

5 Witkin, California Summary 10th Torts § 467, Domestic Violence.

§ 1708.7. Stalking; tort action; damages and equitable remedies

(a) A person is liable for the tort of stalking when the plaintiff proves all of the following elements of the tort:

(1) The defendant engaged in a pattern of conduct the intent of which was to follow, alarm, or harass the plaintiff. In order to establish this element, the plaintiff shall be required to support his or her allegations with independent corroborating evidence.

(2) As a result of that pattern of conduct, the plaintiff reasonably feared for his or her safety, or the safety of an immediate family member. For purposes of this paragraph, "immediate family" means a spouse, parent, child, any person related by consanguinity or affinity within the second degree, or any person who regularly resides, or, within the six months preceding any portion of the pattern of conduct, regularly resided, in the plaintiff's household.

(3) One of the following:

(A) The defendant, as a part of the pattern of conduct specified in paragraph (1), made a credible threat with the intent to place the plaintiff in reasonable fear for his or her safety, or the safety of an immediate family member and, on at least one occasion, the plaintiff clearly and definitively demanded that the defendant cease and abate his or her pattern of conduct and the defendant persisted in his or her pattern of conduct.

(B) The defendant violated a restraining order, including, but not limited to, any order issued pursuant to Section 527.6 of the Code of Civil Procedure, prohibiting any act described in subdivision (a).

(b) For the purposes of this section:

(1) "Pattern of conduct" means conduct composed of a series of acts over a period of time, however short, evidencing a continuity of purpose. Constitutionally protected activity is not included within the meaning of "pattern of conduct."

(2) "Credible threat" means a verbal or written threat, including that communicated by means of an electronic communication device, or a threat implied by a pattern of conduct or a combination of verbal, written, or electronically communicated statements and conduct, made with the intent and apparent ability to carry out the threat so as to cause the person who is the target of the threat to reasonably fear for his or her safety or the safety of his or her immediate family.

(3) "Electronic communication device" includes, but is not limited to, telephones, cellular telephones, computers, video recorders, fax machines, or pagers. "Electronic communication" has the same meaning as the term defined in Subsection 12 of Section 2510 of Title 18 of the United States Code.

(4) "Harass" means a knowing and willful course of conduct directed at a specific person which seriously alarms, annoys, torments, or terrorizes the person, and which serves no legitimate purpose. The course of conduct must be such as would cause a reasonable person to suffer substantial emotional distress, and must actually cause substantial emotional distress to the person.

(c) A person who commits the tort of stalking upon another is liable to that person for damages, including, but not limited to, general damages, special damages, and punitive damages pursuant to Section 3294.

(d) In an action pursuant to this section, the court may grant equitable relief, including, but not limited to, an injunction.

(e) The rights and remedies provided in this section are cumulative and in addition to any other rights and remedies provided by law.

(f) This section shall not be construed to impair any constitutionally protected activity, including, but not limited to, speech, protest, and assembly. *(Added by Stats.1993, c. 582 (A.B.1548), § 1. Amended by Stats.1994, c. 509 (A.B.2676), § 1; Stats.1998, c. 825 (S.B.1796), § 2.)*

Research References

Rutter, Cal. Practice Guide: Civ. Pro. Before Trial Ch. 9(II)-A, A. Injunctions.

11 Witkin, California Summary 10th Husband and Wife § 371, (S 371) Civil Remedies.

5 Witkin, California Summary 10th Torts § 19, in General.

5 Witkin, California Summary 10th Torts § 382, Statutory Actions.

5 Witkin, California Summary 10th Torts § 662, (S 662) Stalking.

§ 1708.8. Physical or constructive invasion of privacy; damages and equitable remedies; employee-employer relationships; defenses

(a) A person is liable for physical invasion of privacy when the defendant knowingly enters onto the land of another person without permission or otherwise committed a trespass in order to physically invade the privacy of the plaintiff with the intent to capture any type of visual image, sound recording, or other physical impression of the plaintiff engaging in a personal or familial activity and the physical invasion occurs in a manner that is offensive to a reasonable person.

(b) A person is liable for constructive invasion of privacy when the defendant attempts to capture, in a manner that is offensive to a reasonable person, any type of visual image, sound recording, or other physical impression of the plaintiff engaging in a personal or familial activity under circumstances in which the plaintiff had a reasonable expectation of privacy, through the use of a visual or auditory enhancing device, regardless of whether there is a physical trespass, if this image, sound recording, or other physical impression could not have been achieved without a trespass unless the visual or auditory enhancing device was used.

(c) An assault or false imprisonment committed with the intent to capture any type of visual image, sound recording, or other physical impression of the plaintiff is subject to subdivisions (d), (e), and (h).

(d) A person who commits any act described in subdivision (a), (b), or (c) is liable for up to three times the amount of any general and special damages that are proximately caused by the violation of this section. This person may also be liable for punitive damages, subject to proof according to Section 3294. If the plaintiff proves that the invasion of privacy was committed for a commercial purpose, the defendant shall also be subject to disgorgement to the plaintiff of any proceeds or other consideration obtained as a result of the violation of this section. A person who comes within the description of this subdivision is also subject to a civil fine of not less than five thousand dollars ($5,000) and not more than fifty thousand dollars ($50,000).

(e) A person who directs, solicits, actually induces, or actually causes another person, regardless of whether there is an employer-employee relationship, to violate any provision of subdivision (a), (b), or (c) is liable for any general, special, and consequential damages resulting from each said violation. In addition, the person that directs, solicits, actually induces, or actually causes another person, regardless of whether there is an employer-employee relationship, to violate this section shall be liable for punitive damages to the extent that an employer would be subject to punitive damages pursuant to subdivision (b) of Section 3294. A person who comes within the description of this subdivision is also subject to a civil fine of not less than five thousand dollars ($5,000) and not more than fifty thousand dollars ($50,000).

(f)(1) The transmission, publication, broadcast, sale, offer for sale, or other use of any visual image, sound recording, or other physical impression that was taken or captured in violation of subdivision (a), (b), or (c) shall not constitute a violation of this section unless the person, in the first transaction following the taking or capture of the visual image, sound recording, or other physical impression, publicly transmitted, published, broadcast, sold or offered for sale, the visual image, sound recording, or other physical impression with actual knowledge that it was taken or captured in violation of subdivision (a), (b), or (c), and provide compensation, consideration, or remuneration, monetary or otherwise, for the rights to the unlawfully obtained visual image, sound recording, or other physical impression.

(2) For the purposes of paragraph (1), "actual knowledge" means actual awareness, understanding, and recognition, obtained prior to the time at which the person purchased or acquired the visual image, sound recording, or other physical impression, that the visual image, sound recording, or other physical impression was taken or captured in violation of subdivision (a), (b), or (c). The plaintiff shall establish actual knowledge by clear and convincing evidence.

(3) Any person that publicly transmits, publishes, broadcasts, sells or offers for sale, in any form, medium, format or work, a visual image, sound recording, or other physical impression that was previously publicly transmitted, published, broadcast, sold or offered for sale, by another person, is exempt from liability under this section.

(4) If a person's first public transmission, publication, broadcast, or sale or offer for sale, of a visual image, sound recording, or other physical impression that was taken or captured in violation of subdivision (a), (b), or (c), does not constitute a violation of this section, that person's subsequent public transmission, publication, broadcast, sale or offer for sale, in any form, medium, format or work, of the visual image, sound recording, or other physical impression, does not constitute a violation of this section.

(5) This section applies only to a visual image, sound recording, or other physical impression that is captured or taken in California in violation of subdivision (a), (b), or (c) after January 1, 2010, and shall not apply to any visual image, sound recording, or other physical impression taken or captured outside of California.

(6) Nothing in this subdivision shall be construed to impair or limit a special motion to strike pursuant to Section 425.16, 425.17, or 425.18 of the Code of Civil Procedure.

(7) This section shall not be construed to limit all other rights or remedies of the plaintiff in law or equity, including, but not limited to, the publication of private facts.

(g) This section shall not be construed to impair or limit any otherwise lawful activities of law enforcement personnel or employees of governmental agencies or other entities, either public or private who, in the course and scope of their employment, and supported by an articulable suspicion, attempt to capture any type of visual image, sound recording, or other physical impression of a person during an investigation, surveillance, or monitoring of any conduct to obtain evidence of suspected illegal activity or other misconduct, the suspected violation of any administrative rule or regulation, a suspected fraudulent conduct, or any activity involving a violation of law or business practices or conduct of public officials adversely affecting the public welfare, health or safety.

(h) In any action pursuant to this section, the court may grant equitable relief, including, but not limited to, an injunction and restraining order against further violations of subdivision (a), (b), or (c).

(i) The rights and remedies provided in this section are cumulative and in addition to any other rights and remedies provided by law.

(j) It is not a defense to a violation of this section that no image, recording, or physical impression was captured or sold.

(k) For the purposes of this section, "for a commercial purpose" means any act done with the expectation of a sale, financial gain, or other consideration. A visual image, sound recording, or other physical impression shall not be found to have been, or intended to have been captured for a commercial purpose unless it is intended to be, or was in fact, sold, published, or transmitted.

(*l*) For the purposes of this section, "personal and familial activity" includes, but is not limited to, intimate details of the plaintiff's personal life, interactions with the plaintiff's family or significant others, or other aspects of the plaintiff's private affairs or concerns. "Personal and familial activity" does not include illegal or otherwise criminal activity as delineated in subdivision (g). However, "personal and familial activity" shall include the activities of victims of crime in circumstances under which subdivision (a), (b), or (c) would apply.

(m)(1) A proceeding to recover the civil fines specified in subdivision (d) or (e) may be brought in any court of competent jurisdiction by a county counsel or city attorney.

(2) Fines collected pursuant to this subdivision shall be allocated, as follows:

(A) One-half shall be allocated to the prosecuting agency.

(B) One-half shall be deposited in the Arts and Entertainment Fund, which is hereby created in the State Treasury.

(3) Funds in the Arts and Entertainment Fund created pursuant to paragraph (2) may be expended by the California Arts Council, upon appropriation by the Legislature, to issue grants pursuant to the Dixon–Zenovich–Maddy California Arts Act of 1975 (Chapter 9 (commencing with Section 8750) of Division 1 of Title 2 of the Government Code).

(4) The rights and remedies provided in this subdivision are cumulative and in addition to any other rights and remedies provided by law.

(n) The provisions of this section are severable. If any provision of this section or its application is held invalid, that invalidity shall not affect other provisions or applications that can be given effect without the invalid provision or application. *(Added by Stats.1998, c. 1000 (S.B.262), § 1. Amended by Stats.2005, c. 424 (A.B.381), § 1; Stats.2009, c. 449 (A.B.524), § 2; Stats.2010, c. 685 (A.B.2479), § 1.)*

Research References

Rutter, Cal. Practice Guide: Civ. Pro. Before Trial Ch. 9(II)-A, A. Injunctions.
5 Witkin, California Summary 10th Torts § 663, (S 663) Capturing Impression of Personal or Familial Activity.

§ 1709. Deceit; damages

FRAUDULENT DECEIT. One who willfully deceives another with intent to induce him to alter his position to his injury or risk, is liable for any damage which he thereby suffers. *(Enacted in 1872.)*

Research References

California Practice Guide: Employment Litigation Ch. 5-A, A. Wrongful Discharge in Violation of Public Policy (Tameny Claims).
Rutter, Cal. Practice Guide: Insurance Litigation Ch. 11-C, C. Fraud.
Rutter, Cal. Practice Guide: Real Prop. Transactions Ch. 11-E, E. Damages for Fraud.
Rutter, Cal. Practice Guide: Prof. Responsibility Ch. 6-D, D. Professional Liability.
Miller and Starr California Real Estate § 3:33, Damages Recoverable by the Principal.
Miller and Starr California Real Estate § 1:124, Definitions; Burden of Proof.
Miller and Starr California Real Estate § 1:137, False Promise (Promissory Fraud).
Miller and Starr California Real Estate § 1:138, Nondisclosure; Duty to Disclose Material Facts; When There is a Duty to Disclose.
Miller and Starr California Real Estate § 1:146, Intent to Induce Reliance.
Miller and Starr California Real Estate § 1:147, Liability to Third Persons.
Miller and Starr California Real Estate § 10:15, Loans Obtained by Fraud.
Miller and Starr California Real Estate § 34:83, General Principles; Election of Remedies.
Miller and Starr California Real Estate § 34:85, Measure of Damages.
Miller and Starr California Real Estate § 34:88, Expenditures in Reliance on the Fraud.
16 NO. 4 Miller & Starr, California Real Estate Newsalert 37, Remedies.
5 Witkin, California Summary 10th Torts § 767, (S 767) Governing Statutes.
5 Witkin, California Summary 10th Torts § 772, (S 772) in General.
5 Witkin, California Summary 10th Torts § 790, (S 790) Representation of Sterility.

5 Witkin, California Summary 10th Torts § 802, in General.

5 Witkin, California Summary 10th Torts § 811, (S 811) Securities Cases.

5 Witkin, California Summary 10th Torts § 816, Pecuniary or Property Loss.

6 Witkin, California Summary 10th Torts § 1714, Elements of Damage.

6 Witkin, California Summary 10th Torts § 1717, (S 1717) Breach of Fiduciary Duty.

§ 1710. Deceit defined

DECEIT, WHAT. A deceit, within the meaning of the last section, is either:

1. The suggestion, as a fact, of that which is not true, by one who does not believe it to be true;

2. The assertion, as a fact, of that which is not true, by one who has no reasonable ground for believing it to be true;

3. The suppression of a fact, by one who is bound to disclose it, or who gives information of other facts which are likely to mislead for want of communication of that fact; or,

4. A promise, made without any intention of performing it. *(Enacted in 1872.)*

Research References

California Practice Guide: Employment Litigation Ch. 5-F, F. Fraud.

California Practice Guide: Employment Litigation Ch. 5-G, G. Negligent Misrepresentation.

Rutter, Cal. Practice Guide: Enforcing Judgments/Debts Form 3:O, Written Notice to Pay Nsf Check Where Drawer Stopped Payment.

Rutter, Cal. Practice Guide: Insurance Litigation Ch. 11-C, C. Fraud.

Rutter, Cal. Practice Guide: Insurance Litigation Ch. 11-D, D. Negligent Misrepresentation.

Rutter, Cal. Practice Guide: Personal Injury Ch. 3-C, C. Specific Items of Compensatory Damages.

Rutter, Cal. Practice Guide: Real Prop. Transactions Ch. 5-D, D. Common Law Environmental Hazards Liability.

Rutter, Cal. Practice Guide: Prof. Responsibility Ch. 2-A, A. Regulations Generally.

Rutter, Cal. Practice Guide: Prof. Responsibility Ch. 6-D, D. Professional Liability.

Miller and Starr California Real Estate § 3:30, Fraud or Misrepresentation (Constructive Fraud).

Miller and Starr California Real Estate § 3:39, Agent's Duty to Disclose; in General--Common Law Duty to Disclose Material Facts.

Miller and Starr California Real Estate § 1:124, Definitions; Burden of Proof.

Miller and Starr California Real Estate § 1:125, Intentional Misrepresentation.

Miller and Starr California Real Estate § 1:126, Negligent Misrepresentation (Negligent Fraud).

Miller and Starr California Real Estate § 1:128, Partial Disclosures; Correction of Prior Errors.

Miller and Starr California Real Estate § 1:136, Misrepresentation of Law as a Representation of Fact.

Miller and Starr California Real Estate § 1:137, False Promise (Promissory Fraud).

Miller and Starr California Real Estate § 1:138, Nondisclosure; Duty to Disclose Material Facts; When There is a Duty to Disclose.

Miller and Starr California Real Estate § 1:142, Duty of Seller of Real Property to Disclose--Disclosure Duty on Sale of Nonresidential Property.

Miller and Starr California Real Estate § 1:146, Intent to Induce Reliance.

Miller and Starr California Real Estate § 1:147, Liability to Third Persons.

Miller and Starr California Real Estate § 29:32, Liability to Third Persons.

Miller and Starr California Real Estate § 29:37, Liability to Third Persons.

Miller and Starr California Real Estate § 29:42, Liability to Third Persons.

Miller and Starr California Real Estate § 34:12, Fraud as Basis for Reformation.

19 NO. 6 Miller & Starr, California Real Estate Newsalert 1, Enforceable Resale Restrictions: Keeping the Doors Open for Long-Term Affordable Housing.

9 Witkin Cal. Proc. 5th Appeal § 894, (S 894) Extraordinary Circumstances Justifying Rejection of Stipulation.

5 Witkin Cal. Proc. 5th Pleading § 727, Distinction: Negligent Misrepresentation.

5 Witkin, California Summary 10th Torts § 767, (S 767) Governing Statutes.

5 Witkin, California Summary 10th Torts § 773, General Requirement that Misrepresentation Must be of Fact.

5 Witkin, California Summary 10th Torts § 781, (S 781) Theory of Misrepresentation of Intention.

5 Witkin, California Summary 10th Torts § 790, (S 790) Representation of Sterility.

5 Witkin, California Summary 10th Torts § 793, (S 793) in General.

5 Witkin, California Summary 10th Torts § 794, in General.

5 Witkin, California Summary 10th Torts § 799, (S 799) Partial Suppression of Facts.

5 Witkin, California Summary 10th Torts § 801, Reckless Misrepresentation.

5 Witkin, California Summary 10th Torts § 811, (S 811) Securities Cases.

5 Witkin, California Summary 10th Torts § 819, (S 819) Tort as Form of Deceit.

5 Witkin, California Summary 10th Torts § 820, (S 820) Scope of Tort.

5 Witkin, California Summary 10th Torts § 821, in General.

6 Witkin, California Summary 10th Torts § 1031, Financial Injury.

§ 1710.1. Removal of manufacturer's distinguishing number or identification mark from mechanical or electrical devices or appliances; liability

Any person who, with intent to defraud, sells or disposes of a radio, piano, phonograph, sewing machine, washing machine, typewriter, adding machine, comptometer, bicycle, firearm, safe, vacuum cleaner, dictaphone, watch, watch movement, watchcase, or any other mechanical or electrical device, appliance, contrivance, material, piece of apparatus or equipment, from which the manufacturer's nameplate, serial number or any other distinguishing number or identification mark has been removed, defaced, covered, altered or destroyed, is civilly liable to the manufacturer in the sum of five hundred dollars ($500) per transaction and civilly liable to the purchaser for treble the actual damages sustained by the purchaser.

This section does not apply to those cases or instances where any of the changes or alterations enumerated in this section have been customarily made or done as an established practice in the ordinary and regular conduct of business by the original manufacturer or his duly appointed direct representative or under specific authorization from the original manufacturer. *(Added by Stats.1971, c. 1713, p. 3654, § 1.)*

Research References

4 Witkin, California Summary 10th Sales § 369, (S 369) Manufacturer's Identification Mark.

6 Witkin, California Summary 10th Torts § 1570, Treble Damages.

§ 1710.2. Occupant of property afflicted with or who died from AIDS; failure to disclose to transferee; no cause of action; state preemption of AIDS disclosure

(a) No cause of action arises against an owner of real property or his or her agent, or any agent of a transferee of real property, for the failure to disclose to the transferee the occurrence of an occupant's death upon the real property or the manner of death where the death has occurred more than three years prior to the date the transferee offers to purchase, lease, or rent the real property, or that an occupant of that property was afflicted with, or died from, Human T-Lymphotropic Virus Type III/Lymphadenopathy-Associated Virus. As used in this section, "agent" includes any person licensed pursuant to Part 1 (commencing with Section 10000) of Division 4 of the Business and Professions

Code. As used in this section, "transferee" includes a purchaser, lessee, or renter of real property.

(b) It is the intention of the Legislature to occupy the field of regulation of disclosure related to deaths occurring upon real property and of AIDS in situations affecting the transfer of real property or any estate or interest in real property.

(c) This section shall not be construed to alter the law relating to disclosure pertaining to any other physical or mental condition or disease, and this section shall not relieve any owner or agent of any obligation to disclose the physical condition of the premises.

(d) Nothing in this section shall be construed to immunize an owner or his or her agent from making an intentional misrepresentation in response to a direct inquiry from a transferee or a prospective transferee of real property, concerning deaths on the real property. *(Added by Stats.1986, c. 498, § 2. Amended by Stats.1987, c. 494, § 1.)*

Research References

Rutter, Cal. Practice Guide: Real Prop. Transactions Ch. 2-C, C. Broker's Relationship and Obligations to Principal and Third Parties.
Miller and Starr California Real Estate § 3:42, Specific Disclosures Required by Statute.
Miller and Starr California Real Estate § 1:144, Duty of Seller of Real Property to Disclose--Statutory Duty of Disclosure.
Miller and Starr California Real Estate § 20:25, Federal Fair Housing Act--Application of the Act.
Miller and Starr California Real Estate § 19:123, Landlord's Duty to Disclose Defects to a Tenant.
5 Witkin, California Summary 10th Torts § 797, Real Estate Transactions.

§ 1711. Deceit to defraud public or particular class

DECEIT UPON THE PUBLIC, ETC. One who practices a deceit with intent to defraud the public, or a particular class of persons, is deemed to have intended to defraud every individual in that class, who is actually misled by the deceit. *(Enacted in 1872.)*

Research References

Miller and Starr California Real Estate § 1:147, Liability to Third Persons.
5 Witkin, California Summary 10th Torts § 805, (S 805) Representation to Public or Class.
5 Witkin, California Summary 10th Torts § 811, (S 811) Securities Cases.

§ 1712. Restoration of thing wrongfully acquired; exceptions

RESTORATION OF THING WRONGFULLY ACQUIRED. One who obtains a thing without the consent of its owner, or by a consent afterwards rescinded, or by an unlawful exaction which the owner could not at the time prudently refuse, must restore it to the person from whom it was thus obtained, unless he has acquired a title thereto superior to that of such other person, or unless the transaction was corrupt and unlawful on both sides. *(Enacted in 1872.)*

§ 1713. Restoration of thing wrongfully acquired; demand

WHEN DEMAND NECESSARY. The restoration required by the last section must be made without demand, except where a thing is obtained by mutual mistake, in which case the party obtaining the thing is not bound to return it until he has notice of the mistake. *(Enacted in 1872.)*

§ 1714. Responsibility for willful acts and negligence; furnishing alcoholic beverages; legislative intent; liability of social hosts; liability of parents, guardians, or adults who furnish alcoholic beverages to minors

(a) Everyone is responsible, not only for the result of his or her willful acts, but also for an injury occasioned to another by his or her want of ordinary care or skill in the management of his or her property or person, except so far as the latter has, willfully or by want of ordinary care, brought the injury upon himself or herself. The design, distribution, or marketing of firearms and ammunition is not exempt from the duty to use ordinary care and skill that is required by this section. The extent of liability in these cases is defined by the Title on Compensatory Relief.

(b) It is the intent of the Legislature to abrogate the holdings in cases such as Vesely v. Sager (1971) 5 Cal.3d 153, Bernhard v. Harrah's Club (1976) 16 Cal.3d 313, and Coulter v. Superior Court (1978) 21 Cal.3d 144 and to reinstate the prior judicial interpretation of this section as it relates to proximate cause for injuries incurred as a result of furnishing alcoholic beverages to an intoxicated person, namely that the furnishing of alcoholic beverages is not the proximate cause of injuries resulting from intoxication, but rather the consumption of alcoholic beverages is the proximate cause of injuries inflicted upon another by an intoxicated person.

(c) Except as provided in subdivision (d), no social host who furnishes alcoholic beverages to any person may be held legally accountable for damages suffered by that person, or for injury to the person or property of, or death of, any third person, resulting from the consumption of those beverages.

(d)(1) Nothing in subdivision (c) shall preclude a claim against a parent, guardian, or another adult who knowingly furnishes alcoholic beverages at his or her residence to a person whom he or she knows, or should have known, to be under 21 years of age, in which case, notwithstanding subdivision (b), the furnishing of the alcoholic beverage may be found to be the proximate cause of resulting injuries or death.

(2) A claim under this subdivision may be brought by, or on behalf of, the person under 21 years of age or by a person who was harmed by the person under 21 years of age. *(Enacted in 1872. Amended by Stats.1978, c. 929, p. 2904, § 2; Stats.2002, c. 906 (A.B.496), § 1; Stats.2002, c. 913 (S.B.682), § 1; Stats.2003, c. 62 (S.B.600), § 15; Stats.2010, c. 154 (A.B.2486), § 1; Stats.2011, c. 410 (A.B.1407), § 1.)*

Research References

Rutter, Cal. Practice Guide: Landlord-Tenant Gen. Matls, Highlights.
Rutter, Cal. Practice Guide: Personal Injury Gen. Matls., Highlights.
Miller and Starr California Real Estate § 14:9, Self-Help for Encroaching Trees.
Miller and Starr California Real Estate § 36:6, Liability to the Borrower for Negligent Disbursement of Loan Funds.
Miller and Starr California Real Estate § 10:53, Waste by the Trustor or a Successor.
Miller and Starr California Real Estate § 22:41, General Rule of Landowner's or Occupier's Duty to Third Persons.
Miller and Starr California Real Estate § 22:42, Liability When Owner Holds Less Than a Fee Interest or a Fractionalized Interest in Property.
Miller and Starr California Real Estate § 22:44, Landowners' Liability for Dangerous Conditions.
Miller and Starr California Real Estate § 22:47, Liability to Persons Injured Due to Dangerous Conditions Off the Premises.
Miller and Starr California Real Estate § 22:49, Landlord's Liability to Persons Injured in the Common Area.
Miller and Starr California Real Estate § 22:51, Liability to a Tenant or Guest Injured in the Premises Leased to the Tenant--Liability of Nonresidential Landlord.
Miller and Starr California Real Estate § 22:53, Liability for Condition Arising After the Tenant Takes Possession.
Miller and Starr California Real Estate § 22:55, Liability of Tenant in Possession.
Miller and Starr California Real Estate § 22:62, Liability for Wrongful or Criminal Conduct of Third Persons--Liability for Injuries Caused by an Intoxicated Customer or Tenant's Invitee.
Miller and Starr California Real Estate § 22:73, Liability to Trespassers.
Miller and Starr California Real Estate § 22:77, Owner's Defenses.
Miller and Starr California Real Estate § 29:53, Negligence, Fraud, and Fiduciary Liabilities.

Miller and Starr California Real Estate § 31:39, Responsibilities of Mobilehome Owners.

Miller and Starr California Real Estate § 10:165, Action Against Third Persons for Fraud or Injury to the Security.

Miller and Starr California Real Estate § 19:121, Tenant's Remedies for Landlord's Breach of the Implied Warranty.

Miller and Starr California Real Estate § 19:132, Landlord's Liability to Persons Injured on the Premises.

Miller and Starr California Real Estate § 34:140, Negligent Interference With Prospective Economic Advantage.

14 NO. 1 Miller & Starr, California Real Estate Newsalert 1, Landlords Beware: the Violent Tenant May Damage Your Pocketbook.

15 NO. 5 Miller & Starr, California Real Estate Newsalert 13, Landowners' Liability.

16 NO. 4 Miller & Starr, California Real Estate Newsalert 1, Premises and Landowner Liability: the Supreme Court Continues Its Expansion of Potential Liability for Personal Injuries.

21 NO. 4 Miller & Starr, California Real Estate Newsalert 35, Landowners' Liability.

22 NO. 3 Miller & Starr, California Real Estate Newsalert 15, Landlord and Tenant.

23 NO. 1 Miller & Starr, California Real Estate Newsalert 16, Landowners' Liability.

3 Witkin Cal. Proc. 5th Actions § 150, Breach of Warranty of Habitability.

12 Witkin, California Summary 10th Real Property § 639, (S 639) Liability Under Foreseeability Test.

5 Witkin, California Summary 10th Torts § 1, (S 1) Definitions and Distinctions.

5 Witkin, California Summary 10th Torts § 24, (S 24) in General.

5 Witkin, California Summary 10th Torts § 343, 911 Calls.

5 Witkin, California Summary 10th Torts § 751, in General.

6 Witkin, California Summary 10th Torts § 833, California Statute.

6 Witkin, California Summary 10th Torts § 982, (S 982) Recovery Limited to Special Damages.

6 Witkin, California Summary 10th Torts § 1070, Statutory Rules.

6 Witkin, California Summary 10th Torts § 1071, Constitutionality of Statutes.

6 Witkin, California Summary 10th Torts § 1073, Furnishing Liquor to Sober Minor.

6 Witkin, California Summary 10th Torts § 1074, Furnishing Liquor to Disabled Person.

6 Witkin, California Summary 10th Torts § 1086, (S 1086) Repudiation of Traditional Classification.

6 Witkin, California Summary 10th Torts § 1097, (S 1097) in General.

6 Witkin, California Summary 10th Torts § 1103, (S 1103) in General.

6 Witkin, California Summary 10th Torts § 1141, No Duty to Comply With Criminal's Demand.

6 Witkin, California Summary 10th Torts § 1152, Near Apartment.

6 Witkin, California Summary 10th Torts § 1157, New Foreseeable Risk Approach.

6 Witkin, California Summary 10th Torts § 1255, (S 1255) Hospital's Liability for Doctor's Negligence.

6 Witkin, California Summary 10th Torts § 1329, (S 1329) Adoption of Doctrine in California.

6 Witkin, California Summary 10th Torts § 1406, Liability for Trespassing Animal.

6 Witkin, California Summary 10th Torts § 1463, Firearms and Ammunition.

6 Witkin, California Summary 10th Torts § 1683, No Recovery by Child.

6 Witkin, California Summary 10th Torts § 859A, (S 859A) (New)-Parking on Shoulder of Interstate Highway.

6 Witkin, California Summary 10th Torts § 1021A, (New)-Defective Product as Source of Emotional Distress.

§ 1714.01. Domestic partners; negligent infliction of emotional distress; damages

(a) Domestic partners shall be entitled to recover damages for negligent infliction of emotional distress to the same extent that spouses are entitled to do so under California law.

(b) For the purpose of this section, "domestic partners" has the meaning provided in Section 297 of the Family Code. *(Added by Stats.2001, c. 893 (A.B.25), § 1.)*

Research References

Rutter, Cal. Practice Guide: Personal Injury Ch. 3-C, C. Specific Items of Compensatory Damages.

Rutter, Cal. Practice Guide: Personal Injury Ch. 3-G, G. Independent Damages Claims.

11 Witkin, California Summary 10th Husband and Wife § 33, Other Rights.

6 Witkin, California Summary 10th Torts § 1020, (S 1020) Unmarried Cohabitant.

§ 1714.1. Liability of parents and guardians for willful misconduct of minor

(a) Any act of willful misconduct of a minor that results in injury or death to another person or in any injury to the property of another shall be imputed to the parent or guardian having custody and control of the minor for all purposes of civil damages, and the parent or guardian having custody and control shall be jointly and severally liable with the minor for any damages resulting from the willful misconduct.

Subject to the provisions of subdivision (c), the joint and several liability of the parent or guardian having custody and control of a minor under this subdivision shall not exceed twenty-five thousand dollars ($25,000) for each tort of the minor, and in the case of injury to a person, imputed liability shall be further limited to medical, dental and hospital expenses incurred by the injured person, not to exceed twenty-five thousand dollars ($25,000). The liability imposed by this section is in addition to any liability now imposed by law.

(b) Any act of willful misconduct of a minor that results in the defacement of property of another with paint or a similar substance shall be imputed to the parent or guardian having custody and control of the minor for all purposes of civil damages, including court costs, and attorney's fees, to the prevailing party, and the parent or guardian having custody and control shall be jointly and severally liable with the minor for any damages resulting from the willful misconduct, not to exceed twenty-five thousand dollars ($25,000), except as provided in subdivision (c), for each tort of the minor.

(c) The amounts listed in subdivisions (a) and (b) shall be adjusted every two years by the Judicial Council to reflect any increases in the cost of living in California, as indicated by the annual average of the California Consumer Price Index. The Judicial Council shall round this adjusted amount up or down to the nearest hundred dollars. On or before July 1 of each odd-numbered year, the Judicial Council shall compute and publish the amounts listed in subdivisions (a) and (b), as adjusted according to this subdivision.

(d) The maximum liability imposed by this section is the maximum liability authorized under this section at the time that the act of willful misconduct by a minor was committed.

(e) Nothing in this section shall impose liability on an insurer for a loss caused by the willful act of the insured for purposes of Section 533 of the Insurance Code. An insurer shall not be liable for the conduct imputed to a parent or guardian by this section for any amount in excess of ten thousand dollars ($10,000). *(Added by Stats.1955, c. 820, p. 1438, § 1. Amended by Stats.1965, c. 407, p. 1719, § 1; Stats.1970, c. 640, p. 1258, § 1; Stats.1972, c. 442, p. 811, § 1; Stats.1974, c. 340, p. 670, § 1; Stats.1979, c. 127, p. 314, § 1; Stats.1983, c. 981, § 1; Stats.1994, c. 568 (A.B.308), § 1; Stats.1994, c. 909 (S.B.1779), § 1; Stats.2007, c. 738 (A.B.1248), § 2.)*

Research References

Rutter, Cal. Practice Guide: Civ. Pro. Before Trial Ch. 3-B, B. Jurisdiction Over Parties-Personal Jurisdiction.

Rutter, Cal. Practice Guide: Insurance Litigation Ch. 7A-G, G. Intentional Acts Limitation.

Rutter, Cal. Practice Guide: Personal Injury Ch. 3-D, D. Mitigating Factors in Reduction of Damages.

2 Witkin Cal. Proc. 5th Courts § 198, (S 198) Additional Elements.

2 Witkin Cal. Proc. 5th Jurisdiction § 155, (S 155) Other Cases.

5 Witkin Cal. Proc. 5th Pleading § 924, Liability of Parent.

10 Witkin, California Summary 10th Parent and Child § 902, (S 902) Restitution to Victim.

10 Witkin, California Summary 10th Parent and Child § 903, (S 903) Liability of Parent or Guardian for Restitution.

10 Witkin, California Summary 10th Parent and Child § 915, in General.

6 Witkin, California Summary 10th Torts § 1229, (S 1229) Nature and Scope of Statute.

6 Witkin, California Summary 10th Torts § 1230, (S 1230) Illustrations.

6 Witkin, California Summary 10th Torts § 1231, (S 1231) Injury to School Students, Personnel, or Property.

6 Witkin, California Summary 10th Torts § 1232, (S 1232) Theft from Merchant or Library.

6 Witkin, California Summary 10th Torts § 1234, (S 1234) California Statute.

6 Witkin, California Summary 10th Torts § 1366, Other Situations.

§ 1714.2. Cardiopulmonary resuscitation; emergency care; immunity from civil liability

(a) In order to encourage citizens to participate in emergency medical services training programs and to render emergency medical services to fellow citizens, no person who has completed a basic cardiopulmonary resuscitation course which complies with the standards adopted by the American Heart Association or the American Red Cross for cardiopulmonary resuscitation and emergency cardiac care, and who, in good faith, renders emergency cardiopulmonary resuscitation at the scene of an emergency, shall be liable for any civil damages as a result of any acts or omissions by such person rendering the emergency care.

(b) This section shall not be construed to grant immunity from civil damages to any person whose conduct in rendering such emergency care constitutes gross negligence.

(c) In order to encourage local agencies and other organizations to train citizens in cardiopulmonary resuscitation techniques, no local agency, entity of state or local government, or other public or private organization which sponsors, authorizes, supports, finances, or supervises the training of citizens in cardiopulmonary resuscitation shall be liable for any civil damages alleged to result from such training programs.

(d) In order to encourage qualified individuals to instruct citizens in cardiopulmonary resuscitation, no person who is certified to instruct in cardiopulmonary resuscitation by either the American Heart Association or the American Red Cross shall be liable for any civil damages alleged to result from the acts or omissions of an individual who received instruction on cardiopulmonary resuscitation by that certified instructor.

(e) This section shall not be construed to grant immunity from civil damages to any person who renders such emergency care to an individual with the expectation of receiving compensation from the individual for providing the emergency care. *(Added by Stats.1977, c. 595, p. 1970, § 1.)*

Research References

5 Witkin, California Summary 10th Torts § 137, Persons or Teams Attempting Resuscitation.

§ 1714.21. Defibrillators; CPR; immunity from civil liability

(a) For purposes of this section, the following definitions shall apply:

(1) "AED" or "defibrillator" means an automated or automatic external defibrillator.

(2) "CPR" means cardiopulmonary resuscitation.

(b) Any person who, in good faith and not for compensation, renders emergency care or treatment by the use of an AED at the scene of an emergency is not liable for any civil damages resulting from any acts or omissions in rendering the emergency care.

(c) A person or entity who provides CPR and AED training to a person who renders emergency care pursuant to subdivision (b) is not liable for any civil damages resulting from any acts or omissions of the person rendering the emergency care.

(d) A person or entity that acquires an AED for emergency use pursuant to this section is not liable for any civil damages resulting from any acts or omissions in the rendering of the emergency care by use of an AED, if that person or entity has complied with subdivision (b) of Section 1797.196 of the Health and Safety Code.

(e) A physician who is involved with the placement of an AED and any person or entity responsible for the site where an AED is located is not liable for any civil damages resulting from any acts or omissions of a person who renders emergency care pursuant to subdivision (b), if that physician, person, or entity has complied with all of the requirements of Section 1797.196 of the Health and Safety Code that apply to that physician, person, or entity.

(f) The protections specified in this section do not apply in the case of personal injury or wrongful death that results from the gross negligence or willful or wanton misconduct of the person who renders emergency care or treatment by the use of an AED.

(g) Nothing in this section shall relieve a manufacturer, designer, developer, distributor, installer, or supplier of an AED or defibrillator of any liability under any applicable statute or rule of law. *(Added by Stats.1999, c. 163 (S.B.911), § 2. Amended by Stats.2002, c. 718 (A.B.2041), § 1.)*

Research References

5 Witkin, California Summary 10th Torts § 137, Persons or Teams Attempting Resuscitation.

§ 1714.22. Opioid antagonist; prescription and dispensing permitted by authorized licensed health care providers to persons at risk of opioid-related overdose or persons in position to assist person at risk; standing distribution orders; overdose prevention and treatment training; immunity from liability

(a) For purposes of this section, the following definitions shall apply:

(1) "Opioid antagonist" means naloxone hydrochloride that is approved by the federal Food and Drug Administration for the treatment of * * * an opioid overdose.

(2) "Opioid overdose prevention and treatment training program" * * * means any program operated by a local health jurisdiction or that is registered by a local health jurisdiction to train individuals to prevent, recognize, and respond to an opiate overdose, and that provides, at a minimum, training in all of the following:

(A) The causes of an opiate overdose.

(B) Mouth to mouth resuscitation.

(C) How to contact appropriate emergency medical services.

(D) How to administer an opioid antagonist.

(b) A licensed health care provider who is authorized by law to prescribe an opioid antagonist may, if acting with reasonable care, prescribe and subsequently dispense or distribute an opioid antagonist * * * to a person at risk of an opioid-related overdose or to a family member, friend, or other person in a position to assist a person at risk of an opioid-related overdose.

(c) * * * (1) A licensed * * * health care provider who is authorized by law to prescribe an opioid antagonist may * * * issue standing orders for the distribution of an opioid antagonist * * * to a person at risk of an opioid-related overdose or to a family member, friend, or other person in a position to assist a person at risk of an opioid-related overdose.

* * *

(2) A licensed health care provider who is authorized by law to prescribe an opioid antagonist may issue standing orders for the administration of an opioid antagonist to a person at risk of an opioid-related overdose by a family member, friend, or other person in a position to assist a person experiencing or reasonably suspected of experiencing an opioid overdose.

(d)(1) A person who is prescribed or possesses an opioid antagonist pursuant to a standing order shall receive the training provided by an opioid overdose prevention and treatment training program.

(2) A person who is prescribed an opioid antagonist directly from a licensed prescriber shall not be required to receive training from an opioid prevention and treatment training program.

(e) A licensed health care provider who acts with reasonable care shall not be subject to professional review, be liable in a civil action, or be subject to criminal prosecution for issuing a prescription or order pursuant to subdivision (b) or (c).

(f) Notwithstanding any other law, a person who possesses or distributes an opioid antagonist pursuant to a prescription or standing order shall not be subject to professional review, be liable in a civil action, or be subject to criminal prosecution for this possession or distribution. Notwithstanding any other law, a person not otherwise licensed to administer an opioid antagonist, but trained as required under paragraph (1) of subdivision (d), who acts with reasonable care in administering an opioid antagonist, in good faith and not for compensation, to a person who is experiencing or is suspected of experiencing an overdose shall not be subject to professional review, be liable in a civil action, or be subject to criminal prosecution for this administration. *(Added by Stats.2007, c. 477 (S.B.767), § 2. Amended by Stats.2010, c. 545 (A.B.2145), § 1; Stats.2013, c. 707 (A.B.635), § 1.)*

Research References

5 Witkin, California Summary 10th Torts § 186A, (New)-Prescription of Controlled Substance Pursuant to Drug Overdose Program.

§ 1714.23. Administration of epinephrine auto-injector; liability for civil damages; requirements for immunity

(a) For purposes of this section, the following definitions shall apply:

(1) "Anaphylaxis" means a potentially life-threatening hypersensitivity or allergic reaction to a substance.

(A) Symptoms of anaphylaxis may include shortness of breath, wheezing, difficulty breathing, difficulty talking or swallowing, hives, itching, swelling, shock, or asthma.

(B) Causes of anaphylaxis may include, but are not limited to, insect stings or bites, foods, drugs, and other allergens, as well as idiopathic or exercise-induced anaphylaxis.

(2) "Epinephrine auto-injector" means a disposable drug delivery system with a spring-activated concealed needle that is designed for emergency administration of epinephrine to provide rapid, convenient first aid for persons suffering from anaphylaxis.

(b) Any person described in subdivision (b) of Section 1797.197a of the Health and Safety Code who administers an epinephrine auto-injector, in good faith and not for compensation, to another person who appears to be experiencing anaphylaxis at the scene of an emergency situation is not liable for any civil damages resulting from his or her acts or omissions in administering the epinephrine auto-injector, if that person has complied with the requirements and standards of Section 1797.197a of the Health and Safety Code.

(c) The protection specified in subdivision (b) shall not apply in a case of personal injury or wrongful death that results from the gross negligence or willful or wanton misconduct of the person who renders emergency care treatment by the use of an epinephrine auto-injector.

(d) Nothing in this section relieves a manufacturer, designer, developer, distributor, or supplier of an epinephrine auto-injector of liability under any other applicable law. *(Added by Stats.2013, c. 725 (S.B.669), § 2.)*

§ 1714.25. Donations by food facilities to nonprofit charitable organizations; immunity

(a) Except for injury resulting from negligence or a willful act in the preparation or handling of donated food, no food facility that donates any food that is fit for human consumption at the time it was donated to a nonprofit charitable organization or a food bank shall be liable for any damage or injury resulting from the consumption of the donated food.

The immunity from civil liability provided by this subdivision applies regardless of compliance with any laws, regulations, or ordinances regulating the packaging or labeling of food, and regardless of compliance with any laws, regulations, or ordinances regulating the storage or handling of the food by the donee after the donation of the food.

(b) A nonprofit charitable organization or a food bank that, in good faith, receives and distributes food without charge that is fit for human consumption at the time it was distributed is not liable for an injury or death due to the food unless the injury or death is a direct result of the negligence, recklessness, or intentional misconduct of the organization.

(c) For the purposes of this section:

(1) "Nonprofit charitable organization" has the meaning defined in Section 114440 of the Health and Safety Code.

(2) "Food bank" has the meaning defined in Section 114445 of the Health and Safety Code. *(Added by Stats.1988, c. 735, § 1. Amended by Stats.1996, c. 1023 (S.B.1497), § 27, eff. Sept. 29, 1996.)*

Research References

2 Witkin, California Summary 10th Insurance § 172, (S 172) Exception of Designated Users.

5 Witkin, California Summary 10th Torts § 43, Liability to Beneficiaries.

§ 1714.26. Vision screenings and eyeglasses provided by nonprofit charitable organizations and licensed optometrists, ophthalmologists, or trained volunteers working with such organizations; limitation of liability; exceptions

(a) Except for damage or injury resulting from gross negligence or a willful act, there is no liability for any damage or injury on the part of a nonprofit charitable organization that provides vision screenings and, if applicable, provides donated or recycled eyeglasses, or a participating licensed optometrist, ophthalmologist, or trained volunteer who works with such a nonprofit charitable organization in the performance of vision screenings, if all of the following conditions are met:

(1) The vision screening is provided to address ocular health concerns and, if applicable, to provide a temporary solution in the form of donated or recycled eyeglasses until the patient can get a full examination and eyeglasses.

(2) The vision screening is not intended to replace a full ocular health examination provided by a licensed optometrist or ophthalmologist.

(3) The patient signs a waiver acknowledging that the services provided are a temporary solution until the patient can get a full examination by a licensed optometrist or ophthalmologist.

(4) Each vision screening is supervised by an attending licensed optometrist or ophthalmologist.

(5) The eyeglass prescription determinations and ocular health recommendations are provided by an attending licensed optometrist or ophthalmologist.

(6) A written prescription is not provided to the patient.

(7) The eyeglasses provided to the patients are a close or approximate match, within tolerances allowed by the attending licensed optometrist or ophthalmologist, to the prescription determined during the vision screening.

(8) The vision screening and eyeglasses are provided without a charge.

(9) The optometrist, ophthalmologist, or volunteer is authorized by the nonprofit organization to provide the vision screening and eyeglasses on behalf of the nonprofit organization and is acting within the scope of his or her authorized responsibilities and the guidelines of the nonprofit charitable organization when providing the vision screening or eyeglasses.

(10) The nonprofit charitable organization provides procedural, risk management, and quality control training, as applicable, to the participating optometrist, ophthalmologist, or volunteer who provides the vision screening or eyeglasses.

(b) The limitation of liability provided in subdivision (a) is not applicable if an action is brought by an officer of a state or local government pursuant to state or local law.

(c) The limitation of liability provided in subdivision (a) is not applicable if the conduct of the nonprofit charitable organization, optometrist, ophthalmologist, or volunteer includes any of the following types of misconduct:

(1) A crime of violence.

(2) A hate crime.

(3) An act involving a sexual offense.

(4) An act involving misconduct in violation of federal or state civil rights laws.

(5) An act performed while the defendant was under the influence of drugs or alcohol.

(d) For the purposes of this section:

(1) "Nonprofit charitable organization" means an organization exempt from federal income tax as an organization described in Section 501(c)(3) of the Internal Revenue Code.[1]

(2) "Vision screening" means a test or examination of an individual using a portion of the usual examination procedures in a comprehensive eye examination and refraction, that are selected or directed by an attending licensed optometrist or ophthalmologist, and are within the guidelines of the nonprofit charitable organization. *(Added by Stats.2013, c. 68 (S.B.724), § 1.)*

[1] Internal Revenue Code sections are in Title 26 of the U.S.C.A.

§ 1714.3. Liability of parent or guardian for injury to person or property caused by discharge of firearm by minor under 18

Civil liability for any injury to the person or property of another proximately caused by the discharge of a firearm by a minor under the age of 18 years shall be imputed to a parent or guardian having custody and control of the minor for all purposes of civil damages, and such parent or guardian shall be jointly and severally liable with such minor for any damages resulting from such act, if such parent or guardian either permitted the minor to have the firearm or left the firearm in a place accessible to the minor.

The liability imposed by this section is in addition to any liability otherwise imposed by law. However, no person, or group of persons collectively, shall incur liability under this section in any amount exceeding thirty thousand dollars ($30,-000) for injury to or death of one person as a result of any one occurrence or, subject to the limit as to one person, exceeding sixty thousand dollars ($60,000) for injury to or death of all persons as a result of any one such occurrence. *(Added by Stats.1970, c. 843, p. 1576, § 1. Amended by Stats.1977, c. 87, p. 505, § 1; Stats.1986, c. 1099, § 1.)*

Research References

Rutter, Cal. Practice Guide: Personal Injury Ch. 3-D, D. Mitigating Factors in Reduction of Damages.
5 Witkin Cal. Proc. 5th Pleading § 924, Liability of Parent.
10 Witkin, California Summary 10th Parent and Child § 903, (S 903) Liability of Parent or Guardian for Restitution.
6 Witkin, California Summary 10th Torts § 1230, (S 1230) Illustrations.
6 Witkin, California Summary 10th Torts § 1234, (S 1234) California Statute.

§ 1714.4. Knowingly assisting child support obligor escape, evade, or avoid paying court-ordered or court-approved child support; application to financial institutions

(a) Any person or business entity that knowingly assists a child support obligor who has an unpaid child support obligation to escape, evade, or avoid paying court-ordered or court-approved child support shall be liable for three times the value of the assistance provided, such as the fair market value of the obligor's assets transferred or hidden. The maximum liability imposed by this section shall not exceed the entire child support obligation due. Any funds or assets collected pursuant to this section shall be paid to the child support obligee, and shall not reduce the amount of the unpaid child support obligation. Upon the satisfaction of the unpaid child support obligation, this section shall not apply.

(b) For purposes of this section, actions taken to knowingly assist a child support obligor to escape, evade, or avoid paying court-ordered or court-approved child support include, with actual knowledge of the child support obligation, helping to hide or transfer assets of the child support obligor.

(c) This section shall not apply to a financial institution unless the financial institution has actual knowledge of the child support obligation and, with that knowledge, knowingly assists the obligor to escape, evade, or avoid paying the child support obligation. However, a financial institution with knowledge of an asset transfer has no duty to inquire into the rightfulness of the transaction, nor shall it be deemed to have knowingly assisted an obligor to escape, evade, or avoid paying the child support obligation if that assistance is provided by an employee or agent of the financial institution acting outside the terms and conditions of employment or agency without the actual knowledge of the financial institution. *(Added by Stats.2006, c. 820 (A.B.2440), § 2.)*

Research References

Rutter, Cal. Practice Guide: Family Law Ch. 6-A, A. Child Support.
10 Witkin, California Summary 10th Parent and Child § 390A, (S 390A) (New)-Liability of Person Assisting Evasion.
6 Witkin, California Summary 10th Torts § 1463, Firearms and Ammunition.

§ 1714.41. Knowingly assisting a child support obligor to escape, evade, or avoid paying child support; included actions

(a) Any person or business entity that knowingly assists a child support obligor who has an unpaid child support obligation to escape, evade, or avoid paying court-ordered or court-approved child support shall be liable for three times the value of the assistance provided, such as the fair market value of the assets transferred or hidden, or the amount of the wages or other compensation paid to the child support obligor but not reported. The maximum liability imposed by this section shall not exceed the entire child support obligation due. Any funds or assets collected pursuant to this section shall be paid to the child support obligee, and shall not reduce the amount of the unpaid child support obligation. Upon the satisfaction of the unpaid child support obligation, this section shall not apply.

(b) For purposes of this section, actions taken to knowingly assist a child support obligor to escape, evade, or avoid paying court-ordered or court-approved child support include, but are not limited to, any of the following actions taken when the individual or entity knew or should have known of the child support obligation:

(1) Hiring or employing the child support obligor as an employee in a trade or business and failing to timely file a report of new employees with the California New Employee Registry maintained by the Employment Development Department.

(2) Engaging the child support obligor as a service provider and failing to timely file a report with the Employment Development Department as required by Section 1088.8 of the Unemployment Insurance Code.

(3) When engaged in a trade or business, paying wages or other forms of compensation for services rendered by a child support obligor that are not reported to the Employment Development Department as required, including, but not limited to, payment in cash or via barter or trade. *(Added by Stats.2006, c. 820 (A.B.2440), § 3.)*

Research References

Rutter, Cal. Practice Guide: Family Law Ch. 6-A, A. Child Support.
10 Witkin, California Summary 10th Parent and Child § 390A, (S 390A) (New)-Liability of Person Assisting Evasion.

§ 1714.43. Retailers to disclose efforts to eradicate slavery and human trafficking from direct supply chain for tangible goods; definitions; posting on Internet Website; contents; injunctive relief for violation

(a)(1) Every retail seller and manufacturer doing business in this state and having annual worldwide gross receipts that exceed one hundred million dollars ($100,000,000) shall disclose, as set forth in subdivision (c), its efforts to eradicate slavery and human trafficking from its direct supply chain for tangible goods offered for sale.

(2) For the purposes of this section, the following definitions shall apply:

(A) "Doing business in this state" shall have the same meaning as set forth in Section 23101 of the Revenue and Taxation Code.

(B) "Gross receipts" shall have the same meaning as set forth in Section 25120 of the Revenue and Taxation Code.

(C) "Manufacturer" means a business entity with manufacturing as its principal business activity code, as reported on the entity's tax return filed under Part 10.2 (commencing with Section 18401) of Division 2 of the Revenue and Taxation Code.

(D) "Retail seller" means a business entity with retail trade as its principal business activity code, as reported on the entity's tax return filed under Part 10.2 (commencing with Section 18401) of Division 2 of the Revenue and Taxation Code.

(b) The disclosure described in subdivision (a) shall be posted on the retail seller's or manufacturer's Internet Web site with a conspicuous and easily understood link to the required informa-

tion placed on the business' homepage. In the event the retail seller or manufacturer does not have an Internet Web site, consumers shall be provided the written disclosure within 30 days of receiving a written request for the disclosure from a consumer.

(c) The disclosure described in subdivision (a) shall, at a minimum, disclose to what extent, if any, that the retail seller or manufacturer does each of the following:

(1) Engages in verification of product supply chains to evaluate and address risks of human trafficking and slavery. The disclosure shall specify if the verification was not conducted by a third party.

(2) Conducts audits of suppliers to evaluate supplier compliance with company standards for trafficking and slavery in supply chains. The disclosure shall specify if the verification was not an independent, unannounced audit.

(3) Requires direct suppliers to certify that materials incorporated into the product comply with the laws regarding slavery and human trafficking of the country or countries in which they are doing business.

(4) Maintains internal accountability standards and procedures for employees or contractors failing to meet company standards regarding slavery and trafficking.

(5) Provides company employees and management, who have direct responsibility for supply chain management, training on human trafficking and slavery, particularly with respect to mitigating risks within the supply chains of products.

(d) The exclusive remedy for a violation of this section shall be an action brought by the Attorney General for injunctive relief. Nothing in this section shall limit remedies available for a violation of any other state or federal law.

(e) The provisions of this section shall take effect on January 1, 2012. *(Added by Stats.2010, c. 556 (S.B.657), § 3, operative Jan. 1, 2012.)*

Research References

5 Witkin, California Summary 10th Torts § 468A, (New)-Human Trafficking.

§ 1714.45. Products liability; consumer products known by consumers to be inherently unsafe

(a) In a product liability action, a manufacturer or seller shall not be liable if both of the following apply:

(1) The product is inherently unsafe and the product is known to be unsafe by the ordinary consumer who consumes the product with the ordinary knowledge common to the community.

(2) The product is a common consumer product intended for personal consumption, such as sugar, castor oil, alcohol, and butter, as identified in comment i to Section 402A of the Restatement (Second) of Torts.

(b) This section does not exempt the manufacture or sale of tobacco products by tobacco manufacturers and their successors in interest from product liability actions, but does exempt the sale or distribution of tobacco products by any other person, including, but not limited to, retailers or distributors.

(c) For purposes of this section, the term "product liability action" means any action for injury or death caused by a product, except that the term does not include an action based on a manufacturing defect or breach of an express warranty.

(d) This section is intended to be declarative of and does not alter or amend existing California law, including Cronin v. J.B.E. Olson Corp. (1972), 8 Cal.3d 121, and shall apply to all product liability actions pending on, or commenced after, January 1, 1988.

(e) This section does not apply to, and never applied to, an action brought by a public entity to recover the value of benefits provided to individuals injured by a tobacco-related illness caused by the tortious conduct of a tobacco company or its successor in interest, including, but not limited to, an action brought pursuant to Section 14124.71 of the Welfare and Institutions Code. In the action brought by a public entity, the fact that the injured individual's claim against the defendant may be barred by a prior version of this section shall not be a defense. This subdivision does not constitute a change in, but is declaratory of, existing law relating to tobacco products.

(f) It is the intention of the Legislature in enacting the amendments to subdivisions (a) and (b) of this section adopted at the 1997–98 Regular Session to declare that there exists no statutory bar to tobacco-related personal injury, wrongful death, or other tort claims against tobacco manufacturers and their successors in interest by California smokers or others who have suffered or incurred injuries, damages, or costs arising from the promotion, marketing, sale, or consumption of tobacco products. It is also the intention of the Legislature to clarify that those claims that were or are brought shall be determined on their merits, without the imposition of any claim of statutory bar or categorical defense.

(g) This section shall not be construed to grant immunity to a tobacco industry research organization. *(Added by Stats.1987, c. 1498, § 3. Amended by Stats.1997, c. 25 (A.B.1603), § 2, eff. June 12, 1997; Stats.1997, c. 570 (S.B.67), § 1; Stats.1998, c. 485 (A.B.2803), § 38.)*

Research References

3 Witkin Cal. Proc. 5th Actions § 461, (S 461) Construction to Avoid Retroactivity.
3 Witkin Cal. Proc. 5th Actions § 560, (S 560) Wrongful Death.
5 Witkin, California Summary 10th Torts § 57, Between Tortfeasors Subject and Not Subject to Liability.
6 Witkin, California Summary 10th Torts § 1534, in General.
6 Witkin, California Summary 10th Torts § 1535, Revocation of Immunity for Tobacco Manufacturers.
6 Witkin, California Summary 10th Torts § 1536, Retroactivity.

§ 1714.5. Defense shelters or other necessary facility for emergency purposes

(a) There shall be no liability on the part of one, including the State of California, county, city and county, city or any other political subdivision of the State of California, who owns or maintains any building or premises which have been designated as a shelter from destructive operations or attacks by enemies of the United States by any disaster council or any public office, body, or officer of this state or of the United States, or which have been designated or are used as mass care centers, first aid stations, temporary hospital annexes, or as other necessary facilities for mitigating the effects of a natural, manmade, or war-caused emergency, for any injuries arising out of the use thereof for such purposes sustained by any person while in or upon said building or premises as a result of the condition of said building or premises or as a result of any act or omission, or in any way arising from the designation of such premises as a shelter, or the designation or use thereof as a mass care center, first aid station, temporary hospital annex, or other necessary facility for emergency purposes, except a willful act, of such owner or occupant or his or her servants, agents or employees when such person has entered or gone upon or into said building or premises for the purpose of seeking refuge, treatment, care, or assistance therein during destructive operations or attacks by enemies of the United States or during tests ordered by lawful authority or during a natural or manmade emergency.

(b) Notwithstanding any other provision of law, no disaster service worker who is performing disaster services during a state of war emergency, a state of emergency, or a local emergency, as such emergencies are defined in Section 8558 of the Government Code, shall be liable for civil damages on account of personal injury to or death of any person or damage to property resulting from any act or omission while performing disaster services anywhere within any jurisdiction covered by such emergency, except one that is willful.

(c) For purposes of this subdivision, a disaster service worker shall be performing disaster services when acting within the scope of the disaster service worker's responsibilities under the authority of the governmental emergency organization.

(d) For purposes of this subdivision, "governmental emergency organization" shall mean the emergency organization of any state, city, city and county, county, district, or other local governmental agency or public agency, which is authorized pursuant to the California Emergency Services Act (Chapter 7 (commencing with Section 8550) of Division 1 of Title 2 of the Government Code).

(e) Nothing in this section shall be construed to alter any existing legal duties or obligations. The amendments to this section made by the act amending this section shall apply exclusively to any legal action filed on or after the effective date of the act. *(Added by Stats.1943, c. 463, p. 1998, § 1. Amended by Stats.1951, c. 247, p. 507, § 1; Stats.1955, c. 1777, p. 3283, § 1; Stats.1971, c. 38, p. 48, § 1; Stats.1974, c. 1158, p. 2464, § 1; Stats.2009, c. 27 (S.B.39), § 1, eff. Aug. 6, 2009.)*

Research References

5 Witkin, California Summary 10th Torts § 132, (S 132) In General.
5 Witkin, California Summary 10th Torts § 136, in General.
5 Witkin, California Summary 10th Torts § 250, (S 250) Property Covered.

§ 1714.55. Retail or wholesale telecommunications service provider of 9–1–1 service; liability for civil claim, damage, or loss; definitions

(a) A retail or wholesale service provider of telecommunications service, or other service, involved in providing 9–1–1 service in accordance with the Warren–911–Emergency Assistance Act (Article 6 (commencing with Section 53100) of Chapter 1 of Part 1 of Division 2 of Title 5 of the Government Code), shall not be liable for any civil claim, damage, or loss caused by an act or omission in the design, development, installation, maintenance, or provision of 9–1–1 service, unless the act or omission that proximately caused the claim, damage, or loss constituted gross negligence, wanton or willful misconduct, or intentional misconduct.

(b) For purposes of this section:

(1) "Public safety agency" means a public safety agency as defined in accordance with the Warren–911–Emergency Assistance Act (Article 6 (commencing with Section 53100) of Chapter 1 of Part 1 of Division 2 of Title 5 of the Government Code).

(2) "9–1–1 service" means a telecommunications service, or other wireline or wireless service, that provides to the user of the public telephone system the ability to reach a public safety agency by utilizing the digits 9–1–1 or otherwise facilitates the provision of emergency services pursuant to the Warren–911–Emergency Assistance Act (Article 6 (commencing with Section 53100) of Chapter 1 of Part 1 of Division 2 of Title 5 of the Government Code). "9–1–1 service" includes a 9–1–1 service that utilizes in whole or in part an Internet Protocol.

(c) This section shall not apply to services provided under tariff.

(d) This section shall not be construed to modify the liability of a manufacturer, distributor, or other person arising from a claim, damage, or loss, related to the operation or performance of an end-user device that is not related to the provision of 9–1–1 service. *(Added by Stats.2011, c. 297 (A.B.1074), § 1, eff. Sept. 21, 2011.)*

Research References

Rutter, Cal. Practice Guide: Personal Injury Gen. Matls., Highlights.
5 Witkin, California Summary 10th Torts § 138A, (S 138A) (New)-Providers of 911 Service.

§ 1714.6. Compliance with military orders or regulations under Emergency Services Act; suspension of civil and criminal liability

The violation of any statute or ordinance shall not establish negligence as a matter of law where the act or omission involved was required in order to comply with an order or proclamation of any military commander who is authorized to issue such orders or proclamations; nor when the act or omission involved is required in order to comply with any regulation, directive, or order of the Governor promulgated under the California Emergency Services Act.[1] No person shall be prosecuted for a violation of any statute or ordinance when violation of such statute or ordinance is required in order to comply with an order or proclamation of any military commander who is authorized to issue such orders or proclamations; nor shall any person be prosecuted for a violation of any statute or ordinance when violation of such statute or ordinance is required in order to comply with any regulation, directive, or order of the Governor promulgated under the California Emergency Services Act. The provisions of this section shall apply to such acts or omissions whether occurring prior to or after the effective date of this section. *(Formerly § 1714.5, added by Stats.1943, c. 895, p. 2741, § 1. Renumbered § 1714.6 and amended by Stats.1951, c. 514, p. 1661, § 1. Amended by Stats.1971, c. 438, p. 857, § 15.)*

[1] Government Code § 8550 et seq.

Research References

6 Witkin, California Summary 10th Torts § 875, (S 875) Statute or Ordinance.

§ 1714.7. Injury while getting on, riding on, or getting off, moving locomotive or railroad car without authority; exemption of owner or operator from liability; exception

No person who is injured while getting on, or attempting to get on, a moving locomotive or railroad car, without authority from the owner or operator of the railroad, or who, having gotten on a locomotive or railroad car while in motion without such authority, is injured while so riding or getting off, shall recover any damages from the owner or operator thereof for such injuries unless proximately caused by an intentional act of such owner or operator with knowledge that serious injury is the probable result of such act, or with a wanton and reckless disregard of the probable result of such act. *(Added by Stats.1971, c. 1554, p. 3067, § 1.)*

Research References

6 Witkin, California Summary 10th Torts § 1097, (S 1097) in General.
6 Witkin, California Summary 10th Torts § 1098, (S 1098) Authority Must be Express.

§ 1714.8. Health care providers; professional negligence or malpractice; exemption from liability; definition

(a) No health care provider shall be liable for professional negligence or malpractice for any occurrence or result solely on the basis that the occurrence or result was caused by the natural course of a disease or condition, or was the natural or expected result of reasonable treatment rendered for the disease or condition. This section shall not be construed so as to limit liability for the failure to inform of the risks of treatment or

failure to accept treatment, or for negligent diagnosis or treatment or the negligent failure to diagnose or treat.

(b) As used in this section, "health care provider" means any person licensed or certified pursuant to Division 2 (commencing with Section 500) of the Business and Professions Code, or licensed pursuant to the Osteopathic Initiative Act or the Chiropractic Initiative Act, or certified pursuant to Chapter 2.5 (commencing with Section 1440) of Division 2 of the Health and Safety Code, and any clinic, health dispensary, or health facility licensed pursuant to Division 2 (commencing with Section 1200) of the Health and Safety Code. *(Added by Stats.1978, c. 1358, p. 4510, § 1.)*

Research References

6 Witkin, California Summary 10th Torts § 936, (S 936) Health Care Provider.
6 Witkin, California Summary 10th Torts § 942, Statutory Provisions.

§ 1714.9. Responsibility for willful acts or want of ordinary care causing injury to peace officers, firefighters or emergency service personnel; circumstances; comparative fault; subrogation; exception

(a) Notwithstanding statutory or decisional law to the contrary, any person is responsible not only for the results of that person's willful acts causing injury to a peace officer, firefighter, or any emergency medical personnel employed by a public entity, but also for any injury occasioned to that person by the want of ordinary care or skill in the management of the person's property or person, in any of the following situations:

(1) Where the conduct causing the injury occurs after the person knows or should have known of the presence of the peace officer, firefighter, or emergency medical personnel.

(2) Where the conduct causing injury violates a statute, ordinance, or regulation, and the conduct causing injury was itself not the event that precipitated either the response or presence of the peace officer, firefighter, or emergency medical personnel.

(3) Where the conduct causing the injury was intended to injure the peace officer, firefighter, or emergency medical personnel.

(4) Where the conduct causing the injury is arson as defined in Section 451 of the Penal Code.

(b) This section does not preclude the reduction of an award of damages because of the comparative fault of the peace officer, firefighter, or emergency medical personnel in causing the injury.

(c) The employer of a firefighter, peace officer or emergency medical personnel may be subrogated to the rights granted by this section to the extent of the worker's compensation benefits, and other liabilities of the employer, including all salary, wage, pension, or other emolument paid to the employee or the employee's dependents.

(d) The liability imposed by this section shall not apply to an employer of a peace officer, firefighter, or emergency medical personnel.

(e) This section is not intended to change or modify the common law independent cause exception to the firefighter's rule as set forth in Donohue v. San Francisco Housing Authority (1993) 16 Cal.App.4th 658. *(Added by Stats.1982, c. 258, p. 836, § 1. Amended by Stats.1983, c. 136, § 1; Stats.2001, c. 140 (S.B.448), § 2.)*

Research References

Rutter, Cal. Practice Guide: Personal Injury Ch. 3-D, D. Mitigating Factors in Reduction of Damages.
Miller and Starr California Real Estate § 22:74, Injuries to Police Officer or Firefighter.

9 Witkin Cal. Proc. 5th Appeal § 800, Use of Traditional Gender-Specific Terms.

6 Witkin, California Summary 10th Torts § 847, Off-Duty Officer.

6 Witkin, California Summary 10th Torts § 852, Extension of Firefighter's Rule to All Public Safety Personnel.

6 Witkin, California Summary 10th Torts § 854, (S 854) Police Officer Cases.

6 Witkin, California Summary 10th Torts § 855, (S 855) Firefighter Cases.

6 Witkin, California Summary 10th Torts § 856, (S 856) Police Officer Cases.

6 Witkin, California Summary 10th Torts § 857, (S 857) in General.

6 Witkin, California Summary 10th Torts § 858, (S 858) Exception Applicable.

6 Witkin, California Summary 10th Torts § 859, (S 859) Exception Not Applicable.

§ 1714.10. Attorney client civil conspiracy; proof and court determination prior to pleading; defense; limitations; appeal

(a) No cause of action against an attorney for a civil conspiracy with his or her client arising from any attempt to contest or compromise a claim or dispute, and which is based upon the attorney's representation of the client, shall be included in a complaint or other pleading unless the court enters an order allowing the pleading that includes the claim for civil conspiracy to be filed after the court determines that the party seeking to file the pleading has established that there is a reasonable probability that the party will prevail in the action. The court may allow the filing of a pleading claiming liability based upon such a civil conspiracy following the filing of a verified petition therefor accompanied by the proposed pleading and supporting affidavits stating the facts upon which the liability is based. The court shall order service of the petition upon the party against whom the action is proposed to be filed and permit that party to submit opposing affidavits prior to making its determination. The filing of the petition, proposed pleading, and accompanying affidavits shall toll the running of any applicable statute of limitations until the final determination of the matter, which ruling, if favorable to the petitioning party, shall permit the proposed pleading to be filed.

(b) Failure to obtain a court order where required by subdivision (a) shall be a defense to any action for civil conspiracy filed in violation thereof. The defense shall be raised by the attorney charged with civil conspiracy upon that attorney's first appearance by demurrer, motion to strike, or such other motion or application as may be appropriate. Failure to timely raise the defense shall constitute a waiver thereof.

(c) This section shall not apply to a cause of action against an attorney for a civil conspiracy with his or her client, where (1) the attorney has an independent legal duty to the plaintiff, or (2) the attorney's acts go beyond the performance of a professional duty to serve the client and involve a conspiracy to violate a legal duty in furtherance of the attorney's financial gain.

(d) This section establishes a special proceeding of a civil nature. Any order made under subdivision (a), (b), or (c) which determines the rights of a petitioner or an attorney against whom a pleading has been or is proposed to be filed, shall be appealable as a final judgment in a civil action.

(e) Subdivision (d) does not constitute a change in, but is declaratory of, the existing law. *(Added by Stats.1988, c. 1052, § 1. Amended by Stats.1991, c. 916 (S.B.820), § 1; Stats.1992, c. 427 (A.B.3355), § 12; Stats.1993, c. 645 (S.B.764), § 1; Stats. 2000, c. 472 (A.B.2069), § 2.)*

Research References

Rutter, Cal. Practice Guide: Civil Appeals & Writs Ch. 2-B, B. Appealable Judgments and Orders.

Rutter, Cal. Practice Guide: Civil Appeals & Writs Ch. 2-C, C. Nonappealable Orders.

Rutter, Cal. Practice Guide: Civ. Pro. Before Trial Ch. 1-G, G. Prior Court Order Required for Certain Pleadings.

Rutter, Cal. Practice Guide: Civ. Pro. Before Trial Ch. 6-B, B. Complaints.

Rutter, Cal. Practice Guide: Insurance Litigation Ch. 11-I, I. Conspiracy.

Rutter, Cal. Practice Guide: Insurance Litigation Ch. 12A-E, E. Persons Who May be Sued for Tortious Breach of Implied Covenant (Proper Defendants).

Rutter, Cal. Practice Guide: Personal Injury Ch. 5-E, E. Selected Pleading Issues.

Rutter, Cal. Practice Guide: Prof. Responsibility Ch. 6-D, D. Professional Liability.

3 Witkin Cal. Proc. 5th Actions § 211, in General.

3 Witkin Cal. Proc. 5th Actions § 212, Procedure.

9 Witkin Cal. Proc. 5th Appeal § 139, (S 139) in General.

1 Witkin Cal. Proc. 5th Attorneys § 287, (S 287) Liability for Conspiracy With Client.

1 Witkin Cal. Proc. 5th Attorneys § 304, (S 304) Misrepresentation to Third Party's Attorney.

7 Witkin Cal. Proc. 5th Judgment § 372, (S 372) Judgment Without Trial on Facts.

2 Witkin Cal. Proc. 5th Jurisdiction § 290, (S 290) Procedural Error or Omission.

5 Witkin Cal. Proc. 5th Pleading § 1034, (S 1034) in General.

§ 1714.11. Donation of fire protection apparatus or equipment; immunity from liability for damage or injury resulting from use; conditions

(a) Except for damage or injury proximately caused by a grossly negligent act or omission or willful or wanton misconduct of the donor, no public employee or public entity, including, but not limited to, a fire department, a fire protection district, or the Department of Forestry and Fire Protection, that donates fire protection apparatus or equipment to a volunteer fire department, volunteer fire protection district, or volunteer fire company is liable for any damage or injury that results from the use of that apparatus or equipment by the recipient fire department, fire protection district, or fire company.

(b)(1) The immunity provided by this section only shall apply if the donor of the fire protection apparatus or equipment discloses in writing to the recipient fire department, fire protection district, or fire company any known damage to, or deficiencies in, the apparatus and equipment.

(2) A volunteer fire department, volunteer fire protection district, or volunteer fire company that receives donated fire protection apparatus or equipment shall inspect and repair the apparatus and equipment prior to use for public safety purposes. *(Added by Stats.2002, c. 388 (A.B.1821), § 1.)*

Research References

5 Witkin, California Summary 10th Torts § 159, Donated Fire Protection Equipment.

§ 1715. Other obligations

OTHER OBLIGATIONS. Other obligations are prescribed by Divisions I [1] and II [2] of this Code. *(Enacted in 1872.)*

[1] Civil Code § 25 et seq.

[2] Civil Code § 654 et seq.

§ 1716. Solicitations for orders; notice or disclaimer; penalties

(a) It is unlawful for a person to solicit payment of money by another by means of a written statement or invoice, or any writing that reasonably could be considered a bill, invoice, or statement of account due, but is in fact a solicitation for an order, unless the solicitation conforms to subdivisions (b) to (f), inclusive.

(b) A solicitation described in subdivision (a) shall bear on its face either the disclaimer prescribed by subparagraph (A) of paragraph (2) of subsection (d) of Section 3001 of Title 39 of the United States Code or the following notice:

"THIS IS NOT A BILL. THIS IS A SOLICITATION. YOU ARE UNDER NO OBLIGATION TO PAY THE AMOUNT STATED ABOVE UNLESS YOU ACCEPT THIS OFFER."

The statutory disclaimer or the alternative notice shall be displayed in conspicuous boldface capital letters of a color prominently contrasting with the background against which they appear, including all other print on the face of the solicitation and shall be at least as large, bold, and conspicuous as any other print on the face of the solicitation but no smaller than 30–point type.

(c) The notice or disclaimer required by this section shall be displayed conspicuously apart from other print on the page and immediately below each portion of the solicitation that reasonably could be construed to specify a monetary amount due and payable by the recipient. The notice or disclaimer shall not be preceded, followed, or surrounded by words, symbols, or other matter that reduces its conspicuousness or that introduces, modifies, qualifies, or explains the required text, such as "legal notice required by law."

(d) The notice or disclaimer may not, by folding or any other device, be rendered unintelligible or less prominent than any other information on the face of the solicitation.

(e) If a solicitation consists of more than one page or if any page is designed to be separated into portions, such as by tearing along a perforated line, the notice or disclaimer shall be displayed in its entirety on the face of each page or portion of a page that reasonably might be considered a bill, invoice, or statement of account due as required by subdivisions (b) and (c).

(f) For the purposes of this section, "color" includes black and "color prominently contrasting" excludes any color, or any intensity of an otherwise included color, that does not permit legible reproduction by ordinary office photocopying equipment used under normal operating conditions, and that is not at least as vivid as any other color on the face of the solicitation.

(g) Any person damaged by noncompliance with this section, in addition to other remedies, is entitled to damages in an amount equal to three times the sum solicited.

(h) Any person who violates this section shall be liable for a civil penalty not to exceed ten thousand dollars ($10,000) for each violation, which shall be assessed and recovered in a civil action brought in the name of the people of the State of California by the Attorney General or by any district attorney, county counsel, or city attorney in any court of competent jurisdiction. If the action is brought by the Attorney General, one-half of the penalty collected shall be paid to the treasurer of the county in which the judgment was entered and one-half to the State Treasurer. If brought by a district attorney or county counsel, the entire amount of the penalty collected shall be paid to the treasurer of the county in which the judgment was entered. If brought by a city attorney or city prosecutor, one-half of the penalty shall be paid to the treasurer of the county and one-half to the city.

(i) A violation of this section is a misdemeanor punishable by imprisonment in a county jail not exceeding six months, by a fine not exceeding two thousand five hundred dollars ($2,500), or by both that fine and imprisonment. *(Added by Stats.1967, c. 346, p. 1545, § 1. Amended by Stats.1978, c. 492, p. 1624, § 1; Stats.1996, c. 397 (S.B.1530), § 1.)*

Research References

4 Witkin, California Summary 10th Sales § 328, (S 328) Solicitation in Form of Invoice.

§ 1717. Action on contract; award of attorney's fees and costs; prevailing party; deposit of amounts in insured, interest-bearing account; damages not based on contract

(a) In any action on a contract, where the contract specifically provides that attorney's fees and costs, which are incurred to enforce that contract, shall be awarded either to one of the parties or to the prevailing party, then the party who is determined to be the party prevailing on the contract, whether he or she is the party specified in the contract or not, shall be entitled to reasonable attorney's fees in addition to other costs.

Where a contract provides for attorney's fees, as set forth above, that provision shall be construed as applying to the entire contract, unless each party was represented by counsel in the negotiation and execution of the contract, and the fact of that representation is specified in the contract.

Reasonable attorney's fees shall be fixed by the court, and shall be an element of the costs of suit.

Attorney's fees provided for by this section shall not be subject to waiver by the parties to any contract which is entered into after the effective date of this section. Any provision in any such contract which provides for a waiver of attorney's fees is void.

(b)(1) The court, upon notice and motion by a party, shall determine who is the party prevailing on the contract for purposes of this section, whether or not the suit proceeds to final judgment. Except as provided in paragraph (2), the party prevailing on the contract shall be the party who recovered a greater relief in the action on the contract. The court may also determine that there is no party prevailing on the contract for purposes of this section.

(2) Where an action has been voluntarily dismissed or dismissed pursuant to a settlement of the case, there shall be no prevailing party for purposes of this section.

Where the defendant alleges in his or her answer that he or she tendered to the plaintiff the full amount to which he or she was entitled, and thereupon deposits in court for the plaintiff, the amount so tendered, and the allegation is found to be true, then the defendant is deemed to be a party prevailing on the contract within the meaning of this section.

Where a deposit has been made pursuant to this section, the court shall, on the application of any party to the action, order the deposit to be invested in an insured, interest-bearing account. Interest on the amount shall be allocated to the parties in the same proportion as the original funds are allocated.

(c) In an action which seeks relief in addition to that based on a contract, if the party prevailing on the contract has damages awarded against it on causes of action not on the contract, the amounts awarded to the party prevailing on the contract under this section shall be deducted from any damages awarded in favor of the party who did not prevail on the contract. If the amount awarded under this section exceeds the amount of damages awarded the party not prevailing on the contract, the net amount shall be awarded the party prevailing on the contract and judgment may be entered in favor of the party prevailing on the contract for that net amount. *(Added by Stats.1968, c. 266, p. 578, § 1. Amended by Stats.1981, c. 888, p. 3399, § 1; Stats. 1983, c. 1073, § 1; Stats.1986, c. 377, § 1; Stats.1986, c. 785, § 1; Stats.1987, c. 1080, § 1.)*

Research References

California Real Estate Forms (Miller & Starr) § 3:7, Promissory Note.

California Real Estate Forms (Miller & Starr) § 3:8, Deed of Trust, Security Agreement, and Fixture Filing With Assignment of Rents and Agreements.

California Real Estate Forms (Miller & Starr) § 4:3, Construction Contract—Small Project (Owner-Oriented).

California Real Estate Forms (Miller & Starr) § 4:6, Construction Contract—Fixed Price—Commercial Project.

California Real Estate Forms (Miller & Starr) § 4:7, Construction Contract—Turnkey Industrial Project (Lump-Sum).

California Real Estate Forms (Miller & Starr) § 5:5, Design Services Agreement.

California Real Estate Forms (Miller & Starr) § 5:6, Consulting Agreement for Project Development.

California Real Estate Forms (Miller & Starr) § 5:7, General Conditions to Consultant Agreement.

California Real Estate Forms (Miller & Starr) § 1:13, Right of First Refusal Agreement.

California Real Estate Forms (Miller & Starr) § 1:14, Right of First Offer Agreement.

California Real Estate Forms (Miller & Starr) § 1:15, Option Agreement—Long Form.

California Real Estate Forms (Miller & Starr) § 1:16, Option Agreement—Short Form.

California Real Estate Forms (Miller & Starr) § 1:17, Purchase and Sale Agreement—Unimproved Real Property—With Escrow Instructions.

California Real Estate Forms (Miller & Starr) § 1:18, Purchase and Sale Agreement—Raw Land.

California Real Estate Forms (Miller & Starr) § 1:19, Agreement for Purchase and Sale of Realty—Build-To-Suit.

California Real Estate Forms (Miller & Starr) § 1:20, Purchase and Sale Agreement—Small Commercial Properties Subject to Tenant Leases.

California Real Estate Forms (Miller & Starr) § 1:21, Purchase and Sale Agreement—Commercial Property Subject to Tenant Leases.

California Real Estate Forms (Miller & Starr) § 1:22, Agreement of Purchase and Sale—Multi-Property.

California Real Estate Forms (Miller & Starr) § 1:23, Purchase and Sale Agreement—Residential Project.

California Real Estate Forms (Miller & Starr) § 1:24, Combination Purchase and Option Agreement—Residential Lots Being Acquired from a Bankrupt Seller.

California Real Estate Forms (Miller & Starr) § 1:25, Purchase and Sale Agreement—Multi-Tenant Residential Property (With Lease-Back).

California Real Estate Forms (Miller & Starr) § 1:26, Purchase and Sale Agreement—Seller-Oriented Short Form.

California Real Estate Forms (Miller & Starr) § 1:27, Purchase and Sale Agreement—Multitenant Residential Property.

California Real Estate Forms (Miller & Starr) § 1:28, Purchase and Sale Agreement—Hotel.

California Real Estate Forms (Miller & Starr) § 1:29, Purchase and Sale Agreement—Seller Oriented With Seller Financing.

California Real Estate Forms (Miller & Starr) § 1:30, Planned Development Deposit Receipt and Agreement of Sale.

California Real Estate Forms (Miller & Starr) § 1:31, Condominium Deposit Receipt and Agreement of Sale.

California Real Estate Forms (Miller & Starr) § 1:32, Hotel Purchase and Sale Agreement With Escrow Instructions.

California Real Estate Forms (Miller & Starr) § 1:33, Real Estate Purchase Contract and Receipt for Deposit—Income Property.

California Real Estate Forms (Miller & Starr) § 1:34, Installment Land Sale Contract With Power of Sale.

California Real Estate Forms (Miller & Starr) § 1:49, Bill of Sale—Warranty.

California Real Estate Forms (Miller & Starr) § 1:50, General Assignment.

California Real Estate Forms (Miller & Starr) § 1:51, Assignment of Leases and Security Deposits.

California Real Estate Forms (Miller & Starr) § 1:52, Assignment of Trade Name.

California Real Estate Forms (Miller & Starr) § 1:53, Assignment of Contracts, Warranties and Guaranties, and Other Intangible Property.

California Real Estate Forms (Miller & Starr) § 1:76, Standard Offer, Agreement and Escrow Instructions for Purchase of Real Estate.

California Real Estate Forms (Miller & Starr) § 2:16, Office Lease—Multistory Office Building.

California Real Estate Forms (Miller & Starr) § 2:17, Office Lease—Mixed Use Building.

California Real Estate Forms (Miller & Starr) § 2:18, Office Lease—Office/Warehouse Building With Four or Fewer Tenants.

California Real Estate Forms (Miller & Starr) § 2:19, Retail Lease—Power Shopping Center.

California Real Estate Forms (Miller & Starr) § 2:20, Retail Lease—Shopping Center With for Profit Parking Garage.

California Real Estate Forms (Miller & Starr) § 2:21, Retail Lease—15,000 RSF to 30,000 RSF (Tenant Oriented).

California Real Estate Forms (Miller & Starr) § 2:22, Retail Lease—Regional Shopping Center.

California Real Estate Forms (Miller & Starr) § 2:23, Retail Lease—Small Strip-Shopping Center

California Real Estate Forms (Miller & Starr) § 2:24, Retail Lease—Restaurant.

California Real Estate Forms (Miller & Starr) § 2:25, Industrial Lease.

California Real Estate Forms (Miller & Starr) § 2:26, Triple Net Lease—Industrial Build-To-Suit Lease.

California Real Estate Forms (Miller & Starr) § 2:27, Ground Lease.

California Real Estate Forms (Miller & Starr) § 2:28, Triple Net Lease—Stand-Alone Building.

California Real Estate Forms (Miller & Starr) § 2:29, Parking Garage Lease.

California Real Estate Forms (Miller & Starr) § 2:32, Gross Lease—Small Commercial Property.

California Real Estate Forms (Miller & Starr) § 2:33, Sublease—With Consent of Master Landlord.

California Real Estate Forms (Miller & Starr) § 2:34, Sublease—Shared Office Space.

California Real Estate Forms (Miller & Starr) § 2:35, Assignment of Lease.

California Real Estate Forms (Miller & Starr) § 2:52, Option to Lease.

California Real Estate Forms (Miller & Starr) § 2:53, Confidentiality Agreement—Tenant's Records.

California Real Estate Forms (Miller & Starr) § 2:62, Standard Industrial/Commercial Multi-Tenant Lease—Net.

California Real Estate Forms (Miller & Starr) § 2:63, Standard Industrial/Commercial Multi-Tenant Lease—Gross.

California Real Estate Forms (Miller & Starr) § 2:65, Residential Lease.

California Real Estate Forms (Miller & Starr) § 2:66, Residential Lease With Purchase Option.

California Real Estate Forms (Miller & Starr) § 3:10, Environmental Certification, Agreement, and Indemnity of Borrower.

California Real Estate Forms (Miller & Starr) § 3:13, Promissory Note Secured by Construction Deed of Trust.

California Real Estate Forms (Miller & Starr) § 3:14, Construction Deed of Trust, Security Agreement, and Fixture Filing With Assignment of Rents and Agreements.

California Real Estate Forms (Miller & Starr) § 3:15, Construction Loan Agreement.

California Real Estate Forms (Miller & Starr) § 3:20, Promissory Note—Conduit Loan.

California Real Estate Forms (Miller & Starr) § 3:21, Deed of Trust, Assignment of Rents, Security Agreement and Fixture Filing—Conduit Loan.

California Real Estate Forms (Miller & Starr) § 3:30, Environmental Indemnity—Conduit Loan.

California Real Estate Forms (Miller & Starr) § 3:36, Contingent Interest Agreement.

California Real Estate Forms (Miller & Starr) § 3:37, Continuing Guaranty.

California Real Estate Forms (Miller & Starr) § 3:38, Completion Guaranty.

California Real Estate Forms (Miller & Starr) § 3:55, Subordination, Nondisturbance, and Attornment Agreement.

California Real Estate Forms (Miller & Starr) § 3:57, Loan Purchase and Sale Agreement.

California Real Estate Forms (Miller & Starr) § 3:66, Deed in Lieu of Foreclosure—Transfer Agreement.

California Real Estate Forms (Miller & Starr) §4:11, Construction Contract—Construction Manager Representing Owner's Interests.

California Real Estate Forms (Miller & Starr) § 4:14, Construction Agreement—Master Agreement for Construction Services.

California Real Estate Forms (Miller & Starr) § 4:15, Development Agreement.

California Real Estate Forms (Miller & Starr) § 4:16, Restaurant Development and Construction Agreement.

California Real Estate Forms (Miller & Starr) § 4:20, Service Contract—Elevators.

California Real Estate Forms (Miller & Starr) § 1:138, Pre-Sale Confidentiality Agreement.

California Real Estate Forms (Miller & Starr) § 1:139, Nondisclosure Agreement.

California Real Estate Forms (Miller & Starr) § 5:200, Bid/Subcontract for Structural Concrete Work.

California Real Estate Forms (Miller & Starr) § 2:18.50, Management Office License Agreement.

Rutter, Cal. Practice Guide: A.D.R. Ch. 2-E, E. Conducting Negotiations.

Rutter, Cal. Practice Guide: A.D.R. Ch. 4-B, B. Judicial Arbitration.

Rutter, Cal. Practice Guide: A.D.R. Ch. 5-G, G. Procedures to Enforce Arbitration.

Rutter, Cal. Practice Guide: A.D.R. Ch. 5-I, I. Arbitrator's Award.

Rutter, Cal. Practice Guide: A.D.R. Ch. 5-K, K. Arbitration of International Commercial Disputes.

Rutter, Cal. Practice Guide: A.D.R. Gen. Matls., Highlights.

Rutter, Cal. Practice Guide: Civil Appeals & Writs Ch. 7-A, A. Overview.

Rutter, Cal. Practice Guide: Civil Appeals & Writs Ch. 7-C, C. Stay by Posting Security (Bond or Undertaking).

Rutter, Cal. Practice Guide: Civil Appeals & Writs Ch. 8-C, C. Standards of Appellate Review.

Rutter, Cal. Practice Guide: Civil Appeals & Writs Ch. 8-D, D. Limits on Assertion of Issues on Appeal.

Rutter, Cal. Practice Guide: Civil Appeals & Writs Ch. 14-B, B. Recovery of Appellate Costs and Attorney Fees.

Rutter, Cal. Practice Guide: Civil Appeals & Writs Ch. 15-E, E. Procedures on Writ Review.

Rutter, Cal. Practice Guide: Civil Appeals & Writs Ch. 14-B, , Outline B.

Rutter, Cal. Practice Guide: Civ. Pro. Before Trial Ch. 1-A, A. Accepting a New Case.

Rutter, Cal. Practice Guide: Civ. Pro. Before Trial Ch. 6-C, C. Answer.

Rutter, Cal. Practice Guide: Civ. Pro. Before Trial Ch. 11-A, A. Voluntary Dismissals.

Rutter, Cal. Practice Guide: Civ. Pro. Before Trial Ch. 13-F, F. Arbitration Award.

Rutter, Cal. Practice Guide: Civ. Pro. Before Trial Ch. 14-C, C. Procedural Issues.

Rutter, Cal. Practice Guide: Civ. Pro. Before Trial Ch. 1-A, Outline a.

Rutter, Cal. Practice Guide: Civ. Pro. Before Trial Gen. Matls., Highlights.

Rutter, Cal. Practice Guide: Civ. Pro. Before Trial Ch. 12(II)-C, C. Statutory Offer to Compromise (CCP § 998).

Rutter, Cal. Practice Guide: Civil Trials & Evidence Ch. 17-D, D. Costs.

Rutter, Cal. Practice Guide: Civil Trials & Evidence Ch. 17-E, E. Attorney Fees as Costs.

Rutter, Cal. Practice Guide: Civil Trials & Evidence Gen. Matls., Highlights.

Rutter, Cal. Practice Guide: Civil Trials & Evidence Ch. 17-E, Outline E.

California Practice Guide: Employment Litigation Ch. 17-H, H. Attorney Fees.

California Practice Guide: Employment Litigation Ch. 18-A, A. Settlement Considerations.

California Practice Guide: Employment Litigation Gen. Matls, Highlights.

Rutter, Cal. Practice Guide: Enforcing Judgments/Debts Ch. 3-C, C. Prelawsuit Considerations.

Rutter, Cal. Practice Guide: Enforcing Judgments/Debts Ch. 4-A, A. Attachment.

Rutter, Cal. Practice Guide: Enforcing Judgments/Debts Ch. 6A-5, Amount Recoverable Under Judgment.

Rutter, Cal. Practice Guide: Enforcing Judgments/Debts Ch. 6D-6, Debtor's Recourse Against Execution Levy.

Rutter, Cal. Practice Guide: Enforcing Judgments/Debts Ch. 6G-4, Creditor's Suit.

Rutter, Cal. Practice Guide: Fed.Civ.Pro. Before Trial Ch. 16-G, G. Voluntary Dismissals.

Rutter, Cal. Practice Guide: Insurance Litigation Ch. 9-F, F. Amount Recoverable by Insurer Under Subrogation.

Rutter, Cal. Practice Guide: Insurance Litigation Ch. 13-B, B. Extracontractual Compensatory Damages.

Rutter, Cal. Practice Guide: Insurance Litigation Ch. 6I-C, C. Surety's Obligations and Rights Upon Default by Principal.

Rutter, Cal. Practice Guide: Insurance Litigation Ch. 6I-C, Outline C.

Rutter, Cal. Practice Guide: Landlord-Tenant Gen. Matls, Highlights.

Rutter, Cal. Practice Guide: Personal Injury Ch. 3-A, A. Introduction.

Rutter, Cal. Practice Guide: Personal Injury Ch. 4-D, D. Techniques Where Settlement Not Forthcoming.

Rutter, Cal. Practice Guide: Personal Injury Ch. 4-F, F. Court-Conducted Settlement Proceedings.

Rutter, Cal. Practice Guide: Personal Injury Ch. 7-I, I. Trial De Novo After Arbitration Award.

Rutter, Cal. Practice Guide: Personal Injury Ch. 9-M, M. Verdicts and Judgment.

Rutter, Cal. Practice Guide: Personal Injury Ch. 3-A, Outline a.

Rutter, Cal. Practice Guide: Real Prop. Transactions Ch. 4-E, E. Drafting the Purchase and Sale Agreement-Terms and Conditions.

Rutter, Cal. Practice Guide: Real Prop. Transactions Ch. 4-F, F. Use of an Escrow.

Rutter, Cal. Practice Guide: Real Prop. Transactions Ch. 5-C, C. Liability Under CERCLA and California Superfund.

Rutter, Cal. Practice Guide: Real Prop. Transactions Ch. 6-F, F. Promissory Note.

Rutter, Cal. Practice Guide: Real Prop. Transactions Ch. 6-H, H. Security for Promissory Note.

Rutter, Cal. Practice Guide: Real Prop. Transactions Ch. 11-A, A. Factors Affecting Choice of Remedies.

Rutter, Cal. Practice Guide: Real Prop. Transactions Ch. 11-C, C. Seller's Remedies Upon Buyer's Breach-Damages and Specific Performance.

Rutter, Cal. Practice Guide: Real Prop. Transactions Ch. 11-D, D. Buyer's Remedies Upon Seller's Breach-Damages and Specific Performance.

Rutter, Cal. Practice Guide: Real Prop. Transactions Ch. 11-E, E. Damages for Fraud.

Rutter, Cal. Practice Guide: Real Prop. Transactions Gen. Matls., Highlights.

Rutter, Cal. Practice Guide: Real Prop. Transactions Ch. 6-H Outline, Outline H.

Rutter, Cal. Practice Guide: Real Prop. Transactions Ch. 11-C Outline, Outline C.

Rutter, Cal. Practice Guide: Prof. Responsibility Ch. 3-B, B. Formation of Relationship.

Rutter, Cal. Practice Guide: Prof. Responsibility Ch. 5-B, B. Types of Fees and Fee Arrangements.

Rutter, Cal. Practice Guide: Prof. Responsibility Ch. 6-D, D. Professional Liability.

Rutter, Cal. Practice Guide: Prof. Responsibility Ch. 5-B, Outline B.

Miller and Starr California Real Estate § 3:8, Warranty of Authority.

Miller and Starr California Real Estate § 6:17, Liability and Measure of Damages to the Parties.

Miller and Starr California Real Estate § 11:48, Pecuniary Loss.

Miller and Starr California Real Estate § 24:30, Rights of Enforcement--Recovery of Attorney's Fees.

Miller and Starr California Real Estate § 27:32, Public Works Competitive Bidding--Bidder Qualifications and Requirements.

Miller and Starr California Real Estate § 29:17, Express and Implied Indemnity.

Miller and Starr California Real Estate § 31:36, Notice of Litigation by a Tenant; Attorney's Fees; Penalties.

Miller and Starr California Real Estate § 34:66, Examples of Actions in Which Fees Can be Recovered.

Miller and Starr California Real Estate § 34:68, Recovery of Fees Pursuant to Contract Provision.

Miller and Starr California Real Estate § 34:70, Recovery in Tort Actions Pursuant to Contract.

Miller and Starr California Real Estate § 34:71, Reciprocity of Attorney Fee Provision.

Miller and Starr California Real Estate § 34:72, Reciprocity in Tort Actions.

Miller and Starr California Real Estate § 34:73, Determining the "Prevailing Party".

Miller and Starr California Real Estate § 34:74, Effect of Dismissal of Action Before Judgment.

Miller and Starr California Real Estate § 34:75, Recovery of Fees by or from a Person Not a Party to the Contract.

Miller and Starr California Real Estate § 34:76, Recovery of Fees in an Action for Indemnity.

Miller and Starr California Real Estate § 34:77, Recovery of Fees After Judgment in Excess of Rejected Settlement Offer.

Miller and Starr California Real Estate § 34:79, Recovery of Fees as an Item of Costs; Procedural Requirements.

Miller and Starr California Real Estate § 34:80, Recovery by Attorney for Self-Representation; House Counsel.

7 Witkin Cal. Proc. 5th Judgment § 201, (S 201) Distinction: Fees Incurred in Defending Noncontract Claims.

7 Witkin Cal. Proc. 5th Judgment § 202, (S 202) Distinction: Voluntary Dismissal of Trial De Novo Following Arbitration.

7 Witkin Cal. Proc. 5th Judgment § 203, (S 203) Distinction: Issue of Entitlement to Costs and Attorneys' Fees Expressly Reserved.

7 Witkin Cal. Proc. 5th Judgment § 204, (S 204) Distinction: Where Prevailing Party's Right to Fees Arises Under Another Statute.

7 Witkin Cal. Proc. 5th Judgment § 205, Settlement Under.

7 Witkin Cal. Proc. 5th Judgment § 206, (S 206) Fees Allowed.

7 Witkin Cal. Proc. 5th Judgment § 207, (S 207) Fees Denied.

7 Witkin Cal. Proc. 5th Judgment § 208, (S 208) Fees Denied.

7 Witkin Cal. Proc. 5th Judgment § 209, (S 209) Fees Allowed.

7 Witkin Cal. Proc. 5th Judgment § 221, (S 221) Actions to Enforce Equitable Servitude.

7 Witkin Cal. Proc. 5th Judgment § 240, Who May Recover.

7 Witkin Cal. Proc. 5th Judgment § 295, (S 295) in General.

7 Witkin Cal. Proc. 5th Judgment § 296, (S 296) Fees Based on Contract.

7 Witkin Cal. Proc. 5th Judgment § 306, Where Contract Does Not Specify Amount.

7 Witkin Cal. Proc. 5th Judgment § 308, Where Contract Specifies "Amount Incurred.".

2 Witkin Cal. Proc. 5th Jurisdiction § 26, (S 26) Attorneys' Fees.

2 Witkin Cal. Proc. 5th Jurisdiction § 227, Motion to Dismiss for Inconvenient Forum.

6 Witkin Cal. Proc. 5th Proceedings Without Trial § 99, (S 99) Judgment on Compromise.

7 Witkin Cal. Proc. 5th Trial § 228, Who May Recover Sanctions.

7 Witkin Cal. Proc. 5th Trial § 233, (S 233) Notice.

12 Witkin, California Summary 10th Real Property § 739, (S 739) Costs and Attorneys' Fees.

1 Witkin Cal. Summ. 10th Contracts § 897, (S 897) Attorneys' Fees.

4 Witkin, California Summary 10th Sales § 260, (S 260) Venue, Attorneys' Fees, and Costs.

6 Witkin, California Summary 10th Torts § 1648, (S 1648) Verdict for Personal Injury and Other Damages.

13 Witkin, California Summary 10th Equity § 27A, (S 27A) (New)- Attorneys' Fees Are Not Incidental to Specific Performance.

§ 1717.5. Action on contract based on book account; award of attorney's fees for the prevailing party; effect of written agreement; scope of application

(a) Except as otherwise provided by law or where waived by the parties to an agreement, in any action on a contract based on a book account, as defined in Section 337a of the Code of Civil Procedure, entered into on or after January 1, 1987, which does not provide for attorney's fees and costs, as provided in Section 1717, the party who is determined to be the party prevailing on the contract shall be entitled to reasonable attorney's fees, as provided below, in addition to other costs. The prevailing party on the contract shall be the party who recovered a greater relief in the action on the contract. The court may determine that there is no party prevailing on the contract for purposes of this section.

Reasonable attorney's fees awarded pursuant to this section for the prevailing party bringing the action on the book account shall be fixed by the court in an amount that shall not exceed the lesser of: (1) eight hundred dollars ($800) for book accounts based upon an obligation owing by a natural person for goods, moneys, or services which were primarily for personal, family, or household purposes; and one thousand dollars ($1,000) for all other book accounts to which this section applies; or (2) 25 percent of the principal obligation owing under the contract.

For the party against whom the obligation on the book account was asserted in the action subject to this section, if that party is found to have no obligation owing on a book account, the court shall award that prevailing party reasonable attorney's fees not to exceed eight hundred dollars ($800) for book accounts based upon an obligation owing by a natural person for goods, moneys, or services which were primarily for personal, family, or household purposes, and one thousand dollars ($1,-

000) for all other book accounts to which this section applies. These attorney's fees shall be an element of the costs of the suit.

If there is a written agreement between the parties signed by the person to be charged, the fees provided by this section may not be imposed unless that agreement contains a statement that the prevailing party in any action between the parties is entitled to the fees provided by this section.

(b) The attorney's fees allowed pursuant to this section shall be the lesser of either the maximum amount allowed by this section, the amount provided by any default attorney's fee schedule adopted by the court applicable to the suit, or an amount as otherwise provided by the court. Any claim for attorney's fees pursuant to this section in excess of the amounts set forth in the default attorney's fee schedule shall be reasonable attorney's fees, as proved by the party, as actual and necessary for the claim that is subject to this section.

(c) This section does not apply to any action in which an insurance company is a party nor shall an insurance company, surety, or guarantor be liable under this section, in the absence of a specific contractual provision, for the attorney's fees and costs awarded a prevailing party against its insured.

This section does not apply to any action in which a bank, a savings association, a federal association, a state or federal credit union, or a subsidiary, affiliate, or holding company of any of those entities, or an authorized industrial loan company, a licensed consumer finance lender, or a licensed commercial finance lender, is a party. *(Added by Stats.1986, c. 884, § 1. Amended by Stats.1987, c. 764, § 4; Stats.1991, c. 406 (S.B.182), § 1; Stats.1992, c. 530 (A.B.2516), § 2; Stats.2004, c. 328 (A.B.2347), § 1.)*

Research References

Rutter, Cal. Practice Guide: Civil Trials & Evidence Ch. 17-E, E. Attorney Fees as Costs.

Rutter, Cal. Practice Guide: Enforcing Judgments/Debts Ch. 3-C, C. Prelawsuit Considerations.

Rutter, Cal. Practice Guide: Enforcing Judgments/Debts Ch. 4-A, A. Attachment.

Rutter, Cal. Practice Guide: Enforcing Judgments/Debts Ch. 6A-5, Amount Recoverable Under Judgment.

Rutter, Cal. Practice Guide: Enforcing Judgments/Debts Ch. 6G-4, Creditor's Suit.

7 Witkin Cal. Proc. 5th Judgment § 174, Contract Action Based on Book Account.

§ 1718. Farm machinery repair shops; invoices; estimates; definitions

(a) As used in this section:

(1) "Farm machinery" means all tools and equipment used in relation to the operation of a farm.

(2) "Farm machinery repair shop" means a business which, for compensation, engages in the operation, on or off its premises, of repairing farm machinery.

(3) "Per-job basis" means each act of maintenance or repair which is performed on farm machinery.

(b) All work done by a farm machinery repair shop, including all warranty work, shall be recorded on an invoice, which shall describe all service work done and parts supplied. If more than one act of maintenance or repair is performed by a farm machinery repair shop, the invoice shall be written in such a way that the labor cost per hour and total labor cost, as well as the specific parts used and their cost, shall be recorded on a per-job basis.

However, where work is done on an agreed total-cost-per-job basis, or the work includes an agreed total cost for component unit replacement, the invoice shall describe the work done on such basis and the total cost for such work.

(c) Each farm machinery repair shop shall give to each customer, upon request, a written estimated price for labor and parts necessary, on a per-job basis. It shall not charge for work done or parts supplied in excess of the estimated price without the consent of the customer, which shall be obtained at some time after it is determined that the estimated price is insufficient and before the work not included in the estimate is done, or the parts not included in the estimate are supplied. Nothing in this section shall be construed to require a farm machinery repair shop to give a written estimated price if the shop does not agree to perform the requested repair.

(d) Any violation of this section is a misdemeanor. *(Added by Stats.1972, c. 302, p. 573, § 1. Amended by Stats.1973, c. 235, p. 621, § 1.)*

Research References

4 Witkin, California Summary 10th Sales § 332, Automobiles and Farm Machinery.

§ 1719. Dishonored checks; liability; demands for payment; stop payments; notice; penalties, damages and service charges; assignees

(a)(1) Notwithstanding any penal sanctions that may apply, any person who passes a check on insufficient funds shall be liable to the payee for the amount of the check and a service charge payable to the payee for an amount not to exceed twenty-five dollars ($25) for the first check passed on insufficient funds and an amount not to exceed thirty-five dollars ($35) for each subsequent check to that payee passed on insufficient funds.

(2) Notwithstanding any penal sanctions that may apply, any person who passes a check on insufficient funds shall be liable to the payee for damages equal to treble the amount of the check if a written demand for payment is mailed by certified mail to the person who had passed a check on insufficient funds and the written demand informs this person of (A) the provisions of this section, (B) the amount of the check, and (C) the amount of the service charge payable to the payee. The person who had passed a check on insufficient funds shall have 30 days from the date the written demand was mailed to pay the amount of the check, the amount of the service charge payable to the payee, and the costs to mail the written demand for payment. If this person fails to pay in full the amount of the check, the service charge payable to the payee, and the costs to mail the written demand within this period, this person shall then be liable instead for the amount of the check, minus any partial payments made toward the amount of the check or the service charge within 30 days of the written demand, and damages equal to treble that amount, which shall not be less than one hundred dollars ($100) nor more than one thousand five hundred dollars ($1,500). When a person becomes liable for treble damages for a check that is the subject of a written demand, that person shall no longer be liable for any service charge for that check and any costs to mail the written demand.

(3) Notwithstanding paragraphs (1) and (2), a person shall not be liable for the service charge, costs to mail the written demand, or treble damages if he or she stops payment in order to resolve a good faith dispute with the payee. The payee is entitled to the service charge, costs to mail the written demand, or treble damages only upon proving by clear and convincing evidence that there was no good faith dispute, as defined in subdivision (b).

(4) Notwithstanding paragraph (1), a person shall not be liable under that paragraph for the service charge if, at any time, he or she presents the payee with written confirmation by his or her financial institution that the check was returned to the payee by the financial institution due to an error on the part of the financial institution.

(5) Notwithstanding paragraph (1), a person shall not be liable under that paragraph for the service charge if the person presents the payee with written confirmation that his or her account had insufficient funds as a result of a delay in the regularly scheduled transfer of, or the posting of, a direct deposit of a social security or government benefit assistance payment.

(6) As used in this subdivision, to "pass a check on insufficient funds" means to make, utter, draw, or deliver any check, draft, or order for the payment of money upon any bank, depository, person, firm, or corporation that refuses to honor the check, draft, or order for any of the following reasons:

(A) Lack of funds or credit in the account to pay the check.

(B) The person who wrote the check does not have an account with the drawee.

(C) The person who wrote the check instructed the drawee to stop payment on the check.

(b) For purposes of this section, in the case of a stop payment, the existence of a "good faith dispute" shall be determined by the trier of fact. A "good faith dispute" is one in which the court finds that the drawer had a reasonable belief of his or her legal entitlement to withhold payment. Grounds for the entitlement include, but are not limited to, the following: services were not rendered, goods were not delivered, goods or services purchased are faulty, not as promised, or otherwise unsatisfactory, or there was an overcharge.

(c) In the case of a stop payment, the notice to the drawer required by this section shall be in substantially the following form:

NOTICE

To: _____

    (name of drawer)

_____ is the payee of a check you wrote

    (name of payee)

for $ _____. The check was not paid because

    (amount)

you stopped payment, and the payee demands payment. You may have a good faith dispute as to whether you owe the full amount. If you do not have a good faith dispute with the payee and fail to pay the payee the full amount of the check in cash, a service charge of an amount not to exceed twenty-five dollars ($25) for the first check passed on insufficient funds and an amount not to exceed thirty-five dollars ($35) for each subsequent check passed on insufficient funds, and the costs to mail this notice within 30 days after this notice was mailed, you could be sued and held responsible to pay at least both of the following:

(1) The amount of the check.

(2) Damages of at least one hundred dollars ($100) or, if higher, three times the amount of the check up to one thousand five hundred dollars ($1,500).

If the court determines that you do have a good faith dispute with the payee, you will not have to pay the service charge, treble damages, or mailing cost. If you stopped payment because you have a good faith dispute with the payee, you should try to work out your dispute with the payee. You can contact the payee at:

_____

    (name of payee)

_____

    (street address)

_____

    (telephone number)

You may wish to contact a lawyer to discuss your legal rights and responsibilities.

(name of sender of notice)

(d) In the case of a stop payment, a court may not award damages or costs under this section unless the court receives into evidence a copy of the written demand that, in that case, shall have been sent to the drawer and a signed certified mail receipt showing delivery, or attempted delivery if refused, of the written demand to the drawer's last known address.

(e) A cause of action under this section may be brought in small claims court by the original payee, if it does not exceed the jurisdiction of that court, or in any other appropriate court. The payee shall, in order to recover damages because the drawer instructed the drawee to stop payment, show to the satisfaction of the trier of fact that there was a reasonable effort on the part of the payee to reconcile and resolve the dispute prior to pursuing the dispute through the courts.

(f) A cause of action under this section may be brought by a holder of the check or an assignee of the payee. A proceeding under this section is a limited civil case. However, if the assignee is acting on behalf of the payee, for a flat fee or a percentage fee, the assignee may not charge the payee a greater flat fee or percentage fee for that portion of the amount collected that represents treble damages than is charged the payee for collecting the face amount of the check, draft, or order. This subdivision shall not apply to an action brought in small claims court.

(g) Notwithstanding subdivision (a), if the payee is the court, the written demand for payment described in subdivision (a) may be mailed to the drawer by the court clerk. Notwithstanding subdivision (d), in the case of a stop payment where the demand is mailed by the court clerk, a court may not award damages or costs pursuant to subdivision (d), unless the court receives into evidence a copy of the written demand, and a certificate of mailing by the court clerk in the form provided for in subdivision (4) of Section 1013a of the Code of Civil Procedure for service in civil actions. For purposes of this subdivision, in courts where a single court clerk serves more than one court, the clerk shall be deemed the court clerk of each court.

(h) The requirements of this section in regard to remedies are mandatory upon a court.

(i) The assignee of the payee or a holder of the check may demand, recover, or enforce the service charge, damages, and costs specified in this section to the same extent as the original payee.

(j)(1) A drawer is liable for damages and costs only if all of the requirements of this section have been satisfied.

(2) The drawer shall in no event be liable more than once under this section on each check for a service charge, damages, or costs.

(k) Nothing in this section is intended to condition, curtail, or otherwise prejudice the rights, claims, remedies, and defenses under Division 3 (commencing with Section 3101) of the Commercial Code of a drawer, payee, assignee, or holder, including a holder in due course as defined in Section 3302 of the Commercial Code, in connection with the enforcement of this section. *(Added by Stats.1983, c. 522, § 1. Amended by Stats.1985, c. 196, § 1; Stats.1986, c. 225, § 1; Stats.1986, c. 708, § 1; Stats.1987, c. 4, § 1, eff. March 17, 1987; Stats.1990, c. 599 (S.B.2130), § 1; Stats.1994, c. 926 (A.B.2533), § 1; Stats.1995, c. 134 (A.B.522), § 1; Stats.1996, c. 1000 (A.B.2643), § 1; Stats. 1998, c. 931 (S.B.2139), § 14, eff. Sept. 28, 1998.)*

Law Revision Commission Comments

Subdivisions (f) and (g) of Section 1719 are amended to accommodate unification of the municipal and superior courts in a county. Cal. Const. art. VI, § 5(e).

A limited civil case is within the original jurisdiction of the municipal court or of the superior court in a county in which there is no municipal court. Cal. Const. art. VI, 10 (superior court jurisdiction); Code Civ. Proc. §§ 85, 85.1 (limited civil cases). See also Code Civ. Proc. §§ 91, 904.2, 1085 (trial procedures and writ and appellate jurisdiction for limited civil cases). [28 Cal.L.Rev.Comm. Reports 51 (1998)].

Research References

Rutter, Cal. Practice Guide: Civil Trials & Evidence Ch. 17-F, F. Prejudgment Interest.
Rutter, Cal. Practice Guide: Enforcing Judgments/Debts Ch. 2-B, B. Statutory Liability and Procedures.
Rutter, Cal. Practice Guide: Enforcing Judgments/Debts Ch. 3-B, B. Collection Without Suit.
Rutter, Cal. Practice Guide: Enforcing Judgments/Debts Ch. 3-C, C. Prelawsuit Considerations.
Rutter, Cal. Practice Guide: Enforcing Judgments/Debts Form 3:N, Written Demand to Pay Nsf Check (No Stop Payment).
Rutter, Cal. Practice Guide: Enforcing Judgments/Debts Form 3:O, Written Notice to Pay Nsf Check Where Drawer Stopped Payment.
Rutter, Cal. Practice Guide: Personal Injury Ch. 3-E, E. Punitive Damages.
Miller and Starr California Real Estate § 2:4, Deposit Receipt as a Contract of Sale--Ownership of the Deposit.
Miller and Starr California Real Estate § 21:1, Policy and Validity of the Usury Law.
Miller and Starr California Real Estate § 10:72, Payment by Check.
Miller and Starr California Real Estate § 19:78, Time and Place of Payment; Late Charges.
Miller and Starr California Real Estate § 34:99, Punitive Damages-- Judicial Review.
6 Witkin, California Summary 10th Torts § 1570, Treble Damages.
3 Witkin, California Summary 10th Agency and Employment § 397, (S 397) Miscellaneous Rules.
4 Witkin, California Summary 10th Negotiable Instruments § 39, Authorized Signature.
4 Witkin, California Summary 10th Negotiable Instruments § 47, (S 47) Additional Liability to Payee or Payee's Assignee.

§ 1720. Failure of obligee to give timely response to inquiry concerning debit or credit applicable to obligation

(a) If an obligee fails to give a timely response to an inquiry of an obligor concerning any debit or credit applicable to an obligation, he shall not be entitled to interest, financing charges, service charges, or any other similar charges thereon, from the date of mailing of the inquiry to the date of mailing of the response.

(b) For the purpose of subdivision (a):

(1) An "inquiry" is a writing which is posted by certified mail to the address of the obligee to which payments are normally tendered, unless another address is specifically indicated on the statement for such purpose, then to such address.

(2) A "response" is a writing which is responsive to an inquiry and mailed to the last known address of the obligor.

(3) A response is "timely" if it is mailed within 60 days from the date on which the inquiry was mailed.

(c) This section shall only apply to an obligation created pursuant to a retail installment account as defined by Section 1802.7. *(Added by Stats.1970, c. 191, p. 446, § 1. Amended by Stats.1971, c. 1019, p. 1958, § 3.)*

Research References

4 Witkin, California Summary 10th Sales § 287, Penalties.

§ 1721. Vandalism at construction site; treble damages and attorney fees

In an action for the intentional and malicious destruction of real or personal property at a site where substantial improvements to real property are under construction, upon judgment in favor of the plaintiff, the court may, in its discretion, award the plaintiff an amount not to exceed three times the amount of actual damages, and may award reasonable attorney's fees. *(Added by Stats.1983. c. 474, § 1.)*

Research References

Miller and Starr California Real Estate § 17:19, Constructive Severance.
4 Witkin, California Summary 10th Sales § 5, Former Uniform Acts.
4 Witkin, California Summary 10th Sales § 22, Sales and Sales Contracts.
6 Witkin, California Summary 10th Torts § 1570, Treble Damages.

§ 1722. Retail sale and delivery, and service or repair transactions; time of delivery, service or repair; delay or inability to deliver; notification; damages for failure to deliver or to commence service or repair; cable television; utilities; void contracts

(a)(1) Whenever a contract is entered into between a consumer and a retailer with 25 or more employees relating to the sale of merchandise which is to be delivered by the retailer or the retailer's agent to the consumer at a later date, and the parties have agreed that the presence of the consumer is required at the time of delivery, the retailer and the consumer shall agree, either at the time of the sale or at a later date prior to the delivery date, on a four-hour time period within which any delivery shall be made. Whenever a contract is entered into between a consumer and a retailer with 25 or more employees for service or repair of merchandise, whether or not the merchandise was sold by the retailer to the consumer, and the parties have agreed that the presence of the consumer is required at the time of service or repair, upon receipt of a request for service or repair under the contract, the retailer and the consumer shall agree, prior to the date of service or repair, on a four-hour period within which the service or repair shall be commenced. Once a delivery, service, or repair time is established, the retailer or the retailer's agent shall deliver the merchandise to the consumer, or commence service or repair of the merchandise, within that four-hour period.

(2) If the merchandise is not delivered, or service or repair are not commenced, within the specified four-hour period, except for delays caused by unforeseen or unavoidable occurrences beyond the control of the retailer, the consumer may bring an action in small claims court against the retailer for lost wages, expenses actually incurred, or other actual damages not exceeding a total of six hundred dollars ($600).

(3) No action shall be considered valid if the consumer was not present at the time, within the specified period, when the retailer or the retailer's agent attempted to make the delivery, service, or repairs or made a diligent attempt to notify the consumer by telephone or in person of its inability to do so because of unforeseen or unavoidable occurrences beyond its control. If notification is by telephone, the retailer or the retailer's agent shall leave a telephone number for a return telephone call by the consumer to the retailer or its agent, to enable the consumer to arrange a new two-hour period for delivery, service, or repair with the retailer or the retailer's agent.

(4) In any small claims action, logs and other business records maintained by the retailer or the retailer's agent in the ordinary course of business shall be prima facie evidence of the time period specified for the delivery, service, or repairs and of the time when the merchandise was delivered, or of a diligent attempt by the retailer or the retailer's agent to notify the consumer of delay caused by unforeseen or unavoidable occurrences.

(5) It shall be a defense to the action if a diligent attempt was made to notify the consumer of the delay caused by unforeseen or unavoidable occurrences beyond the control of the retailer or the retailer's agent, or the retailer or the retailer's agent was unable to notify the consumer of the delay because of the consumer's absence or unavailability during the four-hour period, and, in either instance, the retailer or the retailer's agent makes the delivery, service, or repairs within two hours of a newly agreed upon time or, if the consumer unreasonably declines to arrange a new time for the delivery, service, or repairs.

(b)(1) Cable television companies shall inform their subscribers of their right to service connection or repair within a four-hour period, if the presence of the subscriber is required, by offering the four-hour period at the time the subscriber calls for service connection or repair. Whenever a subscriber contracts with a cable television company for a service connection or repair which is to take place at a later date, and the parties have agreed that the presence of the subscriber is required, the cable company and the subscriber shall agree, prior to the date of service connection or repair, on the time for the commencement of the four-hour period for the service connection or repair.

(2) If the service connection or repair is not commenced within the specified four-hour period, except for delays caused by unforeseen or unavoidable occurrences beyond the control of the company, the subscriber may bring an action in small claims court against the company for lost wages, expenses actually incurred or other actual damages not exceeding a total of six hundred dollars ($600).

(3) No action shall be considered valid if the subscriber was not present at the time, within the specified period, that the company attempted to make the service connection or repair or made a diligent attempt to notify the subscriber by telephone or in person of its inability to do so because of unforeseen or unavoidable occurrences beyond its control. If notification is by telephone, the cable television company or its agent shall leave a telephone number for a return telephone call by the subscriber to the company or its agent, to enable the consumer to arrange a new two-hour period for service connection or repair.

(4) In any small claims action, logs and other business records maintained by the company or its agents in the ordinary course of business shall be prima facie evidence of the time period specified for the commencement of the service connection or repair and the time that the company or its agents attempted to make the service connection or repair, or of a diligent attempt by the company to notify the subscriber in person or by telephone of a delay caused by unforeseen or unavoidable occurrences.

(5) It shall be a defense to the action if a diligent attempt was made to notify the subscriber of a delay caused by unforeseen or unavoidable occurrences beyond the control of the company or its agents, or the company or its agents were unable to notify the subscriber because of the subscriber's absence or unavailability during the four-hour period, and, in either instance, the cable television company commenced service or repairs within a newly agreed upon two-hour period.

(6) No action shall be considered valid against a cable television company pursuant to this section when the franchise or any local ordinance provides the subscriber with a remedy for a delay in commencement of a service connection or repair and the subscriber has elected to pursue that remedy. If a subscriber elects to pursue his or her remedies against a cable television company under this section, the franchising or state or local licensing authority shall be barred from imposing any fine, penalty, or other sanction against the company, arising out of the same incident.

(c)(1) Utilities shall inform their subscribers of their right to service connection or repair within a four-hour period, if the presence of the subscriber is required, by offering the four-hour period at the time the subscriber calls for service connection or repair. Whenever a subscriber contracts with the utility for a service connection or repair, and the parties have agreed that the presence of the subscriber is required, and the subscriber has requested a four-hour appointment, the utility and the subscriber shall agree, prior to the date of service connection or repair, on the time for the commencement of the four-hour period for the service connection or repair.

(2) If the service connection or repair is not commenced within the four-hour period provided under paragraph (1) or another period otherwise agreed to by the utility and the subscriber, except for delays caused by unforeseen or unavoidable circumstances beyond the control of the utility, the subscriber may bring an action in small claims court against the utility for lost wages, expenses actually incurred, or other actual damages not exceeding a total of six hundred dollars ($600).

(3) No action shall be considered valid if the subscriber was not present at the time, within the specified period, that the utility attempted to make the service connection or repair or made a diligent attempt to notify the subscriber by telephone or in person of its inability to do so because of unforeseen or unavoidable occurrences beyond its control. If notification is by telephone, the utility or its agent shall leave a telephone number for a return telephone call by the subscriber to the utility or its agent, to enable the consumer to arrange a new two-hour period for service connection or repair.

(4) In any small claims action, logs and other business records maintained by the utility or its agents in the ordinary course of business shall be prima facie evidence of the time period specified for the commencement of the service connection or repair and of the time that the utility attempted to make the service connection or repair, or of a diligent attempt by a utility to notify the subscriber in person or by telephone of a delay caused by unforeseen or unavoidable occurrences.

(5) It shall be a defense to the action if a diligent attempt was made by the utility to notify the subscriber of a delay caused by unforeseen or unavoidable occurrences beyond the control of the utility, and the utility commenced service within a newly agreed upon two-hour period.

(d) Any provision of a delivery, service, or repair contract in which the consumer or subscriber agrees to modify or waive any of the rights afforded by this section is void as contrary to public policy. *(Added by Stats.1989, c. 1075, § 1. Amended by Stats.1990, c. 193 (S.B.1968), § 1; Stats.1991, c. 394 (A.B.585), § 3; Stats.1992, c. 427 (A.B.3355), § 13; Stats.1992, c. 693 (S.B.1387), § 1; Stats.1993, c. 28 (S.B.47), § 1; Stats.2002, c. 279 (S.B.500), § 1.)*

Research References

4 Witkin, California Summary 10th Sales § 12, Supplementary General Law.
4 Witkin, California Summary 10th Sales § 148, (S 148) Merchandise to Consumer.

§ 1723. Retail sellers; policies of no refund or no exchange; notice; exceptions; violations

(a) Every retail seller which sells goods to the public in this state that has a policy as to any of those goods of not giving full cash or credit refunds, or of not allowing equal exchanges, or any combination thereof, for at least seven days following purchase of the goods if they are returned and proof of their purchase is presented, shall conspicuously display that policy either on signs posted at each cash register and sales counter, at each public entrance, on tags attached to each item sold under that policy, or on the retail seller's order forms, if any. This display shall state the store's policy, including, but not limited to, whether cash refund, store credit, or exchanges will be given for the full amount of the purchase price; the applicable time period; the

types of merchandise which are covered by the policy; and any other conditions which govern the refund, credit, or exchange of merchandise.

(b) This section does not apply to food, plants, flowers, perishable goods, goods marked "as is," "no returns accepted," "all sales final," or with similar language, goods used or damaged after purchase, customized goods received as ordered, goods not returned with their original package, and goods which cannot be resold due to health considerations.

(c)(1) Any retail store which violates this section shall be liable to the buyer for the amount of the purchase if the buyer returns, or attempts to return, the purchased goods on or before the 30th day after their purchase.

(2) Violations of this section shall be subject to the remedies provided in the Consumers Legal Remedies Act (Title 1.5 (commencing with Section 1750) of Part 4).

(3) The duties, rights, and remedies provided in this section are in addition to any other duties, rights, and remedies provided by state law. *(Added by Stats.1990, c. 422 (A.B.3047), § 2.)*

Research References

4 Witkin, California Summary 10th Sales § 381, (S 381) Retail Refund Policies.

§ 1725. Negotiable instruments; identification; credit card as condition of acceptance prohibited

(a) Unless permitted under subdivision (c), no person accepting a negotiable instrument as payment in full or in part for goods or services sold or leased at retail shall do any of the following:

(1) Require the person paying with a negotiable instrument to provide a credit card as a condition of acceptance of the negotiable instrument, or record the number of the credit card.

(2) Require, as a condition of acceptance of the negotiable instrument, or cause the person paying with a negotiable instrument to sign a statement agreeing to allow his or her credit card to be charged to cover the negotiable instrument if returned as no good.

(3) Record a credit card number in connection with any part of the transaction described in this subdivision.

(4) Contact a credit card issuer to determine if the amount of any credit available to the person paying with a negotiable instrument will cover the amount of the negotiable instrument.

(b) For the purposes of this section, the following terms have the following meanings:

(1) "Check guarantee card" means a card issued by a financial institution, evidencing an agreement under which the financial institution will not dishonor a check drawn upon itself, under the terms and conditions of the agreement.

(2) "Credit card" has the meaning specified in Section 1747.02, and does not include a check guarantee card or a card that is both a credit card and a check guarantee card.

(3) "Negotiable instrument" has the meaning specified in Section 3104 of the Commercial Code.

(4) "Retail" means a transaction involving the sale or lease of goods or services or both, between an individual, corporation, or other entity regularly engaged in business and a consumer, for use by the consumer and not for resale.

(c) This section does not prohibit any person from doing any of the following:

(1) Requiring the production of reasonable forms of positive identification, other than a credit card, which may include a driver's license or a California state identification card, or where

one of these is not available, another form of photo identification, as a condition of acceptance of a negotiable instrument.

(2) Requesting, but not requiring, a purchaser to voluntarily display a credit card as an indicia of creditworthiness or financial responsibility, or as an additional identification, provided the only information concerning the credit card which is recorded is the type of credit card displayed, the issuer of the card, and the expiration date of the card. All retailers that request the display of a credit card pursuant to this paragraph shall inform the customer, by either of the following methods, that displaying the credit card is not a requirement for check writing:

(A) By posting the following notice in a conspicuous location in the unobstructed view of the public within the premises where the check is being written, clearly and legibly: "Check writing ID: credit card may be requested but not required for purchases."

(B) By training and requiring the sales clerks or retail employees requesting the credit card to inform all check writing customers that they are not required to display a credit card to write a check.

(3) Requesting production of, or recording, a credit card number as a condition for cashing a negotiable instrument that is being used solely to receive cash back from the person.

(4) Requesting, receiving, or recording a credit card number in lieu of requiring a deposit to secure payment in event of default, loss, damage, or other occurrence.

(5) Requiring, verifying, and recording the purchaser's name, address, and telephone number.

(6) Requesting or recording a credit card number on a negotiable instrument used to make a payment on that credit card account.

(d) This section does not require acceptance of a negotiable instrument whether or not a credit card is presented.

(e) Any person who violates this section is subject to a civil penalty not to exceed two hundred fifty dollars ($250) for a first violation, and to a civil penalty not to exceed one thousand dollars ($1,000) for a second or subsequent violation, to be assessed and collected in a civil action brought by the person paying with a negotiable instrument, by the Attorney General, or by the district attorney or city attorney of the county or city in which the violation occurred. However, no civil penalty shall be assessed for a violation of this section if the defendant shows by a preponderance of the evidence that the violation was not intentional and resulted from a bona fide error made notwithstanding the defendant's maintenance of procedures reasonably adopted to avoid such an error. When collected, the civil penalty shall be payable, as appropriate, to the person paying with a negotiable instrument who brought the action or to the general fund of whichever governmental entity brought the action to assess the civil penalty.

(f) The Attorney General, or any district attorney or city attorney within his or her respective jurisdiction, may bring an action in the superior court in the name of the people of the State of California to enjoin violation of subdivision (a) and, upon notice to the defendant of not less than five days, to temporarily restrain and enjoin the violation. If it appears to the satisfaction of the court that the defendant has, in fact, violated subdivision (a), the court may issue an injunction restraining further violations, without requiring proof that any person has been damaged by the violation. In these proceedings, if the court finds that the defendant has violated subdivision (a), the court may direct the defendant to pay any or all costs incurred by the Attorney General, district attorney, or city attorney in seeking or obtaining injunctive relief pursuant to this subdivision.

(g) Actions for collection of civil penalties under subdivision (e) and for injunctive relief under subdivision (f) may be consolidated. *(Added by Stats.1990, c. 637 (A.B.2880), § 1. Amended by Stats.1991, c. 1089 (A.B.1477), § 1, eff. Oct. 14, 1991; Stats.1995, c. 458 (A.B.1316), § 1.)*

Research References

Miller and Starr California Real Estate § 17:19, Constructive Severance.
4 Witkin, California Summary 10th Sales § 24, Former Law and Commercial Code.
4 Witkin, California Summary 10th Sales § 25, Appropriation and Identification.
4 Witkin, California Summary 10th Negotiable Instruments § 151, (S 151) Condition of Accepting Negotiable Instrument.

Part 4

OBLIGATIONS ARISING FROM PARTICULAR TRANSACTIONS

Title 1

CONSIGNMENT OF FINE ART

CHAPTER 1. DEFINITIONS

Section
1738. Definitions.

§ 1738. Definitions

As used in this title:

(a) "Artist" means the person who creates a work of fine art or, if that person is deceased, that person's heir, legatee, or personal representative.

(b) "Fine art" means a painting, sculpture, drawing, work of graphic art (including an etching, lithograph, offset print, silk screen, or a work of graphic art of like nature), a work of calligraphy, or a work in mixed media (including a collage, assemblage, or any combination of the foregoing art media).

(c) "Art dealer" means a person engaged in the business of selling works of fine art, other than a person exclusively engaged in the business of selling goods at public auction.

(d) "Person" means an individual, partnership, corporation, limited liability company, association or other group, however organized.

(e) "Consignment" means that no title to, estate in, or right to possession of, fine art, superior to that of the consignor shall vest in the consignee, notwithstanding the consignee's power or authority to transfer and convey to a third person all of the right, title and interest of the consignor in and to such fine art. *(Added by Stats.1975, c. 953, p. 2130, § 1. Amended by Stats.1994, c. 1010 (S.B.2053), § 31.)*

Research References

1 Witkin Cal. Summ. 10th Contracts § 875, Damages Exceeding Value of Performance.

4 Witkin, California Summary 10th Sales § 125, (S 125) Agreement of Parties Controlling.

3 Witkin, California Summary 10th Agency and Employment § 2, (S 2) Agent.

CHAPTER 2. GENERAL PROVISIONS

Section
1738.5. Delivery to and acceptance by art dealer; effect.
1738.6. Results of consignment; agency, property in trust, liability and proceeds.
1738.7. Trust property.
1738.8. Waiver by consignor as void.
1738.9. Application of title.

§ 1738.5. Delivery to and acceptance by art dealer; effect

Notwithstanding any custom, practice or usage of the trade to the contrary, whenever an artist delivers or causes to be delivered a work of fine art of the artist's own creation to an art dealer in this state for the purpose of exhibition or sale, or both, on a commission, fee or other basis of compensation, the delivery to and acceptance of such work of fine art by the art dealer shall constitute a consignment, unless the delivery to the art dealer is pursuant to an outright sale for which the artist receives or has received full compensation for the work of fine art upon delivery. *(Added by Stats.1975, c. 953, p. 2130, § 1.)*

§ 1738.6. Results of consignment; agency, property in trust, liability and proceeds

A consignment of a work of fine art shall result in all of the following:

(a) The art dealer, after delivery of the work of fine art, shall constitute an agent of the artist for the purpose of sale or exhibition of the consigned work of fine art within the State of California.

(b) The work of fine art shall constitute property held in trust by the consignee for the benefit of the consignor, and shall not be subject to claim by a creditor of the consignee.

(c) The consignee shall be responsible for the loss of, or damage to, the work of fine art.

(d) The proceeds from the sale of the work of fine art shall constitute funds held in trust by the consignee for the benefit of the consignor. Such proceeds shall first be applied to pay any balance due to the consignor, unless the consignor expressly agrees otherwise in writing. *(Added by Stats.1975, c. 953, p. 2130, § 1.)*

§ 1738.7. Trust property

A work of fine art received as a consignment shall remain trust property, notwithstanding the subsequent purchase thereof by the consignee directly or indirectly for the consignee's own account until the price is paid in full to the consignor. If such work is thereafter resold to a bona fide purchaser before the consignor has been paid in full, the proceeds of the resale received by the consignee shall constitute funds held in trust for the benefit of the consignor to the extent necessary to pay any balance still due to the consignor and such trusteeship shall continue until the fiduciary obligation of the consignee with respect to such transaction is discharged in full. *(Added by Stats.1975, c. 953, p. 2131, § 1.)*

§ 1738.8. Waiver by consignor as void

Any provision of a contract or agreement whereby the consignor waives any provision of this title is void. *(Added by Stats.1975, c. 953, p. 2131, § 1.)*

§ 1738.9. Application of title

This title shall not apply to a written contract executed prior to the effective date of this title, unless either the parties agree by mutual written consent that this title shall apply or such contract is extended or renewed after the effective date of this title.

The provisions of this title shall prevail over any conflicting or inconsistent provisions of the Commercial Code affecting the subject matter of this title. *(Added by Stats.1975, c. 953, p. 2131, § 1.)*

Title 1A

INDEPENDENT WHOLESALE SALES REPRESENTATIVES

§ 1738.10. Legislative findings, declarations and intent

The Legislature finds and declares that independent wholesale sales representatives are a key ingredient to the California economy. The Legislature further finds and declares the wholesale sales representatives spend many hours developing their territory in order to properly market their products, and therefore should be provided unique protection from unjust termination of the territorial market areas. Therefore, it is the intent of the Legislature, in enacting this act to provide security and clarify the contractual relations between manufacturers and their nonemployee sales representatives. *(Added by Stats.1990, c. 964 (A.B.3456), § 1.)*

§ 1738.11. Title of chapter

This chapter shall be known and cited as the Independent Wholesale Sales Representatives Contractual Relations Act of 1990. *(Added by Stats.1990, c. 964 (A.B.3456), § 1.)*

§ 1738.12. Definitions

For purposes of this chapter the following terms have the following meaning:

(a) "Manufacturer" means any organization engaged in the business of producing, assembling, mining, weaving, importing or by any other method of fabrication, a product tangible or intangible, intended for resale to, or use by the consumers of this state.

(b) "Jobber" means any business organization engaged in the business of purchasing products intended for resale and invoicing to purchasers for resale to, or use by, the consumers of this state.

(c) "Distributor" means any business organization engaged in offering for sale products which are shipped from its inventory, or from goods in transit to its inventory, to purchasers and intended for resale to, or use by, the consumers of this state.

(d) "Chargeback" means any deduction taken against the commissions earned by the sales representative which are not required by state or federal law.

(e) "Wholesale sales representative" means any person who contracts with a manufacturer, jobber, or distributor for the purpose of soliciting wholesale orders, is compensated, in whole or part, by commission, but shall not include one who places orders or purchases exclusively for his own account for resale and shall not include one who sells or takes orders for the direct sale of products to the ultimate consumer. *(Added by Stats.1990, c. 964 (A.B.3456), § 1.)*

§ 1738.13. Written contracts required; contents; copies and receipts; information and documentation; waiver

(a) Whenever a manufacturer, jobber, or distributor is engaged in business within this state and uses the services of a wholesale sales representative, who is not an employee of the manufacturer, jobber, or distributor, to solicit wholesale orders at least partially within this state, and the contemplated method of payment involves commissions, the manufacturer, jobber, or distributor shall enter into a written contract with the sales representative.

(b) The written contract shall include all of the following:

(1) The rate and method by which the commission is computed.

(2) The time when commissions will be paid.

(3) The territory assigned to the sales representative.

(4) All exceptions to the assigned territory and customers therein.

(5) What chargebacks will be made against the commissions, if any.

(c) The sales representative and the manufacturer, jobber, or distributor shall each be provided with a signed copy of the written contract and the sales representative shall sign a receipt acknowledging receipt of the signed contract.

(d) The sales representative shall be provided with the following written information and documentation with payment of the commission:

(1) An accounting of the orders for which payment is made, including the customer's name and invoice number.

(2) The rate of commission on each order.

(3) Information relating to any chargebacks included in the accounting.

(e) No contract shall contain any provision which waives any rights established pursuant to this chapter. Any such waiver is deemed contrary to public policy and void. *(Added by Stats. 1990, c. 964 (A.B.3456), § 1.)*

§ 1738.14. Nonresident manufacturers, jobbers or distributors; personal jurisdiction

A manufacturer, jobber, or distributor who is not a resident of this state, and who enters into a contract regulated by this chapter is deemed to be doing business in this state for purposes of personal jurisdiction. *(Added by Stats.1990, c. 964 (A.B.3456), § 1.)*

§ 1738.15. Willful failure to enter contract or pay commissions; treble damages to sales representative

A manufacturer, jobber, or distributor who willfully fails to enter into a written contract as required by this chapter or willfully fails to pay commissions as provided in the written contract shall be liable to the sales representative in a civil action for treble the damages proved at trial. *(Added by Stats.1990, c. 964 (A.B.3456), § 1.)*

§ 1738.16. Attorney's fees and costs

In a civil action brought by the sales representative pursuant to this chapter, the prevailing party shall be entitled to reasonable attorney's fees and costs in addition to any other recovery. *(Added by Stats.1990, c. 964 (A.B.3456), § 1.)*

§ 1738.17. Application of chapter

This chapter shall not apply to any person licensed pursuant to Division 9 (commencing with Section 23000) of the Business and Professions Code. *(Added by Stats.1990, c. 964 (A.B.3456), § 1.)*

Title 1.1

SALE AND MANUFACTURE OF POLITICAL ITEMS

§ 1739. Prohibited offers, advertisements or sales

No person shall sell, advertise for sale, or offer for sale any political item which is purported to be an original political item but which is not in fact an original political item. *(Added by Stats.1977, c. 69, p. 472, § 1.)*

Research References

4 Witkin, California Summary 10th Sales § 25, Appropriation and Identification.
4 Witkin, California Summary 10th Sales § 121, (S 121) Sale on Approval.
4 Witkin, California Summary 10th Sales § 122, (S 122) Sale or Return.
4 Witkin, California Summary 10th Sales § 126, in General.
4 Witkin, California Summary 10th Sales § 127, Identification of Goods.
4 Witkin, California Summary 10th Sales § 128, Delivery to Buyer or Bailee Required.
4 Witkin, California Summary 10th Sales § 375, (S 375) Political Items Sold as Originals.

§ 1739.1. Political item

For purposes of this title, a "political item" is any button, ribbon, poster, sticker, literature, or advertising concerning any candidate or ballot proposition in any electoral campaign. *(Added by Stats.1977, c. 69, p. 472, § 1.)*

Research References

4 Witkin, California Summary 10th Sales § 375, (S 375) Political Items Sold as Originals.

§ 1739.2. Original political item

For purposes of this title, an "original political item" is any political item produced during any electoral campaign for use in support of or in opposition to any candidate or ballot proposition

before the voters in that campaign. *(Added by Stats.1977, c. 69, p. 472, § 1.)*

Research References

4 Witkin, California Summary 10th Sales § 375, (S 375) Political Items Sold as Originals.

§ 1739.3. Copies or reproductions; labeling

No political item which is labeled "copy" or "reproduction" at the time of sale, advertising for sale, or offering for sale shall violate Section 1739. *(Added by Stats.1977, c. 69, p. 472, § 1.)*

Research References

4 Witkin, California Summary 10th Sales § 375, (S 375) Political Items Sold as Originals.

§ 1739.4. Civil actions; treble damages; limitation of actions

(a) A person who offers or sells any political item in violation of this title shall be liable to the person purchasing such political item from him, who may sue to recover the consideration paid for the political item, with interest at the legal rate thereon, upon the tender of the political item.

(b) In any case in which a person knowingly offers or sells a political item in violation of this title, the person purchasing such political item may recover from the person who offers or sells such political item an amount equal to three times the amount required under subdivision (a).

(c) No action shall be maintained to enforce any liability under this section unless brought within one year after discovery of the violation upon which it is based and in no event more than three years after the political item was sold. *(Added by Stats.1977, c. 69, p. 472, § 1.)*

Research References

4 Witkin, California Summary 10th Sales § 375, (S 375) Political Items Sold as Originals.

Title 1.1A

AUTOGRAPHED SPORTS MEMORABILIA

§ 1739.7. Certificates of authenticity; representations; displays or offers; disclosures; civil penalties

(a) As used in this section:

(1) "Autographed" means bearing the actual signature of a personality signed by that individual's own hand.

(2) "Collectible" means an autographed sports item, including, but not limited to, a photograph, book, ticket, plaque, sports program, trading card, item of sports equipment or clothing, or other sports memorabilia sold or offered for sale in or from this state by a dealer to a consumer for five dollars ($5) or more.

(3) "Consumer" means any natural person who purchases a collectible from a dealer for personal, family, or household purposes. "Consumer" also includes a prospective purchaser meeting these criteria.

(4) "Dealer" means a person who is in the business of selling or offering for sale collectibles in or from this state, exclusively or nonexclusively, or a person who by his or her occupation holds himself or herself out as having knowledge or skill peculiar to collectibles, or to whom that knowledge or skill may be attributed by his or her employment of an agent or other intermediary that by his or her occupation holds himself or

herself out as having that knowledge or skill. "Dealer" includes an auctioneer who sells collectibles at a public auction, and also includes persons who are consignors or representatives or agents of auctioneers. "Dealer" includes a person engaged in a mail order, telephone order, or cable television business for the sale of collectibles.

(5) "Description" means any of the following:

(A) Any representation in writing, including, but not limited to, a representation in an advertisement, brochure, catalog, flyer, invoice, sign, or other commercial or promotional material.

(B) Any oral representation.

(C) Any representation included in a radio or television broadcast to the public in or from this state.

(6) "Limited edition" means any collectible that meets all of the following requirements:

(A) A company has produced a specific quantity of a collectible and placed it on the open market.

(B) The producer of the collectible has posted a notice, at its primary place of business, that it will provide any consumer, upon request, with a copy of a notice that states the exact number of a collectible produced in that series of limited editions.

(C) The producer makes available, upon request of a consumer, evidence that the electronic encoding, films, molds, or plates used to create the collectible have been destroyed after the specified number of collectibles have been produced.

(D) The sequence number of the collectible and the number of the total quantity produced in the limited edition are printed on the collectible.

(7) "Mint condition" means any collectible sold on the open market or through a private transaction that meets all of the following requirements:

(A) The item has never been circulated, used, or worn.

(B) The item exhibits little or no sign of aging or degradation caused by oxidation or exposure to sunlight as a result of its display.

(C) The item is otherwise free from creases, blemishes, or marks.

(8) "Promoter" means a person who arranges, holds, organizes, or presents a trade show featuring collectibles, autograph signings, or both.

(9) "Person" means any natural person, partnership, corporation, limited liability company, company, trust, association, or other entity, however organized.

(b) Whenever a dealer, in selling or offering to sell to a consumer a collectible in or from this state, provides a description of that collectible as being autographed, the dealer shall furnish a certificate of authenticity to the consumer at the time of sale. The certificate of authenticity shall be in writing, shall be signed by the dealer or his or her authorized agent, and shall specify the date of sale. The certificate of authenticity shall be in at least 10–point boldface type and shall contain the dealer's true legal name and street address. The dealer shall retain a copy of the certificate of authenticity for not less than seven years. Each certificate of authenticity shall do all of the following:

(1) Describe the collectible and specify the name of the sports personality who autographed it.

(2) Either specify the purchase price and date of sale or be accompanied by a separate invoice setting forth that information.

(3) Contain an express warranty, which shall be conclusively presumed to be part of the bargain, of the authenticity of the collectible. This warranty shall not be negated or limited by reason of the lack of words such as "warranty" or "guarantee" or because the dealer does not have a specific intent or authorization to make the warranty or because any statement relevant to the collectible is or purports to be, or is capable of being, merely the dealer's opinion.

(4) Specify whether the collectible is offered as one of a limited edition and, if so, specify (A) how the collectible and edition are numbered and (B) the size of the edition and the size of any prior or anticipated future edition, if known. If the size of the edition and the size of any prior or anticipated future edition is not known, the certificate shall contain an explicit statement to that effect.

(5) Indicate whether the dealer is surety bonded or is otherwise insured to protect the consumer against errors and omissions of the dealer and, if bonded or insured, provide proof thereof.

(6) Indicate the last four digits of the dealer's resale certificate number from the State Board of Equalization.

(7) Indicate whether the item was autographed in the presence of the dealer and specify the date and location of, and the name of a witness to, the autograph signing.

(8) Indicate whether the item was obtained or purchased from a third party. If so, indicate the name and address of this third party.

(9) Include an identifying serial number that corresponds to an identifying number printed on the collectible item, if any. The serial number shall also be printed on the sales receipt. If the sales receipt is printed electronically, the dealer may manually write the serial number on the receipt.

(c) No dealer shall represent an item as a collectible if it was not autographed by the sports personality in his or her own hand.

(d) No dealer shall display or offer for sale a collectible in this state unless, at the location where the collectible is offered for sale and in close proximity to the collectible merchandise, there is a conspicuous sign that reads as follows:

"SALE OF AUTOGRAPHED SPORTS MEMORABILIA: AS REQUIRED BY LAW, A DEALER WHO SELLS TO A CONSUMER ANY SPORTS MEMORABILIA DESCRIBED AS BEING AUTOGRAPHED MUST PROVIDE A WRITTEN CERTIFICATE OF AUTHENTICITY AT THE TIME OF SALE. THIS DEALER MAY BE SURETY BONDED OR OTHERWISE INSURED TO ENSURE THE AUTHENTICITY OF ANY COLLECTIBLE SOLD BY THIS DEALER."

(e) Any dealer engaged in a mail-order or telephone-order business for the sale of collectibles in or from this state:

(1) Shall include the disclosure specified in subdivision (d), in type of conspicuous size, in any written advertisement relating to a collectible.

(2) Shall include in each television advertisement relating to a collectible the following written on-screen message, which shall be prominently displayed, easily readable, and clearly visible for no less than five seconds, and which shall be repeated for five seconds once during each four-minute segment of the advertisement following the initial four minutes:

"A written certificate of authenticity is provided with each autographed collectible, as required by law. This dealer may be surety bonded or otherwise insured to ensure the authenticity of any collectible sold by this dealer."

(3) Shall include as part of the oral message of each radio advertisement for a collectible the disclosure specified in subdivision (d).

(f) No dealer shall display or offer for sale a collectible in this state at any trade show or similar event primarily featuring sales of collectibles or other sports memorabilia that offers onsite admission ticket sales unless, at each onsite location where admission tickets are sold, there is prominently displayed a specimen example of a certificate of authenticity.

(g) Any consumer injured by the failure of a dealer to provide a certificate of authenticity containing the information required by this section, or by a dealer's furnishing of a certificate of authenticity that is false, shall be entitled to recover, in addition to actual damages, a civil penalty in an amount equal to 10 times actual damages, plus court costs, reasonable attorney's fees, interest, and expert witness fees, if applicable, incurred by the consumer in the action. The court, in its discretion, may award additional damages based on the egregiousness of the dealer's conduct. The remedy specified in this section is in addition to, and not in lieu of, any other remedy that may be provided by law.

(h) No person shall represent himself or herself as a dealer in this state unless he or she possesses a valid resale certificate number from the State Board of Equalization.

(i) A dealer may be surety bonded or otherwise insured for purposes of indemnification against errors and omissions arising from the authentication, sale, or resale of collectibles.

(j) Whenever a promoter arranges or organizes a trade show featuring collectibles and autograph signings, the promoter shall notify, in writing, any dealer who has agreed to purchase or rent space in this trade show what the promoter will do if any laws of this state are violated, including the fact that law enforcement officials will be contacted when those laws are violated. This notice shall be delivered to the dealer, at his or her registered place of business, at the time the agreement to purchase space in the trade show is made. The following language shall be included in each notice:

"As a vendor at this collectibles trade show, you are a professional representative of this hobby. As a result, you will be required to follow the laws of this state, including laws regarding the sale and display of collectibles, as defined in Section 1739.7 of the Civil Code, forged and counterfeit collectibles and autographs, and mint and limited edition collectibles. If you do not obey the laws, you may be evicted from this trade show, be reported to law enforcement, and be held liable for a civil penalty of 10 times the amount of damages." *(Added by Stats.1992, c. 656 (A.B.3113), § 1. Amended by Stats.1994, c. 1010 (S.B.2053), § 32; Stats.1995, c. 360 (A.B.434), § 3; Stats. 1998, c. 494 (S.B.2024), § 1; Stats.1999, c. 83 (S.B.966), § 20.)*

Research References

4 Witkin, California Summary 10th Sales § 385, (S 385) Sports Memorabilia.

Title 1.2

SALE OF FINE PRINTS

CHAPTER 1. GENERAL PROVISIONS

§ 1740. Definitions

As used in this title:

(a) "Fine art multiple" or "multiple" for the purposes of this title means any fine print, photograph (positive or negative), sculpture cast, collage, or similar art object produced in more than one copy. Pages or sheets taken from books and magazines and offered for sale or sold as art objects shall be included, but books and magazines shall be excluded.

(b) "Fine print" or "print" means a multiple produced by, but not limited to, engraving, etching, woodcutting, lithography, and serigraphy, and means multiples produced or developed from photographic negatives, or any combination thereof.

(c) "Master" is used in lieu of and has the same meaning as a printing plate, stone, block, screen, photographic negative, or mold or other process as to a sculpture, which contains an image used to produce fine art objects in multiples.

(d) "Artist" means the person who created the image which is contained in, or constitutes, the master or conceived of, and approved the image which is contained in, or constitutes, the master.

(e) Whether a multiple is "signed" or "unsigned" as these terms are used in this title relating to prints and photographs, depends upon whether or not the multiple was autographed by the artist's own hand, and not by mechanical means, after the multiple was produced, irrespective of whether it was signed or unsigned in the plate.

(f) "Impression" means each individual fine art multiple made by printing, stamping, casting, or any other process.

(g) "Art dealer" means a person who is in the business of dealing, exclusively or nonexclusively, in the fine art multiples to which this title is applicable, or a person who by his or her occupation holds himself or herself out as having knowledge or skill peculiar to these works, or to whom that knowledge or skill may be attributed by his or her employment of an agent or other intermediary who by his or her occupation holds himself or herself out as having that knowledge or skill. The term "art dealer" includes an auctioneer who sells these works at public auction, but excludes persons, not otherwise defined or treated as art dealers herein, who are consignors or principals of auctioneers.

(h) "Limited edition" means fine art multiples produced from a master, all of which are the same image and bear numbers or other markings to denote the limited production thereof to a stated maximum number of multiples, or are otherwise held out as limited to a maximum number of multiples.

(i) "Proofs" means multiples which are the same as, and which are produced from the same master as, the multiples in a limited edition, but which, whether so designated or not, are set aside from and are in addition to the limited edition to which they relate.

(j) "Certificate of authenticity" means a written or printed description of the multiple which is to be sold, exchanged, or consigned by an art dealer. Every certificate shall contain the following statement:

"This is to certify that all information and the statements contained herein are true and correct."

(k) "Person" means an individual, partnership, corporation, limited liability company, association, or other entity, however organized. *(Added by Stats.1970, c. 1223, p. 2141, § 1, operative July 1, 1971. Amended by Stats.1982, c. 1320, p. 4873, § 1; Stats.1988, c. 819, § 1; Stats.1994, c. 1010 (S.B.2053), § 33.)*

Research References

4 Witkin Cal. Proc. 5th Pleading § 302, Statutory Authorization.

4 Witkin, California Summary 10th Sales § 355, (S 355) Fine Prints.

§ 1741. Application of title

This title shall apply to any fine art multiple when offered for sale or sold at wholesale or retail for one hundred dollars ($100) or more, exclusive of any frame. *(Added by Stats.1970, c. 1223, p. 2141, § 1, operative July 1, 1971. Amended by Stats.1982, c. 1320, p. 4875, § 2.)*

Research References

1 Witkin Cal. Summ. 10th Contracts § 402, Scope of Exception.
4 Witkin, California Summary 10th Sales § 123, Sale by Auction.
4 Witkin, California Summary 10th Sales § 355, (S 355) Fine Prints.

CHAPTER 2. FULL DISCLOSURE IN THE SALE OF FINE PRINTS

§ 1742. Certificate of authenticity to be furnished to buyer or consignee; auctions; materials soliciting a direct sale; disclosures

(a) An art dealer shall not sell or consign a multiple into or from this state unless a certificate of authenticity is furnished to the purchaser or consignee, at his or her request, or in any event prior to a sale or consignment, which sets forth as to each multiple, the descriptive information required by Section 1744 for any period. If a prospective purchaser so requests, the certificate shall be transmitted to him or her prior to the payment or placing of an order for a multiple. If payment is made by a purchaser prior to delivery of such a multiple, this certificate shall be supplied at the time of or prior to delivery. With respect to auctions, this information may be furnished in catalogues or other written materials which are made readily available for consultation and purchase prior to sale, provided that a bill of sale, receipt, or invoice describing the transaction is then provided which makes reference to the catalogue and lot number in which this information is supplied. Information supplied pursuant to this subdivision shall be clearly, specifically and distinctly addressed to each of the items listed in Section 1744 unless the required data is not applicable. This section is applicable to transactions by and between art dealers and others considered to be art dealers for the purposes of this title.

(b) An art dealer shall not cause a catalogue, prospectus, flyer, or other written material or advertisement to be distributed in, into, or from this state which solicits a direct sale, by inviting transmittal of payment for a specific multiple, unless it clearly sets forth, in close physical proximity to the place in such material where the multiple is described, the descriptive information required by Section 1744 for any time period. In lieu of this required information, the written material or advertising may set forth the material contained in the following quoted passage, or the passage itself, if the art dealer then supplies the required information prior to or with delivery of the multiple. The nonobservance of the terms within the following passage shall constitute a violation of this title:

"California law provides for disclosure in writing of information concerning certain fine prints, photographs, and sculptures prior to effecting a sale of them. This law requires disclosure of such matters as the identity of the artist, the artist's signature, the medium, whether the multiple is a reproduction, the time when the multiple was produced, use of the plate which produced the multiple, and the number of multiples in a "limited edition." If a prospective purchaser so requests, the information shall be transmitted to him or her prior to payment, or the placing of an order for a multiple. If payment is made by a purchaser prior to delivery of the multiple, this information will be supplied at the time of or prior to delivery, in which case the purchaser is entitled to a refund if, for reasons related to matter contained in such information, he or she returns the multiple in the condition in which received, within 30 days of receiving it. In addition, if after payment and delivery, it is ascertained that the information provided is incorrect, the purchaser may be entitled to certain remedies, including refund upon return of the multiple in the condition in which received."

This requirement is not applicable to general written material or advertising which does not constitute an offer to effect a specific sale.

(c) In each place of business in the state where an art dealer is regularly engaged in sales of multiples, the art dealer shall post in a conspicuous place, a sign which, in a legible format, contains the information included in the following passage:

"California law provides for the disclosure in writing of certain information concerning prints, photographs, and sculpture casts. This information is available to you, and you may request to receive it prior to purchase."

(d) If an art dealer offering multiples by means of a catalogue, prospectus, flyer or other written material or advertisement distributed in, into or from this state disclaims knowledge as to any relevant detail referred to in Section 1744, he or she shall so state specifically and categorically with regard to each such detail to the end that the purchaser shall be enabled to judge the degree of uniqueness or scarcity of each multiple contained in the edition so offered. Describing the edition as an edition of "reproductions" eliminates the need to furnish further informational details unless the edition was allegedly published in a signed, numbered, or limited edition, or any combination thereof, in which case all of the informational details are required to be furnished.

(e) Whenever an artist sells or consigns a multiple of his or her own creation or conception, the artist shall disclose the information required by Section 1744, but an artist shall not otherwise be regarded as an art dealer. *(Added by Stats.1970, c. 1223, p. 2141, § 1, operative July 1, 1971. Amended by Stats.1982, c. 1320, p. 4875, § 3; Stats.1988, c. 819, § 2.)*

Research References

4 Witkin, California Summary 10th Sales § 151, (S 151) Pre-Code Title Theory.
4 Witkin, California Summary 10th Sales § 355, (S 355) Fine Prints.

§ 1742.6. Charitable organizations; exemptions

Any charitable organization which conducts a sale or auction of fine art multiples shall be exempt from the disclosure requirements of this title if it posts in a conspicuous place, at the site of the sale or auction, a disclaimer of any knowledge of the information specified in Section 1744, and includes such a disclaimer in a catalogue, if any, distributed by the organization with respect to the sale or auction of fine art multiples. If a charitable organization uses or employs an art dealer to conduct a sale or auction of fine art multiples, the art dealer shall be subject to all disclosure requirements otherwise required of an art dealer under this title. *(Added by Stats.1982, c. 1320, p. 4876, § 4.)*

§ 1744. Informational detail

(a) Except as provided in subdivisions (c), (d), (e), and otherwise in this title, a certificate of authenticity containing the following informational details shall be required to be supplied in all transactions covered by subdivisions (a), (b), and (e) of Section 1742:

(1) The name of the artist.

(2) If the artist's name appears on the multiple, a statement whether the multiple was signed by the artist.

If the multiple was not signed by the artist, a statement of the source of the artist's name on the multiple, such as whether the artist placed his signature on the multiple or on the master, whether his name was stamped or estate stamped on the multiple or on the master, or was from some other source or in some other manner placed on the multiple or on the master.

(3) A description of the medium or process, and where pertinent to photographic processes, the material used in producing the multiple, such as whether the multiple was produced through the etching, engraving, lithographic, serigraphic, or a particular method or material used in photographic developing processes. If an established term, in accordance with the usage of the trade, cannot be employed accurately to describe the medium or process, a brief, clear description shall be made.

(4) If the multiple or the image on or in the master constitutes, as to prints and photographs, a photomechanical or photographic type of reproduction, or as to sculptures a surmoulage or other form of reproduction of sculpture cases, of an image produced in a different medium, for a purpose other than the creation of the multiple being described, a statement of this information and the respective mediums.

(5) If paragraph (4) is applicable, and the multiple is not signed, a statement whether the artist authorized or approved in writing the multiple or the edition of which the multiple being described is one.

(6) If the purported artist was deceased at the time the master was made which produced the multiple, this shall be stated.

(7) If the multiple is a "posthumous" multiple, that is, if the master was created during the life of the artist but the multiple was produced after the artist's death, this shall be stated.

(8) If the multiple was made from a master which produced a prior limited edition, or from a master which constitutes or was made from a reproduction or surmoulage of a prior multiple or the master which produced the prior limited edition, this shall be stated as shall the total number of multiples, including proofs, of all other editions produced from that master.

(9) As to multiples produced after 1949, the year, or approximate year, the multiple was produced shall be stated. As to multiples produced prior to 1950, state the year, approximate year or period when the master was made which produced the multiple and when the particular multiple being described was produced. The requirements of this subdivision shall be satisfied when the year stated is approximately accurate.

(10) Whether the edition is being offered as a limited edition, and if so: (i) the authorized maximum number of signed or numbered impressions, or both, in the edition; (ii) the authorized maximum number of unsigned or unnumbered impressions, or both, in the edition; (iii) the authorized maximum number of artist's; publisher's or other proofs, if any, outside of the regular edition; and (iv) the total size of the edition.

(11) Whether or not the master has been destroyed, effaced, altered, defaced, or canceled after the current edition.

(b) If the multiple is part of a limited edition, and was printed after January 1, 1983, the statement of the size of the limited edition, as stated pursuant to paragraph (10) of subdivision (a) of

Section 1744 shall also constitute an express warranty that no additional multiples of the same image, including proofs, have been produced in this or in any other limited edition.

(c) If the multiple was produced in the period from 1950 to the effective date of this section, the information required to be supplied need not include the information required by paragraphs (5) and (8) of subdivision (a).

(d) If the multiple was produced in the period from 1900 to 1949, the information required to be supplied need only consist of the information required by paragraphs (1), (2), (3), and (9) of subdivision (a).

(e) If the multiple was produced before the year 1900, the information to be supplied need only consist of the information required by paragraphs (1), (3), and (9) of subdivision (a). *(Added by Stats.1982, c. 1320, p. 4877, § 5. Amended by Stats.1988, c. 819, § 3.)*

Research References

1 Witkin Cal. Summ. 10th Contracts § 33, No Recovery from Bona Fide Purchase.
4 Witkin, California Summary 10th Sales § 355, (S 355) Fine Prints.

§ 1744.7. Express warranties

Whenever an art dealer furnishes the name of the artist pursuant to Section 1744 for any time period after 1949, and otherwise furnishes information required by any of the subdivisions of Section 1744 for any time period, as to transactions including offers, sales, or consignments made to other than art dealers, and to other art dealers, such information shall be a part of the basis of the bargain and shall create express warranties as to the information provided. Such warranties shall not be negated or limited because the art dealer in the written instrument did not use formal words such as "warrant" or "guarantee" or because the art dealer did not have a specific intention or authorization to make a warranty or because any required statement is, or purports to be, or is capable of being merely the seller's opinion. The existence of a basis in fact for information warranted by virtue of this subdivision shall not be a defense in an action to enforce such warranty. However, with respect to photographs and sculptures produced prior to 1950, and other multiples produced prior to 1900, as to information required by paragraphs (3), (4), (5), and (6) of subdivision (a) of Section 1744, the art dealer shall be deemed to have satisfied this section if a reasonable basis in fact existed for the information provided. When information is not supplied as to any subdivision or paragraph of Section 1744 because not applicable, this shall constitute the express warranty that the paragraph is not applicable.

Whenever an art dealer disclaims knowledge as to a particular item about which information is required, such disclaimer shall be ineffective unless clearly, specifically, and categorically stated as to the particular item and contained in the physical context of other language setting forth the required information as to a specific multiple. *(Added by Stats.1982, c. 1320, p. 4878, § 6.)*

Research References

4 Witkin, California Summary 10th Sales § 355, (S 355) Fine Prints.

§ 1744.9. Liability; consignor to purchaser from consignee; art dealer who sells for consignor not art dealer or artist as agent

(a) An artist or art dealer who consigns a multiple to an art dealer for the purpose of effecting a sale of the multiple, shall have no liability to a purchaser under this article if the consignor, as to the consignee, has complied with the provisions of this title.

(b) When an art dealer has agreed to sell a multiple on behalf of a consignor, who is not an art dealer, or an artist has not consigned a multiple to an art dealer but the art dealer has agreed to act as the agent for an artist for the purpose of supplying the information required by this title, the art dealer shall incur the liabilities of other art dealers prescribed by this title, as to a purchaser. *(Added by Stats.1982, c. 1320, p. 4879, § 7.)*

CHAPTER 3. REMEDIES AND PENALTIES

Section
1745.   Violations by art dealer; liability; limitations of actions; costs, and attorneys' and expert witnesses' fees.
1745.5.   Injunctions; civil penalty; penalty surcharge.

§ 1745. Violations by art dealer; liability; limitations of actions; costs, and attorneys' and expert witnesses' fees

(a) An art dealer, including a dealer consignee, who offers or sells a multiple in, into or from this state without providing the certificate of authenticity required in Sections 1742 and 1744 of this title for any time period, or who provides information which is mistaken, erroneous or untrue, except for harmless errors, such as typographical errors, shall be liable to the purchaser of the multiple. The art dealer's liability shall consist of the consideration paid by the purchaser for the multiple, with interest at the legal rate thereon, upon the return of the multiple in the condition in which received by the purchaser.

(b) In any case in which an art dealer, including a dealer consignee, willfully offers or sells a multiple in violation of this title, the person purchasing such multiple may recover from the art dealer, including a dealer consignee, who offers or sells such multiple an amount equal to three times the amount required under subdivision (a).

(c) No action shall be maintained to enforce any liability under this section unless brought within one year after discovery of the violation upon which it is based and in no event more than three years after the multiple was sold.

(d) In any action to enforce any provision of this title, the court may allow the prevailing purchaser the costs of the action together with reasonable attorneys' and expert witnesses' fees. In the event, however, the court determines that an action to enforce was brought in bad faith, it may allow such expenses to the seller as it deems appropriate.

(e) These remedies shall not bar or be deemed inconsistent with a claim for damages or with the exercise of additional remedies otherwise available to the purchaser.

(f) In any proceeding in which an art dealer relies upon a disclaimer of knowledge as to any relevant information set forth in Section 1744 for any time period, such disclaimer shall be effective unless the claimant is able to establish that the art dealer failed to make reasonable inquiries, according to the custom and usage of the trade, to ascertain the relevant information or that such relevant information would have been ascertained as a result of such reasonable inquiries. *(Added by Stats.1970, c. 1223, p. 2142, § 1, operative July 1, 1971. Amended by Stats.1982, c. 1320, p. 4879, § 8; Stats.1988, c. 819, § 4.)*

Research References

4 Witkin, California Summary 10th Sales § 355, (S 355) Fine Prints.

§ 1745.5. Injunctions; civil penalty; penalty surcharge

(a) Any person performing or proposing to perform an act in violation of this title within this state may be enjoined in any court of competent jurisdiction.

(b) Actions for injunction pursuant to this title may be prosecuted by the following persons:

(1) The Attorney General.

(2) Any district attorney.

(3) Any city attorney.

(4) With the consent of the district attorney, a city prosecutor in any city or city and county having a full-time city prosecutor in the name of the people of the State of California upon their own complaint, or upon the complaint of any board, officer, person, corporation, or association.

(5) Any person acting in his or her own interests, or in the interests of the members of a corporation or association, or in the interests of the general public.

(c) Any person who violates any provision of this title may also be liable for a civil penalty not to exceed one thousand dollars ($1,000) for each violation, which may be assessed and recovered in a civil action brought in the name of the people of the State of California by the Attorney General or by any district attorney or any city attorney, and, with the consent of the district attorney, by a city prosecutor in any city or city and county having a full-time city prosecutor in any court of competent jurisdiction.

If the action is brought by the Attorney General, one-half of the penalty collected shall be paid to the treasurer of the county in which the judgment was entered, and one-half to the General Fund. If brought by a district attorney, the penalty collected shall be paid to the treasurer of the county in which the judgment was entered. If brought by a city attorney or city prosecutor, one-half of the penalty collected shall be paid to the treasurer of the city in which the judgment was entered, and one-half to the treasurer of the county in which the judgment was entered.

(d) Any person who violates any provision of this title may also be liable for a civil penalty surcharge not to exceed one thousand dollars ($1,000) for each violation which shall be assessed and recovered in the manner provided in subdivision (c). Any penalty surcharge collected shall be applied to the costs of enforcing this title by the prosecuting officer. *(Added by Stats.1982, c. 1320, p. 4880, § 9. Amended by Stats.1988, c. 819, § 5.)*

Title 1.2A

VIOLENT VIDEO GAMES

Section
1746.   Definitions.
1746.1.   Sale and rental to minors prohibited; affirmative defenses; non-application of prohibition to enumerated relatives or legal guardian.
1746.2.   Package labels.
1746.3.   Penalties.
1746.4.   Violations; reporting.
1746.5.   Severability.

Validity

The sections under this Title 1.2A were held unconstitutional in the decision of Video Software Dealers Ass'n v. Schwarzenegger, C.A.9 (Cal.)2009, 556 F.3d 950, certiorari granted 130 S.Ct. 2398, 559 U.S. 1092, 176 L.Ed.2d 784, affirmed 131 S.Ct. 2729, 180 L.Ed.2d 708.

The sections under this Title 1.2A were held unconstitutional in the decision of Brown v. Entertainment Merchants Ass'n, 2011, 131 S.Ct. 2729, 180 L.Ed.2d 708.

§ 1746. Definitions

For purposes of this title, the following definitions shall apply:

(a) "Minor" means any natural person who is under 18 years of age.

(b) "Person" means any natural person, partnership, firm, association, corporation, limited liability company, or other legal entity.

(c) "Video game" means any electronic amusement device that utilizes a computer, microprocessor, or similar electronic circuitry and its own monitor, or is designed to be used with a television set or a computer monitor, that interacts with the user of the device.

(d)(1) "Violent video game" means a video game in which the range of options available to a player includes killing, maiming, dismembering, or sexually assaulting an image of a human being, if those acts are depicted in the game in a manner that does either of the following:

(A) Comes within all of the following descriptions:

(i) A reasonable person, considering the game as a whole, would find appeals to a deviant or morbid interest of minors.

(ii) It is patently offensive to prevailing standards in the community as to what is suitable for minors.

(iii) It causes the game, as a whole, to lack serious literary, artistic, political, or scientific value for minors.

(B) Enables the player to virtually inflict serious injury upon images of human beings or characters with substantially human characteristics in a manner which is especially heinous, cruel, or depraved in that it involves torture or serious physical abuse to the victim.

(2) For purposes of this subdivision, the following definitions apply:

(A) "Cruel" means that the player intends to virtually inflict a high degree of pain by torture or serious physical abuse of the victim in addition to killing the victim.

(B) "Depraved" means that the player relishes the virtual killing or shows indifference to the suffering of the victim, as evidenced by torture or serious physical abuse of the victim.

(C) "Heinous" means shockingly atrocious. For the killing depicted in a video game to be heinous, it must involve additional acts of torture or serious physical abuse of the victim as set apart from other killings.

(D) "Serious physical abuse" means a significant or considerable amount of injury or damage to the victim's body which involves a substantial risk of death, unconsciousness, extreme physical pain, substantial disfigurement, or substantial impairment of the function of a bodily member, organ, or mental faculty. Serious physical abuse, unlike torture, does not require that the victim be conscious of the abuse at the time it is inflicted. However, the player must specifically intend the abuse apart from the killing.

(E) "Torture" includes mental as well as physical abuse of the victim. In either case, the virtual victim must be conscious of the abuse at the time it is inflicted; and the player must specifically intend to virtually inflict severe mental or physical pain or suffering upon the victim, apart from killing the victim.

(3) Pertinent factors in determining whether a killing depicted in a video game is especially heinous, cruel, or depraved include infliction of gratuitous violence upon the victim beyond that necessary to commit the killing, needless mutilation of the victim's body, and helplessness of the victim. (Added by Stats.2005, c. 638 (A.B.1179), § 2.)

Validity

This section was held unconstitutional in the decision of Video Software Dealers Ass'n v. Schwarzenegger, C.A.9

(Cal.)2009, 556 F.3d 950, certiorari granted 130 S.Ct. 2398, 559 U.S. 1092, 176 L.Ed.2d 784, affirmed 131 S.Ct. 2729, 180 L.Ed.2d 708.

This section was held unconstitutional in the decision of Brown v. Entertainment Merchants Ass'n, 2011, 131 S.Ct. 2729, 180 L.Ed.2d 708.

§ 1746.1. Sale and rental to minors prohibited; affirmative defenses; non-application of prohibition to enumerated relatives or legal guardian

(a) A person may not sell or rent a video game that has been labeled as a violent video game to a minor.

(b) Proof that a defendant, or his or her employee or agent, demanded, was shown, and reasonably relied upon evidence that a purchaser or renter of a violent video game was not a minor or that the manufacturer failed to label a violent video game as required pursuant to Section 1746.2 shall be an affirmative defense to any action brought pursuant to this title. That evidence may include, but is not limited to, a driver's license or an identification card issued to the purchaser or renter by a state or by the Armed Forces of the United States.

(c) This section shall not apply if the violent video game is sold or rented to a minor by the minor's parent, grandparent, aunt, uncle, or legal guardian. (Added by Stats.2005, c. 638 (A.B.1179), § 2.)

Validity

This section was held unconstitutional in the decision of Video Software Dealers Ass'n v. Schwarzenegger, C.A.9 (Cal.)2009, 556 F.3d 950, certiorari granted 130 S.Ct. 2398, 559 U.S. 1092, 176 L.Ed.2d 784, affirmed 131 S.Ct. 2729, 180 L.Ed.2d 708.

This section was held unconstitutional in the decision of Brown v. Entertainment Merchants Ass'n, 2011, 131 S.Ct. 2729, 180 L.Ed.2d 708.

§ 1746.2. Package labels

Each violent video game that is imported into or distributed in California for retail sale shall be labeled with a solid white "18" outlined in black. The "18" shall have dimensions of no less than 2 inches by 2 inches. The "18" shall be displayed on the front face of the video game package. (Added by Stats.2005, c. 638 (A.B.1179), § 2.)

Validity

This section was held unconstitutional in the decision of Video Software Dealers Ass'n v. Schwarzenegger, C.A.9 (Cal.)2009, 556 F.3d 950, certiorari granted 130 S.Ct. 2398, 559 U.S. 1092, 176 L.Ed.2d 784, affirmed 131 S.Ct. 2729, 180 L.Ed.2d 708.

This section was held unconstitutional in the decision of Brown v. Entertainment Merchants Ass'n, 2011, 131 S.Ct. 2729, 180 L.Ed.2d 708.

§ 1746.3. Penalties

Any person who violates any provision of this title shall be liable in an amount of up to one thousand dollars ($1,000), or a lesser amount as determined by the court. However, this liability shall not apply to any person who violates those provisions if he or she is employed solely in the capacity of a salesclerk or other, similar position and he or she does not have an ownership interest in the business in which the violation occurred and is not employed as a manager in that business. (Added by Stats.2005, c. 638 (A.B.1179), § 2.)

Validity

This section was held unconstitutional in the decision of Video Software Dealers Ass'n v. Schwarzenegger, C.A.9 (Cal.)2009, 556 F.3d 950, certiorari granted 130 S.Ct. 2398, 559 U.S. 1092, 176 L.Ed.2d 784, affirmed 131 S.Ct. 2729, 180 L.Ed.2d 708.

This section was held unconstitutional in the decision of Brown v. Entertainment Merchants Ass'n, 2011, 131 S.Ct. 2729, 180 L.Ed.2d 708.

§ 1746.4. Violations; reporting

A suspected violation of this title may be reported to a city attorney, county counsel, or district attorney by a parent, legal guardian, or other adult acting on behalf of a minor to whom a violent video game has been sold or rented. A violation of this title may be prosecuted by any city attorney, county counsel, or district attorney. *(Added by Stats.2005, c. 638 (A.B.1179), § 2.)*

Validity

This section was held unconstitutional in the decision of Video Software Dealers Ass'n v. Schwarzenegger, C.A.9 (Cal.)2009, 556 F.3d 950, certiorari granted 130 S.Ct. 2398, 559 U.S. 1092, 176 L.Ed.2d 784, affirmed 131 S.Ct. 2729, 180 L.Ed.2d 708.

This section was held unconstitutional in the decision of Brown v. Entertainment Merchants Ass'n, 2011, 131 S.Ct. 2729, 180 L.Ed.2d 708.

§ 1746.5. Severability

The provisions of this title are severable. If any provision of this title or its application is held to be invalid, that invalidity shall not affect other provisions or applications that can be given effect without the invalid provision or application. *(Added by Stats.2005, c. 638 (A.B.1179), § 2.)*

Validity

This section was held unconstitutional in the decision of Video Software Dealers Ass'n v. Schwarzenegger, C.A.9 (Cal.)2009, 556 F.3d 950, certiorari granted 130 S.Ct. 2398, 559 U.S. 1092, 176 L.Ed.2d 784, affirmed 131 S.Ct. 2729, 180 L.Ed.2d 708.

This section was held unconstitutional in the decision of Brown v. Entertainment Merchants Ass'n, 2011, 131 S.Ct. 2729, 180 L.Ed.2d 708.

Title 1.3

CREDIT CARDS

§ 1747. Short title

This title may be cited as the "Song-Beverly Credit Card Act of 1971." *(Added by Stats.1971, c. 1019, p. 1958, § 4.)*

Research References

Rutter, Cal. Practice Guide: Civil Appeals & Writs Ch. 14-D, D. Precedential Effect of Appellate Court Opinions.
Rutter, Cal. Practice Guide: Enforcing Judgments/Debts Ch. 3-A, A. Evaluating the Claim.
4 Witkin Cal. Proc. 5th Pleading § 311, (S 311) Factors Considered by Court.
1 Witkin Cal. Summ. 10th Contracts § 484, (S 484) California Law.
4 Witkin, California Summary 10th Negotiable Instruments § 144, in General.

§ 1747.01. Legislative intent; conformance with federal law

It is the intent of the Legislature that the provisions of this title as to which there are similar provisions in the federal Truth in Lending Act, as amended (15 U.S.C. 1601, et seq.), essentially conform, and be interpreted by anyone construing the provisions of this title to so conform, to the Truth in Lending Act and any rule, regulation, or interpretation promulgated thereunder by the Board of Governors of the Federal Reserve System, and any interpretation issued by an official or employee of the Federal

Reserve System duly authorized to issue such interpretation. *(Added by Stats.1982, c. 545, p. 2480, § 1.)*

Research References

4 Witkin, California Summary 10th Negotiable Instruments § 144, in General.

§ 1747.02. Definitions

As used in this title:

(a) "Credit card" means any card, plate, coupon book, or other single credit device existing for the purpose of being used from time to time upon presentation to obtain money, property, labor, or services on credit. "Credit card" does not mean any of the following:

(1) Any single credit device used to obtain telephone property, labor, or services in any transaction under public utility tariffs.

(2) Any device that may be used to obtain credit pursuant to an electronic fund transfer, but only if the credit is obtained under an agreement between a consumer and a financial institution to extend credit when the consumer's asset account is overdrawn or to maintain a specified minimum balance in the consumer's asset account.

(3) Any key or card key used at an automated dispensing outlet to obtain or purchase petroleum products, as defined in subdivision (c) of Section 13401 of the Business and Professions Code, that will be used primarily for business rather than personal or family purposes.

(b) "Accepted credit card" means any credit card that the cardholder has requested or applied for and received or has signed, or has used, or has authorized another person to use, for the purpose of obtaining money, property, labor, or services on credit. Any credit card issued in renewal of, or in substitution for, an accepted credit card becomes an accepted credit card when received by the cardholder, whether the credit card is issued by the same or a successor card issuer.

(c) "Card issuer" means any person who issues a credit card or the agent of that person for that purpose with respect to the credit card.

(d) "Cardholder" means a natural person to whom a credit card is issued for consumer credit purposes, or a natural person who has agreed with the card issuer to pay consumer credit obligations arising from the issuance of a credit card to another natural person. For purposes of Sections 1747.05, 1747.10, and 1747.20, the term includes any person to whom a credit card is issued for any purpose, including business, commercial, or agricultural use, or a person who has agreed with the card issuer to pay obligations arising from the issuance of that credit card to another person.

(e) "Retailer" means every person other than a card issuer who furnishes money, goods, services, or anything else of value upon presentation of a credit card by a cardholder. "Retailer" shall not mean the state, a county, city, city and county, or any other public agency.

(f) "Unauthorized use" means the use of a credit card by a person, other than the cardholder, (1) who does not have actual, implied, or apparent authority for that use and (2) from which the cardholder receives no benefit. "Unauthorized use" does not include the use of a credit card by a person who has been given authority by the cardholder to use the credit card. Any attempted termination by the cardholder of the person's authority is ineffective as against the card issuer until the cardholder complies with the procedures required by the card issuer to terminate that authority. Notwithstanding the above, following the card issuer's receipt of oral or written notice from a cardholder indicating that it wishes to terminate the authority of a previously authorized user of a credit card, the card issuer shall follow its usual procedures for precluding any further use of a credit card by an unauthorized person.

(g) An "inquiry" is a writing that is posted by mail to the address of the card issuer to which payments are normally tendered, unless another address is specifically indicated on the statement for that purpose, then to that other address, and that is received by the card issuer no later than 60 days after the card issuer transmitted the first periodic statement that reflects the alleged billing error, and that does all of the following:

(1) Sets forth sufficient information to enable the card issuer to identify the cardholder and the account.

(2) Sufficiently identifies the billing error.

(3) Sets forth information providing the basis for the cardholder's belief that the billing error exists.

(h) A "response" is a writing that is responsive to an inquiry and mailed to the cardholder's address last known to the card issuer.

(i) A "timely response" is a response that is mailed within two complete billing cycles, but in no event later than 90 days, after the card issuer receives an inquiry.

(j) A "billing error" means an error by omission or commission in (1) posting any debit or credit, or (2) in computation or similar error of an accounting nature contained in a statement given to the cardholder by the card issuer. A "billing error" does not mean any dispute with respect to value, quality, or quantity of goods, services, or other benefit obtained through use of a credit card.

(k) "Adequate notice" means a printed notice to a cardholder that sets forth the pertinent facts clearly and conspicuously so that a person against whom it is to operate could reasonably be expected to have noticed it and understood its meaning.

(*l*) "Secured credit card" means any credit card issued under an agreement or other instrument that pledges, hypothecates, or places a lien on real property or money or other personal property to secure the cardholder's obligations to the card issuer.

(m) "Student credit card" means any credit card that is provided to a student at a public or private college or university and is provided to that student solely based on his or her enrollment in a public or private university, or is provided to a student who would not otherwise qualify for that credit card on the basis of his or her income. A "student credit card" does not include a credit card issued to a student who has a cocardholder or cosigner who would otherwise qualify for a credit card other than a student credit card.

(n) "Retail motor fuel dispenser" means a device that dispenses fuel that is used to power internal combustion engines, including motor vehicle engines, that processes the sale of fuel through a remote electronic payment system, and that is in a location where an employee or other agent of the seller is not present.

(o) "Retail motor fuel payment island automated cashier" means a remote electronic payment processing station that processes the retail sale of fuel that is used to power internal combustion engines, including motor vehicle engines, that is in a location where an employee or other agent of the seller is not present, and that is located in close proximity to a retail motor fuel dispenser. *(Added by Stats.1971, c. 1019, p. 1958, § 4. Amended by Stats.1979, c. 574, p. 1802, § 1, eff. Sept. 12, 1979; Stats.1982, c. 545, p. 2480, § 2; Stats.1982, c. 646, p. 2659, § 1.5; Stats.1991, c. 608 (A.B.998), § 1; Stats.1992, c. 523 (S.B.1683), § 1; Stats.2001, c. 294 (A.B.521), § 1; Stats.2011, c. 690 (A.B.1219), § 1, eff. Oct. 9, 2011.)*

Research References

4 Witkin, California Summary 10th Negotiable Instruments § 145, Definitions.
4 Witkin, California Summary 10th Negotiable Instruments § 150, (S 150) Personal Identification Information.
4 Witkin, California Summary 10th Negotiable Instruments § 153, Billing Errors and Cardholder Inquiries.
4 Witkin, California Summary 10th Negotiable Instruments § 154, Liability for Unauthorized Use.

§ 1747.03. Electronic fund transfer and purchases of petroleum products by key or card key at automated dispensing outlet; inapplicability of title; exception

(a) Any rights or responsibilities created by this title that are based on the use of a credit card shall have no effect with respect to:

(1) Those transactions that constitute an electronic fund transfer as defined by Regulation E of the Federal Reserve Board (12 CFR, Part 205).

(2) Those transactions involving the use of any key or a card key used at an automated dispensing outlet to obtain or purchase petroleum products, as defined in subdivision (c) of Section 13401 of the Business and Professions Code, which will be used primarily for business rather than personal or family purposes.

(b) Notwithstanding subdivision (a), a person, company, or corporation that has been issued a key or card key described in paragraph (2) of subdivision (a) shall not be liable for losses due to the loss or theft of the key or card key incurred after receipt by the issuer of the key or card key of written or oral notification of the loss or theft. *(Added by Stats.1979, c. 574, p. 1803, § 2, eff. Sept. 12, 1979. Amended by Stats.1982, c. 646, p. 2661, § 2.)*

Research References

Rutter, Cal. Practice Guide: Enforcing Judgments/Debts Ch. 3-A, A. Evaluating the Claim.
4 Witkin, California Summary 10th Negotiable Instruments § 144, in General.

§ 1747.04. Public policy; waiver of rights

Any waiver of the provisions of this title is contrary to public policy, and is void and unenforceable. *(Added by Stats.2002, c. 815 (A.B.2331), § 2.)*

Research References

4 Witkin, California Summary 10th Negotiable Instruments § 144, in General.

§ 1747.05. Limitations on issuance

(a) No credit card shall be issued except:

(1) In response to an oral or written request or application therefor.

(2) As a renewal of, or in substitution for, an accepted credit card whether that card is issued by the same or a successor card issuer.

(b) A credit card issued in substitution for an accepted credit card may be issued only if the card issuer provides an activation process whereby the cardholder is required to contact the card issuer to activate the credit card prior to the first use of the credit card in a credit transaction.

(c) This section does not prohibit the completion of an overdraft protection advance or recurring-charge transaction that a cardholder has previously authorized on an accepted credit card. *(Added by Stats.1971, c. 1019, p. 1960, § 4. Amended by Stats.1982, c. 545, p. 2482, § 3; Stats.2002, c. 862 (S.B.1617), § 1.)*

Research References

4 Witkin, California Summary 10th Negotiable Instruments § 145, Definitions.
4 Witkin, California Summary 10th Negotiable Instruments § 146, (S 146) in General.

§ 1747.06. Offer or solicitation to receive card; completed application returned with different address; verification; liability; address change

(a) A credit card issuer that mails an offer or solicitation to receive a credit card and, in response, receives a completed application for a credit card that lists an address that is different from the address on the offer or solicitation shall verify the change of address by contacting the person to whom the solicitation or offer was mailed.

(b) Notwithstanding any other provision of law, a person to whom an offer or solicitation to receive a credit card is made shall not be liable for the unauthorized use of a credit card issued in response to that offer or solicitation if the credit card issuer does not verify the change of address pursuant to subdivision (a) prior to the issuance of the credit card, unless the credit card issuer proves that this person actually incurred the charge on the credit card.

(c) When a credit card issuer receives a written or oral request for a change of the cardholder's billing address and then receives a written or oral request for an additional credit card within 10 days after the requested address change, the credit card issuer shall not mail the requested additional credit card to the new address or, alternatively, activate the requested additional credit card, unless the credit card issuer has verified the change of address.

(d) This section shall become operative on July 1, 2000. *(Added by Stats.1999, c. 423 (S.B.930), § 1, operative July 1, 2000.)*

Research References

4 Witkin, California Summary 10th Negotiable Instruments § 154, Liability for Unauthorized Use.

§ 1747.08. Personal identification information; prohibition upon collection of data upon credit card transaction form; exemptions; civil penalties and injunctive relief

(a) Except as provided in subdivision (c), no person, firm, partnership, association, or corporation that accepts credit cards for the transaction of business shall do any of the following:

(1) Request, or require as a condition to accepting the credit card as payment in full or in part for goods or services, the cardholder to write any personal identification information upon the credit card transaction form or otherwise.

(2) Request, or require as a condition to accepting the credit card as payment in full or in part for goods or services, the cardholder to provide personal identification information, which the person, firm, partnership, association, or corporation accepting the credit card writes, causes to be written, or otherwise records upon the credit card transaction form or otherwise.

(3) Utilize, in any credit card transaction, a credit card form which contains preprinted spaces specifically designated for filling in any personal identification information of the cardholder.

(b) For purposes of this section "personal identification information," means information concerning the cardholder, other than information set forth on the credit card, and including, but not limited to, the cardholder's address and telephone number.

(c) Subdivision (a) does not apply in the following instances:

(1) If the credit card is being used as a deposit to secure payment in the event of default, loss, damage, or other similar occurrence.

(2) Cash advance transactions.

(3) If any of the following applies:

(A) The person, firm, partnership, association, or corporation accepting the credit card is contractually obligated to provide personal identification information in order to complete the credit card transaction.

(B) The person, firm, partnership, association, or corporation accepting the credit card in a sales transaction at a retail motor fuel dispenser or retail motor fuel payment island automated cashier uses the Zip Code information solely for prevention of fraud, theft, or identity theft.

(C) The person, firm, partnership, association, or corporation accepting the credit card is obligated to collect and record the personal identification information by federal or state law or regulation.

(4) If personal identification information is required for a special purpose incidental but related to the individual credit card transaction, including, but not limited to, information relating to shipping, delivery, servicing, or installation of the purchased merchandise, or for special orders.

(d) This section does not prohibit any person, firm, partnership, association, or corporation from requiring the cardholder, as a condition to accepting the credit card as payment in full or in part for goods or services, to provide reasonable forms of positive identification, which may include a driver's license or a California state identification card, or where one of these is not available, another form of photo identification, provided that none of the information contained thereon is written or recorded on the credit card transaction form or otherwise. If the cardholder pays for the transaction with a credit card number and does not make the credit card available upon request to verify the number, the cardholder's driver's license number or identification card number may be recorded on the credit card transaction form or otherwise.

(e) Any person who violates this section shall be subject to a civil penalty not to exceed two hundred fifty dollars ($250) for the first violation and one thousand dollars ($1,000) for each subsequent violation, to be assessed and collected in a civil action brought by the person paying with a credit card, by the Attorney General, or by the district attorney or city attorney of the county or city in which the violation occurred. However, no civil penalty shall be assessed for a violation of this section if the defendant shows by a preponderance of the evidence that the violation was not intentional and resulted from a bona fide error made notwithstanding the defendant's maintenance of procedures reasonably adopted to avoid that error. When collected, the civil penalty shall be payable, as appropriate, to the person paying with a credit card who brought the action, or to the general fund of whichever governmental entity brought the action to assess the civil penalty.

(f) The Attorney General, or any district attorney or city attorney within his or her respective jurisdiction, may bring an action in the superior court in the name of the people of the State of California to enjoin violation of subdivision (a) and, upon notice to the defendant of not less than five days, to temporarily restrain and enjoin the violation. If it appears to the satisfaction of the court that the defendant has, in fact, violated subdivision (a), the court may issue an injunction restraining further violations, without requiring proof that any person has been damaged by the violation. In these proceedings, if the court finds that the defendant has violated subdivision (a), the court may direct the defendant to pay any or all costs incurred by

the Attorney General, district attorney, or city attorney in seeking or obtaining injunctive relief pursuant to this subdivision.

(g) Actions for collection of civil penalties under subdivision (e) and for injunctive relief under subdivision (f) may be consolidated.

(h) The changes made to this section by Chapter 458 of the Statutes of 1995 apply only to credit card transactions entered into on and after January 1, 1996. Nothing in those changes shall be construed to affect any civil action which was filed before January 1, 1996. *(Formerly § 1747.8, added by Stats.1990, c. 999 (A.B.2920), § 1. Amended by Stats.1991, c. 1089 (A.B. 1477), § 2, eff. Oct. 14, 1991; Stats.1995; c. 458 (A.B.1316), § 2. Renumbered § 1747.08 and amended by Stats.2004, c. 183 (A.B. 3082), § 29. Amended by Stats.2005, c. 22 (S.B.1108), § 14; Stats.2011, c. 690 (A.B.1219), § 2, eff. Oct. 9, 2011.)*

Research References

Rutter, Cal. Practice Guide: Enforcing Judgments/Debts Ch. 3-A, A. Evaluating the Claim.
Rutter, Cal. Practice Guide: Enforcing Judgments/Debts Gen. Matls., Highlights.
3 Witkin Cal. Proc. 5th Actions § 668, (S 668) Exceptions.
4 Witkin Cal. Proc. 5th Pleading § 311, (S 311) Factors Considered by Court.
4 Witkin, California Summary 10th Negotiable Instruments § 150, (S 150) Personal Identification Information.

§ 1747.09. Printing credit or debit card receipts; restrictions

(a) Except as provided in this section, no person, firm, partnership, association, corporation, or limited liability company that accepts credit or debit cards for the transaction of business shall print more than the last five digits of the credit or debit card account number or the expiration date upon any of the following:

(1) Any receipt provided to the cardholder.

(2) Any receipt retained by the person, firm, partnership, association, corporation, or limited liability company, which is printed at the time of the purchase, exchange, refund, or return, and is signed by the cardholder.

(3) Any receipt retained by the person, firm, partnership, association, corporation, or limited liability company, which is printed at the time of the purchase, exchange, refund, or return, but is not signed by the cardholder, because the cardholder used a personal identification number to complete the transaction.

(b) This section shall apply only to receipts that include a credit or debit card account number that are electronically printed and shall not apply to transactions in which the sole means of recording the person's credit or debit card account number is by handwriting or by an imprint or copy of the credit or debit card.

(c) This section shall not apply to documents, other than the receipts described in paragraphs (1) to (3), inclusive, of subdivision (a), used for internal administrative purposes.

(d) Paragraphs (2) and (3) of subdivision (a) shall become operative on January 1, 2009. *(Formerly § 1747.9, added by Stats.1999, c. 423 (S.B.930), § 2. Renumbered § 1747.09 and amended by Stats.2004, c. 183 (A.B.3082), § 30. Amended by Stats.2005, c. 445 (S.B.802), § 1; Stats.2006, c. 682 (S.B.1699), § 1.)*

Research References

4 Witkin, California Summary 10th Negotiable Instruments § 152, (S 152) Contents of Receipt.

§ 1747.10. Limitations on liability for unauthorized credit card use

A cardholder shall be liable for the unauthorized use of a credit card only if all of the following conditions are met:

(a) The card is an accepted credit card.

(b) The liability is not in excess of fifty dollars ($50).

(c) The card issuer gives adequate notice to the cardholder of the potential liability.

(d) The card issuer has provided the cardholder with a description of a means by which the card issuer may be notified of loss or theft of the card.

(e) The unauthorized use occurs before the card issuer has been notified that an unauthorized use of the credit card has occurred or may occur as the result of loss, theft, or otherwise.

(f) The card issuer has provided a method whereby the user of such card can be identified as the person authorized to use it. *(Added by Stats.1982, c. 545, p. 2482, § 5.)*

Research References

Rutter, Cal. Practice Guide: Enforcing Judgments/Debts Ch. 3-A, A. Evaluating the Claim.

4 Witkin, California Summary 10th Negotiable Instruments § 145, Definitions.

4 Witkin, California Summary 10th Negotiable Instruments § 154, Liability for Unauthorized Use.

§ 1747.20. Multiple cards issued for use by employees of an organization; liability for unauthorized use; agreements

If 10 or more credit cards are issued by one card issuer for use by the employees of an organization, Section 1747.10 does not prohibit the card issuer and the organization from agreeing to liability for unauthorized use without regard to Section 1747.10. However, liability for unauthorized use may be imposed on an employee of the organization, by either the card issuer or the organization, only in accordance with Section 1747.10. *(Added by Stats.1982, c. 545, p. 2482, § 7.)*

Research References

4 Witkin, California Summary 10th Negotiable Instruments § 145, Definitions.

4 Witkin, California Summary 10th Negotiable Instruments § 154, Liability for Unauthorized Use.

§ 1747.40. Failure of card issuer to give timely response to inquiry concerning debit or credit applicable to obligation

If a card issuer fails to give a timely response to an inquiry of a cardholder concerning any debit or credit applicable to an obligation incurred through the use of a credit card, he shall not be entitled to interest, finance charges, service charges, or any other charges thereon, from the date of mailing of the inquiry to the date of mailing of the response. *(Added by Stats.1971, c. 1019, p. 1960, § 4.)*

Research References

4 Witkin, California Summary 10th Negotiable Instruments § 153, Billing Errors and Cardholder Inquiries.

§ 1747.50. Correction of billing errors by card issuer; penalty for failure to correct; action

(a) Every card issuer shall correct any billing error made by the card issuer within two complete billing cycles, but in no event later than 90 days, after receiving an inquiry.

(b) Any card issuer who fails to correct a billing error made by the card issuer within the period prescribed by subdivision (a) shall not be entitled to the amount by which the outstanding balance of the cardholder's account is greater than the correct balance, nor any interest, finance charges, service charges, or other charges on the obligation giving rise to the billing error.

(c) Any cardholder who is injured by a willful violation of this section may bring an action for the recovery of damages. Judgment may be entered for three times the amount at which

actual damages are assessed. The cardholder shall be entitled to recover reasonable attorney's fees and costs incurred in the action. *(Added by Stats.1971, c. 1019, p. 1960, § 4. Amended by Stats.1982, c. 545, p. 2483, § 9.)*

Research References

4 Witkin, California Summary 10th Negotiable Instruments § 146, (S 146) in General.

4 Witkin, California Summary 10th Negotiable Instruments § 153, Billing Errors and Cardholder Inquiries.

§ 1747.60. Correction of billing errors by retailer; penalty for failure to correct; action

(a) Every retailer shall correct any billing error made by the retailer within 60 days from the date on which an inquiry concerning a billing error was mailed.

(b) Any retailer who fails to correct a billing error made by the retailer within the period prescribed by subdivision (a) shall be liable to the cardholder in the amount by which the outstanding balance of the cardholder's account is greater than the correct balance, and any interest, finance charges, service charges, or other charges on the obligation giving rise to the billing error.

(c) Any cardholder who is injured by a willful violation of this section may bring an action for the recovery of damages. Judgment may be entered for three times the amount at which actual damages are assessed. The cardholder shall be entitled to recover reasonable attorney's fees and costs incurred in the action.

(d) As used in this section, an "inquiry" is a writing which is posted by mail to the address of the retailer, unless another address is specifically indicated by the retailer for the purpose of mailing inquiries with respect to billing errors, then to such address. *(Added by Stats.1971, c. 1019, p. 1960, § 4.)*

Research References

4 Witkin, California Summary 10th Negotiable Instruments § 153, Billing Errors and Cardholder Inquiries.

§ 1747.65. Card issuer or retailer not liable for billing error made by the other

(a) A card issuer shall not be liable for a billing error made by the retailer.

(b) A retailer shall not be liable for a billing error made by a card issuer. *(Added by Stats.1971, c. 1019, p. 1961, § 4.)*

Research References

4 Witkin, California Summary 10th Negotiable Instruments § 153, Billing Errors and Cardholder Inquiries.

§ 1747.70. Giving of untrue or unfavorable credit information by card issuer; unlawful cancellation or refusal to renew credit card; penalty

(a) No card issuer shall knowingly give any untrue credit information to any other person concerning a cardholder.

(b) No card issuer, after receiving an inquiry from a cardholder regarding a billing error and prior to satisfying the requirements of Section 1747.50, shall communicate unfavorable credit information concerning the cardholder to any person solely because of the cardholder's failure to pay the amount by which the outstanding balance of the cardholder's account is greater than the correct balance.

(c) No card issuer shall cancel or refuse to renew a credit card for the reason that the cardholder has obtained relief under Section 1747.50.

(d) Any cardholder who is injured by a willful violation of this section may bring an action for the recovery of damages. Judgment may be entered for three times the amount at which actual damages are assessed. The cardholder shall be entitled to recover reasonable attorney's fees and costs incurred in the action. *(Added by Stats.1971, c. 1019, p. 1961, § 4.)*

Research References

4 Witkin, California Summary 10th Negotiable Instruments § 146, (S 146) in General.

4 Witkin, California Summary 10th Negotiable Instruments § 153, Billing Errors and Cardholder Inquiries.

§ 1747.80. Refusal to issue credit card for discriminatory reasons; penalty

(a) No card issuer shall refuse to issue a credit card to any person solely because of any characteristic listed or defined in subdivision (b) or (e) of Section 51.

(b) Any card issuer who willfully violates this section is liable for each and every offense for the actual damages, and two hundred fifty dollars ($250) in addition thereto, suffered by any person denied a credit card solely for the reasons set forth in subdivision (a). In addition, that person may petition the court to order the card issuer to issue him or her a credit card upon the terms, conditions, and standards as the card issuer normally utilizes in granting credit to other individuals. *(Added by Stats.1971, c. 1019, p. 1961, § 4. Amended by Stats.2007, c. 568 (A.B.14), § 14.)*

Research References

4 Witkin, California Summary 10th Negotiable Instruments § 146, (S 146) in General.

§ 1747.81. Married women; name on card

(a) If a card issuer has determined in the normal course of business that it will issue a card to a married woman, the card shall be issued bearing either the maiden name or married name of the woman, as the woman may direct.

(b) Card issuers may require that a married woman requesting a card in her maiden name open a new account in that name. *(Added by Stats.1974, c. 1252, p. 2712, § 1.)*

Research References

11 Witkin, California Summary 10th Husband and Wife § 21, in Business Transactions.

4 Witkin, California Summary 10th Negotiable Instruments § 146, (S 146) in General.

§ 1747.85. Cancellation of credit card; notice; exceptions; inactive status; updating information to verify current creditworthiness

Unless requested by the cardholder, no card issuer shall cancel a credit card without having first given the cardholder 30 days' written notice of its intention to do so unless the cardholder is or has been within the last 90 days in default of payment or otherwise in violation of any provision of the agreement between the card issuer and the cardholder governing the cardholder's use of the credit card or unless the card issuer has evidence or reasonable belief that the cardholder is unable or unwilling to repay obligations incurred under the agreement or that an unauthorized use of the card may be made.

Nothing provided herein shall be construed to prohibit a card issuer from placing the account of a cardholder on inactive status if the cardholder has not used the card for a period in excess of 18 months or from requiring that cardholder, upon subsequent reuse of a card, to provide to the card issuer such updated information as will enable the card issuer to verify the current creditworthiness of the cardholder. *(Added by Stats.1976, c. 34, p. 60, § 1. Amended by Stats.1983, c. 1247, § 1.)*

Research References

4 Witkin, California Summary 10th Negotiable Instruments § 149, (S 149) Cancellation.

§ 1747.90. Cardholders' claims and defenses arising from card transactions; assertion against issuer; conditions; amount of claims or defenses

(a)(1) Subject to the limitation contained in subdivision (b), a card issuer who has issued a credit card to a cardholder pursuant to an open-end consumer credit plan shall be subject to all claims and defenses, other than tort claims, arising out of any transaction in which the credit card is used as a method of payment or extension of credit if the following conditions are met:

(A) The cardholder has made a good faith attempt to obtain satisfactory resolution of a disagreement or problem relative to the transaction from the person honoring the credit card.

(B) The amount of the initial transaction exceeds fifty dollars ($50).

(C) The place where the initial transaction occurred was in California, or, if not within California, then within 100 miles from the cardholder's current designated address in California.

(2) The limitations set forth in subparagraphs (B) and (C) of paragraph (1) with respect to a cardholder's right to assert claims and defenses against a card issuer shall not be applicable to any transaction in which the person honoring the credit card satisfies any of the following requirements:

(A) Is the same person as the card issuer.

(B) Is controlled by the card issuer.

(C) Is under direct or indirect common control with the card issuer.

(D) Is a franchised dealer in the card issuer's products or services.

(E) Has obtained the order for such transaction through a mail solicitation made by or participated in by the card issuer in which the cardholder is solicited to enter into such transaction by using the credit card issued by the card issuer.

(b) The amount of claims or defenses asserted by the cardholder may not exceed the amount of credit outstanding with respect to such transaction at the time the cardholder first notifies the card issuer or the person honoring the credit card of such claim or defense. For the purpose of determining the amount of credit outstanding, payments and credits to the cardholder's account are deemed to have been applied, in the order indicated, to the payment of the following:

(1) Late charges in the order of their entry to the account.

(2) Finance charges in order of their entry to the account.

(3) Debits to the account other than those set forth above, in the order in which each debit entry to the account was made.

(c) This section does not apply to the use of a check guarantee card or a debit card in connection with an overdraft credit plan, or to a check guarantee card used in connection with cash advance checks. *(Added by Stats.1982, c. 545, p. 2483, § 11.)*

Research References

Rutter, Cal. Practice Guide: Enforcing Judgments/Debts Ch. 3-A, A. Evaluating the Claim.

Civil

4 Witkin, California Summary 10th Negotiable Instruments § 156, Cardholder's Defenses.

§ 1747.94. Secured credit card disclosures; statement in deed of trust executed in connection with card; applicability of section; violation

(a) In addition to any other disclosures required by law, a card issuer of a secured credit card shall, in every advertisement or solicitation to prospective cardholders, expressly identify the credit instrument offered as a "secured credit card" and prominently disclose that credit extended under the secured credit card is secured, and shall describe the security by item or type.

(b) Any deed of trust executed in connection with a secured credit card shall contain a statement that it is security for a secured credit card obligation. However, failure to include the statement shall not invalidate the deed of trust.

(c) This section does not apply to either of the following:

(1) Any credit card which is issued under an agreement or other instrument creating a purchase money security interest in property purchased with the credit card, but which does not pledge, hypothecate, or place a lien on other property of the cardholder or any co-obligor.

(2) Loans or extensions of credit subject to the Federal Home Equity Loan Consumer Protection Act of 1988 (P.L. 100-709).

(d) Any violation of this section shall constitute unfair competition within the meaning of Section 17200 of the Business and Professions Code. *(Added by Stats.1991, c. 608 (A.B.998), § 2.)*

Research References

4 Witkin, California Summary 10th Negotiable Instruments § 159, Matters to be Disclosed.

§ 1748. Agreements to prohibit discounts for cash payment; invalidity

Any provision in a contract between a card issuer and a retailer which has the effect of prohibiting the retailer from offering price discounts or from charging a different and lower price to customers who pay for goods or services by cash instead of by credit card is contrary to public policy and void. *(Added by Stats.1974, c. 1520, p. 3402, § 1.)*

Research References

4 Witkin, California Summary 10th Negotiable Instruments § 147, (S 147) Cash Discounts and Credit Card Surcharges.

§ 1748.1. Surcharges; violations

(a) No retailer in any sales, service, or lease transaction with a consumer may impose a surcharge on a cardholder who elects to use a credit card in lieu of payment by cash, check, or similar means. A retailer may, however, offer discounts for the purpose of inducing payment by cash, check, or other means not involving the use of a credit card, provided that the discount is offered to all prospective buyers.

(b) Any retailer who willfully violates this section by imposing a surcharge on a cardholder who elects to use a credit card and who fails to pay that amount to the cardholder within 30 days of a written demand by the cardholder to the retailer by certified mail, shall be liable to the cardholder for three times the amount at which actual damages are assessed. The cardholder shall also be entitled to recover reasonable attorney's fees and costs incurred in the action.

A cause of action under this section may be brought in small claims court, if it does not exceed the jurisdiction of that court, or in any other appropriate court.

(c) A consumer shall not be deemed to have elected to use a credit card in lieu of another means of payment for purposes of this section in a transaction with a retailer if only credit cards are accepted by that retailer in payment for an order made by a consumer over a telephone, and only cash is accepted at a public store or other facility of the same retailer.

(d) Charges for third-party credit card guarantee services, when added to the price charged by the retailer if cash were to be paid, shall be deemed surcharges for purposes of this section even if they are payable directly to the third party or are charged separately.

(e) It is the intent of the Legislature to promote the effective operation of the free market and protect consumers from deceptive price increases for goods and services by prohibiting credit card surcharges and encouraging the availability of discounts by those retailers who wish to offer a lower price for goods and services purchased by some form of payment other than credit card.

(f) This section does not apply to charges for payment by credit card or debit card that are made by an electrical, gas, or water corporation and approved by the Public Utilities Commission pursuant to Section 755 of the Public Utilities Code. *(Added by Stats.1985, c. 913, § 1. Amended by Stats.1990, c. 309 (S.B.1763), § 1; Stats.2005, c. 426 (A.B.746), § 1.)*

Research References

Rutter, Cal. Practice Guide: Enforcing Judgments/Debts Ch. 3-A, A. Evaluating the Claim.
4 Witkin Cal. Proc. 5th Pleading § 311, (S 311) Factors Considered by Court.
4 Witkin, California Summary 10th Negotiable Instruments § 147, (S 147) Cash Discounts and Credit Card Surcharges.

§ 1748.5. Finance charges; cardholder information request; frequency; form; application

(a) A cardholder may request, not more frequently than once a year, that the card issuer inform the cardholder of the total amount of finance charges assessed on the account during the preceding calendar year and the card issuer shall provide that information to the cardholder within 30 days of receiving the request, without charge.

If the cardholder's request for the information is made in writing, the card issuer shall provide the information in writing. However, if the card issuer is required to furnish the cardholder with a periodic billing or periodic statement of account or furnishes the billing or statement of account, the requested statement of finance charges may be furnished along with the periodic billing or periodic statement of account.

(b) This section shall not apply to card issuers or cardholders who issue or use credit cards in connection with a retail installment account, as defined by Section 1802.7. *(Added by Stats.1996, c. 180 (S.B.1871), § 2.)*

Research References

4 Witkin, California Summary 10th Negotiable Instruments § 148, (S 148) Statements.

§ 1748.7. Credit card transactions through retailer's account with financial institution or credit card issuer without furnishing of goods or services; exemptions; violations; remedies; penalties

(a) No person shall process, deposit, negotiate, or obtain payment of a credit card charge through a retailer's account with a financial institution or through a retailer's agreement with a financial institution, card issuer, or organization of financial institutions or card issuers if that retailer did not furnish or agree to furnish the goods or services which are the subject of the charge.

(b) No retailer shall permit any person to process, deposit, negotiate, or obtain payment of a credit card charge through the retailer's account with a financial institution or the retailer's agreement with a financial institution, card issuer, or organization of financial institutions or card issuers if that retailer did not furnish or agree to furnish the goods or services which are the subject of the charge.

(c) Subdivisions (a) and (b) do not apply to any of the following:

(1) A person who furnishes goods or services on the business premises of a general merchandise retailer and who processes, deposits, negotiates, or obtains payment of a credit card charge through that general merchandise retailer's account or agreement.

(2) A general merchandise retailer who permits a person described in paragraph (1) to process, deposit, negotiate, or obtain payment of a credit card charge through that general merchandise retailer's account or agreement.

(3) A franchisee who furnishes the cardholder with goods or services that are provided in whole or in part by the franchisor and who processes, deposits, negotiates, or obtains payment of a credit card charge through that franchisor's account or agreement.

(4) A franchisor who permits a franchisee described in paragraph (3) to process, deposit, negotiate, or obtain payment of a credit card charge through that franchisor's account or agreement.

(5) The credit card issuer or a financial institution or a parent, subsidiary, or affiliate of the card issuer or a financial institution.

(6) A person who processes, deposits, negotiates, or obtains payment of less than five hundred dollars ($500) of credit card charges in any one year period through a retailer's account or agreement. The person shall have the burden of producing evidence that the person transacted less than five hundred dollars ($500) in credit card charges during any one year period.

(d) Any person injured by a violation of this section may bring an action for the recovery of damages, equitable relief, and reasonable attorney's fees and costs.

(e) Any person who violates this section shall be guilty of a misdemeanor. Each occurrence in which a person processes, deposits, negotiates, or otherwise seeks to obtain payment of a credit card charge in violation of subdivision (a) constitutes a separate offense.

(f) The penalties and remedies provided in this section are in addition to any other remedies or penalties provided by law.

(g) The exemptions from this title specified in Section 1747.03 do not apply to this section.

(h) As used in this section:

(1) "General merchandise retailer" means any person or entity, regardless of the form of organization, that has continuously offered for sale or lease more than 100 different types of goods or services to the public in this state throughout a period which includes the immediately preceding five years.

(2) "Franchisor" has the same meaning as defined in Section 31007 of the Corporations Code.

(3) "Franchisee" has the same meaning as defined in Section 31006 of the Corporations Code. *(Added by Stats.1989, c. 855, § 1.)*

Research References

4 Witkin, California Summary 10th Negotiable Instruments § 155, Processing of Credit Card Charge Without Furnishing Goods or Services.

§ 1748.9.   Preprinted checks or drafts;   required disclosures

(a)[1] A credit card issuer that extends credit to a cardholder through the use of a preprinted check or draft shall disclose on the front of an attachment that is affixed by perforation or other means to the preprinted check or draft, in clear and conspicuous language, all of the following information:

(1) That "use of the attached check or draft will constitute a charge against your credit account."

(2) The annual percentage rate and the calculation of finance charges, as required by Section 226.16 of Regulation Z of the Code of Federal Regulations, associated with the use of the attached check or draft.

(3) Whether the finance charges are triggered immediately upon the use of the check or draft. *(Added by Stats.1999, c. 171 (S.B.545), § 1, operative July 1, 2000.)*

1 So in enrolled bill.

Research References

4 Witkin, California Summary 10th Negotiable Instruments § 159, Matters to be Disclosed.

§ 1748.95.   Identity theft;   credit card application filed by unauthorized person;   right of victim to receive copies of specified documents from credit card company

(a)(1) Upon the request of a person who has obtained a police report pursuant to Section 530.6 of the Penal Code, a credit card issuer shall provide to the person, or to a law enforcement officer specified by the person, copies of all application forms or application information containing the person's name, address, or other identifying information pertaining to the application filed with the credit card issuer by an unauthorized person in violation of Section 530.5 of the Penal Code.

(2) Before providing copies pursuant to paragraph (1), the credit card issuer shall inform the requesting person of the categories of identifying information that the unauthorized person used to complete the application and shall require the requesting person to provide identifying information in those categories and a copy of the police report.

(3) The credit card issuer shall provide copies of all forms and information required by this section, without charge, within 10 business days of receipt of the person's request and submission of the required copy of the police report and identifying information.

(b)(1) Before a credit card issuer provides copies to a law enforcement officer pursuant to paragraph (1) of subdivision (a), the credit card issuer may require the requesting person to provide them with a signed and dated statement by which the person does all of the following:

(A) Authorizes disclosure for a stated period.

(B) Specifies the name of the agency or department to which the disclosure is authorized.

(C) Identifies the type of records that the person authorizes to be disclosed.

(2) The credit card issuer shall include in the statement to be signed by the requesting person a notice that the person has the right at any time to revoke the authorization.

(c) As used in this section, "law enforcement officer" means a peace officer as defined by Section 830.1 of the Penal Code. *(Added by Stats.2001, c. 493 (S.B.125), § 1.)*

Title 1.3A

CREDIT CARD DISCLOSURE

§ 1748.10.   Short title

This act shall be known and may be cited as the "Areias Credit Card Full Disclosure Act of 1986." *(Added by Stats.1986, c. 1397, § 2. Amended by Stats.2000, c. 375 (A.B.1331), § 2; Stats.2000, c. 977 (A.B.2869), § 1; Stats.2001, c. 159 (S.B.662), § 32.)*

Research References

Rutter, Cal. Practice Guide: Enforcing Judgments/Debts Ch. 3-A, A. Evaluating the Claim.
4 Witkin, California Summary 10th Negotiable Instruments § 157, (S 157) Nature and Purpose of Legislation.

§ 1748.11.   Disclosures to accompany application form; manner of disclosure; "Regulation Z"; additional terms, etc.; federal disclosure requirement; establishment of equal requirements; open-end credit card account application form; application of title

(a) Any application form or preapproved written solicitation for an open-end credit card account to be used for personal, family, or household purposes that is mailed on or after October 1, 1987, to a consumer residing in this state by or on behalf of a creditor, whether or not the creditor is located in this state, other than an application form or solicitation included in a magazine, newspaper, or other publication distributed by someone other than the creditor, shall contain or be accompanied by either of the following disclosures:

(1) A disclosure of each of the following, if applicable:

(A) Any periodic rate or rates that may be applied to the account, expressed as an annual percentage rate or rates. If the account is subject to a variable rate, the creditor may instead either disclose the rate as of a specific date and indicate that the rate may vary, or identify the index and any amount or percentage added to, or subtracted from, that index and used to determine the rate. For purposes of this section, that amount or percentage shall be referred to as the "spread."

(B) Any membership or participation fee that may be imposed for availability of a credit card account, expressed as an annualized amount.

(C) Any per transaction fee that may be imposed on purchases, expressed as an amount or as a percentage of the transaction, as applicable.

(D) If the creditor provides a period during which the consumer may repay the full balance reflected on a billing statement that is attributable to purchases of goods or services from the creditor or from merchants participating in the credit card plan, without the imposition of additional finance charges, the creditor shall either disclose the number of days of that period, calculated from the closing date of the prior billing cycle to the date designated in the billing statement sent to the consumer as the date by which that payment must be received to avoid additional finance charges, or describe the manner in which the period is calculated. For purposes of this section, the period shall be referred to as the "free period" or "free-ride period." If the creditor does not provide this period for purchases, the disclosure shall so indicate.

(2) A disclosure that satisfies the initial disclosure statement requirements of Regulation Z.

(b) A creditor need not present the disclosures required by paragraph (1) of subdivision (a) in chart form or use any specific terminology, except as expressly provided in this section. The following chart shall not be construed in any way as a standard by which to determine whether a creditor who elects not to use such a chart has provided the required disclosures in a manner that satisfies paragraph (1) of subdivision (a). However, disclosures shall be conclusively presumed to satisfy the requirements of paragraph (1) of subdivision (a) if a chart with captions substantially as follows is completed with the applicable terms offered by the creditor, or if the creditor presents the applicable terms in tabular, list, or narrative format using terminology substantially similar to the captions included in the following chart:

THE FOLLOWING INFORMATION IS PROVIDED PURSUANT TO THE AREIAS CREDIT CARD FULL DISCLOSURE ACT OF 1986:

INTEREST RATES, FEES, AND FREE-RIDE PERIOD FOR PURCHASES UNDER THIS CREDIT CARD ACCOUNT

ANNUAL PERCENT-AGE RATE(1)	VARIABLE RATE INDEX AND SPREAD(2)	ANNUAL-IZED MEMBER-SHIP OR PARTICI-PATION FEE	TRANS-ACTION FEE	FREE–RIDE PERIOD(3)

(1) For fixed interest rates. If variable rate, creditor may elect to disclose a rate as of a specified date and indicate that the rate may vary.

(2) For variable interest rates. If fixed rate, creditor may eliminate the column, leave the column blank, or indicate "No" or "None" or "Does not apply."

(3) For example, "30 days" or "Yes, if full payment is received by next billing date" or "Yes, if full new balance is paid by due date."

(c) For purposes of this section, "Regulation Z" has the meaning attributed to it under Section 1802.18, and all of the terms used in this section have the same meaning as attributed to them in federal Regulation Z (12 C.F.R. 226.1 et seq.). For the purposes of this section, "open-end credit card account" does not include an account accessed by a device described in paragraph (2) of subdivision (a) of Section 1747.02.

(d) Nothing in this section shall be deemed or construed to prohibit a creditor from disclosing additional terms, conditions, or information, whether or not relating to the disclosures required under this section, in conjunction with the disclosures required by this section.

(e) If a creditor is required under federal law to make any disclosure of the terms applicable to a credit card account in connection with application forms or solicitations, the creditor shall be deemed to have complied with the requirements of paragraph (1) of subdivision (a) with respect to those application forms or solicitations if the creditor complies with the federal disclosure requirement. For example, in lieu of complying with the requirements of paragraph (1) of subdivision (a), a creditor has the option of disclosing the specific terms required to be disclosed in an advertisement under Regulation Z, if the application forms or solicitations constitute advertisements in which specific terms must be disclosed under Regulation Z.

(f) If for any reason the requirements of this section do not apply equally to creditors located in this state and creditors not located in this state, then the requirements applicable to creditors located in this state shall automatically be reduced to the extent necessary to establish equal requirements for both categories of creditors, until it is otherwise determined by a court of law in a proceeding to which the creditor located in this state is a party.

(g) All application forms for an open-end credit card account distributed in this state on or after October 1, 1987, other than by mail, shall contain a statement in substantially the following form:

"If you wish to receive disclosure of the terms of this credit card, pursuant to the Areias Credit Card Full Disclosure Act of 1986, check here and return to the address on this application."

A box shall be printed in or next to this statement for placement of such a checkmark.

However, this subdivision does not apply if the application contains the disclosures provided for in this title.

(h) This title does not apply to any application form or written advertisement or an open-end credit card account where the credit to be extended will be secured by a lien on real or personal property or both real and personal property.

(i) This title does not apply to any person who is subject to Article 10.5 (commencing with Section 1810.20) of Chapter 1 of Title 2. *(Added by Stats.1986, c. 1397, § 2. Amended by Stats.2000, c. 375 (A.B.1331), § 3; Stats.2001, c. 159 (S.B.662), § 33.)*

Research References

Rutter, Cal. Practice Guide: Enforcing Judgments/Debts Ch. 3-A, A. Evaluating the Claim.

4 Witkin, California Summary 10th Negotiable Instruments § 158, Scope of Requirement.

4 Witkin, California Summary 10th Negotiable Instruments § 159, Matters to be Disclosed.

4 Witkin, California Summary 10th Negotiable Instruments § 160, Methods of Compliance.

4 Witkin, California Summary 10th Negotiable Instruments § 162, Matters to be Disclosed.

4 Witkin, California Summary 10th Negotiable Instruments § 163, Methods of Compliance.

4 Witkin, California Summary 10th Negotiable Instruments § 166, Methods of Compliance.

§ 1748.12. Marketing information disclosure; notice to cardholder of right to prohibit information release; federal requirements

(a) For purposes of this section:

(1) "Cardholder" means any consumer to whom a credit card is issued, provided that, when more than one credit card has been issued for the same account, all persons holding those credit cards may be treated as a single cardholder.

(2) "Credit card" means any card, plate, coupon book, or other single credit device existing for the purpose of being used from time to time upon presentation to obtain money, property, labor, or services on credit. "Credit card" does not mean any of the following:

(A) Any single credit device used to obtain telephone property, labor, or services in any transaction under public utility tariffs.

(B) Any device that may be used to obtain credit pursuant to an electronic fund transfer but only if the credit is obtained under an agreement between a consumer and a financial institution to extend credit when the consumer's asset account is overdrawn or to maintain a specified minimum balance in the consumer's asset account.

(C) Any key or card key used at an automated dispensing outlet to obtain or purchase petroleum products, as defined in subdivision (c) of Section 13401 of the Business and Professions Code, which will be used primarily for business rather than personal or family purposes.

(3) "Marketing information" means the categorization of cardholders compiled by a credit card issuer, based on a cardholder's shopping patterns, spending history, or behavioral characteristics derived from account activity which is provided to a marketer of goods or services or a subsidiary or affiliate organization of the company that collects the information for consideration. "Marketing information" does not include aggregate data that does not identify a cardholder based on the cardholder's shopping patterns, spending history, or behavioral characteristics derived from account activity or any communications to any person in connection with any transfer, processing, billing, collection, chargeback, fraud prevention, credit card recovery, or acquisition of or for credit card accounts.

(b) If the credit card issuer discloses marketing information concerning a cardholder to any person, the credit card issuer shall provide a written notice to the cardholder that clearly and conspicuously describes the cardholder's right to prohibit the disclosure of marketing information concerning the cardholder which discloses the cardholder's identity. The notice shall be in 10-point type and shall advise the cardholder of his or her ability to respond either by completing a preprinted form or a toll-free telephone number that the cardholder may call to exercise this right.

(c) The requirements of subdivision (b) shall be satisfied by furnishing the notice to the cardholder:

(1) At least 60 days prior to the initial disclosure of marketing information concerning the cardholder by the credit card issuer.

(2) For all new credit cards issued on or after April 1, 2002, on the form containing the new credit card when the credit card is delivered to the cardholder.

(3) At least once per calendar year, to every cardholder entitled to receive an annual statement of billings rights pursuant to 12 C.F.R. 226.9 (Regulation Z). The notice required by this paragraph may be included on or with any periodic statement or with the delivery of the renewal card.

(d)(1) The cardholder's election to prohibit disclosure of marketing information shall be effective only with respect to marketing information that is disclosed to any party beginning 30 days after the credit card issuer has received, at the designated address on the form containing the new credit card or on the preprinted form, or by telephone, the cardholder's election to prohibit disclosure. This does not apply to the disclosure of marketing information prior to the cardholder's notification to the credit card issuer of the cardholder's election.

(2) An election to prohibit disclosure of marketing information shall terminate upon receipt by the credit card issuer of notice from the cardholder that the cardholder's election to prohibit disclosure is no longer effective.

(e) The requirements of this section do not apply to any of the following communications of marketing information by a credit card issuer:

(1) Communications to any party to, or merchant specified in, the credit card agreement, or to any person whose name appears on the credit card or on whose behalf the credit card is issued.

(2) Communications to consumer credit reporting agencies, as defined in subdivision (d) of Section 1785.3.

(3) To the extent that the Fair Credit Reporting Act preempts the requirements of this section as to communication by a credit card issuer to a corporate subsidiary or affiliate, the credit card issuer may communicate information about a cardholder to a corporate subsidiary or affiliate to the extent and in the manner permitted under that act.

(4) Communications to a third party when the third party is responsible for conveying information from the card issuer to any of its cardholders.

(f) If the laws of the United States require disclosure to cardholders regarding the use of personal information, compliance with the federal requirements shall be deemed to be compliance with this section.

(g) This section shall become operative on April 1, 2002. *(Added by Stats.2000, c. 977 (A.B.2869), § 3, operative April 1, 2002.)*

Research References

4 Witkin, California Summary 10th Negotiable Instruments § 159, Matters to be Disclosed.

§ 1748.13. Statements to be provided by credit card issuer to cardholder in each billing statement; definitions; limitations on application

(a) A credit card issuer shall, with each billing statement provided to a cardholder in this state, provide the following on the front of the first page of the billing statement in type no smaller than that required for any other required disclosure, but in no case in less than 8–point capitalized type:

(1) A written statement in the following form: "Minimum Payment Warning: Making only the minimum payment will increase the interest you pay and the time it takes to repay your balance."

(2) Either of the following:

(A) A written statement in the form of and containing the information described in clause (i) or (ii), as applicable, as follows:

(i) A written three-line statement, as follows:

"A one thousand dollar ($1,000) balance will take 17 years and three months to pay off at a total cost of two thousand five hundred ninety dollars and thirty-five cents ($2,590.35).

A two thousand five hundred dollar ($2,500) balance will take 30 years and three months to pay off at a total cost of seven thousand seven hundred thirty-three dollars and forty-nine cents ($7,733.49).

A five thousand dollar ($5,000) balance will take 40 years and two months to pay off at a total cost of sixteen thousand three hundred five dollars and thirty-four cents ($16,305.34).

This information is based on an annual percentage rate of 17 percent and a minimum payment of 2 percent or ten dollars ($10), whichever is greater."

In the alternative, a credit card issuer may provide this information for the three specified amounts at the annual percentage rate and required minimum payment which are applicable to the cardholder's account. The statement provided shall be immediately preceded by the statement required by paragraph (1).

(ii) Instead of the information required by clause (i), retail credit card issuers shall provide a written three-line statement to read, as follows:

"A two hundred fifty dollar ($250) balance will take two years and eight months to pay off at a total cost of three hundred twenty-five dollars and twenty-four cents ($325.24).

A five hundred dollar ($500) balance will take four years and five months to pay off at a total cost of seven hundred nine dollars and ninety cents ($709.90).

A seven hundred fifty dollar ($750) balance will take five years and five months to pay off at a total cost of one thousand ninety-four dollars and forty-nine cents ($1,094.49).

This information is based on an annual percentage rate of 21 percent and a minimum payment of 5 percent or ten dollars ($10), whichever is greater."

In the alternative, a retail credit card issuer may provide this information for the three specified amounts at the annual percentage rate and required minimum payment which are applicable to the cardholder's account. The statement provided shall be immediately preceded by the statement required by paragraph (1). A retail credit card issuer is not required to provide this statement if the cardholder has a balance of less than five hundred dollars ($500).

(B) A written statement providing individualized information indicating an estimate of the number of years and months and the approximate total cost to pay off the entire balance due on an open-end credit card account if the cardholder were to pay only the minimum amount due on the open-ended account based upon the terms of the credit agreement. For purposes of this subparagraph only, if the account is subject to a variable rate, the creditor may make disclosures based on the rate for the entire balance as of the date of the disclosure and indicate that the rate may vary. In addition, the cardholder shall be provided with referrals or, in the alternative, with the "800" telephone number of the National Foundation for Credit Counseling through which the cardholder can be referred, to credit counseling services in, or closest to, the cardholder's county of residence. The credit counseling service shall be in good standing with the National Foundation for Credit Counseling or accredited by the Council on Accreditation for Children and Family Services. The creditor is required to provide, or continue to provide, the information required by this paragraph only if the cardholder has not paid more than the minimum payment for six consecutive months, after July 1, 2002.

(3)(A) A written statement in the following form: "For an estimate of the time it would take to repay your balance, making only minimum payments, and the total amount of those payments, call this toll-free telephone number: (Insert toll-free telephone number)." This statement shall be provided immediately following the statement required by subparagraph (A) of paragraph (2). A credit card issuer is not required to provide this statement if the disclosure required by subparagraph (B) of paragraph (2) has been provided.

(B) The toll-free telephone number shall be available between the hours of 8 a.m. and 9 p.m., Pacific standard time, seven days a week, and shall provide consumers with the opportunity to speak with a person, rather than a recording, from whom the information described in subparagraph (A) may be obtained.

(C) The Department of Financial Institutions shall establish a detailed table illustrating the approximate number of months that it would take and the approximate total cost to repay an outstanding balance if the consumer pays only the required minimum monthly payments and if no other additional charges or fees are incurred on the account, such as additional extension of credit, voluntary credit insurance, late fees, or dishonored check fees by assuming all of the following:

(i) A significant number of different annual percentage rates.

(ii) A significant number of different account balances, with the difference between sequential examples of balances being no greater than one hundred dollars ($100).

(iii) A significant number of different minimum payment amounts.

(iv) That only minimum monthly payments are made and no additional charges or fees are incurred on the account, such as additional extensions of credit, voluntary credit insurance, late fees, or dishonored check fees.

(D) A creditor that receives a request for information described in subparagraph (A) from a cardholder through the toll-free telephone number disclosed under subparagraph (A), or who is required to provide the information required by subparagraph (B) of paragraph (2), may satisfy its obligation to disclose an estimate of the time it would take and the approximate total cost to repay the cardholder's balance by disclosing only the information set forth in the table described in subparagraph (C). Including the full chart along with a billing statement does not satisfy the obligation under this section.

(b) For purposes of this section:

(1) "Credit card" has the same meaning as in paragraph (2) of subdivision (a) of Section 1748.12.

(2) "Open-end credit card account" means an account in which consumer credit is granted by a creditor under a plan in which the creditor reasonably contemplates repeated transactions, the creditor may impose a finance charge from time to time on an unpaid balance, and the amount of credit that may be extended to the consumer during the term of the plan is generally made available to the extent that any outstanding balance is repaid and up to any limit set by the creditor.

(3) "Retail credit card" means a credit card is issued by or on behalf of a retailer, or a private label credit card that is limited to customers of a specific retailer.

(c)(1) This section shall not apply in any billing cycle in which the account agreement requires a minimum payment of at least 10 percent of the outstanding balance.

(2) This section shall not apply in any billing cycle in which finance charges are not imposed. *(Added by Stats.2001, c. 711 (A.B.865), § 1. Amended by Stats.2002, c. 664 (A.B.3034), § 39.)*

Research References

4 Witkin, California Summary 10th Negotiable Instruments § 148, (S 148) Statements.

§ 1748.14.   Public policy; waiver of rights

Any waiver of the provisions of this title is contrary to public policy, and is void and unenforceable. *(Added by Stats.2002, c. 815 (A.B.2331), § 3.)*

Research References

4 Witkin, California Summary 10th Negotiable Instruments § 157, (S 157) Nature and Purpose of Legislation.

Title 1.3B

CHARGE CARD DISCLOSURES

§ 1748.20.   Short title

This title may be cited as the "Areias-Robbins Charge Card Full Disclosure Act of 1986." *(Added by Stats.1986, c. 1397, § 3.)*

Research References

4 Witkin, California Summary 10th Negotiable Instruments § 157, (S 157) Nature and Purpose of Legislation.
4 Witkin, California Summary 10th Negotiable Instruments § 161, Scope of Requirement.

§ 1748.21.   Definitions

For the purposes of this title:

(a) "Charge card" means any card, plate, or other credit device pursuant to which the charge card issuer extends credit to the charge cardholder, primarily for personal, family, or household purposes where (1) the credit extended does not subject the charge cardholder to a finance charge and (2) the charge cardholder cannot automatically access credit that is repayable in installments.

(b) "Charge cardholder" means the person to whom a charge card is issued.

(c) "Charge card issuer" means any person that issues a charge card or that person's agent with respect to the card. *(Added by Stats.1986, c. 1397, § 3.)*

Research References

Rutter, Cal. Practice Guide: Enforcing Judgments/Debts Ch. 3-A, A. Evaluating the Claim.
4 Witkin, California Summary 10th Negotiable Instruments § 161, Scope of Requirement.
4 Witkin, California Summary 10th Negotiable Instruments § 167, Consumer Credit and Charge Card Fees.

§ 1748.22.   Disclosures in application form; table of interest rate; additional terms; "Regulation Z"

(a) On and after October 1, 1987, issuers of charge cards shall clearly and conspicuously disclose in any charge card application form or preapproved written solicitation for a charge card mailed to a consumer who resides in this state to apply for a charge card, whether or not the charge card issuer is located in this state, other than an application form or solicitation included in a magazine, newspaper, or other publication distributed by someone other than the charge card issuer, the following information:

(1) Any fee or charge assessed for or which may be assessed for the issuance or renewal of the charge card, expressed as an annualized amount. The fee or charge required to be disclosed pursuant to this paragraph shall be denominated as an "annual fee."

(2) The charge card does not permit the charge cardholder to defer payment of charges incurred by the use of the charge card

upon receipt of a periodic statement of charges from the charge card issuer.

(3) Any fee that may be assessed for an extension of credit to a charge cardholder where the extension of credit is made by the charge card issuer, and is not a credit sale and where the charge cardholder receives the extension of credit in the form of cash or where the charge cardholder obtains the extension of credit through the use of a preprinted check, draft, or similar credit device provided by the charge card issuer to obtain an extension of credit. This fee shall be denominated as a "cash advance fee" in the disclosure required by this paragraph.

(b) A charge card issuer shall be conclusively presumed to have complied with the disclosure requirements of subdivision (a) if the table set out in subdivision (b) of Section 1748.11 is completed with the applicable terms offered by the charge card issuer in a clear and conspicuous manner and the completed table in subdivision (b) of Section 1748.11 is then provided to the person invited to apply for the charge card as a part of or in material which accompanies the charge card application or written advertisement which invites a person to apply for a charge card.

The charge card issuer shall include as part of table set out in subdivision (b) of Section 1748.11 the following sentences in the boxes or in a footnote outside of the boxes that relate to the interest rate disclosure: "This is a charge card which does not permit the charge cardholder to pay for purchases made using this charge card in installments. All charges made by a person to whom the charge card is issued are due and payable upon the receipt of a periodic statement of charges by the charge cardholder."

The inclusion or exclusion of an expiration date with table set out in subdivision (b) of Section 1748.11 or the use of footnotes in the boxes of the table to set out the information required to be disclosed by this section outside of the boxes of the table set out in subdivision (b) of Section 1748.11 shall not affect the conclusive presumption of compliance pursuant to this subdivision. If a charge card issuer does not offer or require one of the selected attributes of credit cards in the table set out in subdivision (b) of Section 1748.11 the charge card issuer shall employ the phrase in the appropriate box or in the appropriate footnote "Not offered" or "Not required" or a substantially similar phrase without losing the conclusive presumption of compliance with the requirements of subdivision (a). If one of the selected attributes of charge cards required to be disclosed pursuant to subdivision (a) is not applicable to the charge card issuer, the charge card issuer may employ in the appropriate box or in the appropriate footnote outside of the box in the table set out in subdivision (b) of Section 1748.11 the phrase "Not applicable" or a substantially similar phrase without losing the conclusive presumption of compliance with the requirements of subdivision (a).

(c) Nothing in this section shall be deemed or construed to prohibit a charge card issuer from disclosing additional terms, conditions, or information, whether or not relating to the disclosures required under this section by subdivision (a) or in connection with the disclosure provided in subdivision (b), in conjunction with the disclosures required by this section.

(d) If the charge card issuer offers to the charge cardholder any program or service under which the charge cardholder may elect to access open-end credit, the charge card issuer shall provide to the charge cardholder, before the charge cardholder has the right to access that credit, the initial disclosure statement required by Regulation Z, as defined in subdivision (c) of Section 1748.10.

(e) All charge card application forms distributed in this state on or after October 1, 1987, other than by mail, shall contain a statement in substantially the following form:

"If you wish to receive disclosure of the terms of this credit card, pursuant to the Areias Charge Card Full Disclosure Act of 1986, check here and return to the address on this application."

A box shall be printed in or next to this statement for placing such a checkmark.

However, this subdivision does not apply if the application contains the disclosures provided for in this title. *(Added by Stats.1986, c. 1397, § 3. Amended by Stats.2000, c. 375 (A.B. 1331), § 4.)*

Research References

Rutter, Cal. Practice Guide: Enforcing Judgments/Debts Ch. 3-A, A. Evaluating the Claim.

4 Witkin, California Summary 10th Negotiable Instruments § 161, Scope of Requirement.

4 Witkin, California Summary 10th Negotiable Instruments § 162, Matters to be Disclosed.

4 Witkin, California Summary 10th Negotiable Instruments § 163, Methods of Compliance.

§ 1748.23. Public policy; waiver of rights

Any waiver of the provisions of this title is contrary to public policy, and is void and unenforceable. *(Added by Stats.2002, c. 815 (A.B.2331), § 4.)*

Research References

4 Witkin, California Summary 10th Negotiable Instruments § 157, (S 157) Nature and Purpose of Legislation.

Title 1.3C

DEBIT CARDS

Section
1748.30. Definitions.
1748.31. Liability for unauthorized use.
1748.32. Public policy; waiver of rights.

§ 1748.30. Definitions

For purposes of this title, the following definitions shall apply:

(a) "Accepted debit card" means any debit card which the debit cardholder has requested and received or has signed, or has used, or has authorized another person to use, for the purpose of obtaining money, property, labor, or services. Any debit card issued in renewal of, or in substitution for, an accepted debit card becomes an accepted debit card when received by the debit cardholder, whether the debit card is issued by the same or by a successor card issuer.

(b) "Account" means a demand deposit (checking), savings, or other consumer asset account, other than an occasional or incidental credit balance in a credit plan, established primarily for personal, family, or household purposes.

(c) "Adequate notice" has the same meaning as found in subdivision (k) of Section 1747.02.

(d) "Debit card" means an accepted debit card or other means of access to a debit cardholder's account that may be used to initiate electronic funds transfers and may be used without unique identifying information such as a personal identification number to initiate access to the debit cardholder's account.

(e) "Debit card issuer" means any person who issues a debit card or the agent of that person for that purpose.

(f) "Debit cardholder" means a natural person to whom a debit card is issued.

(g) "Unauthorized use" means the use of a debit card by a person, other than the debit cardholder, to initiate an electronic fund transfer from the debit cardholder's account without actual authority to initiate the transfer and from which the debit cardholder receives no benefit. The term does not include an electronic fund transfer initiated in any of the following manners:

(1) By a person who was furnished the debit card to the debit cardholder's account by the debit cardholder, unless the debit cardholder has notified the debit card issuer that transfers by that person are no longer authorized.

(2) With fraudulent intent by the debit cardholder or any person acting in concert with the debit cardholder.

(3) By the debit card issuer or its employee. *(Added by Stats.1999, c. 244 (S.B.313), § 1.)*

Research References

Rutter, Cal. Practice Guide: Enforcing Judgments/Debts Ch. 3-A, A. Evaluating the Claim.

§ 1748.31. Liability for unauthorized use

(a) A debit cardholder shall be liable for an unauthorized use of a debit card only if all of the following conditions are met:

(1) The card is an accepted debit card.

(2) Except as provided in subdivision (b), the liability is not in excess of fifty dollars ($50).

(3) The debit card issuer has given adequate notice to the debit cardholder of the potential liability.

(4) The debit card issuer has provided the debit cardholder with a description of the means by which the debit card issuer may be notified of loss or theft of the card.

(5) The unauthorized use occurs before the debit card issuer has been notified by the debit cardholder that an unauthorized use of the debit card has occurred or may occur as a result of loss, theft, or otherwise.

(6) The debit card issuer has provided a means to identify the debit cardholder to whom the debit card was issued.

(b) Notwithstanding subdivision (a), if the debit cardholder fails to report an unauthorized use that appears on a periodic statement within 60 days of the debit card issuer's transmittal of the statement, and if the issuer establishes that an unauthorized use would not have occurred had the debit cardholder notified the issuer within the 60–day period, the debit cardholder shall be liable for the amount of each unauthorized transfer that occurs after the close of the 60 days and before notice to the issuer. If the debit cardholder's delay in notifying the debit card issuer was due to extenuating circumstances beyond the debit cardholder's reasonable control, the time specified above shall be extended by a reasonable period. For the purposes of this subdivision, examples of extenuating circumstances include, but are not limited to, extended travel, the death or serious illness of the debit cardholder or a member of the debit cardholder's family, hospitalization, permanent mental impairment, or serious physical impairment, unless the circumstance did not reasonably contribute to the cardholder's delay in notifying the debit card issuer within the 60–day period.

(c) A debit cardholder shall have no liability for erroneous or fraudulent transfers initiated by a debit card issuer, its agent, or employee. *(Added by Stats.1999, c. 244 (S.B.313), § 1.)*

Research References

Rutter, Cal. Practice Guide: Enforcing Judgments/Debts Ch. 3-A, A. Evaluating the Claim.

4 Witkin, California Summary 10th Negotiable Instruments § 154, Liability for Unauthorized Use.

§ 1748.32. Public policy; waiver of rights

Any waiver of the provisions of this title is contrary to public policy, and is void and unenforceable. *(Added by Stats.2002, c. 815 (A.B.2331), § 5.)*

Research References

4 Witkin, California Summary 10th Negotiable Instruments § 154, Liability for Unauthorized Use.

Title 1.4

LAYAWAY PRACTICES

Section
1749.   Written statement of terms and conditions of agreement; furnishing by retail seller; contents.
1749.1.   Definitions.
1749.2.   Waiver of provisions of title; unenforceability.
1749.3.   Cumulative remedies.
1749.4.   Nonapplicability to credit sales or other legal obligations.

§ 1749. Written statement of terms and conditions of agreement; furnishing by retail seller; contents

Any retail seller which permits consumers to lay away consumer goods shall provide to any consumer entering into a layaway agreement with the seller a written statement of the terms and conditions of the agreement, including the following information:

(1) The amount of the deposit received.

(2) The length of time the goods will be held on layaway which may be expressed as a period of time or as a date when final payment for the goods is due.

(3) A specific description of the goods.

(4) The total purchase price of the goods including a separate listing of any handling or processing charges.

(5) Any other terms and conditions of the layaway agreement.

(6) That the seller will refund any layaway deposit and subsequent payments, if any, when, before the end of the stated layaway period, the goods have for any reason become no longer available in the same condition as at the time of the sale to the consumer. *(Added by Stats.1975, c. 825, p. 1879, § 1.)*

§ 1749.1. Definitions

For purposes of this title, the following terms have the following meanings:

(a) "Consumer good" means any article which is used or bought for use primarily for personal, family, or household purposes.

(b) "Retail seller" means an individual, firm, partnership, corporation, joint stock company, association, organization, or other legal entity which engages in the business of selling consumer goods to retail buyers.

(c) "Layaway" means an agreement by a retail seller with a consumer to retain specified consumer goods for sale to the consumer at a specified price, in earnest of which sale the consumer has deposited with the retail seller an agreed upon sum of money, and any other terms and conditions not contrary to law which are mutually agreed upon. *(Added by Stats.1975, c. 825, p. 1879, § 1.)*

Civil

Research References

Miller and Starr California Real Estate § 21:14, Interest in Excess of Maximum Rate.

§ 1749.2. Waiver of provisions of title; unenforceability

Any waiver by the buyer of consumer goods of the provisions of this title, except as expressly provided in this title, shall be deemed contrary to public policy and shall be unenforceable and void. *(Added by Stats.1975, c. 825, p. 1879, § 1.)*

§ 1749.3. Cumulative remedies

The remedies provided by this title are cumulative and shall not be construed as restricting any remedy that is otherwise available. *(Added by Stats.1975, c. 825, p. 1880, § 1.)*

§ 1749.4. Nonapplicability to credit sales or other legal obligations

Nothing in this title shall be construed to limit or reduce any legal obligations imposed under Title 2 (commencing with Section 1801) of Part 4 of Division 3 or under any other applicable law. *(Added by Stats.1975, c. 825, p. 1880, § 1.)*

Title 1.4A

GIFT CERTIFICATES

Section

§ 1749.45. Definitions; exemption for prepaid calling cards

(a) As used in this title, "gift certificate" includes gift cards, but does not include any gift card usable with multiple sellers of goods or services, provided the expiration date, if any, is printed on the card. This exemption does not apply to a gift card usable only with affiliated sellers of goods or services.

(b) Nothing in this title prohibits those fees or practices expressly permitted by Section 17538.9 of the Business and Professions Code with respect to a prepaid calling card, as defined in that section, that is issued solely to provide an access number and authorization code for prepaid calling services. *(Added by Stats.2003, c. 116 (A.B.1092), § 1.)*

Research References

13 Witkin, California Summary 10th Personal Property § 40, Escheat of Unclaimed Personal Property.
4 Witkin, California Summary 10th Sales § 360, (S 360) Gift Certificates.

§ 1749.5. Prohibited transactions; redemption or replacement; expiration dates; application of section; full refund

(a) It is unlawful for any person or entity to sell a gift certificate to a purchaser that contains any of the following:

(1) An expiration date.

(2) A service fee, including, but not limited to, a service fee for dormancy, except as provided in subdivision (e).

(b)(1) Any gift certificate sold after January 1, 1997, is redeemable in cash for its cash value, or subject to replacement with a new gift certificate at no cost to the purchaser or holder.

(2) Notwithstanding paragraph (1), any gift certificate with a cash value of less than ten dollars ($10) is redeemable in cash for its cash value.

(c) A gift certificate sold without an expiration date is valid until redeemed or replaced.

(d) This section does not apply to any of the following gift certificates issued on or after January 1, 1998, provided the expiration date appears in capital letters in at least 10–point font on the front of the gift certificate:

(1) Gift certificates that are distributed by the issuer to a consumer pursuant to an awards, loyalty, or promotional program without any money or other thing of value being given in exchange for the gift certificate by the consumer.

(2) Gift certificates that are donated or sold below face value at a volume discount to employers or to nonprofit and charitable organizations for fundraising purposes if the expiration date on those gift certificates is not more than 30 days after the date of sale.

(3) Gift certificates that are issued for perishable food products.

(e) Paragraph (2) of subdivision (a) does not apply to a dormancy fee on a gift card that meets all of the following criteria:

(1) The remaining value of the gift card is five dollars ($5) or less each time the fee is assessed.

(2) The fee does not exceed one dollar ($1) per month.

(3) There has been no activity on the gift card for 24 consecutive months, including, but not limited to, purchases, the adding of value, or balance inquiries.

(4) The holder may reload or add value to the gift card.

(5) A statement is printed on the gift card in at least 10–point font stating the amount of the fee, how often the fee will occur, that the fee is triggered by inactivity of the gift card, and at what point the fee will be charged. The statement may appear on the front or back of the gift card, but shall appear in a location where it is visible to any purchaser prior to the purchase thereof.

(f) An issuer of gift certificates may accept funds from one or more contributors toward the purchase of a gift certificate intended to be a gift for a recipient, provided that each contributor is provided with a full refund of the amount that he or she paid toward the purchase of the gift certificate upon the occurrence of all of the following:

(1) The funds are contributed for the purpose of being redeemed by the recipient by purchasing a gift certificate.

(2) The time in which the recipient may redeem the funds by purchasing a gift certificate is clearly disclosed in writing to the contributors and the recipient.

(3) The recipient does not redeem the funds within the time described in paragraph (2).

(g) The changes made to this section by the act adding this subdivision shall apply only to gift certificates issued on or after January 1, 2004.

(h) For purposes of this section, "cash" includes, but is not limited to, currency or check. If accepted by both parties, an electronic funds transfer or an application of the balance to a subscriber's wireless telecommunications account is permissible. *(Added by Stats.1996, c. 933 (A.B.2466), § 1. Amended by Stats.1997, c. 472 (A.B.1054), § 1; Stats.2003, c. 116 (A.B.1092), § 2; Stats.2004, c. 319 (A.B.656), § 1; Stats.2007, c. 640 (S.B.250), § 1.)*

Research References

4 Witkin, California Summary 10th Sales § 360, (S 360) Gift Certificates.

§ 1749.51. Public policy; waiver of rights

Any waiver of the provisions of this title is contrary to public policy, and is void and unenforceable. *(Added by Stats.2002, c. 815 (A.B.2331), § 6.)*

Research References

4 Witkin, California Summary 10th Sales § 360, (S 360) Gift Certificates.

§ 1749.6. Gift certificates; value held in trust; bankruptcy of issuer; limitations of section

(a) A gift certificate constitutes value held in trust by the issuer of the gift certificate on behalf of the beneficiary of the gift certificate. The value represented by the gift certificate belongs to the beneficiary, or to the legal representative of the beneficiary to the extent provided by law, and not to the issuer.

(b) An issuer of a gift certificate who is in bankruptcy shall continue to honor a gift certificate issued prior to the date of the bankruptcy filing on the grounds that the value of the gift certificate constitutes trust property of the beneficiary.

(c)(1) This section does not alter the terms of a gift certificate. The terms of a gift certificate may not make its redemption or other use invalid in the event of a bankruptcy.

(2) This section does not require, unless otherwise required by law, the issuer of a gift certificate to:

(A) Redeem a gift certificate for cash.

(B) Replace a gift certificate that has been lost or stolen.

(C) Maintain a separate account for the funds used to purchase the gift certificate.

(d)(1) This section does not create an interest in favor of the beneficiary of the gift certificate in any specific property of the issuer.

(2) This section does not create a fiduciary or quasi-fiduciary relationship between the beneficiary of the gift certificates and the issuer, unless otherwise provided by law.

(3) The issuer of a gift certificate has no obligation to pay interest on the value of the gift certificate held in trust under this section, unless otherwise provided by law. *(Added by Stats.2002, c. 997 (A.B.2473), § 1.)*

Research References

4 Witkin, California Summary 10th Sales § 360, (S 360) Gift Certificates.

Title 1.4B

SUPERMARKET CLUB CARDS

§ 1749.60. Short title

This title shall be known and may be cited as the "Supermarket Club Card Disclosure Act of 1999." *(Added by Stats.1999, c. 586 (S.B.926), § 1, operative July 1, 2000.)*

Research References

4 Witkin, California Summary 10th Sales § 387, (S 387) Supermarket Club Cards.
13 Witkin, California Summary 10th Equity § 110, Unfair Credit and Debt Collection Practices.

§ 1749.61. Definitions

For purposes of this title:

(a) "Cardholder" means any consumer to whom a supermarket club card is issued, provided that in cases where more than one supermarket club card has been issued for the same account, all persons holding those supermarket club cards may be treated as a single cardholder.

(b) "Supermarket" means any retailer that sells food items.

(c) "Supermarket club card" means any card, plate, coupon book, or other single device existing for the purpose of being used from time to time upon presentation for price discounts on retail products offered by the club card issuer. "Supermarket club card" does not include any credit card that is subject to Section 1748.12.

(d) "Club card issuer" means a supermarket that provides supermarket club cards to consumers, and includes a supermarket's contract information services provider.

(e) "Marketing information" means the categorization of cardholders compiled by a club card issuer, based on a cardholder's shopping patterns, spending history, or behavioral characteristics derived from account activity which is provided to any person or entity for consideration. "Marketing information" does not include aggregate data which does not identify a cardholder based on the cardholder's shopping patterns, spending history, or behavioral characteristics derived from account activity. *(Added by Stats.1999, c. 586 (S.B.926), § 1, operative July 1, 2000.)*

§ 1749.63. Violation of title; unfair competition

A violation of this title constitutes "unfair competition" as defined in Section 17200 of the Business and Professions Code and is punishable as prescribed in Chapter 5 (commencing with Section 17200) of Part 2 of Division 7 of the Business and Professions Code. *(Added by Stats.1999, c. 586 (S.B.926), § 1, operative July 1, 2000.)*

Research References

4 Witkin, California Summary 10th Sales § 387, (S 387) Supermarket Club Cards.
13 Witkin, California Summary 10th Equity § 110, Unfair Credit and Debt Collection Practices.

§ 1749.64. Club card issuer; prohibited from requesting driver's license number or social security number

Notwithstanding any other provision of law, no club card issuer shall request in a supermarket club card application, or require as a condition of obtaining a supermarket club card, that an applicant provide a driver's license number or a social security account number. This section shall not be construed to prohibit a club card issuer from requesting a driver's license number or a social security account number for a supermarket club card that can also be used as identification for check cashing purposes or to debit the checking or savings account of the cardholder. However, no club card issuer shall, as a condition of obtaining a supermarket club card, require a cardholder to obtain a supermarket club card that can also be used as identification for check cashing purposes or to debit the checking or savings account of the cardholder. *(Added by Stats.1999, c. 586 (S.B.926), § 1, operative July 1, 2000.)*

Research References

4 Witkin, California Summary 10th Sales § 387, (S 387) Supermarket
    Club Cards.

§ 1749.65. Club card issuer; prohibited from selling or sharing cardholders' personal identification information

(a) Notwithstanding any other provision of law, no club card issuer may sell or share a cardholder's name, address, telephone number, or other personal identification information.

(b) Nothing in this section is intended to prevent a club card issuer from providing names and addresses of cardholders to a third party for purposes of mailing supermarket club card information to cardholders on behalf of the club card issuer. However, that third party shall not use the information for any other purpose.

(c) Notwithstanding subdivision (a), this section does not prohibit a club card issuer from sharing marketing information that includes cardholder names and addresses if the club card issuer complies with all of the following:

(1) The club card issuer charges an annual fee for its supermarket club card.

(2) The club card issuer requires cardholders to renew supermarket club cards annually and to pay an annual renewal fee.

(3) The club card issuer allows only cardholders, and not members of the public, to make purchases in the supermarket.

(4) The club card issuer provides a privacy statement to the cardholder in the supermarket club card application and in the club card issuer's annual renewal material notifying cardholders that outside companies will be receiving marketing information including names and addresses of cardholders, and the cardholder has agreed to allow the club card issuer to share this information.

(5) Prior to selling or transferring names and addresses of cardholders to an outside company, the club card issuer has obtained a written confidentiality agreement from the outside company that the outside company will not sell or share the information with any other entity. *(Added by Stats.1999, c. 586 (S.B.926), § 1, operative July 1, 2000.)*

Research References

4 Witkin, California Summary 10th Sales § 387, (S 387) Supermarket
    Club Cards.

§ 1749.66. Public policy; waiver of rights

Any waiver of the provisions of this title is contrary to public policy, and is void and unenforceable. *(Added by Stats.2002, c. 815 (A.B.2331), § 7.)*

Research References

4 Witkin, California Summary 10th Sales § 387, (S 387) Supermarket
    Club Cards.

Title 1.5

CONSUMERS LEGAL REMEDIES ACT

CHAPTER 1. GENERAL PROVISIONS

§ 1750. Citation

This title may be cited as the Consumers Legal Remedies Act. *(Added by Stats.1970, c. 1550, p. 3157, § 1.)*

Validity

This section was held preempted by the federal Food, Drug, and Cosmetic Act in the decision of Perez v. Nidek Co. Ltd., S.D.Cal.2009, 657 F.Supp.2d 1156, affirmed 711 F.3d 1109.

This section was held preempted by the Federal Communications Act of 1934 with respect to rates and market entry of commercial mobile service providers in the decision of In re Apple iPhone 3G Products Liability Litigation, N.D.Cal.2010, 728 F.Supp.2d 1065, leave to file for reconsideration denied 2010 WL 3119789.

Research References

Rutter, Cal. Practice Guide: A.D.R. Ch. 5-F, F. Arbitration by and Against Nonsignatories.
Rutter, Cal. Practice Guide: A.D.R. Ch. 5-I, I. Arbitrator's Award.
Rutter, Cal. Practice Guide: A.D.R. Ch. 8-E, E. Special Drafting Considerations Re Arbitration Agreements.
Rutter, Cal. Practice Guide: A.D.R. Gen. Matls., Highlights.
Rutter, Cal. Practice Guide: Civ. Pro. Before Trial Ch. 1-C, C. Prelawsuit Notices, Claims and Demands.
Rutter, Cal. Practice Guide: Civ. Pro. Before Trial Ch. 2-A, A. Standing to Sue-"Real Party in Interest" Requirement.
Rutter, Cal. Practice Guide: Civ. Pro. Before Trial Ch. 3-B, B. Jurisdiction Over Parties-Personal Jurisdiction.
Rutter, Cal. Practice Guide: Civ. Pro. Before Trial Ch. 3-D, D. Venue.
Rutter, Cal. Practice Guide: Civ. Pro. Before Trial Ch. 10-A, A. Introduction.
Rutter, Cal. Practice Guide: Civ. Pro. Before Trial Ch. 11-A, A. Voluntary Dismissals.
Rutter, Cal. Practice Guide: Civ. Pro. Before Trial Ch. 14-A, A. General Considerations.
Rutter, Cal. Practice Guide: Civ. Pro. Before Trial Ch. 14-B, B. Class Action Requirements-In General.
Rutter, Cal. Practice Guide: Civ. Pro. Before Trial Gen. Matls., Highlights.
Rutter, Cal. Practice Guide: Civil Trials & Evidence Ch. 17-E, E. Attorney Fees as Costs.
Rutter, Cal. Practice Guide: Civil Trials & Evidence Ch. 8E-G, G. Parol Evidence Rule.
Rutter, Cal. Practice Guide: Enforcing Judgments/Debts Ch. 3-A, A. Evaluating the Claim.
Rutter, Cal. Practice Guide: Fed.Civ.Pro. Before Trial Ch. 16-G, G. Voluntary Dismissals.
Rutter, Cal. Practice Guide: Insurance Litigation Ch. 11-K, K. Statutory Liability.
Rutter, Cal. Practice Guide: Insurance Litigation Ch. 15-C, C. Arbitration/Appraisal/Mediation.
Rutter, Cal. Practice Guide: Insurance Litigation Ch. 6F-D, D. ERISA Preemption and Remedies.
Rutter, Cal. Practice Guide: Insurance Litigation Ch. 6H-F, F. Damages Recoverable Against Title Insurer.
Rutter, Cal. Practice Guide: Insurance Litigation Ch. 11-K, Outline K.
Miller and Starr California Real Estate § 27:54, Home Solicitation Contracts.
Miller and Starr California Real Estate § 34:82, Amount of Fees; Allocation.
Miller and Starr California Real Estate § 35:33, Classwide Arbitrations.

Miller and Starr California Real Estate § 35:39, Issues Which Cannot be the Subject of Arbitration.

Miller and Starr California Real Estate § 35:53, Unconscionability.

Miller and Starr California Real Estate § 35:83, Authority of the Arbitrators; Issues and Remedies.

14 NO. 1 Miller & Starr, California Real Estate Newsalert 5, Defective Construction.

3 Witkin Cal. Proc. 5th Actions § 888, (S 888) Distinction: Action Under Consumers Legal Remedies Act.

2 Witkin Cal. Proc. 5th Jurisdiction § 356, Illustrations.

4 Witkin Cal. Proc. 5th Pleading § 268, (S 268) California Law and Uniform Act.

4 Witkin Cal. Proc. 5th Pleading § 278, (S 278) in General.

4 Witkin Cal. Proc. 5th Pleading § 302, Statutory Authorization.

4 Witkin Cal. Proc. 5th Pleading § 309, (S 309) Necessity of Notice.

4 Witkin Cal. Proc. 5th Pleading § 311, (S 311) Factors Considered by Court.

6 Witkin Cal. Proc. 5th Proceedings Without Trial § 292, Plaintiff Not Sole Party in Interest.

6 Witkin Cal. Proc. 5th Proceedings Without Trial § 500, Public Policy Considerations.

6 Witkin Cal. Proc. 5th Proceedings Without Trial § 577, (S 577) Review of Remedies Granted by Arbitrator.

7 Witkin Cal. Proc. 5th Trial § 42, (S 42) in General.

2 Witkin, California Summary 10th Insurance § 1, (S 1) in General.

2 Witkin, California Summary 10th Insurance § 6, (S 6) Governing Law.

4 Witkin, California Summary 10th Sales § 296, (S 296) Consumers Legal Remedies Act.

4 Witkin, California Summary 10th Sales § 297, Nature and Scope of Statute.

4 Witkin, California Summary 10th Sales § 381, (S 381) Retail Refund Policies.

4 Witkin, California Summary 10th Sales § 396A, (S 396A) (New)-Used Vehicle Certification Programs.

6 Witkin, California Summary 10th Torts § 1568A, (New)-Disgorgement of Profits.

§ 1751. Waiver; public policy

Any waiver by a consumer of the provisions of this title is contrary to public policy and shall be unenforceable and void. *(Added by Stats.1970, c. 1550, p. 3157, § 1.)*

Research References

Rutter, Cal. Practice Guide: Civ. Pro. Before Trial Ch. 14-A, A. General Considerations.

Rutter, Cal. Practice Guide: Civ. Pro. Before Trial Gen. Matls., Highlights.

1 Witkin Cal. Summ. 10th Contracts § 684, Miscellaneous Substantive Rights.

4 Witkin, California Summary 10th Sales § 296, (S 296) Consumers Legal Remedies Act.

§ 1752. Cumulative remedies; class actions

The provisions of this title are not exclusive. The remedies provided herein for violation of any section of this title or for conduct proscribed by any section of this title shall be in addition to any other procedures or remedies for any violation or conduct provided for in any other law.

Nothing in this title shall limit any other statutory or any common law rights of the Attorney General or any other person to bring class actions. Class actions by consumers brought under the specific provisions of Chapter 3 (commencing with Section 1770) of this title shall be governed exclusively by the provisions of Chapter 4 (commencing with Section 1780); however, this shall not be construed so as to deprive a consumer of any statutory or common law right to bring a class action without resort to this title. If any act or practice proscribed under this title also constitutes a cause of action in common law or a violation of another statute, the consumer may assert such common law or statutory cause of action under the procedures and with the remedies provided for in such law. *(Added by Stats.1970, c. 1550, p. 3157, § 1. Amended by Stats.1975, c. 615, p. 1344, § 1.)*

Research References

4 Witkin Cal. Proc. 5th Pleading § 302, Statutory Authorization.

4 Witkin Cal. Proc. 5th Pleading § 304, Exclusive Criteria of Consumers Act.

§ 1753. Partial invalidity

If any provision of this title or the application thereof to any person or circumstance is held to be unconstitutional, the remainder of the title and the application of such provision to other persons or circumstances shall not be affected thereby. *(Added by Stats.1970, c. 1550, p. 3157, § 1.)*

§ 1754. Exemptions; structures

The provisions of this title shall not apply to any transaction which provides for the construction, sale, or construction and sale of an entire residence or all or part of a structure designed for commercial or industrial occupancy, with or without a parcel of real property or an interest therein, or for the sale of a lot or parcel of real property, including any site preparation incidental to such sale. *(Added by Stats.1970, c. 1550, p. 3157, § 1.)*

Research References

4 Witkin Cal. Proc. 5th Pleading § 302, Statutory Authorization.

§ 1755. Exemptions; advertising media

Nothing in this title shall apply to the owners or employees of any advertising medium, including, but not limited to, newspapers, magazines, broadcast stations, billboards and transit ads, by whom any advertisement in violation of this title is published or disseminated, unless it is established that such owners or employees had knowledge of the deceptive methods, acts or practices declared to be unlawful by Section 1770. *(Added by Stats.1970, c. 1550, p. 3157, § 1.)*

Research References

4 Witkin Cal. Proc. 5th Pleading § 302, Statutory Authorization.

§ 1756. Time of application of title

The substantive and procedural provisions of this title shall only apply to actions filed on or after January 1, 1971. *(Added by Stats.1970, c. 1550, p. 3158, § 1.)*

CHAPTER 2. CONSTRUCTION AND DEFINITIONS

Section
1760. Construction and application.
1761. Definitions.

§ 1760. Construction and application

This title shall be liberally construed and applied to promote its underlying purposes, which are to protect consumers against unfair and deceptive business practices and to provide efficient and economical procedures to secure such protection. *(Added by Stats.1970, c. 1550, p. 3158, § 1.)*

Research References

4 Witkin Cal. Proc. 5th Pleading § 304, Exclusive Criteria of Consumers Act.

§ 1761. Definitions

As used in this title:

(a) "Goods" means tangible chattels bought or leased for use primarily for personal, family, or household purposes, including certificates or coupons exchangeable for these goods, and including goods that, at the time of the sale or subsequently, are to be so affixed to real property as to become a part of real property, whether or not they are severable from the real property.

(b) "Services" means work, labor, and services for other than a commercial or business use, including services furnished in connection with the sale or repair of goods.

(c) "Person" means an individual, partnership, corporation, limited liability company, association, or other group, however organized.

(d) "Consumer" means an individual who seeks or acquires, by purchase or lease, any goods or services for personal, family, or household purposes.

(e) "Transaction" means an agreement between a consumer and another person, whether or not the agreement is a contract enforceable by action, and includes the making of, and the performance pursuant to, that agreement.

(f) "Senior citizen" means a person who is 65 years of age or older.

(g) "Disabled person" means a person who has a physical or mental impairment that substantially limits one or more major life activities.

(1) As used in this subdivision, "physical or mental impairment" means any of the following:

(A) A physiological disorder or condition, cosmetic disfigurement, or anatomical loss substantially affecting one or more of the following body systems: neurological; musculoskeletal; special sense organs; respiratory, including speech organs; cardiovascular; reproductive; digestive; genitourinary; hemic and lymphatic; skin; or endocrine.

(B) A mental or psychological disorder, including intellectual disability, organic brain syndrome, emotional or mental illness, and specific learning disabilities. "Physical or mental impairment" includes, but is not limited to, diseases and conditions that include orthopedic, visual, speech, and hearing impairment, cerebral palsy, epilepsy, muscular dystrophy, multiple sclerosis, cancer, heart disease, diabetes, intellectual disability, and emotional illness.

(2) "Major life activities" means functions that include caring for one's self, performing manual tasks, walking, seeing, hearing, speaking, breathing, learning, and working.

(h) "Home solicitation" means a transaction made at the consumer's primary residence, except those transactions initiated by the consumer. A consumer response to an advertisement is not a home solicitation. (Added by Stats.1970, c. 1550, p. 3157, § 1. Amended by Stats.1988, c. 823, § 2; Stats.1994, c. 1010 (S.B.2053), § 34; Stats.1995, c. 255 (S.B.320), § 1; Stats.2006, c. 538 (S.B.1852), § 44; Stats.2012, c. 448 (A.B.2370), § 4; Stats. 2012, c. 457 (S.B.1381), § 4.)

Research References

Rutter, Cal. Practice Guide: A.D.R. Ch. 7-B, B. Arbitrators.
Rutter, Cal. Practice Guide: Insurance Litigation Ch. 13-C, C. Punitive Damages.
Miller and Starr California Real Estate § 27:54, Home Solicitation Contracts.
4 Witkin, California Summary 10th Sales § 43, (S 43) General Obligations.
4 Witkin, California Summary 10th Sales § 296, (S 296) Consumers Legal Remedies Act.

CHAPTER 3. DECEPTIVE PRACTICES

Section
1770. List of proscribed practices.

§ 1770. List of proscribed practices

(a) The following unfair methods of competition and unfair or deceptive acts or practices undertaken by any person in a transaction intended to result or which results in the sale or lease of goods or services to any consumer are unlawful:

(1) Passing off goods or services as those of another.

(2) Misrepresenting the source, sponsorship, approval, or certification of goods or services.

(3) Misrepresenting the affiliation, connection, or association with, or certification by, another.

(4) Using deceptive representations or designations of geographic origin in connection with goods or services.

(5) Representing that goods or services have sponsorship, approval, characteristics, ingredients, uses, benefits, or quantities which they do not have or that a person has a sponsorship, approval, status, affiliation, or connection which he or she does not have.

(6) Representing that goods are original or new if they have deteriorated unreasonably or are altered, reconditioned, reclaimed, used, or secondhand.

(7) Representing that goods or services are of a particular standard, quality, or grade, or that goods are of a particular style or model, if they are of another.

(8) Disparaging the goods, services, or business of another by false or misleading representation of fact.

(9) Advertising goods or services with intent not to sell them as advertised.

(10) Advertising goods or services with intent not to supply reasonably expectable demand, unless the advertisement discloses a limitation of quantity.

(11) Advertising furniture without clearly indicating that it is unassembled if that is the case.

(12) Advertising the price of unassembled furniture without clearly indicating the assembled price of that furniture if the same furniture is available assembled from the seller.

(13) Making false or misleading statements of fact concerning reasons for, existence of, or amounts of price reductions.

(14) Representing that a transaction confers or involves rights, remedies, or obligations which it does not have or involve, or which are prohibited by law.

(15) Representing that a part, replacement, or repair service is needed when it is not.

(16) Representing that the subject of a transaction has been supplied in accordance with a previous representation when it has not.

(17) Representing that the consumer will receive a rebate, discount, or other economic benefit, if the earning of the benefit is contingent on an event to occur subsequent to the consummation of the transaction.

(18) Misrepresenting the authority of a salesperson, representative, or agent to negotiate the final terms of a transaction with a consumer.

(19) Inserting an unconscionable provision in the contract.

(20) Advertising that a product is being offered at a specific price plus a specific percentage of that price unless (A) the total price is set forth in the advertisement, which may include, but is not limited to, shelf tags, displays, and media advertising, in a size larger than any other price in that advertisement, and (B) the specific price plus a specific percentage of that price represents a markup from the seller's costs or from the wholesale price of the product. This subdivision shall not apply to in-store advertising by businesses which are open only to members or

cooperative organizations organized pursuant to Division 3 (commencing with Section 12000) of Title 1 of the Corporations Code where more than 50 percent of purchases are made at the specific price set forth in the advertisement.

(21) Selling or leasing goods in violation of Chapter 4 (commencing with Section 1797.8) of Title 1.7.

(22)(A) Disseminating an unsolicited prerecorded message by telephone without an unrecorded, natural voice first informing the person answering the telephone of the name of the caller or the organization being represented, and either the address or the telephone number of the caller, and without obtaining the consent of that person to listen to the prerecorded message.

(B) This subdivision does not apply to a message disseminated to a business associate, customer, or other person having an established relationship with the person or organization making the call, to a call for the purpose of collecting an existing obligation, or to any call generated at the request of the recipient.

(23) The home solicitation, as defined in subdivision (h) of Section 1761, of a consumer who is a senior citizen where a loan is made encumbering the primary residence of that consumer for the purposes of paying for home improvements and where the transaction is part of a pattern or practice in violation of either subsection (h) or (i) of Section 1639 of Title 15 of the United States Code or paragraph (e) of Section 226.32 of Title 12 of the Code of Federal Regulations.

A third party shall not be liable under this subdivision unless (A) there was an agency relationship between the party who engaged in home solicitation and the third party or (B) the third party had actual knowledge of, or participated in, the unfair or deceptive transaction. A third party who is a holder in due course under a home solicitation transaction shall not be liable under this subdivision.

(24)(A) Charging or receiving an unreasonable fee to prepare, aid, or advise any prospective applicant, applicant, or recipient in the procurement, maintenance, or securing of public social services.

(B) For purposes of this paragraph, the following definitions shall apply:

(i) "Public social services" means those activities and functions of state and local government administered or supervised by the State Department of Health Care Services, the State Department of Public Health, or the State Department of Social Services, and involved in providing aid or services, or both, including health care services, and medical assistance, to those persons who, because of their economic circumstances or social condition, are in need of that aid or those services and may benefit from them.

(ii) "Public social services" also includes activities and functions administered or supervised by the United States Department of Veterans Affairs or the California Department of Veterans Affairs involved in providing aid or services, or both, to veterans, including pension benefits.

(iii) "Unreasonable fee" means a fee that is exorbitant and disproportionate to the services performed. Factors to be considered, when appropriate, in determining the reasonableness of a fee, are based on the circumstances existing at the time of the service and shall include, but not be limited to, all of the following:

(I) The time and effort required.

(II) The novelty and difficulty of the services.

(III) The skill required to perform the services.

(IV) The nature and length of the professional relationship.

(V) The experience, reputation, and ability of the person providing the services.

(C) This paragraph shall not apply to attorneys licensed to practice law in California, who are subject to the California Rules of Professional Conduct and to the mandatory fee arbitration provisions of Article 13 (commencing with Section 6200) of Chapter 4 of Division 3 of the Business and Professions Code, when the fees charged or received are for providing representation in administrative agency appeal proceedings or court proceedings for purposes of procuring, maintaining, or securing public social services on behalf of a person or group of persons.

(25)(A) Advertising or promoting any event, presentation, seminar, workshop, or other public gathering regarding veterans' benefits or entitlements that does not include the following statement in the same type size and font as the term "veteran" or any variation of that term:

(i) "I am not authorized to file an initial application for Veterans' Aid and Attendance benefits on your behalf, or to represent you before the Board of Veterans' Appeals within the United States Department of Veterans Affairs in any proceeding on any matter, including an application for such benefits. It would be illegal for me to accept a fee for preparing that application on your behalf." The requirements of this clause do not apply to a person licensed to act as an agent or attorney in proceedings before the Agency of Original Jurisdiction and the Board of Veterans' Appeals within the United States Department of Veterans Affairs when that person is offering those services at the advertised event.

(ii) The statement in clause (i) shall also be disseminated, both orally and in writing, at the beginning of any event, presentation, seminar, workshop, or public gathering regarding veterans' benefits or entitlements.

(B) Advertising or promoting any event, presentation, seminar, workshop, or other public gathering regarding veterans' benefits or entitlements which is not sponsored by, or affiliated with, the United States Department of Veterans Affairs, the California Department of Veterans Affairs, or any other congressionally chartered or recognized organization of honorably discharged members of the Armed Forces of the United States, or any of their auxiliaries that does not include the following statement, in the same type size and font as the term "veteran" or the variation of that term:

"This event is not sponsored by, or affiliated with, the United States Department of Veterans Affairs, the California Department of Veterans Affairs, or any other congressionally chartered or recognized organization of honorably discharged members of the Armed Forces of the United States, or any of their auxiliaries. None of the insurance products promoted at this sales event are endorsed by those organizations, all of which offer free advice to veterans about how to qualify and apply for benefits."

(i) The statement in this subparagraph shall be disseminated, both orally and in writing, at the beginning of any event, presentation, seminar, workshop, or public gathering regarding veterans' benefits or entitlements.

(ii) The requirements of this subparagraph shall not apply in a case where the United States Department of Veterans Affairs, the California Department of Veterans Affairs, or other congressionally chartered or recognized organization of honorably discharged members of the Armed Forces of the United States, or any of their auxiliaries have granted written permission to the advertiser or promoter for the use of its name, symbol, or insignia to advertise or promote the event, presentation, seminar, workshop, or other public gathering.

(26) Representing that a product is made in California by using a Made in California label created pursuant to Section 12098.10 of the Government Code, unless the product complies with Section 12098.10 of the Government Code.

(b)(1) It is an unfair or deceptive act or practice for a mortgage broker or lender, directly or indirectly, to use a home improvement contractor to negotiate the terms of any loan that is secured, whether in whole or in part, by the residence of the borrower and which is used to finance a home improvement contract or any portion thereof. For purposes of this subdivision, "mortgage broker or lender" includes a finance lender licensed pursuant to the California Finance Lenders Law (Division 9 (commencing with Section 22000) of the Financial Code), a residential mortgage lender licensed pursuant to the California Residential Mortgage Lending Act (Division 20 (commencing with Section 50000) of the Financial Code), or a real estate broker licensed under the Real Estate Law (Division 4 (commencing with Section 10000) of the Business and Professions Code).

(2) This section shall not be construed to either authorize or prohibit a home improvement contractor from referring a consumer to a mortgage broker or lender by this subdivision. However, a home improvement contractor may refer a consumer to a mortgage lender or broker if that referral does not violate Section 7157 of the Business and Professions Code or any other provision of law. A mortgage lender or broker may purchase an executed home improvement contract if that purchase does not violate Section 7157 of the Business and Professions Code or any other provision of law. Nothing in this paragraph shall have any effect on the application of Chapter 1 (commencing with Section 1801) of Title 2 to a home improvement transaction or the financing thereof. *(Added by Stats.1970, c. 1550, p. 3157, § 1. Amended by Stats.1975, c. 379, p. 853, § 1; Stats.1979, c. 819, p. 2827, § 4, eff. Sept. 19, 1979; Stats.1984, c. 1171, § 1; Stats.1986, c. 1497, § 1; Stats.1990, c. 1641 (A.B.4084), § 1; Stats.1995, c. 255 (S.B.320), § 2; Stats.1996, c. 684 (S.B.2045), § 1; Stats.2008, c. 479 (S.B.1136), § 1; Stats.2009, c. 140 (A.B.1164), § 26; Stats.2011, c. 79 (S.B.180), § 1; Stats.2012, c. 653 (S.B.1170), § 1; Stats.2013, c. 541 (S.B.12), § 1.)*

Validity

This section was held preempted by the Federal Communications Act of 1934 with respect to rates and market entry of commercial mobile service providers in the decision of In re Apple iPhone 3G Products Liability Litigation, N.D.Cal.2010, 728 F.Supp.2d 1065, leave to file for reconsideration denied 2010 WL 3119789.

Research References

Rutter, Cal. Practice Guide: Civ. Pro. Before Trial Ch. 14-B, B. Class Action Requirements-In General.

Rutter, Cal. Practice Guide: Enforcing Judgments/Debts Ch. 3-A, A. Evaluating the Claim.

Rutter, Cal. Practice Guide: Insurance Litigation Ch. 11-K, K. Statutory Liability.

Rutter, Cal. Practice Guide: Prof. Responsibility Ch. 2-D, D. In-Person Solicitation for Profit.

Miller and Starr California Real Estate § 27:54, Home Solicitation Contracts.

4 Witkin Cal. Proc. 5th Pleading § 302, Statutory Authorization.

4 Witkin Cal. Proc. 5th Pleading § 303, Fraud in Sales.

4 Witkin Cal. Proc. 5th Pleading § 304, Exclusive Criteria of Consumers Act.

4 Witkin, California Summary 10th Sales § 296, (S 296) Consumers Legal Remedies Act.

4 Witkin, California Summary 10th Security Transactions in Real Property § 38, (S 38) Other Legislation.

13 Witkin, California Summary 10th Equity § 109, False Advertising.

CHAPTER 4. REMEDIES AND PROCEDURES

§ 1780. Consumer's action; relief; senior citizens or disabled persons; venue; court costs and attorney's fees

(a) Any consumer who suffers any damage as a result of the use or employment by any person of a method, act, or practice declared to be unlawful by Section 1770 may bring an action against that person to recover or obtain any of the following:

(1) Actual damages, but in no case shall the total award of damages in a class action be less than one thousand dollars ($1,000).

(2) An order enjoining the methods, acts, or practices.

(3) Restitution of property.

(4) Punitive damages.

(5) Any other relief that the court deems proper.

(b)(1) Any consumer who is a senior citizen or a disabled person, as defined in subdivisions (f) and (g) of Section 1761, as part of an action under subdivision (a), may seek and be awarded, in addition to the remedies specified therein, up to five thousand dollars ($5,000) where the trier of fact does all of the following:

(A) Finds that the consumer has suffered substantial physical, emotional, or economic damage resulting from the defendant's conduct.

(B) Makes an affirmative finding in regard to one or more of the factors set forth in subdivision (b) of Section 3345.

(C) Finds that an additional award is appropriate.

(2) Judgment in a class action by senior citizens or disabled persons under Section 1781 may award each class member that additional award if the trier of fact has made the foregoing findings.

(c) Whenever it is proven by a preponderance of the evidence that a defendant has engaged in conduct in violation of paragraph (24) of subdivision (a) of Section 1770, in addition to all other remedies otherwise provided in this section, the court shall award treble actual damages to the plaintiff. This subdivision shall not apply to attorneys licensed to practice law in California, who are subject to the California Rules of Professional Conduct and to the mandatory fee arbitration provisions of Article 13 (commencing with Section 6200) of Chapter 4 of Division 3 of the Business and Professions Code, when the fees charged or received are for providing representation in administrative agency appeal proceedings or court proceedings for purposes of procuring, maintaining, or securing public social services on behalf of a person or group of persons.

(d) An action under subdivision (a) or (b) may be commenced in the county in which the person against whom it is brought resides, has his or her principal place of business, or is doing business, or in the county where the transaction or any substantial portion thereof occurred.

In any action subject to this section, concurrently with the filing of the complaint, the plaintiff shall file an affidavit stating facts showing that the action has been commenced in a county described in this section as a proper place for the trial of the action. If a plaintiff fails to file the affidavit required by this section, the court shall, upon its own motion or upon motion of any party, dismiss the action without prejudice.

(e) The court shall award court costs and attorney's fees to a prevailing plaintiff in litigation filed pursuant to this section. Reasonable attorney's fees may be awarded to a prevailing defendant upon a finding by the court that the plaintiff's prosecution of the action was not in good faith. *(Added by Stats.1970, c. 1550, p. 3157, § 1. Amended by Stats.1988, c. 823, § 3; Stats.1988, c. 1343, § 2; Stats.1998, c. 931 (S.B.2139), § 15, eff. Sept. 28, 1998; Stats.2003, c. 449 (A.B.1712), § 3; Stats.2008, c. 479 (S.B.1136), § 2; Stats.2009, c. 140 (A.B.1164), § 27.)*

Validity

This section was held preempted by the Federal Communications Act of 1934 with respect to rates and market entry of commercial mobile service providers in the decision of In re Apple iPhone 3G Products Liability Litigation, N.D.Cal.2010, 728 F.Supp.2d 1065, leave to file for reconsideration denied 2010 WL 3119789.

Law Revision Commission Comments

Section 1780 is amended to reflect elimination of the justice court. Cal. Const. art. VI, §§ 1, 5(b). In a county in which there is no municipal court, the superior court has jurisdiction of matters that would be within the subject matter jurisdiction of the municipal court. Cal. Const. art. VI, 10 (superior court jurisdiction); Code Civ. Proc. §§ 85, 85.1 (limited civil cases). [28 Cal.L.Rev.Comm. Reports 51 (1998)].

Research References

Rutter, Cal. Practice Guide: Civ. Pro. Before Trial Ch. 2-A, A. Standing to Sue-"Real Party in Interest" Requirement.
Rutter, Cal. Practice Guide: Civ. Pro. Before Trial Ch. 3-D, D. Venue.
Rutter, Cal. Practice Guide: Civ. Pro. Before Trial Ch. 9(II)-A, A. Injunctions.
Rutter, Cal. Practice Guide: Civil Trials & Evidence Ch. 17-E, E. Attorney Fees as Costs.
Rutter, Cal. Practice Guide: Enforcing Judgments/Debts Ch. 3-A, A. Evaluating the Claim.
Miller and Starr California Real Estate § 27:54, Home Solicitation Contracts.
Miller and Starr California Real Estate § 34:66, Examples of Actions in Which Fees Can be Recovered.
7 Witkin Cal. Proc. 5th Judgment § 203, (S 203) Distinction: Issue of Entitlement to Costs and Attorneys' Fees Expressly Reserved.
7 Witkin Cal. Proc. 5th Judgment § 224, (S 224) Consumer Protection Actions.
4 Witkin Cal. Proc. 5th Pleading § 302, Statutory Authorization.
4 Witkin Cal. Proc. 5th Pleading § 304, Exclusive Criteria of Consumers Act.
4 Witkin Cal. Proc. 5th Pleading § 472, Limited Civil Cases.
6 Witkin Cal. Proc. 5th Proceedings Without Trial § 206, (S 206) When Summary Judgment is Not Available.
4 Witkin, California Summary 10th Sales § 296, (S 296) Consumers Legal Remedies Act.

§ 1781. Consumer's class action; conditions; notices; judgment

(a) Any consumer entitled to bring an action under Section 1780 may, if the unlawful method, act, or practice has caused damage to other consumers similarly situated, bring an action on behalf of himself and such other consumers to recover damages or obtain other relief as provided for in Section 1780.

(b) The court shall permit the suit to be maintained on behalf of all members of the represented class if all of the following conditions exist:

(1) It is impracticable to bring all members of the class before the court.

(2) The questions of law or fact common to the class are substantially similar and predominate over the questions affecting the individual members.

(3) The claims or defenses of the representative plaintiffs are typical of the claims or defenses of the class.

(4) The representative plaintiffs will fairly and adequately protect the interests of the class.

(c) If notice of the time and place of the hearing is served upon the other parties at least 10 days prior thereto, the court shall hold a hearing, upon motion of any party to the action which is supported by affidavit of any person or persons having knowledge of the facts, to determine if any of the following apply to the action:

(1) A class action pursuant to subdivision (b) is proper.

(2) Published notice pursuant to subdivision (d) is necessary to adjudicate the claims of the class.

(3) The action is without merit or there is no defense to the action.

A motion based upon Section 437c of the Code of Civil Procedure shall not be granted in any action commenced as a class action pursuant to subdivision (a).

(d) If the action is permitted as a class action, the court may direct either party to notify each member of the class of the action. The party required to serve notice may, with the consent of the court, if personal notification is unreasonably expensive or it appears that all members of the class cannot be notified personally, give notice as prescribed herein by publication in accordance with Section 6064 of the Government Code in a newspaper of general circulation in the county in which the transaction occurred.

(e) The notice required by subdivision (d) shall include the following:

(1) The court will exclude the member notified from the class if he so requests by a specified date.

(2) The judgment, whether favorable or not, will include all members who do not request exclusion.

(3) Any member who does not request exclusion, may, if he desires, enter an appearance through counsel.

(f) A class action shall not be dismissed, settled, or compromised without the approval of the court, and notice of the proposed dismissal, settlement, or compromise shall be given in such manner as the court directs to each member who was given notice pursuant to subdivision (d) and did not request exclusion.

(g) The judgment in a class action shall describe those to whom the notice was directed and who have not requested exclusion and those the court finds to be members of the class. The best possible notice of the judgment shall be given in such manner as the court directs to each member who was personally served with notice pursuant to subdivision (d) and did not request exclusion. *(Added by Stats.1970, c. 1550, p. 3157, § 1.)*

Validity

This section was held preempted by the Federal Communications Act of 1934 with respect to rates and market entry of commercial mobile service providers in the decision of In re Apple iPhone 3G Products Liability Litigation, N.D.Cal.2010, 728 F.Supp.2d 1065, leave to file for reconsideration denied 2010 WL 3119789.

Research References

Rutter, Cal. Practice Guide: A.D.R. Ch. 4-B, B. Judicial Arbitration.
Rutter, Cal. Practice Guide: A.D.R. Ch. 5-B, B. Federal vs. State Law Governing.

Rutter, Cal. Practice Guide: Civ. Pro. Before Trial Ch. 2-E, E. Intervention.

Rutter, Cal. Practice Guide: Civ. Pro. Before Trial Ch. 10-A, A. Introduction.

Rutter, Cal. Practice Guide: Civ. Pro. Before Trial Ch. 11-A, A. Voluntary Dismissals.

Rutter, Cal. Practice Guide: Civ. Pro. Before Trial Ch. 14-A, A. General Considerations.

Rutter, Cal. Practice Guide: Civ. Pro. Before Trial Ch. 14-B, B. Class Action Requirements-In General.

Rutter, Cal. Practice Guide: Civ. Pro. Before Trial Ch. 14-C, C. Procedural Issues.

Rutter, Cal. Practice Guide: Civ. Pro. Before Trial Gen. Matls., Highlights.

Miller and Starr California Real Estate § 18:12, Distribution of Unclaimed Class Action Judgments.

8 Witkin Cal. Proc. 5th Extraordinary Writs § 135, Illustrations.

7 Witkin Cal. Proc. 5th Judgment § 29, in General.

4 Witkin Cal. Proc. 5th Pleading § 277, (S 277) Superiority of Pending Federal Action.

4 Witkin Cal. Proc. 5th Pleading § 302, Statutory Authorization.

4 Witkin Cal. Proc. 5th Pleading § 304, Exclusive Criteria of Consumers Act.

4 Witkin Cal. Proc. 5th Pleading § 309, (S 309) Necessity of Notice.

4 Witkin Cal. Proc. 5th Pleading § 319, Allocation of Costs.

4 Witkin Cal. Proc. 5th Pleading § 327, (S 327) Dismissal for Delay in Certification.

6 Witkin Cal. Proc. 5th Proceedings Without Trial § 206, (S 206) When Summary Judgment is Not Available.

6 Witkin Cal. Proc. 5th Proceedings Without Trial § 292, Plaintiff Not Sole Party in Interest.

4 Witkin, California Summary 10th Sales § 296, (S 296) Consumers Legal Remedies Act.

§ 1782. Preliminary notices and demands; defenses; injunctive relief; evidence

(a) Thirty days or more prior to the commencement of an action for damages pursuant to this title, the consumer shall do the following:

(1) Notify the person alleged to have employed or committed methods, acts, or practices declared unlawful by Section 1770 of the particular alleged violations of Section 1770.

(2) Demand that the person correct, repair, replace, or otherwise rectify the goods or services alleged to be in violation of Section 1770.

The notice shall be in writing and shall be sent by certified or registered mail, return receipt requested, to the place where the transaction occurred or to the person's principal place of business within California.

(b) Except as provided in subdivision (c), no action for damages may be maintained under Section 1780 if an appropriate correction, repair, replacement, or other remedy is given, or agreed to be given within a reasonable time, to the consumer within 30 days after receipt of the notice.

(c) No action for damages may be maintained under Section 1781 upon a showing by a person alleged to have employed or committed methods, acts, or practices declared unlawful by Section 1770 that all of the following exist:

(1) All consumers similarly situated have been identified, or a reasonable effort to identify such other consumers has been made.

(2) All consumers so identified have been notified that upon their request the person shall make the appropriate correction, repair, replacement, or other remedy of the goods and services.

(3) The correction, repair, replacement, or other remedy requested by the consumers has been, or, in a reasonable time, shall be, given.

(4) The person has ceased from engaging, or if immediate cessation is impossible or unreasonably expensive under the circumstances, the person will, within a reasonable time, cease to engage, in the methods, act, or practices.

(d) An action for injunctive relief brought under the specific provisions of Section 1770 may be commenced without compliance with subdivision (a). Not less than 30 days after the commencement of an action for injunctive relief, and after compliance with subdivision (a), the consumer may amend his or her complaint without leave of court to include a request for damages. The appropriate provisions of subdivision (b) or (c) shall be applicable if the complaint for injunctive relief is amended to request damages.

(e) Attempts to comply with this section by a person receiving a demand shall be construed to be an offer to compromise and shall be inadmissible as evidence pursuant to Section 1152 of the Evidence Code. Furthermore, these attempts to comply with a demand shall not be considered an admission of engaging in an act or practice declared unlawful by Section 1770. Evidence of compliance or attempts to comply with this section may be introduced by a defendant for the purpose of establishing good faith or to show compliance with this section. *(Added by Stats.1970, c. 1550, p. 3157, § 1. Amended by Stats.1999, c. 1000 (S.B.284), § 10.)*

Research References

Rutter, Cal. Practice Guide: Civ. Pro. Before Trial Ch. 1-C, C. Prelawsuit Notices, Claims and Demands.

Miller and Starr California Real Estate § 27:54, Home Solicitation Contracts.

3 Witkin Cal. Proc. 5th Actions § 227, Miscellaneous Statutory Requirements.

4 Witkin Cal. Proc. 5th Pleading § 302, Statutory Authorization.

4 Witkin Cal. Proc. 5th Pleading § 303, Fraud in Sales.

4 Witkin, California Summary 10th Sales § 296, (S 296) Consumers Legal Remedies Act.

§ 1783. Limitation of actions

Any action brought under the specific provisions of Section 1770 shall be commenced not more than three years from the date of the commission of such method, act, or practice. *(Added by Stats.1970, c. 1550, p. 3157, § 1.)*

Research References

Miller and Starr California Real Estate § 27:54, Home Solicitation Contracts.

4 Witkin, California Summary 10th Sales § 192, (S 192) Action for Price.

4 Witkin, California Summary 10th Sales § 296, (S 296) Consumers Legal Remedies Act.

§ 1784. Damages, defense

No award of damages may be given in any action based on a method, act, or practice declared to be unlawful by Section 1770 if the person alleged to have employed or committed such method, act, or practice (a) proves that such violation was not intentional and resulted from a bona fide error notwithstanding the use of reasonable procedures adopted to avoid any such error and (b) makes an appropriate correction, repair or replacement or other remedy of the goods and services according to the provisions of subdivisions (b) and (c) of Section 1782. *(Added by Stats.1970, c. 1550, p. 3157, § 1.)*

Research References

Miller and Starr California Real Estate § 27:54, Home Solicitation Contracts.

4 Witkin Cal. Proc. 5th Pleading § 302, Statutory Authorization.

4 Witkin, California Summary 10th Sales § 184, (S 184) Identification of Goods to Contract.

4 Witkin, California Summary 10th Sales § 190, (S 190) Based on Market Price.

4 Witkin, California Summary 10th Sales § 191, (S 191) Lost Profits.

Title 1.6

CONSUMER CREDIT REPORTING AGENCIES ACT

CHAPTER 1. GENERAL PROVISIONS

§ 1785.1. Legislative findings and declaration

The Legislature finds and declares as follows:

(a) An elaborate mechanism has been developed for investigating and evaluating the credit worthiness, credit standing, credit capacity, and general reputation of consumers.

(b) Consumer credit reporting agencies have assumed a vital role in assembling and evaluating consumer credit and other information on consumers.

(c) There is a need to insure that consumer credit reporting agencies exercise their grave responsibilities with fairness, impartiality, and a respect for the consumer's right to privacy.

(d) It is the purpose of this title to require that consumer credit reporting agencies adopt reasonable procedures for meeting the needs of commerce for consumer credit, personnel, insurance, hiring of a dwelling unit, and other information in a manner which is fair and equitable to the consumer, with regard to the confidentiality, accuracy, relevancy, and proper utilization of such information in accordance with the requirements of this title.

(e) The Legislature hereby intends to regulate consumer credit reporting agencies pursuant to this title in a manner which will best protect the interests of the people of the State of California.

(f) The extension of credit is a privilege and not a right. Nothing in this title shall preclude a creditor from denying credit to any applicant providing such denial is based on factors not inconsistent with present law.

(g) Any clauses in contracts which prohibit any action required by this title are not in the public interest and shall be considered unenforceable. This shall not invalidate the other terms of such a contract. *(Added by Stats.1975, c. 1271, p. 3369, § 1. Amended by Stats.1976, c. 666, p. 1638, § 1; Stats.1982, c. 1127, p. 4062, § 1.)*

Research References

California Practice Guide: Employment Litigation Ch. 1-A, A. Background.
Miller and Starr California Real Estate § 36:1, Applicable Theories of Liability.
Miller and Starr California Real Estate § 19:217, Restrictions on Access and Reporting of Unlawful Detainer Actions.
14 NO. 2 Miller & Starr, California Real Estate Newsalert 16, Lenders' Liability.
18 NO. 5 Miller & Starr, California Real Estate Newsalert 17, Landlord and Tenant.
1 Witkin Cal. Summ. 10th Contracts § 484, (S 484) California Law.
4 Witkin, California Summary 10th Sales § 297, Nature and Scope of Statute.
5 Witkin, California Summary 10th Torts § 666, (S 666) in General.

§ 1785.2. Short title

This act may be referred to as the Consumer Credit Reporting Agencies Act. *(Added by Stats.1975, c. 1271, p. 3369, § 1.)*

§ 1785.3. Definitions

The following terms as used in this title have the meaning expressed in this section:

(a) "Adverse action" means a denial or revocation of credit, a change in the terms of an existing credit arrangement which is adverse to the interests of the consumer, or a refusal to grant credit in substantially the amount or on substantially the terms requested. "Adverse action" includes all of the following:

(1) Any denial of, increase in any charge for, or reduction in the amount of, insurance for personal, family, or household purposes made in connection with the underwriting of insurance.

(2) Any denial of employment or any other decision made for employment purposes which adversely affects any current or prospective employee.

(3) Any action taken, or determination made, with respect to a consumer (A) for an application for an extension of credit, or an application for the hiring of a dwelling unit, and (B) that is adverse to the interests of the consumer.

"Adverse action" does not include (A) a refusal to extend additional credit to a consumer under an existing credit arrangement if (i) the applicant is delinquent or otherwise in default under that credit arrangement or (ii) the additional credit would exceed a credit limit previously established for the consumer or (B) a refusal or failure to authorize an account transaction at a point of sale.

(b) "Consumer" means a natural individual.

(c) "Consumer credit report" means any written, oral, or other communication of any information by a consumer credit reporting agency bearing on a consumer's credit worthiness, credit standing, or credit capacity, which is used or is expected to be used, or collected in whole or in part, for the purpose of serving as a factor in establishing the consumer's eligibility for: (1) credit to be used primarily for personal, family, or household purposes, or (2) employment purposes, or (3) hiring of a dwelling unit, as defined in subdivision (c) of Section 1940, or (4) other purposes authorized in Section 1785.11.

The term does not include (1) any report containing information solely as to transactions or experiences between the consumer and the person making the report, (2) any communication of that information or information from a credit application by a consumer that is internal within the organization that is the person making the report or that is made to an entity owned by, or affiliated by corporate control with, that person; provided that the consumer is informed by means of a clear and conspicuous written disclosure that information contained in the credit application may be provided to these persons; however, where a credit application is taken by telephone, disclosure shall initially be given orally at the time the application is taken, and a clear and conspicuous written disclosure shall be made to the consumer in the first written communication to that consumer after the application is taken, (3) any authorization or approval of a specific extension of credit directly or indirectly by the issuer of a credit card or similar device, (4) any report by a person conveying a decision whether to make a specific extension of credit directly or indirectly to a consumer in response to a request by a third party, if the third party advises the consumer of the name and address of the person to whom the request was made and the person makes the disclosures to the consumer required under Section 1785.20, (5) any report containing information solely on a consumer's character, general reputation, personal characteristics, or mode of living which is obtained through personal interviews with neighbors, friends, or associates of the consumer reported on, or others with whom he is acquainted or who may have knowledge concerning those items of information, (6) any communication about a consumer in connection with a credit transaction which is not initiated by the consumer, between persons who are affiliated (as defined in Section 150 of the Corporations Code) by common ownership or common corporate control (as defined by Section 160 of the Corporations Code), if either of those persons has complied with paragraph (2) of subdivision (b) of Section 1785.20.1 with respect to a prequalifying report from which the information communicated is taken and provided the consumer has consented to the provision and use of the prequalifying report in writing, or (7) any consumer credit report furnished for use in connection with a transaction which consists of an extension of credit to be used solely for a commercial purpose.

(d) "Consumer credit reporting agency" means any person who, for monetary fees, dues, or on a cooperative nonprofit basis, regularly engages in whole or in part in the business of assembling or evaluating consumer credit information or other information on consumers for the purpose of furnishing consumer credit reports to third parties, but does not include any governmental agency whose records are maintained primarily for traffic safety, law enforcement, or licensing purposes.

(e) "Credit transaction that is not initiated by the consumer" does not include the use of a consumer credit report by an assignee for collection or by a person with which the consumer has an account for purposes of (1) reviewing the account or (2) collecting the account. For purposes of this subdivision, "reviewing the account" includes activities related to account maintenance and monitoring, credit line increases, and account upgrades and enhancements.

(f) "Employment purposes," when used in connection with a consumer credit report, means a report used for the purpose of evaluating a consumer for employment, promotion, reassignment, or retention as an employee.

(g) "File," when used in connection with information on any consumer, means all of the information on that consumer recorded and retained by a consumer credit reporting agency, regardless of how the information is stored.

(h) "Firm offer of credit" means any offer of credit to a consumer that will be honored if, based on information in a consumer credit report on the consumer and other information bearing on the creditworthiness of the consumer, the consumer is determined to meet the criteria used to select the consumer for the offer and the consumer is able to provide any real property collateral specified in the offer. For purposes of this subdivision, the phrase "other information bearing on the creditworthiness of the consumer" means information that the person making the offer is permitted to consider pursuant to any rule, regulation, or formal written policy statement relating to the federal Fair Credit Reporting Act, as amended (15 U.S.C.

Sec. 1681 et seq.), promulgated by the Federal Trade Commission or any federal bank regulatory agency.

(i) "Item of information" means any of one or more informative entries in a credit report which causes a creditor to deny credit to an applicant or increase the cost of credit to an applicant or deny an applicant a checking account with a bank or other financial institution.

(j) "Person" means any individual, partnership, corporation, trust, estate, cooperative, association, government or governmental subdivision or agency, or other entity.

(k) "Prequalifying report" means a report containing the limited information permitted under paragraph (2) of subdivision (b) of Section 1785.11.

(*l*) "State or local child support enforcement agency" means the Department of Child Support Services or local child support agency acting pursuant to Division 17 (commencing with Section 17000) of the Family Code to establish, enforce or modify child support obligations, and any state or local agency or official that succeeds to these responsibilities under a successor statute. (*Added by Stats.1975, c. 1271, p. 3369, § 1. Amended by Stats.1976, c. 666, p. 1638, § 2; Stats.1982, c. 1127, p. 4062, § 2; Stats.1990, c. 1144 (S.B.2751), § 1; Stats.1992, c. 1194 (A.B. 1629), § 1, operative July 1, 1993; Stats.1993, c. 285 (A.B.1340), § 1, eff. Aug. 2, 1993; Stats.1994, c. 225 (S.B.1483), § 1; Stats.1994, c. 1010 (S.B.2053), § 35; Stats.2000, c. 808 (A.B. 1358), § 3, eff. Sept. 28, 2000.*)

Research References

California Practice Guide: Employment Litigation Ch. 5-K, K. Invasion of Privacy.
California Practice Guide: Employment Litigation Gen. Matls, Highlights.
4 Witkin, California Summary 10th Sales § 297, Nature and Scope of Statute.
3 Witkin, California Summary 10th Agency and Employment § 359A, (S 359A) (New)-Consumer Credit Reports.

§ 1785.4. Inapplicability to private detectives; exception

Nothing in this title shall apply to any person licensed pursuant to the provisions of Chapter 11 (commencing with Section 7500) of Division 3 of the Business and Professions Code, or to any employee of such person, unless such person is employed directly by a consumer credit reporting agency. (*Added by Stats.1975, c. 1271, p. 3370, § 1.*)

Research References

4 Witkin, California Summary 10th Sales § 297, Nature and Scope of Statute.

§ 1785.5. Assembly, evaluation or dissemination of information on checking account experiences of financial institution customers

Any person who, for monetary fees, dues, or on a cooperative nonprofit basis, regularly engages in whole or in part in the practice of assembling, evaluating, or disseminating information on the checking account experiences of consumer customers of banks or other financial institutions is, with the exception of compliance with the requirements of Section 1785.10, subdivisions (c), (d), and (e), only with regard to the provision of the address and telephone number, subject to the same laws which govern consumer credit reporting agencies. (*Added by Stats. 1990, c. 1144 (S.B.2751), § 2. Amended by Stats.2001, c. 236 (A.B.488), § 1, operative Jan. 1, 2003.*)

Research References

4 Witkin, California Summary 10th Sales § 297, Nature and Scope of Statute.

§ 1785.6. Consumer notice or disclosure; California addresses

The notices and disclosures to consumers provided for in this title shall be required to be made only to those consumers who have a mailing address in California. *(Added by Stats.1993, c. 285 (A.B.1340), § 2, eff. Aug. 2, 1993.)*

CHAPTER 2. OBLIGATIONS OF CONSUMER CREDIT REPORTING AGENCIES

§ 1785.10.   Inspection of files by consumer; advice to consumer; coded files; availability of information; disclosure of recipients of credit reports and inquiries; reselling report or information; exemptions

(a) Every consumer credit reporting agency shall, upon request and proper identification of any consumer, allow the consumer to visually inspect all files maintained regarding that consumer at the time of the request.

(b) Every consumer reporting agency, upon contact by a consumer by telephone, mail, or in person regarding information which may be contained in the agency files regarding that consumer, shall promptly advise the consumer of his or her rights under Sections 1785.11.8, 1785.19, and 1785.19. 5, and of the obligation of the agency to provide disclosure of the files in person, by mail, or by telephone pursuant to Section 1785.15, including the obligation of the agency to provide a decoded written version of the file or a written copy of the file with an explanation of any code, including any credit score used, and the key factors, as defined in Section 1785.15.1, if the consumer so requests that copy. The disclosure shall be provided in the manner selected by the consumer, chosen from among any reasonable means available to the consumer credit reporting agency.

The agency shall determine the applicability of subdivision (1) of Section 1785.17 and, where applicable, the agency shall inform the consumer of the rights under that section.

(c) All information on a consumer in the files of a consumer credit reporting agency at the time of a request for inspection under subdivision (a), shall be available for inspection, including the names, addresses and, if provided by the sources of information, the telephone numbers identified for customer service for the sources of information.

(d)(1) The consumer credit reporting agency shall also disclose the recipients of any consumer credit report on the consumer which the consumer credit reporting agency has furnished:

(A) For employment purposes within the two-year period preceding the request.

(B) For any other purpose within the 12–month period preceding the request.

(2) Disclosure of recipients of consumer credit reports for purposes of this subdivision shall include the name of the recipient or, if applicable, the fictitious business name under which the recipient does business disclosed in full. The identification shall also include the address and, if provided by the recipient, the telephone number identified for customer service for the recipient.

(e) The consumer credit reporting agency shall also disclose a record of all inquiries received by the agency in the 12–month period preceding the request that identified the consumer in connection with a credit transaction which is not initiated by the consumer. This record of inquiries shall include the name, address and, if provided by the recipient, the telephone number identified for customer service for each recipient making an inquiry.

(f) Any consumer credit reporting agency when it is subject to the provisions of Section 1785.22 is exempted from the requirements of subdivisions (c), (d), and (e), only with regard to the provision of the address and telephone number.

(g) Any consumer credit reporting agency, that provides a consumer credit report to another consumer credit reporting agency that procures the consumer credit report for the purpose of resale and is subject to Section 1785.22, is exempted from the requirements of subdivisions (d) and (e), only with regard to the provision of the address and telephone number regarding each prospective user to which the consumer credit report was sold.

(h) This section shall become operative on January 1, 2003. *(Added by Stats.2002, c. 9 (A.B.1531), § 2, eff. Feb. 19, 2002, operative Jan. 1, 2003.)*

Research References

4 Witkin, California Summary 10th Sales § 298, Disclosure of Information.
5 Witkin, California Summary 10th Torts § 597, (S 597) Credit Report.

§ 1785.10.1. Consumer credit report; adverse action taken by user against consumer; unlawful for agency to prohibit or to dissuade or attempt to dissuade user from furnishing copy of report to consumer; civil penalty

(a) It is unlawful for a consumer credit reporting agency to prohibit in any manner, including, but not limited to, in the terms of a contract enforceable in the state, or to dissuade or attempt to dissuade, a user of a consumer credit report furnished by the credit reporting agency from providing a copy of the consumer's credit report to the consumer, upon the consumer's request, if the user has taken adverse action against the consumer based in whole or in part upon information in the report.

(b) The Attorney General, any district attorney or city attorney, or a city prosecutor in any city or city and county having a full-time city prosecutor, may bring a civil action in any court of competent jurisdiction against any credit reporting agency violating this section for a civil penalty not to exceed five thousand dollars ($5,000) which may be assessed and recovered in a civil action brought in the name of the people of the State of California. *(Added by Stats.2013, c. 433 (A.B.1220), § 1.)*

§ 1785.11. Furnishing consumer report; circumstances

(a) A consumer credit reporting agency shall furnish a consumer credit report only under the following circumstances:

(1) In response to the order of a court having jurisdiction to issue an order.

(2) In accordance with the written instructions of the consumer to whom it relates.

(3) To a person whom it has reason to believe:

(A) Intends to use the information in connection with a credit transaction, or entering or enforcing an order of a court of competent jurisdiction for support, involving the consumer as to whom the information is to be furnished and involving the extension of credit to, or review or collection of an account of, the consumer; or

(B) Intends to use the information for employment purposes; or

(C) Intends to use the information in connection with the underwriting of insurance involving the consumer, or for insurance claims settlements; or

(D) Intends to use the information in connection with a determination of the consumer's eligibility for a license or other benefit granted by a governmental instrumentality required by law to consider the applicant's financial responsibility or status; or

(E) Intends to use the information in connection with the hiring of a dwelling unit, as defined in subdivision (c) of Section 1940; or

(F) Otherwise has a legitimate business need for the information in connection with a business transaction involving the consumer.

(b) A consumer credit reporting agency may furnish information for purposes of a credit transaction specified in subparagraph (A) of paragraph (3) of subdivision (a), where it is a credit transaction that is not initiated by the consumer, only under the circumstances specified in paragraph (1) or (2), as follows:

(1) The consumer authorizes the consumer credit reporting agency to furnish the consumer credit report to the person.

(2) The proposed transaction involves a firm offer of credit to the consumer, the consumer credit reporting agency has complied with subdivision (d), and the consumer has not elected pursuant to paragraph (1) of subdivision (d) to have the consumer's name excluded from lists of names provided by the consumer credit reporting agency for purposes of reporting in connection with the potential issuance of firm offers of credit. A consumer credit reporting agency may provide only the following information pursuant to this paragraph:

(A) The name and address of the consumer.

(B) Information pertaining to a consumer that is not identified or identifiable with a particular consumer.

(c) Except as provided in paragraph (3) of subdivision (a) of Section 1785.15, a consumer credit reporting agency shall not furnish to any person a record of inquiries solely resulting from credit transactions that are not initiated by the consumer.

(d)(1) A consumer may elect to have his or her name and address excluded from any list provided by a consumer credit reporting agency pursuant to paragraph (2) of subdivision (b) by notifying the consumer credit reporting agency, by telephone or in writing, through the notification system maintained by the consumer credit reporting agency pursuant to subdivision (e), that the consumer does not consent to any use of consumer credit reports relating to the consumer in connection with any transaction that is not initiated by the consumer.

(2) An election of a consumer under paragraph (1) shall be effective with respect to a consumer credit reporting agency, and any affiliate of the consumer credit reporting agency, on the date on which the consumer notifies the consumer credit reporting agency.

(3) An election of a consumer under paragraph (1) shall terminate and be of no force or effect following notice from the consumer to the consumer credit reporting agency, through the system established pursuant to subdivision (e), that the election is no longer effective.

(e) Each consumer credit reporting agency that furnishes a prequalifying report pursuant to subdivision (b) in connection with a credit transaction not initiated by the consumer shall establish and maintain a notification system, including a toll-free telephone number, that permits any consumer, with appropriate identification and for which the consumer credit reporting agency has a file, to notify the consumer credit reporting agency of the consumer's election to have the consumer's name removed from any list of names and addresses provided by the consumer credit reporting agency, and by any affiliated consumer credit reporting agency, pursuant to paragraph (2) of subdivision (b). Compliance with the requirements of this subdivision by a consumer credit reporting agency shall constitute compliance with those requirements by any affiliate of that consumer credit reporting agency.

(f) Each consumer credit reporting agency that compiles and maintains files on consumers on a nationwide basis shall establish and maintain a notification system under paragraph (1) of subdivision (e) jointly with its affiliated consumer credit reporting agencies. *(Added by Stats.1975, c. 1271, p. 3371, § 1. Amended by Stats.1982, c. 1127, p. 4063, § 3; Stats.1992, c. 1194 (A.B.1629), § 3, operative July 1, 1993; Stats.1993, c. 285 (A.B.1340), § 4, eff. Aug. 2, 1993; Stats.1994, c. 146 (A.B.3601), § 11; Stats.2000, c. 1012 (S.B.2166), § 1; Stats.2002, c. 664 (A.B.3034), § 40.)*

Research References

Miller and Starr California Real Estate § 19:9, Apartment House as a "Business".

4 Witkin, California Summary 10th Sales § 297, Nature and Scope of Statute.

4 Witkin, California Summary 10th Sales § 299, (S 299) Contents.

4 Witkin, California Summary 10th Sales § 303, Consumer's Remedies.

§ 1785.11.1. Security alerts in credit reports

(a) A consumer may elect to place a security alert in his or her credit report by making a request in writing or by telephone to a consumer credit reporting agency. "Security alert" means a notice placed in a consumer's credit report, at the request of the consumer, that notifies a recipient of the credit report that the consumer's identity may have been used without the consumer's consent to fraudulently obtain goods or services in the consumer's name.

(b) A consumer credit reporting agency shall notify each person requesting consumer credit information with respect to a consumer of the existence of a security alert in the credit report of that consumer, regardless of whether a full credit report, credit score, or summary report is requested.

(c) Each consumer credit reporting agency shall maintain a toll-free telephone number to accept security alert requests from consumers 24 hours a day, seven days a week.

(d) The toll-free telephone number shall be included in any written disclosure by a consumer credit reporting agency to any consumer pursuant to Section 1785.15 and shall be printed in a clear and conspicuous manner.

(e) A consumer credit reporting agency shall place a security alert on a consumer's credit report no later than five business days after receiving a request from the consumer.

(f) The security alert shall remain in place for at least 90 days, and a consumer shall have the right to request a renewal of the security alert.

(g) Any person who uses a consumer credit report in connection with the approval of credit based on an application for an extension of credit, or with the purchase, lease, or rental of goods or non-credit-related services and who receives notification of a security alert pursuant to subdivision (a) may not lend money, extend credit, or complete the purchase, lease, or rental of goods or non-credit-related services without taking reasonable steps to verify the consumer's identity, in order to ensure that the application for an extension of credit or for the purchase, lease, or rental of goods or non-credit-related services is not the result of identity theft. If the consumer has placed a statement with the security alert in his or her file requesting that identity be verified by calling a specified telephone number, any person who receives that statement with the security alert in a consumer's file pursuant to subdivision (a) shall take reasonable steps to verify the identity of the consumer by contacting the consumer using the specified telephone number prior to lending money, extending credit, or completing the purchase, lease, or rental of goods or non-credit-related services. If a person uses a consumer credit report to facilitate the extension of credit or for another permissible purpose on behalf of a subsidiary, affiliate, agent, assignee, or prospective assignee, that person may verify a consumer's identity under this section in lieu of the subsidiary, affiliate, agent, assignee, or prospective assignee.

(h) For purposes of this section, "extension of credit" does not include an increase in the dollar limit of an existing open-end credit plan, as defined in Regulation Z issued by the Board of Governors of the Federal Reserve System (12 C.F.R. 226.2), or any change to, or review of, an existing credit account.

(i) If reasonable steps are taken to verify the identity of the consumer pursuant to subdivision (b) of Section 1785.20.3, those steps constitute compliance with the requirements of this section, except that if a consumer has placed a statement including a telephone number with the security alert in his or her file, his or her identity shall be verified by contacting the consumer using that telephone number as specified pursuant to subdivision (g).

(j) A consumer credit reporting agency shall notify each consumer who has requested that a security alert be placed on his or her consumer credit report of the expiration date of the alert.

(k) Notwithstanding Section 1785.19, any consumer credit reporting agency that recklessly, willfully, or intentionally fails to place a security alert pursuant to this section shall be liable for a penalty in an amount of up to two thousand five hundred dollars ($2,500) and reasonable attorneys' fees. *(Added by Stats.2001, c. 720 (S.B.168), § 1, operative July 1, 2002. Amended by Stats. 2003, c. 533 (S.B.602), § 2; Stats.2003, c. 907 (S.B.25), § 1.5, operative July 1, 2004.)*

Research References

4 Witkin, California Summary 10th Sales § 297, Nature and Scope of Statute.

§ 1785.11.2. Security freeze on credit report

(a) A consumer may elect to place a security freeze on his or her credit report by making a request in writing by mail to a consumer credit reporting agency. "Security freeze" means a notice placed in a consumer's credit report, at the request of the consumer, and subject to certain exceptions, that prohibits the consumer credit reporting agency from releasing the consumer's credit report or any information from it without the express authorization of the consumer. If a security freeze is in place, information from a consumer's credit report may not be released to a third party without prior express authorization from the consumer. This subdivision does not prevent a consumer credit reporting agency from advising a third party that a security freeze is in effect with respect to the consumer's credit report.

(b) A consumer credit reporting agency shall place a security freeze on a consumer's credit report no later than three business days after receiving a written request from the consumer.

(c) The consumer credit reporting agency shall send a written confirmation of the security freeze to the consumer within 10 business days and shall provide the consumer with a unique personal identification number or password to be used by the consumer when providing authorization for the release of his or her credit for a specific party or period of time.

(d) If the consumer wishes to allow his or her credit report to be accessed for a specific party or period of time while a freeze is in place, he or she shall contact the consumer credit reporting agency, request that the freeze be temporarily lifted, and provide the following:

(1) Proper identification, as defined in subdivision (c) of Section 1785.15.

(2) The unique personal identification number or password provided by the credit reporting agency pursuant to subdivision (c).

(3) The proper information regarding the third party who is to receive the credit report or the time period for which the report shall be available to users of the credit report.

(e) A consumer credit reporting agency that receives a request from a consumer to temporarily lift a freeze on a credit report pursuant to subdivision (d) shall comply with the request no later than three business days after receiving the request.

(f) A consumer credit reporting agency may develop procedures involving the use of telephone, fax, the Internet, or other electronic media to receive and process a request from a consumer to temporarily lift a freeze on a credit report pursuant to subdivision (d) in an expedited manner.

(g) A consumer credit reporting agency shall remove or temporarily lift a freeze placed on a consumer's credit report only in the following cases:

(1) Upon consumer request, pursuant to subdivision (d) or (j).

(2) If the consumer's credit report was frozen due to a material misrepresentation of fact by the consumer. If a consumer credit reporting agency intends to remove a freeze upon a consumer's credit report pursuant to this paragraph, the consumer credit reporting agency shall notify the consumer in writing prior to removing the freeze on the consumer's credit report.

(h) A third party who requests access to a consumer credit report in connection with an application for credit or any other use may treat the application as incomplete if a security freeze is in effect and the consumer does not allow his or her credit report to be accessed for that specific party or period of time.

(i) If a consumer requests a security freeze, the consumer credit reporting agency shall disclose the process of placing and temporarily lifting a freeze and the process for allowing access to information from the consumer's credit report for a specific party or period of time while the freeze is in place.

(j) A security freeze shall remain in place until the consumer requests that the security freeze be removed. A consumer credit reporting agency shall remove a security freeze within three business days of receiving a request for removal from the consumer if the consumer provides both of the following:

(1) Proper identification, as defined in subdivision (c) of Section 1785.15.

(2) The unique personal identification number or password provided by the credit reporting agency pursuant to subdivision (c).

(k) A consumer credit reporting agency shall require proper identification, as defined in subdivision (c) of Section 1785.15, of the person making a request to place or remove a security freeze.

(l) The provisions of this section do not apply to the use of a consumer credit report by any of the following:

(1)(A)(i) A person or entity with which the consumer has or had, prior to any assignment, an account or contract, including a demand deposit account, or to which the consumer issued a negotiable instrument, for the purpose of reviewing the account or collecting the financial obligation owing for the account, contract, or negotiable instrument.

(ii) A subsidiary, affiliate, or agent of a person or entity described in clause (i), an assignee of a financial obligation owing by the consumer to such a person or entity, or a prospective assignee of a financial obligation owing by the consumer to such a person or entity in conjunction with the proposed purchase of the financial obligation, for the purpose of reviewing the account or collecting the financial obligation owing for the account, contract, or negotiable instrument.

(B) For purposes of this paragraph, "reviewing the account" includes activities related to account maintenance, monitoring, credit line increases, and account upgrades and enhancements.

(2) A subsidiary, affiliate, agent, assignee, or prospective assignee of a person to whom access has been granted under subdivision (d) for purposes of facilitating the extension of credit or other permissible use.

(3) Any state or local agency, law enforcement agency, trial court, or private collection agency acting pursuant to a court order, warrant, or subpoena.

(4) A child support agency acting pursuant to Chapter 2 (commencing with Section 17400) of Division 17 of the Family Code or Title IV–D of the Social Security Act (42 U.S.C. et seq.).

(5) The State Department of Health Care Services or its agents or assigns acting to investigate Medi–Cal fraud.

(6) The Franchise Tax Board or its agents or assigns acting to investigate or collect delinquent taxes or unpaid court orders or to fulfill any of its other statutory responsibilities.

(7) The use of credit information for the purposes of prescreening as provided for by the federal Fair Credit Reporting Act.

(8) Any person or entity administering a credit file monitoring subscription service to which the consumer has subscribed.

(9) Any person or entity for the purpose of providing a consumer with a copy of his or her credit report upon the consumer's request.

(m)(1) Except as provided in paragraph (2), this title does not prevent a consumer credit reporting agency from charging a fee of no more than ten dollars ($10) to a consumer for the placement of each freeze, the removal of the freeze, the temporary lift of the freeze for a period of time, or the temporary lift of the freeze for a specific party, regarding access to a consumer credit report, except that a consumer credit reporting agency may not charge a fee to a victim of identity theft who has submitted a valid police report or valid Department of Motor Vehicles investigative report that alleges a violation of Section 530.5 of the Penal Code.

(2) With respect to a consumer who is 65 years of age or older and who has provided identification confirming his or her age, a consumer credit reporting agency shall not charge a fee for the placement of an initial security freeze, but may charge a fee not to exceed five dollars ($5) for the removal of the freeze, the temporary lift of the freeze for a period of time, the temporary lift of the freeze for a specific party, or replacing the freeze.

(n) Regardless of the existence of a security freeze, a consumer reporting agency may disclose public record information lawfully obtained by, or for, the consumer reporting agency from an open public record to the extent otherwise permitted by law. This subdivision does not prohibit a consumer reporting agency from electing to apply a valid security freeze to the entire contents of a credit report. *(Added by Stats.2001, c. 720 (S.B.168), § 2, operative Jan. 1, 2003. Amended by Stats.2002, c. 664 (A.B.3034), § 41; Stats.2002, c. 786 (S.B.1730), § 1; Stats. 2003, c. 533 (S.B.602), § 3; Stats.2007, c. 699 (A.B.1298), § 2; Stats.2008, c. 151 (A.B.372), § 1; Stats.2012, c. 645 (A.B.2374), § 1.)*

Validity

A prior version of this section was held unconstitutional as violating free speech in the decision of U.D. Registry, Inc. v. State (App. 2 Dist. 2006) 50 Cal.Rptr.3d 647, 144 Cal.App.4th 405, modified on denial of rehearing, review denied.

Research References

4 Witkin, California Summary 10th Sales § 297, Nature and Scope of Statute.

§ 1785.11.3. Official information in consumer credit report requiring written confirmation where there is a security freeze on the report; security alerts and copies

(a) If a security freeze is in place, a consumer credit reporting agency shall not change any of the following official information in a consumer credit report without sending a written confirmation of the change to the consumer within 30 days of the change being posted to the consumer's file: name, date of birth, social security number, and address. Written confirmation is not required for technical modifications of a consumer's official information, including name and street abbreviations, complete spellings, or transposition of numbers or letters. In the case of an address change, the written confirmation shall be sent to both the new address and to the former address.

(b) If a consumer has placed a security alert, a consumer credit reporting agency shall provide the consumer, upon request, with a free copy of his or her credit report at the time the 90–day security alert period expires. *(Added by Stats.2001, c. 720 (S.B.168), § 3, operative Jan. 1, 2003.)*

§ 1785.11.4. Application of specified provisions to consumer credit reporting agency that acts only as a reseller of credit information; honoring security freezes

The provisions of Sections 1785.11.1, 1785.11.2, and 1785.11.3 do not apply to a consumer credit reporting agency that acts only as a reseller of credit information pursuant to Section 1785.22 by assembling and merging information contained in the data base of another consumer credit reporting agency or multiple consumer credit reporting agencies, and does not maintain a permanent data base of credit information from which new consumer credit reports are produced. However, a consumer credit reporting agency acting pursuant to Section 1785.22 shall honor any security freeze placed on a consumer credit report by another consumer credit reporting agency. *(Added by Stats. 2001, c. 720 (S.B.168), § 4.)*

§ 1785.11.6. Entities not required to place in credit report either a security alert or security freeze

The following entities are not required to place in a credit report either a security alert, pursuant to Section 1785.11.1, or a security freeze, pursuant to Section 1785.11.2:

(a) A check services or fraud prevention services company, which issues reports on incidents of fraud or authorizations for the purpose of approving or processing negotiable instruments, electronic funds transfers, or similar methods of payments.

(b) A deposit account information service company, which issues reports regarding account closures due to fraud, substantial overdrafts, ATM abuse, or similar negative information regarding a consumer, to inquiring banks or other financial institutions for use only in reviewing a consumer request for a deposit account at the inquiring bank or financial institution. *(Added by Stats.2001, c. 720 (S.B.168), § 5. Amended by Stats.2002, c. 786 (S.B.1730), § 2; Stats.2003, c. 907 (S.B.25), § 2.)*

§ 1785.11.8. Election by consumer to remove name from list that consumer credit reporting agency furnishes for credit card solicitations

A consumer may elect that his or her name shall be removed from any list that a consumer credit reporting agency furnishes for credit card solicitations, by notifying the consumer credit reporting agency, by telephone or in writing, pursuant to the notification system maintained by the consumer credit reporting agency pursuant to subdivision (d) of Section 1785.11. The election shall be effective for a minimum of two years, unless otherwise specified by the consumer. *(Added by Stats.2001, c. 354 (A.B.655), § 2.)*

Research References

4 Witkin, California Summary 10th Sales § 298, Disclosure of Information.

§ 1785.12. Report to governmental agency

Notwithstanding the provisions of Section 1785.11, a consumer credit reporting agency may furnish to a governmental agency a consumer's name, address, former address, places of employment, or former places of employment. *(Added by Stats.1975, c. 1271, p. 3371, § 1.)*

Research References

4 Witkin, California Summary 10th Sales § 299, (S 299) Contents.

§ 1785.13. Items of information prohibited; exceptions

(a) No consumer credit reporting agency shall make any consumer credit report containing any of the following items of information:

(1) Bankruptcies that, from the date of the order for relief, antedate the report by more than 10 years.

(2) Suits and judgments that, from the date of entry or renewal, antedate the report by more than seven years or until the governing statute of limitations has expired, whichever is the longer period.

(3) Unlawful detainer actions, unless the lessor was the prevailing party. For purposes of this paragraph, the lessor shall be deemed to be the prevailing party only if (A) final judgment was awarded to the lessor (i) upon entry of the tenant's default, (ii) upon the granting of the lessor's motion for summary judgment, or (iii) following trial, or (B) the action was resolved by a written settlement agreement between the parties that states that the unlawful detainer action may be reported. In any other instance in which the action is resolved by settlement agreement, the lessor shall not be deemed to be the prevailing party for purposes of this paragraph.

(4) Paid tax liens that, from the date of payment, antedate the report by more than seven years.

(5) Accounts placed for collection or charged to profit and loss that antedate the report by more than seven years.

(6) Records of arrest, indictment, information, misdemeanor complaint, or conviction of a crime that, from the date of disposition, release, or parole, antedate the report by more than seven years. These items of information shall no longer be reported if at any time it is learned that in the case of a conviction a full pardon has been granted, or in the case of an arrest, indictment, information, or misdemeanor complaint a conviction did not result.

(7) Any other adverse information that antedates the report by more than seven years.

(b) The seven-year period specified in paragraphs (5) and (7) of subdivision (a) shall commence to run, with respect to any account that is placed for collection (internally or by referral to a third party, whichever is earlier), charged to profit and loss, or subjected to any similar action, upon the expiration of the 180–day period beginning on the date of the commencement of the delinquency that immediately preceded the collection activity, charge to profit and loss, or similar action. Where more than one of these actions is taken with respect to a particular account, the seven-year period specified in paragraphs (5) and (7) shall commence concurrently for all these actions on the date of the first of these actions.

(c) Any consumer credit reporting agency that furnishes a consumer credit report containing information regarding any case involving a consumer arising under the bankruptcy provisions of Title 11 of the United States Code shall include an identification of the chapter of Title 11 of the United States Code under which the case arose if that can be ascertained from what was provided to the consumer credit reporting agency by the source of the information.

(d) A consumer credit report shall not include any adverse information concerning a consumer antedating the report by more than 10 years or that otherwise is prohibited from being included in a consumer credit report.

(e) If a consumer credit reporting agency is notified by a furnisher of credit information that an open-end credit account of the consumer has been closed by the consumer, any consumer credit report thereafter issued by the consumer credit reporting agency with respect to that consumer, and that includes information respecting that account, shall indicate the fact that the consumer has closed the account. For purposes of this subdivision, "open-end credit account" does not include any demand deposit account, such as a checking account, money market account, or share draft account.

(f) Consumer credit reporting agencies shall not include medical information in their files on consumers or furnish medical information for employment, insurance, or credit purposes in a consumer credit report without the consent of the consumer.

(g) A consumer credit reporting agency shall include in any consumer credit report information, if any, on the failure of the consumer to pay overdue child or spousal support, where the information either was provided to the consumer credit reporting agency pursuant to Section 4752 or has been provided to the consumer credit reporting agency and verified by another federal, state, or local governmental agency. *(Added by Stats. 1975, c. 1271, p. 3371, § 1. Amended by Stats.1982, c. 1127, p. 4064, § 4; Stats.1988, c. 900, § 1; Stats.1991, c. 965 (A.B.1796), § 1; Stats.1991, c. 1145 (A.B.2032), § 1.1; Stats.1992, c. 1194 (A.B.1629), § 4, operative July 1, 1993; Stats.1993, c. 285 (A.B.1340), § 5, eff. Aug. 2, 1993; Stats.1994, c. 146 (A.B.3601), § 12; Stats.2000, c. 1012 (S.B.2166), § 2; Stats.2009, c. 500 (A.B.1059), § 10.)*

Validity

A prior version of this section was held unconstitutional as a violation of the First Amendment in the decision of U.D. Registry, Inc. v. State of California (App. 2 Dist. 1995) 40 Cal.Rptr.2d 228, 34 Cal.App.4th 107.

Research References

Miller and Starr California Real Estate § 19:217, Restrictions on Access and Reporting of Unlawful Detainer Actions.
12 Witkin, California Summary 10th Real Property § 703, (S 703) Nature of Remedy.
4 Witkin, California Summary 10th Sales § 299, (S 299) Contents.
7 Witkin, California Summary 10th Constitutional Law § 413, (S 413) Right of Media to Report Proceedings.

§ 1785.135. Consumer credit reports; documents acting as lien or encumbrance

No consumer credit reporting agency shall make any consumer credit report with respect to a document which acts as a lien or other encumbrance, including, but not limited to, a notice of lis pendens, but which has together with it a court order striking or releasing the lien or other encumbrance pursuant to Section 765.030 of the Code of Civil Procedure. *(Added by Stats.1998, c. 779 (S.B.1759), § 1.)*

Research References

4 Witkin, California Summary 10th Sales § 299, (S 299) Contents.

§ 1785.14. Agency procedures; record of purposes; disclosure to consumer; notice to supplier of information regarding obligations under title

(a) Every consumer credit reporting agency shall maintain reasonable procedures designed to avoid violations of Section 1785.13 and to limit furnishing of consumer credit reports to the purposes listed under Section 1785.11. These procedures shall require that prospective users of the information identify themselves, certify the purposes for which the information is sought and certify that the information will be used for no other purposes. From the effective date of this act the consumer credit reporting agency shall keep a record of the purposes as stated by the user. Every consumer credit reporting agency shall make a reasonable effort to verify the identity of a new prospective user and the uses certified by the prospective user prior to furnishing the user a consumer report. No consumer credit reporting agency may furnish a consumer credit report to any person unless the consumer credit reporting agency has reasonable grounds for believing that the consumer credit report will be used by the person for the purposes listed in Section 1785.11. A consumer credit reporting agency does not have reasonable grounds for believing that a consumer credit report will be used by the person for the purposes listed in Section 1785.11 unless all of the following requirements are met:

(1) If the prospective user is a retail seller, as defined in Section 1802.3, and intends to issue credit to a consumer who appears in person on the basis of an application for credit submitted in person, the consumer credit reporting agency shall, with a reasonable degree of certainty, match at least three categories of identifying information within the file maintained by the consumer credit reporting agency on the consumer with the information provided to the consumer credit reporting agency by the retail seller. The categories of identifying information may include, but are not limited to, first and last name, month and date of birth, driver's license number, place of employment, current residence address, previous residence address, or social security number. The categories of information shall not include mother's maiden name.

(2) If the prospective user is a retail seller, as defined in Section 1802.3, and intends to issue credit to a consumer who appears in person on the basis of an application for credit submitted in person, the retail seller certifies, in writing, to the consumer credit reporting agency that it instructs its employees and agents to inspect a photo identification of the consumer at the time the application was submitted in person. This paragraph does not apply to an application for credit submitted by mail.

(3) If the prospective user intends to extend credit by mail pursuant to a solicitation by mail, the extension of credit shall be mailed to the same address as on the solicitation unless the prospective user verifies any address change by, among other methods, contacting the person to whom the extension of credit will be mailed.

(b) Whenever a consumer credit reporting agency prepares a consumer credit report, it shall follow reasonable procedures to assure maximum possible accuracy of the information concerning the individual about whom the report relates. These reasonable procedures shall include, but not be limited to, permanent retention by the consumer credit reporting agency in the consumer's file, or a separately individualized file, of that portion of the data in the file that is used by the consumer credit reporting agency to identify the individual consumer pursuant to paragraph (1) of subdivision (a). This permanently retained data shall be available for use in either a reinvestigation pursuant to subdivision (a) of Section 1785.16, an investigation where the consumer has filed a police report pursuant to subdivision (k) of Section 1785.16, or a restoration of a file involving the consumer. If the permanently retained identifying information is retained in a consumer's file, it shall be clearly identified in the file in order for an individual who reviews the file to easily distinguish between the permanently stored identifying information and any other identifying information that may be a part of the file. This retention requirement shall not apply to data that is reported in error, that is obsolete, or that is found to be inaccurate through the results of a reinvestigation initiated by a consumer pursuant to subdivision (a) of Section 1785.16.

(c) No consumer credit reporting agency may prohibit any user of any consumer credit report furnished by the consumer credit reporting agency from disclosing the contents of the consumer credit report to the consumer who is the subject of the report if adverse action may be taken by the user based in whole or in part on the consumer credit report. The act of disclosure to the consumer by the user of the contents of a consumer credit report shall not be a basis for liability of the consumer credit reporting agency or the user under Section 1785.31.

(d) A consumer credit reporting agency shall provide a written notice to any person who regularly and in the ordinary course of business supplies information to the consumer credit reporting agency concerning any consumer or to whom a consumer credit report is provided by the consumer credit reporting agency. The notice shall specify the person's obligations under this title. Copies of the appropriate code sections shall satisfy the requirement of this subdivision. *(Added by Stats.1975, c. 1271, p. 3372, § 1. Amended by Stats.1992, c. 1194 (A.B.1629), § 5, operative July 1, 1993; Stats.1993, c. 285 (A.B.1340), § 6, eff. Aug. 2, 1993; Stats.1997, c. 768 (A.B.156), § 1, operative July 1, 1998.)*

Research References

4 Witkin, California Summary 10th Sales § 299, (S 299) Contents.

§ 1785.15. Supplying files and information; right to information

(a) A consumer credit reporting agency shall supply files and information required under Section 1785.10 during normal business hours and on reasonable notice. In addition to the disclosure provided by this chapter and any disclosures received by the consumer, the consumer has the right to request and receive all of the following:

(1) Either a decoded written version of the file or a written copy of the file, including all information in the file at the time of the request, with an explanation of any code used.

(2) A credit score for the consumer, the key factors, and the related information, as defined in and required by Section 1785.15.1.

(3) A record of all inquiries, by recipient, that result in the provision of information concerning the consumer in connection with a credit transaction not initiated by the consumer and that were received by the consumer credit reporting agency in the 12–month period immediately preceding the request for disclosure under this section.

(4) The recipients, including end users specified in Section 1785.22, of any consumer credit report on the consumer which the consumer credit reporting agency has furnished:

(A) For employment purposes within the two-year period preceding the request.

(B) For any other purpose within the 12–month period preceding the request.

Identification for purposes of this paragraph shall include the name of the recipient or, if applicable, the fictitious business name under which the recipient does business disclosed in full. If requested by the consumer, the identification shall also include the address of the recipient.

(b) Files maintained on a consumer shall be disclosed promptly as follows:

(1) In person, at the location where the consumer credit reporting agency maintains the trained personnel required by subdivision (d), if he or she appears in person and furnishes proper identification.

(2) By mail, if the consumer makes a written request with proper identification for a copy of the file or a decoded written version of that file to be sent to the consumer at a specified address. A disclosure pursuant to this paragraph shall be deposited in the United States mail, postage prepaid, within five business days after the consumer's written request for the disclosure is received by the consumer credit reporting agency. Consumer credit reporting agencies complying with requests for mailings under this section shall not be liable for disclosures to third parties caused by mishandling of mail after the mailings leave the consumer credit reporting agencies.

(3) A summary of all information contained in files on a consumer and required to be provided by Section 1785.10 shall be provided by telephone, if the consumer has made a written request, with proper identification for telephone disclosure.

(4) Information in a consumer's file required to be provided in writing under this section may also be disclosed in another form if authorized by the consumer and if available from the consumer credit reporting agency. For this purpose, a consumer may request disclosure in person pursuant to Section 1785.10, by telephone upon disclosure of proper identification by the consumer, by electronic means if available from the consumer credit reporting agency, or by any other reasonable means that is available from the consumer credit reporting agency.

(c) "Proper identification," as used in subdivision (b) means that information generally deemed sufficient to identify a person. Only if the consumer is unable to reasonably identify himself or herself with the information described above may a consumer credit reporting agency require additional information concerning the consumer's employment and personal or family history in order to verify his or her identity.

(d) The consumer credit reporting agency shall provide trained personnel to explain to the consumer any information furnished him or her pursuant to Section 1785.10.

(e) The consumer shall be permitted to be accompanied by one other person of his or her choosing, who shall furnish reasonable identification. A consumer credit reporting agency may require the consumer to furnish a written statement granting permission to the consumer credit reporting agency to discuss the consumer's file in that person's presence.

(f) Any written disclosure by a consumer credit reporting agency to any consumer pursuant to this section shall include a written summary of all rights the consumer has under this title and, in the case of a consumer credit reporting agency that compiles and maintains consumer credit reports on a nationwide basis, a toll-free telephone number that the consumer can use to communicate with the consumer credit reporting agency. The written summary of rights required under this subdivision is sufficient if in substantially the following form:

"You have a right to obtain a copy of your credit file from a consumer credit reporting agency. You may be charged a reasonable fee not exceeding eight dollars ($8). There is no fee, however, if you have been turned down for credit, employment, insurance, or a rental dwelling because of information in your credit report within the preceding 60 days. The consumer credit reporting agency must provide someone to help you interpret the information in your credit file.

You have a right to dispute inaccurate information by contacting the consumer credit reporting agency directly. However, neither you nor any credit repair company or credit service organization has the right to have accurate, current, and verifiable information removed from your credit report. Under the Federal Fair Credit Reporting Act, the consumer credit reporting agency must remove accurate, negative information from your report only if it is over seven years old. Bankruptcy information can be reported for 10 years.

If you have notified a consumer credit reporting agency in writing that you dispute the accuracy of information in your file, the consumer credit reporting agency must then, within 30 business days, reinvestigate and modify or remove inaccurate information. The consumer credit reporting agency may not charge a fee for this service. Any pertinent information and copies of all documents you have concerning an error should be given to the consumer credit reporting agency.

If reinvestigation does not resolve the dispute to your satisfaction, you may send a brief statement to the consumer credit reporting agency to keep in your file, explaining why you think the record is inaccurate. The consumer credit reporting agency must include your statement about disputed information in a report it issues about you.

You have a right to receive a record of all inquiries relating to a credit transaction initiated in 12 months preceding your request. This record shall include the recipients of any consumer credit report.

You may request in writing that the information contained in your file not be provided to a third party for marketing purposes.

You have a right to place a "security alert" in your credit report, which will warn anyone who receives information in your credit report that your identity may have been used without your consent. Recipients of your credit report are required to take reasonable steps, including contacting you at the telephone number you may provide with your security alert, to verify your identity prior to lending money, extending credit, or completing the purchase, lease, or rental of goods or services. The security alert may prevent credit, loans, and services from being approved in your name without your consent. However, you should be aware that taking advantage of this right may delay or interfere with the timely approval of any subsequent request or application you make regarding a new loan, credit, mortgage, or cellular phone or other new account, including an extension of credit at point of sale. If you place a security alert on your credit report, you have a right to obtain a free copy of your credit report at the time the 90–day security alert period expires. A security alert may be requested by calling the following toll-free telephone number: (Insert applicable toll-free telephone number). California consumers also have the right to obtain a "security freeze."

You have a right to place a "security freeze" on your credit report, which will prohibit a consumer credit reporting agency from releasing any information in your credit report without your express authorization. A security freeze must be requested in writing by mail. The security freeze is designed to prevent credit, loans, and services from being approved in your name without your consent. However, you should be aware that using a security freeze to take control over who gets access to the personal and financial information in your credit report may delay, interfere with, or prohibit the timely approval of any subsequent request or application you make regarding a new loan, credit, mortgage, or cellular phone or other new account, including an extension of credit at point of sale. When you

place a security freeze on your credit report, you will be provided a personal identification number or password to use if you choose to remove the freeze on your credit report or authorize the release of your credit report for a specific party or period of time after the freeze is in place. To provide that authorization you must contact the consumer credit reporting agency and provide all of the following:

(1) The personal identification number or password.

(2) Proper identification to verify your identity.

(3) The proper information regarding the third party who is to receive the credit report or the period of time for which the report shall be available to users of the credit report.

A consumer credit reporting agency must authorize the release of your credit report no later than three business days after receiving the above information.

A security freeze does not apply when you have an existing account and a copy of your report is requested by your existing creditor or its agents or affiliates for certain types of account review, collection, fraud control, or similar activities.

If you are actively seeking credit, you should understand that the procedures involved in lifting a security freeze may slow your application for credit. You should plan ahead and lift a freeze, either completely if you are shopping around, or specifically for a certain creditor, before applying for new credit.

A consumer credit reporting agency may not charge a fee to a consumer for placing or removing a security freeze if the consumer is a victim of identity theft and submits a copy of a valid police report or valid Department of Motor Vehicles investigative report. A person 65 years of age or older with proper identification shall not be charged a fee for placing an initial security freeze, but may be charged a fee of no more than five dollars ($5) for lifting, removing, or replacing a security freeze. All other consumers may be charged a fee of no more than ten dollars ($10) for each of these steps.

You have a right to bring civil action against anyone, including a consumer credit reporting agency, who improperly obtains access to a file, knowingly or willfully misuses file data, or fails to correct inaccurate file data.

If you are a victim of identity theft and provide to a consumer credit reporting agency a copy of a valid police report or a valid investigative report made by a Department of Motor Vehicles investigator with peace officer status describing your circumstances, the following shall apply:

(1) You have a right to have any information you list on the report as allegedly fraudulent promptly blocked so that the information cannot be reported. The information will be unblocked only if (A) the information you provide is a material misrepresentation of the facts, (B) you agree that the information is blocked in error, or (C) you knowingly obtained possession of goods, services, or moneys as a result of the blocked transactions. If blocked information is unblocked, you will be promptly notified.

(2) You have a right to receive, free of charge and upon request, one copy of your credit report each month for up to 12 consecutive months." *(Added by Stats.1975, c. 1271, p. 3373, § 1. Amended by Stats.1976, c. 666, p. 1639, § 3; Stats.1980, c. 1113, p. 3580, § 2; Stats.1992, c. 1194 (A.B.1629), § 6, operative July 1, 1993; Stats.2000, c. 978 (S.B.1607), § 2, operative July 1, 2001; Stats.2001, c. 720 (S.B.168), § 6; Stats.2002, c. 860 (S.B.1239), § 1; Stats.2003, c. 907 (S.B.25), § 3; Stats.2008, c. 151 (A.B.372), § 2; Stats.2012, c. 645 (A.B.2374), § 2.)*

Research References

4 Witkin, California Summary 10th Sales § 298, Disclosure of Information.

5 Witkin, California Summary 10th Torts § 597, (S 597) Credit Report.

§ 1785.15.1. Credit scores supplied upon request by consumer; key factors

(a) Upon the consumer's request for a credit score, a consumer credit reporting agency shall supply to a consumer a notice which shall include the information described in paragraphs (1) to (5), inclusive, and a statement indicating that the information and credit scoring model may be different than the credit score that may be used by the lender. However, if the consumer requests the credit file and not the credit score, then the consumer shall receive the credit file and a statement that he or she may request and obtain a credit score.

(1) The consumer's current credit score or the consumer's most recent credit score that was previously calculated by the credit reporting agency for a purpose related to the extension of credit.

(2) The range of possible credit scores under the model used.

(3) All the key factors that adversely affected the consumer's credit score in the model used, the total number of which shall not exceed four.

(4) The date the credit score was created.

(5) The name of the person or entity that provided the credit score or credit file upon which the credit score was created.

(b) For purposes of this act, "credit score" means a numerical value or a categorization derived from a statistical tool or modeling system used by a person who makes or arranges a loan to predict the likelihood of certain credit behaviors, including default. The numerical value or the categorization derived from this analysis may also be referred to as a "risk predictor" or "risk score." "Credit score" does not include any mortgage score or rating of an automated underwriting system that considers one or more factors in addition to credit information, including, but not limited to, the loan to value ratio, the amount of down payment, or a consumer's financial assets. "Credit score" does not include other elements of the underwriting process or underwriting decision.

(c) For the purposes of this section, "key factors" means all relevant elements or reasons adversely affecting the credit score for the particular individual listed in the order of their importance based on their effect on the credit score.

(d) The information required by this section shall be provided in the same timeframe and manner as the information described in Section 1785.15.

(e) This section shall not be construed to compel a consumer reporting agency to develop or disclose a score if the agency does not (1) distribute scores that are used in connection with residential real property loans, or (2) develop scores that assist credit providers in understanding a consumer's general credit behavior and predicting his or her future credit behavior.

(f) This section shall not be construed to require a consumer credit reporting agency that distributes credit scores developed by another person or entity to provide a further explanation of them, or to process a dispute arising pursuant to subdivision (a) of Section 1785.16, except that the consumer credit reporting agency shall provide the consumer with the name and address and website for contacting the person or entity who developed the score or developed the methodology of the score. This subdivision does not apply to a consumer credit reporting agency that develops or modifies scores that are developed by another person or entity.

(g) This section shall not be construed to require a consumer reporting agency to maintain credit scores in its files. *(Added by Stats.2000, c. 978 (S.B.1607), § 3, operative July 1, 2001.)*

Research References

4 Witkin, California Summary 10th Sales § 298, Disclosure of Information.

§ 1785.15.2. Credit scoring model

(a) In complying with Section 1785.15.1, a consumer credit reporting agency shall supply the consumer with a credit score that is derived from a credit scoring model that is widely distributed to users by that consumer credit reporting agency in connection with residential real property loans or with a credit score that assists the consumer in understanding the credit scoring assessment of his or her credit behavior and predictions about his or her future credit behavior, and a statement indicating that the information and credit scoring model may be different than that used by the lender.

(b) A consumer credit reporting agency may charge a reasonable fee for providing the information required under Section 1785.15.1. *(Added by Stats.2000, c. 978 (S.B.1607), § 4, operative July 1, 2001.)*

§ 1785.15.3. Statement of rights; monthly credit reports

(a) In addition to any other rights the consumer may have under this title, every consumer credit reporting agency, after being contacted by telephone, mail, or in person by any consumer who has reason to believe he or she may be a victim of identity theft, shall promptly provide to that consumer a statement, written in a clear and conspicuous manner, describing the statutory rights of victims of identity theft under this title.

(b) Every consumer credit reporting agency shall, upon the receipt from a victim of identity theft of a police report prepared pursuant to Section 530. 6 of the Penal Code, or a valid investigative report made by a Department of Motor Vehicles investigator with peace officer status regarding the public offenses described in Section 530.5 of the Penal Code, provide the victim, free of charge and upon request, with up to 12 copies of his or her file during a consecutive 12–month period, not to exceed one copy per month, following the date of the police report. Notwithstanding any other provision of this title, the maximum number of free reports a victim of identity theft is entitled to obtain under this title is 12 per year, as provided by this subdivision.

(c) Subdivision (a) does not apply to a consumer reporting agency that acts only as a reseller of credit information by assembling and merging information contained in the database of another consumer reporting agency or agencies and that does not maintain a permanent database of credit information from which new credit reports are produced.

(d) The provisions of this section shall become effective July 1, 2003. *(Added by Stats.2002, c. 860 (S.B.1239), § 2, operative July 1, 2003.)*

Research References

4 Witkin, California Summary 10th Sales § 298, Disclosure of Information.

§ 1785.16. Disputes as to completeness or accuracy of information in file; reinvestigation and recording of current status; notice of results; deletion and reinsertion of information; statement of dispute; agency procedures; block of information appearing as a result of Penal Code § 530.5; unblocking information

(a) If the completeness or accuracy of any item of information contained in his or her file is disputed by a consumer, and the dispute is conveyed directly to the consumer credit reporting agency by the consumer or user on behalf of the consumer, the consumer credit reporting agency shall within a reasonable period of time and without charge, reinvestigate and record the current status of the disputed information before the end of the 30–business–day period beginning on the date the agency receives notice of the dispute from the consumer or user, unless the consumer credit reporting agency has reasonable grounds to believe and determines that the dispute by the consumer is frivolous or irrelevant, including by reason of a failure of the consumer to provide sufficient information, as requested by the consumer credit reporting agency, to investigate the dispute. Unless the consumer credit reporting agency determines that the dispute is frivolous or irrelevant, before the end of the five-business-day period beginning on the date the consumer credit reporting agency receives notice of dispute under this section, the agency shall notify any person who provided information in dispute at the address and in the manner specified by the person. A consumer credit reporting agency may require that disputes by consumers be in writing.

(b) In conducting that reinvestigation the consumer credit reporting agency shall review and consider all relevant information submitted by the consumer with respect to the disputed item of information. If the consumer credit reporting agency determines that the dispute is frivolous or irrelevant, it shall notify the consumer by mail or, if authorized by the consumer for that purpose, by any other means available to the consumer credit reporting agency, within five business days after that determination is made that it is terminating its reinvestigation of the item of information. In this notification, the consumer credit reporting agency shall state the specific reasons why it has determined that the consumer's dispute is frivolous or irrelevant. If the disputed item of information is found to be inaccurate, missing, or can no longer be verified by the evidence submitted, the consumer credit reporting agency shall promptly add, correct, or delete that information from the consumer's file.

(c) No information may be reinserted in a consumer's file after having been deleted pursuant to this section unless the person who furnished the information certifies that the information is accurate. If any information deleted from a consumer's file is reinserted in the file, the consumer credit reporting agency shall promptly notify the consumer of the reinsertion in writing or, if authorized by the consumer for that purpose, by any other means available to the consumer credit reporting agency. As part of, or in addition to, this notice the consumer credit reporting agency shall, within five business days of reinserting the information, provide the consumer in writing (1) a statement that the disputed information has been reinserted, (2) a notice that the agency will provide to the consumer, within 15 days following a request, the name, address, and telephone number of any furnisher of information contacted or which contacted the consumer credit reporting agency in connection with the reinsertion, (3) the toll-free telephone number of the consumer credit reporting agency that the consumer can use to obtain this name, address, and telephone number, and (4) a notice that the consumer has the right to a reinvestigation of the information reinserted by the consumer credit reporting agency and to add a statement to his or her file disputing the accuracy or completeness of the information.

(d) A consumer credit reporting agency shall provide written notice to the consumer of the results of any reinvestigation under this subdivision, within five days of completion of the reinvestigation. The notice shall include (1) a statement that the reinvestigation is completed, (2) a consumer credit report that is based on the consumer's file as that file is revised as a result of the reinvestigation, (3) a description or indication of any changes made in the consumer credit report as a result of those revisions to the consumer's file and a description of any changes made or sought by the consumer that were not made and an explanation why they were not made, (4) a notice that, if requested by the consumer, a description of the procedure used to determine the accuracy and completeness of the information shall be provided

to the consumer by the consumer credit reporting agency, including the name, business address, and telephone number of any furnisher of information contacted in connection with that information, (5) a notice that the consumer has the right to add a statement to the consumer's file disputing the accuracy or completeness of the information, (6) a notice that the consumer has the right to request that the consumer credit reporting agency furnish notifications under subdivision (h), (7) a notice that the dispute will remain on file with the agency as long as the credit information is used, and (8) a statement about the details of the dispute will be furnished to any recipient as long as the credit information is retained in the agency's data base. A consumer credit reporting agency shall provide the notice pursuant to this subdivision respecting the procedure used to determine the accuracy and completeness of information, not later than 15 days after receiving a request from the consumer.

(e) The presence of information in the consumer's file that contradicts the contention of the consumer shall not, in and of itself, constitute reasonable grounds for believing the dispute is frivolous or irrelevant.

(f) If the consumer credit reporting agency determines that the dispute is frivolous or irrelevant, or if the reinvestigation does not resolve the dispute, or if the information is reinserted into the consumer's file pursuant to subdivision (c), the consumer may file a brief statement setting forth the nature of the dispute. The consumer credit reporting agency may limit these statements to not more than 100 words if it provides the consumer with assistance in writing a clear summary of the dispute.

(g) Whenever a statement of dispute is filed, the consumer credit reporting agency shall, in any subsequent consumer credit report containing the information in question, clearly note that the information is disputed by the consumer and shall include in the report either the consumer's statement or a clear and accurate summary thereof.

(h) Following the deletion of information from a consumer's file pursuant to this section, or following the filing of a statement of dispute pursuant to subdivision (f), the consumer credit reporting agency, at the request of the consumer, shall furnish notification that the item of information has been deleted or that the item of information is disputed. In the case of disputed information, the notification shall include the statement or summary of the dispute filed pursuant to subdivision (f). This notification shall be furnished to any person designated by the consumer who has, within two years prior to the deletion or the filing of the dispute, received a consumer credit report concerning the consumer for employment purposes, or who has, within 12 months of the deletion or the filing of the dispute, received a consumer credit report concerning the consumer for any other purpose, if these consumer credit reports contained the deleted or disputed information. The consumer credit reporting agency shall clearly and conspicuously disclose to the consumer his or her rights to make a request for this notification. The disclosure shall be made at or prior to the time the information is deleted pursuant to this section or the consumer's statement regarding the disputed information is received pursuant to subdivision (f).

(i) A consumer credit reporting agency shall maintain reasonable procedures to prevent the reappearance in a consumer's file and in consumer credit reports of information that has been deleted pursuant to this section and not reinserted pursuant to subdivision (c).

(j) If the consumer's dispute is resolved by deletion of the disputed information within three business days, beginning with the day the consumer credit reporting agency receives notice of the dispute in accordance with subdivision (a), and provided that verification thereof is provided to the consumer in writing within five business days following the deletion, then the consumer credit reporting agency shall be exempt from requirements for further action under subdivisions (d), (f), and (g).

(k) If a consumer submits to a credit reporting agency a copy of a valid police report, or a valid investigative report made by a Department of Motor Vehicles investigator with peace officer status, filed pursuant to Section 530.5 of the Penal Code, the consumer credit reporting agency shall promptly and permanently block reporting any information that the consumer alleges appears on his or her credit report as a result of a violation of Section 530.5 of the Penal Code so that the information cannot be reported. The consumer credit reporting agency shall promptly notify the furnisher of the information that the information has been so blocked. Furnishers of information and consumer credit reporting agencies shall ensure that information is unblocked only upon a preponderance of the evidence establishing the facts required under paragraph (1), (2), or (3). The permanently blocked information shall be unblocked only if: (1) the information was blocked due to a material misrepresentation of fact by the consumer or fraud, or (2) the consumer agrees that the blocked information, or portions of the blocked information, were blocked in error, or (3) the consumer knowingly obtained possession of goods, services, or moneys as a result of the blocked transaction or transactions or the consumer should have known that he or she obtained possession of goods, services, or moneys as a result of the blocked transaction or transactions. If blocked information is unblocked pursuant to this subdivision, the consumer shall be promptly notified in the same manner as consumers are notified of the reinsertion of information pursuant to subdivision (c). The prior presence of the blocked information in the consumer credit reporting agency's file on the consumer is not evidence of whether the consumer knew or should have known that he or she obtained possession of any goods, services, or moneys. For the purposes of this subdivision, fraud may be demonstrated by circumstantial evidence. In unblocking information pursuant to this subdivision, furnishers and consumer credit reporting agencies shall be subject to their respective requirements pursuant to this title regarding the completeness and accuracy of information.

(*l*) In unblocking information as described in subdivision (k), a consumer reporting agency shall comply with all requirements of this section and 15 U. S.C. Sec. 1681i relating to reinvestigating disputed information. In addition, a consumer reporting agency shall accept the consumer's version of the disputed information and correct or delete the disputed item when the consumer submits to the consumer reporting agency documentation obtained from the source of the item in dispute or from public records confirming that the report was inaccurate or incomplete, unless the consumer reporting agency, in the exercise of good faith and reasonable judgment, has substantial reason based on specific, verifiable facts to doubt the authenticity of the documentation submitted and notifies the consumer in writing of that decision, explaining its reasons for unblocking the information and setting forth the specific, verifiable facts on which the decision was based.

(m) Any provision in a contract that prohibits the disclosure of a credit score by a person who makes or arranges loans or a consumer credit reporting agency is void. A lender shall not have liability under any contractual provision for disclosure of a credit score. *(Added by Stats.1975, c. 1271, p. 3373, § 1. Amended by Stats.1976, c. 666, p. 1640, § 4; Stats.1980, c. 1113, p. 3581, § 3; Stats.1990, c. 1315 (S.B.2750), § 1; Stats.1992, c. 1194 (A.B.1629), § 7, operative July 1, 1993; Stats.1993, c. 285 (A.B.1340), § 7, eff. Aug. 2, 1993; Stats.1997, c. 768 (A.B.156), § 2, operative July 1, 1998; Stats.2000, c. 978 (S.B.1607), § 5, operative July 1, 2001; Stats.2001, c. 354 (A.B.655), § 3.)*

Research References

4 Witkin, California Summary 10th Sales § 300, (S 300) Correction of Inaccuracies.

4 Witkin, California Summary 10th Sales § 303, Consumer's Remedies.

§ 1785.16.1. Deletion of inquiries for credit reports from consumer credit report with respect to identity theft

A consumer credit reporting agency shall delete from a consumer credit report inquiries for credit reports based upon credit requests that the consumer credit reporting agency verifies were initiated as the result of identity theft, as defined in Section 1798.92. *(Added by Stats.2001, c. 354 (A.B.655), § 4.)*

§ 1785.16.2. Sale of consumer debt to debt collector; identity theft; subsidiaries or affiliates; interstate commerce requirement

(a) No creditor may sell a consumer debt to a debt collector, as defined in 15 U.S.C. Sec. 1692a, if the consumer is a victim of identity theft, as defined in Section 1798.2, and with respect to that debt, the creditor has received notice pursuant to subdivision (k) of Section 1785.16.

(b) Subdivision (a) does not apply to a creditor's sale of a debt to a subsidiary or affiliate of the creditor, if, with respect to that debt, the subsidiary or affiliate does not take any action to collect the debt.

(c) For the purposes of this section, the requirement in 15 U.S.C. Sec. 1692a, that a person must use an instrumentality of interstate commerce or the mails in the collection of any debt to be considered a debt collector, does not apply. *(Added by Stats.2001, c. 354 (A.B.655), § 4.5. Amended by Stats.2002, c. 1030 (A.B.1068), § 1, eff. Sept. 28, 2002.)*

§ 1785.16.3. Consumer reporting agencies acting as resellers of credit information

The provisions of subdivisions (k) and (*l*) of Section 1785.16 do not apply to a consumer reporting agency that acts only as a reseller of credit information by assembling and merging information contained in the database of another consumer reporting agency or agencies, and that does not maintain a permanent database of credit information from which new credit reports are produced. *(Added by Stats.2002, c. 1029 (A.B.2868), § 2, eff. Sept. 28, 2002.)*

§ 1785.17. Charges to consumer; exceptions

(a) Except as otherwise provided, a consumer credit reporting agency may impose a reasonable charge upon a consumer, as follows:

(1) For making a disclosure pursuant to Section 1785.10 or 1785.15, the consumer credit reporting agency may charge a fee not exceeding eight dollars ($8).

(2) For furnishing a notification, statement, or summary, to any person pursuant to subdivision (h) of Section 1785.16, the consumer credit reporting agency may charge a fee not exceeding the charge that it would impose on each designated recipient for a consumer credit report, and the amount of the charge shall be indicated to the consumer before furnishing the notification, statement, or summary.

(b) A consumer credit reporting agency shall make all disclosures pursuant to Sections 1785.10 and 1785.15 and furnish all consumer reports pursuant to Section 1785.16 without charge, if requested by the consumer within 60 days after receipt by the consumer of a notification of adverse action pursuant to Section 1785.20 or of a notification from a debt collection agency affiliated with the consumer credit reporting agency stating that the consumer's credit rating may be or has been adversely affected.

(c) A consumer credit reporting agency shall not impose any charge for (1) providing notice to a consumer required under Section 1785.16 or (2) notifying a person pursuant to subdivision (h) of Section 1785.16 of the deletion of any information which is found to be inaccurate or which can no longer be verified, if the consumer designates that person to the consumer credit reporting agency before the end of the 30-day period beginning on that date of notice under subdivision (d) of Section 1785.16. *(Added by Stats.1975, c. 1271, p. 3374, § 1. Amended by Stats.1976, c. 666, p. 1641, § 5; Stats.1980, c. 1113, p. 3582, § 4; Stats.1992, c. 651 (A.B.2999), § 1; Stats.1992, c. 1194 (A.B.1629), § 8, operative July 1, 1993.)*

Research References

4 Witkin, California Summary 10th Sales § 298, Disclosure of Information.

§ 1785.18. Matters of public record; source; reports for employment purposes; prohibited information

(a) Each consumer credit reporting agency which compiles and reports items of information concerning consumers which are matters of public record, shall specify in any report containing public record information the source from which that information was obtained, including the particular court, if there be such, and the date that the information was initially reported or publicized.

(b) A consumer credit reporting agency which furnishes a consumer credit report for employment purposes, and which for that purpose compiles and reports items of information on consumers which are matters of public record and are likely to have an adverse effect upon a consumer's ability to obtain employment shall, in addition, maintain strict procedures designed to ensure that whenever public record information which is likely to have an adverse effect on a consumer's ability to obtain employment is reported it is complete and up to date. For purposes of this paragraph, items of public record relating to arrests, indictments, convictions, suits, tax liens, and outstanding judgments shall be considered up to date if the current public record status of the item at the time of the report is reported.

(c) No consumer credit reporting agency which furnishes a consumer credit report for employment purposes shall report information on the age, marital status, race, color, or creed of any consumer. *(Added by Stats.1975, c. 1271, p. 3375, § 1. Amended by Stats.1991, c. 971 (A.B.1102), § 1.)*

Research References

4 Witkin, California Summary 10th Sales § 299, (S 299) Contents.

§ 1785.19. Civil penalties; improperly obtaining or misusing file data; costs; attorney fees

(a) In addition to any other remedy provided by law, a consumer may bring an action for a civil penalty, not to exceed two thousand five hundred dollars ($2,500), against any of the following:

(1) A person who knowingly and willfully obtains access to a file other than as provided in Section 1785.11.

(2) Any person who knowingly and willfully obtains data from a file other than as provided in Section 1785.11.

(3) A person who uses the data received from a file in a manner contrary to an agreement with the consumer credit reporting agency.

Such an action may also be brought by the person or entity responsible for the file accessed. This remedy is in addition to any other remedy which may exist.

(b) If a plaintiff prevails in an action under subdivision (a) he or she shall be awarded the civil penalty, costs, and reasonable attorney fees. *(Added by Stats.1990, c. 842 (A.B.2908), § 2.)*

Research References

4 Witkin, California Summary 10th Sales § 298, Disclosure of Information.
4 Witkin, California Summary 10th Sales § 303, Consumer's Remedies.

§ 1785.19.5. Procedures to prevent report or file data from being provided for marketing purposes or offers of credit

Every consumer credit reporting agency, upon written request and the furnishing of sufficient identification to identify the consumer and the subject file, shall create reasonable procedures to prevent a consumer credit report or information from a consumer's file from being provided to any third party for marketing purposes or for any offer of credit not requested by the consumer. This section does not apply to the use of information by a credit grantor for purposes related to an existing credit relationship. *(Added by Stats.1990, c. 842 (A.B. 2908), § 3.)*

Research References

4 Witkin, California Summary 10th Sales § 298, Disclosure of Information.
4 Witkin, California Summary 10th Sales § 302, (S 302) Prohibitions as to Marketing and Resale.

CHAPTER 3. REQUIREMENTS ON USERS OF CONSUMER CREDIT REPORTS

Section

1785.20. Adverse action based on consumer credit report information; notice and disclosure to consumer; denial of credit or insurance or increase in charge because of information from one other than agency; liability.

1785.20.1. Credit transactions not initiated by consumer; solicitation to consumer; required statement; prequalifying reports; consumer's consent.

1785.20.2. Loans to consumers; use of consumer credit score; information to be provided to consumer; notice and form.

1785.20.3. Consumer credit reports with approval of credit based on application for credit extension; consumer address error with respect to identity theft; verification safeguard; violations.

1785.20.5. Report for employment purposes; prior notice to person involved; contemporaneous copies for user and subject; denial of employment; identity of reporter; notice by user to consumer; liability.

1785.21. Contact of reporter by user at request of consumer; investigation of disputed item of information; report by reporter to user and consumer.

1785.22. Reselling report or information; disclosure to agency; requirements.

§ 1785.20. Adverse action based on consumer credit report information; notice and disclosure to consumer; denial of credit or insurance or increase in charge because of information from one other than agency; liability

(a) If any person takes any adverse action with respect to any consumer, and the adverse action is based, in whole or in part, on any information contained in a consumer credit report, that person shall do all of the following:

(1) Provide written notice of the adverse action to the consumer.

(2) Provide the consumer with the name, address, and telephone number of the consumer credit reporting agency which furnished the report to the person.

(3) Provide a statement that the credit grantor's decision to take adverse action was based in whole or in part upon information contained in a consumer credit report.

(4) Provide the consumer with a written notice of the following rights of the consumer:

(A) The right of the consumer to obtain within 60 days a free copy of the consumer's consumer credit report from the consumer credit reporting agency identified pursuant to paragraph (2) and from any other consumer credit reporting agency which compiles and maintains files on consumers on a nationwide basis.

(B) The right of the consumer under Section 1785.16 to dispute the accuracy or completeness of any information in a consumer credit report furnished by the consumer credit reporting agency.

(b) Whenever credit or insurance for personal, family, or household purposes involving a consumer is denied or the charge for such credit is increased either wholly or in part because of information obtained from a person other than a consumer credit reporting agency bearing upon consumer's credit worthiness or credit standing, the user of that information shall, within a reasonable period of time, and upon the consumer's written request for the reasons for that adverse action received within 60 days after learning of the adverse action, disclose the nature and substance of the information to the consumer. The user of the information shall clearly and accurately disclose to the consumer his or her right to make such a written request at the time the adverse action is communicated to the consumer.

(c) No person shall be held liable for any violation of this section if he or she shows by a preponderance of the evidence that at the time of the alleged violation he or she maintained reasonable procedures to assure compliance with this section.

(d) Nothing in this chapter shall excuse compliance with the requirements of Section 1787.2. *(Added by Stats.1975, c. 1271, p. 3375, § 1. Amended by Stats.1980, c. 1113, p. 3582, § 5; Stats.1982, c. 1127, p. 4065, § 5; Stats.1992, c. 1194 (A.B.1629), § 9, operative July 1, 1993.)*

Research References

California Practice Guide: Employment Litigation Ch. 5-K, K. Invasion of Privacy.
Miller and Starr California Real Estate § 19:9, Apartment House as a "Business".
4 Witkin, California Summary 10th Sales § 301, (S 301) Adverse Use of Report.
5 Witkin, California Summary 10th Torts § 597, (S 597) Credit Report.
3 Witkin, California Summary 10th Agency and Employment § 359, (S 359) Other Regulations.

§ 1785.20.1. Credit transactions not initiated by consumer; solicitation to consumer; required statement; prequalifying reports; consumer's consent

(a) Except as provided in subdivision (b), any person who uses a consumer credit report in connection with any credit transaction not initiated by the consumer and which consists of a firm offer of credit shall provide with any solicitation made to the consumer a clear and conspicuous statement as to all of the following:

(1) Information contained in the consumer's prequalifying report was used in connection with the transaction.

(2) The consumer received the offer of credit, because the consumer satisfied the criteria for creditworthiness under which the consumer was selected for the offer.

(3) Where applicable, the credit may not be extended if, after the consumer responds to the offer, the consumer does not meet the criteria used to select the consumer for the offer.

(4) The consumer has a right to prohibit use of information contained in the consumer's file with any consumer credit reporting agency in connection with any credit transaction that is not initiated by the consumer. The consumer may exercise this right by notifying the notification system or joint notification system established under subdivision (d) or (e) of Section 1785.11.

(b) Subdivision (a) does not apply to any person using a prequalifying report if all of the following conditions are met:

(1) The person using the prequalifying report is affiliated by common ownership or common corporate control with the person who procured the report.

(2) The person who procures the prequalifying report from the consumer credit reporting agency clearly and conspicuously discloses to the consumer to whom the report relates, before the prequalifying report is provided to the person who uses the report, that the prequalifying report might be provided to, and used by, persons affiliated in the manner specified in paragraph (1) with the person that procured the report.

(3) The consumer consents in writing to this provision and use of the prequalifying report.

(c) No person shall be denied credit on the basis of the consumer's refusal to provide consent pursuant to paragraph (3) of subdivision (b), unless that consent is necessary for the extension of credit, related to that transaction, by an affiliate. *(Added by Stats.1992, c. 1194 (A.B.1629), § 9.5, operative July 1, 1993.)*

§ 1785.20.2. Loans to consumers; use of consumer credit score; information to be provided to consumer; notice and form

Any person who makes or arranges loans and who uses a consumer credit score as defined in Section 1785.15.1 in connection with an application initiated or sought by a consumer for a closed end loan or establishment of an open end loan for a consumer purpose that is secured by one to four units of residential real property shall provide the following to the consumer as soon as reasonably practicable:

(a) A copy of the information identified in subdivision (a) of Section 1785.15.1 that was obtained from a credit reporting agency or was developed and used by the user of the information. In addition to the information provided to it by a third party that provided the credit score or scores, a lender is only required to provide the notice contained in subdivision (d).

(b) If a person who is subject to this section uses an automated underwriting system to underwrite a loan, that person may satisfy the obligation to provide a credit score by disclosing a credit score and associated key factors supplied by a consumer credit reporting agency. However, if a numerical credit score is generated by an automated underwriting system used by an enterprise, and that score is disclosed to the person, it shall be disclosed to the consumer consistent with subdivision (c). For purposes of this subdivision, the term "enterprise" shall have the meaning provided in paragraph (6) of Section 4502 of Title 12 of the United States Code.

(c) A person subject to the provisions of this section who uses a credit score other than a credit score provided by a consumer reporting agency may satisfy the obligation to provide a credit score by disclosing a credit score and associated key factors supplied by a consumer credit reporting agency.

(d) A copy of the following notice, which shall include the name, address, and telephone number of each credit bureau providing a credit score that was used:

NOTICE TO THE HOME LOAN APPLICANT

In connection with your application for a home loan, the lender must disclose to you the score that a credit bureau distributed to users and the lender used in connection with your home loan, and the key factors affecting your credit scores.

The credit score is a computer generated summary calculated at the time of the request and based on information a credit bureau or lender has on file. The scores are based on data about your credit history and payment patterns. Credit scores are important because they are used to assist the lender in determining whether you will obtain a loan. They may also be used to determine what interest rate you may be offered on the mortgage. Credit scores can change over time, depending on your conduct, how your credit history and payment patterns change, and how credit scoring technologies change.

Because the score is based on information in your credit history, it is very important that you review the credit-related information that is being furnished to make sure it is accurate. Credit records may vary from one company to another.

If you have questions about your credit score or the credit information that is furnished to you, contact the credit bureau at the address and telephone number provided with this notice, or contact the lender, if the lender developed or generated the credit score. The credit bureau plays no part in the decision to take any action on the loan application and is unable to provide you with specific reasons for the decision on a loan application.

If you have questions concerning the terms of the loan, contact the lender.

(e) This section shall not require any person to do the following:

(1) Explain the information provided pursuant to Section 1785.15.1.

(2) Disclose any information other than a credit score or key factor, as defined in Section 1785.15.1.

(3) Disclose any credit score or related information obtained by the user after a loan has closed.

(4) Provide more than one disclosure per loan transaction.

(5) Provide the disclosure required by this section when another person has made the disclosure to the consumer for that loan transaction.

(f) Any person's obligation pursuant to this section shall be limited solely to providing a copy of the information that was received from the consumer credit reporting agency. No person has liability under this section for the content of that information or for the omission of any information within the report provided by the consumer credit reporting agency.

(g) As used in this section, the term "person" does not include an "enterprise" as defined in paragraph (6) of Section 4502 of Title 12 of the United States Code. *(Added by Stats.2000, c. 978 (S.B.1607), § 6, operative July 1, 2001.)*

Research References

4 Witkin, California Summary 10th Sales § 298, Disclosure of Information.

§ 1785.20.3. Consumer credit reports with approval of credit based on application for credit extension; consumer address error with respect to identity theft; verification safeguard; violations

(a) Any person who uses a consumer credit report in connection with the approval of credit based on an application for an extension of credit, and who discovers that the consumer's first and last name, address, or social security number, on the credit application does not match, within a reasonable degree of certainty, the consumer's first and last name, address or addresses, or social security number listed, if any, on the consumer credit report, shall take reasonable steps to verify the accuracy of the consumer's first and last name, address, or social security number provided on the application to confirm that the extension of credit is not the result of identity theft, as defined in Section 1798.92.

(b) Any person who uses a consumer credit report in connection with the approval of credit based on an application for an extension of credit, and who has received notification pursuant to subdivision (k) of Section 1785.16 that the applicant has been a victim of identity theft, as defined in Section 1798.92, may not lend money or extend credit without taking reasonable steps to verify the consumer's identity and confirm that the application for an extension of credit is not the result of identity theft.

(c) Any consumer who suffers damages as a result of a violation of this section by any person may bring an action in a court of appropriate jurisdiction against that person to recover actual damages, court costs, attorney's fees, and punitive damages of not more than thirty thousand dollars ($30,000) for each violation, as the court deems proper.

(d) As used in this section, "identity theft" has the meaning given in subdivision (b) of Section 1798.92.

(e) For the purposes of this section, "extension of credit" does not include an increase in an existing open-end credit plan, as defined in Regulation Z of the Federal Reserve System (12 C.F.R. 226.2), or any change to or review of an existing credit account.

(f) If a consumer provides initial written notice to a creditor that he or she is a victim of identity theft, as defined in subdivision (d) of Section 1798.92, the creditor shall provide written notice to the consumer of his or her rights under subdivision (k) of Section 1785.16.

(g) The provisions of subdivisions (k) and (*l*) of Section 1785.16 do not apply to a consumer credit reporting agency that acts only as a reseller of credit information by assembling and merging information contained in the database of another consumer credit reporting agency or the databases of multiple consumer credit reporting agencies, and does not maintain a permanent database of credit information from which new credit reports are produced.

(h) This section does not apply if one of the addresses at issue is a United States Army or Air Force post office address or a United States Fleet post office address. *(Added by Stats.2001, c. 354 (A.B.655), § 5. Amended by Stats.2002, c. 1030 (A.B.1068), § 2, eff. Sept. 28, 2002; Stats.2003, c. 41 (A.B.1610), § 1.)*

Operative Effect

For operative effect of Stats.2002, c. 1030 (A.B.1068), with respect to subd. (f), see § 10 of that act.

Research References

4 Witkin, California Summary 10th Sales § 298, Disclosure of Information.

§ 1785.20.5. Report for employment purposes; prior notice to person involved; contemporaneous copies for user and subject; denial of employment; identity of reporter; notice by user to consumer; liability

(a) Prior to requesting a consumer credit report for employment purposes, the user of the report shall provide written notice to the person involved. The notice shall inform the person that a report will be used, and shall identify the specific basis under subdivision (a) of Section 1024.5 of the Labor Code for use of the report. The notice shall also inform the person of the source of the report, and shall contain a box that the person may check off to receive a copy of the credit report. If the consumer indicates that he or she wishes to receive a copy of the report, the user shall request that a copy be provided to the person when the user requests its copy from the credit reporting agency. The report to the user and to the subject person shall be provided contemporaneously and at no charge to the subject person.

(b) Whenever employment involving a consumer is denied either wholly or partly because of information contained in a consumer credit report from a consumer credit reporting agency, the user of the consumer credit report shall so advise the consumer against whom the adverse action has been taken and supply the name and address or addresses of the consumer credit reporting agency making the report. No person shall be held liable for any violation of this section if he or she shows by a preponderance of the evidence that, at the time of the alleged violation, he or she maintained reasonable procedures to assure compliance with this section. *(Added by Stats.1976, c. 666, p. 1643, § 7.5. Amended by Stats.1991, c. 971 (A.B.1102), § 2; Stats.2011, c. 724 (A.B.22), § 1.)*

Research References

California Practice Guide: Employment Litigation Ch. 5-K, K. Invasion of Privacy.
California Practice Guide: Employment Litigation Gen. Matls, Highlights.
4 Witkin, California Summary 10th Sales § 301, (S 301) Adverse Use of Report.

§ 1785.21. Contact of reporter by user at request of consumer; investigation of disputed item of information; report by reporter to user and consumer

(a) A user in its discretion may notify the consumer that upon request the user may contact the consumer reporting agency and request that the consumer reporting agency investigate the current status of an item or items of information contained in the consumer report if the consumer disputes the completeness or accuracy of an item or items of information as provided to the user.

(b) The consumer credit reporting agency may require identification from the user to insure the validity of the request and, in that regard, may require that the request be put in writing with proper identification.

(c) In the event that any such request is made and identification given in the form or manner demanded by the consumer credit reporting agency, such agency shall review the file of the consumer and report the current status of the disputed information to the user and the consumer by the most expeditious means possible.

(d) No user who furnishes information pursuant to this section shall be liable to any person for furnishing such information. *(Added by Stats.1976, c. 666, p. 1643, § 8.)*

Research References

4 Witkin, California Summary 10th Sales § 300, (S 300) Correction of Inaccuracies.

§ 1785.22. Reselling report or information; disclosure to agency; requirements

(a) A person may not procure a consumer credit report for the purpose of reselling the report or any information therein unless the person discloses to the consumer credit reporting agency which issues the report the identity of the ultimate end user and each permissible purpose for which the report is furnished to the end user of the consumer credit report or information therein.

(b) A person that procures a consumer credit report for the purpose of reselling the report or any information therein shall do all of the following:

(1) Establish and comply with reasonable procedures designed to ensure that the consumer credit report or information is resold by the person only for a purpose for which the report may be furnished under this title. These procedures shall include all of the following:

(A) Identification of each prospective user of the resold consumer credit report or information.

(B) Certification of each purpose for which the consumer credit report or information will be used.

(C) Certification that the consumer credit report or information will be used for no other purpose.

(2) Before reselling the consumer credit report or information, the person shall make reasonable efforts to verify the identities and certifications made under paragraph (1). *(Added by Stats.1992, c. 1194 (A.B.1629), § 10, operative July 1, 1993.)*

Research References

4 Witkin, California Summary 10th Sales § 302, (S 302) Prohibitions as to Marketing and Resale.

CHAPTER 3.5. OBLIGATIONS OF FURNISHERS OF CREDIT INFORMATION

§ 1785.25. Incomplete or inaccurate information; knowledge; notification to agency; dispute as to completeness or accuracy; notice; closing of open-end credit account; delinquent accounts; investigation of dispute; liability of furnisher

(a) A person shall not furnish information on a specific transaction or experience to any consumer credit reporting agency if the person knows or should know the information is incomplete or inaccurate.

(b) A person who (1) in the ordinary course of business regularly and on a routine basis furnishes information to one or more consumer credit reporting agencies about the person's own transactions or experiences with one or more consumers and (2) determines that information on a specific transaction or experience so provided to a consumer credit reporting agency is not complete or accurate, shall promptly notify the consumer credit reporting agency of that determination and provide to the consumer credit reporting agency any corrections to that information, or any additional information, that is necessary to make the information provided by the person to the consumer credit reporting agency complete and accurate.

(c) So long as the completeness or accuracy of any information on a specific transaction or experience furnished by any person to a consumer credit reporting agency is subject to a continuing dispute between the affected consumer and that person, the person may not furnish the information to any consumer credit reporting agency without also including a notice that the information is disputed by the consumer.

(d) A person who regularly furnishes information to a consumer credit reporting agency regarding a consumer who has an open-end credit account with that person, and which is closed by the consumer, shall notify the consumer credit reporting agency of the closure of that account by the consumer, in the information regularly furnished for the period in which the account is closed.

(e) A person who places a delinquent account for collection (internally or by referral to a third party), charges the delinquent account to profit or loss, or takes similar action, and subsequently furnishes information to a credit reporting agency regarding that action, shall include within the information furnished the approximate commencement date of the delinquency which gave rise to that action, unless that date was previously reported to the credit reporting agency. Nothing in this provision shall require that a delinquency must be reported to a credit reporting agency.

(f) Upon receiving notice of a dispute noticed pursuant to subdivision (a) of Section 1785.16 with regard to the completeness or accuracy of any information provided to a consumer credit reporting agency, the person that provided the information shall (1) complete an investigation with respect to the disputed information and report to the consumer credit reporting agency the results of that investigation before the end of the 30-business-day period beginning on the date the consumer credit reporting agency receives the notice of dispute from the consumer in accordance with subdivision (a) of Section 1785.16 and (2) review relevant information submitted to it.

(g) A person who furnishes information to a consumer credit reporting agency is liable for failure to comply with this section, unless the furnisher establishes by a preponderance of the evidence that, at the time of the failure to comply with this section, the furnisher maintained reasonable procedures to comply with those provisions. *(Added by Stats.1992, c. 1194 (A.B.1629), § 11, operative July 1, 1993. Amended by Stats.1993, c. 285 (A.B.1340), § 8, eff. Aug. 2, 1993.)*

Validity

This section is recognized as preempted by the federal Fair Credit Reporting Act, in the decision of Buraye v. Equifax, C.D.Cal.2008, 625 F.Supp.2d 894.

This section is recognized as preempted by the federal Fair Credit Reporting Act, in Howard v. Blue Ridge Bank, N.D.Cal.2005, 371 F.Supp.2d 1139.

The investigation provisions contained in subd. (f) of this section were held preempted in the decision of Carvalho v. Equifax Information Services, LLC, C.A.9 (Cal.)2010, 615 F.3d 1217, amended and superseded on denial of rehearing en banc 629 F.3d 876.

Research References

Rutter, Cal. Practice Guide: Enforcing Judgments/Debts Ch. 2-B, B. Statutory Liability and Procedures.
14 NO. 2 Miller & Starr, California Real Estate Newsalert 16, Lenders' Liability.
4 Witkin, California Summary 10th Sales § 297, Nature and Scope of Statute.
4 Witkin, California Summary 10th Sales § 298, Disclosure of Information.

§ 1785.26. Creditor; negative credit information; notification to consumer; form and service of notice; liability of creditor

(a) As used in this section:

(1) "Creditor" includes an agent or assignee of a creditor, including an agent engaged in administering or collecting the creditor's accounts.

(2) "Negative credit information" means information concerning the credit history of a consumer that, because of the consumer's past delinquencies, late or irregular payment history, insolvency, or any form of default, would reasonably be expected to affect adversely the consumer's ability to obtain or maintain credit. "Negative credit information" does not include information or credit histories arising from a nonconsumer transaction or any other credit transaction outside the scope of this title, nor does it include inquiries about a consumer's credit record.

(b) A creditor may submit negative credit information concerning a consumer to a consumer credit reporting agency, only if the creditor notifies the consumer affected. After providing this notice, a creditor may submit additional information to a credit reporting agency respecting the same transaction or extension of credit that gave rise to the original negative credit information without providing additional notice.

(c) The notice shall be in writing and shall be delivered in person or mailed first class, postage prepaid, to the party's last known address, prior to or within 30 days after the transmission of the negative credit information.

(1) The notice may be part of any notice of default, billing statement, or other correspondence, and may be included as preprinted or standard form language in any of these from the creditor to the consumer.

(2) The notice is sufficient if it is in substantially the following form:

"As required by law, you are hereby notified that a negative credit report reflecting on your credit record may be submitted to a credit reporting agency if you fail to fulfill the terms of your credit obligations."

(3) The notice may, in the creditor's discretion, be more specific than the form given in paragraph (2). The notice may include, but shall not be limited to, particular information regarding an account or information respecting the approximate date on which the creditor submitted or intends to submit a negative credit report.

(4) The giving of notice by a creditor as provided in this subdivision does not create any requirement for the creditor to actually submit negative credit information to a consumer credit reporting agency. However, this section shall not be construed to authorize the use of notice as provided in this subdivision in violation of the federal Fair Debt Collection Practices Act (15 U.S.C., Sec. 1592 et seq.).

(d) A creditor is liable for failure to provide notice pursuant to this section, unless the creditor establishes, by a preponderance of the evidence, that at the time of that failure to give notice the creditor maintained reasonable procedures to comply with this section. *(Added by Stats.1992, c. 1194 (A.B.1629), § 11, operative July 1, 1993.)*

Research References

Miller and Starr California Real Estate § 19:9, Apartment House as a "Business".
14 NO. 2 Miller & Starr, California Real Estate Newsalert 16, Lenders' Liability.
4 Witkin, California Summary 10th Sales § 298, Disclosure of Information.

CHAPTER 3.6. ESCROW AGENT RATING SERVICE

Repeal

For repeal of Chapter 3.6, see Civil Code § 1785.28.6.

§ 1785.28. Definitions; compliance with provisions applicable to consumer credit agencies

(a) For the purposes of this section, the following definitions shall apply:

(1) Escrow means any transaction in which one person, for the purpose of effecting the sale, transfer, encumbering, or leasing of real or personal property to another person, delivers any written instrument, money, evidence of title to real or personal property, or other thing of value to a third person to be held by that third person until the happening of a specified event or the performance of a prescribed condition, when it is then to be delivered by that third person to a grantee, grantor, promisee, promisor, obligee, obligor, bailee, bailor, or any agent or employee of any of the latter.

(2) An escrow agent is any of the following:

(A) A natural person who performs escrow services for an entity licensed pursuant to the Escrow Law contained in Division 6 (commencing with Section 17000) of the Financial Code.

(B) A natural person performing escrow services for a title insurer admitted pursuant to Article 3 (commencing with Section 699) of Chapter 1 of Part 2 of Division 1 of the Insurance Code or an underwritten title company licensed pursuant to Article 3.7 (commencing with Section 12389) of Chapter 1 of Part 6 of Division 2 of the Insurance Code.

(C) A natural person performing escrow services for a controlled escrow company, as defined in Section 12340.6 of the Insurance Code.

(D) A natural person licensed pursuant to Division 4 (commencing with Section 10000) of the Business and Professions Code, who performs escrow services, in accordance with Section 17006 of the Financial Code.

(3) An escrow agent rating service is a person or entity that prepares a report, for compensation or in expectation of compensation, for use by a creditor in evaluating the capacity of an escrow agent to perform escrow services in connection with an extension of credit. An escrow agent rating service does not include either of the following:

(A) A creditor or an employee of a creditor evaluating an escrow agent in connection with an extension of credit by that creditor.

(B) An entity described in paragraph (2) for which a natural person performs escrow services as an employee or an independent contractor.

(4) An escrow agent rating service shall be considered a reseller of credit information within the meaning of Section 1785.22 if it assembles and merges information contained in the database or databases maintained by a consumer credit reporting agency.

(5) "Consumer" also means escrow agent.

(b) An escrow agent rating service shall comply with and be subject to the following sections of this title applicable to a consumer credit reporting agency:

(1) Subdivision (a) of Section 1785.10.

(2) Subdivision (b) of Section 1785.10, limited to the obligation to advise a consumer of his or her right to a decoded written version of a file.

(3) Subdivision (d) of Section 1785.10.

(4) Paragraph (2) of subdivision (a) of Section 1785.11.

(5) Section 1785.13.

(6) Section 1785.14.

(7) Paragraph (1) of subdivision (a) of Section 1785.15, limited to the right to request and receive a decoded written version of the file.

(8) Section 1785.16.

(9) Section 1785.18.

(c) An escrow agent rating service that acts as a reseller of credit information as described in paragraph (4) of subdivision (a) shall comply with and be subject to Section 1785.22.

(d) An escrow agent rating service shall establish policies and procedures reasonably intended to safeguard from theft or misuse any personally identifiable information it obtains from an escrow agent.

(e) An escrow agent who suffers damages as a result of the failure of an escrow agent rating service to comply with subdivision (b), (c), or (d) may bring an action in a court of competent jurisdiction pursuant to Section 1785.31 of the Civil Code.

(f) If an escrow agent rating service is also a consumer credit reporting agency as defined in subdivision (d) of Section 1785.3, nothing in this section shall be construed to suggest that an escrow agent reporting service that is also a consumer credit reporting agency is not otherwise required to comply with other provisions of this title applicable to consumer credit reporting agencies.

(g) Nothing in this section shall be construed to authorize a person, who was not otherwise legally authorized to perform escrow services prior to the effective date of this section, to legally perform escrow services.

(h) Nothing in this section is intended to alter the provisions of Section 17420 of the Financial Code, including the legal authority of an escrow agent to compensate an escrow agent rating service for a report prepared pursuant to paragraph (3) of subdivision (a). *(Added by Stats.2013, c. 380 (A.B.1169), § 1.)*

Repeal

For repeal of Chapter 3.6, see Civil Code § 1785.28.6.

§ 1785.28.6. Duration of chapter

This chapter shall remain in effect only until January 1, 2017, and as of that date is repealed, unless a later enacted statute, that is enacted before January 1, 2017, deletes or extends that date. *(Added by Stats.2013, c. 380 (A.B.1169), § 1.)*

CHAPTER 4. REMEDIES

§ 1785.30. Consumer's written demand to correct; correction or deletion

Upon notification of the results of a consumer credit reporting agency's reinvestigation pursuant to Section 1785.16, a consumer may make a written demand on any person furnishing information to the consumer credit reporting agency to correct any information that the consumer believes to be inaccurate. The person upon whom the written demand is made shall acknowledge the demand within 30 days. The consumer may require the consumer credit reporting agency to indicate on any subsequent reports issued during the dispute that the item or items of information are in dispute. If upon investigation the information is found to be inaccurate or incorrect, the consumer may require the consumer credit reporting agency to delete or correct the item or items of information within a reasonable time. If within 90 days the consumer credit reporting agency does not receive any information from the person requested to furnish the same or any communication relative to this information from this person, the consumer credit reporting agency shall delete the information from the report. *(Added by Stats.1976, c. 666, p. 1643, § 10. Amended by Stats.1997, c. 768 (A.B.156), § 3, operative July 1, 1998; Stats.2004, c. 183 (A.B.3082), § 31.)*

Research References

4 Witkin, California Summary 10th Sales § 300, (S 300) Correction of Inaccuracies.

§ 1785.31. Actions for actual and punitive damages; remedies available; class actions; court costs and attorney fees

(a) Any consumer who suffers damages as a result of a violation of this title by any person may bring an action in a court of appropriate jurisdiction against that person to recover the following:

(1) In the case of a negligent violation, actual damages, including court costs, loss of wages, attorney's fees and, when applicable, pain and suffering.

(2) In the case of a willful violation:

(A) Actual damages as set forth in paragraph (1) above;

(B) Punitive damages of not less than one hundred dollars ($100) nor more than five thousand dollars ($5,000) for each violation as the court deems proper;

(C) Any other relief that the court deems proper.

(3) In the case of liability of a natural person for obtaining a consumer credit report under false pretenses or knowingly without a permissible purpose, an award of actual damages pursuant to paragraph (1) or subparagraph (A) of paragraph (2) shall be in an amount of not less than two thousand five hundred dollars ($2,500).

(b) Injunctive relief shall be available to any consumer aggrieved by a violation or a threatened violation of this title whether or not the consumer seeks any other remedy under this section.

(c) Notwithstanding any other provision of this section, any person who willfully violates any requirement imposed under this title may be liable for punitive damages in the case of a class action, in an amount that the court may allow. In determining the amount of award in any class action, the court shall consider among relevant factors the amount of any actual damages awarded, the frequency of the violations, the resources of the violator and the number of persons adversely affected.

(d) Except as provided in subdivision (e), the prevailing plaintiffs in any action commenced under this section shall be entitled to recover court costs and reasonable attorney's fees.

(e) If a plaintiff brings an action pursuant to this section against a debt collector, as defined in subdivision (c) of Section 1788.2, and the basis for the action is related to the collection of a debt, whether issues relating to the debt collection are raised in the same or another proceeding, the debt collector shall be entitled to recover reasonable attorney's fees upon a finding by the court that the action was not brought in good faith.

(f) If a plaintiff only seeks and obtains injunctive relief to compel compliance with this title, court costs and attorney's fees shall be awarded pursuant to Section 1021.5 of the Code of Civil Procedure.

(g) Nothing in this section is intended to affect remedies available under Section 128.5 of the Code of Civil Procedure. *(Added by Stats.1976, c. 666, p. 1644, § 12. Amended by Stats.1992, c. 1194 (A.B.1629), § 12, operative July 1, 1993; Stats.1997, c. 768 (A.B.156), § 4, operative July 1, 1998; Stats. 1999, c. 836 (A.B.758), § 1.)*

Validity

This section is recognized as preempted by the federal Fair Credit Reporting Act, in the decision of Buraye v. Equifax, C.D.Cal.2008, 625 F.Supp.2d 894.

This section is recognized as preempted by the federal Fair Credit Reporting Act, in Howard v. Blue Ridge Bank, N.D.Cal.2005, 371 F.Supp.2d 1139.

Research References

Rutter, Cal. Practice Guide: Enforcing Judgments/Debts Ch. 2-C, C. Tort Liability.
4 Witkin, California Summary 10th Sales § 303, Consumer's Remedies.

§ 1785.32. Actions for defamation, invasion of privacy or negligence; malice or wilful intent to injure

Except as provided in Section 1785.31, no consumer may bring any action or proceeding in the nature of defamation, invasion of privacy or negligence with respect to the reporting of information against any consumer reporting agency, any user of information, or any person who furnishes information to a consumer reporting agency, based on information disclosed pursuant to Section 1785.10, 1785.15 or 1785.20 of this title, except as to false information furnished with malice or willful intent to injure such consumer. *(Formerly § 1785.31, added by Stats.1975, c. 1271, p. 3377, § 1. Renumbered § 1785.32 and amended by Stats.1976, c. 666, p. 1644, § 11.)*

Research References

Rutter, Cal. Practice Guide: Enforcing Judgments/Debts Ch. 2-C, C. Tort Liability.
4 Witkin, California Summary 10th Sales § 303, Consumer's Remedies.
4 Witkin, California Summary 10th Sales § 306, (S 306) Investigative Consumer Reporting Agencies Act.
5 Witkin, California Summary 10th Torts § 597, (S 597) Credit Report.

§ 1785.33. Limitations on action; discovery of misrepresentation

An action to enforce any liability created under this chapter may be brought in any appropriate court of competent jurisdiction within two years from the date the plaintiff knew of, or should have known of, the violation of this title, but not more than seven years from the earliest date on which liability could have arisen, except that where a defendant has materially and willfully misrepresented any information required under this chapter to be disclosed to a consumer and the information so misrepresented is material to the establishment of the defendant's liability to the consumer under this chapter, the action may be brought at any time within two years after the discovery by the consumer of the misrepresentation. *(Formerly § 1785.32, added by Stats.1975, c. 1271, p. 3377, § 1. Renumbered § 1785.33 and amended by Stats.1976, c. 666, p. 1645, § 13.*

Amended by Stats.1997, c. 768 (A.B.156), § 5, operative July 1, 1998.)

§ 1785.34. Action pending under federal law; effect of federal judgment

(a) Any consumer credit reporting agency or user of information against whom an action brought pursuant to Section 1681n or 1681o of Title 15 of the United States Code is pending shall not be subject to suit for the same act or omission under Section 1785.31.

(b) The entry of a final judgment against a consumer credit reporting agency or user of information in an action brought pursuant to the provisions of Section 1681n or 1681o of Title 15 of the United States Code shall be a bar to the maintenance of any action based on the same act or omission which might be brought under this chapter. *(Formerly § 1785.33, added by Stats.1975, c. 1271, p. 3377, § 1. Renumbered § 1785.34 and amended by Stats.1976, c. 666, p. 1645, § 14.)*

§ 1785.35. Application of title

This title does not apply to any consumer credit report that by its terms is limited to disclosures from public records relating to land and land titles and does not apply to any person whose records and files are maintained for the primary purpose of reporting those portions of the public records that impart constructive notice under the law of matters relating to land and land titles. *(Formerly § 1785.34, added by Stats.1975, c. 1271, p. 3377, § 1. Renumbered § 1785.35 and amended by Stats.1976, c. 666, p. 1645, § 15. Amended by Stats.1999, c. 836 (A.B.758), § 2.)*

Research References

4 Witkin, California Summary 10th Sales § 297, Nature and Scope of Statute.

§ 1785.36. Public policy; waiver of rights

Any waiver of the provisions of this title is contrary to public policy, and is void and unenforceable. *(Added by Stats.2002, c. 815 (A.B.2331), § 8.)*

Research References

4 Witkin, California Summary 10th Sales § 297, Nature and Scope of Statute.

Title 1.61

COMMERCIAL CREDIT REPORTS

§ 1785.41. Application of Consumer Credit Reporting Agencies Act

Consumer credit reporting is subject to the regulations of the Consumer Credit Reporting Agencies Act.[1] Commercial credit reports, which differ significantly, are not subject to that act. The circumstances, business practices, and reports themselves differ sufficiently to make it impractical to include commercial credit reports under the Consumer Credit Reporting Agencies Act. *(Added by Stats.1992, c. 101 (S.B.652), § 1.)*

1 See Civil Code § 1785.1 et seq.

Research References

4 Witkin, California Summary 10th Sales § 305, (S 305) Commercial Credit Reports.

§ 1785.42. Definitions

(a) "Commercial credit report" means any report provided to a commercial enterprise for a legitimate business purpose, relating to the financial status or payment habits of a commercial enterprise which is the subject of the report. It does not include a report subject to Title 1.6 (commencing with Section 1785.1), Title 1.6A (commencing with Section 1786), or a report prepared for commercial insurance underwriting, claims, or auditing purposes.

The term does not include (1) any report containing information related to transactions or experiences between the subject and the person making the report; (2) any authorization or approval of a specific extension of credit directly or indirectly by the issuer of a credit card or similar device; or (3) any report in which a person who has been requested by a third party to make a specific extension of credit directly or indirectly to the subject conveys its decision with respect to that request.

(b) "Commercial credit reporting agency" means any person who, for monetary fees, dues, or on a cooperative nonprofit basis, provides commercial credit reports to third parties.

(c) "Subject" means the commercial enterprise about which a commercial credit report has been compiled. *(Added by Stats. 1992, c. 101 (S.B.652), § 1. Amended by Stats.1993, c. 285 (A.B.1340), § 9, eff. Aug. 2, 1993.)*

Research References

18 NO. 5 Miller & Starr, California Real Estate Newsalert 17, Landlord and Tenant.
4 Witkin, California Summary 10th Sales § 305, (S 305) Commercial Credit Reports.

§ 1785.43. Protection of identity of sources of information; copy to subject of report upon request; procedure for correction of inaccuracies

(a) Commercial credit reporting agencies may protect the identity of sources of information to be used in commercial credit reports.

(b) Upon the request of a representative of the subject of a report, the commercial credit reporting agency shall provide one printed copy of the subject's commercial credit report in a format routinely made available to third parties, at a cost no greater than the cost usually charged to third parties.

(c) In the event that the subject of a commercial credit report believes the report contains an inaccurate statement of fact, a representative of the subject of the report may, within 30 days of receipt of the report pursuant to subdivision (b), file with the commercial credit reporting agency a written summary statement of not more than 50 words identifying the particular statement of fact that is disputed, and indicating the nature of the disagreement with the statement in the report. Within 30 days of receipt of a subject's summary statement of disagreement, the commercial credit reporting agency shall either delete the disputed item of information from the report, or include in the report an indication that the subject's summary statement of disagreement will be provided upon request. *(Added by Stats.1992, c. 101 (S.B.652), § 1.)*

Research References

4 Witkin, California Summary 10th Sales § 305, (S 305) Commercial Credit Reports.

§ 1785.44. Public policy; waiver of rights

Any waiver of the provisions of this title is contrary to public policy, and is void and unenforceable. *(Added by Stats.2002, c. 815 (A.B.2331), § 9.)*

Research References

4 Witkin, California Summary 10th Sales § 305, (S 305) Commercial Credit Reports.

Title 1.6A

INVESTIGATIVE CONSUMER REPORTING AGENCIES

ARTICLE 1. GENERAL PROVISIONS

§ 1786. Legislative findings and declaration

The Legislature finds and declares as follows:

(a) Investigative consumer reporting agencies have assumed a vital role in collecting, assembling, evaluating, compiling, reporting, transmitting, transferring, or communicating information on consumers for employment and insurance purposes, and for purposes relating to the hiring of dwelling units, subpoenas and court orders, licensure, and other lawful purposes.

(b) There is a need to insure that investigative consumer reporting agencies exercise their grave responsibilities with fairness, impartiality, and a respect for the consumer's right to privacy.

(c) The crime of identity theft in this new computer era has exploded to become the fastest growing white collar crime in America.

(d) The unique nature of this crime means it can often go undetected for years without the victim being aware his identity has been misused.

(e) Because notice of identity theft is critical before the victim can take steps to stop and prosecute this crime, consumers are best protected if they are automatically given copies of any investigative consumer reports made on them.

(f) It is the purpose of this title to require that investigative consumer reporting agencies adopt reasonable procedures for meeting the needs of commerce for employment, insurance information, and information relating to the hiring of dwelling units in a manner which is fair and equitable to the consumer, with regard to the confidentiality, accuracy, relevancy, and proper utilization of the information in accordance with the requirements of this title.

(g) The Legislature hereby intends to regulate investigative consumer reporting agencies pursuant to this title in a manner which will best protect the interests of the people of the State of California. *(Added by Stats.1975, c. 1272, p. 3378, § 1. Amended by Stats.1982, c. 1127, p. 4065, § 6; Stats.2001, c. 354 (A.B.655), § 6.)*

Research References

California Practice Guide: Employment Litigation Ch. 5-K, K. Invasion of Privacy.
Miller and Starr California Real Estate § 19:217, Restrictions on Access and Reporting of Unlawful Detainer Actions.

4 Witkin, California Summary 10th Sales § 306, (S 306) Investigative Consumer Reporting Agencies Act.
5 Witkin, California Summary 10th Torts § 666, (S 666) in General.

§ 1786.1. Short title

This title may be referred to as the Investigative Consumer Reporting Agencies Act. *(Added by Stats.1975, c. 1272, p. 3378, § 1.)*

Research References

California Practice Guide: Employment Litigation Ch. 1-A, A. Background.
California Practice Guide: Employment Litigation Ch. 10-D, D. Employer Liability for Workplace Harassment.

§ 1786.2. Definitions

The following terms as used in this title have the meaning expressed in this section:

(a) The term "person" means any individual, partnership, corporation, limited liability company, trust, estate, cooperative, association, government or governmental subdivision or agency, or other entity. The term "person" as used in this title shall not be construed to require duplicative reporting by any individual, corporation, trust, estate, cooperative, association, government, or governmental subdivision or agency, or other entity involved in the same transaction.

(b) The term "consumer" means a natural individual who has made application to a person for employment purposes, for insurance for personal, family, or household purposes, or the hiring of a dwelling unit, as defined in subdivision (c) of Section 1940.

(c) The term "investigative consumer report" means a consumer report in which information on a consumer's character, general reputation, personal characteristics, or mode of living is obtained through any means. The term does not include a consumer report or other compilation of information that is limited to specific factual information relating to a consumer's credit record or manner of obtaining credit obtained directly from a creditor of the consumer or from a consumer reporting agency when that information was obtained directly from a potential or existing creditor of the consumer or from the consumer. Notwithstanding the foregoing, for transactions between investigative consumer reporting agencies and insurance institutions, agents, or insurance-support organizations subject to Article 6.6 (commencing with Section 791) of Chapter 1 of Part 2 of Division 1 of the Insurance Code, the term "investigative consumer report" shall have the meaning set forth in * * * Section 791.02 of the Insurance Code.

(d) The term "investigative consumer reporting agency" means any person who, for monetary fees or dues, engages in whole or in part in the practice of collecting, assembling, evaluating, compiling, reporting, transmitting, transferring, or communicating information concerning consumers for the purposes of furnishing investigative consumer reports to third parties, but does not include any governmental agency whose records are maintained primarily for traffic safety, law enforcement, or licensing purposes, or any licensed insurance agent, insurance broker, or solicitor, insurer, or life insurance agent.

(e) The term "file," when used in connection with information on any consumer, means all of the information on that consumer recorded and retained by an investigative consumer reporting agency regardless of how the information is stored.

(f) The term "employment purposes," when used in connection with an investigative consumer report, means a report used for the purpose of evaluating a consumer for employment, promotion, reassignment, or retention as an employee.

(g) The term "medical information" means information on a person's medical history or condition obtained directly or indirectly from a licensed physician, medical practitioner, hospital, clinic, or other medical or medically related facility. *(Added by Stats.1975, c. 1272, p. 3378, § 1. Amended by Stats.1976, c. 1150, p. 5209, § 1; Stats.1982, c. 1127, p. 4066, § 7; Stats.1994, c. 1010 (S.B.2053), § 36; Stats.1998, c. 988 (S.B.1454), § 1; Stats. 2001, c. 354 (A.B.655), § 7; Stats.2013, c. 444 (S.B.138), § 6.)*

Research References

California Practice Guide: Employment Litigation Ch. 5-K, K. Invasion of Privacy.

4 Witkin, California Summary 10th Sales § 306, (S 306) Investigative Consumer Reporting Agencies Act.

ARTICLE 2. OBLIGATIONS OF INVESTIGATIVE CONSUMER REPORTING AGENCIES

Section

1786.10.   Inspection of files by consumer; availability; sources; discovery; identification of recipients; disclosure.
1786.11.   Availability of report to consumer.
1786.12.   Furnishing consumer report; circumstances.
1786.14.   Report to governmental agency.
1786.16.   Procurement or preparation of report; conditions; insurance; employment; dwelling unit hiring; disclosure of nature and scope of investigation.
1786.18.   Items of information prohibited.
1786.20.   Agency reporting procedures; records; identity of user and uses to be made of reports.
1786.22.   Supplying files and information; time; methods.
1786.24.   Disputes as to completeness and accuracy of file; reinvestigation; notice to sources; contents; frivolous or irrelevant dispute; deletion and reinsertion of information; notice to consumer; statement of dispute.
1786.26.   Allowable fees charged to consumer by an investigative consumer reporting agency for making disclosures to consumer; other disclosures without charge.
1786.28.   Matters of public record; source; reports for employment purposes.
1786.29.   Notices to be provided by investigative consumer-reporting agency.
1786.30.   Subsequent reports; verification.
1786.40.   Consumer insurance request denied; notice to consumer of adverse action.

§ 1786.10. Inspection of files by consumer; availability; sources; discovery; identification of recipients; disclosure

(a) Every investigative consumer reporting agency shall, upon request and proper identification of any consumer, allow the consumer to visually inspect all files maintained regarding the consumer at the time of the request.

(b)(1) All items of information shall be available for inspection, except that the sources of information, other than public records and records from databases available for sale, acquired solely for use in preparing an investigative consumer report and actually used for no other purpose need not be disclosed. However, if an action is brought under this title, those sources shall be available to the consumer under appropriate discovery procedures in the court in which the action is brought.

(2) This title shall not be interpreted to mean that investigative consumer reporting agencies are required to divulge to consumers the sources of investigative consumer reports, except in appropriate discovery procedures as outlined in this title.

(c) The investigative consumer reporting agency shall also identify the recipients of any investigative consumer report on the consumer that the investigative consumer reporting agency has furnished for either of the following purposes:

(1) For employment or insurance purposes within the three-year period preceding the request.

(2) For any other purpose within the three-year period preceding the request.

(d) The identification of a recipient under subdivision (c) shall include the name of the recipient or, if applicable, the trade name (written in full) under which the recipient conducts business and, upon request of the consumer, the address and telephone number of the recipient.

(e) The investigative consumer reporting agency shall also disclose the dates, original payees, and amounts of any checks or charges upon which is based any adverse characterization of the consumer, included in the file at the time of the disclosure. *(Added by Stats.1975, c. 1272, p. 3379, § 1. Amended by Stats.1998, c. 988 (S.B.1454), § 2; Stats.2001, c. 354 (A.B.655), § 8; Stats.2006, c. 538 (S.B.1852), § 45.)*

Research References

4 Witkin, California Summary 10th Sales § 306, (S 306) Investigative Consumer Reporting Agencies Act.

§ 1786.11. Availability of report to consumer

Every investigative consumer reporting agency that provides an investigative consumer report to a person other than the consumer shall make a copy of that report available, upon request and proper identification, to the consumer for at least two years after the date that the report is provided to the other person. *(Added by Stats.1998, c. 988 (S.B.1454), § 3. Amended by Stats.2001, c. 354 (A.B.655), § 9; Stats.2002, c. 1029 (A.B. 2868), § 3, eff. Sept. 28, 2002.)*

Research References

4 Witkin, California Summary 10th Sales § 306, (S 306) Investigative Consumer Reporting Agencies Act.

§ 1786.12. Furnishing consumer report; circumstances

An investigative consumer reporting agency shall only furnish an investigative consumer report under the following circumstances:

(a) In response to the order of a court having jurisdiction to issue the order.

(b) In compliance with a lawful subpoena issued by a court of competent jurisdiction.

(c) In accordance with the written instructions of the consumer to whom it relates.

(d) To a person that it has reason to believe:

(1) Intends to use the information for employment purposes; or

(2) Intends to use the information serving as a factor in determining a consumer's eligibility for insurance or the rate for any insurance; or

(3) Intends to use the information in connection with a determination of the consumer's eligibility for a license or other benefit granted by a governmental instrumentality required by law to consider the applicant's financial responsibility or status; or

(4) Intends to use the information in connection with an order of a court of competent jurisdiction to provide support where the imposition or enforcement of the order involves the consumer; or

(5) Intends to use the information in connection with the hiring of a dwelling unit, as defined in subdivision (c) of Section 1940.

(e) An investigative consumer reporting agency shall not prepare or furnish an investigative consumer report to a person described in subdivision (d) unless the agency has received the certification under paragraph (4) of subdivision (a) of Section 1786.16 from the person requesting the report.

(f) An investigative consumer reporting agency shall not furnish an investigative consumer report to a person described in subdivision (d) if that report contains medical information about a consumer, unless the consumer consents to the furnishing of the report. *(Added by Stats.1975, c. 1272, p. 3380, § 1. Amended by Stats.1976, c. 1150, p. 5210, § 2; Stats.1982, c. 1127, p. 4067, § 8; Stats.1998, c. 988 (S.B.1454), § 4.)*

Research References

4 Witkin, California Summary 10th Sales § 306, (S 306) Investigative Consumer Reporting Agencies Act.

§ 1786.14. Report to governmental agency

Notwithstanding the provisions of Section 1786.12 an investigative consumer reporting agency may furnish to a governmental agency a consumer's name, address, former address, places of employment, or former places of employment. *(Added by Stats.1975, c. 1272, p. 3380, § 1.)*

§ 1786.16. Procurement or preparation of report; conditions; insurance; employment; dwelling unit hiring; disclosure of nature and scope of investigation

(a) Any person described in subdivision (d) of Section 1786.12 shall not procure or cause to be prepared an investigative consumer report unless the following applicable conditions are met:

(1) If an investigative consumer report is sought in connection with the underwriting of insurance, it shall be clearly and accurately disclosed in writing at the time the application form, medical form, binder, or similar document is signed by the consumer that an investigative consumer report regarding the consumer's character, general reputation, personal characteristics, and mode of living may be made. If no signed application form, medical form, binder, or similar document is involved in the underwriting transaction, the disclosure shall be made to the consumer in writing and mailed or otherwise delivered to the consumer not later than three days after the report was first requested. The disclosure shall include the name and address of any investigative consumer reporting agency conducting an investigation, plus the nature and scope of the investigation requested, and a summary of the provisions of Section 1786.22.

(2) If, at any time, an investigative consumer report is sought for employment purposes other than suspicion of wrongdoing or misconduct by the subject of the investigation, the person seeking the investigative consumer report may procure the report, or cause the report to be made, only if all of the following apply:

(A) The person procuring or causing the report to be made has a permissible purpose, as defined in Section 1786.12.

(B) The person procuring or causing the report to be made provides a clear and conspicuous disclosure in writing to the consumer at any time before the report is procured or caused to be made in a document that consists solely of the disclosure, that:

(i) An investigative consumer report may be obtained.

(ii) The permissible purpose of the report is identified.

(iii) The disclosure may include information on the consumer's character, general reputation, personal characteristics, and mode of living.

(iv) Identifies the name, address, and telephone number of the investigative consumer reporting agency conducting the investigation.

(v) Notifies the consumer in writing of the nature and scope of the investigation requested, including a summary of the provisions of Section 1786.22.

(vi) Notifies the consumer of the Internet Web site address of the investigative consumer reporting agency identified in clause (iv), or, if the agency has no Internet Web site address, the telephone number of the agency, where the consumer may find information about the investigative reporting agency's privacy practices, including whether the consumer's personal information will be sent outside the United States or its territories and information that complies with subdivision (d) of Section 1786.20. This clause shall become operative on January 1, 2012.

(C) The consumer has authorized in writing the procurement of the report.

(3) If an investigative consumer report is sought in connection with the hiring of a dwelling unit, as defined in subdivision (c) of Section 1940, the person procuring or causing the request to be made shall, not later than three days after the date on which the report was first requested, notify the consumer in writing that an investigative consumer report will be made regarding the consumer's character, general reputation, personal characteristics, and mode of living. The notification shall also include the name and address of the investigative consumer reporting agency that will prepare the report and a summary of the provisions of Section 1786.22.

(4) The person procuring or causing the request to be made shall certify to the investigative consumer reporting agency that the person has made the applicable disclosures to the consumer required by this subdivision and that the person will comply with subdivision (b).

(5) The person procuring the report or causing it to be prepared agrees to provide a copy of the report to the subject of the investigation, as provided in subdivision (b).

(b) Any person described in subdivision (d) of Section 1786.12 who requests an investigative consumer report, in accordance with subdivision (a) regarding that consumer, shall do the following:

(1) Provide the consumer a means by which the consumer may indicate on a written form, by means of a box to check, that the consumer wishes to receive a copy of any report that is prepared. If the consumer wishes to receive a copy of the report, the recipient of the report shall send a copy of the report to the consumer within three business days of the date that the report is provided to the recipient, who may contract with any other entity to send a copy to the consumer. The notice to request the report may be contained on either the disclosure form, as required by subdivision (a), or a separate consent form. The copy of the report shall contain the name, address, and telephone number of the person who issued the report and how to contact them.

(2) Comply with Section 1786.40, if the taking of adverse action is a consideration.

(c) Subdivisions (a) and (b) do not apply to an investigative consumer report procured or caused to be prepared by an employer, if the report is sought for employment purposes due to suspicion held by an employer of wrongdoing or misconduct by the subject of the investigation.

(d) Those persons described in subdivision (d) of Section 1786.12 constitute the sole and exclusive class of persons who may cause an investigative consumer report to be prepared. *(Added by Stats.1975, c. 1272, p. 3380, § 1.   Amended by Stats.1976, c. 1150, p. 5210, § 3; Stats.1982, c. 1127, p. 4067, § 9; Stats.1998, c. 988 (S.B.1454), § 5; Stats.2001, c. 354 (A.B.655), § 10; Stats.2002, c. 1030 (A.B.1068), § 3, eff. Sept. 28, 2002; Stats.2010, c. 481 (S.B.909), § 1.)*

Research References

California Practice Guide: Employment Litigation Ch. 5-K, K. Invasion of Privacy.
4 Witkin, California Summary 10th Sales § 306, (S 306) Investigative Consumer Reporting Agencies Act.

§ 1786.18.   Items of information prohibited

(a) Except as authorized under subdivision (b), an investigative consumer reporting agency may not make or furnish any investigative consumer report containing any of the following items of information:

(1) Bankruptcies that, from the date of the order for relief, antedate the report by more than 10 years.

(2) Suits that, from the date of filing, and satisfied judgments that, from the date of entry, antedate the report by more than seven years.

(3) Unsatisfied judgments that, from the date of entry, antedate the report by more than seven years.

(4) Unlawful detainer actions where the defendant was the prevailing party or where the action is resolved by settlement agreement.

(5) Paid tax liens that, from the date of payment, antedate the report by more than seven years.

(6) Accounts placed for collection or charged to profit and loss that antedate the report by more than seven years.

(7) Records of arrest, indictment, information, misdemeanor complaint, or conviction of a crime that, from the date of disposition, release, or parole, antedate the report by more than seven years. These items of information shall no longer be reported if at any time it is learned that, in the case of a conviction, a full pardon has been granted or, in the case of an arrest, indictment, information, or misdemeanor complaint, a conviction did not result; except that records of arrest, indictment, information, or misdemeanor complaints may be reported pending pronouncement of judgment on the particular subject matter of those records.

(8) Any other adverse information that antedates the report by more than seven years.

(b) The provisions of subdivision (a) are not applicable in either of the following circumstances:

(1) If the investigative consumer report is to be used in the underwriting of life insurance involving, or that may reasonably be expected to involve, an amount of two hundred fifty thousand dollars ($250,000) or more.

(2) If the investigative consumer report is to be used by an employer who is explicitly required by a governmental regulatory agency to check for records that are prohibited by subdivision (a) when the employer is reviewing a consumer's qualification for employment.

(c) Except as otherwise provided in Section 1786.28, an investigative consumer reporting agency shall not furnish an investigative consumer report that includes information that is a matter of public record and that relates to an arrest, indictment, conviction, civil judicial action, tax lien, or outstanding judgment, unless the agency has verified the accuracy of the information during the 30-day period ending on the date on which the report is furnished.

(d) An investigative consumer reporting agency shall not prepare or furnish an investigative consumer report on a consumer that contains information that is adverse to the interest of the consumer and that is obtained through a personal interview with a neighbor, friend, or associate of the consumer or with another person with whom the consumer is acquainted or who has knowledge of the item of information, unless either (1) the investigative consumer reporting agency has followed reasonable procedures to obtain confirmation of the information, from an additional source that has independent and direct knowledge of the information, or (2) the person interviewed is the best possible source of the information. *(Added by Stats.1975, c. 1272, p. 3381, § 1.   Amended by Stats.1982, c. 1127, p. 4068, § 10; Stats.1991, c. 965 (A.B.1796), § 2; Stats.1998, c. 988 (S.B.1454), § 6; Stats.2001, c. 354 (A.B.655), § 11; Stats.2002, c. 1029 (A.B.2868), § 4, eff. Sept. 28, 2002; Stats.2009, c. 500 (A.B.1059), § 11.)*

Research References

California Practice Guide: Employment Litigation Ch. 5-K, K. Invasion of Privacy.
4 Witkin, California Summary 10th Sales § 306, (S 306) Investigative Consumer Reporting Agencies Act.

§ 1786.20.   Agency reporting procedures; records; identity of user and uses to be made of reports

(a) An investigative consumer reporting agency shall maintain reasonable procedures designed to avoid violations of Section 1786.18 and to limit furnishing of investigative consumer reports for the purposes listed under Section 1786.12. These procedures shall require that prospective users of the information identify themselves, certify the purposes for which the information is sought and that the information will be used for no other purposes, and make the certifications described in paragraph (4) of subdivision (a) of Section 1786.16. From the effective date of this title, the investigative consumer reporting agency shall keep a record of the purposes for which information is sought, as stated by the user. The investigative consumer reporting agency may assume that the purpose for which a user seeks information remains the same as that which a user has previously stated. The investigative consumer reporting agency shall inform the user that the user is obligated to notify the agency of any change in the purpose for which information will be used. An investigative consumer reporting agency shall make a reasonable effort to verify the identity of a new prospective user and the uses certified by the prospective user prior to furnishing the user any investigative consumer reports. An investigative consumer reporting agency may not furnish an investigative consumer report to a person unless it has a written agreement that the investigative consumer reports will be used by that person only for purposes listed in Section 1786.12.

(b) Whenever an investigative consumer reporting agency prepares an investigative consumer report, it shall follow reasonable procedures to assure maximum possible accuracy of the information concerning the individual about whom the report relates. An investigative consumer reporting agency shall retain the investigative consumer report for two years after the report is provided.

(c) An investigative consumer reporting agency may not make an inquiry for the purpose of preparing an investigative consumer report on a consumer for employment purposes if the making of the inquiry by an employer or prospective employer of the consumer would violate applicable federal or state equal employment opportunity law or regulation.

(d)(1) An investigative consumer reporting agency doing business in this state shall conspicuously post, as defined in subdivision (b) of Section 22577 of the Business and Professions Code, on its primary Internet Web site information describing its privacy practices with respect to its preparation and processing of investigative consumer reports. If the investigative consumer reporting agency does not have an Internet Web site, it shall, upon request, mail a written copy of the privacy statement to consumers. The privacy statement shall conspicuously include, but not be limited to, both of the following:

(A) A statement entitled "Personal Information Disclosure: United States or Overseas," that indicates whether the personal information will be transferred to third parties outside the United States or its territories.

(B) A separate section that includes the name, mailing address, e-mail address, and telephone number of the investigative consumer reporting agency representatives who can assist a consumer with additional information regarding the investigative consumer reporting agency's privacy practices or policies in the event of a compromise of his or her information.

(2) For purposes of this subdivision, "third party" shall include, but not be limited to, a contractor, foreign affiliate, wholly owned entity, or an employee of the investigative consumer reporting agency.

(e) An investigative consumer reporting agency shall be liable to a consumer who is the subject of a report if the consumer is harmed by any unauthorized access of the consumer's personally identifiable information, act, or omission that occurs outside the United States or its territories as a result of the investigative consumer reporting agency negligently preparing or processing an investigative consumer report, or portion thereof, outside of the United States or its territories. Liability shall be in an amount equal to the sum of (1) any actual damages sustained by the consumer as a result of the unauthorized access, and (2) in the case of any successful action to enforce any liability under this section, the costs of the action together with reasonable attorney's fees, as determined by the court. *(Added by Stats. 1975, c. 1272, p. 3381, § 1. Amended by Stats. 1998, c. 988 (S.B. 1454), § 7; Stats. 2001, c. 354 (A.B. 655), § 12; Stats. 2002, c. 1029 (A.B. 2868), § 5, eff. Sept. 28, 2002; Stats. 2003, c. 146 (A.B. 1399), § 1; Stats. 2010, c. 481 (S.B. 909), § 2.)*

Research References

California Practice Guide: Employment Litigation Ch. 5-K, K. Invasion of Privacy.
4 Witkin, California Summary 10th Sales § 306, (S 306) Investigative Consumer Reporting Agencies Act.

§ 1786.22. Supplying files and information; time; methods

(a) An investigative consumer reporting agency shall supply files and information required under Section 1786.10 during normal business hours and on reasonable notice.

(b) Files maintained on a consumer shall be made available for the consumer's visual inspection, as follows:

(1) In person, if he appears in person and furnishes proper identification. A copy of his file shall also be available to the consumer for a fee not to exceed the actual costs of duplication services provided.

(2) By certified mail, if he makes a written request, with proper identification, for copies to be sent to a specified addressee. Investigative consumer reporting agencies complying with requests for certified mailings under this section shall not be liable for disclosures to third parties caused by mishandling of mail after such mailings leave the investigative consumer reporting agencies.

(3) A summary of all information contained in files on a consumer and required to be provided by Section 1786.10 shall be provided by telephone, if the consumer has made a written request, with proper identification for telephone disclosure, and the toll charge, if any, for the telephone call is prepaid by or charged directly to the consumer.

(c) The term "proper identification" as used in subdivision (b) shall mean that information generally deemed sufficient to identify a person. Such information includes documents such as a valid driver's license, social security account number, military identification card, and credit cards. Only if the consumer is unable to reasonably identify himself with the information described above, may an investigative consumer reporting agency require additional information concerning the consumer's employment and personal or family history in order to verify his identity.

(d) The investigative consumer reporting agency shall provide trained personnel to explain to the consumer any information furnished him pursuant to Section 1786.10.

(e) The investigative consumer reporting agency shall provide a written explanation of any coded information contained in files maintained on a consumer. This written explanation shall be distributed whenever a file is provided to a consumer for visual inspection as required under Section 1786.22.

(f) The consumer shall be permitted to be accompanied by one other person of his choosing, who shall furnish reasonable identification. An investigative consumer reporting agency may require the consumer to furnish a written statement granting permission to the consumer reporting agency to discuss the consumer's file in such person's presence. *(Added by Stats. 1975, c. 1272, p. 3382, § 1. Amended by Stats. 1976, c. 666, p. 1645, § 16.)*

Research References

4 Witkin, California Summary 10th Sales § 306, (S 306) Investigative Consumer Reporting Agencies Act.

§ 1786.24. Disputes as to completeness and accuracy of file; reinvestigation; notice to sources; contents; frivolous or irrelevant dispute; deletion and reinsertion of information; notice to consumer; statement of dispute

(a) If the completeness or accuracy of any item of information contained in his or her file is disputed by a consumer, and the dispute is conveyed directly to the investigative consumer reporting agency by the consumer, the investigative consumer reporting agency shall, without charge, reinvestigate and record the current status of the disputed information or delete the item from the file in accordance with subdivision (c), before the end of the 30-day period beginning on the date on which the agency receives the notice of the dispute from the consumer.

(b) The agency shall notify any person who provided information in dispute at the address and in the manner specified by that person. The notice shall include all relevant information regarding the dispute that the investigative consumer reporting agency has received from the consumer. The agency shall also promptly provide to the person who provided the information in dispute all relevant information regarding the dispute that is received by the agency from the consumer during the reinvestigation.

(c) In conducting a reinvestigation, the investigative consumer reporting agency shall review and consider all relevant information submitted by the consumer with respect to the disputed item of information.

(d) Notwithstanding subdivision (a), an investigative consumer reporting agency may terminate a reinvestigation of information disputed by a consumer if the investigative consumer reporting agency reasonably determines that the dispute is frivolous or irrelevant, including by reason of a failure by a consumer to provide sufficient information to investigate the disputed information. Upon making a determination that a dispute is frivolous or irrelevant, the investigative consumer reporting agency shall notify the consumer, by mail or, if authorized by the consumer for that purpose, by any other means available to the agency. In this notification, the investigative consumer reporting agency shall state the specific reasons why it has determined that the consumer's dispute is frivolous or irrelevant and provide a description of any information required to investigate the disputed information, that may consist of a standardized form describing the general nature of the required information.

(e) If a reinvestigation is made and, after reinvestigation, the disputed item of information is found to be inaccurate, incomplete, or cannot be verified by the evidence submitted, the investigative consumer reporting agency shall promptly delete that information from the consumer's file or modify the information, as appropriate, based on the results of the reinvestigation, and shall notify the consumer that the information has been deleted or modified. The consumer reporting agency shall also notify any and all sources from which the disputed information was obtained and inform them in writing of the reasons and results of the reinvestigation, and send a copy of this notification to the consumer. In accordance with subdivision (b) of Section 1786.10, the copy of the notification sent to the consumer need not reveal the identity of the source of information, unless otherwise required by law.

(f) No information may be reinserted in the file of a consumer after having been deleted pursuant to this section, unless the person who furnished the information verifies that the information is complete and accurate. If any information deleted from the file of a consumer is reinserted in the file, the investigative consumer reporting agency shall promptly notify the consumer of the reinsertion in writing or, if authorized by the consumer for that purpose, by any other means available to the agency. As part of, or in addition to, this notice, the investigative consumer reporting agency shall provide to the consumer in writing (1) a statement that the disputed information has been reinserted, (2) the name, address, and telephone number of any furnisher of information contacted or that contacted the investigative consumer reporting agency in connection with the reinsertion, and the telephone number of the furnisher, if reasonably available, and (3) a notice that the consumer has the right to a reinvestigation of the information reinserted by the investigative consumer reporting agency and to add a statement to his or her file disputing the accuracy or completeness of the information.

(g) An investigative consumer reporting agency shall provide notice to the consumer of the results of any reinvestigation under this section by mail or, if authorized by the consumer for that purpose, by other means available to the agency. The notice shall include (1) a statement that the reinvestigation is completed, (2) an investigative consumer report that is based on the consumer's file as that file is revised as a result of the reinvestigation, (3) a description or indication of any changes made in the investigative consumer report as a result of those revisions to the consumer's file, (4) a notice that, if requested by the consumer, a description of the procedure used to determine the accuracy and completeness of the information shall be provided to the consumer by the investigative consumer reporting agency, including the name, business address, and telephone number of any furnisher of information contacted in connection with that information, (5) a notice that the consumer has the right to add a statement to the consumer's file disputing the accuracy or completeness of the information, and (6) a notice that the consumer has the right to request that the investigative consumer reporting agency furnish notifications under subdivision (k).

(h) The presence of information in the consumer's file that contradicts the contention of the consumer shall not, in and of itself, constitute reasonable grounds for believing the dispute is frivolous or irrelevant.

(i) If the investigative consumer reporting agency determines that the dispute is frivolous or irrelevant, or if the reinvestigation does not resolve the dispute, or if the information is reinserted into the file of a consumer pursuant to subdivision (f), the consumer may file a brief statement setting forth the nature of the dispute. The investigative consumer reporting agency may limit these statements to not more than 500 words if it provides the consumer with assistance in writing a clear summary of the dispute.

(j) If a statement of dispute is filed, the investigative consumer reporting agency shall, in any subsequent investigative consumer report containing the information in question, clearly note that the information is disputed by the consumer and shall include in the report either the statement of the consumer or a clear and accurate summary thereof.

(k) Following the deletion of information from the file of a consumer pursuant to this section, or following the filing of a dispute pursuant to subdivision (i), the investigative consumer reporting agency shall, at the request of the consumer, furnish notification that the item of information has been deleted or that the item of information is disputed. In the case of disputed information, the notification shall include the statement or summary of the dispute filed pursuant to subdivision (i). This notification shall be furnished to any person who has, within two years prior to the deletion or the filing of the dispute, received an investigative consumer report concerning the consumer for employment purposes, or who has, within one year of the deletion or the filing of the dispute, received an investigative consumer report concerning the consumer for any other purpose, if these investigative consumer reports contained the deleted or disputed information, unless the consumer specifically requests in writing that this notification not be given to all persons or to any specified persons. The investigative consumer reporting agency shall clearly and conspicuously disclose to the consumer his or her rights to make a request that this notification not be made.

(*l*) An investigative consumer reporting agency shall maintain reasonable procedures designed to prevent the reappearance in the file of a consumer and in investigative consumer reports information that has been deleted pursuant to this section and not reinserted pursuant to subdivision (f).

(m) If the dispute of a consumer is resolved by deletion of the disputed information within three business days, beginning with the day the investigative consumer reporting agency receives notice of the dispute in accordance with subdivision (a), the investigative consumer reporting agency is exempt from requirements for further action under subdivisions (g), (i), and (j), if the agency: (1) provides prompt notice of the deletion to the consumer by telephone, (2) provides written confirmation of the deletion and a copy of an investigative consumer report of the consumer that is based on the file of a consumer after the deletion, and (3) includes, in the telephone notice or in a written notice that accompanies the confirmation and report, a statement of the consumer's right to request under subdivision (k) that the agency not furnish notifications under that subdivision.

(n) Any investigative consumer reporting agency that compiles and maintains files on consumers on a nationwide basis, as defined in the federal Fair Credit Reporting Act, as amended (15 U.S.C. Sec. 1681 et seq.), shall implement an automated system through which furnishers of information to that agency may report the results of a reinvestigation that finds incomplete or inaccurate information in the file of a consumer to other investigative consumer reporting agencies.

(o) All actions to be taken by an investigative consumer reporting agency under this section are governed by the applicable time periods specified in Section 611 of the federal Fair Credit Reporting Act, as amended (15 U.S.C. Sec. 1681i). *(Added by Stats.1975, c. 1272, p. 3383, § 1. Amended by Stats.1998, c. 988 (S.B.1454), § 8; Stats.2001, c. 354 (A.B.655), § 13; Stats.2002, c. 1029 (A.B.2868), § 6, eff. Sept. 28, 2002; Stats.2002, c. 1030 (A.B.1068), § 4, eff. Sept. 28, 2002; Stats.2004, c. 183 (A.B.3082), § 32.)*

Research References

4 Witkin, California Summary 10th Sales § 306, (S 306) Investigative Consumer Reporting Agencies Act.

§ 1786.26. Allowable fees charged to consumer by an investigative consumer reporting agency for making disclosures to consumer; other disclosures without charge

(a) Except as otherwise provided in subdivision (c), an investigative consumer reporting agency may charge a consumer a fee not exceeding eight dollars ($8) for making disclosures to the consumer pursuant to Sections 1786.10, 1786.11, and 1786.22. Any charges shall be indicated to the consumer prior to disclosure.

(b) An investigative consumer reporting agency shall not impose any charge for providing notice to a consumer required under Section 1786.24, furnishing an investigative consumer report pursuant to Section 1786.24, or notifying a person pursuant to subdivision (k) of Section 1786.24 of the deletion of information that is found to be inaccurate or that cannot be verified.

(c) Upon the request of the consumer, an investigative consumer reporting agency shall make all disclosures pursuant to Section 1786.10 and 1786.22 once during any 12–month period without charge to that consumer if the consumer certifies in writing that he or she (1) is unemployed and intends to apply for employment in the 60–day period beginning on the date the certification is made, (2) is a recipient of public welfare assistance, or (3) has reason to believe that the file on the consumer at the investigative consumer reporting agency contains inaccurate information due to fraud.

(d) An investigative consumer reporting agency shall not impose any charge on a consumer for providing any notification or making any disclosure required by this title, except as authorized by this section. *(Added by Stats.1975, c. 1272, p. 3384, § 1. Amended by Stats.1976, c. 666, p. 1646, § 17; Stats.1977, c. 579, p. 1838, § 31; Stats.1998, c. 988 (S.B.1454), § 9; Stats.2001, c. 354 (A.B.655), § 14.)*

Research References

4 Witkin, California Summary 10th Sales § 306, (S 306) Investigative Consumer Reporting Agencies Act.

§ 1786.28. Matters of public record; source; reports for employment purposes

(a) Each investigative consumer reporting agency that collects, assembles, evaluates, compiles, reports, transmits, transfers, or communicates items of information concerning consumers which are matters of public record shall specify in any report containing public record information the source from which this information was obtained, including the particular court, if applicable, and the date that this information was initially reported or publicized.

(b) A consumer reporting agency which furnishes a consumer report for employment purposes and which for that purpose compiles, collects, assembles, evaluates, reports, transmits, transfers, or communicates items of information on consumers which are matters of public record and are likely to have an adverse effect upon a consumer's ability to obtain employment shall in addition maintain strict procedures designed to insure that whenever public record information which is likely to have an adverse effect on a consumer's ability to obtain employment is reported it is complete and up to date. For purposes of this paragraph, items of public record relating to arrests, indictments, convictions, suits, tax liens, and outstanding judgments shall be considered up to date if the current public record status of the item at the time of the report is reported. *(Added by Stats.1975, c. 1272, p. 3384, § 1. Amended by Stats.2001, c. 354 (A.B.655), § 15.)*

Research References

4 Witkin, California Summary 10th Sales § 306, (S 306) Investigative Consumer Reporting Agencies Act.

§ 1786.29. Notices to be provided by investigative consumer-reporting agency

An investigative consumer reporting agency shall provide the following notices on the first page of an investigative consumer report:

(a) A notice in at least 12–point boldface type setting forth that the report does not guarantee the accuracy or truthfulness of the information as to the subject of the investigation, but only that it is accurately copied from public records, and information generated as a result of identity theft, including evidence of criminal activity, may be inaccurately associated with the consumer who is the subject of the report.

(b) An investigative consumer reporting agency shall provide a consumer seeking to obtain a copy of a report or making a request to review a file, a written notice in simple, plain English and Spanish setting forth the terms and conditions of his or her right to receive all disclosures, as provided in Section 1786.26. *(Added by Stats.2001, c. 354 (A.B.655), § 16. Amended by Stats.2002, c. 1030 (A.B.1068), § 5, eff. Sept. 28, 2002.)*

Research References

4 Witkin, California Summary 10th Sales § 306, (S 306) Investigative Consumer Reporting Agencies Act.

§ 1786.30. Subsequent reports; verification

Whenever an investigative consumer reporting agency prepares an investigative consumer report, no adverse information in the report (other than information that is a matter of public record, the status of which has been updated pursuant to Section 1786.28) may be included in a subsequent investigative consumer report unless that adverse information has been verified in the process of making the subsequent investigative consumer report, or the adverse information was received within the three-month period preceding the date the subsequent report is furnished. *(Added by Stats.1975, c. 1272, p. 3385, § 1. Amended by Stats.1998, c. 988 (S.B.1454), § 10.)*

Research References

4 Witkin, California Summary 10th Sales § 306, (S 306) Investigative Consumer Reporting Agencies Act.

§ 1786.40. Consumer insurance request denied; notice to consumer of adverse action

(a) Whenever insurance for personal, family, or household purposes, employment, or the hiring of a dwelling unit involving a consumer is denied, or the charge for that insurance or the hiring of a dwelling unit is increased, under circumstances in which a report regarding the consumer was obtained from an investigative consumer reporting agency, the user of the investigative consumer report shall so advise the consumer against whom the adverse action has been taken and supply the name and address of the investigative consumer reporting agency making the report.

(b) Whenever insurance for personal, family, or household purposes involving a consumer is denied or the charge for that insurance is increased, either wholly or in part because of information bearing upon the consumer's general reputation, personal characteristics, or mode of living, that was obtained from a person other than an investigative consumer reporting agency, the consumer, or another person related to the consumer and acting on the consumer's behalf, the user of the information shall, within a reasonable period of time, and upon the consumer's written request for the reasons for the adverse action received within 60 days after learning of the adverse action, disclose the nature and substance of the information to the consumer. The user of the information shall clearly and accurately disclose to the consumer his or her right to make this written request at the time the adverse action is communicated to the consumer. *(Added by Stats.2002, c. 1030 (A.B.1068), § 6, eff. Sept. 28, 2002.)*

Research References

California Practice Guide: Employment Litigation Ch. 5-K, K. Invasion of Privacy.
Miller and Starr California Real Estate § 19:82, Modification of the Rent.
4 Witkin, California Summary 10th Sales § 306, (S 306) Investigative Consumer Reporting Agencies Act.

ARTICLE 4. REMEDIES

Section

§ 1786.50. Liability of reporter or user to consumer; actual and punitive damages; costs

(a) An investigative consumer reporting agency or user of information that fails to comply with any requirement under this title with respect to an investigative consumer report is liable to the consumer who is the subject of the report in an amount equal to the sum of all the following:

(1) Any actual damages sustained by the consumer as a result of the failure or, except in the case of class actions, ten thousand dollars ($10,000), whichever sum is greater.

(2) In the case of any successful action to enforce any liability under this chapter, the costs of the action together with reasonable attorney's fees as determined by the court.

(b) If the court determines that the violation was grossly negligent or willful, the court may, in addition, assess, and the consumer may recover, punitive damages.

(c) Notwithstanding subdivision (a), an investigative consumer reporting agency or user of information that fails to comply with any requirement under this title with respect to an investigative

consumer report shall not be liable to a consumer who is the subject of the report where the failure to comply results in a more favorable investigative consumer report than if there had not been a failure to comply. *(Added by Stats.1975, c. 1272, p. 3386, § 1. Amended by Stats.1998, c. 988 (S.B.1454), § 12; Stats.2001, c. 354 (A.B.655), § 18; Stats.2002, c. 1029 (A.B.2868), § 7, eff. Sept. 28, 2002; Stats.2003, c. 146 (A.B.1399), § 2.)*

Research References

California Practice Guide: Employment Litigation Ch. 5-K, K. Invasion of Privacy.
4 Witkin, California Summary 10th Sales § 306, (S 306) Investigative Consumer Reporting Agencies Act.

§ 1786.52. Actions for invasion of privacy or defamation; limitations; discovery of misrepresentation

Nothing in this chapter shall in any way affect the right of any consumer to maintain an action against an investigative consumer reporting agency, a user of an investigative consumer report, or an informant for invasion of privacy or defamation.

An action to enforce any liability created under this title may be brought in any appropriate court of competent jurisdiction within two years from the date of discovery.

(a) Any investigative consumer reporting agency or user of information against whom an action brought pursuant to Section 1681n or 1681o of Title 15 of the United States Code is pending shall not be subject to suit for the same act or omission under Section 1786.50.

(b) The entry of a final judgment against the investigative consumer reporting agency or user of information in an action brought pursuant to the provisions of Section 1681n or 1681o of Title 15 of the United States Code shall be a bar to the maintenance of any action based on the same act or omission which might be brought under this title. *(Added by Stats.1975, c. 1272, p. 3386, § 1. Amended by Stats.2001, c. 354 (A.B.655), § 19.)*

Research References

California Practice Guide: Employment Litigation Ch. 5-K, K. Invasion of Privacy.
4 Witkin, California Summary 10th Sales § 306, (S 306) Investigative Consumer Reporting Agencies Act.

§ 1786.53. Personal information obtained regarding consumer in lieu of using services of an investigative consumer reporting agency; disclosure; definitions; copy of information to consumer

(a) Any person who collects, assembles, evaluates, compiles, reports, transmits, transfers, or communicates information on a consumer's character, general reputation, personnel characteristics, or mode of living, for employment purposes, which are matters of public record, and does not use the services of an investigative consumer reporting agency, shall provide that information to the consumer pursuant to subdivision (b). For purposes of this section:

(1) "Adverse action," as relating to employment, means a denial of employment or any decision made for an employment purpose that adversely affects any current or prospective employee.

(2) The term "person" does not include an agency subject to the Information Practices Act of 1977 (Chapter 1 (commencing with Section 1798) of Title 1.8).

(3) "Public records" means records documenting an arrest, indictment, conviction, civil judicial action, tax lien, or outstanding judgment.

(b)(1) Any person described in subdivision (a), or any person who receives information pursuant to subdivision (a), shall provide a copy of the related public record to the consumer within seven days after receipt of the information, regardless of whether the information is received in a written or oral form.

(2) Any person shall provide on any job application form, or any other written form, a box that, if checked by the consumer, permits the consumer to waive his or her right to receive a copy of any public record obtained pursuant to this section.

(3) If any person obtains a public record pursuant to this section for the purpose of conducting an investigation for suspicion of wrongdoing or misconduct by the subject of the investigation, the person may withhold the information until the completion of the investigation. Upon completion, the person shall provide a copy of the public record pursuant to paragraph (1), unless the consumer waived his or her rights pursuant to paragraph (2).

(4) If any person takes any adverse action as a result of receiving information pursuant to subdivision (a), the person shall provide to the consumer a copy of the public record, regardless of whether the consumer waived his or her rights pursuant to paragraph (2).

(c) Nothing in subdivision (a) or (b) requires any person to provide the same information to any consumer on more than one occasion. *(Added by Stats.2001, c. 354 (A.B.655), § 20. Amended by Stats.2002, c. 1030 (A.B.1068), § 7, eff. Sept. 28, 2002.)*

Research References

California Practice Guide: Employment Litigation Ch. 5-K, K. Invasion of Privacy.
4 Witkin, California Summary 10th Sales § 306, (S 306) Investigative Consumer Reporting Agencies Act.

§ 1786.54. Application of title

This title does not apply to any investigative consumer report which by its terms is limited to disclosures from public records relating to land and land titles or which is a report issued preliminary to the issuance of a policy of title insurance, and it does not apply to any person whose records are maintained for the primary purpose of reporting those portions of public records which impart constructive notice under the law of matters relating to land and land titles and which may be issued as the basis for the issuance of a policy of title insurance. *(Added by Stats.1975, c. 1272, p. 3387, § 1.)*

§ 1786.55. Information obtained by an employer or employment agency without use of investigative consumer reporting agency; attorney-client communications or attorney work product

Nothing in this chapter is intended to modify Section 1198.5 of the Labor Code or existing law concerning information obtained by an employer or employment agency without the use of the services of an investigative consumer reporting agency for employment reference checks, background investigations, credential verifications, or employee investigations, except as provided in Section 1786.53. Nothing in this chapter is intended to change or supersede existing law related to privileged attorney-client communications or attorney work product, or require the production or disclosure of that information. *(Added by Stats. 2002, c. 1030 (A.B.1068), § 8, eff. Sept. 28, 2002.)*

Research References

California Practice Guide: Employment Litigation Ch. 5-K, K. Invasion of Privacy.
California Practice Guide: Employment Litigation Ch. 10-D, D. Employer Liability for Workplace Harassment.

§ 1786.56. Severability

If any provision of this act or the application thereof to any person or circumstances is held invalid, such invalidity shall not affect other provisions or applications of the act which can be given effect without the invalid provision or application, and to this end the provisions of this act are severable. *(Added by Stats.1975, c. 1272, p. 3387, § 1.)*

§ 1786.57. Public policy; waiver of rights

Any waiver of the provisions of this title is contrary to public policy, and is void and unenforceable. *(Added by Stats.2002, c. 815 (A.B.2331), § 10.)*

Research References

4 Witkin, California Summary 10th Sales § 306, (S 306) Investigative Consumer Reporting Agencies Act.

§ 1786.60. Permitted printing of social security numbers on account statements

Notwithstanding subdivision (a) of Section 1798.85, prior to July 1, 2004, any financial institution may print the social security number of an individual on any account statement or similar document mailed to that individual, if the social security number is provided in connection with a transaction governed by the rules of the National Automated Clearing House Association, or a transaction initiated by a federal governmental entity through an automated clearing house network. *(Added by Stats.2002, c. 1030 (A.B.1068), § 9, eff. Sept. 28, 2002. Amended by Stats.2003, c. 907 (S.B.25), § 4.)*

Research References

California Practice Guide: Employment Litigation Ch. 5-K, K. Invasion of Privacy.

Title 1.6B

CONSUMER CREDIT DENIAL

ARTICLE 1. GENERAL PROVISIONS

§ 1787.1. Short title

This title may be cited as "The Holden Credit Denial Disclosure Act of 1976." *(Added by Stats.1976, c. 1072, p. 4834, § 1, operative March 31, 1977.)*

Research References

4 Witkin, California Summary 10th Sales § 307, (S 307) Disclosure of Reasons for Denying Consumer Credit.

§ 1787.2. Notice to applicant of disposition; statement of reasons for denial; definitions

(a) Within 30 days, or at a later reasonable time as specified in federal law or regulations, after receipt of a completed written application for credit, a creditor shall notify the applicant of its action on the application.

(b) Each applicant denied credit shall be entitled to a statement of reasons for such action from the creditor. A creditor satisfies this obligation by:

(1) Providing statements of reasons in writing as a matter of course to applicants denied credit; or

(2) Giving written notification of credit denial which discloses:

(i) The applicant's right to a statement of reasons within 30 days after receipt by the creditor of a request made within 60 days after such notification; and

(ii) The identity and address of the person or office from which the statement of reasons may be obtained.

(3) The statement of reasons may be given orally if the written notification advises the applicant of the right to have the statement of reasons confirmed in writing on written request.

(c) A statement of reasons meets the requirements of this section only if it contains the specific reasons for the credit denial.

(d) Where a creditor has been requested by a third party to make a specific extension of credit directly or indirectly to an applicant, the notification and statement of reasons required by this section may be made directly by such creditor, or indirectly through the third party, provided in either case that the identity of the creditor is disclosed.

(e) For purposes of this section:

(1) The term "applicant" means a natural person who applies for credit primarily for personal, family or household purposes.

(2) The term "credit denial" means a denial or revocation of credit, a change in the terms of an existing credit arrangement, or a refusal to grant credit in substantially the amount or on substantially the terms requested. Such term does not include a refusal to extend additional credit under an existing credit arrangement where the applicant is delinquent or otherwise in default, or where such additional credit would exceed a previously established credit limit without a specific written application or written request for an increase in the credit limit.

(3) The term "creditor" refers only to creditors who regularly extend, or arrange for the extension of, credit whether in connection with loans, sales of property or services, or otherwise.

(f) Nothing in this section shall be construed to limit any authority, derived from other provisions of law, of any state department or agency. *(Added by Stats.1976, c. 1072, p. 4834, § 1, operative March 31, 1977.)*

Research References

4 Witkin, California Summary 10th Sales § 301, (S 301) Adverse Use of Report.
4 Witkin, California Summary 10th Sales § 307, (S 307) Disclosure of Reasons for Denying Consumer Credit.

ARTICLE 2.   REMEDIES

Section
1787.3.   Failure of creditor to comply; liability for actual or punitive damages; costs; attorney's fee; inapplicability to act in good faith under federal rule; limitation of actions.
1787.4.   Public policy; waiver of rights.

§ 1787.3.   Failure of creditor to comply; liability for actual or punitive damages; costs; attorney's fee; inapplicability to act in good faith under federal rule; limitation of actions

(a) Any creditor who fails to comply with any requirement of Section 1787.2 shall be liable for any actual damages sustained by an applicant as a result of such failure.

(b) Any creditor, other than a government or governmental subdivision or agency, who fails to comply with any requirement imposed under this title shall be liable to the aggrieved applicant for punitive damages in an amount not greater than ten thousand dollars ($10,000), in addition to any actual damages provided in subdivision (a), except that in the case of a class

action the total recovery under this subdivision shall not exceed the lesser of five hundred thousand dollars ($500,000) or 1 percent of the net worth of the creditor. In determining the amount of such damages in any action, the court shall consider, among other relevant factors, the amount of any actual damages awarded, the frequency and persistence of failures of compliance by the creditor, the resources of the creditor, the number of persons adversely affected, and the extent to which the creditor's failure of compliance was intentional.

(c) In the case of any action brought by an aggrieved applicant under subdivision (a) or (b), the costs of the action, together with a reasonable attorney's fee as determined by the court, shall be added to any damages awarded by the court.

(d) No provision of this title imposing liability shall apply to any act done or omitted in good faith in conformity with any official rule, regulation, or interpretation thereby by the Board of Governors of the Federal Reserve System or in conformity with any interpretation or approval by an official or employee of the Federal Reserve System duly authorized by the board to issue such interpretations or approvals under such procedures as the board may prescribe therefor, notwithstanding that after such act or omission has occurred, such rule, regulation, interpretation, or approval is amended, rescinded, or determined by judicial or other authority to be invalid for any reason.

(e) Actions alleging a failure to comply with any requirement of Section 1787.2 shall be brought within two years from the date of the occurrence of the violation. *(Added by Stats.1976, c. 1072, p. 4834, § 1, operative March 31, 1977.)*

Research References

4 Witkin, California Summary 10th Sales § 307, (S 307) Disclosure of Reasons for Denying Consumer Credit.

§ 1787.4.   Public policy; waiver of rights

Any waiver of the provisions of this title is contrary to public policy, and is void and unenforceable. *(Added by Stats.2002, c. 815 (A.B.2331), § 11.)*

Research References

4 Witkin, California Summary 10th Sales § 307, (S 307) Disclosure of Reasons for Denying Consumer Credit.

Title 1.6C

FAIR DEBT COLLECTION PRACTICES

ARTICLE 1.   GENERAL PROVISIONS

§ 1788.   Short title

This title may be cited as the Rosenthal Fair Debt Collection Practices Act. *(Added by Stats.1977, c. 907, p. 2771, § 1. Amended by Stats.1999, c. 319 (A.B.969), § 1; Stats.2000, c. 375 (A.B.1331), § 5.)*

Research References

Rutter, Cal. Practice Guide: Civ. Pro. Before Trial Ch. 1-C, C. Prelawsuit Notices, Claims and Demands.

Rutter, Cal. Practice Guide: Enforcing Judgments/Debts Ch. 1-C, C. Efficient Debt Collection Office Procedures.

Rutter, Cal. Practice Guide: Enforcing Judgments/Debts Ch. 2-B, B. Statutory Liability and Procedures.

Rutter, Cal. Practice Guide: Enforcing Judgments/Debts Ch. 6A-8, Federal and State Debt Collection Restrictions; Consumer Debts.

Rutter, Cal. Practice Guide: Real Prop. Transactions Ch. 6-I, I. Real Property Foreclosures and Antideficiency Laws.

8 Witkin Cal. Proc. 5th Enforcement of Judgment § 5, (S 5) Rosenthal Act.

8 Witkin Cal. Proc. 5th Enforcement of Judgment § 15, Duties and Prohibited Acts.

7 Witkin Cal. Proc. 5th Judgment § 311, in General.

6 Witkin Cal. Proc. 5th Provisional Remedies § 316, (S 316) Nature and Scope of Statute.

4 Witkin, California Summary 10th Sales § 209, (S 209) Specific Performance or Replevin.

5 Witkin, California Summary 10th Torts § 458, Collectors' Tactics.

§ 1788.1. Legislative findings

(a) The Legislature makes the following findings:

(1) The banking and credit system and grantors of credit to consumers are dependent upon the collection of just and owing debts. Unfair or deceptive collection practices undermine the public confidence which is essential to the continued functioning of the banking and credit system and sound extensions of credit to consumers.

(2) There is need to ensure that debt collectors and debtors exercise their responsibilities to one another with fairness, honesty and due regard for the rights of the other.

(b) It is the purpose of this title to prohibit debt collectors from engaging in unfair or deceptive acts or practices in the collection of consumer debts and to require debtors to act fairly in entering into and honoring such debts, as specified in this title. (Added by Stats.1977, c. 907, p. 2771, § 1.)

Validity

This section was held to be preempted by the Fair Credit Reporting Act in the decision of Nelson v. Equifax Information Services, LLC, C.D.Cal.2007, 522 F.Supp.2d 1222.

Research References

8 Witkin Cal. Proc. 5th Enforcement of Judgment § 5, (S 5) Rosenthal Act.

§ 1788.2. Definitions

(a) Definitions and rules of construction set forth in this section are applicable for the purpose of this title.

(b) The term "debt collection" means any act or practice in connection with the collection of consumer debts.

(c) The term "debt collector" means any person who, in the ordinary course of business, regularly, on behalf of himself or herself or others, engages in debt collection. The term includes any person who composes and sells, or offers to compose and sell, forms, letters, and other collection media used or intended to be used for debt collection, but does not include an attorney or counselor at law.

(d) The term "debt" means money, property or their equivalent which is due or owing or alleged to be due or owing from a natural person to another person.

(e) The term "consumer credit transaction" means a transaction between a natural person and another person in which property, services or money is acquired on credit by that natural person from such other person primarily for personal, family, or household purposes.

(f) The terms "consumer debt" and "consumer credit" mean money, property or their equivalent, due or owing or alleged to be due or owing from a natural person by reason of a consumer credit transaction.

(g) The term "person" means a natural person, partnership, corporation, limited liability company, trust, estate, cooperative, association or other similar entity.

(h) Except as provided in Section 1788.18, the term "debtor" means a natural person from whom a debt collector seeks to collect a consumer debt which is due and owing or alleged to be due and owing from such person.

(i) The term "creditor" means a person who extends consumer credit to a debtor.

(j) The term "consumer credit report" means any written, oral or other communication of any information by a consumer reporting agency bearing on a consumer's creditworthiness, credit standing, credit capacity, character, general reputation, personal characteristics or mode of living which is used or expected to be used or collected in whole or in part for the purpose of serving as a factor in establishing the consumer's eligibility for (1) credit or insurance to be used primarily for person,[1] family, or household purposes, or (2) employment purposes, or (3) other purposes authorized under any applicable federal or state law or regulation. The term does not include (a) any report containing information solely as to transactions or experiences between the consumer and the person making the report; (b) any authorization or approval of a specific extension of credit directly or indirectly by the issuer of a credit card or similar device; or (c) any report in which a person who has been requested by a third party to make a specific extension of credit directly or indirectly to a consumer conveys his or her decision with respect to that request, if the third party advises the consumer of the name and address of the person to whom the request was made and such person makes the disclosures to the consumer required under any applicable federal or state law or regulation.

(k) The term "consumer reporting agency" means any person which, for monetary fees, dues, or on a cooperative nonprofit basis, regularly engages, in whole or in part, in the practice of assembling or evaluating consumer credit information or other information on consumers for the purpose of furnishing consumer credit reports to third parties, and which uses any means or facility for the purpose of preparing or furnishing consumer credit reports. (Added by Stats.1977, c. 907, p. 2771, § 1. Amended by Stats.1994, c. 1010 (S.B.2053), § 37; Stats.2006, c. 538 (S.B.1852), § 46; Stats.2006, c. 521 (A.B.2043), § 1.)

[1] So in enrolled bill.

Research References

Rutter, Cal. Practice Guide: Enforcing Judgments/Debts Ch. 2-B, B. Statutory Liability and Procedures.

Rutter, Cal. Practice Guide: Prof. Responsibility Ch. 1-E, E. Regulation of Form of Practice.

8 Witkin Cal. Proc. 5th Enforcement of Judgment § 5, (S 5) Rosenthal Act.

8 Witkin Cal. Proc. 5th Enforcement of Judgment § 6, (S 6) Effect of Federal Act.

8 Witkin Cal. Proc. 5th Enforcement of Judgment § 7, (S 7) Automobile Repair Shop is Not Covered.

§ 1788.3. Credit union; information to employer who is an employee, officer, etc. of credit union

Nothing contained in this title shall be construed to prohibit a credit union chartered under Division 5 (commencing with Section 14000) of the Financial Code or under the Federal

Credit Union Act (Chapter 14 (commencing with Section 1751) of Title 12 of the United States Code) from providing information to an employer when the employer is ordinarily and necessarily entitled to receive such information because he is an employee, officer, committee member, or agent of such credit union. *(Added by Stats.1977, c. 907, p. 2771, § 1.)*

Research References

8 Witkin Cal. Proc. 5th Enforcement of Judgment § 5, (S 5) Rosenthal Act.

ARTICLE 2.   DEBT COLLECTOR RESPONSIBILITIES

§ 1788.10.   Threats; unlawful conduct

No debt collector shall collect or attempt to collect a consumer debt by means of the following conduct:

(a) The use, or threat of use, of physical force or violence or any criminal means to cause harm to the person, or the reputation, or the property of any person;

(b) The threat that the failure to pay a consumer debt will result in an accusation that the debtor has committed a crime where such accusation, if made, would be false;

(c) The communication of, or threat to communicate to any person the fact that a debtor has engaged in conduct, other than the failure to pay a consumer debt, which the debt collector knows or has reason to believe will defame the debtor;

(d) The threat to the debtor to sell or assign to another person the obligation of the debtor to pay a consumer debt, with an accompanying false representation that the result of such sale or assignment would be that the debtor would lose any defense to the consumer debt;

(e) The threat to any person that nonpayment of the consumer debt may result in the arrest of the debtor or the seizure, garnishment, attachment or sale of any property or the garnishment or attachment of wages of the debtor, unless such action is in fact contemplated by the debt collector and permitted by the law; or

(f) The threat to take any action against the debtor which is prohibited by this title. *(Added by Stats.1977, c. 907, p. 2771, § 1.)*

Research References

Rutter, Cal. Practice Guide: Enforcing Judgments/Debts Ch. 2-B, B. Statutory Liability and Procedures.
Rutter, Cal. Practice Guide: Enforcing Judgments/Debts Ch. 3-B, B. Collection Without Suit.
Rutter, Cal. Practice Guide: Enforcing Judgments/Debts Ch. 5-D, D. Involuntary Bankruptcy.
Rutter, Cal. Practice Guide: Prof. Responsibility Ch. 1-E, E. Regulation of Form of Practice.
1 Witkin Cal. Proc. 5th Attorneys § 506, Improper Debt Collection Methods.
8 Witkin Cal. Proc. 5th Enforcement of Judgment § 8, (S 8) Prohibited Practices.

§ 1788.11.   Obscene or profane language; use of telephones; unlawful practices

No debt collector shall collect or attempt to collect a consumer debt by means of the following practices:

(a) Using obscene or profane language;

(b) Placing telephone calls without disclosure of the caller's identity, provided that an employee of a licensed collection agency may identify himself by using his registered alias name as long as he correctly identifies the agency he represents;

(c) Causing expense to any person for long distance telephone calls, telegram fees or charges for other similar communications, by misrepresenting to such person the purpose of such telephone call, telegram or similar communication;

(d) Causing a telephone to ring repeatedly or continuously to annoy the person called; or

(e) Communicating, by telephone or in person, with the debtor with such frequency as to be unreasonable and to constitute an harassment to the debtor under the circumstances. *(Added by Stats.1977, c. 907, p. 2771, § 1.)*

Research References

Rutter, Cal. Practice Guide: Enforcing Judgments/Debts Ch. 2-B, B. Statutory Liability and Procedures.
8 Witkin Cal. Proc. 5th Enforcement of Judgment § 8, (S 8) Prohibited Practices.

§ 1788.12.   Communications with third parties; unlawful practices

No debt collector shall collect or attempt to collect a consumer debt by means of the following practices:

(a) Communicating with the debtor's employer regarding the debtor's consumer debt unless such a communication is necessary to the collection of the debt, or unless the debtor or his attorney has consented in writing to such communication. A communication is necessary to the collection of the debt only if it is made for the purposes of verifying the debtor's employment, locating the debtor, or effecting garnishment, after judgment, of the debtor's wages, or in the case of a medical debt for the purpose of discovering the existence of medical insurance. Any such communication, other than a communication in the case of a medical debt by a health care provider or its agent for the purpose of discovering the existence of medical insurance, shall be in writing unless such written communication receives no response within 15 days and shall be made only as many times as is necessary to the collection of the debt. Communications to a debtor's employer regarding a debt shall not contain language that would be improper if the communication were made to the debtor. One communication solely for the purpose of verifying the debtor's employment may be oral without prior written contact.

(b) Communicating information regarding a consumer debt to any member of the debtor's family, other than the debtor's spouse or the parents or guardians of the debtor who is either a minor or who resides in the same household with such parent or guardian, prior to obtaining a judgment against the debtor, except where the purpose of the communication is to locate the debtor, or where the debtor or his attorney has consented in writing to such communication;

(c) Communicating to any person any list of debtors which discloses the nature or existence of a consumer debt, commonly known as "deadbeat lists", or advertising any consumer debt for sale, by naming the debtor; or

(d) Communicating with the debtor by means of a written communication that displays or conveys any information about the consumer debt or the debtor other than the name, address and telephone number of the debtor and the debt collector and which is intended both to be seen by any other person and also to embarrass the debtor.

(e) Notwithstanding the foregoing provisions of this section, the disclosure, publication or communication by a debt collector of information relating to a consumer debt or the debtor to a consumer reporting agency or to any other person reasonably believed to have a legitimate business need for such information shall not be deemed to violate this title. (Added by Stats.1977, c. 907, p. 2771, § 1. Amended by Stats.1978, c. 390, p. 1238, § 1, eff. July 11, 1978.)

Research References

Rutter, Cal. Practice Guide: Enforcing Judgments/Debts Ch. 2-B, B. Statutory Liability and Procedures.
8 Witkin Cal. Proc. 5th Enforcement of Judgment § 8, (S 8) Prohibited Practices.

§ 1788.13. Misrepresentations in communications; unlawful practices

No debt collector shall collect or attempt to collect a consumer debt by means of the following practices:

(a) Any communication with the debtor other than in the name either of the debt collector or the person on whose behalf the debt collector is acting;

(b) Any false representation that any person is an attorney or counselor at law;

(c) Any communication with a debtor in the name of an attorney or counselor at law or upon stationery or like written instruments bearing the name of the attorney or counselor at law, unless such communication is by an attorney or counselor at law or shall have been approved or authorized by such attorney or counselor at law;

(d) The representation that any debt collector is vouched for, bonded by, affiliated with, or is an instrumentality, agent or official of any federal, state or local government or any agency of federal, state or local government, unless the collector is actually employed by the particular governmental agency in question and is acting on behalf of such agency in the debt collection matter;

(e) The false representation that the consumer debt may be increased by the addition of attorney's fees, investigation fees, service fees, finance charges, or other charges if, in fact, such fees or charges may not legally be added to the existing obligation;

(f) The false representation that information concerning a debtor's failure or alleged failure to pay a consumer debt has been or is about to be referred to a consumer reporting agency;

(g) The false representation that a debt collector is a consumer reporting agency;

(h) The false representation that collection letters, notices or other printed forms are being sent by or on behalf of a claim, credit, audit or legal department;

(i) The false representation of the true nature of the business or services being rendered by the debt collector;

(j) The false representation that a legal proceeding has been, is about to be, or will be instituted unless payment of a consumer debt is made;

(k) The false representation that a consumer debt has been, is about to be, or will be sold, assigned, or referred to a debt collector for collection; or

(*l*) Any communication by a licensed collection agency to a debtor demanding money unless the claim is actually assigned to the collection agency. (Added by Stats.1977, c. 907, p. 2771, § 1. Amended by Stats.1980, c. 1126, p. 3626, § 7.)

Research References

Rutter, Cal. Practice Guide: Enforcing Judgments/Debts Ch. 2-B, B. Statutory Liability and Procedures.
Rutter, Cal. Practice Guide: Enforcing Judgments/Debts Ch. 5-D, D. Involuntary Bankruptcy.
8 Witkin Cal. Proc. 5th Enforcement of Judgment § 8, (S 8) Prohibited Practices.

§ 1788.14. Affirmation from debtor; collection of collector's fee and expenses from debtor; communication with debtor instead of debtor's attorney; unlawful practices

No debt collector shall collect or attempt to collect a consumer debt by means of the following practices:

(a) Obtaining an affirmation from a debtor of a consumer debt which has been discharged in bankruptcy, without clearly and conspicuously disclosing to the debtor, in writing, at the time such affirmation is sought, the fact that the debtor is not legally obligated to make such affirmation;

(b) Collecting or attempting to collect from the debtor the whole or any part of the debt collector's fee or charge for services rendered, or other expense incurred by the debt collector in the collection of the consumer debt, except as permitted by law; or

(c) Initiating communications, other than statements of account, with the debtor with regard to the consumer debt, when the debt collector has been previously notified in writing by the debtor's attorney that the debtor is represented by such attorney with respect to the consumer debt and such notice includes the attorney's name and address and a request by such attorney that all communications regarding the consumer debt be addressed to such attorney, unless the attorney fails to answer correspondence, return telephone calls, or discuss the obligation in question. This subdivision shall not apply where prior approval has been obtained from the debtor's attorney, or where the communication is a response in the ordinary course of business to a debtor's inquiry. (Added by Stats.1977, c. 907, p. 2771, § 1. Amended by Stats.2009, c. 500 (A.B.1059), § 12.)

Research References

Rutter, Cal. Practice Guide: Enforcing Judgments/Debts Ch. 2-B, B. Statutory Liability and Procedures.
8 Witkin Cal. Proc. 5th Enforcement of Judgment § 8, (S 8) Prohibited Practices.

§ 1788.15. Judicial proceedings where service of process defective; venue

(a) No debt collector shall collect or attempt to collect a consumer debt by means of judicial proceedings when the debt collector knows that service of process, where essential to jurisdiction over the debtor or his property, has not been legally effected.

(b) No debt collector shall collect or attempt to collect a consumer debt, other than one reduced to judgment, by means of judicial proceedings in a county other than the county in which the debtor has incurred the consumer debt or the county in which the debtor resides at the time such proceedings are instituted, or resided at the time the debt was incurred. *(Added by Stats.1977, c. 907, p. 2771, § 1.)*

Research References

Rutter, Cal. Practice Guide: Enforcing Judgments/Debts Ch. 2-B, B. Statutory Liability and Procedures.
Rutter, Cal. Practice Guide: Enforcing Judgments/Debts Ch. 2-B, Outline B.
8 Witkin Cal. Proc. 5th Enforcement of Judgment § 8, (S 8) Prohibited Practices.

§ 1788.16. Communications simulating legal or judicial process or governmental authorization; unlawful practice in consumer debt collection; misdemeanor; punishment

It is unlawful, with respect to attempted collection of a consumer debt, for a debt collector, creditor, or an attorney, to send a communication which simulates legal or judicial process or which gives the appearance of being authorized, issued, or approved by a governmental agency or attorney when it is not. Any violation of the provisions of this section is a misdemeanor punishable by imprisonment in the county jail not exceeding six months, or by a fine not exceeding two thousand five hundred dollars ($2,500) or by both. *(Added by Stats.1980, c. 1126, p. 3627, § 8.)*

Research References

Rutter, Cal. Practice Guide: Enforcing Judgments/Debts Ch. 2-B, B. Statutory Liability and Procedures.
Rutter, Cal. Practice Guide: Prof. Responsibility Ch. 1-E, E. Regulation of Form of Practice.
8 Witkin Cal. Proc. 5th Enforcement of Judgment § 8, (S 8) Prohibited Practices.

§ 1788.17. Compliance with federal provisions

Notwithstanding any other provision of this title, every debt collector collecting or attempting to collect a consumer debt shall comply with the provisions of Sections 1692b to 1692j, inclusive, of, and shall be subject to the remedies in Section 1692k of, Title 15 of the United States Code. However, subsection (11) of Section 1692e and Section 1692g shall not apply to any person specified in paragraphs (A) and (B) of subsection (6) of Section 1692a of Title 15 of the United States Code or that person's principal. The references to federal codes in this section refer to those codes as they read January 1, 2001. *(Added by Stats.1999, c. 319 (A.B.969), § 2. Amended by Stats.2000, c. 688 (A.B.1669), § 1.)*

Research References

Rutter, Cal. Practice Guide: Enforcing Judgments/Debts Ch. 2-B, B. Statutory Liability and Procedures.
8 Witkin Cal. Proc. 5th Enforcement of Judgment § 8, (S 8) Prohibited Practices.
8 Witkin Cal. Proc. 5th Enforcement of Judgment § 10, (S 10) Collection Where Identity Theft is Claimed.

§ 1788.18. Debtor as an alleged victim of identity theft; sworn statement; inferences and presumptions; duties after collection terminated

(a) Upon receipt from a debtor of all of the following, a debt collector shall cease collection activities until completion of the review provided in subdivision (d):

(1) A copy of a police report filed by the debtor alleging that the debtor is the victim of an identity theft crime, including, but not limited to, a violation of Section 530.5 of the Penal Code, for the specific debt being collected by the debt collector.

(2) The debtor's written statement that the debtor claims to be the victim of identity theft with respect to the specific debt being collected by the debt collector.

(b) The written statement described in paragraph (2) of subdivision (a) shall consist of any of the following:

(1) A Federal Trade Commission's Affidavit of Identity Theft.

(2) A written statement that contains the content of the Identity Theft Victim's Fraudulent Account Information Request offered to the public by the California Office of Privacy Protection.

(3) A written statement that certifies that the representations are true, correct, and contain no material omissions of fact to the best knowledge and belief of the person submitting the certification. A person submitting the certification who declares as true any material matter pursuant to this subdivision that he or she knows to be false is guilty of a misdemeanor. The statement shall contain or be accompanied by the following, to the extent that an item listed below is relevant to the debtor's allegation of identity theft with respect to the debt in question:

(A) A statement that the debtor is a victim of identity theft.

(B) A copy of the debtor's driver's license or identification card, as issued by the state.

(C) Any other identification document that supports the statement of identity theft.

(D) Specific facts supporting the claim of identity theft, if available.

(E) Any explanation showing that the debtor did not incur the debt.

(F) Any available correspondence disputing the debt after transaction information has been provided to the debtor.

(G) Documentation of the residence of the debtor at the time of the alleged debt. This may include copies of bills and statements, such as utility bills, tax statements, or other statements from businesses sent to the debtor, showing that the debtor lived at another residence at the time the debt was incurred.

(H) A telephone number for contacting the debtor concerning any additional information or questions, or direction that further communications to the debtor be in writing only, with the mailing address specified in the statement.

(I) To the extent the debtor has information concerning who may have incurred the debt, the identification of any person whom the debtor believes is responsible.

(J) An express statement that the debtor did not authorize the use of the debtor's name or personal information for incurring the debt.

(K) The certification required pursuant to this paragraph shall be sufficient if it is in substantially the following form:

"I certify the representations made are true, correct, and contain no material omissions of fact.

_____   _____"
(Date and Place)   (Signature)

(c) If a debtor notifies a debt collector orally that he or she is a victim of identity theft, the debt collector shall notify the debtor, orally or in writing, that the debtor's claim must be in writing. If a debtor notifies a debt collector in writing that he or she is a victim of identity theft, but omits information required pursuant to subdivision (a) or, if applicable, the certification required pursuant to paragraph (3) of subdivision (b), if the debt collector does not cease collection activities, the debt collector shall provide written notice to the debtor of the additional information that is required, or the certification required pursuant to paragraph (3) of subdivision (b), as applicable, or send the debtor a copy of the Federal Trade Commission's Affidavit of Identity Theft form.

(d) Upon receipt of the complete statement and information described in subdivision (a), the debt collector shall review and consider all of the information provided by the debtor and other information available to the debt collector in its file or from the creditor. The debt collector may recommence debt collection activities only upon making a good faith determination that the information does not establish that the debtor is not responsible for the specific debt in question. The debt collector's determination shall be made in a manner consistent with the provisions of subsection (1) of Section 1692 of Title 15 of the United States Code, as incorporated by Section 1788.17 of this code. The debt collector shall notify the debtor in writing of that determination and the basis for that determination before proceeding with any further collection activities. The debt collector's determination shall be based on all of the information provided by the debtor and other information available to the debt collector in its file or from the creditor.

(e) No inference or presumption that the debt is valid or invalid, or that the debtor is liable or not liable for the debt, shall arise if the debt collector decides after the review described in subdivision (d) to cease or recommence the debt collection activities. The exercise or nonexercise of rights under this section is not a waiver of any other right or defense of the debtor or debt collector.

(f) The statement and supporting documents that comply with subdivision (a) may also satisfy, to the extent those documents meet the requirements of, the notice requirement of paragraph (5) of subdivision (c) of Section 1798.93.

(g) A debt collector who ceases collection activities under this section and does not recommence those collection activities shall do all of the following:

(1) If the debt collector has furnished adverse information to a consumer credit reporting agency, notify the agency to delete that information.

(2) Notify the creditor that debt collection activities have been terminated based upon the debtor's claim of identity theft.

(h) A debt collector who has possession of documents that the debtor is entitled to request from a creditor pursuant to Section 530.8 of the Penal Code is authorized to provide those documents to the debtor.

(i) Notwithstanding subdivision (h) of Section 1788.2, for the purposes of this section, "debtor" means a natural person, firm, association, organization, partnership, business trust, company, corporation, or limited liability company from which a debt collector seeks to collect a debt that is due and owing or alleged to be due and owing from the person or entity. The remedies provided by this title shall apply equally to violations of this section. *(Added by Stats.2003, c. 287 (A.B.1294), § 1. Amended by Stats.2006, c. 521 (A.B.2043), § 2; Stats.2007, c. 130 (A.B. 299), § 34.)*

Research References

Rutter, Cal. Practice Guide: Enforcing Judgments/Debts Ch. 2-B, B. Statutory Liability and Procedures.
8 Witkin Cal. Proc. 5th Enforcement of Judgment § 10, (S 10) Collection Where Identity Theft is Claimed.

ARTICLE 3. DEBTOR RESPONSIBILITIES

§ 1788.20. Request or application for credit; inability or lack of intention to pay obligation; falsity of or concealment of information

In connection with any request or application for consumer credit, no person shall:

(a) Request or apply for such credit at a time when such person knows there is no reasonable probability of such person's being able, or such person then lacks the intention, to pay the obligation created thereby in accordance with the terms and conditions of the credit extension; or

(b) Knowingly submit false or inaccurate information or willfully conceal adverse information bearing upon such person's credit worthiness, credit standing, or credit capacity. *(Added by Stats.1977, c. 907, p. 2771, § 1.)*

Research References

Rutter, Cal. Practice Guide: Enforcing Judgments/Debts Ch. 2-B, B. Statutory Liability and Procedures.
8 Witkin Cal. Proc. 5th Enforcement of Judgment § 11, Responsibilities of Debtor.

§ 1788.21. Notice of change in name, address or employment; disclosure by creditor of debtor's responsibility

(a) In connection with any consumer credit existing or requested to be extended to a person, such person shall within a reasonable time notify the creditor or prospective creditor of any change in such person's name, address, or employment.

(b) Each responsibility set forth in subdivision (a) shall apply only if and after the creditor clearly and conspicuously in writing discloses such responsibility to such person. *(Added by Stats. 1977, c. 907, p. 2771, § 1.)*

Research References

Rutter, Cal. Practice Guide: Enforcing Judgments/Debts Ch. 2-B, B. Statutory Liability and Procedures.
8 Witkin Cal. Proc. 5th Enforcement of Judgment § 11, Responsibilities of Debtor.

§ 1788.22. Credit extended under an account; duties of debtor disclosure by creditor of debtor's responsibility

(a) In connection with any consumer credit extended to a person under an account:

(1) No such person shall attempt to consummate any consumer credit transaction thereunder knowing that credit privileges under the account have been terminated or suspended.

(2) Each such person shall notify the creditor by telephone, telegraph, letter, or any other reasonable means that an unauthorized use of the account has occurred or may occur as the result of loss or theft of a credit card, or other instrument identifying the account, within a reasonable time after such person's discovery thereof, and shall reasonably assist the creditor in determining the facts and circumstances relating to any unauthorized use of the account.

(b) Each responsibility set forth in subdivision (a) shall apply only if and after the creditor clearly and conspicuously in writing discloses such responsibility to such person. *(Added by Stats. 1977, c. 907, p. 2771, § 1.)*

Research References

Rutter, Cal. Practice Guide: Enforcing Judgments/Debts Ch. 2-B, B. Statutory Liability and Procedures.

8 Witkin Cal. Proc. 5th Enforcement of Judgment § 11, Responsibilities of Debtor.

ARTICLE 4. ENFORCEMENT

§ 1788.30. Liability of debt collector; individual action; actual and punitive damages; costs; cure of violation; venue; defenses

(a) Any debt collector who violates this title with respect to any debtor shall be liable to that debtor only in an individual action, and his liability therein to that debtor shall be in an amount equal to the sum of any actual damages sustained by the debtor as a result of the violation.

(b) Any debt collector who willfully and knowingly violates this title with respect to any debtor shall, in addition to actual damages sustained by the debtor as a result of the violation, also be liable to the debtor only in an individual action, and his additional liability therein to that debtor shall be for a penalty in such amount as the court may allow, which shall not be less than one hundred dollars ($100) nor greater than one thousand dollars ($1,000).

(c) In the case of any action to enforce any liability under this title, the prevailing party shall be entitled to costs of the action. Reasonable attorney's fees, which shall be based on time necessarily expended to enforce the liability, shall be awarded to a prevailing debtor; reasonable attorney's fees may be awarded to a prevailing creditor upon a finding by the court that the debtor's prosecution or defense of the action was not in good faith.

(d) A debt collector shall have no civil liability under this title if, within 15 days either after discovering a violation which is able to be cured, or after the receipt of a written notice of such violation, the debt collector notifies the debtor of the violation, and makes whatever adjustments or corrections are necessary to cure the violation with respect to the debtor.

(e) A debt collector shall have no civil liability to which such debt collector might otherwise be subject for a violation of this title, if the debt collector shows by a preponderance of evidence that the violation was not intentional and resulted notwithstanding the maintenance of procedures reasonably adapted to avoid any such violation.

(f) Any action under this section may be brought in any appropriate court of competent jurisdiction in an individual capacity only, within one year from the date of the occurrence of the violation.

(g) Any intentional violation of the provisions of this title by the debt collector may be raised as a defense by the debt collector, if such violation is pertinent or relevant to any claim or action brought against the debt collector by or on behalf of the debtor. *(Added by Stats.1977, c. 907, p. 2771, § 1.)*

Research References

Rutter, Cal. Practice Guide: Enforcing Judgments/Debts Ch. 2-B, B. Statutory Liability and Procedures.
8 Witkin Cal. Proc. 5th Enforcement of Judgment § 12, Relief for Violation.
8 Witkin Cal. Proc. 5th Enforcement of Judgment § 16, Remedies for Violation of Requirements.

7 Witkin Cal. Proc. 5th Judgment § 224, (S 224) Consumer Protection Actions.
7 Witkin Cal. Proc. 5th Judgment § 311, in General.
7 Witkin Cal. Proc. 5th Judgment § 312, Use of Lodestar Approach.

§ 1788.31. Severability

If any provision of this title, or the application thereof to any person or circumstances, is held invalid, the remaining provisions of this title, or the application of such provisions to other persons or circumstances, shall not be affected thereby. *(Added by Stats.1977, c. 907, p. 2771, § 1.)*

§ 1788.32. Cumulative remedies; effect on existing regulations

The remedies provided herein are intended to be cumulative and are in addition to any other procedures, rights, or remedies under any other provision of law. The enactment of this title shall not supersede existing administrative regulations of the Director of Consumer Affairs except to the extent that those regulations are inconsistent with the provisions of this title. *(Added by Stats.1977, c. 907, p. 2771, § 1.)*

Research References

Rutter, Cal. Practice Guide: Enforcing Judgments/Debts Ch. 2-B, B. Statutory Liability and Procedures.
Rutter, Cal. Practice Guide: Enforcing Judgments/Debts Ch. 6A-8, Federal and State Debt Collection Restrictions; Consumer Debts.
8 Witkin Cal. Proc. 5th Enforcement of Judgment § 12, Relief for Violation.

§ 1788.33. Public policy; waiver of rights

Any waiver of the provisions of this title is contrary to public policy, and is void and unenforceable. *(Added by Stats.2002, c. 815 (A.B.2331), § 12.)*

Research References

8 Witkin Cal. Proc. 5th Enforcement of Judgment § 12, Relief for Violation.

Title 1.6C.5

FAIR DEBT BUYING PRACTICES

§ 1788.50. Definitions; application of title

(a) As used in this title:

(1) "Debt buyer" means a person or entity that is regularly engaged in the business of purchasing charged-off consumer debt for collection purposes, whether it collects the debt itself, hires a third party for collection, or hires an attorney-at-law for collection litigation. "Debt buyer" does not mean a person or

entity that acquires a charged-off consumer debt incidental to the purchase of a portfolio predominantly consisting of consumer debt that has not been charged off.

(2) "Charged-off consumer debt" means a consumer debt that has been removed from a creditor's books as an asset and treated as a loss or expense.

(b) The acquisition by a check services company of the right to collect on a paper or electronic check instrument, including an Automated Clearing House item, that has been returned unpaid to a merchant does not constitute a purchase of delinquent consumer debt under this title.

(c) Terms defined in Title 1.6C (commencing with Section 1788) shall apply to this title.

(d) This title shall apply to debt buyers with respect to all consumer debt sold or resold on or after January 1, 2014. *(Added by Stats.2013, c. 64 (S.B.233), § 2.)*

§ 1788.52. Debt buyer written statements to debtor to attempt debt collection; information that must be provided to debtor; timing requirements; written notice; form; conflict of laws

(a) A debt buyer shall not make any written statement to a debtor in an attempt to collect a consumer debt unless the debt buyer possesses the following information:

(1) That the debt buyer is the sole owner of the debt at issue or has authority to assert the rights of all owners of the debt.

(2) The debt balance at charge off and an explanation of the amount, nature, and reason for all post-charge-off interest and fees, if any, imposed by the charge-off creditor or any subsequent purchasers of the debt. This paragraph shall not be deemed to require a specific itemization, but the explanation shall identify separately the charge-off balance, the total of any post-charge-off interest, and the total of any post-charge-off fees.

(3) The date of default or the date of the last payment.

(4) The name and an address of the charge-off creditor at the time of charge off, and the charge-off creditor's account number associated with the debt. The charge-off creditor's name and address shall be in sufficient form so as to reasonably identify the charge-off creditor.

(5) The name and last known address of the debtor as they appeared in the charge-off creditor's records prior to the sale of the debt. If the debt was sold prior to January 1, 2014, the name and last known address of the debtor as they appeared in the debt owner's records on December 31, 2013, shall be sufficient.

(6) The names and addresses of all persons or entities that purchased the debt after charge off, including the debt buyer making the written statement. The names and addresses shall be in sufficient form so as to reasonably identify each such purchaser.

(b) A debt buyer shall not make any written statement to a debtor in an attempt to collect a consumer debt unless the debt buyer has access to a copy of a contract or other document evidencing the debtor's agreement to the debt. If the claim is based on debt for which no signed contract or agreement exists, the debt buyer shall have access to a copy of a document provided to the debtor while the account was active, demonstrating that the debt was incurred by the debtor. For a revolving credit account, the most recent monthly statement recording a purchase transaction, last payment, or balance transfer shall be deemed sufficient to satisfy this requirement.

(c) A debt buyer shall provide the information or documents identified in subdivisions (a) and (b) to the debtor without charge within 15 calendar days of receipt of a debtor's written request for information regarding the debt or proof of the debt.

If the debt buyer cannot provide the information or documents within 15 calendar days, the debt buyer shall cease all collection of the debt until the debt buyer provides the debtor the information or documents described in subdivisions (a) and (b). Except as provided otherwise in this title, the request by the debtor shall be consistent with the validation requirements contained in Section 1692g of Title 15 of the United States Code. A debt buyer shall provide all debtors with whom it has contact an active postal address to which these requests can be sent. A debt buyer may also provide an active email address to which these requests can be sent and through which information and documents can be delivered, if the parties agree.

(d)(1) A debt buyer shall include with its first written communication with the debtor in no smaller than 12–point type, a separate prominent notice that provides:

"You may request records showing the following: (1) that [insert name of debt buyer] has the right to seek collection of the debt; (2) the debt balance, including an explanation of any interest charges and additional fees; (3) the date of default or the date of the last payment; (4) the name of the charge-off creditor and the account number associated with the debt; (5) the name and last known address of the debtor as it appeared in the charge-off creditor's or debt buyer's records prior to the sale of the debt, as appropriate; and (6) the names of all persons or entities that have purchased the debt. You may also request from us a copy of the contract or other document evidencing your agreement to the debt.

"A request for these records may be addressed to: [insert debt buyer's active mailing address and email address, if applicable]."

(2) When collecting on a time-barred debt where the debt is not past the date for obsolescence provided for in Section 605(a) of the federal Fair Credit Reporting Act (15 U.S.C. Sec. 1681c):

"The law limits how long you can be sued on a debt. Because of the age of your debt, we will not sue you for it. If you do not pay the debt, [insert name of debt buyer] may [continue to] report it to the credit reporting agencies as unpaid for as long as the law permits this reporting."

(3) When collecting on a time-barred debt where the debt is past the date for obsolescence provided for in Section 605(a) of the federal Fair Credit Reporting Act (15 U.S.C. Sec. 1681c):

"The law limits how long you can be sued on a debt. Because of the age of your debt, we will not sue you for it, and we will not report it to any credit reporting agency."

(e) If a language other than English is principally used by the debt buyer in the initial oral contact with the debtor, the notice required by subdivision (d) shall be provided to the debtor in that language within five working days.

(f) In the event of a conflict between the requirements of subdivision (d) and federal law, so that it is impracticable to comply with both, the requirements of federal law shall prevail. *(Added by Stats.2013, c. 64 (S.B.233), § 2.)*

§ 1788.54. Settlement agreements; requirement of written agreement or documentation in open court; monthly and final statement requirements for payments by debtor

(a) All settlement agreements between a debt buyer and a debtor shall be documented in open court or otherwise reduced to writing. The debt buyer shall ensure that a copy of the written agreement is provided to the debtor.

(b) A debt buyer that receives payment on a debt shall provide, within 30 calendar days, a receipt or monthly statement, to the debtor. The receipt or statement shall clearly and conspicuously show the amount and date paid, the name of the entity paid, the current account number, the name of the charge-off creditor, the account number issued by the charge-off creditor, and the remaining balance owing, if any. The receipt or statement may be provided electronically if the parties agree.

(c) A debt buyer that accepts a payment as payment in full, or as a full and final compromise of the debt, shall provide, within 30 calendar days, a final statement that complies with subdivision (b). A debt buyer shall not sell an interest in a resolved debt, or any personal or financial information related to the resolved debt. *(Added by Stats.2013, c. 64 (S.B.233), § 2.)*

§ 1788.56.   Statute of limitations bar to actions

A debt buyer shall not bring suit or initiate an arbitration or other legal proceeding to collect a consumer debt if the applicable statute of limitations on the debt buyer's claim has expired. *(Added by Stats.2013, c. 64 (S.B.233), § 2.)*

§ 1788.58.   Actions brought by debt buyer; contents of complaint; requirements

In an action brought by a debt buyer on a consumer debt:

(a) The complaint shall allege all of the following:

(1) That the plaintiff is a debt buyer.

(2) The nature of the underlying debt and the consumer transaction or transactions from which it is derived, in a short and plain statement.

(3) That the debt buyer is the sole owner of the debt at issue, or has authority to assert the rights of all owners of the debt.

(4) The debt balance at charge off and an explanation of the amount, nature, and reason for all post-charge-off interest and fees, if any, imposed by the charge-off creditor or any subsequent purchasers of the debt. This paragraph shall not be deemed to require a specific itemization, but the explanation shall identify separately the charge-off balance, the total of any post-charge-off interest, and the total of any post-charge-off fees.

(5) The date of default or the date of the last payment.

(6) The name and an address of the charge-off creditor at the time of charge off, and the charge-off creditor's account number associated with the debt. The charge-off creditor's name and address shall be in sufficient form so as to reasonably identify the charge-off creditor.

(7) The name and last known address of the debtor as they appeared in the charge-off creditor's records prior to the sale of the debt. If the debt was sold prior to January 1, 2014, the debtor's name and last known address as they appeared in the debt owner's records on December 31, 2013, shall be sufficient.

(8) The names and addresses of all persons or entities that purchased the debt after charge off, including the plaintiff debt buyer. The names and addresses shall be in sufficient form so as to reasonably identify each such purchaser.

(9) That the debt buyer has complied with Section 1788.52.

(b) A copy of the contract or other document described in subdivision (b) of Section 1788.52, shall be attached to the complaint.

(c) The requirements of this title shall not be deemed to require the disclosure in public records of personal, financial, or medical information, the confidentiality of which is protected by any state or federal law. *(Added by Stats.2013, c. 64 (S.B.233), § 2.)*

§ 1788.60.   Default or other judgment; submissions to establish facts alleged in complaint; dismissal of action

(a) In an action initiated by a debt buyer, no default or other judgment may be entered against a debtor unless business records, authenticated through a sworn declaration, are submitted by the debt buyer to the court to establish the facts required to be alleged by paragraphs (3) to (8), inclusive, of subdivision (a) of Section 1788.58.

(b) No default or other judgment may be entered against a debtor unless a copy of the contract or other document described in subdivision (b) of Section 1788.52, authenticated through a sworn declaration, has been submitted by the debt buyer to the court.

(c) In any action on a consumer debt, if a debt buyer plaintiff seeks a default judgment and has not complied with the requirements of this title, the court shall not enter a default judgment for the plaintiff and may, in its discretion, dismiss the action.

(d) Except as provided in this title, this section is not intended to modify or otherwise amend the procedures established in Section 585 of the Code of Civil Procedure. *(Added by Stats.2013, c. 64 (S.B.233), § 2.)*

§ 1788.62.   Violations of title by debt buyer; liability; damages; court considerations; limitation of actions

(a) In the case of an action brought by an individual or individuals, a debt buyer that violates any provision of this title with respect to any person shall be liable to that person in an amount equal to the sum of the following:

(1) Any actual damages sustained by that person as a result of the violation, including, but not limited to, the amount of any judgment obtained by the debt buyer as a result of a time-barred suit to collect a debt from that person.

(2) Statutory damages in an amount as the court may allow, which shall not be less than one hundred dollars ($100) nor greater than one thousand dollars ($1,000).

(b) In the case of a class action, a debt buyer that violates any provision of this title shall be liable for any statutory damages for each named plaintiff as provided in paragraph (2) of subdivision (a). If the court finds that the debt buyer engaged in a pattern and practice of violating any provision of this title, the court may award additional damages to the class in an amount not to exceed the lesser of five hundred thousand dollars ($500,000) or 1 percent of the net worth of the debt buyer.

(c)(1) In the case of any successful action to enforce liability under this section, the court shall award costs of the action, together with reasonable attorney's fees as determined by the court.

(2) Reasonable attorney's fees may be awarded to a prevailing debt buyer upon a finding by the court that the plaintiff's prosecution of the action was not in good faith.

(d) In determining the amount of liability under subdivision (b), the court shall consider, among other relevant factors, the frequency and persistence of noncompliance by the debt buyer, the nature of the noncompliance, the resources of the debt buyer, and the number of persons adversely affected.

(e) A debt buyer shall have no civil liability under this section if the debt buyer shows by a preponderance of evidence that the violation was not intentional and resulted from a bona fide error, and occurred notwithstanding the maintenance of procedures reasonably adopted to avoid any error.

(f) An action to enforce any liability created by this title shall be brought within one year from the date of the last violation.

(g) Recovery in an action brought under the Rosenthal Fair Debt Collection Practices Act (Title 1.6C (commencing with Section 1788)) or the federal Fair Debt Collection Practices Act (15 U.S.C. Sec. 1692 et seq.) shall preclude recovery for the same acts in an action brought under this title. *(Added by Stats.2013, c. 64 (S.B.233), § 2.)*

§ 1788.64. Waiver of provisions void

Any waiver of the provisions of this title is contrary to public policy, and is void and unenforceable. *(Added by Stats.2013, c. 64 (S.B.233), § 2.)*

Title 1.6D

ELECTRONIC COMMERCE

ARTICLE 1. GENERAL PROVISIONS

§ 1789. Legislative finding and declaration

The Legislature hereby finds and declares that it is in the public interest that consumers have comprehensive knowledge of services available through electronic commerce and to that end hereby enacts the Electronic Commerce Act of 1984. *(Added by Stats.1984, c. 638, § 1.)*

Research References

4 Witkin, California Summary 10th Sales § 167, (S 167) in General.
4 Witkin, California Summary 10th Sales § 198, (S 198) in General.
4 Witkin, California Summary 10th Sales § 203, Statutory Rules.
4 Witkin, California Summary 10th Sales § 204, Illustrations: Economic Loss.
4 Witkin, California Summary 10th Sales § 205, Illustrations: Personal Injury and Property Damage.
4 Witkin, California Summary 10th Sales § 208, Deduction of Damages from Price.
4 Witkin, California Summary 10th Sales § 353, (S 353) Electronic Commerce.

§ 1789.1. Short title

This title may be cited as "The Electronic Commerce Act of 1984." *(Added by Stats.1984, c. 638, § 1.)*

§ 1789.2. Definitions

For the purposes of this title, the following terms have the meanings expressed in this section:

(a) "Electronic commercial service" or "service" means an electronic shopping system to conduct the purchase of goods and services via a telecommunications network, but does not mean conventional voice-only telephone service, one-way television or radio broadcasting, an electronic fund transfer system, or a service provided through an electronic terminal located at a place of business where the sale of goods or services sold through that service otherwise occurs.

(b) "Consumer" means a natural person who purchases goods or services using an electronic commercial service.

(c) "Provider of service" means a person who contracts with consumers to provide an electronic commercial service.

(d) "Goods or services" means tangible items or physical services provided to the consumer, or tickets or vouchers for such tangible items or physical services, but does not mean computerized data delivered to the consumer via a computer terminal or in printed form. *(Added by Stats.1984, c. 638, § 1. Amended by Stats.1987, c. 49, § 1, eff. June 17, 1987.)*

Research References

4 Witkin, California Summary 10th Sales § 353, (S 353) Electronic Commerce.

§ 1789.3. Required information to consumers by providers of service

The provider of an electronic commercial service shall provide to consumers with which it contracts to provide the service, at the time it contracts to provide the service and annually, on or before June 30 of each year thereafter, all of the following information:

(a) The name, address, and telephone number of the provider of service.

(b) Any charges to the consumer imposed by the provider for the use of the service.

(c) The procedures a consumer may follow in order to resolve a complaint regarding the service or to receive further information regarding use of the service, including the telephone number and address of the Complaint Assistance Unit of the Division of Consumer Services of the Department of Consumer Affairs. *(Added by Stats.1984, c. 638, § 1. Amended by Stats.1986, c. 508, § 1.)*

Research References

4 Witkin, California Summary 10th Sales § 353, (S 353) Electronic Commerce.

§ 1789.5. Violation; civil penalty; payment

(a) Any provider who knowingly and willfully violates any provision of this title is liable for a civil penalty not to exceed five thousand dollars ($5,000) which may be assessed and recovered in a civil action brought in the name of the people of the State of California by the Attorney General, by any district attorney or city attorney, or by a city prosecutor in any city or city and county having a full-time city prosecutor, in any court of competent jurisdiction.

(b) If the action is brought by the Attorney General, one-half of the penalty collected shall be paid to the treasurer of the county in which the judgment was entered, and one-half to the General Fund. If the action is brought by a district attorney, the penalty collected shall be paid to the treasurer of the county in which the judgment was entered. If the action is brought by a city attorney or city prosecutor, one-half of the penalty shall be paid to the treasurer of the city in which the judgment was entered, and one-half to the treasurer of the county in which the judgment was entered. *(Added by Stats.1984, c. 638, § 1.)*

Research References

4 Witkin, California Summary 10th Sales § 353, (S 353) Electronic Commerce.

§ 1789.6. Liability of provider for errors or omissions from operation of service

Nothing in this title shall be construed to limit the liability of a provider of service to a consumer for errors or omissions arising from the operation of an electronic commercial service. *(Added by Stats.1984, c. 638, § 1.)*

§ 1789.7. Application of title; federal law or regulation; credit cards; electronic fund transfer

(a) This title does not apply where it is inconsistent with, or infringes upon, federal law or regulation.

(b) This title does not apply to the rights and obligations of a cardholder and a card issuer with respect to the use of a credit card arising from the purchase of goods or services conducted through an electronic commercial service. For the purpose of this subdivision, "cardholder," "card issuer," and "credit card" have the same meaning as those terms are given in the federal Fair Credit Billing Act (15 U.S.C. Sec. 1601 et seq.) and regulations adopted thereunder, or, if applicable, the Song-Beverly Credit Card Act of 1971 (Title 1.3 (commencing with Section 1747)).

(c) This title does not apply to the rights and obligations of a consumer and a financial institution with respect to any electronic fund transfer arising from purchase of goods or services conducted through an electronic commercial service. For the purposes of this subdivision, "consumer," "financial institution," and "electronic fund transfer" have the same meaning as those terms are given in the Electronic Fund Transfer Act (15 U.S.C. Sec. 1601 et seq.) and regulations adopted thereunder. *(Added by Stats.1984, c. 638, § 1.)*

Research References

4 Witkin, California Summary 10th Sales § 353, (S 353) Electronic Commerce.

§ 1789.8. Application of title; transactions on or after July 1, 1985

This title applies to transactions entered into on or after July 1, 1985. *(Added by Stats.1984, c. 638, § 1.)*

§ 1789.9. Public policy; waiver of rights

Any waiver of the provisions of this title is contrary to public policy, and is void and unenforceable. *(Added by Stats.2002, c. 815 (A.B.2331), § 13.)*

Research References

4 Witkin, California Summary 10th Sales § 353, (S 353) Electronic Commerce.

Title 1.6E

CREDIT SERVICES

§ 1789.10. Short title

This title shall be known and may be cited as the "Credit Services Act of 1984." *(Added by Stats.1984, c. 1177, § 1.)*

Research References

Rutter, Cal. Practice Guide: A.D.R. Ch. 5-A, A. General Considerations.
Rutter, Cal. Practice Guide: A.D.R. Ch. 5-B, B. Federal vs. State Law Governing.
Miller and Starr California Real Estate § 35:24, Federal Arbitration Act.
4 Witkin, California Summary 10th Sales § 309, Nature and Scope of Statute.

§ 1789.11. Legislative findings and declarations; purposes; liberal construction

The Legislature finds and declares that:

(a) The ability to obtain and use credit has become of great importance to consumers, who have a vital interest in establishing and maintaining their credit worthiness and credit standing. As a result, consumers who have experienced credit problems may seek assistance from credit services organizations which offer to obtain credit or improve the credit standing of such consumers.

Certain advertising and business practices of some credit services organizations have worked a financial hardship upon the people of this state, often those who are of limited economic means and inexperienced in credit matters. Credit services organizations have significant impact upon the economy and well-being of this state and its people.

(b) The purposes of this title are to provide prospective buyers of services of credit services organizations with the information necessary to make an intelligent decision regarding the purchase of those services and to protect the public from unfair or deceptive advertising and business practices.

(c) This title shall be construed liberally to achieve these purposes. *(Added by Stats.1984, c. 1177, § 1.)*

Research References

4 Witkin, California Summary 10th Sales § 309, Nature and Scope of Statute.

§ 1789.12. Definitions

As used in this title:

(a) "Credit services organization" means a person who, with respect to the extension of credit by others, sells, provides, or performs, or represents that he or she can or will sell, provide or perform, any of the following services, in return for the payment of money or other valuable consideration:

(1) Improving a buyer's credit record, history, or rating.

(2) Obtaining a loan or other extension of credit for a buyer.

(3) Providing advice or assistance to a buyer with regard to either paragraph (1) or (2).

(b) "Credit services organization" does not include any of the following:

(1) Any person holding a license to make loans or extensions of credit pursuant to the laws of this state or the United States who is subject to regulation and supervision with respect to the making of those loans or extensions of credit by an official or agency of this state or the United States and whose business is the making of those loans or extensions of credit.

(2) Any bank, as defined in Section 102 of the Financial Code, or any savings institution, as specified in subdivision (a) or (b) of Section 5102 of the Financial Code, whose deposits or accounts are eligible for insurance by the Federal Deposit Insurance Corporation.

(3) Any person licensed as a prorater by the Department of Corporations when the person is acting within the course and scope of that license.

(4) Any person licensed as a real estate broker performing an act for which a real estate license is required under the Real Estate Law (Pt. 1 (commencing with Sec. 10000), Div. 4, B. & P.C.) and who is acting within the course and scope of that license.

(5) Any attorney licensed to practice law in this state, where the attorney renders services within the course and scope of the practice of law, unless the attorney is an employee of, or otherwise directly affiliated with, a credit services organization.

(6) Any broker-dealer registered with the Securities and Exchange Commission or the Commodity Futures Trading Commission where the broker-dealer is acting within the course and scope of the regulation.

(7) Any nonprofit organization described in Section 501(c)(3) of the Internal Revenue Code that, according to a final ruling or determination by the Internal Revenue Service, is both of the following:

(A) Exempt from taxation under Section 501(a) of the Internal Revenue Code.

(B) Not a private foundation as defined in Section 509 of the Internal Revenue Code.

An advance ruling or determination of tax-exempt or foundation status by the Internal Revenue Service does not meet the requirements of this paragraph.

(c) "Buyer" means any natural person who is solicited to purchase or who purchases the services of a credit services organization.

(d) "Extension of credit" means the right to defer payment of debt or to incur debt and defer its payment, offered or granted primarily for personal, family, or household purposes.

(e) "Consumer credit reporting agency" means a consumer credit reporting agency subject to the Consumer Credit Reporting Agencies Act, Title 1.6 (commencing with Section 1785.1).

(f) "Person" includes an individual, corporation, partnership, joint venture, or any business entity. *(Added by Stats.1984, c. 1177, § 1. Amended by Stats.1992, c. 651 (A.B.2999), § 2; Stats.1994, c. 792 (A.B.1922), § 1; Stats.1994, c. 1010 (S.B.2053), § 38; Stats.1996, c. 648 (A.B.2279), § 1.)*

Research References

4 Witkin, California Summary 10th Sales § 309, Nature and Scope of Statute.

§ 1789.13. Credit services organizations; prohibited activities

A credit services organization and its salespersons, agents, representatives, and independent contractors who sell or attempt to sell the services of a credit services organization shall not do any of the following:

(a) Charge or receive any money or other valuable consideration prior to full and complete performance of the services the credit services organization has agreed to perform for or on behalf of the buyer.

(b) Fail to perform the agreed services within six months following the date the buyer signs the contract for those services.

(c) Charge or receive any money or other valuable consideration for referral of the buyer to a retail seller or other credit grantor who will or may extend credit to the buyer, if either of the following apply:

(1) The credit that is or will be extended to the buyer (A) is upon substantially the same terms as those available to the general public or (B) is upon substantially the same terms that would have been extended to the buyer without the assistance of the credit services organization.

(2) The money or consideration is paid by the credit grantor or is derived from the buyer's payments to the credit grantor for costs, fees, finance charges, or principal.

(d) Make, or counsel or advise a buyer to make, a statement that is untrue or misleading and that is known, or that by the exercise of reasonable care should be known, to be untrue or misleading, to a consumer credit reporting agency or to a person who has extended credit to a buyer or to whom a buyer is applying for an extension of credit, such as statements concerning a buyer's identification, home address, creditworthiness, credit standing, or credit capacity.

(e) Remove, or assist or advise the buyer to remove, adverse information from the buyer's credit record which is accurate and not obsolete.

(f) Create, or assist or advise the buyer to create, a new credit record by using a different name, address, social security number, or employee identification number.

(g) Make or use untrue or misleading representations in the offer or sale of the services of a credit services organization, including either of the following:

(1) Guaranteeing or otherwise stating that the organization is able to delete an adverse credit history, unless the representation clearly discloses, in a manner equally as conspicuous as the guarantee, that this can be done only if the credit history is inaccurate or obsolete and is not claimed to be accurate by the creditor who submitted the information.

(2) Guaranteeing or otherwise stating that the organization is able to obtain an extension of credit, regardless of the buyer's previous credit problems or credit history, unless the representation clearly discloses, in a manner equally as conspicuous as the guarantee, the eligibility requirements for obtaining an extension of credit.

(h) Engage, directly or indirectly, in an act, practice, or course of business that operates or would operate as a fraud or deception upon a person in connection with the offer or sale of the services of a credit services organization.

(i) Advertise or cause to be advertised, in any manner, the services of the credit services organization, without being registered with the Department of Justice.

(j) Fail to maintain an agent for service of process in this state.

(k) Transfer or assign its certificate of registration.

(*l*) Submit a buyer's dispute to a consumer credit reporting agency without the buyer's knowledge.

(m) Use a consumer credit reporting agency's telephone system or toll-free telephone number to represent the caller as the buyer in submitting a dispute of a buyer or requesting disclosure without prior authorization of the buyer.

(n) Directly or indirectly extend credit to a buyer.

(o) Refer a buyer to a credit grantor that is related to the credit services organization by a common ownership, management, or control, including a common owner, director, or officer.

(p) Refer a buyer to a credit grantor for which the credit services organization provides, or arranges for a third party to provide, services related to the extension of credit such as underwriting, billing, payment processing, or debt collection.

(q) Provide a credit grantor with an assurance that a portion of an extension of credit to a buyer referred by the credit services organization will be repaid, including providing a guaranty, letter of credit, or agreement to acquire a part of the credit grantor's financial interest in the extension of credit.

(r) Use a scheme, device, or contrivance to evade the prohibitions contained in this section. *(Added by Stats.1984, c. 1177, § 1. Amended by Stats.1992, c. 651 (A.B.2999), § 3; Stats.1994, c. 792 (A.B.1922), § 2; Stats.2007, c. 91 (S.B.500), § 1; Stats.2008, c. 179 (S.B.1498), § 30.)*

Research References

4 Witkin, California Summary 10th Sales § 310, Prohibited Acts.

§ 1789.14. Information statement; necessity and time of delivery to buyer; acknowledgement of delivery; retention on file

Prior to the execution of a contract or agreement between the buyer and a credit services organization, the credit services organization shall provide the buyer a statement in writing, containing all the information required by Section 1789.15. The credit services organization shall maintain on file or microfilm for a period of two years an exact copy of the statement, personally signed by the buyer, acknowledging receipt of a copy of the statement. *(Added by Stats.1984, c. 1177, § 1. Amended by Stats.1992, c. 651 (A.B.2999), § 4.)*

Research References

4 Witkin, California Summary 10th Sales § 311, Information Statements.

§ 1789.15. Information statement; contents

The information statement shall include all of the following:

(a) A complete and detailed description of the services to be performed by the credit services organization for or on behalf of the buyer and the total amount the buyer will have to pay, or become obligated to pay, for the services.

(b) The buyer's right to proceed against the bond under the circumstances and in the manner set forth in Section 1789.18.

(c) The name and address of the surety company which issued the bond.

(d) A complete and accurate statement of the availability of nonprofit credit counseling services.

The information statement shall be printed in at least 10-point boldface type and shall include the following statement or any substantially equivalent alternative that is approved by the Department of Justice:

"CONSUMER CREDIT FILE RIGHTS UNDER STATE AND FEDERAL LAW

You have a right to obtain a copy of your credit file from a consumer credit reporting agency. You may be charged a reasonable fee not exceeding eight dollars ($8). There is no fee, however, if you have been turned down for credit, employment, insurance, or a rental dwelling because of information in your credit report within the preceding 60 days. The consumer credit reporting agency must provide someone to help you interpret the information in your credit file. You have a right to dispute inaccurate information by contacting the consumer credit reporting agency directly. However, neither you nor any credit repair company or credit services organization has the right to have accurate, current, and verifiable information removed from your credit report. Under the Federal Fair Credit Reporting Act, the consumer credit reporting agency must remove accurate, negative information from your report only if it is over seven years old. Bankruptcy information can be reported for 10 years. If you have notified a credit reporting agency in writing that you dispute the accuracy of information in your credit file, the consumer credit reporting agency must then reinvestigate and modify or remove inaccurate information. The consumer credit reporting agency may not charge a fee for this service. Any pertinent information and copies of all documents you have concerning an error should be given to the consumer credit reporting agency.

If reinvestigation does not resolve the dispute to your satisfaction, you may send a brief statement to the consumer credit reporting agency to keep in your file, explaining why you think the record is inaccurate. The consumer credit reporting agency must include your statement about disputed information in any report it issues about you.

You have a right to cancel the contract for any reason within five working days from the date you signed it. If for any reason you do cancel the contract during this time, you do not owe any money.

You have a right to sue a credit services organization if it misleads you." *(Added by Stats.1984, c. 1177, § 1. Amended by Stats.1992, c. 651 (A.B.2999), § 5.)*

Research References

4 Witkin, California Summary 10th Sales § 311, Information Statements.

§ 1789.16. Contracts; requirements; contents

(a) A credit services organization shall not provide any service to a buyer except pursuant to a written contract that complies with this section. Every contract between the buyer and a credit services organization for the purchase of the services of the credit services organization shall be in writing, shall be dated, signed by the buyer, and include all of the following:

(1) A conspicuous statement in size equal to at least 10-point boldface type, in immediate proximity to the space reserved for the signature of the buyer, as follows: "You, the buyer, may cancel this contract at any time prior to midnight of the fifth day after the date of the transaction. See the attached notice of cancellation form for an explanation of this right."

(2) The terms and conditions of payment, including the total of all payments to be made by the buyer, whether to the credit services organization or to some other person.

(3) A full and detailed description of the services to be performed by the credit services organization for the buyer, including all guarantees and all promises of full or partial refunds, and the estimated date by which the services are to be performed, or the estimated length of time for performing the services not to exceed six months or a shorter period consistent

with the purposes of this title as may be prescribed by the Department of Justice.

(4) The credit services organization's principal business address and the name and address of its agent, other than the Secretary of State, in the State of California, authorized to receive service of process.

(b) The contract shall be accompanied by a completed form in duplicate, captioned "Notice of Cancellation," which shall be attached to the contract and easily detachable, and which shall contain in type of at least 10-point the following statement written in the same language as used in the contract:

"Notice of Cancellation"

"You may cancel this contract, without any penalty or obligation, within five days from the date the contract is signed.

"If you cancel, any payment made by you under this contract must be returned within 15 days following receipt by the seller of your cancellation notice.

"To cancel this contract, mail or deliver a signed and dated copy of this cancellation notice, or any other written notice, to

_____at
                    (name of seller)

_____
(address of seller)   (place of business)

not later than midnight _____.
                        (date)

"I hereby cancel this transaction."

_____   _____
    (date)   (purchaser's signature)

A copy of the fully completed contract and all other documents the credit services organization requires the buyer to sign shall be given to the buyer at the time they are signed. (Added by Stats.1984, c. 1177, § 1. Amended by Stats.1992, c. 651 (A.B.2999), § 6; Stats.1993, c. 285 (A.B.1340), § 10, eff. Aug. 2, 1993; Stats.1994, c. 792 (A.B.1922), § 3.)

Research References

14 NO. 3 Miller & Starr, California Real Estate Newsalert 1, Court of Appeal Finds Title Insurance Arbitration Provision Enforceable, Without Reaching "Unconscionability" Analysis.
4 Witkin, California Summary 10th Sales § 312, Requisites of Contract.

§ 1789.17. Seller's breach of contract or obligation; violation of title

The seller's breach of a contract under this title or of any obligation arising therefrom shall constitute a violation of this title. (Added by Stats.1984, c. 1177, § 1.)

Research References

4 Witkin, California Summary 10th Sales § 313, Remedies and Penalties.

§ 1789.18. Surety bonds; compliance requirements; filing of copy

No credit services organization shall conduct business in this state unless the credit services organization has first obtained a surety bond in the principal amount of one hundred thousand dollars ($100,000) issued by an admitted surety and the bond complies with all of the following:

(a) The bond shall be in favor of the State of California for the benefit of any person who is damaged by any violation of this title. The bond shall also be in favor of any individual damaged by those practices.

(b) Any person claiming against the bond for a violation of this title may maintain an action at law against the credit services organization and against the surety. The surety shall be liable

only for actual damages and not the punitive damages permitted under Section 1789.21. The aggregate liability of the surety to all persons damaged by a credit services organization's violation of this title shall in no event exceed the amount of the bond.

(c) The bond shall be maintained for two years following the date on which the credit services organization ceases to conduct business in this state.

A copy of the bond shall be filed with the Secretary of State. (Added by Stats.1984, c. 1177, § 1. Amended by Stats.1992, c. 651 (A.B.2999), § 7.)

Research References

4 Witkin, California Summary 10th Sales § 311, Information Statements.

§ 1789.19. Waiver of rights by buyer; prohibition; attempt to obtain; violation of title; burden of proof on exemption or exception from definition

(a) Any waiver by a buyer of the provisions of this title shall be deemed contrary to public policy and shall be void and unenforceable. Any attempt by a credit services organization to have a buyer waive rights given by this title shall constitute a violation of this title.

(b) In any proceeding involving this title, the burden of proving an exemption or an exception from a definition is upon the person claiming it. (Added by Stats.1984, c. 1177, § 1.)

Research References

4 Witkin, California Summary 10th Sales § 309, Nature and Scope of Statute.

§ 1789.20. Violations; misdemeanor; injunction; prosecutor

(a) Any person who violates any provision of this title is guilty of a misdemeanor. Any superior court of this state shall have jurisdiction in equity to restrain and enjoin the violation of any provision of this title.

The duty to institute actions for violation of this title, including equity proceedings to restrain and enjoin such a violation, is hereby vested in the Attorney General, district attorneys, and city attorneys. The Attorney General, any district attorney, or any city attorney may prosecute misdemeanor actions or institute equity proceedings, or both.

This section shall not be deemed to prohibit the enforcement by any person of any right provided by this or any other law.

(b) The misdemeanor provision of this section does not apply to a seller's breach of a contract subject to this title. (Added by Stats.1984, c. 1177, § 1.)

Research References

4 Witkin, California Summary 10th Sales § 313, Remedies and Penalties.

§ 1789.21. Actions for recovery of damages or injunctive relief

(a) Any buyer injured by a violation of this title or by the credit services organization's breach of a contract subject to this title may bring any action for recovery of damages, or for injunctive relief, or both. Judgment shall be entered for actual damages, but in no case less than the amount paid by the buyer to the credit services organization, plus reasonable attorney's fees and costs. An award, if the trial court deems it proper, may be entered for punitive damages.

(b) Any person, including, but not limited to, a consumer credit reporting agency, as defined in subdivision (d) of Section 1785.3, and any consumer of, or user of, a consumer credit report under the Consumer Credit Reporting Agencies Act (Title 1.6 (commencing with Section 1785.1)), and any furnisher of credit information under the Consumer Credit Reporting Agencies Act, may bring an action for the recovery of damages or for injunctive relief, or both, for a violation of this title. Any person bringing such an action who prevails in the action shall be entitled to reasonable attorney's fees and costs. *(Added by Stats.1984, c. 1177, § 1. Amended by Stats.1992, c. 651 (A.B. 2999), § 8; Stats.1994, c. 792 (A.B.1922), § 4; Stats.2004, c. 183 (A.B.3082), § 33.)*

§ 1789.22. Application of other laws; remedies as additional

The provisions of this title are not exclusive and do not relieve the parties or the contracts subject thereto from compliance with any other applicable provision of law.

The remedies provided in this title for violation of any section of this title shall be in addition to any other procedures or remedies for any violation or conduct provided for in any other law. *(Added by Stats.1984, c. 1177, § 1.)*

§ 1789.23. Severability

If any provision of this title or if any application thereof to any person or circumstance is held invalid, the remainder of the title and the application of the provision to other persons and circumstances shall not be affected thereby. *(Added by Stats. 1984, c. 1177, § 1.)*

§ 1789.24. Claims against deposits in lieu of bonds; establishment; approval; 240-day period; payment; approval of claims after 240-day period; deposits not subject to attachment, garnishment, or execution

(a) When a deposit has been made in lieu of a bond pursuant to Section 995.710 of the Code of Civil Procedure, the person asserting a claim against the deposit shall, in lieu of proceeding under Section 996.430 of the Code of Civil Procedure, establish the claim by furnishing evidence to the Secretary of State of a money judgment entered by a court, together with evidence that the claimant is a person described in subdivision (b) of Section 1789.18.

(b) When a person has established the claim with the Secretary of State, the Secretary of State shall review and approve the claim and enter the date of approval thereon. The claim shall be designated an "approved claim."

(c) When the first claim against a particular deposit has been approved, it shall not be paid until the expiration of a period of 240 days after the date of its approval by the Secretary of State. Subsequent claims that are approved by the Secretary of State within the same 240–day period shall similarly not be paid until the expiration of the 240–day period. Upon the expiration of the 240–day period, the Secretary of State shall pay all approved claims from that 240–day period in full unless the deposit is insufficient, in which case each approved claim shall be paid a pro rata share of the deposit.

(d) When the Secretary of State approves the first claim against a particular deposit after the expiration of a 240–day period, the date of approval of that claim shall begin a new 240–day period to which subdivision (c) shall apply with respect to any amount remaining in the deposit.

(e) After a deposit is exhausted, no further claims shall be paid by the Secretary of State. Claimants who have had their claims paid in full or in part pursuant to subdivision (c) or (d) shall not be required to return funds received from the deposit for the benefit of other claimants.

(f) When a deposit has been made in lieu of a bond, as specified in subdivision (a), the amount of the deposit shall not be subject to attachment, garnishment, or execution with respect to an action or judgment against the credit services organization, other than as to an amount as no longer needed or required for the purpose of this title which would otherwise be returned to the credit services organization by the Secretary of State.

(g) The Secretary of State shall retain a cash deposit for two years from the date the Secretary of State receives written notification from the assignor of the deposit that the assignor has ceased to engage in the business of a credit services organization or has filed a bond pursuant to Section 1789.18, provided that there are no outstanding claims against the deposit. The written notice shall include all of the following: (1) name, address, and telephone number of the assignor; (2) name, address, and telephone number of the bank at which the deposit is located; (3) account number of the deposit; and (4) a statement whether the assignor is ceasing to engage in the business of a credit services organization or has filed a bond with the Secretary of State. The Secretary of State shall forward an acknowledgment of receipt of the written notice to the assignor at the address indicated therein, specifying the date of receipt of the written notice and anticipated date of release of the deposit.

(h) This section shall apply to all deposits retained by the Secretary of State.

(i) A judge of a superior court may order the return of the deposit prior to the expiration of two years upon evidence satisfactory to the judge that there are no outstanding claims against the deposit or order the Secretary of State to retain the deposit for a sufficient period beyond the two years specified in subdivision (g) to resolve outstanding claims against the deposit account. *(Added by Stats.1985, c. 275, § 1. Amended by Stats.1996, c. 633 (S.B.1978), § 4; Stats.1998, c. 829 (S.B.1652), § 6; Stats.2002, c. 784 (S.B.1316), § 13.)*

§ 1789.25. Registration application; bond; fee; contents; investigation; notification of change in information; expiration of certificate of registration

(a) Every credit services organization shall file a registration application with, and receive a certificate of registration from, the Department of Justice before conducting business in this state. The Department of Justice shall not issue a certificate of registration until the bond required by Section 1789.18 has been filed with the office of the Secretary of State and the department establishes that the organization seeking a certificate satisfies the requirements of subdivision (f). The application shall be accompanied by a registration fee of one hundred dollars ($100). The registration application shall contain all of the following information:

(1) The name and address where business is actually conducted of the credit services organization.

(2) The names, addresses, and driver's license numbers of any and all persons who directly or indirectly own or control 10 percent or more of the outstanding shares of stock in the credit services organization.

(3) Either of the following:

(A) A full and complete disclosure of any litigation commenced against the credit services organization or any resolved or unresolved complaint that relates to the operation of the credit services organization and that is filed with the Attorney General or any other governmental authority of this state, any other state, or the federal government. With respect to each resolved complaint identified by the disclosure, the disclosure shall include a brief description of the resolution.

(B) An acknowledged declaration under penalty of perjury stating that no litigation has been commenced and no unresolved complaint relating to the operation of the organization has been filed with the Attorney General or any other governmental authority of this state, any other state, or the federal government.

(4) Other information that the Department of Justice requires, either at the time of application or thereafter.

(b) The Department of Justice may conduct an investigation to verify the accuracy of the registration application. If the application involves investigation outside this state, the applicant credit services organization may be required by the Department of Justice to advance sufficient funds to pay the actual expenses of the investigation. Any nonresident applying for registration under this section shall designate and maintain a resident of this state as the applicant's agent for the purpose of receipt of service of process.

(c) Each credit services organization shall notify the Department of Justice in writing within 30 days after the date of a change in the information required by subdivision (a), except that 30 days' advance notice and approval by the Department of Justice shall be required before changing the corporate name or address, or persons owning more than 10 percent of the shares of stock in the organization. Each credit services organization registering under this section may use no more than one fictitious or trade name and shall maintain a copy of the registration application in its files. The organization shall allow a buyer to inspect the registration application upon request.

(d) A certificate of registration issued pursuant to this section shall expire annually on the last day of December but may be renewed by filing a renewal application accompanied by a fee not to exceed the Department of Justice's costs of administration.

(e) The credit services organization shall attach to the registration statement a copy of the contract or contracts which the credit services organization intends to execute with its customers and a copy of the required bond.

(f) The Department of Justice shall not issue a certificate of registration under this title to any person who has engaged in, or proposes to engage in, any activity that is in violation of Section 1789.13, any law prohibiting the use of untrue or misleading statements, or any law related to the extension of credit to persons for personal, family, or household purposes. *(Added by Stats.1992, c. 651 (A.B.2999), § 9. Amended by Stats.2007, c. 91 (S.B.500), § 2.)*

Research References

4 Witkin, California Summary 10th Sales § 310, Prohibited Acts.

§ 1789.26. Enforcement; filing fees

(a) The Secretary of State shall enforce the provisions of this title that govern the filing and maintenance of bonds and deposits in lieu of bonds.

(b) The Secretary of State shall charge and collect a filing fee not to exceed the cost of filing the bond or the deposit in lieu of a bond pursuant to Section 995.710 of the Code of Civil Procedure. *(Added by Stats.1996, c. 633 (S.B.1978), § 5.)*

Title 1.6F

CHECK CASHERS

§ 1789.30. Posting of schedule of fees and list of valid identification; return required for checks exceeding ten thousand dollars ($10,000)

(a)(1) Every check casher, as applicable to the services provided, shall post a complete, detailed, and unambiguous schedule of all fees for (A) cashing checks, drafts, money orders, or other commercial paper serving the same purpose, (B) the sale or issuance of money orders, and (C) the initial issuance of any identification card. Each check casher shall also post a list of valid identification which is acceptable in lieu of identification provided by the check casher. The information required by this section shall be clear, legible, and in letters not less than one-half inch in height. The information shall be posted in a conspicuous location in the unobstructed view of the public within the check casher's premises.

(2) A check casher may be required to file a return required by Section 18631.7 of the Revenue and Taxation Code.

(b)(1) Except as provided in paragraph (2), this section shall become operative December 31, 2004.

(2)(A) Except as provided in subparagraph (B), paragraph (2) of subdivision (a) shall apply to checks cashed on or after January 1, 2006.

(B) The amendments to this section made by the act [1] adding this subparagraph shall become operative on January 1, 2008. *(Added by Stats.2004, c. 17 (A.B.971), § 2, eff. Feb. 23, 2004, operative Dec. 31, 2004. Amended by Stats.2005, c. 74 (A.B.139), § 24, eff. July 19, 2005; Stats.2007, c. 341 (A.B.1747), § 1, operative Jan. 1, 2008.)*

[1] Stats.2007, c. 341 (A.B.1747).

Research References

4 Witkin, California Summary 10th Sales § 342, (S 342) Check Cashing Services.

§ 1789.31. Check casher

(a) As used in this title, a "check casher" means a person or entity that for compensation engages, in whole or in part, in the business of cashing checks, warrants, drafts, money orders, or other commercial paper serving the same purpose. "Check casher" does not include a state or federally chartered bank, savings association, credit union, or industrial loan company. "Check casher" also does not include a retail seller engaged primarily in the business of selling consumer goods, including consumables, to retail buyers that cashes checks or issues money orders for a fee not exceeding two dollars ($2) as a service to its customers that is incidental to its main purpose or business.

(b) This section shall become operative December 31, 2004. *(Added by Stats.2002, c. 777 (S.B.898), § 3, operative March 1,*

2004. Amended by Stats.2004, c. 17 (A.B.971), § 4, eff. Feb. 23, 2004, operative Dec. 31, 2004.)

Research References

4 Witkin, California Summary 10th Sales § 342, (S 342) Check Cashing Services.

§ 1789.32. Failure to post information or action contrary to posted information; unfair business practice

Failure to post information as required by this title, or the imposition of fees or identification requirements contrary to the information posted, shall constitute an unfair business practice within the meaning of Section 17200 of the Business and Professions Code. *(Added by Stats.1990, c. 1391 (A.B.3096), § 1.)*

§ 1789.35. Fees relating to check cashing services; identification and receipt requirements; violations and penalties; actions for relief

(a) A check casher shall not charge a fee for cashing a payroll check or government check in excess of 3 percent if identification is provided by the customer, or 3.5 percent without the provision of identification, of the face amount of the check, or three dollars ($3), whichever is greater. Identification, for purposes of this section, is limited to a California driver's license, a California identification card, or a valid United States military identification card.

(b) A check casher may charge a fee of no more than ten dollars ($10) to set up an initial account and issue an optional identification card for providing check cashing services. A replacement optional identification card may be issued at a cost not to exceed five dollars ($5).

(c) A check casher shall provide a receipt to the customer for each transaction.

(d) A check casher may charge a fee for cashing a personal check, as posted pursuant to Section 1789.30, for immediate deposit in an amount not to exceed 12 percent of the face value of the check.

(e) Any person who violates any provision of this section shall be liable for a civil penalty not to exceed two thousand dollars ($2,000) for each violation, which shall be assessed and recovered in a civil action brought in the name of the people of the State of California by the Attorney General in any court of competent jurisdiction. Any action brought pursuant to this subdivision shall be commenced within four years of the date on which the act or transaction upon which the action is based occurred.

(f) A willful violation of this section is a misdemeanor.

(g) Any person who is injured by any violation of this section may bring an action for the recovery of damages, an equity proceeding to restrain and enjoin those violations, or both. The amount awarded may be up to three times the damages actually incurred, but in no event less than the amount paid by the aggrieved consumer to a person subject to this section. If the plaintiff prevails, the plaintiff shall be awarded reasonable attorney's fees and costs. If a court determines by clear and convincing evidence that a breach or violation was willful, the court, in its discretion, may award punitive damages in addition to the amounts set forth above.

(h) This section shall become operative December 31, 2004. *(Added by Stats.2002, c. 777 (S.B.898), § 6, operative March 1, 2004. Amended by Stats.2004, c. 17 (A.B.971), § 7, eff. Feb. 23, 2004, operative Dec. 31, 2004; Stats.2004, c. 28 (S.B.31), § 2, eff. April 1, 2004, operative Dec. 31, 2004.)*

Research References

4 Witkin, California Summary 10th Sales § 342, (S 342) Check Cashing Services.

§ 1789.37. Permits; check cashing business; violations; penalties; deposit of forfeited bail and fines

(a) Every owner of a check casher's business shall obtain a permit from the Department of Justice to conduct a check casher's business.

(b) All applications for a permit to conduct a check casher's business shall be filed with the department in writing, signed by the applicant, if an individual, or by a member or officer authorized to sign, if the applicant is a corporation or other entity, and shall state the name of the business, the type of business engaged in, and the business address. Each applicant shall be fingerprinted.

(c) Each applicant for a permit to conduct a check casher's business shall pay a fee not to exceed the cost of processing the application, fingerprinting the applicant, and checking or obtaining the criminal record of the applicant, at the time of filing the application.

(d) Each applicant shall annually, beginning one year from the date of issuance of a check casher's permit, file an application for renewal of the permit with the department, along with payment of a renewal fee not to exceed the cost of processing the application for renewal and checking or obtaining the criminal record of the applicant.

(e) The department shall deny an application for a permit to conduct a check casher's business, or for renewal of a permit, if the applicant has a felony conviction involving dishonesty, fraud, or deceit, if the crime is substantially related to the qualifications, functions, or duties of a person engaged in the business of check cashing.

(f) The department shall adopt regulations to implement this section and shall determine the amount of the application fees required by this section. The department shall prescribe forms for the applications and permit required by this section, which shall be uniform throughout the state.

(g) In any action brought by a city attorney or district attorney to enforce a violation of this section, an owner of a check casher's business who engages in the business of check cashing without holding a current and valid permit issued by the department pursuant to this section is subject to a civil penalty, as follows:

(1) For the first offense, not more than one thousand dollars ($1,000).

(2) For the second offense, not more than five thousand dollars ($5,000).

(h) Any person who has twice been found in violation of subdivision (g) and who, within 10 years of the date of the first offense, engages in the business of check cashing without holding a current and valid permit issued by the department pursuant to this section is guilty of a misdemeanor punishable by imprisonment in a county jail not exceeding six months, or by a fine not exceeding five thousand dollars ($5,000), or by both that fine and imprisonment.

(i) All civil penalties, forfeited bail, or fines received by any court pursuant to this section shall, as soon as practicable after the receipt thereof, be deposited with the county treasurer of the county in which the court is situated. Fines and forfeitures deposited shall be disbursed pursuant to the Penal Code. Civil penalties deposited shall be paid at least once a month as follows:

(1) Fifty percent to the Treasurer by warrant of the county auditor drawn upon the requisition of the clerk or judge of the

court, to be deposited in the State Treasury on order of the Controller.

(2) Fifty percent to the city treasurer of the city, if the offense occurred in a city, otherwise to the treasurer of the county in which the prosecution is conducted. Any money deposited in the State Treasury under this section that is determined by the Controller to have been erroneously deposited shall be refunded, subject to approval of the California Victim Compensation and Government Claims Board prior to the payment of the refund, out of any money in the State Treasury that is available by law for that purpose.

(j) This section shall become operative December 31, 2004. *(Added by Stats.2004, c. 17 (A.B.971), § 9, eff. Feb. 23, 2004, operative Dec. 31, 2004. Amended by Stats.2006, c. 538 (S.B. 1852), § 47.)*

Research References

1 Witkin Cal. Summ. 10th Contracts § 464, Exemptions.
4 Witkin, California Summary 10th Sales § 342, (S 342) Check Cashing Services.

§ 1789.38. Public policy; waiver of rights

Any waiver of the provisions of this title is contrary to public policy, and is void and unenforceable. *(Added by Stats.2002, c. 815 (A.B.2331), § 14.)*

Research References

4 Witkin, California Summary 10th Sales § 342, (S 342) Check Cashing Services.

Title 1.7

CONSUMER WARRANTIES

CHAPTER 1. CONSUMER WARRANTY PROTECTION

ARTICLE 1. GENERAL PROVISIONS

§ 1790. Short title

This chapter may be cited as the "Song-Beverly Consumer Warranty Act." *(Added by Stats.1970, c. 1333, p. 2478, § 1.)*

Research References

Rutter, Cal. Practice Guide: Civ. Pro. Before Trial Ch. 12(II)-C, C. Statutory Offer to Compromise (CCP § 998).
Rutter, Cal. Practice Guide: Civil Trials & Evidence Ch. 12-D, D. Other Motions During Trial.
Rutter, Cal. Practice Guide: Civil Trials & Evidence Ch. 17-D, D. Costs.
Rutter, Cal. Practice Guide: Civil Trials & Evidence Ch. 17-F, F. Prejudgment Interest.
Rutter, Cal. Practice Guide: Enforcing Judgments/Debts Ch. 3-A, A. Evaluating the Claim.
Miller and Starr California Real Estate § 29:5, Contractor's Liability Based on Implied Warranty.
Miller and Starr California Real Estate § 29:19, Liability of Material Suppliers and Manufacturers.
13 NO. 6 Miller & Starr, California Real Estate Newsalert 5, Defective Construction.
14 NO. 1 Miller & Starr, California Real Estate Newsalert 5, Defective Construction.
3 Witkin Cal. Proc. 5th Actions § 519, (S 519) Contract of Sale: Four Years.
3 Witkin Cal. Proc. 5th Actions § 608, (S 608) Scope of Statute.
5 Witkin Cal. Proc. 5th Pleading § 1059, Where Complaint is Not Verified.
7 Witkin Cal. Proc. 5th Trial § 305, Errors in Content.
4 Witkin, California Summary 10th Sales § 52, Commercial Code, Consumer Warranty Act, and Federal Warranty Law.
4 Witkin, California Summary 10th Sales § 63, (S 63) in General.
4 Witkin, California Summary 10th Sales § 65, Mobilehome Warranties.
4 Witkin, California Summary 10th Sales § 85, Conspicuous Language Requirement.
4 Witkin, California Summary 10th Sales § 98, Modern View.
4 Witkin, California Summary 10th Sales § 203, Statutory Rules.
4 Witkin, California Summary 10th Sales § 314, Scope of Act.

§ 1790.1. Waiver, effect

Any waiver by the buyer of consumer goods of the provisions of this chapter, except as expressly provided in this chapter, shall be deemed contrary to public policy and shall be unenforceable and void. *(Added by Stats.1970, c. 1333, p. 2478, § 1.)*

Research References

4 Witkin, California Summary 10th Sales § 92, Illegal Disclaimer.
4 Witkin, California Summary 10th Sales § 198, (S 198) in General.
4 Witkin, California Summary 10th Sales § 314, Scope of Act.

§ 1790.2. Severability

If any provision of this chapter or the application thereof to any person or circumstance is held unconstitutional, such invalidity shall not affect other provisions or applications of this chapter which can be given effect without the invalid provision or application, and to this end the provisions of this chapter are severable. *(Added by Stats.1970, c. 1333, p. 2478, § 1.)*

§ 1790.3. Law governing; reference to Commercial Code

The provisions of this chapter shall not affect the rights and obligations of parties determined by reference to the Commercial Code except that, where the provisions of the Commercial Code conflict with the rights guaranteed to buyers of consumer goods under the provisions of this chapter, the provisions of this chapter shall prevail. *(Added by Stats.1970, c. 1333, p. 2478, § 1.)*

Research References

Rutter, Cal. Practice Guide: Enforcing Judgments/Debts Ch. 3-A, A. Evaluating the Claim.
4 Witkin, California Summary 10th Sales § 52, Commercial Code, Consumer Warranty Act, and Federal Warranty Law.

§ 1790.4. Cumulative remedies; applicability of other remedies

The remedies provided by this chapter are cumulative and shall not be construed as restricting any remedy that is otherwise available, and, in particular, shall not be construed to supplant the provisions of the Unfair Practices Act.[1] *(Added by Stats. 1971, c. 1523, p. 3000, § 1, operative Jan. 1, 1972. Amended by Stats.1976, c. 416, p. 1068, § 1.)*

[1] Business and Professions Code § 17000 et seq.

Research References

4 Witkin, California Summary 10th Sales § 198, (S 198) in General.

ARTICLE 2. DEFINITIONS

Section
1791.   Definitions.
1791.1. Implied warranty; definition; duration; remedies of buyers.
1791.2. Express warranty; definition.
1791.3. Disclaimer of implied warranties; "as is" or "with all faults" sales.

§ 1791. Definitions

As used in this chapter:

(a) "Consumer goods" means any new product or part thereof that is used, bought, or leased for use primarily for personal, family, or household purposes, except for clothing and consumables. "Consumer goods" shall include new and used assistive devices sold at retail.

(b) "Buyer" or "retail buyer" means any individual who buys consumer goods from a person engaged in the business of manufacturing, distributing, or selling consumer goods at retail. As used in this subdivision, "person" means any individual, partnership, corporation, limited liability company, association, or other legal entity that engages in any of these businesses.

(c) "Clothing" means any wearing apparel, worn for any purpose, including under and outer garments, shoes, and accessories composed primarily of woven material, natural or synthetic yarn, fiber, or leather or similar fabric.

(d) "Consumables" means any product that is intended for consumption by individuals, or use by individuals for purposes of personal care or in the performance of services ordinarily rendered within the household, and that usually is consumed or expended in the course of consumption or use.

(e) "Distributor" means any individual, partnership, corporation, association, or other legal relationship that stands between the manufacturer and the retail seller in purchases, consignments, or contracts for sale of consumer goods.

(f) "Independent repair or service facility" or "independent service dealer" means any individual, partnership, corporation, association, or other legal entity, not an employee or subsidiary of a manufacturer or distributor, that engages in the business of servicing and repairing consumer goods.

(g) "Lease" means any contract for the lease or bailment for the use of consumer goods by an individual, for a term exceeding four months, primarily for personal, family, or household purposes, whether or not it is agreed that the lessee bears the risk of the consumer goods' depreciation.

(h) "Lessee" means an individual who leases consumer goods under a lease.

(i) "Lessor" means a person who regularly leases consumer goods under a lease.

(j) "Manufacturer" means any individual, partnership, corporation, association, or other legal relationship that manufactures, assembles, or produces consumer goods.

(k) "Place of business" means, for the purposes of any retail seller that sells consumer goods by catalog or mail order, the distribution point for consumer goods.

(*l*) "Retail seller," "seller," or "retailer" means any individual, partnership, corporation, association, or other legal relationship that engages in the business of selling or leasing consumer goods to retail buyers.

(m) "Return to the retail seller" means, for the purposes of any retail seller that sells consumer goods by catalog or mail order, the retail seller's place of business, as defined in subdivision (k).

(n) "Sale" means either of the following:

(1) The passing of title from the seller to the buyer for a price.

(2) A consignment for sale.

(*o*) "Service contract" means a contract in writing to perform, over a fixed period of time or for a specified duration, services relating to the maintenance or repair of a consumer product, except that this term does not include a policy of automobile insurance, as defined in Section 116 of the Insurance Code.

(p) "Assistive device" means any instrument, apparatus, or contrivance, including any component or part thereof or accessory thereto, that is used or intended to be used, to assist an individual with a disability in the mitigation or treatment of an injury or disease or to assist or affect or replace the structure or any function of the body of an individual with a disability, except that this term does not include prescriptive lenses and other ophthalmic goods unless they are sold or dispensed to a blind person, as defined in Section 19153 of the Welfare and Institutions Code and unless they are intended to assist the limited vision of the person so disabled.

(q) "Catalog or similar sale" means a sale in which neither the seller nor any employee or agent of the seller nor any person related to the seller nor any person with a financial interest in the sale participates in the diagnosis of the buyer's condition or in the selection or fitting of the device.

(r) "Home appliance" means any refrigerator, freezer, range, microwave oven, washer, dryer, dishwasher, garbage disposal, trash compactor, or room air-conditioner normally used or sold for personal, family, or household purposes.

(s) "Home electronic product" means any television, radio, antenna rotator, audio or video recorder or playback equipment, video camera, video game, video monitor, computer equipment, telephone, telecommunications equipment, electronic alarm system, electronic appliance control system, or other kind of electronic product, if it is normally used or sold for personal, family, or household purposes. The term includes any electronic accessory that is normally used or sold with a home electronic product for one of those purposes. The term excludes any single product with a wholesale price to the retail seller of less than fifty dollars ($50).

(t) "Member of the Armed Forces" means a person on full-time active duty in the Army, Navy, Marine Corps, Air Force, National Guard, or Coast Guard. Full-time active duty shall also include active military service at a military service school designated by law or the Adjutant General of the Military Department concerned.

This section shall become operative on January 1, 2008. *(Added by Stats.1993, c. 1265 (S.B.798), § 12.5, operative Jan. 1, 1998. Amended by Stats.1994, c. 1010 (S.B.2053), § 39.5, operative Jan. 1, 1998; Stats.1995, c. 461 (A.B.40), § 2, operative Jan. 1, 1998; Stats.1997, c. 401 (S.B.780), § 63, operative Jan. 1, 2003; Stats.2002, c. 405 (A.B.2973), § 62, operative Jan. 1, 2008; Stats.2007, c. 151 (S.B.234), § 1, operative Jan. 1, 2008.)*

Research References

14 NO. 1 Miller & Starr, California Real Estate Newsalert 5, Defective Construction.

4 Witkin, California Summary 10th Sales § 13, Variation by Agreement.

4 Witkin, California Summary 10th Sales § 52, Commercial Code, Consumer Warranty Act, and Federal Warranty Law.

4 Witkin, California Summary 10th Sales § 79, Usage or Custom.

4 Witkin, California Summary 10th Sales § 98, Modern View.

4 Witkin, California Summary 10th Sales § 314, Scope of Act.

4 Witkin, California Summary 10th Sales § 317, (S 317) Maintenance of Service and Repair Facilities.

4 Witkin, California Summary 10th Sales § 326, Service Contract in Lieu of Express Warranty.

§ 1791.1. Implied warranty; definition; duration; remedies of buyers

As used in this chapter:

(a) "Implied warranty of merchantability" or "implied warranty that goods are merchantable" means that the consumer goods meet each of the following:

(1) Pass without objection in the trade under the contract description.

(2) Are fit for the ordinary purposes for which such goods are used.

(3) Are adequately contained, packaged, and labeled.

(4) Conform to the promises or affirmations of fact made on the container or label.

(b) "Implied warranty of fitness" means (1) that when the retailer, distributor, or manufacturer has reason to know any particular purpose for which the consumer goods are required, and further, that the buyer is relying on the skill and judgment of the seller to select and furnish suitable goods, then there is an implied warranty that the goods shall be fit for such purpose and (2) that when there is a sale of an assistive device sold at retail in this state, then there is an implied warranty by the retailer that the device is specifically fit for the particular needs of the buyer.

(c) The duration of the implied warranty of merchantability and where present the implied warranty of fitness shall be coextensive in duration with an express warranty which accompanies the consumer goods, provided the duration of the express warranty is reasonable; but in no event shall such implied warranty have a duration of less than 60 days nor more than one year following the sale of new consumer goods to a retail buyer. Where no duration for an express warranty is stated with respect to consumer goods, or parts thereof, the duration of the implied warranty shall be the maximum period prescribed above.

(d) Any buyer of consumer goods injured by a breach of the implied warranty of merchantability and where applicable by a breach of the implied warranty of fitness has the remedies provided in Chapter 6 (commencing with Section 2601) and Chapter 7 (commencing with Section 2701) of Division 2 of the Commercial Code, and, in any action brought under such provisions, Section 1794 of this chapter shall apply. *(Added by Stats.1970, c. 1333, p. 2479, § 1. Amended by Stats.1971, c. 1523, p. 3002, § 3, operative Jan. 1, 1972; Stats.1978, c. 991, p. 3059, § 2; Stats.1979, c. 1023, p. 3494, § 1.5.)*

Research References

Miller and Starr California Real Estate § 29:67, Warranty.

4 Witkin, California Summary 10th Sales § 70, (S 70) Consumer Goods Sold at Retail.

4 Witkin, California Summary 10th Sales § 71, (S 71) "Merchantable" Quality.

4 Witkin, California Summary 10th Sales § 72, in General.

4 Witkin, California Summary 10th Sales § 98, Modern View.

4 Witkin, California Summary 10th Sales § 327, (S 327) Magnuson-Moss Warranty Act.

§ 1791.2. Express warranty; definition

(a) "Express warranty" means:

(1) A written statement arising out of a sale to the consumer of a consumer good pursuant to which the manufacturer, distributor, or retailer undertakes to preserve or maintain the utility or performance of the consumer good or provide compensation if there is a failure in utility or performance; or

(2) In the event of any sample or model, that the whole of the goods conforms to such sample or model.

(b) It is not necessary to the creation of an express warranty that formal words such as "warrant" or "guarantee" be used, but if such words are used then an express warranty is created. An affirmation merely of the value of the goods or a statement purporting to be merely an opinion or commendation of the goods does not create a warranty.

(c) Statements or representations such as expressions of general policy concerning customer satisfaction which are not subject to any limitation do not create an express warranty. *(Added by Stats.1970, c. 1333, p. 2479, § 1. Amended by Stats.1978, c. 991, p. 3060, § 2.5.)*

Research References

13 Witkin, California Summary 10th Personal Property § 194, (S 194) Regulatory Provisions.

4 Witkin, California Summary 10th Sales § 56, Promissory Language.

4 Witkin, California Summary 10th Sales § 58, (S 58) Distinction: Value or Opinion.

4 Witkin, California Summary 10th Sales § 62, Sample or Model.

4 Witkin, California Summary 10th Sales § 315, Language of Warranty.

§ 1791.3. Disclaimer of implied warranties; "as is" or "with all faults" sales

As used in this chapter, a sale "as is" or "with all faults" means that the manufacturer, distributor, and retailer disclaim all implied warranties that would otherwise attach to the sale of consumer goods under the provisions of this chapter. *(Added by Stats.1970, c. 1333, p. 2479, § 1.)*

ARTICLE 3.　SALE WARRANTIES

§ 1792. Implied warranty of merchantability; manufacturers and retail sellers; indemnity

Unless disclaimed in the manner prescribed by this chapter, every sale of consumer goods that are sold at retail in this state shall be accompanied by the manufacturer's and the retail seller's implied warranty that the goods are merchantable. The retail seller shall have a right of indemnity against the manufacturer in the amount of any liability under this section. *(Added by Stats.1970, c. 1333, p. 2480, § 1. Amended by Stats.1971, c. 1523, p. 3003, § 4, operative Jan. 1, 1972; Stats.1978, c. 991, p. 3060, § 3.)*

Research References

4 Witkin, California Summary 10th Sales § 70, (S 70) Consumer Goods Sold at Retail.
4 Witkin, California Summary 10th Sales § 98, Modern View.
4 Witkin, California Summary 10th Sales § 314, Scope of Act.
5 Witkin, California Summary 10th Torts § 666, (S 666) in General.

§ 1792.1. Goods for particular purpose; implied warranty of fitness by manufacturer

Every sale of consumer goods that are sold at retail in this state by a manufacturer who has reason to know at the time of the retail sale that the goods are required for a particular purpose and that the buyer is relying on the manufacturer's skill or judgment to select or furnish suitable goods shall be accompanied by such manufacturer's implied warranty of fitness. *(Added by Stats.1970, c. 1333, p. 2480, § 1. Amended by Stats.1971, c. 1523, p. 3003, § 5, operative Jan. 1, 1972; Stats.1978, c. 991, p. 3060, § 4.)*

Research References

4 Witkin, California Summary 10th Sales § 72, in General.
4 Witkin, California Summary 10th Sales § 98, Modern View.

§ 1792.2. Goods for particular purpose; assistive devices; implied warranty of fitness by retailer or distributor

(a) Every sale of consumer goods that are sold at retail in this state by a retailer or distributor who has reason to know at the time of the retail sale that the goods are required for a particular purpose, and that the buyer is relying on the retailer's or distributor's skill or judgment to select or furnish suitable goods shall be accompanied by such retailer's or distributor's implied warranty that the goods are fit for that purpose.

(b) Every sale of an assistive device sold at retail in this state shall be accompanied by the retail seller's implied warranty that the device is specifically fit for the particular needs of the buyer. *(Added by Stats.1970, c. 1333, p. 2480, § 1. Amended by Stats.1971, c. 1523, p. 3003, § 6, operative Jan. 1, 1972; Stats. 1978, c. 991, p. 3060, § 5; Stats.1979, c. 1023, p. 3494, § 2.)*

Research References

4 Witkin, California Summary 10th Sales § 72, in General.
4 Witkin, California Summary 10th Sales § 90, (S 90) Consumer Warranties.
4 Witkin, California Summary 10th Sales § 98, Modern View.

§ 1792.3. Proscription against waiver of implied warranties; exception

No implied warranty of merchantability and, where applicable, no implied warranty of fitness shall be waived, except in the case of a sale of consumer goods on an "as is" or "with all faults" basis where the provisions of this chapter affecting "as is" or "with all faults" sales are strictly complied with. *(Added by Stats.1970, c. 1333, p. 2480, § 1.)*

Research References

4 Witkin, California Summary 10th Sales § 90, (S 90) Consumer Warranties.

4 Witkin, California Summary 10th Sales § 92, Illegal Disclaimer.

§ 1792.4. Written notice to buyer; disclaimer of implied warranties on "as is" or "with all faults" sales

(a) No sale of goods, governed by the provisions of this chapter, on an "as is" or "with all faults" basis, shall be effective to disclaim the implied warranty of merchantability or, where applicable, the implied warranty of fitness, unless a conspicuous writing is attached to the goods which clearly informs the buyer, prior to the sale, in simple and concise language of each of the following:

(1) The goods are being sold on an "as is" or "with all faults" basis.

(2) The entire risk as to the quality and performance of the goods is with the buyer.

(3) Should the goods prove defective following their purchase, the buyer and not the manufacturer, distributor, or retailer assumes the entire cost of all necessary servicing or repair.

(b) In the event of sale of consumer goods by means of a mail order catalog, the catalog offering such goods shall contain the required writing as to each item so offered in lieu of the requirement of notification prior to the sale. *(Added by Stats.1970, c. 1333, p. 2480, § 1. Amended by Stats.1971, c. 1523, p. 3003, § 6.5, operative Jan. 1, 1972.)*

Research References

4 Witkin, California Summary 10th Sales § 90, (S 90) Consumer Warranties.

§ 1792.5. Sales on "as is" or "with all faults" basis; effect as to buyers

Every sale of goods that are governed by the provisions of this chapter, on an "as is" or "with all faults" basis, made in compliance with the provisions of this chapter, shall constitute a waiver by the buyer of the implied warranty of merchantability and, where applicable, of the implied warranty of fitness. *(Added by Stats.1970, c. 1333, p. 2480, § 1. Amended by Stats.1971, c. 1523, p. 3003, § 6.5, operative Jan. 1, 1972.)*

Research References

4 Witkin, California Summary 10th Sales § 90, (S 90) Consumer Warranties.

§ 1793. Right to make express warranties; limitation, modification or disclaimer of implied warranties

Except as provided in Section 1793.02, nothing in this chapter shall affect the right of the manufacturer, distributor, or retailer to make express warranties with respect to consumer goods. However, a manufacturer, distributor, or retailer, in transacting a sale in which express warranties are given, may not limit, modify, or disclaim the implied warranties guaranteed by this chapter to the sale of consumer goods. *(Added by Stats.1970, c. 1333, p. 2480, § 1. Amended by Stats.1971, c. 1523, p. 3004, § 7, operative Jan. 1, 1972; Stats.1978, c. 991, p. 3061, § 6; Stats.1979, c. 1023, p. 3494, § 3.)*

Research References

4 Witkin, California Summary 10th Sales § 12, Supplementary General Law.
4 Witkin, California Summary 10th Sales § 90, (S 90) Consumer Warranties.

§ 1793.02. Assistive devices sold at retail; written warranty; remedies of buyer

(a) All new and used assistive devices sold at retail in this state shall be accompanied by the retail seller's written warranty which shall contain the following language: "This assistive device is warranted to be specifically fit for the particular needs of you, the buyer. If the device is not specifically fit for your particular needs, it may be returned to the seller within 30 days of the date of actual receipt by you or completion of fitting by the seller, whichever occurs later. If you return the device, the seller will either adjust or replace the device or promptly refund the total amount paid. This warranty does not affect the protections and remedies you have under other laws." In lieu of the words "30 days" the retail seller may specify any longer period.

(b) The language prescribed in subdivision (a) shall appear on the first page of the warranty in at least 10-point bold type. The warranty shall be delivered to the buyer at the time of the sale of the device.

(c) If the buyer returns the device within the period specified in the written warranty, the seller shall, without charge and within a reasonable time, adjust the device or, if appropriate, replace it with a device that is specifically fit for the particular needs of the buyer. If the seller does not adjust or replace the device so that it is specifically fit for the particular needs of the buyer, the seller shall promptly refund to the buyer the total amount paid, the transaction shall be deemed rescinded, and the seller shall promptly return to the buyer all payments and any assistive device or other consideration exchanged as part of the transaction and shall promptly cancel or cause to be canceled all contracts, instruments, and security agreements executed by the buyer in connection with the sale. When a sale is rescinded under this section, no charge, penalty, or other fee may be imposed in connection with the purchase, fitting, financing, or return of the device.

(d) With respect to the retail sale of an assistive device to an individual, organization, or agency known by the seller to be purchasing for the ultimate user of the device, this section and subdivision (b) of Section 1792.2 shall be construed to require that the device be specifically fit for the particular needs of the ultimate user.

(e) This section and subdivision (b) of Section 1792.2 shall not apply to any of the following sales of assistive devices:

(1) A catalog or similar sale, as defined in subdivision (q) of Section 1791, except a sale of a hearing aid.

(2) A sale which involves a retail sale price of less than fifteen dollars ($15).

(3) A surgical implant performed by a physician and surgeon, or a restoration or dental prosthesis provided by a dentist.

(f) The rights and remedies of the buyer under this section and subdivision (b) of Section 1792.2 are not subject to waiver under Section 1792.3. The rights and remedies of the buyer under this section and subdivision (b) of Section 1792.2 are cumulative, and shall not be construed to affect the obligations of the retail seller or any other party or to supplant the rights or remedies of the buyer under any other section of this chapter or under any other law or instrument.

(g) Section 1795.5 shall not apply to a sale of used assistive devices, and for the purposes of the Song-Beverly Consumer Warranty Act the buyer of a used assistive device shall have the same rights and remedies as the buyer of a new assistive device.

(h) The language in subdivision (a) shall not constitute an express warranty for purposes of Sections 1793.2 and 1793.3. *(Added by Stats.1979, c. 1023, p. 3495, § 4. Amended by Stats.1982, c. 619, p. 2610, § 2; Stats.1991, c. 228 (A.B.1889), § 2.)*

Research References

4 Witkin, California Summary 10th Sales § 56, Promissory Language.
4 Witkin, California Summary 10th Sales § 72, in General.

4 Witkin, California Summary 10th Sales § 90, (S 90) Consumer Warranties.

§ 1793.025. Wheelchairs; express warranties

(a) All new and used wheelchairs, including, but not limited to, wheelchairs that are motorized or have been otherwise customized to suit the needs of the user, shall be accompanied by the manufacturer's or lessor's written express warranty that the wheelchair is free of defects. The duration of the warranty shall be for a period of at least one year from the date of the first delivery of a new wheelchair to the consumer, or at least 60 days from the date of the first delivery of a used, refurbished, or reconditioned wheelchair to the consumer. If the written express warranty is not furnished to the consumer, the wheelchair nonetheless shall be deemed to be covered by the express warranty. This section shall not apply to wheelchairs manufactured specifically for athletic, competitive, or off-road use.

(b) The provisions of this chapter for express warranties govern the express warranty described in subdivision (a), whether or not those provisions only apply to the sale, and not the lease, of goods.

(c) A reasonable number of attempts have been made to conform a wheelchair to the express warranty if, within the warranty period or within one year of inception of the warranty, whichever occurs first, (1) the same nonconformity has been subject to repair four or more times by the manufacturer, lessor, or an agent thereof, and continues to exist, or (2) the wheelchair is out of service by reason of repair of nonconformities by the manufacturer, lessor, or an agent thereof, for a cumulative total of more than 30 calendar days since inception of the warranty.

(d) No wheelchair that has been returned to the manufacturer, lessor, or an agent thereof, by the consumer for failure to repair a nonconformity after a reasonable number of attempts, either in this state or in another state pursuant to a similar statute of that state, may be sold or leased again in this state unless the reasons for the return are fully disclosed to the prospective buyer or lessee.

(e) If the wheelchair is out of service for a period of at least 24 hours for the repair of a nonconformity by the manufacturer, lessor, or agent thereof, a temporary replacement wheelchair shall be made available to the consumer, if requested. The provider of the temporary replacement wheelchair may not charge the consumer more than the cost to the provider to make the wheelchair available to the consumer. Nothing in this subdivision is intended to prevent a consumer and a provider from negotiating an agreement in which the provider assumes the cost of providing a temporary replacement wheelchair to the consumer. *(Added by Stats.1993, c. 374 (A.B.1945), § 1. Amended by Stats.1995, c. 461 (A.B.40), § 3.)*

§ 1793.03. Electronic or appliance products; express warranty; service and repair facilities; time

(a) Every manufacturer making an express warranty with respect to an electronic or appliance product described in subdivision (h), (i), (j), or (k) of Section 9801 of the Business and Professions Code, with a wholesale price to the retailer of not less than fifty dollars ($50) and not more than ninety-nine dollars and ninety-nine cents ($99.99), shall make available to service and repair facilities sufficient service literature and functional parts to effect the repair of a product for at least three years after the date a product model or type was manufactured, regardless of whether the three-year period exceeds the warranty period for the product.

(b) Every manufacturer making an express warranty with respect to an electronic or appliance product described in subdivision (h), (i), (j), or (k) of Section 9801 of the Business and Professions Code, with a wholesale price to the retailer of one

hundred dollars ($100) or more, shall make available to service and repair facilities sufficient service literature and functional parts to effect the repair of a product for at least seven years after the date a product model or type was manufactured, regardless of whether the seven-year period exceeds the warranty period for the product. *(Added by Stats.1986, c. 547, § 1.)*

§ 1793.05. Vehicle manufacturers; alteration of vehicles into housecars; assumption of original manufacturer's warranty

Vehicle manufacturers who alter new vehicles into housecars shall, in addition to any new product warranty, assume any warranty responsibility of the original vehicle manufacturer for any and all components of the finished product which are, by virtue of any act of the alterer, no longer covered by the warranty issued by the original vehicle manufacturer. *(Added by Stats. 1977, c. 873, p. 2634, § 1, operative July 1, 1978.)*

§ 1793.1. Language of express warranties; identification of warrantor; statement; warranty or product registration card or form; service and repair facilities

(a)(1) Every manufacturer, distributor, or retailer making express warranties with respect to consumer goods shall fully set forth those warranties in simple and readily understood language, which shall clearly identify the party making the express warranties, and which shall conform to the federal standards for disclosure of warranty terms and conditions set forth in the federal Magnuson-Moss Warranty-Federal Trade Commission Improvement Act (15 U.S.C. Sec. 2301 et seq.), and in the regulations of the Federal Trade Commission adopted pursuant to the provisions of that act. If the manufacturer, distributor, or retailer provides a warranty or product registration card or form, or an electronic online warranty or product registration form, to be completed and returned by the consumer, the card or form shall contain statements, each displayed in a clear and conspicuous manner, that do all of the following:

(A) Informs the consumer that the card or form is for product registration.

(B) Informs the consumer that failure to complete and return the card or form does not diminish his or her warranty rights.

(2) Every work order or repair invoice for warranty repairs or service shall clearly and conspicuously incorporate in 10-point boldface type the following statement either on the face of the work order or repair invoice, or on the reverse side, or on an attachment to the work order or repair invoice: "A buyer of this product in California has the right to have this product serviced or repaired during the warranty period. The warranty period will be extended for the number of whole days that the product has been out of the buyer's hands for warranty repairs. If a defect exists within the warranty period, the warranty will not expire until the defect has been fixed. The warranty period will also be extended if the warranty repairs have not been performed due to delays caused by circumstances beyond the control of the buyer, or if the warranty repairs did not remedy the defect and the buyer notifies the manufacturer or seller of the failure of the repairs within 60 days after they were completed. If, after a reasonable number of attempts, the defect has not been fixed, the buyer may return this product for a replacement or a refund subject, in either case, to deduction of a reasonable charge for usage. This time extension does not affect the protections or remedies the buyer has under other laws."

If the required notice is placed on the reverse side of the work order or repair invoice, the face of the work order or repair invoice shall include the following notice in 10-point boldface type: "Notice to Consumer: Please read important information on back."

A copy of the work order or repair invoice and any attachment shall be presented to the buyer at the time that warranty service or repairs are made.

(b) No warranty or product registration card or form, or an electronic online warranty or product registration form, may be labeled as a warranty registration or a warranty confirmation.

(c) The requirements imposed by this section on the distribution of any warranty or product registration card or form, or an electronic online warranty or product registration form, shall become effective on January 1, 2004.

(d) This section does not apply to any warranty or product registration card or form that was printed prior to January 1, 2004, and was shipped or included with a product that was placed in the stream of commerce prior to January 1, 2004.

(e) Every manufacturer, distributor, or retailer making express warranties and who elects to maintain service and repair facilities within this state pursuant to this chapter shall perform one or more of the following:

(1) At the time of sale, provide the buyer with the name and address of each service and repair facility within this state.

(2) At the time of the sale, provide the buyer with the name and address and telephone number of a service and repair facility central directory within this state, or the toll-free telephone number of a service and repair facility central directory outside this state. It shall be the duty of the central directory to provide, upon inquiry, the name and address of the authorized service and repair facility nearest the buyer.

(3) Maintain at the premises of retail sellers of the warrantor's consumer goods a current listing of the warrantor's authorized service and repair facilities, or retail sellers to whom the consumer goods are to be returned for service and repair, whichever is applicable, within this state. It shall be the duty of every retail seller provided with that listing to provide, on inquiry, the name, address, and telephone number of the nearest authorized service and repair facility, or the retail seller to whom the consumer goods are to be returned for service and repair, whichever is applicable. *(Added by Stats.1970, c. 1333, p. 2481, § 1. Amended by Stats.1971, c. 1523, p. 3004, § 8, operative Jan. 1, 1972; Stats.1972, c. 1293, p. 2584, § 1; Stats.1980, c. 394, p. 776, § 1; Stats.1981, c. 150, p. 953, § 1, eff. July 8, 1981; Stats.1982, c. 381, p. 1709, § 1; Stats.2002, c. 306 (S.B.1765), § 1.)*

Research References

4 Witkin, California Summary 10th Sales § 315, Language of Warranty.

4 Witkin, California Summary 10th Sales § 316, (S 316) Notice of Rights Under Warranty.

4 Witkin, California Summary 10th Sales § 317, (S 317) Maintenance of Service and Repair Facilities.

§ 1793.2. Consumer goods manufacturers; express warranties; service and repair facilities

(a) Every manufacturer of consumer goods sold in this state and for which the manufacturer has made an express warranty shall:

(1)(A) Maintain in this state sufficient service and repair facilities reasonably close to all areas where its consumer goods are sold to carry out the terms of those warranties or designate and authorize in this state as service and repair facilities independent repair or service facilities reasonably close to all areas where its consumer goods are sold to carry out the terms of the warranties.

(B) As a means of complying with this paragraph, a manufacturer may enter into warranty service contracts with independent service and repair facilities. The warranty service contracts may provide for a fixed schedule of rates to be charged for warranty

service or warranty repair work. However, the rates fixed by those contracts shall be in conformity with the requirements of subdivision (c) of Section 1793.3. The rates established pursuant to subdivision (c) of Section 1793.3, between the manufacturer and the independent service and repair facility, do not preclude a good faith discount that is reasonably related to reduced credit and general overhead cost factors arising from the manufacturer's payment of warranty charges direct to the independent service and repair facility. The warranty service contracts authorized by this paragraph may not be executed to cover a period of time in excess of one year, and may be renewed only by a separate, new contract or letter of agreement between the manufacturer and the independent service and repair facility.

(2) In the event of a failure to comply with paragraph (1) of this subdivision, be subject to Section 1793.5.

(3) Make available to authorized service and repair facilities sufficient service literature and replacement parts to effect repairs during the express warranty period.

(b) Where those service and repair facilities are maintained in this state and service or repair of the goods is necessary because they do not conform with the applicable express warranties, service and repair shall be commenced within a reasonable time by the manufacturer or its representative in this state. Unless the buyer agrees in writing to the contrary, the goods shall be serviced or repaired so as to conform to the applicable warranties within 30 days. Delay caused by conditions beyond the control of the manufacturer or its representatives shall serve to extend this 30-day requirement. Where delay arises, conforming goods shall be tendered as soon as possible following termination of the condition giving rise to the delay.

(c) The buyer shall deliver nonconforming goods to the manufacturer's service and repair facility within this state, unless, due to reasons of size and weight, or method of attachment, or method of installation, or nature of the nonconformity, delivery cannot reasonably be accomplished. If the buyer cannot return the nonconforming goods for any of these reasons, he or she shall notify the manufacturer or its nearest service and repair facility within the state. Written notice of nonconformity to the manufacturer or its service and repair facility shall constitute return of the goods for purposes of this section. Upon receipt of that notice of nonconformity, the manufacturer shall, at its option, service or repair the goods at the buyer's residence, or pick up the goods for service and repair, or arrange for transporting the goods to its service and repair facility. All reasonable costs of transporting the goods when a buyer cannot return them for any of the above reasons shall be at the manufacturer's expense. The reasonable costs of transporting nonconforming goods after delivery to the service and repair facility until return of the goods to the buyer shall be at the manufacturer's expense.

(d)(1) Except as provided in paragraph (2), if the manufacturer or its representative in this state does not service or repair the goods to conform to the applicable express warranties after a reasonable number of attempts, the manufacturer shall either replace the goods or reimburse the buyer in an amount equal to the purchase price paid by the buyer, less that amount directly attributable to use by the buyer prior to the discovery of the nonconformity.

(2) If the manufacturer or its representative in this state is unable to service or repair a new motor vehicle, as that term is defined in paragraph (2) of subdivision (e) of Section 1793.22, to conform to the applicable express warranties after a reasonable number of attempts, the manufacturer shall either promptly replace the new motor vehicle in accordance with subparagraph (A) or promptly make restitution to the buyer in accordance with subparagraph (B). However, the buyer shall be free to elect

restitution in lieu of replacement, and in no event shall the buyer be required by the manufacturer to accept a replacement vehicle.

(A) In the case of replacement, the manufacturer shall replace the buyer's vehicle with a new motor vehicle substantially identical to the vehicle replaced. The replacement vehicle shall be accompanied by all express and implied warranties that normally accompany new motor vehicles of that specific kind. The manufacturer also shall pay for, or to, the buyer the amount of any sales or use tax, license fees, registration fees, and other official fees which the buyer is obligated to pay in connection with the replacement, plus any incidental damages to which the buyer is entitled under Section 1794, including, but not limited to, reasonable repair, towing, and rental car costs actually incurred by the buyer.

(B) In the case of restitution, the manufacturer shall make restitution in an amount equal to the actual price paid or payable by the buyer, including any charges for transportation and manufacturer-installed options, but excluding nonmanufacturer items installed by a dealer or the buyer, and including any collateral charges such as sales or use tax, license fees, registration fees, and other official fees, plus any incidental damages to which the buyer is entitled under Section 1794, including, but not limited to, reasonable repair, towing, and rental car costs actually incurred by the buyer.

(C) When the manufacturer replaces the new motor vehicle pursuant to subparagraph (A), the buyer shall only be liable to pay the manufacturer an amount directly attributable to use by the buyer of the replaced vehicle prior to the time the buyer first delivered the vehicle to the manufacturer or distributor, or its authorized service and repair facility for correction of the problem that gave rise to the nonconformity. When restitution is made pursuant to subparagraph (B), the amount to be paid by the manufacturer to the buyer may be reduced by the manufacturer by that amount directly attributable to use by the buyer prior to the time the buyer first delivered the vehicle to the manufacturer or distributor, or its authorized service and repair facility for correction of the problem that gave rise to the nonconformity. The amount directly attributable to use by the buyer shall be determined by multiplying the actual price of the new motor vehicle paid or payable by the buyer, including any charges for transportation and manufacturer-installed options, by a fraction having as its denominator 120,000 and having as its numerator the number of miles traveled by the new motor vehicle prior to the time the buyer first delivered the vehicle to the manufacturer or distributor, or its authorized service and repair facility for correction of the problem that gave rise to the nonconformity. Nothing in this paragraph shall in any way limit the rights or remedies available to the buyer under any other law.

(D) Pursuant to Section 1795.4, a buyer of a new motor vehicle shall also include a lessee of a new motor vehicle.

(e)(1) If the goods cannot practicably be serviced or repaired by the manufacturer or its representative to conform to the applicable express warranties because of the method of installation or because the goods have become so affixed to real property as to become a part thereof, the manufacturer shall either replace and install the goods or reimburse the buyer in an amount equal to the purchase price paid by the buyer, including installation costs, less that amount directly attributable to use by the buyer prior to the discovery of the nonconformity.

(2) With respect to claims arising out of deficiencies in the construction of a new residential dwelling, paragraph (1) shall not apply to either of the following:

(A) A product that is not a manufactured product, as defined in subdivision (g) of Section 896.

(B) A claim against a person or entity that is not the manufacturer that originally made the express warranty for that manufactured product. *(Added by Stats.1970, c. 1333, p. 2481, § 1. Amended by Stats.1971, c. 1523, p. 3004, § 9, operative Jan. 1, 1972; Stats.1976, c. 416, p. 1069, § 2; Stats.1978, c. 991, p. 3058, § 7; Stats.1982, c. 388, p. 1720, § 1; Stats.1986, c. 547, § 2; Stats.1987, c. 1280, § 2, operative Jan. 1, 1988; Stats.1988, c. 697, § 1; Stats.1989, c. 193, § 2; Stats.1991, c. 689 (A.B.211), § 10; Stats.1992, c. 1232 (S.B.1762), § 6; Stats.2004, c. 331 (A.B.2723), § 1; Stats.2011, c. 727 (A.B.242), § 1.)*

Research References

Rutter, Cal. Practice Guide: A.D.R. App. A, Selected Statutes Providing for ADR.

Rutter, Cal. Practice Guide: Enforcing Judgments/Debts Ch. 3-A, A. Evaluating the Claim.

4 Witkin, California Summary 10th Sales § 193, (S 193) in General.

4 Witkin, California Summary 10th Sales § 317, (S 317) Maintenance of Service and Repair Facilities.

4 Witkin, California Summary 10th Sales § 318, in General.

4 Witkin, California Summary 10th Sales § 319, Tanner Consumer Protection Act.

4 Witkin, California Summary 10th Sales § 320, Automotive Consumer Notification Act.

4 Witkin, California Summary 10th Sales § 321, (S 321) in General.

4 Witkin, California Summary 10th Sales § 323, (S 323) Remedies Available Only to New Motor Vehicle Purchasers.

4 Witkin, California Summary 10th Sales § 326, Service Contract in Lieu of Express Warranty.

7 Witkin, California Summary 10th Constitutional Law § 118, Construction in Favor of Constitutionality.

§ 1793.22. Tanner Consumer Protection Act; presumption; third-party dispute resolution

(a) This section shall be known and may be cited as the Tanner Consumer Protection Act.

(b) It shall be presumed that a reasonable number of attempts have been made to conform a new motor vehicle to the applicable express warranties if, within 18 months from delivery to the buyer or 18,000 miles on the odometer of the vehicle, whichever occurs first, one or more of the following occurs:

(1) The same nonconformity results in a condition that is likely to cause death or serious bodily injury if the vehicle is driven and the nonconformity has been subject to repair two or more times by the manufacturer or its agents, and the buyer or lessee has at least once directly notified the manufacturer of the need for the repair of the nonconformity.

(2) The same nonconformity has been subject to repair four or more times by the manufacturer or its agents and the buyer has at least once directly notified the manufacturer of the need for the repair of the nonconformity.

(3) The vehicle is out of service by reason of repair of nonconformities by the manufacturer or its agents for a cumulative total of more than 30 calendar days since delivery of the vehicle to the buyer. The 30-day limit shall be extended only if repairs cannot be performed due to conditions beyond the control of the manufacturer or its agents. The buyer shall be required to directly notify the manufacturer pursuant to paragraphs (1) and (2) only if the manufacturer has clearly and conspicuously disclosed to the buyer, with the warranty or the owner's manual, the provisions of this section and that of subdivision (d) of Section 1793.2, including the requirement that the buyer must notify the manufacturer directly pursuant to paragraphs (1) and (2). The notification, if required, shall be sent to the address, if any, specified clearly and conspicuously by the manufacturer in the warranty or owner's manual. This presumption shall be a rebuttable presumption affecting the burden of proof, and it may be asserted by the buyer in any civil action, including an action in small claims court, or other formal or informal proceeding.

(c) If a qualified third-party dispute resolution process exists, and the buyer receives timely notification in writing of the availability of that qualified third-party dispute resolution process with a description of its operation and effect, the presumption in subdivision (b) may not be asserted by the buyer until after the buyer has initially resorted to the qualified third-party dispute resolution process as required in subdivision (d). Notification of the availability of the qualified third-party dispute resolution process is not timely if the buyer suffers any prejudice resulting from any delay in giving the notification. If a qualified third-party dispute resolution process does not exist, or if the buyer is dissatisfied with that third-party decision, or if the manufacturer or its agent neglects to promptly fulfill the terms of the qualified third-party dispute resolution process decision after the decision is accepted by the buyer, the buyer may assert the presumption provided in subdivision (b) in an action to enforce the buyer's rights under subdivision (d) of Section 1793.2. The findings and decision of a qualified third-party dispute resolution process shall be admissible in evidence in the action without further foundation. Any period of limitation of actions under any federal or California laws with respect to any person shall be extended for a period equal to the number of days between the date a complaint is filed with a third-party dispute resolution process and the date of its decision or the date before which the manufacturer or its agent is required by the decision to fulfill its terms if the decision is accepted by the buyer, whichever occurs later.

(d) A qualified third-party dispute resolution process shall be one that does all of the following:

(1) Complies with the minimum requirements of the Federal Trade Commission for informal dispute settlement procedures as set forth in Part 703 of Title 16 of the Code of Federal Regulations, as those regulations read on January 1, 1987.

(2) Renders decisions which are binding on the manufacturer if the buyer elects to accept the decision.

(3) Prescribes a reasonable time, not to exceed 30 days after the decision is accepted by the buyer, within which the manufacturer or its agent must fulfill the terms of its decisions.

(4) Provides arbitrators who are assigned to decide disputes with copies of, and instruction in, the provisions of the Federal Trade Commission's regulations in Part 703 of Title 16 of the Code of Federal Regulations as those regulations read on January 1, 1987, Division 2 (commencing with Section 2101) of the Commercial Code, and this chapter.

(5) Requires the manufacturer, when the process orders, under the terms of this chapter, either that the nonconforming motor vehicle be replaced if the buyer consents to this remedy or that restitution be made to the buyer, to replace the motor vehicle or make restitution in accordance with paragraph (2) of subdivision (d) of Section 1793.2.

(6) Provides, at the request of the arbitrator or a majority of the arbitration panel, for an inspection and written report on the condition of a nonconforming motor vehicle, at no cost to the buyer, by an automobile expert who is independent of the manufacturer.

(7) Takes into account, in rendering decisions, all legal and equitable factors, including, but not limited to, the written warranty, the rights and remedies conferred in regulations of the Federal Trade Commission contained in Part 703 of Title 16 of the Code of Federal Regulations as those regulations read on January 1, 1987, Division 2 (commencing with Section 2101) of the Commercial Code, this chapter, and any other equitable considerations appropriate in the circumstances. Nothing in this chapter requires that, to be certified as a qualified third-party dispute resolution process pursuant to this section, decisions of the process must consider or provide remedies in the form of

awards of punitive damages or multiple damages, under subdivision (c) of Section 1794, or of attorneys' fees under subdivision (d) of Section 1794, or of consequential damages other than as provided in subdivisions (a) and (b) of Section 1794, including, but not limited to, reasonable repair, towing, and rental car costs actually incurred by the buyer.

(8) Requires that no arbitrator deciding a dispute may be a party to the dispute and that no other person, including an employee, agent, or dealer for the manufacturer, may be allowed to participate substantively in the merits of any dispute with the arbitrator unless the buyer is allowed to participate also. Nothing in this subdivision prohibits any member of an arbitration board from deciding a dispute.

(9) Obtains and maintains certification by the Department of Consumer Affairs pursuant to Chapter 9 (commencing with Section 472) of Division 1 of the Business and Professions Code.

(e) For the purposes of subdivision (d) of Section 1793.2 and this section, the following terms have the following meanings:

(1) "Nonconformity" means a nonconformity which substantially impairs the use, value, or safety of the new motor vehicle to the buyer or lessee.

(2) "New motor vehicle" means a new motor vehicle that is bought or used primarily for personal, family, or household purposes. "New motor vehicle" also means a new motor vehicle with a gross vehicle weight under 10,000 pounds that is bought or used primarily for business purposes by a person, including a partnership, limited liability company, corporation, association, or any other legal entity, to which not more than five motor vehicles are registered in this state. "New motor vehicle" includes the chassis, chassis cab, and that portion of a motor home devoted to its propulsion, but does not include any portion designed, used, or maintained primarily for human habitation, a dealer-owned vehicle and a "demonstrator" or other motor vehicle sold with a manufacturer's new car warranty but does not include a motorcycle or a motor vehicle which is not registered under the Vehicle Code because it is to be operated or used exclusively off the highways. A demonstrator is a vehicle assigned by a dealer for the purpose of demonstrating qualities and characteristics common to vehicles of the same or similar model and type.

(3) "Motor home" means a vehicular unit built on, or permanently attached to, a self-propelled motor vehicle chassis, chassis cab, or van, which becomes an integral part of the completed vehicle, designed for human habitation for recreational or emergency occupancy.

(f)(1) Except as provided in paragraph (2), no person shall sell, either at wholesale or retail, lease, or transfer a motor vehicle transferred by a buyer or lessee to a manufacturer pursuant to paragraph (2) of subdivision (d) of Section 1793.2 or a similar statute of any other state, unless the nature of the nonconformity experienced by the original buyer or lessee is clearly and conspicuously disclosed to the prospective buyer, lessee, or transferee, the nonconformity is corrected, and the manufacturer warrants to the new buyer, lessee, or transferee in writing for a period of one year that the motor vehicle is free of that nonconformity.

(2) Except for the requirement that the nature of the nonconformity be disclosed to the transferee, paragraph (1) does not apply to the transfer of a motor vehicle to an educational institution if the purpose of the transfer is to make the motor vehicle available for use in automotive repair courses. *(Added by Stats.1992, c. 1232 (S.B.1762), § 7. Amended by Stats.1998, c. 352 (A.B.1848), § 1; Stats.1999, c. 83 (S.B.966), § 21; Stats. 1999, c. 448 (A.B.1290), § 1; Stats.2000, c. 679 (S.B.1718), § 1.)*

Research References

4 Witkin, California Summary 10th Sales § 318, in General.
4 Witkin, California Summary 10th Sales § 319, Tanner Consumer Protection Act.
4 Witkin, California Summary 10th Sales § 320, Automotive Consumer Notification Act.
4 Witkin, California Summary 10th Sales § 323, (S 323) Remedies Available Only to New Motor Vehicle Purchasers.

§ 1793.23. Automotive Consumer Notification Act; legislative findings and declaration; reacquisition of vehicles; disclosure

(a) The Legislature finds and declares all of the following:

(1) That the expansion of state warranty laws covering new and used cars has given important and valuable protection to consumers.

(2) That, in states without this valuable warranty protection, used and irreparable motor vehicles are being resold in the marketplace without notice to the subsequent purchaser.

(3) That other states have addressed this problem by requiring notices on the title of these vehicles or other notice procedures to warn consumers that the motor vehicles were repurchased by a dealer or manufacturer because the vehicle could not be repaired in a reasonable length of time or a reasonable number of repair attempts or the dealer or manufacturer was not willing to repair the vehicle.

(4) That these notices serve the interests of consumers who have a right to information relevant to their buying decisions.

(5) That the disappearance of these notices upon the transfer of title from another state to this state encourages the transport of "lemons" to this state for sale to the drivers of this state.

(b) This section and Section 1793.24 shall be known, and may be cited as, the Automotive Consumer Notification Act.

(c) Any manufacturer who reacquires or assists a dealer or lienholder to reacquire a motor vehicle registered in this state, any other state, or a federally administered district shall, prior to any sale, lease, or transfer of the vehicle in this state, or prior to exporting the vehicle to another state for sale, lease, or transfer if the vehicle was registered in this state and reacquired pursuant to paragraph (2) of subdivision (d) of Section 1793.2, cause the vehicle to be retitled in the name of the manufacturer, request the Department of Motor Vehicles to inscribe the ownership certificate with the notation "Lemon Law Buyback," and affix a decal to the vehicle in accordance with Section 11713.12 of the Vehicle Code if the manufacturer knew or should have known that the vehicle is required by law to be replaced, accepted for restitution due to the failure of the manufacturer to conform the vehicle to applicable warranties pursuant to paragraph (2) of subdivision (d) of Section 1793.2, or accepted for restitution by the manufacturer due to the failure of the manufacturer to conform the vehicle to warranties required by any other applicable law of the state, any other state, or federal law.

(d) Any manufacturer who reacquires or assists a dealer or lienholder to reacquire a motor vehicle in response to a request by the buyer or lessee that the vehicle be either replaced or accepted for restitution because the vehicle did not conform to express warranties shall, prior to the sale, lease, or other transfer of the vehicle, execute and deliver to the subsequent transferee a notice and obtain the transferee's written acknowledgment of a notice, as prescribed by Section 1793.24.

(e) Any person, including any dealer, who acquires a motor vehicle for resale and knows or should have known that the vehicle was reacquired by the vehicle's manufacturer in response to a request by the last retail owner or lessee of the vehicle that it be replaced or accepted for restitution because the vehicle did not conform to express warranties shall, prior to the sale, lease, or other transfer, execute and deliver to the subsequent transferee a notice and obtain the transferee's written acknowledgment of a notice, as prescribed by Section 1793.24.

(f) Any person, including any manufacturer or dealer, who sells, leases, or transfers ownership of a motor vehicle when the vehicle's ownership certificate is inscribed with the notation "Lemon Law Buyback" shall, prior to the sale, lease, or ownership transfer of the vehicle, provide the transferee with a disclosure statement signed by the transferee that states:

"THIS VEHICLE WAS REPURCHASED BY ITS MANUFACTURER DUE TO A DEFECT IN THE VEHICLE PURSUANT TO CONSUMER WARRANTY LAWS. THE TITLE TO THIS VEHICLE HAS BEEN PERMANENTLY BRANDED WITH THE NOTATION 'LEMON LAW BUYBACK'."

(g) The disclosure requirements in subdivisions (d), (e), and (f) are cumulative with all other consumer notice requirements and do not relieve any person, including any dealer or manufacturer, from complying with any other applicable law, including any requirement of subdivision (f) of Section 1793.22.

(h) For purposes of this section, "dealer" means any person engaged in the business of selling, offering for sale, or negotiating the retail sale of, a used motor vehicle or selling motor vehicles as a broker or agent for another, including the officers, agents, and employees of the person and any combination or association of dealers. *(Added by Stats.1995, c. 503 (A.B.1381), § 1. Amended by Stats.1998, c. 932 (A.B.1094), § 7.)*

Research References

4 Witkin, California Summary 10th Sales § 320, Automotive Consumer Notification Act.
6 Witkin, California Summary 10th Torts § 1568A, (New)-Disgorgement of Profits.

§ 1793.24. Preparation of notice; contents of disclosure

(a) The notice required in subdivisions (d) and (e) of Section 1793.23 shall be prepared by the manufacturer of the reacquired vehicle and shall disclose all of the following:

(1) Year, make, model, and vehicle identification number of the vehicle.

(2) Whether the title to the vehicle has been inscribed with the notation "Lemon Law Buyback."

(3) The nature of each nonconformity reported by the original buyer or lessee of the vehicle.

(4) Repairs, if any, made to the vehicle in an attempt to correct each nonconformity reported by the original buyer or lessee.

(b) The notice shall be on a form 8½ x 11 inches in size and printed in no smaller than 10–point black type on a white background.

The form shall only contain the following information prior to it being filled out by the manufacturer:

WARRANTY BUYBACK NOTICE

(Check One)

☐ This vehicle was repurchased by the vehicle's manufacturer after the last retail owner or lessee requested its repurchase due to the problem(s) listed below.

☐ THIS VEHICLE WAS REPURCHASED BY ITS MANUFACTURER DUE TO A DEFECT IN THE VEHICLE PURSUANT TO CONSUMER WARRANTY LAWS. THE TITLE TO THIS VEHICLE HAS BEEN PERMANENTLY BRANDED WITH THE NOTATION "LEMON LAW BUYBACK." Under California law, the manufacturer must warrant to you, for a one year period, that the vehicle is free of the problem(s) listed below.

V.I.N.	Year	Make	Model
Problem(s) Reported by Original Owner	Repairs Made, if any, to Correct Reported Problem(s)		

Signature of Manufacturer   Date

Signature of Dealer(s)   Date

Signature of Retail Buyer or Lessee   Date

(c) The manufacturer shall provide an executed copy of the notice to the manufacturer's transferee. Each transferee, including a dealer, to whom the motor vehicle is transferred prior to its sale to a retail buyer or lessee shall be provided an executed copy of the notice by the previous transferor. *(Added by Stats.1995, c. 503 (A.B.1381), § 2.)*

Research References

4 Witkin, California Summary 10th Sales § 320, Automotive Consumer Notification Act.

§ 1793.25. Reimbursement of sales or use tax to manufacturer of vehicle making restitution to buyer or lessee; rules and regulations; application of sales and use tax to tangible personal property transactions; applicable laws; limitation on reimbursement amount

(a) Notwithstanding Part 1 (commencing with Section 6001) of Division 2 of the Revenue and Taxation Code, the State Board of Equalization shall reimburse the manufacturer of a new motor vehicle for an amount equal to the sales tax or use tax which the manufacturer pays to or for the buyer or lessee when providing a replacement vehicle pursuant to subparagraph (A) of paragraph (2) of subdivision (d) of Section 1793.2 or includes in making restitution to the buyer or lessee pursuant to subparagraph (B) of paragraph (2) of subdivision (d) of Section 1793.2, when the manufacturer provides satisfactory proof that it has complied with subdivision (c) of Section 1793.23, and satisfactory proof is provided for one of the following:

(1) The retailer of the motor vehicle for which the manufacturer is making restitution has reported and paid the sales tax on the gross receipts from the sale of that motor vehicle.

(2) The buyer of the motor vehicle has paid the use tax on the sales price for the storage, use, or other consumption of that motor vehicle in this state.

(3) The lessee of the motor vehicle has paid the use tax on the rentals payable from the lease of that motor vehicle.

(b) The State Board of Equalization may adopt rules and regulations to carry out, facilitate compliance with, or prevent circumvention or evasion of, this section.

(c) This section shall not change the application of the sales and use tax to the gross receipts, the rentals payable, and the sales price from the sale, lease, and the storage, use, or other consumption, in this state of tangible personal property pursuant to Part 1 (commencing with Section 6001) of Division 2 of the Revenue and Taxation Code.

(d) The manufacturer's claim for reimbursement and the State Board of Equalization's approval or denial of the claim shall be subject to the provisions of Article 1 (commencing with Section 6901) of Chapter 7 of Part 1 of Division 2 of the Revenue and Taxation Code, except Sections 6907 and 6908, insofar as those provisions are not inconsistent with this section.

(e) For purposes of this section, the amount of use tax that the State Board of Equalization is required to reimburse the manufacturer shall be limited to the amount of use tax the manufacturer is required to pay to or for the lessee pursuant to Section 1793.2. *(Added by Stats.1987, c. 1280, § 3, operative Jan. 1, 1988. Amended by Stats.1995, c. 503 (A.B.1381), § 3; Stats. 2011, c. 727 (A.B.242), § 2.)*

§ 1793.26. Reacquisition of motor vehicle; confidentiality or gag clause imposed upon dispossessed buyer or lessee; prohibitions

(a) Any automobile manufacturer, importer, distributor, dealer, or lienholder who reacquires, or who assists in reacquiring, a motor vehicle, whether by judgment, decree, arbitration award, settlement agreement, or voluntary agreement, is prohibited from doing either of the following:

(1) Requiring, as a condition of the reacquisition of the motor vehicle, that a buyer or lessee who is a resident of this state agree not to disclose the problems with the vehicle experienced by the buyer or lessee or the nonfinancial terms of the reacquisition.

(2) Including, in any release or other agreement, whether prepared by the manufacturer, importer, distributor, dealer, or lienholder, for signature by the buyer or lessee, a confidentiality clause, gag clause, or similar clause prohibiting the buyer or lessee from disclosing information to anyone about the problems with the vehicle, or the nonfinancial terms of the reacquisition of the vehicle by the manufacturer, importer, distributor, dealer, or lienholder.

(b) Any confidentiality clause, gag clause, or similar clause in such a release or other agreement in violation of this section shall be null and void as against the public policy of this state.

(c) Nothing in this section is intended to prevent any confidentiality clause, gag clause, or similar clause regarding the financial terms of the reacquisition of the vehicle. *(Added by Stats.1998, c. 1063 (A.B.2410), § 1. Amended by Stats.2000, c. 258 (A.B.2517), § 1.)*

Research References

4 Witkin, California Summary 10th Sales § 319, Tanner Consumer Protection Act.

§ 1793.3. Return of nonconforming consumer goods; service, repair, replacement or refund; independent repair or service facilities; notice to buyers

If the manufacturer of consumer goods sold in this state for which the manufacturer has made an express warranty does not provide service and repair facilities within this state pursuant to subdivision (a) of Section 1793.2, or does not make available to authorized service and repair facilities service literature and replacement parts sufficient to effect repair during the express warranty period, the buyer of such manufacturer's nonconforming goods may follow the course of action prescribed in either subdivision (a), (b), or (c), below, as follows:

(a) Return the nonconforming consumer goods to the retail seller thereof. The retail seller shall do one of the following:

(1) Service or repair the nonconforming goods to conform to the applicable warranty.

(2) Direct the buyer to a reasonably close independent repair or service facility willing to accept service or repair under this section.

(3) Replace the nonconforming goods with goods that are identical or reasonably equivalent to the warranted goods.

(4) Refund to the buyer the original purchase price less that amount directly attributable to use by the buyer prior to the discovery of the nonconformity.

(b) Return the nonconforming consumer goods to any retail seller of like goods of the same manufacturer within this state who may do one of the following:

(1) Service or repair the nonconforming goods to conform to the applicable warranty.

(2) Direct the buyer to a reasonably close independent repair or service facility willing to accept service or repair under this section.

(3) Replace the nonconforming goods with goods that are identical or reasonably equivalent to the warranted goods.

(4) Refund to the buyer the original purchase price less that amount directly attributable to use by the buyer prior to the discovery of the nonconformity.

(c) Secure the services of an independent repair or service facility for the service or repair of the nonconforming consumer goods, when service or repair of the goods can be economically accomplished. In that event the manufacturer shall be liable to the buyer, or to the independent repair or service facility upon an assignment of the buyer's rights, for the actual and reasonable cost of service and repair, including any cost for parts and any reasonable cost of transporting the goods or parts, plus a reasonable profit. It shall be a rebuttable presumption affecting the burden of producing evidence that the reasonable cost of service or repair is an amount equal to that which is charged by the independent service dealer for like services or repairs rendered to service or repair customers who are not entitled to warranty protection. Any waiver of the liability of a manufacturer shall be void and unenforceable.

The course of action prescribed in this subdivision shall be available to the buyer only after the buyer has followed the course of action prescribed in either subdivision (a) or (b) and such course of action has not furnished the buyer with appropriate relief. In no event, shall the provisions of this subdivision be available to the buyer with regard to consumer goods with a wholesale price to the retailer of less than fifty dollars ($50). In no event shall the buyer be responsible or liable for service or repair costs charged by the independent repair or service facility which accepts service or repair of nonconforming consumer goods under this section. Such independent repair or service facility shall only be authorized to hold the manufacturer liable for such costs.

(d) A retail seller to which any nonconforming consumer good is returned pursuant to subdivision (a) or (b) shall have the option of providing service or repair itself or directing the buyer to a reasonably close independent repair or service facility willing to accept service or repair under this section. In the event the retail seller directs the buyer to an independent repair or service facility, the manufacturer shall be liable for the reasonable cost of repair services in the manner provided in subdivision (c).

(e) In the event a buyer is unable to return nonconforming goods to the retailer due to reasons of size and weight, or method of attachment, or method of installation, or nature of the nonconformity, the buyer shall give notice of the nonconformity to the retailer. Upon receipt of such notice of nonconformity the retailer shall, at its option, service or repair the goods at the buyer's residence, or pick up the goods for service or repair, or arrange for transporting the goods to its place of business. The reasonable costs of transporting the goods shall be at the retailer's expense. The retailer shall be entitled to recover all such reasonable costs of transportation from the manufacturer pursuant to Section 1793.5. The reasonable costs of transporting nonconforming goods after delivery to the retailer until return of the goods to the buyer, when incurred by a retailer, shall be recoverable from the manufacturer pursuant to Section 1793.5. Written notice of nonconformity to the retailer shall constitute return of the goods for the purposes of subdivisions (a) and (b).

(f) The manufacturer of consumer goods with a wholesale price to the retailer of fifty dollars ($50) or more for which the manufacturer has made express warranties shall provide written notice to the buyer of the courses of action available to him under subdivision (a), (b), or (c). *(Added by Stats.1970, c. 1333, p. 2481, § 1. Amended by Stats.1971, c. 1523, p. 3005, § 10, operative Jan. 1, 1972; Stats.1976, c. 416, p. 1070, § 3; Stats.1978, c. 991, p. 3062, § 8; Stats.1986, c. 547, § 3.)*

Research References

4 Witkin, California Summary 10th Sales § 317, (S 317) Maintenance of Service and Repair Facilities.

§ 1793.35. Clothing; consumables; draperies; reimbursement or replacement; implied warranty of merchantability

(a) Where the retail sale of clothing or consumables is accompanied by an express warranty and such items do not conform with the terms of the express warranty, the buyer thereof may return the goods within 30 days of purchase or the period specified in the warranty, whichever is greater. The manufacturer may, in the express warranty, direct the purchaser to return nonconforming goods to a retail seller of like goods of the same manufacturer for replacement.

(b) When clothing or consumables are returned to a retail seller for the reason that they do not conform to an express warranty, the retailer shall replace the nonconforming goods where the manufacturer has directed replacement in the express warranty. In the event the manufacturer has not directed replacement in the express warranty, the retailer may replace the nonconforming goods or reimburse the buyer in an amount equal to the purchase price paid by the buyer for the goods, at the option of the retailer. Costs of reimbursement or replacement are recoverable by a retailer from the manufacturer in the manner provided in Section 1793.5.

(c) Where the retail sale of draperies is not accompanied by an express warranty and the sale of such draperies is accompanied by a conspicuous writing disclaiming the retailer's implied warranty of merchantability on the fabric, the retailer's implied warranty of merchantability shall not apply to the fabric. *(Added by Stats.1971, c. 1523, p. 3006, § 10.5, operative Jan. 1, 1972. Amended by Stats.1978, c. 991, p. 3064, § 8.5.)*

§ 1793.4. Commencement of service and repair within reasonable time; tender of conforming goods within 30 days; extension of time

Where an option is exercised in favor of service and repair under Section 1793.3, such service and repair must be commenced within a reasonable time, and, unless the buyer agrees in writing to the contrary, goods conforming to the applicable express warranties shall be tendered within 30 days. Delay caused by conditions beyond the control of the retail seller or his representative shall serve to extend this 30-day requirement.

Where such a delay arises, conforming goods shall be tendered as soon as possible following termination of the condition giving rise to the delay. *(Added by Stats.1970, c. 1333, p. 2482, § 1. Amended by Stats.1971, c. 1523, p. 3006, § 11, operative Jan. 1, 1972; Stats.1978, c. 991, p. 3064, § 9.)*

§ 1793.5. Liability of manufacturer to retailer

Every manufacturer making express warranties who does not provide service and repair facilities within this state pursuant to subdivision (a) of Section 1793.2 shall be liable as prescribed in this section to every retail seller of such manufacturer's goods who incurs obligations in giving effect to the express warranties that accompany such manufacturer's consumer goods. The amount of such liability shall be determined as follows:

(a) In the event of replacement, in an amount equal to the actual cost to the retail seller of the replaced goods, and cost of transporting the goods, if such costs are incurred plus a reasonable handling charge.

(b) In the event of service and repair, in an amount equal to that which would be received by the retail seller for like service rendered to retail consumers who are not entitled to warranty protection, including actual and reasonable costs of the service and repair and the cost of transporting the goods, if such costs are incurred, plus a reasonable profit.

(c) In the event of reimbursement under subdivision (a) of Section 1793.3, in an amount equal to that reimbursed to the buyer, plus a reasonable handling charge. *(Added by Stats.1970, c. 1333, p. 2482, § 1. Amended by Stats.1971, c. 1523, p. 3006, § 12, operative Jan. 1, 1972.)*

Research References

4 Witkin, California Summary 10th Sales § 317, (S 317) Maintenance of Service and Repair Facilities.

§ 1793.6. Liability of manufacturer to independent service and repair facility

Except as otherwise provided in the terms of a warranty service contract, as specified in subdivision (a) of Section 1793.2, entered into between a manufacturer and an independent service and repair facility, every manufacturer making express warranties whose consumer goods are sold in this state shall be liable as prescribed in this section to every independent serviceman who performs services or incurs obligations in giving effect to the express warranties that accompany such manufacturer's consumer goods whether the independent serviceman is acting as an authorized service and repair facility designated by the manufacturer pursuant to paragraph (1) of subdivision (a) of Section 1793.2 or is acting as an independent serviceman pursuant to subdivisions (c) and (d) of Section 1793.3. The amount of such liability shall be an amount equal to the actual and reasonable costs of the service and repair, including any cost for parts and any reasonable cost of transporting the goods or parts, plus a reasonable profit. It shall be a rebuttable presumption affecting the burden of producing evidence that the reasonable cost of service or repair is an amount equal to that which is charged by the independent serviceman for like services or repairs rendered to service or repair customers who are not entitled to warranty protection. Any waiver of the liability of a manufacturer shall be void and unenforceable. *(Added by Stats.1976, c. 416, p. 1072, § 4.)*

§ 1794. Actions by buyers; measure of damages; civil penalties; costs and expenses; attorney's fees

(a) Any buyer of consumer goods who is damaged by a failure to comply with any obligation under this chapter or under an implied or express warranty or service contract may bring an action for the recovery of damages and other legal and equitable relief.

(b) The measure of the buyer's damages in an action under this section shall include the rights of replacement or reimbursement as set forth in subdivision (d) of Section 1793.2, and the following:

(1) Where the buyer has rightfully rejected or justifiably revoked acceptance of the goods or has exercised any right to cancel the sale, Sections 2711, 2712, and 2713 of the Commercial Code shall apply.

(2) Where the buyer has accepted the goods, Sections 2714 and 2715 of the Commercial Code shall apply, and the measure of damages shall include the cost of repairs necessary to make the goods conform.

(c) If the buyer establishes that the failure to comply was willful, the judgment may include, in addition to the amounts recovered under subdivision (a), a civil penalty which shall not exceed two times the amount of actual damages. This subdivision shall not apply in any class action under Section 382 of the Code of Civil Procedure or under Section 1781, or with respect to a claim based solely on a breach of an implied warranty.

(d) If the buyer prevails in an action under this section, the buyer shall be allowed by the court to recover as part of the judgment a sum equal to the aggregate amount of costs and expenses, including attorney's fees based on actual time expended, determined by the court to have been reasonably incurred by the buyer in connection with the commencement and prosecution of such action.

(e)(1) Except as otherwise provided in this subdivision, if the buyer establishes a violation of paragraph (2) of subdivision (d) of Section 1793.2, the buyer shall recover damages and reasonable attorney's fees and costs, and may recover a civil penalty of up to two times the amount of damages.

(2) If the manufacturer maintains a qualified third-party dispute resolution process which substantially complies with Section 1793.22, the manufacturer shall not be liable for any civil penalty pursuant to this subdivision.

(3) After the occurrence of the events giving rise to the presumption established in subdivision (b) of Section 1793.22, the buyer may serve upon the manufacturer a written notice requesting that the manufacturer comply with paragraph (2) of subdivision (d) of Section 1793.2. If the buyer fails to serve the notice, the manufacturer shall not be liable for a civil penalty pursuant to this subdivision.

(4) If the buyer serves the notice described in paragraph (3) and the manufacturer complies with paragraph (2) of subdivision (d) of Section 1793.2 within 30 days of the service of that notice, the manufacturer shall not be liable for a civil penalty pursuant to this subdivision.

(5) If the buyer recovers a civil penalty under subdivision (c), the buyer may not also recover a civil penalty under this subdivision for the same violation. *(Added by Stats.1982, c. 385, p. 1716, § 2. Amended by Stats.1987, c. 1280, § 4, operative Jan. 1, 1988; Stats.1992, c. 1232 (S.B.1762), § 9.)*

Research References

Rutter, Cal. Practice Guide: Civil Trials & Evidence Ch. 17-D, D. Costs.
Rutter, Cal. Practice Guide: Civil Trials & Evidence Ch. 17-E, E. Attorney Fees as Costs.
Rutter, Cal. Practice Guide: Enforcing Judgments/Debts Ch. 3-A, A. Evaluating the Claim.
Miller and Starr California Real Estate § 29:19, Liability of Material Suppliers and Manufacturers.
Miller and Starr California Real Estate § 31:61, Warranties.
Miller and Starr California Real Estate § 27:127, Treble Damages and Civil Penalties.

14 NO. 1 Miller & Starr, California Real Estate Newsalert 5, Defective Construction.

3 Witkin Cal. Proc. 5th Actions § 519, (S 519) Contract of Sale: Four Years.

3 Witkin Cal. Proc. 5th Actions § 668, (S 668) Exceptions.

7 Witkin Cal. Proc. 5th Judgment § 89, Determining Who is Prevailing Party.

7 Witkin Cal. Proc. 5th Judgment § 112, Plaintiff Fails to Obtain Judgment More Favorable Than Offer.

7 Witkin Cal. Proc. 5th Judgment § 203, (S 203) Distinction: Issue of Entitlement to Costs and Attorneys' Fees Expressly Reserved.

7 Witkin Cal. Proc. 5th Judgment § 224, (S 224) Consumer Protection Actions.

7 Witkin Cal. Proc. 5th Judgment § 311, in General.

7 Witkin Cal. Proc. 5th Judgment § 312, Use of Lodestar Approach.

4 Witkin, California Summary 10th Sales § 10, Liberal and Uniform Construction.

4 Witkin, California Summary 10th Sales § 321, (S 321) in General.

4 Witkin, California Summary 10th Sales § 322, (S 322) Costs and Attorneys' Fees.

4 Witkin, California Summary 10th Sales § 323, (S 323) Remedies Available Only to New Motor Vehicle Purchasers.

6 Witkin, California Summary 10th Torts § 1569, Nature and Validity of Penalties.

6 Witkin, California Summary 10th Torts § 1571, Recovery of Both Penalty and Punitive Damages.

§ 1794.1.   Actions by retailer and independent serviceman

(a) Any retail seller of consumer goods injured by the willful or repeated violation of the provisions of this chapter may bring an action for the recovery of damages. Judgment may be entered for three times the amount at which the actual damages are assessed plus reasonable attorney fees.

(b) Any independent serviceman of consumer goods injured by the willful or repeated violation of the provisions of this chapter may bring an action for the recovery of damages. Judgment may be entered for three times the amount at which the actual damages are assessed plus reasonable attorney fees. *(Added by Stats.1970, c. 1333, p. 2482, § 1. Amended by Stats.1976, c. 416, p. 1072, § 5.)*

Research References

4 Witkin, California Summary 10th Sales § 324, (S 324) Action by Seller or Independent Service Person.

§ 1794.3.   Defect or nonconformity caused by unauthorized or unreasonable use; inapplicability of chapter

The provisions of this chapter shall not apply to any defect or nonconformity in consumer goods caused by the unauthorized or unreasonable use of the goods following sale. *(Added by Stats.1970, c. 1333, p. 2482, § 1. Amended by Stats.1971, c. 1523, p. 3007, § 15, operative Jan. 1, 1972.)*

Research References

4 Witkin, California Summary 10th Sales § 314, Scope of Act.

§ 1794.4.   Service contract; contents

(a) Nothing in this chapter shall be construed to prevent the sale of a service contract to the buyer in addition to or in lieu of an express warranty if that contract fully and conspicuously discloses in simple and readily understood language the terms, conditions, and exclusions of that contract, provided that nothing in this section shall apply to a home protection contract issued by a home protection company that is subject to Part 7 (commencing with Section 12740) of Division 2 of the Insurance Code.

(b) Except as otherwise expressly provided in the service contract, every service contract shall obligate the service contractor to provide to the buyer of the product all of the services and functional parts that may be necessary to maintain proper operation of the entire product under normal operation and service for the duration of the service contract and without additional charge.

(c) The service contract shall contain all of the following items of information:

(1) A clear description and identification of the covered product.

(2) The point in time or event when the term of the service contract commences, and its duration measured by elapsed time or an objective measure of use.

(3) If the enforceability of the service contract is limited to the original buyer or is limited to persons other than every consumer owner of the covered product during the term of the service contract, a description of the limits on transfer or assignment of the service contract.

(4) A statement of the general obligation of the service contractor in the same language set forth in subdivision (b), with equally clear and conspicuous statements of the following:

(A) Any services, parts, characteristics, components, properties, defects, malfunctions, causes, conditions, repairs, or remedies that are excluded from the scope of the service contract.

(B) Any other limits on the application of the language in subdivision (b) such as a limit on the total number of service calls.

(C) Any additional services that the service contractor will provide.

(D) Whether the obligation of the service contractor includes preventive maintenance and, if so, the nature and frequency of the preventive maintenance that the service contractor will provide.

(E) Whether the buyer has an obligation to provide preventive maintenance or perform any other obligations and, if so, the nature and frequency of the preventive maintenance and of any other obligations, and the consequences of any noncompliance.

(5) A step-by-step explanation of the procedure that the buyer should follow in order to obtain performance of any obligation under the service contract including the following:

(A) The full legal and business name of the service contractor.

(B) The mailing address of the service contractor.

(C) The persons or class of persons that are authorized to perform service.

(D) The name or title and address of any agent, employee, or department of the service contractor that is responsible for the performance of any obligations.

(E) The method of giving notice to the service contractor of the need for service.

(F) Whether in-home service is provided or, if not, whether the costs of transporting the product, for service or repairs will be paid by the service contractor.

(G) If the product must be transported to the service contractor, either the place where the product may be delivered for service or repairs or a toll-free telephone number that the buyer may call to obtain that information.

(H) All other steps that the buyer must take to obtain service.

(I) All fees, charges, and other costs that the buyer must pay to obtain service.

(6) An explanation of the steps that the service contractor will take to carry out its obligations under the service contract.

(7) A description of any right to cancel the contract if the buyer returns the product or the product is sold, lost, stolen, or destroyed, or, if there is no right to cancel or the right to cancel is limited, a statement of the fact.

(8) Information respecting the availability of any informal dispute settlement process.

(d) Subdivisions (b) and (c) are applicable to service contracts on new or used home appliances and home electronic products entered into on or after July 1, 1989. They are applicable to service contracts on all other new or used products entered into on and after July 1, 1991.

(e) This section shall become operative on January 1, 2008. *(Added by Stats.1993, c. 1265 (S.B.798), § 13.5, operative Jan. 1, 1998. Amended by Stats.1997, c. 401 (S.B.780), § 65, operative Jan. 1, 2003; Stats.2002, c. 405 (A.B.2973), § 64, operative Jan. 1, 2008.)*

Research References

4 Witkin, California Summary 10th Sales § 326, Service Contract in Lieu of Express Warranty.

§ 1794.41. Service contract provisions

(a) No service contract covering any motor vehicle, home appliance, or home electronic product purchased for use in this state may be offered for sale or sold unless all of the following elements exist:

(1) The contract shall contain the disclosures specified in Section 1794.4 and shall disclose in the manner described in that section the buyer's cancellation and refund rights provided by this section.

(2) The contract shall be available for inspection by the buyer prior to purchase and either the contract, or a brochure which specifically describes the terms, conditions, and exclusions of the contract, and the provisions of this section relating to contract delivery, cancellation, and refund, shall be delivered to the buyer at or before the time of purchase of the contract. Within 60 days after the date of purchase, the contract itself shall be delivered to the buyer. If a service contract for a home appliance or a home electronic product is sold by means of a telephone solicitation, the seller may elect to satisfy the requirements of this paragraph by mailing or delivering the contract to the buyer not later than 30 days after the date of the sale of the contract.

(3) The contract is applicable only to items, costs, and time periods not covered by the express warranty. However, a service contract may run concurrently with or overlap an express warranty if (A) the contract covers items or costs not covered by the express warranty or (B) the contract provides relief to the purchaser not available under the express warranty, such as automatic replacement of a product where the express warranty only provides for repair.

(4) The contract shall be cancelable by the purchaser under the following conditions:

(A) Unless the contract provides for a longer period, within the first 60 days after receipt of the contract, or with respect to a contract covering a used motor vehicle without manufacturer warranties, a home appliance, or a home electronic product, within the first 30 days after receipt of the contract, the full amount paid shall be refunded by the seller to the purchaser if the purchaser provides a written notice of cancellation to the person specified in the contract, and if no claims have been made against the contract. If a claim has been made against the contract either within the first 60 days after receipt of the contract, or with respect to a used motor vehicle without manufacturer warranties, home appliance, or home electronic product, within the first 30 days after receipt of the contract, a pro rata refund, based on either elapsed time or an objective measure of use, such as mileage or the retail value of any service performed, at the seller's option as indicated in the contract, or for a vehicle service contract at the obligor's option as deter-

mined at the time of cancellation, shall be made by the seller to the purchaser if the purchaser provides a written notice of cancellation to the person specified in the contract.

(B) Unless the contract provides for a longer period for obtaining a full refund, after the first 60 days after receipt of the contract, or with respect to a contract covering a used motor vehicle without manufacturer warranties, a home appliance, or a home electronic product, after the first 30 days after the receipt of the contract, a pro rata refund, based on either elapsed time or an objective measure of use, such as mileage or the retail value of any service performed, at the seller's option as indicated in the contract, or for a vehicle service contract at the obligor's option as determined at the time of cancellation, shall be made by the seller to the purchaser if the purchaser provides a written notice of cancellation to the person specified in the contract. In addition, the seller may assess a cancellation or administrative fee, not to exceed 10 percent of the price of the service contract or twenty-five dollars ($25), whichever is less.

(C) If the purchase of the service contract was financed, the seller may make the refund payable to the purchaser, the assignee, or lender of record, or both.

(b) Nothing in this section shall apply to a home protection plan that is issued by a home protection company which is subject to Part 7 (commencing with Section 12740) of Division 2 of the Insurance Code.

(c) If any provision of this section conflicts with any provision of Part 8 (commencing with Section 12800) of Division 2 of the Insurance Code, the provision of the Insurance Code shall apply instead of this section. *(Added by Stats.1985, c. 1047, § 3. Amended by Stats.1988, c. 581, § 3; Stats.1990, c. 1183 (A.B. 2226), § 1; Stats.2003, c. 439 (A.B.984), § 1, operative July 1, 2004; Stats.2010, c. 543 (A.B.2111), § 7.)*

Research References

4 Witkin, California Summary 10th Sales § 326, Service Contract in Lieu of Express Warranty.

§ 1794.45. Service contract; requirements while in effect; exclusions

(a) A retailer that sells a service contract pursuant to Section 1794.4 shall do either of the following during the period that the service contract is in effect:

(1) Maintain contract information that includes a description of the terms and conditions of the service contract, and provide that information to the purchaser of the service contract or other beneficiary upon request.

(2) Upon request from the purchaser of the service contract or other beneficiary, obtain a copy of the service contract, and provide that copy to the requester within 10 business days after receiving the request.

(b) This section shall not apply to a vehicle service contract, as defined in subdivision (c) of Section 12800 of the Insurance Code. *(Added by Stats.2009, c. 74 (A.B.63), § 1.)*

Research References

4 Witkin, California Summary 10th Sales § 326, Service Contract in Lieu of Express Warranty.

§ 1794.5. Suggestions of methods of service and repair by manufacturer

The provisions of this chapter shall not preclude a manufacturer making express warranties from suggesting methods of effecting service and repair, in accordance with the terms and conditions of the express warranties, other than those required by this chapter. *(Added by Stats.1970, c. 1333, p. 2483, § 1.)*

§ 1795. Liability of warrantors other than manufacturers

If express warranties are made by persons other than the manufacturer of the goods, the obligation of the person making such warranties shall be the same as that imposed on the manufacturer under this chapter. *(Added by Stats.1970, c. 1333, p. 2483, § 1.)*

Research References

4 Witkin, California Summary 10th Sales § 31, Applicability of Division 2 to Particular Transactions.

§ 1795.1. Systems designed to heat, cool or condition air; equipment or component; application of chapter

This chapter shall apply to any equipment or mechanical, electrical, or thermal component of a system designed to heat, cool, or otherwise condition air, but, with that exception, shall not apply to the system as a whole where such a system becomes a fixed part of a structure. *(Added by Stats.1971, c. 1523, p. 3007, § 16.5, operative Jan. 1, 1972. Amended by Stats.1978, c. 991, p. 3065, § 11; Stats.1983, c. 728, § 1.)*

Research References

4 Witkin, California Summary 10th Sales § 52, Commercial Code, Consumer Warranty Act, and Federal Warranty Law.

§ 1795.4. Leases of new and used consumer goods; rules applicable

For the purposes of this chapter only, the following rules apply to leases of both new and used consumer goods:

(a) If express warranties are regularly furnished to purchasers of substantially the same kind of goods, (1) those warranties will be deemed to apply to the leased goods and (2) the lessor and lessee shall each be deemed to be the first purchaser of the goods for the purpose of any warranty provision limiting warranty benefits to the original purchaser.

(b) The lessee of goods has the same rights under this chapter against the manufacturer and any person making express warranties that the lessee would have had under this chapter if the goods had been purchased by the lessee, and the manufacturer and any person making express warranties have the same duties and obligations under this chapter with respect to the goods that such manufacturer and other person would have had under this chapter if the goods had been sold to the lessee.

(c) If a lessor leases goods to a lessee from the lessor's inventory, the lessee has the same rights under this chapter against the lessor that the lessee would have had if the goods had been purchased by the lessee, and the lessor has the same duties and obligations under this chapter with respect to the goods that the lessor would have had under this chapter if the goods had been sold to the lessee. For purposes of this section, "inventory" shall include both goods in the lessor's possession prior to negotiation of the lease and goods ordered from another party in order to lease those goods to the lessee where the lessor is a dealer in goods of that type.

(d) If a lessor leases goods to a lessee which the lessor acquires other than from the lessor's inventory, the lessee has the same rights under this chapter against the seller of the goods to the lessor that the lessee would have had under this chapter if the goods had been purchased by the lessee from the seller, and the seller of the goods to the lessor has the same duties and obligations under this chapter with respect to the goods that the seller would have had under this chapter if the goods had been purchased by the lessee from the seller.

(e) A lessor who re-leases goods to a new lessee and does not retake possession of the goods prior to consummation of the re-lease may, notwithstanding the provisions of Section 1793, disclaim as to that lessee any and all warranties created by this chapter by conspicuously disclosing in the lease that these warranties are disclaimed.

(f) A lessor who has obligations to the lessee with relation to warranties in connection with a lease of goods and the seller of goods to a lessor have the same rights and remedies against the manufacturer and any person making express warranties that a seller of the goods would have had if the seller had sold the goods to the lessee. *(Added by Stats.1984, c. 1169, § 2.)*

Research References

4 Witkin, California Summary 10th Sales § 314, Scope of Act.

§ 1795.5. Used goods; obligation of distributor or retail seller; maintenance of service and repair facilities; duration of warranties

Notwithstanding the provisions of subdivision (a) of Section 1791 defining consumer goods to mean "new" goods, the obligation of a distributor or retail seller of used consumer goods in a sale in which an express warranty is given shall be the same as that imposed on manufacturers under this chapter except:

(a) It shall be the obligation of the distributor or retail seller making express warranties with respect to used consumer goods (and not the original manufacturer, distributor, or retail seller making express warranties with respect to such goods when new) to maintain sufficient service and repair facilities within this state to carry out the terms of such express warranties.

(b) The provisions of Section 1793.5 shall not apply to the sale of used consumer goods sold in this state.

(c) The duration of the implied warranty of merchantability and where present the implied warranty of fitness with respect to used consumer goods sold in this state, where the sale is accompanied by an express warranty, shall be coextensive in duration with an express warranty which accompanies the consumer goods, provided the duration of the express warranty is reasonable, but in no event shall such implied warranties have a duration of less than 30 days nor more than three months following the sale of used consumer goods to a retail buyer. Where no duration for an express warranty is stated with respect to such goods, or parts thereof, the duration of the implied warranties shall be the maximum period prescribed above.

(d) The obligation of the distributor or retail seller who makes express warranties with respect to used goods that are sold in this state, shall extend to the sale of all such used goods, regardless of when such goods may have been manufactured. *(Added by Stats.1971, c. 1523, p. 3008, § 17, operative Jan. 1, 1972. Amended by Stats.1974, c. 169, p. 325, § 1; Stats.1978, c. 991, p. 3065, § 12; Stats.1983, c. 728, § 2.)*

Research References

4 Witkin, California Summary 10th Sales § 317, (S 317) Maintenance of Service and Repair Facilities.

§ 1795.51. Buy-here-pay-here dealer; written warranty and receipt for sale or lease of vehicle; prohibited actions; notice of election to cancel; vehicle repairs

(a) No buy-here-pay-here dealer, as that term is defined in Section 241 of the Vehicle Code, shall sell or lease a used vehicle, as defined in Section 665 of the Vehicle Code, at retail price without giving the buyer or lessee a written warranty that shall have a minimum duration of at least 30 days from the date of delivery or when the odometer has registered 1,000 miles from what is shown on the contract, whichever occurs first.

(b) The written warranty shall provide that if the buyer or lessee notifies the buy-here-pay-here dealer that the vehicle does not conform to the written warranty, the buy-here-pay-here dealer shall either repair the vehicle to conform to the written warranty, reimburse the buyer or lessee for the reasonable cost of repairs, or cancel the sale or lease contract and provide the buyer or lessee with a full refund, less a reasonable amount for any damage sustained by the vehicle after the sale or lease, excepting damage caused by any nonconformity with the written warranty.

(c) The written warranty shall provide that the buy-here-pay-here dealer shall pay 100 percent of the cost of labor and parts for any repairs pursuant to the warranty, and may not charge the buyer or lessee for the cost of repairs or for inspecting the vehicle, tearing down the engine or transmission or other part, or for any deductible. Any person performing repairs pursuant to this subdivision shall comply with the requirements of an automotive repair dealer pursuant to Chapter 20.3 (commencing with Section 9880) of Division 3 of the Business and Professions Code.

(d) The buy-here-pay-here dealer or its agent may elect to refund the buyer or lessee a full refund, less a reasonable amount for any damage sustained by the vehicle after the sale or lease, excepting damage caused by any nonconformity with the written warranty, rather than performing a repair. In the event that the buy-here-pay-here dealer cancels the sale or lease, all of the following shall apply:

(1) The buy-here-pay-here dealer shall give written notice to the buyer or lessee of the election to cancel the sale or lease by personal delivery or first-class mail.

(2) The buyer or lessee shall return the vehicle in substantially the same condition as when it was delivered by the buy-here-pay-here dealer, reasonable wear and tear and any nonconformity with the written warranty excepted.

(3) The buy-here-pay-here dealer shall provide the buyer or lessee with a receipt stating all of the following:

(A) The date the vehicle was returned to the buy-here-pay-here dealer.

(B) The vehicle identification number.

(C) The make, year, and model of the vehicle.

(D) The odometer reading at the time that the vehicle was returned to the buy-here-pay-here dealer.

(E) A statement that the buy-here-pay-here dealer has canceled the sale or lease.

(F) The amount of the buyer's or lessee's refund.

(4) The buy-here-pay-here dealer shall not treat the return of the vehicle pursuant to the contract cancellation provisions of this subdivision as a repossession.

(5) The buyer or lessee shall execute the documents necessary to transfer any interest in the vehicle to the buy-here-pay-here dealer or to remove the buyer or lessee from any registration or title documents.

(6) The buy-here-pay-here dealer shall refund to the buyer or lessee, no later than the day after the day on which the buyer or lessee returns the vehicle and the notice of election to cancel is given to the buyer or lessee, all amounts paid under the sale or lease agreement, less a reasonable amount for property damage sustained by the vehicle after the sale or lease, excepting damage caused by any nonconformity with the warranty.

(e) The written warranty shall cover at least the following components:

(1) Engine, including all internally lubricated parts.

(2) Transmission and transaxle.

(3) Front and rear wheel drive components.

(4) Engine cooling system.

(5) Alternator, generator, starter, and ignition system, not including the battery.

(6) Braking system.

(7) Front and rear suspension systems.

(8) Steering system and components.

(9) Seatbelts.

(10) Inflatable restraint systems installed on the vehicle as originally manufactured.

(11) Catalytic converter and other emissions components necessary for the vehicle to pass a California emissions test.

(12) Heater.

(13) Seals and gaskets on components described in this subdivision.

(14) Electrical, electronic, and computer components, to the extent that those components substantially affect the functionality of other components described in this subdivision.

(f) Any Used Car Buyer's Guide displayed on a vehicle offered for sale or lease by a buy-here-pay-here dealer shall list each of the above systems and components and shall specify that the buy-here-pay-here dealer will pay 100 percent of the cost of parts and labor for repairs covered by the warranty.

(g) The buy-here-pay-here dealer shall make the repair or provide a refund notwithstanding the fact that the warranty period has expired if the buyer or lessee notified the buy-here-pay-here dealer of the failure of a covered system or part within the warranty period.

(h) This section shall not apply to any defect or nonconformity caused by the unauthorized or unreasonable use of the vehicle following the sale, or to any property damage not to the vehicle arising out of the failure of a covered part.

(i) In any proceeding in which the exclusion of coverage permitted by subdivision (h) or the deduction allowed by paragraph (6) of subdivision (d) is an issue, the buy-here-pay-here dealer shall have the burden of proof.

(j) A buy-here-pay-here dealer shall not sell or lease any vehicle unless the vehicle meets all of the equipment requirements of Division 12 (commencing with Section 24000) of the Vehicle Code.

(k) Any agreement between a buy-here-pay-here dealer and a buyer or lessee that disclaims, limits, or waives the rights set forth in this section shall be void as contrary to public policy.

(*l*) If a buy-here-pay-here dealer fails to give a buyer a written warranty pursuant to this section, the buy-here-pay-here dealer shall be deemed to have provided the warranty as a matter of law. (Added by Stats.2012, c. 740 (A.B.1447), § 2.)

§ 1795.6. Tolling or expiration of warranty period during time of repairs

(a) Every warranty period relating to an implied or express warranty accompanying a sale or consignment for sale of consumer goods selling for fifty dollars ($50) or more shall automatically be tolled for the period from the date upon which the buyer either (1) delivers nonconforming goods to the manufacturer or seller for warranty repairs or service or (2), pursuant to subdivision (c) of Section 1793.2 or Section 1793.22, notifies the manufacturer or seller of the nonconformity of the goods up to, and including, the date upon which (1) the repaired or serviced goods are delivered to the buyer, (2) the buyer is notified the goods are repaired or serviced and are available for the buyer's possession or (3) the buyer is notified that repairs or service is completed, if repairs or service is made at the buyer's residence.

(b) Notwithstanding the date or conditions set for the expiration of the warranty period, such warranty period shall not be deemed expired if either or both of the following situations occur: (1) after the buyer has satisfied the requirements of subdivision (a), the warranty repairs or service has not been performed due to delays caused by circumstances beyond the control of the buyer or (2) the warranty repairs or service performed upon the nonconforming goods did not remedy the nonconformity for which such repairs or service was performed and the buyer notified the manufacturer or seller of this failure within 60 days after the repairs or service was completed. When the warranty repairs or service has been performed so as to remedy the nonconformity, the warranty period shall expire in accordance with its terms, including any extension to the warranty period for warranty repairs or service.

(c) For purposes of this section only, "manufacturer" includes the manufacturer's service or repair facility.

(d) Every manufacturer or seller of consumer goods selling for fifty dollars ($50) or more shall provide a receipt to the buyer showing the date of purchase. Every manufacturer or seller performing warranty repairs or service on the goods shall provide to the buyer a work order or receipt with the date of return and either the date the buyer was notified that the goods were repaired or serviced or, where applicable, the date the goods were shipped or delivered to the buyer. *(Added by Stats.1974, c. 844, p. 1809, § 1, operative July 1, 1975. Amended by Stats.1980, c. 394, p. 778, § 2; Stats.1983, c. 728, § 3; Stats.1992, c. 1232 (S.B.1762), § 10.)*

Research References

4 Witkin, California Summary 10th Sales § 325, Tolling of Warranty Period.

§ 1795.7. Liability of manufacturer; extension upon tolling of warranty period

Whenever a warranty, express or implied, is tolled pursuant to Section 1795.6 as a result of repairs or service performed by any retail seller, the warranty shall be extended with regard to the liability of the manufacturer to a retail seller pursuant to law. In such event, the manufacturer shall be liable in accordance with the provisions of Section 1793.5 for the period that an express warranty has been extended by virtue of Section 1795.6 to every retail seller who incurs obligations in giving effect to such express warranty. The manufacturer shall also be liable to every retail seller for the period that an implied warranty has been extended by virtue of Section 1795.6, in the same manner as he would be liable under Section 1793.5 for an express warranty. If a manufacturer provides for warranty repairs and service through its own service and repair facilities and through independent repair facilities in the state, its exclusive liability pursuant to this section shall be to such facilities. *(Added by Stats.1974, c. 844, p. 1809, § 2, operative July 1, 1975.)*

Research References

4 Witkin, California Summary 10th Sales § 325, Tolling of Warranty Period.

§ 1795.8. Application of chapter to members of Armed Forces purchasing motor vehicle

Notwithstanding any other provision of law, this chapter shall apply to a purchase in the United States of a motor vehicle, as defined in paragraph (2) of subdivision (e) of Section 1793.22, with a manufacturer's express warranty by a member of the Armed Forces regardless of in which state his or her motor vehicle is purchased or registered, if both of the following apply:

(a) The member of the Armed Forces purchases a motor vehicle, as defined in paragraph (2) of subdivision (e) of Section 1793.22, with a manufacturer's express warranty from a manufac-

turer who sells motor vehicles in this state or from an agent or representative of that manufacturer.

(b) The member of the Armed Forces was stationed in or a resident of this state at the time he or she purchased the motor vehicle or at the time he or she filed an action pursuant to this chapter. *(Added by Stats.2007, c. 151 (S.B.234), § 2.)*

Research References

4 Witkin, California Summary 10th Sales § 314, Scope of Act.

CHAPTER 1.5. MOTOR VEHICLE WARRANTY ADJUSTMENT PROGRAMS

§ 1795.90. Definitions

For purposes of this chapter:

(a) "Consumer" means the purchaser, other than for purposes of resale, of a motor vehicle, a lessee of a motor vehicle, any person to whom the motor vehicle is transferred during the duration of an express warranty applicable to that motor vehicle, and any person entitled by the terms of the warranty to enforce the obligations of the warranty.

(b) "Manufacturer" means any person, firm, or corporation, whether resident or nonresident, that manufactures or assembles motor vehicles for sale or distribution in this state. In the case of motor vehicles not manufactured in the United States, the term "manufacturer" shall also include any person, firm, or corporation that is engaged in the business of importing motor vehicles.

(c) "Dealer" means any person, firm, or corporation selling or agreeing to sell in this state one or more new motor vehicles under a retail agreement with a manufacturer, manufacturer branch, distributor, distributor branch, or agent of any of them.

(d) "Adjustment program" means any program or policy that expands or extends the consumer's warranty beyond its stated limit or under which a manufacturer offers to pay for all or any part of the cost of repairing, or to reimburse consumers for all or any part of the cost of repairing, any condition that may substantially affect vehicle durability, reliability, or performance, other than service provided under a safety or emission-related recall campaign. "Adjustment program" does not include ad hoc adjustments made by a manufacturer on a case-by-case basis.

(e) "Motor vehicle" means a motor vehicle, excluding motorcycles, motor homes, and off-road vehicles, which is registered in this state.

(f) "Lessee" means any person who leases a motor vehicle pursuant to a written lease which provides that the lessee is responsible for repairs to the motor vehicle.

(g) "Service bulletin" means any notice issued by a manufacturer and filed with the National Highway Traffic Safety Administration relating to vehicle durability, reliability, or performance. *(Added by Stats.1993, c. 814 (S.B.486), § 1.)*

Research References

4 Witkin, California Summary 10th Sales § 64, (S 64) Adjustment Programs.

§ 1795.91. Dealers; duties

Dealers shall have the following duties:

(a) A dealer shall provide notice to prospective purchasers and lessees that provides information on how to get copies of service bulletins. Nothing in this notice shall be construed as an admission by the dealer or manufacturer of the existence or nonexistence of a vehicle defect.

The notice shall be deemed sufficient if posted in the showroom or other area conspicuous to motor vehicle purchasers and written in the following form:

FEDERAL LAW REQUIRES MANUFACTURERS TO FURNISH THE NATIONAL HIGHWAY TRAFFIC SAFETY ADMINISTRATION (N.H.T.S.A.) WITH BULLETINS DESCRIBING ANY DEFECTS IN THEIR VEHICLES.

YOU MAY OBTAIN COPIES OF THESE BULLETINS, FOR A FEE, FROM EITHER OF THE FOLLOWING:

THE MANUFACTURER (ASK YOUR DEALER FOR THE TOLL-FREE NUMBER)

N.H.T.S.A.—TECHNICAL REFERENCE DIVISION

      400 SEVENTH STREET, S.W.
      ROOM 5110
      WASHINGTON, D.C. 20590
      202-366-2768

IN ADDITION, CERTAIN CONSUMER PUBLICATIONS PUBLISH THESE BULLETINS AND SOME COMPANIES WILL SEND THEM TO YOU, FOR A FEE.

(b) A dealer shall disclose to a consumer seeking repairs for a particular condition at its repair shop, the principal terms and conditions of the manufacturer's adjustment program covering the condition if the dealer has received a service bulletin concerning the adjustment program. *(Added by Stats.1993, c. 814 (S.B.486), § 1.)*

Research References

4 Witkin, California Summary 10th Sales § 64, (S 64) Adjustment Programs.

§ 1795.92. Manufacturers; duties

Manufacturers shall have the following duties:

(a) A manufacturer shall, within 90 days of the adoption of an adjustment program, subject to priority for safety or emission-related recalls, notify by first-class mail all owners or lessees of motor vehicles eligible under the program of the condition giving rise to and the principal terms and conditions of the program.

(b) Copies of all notices mailed in accordance with subdivision (a) shall be sent to the New Motor Vehicle Board within the Department of Motor Vehicles and made available for public inquiries.

(c) A manufacturer shall, within 30 days of the adoption of any new adjustment program, notify its dealers, in writing, of all the terms and conditions thereof.

(d) A manufacturer who establishes an adjustment program shall implement procedures to assure reimbursement of each consumer eligible under an adjustment program who incurs expenses for repair of a condition subject to the program prior to acquiring knowledge of the program. The reimbursement shall be consistent with the terms and conditions of the particular program. The manufacturer shall notify the consumer within 21 business days of receiving a claim for reimbursement whether the claim will be allowed or denied. If the claim is denied, the specific reasons for the denial shall be stated in writing.

(e) Any consumer who, prior to acquiring knowledge of an adjustment program, incurs expenses for repair of a condition subject to the adjustment program may file a claim for reimbursement under subdivision (d). The claim shall be made in writing to the manufacturer within two years of the date of the consumer's payment for repair of the condition. *(Added by Stats.1993, c. 814 (S.B.486), § 1.)*

Research References

4 Witkin, California Summary 10th Sales § 64, (S 64) Adjustment Programs.

§ 1795.93. Consumer or lessee remedies; construction of chapter

Nothing in this chapter shall be construed to exclude, modify, or otherwise limit any other remedy provided by law to a consumer or lessee. *(Added by Stats.1993, c. 814 (S.B.486), § 1.)*

CHAPTER 2. STANDARDS FOR WARRANTY WORK

Section
1796.   Installation of consumer goods; duty owed to buyers.
1796.5.   Service or repair to consumer goods; duty owed to purchasers.

§ 1796. Installation of consumer goods; duty owed to buyers

Any individual, partnership, corporation, association, or other legal relationship which engages in the business of installing new or used consumer goods, has a duty to the buyer to install them in a good and workmanlike manner. *(Added by Stats.1978, c. 991, p. 3065, § 13.)*

Research References

Rutter, Cal. Practice Guide: Enforcing Judgments/Debts Ch. 3-A, A. Evaluating the Claim.
4 Witkin, California Summary 10th Sales § 16, Value.
4 Witkin, California Summary 10th Sales § 31, Applicability of Division 2 to Particular Transactions.
4 Witkin, California Summary 10th Sales § 127, Identification of Goods.
4 Witkin, California Summary 10th Sales § 229, General Principles.
4 Witkin, California Summary 10th Sales § 317, (S 317) Maintenance of Service and Repair Facilities.

§ 1796.5. Service or repair to consumer goods; duty owed to purchasers

Any individual, partnership, corporation, association, or other legal relationship which engages in the business of providing service or repair to new or used consumer goods has a duty to the purchaser to perform those services in a good and workmanlike manner. *(Added by Stats.1978, c. 991, p. 3065, § 13.)*

Research References

4 Witkin, California Summary 10th Sales § 317, (S 317) Maintenance of Service and Repair Facilities.

CHAPTER 3. MOBILEHOME WARRANTIES

Section
1797.   Necessity of warranty.
1797.1.   Definitions.
1797.2.   Application; warranty coverage; responsibility on sale to public agency.
1797.3.   Written warranty; contents.
1797.4.   Cumulative remedies; proscription against waiver.
1797.5.   Copy of warranty provisions; display; posting.
1797.6.   Records.
1797.7.   Warranty service to be completed within specified time.

§ 1797. Necessity of warranty

All new mobilehomes and manufactured homes sold to a buyer shall be covered by the warranty set forth in this chapter. *(Added by Stats.1971, c. 1492, p. 2944, § 1. Amended by Stats.1982, c. 730, p. 2904, § 1.)*

Research References

Rutter, Cal. Practice Guide: Enforcing Judgments/Debts Ch. 3-A, A. Evaluating the Claim.
Miller and Starr California Real Estate § 31:59, Recovery of Damages and Restitution.
12 Witkin, California Summary 10th Real Property § 761, (S 761) Governing Law.
4 Witkin, California Summary 10th Sales § 65, Mobilehome Warranties.
6 Witkin, California Summary 10th Torts § 1571, Recovery of Both Penalty and Punitive Damages.

§ 1797.1. Definitions

As used in this chapter:

(a) "Contractor" means any person who is a general building contractor within the meaning of Section 7057 of the Business and Professions Code.

(b) "Dealer" means any person who is a dealer within the meaning of Section 18002.6 of the Health and Safety Code.

(c) "Mobilehome" and "manufactured home" have the meanings, respectively, defined in Sections 18007 and 18008 of the Health and Safety Code.

(d) "Substantial defects in materials and workmanship" means defects objectively manifested by broken, ripped, cracked, stained, or missing parts or components, or workmanship resulting in improper function of materials, components, appliances, or systems as installed or manufactured by the contractor, dealer, or manufacturer. *(Added by Stats.1971, c. 1492, p. 2944, § 1. Amended by Stats.1982, c. 730, p. 2904, § 2; Stats.1985, c. 763, § 1; Stats.1988, c. 793, § 1; Stats.1993, c. 458 (A.B.247), § 1.)*

Research References

Miller and Starr California Real Estate § 31:53, License Requirements.
4 Witkin, California Summary 10th Sales § 65, Mobilehome Warranties.

§ 1797.2. Application; warranty coverage; responsibility on sale to public agency

(a) The warranty provided for in this chapter shall apply to the manufacturer of the mobilehome or the manufactured home as well as to the contractor or dealer who sells the mobilehome or the manufactured home to the buyer. The warranty shall cover the electrical, plumbing, heating, cooling, fire safety, and structural systems, and all appliances of the mobilehome or manufactured home as installed or manufactured by the contractor, dealer, or manufacturer.

(b) Where a manufacturer sells a mobilehome or manufactured home directly to a city, city and county, or other public agency pursuant to the exception established in Section 18015.7, the manufacturer shall be responsible for providing the warranty required by this chapter. *(Added by Stats.1971, c. 1492, p. 2944, § 1. Amended by Stats.1982, c. 730, p. 2904, § 3; Stats.1985, c. 763, § 2; Stats.1993, c. 458 (A.B.247), § 2; Stats.1995, c. 185 (A.B.431), § 1.)*

Research References

Miller and Starr California Real Estate § 31:61, Warranties.
4 Witkin, California Summary 10th Sales § 65, Mobilehome Warranties.

§ 1797.3. Written warranty; contents

The mobilehome/manufactured home warranty from the contractor, manufacturer, or dealer to the buyer shall be set forth in a separate written document that reprints all of the provisions of this chapter and shall be delivered to the buyer by the contractor or dealer at the time the contract of sale is signed, and shall contain, but is not limited to, the following terms:

(a) That the mobilehome or manufactured home is free from any substantial defects in materials or workmanship.

(b) That the contractor, manufacturer, or dealer or any or all of them shall take appropriate corrective action at the site of the mobilehome or manufactured home in instances of substantial defects in materials or workmanship which become evident within one year from the date of delivery of the mobilehome or manufactured home to the buyer, provided the buyer or his or her transferee gives written notice of those defects to the contractor, manufacturer, or dealer at their business address not later than one year and 10 days after date of delivery.

(c) That the manufacturer and the contractor or dealer shall be jointly and severally liable to the buyer for the fulfillment of the terms of warranty, and that the buyer may notify either one or both of the need for appropriate corrective action in instances of substantial defects in materials or workmanship.

(d) That the address and the phone number of where to mail or deliver written notices of defects shall be set forth in the document.

(e) That the one-year warranty period applies to the plumbing, heating, electrical, cooling, fire safety, and structural systems and all appliances of the mobilehome or manufactured home.

(f) That, while the manufacturers of any or all appliances may also issue their own warranties, the primary responsibility for appropriate corrective action under the warranty rests with the contractor or dealer and the manufacturer, and the buyer should report all complaints to the contractor or dealer and the manufacturer initially.

(g) That, if corrective action taken by the manufacturer or the contractor or dealer fails to eliminate a substantial defect, then the material, system, appliance, or component shall be replaced in kind. As used in this subdivision, "replaced in kind" means (1) replacement with the identical material, system, appliance, or component, and, if not available (2) replacement with a comparable or better material, system, appliance, or component. *(Added by Stats.1971, c. 1492, p. 2944, § 1. Amended by Stats.1973, c. 807, p. 1441, § 1; Stats.1982, c. 730, p. 2904, § 4; Stats.1985, c. 763, § 3; Stats.1990, c. 765 (A.B.4079), § 1; Stats.1993, c. 458 (A.B.247), § 3.)*

Research References

Miller and Starr California Real Estate § 31:56, Contract Requirements.
Miller and Starr California Real Estate § 31:61, Warranties.
4 Witkin, California Summary 10th Sales § 65, Mobilehome Warranties.

§ 1797.4. Cumulative remedies; proscription against waiver

The warranty under this chapter shall be in addition to, and not in derogation of, all other rights and privileges which the buyer may have under any other law or instrument. The contractor, manufacturer, or dealer shall not require the buyer to waive his or her rights under this chapter, and any waiver of these rights shall be deemed contrary to public policy and shall be unenforceable and void. *(Added by Stats.1971, c. 1492, p. 2945, § 1. Amended by Stats.1993, c. 458 (A.B.247), § 4.)*

Research References

4 Witkin, California Summary 10th Sales § 65, Mobilehome Warranties.

§ 1797.5. Copy of warranty provisions; display; posting

Every contractor or dealer shall display a copy of all of the warranty provisions required by this chapter. The copy of the warranty provisions required by this chapter shall be posted in each area where purchase orders and conditional sales contracts are written. *(Added by Stats.1974, c. 1286, p. 2792, § 1, operative July 1, 1975. Amended by Stats.1990, c. 765 (A.B.4079), § 2; Stats.1993, c. 458 (A.B.247), § 5.)*

Research References

4 Witkin, California Summary 10th Sales § 65, Mobilehome Warranties.

§ 1797.6. Records

Manufacturers, contractors, and dealers shall keep records of all actions taken pursuant to this chapter, including all correspondence to or from the buyer for a period of three years from the date of delivery. *(Added by Stats.1985, c. 763, § 4. Amended by Stats.1993, c. 458 (A.B.247), § 6.)*

Research References

Miller and Starr California Real Estate § 31:61, Warranties.
4 Witkin, California Summary 10th Sales § 65, Mobilehome Warranties.

§ 1797.7. Warranty service to be completed within specified time

The contractor, dealer, or manufacturer shall complete warranty service to correct all substantial defects within 90 days of receiving the buyer's written notice specified in subdivision (b) of Section 1797.3, unless there are circumstances which are beyond the control of the contractor, dealer, or manufacturer. *(Added by Stats.1988, c. 793, § 2. Amended by Stats.1993, c. 458 (A.B.247), § 7.)*

Research References

Miller and Starr California Real Estate § 31:53, License Requirements.
Miller and Starr California Real Estate § 31:61, Warranties.
4 Witkin, California Summary 10th Sales § 65, Mobilehome Warranties.

CHAPTER 4. GREY MARKET GOODS

§ 1797.8. Definitions

(a) As used in this chapter, the term "grey market goods" means consumer goods bearing a trademark and normally accompanied by an express written warranty valid in the United States of America which are imported into the United States through channels other than the manufacturer's authorized United States distributor and which are not accompanied by the manufacturer's express written warranty valid in the United States.

(b) As used in this chapter, the term "sale" includes a lease of more than four months. *(Added by Stats.1986, c. 1497, § 2.)*

Research References

Rutter, Cal. Practice Guide: Enforcing Judgments/Debts Ch. 3-A, A. Evaluating the Claim.

§ 1797.81. Retail sellers; disclosures; signs; tickets, labels or tags

(a) Every retail seller who offers grey market goods for sale shall post a conspicuous sign at the product's point of display and affix to the product or its package a conspicuous ticket, label, or tag disclosing any or all of the following, whichever is applicable:

(1) The item is not covered by a manufacturer's express written warranty valid in the United States (however, any implied warranty provided by law still exists).

(2) The item is not compatible with United States electrical currents.

(3) The item is not compatible with United States broadcast frequencies.

(4) Replacement parts are not available through the manufacturer's United States distributors.

(5) Compatible accessories are not available through the manufacturer's United States distributors.

(6) The item is not accompanied by instructions in English.

(7) The item is not eligible for a manufacturer's rebate.

(8) Any other incompatibility or nonconformity with relevant domestic standards known to the seller.

(b) The disclosure described in paragraph (1) of subdivision (a) shall not be required to be made by a retail seller with respect to grey market goods that are accompanied by an express written warranty provided by the retail seller, provided that each of the following conditions is satisfied:

(1) The protections and other benefits that are provided to the buyer by the express written warranty provided by the retail seller are equal to or better than the protections and other benefits that are provided to buyers in the United States of America by the manufacturer's express written warranty that normally accompanies the goods.

(2) The express written warranty conforms to the requirements of the Song-Beverly Consumer Warranty Act, (Chapter 1 (commencing with Section 1790)), including, but not limited to, the warranty disclosure standards specified in Section 1793.1, and the standards applicable to service and repair facilities specified in Section 1793.2.

(3) The retail seller has posted a conspicuous sign at the product's point of sale or display, or has affixed to the product or its package a conspicuous ticket, label, or tag that informs prospective buyers that copies of all of the warranties applicable to the products offered for sale by the retail seller are available to prospective buyers for inspection upon request.

(4) The retail seller has complied with the provisions on presale availability of written warranties set forth in the regulations of the Federal Trade Commission adopted pursuant to the federal Magnuson-Moss Warranty-Federal Trade Commission Improvement Act (see 15 U.S.C.A. Sec. 2302(b)(1)(A) and 16 C.F.R. 702.1 et seq.).

(c) Nothing in subdivision (b) shall affect the obligations of a retail seller to make the disclosures, if any, required by any other paragraph of subdivision (a). *(Added by Stats.1986, c. 1497, § 2.)*

§ 1797.82. Retail dealers; disclosures in advertisements

Every retail dealer who offers for sale grey market goods shall be required to disclose in any advertisement of those goods the disclosures required by Section 1797.81. The disclosure shall be made in a type of conspicuous size. *(Added by Stats.1986, c. 1497, § 2.)*

§ 1797.83. Equivalent language

In making the disclosures prescribed by this chapter, the retail seller may use reasonably equivalent language if necessary or appropriate to achieve a clearer, or more accurate, disclosure. *(Added by Stats.1986, c. 1497, § 2.)*

§ 1797.84. Construction with other laws

Nothing in this chapter shall be construed to authorize any sale of goods which is specifically prohibited by a federal or state statute or regulation or a local ordinance or regulation, or to relieve the seller of any responsibility for bringing the goods into compliance with any applicable federal or state statute or regulation or local ordinance or regulation. *(Added by Stats. 1986, c. 1497, § 2.)*

§ 1797.85. Retail sellers; violations; liability to buyer

Any retail seller who violates this chapter shall be liable to the buyer who returns the product for a refund, or credit on credit purchases, if the product purchased has not been used in a manner inconsistent with any printed instructions provided by the seller. *(Added by Stats.1986, c. 1497, § 2.)*

§ 1797.86. Violations; unfair competition; grounds for rescission

Any violation of this chapter constitutes unfair competition under Section 17200 of the Business and Professions Code, grounds for rescission under Section 1689 of this code, and an unfair method of competition or deceptive practice under Section 1770 of this code. *(Added by Stats.1986, c. 1497, § 2.)*

Research References

Rutter, Cal. Practice Guide: Enforcing Judgments/Debts Ch. 3-A, A. Evaluating the Claim.

CHAPTER 5. HOME ROOF WARRANTIES

Section

§ 1797.90. Application of chapter

This chapter shall apply to all contracts and warranties for roofing materials used on a residential structure, including, but not limited to, a manufactured home or mobilehome, and to all contracts and warranties for the installation, repair, or replacement of all or any portion of the roof of a residential structure, including, but not limited to, a manufactured home or mobilehome. *(Added by Stats.1993, c. 835 (S.B.409), § 1.)*

Research References

Rutter, Cal. Practice Guide: Enforcing Judgments/Debts Ch. 3-A, A. Evaluating the Claim.
Rutter, Cal. Practice Guide: Real Prop. Transactions Ch. 4-E, E. Drafting the Purchase and Sale Agreement-Terms and Conditions.
4 Witkin, California Summary 10th Sales § 66, Home Roof Warranties.

§ 1797.91. Contract for roofing materials or roof; warranty; writing requirement

Any contract for roofing materials, or for the installation, repair, or replacement of all or any portion of the roof of a residential structure, including, but not limited to, a manufactured home or mobilehome, shall be in writing if the contract includes any warranty of the materials or workmanship that extends for any period of time beyond completion of the work. *(Added by Stats.1993, c. 835 (S.B.409), § 1.)*

Research References

Miller and Starr California Real Estate § 29:5, Contractor's Liability Based on Implied Warranty.
Miller and Starr California Real Estate § 27:42, Contract Terms--General Requirements.
4 Witkin, California Summary 10th Sales § 66, Home Roof Warranties.

§ 1797.92. Contracts on or after January 1, 1994; transferability of warranty

For any contract subject to this chapter that is entered into on or after January 1, 1994, the warranty obligations shall inure to the benefit of, and shall be directly enforceable by, all subsequent purchasers and transferees of the residential structure, without limitation, unless the contract contains a clear and conspicuous provision limiting transferability of the warranty. *(Added by Stats.1993, c. 835 (S.B.409), § 1.)*

Research References

Miller and Starr California Real Estate § 29:5, Contractor's Liability Based on Implied Warranty.
Miller and Starr California Real Estate § 27:42, Contract Terms--General Requirements.
4 Witkin, California Summary 10th Sales § 66, Home Roof Warranties.

§ 1797.93. Lifetime warranty; disclosure of life to which it refers

If any warranty subject to this chapter, uses the term "lifetime," "life," or a similar representation to describe the duration of the warranty, then the warranty shall disclose with such clarity and prominence as will be noticed and understood by prospective purchasers, the life to which the representation refers. *(Added by Stats.1993, c. 835 (S.B.409), § 1.)*

Research References

Miller and Starr California Real Estate § 27:42, Contract Terms--General Requirements.
4 Witkin, California Summary 10th Sales § 66, Home Roof Warranties.

§ 1797.94. Limit on transferability; form of provision

Any warranty subject to this chapter, shall inure to the benefit of, and shall be directly enforceable by, all subsequent purchasers and transferees of the residential structure, without limitation, unless the warranty contains a provision limiting transferability of the warranty. A provision limiting transferability shall be set forth at the top of the first page of the warranty in 14-point boldface type, and shall be enclosed in a rectangular box in at least 4-point type.

(b)[1] Any disclosure required by Section 1797.93 shall also be set forth at the top of the first page of the warranty in 14-point boldface type, and shall be enclosed in a rectangular box in at least 4-point type. This disclosure may be included in a disclosure required under subdivision (a). *(Added by Stats.1993, c. 835 (S.B.409), § 1.)*

[1] Chaptered law did not contain a subdivision (a) designation.

Research References

Miller and Starr California Real Estate § 29:5, Contractor's Liability Based on Implied Warranty.
Miller and Starr California Real Estate § 27:42, Contract Terms--General Requirements.
4 Witkin, California Summary 10th Sales § 66, Home Roof Warranties.

§ 1797.95. Roof warranties; standardization to meet requirements in other states

A warrantor who provides roof warranties in multiple states may standardize the warranty to meet warranty requirements of other states. However, those standardized warranties shall meet requirements which are no less than those imposed by this chapter. *(Added by Stats.1993, c. 835 (S.B.409), § 1.)*

§ 1797.96. Newly constructed residential structure; provision of warranty disclosures prior to close of escrow

Where a warranty subject to this chapter is provided for the benefit of the purchaser of a newly constructed residential structure, the seller shall provide the warranty disclosures required by this chapter to the purchaser prior to the close of escrow. No transfer shall be invalidated for failure to comply with this section. *(Added by Stats.1993, c. 835 (S.B.409), § 1.)*

Research References

Rutter, Cal. Practice Guide: Real Prop. Transactions Ch. 4-E, E. Drafting the Purchase and Sale Agreement-Terms and Conditions.
Miller and Starr California Real Estate § 29:5, Contractor's Liability Based on Implied Warranty.
Miller and Starr California Real Estate § 27:42, Contract Terms--General Requirements.

Title 1.8

PERSONAL DATA

CHAPTER 1. INFORMATION PRACTICES ACT OF 1977

ARTICLE 1. GENERAL PROVISIONS AND LEGISLATIVE FINDINGS

§ 1798. Citation of chapter

This chapter shall be known and may be cited as the Information Practices Act of 1977. *(Added by Stats.1977, c. 709, p. 2269, § 1, operative July 1, 1978.)*

Research References

Rutter, Cal. Practice Guide: Civil Trials & Evidence Ch. 8E-A, A. Privileges.
California Practice Guide: Employment Litigation Ch. 19-F, F. Discovery.
Miller and Starr California Real Estate § 4:43, Disciplinary Process--Penalties and Other Remedies.
Miller and Starr California Real Estate § 4:96, State Regulation of Appraisers--Disciplinary Procedures and Penalties.
Miller and Starr California Real Estate § 19:100, Administration; Authority and Duty of the Rent Board.
7 Witkin Cal. Proc. 5th Judgment § 312, Use of Lodestar Approach.

10 Witkin, California Summary 10th Parent and Child § 150, Confidentiality of Information.
5 Witkin, California Summary 10th Torts § 289, (S 289) Tax Collection or Administration.
5 Witkin, California Summary 10th Torts § 666, (S 666) in General.
5 Witkin, California Summary 10th Torts § 667, (S 667) Information Practices Act.
3 Witkin, California Summary 10th Agency and Employment § 357, (S 357) Inspection of Personnel Files.
3 Witkin, California Summary 10th Agency and Employment § 675, (S 675) Actions Between Employers and Unions.
7 Witkin, California Summary 10th Constitutional Law § 604, (S 604) Information Practices Act.

§ 1798.1. Legislative declaration and findings

The Legislature declares that the right to privacy is a personal and fundamental right protected by Section 1 of Article I of the Constitution of California and by the United States Constitution and that all individuals have a right of privacy in information pertaining to them. The Legislature further makes the following findings:

(a) The right to privacy is being threatened by the indiscriminate collection, maintenance, and dissemination of personal information and the lack of effective laws and legal remedies.

(b) The increasing use of computers and other sophisticated information technology has greatly magnified the potential risk to individual privacy that can occur from the maintenance of personal information.

(c) In order to protect the privacy of individuals, it is necessary that the maintenance and dissemination of personal information be subject to strict limits. *(Added by Stats.1977, c. 709, p. 2269, § 1, operative July 1, 1978.)*

Research References

7 Witkin, California Summary 10th Constitutional Law § 604, (S 604) Information Practices Act.

ARTICLE 2. DEFINITIONS

§ 1798.3. Definitions

As used in this chapter:

(a) The term "personal information" means any information that is maintained by an agency that identifies or describes an individual, including, but not limited to, his or her name, social security number, physical description, home address, home telephone number, education, financial matters, and medical or employment history. It includes statements made by, or attributed to, the individual.

(b) The term "agency" means every state office, officer, department, division, bureau, board, commission, or other state agency, except that the term agency shall not include:

(1) The California Legislature.

(2) Any agency established under Article VI of the California Constitution.

(3) The State Compensation Insurance Fund, except as to any records which contain personal information about the employees of the State Compensation Insurance Fund.

(4) A local agency, as defined in subdivision (a) of Section 6252 of the Government Code.

(c) The term "disclose" means to disclose, release, transfer, disseminate, or otherwise communicate all or any part of any record orally, in writing, or by electronic or any other means to any person or entity.

(d) The term "individual" means a natural person.

(e) The term "maintain" includes maintain, acquire, use, or disclose.

(f) The term "person" means any natural person, corporation, partnership, limited liability company, firm, or association.

(g) The term "record" means any file or grouping of information about an individual that is maintained by an agency by reference to an identifying particular such as the individual's name, photograph, finger or voice print, or a number or symbol assigned to the individual.

(h) The term "system of records" means one or more records, which pertain to one or more individuals, which is maintained by any agency, from which information is retrieved by the name of an individual or by some identifying number, symbol or other identifying particular assigned to the individual.

(i) The term "governmental entity," except as used in Section 1798.26, means any branch of the federal government or of the local government.

(j) The term "commercial purpose" means any purpose which has financial gain as a major objective. It does not include the gathering or dissemination of newsworthy facts by a publisher or broadcaster.

(k) The term "regulatory agency" means the Department of * * * Business Oversight, the Department of Insurance, the Bureau of Real Estate, and agencies of the United States or of any other state responsible for regulating financial institutions. *(Added by Stats.1977, c. 709, p. 2269, § 1, operative July 1, 1978. Amended by Stats.1978, c. 874, p. 2741, § 1, eff. Sept. 19, 1978; Stats.1979, c. 143, p. 330, § 1, eff. June 22, 1979; Stats.1980, c. 174, p. 391, § 1; Stats.1982, c. 604, p. 2579, § 1; Stats.1985, c. 595, § 2; Stats.1987, c. 1453, § 1; Stats.1994, c. 1010 (S.B.2053), § 40; Stats.1996, c. 1064 (A.B.3351), § 4, operative July 1, 1997; Stats.2005, c. 677 (S.B.512), § 1, eff. Oct. 7, 2005; Stats.2013, c. 352 (A.B.1317), § 52, eff. Sept. 26, 2013, operative July 1, 2013.)*

Research References

Rutter, Cal. Practice Guide: Civ. Pro. Before Trial Ch. 8E-6, Subpoena to Nonparty Deponent or Business Records Custodian.
Rutter, Cal. Practice Guide: Civil Trials & Evidence Ch. 1-C, C. Marshalling the Evidence.
7 Witkin, California Summary 10th Constitutional Law § 604, (S 604) Information Practices Act.

ARTICLE 5. AGENCY REQUIREMENTS

§ 1798.14. Contents of records

Each agency shall maintain in its records only personal information which is relevant and necessary to accomplish a purpose of the agency required or authorized by the California Constitution or statute or mandated by the federal government. *(Added by Stats.1977, c. 709, p. 2269, § 1, operative July 1, 1978. Amended by Stats.1985, c. 595, § 5.)*

Research References

7 Witkin, California Summary 10th Constitutional Law § 604, (S 604) Information Practices Act.

§ 1798.15. Sources of information

Each agency shall collect personal information to the greatest extent practicable directly from the individual who is the subject of the information rather than from another source. *(Added by Stats.1977, c. 709, p. 2269, § 1, operative July 1, 1978. Amended by Stats.1985, c. 595, § 6.)*

Research References

7 Witkin, California Summary 10th Constitutional Law § 604, (S 604) Information Practices Act.

§ 1798.16. Personal information; maintaining sources of information

(a) Whenever an agency collects personal information, the agency shall maintain the source or sources of the information, unless the source is the data subject or he or she has received a copy of the source document, including, but not limited to, the name of any source who is an individual acting in his or her own private or individual capacity. If the source is an agency, governmental entity or other organization, such as a corporation or association, this requirement can be met by maintaining the name of the agency, governmental entity, or organization, as long as the smallest reasonably identifiable unit of that agency, governmental entity, or organization is named.

(b) On or after July 1, 2001, unless otherwise authorized by the Department of Information Technology pursuant to Executive Order D–3–99, whenever an agency electronically collects personal information, as defined by Section 11015.5 of the Government Code, the agency shall retain the source or sources or any intermediate form of the information, if either are created or possessed by the agency, unless the source is the data subject that has requested that the information be discarded or the data subject has received a copy of the source document.

(c) The agency shall maintain the source or sources of the information in a readily accessible form so as to be able to provide it to the data subject when they inspect any record pursuant to Section 1798.34. This section shall not apply if the source or sources are exempt from disclosure under the provisions of this chapter. *(Added by Stats.1977, c. 709, p. 2269, § 1, operative July 1, 1978. Amended by Stats.1998, c. 429 (S.B.1386), § 1; Stats.1999, c. 784 (A.B.724), § 7, eff. Oct. 10, 1999.)*

Research References

7 Witkin, California Summary 10th Constitutional Law § 604, (S 604) Information Practices Act.

§ 1798.17. Notice; periodic provision; contents

Each agency shall provide on or with any form used to collect personal information from individuals the notice specified in this section. When contact with the individual is of a regularly recurring nature, an initial notice followed by a periodic notice of not more than one-year intervals shall satisfy this requirement. This requirement is also satisfied by notification to individuals of the availability of the notice in annual tax-related pamphlets or booklets provided for them. The notice shall include all of the following:

(a) The name of the agency and the division within the agency that is requesting the information.

(b) The title, business address, and telephone number of the agency official who is responsible for the system of records and who shall, upon request, inform an individual regarding the location of his or her records and the categories of any persons who use the information in those records.

(c) The authority, whether granted by statute, regulation, or executive order which authorizes the maintenance of the information.

(d) With respect to each item of information, whether submission of such information is mandatory or voluntary.

(e) The consequences, if any, of not providing all or any part of the requested information.

(f) The principal purpose or purposes within the agency for which the information is to be used.

(g) Any known or foreseeable disclosures which may be made of the information pursuant to subdivision (e) or (f) of Section 1798.24.

(h) The individual's right of access to records containing personal information which are maintained by the agency.

This section does not apply to any enforcement document issued by an employee of a law enforcement agency in the performance of his or her duties wherein the violator is provided an exact copy of the document, or to accident reports whereby the parties of interest may obtain a copy of the report pursuant to Section 20012 of the Vehicle Code.

The notice required by this section does not apply to agency requirements for an individual to provide his or her name, identifying number, photograph, address, or similar identifying information, if this information is used only for the purpose of identification and communication with the individual by the agency, except that requirements for an individual's social security number shall conform with the provisions of the Federal Privacy Act of 1974 (Public Law 93–579). *(Added by Stats.1977, c. 709, p. 2269, § 1, operative July 1, 1978. Amended by Stats.1978, c. 874, p. 2744, § 3.5, eff. Sept. 19, 1978; Stats.1982, c. 604, p. 2582, § 2.5; Stats.1985, c. 595, § 7.)*

Research References

7 Witkin, California Summary 10th Constitutional Law § 604, (S 604) Information Practices Act.

§ 1798.18. Maintenance of records; standards; transfers of records outside state government

Each agency shall maintain all records, to the maximum extent possible, with accuracy, relevance, timeliness, and completeness.

Such standard need not be met except when such records are used to make any determination about the individual. When an agency transfers a record outside of state government, it shall correct, update, withhold, or delete any portion of the record that it knows or has reason to believe is inaccurate or untimely. *(Added by Stats.1977, c. 709, p. 2269, § 1, operative July 1, 1978.)*

Research References

7 Witkin, California Summary 10th Constitutional Law § 604, (S 604) Information Practices Act.

§ 1798.19. Contracts for the operation or maintenance of records; requirements of chapter; employees of agency

Each agency when it provides by contract for the operation or maintenance of records containing personal information to accomplish an agency function, shall cause, consistent with its authority, the requirements of this chapter to be applied to those records. For purposes of Article 10 (commencing with Section 1798.55), any contractor and any employee of the contractor, if the contract is agreed to on or after July 1, 1978, shall be considered to be an employee of an agency. Local government

functions mandated by the state are not deemed agency functions within the meaning of this section. *(Added by Stats.1977, c. 709, p. 2269, § 1, operative July 1, 1978. Amended by Stats.1978, c. 874, p. 2744, § 4, eff. Sept. 19, 1978; Stats.1985, c. 595, § 8.)*

§ 1798.20. Rules of conduct; instruction

Each agency shall establish rules of conduct for persons involved in the design, development, operation, disclosure, or maintenance of records containing personal information and instruct each such person with respect to such rules and the requirements of this chapter, including any other rules and procedures adopted pursuant to this chapter and the remedies and penalties for noncompliance. *(Added by Stats.1977, c. 709, p. 2269, § 1, operative July 1, 1978. Amended by Stats.1985, c. 595, § 9.)*

§ 1798.21. Safeguards; administrative, technical and physical

Each agency shall establish appropriate and reasonable administrative, technical, and physical safeguards to ensure compliance with the provisions of this chapter, to ensure the security and confidentiality of records, and to protect against anticipated threats or hazards to their security or integrity which could result in any injury. *(Added by Stats.1977, c. 709, p. 2269, § 1, operative July 1, 1978.)*

§ 1798.22. Designation of employee responsible for agency compliance

Each agency shall designate an agency employee to be responsible for ensuring that the agency complies with all of the provisions of this chapter. *(Added by Stats.1977, c. 709, p. 2269, § 1, operative July 1, 1978.)*

§ 1798.23. Department of Justice; periodic review of personal information; exemption from access

The Department of Justice shall review all personal information in its possession every five years commencing July 1, 1978, to determine whether it should continue to be exempt from access pursuant to Section 1798.40. *(Added by Stats.1977, c. 709, p. 2269, § 1, operative July 1, 1978. Amended by Stats.1985, c. 595, § 10.)*

ARTICLE 6. CONDITIONS OF DISCLOSURE

§ 1798.24. Personal information

No agency may disclose any personal information in a manner that would link the information disclosed to the individual to whom it pertains unless the information is disclosed, as follows:

(a) To the individual to whom the information pertains.

(b) With the prior written voluntary consent of the individual to whom the record pertains, but only if that consent has been obtained not more than 30 days before the disclosure, or in the time limit agreed to by the individual in the written consent.

(c) To the duly appointed guardian or conservator of the individual or a person representing the individual if it can be proven with reasonable certainty through the possession of agency forms, documents or correspondence that this person is the authorized representative of the individual to whom the information pertains.

(d) To those officers, employees, attorneys, agents, or volunteers of the agency that has custody of the information if the disclosure is relevant and necessary in the ordinary course of the performance of their official duties and is related to the purpose for which the information was acquired.

(e) To a person, or to another agency where the transfer is necessary for the transferee agency to perform its constitutional or statutory duties, and the use is compatible with a purpose for which the information was collected and the use or transfer is accounted for in accordance with Section 1798.25. With respect to information transferred from a law enforcement or regulatory agency, or information transferred to another law enforcement or regulatory agency, a use is compatible if the use of the information requested is needed in an investigation of unlawful activity under the jurisdiction of the requesting agency or for licensing, certification, or regulatory purposes by that agency.

(f) To a governmental entity when required by state or federal law.

(g) Pursuant to the California Public Records Act (Chapter 3.5 (commencing with Section 6250) of Division 7 of Title 1 of the Government Code).

(h) To a person who has provided the agency with advance, adequate written assurance that the information will be used solely for statistical research or reporting purposes, but only if the information to be disclosed is in a form that will not identify any individual.

(i) Pursuant to a determination by the agency that maintains information that compelling circumstances exist that affect the health or safety of an individual, if upon the disclosure notification is transmitted to the individual to whom the information pertains at his or her last known address. Disclosure shall not be made if it is in conflict with other state or federal laws.

(j) To the State Archives as a record that has sufficient historical or other value to warrant its continued preservation by the California state government, or for evaluation by the Director of General Services or his or her designee to determine whether the record has further administrative, legal, or fiscal value.

(k) To any person pursuant to a subpoena, court order, or other compulsory legal process if, before the disclosure, the agency reasonably attempts to notify the individual to whom the record pertains, and if the notification is not prohibited by law.

(*l*) To any person pursuant to a search warrant.

(m) Pursuant to Article 3 (commencing with Section 1800) of Chapter 1 of Division 2 of the Vehicle Code.

(n) For the sole purpose of verifying and paying government health care service claims made pursuant to Division 9 (commencing with Section 10000) of the Welfare and Institutions Code.

(*o*) To a law enforcement or regulatory agency when required for an investigation of unlawful activity or for licensing, certification, or regulatory purposes, unless the disclosure is otherwise prohibited by law.

(p) To another person or governmental organization to the extent necessary to obtain information from the person or governmental organization as necessary for an investigation by the agency of a failure to comply with a specific state law that the agency is responsible for enforcing.

(q) To an adopted person and is limited to general background information pertaining to the adopted person's natural parents, provided that the information does not include or reveal the identity of the natural parents.

(r) To a child or a grandchild of an adopted person and disclosure is limited to medically necessary information pertaining to the adopted person's natural parents. However, the information, or the process for obtaining the information, shall not include or reveal the identity of the natural parents. The State Department of Social Services shall adopt regulations governing the release of information pursuant to this subdivision by July 1, 1985. The regulations shall require licensed adoption agencies to provide the same services provided by the department as established by this subdivision.

(s) To a committee of the Legislature or to a Member of the Legislature, or his or her staff when authorized in writing by the member, where the member has permission to obtain the information from the individual to whom it pertains or where the member provides reasonable assurance that he or she is acting on behalf of the individual.

(t)(1) To the University of California, a nonprofit educational institution, or, in the case of education-related data, another nonprofit entity, conducting scientific research, provided the request for information is approved by the Committee for the Protection of Human Subjects (CPHS) for the California Health and Human Services Agency (CHHSA) or an institutional review board, as authorized in paragraphs (4) and (5). The approval required under this subdivision shall include a review and determination that all the following criteria have been satisfied:

(A) The researcher has provided a plan sufficient to protect personal information from improper use and disclosures, including sufficient administrative, physical, and technical safeguards to protect personal information from reasonable anticipated threats to the security or confidentiality of the information.

(B) The researcher has provided a sufficient plan to destroy or return all personal information as soon as it is no longer needed for the research project, unless the researcher has demonstrated an ongoing need for the personal information for the research project and has provided a long-term plan sufficient to protect the confidentiality of that information.

(C) The researcher has provided sufficient written assurances that the personal information will not be reused or disclosed to any other person or entity, or used in any manner, not approved in the research protocol, except as required by law or for authorized oversight of the research project.

(2) The CPHS or institutional review board shall, at a minimum, accomplish all of the following as part of its review and approval of the research project for the purpose of protecting personal information held in agency databases:

(A) Determine whether the requested personal information is needed to conduct the research.

(B) Permit access to personal information only if it is needed for the research project.

(C) Permit access only to the minimum necessary personal information needed for the research project.

(D) Require the assignment of unique subject codes that are not derived from personal information in lieu of social security numbers if the research can still be conducted without social security numbers.

(E) If feasible, and if cost, time, and technical expertise permit, require the agency to conduct a portion of the data processing for the researcher to minimize the release of personal information.

(3) Reasonable costs to the agency associated with the agency's process of protecting personal information under the conditions of CPHS approval may be billed to the researcher, including, but not limited to, the agency's costs for conducting a portion of the data processing for the researcher, removing personal information, encrypting or otherwise securing personal information, or assigning subject codes.

(4) The CPHS may enter into written agreements to enable other institutional review boards to provide the data security approvals required by this subdivision, provided the data security requirements set forth in this subdivision are satisfied.

(5) Pursuant to paragraph (4), the CPHS shall enter into a written agreement with the institutional review board established pursuant to Section 49079.5 of the Education Code. The agreement shall authorize, commencing July 1, 2010, or the date upon which the written agreement is executed, whichever is later, that board to provide the data security approvals required by this subdivision, provided the data security requirements set forth in this subdivision and the act specified in paragraph (1) of subdivision (a) of Section 49079.5 are satisfied.

(u) To an insurer if authorized by Chapter 5 (commencing with Section 10900) of Division 4 of the Vehicle Code.

(v) Pursuant to Section 280, 282, 8009, or 18396 of the Financial Code.

This article shall not be construed to require the disclosure of personal information to the individual to whom the information pertains when that information may otherwise be withheld as set forth in Section 1798.40. *(Added by Stats.1977, c. 709, p. 2269, § 1, operative July 1, 1978. Amended by Stats.1978, c. 874, p. 2745, § 5, eff. Sept. 19, 1978; Stats.1979, c. 143, p. 332, § 2, eff. June 22, 1979; Stats.1982, c. 604, p. 2583, § 3; Stats.1982, c. 957, p. 3454, § 1; Stats.1984, c. 2, § 1; Stats.1984, c. 724, § 1; Stats.1985, c. 595, § 11; Stats.1987, c. 1453, § 2; Stats.1991–1992, 1st Ex.Sess., c. 21 (A.B.66), § 33.5; Stats.1995, c. 480 (A.B.1482), § 1.1, eff. Oct. 2, 1995, operative Oct. 2, 1995; Stats.2005, c. 241 (S.B.13), § 2; Stats.2006, c. 567 (A.B.2303), § 2.5; Stats.2008, c. 501 (A.B.2749), § 1; Stats.2009–2010, 5th Ex.Sess., c. 1 (S.B.2), § 1, eff. April 12, 2010; Stats.2010, c. 725 (A.B.1612), § 1, eff. Oct. 19, 2010.)*

Research References

10 Witkin, California Summary 10th Parent and Child § 150, Confidentiality of Information.

5 Witkin, California Summary 10th Torts § 667, (S 667) Information Practices Act.

7 Witkin, California Summary 10th Constitutional Law § 604, (S 604) Information Practices Act.

§ 1798.24a. Exception; screening of prospective concessionaires

Notwithstanding Section 1798.24, information may be disclosed to any city, county, city and county, or district, or any officer or official thereof, if a written request is made to a local law enforcement agency and the information is needed to assist in the screening of a prospective concessionaire, and any affiliate or associate thereof, as these terms are defined in subdivision (k) of Section 432.7 of the Labor Code for purposes of consenting to, or approving of, the prospective concessionaire's application for, or acquisition of, any beneficial interest in a concession, lease, or other property interest. However, any summary criminal history information that may be disclosed pursuant to this section shall be limited to information pertaining to criminal convictions. *(Added by Stats.1992, c. 1026 (S.B.1769), § 2.)*

§ 1798.24b. Disclosure of information to protection and advocacy agency for rights of persons with disabilities

(a) Notwithstanding Section 1798.24, except subdivision (v) thereof, information shall be disclosed to the protection and advocacy agency designated by the Governor in this state pursuant to federal law to protect and advocate for the rights of people with disabilities, as described in Division 4.7 (commencing with Section 4900) of the Welfare and Institutions Code.

(b) Information that shall be disclosed pursuant to this section includes all of the following information:

(1) Name.

(2) Address.

(3) Telephone number.

(4) Any other information necessary to identify that person whose consent is necessary for either of the following purposes:

(A) To enable the protection and advocacy agency to exercise its authority and investigate incidents of abuse or neglect of people with disabilities.

(B) To obtain access to records pursuant to Section 4903 of the Welfare and Institutions Code. *(Added by Stats.1991, c. 534 (S.B.1088), § 2. Amended by Stats.2003, c. 878 (S.B.577), § 2.)*

ARTICLE 7. ACCOUNTING OF DISCLOSURES

§ 1798.25. Accounting for disclosure to law enforcement or regulatory agency; contents; routine disclosures

Each agency shall keep an accurate accounting of the date, nature, and purpose of each disclosure of a record made pursuant to subdivision (i), (k), (*l*), (*o*), or (p) of Section 1798.24. This accounting shall also be required for disclosures made pursuant to subdivision (e) or (f) of Section 1798.24 unless notice of the type of disclosure has been provided pursuant to Sections 1798.9 and 1798.10. The accounting shall also include the name, title, and business address of the person or agency to whom the disclosure was made. For the purpose of an accounting of a disclosure made under subdivision (*o*) of Section 1798.24, it shall be sufficient for a law enforcement or regulatory agency to record the date of disclosure, the law enforcement or regulatory agency requesting the disclosure, and whether the purpose of the disclosure is for an investigation of unlawful activity under the jurisdiction of the requesting agency, or for licensing, certification, or regulatory purposes by that agency.

Routine disclosures of information pertaining to crimes, offenders, and suspected offenders to law enforcement or regulatory agencies of federal, state, and local government shall be deemed to be disclosures pursuant to subdivision (e) of Section 1798.24 for the purpose of meeting this requirement. *(Added by Stats.1977, c. 709, p. 2269, § 1, operative July 1, 1978. Amended by Stats.1978, c. 874, p. 2747, § 6, eff. Sept. 19, 1978; Stats.1985, c. 595, § 12; Stats.1987, c. 1453, § 3.)*

Research References

7 Witkin, California Summary 10th Constitutional Law § 604, (S 604) Information Practices Act.

§ 1798.26. Motor vehicles; sale of registration information or information from drivers' licenses files; administrative procedures

With respect to the sale of information concerning the registration of any vehicle or the sale of information from the files of drivers' licenses, the Department of Motor Vehicles shall, by regulation, establish administrative procedures under which any person making a request for information shall be required to identify himself or herself and state the reason for making the request. These procedures shall provide for the verification of the name and address of the person making a request for the information and the department may require the person to produce the information as it determines is necessary in order to ensure that the name and address of the person are his or her true name and address. These procedures may provide for a 10-day delay in the release of the requested information. These procedures shall also provide for notification to the person to whom the information primarily relates, as to what information was provided and to whom it was provided. The department shall, by regulation, establish a reasonable period of time for which a record of all the foregoing shall be maintained.

The procedures required by this subdivision do not apply to any governmental entity, any person who has applied for and has been issued a requester code by the department, or any court of competent jurisdiction. *(Added by Stats.1977, c. 709, p. 2269, § 1, operative July 1, 1978. Amended by Stats.1987, c. 961, § 1; Stats.1989, c. 1213, § 2.)*

§ 1798.27. Retention of accounting and original documents

Each agency shall retain the accounting made pursuant to Section 1798.25 for at least three years after the disclosure for which the accounting is made, or until the record is destroyed, whichever is shorter.

Nothing in this section shall be construed to require retention of the original documents for a three-year period, providing that the agency can otherwise comply with the requirements of this section. *(Added by Stats.1977, c. 709, p. 2269, § 1, operative July 1, 1978.)*

§ 1798.28. Correction of errors; notation of disputes; notice

Each agency, after July 1, 1978, shall inform any person or agency to whom a record containing personal information has been disclosed during the preceding three years of any correction of an error or notation of dispute made pursuant to Sections 1798.35 and 1798.36 if (1) an accounting of the disclosure is required by Section 1798.25 or 1798.26, and the accounting has not been destroyed pursuant to Section 1798.27, or (2) the information provides the name of the person or agency to whom the disclosure was made, or (3) the person who is the subject of the disclosed record provides the name of the person or agency to whom the information was disclosed. *(Added by Stats.1977, c. 709, p. 2269, § 1, operative July 1, 1978. Amended by Stats.1985, c. 595, § 13.)*

§ 1798.29. Agencies owning, licensing, or maintaining computerized data including personal information; disclosure of security breach; notice requirements

(a) Any agency that owns or licenses computerized data that includes personal information shall disclose any breach of the security of the system following discovery or notification of the breach in the security of the data to any resident of California whose unencrypted personal information was, or is reasonably believed to have been, acquired by an unauthorized person. The disclosure shall be made in the most expedient time possible and without unreasonable delay, consistent with the legitimate needs of law enforcement, as provided in subdivision (c), or any measures necessary to determine the scope of the breach and restore the reasonable integrity of the data system.

(b) Any agency that maintains computerized data that includes personal information that the agency does not own shall notify the owner or licensee of the information of any breach of the security of the data immediately following discovery, if the personal information was, or is reasonably believed to have been, acquired by an unauthorized person.

(c) The notification required by this section may be delayed if a law enforcement agency determines that the notification will impede a criminal investigation. The notification required by this section shall be made after the law enforcement agency determines that it will not compromise the investigation.

(d) Any agency that is required to issue a security breach notification pursuant to this section shall meet all of the following requirements:

(1) The security breach notification shall be written in plain language.

(2) The security breach notification shall include, at a minimum, the following information:

(A) The name and contact information of the reporting agency subject to this section.

(B) A list of the types of personal information that were or are reasonably believed to have been the subject of a breach.

(C) If the information is possible to determine at the time the notice is provided, then any of the following: (i) the date of the breach, (ii) the estimated date of the breach, or (iii) the date range within which the breach occurred. The notification shall also include the date of the notice.

(D) Whether the notification was delayed as a result of a law enforcement investigation, if that information is possible to determine at the time the notice is provided.

(E) A general description of the breach incident, if that information is possible to determine at the time the notice is provided.

(F) The toll-free telephone numbers and addresses of the major credit reporting agencies, if the breach exposed a social security number or a driver's license or California identification card number.

(3) At the discretion of the agency, the security breach notification may also include any of the following:

(A) Information about what the agency has done to protect individuals whose information has been breached.

(B) Advice on steps that the person whose information has been breached may take to protect himself or herself.

(4) In the case of a breach of the security of the system involving personal information defined in paragraph (2) of subdivision (g) for an online account, and no other personal information defined in paragraph (1) of subdivision (g), the agency may comply with this section by providing the security breach notification in electronic or other form that directs the person whose personal information has been breached to promptly change his or her password and security question or answer, as applicable, or to take other steps appropriate to protect the online account with the agency and all other online accounts for which the person uses the same user name or email address and password or security question or answer.

(5) In the case of a breach of the security of the system involving personal information defined in paragraph (2) of subdivision (g) for login credentials of an email account furnished by the agency, the agency shall not comply with this section by providing the security breach notification to that email address, but may, instead, comply with this section by providing notice by another method described in subdivision (i) or by clear and conspicuous notice delivered to the resident online when the resident is connected to the online account from an Internet Protocol address or online location from which the agency knows the resident customarily accesses the account.

(e) Any agency that is required to issue a security breach notification pursuant to this section to more than 500 California residents as a result of a single breach of the security system shall electronically submit a single sample copy of that security breach notification, excluding any personally identifiable information, to the Attorney General. A single sample copy of a security breach notification shall not be deemed to be within subdivision (f) of Section 6254 of the Government Code.

(f) For purposes of this section, "breach of the security of the system" means unauthorized acquisition of computerized data that compromises the security, confidentiality, or integrity of personal information maintained by the agency. Good faith acquisition of personal information by an employee or agent of the agency for the purposes of the agency is not a breach of the security of the system, provided that the personal information is not used or subject to further unauthorized disclosure.

(g) For purposes of this section, "personal information" means either of the following:

(1) An individual's first name or first initial and last name in combination with any one or more of the following data elements, when either the name or the data elements are not encrypted:

(A) Social security number.

(B) Driver's license number or California identification card number.

(C) Account number, credit or debit card number, in combination with any required security code, access code, or password that would permit access to an individual's financial account.

(D) Medical information.

(E) Health insurance information.

(2) A user name or email address, in combination with a password or security question and answer that would permit access to an online account.

(h)(1) For purposes of this section, "personal information" does not include publicly available information that is lawfully made available to the general public from federal, state, or local government records.

(2) For purposes of this section, "medical information" means any information regarding an individual's medical history, mental or physical condition, or medical treatment or diagnosis by a health care professional.

(3) For purposes of this section, "health insurance information" means an individual's health insurance policy number or subscriber identification number, any unique identifier used by a health insurer to identify the individual, or any information in an individual's application and claims history, including any appeals records.

(i) For purposes of this section, "notice" may be provided by one of the following methods:

(1) Written notice.

(2) Electronic notice, if the notice provided is consistent with the provisions regarding electronic records and signatures set forth in Section 7001 of Title 15 of the United States Code.

(3) Substitute notice, if the agency demonstrates that the cost of providing notice would exceed two hundred fifty thousand dollars ($250,000), or that the affected class of subject persons to be notified exceeds 500,000, or the agency does not have sufficient contact information. Substitute notice shall consist of all of the following:

(A) Email notice when the agency has an email address for the subject persons.

(B) Conspicuous posting of the notice on the agency's Internet Web site page, if the agency maintains one.

(C) Notification to major statewide media and the Office of Information Security within the * * * Department of Technology * * *.

(j) Notwithstanding subdivision (i), an agency that maintains its own notification procedures as part of an information security policy for the treatment of personal information and is otherwise consistent with the timing requirements of this part shall be deemed to be in compliance with the notification requirements of this section if it notifies subject persons in accordance with its policies in the event of a breach of security of the system.

(k) Notwithstanding the exception specified in paragraph (4) of subdivision (b) of Section 1798.3, for purposes of this section, "agency" includes a local agency, as defined in subdivision (a) of Section 6252 of the Government Code. *(Added by Stats.2002, c. 1054 (A.B.700), § 2, operative July 1, 2003. Amended by Stats.2007, c. 699 (A.B.1298), § 4; Stats.2011, c. 197 (S.B.24), § 1; Stats.2013, c. 395 (A.B.1149), § 1; Stats.2013, c. 396 (S.B.46), § 1.5.)*

Research References

5 Witkin, California Summary 10th Torts § 666, (S 666) in General.
5 Witkin, California Summary 10th Torts § 671, (S 671) Breach of Security for Computerized Personal Information.
7 Witkin, California Summary 10th Constitutional Law § 607, (S 607) Other Privacy Statutes.

ARTICLE 8. ACCESS TO RECORDS AND ADMINISTRATIVE REMEDIES

§ 1798.30. Regulations or guidelines; procedure for implementation of article

Each agency shall either adopt regulations or publish guidelines specifying procedures to be followed in order fully to implement each of the rights of individuals set forth in this article. *(Added by Stats.1977, c. 709, p. 2269, § 1, operative July 1, 1978. Amended by Stats.1978, c. 874, p. 2747, § 7, eff. Sept. 19, 1978.)*

§ 1798.32. Maintenance of records; rights of inquiry and notice; contents of notice; rules and regulations

Each individual shall have the right to inquire and be notified as to whether the agency maintains a record about himself or herself. Agencies shall take reasonable steps to assist individuals in making their requests sufficiently specific.

Any notice sent to an individual which in any way indicates that the agency maintains any record concerning that individual shall include the title and business address of the agency official responsible for maintaining the records, the procedures to be followed to gain access to the records, and the procedures to be followed for an individual to contest the contents of these records unless the individual has received this notice from the agency during the past year.

In implementing the right conferred by this section, an agency may specify in its rules or regulations reasonable times, places, and requirements for identifying an individual who requests access to a record, and for disclosing the contents of a record. *(Added by Stats.1977, c. 709, p. 2269, § 1, operative July 1, 1978. Amended by Stats.1978, c. 874, p. 2747, § 8, eff. Sept. 19, 1978; Stats.1991–1992, 1st Ex.Sess., c. 21 (A.B.66), § 33.6, eff. March 1, 1993.)*

Research References

7 Witkin, California Summary 10th Constitutional Law § 604, (S 604) Information Practices Act.

§ 1798.33. Copies of records; fees

Each agency may establish fees to be charged, if any, to an individual for making copies of a record. Such fees shall exclude the cost of any search for and review of the record, and shall not exceed ten cents ($0.10) per page, unless the agency fee for copying is established by statute. *(Added by Stats.1977, c. 709, p. 2269, § 1, operative July 1, 1978. Amended by Stats.1978, c. 874, p. 2747, § 9, eff. Sept. 19, 1978.)*

Research References

7 Witkin, California Summary 10th Constitutional Law § 604, (S 604) Information Practices Act.

§ 1798.34. Inspection of personal information in records and accounting; time; copies; form; availability

(a) Except as otherwise provided in this chapter, each agency shall permit any individual upon request and proper identification to inspect all the personal information in any record containing personal information and maintained by reference to an identifying particular assigned to the individual within 30 days of the agency's receipt of the request for active records, and within 60 days of the agency's receipt of the request for records that are geographically dispersed or which are inactive and in central storage. Failure to respond within these time limits shall be deemed denial. In addition, the individual shall be permitted to inspect any personal information about himself or herself where it is maintained by reference to an identifying particular other than that of the individual, if the agency knows or should know that the information exists. The individual also shall be permitted to inspect the accounting made pursuant to Article 7 (commencing with Section 1798.25).

(b) The agency shall permit the individual, and, upon the individual's request, another person of the individual's own choosing to inspect all the personal information in the record and have an exact copy made of all or any portion thereof within 15 days of the inspection. It may require the individual to furnish a written statement authorizing disclosure of the individual's record to another person of the individual's choosing.

(c) The agency shall present the information in the record in a form reasonably comprehensible to the general public.

(d) Whenever an agency is unable to access a record by reference to name only, or when access by name only would impose an unreasonable administrative burden, it may require the individual to submit such other identifying information as will facilitate access to the record.

(e) When an individual is entitled under this chapter to gain access to the information in a record containing personal information, the information or a true copy thereof shall be made available to the individual at a location near the residence of the individual or by mail, whenever reasonable. *(Added by Stats.1977, c. 709, p. 2269, § 1, operative July 1, 1978. Amended by Stats.1982, c. 604, p. 2584, § 4; Stats.1985, c. 595, § 15.)*

Research References

7 Witkin, California Summary 10th Constitutional Law § 604, (S 604) Information Practices Act.

§ 1798.35. Amendment of records; procedure; notice

Each agency shall permit an individual to request in writing an amendment of a record and, shall within 30 days of the date of receipt of such request:

(a) Make each correction in accordance with the individual's request of any portion of a record which the individual believes is not accurate, relevant, timely, or complete and inform the individual of the corrections made in accordance with their request; or

(b) Inform the individual of its refusal to amend the record in accordance with such individual's request, the reason for the refusal, the procedures established by the agency for the individual to request a review by the head of the agency or an official specifically designated by the head of the agency of the refusal to amend, and the name, title, and business address of the reviewing official. *(Added by Stats.1977, c. 709, p. 2269, § 1, operative July 1, 1978.)*

Research References

7 Witkin, California Summary 10th Constitutional Law § 604, (S 604) Information Practices Act.

§ 1798.36. Refusal to amend records; review; final determination; time; statement of individual's disagreement

Each agency shall permit any individual who disagrees with the refusal of the agency to amend a record to request a review of such refusal by the head of the agency or an official specifically designated by the head of such agency, and, not later than 30 days from the date on which the individual requests such review, complete such review and make a final determination unless, for good cause shown, the head of the agency extends such review period by 30 days. If, after such review, the reviewing official refuses to amend the record in accordance with the request, the agency shall permit the individual to file with the agency a statement of reasonable length setting forth the reasons for the individual's disagreement. *(Added by Stats.1977, c. 709, p. 2269, § 1, operative July 1, 1978.)*

Research References

7 Witkin, California Summary 10th Constitutional Law § 604, (S 604) Information Practices Act.

§ 1798.37. Disputed records; statements of individual's disagreement and rationale of agency for refusal of amendment; notation of disputed portions; copies

The agency, with respect to any disclosure containing information about which the individual has filed a statement of disagreement, shall clearly note any portion of the record which is disputed and make available copies of such individual's statement and copies of a concise statement of the reasons of the agency for not making the amendment to any person or agency to whom the disputed record has been or is disclosed. *(Added by Stats.1977, c. 709, p. 2269, § 1, operative July 1, 1978.)*

Research References

7 Witkin, California Summary 10th Constitutional Law § 604, (S 604) Information Practices Act.

§ 1798.38. Promises or understandings concerning confidentiality of source; specified information in possession of agencies; protection of identity

If information, including letters of recommendation, compiled for the purpose of determining suitability, eligibility, or qualifications for employment, advancement, renewal of appointment or promotion, status as adoptive parents, or for the receipt of state contracts, or for licensing purposes, was received with the promise or, prior to July 1, 1978, with the understanding that the identity of the source of the information would be held in confidence and the source is not in a supervisory position with respect to the individual to whom the record pertains, the agency shall fully inform the individual of all personal information about that individual without identification of the source. This may be done by providing a copy of the text of the material with only such deletions as are necessary to protect the identity of the source or by providing a comprehensive summary of the substance of the material. Whichever method is used, the agency shall insure that full disclosure is made to the subject of any personal information that could reasonably in any way reflect or convey anything detrimental, disparaging, or threatening to an individual's reputation, rights, benefits, privileges, or qualifications, or be used by an agency to make a determination that would affect an individual's rights, benefits, privileges, or qualifications. In institutions of higher education, "supervisory positions" shall not be deemed to include chairpersons of academic departments. *(Added by Stats.1977, c. 709, p. 2269, § 1, operative July 1, 1978. Amended by Stats.1985, c. 595, § 16.)*

§ 1798.39. Records evidencing property rights

Sections 1798.35, 1798.36, and 1798.37 shall not apply to any record evidencing property rights. *(Added by Stats.1977, c. 709, p. 2269, § 1, operative July 1, 1978.)*

Research References

7 Witkin, California Summary 10th Constitutional Law § 604, (S 604) Information Practices Act.

§ 1798.40. Nondisclosure of personal information to individual to whom information pertains; criteria

This chapter shall not be construed to require an agency to disclose personal information to the individual to whom the information pertains, if the information meets any of the following criteria:

(a) Is compiled for the purpose of identifying individual criminal offenders and alleged offenders and consists only of identifying data and notations of arrests, the nature and disposition of criminal charges, sentencing, confinement, release, and parole and probation status.

(b) Is compiled for the purpose of a criminal investigation of suspected criminal activities, including reports of informants and investigators, and associated with an identifiable individual.

(c) Is contained in any record which could identify an individual and which is compiled at any stage of the process of enforcement of the criminal laws, from the arrest or indictment stage through release from supervision and including the process of extradition or the exercise of executive clemency.

(d) Is maintained for the purpose of an investigation of an individual's fitness for licensure or public employment, or of a grievance or complaint, or a suspected civil offense, so long as

the information is withheld only so as not to compromise the investigation, or a related investigation. The identities of individuals who provided information for the investigation may be withheld pursuant to Section 1798.38.

(e) Would compromise the objectivity or fairness of a competitive examination for appointment or promotion in public service, or to determine fitness for licensure, or to determine scholastic aptitude.

(f) Pertains to the physical or psychological condition of the individual, if the agency determines that disclosure would be detrimental to the individual. The information shall, upon the individual's written authorization, be disclosed to a licensed medical practitioner or psychologist designated by the individual.

(g) Relates to the settlement of claims for work related illnesses or injuries and is maintained exclusively by the State Compensation Insurance Fund.

(h) Is required by statute to be withheld from the individual to whom it pertains.

This section shall not be construed to deny an individual access to information relating to him or her if access is allowed by another statute or decisional law of this state. *(Added by Stats.1985, c. 595, § 18.)*

Research References

7 Witkin, California Summary 10th Constitutional Law § 604, (S 604) Information Practices Act.

§ 1798.41. Finding that requested information is exempt from access; written notice; review; ex parte orders authorizing responses of no maintenance

(a) Except as provided in subdivision (c), if the agency determines that information requested pursuant to Section 1798.34 is exempt from access, it shall inform the individual in writing of the agency's finding that disclosure is not required by law.

(b) Except as provided in subdivision (c), each agency shall conduct a review of its determination that particular information is exempt from access pursuant to Section 1798.40, within 30 days from the receipt of a request by an individual directly affected by the determination, and inform the individual in writing of the findings of the review. The review shall be conducted by the head of the agency or an official specifically designated by the head of the agency.

(c) If the agency believes that compliance with subdivision (a) would seriously interfere with attempts to apprehend persons who are wanted for committing a crime or attempts to prevent the commission of a crime or would endanger the life of an informant or other person submitting information contained in the record, it may petition the presiding judge of the superior court of the county in which the record is maintained to issue an ex parte order authorizing the agency to respond to the individual that no record is maintained. All proceedings before the court shall be in camera. If the presiding judge finds that there are reasonable grounds to believe that compliance with subdivision (a) will seriously interfere with attempts to apprehend persons who are wanted for committing a crime or attempts to prevent the commission of a crime or will endanger the life of an informant or other person submitting information contained in the record, the judge shall issue an order authorizing the agency to respond to the individual that no record is maintained by the agency. The order shall not be issued for longer than 30 days but can be renewed at 30-day intervals. If a request pursuant to this section is received after the expiration of the order, the agency must either respond pursuant to subdivision (a) or seek a new order pursuant to this subdivision. *(Formerly § 1798.40, added by Stats.1977, c. 709, p. 2269, § 1, operative July 1, 1978. Amended by Stats.1982, c. 604, p. 2585, § 5. Renumbered § 1798.41 and amended by Stats.1985, c. 595, § 17.)*

Research References

7 Witkin, California Summary 10th Constitutional Law § 604, (S 604) Information Practices Act.

§ 1798.42.　Disclosure of personal information relating to others; deletions

In disclosing information contained in a record to an individual, an agency shall not disclose any personal information relating to another individual which may be contained in the record. To comply with this section, an agency shall, in disclosing information, delete from disclosure such information as may be necessary. This section shall not be construed to authorize withholding the identities of sources except as provided in Sections 1798.38 and 1798.40. *(Formerly § 1798.41, added by Stats.1977, c. 709, p. 2269, § 1, operative July 1, 1978. Amended by Stats.1982, c. 604, p. 2586, § 6. Renumbered § 1798.42 and amended by Stats.1985, c. 595, § 19.)*

Research References

7 Witkin, California Summary 10th Constitutional Law § 604, (S 604) Information Practices Act.

§ 1798.43.　Disclosure of personal information to individual to whom information pertains; deletion of exempt information

In disclosing information contained in a record to an individual, an agency need not disclose any information pertaining to that individual which is exempt under Section 1798.40. To comply with this section, an agency may, in disclosing personal information contained in a record, delete from the disclosure any exempt information. *(Formerly § 1798.42, added by Stats.1977, c. 709, p. 2269, § 1, operative July 1, 1978. Amended by Stats.1982, c. 604, p. 2586, § 7. Renumbered § 1798.43 and amended by Stats.1985, c. 595, § 20.)*

Research References

7 Witkin, California Summary 10th Constitutional Law § 604, (S 604) Information Practices Act.

§ 1798.44.　Application of article

This article applies to the rights of an individual to whom personal information pertains and not to the authority or right of any other person, agency, other state governmental entity, or governmental entity to obtain this information. *(Formerly § 1798.43, added by Stats.1978, c. 874, p. 2747, § 10, eff. Sept. 19, 1978. Renumbered § 1798.44 and amended by Stats.1985, c. 595, § 21.)*

ARTICLE 9.　CIVIL REMEDIES

§ 1798.45.　Civil actions against agencies; grounds

An individual may bring a civil action against an agency whenever such agency does any of the following:

(a) Refuses to comply with an individual's lawful request to inspect pursuant to subdivision (a) of Section 1798.34.

(b) Fails to maintain any record concerning any individual with such accuracy, relevancy, timeliness, and completeness as is necessary to assure fairness in any determination relating to the qualifications, character, rights, opportunities of, or benefits to the individual that may be made on the basis of such record, if, as a proximate result of such failure, a determination is made which is adverse to the individual.

(c) Fails to comply with any other provision of this chapter, or any rule promulgated thereunder, in such a way as to have an adverse effect on an individual. *(Added by Stats.1977, c. 709, p. 2269, § 1, operative July 1, 1978.)*

Research References

5 Witkin, California Summary 10th Torts § 667, (S 667) Information Practices Act.
7 Witkin, California Summary 10th Constitutional Law § 604, (S 604) Information Practices Act.

§ 1798.46.　Actions for refusal to comply with requests for inspection; injunctions; proceedings de novo; in camera examination of records; attorney fees and costs

In any suit brought under the provisions of subdivision (a) of Section 1798.45:

(a) The court may enjoin the agency from withholding the records and order the production to the complainant of any agency records improperly withheld from the complainant. In such a suit the court shall determine the matter de novo, and may examine the contents of any agency records in camera to determine whether the records or any portion thereof may be withheld as being exempt from the individual's right of access and the burden is on the agency to sustain its action.

(b) The court shall assess against the agency reasonable attorney's fees and other litigation costs reasonably incurred in any suit under this section in which the complainant has prevailed. A party may be considered to have prevailed even though he or she does not prevail on all issues or against all parties. *(Added by Stats.1977, c. 709, p. 2269, § 1, operative July 1, 1978. Amended by Stats.1985, c. 595, § 22.)*

§ 1798.47.　Injunctions; orders and judgments

Any agency that fails to comply with any provision of this chapter may be enjoined by any court of competent jurisdiction. The court may make any order or judgment as may be necessary to prevent the use or employment by an agency of any practices which violate this chapter.

Actions for injunction under this section may be prosecuted by the Attorney General, or any district attorney in this state, in the name of the people of the State of California whether upon his or her own complaint, or of a member of the general public, or by any individual acting in his or her own behalf. *(Added by Stats.1977, c. 709, p. 2269, § 1, operative July 1, 1978. Amended by Stats.1991–1992, 1st Ex.Sess., c. 21 (A.B.66), § 33.7, eff. March 1, 1993.)*

§ 1798.48. Failure to maintain records properly; noncompliance with provisions of chapter and rules; actual damages; costs; attorney fees

In any suit brought under the provisions of subdivision (b) or (c) of Section 1798.45, the agency shall be liable to the individual in an amount equal to the sum of:

(a) Actual damages sustained by the individual, including damages for mental suffering.

(b) The costs of the action together with reasonable attorney's fees as determined by the court. *(Added by Stats.1977, c. 709, p. 2269, § 1, operative July 1, 1978.)*

§ 1798.49. Jurisdiction; limitation of actions; nonexclusive rights and remedies

An action to enforce any liability created under Sections 1798.45 to 1798.48, inclusive, may be brought in any court of competent jurisdiction in the county in which the complainant resides, or has his principal place of business, or in which the defendant's records are situated, within two years from the date on which the cause of action arises, except that where a defendant has materially and willfully misrepresented any information required under this section to be disclosed to an individual who is the subject of the information and the information so misrepresented is material to the establishment of the defendant's liability to that individual under this section, the action may be brought at any time within two years after discovery by the complainant of the misrepresentation. Nothing in Sections 1798.45 to 1798.48, inclusive, shall be construed to authorize any civil action by reason of any injury sustained as the result of any information practice covered by this chapter prior to July 1, 1978.

The rights and remedies set forth in this chapter shall be deemed to be nonexclusive and are in addition to all those rights and remedies which are otherwise available under any other provision of law. *(Added by Stats.1977, c. 709, p. 2269, § 1, operative July 1, 1978.)*

§ 1798.50. Personnel actions; qualifications of individuals; subjective opinions; liability

A civil action shall not lie under this article based upon an allegation that an opinion which is subjective in nature, as distinguished from a factual assertion, about an individual's qualifications, in connection with a personnel action concerning such an individual, was not accurate, relevant, timely, or complete. *(Added by Stats.1977, c. 709, p. 2269, § 1, operative July 1, 1978.)*

§ 1798.51. Lapse of time; corrections to records

Where a remedy other than those provided in Articles 8 and 9 is provided by law but is not available because of lapse of time an individual may obtain a correction to a record under this chapter but such correction shall not operate to revise or restore a right or remedy not provided by this chapter that has been barred because of lapse of time. *(Added by Stats.1977, c. 709, p. 2269, § 1, operative July 1, 1978.)*

§ 1798.53. Invasion of privacy; intentional disclosure of personal information; state or federal records; exemplary damages; attorney fees and costs

Any person, other than an employee of the state or of a local government agency acting solely in his or her official capacity, who intentionally discloses information, not otherwise public, which they know or should reasonably know was obtained from personal information maintained by a state agency or from "records" within a "system of records" (as these terms are defined in the Federal Privacy Act of 1974 (P.L. 93–579; 5 U.S.C. 552a)) maintained by a federal government agency, shall be subject to a civil action, for invasion of privacy, by the individual to whom the information pertains.

In any successful action brought under this section, the complainant, in addition to any special or general damages awarded, shall be awarded a minimum of two thousand five hundred dollars ($2,500) in exemplary damages as well as attorney's fees and other litigation costs reasonably incurred in the suit.

The right, remedy, and cause of action set forth in this section shall be nonexclusive and is in addition to all other rights, remedies, and causes of action for invasion of privacy, inherent in Section 1 of Article I of the California Constitution. *(Added by Stats.1977, c. 709, p. 2269, § 1, operative July 1, 1978. Amended by Stats.1985, c. 595, § 23.)*

ARTICLE 10. PENALTIES

§ 1798.55. Intentional violations; agency officers and employees; discipline; termination of employment

The intentional violation of any provision of this chapter or of any rules or regulations adopted thereunder, by an officer or employee of any agency shall constitute a cause for discipline, including termination of employment. *(Added by Stats.1977, c. 709, p. 2269, § 1, operative July 1, 1978.)*

§ 1798.56. False pretenses; requesting or obtaining records; misdemeanor

Any person who willfully requests or obtains any record containing personal information from an agency under false pretenses shall be guilty of a misdemeanor and fined not more than five thousand dollars ($5,000), or imprisoned not more than one year, or both. *(Added by Stats.1977, c. 709, p. 2269, § 1, operative July 1, 1978. Amended by Stats.1985, c. 595, § 24.)*

Research References

7 Witkin, California Summary 10th Constitutional Law § 604, (S 604) Information Practices Act.

§ 1798.57. Wrongful disclosure of medical, psychiatric, or psychological information; economic loss or personal injury; misdemeanor

Except for disclosures which are otherwise required or permitted by law, the intentional disclosure of medical, psychiatric, or psychological information in violation of the disclosure provisions of this chapter is punishable as a misdemeanor if the wrongful disclosure results in economic loss or personal injury to the individual to whom the information pertains. *(Added by Stats.1986, c. 94, § 1, eff. May 13, 1986.)*

Research References

7 Witkin, California Summary 10th Constitutional Law § 604, (S 604) Information Practices Act.

ARTICLE 11. MISCELLANEOUS PROVISIONS

§ 1798.60. Names and addresses; distribution for commercial purposes, sale or rental

An individual's name and address may not be distributed for commercial purposes, sold, or rented by an agency unless such action is specifically authorized by law. *(Added by Stats.1977, c. 709, p. 2269, § 1, operative July 1, 1978.)*

§ 1798.61. Release of licensees' and applicants' names and addresses

(a) Nothing in this chapter shall prohibit the release of only names and addresses of persons possessing licenses to engage in professional occupations.

(b) Nothing in this chapter shall prohibit the release of only names and addresses of persons applying for licenses to engage in professional occupations for the sole purpose of providing those persons with informational materials relating to available professional educational materials or courses. *(Added by Stats. 1977, c. 709, p. 2269, § 1, operative July 1, 1978. Amended by Stats.1978, c. 874, p. 2747, § 11, eff. Sept. 19, 1978; Stats.1979, c. 143, p. 333, § 3, eff. June 22, 1979; Stats.1982, c. 1001, p. 3686, § 1; Stats.2000, c. 962 (A.B.1965), § 1.)*

Research References

Rutter, Cal. Practice Guide: Personal Injury Ch. 5-A, A. Prelawsuit Filings.

§ 1798.62. Mailing lists; agencies; removal of names and addresses

Upon written request of any individual, any agency which maintains a mailing list shall remove the individual's name and address from such list, except that such agency need not remove the individual's name if such name is exclusively used by the agency to directly contact the individual. *(Added by Stats.1977, c. 709, p. 2269, § 1, operative July 1, 1978.)*

§ 1798.63. Construction of chapter

The provisions of this chapter shall be liberally construed so as to protect the rights of privacy arising under this chapter or under the Federal or State Constitution. *(Added by Stats.1977, c. 709, p. 2269, § 1, operative July 1, 1978.)*

Research References

7 Witkin, California Summary 10th Constitutional Law § 604, (S 604) Information Practices Act.

§ 1798.64. Director of General Services; storage, processing and servicing of records; state archives; maintenance

(a) Each agency record which is accepted by the Director of General Services for storage, processing, and servicing in accordance with provisions of the State Administrative Manual for the purposes of this chapter shall be considered to be maintained by the agency which deposited the record and shall continue to be subject to the provisions of this chapter. The Director of General Services shall not disclose the record except to the agency which maintains the record, or pursuant to rules established by such agency which are not inconsistent with the provisions of this chapter.

(b) Each agency record pertaining to an identifiable individual which was or is transferred to the State Archives as a record which has sufficient historical or other value to warrant its continued preservation by the California state government, prior to or after July 1, 1978, shall, for the purposes of this chapter, be considered to be maintained by the archives. *(Added by Stats.1977, c. 709, p. 2269, § 1, operative July 1, 1978.)*

§ 1798.66. Access to records; time limitations; extension

The time limits specified in Article 8 (commencing with Section 1798.30) may be extended to 60 days by the Franchise Tax Board if the following conditions exist:

(a) The request is made during the period January 1 through June 30; and

(b) The records requested are stored on magnetic tape. *(Added by Stats.1977, c. 709, p. 2269, § 1, operative July 1, 1978.)*

§ 1798.67. Liens or encumbrances; state; disclosure of information relating to identity

Where an agency has recorded a document creating a lien or encumbrance on real property in favor of the state, nothing herein shall prohibit any such agency from disclosing information relating to the identity of the person against whom such lien or encumbrance has been recorded for the purpose of distinguishing such person from another person bearing the same or a similar name. *(Added by Stats.1977, c. 709, p. 2269, § 1, operative July 1, 1978.)*

§ 1798.68. Disclosure of personal or confidential information to district attorney; petition to disclose

(a) Information which is permitted to be disclosed under the provisions of subdivision (e), (f), or (o), of Section 1798.24 shall be provided when requested by a district attorney.

A district attorney may petition a court of competent jurisdiction to require disclosure of information when an agency fails or refuses to provide the requested information within 10 working days of a request. The court may require the agency to permit inspection unless the public interest or good cause in withholding such records clearly outweighs the public interest in disclosure.

(b) Disclosure of information to a district attorney under the provisions of this chapter shall effect no change in the status of the records under any other provision of law. *(Added by Stats.1979, c. 601, p. 1873, § 1.)*

§ 1798.69. Release of names and addresses; State Board of Equalization

(a) Except as provided in subdivision (b), the State Board of Equalization may not release the names and addresses of individuals who are registered with, or are holding licenses or permits issued by, the State Board of Equalization except to the extent necessary to verify resale certificates or to administer the tax and fee provisions of the Revenue and Taxation Code.

(b) Nothing in this section shall prohibit the release by the State Board of Equalization to, or limit the use by, any federal or state agency, or local government, of any data collected by the board that is otherwise authorized by law. *(Added by Stats.2000, c. 962 (A.B.1965), § 2.)*

ARTICLE 12. CONSTRUCTION WITH OTHER LAWS

Section

§ 1798.70. Superseding other provisions of state law

This chapter shall be construed to supersede any other provision of state law, including Section 6253.5 of the Government Code, or any exemption in Section 6254 or 6255 of the Government Code, which authorizes any agency to withhold from an individual any record containing personal information which is otherwise accessible under the provisions of this chapter. *(Added by Stats.1977, c. 709, p. 2269, § 1, operative July 1, 1978. Amended by Stats.1978, c. 874, p. 2748, § 12, eff. Sept. 19, 1978.)*

Research References

7 Witkin, California Summary 10th Constitutional Law § 604, (S 604) Information Practices Act.

§ 1798.71. Discovery; rights of litigants

This chapter shall not be deemed to abridge or limit the rights of litigants, including parties to administrative proceedings, under the laws, or case law, of discovery of this state. *(Added by Stats.1977, c. 709, p. 2269, § 1, operative July 1, 1978.)*

§ 1798.72. Personal information; disclosure of records to other than the subject; violation of other law

Nothing in this chapter shall be construed to authorize the disclosure of any record containing personal information, other than to the subject of such records, in violation of any other law. *(Added by Stats.1977, c. 709, p. 2269, § 1, operative July 1, 1978.)*

§ 1798.73. Privacy; constitutional rights

Nothing in this chapter shall be construed to deny or limit any right of privacy arising under Section 1 of Article I of the California Constitution. *(Added by Stats.1977, c. 709, p. 2269, § 1, operative July 1, 1978.)*

§ 1798.74. Student records

The provisions of Chapter 13 (commencing with Section 67110) [1] of Part 40 of the Education Code shall, with regard to student records, prevail over the provisions of this chapter. *(Added by Stats.1977, c. 709, p. 2269, § 1, operative July 1, 1978.)*

[1] So in chaptered copy.

§ 1798.75. Inspection of public records

This chapter shall not be deemed to supersede Chapter 3.5 (commencing with Section 6250) of Division 7 of Title 1 of the Government Code, except as to the provisions of Sections 1798.60, 1798.69, and 1798.70. *(Added by Stats.1977, c. 709, p. 2269, § 1, operative July 1, 1978. Amended by Stats.1979, c. 143, p. 334, § 4, eff. June 22, 1979; Stats.2000, c. 962 (A.B.1965), § 3.)*

§ 1798.76. Law enforcement records; discovery in criminal or civil litigation

Nothing in this chapter shall be construed to revoke, modify, or alter in any manner any statutory provision or any judicial decision which (a) authorizes an individual to gain access to any law enforcement record, or (b) authorizes discovery in criminal or civil litigation. *(Added by Stats.1977, c. 709, p. 2269, § 1, operative July 1, 1978.)*

§ 1798.77. Modification, transfer, or destruction of records to avoid compliance with chapter prohibited; civil action; removal or destruction of requested information before access prohibited

Each agency shall ensure that no record containing personal information shall be modified, transferred, or destroyed to avoid compliance with any of the provisions of this chapter. In the event that an agency fails to comply with the provisions of this section, an individual may bring a civil action and seek the appropriate remedies and damages in accordance with the provisions of Article 9 (commencing with Section 1798.45).

An agency shall not remove or destroy personal information about an individual who has requested access to the information before allowing the individual access to the record containing the information. *(Added by Stats.1985, c. 595, § 26.)*

Research References

7 Witkin, California Summary 10th Constitutional Law § 604, (S 604) Information Practices Act.

§ 1798.78. Chapter deemed not to supersede Chapter 1299 of Statutes of 1976

This chapter shall not be deemed to supersede the provisions of Chapter 1299 of the Statutes of 1976.[1] *(Added by Stats.1985, c. 595, § 27.)*

[1] Stats.1976, c. 1299, added Education Code 1959, § 24317. See Education Code § 89546.

Title 1.80

IDENTIFICATION DOCUMENTS

Section

§ 1798.79. Intentional reading or attempts to remotely read a person's identification document using radio frequency identification; disclosure of operational systems in a contactless identification system; penalties; application

(a) Except as provided in this section, a person or entity that intentionally remotely reads or attempts to remotely read a person's identification document using radio frequency identification (RFID), for the purpose of reading that person's identification document without that person's knowledge and prior consent, shall be punished by imprisonment in a county jail for up to one year, a fine of not more than one thousand five hundred dollars ($1,500), or both that fine and imprisonment.

(b) A person or entity that knowingly discloses, or causes to be disclosed, the operational system keys used in a contactless identification document system shall be punished by imprisonment in a county jail for up to one year, a fine of not more than one thousand five hundred dollars ($1,500), or both that fine and imprisonment.

(c) Subdivision (a) shall not apply to:

(1) The reading of a person's identification document for triage or medical care during a disaster and immediate hospitalization or immediate outpatient care directly related to a disaster, as defined by the local emergency medical services agency organized under Section 1797.200 of the Health and Safety Code.

(2) The reading of a person's identification document by a health care professional for reasons relating to the health or safety of that person or an identification document issued to a patient by emergency services.

(3) The reading of an identification document of a person who is incarcerated in the state prison or a county jail, detained in a juvenile facility operated by the Division of Juvenile Facilities in the Department of Corrections and Rehabilitation, or housed in a mental health facility, pursuant to a court order after having been charged with a crime, or to a person pursuant to a court-ordered electronic monitoring.

(4) Law enforcement or government personnel who need to read a lost identification document when the owner is unavailable for notice, knowledge, or consent, or those parties specifically authorized by law enforcement or government personnel for the limited purpose of reading a lost identification document when the owner is unavailable for notice, knowledge, or consent.

(5) Law enforcement personnel who need to read a person's identification document after an accident in which the person is unavailable for notice, knowledge, or consent.

(6) Law enforcement personnel who need to read a person's identification document pursuant to a search warrant.

(d) Subdivision (a) shall not apply to a person or entity that unintentionally remotely reads a person's identification document using RFID in the course of operating a contactless identification document system unless it knows it unintentionally read the document and thereafter intentionally does any of the following acts:

(1) Discloses what it read to a third party whose purpose is to read a person's identification document, or any information derived therefrom, without that person's knowledge and consent.

(2) Stores what it read for the purpose of reading a person's identification document, or any information derived therefrom, without that person's knowledge and prior consent.

(3) Uses what it read for the purpose of reading a person's identification document, or any information derived therefrom, without that person's knowledge and prior consent.

(e) Subdivisions (a) and (b) shall not apply to the reading, storage, use, or disclosure to a third party of a person's identification document, or information derived therefrom, in the course of an act of good faith security research, experimentation, or scientific inquiry, including, but not limited to, activities useful in identifying and analyzing security flaws and vulnerabilities.

(f) Nothing in this section shall affect the existing rights of law enforcement to access data stored electronically on driver's licenses.

(g) The penalties set forth in subdivisions (a) and (b) are independent of, and do not supersede, any other penalties provided by state law, and in the case of any conflict, the greater penalties shall apply. *(Added by Stats.2008, c. 746 (S.B.31), § 2. Amended by Stats.2009, c. 54 (S.B.544), § 5.)*

Research References

7 Witkin, California Summary 10th Constitutional Law § 607, (S 607) Other Privacy Statutes.

§ 1798.795. Definitions

For purposes of this title, the following definitions shall apply:

(a) "Contactless identification document system" means a group of identification documents issued and operated under a single authority that use RFID to transmit data remotely to readers intended to read that data. In a contactless identification document system, every reader must be able to read every identification document in the system.

(b) "Data" means any information stored or transmitted on an identification document in machine-readable form.

(c) "Identification document" means any document containing data that is issued to an individual and which that individual, and only that individual, uses alone or in conjunction with any other information for the primary purpose of establishing his or her identity. Identification documents specifically include, but are not limited to, the following:

(1) Driver's licenses or identification cards issued pursuant to Section 13000 of the Vehicle Code.

(2) Identification cards for employees or contractors.

(3) Identification cards issued by educational institutions.

(4) Health insurance or benefit cards.

(5) Benefit cards issued in conjunction with any government-supported aid program.

(6) Licenses, certificates, registration, or other means to engage in a business or profession regulated by the Business and Professions Code.

(7) Library cards issued by any public library.

(d) "Key" means a string of bits of information used as part of a cryptographic algorithm used in encryption.

(e) "Radio frequency identification" or "RFID" means the use of electromagnetic radiating waves or reactive field coupling in the radio frequency portion of the spectrum to communicate to or from an identification document through a variety of modulation and encoding schemes.

(f) "Reader" means a scanning device that is capable of using RFID to communicate with an identification document and read the data transmitted by that identification document.

(g) "Remotely" means that no physical contact between the identification document and a reader is necessary in order to transmit data using RFID. *(Added by Stats.2008, c. 746 (S.B.31), § 2.)*

Research References

7 Witkin, California Summary 10th Constitutional Law § 607, (S 607) Other Privacy Statutes.

Title 1.807

DOMESTIC VIOLENCE, SEXUAL ASSAULT, AND STALKING: PERSONAL INFORMATION

Section

§ 1798.79.8. Definitions

For purposes of this title:

(a) "Person or entity" means any individual, corporation, partnership, joint venture, or any business entity, or any state or local agency.

(b) "Personally identifying information" means:

(1) First and last name or last name only.

(2) Home or other physical address, including, but not limited to, a street name or ZIP Code, other than an address obtained pursuant to the California Safe At Home program or a business mailing address for the victim service provider.

(3) Electronic mail address or other online contact information, such as an instant messaging user identifier or a screen name that reveals an individual's electronic mail address.

(4) Telephone number, other than a business telephone number for the victim service provider.

(5) Social security number.

(6) Date of birth, with the exception of the year of birth.

(7) Internet protocol address or host name that identifies an individual.

(8) Any other information, including, but not limited to, the first and last names of children and relatives, racial or ethnic background, or religious affiliation, that, in combination with any other nonpersonally identifying information, would serve to identify any individual.

(c) "Victim service provider" means a nongovernmental organization or entity that provides shelter, programs, or services at low cost, no cost, or on a sliding scale to victims of domestic violence, dating violence, sexual assault, or stalking, or their children, either directly or through other contractual arrangements, including rape crisis centers, domestic violence shelters, domestic violence transitional housing programs, and other programs with the primary mission to provide services to victims of domestic violence, dating violence, sexual assault, or stalking, or their children, whether or not that program exists in an agency that provides additional services. *(Added by Stats.2006, c. 54 (S.B.1491), § 1.)*

Research References

Rutter, Cal. Practice Guide: Civ. Pro. Before Trial Ch. 8E-6, Subpoena to Nonparty Deponent or Business Records Custodian.

Rutter, Cal. Practice Guide: Civil Trials & Evidence Ch. 1-C, C. Marshalling the Evidence.

§ 1798.79.9. Prohibition on collection of personal identification information of clients from victim services providers receiving grants; statistical information excluded

(a) In the course of awarding grants, including, but not limited to, requests for proposals, contracts, or billing procedures, implementing programs, or providing financial support or assistance for the purpose of providing shelter, programs, or services at low cost, no cost, or on a sliding scale to victims of domestic violence, dating violence, sexual assault, or stalking, or their children, to any victim service provider, it is unlawful for any person or entity to request or require that victim service provider to provide personally identifying information regarding any of the persons to whom it is providing services, it has provided services, or it has considered or is considering providing services.

(b) In the course of awarding grants, including, but not limited to, requests for proposals, contracts, or billing procedures, implementing programs, or providing financial support or assistance for the purpose of providing shelter, programs, or services at low cost, no cost, or on a sliding scale to victims of domestic violence, dating violence, sexual assault, or stalking, or their children, to any victim service provider, it is unlawful for any person or entity to request or require that victim service provider to use any computer software, computer program, computer protocol, or other computer system that requires the disclosure of personally identifying information regarding any of the persons to whom it is providing services, it has provided services, or it has considered or is considering providing services.

(c) Nothing in this section is intended to prevent the collection of information for statistical purposes that are necessary for the proper administration of the grant, program, or financial assistance, provided that collection does not require the disclosure of information that would serve to identify any specific individual. *(Added by Stats.2006, c. 54 (S.B.1491), § 1.)*

§ 1798.79.95. Violations of title; injunctive relief; recovery of costs and attorney's fees; notice requirements

Injunctive relief shall be available to any victim service provider aggrieved by a violation of this title. The prevailing plaintiff in any action commenced under this section shall be entitled to recover court costs and reasonable attorney's fees if the victim service provider has provided notice of this section and the asserted violation of this section to the defendant and the defendant has failed to cease the violation within five business days of receiving that notice. *(Added by Stats.2006, c. 54 (S.B.1491), § 1.)*

Title 1.81

CUSTOMER RECORDS

Section

Section

doned records containing personal information; attorney's fees and costs.

§ 1798.80. Definitions

The following definitions apply to this title:

(a) "Business" means a sole proprietorship, partnership, corporation, association, or other group, however organized and whether or not organized to operate at a profit, including a financial institution organized, chartered, or holding a license or authorization certificate under the law of this state, any other state, the United States, or of any other country, or the parent or the subsidiary of a financial institution. The term includes an entity that disposes of records.

(b) "Records" means any material, regardless of the physical form, on which information is recorded or preserved by any means, including in written or spoken words, graphically depicted, printed, or electromagnetically transmitted. "Records" does not include publicly available directories containing information an individual has voluntarily consented to have publicly disseminated or listed, such as name, address, or telephone number.

(c) "Customer" means an individual who provides personal information to a business for the purpose of purchasing or leasing a product or obtaining a service from the business.

(d) "Individual" means a natural person.

(e) "Personal information" means any information that identifies, relates to, describes, or is capable of being associated with, a particular individual, including, but not limited to, his or her name, signature, social security number, physical characteristics or description, address, telephone number, passport number, driver's license or state identification card number, insurance policy number, education, employment, employment history, bank account number, credit card number, debit card number, or any other financial information, medical information, or health insurance information. "Personal information" does not include publicly available information that is lawfully made available to the general public from federal, state, or local government records. *(Added by Stats.2000, c. 1039 (A.B.2246), § 1. Amended by Stats.2009, c. 134 (A.B.1094), § 1.)*

Research References

California Real Estate Forms (Miller & Starr) § 2:16, Office Lease—Multistory Office Building.
California Real Estate Forms (Miller & Starr) § 2:17, Office Lease—Mixed Use Building.
California Real Estate Forms (Miller & Starr) § 2:18, Office Lease—Office/Warehouse Building With Four or Fewer Tenants.
California Real Estate Forms (Miller & Starr) § 2:19, Retail Lease—Power Shopping Center.
California Real Estate Forms (Miller & Starr) § 2:20, Retail Lease—Shopping Center With for Profit Parking Garage.
California Real Estate Forms (Miller & Starr) § 2:21, Retail Lease—15,000 RSF to 30,000 RSF (Tenant Oriented).
California Real Estate Forms (Miller & Starr) § 2:22, Retail Lease—Regional Shopping Center.
California Real Estate Forms (Miller & Starr) § 2:23, Retail Lease—Small Strip-Shopping Center.
California Real Estate Forms (Miller & Starr) § 2:24, Retail Lease—Restaurant.
California Real Estate Forms (Miller & Starr) § 2:25, Industrial Lease.
California Real Estate Forms (Miller & Starr) § 2:26, Triple Net Lease—Industrial Build-To-Suit Lease.
California Real Estate Forms (Miller & Starr) § 2:27, Ground Lease.
California Real Estate Forms (Miller & Starr) § 2:28, Triple Net Lease—Stand-Alone Building.
California Real Estate Forms (Miller & Starr) § 2:29, Parking Garage Lease.
California Real Estate Forms (Miller & Starr) § 2:31, Rental Agreement—Self Storage.

California Real Estate Forms (Miller & Starr) § 2:32, Gross Lease—Small Commercial Property.
California Real Estate Forms (Miller & Starr) § 2:34, Sublease—Shared Office Space.
California Real Estate Forms (Miller & Starr) § 2:18.50, Management Office License Agreement.
20 NO. 4 Miller & Starr, California Real Estate Newsalert 13, Landlord and Tenant.
5 Witkin, California Summary 10th Torts § 666, (S 666) in General.
5 Witkin, California Summary 10th Torts § 670, (S 670) Failure to Destroy Consumer Records.
7 Witkin, California Summary 10th Constitutional Law § 607, (S 607) Other Privacy Statutes.

§ 1798.81. Reasonable steps for disposal of customer records

A business shall take all reasonable steps to dispose, or arrange for the disposal, of customer records within its custody or control containing personal information when the records are no longer to be retained by the business by (a) shredding, (b) erasing, or (c) otherwise modifying the personal information in those records to make it unreadable or undecipherable through any means. *(Added by Stats.2000, c. 1039 (A.B.2246), § 1. Amended by Stats.2009, c. 134 (A.B.1094), § 2.)*

Research References

California Real Estate Forms (Miller & Starr) § 2:16, Office Lease—Multistory Office Building.
California Real Estate Forms (Miller & Starr) § 2:17, Office Lease—Mixed Use Building.
California Real Estate Forms (Miller & Starr) § 2:18, Office Lease—Office/Warehouse Building With Four or Fewer Tenants.
California Real Estate Forms (Miller & Starr) § 2:19, Retail Lease—Power Shopping Center.
California Real Estate Forms (Miller & Starr) § 2:20, Retail Lease—Shopping Center With for Profit Parking Garage.
California Real Estate Forms (Miller & Starr) § 2:21, Retail Lease—15,000 RSF to 30,000 RSF (Tenant Oriented).
California Real Estate Forms (Miller & Starr) § 2:22, Retail Lease—Regional Shopping Center.
California Real Estate Forms (Miller & Starr) § 2:23, Retail Lease—Small Strip-Shopping Center.
California Real Estate Forms (Miller & Starr) § 2:24, Retail Lease—Restaurant.
California Real Estate Forms (Miller & Starr) § 2:25, Industrial Lease.
California Real Estate Forms (Miller & Starr) § 2:26, Triple Net Lease—Industrial Build-To-Suit Lease.
California Real Estate Forms (Miller & Starr) § 2:27, Ground Lease.
California Real Estate Forms (Miller & Starr) § 2:28, Triple Net Lease—Stand-Alone Building.
California Real Estate Forms (Miller & Starr) § 2:29, Parking Garage Lease.
California Real Estate Forms (Miller & Starr) § 2:31, Rental Agreement—Self Storage.
California Real Estate Forms (Miller & Starr) § 2:32, Gross Lease—Small Commercial Property.
California Real Estate Forms (Miller & Starr) § 2:34, Sublease—Shared Office Space.
California Real Estate Forms (Miller & Starr) § 2:18.50, Management Office License Agreement.
20 NO. 4 Miller & Starr, California Real Estate Newsalert 13, Landlord and Tenant.
5 Witkin, California Summary 10th Torts § 670, (S 670) Failure to Destroy Consumer Records.

§ 1798.81.5. Security procedures and practices with respect to personal information about California residents

(a) It is the intent of the Legislature to ensure that personal information about California residents is protected. To that end, the purpose of this section is to encourage businesses that own or license personal information about Californians to provide reasonable security for that information. For the purpose of this section, the phrase "owns or licenses" is intended to include, but is not limited to, personal information that a business retains as part of the business' internal customer account or for the purpose of using that information in transactions with the person to whom the information relates.

(b) A business that owns or licenses personal information about a California resident shall implement and maintain reasonable security procedures and practices appropriate to the nature of the information, to protect the personal information from unauthorized access, destruction, use, modification, or disclosure.

(c) A business that discloses personal information about a California resident pursuant to a contract with a nonaffiliated third party shall require by contract that the third party implement and maintain reasonable security procedures and practices appropriate to the nature of the information, to protect the personal information from unauthorized access, destruction, use, modification, or disclosure.

(d) For purposes of this section, the following terms have the following meanings:

(1) "Personal information" means an individual's first name or first initial and his or her last name in combination with any one or more of the following data elements, when either the name or the data elements are not encrypted or redacted:

(A) Social security number.

(B) Driver's license number or California identification card number.

(C) Account number, credit or debit card number, in combination with any required security code, access code, or password that would permit access to an individual's financial account.

(D) Medical information.

(2) "Medical information" means any individually identifiable information, in electronic or physical form, regarding the individual's medical history or medical treatment or diagnosis by a health care professional.

(3) "Personal information" does not include publicly available information that is lawfully made available to the general public from federal, state, or local government records.

(e) The provisions of this section do not apply to any of the following:

(1) A provider of health care, health care service plan, or contractor regulated by the Confidentiality of Medical Information Act (Part 2.6 (commencing with Section 56) of Division 1).

(2) A financial institution as defined in Section 4052 of the Financial Code and subject to the California Financial Information Privacy Act (Division 1.2 (commencing with Section 4050) of the Financial Code.

(3) A covered entity governed by the medical privacy and security rules issued by the federal Department of Health and Human Services, Parts 160 and 164 of Title 45 of the Code of Federal Regulations, established pursuant to the Health Insurance Portability and Availability Act of 1996 (HIPAA).

(4) An entity that obtains information under an agreement pursuant to Article 3 (commencing with Section 1800) of Chapter 1 of Division 2 of the Vehicle Code and is subject to the confidentiality requirements of the Vehicle Code.

(5) A business that is regulated by state or federal law providing greater protection to personal information than that provided by this section in regard to the subjects addressed by this section. Compliance with that state or federal law shall be deemed compliance with this section with regard to those subjects. This paragraph does not relieve a business from a duty to comply with any other requirements of other state and federal law regarding the protection and privacy of personal information. *(Added by Stats.2004, c. 877 (A.B.1950), § 1. Amended by Stats.2005, c. 22 (S.B.1108), § 15.)*

Research References

5 Witkin, California Summary 10th Torts § 666, (S 666) in General.
5 Witkin, California Summary 10th Torts § 669, (S 669) Failure to Protect Security of Personal Information.
7 Witkin, California Summary 10th Constitutional Law § 607, (S 607) Other Privacy Statutes.

§ 1798.82. Person or business who owns or licenses computerized data including person information; breach of security of the system; disclosure requirements

(a) Any person or business that conducts business in California, and that owns or licenses computerized data that includes personal information, shall disclose any breach of the security of the system following discovery or notification of the breach in the security of the data to any resident of California whose unencrypted personal information was, or is reasonably believed to have been, acquired by an unauthorized person. The disclosure shall be made in the most expedient time possible and without unreasonable delay, consistent with the legitimate needs of law enforcement, as provided in subdivision (c), or any measures necessary to determine the scope of the breach and restore the reasonable integrity of the data system.

(b) Any person or business that maintains computerized data that includes personal information that the person or business does not own shall notify the owner or licensee of the information of any breach of the security of the data immediately following discovery, if the personal information was, or is reasonably believed to have been, acquired by an unauthorized person.

(c) The notification required by this section may be delayed if a law enforcement agency determines that the notification will impede a criminal investigation. The notification required by this section shall be made after the law enforcement agency determines that it will not compromise the investigation.

(d) Any person or business that is required to issue a security breach notification pursuant to this section shall meet all of the following requirements:

(1) The security breach notification shall be written in plain language.

(2) The security breach notification shall include, at a minimum, the following information:

(A) The name and contact information of the reporting person or business subject to this section.

(B) A list of the types of personal information that were or are reasonably believed to have been the subject of a breach.

(C) If the information is possible to determine at the time the notice is provided, then any of the following: (i) the date of the breach, (ii) the estimated date of the breach, or (iii) the date range within which the breach occurred. The notification shall also include the date of the notice.

(D) Whether notification was delayed as a result of a law enforcement investigation, if that information is possible to determine at the time the notice is provided.

(E) A general description of the breach incident, if that information is possible to determine at the time the notice is provided.

(F) The toll-free telephone numbers and addresses of the major credit reporting agencies if the breach exposed a social security number or a driver's license or California identification card number.

(3) At the discretion of the person or business, the security breach notification may also include any of the following:

(A) Information about what the person or business has done to protect individuals whose information has been breached.

(B) Advice on steps that the person whose information has been breached may take to protect himself or herself.

(4) In the case of a breach of the security of the system involving personal information defined in paragraph (2) of subdivision (h) for an online account, and no other personal information defined in paragraph (1) of subdivision (h), the person or business may comply with this section by providing the security breach notification in electronic or other form that directs the person whose personal information has been breached promptly to change his or her password and security question or answer, as applicable, or to take other steps appropriate to protect the online account with the person or business and all other online accounts for which the person whose personal information has been breached uses the same user name or email address and password or security question or answer.

(5) In the case of a breach of the security of the system involving personal information defined in paragraph (2) of subdivision (h) for login credentials of an email account furnished by the person or business, the person or business shall not comply with this section by providing the security breach notification to that email address, but may, instead, comply with this section by providing notice by another method described in subdivision (j) or by clear and conspicuous notice delivered to the resident online when the resident is connected to the online account from an Internet Protocol address or online location from which the person or business knows the resident customarily accesses the account.

(e) A covered entity under the federal Health Insurance Portability and Accountability Act of 1996 (42 U.S.C. Sec. 1320d et seq.) will be deemed to have complied with the notice requirements in subdivision (d) if it has complied completely with Section 13402(f) of the federal Health Information Technology for Economic and Clinical Health Act (Public Law 111–5). However, nothing in this subdivision shall be construed to exempt a covered entity from any other provision of this section.

(f) Any person or business that is required to issue a security breach notification pursuant to this section to more than 500 California residents as a result of a single breach of the security system shall electronically submit a single sample copy of that security breach notification, excluding any personally identifiable information, to the Attorney General. A single sample copy of a security breach notification shall not be deemed to be within subdivision (f) of Section 6254 of the Government Code.

(g) For purposes of this section, "breach of the security of the system" means unauthorized acquisition of computerized data that compromises the security, confidentiality, or integrity of personal information maintained by the person or business. Good faith acquisition of personal information by an employee or agent of the person or business for the purposes of the person or business is not a breach of the security of the system, provided that the personal information is not used or subject to further unauthorized disclosure.

(h) For purposes of this section, "personal information" means either of the following:

(1) An individual's first name or first initial and last name in combination with any one or more of the following data elements, when either the name or the data elements are not encrypted:

(A) Social security number.

(B) Driver's license number or California identification card number.

(C) Account number, credit or debit card number, in combination with any required security code, access code, or password that would permit access to an individual's financial account.

(D) Medical information.

(E) Health insurance information.

(2) A user name or email address, in combination with a password or security question and answer that would permit access to an online account.

(i)(1) For purposes of this section, "personal information" does not include publicly available information that is lawfully made available to the general public from federal, state, or local government records.

(2) For purposes of this section, "medical information" means any information regarding an individual's medical history, mental or physical condition, or medical treatment or diagnosis by a health care professional.

(3) For purposes of this section, "health insurance information" means an individual's health insurance policy number or subscriber identification number, any unique identifier used by a health insurer to identify the individual, or any information in an individual's application and claims history, including any appeals records.

(j) For purposes of this section, "notice" may be provided by one of the following methods:

(1) Written notice.

(2) Electronic notice, if the notice provided is consistent with the provisions regarding electronic records and signatures set forth in Section 7001 of Title 15 of the United States Code.

(3) Substitute notice, if the person or business demonstrates that the cost of providing notice would exceed two hundred fifty thousand dollars ($250,000), or that the affected class of subject persons to be notified exceeds 500,000, or the person or business does not have sufficient contact information. Substitute notice shall consist of all of the following:

(A) Email notice when the person or business has an email address for the subject persons.

(B) Conspicuous posting of the notice on the Internet Web site page of the person or business, if the person or business maintains one.

(C) Notification to major statewide media * * *.

(k) Notwithstanding subdivision (j), a person or business that maintains its own notification procedures as part of an information security policy for the treatment of personal information and is otherwise consistent with the timing requirements of this part, shall be deemed to be in compliance with the notification requirements of this section if the person or business notifies subject persons in accordance with its policies in the event of a breach of security of the system. *(Added by Stats.2002, c. 1054 (A.B.700), § 4, operative July 1, 2003. Amended by Stats.2007, c. 699 (A.B.1298), § 6; Stats.2011, c. 197 (S.B.24), § 2; Stats.2013, c. 396 (S.B.46), § 2.)*

Research References

California Practice Guide: Employment Litigation Ch. 5-K, K. Invasion of Privacy.
5 Witkin, California Summary 10th Torts § 666, (S 666) in General.
5 Witkin, California Summary 10th Torts § 671, (S 671) Breach of Security for Computerized Personal Information.
7 Witkin, California Summary 10th Constitutional Law § 607, (S 607) Other Privacy Statutes.

§ 1798.83. Personal information; disclosure to direct marketers

(a) Except as otherwise provided in subdivision (d), if a business has an established business relationship with a customer and has within the immediately preceding calendar year disclosed personal information that corresponds to any of the categories of personal information set forth in paragraph (6) of subdivision (e) to third parties, and if the business knows or reasonably should know that the third parties used the personal information for the third parties' direct marketing purposes, that business shall, after the receipt of a written or electronic mail request, or, if the business chooses to receive requests by toll-free telephone or facsimile numbers, a telephone or facsimile request from the customer, provide all of the following information to the customer free of charge:

(1) In writing or by electronic mail, a list of the categories set forth in paragraph (6) of subdivision (e) that correspond to the personal information disclosed by the business to third parties for the third parties' direct marketing purposes during the immediately preceding calendar year.

(2) In writing or by electronic mail, the names and addresses of all of the third parties that received personal information from the business for the third parties' direct marketing purposes during the preceding calendar year and, if the nature of the third parties' business cannot reasonably be determined from the third parties' name, examples of the products or services marketed, if known to the business, sufficient to give the customer a reasonable indication of the nature of the third parties' business.

(b)(1) A business required to comply with this section shall designate a mailing address, electronic mail address, or, if the business chooses to receive requests by telephone or facsimile, a toll-free telephone or facsimile number, to which customers may deliver requests pursuant to subdivision (a). A business required to comply with this section shall, at its election, do at least one of the following:

(A) Notify all agents and managers who directly supervise employees who regularly have contact with customers of the designated addresses or numbers or the means to obtain those addresses or numbers and instruct those employees that customers who inquire about the business's privacy practices or the business's compliance with this section shall be informed of the designated addresses or numbers or the means to obtain the addresses or numbers.

(B) Add to the home page of its Web site a link either to a page titled "Your Privacy Rights" or add the words "Your Privacy Rights" to the home page's link to the business's privacy policy. If the business elects to add the words "Your Privacy Rights" to the link to the business's privacy policy, the words "Your Privacy Rights" shall be in the same style and size as the link to the business's privacy policy. If the business does not display a link to its privacy policy on the home page of its Web site, or does not have a privacy policy, the words "Your Privacy Rights" shall be written in larger type than the surrounding text, or in contrasting type, font, or color to the surrounding text of the same size, or set off from the surrounding text of the same size by symbols or other marks that call attention to the language. The first page of the link shall describe a customer's rights pursuant to this section and shall provide the designated mailing address, e-mail address, as required, or toll-free telephone number or facsimile number, as appropriate. If the business elects to add the words "Your California Privacy Rights" to the home page's link to the business's privacy policy in a manner that complies with this subdivision, and the first page of the link describes a customer's rights pursuant to this section, and provides the designated mailing address, electronic mailing address, as required, or toll-free telephone or facsimile number, as appropriate, the business need not respond to requests that are not received at one of the designated addresses or numbers.

(C) Make the designated addresses or numbers, or means to obtain the designated addresses or numbers, readily available upon request of a customer at every place of business in California where the business or its agents regularly have contact with customers.

The response to a request pursuant to this section received at one of the designated addresses or numbers shall be provided within 30 days. Requests received by the business at other than one of the designated addresses or numbers shall be provided within a reasonable period, in light of the circumstances related to how the request was received, but not to exceed 150 days from the date received.

(2) A business that is required to comply with this section and Section 6803 of Title 15 of the United States Code may comply with this section by providing the customer the disclosure required by Section 6803 of Title 15 of the United States Code, but only if the disclosure also complies with this section.

(3) A business that is required to comply with this section is not obligated to provide information associated with specific individuals and may provide the information required by this section in standardized format.

(c)(1) A business that is required to comply with this section is not obligated to do so in response to a request from a customer more than once during the course of any calendar year. A business with fewer than 20 full-time or part-time employees is exempt from the requirements of this section.

(2) If a business that is required to comply with this section adopts and discloses to the public, in its privacy policy, a policy of not disclosing personal information of customers to third parties for the third parties' direct marketing purposes unless the customer first affirmatively agrees to that disclosure, or of not disclosing the personal information of customers to third parties for the third parties' direct marketing purposes if the customer has exercised an option that prevents that information from being disclosed to third parties for those purposes, as long as the business maintains and discloses the policies, the business may comply with subdivision (a) by notifying the customer of his or her right to prevent disclosure of personal information, and providing the customer with a cost- free means to exercise that right.

(d) The following are among the disclosures not deemed to be disclosures of personal information by a business for a third party's direct marketing purposes for purposes of this section:

(1) Disclosures between a business and a third party pursuant to contracts or arrangements pertaining to any of the following:

(A) The processing, storage, management, or organization of personal information, or the performance of services on behalf of the business during which personal information is disclosed, if the third party that processes, stores, manages, or organizes the personal information does not use the information for a third party's direct marketing purposes and does not disclose the information to additional third parties for their direct marketing purposes.

(B) Marketing products or services to customers with whom the business has an established business relationship where, as a part of the marketing, the business does not disclose personal information to third parties for the third parties' direct marketing purposes.

(C) Maintaining or servicing accounts, including credit accounts and disclosures pertaining to the denial of applications for credit or the status of applications for credit and processing bills or insurance claims for payment.

(D) Public record information relating to the right, title, or interest in real property or information relating to property characteristics, as defined in Section 408.3 of the Revenue and Taxation Code, obtained from a governmental agency or entity or from a multiple listing service, as defined in Section 1087, and not provided directly by the customer to a business in the course of an established business relationship.

(E) Jointly offering a product or service pursuant to a written agreement with the third party that receives the personal information, provided that all of the following requirements are met:

(i) The product or service offered is a product or service of, and is provided by, at least one of the businesses that is a party to the written agreement.

(ii) The product or service is jointly offered, endorsed, or sponsored by, and clearly and conspicuously identifies for the customer, the businesses that disclose and receive the disclosed personal information.

(iii) The written agreement provides that the third party that receives the personal information is required to maintain the confidentiality of the information and is prohibited from disclosing or using the information other than to carry out the joint offering or servicing of a product or service that is the subject of the written agreement.

(2) Disclosures to or from a consumer reporting agency of a customer's payment history or other information pertaining to transactions or experiences between the business and a customer if that information is to be reported in, or used to generate, a consumer report as defined in subdivision (d) of Section 1681a of Title 15 of the United States Code, and use of that information is limited by the federal Fair Credit Reporting Act (15 U.S.C. Sec. 1681 et seq.).

(3) Disclosures of personal information by a business to a third party financial institution solely for the purpose of the business obtaining payment for a transaction in which the customer paid the business for goods or services with a check, credit card, charge card, or debit card, if the customer seeks the information required by subdivision (a) from the business obtaining payment, whether or not the business obtaining payment knows or reasonably should know that the third party financial institution has used the personal information for its direct marketing purposes.

(4) Disclosures of personal information between a licensed agent and its principal, if the personal information disclosed is necessary to complete, effectuate, administer, or enforce transactions between the principal and the agent, whether or not the licensed agent or principal also uses the personal information for direct marketing purposes, if that personal information is used by each of them solely to market products and services directly to customers with whom both have established business relationships as a result of the principal and agent relationship.

(5) Disclosures of personal information between a financial institution and a business that has a private label credit card, affinity card, retail installment contract, or cobranded card program with the financial institution, if the personal information disclosed is necessary for the financial institution to maintain or service accounts on behalf of the business with which it has a private label credit card, affinity card, retail installment contract, or cobranded card program, or to complete, effectuate, administer, or enforce customer transactions or transactions between the institution and the business, whether or not the institution or the business also uses the personal information for direct marketing purposes, if that personal information is used solely to market products and services directly to customers with whom both the business and the financial institution have established business relationships as a result of the private label credit card, affinity card, retail installment contract, or cobranded card program.

(e) For purposes of this section, the following terms have the following meanings:

(1) "Customer" means an individual who is a resident of California who provides personal information to a business during the creation of, or throughout the duration of, an established business relationship if the business relationship is primarily for personal, family, or household purposes.

(2) "Direct marketing purposes" means the use of personal information to solicit or induce a purchase, rental, lease, or exchange of products, goods, property, or services directly to individuals by means of the mail, telephone, or electronic mail for their personal, family, or household purposes. The sale, rental, exchange, or lease of personal information for consideration to businesses is a direct marketing purpose of the business that sells, rents, exchanges, or obtains consideration for the personal information. "Direct marketing purposes" does not include the use of personal information (A) by bona fide tax exempt charitable or religious organizations to solicit charitable contributions, (B) to raise funds from and communicate with individuals regarding politics and government, (C) by a third party when the third party receives personal information solely as a consequence of having obtained for consideration permanent ownership of accounts that might contain personal information, or (D) by a third party when the third party receives personal information solely as a consequence of a single transaction where, as a part of the transaction, personal information had to be disclosed in order to effectuate the transaction.

(3) "Disclose" means to disclose, release, transfer, disseminate, or otherwise communicate orally, in writing, or by electronic or any other means to any third party.

(4) "Employees who regularly have contact with customers" means employees whose contact with customers is not incidental to their primary employment duties, and whose duties do not predominantly involve ensuring the safety or health of the business's customers. It includes, but is not limited to, employees whose primary employment duties are as cashier, clerk, customer service, sales, or promotion. It does not, by way of example, include employees whose primary employment duties consist of food or beverage preparation or service, maintenance and repair of the business's facilities or equipment, direct involvement in the operation of a motor vehicle, aircraft, watercraft, amusement ride, heavy machinery or similar equipment, security, or participation in a theatrical, literary, musical, artistic, or athletic performance or contest.

(5) "Established business relationship" means a relationship formed by a voluntary, two-way communication between a business and a customer, with or without an exchange of consideration, for the purpose of purchasing, renting, or leasing real or personal property, or any interest therein, or obtaining a product or service from the business, if the relationship is ongoing and has not been expressly terminated by the business or the customer, or if the relationship is not ongoing, but is solely established by the purchase, rental, or lease of real or personal property from a business, or the purchase of a product or service, and no more than 18 months have elapsed from the date of the purchase, rental, or lease.

(6)(A) The categories of personal information required to be disclosed pursuant to paragraph (1) of subdivision (a) are all of the following:

(i) Name and address.

(ii) Electronic mail address.

(iii) Age or date of birth.

(iv) Names of children.

(v) Electronic mail or other addresses of children.

(vi) Number of children.

(vii) The age or gender of children.

(viii) Height.

(ix) Weight.

(x) Race.

(xi) Religion.

(xii) Occupation.

(xiii) Telephone number.

(xiv) Education.

(xv) Political party affiliation.

(xvi) Medical condition.

(xvii) Drugs, therapies, or medical products or equipment used.

(xviii) The kind of product the customer purchased, leased, or rented.

(xix) Real property purchased, leased, or rented.

(xx) The kind of service provided.

(xxi) Social security number.

(xxii) Bank account number.

(xxiii) Credit card number.

(xxiv) Debit card number.

(xxv) Bank or investment account, debit card, or credit card balance.

(xxvi) Payment history.

(xxvii) Information pertaining to the customer's creditworthiness, assets, income, or liabilities.

(B) If a list, description, or grouping of customer names or addresses is derived using any of these categories, and is disclosed to a third party for direct marketing purposes in a manner that permits the third party to identify, determine, or extrapolate any other personal information from which the list was derived, and that personal information when it was disclosed identified, described, or was associated with an individual, the categories set forth in this subdivision that correspond to the personal information used to derive the list, description, or grouping shall be considered personal information for purposes of this section.

(7) "Personal information" as used in this section means any information that when it was disclosed identified, described, or was able to be associated with an individual and includes all of the following:

(A) An individual's name and address.

(B) Electronic mail address.

(C) Age or date of birth.

(D) Names of children.

(E) Electronic mail or other addresses of children.

(F) Number of children.

(G) The age or gender of children.

(H) Height.

(I) Weight.

(J) Race.

(K) Religion.

(L) Occupation.

(M) Telephone number.

(N) Education.

(O) Political party affiliation.

(P) Medical condition.

(Q) Drugs, therapies, or medical products or equipment used.

(R) The kind of product the customer purchased, leased, or rented.

(S) Real property purchased, leased, or rented.

(T) The kind of service provided.

(U) Social security number.

(V) Bank account number.

(W) Credit card number.

(X) Debit card number.

(Y) Bank or investment account, debit card, or credit card balance.

(Z) Payment history.

(AA) Information pertaining to creditworthiness, assets, income, or liabilities.

(8) "Third party" or "third parties" means one or more of the following:

(A) A business that is a separate legal entity from the business that has an established business relationship with a customer.

(B) A business that has access to a database that is shared among businesses, if the business is authorized to use the database for direct marketing purposes, unless the use of the database is exempt from being considered a disclosure for direct marketing purposes pursuant to subdivision (d).

(C) A business not affiliated by a common ownership or common corporate control with the business required to comply with subdivision (a).

(f)(1) Disclosures of personal information for direct marketing purposes between affiliated third parties that share the same brand name are exempt from the requirements of paragraph (1) of subdivision (a) unless the personal information disclosed corresponds to one of the following categories, in which case the customer shall be informed of those categories listed in this subdivision that correspond to the categories of personal information disclosed for direct marketing purposes and the third party recipients of personal information disclosed for direct marketing purposes pursuant to paragraph (2) of subdivision (a):

(A) Number of children.

(B) The age or gender of children.

(C) Electronic mail or other addresses of children.

(D) Height.

(E) Weight.

(F) Race.

(G) Religion.

(H) Telephone number.

(I) Medical condition.

(J) Drugs, therapies, or medical products or equipment used.

(K) Social security number.

(L) Bank account number.

(M) Credit card number.

(N) Debit card number.

(O) Bank or investment account, debit card, or credit card balance.

(2) If a list, description, or grouping of customer names or addresses is derived using any of these categories, and is disclosed to a third party or third parties sharing the same brand name for direct marketing purposes in a manner that permits the third party to identify, determine, or extrapolate the personal information from which the list was derived, and that personal information when it was disclosed identified, described, or was associated with an individual, any other personal information that corresponds to the categories set forth in this subdivision used to derive the list, description, or grouping shall be considered personal information for purposes of this section.

(3) If a business discloses personal information for direct marketing purposes to affiliated third parties that share the same brand name, the business that discloses personal information for direct marketing purposes between affiliated third parties that share the same brand name may comply with the requirements of paragraph (2) of subdivision (a) by providing the overall number of affiliated companies that share the same brand name.

(g) The provisions of this section are severable. If any provision of this section or its application is held invalid, that invalidity shall not affect other provisions or applications that can be given effect without the invalid provision or application.

(h) This section does not apply to a financial institution that is subject to the California Financial Information Privacy Act (Division 1.2 (commencing with Section 4050) of the Financial Code) if the financial institution is in compliance with Sections 4052, 4052.5, 4053, 4053.5, and 4054.6 of the Financial Code, as those sections read when they were chaptered on August 28, 2003, and as subsequently amended by the Legislature or by initiative.

(i) This section shall become operative on January 1, 2005. *(Added by Stats.2003, c. 505 (S.B.27), § 3, operative Jan. 1, 2005. Amended by Stats.2004, c. 183 (A.B.3082), § 34, operative Jan. 1, 2005; Stats.2005, c. 22 (S.B.1108), § 16.)*

Research References

5 Witkin, California Summary 10th Torts § 670, (S 670) Failure to Destroy Consumer Records.
7 Witkin, California Summary 10th Constitutional Law § 607, (S 607) Other Privacy Statutes.

§ 1798.84. Waiver and violations of provisions of this title; civil actions and penalties; disposal of abandoned records containing personal information; attorney's fees and costs

(a) Any waiver of a provision of this title is contrary to public policy and is void and unenforceable.

(b) Any customer injured by a violation of this title may institute a civil action to recover damages.

(c) In addition, for a willful, intentional, or reckless violation of Section 1798.83, a customer may recover a civil penalty not to exceed three thousand dollars ($3,000) per violation; otherwise, the customer may recover a civil penalty of up to five hundred dollars ($500) per violation for a violation of Section 1798.83.

(d) Unless the violation is willful, intentional, or reckless, a business that is alleged to have not provided all the information required by subdivision (a) of Section 1798.83, to have provided inaccurate information, failed to provide any of the information required by subdivision (a) of Section 1798.83, or failed to provide information in the time period required by subdivision (b) of Section 1798.83, may assert as a complete defense in any action in law or equity that it thereafter provided regarding the information that was alleged to be untimely, all the information, or accurate information, to all customers who were provided incomplete or inaccurate information, respectively, within 90 days of the date the business knew that it had failed to provide the information, timely information, all the information, or the accurate information, respectively.

(e) Any business that violates, proposes to violate, or has violated this title may be enjoined.

(f)(1) A cause of action shall not lie against a business for disposing of abandoned records containing personal information by shredding, erasing, or otherwise modifying the personal information in the records to make it unreadable or undecipherable through any means.

(2) The Legislature finds and declares that when records containing personal information are abandoned by a business, they often end up in the possession of a storage company or commercial landlord. It is the intent of the Legislature in paragraph (1) to create a safe harbor for such a record custodian who properly disposes of the records in accordance with paragraph (1).

(g) A prevailing plaintiff in any action commenced under Section 1798.83 shall also be entitled to recover his or her reasonable attorney's fees and costs.

(h) The rights and remedies available under this section are cumulative to each other and to any other rights and remedies available under law. *(Formerly § 1798.82, added by Stats.2000, c. 1039 (A.B.2246), § 1. Renumbered § 1798.84 and amended by Stats.2002, c. 915 (S.B.1386), § 3, operative July 1, 2003; Stats. 2002, c. 1054 (A.B.700), § 3, operative July 1, 2003. Amended by Stats.2003, c. 505 (S.B.27), § 4; Stats.2009, c. 134 (A.B.1094), § 3.)*

Research References

20 NO. 4 Miller & Starr, California Real Estate Newsalert 13, Landlord and Tenant.
5 Witkin, California Summary 10th Torts § 669, (S 669) Failure to Protect Security of Personal Information.
5 Witkin, California Summary 10th Torts § 670, (S 670) Failure to Destroy Consumer Records.
5 Witkin, California Summary 10th Torts § 671, (S 671) Breach of Security for Computerized Personal Information.
7 Witkin, California Summary 10th Constitutional Law § 607, (S 607) Other Privacy Statutes.

Title 1.81.1

CONFIDENTIALITY OF SOCIAL SECURITY NUMBERS

§ 1798.85. Prohibited actions with respect to social security numbers; application and exceptions; operative dates with respect to specified entities

(a) Except as provided in this section, a person or entity may not do any of the following:

(1) Publicly post or publicly display in any manner an individual's social security number. "Publicly post" or "publicly display" means to intentionally communicate or otherwise make available to the general public.

(2) Print an individual's social security number on any card required for the individual to access products or services provided by the person or entity.

(3) Require an individual to transmit his or her social security number over the Internet, unless the connection is secure or the social security number is encrypted.

(4) Require an individual to use his or her social security number to access an Internet Web site, unless a password or unique personal identification number or other authentication device is also required to access the Internet Web site.

(5) Print an individual's social security number on any materials that are mailed to the individual, unless state or federal law requires the social security number to be on the document to be mailed. Notwithstanding this paragraph, social security numbers may be included in applications and forms sent by mail,

including documents sent as part of an application or enrollment process, or to establish, amend or terminate an account, contract or policy, or to confirm the accuracy of the social security number. A social security number that is permitted to be mailed under this section may not be printed, in whole or in part, on a postcard or other mailer not requiring an envelope, or visible on the envelope or without the envelope having been opened.

(b) This section does not prevent the collection, use, or release of a social security number as required by state or federal law or the use of a social security number for internal verification or administrative purposes.

(c) This section does not prevent an adult state correctional facility, an adult city jail, or an adult county jail from releasing an inmate's social security number, with the inmate's consent and upon request by the county veterans service officer or the United States Department of Veterans Affairs, for the purposes of determining the inmate's status as a military veteran and his or her eligibility for federal, state, or local veterans' benefits or services.

(d) This section does not apply to documents that are recorded or required to be open to the public pursuant to Chapter 3.5 (commencing with Section 6250), Chapter 14 (commencing with Section 7150) or Chapter 14.5 (commencing with Section 7220) of Division 7 of Title 1 of, Article 9 (commencing with Section 11120) of Chapter 1 of Part 1 of Division 3 of Title 2 of, or Chapter 9 (commencing with Section 54950) of Part 1 of Division 2 of Title 5 of, the Government Code. This section does not apply to records that are required by statute, case law, or California Rule of Court, to be made available to the public by entities provided for in Article VI of the California Constitution.

(e)(1) In the case of a health care service plan, a provider of health care, an insurer or a pharmacy benefits manager, a contractor as defined in Section 56.05, or the provision by any person or entity of administrative or other services relative to health care or insurance products or services, including third-party administration or administrative services only, this section shall become operative in the following manner:

(A) On or before January 1, 2003, the entities listed in paragraph (1) shall comply with paragraphs (1), (3), (4), and (5) of subdivision (a) as these requirements pertain to individual policyholders or individual contractholders.

(B) On or before January 1, 2004, the entities listed in paragraph (1) shall comply with paragraphs (1) to (5), inclusive, of subdivision (a) as these requirements pertain to new individual policyholders or new individual contractholders and new groups, including new groups administered or issued on or after January 1, 2004.

(C) On or before July 1, 2004, the entities listed in paragraph (1) shall comply with paragraphs (1) to (5), inclusive, of subdivision (a) for all individual policyholders and individual contractholders, for all groups, and for all enrollees of the Healthy Families and Medi–Cal programs, except that for individual policyholders, individual contractholders and groups in existence prior to January 1, 2004, the entities listed in paragraph (1) shall comply upon the renewal date of the policy, contract, or group on or after July 1, 2004, but no later than July 1, 2005.

(2) A health care service plan, a provider of health care, an insurer or a pharmacy benefits manager, a contractor, or another person or entity as described in paragraph (1) shall make reasonable efforts to cooperate, through systems testing and other means, to ensure that the requirements of this article are implemented on or before the dates specified in this section.

(3) Notwithstanding paragraph (2), the Director of the Department of Managed Health Care, pursuant to the authority granted under Section 1346 of the Health and Safety Code, or the Insurance Commissioner, pursuant to the authority granted under Section 12921 of the Insurance Code, and upon a determination of good cause, may grant extensions not to exceed six months for compliance by health care service plans and insurers with the requirements of this section when requested by the health care service plan or insurer. Any extension granted shall apply to the health care service plan or insurer's affected providers, pharmacy benefits manager, and contractors.

(f) If a federal law takes effect requiring the United States Department of Health and Human Services to establish a national unique patient health identifier program, a provider of health care, a health care service plan, a licensed health care professional, or a contractor, as those terms are defined in Section 56.05, that complies with the federal law shall be deemed in compliance with this section.

(g) A person or entity may not encode or embed a social security number in or on a card or document, including, but not limited to, using a barcode, chip, magnetic strip, or other technology, in place of removing the social security number, as required by this section.

(h) This section shall become operative, with respect to the University of California, in the following manner:

(1) On or before January 1, 2004, the University of California shall comply with paragraphs (1), (2), and (3) of subdivision (a).

(2) On or before January 1, 2005, the University of California shall comply with paragraphs (4) and (5) of subdivision (a).

(i) This section shall become operative with respect to the Franchise Tax Board on January 1, 2007.

(j) This section shall become operative with respect to the California community college districts on January 1, 2007.

(k) This section shall become operative with respect to the California State University system on July 1, 2005.

(l) This section shall become operative, with respect to the California Student Aid Commission and its auxiliary organization, in the following manner:

(1) On or before January 1, 2004, the commission and its auxiliary organization shall comply with paragraphs (1), (2), and (3) of subdivision (a).

(2) On or before January 1, 2005, the commission and its auxiliary organization shall comply with paragraphs (4) and (5) of subdivision (a). *(Added by Stats.2001, c. 720 (S.B.168), § 7. Amended by Stats.2002, c. 664 (A.B.3034), § 42; Stats.2002, c. 786 (S.B.1730), § 3; Stats.2003, c. 532 (A.B.763), § 1; Stats. 2003, c. 907 (S.B.25), § 5.5; Stats.2004, c. 183 (A.B.3082), § 35; Stats.2004, c. 282 (A.B.3016), § 1, operative July 1, 2006; Stats. 2013, c. 103 (A.B.555), § 1.)*

Operative Effect

For operative effect of this section, see its terms.

Research References

California Practice Guide: Employment Litigation Ch. 5-K, K. Invasion of Privacy.

7 Witkin, California Summary 10th Constitutional Law § 607, (S 607) Other Privacy Statutes.

§ 1798.86. Public policy; waiver of rights

Any waiver of the provisions of this title is contrary to public policy, and is void and unenforceable. *(Added by Stats.2002, c. 815 (A.B.2331), § 16.)*

Research References

California Practice Guide: Employment Litigation Ch. 5-K, K. Invasion of Privacy.

§ 1798.89. Recording or filing of documents; social security numbers; due diligence in using truncated social security numbers

(a) Unless otherwise required to do so by state or federal law, no person, entity, or governmental agency shall present for recording or filing with a county recorder a document that is required by any provision of law to be open to the public if that record displays more than the last four digits of a social security number. Unless otherwise authorized by state or federal law, a document containing more than the last four digits of a social security number is not entitled for recording.

(b) A recorder shall be deemed to be in compliance with the requirements of this section if he or she uses due diligence to truncate social security numbers in documents recorded, as provided in Article 3.5 (commencing with Section 27300) of Chapter 6 of Part 3 of Division 2 of Title 3 of the Government Code.

(c) This section shall not apply to documents created prior to January 1, 2010. *(Added by Stats.2009, c. 552 (S.B.40), § 2.)*

Research References

7 Witkin, California Summary 10th Constitutional Law § 607, (S 607) Other Privacy Statutes.

Title 1.81.15

READER PRIVACY ACT

Section

1798.90.   Short title; definitions; restrictions on disclosure of personal information of book service users; orders compelling disclosure; preservation of records and evidence; admissibility of evidence; penalties; defense; reports; actions by operators of certain commercial Web sites and online services.

1798.90.05.   Authority to obtain search warrants for personal information of book service users; provider compliance with proper search warrants.

§ 1798.90. Short title; definitions; restrictions on disclosure of personal information of book service users; orders compelling disclosure; preservation of records and evidence; admissibility of evidence; penalties; defense; reports; actions by operators of certain commercial Web sites and online services

(a) This title shall be known and may be cited as the Reader Privacy Act.

(b) For purposes of this section:

(1) "Book" means paginated or similarly organized content in printed, audio, electronic, or other format, including fiction, nonfiction, academic, or other works of the type normally published in a volume or finite number of volumes, excluding serial publications such as a magazine or newspaper.

(2) "Book service" means a service that, as its primary purpose, provides the rental, purchase, borrowing, browsing, or viewing of books. "Book service" does not include a store that sells a variety of consumer products when the book service sales do not exceed 2 percent of the store's total annual gross sales of consumer products sold in the United States.

(3) "Government entity" means any state or local agency, including, but not limited to, a law enforcement entity or any other investigative entity, agency, department, division, bureau, board, or commission, or any individual acting or purporting to act for or on behalf of a state or local agency.

(4) "Law enforcement entity" means a district attorney, a district attorney's office, a municipal police department, a sheriff's department, a county probation department, a county social services agency, the Department of Justice, the Department of Corrections and Rehabilitation, the Department of Corrections and Rehabilitation Division of Juvenile Facilities, the Department of the California Highway Patrol, the police department of a campus of a community college, the University of California, or the California State University, or any other department or agency of the state authorized to investigate or prosecute the commission of a crime.

(5) "Personal information" means all of the following:

(A) Any information that identifies, relates to, describes, or is associated with a particular user, including, but not limited to, the information specifically listed in Section 1798.80.

(B) A unique identifier or Internet Protocol address, when that identifier or address is used to identify, relate to, describe, or be associated with a particular user or book, in whole or in partial form.

(C) Any information that relates to, or is capable of being associated with, a particular user's access to or use of a book service or a book, in whole or in partial form.

(6) "Provider" means any commercial entity offering a book service to the public.

(7) "User" means any person or entity that uses a book service.

(c) A provider shall not knowingly disclose to any government entity, or be compelled to disclose to any person, private entity, or government entity, any personal information of a user, except under any of the following circumstances:

(1) A provider shall disclose personal information of a user to a law enforcement entity only pursuant to a court order issued by a duly authorized court with jurisdiction over an offense that is under investigation and only if all of the following conditions are met:

(A) The court issuing the order finds that probable cause exists to believe the personal information requested is relevant evidence to the investigation of an offense and any of the grounds in Section 1524 of the Penal Code is satisfied.

(B) The court issuing the order finds that the law enforcement entity seeking disclosure has a compelling interest in obtaining the personal information sought.

(C) The court issuing the order finds that the personal information sought cannot be obtained by the law enforcement entity seeking disclosure through less intrusive means.

(D) Prior to issuance of the court order, the law enforcement entity seeking disclosure provides, in a timely manner, the provider with reasonable notice of the proceeding to allow the provider the opportunity to appear and contest issuance of the order.

(E) The law enforcement entity seeking disclosure has informed the provider that it has given notice of the court order to the user contemporaneously with the execution of the order, unless there is a judicial determination of a strong showing of necessity to delay that notification for a reasonable period of time, not to exceed 90 days.

(2)(A) A provider shall disclose personal information of a user to any of the following only if all of the conditions listed in subparagraph (B) are satisfied:

(i) A government entity, other than a law enforcement entity, pursuant to a court order issued by a court having jurisdiction over an offense under investigation by that government entity.

(ii) A government entity, other than a law enforcement entity, or a person or private entity pursuant to a court order in a pending action brought by the government entity or by the person or private entity.

(B) A provider shall disclose personal information of a user pursuant to subparagraph (A) only if all of the following conditions are satisfied:

(i) The court issuing the order finds that the person or entity seeking disclosure has a compelling interest in obtaining the personal information sought.

(ii) The court issuing the order finds that the personal information sought cannot be obtained by the person or entity seeking disclosure through less intrusive means.

(iii) Prior to issuance of the court order, the person or entity seeking disclosure provides, in a timely manner, the provider with reasonable notice of the proceeding to allow the provider the opportunity to appear and contest the issuance of the court order.

(iv) The provider refrains from disclosing any personal information pursuant to the court order until it provides, in a timely manner, notice to the user about the issuance of the order and the ability to appear and quash the order, and the user has been given a minimum of 35 days prior to disclosure of the information within which to appear and quash the order.

(3) A provider shall disclose the personal information of a user to any person, private entity, or government entity if the user has given his or her informed, affirmative consent to the specific disclosure for a particular purpose.

(4) A provider may disclose personal information of a user to a government entity, if the government entity asserts, and the provider in good faith believes, that there is an imminent danger of death or serious physical injury requiring the immediate disclosure of the requested personal information and there is insufficient time to obtain a court order. The government entity seeking the disclosure shall provide the provider with a written statement setting forth the facts giving rise to the emergency upon request or no later than 48 hours after seeking disclosure.

(5) A provider may disclose personal information of a user to a government entity if the provider in good faith believes that the personal information is evidence directly related and relevant to a crime against the provider or that user.

(d)(1) Any court issuing a court order requiring the disclosure of personal information of a user shall impose appropriate safeguards against the unauthorized disclosure of personal information by the provider and by the person, private entity, or government entity seeking disclosure pursuant to the order.

(2) The court may, in its discretion, quash or modify a court order requiring the disclosure of the user's personal information upon a motion made by the user, provider, person, or entity seeking disclosure.

(e) A provider, upon the request of a law enforcement entity, shall take all necessary steps to preserve records and other evidence in its possession of a user's personal information related to the use of a book or part of a book, pending the issuance of a court order or a warrant pursuant to this section or Section 1798.90.05. The provider shall retain the records and evidence for a period of 90 days from the date of the request by the law enforcement entity, which shall be extended for an additional 90–day period upon a renewed request by the law enforcement entity.

(f) Except in an action for a violation of this section, no evidence obtained in violation of this section shall be admissible in any civil or administrative proceeding.

(g)(1) Violations of this section shall be subject to the following penalties:

(A) Any provider that knowingly provides personal information about a user to a government entity in violation of this section shall be subject to a civil penalty not to exceed five hundred dollars ($500) for each violation, which shall be paid to the user in a civil action brought by the user.

(B) Any provider that knowingly provides personal information about a user to a government entity in violation of this section shall, in addition to the penalty prescribed by subparagraph (A), be subject to a civil penalty not to exceed five hundred dollars ($500) for each violation, which may be assessed and recovered in a civil action brought by the Attorney General, by any district attorney or city attorney, or by a city prosecutor in any city having a full-time city prosecutor, in any court of competent jurisdiction.

(2) If an action is brought by the Attorney General, one-half of the penalty collected shall be paid to the treasurer of the county in which the judgment was entered, and one-half to the General Fund. If the action is brought by a district attorney, the penalty collected shall be paid to the treasurer of the county in which the judgment was entered. If the action is brought by a city attorney or city prosecutor, one-half of the penalty shall be paid to the treasurer of the city in which the judgment was entered, and one-half to the treasurer of the county in which the judgment was entered.

(3) The penalties provided by this section are not the exclusive remedy and do not affect any other relief or remedy provided by law.

(4) A civil action brought pursuant to this section shall be commenced within two years after the date upon which the claimant first discovered the violation.

(h) An objectively reasonable reliance by the provider on a warrant or court order for the disclosure of personal information of a user, or on any of the enumerated exceptions to the confidentiality of a user's personal information set forth in this section, is a complete defense to any civil action for the violation of this section.

(i)(1) Unless disclosure of information pertaining to a particular request or set of requests is specifically prohibited by law, a provider shall prepare a report including all of the following information, to the extent it can be reasonably determined:

(A) The number of federal and state warrants, federal and state grand jury subpoenas, federal and state civil and administrative subpoenas, federal and state civil and criminal court orders, and requests for information made with the informed consent of the user as described in paragraph (3) of subdivision (c), seeking disclosure of any personal information of a user related to the access or use of a book service or book, received by the provider from January 1 to December 31, inclusive, of the previous year.

(B) The number of disclosures made by the provider pursuant to paragraphs (4) and (5) of subdivision (c) from January 1 to December 31, inclusive, of the previous year.

(C) For each category of demand or disclosure, the provider shall include all of the following information:

(i) The number of times notice of a court order in a criminal, civil, or administrative action has been provided by the provider and the date the notice was provided.

(ii) The number of times personal information has been disclosed by the provider.

(iii) The number of times no personal information has been disclosed by the provider.

(iv) The number of times the provider contests the demand.

(v) The number of times the user contests the demand.

(vi) The number of users whose personal information was disclosed by the provider.

(vii) The type of personal information that was disclosed and the number of times that type of personal information was disclosed.

(2) Notwithstanding paragraph (1), a provider is not required to prepare a report pursuant to this subdivision unless it has disclosed personal information related to the access or use of a book service or book of more than 30 total users consisting of users located in this state or users whose location is unknown or of both types of users.

(3) The reporting requirements of this subdivision shall not apply to information disclosed to a government entity that is made by a provider serving a postsecondary educational institution when the provider is required to disclose the information in order to be reimbursed for the sale or rental of a book that was purchased or rented by a student using book vouchers or other financial aid subsidies for books.

(j) Reports prepared pursuant to subdivision (i) shall be made publicly available in an online, searchable format on or before March 1 of each year. If the provider does not have an Internet Web site, the provider shall post the reports prominently on its premises or send the reports to the Office of Privacy Protection on or before March 1 of each year.

(k) On or before March 1 of each year, a provider subject to Section 22575 of the Business and Professions Code shall complete one of the following actions:

(1) Create a prominent hyperlink to its latest report prepared pursuant to subdivision (i) in the disclosure section of its privacy policy applicable to its book service.

(2) Post the report prepared pursuant to subdivision (i) in the section of its Internet Web site explaining the way in which user information and privacy issues related to its book service are addressed.

(3) State on its Internet Web site in one of the areas described in paragraphs (1) and (2) that no report prepared pursuant to subdivision (i) is available because the provider is exempt from the reporting requirement pursuant to paragraph (2) of subdivision (i).

(*l*) Nothing in this section shall otherwise affect the rights of any person under the California Constitution or any other law or be construed as conflicting with the federal Privacy Protection Act of 1980 (42 U.S.C. 2000aa et seq.). *(Added by Stats.2011, c. 424 (S.B.602), § 1.)*

Research References

7 Witkin, California Summary 10th Constitutional Law § 607, (S 607) Other Privacy Statutes.

§ 1798.90.05. Authority to obtain search warrants for personal information of book service users; provider compliance with proper search warrants

Section 1798.90 does not make it unlawful for a law enforcement entity subject to Section 2000aa of Title 42 of the United States Code to obtain a search warrant for the personal information of a user pursuant to otherwise applicable law in connection with the investigation or prosecution of a criminal offense when probable cause exists to believe that the person possessing the personal information has committed, or is committing, a criminal offense involving the production, possession, receipt, mailing, sale, distribution, shipment, or transportation of child pornography, the sexual exploitation of children, or the sale or purchase of children prohibited by Sections 2251, 2251A, 2252, and 2252A of Title 18 of the United States Code. Nothing in Section 1798.90 shall prevent a provider from complying with a proper search warrant issued by a duly authorized court in connection with the investigation or prosecution of any of those offenses. *(Added by Stats.2011, c. 424 (S.B.602), § 1.)*

Title 1.81.2

CONFIDENTIALITY OF DRIVER'S LICENSE INFORMATION

Section

1798.90.1. Information encoded on driver's license; authorization for use by businesses in electronic devices; purpose; prohibited uses; violations; penalty.

§ 1798.90.1. Information encoded on driver's license; authorization for use by businesses in electronic devices; purpose; prohibited uses; violations; penalty

(a)(1) Any business may swipe a driver's license or identification card issued by the Department of Motor Vehicles in any electronic device for the following purposes:

(A) To verify age or the authenticity of the driver's license or identification card.

(B) To comply with a legal requirement to record, retain, or transmit that information.

(C) To transmit information to a check service company for the purpose of approving negotiable instruments, electronic funds transfers, or similar methods of payments, provided that only the name and identification number from the license or the card may be used or retained by the check service company.

(D) To collect or disclose personal information that is required for reporting, investigating, or preventing fraud, abuse, or material misrepresentation.

(2) A business may not retain or use any of the information obtained by that electronic means for any purpose other than as provided herein.

(b) As used in this section, "business" means a proprietorship, partnership, corporation, or any other form of commercial enterprise.

(c) A violation of this section constitutes a misdemeanor punishable by imprisonment in a county jail for no more than one year, or by a fine of no more than ten thousand dollars ($10,000), or by both. *(Added by Stats.2003, c. 533 (S.B.602), § 4.)*

Title 1.81.25

CONSUMER PRIVACY PROTECTION

Section

1798.91. Definitions; oral and written requests by businesses for medical information; requirements; health care providers or contractors; insurance institutions, agents, or support organizations; telephone corporations.

§ 1798.91. Definitions; oral and written requests by businesses for medical information; requirements; health care providers or contractors; insurance institutions, agents, or support organizations; telephone corporations

(a) For purposes of this title, the following definitions shall apply:

(1) "Direct marketing purposes" means the use of personal information for marketing or advertising products, goods, or services directly to individuals. "Direct marketing purposes" does not include the use of personal information (A) by bona fide tax exempt charitable or religious organizations to solicit charitable contributions or (B) to raise funds from and communicate with individuals regarding politics and government.

(2) "Medical information" means any individually identifiable information, in electronic or physical form, regarding the individual's medical history, or medical treatment or diagnosis by a health care professional. "Individually identifiable" means that the medical information includes or contains any element of personal identifying information sufficient to allow identification of the individual, such as the individual's name, address, electronic mail address, telephone number, or social security number, or other information that, alone or in combination with other publicly available information, reveals the individual's identity. For purposes of this section, "medical information" does not mean a subscription to, purchase of, or request for a periodical, book, pamphlet, video, audio, or other multimedia product or nonprofit association information.

(3) "Clear and conspicuous" means in larger type than the surrounding text, or in contrasting type, font, or color to the surrounding text of the same size, or set off from the surrounding text of the same size by symbols or other marks that call attention to the language.

(4) For purposes of this section, the collection of medical information online constitutes "in writing." For purposes of this section, "written consent" includes consent obtained online.

(b) A business may not orally request medical information directly from an individual regardless of whether the information pertains to the individual or not, and use, share, or otherwise disclose that information for direct marketing purposes, without doing both of the following prior to obtaining that information:

(1) Orally disclosing to the individual in the same conversation during which the business seeks to obtain the information, that it is obtaining the information to market or advertise products, goods, or services to the individual.

(2) Obtaining the consent of either the individual to whom the information pertains or a person legally authorized to consent for the individual, to permit his or her medical information to be used or shared to market or advertise products, goods, or services to the individual, and making and maintaining for two years after the date of the conversation, an audio recording of the entire conversation.

(c) A business may not request in writing medical information directly from an individual regardless of whether the information pertains to the individual or not, and use, share, or otherwise disclose that information for direct marketing purposes, without doing both of the following prior to obtaining that information:

(1) Disclosing in a clear and conspicuous manner that it is obtaining the information to market or advertise products, goods, or services to the individual.

(2) Obtaining the written consent of either the individual to whom the information pertains or a person legally authorized to consent for the individual, to permit his or her medical information to be used or shared to market or advertise products, goods, or services to the individual.

(d) This section does not apply to a provider of health care, health care service plan, or contractor, as defined in Section 56.05.

(e) This section shall not apply to an insurance institution, agent, or support organization, as defined in Section 791.02 of the Insurance Code, when engaged in an insurance transaction, as defined in * * * Section 791.02 of the Insurance Code, pursuant to all the requirements of Article 6.6 (commencing with Section 791) of Chapter 1 of Part 2 of Division 1 of the Insurance Code, and the regulations promulgated thereunder.

(f) This section does not apply to a telephone corporation, as defined in Section 234 of the Public Utilities Code, when that corporation is engaged in providing telephone services and products pursuant to Sections 2881, 2881. 1, and 2881.2 of the Public Utilities Code, if the corporation does not share or disclose medical information obtained as a consequence of complying with those sections of the Public Utilities Code, to third parties for direct marketing purposes. *(Added by Stats. 2004, c. 861 (S.B.1633), § 1. Amended by Stats.2013, c. 444 (S.B.138), § 7.)*

Research References

5 Witkin, California Summary 10th Torts § 666, (S 666) in General.
7 Witkin, California Summary 10th Constitutional Law § 580, (S 580) in General.

Title 1.81.3

IDENTITY THEFT

§ 1798.92. Definitions

For the purposes of this title:

(a) "Claimant" means a person who has or purports to have a claim for money or an interest in property in connection with a transaction procured through identity theft.

(b) "Identity theft" means the unauthorized use of another person's personal identifying information to obtain credit, goods, services, money, or property.

(c) "Personal identifying information" means a person's name, address, telephone number, driver's license number, social security number, place of employment, employee identification number, mother's maiden name, demand deposit account number, savings account number, or credit card number.

(d) "Victim of identity theft" means a person who had his or her personal identifying information used without authorization by another to obtain credit, goods, services, money, or property, and did not use or possess the credit, goods, services, money, or property obtained by the identity theft, and filed a police report in this regard pursuant to Section 530.5 of the Penal Code. *(Added by Stats.2001, c. 354 (A.B.655), § 21.)*

Research References

3 Witkin Cal. Proc. 5th Actions § 214, Steps by Defendant.

5 Witkin, California Summary 10th Torts § 668, (S 668) Identity Theft.

§ 1798.93.   Actions and judgment for identity theft

(a) A person may bring an action against a claimant to establish that the person is a victim of identity theft in connection with the claimant's claim against that person. If the claimant has brought an action to recover on its claim against the person, the person may file a cross-complaint to establish that the person is a victim of identity theft in connection with the claimant's claim.

(b) A person shall establish that he or she is a victim of identity theft by a preponderance of the evidence.

(c) A person who proves that he or she is a victim of identity theft, as defined in Section 530.5 of the Penal Code, as to a particular claim, shall be entitled to a judgment providing all of the following, as appropriate:

(1) A declaration that he or she is not obligated to the claimant on that claim.

(2) A declaration that any security interest or other interest the claimant had purportedly obtained in the victim's property in connection with that claim is void and unenforceable.

(3) An injunction restraining the claimant from collecting or attempting to collect from the victim on that claim, from enforcing or attempting to enforce any security interest or other interest in the victim's property in connection with that claim, or from enforcing or executing on any judgment against the victim on that claim.

(4) If the victim has filed a cross-complaint against the claimant, the dismissal of any cause of action in the complaint filed by the claimant based on a claim which arose as a result of the identity theft.

(5) Actual damages, attorney's fees, and costs, and any equitable relief that the court deems appropriate. In order to recover actual damages or attorney's fees in an action or cross-complaint filed by a person alleging that he or she is a victim of identity theft, the person shall show that he or she provided written notice to the claimant that a situation of identity theft might exist, including, upon written request of the claimant, a valid copy of the police report or the Department of Motor Vehicles investigative report promptly filed pursuant to Section 530.5 of the Penal Code at least 30 days prior to his or her filing of the action, or within his or her cross-complaint pursuant to this section.

(6) A civil penalty, in addition to any other damages, of up to thirty thousand dollars ($30,000) if the victim establishes by clear and convincing evidence all of the following:

(A) That at least 30 days prior to filing an action or within the cross-complaint pursuant to this section, he or she provided written notice to the claimant at the address designated by the claimant for complaints related to credit reporting issues that a situation of identity theft might exist and explaining the basis for that belief.

(B) That the claimant failed to diligently investigate the victim's notification of a possible identity theft.

(C) That the claimant continued to pursue its claim against the victim after the claimant was presented with facts that were later held to entitle the victim to a judgment pursuant to this section. *(Added by Stats.2001, c. 354 (A.B.655), § 21.)*

Research References

8 Witkin Cal. Proc. 5th Enforcement of Judgment § 10, (S 10) Collection Where Identity Theft is Claimed.

6 Witkin Cal. Proc. 5th Provisional Remedies § 291, (S 291) Special Statutes.

6 Witkin Cal. Proc. 5th Provisional Remedies § 311, Action or Cross-Complaint by Victim of Identity Theft.

5 Witkin, California Summary 10th Torts § 668, (S 668) Identity Theft.

§ 1798.94.   Actions or cross-complaints joining other claimants as defendants in same action or cross-complaint; compliance with Code of Civil Procedure

An action or cross-complaint brought under this title that joins other claimants as defendants in the same action or cross-complaint shall be deemed to comply with Section 379 of the Code of Civil Procedure. *(Added by Stats.2001, c. 354 (A.B.655), § 21.)*

§ 1798.95.   Jurisdiction over action or cross-complaint filed pursuant to this title; joinder

A court shall have continuing jurisdiction over an action or cross-complaint filed pursuant to this title in order to provide for the joinder of related causes of action based on the theft of the same person's identity and the joinder of further defendants based upon the theft of the same person's identity, regardless of whether a final judgment has been entered as to any defendant. The court's continuing jurisdiction shall terminate 10 years after filing of the original action unless the court, prior to that date, finds good cause to extend jurisdiction over the matter. *(Added by Stats.2001, c. 354 (A.B.655), § 21.)*

Research References

5 Witkin, California Summary 10th Torts § 668, (S 668) Identity Theft.

§ 1798.96.   Statute of limitations

Any action brought pursuant to this title or any joinder of a defendant pursuant to Section 1798.82 may be brought within four years of the date the person who alleges that he or she is a victim of identity theft knew or, in the exercise of reasonable diligence, should have known of the existence of facts which would give rise to the bringing of the action or joinder of the defendant. *(Added by Stats.2001, c. 354 (A.B.655), § 21.)*

Research References

5 Witkin, California Summary 10th Torts § 668, (S 668) Identity Theft.

§ 1798.97.   Limits on application of identity theft actions; cumulative nature of title

(a) This title does not apply to a transaction subject to Section 1747.10.

(b) Nothing is this title shall be construed to affect a claimant's rights and remedies against a person who perpetrates identity theft or against any person who used or possessed the credit, goods, services, or property obtained by identity theft.

(c) This title is cumulative to the rights and remedies provided under other laws. *(Added by Stats.2001, c. 354 (A.B.655), § 21.)*

Title 1.81.4

PRIVACY OF CUSTOMER ELECTRICAL OR NATURAL GAS USAGE DATA

§ 1798.98. Definitions; prohibition on sharing, disclosing, or making customer's data accessible to third parties without consent; required data security procedures and practices; incentives or discounts for accessing data without prior consent prohibited; disposal of customer data; exemptions

(a) For the purposes of this title, the following definitions shall apply:

(1) "Business" means a sole proprietorship, partnership, corporation, association, or other group, however organized and whether or not organized to operate at a profit, including a financial institution organized, chartered, or holding a license or authorization certificate under the law of this state, any other state, the United States, or of any other country, or the parent or the subsidiary of a financial institution.

(2) "Customer" means a customer of an electrical or gas corporation or a local publicly owned electric utility that permits a business to have access to data in association with purchasing or leasing a product or obtaining a service from the business.

(3) "Data" means a customer's electrical or natural gas usage that is made available to the business as part of an advanced metering infrastructure provided by an electrical corporation, a gas corporation, or a local publicly owned electric utility, and includes the name, account number, or physical address of the customer.

(4) "Electrical corporation" has the same meaning as in Section 218 of the Public Utilities Code.

(5) "Gas corporation" has the same meaning as in Section 222 of the Public Utilities Code.

(6) "Local publicly owned electric utility" has the same meaning as in Section 224.3 of the Public Utilities Code.

(b) Unless otherwise required or authorized by federal or state law, a business shall not share, disclose, or otherwise make accessible to any third party a customer's data without obtaining the express consent of the customer and conspicuously disclosing to whom the disclosure will be made and how the data will be used.

(c) A business that discloses data, with the express consent of the customer, pursuant to a contract with a nonaffiliated third party, shall require by contract that the third party implement and maintain reasonable security procedures and practices appropriate to the nature of the information, to protect the data from unauthorized access, destruction, use, modification, or disclosure.

(d) A business shall implement and maintain reasonable security procedures and practices appropriate to the nature of the information to protect the data from unauthorized access, destruction, use, modification, or disclosure.

(e) A business shall not provide an incentive or discount to the customer for accessing the data without the prior consent of the customer.

(f) A business shall take all reasonable steps to dispose, or arrange for the disposal, of customer data within its custody or control when the records are no longer to be retained by the business by (1) shredding, (2) erasing, or (3) otherwise modifying the data in those records to make it unreadable or undecipherable through any means.

(g) The provisions of this section do not apply to an electrical corporation, a gas corporation, or a local publicly owned electric utility or a business that secures the data as a result of a contract with an electrical or gas corporation or a local publicly owned electric utility under the provisions of subdivision (e) of Section 8380 or subdivision (e) of 8381 of the Public Utilities Code. *(Added by Stats.2013, c. 597 (A.B.1274), § 1.)*

§ 1798.99. Civil actions; limitation on damages; other rights, remedies, or penalties; enforcement authority of Attorney General

(a) A customer harmed by the release or unauthorized use of his or her customer data, in violation of Section 1798.98, may bring a civil action to recover actual damages in an amount not to exceed five hundred dollars ($500) for each willful violation.

(b) The rights, remedies, and penalties established by this title are in addition to the rights, remedies, or penalties established under any other law.

(c) Nothing in this title shall abrogate any authority of the Attorney General to enforce existing law. *(Added by Stats.2013, c. 597 (A.B.1274), § 1.)*

Title 1.82

BUSINESS RECORDS

CHAPTER 1. DEFINITIONS

Section
1799.   Bookkeeping services; business entity; individual; person; record.

§ 1799. Bookkeeping services; business entity; individual; person; record

As used in this title:

(a) The term "bookkeeping services" means keeping books, making trial balances, preparing statements, making audits, or preparing reports, all as a part of bookkeeping operations, provided that such trial balances, statements, or reports are not issued over the name of such person as having been prepared or examined by a certified public accountant or public accountant.

(b) The term "business entity" means a sole proprietorship, partnership, corporation, association or other group, however organized and whether or not organized to operate at a profit, but does not mean a financial institution organized, chartered, or holding a license or authorization certificate under a law of this state or the United States to make loans or extend credit and subject to supervision by an official or agency of this state or the United States, nor the parent of any such financial institution, nor any subsidiary of any such financial institution or parent.

(c) The term "individual" means a natural person.

(d) The term "person" means any natural person, corporation, partnership, limited liability company, firm, association, or governmental entity.

(e) The term "record" means any item, collection, or grouping of information about an individual or business entity. *(Added by Stats.1977, c. 221, p. 1017, § 1. Amended by Stats.1994, c. 1010 (S.B.2053), § 41.)*

Research References

7 Witkin, California Summary 10th Constitutional Law § 607, (S 607) Other Privacy Statutes.

CHAPTER 2. DISCLOSURES

Section
1799.1.   Prohibition against disclosure except upon written consent; application of section.

Section
1799.1a.   Income tax returns.
1799.1b.   Credit card holders and telephone accountholders; change of address requests; requirements and restrictions for credit card issuers and business entities providing telephone accounts; change of address notifications.

§ 1799.1. Prohibition against disclosure except upon written consent; application of section

(a) No business entity which performs bookkeeping services shall disclose in whole or in part the contents of any record, including the disclosure of information in the record in any composite of information, which is prepared or maintained by such business entity to any person, other than the individual or business entity which is the subject of the record, without the express written consent of such individual or business entity.

(b) This section shall not apply to the following:

(1) To a disclosure to any person pursuant to a subpoena or court order.

(2) To a disclosure which is discoverable.

(3) To a disclosure to any person acting pursuant to a lawful search warrant.

(4) To a disclosure to a law enforcement agency when required for investigations of criminal activity, unless such disclosure is prohibited by law.

(5) To a disclosure to a taxing agency for purposes of tax administration. *(Added by Stats.1977, c. 221, p. 1017, § 1.)*

Research References

5 Witkin, California Summary 10th Torts § 666, (S 666) in General.

§ 1799.1a. Income tax returns

(a) No person, including an individual, firm, corporation, association, partnership, or joint venture, or any employee or agent thereof, shall disclose information obtained from a federal or state income tax return or any information obtained from a tax schedule submitted with the return by a consumer in connection with a financial or other business-related transaction unless the disclosure is within any of the following:

(1) Consented to in writing by the consumer in a separate document that states to whom the disclosure will be made and how the information will be used. If the consumer agrees, this separate consent document may be in the form of an electronic record, executed by an electronic signature as provided by Title 2.5 (commencing with Section 1633.1) of Part 2 of Division 3 of the Civil Code.

(2) Authorized or required by state or federal law.

(3) Necessary to complete or service the financial or business-related transaction or to effect, administer, or enforce a financial or business-related transaction requested by the consumer.

(4) Pursuant to court order.

(5) Required to complete any of the transactions described in subparagraphs (A) to (D), inclusive, by a person, including an individual, firm, corporation, association, partnership or joint venture, if the disclosure is made solely for that purpose. The provisions of this section apply to any person, including an individual, firm, corporation, association, partnership, or joint venture, and any employee or agent thereof, receiving information as a result of a disclosure authorized by this paragraph.

(A) A proposed or actual sale, merger, transfer, or exchange of all or a portion of a business or operating unit.

(B) A proposed or actual securitization or secondary market sale, including the sale of servicing rights.

(C) To provide information to insurance rate advisory organizations, guaranty funds or agencies, rating agencies, and other persons assessing compliance with industry standards.

(D) To protect against or to prevent actual or potential fraud and unauthorized transactions and claims and for institutional risk control activities.

(b) No unrelated use shall be made of a federal or state tax return or any information obtained therefrom or any information submitted with the return by a consumer in connection with a financial or other business-related transaction. "Unrelated use" means any use that is not necessary to effect, administer, or enforce the financial or other business-related transaction with the consumer or that is beyond the scope of the stated purpose to which the consumer consented for the use of the return or any other information he or she submitted.

(c)(1) For purposes of this section, the following definitions shall apply:

(A) "Affiliate" means any entity that, directly or indirectly, through one or more intermediaries, controls, is controlled by, or is under common control with, another entity.

(B) "Consumer" means an individual who requests or obtains financial or other business-related services.

(C) "Tax return" means a return, declaration, statement, refund claim, or other document required to be made or to be filed in connection with state or federal income taxes or state bank and corporation franchise taxes.

(2) A disclosure prohibited by this section includes a disclosure made internally within the entity or by that entity to any of its subsidiaries or affiliates.

(3) The information described in subdivision (a) includes that information obtained through an electronic medium.

(d) No person, including an individual, firm, corporation, association, partnership, or joint venture, or any employee or agent thereof, shall dispose of any of the information described in subdivision (a) in a manner in which the identity of the consumer may be determined from the disposed information alone or in combination with other publicly available information. This subdivision shall not become operative if Assembly Bill 2246 of the 1999–2000 Regular Session is enacted and becomes effective on or before January 1, 2001.

(e) The civil remedies in Chapter 3 (commencing with Section 1799.2) shall be applicable to a violation of this section. Each violation of this section shall constitute a separate cause of action for which damages are recoverable.

(f) The treatment of tax returns by tax preparers, as defined in Section 22251 of the Business and Professions Code, shall be governed by Section 17530.5 of the Business and Professions Code. *(Added by Stats.2000, c. 1084 (S.B.1724), § 5.)*

Research References

5 Witkin, California Summary 10th Torts § 666, (S 666) in General.

§ 1799.1b. Credit card holders and telephone accountholders; change of address requests; requirements and restrictions for credit card issuers and business entities providing telephone accounts; change of address notifications

(a) Any credit card issuer that receives a change of address request, other than for a correction of a typographical error, from a cardholder who orders a replacement credit card within 60 days before or after that request is received shall send to that cardholder a change of address notification that is addressed to the cardholder at the cardholder's previous address of record. If the replacement credit card is requested prior to the effective date of the change of address, the notification shall be sent within 30 days of the change of address request. If the replacement credit card is requested after the effective date of the change of address, the notification shall be sent within 30 days of the request for the replacement credit card.

(b) Any business entity that provides telephone accounts that receives a change of address request, other than for a correction of a typographical error, from an accountholder who orders new service, shall send to that accountholder a change of address notification that is addressed to the accountholder at the accountholder's previous address of record. The notification shall be sent within 30 days of the request for new service.

(c) The notice required pursuant to subdivision (a) or (b) may be given by telephone or e-mail communication if the credit card issuer or business entity that provides telephone accounts reasonably believes that it has the current telephone number or e-mail address for the accountholder or cardholder who has requested a change of address. If the notification is in writing it may not contain the consumer's account number, social security number, or other personal identifying information, but may contain the consumer's name, previous address, and new address of record. For business entities described in subdivision (b), the notification may also contain the accountholder's telephone number.

(d) A credit card issuer or a business entity that provides telephone accounts is not required to send a change of address notification when a change of address request is made in person by a consumer who has presented valid identification, or is made by telephone and the requester has provided a unique alpha-numeric password.

(e) The following definitions shall apply to this section:

(1) "Credit account" has the same meaning as "credit card," as defined in subdivision (a) of Section 1747.02.

(2) "Telephone account" means an account with a telephone corporation, as defined in Section 234 of the Public Utilities Code. *(Added by Stats.2003, c. 533 (S.B.602), § 5. Amended by Stats.2004, c. 183 (A.B.3082), § 36.)*

CHAPTER 3. CIVIL REMEDIES

Section
1799.2.   Initiation of civil action; liability for damages; limitation.
1799.3.   Prohibition of disclosure by persons providing video recording sales or rentals without written consent; exceptions; violations; penalties.

§ 1799.2. Initiation of civil action; liability for damages; limitation

(a) A person may initiate a civil action against a business entity in accordance with state law whenever a business entity violates the provisions of Section 1799.1.

(b) In any suit brought pursuant to the provisions of subdivision (a) a business entity which has violated Section 1799.1 shall be liable to the person in an amount equal to the actual damages sustained by the person as a result of such violation, but in no case less than five hundred dollars ($500), and the attendant court costs and reasonable attorneys' fees.

(c) An action to enforce any liability created under this section may be brought in any court of competent jurisdiction within two years from the date on which the cause of action arose. *(Added by Stats.1977, c. 221, p. 1017, § 1.)*

Research References

5 Witkin, California Summary 10th Torts § 666, (S 666) in General.

§ 1799.3. Prohibition of disclosure by persons providing video recording sales or rentals without written consent; exceptions; violations; penalties

(a) No person providing video recording sales or rental services shall disclose any personal information or the contents of any record, including sales or rental information, which is prepared or maintained by that person, to any person, other than the individual who is the subject of the record, without the written consent of that individual.

(b) This section does not apply to any of the following:

(1) To a disclosure to any person pursuant to a subpoena or court order.

(2) To a disclosure that is in response to the proper use of discovery in a pending civil action.

(3) To a disclosure to any person acting pursuant to a lawful search warrant.

(4) To a disclosure to a law enforcement agency when required for investigations of criminal activity, unless that disclosure is prohibited by law.

(5) To a disclosure to a taxing agency for purposes of tax administration.

(6) To a disclosure of names and addresses only for commercial purposes.

(c) Any willful violation of this section shall be subject to a civil penalty not to exceed five hundred dollars ($500) for each violation, which may be recovered in a civil action brought by the person who is the subject of the records.

(d)(1) Any person who willfully violates this section on three or more occasions in any six-month period shall, in addition, be subject to a civil penalty not to exceed five hundred dollars ($500) for each violation, which may be assessed and recovered in a civil action brought in the name of the people of the State of California by the Attorney General, by any district attorney or city attorney, or by a city prosecutor in any city or city and county having a full-time city prosecutor, in any court of competent jurisdiction.

(2) If the action is brought by the Attorney General, one-half of the penalty collected shall be paid to the treasurer of the county in which the judgment was entered, and one-half to the General Fund. If the action is brought by a district attorney, the penalty collected shall be paid to the treasurer of the county in which the judgment was entered. If the action is brought by a city attorney or city prosecutor, one-half of the penalty shall be paid to the treasurer of the city in which the judgment was entered, and one-half to the treasurer of the county in which the judgment was entered.

(e) The penalty provided by this section is not an exclusive remedy, and does not affect any other relief or remedy provided by law. *(Added by Stats.1988, c. 1050, § 1. Amended by Stats.2009, c. 88 (A.B.176), § 14.)*

Law Revision Commission Comments

Subdivision (a) of Section 1799.3 is amended to reflect advances in recording technology and for consistency of terminology. For a similar reform, see 2002 Cal. Stat. ch. 1068 (replacing numerous references to "audiotape" in Civil Discovery Act with either "audio technology," "audio recording," or "audio record," as context required). [37 Cal. L. Revision Comm'n Reports 211 (2007)].

Research References

5 Witkin, California Summary 10th Torts § 666, (S 666) in General.

5 Witkin, California Summary 10th Torts § 672, (S 672) Disclosure by Videotape Provider.

Title 1.83

PRECOMPUTED INTEREST

Section

§ 1799.5. Definition; limitation of duration of loan for personal, family or household purposes; written statement of intended purpose; signature; date of application

(a) "Precomputed interest" means interest, as that term is contemplated by the Truth in Lending Act, 15 United States Code 1605(a)(1), which is (1) computed by multiplying the original balance of the loan by a rate and multiplying that product by the number of payment periods elapsing between the date of the loan and the date of the last scheduled payment and (2) either added to the original principal balance of the loan in advance or subtracted from the loan proceeds.

(b) No loan which is made to a natural person primarily for personal, family, or household purposes shall provide for the payment of precomputed interest if the date on which the final installment is due, according to the original terms of the loan, is more than 62 months after the date of the loan.

(c) For purposes of determining whether a loan is covered by this title, the lender may conclusively rely on any written statement of intended purpose signed by the borrower. Such written statement may be a separate statement signed by the borrower or may be contained in a loan application or other document signed by the borrower.

(d) For purposes of this title, the term "loan" does not include the forbearance of a debt arising from a sale or lease of property and does not include any loan arising under an open end credit plan.

(e) This title shall apply only to loans made on or after January 1, 1983. *(Added by Stats.1979, c. 805, p. 2769, § 1. Amended by Stats.1980, c. 1380, p. 5005, § 2, eff. Oct. 1, 1980.)*

Research References

4 Witkin, California Summary 10th Sales § 378, (S 378) Precomputed Interest in Personal Loan.

§ 1799.6. Public policy; waiver of rights

Any waiver of the provisions of this title is contrary to public policy, and is void and unenforceable. *(Added by Stats.2002, c. 815 (A.B.2331), § 17.)*

Research References

4 Witkin, California Summary 10th Sales § 378, (S 378) Precomputed Interest in Personal Loan.

Title 1.84

PRECOMPUTED FINANCE CHARGE CONTRACT

Section

Section

§ 1799.8. Definitions; limitation of duration of contract for personal, family or household purposes; written statement of purpose; signature; date of application

(a) "Precomputed finance charge" means a finance charge which is (1) computed by multiplying the original contract balance by a rate and multiplying that product by the number of payment periods elapsing between the date of the contract and the date of the last scheduled payment and (2) either added to the original contract balance in advance or subtracted from the contract balance.

(b) "Contract" means any agreement (1) providing for the construction, sale, or construction and sale of an entire residence, with or without a parcel of real property or an interest therein, or for the sale of a lot or parcel of real property, including any site preparation incidental to such sale, and (2) where the purchaser is a natural person who enters into such agreement primarily for personal, family, or household purposes.

(c) No contract as defined in subdivision (b) shall provide for the payment of a precomputed finance charge if the date on which the final installment is due, according to the original terms of the contract, is more than 62 months after the date of the contract.

(d) For purposes of determining whether a contract is covered by this title, the seller may conclusively rely on any written statement of intended purpose signed by the purchaser. Such written statement may be a separate statement signed by the purchaser or may be contained in a credit application or other document signed by the purchaser.

(e) This title shall apply only to contracts entered into on or after January 1, 1983. *(Added by Stats.1979, c. 805, p. 2770, § 2.)*

Research References

4 Witkin, California Summary 10th Sales § 377, (S 377) Precomputed Finance Charges in Residential Sale.

§ 1799.85. Public policy; waiver of rights

Any waiver of the provisions of this title is contrary to public policy, and is void and unenforceable. *(Added by Stats.2002, c. 815 (A.B.2331), § 18.)*

Research References

4 Witkin, California Summary 10th Sales § 377, (S 377) Precomputed Finance Charges in Residential Sale.

Title 1.85

CONSUMER CREDIT CONTRACTS

Section

§ 1799.90. Definitions

As used in this title:

(a) "Consumer credit contract" means any of the following obligations to pay money on a deferred payment basis, where the money, property, services or other consideration which is the subject matter of the contract is primarily for personal, family or household purposes:

(1) Retail installment contracts, as defined in Section 1802.6.

(2) Retail installment accounts, as defined in Section 1802.7.

(3) Conditional sales contracts, as defined in Section 2981.

(4) Loans or extensions of credit secured by other than real property, or unsecured, for use primarily for personal, family or household purposes.

(5) Loans or extensions of credit for use primarily for personal, family or household purposes where such loans or extensions of credit are subject to the provisions of Article 7 (commencing with Section 10240) of Chapter 3 of Part I of Division 4 of the Business and Professions Code, Division 7 (commencing with Section 18000), Division 9 (commencing with Section 22000), or Division 10 (commencing with Section 24000) of the Financial Code, whether secured by real property or otherwise.

(6) Lease contracts, as defined in Section 2985.7.

(b) "Creditor" means an individual, partnership, corporation, association or other entity, however designated, who enters into or arranges for consumer credit contracts in the ordinary course of business. *(Added by Stats.1975, c. 847, p. 1912, § 1, operative April 1, 1976. Amended by Stats.1984, c. 890, § 1; Stats.1997, c. 800 (S.B.1291), § 1.)*

Research References

Rutter, Cal. Practice Guide: Real Prop. Transactions Ch. 6-D, D. Mortgage Loan Brokers and Mortgage Loan Broker Agreements.

§ 1799.91. Multiple signatures on consumer credit contracts; delivery of notice of liability to each signatory who does not receive any of the subject matter of the contract

(a) Unless the persons are married to each other, each creditor who obtains the signature of more than one person on a consumer credit contract shall deliver to each person who does not in fact receive any of the money, property, or services which

are the subject matter of the consumer credit contract, prior to that person's becoming obligated on the consumer credit contract, a notice in English and Spanish in at least 10–point type as follows:

NOTICE TO COSIGNER (Traducción en Inglés Se Requiere Por La Ley)

You are being asked to guarantee this debt. Think carefully before you do. If the borrower doesn't pay the debt, you will have to. Be sure you can afford to pay if you have to, and that you want to accept this responsibility.

You may have to pay up to the full amount of the debt if the borrower does not pay. You may also have to pay late fees or collection costs, which increase this amount.

The creditor can collect this debt from you without first trying to collect from the borrower. The creditor can use the same collection methods against you that can be used against the borrower, such as suing you, garnishing your wages, etc. If this debt is ever in default, that fact may become a part of *your* credit record.

This notice is not the contract that makes you liable for the debt.

AVISO PARA EL FIADOR (Spanish Translation Required By Law)

Se le está pidiendo que garantice esta deuda. Piénselo con cuidado antes de ponerse de acuerdo. Si la persona que ha pedido este préstamo no paga la deuda, usted tendrá que pagarla. Esté seguro de que usted podrá pagar si sea obligado a pagarla y de que usted desea aceptar la responsabilidad.

Si la persona que ha pedido el préstamo no paga la deuda, es posible que usted tenga que pagar la suma total de la deuda, mas los cargos por tardarse en el pago o el costo de cobranza, lo cual aumenta el total de esta suma.

El acreedor (financiero) puede cobrarle a usted sin, primeramente, tratar de cobrarle al deudor. Los mismos metodos de cobranza que pueden usarse contra el deudor, podran usarse contra usted, tales como presentar una demanda en corte, quitar parte de su sueldo, etc. Si alguna vez no se cumpla con la obligación de pagar esta deuda, se puede incluir esa información en la historia de credito de usted.

Este aviso no es el contrato mismo en que se le echa a usted la responsabilidad de la deuda.

(b) Whenever notice is required to be given under subdivision (a) or (d) and the consumer credit contract is written in a language other than English or Spanish, the creditor shall deliver the notice as required in subdivision (a) or (d) in English and, in addition to or in lieu of Spanish, in the language in which the consumer contract is written.

(c) The requirements of subdivisions (a) and (b) do not apply to a creditor offering or extending open-end credit, as defined in Regulation Z, to joint applicants if all of the following conditions are satisfied:

(1) The application or agreement signed by each applicant clearly and conspicuously discloses that after credit approval each applicant shall have the right to use the open-end credit plan to the extent of any limit set by the creditor and may be liable for all amounts extended under the plan to any joint applicant.

(2) After credit approval, the creditor issues for the use of each applicant any credit device such as a credit card which may be used to obtain credit under the open-end credit plan and sends the credit device to the address specified in the application or otherwise delivers the credit device in a manner specified in the application or agreement signed by each applicant.

This paragraph does not apply to a creditor who does not issue a credit card or other credit device in order to obtain credit under the creditor's open-end credit plan.

(d) Unless the persons are married to each other, a lessor under a lease shall deliver to each person who does not in fact receive the vehicle which is the subject of the lease contract, prior to that person becoming liable on the lease contract, the following notice in English and Spanish in at least 10–point type in lieu of the notice required by subdivision (a):

NOTICE TO COSIGNER (Traducción en Inglés Se Requiere Por La Ley)

You are being asked to guarantee this lease. Think carefully before you do. If the lessee doesn't pay, you will have to. Be sure you can afford to pay if you have to, and that you want to accept this responsibility.

You may have to pay up to the full amount owed on the lease if the lessee does not pay. You may also have to pay late fees or other collection costs, which increase this amount.

The lessor can collect on the lease from you without first trying to collect from the lessee. The lessor can use the same collection methods against you that can be used against the lessee, such as suing you, garnishing your wages, etc. If this lease is ever in default, that fact may become part of *your* credit record.

This notice is not the contract that makes you liable for the lease obligation.

AVISO PARA EL FIADOR (Spanish Translation Required By Law)

Se le está piediendo que garantice este arrendamiento. Piénselo con cuidado antes de ponerse de acuerdo. Si el arrendatario no paga, usted tendrá que pagar. Esté seguro de que usted podrá pagar si sea obligado a pagar y de que usted desea aceptar la responsabilidad.

Si el arrendatario no paga, es posible que usted tenga que pagar la suma total debida en el contrato de arrendamiento, más los cargos por tardarse en el pago o el costo de cobranza, los cuales aumentan el total de esta suma.

La compañía arrendadora puede cobrarle a usted por la suma debida en el arrendamiento, sin, primeramente, tratar de cobrarle al arrendatario. Los mismos métodos de cobranza que pueden usarse contra el arrendatario, podrán usarse contra usted, tales como presentar una demanda en corte, quitar parte de su sueldo, etc. Si alguna vez no se cumpla con la obligación del arrendamiento, se puede incluir esa información en la historia de credito de usted.

Este aviso no es el contrato mismo en que se le echa a usted la responsabilidad del arrendamiento.

(e) "Regulation Z" has the meaning set forth in Section 1802.18.

(f) The word "your" in the last sentence of the third paragraph of the notice in English set forth in subdivisions (a) and (d) shall be italicized. *(Added by Stats.1975, c. 847, p. 1912, § 1, operative April 1, 1976. Amended by Stats.1985, c. 987, § 1; Stats.1986, c. 280, § 1; Stats.1987, c. 295, § 1, eff. July 30, 1987; Stats.1997, c. 800 (S.B.1291), § 2.)*

Research References

Rutter, Cal. Practice Guide: Enforcing Judgments/Debts Ch. 3-A, A. Evaluating the Claim.
Rutter, Cal. Practice Guide: Real Prop. Transactions Ch. 6-D, D. Mortgage Loan Brokers and Mortgage Loan Broker Agreements.

Miller and Starr California Real Estate § 4:63, Requirements in Making or Arranging a Loan--Special Notice to Cosigners in Consumer Credit Transactions.
Miller and Starr California Real Estate § 10:10, Requirement of Some Debt or Obligation.
3 Witkin Cal. Proc. 5th Actions § 674, (S 674) Action Alleging Multiple Claims.

§ 1799.92. Notice; method of inclusion in contract

(a) If the notice required by Section 1799.91 is included with the text of the consumer credit contract or with any other document establishing the liability of the person, the statement shall appear immediately above the space reserved for that person's signature or above or adjacent to any other notices required by law to be placed immediately above the signature space and shall be contained in a box formed by a heavy line.

(b) If the notice required by Section 1799.91 is not included with the text of the consumer credit contract it shall be on a separate sheet which shall not contain any other text except as is necessary to identify the creditor and consumer credit contract to which the statement refers and to provide for the date and the person's acknowledgment of receipt. *(Added by Stats.1975, c. 847, p. 1914, § 1, operative April 1, 1976. Amended by Stats.1985, c. 987, § 2.)*

Research References

Miller and Starr California Real Estate § 4:63, Requirements in Making or Arranging a Loan--Special Notice to Cosigners in Consumer Credit Transactions.

§ 1799.93. Obtaining signatures on consumer credit contract containing blank spaces prohibited; notice; documents given to persons receiving notice

(a) The creditor shall not obtain the signature of any person entitled to notice under Section 1799.91 if the consumer credit contract contains blank spaces to be filled in after the person's signature has been obtained.

(b) The creditor shall give each person entitled to notice under Section 1799.91 a copy of the debt instrument and security agreement or deed of trust, if any, evidencing the consumer credit contract and, if separate therefrom, a copy of the notice required by Section 1799.91 and a copy of the document evidencing that person's obligations. *(Added by Stats.1975, c. 847, p. 1914, § 1, operative April 1, 1976. Amended by Stats.1985, c. 987, § 3.)*

Research References

Miller and Starr California Real Estate § 4:63, Requirements in Making or Arranging a Loan--Special Notice to Cosigners in Consumer Credit Transactions.

§ 1799.94. Rights and obligations of parties; nonapplication of statement

The text of the statement required by Section 1799.91 of this title shall not be construed to alter or affect the rights and obligations of the parties to any consumer credit contract. *(Added by Stats.1975, c. 847, p. 1914, § 1, operative April 1, 1976.)*

§ 1799.95. Action or enforcement by creditor or assignee against any person not in receipt of subject matter of contract without compliance with title; prohibition

No action shall be brought, nor shall any security interest be enforced, by any creditor or any assignee of a creditor on any consumer credit contract which fails to comply with this title against any person, however designated, who is entitled to notice under Section 1799.91 and who does not in fact receive any of the money, property or services which are the subject matter of the consumer credit contract.

Nothing herein shall affect the rights of any bona fide purchaser for value of property sold pursuant to the enforcement of a security interest if the purchase was made without notice of any facts constituting a violation of this title. *(Added by Stats.1975, c. 847, p. 1914, § 1, operative April 1, 1976. Amended by Stats.1985, c. 987, § 4.)*

Research References

Rutter, Cal. Practice Guide: Enforcing Judgments/Debts Ch. 3-A, A. Evaluating the Claim.
Rutter, Cal. Practice Guide: Real Prop. Transactions Ch. 6-D, D. Mortgage Loan Brokers and Mortgage Loan Broker Agreements.
Miller and Starr California Real Estate § 4:63, Requirements in Making or Arranging a Loan--Special Notice to Cosigners in Consumer Credit Transactions.

§ 1799.96. Notice required by federal law; substitution

If federal law or regulations require or permit the use of a notice substantially similar to that required by Section 1799.91, the use of such federally sanctioned notice and an accurate Spanish translation thereof shall constitute compliance with Section 1799.91. However, the other provisions of this title shall remain unaffected. *(Added by Stats.1975, c. 847, p. 1914, § 1, operative April 1, 1976.)*

§ 1799.97. Security interests in religious books, artifacts or materials

(a) No consumer credit contract shall provide for a security interest in any religious books, religious artifacts, or religious materials, valued at less than five hundred dollars ($500), unless the religious books, artifacts, or materials are specifically pledged as collateral.

(b) Any provision in any contract which provides for a security interest in violation of subdivision (a) shall be void and unenforceable. *(Added by Stats.1984, c. 732, § 1.)*

§ 1799.98. Application of provisions of title; evidentiary effect of delivery of notice to contract signatory

(a) Nothing in this title shall be construed to make applicable or affect or operate as a waiver of any of the provisions of any of the following:

(1) Title 13 (commencing with Section 2787) of Part 4 of Division 3 of this code.

(2) Parts 1 (commencing with Section 700), 2 (commencing with Section 760), 3 (commencing with Section 900), and 4 (commencing with Section 1100) of Division 4 of the Family Code.

(3) Sections 4301 and 4302 of the Family Code.

(b) The delivery of notice pursuant to Section 1799.91 is not evidence that the person to whom the notice was delivered entered or did not enter the transaction in the capacity of a surety. *(Added by Stats.1985, c. 987, § 5. Amended by Stats. 1992, c. 163 (A.B.2641), § 10, operative Jan. 1, 1994; Stats.1993, c. 219 (A.B.1500), § 28.5.)*

Law Revision Commission Comments

Section 1799.98 is amended to substitute references to the Family Code provisions that replaced the former Civil Code provisions. [23 Cal.L.Rev. Comm. Reports 1 (1993)].

Research References

Rutter, Cal. Practice Guide: Enforcing Judgments/Debts Ch. 3-A, A. Evaluating the Claim.

§ 1799.99. Transactions other than consumer credit contracts; action or enforcement against persons not receiving notice in manner prescribed; prohibition

(a) This section applies to transactions, other than consumer credit contracts as defined in Section 1799.90, which are subject to 16 C.F.R. 444.3, 12 C.F.R. 227.14, or 12 C.F.R. 535.3, whichever is applicable to the creditor.

(b) Unless the persons who are obligated under the transaction are married to each other, no action shall be brought, nor shall any security interest be enforced, against any person entitled to receive notice under 16 C.F.R. 444.3, 12 C.F.R. 227.14, or 12 C.F.R. 535.3, whichever is applicable to the creditor, if that person did not receive the notice in the manner prescribed by the applicable regulation and an accurate Spanish translation of the notice. *(Added by Stats.1985, c. 987, § 6. Amended by Stats.1988, c. 160, § 15.)*

§ 1799.100. Taking of security interest in household goods with consumer credit contract; statement of description; enforcement; civil action

(a) It is unlawful for any person to take a security interest in any household goods, as defined in subdivision (g), in connection with a consumer credit contract or other credit obligation incurred primarily for personal, family, or household purposes unless (1) the person takes possession of the household goods or (2) the purchase price of the household goods was financed through the consumer credit contract or credit obligation.

(b) An agreement or other document creating a nonpossessory security interest in personal property as defined in subdivision (d) in connection with a consumer credit contract or other credit obligation incurred primarily for personal, family, or household purposes shall contain a statement of description reviewed and signed by the consumer indicating each specific item of the personal property in which the security interest is taken. A consumer credit contract or other credit obligation subject to the Unruh Act (Chapter 1 (commencing with Section 1801) of Title 2) that complies with the provisions of subdivision (a) of Section 1803.3, or of subdivision (f) of Section 1810.1, shall be deemed to comply with this subdivision.

(c) Notwithstanding any other provision of law, a person who has a nonpossessory security interest in personal property, described in subdivision (d), taken in connection with a consumer credit contract or other credit obligation incurred primarily for personal, family, or household purposes shall only enforce the security interest by judicial action unless the property is abandoned or freely and voluntarily surrendered by the consumer.

(d) The provisions of subdivisions (b) and (c) apply only to the following types of personal property:

(1) Any goods, as defined in paragraph (44) of subdivision (a) of Section 9102 of the Commercial Code, except for vessels, vehicles, and aircraft, that are used or bought for use primarily for personal, family, or household purposes and that has a fair market value of less than one thousand dollars ($1,000) per individual item at the time the security interest is created.

(2) The property described in Section 704.050 and subdivision (a) of Section 704.060 of the Code of Civil Procedure, except for vessels, vehicles, and aircraft.

(e) Any security interest taken in violation of either subdivision (a) or (b) is void and unenforceable.

(f) Any person injured by a violation of this section may bring a civil action for the recovery of damages, equitable relief, and attorney's fees and costs.

(g) For the purpose of this section:

(1) "Household goods" means and includes clothing, furniture, appliances, one radio, one television, linens, china, crockery, kitchenware, personal effects, and wedding rings. "Household goods" does not include works of art, electronic entertainment equipment (except one radio and one televi-

sion), items acquired as antiques, and jewelry (except wedding rings).

(2) "Antique" means any item over one hundred years of age, including such items that have been repaired or renovated without changing their original form or character. *(Added by Stats.1989, c. 525, § 1. Amended by Stats.1990, c. 31 (A.B.1259), § 1, eff. March 26, 1990; Stats.1999, c. 991 (S.B.45), § 3.5, operative July 1, 2001.)*

Research References

Rutter, Cal. Practice Guide: Enforcing Judgments/Debts Ch. 2-B, B. Statutory Liability and Procedures.
Rutter, Cal. Practice Guide: Enforcing Judgments/Debts Ch. 3-A, A. Evaluating the Claim.
4 Witkin, California Summary 10th Secured Transactions in Personal Property § 48, Description of Collateral.

§ 1799.101. Cosigners; delinquency; adverse information provided by creditor to consumer reporting agency; notice to cosigner; curing delinquency; operative date

(a) For the purposes of this section, the following terms are defined as follows:

(1) "Adverse information" means information directly or indirectly indicating that a delinquency has occurred, because a cosigner has not complied with the contractual provisions of a consumer credit contract.

(2) "Collection action" means requesting a cosigner to pay all or part of the obligation on a consumer credit contract.

(3) "Cosigner" means a natural person, other than the primary obligor or the spouse of the primary obligor, who renders himself or herself liable for the obligation on a consumer credit contract without compensation. The term includes a person whose signature is requested by a creditor as a condition to granting credit to another person. A person who does not receive goods, services, or money in return for executing a consumer credit contract does not receive compensation within the meaning of this section. "Cosigner" does not include a joint applicant for open-end credit pursuant to subdivision (c) of Section 1799.91. A person is a cosigner within the meaning of this section whether or not he or she is designated as such on a consumer credit contract or other document creating the consumer credit contract obligation for the cosigner.

(4) "Delinquency" means a failure to make timely payment to the creditor of all or a portion of any installment under a consumer credit contract.

(5) "Notice" means a writing which describes, recites, or otherwise refers to a delinquency.

(6) "Obligation" means an indebtedness incurred by an individual for personal, family, or household purposes.

(7) "Person" means an individual, firm, partnership, association, limited liability company, or corporation.

(8) "Primary obligor" means one or more persons, other than a cosigner, who sign a consumer credit contract and assume an obligation as debtor under that contract.

(b) Except as provided in subdivisions (d) and (e), no creditor shall provide any adverse information with respect to any cosigner, to a consumer credit reporting agency regarding a delinquency on a consumer credit contract entered into on or after July 1, 1992, unless, at or before the time the information is provided to the consumer credit reporting agency, written notice of the delinquency is provided to the cosigner.

(c) No creditor shall provide any information regarding the cosigner's obligation on a consumer credit contract to a debt collector, as defined in subdivision (c) of Section 1788.2, until notice has been provided to the cosigner under subdivision (b).

(d) The notice requirements of subdivisions (b) and (c) do not apply to any cosigner whose address, as shown in the creditor's records respecting the consumer credit contract, is the same as the primary obligor.

(e) The notice requirements of subdivisions (b) and (c) shall be satisfied by mailing a copy of the required notice to the cosigner at the cosigner's address, as shown in the creditor's records respecting the consumer credit contract. However, if more than one cosigner reside at the same address, as shown in the creditor's records respecting the consumer credit contract, a notice addressed to any cosigner at that address shall be deemed notice to all the cosigners residing at that address.

(f) Nothing in this section shall require any particular form or language with respect to a notice of delinquency sent to either a primary obligor or cosigner.

(g) Within a reasonable time after a creditor has reported to a credit reporting agency that a delinquency or delinquencies that have been reported to the consumer credit reporting agency and included in the cosigner's file maintained by the consumer credit reporting agency have been cured, the consumer credit reporting agency shall indicate in the file that the payment was made.

(h) Nothing in this section shall be construed to require notice of a delinquency to be provided to a cosigner in any instance not expressly specified in this section, or to provide notice to persons other than cosigners.

(i) This section shall become operative on July 1, 1992. *(Added by Stats.1990, c. 1549 (A.B.2729), § 1, operative July 1, 1992. Amended by Stats.1991, c. 131 (A.B.956), § 1, operative July 1, 1992; Stats.1994, c. 1010 (S.B.2053), § 42.)*

Research References

Rutter, Cal. Practice Guide: Enforcing Judgments/Debts Ch. 3-A, A. Evaluating the Claim.
4 Witkin, California Summary 10th Sales § 304, Cosigner's Rights.

§ 1799.102. Action by cosigner; amount; attorney fees; notification; resolution; operative date

(a) A cosigner who suffers a loss as a result of a violation of Section 1799.101 may bring an action to recover actual damages or two hundred fifty dollars ($250), whichever is greater, and reasonable attorney fees.

(b) The cosigner shall, not less than 30 days prior to bringing an action pursuant to subdivision (a), notify the person alleged to have violated Section 1799.101 of the cosigner's intention to bring an action. The notice shall include a statement of the specific evidence that proves the loss suffered by the cosigner. If within 25 days after the date of receiving the notice, the person alleged to have violated Section 1799.101 tenders to the cosigner an amount equal to the loss, or otherwise resolves the matter to the cosigner's satisfaction, the cosigner shall be barred from further recovery of that loss, including reasonable attorney fees.

(c) This section shall become operative on July 1, 1992. *(Added by Stats.1990, c. 1549 (A.B.2729), § 2, operative July 1, 1992.)*

Research References

Rutter, Cal. Practice Guide: Enforcing Judgments/Debts Ch. 3-A, A. Evaluating the Claim.
4 Witkin, California Summary 10th Sales § 304, Cosigner's Rights.

§ 1799.103. Security interests in investment property pledged as collateral; conditions for provision in consumer credit contract or guarantee thereof

No consumer credit contract or guarantee of a consumer credit contract shall provide for a security interest in any investment property, as defined in paragraph (49) of subdivision

(a) of Section 9102 of the Commercial Code, that is pledged as collateral, unless (a) the contract either specifically identifies the investment property as collateral or (b) the secured party is a securities intermediary, as defined in paragraph (14) of subdivision (a) of Section 8102 of the Commercial Code, or commodity intermediary, as defined in paragraph (17) of subdivision (a) of Section 9102 of the Commercial Code, with respect to the investment property. The identification of an account shall include the name of the holder, account number, and name of the institute holding the investment property. In the event that a consumer credit contract or guarantee does not comply with this section, the security interest in the investment property is void. *(Added by Stats.1996, c. 497 (S.B.1591), § 1, operative Jan. 1, 1997. Amended by Stats.1999, c. 991 (S.B.45), § 4, operative July 1, 2001.)*

Research References

4 Witkin, California Summary 10th Secured Transactions in Personal Property § 48, Description of Collateral.

§ 1799.104. Public policy; waiver of rights

Any waiver of the provisions of this title is contrary to public policy, and is void and unenforceable. *(Added by Stats.2002, c. 815 (A.B.2331), § 19.)*

Research References

4 Witkin, California Summary 10th Sales § 304, Cosigner's Rights.

Title 1.86

CONSUMER CONTRACT AWARENESS ACT OF 1990

§ 1799.200. Short title

This title shall be known and may be cited as the Consumer Contract Awareness Act of 1990. *(Added by Stats.1990, c. 1079 (S.B.1107), § 1, operative July 1, 1991.)*

Research References

Rutter, Cal. Practice Guide: Enforcing Judgments/Debts Ch. 3-A, A. Evaluating the Claim.
4 Witkin, California Summary 10th Sales § 308, (S 308) Consumer Contract Awareness Act.

§ 1799.201. Definitions

As used in this title:

(a) "Consumer" means a natural person who has entered into a consumer contract with a seller.

(b) "Consumer contract" means a writing prepared by a seller and, except as provided in subdivision (c) of Section 1799.202, signed, or to be signed, by a consumer, which provides (1) for the sale or lease of goods or services that are purchased or leased primarily for personal, family, or household purposes, or (2) for extension of credit, the proceeds of which are used primarily for

personal, family, or household purposes. Without affecting the enforceability of any incidental provision contained therein, an application for credit shall not be considered to be a consumer contract for purposes of this section even if it contains incidental provisions, such as the consumer's consent to a credit review, a certification of the accuracy of the information furnished, or the consumer's agreement to the terms that will be furnished to the consumer pursuant to this title.

(c) "Consumer contract guaranty" means a writing prepared by a seller and signed, or to be signed, by a guarantor which guarantees the obligation of a consumer under a consumer contract.

(d) "Copy" means a reproduction, facsimile, or duplicate.

(e) "Days" means calendar days.

(f) "Goods" means tangible and intangible personal property.

(g) "Guarantor" means a person who guarantees the obligation of a consumer under a consumer contract by signing a consumer contract guaranty.

(h) "Seller" means a person who has entered into a consumer contract with a consumer.

(i) "Services" means work, labor, and services, including depository services and other banking services.

(j) "Financial institution" means any commercial bank, trust company, savings and loan association, credit union, industrial loan company, insurance company, or person engaged in the business of lending money. *(Added by Stats.1990, c. 1079 (S.B.1107), § 1, operative July 1, 1991. Amended by Stats.1991, c. 1129 (S.B.108), § 1; Stats.1992, c. 879 (A.B.3468), § 1.)*

Research References

4 Witkin, California Summary 10th Sales § 308, (S 308) Consumer Contract Awareness Act.

§ 1799.202. Contract; mailing or delivery; copies

(a) Except as otherwise provided in this title, a seller shall deliver a copy of a consumer contract to the consumer at the time it is signed by the consumer if the consumer contract is signed at a place of business of the seller. If the consumer contract is not signed by the consumer at a place of business of the seller, and the seller has not provided a copy of the consumer contract for the consumer which the consumer is instructed to keep, the seller shall mail or deliver a copy of it to the consumer within 10 calendar days after the seller receives the signed consumer contract. In any case, the copy of the contract provided to the consumer shall not contain any blank spaces to be completed after the consumer signs the contract, shall contain the signature of the seller if it provides for that signature, and may also contain the signature of the consumer.

(b) A seller that is a financial institution need not deliver to the consumer, pursuant to subdivision (a), any writing which the consumer contract incorporates by reference if either of the following conditions apply:

(1) The writing was previously delivered or mailed to the consumer.

(2) The writing was not prepared by the seller.

(c) If the consumer contract (1) is wholly or partly contained on a card or other writing which is used to identify the consumer in connection with a deposit account, safe deposit box, safekeeping agreement, or other service offered by a financial institution, and (2) contains information particular to the consumer's account, box, or other arrangement that, if known by a third party, could be used by the third party to cause loss to the consumer or financial institution, the copy of the contract furnished to the consumer need not contain the consumer's signature or any of the identifying information particular to the consumer's account, box, or other arrangement.

For purposes of this subdivision, a document which includes the same terms as those contained in the consumer contract shall be deemed a copy.

(d) Within a reasonable time after receipt of a written request from a consumer, a seller or financial institution shall mail a copy of the consumer's completed consumer credit application, which may, but need not, contain any information completed or added by the seller or financial institution, to the consumer at the address indicated on the request. By making a written request, the consumer shall conclusively be deemed to have waived any action against the seller or financial institution, as well as its employees or agents, on any theory, at law or in equity, arising directly or indirectly out of the mailing or other delivery of the copy, including any information added to the application by the seller or financial institution and included in the copy. The seller or financial institution may specify the address to which such a request may be sent, may charge the consumer a reasonable copying fee, and shall not be obligated to provide the copy until the fee is paid. *(Added by Stats.1990, c. 1079 (S.B.1107), § 1, operative July 1, 1991. Amended by Stats.1991, c. 1129 (S.B.108), § 2; Stats.1992, c. 879 (A.B.3468), § 2.)*

Research References

Rutter, Cal. Practice Guide: Enforcing Judgments/Debts Ch. 3-A, A. Evaluating the Claim.
4 Witkin, California Summary 10th Sales § 308, (S 308) Consumer Contract Awareness Act.

§ 1799.203. Compliance with and application of § 1799.202

(a) It shall be deemed compliance with Section 1799.202 if a copy of any consumer contract which is subject to Article 10 (commencing with Section 1810.1) of Chapter 1 of Title 2, or which is an open-end consumer credit plan subject to Section 127 of the federal Truth in Lending Act (15 U.S.C. 1637), is delivered or mailed to the consumer before the consumer enters into a transaction covered and permitted by the consumer contract.

(b) Section 1799.202 does not apply to any of the following:

(1) A consumer contract for the purchase of goods by mail if the seller permits the consumer to examine the goods for seven calendar days and cancel the consumer contract and receive a full refund within 30 calendar days for returned unused and undamaged goods.

(2) A written contract created by, and consisting of, an exchange of letters by mail.

(3) Any consumer contract which is required to be mailed or delivered at a time prescribed by another law of this state or the United States. *(Added by Stats.1990, c. 1079 (S.B.1107), § 1, operative July 1, 1991. Amended by Stats.1991, c. 1129 (S.B.108), § 3.)*

Research References

4 Witkin, California Summary 10th Sales § 308, (S 308) Consumer Contract Awareness Act.

§ 1799.204. Contract signed by more than one consumer; mailing or delivery

If more than one consumer has signed a consumer contact[1], the seller may comply with Section 1799.202 by mailing or delivering the copy to any one of the consumers who reside at the same address. A copy shall also be mailed or delivered to any other consumer who has signed the consumer contract and

who does not reside at the same address. *(Added by Stats.1990, c. 1079 (S.B.1107), § 1, operative July 1, 1991.)*

[1]So in enrolled bill.

Research References

4 Witkin, California Summary 10th Sales § 308, (S 308) Consumer Contract Awareness Act.

§ 1799.205. Failure to comply; liability; remedies; basis for rescission

(a) A seller who fails to comply with Section 1799.202 is liable to the consumer for any actual damages suffered by the consumer as the result of that failure. The remedy provided by this subdivision is nonexclusive and is in addition to any other remedies or penalties available under other laws of this state.

(b) Failure to comply with Section 1799.202 does not create an independent basis for the rescission, but is admissible to establish a basis for the rescission of the contract otherwise authorized by law. *(Added by Stats.1990, c. 1079 (S.B.1107), § 1, operative July 1, 1991. Amended by Stats.1991, c. 1129 (S.B.108), § 4.)*

Research References

Rutter, Cal. Practice Guide: Enforcing Judgments/Debts Ch. 3-A, A. Evaluating the Claim.
4 Witkin, California Summary 10th Sales § 308, (S 308) Consumer Contract Awareness Act.

§ 1799.206. Delivery of copy to guarantor; failure to comply with section; liability; basis for rescission

(a) Except as otherwise provided in this section, a seller shall deliver a copy of the consumer contract guaranty to the guarantor at the time the consumer contract guaranty is signed by the guarantor if the consumer contract guaranty is signed by the guarantor at a place of business of the seller. If the consumer contract guaranty is not signed by the guarantor at a place of business of the seller, and the seller has not provided a copy of the consumer contract guaranty for the guarantor which the guarantor is able to keep, the seller shall mail or deliver a copy of the consumer contract guaranty to the guarantor within 10 calendar days after the seller receives the signed consumer contract guaranty. In any case, the copy of the consumer contract guaranty provided to the guarantor shall not contain any blank spaces to be completed after the guarantor signs the guaranty, shall contain the signature of the seller if it provides for that signature, and may also contain the signature of the guarantor.

(b) If more than one guarantor has signed the consumer contract guaranty, the seller may comply with subdivision (a) by mailing or delivering the copy to any one of the guarantors who reside at the same address. A copy shall also be mailed or delivered to any guarantor who has signed the consumer contract guaranty and who does not reside at the same address.

(c) A seller that fails to comply with this section is liable to the guarantor for any actual damages suffered by the guarantor as the result of that failure. The remedy provided by this subdivision is nonexclusive and in addition to any other remedies or penalties available under other laws of this state.

(d) Failure to comply with this section does not create a new basis for rescission, but is admissible to establish a basis for rescission of the consumer contract guaranty otherwise authorized by law. *(Added by Stats.1990, c. 1079 (S.B.1107), § 1, operative July 1, 1991. Amended by Stats.1991, c. 1129 (S.B.108), § 5; Stats.1992, c. 879 (A.B.3468), § 3.)*

Research References

Rutter, Cal. Practice Guide: Enforcing Judgments/Debts Ch. 3-A, A. Evaluating the Claim.

4 Witkin, California Summary 10th Sales § 308, (S 308) Consumer Contract Awareness Act.

§ 1799.207. Public policy; waiver of rights

Any waiver of the provisions of this title is contrary to public policy, and is void and unenforceable. *(Added by Stats.2002, c. 815 (A.B.2331), § 20.)*

Research References

4 Witkin, California Summary 10th Sales § 308, (S 308) Consumer Contract Awareness Act.

Title 2

CREDIT SALES

CHAPTER 1. RETAIL INSTALLMENT SALES

ARTICLE 1. GENERAL PROVISIONS

§ 1801. Citation

This chapter may be cited as the "Unruh Act." *(Added by Stats.1959, c. 201, p. 2092, § 1, operative Jan. 1, 1960.)*

Research References

Rutter, Cal. Practice Guide: Enforcing Judgments/Debts Ch. 3-A, A. Evaluating the Claim.

Rutter, Cal. Practice Guide: Enforcing Judgments/Debts Ch. 3-B, B. Collection Without Suit.

Rutter, Cal. Practice Guide: Enforcing Judgments/Debts Ch. 4-B, B. Claim and Delivery.

Miller and Starr California Real Estate § 27:56, Home Improvement Contracts--Contracts for Installment Payments, Cash Discounts, or Finance Charges.

2 Witkin Cal. Proc. 5th Courts § 275, Exceptions.

1 Witkin Cal. Summ. 10th Contracts § 124, (S 124) of Translation.

1 Witkin Cal. Summ. 10th Contracts § 484, (S 484) California Law.

1 Witkin Cal. Summ. 10th Contracts § 896, Rate of Interest.

4 Witkin, California Summary 10th Sales § 263, (S 263) Nature of Act.

4 Witkin, California Summary 10th Sales § 371, (S 371) Membership Camping Contracts.

4 Witkin, California Summary 10th Secured Transactions in Personal Property § 49, Effectiveness of Security Agreement.

8 Witkin, California Summary 10th Constitutional Law § 898, in General.

§ 1801.1. Waiver of provisions

Any waiver by the buyer of the provisions of this chapter shall be deemed contrary to public policy and shall be unenforceable and void. *(Added by Stats.1959, c. 201, p. 2092, § 1. Amended by Stats.1963, c. 1603, p. 3181, § 1.)*

Research References

1 Witkin Cal. Summ. 10th Contracts § 684, Miscellaneous Substantive Rights.

4 Witkin, California Summary 10th Sales § 263, (S 263) Nature of Act.

§ 1801.2. Partial invalidity

If any provision of this chapter or the application thereof to any person or circumstances is held unconstitutional, the remainder of the chapter and the application of such provision to other persons or circumstances shall not be affected thereby. *(Added by Stats.1959, c. 201, p. 2092, § 1, operative Jan. 1, 1960.)*

§ 1801.4. Application of chapter

The provisions of this chapter shall not apply to any contract or series of contracts providing for: (a) the construction, sale, or construction and sale of an entire residence, including a mobile-home, or all or part of a structure designed for commercial or industrial occupancy, with or without a parcel of real property or an interest therein, (b) for the sale of a lot or parcel of real property, including any site preparation incidental to such sale, (c) the sale of any aircraft required to be registered under the Federal Aviation Act of 1958, or (d) the sale of any vessel as defined in subdivision (a) of Section 9840 of the Vehicle Code if the cash price of such vessel, including accessories and equipment sold in conjunction therewith, exceeds twenty-five thousand dollars ($25,000). *(Added by Stats.1969, c. 554, p. 1180, § 1. Amended by Stats.1980, c. 437, p. 922, § 1; Stats.1980, c. 1149, p. 3722, § 6.)*

Research References

4 Witkin, California Summary 10th Sales § 269, Inapplicable to Real Property.

4 Witkin, California Summary 10th Sales § 270, Inapplicable to Aircraft or Vessel.

§ 1801.5. Regulation Z; disclosures

Notwithstanding any other provision of this chapter to the contrary, any information required to be disclosed in a retail installment contract or other document under this chapter may be disclosed in any manner, method, or terminology required or permitted under Regulation Z, as in effect at the time such disclosure is made, except that permitted by paragraph (2) of subdivision (c) of Section 226.18 of Regulation Z, provided that all of the requirements and limitations set forth in subdivision (b) of Section 1803.3 are satisfied. Nothing contained in this chapter shall be deemed to prohibit the disclosure in such contract or other document of additional information required or permitted under Regulation Z, as in effect at the time such disclosure is made. *(Added by Stats.1970, c. 546, p. 1041, § 1. Amended by Stats.1979, c. 805, p. 2770, § 3; Stats.1981, c. 1075, p. 4114, § 1, operative Oct. 1, 1982.)*

Research References

1 Witkin Cal. Summ. 10th Contracts § 484, (S 484) California Law.
4 Witkin, California Summary 10th Sales § 275, Compliance With Regulation Z.

§ 1801.6. Legislative finding and purpose; application of chapter; loans by supervised financial organization

(a) The Legislature finds that the decisional law of this state regarding the characterization of credit transactions as either loans or credit sales has been made unclear by the holding in King v. Central Bank, 18 Cal.3d 840. It is the purpose of subdivision (b) to clarify such law by establishing standards for determining whether a transaction is subject to the Unruh Act. However, subdivision (b) is not intended to abrogate the judicial principle that the substance of a transaction rather than its form is determinative of its characterization as a loan or credit sale as exemplified by such decisions as Verbeck v. Clymer, 202 Cal. 557, Milana v. Credit Discount Co., 27 Cal.2d 335, and Boerner v. Colwell Co., 21 Cal.3d 37. Subdivision (b) also is not intended to abrogate the decision in Morgan v. Reasor Corp., 69 Cal.2d 881, to the extent such decision has not been modified by Chapter 554 of the Statutes of 1969 or other legislative amendments to the Unruh Act.

(b) The provisions of this chapter shall not apply to any transaction in the form of a loan made by a supervised financial organization to a buyer of goods or services where all or a portion of the loan proceeds are used to purchase such goods or services, whether or not the seller of such goods or services arranges the loan or participates in the preparation of the loan documents, unless the supervised financial organization and the seller:

(1) Are related by common ownership and control and the relationship was a material factor in the loan transaction; or

(2) Share in the profits and losses of either or both the sale and the loan.

(c) For purposes of this section:

(1) The term "supervised financial organization" means a person organized, chartered, or holding a license or authorization certificate to make loans pursuant to the laws of this state or the United States who is subject to supervision by an official or agency of this state or the United States.

(2) Receipt of a loan commission, brokerage or referral fee by a seller from a supervised financial organization shall not constitute a sharing of profits of the supervised financial organization, provided that such payment (i) is reasonable under the circumstances existing at the time the loan is consummated, and (ii) is not refundable or is wholly or partly refundable only if the loan is voluntarily paid in full prior to its scheduled maturity. For purposes of this paragraph, a loan commission, brokerage or referral fee not exceeding the greater of 1 percent of the amount financed (as that term is defined by Regulation Z with respect to loans), or twenty dollars ($20), is reasonable under the circumstances existing at the time the loan is consummated.

(3) Payment of money by a seller to a supervised financial organization pursuant to an actual or alleged contractual or statutory obligation to indemnify a supervised financial organization for losses incurred as a result of the assertion by a buyer of claims or defenses with respect to goods or services purchased with loan proceeds shall not constitute participation in or sharing of loan losses by the seller. *(Added by Stats.1979, c. 1151, p. 4221, § 1. Amended by Stats.1980, c. 438, p. 922, § 1.)*

Research References

4 Witkin, California Summary 10th Sales § 269, Inapplicable to Real Property.
4 Witkin, California Summary 10th Sales § 271, Loan by Supervised Financial Organization.
4 Witkin, California Summary 10th Sales § 277, (S 277) Prohibited Terms and Acts.

§ 1801.7. Application of chapter; premium finance agreements entered into by industrial loan company

The provisions of this chapter shall not apply to any premium finance agreement entered into by an industrial loan company pursuant to Chapter 8 (commencing with Section 18560) of Division 7 of the Financial Code. *(Added by Stats.1979, c. 1151, p. 4221, § 2.)*

Research References

4 Witkin, California Summary 10th Sales § 269, Inapplicable to Real Property.
4 Witkin, California Summary 10th Sales § 271, Loan by Supervised Financial Organization.

ARTICLE 2. DEFINITIONS

§ 1802. Construction of chapter

Unless the context or subject matter otherwise requires, the definitions given in this article govern the construction of this chapter. *(Added by Stats.1959, c. 201, p. 2092, § 1, operative Jan. 1, 1960.)*

§ 1802.1. Goods

"Goods" means tangible chattels bought for use primarily for personal, family or household purposes, including certificates or coupons exchangeable for such goods, and including goods which, at the time of the sale or subsequently are to be so affixed to real property as to become a part of such real property whether or not severable therefrom, but does not include any vehicle required to be registered under the Vehicle Code, nor any goods sold or leased with such a vehicle if sold under a contract governed by Section 2982 or leased under a contract governed by Section 2985.7. "Goods" also includes a trailer which is sold in conjunction with a vessel, as defined in subdivision (a) of Section 9840 of the Vehicle Code, unless the sales transaction is exempted under Section 1801.4. As used in this section, "trailer" means a vehicle designed solely for carrying vessels. *(Added by Stats.1959, c. 201, p. 2092, § 1, operative Jan. 1, 1960. Amended by Stats.1984, c. 1114, § 1; Stats.1985, c. 1186, § 1.)*

Research References

4 Witkin, California Summary 10th Sales § 240, Scope and Exclusions.
4 Witkin, California Summary 10th Sales § 268, Inapplicable to Commercial Sales.
4 Witkin, California Summary 10th Sales § 269, Inapplicable to Real Property.

§ 1802.2. Services

"Services" means work, labor and services, for other than a commercial or business use, including services furnished in connection with the sale or repair of goods as defined in Section 1802.1 or furnished in connection with the repair of motor vehicles (except for service contracts as defined by subdivision (p) of Section 2981 which are sold in conjunction with the sale or lease of a vehicle required to be registered under the Vehicle Code) or in connection with the improvement of real property or the providing of insurance, but does not include the services of physicians or dentists, nor services for which the tariffs, rates, charges, costs or expenses, including in each instance the deferred payment price, are required by law to be filed with and approved by the federal government or any official, department, division, commission or agency of the United States. *(Added by Stats.1959, c. 201, p. 2092, § 1, operative Jan. 1, 1960. Amended by Stats.1968, c. 48, p. 188, § 1; Stats.1970, c. 546, p. 1041, § 2; Stats.1980, c. 1380, p. 5005, § 3, eff. Oct. 1, 1980; Stats.1981, c. 1075, p. 4114, § 1.5, operative Oct. 1, 1982; Stats.1984, c. 1114, § 2.)*

Research References

4 Witkin, California Summary 10th Sales § 265, Services.
4 Witkin, California Summary 10th Sales § 269, Inapplicable to Real Property.
4 Witkin, California Summary 10th Sales § 271, Loan by Supervised Financial Organization.

§ 1802.3. Retail seller; seller

"Retail seller" or "seller" means a person engaged in the business of selling goods or furnishing services to retail buyers. *(Added by Stats.1959, c. 201, p. 2093, § 1, operative Jan. 1, 1960.)*

Research References

4 Witkin, California Summary 10th Sales § 271, Loan by Supervised Financial Organization.

§ 1802.4. Retail buyer; buyer

"Retail buyer" or "buyer" means a person who buys goods or obtains services from a retail seller in a retail installment sale and not principally for the purpose of resale. *(Added by Stats.1959, c. 201, p. 2093, § 1, operative Jan. 1, 1960.)*

§ 1802.5. Retail installment sale; sale

"Retail installment sale" or "sale" means the sale of goods or the furnishing of services by a retail seller to a retail buyer for a deferred payment price payable in installments. *(Added by Stats.1959, c. 201, p. 2093, § 1, operative Jan. 1, 1960. Amended by Stats.1970, c. 546, p. 1041, § 3.)*

Research References

Rutter, Cal. Practice Guide: Enforcing Judgments/Debts Ch. 3-A, A. Evaluating the Claim.

§ 1802.6. Retail installment contract; contract

"Retail installment contract" or "contract" means any contract for a retail installment sale between a buyer and seller, entered into or performed in this state, which provides for (a) repayment in installments, whether or not such contract contains a title retention provision, and in which the buyer agrees to pay a finance charge, or in which the buyer does not agree to pay a finance charge but the goods or services are available at a lesser price if paid for by either cash or credit card, or in which the buyer would have received any additional goods or services or any higher quality goods or services at no added cost over the total amount payable in installments if the sale had been for cash, or (b) which provides for payment in more than four installments. When taken or given in connection with a retail installment sale, the term includes but is not limited to a security agreement and a contract for the bailment or leasing of goods by which the bailee or lessee contracts to pay as compensation for their use a sum substantially equivalent to or in excess of their value and by which it is agreed that the bailee or lessee will become, or for no other or for a nominal consideration has the option of becoming, the owner of the goods upon full compliance with the terms of the contract. *(Added by Stats.1959, c. 201, p. 2093, § 1. Amended by Stats.1961, c. 1214, p. 2948, § 1; Stats.1963, c. 819, p. 1998, § 6, eff. Jan. 1, 1965; Stats.1969, c. 1192, p. 2322, § 1; Stats.1970, c. 546, p. 1041, § 4; Stats.1979, c. 805, p. 2771, § 4.)*

Research References

Rutter, Cal. Practice Guide: Enforcing Judgments/Debts Ch. 3-A, A. Evaluating the Claim.
Miller and Starr California Real Estate § 27:56, Home Improvement Contracts--Contracts for Installment Payments, Cash Discounts, or Finance Charges.
4 Witkin, California Summary 10th Sales § 132, (S 132) Pre-Code Case Law.
4 Witkin, California Summary 10th Sales § 264, Retail Installment Contract.

§ 1802.7. Retail installment account; installment account; revolving account

"Retail installment account" or "installment account" or "revolving account" means an account established by an agreement entered into in this state, pursuant to which the buyer promises to pay, in installments, to a retail seller, his outstanding balance incurred in retail installment sales, whether or not a security interest in the goods sold is retained by the seller, and which provides for a finance charge which is expressed as a percent of the periodic balances to accrue thereafter providing such charge is not capitalized or stated as a dollar amount in such agreement. *(Added by Stats.1959, c. 201, p. 2093, § 1, operative Jan. 1, 1960. Amended by Stats.1970, c. 546, p. 1042, § 5.)*

Research References

Rutter, Cal. Practice Guide: Enforcing Judgments/Debts Ch. 3-A, A. Evaluating the Claim.
4 Witkin, California Summary 10th Sales § 264, Retail Installment Contract.

§ 1802.8. Cash price

"Cash price" means the cash price stated in a retail installment contract for which the seller would sell or furnish to the buyer and the buyer would buy or obtain from the seller the goods or services which are the subject matter of a retail installment contract if the sale were a sale for cash instead of a retail installment sale. The cash price shall include any taxes and cash prices for accessories and services, if any, included in a retail installment sale. *(Added by Stats.1959, c. 201, p. 2093, § 1, operative Jan. 1, 1960. Amended by Stats.1969, c. 625, p. 1264, § 1; Stats.1981, c. 1075, p. 4115, § 2, operative Oct. 1, 1982.)*

§ 1802.9.   Total sale price

"Total sale price" means the total of the cash price of the goods or services, the amounts, if any, included for insurance, official fees, and the finance charge. *(Added by Stats.1959, c. 201, p. 2094, § 1, operative Jan. 1, 1960. Amended by Stats.1969, c. 625, p. 1264, § 2; Stats.1970, c. 546, p. 1042, § 6; Stats.1981, c. 1075, p. 4115, § 3, operative Oct. 1, 1982.)*

§ 1802.10.   Finance charge

"Finance charge" means the amount however denominated or expressed which the retail buyer contracts to pay or pays for the privilege of purchasing goods or services to be paid for by the buyer in installments. "Finance charge" does not include the amounts, if any, charged for insurance premiums, including premiums of the kind and to the extent described in paragraph (2) of subsection (e) of Section 226.4 of Regulation Z, delinquency charges, attorney's fees, court costs, collection expenses, official fees, extension or deferral agreement charges as provided by Section 1807.1, or amounts for insurance, repairs to or preservation of the goods, or preservation of the holder's security interest therein advanced by the holder subsequent to the execution of a contract. *(Added by Stats.1959, c. 201, p. 2094, § 1, operative Jan. 1, 1960. Amended by Stats.1969, c. 625, p. 1265, § 3; Stats.1970, c. 546, p. 1042, § 7; Stats.1980, c. 1380, p. 5005, § 4, eff. Oct. 1, 1980; Stats.1984, c. 199, § 1.)*

§ 1802.11.   Amount financed; unpaid balance

(a) "Amount financed" means the amount required to be disclosed pursuant to paragraph (7) of subdivision (c) of Section 1803.3.

(b) "Unpaid balance" means the cash price of the goods or services which are the subject matter of the retail installment sale, plus the amounts, if any, included in a retail installment sale for insurance and official fees, minus the amount of the buyer's downpayment in money or goods. *(Added by Stats.1959, c. 201, p. 2094, § 1, operative Jan. 1, 1960. Amended by Stats.1969, c. 625, p. 1265, § 4; Stats.1970, c. 546, p. 1042, § 8; Stats.1980, c. 1380, p. 5006, § 5, eff. Oct. 1, 1980; Stats.1981, c. 1075, p. 4115, § 4, operative Oct. 1, 1982.)*

§ 1802.12.   Total of payments

"Total of payments" means the amount required to be disclosed pursuant to subdivision (h) of Section 226.18 of Regulation Z. The term includes any portion of the downpayment deferred until not later than the second otherwise scheduled payment and which is not subject to a finance charge. *(Added by Stats.1959, c. 201, p. 2094, § 1, operative Jan. 1, 1960. Amended by Stats.1970, c. 546, p. 1042, § 9; Stats.1981, c. 1075, p. 4115, § 5, operative Oct. 1, 1982.)*

§ 1802.13.   Holder

"Holder" means the retail seller who acquires a retail installment contract or installment account executed, incurred or entered into by a retail buyer, or if the contract or installment account is purchased by a financing agency or other assignee, the financing agency or other assignee. The term does not include the pledgee of or the holder of a security interest in an aggregate number of such contracts or installment accounts to secure a bona fide loan thereon. *(Added by Stats.1959, c. 201, p. 2094, § 1, operative Jan. 1, 1960.)*

§ 1802.14.   Official fees

"Official fees" means the fees required by law and actually to be paid to the appropriate public officer to perfect a lien or other security interest, on or in goods, retained or taken by a seller under a retail installment contract or installment account, and license, certificate of title, and registration fees imposed by law.

(Added by Stats.1959, c. 201, p. 2094, § 1, operative Jan. 1, 1960. Amended by Stats.1970, c. 546, p. 1043, § 10.)

§ 1802.15.   Person

"Person" means an individual, partnership, corporation, limited liability company, association or other group, however organized. *(Added by Stats.1959, c. 201, p. 2094, § 1, operative Jan. 1, 1960. Amended by Stats.1994, c. 1010 (S.B.2053), § 43.)*

§ 1802.16.   Financing agency

"Financing agency" means a person engaged in this State in whole or in part in the business of purchasing retail installment contracts, or installment accounts from one or more retail sellers. The term includes but is not limited to a bank, trust company, private banker, or investment company, if so engaged. *(Added by Stats.1959, c. 201, p. 2094, § 1, operative Jan. 1, 1960.)*

§ 1802.17.   Billing cycle

"Billing cycle" means the time interval between regular monthly billing statement dates. *(Added by Stats.1970, c. 546, p. 1043, § 12.)*

§ 1802.18.   Regulation Z

"Regulation Z" means any rule, regulation, or interpretation promulgated by the Board of Governors of the Federal Reserve System ("Board") under the Federal Truth in Lending Act, as amended (15 U.S.C. 1601, et seq.), and any interpretation or approval issued by an official or employee of the Federal Reserve System duly authorized by the board under the Truth in Lending Act, as amended, to issue such interpretations or approvals. *(Added by Stats.1970, c. 546, p. 1043, § 13. Amended by Stats.1979, c. 805, p. 2771, § 5.)*

Research References

4 Witkin, California Summary 10th Sales § 275, Compliance With Regulation Z.

§ 1802.19.   Contracts and accounts; offer or agreement to sell or buy in this state; application of chapter

(a) For the purposes of this chapter, a retail installment contract, contract, retail installment account, installment account, or revolving account shall be deemed to have been made in this state and, therefore, subject to the provisions of this chapter, if either the seller offers or agrees in this state to sell to a buyer who is a resident of this state or if such buyer accepts or makes the offer in this state to buy, regardless of the situs of the contract as specified therein.

(b) Any solicitation or communication to sell, oral or written, originating outside of this state, but forwarded to, and received in this state by, a buyer who is a resident of this state, shall be deemed to be an offer or agreement to sell in this state.

(c) Any solicitation or communication to buy, oral or written, originating within this state, from a buyer who is a resident of this state, but forwarded to, and received by, a retail seller outside of this state, shall be deemed to be an acceptance or offer to buy in this state. *(Added by Stats.1976, c. 508, p. 1258, § 1.)*

Research References

4 Witkin, California Summary 10th Sales § 266, Purchases from Out of State.

§ 1802.20.   Simple-interest basis

"Simple-interest basis" means the determination of a finance charge, other than an administrative finance charge, by applying a constant rate to the unpaid balance as it changes from time to time, either:

(a) Calculated on the basis of a 365-day year and actual days elapsed (although the seller may, but need not, adjust its calculations to account for leap years); reference in this chapter to the "365-day basis" shall mean this method of determining the finance charge, or

(b) For contracts entered into prior to January 1, 1988, calculated on the basis of a 360-day year consisting of 12 months of 30 days each and on the assumption that all payments will be received by the seller on their respective due dates; reference in this chapter to the "360-day basis" shall mean this method of determining the finance charge. *(Added by Stats.1979, c. 805, p. 2771, § 6.)*

Research References

4 Witkin, California Summary 10th Sales § 278, (S 278) Limitation of Charges.

§ 1802.21. Precomputed basis

"Precomputed basis" means the determination of a finance charge by multiplying the original unpaid balance of the contract by a rate and multiplying that product by the number of payment periods elapsing between the date on which the finance charge begins to be assessed and the date of the last scheduled payment. *(Added by Stats.1979, c. 805, p. 2771, § 7.)*

Research References

4 Witkin, California Summary 10th Sales § 278, (S 278) Limitation of Charges.

ARTICLE 3. PROVISIONS OF RETAIL INSTALLMENT CONTRACTS

Section
1803.1.   Date; writing; size of type.
1803.2.   Single document; contents.
1803.3.   Contract; contents.
1803.4.   Obtaining signature of buyer to contract containing blank spaces.
1803.5.   Cost of insurance included in contract and separate charge made to buyer.
1803.6.   Delinquency charges; costs of collection.
1803.7.   Delivery of copy of completed contract or other document to buyer; penalties; acknowledgment of delivery; rebuttable presumption.
1803.8.   Negotiation of sales by mail or telephone.
1803.9.   Contract contingent on loan to be obtained by buyer; rescission upon failure; time; return of consideration.
1803.10.   Rebates, discounts, commissions, or other consideration.
1803.11.   Advertisements; solicitation to enter into contract without intent to sell contract to financing agency or assignee; requirements.

§ 1803.1. Date; writing; size of type

A retail installment contract shall be dated and in writing; the printed portion thereof shall be in at least eight-point type. *(Added by Stats.1959, c. 201, p. 2094, § 1, operative Jan. 1, 1960.)*

Research References

Rutter, Cal. Practice Guide: Enforcing Judgments/Debts Ch. 3-A, A. Evaluating the Claim.
Miller and Starr California Real Estate § 27:56, Home Improvement Contracts--Contracts for Installment Payments, Cash Discounts, or Finance Charges.

4 Witkin, California Summary 10th Sales § 272, Written and Signed.

§ 1803.2. Single document; contents

Except as provided in Section 1808.3, every retail installment contract shall be contained in a single document that shall contain:

(a) The entire agreement of the parties with respect to the cost and terms of payment for the goods and services, including any promissory notes or any other evidences of indebtedness between the parties relating to the transaction.

(b)(1) At the top of the contract the words "Security Agreement" shall appear in at least 12–point bold type where a security interest in the goods is retained or a security interest on other goods or realty is obtained by the seller as security for the goods or services purchased.

(2) At the top of the contract the words "Retail Installment Contract" shall appear in at least 12–point bold type where a security interest is not retained or obtained by the seller as security for the goods or services purchased.

(3) Any contract for goods or services that provides for a security interest in real property shall also provide the following notice, written in the same language, e.g., Spanish, as used in the contract: "WARNING TO BUYER: IF YOU SIGN THIS CONTRACT, YOU WILL BE PUTTING UP YOUR HOME AS SECURITY. THIS MEANS THAT YOUR HOME COULD BE SOLD WITHOUT YOUR PERMISSION AND WITHOUT ANY COURT ACTION IF YOU MISS ANY PAYMENT AS REQUIRED BY THIS CONTRACT." This notice shall be printed in at least 14–point boldface type, shall be set apart from the rest of the contract by a border, and shall appear directly above the space reserved for the signature of the buyer. A security interest created in any contract described in this paragraph that does not provide the notice as required by this paragraph shall be void and unenforceable.

As used in this subdivision, the term "security interest" refers to a contractual interest in property and not to a mechanic's lien or other interest in property arising by operation of law.

(c) Where the contract includes a finance charge that is determined on the precomputed basis and provides that the unearned portion of the finance charge to be refunded upon full prepayment of the contract is to be determined by a method other than actuarial, a notice in at least 10–point bold type if the contract is printed reading as follows: "Notice to buyer: (1) Do not sign this agreement before you read it or if it contains any blank spaces to be filled in. (2) You are entitled to a completely filled-in copy of this agreement. (3) You can prepay the full amount due under this agreement at any time and obtain a partial refund of the finance charge if it is $1 or more. Because of the way the amount of this refund will be figured, the time when you prepay could increase the ultimate cost of credit under this agreement. (4) If you desire to pay off in advance the full amount due, the amount of the refund you are entitled to, if any, will be furnished upon request."

(d) Where the contract includes a finance charge that is determined on the precomputed basis and provides for the actuarial method for computing the unearned portion of the finance charge upon prepayment in full, a notice in at least 10–point bold type if the contract is printed reading as follows: "Notice to buyer: (1) Do not sign this agreement before you read it or if it contains any blank spaces to be filled in. (2) You are entitled to a completely filled-in copy of this agreement. (3) You can prepay the full amount due under this agreement at any time and obtain a partial refund of the finance charge if it is $1 or more. (4) If you desire to pay off in advance the full amount due, the amount of the refund you are entitled to, if any, will be furnished upon request."

(e) Where the contract includes a finance charge that is determined on the simple-interest basis, a notice in at least 10–point bold type if the contract is printed reading as follows: "Notice to buyer: (1) Do not sign this agreement before you read it or if it contains any blank spaces to be filled in. (2) You are entitled to a completely filled-in copy of this agreement. (3) You can prepay the full amount due under this agreement at any time. (4) If you desire to pay off in advance the full amount due, the amount which is outstanding will be furnished upon request."

(f) This section shall become operative on October 1, 1995.

(g) The form specified in this section may be used before October 1, 1995, to comply with the provisions of this section as amended and repealed by Section 2 of Chapter 888 of the Statutes of 1994. *(Added by Stats.1994, c. 888 (A.B.3269), § 3, operative Oct. 1, 1995. Amended by Stats.1995, c. 91 (S.B.975), § 17, operative Oct. 1, 1995; Stats.1995, c. 153 (A.B.1635), § 1, eff. July 24, 1995, operative Oct. 1, 1995.)*

Research References

Miller and Starr California Real Estate § 27:56, Home Improvement Contracts--Contracts for Installment Payments, Cash Discounts, or Finance Charges.
1 Witkin Cal. Summ. 10th Contracts § 545, (S 545) Residential Property: in General.
4 Witkin, California Summary 10th Sales § 272, Written and Signed.
4 Witkin, California Summary 10th Sales § 274, Notice to Buyer.
4 Witkin, California Summary 10th Sales § 287, Penalties.

§ 1803.3. Contract; contents

Except as provided in Article 8 (commencing with Section 1808.1) of this chapter, a contract shall contain the following:

(a) The names of the seller and the buyer, the place of business of the seller, the residence or place of business of the buyer as specified by the buyer and a description of the goods or services sufficient to identify them. Services or multiple items of goods may be described in general terms and may be described in detail sufficient to identify them in a separate writing.

(b) Every contract subject to this chapter shall contain the disclosures required by Regulation Z whether or not Regulation Z applies to the transaction. In addition, to the extent applicable, the contract shall contain the other disclosures and notices required by, and shall satisfy the requirements and limitations of, this section. The disclosures required by subdivision (c) may be itemized or subtotaled to a greater extent than as required by that subdivision and shall be made together and in the sequence set forth in that subdivision. No particular terminology is required to disclose the items set forth in subdivision (c) except as therein expressly provided. Except as otherwise provided by this subdivision (b), these disclosures and notices may appear in the contract in any location or sequence and may be combined or interspersed with other provisions of the contract.

(c) The contract shall contain the following disclosures, as applicable, which shall be labeled "itemization of the amount financed":

(1)(A) The cash price, exclusive of taxes imposed on the sale.

(B) Taxes imposed on the sale.

(C) The total of the above.

(2) An itemization of the amount to be paid to any public officer for official fees.

(3) The aggregate amount of premiums agreed, upon execution of the contract, to be paid for policies of insurance included in the contract, excluding the amount of any insurance premium included in the finance charge.

(4) A subtotal representing the sum of the foregoing items.

(5) The amount of the buyer's downpayment, which downpayment shall not include any administrative finance charge charged, received, or collected by the seller pursuant to subdivision (c) of Section 1805.1 and as shown as item (6), itemized to show the following:

(A) The net agreed value of the property being traded in.

(B) The amount of any portion of downpayment to be deferred until not later than the due date of the second regularly scheduled installment under the contract and which is not subject to a finance charge.

(C) The amount of any manufacturer's rebate applied or to be applied to the downpayment.

(D) The remaining amount paid or to be paid by the buyer as a downpayment.

(6) The amount of any administrative finance charge, labeled "prepaid finance charge."

(7) The difference between item (4) and the sum of items (5) and (6), labeled "amount financed."

(d) If the payment of all or a portion of the downpayment is to be deferred, the deferred payment shall be reflected in the payment schedule disclosed pursuant to Regulation Z.

(e) If the downpayment includes property being traded in, the contract shall contain a brief description of that property.

(f)(1) Where the contract includes a finance charge determined on the precomputed basis, the contract shall identify the method of computing the unearned portion of the finance charge in the event of prepayment in full of the buyer's obligation and contain a statement of the amount or method of computation of any charge that may be deducted from the amount of any such unearned finance charge in computing the amount that will be credited to the obligation or refunded to the buyer. Reference to the Rule of 78's, the sum of the digits, the sum of the periodic time balances or the actuarial method shall constitute a sufficient identification of the method of computing the unearned portion of the finance charge.

(2) Where the contract includes a finance charge which is determined on the simple-interest basis but provides for a minimum finance charge in the event of prepayment in full, the contract shall contain a statement of that fact and the amount of the minimum finance charge or its method of calculation.

(g) The contract shall contain an itemization of any insurance included as part of the amount financed disclosed pursuant to paragraph (3) of subdivision (c) and of any insurance included as part of the finance charge. The itemization shall identify the type of insurance coverage and the premium charged therefor, and, if the insurance expires before the date of the last scheduled installment included in the repayment schedule, the term of the insurance shall be stated. *(Added by Stats.1959, c. 201, p. 2095, § 1, operative Jan. 1, 1960. Amended by Stats.1969, c. 625, p. 1266, § 6; Stats.1970, c. 546, p. 1044, § 15; Stats.1979, c. 805, p. 2774, § 8; Stats.1980, c. 1380, p. 5009, § 8, eff. Oct. 1, 1980; Stats.1981, c. 1075, p. 4115, § 6, operative Oct. 1, 1982.)*

Research References

Miller and Starr California Real Estate § 27:56, Home Improvement Contracts--Contracts for Installment Payments, Cash Discounts, or Finance Charges.
4 Witkin, California Summary 10th Sales § 273, Disclosure of Cost Items.
4 Witkin, California Summary 10th Sales § 275, Compliance With Regulation Z.
4 Witkin, California Summary 10th Sales § 276, (S 276) Copy to Buyer.

4 Witkin, California Summary 10th Sales § 278, (S 278) Limitation of Charges.

§ 1803.4. Obtaining signature of buyer to contract containing blank spaces

The seller shall not obtain the signature of the buyer to a contract when it contains blank spaces to be filled in after it has been signed. *(Added by Stats.1959, c. 201, p. 2096, § 1, operative Jan. 1, 1960.)*

Research References

Miller and Starr California Real Estate § 27:56, Home Improvement Contracts--Contracts for Installment Payments, Cash Discounts, or Finance Charges.
4 Witkin, California Summary 10th Sales § 272, Written and Signed.

§ 1803.5. Cost of insurance included in contract and separate charge made to buyer

If the cost of any insurance is included in the contract and a separate charge is made to the buyer for such insurance:

(a) The contract shall state whether the insurance is to be procured by the buyer or the seller.

(b) The amount, included for such insurance, shall not exceed the premiums chargeable in accordance with rate fixed for such insurance by the insurer.

(c) If the insurance is to be procured by the seller or holder, he shall, within 45 days after delivery of the goods or furnishing of the services under the contract, deliver, mail or cause to be mailed to the buyer, at his address as specified in the contract, a notice thereof or a copy of the policy or policies of insurance or a certificate or certificates of the insurance so procured.

(d) The provisions of Insurance Code Section 1668 shall apply to any violation of this section. *(Added by Stats.1959, c. 201, p. 2096, § 1, operative Jan. 1, 1960.)*

Research References

4 Witkin, California Summary 10th Sales § 276, (S 276) Copy to Buyer.
4 Witkin, California Summary 10th Sales § 278, (S 278) Limitation of Charges.

§ 1803.6. Delinquency charges; costs of collection

(a) A contract may provide that for each installment in default the buyer shall pay a delinquency charge not in excess of one of the following amounts:

(1) For a period in default of not less than 10 days, an amount not in excess of ten dollars ($10).

(2) For a period in default of not less than 15 days, an amount not in excess of fifteen dollars ($15).

(b) Only one delinquency charge may be collected on any installment regardless of the period during which it remains in default. Payments timely received by the seller under a written extension or deferral agreement shall not be subject to any delinquency charge. The contract may also provide for payment of any actual and reasonable costs of collection occasioned by removal of the goods from the state without written permission of the holder, or by the failure of the buyer to notify the holder of any change of residence, or by the failure of the buyer to communicate with the holder for a period of 45 days after any default in making payments due under the contract. *(Added by Stats.1959, c. 201, p. 2096, § 1, operative Jan. 1, 1960. Amended by Stats.1980, c. 1380, p. 5011, § 9, eff. Oct. 1, 1980; Stats.1994, c. 168 (S.B.1583), § 1; Stats.1996, c. 301 (S.B.2050), § 1.)*

Research References

4 Witkin, California Summary 10th Sales § 278, (S 278) Limitation of Charges.

4 Witkin, California Summary 10th Sales § 280, (S 280) Right to Pay Before Maturity.

§ 1803.7. Delivery of copy of completed contract or other document to buyer; penalties; acknowledgment of delivery; rebuttable presumption

The seller shall deliver to the buyer at the time of the buyer's signature a legible copy of the contract or of any other document which the seller has required or requested the buyer to sign, and which he has signed, during the contract negotiation. In addition to the penalties provided under Article 12.2 (commencing with Section 1812.6) of this chapter, until the seller delivers such documents, the buyer shall be obligated to pay only the cash price. Any acknowledgment by the buyer of delivery of a copy of such documents shall be printed or written in a size equal to at least 10-point bold type and, if contained in the contract shall also appear directly above the space reserved for the buyer's signature. The buyer's written acknowledgment, conforming to the requirements of this section of delivery of a copy of such documents shall be a rebuttable presumption of such delivery and of compliance with this section and Section 1803.4, in any action or proceeding by or against an assignee of the contract without knowledge to the contrary when he purchases the contract. If the holder furnishes the buyer a copy of such documents, or a notice containing the items required by Section 1803.3 and stating that the buyer should notify the holder in writing within 30 days if he was not furnished a copy of the contract or of any other document which the seller had required or requested the buyer to sign, and which he did sign, during the contract negotiation, and no such notification is given, it shall be conclusively presumed in favor of the third party that copies of such documents were furnished as required by Sections 1803.4 and 1803.7. *(Added by Stats.1959, c. 201, p. 2096, § 1. Amended by Stats.1961, c. 1214, p. 2950, § 3; Stats.1969, c. 353, p. 730, § 1; Stats.1970, c. 546, p. 1044, § 16.)*

Research References

Miller and Starr California Real Estate § 27:56, Home Improvement Contracts--Contracts for Installment Payments, Cash Discounts, or Finance Charges.
1 Witkin Cal. Summ. 10th Contracts § 545, (S 545) Residential Property: in General.
4 Witkin, California Summary 10th Sales § 276, (S 276) Copy to Buyer.

§ 1803.8. Negotiation of sales by mail or telephone

Retail installment sales negotiated and entered into by mail or telephone without personal solicitation by a salesman or other representative of the seller, where the seller's cash and deferred payment prices and other terms are clearly set forth in a catalog or other printed solicitation of business which is generally available to the public, may be made as hereinafter provided. All of the provisions of this chapter shall apply to such sales except that the seller shall not be required to deliver a copy of the contract to the buyer as provided in Section 1803.7, and if, when the proposed retail installment sale contract is received by the seller from the buyer, there are blank spaces to be filled in, the seller may insert in the appropriate blank spaces the amounts of money and other terms which are set forth in the seller's catalog which is then in effect. In lieu of the copy of the contract provided for in Section 1803.7 the seller shall, within 15 days from the date of shipment of goods, furnish to the buyer a written statement of the items inserted in such blank spaces. *(Added by Stats.1959, c. 201, p. 2097, § 1, operative Jan. 1, 1960.)*

Research References

4 Witkin, California Summary 10th Sales § 276, (S 276) Copy to Buyer.

§ 1803.9. Contract contingent on loan to be obtained by buyer; rescission upon failure; time; return of consideration

If it is explicitly understood between the seller and the buyer that all or any part of the cash price will be paid from the proceeds of a loan to be obtained by the buyer from a third party, the contract of sale or purchase order may be rescinded at the election of the buyer, and all considerations thereupon shall be returned by the respective parties without further demand, if the buyer is unable to obtain such third-party financing upon reasonable terms after having made a reasonable effort to obtain it, and buyer notifies the seller of the rescission within three business days. *(Added by Stats.1979, c. 1151, p. 4222, § 3.)*

Research References

4 Witkin, California Summary 10th Sales § 269, Inapplicable to Real Property.
4 Witkin, California Summary 10th Sales § 279, (S 279) Right to Rescind If Financing Unavailable.

§ 1803.10. Rebates, discounts, commissions, or other consideration

It shall be unlawful for any seller to induce or attempt to induce any person to enter into a contract subject to this act by offering a rebate, discount, commission, or other consideration, contingent upon the happening of a future event, on the condition that the buyer either sells, or gives information or assistance for the purpose of leading to a sale by the seller of, the same or related goods. *(Added by Stats.1968, c. 452, p. 1074, § 2.)*

Research References

Rutter, Cal. Practice Guide: Enforcing Judgments/Debts Ch. 3-A, A. Evaluating the Claim.
4 Witkin, California Summary 10th Sales § 277, (S 277) Prohibited Terms and Acts.

§ 1803.11. Advertisements; solicitation to enter into contract without intent to sell contract to financing agency or assignee; requirements

It shall be unlawful for any seller to solicit buyers, in any advertisement, to enter into a retail installment contract with it if the seller does not intend to sell that retail installment contract to a financing agency or other assignee, unless the advertisement clearly states the periodic rate or range of periodic rates, expressed as an annual percentage rate or a range of annual percentage rates that will be used to determine the finance charge imposed on the retail installment contract. *(Added by Stats.1991, c. 819 (S.B.1105), § 1.)*

Research References

4 Witkin, California Summary 10th Sales § 278, (S 278) Limitation of Charges.

ARTICLE 4. RESTRICTIONS ON RETAIL INSTALLMENT CONTRACTS

Section
1804.1. Prohibited provisions.
1804.2. Assignment of seller's rights; recourse.
1804.3. Security interest in goods paid for or not sold; security interest in real property for sale of unattached goods.
1804.4. Invalidity of prohibited provisions; effect upon contract.

§ 1804.1. Prohibited provisions

No contract or obligation shall contain any provision by which:

(a) The buyer agrees not to assert against a seller a claim or defense arising out of the sale or agrees not to assert against an assignee such a claim or defense other than as provided in Section 1804.2.

(b) In the absence of the buyer's default in the performance of any of his or her obligations, the holder may accelerate the maturity of any part or all of the amount owing thereunder.

(c) A power of attorney is given to confess judgment in this state, or an assignment of wages is given; provided, that nothing herein contained shall prohibit the giving of an assignment of wages contained in a separate instrument, executed pursuant to Section 300 of the Labor Code.

(d) The seller or holder of the contract or other person acting on his or her behalf is given authority to enter upon the buyer's premises unlawfully or to commit any breach of the peace in the repossession of goods.

(e) The buyer waives any right of action against the seller or holder of the contract or other person acting on his or her behalf, for any illegal act committed in the collection of payments under the contract or in the repossession of goods.

(f) The buyer executes a power of attorney appointing the seller or holder of the contract, or other person acting on his or her behalf, as the buyer's agent in collection of payments under the contract or in the repossession of goods.

(g) The buyer relieves the seller from liability for any legal remedies which the buyer may have against the seller under the contract or any separate instrument executed in connection therewith.

(h) The buyer agrees to the payment of any charge by reason of the exercise of his or her right to rescind or void the contract.

(i) The seller or holder of the contract is given the right to commence an action on a contract under the provisions of this chapter in a county other than the county in which the contract was in fact signed by the buyer, the county in which the buyer resides at the commencement of the action, the county in which the buyer resided at the time that the contract was entered into, or in the county in which the goods purchased pursuant to the contract have been so affixed to real property as to become a part of such real property.

(j) The seller takes a security interest, other than a mechanics' lien, in the buyer's real property which is the buyer's primary residence where the buyer is a person who is 65 years of age or older and the contract is for a home improvement, as defined in Section 7151.2 of the Business and Professions Code. *(Added by Stats.1959, c. 201, p. 2097, § 1. Amended by Stats.1961, c. 1214, p. 2950, § 4; Stats.1963, c. 1310, p. 2833, § 1; Stats.1965, c. 776, p. 2361, § 1; Stats.1999, c. 512 (S.B.187), § 2.)*

Research References

Rutter, Cal. Practice Guide: Enforcing Judgments/Debts Ch. 3-A, A. Evaluating the Claim.
Miller and Starr California Real Estate § 27:56, Home Improvement Contracts--Contracts for Installment Payments, Cash Discounts, or Finance Charges.
3 Witkin Cal. Proc. 5th Actions § 786, (S 786) Distinctions and Exceptions.
3 Witkin Cal. Proc. 5th Actions § 845, Actions on Installment Contracts.
4 Witkin, California Summary 10th Sales § 277, (S 277) Prohibited Terms and Acts.
4 Witkin, California Summary 10th Sales § 289, Venue, Attorneys' Fees, and Costs.

§ 1804.2. Assignment of seller's rights; recourse

(a) An assignee of the seller's rights is subject to all equities and defenses of the buyer against the seller arising out of the sale, notwithstanding an agreement to the contrary, but the assignee's liability may not exceed the amount of the debt owing to the assignee at the time of the assignment.

(b) The assignee shall have recourse against the seller to the extent of any liability incurred by the assignee pursuant to this section regardless of whether the assignment was with or without recourse. *(Added by Stats.1967, c. 1294, p. 3099, § 2. Amended by Stats.1971, c. 999, p. 1917, § 1; Stats.1975, c. 66, p. 128, § 1.)*

Research References

Rutter, Cal. Practice Guide: Enforcing Judgments/Debts Ch. 3-A, A. Evaluating the Claim.

Miller and Starr California Real Estate § 27:56, Home Improvement Contracts--Contracts for Installment Payments, Cash Discounts, or Finance Charges.

1 Witkin Cal. Summ. 10th Contracts § 735, in General.

4 Witkin, California Summary 10th Sales § 247, (S 247) Assignment by Seller.

4 Witkin, California Summary 10th Sales § 277, (S 277) Prohibited Terms and Acts.

4 Witkin, California Summary 10th Sales § 281, (S 281) Assignment by Seller.

4 Witkin, California Summary 10th Sales § 287, Penalties.

§ 1804.3. Security interest in goods paid for or not sold; security interest in real property for sale of unattached goods

(a) No contract other than one for services shall provide for a security interest in any goods theretofore fully paid for or which have not been sold by the seller.

(b) Any contract for goods which provides for a security interest in real property where the primary goods sold are not to be attached to the real property shall be a violation of this chapter and subject to the penalties set forth in Article 12.2 (commencing with Section 1812.6).

(c) This section shall become operative October 1, 1982. *(Added by Stats.1980, c. 1380, p. 5012, § 11, eff. Oct. 1, 1980. Amended by Stats.1981, c. 107, p. 817, § 4, eff. June 29, 1981, operative April 1, 1982; Stats.1982, c. 129, p. 403, § 4, eff. March 25, 1982, operative Oct. 1, 1982.)*

Research References

Miller and Starr California Real Estate § 17:6, in General; Personal Property Secured Transactions.

Miller and Starr California Real Estate § 27:56, Home Improvement Contracts--Contracts for Installment Payments, Cash Discounts, or Finance Charges.

4 Witkin, California Summary 10th Sales § 277, (S 277) Prohibited Terms and Acts.

§ 1804.4. Invalidity of prohibited provisions; effect upon contract

Any provision in a contract which is prohibited by this chapter shall be void but shall not otherwise affect the validity of the contract. *(Added by Stats.1959, c. 201, p. 2098, § 1, operative Jan. 1, 1960.)*

Research References

Rutter, Cal. Practice Guide: Enforcing Judgments/Debts Ch. 3-A, A. Evaluating the Claim.

4 Witkin, California Summary 10th Sales § 277, (S 277) Prohibited Terms and Acts.

ARTICLE 5. FINANCE CHARGE LIMITATION

§ 1805.1. Rates; prohibition of annual fee or charge in retail installment contract

The holder of the contract shall not charge, collect, or receive a finance charge which exceeds the dollar amount shown pursuant to subdivision (b) of Section 1803.3, except to the extent (a) caused by the holder's receipt of one or more payments under a contract which provides for determination of the finance charge or a portion thereof on the 365-day basis at a time or times other than as originally scheduled, whether or not the parties enter into an agreement pursuant to Section 1807.1, (b) permitted by paragraph (2), (3), or (4) of subdivision (c) of Section 226.17 of Regulation Z, or (3) permitted by Section 1805.8.

No annual fee or charge shall be made in any retail installment contract. *(Added by Stats.1982, c. 129, p. 405, § 10, eff. March 25, 1982, operative Oct. 1, 1982. Amended by Stats.1982, c. 1611, p. 6443, § 2, eff. Sept. 30, 1982, operative Jan. 1, 1984; Stats.1983, c. 1157, § 2, operative Jan. 1, 1986; Stats.1985, c. 227, § 2, operative Jan. 1, 1988; Stats.1988, c. 479, § 1; Stats.1991, c. 819 (S.B.1105), § 2.)*

Research References

Rutter, Cal. Practice Guide: Enforcing Judgments/Debts Ch. 3-A, A. Evaluating the Claim.

Miller and Starr California Real Estate § 21:35, Who is Liable for Usury Penalties--Other Exemptions.

4 Witkin, California Summary 10th Sales § 278, (S 278) Limitation of Charges.

§ 1805.2. Installment payments

Contracts may be payable in successive monthly, semimonthly or weekly installments. *(Added by Stats.1959, c. 201, p. 2098, § 1, operative Jan. 1, 1960.)*

§ 1805.4. Inclusive charge; additional fee for return of dishonored check, negotiable order of withdrawal or share draft

The finance charge shall be inclusive of all charges incident to investigating and making the contract and for the extension of the credit provided for in the contract, and no fee, expense or other charge whatsoever shall be taken, received, reserved or contracted for except as otherwise provided in this chapter.

The seller or holder of a retail installment contract may charge and collect a fee not to exceed fifteen dollars ($15) for the return by a depository institution of a dishonored check, negotiable order of withdrawal, or share draft issued in connection with the retail installment contract. The fee is not included in charges as defined in this chapter or in determining the applicable charges which may be made under this chapter. *(Added by Stats.1959, c. 201, p. 2098, § 1, operative Jan. 1, 1960. Amended by Stats.1970, c. 546, p. 1046, § 20; Stats.1982, c. 512, p. 2289, § 1; Stats.1993, c. 101 (S.B.329), § 1.)*

Research References

4 Witkin, California Summary 10th Sales § 278, (S 278) Limitation of Charges.

§ 1805.6. Undelivered goods

(a) Notwithstanding the provisions of any contract to the contrary, except as provided in subdivision (b) or (c), no retail seller shall assess any finance charge for goods purchased under a retail installment contract until the goods are in the buyer's possession.

(b) A finance charge may be assessed for such undelivered goods, as follows:

(1) From the date when such goods are available for pickup by the buyer and the buyer is notified of their availability, or

(2) From the date of purchase, when such goods are delivered or available for pickup by the buyer within 10 days of the date of purchase.

(c) In the case of a home improvement contract as defined in Section 7151.2 of the Business and Professions Code, a finance charge may be assessed from the approximate date of commencement of the work as set forth in the home improvement contract. *(Added by Stats.1975, c. 1041, p. 2455, § 1. Amended by Stats.1976, c. 1271, p. 5625, § 3, eff. Sept. 28, 1976, operative Jan. 1, 1978; Stats.1977, c. 868, p. 2622, § 3; Stats.1979, c. 1000, p. 3400, § 4; Stats.1980, c. 1380, p. 5015, § 15, eff. Oct. 1, 1980; Stats.1981, c. 1075, p. 4120, § 8, operative Oct. 1, 1982.)*

Research References

4 Witkin, California Summary 10th Sales § 278, (S 278) Limitation of Charges.

§ 1805.7. Finance charge; calculation after January 1, 1983

All contracts entered into between a buyer and a seller on or after January 1, 1983, shall provide for the calculation of the finance charge contemplated by item (1) of subdivision (a) of Section 1805.1 on the simple-interest basis if the date on which the final installment is due, according to the original terms of the contract, is more than 62 months after the date of the contract. *(Added by Stats.1979, c. 805, p. 2776, § 11.)*

Research References

4 Witkin, California Summary 10th Sales § 278, (S 278) Limitation of Charges.

§ 1805.8. Amounts advanced subsequent to execution of contract; maximum rate of finance charge

The maximum rate of finance charge which may be imposed on amounts advanced by the holder subsequent to the execution of the contract for insurance, repairs to or preservation of the goods, or preservation of the holder's security interest therein, shall not exceed the annual percentage rate disclosed pursuant to item (b) of Section 1803.3. *(Added by Stats.1979, c. 805, p. 2776, § 11.5. Amended by Stats.1981, c. 1075, p. 4120, § 9, operative Oct. 1, 1982.)*

Research References

4 Witkin, California Summary 10th Sales § 278, (S 278) Limitation of Charges.

§ 1805.9. Determination of finance charge on precomputed and simple-interest bases; exception

No contract shall provide for a finance charge which is determined in part by the precomputed basis and in part by the simple-interest basis, except for any finance charge permitted by Section 1805.8. *(Added by Stats.1979, c. 805, p. 2776, § 11.7.)*

Research References

Rutter, Cal. Practice Guide: Enforcing Judgments/Debts Ch. 3-A, A. Evaluating the Claim.
4 Witkin, California Summary 10th Sales § 278, (S 278) Limitation of Charges.

ARTICLE 6. PAYMENTS

Section

§ 1806.1. Payment to last known holder of contract or installment account; discharge of obligation

Unless the buyer has notice of actual or intended assignment of a contract or installment account, payment thereunder made by the buyer to the last known holder of such contract or installment account, shall to the extent of the payment, discharge the buyer's obligation. *(Added by Stats.1959, c. 201, p. 2099, § 1, operative Jan. 1, 1960.)*

§ 1806.2. Statement of unpaid balance

At any time after its execution, but not later than one year after the last payment thereunder, the holder of a contract shall, upon written request of the buyer made in good faith, promptly give or forward to the buyer a detailed written statement which will state with accuracy the total amount, if any, unpaid thereunder. Such a statement shall be supplied by the holder once each year without charge; if any additional statement is requested by the buyer, the holder shall supply such statement to the buyer at a charge not exceeding one dollar ($1) for each additional statement supplied to the buyer. The provisions of this section shall apply only to those transactions wherein, instead of periodic statements of account, the buyer is provided with a passbook or payment book in which all payments, credits, charges and the unpaid balance is entered. *(Added by Stats. 1959, c. 201, p. 2099, § 1, operative Jan. 1, 1960. Amended by Stats.1969, c. 625, p. 1266, § 7.)*

Research References

4 Witkin, California Summary 10th Sales § 280, (S 280) Right to Pay Before Maturity.

§ 1806.3. Payment or satisfaction before maturity; refund credit

(a) Notwithstanding any provision of a contract to the contrary, the buyer may pay at any time before maturity the entire indebtedness evidenced by the contract without penalty. In the event of prepayment in full:

(1) If the finance charge was determined on the precomputed basis, the amount required to repay the contract shall be the outstanding contract balance as of that date, provided, however, that the buyer shall be entitled to a refund credit in the amount of the unearned portion of the finance charge. The amount of the unearned portion of the finance charge shall be at least as great a proportion of the finance charge, or if the contract has been extended, deferred, or refinanced, of the additional charge therefor, as the sum of the periodic monthly time balances payable more than 15 days after the date of prepayment bears to the sum of all the periodic monthly time balances under the schedule of installments in the contract or, if the contract has been extended, deferred or refinanced, as so extended, deferred or refinanced. Where the amount of the refund credit is less than one dollar ($1), no refund credit need be made by the holder. Any refund credit in the amount of one dollar ($1) or more may be made in cash or credited to the outstanding obligations of the buyer under the contract.

(2) If the finance charge or a portion thereof was determined on the simple-interest basis, the amount required to prepay the contract shall be the outstanding contract balance as of that date, including any earned finance charges which are unpaid as of that date, and provided further that in cases where the finance charge or a portion thereof is determined on the 360-day basis, the payments theretofore received will be assumed to have been

received on their respective due dates regardless of the actual dates on which those payments were received.

(b) Notwithstanding any provision of a contract to the contrary, whenever the indebtedness created by any retail installment contract is satisfied prior to its maturity through surrender of the collateral, repossession of the collateral, redemption of the collateral after repossession, or any judgment, the outstanding obligation of the buyer shall be determined as provided in subdivision (a); provided further that the buyer's outstanding obligation shall be computed by the holder as of the date the holder recovers the value of the collateral through disposition thereof or judgment is entered or, if the holder elects to keep the collateral in satisfaction of the buyer's indebtedness, as of the date the holder takes possession of the collateral.

(c) This section does not preclude the collection or retention by the holder of any delinquency charge made pursuant to Section 1803.6. *(Added by Stats.1959, c. 201, p. 2099, § 1, operative Jan. 1, 1960. Amended by Stats.1970, c. 546, p. 1046, § 22; Stats.1973, c. 793, p. 1409, § 1; Stats.1979, c. 805, p. 2777, § 12; Stats.1980, c. 1380, p. 5015, § 16, eff. Oct. 1, 1980; Stats.1988, c. 479, § 5; Stats.1991, c. 819 (S.B.1105), § 7.)*

Research References

4 Witkin, California Summary 10th Sales § 280, (S 280) Right to Pay Before Maturity.

§ 1806.4. Acknowledgment of payments; release of security

After the payment of all sums for which the buyer is obligated under a contract and upon demand made by the buyer, the holder shall deliver, or mail to the buyer at his last known address, such one or more good and sufficient instruments as may be necessary to acknowledge payment in full and to release all security in the goods under such contract. *(Added by Stats.1959, c. 201, p. 2099, § 1, operative Jan. 1, 1960.)*

ARTICLE 7.   REFINANCING AND CONSOLIDATION

Section
1807.1.   Extension of due date or deferment of payment; agreement; charge.
1807.2.   Refinancing; agreement; charge; provisions applicable to consolidation of contracts.
1807.3.   Installment more than double amount of regularly scheduled equal payment; balloon payment; right to new payment schedule; necessary provision.

§ 1807.1.   Extension of due date or deferment of payment; agreement; charge

(a) The holder of a retail installment contract may, upon agreement with the buyer, extend the scheduled due date or defer the scheduled payment of all or of any part of any installment or installments payable thereunder. No charge shall be made for any such extension or deferment unless the agreement for such extension or deferment is in writing and signed by the parties thereto.

(b) Where the contract includes a finance charge determined on the precomputed basis, the holder may charge and contract for the payment of an extension or deferral agreement charge by the buyer and collect and receive the same, but such charge may not exceed an amount equal to 1 percent per month simple interest on the amount of the installment or installments, or part thereof, extended or deferred for the period of extension or deferral. Such period shall not exceed the period from the date when such extended or deferred installment or installments, or part thereof, would have been payable in the absence of such extension or deferral, to the date when such installment or installments, or part thereof, are made payable under the

agreement of extension or deferment; except that a minimum charge of one dollar ($1) for the period of extension or deferral may be made in any case where the extension or deferral agreement charge, when computed at such rate, amounts to less than one dollar ($1).

(c) Where the contract includes a finance charge determined on the simple-interest basis, the holder may charge and contract for the payment of an extension or deferral agreement charge by the buyer and collect and receive the same, but the charge for the extension or deferral agreement may not exceed the lesser of twenty-five dollars ($25) or 10 percent of the then unpaid balance of the contract. Such charge shall be in addition to any finance charges which accrue because such extended or deferred payments are received at a time other than as originally scheduled.

(d) An extension or deferral agreement may also provide for the payment by the buyer of the additional cost to the holder of the contract of premiums for continuing in force, until the end of such period of extension or deferral, any insurance coverages provided for in the contract, subject to the provisions of Section 1803.5. *(Added by Stats.1959, c. 201, p. 2100, § 1, operative Jan. 1, 1960. Amended by Stats.1980, c. 1380, p. 5016, § 17, eff. Oct. 1, 1980.)*

§ 1807.2.   Refinancing; agreement; charge; provisions applicable to consolidation of contracts

The holder of a retail installment contract or contracts may, upon agreement in writing with the buyer, refinance the remaining amount owing on the contract or contracts by providing for a new schedule of installment payments. The holder may charge and contract for the payment of a refinance charge by the buyer and collect and receive the same, but such refinance charge shall be based upon the amount refinanced, plus any additional cost of insurance and of official fees incident to the refinancing, after the deduction of a refund credit in an amount equal to that to which the buyer would have been entitled under Section 1806.3 if he or she had prepaid in full his or her obligations under the contract or contracts. The agreement for refinancing may also provide for the payment by the buyer of the additional cost to the holder of the contract or contracts of premiums for continuing in force, until the maturity of the contract or contracts as refinanced, any insurance coverages provided for therein, subject to Section 1803.5. The refinancing agreement shall set forth:

(a) The amount of the existing outstanding balance to be refinanced, which consists of the remaining amount owing to be refinanced.

(b) The amount of any refund credit.

(c) The difference between subdivisions (a) and (b), which is the net outstanding balance to be refinanced.

(d) Any additional cost of insurance and of official fees to the buyer.

(e) The sum of subdivisions (c) and (d), which is the amount financed.

(f) The finance charge (1) as expressed as the annual percentage rate as defined in Regulation Z and (2) expressed in dollars.

(g) The number amount, and due dates or periods of payments scheduled to repay the indebtedness and the sum of those payments.

The items need not be stated in the sequence or order set forth above; additional items may be included to explain the computations made in determining the amount to be paid by the buyer. Where there is a consolidation of two or more contracts then Sections 1808.1 and 1808.2 shall apply. If the finance charge or any portion thereof is calculated on the 365-day basis, the amount of the finance charge shown pursuant to subdivision (f) shall be that amount which will be incurred by the buyer if all payments are received by the seller on their respective due dates. *(Added by Stats.1959, c. 201, p. 2100, § 1, operative Jan. 1, 1960. Amended by Stats.1970, c. 546, p. 1046, § 23; Stats.1979, c. 805, p. 2777, § 13; Stats.1981, c. 1075, p. 4120, § 10, operative Oct. 1, 1982; Stats.1988, c. 479, § 6; Stats.1991, c. 819 (S.B.1105), § 9.)*

Research References

4 Witkin, California Summary 10th Sales § 278, (S 278) Limitation of Charges.

§ 1807.3. Installment more than double amount of regularly scheduled equal payment; balloon payment; right to new payment schedule; necessary provision

(a) If any payment, other than a deferred downpayment, under a contract or refinancing agreement is more than twice the amount of an otherwise regularly scheduled equal payment, the contract or refinancing agreement shall contain the following provision:

"The payment schedule contained in this contract requires that you make a balloon payment of $_____ which is a payment more than double the amount of the regular payments. You have an absolute right to obtain a new payment schedule if you default in the payment of any balloon payment."

(Amount of balloon payment)

(b) If the buyer defaults in the payment of any balloon payment, he or she shall be given an absolute right to obtain a new payment schedule. Unless agreed to by the buyer, the periodic payments under the new schedule shall not be substantially greater than the average of the preceding installments. *(Added by Stats.1959, c. 201, p. 2101, § 1, operative Jan. 1, 1960. Amended by Stats.1969, c. 625, p. 1267, § 8; Stats.1970, c. 546, p. 1047, § 23.5; Stats.1981, c. 1075, p. 4121, § 11, operative Oct. 1, 1982.)*

ARTICLE 8.   ADD–ON SALES

Section
1808.1.   Contract provisions.
1808.2.   Subsequent purchase; memorandum; contents; delivery to buyer.
1808.3.   Series of transactions; memorandum; contents; delivery to buyer.
1808.4.   Obligation of buyer prior to delivery of memorandum.
1808.5.   Finance charge; determination.

§ 1808.1.   Contract provisions

A retail installment contract, which otherwise conforms to the requirements of this chapter, may contain the provision that the seller may at his option add subsequent purchases made by the buyer to the contract, and that the total price of the goods or services covered by the contract shall be increased by the price of such additional goods or services, and that all finance charges and installment payments may at the seller's option be increased proportionately, and that all terms and conditions of the contract shall apply equally to such additional goods or services. The contract may also provide that the goods purchased under the previous contract or contracts shall be security for the goods purchased under the subsequent contract but only until such time as the total of payments under the previous contract or contracts is fully paid. *(Added by Stats.1959, c. 201, p. 2101, § 1,*

operative Jan. 1, 1960. Amended by Stats.1969, c. 625, p. 1267, § 9; Stats.1970, c. 546, p. 1047, § 24.)

Research References

4 Witkin, California Summary 10th Sales § 278, (S 278) Limitation of Charges.
4 Witkin, California Summary 10th Sales § 287, Penalties.

§ 1808.2.   Subsequent purchase; memorandum; contents; delivery to buyer

When a subsequent purchase is made, the entire amount of all payments made previous thereto shall be deemed to have been applied toward the payment of the previous deferred payment price or deferred payment prices. Each payment thereafter received shall be deemed to be allocated to all of the various deferred payment prices in the same proportion or ratio as the original cash sale prices of the various purchases bear to one another; where the amount of each installment payment is increased in connection with the subsequent purchase, the subsequent payments (at the seller's election) may be deemed to be allocated as follows: an amount equal to the original payment to the previous deferred payment price, and an amount equal to the increase, to the subsequent deferred payment price. However, the amount of any initial or downpayment on the subsequent purchase shall be deemed to be allocated in its entirety to such purchase.

When a subsequent purchase under this section is made the seller shall deliver to the buyer, prior to the due date of the first installment, a memorandum which shall set forth the following:

(a) The names of the seller and the buyer, the place of business of the seller, the residence or place of business of the buyer as specified by the buyer and a description of the goods and services sufficient to identify them. Services or multiple items of goods may be described in general terms and may be described in detail in a separate writing.

(b) The cash price of the goods, services and accessories which are the subject matter of the new retail installment sale.

(c) The amount of the buyer's downpayment, itemizing the amounts paid in money and in goods and containing a brief description of the goods, if any, traded in.

(d) The difference between item (b) and item (c) which is the unpaid balance of cash price.

(e) The amount of the existing outstanding balance to be consolidated, which consists of the unpaid time balance or balances of the prior contract or contracts to be consolidated.

(f) The amount of any unearned finance charge, determined by deducting from the amount of item (e) any then unearned finance charge in an amount not less than the refund credit provided for in Article 6 (commencing with Section 1806.1) of this chapter (computed, however, without the allowance of any minimum earned finance charge).

(g) The difference between items (e) and (f), which is the net outstanding balance to be consolidated.

(h) The amount, if any, included for insurance, specifying the coverages.

(i) The amount, if any, of official fees.

(j) The unpaid balance, which is the sum of items (d), (g), (h) and (i).

(k) The finance charge (1) expressed as the annual percentage rate as defined in Regulation Z and (2) expressed in dollars, and computed in conformity with Section 1808.5.

(*l*) The number, amount, and due dates or periods of payment scheduled to repay the indebtedness and the sum of such payments.

(m) Any "balloon payments" as described in Section 1807.3.

The items need not be stated in the sequence or order set forth above; additional items may be included to explain the computations made in determining the amount to be paid by the buyer. If the finance charge or any portion thereof is calculated on the 365-day basis, the amount of the finance charge shown pursuant to item (k) shall be that amount which will be incurred by the buyer if all payments are received by the seller on their respective due dates. *(Added by Stats.1959, c. 201, p. 2101, § 1, operative Jan. 1, 1960. Amended by Stats.1969, c. 625, p. 1267, § 10; Stats.1970, c. 546, p. 1048, § 25; Stats.1979, c. 805, p. 2778, § 14.)*

§ 1808.3. Series of transactions; memorandum; contents; delivery to buyer

If a credit sale is one of a series of transactions made pursuant to an agreement providing for the addition of the amount financed plus the finance charge for the current sale to an existing outstanding balance, and the disclosures required under this article for the initial sale and each subsequent sale are delayed until some date prior to the date the first payment for that particular sale is due; and

(1) The customer has approved in writing both the annual percentage rate or rates and the method of treating any unearned finance charge on an existing outstanding balance in computing the finance charge or charges; and

(2) The seller retains no security interest in any property as to which he has received payments aggregating the amount of the sale price including any finance charges attributable thereto; then, for the purposes of this section, in the case of items purchased on different dates, the first purchased shall be deemed first paid for, and in the case of items purchased on the same date the lowest priced shall be deemed first paid for.

When a credit sale under this section is made, the seller shall deliver to the buyer, prior to the due date of the first installment, a memorandum which shall set forth the following:

(a) The names of the seller and the buyer, the place of business of the seller, the residence or place of business of the buyer as specified by the buyer and a description of the goods and services sufficient to identify them. Services or multiple items of goods may be described in general terms and may be described in detail in a separate writing.

(b) The cash price of the goods, services and accessories which are the subject matter of the new retail installment sale.

(c) The amount of the buyer's downpayment, itemizing the amounts paid in money and in goods and containing a brief description of the goods, if any, traded in.

(d) The difference between item (b) and item (c), which is the unpaid balance of cash price.

(e) The amount, if any, included for insurance, specifying the coverages.

(f) The amount, if any, of official fees.

(g) The amount financed, which is the sum of items (d), (e) and (f).

(h) The amount of the finance charge (1) expressed as the annual percentage rate as defined in Regulation Z and (2) expressed in dollars, which is to be computed in accordance with this chapter.

(i) The deferred payment price, which is the sum of the amounts determined under items (b), (e), (f) and (h).

(j) The previous balance, which is the amount owing on prior purchases.

(k) The number, amount, and due dates or periods of payments scheduled to repay the indebtedness and the sum of such payments.

(*l*) Any "balloon payments," as described in Section 1807.3.

The items need not be stated in the sequence or order set forth above; additional items may be included to explain the computations made in determining the amount to be paid by the buyer. If the finance charge or any portion thereof is calculated on the 365-day basis, the amount of the finance charge shown pursuant to item (h) shall be that amount which will be incurred by the buyer if all payments are received by the seller on their respective due dates. *(Added by Stats.1959, c. 201, p. 2102, § 1, operative Jan. 1, 1960. Amended by Stats.1969, c. 625, p. 1268, § 11; Stats.1970, c. 546, p. 1049, § 26; Stats.1979, c. 805, p. 2779, § 15.)*

§ 1808.4. Obligation of buyer prior to delivery of memorandum

Until the seller delivers to the buyer the memorandum as provided in Sections 1808.2 and 1808.3, the buyer shall be obligated to pay only the cash price of the subsequent purchase. *(Added by Stats.1959, c. 201, p. 2102, § 1, operative Jan. 1, 1960. Amended by Stats.1970, c. 546, p. 1050, § 27.)*

§ 1808.5. Finance charge; determination

Subject to the other provisions of Article 5 (commencing with Section 1805.1), the finance charge to be included in a consolidated total of payments under subdivision (*l*) of Section 1808.2 shall be determined by applying the finance charge at the applicable rate to the unpaid balance under subdivision (j) of Section 1808.2, for the period from the date of the consolidation to and including the date when the final installment of the consolidated total is payable. *(Added by Stats.1959, c. 201, p. 2102, § 1, operative Jan. 1, 1960. Amended by Stats.1970, c. 546, p. 1050, § 28; Stats.1979, c. 805, p. 2781, § 16; Stats.1988, c. 479, § 7; Stats.1991, c. 819 (S.B.1105), § 11.)*

ARTICLE 9. TERMS OF PURCHASE BY FINANCING AGENCY

Section
1809.1.   Authority to purchase; terms; conditions and price.

§ 1809.1. Authority to purchase; terms; conditions and price

Notwithstanding any contrary provision of this title a financing agency may purchase a retail installment contract or installment account from a seller on such terms and conditions and for such price as may be mutually agreed upon. No filing of notice or of the assignment, no notice to the buyer of the assignment, and no requirement that the seller be deprived of dominion over payments upon the contract or installment account or over the goods if repossessed by the seller, shall be necessary to the validity of a written assignment of a contract or installment account as against creditors, subsequent purchasers, pledgees, mortgagees or encumbrancers of the seller, except as may otherwise be required by law. *(Added by Stats.1959, c. 201, p. 2103, § 1, operative Jan. 1, 1960.)*

ARTICLE 10. RETAIL INSTALLMENT ACCOUNTS

§ 1810. Agreements; acceptance by buyer; disclosures; notices of change

For the purposes of this article, a retail installment account agreement shall be deemed to be accepted by the buyer if (1) the buyer signs the agreement, including signing an application containing the terms of the agreement, or (2) the account is used by the buyer or a person who has been authorized by the buyer to use the account, and the buyer has been notified in writing that the use of the credit card will mean that the agreement has been accepted by the buyer. The agreement shall not become effective unless and until the buyer has been given or provided with the disclosures required pursuant to Section 1810.1, and has accepted the agreement as provided in this section. A subsequent change in any term of the agreement shall not become effective until the seller has given notice of the change and complies with the provisions of subdivision (d) of Section 1810.3. *(Added by Stats.1995, c. 566 (S.B.538), § 1.)*

Research References

Miller and Starr California Real Estate § 21:35, Who is Liable for Usury Penalties--Other Exemptions.

4 Witkin, California Summary 10th Sales § 282, (S 282) Required Disclosures.

4 Witkin, California Summary 10th Sales § 283, (S 283) Limitation of Charges.

§ 1810.1. Written statement by creditor; contents

Notwithstanding any other provisions of this article to the contrary, before the first transaction is made on any retail installment account, the seller shall disclose to the buyer in a single written statement, which the buyer may retain, in terminology consistent with the requirements of Section 1810.3, each of the following items, to the extent applicable:

(a) The conditions under which a finance charge may be imposed, including an explanation of the time period, if any, within which any credit extended may be paid without incurring a finance charge.

(b) The method of determining the balance upon which a finance charge may be imposed.

(c) The method of determining the amount of the finance charge, including the method of determining any minimum, charge which may be imposed as a finance charge.

(d) Where one or more periodic rates may be used to compute the finance charge, each such rate, the range of balances to which it is applicable, and the corresponding annual percentage rate determined by multiplying the periodic rate by the number of periods in a year.

(e) The conditions under which any other charges may be imposed, and the method by which they will be determined.

(f) The conditions under which the creditor may retain or acquire any security interest in any property to secure the payment of any credit extended on the account, and a description or identification of the type of the interest or interests which may be so retained, or acquired.

(g) The minimum periodic payment required.

In addition to the penalties provided under Article 12.2 (commencing with Section 1812.6) of this chapter, until the seller delivers the written statement required by this section, the buyer shall be obligated to pay only the cash price of the goods or services. *(Added by Stats.1969, c. 625, p. 1269, § 13. Amended by Stats.1970, c. 304, p. 698, § 1, operative Jan. 1, 1971; Stats.1970, c. 546, p. 1051, § 29.5, operative Jan. 1, 1971.)*

Research References

Rutter, Cal. Practice Guide: Enforcing Judgments/Debts Ch. 3-A, A. Evaluating the Claim.

4 Witkin, California Summary 10th Sales § 282, (S 282) Required Disclosures.

4 Witkin, California Summary 10th Sales § 308, (S 308) Consumer Contract Awareness Act.

§ 1810.2. Finance charge

Subject to the other provisions of this article, the seller or holder of a retail installment account may charge, receive and collect a finance charge as disclosed to the buyer pursuant to Section 1810.3. *(Added by Stats.1980, c. 1381, p. 5047, § 6, operative April 1, 1982. Amended by Stats.1981, c. 26, p. 61, § 2, eff. April 30, 1981, operative Oct. 1, 1982; Stats.1982, c. 1611, p. 6445, § 4, eff. Sept. 30, 1982, operative Jan. 1, 1984; Stats.1983, c. 1157, § 4, operative Jan. 1, 1986; Stats.1985, c. 227, § 4, operative Jan. 1, 1988; Stats.1988, c. 479, § 9; Stats.1991, c. 819 (S.B. 1105), § 14.)*

Research References

Miller and Starr California Real Estate § 21:35, Who is Liable for Usury Penalties--Other Exemptions.

4 Witkin, California Summary 10th Sales § 283, (S 283) Limitation of Charges.

§ 1810.3. Periodic statement; contents; disclosure of change in terms; credit balances; notice; disposition

(a) Except in the case of an account which the seller deems to be uncollectible or with respect to which delinquency collection procedures have been instituted, the seller of any retail installment account shall mail or deliver to the buyer for each billing cycle at the end of which there is an outstanding debit balance in excess of one dollar ($1) in that account or with respect to which a finance charge is imposed, a statement or statements which the buyer may retain, setting forth in accordance with subdivision (c) each of the following items to the extent applicable:

(1) The outstanding balance in the account at the beginning of the billing cycle, using the term "previous balance."

(2) The amount and date of each extension of credit or the date the extension of credit is debited to the account during the billing cycle and, unless previously furnished, a brief identification of any goods or services purchased or other extension of credit.

(3) The total amounts credited to the account during the billing cycle for payments, using the term "payment," and for other credits, including returns, rebates of finance charges, and adjustments, using the term "credits," and unless previously furnished, a brief identification of each of the items included in the other credits.

(4) The amount of any finance charge, using the term "finance charge," debited to the account during the billing cycle, itemized and identified to show the amounts, if any, due to the

application of periodic rates and the amount of any other charge included in the finance charge, such as a minimum charge, using appropriate descriptive terminology.

(5) Each periodic rate, using the term "periodic rate" (or "rates"), that may be used to compute the finance charge (whether or not applied during the billing cycle), and the range of balances to which it is applicable.

(6) The balance on which the finance charge was computed, and a statement of how that balance was determined. If any balance is determined without first deducting all credits during the billing cycle, that fact and the amount of the credits shall also be disclosed.

(7) The closing date of the billing cycle and the outstanding balance in the account on that date, using the term "new balance," accompanied by the statement of the date by which, or the period, if any, within which, payment must be made to avoid additional finance charges.

(b) The seller shall mail or deliver the statements required by subdivision (a) at least 14 days prior to any date or the end of any time period required to be disclosed under paragraph (7) of subdivision (a) in order for the consumer to avoid an additional finance or other charge. A seller that fails to meet this requirement shall not collect any finance or other charges imposed as a result of the failure.

(c) The disclosures required by subdivision (a) may be made on the face of the periodic statement or on its reverse side. In addition, the disclosures required by subdivision (a) may be made on the periodic statement supplemented by separate statement forms if they are enclosed together and delivered to the customer at the same time and if all of the following conditions are met:

(1) The disclosures required by paragraph (1) of subdivision (a) shall appear on the face of the periodic statement. If the amounts and dates of the charges and credits required to be disclosed under paragraphs (2) and (3) of subdivision (a) are not itemized on the face or reverse side of the periodic statement, they shall be disclosed on a separate statement or separate slips which shall accompany the periodic statement and identify each charge and credit and show the date and amount thereof. Identification of goods or services purchased may be made on an accompanying slip or by symbol relating to an identification list printed on the statement. If the disclosures required under paragraph (4) of subdivision (a) are not itemized on the face or reverse side of the periodic statement, they shall be disclosed on a separate statement which shall accompany the periodic statement.

(2) The disclosures required by paragraph (5) of subdivision (a) and a reference to the amounts required to be disclosed under paragraphs (4) and (6) of subdivision (a), if not disclosed together on the face or the reverse side of the periodic statement, shall appear together on the face of a single supplemental statement which shall accompany the periodic statement.

(3) The face of the periodic statement shall contain one of the following notices, as applicable: "NOTICE: See reverse side for important information" or "NOTICE: See accompanying statement(s) for important information" or "NOTICE: See reverse side and accompanying statement(s) for important information."

(4) The disclosures shall not be separated so as to confuse or mislead the customer, or to obscure or detract attention from the information required to be disclosed.

(d) If any change is to be made in terms of a retail installment account previously disclosed to the buyer, the seller shall mail or deliver to the buyer written disclosure of the proposed change not less than 30 days prior to the effective date of the change or 30 days prior to the beginning of the billing cycle within which the change will become effective, whichever is the earlier date. When the change involves a reduction of any component of a finance charge or other charge, the notice shall be sufficient if it appears on or accompanies the periodic statements mailed or delivered to buyers receiving periodic statements in the ordinary course of business. When the change involves an increase in any component of a finance charge, as defined in Section 1802.10, or involves a change in a charge permitted by Section 1810.4 or a change in the attorney's fee provision in the agreement pursuant to Section 1810.4, the change shall be effective only with respect to purchases made on or after the effective date of the change.

(e)(1) If any outstanding credit balance in excess of one dollar ($1) exists in a retail installment account, the seller shall mail or deliver to the buyer at the end of the billing cycle in which the credit balance is created either of the following:

(A) A cash refund in the amount of the outstanding credit.

(B) A statement setting forth the credit balance, and thereafter shall mail or deliver to the buyer a statement setting forth the credit balance no fewer than two additional times during the six-month period following creation of the credit balance.

(2) If the credit balance exists for a period of 90 days, the seller shall, at his or her option, do either of the following:

(A) Notify the buyer of his or her right to request and receive a cash refund in the amount of the outstanding credit balance in two successive statements covering, respectively, each of the two successive billing cycles immediately following the 90–day period. The notice is to be accomplished by a clear and conspicuous disclosure on or enclosed with each of the two successive statements, each of which shall be accompanied by a self-addressed return envelope. The disclosure shall contain the following information and may be in the following form:

"We owe you ____. Your credit balance will be refunded on request. If you don't request a refund, six months from the first appearance of a 'credit balance' on your bill, your credit balance will be refunded automatically.

"If your credit balance is $1.00 or less, it will not be refunded unless requested, and after 6 months, it will not be credited against future purchases.

"You may obtain a refund of your credit balance by mail by presenting your statement at our store or by returning the top half of your statement in the enclosed envelope."

If between the sending of the first notice and the sending of the second notice required by this subparagraph, the outstanding credit balance is refunded to the buyer or otherwise disposed of, the sending of the second notice shall not be required.

(B) Refund to the buyer the outstanding credit balance at any time after the credit balance is created in the buyer's account and prior to the date by which the first notice of the outstanding balance would have been sent had the seller elected to proceed under subparagraph (A).

(f)(1) If a retail installment account with an outstanding credit balance in excess of one dollar ($1) which has been determined to be correct by the seller is dormant for a period of 180 days after the credit balance is created in the buyer's account, the seller shall mail or deliver a refund in the amount of the outstanding credit balance to the buyer at the buyer's last known address.

(2) If any refund is returned to the seller with a notification to the effect that the addressee is not located at the address to which it was sent, the seller shall make one remailing of the refund with an address correction request, and shall mail the refund to the corrected address, if it is obtained.

(3) If the refund reflecting an outstanding credit balance in excess of twenty-five dollars ($25) is again returned, the seller shall reinstate the full amount of the outstanding credit balance on the buyer's account to be retained and credited against future purchases for one year from the date on which the remailed refund was returned. The seller may continue to attempt to obtain a current mailing address for the buyer by whatever means the seller deems appropriate. Except as provided in subdivision (g), the seller shall not be required to take any further action with respect to sending any statement of the credit balance or otherwise with respect to the credit balance, unless the buyer of the account thereafter requests a refund of the credit balance, in which event the seller shall either make the refund or provide a written explanation as provided in paragraph (5) of this subdivision.

(4) If a remailed refund reflecting an outstanding credit balance of twenty-five dollars ($25) or less is again returned, the seller, except as provided in subdivision (g), shall not be required to take any further action with respect to sending any statement of the credit balance to the buyer or otherwise with respect to the credit balance, unless the buyer of the account thereafter requests a refund of the credit balance, in which event the seller shall either make the refund or provide a written explanation as provided in paragraph (5) of this subdivision.

(5) If a buyer requests, in person or by mail, a refund of a credit balance in any amount which has been reflected at any time on the buyer's account, the seller shall, within 30 days of receipt of the request, either refund the amount requested, or furnish the customer with a written explanation, with supporting documentation when available, of the reasons for refusing to refund the amount requested.

(6) If a buyer, in writing, requests a seller to retain an outstanding credit balance on his or her account, the seller shall not be required to give notification as otherwise required by subdivisions (e) and (f).

(g) If an outstanding credit balance remains unrefundable for three years from the date it was created in the buyer's account, then the amount of the buyer's outstanding credit balance shall escheat to the state as property included within Section 1520 of the Code of Civil Procedure. Those funds shall be paid or delivered to the Controller, and may thereafter be claimed, as specified in Chapter 7 (commencing with Section 1500) of Title 10 of Part 4 of the Code of Civil Procedure.

(h) For the purposes of this section, an outstanding credit balance is created at the end of the billing cycle in which the credit balance is first recorded on a buyer's account and is created anew at the end of the billing cycle in which the recorded amount of an existing credit balance is changed because of the buyer's use of his or her account. *(Formerly § 1810.5, added by Stats.1959, c. 201, p. 2104, § 1, operative Jan. 1, 1960. Renumbered § 1810.3 and amended by Stats.1969, c. 625, p. 1270, § 17. Amended by Stats.1970, c. 546, p. 1052, § 31; Stats.1975, c. 947, p. 2117, § 1; Stats.1981, c. 452, p. 1700, § 1; Stats.1988, c. 1402, § 1; Stats.1995, c. 566 (S.B.538), § 2; Stats.1996, c. 762 (S.B. 2014), § 1.)*

Research References

4 Witkin, California Summary 10th Sales § 282, (S 282) Required Disclosures.
4 Witkin, California Summary 10th Sales § 283, (S 283) Limitation of Charges.

§ 1810.4. Finance charge as inclusive of all incidental charges; agreement for payment of attorney's fees and costs; annual fee for credit cards; fee for dishonored checks

The finance charge shall include all charges incident to investigating and making the retail installment account. No fee, expense, delinquency, collection, or other charge whatsoever shall be taken, received, reserved, or contracted by the seller or holder of a retail installment account except as provided in this section. A seller may, however, in an agreement which is accepted by the buyer and of which a copy is given or furnished to the buyer provide for the payment of attorney's fees and costs in conformity with Article 11 (commencing with Section 1811.1). Any subsequent change in any term of the agreement shall not become effective until the seller has given notice of the change and complies with the provisions of subdivision (d) of Section 1810.3. When credit cards are issued in connection with a retail installment account, the seller, either in the agreement or after giving the notice required by subdivision (d) of Section 1810.3, may require the payment of an annual fee of not more than fifteen dollars ($15) for membership in the credit card plan, which fee shall not be deemed a finance charge or interest for any purpose of the law.

The seller or holder of a retail installment account may charge and collect a fee not to exceed fifteen dollars ($15) for the return by a depository institution of a dishonored check, negotiable order of withdrawal, or share draft issued in connection with the retail installment account. The fee is not included in charges as defined in this chapter or in determining the applicable charges which may be made under this chapter. *(Formerly § 1810.6, added by Stats.1959, c. 201, p. 2105, § 1, operative Jan. 1, 1960. Renumbered § 1810.4 and amended by Stats.1969, c. 625, p. 1272, § 18. Amended by Stats.1970, c. 546, p. 1054, § 32; Stats.1982, c. 371, p. 1690, § 1; Stats.1982, c. 512, p. 2290, § 3; Stats.1993, c. 101 (S.B.329), § 2; Stats.1995, c. 566 (S.B.538), § 3.)*

Research References

4 Witkin, California Summary 10th Sales § 282, (S 282) Required Disclosures.
4 Witkin, California Summary 10th Sales § 283, (S 283) Limitation of Charges.
4 Witkin, California Summary 10th Sales § 289, Venue, Attorneys' Fees, and Costs.

§ 1810.5. Cost of insurance separately charged to buyer; agreement

If the cost of any insurance is to be separately charged to the buyer, there shall be an agreement to this effect, signed by both the buyer and the seller, a copy of which shall be given or furnished to the buyer. Such agreement shall state whether the insurance is to be procured by the buyer or the seller or holder. If the insurance is to be procured by the seller or holder, the seller or holder shall comply with the provisions of Section 1803.5. *(Formerly § 1810.7, added by Stats.1959, c. 201, p. 2105, § 1, operative Jan. 1, 1960. Renumbered § 1810.5 and amended by Stats.1969, c. 625, p. 1272, § 19.)*

Research References

4 Witkin, California Summary 10th Sales § 283, (S 283) Limitation of Charges.
4 Witkin, California Summary 10th Sales § 284, (S 284) Other Regulations.

§ 1810.6. Retention by seller of security interest in goods; allocation of payments

Nothing in this article prohibits the execution of an agreement between a buyer and seller whereby the seller retains a security interest in goods sold to the buyer until full payment therefor has been made. For purposes of release of the security interests, in the case of goods or services purchased on different dates, the first purchased shall be deemed first paid for, and in the case of goods or services purchased on the same date, the lowest priced shall be deemed first paid for, and all amounts allocated to payment of these goods or services shall be applied to accomplish that result. However, any downpayment on a specific purchase shall be deemed to be allocated in its entirety to such purchase. *(Formerly § 1810.8, added by Stats.1959, c. 201, p. 2105, § 1, operative Jan. 1, 1960. Renumbered § 1810.6 and amended by Stats.1969, c. 625, p. 1272, § 20. Amended by Stats.1974, c. 563, p. 1382, § 1; Stats.1981, c. 26, p. 61, § 3, eff. April 30, 1981.)*

Research References

4 Witkin, California Summary 10th Sales § 284, (S 284) Other Regulations.

§ 1810.7. Execution of notes or series of notes

No retail installment account shall require or entail the execution of any note or series of notes by the buyer which when separately negotiated will cut off as to third parties any right of action or defense which the buyer may have against the seller. *(Formerly § 1810.9, added by Stats.1959, c. 201, p. 2105, § 1, operative Jan. 1, 1960. Renumbered § 1810.7 and amended by Stats.1969, c. 625, p. 1272, § 21.)*

Research References

Rutter, Cal. Practice Guide: Enforcing Judgments/Debts Ch. 3-A, A. Evaluating the Claim.
4 Witkin, California Summary 10th Sales § 284, (S 284) Other Regulations.

§ 1810.8. Applicability of provisions relating to payments

The provisions of Sections 1806.1 and 1806.4 shall be applicable to retail installment accounts. *(Formerly § 1810.10, added by Stats.1959, c. 201, p. 2105, § 1, operative Jan. 1, 1960. Renumbered § 1810.8 and amended by Stats.1969, c. 625, p. 1272, § 22.)*

Research References

Rutter, Cal. Practice Guide: Enforcing Judgments/Debts Ch. 3-A, A. Evaluating the Claim.

§ 1810.10. Finance charge on undelivered goods

(a) Notwithstanding the provision of any contract to the contrary, except as provided in subdivision (b) or (c), no retail seller shall assess any finance charge against the outstanding balance for goods purchased under a retail installment account until the goods are in the buyer's possession.

(b) A finance charge may be assessed against the outstanding balance for such undelivered goods, as follows:

(1) From the date when such goods are available for pickup by the buyer and the buyer is notified of their availability, or

(2) From the date of purchase, when such goods are delivered or available for pickup by the buyer within 10 days of the date of purchase.

(c) In the case of a home improvement contract as defined in Section 7151.2 of the Business and Professions Code, a finance charge may be assessed against the amount financed from the approximate date of commencement of the work as set forth in the home improvement contract. *(Added by Stats.1975, c. 1041, p. 2455, § 2. Amended by Stats.1976, c. 1271, p. 5626, § 5, eff. Sept. 28, 1976, operative Jan. 1, 1978; Stats.1977, c. 868, p. 2622, § 5; Stats.1979, c. 1000, p. 3400, § 6.)*

Research References

Rutter, Cal. Practice Guide: Enforcing Judgments/Debts Ch. 3-A, A. Evaluating the Claim.
4 Witkin, California Summary 10th Sales § 283, (S 283) Limitation of Charges.

§ 1810.11. Statement of finance charges; request; form; time

The buyer may request, not more frequently than once a year, that the seller inform the buyer of the total amount of finance charges assessed on the account during the preceding calendar year and the seller shall provide that information to the buyer within 30 days of receiving the request, without charge.

If the buyer's request for the information is made in writing, the seller shall provide the information in writing, provided, however, that if the seller is required to furnish the buyer with a periodic billing or periodic statement of account or furnishes the billing or statement of account, the requested statement of finance charges may be furnished along with the periodic billing or periodic statement of account.

"Seller," for the purposes of this section, means a person engaged in the business of selling goods or furnishing services to retail buyers whose annual sales pursuant to retail installment accounts in California have exceeded one hundred fifty million dollars ($150,000,000) in the seller's last two consecutive years. *(Added by Stats.1995, c. 693 (S.B.539), § 2.)*

Research References

Miller and Starr California Real Estate § 27:56, Home Improvement Contracts--Contracts for Installment Payments, Cash Discounts, or Finance Charges.
4 Witkin, California Summary 10th Sales § 282, (S 282) Required Disclosures.
4 Witkin, California Summary 10th Negotiable Instruments § 148, (S 148) Statements.

§ 1810.12. Delinquency charge for default in payment of installment; agreement with and copy to buyer; collection cost

(a) Notwithstanding Section 1810.4, a seller or holder of a retail installment account may, subject to subdivision (d) of Section 1810.3, provide that for each installment in default the buyer shall pay a delinquency charge not in excess of one of the following amounts:

(1) For a period in default of not less than 10 days, an amount not in excess of ten dollars ($10).

(2) For a period in default of not less than 15 days, an amount not in excess of fifteen dollars ($15).

(b) Only one delinquency charge may be collected on any installment regardless of the period during which it remains in default. No delinquency charge shall be imposed for any default of payment on any payment due prior to the mailing or delivery to the buyer of the written disclosure concerning the delinquency charge provided by the seller or holder of a retail installment account pursuant to subdivision (d) of Section 1810.3. Payments timely received by the seller under a written extension or deferral agreement shall not be subject to any delinquency charge. The agreement may also provide for payment of any actual and reasonable costs of collection occasioned by removal of the goods from the state without written permission of the holder, or by the failure of the buyer to notify the holder of any change of residence, or by the failure of the buyer to communicate with the holder for a period of 45 days after any default in making payments due under the agreement.

(c) Notwithstanding subdivision (b) of Section 1810.3, the seller or holder of a retail installment account shall provide a minimum of 20 days between the monthly billing date and the date upon which the minimum payment is due, exclusive of the applicable grace period provided in subdivision (a). *(Added by Stats.1983, c. 763, § 1. Amended by Stats.1988, c. 1402, § 3; Stats.1994, c. 168 (S.B.1583), § 2; Stats.1996, c. 301 (S.B.2050), § 2.)*

Research References

Rutter, Cal. Practice Guide: Enforcing Judgments/Debts Ch. 3-A, A. Evaluating the Claim.
Miller and Starr California Real Estate § 21:35, Who is Liable for Usury Penalties--Other Exemptions.

4 Witkin, California Summary 10th Sales § 283, (S 283) Limitation of
Charges.

ARTICLE 10.5. RETAIL INSTALLMENT ACCOUNT CREDIT CARD PERIODIC RATE DISCLOSURES

Section
1810.20.   Short title.
1810.21.   Disclosures to accompany application form; manner
of disclosure; "Regulation Z"; additional terms,
etc.; federal disclosure requirement; statement
offering disclosures; application of article.

§ 1810.20.   Short title

This article shall be known and may be cited as the " Areias
Retail Installment Account Full Disclosure Act of 1986." *(Added by Stats.1986, c. 1397, § 4. Amended by Stats.2000, c. 375
(A.B.1331), § 6.)*

Research References

Rutter, Cal. Practice Guide: Enforcing Judgments/Debts Ch. 3-A, A.
Evaluating the Claim.
4 Witkin, California Summary 10th Negotiable Instruments § 157, (S 157)
Nature and Purpose of Legislation.
4 Witkin, California Summary 10th Negotiable Instruments § 158, Scope
of Requirement.

§ 1810.21.   Disclosures to accompany application form; manner of disclosure; "Regulation Z"; additional terms, etc.; federal disclosure requirement; statement offering disclosures; application of article

(a) Any application form or preapproved written solicitation
for a credit card issued in connection with a retail installment
account that is mailed on or after October 1, 1987, to a retail
buyer residing in this state by or on behalf of a retail seller,
whether or not the retail seller is located in this state, other than
an application form or solicitation included in a magazine,
newspaper, or other publication distributed by someone other
than the retail seller, shall contain or be accompanied by either
of the following disclosures:

(1) A disclosure of each of the following, if applicable:

(A) Any periodic rate or rates that will be used to determine
the finance charge imposed on the balance due under the terms
of a retail installment account, expressed as an annual percentage rate or rates.

(B) Any membership or participation fee that will be imposed
for availability of a retail installment account in connection with
which a credit card is issued expressed as an annualized amount.

(C) If the retail seller provides a period during which the
retail buyer may repay the full balance reflected on a billing
statement that is attributable to purchases of goods or services
from the retail seller without the imposition of additional finance
charges, the retail seller shall either disclose the minimum
number of days of that period, calculated from the closing date
of the prior billing cycle to the date designated in the billing
statement sent to the retail buyer as the date by which that
payment must be received to avoid additional finance charges, or
describe the manner in which the period is calculated. For
purposes of this section, the period shall be referred to as the
"free period" or "free-ride period." If the retail seller does not
provide this period for purchases, the disclosure shall so indicate.

(2) A disclosure that satisfies the initial disclosure statement
requirements of Regulation Z (12 C.F.R. 226.6).

(b) In the event that an unsolicited application form is mailed
or otherwise delivered to retail buyers in more than one state,
the requirements of subdivision (a) shall be satisfied if on the
application form or the soliciting material there is a notice that
credit terms may vary from state to state and that provides either
the disclosures required by subdivision (a) or an address or
phone number for the customer to use to obtain the disclosure.
The notice shall be in boldface type no smaller than the largest
type used in the narrative portion, excluding headlines, of the
material soliciting the application. Any person responding to
the notice shall be given the disclosures required by subdivision
(a).

(c) A retail seller need not present the disclosures required by
paragraph (1) of subdivision (a) in chart form or use any specific
terminology, except as expressly provided in this section. The
following chart shall not be construed in any way as a standard by
which to determine whether a retail seller who elects not to use
the chart has provided the required disclosures in a manner
which satisfies paragraph (1) of subdivision (a). However,
disclosures shall be conclusively presumed to satisfy the requirements of paragraph (1) of subdivision (a) if a chart with captions
substantially as follows is completed with the applicable terms
offered by the retail seller, or if the retail seller presents the
applicable terms in tabular, list, or narrative format using
terminology substantially similar to the captions included in the
following chart:

THE FOLLOWING INFORMATION IS PROVIDED PURSUANT TO THE AREIAS RETAIL INSTALLMENT
ACCOUNT FULL DISCLOSURE ACT OF 1986:

CREDIT CARD TERMS VARY AMONG RETAIL SELLERS—SELECTED TERMS FOR PURCHASES UNDER
THIS RETAIL INSTALLMENT ACCOUNT ARE SET
OUT BELOW

PERIODIC RATES (as APRs)	ANNUAL FEES	FREE–RIDE PERIOD

(d) For purposes of this section, "Regulation Z" has the
meaning attributed to it under Section 1802.18, and all of the
terms used in this section have the same meaning as attributed to
them in federal Regulation Z (12 C.F.R. 226.1 et seq.).

(e) Nothing in this section shall be deemed or construed to
prohibit a retail seller from disclosing additional terms, conditions, or information, whether or not relating to the disclosures
required under this section, in conjunction with the disclosures
required by this section. Notwithstanding subdivision (g) of
Section 1748.11, a retail seller that complies with the requirements of Section 1748.11 shall be deemed to have complied with
the requirements of this section.

(f) If a retail seller is required under federal law to make any
disclosure of the terms applicable to a retail installment account
in connection with application forms or solicitations, the retail
seller shall be deemed to have complied with the requirements of
paragraph (1) of subdivision (a) with respect to those application
forms or solicitations if the retail seller complies with the federal
disclosure requirement.

(g) If the disclosure required by this section does not otherwise appear on an application form or an accompanying retail
installment agreement distributed in this state on or after

October 1, 1987, other than by mail, the application form shall include a statement in substantially the following form:

"If you wish to receive disclosure of the terms of this retail installment account, pursuant to the Areias Retail Installment Account Full Disclosure Act of 1986, check here and return to the address on this form."

A box shall be printed in or next to this statement for placing such a checkmark.

(h) This article does not apply to (1) any application form or preapproved written solicitation for a retail installment account credit card where the credit to be extended will be secured by a lien on real or personal property, or both real and personal property, (2) any application form or written solicitation that invites a person or persons to apply for a retail installment account credit card and which is included as part of a catalog which is sent to one or more persons by a creditor in order to facilitate a credit sale of goods offered in the catalog, (3) any advertisement which does not invite, directly or indirectly, an application for a retail installment account credit card, and (4) any application form or written advertisement included in a magazine, newspaper, or other publication distributed in more than one state by someone other than the creditor. *(Added by Stats.1986, c. 1397, § 4. Amended by Stats.2000, c. 375 (A.B. 1331), § 7; Stats.2001, c. 159 (S.B.662), § 34.)*

Research References

Rutter, Cal. Practice Guide: Enforcing Judgments/Debts Ch. 3-A, A. Evaluating the Claim.
4 Witkin, California Summary 10th Negotiable Instruments § 157, (S 157) Nature and Purpose of Legislation.
4 Witkin, California Summary 10th Negotiable Instruments § 164, Scope of Requirement.
4 Witkin, California Summary 10th Negotiable Instruments § 165, Matters to be Disclosed.
4 Witkin, California Summary 10th Negotiable Instruments § 166, Methods of Compliance.

ARTICLE 11.　ATTORNEY'S FEES AND COURT COSTS

Section
1811.1.　Award to prevailing party.

§ 1811.1.　Award to prevailing party

Reasonable attorney's fees and costs shall be awarded to the prevailing party in any action on a contract or installment account subject to the provisions of this chapter regardless of whether such action is instituted by the seller, holder or buyer. Where the defendant alleges in his answer that he tendered to the plaintiff the full amount to which he was entitled, and thereupon deposits in court, for the plaintiff, the amount so tendered, and the allegation is found to be true, then the defendant is deemed to be a prevailing party within the meaning of this article. *(Added by Stats.1959, c. 201, p. 2105, § 1. Amended by Stats.1961, c. 1214, p. 2951, § 6.)*

Research References

Rutter, Cal. Practice Guide: Enforcing Judgments/Debts Ch. 3-C, C. Prelawsuit Considerations.
Miller and Starr California Real Estate § 27:56, Home Improvement Contracts--Contracts for Installment Payments, Cash Discounts, or Finance Charges.
7 Witkin Cal. Proc. 5th Judgment § 95, (S 95) Prevailing Party in Specified Actions.
7 Witkin Cal. Proc. 5th Judgment § 180, Action Where No Contract was Formed.
7 Witkin Cal. Proc. 5th Judgment § 224, (S 224) Consumer Protection Actions.

4 Witkin, California Summary 10th Sales § 289, Venue, Attorneys' Fees, and Costs.

ARTICLE 12.1.　REPOSSESSION AND RESALE

Section
1812.2.　Default by buyer; rights of holder; notice of sale or retention of goods; redemption; statement of sum due.
1812.3.　Notice; contents; service.
1812.4.　Application of proceeds of resale.
1812.5.　Recovery of deficiency prohibited.

§ 1812.2.　Default by buyer; rights of holder; notice of sale or retention of goods; redemption; statement of sum due

In the event of any default by the buyer in the performance of his obligations under a contract or installment account, the holder, pursuant to any rights granted therein, may proceed to recover judgment for the balance due without retaking the goods, or he may retake the goods and proceed as hereinafter provided. If he retakes the goods, he shall, within 10 days, give notice to the buyer of his intention to sell the goods at public sale or give notice to the buyer of his intention to retain the goods in satisfaction of the balance due. The notice must state the amount of the overdue payments, that the buyer must pay, if he pays within 10 days of the notice, in order to redeem the goods. In either case the buyer shall have an absolute right to redeem the goods within 10 days after the notice is given by paying or tendering the amount owing under the contract. If the holder gives notice of election to sell the goods the buyer shall also have the absolute right to redeem the goods at any time before sale by paying or tendering the amounts specified above and also any expense reasonably incurred by the seller or holder in good faith in repairing, reconditioning the goods or preparing them for sale. If the holder gives notice of his intention to retain the goods in satisfaction of the indebtedness he shall be deemed to have done so at the end of the 10-day period if the goods are not redeemed; at the time the notice is given, the holder shall furnish the buyer a written statement of the sum due under the contract and the expenses provided for in this section. For failure to render such a statement the holder shall forfeit to the buyer ten dollars ($10) and also be liable to him for all damages suffered because of such failure. *(Added by Stats.1959, c. 201, p. 2106, § 1. Amended by Stats.1961, c. 1214, p. 2951, § 7; Stats.1963, c. 1952, p. 4017, § 1.)*

Research References

Rutter, Cal. Practice Guide: Enforcing Judgments/Debts Ch. 3-A, A. Evaluating the Claim.
Rutter, Cal. Practice Guide: Enforcing Judgments/Debts Ch. 3-B, B. Collection Without Suit.
Miller and Starr California Real Estate § 27:56, Home Improvement Contracts--Contracts for Installment Payments, Cash Discounts, or Finance Charges.
4 Witkin, California Summary 10th Sales § 285, (S 285) in General.

§ 1812.3.　Notice; contents; service

The notice provided for in Section 1812.2 shall be given to the buyer and any other person liable by causing it to be delivered personally or to be deposited in the United States mail addressed to the buyer or to such other person at his last known address and shall advise the buyer or such other person of his right to redeem as provided for in Section 1812.2. If the holder determines to sell the goods at public sale he shall give notice of the time and place of sale at least 10 days before the date of sale by delivering a copy of the notice personally to the buyer or other person liable or depositing the same in the United States mail addressed to the buyer or such other person at his last known address. *(Added by Stats.1959, c. 201, p. 2106, § 1. Amended by Stats.1961, c. 1214, p. 2952, § 8.)*

Research References

Rutter, Cal. Practice Guide: Enforcing Judgments/Debts Ch. 3-B, B. Collection Without Suit.
Miller and Starr California Real Estate § 27:56, Home Improvement Contracts--Contracts for Installment Payments, Cash Discounts, or Finance Charges.
4 Witkin, California Summary 10th Sales § 285, (S 285) in General.

§ 1812.4. Application of proceeds of resale

The proceeds of a resale shall be applied (1) to the payment of the expenses thereof, (2) to the payment of any expenses of retaking, including reasonable attorney's fees actually incurred, and of any expenses of keeping, storing, repairing, reconditioning or preparing the goods for sale to which the holder may be entitled, (3) to the satisfaction of the balance due under the contract. Any sum remaining after the satisfaction of such claims shall be paid to the buyer. *(Added by Stats.1959, c. 201, p. 2107, § 1, operative Jan. 1, 1960.)*

Research References

Miller and Starr California Real Estate § 27:56, Home Improvement Contracts--Contracts for Installment Payments, Cash Discounts, or Finance Charges.
4 Witkin, California Summary 10th Sales § 285, (S 285) in General.

§ 1812.5. Recovery of deficiency prohibited

If the proceeds of the sale are not sufficient to cover items (1), (2) and (3) of Section 1812.4, the holder may not recover the deficiency from the buyer or from anyone who has succeeded to the obligations of the buyer. *(Added by Stats.1959, c. 201, p. 2107, § 1. Amended by Stats.1963, c. 1952, p. 4018, § 2.)*

Research References

Miller and Starr California Real Estate § 27:56, Home Improvement Contracts--Contracts for Installment Payments, Cash Discounts, or Finance Charges.
4 Witkin, California Summary 10th Sales § 285, (S 285) in General.
4 Witkin, California Summary 10th Secured Transactions in Personal Property § 200, Consumer Transactions.

ARTICLE 12.2. PENALTIES

Section
1812.6. Violation; misdemeanor.
1812.7. Noncompliance with provisions as barring right of recovery; remedy of buyer.
1812.8. Correction of failure to comply with provisions.
1812.9. Willful violation; triple damages.

§ 1812.6. Violation; misdemeanor

Any person who shall willfully violate any provision of this chapter shall be guilty of a misdemeanor. *(Added by Stats.1959, c. 201, p. 2107, § 1, operative Jan. 1, 1960.)*

Research References

Rutter, Cal. Practice Guide: Enforcing Judgments/Debts Ch. 3-A, A. Evaluating the Claim.
Miller and Starr California Real Estate § 27:56, Home Improvement Contracts--Contracts for Installment Payments, Cash Discounts, or Finance Charges.
4 Witkin, California Summary 10th Sales § 277, (S 277) Prohibited Terms and Acts.

4 Witkin, California Summary 10th Sales § 287, Penalties.

§ 1812.7. Noncompliance with provisions as barring right of recovery; remedy of buyer

In case of failure by any person to comply with the provisions of this chapter, such person or any person who acquires a contract or installment account with knowledge of such noncompliance is barred from recovery of any finance charge or of any delinquency, collection, extension, deferral or refinance charge imposed in connection with such contract or installment account and the buyer shall have the right to recover from such person an amount equal to any of such charges paid by the buyer. *(Added by Stats.1959, c. 201, p. 2107, § 1, operative Jan. 1, 1960. Amended by Stats.1970, c. 546, p. 1054, § 33.)*

Research References

Rutter, Cal. Practice Guide: Enforcing Judgments/Debts Ch. 3-A, A. Evaluating the Claim.
Miller and Starr California Real Estate § 27:56, Home Improvement Contracts--Contracts for Installment Payments, Cash Discounts, or Finance Charges.
4 Witkin, California Summary 10th Sales § 267, Application to Financing Agency.
4 Witkin, California Summary 10th Sales § 269, Inapplicable to Real Property.
4 Witkin, California Summary 10th Sales § 287, Penalties.

§ 1812.8. Correction of failure to comply with provisions

Notwithstanding the provisions of this article, any failure to comply with any provision of this chapter may be corrected by the holder in accordance with the provisions of this section, provided that a willful violation may not be corrected, and a correction which will increase the amount owed by the buyer or the amount of any payment shall not be effective unless the buyer concurs in writing to the correction. If a violation is corrected by the holder in accordance with the provisions of this section, neither the seller nor the holder shall be subject to any penalty under this article. The correction shall be made by delivery to the buyer of a corrected copy of the contract within 30 days of the execution of the original contract by the buyer. Any amount improperly collected from the buyer shall be credited against the indebtedness evidenced by the contract. *(Added by Stats.1959, c. 201, p. 2107, § 1. Amended by Stats.1961, c. 1214, p. 2952, § 9.)*

Research References

Rutter, Cal. Practice Guide: Enforcing Judgments/Debts Ch. 3-A, A. Evaluating the Claim.
Miller and Starr California Real Estate § 27:56, Home Improvement Contracts--Contracts for Installment Payments, Cash Discounts, or Finance Charges.
4 Witkin, California Summary 10th Sales § 288, Correction.

§ 1812.9. Willful violation; triple damages

In any case in which a person willfully violates any provision of this chapter in connection with the imposition, computation or disclosures of or relating to a finance charge on a consolidated total of two or more contracts under the provisions of Article 8 (commencing with Section 1808.1) of this chapter, the buyer may recover from such person an amount equal to three times the total of the finance charges and any delinquency, collection, extension, deferral or refinance charges imposed, contracted for or received on all contracts included in the consolidated total and the seller shall be barred from the recovery of any such charges. *(Added by Stats.1959, c. 201, p. 2108, § 1. Amended by Stats.1961, c. 1214, p. 2953, § 10; Stats.1970, c. 546, p. 1054, § 34.)*

Research References

Rutter, Cal. Practice Guide: Enforcing Judgments/Debts Ch. 3-A, A. Evaluating the Claim.

Miller and Starr California Real Estate § 27:56, Home Improvement Contracts--Contracts for Installment Payments, Cash Discounts, or Finance Charges.

4 Witkin, California Summary 10th Sales § 287, Penalties.

ARTICLE 12.3.   ACTIONS

Section

1812.10.   Venue; jurisdiction.

§ 1812.10.   Venue; jurisdiction

(a) An action on a contract or installment account under this chapter shall be tried in the superior court in the county where the contract was in fact signed by the buyer, where the buyer resided at the time the contract was entered into, where the buyer resides at the commencement of the action, or where the goods purchased pursuant to the contract have been so affixed to real property as to become a part of that real property.

(b) In the superior court designated as the proper court in subdivision (a), the proper court location for trial of an action under this chapter is the location where the court tries that type of action that is nearest or most accessible to where the contract was in fact signed by the buyer, where the buyer resided at the time the contract was entered into, where the buyer resides at the commencement of the action, or where the goods purchased pursuant to the contract have been so affixed to real property as to become a part of that real property. Otherwise, any location of the superior court designated as the proper court in subdivision (a) is the proper court location for the trial of the action. The court may specify by local rule the nearest or most accessible court location where the court tries that type of case.

(c) In any action subject to this section, concurrently with the filing of the complaint, the plaintiff shall file an affidavit stating facts showing that the action has been commenced in a superior court and court location described in this section as a proper place for the trial of the action. Those facts may be stated in a verified complaint and shall not be stated on information or belief. When that affidavit is filed with the complaint, a copy thereof shall be served with the summons. If a plaintiff fails to file the affidavit or state facts in a verified complaint required by this section, no further proceedings may occur, but the court shall, upon its own motion or upon motion of any party, dismiss the action without prejudice. The court may, on terms that are just, permit the affidavit to be filed subsequent to the filing of the complaint and a copy of the affidavit shall be served on the defendant. The time to answer or otherwise plead shall date from that service. *(Added by Stats.1965, c. 792, p. 2382, § 1. Amended by Stats.1968, c. 743, p. 1446, § 1; Stats.1969, c. 186, p. 466, § 1; Stats.1970, c. 725, p. 1352, § 1; Stats.1971, c. 1529, p. 3020, § 1; Stats.1998, c. 931 (S.B.2139), § 16, eff. Sept. 28, 1998; Stats.2002, c. 806 (A.B.3027), § 1.)*

Law Revision Commission Comments

Section 1812.10 is amended to reflect elimination of the justice court. Cal. Const. art. VI, §§ 1, 5(b). In a county in which there is no municipal court, the superior court has jurisdiction of matters that would be within the subject matter jurisdiction of the municipal court. Cal. Const. art. VI, 10 (superior court jurisdiction); Code Civ. Proc. §§ 85, 85.1 (limited civil cases). [28 Cal.L.Rev.Comm. Reports 51 (1998)].

Research References

Rutter, Cal. Practice Guide: Civ. Pro. Before Trial Ch. 3-D, D. Venue.

Rutter, Cal. Practice Guide: Civ. Pro. Before Trial Ch. 5-G, G. Relief from Default.

Rutter, Cal. Practice Guide: Civ. Pro. Before Trial Ch. 6-B, B. Complaints.

Rutter, Cal. Practice Guide: Enforcing Judgments/Debts Ch. 3-C, C. Prelawsuit Considerations.

Rutter, Cal. Practice Guide: Enforcing Judgments/Debts Ch. 4-B, B. Claim and Delivery.

3 Witkin Cal. Proc. 5th Actions § 845, Actions on Installment Contracts.

4 Witkin Cal. Proc. 5th Pleading § 472, Limited Civil Cases.

5 Witkin Cal. Proc. 5th Pleading § 762, Filing at Improper Venue.

6 Witkin Cal. Proc. 5th Proceedings Without Trial § 161, (S 161) Application and Affidavit.

4 Witkin, California Summary 10th Sales § 277, (S 277) Prohibited Terms and Acts.

4 Witkin, California Summary 10th Sales § 289, Venue, Attorneys' Fees, and Costs.

5 Witkin, California Summary 10th Torts § 525, Action Disregarding Venue Statutes.

ARTICLE 12.4.   FINANCING RETAIL PURCHASES

Section

1812.20.   Requirement that purchaser obtain financing from particular source; prohibition; penalty.

§ 1812.20.   Requirement that purchaser obtain financing from particular source; prohibition; penalty

Notwithstanding Section 1801.6, no person shall require a purchaser of goods or services to obtain financing from any particular source. Any person who violates this section shall be subject to the penalty provided in Section 1812.6. *(Added by Stats.1979, c. 1151, p. 4222, § 4.)*

Research References

4 Witkin, California Summary 10th Sales § 269, Inapplicable to Real Property.

4 Witkin, California Summary 10th Sales § 277, (S 277) Prohibited Terms and Acts.

CHAPTER 2.   CREDIT TRANSACTIONS REGARDING WOMEN

Section

1812.30.   Denial of credit to person regardless of marital status; prohibition; conditions; reporting agency.

1812.31.   Right of action; damages; individual and class suits.

1812.32.   Injunction.

1812.33.   Civil penalties; precedence of action; distribution of proceeds.

1812.34.   Costs and attorney fees.

1812.35.   Commencement of action; limitations.

§ 1812.30.   Denial of credit to person regardless of marital status; prohibition; conditions; reporting agency

(a) No person, regardless of marital status, shall be denied credit in his or her own name if the earnings and other property over which he or she has management and control are such that a person of the opposite sex managing and controlling the same amount of earnings and other property would receive credit.

(b) No person, regardless of marital status, managing and controlling earnings and other property shall be offered credit on terms less favorable than those offered to a person of the opposite sex seeking the same type of credit and managing and controlling the same amount of earnings and other property.

(c) No unmarried person shall be denied credit if his or her earnings and other property are such that a married person managing and controlling the same amount of earnings and other property would receive credit.

(d) No unmarried person shall be offered credit on terms less favorable than those offered to a married person managing and controlling the same amount of earnings and other property.

(e) For accounts established after January 1, 1977 or for accounts in existence on January 1, 1977 where information on that account is received after January 1, 1977, a credit reporting agency which in its normal course of business receives information on joint credit accounts identifying the persons responsible for such accounts, or receives information which reflects the participation of both spouses, shall: (1) at the time such information is received file such information separately under the names of each person or spouse, or file such information in another manner which would enable either person or spouse to automatically gain access to the credit history without having in any way to list or refer to the name of the other person, and (2) provide access to all information about the account in the name of each person or spouse.

(f) For all accounts established prior to January 1, 1977, a credit reporting agency shall at any time upon the written or personal request of a person who is or has been married, verify the contractual liability, liability by operation of law, or authorized use by such person, of joint credit accounts appearing in the file of the person's spouse or former spouse, and, if applicable, shall file such information separately and thereafter continue to do so under the names of each person responsible for the joint account or in another manner which would enable either person responsible for the joint account to automatically gain access to the credit history without having in any way to list or refer to the name of the other person.

(g) For the purposes of this chapter "credit" means obtainment of money, property, labor, or services on a deferred-payment basis.

(h) For the purposes of this chapter, earnings shall include, but not be limited to, spousal, family, and child support payments, pensions, social security, disability or survivorship benefits. Spousal, family, and child support payments shall be considered in the same manner as earnings from salary, wages, or other sources where the payments are received pursuant to a written agreement or court decree to the extent that the reliability of such payments is established. The factors which a creditor may consider in evaluating the reliability of such payments are the length of time payments have been received; the regularity of receipt; and whether full or partial payments have been made.

(i) Nothing in this chapter shall be construed to prohibit a person from: (1) utilizing an evaluation of the reliability of earnings provided that such an evaluation is applied to persons without regard to their sex or marital status; or (2) inquiring into and utilizing an evaluation of the obligations for which community property is liable pursuant to the Family Code for the sole purpose of determining the creditor's rights and remedies with respect to the particular extension of credit, provided that such is done with respect to all applicants without regard to their sex; or (3) utilizing any other relevant factors or methods in determining whether to extend credit to an applicant provided that such factors or methods are applicable to all applicants without regard to their sex or marital status. For the purpose of this subdivision, the fact that an applicant is of childbearing age is not a relevant factor.

(j) Credit applications for the obtainment of money, goods, labor, or services shall clearly specify that the applicant, if married, may apply for a separate account. *(Added by Stats. 1973, c. 999, p. 1987, § 1. Amended by Stats.1975, c. 332, p. 778, § 1; Stats.1976, c. 1361, p. 6203, § 1; Stats.1992, c. 163 (A.B.2641), § 11, operative Jan. 1, 1994.)*

Law Revision Commission Comments

Section 1812.30 is amended to add a reference to "family" support in subdivision (h) and to replace the reference to the former Civil Code provisions in subdivision (i) with a reference to the Family Code. [22 Cal.L.Rev.Comm.Reports 1 (1992)].

Research References

11 Witkin, California Summary 10th Husband and Wife § 22, Statutory Prohibitions.

11 Witkin, California Summary 10th Husband and Wife § 23, Remedies and Penalties.

11 Witkin, California Summary 10th Husband and Wife § 24, Permissible Evaluations and Credit Reports.

8 Witkin, California Summary 10th Constitutional Law § 897, Other Discrimination Statutes.

§ 1812.31. Right of action; damages; individual and class suits

(a) Whoever violates Section 1812.30 shall be liable to the aggrieved person in an amount equal to the sum of any actual damages sustained by such person acting either in an individual capacity or as a representative of a class.

(b) Whoever violates Section 1812.30 shall be liable to the aggrieved person for punitive damages in an amount not greater than ten thousand dollars ($10,000), as determined by the court, in addition to any actual damages provided in subdivision (a); provided, however, that in pursuing the recovery allowed under this subdivision, the aggrieved person may proceed only in an individual capacity and not as a representative of a class.

(c) Notwithstanding subdivision (b), whoever violates Section 1812.30 may be liable for punitive damages in the case of a class action in such amount as the court may allow, except that as to each member of the class no minimum recovery shall be applicable, and the total recovery in such action shall not exceed the lesser of one hundred thousand dollars ($100,000) or one percent (1%) of the net worth of the creditor. In determining the amount of the award in any class action, the court shall consider, among other relevant factors, the amount of any actual damages awarded, the frequency and persistence of violations, the resources of the creditor, the number of persons adversely affected, and the extent to which the creditor's violation was intentional. *(Added by Stats.1973, c. 999, p. 1987, § 1. Amended by Stats.1975, c. 332, p. 779, § 2.)*

Research References

11 Witkin, California Summary 10th Husband and Wife § 23, Remedies and Penalties.

§ 1812.32. Injunction

Any person, corporation, firm, partnership, joint stock company, or any other association or organization which violates or proposes to violate this chapter may be enjoined by any court of competent jurisdiction. Actions for injunction under this section may be prosecuted by the Attorney General or any district attorney, county counsel, city attorney, or city prosecutor in this state in the name of the people of the State of California or by any person denied credit or offered credit in violation of Section 1812.30. *(Added by Stats.1975, c. 332, p. 780, § 3.)*

Research References

11 Witkin, California Summary 10th Husband and Wife § 22, Statutory Prohibitions.

11 Witkin, California Summary 10th Husband and Wife § 23, Remedies and Penalties.

§ 1812.33. Civil penalties; precedence of action; distribution of proceeds

(a) Any person who intentionally violates any injunction issued pursuant to this chapter shall be liable for a civil penalty not to exceed two thousand five hundred dollars ($2,500) for each day that such person violates the injunction.

(b) The civil penalty prescribed by this section shall be assessed and recovered in a civil action brought in the name of the people of the State of California by the Attorney General or by any district attorney, county counsel, or city attorney in any court of competent jurisdiction. An action brought pursuant to this section to recover such civil penalties shall take special precedence over all civil matters on the calendar of the court except those matters to which equal precedence on the calendar is granted by law.

(c) If such an action is brought by the Attorney General, one-half of the penalty collected pursuant to this section shall be paid to the treasurer of the county in which the judgment was entered, and one-half to the State Treasurer. If brought by a district attorney or county counsel, the entire amount of the penalty collected shall be paid to the treasurer of the county in which the judgment was entered. If brought by a city attorney or city prosecutor, one-half of the penalty shall be paid to the treasurer of the county in which the judgment was entered and one-half to the city. *(Added by Stats.1975, c. 332, p. 780, § 4.)*

Research References

11 Witkin, California Summary 10th Husband and Wife § 23, Remedies and Penalties.

§ 1812.34. Costs and attorney fees

Any person denied credit or offered credit in violation of Section 1812.30 who brings an action pursuant to Section 1812.31 or 1812.32 of this code may petition the court for award of costs and reasonable attorney's fees which the court shall award if the action is successful. *(Added by Stats.1975, c. 332, p. 781, § 5.)*

Research References

11 Witkin, California Summary 10th Husband and Wife § 23, Remedies and Penalties.

§ 1812.35. Commencement of action; limitations

Any action commenced pursuant to Section 1812.31 shall be commenced within two years from the date on which the person is denied credit or is offered credit in violation of Section 1812.30. *(Added by Stats.1975, c. 332, p. 781, § 6.)*

Research References

3 Witkin Cal. Proc. 5th Actions § 482, (S 482) Two Years.
11 Witkin, California Summary 10th Husband and Wife § 23, Remedies and Penalties.

Title 2.4

CONTRACTS FOR DANCE STUDIO LESSONS AND OTHER SERVICES

§ 1812.50. Legislative findings; purpose

(a) The Legislature finds that there exists in connection with a substantial number of contracts for dance studio lessons and other services, sales practices, and business and financing methods which have worked a fraud, deceit, imposition, and financial hardship upon the people of this state; that existing legal remedies are inadequate to correct these abuses; that the dance studio industry has a significant impact upon the economy and well-being of this state and its local communities; and that the provisions of this title relating to these contracts are necessary for the public welfare.

(b) The Legislature declares that the purpose of this title is to safeguard the public against fraud, deceit, imposition, and financial hardship, and to foster and encourage competition, fair dealing, and prosperity in the field of dance studio lessons and other services by prohibiting or restricting false or misleading advertising, onerous contract terms, harmful financial practices, and other unfair, dishonest, deceptive, destructive, unscrupulous, fraudulent, and discriminatory practices by which the public has been injured in connection with contracts for dance studio lessons and other services. *(Added by Stats.1969, c. 1571, p. 3190, § 1. Amended by Stats.1987, c. 449, § 2; Stats.1988, c. 1043, § 2.)*

Research References

4 Witkin, California Summary 10th Sales § 362, (S 362) Health and Dance Services Contracts.

§ 1812.51. Contract for dance studio lessons and other services; exceptions from application of title

As used in this title, "contract for dance studio lessons and other services" means a contract for instruction in ballroom or other types of dancing, and includes lessons and other services, whether given to students individually or in groups. This title does not include contracts for professional services rendered or furnished by a person licensed under Division 2 (commencing with Section 500) of the Business and Professions Code, or contracts for instruction at schools operating pursuant to the Education Code. *(Added by Stats.1969, c. 1571, p. 3190, § 1. Amended by Stats.1987, c. 449, § 3; Stats.1988, c. 1043, § 3.)*

§ 1812.52. Written contract required

Every contract for dance studio lessons and other services shall be in writing and shall be subject to this title. A copy of the written contract shall be given to the customer at the time he or she signs the contract. *(Added by Stats.1969, c. 1571, p. 3190, § 1. Amended by Stats.1987, c. 449, § 5; Stats.1988, c. 1043, § 5.)*

Research References

4 Witkin, California Summary 10th Sales § 362, (S 362) Health and Dance Services Contracts.

§ 1812.53. Limitation on payment period; prohibition against life contract; permissible service period; single contract

(a) No contract for dance studio lessons and other services shall require payments or financing by the buyer over a period in excess of one year from the date the contract is entered into, nor shall the term of any contract be measured by the life of the buyer. However, the lessons and other services to be rendered to the buyer under the contract may extend over a period not to exceed seven years from the date the contract is entered into.

(b) All contracts for dance studio lessons and other services that may be in effect between the same seller and the same buyer, the terms of which overlap for any period, shall be considered as one contract for the purposes of this title. *(Added by Stats.1969, c. 1571, p. 3190, § 1. Amended by Stats.1983, c. 259, § 1; Stats.1987, c. 449, § 6; Stats.1988, c. 1043, § 6; Stats.1999, c. 1024 (A.B.648), § 1.)*

Research References

4 Witkin, California Summary 10th Sales § 362, (S 362) Health and Dance Services Contracts.

§ 1812.54. Performance of contract; cancellation and refund; statement of hourly rate and on bond of studio

(a) Every contract for dance studio lessons and other services shall provide that performance of the agreed-upon lessons will begin within six months from the date the contract is entered into.

(b) A contract for dance studio lessons and other services may be canceled by the student at any time provided he or she gives written notice to the dance studio at the address specified in the contract. When a contract for dance studio lessons and other services is canceled the dance studio shall calculate the refund on the contract, if any, on a pro rata basis. The dance studio shall refund any moneys owed to the student within 10 days of receiving the cancellation notice, unless the student owes the dance studio money for studio lessons or other services received prior to the cancellation, in which case any moneys owed the dance studio shall be deducted by the dance studio from the refund owed to the student and the balance, if any, shall be refunded as specified above. A dance studio shall not charge a cancellation fee, or other fee, for cancellation of the contract by the student.

(c) Every contract for dance studio lessons and other services shall contain a written statement of the hourly rate charged for each type of lesson for which the student has contracted. If the contract includes dance studio lessons that are sold at different per-hour rates, the contract shall contain separate hourly rates for each different type of lesson sold. All other services for which the student has contracted that are not capable of a per-hour charge shall be set forth in writing in specific terms. The statement shall be contained in the dance studio contract before the contract is signed by the buyer.

(d) Every dance studio subject to Sections 1812.64 and 1812.65 shall include in every contract for dance studio lessons or other services a statement that the studio is bonded and that information concerning the bond may be obtained by writing to the office of the Secretary of State. *(Added by Stats.1969, c. 1571, p. 3191, § 1. Amended by Stats.1976, c. 1200, p. 5474, § 1; Stats.1982, c. 517, p. 2321, § 58; Stats.1983, c. 259, § 2; Stats.1987, c. 449, § 7; Stats.1988, c. 1043, § 7; Stats.1997, c. 112 (S.B.338), § 1; Stats.1998, c. 829 (S.B.1652), § 7; Stats.1999, c. 1024 (A.B.648), § 2.)*

Law Revision Commission Comments

The changes in Section 1812.54 are technical. [16 Cal.L.Rev.Comm. Reports 501 (1981)].

Research References

4 Witkin, California Summary 10th Sales § 362, (S 362) Health and Dance Services Contracts.

§ 1812.55. Prohibition of notes cutting off, as to third parties, buyer's right of action or defense against seller

No contract for dance studio lessons and other services shall require or entail the execution of any note or series of notes by the buyer which, when separately negotiated, will cut off as to third parties any right of action or defense which the buyer may have against the seller. *(Added by Stats.1969, c. 1571, p. 3191, § 1. Amended by Stats.1987, c. 449, § 8; Stats.1988, c. 1043, § 8.)*

§ 1812.56. Prohibition against assignment of contract cutting off buyer's right of action or defense against seller; conditions

No right of action or defense arising out of a contract for dance studio lessons and other services which the buyer has against the seller, and which would be cut off by assignment, shall be cut off by assignment of the contract to any third party whether or not he or she acquires the contract in good faith and for value unless the assignee gives notice of the assignment to the buyer as provided in this section and, within 30 days of the mailing of notice, receives no written notice of the facts giving rise to the claim or defense of the buyer. A notice of assignment shall be in writing addressed to the buyer at the address shown on the contract and shall identify the contract and inform the buyer that he or she shall, within 30 days of the date of mailing of the notice, notify the assignee in writing of any facts giving rise to a claim or defense which he or she may have. The notice of assignment shall state the name of the seller and buyer, a description of the lessons and other services, the contract balance, and the number and amount of the installments. *(Added by Stats.1969, c. 1571, p. 3191, § 1. Amended by Stats.1987, c. 449, § 9; Stats.1988, c. 1043, § 9.)*

§ 1812.57. Relief from payment upon death or disability

(a) Every contract for dance studio lessons and other services shall contain a clause providing that if, by reason of death or disability, the person agreeing to receive lessons and other services is unable to receive all lessons and other services for which he or she has contracted, the person and his or her estate shall be relieved from the obligation of making payment for lessons and other services other than those received prior to death or the onset of disability, and that if the buyer has prepaid any sum for lessons and other services so much of that sum as is allocable to lessons and other services he or she has not taken shall be promptly refunded to the buyer or his or her representative.

(b) Notwithstanding the provisions of any contract to the contrary, whenever the contract price is payable in installments and the buyer is relieved from making further payments or entitled to a refund under this section, the buyer shall be entitled to receive a refund or refund credit of so much of the cash price as is allocable to the lessons or other services not actually received by the buyer. The refund of the finance charge shall be computed according to the "sum of the balances method," also known as the "Rule of 78". *(Added by Stats.1969, c. 1571, p. 3192, § 1. Amended by Stats.1976, c. 1200, p. 5475, § 2; Stats.1987, c. 449, § 10; Stats.1988, c. 1043, § 10.)*

Research References

4 Witkin, California Summary 10th Sales § 362, (S 362) Health and Dance Services Contracts.

§ 1812.58. Provisions not exclusive

The provisions of this title are not exclusive and do not relieve the parties or the contracts subject thereto from compliance with all other applicable provisions of law. *(Added by Stats.1969, c. 1571, p. 3192, § 1.)*

§ 1812.59. Noncomplying contracts void

Any contract for dance studio lessons and other services which does not comply with the applicable provisions of this title shall be void and unenforceable as contrary to public policy. *(Added by Stats.1969, c. 1571, p. 3192, § 1. Amended by Stats.1987, c. 449, § 11; Stats.1988, c. 1043, § 11.)*

Research References

4 Witkin, California Summary 10th Sales § 362, (S 362) Health and Dance Services Contracts.

§ 1812.60. Fraud rendering contract void

Any contract for dance studio lessons and other services entered into in reliance upon any willful and false, fraudulent, or misleading information, representation, notice, or advertisement of the seller shall be void and unenforceable. *(Added by Stats.1969, c. 1571, p. 3192, § 1. Amended by Stats.1987, c. 449, § 12; Stats.1988, c. 1043, § 12.)*

§ 1812.61. Waiver of provisions

Any waiver of the buyer of the provisions of this title shall be deemed contrary to public policy and shall be void and unenforceable. *(Added by Stats.1969, c. 1571, p. 3192, § 1.)*

§ 1812.62. Recovery of triple damages and attorney fee; correction of contract; holder defined

(a) Any buyer injured by a violation of this title may bring an action for the recovery of damages. Judgment may be entered for three times the amount at which the actual damages are assessed plus reasonable attorney fees.

(b) Notwithstanding the provisions of this title, any failure to comply with any provision of this title may be corrected within 30 days after the execution of the contract by the buyer, and, if so corrected, neither the seller nor the holder shall be subject to any penalty under this title, provided that any correction which increases any monthly payment, the number of payments, or the total amount due, must be concurred in, in writing, by the buyer. "Holder" includes the seller who acquires the contract, or, if the contract is purchased by a financing agency or other assignee, the financing agency or other assignee. *(Added by Stats.1969, c. 1571, p. 3193, § 1.)*

Research References

3 Witkin Cal. Proc. 5th Actions § 664, (S 664) in General.
3 Witkin Cal. Proc. 5th Actions § 668, (S 668) Exceptions.

§ 1812.63. Violation of provisions; offense; injunction; duty to institute actions

Any person who violates any provision of this title relating to dance studio contracts is guilty of a misdemeanor. Any superior court of this state has jurisdiction in equity to restrain and enjoin the violation of any of the provisions of this title relating to dance studio contracts.

The duty to institute actions for violation of those provisions of this title, including equity proceedings to restrain and enjoin violations, is hereby vested in the Attorney General, district attorneys, and city attorneys. The Attorney General, any district attorney, or any city attorney may prosecute misdemeanor actions or institute equity proceedings, or both.

This section shall not be deemed to prohibit the enforcement by any person of any right provided by this or any other law. *(Added by Stats.1969, c. 1571, p. 3193, § 1. Amended by Stats.1987, c. 449, § 13; Stats.1988, c. 1043, § 13.)*

§ 1812.64. Bond; amount; filing

Every dance studio shall maintain a bond issued by a surety company admitted to do business in this state. The principal sum of the bond shall be 25 percent of the dance studio's gross income from the studio business in this state during the studio's last fiscal year, except that the principal sum of the bond shall not be less than twenty-five thousand dollars ($25,000) in the first or any subsequent year of operation.

A copy of the bond shall be filed with the Secretary of State, together with a declaration under penalty of perjury signed by the owner of the studio stating the dance studio's gross income from the dance studio business in this state during the last fiscal year. The information contained in the declaration shall not be subject to public inspection. If the person in whose name the bond is issued severs his or her relationship with the bonded dance studio, the new owner shall, as a condition of doing business, notify the Secretary of State of the change of ownership and of proof of compliance with Sections 1812.64 and 1812.65. *(Added by Stats.1969, c. 1571, p. 3193, § 1. Amended by Stats.1976, c. 1200, p. 5476, § 3; Stats.1987, c. 449, § 14; Stats.1988, c. 1043, § 14; Stats.1999, c. 1024 (A.B.648), § 3.)*

Research References

4 Witkin, California Summary 10th Sales § 362, (S 362) Health and Dance Services Contracts.

§ 1812.65. Bond; persons protected

The bond required by Section 1812.64 shall be in favor of the State of California for the benefit of any person who, after entering into a contract for dance studio lessons and other services with the dance studio, is damaged by fraud or dishonesty or failure to provide the services of the studio in performance of the contract. *(Added by Stats.1969, c. 1571, p. 3193, § 1. Amended by Stats.1982, c. 517, p. 2322, § 59; Stats.1987, c. 449, § 15; Stats.1988, c. 1043, § 15.)*

Law Revision Commission Comments

Section 1812.65 is amended to delete provisions duplicated in the Bond and Undertaking Law. See Code Civ.Proc. §§ 995.850 (enforcement by or for benefit of persons interested) and 996.470 (limitation on liability of surety). [16 Cal.L.Rev.Comm. Reports 501 (1981)].

Research References

Rutter, Cal. Practice Guide: Insurance Litigation Ch. 6I-B, B. Particular Surety Bond Coverages.

§ 1812.67. Exclusions from application of certain sections

(a) Sections 1812.64 and 1812.65 do not apply to any dance studio which requires or receives less than fifty dollars ($50) in advance payments from or on behalf of each student for dance studio lessons or other services which are to be rendered by the studio in the future and such advance payments are not required or received by the studio from each student more frequently than once every 30 days.

(b) Sections 1812.53, 1812.54, 1812.64, and 1812.65 do not apply to a dance studio which only offers instruction in ballet, modern, jazz, tap dance, or any combination thereof, to persons under 21 years of age pursuant to a contract for dance studio lessons that provides all of the following: (1) a total payment of less than five hundred dollars ($500), (2) that all agreed-upon lessons will be offered within four months from the date the contract is entered, and (3) that the contract may be canceled and all money paid for instruction not yet received will be refunded within 10 days of cancellation, if the dance student cancels within three days after receiving the first lesson, or if the dance student cancels at any time after moving his or her residence to a location more than 15 miles from the location of the dance studio.

(c) Sections 1812.53, 1812.54, 1812.64, and 1812.65 do not apply to any organization that has qualified for a tax exemption under Section 501(c)(3) of the Internal Revenue Code and which receives a direct grant of funds from the California Arts Council. *(Added by Stats.1969, c. 1571, p. 3190, § 1. Amended by Stats.1971, c. 903, p. 1752, § 2; Stats.1976, c. 1200, p. 5476, § 4; Stats.1982, c. 517, p. 2322, § 61; Stats.1987, c. 449, § 16; Stats.1988, c. 1043, § 16.)*

Law Revision Commission Comments

Section 1812.67 is amended to correct a section reference. [16 Cal.L.Rev.Comm. Reports 501 (1981)].

§ 1812.68. Severability clause

If any provision of this title or the application thereof to any person or circumstances is held unconstitutional, the remainder of the title and the application of such provision to other persons and circumstances shall not be affected thereby. *(Added by Stats.1969, c. 1571, p. 3194, § 1.)*

Research References

Rutter, Cal. Practice Guide: Insurance Litigation Ch. 6I-B, B. Particular Surety Bond Coverages.

§ 1812.69. Enforcement; filing fees

(a) The Secretary of State shall enforce the provisions of this title that govern the filing and maintenance of bonds.

(b) The Secretary of State shall charge a filing fee not to exceed the cost of filing the bond. *(Added by Stats.1996, c. 633 (S.B.1978), § 7. Amended by Stats.1999, c. 1024 (A.B.648), § 5.)*

Title 2.5

CONTRACTS FOR HEALTH STUDIO SERVICES

§ 1812.80. Purpose

(a) The Legislature finds that the health studio industry has a significant impact upon the economy and well-being of this state and its local communities; and that the provisions of this title relating to contracts for health studio services are necessary for the public welfare.

(b) The Legislature declares that the purpose of this title is to safeguard the public against fraud, deceit, imposition and financial hardship, and to foster and encourage competition, fair dealing, and prosperity in the field of health studio services by prohibiting or restricting false or misleading advertising, onerous contract terms, harmful financial practices, and other unfair, dishonest, deceptive, destructive, unscrupulous, fraudulent, and discriminatory practices by which the public has been injured in connection with contracts for health studio services. *(Added by Stats.1961, c. 1675, p. 3641, § 1. Amended by Stats.1969, c. 1571, p. 3194, § 3; Stats.2005, c. 439 (S.B.581), § 1.)*

Research References

4 Witkin, California Summary 10th Sales § 362, (S 362) Health and Dance Services Contracts.

§ 1812.81. Contract for health studio services defined

As used in this title, "contract for health studio services" means a contract for instruction, training or assistance in physical culture, body building, exercising, reducing, figure development, or any other such physical skill, or for the use by an individual patron of the facilities of a health studio, gymnasium or other facility used for any of the above purposes, or for membership in any group, club, association or organization formed for any of the above purposes; but does not include (a) contracts for professional services rendered or furnished by a person licensed under the provisions of Division 2 (commencing with Section 500) of the Business and Professions Code, (b) contracts for instruction at schools operating pursuant to the provisions of the Education Code, or (c) contracts for instruction, training, or assistance relating to diet or control of eating habits not involving physical culture, body building, exercising, figure development, or any other such physical skill. *(Added by Stats.1961, c. 1675, p. 3642, § 1. Amended by Stats.1969, c. 1571, p. 3195, § 4; Stats.1980, c. 690, p. 2081, § 1.)*

Research References

4 Witkin, California Summary 10th Sales § 398, (S 398) Weight Loss Contracts.

§ 1812.82. Written contract required; copy to customer

Every contract for health studio services shall be in writing and shall be subject to the provisions of this title. A copy of the written contract shall be given to the customer at the time he signs the contract. *(Added by Stats.1961, c. 1675, p. 3642, § 1. Amended by Stats.1969, c. 611, p. 1251, § 1; Stats.1969, c. 1571, p. 3195, § 5.)*

Research References

4 Witkin, California Summary 10th Sales § 362, (S 362) Health and Dance Services Contracts.

§ 1812.83. Overlapping contracts; consideration as one

All contracts for health studio services, which may be in effect between the same seller and the same buyer, the terms of which overlap for any period, shall be considered as one contract for the purposes of this title. *(Added by Stats.1961, c. 1675, p. 3642, § 1. Amended by Stats.1969, c. 1571, p. 3195, § 6.)*

Research References

4 Witkin, California Summary 10th Sales § 362, (S 362) Health and Dance Services Contracts.

§ 1812.84. Payment period and contract term limitations; statement disclosing length of term

(a) A contract for health studio services may not require payments or financing by the buyer to exceed the term of the contract, nor may the term of the contract exceed three years. This subdivision does not apply to a member's obligation to pay valid, outstanding moneys due under the contract, including moneys to be paid pursuant to a termination notice period in the contract in which the termination notice period does not exceed 30 days.

(b) A contract for health studio services shall include a statement printed in a size at least 14–point type that discloses the length of the term of the contract. This statement shall be placed above the space reserved for the signature of the buyer. *(Added by Stats.1961, c. 1675, p. 3642, § 1. Amended by Stats.1969, c. 1571, p. 3195, § 7; Stats.1980, c. 651, p. 1825, § 1; Stats.1993, c. 339 (A.B.626), § 1; Stats.2001, c. 233 (S.B.85), § 1; Stats.2005, c. 439 (S.B.581), § 2; Stats.2006, c. 219 (A.B.2664), § 1.)*

Research References

4 Witkin, California Summary 10th Sales § 362, (S 362) Health and Dance Services Contracts.

§ 1812.85. Time for beginning performance of services; grounds for cancellation and refunds; statement and notice of cancellation; consumer liability

(a) Every contract for health studio services shall provide that performance of the agreed-upon services will begin within six months after the date the contract is entered into. The consumer may cancel the contract and receive a pro rata refund if the health studio fails to provide the specific facilities advertised or offered in writing by the time indicated. If no time is indicated in the contract, the consumer may cancel the contract within six months after the execution of the contract and shall receive a pro rata refund. If a health studio fails to meet a timeline set forth in this section, the consumer may cancel the contract at any time after the expiration of the timeline. However, if following the expiration of the timeline, the health studio provides the advertised or agreed-upon services, the consumer may cancel the contract up to 10 days after those services are provided.

(b)(1) Every contract for health studio services shall, in addition, contain on its face, and in close proximity to the space reserved for the signature of the buyer, a conspicuous statement in a size equal to at least 10–point boldface type, as follows:

"You, the buyer, may cancel this agreement at any time prior to midnight of the fifth business day of the health studio after the date of this agreement, excluding Sundays and holidays. To cancel this agreement, mail or deliver a signed and dated notice, or send a telegram which states that you, the buyer, are canceling this agreement, or words of similar effect. The notice shall be sent to,

_____

(Name of health studio operator)

at_____

(Address of health studio operator)."

(2) The contract for health studio services shall contain on the first page, in a type size no smaller than that generally used in the body of the document, the following: (A) the name and address of the health studio operator to which the notice of cancellation is to be mailed, and (B) the date the buyer signed the contract.

(3) The contract shall provide a description of the services, facilities, and hours of access to which the consumer is entitled. Any services, facilities, and hours of access that are not described in the contract shall be considered optional services, and these optional services shall be considered as separate contracts for the purposes of this title and Section 1812.83.

(4) Until the health studio operator has complied with this section, the buyer may cancel the contract for health studio services.

(5) All moneys paid pursuant to a contract for health studio services shall be refunded within 10 days after receipt of the notice of cancellation, except that payment shall be made for any health studio services received prior to cancellation.

(c) If at any time during the term of the contract, including a transfer of the contractual obligation, the health studio eliminates or substantially reduces the scope of the facilities, such as swimming pools or tennis courts, that were described in the contract, in an advertisement relating to the specific location, or in a written offer, and available to the consumer upon execution of the contract, the consumer may cancel the contract and receive a pro rata refund. The consumer may not cancel the contract pursuant to this subdivision if the health studio, after giving reasonable notice to its members, temporarily takes facilities out of operation for reasonable repairs, modifications, substitutions, or improvements. This subdivision shall not be interpreted to give the consumer the right to cancel a contract because of changes to the type or quantity of classes or equipment offered, provided the consumer is informed in the contract that the health studio reserves the right to make changes to the type or quantity of classes or equipment offered and the changes to the type or quantity of classes or equipment offered are reasonable under the circumstances.

(d)(1) If a contract for health studio services requires payment of one thousand five hundred dollars ($1,500) to two thousand dollars ($2,000), inclusive, including initiation fees or initial membership fees, by the person receiving the services or the use of the facility, the person shall have the right to cancel the contract within 20 days after the contract is executed.

(2) If a contract for health studio services requires payment of two thousand one dollars ($2,001) to two thousand five hundred dollars ($2,500), inclusive, including initiation fees or initial membership fees, by the person receiving the services or the use of the facility, the person shall have the right to cancel the contract within 30 days after the contract is executed.

(3) If a contract for health studio services requires payment of two thousand five hundred one dollars ($2,501) or more, including initiation fees or initial membership fees, by the person receiving the services or the use of the facility, the person shall have the right to cancel the contract within 45 days after the contract is executed.

(4) The right of cancellation provided in this subdivision shall be set out in the membership contract.

(5) The rights and remedies under this paragraph are cumulative to any rights and remedies under other law.

(6) A health studio entering into a contract for health studio services that requires a payment of less than one thousand five hundred dollars ($1,500), including initiation or initial membership fees and exclusive of interest or finance charges, by the

person receiving the services or the use of the facilities, is not required to comply with paragraph (1), (2), or (3).

(e) Upon cancellation, the consumer shall be liable only for that portion of the total contract payment, including initiation fees and other charges however denominated, that has been available for use by the consumer, based upon a pro rata calculation over the term of the contract. The remaining portion of the contract payment shall be returned to the consumer by the health studio. *(Added by Stats.1961, c. 1675, p. 3642, § 1. Amended by Stats.1967, c. 1613, p. 3854, § 1; Stats.1969, c. 611, p. 1251, § 2; Stats.1969, c. 1571, p. 3195, § 8; Stats.1980, c. 651, p. 1825, § 2; Stats.2005, c. 439 (S.B.581), § 3; Stats.2006, c. 538 (S.B.1852), § 48; Stats.2006, c. 219 (A.B.2664), § 2.)*

Research References

1 Witkin Cal. Summ. 10th Contracts § 123, (S 123) in General.
4 Witkin, California Summary 10th Sales § 362, (S 362) Health and Dance Services Contracts.

§ 1812.86.　Limitation on amount of payment

(a) No contract for health studio services shall require payment by the person receiving the services or the use of the facilities of a total amount in excess of the amount specified in subdivision (b) or (c).

(b) The limit specified in subdivision (a) shall, on and after January 1, 2006, be three thousand dollars ($3,000), inclusive of initiation or initial membership fees and exclusive of interest or finance charges.

(c) The limit in subdivision (a) shall, on and after January 1, 2010, be four thousand four hundred dollars ($4,400), inclusive of initiation or initial membership fees and exclusive of interest or finance charges. *(Added by Stats.1961, c. 1675, p. 3642, § 1. Amended by Stats.1967, c. 1613, p. 3855, § 2; Stats.1969, c. 1571, p. 3195, § 9; Stats.1980, c. 651, p. 1825, § 3; Stats.2005, c. 439 (S.B.581), § 4.)*

§ 1812.87.　Prohibition of notes cutting off, as to third parties, buyer's right of action or defense against seller

No contract for health studio services shall require or entail the execution of any note or series of notes by the buyer which when separately negotiated will cut off as to third parties any right of action or defense which the buyer may have against the seller. *(Added by Stats.1961, c. 1675, p. 3642, § 1. Amended by Stats.1969, c. 1571, p. 3195, § 10.)*

Research References

4 Witkin, California Summary 10th Sales § 362, (S 362) Health and Dance Services Contracts.

§ 1812.88.　Prohibition against assignment of contract cutting off buyer's right of action or defense against seller; conditions

No right of action or defense arising out of a contract for health studio services which the buyer has against the seller, and which would be cut off by assignment, shall be cut off by assignment of the contract to any third party whether or not he acquires the contract in good faith and for value unless the assignee gives notice of the assignment to the buyer as provided in this section and within 30 days of the mailing of notice receives no written notice of the facts giving rise to the claim or defense of the buyer. A notice of assignment shall be in writing addressed to the buyer at the address shown on the contract and shall identify the contract and inform the buyer that he must, within 30 days of the date of mailing of the notice, notify the assignee in writing of any facts giving rise to a claim or defense which he may have. The notice of assignment shall state the name of the seller and buyer, a description of the services, the

contract balance and the number and amount of the installments. *(Added by Stats.1961, c. 1675, p. 3643, § 1. Amended by Stats.1969, c. 1571, p. 3196, § 11.)*

§ 1812.89.　Relief from payment upon death, disability or movement; refund of prepayments; predetermined fee

(a)(1) Every contract for health studio services shall contain a clause providing that if, by reason of death or disability, the person agreeing to receive services is unable to receive all services for which he has contracted, he and his estate shall be relieved from the obligation of making payment for services other than those received prior to death or the onset of disability, and that if he has prepaid any sum for services, so much of such sum as is allocable to services he has not taken shall be promptly refunded to him or his representative.

(2) In every case in which a person has prepaid a sum for services under a contract for health studio services, and by reason of death or disability, is unable to receive all such services, the party agreeing to furnish such services shall, on request, immediately refund to such person or his personal representative such amount of the sum prepaid as is proportionate to the amount of services not received.

(3) For the purposes of this section, "disability" means a condition which precludes the buyer from physically using the facilities and the condition is verified by a physician.

(4) Notwithstanding the provisions of any contract to the contrary, whenever the contract price is payable in installments and the buyer is relieved from making further payments or entitled to a refund under this section, the amount of the contract price allocable to services not received shall represent at least as great a proportion of the total contract price as the sum of the periodic monthly balances not yet due bears to the sum of all the periodic monthly balances under the schedule of installments in the contract.

(b)(1) Except as provided in paragraph (2), every contract for health studio services shall contain a clause providing that if the person agreeing to receive health studio services moves further than 25 miles from the health studio and is unable to transfer the contract to a comparable facility, such person shall be relieved from the obligation of making payment for services other than those received prior to the move, and if such person has prepaid any sum for health studio services, so much of such sum as is allocable to services he or she has not taken shall be promptly refunded.

(2) Notwithstanding paragraph (1), a contract for health studio services may contain a clause providing that if the person agreeing to receive health studio services moves further than 25 miles from the health studio and is unable to transfer the contract to a comparable facility, such person may be charged a predetermined fee not exceeding one hundred dollars ($100), or, if more than half the life of the contract has expired, such person may be charged a predetermined fee not exceeding fifty dollars ($50). *(Added by Stats.1961, c. 1675, p. 3643, § 1. Amended by Stats.1969, c. 1571, p. 3196, § 12; Stats.1980, c. 651, p. 1826, § 4.)*

Research References

4 Witkin, California Summary 10th Sales § 362, (S 362) Health and Dance Services Contracts.

§ 1812.90.　Provisions not exclusive

The provisions of this title are not exclusive and do not relieve the parties or the contracts subject thereto from compliance with all other applicable provisions of law. *(Added by Stats.1961, c. 1675, p. 3643, § 1.)*

§ 1812.91. Noncomplying contracts void

Any contract for health studio services which does not comply with the applicable provisions of this title shall be void and unenforceable as contrary to public policy. *(Added by Stats. 1961, c. 1675, p. 3643, § 1. Amended by Stats.1969, c. 1571, p. 3197, § 13.)*

Research References

4 Witkin, California Summary 10th Sales § 362, (S 362) Health and Dance Services Contracts.

§ 1812.92. Fraud rendering contract void

Any contract for health studio services entered into in reliance upon any willful and false, fraudulent, or misleading information, representation, notice or advertisement of the seller shall be void and unenforceable. *(Added by Stats.1961, c. 1675, p. 3644, § 1. Amended by Stats.1969, c. 1571, p. 3197, § 14.)*

§ 1812.93. Waiver of provisions

Any waiver of the buyer of the provisions of this title shall be deemed contrary to public policy and shall be void and unenforceable. *(Added by Stats.1961, c. 1675, p. 3644, § 1.)*

§ 1812.94. Recovery of triple damages and attorney fee; correction of contract; holder defined

(a) Any buyer injured by a violation of this title may bring an action for the recovery of damages. Judgment may be entered for three times the amount at which the actual damages are assessed plus reasonable attorney fees.

(b) Notwithstanding the provisions of this title, any failure to comply with any provision of this title may be corrected within 30 days after the execution of the contract by the buyer, and, if so corrected, neither the seller nor the holder shall be subject to any penalty under this title, provided that any correction which increases any monthly payment, the number of payments, or the total amount due, must be concurred in, in writing, by the buyer. "Holder" includes the seller who acquires the contract or, if the contract is purchased by a financing agency or other assignee, the financing agency or other assignee. *(Added by Stats.1961, c. 1675, p. 3644, § 1. Amended by Stats.1963, c. 299, p. 1072, § 1.)*

§ 1812.95. Severability clause

If any provision of this title or the application thereof to any person or circumstances is held unconstitutional, the remainder of the title and the application of such provision to other persons and circumstances shall not be affected thereby. *(Added by Stats.1961, c. 1675, p. 3644, § 1.)*

§ 1812.96. Money to be held in trust until business opens; use of funds; cancellation rights

(a) Except as provided in subdivision (c) or (d), all money received by the seller of health studio services from a consumer for a health studio facility that has not yet opened for business shall be held in trust and shall be deposited in a trust account established in a state or federally chartered bank or savings association. The seller shall not draw, transfer, or encumber any of the money held in trust until five business days after the health studio facility has opened and the seller has fully paid refunds to consumers who canceled their contracts as provided in subdivision (b) or in Section 1812.85.

(b) In addition to any other cancellation rights, a consumer who pays any money under a contract for health studio services for a health studio facility that has not yet opened for business has the right to cancel the contract and receive a full refund at any time prior to midnight of the fifth business day after the date the health studio opens for business. The cancellation right

shall be set forth in the contract. The refund shall be paid within 10 days of receipt of notice of cancellation.

(c) Notwithstanding subdivision (a), a seller of health studio services may draw on money held in trust to pay refunds or may draw, transfer, or encumber funds to the extent that the amount is offset by a bond of equal or greater amount than satisfies this subdivision. The bond shall be issued by a surety insurer admitted to do business in this state and shall be filed with the Secretary of State. The bond shall be in favor of the State of California for the benefit of consumers harmed by a violation of this title.

(d) Subdivision (a) does not apply to a seller of health studio services that is, at the time money is received from the consumer, operating at least five health studio facilities in this state that have been in operation for a period of at least five years, and that has an excess of current assets over current liabilities of at least one million dollars ($1,000,000). *(Added by Stats.2005, c. 439 (S.B.581), § 5.)*

§ 1812.97. Editorial Note

For a section of this number as added by Stats.1986, c. 565, § 1, see Civil Code § 1812.97 under Title 2.55.

Research References

4 Witkin, California Summary 10th Sales § 337, (S 337) Anabolic Steroids.

§ 1812.98. Month-to-month contracts; declaration of existing law

Nothing in this title is intended to prohibit month-to-month contracts. This section is declaratory of existing law. *(Formerly § 1812.97, added by Stats.2005, c. 439 (S.B.581), § 6. Renumbered § 1812.98 and amended by Stats.2006, c. 538 (S.B.1852), § 49.)*

Title 2.55

CONTRACTS FOR THE LEASE OR RENTAL OF ATHLETIC FACILITIES

Section

§ 1812.97. Warning statement; posting; athletic facilities; anabolic steroids

(a) Every contract which has as its purpose the lease or rental of athletic facilities for instruction, training, or assistance in physical culture, body building, exercising, reducing, figure development, or any other related physical skill, or for baseball, football, tennis, basketball, gymnastics, track and field, hockey, ice skating, weightlifting, wrestling, or bicycling shall contain the following warning statement in 10-point bold type:

Warning: Use of steroids to increase strength or growth can cause serious health problems. Steroids can keep teenagers from growing to their full height; they can also cause heart disease, stroke, and damaged liver function. Men and women using steroids may develop fertility problems, personality changes, and acne. Men can also experience premature balding and development of breast tissue. These health hazards are in addition to the civil and criminal penalties for unauthorized sale, use, or exchange of anabolic steroids.

(b) Commencing June 1, 1990, the warning statement required pursuant to subdivision (a) shall be conspicuously posted in all athletic facilities in this state which have locker rooms. At least one warning statement shall be posted in every locker room of the athletic facility.

(c) As used in this section, "athletic facilities" includes a health studio regulated pursuant to Title 2.5 (commencing with Section 1812.80), a professional boxers' training gymnasium, as defined in Section 18685 of the Business and Professions Code, any privately owned sports facility or stadium in this state which is open to the general public, and any publicly owned sports facility or stadium in this state, including facilities in institutions of higher learning and schools that include any or all grades 7 to 12, inclusive.

(d) As used in this section, "anabolic steroids" include, but are not limited to, the following:

(1) Dianabol (methandrostenelone).

(2) Winstrol (stabozalol).

(3) Maxibolin (ethyl estrenol).

(4) Durabolin (nandrolone phenpropionate).

(5) Deca-Durabolin (nandrolone decanote).

(6) Testosterone propionate.

(7) Pregnyl (chorionic gonadotropin).

(8) Anavar (toxandroprione).

(e) When an athletic facility seeks to renew an operating license, if it can be demonstrated by a preponderance of the evidence that an athletic facility has not posted the sign required pursuant to this section, the licensing agency may impose a fine in the amount of fifty dollars ($50) per day for each day that the violation occurred, as a condition of obtaining the license renewal. *(Added by Stats.1986, c. 565, § 1. Amended by Stats.1989, c. 807, § 2, operative June 1, 1990.)*

Research References

4 Witkin, California Summary 10th Sales § 337, (S 337) Anabolic Steroids.

§ 1812.98. Editorial Note

For a section of this number as added by Stats.2005, c. 439 (S.B.581), § 6, see Civil Code § 1812.98 under Title 2.5.

Title 2.6

CONTRACTS FOR DISCOUNT BUYING SERVICES

§ 1812.100. Legislative findings; purpose

(a) The Legislature finds that there exist in connection with a substantial number of contracts for discount buying services, sales practices and business and financing practices which result in fraud, deceit, and financial hardships being perpetrated on the people of the state; that existing legal remedies are inadequate to correct these abuses; that the discount buying industry has a significant impact upon the economy and well-being of the state and its local communities; and that the provisions of this title relating to such contracts are necessary for the public welfare.

(b) The purpose of this title is to safeguard the public against fraud, deceit, and financial hardship, and to foster and encourage competition, fair dealing, and prosperity in the field of discount buying services by prohibiting or restricting false or misleading advertising, unfair contract terms, harmful financial practices, and other unfair, deceptive, destructive, unscrupulous, fraudulent and discriminatory practices by which the public has been endangered and by which the public may in the future be harmed in connection with contracts for discount buying services. This title shall be construed liberally in order to achieve the foregoing purposes. *(Added by Stats.1976, c. 237, p. 447, § 1.)*

Research References

Miller and Starr California Real Estate § 25C:66, Regulation of Time-Shares; in General.

§ 1812.101. Definitions

For the purpose of this title, the following definitions shall be used:

(a) "Discount buying organization" means any person or persons, corporation, unincorporated association, or other organization which, for a consideration, provides or purports to provide its clients or the clients or members of any other discount buying organization with the ability to purchase goods or services at discount prices, except that a discount buying organization does not include any of the following:

(1) Any discount buying organization in which the total consideration paid by each client or member in any manner whatsoever for the purchase of discount buying services from the organization that either:

(A) Does not exceed a one-time fee of fifty dollars ($50) or an annual fee of twenty-five dollars ($25) to be paid on a yearly basis.

(B) Does not exceed a one-time or annual fee of fifty dollars ($50) and the organization provides a majority of the goods and services through purchases by members who walk in to a fixed location operated by the organization.

(2) Any discount buying organization in which the total consideration paid by each client or member in any manner whatsoever for the purchase of discount buying services from the organization does not exceed a one-time or annual fee of one hundred dollars ($100) and the organization does all of the following in subparagraphs (A) to (F), inclusive, and subject to subparagraph (G):

(A) Offers buying services to clients or members through toll-free telephone access, computer access, or video shopping terminals.

(B) (i) During the first year of membership of each member, upon the request of the member, provides a full refund of membership fees, exclusive of any fees, however designated, not exceeding ten dollars ($10) in the aggregate, without conditions other than the surrender or destruction of materials which allow the member to access or use the service.

(ii)(I) The organization shall establish an escrow account of fifty thousand dollars ($50,000) for the purpose of providing refunds to members, pursuant to clause (i). If the fifty thousand dollars ($50,000) deposited in escrow is depleted during the first year of the existence of the escrow account, the organization shall within three business days of depletion replenish the account in the amount of fifty thousand dollars ($50,000). For each calendar year thereafter, the organization shall deposit in the account an amount equal to refunds made from the account in the prior calendar year, but not less than fifty thousand dollars ($50,000). At any time the balance in the escrow account decreases to 50 percent of the amount funded that year, the organization shall within three business days replenish the account back to the balance required at the beginning of that calendar year. The organization shall provide proof of the establishment of the escrow account to the Secretary of State and shall maintain records of all member requests for refunds and refunds made pursuant to this clause. The records shall be made available for review upon request by the Attorney General, any district attorney, or the Department of Justice.

(II) The escrow account shall be established and maintained at a federally insured bank or federally insured financial institution independent of the organization with escrow instructions making the bank or financial institution or an officer or employee thereof the escrow trustee.

(III) Refunds shall be made from the escrow account to any member who provides proof of membership while a California resident and requests, in writing, a membership refund, and has not previously been refunded his or her membership fee. The escrow trustee shall issue the refund within 10 days of the date the written request is received by the escrow trustee. In addition, requests for refunds may be made directly to and paid directly by the organization.

(IV) Proof of creation of the escrow account, and membership refund information, shall be provided to the members in the following form:

"The _____ (organization) has established an escrow account for the refund of membership fees at _____ (financial institution). Refunds from the escrow account may, in addition to other remedies and sources available to you, be obtained by mailing a written request along with proof of membership to _____ (escrow trustee). This refund request

shall not affect or limit any other remedy at law available to you."

(C) Provides at least 15 toll-free service lines to California consumers devoted exclusively to customer service questions and complaints.

(D) Maintains a bond which meets the requirements of Sections 1812.103 and 1812.104, except that the principal sum of the bond need only be twenty thousand dollars ($20,000).

(E)(i) Possesses an unrevoked acknowledgment from the Attorney General that the organization has provided to the Attorney General, to the Attorney General's reasonable satisfaction, marketing procedures and documents that clearly explain membership fee cancellation and refund terms which include:

(I) The amount of the initial membership fee and how and when it will be collected.

(II) If applicable, that a member must be advised, before any charges are applied, that they need not provide billing information in order to be charged a membership fee, in circumstances in which the telemarketing firm has prior access to the member's billing information.

(III) In the case of trial membership offers, the duration of the trial period and that if the member does not cancel within the trial period he or she will automatically be charged the membership fee.

(IV) Specifically how the member may cancel membership.

(V) The written disclosure, printed in capital letters with a minimum 14–point boldface type, indicating who to contact, both directly through the company and through the escrow account, for a refund.

(VI) The written disclosure made at the time of solicitation and at the time an enrollment package is sent to consumers.

(ii) When an organization provides documentation that clearly explains membership fee cancellation and refund terms to the Attorney General's reasonable satisfaction, which includes the information required by subclauses (I) to (VI), inclusive, of clause (i) of subparagraph (E), the Attorney General shall issue a revocable acknowledgment to the organization for it to obtain this exception. The acknowledgment issued by the Attorney General is not evidence of the adequacy or accuracy of the organization's actual disclosures and representations provided to consumers. No organization in any marketing to consumers may make any reference to an acknowledgment issued by the Attorney General under this clause.

(F) Provides the disclosures listed in subclauses (I) to (VI), inclusive, of clause (i) of subparagraph (E) to every prospective member.

(G) The exemption is null and void if the organization fails to comply with the conditions set forth in this section or if the Attorney General's office revokes the exemption due to a organization not being in full compliance with all of the provisions of this section.

(3) Any discount buying organization in which persons receive discount buying services incidentally as part of a package of services provided to or available to the individual on account of his or her membership in the organization, which is not organized for the profit of any person or organization, and which does not have as one of its primary purposes or businesses, the provision of discount buying services.

(4) Any person, corporation, unincorporated association, or other organization, which, for a consideration collected from another entity, provides or purports to provide the clients of the other entity with the ability to purchase goods or services at discount prices, if the clients of the other entity do not order from, or pay any money to, that person, corporation, unincorpo-

rated association, or other organization; however, the entity, from which the customer purchases the right to obtain goods or services at discount prices, shall comply with the requirements of this title.

(b) "Contract for discount buying services" means a contract between one party (hereinafter referred to as the "buyer") who is purchasing the service for personal or family use, and a discount buying organization, whereby the buyer for a consideration receives the right to obtain goods or services from the discount buying organization, or to utilize the discount buying organization services in obtaining goods and services, at discount prices.

(c) "Discount prices" means prices which are represented to be lower on most or all offered goods or services than those generally charged for the items in the locality in which the representation is made.

This definition is not intended to affect the degree of savings which must be offered on an item or selection of items in order to truthfully and without misleading consumers represent an item, selection of items, or entire store as being "discount" or "discounted." *(Added by Stats.1976, c. 237, p. 447, § 1. Amended by Stats.1985, c. 558, § 1; Stats.1986, c. 345, § 1, eff. July 15, 1986; Stats.1992, c. 304 (A.B.2859), § 1; Stats.2001, c. 178 (S.B.916), § 1.)*

Research References
Rutter, Cal. Practice Guide: Insurance Litigation Ch. 6I-B, B. Particular Surety Bond Coverages.
4 Witkin, California Summary 10th Sales § 351, (S 351) Discount Buying Services.

§ 1812.103. Bond; amount; copy

Every discount buying organization shall maintain a bond issued by a surety company admitted to do business in this state. The principal sum of the bond shall be twenty thousand dollars ($20,000). A copy of such bond shall be filed with the Secretary of State. *(Added by Stats.1976, c. 237, p. 447, § 1. Amended by Stats.1996, c. 633 (S.B.1978), § 8.)*

Research References
4 Witkin, California Summary 10th Sales § 351, (S 351) Discount Buying Services.

§ 1812.104. Bond; beneficiaries; liability

The bond required by Section 1812.103 shall be in favor of the State of California for the benefit of any person who is damaged by any violation of this title or by fraud or dishonesty or failure to provide the services of the discount buying organization in performance of the contract. The surety shall be liable only for the actual damages plus restitution and not the treble damages permitted under subdivision (a) of Section 1812.123. *(Added by Stats.1976, c. 237, p. 447, § 1. Amended by Stats.1982, c. 517, p. 2322, § 62.)*

Law Revision Commission Comments
Section 1812.104 is amended to delete provisions duplicated in the Bond and Undertaking Law. See Code Civ.Proc. §§ 995.850 (enforcement by or for benefit of persons interested) and 996.470 (limitation on liability of surety). [16 Cal.L.Rev.Comm. Reports 501 (1981)].

§ 1812.105. Deposit in lieu of bond; claim against deposit; review and approval; payment; attachment, garnishment, or execution

(a) When a deposit has been made in lieu of a bond pursuant to Section 995.710 of the Code of Civil Procedure, the person asserting a claim against the deposit shall, in lieu of Section 996.430 of the Code of Civil Procedure, establish the claim by furnishing evidence to the Secretary of State of a money judgment entered by a court together with evidence that the claimant is a person described in Section 1812.104.

(b) When a person has established the claim with the Secretary of State, the Secretary of State shall review and approve the claim and enter the date of approval on the claim. The claim shall be designated an "approved claim."

(c) When the first claim against a particular deposit has been approved, it shall not be paid until the expiration of a period of 240 days after the date of its approval by the Secretary of State. Subsequent claims that are approved by the Secretary of State within the same 240–day period shall similarly not be paid until the expiration of the 240–day period. Upon the expiration of the 240–day period, the Secretary of State shall pay all approved claims from that 240–day period in full unless the deposit is insufficient, in which case each approved claim shall be paid a pro rata share of the deposit.

(d) When the Secretary of State approves the first claim against a particular deposit after the expiration of a 240–day period, the date of approval of that claim shall begin a new 240–day period to which subdivision (c) shall apply with respect to the amount remaining in the deposit.

(e) After a deposit is exhausted, no further claims shall be paid by the Secretary of State. Claimants who have had their claims paid in full or in part pursuant to subdivisions (c) and (d) shall not be required to return funds received from the deposit for the benefit of other claimants.

(f) When a deposit has been made in lieu of a bond, the amount of the deposit shall not be subject to attachment, garnishment, or execution with respect to an action or judgment against the discount buying organization, other than as to an amount as no longer needed or required for the purpose of this title that would otherwise be returned to the discount buying organization by the Secretary of State.

(g) The Secretary of State shall retain a cash deposit for two years from the date the Secretary of State receives written notification from the assignor of the deposit that the assignor has ceased to engage in the business of a discount buying organization or has filed a bond pursuant to Section 1812.103, provided that there are no outstanding claims against the deposit. This written notice shall include all of the following: (1) name, address, and telephone number of the assignor; (2) name, address, and telephone number of the bank at which the deposit is located; (3) account number of the deposit; and (4) a statement whether the assignor is ceasing to engage in the business of a discount buying organization or has filed a bond with the Secretary of State. The Secretary of State shall forward an acknowledgment of receipt of the written notice to the assignor at the address indicated therein, specifying the date of receipt of the written notice and anticipated date of release of the deposit, provided there are no outstanding claims against the deposit.

(h) A judge of a superior court may order the return of the deposit prior to the expiration of two years upon evidence satisfactory to the judge that there are no outstanding claims against the deposit or order the Secretary of State to retain the deposit for a sufficient period beyond the two years specified in subdivision (g) to resolve outstanding claims against the deposit. *(Added by Stats.1984, c. 545, § 3. Amended by Stats.1996, c. 633 (S.B.1978), § 9; Stats.1998, c. 829 (S.B.1652), § 9; Stats.2002, c. 784 (S.B.1316), § 14.)*

Law Revision Commission Comments
Subdivision (h) of Section 1812.105 is amended to reflect unification of the municipal and superior courts pursuant to Article VI, Section 5(e), of the California Constitution. [32 Cal.L.Rev.Comm. Reports 70 (2002)].

Research References

Rutter, Cal. Practice Guide: Enforcing Judgments/Debts Ch. 4-A, A. Attachment.

Rutter, Cal. Practice Guide: Insurance Litigation Ch. 6I-B, B. Particular Surety Bond Coverages.

§ 1812.106. Disclosures by buying organization; nature of services; listing of items; warranties or guarantees; charges; criminal or civil actions

Every discount buying organization, before obtaining the signature of a potential buyer on any application or contract for discount buying services, shall provide to the buyer, and shall allow the buyer to retain, the following written disclosures:

(a) The exact nature of the services it provides, specifying the general categories of goods that are available at the discount buying organization's place of business or warehouse, those categories of goods, if any, that must be ordered or obtained through stores to which the discount buying organization will refer the customer, and those categories of goods, if any, that must be ordered or obtained through the mail.

(b) A list, current within the previous 60 days, of at least 100 items that are sold by or through the organization or available to those who contract with the organization, identified by brand name, model, and total price including a reasonable estimate of freight charges, if any are to be imposed; a reasonable estimate of delivery charges, if any are to be imposed; a reasonable estimate of setup charges, if any are to be imposed; the discount buying organization's price markup; and a reasonable estimate of any other charges the discount buying organization imposes. These items shall be reasonably representative as to the type of goods available. In lieu of providing this list, the discount buying organization shall provide and allow the buyer to retain a list of at least 100 items that were purchased by its members through the discount buying organization during the preceding 60 days. This list shall identify the items by brand name, model, and total selling price including freight charges, if any; delivery charges, if any; setup charges, if any; the discount buying organization's price markup; and any other charges imposed by the discount buying organization, and shall be representative as to the type of goods sold and the prices charged for the listed goods sold during that period. If the maximum number of items available through a discount buying organization is fewer than 100 in number, it may comply with this section by furnishing a list of the total items available, identified as described above with a statement that those are the only goods presently available. Any list required by this subdivision shall state the date on which it was prepared.

(c) A statement of the discount buying organization's policy with respect to warranties or guarantees on goods ordered, and the policy with respect to the return of ordered goods, cancellation of orders by the buyer, and refunds for cancellation or return.

(d) A description of any charges, such as freight charges, delivery charges, setup charges, seller's markup, and any other charges that are incidental to the purchase of goods through the discount buying organization and are to be paid by the buyer. A disclosure of these costs in specific monetary amounts shall also be made on each order placed through the discount buying organization.

(e) If any stockholder, director, officer, or general or limited partner of the discount buying organization, as the case may be:

(1) Has been convicted of a felony or misdemeanor or pleaded nolo contendere to a felony or misdemeanor charge, if the felony or misdemeanor involved fraud, embezzlement, fraudulent conversion, misappropriation of property, or a violation of this title.

(2) Has been held liable in a civil action by final judgment or consented to the entry of a stipulated judgment if the civil action alleged fraud, embezzlement, fraudulent conversion, or misappropriation of property, a violation of this title, the use of untrue or misleading representations in an attempt to sell or dispose of real or personal property, or the use of unfair, unlawful, or deceptive business practices.

(3) Is subject to any currently effective injunction or restrictive order relating to business activity as the result of an action brought by a public agency or department, including, but not limited to, an action affecting any vocational license, a statement so stating, and including the name of the court, the date of the conviction, judgment, order, or injunction and, if applicable, the name of the governmental agency that filed the action resulting in the conviction, judgment, order, or injunction. *(Added by Stats.1976, c. 237, p. 447, § 1. Amended by Stats.1980, c. 1001, p. 3190, § 1, eff. Sept. 21, 1980; Stats.2006, c. 538 (S.B.1852), § 50.)*

§ 1812.107. Written contract; contents

Every contract for discount buying services shall be in writing and shall be subject to the provisions of this title. The address of the seller's discount buying facility and the residence address of the buyer shall be clearly indicated on the face of the contract. A copy of the written contract shall be given to the buyer at the time he signs the contract. All blank spaces in the contract shall be filled in before the contract is signed by the buyer. Provisions or terms written by hand on the buyer's copy shall be legible. The contract shall disclose that a bond has been obtained by the discount buying organization and that a copy of such bond is on file with the Secretary of State. The contract shall be specific as to the period of time for which the discount buying services will be available to the buyer. This time period shall not be measured by the life of the buyer. *(Added by Stats.1976, c. 237, p. 447, § 1.)*

Research References

4 Witkin, California Summary 10th Sales § 351, (S 351) Discount Buying Services.

§ 1812.108. Overlapping contracts; consideration as one

All contracts for discount buying services, which may be in effect between a seller or related sellers and a buyer, the terms of which overlap for any period of time, shall be considered as one contract for the purpose of this title. *(Added by Stats.1976, c. 237, p. 447, § 1.)*

§ 1812.109. Payment or financing period; limitation

No contract for discount buying services shall require payments or financing by the buyer over a period in excess of two years from the date the contract was entered into. *(Added by Stats.1976, c. 237, p. 447, § 1.)*

§ 1812.110. Availability of services; time

Every contract for discount buying services shall provide that the buying services shall become available to the buyer within seven days from the date the contract was entered into. *(Added by Stats.1976, c. 237, p. 447, § 1.)*

§ 1812.113. Prohibition of notes cutting off, as to third parties, buyer's right of action or defense against seller

No contract for discount buying services shall require or entail the execution of any note or series of notes by the buyer which, when separately negotiated, will cut off as to any third party any right of action or defense which the buyer may have against the seller. *(Added by Stats.1976, c. 237, p. 447, § 1.)*

§ 1812.114. Prohibition against assignment or transfer of contract cutting off buyer's right of action or defense against organization

No right of action or defense arising out of a contract for discount buying services which the buyer has against the discount buying organization shall be cut off by assignment or transfer of the contract to any third party. *(Added by Stats.1976, c. 237, p. 447, § 1.)*

§ 1812.116. Receipt of payment or funds; delivery or availability of goods; time; refund; trust account; deposits and withdrawals

(a) Every contract for discount buying services shall provide that if any goods ordered by the buyer from the seller are not delivered to the buyer or available for pickup by the buyer at a location within his county of residence within six weeks from the date the buyer placed an order for such goods, then any moneys paid by the buyer for such goods in advance of delivery shall, upon the buyer's request, be fully refunded unless a predetermined delivery date has been furnished to the buyer in writing at the time he ordered such goods and the goods are delivered to the buyer or are available for pickup by that date.

(b) Prior to receiving from a buyer any payments pursuant to the terms of a contract for discount buying services, the discount buying organization shall establish a trust account at a federally insured bank or savings and loan association for the deposit, except for the first fifty dollars ($50) of a downpayment, of the contract payments as they are received.

If the discount buying organization sells or assigns the contract for discount buying services to a third party and such third party pays the discount buying organization as consideration an amount which is commercially reasonable for the sale or assignment of the contract, the discount buying organization shall deposit all funds received from the third party into the trust account.

If the discount buying organization in any manner transfers the contract for discount buying services to a third party which is to act as the recipient of contract payments from the buyer and such third party does not pay the discount buying organization as consideration for such transfer an amount which is commercially reasonable, then all sums received by the third party from the buyer shall be deposited in the discount buying organization's trust account for contract payments.

As to each buyer, during the first one-fourth or first six months of the buyer's membership period, whichever is shorter, funds representing no more than one-fourth of the contract price may be withdrawn from the trust account. During each subsequent one-fourth or six-month period, whichever is shorter, funds representing an additional one-fourth of the contract price may be withdrawn from the trust account.

(c)(1) Prior to receiving funds for an order of goods or services from any buyer, the discount buying organization shall establish a trust account at a federally insured bank or savings and loan association for the deposit of the funds. The discount buying organization shall deposit into the account all funds received from buyers for orders of goods or services regardless of how the funds are styled, including but not limited to, down payment, partial payment, payment in full, freight charge, or any other terms. If the total cost of goods or services ordered by a buyer on any one day does not exceed fifty dollars ($50), including taxes, freight charges, delivery charges, markup and all other charges collected by the discount buying organization, then the funds received from the buyer need not be deposited in the trust account.

(2) The trust account required by this section shall be created and maintained for the benefit of buyers who order goods or

services from or through the discount buying organization. The discount buying organization shall not in any manner encumber the corpus of the account and shall not withdraw money deposited therein on behalf of a buyer except: (i) in partial or full payment to the discount buying organization's source for the goods or services ordered by the buyer, or (ii) to make a refund to the buyer. After the withdrawal of money from a buyer's deposit pursuant to (i) or (ii) above, only that portion of the remainder of the deposit which represents compensation to the discount buying organization may be withdrawn. *(Added by Stats.1976, c. 237, p. 447, § 1. Amended by Stats.1980, c. 1001, p. 3191, § 2, eff. Sept. 21, 1980.)*

§ 1812.117. Trust account withdrawal provisions; conditions for compliance with alternate trust account provisions; bond requirements: letter of credit; enforcement

(a) An affiliate discount buying organization may, at its option, and with the express written consent of its parent, comply with the trust account withdrawal provisions set forth in subdivision (b), in lieu of those contained in subdivision (b) of Section 1812.116.

(b) The affiliate shall comply with the trust account provisions of subdivision (b) of Section 1812.116, except that:

(1) As to each buyer, during the first one-fourth or first six months of the buyer's membership period, whichever is shorter, funds representing no more than one-half of the contract price may be withdrawn from the trust account.

(2) During the subsequent one-fourth or six-month period of the buyer's membership period, whichever is shorter, the remaining balance of the contract price may be withdrawn from the trust account.

(c) To qualify for the provisions set forth in subdivision (b), (1) the affiliate shall maintain a surety bond of two hundred fifty thousand dollars ($250,000), and (2) the parent shall maintain an aggregate surety bond of two million five hundred thousand dollars ($2,500,000) and a letter of credit, as set forth in subdivision (d), for all of its affiliates that qualify for the withdrawal provisions of subdivision (b). The bonds shall be issued by a surety company admitted to do business in this state. A copy of each bond shall be filed with the Secretary of State, with a copy provided to the Attorney General. The affiliate's bond shall be in lieu of the bond required by subdivision (a) of Section 1812.103. The surety bonds shall comply with the requirements of this section and shall be in favor of the State of California for the benefit of consumers harmed by any violation of this title by the affiliate, the failure of the affiliate to comply with the terms of its membership contracts with consumers, and the failure of the affiliate to comply with the terms of any agreement with consumers for the purchase of goods or services, provided the bonds shall cover only pecuniary loss and not exemplary damages or treble damages permitted under subdivision (a) of Section 1812.123, and provided further the parent's bond shall not be drawn on until the affiliate's bond is exhausted.

(d) The parent shall continuously maintain and provide to the Attorney General as beneficiary an irrevocable letter of credit issued by a California state chartered bank or a national bank with its principal place of business in the State of California, in the amount of one million dollars ($1,000,000), in a form satisfactory to the Attorney General. After the bonds described in subdivision (c) have been exhausted, only the Attorney General, by and through the Attorney General's deputy or assistant, may draw on the letter of credit for the satisfaction of any final judgments based on any violation of this title by the affiliate, the failure of the affiliate to comply with the terms of its membership contracts with consumers, or the failure of an affiliate to comply with the terms of any agreement with consumers for the purchase of goods or services, provided the liability is established by final judgment of a court of competent jurisdiction and the time for appeal has expired or, if an appeal is taken, the appeal is finally determined and the judgment is affirmed, and provided further the letter of credit shall cover only pecuniary loss and not exemplary damages or treble damages permitted under subdivision (a) of Section 1812.123. The letter of credit shall provide that payment shall be made to the Attorney General upon presentation to the issuer of a sight draft stating only the amount drawn and signed by the Attorney General or by an Assistant or Deputy Attorney General. Any amount received by the Attorney General under the letter of credit shall be used exclusively to satisfy final judgments as described in this subdivision. The Attorney General may apply to the court for orders as desired or needed to carry out the provisions of this subdivision.

(e) In addition to other lawful means for the enforcement of the surety's liability on the bonds required by this section, the surety's liability may be enforced by motion after a final judgment has been obtained against an affiliate based on any violation of this title by the affiliate, the failure of the affiliate to comply with the terms of its membership contracts with consumers, or the failure of the affiliate to comply with the terms of any agreement with consumers for the purchase of goods or services. The bond of the parent shall not be drawn on until the bond of the affiliate has been exhausted, as provided in subdivisions (c) and (d). The motion may be filed by the Attorney General, a public prosecutor, or any person who obtained the judgment without first attempting to enforce the judgment against any party liable under the judgment. The notice of motion, motion, and a copy of the judgment shall be served on the surety as provided in Chapter 5 (commencing with Section 1010) of Title 14 of Part 2 of the Code of Civil Procedure. The notice shall set forth the amount of the claim, a brief statement indicating that the claim is covered by the bond, and, if the motion is to enforce liability under the bond provided by the parent, a statement that the bond provided by the affiliate has been exhausted or will be exhausted if the motion is granted. Service shall also be made on the Attorney General directed to the Consumer Law section. The court shall grant the motion unless the surety establishes that the claim is not covered by the bond or unless the court sustains an objection made by the Attorney General that the grant of the motion might impair the rights of actual or potential claimants or is not in the public interest. The court may, in the interest of justice, order a pro rata or other equitable distribution of the bond proceeds.

(f)(1) The bond required by subdivision (c) for an affiliate shall be continuously maintained by the affiliate until the date the affiliate ceases to make the election under subdivision (a) or ceases to engage in the business of a discount buying organization. The bond required by subdivision (c) for the parent shall be continuously maintained by the parent until the date all affiliates cease to make the election under subdivision (a) or all affiliates cease to engage in the business of a discount buying organization.

(2) Notwithstanding the expiration or termination of any bond required under this section, the bond remains in full force and effect for all liabilities incurred before, and for acts, omissions, and causes existing or which arose before, the expiration or termination of the bond. Legal proceedings may be had therefor in all respects as though the bond were in effect.

(3) The letter of credit required under subdivisions (c) and (d) shall be continuously maintained for a period of four years after all affiliates cease to make the election under subdivision (a) or cease to engage in the business of a discount buying organization, provided the period shall be extended until there is a final judgment, as described in subdivision (d), entered in each action seeking relief that may be covered by the letter of credit if the action was filed before the expiration of the four-year period.

(g) Subdivision (a) of Section 1812.121 does not apply to a discount buying organization that offers substantially equivalent alternative at-home ordering service through other generally available channels of communications, such as the Internet, for the same categories of goods and services, provided the ordered goods are shipped either to the home or to a freight receiver within 20 miles of the buyer's residence at the time the buyer entered into the contract for discount buying services.

(h) For purposes of this section, the following terms apply:

(1) "Affiliate" or "affiliate discount buying organization" means a discount buying organization that is a subsidiary of a parent, as defined in paragraph (4), or operates under a franchise, as defined in paragraph (3), granted by a parent.

(2) "Consumer" or "buyer" means and includes a client or member of an affiliate discount buying organization.

(3) "Franchise" has the same meaning as in Section 31005 of the Corporations Code.

(4) "Parent" means a business entity that directly or indirectly has franchised or operated 25 or more discount buying organizations for 10 years or more. *(Added by Stats.2004, c. 451 (A.B.2613), § 1.)*

§ 1812.118.   Cancellation of contract; time

Every contract for discount buying services shall further provide that such contract may be canceled at any time within three days after the date of receipt by the buyer of a copy of the contract by written notice to the seller at the address specified in the contract. If such cancellation is made, all moneys paid pursuant to the contract shall be refunded. Every contract for discount buying services shall be subject to the cancellation privileges and comply with the requirements of Sections 1689.6 and 1689.7 of this code. *(Added by Stats.1976, c. 237, p. 447, § 1.)*

§ 1812.119.   Voidable contracts; reference to compliance with title

(a) Any contract for discount buying services which does not comply with the applicable provisions of this title shall be voidable by the buyer.

(b) No discount buying organization shall make or authorize the making of any reference to its compliance with this title. *(Added by Stats.1976, c. 237, p. 447, § 1. Amended by Stats.1980, c. 1001, p. 3193, § 3, eff. Sept. 21, 1980.)*

§ 1812.120.   Misrepresentation; contract void and unenforceable

Any untrue or misleading information, representation, notice or advertisement of the seller which has been received by or made to the buyer prior to his signing a contract for discount buying services shall render the contract for discount buying services void and unenforceable by the seller. No seller shall make or disseminate such information, representations, notices or advertisements. The phrase "untrue or misleading information, representation, notice, or advertisement" shall include any acts which constitute violations of Chapter 1 (commencing with Section 17500) of Part 3 of Division 7 of the Business and Professions Code. However, neither this section nor any other section of this title shall operate to exempt discount buying services from any other provisions of law, including the penalty provisions of Section 17536 of the Business and Professions Code and Section 3370.1 of this code. *(Added by Stats.1976, c. 237, p. 447, § 1.)*

§ 1812.121. Rescission and pro rata refund; removal of place of business; discontinuance of goods or services

(a) If a discount buying organization removes its place of business or, if it conducts business at more than one location, that place of business which is geographically closest to the buyer's residence indicated on the face of the contract, more than 20 miles farther from the buyer's residence than it was at the time the contract for discount buying services was entered into, the organization shall offer rescission and a pro rata refund to each buyer affected, based upon the amount of time for which the buyer has been a member of the organization.

(b) If a discount buying organization discontinues providing any category of goods or services disclosed in compliance with Section 1812.106 or otherwise represented to the buyer to be available at or before the buyer's signing of the contract for discount buying services, the organization shall offer rescission and a pro rata refund based upon the amount of time for which the buyer has been a member of the organization, to each buyer who was informed of the availability of the category of goods or services to be discontinued and signed a contract for discount buying services within the six months immediately preceding the discontinuance of said category of goods or services. *(Added by Stats.1976, c. 237, p. 447, § 1.)*

§ 1812.122. Transfer to another entity of duty or obligation to provide services; defense in action for enforcement or collection on contract

Any transfer by a discount buying organization of its duty or obligation to provide services to buyers under its contracts for discount buying services to another individual, corporation, or other business entity, as a result of which a buyer shall have available substantially fewer goods and services, shall constitute a complete defense to an action for further enforcement of or collection on such a contract for discount buying services which may be asserted by any buyer who did not consent in writing, after a full and fair disclosure of the categories of goods and services to be provided by the new discount buying organization, to such transfer of the duty or obligation of performance, and shall entitle such a nonconsenting individual to rescind the contract and obtain a pro rata refund from the transferor. *(Added by Stats.1976, c. 237, p. 447, § 1.)*

§ 1812.123. Action for damages and restitution of moneys paid; treble damages and attorney fees and costs; correction of contract; transferee defined

(a) Any buyer injured by a violation of this title may bring an action for the recovery of damages and return of all moneys paid by the buyer to the seller. Judgment shall be entered for three times the amount at which the actual damages, plus such restitution, are assessed plus reasonable attorney's fees and costs. In the event that the court finds a violation of Section 1812.120 relating to untrue or misleading statements, judgment shall be entered for one thousand dollars ($1,000) plus reasonable attorney's fees or three times the amount of actual damages plus restitution plus reasonable attorney's fees, whichever is greater.

(b) Notwithstanding any other provision of this title, any failure to comply with any provision of this title except Section 1812.120 may be corrected within 30 days after the execution of the contract by the buyer, and if so corrected, neither the seller nor his transferee shall be subject to any liability under this title except that of a suit for actual damages plus reasonable attorney's fees and costs, provided that any correction must be concurred in, in writing, by the buyer, or the contract shall be void and unenforceable by the seller, who shall forthwith tender to the buyer a full refund. "Transferee" includes holders and assignees. *(Added by Stats.1976, c. 237, p. 447, § 1.)*

Research References

4 Witkin, California Summary 10th Sales § 351, (S 351) Discount Buying Services.

§ 1812.125. Violations; punishment; misdemeanor

(a) Any person who violates subdivision (b) or (c) of Section 1812.116 shall, upon conviction, be fined not more than ten thousand dollars ($10,000) for each violation, or imprisoned pursuant to subdivision (h) of Section 1170 of the Penal Code, or imprisoned in a county jail for not more than one year, or be punished by both that fine and imprisonment.

(b) Any person who violates any other provision of this title shall be guilty of a misdemeanor. *(Added by Stats.1976, c. 237, p. 447, § 1. Amended by Stats.1980, c. 1001, p. 3193, § 4, eff. Sept. 21, 1980; Stats.2011, c. 15 (A.B.109), § 33, eff. April 4, 2011, operative Oct. 1, 2011.)*

Research References

4 Witkin, California Summary 10th Sales § 351, (S 351) Discount Buying Services.

§ 1812.126. Provisions not exclusive

The prohibitions [1] of this title are not exclusive and do not relieve the parties or the contracts subject thereto from compliance with any other applicable provision of law. *(Added by Stats.1976, c. 237, p. 447, § 1.)*

1 Probably should read "provisions".

§ 1812.127. Waiver

Any waiver by the buyer of the provisions of this title shall be deemed contrary to public policy and shall be void and unenforceable. *(Added by Stats.1976, c. 237, p. 447, § 1.)*

§ 1812.128. Severability

If any provision of this title or the application thereof to any person or circumstances is held invalid, such invalidity shall not affect other provisions or applications of the title which can be given effect without the invalid provision or application, and to this end the provisions of this title are severable. *(Added by Stats.1976, c. 237, p. 447, § 1.)*

§ 1812.129. Enforcement; filing fees

(a) The Secretary of State shall enforce the provisions of this title that govern the filing and maintenance of bonds and deposits in lieu of bonds.

(b) The Secretary of State shall charge a filing fee not to exceed the cost of filing the bond or the deposit in lieu of a bond pursuant to Section 995.710 of the Code of Civil Procedure. *(Added by Stats.1996, c. 633 (S.B.1978), § 10. Amended by Stats.1998, c. 829 (S.B.1652), § 10.)*

Research References

Miller and Starr California Real Estate § 25C:66, Regulation of Time-Shares; in General.

Title 2.7

CONTRACTS FOR SELLER ASSISTED MARKETING PLANS

§ 1812.200.   Legislative finding and intent

(a) The Legislature finds and declares that the widespread sale of seller assisted marketing plans, often connected with the sale of vending machines, racks or work-at-home paraphernalia, has created numerous problems in California for purchasers which are inimical to good business practice. Often purchasers of seller assisted marketing plans are individuals inexperienced in business matters who use their life savings to purchase the seller assisted marketing plan in the hope that they will earn enough money in addition to retirement income or salary to become or remain self-sufficient. Many purchasers are the elderly who are seeking a way to supplement their fixed incomes. The initial payment is usually in the form of a purchase of overpriced equipment or products. California purchasers have suffered substantial losses when they have failed to receive full and complete information regarding the seller assisted marketing plan, the amount of money they can reasonably expect to earn, and the previous experience of the seller assisted marketing plan seller. Seller assisted marketing plan sellers have a significant impact upon the economy and well-being of this state and its local communities. The provisions of this title relating to seller assisted marketing plans are necessary for the public welfare.

(b) It is the intent of this title to provide each prospective seller assisted marketing plan purchaser with the information necessary to make an intelligent decision regarding seller assisted marketing plans being offered; to safeguard the public against deceit and financial hardship; to insure, foster and encourage competition and fair dealing in the sale of seller assisted marketing plans by requiring adequate disclosure; to prohibit representations that tend to mislead; and to prohibit or restrict unfair contract terms. This title shall be construed liberally in order to achieve the foregoing purposes. *(Added by Stats.1978, c. 876, p. 2749, § 1.)*

Research References

4 Witkin, California Summary 10th Sales § 382, (S 382) Seller Assisted
    Marketing Plans.

§ 1812.201.   Definitions

For the purposes of this title, the following definitions shall apply:

(a) "Seller assisted marketing plan" means any sale or lease or offer to sell or lease any product, equipment, supplies, or services that requires a total initial payment exceeding five hundred dollars ($500), but requires an initial cash payment of less than fifty thousand dollars ($50,000), that will aid a purchaser or will be used by or on behalf of the purchaser in connection with or incidental to beginning, maintaining, or operating a business when the seller assisted marketing plan seller has advertised or in any other manner solicited the purchase or lease of the seller assisted marketing plan and done any of the following acts:

(1) Represented that the purchaser will earn, is likely to earn, or can earn an amount in excess of the initial payment paid by the purchaser for participation in the seller assisted marketing plan.

(2) Represented that there is a market for the product, equipment, supplies, or services, or any product marketed by the user of the product, equipment, supplies, or services sold or leased or offered for sale or lease to the purchaser by the seller, or anything, be it tangible or intangible, made, produced, fabricated, grown, bred, modified, or developed by the purchaser using, in whole or in part, the product, supplies, equipment, or services that were sold or leased or offered for sale or lease to the purchaser by the seller assisted marketing plan seller.

(3) Represented that the seller will buy back or is likely to buy back any product made, produced, fabricated, grown, or bred by the purchaser using, in whole or in part, the product, supplies, equipment, or services that were initially sold or leased or offered for sale or lease to the purchaser by the seller assisted marketing plan seller.

(b) A "seller assisted marketing plan" shall not include:

(1) A security, as defined in the Corporate Securities Law of 1968 (Division 1 (commencing with Section 25000) of Title 4 of the Corporations Code), that has been qualified for sale by the Department of Corporations, or is exempt under Chapter 1 (commencing with Section 25100) of Part 2 of Division 1 of Title 4 of the Corporations Code from the necessity to qualify.

(2) A franchise defined by the Franchise Investment Law (Division 5 (commencing with Section 31000) of Title 4 of the Corporations Code) that is registered with the Department of Corporations or is exempt under Chapter 1 (commencing with Section 31100) of Part 2 of Division 5 of Title 4 of the Corporations Code from the necessity of registering.

(3) Any transaction in which either the seller or purchaser or the lessor or lessee is licensed pursuant to and the transaction is governed by the Real Estate Law, Division 4 (commencing with Section 10000) of the Business and Professions Code.

(4) A license granted by a general merchandise retailer that allows the licensee to sell goods, equipment, supplies, products, or services to the general public under the retailer's trademark, trade name, or service mark if all of the following criteria are satisfied:

(A) The general merchandise retailer has been doing business in this state continually for five years prior to the granting of the license.

(B) The general merchandise retailer sells diverse kinds of goods, equipment, supplies, products, or services.

(C) The general merchandise retailer also sells the same goods, equipment, supplies, products, or services directly to the general public.

(D) During the previous 12 months the general merchandise retailer's direct sales of the same goods, equipment, supplies, products, or services to the public account for at least 50 percent of its yearly sales of these goods, equipment, supplies, products, or services made under the retailer's trademark, trade name, or service mark.

(5) A newspaper distribution system distributing newspapers as defined in Section 6362 of the Revenue and Taxation Code.

(6) A sale or lease to an existing or beginning business enterprise that also sells or leases equipment, products, supplies, or performs services that are not supplied by the seller and that the purchaser does not utilize with the equipment, products, supplies, or services of the seller, if the equipment, products, supplies, or services not supplied by the seller account for more than 25 percent of the purchaser's gross sales.

(7) The sale in the entirety of an "ongoing business." For purposes of this paragraph, an "ongoing business" means a business that for at least six months previous to the sale has been operated from a particular specific location, has been open for business to the general public, and has had all equipment and supplies necessary for operating the business located at that location. The sale shall be of the entire "ongoing business" and not merely a portion of the ongoing business.

(8) A sale or lease or offer to sell or lease to a purchaser (A) who has for a period of at least six months previously bought products, supplies, services, or equipment that were sold under the same trademark or trade name or that were produced by the seller and, (B) who has received on resale of the product, supplies, services, or equipment an amount that is at least equal to the amount of the initial payment.

(9) The renewal or extension of an existing seller assisted marketing plan contract.

(10) A product distributorship that meets each of the following requirements:

(A) The seller sells products to the purchaser for resale by the purchaser, and it is reasonably contemplated that substantially all of the purchaser's sales of the product will be at wholesale.

(B) The agreement between the parties does not require that the purchaser pay the seller, or any person associated with the seller, a fee or any other payment for the right to enter into the agreement, and does not require the purchaser to buy a minimum or specified quantity of the products, or to buy products for a minimum or specified period of time. For purposes of this paragraph, a "person associated with the seller" means a person, including an individual or a business entity, controlling, controlled by, or under the same control as the seller.

(C) The seller is a corporation, partnership, limited liability company, joint venture, or any other business entity.

(D) The seller has a net worth of at least ten million dollars ($10,000,000) according to audited financial statements of the seller done during the 18 months preceding the date of the initial sale of products to the purchaser. Net worth may be determined on a consolidated basis if the seller is a subsidiary of another business entity that is permitted by generally accepted accounting standards to prepare financial statements on a consolidated basis and that business entity absolutely and irrevocably agrees in writing to guarantee the seller's obligations to the purchaser. The seller's net worth shall be verified by a certification to the Attorney General from an independent certified public accountant that the audited financial statement reflects a net worth of at least ten million dollars ($10,000,000). This certification shall be provided within 30 days following receipt of a written request from the Attorney General.

(E) The seller grants the purchaser a license to use a trademark that is registered under federal law.

(F) It is not an agreement or arrangement encouraging a distributor to recruit others to participate in the program and compensating the distributor for recruiting others into the program or for sales made by others recruited into the program.

(c) "Person" includes an individual, corporation, partnership, limited liability company, joint venture, or any business entity.

(d) "Seller" means a person who sells or leases or offers to sell or lease a seller assisted marketing plan and who meets either of the following conditions:

(1) Has sold or leased or represents or implies that the seller has sold or leased, whether in California or elsewhere, at least five seller assisted marketing plans within 24 months prior to a solicitation.

(2) Intends or represents or implies that the seller intends to sell or lease, whether in California or elsewhere, at least five seller assisted marketing plans within 12 months following a solicitation.

For purposes of this title, the seller is the person to whom the purchaser becomes contractually obligated. A "seller" does not include a licensed real estate broker or salesman who engages in the sale or lease of a "business opportunity" as that term is used in Sections 10000 to 10030, inclusive, of the Business and Professions Code, or elsewhere in Chapter 1 (commencing with Section 10000), Chapter 2 (commencing with Section 10050), or Chapter 6 (commencing with Section 10450) of Part 1 of Division 4 of the Business and Professions Code.

(e) "Purchaser" means a person who is solicited to become obligated or does become obligated on a seller assisted marketing plan contract.

(f) "Equipment" includes machines, all electrical devices, video or audio devices, molds, display racks, vending machines, coin operated game machines, machines that dispense products, and display units of all kinds.

(g) "Supplies" includes any and all materials used to produce, grow, breed, fabricate, modify, develop, or make any product or item.

(h) "Product" includes any tangible chattel, including food or living animals, that the purchaser intends to:

(1) Sell or lease.

(2) Use to perform a service.

(3) Resell or attempt to resell to the seller assisted marketing plan seller.

(4) Provide or attempt to provide to the seller assisted marketing plan seller or to any other person whom the seller suggests the purchaser contact so that the seller assisted marketing plan seller or that other person may assist, either directly or indirectly, the purchaser in distributing, selling, leasing, or otherwise disposing of the product.

(i) "Services" includes any assistance, guidance, direction, work, labor, or services provided by the seller to initiate or maintain or assist in the initiation or maintenance of a business.

(j) "Seller assisted marketing plan contract" or "contract" means any contract or agreement that obligates a purchaser to a seller.

(k) "Initial payment" means the total amount a purchaser is obligated to pay to the seller under the terms of the seller assisted marketing plan contract prior to or at the time of delivery of the equipment, supplies, products, or services or within six months of the purchaser commencing operation of the seller assisted marketing plan. If the contract sets forth a specific total sale price for purchase of the seller assisted marketing plan which total price is to be paid partially as a downpayment and then in specific monthly payments, the "initial payment" means the entire total sale price.

(*l*) "Initial cash payment" or "downpayment" means that portion of the initial payment that the purchaser is obligated to pay to the seller prior to or at the time of delivery of equipment, supplies, products, or services. It does not include any amount financed by or for which financing is to be obtained by the seller, or financing that the seller assists in obtaining.

(m) "Buy–back" or "secured investment" means any representation that implies in any manner that the purchaser's initial payment is protected from loss. These terms include a representation or implication of any of the following:

(1) That the seller may repurchase either all or part of what it sold to the purchaser.

(2) That the seller may at some future time pay the purchaser the difference between what has been earned and the initial payment.

(3) That the seller may in the ordinary course buy from the purchaser items made, produced, fabricated, grown, bred, modified, or developed by the purchaser using, in whole or in part, the product, supplies, equipment, or services that were initially sold or leased to the purchaser by the seller.

(4) That the seller or a person to whom the seller will refer the purchaser may in the ordinary course sell, lease, or distribute the items the purchaser has for sale or lease. (*Added by Stats.1978, c. 876, p. 2749, § 1. Amended by Stats.1980, c. 567, p. 1554, § 1; Stats.1981, c. 258, p. 1324, § 1; Stats.1989, c. 1021, § 1; Stats.1990, c. 216 (S.B.2510), § 6; Stats.1994, c. 1010 (S.B.2053), § 44; Stats.2000, c. 413 (A.B.2699), § 1.*)

Research References

4 Witkin, California Summary 10th Sales § 382, (S 382) Seller Assisted Marketing Plans.

§ 1812.202. Offer in state

(a) An offer to sell or offer to lease a seller assisted marketing plan shall occur in this state whenever:

(1) The offer to sell or offer to lease is made in this state;

(2) The purchaser resides in this state at the time of the offer; or

(3) The offer to sell or offer to lease either originates from this state or is directed by the seller or lessor to this state and received at the place to which it is directed.

(b) A sale or lease of a seller assisted marketing plan shall occur in this state whenever:

(1) The offer to sell or offer to lease is accepted in this state;

(2) The purchaser resides in this state at the time of the sale; or

(3) The acceptance is communicated to a seller situated in this state. (*Added by Stats.1978, c. 876, p. 2749, § 1.*)

§ 1812.203. Filing disclosure statements and lists of salespersons; notice of intent to issue stop orders; refutation

(a) The seller of any seller assisted marketing plan shall pay an annual fee in the amount of one hundred dollars ($100) and annually file with the Attorney General a copy of the disclosure statements required under Sections 1812.205 and 1812.206, as well as a list of the names and resident addresses of those individuals who sell the seller assisted marketing plan on behalf of the seller. The first filing shall be made at least 30 days prior to placing any advertisement or making any other representations to prospective purchasers. The first filing shall not be deemed to be effective until a notice of filing has been issued by the Attorney General. The seller may not make any advertisement or other representation to prospective purchasers until a notice of filing has been issued by the Attorney General. The

disclosure statements on file shall be updated through a new filing and payment of a fee in the amount of thirty dollars ($30), whenever material changes occur during the year following the annual filing and the updated filing shall include all disclosure statements required by Sections 1812.205 and 1812.206 and a list of the names and resident addresses of all current salespersons and all salespersons who have acted on behalf of the seller since the previous filing, whether the annual filing or an updated filing, indicating which salespersons are still active and which no longer act on behalf of the seller. Each seller of a seller assisted marketing plan shall file the annual renewal filing, whether or not any update filings have been made, at least 10 days before one year has elapsed from the date of the notice of filing issued by the Attorney General, and at least 10 days before the same date every year thereafter. The annual renewal filing shall include all disclosure statements required by Sections 1812.205 and 1812.206 and a list of the names and addresses of the residences of all current salespersons and all salespersons who have acted on behalf of the seller since the previous filing (whether the annual filing or an updated filing), indicating which salespersons are still active and which no longer act on behalf of the seller. The annual renewal filing fee shall be one hundred dollars ($100). If an annual renewal filing is not filed as required, the previous filing shall be deemed to have lapsed and the seller shall be prohibited from placing any seller assisted marketing plan advertisements or making any other representations to prospective purchasers of seller assisted marketing plan until a new annual filing is made and a new notice of filing has been issued by the Attorney General.

(b) The Attorney General may send by certified mail to the address set forth in the seller assisted marketing plan filing an intent to issue a stop order denying the effectiveness of or suspending or revoking the effectiveness of any filing if he or she finds the following:

(1) That there has been a failure to comply with any of the provisions of this title.

(2) That the offer or sale of the seller assisted marketing plan would constitute a misrepresentation to, or deceit of, or fraud on, the purchaser.

(3) That any person identified in the filing has been convicted of an offense under paragraph (1) of subdivision (b) of Section 1812.206, or is subject to an order or has had a civil judgment entered against him or her as described in paragraphs (2) and (3) of subdivision (b) of Section 1812.206, and the involvement of that person in the sale or management of the seller assisted marketing plan creates an unreasonable risk to prospective purchasers.

(c) The notice referred to shall include facts supporting a suspension or revocation. If the seller assisted marketing plan does not submit to the Attorney General, under penalties of perjury signed by an owner or officer of the seller assisted marketing plan, within 10 days of receipt of the intent to issue a stop order, a refutation of each and every supporting fact set forth in the notice, and each fact not refuted shall be deemed, for purposes of issuance of the order, an admission that the fact is true. If, in the opinion of the Attorney General, and based upon supporting facts not refuted by the seller assisted marketing plan, the plan is offered to the public without compliance with this title, the Attorney General may order the seller to desist and refrain from the further sale or attempted sale of the seller assisted marketing plan unless and until a notice of filing has been issued pursuant to this section. Until that time, the registration shall be void. The order shall be in effect until and unless the seller assisted marketing plan files a proceeding in superior court pursuant to Section 1085 or 1094.5 of the Code of Civil Procedure or seeks other judicial relief and serves a copy of the proceeding upon the Attorney General. (*Added by Stats.*

1978, c. 876, p. 2749, § 1.   Amended by Stats.1989, c. 1021, § 2; Stats.1990, c. 1491, (A.B.3765), § 2; Stats.1998, c. 595 (A.B. 1830), § 1.)

§ 1812.204.   Prohibited representations and activities

In selling, leasing, or offering to sell or lease a seller assisted marketing plan in this state, sellers shall not:

(a) Use the phrase "buy-back" or "secured investment" or similar phrase orally or in writing when soliciting, offering, leasing, or selling a seller assisted marketing plan if the "security" is the value of the equipment, supplies, products or services supplied by the seller to the purchaser.

(b) Use the phrase "buy-back" or "secured investment" or similar phrase orally or in writing when soliciting, offering, leasing, or selling a seller assisted marketing plan unless there are no restrictions or qualifications whatsoever preventing or limiting a purchaser from being able to invoke the "buy-back" or "secured" portion of the seller assisted marketing plan contract at any time the purchaser desires during the one-year period following the contract date. Upon invocation of the "buy-back" or "security" provision, the minimum amount a purchaser shall be entitled to have returned to him is the full amount of his initial payment, less the amount actually received by him from the operation of the seller assisted marketing plan. The "amount actually received" means either the amount the purchaser actually obtained from the seller for any product resold to the seller or the amount of money the purchaser received for use of the purchaser's product, equipment, supplies or services, less any amount: (1) the purchaser has paid the owner or manager of the location at which the purchaser's products, equipment, supplies or services are placed; and (2) the purchaser has paid to obtain other items needed in order to sell, make, produce, fabricate, grow, breed, modify, or develop the item which the seller assisted marketing plan purchaser intends to sell, lease, distribute, or otherwise dispose of.

(c) Represent that a purchaser's initial payment is "secured" in any manner or to any degree or that the seller provides a "buy-back" arrangement unless the seller has, in conformity with subdivision (b) of Section 1812.214, either obtained a surety bond issued by a surety company admitted to do business in this state or established a trust account at a federally insured bank or savings and loan association located in this state.

(d) Represent that the seller assisted marketing plan provides income or earning potential of any kind unless the seller has data to substantiate the claims of income or earning potential and discloses this data to the purchaser at the time the claim is made, if made in person, or if made through written or telephonic communication, at the first in-person communication thereafter and, when disclosed, the data is left with the purchaser. A mathematical computation of the number of sales multiplied by the amount of profit per sale to reach a projected income figure is not sufficient data to substantiate an income or earning potential claim. Income or earning potential claims cannot be made or implied at all unless they are based on the experience of at least 10 purchasers from the seller assisted marketing plan being offered. The data left by the seller must, at a minimum, disclose:

(1) The length of time the seller has been selling the particular seller assisted marketing plan being offered;

(2) The number of purchasers from the seller known to the seller to have made at least the same sales, income or profits as those represented; and

(3) The percentage the number represents of the total number of purchasers from the seller.

(e) Use the trademark, service mark, trade name, logotype, advertising or other commercial symbol of any business which does not either control the ownership interest in the seller or accept responsibility for all representations made by the seller in regard to the seller assisted marketing plan, unless the nature of the seller's relationship to such other business entity is set forth immediately adjacent to and in type size equal to or larger than that used to depict the commercial symbol of such other business. If a member of a trade association, the seller may use the logo or registration mark of the trade association in advertisements and materials without regard to this subdivision.

(f) Place or cause to be placed any advertisement for a seller assisted marketing plan which does not include the actual business name of the seller, and if it differs, the name under which the seller assisted marketing plan is operated and the street address of the principal place of business of the seller. (Added by Stats.1978, c. 876, p. 2749, § 1. Amended by Stats.1981, c. 258, p. 1327, § 2.)

§ 1812.205.   Disclosure statement

At the first in-person communication with a potential purchaser or in the first written response to an inquiry by a potential purchaser, whichever occurs first, wherein the seller assisted marketing plan is described, the seller or his or her representative shall provide the prospective purchaser a written document, the cover sheet of which is entitled in at least 16-point boldface capital letters "DISCLOSURE REQUIRED BY CALIFORNIA LAW." Under the title shall appear in boldface of at least 10-point type, the statement: "The State of California has not reviewed and does not approve, recommend, endorse or sponsor any seller assisted marketing plan. The information contained in this disclosure has not been checked by the state. If you have any questions about this purchase, see an attorney or other financial adviser before you sign a contract or agreement." Nothing shall appear on the cover sheet except the title and the statement required above. The disclosure document shall contain the following information:

(a) The name of the seller, the name under which the seller is doing or intends to do business and the name of any parent or affiliated company that will engage in business transactions with purchasers or accept responsibility for statements made by the seller.

(b) A statement of the initial payment to be paid by the purchaser to the seller, or when not known, a statement of the approximate initial payment charged, the amount of the initial payment to be paid to a person inducing, directly or indirectly, a purchaser to contract for the seller assisted marketing plan.

(c) A full and detailed description of the actual services the seller will undertake to perform for the purchaser.

(d) When the seller makes any statement concerning earnings or range of earnings that may be made through the seller assisted marketing plan, he must comply with subdivision (d) of Section 1812.204 and set forth in complete form in this disclosure statement the following:

"No guarantee of earnings or ranges of earnings can be made. The number of purchasers who have earned through this business an amount in excess of the amount of their initial payment is at least _____, which represents _____ percent of the total number of purchasers of this seller assisted marketing plan."

(e) If training of any type is promised by the seller, a complete description of the training and the length of the training.

(f) If the seller promises services to be performed in connection with the placement of the equipment, product or supplies at a location from which they will be sold or used, the full nature of those services as well as the nature of the agreements to be made with the owner or manager of the location at which the purchaser's equipment, product or supplies will be placed, must be set forth.

(g) If the seller represents orally or in writing when soliciting or offering for sale or lease or selling or leasing a seller assisted marketing plan that there is a "buy-back" arrangement or that the initial payment is in some manner protected from loss or "secured," the entire and precise nature of the "buy-back", "protection" or "security" arrangement shall be completely and clearly disclosed. *(Added by Stats.1978, c. 876, p. 2749, § 1. Amended by Stats.1981, c. 258, p. 1329, § 3.)*

§ 1812.206. Information sheet

At least 48 hours prior to the execution of a seller assisted marketing plan contract or agreement or at least 48 hours prior to the receipt of any consideration, whichever occurs first, the seller or his or her representative shall provide to the prospective purchaser in writing a document entitled "SELLER ASSISTED MARKETING PLAN INFORMATION SHEET." The seller may combine the information required under this section with the information required under Section 1812.205 and, if done, shall utilize the single title "DISCLOSURES REQUIRED BY CALIFORNIA LAW," and the title page required by Section 1812.205. If a combined document is used, it shall be given at the time required by Section 1812.205, provided that this time meets the 48–hour test of this section. The information sheet required by this section shall contain the following:

(a) The name of and the office held by the seller's owners, officers, directors, trustees and general or limited partners, as the case may be, and the names of those individuals who have management responsibilities in connection with the seller's business activities.

(b) A statement whether the seller, any person identified in subdivision (a), and any other company managed by a person identified in subdivision (a):

(1) Has been convicted of a felony or misdemeanor or pleaded nolo contendere to a felony or misdemeanor charge if the felony or misdemeanor involved an alleged violation of this title, fraud, embezzlement, fraudulent conversion or misappropriation of property.

(2) Has been held liable in a civil action by final judgment or consented to the entry of a stipulated judgment if the civil action alleged a violation of this title, fraud, embezzlement, fraudulent conversion or misappropriation of property or the use of untrue or misleading representations in an attempt to sell or dispose of real or personal property or the use of unfair, unlawful or deceptive business practices.

(3) Is subject to any currently effective agreement, injunction, or restrictive order, including, but not limited to, a "cease and desist" order, an "assurance of discontinuance," or other comparable agreement or order, relating to business activity as the result of an action or investigation brought by a public agency or department, including, but not limited to, an action affecting any vocational license.

The statements required by paragraphs (1), (2) and (3) of this subdivision shall set forth the terms of the agreement, or the court, the docket number of the matter, the date of the conviction or of the judgment and, when involved, the name of the governmental agency that initiated the investigation or brought the action resulting in the conviction or judgment.

(4) Has at any time during the previous seven fiscal years been the subject of an order for relief in bankruptcy, been reorganized due to insolvency, or been a principal, director, officer, trustee, general or limited partner, or had management responsibilities of any other person, as defined in subdivision (b) of Section 1812.201, that has so filed or was so reorganized, during or within one year after the period that the individual

held that position. If so, the name and location of the person having so filed, or having been so reorganized, the date thereof, the court which exercised jurisdiction, and the docket number of the matter shall be set forth.

(c) The length of time the seller:

(1) Has sold seller assisted marketing plans.

(2) Has sold the specific seller assisted marketing plan being offered to the purchaser.

(d) If the seller is required to secure a bond or establish a trust account pursuant to the requirements of Section 1812.204, the information sheet shall state either:

(1) "Seller has secured a bond issued by

_____

(name and address of surety company)

a surety company admitted to do business in this state. Before signing a contract to purchase this seller assisted marketing plan, you should check with the surety company to determine the bond's current status," or

(2) "Seller has deposited with the office of the Attorney General information regarding its trust account. Before signing a contract to purchase this seller assisted marketing plan, you should check with the Attorney General to determine the current status of the trust account."

(e) A copy of a recent, not more than 12 months old, financial statement of the seller, together with a statement of any material changes in the financial condition of the seller from the date thereof. That financial statement shall either be audited or be under penalty of perjury signed by one of the seller's officers, directors, trustees or general or limited partners. The declaration under penalty of perjury shall indicate that to the best of the signatory's knowledge and belief the information in the financial statement is true and accurate; the date of signature and the location where signed shall also be indicated. Provided, however, that where a seller is a subsidiary of another corporation which is permitted by generally accepted accounting standards to prepare financial statements on a consolidated basis, the above information may be submitted in the same manner for the parent if the corresponding financial statement of the seller is also provided and the parent absolutely and irrevocably has agreed to guarantee all obligations of the seller.

(f) An unexecuted copy of the entire seller assisted marketing plan contract.

(g) For purposes of this section, "seller's owners" means any individual who holds an equity interest of at least 10 percent in the seller. *(Added by Stats.1978, c. 876, p. 2749, § 1. Amended by Stats.1981, c. 258, p. 1330, § 4; Stats.1989, c. 1021, § 3; Stats.1997, c. 377 (A.B.1548), § 1; Stats.1998, c. 595 (A.B.1830), § 2; Stats.2009, c. 500 (A.B.1059), § 13.)*

§ 1812.207. Written contracts; delivery of copies

Every contract for sale or lease of a seller assisted marketing plan in this state shall be in writing and shall be subject to the provisions of this title. A copy of the fully completed contract and all other documents the seller requires the purchaser to sign shall be given to the purchaser at the time they are signed. *(Added by Stats.1978, c. 876, p. 2749, § 1.)*

§ 1812.208. Right to cancel; time; notice

The purchaser shall have the right to cancel a seller assisted marketing plan contract for any reason at any time within three business days of the date the purchaser and the seller sign the contract. The notice of the right to cancel and the procedures to be followed when a contract is canceled shall comply with Section 1812.209. *(Added by Stats.1978, c. 876, p. 2749, § 1.)*

§ 1812.209.　Mandatory contract provisions

Every seller assisted marketing plan contract shall set forth in at least 10-point type or equivalent size if handwritten, all of the following:

(a) The terms and conditions of payment including the initial payment, additional payments, and downpayment required. If the contract provides for the seller to receive more than 20 percent of the initial payment before delivery to the purchaser of the equipment, supplies or products or services to be furnished under the terms of the contract, the contract shall clearly set forth for the escrow account established pursuant to subdivision (b) of Section 1812.210 and the name and address of the escrow account holder, as well as the institution, branch, and account number of the escrow account. If the contract provides for payment of any amount in excess of 20 percent of the initial payment prior to delivery of the equipment, supplies or products or services to be furnished under the terms of the contract, the contract shall set forth that payment of the amount in excess of 20 percent shall be by separate instrument made payable to the escrow account.

(b) Immediately above the place at which the purchaser signs the contract the following notification, in boldface type, of the purchaser's right to cancel the contract:

"You have three business days in which you may cancel this contract for any reason by mailing or delivering written notice to the seller assisted marketing plan seller. The three business days shall expire on

_____

(last date to mail or deliver notice)
and notice of cancellation should be mailed or delivered to

_____

_____.

(seller assisted marketing plan seller's
name and business street address)

If you choose to mail your notice, it must be placed in the United States mail properly addressed, first-class postage prepaid, and postmarked before midnight of the above date. If you choose to deliver your notice to the seller directly, it must be delivered to him by the end of his normal business day on the above date. Within five business days of receipt of the notice of cancellation, the seller shall return to the purchaser all sums paid by the purchaser to the seller pursuant to this contract. Within five business days after receipt of all such sums, the purchaser shall make available at his address or at the place at which they were caused to be located, all equipment, products and supplies provided to the purchaser pursuant to this contract. Upon demand of the seller, such equipment, products and supplies shall be made available at the time the purchaser receives full repayment by cash, money order or certified check."

(c) A full and detailed description of the acts or services the seller will undertake to perform for the purchaser.

(d) The seller's principal business address and the name and the address of its agent, other than the Secretary of State, in the State of California authorized to receive service of process.

(e) The business form of the seller, whether corporate, partnership or otherwise.

(f) The delivery date or, when the contract provides for a staggered delivery of items to the purchaser, the approximate delivery date of those products, equipment or supplies the seller is to deliver to the purchaser to enable the purchaser to begin or maintain his business and whether the products, equipment or supplies are to be delivered to the purchaser's home or business

address or are to be placed or caused to be placed by the seller at locations owned or managed by persons other than the purchaser.

(g) A complete description of the nature of the "buy-back", "protection", or "security" arrangement, if the seller has represented orally or in writing when selling or leasing, soliciting or offering a seller assisted marketing plan that there is a "buy-back" or that the initial payment or any part of it is "protected" or "secured."

(h) A statement which accurately sets forth a purchaser's right to void the contract under the circumstances and in the manner set forth in subdivisions (a) and (b) of Section 1812.215.

(i) The name of the supplier and the address of such supplier of the products, equipment, or supplies the seller is to deliver to the purchaser to enable the purchaser to begin or maintain his business. *(Added by Stats.1978, c. 876, p. 2749, § 1. Amended by Stats.1981, c. 258, p. 1332, § 5; Stats.1989, c. 1021, § 4.)*

§ 1812.210.　Notes; downpayment restrictions; escrow

(a) No seller assisted marketing plan contract shall require or entail the execution of any note or series of notes by the purchaser which, when separately negotiated, will cut off as to third parties any right of action or defense which the purchaser may have against the seller.

(b) If the contract referred to in Section 1812.209 provides for a downpayment to be paid to the seller, the downpayment shall not exceed 20 percent of the initial payment amount. In no event shall the contract payment schedule provide for the seller to receive more than 20 percent of the initial payment before delivery to the purchaser, or to the place at which they are to be located, the equipment, supplies or products, unless all sums in excess of 20 percent are placed in an escrow account as provided for in subdivision (c) of Section 1812.214. Funds placed in an escrow account shall not be released until the purchaser notifies the escrow holder in writing of the delivery of such equipment, supplies or products within the time limits set forth in the seller assisted marketing plan contract. Notification of delivery by the purchaser to the escrow holder shall not be unreasonably withheld. *(Added by Stats.1978, c. 876, p. 2749, § 1. Amended by Stats.1981, c. 258, p. 1333, § 6; Stats.1989, c. 1021, § 5.)*

§ 1812.211.　Rights of purchaser against seller's assignee

Any assignee of the seller assisted marketing plan contract or the seller's rights is subject to all equities, rights and defenses of the purchaser against the seller. *(Added by Stats.1978, c. 876, p. 2749, § 1.)*

§ 1812.212.　Reference to compliance

No seller shall make or authorize the making of any reference to its compliance with this title. *(Added by Stats.1978, c. 876, p. 2749, § 1.)*

§ 1812.213.　Books, records and accounts; preservation of documents

Every seller shall at all times keep and maintain a complete set of books, records and accounts of seller assisted marketing plan sales made by the seller. All documents relating to each specific seller assisted marketing plan sold or leased shall be maintained for four years after the date of the seller assisted marketing plan contract. *(Added by Stats.1978, c. 876, p. 2749, § 1.)*

§ 1812.214.　Attorney to receive process; service of process; bond or trust accounts; escrow account procedures

(a) Every seller of seller-assisted marketing plans other than a California corporation shall file with the Attorney General an irrevocable consent appointing the Secretary of State or successor in office to act as the seller's attorney to receive service or any lawful process in any noncriminal suit, action or proceeding against the seller or the seller's successor, executor or administrator, which may arise under this title. When service is made upon the Secretary of State, it shall have the same force and validity as if served personally on the seller. Service may be made by leaving a copy of the process in the office of the Secretary of State, but it shall not be effective unless:

(1) The plaintiff forthwith sends by first-class mail a notice of the service upon the Secretary of State and a copy of the process to the defendant or respondent at the last address on file with the Attorney General; and

(2) The plaintiff's affidavit of compliance with this section is filed in the case on or before the return date of the process, if any, or within such further time as the court allows.

(b) If, pursuant to subdivision (c) of Section 1812.204, a seller must obtain a surety bond or establish a trust account, the following procedures apply:

(1) If a bond is obtained, a copy of it shall be filed with the Attorney General; if a trust account is established, notification of the depository, the trustee and the account number shall be filed with the Attorney General.

(2) The bond or trust account required shall be in favor of the State of California for the benefit of any person who is damaged by any violation of this title or by the seller's breach of a contract subject to this title or of any obligation arising therefrom. The trust account shall also be in favor of any person damaged by these practices.

(3) Any person claiming against the trust account for a violation of this title may maintain an action at law against the seller and the trustee. The surety or trustee shall be liable only for actual damages and not the punitive damages permitted under Section 1812.218. The aggregate liability of the trustee to all persons damaged by a seller's violation of this title shall in no event exceed the amount of the trust account.

(4) The bond or the trust account shall be in an amount equal to the total amount of the "initial payment" section of all seller-assisted marketing plan contracts the seller has entered into during the previous year or three hundred thousand dollars ($300,000), whichever is less, but in no case shall the amount be less than fifty thousand dollars ($50,000). The amount required shall be adjusted twice a year, no later than the tenth day of the first month of the seller's fiscal year and no later than the tenth day of the seventh month of the seller's fiscal year. A seller need only establish a bond or trust account in the amount of fifty thousand dollars ($50,000) at the commencement of business and during the first six months the seller is in business. By the tenth day of the seller's seventh month in business, the amount of the bond or trust account shall be established as provided for herein as if the seller had been in business for a year.

(c) If, pursuant to subdivision (b) of Section 1812.210, a seller utilizes an escrow account to receive those portions of the downpayment in excess of 20 percent of the initial payment before delivery to the purchaser of the equipment, supplies or products or services to be furnished under the terms of the contract, the following procedures shall apply:

(1) The holder of the escrow account shall be independent of the seller, and the seller shall not have any authority to direct disbursements from the escrow account by the holder except upon written notification by the purchaser to the holder of the escrow account of the delivery of the equipment, supplies, or products as required by and within the time limits set forth in the seller assisted marketing plan contract.

(2) The name and address of the escrow account holder, the name of the institution, the branch and account number of the escrow account shall be reported to the Attorney General by the seller.

(3) Any person claiming against the escrow account for a violation of this title may maintain an action at law against the seller and the escrow account holder. The escrow account holder shall be liable only for actual damages and not the punitive damages permitted under Section 1812.218. The aggregate liability of the escrow account holder to all persons damaged by a seller's violation of this title shall in no event exceed the amount of the escrow account. *(Added by Stats.1978, c. 876, p. 2749, § 1. Amended by Stats.1981, c. 258, p. 1333, § 7; Stats.1982, c. 517, p. 2322, § 64; Stats.1989, c. 1021, § 6; Stats.1990, c. 1491 (A.B.3765), § 3.)*

Law Revision Commission Comments

Section 1812.214 is amended to delete provisions duplicated in the general provisions governing bonds. See Code Civ.Proc. §§ 995.850 (enforcement by or for benefit of persons interested) and 996.470 (limitation on liability of surety). The other changes in Section 1812.214 are technical. [16 Cal.L.Rev.Comm. Reports 501 (1981)].

§ 1812.215. Purchaser's right to void contract

(a) If a seller uses any untrue or misleading statements to sell or lease a seller assisted marketing plan, or fails to comply with Section 1812.203, or fails to give the disclosure documents or disclose any of the information required by Sections 1812.205 and 1812.206, or the contract does not comply with the requirements of this title, then within one year of the date of the contract at the election of the purchaser upon written notice to the seller, the contract shall be voidable by the purchaser and unenforceable by the seller or his assignee as contrary to public policy and the purchaser shall be entitled to receive from the seller all sums paid to the seller when the purchaser is able to return all equipment, supplies or products delivered by the seller; when such complete return cannot be made, the purchaser shall be entitled to receive from the seller all sums paid to the seller less the fair market value at the time of delivery of the equipment, supplies or products not returned by the purchaser, but delivered by the seller. Upon the receipt of such sums, the purchaser shall make available to the seller at the purchaser's address or at the places at which they are located at the time the purchaser gives notice pursuant to this section, the products, equipment or supplies received by the purchaser from the seller. Provided, however, if the seller inadvertently has failed to make any of the disclosures required by Section 1812.205 or 1812.206 or the contract inadvertently fails to comply with the requirements of this title, the seller may cure such inadvertent defect by providing the purchaser with the correct disclosure statements or contract if at the time of providing such correct disclosures or contract the seller also informs the purchaser in writing that because of the seller's error, the purchaser has an additional 15-day period after receipt of the correct disclosures or contract within which to cancel the contract and receive a full return of all moneys paid in exchange for return of whatever equipment, supplies or products the purchaser has. If the purchaser does not cancel the contract within 15 days after receipt of the correct disclosures or contract, he may not in the future exercise his right to void the contract under this section due to such noncompliance with the disclosure or contract requirements of this title.

(b) If a seller fails to deliver the equipment, supplies or product within 30 days of the delivery date stated in the contract, unless such delivery delay is beyond the control of the seller, then at any time prior to delivery or within 30 days after delivery, at the election of the purchaser upon written notice to the seller, the contract shall be voidable by the purchaser and unenforceable by the seller or his assignee as contrary to public policy.

The rights of the purchaser set forth in this section shall be cumulative to all other rights under this title or otherwise.

(Added by Stats.1978, c. 876, p. 2749, § 1. Amended by Stats.1981, c. 258, p. 1334, § 8.)

§ 1812.216. Waiver of rights by purchaser; burden of proving exemption or exception from definitions

(a) Any waiver by a purchaser of the provisions of this title shall be deemed contrary to public policy and shall be void and unenforceable. Any attempt by a seller to have a purchaser waive rights given by this title shall be a violation of this title.

(b) In any proceeding involving this title, the burden of proving an exemption or an exception from a definition is upon the person claiming it. *(Added by Stats.1978, c. 876, p. 2749, § 1. Amended by Stats.1981, c. 258, p. 1335, § 9.)*

§ 1812.217. Violations; punishment

Any person, including, but not limited to, the seller, a salesman, agent or representative of the seller or an independent contractor who attempts to sell or lease or sells or leases a seller assisted marketing plan, who willfully violates any provision of this title or employs, directly or indirectly, any device, scheme or artifice to deceive in connection with the offer or sale of any seller assisted marketing plan, or willfully engages, directly or indirectly, in any act, practice or course of business which operates or would operate as a fraud or deceit upon any person in connection with the offer, purchase, lease or sale of any seller assisted marketing plan shall, upon conviction, be fined not more than ten thousand dollars ($10,000) for each unlawful transaction, or imprisoned pursuant to subdivision (h) of Section 1170 of the Penal Code, or imprisoned in a county jail for not more than one year, or be punished by both that fine and imprisonment. *(Added by Stats.1978, c. 876, p. 2749, § 1. Amended by Stats.2011, c. 15 (A.B.109), § 34, eff. April 4, 2011, operative Oct. 1, 2011.)*

§ 1812.218. Damages

Any purchaser injured by a violation of this title or by the seller's breach of a contract subject to this title or of any obligation arising from the sale or lease of the seller assisted marketing plan may bring any action for recovery of damages. Judgment shall be entered for actual damages, plus reasonable attorney's fees and costs, but in no case shall the award of damages be less than the amount of the initial payment provided the purchaser is able to return all the equipment, supplies or products delivered by the seller; when such complete return cannot be made, the minimum award shall be no less than the amount of the initial payment less the fair market value at the time of delivery of the equipment, supplies or products that cannot be returned but were actually delivered by the seller. An award, if the trial court deems it proper, may be entered for punitive damages. *(Added by Stats.1978, c. 876, p. 2749, § 1.)*

§ 1812.219. Additional remedies

The provisions of this title are not exclusive. The remedies provided herein for violation of any section of this title or for conduct proscribed by any section of this title shall be in addition to any other procedures or remedies for any violation or conduct provided for in any other law.

Nothing in this title shall limit any other statutory or any common law rights of the Attorney General, any district attorney or city attorney, or any other person. If any act or practice proscribed under this title also constitutes a cause of action in common law or a violation of another statute, the purchaser may assert such common law or statutory cause of action under the procedures and with the remedies provided for in such other law. *(Added by Stats.1978, c. 876, p. 2749, § 1.)*

§ 1812.220. Partial invalidity

If any provision of this act or if any application thereof to any person or circumstance is held unconstitutional, the remainder of the title and the application of such provision to other persons and circumstances shall not be affected thereby. *(Added by Stats.1978, c. 876, p. 2749, § 1.)*

§ 1812.221. Deposit in lieu of bond; claim against deposit; review and approval; payment; attachment, garnishment, or execution

(a) When a deposit has been made in lieu of bond pursuant to paragraph (1) of subdivision (b) of Section 1812.214 and Section 995.710 of the Code of Civil Procedure, the person asserting a claim against the deposit shall, in lieu of the provisions of Section 996.430 of the Code of Civil Procedure, establish the claim by furnishing evidence to the Attorney General of a money judgment entered by a court together with evidence that the claimant is a person described in paragraph (2) of subdivision (b) of Section 1812.214.

(b) When a person has completely established the claim with the Attorney General, the Attorney General shall forthwith review and approve the claim and enter the date of approval thereon. The claim shall be designated an "approved claim."

(c) When the first claim against a particular deposit account has been approved, it shall not be paid until the expiration of a period of 240 days after the date of its approval by the Attorney General. Subsequent claims which are approved by the Attorney General within the same 240-day period shall similarly not be paid until the expiration of the 240-day period. Forthwith upon the expiration of the 240-day period, the Attorney General shall pay all approved claims from that 240-day period in full unless there are insufficient funds in the deposit account in which case each approved claim shall be paid a proportionate amount to exhaust the deposit account.

(d) When the Attorney General approves the first claim against a particular deposit account after the expiration of a 240-day period, the date of approval of that claim shall begin a new 240-day period to which subdivision (c) shall apply with respect to the amount remaining in the deposit account.

(e) After a deposit account is exhausted, no further claims shall be paid by the Attorney General. Claimants who have had their claims paid in full or in part pursuant to subdivisions (c) and (d) shall not be required to make a contribution back to the deposit account for the benefit of other claimants.

(f) When a deposit has been made in lieu of bond, the amount of the deposit shall not be subject to attachment, garnishment, or execution with respect to an action or judgment against the seller, other than as to an amount as no longer needed or required for the purpose of this title which would otherwise be returned to the seller by the Attorney General. *(Added by Stats.1984, c. 545, § 4. Amended by Stats.1989, c. 1021, § 7.)*

Title 2.8

MEMBERSHIP CAMPING CONTRACTS

§ 1812.300.   Definitions

For the purposes of this title:

(a) "Membership camping operator" means any enterprise, other than one that is tax exempt under Section 501(c)(3) of the Internal Revenue Code of 1954, as amended, that has as one of its purposes the ownership or operation of campgrounds which include or may include use of camping sites, that solicits membership paid for by a fee or periodic payments, such as annual dues, and the contractual members are the primary intended users. "Membership camping operator" does not include camping or recreational trailer parks, as defined in Section 18215 of the Health and Safety Code, which are open to the general public and which contain camping sites rented for a per use fee, or a "mobilehome park," as defined in either Section 798.4 of the Civil Code or Section 18214 of the Health and Safety Code.

As used in this title, "seller" means membership camping operator.

(b) "Membership camping contract" means an agreement offered or sold within the State of California by a membership camping operator or membership camping broker evidencing a purchaser's right or license to use for more than 14 days in a year, the campgrounds of a membership camping operator and includes a membership which provides for this use.

(c) "Camping site" means a space designed and promoted for the purpose of locating a trailer, tent, tent trailer, pickup camper, or other similar device used for camping.

(d) "Offer" means any solicitation reasonably designed to result in entering into a membership camping contract.

(e) "Person" means any individual, corporation, partnership, limited liability company, trust, association, or other organization other than a government or a subdivision thereof.

(f) "Purchaser" means a person who enters into a membership camping contract and thereby obtains the right to use the campgrounds of a membership camping operator.

(g) "Sale" or "sell" means entering into, or other disposition, of a membership camping contract for value. The term "value" does not include a reasonable fee to offset the administrative costs of transfer of a membership camping contract.

(h) "Campground" means real property within this state owned or operated by a membership camping operator and designated in whole or in part by the membership camping operator as available for camping or outdoor recreation by purchasers of membership camping contracts.

(i) "Blanket encumbrance" means any mortgage, deed of trust, option to purchase, vendor's lien or interest under a contract or agreement of sale, or other financing lien or encumbrance granted by the membership camping operator or affiliate which secures or evidences the obligation to pay money or to sell or convey any campgrounds made available to purchasers by the membership camping operator or any portion thereof, and which authorizes, permits, or requires the foreclosure or other disposition of the campground.

(j) "Nondisturbance agreement" means an instrument in recordable form by which the holder of a blanket encumbrance agrees to all of the following:

(1) The holder's rights in any campground made available to purchasers, prior or subsequent to the agreement, by the membership camping operator shall be subordinate to the rights of purchasers from and after the recordation of the nondisturbance agreement.

(2) The holder and all successors and assignees of the holder, and any person who acquires the campground through foreclosure or by deed in lieu of foreclosure of the blanket encumbrance shall take the campground subject to the rights of purchasers.

(3) The holder or any successor acquiring the campground through the blanket encumbrance shall not use or cause the campground to be used in a manner which would materially prevent purchasers from using or occupying the campground in a manner contemplated by the purchasers' membership camping contracts. However, the holder shall have no obligation to, and no liability for failure to assume the responsibilities or obligations of, the membership camping operator under the membership camping contracts.

(k) "Membership camping contract broker" means a person who, for compensation, resells or offers to resell a membership camping contract to a new purchaser on behalf of a prior purchaser. Membership camping contract broker does not include a membership camping operator or its employees or agents. (Added by Stats.1983, c. 847, § 1. Amended by Stats. 1990, c. 1529, (S.B.2203), § 4; Stats.1994, c. 1010 (S.B.2053), § 45.)

Research References

4 Witkin, California Summary 10th Sales § 371, (S 371) Membership Camping Contracts.

§ 1812.301.   Unruh Act; application to contracts and persons covered by the title

The membership camping contracts and persons covered by this title shall be subject to Chapter 5 (commencing with Section 17200) of Part 2 of Division 7 and Article 1 (commencing with Section 17500) of Chapter 1 of Part 3 of Division 7 of the Business and Professions Code and the Unruh Act (Chapter 1 (commencing with Section 1801) of Title 2 of Part 4 of Division 3). (Added by Stats.1983, c. 847, § 1. Amended by Stats.1990, c. 1529 (S.B.2203), § 5.)

Research References

4 Witkin, California Summary 10th Sales § 371, (S 371) Membership Camping Contracts.

§ 1812.302.   Written disclosures by operator to purchaser

A membership camping operator shall provide to a purchaser the following written disclosures in any format which clearly communicates the following reasonably current information before the purchaser signs a membership camping contract, or gives any money or thing of value for the purchase of a membership camping contract. The written disclosures shall be included in or attached to the contract before the time the contract is signed. The following information shall be updated once a year.

(a) The name and address of the membership camping operator and any material affiliate membership camping operator.

(b) A brief description of the membership camping operator's experience in the membership camping business, including the number of years the operator has been in the membership camping business; a brief description of the past five years' business experience of the chairman, the president and chief executive officer, and if other than the foregoing, the person in charge of marketing of the membership camping operator, or persons in comparable positions in noncorporate operators, including the number of other membership camping operators with which the executive has been associated and the length of time with each.

(c) A brief description of the nature of the purchaser's right or license to use the membership camping operator's property or facilities.

(d) The location of each of the membership camping operator's campgrounds and a brief description for each campground of the significant facilities then available for use by purchasers and those which are represented to purchasers as being planned, together with a brief description of any significant facilities that are or will be available to nonpurchasers or nonmembers.

"Significant facilities" shall include, but are not limited to, each of the following: the number of campsites, in each campground; the number of campsites in each campground with full or partial hookups; swimming pools; tennis courts; recreation buildings; restrooms and showers; laundry rooms; trading posts; or grocery stores. "Partial hookups" mean those hookups with at least one of the following connections: electricity, water, or sewer connections.

Following such description there shall appear in 10-point bold type the following disclosure:

NOTICE: PURCHASE A MEMBERSHIP CAMPING CONTRACT ONLY ON THE BASIS OF EXISTING FACILITIES. CONSTRUCTION OF PLANNED FACILITIES IS SOMETIMES DEFERRED OR REVISED FOR A VARIETY OF REASONS. SHOULD THE SALESPERSON DESCRIBE A SIGNIFICANT FACILITY WHICH IS NEITHER LISTED AS EXISTING NOR PLANNED, TELEPHONE COLLECT OR TOLL FREE DURING WEEKDAY BUSINESS HOURS TO [insert headquarter's telephone number] TO VERIFY THE OPERATOR'S PLAN FOR SUCH A FACILITY.

(e) A brief description of the membership camping operator's ownership of, or other right to use, the campgrounds represented to be available for use by purchasers, together with the duration and expiration date of any lease, license, franchise, or reciprocal agreement entitling the membership camping operator to use the campgrounds, and any material provisions of any agreements, land use permits, or operating licenses which could materially restrict a purchaser's use of the campgrounds under the terms of the purchaser's camping contract.

(f) A summary or copy of the rules, restrictions, or covenants regulating the purchaser's use of the membership camping operator's properties, including a statement of whether and how the rules, restrictions, or covenants may be changed.

(g) A brief description of all payments of a purchaser under a membership camping contract, including initial fees and any further fees, charges, or assessments, together with any provisions for changing the payments.

(h) A description of any restraints on the transfer of the membership camping contract.

(i) A brief description of the policies relating to the availability of camping sites and whether reservations are required.

(j) A brief description of any grounds for forfeiture of a purchaser's membership camping contract.

(k) A copy of the membership camping contract form. *(Added by Stats.1983, c. 847, § 1. Amended by Stats.1990, c. 1529 (S.B.2203), § 6.)*

Research References

4 Witkin, California Summary 10th Sales § 371, (S 371) Membership Camping Contracts.

§ 1812.303. Language of contract; date and signature; notice of cancellation; refunds after cancellation

(a) A membership camping contract shall be written in the same language as that principally used in any oral sales presentation (e.g., Spanish). A membership camping contract shall be dated, signed by the purchaser, and contain, in immediate proximity to the space reserved for the signature of the purchaser, a conspicuous statement in a size equal to at least 10-point bold type, as follows: "You, the purchaser, may cancel this contract at any time prior to midnight of the third business day after the date of the transaction. See an explanation of this right as set forth in this contract or on the attached notice of cancellation form." In the alternative the notice of cancellation as set forth in subdivision (b) may be placed in immediate proximity to the signature line of the contract in lieu of the foregoing statement.

(b) The contract shall be accompanied by a completed form in duplicate, captioned "Notice of Cancellation", which shall be attached to the contract and easily detachable. In the alternative, the seller may include all of the cancellation information on the contract and provide the consumer with a carbon copy which may be retained after cancellation. Both shall contain, in type of at least 10-point, the following statement written in the same language as used in the contract:

"Notice of Cancellation"

"You may cancel this contract, without any penalty or obligation, within three business days from the date the contract is executed.

"To cancel this contract, mail or deliver a signed and dated copy of this cancellation notice or a copy of this contract if it contains the cancellation instructions, or any other written notice, or send a telegram to

_____, at
                    (Name of seller)

_____
        (Address of seller's place of business)
not later than midnight of _____.
                                      (Date)
I hereby cancel this transaction _____.
                                           (Date)

_____
              (Purchaser's signature)

"With the notice of cancellation, or separately if a telegram is sent, you must return the original membership camping contract, membership card and all other evidence of membership to the seller. You should promptly return these documents with the notice of cancellation, or separately if a telegram is sent. Failure to send the documents promptly could delay your refund. You should retain for your records one copy of the cancellation notice, or a carbon of the contract when it provides the cancellation information, or other writing showing intent to cancel. Mailing by ordinary mail is adequate but certified mail return receipt requested is recommended."

(c) On the date of purchase the membership camping operator shall provide the purchaser with a copy of the contract and duplicate of the notice of cancellation. The membership camping operator shall inform the purchaser orally of the right to cancel at the time the contract is executed.

(d) Within 20 days after the membership camping operator receives a notice of cancellation, the membership camping contract, the membership card and all other evidence of purchase or membership, the membership camping operator shall refund to the purchaser any sums paid as a deposit, downpayment or other payment therefor. If the purchaser does not promptly return the evidence of membership, the 20-day period shall be extended until such evidence of membership is returned.

(e) Until the membership camping operator has complied with this section, the purchaser shall have the right to cancel the contract.

(f) "Business day" means any calendar day except Sunday, or the following business holidays: New Year's Day, Washington's Birthday, Memorial Day, Independence Day, Labor Day, Columbus Day, Veteran's Day, Thanksgiving Day, and Christmas Day. *(Added by Stats.1983, c. 847, § 1. Amended by Stats.1990, c. 1529 (S.B.2203), § 7.)*

Research References

4 Witkin, California Summary 10th Sales § 371, (S 371) Membership Camping Contracts.

§ 1812.304. Notice of cancellation rights to purchaser failing to inspect campgrounds; return of payment and negotiable instruments upon cancellation

(a) If the purchaser has not inspected at least one of the membership camping operator's campgrounds prior to purchase of a membership camping contract, the notice shall contain the following additional language:

"If you sign this contract without having first inspected one of the membership camping operator's campgrounds, you may also cancel this contract at any time prior to midnight of the 10th business day after date of purchase by mailing or delivering the signed and dated attached written notice of cancellation or a copy of the contract when that contains the cancellation instructions together with the original camping club contract, membership card and any other evidence of membership."

(b) The seller shall return any payment made by the purchaser under the contract or offer to purchase, and any negotiable instrument executed by the purchaser, within 10 days of the return of evidence of membership and cancellation of the contract by the purchaser. If the purchaser does not promptly return the evidence of membership, the 10-day period shall be extended until the evidence of membership is returned. *(Added by Stats.1983, c. 847, § 1. Amended by Stats.1990, c. 1529 (S.B.2203), § 8.)*

Research References

4 Witkin, California Summary 10th Sales § 371, (S 371) Membership Camping Contracts.

§ 1812.305. Exempt transactions

The following transactions are exempt from the provisions of this title.

(a) An offer, sale or transfer by any one person of not more than one membership camping contract for any given membership camping operator in any 12-month period.

(b) An offer or sale by a government or governmental agency.

(c) A bona fide pledge of a membership camping contract. *(Added by Stats.1983, c. 847, § 1.)*

§ 1812.306. Remedy of purchaser for errors or omissions; attorney's fees; corrections

(a) A purchaser's remedy for errors in or omissions from the membership camping contract of any of the disclosures or requirements of Sections 1812.302 to 1812.304, inclusive, shall be limited to a right of rescission and refund. Reasonable attorney's fees shall be awarded to the prevailing party in any action under this title. This limitation does not apply to errors or omissions from the contract, or disclosures or other requirements of this title, which are a part of a scheme to willfully misstate or omit the information required, or other requirements imposed by this title.

(b) Any failure, except a willful or material failure, to comply with any provision of Sections 1812.302 to 1812.304, inclusive, may be corrected within 30 days after receipt of written notice to the membership camping operator from the purchaser, and, if so corrected, there shall be no right of rescission. The membership camping operator or the holder shall not be subject to any penalty under this title. However, there can be no correction that increases any monthly payment, the number of payments, or the total amount due, unless concurred to, in writing, by the purchaser. "Holder" includes the seller who acquires the contract, or if the contract is purchased, a financing agency or other assignee who purchases the contract. *(Added by Stats. 1983, c. 847, § 1. Amended by Stats.2006, c. 538 (S.B.1852), § 51.)*

Research References

4 Witkin, California Summary 10th Sales § 371, (S 371) Membership Camping Contracts.

§ 1812.307. Withdrawal of campgrounds; conditions

No membership camping operator shall withdraw from the use by purchasers of membership camping contracts any campground unless one of the following conditions is satisfied:

(a) Adequate provision is made to provide within a reasonable time, a substitute campground in the same general area that is as desirable for the purpose of camping and outdoor recreation.

(b) The campground is withdrawn from use because, despite good faith efforts by the membership camping operator, a person not affiliated with the membership camping operator has exercised a superior right to possession (such as the right of a lessor to take possession following expiration of a lease of the property) and the terms and date of the withdrawal were disclosed in writing to all purchasers at or prior to the time of any sale of a membership camping contract after the membership camping operator represented to purchasers that the campground would be available for camping or recreation purposes.

(c) The rights of all purchasers of membership camping contracts who are entitled to use the campground have expired or have been lawfully terminated. *(Added by Stats.1990, c. 1529 (S.B.2203), § 10.)*

Research References

4 Witkin, California Summary 10th Sales § 371, (S 371) Membership Camping Contracts.

§ 1812.308. Sale, lease, assignment or transfer of campground

(a) Except in the case of a membership camping operator substituting a campground in accordance with Section 1812.307, no membership camping operator or owner of the underlying fee shall sell, lease, assign, or otherwise transfer his or her interest in a campground except by an instrument evidencing the transfer recorded in the office of the county recorder for the county in which the campground is located. The instrument shall be in recordable form and be executed by both the transferor and transferee and shall state each of the following:

(1) That the instrument is intended to protect the rights of all purchasers of membership camping contracts.

(2) That its terms may be enforced by any prior or subsequent purchaser so long as that purchaser is not in default on his or her obligations under the membership camping contract.

(3) That the transferee shall fully honor the rights of the purchasers to occupy and use the campground as provided in the purchaser's original membership camping contracts.

(4) That the transferee shall fully honor all rights of purchasers to cancel their contracts and receive appropriate refunds.

(5) That the obligations of the transferee under the instrument will continue to exist despite any cancellation or rejection of the contracts between the membership camping operator and purchaser arising out of bankruptcy proceedings.

(b) If any transfer of the interest of the membership camping operator or owner of the underlying fee occurs in a manner which is not in compliance with this section, the terms set forth in this section shall be presumed to be a part of the transfer and shall be deemed to be included in the instrument of transfer. Notice of the transfer shall be mailed to each purchaser within 30 days of the transfer. Persons who hold blanket encumbrances on a campground shall not be considered transferees for the purposes of this section. *(Added by Stats.1990, c. 1529 (S.B. 2203), § 12.)*

Research References

4 Witkin, California Summary 10th Sales § 371, (S 371) Membership Camping Contracts.

§ 1812.309. Availability of campgrounds for use; conditions

(a) Campgrounds subject to this section include any campground which is offered or made available by an operator for the first time after January 1, 1991, or any campground which becomes subject to a new or refinanced blanket encumbrance after January 1, 1991. A membership camping operator shall not offer or represent that any campground subject to this section is available for use by the purchasers of its camping contracts unless one of the following conditions has been satisfied:

(1) The membership camping operator obtains and records a nondisturbance agreement from each holder of a blanket encumbrance. The nondisturbance agreement is executed by the membership camping operator and each holder of the blanket encumbrance and includes the provisions set forth in subdivision (j) of Section 1812.300 and each of the following:

(A) The instrument may be enforced by purchasers of membership camping contracts. If the membership camping operator is not in default under its obligations to the holder of the blanket encumbrance, the agreement may be enforced by both the membership camping operator and the purchasers.

(B) The nondisturbance agreement is effective as between each purchaser and the holder of the blanket encumbrance despite any rejection or cancellation of the purchaser's contract during any bankruptcy proceedings of the membership camping operator.

(C) The agreement is binding upon the successors in the interest of both the membership camping operator and the holder of the blanket encumbrance.

(D) A holder of the blanket encumbrance who obtains title or possession, or who causes a change in title or possession in a campground by foreclosure or otherwise, and who does not continue to operate the campground upon conditions no less

favorable to members than existed prior to the change of title or possession shall either:

(i) Offer the title or possession of the campground to an association of members to operate the campground.

(ii) Obtain a commitment from another entity which obtains title or possession to undertake the responsibility of operating the campground.

(2) The membership camping operator posts a surety bond or irrevocable letter of credit with a trustee in favor of purchasers and which guarantees that the payments on the blanket encumbrance are made as they become due. A trustee shall be either a corporate trustee or an attorney licensed to practice law in this state.

(3) The membership camping operator delivers to a trustee an encumbrance trust agreement which contains each of the following provisions:

(A) The membership camping operator shall collaterally assign to the trustee all of its membership camping contracts receivable or other receivables of the membership camping operator in an amount calculated in accordance with subparagraph (B). The membership camping operator shall provide the trustee with a security interest in the receivables and all proceeds therefrom. For purposes of this section, the membership camping operator shall be credited with 100 percent of the outstanding principal balance of each receivable assigned to the trustee. All proceeds of the receivables shall be held in a trust account by the trustee subject to this section for the use and benefit of the purchasers to make the payments of principal and interest due under the blanket encumbrance. However, if the proceeds of the receivables during any calendar year exceed the amount due under the blanket encumbrance in the following calendar quarter, these excess funds shall be returned by the trustee to the membership camping operator.

(B) The amount of membership camping contracts receivable or other receivables to be collaterally assigned as described in subparagraph (A) shall be calculated based upon the maximum number of contracts per camping site to be offered on or after January 1, 1991, in connection with the campground in question, which number of contracts per camping site shall not exceed 15 multiplied by the total number of camping sites available at the campground thereby yielding the anticipated total number of contracts to be sold in connection with the campground. The outstanding balance due under the blanket encumbrance shall then be divided by the anticipated total number of contracts to arrive at the amount per contract sold to be paid over to the trustee in the form of collaterally assigned receivables as described in subparagraph (A). The membership camping operator shall make the required collateral assignments to the trustee on a quarterly basis based upon the actual sales of contracts at the campground in question during the previous calendar quarter. However, the membership camping operator's obligation to collaterally assign receivables to the trustee shall cease when the membership camping operator has collaterally assigned to the trustee an aggregate principal amount of receivables equal to 100 percent of the aggregate principal indebtedness remaining due under the blanket encumbrance.

(C) If the outstanding balance due under the blanket encumbrance at the time of execution of the encumbrance trust agreement exceeds the anticipated gross revenue based upon the membership camping operator's price list to be generated by the sale of the anticipated total number of contracts as calculated in subparagraph (B), the membership camping operator shall meet the conditions specified in paragraph (1), (2), or (4) of this subdivision as to the full amount of the excess.

(D) It may be terminated by the membership camping operator if the membership camping operator has satisfied the obligation secured by the blanket encumbrance in full or has complied with paragraph (1), (2), or (4) of this subdivision. Upon termination of the agreement, all receivables and proceeds thereof held by the trustee shall be immediately assigned and delivered to the membership camping operator. All costs of administering this trust, filing, and perfecting the security interest, and foreclosing the lien shall be borne by the membership camping operator.

(4) Any financial institution which has made a hypothecation loan to the membership camping operator (a "hypothecation lender") shall have a lien on, or security interest in, the membership camping operator's interest in the campground, and the hypothecation lender shall have executed and recorded a nondisturbance agreement at the county recorder's office for the county in which the campground is located. Each person holding an interest in a blanket encumbrance superior to the interest held by the hypothecation lender shall execute and record at the county recorder's office, an instrument stating that the person shall give the hypothecation lender notice of, and at least 30 days to cure, any default under the blanket encumbrance before the person commences any foreclosure action affecting the campground. For the purposes of this paragraph, a "hypothecation loan to a membership camping operator" means a loan or line of credit secured by membership camping contracts receivable arising from the sale of membership camping contracts by the membership camping operator, which exceeds in the aggregate all outstanding indebtedness secured by blanket encumbrances superior to the interest held by the hypothecation lender.

A hypothecation lender who obtains title or possession, or who causes a change in title or possession, in a campground, by foreclosure or otherwise, and who does not continue to operate the campground upon conditions no less favorable to purchasers than existed prior to the change of title or possession shall either:

(A) Offer the title or possession to an association of members to operate the campground.

(B) Obtain a commitment from another entity which obtains title to, or possession of, the campground to undertake the responsibility of operating the campground.

(b) Any membership camping operator which does not comply at all times with subdivision (a) with regard to any blanket encumbrance in connection with any campground subject to that subdivision is prohibited from offering any membership camping contracts for sale during the period of noncompliance. *(Added by Stats.1990, c. 1529 (S.B.2203), § 13.)*

§ 1812.314. Membership camping contract brokers; fees; escrows; disclosures to new purchaser; notice of cancellation to purchaser

(a) All money received from the owner of a membership camping contract or the prospective purchaser thereof, by a membership camping contract broker in advance of the completion of any membership camping contract resale, including, but not limited to, listing fees, and fees for services, shall be deposited into an escrow account. The money shall not be disbursed until the transaction is complete, or until the escrow agent has received written instructions to disburse the funds signed by the owner of the membership camping contract or the prospective purchaser and the broker. For purposes of this section, a transaction is complete when ownership of the membership camping contract has been transferred from the prior purchaser to the new purchaser in the manner required by the terms of the membership camping contract, all documents necessary to complete the transfer have been fully executed, and the new purchaser has not exercised the right to cancel provided in paragraph (2) of subdivision (c).

(b) The broker shall inform the new purchaser in writing of the following:

(1) The risks of purchasing a membership camping contract without visiting at least one of the membership camping operator's campgrounds.

(2) That the membership camping operator may have a valid reason for not transferring the contract to the new purchaser such as a default in payment on contract or annual dues, or that the new purchaser does not meet the same credit standards applied to other new purchasers.

(3) That there may have been changes in the rules or regulations concerning the rights and obligations of the membership camping operator or its members including changes with respect to annual dues, fees, assessments, use restrictions or that some campgrounds may have been withdrawn.

(4) Any material changes or risks to the purchaser known to the broker.

(c)(1) Every broker shall provide in writing the following notice of cancellation to the new purchaser:

"You may cancel your contract of purchase, without any penalty or obligation, within 10 business days from the above date of purchase by mailing notice of cancellation together with the membership camping contract, if any, any contract for transfer, membership card or other evidence of membership to

_____,
(Name and address of broker)
the membership camping operator

_____
(Name and address of membership camping operator)
and the escrow company

_____,
(Name and address of escrow company)
if any, not later than midnight of _____.
(Date)
I hereby cancel this transaction _____
_____
(Purchaser's signature)
_____
(Date)

Notice by ordinary mail is adequate but certified mail return receipt requested is recommended."

(2) Any escrow company which receives a notice of cancellation from a purchaser shall, within 72 hours of receipt of the notice, notify the membership camping operator of the cancellation and shall refund any sums paid by the purchaser of the contract within 10 days of receipt of the notice of the cancellation and other documents. The escrow company shall incur no liability to the seller, purchaser, or broker as a result of its compliance with this section. *(Formerly § 1812.307, added by Stats.1983, c. 847, § 1. Renumbered § 1812.314 and amended by Stats.1990, c. 1529 (S.B.2203), § 9.)*

Research References

4 Witkin, California Summary 10th Sales § 371, (S 371) Membership Camping Contracts.

§ 1812.315. Severability

If any provision of this title or the application thereof to any person or circumstances is held invalid, the invalidity shall not affect other provisions or applications of this title which can be given effect without the invalid provision or application, and to this end the provisions of this title are severable. *(Formerly § 1812.308, added by Stats.1983, c. 847, § 1. Renumbered § 1812.315 and amended by Stats.1990, c. 1529 (S.B.2203), § 11.)*

§ 1812.316. Public policy; waiver of rights

Any waiver of the provisions of this title is contrary to public policy, and is void and unenforceable. *(Added by Stats.2002, c. 815 (A.B.2331), § 21.)*

Research References

4 Witkin, California Summary 10th Sales § 371, (S 371) Membership Camping Contracts.

Title 2.9

CREDITOR REMEDIES: DISABILITY INSURANCE

§ 1812.400. Legislative findings and declaration

The Legislature finds and declares that it is unfair for a creditor who has directly participated in, arranged, or received a commission or other compensation for the sale of credit disability insurance to the debtor, or that creditor's successor in interest, to invoke a creditor's remedy because of a debtor's nonpayment of any sum which has become due during a period of disability until a reasonable time has passed for the disability insurance claim to be filed, verified and processed. *(Added by Stats.1983, c. 973, § 1.)*

Research References

Rutter, Cal. Practice Guide: Enforcing Judgments/Debts Ch. 3-A, A. Evaluating the Claim.
Miller and Starr California Real Estate § 10:134, Nature of Default.
Miller and Starr California Real Estate § 10:136, Failure to Pay Principal or Interest When Due.

§ 1812.401. Definitions

For the purposes of this title:

(a) "Credit disability insurance" means insurance of a debtor to provide indemnity for payments becoming due on a specific loan or other credit transaction while the debtor is disabled as defined in the policy.

(b) "Creditor" means the lender of money or vendor or lessor of goods, services, property, rights, or privileges, for which payment is arranged through a credit transaction, who has directly participated in, arranged, or received a commission or other compensation for the sale of credit disability insurance to the debtor, or any successor to the right, title, or interest of any such lender, vendor, or lessor, and an affiliate, associate, or subsidiary of any of them or any director, officer, or employee of any of them, or any other person in any way associated with any of them.

(c) "Debtor" means a borrower of money or a purchaser or lessee of goods, services, property, rights, or privileges for which payment is arranged through a credit transaction.

(d) "Creditor's remedy" means and includes the imposition of any late charge or penalty, the acceleration of the maturity of all or any part of the indebtedness, the collection or assignment for the collection of all or any part of the indebtedness, the commencement of any action or special proceeding, or the enforcement of any security interest in any manner, including, but not limited to, repossession, foreclosure, or the exercise of a power of sale contained in a deed of trust or mortgage.

(e) "Disability claim period" or "claim period" means the period beginning on the due date of the first payment not paid by the debtor for which the debtor claims disability coverage arising from a then current disability and continuing until three calendar months thereafter or until the insurer pays or rejects the claim, whichever occurs sooner.

(f) "Notice" to a creditor means written notice deposited in the United States mail, postage prepaid, addressed to the creditor at the location where payments on the loan or credit transaction are normally required to be sent by the debtor. A creditor may elect to require that written notice, otherwise complying with the requirements of this subdivision, be sent to a different location or may elect to accept telephonic notice to a telephone number specified by the creditor, in either case in lieu of notice being sent to the location where payments are regularly required to be sent, if that location or telephone number is clearly and conspicuously disclosed as the proper place to direct any notice to the creditor relating to any claim of disability on each monthly billing, or on or in each payment coupon book (by adhesive attachment, republication, or otherwise), as the case may be, or (if payments are automatically deducted from an account of the debtor) on the annual statement of loan activity. In any particular instance a creditor may waive the requirement that notice be in writing and accept oral notice. *(Added by Stats.1983, c. 973, § 1. Amended by Stats.1984, c. 1200, § 1, eff. Sept. 17, 1984.)*

Research References

Miller and Starr California Real Estate § 10:136, Failure to Pay Principal or Interest When Due.

§ 1812.402. Prohibition of invocation of creditor's remedies because of nonpayment of sum due during any credit insurance disability claim period; prior indebtedness; foreclosure of lien; payments; disclosure; cumulative rights and remedies

(a) No creditor, as defined in Section 1812.401, shall invoke any creditor's remedy against a debtor because of the debtor's nonpayment of any sum which becomes due during any disability claim period and for which credit disability insurance coverage, subject to this title, is provided.

(b) Upon initially receiving notice, as defined in subdivision (f) of Section 1812.401, of the debtor's claim of disability, the creditor shall inform the debtor in writing of the name, address, and telephone number of the insurer or its designated representative from whom the debtor may obtain claim forms. Upon receiving notice of the disability claim, the insurer or its designated representative shall send necessary claim forms to the debtor. The debtor shall submit the claim to the insurer or its designated representative and shall notify the creditor, as specified in subdivision (f) of Section 1812.401, that a claim has been submitted.

This subdivision shall apply to the original creditor who sold the disability insurance and shall not apply to that creditor's successor in interest if the successor in interest (1) is not related by common ownership or control to that creditor and (2) has no information regarding the name, address, and telephone number of the insurer or its designated representative.

(c) Nothing in this section prohibits a creditor from invoking any creditor's remedy during or after the claim period for the debtor's nonpayment of any sum due prior to the claim period, whether or not the nonpayment is related to the claimed disability, or for the debtor's nonpayment of any interest, finance charge, or late charge accruing during the claim period of any sum due prior to the period.

(d) Nothing in this section prohibits a creditor from foreclosing a lien on any property to protect that creditor's security interest if a senior lienholder on that property (1) has initiated the foreclosure of its lien, (2) is not prohibited from continuing the foreclosure by any law or order of court, or (3) will not otherwise suspend or delay its foreclosure proceeding until after the disability claim period.

(e) If the insurer pays the claim within the disability claim period, the creditor shall treat each payment made by the insurer as though it were timely made by the debtor. If the insurer rejects the claim within the disability claim period or accepts the claim within the claim period as a partial disability which results in a payment of less than the full benefit which would be paid for the total disability, the debtor shall have the opportunity to pay the entire amount which became due during the claim period or the difference between the amount which became due during the claim period and the amount paid by the insurer for the partial disability without being subject to any creditor's remedy, except the imposition of late charges, for 35 days following the date on which the insurer sends notice of the rejection of the claim or acceptance of the claim as a partial disability. In the event the debtor does not pay the entire amount which became due during the claim period plus any accrued late charges within 35 days from that date, the creditor may then invoke any creditor's remedy.

(f) The obligations of the creditor and debtor pursuant to this section shall be disclosed in writing in at least 10-point type by the creditor to the debtor at the time the creditor sells the insurance, in the manner provided in paragraph (1), and by the insurer to the debtor at the time the insurer sends claim forms pursuant to subdivision (b), in the manner provided in paragraph (2).

(1) The disclosure required by the creditor shall be substantially in the following form:

CLAIM PROCEDURE

If you become disabled, tell us (your creditor) right away. (We advise you to send this information to the same address to which you are normally required to send your payments, unless a different address or telephone number is given to you in writing by us as the location where we would like to be notified.) We will tell you where to get claim forms. Send in the completed form to the insurance company as soon as possible and tell us as soon as you do.

If your disability insurance covers all of your missed payment, WE CANNOT TRY TO COLLECT WHAT YOU OWE OR FORECLOSE UPON OR REPOSSESS ANY COLLATERAL UNTIL THREE CALENDAR MONTHS AFTER your first missed payment is due or until the insurance company pays or rejects your claim, whichever comes first. We can, however, try to collect, foreclose, or repossess if you have money due and owing us or are otherwise in default when your disability claim is made or if a senior mortgage or lienholder is foreclosing.

If the insurance company pays the claim within the three calendar months, we must accept the money as though you paid on time. If the insurance company rejects the claim within the three calendar months or accepts the claim within the three calendar months as a partial disability and pays less than for a total disability, you will have 35 days from the date that the rejection or the acceptance of the partial disability claim is sent to pay past due payments, or the difference between past due payments and what the insurance company pays for the partial disability, plus late charges. You can contact us, and we will tell you how much you owe. After that time, we can take action to collect or foreclose or repossess any collateral you may have given.

If the insurance company accepts your claim but requires that you send in additional forms to remain eligible for continued payments, you should send in these completed additional forms no later than required. If you do not send in these forms on time, the insurance company may stop paying, and we will then be able to take action to collect or foreclose or repossess any collateral you may have given.

(2) The disclosure required by the insurer shall be substantially in the following form:

CLAIM PROCEDURE

Send in the completed form to the insurance company as soon as possible and tell your creditor as soon as you do. (Your creditor has already advised you of the address or telephone number to use to confirm that you have submitted your completed form to the insurance company.)

If your disability insurance covers all of your missed payments, YOUR CREDITOR CANNOT TRY TO COLLECT WHAT YOU OWE OR FORECLOSE UPON OR REPOSSESS ANY COLLATERAL UNTIL THREE CALENDAR MONTHS AFTER your first missed payment is due or until the insurance company pays or rejects your claim, whichever comes first. Your creditor can, however, try to collect, foreclose, or repossess if you have money due and owing or are otherwise in default when your disability claim is made or if a senior mortgage or lienholder is foreclosing.

If the insurance company pays the claim within the three calendar months, your creditor must accept the money as though you paid on time. If the insurance company rejects the claim within the three calendar months or accepts the claim within the three calendar months as a partial disability and pays less than for a total disability, you will have 35 days from the date that the rejection or the acceptance of the partial disability claim was sent to pay past due payments, or the difference between past due payments and what the insurance company pays for the partial disability, plus late charges. You can contact your creditor who will tell you how much you owe. After that time, your creditor can take action to collect or foreclose or repossess any collateral you may have given.

If the insurance company accepts your claim, but requires that you send in additional forms to remain eligible for continued payments, you should send in these completed additional forms no later than required. If you do not send in these forms on time, the insurance company may stop paying, and your creditor will then be able to take action to collect or foreclose or repossess any collateral you have given.

(g) If a debtor does not make a payment for which the debtor claims disability coverage arising from a then current disability and if the creditor, after sending the debtor notice of the debtor's delinquency, invokes any creditor's remedy because of the nonpayment without knowledge of the debtor's claim of disability coverage, subject to this title, the following provisions apply:

(1) Upon receiving notice of the debtor's claim, the creditor shall not invoke any further creditor's remedy during the remainder of the claim period and the period provided in subdivision (e).

(2) Upon receiving notice, as specified in subdivision (f) of Section 1812.401, of the debtor's claim, the creditor shall rescind every creditor's remedy that has been invoked relating to the delinquency for which coverage is claimed, except that the creditor shall not be obligated to restore property which has been sold in a bona fide lawful sale to any person not related by common ownership or control to the creditor.

(3) The debtor shall be liable for costs and expenses actually incurred in connection with the invocation or rescission of any creditor's remedy.

(4) The creditor shall not be in violation of this title and shall not be liable under subdivision (i) provided the creditor complies with paragraphs (1) and (2) of this subdivision.

(h) The rights and remedies afforded debtors by this title shall be cumulative to each other and to all other rights and remedies which the debtors may have under other laws.

(i) The debtor may bring an action for damages, equitable relief, or other relief for any violation of this title. (Added by Stats.1983, c. 973, § 1. Amended by Stats.1984, c. 1200, § 2, eff. Sept. 17, 1984.)

Research References

Miller and Starr California Real Estate § 10:136, Failure to Pay Principal or Interest When Due.

§ 1812.403. Invocation of creditor's remedies; cessation of payment of claim because of debtor's failure to timely submit forms to credit insurer

A creditor may invoke any creditor's remedy 15 days after receiving notice that the insurer has ceased making payments on a credit disability insurance claim because of the debtor's failure to timely submit any forms required by the insurer for recertification of a temporary disability. (Added by Stats.1983, c. 973, § 1.)

Research References

Miller and Starr California Real Estate § 10:136, Failure to Pay Principal or Interest When Due.

§ 1812.404. Application of title; creditors arranging or participating in sale or receiving commission or compensation for sale of credit disability insurance to debtor

This title shall apply to a creditor only if the creditor, the predecessor to the right, title, or interest of the creditor, or the representative of either of them directly arranges or participates in the sale or receives a commission or other compensation for the sale of credit disability insurance to the debtor. (Added by Stats.1983, c. 973, § 1.)

§ 1812.405. Invocation of creditor's remedies; nonpayment of amount due under open-end credit plan

This title shall not prohibit a creditor from invoking any creditor's remedy as a result of a debtor's nonpayment when due of any amount obtained under an open-end credit plan, as hereafter defined, after the debtor has given notice of a disability claim unless the nonpayment is related to a covered disability then affecting the debtor other than the disability previously claimed. The creditor's termination of the open-end credit plan because the debtor does not meet the creditor's customary credit standards at the time the debtor notifies the creditor of the disability claim is not a creditor's remedy.

An "open-end credit plan" means credit extended by a creditor under a plan in which the creditor reasonably contemplates repeated transactions, the creditor may impose a finance charge from time to time on an outstanding unpaid balance, and the amount of credit that may be extended to the debtor during the term of the plan (up to any limit set by the creditor) is generally made available to the extent that any outstanding balance is repaid. (Added by Stats.1983, c. 973, § 1.)

§ 1812.406. Application of title; credit insurance covering key person; certain loans or transactions secured by mortgage or deed of trust

(a) This title does not apply to credit disability insurance covering a key person, as hereinafter defined, which a creditor requires as a condition to making a loan of at least twenty-five thousand dollars ($25,000) to be used in the operation of a business in which the key person is employed or has an ownership interest.

For the purposes of this subdivision, a "key person" is a person who the creditor and the debtor or debtors mutually agree must be involved in the operation of the business to assure its success.

(b) This title does not apply to a loan or other credit transaction (including an open line of credit) of more than 10 years' duration which is secured by a mortgage or deed of trust unless (1) the principal purpose of the loan or credit transaction is for the construction (other than initial construction), rehabilitation, or improvement (including "home improvement" as defined in Section 7151 of the Business and Professions Code) of real property consisting of four or fewer residential units, and (2) any document incident to the loan or credit transaction at the time the loan or extension of credit is made, or any course of dealing between the creditor and a contractor or material supplier assisting the borrower in obtaining the loan or extension of credit, would indicate that purpose.

(c) Subdivision (b) shall not apply to debtors who were entitled to receive notice from the creditor pursuant to subdivision (f) of Section 1812.402 on or after January 1, 1984, and prior to the effective date of the act which added this subdivision, unless the debtor receives written notice that the remedies provided in this title are revoked, the debtor is given an opportunity to cancel the coverage, and no claim has been made or notice provided as specified in Section 1812.401. If the debtor fails to cancel the insurance following receipt of the notice required under this subdivision, subdivision (b) shall apply to that policy upon payment by the debtor of the next installment of premium, whether to the insurer or to a creditor pursuant to a premium finance agreement. (Added by Stats.1983, c. 973, § 1. Amended by Stats.1984, c. 1200, § 3, eff. Sept. 17, 1984.)

Research References

Miller and Starr California Real Estate § 10:136, Failure to Pay Principal or Interest When Due.

§ 1812.407. Application of title; nonpayment of sums due after April 1, 1984

The provisions of this title shall apply to the nonpayment of any sum which becomes due on or after April 1, 1984, and for which the debtor claims disability coverage. (Added by Stats. 1983, c. 973, § 1.)

§ 1812.408. Waiver by debtor; invalidity

Any waiver by the debtor of the provisions of this title shall be void and unenforceable. (Added by Stats.1983, c. 973, § 1.)

Research References

Miller and Starr California Real Estate § 10:136, Failure to Pay Principal or Interest When Due.

§ 1812.409. Effect of title; after-acquired property interest by bona fide purchaser or encumbrancer

This title shall not affect or defeat an interest in the debtor's property, acquired after the creditor invokes a creditor's remedy in violation of this title, by a bona fide purchaser or encumbrancer for value and without notice of facts that constitute a violation of this title. (*Added by Stats.1984, c. 1200, § 4, eff. Sept. 17, 1984.*)

Research References

Miller and Starr California Real Estate § 10:136, Failure to Pay Principal or Interest When Due.

§ 1812.410. Severability

If any provision of this title or the application thereof to any person or circumstance is held to be unconstitutional, the remainder of the title and the application of the provision to other persons and circumstances shall not be affected thereby. (*Formerly § 1812.409, added by Stats.1983, c. 973, § 1. Renumbered § 1812.410 and amended by Stats.1984, c. 1200, § 5, eff. Sept. 17, 1984.*)

Research References

Rutter, Cal. Practice Guide: Enforcing Judgments/Debts Ch. 3-A, A. Evaluating the Claim.

Title 2.91

EMPLOYMENT AGENCY, EMPLOYMENT COUNSELING, AND JOB LISTING SERVICES ACT

CHAPTER 1. GENERAL PROVISIONS

§ 1812.500. Citation of title

This title shall be known and cited as the Employment Agency, Employment Counseling, and Job Listing Services Act. (*Added by Stats.1989, c. 704, § 2.*)

Research References

3 Witkin, California Summary 10th Agency and Employment § 430, (S 430) Nature and Scope of Act.

§ 1812.501. Definitions

(a)(1) "Employment agency" or "agency" means:

(A) Any person who, for a fee or other valuable consideration to be paid, directly or indirectly by a jobseeker, performs, offers to perform, or represents it can or will perform any of the following services:

(i) Procures, offers, promises, or attempts to procure employment or engagements for others or employees for employers.

(ii) Registers persons seeking to procure or retain employment or engagement.

(iii) Gives information as to where and from whom this help, employment, or engagement may be procured.

(iv) Provides employment or engagements.

(B) Any person who offers, as one of its main objects or purposes, to procure employment for any person who will pay for its services, or that collects dues, tuition, or membership or registration fees of any sort, if the main object of the person paying those fees is to secure employment.

(C) Any person who, for a fee or other valuable consideration, procures, offers, promises, provides, or attempts to procure babysitting or domestic employment for others or domestics or babysitters for others.

(2) "Employment agency" or "agency" shall not include any employment counseling service or any job listing service.

(b)(1) "Employment counseling service" means any person who offers, advertises, or represents it can or will provide any of the following services for a fee: career counseling, vocational guidance, aptitude testing, executive consulting, personnel consulting, career management, evaluation, or planning, or the development of résumés and other promotional materials relating to the preparation for employment. "Employment counseling service" shall not include persons who provide services strictly on an hourly basis with no financial obligation required of the consumer beyond the hourly fee for services rendered. An "employment counseling service" does not include the functions of an "employment agency" as defined in subdivision (a).

(2) "Employment counseling service" does not include:

(A) Businesses that are retained by, act solely on behalf of, and are compensated solely by prior or current employers that do not require any "customer" to sign a contract and do not in any way hold any "customer" liable for fees.

(B)(i) Any provider of vocational rehabilitation in which the counseling services are paid for by insurance benefits, if the counseling is provided as a result of marital dissolution or separation proceedings to prepare one of the spouses for reentry into the job market and if the fees are paid by some party other than the person receiving the counseling services.

(ii) The exemption provided in this subparagraph does not apply to any vocational rehabilitation counselor who receives any payments directly from the individual customer receiving the counseling.

(C) Any person who engages solely in the preparation of résumés and cover letters, provided that the résumé writing service does not advertise or hold itself out as offering other job seeking or placement services and does not charge more than three hundred dollars ($300) for any résumé, cover letter, or combination of both to any single customer in any individual transaction.

(D) Any public educational institution.

(E) Any private educational institution established solely for educational purposes that, as a part of its curriculum, offers employment counseling to its student body and conforms to the requirements of Article 3.5 (commencing with Section 94760) of Chapter 7 of Part 59 of the Education Code.

(F) A psychologist or psychological corporation licensed pursuant to Chapter 6.6 (commencing with Section 2900) of Division 2 of the Business and Professions Code, providing psychological assessment, career or occupational counseling, or consultation and related professional services within his, her, or its scope of practice.

(G) An educational psychologist licensed pursuant to Article 5 (commencing with Section 4986) of Chapter 13 of Division 2 of the Business and Professions Code, providing counseling services within his or her scope of practice.

(c) "Job listing service" means any person who provides, offers, or represents it can or will provide any of the following services, for a fee or other valuable consideration to be paid, directly or indirectly, by the jobseeker in advance of, or contemporaneously with, performance of these services: matches jobseekers with employment opportunities, providing or offering to provide jobseekers lists of employers or lists of job openings or like publications, or preparing résumés or lists of jobseekers for distribution to potential employers.

(d) A "nurses' registry" as defined in subdivision (b) of Section 1812.524 is an employment agency. However, unless otherwise provided for in this title, a nurses' registry shall not be required to comply with Chapter 2 (commencing with Section 1812.503) regulating employment agencies but, instead, shall be required to comply with Chapter 7 (commencing with Section 1812.524).

(e) "Jobseeker" means a person seeking employment.

(f) "Employer" means any individual, company, partnership, association, corporation, agent, employee, or representative for whom or for which an employment agency or job listing service attempts to obtain an employee or to place a jobseeker.

(g) "Job order" means any written or oral instruction, direction, or permission granted by an employer or its agent to an employment agency or job listing service to refer jobseekers for a specified job.

(h) "Domestic agency" means any agency that provides, or attempts to provide, employment by placement of domestic help in private homes.

(i) "Deposit" means any money or valuable consideration received by an employment agency or job listing service from a jobseeker for referring the jobseeker to a position of employment prior to the jobseeker's acceptance of a position.

(j) "Fee" means:

(1) Any money or other valuable consideration paid, or promised to be paid, for services rendered or to be rendered by any person conducting an employment agency, employment counseling service, or job listing service under this title.

(2) Any money received by any person in excess of that which has been paid out by him or her for transportation, transfer of baggage, or board and lodging for any applicant for employment.

(k) "Registration fee" means any charge made, or attempted to be made, by an employment agency for registering or listing an applicant for employment, for letter writing, or any charge of a like nature made, or attempted to be made without having a bona fide order for the placement of the applicant in a position.

(*l*) "Person" means any individual, corporation, partnership, limited liability company, trust, association, or other organization.

(m) This section shall become operative on January 1, 1997. *(Added by Stats.1995, c. 758 (A.B.446), § 8.5, operative Jan. 1, 1997. Amended by Stats.2006, c. 538 (S.B.1852), § 52.)*

Research References

3 Witkin, California Summary 10th Agency and Employment § 430, (S 430) Nature and Scope of Act.
3 Witkin, California Summary 10th Agency and Employment § 434, in General.
3 Witkin, California Summary 10th Agency and Employment § 437, in General.
3 Witkin, California Summary 10th Agency and Employment § 440, in General.
3 Witkin, California Summary 10th Agency and Employment § 443, in General.

§ 1812.502. Application of title; person charging employer exclusively; nonprofit corporation; labor organization; nursing, business, or vocational school; job listing service

(a) This title does not apply to any person who provides any of the services described in subdivision (a) of Section 1812.501 and who charges fees exclusively to employers for those services. The exemption from regulation provided by this subdivision does not apply to any person who provides babysitting or domestic employment for others. This subdivision does not apply to an employment counseling service as defined in subdivision (b) of Section 1812.501.

(b) This title shall not apply to any nonprofit corporation, organized for the purpose of economic adjustment, civic betterment, and the giving of vocational guidance and placement to its members, or others, including employment counseling services, when all of the following conditions exist:

(1) None of the directors, officers, or employees thereof receive any profit other than a nominal salary for services performed for the organization or corporation.

(2) No fee is charged for those services, though a voluntary contribution may be requested.

(3) Membership dues or fees charged are used solely for maintenance of the organization or corporation.

(c) Nothing in this title shall apply to a nonprofit corporation which has been formed in good faith for the promotion and advancement of the general professional interests of its members and which maintains a placement service principally engaged in securing employment for such members with the state or any county, city, district or other public agency under contracts providing employment for one year or longer, or any nonprofit corporation exempted by subdivision (b).

(d) This title shall not apply to a labor organization as defined in Section 1117 of the Labor Code, a newspaper of general circulation, bona fide newsletter, magazine, trade or professional journal, or other publication of general circulation, the main purpose of which is dissemination of news, reports, trade or professional information, or information not intended to assist in locating, securing, or procuring employment or assignments for others.

(e) As used in this title, "employment agency" or "agency" does not include a nursing school, business school, or vocational school, except that if such a school charges a fee for placement, the school shall be an employment agency within the meaning of this title.

(f)(1) A job listing service which meets the requirements specified in paragraph (2) or (3) shall not be subject to any of the following: Sections 1812.515, 1812.516, 1812.517, and 1812.518; subdivisions (a) and (b), and paragraph (3) of subdivision (c), and subdivision (d) of Section 1812.519; paragraph (2) of subdivision (b), and subdivisions (c), (d), (e), and (f) of Section 1812.520; and Section 1812.521.

(2) A job listing service shall be exempt pursuant to paragraph (1) if it complies with all of the following:

(A) Does not provide, offer, or imply the offer of, services related to employment.

(B) Does not offer or sell lists of employers or job openings to jobseekers on an in-person basis.

(C) Maintains records of all its advertisements, identified by date and publication, and the sources of information used for the preparation of lists of employers and job openings, from which can be determined the accuracy of any statistics regarding success rate or similar statistics used in its advertising, promotional materials, or oral or written statements to jobseekers.

(D) Identifies, on each list of employers and job openings, its general source of information for jobs included on that list when the source of information is a publication or other public record.

(E) Provides, at or before the time of delivery of the list, a prominent written statement to the jobseeker granting the jobseeker a right to return the list for an immediate refund of the purchase price during a stated period of time which expires not less than 10 days from the date of delivery of the list. The list shall be deemed returned upon delivery to the address from which it was obtained or upon deposit in the mail properly addressed to that address, with postage prepaid.

(3) A job listing service shall be exempt pursuant to paragraph (1) if it complies with all of the following:

(A) A majority interest in the job listing service is owned by one or more colleges or universities, or alumni associations affiliated therewith, and each college or university is accredited by both (i) an accrediting agency recognized as such by the United States Department of Education and (ii) a member organization of the Council of Postsecondary Accreditation.

(B) The job listing service provides services related to employment exclusively for jobseekers who are the alumni of colleges or universities specified in subparagraph (A).

(C) The job listing service does not require, as a condition to receiving employment services, that the applicant have completed courses or examinations beyond the requirements for graduation from the college or university specified in subparagraph (A).

(D) More than 50 percent of the annual revenues received by the job listing service are derived from paid subscriptions of prospective employers. *(Added by Stats.1989, c. 704, § 2. Amended by Stats.1990, c. 1256 (A.B.2649), § 4.)*

Research References

3 Witkin, California Summary 10th Agency and Employment § 430, (S 430) Nature and Scope of Act.

3 Witkin, California Summary 10th Agency and Employment § 434, in General.

3 Witkin, California Summary 10th Agency and Employment § 440, in General.

CHAPTER 2. EMPLOYMENT AGENCIES

§ 1812.503. Bond; deposit in lieu of bond

(a) Every employment agency subject to this title shall maintain a bond issued by a surety company admitted to do business in this state. The principal sum of the bond shall be three thousand dollars ($3,000). A copy of the bond shall be filed with the Secretary of State.

(b) The bond required by this section shall be in favor of, and payable to, the people of the State of California and shall be conditioned that the person obtaining the bond will comply with this title and will pay all sums due any individual or group of individuals when the person or his or her representative, agent, or employee has received those sums. The bond shall be for the benefit of any person or persons damaged by any violation of this title or by fraud, dishonesty, misstatement, misrepresentation, deceit, unlawful acts or omissions, or failure to provide the services of the employment agency in performance of the contract with the jobseeker, by the employment agency or its agents, representatives, or employees while acting within the scope of their employment.

(c)(1) No employment agency shall conduct any business without having a current surety bond in the amount prescribed by this title and filing a copy of the bond with the Secretary of State.

(2) Thirty days prior to the cancellation or termination of any surety bond required by this section, the surety shall send a written notice of that cancellation or termination to both the employment agency and the Secretary of State, identifying the bond and the date of cancellation or termination.

(3) If any employment agency fails to obtain a new bond and file a copy of that bond with the Secretary of State by the effective date of the cancellation or termination of the former bond, the employment agency shall cease to conduct any business unless and until a new surety bond is obtained and a copy of that bond is filed with the Secretary of State.

(d) When a deposit has been made in lieu of the bond pursuant to Section 995.710 of the Code of Civil Procedure, the person asserting a claim against the deposit shall, in lieu of Section 996.430 of the Code of Civil Procedure, establish the claim by furnishing evidence to the Secretary of State of a money judgment entered by a court together with evidence that the claimant is a person described in subdivision (b).

(e) When a claimant has established the claim with the Secretary of State, the Secretary of State shall review and approve the claim and enter the date of approval thereon. The claim shall be designated an "approved claim."

(f) When the first claim against a particular deposit has been approved, it shall not be paid until the expiration of a period of 240 days after the date of its approval by the Secretary of State. Subsequent claims that are approved by the Secretary of State within the same 240-day period shall similarly not be paid until the expiration of the 240-day period. Upon the expiration of the 240-day period, the Secretary of State shall pay all approved claims from that 240-day period in full unless the deposit is insufficient, in which case each approved claim shall be paid a pro rata share of the deposit.

(g) When the Secretary of State approves the first claim against a particular deposit after the expiration of a 240-day period, the date of approval of that claim shall begin a new 240-

day period to which subdivision (f) shall apply with respect to any amount remaining in the deposit.

(h) After a deposit is exhausted, no further claims shall be paid by the Secretary of State. Claimants who have had their claims paid in full or in part pursuant to subdivision (f) or (g) shall not be required to return funds received from the deposit for the benefit of other claimants.

(i) When a deposit has been made in lieu of a bond, the amount of the deposit shall not be subject to attachment, garnishment, or execution with respect to an action or judgment against the employment agency, other than as to an amount as no longer needed or required for the purpose of this title that would otherwise be returned to the employment agency by the Secretary of State.

(j) The Secretary of State shall retain a cash deposit for two years from the date the Secretary of State receives written notification from the assignor of the deposit that the assignor has ceased to engage in the business of an employment agency or has filed a bond pursuant to subdivision (a), provided that there are no outstanding claims against the deposit. This written notice shall include all of the following: (1) name, address, and telephone number of the assignor; (2) name, address, and telephone number of the bank at which the deposit is located; (3) account number of the deposit; and (4) a statement whether the assignor is ceasing to engage in the business of an employment agency or has filed a bond with the Secretary of State. The Secretary of State shall forward an acknowledgment of receipt of the written notice to the assignor at the address indicated therein, specifying the date of receipt of the written notice and anticipated date of release of the deposit, provided there are no outstanding claims against the deposit.

(k) A judge of a superior court may order the return of the deposit prior to the expiration of two years upon evidence satisfactory to the judge that there are no outstanding claims against the deposit or order the Secretary of State to retain the deposit for a sufficient period beyond the two years pursuant to subdivision (j) to resolve outstanding claims against the deposit account.

(l) The Secretary of State shall charge a filing fee not to exceed the cost of filing the bond or deposit filed in lieu of a bond as set forth in Section 995.710 of the Code of Civil Procedure.

(m) The Secretary of State shall enforce the provisions of this chapter that govern the filing and maintenance of bonds and deposits in lieu of bonds. (Added by Stats.1989, c. 704, § 2. Amended by Stats.1996, c. 633 (S.B.1978), § 11; Stats.1998, c. 829 (S.B.1652), § 11; Stats.2002, c. 784 (S.B.1316), § 15.)

Law Revision Commission Comments

Subdivision (k) of Section 1812.503 is amended to reflect unification of the municipal and superior courts pursuant to Article VI, Section 5(e), of the California Constitution. [32 Cal.L.Rev.Comm. Reports 72 (2002)].

Research References

Rutter, Cal. Practice Guide: Enforcing Judgments/Debts Ch. 4-A, A. Attachment.
Rutter, Cal. Practice Guide: Insurance Litigation Ch. 6I-B, B. Particular Surety Bond Coverages.
3 Witkin, California Summary 10th Agency and Employment § 433, (S 433) Bond or Deposit.

§ 1812.504. Contract

(a) Every employment agency shall give a written contract to every jobseeker from whom a fee or deposit is to be received, whether directly or indirectly. The original of the contract shall be given to the jobseeker at the time the jobseeker signs the contract and before the employment agency accepts any fee or deposit or the jobseeker becomes obligated to pay any such fee or deposit. The contract shall contain all of the following:

(1) The name, address, and telephone number of the employment agency, and, if the employment agency has more than one office or location, the address and telephone number of the principal office or location providing services to the jobseeker.

(2) The name and address of the person giving the order for help, the date and consecutive number of the receipt of the order by the agency, and its manner of transmission.

(3) The name of the jobseeker, the name and address of the person to whom the jobseeker is sent for employment, and the address where the jobseeker is to report for employment.

(4) The date and consecutive number of the contract.

(5) The amount of the fee to be charged and to be collected from the jobseeker, including a statement that if the employment is terminated, the fee may not exceed gross earnings of the jobseeker in that employment, and the amount of the fee paid or advanced by the prospective employer and by whom paid or advanced.

(6) The kind of work or employment.

(7) The daily hours of work; the wages or salary, including any consideration or privilege; the benefits; and any other conditions of employment.

(8) If any labor trouble exists at the place of employment, that fact shall be stated in the contract.

(9) A contract expiration date which shall not be later than 180 days from the date of the referral or signing of the contract, whichever occurs first; however, a domestic agency operating as a registry may enter into a continuing contract subject to termination by written notice by either the domestic worker or the agency.

(10) Any other term, condition, or understanding agreed upon between the agency and the jobseeker.

(11) The following statement, with the caption in type no smaller than 10-point boldfaced type and the remainder in a size no smaller than that generally used throughout the contract, and in full capitals, boldface, or italics:

RIGHT TO REFUND

"If you pay all or any portion of a fee and fail to accept employment, the employment agency shall, upon your request, return the amount paid to you within 48 hours after your request for a refund.

"If you leave employment for just cause or are discharged for reasons other than misconduct connected with your work within 90 days from the starting date of employment, the agency shall reduce your fee to that payable for temporary employment and shall refund any excess paid within 10 days of your request for a refund.

"No fee larger than that for temporary employment may be charged to you for employment lasting 90 days or less unless the agency's fee schedules, contracts, and agreements provide for a further charge if you leave employment without just cause or are discharged for misconduct in connection with your work.

"If any refund due is not made within the time limits set forth above, the employment agency shall pay you an additional sum equal to the amount of the refund."

(b) All contracts shall be dated and shall be made and numbered consecutively, both copies to be signed by the jobseeker and the person acting for the employment agency. The original shall be given to the jobseeker and one copy shall be kept on file at the employment agency.

(c) The full agreement between the parties shall be contained in a single document containing those elements set forth in this section.

(d) When a referral is made by telephone the agency shall execute the contract or receipt in triplicate and shall mail the original and duplicate to the jobseeker on the day the referral is made, with instructions that they be signed by the jobseeker and the duplicate returned to the agency. The date of mailing the contract or receipt to the jobseeker shall be entered thereon by the agency. The same contract or receipt shall not be used for more than one referral.

(e) For purposes of this section, a "domestic agency operating as a registry" means a domestic agency that engages in the business of obtaining and filling commitments for domestic help. *(Added by Stats.1989, c. 704, § 2. Amended by Stats.1996, c. 102 (S.B.2030), § 1.)*

Research References

3 Witkin, California Summary 10th Agency and Employment § 435, Contracts and Fees.

§ 1812.505. Fees; schedule; payment terms; notice; change; confession of judgment, note, or wage assignment as payment; deposit; termination of employment; interagency disputes; splitting; employer interest in agency

(a)(1) An employment agency shall provide a copy of the agency's jobseeker fee schedule and payment terms to any jobseeker from whom a fee or deposit is to be received, prior to the jobseeker being interviewed by a counselor. The jobseeker fee schedule shall indicate the percentage of both the projected annual and first month's total gross earnings represented by those fees.

(2) In the schedule, the various employments or salary ranges by which the fee is to be computed or determined shall be classified, and in each class the maximum fee shall be fixed and shall include the charges of every kind rendered by the agency in each case or transaction on behalf of the prospective employee. Changes in the schedule may be made, but no change shall become effective until posted for not less than seven days in a conspicuous place in the agency.

(3) A copy of the schedule in effect shall be kept posted in the employment agency in a conspicuous place, and the posted schedule and the changes therein shall be in lettering or printing of not less than standard pica capitals. The date of the taking effect of the schedule and of each change therein shall appear on the posted copies.

(4) A copy of all fee schedules, and of all changes therein, shall be kept on file at the employment agency, retrospectively, for a period of one year.

(b) No fee charged or collected shall be in excess of the fee as scheduled.

(c) No employment agency shall accept, directly or indirectly, a registration fee of any kind.

(d) No employment agency may take from a jobseeker a confession of judgment, a promissory note or notes, or an assignment of wages to cover its fees.

(e) The employment agency shall give a receipt to every jobseeker from whom a deposit is received. No other deposit or prepayment of any kind may be required by an agency. If the jobseeker accepts employment, the deposit shall be applied to the fee to be paid by the jobseeker.

(f)(1) If a jobseeker leaves employment for just cause or is discharged for reasons other than misconduct connected with the jobseeker's work within 90 days from the starting date of employment, the agency shall reduce the fee payable by the jobseeker to that payable for temporary employment under subdivision (g) and shall refund any fee paid in excess of that amount.

(2) No charge may be made to or obligation to pay incurred by any jobseeker beyond that authorized by subdivision (g) for employment lasting 90 days or less, unless the agency's fee schedules, contracts, and agreements specifically provide for a further charge if the jobseeker leaves employment without just cause or is discharged for misconduct in connection with his or her work, and then only if lack of just cause or misconduct exists. Otherwise, the agency shall retain or charge only the fee for temporary employment for any employment lasting 90 days or less from the starting date of employment.

(3) Notwithstanding subdivision (a) and this subdivision, in no instance in which the employment accepted is subsequently terminated shall the fee charged or obligation to pay incurred by a jobseeker be greater than the total gross earnings of the jobseeker in that employment. This provision shall be stated in all agency contracts issued pursuant to Section 1812.504.

(g) The fee payable by the jobseeker for temporary employment shall not exceed ⅟₉₀ of the fee for permanent employment for each consecutive calendar day during the period that the jobseeker is employed or compensated as though employed.

(h)(1) If a jobseeker accepts employment in which the jobseeker is to be paid on the basis of straight commissions, or a drawing account against commissions, or either a drawing account or salary plus commissions, the fee payable by the jobseeker may be predicated upon the projected total gross earnings during the first year of employment as estimated by the employer.

(2) Upon the conclusion of a jobseeker's first 12 months of employment, a computation of his or her actual total gross earnings may be provided by the jobseeker to the agency, and, predicated upon appropriate proof of earnings, an adjustment in the fee shall be made in which either the agency shall refund to the jobseeker any excess fee paid by him or her or the jobseeker shall pay to the agency any deficiency thereon.

(3) If the jobseeker's employment is terminated prior to the conclusion of the first 12 months of employment, the actual total gross earnings of the jobseeker for the period of employment shall be projected to 12 months on a pro rata basis as though the jobseeker had been employed for the entire period of 12 months, and a computation shall be made thereon. The fee paid or payable by the jobseeker shall be predicated upon that computation as though the jobseeker had been so employed.

(i) If an employment agency sends a jobseeker for employment and the jobseeker accepts employment other than that position specified in the bona fide order for employment to which the jobseeker was sent, but with the same employer, then the agency shall be entitled to a fee for the employment of the jobseeker, payable by the jobseeker, computed under the terms of the fee schedule in effect in the agency at the time of referral, provided that the jobseeker accepts employment within 180 days of the date of referral. The expiration date of the referral shall be stated in the contract.

In interagency disputes concerning the earning of a fee for placement of a jobseeker, the fee shall be earned by the agency responsible for the jobseeker being placed. A reasonable effort shall be made by the billing agency that it is entitled to the fee. The jobseeker shall be responsible for only one full fee for any single placement, and that fact shall be so stated in the contract.

(j)(1) No employment agency shall divide fees with an employer, an agent, or other employee of an employer or person to whom help is furnished.

(2) No employment agency shall charge any jobseeker a fee for accepting employment with such employment agency or any subsidiary of that agency.

(3) No employment agency shall charge any jobseeker a fee when help is furnished to an employer, an agent, any employee of an employer, a member, or person who has a financial interest in the employment agency. *(Added by Stats.1989, c. 704, § 2.)*

Research References

3 Witkin, California Summary 10th Agency and Employment § 435, Contracts and Fees.

§ 1812.506. Fees; deposit; return; delay; notice; permanent employment; termination of employment; refusal to refund

(a) If a jobseeker paying or becoming obligated to pay a fee, or making a deposit on a fee for placement fails to accept employment, the employment agency shall, upon request by the jobseeker, repay the amount of the deposit or fee to the jobseeker. Unless the deposit is returned within 48 hours after request, the employment agency shall pay to the jobseeker an additional sum equal to the amount of the deposit. A notice to this effect shall be inserted in all contracts between the agency and the jobseeker, and in all receipts given to the jobseeker for cash payment in advance of employment, and in the schedule of fees posted in the office of the agency.

(b)(1) All employment provided by any employment agency to any jobseeker from whom a fee is to be received shall be considered permanent only if it lasts longer than 90 days. If a jobseeker leaves the job or is discharged within the first 90 days of employment, the agency shall make a refund or reduction of the fee to the temporary fee amount unless the agency's fee schedules, contracts, and agreements specifically provide for a further charge if the jobseeker leaves employment without just cause or is discharged for misconduct in connection with his or her work.

(2) "Just cause" or "discharge for reasons other than misconduct" includes, but is not limited to, the following:

(A) Wages or salary less than that agreed upon between the jobseeker and the employer.

(B) Receiving a payroll check which is not honored by the bank upon which it was drawn.

(C) Working hours, working days, or working shifts significantly different than those agreed upon between the jobseeker and the employer.

(D) Receiving a work assignment, subsequent to accepting the job, which is substantially different from that agreed upon between the jobseeker and the employer.

(E) Being assigned to a job location different from that which was agreed upon between the jobseeker and the employer.

(F) The jobseeker's lack of physical ability to perform duties connected with the position agreed upon between the jobseeker and the employer unless the provisions of subparagraph (E) of paragraph (3) apply.

(G) A lockout or strike causing loss of pay.

(H) The jobseeker's lack of physical ability to perform duties connected with the position unless the provisions of subparagraph (E) of paragraph (3) apply.

(J)[1] The jobseeker's entry into active service in the armed forces.

(K) Physical or economic destruction of the business.

(L) The death of the jobseeker (any refund in that case shall be paid to the estate of the jobseeker).

(3) "Lack of just cause" or a discharge for "misconduct" includes, but is not limited to:

(A) Abandonment of the job by the jobseeker.

(B) Conviction of the jobseeker, subsequent to employment, of a crime when conviction temporarily or permanently prevents the jobseeker from fulfilling the terms of employment.

(C) Willful violation of lawful company policies or rules by the jobseeker.

(D) Willful failure to perform lawful duties appropriate to employment by the jobseeker.

(E) Acts of the jobseeker constituting misrepresentation or withholding of information directly related to education, work experience, responsibility, physical ability, or training, that would have caused the employer to refuse employment.

(c)(1) Except as otherwise provided in subdivision (a), a refund when due shall be made within 10 working days after request therefor from the jobseeker.

(2) Alternatively, if the decision of the agency is not to make a refund, the agency shall notify the jobseeker in writing, within the 10-day working period specified in paragraph (1), as to the specific reasons why the refund is not being made.

(3) If the agency fails to properly notify the jobseeker pursuant to paragraph (2) or fails to tender a refund within the time allowed, the agency shall be liable to the jobseeker in the amount of an additional sum equal to the amount of the refund. *(Added by Stats.1989, c. 704, § 2.)*

1 No (I) in enrolled copy.

Research References

3 Witkin, California Summary 10th Agency and Employment § 435, Contracts and Fees.

§ 1812.507. Job order; referring jobseeker

(a) No employment agency shall accept a fee from any jobseeker, or send any jobseeker for employment, without having obtained, orally or in writing, a bona fide job order for employment.

(b) An agency shall identify itself as an employment agency to the employer in all instances in which it contacts an employer for the purpose of soliciting a job order. All job orders shall be recorded in writing. A job order for employment shall be considered to have been given by an employer to an employment agency under the following conditions:

(1) The employer, or his or her agent, orally or in writing, registers a request or gives permission that the agency recruit or refer jobseekers who meet the employer's stated job specifications and the employer furnishes such information as required by subdivision (a) of Section 1812.504. A job order is valid for the referral of any qualified jobseeker until it is filled or canceled by the employer, and may serve as the basis for agency advertising. The agency is required to recontact the employer within 30 days to ensure that the position is still vacant prior to any additional advertising or referral of jobseekers.

(2) When an agency has brought the qualifications of a specific jobseeker to the attention of an employer and the employer has expressed interest in that jobseeker either by agreeing to interview the jobseeker, or by requesting that the agency furnish him or her with the jobseeker's resumé or other written history or data, or by initiating direct contact with the jobseeker as a result of information furnished by the agency, that action by the employer shall constitute a job order only for the jobseeker discussed and is not valid for advertisement, unless the contact by the agency resulted in a job order for a specific position sufficient under paragraph (1). If the employer has no position open but merely wishes to explore the possible employment of the jobseeker and the jobseeker is to be responsible for

the placement fee, that fact shall be indicated on the jobseeker's referral contract.

(c) No employment agency shall refer a jobseeker to a job knowing or having reason to know that:

(1) The job does not exist or the jobseeker is not qualified for the job.

(2) The job has been described or advertised by or on behalf of the agency in a false, misleading, or deceptive manner.

(3) The agency has not obtained written or oral permission to list the job from the employer or an authorized agent of the employer. *(Added by Stats.1989, c. 704, § 2.)*

§ 1812.508. False or misleading representations; advertisements; name, address, and telephone number; designation in name; fee; records

(a) No employment agency shall make, or cause to be made, any false, misleading, or deceptive advertisements or representations concerning the services that the agency will provide to jobseekers.

(b)(1) No employment agency shall publish or cause to be published any false, fraudulent, or misleading information, representation, notice, or advertisements.

(2) All advertisements of an employment agency shall contain the correct name of the employment agency and one of the following:

(A) The street address of the agency's place of business.

(B) The correct telephone number of the agency at its place of business.

(3) Every employment agency, except a nurses' registry shall use, as part of its name, either the designation "agency" or "personnel service."

(4) No employment agency shall give any false information or make any false promises or representations concerning an engagement or employment to any jobseeker who registers or applies for an engagement or employment or help.

(5) No employment agency shall, by its name, advertisement, or any other representation, represent itself to be a home health agency, as defined by subdivision (a) of Section 1727 of the Health and Safety Code, or to perform the services of a home health agency. An employment agency shall provide a written disclosure to each individual receiving nursing services in his or her place of residence stating that it does not perform the services of a home health agency and clearly describing that it is an employment agency only and that any complaints against personnel providing nursing services who are neither licensed nor certified shall be submitted to the local district attorney, complaints against certified nursing assistants and certified home health aides providing nursing services shall be submitted to the local district attorney and the State Department of Health Services, and complaints against licensed personnel providing nursing services shall be submitted to the local district attorney and the Department of Consumer Affairs. The address and telephone number of each agency and board to which complaints are required to be submitted shall be provided by the employment agency to all patients prior to the time they are under the care of any nursing services personnel.

(6) Any person may refer complaints concerning employment agencies to the proper law enforcement agency for action.

(c)(1) Where an employment agency job advertisement includes a description of the placement fee associated with the advertised job, the employment agency shall describe the placement fee in a manner which either clearly indicates whether or not a jobseeker shall be responsible for the placement fee or in accordance with the following terms and provisions:

(A) "FEE" means the jobseeker pays the entire placement fee.

(B) "NO FEE" means the jobseeker pays no portion of the placement fee.

(2) Where "NO FEE" jobs are advertised and the agency also administers placement for "FEE" jobs, the advertisement shall state "ALSO FEE JOBS" in type of equal size, prominence, and boldness as "NO FEE" notations.

(3) A group job advertisement which includes a description of the placement fee shall describe the placement fee either separately for each job, or by use of the proper term as a heading under which all applicable jobs shall be listed. All those headings shall be in type and of the same size, prominence, and boldness.

(d) Special requirements not usually associated with a job shall be specified in any advertisement. When the location of the position advertised is more than 50 miles from the employment agency office responsible for the advertisement, it shall state either the location or that the job is "nonlocal." Special benefits of the job, if advertised, shall be specifically described and substitute terms or symbols such as "extras" or "+" shall not be sufficient.

(e) An advertised salary shall be based upon the starting salary contained in the job order. An advertised range of starting salaries shall be specified by preceding the minimum salary and maximum salary by the terms "from" and "to" respectively. When the job order contains only the maximum amount of a salary range, that advertised salary shall be preceded by the word "to." If a maximum salary is dependent upon the jobseeker's experience, the advertised salary may be described by listing the minimum salary and the term "up Depending on Experience" or "up D.O.E." The words "open" and "negotiable" or words or symbols of like import shall not be used as a substitute for the salary. If an advertised salary is based in whole or in part on commissions, that fact shall be indicated in the advertisement.

(f) All employment agencies shall maintain a record of all advertised jobs, correlated to show the date and the publication in which the advertisement appeared and the job order number of each job advertised, retrospectively for a period of one year. *(Added by Stats.1989, c. 704, § 2. Amended by Stats.1990, c. 761 (A.B.3924), § 1.)*

§ 1812.509. Employment of minors; notification required to be given to jobseekers; necessity of personal interview

(a) No employment agency shall, when employment would be in violation of Chapter 1 (commencing with Section 1171) of Part 4 of Division 2 of the Labor Code or Part 27 (commencing with Section 48000) of the Education Code, accept any application for employment made by, or on behalf of, any minor, or place or assist in placing any minor in that employment.

(b) Every employment agency shall notify each jobseeker before sending the jobseeker in response to a request for employment whether a labor contract is in existence at the establishment to which the jobseeker is being sent, and whether union membership is required.

(c) No employment agency shall send a jobseeker to any place where a strike, lockout, or other labor trouble exists without notifying the jobseeker of that fact and shall in addition thereto enter a statement of those conditions upon the contract or receipt given to the jobseeker.

(d) No babysitting, domestic, or other employment agency which procures babysitting or domestic employment for employers shall refer babysitters or domestics for any employment without first conducting a personal interview of the jobseeker and making a reasonable effort to verify the experience or training of the jobseeker.

(e) No employment agency that procures temporary employment for long-term health care employers shall refer certified nurse assistants or licensed nursing staff as defined in Section 1812.540, for any employment without first conducting a personal interview of the individual, verifying the experience, training, and references of the individual, and verifying that the individual is in good standing with the appropriate licensing or certification board, including verification that the individual has successfully secured a criminal record clearance. *(Added by Stats.1989, c. 704, § 2. Amended by Stats.1990, c. 1256 (A.B.2649), § 5; Stats.2001, c. 326 (A.B.1643), § 1.)*

Research References

3 Witkin, California Summary 10th Agency and Employment § 434, in General.
3 Witkin, California Summary 10th Agency and Employment § 446, Requirements.

§ 1812.5093. Child care provider referral; disclosure

(a) Every employment agency that refers a child care provider to an employer who is not required to be a licensed child day care facility pursuant to Section 1596.792 of the Health and Safety Code shall provide the employer with all the following:

(1) A description of the child care provider trustline registry established pursuant to Chapter 3.35 (commencing with Section 1596.60) of Division 2 of the Health and Safety Code that provides criminal history checks on child care providers.

(2) An explanation of how an employer may obtain more information about the child care provider trustline registry.

(3) A statement that an employment agency is prohibited by law from placing a child care provider unless the provider is a trustline applicant or a registered child care provider.

(4) An explanation of how the employer may verify the prospective child care provider's trustline registry registration.

(b) Receipt of the information required to be provided pursuant to subdivision (a) shall be verified in writing by the employer. *(Added by Stats.1998, c. 287 (A.B.2001), § 1.)*

Research References

3 Witkin, California Summary 10th Agency and Employment § 434, in General.

§ 1812.5095. Domestic worker; relationship with employment agency; agency referral authority and duties

(a) For purposes of this section, the term "employment agency" means an employment agency, as defined in paragraph (3) of subdivision (a) of Section 1812.501, or a domestic agency, as defined in subdivision (h) of Section 1812.501.

(b) An employment agency is not the employer of a domestic worker for whom it procures, offers, refers, provides, or attempts to provide work, if all of the following factors characterize the nature of the relationship between the employment agency and the domestic worker for whom the agency procures, offers, refers, provides, or attempts to provide domestic work:

(1) There is a signed contract or agreement between the employment agency and the domestic worker that contains, at a minimum, provisions that specify all of the following:

(A) That the employment agency shall assist the domestic worker in securing work.

(B) How the employment agency's referral fee shall be paid.

(C) That the domestic worker is free to sign an agreement with other employment agencies and to perform domestic work for persons not referred by the employment agency.

(2) The domestic worker informs the employment agency of any restrictions on hours, location, conditions, or type of work he or she will accept and the domestic worker is free to select or reject any work opportunity procured, offered, referred, or provided by the employment agency.

(3) The domestic worker is free to renegotiate with the person hiring him or her the amount proposed to be paid for the work.

(4) The domestic worker does not receive any training from the employment agency with respect to the performance of domestic work. However, an employment agency may provide a voluntary orientation session in which the relationship between the employment agency and the domestic worker, including the employment agency's administrative and operating procedures, and the provisions of the contract or agreement between the employment agency and the domestic worker are explained.

(5) The domestic worker performs domestic work without any direction, control, or supervision exercised by the employment agency with respect to the manner and means of performing the domestic work. An employment agency shall not be deemed to be exercising direction, control, or supervision when it takes any of the following actions:

(A) Informs the domestic worker about the services to be provided and the conditions of work specified by the person seeking to hire a domestic worker.

(B) Contacts the person who has hired the domestic worker to determine whether that person is satisfied with the agency's referral service.

(C) Informs the domestic worker of the time during which new referrals are available.

(D) Requests the domestic worker to inform the employment agency if the domestic worker is unable to perform the work accepted.

(6) The employment agency does not provide tools, supplies, or equipment necessary to perform the domestic work.

(7) The domestic worker is not obligated to pay the employment agency's referral fee, and the employment agency is not obligated to pay the domestic worker if the person for whom the services were performed fails or refuses to pay for the domestic work.

(8) Payments for domestic services are made directly to either the domestic worker or to the employment agency. Payments made directly to the employment agency shall be deposited into a trust account until payment can be made to the domestic worker.

(9) The relationship between a domestic worker and the person for whom the domestic worker performs services may only be terminated by either of those parties and not by the employment agency that referred the domestic worker. However, an employment agency may decline to make additional referrals to a particular domestic worker, and the domestic worker may decline to accept a particular referral.

(c) The fee charged by an employment agency for its services shall be reasonable, negotiable, and based on a fixed percentage of the job cost.

(d) An employment agency referring a domestic worker to a job shall inform that domestic worker, in writing, on or before the signing of the contract pursuant to paragraph (1) of subdivision (b), that the domestic worker may be obligated to obtain business permits or licenses, where required by any state or local law, ordinance, or regulation, and that he or she is not eligible for unemployment insurance, state disability insurance, social security, or workers' compensation benefits through an employment agency complying with subdivision (b). The employment agency referring a domestic worker shall also inform that domestic worker, if the domestic worker is self-employed, that he or she is required to pay self-employment tax, state tax, and federal income taxes.

(e) An employment agency referring a domestic worker to a job shall verify the worker's legal status or authorization to work prior to providing referral services in accordance with procedures established under federal law.

(f) An employment agency referring a domestic worker to a job shall orally communicate to the person seeking domestic services the disclosure set forth below prior to the referral of the domestic worker the following disclosure statement:

"(Name of agency) is not the employer of the domestic worker it referred to you. Depending on your arrangement with the domestic worker, you may have employer responsibilities."

Within three business days after the employment agency refers a domestic worker to the person seeking domestic services, the following statement printed in not less than 10-point type shall be mailed to the person seeking domestic services:

"(Name of agency) is not the employer of the domestic worker it referred to you. The domestic worker may be your employee or an independent contractor depending on the relationship you have with him or her. If you direct and control the manner and means by which the domestic worker performs his or her work you may have employer responsibilities, including employment taxes and workers' compensation, under state and federal law. For additional information contact your local Employment Development Department and the Internal Revenue Service."

(g) An employment agency referring a domestic worker to a job shall not specify that a worker is self-employed or an independent contractor in any notice, advertisement, or brochure provided to either the worker or the customer.

(h) Every employment agency referring a domestic worker to a job and who is not the employer of the domestic worker being referred, shall in any paid telephone directory advertisement or any other promotional literature or advertising distributed or placed by such an employment agency, on or after January 1, 1995, insert the following statement, in no less than 6-point type which shall be in print which contrasts with the background of the advertisement so as to be easily legible:

"(Name of agency) is a referral agency."

(i) An employment agency may not refer, in its advertising, soliciting, or other presentments to the public, to any bond required to be filed pursuant to this chapter.

(j) An employment agency may not refer, in its advertising, soliciting, or other presentments to the public, to any licensure acquired by the agency.

(k) Any violation of this section with the intent to directly or indirectly mislead the public on the nature of services provided by an employment agency shall constitute unfair competition which includes any unlawful, unfair, or fraudulent business acts or practices and unfair, deceptive, untrue, or misleading advertising. Any person or entity that engages in unfair competition shall be liable for a civil penalty not to exceed two thousand five hundred dollars ($2,500) for each violation. *(Added by Stats. 1993, c. 1275 (A.B.1370), § 1. Amended by Stats.1994, c. 1081 (S.B.1418), § 1.)*

Research References

3 Witkin, California Summary 10th Agency and Employment § 434, in General.

2 Witkin Cal. Summ. 10th Workers' Compensation § 159, (S 159) in General.

CHAPTER 3. EMPLOYMENT COUNSELING SERVICES

§ 1812.510. Bond; deposit in lieu of bond

(a) Every employment counseling service subject to this title shall maintain a bond issued by a surety company admitted to do business in this state. The principal sum of the bond shall be ten thousand dollars ($10,000). A copy of the bond shall be filed with the Secretary of State.

(b) The bond required by this section shall be in favor of, and payable to, the people of the State of California, and shall be conditioned that the person obtaining the bond will comply with this title and will pay all sums due any individual or group of individuals when the person or his or her representative, agent, or employee has received those sums. The bond shall be for the benefit of any person or persons damaged by any violation of this title or by fraud, dishonesty, misstatement, misrepresentation, deceit, unlawful acts or omissions, or failure to provide the services of the employment counseling service in performance of the contract with the customer by the employment counseling service or its agents, representatives, or employees while acting within the scope of their employment.

(c)(1) No employment counseling service shall conduct any business without having a current surety bond in the amount prescribed by this title and filing a copy of the bond with the Secretary of State.

(2) Thirty days prior to the cancellation or termination of any surety bond required by this section, the surety shall send a written notice of that cancellation or termination to both the employment counseling service and the Secretary of State, identifying the bond and the date of cancellation or termination.

(3) If any employment counseling service fails to obtain a new bond and file a copy of that bond with the Secretary of State by the effective date of the cancellation or termination of the former bond, the employment counseling service shall cease to conduct any business unless and until a new surety bond is obtained and a copy of that bond is filed with the Secretary of State.

(d) When a deposit has been made in lieu of the bond pursuant to Section 995.710 of the Code of Civil Procedure, the person asserting a claim against the deposit shall, in lieu of Section 996.430 of the Code of Civil Procedure, establish the claim by furnishing evidence to the Secretary of State of a money judgment entered by a court together with evidence that the claimant is a person described in subdivision (b).

(e) When a person has established the claim with the Secretary of State, the Secretary of State shall immediately review and approve the claim and enter the date of approval on the claim. The claim shall be designated an "approved claim."

(f) When the first claim against a particular deposit has been approved, it shall not be paid until the expiration of a period of 240 days after the date of its approval by the Secretary of State. Subsequent claims that are approved by the Secretary of State within the same 240–day period shall similarly not be paid until the expiration of the 240–day period. Upon the expiration of the 240–day period, the Secretary of State shall pay all approved claims from that 240–day period in full unless the deposit is insufficient, in which case each approved claim shall be paid a pro rata share of the deposit.

(g) When the Secretary of State approves the first claim against a particular deposit account after the expiration of the 240–day period, the date of approval of that claim shall begin a new 240–day period to which subdivision (f) shall apply with respect to the amount remaining in the deposit account.

(h) After a deposit account is exhausted, no further claims shall be paid by the Secretary of State. Claimants who have had their claims paid in full or in part pursuant to subdivisions (f) and (g) shall not be required to return funds received from the deposit for the benefit of other claimants.

(i) When a deposit has been made in lieu of a bond, the amount of the deposit shall not be subject to attachment, garnishment, or execution with respect to an action or judgment against the employment counseling service, other than as to an amount as no longer needed or required for the purpose of this title that would otherwise be returned to the employment counseling service by the Secretary of State.

(j) The Secretary of State shall retain a cash deposit for two years from the date the Secretary of State receives written notification from the assignor of the deposit that the assignor has ceased to engage in the business of a counseling service or has filed a bond pursuant to subdivision (a), provided that there are no outstanding claims against the deposit. Written notification to the Secretary of State shall include all of the following: (1) name, address, and telephone number of the assignor; (2) name, address, and telephone number of the bank at which the deposit is located; (3) account number of the deposit; and (4) a statement whether the assignor is ceasing to engage in the business of a counseling service or has filed a bond with the Secretary of State. The Secretary of State shall forward an acknowledgment of receipt of the written notice to the assignor at the address indicated in the notice, specifying the date of receipt of the written notice and anticipated date of release of the deposit, provided there are no outstanding claims against the deposit account.

(k) A judge of a superior court may order the return of the deposit prior to the expiration of two years upon evidence satisfactory to the judge that there are no outstanding claims against the deposit or order the Secretary of State to retain the deposit for a sufficient period beyond the two years pursuant to subdivision (j) to resolve outstanding claims against the deposit account.

(l) The Secretary of State shall charge a filing fee not to exceed the cost of filing the bond or the deposit filed in lieu of a bond pursuant to Section 995.710 of the Code of Civil Procedure.

(m) The Secretary of State shall enforce the provisions of this chapter that govern the filing and maintenance of bonds and deposits in lieu of bonds. *(Added by Stats.1989, c. 704, § 2. Amended by Stats.1996, c. 633 (S.B.1978), § 12; Stats.1998, c. 829 (S.B.1652), § 12; Stats.2002, c. 784 (S.B.1316), § 16.)*

Law Revision Commission Comments

Subdivision (b) of Section 1812.510 is amended to make a technical change.

Subdivision (k) is amended to reflect unification of the municipal and superior courts pursuant to Article VI, Section 5(e), of the California Constitution. [32 Cal.L.Rev.Comm. Reports 75 (2002)].

Research References

Rutter, Cal. Practice Guide: Enforcing Judgments/Debts Ch. 4-A, A. Attachment.
Rutter, Cal. Practice Guide: Insurance Litigation Ch. 6I-B, B. Particular Surety Bond Coverages.
3 Witkin, California Summary 10th Agency and Employment § 433, (S 433) Bond or Deposit.

§ 1812.511. Contract; cancellation

(a) Every contract for employment counseling services shall be in writing. An original and one copy of the contract shall be given to the customer at the time the customer signs the contract and before the employment counseling service accepts any fee or deposit or the customer becomes obligated to pay any such fee or deposit. The contract shall contain all of the following:

(1) The name, address, and telephone number of the employment counseling service.

(2) The name and address of the person signing the contract and the person to whom the employment counseling services are to be provided.

(3) A description of the services to be provided; a statement when those services are to be provided; the duration of the contract; and refund provisions as appropriate, to be applicable if the described services are not provided according to the contract.

(4) The amount of the fee to be charged to or collected from the person receiving the services or any other person, and the date or dates when that fee is required to be paid.

(5) The following statement, in type no smaller than 10-point boldfaced type:

"No verbal or written promise or guarantee of any job or employment is made or implied under the terms of this contract."

(6) The following statement, in immediate proximity to the space reserved for the customer's signature, in type no smaller than 10-point boldfaced type:

YOUR RIGHT TO CANCEL

/enter date of transaction/

"You may cancel this contract for employment counseling services, without any penalty or obligation, if notice of cancellation is given, in writing, within three business days from the above date.

"To cancel this contract, just mail or deliver a signed and dated copy of the following cancellation notice or any other written notice of cancellation, or send a telegram containing a notice of cancellation, to (name of employment counseling service) at (address of its place of business), NOT LATER THAN MIDNIGHT OF /date/."

CANCELLATION NOTICE

I hereby cancel this contract.

Dated: _____

_____ Customer's Signature"

Until the employment counseling service has complied with this section the customer may cancel the employment counseling services contract.

(b) All contracts shall be dated and shall be made and numbered consecutively in triplicate, the original and each copy to be signed by the customer and the person acting for the employment counseling service. The original and one copy shall be given to the customer and the other copy shall be kept on file at the employment counseling service.

(c) The full agreement between the parties shall be contained in a single document containing those elements set forth in this section. *(Added by Stats.1989, c. 704, § 2.)*

Research References

3 Witkin, California Summary 10th Agency and Employment § 438, Contracts and Fees.

§ 1812.512. Fees; schedule; payment terms; notice; change; confession of judgment, note, or wage assignment as payment

(a)(1) An employment counseling service shall provide a copy of its fee schedule and payment terms to any customer from whom a fee or deposit is to be received, prior to the customer being interviewed by a counselor, agent, or employee.

(2) In the schedule, the maximum fee shall be fixed and shall include the charges of every kind rendered by the employment counseling service in each case or transaction on behalf of the prospective employee. Changes in the fee schedule may be made, but no change shall become effective until posted for not less than seven days in a conspicuous place in the employment counseling service.

(3) A copy of the schedule in effect shall be kept posted in the employment counseling service in a conspicuous place, and the posted schedule and the changes therein shall be in lettering or printing of not less than standard pica capitals. The date of the taking effect of the schedule and of each change therein shall appear on the posted copies.

(4) A copy of all fee schedules, and of all changes therein, shall be kept on file at the employment counseling service, retrospectively for a period of one year.

(b) No fee charged or collected shall be in excess of the fee as scheduled.

(c) No employment counseling service shall accept, directly or indirectly, a registration fee of any kind.

(d) No employment counseling service may take from a customer a confession of judgment, a promissory note or notes, or an assignment of wages to cover its fees. *(Added by Stats.1989, c. 704, § 2.)*

Research References

3 Witkin, California Summary 10th Agency and Employment § 438, Contracts and Fees.

§ 1812.513. False or misleading representations; advertisements; name, address, and telephone number; guarantee; records

(a) No employment counseling service shall make or cause to be made any false, misleading, or deceptive advertisements or representations concerning the services that the employment counseling service will provide to customers.

(b)(1) No employment counseling service shall publish or cause to be published any false, fraudulent, or misleading information, representation, notice, or advertisements.

(2) All advertisements of an employment counseling service shall contain the correct name of the employment counseling service and one of the following:

(A) The street address of the employment counseling service's place of business.

(B) The correct telephone number of the employment counseling service at its place of business.

(c) No employment counseling service shall give any false information or make any false promises or representations concerning engagement or employment to any customer, or make any verbal or written promise or guarantee of any job or employment.

(d) An employment counseling service shall maintain a record of all advertisements for the service, correlated to show the date and the publication in which the advertisement appeared, retrospectively, for a period of one year.

(e) No employment counseling service shall, by its choice of name or by advertisement or representation, represent itself to be an employment agency or to perform the job placement services of an employment agency. *(Added by Stats.1989, c. 704, § 2.)*

Research References

3 Witkin, California Summary 10th Agency and Employment § 439, Advertisements.

CHAPTER 4. JOB LISTING SERVICES

§ 1812.515. Bond; deposit in lieu of bond

(a) Every job listing service subject to this title shall maintain a bond issued by a surety company admitted to do business in this state. The principal sum of the bond shall be ten thousand dollars ($10,000) for each location. A copy of the bond shall be filed with the Secretary of State.

(b) The bond required by this section shall be in favor of, and payable to, the people of the State of California, and shall be conditioned that the person obtaining the bond will comply with this title and will pay all sums due any individual or group of individuals when the person or his or her representative, agent, or employee has received those sums. The bond shall be for the benefit of any person or persons damaged by any violation of misrepresentation, deceit, unlawful acts of omissions, or failure to provide the services of the job listing service in performance of the contract with the jobseeker, by the job listing service or its agent, representatives, or employees while acting within the scope of their employment.

(c)(1) No job listing service shall conduct any business without having a current surety bond in the amount prescribed by this chapter and filing a copy of the bond with the Secretary of State, identifying the bond and the date of cancellation or termination.

(2) Thirty days prior to the cancellation or termination of any surety bond required by this section, the surety shall send a written notice of that cancellation or termination to both the job listing service and the Secretary of State, identifying the bond and the date of cancellation or termination.

(3) If any job listing service fails to obtain a new bond and file a copy of that bond with the Secretary of State by the effective date of the cancellation or termination of the former bond, the job listing service shall cease to conduct any business unless and until a new surety bond is obtained and a copy of that bond is filed with the Secretary of State.

(d) When a deposit has been made in lieu of a bond pursuant to Section 995.710 of the Code of Civil Procedure, the person asserting a claim against the deposit shall, in lieu of Section 996.430 of the Code of Civil Procedure, establish the claim by furnishing evidence to the Secretary of State of a money judgment entered by a court together with evidence that the claimant is a person described in subdivision (b).

(e) When a person has established the claim with the Secretary of State, the Secretary of State shall review and approve the claim and enter the date of approval on the claim. The claim shall be designated an "approved claim."

(f) When the first claim against a particular deposit has been approved, it shall not be paid until the expiration of a period of 240 days after the date of its approval by the Secretary of State. Subsequent claims that are approved by the Secretary of State within the same 240–day period shall similarly not be paid until the expiration of the 240–day period. Upon the expiration of the 240–day period, the Secretary of State shall pay all approved claims from that 240–day period in full unless the deposit is insufficient, in which case each approved claim shall be paid in a pro rata share of the deposit.

(g) When the Secretary of State approves the first claim against a particular deposit after the expiration of the 240–day period, the date of approval of that claim shall begin a new 240–day period to which subdivision (f) shall apply with respect to the amount remaining in the deposit.

(h) After a deposit is exhausted, no further claims shall be paid by the Secretary of State. Claimants who have had their claims paid in full or in part pursuant to subdivisions (f) and (g) shall not be required to return funds received from the deposit for the benefit of other claimants.

(i) When a deposit has been made in lieu of a bond, the amount of the deposit shall not be subject to attachment, garnishment, or execution with respect to an action or judgment against the job listing service, other than as to an amount as no longer needed or required for the purpose of this title that would otherwise be returned to the job listing service by the Secretary of State.

(j) The Secretary of State shall retain a cash deposit for two years from the date the Secretary of State receives written notification from the assignor of the deposit that the assignor has ceased to engage in the business of a job listing service or has filed a bond pursuant to subdivision (a), provided that there are no outstanding claims against the deposit. Written notification to the Secretary of State shall include all of the following: (1) name, address, and telephone number of the assignor; (2) name, address, and telephone number of the bank at which the deposit is located; (3) account number of the deposit; and (4) a statement whether the assignor is ceasing to engage in the business of a job listing service or has filed a bond with the Secretary of State. The Secretary of State shall forward an acknowledgment of receipt of the written notice to the assignor at the address indicated therein, specifying the date of receipt of the written notice and anticipated date of release of the deposit, provided there are no outstanding claims against the deposit.

(k) A judge of a superior court may order the return of the deposit prior to the expiration of two years upon evidence satisfactory to the judge that there are no outstanding claims against the deposit or order the Secretary of State to retain the deposit for a specified period beyond the two years pursuant to

subdivision (j) to resolve outstanding claims against the deposit account.

(*l*) The Secretary of State shall charge a filing fee not to exceed the cost of filing the bond or deposit filed in lieu of a bond pursuant to Section 995.710 of the Code of Civil Procedure.

(m) The Secretary of State shall enforce the provisions of this chapter that govern the filing and maintenance of bonds and deposits in lieu of bonds. *(Added by Stats.1989, c. 704, § 2. Amended by Stats.1996, c. 633 (S.B.1978), § 13; Stats.1998, c. 829 (S.B.1652), § 13; Stats.2002, c. 784 (S.B.1316), § 17.)*

Law Revision Commission Comments

Subdivision (k) of Section 1812.515 is amended to reflect unification of the municipal and superior courts pursuant to Article VI, Section 5(e), of the California Constitution. [32 Cal.L.Rev.Comm. Reports 78 (2002)].

Research References

Rutter, Cal. Practice Guide: Enforcing Judgments/Debts Ch. 4-A, A. Attachment.
Rutter, Cal. Practice Guide: Insurance Litigation Ch. 6I-B, B. Particular Surety Bond Coverages.
3 Witkin, California Summary 10th Agency and Employment § 433, (S 433) Bond or Deposit.

§ 1812.516.　Contracts; cancellation

(a) Every job listing service shall give a written contract to every jobseeker from whom a fee or deposit is to be received, whether directly or indirectly. The original and one copy of the contract shall be given to the jobseeker at the time the jobseeker signs the contract and before the job listing service accepts any fee or deposit or the jobseeker becomes obligated to pay any such fee or deposit. The contract shall contain all of the following:

(1) The name of the job listing service and the addresses and telephone numbers of the principal office of the job listing service and the location providing the listing services to the jobseeker.

(2) The amount of the fee to be charged and to be collected from the jobseeker.

(3) A description of the service to be performed by the job listing service, including significant conditions, restrictions, and limitations where applicable.

(4) A description of the jobseeker's specifications for the employment opportunity in clear language understandable to the jobseeker, including, but not limited to, the following:

(A) Kind of work or employment.

(B) Interests of jobseeker.

(C) Qualifications of jobseeker.

(D) Daily hours of work, the wages or salary, benefits, and other conditions of employment.

(E) Location of job.

(5) The contract expiration date, which shall not be later than 90 days from the date of execution of the contract.

(6) The following statement, in immediate proximity to the space reserved for the jobseeker's signature, in type no smaller than 10-point boldfaced type:

YOUR RIGHT TO CANCEL

/enter date of transaction/

"You may cancel this contract for job listing services without any penalty or obligation, if notice of cancellation is given, in writing, within three business days from the above date.

"To cancel this contract, just mail or deliver a signed and dated copy of the following cancellation notice or any other written notice of cancellation, to (name of job listing service) at (address of its place of business), NOT LATER THAN MID-NIGHT OF /date/."

CANCELLATION NOTICE

I hereby cancel this contract.

Dated: _____

_____ Customer's Signature"

Until the job listing service has complied with this section the jobseeker may cancel the job listing service's contract.

(7) The following statement, with the caption in type no smaller than 10-point boldfaced type and the remainder in a size no smaller than that generally used throughout the contract, and in full capitals, boldface, or italics:

"RIGHT TO REFUND"

"If, within seven business days after payment of a fee or deposit, the job listing service has not supplied you with at least three available employment opportunities meeting the specifications of the contract as to type of job; interests of jobseeker; qualifications of jobseeker; hours, salary, benefits, and other conditions of employment; location of job; and any other specifications expressly set forth in the contract, the full amount of the fee or deposit paid shall be refunded to you upon your request.

"If you do not obtain a job through the services of the job listing service, or if you obtain employment which lasts less than 90 days, any amount paid in fees or deposits in excess of a twenty-five dollar ($25) service charge shall be refunded to you, upon your request after expiration of the contract.

"Any refund due must be made to you within 10 days of your request. If the refund is not made in that time, the job listing service must pay to you an additional sum equal to the amount of your fee or deposit."

(8) If any labor trouble exists at the place of employment, that fact shall be stated in the listing of that employment provided to the jobseeker.

(b) All contracts shall be dated and shall be made and numbered consecutively in triplicate, the original and each copy to be signed by the jobseeker and the person acting for the job listing service. The original and one copy shall be given to the jobseeker and the other copy shall be kept on file at the job listing service.

(c) The full agreement between the parties shall be contained in a single document containing those elements set forth in this section. *(Added by Stats.1989, c. 704, § 2. Amended by Stats.1990, c. 1256 (A.B.2649), § 6.)*

Research References

3 Witkin, California Summary 10th Agency and Employment § 441, Contracts and Fees.

§ 1812.517. Fees; schedule; payment terms; notice; change; confession of judgment, note, or wage assignment as payment; splitting

(a)(1) A job listing service shall provide a copy of the service's fee schedule and payment terms to any jobseeker from whom a fee or deposit is to be received, prior to the jobseeker being interviewed by a counselor or other agent or employee.

(2) In the schedule, the maximum fee shall be fixed and shall include the charges of every kind rendered by the job listing service in each case or transaction on behalf of the prospective employee. Changes in the fee schedule may be made, but no change shall become effective until posted for not less than seven days in a conspicuous place in the job listing service.

(3) A copy of the schedule in effect shall be kept posted in the job listing service in a conspicuous place, and the posted schedule and the changes therein shall be in lettering or printing of not less than standard pica capitals. The date of the taking effect of the schedule and of each change therein shall appear on the posted copies.

(4) A copy of all fee schedules, and of all changes therein, shall be kept on file at the job listing service, retrospectively, for a period of one year.

(b) No fee charged or collected shall be in excess of the fee as scheduled.

(c) No job listing service may take from a jobseeker a confession of judgment, a promissory note or notes, or an assignment of wages to cover its fees.

(d) The fee charged shall not be based on a portion or percentage of the salary or wages earned or to be earned in the employment obtained through use of the job listing service.

(e)(1) No job listing service shall divide fees with an employer, an agent, or other employee of any employer or person to whom help is furnished.

(2) No job listing service shall charge any jobseeker a fee for accepting employment with that job listing service or any subsidiary of that service.

(3) No job listing service shall charge any jobseeker a fee when help is furnished to an employer, an agent, any employee of any employer, a member, or person who has a financial interest in the job listing service. *(Added by Stats.1989, c. 704, § 2.)*

Research References

3 Witkin, California Summary 10th Agency and Employment § 441, Contracts and Fees.

§ 1812.518. Refunds; failure to meet contract specifications; job not obtained or lasting less than 90 days; penalty

(a)(1) A job listing service shall refund in full any advance fee paid and cancel any other obligation incurred by the jobseeker if the job listing service does not, within seven business days after execution of the contract, supply at least three employment opportunities then available to the jobseeker and meeting the specifications of the contract.

(2) A job listing service will be deemed to have supplied information meeting the specifications of the jobseeker if the information supplied meets the contract specifications with reference to: type of job; interests of jobseeker; qualifications of jobseeker; hours, salary, benefits, and other conditions of employment; location of job; and any other specifications expressly set forth in the contract.

(b) A job listing service shall refund any amount over and above a twenty-five dollar ($25) service charge and cancel any other obligation incurred by the jobseeker if the jobseeker does not obtain a job, or if employment, once obtained, lasts less than 90 days.

(c) A job listing service shall make all refunds required under this section within 10 days after the jobseeker requests such refund. Unless the refund is made within that time, the job listing service shall pay the jobseeker an additional sum equal to the amount of the deposit. *(Added by Stats.1989, c. 704, § 2.)*

Research References

3 Witkin, California Summary 10th Agency and Employment § 441, Contracts and Fees.

§ 1812.519. Job order; prerequisite to fee acceptance; conditions; referrals; exchange with employment agency

(a) No job listing service shall accept a fee from any jobseeker, or send any jobseeker for employment, without having obtained, in writing, a bona fide job order for employment.

(b) A job listing service shall identify itself as a job listing service to the employer in all instances in which it contacts an employer for the purposes of soliciting a job order. All job orders shall be recorded in writing. A job order for employment shall be considered to have been given by an employer to a job listing service under the following conditions:

(1) The employer, or his or her agent, in writing, registers a request or gives permission that the job listing service recruit or refer jobseekers who meet the employer's stated job specifications and the employer furnishes such information as required by subdivision (a) of Section 1812.516.

(2) A job order is valid for the referral of any qualified jobseeker until it is filled or canceled by the employer, and may serve as the basis for job listing service advertising. The job listing service is required to recontact the employer within the four-day period immediately preceding dissemination of the job listing information to ensure that the position is still vacant prior to any additional advertising or referral of jobseekers.

(c) No job listing service shall refer a jobseeker to a job knowing or having reason to know that:

(1) The job does not exist or the jobseeker is not qualified for the job.

(2) The job has been described or advertised by or on behalf of the job listing service in a false, misleading, or deceptive manner.

(3) The job listing service has not obtained written permission to list the job from the employer or an authorized agent of the employer.

(d) No job listing service shall exchange job orders with an employment agency which charges a placement fee. *(Added by Stats.1989, c. 704, § 2. Amended by Stats.1991, c. 654 (A.B. 1893), § 51.)*

Research References

3 Witkin, California Summary 10th Agency and Employment § 442, Job Orders and Advertisements.

§ 1812.520. False or misleading representations; advertisements; contents; records

(a) No job listing service shall make or cause to be made any false, misleading or deceptive advertisements or representations concerning the services that the job listing service will provide to jobseekers.

(b)(1) No job listing service shall publish or cause to be published any false, fraudulent, or misleading information, representation, notice, or advertisements.

(2) All advertisements of a job listing service shall contain the correct name of the job listing service and one of the following:

(A) The street address of the job listing service's place of business.

(B) The correct telephone number of the job listing service at its place of business.

(3) No job listing service shall give any false information or make any false promises or representations concerning an engagement or employment to any jobseeker.

(4) No job listing service shall, by its choice of name or by advertisement or representation, represent itself to be an employment agency or to perform the services of an employment agency.

(c) Special requirements not usually associated with a job shall be specified in any advertisement. When the location of the position advertised is more than 50 miles from the job listing service office responsible for the advertisement, it shall state either the location or that the job is "nonlocal." Special benefits of the job, if advertised, shall be specifically described and substitute terms or symbols such as "extras" or "+" shall not be sufficient.

(d) An advertised salary shall be based upon the starting salary contained in the job order. An advertised range of starting salaries shall be specified by preceding the minimum salary and maximum salary by terms "from" and "to" respectively. When the job order contains only the maximum amount of a salary range, that advertised salary shall be preceded by the word "to." If a maximum salary is dependent upon the jobseeker's experience, the advertised salary may be described by listing the minimum salary and the term "up Depending on Experience" or "up D.O.E." The words "open" and "negotiable" or words or symbols of like import shall not be used as a substitute for the salary. If an advertised salary is based in whole or in part on commissions, that fact shall be indicated in the advertisement.

(e) All job listing services shall maintain a record of all advertised jobs, correlated to show the date and the publication in which the advertisement appeared and the job order number of each job advertised, retrospectively for a period of one year. *(Added by Stats.1989, c. 704, § 2. Amended by Stats.1990, c. 1256, (A.B.2649), § 7.)*

Research References

3 Witkin, California Summary 10th Agency and Employment § 442, Job Orders and Advertisements.

§ 1812.521. Illegal employment; minors; labor contract; union membership; labor trouble; notice

(a) No job listing service shall, when employment would be in violation of Chapter 1 (commencing with Section 1171) of Part 4 of Division 2 of the Labor Code or Part 27 (commencing with Section 48000) of the Education Code, accept any application for employment made by, or on behalf of, any minor, or place or assist in placing any minor in that employment.

(b) Every job listing service shall notify each jobseeker before sending the jobseeker in response to a request for employment whether a labor contract is in existence at the establishment to which the jobseeker is being sent, and whether union membership is required.

(c) No job listing service shall send a jobseeker to any place where a strike, lockout, or other labor trouble exists without notifying the jobseeker of that fact and shall in addition thereto enter a statement of those conditions upon the contract or receipt given to the jobseeker. *(Added by Stats.1989, c. 704, § 2. Amended by Stats.1990, c. 1256, (A.B.2649), § 8.)*

Research References

3 Witkin, California Summary 10th Agency and Employment § 440, in General.

CHAPTER 5. RECORDS

Section
1812.522. Inspection; reports; separation from records of other business.

§ 1812.522. Inspection; reports; separation from records of other business

(a) All books, records, files, the schedules, and other papers required by this title to be kept by any employment agency, employment counseling service, or job listing service shall be open at all reasonable hours to the inspection of the representative of the Attorney General, any district attorney, or any city attorney. Every employment agency, employment counseling service, and job listing service shall furnish to the representative of the Attorney General, any district attorney, or any city attorney upon request a true copy of those books, records, files, the schedules, and papers or any portion thereof, and shall make such reports as the Attorney General prescribes.

(b) If any employment agency, employment counseling service, or job listing service also engages in any other business which is not subject to this title, the records of the agency or service pertaining to matters under the jurisdictions of this title shall be kept separate and apart from the records of that other business. *(Added by Stats.1989, c. 704, § 2.)*

Research References

3 Witkin, California Summary 10th Agency and Employment § 432, (S 432) Access to Records.

CHAPTER 6. REMEDIES AND ENFORCEMENT

Section
1812.523. Misdemeanors; civil actions and proceedings; false or misleading representation voiding contract; refund; damages; attorney fees; costs; other laws; waiver of provisions; severability.

§ 1812.523. Misdemeanors; civil actions and proceedings; false or misleading representation voiding contract; refund; damages; attorney fees; costs; other laws; waiver of provisions; severability

(a) Any person who violates any provision of this title is guilty of a misdemeanor. The Attorney General, any district attorney, or any city attorney may prosecute misdemeanor actions.

(b) Actions for violation of this title, including, but not limited to, equity proceedings to restrain and enjoin such a violation, may be instituted by the Attorney General, any district attorney, or any city attorney. This section shall not be deemed to prohibit the enforcement by any person of any right provided by this or any other law.

(c) If any person uses any untrue or misleading statement, information, or advertisement to sell its services or fails to comply with the applicable provisions of this title, or the contract does not comply with the applicable provisions of this title, then the contract shall be void and unenforceable as contrary to public policy and the jobseeker, customer, or nurse shall be entitled to the return of all sums paid.

(d) Any person who is injured by any violation of this title or by the breach of a contract subject to this title may bring an action for the recovery of damages, an equity proceeding to restrain and enjoin those violations, or both. The amount awarded may be up to three times the damages actually incurred, but in no event less than the amount paid by the jobseeker, customer, or nurse to the person subject to this title. If the person subject to this title refuses or is unwilling to pay the damages awarded, the amount awarded may be satisfied out of the security required by this title. If the plaintiff prevails, the plaintiff shall be awarded a reasonable attorney's fee and costs. If the court determines that the breach or violation was willful, by clear and convincing evidence, the court, in its discretion, may award punitive damages in addition to the amounts set forth above.

(e) The provisions of this title are not exclusive and do not relieve the parties subject to this title from the duty to comply with all other applicable laws.

(f) The remedies provided in this title are not exclusive and shall be in addition to any other remedies or procedures provided in any other law.

(g) Any waiver by the consumer, jobseeker, or nurse of the provisions of this title shall be deemed contrary to public policy and shall be void and unenforceable. Any attempt by a person subject to this title to have a jobseeker, customer, or nurse waive rights given by this title shall constitute a violation of this title.

(h) If any provisions of this title or the application thereof to any person or circumstances is held unconstitutional, the remainder of the title and the application of that provision to other persons and circumstances shall not be affected thereby. *(Added by Stats.1989, c. 704, § 2.)*

Research References

3 Witkin, California Summary 10th Agency and Employment § 431, (S 431) Remedies and Enforcement.

CHAPTER 7. NURSES' REGISTRIES

Section
1812.524. Definitions.
1812.525. Bond; deposit in lieu of bond.
1812.526. Continuing contract; contents.
1812.527. Fees; schedule; payment terms; notice; change.
1812.528. Experience, training, license; verification.
1812.529. Records.
1812.530. Registration fee; confession of judgment, note, or wage assignment as fee payment.
1812.531. Splitting fees.
1812.532. Failure to obtain or be paid for assignment; refund; delay; penalty.
1812.533. False or misleading representations; advertisements; contents.

§ 1812.524. Definitions

(a) "Nursing service" means the assignment of a nurse, as a private duty, self-employed, licensed registered nurse, licensed vocational nurse, or practical nurse to render service to a patient under the direction or supervision of a physician or surgeon registered to practice in this state.

(b) "Nurses' registry" means a person who engages in the business of obtaining and filling commitments for nursing service. A nurses' registry which makes or plans to make referrals for nurses' employment other than private duty nursing shall comply with Chapters 1 (commencing with Section 1812.500) and 2 (commencing with Section 1812.503) of this title with respect to those referrals.

(c) "Private duty nurse" means a self-employed nurse rendering service in the care of either a physically or mentally ill patient under the direction of a physician or surgeon, but who is paid by either the patient or the designated agent of the patient and who accepts the responsibilities of a self-employed private contractor. *(Added by Stats.1989, c. 704, § 2. Amended by Stats.1990, c. 1256, (A.B.2649), § 9.)*

Research References

3 Witkin, California Summary 10th Agency and Employment § 443, in General.

§ 1812.525. Bond; deposit in lieu of bond

(a) Every nurses' registry subject to this title shall maintain a bond issued by a surety company admitted to do business in this state. The principal sum of the bond shall be three thousand dollars ($3,000). A copy of the bond shall be filed with the Secretary of State.

(b) The bond required by this section shall be in favor of, and payable to, the people of the State of California, and shall be conditioned that the person obtaining the bond will comply with this title and will pay all sums due any individual or group of individuals when the person or his or her representative, agent, or employee has received those sums. The bond shall be for the benefit of any person or persons damaged by any violation of this title or by fraud, dishonesty, misstatement, misrepresentation, deceit, unlawful acts or omissions, or failure to provide the services of the nurses' registry in performance of the contract with the nurse by the nurses' registry or its agents, representatives, or employees while acting within the scope of their employment.

(c)(1) No nurses' registry shall conduct any business without having a current surety bond in the amount prescribed by this title and filing a copy of the bond with the Secretary of State.

(2) Thirty days prior to the cancellation or termination of any surety bond required by this section, the surety shall send a written notice of that cancellation or termination to both the nurses' registry and the Secretary of State, identifying the bond and the date of cancellation or termination.

(3) If any nurses' registry fails to obtain a new bond and file a copy of that bond with the Secretary of State by the effective date of the cancellation or termination of the former bond, the nurses' registry shall cease to conduct any business unless and until a new surety bond is obtained and a copy of that bond is filed with the Secretary of State.

(d) When a deposit has been made in lieu of a bond pursuant to Section 995.710 of the Code of Civil Procedure, the person asserting a claim against the deposit shall, in lieu of Section 996.430 of the Code of Civil Procedure, establish the claim by furnishing evidence to the Secretary of State of a money judgment entered by a court together with evidence that the claimant is a person described in subdivision (b).

(e) When a person has established the claim with the Secretary of State, the Secretary of State shall review and approve the claim and enter the date of approval on the claim. The claim shall be designated an "approved claim."

(f) When the first claim against a particular deposit has been approved, it shall not be paid until the expiration of a period of 240 days after the date of its approval by the Secretary of State. Subsequent claims that are approved by the Secretary of State within the same 240–day period shall similarly not be paid until the expiration of the 240–day period. Upon the expiration of the 240–day period, the Secretary of State shall pay all approved claims from that 240–day period in full unless the deposit is insufficient, in which case each approved claim shall be paid a pro rata share of the deposit.

(g) When the Secretary of State approves the first claim against a particular deposit after the expiration of a 240–day period, the date of approval of that claim shall begin a new 240–day period to which subdivision (f) shall apply with respect to the amount remaining in the deposit.

(h) After a deposit is exhausted, no further claims shall be paid by the Secretary of State. Claimants who have had their claims paid in full or in part pursuant to subdivisions (f) and (g) shall not be required to return funds received from the deposit for the benefit of other claimants.

(i) When a deposit has been made in lieu of a bond, the amount of the deposit shall not be subject to attachment, garnishment, or execution with respect to an action or judgment against the nurses' registry, other than as to an amount as no longer needed or required for the purpose of this title that would otherwise be returned to the nurses' registry by the Secretary of State.

(j) The Secretary of State shall retain a cash deposit for two years from the date the Secretary of State receives written notification from the assignor of the deposit that the assignor has ceased to engage in the business of a nurses' registry or has filed a bond pursuant to subdivision (a), provided that there are no outstanding claims against the deposit. The written notice to the Secretary of State shall include all of the following: (1) name, address, and telephone number of the assignor; (2) name, address, and telephone number of the bank at which the deposit is located; (3) account number of the deposit; and (4) a statement whether the assignor is ceasing to engage in the business of a nurses' registry or has filed a bond with the Secretary of State. The Secretary of State shall forward an acknowledgment of receipt of the written notice to the assignor at the address indicated therein, specifying the date of receipt of the written notice and anticipated date of release of the deposit, provided there are no outstanding claims against the deposit.

(k) A judge of a superior court may order the return of the deposit prior to the expiration of two years upon evidence satisfactory to the judge that there are no outstanding claims against the deposit or order the Secretary of State to retain the deposit for a specified period beyond the two years pursuant to subdivision (j) to resolve outstanding claims against the deposit.

(*l*) The Secretary of State shall charge a filing fee not to exceed the cost of filing the bond or deposit filed in lieu of a bond pursuant to Section 995.710 of the Code of Civil Procedure.

(m) The Secretary of State shall enforce the provisions of this chapter that govern the filing and maintenance of bonds and deposits in lieu of bonds. *(Added by Stats.1989, c. 704, § 2. Amended by Stats.1996, c. 633 (S.B.1978), § 14; Stats.1998, c. 829 (S.B.1652), § 14; Stats.2002, c. 784 (S.B.1316), § 18.)*

Law Revision Commission Comments

Subdivision (k) of Section 1812.525 is amended to reflect unification of the municipal and superior courts pursuant to Article VI, Section 5(e), of the California Constitution. [32 Cal.L.Rev.Comm. Reports 80 (2002)].

Research References

Rutter, Cal. Practice Guide: Enforcing Judgments/Debts Ch. 4-A, A. Attachment.

Rutter, Cal. Practice Guide: Insurance Litigation Ch. 6I-B, B. Particular Surety Bond Coverages.

3 Witkin, California Summary 10th Agency and Employment § 433, (S 433) Bond or Deposit.

§ 1812.526. Continuing contract; contents

Nurses' registries may enter into a continuing contract with private duty nurses covering the assignment of those nurses by the nurses' registries. The continuing contract shall state:

(a) The name, address, and telephone number of the nurses' registry.

(b) The name, address, and telephone number of the nurse.

(c) The current fee schedule of the nurses' registry.

(d) The date of its execution by the nurses' registry and the nurse.

(e) The contract shall specify that the provisions thereof are to govern only the assignment of private duty nurses and shall do all of the following:

(1) Designate the nurses' registry as the continuous agent of the nurse for purposes of assignment.

(2) Provide that the contract in effect may be terminated at any time by written notice given by one to the other for any future assignment.

(3) Provide for delivery to the nurse at the time of the execution of the contract a written schedule of the rates of nurses' charges currently agreed to between the nurses' registry and the nurse for the nurse's services to the patient.

(4) State that the nurses' registry will immediately notify the nurse in writing of all subsequent changes in the rates to be charged the patient for services, and that the nurse shall agree to abide by these rates.

(5) Contain express undertakings by the nurses' registry that it shall continuously maintain true and correct records of orders and assignments as provided in this title.

(6) Provide that the nurses' registry shall periodically and at least once each month render to the nurse a written statement of all fees claimed to be due the nurses' registry, and further that the statement shall adequately identify each assignment as to the inception date and period of service covered by the claim, including the name of the patient and the amount of service fee claimed.

(7) Contain appropriate wording advising the nurse of his or her right to dispute the correctness of any service fee claimed by the nurses' registry in the written statement referred to above, and that in the absence of objections within a reasonable time, any such service fee may be presumed to be correctly charged.

(8) Include any other term, condition, or understanding agreed upon between the nurses' registry and the nurse.

(f) Each contract shall be numbered consecutively in original and duplicate, both to be signed by the nurse and the nurses' registry. The original shall be given to the nurse and the duplicate shall be kept on file at the nurses' registry within the nurse's records.

(g) The full agreement between the parties shall be contained in a single document containing those elements set forth in this section. *(Added by Stats.1989, c. 704, § 2. Amended by Stats.1990, c. 1256, (A.B.2649), § 10.)*

Research References

3 Witkin, California Summary 10th Agency and Employment § 444, Contracts and Fees.

§ 1812.527. Fees; schedule; payment terms; notice; change

(a)(1)[1] A nurses' registry shall provide a copy of the registry's fee schedule and payment terms to any nurse from whom a fee or deposit is to be received, prior to the nurse being interviewed by the registry.

(2) In the schedule, the maximum fee shall be fixed and shall include the charges of every kind rendered by the nurses' registry in each case or transaction on behalf of the nurse. Changes in the fee schedule may be made, but no change shall become effective until posted for not less than seven days in a conspicuous place in the nurses' registry.

(3) A copy of the schedule in effect shall be kept posted in the nurses' registry in a conspicuous place, and the posted schedule and the changes therein shall be in lettering or printing of not less than standard pica capitals. The date of the taking effect of the schedule and of each change therein shall appear on the posted copies.

(4) A copy of all fee schedules, and of all changes therein, shall be kept on file at the nurses' registry, retrospectively for a period of one year. *(Added by Stats.1989, c. 704, § 2.)*

[1] So in enrolled bill.

Research References

3 Witkin, California Summary 10th Agency and Employment § 444, Contracts and Fees.

§ 1812.528. Experience, training, license; verification

It shall be the duty of the nurses' registry to verify in writing the claims as to the experience or training listed on the application and to keep a file of those records in the nurse's folder within the nurses' registry. It shall also be the duty of the person interviewing the jobseeker to require the jobseeker to exhibit his or her license as issued by the Board of Registered Nursing or the Board of Vocational Nurse and Psychiatric Technician Examiners, with a notation to be made on the application by the interviewer that the license has been inspected and the date of expiration of the license. *(Added by Stats.1989, c. 704, § 2.)*

Research References

3 Witkin, California Summary 10th Agency and Employment § 443, in General.

§ 1812.529. Records

Each nurses' registry shall continuously maintain in its offices true and correct permanent log sheets and other records which shall disclose, in addition to the other information required, the date and hour of the receipt by the nurses' registry of each order for a private duty nurse, and the date and hour of the making or giving of each assignment to the nurse by the nurses' registry, the name of the nurse assigned, the name of the patient and the address where the nurse is assigned, the name of the attending physician, the date the assignment is to start, the period of actual service for each assignment, and the amount of the fee charged for each assignment. No nurses' registry, his or her agent or employees, shall make any false entry in those records. The nurses' registry shall maintain the log sheets and records required by this section respectively for a period of one year. *(Added by Stats.1989. c. 704, § 2.)*

Research References

3 Witkin, California Summary 10th Agency and Employment § 443, in General.

§ 1812.530. Registration fee; confession of judgment, note, or wage assignment as fee payment

(a) No nurses' registry shall accept, directly or indirectly, a registration fee of any kind.

(b) No nurses' registry may take from a nurse a confession of judgment, or promissory note, or an assignment of wages to cover its fees. *(Added by Stats.1989, c. 704, § 2.)*

Research References

3 Witkin, California Summary 10th Agency and Employment § 444, Contracts and Fees.

§ 1812.531. Splitting fees

No nurses' registry shall divide fees with any physician and surgeon, nurse, hospital, patient, or any agent or employee of any of these. *(Added by Stats.1989, c. 704, § 2.)*

Research References

3 Witkin, California Summary 10th Agency and Employment § 444, Contracts and Fees.

§ 1812.532. Failure to obtain or be paid for assignment; refund; delay; penalty

In the event that a nurses' registry collects from a nurse a fee or expenses for an assignment, and the nurse fails to obtain the assignment, or the nurse fails to be paid for the assignment, the nurses' registry shall upon demand therefor, repay to the nurse the fee and expenses so collected. Unless repayment is made within 48 hours after demand, the nurses' registry shall pay to the nurse an additional sum equal to the amount of the fee. *(Added by Stats.1989, c. 704, § 2.)*

Research References

3 Witkin, California Summary 10th Agency and Employment § 444, Contracts and Fees.

§ 1812.533. False or misleading representations; advertisements; contents

(a) No nurses' registry shall make, or cause to be made, any false, misleading, or deceptive advertisements or representations concerning the services that registry will provide to nurses.

(b)(1) No nurses' registry shall publish or cause to be published any false, fraudulent, or misleading information, representation, notice, or advertisements.

(2) All advertisements of a nurses' registry shall contain the correct name of the nurses' registry and one of the following:

(A) The street address of the registry's place of business.

(B) The correct telephone number of the registry at its place of business.

(3) No nurses' registry shall give any false information or make any false promises or representations concerning an assignment or employment to any nurse who registers or applies for an assignment or employment.

(4) No nurses' registry shall, by its name, advertisement, or any other representation, represent itself to be a home health agency, as defined by subdivision (a) of Section 1727 of the Health and Safety Code, or to perform the services of a home health agency. A nurses' registry shall provide a written disclosure to each individual receiving nursing services, as defined in subdivision (a) of Section 1812.524, in his or her place of residence stating that it does not perform the services of a home health agency and clearly describing that it is a nurses' registry only and that any complaints against licensed personnel providing a nursing service shall be brought to the local district attorney and the Department of Consumer Affairs. The address and telephone number of each agency and board to which complaints are required to be submitted shall be provided to all patients prior to the time they are under the care of any nursing services personnel.

(5) Any person may refer complaints concerning nurses' registries to the proper law enforcement agency for action.

(c) Every nurses' registry shall maintain a record of all advertisements, correlated to show the date and the publication in which the advertisement appeared, retrospectively for a period of one year. *(Added by Stats.1989, c. 704, § 2. Amended by Stats.1990, c. 761, (A.B.3924), § 2.)*

Research References

3 Witkin, California Summary 10th Agency and Employment § 443, in General.

CHAPTER 8. LONG–TERM CARE FACILITIES

§ 1812.540. Definitions

For purposes of this chapter, the following definitions shall apply:

(a) "Direct care service" means the temporary assignment of certified nurse assistants to render basic care services directed at the safety, comfort, personal hygiene, or protection of a patient who is a resident of a long-term health care facility.

(b) "Nursing service" means the temporary assignment of a licensed registered nurse, licensed vocational nurse, or psychiatric technician to render nursing and basic care services to a patient who is a resident of a long-term health care facility.

(c) "Licensed nursing staff" means a licensed registered nurse, licensed vocational nurse, or psychiatric technician.

(d) "Long-term health care facility" means a licensed facility, as defined in Section 1418 of the Health and Safety Code. *(Added by Stats.2001, c. 326 (A.B.1643), § 2.)*

Research References

3 Witkin, California Summary 10th Agency and Employment § 445, in General.

§ 1812.541. Information or material to be provided to long-term health care facility with respect to the referral of a temporary certified nurse assistant

Every employment agency that refers temporary certified nurse assistants to an employer that is a long-term health care facility shall provide the employer with all of the following:

(a) Written verification that the employment agency has verified that any certified nurse assistant referred by the agency is registered on the state registry of certified nurse assistants and is in good standing. The employment agency shall provide to the employer the certified nurse assistant's professional certification number and date of expiration.

(b) A statement that the certified nurse assistant has at least six months of experience working in a long-term health care facility.

(c) A statement that the certified nurse assistant has had a health examination within 90 days prior to employment with the employment agency or seven days after employment with the employment agency and at least annually thereafter by a person lawfully authorized to perform that procedure. Each examination shall include a medical history and physical evaluation. The employment agency shall also provide verification that the individual has had tuberculosis screening within 90 days prior to employment and annually thereafter.

(d) A statement that the certified nurse assistant will participate in the facility's orientation program and any in-service training programs at the request of the long-term health care employer.

(e) A statement that a certified nurse assistant is in compliance with the in-service training requirements of paragraph (1) of subdivision (a) of Section 1337.6 of the Health and Safety Code. *(Added by Stats.2001, c. 326 (A.B.1643), § 2.)*

§ 1812.542. Information or material to be provided to long-term health care facility with respect to the referral of a temporary licensed nursing staff

Every employment agency that refers temporary licensed nursing staff to an employer who is a licensed long-term health care facility shall provide the employer with all of the following:

(a) Written verification that the individual is in good standing with the Board of Registered Nursing or the Board of Vocational Nursing and Psychiatric Technicians, as applicable, and has successfully secured a criminal record clearance. The employment agency shall provide to the employer the individual's professional license and registration number and date of expiration.

(b) A statement that the licensed nursing staff person has had a health examination within 90 days prior to employment with the employment agency or seven days after employment with the employment agency and at least annually thereafter by a person lawfully authorized to perform that procedure. Each examination shall include a medical history and physical evaluation. The employment agency shall also provide verification that the individual has had tuberculosis screening within 90 days prior to employment and annually thereafter. *(Added by Stats.2001, c. 326 (A.B.1643), § 2.)*

§ 1812.543. Adoption of policies and procedures by employment agency regarding prevention of resident or patient abuse by temporary staff

(a) An employment agency that makes referrals of licensed nursing staff or certified nurse assistants for temporary employment in a long-term health care facility shall adopt policies and procedures regarding prevention of resident or patient abuse by temporary staff.

(b) The employment agency shall provide written verification to the long-term health care facility that any certified nurse assistants or licensed nursing staff referred by the agency do not have any unresolved allegations against them involving the mistreatment, neglect, or abuse of a patient, including injuries of unknown source and misappropriation of resident property.

(c) No temporary staff person referred by an employment agency may be solely responsible for a unit unless that person has received a full orientation to the facility and the applicable unit for which he or she is assigned.

(d) Upon the request of the State Department of Health Services, an employment agency shall provide a list of temporary employees who have been referred to a specified facility during the period in which the facility is involved in a labor action.

(e) An employment agency shall require that any employee referred to a long-term care facility be identified as a temporary staff person in the facility's daily staffing levels required to be posted in accordance with the standards set forth in Section 941 of Appendix F of Public Law 106–554 (42 U.S.C. Sec. 1395i–3(b)(8) and 42 U.S.C. Sec. 1395r(b)(8)). *(Added by Stats.2001, c. 326 (A.B.1643), § 2.)*

§ 1812.544. Maintaining records of all advertisements by employment agencies making referrals of licensed nursing staff or certified nurse assistants for temporary employment in a long-term health care facility

(a) Every employment agency that makes referrals of licensed nursing staff or certified nurse assistants for temporary employment in a long-term health care facility shall maintain a record of all advertisements, showing the date of publication and the publication in which the advertisement appeared, for a period of one year from the date of the advertisement.

(b) No employment agency that makes referrals for employment to a long-term health care facility shall, by its name, advertisement, or any other representation, represent itself to be a home health agency, as defined by subdivision (a) of Section 1727 of the Health and Safety Code, or to perform the services of a home health agency. The employment agency shall provide a written disclosure to each employer stating that it does not perform the services of a home health agency and clearly describing that it is an employment agency only.

(c) Any facility or individual may refer complaints concerning employment agencies which place licensed nursing staff or certified nurse assistants in long-term health care facilities to the appropriate licensing, certification, ombudsman, adult protective services, or proper law enforcement agency for action. *(Added by Stats.2001, c. 326 (A.B.1643), § 2.)*

Title 2.95

AUCTIONEER AND AUCTION COMPANIES

§ 1812.600. Necessity of surety bond; amount; cancellation; deposits in lieu of bonds; enforcement; civil penalties; attorney fees

(a) Every auctioneer and auction company shall maintain a bond issued by a surety company admitted to do business in this state. The principal sum of the bond shall be twenty thousand dollars ($20,000). A copy of the bond shall be filed with the Secretary of State.

(b) The bond required by this section shall be in favor of, and payable to, the people of the State of California and shall be for the benefit of any person or persons damaged by any fraud, dishonesty, misstatement, misrepresentation, deceit, unlawful acts or omissions, or failure to provide the services of the auctioneer or auction company in performance of the auction by the auctioneer or auction company or its agents, representatives, or employees while acting within the scope of their employment.

(c)(1) No auctioneer or auction company shall conduct any business without having a current surety bond in the amount prescribed by this section and without filing a copy of the bond with the Secretary of State.

(2) Thirty days prior to the cancellation or termination of any surety bond required by this section, the surety shall send a written notice of that cancellation or termination to both the auctioneer or auction company and the Secretary of State, identifying the bond and the date of cancellation or termination.

(3) If any auctioneer or auction company fails to obtain a new bond and file a copy of that bond with the Secretary of State by the effective date of the cancellation or termination of the former bond, the auctioneer or auction company shall cease to conduct any business unless and until that time as a new surety bond is obtained and a copy of that bond is filed with the Secretary of State.

(d) A deposit may be made in lieu of a bond as set forth in Section 995.710 of the Code of Civil Procedure. When a deposit is made in lieu of the bond, the person asserting the claim against the deposit shall establish the claim by furnishing evidence to the Secretary of State of a money judgment entered by a court together with evidence that the claimant is a person described in subdivision (b).

(e) When a claimant has established the claim with the Secretary of State, the Secretary of State shall review and approve the claim and enter the date of approval on the claim. The claim shall be designated an "approved claim."

(f) When the first claim against a particular deposit has been approved, it shall not be paid until the expiration of a period of 240 days after the date of its approval by the Secretary of State. Subsequent claims that are approved by the Secretary of State within the same 240–day period shall similarly not be paid until the expiration of the 240–day period. Upon expiration of the 240–day period, the Secretary of State shall pay all approved claims from that 240–day period in full unless the deposit is insufficient, in which case each approved claim shall be paid a pro rata share of the deposit.

(g) When the Secretary of State approves the first claim against a particular deposit after the expiration of a 240–day period, the date of approval of that claim shall begin a new 240–day period to which subdivision (f) shall apply with respect to any amount remaining in the deposit.

(h) After a deposit is exhausted, no further claims shall be paid by the Secretary of State. Claimants who have had their claims paid in full or in part pursuant to subdivision (f) or (g) shall not be required to return funds received from the deposit for the benefit of other claimants.

(i) When a deposit has been made in lieu of a bond, the amount of the deposit shall not be subject to attachment, garnishment, or execution with respect to an action or judgment against the auctioneer or auction company, other than as to that amount that is no longer needed or required for the purpose of this section that otherwise would be returned to the auctioneer or auction company by the Secretary of State.

(j) The Secretary of State shall retain a cash deposit for two years from the date the Secretary of State receives written notification from the assignor of the deposit that the assignor has ceased to engage in the business of an auctioneer or auction company or has filed a bond pursuant to subdivision (a), provided that there are no outstanding claims against the deposit. Written notification to the Secretary of State shall include all of the following: (1) name, address, and telephone number of the assignor; (2) name, address, and telephone number of the bank at which the deposit is located; (3) account number of the deposit; and (4) a statement whether the assignor is ceasing to engage in the business of an auctioneer or auction company or has filed a bond with the Secretary of State. The Secretary of State shall forward an acknowledgment of receipt of the written notice to the assignor at the address indicated in the notice, specifying the date of receipt of the written notice and anticipated date of release of the deposit, provided there are no outstanding claims against the deposit.

(k) A judge of a superior court may order the return of the deposit prior to the expiration of two years upon evidence satisfactory to the judge that there are no outstanding claims against the deposit or order the Secretary of State to retain the deposit for a specified period beyond the two years pursuant to subdivision (j) to resolve outstanding claims against the deposit.

(*l*) If an auctioneer or auction company fails to perform any of the duties specifically imposed upon him or her pursuant to this title, any person may maintain an action for enforcement of those duties or to recover a civil penalty in the amount of one thousand dollars ($1,000), or for both enforcement and recovery.

(m) In any action to enforce these duties or to recover civil penalties, or for both enforcement and recovery, the prevailing plaintiff shall be entitled to reasonable attorney's fees and costs, in addition to the civil penalties provided under subdivision (*l*).

(n) Notwithstanding the repeal of Chapter 3.7 (commencing with Section 5700) of Division 3 of the Business and Professions Code by the act adding this chapter, any cash security in lieu of the surety bond formerly required and authorized by former Chapter 3.7 (commencing with Section 5700) of Division 3 of the Business and Professions Code, shall be transferred to, and maintained by, the Secretary of State.

(*o*) The Secretary of State shall charge and collect a filing fee not to exceed the cost of filing the bond or deposit filed in lieu of a bond as set forth in Section 995.710 of the Code of Civil Procedure.

(p) The Secretary of State shall enforce the provisions of this chapter that govern the filing and maintenance of bonds and deposits in lieu of bonds. *(Added by Stats.1993, c. 1170 (A.B.259), § 2, eff. Oct. 11, 1993. Amended by Stats.1996, c. 633 (S.B.1978), § 15; Stats.1998, c. 829 (S.B.1652), § 15; Stats.2002, c. 784 (S.B.1316), § 19.)*

Law Revision Commission Comments

Subdivision (k) of Section 1812.600 is amended to reflect unification of the municipal and superior courts pursuant to Article VI, Section 5(e), of the California Constitution. [32 Cal.L.Rev.Comm. Reports 83 (2002)].

Research References

Rutter, Cal. Practice Guide: Enforcing Judgments/Debts Ch. 4-A, A. Attachment.
3 Witkin, California Summary 10th Agency and Employment § 43, Auctioneers.
14 Witkin, California Summary 10th Wills and Probate § 679, (S 679) Auctioneer.

§ 1812.601. Definitions

(a) "Advertisement" means any of the following:

(1) Any written or printed communication for the purpose of soliciting, describing, or offering to act as an auctioneer or provide auction company services, including any brochure, pamphlet, newspaper, periodical, or publication.

(2) A telephone or other directory listing caused or permitted by an auctioneer or auction company to be published that indicates the offer to practice auctioneering or auction company services.

(3) A radio, television, or similar airwave transmission that solicits or offers the practice of auctioneering or auction company services.

(b) "Auction" means a sale transaction conducted by means of oral or written exchanges, which include exchanges made in person or through electronic media, between an auctioneer and the members of his or her audience, which exchanges consist of a series of invitations for offers for the purchase of goods made by the auctioneer and offers to purchase made by members of the audience and culminate in the acceptance by the auctioneer of the highest or most favorable offer made by a member of the participating audience. However, auction does not include either of the following:

(1) A wholesale motor vehicle auction subject to regulation by the Department of Motor Vehicles.

(2) A sale of real estate or a sale in any sequence of real estate with personal property or fixtures or both in a unified sale pursuant to subparagraph (B) of paragraph (1) of subdivision (a) of Section 9604 of the Commercial Code.

(c) "Auction company" means any person who arranges, manages, sponsors, advertises, accounts for the proceeds of, or carries out auction sales at locations, including, but not limited to, any fixed location, including an auction barn, gallery place of business, sale barn, sale yard, sale pavilion, and the contiguous surroundings of each.

(d) "Auctioneer" means any individual who is engaged in, or who by advertising or otherwise holds himself or herself out as being available to engage in, the calling for, the recognition of, and the acceptance of, offers for the purchase of goods at an auction.

(e) "Employee" means an individual who works for an employer, is listed on the employer's payroll records, and is under the employer's control.

(f) "Employer" means a person who employs an individual for wages or salary, lists the individual on the person's payroll records, and withholds legally required deductions and contributions.

(g) "Goods" means any goods, wares, chattels, merchandise, or other personal property, including domestic animals and farm products.

(h) "Person" means an individual, corporation, partnership, trust, including a business trust, firm, association, organization, or any other form of business enterprise. *(Added by Stats.1993, c. 1170 (A.B.259), § 2, eff. Oct. 11, 1993. Amended by Stats.1994, c. 1010 (S.B.2053), § 46.1; Stats.1994, c.180 (A.B.375), § 2, eff. July 11, 1994; Stats.1999, c. 991 (S.B.45), § 5, operative July 1, 2001; Stats.2004, c. 194 (S.B.1832), § 1.)*

Research References

15 NO. 4 Miller & Starr, California Real Estate Newsalert 15, Recording and Priorities.

§ 1812.602. Restraining order; injunction

The superior court for the county in which any person has engaged or is about to engage in any act that constitutes a violation of this title may, upon a petition filed by any person, issue an injunction or other appropriate order restraining the violative conduct. Proceedings under this section shall be governed by Chapter 3 (commencing with Section 525) of Title 7 of Part 2 of the Code of Civil Procedure, except that no undertaking shall be required. *(Added by Stats.1993, c. 1170 (A.B.259), § 2, eff. Oct. 11, 1993.)*

Research References

3 Witkin, California Summary 10th Agency and Employment § 43, Auctioneers.

§ 1812.603. Restitution order; reimbursement for expenses; additional remedies

(a) The superior court for the county in which any person has engaged in any act that constitutes a violation of this title may, upon a petition filed by any person, order the person who committed the violation to make restitution to any person injured as a result of the violation.

(b) The court may order any person against whom an injunction or restraining order pursuant to subdivision (a), or an order requiring restitution pursuant to subdivision (b), is directed, to reimburse the petitioner for expenses incurred in the investigation related to its petition.

(c) The remedies set forth in this section are in addition to, and not a limitation on, the authority provided for in any other section of this code. *(Added by Stats.1993, c. 1170 (A.B.259), § 2, eff. Oct. 11, 1993.)*

Research References

3 Witkin, California Summary 10th Agency and Employment § 43, Auctioneers.

§ 1812.604. Violations; misdemeanor; punishment

Except as otherwise provided in this title, any person who violates any provision of this title is guilty of a misdemeanor, which offense is punishable by a fine not exceeding one thousand dollars ($1,000), or by imprisonment in a county jail for not more than one year, or by both that fine and imprisonment. In addition, upon a conviction of any violation of this chapter, or of any crime related to the conduct of an auctioneer, the court may issue an injunction and prohibit the convicted person from acting as an auctioneer or an auction company in this state, in which case the court shall inform the Secretary of State of that action. *(Added by Stats.1993, c. 1170 (A.B.259), § 2, eff. Oct. 11, 1993.)*

Research References

3 Witkin, California Summary 10th Agency and Employment § 43, Auctioneers.

§ 1812.605. Business of auctioneering; requirements

In conducting the business of auctioneering, each auctioneer and auction company, and the company's owners, partners, officers, agents, and employees, shall do all of the following:

(a) Follow all lawful requests of the owner or consignor of the goods being sold at auction with regard to the sale of those goods.

(b) Perform his or her duties so that the highest or most favorable offer made by a member of his or her audience is accepted, except to the extent that any item or sale is offered with reserve or subject to confirmation.

(c) Truthfully represent the goods to be auctioned.

(d) Otherwise perform his or her duties in accordance with the laws of this state. *(Added by Stats.1993, c. 1170 (A.B.259), § 2, eff. Oct. 11, 1993.)*

Research References

3 Witkin, California Summary 10th Agency and Employment § 43, Auctioneers.

§ 1812.606. Auctioneer or auction company; liability

Every auctioneer who operates his or her own auction company as a sole proprietor, and every auction company, together with its owners, partners, and officers, that employs an auctioneer, shall be responsible for all violations committed by the auctioneer or by any company employee in the conduct of auction business. An auctioneer who is employed by an auctioneer or auction company shall be responsible for all violations committed by him or her in the conduct of auction business.

It is a violation of this title for any auctioneer or auction company, or the company's owners, partners, and officers, to direct or knowingly permit any violation of this title by any auctioneer employed by or under contract with that auctioneer or auction company, or by any owner, partner, officer, agent, or employee of the auction company. *(Added by Stats.1993, c. 1170 (A.B.259), § 2, eff. Oct. 11, 1993.)*

Research References

3 Witkin, California Summary 10th Agency and Employment § 43, Auctioneers.

§ 1812.607. Requirements of auctioneer or auction company; punishment

Every auction company and auctioneer shall do all of the following:

(a) Disclose his or her name, trade or business name, telephone number, and bond number in all advertising of auctions. A first violation of this subdivision is an infraction subject to a fine of fifty dollars ($50); a second violation is subject to a fine of seventy-five dollars ($75); and a third or subsequent violation is subject to a fine of one hundred dollars ($100). This section shall not apply to business cards, business stationery, or to any advertisement that does not specify an auction date.

(b) Post a sign, the dimensions of which shall be at least 18 inches by 24 inches, at the main entrance to each auction, stating that the auction is being conducted in compliance with Section 2328 of the Commercial Code, Section 535 of the Penal Code, and the provisions of the California Civil Code. A first violation of this subdivision is an infraction subject to a fine of fifty dollars ($50); a second violation is subject to a fine of seventy-five dollars ($75); and a third or subsequent violation is subject to a fine of one hundred dollars ($100).

(c) Post or distribute to the audience the terms, conditions, restrictions, and procedures whereby goods will be sold at the auction, and announce any changes to those terms, conditions, restrictions, and procedures prior to the beginning of the auction sale. A first violation of this subdivision is an infraction subject to a fine of fifty dollars ($50); a second violation is subject to a fine of one hundred dollars ($100); and a third or subsequent violation is subject to a fine of two hundred fifty dollars ($250).

(d) Notify the Secretary of State of any change in address of record within 30 days of the change. A violation of this subdivision is an infraction subject to a fine of fifty dollars ($50).

(e) Notify the Secretary of State of any change in the officers of a corporate license within 30 days of the change. A violation of this subdivision is an infraction subject to a fine of fifty dollars ($50).

(f) Notify the Secretary of State of any change in the business or trade name of the auctioneer or auction company within 30 days of the change. A violation of this subdivision is an infraction subject to a fine of fifty dollars ($50).

(g) Keep and maintain, at the auctioneer's or auction company's address of record, complete and correct records and accounts pertaining to the auctioneer's or auction company's activity for a period of not less than two years. The records shall include the name and address of the owner or consignor and of any buyer of goods at any auction sale engaged in or conducted by the auctioneer or auction company, a description of the goods, the terms and conditions of the acceptance and sale of the goods, all written contracts with owners and consignors, and accounts of all moneys received and paid out, whether on the auctioneer's or auction company's own behalf or as agent, as a result of those activities. A first violation of this subdivision is a misdemeanor subject to a fine of five hundred dollars ($500); and a second or subsequent violation is subject to a fine of one thousand dollars ($1,000).

(h) Within 30 working days after the sale transaction, provide, or cause to be provided, an account to the owner or consignor of all goods that are the subject of an auction engaged in or conducted by the auctioneer or auction company. A first violation of this subdivision is a misdemeanor subject to a fine of five hundred dollars ($500); and a second or subsequent violation is subject to a fine of one thousand dollars ($1,000).

(i) Within 30 working days after a sale transaction of goods, pay or cause to be paid all moneys and proceeds due to the owner or the consignor of all goods that were the subject of an auction engaged in or conducted by the auctioneer or auction company, unless delay is compelled by legal proceedings or the inability of the auctioneer or auction company, through no fault of his or her own, to transfer title to the goods or to comply with any provision of this chapter, the Commercial Code, or the Code of Civil Procedure, or with any other applicable provision of law. A first violation of this subdivision is a misdemeanor subject to a fine of one thousand dollars ($1,000); a second violation is subject to a fine of one thousand five hundred dollars ($1,500); and a third or subsequent violation is subject to a fine of two thousand dollars ($2,000).

(j) Maintain the funds of all owners, consignors, buyers, and other clients and customers separate from his or her personal funds and accounts. A violation of this subdivision is an infraction subject to a fine of two hundred fifty dollars ($250).

(k) Immediately prior to offering any item for sale, disclose to the audience the existence and amount of any liens or other encumbrances on the item, unless the item is sold as free and clear. For the purposes of this subdivision, an item is "free and clear" if all liens and encumbrances on the item are to be paid prior to the transfer of title. A violation of this subdivision is an infraction subject to a fine of two hundred fifty dollars ($250) in addition to the requirement that the buyer be refunded, upon demand, the amount paid for any item that is the subject of the violation.

(*l*) Within two working days after an auction sale, return the blank check or deposit of each buyer who purchased no goods at the sale. A first violation of this subdivision is an infraction subject to a fine of one hundred dollars ($100); and a second or subsequent violation is subject to a fine of two hundred fifty dollars ($250).

(m) Within 30 working days of any auction sale, refund that portion of the deposit of each buyer that exceeds the cost of the goods purchased, unless delay is compelled by legal proceedings or the inability of the auctioneer or auction company, through no fault of his or her own, to transfer title to the goods or to comply with any provision of this chapter, the Commercial Code, or the Code of Civil Procedure, or with other applicable provisions of law, or unless the buyer violated the terms of a written agreement that he or she take possession of purchased goods within a specified period of time. A first violation of this subdivision is an infraction subject to a fine of one hundred dollars ($100); and a second or subsequent violation is subject to a fine of two hundred fifty dollars ($250). *(Formerly § 1861.607, added by Stats.1993, c. 1170 (A.B.259), § 2, eff. Oct. 11, 1993. Renumbered § 1812.607 and amended by Stats.1997, c. 17 (S.B. 947), § 16.)*

Research References

Miller and Starr California Real Estate § 10:202, Conduct of the Sale.

3 Witkin, California Summary 10th Agency and Employment § 43, Auctioneers.

§ 1812.608. Additional violations; punishment

In addition to other requirements and prohibitions of this title, it is a violation of this title for any person to do any of the following:

(a) Fail to comply with any provision of this code, or with any provision of the Vehicle Code, the Commercial Code, any regulation of the Secretary of State, the Code of Civil Procedure, the Penal Code, or any law administered by the State Board of Equalization, relating to the auctioneering business, including, but not limited to, sales and the transfer of title of goods.

(b) Aid or abet the activity of any other person that violates any provision of this title. A violation of this subdivision is a misdemeanor subject to a fine of one thousand dollars ($1,000).

(c) Place or use any misleading or untruthful advertising or statements or make any substantial misrepresentation in conducting auctioneering business. A first violation of this subdivision is a misdemeanor subject to a fine of five hundred dollars ($500); and a second or subsequent violation is subject to a fine of one thousand dollars ($1,000).

(d) Sell goods at auction before the auctioneer or auction company involved has first entered into a written contract with the owner or consignor of the goods, which contract sets forth the terms and conditions upon which the auctioneer or auction company accepts the goods for sale. The written contract shall include all of the following:

(1) The auctioneer's or auction company's name, trade or business name, business address, and business telephone number.

(2) An inventory of the item or items to be sold at auction.

(3) A description of the services to be provided and the agreed consideration for the services, which description shall explicitly state which party shall be responsible for advertising and other expenses.

(4) The approximate date or dates when the item or items will be sold at auction.

(5) A statement as to which party shall be responsible for insuring the item or items against loss by theft, fire, or other means.

(6) A disclosure that the auctioneer or auction company has a bond on file with the Secretary of State. A first violation of this subdivision is an infraction subject to a fine of two hundred fifty dollars ($250); a second violation is subject to a fine of five hundred dollars ($500); and a third or subsequent violation is subject to a fine of one thousand dollars ($1,000).

(e) Sell goods at auction before the auctioneer or auction company involved has first entered into a written contract with the auctioneer who is to conduct the auction. A first violation of this subdivision is an infraction subject to a fine of one hundred dollars ($100); and a second or subsequent violation is subject to a fine of two hundred fifty dollars ($250).

(f) Fail to reduce to writing all amendments or addenda to any written contract with an owner or consignor or an auctioneer. A first violation of this subdivision is an infraction subject to a fine of one hundred dollars ($100); and a second or subsequent violation is subject to a fine of two hundred fifty dollars ($250).

(g) Fail to abide by the terms of any written contract required by this section. A first violation of this subdivision is an infraction subject to a fine of one hundred dollars ($100); and a second or subsequent violation is subject to a fine of two hundred fifty dollars ($250).

(h) Cause or allow any person to bid at a sale for the sole purpose of increasing the bid on any item or items being sold by the auctioneer, except as authorized by Section 2328 of the Commercial Code or by this title. A violation of this subdivision includes, but is not limited to, either of the following:

(1) Stating any increased bid greater than that offered by the last highest bidder when, in fact, no person has made such a bid.

(2) Allowing the owner, consignor, or agent thereof, of any item or items to bid on the item or items, without disclosing to the audience that the owner, consignor, or agent thereof has reserved the right to so bid.

A violation of this subdivision is an infraction subject to a fine of one hundred dollars ($100).

(i) Knowingly misrepresent the nature of any item or items to be sold at auction, including, but not limited to, age, authenticity, value, condition, or origin. A violation of this subdivision is an infraction subject to a fine of two hundred fifty dollars ($250). In addition, it shall be required that the buyer of the misrepresented item be refunded the purchase price of the item or items within 24 hours of return to the auctioneer or auction company of the item by the buyer, provided that the item is returned within five days after the date of the auction sale.

(j) Misrepresent the terms, conditions, restrictions, or procedures under which goods will be sold at auction. A violation of this subdivision is an infraction subject to a fine of seventy-five dollars ($75).

(k) Sell any item subject to sales tax without possessing a valid and unrevoked seller's permit from the State Board of Equalization. A violation of this subdivision is an infraction subject to a fine of five hundred dollars ($500). *(Formerly § 1861.608, added by Stats.1993, c. 1170 (A.B.259), § 2, eff. Oct. 11, 1993. Renumbered § 1812.608 and amended by Stats.1997, c. 17 (S.B.947), § 17.)*

Research References

3 Witkin, California Summary 10th Agency and Employment § 43, Auctioneers.

§ 1812.609. Public policy; waiver of rights

Any waiver of the provisions of this title is contrary to public policy, and is void and unenforceable. *(Added by Stats.2002, c. 815 (A.B.2331), § 22.)*

Research References

3 Witkin, California Summary 10th Agency and Employment § 43, Auctioneers.

Title 2.96

CALIFORNIA RENTAL-PURCHASE ACT

Section

§ 1812.620. Short title

This title shall be known and may be cited as the Karnette Rental-Purchase Act. *(Added by Stats.1994, c. 1026 (A.B.722), § 1.)*

Research References

Rutter, Cal. Practice Guide: Enforcing Judgments/Debts Ch. 3-A, A. Evaluating the Claim.
4 Witkin, California Summary 10th Sales § 380, (S 380) Rental-Purchase Agreements.

§ 1812.621. Legislative findings, declarations and intent

The Legislature hereby finds and declares that consumers enter into rental-purchase contracts that do not adequately disclose the actual terms and cost of the transaction or the consumer's liability for certain breaches of the contract, and that contain unfair provisions, including unfair terms related to fees and charges, the exercise or the termination of purchase option rights, property loss and damage, and the repair or replacement of improperly functioning rental property.

It is, therefore, the intent of the Legislature in enacting this title to ensure that consumers are protected from misrepresentations and unfair dealings by ensuring that consumers are adequately informed of all relevant terms, including the cash price, periodic payments, total purchase price, and other applicable charges or fees, before they enter into rental-purchase contracts.

It is further the intent of the Legislature to (a) prohibit unfair or unconscionable conduct toward consumers in connection with rental-purchase transactions, (b) prohibit unfair contract terms, including unreasonable charges, (c) prevent the forfeiture of contract rights by consumers, (d) provide a right of reinstatement and a reasonable formula for the exercise of purchase option rights under a rental-purchase contract, (e) provide reasonable requirements for the servicing, repair, and replacement of improperly functioning rental property, and (f) cover rental-purchase transactions under existing laws, including laws governing debt collection, cosigners, home solicitation contracts, and warranties. This title shall be liberally construed to achieve its remedial objectives. *(Added by Stats.1994, c. 1026 (A.B.722), § 1.)*

§ 1812.622. Definitions

As used in this title:

(a) "Advertisement" means a commercial message in any medium that directly or indirectly solicits or promotes one or more specific rental-purchase transactions, excluding instore merchandising aids. This definition does not limit or alter the application of other laws, including Chapter 5 (commencing with Section 17200) of Part 2 and Chapter 1 (commencing with Section 17500) of Part 3, of Division 7 of the Business and Professions Code, to rental-purchase transactions.

(b) "Consumer" means a natural person or persons who rent or lease personal property from a lessor pursuant to a rental-purchase agreement or to whom a lessor offers personal property for use pursuant to a rental-purchase agreement.

(c) "Lessor" means any person or entity that provides or offers to provide personal property for use by consumers pursuant to a rental-purchase agreement.

(d) "Rental-purchase agreement," except as otherwise provided in this subdivision, means an agreement between a lessor and a consumer pursuant to which the lessor rents or leases, for valuable consideration, personal property for use by a consumer for personal, family, or household purposes for an initial term not exceeding four months that may be renewed or otherwise extended, if under the terms of the agreement the consumer acquires an option or other legally enforceable right to become owner of the property. A rental-purchase agreement is a lease subject to Title 1.5 (commencing with Section 1750) and Title 1.7 (commencing with Section 1790).

"Rental-purchase agreement" shall not be construed to be, nor be governed by, and shall not apply to, any of the following:

(1) A retail installment sale, as defined in Section 1802.5.

(2) A retail installment contract, as defined in Section 1802.6.

(3) A retail installment account, as defined in Section 1802.7.

(4) A lease or agreement that constitutes a security interest, as defined in Section 1201 of the Commercial Code.

(5) A consumer credit contract, as defined in Section 1799.90.

(e) "Cash price" means the price of the personal property described in the rental-purchase agreement that the consumer may pay in cash to the lessor at the inception of the rental-purchase agreement to acquire ownership of that personal property.

(f) "Cost of rental" means the difference between the total of all periodic payments necessary to acquire ownership under the rental-purchase agreement and the cash price of the rental property that is subject to the rental-purchase agreement.

(g) "Fee" means any payment, charge, fee, cost, or expense, however denominated, other than a rental payment.

(h) "Appliance" means and includes any refrigerator, freezer, range including any cooktop or oven, microwave oven, washer, dryer, dishwasher, or room air conditioner or air purifier.

(i) "Electronic set" means and includes any television, radio, camera, video game, or any type of device for the recording, storage, copying, printing, transmission, display, or playback of any sound or image, but does not include any item that is part of a computer system.

(j) "Computer system" means a computer processor and a video monitor, printer, and peripheral items primarily designed for use with a computer. Audio and video devices, which are commonly used for entertainment and into which data may be downloaded from a computer, are not part of a computer system.

(k) "Lessor's cost" means the documented actual cost, including actual freight charges, of the rental property to the lessor from a wholesaler, distributor, supplier, or manufacturer and net of any discounts, rebates, and incentives.

(*l*) "Total of payments" means the total amount of periodic payments necessary to acquire ownership of the property that is the subject of the rental-purchase agreement if the consumer makes all regularly scheduled payments. *(Added by Stats.1994, c. 1026 (A.B.722), § 1. Amended by Stats.2006, c. 254 (S.B. 1481), § 2; Stats.2006, c. 410 (A.B.594), § 1.)*

Research References

4 Witkin, California Summary 10th Sales § 380, (S 380) Rental-Purchase Agreements.

§ 1812.623. Rental-purchase agreement; form; contents

(a) Every rental-purchase agreement shall be contained in a single document which shall set forth all of the agreements of the lessor and the consumer with respect to the rights and obligations of each party. Every rental-purchase agreement shall be written in at least 10–point type in the same language as principally used in any oral sales presentation or negotiations leading to the execution of the agreement, and shall clearly and conspicuously disclose all of the following:

(1) The names of the lessor and the consumer, the lessor's business address and telephone number, the consumer's address, the date on which the agreement is executed, and a description of the property sufficient to identify it.

(2) Whether the property subject to the rental-purchase agreement is new or used. If the property is new, the lessor shall disclose the model year or, if the model year is not known by the lessor, the date of the lessor's acquisition of the property. If the property is used, the age or the model year shall be disclosed if known by the lessor.

(3) The minimum period for which the consumer is obligated under the rental-purchase agreement; the duration of the rental-purchase agreement if all regularly scheduled periodic payments are made, designated as the "rental period"; and the amount of each periodic payment.

(4) The total of payments and the total number of periodic payments necessary to acquire ownership of the property if the renter makes all regularly scheduled periodic payments.

(5) The cash price of the property subject to the rental purchase agreement.

(6) The cost of rental.

(7) The amount and purpose of any other payment or fee permitted by this title in addition to those specified pursuant to paragraphs (3) and (4), including any late payment fee.

(8) A statement that the total number and dollar amount of payments necessary to acquire ownership of the rental property disclosed under paragraph (4) does not include other fees permitted by this title, such as late payment fees, and that the consumer should read the rental-purchase agreement for an explanation of any applicable additional fees.

(9) Whether the consumer is liable for loss or damage to the rental property and, if so, the maximum amount for which the consumer may be liable as provided in subdivision (a) of Section 1812.627.

(10) The following notice:

NOTICE

You are renting this property. You will not own it until you make all of the regularly scheduled payments or you use the early purchase option.

You do not have the right to keep the property if you do not make required payments or do not use the early purchase option. If you miss a payment, the lessor can repossess the property, but, you may have the right to the return of the same or similar property.

See the contract for an explanation of your rights.

(11) A description of the consumer's right to acquire ownership of the property before the end of the rental period as provided in subdivisions (a) and (b) of Section 1812.632.

(12) A description of the consumer's reinstatement rights as provided in Section 1812.631.

(13) If warranty coverage is transferable to a consumer who acquires ownership of the property, a statement that the unexpired portion of all warranties provided by the manufacturer, distributor, or seller of the property that is the subject of the rental-purchase agreement will be transferred by the lessor to the consumer at the time the consumer acquires ownership of the property from the lessor.

(14) A description of the lessor's obligation to maintain the rental property and to repair or replace rental property that is not operating properly, as provided in Section 1812.633.

(b)(1) The disclosures required by paragraphs (3), (4), (5), and (6) of subdivision (a) shall be printed in at least 10–point boldface type or capital letters if typed and shall be grouped together in a box formed by a heavy line in the following form:

TOTAL OF PAYMENTS	COST OF RENTAL	CASH PRICE	
$	$ Amount over cash price you will pay if you make all regular payments.	$ Property available at this price for cash from the lessor. See about your early purchase option rights. rights.	
You must pay this amount to own the property if you make all	AMOUNT OF EACH PAYMENT	NUMBER OF PAYMENTS	RENTAL PERIOD

the regular payments.		
You can buy the property for less under the early purchase option.	$	per
		_____
		(insert period)

(2) The box described in paragraph (1) shall appear immediately above the space reserved for the buyer's signature.

(c) The disclosures required by paragraphs (3), (4), (5), and (6) of subdivision (a) shall be grouped together in a box formed by a heavy line in the form prescribed in subdivision (b) and shall be clearly and conspicuously placed on a tag or sticker affixed to the property available for rental-purchase. If the property available for rental-purchase is not displayed at the lessor's place of business but appears in a photograph or catalog shown to consumers, a tag or sticker shall be affixed to the photograph of the property or catalog shown to consumers or shall be given to consumers. The disclosure required by paragraph (2) of subdivision (a) also shall be clearly and conspicuously placed on the tag or sticker.

(d) All disclosures required by this section shall be printed or typed in a color or shade that clearly contrasts with the background. *(Added by Stats.1994, c. 1026 (A.B.722), § 1. Amended by Stats.1997, c. 112 (S.B.338), § 2; Stats.2006, c. 410 (A.B.594), § 2.)*

Research References

4 Witkin, California Summary 10th Sales § 380, (S 380) Rental-Purchase Agreements.

§ 1812.624. Prohibited provisions; effect

(a) No rental-purchase agreement or any document that the lessor requests the consumer to sign shall contain any provision by which:

(1) A power of attorney is given to confess judgment in this state or to appoint the lessor, its agents, or its successors in interest as the consumer's agent in the collection of payments or the repossession of the rental property.

(2) The consumer authorizes the lessor or its agent to commit any breach of the peace in repossessing the rental property or to enter the consumer's dwelling or other premises without obtaining the consumer's consent at the time of entry.

(3) The consumer agrees to purchase from the lessor insurance or a liability waiver against loss or damage to the rental property.

(4) The consumer waives or agrees to waive any defense, counterclaim, or right the consumer may have against the lessor, its agent, or its successor in interest.

(5) The consumer is required to pay any fee in connection with reinstatement except as provided in Section 1812.631.

(6) The consumer is required to pay a fee in connection with the pickup of the property or the termination or rescission of the rental-purchase agreement.

(7) The consumer is required to pay any fee permitted by the rental-purchase agreement and this title that is not reasonable and actually incurred by the lessor. The lessor has the burden of proof to establish that a fee was reasonable and was an actual cost incurred by the lessor.

(8) The consumer is required to pay a downpayment, more than one advance periodic rental payment, or any other payment except a security deposit permitted under Section 1812.625.

(9) Except to the extent permitted by subdivision (b) of Section 1812.627, the consumer waives any rights under Sections 1928 or 1929.

(10) The consumer grants a security interest in any property.

(11) The consumer's liability for loss or damage to the property which is the subject of the rental-purchase agreement may exceed the maximum described in subdivision (a) of Section 1812.627.

(12) Except under the circumstances authorized by subdivision (a) or (b) of Section 1812.632, the consumer is obligated to make any balloon payment. A "balloon payment" is any payment for the purchase or use of the rental property which is more than the regularly scheduled periodic payment amount.

(13) The consumer is required to pay a late payment fee that is not permitted under Section 1812.626.

(14) The consumer is required to pay both a late payment fee and a fee for the lessor's collection of a past due payment at the consumer's home or other location.

(15) The consumer waives or offers to waive any right or remedy against the lessor, its agents, or its successors in interest for any violation of this title or any other illegal act. This subdivision does not apply to a document executed in connection with the bona fide settlement, compromise, or release of a specific disputed claim.

(16) The lessor, its agents, or its successors in interest may commence any judicial action against the consumer in a county other than the county in which (A) the rental-purchase agreement was signed or (B) the consumer resides at the time the action is commenced.

(17) The amount stated as the cash price for any item of personal property exceeds the cash price permitted under Section 1812.644.

(18) The total of payments exceeds the amount permitted under Section 1812.644.

(b) Any provision in a rental-purchase agreement that is prohibited by this title shall be void and unenforceable and a violation of this title. A rental-purchase agreement which contains any provision that is prohibited by this title is voidable by the consumer. *(Added by Stats.1994, c. 1026 (A.B.722), § 1. Amended by Stats.2006, c. 410 (A.B.594), § 3.)*

Research References

4 Witkin, California Summary 10th Sales § 380, (S 380) Rental-Purchase Agreements.

§ 1812.625. Security deposits; amount; purpose; return

(a) The lessor may require the consumer to pay a security deposit, however denominated, in an amount not to exceed the equivalent of one month's rental only for the purpose of satisfying any lawful claim by the lessor, up to the maximum described in subdivision (a) of Section 1812.627, for those amounts reasonably necessary to pay for the loss of the property or the repair of damage, exclusive of reasonable wear and tear.

(b) Within two weeks after the lessor has taken possession of the property from the consumer, the lessor shall deliver to the consumer the amount of the security deposit less the amount, if any, deducted for loss or repair as permitted by this title. If any amount is deducted, the lessor shall also deliver to the consumer at that time a copy of an itemized statement indicating the amount of the security deposit, the amount deducted for loss or repair, and a detailed statement of the basis for the deduction. Delivery may be made by personal delivery or by first-class mail, postage prepaid. *(Added by Stats.1994, c. 1026 (A.B.722), § 1.)*

Research References

4 Witkin, California Summary 10th Sales § 380, (S 380) Rental-Purchase Agreements.

§ 1812.626. Late payment fee; conditions; limit

(a) The lessor may assess a late payment fee if the late payment fee is specified in the rental-purchase agreement and is permitted by this section.

(b) No fee shall be assessed for a payment which is less than three days late if the rental-purchase agreement specifies weekly periodic payments.

(c) No fee shall be assessed for a payment which is less than 7 days late if the rental-purchase agreement specifies longer than weekly periodic payments.

(d) The lessor may assess more than one late fee for a particular late payment if the total of all fees assessed for that late payment does not exceed the maximum provided in subdivision (e). If the maximum total late payment fee has been imposed for a particular payment, no additional late payment fee may be imposed for that payment.

(e) The total of all fees for a late payment shall not exceed the lesser of 5 percent of the payment or five dollars ($5), except that a minimum total fee of two dollars ($2) may be required. *(Added by Stats.1994, c. 1026 (A.B.722), § 1.)*

Research References

4 Witkin, California Summary 10th Sales § 380, (S 380) Rental-Purchase Agreements.

§ 1812.627. Consumer's liability for loss or damage to the property; limit

(a) The consumer's liability for loss or damage to the property which is the subject of the rental-purchase agreement shall in no event exceed the lesser of (1) the fair market value at the time of the loss or damage or (2) the amount that would be necessary for the renter to exercise the purchase option provided in subdivision (a) of Section 1812.632.

(b) A lessor and a consumer may agree that the consumer may be liable for loss only up to the maximum amount described in subdivision (a) and only for one of the following:

(1) Loss caused by the consumer's negligent, reckless, or intentional acts.

(2) Loss caused by the theft of the property subject to the rental-purchase agreement unless one of the following is applicable:

(A) There is evidence of a burglary of the premises in which the property is located, such as physical evidence or an official report filed by the consumer with the police or other law enforcement agency.

(B) The consumer establishes by the preponderance of the evidence that the consumer has not committed or aided or abetted in the commission of the theft of the property. *(Added by Stats.1994, c. 1026 (A.B.722), § 1.)*

Research References

4 Witkin, California Summary 10th Sales § 380, (S 380) Rental-Purchase Agreements.

§ 1812.628. Right of cancellation

(a) In addition to the circumstances described in subdivision (a) of Section 1689.5, a rental-purchase agreement regardless of the amount involved shall be deemed a home solicitation contract or offer if the rental-purchase agreement has an initial term that exceeds one week and was made at other than appropriate trade premises, as defined in subdivision (b) of Section 1689.5.

(b) In addition to any other right of cancellation, a consumer has the right to cancel a rental-purchase agreement, without penalty or obligation if the consumer has not taken possession of the property. *(Added by Stats.1994, c. 1026 (A.B.722), § 1.)*

§ 1812.629. Information and documents to be provided to consumer; execution of rental-purchase agreement; receipts

(a) Upon the request of the consumer, the lessor shall provide the information as required by subdivision (b) of Section 1812.623 in an exemplar of the rental-purchase agreement covering the property specified by the consumer and shall provide the consumer with a copy of the proposed rental-purchase agreement prior to its execution. The consumer may take this copy from the lessor's premises.

(b) The lessor shall not obtain the consumer's signature to a rental-purchase agreement if it contains blank spaces to be filled in after it has been signed.

(c) A copy of the fully completed rental-purchase agreement and all other documents which the lessor requests the consumer to sign shall be given to the consumer at the time they are signed. The rental-purchase agreement shall not be enforceable against the consumer until the consumer has received a signed copy.

(d) The lessor shall deliver to the consumer a written receipt for each payment made by the consumer. *(Added by Stats.1994, c. 1026 (A.B.722), § 1.)*

§ 1812.630. Advertisements

(a)(1) Any advertisement of a rental-purchase agreement that states the amount of any payment shall clearly and conspicuously disclose all of the following in the same language used in the advertisement:

(A) That the agreement advertised is a rental-purchase agreement.

(B) That the property is used if that is the case.

(C) That ownership is not acquired until all of the payments necessary to acquire ownership have been made.

(D) The total amount and number of periodic payments necessary to acquire ownership.

(2) If more than one item is advertised in one print advertisement, the lessor may comply with paragraph (1) by clearly and conspicuously including in the advertisement a table or schedule sufficient in detail to permit determination of the total amount and number of periodic payments necessary to acquire ownership of the items advertised having the highest and lowest total amount of periodic payments necessary to acquire ownership.

(b) A lessor who advertises "no credit check" or otherwise states or implies that no inquiry will be made of a consumer's credit history or creditworthiness shall not (1) make any inquiry or request a consumer to complete any document concerning the consumer's assets or credit history, (2) obtain a consumer credit report as defined in subdivision (c) of Section 1785.3, or (3) obtain an investigative consumer report as defined in subdivision

(c) of Section 1786.2. *(Added by Stats.1994, c. 1026 (A.B.722), § 1.)*

§ 1812.631. Default; reinstatement

(a) A consumer may be deemed in default under the rental-purchase agreement if either of the following applies:

(1) The rental-purchase agreement requires weekly periodic rental payments and the consumer has not made a payment by the end of the seventh day after its due date.

(2) The rental-purchase agreement requires rental payments in periodic intervals longer than one week and the consumer has not made a payment by the end of the 10th day after its due date.

(b) A consumer who is in default under a rental-purchase agreement requiring weekly periodic rental payments may reinstate the rental-purchase agreement, without losing any rights or options under that agreement, by paying all past due payments, including late payment fees, by the end of the seventh day after the due date of the payment in default if the consumer retains possession of the property and within one year after the due date of the payment in default if the consumer returns or tenders the property to the lessor, unless the lessor permits the consumer to retain the property during this period.

(c) A consumer who is in default under a rental-purchase agreement requiring rental payments in periodic intervals longer than one week may reinstate the rental-purchase agreement, without losing any rights or options under that agreement, by paying all past due payments, including late payment fees, by the end of the 10th day after the due date of the payment in default if the consumer retains possession of the property and within one year after the due date of the payment in default if the consumer returns or tenders the property to the lessor, unless the lessor permits the consumer to retain the property during this period.

(d) Upon reinstatement, the lessor shall provide the consumer with the same rental property, if available, or substitute property of the same brand, if available, and comparable quality, age, condition, and warranty coverage. If substitute property is provided, the lessor shall provide the lessee with the disclosures required in paragraph (2) of subdivision (a) of Section 1812.623.

(e)(1) Except as provided in paragraph (2), a lessor shall not deny a consumer the right of reinstatement provided in this section.

(2) This section does not apply to a consumer who has (A) stolen or unlawfully disposed of the property, (B) damaged the property as the result of the consumer's intentional, willful, wanton, or reckless conduct, or (C) defaulted in making payments as described in subdivision (a) on three consecutive occasions.

(3) If the lessor denies a consumer the right to reinstate pursuant to paragraph (2), the lessor has the burden of proof to establish that the denial was in good faith and was permitted under paragraph (2).

(f) Nothing in this subdivision prohibits the lessor from contacting the consumer provided that the lessor does not violate Section 1812.638. *(Added by Stats.1994, c. 1026 (A.B.722), § 1.)*

§ 1812.632. Acquisition of ownership; reduction of periodic rental payment

(a)(1) The consumer has the right to acquire ownership of the property within three months of the date on which the consumer executed the rental-purchase agreement by tendering to the lessor an amount equal to the cash price and any past due fees less all periodic payments that the consumer has paid.

(2) Within 10 days after the consumer executes the rental purchase agreement, the lessor shall personally deliver or send by first-class mail to the consumer a notice informing the

consumer of the right described in paragraph (1), including the amount the consumer must pay to acquire ownership and the date by which payment must be made. The statement shall not be accompanied by any other written information including solicitations for other rental-purchase agreements.

(b) After the expiration of the three-month period following the execution of the rental-purchase agreement, the consumer has the right to acquire ownership of the property at any time by tendering to the lessor all past due payments and fees and an amount equal to the cash price stated in the rental-purchase agreement multiplied by a fraction that has as its numerator the number of periodic payments remaining under the agreement and that has as its denominator the total number of periodic payments.

(c)(1) The lessor shall, in connection with a consumer's rights under subdivision (b), provide the consumer with a written statement in the manner set forth in paragraph (2) below that clearly states (A) the total amount the consumer would have to pay to acquire ownership of the rental property if the consumer makes all regularly scheduled payments remaining under the rental-purchase agreement and (B) the total amount the consumer would have to pay to acquire ownership of that property pursuant to subdivision (a).

(2) The statement required by paragraph (1) shall be personally delivered or sent by first-class mail to the consumer within seven days after (A) the date the consumer requests information about the amount required to purchase the rental property and (B) the date the consumer has made one-half of the total number of periodic payments required to acquire ownership of the rental property. The statement shall not be accompanied by any other written information including solicitations for other rental-purchase agreements.

(d)(1) Subject to paragraph (2), if any consumer who has signed the rental-purchase agreement has experienced an interruption or reduction of 25 percent or more of income due to involuntary job loss, involuntary reduced employment, illness, pregnancy, or disability after one-half or more of the total amount of the periodic payments necessary to acquire ownership under the agreement has been paid, the lessor shall reduce the amount of each periodic rental payment by (A) the percentage of the reduction in the consumer's income or (B) 50 percent, whichever is less, for the period during which the consumer's income is interrupted or reduced. If payments are reduced, the total dollar amount of payments necessary to acquire ownership shall not be increased, and the rights and duties of the lessor and the consumer shall not otherwise be affected. When the consumer's income is restored, the lessor may increase the amount of rental payments, but in no event shall rental payments exceed the originally scheduled amount of rental payments.

(2) Paragraph (1) applies only after the consumer provides to the lessor some evidence of the amount and cause of the interruption or reduction of income. *(Added by Stats.1994, c. 1026 (A.B.722), § 1. Amended by Stats.2006, c. 410 (A.B.594), § 4.)*

Research References

4 Witkin, California Summary 10th Sales § 380, (S 380) Rental-Purchase Agreements.

§ 1812.633. Lessor's duty to maintain the property

(a) The lessor shall maintain the property subject to the rental-purchase agreement in good working order while the agreement is in effect without charging any fee to the consumer in addition to the regularly scheduled rental payments set forth in the rental-purchase agreement.

(b) By the end of the second business day following the day on which the lessor received notice from the consumer that the property is not operating properly, the lessor shall repair or replace the property without any fee to the consumer in addition to the regularly scheduled rental payments set forth in the rental-purchase agreement.

(c) If a repair or replacement cannot be immediately effected, the lessor shall temporarily substitute property of comparable quality and condition while repairs are being effected. If repairs cannot be completed to the reasonable satisfaction of the consumer within 30 days after the lessor receives notice from the consumer or within a longer period voluntarily agreed to by the consumer, the lessor shall permanently replace the property.

(d) All replacement property shall be the same brand, if available, and comparable in quality, age, condition, and warranty coverage to the replaced property. If the same brand is not available, the brand of the replacement property shall be agreeable to the consumer.

(e) All of the consumer's and lessor's rights and obligations under the rental-purchase agreement and this title that applied to the property originally subject to the rental-purchase agreement shall apply to any replacement property.

(f) The consumer shall not be charged, or held liable for, any rental fee for any period of time during which the property that is the subject of the rental-purchase agreement or any property substituted for it pursuant to this section is not in good working order.

(g) This section does not apply to the repair of damage resulting from the consumer's intentional, willful, wanton, reckless, or negligent conduct. If the lessor does not comply with this section because of this subdivision, the lessor has the burden of proof to establish that noncompliance was justified and in good faith.

(h) A lessor shall not deliver to a consumer any property which the lessor knows or has reason to know is defective. *(Added by Stats.1994, c. 1026 (A.B.722), § 1.)*

§ 1812.634. Transfer of warranties

When the lessor transfers ownership of the rental property, the lessor shall also transfer to the consumer the unexpired portion of any transferable warranties provided by the manufacturer, distributor, or seller of the rental property, and these warranties shall apply as if the consumer were the original purchaser of the goods. *(Added by Stats.1994, c. 1026 (A.B.722), § 1.)*

§ 1812.635. Service contracts

(a) A lessor shall not sell, or offer for sale, a service contract for the rental property if that service contract provides any coverage while the rental-purchase agreement is in effect.

(b) A lessor may sell, or offer for sale, a service contract providing coverage for the rental property after the consumer acquires ownership of that property, if both of the following conditions are satisfied:

(1) The lessor does not sell, or offer to sell, the service contract before (A) the consumer pays at least one-half of the total number of periodic payments necessary to acquire ownership of the property or (B) the consumer acquires ownership of the property, as provided in Section 1812.632, whichever occurs first.

(2) The lessor clearly and conspicuously indicates to the consumer in writing before the consumer's purchase of the service contract that the purchase is optional.

(c) If the consumer chooses to purchase a service contract before the expiration of the rental-purchase agreement and defaults or otherwise does not make all payments necessary to acquire ownership within the rental period specified in the

agreement, the lessor shall refund all consideration paid for the service contract to the consumer within two weeks after the lessor has received the consumer's last rental payment. This subdivision does not limit or alter any of the consumer's cancellation or refund rights under the service contract or under other provisions of law.

(d) "Service contract" has the meaning set forth in subdivision *(o)* of Section 1791. *(Added by Stats.1994, c. 1026 (A.B.722), § 1.)*

Research References

4 Witkin, California Summary 10th Sales § 380, (S 380) Rental-Purchase Agreements.

§ 1812.636. Violations; damages; fees and costs; equitable relief

(a) A consumer damaged by a violation of this title by a lessor is entitled to recover all of the following:

(1) Actual damages.

(2) Twenty-five percent of an amount equal to the total amount of payments required to obtain ownership if all payments were made under the rental-purchase agreement, but not less than one hundred dollars ($100) nor more than one thousand dollars ($1,000).

(3) The consumer's reasonable attorney's fees and court costs.

(4) Exemplary damages, in the amount the court deems proper, for intentional or willful violations of this title.

(5) Equitable relief as the court deems proper.

(b) Where more than one consumer is a party to a rental-purchase agreement, the limitations of subdivision (a) shall apply to all those consumers in the aggregate, and no more than one recovery shall be permitted for each violation. *(Added by Stats.1994, c. 1026 (A.B.722), § 1.)*

Research References

4 Witkin, California Summary 10th Sales § 380, (S 380) Rental-Purchase Agreements.

§ 1812.637. Bona fide errors

(a) A lessor is not liable for a violation of this title if, before the 30th calendar day after the date the lessor discovers a bona fide error and before an action under this title is filed or written notice of the error is received by the lessor from the consumer, the lessor gives the consumer written notice of the error. "Bona fide error," as used in this section, means a violation that was not intentional and resulted from a bona fide error notwithstanding the maintenance of procedures reasonably adapted to avoid that error. Examples of a bona fide error include clerical errors, calculation errors, errors due to unintentionally improper computer programming or data entry, and printing errors, but does not include an error of legal judgment with respect to a lessor's obligations under this title.

(b) Notwithstanding subdivision (a), if the lessor notifies the consumer of a bona fide error the correction of which would increase the amount of any payment, the lessor may not collect the amount of the increase, and the consumer may enforce the rental-purchase agreement as initially written.

(c) Notwithstanding subdivision (a), if the lessor notifies the consumer of a bona fide error the correction of which would lower the amount of any payment, the lessor shall immediately refund to the consumer the difference between what the consumer paid and what the consumer should have paid if the agreement were correct at the inception of the transaction. *(Added by Stats.1994, c. 1026 (A.B.722), § 1.)*

§ 1812.638. Unfair, unlawful or deceptive conduct; collection or repossession; communications to locate consumer or rental property; communications with consumer; harassment

(a) A lessor shall not engage in any unfair, unlawful, or deceptive conduct, or make any untrue or misleading statement in connection with the collection of any payment owed by a consumer or the repossession of any property or attempt to collect or collect any payment in a manner that would be unlawful to collect a debt pursuant to Title 1.6C (commencing with Section 1788).

(b) All of the following apply to any communication by a lessor with any person other than the consumer for the purpose of acquiring information about the location of a consumer or of any rental property:

(1) The lessor shall identify itself and state that the lessor is confirming or correcting location information concerning the consumer.

(2) The lessor shall not communicate with any person more than once unless requested to do so by the person or unless the lessor reasonably believes that the earlier response is erroneous or incomplete and that the person now has correct or complete location information.

(3) The lessor shall not communicate by postcard.

(4) The lessor shall not use any language or symbol on any envelope or in the contents of any communication that indicates that the communication relates to the collection of any payment or the recovery or repossession of rental property.

(5) The lessor shall not communicate with any person other than the consumer's attorney, after the lessor knows the consumer is represented by an attorney with regard to the rental-purchase agreement and has knowledge of, or can readily ascertain, the attorney's name and address, unless the attorney fails to respond within a reasonable period of time to communication from the lessor or unless the attorney consents to direct communication with the consumer.

(c) Without the prior consent of the consumer given directly to the lessor or the express permission of a court of competent jurisdiction, a lessor shall not communicate with a consumer in connection with the collection of any payment or the recovery or repossession of rental property at any of the following:

(1) The consumer's place of employment.

(2) Any unusual time or place or a time or place known or that should be known to be inconvenient to the consumer. In the absence of knowledge of circumstances to the contrary, a lessor shall assume that the convenient time for communicating with a consumer is after 8 a.m. and before 9 p.m., local time at the consumer's location.

(d) A lessor shall not communicate, in connection with the rental-purchase agreement, with any person other than the consumer, the consumer's attorney, or the lessor's attorney, except to the extent the communication is any of the following:

(1) Reasonably necessary to acquire location information concerning the consumer or the rental property, as provided in subdivision (b).

(2) Upon the prior consent of the consumer given directly to the lessor.

(3) Upon the express permission of a court of competent jurisdiction.

(4) Reasonably necessary to effectuate a postjudgment judicial remedy.

(e) If a consumer notifies the lessor in writing that the consumer wishes the lessor to cease further communication with the consumer, the lessor shall not communicate further with the consumer with respect to the rental-purchase agreement, except for any of the following:

(1) To advise the consumer that the lessor's further efforts are being terminated.

(2) To notify the consumer that the lessor may invoke specified remedies allowable by law which are ordinarily invoked by the lessor.

(3) Where necessary to effectuate any postjudgment remedy.

(f) A lessor shall not harass, oppress, or abuse any person in connection with a rental-purchase agreement, including engaging in any of the following conduct:

(1) Using or threatening the use of violence or any criminal means to harm the physical person, reputation, or property of any person.

(2) Using obscene, profane, or abusive language.

(3) Causing a telephone to ring, or engaging any person in telephone conversation repeatedly or continuously with intent to annoy, abuse, or harass any person.

(4) Placing telephone calls without disclosure of the caller's identity. *(Added by Stats.1994, c. 1026 (A.B.722), § 1.)*

§ 1812.639. Unfair, unlawful or deceptive conduct; untrue or misleading statements; rental-purchase agreement

A lessor shall not engage in any unfair, unlawful, or deceptive conduct or make any untrue or misleading statement in connection with a rental-purchase agreement, including any violation of this title. *(Added by Stats.1994, c. 1026 (A.B.722), § 1.)*

§ 1812.640. Report of late payment, default or repossession to consumer credit reporting agency or investigative consumer reporting agency

A lessor shall not report any late payment, default, or repossession to a consumer credit reporting agency, as defined in subdivision (d) of Section 1785.3, or to an investigative consumer reporting agency, as defined in subdivision (d) of Section 1786.2 if the lessor (a) advertises "no credit check" or otherwise states or implies that no inquiry will be made of a consumer's credit history or creditworthiness or (b) does not obtain a consumer credit report or investigative consumer report on a consumer before entering into a rental-purchase agreement with that consumer. *(Added by Stats.1994, c. 1026 (A.B.722), § 1.)*

§ 1812.641. Solicitation or promotional material to consumer reference to verify consumer's income, assets, credit history or residence

(a) A lessor shall not send any solicitation or other promotional material to a person identified by the consumer as a reference to verify the consumer's income, assets, credit history, or residence unless all of the following occur:

(1) The lessor clearly discloses in the rental-purchase agreement or application that (A) the lessor may send solicitations or other promotional material to references provided by the consumer unless the consumer objects and (B) the consumer has the right to object without incurring any additional rental charge or fee or any loss of contractual rights.

(2) A space on the rental-purchase agreement or application adjacent to the disclosure described in paragraph (1) is provided for the consumer to indicate the consumer's approval or disapproval of the lessor's sending solicitations or other promotional material.

(3) The consumer affirmatively indicates approval.

(4) The lessor does not vary any term required to be disclosed pursuant to Section 1812.623 depending on whether the consum-

er approves or disapproves of the lessor's sending of solicitations or other promotional material to references.

(b) The first solicitation or other promotional material directed to a person whom the consumer has identified as a reference shall clearly offer the reference the opportunity, without cost, to instruct the lessor to refrain from sending further solicitations or other promotional material to the reference. If so instructed, the lessor shall not send any further solicitations or other promotional material to the reference and shall remove the reference's name and address from the lessor's mailing list.

(c) This section shall not apply to solicitations or other promotional material sent generally to people solely on the basis of demographic, geographic, or postal zip code criteria and without regard to whether the people have been identified as references by consumers. *(Added by Stats.1994, c. 1026 (A.B. 722), § 1.)*

§ 1812.642. Discrimination against prospective consumers

A lessor shall not discriminate against a prospective consumer on any ground that would be a prohibited basis for a creditor to discriminate against an applicant for credit as provided in the Equal Credit Opportunity Act (15 U.S.C. Sec. 1691 et seq.) and Regulation B (12 C.F.R. Part 202) as if they applied to a rental-purchase agreement. Nothing in this section shall be construed in any manner to mean that a rental-purchase agreement is a credit transaction. *(Added by Stats.1994, c. 1026 (A.B.722), § 1.)*

§ 1812.643. Notice to joint signers of rental-purchase agreement

(a) Except as provided in subdivision (b), a lessor who obtains the signature of more than one person on a rental-purchase agreement shall deliver the notice set forth in subdivision (c) to each person before that person signs the agreement.

(b) This section does not apply if the persons signing the agreement are married to each other or in fact receive possession of the property described in the agreement.

(c) The notice required by this section is as follows:

"NOTICE TO COSIGNER

If you sign this contract, you will have the same responsibility for the property and the same obligation to make payments that every renter has.

If any renter does not pay, you may have to pay the full amount owed, including late fees, and you may have to pay for certain loss or damage to the property.

The lessor may collect from you without first trying to collect from any other renter. The lessor can use the same collection methods against you that can be used against any renter, such as suing you or garnishing your wages.

This notice is not the contract that makes you responsible.

Before you sign, be sure you can afford to pay if you have to, and that you want to accept this responsibility."

(d) The notice required by subdivision (c) shall be printed in at least 10-point boldface type in English and Spanish. If the rental-purchase agreement is required to be written in a language other than English or Spanish, the notice shall be written in English and, in addition or in lieu of Spanish, in that other language.

(e) If the notice set forth in subdivision (c) is included with the text of the rental-purchase agreement, the notice shall appear immediately above or adjacent to the disclosures required by subdivision (b) of Section 1812.623. If the notice is not included with the text of the agreement, the notice shall be on a separate sheet which shall not contain any other text except as is necessary to identify the lessor and agreement to which the notice refers and to provide for the date and the person's acknowledgment of receipt.

(f) The lessor shall give each person entitled to notice under this section a copy of the completed rental-purchase agreement before obtaining that person's signature.

(g) If a person entitled to receive notice and a copy of the rental-purchase agreement under this section does not receive the notice or agreement in the manner required, that person has no liability in connection with the rental-purchase transaction. *(Added by Stats.1994, c. 1026 (A.B.722), § 1.)*

§ 1812.644. Records of lessor's cost; maximum cash price; maximum total of payments

(a) A lessor shall maintain records that establish the lessor's cost, as defined in subdivision (k) of Section 1812.622, for each item of personal property that is the subject of the rental-purchase agreement. A copy of each rental-purchase agreement and of the records required by this subdivision shall be maintained for two years following the termination of the agreement.

(b) The maximum cash price for the lessor's first rental of the property that is the subject of the rental-purchase agreement may not exceed 1.65 times the lessor's cost for computer systems and appliances, 1.7 times the lessor's cost for electronic sets, 1.9 times the lessor's cost for automotive accessories, furniture, jewelry, and musical instruments, and 1.65 times the lessor's cost for all other items.

(c) The maximum total of payments may not exceed 2.25 times the maximum cash price that could have been charged for the first rental of the property under subdivision (b).

(d) The maximum total of payments for the lessor's second and subsequent rental of the property that is the subject of the rental-purchase agreement may not exceed the maximum total of payments permitted under subdivision (c) for the first rental of that property less (1) for appliances and electronic sets, one-third the amount of all rental payments paid to the lessor by consumers who previously rented that property or (2) for furniture, computer systems, and all other items, one-half the amount of all rental payments paid to the lessor by consumers who previously rented that property.

(e) The maximum cash price for property on its second or subsequent rental may not exceed the maximum total of payments for that property as permitted under subdivision (d) divided by 2.25.

(f) Upon the written request of the Attorney General, any district attorney or city attorney, or the Director of the Department of Consumer Affairs, a lessor shall provide copies of the records described in this section.

(g) If a lessor willfully discloses a cash price or a total of payments that exceeds the amount permitted by this section, the rental-purchase agreement is void, the consumer shall retain the property without any obligation, and the lessor shall refund to the consumer all amounts paid. *(Added by Stats.1994, c. 1026 (A.B.722), § 1. Amended by Stats.2006, c. 410 (A.B.594), § 5.)*

§ 1812.645. Action on rental-purchase agreement; venue

An action on a rental-purchase agreement shall be tried in the county in which the rental-purchase agreement was signed or the consumer resides at the time the action is commenced. *(Added by Stats.1994, c. 1026 (A.B.722), § 1.)*

§ 1812.646. Waiver or modification of provisions of title

Any waiver or modification of the provisions of this title by the consumer or lessor shall be void and unenforceable as contrary to public policy. *(Added by Stats.1994, c. 1026 (A.B.722), § 1.)*

§ 1812.647. Violation; punishment

Any person who willfully violates any provision of this title is guilty of a misdemeanor. *(Added by Stats.1994, c. 1026 (A.B. 722), § 1.)*

Research References

4 Witkin, California Summary 10th Sales § 380, (S 380) Rental-Purchase Agreements.

§ 1812.648. Cumulative remedies

The rights, remedies, and penalties established by this title are cumulative to the rights, remedies, or penalties established under other laws. *(Added by Stats.1994, c. 1026 (A.B.722), § 1.)*

§ 1812.649. Severability

If any provision of this title or the application thereof to any person or circumstances is held invalid, that invalidity shall not affect other provisions or applications of the title that can be given effect without the invalid provision or application, and to this end the provisions of this title are severable. *(Added by Stats.1994, c. 1026 (A.B.722), § 1.)*

Title 2.97

CONSUMER COLLECTION NOTICE

§ 1812.700. Notice to be provided to debtors by third-party collectors subject to federal Fair Debt Collection Practices Act

(a) In addition to the requirements imposed by Article 2 (commencing with Section 1788.10) of Title 1.6C, third-party debt collectors subject to the federal Fair Debt Collection Practices Act (15 U.S.C. Sec. 1692 et seq.) shall provide a notice to debtors that shall include the following description of debtor rights:

"The state Rosenthal Fair Debt Collection Practices Act and the federal Fair Debt Collection Practices Act require that, except under unusual circumstances, collectors may not contact you before 8 a.m. or after 9 p.m. They may not harass you by using threats of violence or arrest or by using obscene language. Collectors may not use false or misleading statements or call you at work if they know or have reason to know that you may not receive personal calls at work. For the most part, collectors may not tell another person, other than your attorney or spouse, about your debt. Collectors may contact another person to confirm your location or enforce a judgment. For more information about debt collection activities, you may contact the Federal Trade Commission at 1–877–FTC–HELP or www.ftc. gov."

(b) The notice shall be included with the first written notice initially addressed to a California address of a debtor in connection with collecting the debt by the third-party debt collector.

(c) If a language other than English is principally used by the third-party debt collector in the initial oral contact with the debtor, a notice shall be provided to the debtor in that language within five working days. *(Added by Stats.2003, c. 259 (S.B. 1022), § 1, operative July 1, 2004.)*

Research References

Rutter, Cal. Practice Guide: Enforcing Judgments/Debts Ch. 2-B, B. Statutory Liability and Procedures.
8 Witkin Cal. Proc. 5th Enforcement of Judgment § 9, (S 9) Notice to Debtor of Rights.

§ 1812.701. Change in notice; type-sized used

(a) The notice required in this title may be changed only as necessary to reflect changes under the federal Fair Debt Collection Practices Act (15 U.S.C. Sec. 1692 et seq.) that would otherwise make the disclosure inaccurate.

(b) The type-size used in the disclosure shall be at least the same type-size as that used to inform the debtor of his or her specific debt, but is not required to be larger than 12–point type. *(Added by Stats.2003, c. 259 (S.B.1022), § 1, operative July 1, 2004. Amended by Stats.2004, c. 183 (A.B.3082), § 37.)*

Research References

Rutter, Cal. Practice Guide: Enforcing Judgments/Debts Ch. 2-B, B. Statutory Liability and Procedures.
8 Witkin Cal. Proc. 5th Enforcement of Judgment § 9, (S 9) Notice to Debtor of Rights.

§ 1812.702. Violations

Any violation of this act shall be considered a violation of the Rosenthal Fair Debt Collection Practices Act (Title 1.6C (commencing with Section 1788)). *(Added by Stats.2003, c. 259 (S.B.1022), § 1, operative July 1, 2004.)*

Research References

Rutter, Cal. Practice Guide: Enforcing Judgments/Debts Ch. 2-B, B. Statutory Liability and Procedures.
8 Witkin Cal. Proc. 5th Enforcement of Judgment § 9, (S 9) Notice to Debtor of Rights.

Title 3

DEPOSIT

CHAPTER 1. DEPOSIT IN GENERAL

ARTICLE 1. NATURE AND CREATION OF DEPOSIT

§ 1813. Kinds of deposit

A deposit may be voluntary or involuntary; and for safe keeping or for exchange. *(Enacted in 1872.)*

Miller and Starr California Real Estate § 10:71, Payment or Performance of the Secured Obligation.
Miller and Starr California Real Estate § 19:236, Tenant's Personal Property--Residential Landlord's Lien.
12 Witkin, California Summary 10th Real Property § 250, (S 250) Statutory Limitations.
13 Witkin, California Summary 10th Personal Property § 156, (S 156) Nature and Types.

§ 1814. Voluntary deposit; depositor and depositary defined

A voluntary deposit is made by one giving to another, with his consent, the possession of personal property to keep for the benefit of the former, or of a third party. The person giving is called the depositor, and the person receiving the depositary. *(Enacted in 1872.)*

13 Witkin, California Summary 10th Personal Property § 156, (S 156) Nature and Types.

§ 1815. Involuntary deposit

An involuntary deposit is made:

(a) By the accidental leaving or placing of personal property in the possession of any person, without negligence on the part of its owner.

(b) In cases of fire, shipwreck, inundation, insurrection, riot, or like extraordinary emergencies, by the owner of personal property committing it, out of necessity, to the care of any person.

(c) By the delivery to, or picking up by, and the holding of, a stray live animal by any person or public or private entity.

(d) By the abandonment or leaving of a live animal, as proscribed by Section 597.1 of the Penal Code, in or about any premises or real property that has been vacated upon, or immediately preceding, the termination of a lease or other rental agreement or foreclosure of the property. *(Enacted in 1872. Amended by Stats.1998, c. 752 (S.B.1785), § 2; Stats.1999, c. 83 (S.B.966), § 22; Stats.2008, c. 265 (A.B.2949), § 1.)*

12 Witkin, California Summary 10th Real Property § 749, Nature of Statute.
13 Witkin, California Summary 10th Personal Property § 156, (S 156) Nature and Types.

§ 1816. Involuntary deposit; animal control notification; duty of depositary

(a) The person or private entity with whom a thing is deposited in the manner described in Section 1815 is bound to take charge of it, if able to do so.

(b) Any person or private entity with whom a live animal is deposited in the manner described in subdivision (d) of Section 1815 shall immediately notify animal control officials for the purpose of retrieving the animal pursuant to Section 597.1 of the Penal Code. Animal control officers who respond shall be entitled to exercise the right afforded them pursuant to that section to secure a lien for the purpose of recovering the costs of attempting to rescue the animal. Nothing in this subdivision shall impose any new or additional civil or criminal liability upon a depositary who complies with this subdivision.

(c) A public agency or shelter with whom an abandoned animal is deposited in the manner described in Section 1815 is bound to take charge of it, as provided in Section 597.1 of the Penal Code.

(d) The person in possession of the abandoned animal is subject to all local ordinances and state laws that govern the proper care and treatment of those animals.

(e) For purposes of this section, the person or private entity that notifies animal control officials to retrieve the animal or the successor property owner shall not be considered the keeper of the animal or the agent of the animal's owner as those terms are used in Section 597.1 of the Penal Code. *(Enacted in 1872. Amended by Stats.1998, c. 752 (S.B.1785), § 3; Stats.2008, c. 265 (A.B.2949), § 2.)*

13 Witkin, California Summary 10th Personal Property § 156, (S 156) Nature and Types.

§ 1817. Deposit for keeping defined

A deposit for keeping is one in which the depositary is bound to return the identical thing deposited. *(Enacted in 1872.)*

§ 1818. Deposit for exchange defined

A deposit for exchange is one in which the depositary is only bound to return a thing corresponding in kind to that which is deposited. *(Enacted in 1872.)*

13 Witkin, California Summary 10th Personal Property § 157, (S 157) Title and Estoppel to Deny.

ARTICLE 2. OBLIGATIONS OF THE DEPOSITARY

Section
1822. Delivery on demand.
1823. Necessity of demand.
1824. Place of delivery.
1825. Adverse claims; notice to beneficiary of deposit.
1826. Notice of deposit to true owner.
1827. Delivery to co-owners.
1828. Joint tenancy deposits; delivery.

§ 1822. Delivery on demand

A depositary must deliver the thing to the person for whose benefit it was deposited, on demand, whether the deposit was made for a specified time or not, unless he has a lien upon the thing deposited, or has been forbidden or prevented from doing so by the real owner thereof, or by the act of the law, and has given the notice required by Section 1825. *(Enacted in 1872.)*

13 Witkin, California Summary 10th Personal Property § 165, in General.
13 Witkin, California Summary 10th Personal Property § 166, Where Third Party Claims Goods.

§ 1823. Necessity of demand

A depositary is not bound to deliver a thing deposited without demand, even where the deposit is made for a specified time. *(Enacted in 1872.)*

Rutter, Cal. Practice Guide: Civ. Pro. Before Trial Ch. 1-C, C. Prelawsuit Notices, Claims and Demands.
13 Witkin, California Summary 10th Personal Property § 165, in General.

§ 1824. Place of delivery

A depositary must deliver the thing deposited at his residence or place of business, as may be most convenient for him. *(Enacted in 1872.)*

§ 1825. Adverse claims; notice to beneficiary of deposit

A depositary must give prompt notice to the person for whose benefit the deposit was made, of any proceedings taken adversely to his interest in the thing deposited, which may tend to excuse the depositary from delivering the thing to him. *(Enacted in 1872.)*

Research References

3 Witkin Cal. Proc. 5th Actions § 214, Steps by Defendant.
13 Witkin, California Summary 10th Personal Property § 166, Where Third Party Claims Goods.

§ 1826. Notice of deposit to true owner

A depositary, who believes that a thing deposited with him is wrongfully detained from its true owner, may give him notice of the deposit; and if within a reasonable time afterwards he does not claim it, and sufficiently establish his right thereto, and indemnify the depositary against the claim of the depositor, the depositary is exonerated from liability to the person to whom he gave the notice, upon returning the thing to the depositor, or assuming, in good faith, a new obligation changing his position in respect to the thing, to his prejudice. *(Enacted in 1872.)*

Research References

13 Witkin, California Summary 10th Personal Property § 166, Where Third Party Claims Goods.

§ 1827. Delivery to co-owners

If a thing deposited is owned jointly or in common by persons who cannot agree upon the manner of its delivery, the depositary may deliver to each his proper share thereof, if it can be done without injury to the thing. *(Enacted in 1872.)*

§ 1828. Joint tenancy deposits; delivery

When a deposit is made in the name of two or more persons, deliverable or payable to either or to their survivor or survivors, such deposit or any part thereof, or increase thereof, may be delivered or paid to either of said persons or to the survivor or survivors in due course of business. *(Added by Stats.1907, c. 75, p. 92, § 1.)*

CHAPTER 2.　DEPOSIT FOR KEEPING

ARTICLE 1.　GENERAL PROVISIONS

§ 1833. Indemnification of depositary

A depositor must indemnify the depositary:

1.　For all damage caused to him by the defects or vices of the thing deposited; and,

2.　For all expenses necessarily incurred by him about the thing, other than such as are involved in the nature of the undertaking. *(Enacted in 1872.)*

§ 1834. Depositary of animals; duties

A depositary of living animals shall provide the animals with necessary and prompt veterinary care, nutrition, and shelter, and treat them kindly. Any depositary that fails to perform these duties may be liable for civil damages as provided by law. *(Enacted in 1872. Amended by Stats.1998, c. 752 (S.B.1785), § 4.)*

§ 1834.4. Euthanasia

(a) It is the policy of the state that no adoptable animal should be euthanized if it can be adopted into a suitable home. Adoptable animals include only those animals eight weeks of age or older that, at or subsequent to the time the animal is impounded or otherwise taken into possession, have manifested no sign of a behavioral or temperamental defect that could pose a health or safety risk or otherwise make the animal unsuitable for placement as a pet, and have manifested no sign of disease, injury, or congenital or hereditary condition that adversely affects the health of the animal or that is likely to adversely affect the animal's health in the future.

(b) It is the policy of the state that no treatable animal should be euthanized. A treatable animal shall include any animal that is not adoptable but that could become adoptable with reasonable efforts. This subdivision, by itself, shall not be the basis of liability for damages regarding euthanasia. *(Added by Stats. 1998, c. 752 (S.B.1785), § 5.)*

§ 1834.5. Abandoned animals; disposition; notice

Notwithstanding any other provision of law, whenever any animal is delivered to any veterinarian, dog kennel, cat kennel, pet-grooming parlor, animal hospital, or any other animal care facility pursuant to any written or oral agreement entered into after the effective date of this section, and the owner of such animal does not pick up the animal within 14 calendar days after the day the animal was due to be picked up, the animal shall be deemed to be abandoned. The person into whose custody the animal was placed for care shall first try for a period of not less than 10 days to find a new owner for the animal, and, if unable to place the animal with a new owner, shall thereafter humanely destroy the animal so abandoned.

If an animal so abandoned was left with a veterinarian or with a facility which has a veterinarian, and a new owner cannot be found pursuant to this section, such veterinarian shall humanely destroy the animal.

There shall be a notice posted in a conspicuous place, or in conspicuous type in a written receipt given, to warn each person depositing an animal at such animal care facilities of the provisions of this section. *(Added by Stats.1969, c. 1138, p. 2205,*

§ 1. Amended by Stats.1970, c. 1166, p. 2071, § 1; Stats.1971, c. 477, p. 962, § 1.)

Research References

13 Witkin, California Summary 10th Personal Property § 39, (S 39) Other Statutes Dealing With Unclaimed Property.

§ 1834.6. Use of abandoned animals for scientific or other experimentation prohibited

An abandoned animal, as described in Section 1834.5, shall not be used for scientific or any other type of experimentation, nor shall such an abandoned animal be turned over to a pound or animal regulation department of a public agency. *(Added by Stats.1969, c. 1138, p. 2205, § 2.)*

Research References

13 Witkin, California Summary 10th Personal Property § 39, (S 39) Other Statutes Dealing With Unclaimed Property.

§ 1834.7. Use of animals turned over to pound or animal regulation department for biological supply or research facility; sign on pound or animal regulation department

(a) In any pound or animal regulation department of a public or private agency where animals are turned over dead or alive to a biological supply facility or a research facility, a sign (measuring a minimum of 28 x 21 cm—11 x 8 ½ inches—with lettering of a minimum of 3.2 cm high and 1.2 cm wide—1 ¼ x ½ inch—(91 point)) stating:

"Animals Turned In To This Shelter May Be Used For Research Purposes or to Supply Blood, Tissue, or Other Biological Products" shall be posted in a place where it will be clearly visible to a majority of persons when turning animals over to the shelter. This statement shall also be included on owner surrender forms. The owner surrender forms shall also include the definition of "biological supply facility" contained in subdivision (c).

(b) For purposes of this section, "animal research facility" includes any laboratory, firm, association, corporation, copartnership, and educational institution.

(c) For purposes of this section, "biological supply facility" includes any blood bank, laboratory, firm, association, corporation, copartnership, or educational institution that sells biological materials such as blood or animals, either alive or dead, to research facilities, educational institutions, or veterinarians. *(Added by Stats.1978, c. 777, p. 2484, § 1. Amended by Stats.1980, c. 676, p. 1896, § 50; Stats.2001, c. 139 (S.B.338), § 1, operative July 1, 2002.)*

§ 1834.8. Public auctions or sales of equines; notice of sale for slaughter; minimum bids; posting of slaughter prices

(a) At any public auction or sale where equines are sold, the management of the auction or sale shall post a sign (measuring a minimum of 15 x 9 inches with lettering of a minimum of 1 ¼ x ½ (91 point)) or shall insert into its consignment agreement with the seller in boldface type the notice stated in subdivision (b). If a sign is posted, it shall be posted in a conspicuous place so that it will be clearly visible to a majority of persons attending the sale. If the notice is inserted into the consignment agreement, space shall be provided adjacent to the notice for the seller to initial his or her acknowledgment of the notice.

(b) The notice required by subdivision (a) shall read as follows:

"WARNING

Horses sold on these premises may be purchased for slaughter.

As a possible safeguard, seller can set minimum bid above current slaughter prices."

(c) For the purposes of this section, the management of the auction or sale shall post current slaughter prices or make them available to sellers upon request. *(Added by Stats.1995, c. 99 (S.B.1219), § 1. Amended by Stats.2006, c. 538 (S.B.1852), § 53.)*

§ 1834.9. Alternative animal test methods; required use by manufacturers and contract testing facilities

(a) Manufacturers and contract testing facilities shall not use traditional animal test methods within this state for which an appropriate alternative test method has been scientifically validated and recommended by the Inter-Agency Coordinating Committee for the Validation of Alternative Methods (IC-CVAM) and adopted by the relevant federal agency or agencies or program within an agency responsible for regulating the specific product or activity for which the test is being conducted.

(b) Nothing in this section shall prohibit the use of any alternative nonanimal test method for the testing of any product, product formulation, chemical, or ingredient that is not recommended by ICCVAM.

(c) Nothing in this section shall prohibit the use of animal tests to comply with requirements of state agencies. Nothing in this section shall prohibit the use of animal tests to comply with requirements of federal agencies when the federal agency has approved an alternative nonanimal test pursuant to subdivision (a) and the federal agency staff concludes that the alternative nonanimal test does not assure the health or safety of consumers.

(d) Notwithstanding any other provision of law, the exclusive remedy for enforcing this section shall be a civil action for injunctive relief brought by the Attorney General, the district attorney of the county in which the violation is alleged to have occurred, or a city attorney of a city or a city and county having a population in excess of 750,000 and in which the violation is alleged to have occurred. If the court determines that the Attorney General or district attorney is the prevailing party in the enforcement action, the official may also recover costs, attorney fees, and a civil penalty not to exceed five thousand dollars ($5,000) in that action.

(e) This section shall not apply to any animal test performed for the purpose of medical research.

(f) For the purposes of this section, these terms have the following meanings:

(1) "Animal" means vertebrate nonhuman animal.

(2) "Manufacturer" means any partnership, corporation, association, or other legal relationship that produces chemicals, ingredients, product formulations, or products in this state.

(3) "Contract testing facility" means any partnership, corporation, association, or other legal relationship that tests chemicals, ingredients, product formulations, or products in this state.

(4) "ICCVAM" means the Inter-Agency Coordinating Committee for the Validation of Alternative Methods, a federal committee comprised of representatives from 14 federal regulatory or research agencies, including the Food and Drug Administration, Environmental Protection Agency, and Consumer Products Safety Commission, that reviews the validity of alternative test methods. The committee is the federal mechanism for recommending appropriate, valid test methods to relevant federal agencies.

(5) "Medical research" means research related to the causes, diagnosis, treatment, control, or prevention of physical or mental diseases and impairments of humans and animals or related to the development of biomedical products, devices, or drugs as defined in Section 321(g)(1) of Title 21 of the United States Code. Medical research does not include the testing of an ingredient that was formerly used in a drug, tested for the drug use with traditional animal methods to characterize the ingredient and to substantiate its safety for human use, and is now proposed for use in a product other than a biomedical product, medical device, or drug.

(6) "Traditional animal test method" means a process or procedure using animals to obtain information on the characteristics of a chemical or agent. Toxicological test methods generate information regarding the ability of a chemical or agent to produce a specific biological effect under specified conditions.

(7) "Validated alternative test method" means a test method that does not use animals, or in some cases reduces or refines the current use of animals, for which the reliability and relevance for a specific purpose has been established in validation studies as specified in the ICCVAM report provided to the relevant federal agencies.

(8) "Person" means an individual with managerial control, or a partnership, corporation, association, or other legal relationship.

(9) "Adopted by a federal agency" means a final action taken by an agency, published in the Federal Register, for public notice. (Formerly § 1834.8, added by Stats.2000, c. 476 (S.B. 2082), § 1. Renumbered § 1834.9 and amended by Stats.2001, c. 159 (S.B.662), § 34.5.)

§ 1835. Use of thing deposited; opening fastened thing

A depositary may not use the thing deposited, or permit it to be used, for any purpose, without the consent of the depositor. He may not, if it is purposely fastened by the depositor, open it without the consent of the latter, except in case of necessity. (Enacted in 1872.)

Research References

13 Witkin, California Summary 10th Personal Property § 164, (S 164) Bailee's Liability for Unauthorized Use (Deviation).

§ 1836. Wrongful use; damages

A depositary is liable for any damage happening to the thing deposited, during his wrongful use thereof, unless such damage must inevitably have happened though the property had not been thus used. (Enacted in 1872.)

Research References

13 Witkin, California Summary 10th Personal Property § 164, (S 164) Bailee's Liability for Unauthorized Use (Deviation).

§ 1837. Sale of thing in danger of perishing

If a thing deposited is in actual danger of perishing before instructions can be obtained from the depositor, the depositary may sell it for the best price obtainable, and retain the proceeds as a deposit, giving immediate notice of his proceedings to the depositor. (Enacted in 1872.)

§ 1838. Loss of or injury to thing deposited

If a thing is lost or injured during its deposit, and the depositary refuses to inform the depositor of the circumstances under which the loss or injury occurred, so far as he has information concerning them, or willfully misrepresents the circumstances to him, the depositary is presumed to have willfully, or by gross negligence, permitted the loss or injury to occur. (Enacted in 1872.)

§ 1839. Services by depositary

So far as any service is rendered by a depositary, or required from him, his duties and liabilities are prescribed by the Title on Employment and Service. (Enacted in 1872.)

§ 1840. Negligence; limitation of liability

The liability of a depositary for negligence cannot exceed the amount which he is informed by the depositor, or has reason to suppose, the thing deposited to be worth. (Enacted in 1872. Amended by Code Am.1873–74, c. 612, p. 244, § 200.)

Research References

13 Witkin, California Summary 10th Personal Property § 162, (S 162) Limitation of Liability to Apparent Value.
13 Witkin, California Summary 10th Personal Property § 171, (S 171) What Constitutes Written Consent.

ARTICLE 2. GRATUITOUS DEPOSIT

Section

§ 1844. Gratuitous deposit defined

Gratuitous deposit is a deposit for which the depositary receives no consideration beyond the mere possession of the thing deposited. (Enacted in 1872.)

§ 1845. Involuntary deposit

An involuntary deposit is gratuitous, the depositary being entitled to no reward. However, an involuntary depositary of any live animal may accept advertised rewards or rewards freely offered by the owner of the animal. (Enacted in 1872. Amended by Stats.1998, c. 752 (S.B.1785), § 6.)

Research References

13 Witkin, California Summary 10th Personal Property § 156, (S 156) Nature and Types.
13 Witkin, California Summary 10th Personal Property § 159, in General.

§ 1846. Degree of care required

(a) A gratuitous depositary must use, at least, slight care for the preservation of the thing deposited.

(b) A gratuitous depositary of a living animal shall provide the animal with necessary and prompt veterinary care, adequate nutrition and water, and shelter, and shall treat it humanely and, if the animal has any identification, make reasonable attempts to notify the owner of the animal's location. Any gratuitous depositary that does not have sufficient resources or desire to provide that care shall promptly turn the animal over to an appropriate care facility.

(c) If the gratuitous depositary of a living animal is a public pound, shelter operated by a society for the prevention of cruelty to animals, or humane shelter, the depositary shall comply with all other requirements of the Food and Agricultural Code regarding the impounding of live animals. (Enacted in 1872. Amended by Stats.1998, c. 752 (S.B.1785), § 7.)

Research References

13 Witkin, California Summary 10th Personal Property § 159, in General.
13 Witkin, California Summary 10th Personal Property § 163, Gratuitous Bailment.
6 Witkin, California Summary 10th Torts § 869, (S 869) Degrees of Care and Negligence.

14 Witkin, California Summary 10th Wills and Probate § 18, (S 18) Nature and Scope of Deposit Agreement.

§ 1847. Termination of duties of depositary

The duties of a gratuitous depositary cease:

(a) Upon restoration by the depositary of the thing deposited to its owner.

(b) Upon reasonable notice given by the depositary to the owner to remove it, and the owner failing to do so within a reasonable time. But an involuntary depositary, under subdivision (b) of Section 1815, may not give notice until the emergency that gave rise to the deposit is past. This subdivision shall not apply to a public pound, a shelter operated by a society for the prevention of cruelty to animals, or a humane shelter. The duty to provide care, as required by Section 1846, continues until the public pound or private shelter is lawfully relieved of responsibility for the animal. *(Enacted in 1872. Amended by Stats.1998, c. 752 (S.B.1785), § 8.)*

ARTICLE 3. STORAGE

Section
1851. Storage; deposit for hire.
1852. Degree of care required.
1853. Hire for fraction of week or month.
1854. Termination of deposit.
1855. Termination of deposit; agreement respecting time.
1856. Depositary's lien.
1857. Depositary's lien; sale.

§ 1851. Storage; deposit for hire

A deposit not gratuitous is called storage. The depositary in such case is called a depositary for hire. *(Enacted in 1872.)*

§ 1852. Degree of care required

A depositary for hire must use at least ordinary care for the preservation of the thing deposited. *(Enacted in 1872.)*

Research References

13 Witkin, California Summary 10th Personal Property § 159, in General.
13 Witkin, California Summary 10th Personal Property § 161, (S 161) Kind of Care and Burden of Proof.
6 Witkin, California Summary 10th Torts § 869, (S 869) Degrees of Care and Negligence.
14 Witkin, California Summary 10th Wills and Probate § 18, (S 18) Nature and Scope of Deposit Agreement.

§ 1853. Hire for fraction of week or month

In the absence of a different agreement or usage, a depositary for hire is entitled to one week's hire for the sustenance and shelter of living animals during any fraction of a week, and to half a month's hire for the storage of any other property during any fraction of a half month. *(Enacted in 1872.)*

§ 1854. Termination of deposit

In the absence of an agreement as to the length of time during which a deposit is to continue, it may be terminated by the depositor at any time, and by the depositary upon reasonable notice. *(Enacted in 1872.)*

§ 1855. Termination of deposit; agreement respecting time

Notwithstanding an agreement respecting the length of time during which a deposit is to continue, it may be terminated by the depositor on paying all that would become due to the depositary in case of the deposit so continuing. *(Enacted in 1872.)*

§ 1856. Depositary's lien

A depositary for hire has a lien for storage charges and for advances and insurance incurred at the request of the bailor, and for money necessarily expended in and about the care, preservation and keeping of the property stored, and he also has a lien for money advanced at the request of the bailor, to discharge a prior lien, and for the expenses of a sale where default has been made in satisfying a valid lien. The rights of the depositary for hire to such lien are regulated by the title on liens. *(Added by Stats.1891, c. 249, p. 470, § 1. Amended by Stats.1909, c. 664, p. 1001, § 1.)*

Research References

Miller and Starr California Real Estate § 1:60, Parol Evidence; Extrinsic Evidence Rules.
13 Witkin, California Summary 10th Personal Property § 228, Nature and Effect.

§ 1857. Depositary's lien; sale

If from any cause other than want of ordinary care and diligence on his part, a depositary for hire is unable to deliver perishable property, baggage, or luggage received by him for storage, or to collect his charges for storage due thereon, he may cause such property to be sold, in open market, to satisfy his lien for storage; *provided,* that no property except perishable property shall be sold, under the provisions of this section, upon which storage charges shall not be due and unpaid for one year at the time of such sale.

All Acts and parts of Acts in conflict with the provisions of this Act are hereby repealed.

This Act shall take effect from and after its passage. *(Added by Stats.1891, c. 249, p. 470, § 2.)*

ARTICLE 3.5. DEPOSITS FOR REPAIR, ALTERATION OR SALE

Section
1858. Definitions.
1858.1. Customer's receipt; contents.
1858.2. Failure to furnish receipt; strict liability.
1858.3. Insurance protection.

§ 1858. Definitions

As used in this article:

(a) "Customer" means a natural person who deals with a depositary.

(b) "Depositary" means a person who in the ordinary course of business regularly receives property from customers for the purpose of repair or alteration.

(c) "Property" means personal property used for or intended for personal, family, or household purposes, but does not include any motor vehicle within the meaning of Section 415 of the Vehicle Code. *(Added by Stats.1970, c. 1185, p. 2093, § 1. Amended by Stats.1971, c. 180, p. 247, § 1, eff. June 25, 1971.)*

Research References

4 Witkin, California Summary 10th Sales § 333, Electronic Equipment and Appliances.

§ 1858.1. Customer's receipt; contents

Every depositary shall, upon accepting property from a customer, present the customer with written receipt which shall include a statement, if such is the case, that such deposited property is not insured or protected to the amount of the actual cash value thereof by the depositary against loss occasioned by theft, fire, and vandalism while such property remains with the depositary. *(Added by Stats.1970, c. 1185, p. 2093, § 1.)*

Research References

13 Witkin, California Summary 10th Personal Property § 159, in General.

§ 1858.2.   Failure to furnish receipt; strict liability

Every depositary who fails to furnish the receipt, or a statement thereon as required by Section 1858.1, or who makes any misrepresentation in such receipt, shall be strictly liable to the customer for any loss occasioned by theft, fire, or vandalism while such property remains with the depositary and shall forfeit any lien or other right to hold the property arising from services rendered in holding, repairing, altering, or selling the property. When liability is imposed upon a depositary under this section it shall be deemed as having been imposed for the commission of a willful act for the purposes of Section 533 of the Insurance Code. *(Added by Stats.1970, c. 1185, p. 2093, § 1.)*

Research References

13 Witkin, California Summary 10th Personal Property § 159, in General.

§ 1858.3.   Insurance protection

If the depositary by insurance or by self-insurance does protect property deposited by customers for loss or damage occasioned by theft, fire or vandalism while such property remains with the depositary, such depositary need not make or deliver to customer any notice thereof. *(Added by Stats.1970, c. 1185, p. 2093, § 1.)*

ARTICLE 4.   INNKEEPERS

§ 1859.   Innkeepers, etc., liability as depositaries for hire; limit of liability; special contracts

The liability of an innkeeper, hotelkeeper, operator of a licensed hospital, rest home or sanitarium, furnished apartment house keeper, furnished bungalow court keeper, boardinghouse or lodginghouse keeper, for losses of or injuries to personal property, is that of a depositary for hire; provided, however, that in no case shall such liability exceed the sum of one thousand dollars ($1,000) in the aggregate. In no case shall liability exceed, for each item of described property, the respective sums of five hundred dollars ($500) for each trunk and its contents, two hundred fifty dollars ($250) for each valise or traveling bag and its contents, two hundred fifty dollars ($250) for each box, bundle or package and its contents, and two hundred fifty dollars ($250) for all other personal property of any kind, unless he shall have consented in writing with the owner thereof to assume a greater liability. *(Enacted in 1872. Amended by Stats.1895, c. 47, p. 49, § 1; Stats.1921, c. 151, p. 149, § 1; Stats.1927, c. 593, p. 1028, § 1; Stats.1931, c. 1190, p. 2501, § 1; Stats.1943, c. 363, p. 1599, § 1; Stats.1957, c. 1251, p. 2557, § 1; Stats.1979, c. 705, p. 2183, § 1.)*

Research References

Miller and Starr California Real Estate § 19:7, Other Interests Distinguished--Eviction of a Guest or Lodger.

Miller and Starr California Real Estate § 19:235, Tenant's Personal Property--Innkeeper's Lien.

3 Witkin Cal. Proc. 5th Actions § 621, Action for Recovery or Conversion of Personal Property Left in Hotel and Similar Establishments.

13 Witkin, California Summary 10th Personal Property § 163, Gratuitous Bailment.

13 Witkin, California Summary 10th Personal Property § 168, Liability: in General.

13 Witkin, California Summary 10th Personal Property § 170, (S 170) Statutory Limitation to Fixed Sums.

13 Witkin, California Summary 10th Personal Property § 171, (S 171) What Constitutes Written Consent.

13 Witkin, California Summary 10th Personal Property § 172, Liability for Acts of Employees.

§ 1860.   Fireproof safe; notice of nonliability; limit of liability

If an innkeeper, hotelkeeper, operator of a licensed hospital, rest home or sanitarium, boardinghouse or lodginghouse keeper, keeps a fireproof safe and gives notice to a guest, patient, boarder or lodger, either personally or by putting up a printed notice in a prominent place in the office or the room occupied by the guest, patient, boarder, or lodger, that he keeps such a safe and will not be liable for money, jewelry, documents, furs, fur coats and fur garments, or other articles of unusual value and small compass, unless placed therein, he is not liable, except so far as his own acts shall contribute thereto, for any loss of or injury to such articles, if not deposited with him to be placed therein, nor in any case for more than the sum of five hundred dollars ($500) for any or all such property of any individual guest, patient, boarder, or lodger, unless he shall have given a receipt in writing therefor to such guest, patient, boarder or lodger. *(Enacted in 1872. Amended by Stats.1895, c. 47, p. 50, § 2; Stats.1921, c. 150, p. 149, § 1; Stats.1943, c. 363, p. 1600, § 2; Stats.1957, c. 1251, p. 2557, § 2; Stats.1979, c. 705, p. 2183, § 2.)*

Research References

Miller and Starr California Real Estate § 19:7, Other Interests Distinguished--Eviction of a Guest or Lodger.
Miller and Starr California Real Estate § 19:235, Tenant's Personal Property--Innkeeper's Lien.
12 Witkin, California Summary 10th Real Property § 514, Statutory Rights of Lodger.
13 Witkin, California Summary 10th Personal Property § 169, (S 169) Exemption: Fireproof Safe and Notice.
13 Witkin, California Summary 10th Personal Property § 170, (S 170) Statutory Limitation to Fixed Sums.
13 Witkin, California Summary 10th Personal Property § 171, (S 171) What Constitutes Written Consent.
13 Witkin, California Summary 10th Personal Property § 172, Liability for Acts of Employees.

§ 1861. Innkeeper's lien; enforcement; writ of possession; third party claims; exemptions

Hotel, motel, inn, boardinghouse, and lodginghouse keepers shall have a lien upon the baggage and other property belonging to or legally under the control of their guests, boarders, tenants, or lodgers which may be in such hotel, motel, inn, or boarding or lodging house for the proper charges due from such guests, boarders, tenants, or lodgers, for their accommodation, board and lodging and room rent, and such extras as are furnished at their request, and for all money paid for or advanced to such guests, boarders, tenants, or lodgers, and for the costs of enforcing such lien. The lien may be enforced only after final judgment in an action brought to recover such charges or moneys. During the pendency of the proceeding, the plaintiff may take possession of the baggage and property pursuant to a writ of possession as provided by Sections 1861.1 to 1861.27, inclusive. However, if any baggage or property becoming subject to the lien herein provided for does not belong to the guest, lodger, tenant, or boarder who incurred the charges or indebtedness secured thereby, at the time when such charges or indebtedness was incurred, and if the hotel, motel, inn, boarding or lodging house keeper entitled to such lien receives notice of such fact at any time before the sale of such baggage or property hereunder, then, and in that event, such baggage and property which is subject to said lien and did not belong to said guest, boarder, tenant, or lodger at the time when such charges or indebtedness was incurred shall not be subject to this lien.

Any property which is exempt from enforcement of a money judgment is not subject to the lien provided for in this section. *(Added by Code Am.1875–76, c. 486, p. 78, § 1. Amended by Stats.1915, c. 650, p. 1285, § 1; Stats.1939, c. 483, p. 1829, § 1; Stats.1953, c. 261, p. 1417, § 1; Stats.1957, c. 42, p. 600, § 1; Stats.1957, c. 591, p. 1686, § 1; Stats.1965, c. 1540, p. 3632, § 1; Stats.1967, c. 1387, p. 3246, § 1; Stats.1968, c. 1182, p. 2240, § 1; Stats.1970, c. 1247, p. 2237, § 1; Stats.1974, c. 546, p. 1357, § 13; Stats.1979, c. 964, p. 3309, § 1.5; Stats.1982, c. 497, p. 2137, § 9, operative July 1, 1983.)*

Research References

Miller and Starr California Real Estate § 19:7, Other Interests Distinguished--Eviction of a Guest or Lodger.
Miller and Starr California Real Estate § 19:235, Tenant's Personal Property--Innkeeper's Lien.

2 Witkin Cal. Proc. 5th Courts § 344, (S 344) Statutory Duties.
13 Witkin, California Summary 10th Personal Property § 222, Nature and Scope.
13 Witkin, California Summary 10th Personal Property § 223, Exemptions.
13 Witkin, California Summary 10th Personal Property § 224, (S 224) in General.
13 Witkin, California Summary 10th Personal Property § 225, (S 225) Landlord's Possession During Pendency of Action.

§ 1861.1. Definitions

Definitions for purposes of Sections 1861 through 1861.27 include the following:

(a) "Hotel", "motel", "inn", "boardinghouse", and "lodginghouse keeper" means any person, corporation, partnership, unincorporated association, public entity, or agent of any of the aforementioned, who offers and accepts payment for rooms, sleeping accommodations, or board and lodging and retains the right of access to, and control of, the dwelling unit.

(b) "Levying officer" means the sheriff or marshal who is directed to execute a writ of possession issued pursuant to this article.

(c) "Plaintiff" means any party filing a complaint or cross complaint.

(d) "Probable validity" means that the plaintiff, more likely than not, will obtain a judgment against the defendant on the plaintiff's claim. *(Added by Stats.1979, c. 964, p. 3310, § 2. Amended by Stats.1996, c. 872 (A.B.3472), § 23.)*

§ 1861.5. Application for writ of possession

(a) Upon the filing of a complaint, or at any time thereafter, the plaintiff may apply, pursuant to this article, for a writ of possession by filing an application for the writ with the court in which the action was filed.

(b) The application shall be executed under oath and shall include all of the following:

(1) A showing of the basis of the plaintiff's claim, including a showing that the plaintiff is entitled to possession of the property claimed pursuant to an innkeepers' lien.

(2) A general description of the property and a statement of its value.

(3) A statement of the amount of money claimed to be owed by the guest, lodger, tenant, or boarder.

(c) The requirements of subdivision (b) may be satisfied by one or more affidavits filed with the application. *(Added by Stats.1979, c. 964, p. 3310, § 3.)*

Research References

Rutter, Cal. Practice Guide: Civ. Pro. Before Trial Ch. 3-A, A. Subject Matter Jurisdiction (Competency).
Miller and Starr California Real Estate § 19:7, Other Interests Distinguished--Eviction of a Guest or Lodger.
Miller and Starr California Real Estate § 19:235, Tenant's Personal Property--Innkeeper's Lien.
2 Witkin Cal. Proc. 5th Courts § 282, (S 282) Particular Actions.
13 Witkin, California Summary 10th Personal Property § 226, Application, Writ, and Restraining Order.

§ 1861.6. Writ of possession; hearing; issuance; probable cause; conditions; papers served with writ; motion to quash; damages

(a) Except as otherwise provided in this section, no writ shall be issued under this article except after a hearing on a noticed motion.

(b) A writ of possession may be issued ex parte pursuant to this subdivision, if probable cause appears that the following conditions exist:

(1) The property is not necessary for the support of the defendant or his family;

(2) There is an immediate danger that the property will become unavailable to levy, by reason of being transferred, concealed, or removed from the state, or the premises of the motel, hotel, inn, boardinghouse, or lodginghouse, or will become substantially impaired in value by acts of destruction or by failure to take care of the property in a reasonable manner; and

(3) The ex parte issuance of a writ of possession is necessary to protect the property.

(4) The plaintiff establishes the probable validity of the plaintiff's claim.

The plaintiff's application for the writ shall satisfy the requirements of Section 1861.5 and, in addition, shall include a showing that the conditions required by this subdivision exist. A writ of possession may issue if the court finds that the conditions required by this subdivision exist, and the requirements of Section 1861.5 are met. Where a writ of possession has been issued pursuant to this subdivision, a copy of the summons and complaint, a copy of the application and any affidavit in support thereof, and a notice which satisfies the requirements of subdivisions (b) and (c) of Section 1861.8 and informs the defendant of his rights under this subdivision shall be served upon the defendant, and any other person required by Section 1861.8 to be served with a writ of possession. Any defendant whose property has been taken pursuant to a writ of possession issued under this subdivision may apply for an order that the writ be quashed, and any property levied on pursuant to the writ be released. Such application shall be made by noticed motion, and the provisions of Section 1861.9 shall apply. Pending the hearing of the defendant's application, the court may order that delivery pursuant to Section 1861.19 of any property previously levied upon be stayed. If the court determines that the plaintiff is not entitled to a writ of possession, the court shall quash the writ of possession and order the release and redelivery of any property previously levied upon, and shall award the defendant any damages sustained by the defendant which were proximately caused by the levy of the writ of possession and the loss of possession of the property pursuant to such levy. *(Added by Stats.1979, c. 964, p. 3310, § 4.)*

Research References

Miller and Starr California Real Estate § 19:235, Tenant's Personal Property--Innkeeper's Lien.
13 Witkin, California Summary 10th Personal Property § 226, Application, Writ, and Restraining Order.

§ 1861.7. Documents to be served

Prior to the hearing required by subdivision (a) of Section 1861.6, the defendant shall be served with all of the following:

(a) A copy of the summons and complaint.

(b) Notice of application and hearing.

(c) A copy of the application and any affidavit filed in support thereof. *(Added by Stats.1979, c. 964, p. 3311, § 5.)*

Research References

Miller and Starr California Real Estate § 19:235, Tenant's Personal Property--Innkeeper's Lien.
13 Witkin, California Summary 10th Personal Property § 226, Application, Writ, and Restraining Order.

§ 1861.8. Notice of Application and Hearing

The "Notice of Application and Hearing" shall inform the defendant of all of the following:

(a) The hearing will be held at a place and at a time, to be specified in the notice, on plaintiff's application for writ of possession.

(b) The writ shall be issued if the court finds that the plaintiff's claim has probable validity and the other requirements for issuing the writ are established. The hearing is not for the purpose of determining whether the claim is actually valid; such determination shall be made in subsequent proceedings in the action.

(c) If the defendant desires to oppose the issuance of the writ, he shall file with the court either an affidavit providing evidence sufficient to defeat the plaintiff's right to issuance of the writ, or an undertaking to stay the delivery of the property in accordance with Section 1861.22.

(d) The notice shall contain the following statement in 10-point bold type:

"If you believe the plaintiff may not be entitled to possession of the property claimed, you may wish to seek the advice of an attorney. Such attorney should be consulted promptly so that he may assist you before the time set for the hearing." *(Added by Stats.1979, c. 964, p. 3311, § 6.)*

Research References

Miller and Starr California Real Estate § 19:235, Tenant's Personal Property--Innkeeper's Lien.
13 Witkin, California Summary 10th Personal Property § 226, Application, Writ, and Restraining Order.

§ 1861.9. Affidavits; points and authorities; basis for determination; continuance; additional evidence

Each party shall file with the court and serve upon the other party within the time prescribed by rule, any affidavits and points and authorities intended to be relied upon at the hearing. At the hearing, the court shall make its determination upon the basis of the pleadings and other papers in the record; but, upon good cause shown, the court may receive and consider additional evidence and authority produced at the hearing, or may continue the hearing for the production of additional evidence, oral or documentary, and the filing of other affidavits or points and authorities. *(Added by Stats.1979, c. 964, p. 3312, § 7.)*

Research References

Miller and Starr California Real Estate § 19:235, Tenant's Personal Property--Innkeeper's Lien.
13 Witkin, California Summary 10th Personal Property § 226, Application, Writ, and Restraining Order.

§ 1861.10. Issuance of writ of possession; required findings

(a) At the hearing a writ of possession shall issue if all of the following are found:

(1) The plaintiff has established the probable validity of his claim to possession of the property of the tenant, boarder, or lodger.

(2) That the property which is described within the application for the writ is located on the premises of the motel, hotel, boardinghouse or lodginghouse.

(3) The plaintiff has provided an undertaking as required by Section 1861.21.

(b) No writ directing the levying officer to enter any premises to take possession of any property shall be issued unless the plaintiff has established that there is probable cause to believe that such property is located there. *(Added by Stats.1979, c. 964, p. 3312, § 8.)*

Research References

Miller and Starr California Real Estate § 19:235, Tenant's Personal Property--Innkeeper's Lien.
2 Witkin Cal. Proc. 5th Courts § 282, (S 282) Particular Actions.
13 Witkin, California Summary 10th Personal Property § 226, Application, Writ, and Restraining Order.

§ 1861.12.   Writ of possession; requirements

The writ of possession shall meet all of the following requirements:

(a) Be directed to the levying officer within whose jurisdiction the property is located.

(b) Generally describe the property to be seized.

(c) Specify the apartment, motel, or other boarding premises that may be entered to take possession of the property, or some part of it.

(d) Direct the levying officer to levy on the property pursuant to Section 1861.18 if found on the described premises, and to retain custody of it until released or sold pursuant to Section 1861.19.

(e) Inform the defendant of the right to object to the plaintiff's undertaking, a copy of which shall be attached to the writ, or to obtain the delivery of the property by filing an undertaking as prescribed by Section 1861.22. *(Added by Stats.1979, c. 964, p. 3312, § 9. Amended by Stats.1982, c. 517, p. 2323, § 65.)*

Law Revision Commission Comments

Section 1861.12 is amended for consistency with the Bond and Undertaking Law. See Code Civ.Proc. § 995.910 (objections to undertakings). The other changes in Section 1861.12 are technical. [16 Cal.L.Rev.Comm. Reports 501 (1981)].

Research References

13 Witkin, California Summary 10th Personal Property § 226, Application, Writ, and Restraining Order.

§ 1861.13.   Effect of failure to defend

Neither the failure of the defendant to oppose the issuance of a writ of possession under this article, nor his failure to rebut any evidence produced by the plaintiff in connection with proceedings under this article, shall constitute a waiver of any defense to the plaintiff's claim in the action, or any other action, or have any effect on the right of the defendant to produce or exclude evidence at the trial of any such action. *(Added by Stats.1979, c. 964, p. 3313, § 10.)*

Research References

Miller and Starr California Real Estate § 19:235, Tenant's Personal Property--Innkeeper's Lien.
13 Witkin, California Summary 10th Personal Property § 226, Application, Writ, and Restraining Order.

§ 1861.14.   Effect of determinations

The determinations of the court under this article shall have no effect on the determination of any issues in the action, other than the issues relevant to proceedings under this article, nor shall they affect the rights of any party in any other action arising out of the same claim. The determinations of the court under this article shall not be given in evidence, or referred to in the trial. *(Added by Stats.1979, c. 964, p. 3313, § 11.)*

Research References

Miller and Starr California Real Estate § 19:235, Tenant's Personal Property--Innkeeper's Lien.

13 Witkin, California Summary 10th Personal Property § 226, Application, Writ, and Restraining Order.

§ 1861.15.   Failure to recover judgment; redelivery of property; liability for damages

If the plaintiff fails to recover judgment in the action, he shall redeliver the property to the defendant, and be liable for all damages sustained by the defendant, which are proximately caused by operation of the temporary restraining order and preliminary injunction, if any, the levy of the writ of possession, and the loss of possession of the property pursuant to the levy of the writ of possession. *(Added by Stats.1979, c. 964, p. 3313, § 12.)*

Research References

Miller and Starr California Real Estate § 19:235, Tenant's Personal Property--Innkeeper's Lien.
13 Witkin, California Summary 10th Personal Property § 227, Levy on Property.

§ 1861.16.   Temporary restraining order; preliminary injunction

(a) At or after the time he files an application for a writ of possession, the plaintiff may apply for a temporary restraining order by setting forth in the application a statement of grounds justifying the issuance of such order.

(b) A temporary restraining order may issue ex parte if all the following are found:

(1) The plaintiff has established the probable validity of his claim and entitlement to possession of the property, pursuant to an innkeepers' lien.

(2) The plaintiff has provided an undertaking as required by Section 1861.21.

(3) The plaintiff has established the probable validity that there is an immediate danger that the property claimed may become unavailable to levy by reason of being transferred, concealed, or removed, or may become substantially impaired in value.

(c) If at the hearing on the issuance of the writ of possession the court determines that the plaintiff is not entitled to a writ of possession, the court shall dissolve any temporary restraining order; otherwise, the court may issue a preliminary injunction to remain in effect until the property claimed is seized pursuant to the writ of possession. *(Added by Stats.1979, c. 964, p. 3313, § 13.)*

Research References

Miller and Starr California Real Estate § 19:235, Tenant's Personal Property--Innkeeper's Lien.
13 Witkin, California Summary 10th Personal Property § 226, Application, Writ, and Restraining Order.

§ 1861.17.   Scope of temporary restraining order

In the discretion of the court, the temporary restraining order may prohibit the defendant from doing any or all of the following:

(a) Transferring any interest in the property by sale, pledge, or grant of security interest, or otherwise disposing of, or encumbering, the property.

(b) Concealing or otherwise removing the property in such a manner as to make it less available to seizure by the levying officer.

(c) Impairing the value of the property either by acts of destruction or by failure to care for the property in a reasonable manner. *(Added by Stats.1979, c. 964, p. 3314, § 14.)*

Research References

Miller and Starr California Real Estate § 19:235, Tenant's Personal Property--Innkeeper's Lien.

13 Witkin, California Summary 10th Personal Property § 226, Application, Writ, and Restraining Order.

§ 1861.18.   Service by levying officer

(a) At the time of levy, the levying officer shall deliver to the person in possession of the property a copy of the writ of possession, with a copy of the plaintiff's undertaking attached.

(b) If no one is in possession of the property at the time of levy, the levying officer shall subsequently serve the writ and attached undertaking on the defendant. If the defendant has appeared in the action, service shall be accomplished in the manner provided by Chapter 5 (commencing with Section 1010) of Title 14 of Part 2. If the defendant has not appeared in the action, service shall be accomplished in the manner provided for the service of summons and complaint by Article 3 (commencing with Section 415.10) of Chapter 4 of Title 5 of Part 2. *(Added by Stats.1979, c. 964, p. 3314, § 15.)*

Research References

13 Witkin, California Summary 10th Personal Property § 227, Levy on Property.

§ 1861.19.   Duties of levying officer; undertaking for redelivery; objection; perishables

(a) After the levying officer takes possession pursuant to the writ of possession, the levying officer shall keep the property in a secure place. Except as otherwise provided in Section 1861.6:

(1) If notice of the filing of an undertaking for redelivery or notice of objection to the undertaking is not received by the levying officer within 10 days after levy of the writ of possession, the levying officer shall deliver the property to plaintiff, upon receiving the fees for taking, and necessary expenses for keeping, the property.

(2) If notice of the filing of an undertaking for redelivery is received by the levying officer within 10 days after levy of the writ of possession, and no objection is made to the defendant's undertaking, the levying officer shall redeliver the property to defendant upon expiration of the time to object, upon receiving the fees for taking and necessary expenses for keeping the property not already paid or advanced by the plaintiff.

(3) If notice of objection to the plaintiff's undertaking or notice of the filing of an undertaking for redelivery is received within 10 days after levy of the writ of possession, and objection is made to the defendant's undertaking, the levying officer shall not deliver or redeliver the property until the time provided in Section 1861.23.

(b) Notwithstanding subdivision (a), when not otherwise provided by contract, and where an undertaking for redelivery has not been filed, upon a showing that the property is perishable, or will greatly deteriorate or depreciate in value, or for some other reason that the interest of the parties will be best served thereby, the court may order that the property be sold and the proceeds deposited in the court to abide the judgment in the action. *(Added by Stats.1979, c. 964, p. 3314, § 16. Amended by Stats.1982, c. 517, p. 2323, § 66.)*

Law Revision Commission Comments

Section 1861.19 is amended for consistency with the Bond and Undertaking Law. See Code Civ.Proc. § 995.910 (objections to undertakings). The other changes in Section 1861.19 are technical. [16 Cal.L.Rev.Comm. Reports 501 (1981)].

Research References

Miller and Starr California Real Estate § 19:235, Tenant's Personal Property--Innkeeper's Lien.

13 Witkin, California Summary 10th Personal Property § 226, Application, Writ, and Restraining Order.

13 Witkin, California Summary 10th Personal Property § 227, Levy on Property.

§ 1861.20.   Return of writ of possession; time

The levying officer shall return the writ of possession, with his proceedings thereon, to the court in which the action is pending, within 30 days after a levy, but in no event more than 60 days after the writ is issued. *(Added by Stats.1979, c. 964, p. 3315, § 17.)*

Research References

13 Witkin, California Summary 10th Personal Property § 227, Levy on Property.

§ 1861.21.   Plaintiff's undertaking

The court shall not issue a temporary restraining order or a writ of possession until the plaintiff has filed with the court an undertaking. The undertaking shall provide that the sureties are bound to the defendant in the amount of the undertaking for the return of the property to the defendant, if the return thereof be ordered, and for the payment to the defendant of any sum recovered against plaintiff. The undertaking shall be in an amount not less than twice the value of the property. *(Added by Stats.1979, c. 964, p. 3315, § 18. Amended by Stats.1982, c. 517, p. 2324, § 67.)*

Law Revision Commission Comments

Section 1861.21 is amended to delete provisions duplicated in the Bond and Undertaking Law. See Code Civ.Proc. §§ 995.310 (number of sureties), 995.320 (contents of undertaking). See also Code Civ.Proc. § 995.910 (objections to undertakings). [16 Cal.L.Rev.Comm. Reports 501 (1981)].

Research References

Miller and Starr California Real Estate § 19:235, Tenant's Personal Property--Innkeeper's Lien.

13 Witkin, California Summary 10th Personal Property § 226, Application, Writ, and Restraining Order.

§ 1861.22.   Defendant's undertaking

(a) The defendant may prevent the plaintiff from taking possession of property, pursuant to a writ of possession, or regain possession of property so taken, by filing with the court in which the action was brought an undertaking in an amount equal to the amount of the plaintiff's undertaking required by Section 1861.21. The undertaking shall state that, if the plaintiff recovers judgment on the action, the defendant shall pay all costs awarded to the plaintiff and all damages that the plaintiff may sustain by reason of the loss of possession of the property, not exceeding the amount of the undertaking.

(b) The defendant's undertaking may be filed at any time before or after the levy of the writ of possession. The defendant shall mail a copy of the undertaking to the levying officer.

(c) If an undertaking for redelivery is filed, and no objection is made to the undertaking, the levying officer shall deliver the property to the defendant, or, if the plaintiff has previously been given possession of the property, the plaintiff shall deliver the property to the defendant. If an undertaking for redelivery is filed and an objection to the undertaking is made, the provisions of Section 1861.23 apply. *(Added by Stats.1979, c. 964, p. 3315, § 19. Amended by Stats.1982, c. 517, p. 2324, § 68.)*

Law Revision Commission Comments

Section 1861.22 is amended to delete provisions duplicated in the Bond and Undertaking Law. See Code Civ.Proc. §§ 995.310 (number of sureties), 995.320 (contents of undertaking), 995.370 (service of copy of undertaking); see also Code Civ.Proc. § 995.910 (objections to undertakings). [16 Cal.L.Rev.Comm. Reports 501 (1981)].

Research References

Miller and Starr California Real Estate § 19:235, Tenant's Personal Property--Innkeeper's Lien.
13 Witkin, California Summary 10th Personal Property § 227, Levy on Property.

§ 1861.23. Objections to undertakings; time; notice; determination of sufficiency; order of court

(a) The defendant may object to the plaintiff's undertaking not later than 10 days after levy of the writ of possession. The defendant shall mail notice of objection to the levying officer.

(b) The plaintiff may object to the defendant's undertaking not later than 10 days after the defendant's undertaking is filed. The plaintiff shall mail notice of objection to the levying officer.

(c) If the court determines that the plaintiff's undertaking is not sufficient and a sufficient undertaking is not given within the time provided by statute, the court shall vacate the temporary restraining order or preliminary injunction, if any, and the writ of possession and, if levy has occurred, order the levying officer or the plaintiff to return the property to the defendant. If the court determines that the plaintiff's undertaking is sufficient, the court shall order the levying officer to deliver the property to the plaintiff.

(d) If the court determines that the defendant's undertaking is not sufficient and a sufficient undertaking is not given within the time required by statute, the court shall order the levying officer to deliver the property to the plaintiff, or, if the plaintiff has previously been given possession of the property, the plaintiff shall retain possession. If the court determines the defendant's undertaking is sufficient, the court shall order the levying officer or the plaintiff to deliver the property to the defendant. *(Formerly § 1821.23, added by Stats.1979, c. 964, p. 3316, § 20. Renumbered § 1861.23 and amended by Stats.1981, c. 714, p. 2591, § 53. Amended by Stats.1982, c. 517, p. 2325, § 69.)*

Law Revision Commission Comments

Section 1861.23 is amended to delete provisions duplicated in the Bond and Undertaking Law. See Code Civ.Proc. §§ 995.910–995.960 (objections to undertakings). [16 Cal.L.Rev.Comm. Reports 501 (1981)].

Research References

Miller and Starr California Real Estate § 19:235, Tenant's Personal Property--Innkeeper's Lien.
13 Witkin, California Summary 10th Personal Property § 226, Application, Writ, and Restraining Order.
13 Witkin, California Summary 10th Personal Property § 227, Levy on Property.

§ 1861.24. Nonpayment of judgment; sale of baggage or property; procedure; distribution of proceeds

Unless the judgment is paid within 30 days from the date it becomes final, the plaintiff may sell the baggage and property at public auction to the highest bidder, after giving notice of the sale by publication. The notice shall contain the name of the debtor, the amount due, a brief description of the property to be sold, and the time and place of sale, in the manner required by Section 6061 of the Government Code in the county in which the premises are situated. A copy of the notice shall be mailed, at least 15 days prior to the date of sale, to the tenant or guest at his or her residence or other known address, and if not known, to the tenant or guest at the place where the premises are situated. After satisfying the lien out of the proceeds of the sale, together with any reasonable costs that may have been incurred in enforcing the lien, the balance of the proceeds of the sale, if any, which have not been claimed by the tenant or guest shall, within 30 days from the date of the sale, be paid into the treasury of the county in which the sale took place. If that balance is not claimed by the owner thereof, or his legal representative, within one year thereafter, by making application to the treasurer or other official designated by the county, it shall be paid into the general fund of the county. Any sale conducted pursuant to this section shall be a bar to any action against the plaintiff for the recovery of the baggage or property, or of the value thereof, or for any damages arising out of the failure of the tenant or guest to receive the baggage or property. *(Added by Stats.1979, c. 964, p. 3316, § 21.)*

Research References

Miller and Starr California Real Estate § 19:235, Tenant's Personal Property--Innkeeper's Lien.

§ 1861.25. Application of rules and proceedings applicable to third-party claims

Where the property taken is claimed by a third person, the rules and proceedings applicable in cases of third-party claims under Division 4 (commencing with Section 720.010) of Title 9 of Part 2 of the Code of Civil Procedure apply. *(Added by Stats.1982, c. 497, p. 2139, § 10.5, operative July 1, 1983.)*

Research References

8 Witkin Cal. Proc. 5th Enforcement of Judgment § 364, (S 364) Nature and Scope of Remedy.
13 Witkin, California Summary 10th Personal Property § 227, Levy on Property.

§ 1861.27. Affidavits; particularity; qualifications of affiant; verified complaint

The facts stated in each affidavit filed pursuant to this article shall be set forth with particularity. Except where matters are specifically permitted by this article to be shown by information and belief, each affidavit shall show affirmatively that the affiant, if sworn as a witness, can testify competently to the facts stated therein. The affiant may be any person, whether or not a party to this action, who has knowledge of the facts. A verified complaint that satisfies the requirements of this section may be used in lieu of, or in addition to, an ordinary affidavit. *(Added by Stats.1979, c. 964, p. 3317, § 22.)*

Research References

Miller and Starr California Real Estate § 19:7, Other Interests Distinguished--Eviction of a Guest or Lodger.
Miller and Starr California Real Estate § 19:235, Tenant's Personal Property--Innkeeper's Lien.
13 Witkin, California Summary 10th Personal Property § 226, Application, Writ, and Restraining Order.

§ 1861.28. Subordinate judicial duties

The judicial duties to be performed under this article are "subordinate judicial duties" within the meaning of Section 22 of Article VI of the California Constitution, and may be performed by appointed officers such as court commissioners. *(Added by Stats.1979, c. 964, p. 3317, § 23.)*

Research References

Miller and Starr California Real Estate § 19:235, Tenant's Personal Property--Innkeeper's Lien.
2 Witkin Cal. Proc. 5th Courts § 344, (S 344) Statutory Duties.

13 Witkin, California Summary 10th Personal Property § 226, Application, Writ, and Restraining Order.

§ 1861a. Keepers of apartment houses, etc.; lien; enforcement procedure; disposition of proceeds; exemptions

Keepers of furnished and unfurnished apartment houses, apartments, cottages, or bungalow courts shall have a lien upon the baggage and other property of value belonging to their tenants or guests, and upon all the right, title and interest of their tenants or guests in and to all property in the possession of such tenants or guests which may be in such apartment house, apartment, cottage, or bungalow court, for the proper charges due from such tenants or guests, for their accommodation, rent, services, meals, and such extras as are furnished at their request, and for all moneys expended for them, at their request, and for the costs of enforcing such lien.

Such lien may be enforced only after final judgment in an action brought to recover such charges or moneys. During the pendency of the proceeding, the plaintiff may take possession of such baggage and property upon an order issued by the court, where it appears to the satisfaction of the court from an affidavit filed by or on behalf of the plaintiff that the baggage or property is about to be destroyed, substantially devalued, or removed from the premises. Ten days written notice of the hearing on the motion for such order shall be served on the defendant and shall inform the defendant that the defendant may file affidavits on the defendant's behalf and present testimony in the defendant's behalf and that if the defendant fails to appear the plaintiff will apply to the court for such order. The plaintiff shall file an undertaking with good and sufficient sureties, to be approved by the court, in such sum as may be fixed by the court.

Upon such order, the plaintiff shall have the right to enter peaceably the unfurnished apartment house, apartment, cottage, or bungalow court used by the guest or tenant without liability to the guest or tenant, including any possible claim of liability for conversion, trespass, or forcible entry. The plaintiff shall have the same duties and liabilities as a depository for hire as to property which the plaintiff takes into possession. An entry shall be considered peaceable when accomplished with a key or passkey or through an unlocked door during the hours between sunrise and sunset. Unless the judgment shall be paid within 30 days from the date when it becomes final, the plaintiff may sell the baggage and property, at public auction to the highest bidder, after giving notice of such sale by publication of a notice containing the name of the debtor, the amount due, a brief description of the property to be sold, and the time and place of such sale, pursuant to Section 6064 of the Government Code in the county in which said apartment house, apartment, cottage, or bungalow court is situated, and after by mailing, at least 15 days prior to the date of sale, a copy of such notice addressed to such tenant or guest at the residence or other known address of the tenant or guest, and if not known, such notice shall be addressed to the tenant or guest at the place where such apartment house, apartment, cottage, or bungalow court is situated; and, after satisfying such lien out of the proceeds of such sale, together with any reasonable costs, that may have been incurred in enforcing said lien, the residue of said proceeds of sale, if any, shall, upon demand made within six months after such sale, be paid to such tenant or guest; and if not demanded within six months from the date of such sale, said residue, if any, shall be paid into the treasury of the county in which such sale took place; and if the same be not claimed by the owner thereof, or the owner's legal representative within one year thereafter, it shall be paid into the general fund of the county; and such sale shall be a perpetual bar to any action against said keeper for the recovery of such baggage or property, or of the value thereof, or for any damages, growing out of the failure of such tenant or guest to receive such baggage or property.

When the baggage and property are not in the possession of the keeper as provided herein, such lien shall be enforced only in the manner provided for enforcement of a money judgment.

Any property which is exempt from enforcement of a money judgment is not subject to the lien provided for in this section. *(Added by Stats.1917, c. 794, p. 1662, § 1. Amended by Stats.1933, c. 900, p. 2341, § 1; Stats.1939, c. 483, p. 1831, § 2; Stats.1941, c. 515, p. 1825, § 1; Stats.1953, c. 250, p. 1385, § 1; Stats.1953, c. 1453, p. 3051, § 1; Stats.1957, c. 454, p. 1306, § 1; Stats.1961, c. 2041, p. 4258, § 1; Stats.1965, c. 1540, p. 3634, § 1.5; Stats.1967, c. 1387, p. 3247, § 2; Stats.1968, c. 1182, p. 2242, § 2; Stats.1970, c. 1247, p. 2238, § 2; Stats.1982, c. 517, p. 2325, § 70; Stats.1982, c. 497, p. 2139, § 10, operative July 1, 1983.)*

Law Revision Commission Comments

Section 1861a is amended to conform to Title 9 (commencing with Section 680.010) of Part 2 of the Code of Civil Procedure (Enforcement of Judgments Law). The provision concerning the rights of chattel mortgagees and conditional sellers is not continued because it is unnecessary. See, e.g., Com. Code §§ 9301 (rights of lien creditor), 9310 (priority of certain liens arising by operation of law). The last paragraph of Section 1861a is revised to read the same as the last paragraph of revised Section 1861. See the Comment to that section. [16 Cal.L.Rev.Comm. Reports 1001 (1982)].

Research References

Miller and Starr California Real Estate § 19:236, Tenant's Personal Property--Residential Landlord's Lien.

12 Witkin, California Summary 10th Real Property § 759, Where Landlord Has Lien.

13 Witkin, California Summary 10th Personal Property § 222, Nature and Scope.

13 Witkin, California Summary 10th Personal Property § 223, Exemptions.

13 Witkin, California Summary 10th Personal Property § 224, (S 224) in General.

13 Witkin, California Summary 10th Personal Property § 225, (S 225) Landlord's Possession During Pendency of Action.

5 Witkin, California Summary 10th Torts § 697, Other Privileged Entries.

5 Witkin, California Summary 10th Torts § 719, (S 719) Defense of Privilege.

§ 1862.5. Unclaimed property in hospital; sale; notice; expenses; surplus

Whenever any personal property has heretofore been found in or deposited with, or is hereafter found in or deposited with any licensed hospital and has remained or shall remain unclaimed for a period of 180 days following the departure of the owner from the hospital, such hospital may proceed to sell the same at public auction, and out of the proceeds of such sale may retain the charges for storage, if any, the reasonable expenses of sale thereof and all sums due the hospital from the last known owner. No such sale shall be made until the expiration of four weeks from the time written notice of such sale is given to the last known owner. Said notice shall contain a description of each item of personal property to be sold, the name of the last owner, the name of the hospital and the time and place of sale and may be sent by regular mail, postage prepaid, to the last known owner at his last known address. In case there should be any balance from such sale after the deductions herein provided for, and such balance shall not be claimed by the rightful owner or his legal representative within one week of said sale, the same shall be paid into the treasury of the county wherein said hospital is located; and if the same be not claimed by the owner thereof, or his legal representative within one year thereafter, the same shall be paid into the general fund of said county. Proceedings in substantial compliance with this section shall exonerate the hospital from any liability for property so sold. This section shall not be construed as limiting or in any way amending any other provision of law limiting the liabilities of any licensed hospital. *(Added by Stats.1963, c. 810, p. 1840, § 1.)*

Research References

12 Witkin, California Summary 10th Real Property § 749, Nature of Statute.
12 Witkin, California Summary 10th Real Property § 754A, (New)-Scope of Statute.
13 Witkin, California Summary 10th Personal Property § 39, (S 39) Other Statutes Dealing With Unclaimed Property.

§ 1863. Rates of charges; posting

(a) Every keeper of a hotel, inn, boardinghouse or lodging-house, shall post in a conspicuous place in the office or public room, and in every bedroom of said hotel, boardinghouse, inn, or lodginghouse, a printed copy of this section, and a statement of rate or range of rates by the day for lodging.

(b) No charge or sum shall be collected or received for any greater sum than is specified in subdivision (a). For any violation of this subdivision, the offender shall forfeit to the injured party one hundred dollars ($100) or three times the amount of the sum charged in excess of what he is entitled to, whichever is greater. There shall be no forfeiture under this subdivision unless notice be given of the overcharge to such keeper within 30 days after payment of such charges and such keeper shall fail or refuse to make proper adjustment of such overcharge. *(Added by Code Am.1875–76, c. 486, p. 79, § 1. Amended by Stats.1969, c. 826, p. 1655, § 1.)*

Research References

Miller and Starr California Real Estate § 19:7, Other Interests Distinguished--Eviction of a Guest or Lodger.
3 Witkin Cal. Proc. 5th Actions § 227, Miscellaneous Statutory Requirements.

§ 1864. Solicitation or acceptance of reservations or money for transient occupancies in certain dwelling units; duties

Any person or entity, including a person employed by a real estate broker, who, on behalf of another or others, solicits or arranges, or accepts reservations or money, or both, for transient occupancies described in paragraphs (1) and (2) of subdivision (b) of Section 1940, in a dwelling unit in a common interest development, as defined in Section 4100, in a dwelling unit in an apartment building or complex, or in a single-family home, shall do each of the following:

(a) Prepare and maintain, in accordance with a written agreement with the owner, complete and accurate records and books of account, kept in accordance with generally accepted accounting principles, of all reservations made and money received and spent with respect to each dwelling unit. All money received shall be kept in a trust account maintained for the benefit of owners of the dwelling units.

(b) Render, monthly, to each owner of the dwelling unit, or to that owner's designee, an accounting for each month in which there are any deposits or disbursements on behalf of that owner, however, in no event shall this accounting be rendered any less frequently than quarterly.

(c) Make all records and books of account with respect to a dwelling unit available, upon reasonable advance notice, for inspection and copying by the dwelling unit's owner. The records shall be maintained for a period of at least three years.

(d) Comply fully with all collection, payment, and recordkeeping requirements of a transient occupancy tax ordinance, if any, applicable to the occupancy.

(e) In no event shall any activities described in this section subject the person or entity performing those activities in any manner to Part 1 (commencing with Section 10000) of Division 4

of the Business and Professions Code. However, a real estate licensee subject to this section may satisfy the requirements of this section by compliance with the Real Estate Law. *(Added by Stats.1992, c. 134 (A.B.814), § 2. Amended by Stats.2012, c. 181 (A.B.806), § 37, operative Jan. 1, 2014.)*

Law Revision Commission Comments

Section 1864 is amended to correct a cross-reference to former Section 1351(c). [40 Cal.L.Rev.Comm. Reports 235 (2010)].

Research References

Miller and Starr California Real Estate § 4:10, Property Management.
13 Witkin, California Summary 10th Personal Property § 118, Former Law and Revision.

§ 1865. Distribution of handbills in hotels without permission

(a) For purposes of this section, "hotel" means any hotel, motel, bed and breakfast inn, or other similar transient lodging establishment, but it shall not include any residential hotel as defined in Section 50519 of the Health and Safety Code. "Innkeeper" means the owner or operator of a hotel, or the duly authorized agent or employee of the owner or operator.

(b) For purposes of this section, "guest" means, and is specifically limited to, an occupant of a hotel whose occupancy is exempt, pursuant to subdivision (b) of Section 1940, from Chapter 2 (commencing with Section 1940) of Title 5 of Part 4 of Division 3.

(c) In addition to, and not in derogation of, any other provision of law, every innkeeper shall have the right to evict a guest in the manner specified in this subdivision if the guest refuses or otherwise fails to fully depart the guest room at or before the innkeeper's posted checkout time on the date agreed to by the guest, but only if both of the following conditions are met:

(1) If the guest is provided written notice, at the time that he or she was received and provided accommodations by the innkeeper, that the innkeeper needs that guest's room to accommodate an arriving person with a contractual right thereto, and that if the guest fails to fully depart at the time agreed to the innkeeper may enter the guest's guest room, take possession of the guest's property, re-key the door to the guest room, and make the guest room available to a new guest. The written notice shall be signed by the guest.

(2) At the time that the innkeeper actually undertakes to evict the guest as specified in this subdivision, the innkeeper in fact has a contractual obligation to provide the guest room to an arriving person.

In the above cases, the innkeeper may enter the guest's guest room, take possession of the guest's property, re-key the door to the guest room, and make the guest room available to a new guest. The evicted guest shall be entitled to immediate possession of his or her property upon request therefor, subject to the rights of the innkeeper pursuant to Sections 1861 to 1861.28, inclusive.

(d) As pertains to a minor, the rights of an innkeeper include, but are not limited to, the following:

(1) Where a minor unaccompanied by an adult seeks accommodations, the innkeeper may require a parent or guardian of the minor, or another responsible adult, to assume, in writing, full liability for any and all proper charges and other obligations incurred by the minor for accommodations, food and beverages, and other services provided by or through the innkeeper, as well as for any and all injuries or damage caused by the minor to any person or property.

(2) Where a minor is accompanied by an adult, the innkeeper may require the adult to agree, in writing, not to leave any minor

12 years of age or younger unattended on the innkeeper's premises at any time during their stay, and to control the minor's behavior during their stay so as to preserve the peace and quiet of the innkeeper's other guests and to prevent any injury to any person and damage to any property. *(Added by Stats.1999, c. 354 (S.B.1171), § 2. Amended by Stats.2004, c. 183 (A.B.3082), § 38.)*

Research References

Miller and Starr California Real Estate § 19:6, Other Interests Distinguished--Occupation by a Guest or Lodger.

Miller and Starr California Real Estate § 19:7, Other Interests Distinguished--Eviction of a Guest or Lodger.

§ 1866. Special occupancy parks; eviction; possession and removal of property; rights of minors

(a) For purposes of this section, the following definitions apply:

(1) "Camping cabin" has the same meaning as in Section 18862.5 of the Health and Safety Code.

(2) "Campsite" has the same meaning as in Section 18862.9 of the Health and Safety Code.

(3) "Guest" is interchangeable with "occupant" and has the same meaning as used in Chapter 2.6 (commencing with Section 799.20) of Title 2 of Part 2 of Division 1.

(4) "Lot" has the same meaning as in Section 18862.23 of the Health and Safety Code.

(5) "Motor vehicle" has the same meaning as in Section 415 of the Vehicle Code.

(6) "Occupant" is interchangeable with "guest" and has the same meaning as used in Chapter 2.6 (commencing with Section 799.20) of Title 2 of Part 2 of Division 1.

(7) "Park trailer" has the same meaning as in Section 18009.3 of the Health and Safety Code.

(8) "Recreational vehicle" has the same meaning as in Section 18010 of the Health and Safety Code.

(9) "Site" means the campsite, camping cabin, lot, or rental unit.

(10) "Special occupancy park" has the same meaning as in Section 18862.43 of the Health and Safety Code.

(11) "Tent" has the same meaning as in Section 18862.49 of the Health and Safety Code.

(b)(1) Notwithstanding any other provision of law, the park management of a special occupancy park shall have the right to evict a guest if the guest refuses or otherwise fails to fully depart from the campsite, camping cabin, lot, or other rental unit at the park management's posted checkout time on the date agreed to by the guest, but only if the following conditions are met:

(A) The guest is provided with written notice, at the time that he or she was provided accommodations by the park management, that the park management needs that guest's campsite, camping cabin, lot, or rental unit to accommodate an arriving person with a contractual right thereto, and that if the guest fails to fully depart at the time agreed to, the park management may take possession of the guest's property left in the site, subject to the limits of paragraph (2), including any tent, park trailer, or recreational vehicle, and make the campsite, camping cabin, lot, or rental unit available to new guests. The written notice shall be signed by the guest.

(B)(i) At the time that the park management actually undertakes to evict the guest as specified in this subdivision, the park management has a contractual obligation to provide the guest's campsite, camping cabin, lot, or rental unit to an arriving person

and there are no other substantially similar campsites, camping cabins, lots, or rental units available for the arriving person.

(ii) Subject to the same requirements described in subparagraph (i), a guest may be provided with the notice described in subparagraph (A) subsequent to the time he or she was provided accommodations by park management, if the notice is provided at least 24 hours prior to the guest's scheduled checkout time. If park management provides a notice under this subparagraph in bad faith or with the knowledge that the contractual obligation is not a bona fide obligation, it shall be liable to the evicted guest for actual damages, plus a civil penalty of two hundred fifty dollars ($250).

(C) At the time that the park management actually undertakes to evict the guest as specified in this subdivision, the park management offers another campsite, camping cabin, lot, or rental unit to the guest, if one is available.

(2) In addition to the requirements of paragraph (1), in order for management to remove a recreational vehicle or motor vehicle, the park management shall do all of the following:

(A) Management shall have an oral, face-to-face communication with the registered guest after the guest has held over that does all of the following:

(i) Alerts the guest that he or she is in violation of the terms of the reservation because he or she has failed to depart the site at the agreed-upon time.

(ii) Reminds the guest that failure to remove a recreational vehicle, motor vehicle, or any other property from the space within two hours may result in the park management removing the recreational vehicle, motor vehicle, or any other property.

(iii) Discloses that the cost of towing a recreational vehicle or motor vehicle is substantial and that these costs will be incurred by the guest.

(iv) Identifies another location in the park to which the guest may temporarily move his or her recreational vehicle or motor vehicle.

(B) The park management gives the guest two hours after the park management has communicated with the guest, pursuant to subparagraph (A), to remove the guest's recreational vehicle, motor vehicle, or other property from the site.

(c) Except as provided in subdivision (f), if the conditions specified in subdivision (b) are met, the park management may take possession of the guest's property left at the site and have the guest's recreational vehicle or motor vehicle towed from the special occupancy park and make the guest's campsite, camping cabin, lot, or rental unit available to a new guest. Park management may enter a campsite, camping cabin, park trailer, lot, or rental unit owned by the park management to take possession of the guest's possessions. The evicted guest shall be entitled to immediate possession of his or her property upon request, subject to the enforcement rights of the park management, which are the same as those accorded to a hotel, motel, inn, boarding house, or lodging housekeeper, pursuant to Sections 1861 to 1861.28, inclusive. If a guest's recreational vehicle or motor vehicle has been towed from the premises, the guest shall be entitled to immediate possession of his or her vehicle upon request, subject to the conditions of the towing company.

(d) When the park management moves or causes the removal of a guest's recreational vehicle, motor vehicle, or other property, the management and the individual or entity that removes the recreational vehicle, motor vehicle, or other property shall exercise reasonable and ordinary care in removing the recreational vehicle, motor vehicle, or other property.

(e) This section does not apply to a manufactured home, as defined in Section 18007 of the Health and Safety Code, or a mobilehome, as defined in Section 18008 of the Health and Safety Code.

(f) In the event that a guest is incapable of removing his or her recreational vehicle or motor vehicle from the lot because of: (1) a physical incapacity, (2) the recreational vehicle or motor vehicle is not motorized and cannot be moved by the guest's vehicle, or (3) the recreational vehicle or motor vehicle is inoperable due to mechanical difficulties, the guest shall be provided with 72 hours in which to remove the vehicle. If the guest has not removed the vehicle within 72 hours, park management may remove the vehicle without further notice.

(g) As pertains to a minor, the rights of guests include, but are not limited to, the following:

(1) If a minor who is unaccompanied by an adult seeks accommodations, the park management may require a parent or guardian of the minor, or another responsible adult, to assume, in writing, full liability for any and all proper charges and other obligations incurred by the minor for accommodations, food and beverages, and other services provided by or through the park management, as well as for any and all injuries or damage caused by the minor to any person or property.

(2) If a minor is accompanied by an adult, the park management may require the adult to agree, in writing, not to leave any minor 12 years of age or younger unattended on the park management's premises at any time during their stay, and to control the minor's behavior during their stay so as to preserve the peace and quiet of the other guests and to prevent any injury to any person and damage to any property. *(Added by Stats. 2004, c. 530 (A.B.1964), § 4.)*

§ 1867. Special occupancy parks; movement of guest if imminent danger

(a) The park management of a special occupancy park may require a guest to move from a space in the special occupancy park to a different space in the special occupancy park if an imminent danger is present, as determined by the park management. If possible, the park management shall offer to return the guest to his or her original space once the park management has determined that the imminent danger is removed or resolved.

(b) For purposes of this section, the following definitions apply:

(1) "Imminent danger" means a danger that poses an immediate and likely risk to the health or safety of a guest or guests in the special occupancy park.

(2) "Space" means any of the following:

(A) "Camping cabin," as defined in Section 18862.5 of the Health and Safety Code.

(B) "Campsite," as defined in Section 18862.9 of the Health and Safety Code.

(C) "Lot," as defined in Section 18862.23 of the Health and Safety Code, or other rental unit.

(3) "Special occupancy park" has the same meaning as in Section 18862.43 of the Health and Safety Code. *(Added by Stats.2004, c. 530 (A.B.1964), § 5.)*

CHAPTER 3. DEPOSIT FOR EXCHANGE

§ 1878. Transfer of title; relationship between parties

A deposit for exchange transfers to the depositary the title to the thing deposited, and creates between him and the depositor the relation of debtor and creditor merely. *(Enacted in 1872.)*

Research References

13 Witkin, California Summary 10th Personal Property § 157, (S 157) Title and Estoppel to Deny.

CHAPTER 4. PRIVATE BULK STORAGE OF GRAIN

§ 1880. Short title

This chapter may be cited as the Private Bulk Grain Storage Law. *(Added by Stats.1944, 4th Ex.Sess., c. 54, p. 211, § 1.)*

§ 1880.1. Definitions

As used in this chapter:

(a) "Grain" includes barley, corn, flax, hay, grain sorghums, oats, rice, rye, and wheat.

(b) "Seller" means a producer of grain who continues to store grain after sale thereof by him in storage facilities owned, operated, or controlled by him.

(c) "Storage facilities" means any bin, building, elevator, protected enclosure, or other structure owned, operated, or controlled by the seller of the grain stored therein.

(d) "Private bulk storage" means the storage of grain in storage facilities after sale of such grain by a seller.

(e) "Buyer" means a purchaser of grain which is thereafter stored in private bulk storage, and includes the assigns and successors in interest of such buyer.

(f) "Bill of sale" means a written instrument, conforming to the requirements of this chapter, which evidences a transfer of grain. *(Added by Stats.1944, 4th Ex.Sess., c. 54, p. 211, § 1.)*

§ 1880.2. Storage facilities; marking

The seller shall conspicuously mark on all storage facilities "Private bulk storage only" and with a designating number on each such facility and such markings shall be maintained at all times during which grain remains in private bulk storage therein. *(Added by Stats.1944, 4th Ex.Sess., c. 54, p. 212, § 1.)*

§ 1880.3. Sale by bill of sale without delivery

Grain in private bulk storage facilities may be sold in conformity with this chapter by bill of sale without delivery and no provision of Section 3440 of this code or of any other law requiring delivery or actual and continued change of possession shall be applicable to grain so sold. *(Added by Stats.1944, 4th Ex.Sess., c. 54, p. 212, § 1.)*

§ 1880.4. Bill of sale; contents

Upon sale of grain which is to remain in private bulk storage the seller shall execute and deliver to the buyer a bill of sale which shall contain all of the following:

(a) The date and place where made.

(b) The names of the seller and the buyer.

(c) A statement of the estimated quantity and kind of grain.

(d) A statement of the location and designating numbers of the storage facilities in which the grain is stored.

(e) A statement of the price per unit and a statement of the amount received by the seller. *(Added by Stats.1944, 4th Ex.Sess., c. 54, p. 212, § 1.)*

§ 1880.5. Bill of sale; optional contracts

The bill of sale may contain other provisions, including reference to or provision for any one or more of the following:

(a) Provision that the total price is based upon the estimated weight and that the total price may be adjusted in accordance with the outturn weight.

(b) A statement that the buyer may have free use of the designated storage facilities until a specified date and that any extension beyond the specified date granted by seller must be endorsed under the signature of seller on the bill of sale.

(c) A statement that seller has the legal right to extend to buyer the use of designated storage facilities.

(d) A statement that actual possession of the grain by the buyer is to be taken on board trucks at the storage facility, or on railroad cars, or in the storage facility, or as may be agreed upon.

(e) A statement that if actual possession be not taken within the time specified, due to any cause not chargeable to seller, the seller may consign the same at buyer's risk and expense to a specified destination. *(Added by Stats.1944, 4th Ex.Sess., c. 54, p. 212, § 1.)*

§ 1880.6. Bill of sale; title passing by delivery and endorsement

Execution and delivery by a seller of a bill of sale shall pass seller's title to the grain covered thereby to the buyer and such title passes to the assignees of the buyer upon further endorsement and delivery of the bill of sale. *(Added by Stats.1944, 4th Ex.Sess., c. 54, p. 212, § 1.)*

§ 1880.7. Notice of sale; posting; form

Upon the issuance of any such bill of sale, the seller shall immediately post upon the storage facilities containing the grain a notice in substantially the following form:

"Notice of Sale

On this _____ day of _____, 19__, grain in this storage facility numbered _____, estimated to be _____ bushels of _____ (designating the kind of grain) was transferred and sold as follows:

Name of Seller _____   Name of original Buyer __
Address of Seller _____   Address of Buyer _____

Grain to be removed by buyer on or before _____, 19___, (If date extended such fact and the date to which extended must appear on the notice)."

Such notice shall be maintained by seller in a conspicuous place upon the storage facility at all times during which the grain involved continues to be stored therein. *(Added by Stats.1944, 4th Ex.Sess., c. 54, p. 212, § 1.)*

§ 1880.8. Delivery; necessity of presenting bill of sale; endorsement of amount delivered

No delivery shall be made of any portion of the grain so privately stored unless the bill of sale therefor is presented to the seller, or other person in charge of the storage facility, and the amount of grain so delivered plainly endorsed upon the bill of sale; but this provision shall not apply to any consignment of the grain by the seller to the buyer upon the expiration of the time for delivery specified in the bill of sale. *(Added by Stats.1944, 4th Ex.Sess., c. 54, p. 213, § 1.)*

§ 1880.9. Bill of sale; presumptive evidence of right to delivery

The presentment of the bill of sale by the holder to seller shall be presumptive evidence that the person presenting it is entitled to delivery of the grain described therein unless the seller has knowledge of facts or circumstances sufficient to place him on notice that the possession of the instrument by such person is unlawful. *(Added by Stats.1944, 4th Ex.Sess., c. 54, p. 213, § 1.)*

§ 1881. Storage after delivery date

If any grain in private bulk storage is not removed or delivered on or before the original date of delivery specified in the bill of sale and in the notice of sale, it shall be lawful for the seller to continue to store such grain to the order of the buyer upon such terms as may be agreed upon. *(Added by Stats.1944, 4th Ex.Sess., c. 54, p. 213, § 1.)*

§ 1881.1. Offense and punishment; irregularity of notice or posting, effect on sale

A seller who shall willfully fail to comply with the requirements of notice and posting as provided for in Section 1880.2 or in Section 1880.7 shall be guilty of a misdemeanor and punishable by imprisonment in the county jail not exceeding six months, or by fine not exceeding one thousand dollars ($1,000), or by both. No sale of grain shall be invalidated by reason of any lack or irregularity in connection with such notice or posting. *(Added by Stats.1944, 4th Ex.Sess., c. 54, p. 213, § 1. Amended by Stats.1983, c. 1092, § 66, eff. Sept. 27, 1983, operative Jan. 1, 1984.)*

§ 1881.2. Depositary; legal status

The storage of grain pursuant to this chapter shall not constitute the depositary a warehouseman or storer of goods for hire and no storage facility shall be deemed to constitute a warehouse or public place of storage. *(Added by Stats.1944, 4th Ex.Sess., c. 54, p. 213, § 1.)*

Title 3.5

UTILITY SERVICES

§ 1882. Definitions

Unless the context requires otherwise, the following definitions govern the construction of this title:

(a) "Customer" means the person in whose name a utility service is provided.

(b) "Divert" means to change the intended course or path of electricity, gas, or water without the authorization or consent of the utility.

(c) "Person" means any individual, a partnership, firm, association, limited liability company, or corporation.

(d) "Reconnection" means the commencement of utility service to a customer or other person after service has been lawfully discontinued by the utility.

(e) "Tamper" means to rearrange, injure, alter, interfere with, or otherwise to prevent from performing normal or customary function.

(f) "Utility" means any electrical, gas, or water corporation as those terms are defined in the Public Utilities Code and includes any electrical, gas, or water system operated by any public agency.

(g) "Utility service" means the provision of electricity, gas, water, or any other service or commodity furnished by the utility for compensation. (*Added by Stats.1981, c. 981, p. 3807, § 1. Amended by Stats.1994, c. 1010 (S.B.2053), § 47.*)

Research References

6 Witkin, California Summary 10th Torts § 1570, Treble Damages.

§ 1882.1. Civil actions for diversion, unauthorized connections, tampering with meter, etc.

A utility may bring a civil action for damages against any person who commits, authorizes, solicits, aids, abets, or attempts any of the following acts:

(a) Diverts, or causes to be diverted, utility services by any means whatsoever.

(b) Makes, or causes to be made, any connection or reconnection with property owned or used by the utility to provide utility service without the authorization or consent of the utility.

(c) Prevents any utility meter, or other device used in determining the charge for utility services, from accurately performing its measuring function by tampering or by any other means.

(d) Tampers with any property owned or used by the utility to provide utility services.

(e) Uses or receives the direct benefit of all, or a portion, of the utility service with knowledge of, or reason to believe that, the diversion, tampering, or unauthorized connection existed at the time of the use, or that the use or receipt, was without the authorization or consent of the utility. (*Added by Stats.1981, c. 981, p. 3807, § 1.*)

§ 1882.2. Treble damages; costs; attorney fees

In any civil action brought pursuant to Section 1882.1, the utility may recover as damages three times the amount of actual damages, if any, plus the cost of the suit and reasonable attorney's fees. (*Added by Stats.1981, c. 981, p. 3807, § 1.*)

§ 1882.3. Presumptions; certain apparatus or altered meter found on premises

There is a rebuttable presumption that there is a violation of Section 1882.1 if, on premises controlled by the customer or by the person using or receiving the direct benefit of utility service, there is either, or both, of the following:

(a) Any instrument, apparatus, or device primarily designed to be used to obtain utility service without paying the full lawful charge therefor.

(b) Any meter that has been altered, tampered with, or bypassed so as to cause no measurement or inaccurate measurement of utility services. (*Added by Stats.1981, c. 981, p. 3807, § 1.*)

§ 1882.4. Action to enjoin or restrain unauthorized use permitted; damages recoverable in same action

A utility may, in accordance with Chapter 3 (commencing with Section 525) of Title 7 of Part 2 of the Code of Civil Procedure, bring an action to enjoin and restrain any of the acts specified in Section 1882.1.

The utility may, in the same action, seek damages for any of the acts specified in Section 1882.1. (*Added by Stats.1981, c. 981, p. 3807, § 1.*)

§ 1882.5. Action to enjoin or restrain unauthorized use; monetary damages or threat thereof not a prerequisite

It is not a necessary prerequisite to an action pursuant to Section 1882.4 that the utility have suffered, or be threatened with, monetary damages. (*Added by Stats.1981, c. 981, p. 3807, § 1.*)

§ 1882.6. Damages exceeding actual loss; consideration in establishing utility rates

Any damages recovered pursuant to this title in excess of the actual damages sustained by the utility may be taken into account by the Public Utilities Commission or other applicable ratemaking agency in establishing utility rates. (*Added by Stats.1981, c. 981, p. 3807, § 1.*)

Title 4

LOAN

CHAPTER 1. LOAN FOR USE

§ 1884.   Loan for use defined

A loan for use is a contract by which one gives to another the temporary possession and use of personal property, and the latter agrees to return the same thing to him at a future time, without reward for its use. *(Enacted in 1872.)*

§ 1885.   Title and increase of thing lent

A loan for use does not transfer the title to the thing; and all its increase during the period of the loan belongs to the lender. *(Enacted in 1872.)*

§ 1886.   Borrower; degree of care

A borrower for use must use great care for the preservation in safety and in good condition of the thing lent. *(Enacted in 1872.)*

Research References

13 Witkin, California Summary 10th Personal Property § 159, in General.

§ 1887.   Borrower; treatment of animals

One who borrows a living animal for use, must treat it with great kindness, and provide everything necessary and suitable for it. *(Enacted in 1872.)*

§ 1888.   Borrower; degree of skill

A borrower for use is bound to have and to exercise such skill in the care of the thing lent as he causes the lender to believe him to possess. *(Enacted in 1872.)*

§ 1889.   Repairs

A borrower for use must repair all deteriorations or injuries to the thing lent, which are occasioned by his negligence, however slight. *(Enacted in 1872.)*

§ 1890.   Use of thing; purposes

The borrower of a thing for use may use it for such purposes only as the lender might reasonably anticipate at the time of lending. *(Enacted in 1872.)*

§ 1891.   Relending

The borrower of a thing for use must not part with it to a third person, without the consent of the lender. *(Enacted in 1872.)*

§ 1892.   Expenses of thing lent

The borrower of a thing for use must bear all its expenses during the loan, except such as are necessarily incurred by him to preserve it from unexpected and unusual injury. For such expenses he is entitled to compensation from the lender, who may, however, exonerate himself by surrendering the thing to the borrower. *(Enacted in 1872.)*

§ 1893.   Concealed defects; lender's liability

The lender of a thing for use must indemnify the borrower for damage caused by defects or vices in it, which he knew at the time of lending, and concealed from the borrower. *(Enacted in 1872.)*

§ 1894.   Return of thing; time; indemnification for loss

The lender of a thing for use may at any time require its return, even though he lent it for a specified time or purpose. But if, on the faith of such an agreement, the borrower has made such arrangements that a return of the thing before the period agreed upon would cause him loss, exceeding the benefit derived by him from the loan, the lender must indemnify him for such loss, if he compels such return, the borrower not having in any manner violated his duty. *(Enacted in 1872.)*

§ 1895.   Return of thing; demand

If a thing is lent for use for a specified time or purpose, it must be returned to the lender without demand, as soon as the time has expired, or the purpose has been accomplished. In other cases it need not be returned until demanded. *(Enacted in 1872.)*

§ 1896.   Return of thing; place

The borrower of a thing for use must return it to the lender, at the place contemplated by the parties at the time of lending; or if no particular place was so contemplated by them, then at the place where it was at that time. *(Enacted in 1872.)*

CHAPTER 1.5.   LOANS TO MUSEUMS FOR INDEFINITE OR LONG TERMS

§ 1899.   Legislative findings and declarations

The Legislature finds and declares as follows:

(a) Many museums have benefited greatly from having property loaned to them for study or display. Problems have arisen, however, in connection with loans for indefinite or long terms, when museums and lenders have failed to maintain contact. Many of these problems could be avoided by a clarification and regularization of the rights and obligations of the parties to loans for indefinite or long terms.

(b) An existing law, the Unclaimed Property Law (commencing with Section 1500 of the Code of Civil Procedure), is technically applicable to property on loan to a museum which has been left unclaimed by its owner for at least seven years.

(c) While the Unclaimed Property Law addresses problems similar to those which arise in the museum context when the parties to loans fail to maintain contact, there is need for an alternative method of dealing with unclaimed property in the hands of museums, one tailored to the unique circumstances of unclaimed loans to museums. These circumstances include the likelihood that the unclaimed property has significant scientific, historical, aesthetic, or cultural value but does not have great monetary value; that the public's interest in the intangible values of unclaimed property loaned to museums can best be realized if title is transferred to the museums holding the property; that often lenders intend eventually to donate property but place it on indefinite or long term loan initially for tax and other reasons; and that many museums have incurred unreimbursed expenses in caring for and storing unclaimed loaned property.

(d) There is an inherent tendency for the condition of tangible property to change over time. Loaned property often requires conservation work and conservation measures may be expensive or potentially detrimental to the property. Organic materials and specimens may serve as breeding grounds for insects, fungi, or diseases which threaten other more valuable property.

(e) Museums cannot reasonably be expected to make decisions regarding conservation or disposition of loaned property at their own risk and expense. Over time, however, lenders die or move, and museums and lenders lose contact. If a lender has failed to maintain contact with a museum, it is often impossible to locate the lender so that the lender can make decisions regarding conservation or disposition of loaned property.

(f) Since museums rarely relocate, it is easier for lenders, and those who claim through them, to notify museums of address or ownership changes so that museums can readily contact lenders when decisions must be made regarding conservation or disposition of loaned property.

(g) The best evidence of ownership of property on loan to a museum is generally the original loan receipt. The longer property remains on loan, the less likely it is that the original lender will claim it, and the more likely it is that any claim which is made will be made by someone who does not have the original loan receipt or other clear evidence of ownership. The state has a substantial interest in cutting off stale and uncertain claims to tangible personal property loaned to nonprofit and public museums.

(h) Most of the tangible personal property which escheats to the state under the Unclaimed Property Law is found in safe deposit boxes. Although 40–50 percent of the intangible property which escheats to the state is subsequently claimed, less than 1 percent of escheated tangible personal property is claimed. Of the few claims which are presented to the Controller for tangible personal property, most are presented within two years of the date the Controller gives notice of the escheat.

(i) The public interest is served by requiring lenders to notify museums of changes in address or ownership of loaned property, by establishing a uniform procedure for lenders to preserve their interests in property loaned to museums for indefinite or long terms, and by vesting title to unclaimed property on loan to museums in the museums which have custody of the property. *(Added by Stats.1983, c. 61, § 1.)*

Research References

13 Witkin, California Summary 10th Personal Property § 39, (S 39) Other Statutes Dealing With Unclaimed Property.

§ 1899.1. Definitions

For the purposes of this chapter:

(a) A "museum" is an institution located in California and operated by a nonprofit corporation or public agency, primarily educational, scientific, or aesthetic in purpose, which owns, borrows, or cares for, and studies, archives, or exhibits property.

(b) A "lender's address" is the most recent address as shown on the museum's records pertaining to the property on loan from the lender.

(c) The terms "loan," "loaned," and "on loan" include all deposits of property with a museum which are not accompanied by a transfer of title to the property.

(d) "Property" includes all tangible objects, animate and inanimate, under a museum's care which have intrinsic value to science, history, art, or culture, except that it does not include botanical or zoological specimens loaned to a museum for scientific research purposes. *(Added by Stats.1983, c. 61, § 1.)*

§ 1899.2. Notice to lender; manner; contents; location of museum

(a) When a museum is required to give a lender notice pursuant to the provisions of this chapter, the museum shall be deemed to have given a lender notice if the museum mails the notice to the lender at the lender's address and proof of receipt is received by the museum within 30 days from the date the notice was mailed. If the museum does not have an address for the lender, or if proof of receipt is not received by the museum, notice shall be deemed given if the museum publishes notice at least once a week for three successive weeks in a newspaper of general circulation in both the county in which the museum is located and the county of the lender's address, if any.

(b) In addition to any other information prescribed in this chapter, notices given pursuant to it shall contain the lender's name, the lender's address, if known, the date of the loan and, if the notice is being given by the museum, the name, address, and telephone number of the appropriate office or official to be contacted at the museum for information regarding the loan.

(c) For the purposes of this section, a museum is "located" in the county of a branch of the museum to which a loan is made. In all other instances, a museum is located in the county in which it has its principal place of business. *(Added by Stats.1983, c. 61, § 1.)*

§ 1899.3. Notice of provisions of chapter; retention of claimant notices; receipts for notices of intent to preserve interest; notice of injury or loss

(a) If, on or after January 1, 1984, a museum accepts a loan of property for an indefinite term, or for a term in excess of seven years, the museum shall inform the lender in writing at the time of the loan of the provisions of this chapter. A copy of the form notice prescribed in Section 1899.5, or a citation to this chapter, is adequate for this purpose.

(b) Unless the loaned property is returned to the claimant, the museum shall retain for a period of not less than 25 years the original or an accurate copy of each notice filed by a claimant pursuant to Section 1899.4.

(c) The museum shall furnish anyone who files a notice of intent to preserve an interest in property on loan proof of receipt of the notice by mailing an original receipt or a copy of the receipt portion of the form notice prescribed in Section 1899.5 to the lender or other claimant at the address given on the notice within 30 days of receiving the notice.

(d) A museum shall give a lender prompt notice of any known injury to or loss of property on loan. *(Added by Stats.1983, c. 61, § 1.)*

Research References

13 Witkin, California Summary 10th Personal Property § 39, (S 39) Other Statutes Dealing With Unclaimed Property.

§ 1899.4. Property owners' notices; change of address or ownership; intent to preserve an interest in property; effect

(a) It is the responsibility of the owner of property on loan to a museum to notify the museum promptly in writing of any change of address or change in ownership of the property.

Failure to notify the museum of these changes may result in the owner's loss of rights in the property.

(b) The owner of property on loan to a museum may file with the museum a notice of intent to preserve an interest in the property as provided for in Section 1899.5. The filing of a notice of intent to preserve an interest in property on loan to a museum does not validate or make enforceable any claim which would be extinguished under the terms of a written loan agreement, or which would otherwise be invalid or unenforceable. *(Added by Stats.1983, c. 61, § 1.)*

Research References

13 Witkin, California Summary 10th Personal Property § 39, (S 39) Other Statutes Dealing With Unclaimed Property.

§ 1899.5. Notice of intent to preserve an interest in property; requirements; retention by museum; form; disclosure

(a) A notice of intent to preserve an interest in property on loan to a museum filed pursuant to this chapter shall be in writing, shall contain a description of the property adequate to enable the museum to identify the property, shall be accompanied by documentation sufficient to establish the claimant as owner of the property, and shall be signed under penalty of perjury by the claimant or by a person authorized to act on behalf of the claimant.

(b) The museum need not retain a notice which does not meet the requirements set forth in subdivision (a). If, however, the museum does not intend to retain a notice for this reason, the museum shall promptly notify the claimant at the address given on the notice that it believes the notice is ineffective to preserve an interest, and the reasons therefor. The fact that the museum retains a notice shall not be construed to mean that the museum accepts the sufficiency or accuracy of the notice or that the notice is effective to preserve an interest in property on loan to the museum.

(c) A notice of intent to preserve an interest in property on loan to a museum which is in substantially the following form, and contains the information and attachments described, satisfies the requirements of subdivision (a):

NOTICE OF INTENT TO PRESERVE AN INTEREST IN PROPERTY ON LOAN TO A MUSEUM

TO THE LENDER: Section 1899.4 of the California Civil Code requires that you notify the museum promptly in writing of any change of address or ownership of the property. If the museum is unable to contact you regarding your loan, you may lose rights in the loaned property. If you choose to file this form with the museum to preserve your interest in the property, the museum is required to maintain it, or a copy of it, for 25 years. For full details, see Section 1899, et seq. of the California Civil Code.

TO THE MUSEUM: You are hereby notified that the undersigned claims an interest in the property described herein.

Claimant

Name: _____

Address: _____

_____

_____

Telephone: _____

Social Security Number (optional): _____

Museum Name: _____

Date Property Loaned: _____

Interest in Property:

If you are not the original lender, describe the origin of your interest in the property and attach a copy of any document creating your interest:

_____

_____

_____

_____

Description of Property:

Unless an accurate, legible copy of the original loan receipt is attached, give a detailed description of the claimed property, including its nature and general characteristics and the museum registration number assigned to the property, if known, and attach any documentary evidence you have establishing the loan:

Registration # _____

Description: _____

_____

_____

_____

_____

(Attach additional sheets if necessary.)

I understand that I must promptly notify the museum in writing of any change of address or change in ownership of the loaned property.

I declare under penalty of perjury that to the best of my knowledge the information contained in this notice is true.

Signed: _____ Date: _____

      (claimant)

OR

I declare under penalty of perjury that I am authorized to act on behalf of the claimant and am informed and believe that the information contained in this notice is true.

Signed: _____ Date: _____

   (claimant's representative)

RECEIPT FOR NOTICE OF INTENT TO PRESERVE AN INTEREST IN PROPERTY

Notice received by: _____

Date of receipt: _____

Copy of receipt returned to claimant:

By _____

Date: _____

(d) Notices of intent to preserve an interest in property on loan to a museum filed pursuant to this chapter are exempt from the disclosure requirements of the California Public Records Act (commencing with Section 6250 of the Government Code). *(Added by Stats.1983, c. 61, § 1.)*

Research References

13 Witkin, California Summary 10th Personal Property § 39, (S 39) Other Statutes Dealing With Unclaimed Property.

§ 1899.6. Conservation or disposal of loaned property without permission; conditions; lien; liability of museum

(a) Unless there is a written loan agreement to the contrary, a museum may apply conservation measures to or dispose of property on loan to the museum without a lender's permission if:

(1) Immediate action is required to protect the property on loan or to protect other property in the custody of the museum,

or because the property on loan has become a hazard to the health and safety of the public or of the museum's staff, and:

(A) The museum is unable to reach the lender at the lender's last address of record so that the museum and the lender can promptly agree upon a solution; or

(B) The lender will not agree to the protective measures the museum recommends, yet is unwilling or unable to terminate the loan and retrieve the property.

(2) In the case of a lender who cannot be contacted in person, the museum publishes a notice containing the information described in subdivision (a) of Section 1899.7 and there is no response for 120 days.

(b) If a museum applies conservation measures to or disposes of property pursuant to subdivision (a):

(1) The museum shall have a lien on the property and on the proceeds from any disposition thereof for the costs incurred by the museum; and

(2) The museum shall not be liable for injury to or loss of the property:

(A) If the museum had a reasonable belief at the time the action was taken that the action was necessary to protect the property on loan or other property in the custody of the museum, or that the property on loan constituted a hazard to the health and safety of the public or of the museum's staff; and

(B) If the museum applied conservation measures, the museum exercised reasonable care in the choice and application of the conservation measures. *(Added by Stats.1983, c. 61, § 1.)*

Research References

13 Witkin, California Summary 10th Personal Property § 39, (S 39) Other Statutes Dealing With Unclaimed Property.

§ 1899.7. Publication of statement in lieu of notice of injury or loss; informing claimant; time limit

(a) Except as provided in subdivision (b), if a museum is unable to give the lender the notice required by subdivision (d) of Section 1899.3 of injury to or loss of property on loan by mail, the museum shall be deemed to have given the lender notice of any injury or loss if in addition to the information required by subdivision (b) of Section 1899.2 the published notice includes a statement containing substantially the following information:

> "The records of _____
> (name of museum)
> indicate that you have property on loan to it.
> Your failure to notify it in writing of a change of
> address or ownership of property on loan or to
> contact it in writing regarding the loan may result
> in the loss of rights in the loaned property. See
> California Civil Code Sections 1899, et seq."

(b) If, within three years of giving notice of injury to or loss of loaned property by publishing the notice set forth in subdivision (a), the museum receives a notice from a claimant pursuant to Section 1899.4, the museum shall promptly advise the claimant in writing of the nature of the injury to or the fact of the loss of property on loan and the approximate date thereof. For the purposes of the limitation period in Section 1899.8, if the museum mails the information to the claimant within 30 days of the date the museum receives the notice from the claimant, the museum shall be deemed to have given the claimant notice of the injury to or loss of property on loan on the date notice by publication pursuant to subdivision (a) was completed. *(Added by Stats.1983, c. 61, § 1.)*

Research References

13 Witkin, California Summary 10th Personal Property § 39, (S 39) Other Statutes Dealing With Unclaimed Property.

§ 1899.8. Limitations of actions

Effective January 1, 1985, no action shall be brought against a museum for damages because of injury to or loss of property loaned to the museum more than (1) three years from the date the museum gives the lender notice of the injury or loss, or (2) ten years from the date of the injury or loss, whichever occurs earlier. *(Added by Stats.1983, c. 61, § 1.)*

Research References

13 Witkin, California Summary 10th Personal Property § 39, (S 39) Other Statutes Dealing With Unclaimed Property.

§ 1899.9. Intent to terminate loan; form; transformation of specified term to indefinite term

(a) A museum may give the lender notice of the museum's intent to terminate a loan which was made for an indefinite term, or which was made on or after January 1, 1984, for a term in excess of seven years.

A notice of intent to terminate a loan given pursuant to this section shall include a statement containing substantially the following information:

> "The records of _____
> (name of museum)
> indicate that you have property on loan to it. The
> institution wishes to terminate the loan. You must
> contact the institution, establish your ownership of
> the property, and make arrangements to collect the
> property. If you fail to do so promptly, you will be
> deemed to have donated the property to the
> institution. See California Civil Code Sections
> 1899, et seq."

(b) For the purposes of this chapter, a loan for a specified term becomes a loan for an indefinite term if the property remains in the custody of the museum when the specified term expires. *(Added by Stats.1983, c. 61, § 1.)*

Research References

13 Witkin, California Summary 10th Personal Property § 39, (S 39) Other Statutes Dealing With Unclaimed Property.

§ 1899.10. Action to recover property; limitations; donation presumed; title of purchaser

(a) The three-year limitation on actions to recover personal property prescribed in Code of Civil Procedure Section 338.3 shall run from the date the museum gives the lender notice of its intent to terminate the loan pursuant to Section 1899.9.

(b) Except as provided in subdivision (e), effective January 1, 1985, no action shall be brought against a museum to recover property on loan when more than 25 years have passed from the date of the last written contact between the lender and the museum, as evidenced in the museum's records.

(c) A lender shall be deemed to have donated loaned property to a museum if the lender fails to file an action to recover the property on loan to the museum within the periods specified in subdivisions (a) and (b).

(d) One who purchases property from a museum acquires good title to the property if the museum represents that it has acquired title to the property pursuant to subdivision (c).

(e) Notwithstanding subdivisions (b) and (c), a lender who was not given notice that the museum intended to terminate a loan and who proves that the museum received a notice of intent to preserve an interest in loaned property within the 25 years immediately preceding the date on which the lender's right to recover the property otherwise expired under subdivision (b) may recover the property or, if the property has been disposed of, the reasonable value of the property at the time the property was disposed of with interest at the rate on judgments set by the Legislature pursuant to Section 1 of Article XV of the California Constitution. *(Added by Stats.1983, c. 61, § 1. Amended by Stats.1984, c. 541, § 1, eff. July 17, 1984.)*

Research References

13 Witkin, California Summary 10th Personal Property § 39, (S 39) Other Statutes Dealing With Unclaimed Property.

§ 1899.11. Construction with Unclaimed Property Law; notice of intent to report property to controller

(a) The provisions of this chapter supersede the provisions of the Unclaimed Property Law (commencing with Section 1500 of the Code of Civil Procedure) except that at its option, a museum may report property which has been on loan unclaimed by its owner for more than seven years to the Controller pursuant to Section 1530 of the Code of Civil Procedure for disposition in accordance with the provisions of the Unclaimed Property Law.

(b) Not less than six months or more than 12 months before reporting any loaned property to the Controller, a museum shall mail to the lender at the lender's address, if known, a notice of intent to report the property to the Controller. The notice shall include a statement containing substantially the following information:

> "The records of _____
> (name of museum)
> indicate that you have property on loan to the institution. The institution wishes to terminate the loan. You must contact the institution, establish your ownership of the property and make arrangements to collect the property before _____
> (fill in date)
> or the property will be disposed of in accordance with the provisions of the Unclaimed Property Law (commencing with Section 1500 of the Code of Civil Procedure)."

(Added by Stats.1983, c. 61, § 1.)

Research References

13 Witkin, California Summary 10th Personal Property § 39, (S 39) Other Statutes Dealing With Unclaimed Property.

CHAPTER 2. LOAN FOR EXCHANGE

Section
1902. Loan for exchange defined.
1903. Optional loan; application of chapter.
1904. Title, expense and increase of thing lent.
1905. Modification of contract.
1906. Applicability of other sections.

§ 1902. Loan for exchange defined

A loan for exchange is a contract by which one delivers personal property to another, and the latter agrees to return to the lender a similar thing at a future time, without reward for its use. *(Enacted in 1872.)*

§ 1903. Optional loan; application of chapter

A loan, which the borrower is allowed by the lender to treat as a loan for use, or for exchange, at his option, is subject to all the provisions of this Chapter. *(Enacted in 1872.)*

§ 1904. Title, expense and increase of thing lent

By a loan for exchange the title to the thing lent is transferred to the borrower, and he must bear all its expenses, and is entitled to all its increase. *(Enacted in 1872.)*

§ 1905. Modification of contract

A lender for exchange cannot require the borrower to fulfill his obligations at a time, or in a manner, different from that which was originally agreed upon. *(Enacted in 1872.)*

§ 1906. Applicability of other sections

Sections 1893, 1895 and 1896, apply to a loan for exchange. *(Enacted in 1872.)*

CHAPTER 3. LOAN OF MONEY

Section
1912. Loan of money defined.
1913. Payment in current money.
1914. Interest; presumption.
1915. Interest defined.
1916. Interest; annual rate.
1916.1. Constitutional restrictions; application to loans secured by real property; licensed real estate brokers; arrangement of loan or forbearance.
1916.2. Constitutional restrictions; application to loans by out-of-state public retirement or pension systems; exemption.
1916.5. Variable interest; requirements.
1916.6. Variable interest; change; five year period.
1916.7. Adjustable-payment, adjustable-rate loan secured by owner occupied real property; exemption from other laws; disclosure notice.
1916.8. Renegotiable rate mortgage loans; interest rate changes at renewal; costs or fees; notice to borrower; disclosure to applicant.
1916.9. Offer of fixed rate mortgage loan as alternative to renegotiable rate mortgage loan.
1916.11. Lien of mortgage or deed of trust; validity.
1916.12. Legislative findings; purpose; mortgage parity between state and federal institutions; rules and regulations.
1916–1. Legal rate of interest; contract rate.
1916–2. Maximum rate of interest; compound interest; effect of contract provisions for excessive interest.
1916–3. Civil and criminal liability for violations.
1916–4. Repeals.
1916–5. Usury Law, citation.

§ 1912. Loan of money defined

A loan of money is a contract by which one delivers a sum of money to another, and the latter agrees to return at a future time a sum equivalent to that which he borrowed. A loan for mere use is governed by the Chapter on Loan for Use. *(Enacted in 1872.)*

Research References

California Real Estate Forms (Miller & Starr) § 3:21, Deed of Trust, Assignment of Rents, Security Agreement and Fixture Filing— Conduit Loan.

Miller and Starr California Real Estate § 21:3, Loan or Forbearance of Money.

22 NO. 3 Miller & Starr, California Real Estate Newsalert 1, Show Me Your Papers: Sales and Assignments of Secured Real Estate Loans and the California Foreclosure Process.

§ 1913. Payment in current money

A borrower of money, unless there is an express contract to the contrary, must pay the amount due in such money as is current at the time when the loan becomes due, whether such money is worth more or less than the actual money lent. *(Enacted in 1872.)*

§ 1914. Interest; presumption

Whenever a loan of money is made, it is presumed to be made upon interest, unless it is otherwise expressly stipulated at the time in writing. *(Enacted in 1872. Amended by Code Am.1873–74, c. 612, p. 244, § 201.)*

Research References

Miller and Starr California Real Estate § 21:1, Policy and Validity of the Usury Law.
22 NO. 3 Miller & Starr, California Real Estate Newsalert 1, Show Me Your Papers: Sales and Assignments of Secured Real Estate Loans and the California Foreclosure Process.

§ 1915. Interest defined

Interest is the compensation allowed by law or fixed by the parties for the use, or forbearance, or detention of money. *(Enacted in 1872. Amended by Code Am.1873–74, c. 612, p. 245, § 202.)*

Research References

Rutter, Cal. Practice Guide: Enforcing Judgments/Debts Ch. 3-C, C. Prelawsuit Considerations.
Miller and Starr California Real Estate § 21:15, Interest Defined; Method of Calculation.
2 Witkin Cal. Proc. 5th Jurisdiction § 25, (S 25) Interest and Costs.

§ 1916. Interest; annual rate

When a rate of interest is prescribed by a law or contract, without specifying the period of time by which such rate is to be calculated, it is to be deemed an annual rate. *(Enacted in 1872.)*

Research References

Miller and Starr California Real Estate § 21:2, Essential Elements of Usury.
Miller and Starr California Real Estate § 21:17, Term of Loan; Prepayment.

§ 1916.1. Constitutional restrictions; application to loans secured by real property; licensed real estate brokers; arrangement of loan or forbearance

The restrictions upon rates of interest contained in Section 1 of Article XV of the California Constitution shall not apply to any loan or forbearance made or arranged by any person licensed as a real estate broker by the State of California, and secured, directly or collaterally, in whole or in part by liens on real property. For purposes of this section, a loan or forbearance is arranged by a person licensed as a real estate broker when the broker (1) acts for compensation or in expectation of compensation for soliciting, negotiating, or arranging the loan for another, (2) acts for compensation or in expectation of compensation for selling, buying, leasing, exchanging, or negotiating the sale, purchase, lease, or exchange of real property or a business for another and (A) arranges a loan to pay all or any portion of the purchase price of, or of an improvement to, that property or business or (B) arranges a forbearance, extension, or refinancing of any loan in connection with that sale, purchase, lease, exchange of, or an improvement to, real property or a business, or (3) arranges or negotiates for another a forbearance, extension, or refinancing of any loan secured by real property in connection with a past transaction in which the broker had acted for compensation or in expectation of compensation for selling, buying, leasing, exchanging, or negotiating the sale, purchase,

lease, or exchange of real property or a business. The term "made or arranged" includes any loan made by a person licensed as a real estate broker as a principal or as an agent for others, and whether or not the person is acting within the course and scope of such license. *(Added by Stats.1983, c. 307, § 1. Amended by Stats.1985, c. 489, § 1.)*

Research References

Rutter, Cal. Practice Guide: Real Prop. Transactions Ch. 2-B, B. Licensing and Regulatory Requirements.
Rutter, Cal. Practice Guide: Real Prop. Transactions Ch. 6-F, F. Promissory Note.
Miller and Starr California Real Estate § 1:64, Unconscionability as a Defense to Enforcement.
Miller and Starr California Real Estate § 3:43, Negligence Liability.
Miller and Starr California Real Estate § 21:28, Mistake and Reformation.
Miller and Starr California Real Estate § 21:34, Who is Liable for Usury Penalties--Loans "Made or Arranged" by a Licensed Real Estate Broker.
15 NO. 3 Miller & Starr, California Real Estate Newsalert 19, Usury.
18 NO. 2 Miller & Starr, California Real Estate Newsalert 25, Usury.
1 Witkin Cal. Summ. 10th Contracts § 458, Real Estate Brokers.

§ 1916.2. Constitutional restrictions; application to loans by out-of-state public retirement or pension systems; exemption

The restrictions upon rates of interest contained in Section 1 of Article XV of the California Constitution do not apply to any loans made by, or forbearances of, a public retirement or pension system that is created, authorized, and regulated by the laws of a state other than California, or the laws of a local agency of a state other than California.

This section establishes as an exempt class of persons pursuant to Section 1 of Article XV of the California Constitution, any public retirement or pension system that is created, authorized, and regulated by the laws of a state other than California, or the laws of a local agency of a state other than California. *(Added by Stats.1987, c. 764, § 5.)*

Research References

Miller and Starr California Real Estate § 21:35, Who is Liable for Usury Penalties--Other Exemptions.

§ 1916.5. Variable interest; requirements

(a) No increase in interest provided for in any provision for a variable interest rate contained in a security document, or evidence of debt issued in connection therewith, by a lender other than a supervised financial organization is valid unless that provision is set forth in the security document, and in any evidence of debt issued in connection therewith, and the document or documents contain the following provisions:

(1) A requirement that when an increase in the interest rate is required or permitted by a movement in a particular direction of a prescribed standard an identical decrease is required in the interest rate by a movement in the opposite direction of the prescribed standard.

(2) The rate of interest shall not change more often than once during any semiannual period, and at least six months shall elapse between any two changes.

(3) The change in the interest rate shall not exceed one-fourth of 1 percent in any semiannual period, and shall not result in a rate more than 2.5 percentage points greater than the rate for the first loan payment due after the closing of the loan.

(4) The rate of interest shall not change during the first semiannual period.

(5) The borrower is permitted to prepay the loan in whole or in part without a prepayment charge within 90 days of notification of any increase in the rate of interest.

(6) A statement attached to the security document and to any evidence of debt issued in connection therewith printed or written in a size equal to at least 10–point boldface type, consisting of the following language:

NOTICE TO BORROWER: THIS DOCUMENT CONTAINS PROVISIONS FOR A VARIABLE INTEREST RATE.

(b)(1) This section shall be applicable only to a mortgage contract, deed of trust, real estate sales contract, or any note or negotiable instrument issued in connection therewith, when its purpose is to finance the purchase or construction of real property containing four or fewer residential units or on which four or fewer residential units are to be constructed.

(2) This section does not apply to unamortized construction loans with an original term of two years or less or to loans made for the purpose of the purchase or construction of improvements to existing residential dwellings.

(c) Regulations setting forth the prescribed standard upon which variations in the interest rate shall be based may be adopted by the Commissioner of Financial Institutions with respect to savings associations and by the Insurance Commissioner with respect to insurers. Regulations adopted by the Commissioner of Financial Institutions shall apply to all loans made by savings associations pursuant to this section prior to January 1, 1990.

(d) As used in this section:

(1) "Supervised financial organization" means a state or federally regulated bank, savings association, savings bank, or credit union, or state regulated industrial loan company, a licensed finance lender under the California Finance Lenders Law, [1] a licensed residential mortgage lender under the California Residential Mortgage Lending Act, [2] or holding company, affiliate, or subsidiary thereof, or institution of the Farm Credit System, as specified in 12 U.S.C. Sec. 2002.

(2) "Insurer" includes, but is not limited to, a nonadmitted insurance company.

(3) "Semiannual period" means each of the successive periods of six calendar months commencing with the first day of the calendar month in which the instrument creating the obligation is dated.

(4) "Security document" means a mortgage contract, deed of trust, or real estate sales contract.

(5) "Evidence of debt" means a note or negotiable instrument.

(e) This section is applicable only to instruments executed on and after the effective date of this section.

(f) This section does not apply to nonprofit public corporations.

(g) This section is not intended to apply to a loan made where the rate of interest provided for is less than the then current market rate for a similar loan in order to accommodate the borrower because of a special relationship, including, but not limited to, an employment or business relationship, of the borrower with the lender or with a customer of the lender and the sole increase in interest provided for with respect to the loan will result only by reason of the termination of that relationship or upon the sale, deed, or transfer of the property securing the loan to a person not having that relationship. *(Added by Stats.1970, c. 1584, p. 3300, § 1. Amended by Stats.1971, c. 1265, p. 2482, § 1; Stats.1975, c. 338, p. 787, § 1; Stats.1980, c. 1139, p. 3681, § 1; Stats.1982, c. 1307, p. 4816, § 1; Stats.1984, c. 975,*

§ 1; Stats.1989, c. 188, § 1; Stats.1990, c. 157 (A.B.2728), § 1; Stats.1996, c. 1064 (A.B.3351), § 5, operative July 1, 1997; Stats.2004, c. 939 (A.B.1979), § 1; Stats.2004, c. 940 (A.B.2693), § 3.)

[1] Financial Code § 22000 et seq.
[2] Financial Code § 50000 et seq.

Research References

Rutter, Cal. Practice Guide: Real Prop. Transactions Ch. 6-F, F. Promissory Note.
Miller and Starr California Real Estate § 10:83, Regulation of Variable Interest Rate Loans.
Miller and Starr California Real Estate § 10:84, Adjustable-Payment, Adjustable-Rate Loan.
Miller and Starr California Real Estate § 10:96, Statutory Prohibitions Against Restricting Prepayment.
Miller and Starr California Real Estate § 10:236, Policy Objectives; the "Standard" Transaction.
15 NO. 4 Miller & Starr, California Real Estate Newsalert 7, Deeds.
15 NO. 4 Miller & Starr, California Real Estate Newsalert 16, Regulation of the Real Estate Industry.
1 Witkin Cal. Summ. 10th Contracts § 484, (S 484) California Law.
4 Witkin, California Summary 10th Security Transactions in Real Property § 42, (S 42) Alternative Mortgage Transactions for Residential Loans.

§ 1916.6. Variable interest; change; five year period

A security document, or evidence of debt issued in connection therewith, executed pursuant to Section 1916.5 may provide that the rate of interest shall not change until five years after execution of such document or documents, and not more frequently than every five years thereafter. In every security document, or evidence of debt issued in connection therewith, executed pursuant to this section all the provisions of Section 1916.5 shall be applicable, except those provisions specifying the frequency of interest rate changes and limiting rate changes to one-fourth of 1 percent in any semiannual period. For the purposes of this section "five years" means each of the successive periods of five years commencing with the first day of the calendar month in which the instrument creating the obligation is dated. *(Added by Stats.1977, c. 575, p. 1821, § 1.)*

Research References

Miller and Starr California Real Estate § 10:83, Regulation of Variable Interest Rate Loans.
4 Witkin, California Summary 10th Security Transactions in Real Property § 42, (S 42) Alternative Mortgage Transactions for Residential Loans.

§ 1916.7. Adjustable-payment, adjustable-rate loan secured by owner occupied real property; exemption from other laws; disclosure notice

(a) Sections 1916.5, 1916.6, 1916.8, and 1916.9 of the Civil Code, and any other provision of law restricting or setting forth requirements for changes in the rate of interest on loans, shall not be applicable to loans made pursuant to this section.

(b) A mortgage loan made pursuant to the provisions of this section is an adjustable-payment, adjustable-rate loan, on the security of real property occupied or intended to be occupied by the borrower containing four or fewer residential units and incorporating terms substantially as follows:

(1) The term of the loan shall be not less than 29 years, repayable in monthly installments amortized over a period of not less than 30 years.

(2) Monthly payments may be adjusted to reflect changes in the variable interest rate of the loan. Changes in interest and monthly payment shall not occur more often than twice during any annual period and at least six months shall elapse between any two changes. The rate of interest and monthly payments

shall not change during the first semiannual period. The amount of any increase in monthly payment shall not exceed 7.5 percent annually.

(3) Monthly payments may also be established on a graduated basis within the parameters of a loan originated pursuant to the provisions of this section. A graduated payment adjustable mortgage loan shall meet all the requirements of this section and shall set forth in the note, at the time of origination, limitations on the rate of increase in the scheduled payments due both to graduation and to changes in the interest rate.

(4) Whenever any monthly installment is less than the amount of interest accrued during the month with respect to which the installment is payable, the borrower shall have the option to select one, or any combination of, the following:

(A) Notwithstanding paragraph (2) of subdivision (b), increase the monthly installment in an amount which at least covers the increase in interest.

(B) Have the difference added to the principal of the loan as of the due date of the installment and thereafter shall bear interest as part of the principal. In no instance shall the difference which is added to the principal be an amount which causes the resulting loan-to-value ratio to exceed the loan-to-value ratio at the time of loan origination.

(C) Extend the term of the loan up to, but not exceeding, 40 years.

(5) Changes in the rate of interest on the loan shall reflect the movement, in reference to the date of the original loan, of a periodically published index selected by the lender which may be either of the following:

(A) The contract interest rate on the purchase of previously occupied homes in the most recent monthly national average mortgage rate index for all major lenders published periodically by the Federal Home Loan Bank Board.

(B) The weighted average cost of funds for California Associations of the Eleventh District Savings and Loan Associations as published periodically by the Federal Home Loan Bank of San Francisco.

(6) Any change in the interest rate shall not exceed the limit, specified by the lender in the loan contract, for rate increases in any semiannual period and shall not exceed the limit, specified by the lender in the loan contract, for rate increases greater than the base index rate.

(7) Notwithstanding any change in the interest rate indicated by a movement of the index, increases in the interest rate shall be optional with the lender, while decreases are mandatory. Such decreases, upon the option of the borrower, shall be used (1) to pay off any negative amortization accrued when the interest rate was increased, or (2) to decrease the monthly payment as reflected in the decrease in the interest rate.

(8) The borrower is permitted to prepay the loan in whole or in part without a prepayment charge at any time, and no fee or other charge may be required by the lender of the borrower as a result of any change in the interest rate or the exercise of any option or election extended to the borrower pursuant to this section.

(9) The borrower, after initiation of the loan, shall not be subsequently required to demonstrate his or her qualification for the loan, except that this paragraph shall not limit any remedy available to the lender by law for default or other breach of contract.

(10) In the event the remaining principal due on a loan made pursuant to this section will not be paid off during the current term, within 90 days of expiration of the term a borrower may elect in writing to repay the remaining balance in full or in substantially equal installments of principal and interest over an additional period not to exceed 10 years, during which period the interest rate shall remain fixed.

(c) An applicant for a loan originated pursuant to the provisions of this section must be given, at the time he or she requests an application, a disclosure notice in the following form:

NOTICE TO BORROWER

IMPORTANT INFORMATION ABOUT
THE ADJUSTABLE–PAYMENT,
ADJUSTABLE–RATE LOAN

PLEASE READ CAREFULLY

(at least 10-point bold type)

You have received an application form for an adjustable-payment, adjustable-rate mortgage loan. This loan may differ from other mortgages with which you are familiar.

I. GENERAL DESCRIPTION OF ADJUSTABLE–PAYMENT, ADJUSTABLE–RATE LOAN

The adjustable-payment, adjustable-rate mortgage loan is a flexible loan instrument. This means that the interest, monthly payment and/or the length of the loan may be changed during the course of the loan contract.

The first flexible feature of this loan is the interest rate. The interest rate on the loan may be changed by the lender every six months. Changes in the interest rate must reflect the movement of an index that is selected by the lender. Changes in the interest rate may result in increases or decreases in your monthly payment, in the outstanding principal loan balance, in the loan term, or in all three.

The lender is required by law to limit the amount that the interest can change at any one time or over the life of the loan. The law does not specify what these limits are. That is a matter you should negotiate with the lender.

You may also want to make inquiries concerning the lending terms offered by other lenders on adjustable-payment, adjustable-rate mortgage loans to compare the terms and conditions.

Another flexible feature of the adjustable-payment, adjustable-rate mortgage loan is the monthly payment. The amount of the monthly payment may be increased or decreased by the lender every six months to reflect the changes in the interest rate. State law prohibits the lender from increasing your monthly payment by more than 7.5 percent per year. There may be circumstances, however, in which you, the borrower, may want to increase the amount of your monthly payment beyond the 7.5 percent limit. This option would be available to you whenever changes in the interest rate threaten to increase the outstanding principal loan balance on the loan.

A third flexible feature of the adjustable-payment, adjustable-rate mortgage loan is that the outstanding principal loan balance (the total amount you owe) may be increased from time to time. This situation, called "negative amortization," can occur when rising interest rates make the monthly payment too small to cover the interest due on the loan. The difference between the monthly payment and the actual amount due in interest is added to the outstanding loan balance.

Under the terms of this mortgage, you as a borrower would always have the option of either incurring additions to the amount you owe on the loan or voluntarily increasing your monthly payments beyond the 7.5 percent annual limit to an amount needed to pay off the rising interest costs.

Continual increases in the outstanding loan balance may cause a situation in which the loan balance is not entirely paid off at the end of the 30-year loan term. If this occurs, you may elect in writing to repay the outstanding principal all at once, or with a series of fixed payments at a fixed rate of interest for up to 10 years.

The final flexible feature of the adjustable-payment, adjustable-rate mortgage loan is that you may lengthen the loan term from 30 to up to 40 years. Extending the loan term will lower your monthly payment slightly less than they would have been had the loan term not been extended.

II. INDEX

Adjustments to the interest rate of an adjustable-payment, adjustable-rate mortgage loan must correspond directly to the movement of an index which is selected, but not controlled, by the lender. Any adjustments to the interest rate are subject to limitations provided in the loan contract.

If the index moves down, the lender must reduce the interest rate by at least the decrease in the index. If the index moves up, the lender has the right to increase the interest rate by that amount. Although making such an increase is optional by the lender, you should be aware that the lender has this right and may be contractually obligated to exercise it.

The index used is [Name and description of index to be used for applicant's loan, initial index value (if known) and date of initial index value, a source or sources where the index may be readily obtained by the borrower, and the high and low index rates during the previous calendar year].

III. KEY PROVISIONS OF [Name of Institution]

ADJUSTABLE–PAYMENT, ADJUSTABLE–RATE MORTGAGE LOAN

The following information is a summary of the basic terms on the mortgage loan being offered to you. This summary is intended for reference purposes only. Important information relating specifically to your loan will be contained in the loan agreement.

[Provide a summary of basic terms of the loan, including the loan term, the frequency of rate changes, the frequency of payment changes, the maximum rate change at any one time, the maximum rate change over the life of the loan, the maximum annual payment change, and whether additions to the principal loan balance are possible, in the following format:]

LOAN TERM

FREQUENCY OF RATE CHANGES

FREQUENCY OF PAYMENT CHANGES

IV. HOW YOUR ADJUSTABLE–PAYMENT, ADJUSTABLE–RATE MORTGAGE LOAN WOULD WORK

A. INITIAL INTEREST RATE

The initial interest rate offered by [Name of Institution] on your adjustable-payment, adjustable-rate mortgage loan will be established and disclosed to you on [commitment date, etc.] based on market conditions at that time.

[Insert a short description of each of the key provisions of the loan to be offered to the borrower, using headings where appropriate.]

B. NOTICE OF PAYMENT ADJUSTMENTS

[Name of Institution] will send you notice of an adjustment to the payment amount at least 60 days before it becomes effective. [Describe what information the notice will contain.]

C. PREPAYMENT PENALTY

You may prepay your adjustable-payment, adjustable-rate mortgage in whole or in part without penalty at any time during the term of the loan.

D. FEES

You will be charged fees by [Name of Institution] and by other persons in connection with the origination of your loan. The association will give you an estimate of these fees after receiving your loan application. However, you will not be charged any costs of fees in connection with any regularly scheduled adjustment to the interest rate, the payment, the outstanding principal loan balance, or the loan term.

V. EXAMPLE OF OPERATION OF YOUR ADJUSTABLE–PAYMENT, ADJUSTABLE–RATE MORTGAGE LOAN

[Set out an example of the operation of the mortgage loan, including the use of a table. In at least one of the examples, create a situation showing how negative amortization could occur.]

(d) At least 60 days prior to the due date of a monthly installment to be revised due to a change in the interest rate, notice shall be mailed to the borrower of the following:

(1) The base index.

(2) The most recently published index at the date of the change in the rate.

(3) The interest rate in effect as a result of the change.

(4) The amount of the unpaid principal balance.

(5) If the interest scheduled to be paid on the due date exceeds the amount of the installment, a statement to that effect, including the amount of excess and extent of borrower options as described in paragraph (4) of subdivision (b).

(6) The amount of the revised monthly installment.

(7) The borrower's right to prepayment under paragraph (8) of subdivision (b).

(8) The address and telephone number of the office of the lender to which inquiries may be made.

(e) As used in this section:

(1) "Base index" means the last published index at the date of the note.

(2) "Base index rate" means the interest rate initially applicable to the loan as specified in the note.

(3) "Graduated Payment Adjustable Mortgage Loan" means a loan on which the monthly payments begin at a level lower than that necessary to pay off the remaining principal balance over an amortization period of not less than 30 years. During a period the length of which is fixed at loan origination (the "graduation period"), the scheduled payments gradually rise to a level sufficient to pay off the remaining principal balance over the stipulated amortization period. Limitations on the rate of increase in the scheduled payments due both to graduation and to changes in the interest rate are also fixed at loan origination.

(4) "Note" means the note or other loan contract evidencing an adjustable-payment, adjustable-rate mortgage loan. (*Added by Stats.1981, c. 1079, p. 4152, § 1.*)

Research References

Miller and Starr California Real Estate § 10:84, Adjustable-Payment, Adjustable-Rate Loan.
4 Witkin, California Summary 10th Security Transactions in Real Property § 42, (S 42) Alternative Mortgage Transactions for Residential Loans.

§ 1916.8. Renegotiable rate mortgage loans; interest rate changes at renewal; costs or fees; notice to borrower; disclosure to applicant

Any lender may make, purchase or participate in a renegotiable rate mortgage loan under this section if the loan complies with the provisions of this section pertaining to one- to four-family home loans.

(a) For purposes of this section, a renegotiable rate mortgage loan is a loan issued for a term of three, four or five years, secured by a long-term mortgage or deed of trust of up to 30 years, and automatically renewable at equal intervals except as provided in paragraph (1) of subdivision (b). The loan must be repayable in equal monthly installments of principal and interest during the loan term, in an amount at least sufficient to amortize a loan with the same principal and at the same interest rate over the remaining term of the mortgage or deed of trust. Only one of the indices described in paragraph (1) of subdivision (b) shall be used and no other index shall be used during the term of the mortgage or deed of trust securing the loan. At renewal, no change other than in the interest rate may be made in the terms or conditions of the initial loan. Prepayment in full or in part of the loan balance secured by the mortgage or deed of trust may be made without penalty at any time after the beginning of the minimum notice period for the first renewal, or at any earlier time specified in the loan contract.

(b) Interest rate changes at renewal shall be determined as follows:

(1) Subject to the provisions of subdivision (a) the interest rate offered at renewal shall reflect the movement, in reference to the date of the original loan, of an index, which may be either (i) the contract interest rate on the purchase of previously occupied homes in the most recent monthly national average mortgage rate index for all major lenders published by the Federal Home Loan Bank Board, or (ii) the weighted average cost of funds for the 11th District Savings and Loan Associations as computed by the Federal Home Loan Bank of San Francisco; provided that a lender may extend the initial terms of loans for a period less than six months so that they may mature on the same date three, four or five years after the end of such period of extension, in which case the interest rate offered at renewal shall reflect the movement of the index from the end of such period so that loans may be grouped as though all loans of such group had originated at the end of the extension period.

(2) The maximum rate increase or decrease shall be ½ of 1 percentage point per year multiplied by the number of years in the loan term, with a maximum increase or decrease of 5 percentage points over the life of the mortgage or deed of trust. The lender may offer a borrower a renegotiable rate mortgage loan with maximum annual and total interest rate decreases smaller than the maximum set out in this paragraph, except that in such a case the maximum annual and total interest rate increases offered shall not exceed the maximum annual and total decreases set out in the loan contract.

(3) Interest rate decreases from the previous loan term shall be mandatory. Interest rate increases are optional with the lender, but the lender may obligate itself to a third party to take the maximum increase permitted by this paragraph.

(c) The borrower may not be charged any costs or fees in connection with the renewal of such loan.

(d) At least 90 days before the due date of the loan, the lender shall send written notification in the following form to the borrower:

NOTICE

Your loan with [name of lender], secured by a [mortgage/deed of trust] on property located at [address], is due and payable on [90 days from the date of notice].

If you do not pay by that date, your loan will be renewed automatically for _____ years, upon the same terms and conditions as the current loan, except that the interest rate will be _____%. (See accompanying Truth-In-Lending statement for further credit information.)

Your monthly payment, based on that rate, will be $_____, beginning with the payment due on _____, 19___.

You may pay off the entire loan or a part of it without penalty at any time.

If you have questions about this notice, please contact [title and telephone number of lender's employee].

(e) An applicant for a renegotiable rate mortgage loan must be given, at the time he or she requests an application, a disclosure notice in the following form:

INFORMATION ABOUT THE RENEGOTIABLE-RATE MORTGAGE

You have received an application form for a renegotiable-rate mortgage ("RRM"). The RRM differs from the fixed-rate mortgage with which you may be familiar. In the fixed-rate mortgage the length of the loan and the length of the underlying mortgage are the same, but in the RRM the loan is short-term (3–5 years) and is automatically renewable for a period equal to the mortgage (up to 30 years). Therefore, instead of having an interest rate that is set at the beginning of the mortgage and remains the same, the RRM has an interest rate that may increase or decrease at each renewal of the short-term loan. This means that the amount of your monthly payment may also increase or decrease.

The term of the RRM loan is _____ years, and the length of the underlying mortgage is _____ years. The initial loan term may be up to six months longer than later terms.

The lender must offer to renew the loan, and the only loan provision that may be changed at renewal is the interest rate. The interest rate offered at renewal is based on changes in an index rate. The index used is (either of the following statements shall be given): [computed monthly by the Federal Home Loan Bank Board, an agency of the federal government. The index is based on the national average contract rate for all major lenders for the purchase of previously occupied, single-family homes.] [the weighted average cost of savings, borrowings and Federal Home Loan Bank advances to California members of the Federal Home Loan Bank Board of San Francisco as computed from statistics tabulated by the Federal Home Loan Bank of San Francisco. The index used is computed by the Federal Home Loan Bank of San Francisco.]

At renewal, if the index has moved higher than it was at the beginning of the mortgage, the lender has the right to offer a renewal of the loan at an interest rate equaling the original interest rate plus the increase in the index rate. This is the maximum increase permitted to the lender. Although taking such an increase is optional with the lender, you should be aware that the lender has this right and may become contractually obligated to exercise it.

If the index has moved down, the lender must at renewal reduce the original interest rate by the decrease in the index rate. No matter how much the index rate increases or decreases, THE LENDER, AT RENEWAL, MAY NOT INCREASE OR DECREASE THE INTEREST RATE ON YOUR RRM LOAN BY AN AMOUNT GREATER THAN _____ OF

ONE PERCENTAGE POINT PER YEAR OF THE LOAN, AND THE TOTAL INCREASE OR DECREASE OVER THE LIFE OF THE MORTGAGE MAY NOT BE MORE THAN _____ PERCENTAGE POINTS.

As the borrower, you have the right to decline the lender's offer of renewal. If you decide not to renew, you will have to pay off the remaining balance of the mortgage. Even if you decide to renew, you have the right to prepay the loan in part or in full without penalty at any time after the beginning of the minimum notice period for the first renewal. To give you enough time to make this decision, the lender, 90 days before renewal, will send a notice stating the due date of the loan, the new interest rate and the monthly payment amount. If you do not respond to the notice, the loan will be automatically renewed at the new rate. You will not have to pay any fees or charges at renewal time.

The maximum interest rate increase at the first renewal is _____ percentage points. On a $50,000 mortgage with a loan term of _____ years and an original interest rate of [lender's current commitment rate] percent, this rate change would increase the monthly payment (principal and interest) from $_____ to $_____. Using the same example, the highest rate you might have to pay over the life of the mortgage would be _____ percent, and the lowest would be _____ percent. *(Added by Stats.1980, c. 1139, p. 3681, § 2.)*

Research References

Miller and Starr California Real Estate § 10:85, Renegotiable Rate Loan.
Miller and Starr California Real Estate § 10:236, Policy Objectives; the "Standard" Transaction.
4 Witkin, California Summary 10th Security Transactions in Real Property § 42, (S 42) Alternative Mortgage Transactions for Residential Loans.

§ 1916.9. Offer of fixed rate mortgage loan as alternative to renegotiable rate mortgage loan

(a) Every lender who offers a renegotiable rate mortgage loan pursuant to Section 1916.8 to a borrower who occupies or intends to occupy the property which is security for the loan shall also offer to such borrower a fixed rate mortgage loan in the same amount with a term of at least 29 years.

(b) Nothing in this section shall require that the terms of such alternative loans, including the rates of interest thereon, must be the same as those terms offered with regard to the fixed-payment adjustable-rate loan or the renegotiable rate mortgage loan also offered.

(c) This section does not apply to any lender who makes less than 10 loans per year. *(Added by Stats.1980, c. 1139, p. 3685, § 3.)*

Research References

Miller and Starr California Real Estate § 10:85, Renegotiable Rate Loan.
4 Witkin, California Summary 10th Security Transactions in Real Property § 42, (S 42) Alternative Mortgage Transactions for Residential Loans.

§ 1916.11. Lien of mortgage or deed of trust; validity

Notwithstanding any other remedy a borrower may have based on an alleged failure to comply with Sections 1916.5 through 1916.9, the lien of the mortgage or deed of trust shall be valid. *(Added by Stats.1981, c. 274, p. 1370, § 2, eff. Aug. 27, 1981.)*

Research References

Miller and Starr California Real Estate § 10:83, Regulation of Variable Interest Rate Loans.

§ 1916.12. Legislative findings; purpose; mortgage parity between state and federal institutions; rules and regulations

(a) The Legislature finds that the economic environment of financial institutions has become increasingly volatile as a result of regulatory revisions enacted by the United States Congress and federal agencies <u>including</u>, but not necessarily limited to, the Comptroller of the Currency, the Federal Home Loan Bank Board, Federal Reserve Board, and the Depository Institutions Deregulation Committee. The Legislature further finds that deposit rate ceilings are being phased out while the cost of and competition for funds have escalated. It is the purpose of this section to maintain the quality of competition between state-licensed and federally regulated financial institutions in the field of mortgage lending, as well as promote the convenience, advantage and best interests of California residents in their pursuit of adequate and available housing. In order to remain competitive and provide the optimum housing environment for the citizens of California, state institutions require the ability to respond in a timely manner to changes in mortgage lending parameters initiated at the federal level. Local regulatory guidelines must promote continued parity between the state and federal levels in order to avoid creation of discriminatory burdens upon state institutions and to protect interests held by California citizens. It is the intent of the Legislature to eliminate past and prevent future inequities between state and federal financial institutions doing business in the State of California by creating a sensitive and responsive mortgage parity procedure.

(b) The Secretary of the Business, * * * <u>Consumer Services,</u> and Housing Agency, or the secretary's designee as defined by subdivision (c) of Section 1918.5 of the Civil Code, shall have the authority to prescribe rules and regulations extending to lenders who make loans upon the security of residential real property any right, power, privilege or duty relating to mortgage instruments that is equivalent to authority extended to <u>federally regulated</u> financial institutions by federal statute or regulation.

(c) In order to grant equivalent mortgage lending authority to state financial institutions to that which has been extended to federal financial institutions, the secretary or the secretary's designee shall adopt such regulations within 60 days of the effective date of the statute or regulation extending the comparable right, power, privilege, or duty to federally regulated financial institutions.

(d) The provisions of Sections 1916.5, 1916.6, 1916.7, 1916.8, <u>and</u> 1916.9, * * * and any other provisions of law relating to the requirements for changes in the rate of interest on loans, shall not be applicable to loans made pursuant to the provisions of this section and regulations promulgated thereunder.

(e) Any regulations adopted pursuant to this section shall expire on January 1 of the second succeeding year following the end of the calendar year in which the regulation was promulgated. Subsequent amendments to these regulations cannot extend this expiration date.

(f) This section shall become operative on December 31, 1983. *(Added by Stats.1981, c. 1079, p. 4151, § 3, operative Dec. 31, 1983. Amended by Stats.2013, c. 353 (S.B.820), § 10, eff. Sept. 26, 2013, operative July 1, 2013.)*

Research References

Miller and Starr California Real Estate § 10:84, Adjustable-Payment, Adjustable-Rate Loan.
4 Witkin, California Summary 10th Security Transactions in Real Property § 42, (S 42) Alternative Mortgage Transactions for Residential Loans.

§ 1916–1. Legal rate of interest; contract rate

The rate of interest upon the loan or forbearance of any money, goods or things in action or on accounts after demand or judgments rendered in any court of this state, shall be seven dollars upon the one hundred dollars for one year and at that rate for a greater or less sum or for a longer or a shorter time;

but it shall be competent for parties to contract for the payment and receipt of a rate of interest not exceeding twelve dollars on the one hundred dollars for one year and not exceeding that rate for a greater or less sum or for a longer or shorter time, in which case such rate exceeding seven dollars on one hundred dollars shall be clearly expressed in writing. *(Initiative Measure, Stats. 1919, p. lxxxiii, § 1.)*

Research References

Rutter, Cal. Practice Guide: Real Prop. Transactions Form 9:A, Sample Opinion Letter (By Borrower's Counsel).
Miller and Starr California Real Estate § 21:1, Policy and Validity of the Usury Law.
1 Witkin Cal. Summ. 10th Contracts § 455, Usury Law.

§ 1916–2. Maximum rate of interest; compound interest; effect of contract provisions for excessive interest

No person, company, association or corporation shall directly or indirectly take or receive in money, goods or things in action, or in any other manner whatsoever, any greater sum or any greater value for the loan or forbearance of money, goods or things in action than at the rate of twelve dollars upon one hundred dollars for one year; and in the computation of interest upon any bond, note, or other instrument or agreement, interest shall not be compounded, nor shall the interest thereon be construed to bear interest unless an agreement to that effect is clearly expressed in writing and signed by the party to be charged therewith. Any agreement or contract of any nature in conflict with the provisions of this section shall be null and void as to any agreement or stipulation therein contained to pay interest and no action at law to recover interest in any sum shall be maintained and the debt can not be declared due until the full period of time it was contracted for has elapsed. *(Initiative Measure, Stats.1919, p. lxxxiii, § 2.)*

Research References

Rutter, Cal. Practice Guide: Real Prop. Transactions Ch. 6-F, F. Promissory Note.
1 Witkin Cal. Summ. 10th Contracts § 455, Usury Law.
1 Witkin Cal. Summ. 10th Contracts § 475, Forbearance.

§ 1916–3. Civil and criminal liability for violations

(a) Every person, company, association or corporation, who for any loan or forbearance of money, goods or things in action shall have paid or delivered any greater sum or value than is allowed to be received under the preceding sections, one and two, may either in person or his or its personal representative, recover in an action at law against the person, company, association or corporation who shall have taken or received the same, or his or its personal representative, treble the amount of the money so paid or value delivered in violation of said sections, providing such action shall be brought within one year after such payment or delivery.

(b) Any person who willfully makes or negotiates, for himself or another, a loan of money, credit, goods, or things in action, and who directly or indirectly charges, contracts for, or receives with respect to any such loan any interest or charge of any nature, the value of which is in excess of that allowed by law, is guilty of loan-sharking, a felony, and is punishable by imprisonment in the state prison for not more than five years or in the county jail for not more than one year. This subdivision shall not apply to any person licensed to make or negotiate, for himself or another, loans of money, credit, goods, or things in action, or expressly exempted from compliance by the laws of this state with respect to such licensure or interest or other charge, or to any agent or employee of such person when acting within the scope of his agency or employment. *(Initiative Measure, Stats.1919, p. lxxxiii, § 3. Amended by Stats.1970, c. 784, p. 1497, § 1.)*

Research References

Rutter, Cal. Practice Guide: Real Prop. Transactions Ch. 6-F, F. Promissory Note.
Miller and Starr California Real Estate § 21:1, Policy and Validity of the Usury Law.
22 NO. 1 Miller & Starr, California Real Estate Newsalert 25, Usury.
1 Witkin Cal. Summ. 10th Contracts § 455, Usury Law.
1 Witkin Cal. Summ. 10th Contracts § 469, Penalty of Treble Interest.

§ 1916–4. Repeals

Sections one thousand nine hundred seventeen, one thousand nine hundred eighteen, one thousand nine hundred nineteen and one thousand nine hundred twenty of the Civil Code and all acts and parts of acts in conflict with this act are hereby repealed. *(Initiative Measure, Stats.1919, p. lxxxiv, § 4.)*

§ 1916–5. Usury Law, citation

This act whenever cited, referred to, or amended may be designated simply as the "usury law." *(Initiative Measure, Stats.1919, p. lxxxiv, § 5.)*

CHAPTER 3.5. SHARED APPRECIATION LOANS

§ 1917. Definitions; contingent deferred interest; shared appreciation loan

For purposes of this chapter:

(a) "Contingent deferred interest" means the sum a borrower is obligated to pay to a lender pursuant to the documentation of a shared appreciation loan as a share of (1) the appreciation in the value of the security property (2) rents and profits attributable to the subject property, or (3) both.

(b) A "shared appreciation loan" means any loan made upon the security of an interest in real property which additionally obligates the borrower to pay to the lender contingent deferred interest pursuant to the loan documentation. "Shared appreciation loan" does not include any loan made upon the security of an interest in real property containing one to four residential units at least one of which at the time the loan is made is or is to be occupied by the borrower. *(Added by Stats.1987, c. 652, § 1.)*

Research References

California Real Estate Forms (Miller & Starr) § 3:36, Contingent Interest Agreement.
Rutter, Cal. Practice Guide: Real Prop. Transactions Ch. 6-B, B. Sources and Kinds of Financing.
Miller and Starr California Real Estate § 10:86, Shared Appreciation Loan.
Miller and Starr California Real Estate § 21:13, Participation in Profits; Shared Appreciation Loans.
18 NO. 2 Miller & Starr, California Real Estate Newsalert 25, Usury.
4 Witkin, California Summary 10th Security Transactions in Real Property § 42, (S 42) Alternative Mortgage Transactions for Residential Loans.

§ 1917.001. Relationship of borrower and lender

The relationship of the borrower and the lender in a shared appreciation loan transaction is that of debtor and creditor and shall not be, or be construed to be, a joint venture, equity venture, partnership, or other relationship. *(Added by Stats. 1987, c. 652, § 1.)*

Research References

Rutter, Cal. Practice Guide: Real Prop. Transactions Ch. 6-B, B. Sources and Kinds of Financing.
Miller and Starr California Real Estate § 10:86, Shared Appreciation Loan.
Miller and Starr California Real Estate § 21:13, Participation in Profits; Shared Appreciation Loans.

§ 1917.002. Statutes governing variable, adjustable, or renegotiable interest rate instruments; application

A shared appreciation loan shall not be subject to any provisions of this code or the Financial Code which limits the interest rate or change of interest rate of variable, adjustable, or renegotiable interest instruments, or which requires particular language or provisions in security instruments securing variable, adjustable, or renegotiable rate obligations or in evidences of such debts except for those specifically imposed by Chapter 4 (commencing with Section 1917.010) or Chapter 7 (commencing with Section 1917.320) for loans subject to those chapters. This section is declaratory of existing law. *(Added by Stats.1987, c. 652, § 1.)*

Research References

Rutter, Cal. Practice Guide: Real Prop. Transactions Ch. 6-B, B. Sources and Kinds of Financing.
Miller and Starr California Real Estate § 10:86, Shared Appreciation Loan.
Miller and Starr California Real Estate § 21:13, Participation in Profits; Shared Appreciation Loans.

§ 1917.003. Liens of deeds of trust; included amounts

The lien or liens of a deed or deeds of trust securing a shared appreciation loan shall include and secure the principal amount of the shared appreciation loan, and all interest, whether accrued or to be accrued, including all amounts of contingent deferred interest. *(Added by Stats.1987, c. 652, § 1. Amended by Stats.1989, c. 1416, § 5.)*

Research References

Miller and Starr California Real Estate § 10:86, Shared Appreciation Loan.
Miller and Starr California Real Estate § 21:13, Participation in Profits; Shared Appreciation Loans.

§ 1917.004. Lien of deed of trust securing loan; attachment; priority; indication of type of loan on document

(a) The lien of a shared appreciation loan, including the principle[1] amount and all interest, whether accrued or to be accrued, and all amounts of contingent deferred interest, shall attach from the time of the recordation of the deed of trust securing the loan, and the lien, including the lien of the interest accrued, or to be accrued, and of the contingent deferred interest, shall have priority over any other lien or encumbrance affecting the property encumbered by the shared appreciation deed of trust which is recorded after the time of recordation of the shared appreciation deed of trust. Nothing in this section shall preclude a junior or subordinate lien to the deed of trust securing the shared appreciation loan.

(b) Any deed of trust that acts as security for a shared appreciation loan shall indicate on the document that the deed of trust secures a shared appreciation loan. *(Added by Stats. 1987, c. 652, § 1.)*

1 Probably should read "principal".

Research References

California Real Estate Forms (Miller & Starr) § 3:8, Deed of Trust, Security Agreement, and Fixture Filing With Assignment of Rents and Agreements.
California Real Estate Forms (Miller & Starr) § 3:14, Construction Deed of Trust, Security Agreement, and Fixture Filing With Assignment of Rents and Agreements.
California Real Estate Forms (Miller & Starr) § 3:21, Deed of Trust, Assignment of Rents, Security Agreement and Fixture Filing—Conduit Loan.
California Real Estate Forms (Miller & Starr) § 3:35, Long Form Deed of Trust and Assignment of Rents.
Rutter, Cal. Practice Guide: Real Prop. Transactions Ch. 6-B, B. Sources and Kinds of Financing.
Miller and Starr California Real Estate § 10:11, Future Advances Secured.
Miller and Starr California Real Estate § 10:86, Shared Appreciation Loan.
Miller and Starr California Real Estate § 21:13, Participation in Profits; Shared Appreciation Loans.
Miller and Starr California Real Estate § 11:106, Liens for Future Advances--In General.

§ 1917.005. Usury exemption

Lenders shall be exempt from the usury provisions of Article XV of the California Constitution with respect to shared appreciation loan transactions. This section is declaratory of existing law. *(Added by Stats.1987, c. 652, § 1.)*

Research References

Rutter, Cal. Practice Guide: Real Prop. Transactions Ch. 6-B, B. Sources and Kinds of Financing.
Miller and Starr California Real Estate § 10:86, Shared Appreciation Loan.
Miller and Starr California Real Estate § 21:13, Participation in Profits; Shared Appreciation Loans.
Miller and Starr California Real Estate § 21:35, Who is Liable for Usury Penalties--Other Exemptions.

§ 1917.006. Definitions; shared appreciation loan; local public entity; owner-occupied residence

For purposes of this chapter:

(a) "Shared appreciation loan" means, in addition to the meaning defined in Section 1917, a loan that obligates the borrower to pay to the lender contingent deferred interest pursuant to the loan documentation and that is made upon the security of an interest in real property that is an owner-occupied residence in compliance with all of the following conditions:

(1) The loan is made by, and all contingent deferred interest paid with respect to the loan is used by, a local public entity to provide financial assistance in the acquisition of housing that is affordable to persons and families of low or moderate income, as defined in Section 50093 of the Health and Safety Code.

(2) The loan is made or acquired with assets of the local public entity other than the proceeds of a bond meeting the requirements of Section 143 of the United States Internal Revenue Code of 1986.

(3) The loan documentation assures that the obligation to pay contingent deferred interest is subject to a superior right of the borrower, upon termination of the loan, to receive repayment of money paid by the borrower for purchase of the security property (including downpayment, installment payments of mortgage principal, escrow fees, transfer taxes, recording fees, brokerage commissions and similar costs of acquisition actually paid by the borrower) and money paid by the borrower for

capital improvements to the security property, plus not less than the legal rate of interest on those cash payments.

(4) The loan documentation assures that the amount of contingent deferred interest shall not exceed that percentage of the appreciation in appraised fair market value of the security property that equals the local public entity's proportionate share of the total initial equity in the security property. The amount of the total initial equity and of the local public entity's share of the initial equity shall be agreed upon by the borrower and the local public entity at the time of executing the shared appreciation loan and shall include the local public entity's cash investment, the difference between the price of land provided by the local public entity and the fair market value of the land, the amount of fees waived by the local public entity, and the value of in-kind contributions made by or on behalf of the local public entity. Funds borrowed by the borrower, the repayment of which are secured by the security property, shall not be included in the calculation of total initial equity of the borrower.

(5) At least 30 days in advance of executing the loan documentation, the borrower receives full disclosure of the terms and conditions of the loan, including the economic consequences to the borrower of the obligation to pay contingent deferred interest.

(b) "Local public entity" means a city and county, or a housing authority or redevelopment agency of a city and county.

(c) "Owner-occupied residence" means real property containing one to four residential units at least one of which at the time the loan is made is, or is to be, occupied by the borrower. *(Added by Stats.1990, c. 1606 (S.B.2716), § 1.)*

Research References

Miller and Starr California Real Estate § 21:13, Participation in Profits; Shared Appreciation Loans.

CHAPTER 4. SHARED APPRECIATION LOANS OF E.R.I.S.A. PENSION FUNDS [INOPERATIVE]

ARTICLE 1. LEGISLATIVE FINDINGS AND DECLARATIONS [INOPERATIVE]

Section
1917.010. Legislative findings and declarations.

Operative Effect

Chapter 4 became inoperative January 1, 1990 pursuant to Stats.1982, c. 466, § 11.5. For continuing application of Chapter 4, see Historical and Statutory Notes under Civil Code § 1917.010.

§ 1917.010. Legislative findings and declarations

The Legislature hereby finds and declares that:

(a) It is necessary and essential that the state provide and promote alternative means of supplying affordable housing to the citizens of the state.

(b) High interest rates have caused payment schedules for new long-term, fixed-rate and adjustable-rate mortgages to exceed affordable levels for the vast majority of the state's households.

(c) Because of current economic conditions, including high and volatile interest rates, alternative mortgage instruments must be developed to supplement the standard long-term, fixed-rate mortgage.

(d) Because the interest to which the lender is entitled under a shared appreciation mortgage includes a share of the appreciated value of the property securing the loan, the periodic payments under a shared appreciation mortgage are lower and, therefore, more affordable to borrowers than under a mortgage in which the lender's interest does not include a share of the appreciated value of the property. State authorization of the shared appreciation loan for pension fund lenders will serve the need to develop alternative and more affordable means of financing the construction of new housing and the subsequent marketing of new homes, and to create vitally needed jobs in the construction industry.

(e) Pension funds may find shared appreciation loans suited to their investment needs since yields are keyed to appreciation in property values, which may serve as a hedge against inflation. *(Added by Stats.1982, c. 466, p. 1975, § 11.)*

Operative Effect

Chapter 4 became inoperative January 1, 1990 pursuant to Stats.1982, c. 466, § 11.5. For continuing application of Chapter 4, see Historical and Statutory Notes under this section.

Research References

4 Witkin, California Summary 10th Security Transactions in Real Property § 42, (S 42) Alternative Mortgage Transactions for Residential Loans.

ARTICLE 2. DEFINITIONS [INOPERATIVE]

Section
1917.020. Definitions.

Operative Effect

Chapter 4 became inoperative January 1, 1990 pursuant to Stats.1982, c. 466, § 11.5. For continuing application of Chapter 4, see Historical and Statutory Notes under Civil Code § 1917.010.

§ 1917.020. Definitions

For purposes of this chapter:

(a) "Adjusted fair market value" means all of the following:

(1) The net sale price, in the case of a bona fide sale made in good faith prior to the maturity date of the shared appreciation loan, but excluding any sale upon a foreclosure or trustee's sale pursuant to Section 726 of the Code of Civil Procedure or Section 2924.

(2) In all other cases, the amount of value of the property specified in the most recent annual appraisal performed pursuant to Section 1917.040 or 1917.042.

(b) "Borrower's cost of the property" means the total cost to the borrower incident to the purchase of the property, including documentary transfer taxes, escrow and recording fees, and title insurance premiums.

(c) "Contingent deferred interest" means the sum resulting upon multiplying the net appreciated value by one-third.

(d) "Cost of capital improvements" means the amount of the credit, if any, determined pursuant to Article 5 (commencing with Section 1917.050).

(e) "Lender" means any person who makes a shared appreciation loan on behalf of a pension fund specified in Section 1917.030. Subsequent to an assignment of a shared appreciation loan to a pension fund pursuant to Section 1917.030, "lender" shall mean the pension fund assignee (or any subsequent assignee) and its agents designated to service the shared appreciation loan.

(f) "Net appreciated value" means the adjusted fair market value less the sum of the borrower's cost of the property and the cost of capital improvements.

(g) "Net sale price" means the gross sale price less expenses of sale actually paid by the borrower, including real estate commissions, advertising, documentary transfer taxes, legal, escrow and recording fees, and title insurance premiums.

(h) "Prevailing rate" means the weighted average yield accepted by the Federal National Mortgage Association in its most recent free market system auction for four-month conventional mortgage commitments or, if the Federal National Mortgage Association alters its free market system auction, then the system which is adopted by the Federal National Mortgage Association which substantially replaces or supersedes the present free market system auction for four-month commitments, or if no auction or equivalent thereof has been conducted within the six months immediately preceding the date the application for a shared appreciation mortgage loan is executed, the weighted average cost of funds for the 11th District Savings and Loan Associations as computed by the Federal Home Loan Bank of San Francisco.

(i) "Shared appreciation loan" means any loan made pursuant to this chapter upon the security of owner-occupied real property of a type specified in Section 1917.030, and in connection with which the lender has a right to receive a share of the appreciation in the value of the security property. "Shared appreciation loan" includes a deed of trust and any evidence of debt issued in connection with the loan. *(Added by Stats.1982, c. 466, p. 1975, § 11. Amended by Stats.1984, c. 1267, § 1.)*

Operative Effect

Chapter 4 became inoperative January 1, 1990 pursuant to Stats.1982, c. 466, § 11.5. For continuing application of Chapter 4, see Historical and Statutory Notes under Civil Code § 1917.010.

ARTICLE 3. TERMS AND CONDITIONS [INOPERATIVE]

Operative Effect

Chapter 4 became inoperative January 1, 1990 pursuant to Stats.1982, c. 466, § 11.5. For continuing application of Chapter 4, see Historical and Statutory Notes under Civil Code § 1917.010.

§ 1917.030. Authority to make loans on owner-occupied property; pension funds

Lenders may make shared appreciation loans pursuant to this chapter for the purchase of real property improved with one- to four-family dwelling units, including structures ancillary to such dwelling units and including attached single-family dwelling units, single-family mobilehome units placed upon permanent foundations, residential condominium units and dwelling units within a planned unit development. Shared appreciation loans shall be made to finance only owner-occupied dwelling units, but in the case of two- to four-unit dwellings financed under this chapter only one of the units need be owner-occupied. The original recipient of a shared appreciation loan shall certify in writing to the lender that he or she will occupy the security property as his or her principal residence, provided that failure to so occupy the security property shall not void a shared appreciation loan, but at the option of the lender the loan may be accelerated in accordance with the terms and conditions provided in the shared appreciation loan. All shared appreciation loans shall be originated by the lender on behalf of a pension fund which is subject to the Employee Retirement Income Security Act of 1974 (P.L. 93–406, 88 Stat. 829),[1] pursuant to a prior written commitment to purchase the loan. *(Added by Stats.1982, c. 466, p. 1975, § 11.)*

[1] 29 U.S.C.A. § 1001 et seq.

Operative Effect

Chapter 4 became inoperative January 1, 1990 pursuant to Stats.1982, c. 466, § 11.5. For continuing application of Chapter 4, see Historical and Statutory Notes under Civil Code § 1917.010.

Research References

Miller and Starr California Real Estate § 10:236, Policy Objectives; the "Standard" Transaction.

§ 1917.031. General terms and conditions

A shared appreciation loan shall include the following terms and conditions:

(a) The term of the loan, excluding refinancing under Section 1917.033, shall be at least seven years, but not more than 30 years.

(b) The repayment schedule for the loan, excluding refinancing under Section 1917.033, shall be cast so that full amortization of the principal amount of the loan would occur in 30 years, regardless of the actual term of the loan. Any principal balance remaining at maturity shall be due and payable at that time, unless refinanced as provided in Section 1917.033. Monthly installment payments shall be equal in amount and in addition to amortization of principal, shall include fixed interest pursuant to subdivision (d).

(c) The loan shall be secured by a deed of trust or mortgage on the real property financed.

(d) The loan shall bear interest at a fixed rate, which shall be one-third below the prevailing rate in effect 90 days prior to the loan closing, or at another date between that date and the loan closing if mutually agreed by the lender and borrower.

(e) The borrower shall additionally be obligated to pay contingent deferred interest in the amount of one-third of the net appreciated value of the real property which secures the loan, at the time the property is sold (including a sale pursuant to a land sale contract), when title is transferred, other than a transfer specified in Section 2924.6, when a lease with an option to purchase is entered into, when a partnership is formed which in effect transfers the beneficial ownership to another person, when a trust is created which affects title to the property, upon a judicial or nonjudicial foreclosure sale, at the time the loan is prepaid in full, or upon the maturity of the loan, whichever first occurs. *(Added by Stats.1982, c. 466, p. 1975, § 11.)*

Operative Effect

Chapter 4 became inoperative January 1, 1990 pursuant to Stats.1982, c. 466, § 11.5. For continuing application of Chapter 4, see Historical and Statutory Notes under Civil Code § 1917.010.

§ 1917.032. Right to prepay; prepayment charge

(a) The borrower shall have the right to prepay, at any time, in full or in part, the principal loan balance of the shared appreciation loan, together with accrued interest, including deferred contingent interest.

(b) Nothing in this chapter shall prevent a borrower from obligating himself or herself, by an agreement in writing, to pay a prepayment charge, as authorized by this section, upon prepayment of the loan, in full or in part, within five years of the date of execution of the shared appreciation loan.

(c) Any prepayment charge imposed upon the prepayment of a shared appreciation loan shall not exceed the amount authorized and specified in subdivision (b) of Section 2954.9.

(d) No prepayment charge shall be imposed as to any portion of the contingent deferred interest. *(Added by Stats.1982, c. 466, p. 1975, § 11.)*

Operative Effect

Chapter 4 became inoperative January 1, 1990 pursuant to Stats.1982, c. 466, § 11.5. For continuing application of Chapter 4, see Historical and Statutory Notes under Civil Code § 1917.010.

§ 1917.033. Refinancing

(a) If the shared appreciation loan is not prepaid in full or the real property securing the loan is not sold or transferred prior to maturity of the loan, the lender shall offer to the original borrower refinancing of the unpaid balance of the loan and all contingent deferred interest.

(b) The term of the refinancing loan shall be at least 30 years from the date of the refinancing, provided that if the interest rate of the refinancing loan is not adjustable or variable during the term of such loan, the loan may contain a call provision giving the lender an option to accelerate the principal loan balance making it, together with accrued interest, payable in full at a date specified in the shared appreciation loan, which shall be no earlier than seven years following the date of refinancing under this section. If such a call provision is included in the refinancing loan, a concise description thereof shall be included in upper case print in the disclosures on refinancing required by Section 1917.071.

(c) The interest rate for the refinancing loan shall not exceed the prevailing rate existing at maturity of the shared appreciation loan.

(d) The lender may require as a condition of the refinancing loan that it be secured by a deed of trust or mortgage of first priority on the property financed.

(e) The terms and conditions of refinancing pursuant to this section shall be specified in the shared appreciation loan, shall be a part of the shared appreciation loan contract, and shall be subject to the applicable laws in effect on the date of execution of the shared appreciation loan. The refinancing shall be fully amortizing and the interest rate may be either fixed or adjustable as permitted by law for home financing offered by banks or savings and loan associations doing business in this state to the public for financing housing similar to the borrower's property, provided that nothing in this section shall preclude such other lawful refinancing terms as may be mutually acceptable to the borrower and lender. If the lender offers more than one form of refinancing, the borrower may select from among the types of refinancing offered by the lender. *(Added by Stats.1982, c. 466, p. 1975, § 11.)*

Operative Effect

Chapter 4 became inoperative January 1, 1990 pursuant to Stats.1982, c. 466, § 11.5. For continuing application of Chapter 4, see Historical and Statutory Notes under Civil Code § 1917.010.

§ 1917.034. Alternative refinancing

Nothing in this chapter shall preclude the borrower from obtaining any other financing, in lieu of the refinancing provided for in Section 1917.033, including refinancing on other terms that are mutually agreeable to the borrower and lender. *(Added by Stats.1982, c. 466, p. 1975, § 11.)*

Operative Effect

Chapter 4 became inoperative January 1, 1990 pursuant to Stats.1982, c. 466, § 11.5. For continuing application of Chapter 4, see Historical and Statutory Notes under Civil Code § 1917.010.

ARTICLE 4. ANNUAL APPRAISALS [INOPERATIVE]

Operative Effect

Chapter 4 became inoperative January 1, 1990 pursuant to Stats.1982, c. 466, § 11.5. For continuing application of Chapter 4, see Historical and Statutory Notes under Civil Code § 1917.010.

§ 1917.040. Appraisal for lender; time; copy for borrower; notice; payment of cost

The fair market value of the real property securing a shared appreciation loan shall be determined annually as provided in this article. The lender shall select an independent appraiser annually to perform an appraisal of the property subject to a shared appreciation loan. The appraisal shall be performed within 30 days preceding the anniversary date of the loan and a copy of the current appraisal shall be sent by first-class mail to the borrower no later than five days following the anniversary date of the loan, together with a notice informing the borrower that the appraisal will constitute a final and conclusive determination of the value of the property for certain purposes and that if the borrower disputes the amount of the appraisal, the borrower may procure an independent appraisal as provided in Section 1917.041. The lender may require the borrower to pay for the cost of the appraisal. *(Added by Stats.1982, c. 466, p. 1975, § 11.)*

Chapter 4 became inoperative January 1, 1990 pursuant to Stats.1982, c. 466, § 11.5. For continuing application of Chapter 4, see Historical and Statutory Notes under Civil Code § 1917.010.

§ 1917.041. Appraisal for borrower; time; copy to lender

If the borrower disputes the amount of the appraisal, the borrower, within 30 days of the anniversary date of the loan, may procure an appraisal of the property at the borrower's expense by a qualified independent appraiser, and a copy of the appraisal shall be sent by first-class mail to the lender within the 30-day period. *(Added by Stats.1982, c. 466, p. 1975, § 11.)*

Chapter 4 became inoperative January 1, 1990 pursuant to Stats.1982, c. 466, § 11.5. For continuing application of Chapter 4, see Historical and Statutory Notes under Civil Code § 1917.010.

§ 1917.042. Differing appraisals; determination of amount

If the appraisal by the appraiser selected by the borrower is lower in amount than the appraisal by the appraiser selected by the lender, the amount to be used to calculate the annual adjustment shall be one-half of the sum of the two appraisals. *(Added by Stats.1982, c. 466, p. 1975, § 11.)*

Chapter 4 became inoperative January 1, 1990 pursuant to Stats.1982, c. 466, § 11.5. For continuing application of Chapter 4, see Historical and Statutory Notes under Civil Code § 1917.010.

§ 1917.043. Value of property; determination of adjusted fair market value

The appraisal amount, as determined pursuant to Section 1917.040 if the borrower does not dispute the appraisal amount, or 1917.042 if the borrower disputes the appraisal amount, shall constitute the value of the property from and after the anniversary date of the loan for the purpose of determining the property's adjusted fair market value under Section 1917.020. *(Added by Stats.1982, c. 466, p. 1975, § 11.)*

Chapter 4 became inoperative January 1, 1990 pursuant to Stats.1982, c. 466, § 11.5. For continuing application of Chapter 4, see Historical and Statutory Notes under Civil Code § 1917.010.

§ 1917.044. Qualifications of appraisers; specification by loan terms

The qualifications of the appraisers may be specified by the terms of the shared appreciation loan for purposes of this article and Article 5 (commencing with Section 1917.050). *(Added by Stats.1982, c. 466, p. 1975, § 11.)*

Chapter 4 became inoperative January 1, 1990 pursuant to Stats.1982, c. 466, § 11.5. For continuing application of Chapter 4, see Historical and Statutory Notes under Civil Code § 1917.010.

ARTICLE 5. IMPROVEMENTS [INOPERATIVE]

Section
1917.050. Addition of cost of improvements to borrower's cost in determining contingent deferred interest; procedure.

Chapter 4 became inoperative January 1, 1990 pursuant to Stats.1982, c. 466, § 11.5. For continuing application of Chapter 4, see Historical and Statutory Notes under Civil Code § 1917.010.

§ 1917.050. Addition of cost of improvements to borrower's cost in determining contingent deferred interest; procedure

The borrower may have the cost of capital improvements to the security property completed within any 12-month period, and with an appraised value in excess of two thousand five hundred dollars ($2,500), added to the borrower's cost of the property, for purposes of determining the contingent deferred interest, but only if the procedures set forth in this article are followed.

(a) Within 60 days following the completion of the improvements, the borrower shall send by first-class mail a notice of the completion of the improvements to the lender and shall submit proof of cost of the improvements.

(b) Within 90 days following the completion of the improvements, the lender shall select an appraiser to perform an appraisal to determine the increase in value of the property, if any, by reason of the improvements. A copy of the appraisal shall be sent by first-class mail to the borrower, together with a notice informing the borrower that the appraisal will constitute a final and conclusive determination of the increase in the value of the property by reason of the improvement for purposes of computing the net appreciated value of the property, and that if the borrower disputes the amount of the appraisal, the borrower may procure an independent appraisal as provided in subdivision (c). The lender may require the borrower to pay for the cost of the appraisal.

(c) If the borrower disputes the amount of the appraisal, the borrower, within 120 days of the completion of the improvements, may secure at borrower's expense, a qualified, independent appraiser to perform an appraisal to determine the increase in value of the property, if any, by reason of the improvements, and a copy of the appraisal shall be sent by first-class mail to the lender within that period of time.

(d) If the appraisal of the appraiser selected by the borrower is greater in amount than the appraisal by the appraiser selected by the lender, the amount of the appraisal, for the purposes of this section, shall be one-half of the sum of the two appraisals.

(e) The lesser of the borrower's actual cost or the appraised increase in the value of the property by reason of the improvements shall be available as a credit to the buyer for purposes of determining net appreciated value, except as provided in subdivision (f).

(f) If 50 percent or more of the value of the labor or other work on the improvements was performed by the borrower, then the appraised increase in the value of the property by reason of the improvements shall be the cost of capital improvements for purposes of establishing the credit under this section. *(Added by Stats.1982, c. 466, p. 1975, § 11.)*

Chapter 4 became inoperative January 1, 1990 pursuant to Stats.1982, c. 466, § 11.5. For continuing application of Chapter 4, see Historical and Statutory Notes under Civil Code § 1917.010.

ARTICLE 6. GENERAL PROVISIONS [INOPERATIVE]

Operative Effect

Chapter 4 became inoperative January 1, 1990 pursuant to Stats.1982, c. 466, § 11.5. For continuing application of Chapter 4, see Historical and Statutory Notes under Civil Code § 1917.010.

§ 1917.060. Relationship of borrower and lender

The relationship of the borrower and the lender, as to a shared appreciation loan, is that of debtor and creditor and shall not be, or be construed to be, a joint venture, equity venture, partnership, or other relationship. *(Added by Stats.1982, c. 466, p. 1975, § 11.)*

Operative Effect

Chapter 4 became inoperative January 1, 1990 pursuant to Stats.1982, c. 466, § 11.5. For continuing application of Chapter 4, see Historical and Statutory Notes under Civil Code § 1917.010.

§ 1917.061. Waiver of borrower's rights; prohibition

Any waiver of any right of a borrower under the provisions of this chapter shall be void and unenforceable. *(Added by Stats.1982, c. 466, p. 1975, § 11.)*

Operative Effect

Chapter 4 became inoperative January 1, 1990 pursuant to Stats.1982, c. 466, § 11.5. For continuing application of Chapter 4, see Historical and Statutory Notes under Civil Code § 1917.010.

§ 1917.062. Acceleration of maturity upon sale or transfer

(a) Notwithstanding Section 711, a provision in a shared appreciation loan (not including the refinancing obligation) permitting the lender to accelerate the maturity date of the principal and accrued interest on the loan upon a sale or other transfer of the property, as specified in subdivision (e) of Section 1917.031, shall be valid and enforceable against the borrower, except as may be precluded by Section 2924.6.

(b) The Legislature finds and declares that potential exposure to liability for enforcement of a "due-on-sale" clause consistent with Section 711, as interpreted by the courts, makes use of such a provision impractical. Moreover, the additional risks to the lender inherent in shared appreciation financing are greater with longer loan terms (which are more desirable from the standpoint of housing affordability), but this risk is reduced with an enforceable "due-on-sale" clause. Therefore, in order to facilitate shared appreciation financing, it is necessary to establish the exception specified in subdivision (a). *(Added by Stats.1982, c. 466, p. 1975, § 11.)*

Operative Effect

Chapter 4 became inoperative January 1, 1990 pursuant to Stats.1982, c. 466, § 11.5. For continuing application of Chapter 4, see Historical and Statutory Notes under Civil Code § 1917.010.

§ 1917.063. Conformity of loan terms and conditions to chapter; application

This chapter facilitates the making of shared appreciation financing in this state which conforms to the provisions of this chapter. The terms and conditions of any shared appreciation loan made pursuant to this chapter shall be consistent with this chapter. This chapter does not, however, apply to or limit shared appreciation financing of real property of a type specified in Section 1917.030 that is made pursuant to other provisions of law, or which is not otherwise unlawful. Nothing in this chapter shall be construed to in any way affect shared appreciation financing of commercial property or residential property not meeting the criteria specified in Section 1917.030.

Nothing in this chapter precludes a pension fund specified in Section 1917.030 from providing shared appreciation financing pursuant to Chapter 5 (commencing with Section 1917.110) or any other provision of law, or which is not otherwise unlawful. *(Added by Stats.1982, c. 1346, p. 5032, § 5.)*

Operative Effect

Chapter 4 became inoperative January 1, 1990 pursuant to Stats.1982, c. 466, § 11.5. For continuing application of Chapter 4, see Historical and Statutory Notes under Civil Code § 1917.010.

§ 1917.064. Exemption of loans under this chapter from laws applicable to other loans

A shared appreciation loan shall not be subject to any provision of this code or the Financial Code which limits the interest rate or change of interest rate of variable, adjustable, or renegotiable interest instruments, or which requires particular language or provisions in security instruments securing variable, adjustable, or renegotiable rate obligations or in evidences of such debts.

This section is declaratory of existing law. *(Added by Stats. 1982, c. 466, p. 1981, § 11.)*

Operative Effect

Chapter 4 became inoperative January 1, 1990 pursuant to Stats.1982, c. 466, § 11.5. For continuing application of Chapter 4, see Historical and Statutory Notes under Civil Code § 1917.010.

§ 1917.065. Scope of lien

The lien of a deed of trust securing a shared appreciation loan shall include and secure the principal amount of the shared appreciation loan, and all interest, whether accrued or to be accrued, including all amounts of contingent deferred interest. *(Added by Stats.1982, c. 466, p. 1982, § 11.)*

Operative Effect

Chapter 4 became inoperative January 1, 1990 pursuant to Stats.1982, c. 466, § 11.5. For continuing application of Chapter 4, see Historical and Statutory Notes under Civil Code § 1917.010.

§ 1917.066. Lien; time of attachment; priority; junior lien

The lien of a shared appreciation loan, including the principal amount and all interest, whether accrued or to be accrued, and all amounts of contingent deferred interest, shall attach from the time of the recordation of the deed of trust securing the loan, and the lien, including the lien of the interest accrued or to be accrued and of the contingent deferred interest, shall have priority over any other lien or encumbrance affecting the property secured by the shared appreciation instrument which is recorded after the time of recordation of the shared appreciation instrument. However, nothing in this section or Section 1917.165 shall preclude a junior lien or encumbrance subordinate to the obligation of the shared appreciation loan. *(Added by Stats.1982, c. 466, p. 1982, § 11.)*

Operative Effect

Chapter 4 became inoperative January 1, 1990 pursuant to Stats.1982, c. 466, § 11.5. For continuing application of Chapter 4, see Historical and Statutory Notes under Civil Code § 1917.010.

§ 1917.067. Usury exemption

Lenders shall be exempt from the usury provisions of Article XV of the California Constitution with respect to shared appreciation loans made pursuant to this chapter.

This section is declaratory of existing law. *(Added by Stats. 1982, c. 466, p. 1982, § 11. Amended by Stats.1983, c. 557, § 1.)*

Operative Effect

Chapter 4 became inoperative January 1, 1990 pursuant to Stats.1982, c. 466, § 11.5. For continuing application of Chapter 4, see Historical and Statutory Notes under Civil Code § 1917.010.

Research References

1 Witkin Cal. Summ. 10th Contracts § 457, in General.

§ 1917.068. Exemption from qualification requirements for corporate securities

The qualification requirements of Sections 25110, 25120, and 25130 of the Corporations Code shall not apply to a shared appreciation loan, provided (1) the loan obligation is evidenced by one promissory note secured by a deed of trust which is not one of a series of notes secured by interests in the same real property and (2) the loan obligation is not evidenced by fractional undivided interests in one promissory note secured by interests in the same real property. *(Added by Stats.1982, c. 466, p. 1982, § 11.)*

Operative Effect

Chapter 4 became inoperative January 1, 1990 pursuant to Stats.1982, c. 466, § 11.5. For continuing application of Chapter 4, see Historical and Statutory Notes under Civil Code § 1917.010.

§ 1917.069. Fees and charges

The aggregate amount of any fee charged to the borrower for processing an application and preparing any necessary documents in connection with originating a shared appreciation loan shall not exceed the reasonable cost of providing the service. No prepaid interest shall be charged to the borrower, but nothing in this chapter shall preclude a lender from requiring a fee for providing commitments for shared appreciation loans to builders or others who will not be the ultimate borrower. *(Added by Stats.1982, c. 466, p. 1982, § 11.)*

Operative Effect

Chapter 4 became inoperative January 1, 1990 pursuant to Stats.1982, c. 466, § 11.5. For continuing application of Chapter 4, see Historical and Statutory Notes under Civil Code § 1917.010.

ARTICLE 7. NOTICES AND DISCLOSURES [INOPERATIVE]

Section
1917.070.   Exemption from disclosures required by other laws; exceptions; use of equivalent language.
1917.071.   Initial disclosure; time; form.
1917.072.   Disclosures required by federal regulations.
1917.073.   Statement to be given prospective borrower.
1917.074.   Statement in deed of trust and evidence of debt.
1917.075.   Interest disclosure.

Operative Effect

Chapter 4 became inoperative January 1, 1990 pursuant to Stats.1982, c. 466, § 11.5. For continuing application of Chapter 4, see Historical and Statutory Notes under Civil Code § 1917.010.

§ 1917.070. Exemption from disclosures required by other laws; exceptions; use of equivalent language

(a) The disclosures made pursuant to this chapter, as required, shall be the only disclosures required to be made pursuant to state law for shared appreciation loans, notwithstanding any contrary provisions applicable to loans not made under this chapter, except those, if any, that may be required by reason of the application of Division 1 (commencing with Section 25000) of the Corporations Code, or Chapter 1 (commencing with Section 11000) of Part 2 of Division 4 of the Business and Professions Code. A lender may, but shall not be required to, supplement the disclosures required by this article with additional disclosures that are not inconsistent with the disclosures required by this article.

(b) When very specific language is prescribed by this chapter, substantially the same language shall be utilized if possible, but reasonably equivalent language may be used to the extent necessary or appropriate to achieve a clearer or more accurate disclosure. *(Added by Stats.1982, c. 466, p. 1982, § 11.)*

Operative Effect

Chapter 4 became inoperative January 1, 1990 pursuant to Stats.1982, c. 466, § 11.5. For continuing application of Chapter 4, see Historical and Statutory Notes under Civil Code § 1917.010.

§ 1917.071. Initial disclosure; time; form

(a) Each lender offering shared appreciation loans shall furnish to a prospective borrower, on the earlier of the date on which the lender first provides written information concerning shared appreciation loans from such lender or provides a loan application form to the prospective borrower, a written disclosure as provided in this section.

(b) The disclosure shall be entitled "INFORMATION ABOUT THE (Name of Lender) SHARED APPRECIATION LOAN," and shall describe the operation and effect of the shared appreciation loan including a brief summary of its terms and conditions, together with a statement consisting of substantially the following language, to the extent applicable to such loan:

INFORMATION ABOUT THE [Name of Lender]
SHARED APPRECIATION LOAN

(Name of Lender) is pleased to offer you the opportunity to finance your home through a shared appreciation loan.

Because the shared appreciation loan differs from the usual mortgage loan, the law requires that you should read and understand before you sign the loan documents.

The loan will bear a stated rate of interest which will be one-third below the prevailing market interest rate. In exchange for a stated interest rate which is below the prevailing rate, you will be obligated to pay us additional interest later. This additional interest is called "contingent deferred interest."

Contingent Deferred Interest

This loan provides that you, as borrower, must pay to us, as lender, as contingent deferred interest, one-third of the net appreciated value of the real property which secures the loan. This contingent interest is due and payable when the property is sold or transferred, when the loan is paid in full, upon any acceleration of the loan upon default, or at the end of the term of the loan, whichever first occurs. The dollar amount of contingent interest which you will be required to pay cannot be determined at this time. If the property does not appreciate, you will owe us nothing.

Your obligation to pay contingent interest will reduce the amount of the appreciation, if any, that you will realize on the property. This appreciation will not produce a real gain in your equity in the property, unless the appreciation rate exceeds the general inflation rate, but you will be required to pay a portion of the appreciation as contingent interest without regard to whether the appreciation has resulted in a real gain.

When you sell or refinance your home, you normally will receive enough cash to pay the shared appreciation loan balance, accrued interest, prepayment penalty (if applicable), the contingent interest, and expenses of sale. However, if you sell with only a small downpayment, you may possibly not receive enough cash to pay the contingent interest, and, in that event, it will be necessary for you to provide cash from other funds.

If you do not sell the property before the end of the term of this loan, you will need to refinance this loan at that time. The term of this loan is (duration) years. We will offer to refinance the outstanding obligation, including any contingent interest, at that time. If you refinance this loan, your monthly payments may increase substantially if the property appreciates significantly or if the interest rate on the refinancing loan is much higher than today's prevailing rates. In general, the more your property appreciated, the larger will be the amount of the contingent interest that you will have an obligation to pay or refinance.

The contingent interest will not become due if title to the property is transferred on your death to a spouse, or where a transfer results from a decree of dissolution of a marriage and a spouse becomes the sole owner.

Calculating the Contingent Interest

Contingent interest will be calculated as follows:

FAIR MARKET VALUE OF THE PROPERTY
(Sale price or amount of value determined by appraisal.)
- (less)   BORROWER'S COST OF THE PROPERTY
(This amount includes certain costs paid by you incident to the purchase.)
- (less)   COST OF CAPITAL IMPROVEMENTS MADE BY YOU IN ANY 12–MONTH PERIOD
(Must exceed $2,500 in value. The actual

amount may be the lesser of actual cost or appraised value.)
- = (equals)   NET APPRECIATED VALUE
- × (times)   ONE–THIRD PERCENTAGE OWED TO LENDER
- = (equals)   TOTAL CONTINGENT INTEREST

Determining Net Appreciated Value

We are entitled to receive one-third of the net appreciated value of the property as contingent interest. As explained above, net appreciated value equals (1) the fair market value of the property at the time of the sale or appraisal, less (2) your cost of the property, less (3) the value of any capital improvements for which you are entitled to credit.

Determining Fair Market Value

Fair market value is the sale price of the property in the case of a bona fide sale of the property made before the maturity of the shared appreciation loan, excluding certain foreclosure related sales. In all other cases, fair market value is determined by our most recent annual appraisal of the property. If you desire to contest the amount of our annual appraisal, you may obtain another appraisal by a qualified independent appraiser within 30 days after the anniversary date of the loan and send a copy of the appraisal to us by first-class mail within that 30-day period. If your appraiser's appraisal is lower than our appraisal, the annual appraisal shall equal one-half the sum of the two appraisals.

Determining Value of Capital Improvements

The cost or value of certain capital improvements (but no maintenance or repair costs) may be added to your cost of the property for the purpose of determining the net appreciated value, but only if the procedures set forth in the shared appreciation loan documents are followed. It is important to note that capital improvements completed and for which a credit is claimed in any 12-month period must cost or be appraised at more than two thousand five hundred dollars ($2,500). The lesser of the cost or appraised value will control. However, if you have performed at least half the value of the labor or other work involved, then the appraised value of the improvements will control. The appraised value of the improvements shall be considered to be the increase in the value of the property resulting from the improvements. You will receive no credit for improvements that are not appraised at more than two thousand five hundred dollars ($2,500).

Cost of Appraisals

The terms of this loan call for annual appraisals of the property, and for additional appraisals to value improvements or in the event of a dispute regarding the value of the property or improvements. The cost of the appraisals will be paid as follows:

Your Right to Refinance This Loan

If the property is not sold or transferred prior to the maturity of the loan, we will offer to refinance the outstanding obligation on the loan, including any contingent interest. We will offer refinancing at the then prevailing interest rate either directly or through another mortgage lender.

The terms of the refinancing loan will be like home loans offered at that time by banks or savings and loan associations, but you are assured that at least one of the options will be a fully amortizing 30-year loan. The interest rate on the refinancing loan may be either fixed or adjustable, as provided in your shared appreciation loan.

We will not be permitted to look to the forecast of your income in offering to refinance. The interest rate and monthly payment upon refinancing cannot be determined at this time. They may be either more or less burdensome to you than the currently prevailing rates and terms.

Tax Consequences

Use of the shared appreciation loan will have income tax or estate planning consequences which will depend upon your own financial and tax situation. FOR FURTHER INFORMATION, YOU ARE URGED TO CONSULT YOUR OWN ACCOUNTANT, ATTORNEY OR OTHER FINANCIAL ADVISER. THE QUESTIONS YOU SHOULD DISCUSS INCLUDE THE TAX DEDUCTIBILITY OF THE CONTINGENT INTEREST PAYMENT, YOUR RIGHT TO UTILIZE THAT DEDUCTION IN YEARS OTHER THAN THE YEAR IT IS PAID, AND THE EFFECT OF THE LOSS OF TAX BENEFITS BEFORE THAT TIME.

Other Important Information

(Here insert additional description, if necessary, of the operation and effect of the shared appreciation loan.)

The foregoing describes our shared appreciation loan, includes a summary of all of its important provisions, and informs you of some of the risks of a shared appreciation loan.

If your loan application is accepted by us, we will provide you with more information about your particular shared appreciation loan, which will include a comparison with conventional mortgages, an illustration of the possible increase in your monthly payments upon refinancing, and other important information.

Before you enter into a shared appreciation loan with us, we recommend that you and your attorney or tax accountant review the loan documents for the full text of all of the terms and conditions which will govern the loan. *(Added by Stats.1982, c. 466, p. 1983, § 11.)*

Operative Effect

Chapter 4 became inoperative January 1, 1990 pursuant to Stats.1982, c. 466, § 11.5. For continuing application of Chapter 4, see Historical and Statutory Notes under Civil Code § 1917.010.

§ 1917.072. Disclosures required by federal regulations

(a) Each lender making a shared appreciation loan shall also furnish to the prospective borrower, prior to the consummation of the loan, the disclosures required by Subpart C of Federal Reserve Board Regulation Z (12 CFR Part 226), including 12 CFR Section 226.18(f), to the extent applicable to the transaction.

(b) The disclosure made pursuant to paragraph (a) and Regulation Z shall be based on the fixed interest rate of the shared appreciation loan, and shall include a description of the shared appreciation feature, including (1) the conditions for its imposition, the time at which it would be collected, and the limitations on the lender's share, as required by the Federal Reserve Board in the information published by the Board at 46 Federal Register 20877 and 20878 (April 7, 1981), and (2) the lender's share of the net appreciated value and the prevailing interest rate as defined in Section 1917.120(h).

(c) The disclosure made pursuant to paragraph (a) and Regulation Z shall be accompanied by (1) one or more transaction-specific examples of the operation and effect the shared appreciation loan, and (2) the following charts, comparing the shared appreciation loan and a conventional loan made at the prevailing interest rate, and illustrating the possible increase in the monthly payments, and the possible annual

percentage rate of finance charge, on the assumptions therein stated:

Chart 1

CONVENTIONAL MORTGAGE AT __%
If the same loan balance were financed under a conventional, 30-year, fixed-rate, level-payment mortgage, your monthly payments would be:
Years 1–30
$_____/mo.

Chart 2

IF YOU REFINANCE THIS TRANSACTION at __%
If your property appreciates at 10% per year, and if your loan balance (including contingent deferred interest due) at the end of ____ years is refinanced at __% (the prevailing market interest rate now), your monthly payments will be:

Years 1-____	Refinancing loan
$_____/mo.	$_____/mo.*

* Refinancing loan, assuming a conventional, 30-year, fixed-rate level-payment mortgage. Other mortgage instruments, e.g., graduated-payment or shared appreciation, if available, may result in lower payments.

Chart 3

APR IF PROPERTY APPRECIATES AT 10%
If your property appreciates at 10% per year, the total finance charge on your shared appreciation loan (including contingent interest) will equal $_____, and the annual percentage rate of the total finance charge (including contingent interest) will equal _____%.

(d) The disclosures required by paragraph (c) shall be separated from the disclosures required by Regulation Z, and may be presented in the document containing the disclosures required by Regulation Z or in one or more separate documents.

(e) Except to the extent that this section requires disclosure of additional information not required by Regulation Z, compliance with the applicable credit disclosure requirements of Regulation Z shall constitute compliance with the requirements of this section.

(f) The disclosures prescribed in Section 1917.171 shall be physically attached to the disclosures required by this section and Regulation Z at the time such disclosures are furnished to the borrower.

(g) In the event federal law is amended so that this section is inconsistent therewith, the federal law shall prevail as to the disclosures required by this section. (*Added by Stats.1982, c. 466, p. 1986, § 11.*)

Operative Effect

Chapter 4 became inoperative January 1, 1990 pursuant to Stats.1982, c. 466, § 11.5. For continuing application of Chapter 4, see Historical and Statutory Notes under Civil Code § 1917.010.

§ 1917.073. Statement to be given prospective borrower

Each lender making a shared appreciation loan shall additionally furnish to the prospective borrower, prior to the consummation of the loan, a statement containing the following information:

IMPORTANT INFORMATION ABOUT YOUR SHARED APPRECIATION LOAN

You are being offered a shared appreciation loan. Before you decide to accept this loan read this statement, which is designed to provide important information that you should consider.

1. Prevailing interest rate: ____%.

2. Fixed interest rate on this loan: ____%.

3. Lender's share of net appreciated value: one-third.

4. Amount of this loan: $____.

5. Amount of the monthly payments: $____.

6. Term of this loan: ____ years.

7. Amortization period on which payments are calculated: 30 years.

8. Prepayment penalty (if any) ____. (*Added by Stats.1982, c. 466, p. 1988, § 11.*)

Operative Effect

Chapter 4 became inoperative January 1, 1990 pursuant to Stats.1982, c. 466, § 11.5. For continuing application of Chapter 4, see Historical and Statutory Notes under Civil Code § 1917.010.

§ 1917.074. Statement in deed of trust and evidence of debt

Each deed of trust and evidence of debt executed in connection with a shared appreciation loan shall contain a statement, printed or written in a size equal to at least 12-point bold type, consisting of substantially the following language: "THIS IS A [DURATION] SHARED APPRECIATION LOAN. THE LENDER'S INTEREST INCLUDES ONE–THIRD OF THE NET APPRECIATED VALUE OF THE PROPERTY. FOR FURTHER INFORMATION, READ THE FLYER 'INFORMATION ABOUT THE [NAME OF LENDER] SHARED APPRECIATION LOAN.'" The notice required by this section shall be completed to state the term of the shared appreciation loan. (*Added by Stats.1982, c. 466, p. 1989, § 11.*)

Operative Effect

Chapter 4 became inoperative January 1, 1990 pursuant to Stats.1982, c. 466, § 11.5. For continuing application of Chapter 4, see Historical and Statutory Notes under Civil Code § 1917.010.

§ 1917.075. Interest disclosure

Where, pursuant to any provision of law, the lender is required to disclose the amount of interest due or to be due under a shared appreciation loan and the amount of contingent deferred interest due or to be due is not known, the lender may disclose that fact and specify in the disclosure the method for calculating contingent deferred interest. (*Added by Stats.1982, c. 466, p. 1989, § 11.*)

Operative Effect

Chapter 4 became inoperative January 1, 1990 pursuant to Stats.1982, c. 466, § 11.5. For continuing application of Chapter 4, see Historical and Statutory Notes under Civil Code § 1917.010.

CHAPTER 5. SHARED APPRECIATION LOANS [INOPERATIVE]

ARTICLE 1. LEGISLATIVE FINDINGS AND DECLARATIONS [INOPERATIVE]

Operative Effect

Chapter 5 became inoperative January 1, 1987 pursuant to Stats.1982, c. 466, § 12.5. For continuing application of Chapter 5, see Historical and Statutory Notes under Civil Code § 1917.110.

§ 1917.110. Legislative findings and declarations

The Legislature hereby finds and declares that:

(a) It is necessary and essential that the state provide and promote alternative means of supplying affordable housing to the citizens of the state.

(b) Because of current economic conditions, including the unprecedented fluctuation in interest rates, alternative mortgage instruments must be developed to supplement the standard long-term, fixed-rate mortgage.

(c) State facilitation of the shared appreciation loan will serve the need to develop alternative means of financing housing, particularly new homes, and will help to create vitally needed jobs in the construction industry. (*Added by Stats.1982, c. 466, p. 1989, § 12.*)

Operative Effect

Chapter 5 became inoperative January 1, 1987 pursuant to Stats.1982, c. 466, § 12.5. For continuing application of Chapter 5, see Historical and Statutory Notes under this section.

ARTICLE 2. DEFINITIONS [INOPERATIVE]

Section
1917.120. Definitions.

Operative Effect

Chapter 5 became inoperative January 1, 1987 pursuant to Stats.1982, c. 466, § 12.5. For continuing application of Chapter 5, see Historical and Statutory Notes under Civil Code § 1917.110.

§ 1917.120. Definitions

For purposes of this chapter:

(a) "Borrower" means the recipient or recipients of a shared appreciation loan and includes any successor in interest to the borrower under a shared appreciation loan, to the extent such succession is permitted by law or by the terms of the shared appreciation loan.

(b) "Borrower's cost of the property" means the price paid by the borrower for the purchase of the property to be financed with a shared appreciation loan and also includes documentary transfer taxes, escrow and recording fees, title insurance premiums, and any other fees directly paid by the borrower as a necessary or customary cost of consummating acquisition of the property. However, if the purchase price to be paid for the property does not reasonably reflect the true value of the property, the borrower may request that, in lieu of the actual price paid, the "borrower's cost of the property" be established at an amount mutually agreed by the lender and borrower or be established by averaging two appraisals in the same manner as specified in Section 1917.142 for determination of fair market value. Nothing in this subdivision shall be construed to require a lender to make shared appreciation loans with the borrower's cost of the property established on the basis of appraisals.

(c) "Contingent deferred interest" means the lender's share of net appreciated value, calculated as the sum resulting upon multiplying the net appreciated value by a percentage agreed by the lender and borrower, not to exceed 50 percent.

(d) "Fair market value" means the highest price on the date of valuation that would be agreed to by a seller, being willing to sell but under no particular or urgent necessity for so doing, nor obliged to sell, and a buyer, being ready, willing, and able to buy but under no particular necessity for so doing, each dealing with the other with full knowledge of all the uses and purposes for which the property is reasonably adaptable and available.

Fair market value shall be determined pursuant to Article 4 (commencing with Section 1917.140).

(e) "Lender" means any person who makes a shared appreciation loan or the successor in interest to any such person.

(f) "Net appreciated value" means the fair market value less the sum of the borrower's cost of the property and the value of capital improvements. Nothing in this chapter shall, however, preclude a shared appreciation loan from additionally including a provision requiring deduction of any or all of the borrower's costs of selling the property from fair market value in determining, "net appreciated value," and if such a provision is included, the disclosures required by Section 1917.171 shall be modified accordingly.

(g) "Prevailing rate" means the weighted average yield accepted by the Federal National Mortgage Association in its most recent free market system auction for four-month conventional mortgage commitments. In the event that the Federal National Mortgage Association discontinues or substantially alters its free market system auction for conventional mortgages then the "prevailing rate" shall be the average yield established at the most recent immediate delivery auction of the Federal Home Loan Mortgage Corporation, or if the auction has been discontinued, then the "prevailing rate" shall be specified in the shared appreciation loan as either (1) the most recently published Federal Home Loan Bank Board mortgage contract rate or (2) the average single-family home mortgage rate for the 10 largest savings and loan associations with principal offices in this state.

(h) "Property" means the property financed by the shared appreciation loan.

(i) "Sale" means any transfer of title to the property and additionally includes the execution of an installment sale contract giving the purchaser a right to possess the property before transfer of title, refinancing, judicial sale on execution or other legal process of foreclosure or trustee's sale (regardless of whether initiated by the lender), but "sale" does not include a transfer specified in Section 2924.6.

(j) "Shared appreciation loan" means any loan made pursuant to this chapter upon the security of owner-occupied real property of a type specified in Section 1917.130, and in connection with which the lender has a right to receive a share of the appreciation in the value of the security property. "Shared appreciation loan" includes a deed of trust and any evidence of debt issued in connection with the loan.

(k) "Value of capital improvements" means the amount of the credit or credits for capital improvements, if any, determined pursuant to Article 5 (commencing with Section 1917.150). (Added by Stats.1982, c. 466, p. 1989, § 12.)

Operative Effect

Chapter 5 became inoperative January 1, 1987 pursuant to Stats.1982, c. 466, § 12.5. For continuing application of Chapter 5, see Historical and Statutory Notes under Civil Code § 1917.110.

ARTICLE 3. TERMS AND CONDITIONS [INOPERATIVE]

Section
1917.130. Authority to make loans on owner-occupied property.
1917.131. General terms and conditions.
1917.132. Right to prepay; prepayment charge.
1917.133. Refinancing.
1917.134. Laws applicable to refinancing.
1917.135. Alternative refinancing.

Operative Effect

Chapter 5 became inoperative January 1, 1987 pursuant to Stats.1982, c. 466, § 12.5. For continuing application of Chapter 5, see Historical and Statutory Notes under Civil Code § 1917.110.

§ 1917.130. Authority to make loans on owner-occupied property

Lenders may make shared appreciation loans pursuant to this chapter for the purchase of real property improved with one- to four-dwelling units, including structures ancillary to such dwelling units and including attached single-family dwelling units, single-family mobilehome units placed upon permanent foundations, residential condominium units, and dwelling units within a planned unit development. Shared appreciation loans shall be made to finance only owner-occupied dwelling units, but in the case of two- to four-unit dwellings financed under this chapter only one of the units need be owner-occupied. A dwelling unit shall be conclusively deemed to be owner-occupied for purposes of this chapter if an original recipient of the shared appreciation loan certifies in writing to the lender at the time the loan is made that he or she will occupy the property. *(Added by Stats.1982, c. 466, p. 1991, § 12.)*

Operative Effect

Chapter 5 became inoperative January 1, 1987 pursuant to Stats.1982, c. 466, § 12.5. For continuing application of Chapter 5, see Historical and Statutory Notes under Civil Code § 1917.110.

§ 1917.131. General terms and conditions

A shared appreciation loan shall include the following terms and conditions:

(a) The term of the loan, excluding any refinancing under Section 1917.133, shall be at least seven years, but not more than 30 years.

(b) The repayment schedule for the loan, excluding any refinancing under Section 1917.133, shall be cast so that full amortization of the principal amount of the loan would occur in not less than 30 nor more than 40 years, regardless of the actual term of the loan. Any principal balance remaining at maturity shall be due and payable at that time, unless refinanced as provided in Section 1917.133. Monthly installment payments shall be equal in amount, except for the final payment when a principal balance is remaining at maturity, and in addition to amortization of principal shall include fixed interest pursuant to subdivision (d).

(c) The loan shall be secured by a deed of trust on the real property financed.

(d) The loan shall bear interest at a fixed rate, which shall be established in relation to the prevailing rate (1) in effect 90 days prior to the loan closing, (2) in effect at another date between that date and the loan closing if and as mutually agreed by the lender and borrower, or (3) in effect at the time of the lender's loan commitment given to the borrower or to the person from whom the borrower purchases the property. The percentage by which the fixed interest rate is reduced below the applicable prevailing rate shall be at least one-half the lender's percentage share of net appreciated value which is contingent deferred interest, except that if the shared appreciation loan is for less than 80 percent of the borrower's purchase price of the property, the percentage by which the fixed interest rate is reduced below the applicable prevailing rate shall be at least two-thirds the lender's percentage share of net appreciated value which is contingent deferred interest.

(e) The borrower shall additionally be obligated to pay to the lender contingent deferred interest (1) at the time of sale of the property if the lender accelerates the principal balance of the loan in accordance with a provision in the shared appreciation loan authorized by Section 1917.162, (2) at the time the loan is prepaid in full, upon acceleration of the loan upon default, or (3) upon the maturity of the loan, whichever first occurs.

(f) The aggregate amount of any fee charged to the borrower by the lender for processing an application, preparing any necessary documents, obtaining a credit report, or any other costs incurred by the lender in connection with originating a shared appreciation loan shall not exceed two percent of the principal amount of the loan or five hundred dollars ($500), whichever is greater. No prepaid interest shall be charged to the borrower, but nothing in this chapter shall preclude a lender from requiring a fee for providing commitments for shared appreciation loans to builders or others who purchase such commitments and who will not be the ultimate borrower. *(Added by Stats.1982, c. 466, p. 1991, § 12.)*

Operative Effect

Chapter 5 became inoperative January 1, 1987 pursuant to Stats.1982, c. 466, § 12.5. For continuing application of Chapter 5, see Historical and Statutory Notes under Civil Code § 1917.110.

§ 1917.132. Right to prepay; prepayment charge

(a) The borrower shall have the right to prepay, at any time, in full or in part, the principal loan balance of the shared appreciation loan, together with accrued interest, including contingent deferred interest.

(b) Nothing in this chapter shall prevent a borrower from obligating himself or herself, by an agreement in writing, to pay a prepayment charge upon prepayment of the loan, in full or in part, made within five years of the date of execution of the shared appreciation loan.

(c) Any prepayment charge imposed upon the prepayment of a shared appreciation loan shall not exceed the amount authorized and specified in subdivision (b) of Section 2954.9.

(d) No prepayment charge shall be imposed as to any portion of the contingent deferred interest. *(Added by Stats.1982, c. 466, p. 1992, § 12.)*

Operative Effect

Chapter 5 became inoperative January 1, 1987 pursuant to Stats.1982, c. 466, § 12.5. For continuing application of Chapter 5, see Historical and Statutory Notes under Civil Code § 1917.110.

§ 1917.133. Refinancing

(a) If a shared appreciation loan with an original term of less than 10 years is not prepaid in full or the property is not sold or transferred prior to maturity of the loan, and provided the borrower is not then in default, the lender shall offer or arrange for refinancing of the unpaid balance of the loan upon maturity and all contingent deferred interest. The refinancing may be provided directly by the lender or another mortgage lender, or the lender may arrange at the time of making the shared appreciation loan for the refinancing to be provided by a federally or state chartered bank or savings and loan association doing business in this state or by a qualified mortgage banker. As used in this section "qualified mortgage banker" means a lender (1) meeting the criteria established by the Government National Mortgage Association for lenders selling over ten million dollars ($10,000,000) in mortgage loans to that organization annually and (2) which either has conducted an ongoing business of mortgage lending in this state for not less than five years immediately preceding the making of the shared appreciation loans, or made over fifty million dollars ($50,000,000) in mortgage loans in this state during the 12 months immediately preceding the making of the shared appreciation loan. If a refinancing commitment is arranged by the lender upon origination of the shared appreciation loan, this fact shall be fully and fairly disclosed to the borrower, a copy of the lender's contract with the bank, savings and loan association or qualified mortgage banker making the commitment shall be supplied to the borrower at such time, and the contract shall be fully enforceable by the borrower as a third-party beneficiary thereto, but the lender shall not be a guarantor of the obligation of the bank, savings and loan association, or qualified mortgage banker to provide refinancing.

If the original lender is a bank or savings and loan association doing business in this state or a qualified mortgage banker, it may provide the refinancing commitment to the borrower required by this section and assignees or successors in interest of the original lender shall not be guarantors of the refinancing obligation, provided the shared appreciation loan contains this limitation, which is fully and fairly disclosed to the borrower, and the original lender's refinancing commitment is fully enforceable by the borrower.

(b) The term of the loan for refinancing shall be established so that the borrower's repayment schedule provides for the final installment payment not less than 30 years from the date of origination of the shared appreciation loan. However, if loans at that duration are not available, within the meaning of subdivision (d), the lender or other obligor shall give the borrower a choice of any form of loan and maturity for that type of loan which is available at the time of refinancing, within the meaning of subdivision (d). The lender or other obligor shall inform the borrower of the types of loans (and maturities) available for refinancing under this section not less than 60 days prior to maturity of the shared appreciation loan.

(c) The interest rate for the refinancing loan shall not exceed rates generally available in the market for the type of loan instrument provided under subdivision (d) at the time of maturity of the shared appreciation loan. No loan origination fees shall be required of the borrower, either as prepaid interest or for processing services, as a condition of obtaining a refinancing loan pursuant to this section, but the borrower may be required to pay the costs of obtaining a policy of title insurance in accordance with the lender's requirements. The refinancing loan need not be a fixed interest rate loan, subject to the limitations of subdivision (d).

(d) The refinancing loan may be any form of loan which, at the time of refinancing, is generally offered to and utilized by the public for financing housing like the borrower's property by banks or savings and loan associations doing business in this state.

(e) The lender may require as a condition of the refinancing loan that it be secured by a deed of trust having a lien of first priority. *(Added by Stats.1982, c. 466, p. 1993, § 12.)*

Operative Effect

Chapter 5 became inoperative January 1, 1987 pursuant to Stats.1982, c. 466, § 12.5. For continuing application of Chapter 5, see Historical and Statutory Notes under Civil Code § 1917.110.

§ 1917.134.   Laws applicable to refinancing

Except as provided in this article, the terms and conditions of the refinancing loan shall be subject to all laws applicable to loans in effect on the date of refinancing. *(Added by Stats.1982, c. 466, p. 1994, § 12.)*

Operative Effect

Chapter 5 became inoperative January 1, 1987 pursuant to Stats.1982, c. 466, § 12.5. For continuing application of Chapter 5, see Historical and Statutory Notes under Civil Code § 1917.110.

§ 1917.135.   Alternative refinancing

Nothing in this chapter shall preclude the borrower from obtaining any other financing, in lieu of the refinancing provided for in Section 1917.133, including refinancing on other terms mutually agreeable to the borrower and lender. *(Added by Stats.1982, c. 466, p. 1994, § 12.)*

Operative Effect

Chapter 5 became inoperative January 1, 1987 pursuant to Stats.1982, c. 466, § 12.5. For continuing application of Chapter 5, see Historical and Statutory Notes under Civil Code § 1917.110.

ARTICLE 4.   DETERMINATION OF FAIR MARKET VALUE [INOPERATIVE]

Operative Effect

Chapter 5 became inoperative January 1, 1987 pursuant to Stats.1982, c. 466, § 12.5. For continuing application of Chapter 5, see Historical and Statutory Notes under Civil Code § 1917.110.

§ 1917.140.   Lender's estimate; good faith

The borrower may, at any time for the purpose of facilitating a sale of the property, request the lender to stipulate the minimum amount which the lender considers to be the fair market value of the property for the purposes of this chapter. The lender shall advise the borrower within 10 working days of the receipt of such request of the lender's estimate of the minimum fair market value. The estimate shall remain effective for purposes of this section for 90 days. For the purposes of this section and Section 1917.141, a sale of the property shall be deemed to have occurred within the 90-day period if there is a valid contract entered by an offer and acceptance within the 90-day period for the sale of the property. The lender's stipulation shall remain effective for an additional 60 days following execution of the sale contract to permit completion of the sale and close of escrow.

The lender shall not be liable to the borrower or any other party on account of damages alleged as a result of providing the stipulation or estimate required by this section if such stipulation or estimate is made in good faith. Evidence of lack of good faith shall include, but not be limited to, a showing that the lender has willfully or repeatedly overrepresented the fair market value of other properties in similar situations, applying equitable principles to those determinations. The lender shall be conclusively presumed to have acted in good faith and no action may be brought or maintained against a lender which arises out of the provision by the lender of such stipulation or estimate, if the lender relied upon an appraisal of an independent appraiser approved by the Federal National Mortgage Association. *(Added by Stats.1982, c. 466, p. 1994, § 12.)*

Operative Effect

Chapter 5 became inoperative January 1, 1987 pursuant to Stats.1982, c. 466, § 12.5. For continuing application of Chapter 5, see Historical and Statutory Notes under Civil Code § 1917.110.

§ 1917.141.   Cash sale; challenge to reasonableness of price

(a) In the case of a sale for cash within 90 days after the lender stipulates, under the provisions of Section 1917.140, a minimum amount which the lender considers to be the fair market value of the property, the fair market value shall be the gross sale price, unless the gross sales price is below the minimum amount stipulated by the lender and the lender contests in writing the reasonableness of the gross sale price in relation to the fair market value within 10 working days of the lender's receipt of notice of the gross sale price from borrower, in which case fair market value shall be the greater of gross sale price or the amount determined under Section 1917.142.

(b) In the case of a sale for cash where the borrower has not requested the lender under the provisions of Section 1917.140 to stipulate to the minimum amount which the lender considers to be the fair market value of the property or where the stipulated minimum amount was provided by the lender more than 90 days prior to the date of sale, fair market value shall be the gross sale price, unless lender contests in writing the reasonableness of the gross sale price in relation to the fair market value within 10 working days of the lender's receipt of notice of the gross sale price from borrower, in which case fair market value shall be the greater of gross sale price or the amount determined under Section 1917.142.

(c) In the case of a sale which includes consideration to the seller other than cash, fair market value shall be as determined under Section 1917.142.

(d) In the case the shared appreciation loan is prepaid in full, or upon acceleration of the shared appreciation loan upon default, or upon maturity of the shared appreciation loan, fair market value shall be as determined under Section 1917.142. *(Added by Stats.1982, c. 466, p. 1995, § 12.)*

Operative Effect

Chapter 5 became inoperative January 1, 1987 pursuant to Stats.1982, c. 466, § 12.5. For continuing application of Chapter 5, see Historical and Statutory Notes under Civil Code § 1917.110.

§ 1917.142. Average of two appraisals; selection and qualifications of appraisers; costs

When Section 1917.141 requires the application of this section, the fair market value shall be determined as the average of two appraisals of the property performed as described in this section. If possible, the appraisals shall be based on the sale prices of comparable properties in the market area sold within the preceding three-month period. The appraisals shall be made upon request of the lender by two independent residential appraisers, one to be selected by the lender and one by the borrower. Each appraiser shall be approved by the Federal National Mortgage Association. The cost of the appraiser selected by the lender shall be borne by the lender, and the cost of the appraiser selected by the borrower shall be borne by the borrower, unless the average of the two appraisals equals or is less than the gross sale price of the property, in which case the lender shall also pay the fee of the borrower's appraiser up to two hundred dollars ($200). If either of the appraisers determines that the gross sale price does not reasonably reflect the fair market value of the property, or, in the case of a sale for which appraisal is required by this section, then the fair market value of the property shall be determined as the average of the two appraisals. If the borrower fails to select a qualified appraiser within 15 days after the lender has notified the borrower in writing of the lender's request for an appraisal of the property, the reasons therefor, and the borrower's option to select an independent appraiser within 15 days after the lender's request is submitted to the borrower, the lender may designate the second appraiser, provided the lender's request informs the borrower of this time limitation, and that the lender will select an appraiser on behalf of the borrower in the event the borrower fails to designate an appraiser, with consequent cost to the borrower. If pursuant to this section the lender designates the second appraiser, the cost of both appraisals shall be borne equally by the borrower and lender. If in any case the property has been damaged (other than normal wear and tear) and the damage has not been fully repaired, the determination of fair market value shall be based on the condition of the property not including the damage.

Nothing in this section shall preclude the borrower and lender from establishing the fair market value of the property by mutual agreement in lieu of appraisals pursuant to this section. *(Added by Stats.1982, c. 466, p. 1995, § 12.)*

Operative Effect

Chapter 5 became inoperative January 1, 1987 pursuant to Stats.1982, c. 466, § 12.5. For continuing application of Chapter 5, see Historical and Statutory Notes under Civil Code § 1917.110.

ARTICLE 5. IMPROVEMENTS [INOPERATIVE]

Operative Effect

Chapter 5 became inoperative January 1, 1987 pursuant to Stats.1982, c. 466, § 12.5. For continuing application of Chapter 5, see Historical and Statutory Notes under Civil Code § 1917.110.

§ 1917.150. Addition of value of improvements to borrower's cost; appraisal

The borrower may have the value of capital improvements added to the borrower's cost of the property, for purposes of determining net appreciated value and the amount of contingent deferred interest, but only if the procedures set forth in this article are followed.

(a) Within 60 days following the completion of capital improvements during any 12-month period with a cost in excess of two thousand five hundred dollars ($2,500), the borrower shall send by first-class mail a notice of the completion of the improvements to the lender and shall submit proof of cost and an estimate of the increase in value of the property by reason of the improvements.

(b) If, within 30 days of receipt of the notice, the lender questions the claimed increase in value of the property by reason of the improvements, the lender and the borrower may, by mutual agreement, establish the value of the capital improvements or the lender may require appraisal of the property. An appraisal shall be made to determine the increase in value of the property, if any, by reason of the improvements, by two appraisers selected in the same manner specified in Section 1917.142. If appraisals are performed, the increase in value resulting from the improvements for the purposes of this section, shall be one-half of the sum of the two appraisals. The cost of the appraiser selected by the borrower shall be borne by the borrower, and the cost of the appraiser selected by the lender shall be borne by the lender.

(c) A credit for the value of capital improvements shall be provided if the increase in value of the property resulting therefrom is determined pursuant to subdivision (b) to exceed two thousand five hundred dollars ($2,500).

(d) If 50 percent or more of the value of the labor or other work on the improvements was performed by the borrower, then the actual cost of the improvements need not exceed two thousand five hundred dollars ($2,500) for purposes of making application under subdivision (a). *(Added by Stats.1982, c. 466, p. 1996, § 12.)*

Operative Effect

Chapter 5 became inoperative January 1, 1987 pursuant to Stats.1982, c. 466, § 12.5. For continuing application of Chapter 5, see Historical and Statutory Notes under Civil Code § 1917.110.

§ 1917.151.   Additional credit

Nothing in this article shall preclude a shared appreciation loan from providing the borrower with a greater credit for improvements than specified in this article, provided the relevant disclosures required by Article 7 (commencing with Section 1917.170) are appropriately modified to accurately disclose the terms of the credit. *(Added by Stats.1982, c. 466, p. 1997, § 12.)*

Operative Effect

Chapter 5 became inoperative January 1, 1987 pursuant to Stats.1982, c. 466, § 12.5. For continuing application of Chapter 5, see Historical and Statutory Notes under Civil Code § 1917.110.

ARTICLE 6.   GENERAL PROVISIONS [INOPERATIVE]

Section
1917.160.   Relationship of borrower and lender.
1917.161.   Waiver of borrower's rights; prohibition.
1917.162.   Acceleration of maturity upon sale or transfer.
1917.163.   Conformity of loan terms and conditions to chapter; application of chapter.
1917.164.   Exemption of loans under this chapter from interest laws applicable to other loans.
1917.165.   Scope of lien.
1917.166.   Lien; time of attachment; priority; junior lien.
1917.167.   Usury exemption.
1917.168.   Exemption from qualification requirements for corporate securities.

Operative Effect

Chapter 5 became inoperative January 1, 1987 pursuant to Stats.1982, c. 466, § 12.5. For continuing application of Chapter 5, see Historical and Statutory Notes under Civil Code § 1917.110.

§ 1917.160.   Relationship of borrower and lender

The relationship of the borrower and the lender, as to a shared appreciation loan, is that of debtor and creditor and shall not be, or be construed to be, a joint venture, equity venture, partnership, or other relationship. *(Added by Stats.1982, c. 466, p. 1997, § 12.)*

Operative Effect

Chapter 5 became inoperative January 1, 1987 pursuant to Stats.1982, c. 466, § 12.5. For continuing application of Chapter 5, see Historical and Statutory Notes under Civil Code § 1917.110.

§ 1917.161.   Waiver of borrower's rights; prohibition

Any waiver of any right of a borrower under the provisions of this chapter shall be void and unenforceable. *(Added by Stats.1982, c. 466, p. 1997, § 12.)*

Operative Effect

Chapter 5 became inoperative January 1, 1987 pursuant to Stats.1982, c. 466, § 12.5. For continuing application of Chapter 5, see Historical and Statutory Notes under Civil Code § 1917.110.

§ 1917.162.   Acceleration of maturity upon sale or transfer

(a) Notwithstanding Section 711, a provision in a shared appreciation loan made pursuant to this chapter permitting the lender to accelerate the maturity date of the principal and accrued interest on the loan upon sale of the property shall be valid and enforceable against the borrower, except as may be precluded by Section 2924.6.

(b) The Legislature finds and declares that potential exposure to liability for enforcement of a "due-on-sale" clause consistent with Section 711, as interpreted by the courts, makes use of such a provision impractical. Moreover, the additional risks to the lender inherent in shared appreciation financing are greater with longer loan terms (which are more desirable from the standpoint of housing affordability), but this risk is reduced with an enforceable "due-on-sale" clause. Therefore, in order to facilitate shared appreciation financing, it is necessary to establish the exception specified in subdivision (a). *(Added by Stats.1982, c. 466, p. 1997, § 12.)*

Operative Effect

Chapter 5 became inoperative January 1, 1987 pursuant to Stats.1982, c. 466, § 12.5. For continuing application of Chapter 5, see Historical and Statutory Notes under Civil Code § 1917.110.

§ 1917.163.   Conformity of loan terms and conditions to chapter; application of chapter

This chapter facilitates the making of shared appreciation financing in this state which conforms to the provisions of this chapter. The terms and conditions of any shared appreciation loan made pursuant to this chapter shall be consistent with this chapter. This chapter does not, however, apply to or limit shared appreciation financing of real property of a type specified in Section 1917.130 that is made pursuant to other provisions of law, or which is not otherwise unlawful. Nothing in this chapter shall be construed to in any way affect shared appreciation financing of commercial property or residential property not meeting the criteria specified in Section 1917.130. *(Added by Stats.1982, c. 466, p. 1997, § 12.)*

Operative Effect

Chapter 5 became inoperative January 1, 1987 pursuant to Stats.1982, c. 466, § 12.5. For continuing application of Chapter 5, see Historical and Statutory Notes under Civil Code § 1917.110.

§ 1917.164.   Exemption of loans under this chapter from interest laws applicable to other loans

A shared appreciation loan shall not be subject to any provision of this code or the Financial Code which limits the interest rate or change of interest rate of variable interest rate or renegotiable interest instruments, or which requires particular language or provisions in security instruments securing variable or renegotiable rate obligations or in evidences of those debts.

This section is declaratory of existing law. *(Added by Stats. 1982, c. 466, p. 1998, § 12.)*

Operative Effect

Chapter 5 became inoperative January 1, 1987 pursuant to Stats.1982, c. 466, § 12.5. For continuing application of Chapter 5, see Historical and Statutory Notes under Civil Code § 1917.110.

§ 1917.165.   Scope of lien

The lien of a deed of trust securing a shared appreciation loan shall include and secure the principal amount of the shared appreciation loan, and all interest, whether accrued or to be accrued, including all amounts of contingent deferred interest. *(Added by Stats.1982, c. 466, p. 1998, § 12.)*

Operative Effect

Chapter 5 became inoperative January 1, 1987 pursuant to Stats.1982, c. 466, § 12.5. For continuing application of Chapter 5, see Historical and Statutory Notes under Civil Code § 1917.110.

§ 1917.166. Lien; time of attachment; priority; junior lien

The lien of a shared appreciation loan, including the principal amount and all interest, whether accrued or to be accrued, and all amounts of contingent deferred interest, shall attach from the time of the recordation of the deed of trust securing the loan, and the lien, including the lien of the interest accrued or to be accrued and of the contingent deferred interest, shall have priority over any other lien or encumbrance affecting the property secured by the shared appreciation instrument, recorded after the time of recordation of the shared appreciation instrument. However, nothing in this section or Section 1917.165 shall preclude a junior lien or encumbrance subordinate to the obligation of the shared appreciation loan. In no case may a junior lien achieve priority over the lien securing the obligation of the shared appreciation loan, provided that nothing in this section shall be construed to supersede Section 8450. *(Added by Stats.1982, c. 466, p. 1998, § 12. Amended by Stats.2010, c. 697 (S.B.189), § 11, operative July 1, 2012.)*

Operative Effect

Chapter 5 became inoperative January 1, 1987 pursuant to Stats.1982, c. 466, § 12.5. For continuing application of Chapter 5, see Historical and Statutory Notes under Civil Code § 1917.110.

Law Revision Commission Comments

Section 1917.166 is amended to correct a cross-reference. [37 Cal. L.Rev.Comm. Reports 527 (2007)].

§ 1917.167. Usury exemption

A shared appreciation loan which at origination bears a fixed interest rate complying with the usury provisions of Article XV of the California Constitution shall not be deemed to become usurious by reason of the payment of contingent deferred interest pursuant to this chapter. *(Added by Stats.1982, c. 466, p. 1998, § 12.)*

Operative Effect

Chapter 5 became inoperative January 1, 1987 pursuant to Stats.1982, c. 466, § 12.5. For continuing application of Chapter 5, see Historical and Statutory Notes under Civil Code § 1917.110.

§ 1917.168. Exemption from qualification requirements for corporate securities

The qualification requirements of Sections 25110, 25120, and 25130 of the Corporations Code do not apply to a shared appreciation loan to the extent the exemption afforded by subdivision (p) of Section 25100 of that code is applicable. *(Added by Stats.1982, c. 466, p. 1998, § 12.)*

Operative Effect

Chapter 5 became inoperative January 1, 1987 pursuant to Stats.1982, c. 466, § 12.5. For continuing application of Chapter 5, see Historical and Statutory Notes under Civil Code § 1917.110.

ARTICLE 7. NOTICES AND DISCLOSURES [INOPERATIVE]

Section

1917.170. Exemption from disclosures required by other laws; exceptions; use of equivalent language.
1917.171. Initial disclosure; time; form.
1917.172. Disclosures required by federal regulation.
1917.173. Statement to be given prospective borrower.
1917.174. Statement in deed of trust and evidence of debt.
1917.175. Interest disclosure.

Operative Effect

Chapter 5 became inoperative January 1, 1987 pursuant to Stats.1982, c. 466, § 12.5. For continuing application of Chapter 5, see Historical and Statutory Notes under Civil Code § 1917.110.

§ 1917.170. Exemption from disclosures required by other laws; exceptions; use of equivalent language

(a) The disclosures made pursuant to this chapter, as required, shall be the only disclosures required to be made pursuant to state law for shared appreciation loans, notwithstanding any contrary provision applicable to loans not made under this chapter, except those, if any, that may be required by reason of the application of Division 1 (commencing with Section 25000) of the Corporations Code, or Chapter 1 (commencing with Section 11000) of Part 2 of Division 4 of the Business and Professions Code. However, a lender shall not be precluded from supplementing the disclosures required by this chapter with additional disclosures that are not inconsistent with the disclosures required by this chapter.

(b) Whenever specific language is prescribed by this chapter, substantially the same language shall be utilized if possible, but reasonably equivalent language may be used to the extent necessary or appropriate to achieve a clearer or more accurate disclosure. *(Added by Stats.1982, c. 466, p. 1998, § 12.)*

Operative Effect

Chapter 5 became inoperative January 1, 1987 pursuant to Stats.1982, c. 466, § 12.5. For continuing application of Chapter 5, see Historical and Statutory Notes under Civil Code § 1917.110.

§ 1917.171. Initial disclosure; time; form

(a) Each lender offering shared appreciation loans shall furnish to a prospective borrower, on the earlier of the dates on which the lender first provides written information concerning shared appreciation loans from the lender or provides a loan application form to the prospective borrower, a written disclosure as provided in this section.

(b) The disclosure shall be entitled "INFORMATION ABOUT THE (Name of Lender) SHARED APPRECIATION LOAN," and shall describe the operation and effect of the shared appreciation loan including a brief summary of its terms and conditions, together with a statement consisting of substantially the following language, to the extent applicable to such loan:

INFORMATION ABOUT THE (Name of Lender) SHARED APPRECIATION LOAN

(Name of Lender) is pleased to offer you the opportunity to finance your home through a shared appreciation loan.

Because the shared appreciation loan differs from the usual mortgage loan, the law requires that you have a detailed explanation of the special features of the loan before you apply.

Before you sign your particular shared appreciation loan documents, you will receive more information about your particular shared appreciation loan, which you should read and understand before you sign the loan documents.

The loan will bear a stated rate of interest which will be (percent) below the prevailing market interest rate. In exchange for a stated interest rate which is below the prevailing rate, you will be obligated to pay us additional interest later. This additional interest is called "contingent interest."

The loan will require a balloon payment at the end of the _____ year. Thus, if you do not sell the property before that time, you will need to refinance the loan at that time.

Contingent Interest

This loan provides that you, as borrower, must pay to us, as lender, as contingent interest, (percent) of the net appreciated value of the real property which secures the loan. This contingent interest is due and payable when the property is sold or transferred, when the loan is paid in full, upon any acceleration of the loan upon default, or at the end of the term of the loan, whichever first occurs. The dollar amount of contingent interest, if any, which you will be required to pay cannot be determined at this time. If the property does not appreciate, you will owe us nothing. The contingent interest will not become due if title to the property is transferred on your death to a spouse, or where a transfer results from a decree of dissolution of a marriage and a spouse becomes the sole owner.

Your obligation to pay contingent interest will reduce the amount of the appreciation, if any, that you will realize on the property. This appreciation will not produce a real gain in your equity in the property, unless the appreciation rate exceeds the general inflation rate, but you will be required to pay a portion of the appreciation as contingent interest without regard to whether the appreciation has resulted in a real gain.

When you sell or refinance your home, you normally will receive enough cash to pay the shared appreciation loan balance, accrued interest, prepayment charge (if applicable), contingent interest, and expenses of sale. However, if you sell with only a small downpayment, you may possibly not receive enough cash to pay the contingent interest, and, in that event, it will be necessary for you to provide cash from other funds.

Calculating the Contingent Interest

Contingent interest will be calculated as follows:

	FAIR MARKET VALUE OF THE PROPERTY (Sale price or appraised value.)
− (less)	BORROWER'S COST OF THE PROPERTY (This amount includes certain costs paid by you incident to the purchase.)
− (less)	VALUE OF CAPITAL IMPROVEMENTS MADE BY YOU (Must exceed $2,500 in value. Must also exceed $2,500 in cost unless you perform more than 50% of the value of the labor or work on the improvement.)
= (equals)	NET APPRECIATED VALUE
× (times)	_____ PERCENT OWED TO LENDER
= (equals)	TOTAL CONTINGENT INTEREST

Determining Fair Market Value

If you sell your property for cash before maturity of your shared appreciation loan, the gross sale price will be the fair market value of the property, unless appraisals are requested by us and the appraisals average more than the gross sale price. However, at your request, we also will tell you what we consider to be the fair market value of the property. If you sell for cash

for a gross sale price that equals or exceeds that amount, the gross sale price will control and appraisals will not be needed.

Fair market value is determined by appraisals in the event of sales involving a consideration other than cash, prepayment of the loan in full, or maturity of the loan.

When appraisals are required, fair market value is determined by averaging two independent appraisals of the property. You may select one of the two appraisers from a list approved by the Federal National Mortgage Association. If appraisals are requested by us, we will provide you with full information on how to select an appraiser.

In lieu of appraisals, we may establish fair market value at an agreed amount if an agreement can be reached between you and us.

Determining Value of Capital Improvements

Capital improvements with a value exceeding $2,500 (but no maintenance or repair costs) may be added to your cost of the property for the purpose of determining the net appreciated value, but only if the procedures set forth in the shared appreciation loan documents are followed. It is important to note that capital improvements completed and claimed in any 12-month period must add more than $2,500 in value to the property and must generally also cost more than $2,500. However, if you have performed at least half the value of the labor or other work involved, then the cost of the improvements will not be considered. The appraised value of the improvements will be the increase in the value of the property resulting from the improvements. You will receive no credit for minor or major repairs or for improvements that are not appraised at more than $2,500, but the lender will acquire a share of any resulting appreciation in the value of the property.

Determining Net Appreciated Value

We are entitled to receive _____ percent of the net appreciated value of the property as contingent interest. As shown in the chart above, net appreciated value equals (1) the fair market value of the property at the time of the sale or appraisal, less (2) your cost of the property, less (3) the value of any capital improvements for which you are entitled to credit.

Balloon Payment of Principal

If you do not sell the property before the end of the term of this loan, you will need to refinance this loan at that time. The term of this loan is (duration) years. We [are not obligated to refinance either the unpaid balance of the loan or the contingent interest at that time; you alone will be responsible for obtaining refinancing] [will offer or arrange with another lender to refinance the outstanding obligation, including any contingent interest, at that time]. If you refinance this loan, your monthly payments may increase substantially if the property appreciates significantly or if the interest rate on the refinancing loan is much higher than today's prevailing rates. In general, the more your property appreciates, the larger will be the amount of the contingent interest that you will have an obligation to pay or refinance.

Your Right to Refinance This Loan

(For loans with a refinancing obligation)

If the property is not sold or transferred prior to the maturity of the loan, we will offer or arrange with another lender to refinance the outstanding obligation of the loan, including any contingent interest. The refinancing will be at the then prevailing interest rate.

The terms of the refinancing loan will be like those of home loans offered at that time by banks or savings and loan associations. If at the time of refinancing, banks or savings and loan associations in this state offer loans of sufficient duration, you are assured that the combined length of your shared appreciation loan and refinancing loan will be at least 30 years. However, if loans of sufficient duration are not then offered by banks or savings and loan associations, you may elect any type and maturity of loan then offered by banks or savings and loan associations.

We will not be permitted to look to the forecast of your income in offering or arranging for your refinancing loan. The interest rate and specific terms of any refinancing loan will be subject to then-prevailing market conditions. The interest rate and monthly payment upon refinancing cannot be determined at this time. They may be either more or less burdensome to you than the currently prevailing rates and terms.

Tax Consequences

(For all loans)

USE OF THE SHARED APPRECIATION LOAN WILL HAVE INCOME TAX OR ESTATE PLANNING CONSEQUENCES WHICH WILL DEPEND UPON YOUR OWN FINANCIAL AND TAX SITUATION. FOR FURTHER INFORMATION, YOU ARE URGED TO CONSULT YOUR OWN ACCOUNTANT, ATTORNEY, OR OTHER FINANCIAL ADVISOR.

THE QUESTIONS YOU SHOULD DISCUSS INCLUDE THE TAX DEDUCTIBILITY OF THE CONTINGENT INTEREST PAYMENT, YOUR RIGHT TO UTILIZE THAT DEDUCTION IN YEARS OTHER THAN THE YEAR IT IS PAID, AND THE EFFECT OF THE LOSS OF TAX BENEFITS BEFORE THAT TIME.

Other Important Information

(Here insert additional description, if necessary, of the operation and effect of the shared appreciation loan.)

The foregoing describes our shared appreciation loan, includes a summary of all of its important provisions, and informs you of some of the risks of a shared appreciation loan.

If your loan application is accepted by us, we will provide you with more information about your particular shared appreciation loan, which will include a comparison with conventional mortgages, an illustration of the possible increase in your monthly payments upon refinancing, and other important information.

Before you enter into a shared appreciation loan with us, we recommend that you and your attorney or tax accountant review the loan documents for the full text of all of the terms and conditions which will govern the loan. *(Added by Stats.1982, c. 466, p. 1999, § 12.)*

Operative Effect

Chapter 5 became inoperative January 1, 1987 pursuant to Stats.1982, c. 466, § 12.5. For continuing application of Chapter 5, see Historical and Statutory Notes under Civil Code § 1917.110.

§ 1917.172. Disclosures required by federal regulation

(a) Each lender making a shared appreciation loan shall also furnish to the prospective borrower, prior to the consummation of the loan, the disclosures required by Subpart C of Federal Reserve Board Regulation Z (12 CFR Part 226), including 12 CFR Section 226.18(f), to the extent applicable to the transaction.

(b) The disclosure made pursuant to subdivision (a) and Regulation Z shall be based on the fixed interest rate of the shared appreciation loan, and shall include a description of the shared appreciation feature, including (1) the conditions for its imposition, the time at which it would be collected, and the limitations on the lender's share, as required by the Federal Reserve Board in the information published by the board in 46 Federal Register 20877–78 (April 7, 1981), and (2) the lender's share of the net appreciated value and the prevailing interest rate as defined in Section 1917.120 of the Civil Code.

(c) The disclosure made pursuant to subdivision (a) and Regulation Z shall be accompanied by (1) one or more transaction-specific examples of the operation and effect of the shared appreciation loan and (2) the following charts comparing the shared appreciation loan and a conventional loan made at the prevailing interest rate, and illustrating the possible increase in the monthly payments, and the possible annual percentage rate of finance charge, on the assumptions therein stated:

Chart 1

CONVENTIONAL MORTGAGE AT __%
If the same loan balance were financed under a conventional, 30-year, fixed-rate, level-payment mortgage, your monthly payments would be:
Years 1-30
$_____/mo.

Chart 2

IF YOU REFINANCE THIS TRANSACTION at __%	
If your property appreciates at 10% per year, and if your loan balance (including contingent interest due) at the end of ____ years is refinanced at __% (the prevailing market interest rate now), your monthly payments will be:	
Years 1-__	Refinancing loan
$_____/mo.	$_____/mo.*

* Refinancing loan, assuming a conventional 30-year fixed-rate, level-payment mortgage. Other mortgage instruments, e.g., graduated-payment or shared-appreciation, if available, may result in lower payments.

Chart 3

APR IF PROPERTY APPRECIATES AT 10%
If your property appreciates at 10% per year, and if your loan balance on your shared appreciation loan (including contingent interest) will equal $_____, and the annual

percentage rate of the total finance charge (including contingent interest) will equal _____%.

(d) The disclosures required by subdivision (c) shall be separate from the disclosures required by Regulation Z, and may be presented in the document containing the disclosures required by Regulation Z or in one or more separate documents.

(e) Except to the extent that this section requires disclosure of additional information not required by Regulation Z, compliance with the applicable credit disclosure requirements of Regulation Z shall constitute compliance with the requirements of this section.

(f) The disclosure prescribed in Section 1917.171 shall be physically attached to the disclosures required by this section and Regulation Z at the time the Regulation Z disclosures are furnished to the borrower.

(g) In the event federal law is amended so that this section is inconsistent therewith, the federal law shall prevail as to the disclosures required by this section. *(Added by Stats.1982, c. 466, p. 2003, § 12.)*

Operative Effect

Chapter 5 became inoperative January 1, 1987 pursuant to Stats.1982, c. 466, § 12.5. For continuing application of Chapter 5, see Historical and Statutory Notes under Civil Code § 1917.110.

§ 1917.173. Statement to be given prospective borrower

Each lender making a shared appreciation loan shall additionally furnish to the prospective borrower, prior to consummation of the loan, a statement containing the following information:

IMPORTANT INFORMATION ABOUT YOUR SHARED APPRECIATION LOAN

You are being offered a shared appreciation loan. Before you decide to accept this loan, read this statement, which is designed to provide important information you should consider.

1. Prevailing interest rate: _____%.

2. Interest rate on this loan: _____%.

3. Lender's share of net appreciated value: _____%.

4. Amount of this loan: $_____.

5. Amount of the monthly payments: $_____.

6. Term of this loan: _____ years.

7. Amortization period on which payments are calculated: _____ years.

8. Prepayment charge (if any): _____. *(Added by Stats.1982, c. 466, p. 2005, § 12.)*

Operative Effect

Chapter 5 became inoperative January 1, 1987 pursuant to Stats.1982, c. 466, § 12.5. For continuing application of Chapter 5, see Historical and Statutory Notes under Civil Code § 1917.110.

§ 1917.174. Statement in deed of trust and evidence of debt

Each deed of trust and evidence of debt executed in connection with a shared appreciation loan shall contain a statement, printed or written in a size equal to at least 12-point bold type, consisting of substantially the following language: "THIS IS A [DURATION] SHARED APPRECIATION LOAN. THE LENDER'S INTEREST INCLUDES [PERCENT] OF THE NET APPRECIATED VALUE OF THE PROPERTY. A BALLOON PAYMENT OF PRINCIPAL WILL BE REQUIRED. FOR FURTHER INFORMATION, READ THE FLYER ENTITLED 'INFORMATION ABOUT THE [NAME OF LENDER] SHARED APPRECIATION LOAN.' " The notice required by this section shall be completed to state the terms of the shared appreciation loan and the lender's share of the net appreciated value. *(Added by Stats.1982, c. 466, p. 2005, § 12.)*

Operative Effect

Chapter 5 became inoperative January 1, 1987 pursuant to Stats.1982, c. 466, § 12.5. For continuing application of Chapter 5, see Historical and Statutory Notes under Civil Code § 1917.110.

§ 1917.175. Interest disclosure

Where, pursuant to any provision of law, the lender is required to disclose the amount of interest due or to be due under a shared appreciation loan and the amount of contingent deferred interest due or to be due is not known, the lender may disclose that fact and specify in the disclosure the method for calculating contingent deferred interest. *(Added by Stats.1982, c. 466, p. 2005, § 12.)*

Operative Effect

Chapter 5 became inoperative January 1, 1987 pursuant to Stats.1982, c. 466, § 12.5. For continuing application of Chapter 5, see Historical and Statutory Notes under Civil Code § 1917.110.

CHAPTER 6. LOANS OF E.R.I.S.A. PENSION FUNDS

§ 1917.210. License or certificate; exemption

Each pension fund or retirement system which is subject to the Employee Retirement Income Security Act of 1974 (P.L. 93–406),[1] shall not be required to obtain any license or certificate in order to provide funds for any type of loan transaction permitted by law. *(Added by Stats.1983, c. 557, § 2.)*

1 29 U.S.C.A. § 1001 et seq.

§ 1917.220. Usury exemption

Pursuant to the authority contained in Section 1 of Article XV of the California Constitution, the restrictions upon rates of interest contained in Section 1 of Article XV of the California Constitution shall not apply to any obligation of, loan made by, or forbearance of, any pension fund or retirement system which is subject to the Employee Retirement Income Security Act of 1974 (P.L. 93–406).[1]

This section creates and authorizes pension funds or retirement systems subject to the Employee Retirement Income Security Act of 1974 (P.L. 93–406) as an exempt class of persons pursuant to Section 1 of Article XV of the Constitution. *(Added by Stats.1983, c. 557, § 2.)*

1 29 U.S.C.A. § 1001 et seq.

Research References

Rutter, Cal. Practice Guide: Real Prop. Transactions Ch. 6-F, F. Promissory Note.
Miller and Starr California Real Estate § 21:35, Who is Liable for Usury Penalties--Other Exemptions.

1 Witkin Cal. Summ. 10th Contracts § 457, in General.

CHAPTER 7. SHARED APPRECIATION
LOANS FOR SENIORS

ARTICLE 1. DEFINITIONS

Section
1917.320. Definitions.

§ 1917.320. Definitions

For the purposes of this chapter:

(a) "Actual contingent interest" means the lender's appreciation share of the net appreciated amount. In no event, however, shall the rate of appreciation upon which actual contingent interest is calculated at the end of the loan term exceed 2 ½ times the rate at which projected contingent interest had been calculated.

(b) "Actual life expectancy" shall be calculated based upon actuarial tables for women only, regardless of the sex of the borrower, and acceptable to both the state and the insurance industry.

(c) "Annuity base amount" means the projected loan amount less (1) the initial advance and (2) the projected contingent interest based on the reasonable appreciation rate used in calculating the projected loan amount.

(d) "Borrower" means the recipient or recipients of a shared appreciation loan for seniors who is obligated by execution of a promissory note and who is at least 65 years of age.

(e) "Borrower's life expectancy" means the actual life expectancy of the borrower plus no more than five years. In the case of a loan executed by two borrowers, the actual life expectancy shall be based upon the youngest of the two.

(f) "Cessation of occupancy" means the rental to a third party of the right of exclusive occupancy of the subject property, or the abandonment by all coborrowers of the property as his or her residence.

(g) "Lender" means any corporation organized as a public benefit corporation pursuant to the Nonprofit Corporation Law (Part 2 (commencing with Section 5110), Div. 2, Title 1, Corp. C.).

(h) "Lender's appreciation share" means a proportion not to exceed 25 percent of the appreciation of the property securing the loan calculated in accordance with this chapter.

(i) "Shared appreciation loan for seniors" means any loan made pursuant to this chapter upon the security of owner-occupied real property of a type specified in Section 1917.330, and in connection with which the lender has a right to receive a share of the appreciation in the value of the security property. "Shared appreciation loan" includes a deed of trust and any evidence of debt issued in connection with the loan.

(j) "Maturity event" means the earliest of any of the following:

(1) The death of the borrower. In the case of a married couple who are coborrowers, the death of the surviving spouse.

(2) The date of sale.

(3) The date a loan made pursuant to this chapter is refinanced or repaid in full.

(4) Cessation of occupancy.

(k) "Monthly annuity" means an amount paid in equal monthly installments to the borrower which, together with interest calculated at the stated rate, shall exhaust the annuity base amount during the borrower's life expectancy.

In the event that the calculated monthly annuity exceeds the cap or ceiling determined in accordance with this subdivision, the lender may limit the actual monthly annuity payment to an amount not lower than the cap. If the cap is imposed, the lender's appreciation share shall be limited to 25 percent times the ratio between the actual capped monthly payment and the monthly payment calculated in accordance with the first sentence of this subdivision. For example, if the monthly payment calculated in the first sentence is five thousand dollars ($5,000), but the lender applies a two thousand five hundred dollar ($2,500) ceiling, the lender's share of the home's appreciation shall be likewise reduced by 50 percent.

The minimum cap shall be two thousand five hundred dollars ($2,500) for loans made during the calendar year 1989. In subsequent calendar years, the minimum cap shall be two thousand five hundred dollars ($2,500) increased to reflect the proportional increase in the Consumer Price Index for the State of California, as determined by the United States Bureau of Labor Statistics, for the period from January 1, 1989, until the November monthly index figure for the year prior to the year in which the loan agreement is entered into.

(l) "Net advance" means any lump-sum advance of funds by the lender to the borrower made at the time of the loan closing. Net advance shall not exceed 15 percent of the projected loan amount.

(m) "Net appreciated value" means the difference between the fair market value of the property securing the loan at the time the loan is made and the fair market value of the property securing the loan at the time of the maturity event, less any credit for approved improvements made during the term of the loan.

(n) "Prevailing rate" means the yield of a 30–year mortgage commitment for delivery within 30 days for a standard conventional fixed rate mortgage of the Federal Home Loan Mortgage Corporation.

(o) "Projected contingent interest" means the lender's appreciation share of the projected appreciation of the property securing the loan from the date of the loan until the end of the borrower's life expectancy, using the same reasonable projection of annual appreciation used in determining the projected loan amount.

(p) "Projected loan amount" means not less than 75 percent of the estimated fair market value of the borrower's home at the end of the borrower's life expectancy, calculated by applying to the fair market value a reasonable projection of appreciation over the borrower's life expectancy based on a reasonable projected annual appreciation rate of the fair market value of the home.

(q) "Sale" means any transfer of title to the property and includes the execution of an installment sale contract giving the purchaser a right to possess the property before transfer of title, refinancing, judicial sale on execution, or other legal process of foreclosure or trustee's sale, but "sale" does not include a transfer specified in Section 2924.6 if any spouse to whom the property is transferred is also a coborrower.

(r) "Stated interest rate" means a total interest rate of not more than four-fifths of the prevailing rate.

(s) "Total loan obligation" means the net original loan and the sum total of all monthly annuity payments received by the borrower, with interest on all outstanding amounts calculated no more often than monthly at the stated interest rate, and actual contingent interest plus interest at the prevailing rate as disclosed to the borrower at the time the loan was entered into on all of the above amounts from the date of any maturity event until the outstanding loan obligation is repaid in full. In no event shall the total loan obligation exceed the actual fair market value of the home on the date of the maturity event. *(Added by Stats.1984, c. 1701, § 1. Amended by Stats.1988, c. 1406, § 1.)*

Research References

Miller and Starr California Real Estate § 10:86, Shared Appreciation Loan.
4 Witkin, California Summary 10th Security Transactions in Real Property § 42, (S 42) Alternative Mortgage Transactions for Residential Loans.

ARTICLE 2.　TERMS AND CONDITIONS

§ 1917.330.　Refinancing real property improved with one- to four-dwelling units; owner-occupied dwelling units

Lenders may make shared appreciation loans for seniors pursuant to this chapter for the refinancing of real property improved with one- to four-dwelling units, including structures ancillary to such dwelling units and including attached single-family dwelling units, single-family mobilehome units, residential condominium units, and dwelling units within a planned unit development. Shared appreciation loans shall be made to refinance only owner-occupied dwelling units, but in the case of two- to four-unit dwellings financed under this chapter, only one of the units need be owner-occupied. A dwelling unit shall be conclusively deemed to be owner-occupied for purposes of this chapter with respect to initial qualification for participation in the loan program if a borrower certifies in writing to the lender at the time the loan is made that he or she will occupy the property.

Nothing contained herein shall be deemed or interpreted to restrict a lender from providing a shared appreciation loan based solely upon the value of the real property upon which the borrower's dwelling is situated, secured only by that real property and not by the improvements thereon. In that case, the lender's actual contingent interest, and any other necessary calculations, shall be based upon the land value alone, not taking into account any improvements thereon. This paragraph is declaratory of existing law. *(Added by Stats.1984, c. 1701, § 1. Amended by Stats.1988, c. 1406, § 2.)*

Research References

Miller and Starr California Real Estate § 10:86, Shared Appreciation Loan.

§ 1917.331.　Terms and conditions; security; fee

(a) A shared appreciation loan for seniors shall include all of the following:

(1) The term of the loan shall be for an open-ended term, terminating upon the occurrence of a maturity event, or the failure of the borrower to meet the terms of a deed of trust granted by the borrower to the lender which are normally and customarily used by mortgage lenders in this state for loans secured by residential real property. However, if the maturity event is either cessation of occupancy of the property by the borrower or death of the borrower, the term shall be extended until the earlier of the sale or refinancing of the property or 12 months after the occurrence of the maturity event.

(2) An initial advance, if desired by the borrower.

(3) Monthly annuity payments which shall continue until the occurrence of a maturity event, or earlier termination in accordance with paragraph (1).

(4) Interest on (2) and (3), calculated no more often than monthly at the stated interest rate.

(5) Actual contingent interest.

(6) Interest on paragraphs (2) to (5), inclusive, compounded no more often than monthly, from the date of a maturity event until the loan is repaid in full.

(b) The loan shall be secured by a deed of trust on the real property financed.

(c) The aggregate amount of any fee charged to the borrower by the lender for processing an application, preparing any necessary documents, obtaining a credit report, or any other costs incurred by the lender in connection with originating a shared appreciation loan for seniors shall not exceed five hundred dollars ($500). No prepaid interest shall be charged to the borrower. *(Added by Stats.1984, c. 1701, § 1. Amended by Stats.1988, c. 1406, § 3.)*

Research References

Miller and Starr California Real Estate § 10:86, Shared Appreciation Loan.

§ 1917.332.　Discontinuation or termination of monthly annuity

Any provision in any loan made pursuant to this chapter for the discontinuation or termination of a monthly annuity other than upon the occurrence of a maturity event is void and unenforceable. *(Added by Stats.1984, c. 1701, § 1.)*

§ 1917.333.　Right to prepay

(a)[1] The borrower shall have the right to prepay, at any time, in full or in part, the total loan obligation. *(Added by Stats.1984, c. 1701, § 1.)*

[1] So in enrolled bill.

§ 1917.334.　Laws applicable

Except as provided in this article, the terms and conditions of the shared appreciation loan for seniors shall be subject to all laws applicable to loans in effect on the date the loan is made. *(Added by Stats.1984, c. 1701, § 1.)*

ARTICLE 3.　DETERMINATION OF FAIR MARKET VALUE

§ 1917.410.　Lender's estimate of minimum fair market value

The borrower, at any time for the purpose of facilitating a sale of the property or prepaying or refinancing the loan, may request the lender to stipulate the minimum amount which the lender considers to be the fair market value of the property for the purposes of this chapter. The lender shall advise the borrower within 10 working days of the receipt of such request of the lender's estimate of the minimum fair market value. The estimate shall remain effective for purposes of this section for 90 days. For the purposes of this section and Section 1917.411, a sale of the property shall be deemed to have occurred within the 90-day period if there is a valid contract entered by an offer and acceptance within the 90-day period for the sale of the property. The lender's stipulation shall remain effective for an additional 60 days following execution of the sale contract to permit completion of the sale and close of escrow.

The lender shall not be liable to the borrower or any other party on account of damages alleged as a result of providing the stipulation or estimate required by this section if such stipulation or estimate is made in good faith. Evidence of lack of good faith shall include, but not be limited to, a showing that the lender has willfully or repeatedly overrepresented the fair market value of other properties in similar situations, applying equitable principles to those determinations. The lender shall be conclusively presumed to have acted in good faith and no action may be brought or maintained against a lender which arises out of the provision by the lender of such stipulation or estimate, if the lender relied upon an appraisal of an independent appraiser approved by the Federal National Mortgage Association. *(Added by Stats.1984, c. 1701, § 1.)*

§ 1917.411. Sales for cash; sale including consideration other than cash; prepaid in full or upon occurrence of maturity event

(a) In the case of a sale for cash within 90 days after the lender stipulates, under the provisions of Section 1917.410, a minimum amount which the lender considers to be the fair market value of the property, the fair market value shall be the gross sale price, unless the gross sale price is below the minimum amount stipulated by the lender and the lender contests in writing the reasonableness of the gross sale price in relation to the fair market value within 10 working days of the lender's receipt of notice of the gross sale price from the borrower, in which case fair market value shall be the greater of gross sale price or the amount determined under Section 1917.412.

(b) In the case of a sale for cash where the borrower has not requested the lender under the provisions of Section 1917.410 to stipulate to the minimum amount which the lender considers to be the fair market value of the property or where the stipulated minimum amount was provided by the lender more than 90 days prior to the date of sale, fair market value shall be the gross sale price, unless the lender contests in writing the reasonableness of the gross sale price in relation to the fair market value within 10 working days of the lender's receipt of notice of the gross sale price from borrower, in which case fair market value shall be the greater of the gross sale price or the amount determined under Section 1917.412.

(c) In the case of a sale which includes consideration to the seller other than cash, fair market value shall be as determined under Section 1917.412.

(d) If the shared appreciation loan is prepaid in full, or upon the occurrence of a maturity event, fair market value shall be as determined under Section 1917.412. *(Added by Stats.1984, c. 1701, § 1.)*

§ 1917.412. Appraisals; mutual agreement

When Section 1917.411 requires the application of this section, the fair market value shall be determined by averaging two appraisals of the property performed as described in this section. If possible, the appraisals shall be based on the sale prices of comparable properties in the market area sold within the preceding three-month period. The appraisals shall be made upon request of the lender by two independent residential appraisers, one to be selected by the lender and one by the borrower. Each appraiser shall be approved by the Federal National Mortgage Association. The cost of the appraiser selected by the lender shall be borne by the lender, and the cost of the appraiser selected by the borrower shall be borne by the borrower, unless the average of the two appraisals equals or is less than the gross sale price of the property, in which case the lender shall also pay the fee of the borrower's appraiser up to two hundred dollars ($200). If either of the appraisers determines that the gross sale price does not reasonably reflect the fair market value of the property, or, in the case of a sale for which appraisal is required by this section, then the fair market value of the property shall be determined as the average of the two appraisals. If the borrower fails to select a qualified appraiser within 15 days after the lender has notified the borrower in writing of the lender's request for an appraisal of the property, the reasons therefor, and the borrower's option to select an independent appraiser within 15 days after the lender's request is submitted to the borrower, the lender may designate the second appraiser, provided the lender's request informs the borrower of this time limitation, and that the lender will select an appraiser on behalf of the borrower in the event the borrower fails to designate an appraiser, with consequent cost to the borrower. If pursuant to this section the lender designates the second appraiser, the cost of both appraisals shall be borne equally by the borrower and lender. If in any case the property has been damaged (other than normal wear and tear) and the damage has not been fully repaired, the determination of fair market value shall be based on the condition of the property not including the damage.

Nothing in this section shall preclude the borrower and lender from establishing the fair market value of the property by mutual agreement in lieu of appraisals pursuant to this section. *(Added by Stats.1984, c. 1701, § 1.)*

ARTICLE 4. IMPROVEMENTS

§ 1917.510. Procedures for adding value of capital improvements to fair market value

The borrower may have the value of capital improvements added to the fair market value of the borrower's property, for purposes of determining the total loan obligation, but only if the procedures set forth in this article are followed.

(a) Within 60 days following the completion of capital improvements during any 12-month period with a cost in excess of one thousand dollars ($1,000), the borrower shall send by first-class mail a notice of the completion of the improvements to the lender and shall submit proof of cost and an estimate of the increase in value of the property by reason of the improvements.

(b) If, within 30 days of receipt of the notice, the lender questions the claimed increase in value of the property by reason of the improvements, the lender and the borrower may, by mutual agreement, establish the value of the capital improvements or the lender may require appraisal of the property. An appraisal shall be made to determine the increase in value of the property, if any, by reason of the improvements, by two appraisers selected in the same manner specified in Section 1917.412. If appraisals are performed, the increase in value resulting from the improvements for the purposes of this section, shall be one-half of the sum of the two appraisals. The cost of the appraiser selected by the borrower shall be borne by the borrower, and the cost of the appraiser selected by the lender shall be borne by the lender.

(c) A credit for the value of capital improvements shall be provided if the increase in value of the property resulting therefrom is determined pursuant to subdivision (b) to exceed one thousand dollars ($1,000).

(d) If 50 percent or more of the value of the labor or other work on the improvements was performed by the borrower, then the actual cost of the improvements need not exceed one thousand dollars ($1,000) for purposes of making application under subdivision (a). *(Added by Stats.1984, c. 1701, § 1.)*

§ 1917.511. Greater credit for improvements than specified in article

Nothing in this article shall preclude a shared appreciation loan for seniors from providing the borrower with a greater credit for improvements than specified in this article, provided the relevant disclosures required by Article 7 (commencing with Section 1917.710) are appropriately modified to accurately disclose the terms of the credit. *(Added by Stats.1984, c. 1701, § 1.)*

ARTICLE 5. GENERAL PROVISIONS

§ 1917.610. Relationship of borrower and lender; debtor and creditor

The relationship of the borrower and the lender of a shared appreciation loan for seniors is that of debtor and creditor and shall not be, or be construed to be, a joint venture, an equity venture, a partnership, or other relationship. *(Added by Stats. 1984, c. 1701, § 1.)*

Research References

Miller and Starr California Real Estate § 10:86, Shared Appreciation Loan.

§ 1917.611. Waiver of borrower's rights; void and unenforceable

Any waiver of any right of a borrower under the provisions of this chapter shall be void and unenforceable. *(Added by Stats.1984, c. 1701, § 1.)*

§ 1917.612. Terms and conditions of loans made pursuant to chapter to be consistent with chapter; other shared appreciation financing, application and effect of chapter

This chapter facilitates one method of making shared appreciation loans to senior citizens in this state. The terms and conditions of any shared appreciation loan for seniors made pursuant to this chapter shall be consistent with this chapter. This chapter does not, however, apply to or limit shared appreciation financing of real property of a type made pursuant to other provisions of law, or which is not otherwise unlawful. Nothing in this chapter shall be construed in any way to affect shared appreciation financing of residential property of senior citizens not meeting the criteria specified in this chapter. *(Added by Stats.1984, c. 1701, § 1.)*

§ 1917.613. Application of interest rate provisions

A shared appreciation loan for seniors shall not be subject to any provision of this code or the Financial Code which limits the interest rate or change of interest rate of variable interest rate or renegotiable interest instruments, or which requires particular language or provisions in security instruments securing variable or renegotiable rate obligations or in evidences of those debts.

This section is declaratory of existing law. *(Added by Stats. 1984, c. 1701, § 1.)*

Research References

Miller and Starr California Real Estate § 10:86, Shared Appreciation Loan.

§ 1917.614. Lien of deed of trust securing loan

The lien of a deed of trust securing a shared appreciation loan for seniors shall include and secure the total loan obligation of the shared appreciation loan for seniors. *(Added by Stats.1984, c. 1701, § 1.)*

§ 1917.615. Lien; attachment, priority

The lien of a shared appreciation loan for seniors, including the total loan obligation, shall attach from the time of the recordation of the deed of trust securing the loan, and the lien, including the lien of the total loan obligation accrued or to be accrued, shall have priority over any other lien or encumbrance affecting the property secured by the shared appreciation instrument and recorded after the time of recordation of the shared appreciation instrument. However, nothing in this section or Section 1917.614 shall preclude a junior lien or encumbrance subordinate to the total loan obligation of the shared appreciation loan for seniors. In no case may a junior lien achieve priority over the lien securing the total loan obligation of the shared appreciation loan for seniors, provided that nothing in this section shall be construed to supersede Section 8450. *(Added by Stats.1984, c. 1701, § 1. Amended by Stats.2010, c. 697 (S.B.189), § 12, operative July 1, 2012.)*

Law Revision Commission Comments

Section 1917.615 is amended to correct a cross-reference. [37 Cal. L.Rev.Comm. Reports 527 (2007)].

Research References

Miller and Starr California Real Estate § 10:86, Shared Appreciation Loan.

§ 1917.616. Contingent interest; usury

A shared appreciation loan for seniors which bears a fixed interest rate complying with the usury provisions of Article XV of the California Constitution shall not be deemed to become usurious by reason of the payment of actual contingent interest pursuant to this chapter; provided, however, that in no event may the amount of actual contingent interest received by the lender, plus the stated interest received by the lender, result in an annual percentage rate in excess of 1.5 times the applicable usury rate calculated pursuant to Article XV of the California Constitution, when all of such interest is applied over the actual term of the loan. *(Added by Stats.1984, c. 1701, § 1.)*

Research References

Miller and Starr California Real Estate § 10:86, Shared Appreciation Loan.

§ 1917.617. Application of qualification requirements of Corp. C. §§ 25110, 25120, and 25130

The qualification requirements of Sections 25110, 25120, and 25130 of the Corporations Code do not apply to a shared appreciation loan for seniors to the extent the exemption afforded by subdivision (p) of Section 25100 of that code is applicable. *(Added by Stats.1984, c. 1701, § 1.)*

§ 1917.618. Loans subject to C.C.P. § 580b

Any loan made pursuant to this chapter shall be subject to Section 580b of the Code of Civil Procedure. *(Added by Stats.1984, c. 1701, § 1.)*

§ 1917.619. Nonapplication of interest rate restrictions contained in Const. Art. XV, § 1

Pursuant to the authority contained in Section 1 of Article XV of the California Constitution, the restrictions upon rates of interest contained in Section 1 of Article XV of the California Constitution shall not apply to any obligation of any loan made by any lender pursuant to this chapter.

This section creates and authorizes lenders under this chapter as an exempt class of persons pursuant to Section 1 of Article XV of the Constitution. *(Added by Stats.1984, c. 1701, § 1.)*

Research References

Miller and Starr California Real Estate § 10:86, Shared Appreciation Loan.

ARTICLE 6. NOTICES AND DISCLOSURES

§ 1917.710. Required disclosures; additional disclosures; language

(a) The disclosures made pursuant to this chapter, as required, shall be the only disclosures required to be made pursuant to state law for shared appreciation loans for seniors, notwithstanding any contrary provision applicable to loans not made under this chapter, except those, if any, that may be required by reason of the application of Division 1 (commencing with Section 25000) of the Corporations Code, or Chapter 1 (commencing with Section 11000) of Part 2 of Division 4 of the Business and Professions Code. However, a lender shall not be precluded from supplementing the disclosures required by this chapter with additional disclosures that are not inconsistent with the disclosures required by this chapter.

(b) Whenever specific language is prescribed by this chapter, substantially the same language shall be utilized if possible, but reasonably equivalent language may be used to the extent necessary or appropriate to achieve a clearer or more accurate disclosure. *(Added by Stats.1984, c. 1701, § 1.)*

Research References

Miller and Starr California Real Estate § 10:86, Shared Appreciation Loan.

§ 1917.711. Written disclosure to prospective borrower; "Information About the Shared Appreciation Loans For Seniors"

(a) Each lender offering shared appreciation loans for seniors shall furnish to a prospective borrower, on the earlier of the dates on which the lender first provides written information concerning shared appreciation loans for seniors by the lender or provides a loan application form to the prospective borrower, a written disclosure as provided in this section, in type of not less than 10 point.

(b) The disclosure shall be entitled "INFORMATION ABOUT THE (Name of Lender) SHARED APPRECIATION LOAN FOR SENIORS," and shall describe the operation and effect of the shared appreciation loan for seniors, including a brief summary of its terms and conditions, together with a statement consisting of substantially the following language, to the extent applicable to such loan:

INFORMATION ABOUT THE SHARED APPRECIATION LOANS FOR SENIORS

Your lender is pleased to offer you the opportunity to borrow against the equity in your home through a Shared Appreciation Loan for Seniors.

Because the Shared Appreciation Loan for Seniors differs from the usual mortgage loan, the law requires that you have a detailed explanation of the special features of the loan before you apply. Before you sign your particular Shared Appreciation Loan for Seniors documents, you will receive more information about your particular Shared Appreciation Loan for Seniors, which you should read and understand before you sign the loan documents.

Receipt of shared appreciation loan proceeds could be considered income, thereby reducing payments received under government benefit programs, such as Supplemental Security Income (SSI). If this income is accumulated, the payments will be considered a resource, and could terminate your eligibility for SSI or Medi–Cal. See your legal adviser for more information.

I

GENERAL TERMS

A Shared Appreciation Loan for Seniors will provide you with funds to pay off any existing indebtedness on your home and to pay the closing costs for the loan, and will then advance funds to you each month (monthly annuity) (1) for so long as you or your spouse who is a coborrower live; or (2) until you sell the house; or (3) until you decide to refinance the property and pay off your Shared Appreciation Loan for Seniors; or (4) until you cease to occupy the property as your residence, meaning either that the property has been rented out for exclusive use by a nonborrower, or the abandonment by all coborrowers of the property as their residence. Any of these four events are considered "maturity events," and will constitute the end of the obligation to advance funds to you. The maturity events are described more fully in the promissory note. Your monthly annuity is calculated according to the method described in Section II, below. You will also be required to fulfill any customary terms or conditions included in the deed of trust encumbering your property.

Each advance of funds you receive, including both initial advances (net original loan) and each monthly annuity, will be considered outstanding principal on your loan and will bear a stated interest rate which will be not more than 80 percent of the prevailing rate of interest in the locality in which you live. No payments on your total loan obligation need be made by you until the occurrence of one of the four maturity events described above.

In exchange for a stated interest rate which is below the prevailing rate, you will be obligated to pay us additional interest later, in the form of a share of the appreciation of your home between the time you execute the promissory note and the occurrence of a maturity event. This additional interest is called "actual contingent interest" and is described more fully below at Section III. Once a maturity event has occurred, interest at the prevailing rate compounded not more often than monthly shall accrue on the entire outstanding loan balance, including the actual contingent interest, until repayment in full of the loan.

Balloon Payment of Principal. If you do not sell the property before the occurrence of a maturity event, you or your successors will need to refinance or pay this loan at that time. The term of this loan is until occurrence of a maturity event. However, if the maturity event is cessation of occupancy or death of the borrowers, the term shall be extended until the earlier of the sale or refinancing of the property, or 12 months after occurrence of the maturity event. We will not refinance either the unpaid balance of the loan or the contingent interest at that time; you or your successors alone will be responsible for obtaining refinancing. If you refinance this loan, your monthly payments may increase substantially if the property has appreciated significantly or if the interest rate on the refinancing loan is much higher than today's prevailing rates. In general, the more your property appreciates, the larger will be the amount of the actual contingent interest that you will have an obligation to pay or refinance.

Tax and Estate Consequences. USE OF THE SHARED APPRECIATION LOAN FOR SENIORS WILL HAVE INCOME TAX OR ESTATE PLANNING CONSEQUENCES WHICH WILL DEPEND UPON YOUR OWN FINANCIAL AND TAX SITUATION. FOR FURTHER INFORMATION, YOU ARE URGED TO CONSULT YOUR OWN ACCOUNTANT, ATTORNEY, OR OTHER FINANCIAL ADVISER.

THE QUESTIONS YOU SHOULD DISCUSS INCLUDE THE TAX DEDUCTIBILITY OF THE CONTINGENT INTEREST PAYMENT, YOUR RIGHT TO UTILIZE THAT DEDUCTION IN YEARS OTHER THAN THE YEAR IT IS PAID, AND THE EFFECT OF THE LOSS OF TAX BENEFITS BEFORE THAT TIME. BECAUSE YOU WILL BE BORROWING A SIGNIFICANT AMOUNT OF THE EQUITY IN YOUR HOME, WHEN A MATURITY EVENT OCCURS AND YOUR LOAN IS REPAID, LITTLE OR NO EQUITY MAY REMAIN FOR YOU OR YOUR HEIRS.

Determining Fair Market Value. If you sell your property, the gross sale price will be the fair market value of the property, unless appraisals are requested by us and the appraisals average more than the gross sale price. However, at your request, you also will tell you what we consider to be the fair market value of the property. If you sell for cash for a gross sale price that equals or exceeds that amount, the gross sale price will control and appraisals will not be needed.

Fair market value is determined by appraisals in the event of sales involving a consideration other than cash, prepayment of the loan in full, or any other maturity event.

When appraisals are required, fair market value is determined by averaging two independent appraisals of the property. You may select one of the two appraisers from a list approved by the Federal National Mortgage Association. If appraisals are requested by us, we will provide you with full information on how to select an appraiser.

In lieu of appraisals, we may establish fair market value at an agreed amount if an agreement can be reached between you and us.

Determining Value of Capital Improvements. Capital improvements with a value exceeding one thousand dollars ($1,000) (but no maintenance or repair costs) may be added to the value of the property for the purpose of determining the net appreciated value, but only if the procedures set forth in the shared appreciation loan documents are followed. It is important to note that capital improvements completed and claimed in any 12-month period must add more than one thousand dollars ($1,000) in value to the property and must generally also cost more than one thousand dollars ($1,000). However, if you have performed at least one-half the value of the labor or other work involved, then the cost of the improvements will not be considered. The appraised value of the improvements will be the increase in the value of the property resulting from the improvements. You will receive no credit for minor or major repairs or for improvements that are not appraised at more than one thousand dollars ($1,000), but the lender will acquire a share of any resulting appreciation in the value of the property.

II

CALCULATION OF MONTHLY ANNUITY

Your Shared Appreciation Loan for Seniors consists of two components: first, an initial advance to cover the cost of paying off any existing liens which you wish to pay off, and to cover closing costs; and second, a monthly annuity.

Your Shared Appreciation Loan for Seniors is designed to provide a monthly stream of funds for the remainder of the lives of the borrowers, with no payments on the loan due at any time during the lives of the borrowers unless the property is sold or the loan is refinanced or repaid in full or until you cease to occupy the property. In determining the amount that it is able to lend, the lender estimates what at least 75 percent of the value of the borrower's home is likely to be at the end of the borrower's life expectancy, based on a reasonable projected appreciation rate per year. Borrowers' estimated life spans are predicted on the basis of "actuarial tables" prepared by the government and the insurance industry; and are based only upon estimated female life span, plus up to five years, to avoid any discriminatory effect between the sexes in determining loan amounts and for conservative lending practices. Once the maximum amount which may be loaned has been determined, the amount necessary to pay off existing liens and for closing costs, plus interest at the stated interest rate on that amount for the borrower's life expectancy, is subtracted. The "projected contingent interest" that is predicted to have been earned at the end of the estimated life span is also subtracted. A monthly annuity is then calculated on the remaining amount, based on the stated interest and the borrower's life expectancy.

This complex calculation is illustrated by the following example:

Mr. and Mrs. Smith, who are 73 and 71 years of age, respectively, live in a home with a current value of one hundred fifty thousand dollars ($150,000), and apply for a Shared Appreciation Loan for Seniors. According to acceptable actuarial tables, Mrs. Smith, the younger of the two, has a remaining actuarial life span of 18 years. At the end of the 18 years, at a 4 percent per year projected appreciation rate, the house would be worth three hundred thousand dollars ($300,000), 80 percent of which equals two hundred forty thousand dollars ($240,000) (the lender could have based the calculation on as little as 75 percent of the three hundred thousand dollar ($300,000) projected value). The house currently has a fifteen thousand dollar ($15,000) first mortgage, and closing costs will be approximately two thousand dollars ($2,000), and the Smiths' wish to receive an initial advance to pay off the mortgage and to cover closing costs.

At the time the Smiths apply, the average of the 30–year fixed interest rate for home mortgages of the Federal Home Loan Mortgage Corporation is 13 percent, which is the "prevailing rate." The "stated interest rate" on the Smiths' loan will be 75 percent of the "prevailing rate," or 9 ¾ percent (the lender could have charged up to 80 percent of the prevailing rate).

The Smiths' payments will be calculated so that at the end of the projected loan term of 18 years, the total of all payments owed to the lender will be two hundred forty thousand dollars ($240,000), 80 percent of the estimated value of the Smiths' home after 18 years.

Two items must be subtracted from the two hundred forty thousand dollar ($240,000) future value before the Smiths' payment can be calculated:

(a) Since the Smiths' are requesting an advance of seventeen thousand dollars ($17,000) to pay off their existing mortgage and for closing costs, seventeen thousand dollars ($17,000), plus interest on seventeen thousand dollars ($17,000) at 9 ¾ percent for 18 years, for a total of ninety-six thousand fifty-seven dollars ($96,057), must be subtracted from the two hundred forty thousand dollars ($240,000) available for lending. This leaves one hundred forty-three thousand nine hundred forty-three dollars ($143,943).

(b) The lender's share of appreciation of the value of the home is also subtracted before calculating the monthly payment. Since the home is projected to increase in value by one hundred fifty thousand dollars ($150,000), the lender's share, 25 percent, equals thirty-seven thousand five hundred dollars ($37,500). When subtracted from one hundred forty-three thousand nine hundred forty-three dollars ($143,943), this leaves one hundred six thousand four hundred forty-three dollars ($106,443) for monthly payments.

The monthly payment is calculated on the basis of one hundred six thousand four hundred forty-three dollars ($106,-443), over an 18–year term with interest at 9 ¾ percent. This equals one hundred eighty-four dollars ($184) per month. The Smiths' will receive one hundred eighty-four dollars ($184) per month until a maturity event occurs.

At the time of occurrence of a maturity event, the Smiths, or their successors, if they are both deceased, will owe the seventeen thousand dollars ($17,000) advanced initially, plus the sum of all the monthly payments of one hundred eighty-four dollars ($184) received by them until the occurrence of the maturity event, plus interest at 9 ¾ percent on all of the above from the time the funds were advanced until occurrence of the maturity event, plus actual contingent interest calculated as described in Section III below. Interest, compounded no more often than monthly, on all of the above shall accrue at the prevailing rate from the date of any maturity event until the loan is paid in full.

Because interest accumulates rapidly, when a large initial advance is received, or the projected loan term is relatively long, the monthly payment is significantly lower. For instance, if the Smiths' were 80 years old, and received no lump-sum advance, their monthly payment would be seven hundred forty-nine dollars ($749) per month.

The longer the loan has been in effect, of course, the greater the amount that will be owed, as monthly payments and interest

accumulate, and as the home appreciates in value. Unless the borrowers choose to sell the home or refinance the loan, monthly payments will continue until both are deceased, no matter how long they live so long as they continue to occupy the property. Thus, the total loan obligation is not limited to the projected life span of the borrowers, nor to any set dollar amount, regardless of the projected maximum. Regardless of how much principal has been advanced by Shared Appreciation Loans for Seniors, and regardless of how much stated interest and actual contingent interest have accumulated or been earned, payments will continue. If the borrower lives substantially longer than the actuarial prediction, it is possible that the total of principal and acquired stated interest plus actual contingent interest, may exceed the value of the home. IN NO EVENT, HOWEVER, WILL A BORROWER OR A BORROWER'S ESTATE BE LIABLE ON THE SHARED APPRECIATION LOAN FOR SENIORS IN AN AMOUNT GREATER THAN THE VALUE OF THE HOME.

The Smith example can be illustrated as follows:

A. $150,000 = Value of home at time of loan.
B. $300,000 = Estimated value of home at end of life expectancy (18 years, 4% annual appreciation).
C. $240,000 = Loan (80% of B).
D. $150,000 = Total appreciation (B less A).
E. $ 37,500 = Lender's share of appreciation (25% × D).
F. $ 96,057 = Payoff of preexisting mortgage, plus interest.
G. $106,443 = Amount from which monthly payment is calculated (C less E less F).
H. $ 184 = Monthly payment (based on G) to the Smiths. At death or other maturity event, the sum of all monthly payments, plus interest, plus the lender's share of appreciation, plus the amount owing from payoff of the old mortgage, must be paid to the lender.

III

ACTUAL CONTINGENT INTEREST

This Shared Appreciation Loan for Seniors provides that you, as borrower, must pay to the lender, as actual contingent interest, a share of up to 25 percent of the net appreciated value of the real property which secures the loan. This actual contingent interest is due and payable whenever a maturity event occurs. The dollar amount of actual contingent interest, if any, which you will be required to pay cannot be determined at this time. If the property does not appreciate, you will owe us nothing as actual contingent interest, and will only have to repay principal and stated interest. Actual contingent interest will not become due if title to the property is transferred on your death to a spouse who is a coborrower, or where a transfer results from a decree of dissolution of a marriage and a spouse who is a coborrower becomes the sole owner.

Your obligation to pay actual contingent interest and stated interest will reduce the amount of the appreciation, if any, that you will realize on the property over and above its value today. Appreciation will not produce a real gain in your equity in the property unless the appreciation rate exceeds the general inflation rate, but you will be required to pay a portion of the appreciation as actual contingent interest without regard to whether the appreciation has resulted in a real gain.

When your home is sold or refinanced, you normally will receive enough cash to pay the total loan obligation. However, if you sell and provide financing to the buyer, you may possibly not receive enough cash to pay the actual contingent interest, and, in that event, it will be necessary for you to provide cash from other funds. In no event, however, will your total loan obligation exceed the value of your home at the time of occurrence of a maturity event, unless you have willfully caused damage to the property.

Calculating the actual contingent interest. Actual contingent interest will be calculated as follows:

FAIR MARKET VALUE OF THE PROPERTY
ON DATE OF MATURITY EVENT
(Sale Price or Appraised Value)

– (less)   CURRENT VALUE OF THE PROPERTY

– (less)   VALUE OF CAPITAL IMPROVEMENTS
MADE BY YOU
(Must exceed $1,000 in cost.)

× (times)   LENDER'S APPRECIATION SHARE (up to 25%)

= (equals) ACTUAL CONTINGENT INTEREST

Below are answers to two frequently asked questions about the Shared Appreciation Loans for Seniors program. If you have any further questions, feel free to call the lender at _____, or write to the lender at _____.

Question. What if I marry, or my spouse is not a coborrower?

Answer. Your Shared Appreciation Loan for Seniors will be due upon the death of the last surviving coborrower. Your lender will be happy to include a new or present spouse as a coborrower, provided the new spouse is over age _____ at the time he or she becomes a coborrower. Because the monthly payment annuity is based upon the projected life span of the youngest coborrower, the annuity will be readjusted if a new, younger coborrower is added. The annuity will be adjusted to reflect the annuity that would have existed had the new coborrower been a coborrower from the beginning of the loan period. Since the monthly annuity is based on a fixed "lendable amount" derived from projected appreciation of the home (see Section II, above), a longer projected loan period, because of the younger age of the new coborrower, will result in a decrease in the size of the monthly annuity.

Question. Can I obtain an additional advance for home improvements?

Answer. Yes, provided your lender approves of the improvement. Your lender will act reasonably in reviewing your request. At the time the advance is made, your lender will calculate the amount of interest at the stated interest rate that will accrue through the projected life of the loan, as it was determined at the time the loan was made. This amount will be deducted from the original lendable amount, and a new annuity calculated, based upon the calculations described in Section II. The effect is the same as if the advance had been made at the outset of the loan, except, of course, you will not be responsible for any interest until the funds are actually advanced. Your annuity will, however, be smaller. *(Added by Stats.1984, c. 1701, § 1. Amended by Stats.1988, c. 1406, § 4.)*

§ 1917.712. Disclosures required by Subpart C of Federal Reserve Board Regulation Z

(a) Each lender making a shared appreciation loan for seniors shall also furnish to the prospective borrower, prior to the consummation of the loan, the disclosures required by Subpart C of Federal Reserve Board Regulation Z (12 C.F.R. Part 226), including 12 C.F.R. Section 226.18(f), to the extent applicable to the transaction.

(b) The disclosure made pursuant to subdivision (a) and Regulation Z shall be based on the fixed interest rate of the shared appreciation loan for seniors, and shall include a description of the shared appreciation feature, including (1) the conditions for its imposition, the time at which it would be collected, and the limitations on the lender's share, as required by the Federal Reserve Board in the information published by the board in 46 Federal Register 20877–78 (April 7, 1981), and (2) the lender's share of the appreciated value and the prevailing interest rate as defined in Section 1917.320.

(c) The disclosure made pursuant to subdivision (a) and Regulation Z shall be accompanied by (1) several transaction-specific examples of the operation and effect of the shared appreciation loan and (2) the following charts comparing the shared appreciation loan and a conventional loan made at the prevailing interest rate, and illustrating the possible increase in the monthly payments, and the possible annual percentage rate of finance charge, on the assumptions therein stated:

Chart 1

CONVENTIONAL MORTGAGE AT ___%

If the same loan balance were financed under a conventional, 30-year, fixed-rate, level-payment mortgage, your monthly payments would be:

Years 1–30

$_____/mo.

Chart 2

IF YOU REFINANCE THIS TRANSACTION AT ___%

If your property appreciates at 10% per year, and if your total loan obligation (including actual contingent interest due) at the end of ___ years is refinanced at ___% (the prevailing market interest rate now), your monthly payments will be:

Years 1–___   Refinancing loan

$_____/mo. $_____/mo.*

---

* Refinancing loan, assuming a conventional 30-year, fixed-rate, level-payment mortgage. Other mortgage instruments, e.g., graduated-payment or shared-appreciation, if available, may result in lower payments.

Chart 3

APR IF PROPERTY APPRECIATES AT 10%

If your property appreciates at 10% per year, the total finance charge on your shared appreciation loan for seniors (including actual contingent interest) will equal $_____, and the annual percentage rate of the total finance charge (including actual contingent interest) will equal _____%.

(d) The disclosures required by subdivision (c) shall be separate from the disclosures required by Regulation Z, and may be presented in the document containing the disclosures required by Regulation Z or in one or more separate documents.

(e) Except to the extent that this section requires disclosure of additional information not required by Regulation Z, compliance with the applicable credit disclosure requirements of Regulation Z shall constitute compliance with the requirements of this section.

(f) The disclosure prescribed in Section 1917.711 shall be physically attached to the disclosures required by this section and Regulation Z at the time the Regulation Z disclosures are furnished to the borrower.

(g) In the event federal law is amended so that this section is inconsistent therewith, the federal law shall prevail as to the disclosures required by this section. *(Added by Stats.1984, c. 1701, § 1.)*

§ 1917.713. Statement furnished to prospective borrower prior to consummation of loan

Each lender making a shared appreciation loan for seniors shall additionally furnish to the prospective borrower, prior to consummation of the loan, a statement containing the following information:

IMPORTANT INFORMATION ABOUT YOUR SHARED APPRECIATION LOAN FOR SENIORS

You are being offered a shared appreciation loan. Before you decide to accept this loan, read this statement, which is designed to provide important information you should consider.

    1. Prevailing interest rate: ____%.

    2. Stated interest rate on this loan: ____%.

    3. Projected contingent interest: ____%.

    4. Initial amount of this loan: $____.

    5. Amount of the monthly annuity payments you will receive: $____.

    6. Projected term of this loan: ____ years.

    7. Projected total loan obligation you will have to pay, assuming the loan continues to the end of the "borrower's" life expectancy: $____.

(Added by Stats.1984, c. 1701, § 1.)

§ 1917.714. Statement in deed of trust and evidence of debt; notice stating terms and lender's share of net appreciated value

Each deed of trust and evidence of debt executed in connection with a shared appreciation loan for seniors shall contain a statement, printed or written in a size equal to at least 12-point bold type, consisting of substantially the following language: "THIS IS A [DURATION] SHARED APPRECIATION LOAN FOR SENIORS. THE LENDER'S INTEREST INCLUDES [PERCENT] OF THE NET APPRECIATED VALUE OF THE PROPERTY. A BALLOON PAYMENT OF PRINCIPAL WILL BE REQUIRED. FOR FURTHER INFORMATION, READ THE FLYER ENTITLED 'INFORMATION ABOUT THE [NAME OF LENDER] SHARED APPRECIATION LOAN FOR SENIORS.' " The notice required by this section shall be completed to state the terms of the shared appreciation loan and the lender's share of the net appreciated value. *(Added by Stats.1984, c. 1701, § 1.)*

CHAPTER 7.5. MORTGAGE LOANS

Section
1918.5.   Definitions.
1920.   Requirements of mortgage instrument.
1921.   Definitions; providing prospective borrowers with publications on adjustable-rate mortgages; failure of lender to comply; liability for damages.

§ 1918.5. Definitions

As used in this chapter:

(a) "Evidence of debt" means a note or negotiable instrument.

(b) "Secretary" means the Secretary of the Business, * * * Consumer Services, and Housing * * *.

(c) "Secretary's designee" means the director of a department within the agency that licenses or regulates the institutions, organizations, or persons engaged in a business related to or affecting compliance with this chapter.

(d) "Security document" means a mortgage contract, deed of trust, real estate sales contract, or any note or negotiable instrument issued in connection therewith, when its purpose is to finance the purchase or construction of real property occupied or intended to be occupied by the borrower, containing four or fewer residential units or on which four or fewer residential units are to be constructed. *(Added by Stats.1981, c. 1079, p. 4159, § 4, operative Jan. 1, 1983. Amended by Stats.2013, c. 353 (S.B.820), § 11, eff. Sept. 26, 2013, operative July 1, 2013.)*

§ 1920. Requirements of mortgage instrument

Any mortgage instrument that is made pursuant to the provisions of this chapter shall meet the following requirements:

(a) Standards for the adjustment of interest rates or monthly payments shall consider factors which can reasonably be deemed to affect the ability of borrowers to meet their mortgage obligations.

(b) No change in interest provided for in any provision for a variable interest rate contained in a security document, or evidence of debt issued in connection therewith, shall be valid unless the provision is set forth in the security document, and in any evidence of debt issued in connection therewith, and the document or documents contain the following provisions:

(1) A statement attached to the security document and to any evidence of debt issued in connection therewith printed or written in a size equal to at least 10–point bold type, consisting of language authorized by the secretary or the secretary's designee notifying the borrower that the mortgage may provide for changes in interest, principal loan balance, payment, or the loan term.

(2) Before the due date of the first monthly installment following each change in the interest rate, notice shall be mailed to the borrower of the following:

(A) The base index.

(B) The most recently published index at the date of the change in the rate.

(C) The interest rate in effect as a result of the change.

(D) Any change in the monthly installment.

(E) The amount of the unpaid principal balance.

(F) If the interest scheduled to be paid on the due date exceeds the amount of the installment, a statement to that effect and the amount of the excess, and the address and telephone number of the office of the lender to which inquiries may be made.

(c) The borrower is permitted to prepay the loan in whole or in part without a prepayment charge at any time, and no fee or other charge may be required by the lender of the borrower as a result of any change in the interest rate, the payment, the outstanding principal loan balance, or the loan term.

(d) Changes in the rate of interest on the loan shall reflect the movement of an index, which shall be authorized by the secretary or the secretary's designee.

(e) To the extent that any monthly installment is less than the amount of interest accrued during the month with respect to which the installment is payable, the borrower shall be notified of such instance in a form and manner prescribed by the secretary or the secretary's designee. Such notice shall include, but not be limited to, the amount of interest exceeding the monthly installment, and any borrower options under these circumstances.

(f) The lender shall provide to the borrower, prior to the execution by the borrower of any mortgage payment instrument authorized pursuant to this chapter, full and complete disclosure, as specified by the secretary or the secretary's designee, of the nature and effect of the mortgage payment instrument, and all costs or savings attributed to the mortgage instrument. *(Added by Stats.1981, c. 1079, p. 4159, § 4, operative Jan. 1, 1983. Amended by Stats.1997, c. 232 (A.B.447), § 24.)*

Research References
Miller and Starr California Real Estate § 10:83, Regulation of Variable Interest Rate Loans.
4 Witkin, California Summary 10th Security Transactions in Real Property § 42, (S 42) Alternative Mortgage Transactions for Residential Loans.

§ 1921. Definitions; providing prospective borrowers with publications on adjustable-rate mortgages; failure of lender to comply; liability for damages

(a) As used in this section:

(1) "Adjustable-rate residential mortgage loan" means any loan or credit sale which is primarily for personal, family, or household purposes which bears interest at a rate subject to change during the term of the loan, whether predetermined or otherwise, and which is made upon the security of real property containing not less than one nor more than four dwelling units.

(2) "Lender" means any person, association, corporation, partnership, limited partnership, or other business entity making, in any 12–month period, more than 10 loans or credit sales upon the security of residential real property containing not less than one nor more than four dwelling units.

(b) Any lender offering adjustable-rate residential mortgage loans shall provide to prospective borrowers a copy of the most recent available publication of the Federal Reserve Board that is designed to provide the public with descriptive information concerning adjustable-rate mortgages (currently entitled "Consumer Handbook on Adjustable Rate Mortgages"), either upon the prospective borrower's request or at the same time the lender first provides written information, other than direct-mail advertising, concerning any adjustable-rate residential mortgage loan or credit sale to the prospective borrower, whichever is earlier. Any lender who fails to comply with the requirements of this section may be enjoined by any court of competent jurisdiction and shall be liable for actual damages, the costs of the action, and reasonable attorney's fees as determined by the court. The court may make those orders as may be necessary to prevent future violations of this section.

(c) A lender that makes adjustable-rate mortgage loan disclosures pursuant to either Part 29 of Chapter I of, or Part 563 of Chapter V of, Title 12 of the Code of Federal Regulations, may comply with this section by providing the descriptive information required by subdivision (b) at the same time and under the same circumstances that it makes disclosures in accordance with those federal regulations. Such a lender shall also display and make the descriptive information available to the public in an area of the lender's office that is open to the public. *(Added by Stats.1985, c. 1284, § 1. Amended by Stats.1987, c. 56, § 19.)*

Research References
Miller and Starr California Real Estate § 10:83, Regulation of Variable Interest Rate Loans.
4 Witkin, California Summary 10th Security Transactions in Real Property § 42, (S 42) Alternative Mortgage Transactions for Residential Loans.

CHAPTER 8. REVERSE MORTGAGES

§ 1923. Reverse mortgage; defining criteria

For purposes of this chapter, "reverse mortgage" means a nonrecourse loan secured by real property that meets all of the following criteria:

(a) The loan provides cash advances to a borrower based on the equity or the value in a borrower's owner-occupied principal residence.

(b) The loan requires no payment of principal or interest until the entire loan becomes due and payable.

(c) The loan is made by a lender licensed or chartered pursuant to the laws of this state or the United States. *(Added by Stats.1997, c. 797 (A.B.456), § 1.)*

Research References
Rutter, Cal. Practice Guide: Landlord-Tenant Form 2:C, Office Lease.
Rutter, Cal. Practice Guide: Real Prop. Transactions Ch. 6-B, B. Sources and Kinds of Financing.
Miller and Starr California Real Estate § 10:3, Parties.
Miller and Starr California Real Estate § 10:87, Reverse Mortgages.
4 Witkin, California Summary 10th Security Transactions in Real Property § 23, Reverse Mortgage.
4 Witkin, California Summary 10th Security Transactions in Real Property § 42, (S 42) Alternative Mortgage Transactions for Residential Loans.

§ 1923.2. Reverse mortgage loans; requirements

A reverse mortgage loan shall comply with all of the following requirements:

(a) Prepayment, in whole or in part, shall be permitted without penalty at any time during the term of the reverse mortgage loan. For the purposes of this section, penalty does not include any fees, payments, or other charges that would have otherwise been due upon the reverse mortgage being due and payable.

(b) A reverse mortgage loan may provide for a fixed or adjustable interest rate or combination thereof, including compound interest, and may also provide for interest that is contingent on the value of the property upon execution of the loan or at maturity, or on changes in value between closing and maturity.

(c) A reverse mortgage may include costs and fees that are charged by the lender, or the lender's designee, originator, or servicer, including costs and fees charged upon execution of the loan, on a periodic basis, or upon maturity.

(d) If a reverse mortgage loan provides for periodic advances to a borrower, these advances shall not be reduced in amount or number based on any adjustment in the interest rate.

(e) A lender who fails to make loan advances as required in the loan documents, and fails to cure an actual default after notice as specified in the loan documents, shall forfeit to the borrower treble the amount wrongfully withheld plus interest at the legal rate.

(f) The reverse mortgage loan may become due and payable upon the occurrence of any one of the following events:

(1) The home securing the loan is sold or title to the home is otherwise transferred.

(2) All borrowers cease occupying the home as a principal residence, except as provided in subdivision (g).

(3) Any fixed maturity date agreed to by the lender and the borrower occurs.

(4) An event occurs which is specified in the loan documents and which jeopardizes the lender's security.

(g) Repayment of the reverse mortgage loan shall be subject to the following additional conditions:

(1) Temporary absences from the home not exceeding 60 consecutive days shall not cause the mortgage to become due and payable.

(2) Extended absences from the home exceeding 60 consecutive days, but less than one year, shall not cause the mortgage to become due and payable if the borrower has taken prior action which secures and protects the home in a manner satisfactory to the lender, as specified in the loan documents.

(3) The lender's right to collect reverse mortgage loan proceeds shall be subject to the applicable statute of limitations for written loan contracts. Notwithstanding any other provision of law, the statute of limitations shall commence on the date that the reverse mortgage loan becomes due and payable as provided in the loan agreement.

(4) The lender shall prominently disclose in the loan agreement any interest rate or other fees to be charged during the period that commences on the date that the reverse mortgage loan becomes due and payable, and that ends when repayment in full is made.

(h) The first page of any deed of trust securing a reverse mortgage loan shall contain the following statement in 10–point boldface type: "This deed of trust secures a reverse mortgage loan."

(i) A lender or any other person that participates in the origination of the mortgage shall not require an applicant for a reverse mortgage to purchase an annuity as a condition of obtaining a reverse mortgage loan.

(1) The lender or any other person that participates in the origination of the mortgage shall not do either of the following:

(A) Participate in, be associated with, or employ any party that participates in or is associated with any other financial or insurance activity, unless the lender maintains procedural safeguards designed to ensure that individuals participating in the origination of the mortgage shall have no involvement with, or

incentive to provide the prospective borrower with, any other financial or insurance product.

(B) Refer the borrower to anyone for the purchase of an annuity or other financial or insurance product prior to the closing of the reverse mortgage or before the expiration of the right of the borrower to rescind the reverse mortgage agreement.

(2) This subdivision does not prevent a lender from offering or referring borrowers for title insurance, hazard, flood, or other peril insurance, or other similar products that are customary and normal under a reverse mortgage loan.

(3) A lender or any other person who participates in the origination of a reverse mortgage loan to which this subdivision would apply, and who complies with paragraph (1) of subsection (n), and with subsection (o), of Section 1715z–20 of Title 12 of the United States Code, and any regulations and guidance promulgated under that section, as amended from time to time, in offering the loan, regardless of whether the loan is originated pursuant to the program authorized under Section 1715z–20 of Title 12 of the United States Code, and any regulations and guidance promulgated under that section, shall be deemed to have complied with this subdivision.

(j) Prior to accepting a final and complete application for a reverse mortgage the lender shall provide the borrower with a list of not fewer than 10 counseling agencies that are approved by the United States Department of Housing and Urban Development to engage in reverse mortgage counseling as provided in Subpart B of Part 214 of Title 24 of the Code of Federal Regulation. The counseling agency shall not receive any compensation, either directly or indirectly, from the lender or from any other person or entity involved in originating or servicing the mortgage or the sale of annuities, investments, long-term care insurance, or any other type of financial or insurance product. This subdivision does not prevent a counseling agency from receiving financial assistance that is unrelated to the offering or selling of a reverse mortgage loan and that is provided by the lender as part of charitable or philanthropic activities.

(k) A lender shall not accept a final and complete application for a reverse mortgage loan from a prospective applicant or assess any fees upon a prospective applicant without first receiving certification from the applicant or the applicant's authorized representative that the applicant has received counseling from an agency as described in subdivision (j) and that the counseling was conducted in person, unless the certification specifies that the applicant elected to receive the counseling in a manner other than in person. The certification shall be signed by the borrower and the agency counselor, and shall include the date of the counseling and the name, address, and telephone number of both the counselor and the applicant. Electronic facsimile copy of the housing counseling certification satisfies the requirements of this subdivision. The lender shall maintain the certification in an accurate, reproducible, and accessible format for the term of the reverse mortgage.

(l) A lender shall not make a reverse mortgage loan without first complying with, or in the case of brokered loans ensuring compliance with, the requirements of Section 1632, if applicable. (*Added by Stats.1997, c. 797 (A.B.456), § 1. Amended by Stats.2006, c. 202 (S.B.1609), § 2; Stats.2009, c. 236 (A.B.329), § 3; Stats.2012, c. 641 (A.B.2010), § 1.*)

Research References

Rutter, Cal. Practice Guide: Real Prop. Transactions Ch. 6-B, B. Sources and Kinds of Financing.

Rutter, Cal. Practice Guide: Real Prop. Transactions Ch. 6-F, F. Promissory Note.

Miller and Starr California Real Estate § 10:87, Reverse Mortgages.

Miller and Starr California Real Estate § 19:218, Required Relationship
  of the Parties.
20 NO. 4 Miller & Starr, California Real Estate Newsalert 6, Deeds of
  Trust.
20 NO. 4 Miller & Starr, California Real Estate Newsalert 13, Landlord
  and Tenant.
4 Witkin, California Summary 10th Security Transactions in Real Property
  § 23, Reverse Mortgage.

§ 1923.3. Reverse mortgages constituting lien against subject property

A reverse mortgage shall constitute a lien against the subject
property to the extent of all advances made pursuant to the
reverse mortgage and all interest accrued on these advances, and
that lien shall have priority over any lien filed or recorded after
recordation of a reverse mortgage loan. *(Added by Stats.1997, c.
797 (A.B.456), § 1.)*

Research References

Rutter, Cal. Practice Guide: Real Prop. Transactions Ch. 6-B, B. Sources
  and Kinds of Financing.
Miller and Starr California Real Estate § 10:87, Reverse Mortgages.
4 Witkin, California Summary 10th Security Transactions in Real Property
  § 23, Reverse Mortgage.

§ 1923.4. Property deemed to be owner-occupied; occupant as trust beneficiary

For the purposes of this chapter, a property shall be deemed
to be owner-occupied, notwithstanding that the legal title to the
property is held in the name of a trust, provided that the
occupant of the property is a beneficiary of that trust. *(Added by
Stats.1997, c. 797 (A.B.456), § 1.)*

Research References

Rutter, Cal. Practice Guide: Real Prop. Transactions Ch. 6-B, B. Sources
  and Kinds of Financing.
Miller and Starr California Real Estate § 10:87, Reverse Mortgages.

§ 1923.5. Reverse mortgage loan application; plain language statement

(a) No reverse mortgage loan application shall be taken by a
lender unless the loan applicant, prior to receiving counseling,
has received from the lender the following plain language
statement in conspicuous 16–point type or larger, advising the
prospective borrower about counseling prior to obtaining the
reverse mortgage loan:

IMPORTANT NOTICE TO REVERSE MORTGAGE LOAN APPLICANT

A REVERSE MORTGAGE IS A COMPLEX FINANCIAL
TRANSACTION. IF YOU DECIDE TO OBTAIN A RE-
VERSE MORTGAGE LOAN, YOU WILL SIGN BINDING
LEGAL DOCUMENTS THAT WILL HAVE IMPORTANT
LEGAL AND FINANCIAL IMPLICATIONS FOR YOU AND
YOUR ESTATE. IT IS THEREFORE IMPORTANT TO
UNDERSTAND THE TERMS OF THE REVERSE MORT-
GAGE AND ITS EFFECT. BEFORE ENTERING INTO
THIS TRANSACTION, YOU ARE REQUIRED TO CON-
SULT WITH AN INDEPENDENT LOAN COUNSELOR. A
LIST OF APPROVED COUNSELORS WILL BE PROVID-
ED TO YOU BY THE LENDER.

SENIOR CITIZEN ADVOCACY GROUPS ADVISE
AGAINST USING THE PROCEEDS OF A REVERSE
MORTGAGE TO PURCHASE AN ANNUITY OR RELAT-
ED FINANCIAL PRODUCTS. IF YOU ARE CONSIDER-
ING USING YOUR PROCEEDS FOR THIS PURPOSE,
YOU SHOULD DISCUSS THE FINANCIAL IMPLICA-
TIONS OF DOING SO WITH YOUR COUNSELOR AND
FAMILY MEMBERS.

(b)(1) In addition to the plain statement notice described in
subdivision (a), no reverse mortgage loan application shall be
taken by a lender unless the lender provides the prospective
borrower, prior to his or her meeting with a counseling agency
on reverse mortgages, with a written checklist, or in the event
that the prospective borrower seeks counseling prior to requesting a reverse mortgage loan application from the reverse
mortgage lender, the counseling agency shall provide the prospective borrower with a written checklist. The written checklist
shall conspicuously alert the prospective borrower, in 12–point
type or larger, that he or she should discuss with the agency
counselor the following issues:

(A) How unexpected medical or other events that cause the
prospective borrower to move out of the home, either permanently or for more than one year, earlier than anticipated will
impact the total annual loan cost of the mortgage.

(B) The extent to which the prospective borrower's financial
needs would be better met by options other than a reverse
mortgage, including, but not limited to, less costly home equity
lines of credit, property tax deferral programs, or governmental
aid programs.

(C) Whether the prospective borrower intends to use the
proceeds of the reverse mortgage to purchase an annuity or
other insurance products and the consequences of doing so.

(D) The effect of repayment of the loan on nonborrowing
residents of the home after all borrowers have died or permanently left the home.

(E) The prospective borrower's ability to finance routine or
catastrophic home repairs, especially if maintenance is a factor
that may determine when the mortgage becomes payable.

(F) The impact that the reverse mortgage may have on the
prospective borrower's tax obligations, eligibility for government
assistance programs, and the effect that losing equity in the
home will have on the borrower's estate and heirs.

(G) The ability of the borrower to finance alternative living
accommodations, such as assisted living or long-term care
nursing home registry, after the borrower's equity is depleted.

(2) The checklist required in paragraph (1) shall be signed by
the agency counselor, if the counseling is done in person, and by
the prospective borrower and returned to the lender along with
the certification of counseling required under subdivision (k) of
Section 1923.2, and the loan application shall not be approved
until the signed checklist is provided to the lender. A copy of
the checklist shall be provided to the borrower. *(Added by
Stats.1997, c. 797 (A.B.456), § 1. Amended by Stats.2006, c. 202
(S.B.1609), § 3; Stats.2009, c. 236 (A.B.329), § 4.)*

Research References

Rutter, Cal. Practice Guide: Real Prop. Transactions Ch. 6-B, B. Sources
  and Kinds of Financing.
Miller and Starr California Real Estate § 10:87, Reverse Mortgages.
Miller and Starr California Real Estate § 19:218, Required Relationship
  of the Parties.
20 NO. 4 Miller & Starr, California Real Estate Newsalert 6, Deeds of
  Trust.
20 NO. 4 Miller & Starr, California Real Estate Newsalert 13, Landlord
  and Tenant.
4 Witkin, California Summary 10th Security Transactions in Real Property
  § 23, Reverse Mortgage.

§ 1923.6. Disclosure statement

The lender shall be presumed to have satisfied any disclosure
duty imposed by this chapter if the lender provides a disclosure
statement in the same form as provided in this chapter. *(Added
by Stats.1997, c. 797 (A.B.456), § 1.)*

Miller and Starr California Real Estate § 10:87, Reverse Mortgages.

Research References

Rutter, Cal. Practice Guide: Real Prop. Transactions Ch. 6-B, B. Sources and Kinds of Financing.
Miller and Starr California Real Estate § 10:87, Reverse Mortgages.

§ 1923.7. Failure of lender to comply with requirements; effect on liens

No arrangement, transfer, or lien subject to this chapter shall be invalidated solely because of the failure of a lender to comply with any provision of this chapter. However, nothing in this section shall preclude the application of any other existing civil remedies provided by law. *(Added by Stats.1997, c. 797 (A.B. 456), § 1.)*

Research References

Rutter, Cal. Practice Guide: Real Prop. Transactions Ch. 6-B, B. Sources and Kinds of Financing.
Miller and Starr California Real Estate § 10:3, Parties.
Miller and Starr California Real Estate § 10:84, Adjustable-Payment, Adjustable-Rate Loan.
Miller and Starr California Real Estate § 10:87, Reverse Mortgages.

§ 1923.9. Reverse mortgage loan payments; treatment for means-tested programs of aid to individuals

(a) To the extent that implementation of this section does not conflict with federal law resulting in the loss of federal funding, reverse mortgage loan payments made to a borrower shall be treated as proceeds from a loan and not as income for the purpose of determining eligibility and benefits under means-tested programs of aid to individuals.

(b) Undisbursed reverse mortgage funds shall be treated as equity in the borrower's home and not as proceeds from a loan, resources, or assets for the purpose of determining eligibility and benefits under means-tested programs of aid to individuals.

(c) This section applies to any law or program relating to payments, allowances, benefits, or services provided on a means-tested basis, by this state, including, but not limited to, optional state supplements to the federal supplemental security income program, low-income energy assistance, property tax relief, general assistance, and medical assistance only to the extent this section does not conflict with Title 19 of the federal Social Security Act.

(d) For the purposes of this section, "means-tested programs and aid to individuals" includes, but is not limited to, programs set forth in Chapter 2 (commencing with Section 11200) of Part 3 of Division 9, and Part 5 (commencing with Section 17000) of Division 9, of the Welfare and Institutions Code. *(Added by Stats.1997, c. 797 (A.B.456), § 1.)*

Research References

Miller and Starr California Real Estate § 10:3, Parties.
Miller and Starr California Real Estate § 10:87, Reverse Mortgages.
4 Witkin, California Summary 10th Security Transactions in Real Property § 23, Reverse Mortgage.

§ 1923.10. Application of chapter

This chapter shall only apply to those reverse mortgage loans executed on or after January 1, 1998. *(Added by Stats.1997, c. 797 (A.B.456), § 1.)*

Research References

Rutter, Cal. Practice Guide: Real Prop. Transactions Ch. 6-B, B. Sources and Kinds of Financing.

Miller and Starr California Real Estate § 10:87, Reverse Mortgages.

Title 5

HIRING

CHAPTER 1. HIRING IN GENERAL

§ 1925. Hiring defined

Hiring is a contract by which one gives to another the temporary possession and use of property, other than money, for reward, and the latter agrees to return the same to the former at a future time. *(Enacted in 1872.)*

Research References

Rutter, Cal. Practice Guide: Insurance Litigation Ch. 7D-B, B. Liability Based on Use or Maintenance of Vehicle.

Miller and Starr California Real Estate § 19:19, Lease as a Contract and Conveyance.

2 Witkin, California Summary 10th Insurance § 165, Vehicles Insured.

12 Witkin, California Summary 10th Real Property § 517, Dual Nature.

12 Witkin, California Summary 10th Real Property § 599, Other Acts and Powers of Entity Are Not Affected.

13 Witkin, California Summary 10th Personal Property § 188, (S 188) in General.

§ 1926. Title to products of thing hired

The products of a thing hired, during the hiring, belong to the hirer. *(Enacted in 1872.)*

Research References

Miller and Starr California Real Estate § 17:36, Crops--Lease of the Realty.

§ 1927. Quiet possession of hire

An agreement to let upon hire binds the letter to secure to the hirer the quiet possession of the thing hired during the term of the hiring, against all persons lawfully claiming the same. *(Enacted in 1872.)*

Research References

Miller and Starr California Real Estate § 19:156, Covenant of Quiet Enjoyment and Possession.

Miller and Starr California Real Estate § 19:157, Covenant of Quiet Enjoyment and Possession--Wrongful Actual or Constructive Eviction.

3 Witkin Cal. Proc. 5th Actions § 597, General Rule: Accrual on Date of Wrongful Act.

12 Witkin, California Summary 10th Real Property § 610, (S 610) Actual Eviction.

12 Witkin, California Summary 10th Real Property § 616, Landlord's Use of Theft, Extortion, or Force.

12 Witkin, California Summary 10th Real Property § 683A, (New)-Domestic Violence or Sexual Assault Against Tenant.

§ 1928. Degree of care

The hirer of a thing must use ordinary care for its preservation in safety and in good condition. *(Enacted in 1872.)*

Research References

Miller and Starr California Real Estate § 2:19, Right to Possession; Waste.

Miller and Starr California Real Estate § 19:122, Maintenance Obligations of the Landlord--Nonresidential Premises.

Miller and Starr California Real Estate § 19:124, Maintenance Obligations of the Tenant--Residential.

Miller and Starr California Real Estate § 19:126, Waste.

12 Witkin, California Summary 10th Real Property § 632, Nature of Covenant.

§ 1929. Repairs

The hirer of a thing must repair all deteriorations or injuries thereto occasioned by his want of ordinary care. *(Enacted in 1872. Amended by Stats.1905, c. 454, p. 614, § 1.)*

Research References

Miller and Starr California Real Estate § 2:19, Right to Possession; Waste.

Miller and Starr California Real Estate § 19:117, Landlord's Statutory Duty of Maintenance.

Miller and Starr California Real Estate § 19:122, Maintenance Obligations of the Landlord--Nonresidential Premises.

Miller and Starr California Real Estate § 19:124, Maintenance Obligations of the Tenant--Residential.

4 Witkin Cal. Proc. 5th Pleading § 415, (S 415) Contract, Quasi-Contract, and Tort Theories.

12 Witkin, California Summary 10th Real Property § 620, Tenant's Remedies.

12 Witkin, California Summary 10th Real Property § 632, Nature of Covenant.

12 Witkin, California Summary 10th Real Property § 736, Trial.

13 Witkin, California Summary 10th Personal Property § 188, (S 188) in General.

§ 1930. Use of thing lent for particular purpose; damages

When a thing is let for a particular purpose the hirer must not use it for any other purpose; and if he does, he is liable to the letter for all damages resulting from such use, or the letter may treat the contract as thereby rescinded. *(Enacted in 1872. Amended by Stats.1905, c. 454, p. 614, § 2.)*

Research References

Miller and Starr California Real Estate § 19:111, Specification or Restriction of Use.

12 Witkin, California Summary 10th Real Property § 503, Statutory Framework.

12 Witkin, California Summary 10th Real Property § 663, (S 663) in General.

12 Witkin, California Summary 10th Real Property § 667, in General.

13 Witkin, California Summary 10th Personal Property § 191, Liability of Lessee (Hirer or Bailee).

§ 1931. Termination of hiring by letter

The letter of a thing may terminate the hiring and reclaim the thing before the end of the term agreed upon:

1. When the hirer uses or permits a use of the thing hired in a manner contrary to the agreement of the parties; or,

2. When the hirer does not, within a reasonable time after request, make such repairs as he is bound to make. *(Enacted in 1872.)*

Research References

Miller and Starr California Real Estate § 19:111, Specification or Restriction of Use.

Miller and Starr California Real Estate § 19:130, Landlord's Remedies.

Miller and Starr California Real Estate § 19:200, Termination for Cause or Default.

13 Witkin, California Summary 10th Personal Property § 191, Liability of Lessee (Hirer or Bailee).

13 Witkin, California Summary 10th Equity § 30, (S 30) Contract Concerning Personal Property.

§ 1932. Termination of hiring by hirer

The hirer of a thing may terminate the hiring before the end of the term agreed upon:

1. When the letter does not, within a reasonable time after request, fulfill his obligations, if any, as to placing and securing the hirer in the quiet possession of the thing hired, or putting it into good condition, or repairing; or,

2. When the greater part of the thing hired, or that part which was and which the letter had at the time of the hiring reason to believe was the material inducement to the hirer to enter into the contract, perishes from any other cause than the want of ordinary care of the hirer. *(Enacted in 1872. Amended by Stats.1905, c. 454, p. 614, § 3.)*

Research References

California Real Estate Forms (Miller & Starr) 2:17, Office Lease—Mixed Use Building.

California Real Estate Forms (Miller & Starr) 2:18, Office Lease—Office/Warehouse Building With Four or Fewer Tenants.

California Real Estate Forms (Miller & Starr) § 2:19, Retail Lease—Power Shopping Center.

California Real Estate Forms (Miller & Starr) § 2:20, Retail Lease—Shopping Center With for Profit Parking Garage.

California Real Estate Forms (Miller & Starr) § 2:27, Ground Lease.

California Real Estate Forms (Miller & Starr) § 2:29, Parking Garage Lease.

California Real Estate Forms (Miller & Starr) § 2:30, Storage Lease—Office Building.

California Real Estate Forms (Miller & Starr) § 2:32, Gross Lease—Small Commercial Property.

California Real Estate Forms (Miller & Starr) § 2:78, Damage and Destruction.

Rutter, Cal. Practice Guide: Landlord-Tenant Form 2:B, Standard Shopping Center Lease.

Rutter, Cal. Practice Guide: Real Prop. Transactions Form 7:A, Ground Lease.

Miller and Starr California Real Estate § 19:122, Maintenance Obligations of the Landlord--Nonresidential Premises.

Miller and Starr California Real Estate § 19:160, Covenant of Quiet Enjoyment and Possession--Tenant's Remedies for Breach of the Covenant.

Miller and Starr California Real Estate § 19:175, Destruction of the Premises.

Miller and Starr California Real Estate § 19:200, Termination for Cause or Default.

12 Witkin, California Summary 10th Real Property § 635, Factors for Determining Responsibility.

12 Witkin, California Summary 10th Real Property § 665, in General.

§ 1933. Termination of hiring

The hiring of a thing terminates:

1. At the end of the term agreed upon;

2. By the mutual consent of the parties;

3. By the hirer acquiring a title to the thing hired superior to that of the letter; or,

4. By the destruction of the thing hired. *(Enacted in 1872.)*

Research References

California Real Estate Forms (Miller & Starr) § 2:17, Office Lease—Mixed Use Building.

California Real Estate Forms (Miller & Starr) § 2:18, Office Lease—Office/Warehouse Building With Four or Fewer Tenants.

California Real Estate Forms (Miller & Starr) § 2:19, Retail Lease—Power Shopping Center.

California Real Estate Forms (Miller & Starr) § 2:20, Retail Lease—Shopping Center With for Profit Parking Garage.

California Real Estate Forms (Miller & Starr) § 2:27, Ground Lease.

California Real Estate Forms (Miller & Starr) § 2:29, Parking Garage Lease.

California Real Estate Forms (Miller & Starr) § 2:30, Storage Lease—Office Building.

California Real Estate Forms (Miller & Starr) § 2:32, Gross Lease—Small Commercial Property.

California Real Estate Forms (Miller & Starr) § 2:78, Damage and Destruction.

Rutter, Cal. Practice Guide: Landlord-Tenant Form 2:B, Standard Shopping Center Lease.

Rutter, Cal. Practice Guide: Landlord-Tenant Form 2:C, Office Lease.

Rutter, Cal. Practice Guide: Real Prop. Transactions Form 7:A, Ground Lease.

Miller and Starr California Real Estate § 15:75, Merger.

Miller and Starr California Real Estate § 19:28, Tenancy for Fixed Term.

Miller and Starr California Real Estate § 19:135, Exercise of the Option.

Miller and Starr California Real Estate § 19:139, Summary of Causes for Termination.

Miller and Starr California Real Estate § 19:175, Destruction of the Premises.

Miller and Starr California Real Estate § 19:177, Merger of Estates.

Miller and Starr California Real Estate § 19:188, Notice Required by Statute.

12 Witkin, California Summary 10th Real Property § 664, (S 664) Expiration of Term.

12 Witkin, California Summary 10th Real Property § 665, in General.

§ 1934. Death or incapacity of party; effect

If the hiring of a thing is terminable at the pleasure of one of the parties, it is terminated by notice to the other of his death or incapacity to contract. In other cases it is not terminated thereby. *(Enacted in 1872.)*

Research References

Miller and Starr California Real Estate § 19:85, Persons Liable for Payment of Rent.

Miller and Starr California Real Estate § 19:178, Death of a Party.

12 Witkin, California Summary 10th Real Property § 663, (S 663) in General.

§ 1934.5. Accommodations from month to month in nursing or convalescent home; termination on death of patient

Notwithstanding the provisions of Section 1934, the hiring of accommodations from month to month in a nursing or convalescent home shall be terminated by the death of the patient by or for whom the hiring was made. The hirer or his heir, legatee, or personal representative shall not be liable for any rent due for such accommodations under the hiring agreement beyond that rent due for the date on which such patient died. No advance payment of rent made by the hirer shall be subject to the claim of, or retention by, the nursing or convalescent home and shall be returned to the heir, legatee, or personal representative no later than two weeks after such patient has died. Any provision in the hiring agreement by which the hirer agrees to modify or waive any of his rights under this section shall be void as contrary to public policy.

The provisions of this section shall be applicable to all hiring agreements executed on or after January 1, 1979. *(Added by Stats.1978, c. 628, p. 2081, § 1.)*

Research References

12 Witkin, California Summary 10th Real Property § 663, (S 663) in General.

§ 1935. Termination of hiring; apportionment of hire

When the hiring of a thing is terminated before the time originally agreed upon, the hirer must pay the due proportion of the hire for such use as he has actually made of the thing, unless such use is merely nominal, and of no benefit to him. *(Enacted in 1872.)*

Research References

Miller and Starr California Real Estate § 19:87, Termination of the Obligation to Pay Rent--Apportionment of Rent on Premature Termination of the Lease.

Miller and Starr California Real Estate § 19:199, Surrender--Effect of a Surrender.

12 Witkin, California Summary 10th Real Property § 213, Public Property.

12 Witkin, California Summary 10th Real Property § 570, (S 570) General Rule Against Apportionment.

12 Witkin, California Summary 10th Real Property § 571, (S 571) When Apportionment is Authorized.

1 Witkin Cal. Summ. 10th Contracts § 752, Applicable Laws Become Part of Contract.

§ 1936. Vehicle rental agreements; losses; liability; remedies

Section operative until Jan. 1, 2015. See, also, section operative Jan. 1, 2015.

(a) For the purpose of this section, the following definitions shall apply:

(1) "Rental company" means a person or entity in the business of renting passenger vehicles to the public.

(2) "Renter" means any person in a manner obligated under a contract for the lease or hire of a passenger vehicle from a rental company for a period of less than 30 days.

(3) "Authorized driver" means (A) the renter, (B) the renter's spouse if that person is a licensed driver and satisfies the rental company's minimum age requirement, (C) the renter's employer or coworker if he or she is engaged in business activity with the renter, is a licensed driver, and satisfies the rental company's minimum age requirement, and (D) a person expressly listed by the rental company on the renter's contract as an authorized driver.

(4)(A) "Customer facility charge" means any fee, including an alternative fee, required by an airport to be collected by a rental company from a renter for any of the following purposes:

(i) To finance, design, and construct consolidated airport car rental facilities.

(ii) To finance, design, construct, and operate common-use transportation systems that move passengers between airport terminals and those consolidated car rental facilities, and acquire vehicles for use in that system.

(iii) To finance, design, and construct terminal modifications solely to accommodate and provide customer access to common-use transportation systems.

(B) The aggregate amount to be collected shall not exceed the reasonable costs, as determined by an * * * audit, by an independent auditor, paid for by the airport, to finance, design, and construct those facilities. The auditor shall independently examine and substantiate the necessity for and the amount of the customer facility charge, including whether the airport's actual or projected costs are supported and justified, any steps the airport may take to limit costs, potential alternatives for meeting the airport's revenue needs other than the collection of the fee, and whether and to what extent car rental companies or other businesses or individuals using the facility or common-use transportation system may pay for the costs associated with these facilities and systems other than the fee from rental customers, or whether the airport did not comply with any provision of this subparagraph. Copies of the audit shall be provided to the Assembly and Senate Committees on Judiciary, the Assembly Committee on Transportation, and the Senate Committee on Transportation and Housing and shall be posted on the airport's Internet Web site. In the case of a customer facility charge for a common-use transportation system, the audit also shall consider the reasonable costs of providing the transit system or busing network pursuant to clause (ii) of subparagraph (A). Any audit required by this subparagraph may be included as a part of an audit of an airport's finances. Notwithstanding clause (iii) of subparagraph (A), the fees designated as a customer facility charge shall not be used to pay for terminal expansion, gate expansion, runway expansion, changes in hours of operation, or changes in the number of flights arriving or departing from the airport.

(C) Except as provided in subparagraph (D), the authorization given pursuant to this section for an airport to impose a customer facility charge shall become inoperative when the bonds used for financing are paid.

(D) If a bond or other form of indebtedness is not used for financing, or the bond or other form of indebtedness used for financing has been paid, the Oakland International Airport may require the collection of a customer facility charge for a period of up to 10 years from the imposition of the charge for the purposes allowed by, and subject to the conditions imposed by, this section.

(5) "Damage waiver" means a rental company's agreement not to hold a renter liable for all or any portion of any damage or loss related to the rented vehicle, any loss of use of the rented

vehicle, or any storage, impound, towing, or administrative charges.

(6) "Electronic surveillance technology" means a technological method or system used to observe, monitor, or collect information, including telematics, Global Positioning System (GPS), wireless technology, or location-based technologies. "Electronic surveillance technology" does not include event data recorders (EDR), sensing and diagnostic modules (SDM), or other systems that are used either:

(A) For the purpose of identifying, diagnosing, or monitoring functions related to the potential need to repair, service, or perform maintenance on the rental vehicle.

(B) As part of the vehicle's airbag sensing and diagnostic system in order to capture safety systems-related data for retrieval after a crash has occurred or in the event that the collision sensors are activated to prepare the decisionmaking computer to make the determination to deploy or not to deploy the airbag.

(7) "Estimated time for replacement" means the number of hours of labor, or fraction thereof, needed to replace damaged vehicle parts as set forth in collision damage estimating guides generally used in the vehicle repair business and commonly known as "crash books."

(8) "Estimated time for repair" means a good faith estimate of the reasonable number of hours of labor, or fraction thereof, needed to repair damaged vehicle parts.

(9) "Membership program" means a service offered by a rental company that permits customers to bypass the rental counter and go directly to the car previously reserved. A membership program shall meet all of the following requirements:

(A) The renter initiates enrollment by completing an application on which the renter can specify a preference for type of vehicle and acceptance or declination of optional services.

(B) The rental company fully discloses, prior to the enrollee's first rental as a participant in the program, all terms and conditions of the rental agreement as well as all required disclosures.

(C) The renter may terminate enrollment at any time.

(D) The rental company fully explains to the renter that designated preferences, as well as acceptance or declination of optional services, may be changed by the renter at any time for the next and future rentals.

(E) An employee designated to receive the form specified in subparagraph (C) of paragraph (1) of subdivision (t) is present at the lot where the renter takes possession of the car, to receive any change in the rental agreement from the renter.

(10) "Passenger vehicle" means a passenger vehicle as defined in Section 465 of the Vehicle Code.

(b) Except as limited by subdivision (c), a rental company and a renter may agree that the renter will be responsible for no more than all of the following:

(1) Physical or mechanical damage to the rented vehicle up to its fair market value, as determined in the customary market for the sale of that vehicle, resulting from collision regardless of the cause of the damage.

(2) Loss due to theft of the rented vehicle up to its fair market value, as determined in the customary market for the sale of that vehicle, provided that the rental company establishes by clear and convincing evidence that the renter or the authorized driver failed to exercise ordinary care while in possession of the vehicle. In addition, the renter shall be presumed to have no liability for any loss due to theft if (A) an authorized driver has possession of the ignition key furnished by the rental company or an author-

ized driver establishes that the ignition key furnished by the rental company was not in the vehicle at the time of the theft, and (B) an authorized driver files an official report of the theft with the police or other law enforcement agency within 24 hours of learning of the theft and reasonably cooperates with the rental company and the police or other law enforcement agency in providing information concerning the theft. The presumption set forth in this paragraph is a presumption affecting the burden of proof which the rental company may rebut by establishing that an authorized driver committed, or aided and abetted the commission of, the theft.

(3) Physical damage to the rented vehicle up to its fair market value, as determined in the customary market for the sale of that vehicle, resulting from vandalism occurring after, or in connection with, the theft of the rented vehicle. However, the renter shall have no liability for any damage due to vandalism if the renter would have no liability for theft pursuant to paragraph (2).

(4) Physical damage to the rented vehicle up to a total of five hundred dollars ($500) resulting from vandalism unrelated to the theft of the rented vehicle.

(5) Actual charges for towing, storage, and impound fees paid by the rental company if the renter is liable for damage or loss.

(6) An administrative charge, which shall include the cost of appraisal and all other costs and expenses incident to the damage, loss, repair, or replacement of the rented vehicle.

(c) The total amount of the renter's liability to the rental company resulting from damage to the rented vehicle shall not exceed the sum of the following:

(1) The estimated cost of parts which the rental company would have to pay to replace damaged vehicle parts. All discounts and price reductions or adjustments that are or will be received by the rental company shall be subtracted from the estimate to the extent not already incorporated in the estimate, or otherwise promptly credited or refunded to the renter.

(2) The estimated cost of labor to replace damaged vehicle parts, which shall not exceed the product of (A) the rate for labor usually paid by the rental company to replace vehicle parts of the type that were damaged and (B) the estimated time for replacement. All discounts and price reductions or adjustments that are or will be received by the rental company shall be subtracted from the estimate to the extent not already incorporated in the estimate, or otherwise promptly credited or refunded to the renter.

(3)(A) The estimated cost of labor to repair damaged vehicle parts, which shall not exceed the lesser of the following:

(i) The product of the rate for labor usually paid by the rental company to repair vehicle parts of the type that were damaged and the estimated time for repair.

(ii) The sum of the estimated labor and parts costs determined under paragraphs (1) and (2) to replace the same vehicle parts.

(B) All discounts and price reductions or adjustments that are or will be received by the rental company shall be subtracted from the estimate to the extent not already incorporated in the estimate, or otherwise promptly credited or refunded to the renter.

(4) For the purpose of converting the estimated time for repair into the same units of time in which the rental rate is expressed, a day shall be deemed to consist of eight hours.

(5) Actual charges for towing, storage, and impound fees paid by the rental company.

(6) The administrative charge described in paragraph (6) of subdivision (b) shall not exceed (A) fifty dollars ($50) if the total estimated cost for parts and labor is more than one hundred dollars ($100) up to and including five hundred dollars ($500), (B) one hundred dollars ($100) if the total estimated cost for parts and labor exceeds five hundred dollars ($500) up to and including one thousand five hundred dollars ($1,500), and (C) one hundred fifty dollars ($150) if the total estimated cost for parts and labor exceeds one thousand five hundred dollars ($1,500). An administrative charge shall not be imposed if the total estimated cost of parts and labor is one hundred dollars ($100) or less.

(d)(1) The total amount of an authorized driver's liability to the rental company, if any, for damage occurring during the authorized driver's operation of the rented vehicle shall not exceed the amount of the renter's liability under subdivision (c).

(2) A rental company shall not recover from the renter or other authorized driver an amount exceeding the renter's liability under subdivision (c).

(3) A claim against a renter resulting from damage or loss, excluding loss of use, to a rental vehicle shall be reasonably and rationally related to the actual loss incurred. A rental company shall mitigate damages where possible and shall not assert or collect a claim for physical damage which exceeds the actual costs of the repairs performed or the estimated cost of repairs, if the rental company chooses not to repair the vehicle, including all discounts and price reductions. However, if the vehicle is a total loss vehicle, the claim shall not exceed the total loss vehicle value established in accordance with procedures that are customarily used by insurance companies when paying claims on total loss vehicles, less the proceeds from salvaging the vehicle, if those proceeds are retained by the rental company.

(4) If insurance coverage exists under the renter's applicable personal or business insurance policy and the coverage is confirmed during regular business hours, the renter may require that the rental company submit any claims to the renter's applicable personal or business insurance carrier. The rental company shall not make any written or oral representations that it will not present claims or negotiate with the renter's insurance carrier. For purposes of this paragraph, confirmation of coverage includes telephone confirmation from insurance company representatives during regular business hours. Upon request of the renter and after confirmation of coverage, the amount of claim shall be resolved between the insurance carrier and the rental company. The renter shall remain responsible for payment to the rental car company for any loss sustained that the renter's applicable personal or business insurance policy does not cover.

(5) A rental company shall not recover from the renter or other authorized driver for an item described in subdivision (b) to the extent the rental company obtains recovery from another person.

(6) This section applies only to the maximum liability of a renter or other authorized driver to the rental company resulting from damage to the rented vehicle and not to the liability of another person.

(e)(1) Except as provided in subdivision (f), a damage waiver shall provide or, if not expressly stated in writing, shall be deemed to provide that the renter has no liability for a damage, loss, loss of use, or a cost or expense incident thereto.

(2) Except as provided in subdivision (f), every limitation, exception, or exclusion to a damage waiver is void and unenforceable.

(f) A rental company may provide in the rental contract that a damage waiver does not apply under any of the following circumstances:

(1) Damage or loss results from an authorized driver's (A) intentional, willful, wanton, or reckless conduct, (B) operation of

the vehicle under the influence of drugs or alcohol in violation of Section 23152 of the Vehicle Code, (C) towing or pushing anything, or (D) operation of the vehicle on an unpaved road if the damage or loss is a direct result of the road or driving conditions.

(2) Damage or loss occurs while the vehicle is (A) used for commercial hire, (B) used in connection with conduct that could be properly charged as a felony, (C) involved in a speed test or contest or in driver training activity, (D) operated by a person other than an authorized driver, or (E) operated outside the United States.

(3) An authorized driver who has (A) provided fraudulent information to the rental company, or (B) provided false information and the rental company would not have rented the vehicle if it had instead received true information.

(g)(1) A rental company that offers or provides a damage waiver for any consideration in addition to the rental rate shall clearly and conspicuously disclose the following information in the rental contract or holder in which the contract is placed and, also, in signs posted at the place, such as the counter, where the renter signs the rental contract, and, for renters who are enrolled in the rental company's membership program, in a sign that shall be posted in a location clearly visible to those renters as they enter the location where their reserved rental cars are parked or near the exit of the bus or other conveyance that transports the enrollee to a reserved car: (A) the nature of the renter's liability, such as liability for all collision damage regardless of cause, (B) the extent of the renter's liability, such as liability for damage or loss up to a specified amount, (C) the renter's personal insurance policy or the credit card used to pay for the car rental transaction may provide coverage for all or a portion of the renter's potential liability, (D) the renter should consult with his or her insurer to determine the scope of insurance coverage, including the amount of the deductible, if any, for which the renter is obligated, (E) the renter may purchase an optional damage waiver to cover all liability, subject to whatever exceptions the rental company expressly lists that are permitted under subdivision (f), and (F) the range of charges for the damage waiver.

(2) In addition to the requirements of paragraph (1), a rental company that offers or provides a damage waiver shall orally disclose to all renters, except those who are participants in the rental company's membership program, that the damage waiver may be duplicative of coverage that the customer maintains under his or her own policy of motor vehicle insurance. The renter's receipt of the oral disclosure shall be demonstrated through the renter's acknowledging receipt of the oral disclosure near that part of the contract where the renter indicates, by the renter's own initials, his or her acceptance or declination of the damage waiver. Adjacent to that same part, the contract also shall state that the damage waiver is optional. Further, the contract for these renters shall include a clear and conspicuous written disclosure that the damage waiver may be duplicative of coverage that the customer maintains under his or her own policy of motor vehicle insurance.

(3) The following is an example, for purposes of illustration and not limitation, of a notice fulfilling the requirements of paragraph (1) for a rental company that imposes liability on the renter for collision damage to the full value of the vehicle:

"NOTICE ABOUT YOUR FINANCIAL RESPONSIBILITY AND OPTIONAL DAMAGE WAIVER

You are responsible for all collision damage to the rented vehicle even if someone else caused it or the cause is unknown. You are responsible for the cost of repair up to the value of the vehicle, and towing, storage, and impound fees.

Your own insurance, or the issuer of the credit card you use to pay for the car rental transaction, may cover all or part of your financial responsibility for the rented vehicle. You should check with your insurance company, or credit card issuer, to find out about your coverage and the amount of the deductible, if any, for which you may be liable.

Further, if you use a credit card that provides coverage for your potential liability, you should check with the issuer to determine if you must first exhaust the coverage limits of your own insurance before the credit card coverage applies.

The rental company will not hold you responsible if you buy a damage waiver. But a damage waiver will not protect you if (list exceptions)."

(A) When the above notice is printed in the rental contract or holder in which the contract is placed, the following shall be printed immediately following the notice:

"The cost of an optional damage waiver is $____ for every (day or week)."

(B) When the above notice appears on a sign, the following shall appear immediately adjacent to the notice:

"The cost of an optional damage waiver is $____ to $____ for every (day or week), depending upon the vehicle rented."

(h) Notwithstanding any other provision of law, a rental company may sell a damage waiver subject to the following rate limitations for each full or partial 24–hour rental day for the damage waiver.

(1) For rental vehicles that the rental company designates as an "economy car," "subcompact car," "compact car," or another term having similar meaning when offered for rental, or another vehicle having a manufacturer's suggested retail price of nineteen thousand dollars ($19,000) or less, the rate shall not exceed nine dollars ($9).

(2) For rental vehicles that have a manufacturer's suggested retail price from nineteen thousand one dollars ($19,001) to thirty-four thousand nine hundred ninety-nine dollars ($34,999), inclusive, and that are also either vehicles of next year's model, or not older than the previous year's model, the rate shall not exceed fifteen dollars ($15). For those rental vehicles older than the previous year's model-year, the rate shall not exceed nine dollars ($9).

(i) The manufacturer's suggested retail prices described in subdivision (h) shall be adjusted annually to reflect changes from the previous year in the Consumer Price Index. For the purposes of this section, "Consumer Price Index" means the United States Consumer Price Index for All Urban Consumers, for all items.

(j) A rental company that disseminates in this state an advertisement containing a rental rate shall include in that advertisement a clearly readable statement of the charge for a damage waiver and a statement that a damage waiver is optional.

(k)(1) A rental company shall not require the purchase of a damage waiver, optional insurance, or another optional good or service.

(2) A rental company shall not engage in any unfair, deceptive, or coercive conduct to induce a renter to purchase the damage waiver, optional insurance, or another optional good or service, including conduct such as, but not limited to, refusing to honor the renter's reservation, limiting the availability of vehicles, requiring a deposit, or debiting or blocking the renter's credit card account for a sum equivalent to a deposit if the renter declines to purchase the damage waiver, optional insurance, or another optional good or service.

(l)(1) In the absence of express permission granted by the renter subsequent to damage to, or loss of, the vehicle, a rental company shall not seek to recover any portion of a claim arising out of damage to, or loss of, the rented vehicle by processing a credit card charge or causing a debit or block to be placed on the renter's credit card account.

(2) A rental company shall not engage in any unfair, deceptive, or coercive tactics in attempting to recover or in recovering on any claim arising out of damage to, or loss of, the rented vehicle.

(m)(1) A customer facility charge may be collected by a rental company under the following circumstances:

(A) Collection of the fee by the rental company is required by an airport operated by a city, a county, a city and county, a joint powers authority, a special district, or the San Diego County Regional Airport Authority formed pursuant to Division 17 (commencing with Section 170000) of the Public Utilities Code.

(B) The fee is calculated on a per contract basis or as provided in paragraph (2).

(C) The fee is a user fee, not a tax imposed upon real property or an incidence of property ownership under Article XIII D of the California Constitution.

(D) Except as otherwise provided in subparagraph (E), the fee shall be ten dollars ($10) per contract or the amount provided in paragraph (2).

(E) The fee for a consolidated rental car facility shall be collected only from customers of on-airport rental car companies. If the fee imposed by the airport is for both a consolidated rental car facility and a common-use transportation system, the fee collected from customers of on-airport rental car companies shall be ten dollars ($10) or the amount provided in paragraph (2), but the fee imposed on customers of off-airport rental car companies who are transported on the common-use transportation system is proportionate to the costs of the common-use transportation system only. The fee is uniformly applied to each class of on-airport or off-airport customers, provided that the airport requires off-airport customers to use the common-use transportation system. For purposes of this subparagraph, "on-airport rental car company" means a rental company operating under an airport property lease or an airport concession or license agreement whose customers use or will use the consolidated rental car facility and the collection of the fee as to those customers is consistent with subparagraph (C).

(F) Revenues collected from the fee do not exceed the reasonable costs of financing, designing, and constructing the facility and financing, designing, constructing, and operating any common-use transportation system, or acquiring vehicles for use in that system, and shall not be used for any other purpose.

(G) The fee is separately identified on the rental agreement.

(H) This paragraph does not apply to fees which are governed by Section 50474.1 of the Government Code or Section 57.5 of the San Diego Unified Port District Act.

(I) For any airport seeking to require rental car companies to collect an alternative customer facility charge pursuant to paragraph (2), the following provisions apply:

(i) Notwithstanding Section 10231.5 of the Government Code, the airport shall provide reports on an annual basis to the Senate and Assembly Committees on Judiciary detailing all of the following:

(I) The total amount of the customer facility charge collected.

(II) How the funds are being spent.

(III) The amount of and reason for any changes in the airport's budget or financial needs for the facility or common-use transportation system.

(IV) Whether airport concession fees authorized by Section 1936.01 have increased since the prior report, if any.

(ii)(I) The airport shall complete the * * * audit required by subparagraph (B) of paragraph (4) of subdivision (a) prior to initial collection of the customer facility charge * * *. Notwithstanding Section 10231.5 of the Government Code, copies of the audit shall be provided to the Assembly and Senate Committees on Judiciary, the Assembly Committee on Transportation, and the Senate Committee on Transportation and Housing and shall be posted on the airport's Internet Web site.

(II) Prior to any increase pursuant to paragraph (2), * * * the airport shall update the information provided in the initial collection audit pursuant to subclause (I). Notwithstanding Section 10231.5 of the Government Code, copies of the updated audit shall be provided to the Assembly and Senate Committees on Judiciary, the Assembly Committee on Transportation, and the Senate Committee on Transportation and Housing and shall be posted on the airport's Internet Web site.

(III) An audit shall be completed every three years after initial collection * * * only if the customer facility charge is collected for the purpose of operating a common-use transportation system or to acquire vehicles for use in such a system pursuant to clause (ii) of subparagraph (A) of paragraph (4) of subdivision (a). A regularly conducted audit of airport finances that includes the customer facility charge information, that satisfies the requirements of subparagraph (B) of paragraph (4) of subdivision (a), and is produced in accordance with the generally accepted accounting principles of the Government Accounting Standards Board, shall satisfy the requirements of this subclause. This obligation shall continue until the fee authorization becomes inoperative pursuant to subparagraph (C) of paragraph (4) of subdivision (a). Notwithstanding Section 10231.5 of the Government Code, the information reported pursuant to this subclause shall be compiled into one document, shall be provided to the Assembly and Senate Committees on Judiciary, the Assembly Committee on Transportation, and the Senate Committee on Transportation and Housing and shall be posted on the airport's Internet Web site accessible to the public. The information reported shall be contained within one easily accessible page contained within the airport's Internet Web site.

(IV) This section shall not be construed to require an airport to audit a common-use transportation system not financed by a customer facility charge and used for the purposes permitted pursuant to clause (ii) of subparagraph (A) of paragraph(4) of subdivision (a).

(V) The airport shall post on the airport's Internet Web site copies of the completed audits required by this clause for a period of six years following the audit's completion.

(iii) Use of the bonds shall be limited to construction and design of the consolidated rental car facility, terminal modifications, and operating costs of the common-use transportation system, as specified in paragraph (4) of subdivision (a).

(2) Any airport may require rental car companies to collect an alternative customer facility charge under the following conditions:

(A) The airport first conducts a publicly noticed hearing pursuant to the Ralph M. Brown Act (Chapter 9 (commencing with Section 54950) of Part 1 of Division 2 of Title 5 of the Government Code) to review the costs of financing the design and construction of a consolidated rental car facility and the design, construction, and operation of any common-use transportation system in which all of the following occur:

(i) The airport establishes the amount of revenue necessary to finance the reasonable cost to design and construct a consolidated rental car facility and to design, construct, and operate any common-use transportation system, or acquire vehicles for use in that system, based on evidence presented during the hearing.

(ii) The airport finds, based on evidence presented during the hearing, that the fee authorized in paragraph (1) will not generate sufficient revenue to finance the reasonable costs to design and construct a consolidated rental car facility and to design, construct, and operate any common-use transportation system, or acquire vehicles for use in that system.

(iii) The airport finds that the reasonable cost of the project requires the additional amount of revenue that would be generated by the proposed daily rate, including any rate increase, authorized pursuant to this paragraph.

(iv) The airport outlines each of the following:

(I) Steps it has taken to limit costs.

(II) Other potential alternatives for meeting its revenue needs other than the collection of the fee.

(III) The extent to which rental car companies or other businesses or individuals using the facility or common-use transportation system will pay for the costs associated with these facilities and systems other than the fee from rental customers.

(B) The airport may not require the fee authorized in this paragraph to be collected at any time that the fee authorized in paragraph (1) of this subdivision is being collected.

(C) Pursuant to the procedure set forth in this subdivision, the fee may be collected at a rate charged on a per-day basis subject to the following conditions:

(i) Commencing January 1, 2011, the amount of the fee may not exceed six dollars ($6) per day.

(ii) Commencing January 1, 2014, the amount of the fee may not exceed seven dollars and fifty cents ($7.50) per day.

(iii) Commencing January 1, 2017, and thereafter, the amount of the fee may not exceed nine dollars ($9) per day.

(iv) At no time shall the fee authorized in this paragraph be collected from any customer for more than five days for each individual rental car contract.

(v) An airport subject to this paragraph shall initiate the process for obtaining the authority to require or increase the alternative fee no later than January 1, 2018. Any airport that obtains the authority to require or increase an alternative fee shall be authorized to continue collecting that fee until the fee authorization becomes inoperative pursuant to subparagraph (C) of paragraph (4) of subdivision (a).

(3) Notwithstanding any other provision of law, including, but not limited to, Part 1 (commencing with Section 6001) to Part 1.7 (commencing with Section 7280), inclusive, of Division 2 of the Revenue and Taxation Code, the fees collected pursuant to this section, or another law whereby a local agency operating an airport requires a rental car company to collect a facility financing fee from its customers, are not subject to sales, use, or transaction taxes.

(n)(1) A rental company shall only advertise, quote, and charge a rental rate that includes the entire amount except taxes, a customer facility charge, if any, and a mileage charge, if any, that a renter must pay to hire or lease the vehicle for the period of time to which the rental rate applies. A rental company shall not charge in addition to the rental rate, taxes, a customer facility charge, if any, and a mileage charge, if any, any fee that is required to be paid by the renter as a condition of hiring or leasing the vehicle, including, but not limited to, required fuel or airport surcharges other than customer facility charges, nor a fee for transporting the renter to the location where the rented vehicle will be delivered to the renter.

(2) In addition to the rental rate, taxes, customer facility charges, if any, and mileage charges, if any, a rental company may charge for an item or service provided in connection with a particular rental transaction if the renter could have avoided incurring the charge by choosing not to obtain or utilize the optional item or service. Items and services for which the rental company may impose an additional charge include, but are not limited to, optional insurance and accessories requested by the renter, service charges incident to the renter's optional return of the vehicle to a location other than the location where the vehicle was hired or leased, and charges for refueling the vehicle at the conclusion of the rental transaction in the event the renter did not return the vehicle with as much fuel as was in the fuel tank at the beginning of the rental. A rental company also may impose an additional charge based on reasonable age criteria established by the rental company.

(3) A rental company shall not charge a fee for authorized drivers in addition to the rental charge for an individual renter.

(4) If a rental company states a rental rate in print advertisement or in a telephonic, in-person, or computer-transmitted quotation, the rental company shall disclose clearly in that advertisement or quotation the terms of mileage conditions relating to the advertised or quoted rental rate, including, but not limited to, to the extent applicable, the amount of mileage and gas charges, the number of miles for which no charges will be imposed, and a description of geographic driving limitations within the United States and Canada.

(5)(A) When a rental rate is stated in an advertisement, quotation, or reservation in connection with a car rental at an airport where a customer facility charge is imposed, the rental company shall disclose clearly the existence and amount of the customer facility charge. For purposes of this subparagraph, advertisements include radio, television, other electronic media, and print advertisements. For purposes of this subparagraph, quotations and reservations include those that are telephonic, in-person, and computer-transmitted. If the rate advertisement is intended to include transactions at more than one airport imposing a customer facility charge, a range of fees may be stated in the advertisement. However, all rate advertisements that include car rentals at airport destinations shall clearly and conspicuously include a toll-free telephone number whereby a customer can be told the specific amount of the customer facility charge to which the customer will be obligated.

(B) If a person or entity other than a rental car company, including a passenger carrier or a seller of travel services, advertises or quotes a rate for a car rental at an airport where a customer facility charge is imposed, that person or entity shall, provided that he, she, or it is provided with information about the existence and amount of the fee, to the extent not specifically prohibited by federal law, clearly disclose the existence and amount of the fee in any telephonic, in-person, or computer-transmitted quotation at the time of making an initial quotation of a rental rate and at the time of making a reservation of a rental car. If a rental car company provides the person or entity with rate and customer facility charge information, the rental car company is not responsible for the failure of that person or entity to comply with this subparagraph when quoting or confirming a rate to a third person or entity.

(6) If a rental company delivers a vehicle to a renter at a location other than the location where the rental company normally carries on its business, the rental company shall not charge the renter an amount for the rental for the period before the delivery of the vehicle. If a rental company picks up a rented vehicle from a renter at a location other than the location where the rental company normally carries on its business, the rental company shall not charge the renter an amount for the

rental for the period after the renter notifies the rental company to pick up the vehicle.

(*o*) A rental company shall not use, access, or obtain any information relating to the renter's use of the rental vehicle that was obtained using electronic surveillance technology, except in the following circumstances:

(1)(A) When the equipment is used by the rental company only for the purpose of locating a stolen, abandoned, or missing rental vehicle after one of the following:

(i) The renter or law enforcement has informed the rental company that the vehicle is missing or has been stolen or abandoned.

(ii) The rental vehicle has not been returned following one week after the contracted return date, or by one week following the end of an extension of that return date.

(iii) The rental company discovers the rental vehicle has been stolen or abandoned, and, if stolen, it shall report the vehicle stolen to law enforcement by filing a stolen vehicle report, unless law enforcement has already informed the rental company that the vehicle is missing or has been stolen or abandoned.

(B) If electronic surveillance technology is activated pursuant to subparagraph (A), a rental company shall maintain a record, in either electronic or written form, of information relevant to the activation of that technology. That information shall include the rental agreement, including the return date, and the date and time the electronic surveillance technology was activated. The record shall also include, if relevant, a record of written or other communication with the renter, including communications regarding extensions of the rental, police reports, or other written communication with law enforcement officials. The record shall be maintained for a period of at least 12 months from the time the record is created and shall be made available upon the renter's request. The rental company shall maintain and furnish explanatory codes necessary to read the record. A rental company shall not be required to maintain a record if electronic surveillance technology is activated to recover a rental vehicle that is stolen or missing at a time other than during a rental period.

(2) In response to a specific request from law enforcement pursuant to a subpoena or search warrant.

(3) This subdivision does not prohibit a rental company from equipping rental vehicles with GPS–based technology that provides navigation assistance to the occupants of the rental vehicle, if the rental company does not use, access, or obtain information relating to the renter's use of the rental vehicle that was obtained using that technology, except for the purposes of discovering or repairing a defect in the technology and the information may then be used only for that purpose.

(4) This subdivision does not prohibit a rental company from equipping rental vehicles with electronic surveillance technology that allows for the remote locking or unlocking of the vehicle at the request of the renter, if the rental company does not use, access, or obtain information relating to the renter's use of the rental vehicle that was obtained using that technology, except as necessary to lock or unlock the vehicle.

(5) This subdivision does not prohibit a rental company from equipping rental vehicles with electronic surveillance technology that allows the company to provide roadside assistance, such as towing, flat tire, or fuel services, at the request of the renter, if the rental company does not use, access, or obtain information relating to the renter's use of the rental vehicle that was obtained using that technology except as necessary to provide the requested roadside assistance.

(6) This subdivision does not prohibit a rental company from obtaining, accessing, or using information from electronic surveillance technology for the sole purpose of determining the date and time the vehicle is returned to the rental company, and the total mileage driven and the vehicle fuel level of the returned vehicle. This paragraph, however, shall apply only after the renter has returned the vehicle to the rental company, and the information shall only be used for the purpose described in this paragraph.

(p) A rental company shall not use electronic surveillance technology to track a renter in order to impose fines or surcharges relating to the renter's use of the rental vehicle.

(q) A renter may bring an action against a rental company for the recovery of damages and appropriate equitable relief for a violation of this section. The prevailing party shall be entitled to recover reasonable attorney's fees and costs.

(r) A rental company that brings an action against a renter for loss due to theft of the vehicle shall bring the action in the county in which the renter resides or, if the renter is not a resident of this state, in the jurisdiction in which the renter resides.

(s) A waiver of any of the provisions of this section shall be void and unenforceable as contrary to public policy.

(t)(1) A rental company's disclosure requirements shall be satisfied for renters who are enrolled in the rental company's membership program if all of the following conditions are met:

(A) Prior to the enrollee's first rental as a participant in the program, the renter receives, in writing, the following:

(i) All of the disclosures required by paragraph (1) of subdivision (g), including the terms and conditions of the rental agreement then in effect.

(ii) An Internet Web site address, as well as a contact number or address, where the enrollee can learn of changes to the rental agreement or to the laws of this state governing rental agreements since the effective date of the rental company's most recent restatement of the rental agreement and distribution of that restatement to its members.

(B) At the commencement of each rental period, the renter is provided, on the rental record or the folder in which it is inserted, with a printed notice stating that he or she had either previously selected or declined an optional damage waiver and that the renter has the right to change preferences.

(C) At the commencement of each rental period, the rental company provides, on the rearview mirror, a hanger on which a statement is printed, in a box, in at least 12–point boldface type, notifying the renter that the collision damage waiver offered by the rental company may be duplicative of coverage that the customer maintains under his or her own policy of motor vehicle insurance. If it is not feasible to hang the statement from the rearview mirror, it shall be hung from the steering wheel.

The hanger shall provide the renter a box to initial if he or she (not his or her employer) has previously accepted or declined the collision damage waiver and that he or she now wishes to change his or her decision to accept or decline the collision damage waiver, as follows:

"☐ If I previously accepted the collision damage waiver, I now decline it.

☐ If I previously declined the collision damage waiver, I now accept it."

The hanger shall also provide a box for the enrollee to indicate whether this change applies to this rental transaction only or to all future rental transactions. The hanger shall also notify the renter that he or she may make that change, prior to leaving the lot, by returning the form to an employee designated to receive the form who is present at the lot where the renter takes possession of the car, to receive any change in the rental agreement from the renter.

(2)(A) This subdivision is not effective unless the employee designated pursuant to subparagraph (E) of paragraph (8) of subdivision (a) is actually present at the required location.

(B) This subdivision does not relieve the rental company from the disclosures required to be made within the text of a contract or holder in which the contract is placed; in or on an advertisement containing a rental rate; or in a telephonic, in-person, or computer-transmitted quotation or reservation.

(u) The amendments made to this section during the 2001–02 Regular Session of the Legislature do not affect litigation pending on or before January 1, 2003, alleging a violation of Section 22325 of the Business and Professions Code as it read at the time the action was commenced.

(v)(1) When a rental company enters into a rental agreement in the state for the rental of a vehicle to any renter who is not a resident of this country and, as part of, or associated with, the rental agreement, the renter purchases liability insurance, as defined in subdivision (b) of Section 1758.85 of the Insurance Code, from the rental company in its capacity as a rental car agent for an authorized insurer, the rental company shall be authorized to accept, and, if served as set forth in this subdivision, shall accept, service of a summons and complaint and any other required documents against the foreign renter for any accident or collision resulting from the operation of the rental vehicle within the state during the rental period. If the rental company has a registered agent for service of process on file with the Secretary of State, process shall be served on the rental company's registered agent, either by first-class mail, return receipt requested, or by personal service.

(2) Within 30 days of acceptance of service of process, the rental company shall * * * provide a copy of the summons and complaint and any other required documents served in accordance with this subdivision to the foreign renter by first-class mail, return receipt requested.

(3) Any plaintiff, or his or her representative, who elects to serve the foreign renter by delivering a copy of the summons and complaint and any other required documents to the rental company pursuant to paragraph (1) shall agree to limit his or her recovery against the foreign renter and the rental company to the limits of the protection extended by the liability insurance.

(4) Notwithstanding the requirements of Sections 17450 to 17456, inclusive, of the Vehicle Code, service of process in compliance with paragraph (1) shall be deemed valid and effective service.

(5) Notwithstanding any other provision of law, the requirement that the rental company accept service of process pursuant to paragraph (1) shall not create any duty, obligation, or agency relationship other than that provided in paragraph (1).

(w) This section shall remain in effect only until January 1, 2015, and as of that date is repealed, unless a later enacted statute, that is enacted before January 1, 2015, deletes or extends that date. *(Added by Stats.1996, c. 992 (S.B.1070), § 2, operative Jan. 1, 2002. Amended by Stats.2001, c. 661 (A.B.491), § 1, operative Jan. 1, 2002; Stats.2002, c. 664 (A.B.3034), § 43; Stats.2002, c. 948 (A.B.2457), § 2; Stats.2004, c. 317 (A.B.2840), § 1; Stats.2005, c. 22 (S.B.1108), § 17; Stats.2005, c. 82 (A.B. 987), § 2; Stats.2007, c. 44 (S.B.641), § 1; Stats.2008, c. 179 (S.B.1498), § 31; Stats.2008, c. 228 (A.B.2142), § 1; Stats.2008, c. 620 (S.B.1510), § 1; Stats.2009, c. 140 (A.B.1164), § 28; Stats.2010, c. 642 (S.B.1192), § 1; Stats.2011, c. 531 (A.B.621), § 1; Stats.2012, c. 32 (S.B.1006), § 2, eff. June 27, 2012; Stats.2013, c. 549 (A.B.359), § 1.)*

Repeal

For repeal of this section, see its terms.

Research References

Rutter, Cal. Practice Guide: Insurance Litigation Ch. 1-A, A. Insurance-In General.

Miller and Starr California Real Estate § 20:5, The Unruh Civil Rights Act--Age Discrimination.

13 Witkin, California Summary 10th Equity § 116, Rental Car Company Practices.

13 Witkin, California Summary 10th Equity § 121, Rental Car Company Practices.

§ 1936. Vehicle rental agreements; losses; liability; remedies

Section operative Jan. 1, 2015. See, also, section operative until Jan. 1, 2015.

(a) For the purpose of this section, the following definitions shall apply:

(1) "Rental company" means a person or entity in the business of renting passenger vehicles to the public.

(2) "Renter" means any person in a manner obligated under a contract for the lease or hire of a passenger vehicle from a rental company for a period of less than 30 days.

(3) "Authorized driver" means (A) the renter, (B) the renter's spouse if that person is a licensed driver and satisfies the rental company's minimum age requirement, (C) the renter's employer or coworker if he or she is engaged in business activity with the renter, is a licensed driver, and satisfies the rental company's minimum age requirement, and (D) a person expressly listed by the rental company on the renter's contract as an authorized driver.

(4)(A) "Customer facility charge" means any fee, including an alternative fee, required by an airport to be collected by a rental company from a renter for any of the following purposes:

(i) To finance, design, and construct consolidated airport car rental facilities.

(ii) To finance, design, construct, and operate common-use transportation systems that move passengers between airport terminals and those consolidated car rental facilities, and acquire vehicles for use in that system.

(iii) To finance, design, and construct terminal modifications solely to accommodate and provide customer access to common-use transportation systems.

(B) The aggregate amount to be collected shall not exceed the reasonable costs, as determined by an * * * audit, by an independent auditor, paid for by the airport, to finance, design, and construct those facilities. The auditor shall independently examine and substantiate the necessity for and the amount of the customer facility charge, including whether the airport's actual or projected costs are supported and justified, any steps the airport may take to limit costs, potential alternatives for meeting the airport's revenue needs other than the collection of the fee, and whether and to what extent car rental companies or other businesses or individuals using the facility or common-use transportation system may pay for the costs associated with these facilities and systems other than the fee from rental customers, or whether the airport did not comply with any provision of this subparagraph. Copies of the audit shall be provided to the Assembly and Senate Committees on Judiciary, the Assembly Committee on Transportation, and the Senate Committee on Transportation and Housing and shall be posted on the airport's Internet Web site. In the case of a customer facility charge for a common-use transportation system, the audit also shall consider the reasonable costs of providing the transit system or busing network pursuant to clause (ii) of subparagraph (A). Any audit required by this subparagraph may be included as a part of an audit of an airport's finances. Notwithstanding clause (iii) of subparagraph (A), the fees designated as a customer facility charge shall not be used to pay for terminal expansion, gate expansion, runway expansion, changes in hours of operation, or changes in the number of flights arriving or departing from the airport.

(C) Except as provided in subparagraph (D), the authorization given pursuant to this section for an airport to impose a customer facility charge shall become inoperative when the bonds used for financing are paid.

(D) If a bond or other form of indebtedness is not used for financing, or the bond or other form of indebtedness used for financing has been paid, the Oakland International Airport may require the collection of a customer facility charge for a period of up to 10 years from the imposition of the charge for the purposes allowed by, and subject to the conditions imposed by, this section.

(5) "Damage waiver" means a rental company's agreement not to hold a renter liable for all or any portion of any damage or loss related to the rented vehicle, any loss of use of the rented vehicle, or any storage, impound, towing, or administrative charges.

(6) "Electronic surveillance technology" means a technological method or system used to observe, monitor, or collect information, including telematics, Global Positioning System (GPS), wireless technology, or location-based technologies. "Electronic surveillance technology" does not include event data recorders (EDR), sensing and diagnostic modules (SDM), or other systems that are used either:

(A) For the purpose of identifying, diagnosing, or monitoring functions related to the potential need to repair, service, or perform maintenance on the rental vehicle.

(B) As part of the vehicle's airbag sensing and diagnostic system in order to capture safety systems-related data for retrieval after a crash has occurred or in the event that the collision sensors are activated to prepare the decisionmaking computer to make the determination to deploy or not to deploy the airbag.

(7) "Estimated time for replacement" means the number of hours of labor, or fraction thereof, needed to replace damaged vehicle parts as set forth in collision damage estimating guides generally used in the vehicle repair business and commonly known as "crash books."

(8) "Estimated time for repair" means a good faith estimate of the reasonable number of hours of labor, or fraction thereof, needed to repair damaged vehicle parts.

(9) "Membership program" means a service offered by a rental company that permits customers to bypass the rental counter and go directly to the car previously reserved. A membership program shall meet all of the following requirements:

(A) The renter initiates enrollment by completing an application on which the renter can specify a preference for type of vehicle and acceptance or declination of optional services.

(B) The rental company fully discloses, prior to the enrollee's first rental as a participant in the program, all terms and conditions of the rental agreement as well as all required disclosures.

(C) The renter may terminate enrollment at any time.

(D) The rental company fully explains to the renter that designated preferences, as well as acceptance or declination of optional services, may be changed by the renter at any time for the next and future rentals.

(E) An employee designated to receive the form specified in subparagraph (C) of paragraph (1) of subdivision (t) is present at the lot where the renter takes possession of the car, to receive any change in the rental agreement from the renter.

(10) "Passenger vehicle" means a passenger vehicle as defined in Section 465 of the Vehicle Code.

(b) Except as limited by subdivision (c), a rental company and a renter may agree that the renter will be responsible for no more than all of the following:

(1) Physical or mechanical damage to the rented vehicle up to its fair market value, as determined in the customary market for the sale of that vehicle, resulting from collision regardless of the cause of the damage.

(2) Loss due to theft of the rented vehicle up to its fair market value, as determined in the customary market for the sale of that vehicle, provided that the rental company establishes by clear and convincing evidence that the renter or the authorized driver failed to exercise ordinary care while in possession of the vehicle. In addition, the renter shall be presumed to have no liability for any loss due to theft if (A) an authorized driver has possession of the ignition key furnished by the rental company or an authorized driver establishes that the ignition key furnished by the rental company was not in the vehicle at the time of the theft, and (B) an authorized driver files an official report of the theft with the police or other law enforcement agency within 24 hours of learning of the theft and reasonably cooperates with the rental company and the police or other law enforcement agency in providing information concerning the theft. The presumption set forth in this paragraph is a presumption affecting the burden of proof which the rental company may rebut by establishing that an authorized driver committed, or aided and abetted the commission of, the theft.

(3) Physical damage to the rented vehicle up to its fair market value, as determined in the customary market for the sale of that vehicle, resulting from vandalism occurring after, or in connection with, the theft of the rented vehicle. However, the renter shall have no liability for any damage due to vandalism if the renter would have no liability for theft pursuant to paragraph (2).

(4) Physical damage to the rented vehicle up to a total of five hundred dollars ($500) resulting from vandalism unrelated to the theft of the rented vehicle.

(5) Actual charges for towing, storage, and impound fees paid by the rental company if the renter is liable for damage or loss.

(6) An administrative charge, which shall include the cost of appraisal and all other costs and expenses incident to the damage, loss, repair, or replacement of the rented vehicle.

(c) The total amount of the renter's liability to the rental company resulting from damage to the rented vehicle shall not exceed the sum of the following:

(1) The estimated cost of parts which the rental company would have to pay to replace damaged vehicle parts. All discounts and price reductions or adjustments that are or will be received by the rental company shall be subtracted from the estimate to the extent not already incorporated in the estimate, or otherwise promptly credited or refunded to the renter.

(2) The estimated cost of labor to replace damaged vehicle parts, which shall not exceed the product of (A) the rate for labor usually paid by the rental company to replace vehicle parts of the type that were damaged and (B) the estimated time for replacement. All discounts and price reductions or adjustments that are or will be received by the rental company shall be subtracted from the estimate to the extent not already incorporated in the estimate, or otherwise promptly credited or refunded to the renter.

(3)(A) The estimated cost of labor to repair damaged vehicle parts, which shall not exceed the lesser of the following:

(i) The product of the rate for labor usually paid by the rental company to repair vehicle parts of the type that were damaged and the estimated time for repair.

(ii) The sum of the estimated labor and parts costs determined under paragraphs (1) and (2) to replace the same vehicle parts.

(B) All discounts and price reductions or adjustments that are or will be received by the rental company shall be subtracted from the estimate to the extent not already incorporated in the estimate, or otherwise promptly credited or refunded to the renter.

(4) For the purpose of converting the estimated time for repair into the same units of time in which the rental rate is expressed, a day shall be deemed to consist of eight hours.

(5) Actual charges for towing, storage, and impound fees paid by the rental company.

(6) The administrative charge described in paragraph (6) of subdivision (b) shall not exceed (A) fifty dollars ($50) if the total estimated cost for parts and labor is more than one hundred dollars ($100) up to and including five hundred dollars ($500), (B) one hundred dollars ($100) if the total estimated cost for parts and labor exceeds five hundred dollars ($500) up to and including one thousand five hundred dollars ($1,500), and (C) one hundred fifty dollars ($150) if the total estimated cost for parts and labor exceeds one thousand five hundred dollars ($1,500). An administrative charge shall not be imposed if the total estimated cost of parts and labor is one hundred dollars ($100) or less.

(d)(1) The total amount of an authorized driver's liability to the rental company, if any, for damage occurring during the authorized driver's operation of the rented vehicle shall not exceed the amount of the renter's liability under subdivision (c).

(2) A rental company shall not recover from the renter or other authorized driver an amount exceeding the renter's liability under subdivision (c).

(3) A claim against a renter resulting from damage or loss, excluding loss of use, to a rental vehicle shall be reasonably and rationally related to the actual loss incurred. A rental company shall mitigate damages where possible and shall not assert or collect a claim for physical damage which exceeds the actual costs of the repairs performed or the estimated cost of repairs, if the rental company chooses not to repair the vehicle, including all discounts and price reductions. However, if the vehicle is a total loss vehicle, the claim shall not exceed the total loss vehicle value established in accordance with procedures that are customarily used by insurance companies when paying claims on total loss vehicles, less the proceeds from salvaging the vehicle, if those proceeds are retained by the rental company.

(4) If insurance coverage exists under the renter's applicable personal or business insurance policy and the coverage is confirmed during regular business hours, the renter may require that the rental company submit any claims to the renter's applicable personal or business insurance carrier. The rental company shall not make any written or oral representations that it will not present claims or negotiate with the renter's insurance carrier. For purposes of this paragraph, confirmation of coverage includes telephone confirmation from insurance company representatives during regular business hours. Upon request of the renter and after confirmation of coverage, the amount of claim shall be resolved between the insurance carrier and the rental company. The renter shall remain responsible for payment to the rental car company for any loss sustained that the renter's applicable personal or business insurance policy does not cover.

(5) A rental company shall not recover from the renter or other authorized driver for an item described in subdivision (b) to the extent the rental company obtains recovery from another person.

(6) This section applies only to the maximum liability of a renter or other authorized driver to the rental company resulting from damage to the rented vehicle and not to the liability of another person.

(e)(1) Except as provided in subdivision (f), a damage waiver shall provide or, if not expressly stated in writing, shall be deemed to provide that the renter has no liability for a damage, loss, loss of use, or a cost or expense incident thereto.

(2) Except as provided in subdivision (f), every limitation, exception, or exclusion to a damage waiver is void and unenforceable.

(f) A rental company may provide in the rental contract that a damage waiver does not apply under any of the following circumstances:

(1) Damage or loss results from an authorized driver's (A) intentional, willful, wanton, or reckless conduct, (B) operation of the vehicle under the influence of drugs or alcohol in violation of Section 23152 of the Vehicle Code, (C) towing or pushing anything, or (D) operation of the vehicle on an unpaved road if the damage or loss is a direct result of the road or driving conditions.

(2) Damage or loss occurs while the vehicle is (A) used for commercial hire, (B) used in connection with conduct that could be properly charged as a felony, (C) involved in a speed test or contest or in driver training activity, (D) operated by a person other than an authorized driver, or (E) operated outside the United States.

(3) An authorized driver who has (A) provided fraudulent information to the rental company, or (B) provided false information and the rental company would not have rented the vehicle if it had instead received true information.

(g)(1) A rental company that offers or provides a damage waiver for any consideration in addition to the rental rate shall clearly and conspicuously disclose the following information in the rental contract or holder in which the contract is placed and, also, in signs posted at the place, such as the counter, where the renter signs the rental contract, and, for renters who are enrolled in the rental company's membership program, in a sign that shall be posted in a location clearly visible to those renters as they enter the location where their reserved rental cars are parked or near the exit of the bus or other conveyance that transports the enrollee to a reserved car: (A) the nature of the renter's liability, such as liability for all collision damage regardless of cause, (B) the extent of the renter's liability, such as liability for damage or loss up to a specified amount, (C) the renter's personal insurance policy or the credit card used to pay for the car rental transaction may provide coverage for all or a portion of the renter's potential liability, (D) the renter should consult with his or her insurer to determine the scope of insurance coverage, including the amount of the deductible, if any, for which the renter is obligated, (E) the renter may purchase an optional damage waiver to cover all liability, subject to whatever exceptions the rental company expressly lists that are permitted under subdivision (f), and (F) the range of charges for the damage waiver.

(2) In addition to the requirements of paragraph (1), a rental company that offers or provides a damage waiver shall orally disclose to all renters, except those who are participants in the rental company's membership program, that the damage waiver may be duplicative of coverage that the customer maintains

under his or her own policy of motor vehicle insurance. The renter's receipt of the oral disclosure shall be demonstrated through the renter's acknowledging receipt of the oral disclosure near that part of the contract where the renter indicates, by the renter's own initials, his or her acceptance or declination of the damage waiver. Adjacent to that same part, the contract also shall state that the damage waiver is optional. Further, the contract for these renters shall include a clear and conspicuous written disclosure that the damage waiver may be duplicative of coverage that the customer maintains under his or her own policy of motor vehicle insurance.

(3) The following is an example, for purposes of illustration and not limitation, of a notice fulfilling the requirements of paragraph (1) for a rental company that imposes liability on the renter for collision damage to the full value of the vehicle:

"NOTICE ABOUT YOUR FINANCIAL RESPONSIBILITY AND OPTIONAL DAMAGE WAIVER

You are responsible for all collision damage to the rented vehicle even if someone else caused it or the cause is unknown. You are responsible for the cost of repair up to the value of the vehicle, and towing, storage, and impound fees.

Your own insurance, or the issuer of the credit card you use to pay for the car rental transaction, may cover all or part of your financial responsibility for the rented vehicle. You should check with your insurance company, or credit card issuer, to find out about your coverage and the amount of the deductible, if any, for which you may be liable.

Further, if you use a credit card that provides coverage for your potential liability, you should check with the issuer to determine if you must first exhaust the coverage limits of your own insurance before the credit card coverage applies.

The rental company will not hold you responsible if you buy a damage waiver. But a damage waiver will not protect you if (list exceptions)."

(A) When the above notice is printed in the rental contract or holder in which the contract is placed, the following shall be printed immediately following the notice:

"The cost of an optional damage waiver is $____ for every (day or week)."

(B) When the above notice appears on a sign, the following shall appear immediately adjacent to the notice:

"The cost of an optional damage waiver is $____ to $____ for every (day or week), depending upon the vehicle rented."

(h) Notwithstanding any other provision of law, a rental company may sell a damage waiver subject to the following rate limitations for each full or partial 24–hour rental day for the damage waiver.

(1) For rental vehicles that the rental company designates as an "economy car," "subcompact car," "compact car," or another term having similar meaning when offered for rental, or another vehicle having a manufacturer's suggested retail price of nineteen thousand dollars ($19,000) or less, the rate shall not exceed nine dollars ($9).

(2) For rental vehicles that have a manufacturer's suggested retail price from nineteen thousand one dollars ($19,001) to thirty-four thousand nine hundred ninety-nine dollars ($34,999), inclusive, and that are also either vehicles of next year's model, or not older than the previous year's model, the rate shall not exceed fifteen dollars ($15). For those rental vehicles older than the previous year's model-year, the rate shall not exceed nine dollars ($9).

(i) The manufacturer's suggested retail prices described in subdivision (h) shall be adjusted annually to reflect changes from the previous year in the Consumer Price Index. For the purposes of this section, "Consumer Price Index" means the United States Consumer Price Index for All Urban Consumers, for all items.

(j) A rental company that disseminates in this state an advertisement containing a rental rate shall include in that advertisement a clearly readable statement of the charge for a damage waiver and a statement that a damage waiver is optional.

(k)(1) A rental company shall not require the purchase of a damage waiver, optional insurance, or another optional good or service.

(2) A rental company shall not engage in any unfair, deceptive, or coercive conduct to induce a renter to purchase the damage waiver, optional insurance, or another optional good or service, including conduct such as, but not limited to, refusing to honor the renter's reservation, limiting the availability of vehicles, requiring a deposit, or debiting or blocking the renter's credit card account for a sum equivalent to a deposit if the renter declines to purchase the damage waiver, optional insurance, or another optional good or service.

(*l*)(1) In the absence of express permission granted by the renter subsequent to damage to, or loss of, the vehicle, a rental company shall not seek to recover any portion of a claim arising out of damage to, or loss of, the rented vehicle by processing a credit card charge or causing a debit or block to be placed on the renter's credit card account.

(2) A rental company shall not engage in any unfair, deceptive, or coercive tactics in attempting to recover or in recovering on any claim arising out of damage to, or loss of, the rented vehicle.

(m)(1) A customer facility charge may be collected by a rental company under the following circumstances:

(A) Collection of the fee by the rental company is required by an airport operated by a city, a county, a city and county, a joint powers authority, a special district, or the San Diego County Regional Airport Authority formed pursuant to Division 17 (commencing with Section 170000) of the Public Utilities Code.

(B) The fee is calculated on a per contract basis or as provided in paragraph (2).

(C) The fee is a user fee, not a tax imposed upon real property or an incidence of property ownership under Article XIII D of the California Constitution.

(D) Except as otherwise provided in subparagraph (E), the fee shall be ten dollars ($10) per contract or the amount provided in paragraph (2).

(E) The fee for a consolidated rental car facility shall be collected only from customers of on-airport rental car companies. If the fee imposed by the airport is for both a consolidated rental car facility and a common-use transportation system, the fee collected from customers of on-airport rental car companies shall be ten dollars ($10) or the amount provided in paragraph (2), but the fee imposed on customers of off-airport rental car companies who are transported on the common-use transportation system is proportionate to the costs of the common-use transportation system only. The fee is uniformly applied to each class of on-airport or off-airport customers, provided that the airport requires off-airport customers to use the common-use transportation system. For purposes of this subparagraph, "on-airport rental car company" means a rental company operating under an airport property lease or an airport concession or license agreement whose customers use or will use the consolidated rental car facility and the collection of the fee as to those customers is consistent with subparagraph (C).

(F) Revenues collected from the fee do not exceed the reasonable costs of financing, designing, and constructing the facility and financing, designing, constructing, and operating any common-use transportation system, or acquiring vehicles for use in that system, and shall not be used for any other purpose.

(G) The fee is separately identified on the rental agreement.

(H) This paragraph does not apply to fees which are governed by Section 50474.1 of the Government Code or Section 57.5 of the San Diego Unified Port District Act.

(I) For any airport seeking to require rental car companies to collect an alternative customer facility charge pursuant to paragraph (2), the following provisions apply:

(i) Notwithstanding Section 10231.5 of the Government Code, the airport shall provide reports on an annual basis to the Senate and Assembly Committees on Judiciary detailing all of the following:

(I) The total amount of the customer facility charge collected.

(II) How the funds are being spent.

(III) The amount of and reason for any changes in the airport's budget or financial needs for the facility or common-use transportation system.

(IV) Whether airport concession fees authorized by Section 1936.01 have increased since the prior report, if any.

(ii)(I) The airport shall complete the * * * audit required by subparagraph (B) of paragraph (4) of subdivision (a) prior to initial collection of the customer facility charge * * *. Notwithstanding Section 10231.5 of the Government Code, copies of the audit shall be provided to the Assembly and Senate Committees on Judiciary, the Assembly Committee on Transportation, and the Senate Committee on Transportation and Housing and shall be posted on the airport's Internet Web site.

(II) Prior to any increase pursuant to paragraph (2), * * * the airport shall update the information provided in the initial collection audit pursuant to subclause (I). Notwithstanding Section 10231.5 of the Government Code, copies of the updated audit shall be provided to the Assembly and Senate Committees on Judiciary, the Assembly Committee on Transportation, and the Senate Committee on Transportation and Housing and shall be posted on the airport's Internet Web site.

(III) An audit shall be completed every three years after initial collection * * * only if the customer facility charge is collected for the purpose of operating a common-use transportation system or to acquire vehicles for use in such a system pursuant to clause (ii) of subparagraph (A) of paragraph (4) of subdivision (a). A regularly conducted audit of airport finances that includes the customer facility charge information, that satisfies the requirements of subparagraph (B) of paragraph (4) of subdivision (a), and is produced in accordance with the generally accepted accounting principles of the Government Accounting Standards Board, shall satisfy the requirements of this subclause. This obligation shall continue until the fee authorization becomes inoperative pursuant to subparagraph (C) of paragraph (4) of subdivision (a). Notwithstanding Section 10231.5 of the Government Code, the information reported pursuant to this subclause shall be compiled into one document, shall be provided to the Assembly and Senate Committees on Judiciary, the Assembly Committee on Transportation, and the Senate Committee on Transportation and Housing and shall be posted on the airport's Internet Web site accessible to the public. The information reported shall be contained within one easily accessible page contained within the airport's Internet Web site.

(IV) This section shall not be construed to require an airport to audit a common-use transportation system not financed by a customer facility charge and used for the purposes permitted pursuant to clause (ii) of subparagraph (A) of paragraph (4) of subdivision (a).

(V) The airport shall post on the airport's Internet Web site copies of the completed audits required by this clause for a period of six years following the audit's completion.

(iii) Use of the bonds shall be limited to construction and design of the consolidated rental car facility, terminal modifications, and operating costs of the common-use transportation system, as specified in paragraph (4) of subdivision (a).

(2) Any airport may require rental car companies to collect an alternative customer facility charge under the following conditions:

(A) The airport first conducts a publicly noticed hearing pursuant to the Ralph M. Brown Act (Chapter 9 (commencing with Section 54950) of Part 1 of Division 2 of Title 5 of the Government Code) to review the costs of financing the design and construction of a consolidated rental car facility and the design, construction, and operation of any common-use transportation system in which all of the following occur:

(i) The airport establishes the amount of revenue necessary to finance the reasonable cost to design and construct a consolidated rental car facility and to design, construct, and operate any common-use transportation system, or acquire vehicles for use in that system, based on evidence presented during the hearing.

(ii) The airport finds, based on evidence presented during the hearing, that the fee authorized in paragraph (1) will not generate sufficient revenue to finance the reasonable costs to design and construct a consolidated rental car facility and to design, construct, and operate any common-use transportation system, or acquire vehicles for use in that system.

(iii) The airport finds that the reasonable cost of the project requires the additional amount of revenue that would be generated by the proposed daily rate, including any rate increase, authorized pursuant to this paragraph.

(iv) The airport outlines each of the following:

(I) Steps it has taken to limit costs.

(II) Other potential alternatives for meeting its revenue needs other than the collection of the fee.

(III) The extent to which rental car companies or other businesses or individuals using the facility or common-use transportation system will pay for the costs associated with these facilities and systems other than the fee from rental customers.

(B) The airport may not require the fee authorized in this paragraph to be collected at any time that the fee authorized in paragraph (1) of this subdivision is being collected.

(C) Pursuant to the procedure set forth in this subdivision, the fee may be collected at a rate charged on a per-day basis subject to the following conditions:

(i) Commencing January 1, 2011, the amount of the fee may not exceed six dollars ($6) per day.

(ii) Commencing January 1, 2014, the amount of the fee may not exceed seven dollars and fifty cents ($7.50) per day.

(iii) Commencing January 1, 2017, and thereafter, the amount of the fee may not exceed nine dollars ($9) per day.

(iv) At no time shall the fee authorized in this paragraph be collected from any customer for more than five days for each individual rental car contract.

(v) An airport subject to this paragraph shall initiate the process for obtaining the authority to require or increase the alternative fee no later than January 1, 2018. Any airport that obtains the authority to require or increase an alternative fee shall be authorized to continue collecting that fee until the fee authorization becomes inoperative pursuant to subparagraph (C) of paragraph (4) of subdivision (a).

(3) Notwithstanding any other provision of law, including, but not limited to, Part 1 (commencing with Section 6001) to Part 1.7 (commencing with Section 7280), inclusive, of Division 2 of the Revenue and Taxation Code, the fees collected pursuant to this section, or another law whereby a local agency operating an airport requires a rental car company to collect a facility financing fee from its customers, are not subject to sales, use, or transaction taxes.

(n)(1) A rental company shall only advertise, quote, and charge a rental rate that includes the entire amount except taxes, a customer facility charge, if any, and a mileage charge, if any, that a renter must pay to hire or lease the vehicle for the period of time to which the rental rate applies. A rental company shall not charge in addition to the rental rate, taxes, a customer facility charge, if any, and a mileage charge, if any, any fee that is required to be paid by the renter as a condition of hiring or leasing the vehicle, including, but not limited to, required fuel or airport surcharges other than customer facility charges, nor a fee for transporting the renter to the location where the rented vehicle will be delivered to the renter.

(2) In addition to the rental rate, taxes, customer facility charges, if any, and mileage charges, if any, a rental company may charge for an item or service provided in connection with a particular rental transaction if the renter could have avoided incurring the charge by choosing not to obtain or utilize the optional item or service. Items and services for which the rental company may impose an additional charge include, but are not limited to, optional insurance and accessories requested by the renter, service charges incident to the renter's optional return of the vehicle to a location other than the location where the vehicle was hired or leased, and charges for refueling the vehicle at the conclusion of the rental transaction in the event the renter did not return the vehicle with as much fuel as was in the fuel tank at the beginning of the rental. A rental company also may impose an additional charge based on reasonable age criteria established by the rental company.

(3) A rental company shall not charge a fee for authorized drivers in addition to the rental charge for an individual renter.

(4) If a rental company states a rental rate in print advertisement or in a telephonic, in-person, or computer-transmitted quotation, the rental company shall disclose clearly in that advertisement or quotation the terms of mileage conditions relating to the advertised or quoted rental rate, including, but not limited to, to the extent applicable, the amount of mileage and gas charges, the number of miles for which no charges will be imposed, and a description of geographic driving limitations within the United States and Canada.

(5)(A) When a rental rate is stated in an advertisement, quotation, or reservation in connection with a car rental at an airport where a customer facility charge is imposed, the rental company shall disclose clearly the existence and amount of the customer facility charge. For purposes of this subparagraph, advertisements include radio, television, other electronic media, and print advertisements. For purposes of this subparagraph, quotations and reservations include those that are telephonic, in-person, and computer-transmitted. If the rate advertisement is intended to include transactions at more than one airport imposing a customer facility charge, a range of fees may be stated in the advertisement. However, all rate advertisements that include car rentals at airport destinations shall clearly and conspicuously include a toll-free telephone number whereby a customer can be told the specific amount of the customer facility charge to which the customer will be obligated.

(B) If a person or entity other than a rental car company, including a passenger carrier or a seller of travel services, advertises or quotes a rate for a car rental at an airport where a customer facility charge is imposed, that person or entity shall,

provided that he, she, or it is provided with information about the existence and amount of the fee, to the extent not specifically prohibited by federal law, clearly disclose the existence and amount of the fee in any telephonic, in-person, or computer-transmitted quotation at the time of making an initial quotation of a rental rate and at the time of making a reservation of a rental car. If a rental car company provides the person or entity with rate and customer facility charge information, the rental car company is not responsible for the failure of that person or entity to comply with this subparagraph when quoting or confirming a rate to a third person or entity.

(6) If a rental company delivers a vehicle to a renter at a location other than the location where the rental company normally carries on its business, the rental company shall not charge the renter an amount for the rental for the period before the delivery of the vehicle. If a rental company picks up a rented vehicle from a renter at a location other than the location where the rental company normally carries on its business, the rental company shall not charge the renter an amount for the rental for the period after the renter notifies the rental company to pick up the vehicle.

(o) A rental company shall not use, access, or obtain any information relating to the renter's use of the rental vehicle that was obtained using electronic surveillance technology, except in the following circumstances:

(1)(A) When the equipment is used by the rental company only for the purpose of locating a stolen, abandoned, or missing rental vehicle after one of the following:

(i) The renter or law enforcement has informed the rental company that the vehicle is missing or has been stolen or abandoned.

(ii) The rental vehicle has not been returned following one week after the contracted return date, or by one week following the end of an extension of that return date.

(iii) The rental company discovers the rental vehicle has been stolen or abandoned, and, if stolen, it shall report the vehicle stolen to law enforcement by filing a stolen vehicle report, unless law enforcement has already informed the rental company that the vehicle is missing or has been stolen or abandoned.

(B) If electronic surveillance technology is activated pursuant to subparagraph (A), a rental company shall maintain a record, in either electronic or written form, of information relevant to the activation of that technology. That information shall include the rental agreement, including the return date, and the date and time the electronic surveillance technology was activated. The record shall also include, if relevant, a record of written or other communication with the renter, including communications regarding extensions of the rental, police reports, or other written communication with law enforcement officials. The record shall be maintained for a period of at least 12 months from the time the record is created and shall be made available upon the renter's request. The rental company shall maintain and furnish explanatory codes necessary to read the record. A rental company shall not be required to maintain a record if electronic surveillance technology is activated to recover a rental vehicle that is stolen or missing at a time other than during a rental period.

(2) In response to a specific request from law enforcement pursuant to a subpoena or search warrant.

(3) This subdivision does not prohibit a rental company from equipping rental vehicles with GPS–based technology that provides navigation assistance to the occupants of the rental vehicle, if the rental company does not use, access, or obtain information relating to the renter's use of the rental vehicle that was obtained using that technology, except for the purposes of discovering or

repairing a defect in the technology and the information may then be used only for that purpose.

(4) This subdivision does not prohibit a rental company from equipping rental vehicles with electronic surveillance technology that allows for the remote locking or unlocking of the vehicle at the request of the renter, if the rental company does not use, access, or obtain information relating to the renter's use of the rental vehicle that was obtained using that technology, except as necessary to lock or unlock the vehicle.

(5) This subdivision does not prohibit a rental company from equipping rental vehicles with electronic surveillance technology that allows the company to provide roadside assistance, such as towing, flat tire, or fuel services, at the request of the renter, if the rental company does not use, access, or obtain information relating to the renter's use of the rental vehicle that was obtained using that technology except as necessary to provide the requested roadside assistance.

(6) This subdivision does not prohibit a rental company from obtaining, accessing, or using information from electronic surveillance technology for the sole purpose of determining the date and time the vehicle is returned to the rental company, and the total mileage driven and the vehicle fuel level of the returned vehicle. This paragraph, however, shall apply only after the renter has returned the vehicle to the rental company, and the information shall only be used for the purpose described in this paragraph.

(p) A rental company shall not use electronic surveillance technology to track a renter in order to impose fines or surcharges relating to the renter's use of the rental vehicle.

(q) A renter may bring an action against a rental company for the recovery of damages and appropriate equitable relief for a violation of this section. The prevailing party shall be entitled to recover reasonable attorney's fees and costs.

(r) A rental company that brings an action against a renter for loss due to theft of the vehicle shall bring the action in the county in which the renter resides or, if the renter is not a resident of this state, in the jurisdiction in which the renter resides.

(s) A waiver of any of the provisions of this section shall be void and unenforceable as contrary to public policy.

(t)(1) A rental company's disclosure requirements shall be satisfied for renters who are enrolled in the rental company's membership program if all of the following conditions are met:

(A) Prior to the enrollee's first rental as a participant in the program, the renter receives, in writing, the following:

(i) All of the disclosures required by paragraph (1) of subdivision (g), including the terms and conditions of the rental agreement then in effect.

(ii) An Internet Web site address, as well as a contact number or address, where the enrollee can learn of changes to the rental agreement or to the laws of this state governing rental agreements since the effective date of the rental company's most recent restatement of the rental agreement and distribution of that restatement to its members.

(B) At the commencement of each rental period, the renter is provided, on the rental record or the folder in which it is inserted, with a printed notice stating that he or she had either previously selected or declined an optional damage waiver and that the renter has the right to change preferences.

(C) At the commencement of each rental period, the rental company provides, on the rearview mirror, a hanger on which a statement is printed, in a box, in at least 12–point boldface type, notifying the renter that the collision damage waiver offered by the rental company may be duplicative of coverage that the customer maintains under his or her own policy of motor vehicle

insurance. If it is not feasible to hang the statement from the rearview mirror, it shall be hung from the steering wheel.

The hanger shall provide the renter a box to initial if he or she (not his or her employer) has previously accepted or declined the collision damage waiver and that he or she now wishes to change his or her decision to accept or decline the collision damage waiver, as follows:

"☐ If I previously accepted the collision damage waiver, I now decline it.

☐ If I previously declined the collision damage waiver, I now accept it."

The hanger shall also provide a box for the enrollee to indicate whether this change applies to this rental transaction only or to all future rental transactions. The hanger shall also notify the renter that he or she may make that change, prior to leaving the lot, by returning the form to an employee designated to receive the form who is present at the lot where the renter takes possession of the car, to receive any change in the rental agreement from the renter.

(2)(A) This subdivision is not effective unless the employee designated pursuant to subparagraph (E) of paragraph (8) of subdivision (a) is actually present at the required location.

(B) This subdivision does not relieve the rental company from the disclosures required to be made within the text of a contract or holder in which the contract is placed; in or on an advertisement containing a rental rate; or in a telephonic, in-person, or computer-transmitted quotation or reservation.

(u) The amendments made to this section during the 2001–02 Regular Session of the Legislature do not affect litigation pending on or before January 1, 2003, alleging a violation of Section 22325 of the Business and Professions Code as it read at the time the action was commenced.

(v) This section shall become operative on January 1, 2015. *(Added by Stats.2011, c. 531 (A.B.621), § 2, operative Jan. 1, 2015. Amended by Stats.2012, c. 32 (S.B.1006), § 3, eff. June 27, 2012, operative Jan. 1, 2015; Stats.2013, c. 549 (A.B.359), § 2, operative Jan. 1, 2015.)*

Research References

Rutter, Cal. Practice Guide: Insurance Litigation Ch. 1-A, A. Insurance-In General.

Miller and Starr California Real Estate § 20:5, The Unruh Civil Rights Act--Age Discrimination.

13 Witkin, California Summary 10th Equity § 116, Rental Car Company Practices.

13 Witkin, California Summary 10th Equity § 121, Rental Car Company Practices.

§ 1936.01. Vehicle rentals; advertised rates; quoted or stated rates; actions against rental company for violation; waiver

(a) For the purpose of this section, the following definitions shall apply:

(1) "Airport concession fee" means a charge collected by a rental company from a renter that is the renter's proportionate share of the amount paid by the rental company to the owner or operator of an airport for the right or privilege of conducting a vehicle rental business on the airport's premises.

(2) "Quote" means an estimated cost of rental provided by a rental company or a third party to a potential customer by telephone, in-person, computer-transmission, or other means, that is based on information provided by the potential customer and used to generate an estimated cost of rental, including, but not limited to, any of the following: potential dates of rental, locations, or classes of car.

(3) "Tourism commission assessment" means the charge collected by a rental company from a renter that has been

established by the California Travel and Tourism Commission pursuant to Section 13995.65 of the Government Code.

(b) Notwithstanding subdivision (n) of Section 1936, the following provisions shall apply:

(1) A rental company shall only advertise a rental rate that includes the entire amount, except taxes, a customer facility charge, if any, and a mileage charge, if any, that a renter must pay to hire or lease the vehicle for the period of time to which the rental rate applies.

(2) When providing a quote, or imposing charges for a rental, the rental company may separately state the rental rate, taxes, customer facility charge, if any, airport concession fee, if any, tourism commission assessment, if any, and a mileage charge, if any, that a renter must pay to hire or lease the vehicle for the period of time to which the rental rate applies. A rental company may not charge in addition to the rental rate, taxes, a customer facility charge, if any, airport concession fee, if any, tourism commission assessment, if any, and a mileage charge, if any, any fee that must be paid by the renter as a condition of hiring or leasing the vehicle, such as, but not limited to, required fuel or airport surcharges other than customer facility charges and airport concession fees.

(3) If customer facility charges, airport concession fees, or tourism commission assessments are imposed, the rental company shall do each of the following:

(A) At the time the quote is given, provide the person receiving the quote with a good faith estimate of the rental rate, taxes, customer facility charge, if any, airport concession fee, if any, and tourism commission assessment, if any, as well as the total charges for the entire rental. The total charges, if provided on an Internet Web site, shall be displayed in a typeface at least as large as any rental rate disclosed on that page and shall be provided on a page that the person receiving the quote may reach by following links through no more than two Internet Web site pages, including the page on which the rental rate is first provided. The good faith estimate may exclude mileage charges and charges for optional items that cannot be determined prior to completing the reservation based upon the information provided by the person.

(B) At the time and place the rental commences, clearly and conspicuously disclose in the rental contract, or that portion of the contract that is provided to the renter, the total of the rental rate, taxes, customer facility charge, if any, airport concession fee, if any, and tourism commission assessment, if any, for the entire rental, exclusive of charges that cannot be determined at the time the rental commences. Charges imposed pursuant to this subparagraph shall be no more than the amount of the quote provided in a confirmed reservation, unless the person changes the terms of the rental contract subsequent to making the reservation.

(C) Provide each person, other than those persons within the rental company, offering quotes to actual or prospective customers access to information about customer facility charges, airport concession fees, and tourism commission assessments as well as access to information about when those charges apply. Any person providing quotes to actual or prospective customers for the hire or lease of a vehicle from a rental company shall provide the quotes in the manner described in subparagraph (A).

(4) In addition to the rental rate, taxes, customer facility charges, if any, airport concession fees, if any, tourism commission assessments, if any, and mileage charges, if any, a rental company may charge for an item or service provided in connection with a particular rental transaction if the renter could have avoided incurring the charge by choosing not to obtain or utilize the optional item or service. Items and services for which the rental company may impose an additional charge, include,

but are not limited to, optional insurance and accessories requested by the renter, service charges incident to the renter's optional return of the vehicle to a location other than the location where the vehicle was hired or leased, and charges for refueling the vehicle at the conclusion of the rental transaction in the event the renter did not return the vehicle with as much fuel as was in the fuel tank at the beginning of the rental. A rental company also may impose an additional charge based on reasonable age criteria established by the rental company.

(5) A rental company may not charge any fee for authorized drivers in addition to the rental charge for an individual renter.

(6) If a rental company states a rental rate in print advertisement or in a telephonic, in-person, or computer-transmitted quote, the rental company shall clearly disclose in that advertisement or quote the terms of any mileage conditions relating to the rental rate disclosed in the advertisement or quote, including, but not limited to, to the extent applicable, the amount of mileage and gas charges, the number of miles for which no charges will be imposed, and a description of geographic driving limitations within the United States and Canada.

(7)(A) When a rental rate is stated in an advertisement, in connection with a car rental at an airport where a customer facility charge is imposed, the rental company shall clearly disclose the existence and amount of the customer facility charge. For the purposes of this subparagraph, advertisements include radio, television, other electronic media, and print advertisements. If the rental rate advertisement is intended to include transactions at more than one airport imposing a customer facility charge, a range of charges may be stated in the advertisement. However, all rental rate advertisements that include car rentals at airport destinations shall clearly and conspicuously include a toll-free telephone number whereby a customer can be told the specific amount of the customer facility charge to which the customer will be obligated.

(B) If any person or entity other than a rental car company, including a passenger carrier or a seller of travel services, advertises a rental rate for a car rental at an airport where a customer facility charge is imposed, that person or entity shall, provided they are provided with information about the existence and amount of the charge, to the extent not specifically prohibited by federal law, clearly disclose the existence and amount of the charge. If a rental car company provides the person or entity with rental rate and customer facility charge information, the rental car company is not responsible for the failure of that person or entity to comply with this subparagraph.

(8) If a rental company delivers a vehicle to a renter at a location other than the location where the rental company normally carries on its business, the rental company may not charge the renter any amount for the rental for the period before the delivery of the vehicle. If a rental company picks up a rented vehicle from a renter at a location other than the location where the rental company normally carries on its business, the rental company may not charge the renter any amount for the rental for the period after the renter notifies the rental company to pick up the vehicle.

(9) Except as otherwise permitted pursuant to the customer facility charge, a rental company may not separately charge, in addition to the rental rate, a fee for transporting the renter to the location where the rented vehicle will be delivered to the renter.

(c) A renter may bring an action against a rental company for the recovery of damages and appropriate equitable relief for a violation of this section. The prevailing party shall be entitled to recover reasonable attorney's fees and costs.

(d) Any waiver of any of the provisions of this section shall be void and unenforceable as contrary to public policy.

(e) This section shall become operative only if the Secretary of Business, Transportation and Housing provides notice to the Legislature and the Secretary of State and posts notice on its Internet Web site that the conditions described in Section 13995.92 of the Government Code have been satisfied. *(Added by Stats.2006, c. 790 (A.B.2592), § 1.)*

§ 1936.015. Vehicle license fee; definitions; advertisement of vehicle rental rate, quotes and contracts; permitted fees and charges

(a) For the purposes of this section, the following definitions shall apply:

(1) "Vehicle license fee" has the same meaning as in Sections 10751 and 10752 of the Revenue and Taxation Code, as that fee existed on January 1, 2009.

(2) "Increased vehicle license fee" means the amount of the fee increase in the vehicle license fee above 0.65 percent of the value of the vehicle.

(3) "Increased vehicle license recovery fee" means a charge that seeks to recover the amount of increased vehicle license fees actually paid by a rental company for the particular class of vehicle being rented. The increased vehicle license recovery fee shall be calculated as provided in paragraph (1) of subdivision (b).

(b) Notwithstanding subdivision (n) of Section 1936 or subdivision (b) of Section 1936.01, upon an increase of the vehicle license fee above 0.65 percent of the value of the vehicle pursuant to legislation enacted with the Budget Act of 2009, the following provisions shall apply with respect to the increased vehicle license fee:

(1) A rental company shall calculate the amount of the increased vehicle license recovery fee in the following manner:

(A) The initial calculation required by this section shall be made as of August 21, 2009, and shall include the three-month period of May 21, 2009, to August 21, 2009, inclusive. Subsequent calculations shall be made every three months thereafter.

(B) The rental company shall determine the total amount of the increased vehicle license fee actually paid during the twelve months preceding the calculation date, for each particular class of vehicle being rented.

(C) The total amount of increased vehicle license fee actually paid for each class of vehicle shall be divided by the number of vehicles in the class, to determine the average increased vehicle license fee for each class.

(D) The average increased vehicle license fee for vehicles in each class shall be prorated at one three-hundred-and-sixty-fifth, to determine the daily increased vehicle license recovery fee for vehicles in each particular class of vehicle, to be charged for each full or partial 24–hour rental day that the vehicle is rented.

(2) As of November 21, 2009, and annually as of each November 21 thereafter, a rental company shall reconcile the amount of increased vehicle license fees actually paid by the rental company during the preceding 12 months for each class of vehicle and the amount of increased vehicle license recovery fees charged to customers during that same 12–month period for rental of vehicles in those classes. The rental company shall post that information on its Internet Web site by December 31 of each year.

(3) The total of all increased vehicle license fees charged to customers by the rental company for each class of vehicle shall not exceed the total of increased vehicle license recovery fees actually paid for vehicles in those classes on an annual basis.

(4) A rental company shall only advertise a rental rate that includes the entire amount, except taxes, the increased vehicle license recovery fee, a customer facility charge, if any, and a mileage charge, if any, that a renter must pay to hire or lease the vehicle for the period of time to which the rental rate applies.

(5) When providing a quote, or imposing charges for a rental, the rental company may separately state the rental rate, taxes, the increased vehicle license recovery fee, customer facility charge, if any, airport concession fee, if any, tourism commission assessment, if any, and a mileage charge, if any, that a renter must pay to hire or lease the vehicle for the period of time to which the rental rate applies. A rental company may not charge in addition to the rental rate, taxes, the increased vehicle license recovery fee, a customer facility charge, if any, airport concession fee, if any, tourism commission assessment, if any, and a mileage charge, if any, any fee that must be paid by the renter as a condition of hiring or leasing the vehicle, such as, but not limited to, required fuel or airport surcharges other than customer facility charges and airport concession fees.

(6) If customer facility charges, airport concession fees, or tourism commission assessments are imposed, the rental company shall do each of the following:

(A) At the time the quote is given, provide the person receiving the quote with a good faith estimate of the rental rate, taxes, the increased vehicle license recovery fee, customer facility charge, if any, airport concession fee, if any, and tourism commission assessment, if any, as well as the total charges for the entire rental. The total charges, if provided on an Internet Web site, shall be displayed in a typeface at least as large as any rental rate disclosed on that page and shall be provided on a page that the person receiving the quote may reach by following links through no more than two Internet Web site pages, including the page on which the rental rate is first provided. The good faith estimate may exclude mileage charges and charges for optional items that cannot be determined prior to completing the reservation based upon the information provided by the person.

(B) At the time and place the rental commences, clearly and conspicuously disclose in the rental contract, or that portion of the contract that is provided to the renter, the total of the rental rate, taxes, the increased vehicle license recovery fee, customer facility charge, if any, airport concession fee, if any, and tourism commission assessment, if any, for the entire rental, exclusive of charges that cannot be determined at the time the rental commences. Charges imposed pursuant to this subparagraph shall be no more than the amount of the quote provided in a confirmed reservation, unless the person changes the terms of the rental contract subsequent to making the reservation.

(C) Provide each person, other than those persons within the rental company, offering quotes to actual or prospective customers access to information about the increased vehicle license recovery fee, customer facility charges, airport concession fees, and tourism commission assessments as well as access to information about when those charges apply. Any person providing quotes to actual or prospective customers for the hire or lease of a vehicle from a rental company shall provide the quotes in the manner described in subparagraph (A).

(7) In addition to the rental rate, taxes, the increased vehicle license recovery fee, customer facility charges, if any, airport concession fees, if any, tourism commission assessments, if any, and mileage charges, if any, a rental company may charge for an item or service provided in connection with a particular rental transaction if the renter could have avoided incurring the charge by choosing not to obtain or utilize the optional item or service. Items and services for which the rental company may impose an additional charge, include, but are not limited to, optional insurance and accessories requested by the renter, service charges incident to the renter's optional return of the vehicle to a location other than the location where the vehicle was hired or leased, and charges for refueling the vehicle at the conclusion of

the rental transaction in the event the renter did not return the vehicle with as much fuel as was in the fuel tank at the beginning of the rental. A rental company also may impose an additional charge based on reasonable age criteria established by the rental company.

(8) A rental company may not charge any fee for authorized drivers in addition to the rental charge for an individual renter.

(9) If a rental company states a rental rate in print advertisement or in a telephonic, in-person, or computer-transmitted quote, the rental company shall clearly disclose in that advertisement or quote the terms of any mileage conditions relating to the rental rate disclosed in the advertisement or quote, including, but not limited to, to the extent applicable, the amount of mileage and gas charges, the number of miles for which no charges will be imposed, and a description of geographic driving limitations within the United States and Canada.

(10)(A) When a rental rate is stated in an advertisement, in connection with a car rental at an airport where a customer facility charge is imposed, the rental company shall clearly disclose the existence and amount of the customer facility charge. For the purposes of this subparagraph, advertisements include radio, television, other electronic media, and print advertisements. If the rental rate advertisement is intended to include transactions at more than one airport imposing a customer facility charge, a range of charges may be stated in the advertisement. However, all rental rate advertisements that include car rentals at airport destinations shall clearly and conspicuously include a toll-free telephone number whereby a customer can be told the specific amount of the customer facility charge to which the customer will be obligated.

(B) If any person or entity other than a rental company, including a passenger carrier or a seller of travel services, advertises a rental rate for a car rental at an airport where a customer facility charge is imposed, that person or entity shall, provided they are provided with information about the existence and amount of the charge, to the extent not specifically prohibited by federal law, clearly disclose the existence and amount of the charge. If a rental company provides the person or entity with rental rate and customer facility charge information, the rental company is not responsible for the failure of that person or entity to comply with this subparagraph.

(11) If a rental company delivers a vehicle to a renter at a location other than the location where the rental company normally carries on its business, the rental company may not charge the renter any amount for the rental for the period before the delivery of the vehicle. If a rental company picks up a rented vehicle from a renter at a location other than the location where the rental company normally carries on its business, the rental company may not charge the renter any amount for the rental for the period after the renter notifies the rental company to pick up the vehicle.

(12) Except as otherwise permitted pursuant to the customer facility charge, a rental company may not separately charge, in addition to the rental rate, a fee for transporting the renter to the location where the rented vehicle will be delivered to the renter.

(c) A renter may bring an action against a rental company for the recovery of damages and appropriate equitable relief for a violation of this section. The prevailing party shall be entitled to recover reasonable attorney's fees and costs.

(d) Any waiver of any of the provisions of this section shall be void and unenforceable as contrary to public policy.

(e)(1) This section shall become operative only if Senate Bill 3 or Assembly Bill 3 [1] of the 2009–10 Third Extraordinary Session of the Legislature is enacted and increases the vehicle license fee above 0.65 percent of the value of the vehicle and shall cease to become operative 12 months after the restoration of the vehicle license fee to no more than 0.65 percent of the value of the vehicle.

(2) Provisions of this section relating to the disclosure and separately stated charges for a customer facility charge or an airport concession fee shall remain operative so long as the Secretary of Business, Transportation and Housing provides notice to the Legislature and the Secretary of State and posts notice on its Internet Web site that the conditions described in Section 13995.92 of the Government Code have been satisfied. *(Added by Stats.2009–2010, 2nd Ex.Sess., c. 8 (S.B.10), § 1, eff. May 21, 2009. Amended by Stats.2009, c. 156 (S.B.348), § 1, eff. Aug. 21, 2009.)*

1 Stats.2009–2010, 3rd Ex.Sess., c. 18 (A.B.3), eff. Feb. 20, 2009.

Operative Effect

For operative effect of this section, see its terms.

§ 1936.05. Vehicle rental agreements; qualified business rentals

(a) For purposes of this section:

(1) "Additional charges" means charges other than a per period base rental rate established by the business program.

(2) "Business program" means (A) a contract between a rental company and a business program sponsor that has established the per period base rental rate, and any other material terms relating to additional charges, on which the rental company will rent passenger vehicles to persons authorized by the sponsor, or (B) a plan, program, or other arrangement established by a rental company at the request of, or with the consent of, a business program sponsor under which the rental company offers to rent passenger vehicles to persons authorized by the sponsor at per period base rental rates, and any other material terms relating to additional charges, that are not the same as those generally offered by the rental company to the public.

(3) "Business program sponsor" means a legal entity, other than a natural person, that is a corporation, limited liability company, or partnership.

(4) "Business renter" means, for any business program sponsor, a person who is authorized by the sponsor, through the use of an identifying number or program name or code, to enter into a rental contract under the sponsor's business program. In no case shall the term "business renter" include a person renting as: (A) a nonemployee member of a not-for-profit organization, (B) the purchaser of a voucher or other prepaid rental arrangement from a person, including a tour operator, engaged in the business of reselling those vouchers or prepaid rental arrangements to the general public, (C) an individual whose car rental is eligible for reimbursement in whole or in part as a result of the person being insured or provided coverage under a policy of insurance issued by an insurance company, or (D) an individual whose car rental is eligible for reimbursement in whole or in part as a result of the person purchasing passenger vehicle repair services from a person licensed to perform such services.

(5) "Qualified business rental" under a business program established for a business program sponsor by a rental company means the rental of a passenger vehicle under the business program if either (A) in the 12–month period ending on the date of the rental or in the calendar year immediately preceding the year in which the rental occurs, the rentals under all business programs established by the rental company for the business program sponsor and its affiliates produced gross rental revenues in excess of twenty-five thousand dollars ($25,000) or (B) the rental company in good faith estimates that rentals under all the business programs established by the rental company for the

business program sponsor and its affiliates will produce gross rental revenues in excess of twenty-five thousand dollars ($25,-000) in the 12–month period commencing with the date of the rental or in the calendar year in which the rental occurs. The rental company has the burden of establishing by objectively verifiable evidence that the rental was a qualified business rental.

(6) "Quote" means telephonic, in-person, and computer-transmitted quotations.

(b) Notwithstanding any provision to the contrary contained in paragraph (1) of subdivision (n) of Section 1936, a rental car company may, in connection with the qualified business rental of a passenger vehicle to a business renter of a business program sponsor under the sponsor's business program, do both of the following:

(1) Separately quote additional charges for the rental if, at the time the quote is provided, the person receiving the quote is also provided a good faith estimate of the total of all the charges for the entire rental. The estimate may exclude mileage charges and charges for optional items and services that cannot be determined prior to completing the reservation based upon the information provided by the renter.

(2) Separately impose additional charges for the rental, if the rental contract, or another document provided to the business renter at the time and place the rental commences, clearly and conspicuously discloses the total of all the charges for the entire rental, exclusive of charges that cannot be determined at the time the rental commences.

(c) A renter may bring an action against a rental company for the recovery of damages and appropriate equitable relief for a violation of this section. The prevailing party shall be entitled to recover reasonable attorney's fees and costs.

(d) Any waiver of any of the provisions of this section shall be void and unenforceable as contrary to public policy.

(e) Nothing in this section shall be interpreted to mean that a rental company is not required to comply with the requirements of paragraphs (2) to (6), inclusive, of subdivision (n) of Section 1936. *(Added by Stats.2004, c. 536 (A.B.2761), § 1.)*

§ 1936.1.   15–passenger vans; renter documentation

(a)(1) A rental company shall provide a renter of a 15–passenger van with a copy of the United States Department of Transportation, National Highway Traffic Safety Administration's consumer advisory for 15–passenger vans titled "Reducing the Risk of Rollover Crashes" or, if that advisory is updated, a copy of the updated advisory. The renter shall acknowledge receipt of that copy by signing an acknowledgment of receipt on the rental agreement or on an attached form.

(2) If the rental of that 15–passenger van is for a business purpose or use, the rental company shall also provide on the document described in paragraph (1) that only an employee with the proper licensing may drive that vehicle. The renter shall acknowledge the receipt thereof in the same manner as described in paragraph (1).

(b)(1) Except as provided in paragraph (2), for purposes of this section, a "15–passenger van" means any van manufactured to accommodate 15 passengers, including the driver, regardless of whether that van has been altered to accommodate fewer than 15 passengers.

(2) For purposes of this section, a "15–passenger van" does not mean a 15–passenger van with dual rear wheels that has a gross weight rating equal to, or greater than, 11,500 pounds. *(Added by Stats.2004, c. 883 (A.B.2503), § 1.)*

§ 1936.5.   Rental company not subject to specified vehicle rental requirements; conditions

Section added by Stats.2012, c. 406 (A.B.2659), § 1. See, also, another section of the same number added by Stats.2012, c. 862 (A.B.2189), § 1.

A "rental company" as defined in paragraph (1) of subdivision (a) of Section 1936 is not subject to the requirements of Section 14608 of the Vehicle Code if the rental is subject to the terms of a membership agreement that allows the renter to gain physical access to a car without a key through use of a code, use of a key card, or by other means that allow the car to be accessed at a remote location, or at a business location of the rental company outside of that location's regular hours of operation. *(Added by Stats.2012, c. 406 (A.B.2659), § 1.)*

§ 1936.5.   Rental company not subject to specified vehicle rental requirements; conditions

Section added by Stats.2012, c. 862 (A.B.2189), § 1. See, also, another section of the same number added by Stats.2012, c. 406 (A.B.2659), § 1.

A "rental company" as defined in paragraph (1) of subdivision (a) of Section 1936 is not subject to the requirements of Section 14608 of the Vehicle Code if the rental is subject to the terms of a membership agreement that allows the renter to gain physical access to a car without a key through use of a code, key card, or by other means that allow the car to be accessed at a remote location, or at a business location of the rental company outside of that location's regular hours of operation. *(Added by Stats.2012, c. 862 (A.B.2189), § 1.)*

§ 1938.   Commercial property lease form or rental agreement; statement regarding Certified Access Specialist (CASp) inspection and construction-related accessibility standards

A commercial property owner or lessor shall state on every lease form or rental agreement executed on or after July 1, 2013, whether the property being leased or rented has undergone inspection by a Certified Access Specialist (CASp), and, if so, whether the property has or has not been determined to meet all applicable construction-related accessibility standards pursuant to Section 55.53. *(Added by Stats.2012, c. 383 (S.B.1186), § 12, eff. Sept. 19, 2012.)*

CHAPTER 2.   HIRING OF REAL PROPERTY

Section

1954.1.   Assignment for the benefit of creditors; right of assignee to occupy business premises; payment of rent; time.

§ 1940. Application of chapter; "persons who hire" and "dwelling unit"

(a) Except as provided in subdivision (b), this chapter shall apply to all persons who hire dwelling units located within this state including tenants, lessees, boarders, lodgers, and others, however denominated.

(b) The term "persons who hire" shall not include a person who maintains either of the following:

(1) Transient occupancy in a hotel, motel, residence club, or other facility when the transient occupancy is or would be subject to tax under Section 7280 of the Revenue and Taxation Code. The term "persons who hire" shall not include a person to whom this paragraph pertains if the person has not made valid payment for all room and other related charges owing as of the last day on which his or her occupancy is or would be subject to tax under Section 7280 of the Revenue and Taxation Code.

(2) Occupancy at a hotel or motel where the innkeeper retains a right of access to and control of the dwelling unit and the hotel or motel provides or offers all of the following services to all of the residents:

(A) Facilities for the safeguarding of personal property pursuant to Section 1860.

(B) Central telephone service subject to tariffs covering the same filed with the California Public Utilities Commission.

(C) Maid, mail, and room services.

(D) Occupancy for periods of less than seven days.

(E) Food service provided by a food establishment, as defined in Section 113780 of the Health and Safety Code, located on or adjacent to the premises of the hotel or motel and owned or operated by the innkeeper or owned or operated by a person or entity pursuant to a lease or similar relationship with the innkeeper or person or entity affiliated with the innkeeper.

(c) "Dwelling unit" means a structure or the part of a structure that is used as a home, residence, or sleeping place by one person who maintains a household or by two or more persons who maintain a common household.

(d) Nothing in this section shall be construed to limit the application of any provision of this chapter to tenancy in a dwelling unit unless the provision is so limited by its specific terms. *(Added by Stats.1976, c. 712, p. 1727, § 1. Amended by Stats.1994, c. 680 (S.B.2088), § 1; Stats.1996, c. 1023 (S.B.1497), § 28, eff. Sept. 29, 1996.)*

Research References

Rutter, Cal. Practice Guide: Real Prop. Transactions Ch. 2-B, B. Licensing and Regulatory Requirements.

Miller and Starr California Real Estate § 19:6, Other Interests Distinguished--Occupation by a Guest or Lodger.

Miller and Starr California Real Estate § 19:7, Other Interests Distinguished--Eviction of a Guest or Lodger.

Miller and Starr California Real Estate § 19:156, Covenant of Quiet Enjoyment and Possession.

Miller and Starr California Real Estate § 19:157, Covenant of Quiet Enjoyment and Possession--Wrongful Actual or Constructive Eviction.

Miller and Starr California Real Estate § 19:162, Elements of the Offense--Forcible Entry.

Miller and Starr California Real Estate § 19:188, Notice Required by Statute.

12 Witkin, California Summary 10th Real Property § 503, Statutory Framework.

12 Witkin, California Summary 10th Real Property § 514, Statutory Rights of Lodger.

12 Witkin, California Summary 10th Real Property § 599, Other Acts and Powers of Entity Are Not Affected.

12 Witkin, California Summary 10th Real Property § 610, (S 610) Actual Eviction.

12 Witkin, California Summary 10th Real Property § 615, Expanded Statute.

12 Witkin, California Summary 10th Real Property § 616, Landlord's Use of Theft, Extortion, or Force.

12 Witkin, California Summary 10th Real Property § 620, Tenant's Remedies.

12 Witkin, California Summary 10th Real Property § 712, Retaliatory Acts Prohibited.

12 Witkin, California Summary 10th Real Property § 715, Tenant's Remedies.

12 Witkin, California Summary 10th Real Property § 722, (S 722) Commercial Tenant's Tender of Rent in Response.

12 Witkin, California Summary 10th Real Property § 754, Alternative Procedure on Tenant's Request.

§ 1940.1. Occupants of residential hotels; moving or checking out and reregistering

(a) No person may require an occupant of a residential hotel, as defined in Section 50519 of the Health and Safety Code, to move, or to check out and reregister, before the expiration of 30 days occupancy if a purpose is to have that occupant maintain transient occupancy status pursuant to paragraph (1) of subdivision (b) of Section 1940. Evidence that an occupant was required to check out and reregister shall create a rebuttable presumption, which shall affect solely the burden of producing evidence, of the purpose referred to in this subdivision.

(b) In addition to any remedies provided by local ordinance, any violation of subdivision (a) is punishable by a civil penalty of five hundred dollars ($500). In any action brought pursuant to this section, the prevailing party shall be entitled to reasonable attorney's fees.

(c) Nothing in this section shall prevent a local governing body from establishing inspection authority or reporting or recordkeeping requirements to ensure compliance with this section. *(Added by Stats.1990, c. 1235 (A.B.3926), § 1. Amended by Stats.1991, c. 245 (A.B.537), § 1, eff. July 29, 1991; Stats.2004, c. 950 (A.B.2867), § 1.)*

Research References

Rutter, Cal. Practice Guide: Civil Trials & Evidence Ch. 8G-C, C. Presumptions.

Miller and Starr California Real Estate § 19:7, Other Interests Distinguished--Eviction of a Guest or Lodger.

12 Witkin, California Summary 10th Real Property § 514, Statutory Rights of Lodger.

§ 1940.2. Unlawful actions by landlord to influence tenant to vacate; civil penalties; oral or written notice of violations of lease

(a) It is unlawful for a landlord to do any of the following for the purpose of influencing a tenant to vacate a dwelling:

(1) Engage in conduct that violates subdivision (a) of Section 484 of the Penal Code.

(2) Engage in conduct that violates Section 518 of the Penal Code.

(3) Use, or threaten to use, force, willful threats, or menacing conduct constituting a course of conduct that interferes with the tenant's quiet enjoyment of the premises in violation of Section 1927 that would create an apprehension of harm in a reasonable person. Nothing in this paragraph requires a tenant to be actually or constructively evicted in order to obtain relief.

(4) Commit a significant and intentional violation of Section 1954.

(b) A tenant who prevails in a civil action, including an action in small claims court, to enforce his or her rights under this section is entitled to a civil penalty in an amount not to exceed two thousand dollars ($2,000) for each violation.

(c) An oral or written warning notice, given in good faith, regarding conduct by a tenant, occupant, or guest that violates, may violate, or violated the applicable rental agreement, rules, regulations, lease, or laws, is not a violation of this section. An oral or written explanation of the rental agreement, rules, regulations, lease, or laws given in the normal course of business is not a violation of this section.

(d) Nothing in this section shall enlarge or diminish a landlord's right to terminate a tenancy pursuant to existing state or local law; nor shall this section enlarge or diminish any ability of local government to regulate or enforce a prohibition against a landlord's harassment of a tenant. *(Added by Stats.2003, c. 542 (A.B.1059), § 1.)*

Research References

Miller and Starr California Real Estate § 19:225, Cross-Complaint; Affirmative Defenses--Retaliatory Eviction.
14 NO. 4 Miller & Starr, California Real Estate Newsalert 10, Landlord and Tenant.
12 Witkin, California Summary 10th Real Property § 616, Landlord's Use of Theft, Extortion, or Force.

§ 1940.3. Immigration or citizenship status; city and county legislation prohibited; unlawful actions by landlord

(a) No city, county, or city and county shall, by statute, ordinance, or regulation, or by administrative action implementing any statute, ordinance, or regulation, compel a landlord or any agent of the landlord to make any inquiry, compile, disclose, report, or provide any information, prohibit offering or continuing to offer, accommodations in the property for rent or lease, or otherwise take any action regarding or based on the immigration or citizenship status of a tenant, prospective tenant, occupant, or prospective occupant of residential rental property.

(b) No landlord or any agent of the landlord shall do any of the following:

(1) Make any inquiry regarding or based on the immigration or citizenship status of a tenant, prospective tenant, occupant, or prospective occupant of residential rental property.

(2) Require that any tenant, prospective tenant, occupant, or prospective occupant of the rental property make any statement, representation, or certification concerning his or her immigration or citizenship status.

(c) Nothing in this section shall prohibit a landlord from either:

(1) Complying with any legal obligation under federal law.

(2) Requesting information or documentation necessary to determine or verify the financial qualifications of a prospective tenant, or to determine or verify the identity of a prospective tenant or prospective occupant. *(Added by Stats.2007, c. 403 (A.B.976), § 1.)*

Research References

Miller and Starr California Real Estate § 19:139, Summary of Causes for Termination.
18 NO. 4 Miller & Starr, California Real Estate Newsalert 16, Landlord and Tenant.
18 NO. 4 Miller & Starr, California Real Estate Newsalert 45, Table of Statutes (Newsalert Vol 18).

12 Witkin, California Summary 10th Real Property § 616A, (New)- Inquiries Regarding Immigration Status.

§ 1940.4. Posting or displaying political signs by tenant; landlord not to prohibit; exceptions; location; time limit; notice and enforcement of changes in terms of tenancy

(a) Except as provided in subdivision (c), a landlord shall not prohibit a tenant from posting or displaying political signs relating to any of the following:

(1) An election or legislative vote, including an election of a candidate to public office.

(2) The initiative, referendum, or recall process.

(3) Issues that are before a public commission, public board, or elected local body for a vote.

(b) Political signs may be posted or displayed in the window or on the door of the premises leased by the tenant in a multifamily dwelling, or from the yard, window, door, balcony, or outside wall of the premises leased by a tenant of a single-family dwelling.

(c) A landlord may prohibit a tenant from posting or displaying political signs in the following circumstances:

(1) The political sign is more than six square feet in size.

(2) The posting or displaying would violate a local, state, or federal law.

(3) The posting or displaying would violate a lawful provision in a common interest development governing a document that satisfies the criteria of Section 1353.6.

(d) A tenant shall post and remove political signs in compliance with the time limits set by the ordinance for the jurisdiction where the premises are located. A tenant shall be solely responsible for any violation of a local ordinance. If no local ordinance exists or if the local ordinance does not include a time limit for posting and removing political signs on private property, the landlord may establish a reasonable time period for the posting and removal of political signs. A reasonable time period for this purpose shall begin at least 90 days prior to the date of the election or vote to which the sign relates and end at least 15 days following the date of the election or vote.

(e) Notwithstanding any other provision of law, any changes in the terms of a tenancy that are made to implement the provisions of this section and are noticed pursuant to Section 827 shall not be deemed to cause a diminution in housing services, and may be enforced in accordance with Section 1161 of the Code of Civil Procedure. *(Added by Stats.2011, c. 383 (S.B.337), § 1.)*

Research References

Rutter, Cal. Practice Guide: Landlord-Tenant Gen. Matls, Highlights.
Miller and Starr California Real Estate § 19:111, Specification or Restriction of Use.
22 NO. 4 Miller & Starr, California Real Estate Newsalert 15, Landlord and Tenant.
12 Witkin, California Summary 10th Real Property § 616B, (New)- Prohibition Against Posting or Displaying Political Sign.

§ 1940.5. Refusal to rent to otherwise qualified tenant on basis of possession of waterbed prohibited; requirements and conditions

An owner or an owner's agent shall not refuse to rent a dwelling unit in a structure which received its valid certificate of occupancy after January 1, 1973, to an otherwise qualified prospective tenant or refuse to continue to rent to an existing tenant solely on the basis of that tenant's possession of a waterbed or other bedding with liquid filling material where all of the following requirements and conditions are met:

(a) A tenant or prospective tenant furnishes to the owner, prior to installation, a valid waterbed insurance policy or certificate of insurance for property damage. The policy shall be issued by a company licensed to do business in California and possessing a Best's Insurance Report rating of "B" or higher. The insurance policy shall be maintained in full force and effect until the bedding is permanently removed from the rental premises. The policy shall be written for no less than one hundred thousand dollars ($100,000) of coverage. The policy shall cover, up to the limits of the policy, replacement value of all property damage, including loss of use, incurred by the rental property owner or other caused by or arising out of the ownership, maintenance, use, or removal of the waterbed on the rental premises only, except for any damage caused intentionally or at the direction of the insured, or for any damage caused by or resulting from fire. The owner may require the tenant to produce evidence of insurance at any time. The carrier shall give the owner notice of cancellation or nonrenewal 10 days prior to this action. Every application for a policy shall contain the information as provided in subdivisions (a), (b), and (c) of Section 1962 and Section 1962.5.

(b) The bedding shall conform to the pounds-per-square foot weight limitation and placement as dictated by the floor load capacity of the residential structure. The weight shall be distributed on a pedestal or frame which is substantially the dimensions of the mattress itself.

(c) The tenant or prospective tenant shall install, maintain and remove the bedding, including, but not limited to, the mattress and frame, according to standard methods of installation, maintenance, and removal as prescribed by the manufacturer, retailer, or state law, whichever provides the higher degree of safety. The tenant shall notify the owner or owner's agent in writing of the intent to install, remove, or move the waterbed. The notice shall be delivered 24 hours prior to the installation, removal, or movement. The owner or the owner's agent may be present at the time of installation, removal, or movement at the owner's or the owner's agent's option. If the bedding is installed or moved by any person other than the tenant or prospective tenant, the tenant or prospective tenant shall deliver to the owner or to the owner's agent a written installation receipt stating the installer's name, address, and business affiliation where appropriate.

(d) Any new bedding installation shall conform to the owner's or the owner's agent's reasonable structural specifications for placement within the rental property and shall be consistent with floor capacity of the rental dwelling unit.

(e) The tenant or prospective tenant shall comply with the minimum component specification list prescribed by the manufacturer, retailer, or state law, whichever provides the higher degree of safety.

(f) Subject to the notice requirements of Section 1954, the owner, or the owner's agent, shall have the right to inspect the bedding installation upon completion, and periodically thereafter, to insure its conformity with this section. If installation or maintenance is not in conformity with this section, the owner may serve the tenant with a written notice of breach of the rental agreement. The owner may give the tenant three days either to bring the installation into conformity with those standards or to remove the bedding, unless there is an immediate danger to the structure, in which case there shall be immediate corrective action. If the bedding is installed by any person other than the tenant or prospective tenant, the tenant or prospective tenant shall deliver to the owner or to the owner's agent a written installation receipt stating the installer's name and business affiliation where appropriate.

(g) Notwithstanding Section 1950.5, an owner or owner's agent is entitled to increase the security deposit on the dwelling unit in an amount equal to one-half of one months' rent. The owner or owner's agent may charge a tenant, lessee, or sublessee a reasonable fee to cover administration costs. In no event does this section authorize the payment of a rebate of premium in violation of Article 5 (commencing with Section 750) of Chapter 1 of Part 2 of Division 1 of the Insurance Code.

(h) Failure of the owner, or owner's agent, to exercise any of his or her rights pursuant to this section does not constitute grounds for denial of an insurance claim.

(i) As used in this section, "tenant" includes any lessee, and "rental" means any rental or lease. *(Added by Stats.1987, c. 1503, § 1. Amended by Stats.1996, c. 1137 (S.B.1077), § 52.)*

Research References

California Real Estate Forms (Miller & Starr) § 2:65, Residential Lease.

California Real Estate Forms (Miller & Starr) § 2:66, Residential Lease With Purchase Option.

Rutter, Cal. Practice Guide: Landlord-Tenant Form 2:A, Residential Rental Agreement.

Miller and Starr California Real Estate § 19:112, Restrictions on Occupancy.

12 Witkin, California Summary 10th Real Property § 632, Nature of Covenant.

§ 1940.6. Demolition of residential dwelling unit; notice to prospective tenants; contents; remedies and civil penalties for noncompliance; attorney's fees

(a) The owner of a residential dwelling unit or the owner's agent who applies to any public agency for a permit to demolish that residential dwelling unit shall give written notice of that fact to:

(1) A prospective tenant prior to the occurrence of any of the following actions by the owner or the owner's agent:

(A) Entering into a rental agreement with a prospective tenant.

(B) Requiring or accepting payment from the prospective tenant for an application screening fee, as provided in Section 1950.6.

(C) Requiring or accepting any other fees from a prospective tenant.

(D) Requiring or accepting any writings that would initiate a tenancy.

(2) A current tenant, including a tenant who has entered into a rental agreement but has not yet taken possession of the dwelling unit, prior to applying to the public agency for the permit to demolish that residential dwelling unit.

(b) The notice shall include the earliest possible approximate date on which the owner expects the demolition to occur and the approximate date on which the owner will terminate the tenancy. However, in no case may the demolition for which the owner or the owner's agent has applied occur prior to the earliest possible approximate date noticed.

(c) If a landlord fails to comply with subdivision (a) or (b), a tenant may bring an action in a court of competent jurisdiction. The remedies the court may order shall include, but are not limited to, the following:

(1) In the case of a prospective tenant who moved into a residential dwelling unit and was not informed as required by subdivision (a) or (b), the actual damages suffered, moving expenses, and a civil penalty not to exceed two thousand five hundred dollars ($2,500) to be paid by the landlord to the tenant.

(2) In the case of a current tenant who was not informed as required by subdivision (a) or (b), the actual damages suffered, and a civil penalty not to exceed two thousand five hundred dollars ($2,500) to be paid by the landlord to the tenant.

(3) In any action brought pursuant to this section, the prevailing party shall be entitled to reasonable attorney's fees.

(d) The remedies available under this section are cumulative to other remedies available under law.

(e) This section shall not be construed to preempt other laws regarding landlord obligations or disclosures, including, but not limited to, those arising pursuant to Chapter 12.75 (commencing with Section 7060) of Division 7 of Title 1 of the Government Code.

(f) For purposes of this section:

(1) "Residential dwelling unit" has the same meaning as that contained in Section 1940.

(2) "Public agency" has the same meaning as that contained in Section 21063 of the Public Resources Code. *(Added by Stats.2002, c. 285 (S.B.1576), § 1.)*

Research References

Miller and Starr California Real Estate § 19:20, Lease as a Contract and Conveyance--Form, Execution, Delivery, and Recordation.
Miller and Starr California Real Estate § 19:123, Landlord's Duty to Disclose Defects to a Tenant.
13 NO. 4 Miller & Starr, California Real Estate Newsalert 14, Landlord and Tenant.
12 Witkin, California Summary 10th Real Property § 604, (S 604) by Owner Who Demolishes Property.

§ 1940.7. Disclosure of former federal or state ordnance locations

(a) The Legislature finds and declares that the December 10, 1983, tragedy in Tierra Santa, in which lives were lost as a result of a live munition exploding in a residential area that was formerly a military ordnance location, has demonstrated (1) the unique and heretofore unknown risk that there are other live munitions in former ordnance locations in California, (2) that these former ordnance locations need to be identified by the federal, state, or local authorities, and (3) that the people living in the neighborhood of these former ordnance locations should be notified of their existence. Therefore, it is the intent of the Legislature that the disclosure required by this section is solely warranted and limited by (1) the fact that these former ordnance locations cannot be readily observed or discovered by landlords and tenants, and (2) the ability of a landlord who has actual knowledge of a former ordnance location within the neighborhood of his or her rental property to disclose this information for the safety of the tenant.

(b) The landlord of a residential dwelling unit who has actual knowledge of any former federal or state ordnance locations in the neighborhood area shall give written notice to a prospective tenant of that knowledege [1] prior to the execution of a rental agreement. In cases of tenancies in existence on January 1, 1990, this written notice shall be given to tenants as soon as practicable thereafter.

(c) For purposes of this section:

(1) "Former federal or state ordnance location" means an area identified by an agency or instrumentality of the federal or state government as an area once used for military training purposes and which may contain potentially explosive munitions.

(2) "Neighborhood area" means within one mile of the residential dwelling. *(Added by Stats.1989, c. 294, § 2.)*

[1] So in chaptered bill.

Research References

Miller and Starr California Real Estate § 1:144, Duty of Seller of Real Property to Disclose--Statutory Duty of Disclosure.
Miller and Starr California Real Estate § 19:123, Landlord's Duty to Disclose Defects to a Tenant.

12 Witkin, California Summary 10th Real Property § 493, (S 493) Military, Industrial, and Airport Influences.
12 Witkin, California Summary 10th Real Property § 617, (S 617) in General.

§ 1940.8. Pest control company notices

A landlord of a residential dwelling unit shall provide each new tenant that occupies the unit with a copy of the notice provided by a registered structural pest control company pursuant to Section 8538 of the Business and Professions Code, if a contract for periodic pest control service has been executed. *(Added by Stats.2000, c. 234 (S.B.2143), § 2.)*

§ 1940.9. Gas and electric meters; notice to tenant when meter serves area outside tenant's dwelling unit; cost of services; remedies

(a) If the landlord does not provide separate gas and electric meters for each tenant's dwelling unit so that each tenant's meter measures only the electric or gas service to that tenant's dwelling unit and the landlord or his or her agent has knowledge that gas or electric service provided through a tenant's meter serves an area outside the tenant's dwelling unit, the landlord, prior to the inception of the tenancy or upon discovery, shall explicitly disclose that condition to the tenant and shall do either of the following:

(1) Execute a mutual written agreement with the tenant for payment by the tenant of the cost of the gas or electric service provided through the tenant's meter to serve areas outside the tenant's dwelling unit.

(2) Make other arrangements, as are mutually agreed in writing, for payment for the gas or electric service provided through the tenant's meter to serve areas outside the tenant's dwelling unit. These arrangements may include, but are not limited to, the landlord becoming the customer of record for the tenant's meter, or the landlord separately metering and becoming the customer of record for the area outside the tenant's dwelling unit.

(b) If a landlord fails to comply with subdivision (a), the aggrieved tenant may bring an action in a court of competent jurisdiction. The remedies the court may order shall include, but are not limited to, the following:

(1) Requiring the landlord to be made the customer of record with the utility for the tenant's meter.

(2) Ordering the landlord to reimburse the tenant for payments made by the tenant to the utility for service to areas outside of the tenant's dwelling unit. Payments to be reimbursed pursuant to this paragraph shall commence from the date the obligation to disclose arose under subdivision (a).

(c) Nothing in this section limits any remedies available to a landlord or tenant under other provisions of this chapter, the rental agreement, or applicable statutory or common law. *(Added by Stats.1989, c. 861, § 1.)*

Research References

California Real Estate Forms (Miller & Starr) § 2:65, Residential Lease.
California Real Estate Forms (Miller & Starr) § 2:66, Residential Lease With Purchase Option.
Miller and Starr California Real Estate § 19:81, Amount; Percentage Rent--Payment for Utilities.
12 Witkin, California Summary 10th Real Property § 619, Nature of Duty.

§ 1941. Buildings for human occupancy; fitness; repairs

The lessor of a building intended for the occupation of human beings must, in the absence of an agreement to the contrary, put it into a condition fit for such occupation, and repair all subsequent dilapidations thereof, which render it untenantable, except such as are mentioned in section nineteen hundred and twenty-nine. *(Enacted in 1872. Amended by Code Am.1873–74, c. 612, p. 245, § 205.)*

Research References

California Real Estate Forms (Miller & Starr) § 2:5, Drafting Checklist—Landlord Oriented.

California Real Estate Forms (Miller & Starr) § 2:16, Office Lease—Multistory Office Building.

California Real Estate Forms (Miller & Starr) § 2:17, Office Lease—Mixed Use Building.

California Real Estate Forms (Miller & Starr) § 2:18, Office Lease—Office/Warehouse Building With Four or Fewer Tenants.

California Real Estate Forms (Miller & Starr) § 2:19, Retail Lease—Power Shopping Center.

California Real Estate Forms (Miller & Starr) § 2:22, Retail Lease—Regional Shopping Center.

California Real Estate Forms (Miller & Starr) § 2:23, Retail Lease—Small Strip-Shopping Center.

California Real Estate Forms (Miller & Starr) § 2:24, Retail Lease—Restaurant.

California Real Estate Forms (Miller & Starr) § 2:25, Industrial Lease.

California Real Estate Forms (Miller & Starr) § 2:27, Ground Lease.

California Real Estate Forms (Miller & Starr) § 2:28, Triple Net Lease—Stand-Alone Building.

California Real Estate Forms (Miller & Starr) § 2:29, Parking Garage Lease.

California Real Estate Forms (Miller & Starr) § 2:32, Gross Lease—Small Commercial Property.

California Real Estate Forms (Miller & Starr) § 2:65, Residential Lease.

California Real Estate Forms (Miller & Starr) § 2:66, Residential Lease With Purchase Option.

Rutter, Cal. Practice Guide: A.D.R. Ch. 5-A, A. General Considerations.

Rutter, Cal. Practice Guide: A.D.R. App. D Form 67, Lease Provision for Arbitration of Disputes Re Disputes Re Habitability.

Rutter, Cal. Practice Guide: Landlord-Tenant Form 2:B, Standard Shopping Center Lease.

Rutter, Cal. Practice Guide: Landlord-Tenant Form 2:C, Office Lease.

Miller and Starr California Real Estate § 19:117, Landlord's Statutory Duty of Maintenance.

Miller and Starr California Real Estate § 19:122, Maintenance Obligations of the Landlord--Nonresidential Premises.

Miller and Starr California Real Estate § 19:124, Maintenance Obligations of the Tenant--Residential.

Miller and Starr California Real Estate § 19:154, Landlord's Right of Entry.

22 NO. 3 Miller & Starr, California Real Estate Newsalert 15, Landlord and Tenant.

3 Witkin Cal. Proc. 5th Actions § 150, Breach of Warranty of Habitability.

7 Witkin Cal. Proc. 5th Judgment § 95, (S 95) Prevailing Party in Specified Actions.

12 Witkin, California Summary 10th Real Property § 503, Statutory Framework.

12 Witkin, California Summary 10th Real Property § 619, Nature of Duty.

12 Witkin, California Summary 10th Real Property § 621, When Dwelling is Deemed Untenantable.

12 Witkin, California Summary 10th Real Property § 622, When Tenant's Violation Excuses Duty.

12 Witkin, California Summary 10th Real Property § 623, Waiver and Arbitration.

12 Witkin, California Summary 10th Real Property § 625, (S 625) Doctrine as Defense to Unlawful Detainer Action.

12 Witkin, California Summary 10th Real Property § 649, Violation of Safety Law.

12 Witkin, California Summary 10th Real Property § 687, (S 687) State Requirements.

12 Witkin, California Summary 10th Real Property § 706, Nature of Defense.

12 Witkin, California Summary 10th Real Property § 707, Tenant's Cause of Action.

12 Witkin, California Summary 10th Real Property § 736, Trial.

12 Witkin, California Summary 10th Real Property § 737, (S 737) Restoration of Possession.

§ 1941.1. Untenantable dwellings; program assistance for heating or hot water system repairs or replacement

(a) A dwelling shall be deemed untenantable for purposes of Section 1941 if it substantially lacks any of the following affirmative standard characteristics or is a residential unit described in Section 17920.3 or 17920.10 of the Health and Safety Code:

(1) Effective waterproofing and weather protection of roof and exterior walls, including unbroken windows and doors.

(2) Plumbing or gas facilities that conformed to applicable law in effect at the time of installation, maintained in good working order.

(3) A water supply approved under applicable law that is under the control of the tenant, capable of producing hot and cold running water, or a system that is under the control of the landlord, that produces hot and cold running water, furnished to appropriate fixtures, and connected to a sewage disposal system approved under applicable law.

(4) Heating facilities that conformed with applicable law at the time of installation, maintained in good working order.

(5) Electrical lighting, with wiring and electrical equipment that conformed with applicable law at the time of installation, maintained in good working order.

(6) Building, grounds, and appurtenances at the time of the commencement of the lease or rental agreement, and all areas under control of the landlord, kept in every part clean, sanitary, and free from all accumulations of debris, filth, rubbish, garbage, rodents, and vermin.

(7) An adequate number of appropriate receptacles for garbage and rubbish, in clean condition and good repair at the time of the commencement of the lease or rental agreement, with the landlord providing appropriate serviceable receptacles thereafter and being responsible for the clean condition and good repair of the receptacles under his or her control.

(8) Floors, stairways, and railings maintained in good repair.

(9) A locking mail receptacle for each residential unit in a residential hotel, as required by Section 17958.3 of the Health and Safety Code. This subdivision shall become operative on July 1, 2008.

(b) Nothing in this section shall be interpreted to prohibit a tenant or owner of rental properties from qualifying for a utility energy savings assistance program, or any other program assistance, for heating or hot water system repairs or replacement, or a combination of heating and hot water system repairs or replacements, that would achieve energy savings. *(Added by Stats.1970, c. 1280, p. 2314, § 1. Amended by Stats.1979, c. 307, p. 1125, § 1; Stats.2002, c. 931 (S.B.460), § 1; Stats.2007, c. 599 (A.B.607), § 1; Stats.2012, c. 600 (A.B.1124), § 1.)*

Research References

California Real Estate Forms (Miller & Starr) § 2:65, Residential Lease.

California Real Estate Forms (Miller & Starr) § 2:66, Residential Lease With Purchase Option.

Rutter, Cal. Practice Guide: Landlord-Tenant Form 3:A, Letter Advising Landlord of Uninhabitable Condition.

Miller and Starr California Real Estate § 22:32, Recovery of Abatement Costs.

Miller and Starr California Real Estate § 19:117, Landlord's Statutory Duty of Maintenance.

Miller and Starr California Real Estate § 19:120, Landlord's Common-Law Duty of Maintenance; Implied Warranty of Habitability.

Miller and Starr California Real Estate § 19:121, Tenant's Remedies for Landlord's Breach of the Implied Warranty.

Miller and Starr California Real Estate § 19:224, Cross-Complaint; Affirmative Defenses--Breach of the Warranty of Habitability.

22 NO. 3 Miller & Starr, California Real Estate Newsalert 15, Landlord and Tenant.

12 Witkin, California Summary 10th Real Property § 620, Tenant's Remedies.

12 Witkin, California Summary 10th Real Property § 621, When Dwelling is Deemed Untenantable.

12 Witkin, California Summary 10th Real Property § 687, (S 687) State Requirements.

12 Witkin, California Summary 10th Real Property § 736, Trial.

§ 1941.2. Tenant's affirmative obligations

(a) No duty on the part of the landlord to repair a dilapidation shall arise under Section 1941 or 1942 if the tenant is in substantial violation of any of the following affirmative obligations, provided the tenant's violation contributes substantially to the existence of the dilapidation or interferes substantially with the landlord's obligation under Section 1941 to effect the necessary repairs:

(1) To keep that part of the premises which he occupies and uses clean and sanitary as the condition of the premises permits.

(2) To dispose from his dwelling unit of all rubbish, garbage and other waste, in a clean and sanitary manner.

(3) To properly use and operate all electrical, gas and plumbing fixtures and keep them as clean and sanitary as their condition permits.

(4) Not to permit any person on the premises, with his permission, to willfully or wantonly destroy, deface, damage, impair or remove any part of the structure or dwelling unit or the facilities, equipment, or appurtenances thereto, nor himself do any such thing.

(5) To occupy the premises as his abode, utilizing portions thereof for living, sleeping, cooking or dining purposes only which were respectively designed or intended to be used for such occupancies.

(b) Paragraphs (1) and (2) of subdivision (a) shall not apply if the landlord has expressly agreed in writing to perform the act or acts mentioned therein. *(Added by Stats.1970, c. 1280, p. 2315, § 2. Amended by Stats.1979, c. 307, p. 1125, § 2.)*

Research References

Miller and Starr California Real Estate § 19:117, Landlord's Statutory Duty of Maintenance.

Miller and Starr California Real Estate § 19:124, Maintenance Obligations of the Tenant--Residential.

12 Witkin, California Summary 10th Real Property § 620, Tenant's Remedies.

12 Witkin, California Summary 10th Real Property § 622, When Tenant's Violation Excuses Duty.

12 Witkin, California Summary 10th Real Property § 687, (S 687) State Requirements.

12 Witkin, California Summary 10th Real Property § 736, Trial.

§ 1941.3. Buildings intended for human habitation; landlord's duties; tenants' duties; violations; exempt buildings

(a) On and after July 1, 1998, the landlord, or his or her agent, of a building intended for human habitation shall do all of the following:

(1) Install and maintain an operable dead bolt lock on each main swinging entry door of a dwelling unit. The dead bolt lock shall be installed in conformance with the manufacturer's specifications and shall comply with applicable state and local codes including, but not limited to, those provisions relating to fire and life safety and accessibility for the disabled. When in the locked position, the bolt shall extend a minimum of $\frac{13}{16}$ of an inch in length beyond the strike edge of the door and protrude into the doorjamb.

This section shall not apply to horizontal sliding doors. Existing dead bolts of at least one-half inch in length shall satisfy the requirements of this section. Existing locks with a thumbturn deadlock that have a strike plate attached to the doorjamb and a latch bolt that is held in a vertical position by a guard bolt, a plunger, or an auxiliary mechanism shall also satisfy the requirements of this section. These locks, however, shall be replaced with a dead bolt at least $\frac{13}{16}$ of an inch in length the first time after July 1, 1998, that the lock requires repair or replacement.

Existing doors which cannot be equipped with dead bolt locks shall satisfy the requirements of this section if the door is equipped with a metal strap affixed horizontally across the midsection of the door with a dead bolt which extends $\frac{13}{16}$ of an inch in length beyond the strike edge of the door and protrudes into the doorjamb. Locks and security devices other than those described herein which are inspected and approved by an appropriate state or local government agency as providing adequate security shall satisfy the requirements of this section.

(2) Install and maintain operable window security or locking devices for windows that are designed to be opened. Louvered windows, casement windows, and all windows more than 12 feet vertically or six feet horizontally from the ground, a roof, or any other platform are excluded from this subdivision.

(3) Install locking mechanisms that comply with applicable fire and safety codes on the exterior doors that provide ingress or egress to common areas with access to dwelling units in multifamily developments. This paragraph does not require the installation of a door or gate where none exists on January 1, 1998.

(b) The tenant shall be responsible for notifying the owner or his or her authorized agent when the tenant becomes aware of an inoperable dead bolt lock or window security or locking device in the dwelling unit. The landlord, or his or her authorized agent, shall not be liable for a violation of subdivision (a) unless he or she fails to correct the violation within a reasonable time after he or she either has actual notice of a deficiency or receives notice of a deficiency.

(c) On and after July 1, 1998, the rights and remedies of tenant for a violation of this section by the landlord shall include those available pursuant to Sections 1942, 1942.4, and 1942.5, an action for breach of contract, and an action for injunctive relief pursuant to Section 526 of the Code of Civil Procedure. Additionally, in an unlawful detainer action, after a default in the payment of rent, a tenant may raise the violation of this section as an affirmative defense and shall have a right to the remedies provided by Section 1174.2 of the Code of Civil Procedure.

(d) A violation of this section shall not broaden, limit, or otherwise affect the duty of care owed by a landlord pursuant to existing law, including any duty that may exist pursuant to Section 1714. The delayed applicability of the requirements of subdivision (a) shall not affect a landlord's duty to maintain the premises in safe condition.

(e) Nothing in this section shall be construed to affect any authority of any public entity that may otherwise exist to impose any additional security requirements upon a landlord.

(f) This section shall not apply to any building which has been designated as historically significant by an appropriate local, state, or federal governmental jurisdiction.

(g) Subdivisions (a) and (b) shall not apply to any building intended for human habitation which is managed, directly or indirectly, and controlled by the Department of Transportation. This exemption shall not be construed to affect the duty of the Department of Transportation to maintain the premises of these buildings in a safe condition or abrogate any express or implied statement or promise of the Department of Transportation to provide secure premises. Additionally, this exemption shall not apply to residential dwellings acquired prior to July 1, 1997, by the Department of Transportation to complete construction of state highway routes 710 and 238 and related interchanges. *(Added by Stats.1997, c. 537 (S.B.548), § 1.)*

Research References

Miller and Starr California Real Estate § 19:117, Landlord's Statutory Duty of Maintenance.
Miller and Starr California Real Estate § 19:119, Tenant's Right to Repair and Deduct.
Miller and Starr California Real Estate § 19:120, Landlord's Common-Law Duty of Maintenance; Implied Warranty of Habitability.
12 Witkin, California Summary 10th Real Property § 619, Nature of Duty.

§ 1941.4. Residential buildings; lessors' responsibilities; inside telephone wiring

The lessor of a building intended for the residential occupation of human beings shall be responsible for installing at least one usable telephone jack and for placing and maintaining the inside telephone wiring in good working order, shall ensure that the inside telephone wiring meets the applicable standards of the most recent California Electrical Code * * *, and shall make any required repairs. The lessor shall not restrict or interfere with access by the telephone utility to its telephone network facilities up to the demarcation point separating the inside wiring.

"Inside telephone wiring" for purposes of this section, means that portion of the telephone wire that connects the telephone equipment at the customer's premises to the telephone network at a demarcation point determined by the telephone corporation in accordance with orders of the Public Utilities Commission. *(Added by Stats.1991, c. 1001 (S.B.841), § 2. Amended by Stats.2013, c. 183 (S.B.745), § 5.)*

Research References

Miller and Starr California Real Estate § 19:117, Landlord's Statutory Duty of Maintenance.
12 Witkin, California Summary 10th Real Property § 619, Nature of Duty.

§ 1941.5. Tenant protected by restraining order against nontenant; change of locks on dwelling unit; definitions

(a) This section shall apply if a person who is restrained from contact with the protected tenant under a court order or is named in a police report is not a tenant of the same dwelling unit as the protected tenant.

(b) A landlord shall change the locks of a protected tenant's dwelling unit upon written request of the protected tenant not later than 24 hours after the protected tenant gives the landlord a copy of a court order or police report, and shall give the protected tenant a key to the new locks.

(c)(1) If a landlord fails to change the locks within 24 hours, the protected tenant may change the locks without the landlord's permission, notwithstanding any provision in the lease to the contrary.

(2) If the protected tenant changes the locks pursuant to this subdivision, the protected tenant shall do all of the following:

(A) Change the locks in a workmanlike manner with locks of similar or better quality than the original lock.

(B) Notify the landlord within 24 hours that the locks have been changed.

(C) Provide the landlord with a key by any reasonable method agreed upon by the landlord and protected tenant.

(3) This subdivision shall apply to leases executed on or after the date the act that added this section takes effect.

(d) For the purposes of this section, the following definitions shall apply:

(1) "Court order" means a court order lawfully issued within the last 180 days pursuant to Section 527.6 of the Code of Civil Procedure, Part 3 (commencing with Section 6240), Part 4 (commencing with Section 6300), or Part 5 (commencing with Section 6400) of Division 10 of the Family Code, Section 136.2 of the Penal Code, or Section 213.5 of the Welfare and Institutions Code.

(2) "Locks" means any exterior lock that provides access to the dwelling.

(3) "Police report" means a written report, written within the last 180 days, by a peace officer employed by a state or local law enforcement agency acting in his or her official capacity, stating that the protected tenant or a household member has filed a report alleging that the protected tenant or the household member is a victim of domestic violence, sexual assault, or stalking.

(4) "Protected tenant" means a tenant who has obtained a court order or has a copy of a police report.

(5) "Tenant" means tenant, subtenant, lessee, or sublessee. *(Added by Stats.2010, c. 626 (S.B.782), § 2.)*

Research References

Miller and Starr California Real Estate § 19:86, Termination of the Obligation to Pay Rent.
21 NO. 4 Miller & Starr, California Real Estate Newsalert 14, Landlord and Tenant.
12 Witkin, California Summary 10th Real Property § 619, Nature of Duty.

§ 1941.6. Tenant protected by restraining order against another tenant; change of locks on dwelling unit; liability regarding person excluded; definitions

(a) This section shall apply if a person who is restrained from contact with a protected tenant under a court order is a tenant of the same dwelling unit as the protected tenant.

(b) A landlord shall change the locks of a protected tenant's dwelling unit upon written request of the protected tenant not later than 24 hours after the protected tenant gives the landlord a copy of a court order that excludes from the dwelling unit the restrained person referred to in subdivision (a). The landlord shall give the protected tenant a key to the new locks.

(c)(1) If a landlord fails to change the locks within 24 hours, the protected tenant may change the locks without the landlord's permission, notwithstanding any provision in the lease to the contrary.

(2) If the protected tenant changes the locks pursuant to this subdivision, the protected tenant shall do all of the following:

(A) Change the locks in a workmanlike manner with locks of similar or better quality than the original lock.

(B) Notify the landlord within 24 hours that the locks have been changed.

(C) Provide the landlord with a key by any reasonable method agreed upon by the landlord and protected tenant.

(3) This subdivision shall apply to leases executed on or after the date the act that added this section takes effect.

(d) Notwithstanding Section 789.3, if the locks are changed pursuant to this section, the landlord is not liable to a person excluded from the dwelling unit pursuant to this section.

(e) A person who has been excluded from a dwelling unit under this section remains liable under the lease with all other tenants of the dwelling unit for rent as provided in the lease.

(f) For the purposes of this section, the following definitions shall apply:

(1) "Court order" means a court order lawfully issued within the last 180 days pursuant to Section 527.6 of the Code of Civil Procedure, Part 3 (commencing with Section 6240), Part 4 (commencing with Section 6300), or Part 5 (commencing with Section 6400) of Division 10 of the Family Code, Section 136.2 of the Penal Code, or Section 213.5 of the Welfare and Institutions Code.

(2) "Locks" means any exterior lock that provides access to the dwelling.

(3) "Protected tenant" means a tenant who has obtained a court order.

(4) "Tenant" means tenant, subtenant, lessee, or sublessee. *(Added by Stats.2010, c. 626 (S.B.782), § 3.)*

Research References

Miller and Starr California Real Estate § 19:86, Termination of the Obligation to Pay Rent.
21 NO. 4 Miller & Starr, California Real Estate Newsalert 14, Landlord and Tenant.
12 Witkin, California Summary 10th Real Property § 619, Nature of Duty.

§ 1942. Repairs by tenant; rent deduction or vacation of premises; presumption; limit; nonavailability of remedy; additional remedy

(a) If within a reasonable time after written or oral notice to the landlord or his agent, as defined in subdivision (a) of Section 1962, of dilapidations rendering the premises untenantable which the landlord ought to repair, the landlord neglects to do so, the tenant may repair the same himself where the cost of such repairs does not require an expenditure more than one month's rent of the premises and deduct the expenses of such repairs from the rent when due, or the tenant may vacate the premises, in which case the tenant shall be discharged from further payment of rent, or performance of other conditions as of the date of vacating the premises. This remedy shall not be available to the tenant more than twice in any 12-month period.

(b) For the purposes of this section, if a tenant acts to repair and deduct after the 30th day following notice, he is presumed to have acted after a reasonable time. The presumption established by this subdivision is a rebuttable presumption affecting the burden of producing evidence and shall not be construed to prevent a tenant from repairing and deducting after a shorter notice if all the circumstances require shorter notice.

(c) The tenant's remedy under subdivision (a) shall not be available if the condition was caused by the violation of Section 1929 or 1941.2.

(d) The remedy provided by this section is in addition to any other remedy provided by this chapter, the rental agreement, or other applicable statutory or common law. *(Enacted in 1872. Amended by Code Am.1873–74, c. 612, p. 246, § 206; Stats.1970, c. 1280, p. 2315, § 3; Stats.1979, c. 307, p. 1126, § 3.)*

Research References

California Real Estate Forms (Miller & Starr) § 2:5, Drafting Checklist—Landlord Oriented.
California Real Estate Forms (Miller & Starr) § 2:16, Office Lease—Multistory Office Building.
California Real Estate Forms (Miller & Starr) § 2:17, Office Lease—Mixed Use Building.
California Real Estate Forms (Miller & Starr) § 2:18, Office Lease—Office/Warehouse Building With Four or Fewer Tenants.
California Real Estate Forms (Miller & Starr) § 2:19, Retail Lease—Power Shopping Center.
California Real Estate Forms (Miller & Starr) § 2:20, Retail Lease—Shopping Center With for Profit Parking Garage.
California Real Estate Forms (Miller & Starr) § 2:22, Retail Lease—Regional Shopping Center.
California Real Estate Forms (Miller & Starr) § 2:23, Retail Lease—Small Strip-Shopping Center.
California Real Estate Forms (Miller & Starr) § 2:24, Retail Lease—Restaurant.
California Real Estate Forms (Miller & Starr) § 2:25, Industrial Lease.
California Real Estate Forms (Miller & Starr) § 2:27, Ground Lease
California Real Estate Forms (Miller & Starr) § 2:28, Triple Net Lease—Stand-Alone Building.
California Real Estate Forms (Miller & Starr) § 2:29, Parking Garage Lease.

California Real Estate Forms (Miller & Starr) § 2:32, Gross Lease—Small Commercial Property.
California Real Estate Forms (Miller & Starr) § 2:65, Residential Lease.
California Real Estate Forms (Miller & Starr) § 2:66, Residential Lease With Purchase Option.
Rutter, Cal. Practice Guide: Landlord-Tenant Form 2:B, Standard Shopping Center Lease.
Rutter, Cal. Practice Guide: Landlord-Tenant Form 2:C, Office Lease.
Miller and Starr California Real Estate § 19:119, Tenant's Right to Repair and Deduct.
Miller and Starr California Real Estate § 19:121, Tenant's Remedies for Landlord's Breach of the Implied Warranty.
Miller and Starr California Real Estate § 19:122, Maintenance Obligations of the Landlord--Nonresidential Premises.
Miller and Starr California Real Estate § 19:124, Maintenance Obligations of the Tenant--Residential.
8 Witkin Cal. Proc. 5th Extraordinary Writs § 111, Exercise of Discretion in Decision.
12 Witkin, California Summary 10th Real Property § 620, Tenant's Remedies.
12 Witkin, California Summary 10th Real Property § 621, When Dwelling is Deemed Untenantable.
12 Witkin, California Summary 10th Real Property § 622, When Tenant's Violation Excuses Duty.
12 Witkin, California Summary 10th Real Property § 623, Waiver and Arbitration.
12 Witkin, California Summary 10th Real Property § 628, Occupancy With Knowledge Does Not Waive Warranty.
12 Witkin, California Summary 10th Real Property § 649, Violation of Safety Law.
12 Witkin, California Summary 10th Real Property § 706, Nature of Defense.
12 Witkin, California Summary 10th Real Property § 707, Tenant's Cause of Action.
12 Witkin, California Summary 10th Real Property § 713, Restrictions on Lessee's Defense.
1 Witkin Cal. Summ. 10th Contracts § 680, Other Rights.

§ 1942.1. Waiver of rights; public policy; arbitration of untenantability

Any agreement by a lessee of a dwelling waiving or modifying his rights under Section 1941 or 1942 shall be void as contrary to public policy with respect to any condition which renders the premises untenantable, except that the lessor and the lessee may agree that the lessee shall undertake to improve, repair or maintain all or stipulated portions of the dwelling as part of the consideration for rental.

The lessor and lessee may, if an agreement is in writing, set forth the provisions of Sections 1941 to 1942.1, inclusive, and provide that any controversy relating to a condition of the premises claimed to make them untenantable may by application of either party be submitted to arbitration, pursuant to the provisions of Title 9 (commencing with Section 1280), Part 3 of the Code of Civil Procedure, and that the costs of such arbitration shall be apportioned by the arbitrator between the parties. *(Added by Stats.1970, c. 1280, p. 2316, § 4.)*

Research References

Rutter, Cal. Practice Guide: A.D.R. Ch. 5-A, A. General Considerations.
Rutter, Cal. Practice Guide: A.D.R. Ch. 5-C, C. Enforceability of Arbitration Agreements-In General.
Rutter, Cal. Practice Guide: A.D.R. App. D Form 67, Lease Provision for Arbitration of Disputes Re Disputes Re Habitability.
Miller and Starr California Real Estate § 19:88, Termination of the Obligation to Pay Rent--Eviction; Landlord's Failure to Maintain.
Miller and Starr California Real Estate § 35:39, Issues Which Cannot be the Subject of Arbitration.
Miller and Starr California Real Estate § 19:119, Tenant's Right to Repair and Deduct.
14 NO. 2 Miller & Starr, California Real Estate Newsalert 14, Landlord and Tenant.
12 Witkin, California Summary 10th Real Property § 567, (S 567) Restrictions on Waivers of Tenants' Rights.

12 Witkin, California Summary 10th Real Property § 623, Waiver and
    Arbitration.
1 Witkin Cal. Summ. 10th Contracts § 683, Waivers by Tenants.

§ 1942.2. Deduction of utility payment

A tenant who has made a payment to a utility pursuant to
Section 777, 777.1, 10009, 10009.1, 12822, 12822.1, 16481, or
16481.1 of the Public Utilities Code may deduct the payment
from the rent as provided in that section. *(Added by Stats.2009,
c. 560 (S.B.120), § 1.)*

Research References

Miller and Starr California Real Estate § 19:81, Amount; Percentage
    Rent--Payment for Utilities.
Miller and Starr California Real Estate § 31:22, Utility Services.
20 NO. 4 Miller & Starr, California Real Estate Newsalert 13, Landlord
    and Tenant.
12 Witkin, California Summary 10th Real Property § 569, (S 569) Form
    and Determination of Payment.

§ 1942.3. Unlawful detainer; burden of proof; rebuttable presumption landlord breached habitability requirements; conditions

(a) In any unlawful detainer action by the landlord to recover
possession from a tenant, a rebuttable presumption affecting the
burden of producing evidence that the landlord has breached the
habitability requirements in Section 1941 is created if all of the
following conditions exist:

(1) The dwelling substantially lacks any of the affirmative
standard characteristics listed in Section 1941.1, is deemed and
declared substandard pursuant to Section 17920.3 of the Health
and Safety Code, or contains lead hazards as defined in Section
17920.10 of the Health and Safety Code.

(2) A public officer or employee who is responsible for the
enforcement of any housing law has notified the landlord, or an
agent of the landlord, in a written notice issued after inspection
of the premises which informs the landlord of his or her
obligation to abate the nuisance or repair the substandard or
unsafe conditions identified under the authority described in
paragraph (1).

(3) The conditions have existed and have not been abated 60
days beyond the date of issuance of the notice specified in
paragraph (2) and the delay is without good cause.

(4) The conditions were not caused by an act or omission of
the tenant or lessee in violation of Section 1929 or 1941.2.

(b) The presumption specified in subdivision (a) does not
arise unless all of the conditions set forth therein are proven, but
failure to so establish the presumption shall not otherwise affect
the right of the tenant to raise and pursue any defense based on
the landlord's breach of the implied warranty of habitability.

(c) The presumption provided in this section shall apply only
to rental agreements or leases entered into or renewed on or
after January 1, 1986. *(Added by Stats.1985, c. 1279, § 1.
Amended by Stats.2005, c. 595 (S.B.253), § 2.)*

Research References

Miller and Starr California Real Estate § 19:120, Landlord's Common-
    Law Duty of Maintenance; Implied Warranty of Habitability.
Miller and Starr California Real Estate § 19:224, Cross-Complaint;
    Affirmative Defenses--Breach of the Warranty of Habitability.
16 NO. 4 Miller & Starr, California Real Estate Newsalert 13, Landlord
    and Tenant.
16 NO. 5 Miller & Starr, California Real Estate Newsalert 26, State Board
    of Equalization Issues Comprehensive Summary and Qs and As for
    Transfers of Base Year Values of Principal Residences.

12 Witkin, California Summary 10th Real Property § 736, Trial.

§ 1942.4. Demand, collection or increase of rent under certain enumerated conditions; landlord liability; attorney's fees; abatement and repair; additional remedies

(a) A landlord of a dwelling may not demand rent, collect
rent, issue a notice of a rent increase, or issue a three-day notice
to pay rent or quit pursuant to subdivision (2) of Section 1161 of
the Code of Civil Procedure, if all of the following conditions
exist prior to the landlord's demand or notice:

(1) The dwelling substantially lacks any of the affirmative
standard characteristics listed in Section 1941.1 or violates
Section 17920.10 of the Health and Safety Code, or is deemed
and declared substandard as set forth in Section 17920.3 of the
Health and Safety Code because conditions listed in that section
exist to an extent that endangers the life, limb, health, property,
safety, or welfare of the public or the occupants of the dwelling.

(2) A public officer or employee who is responsible for the
enforcement of any housing law, after inspecting the premises,
has notified the landlord or the landlord's agent in writing of his
or her obligations to abate the nuisance or repair the substandard conditions.

(3) The conditions have existed and have not been abated 35
days beyond the date of service of the notice specified in
paragraph (2) and the delay is without good cause. For
purposes of this subdivision, service shall be complete at the time
of deposit in the United States mail.

(4) The conditions were not caused by an act or omission of
the tenant or lessee in violation of Section 1929 or 1941.2.

(b)(1) A landlord who violates this section is liable to the
tenant or lessee for the actual damages sustained by the tenant
or lessee and special damages of not less than one hundred
dollars ($100) and not more than five thousand dollars ($5,000).

(2) The prevailing party shall be entitled to recovery of
reasonable attorney's fees and costs of the suit in an amount
fixed by the court.

(c) Any court that awards damages under this section may
also order the landlord to abate any nuisance at the rental
dwelling and to repair any substandard conditions of the rental
dwelling, as defined in Section 1941.1, which significantly or
materially affect the health or safety of the occupants of the
rental dwelling and are uncorrected. If the court orders repairs
or corrections, or both, the court's jurisdiction continues over the
matter for the purpose of ensuring compliance.

(d) The tenant or lessee shall be under no obligation to
undertake any other remedy prior to exercising his or her rights
under this section.

(e) Any action under this section may be maintained in small
claims court if the claim does not exceed the jurisdictional limit
of that court.

(f) The remedy provided by this section may be utilized in
addition to any other remedy provided by this chapter, the rental
agreement, lease, or other applicable statutory or common law.
Nothing in this section shall require any landlord to comply with
this section if he or she pursues his or her rights pursuant to
Chapter 12.75 (commencing with Section 7060) of Division 7 of
Title 1 of the Government Code. *(Added by Stats.1985, c. 1279,
§ 2. Amended by Stats.1990, c. 1305 (S.B.2627), § 1; Stats.1992,
c. 488 (A.B.2574), § 1; Stats.1993, c. 589 (A.B.2211), § 23;
Stats.2003, c. 109 (A.B.647), § 1.)*

Research References

Miller and Starr California Real Estate § 19:119, Tenant's Right to
    Repair and Deduct.

§ 1942.5. Retaliation; prohibited acts; violations; remedies; penalties

(a) If the lessor retaliates against the lessee because of the exercise by the lessee of his rights under this chapter or because of his complaint to an appropriate agency as to tenantability of a dwelling, and if the lessee of a dwelling is not in default as to the payment of his rent, the lessor may not recover possession of a dwelling in any action or proceeding, cause the lessee to quit involuntarily, increase the rent, or decrease any services within 180 days of any of the following:

(1) After the date upon which the lessee, in good faith, has given notice pursuant to Section 1942, or has made an oral complaint to the lessor regarding tenantability.

(2) After the date upon which the lessee, in good faith, has filed a written complaint, or an oral complaint which is registered or otherwise recorded in writing, with an appropriate agency, of which the lessor has notice, for the purpose of obtaining correction of a condition relating to tenantability.

(3) After the date of an inspection or issuance of a citation, resulting from a complaint described in paragraph (2) of which the lessor did not have notice.

(4) After the filing of appropriate documents commencing a judicial or arbitration proceeding involving the issue of tenantability.

(5) After entry of judgment or the signing of an arbitration award, if any, when in the judicial proceeding or arbitration the issue of tenantability is determined adversely to the lessor.

In each instance, the 180–day period shall run from the latest applicable date referred to in paragraphs (1) to (5), inclusive.

(b) A lessee may not invoke subdivision (a) more than once in any 12–month period.

(c) It is unlawful for a lessor to increase rent, decrease services, cause a lessee to quit involuntarily, bring an action to recover possession, or threaten to do any of those acts, for the purpose of retaliating against the lessee because he or she has lawfully organized or participated in a lessees' association or an organization advocating lessees' rights or has lawfully and peaceably exercised any rights under the law. In an action brought by or against the lessee pursuant to this subdivision, the lessee shall bear the burden of producing evidence that the lessor's conduct was, in fact, retaliatory.

(d) Nothing in this section shall be construed as limiting in any way the exercise by the lessor of his or her rights under any lease or agreement or any law pertaining to the hiring of property or his or her right to do any of the acts described in subdivision (a) or (c) for any lawful cause. Any waiver by a lessee of his or her rights under this section is void as contrary to public policy.

(e) Notwithstanding subdivisions (a) to (d), inclusive, a lessor may recover possession of a dwelling and do any of the other acts described in subdivision (a) within the period or periods prescribed therein, or within subdivision (c), if the notice of termination, rent increase, or other act, and any pleading or statement of issues in an arbitration, if any, states the ground upon which the lessor, in good faith, seeks to recover possession, increase rent, or do any of the other acts described in subdivision (a) or (c). If the statement is controverted, the lessor shall establish its truth at the trial or other hearing.

(f) Any lessor or agent of a lessor who violates this section shall be liable to the lessee in a civil action for all of the following:

(1) The actual damages sustained by the lessee.

(2) Punitive damages in an amount of not less than one hundred dollars ($100) nor more than two thousand dollars ($2,000) for each retaliatory act where the lessor or agent has been guilty of fraud, oppression, or malice with respect to that act.

(g) In any action brought for damages for retaliatory eviction, the court shall award reasonable attorney's fees to the prevailing party if either party requests attorney's fees upon the initiation of the action.

(h) The remedies provided by this section shall be in addition to any other remedies provided by statutory or decisional law. (*Added by Stats.1979, c. 652, p. 2005, § 2. Amended by Stats.2003, c. 542 (A.B.1059), § 2.*)

Research References

12 Witkin, California Summary 10th Real Property § 739, (S 739) Costs and Attorneys' Fees.

§ 1942.6. Entry on property for purposes of tenants' rights

Any person entering onto residential real property, upon the invitation of an occupant, during reasonable hours or because of emergency circumstances, for the purpose of providing information regarding tenants' rights or to participate in a lessees' association or association of tenants or an association that advocates tenants' rights shall not be liable in any criminal or civil action for trespass.

The Legislature finds and declares that this section is declaratory of existing law. Nothing in this section shall be construed to enlarge or diminish the rights of any person under existing law. *(Added by Stats.1999, c. 590 (S.B.1098), § 1.)*

Research References

Miller and Starr California Real Estate § 19:114, Use of the Common Areas.
12 Witkin, California Summary 10th Real Property § 712, Retaliatory Acts Prohibited.

§ 1942.7. Conditions on occupancy based on declawing or devocalizing animals allowed on the premises; restrictions on persons or corporations occupying, owning, managing, or providing services in connection with real property; declaratory or injunctive relief; civil penalties

(a) A person or corporation that occupies, owns, manages, or provides services in connection with any real property, including the individual's or corporation's agents or successors in interest, and that allows an animal on the premises, shall not do any of the following:

(1) Advertise, through any means, the availability of real property for occupancy in a manner designed to discourage application for occupancy of that real property because an applicant's animal has not been declawed or devocalized.

(2) Refuse to allow the occupancy of any real property, refuse to negotiate the occupancy of any real property, or otherwise make unavailable or deny to any other person the occupancy of any real property because of that person's refusal to declaw or devocalize any animal.

(3) Require any tenant or occupant of real property to declaw or devocalize any animal allowed on the premises.

(b) For purposes of this section, the following definitions apply:

(1) "Animal" means any mammal, bird, reptile, or amphibian.

(2) "Application for occupancy" means all phases of the process of applying for the right to occupy real property, including, but not limited to, filling out applications, interviewing, and submitting references.

(3) "Claw" means a hardened keratinized modification of the epidermis, or a hardened keratinized growth, that extends from the end of the digits of certain mammals, birds, reptiles, and amphibians, often commonly referred to as a "claw," "talon," or "nail."

(4) "Declawing" means performing, procuring, or arranging for any procedure, such as an onychectomy, tendonectomy, or phalangectomy, to remove or to prevent the normal function of an animal's claw or claws.

(5) "Devocalizing" means performing, procuring, or arranging for any surgical procedure such as a vocal cordectomy, to remove an animal's vocal cords or to prevent the normal function of an animal's vocal cords.

(6) "Owner" means any person who has any right, title, or interest in real property.

(c)(1) A city attorney, district attorney, or other law enforcement prosecutorial entity has standing to enforce this section and may sue for declaratory relief or injunctive relief for a violation of this section, and to enforce the civil penalties provided in paragraphs (2) and (3).

(2) In addition to any other penalty allowed by law, a violation of paragraph (1) of subdivision (a) shall result in a civil penalty of not more than one thousand dollars ($1,000) per advertisement, to be paid to the entity that is authorized to bring the action under this section.

(3) In addition to any other penalty allowed by law, a violation of paragraph (2) or (3) of subdivision (a) shall result in a civil penalty of not more than one thousand dollars ($1,000) per animal, to be paid to the entity that is authorized to bring the action under this section. *(Added by Stats.2012, c. 596 (S.B. 1229), § 2.)*

§ 1943. Term of hiring; presumption

A hiring of real property, other than lodgings and dwelling-houses, in places where there is no custom or usage on the subject, is presumed to be a month to month tenancy unless otherwise designated in writing; except that, in the case of real property used for agricultural or grazing purposes a hiring is presumed to be for one year from its commencement unless otherwise expressed in the hiring. *(Enacted in 1872. Amended by Stats.1953, c. 1541, p. 3212, § 1.)*

Research References

Miller and Starr California Real Estate § 19:30, Periodic Tenancy.
Miller and Starr California Real Estate § 19:33, Contract Term Provided in the Lease.
12 Witkin, California Summary 10th Real Property § 524, Specification in Instrument.

§ 1944. Term of hiring; presumption; lodgings or dwelling house

A hiring of lodgings or a dwelling house for an unspecified term is presumed to have been made for such length of time as the parties adopt for the estimation of the rent. Thus a hiring at a monthly rate of rent is presumed to be for one month. In the absence of any agreement respecting the length of time or the rent, the hiring is presumed to be monthly. *(Enacted in 1872.)*

Research References

Rutter, Cal. Practice Guide: Civil Trials & Evidence Ch. 8G-C, C. Presumptions.
Miller and Starr California Real Estate § 19:30, Periodic Tenancy.
Miller and Starr California Real Estate § 19:31, Tenancy at Will.
Miller and Starr California Real Estate § 19:33, Contract Term Provided in the Lease.
12 Witkin, California Summary 10th Real Property § 524, Specification in Instrument.

§ 1945. Renewal by continued possession and acceptance of rent

If a lessee of real property remains in possession thereof after the expiration of the hiring, and the lessor accepts rent from him, the parties are presumed to have renewed the hiring on the same terms and for the same time, not exceeding one month when the rent is payable monthly, nor in any case one year. *(Enacted in 1872.)*

Research References

Rutter, Cal. Practice Guide: Civil Trials & Evidence Ch. 8G-C, C. Presumptions.
Miller and Starr California Real Estate § 17:54, Landlords and Tenants--Termination of Right of Removal.
Miller and Starr California Real Estate § 19:32, Tenancy at Sufferance.

Miller and Starr California Real Estate § 19:33, Contract Term Provided
in the Lease.
Miller and Starr California Real Estate § 19:39, Automatic Extension or
Renewal.
Miller and Starr California Real Estate § 19:43, Presumption of Nature of
Holdover Tenancy.
Miller and Starr California Real Estate § 11:101, Effect of Foreclosure on
Rights of Tenants in Possession.
21 NO. 6 Miller & Starr, California Real Estate Newsalert 15, Landlord
and Tenant.
22 NO. 1 Miller & Starr, California Real Estate Newsalert 20, Landlord
and Tenant.
12 Witkin, California Summary 10th Real Property § 509, Landlord's
Election.
12 Witkin, California Summary 10th Real Property § 532, Provision for
Automatic Renewal.
12 Witkin, California Summary 10th Real Property § 680, Periodic
Tenancy.

§ 1945.5.　Automatic renewal or extension; recitals in contract; size of type, etc.

Notwithstanding any other provision of law, any term of a lease executed after the effective date of this section for the hiring of residential real property which provides for the automatic renewal or extension of the lease for all or part of the full term of the lease if the lessee remains in possession after the expiration of the lease or fails to give notice of his intent not to renew or extend before the expiration of the lease shall be voidable by the party who did not prepare the lease unless such renewal or extension provision appears in at least eight-point boldface type, if the contract is printed, in the body of the lease agreement and a recital of the fact that such provision is contained in the body of the agreement appears in at least eight-point boldface type, if the contract is printed, immediately prior to the place where the lessee executes the agreement. In such case, the presumption in Section 1945 of this code shall apply.

Any waiver of the provisions of this section is void as against public policy. (Added by Stats.1965, c. 1664, p. 3779, § 1, operative June 30, 1966. Amended by Stats.1976, c. 1107, p. 4991, § 1.)

Research References

Miller and Starr California Real Estate § 19:39, Automatic Extension or
Renewal.
12 Witkin, California Summary 10th Real Property § 532, Provision for
Automatic Renewal.
1 Witkin Cal. Summ. 10th Contracts § 683, Waivers by Tenants.

§ 1946.　Renewable hiring; notice of termination

A hiring of real property, for a term not specified by the parties, is deemed to be renewed as stated in Section 1945, at the end of the term implied by law unless one of the parties gives written notice to the other of his or her intention to terminate the same, at least as long before the expiration thereof as the term of the hiring itself, not exceeding 30 days; provided, however, that as to tenancies from month to month either of the parties may terminate the same by giving at least 30 days' written notice thereof at any time and the rent shall be due and payable to and including the date of termination. It shall be competent for the parties to provide by an agreement at the time the tenancy is created that a notice of the intention to terminate the same may be given at any time not less than seven days before the expiration of the term thereof. The notice herein required shall be given in the manner prescribed in Section 1162 of the Code of Civil Procedure or by sending a copy by certified or registered mail addressed to the other party. In addition, the lessee may give the notice by sending a copy by certified or registered mail addressed to the agent of the lessor to whom the lessee has paid the rent for the month prior to the date of the notice or by delivering a copy to the agent personally. The

notice given by the lessor shall also contain, in substantially the same form, the following:

"State law permits former tenants to reclaim abandoned personal property left at the former address of the tenant, subject to certain conditions. You may or may not be able to reclaim property without incurring additional costs, depending on the cost of storing the property and the length of time before it is reclaimed. In general, these costs will be lower the sooner you contact your former landlord after being notified that property belonging to you was left behind after you moved out."

(Enacted in 1872. Amended by Stats.1931, c. 643, p. 1385, § 1; Stats.1937, c. 354, p. 773, § 1; Stats.1941, c. 784, p. 2325, § 1; Stats.1947, c. 676, p. 1709, § 2; Stats.1969, c. 442, p. 993, § 1; Stats.1973, c. 167, p. 468, § 10; Stats.2012, c. 560 (A.B. 2521), § 1.)

Research References

California Real Estate Forms (Miller & Starr) § 2:17, Office Lease—
Mixed Use Building.
California Real Estate Forms (Miller & Starr) § 2:34, Sublease—Shared
Office Space.
California Real Estate Forms (Miller & Starr) § 2:65, Residential Lease.
California Real Estate Forms (Miller & Starr) § 2:66, Residential Lease
With Purchase Option.
Rutter, Cal. Practice Guide: Landlord-Tenant Form 2:A, Residential
Rental Agreement.
Rutter, Cal. Practice Guide: Landlord-Tenant Form 7:C, Thirty/Sixty-Day
Notice to Terminate.
Miller and Starr California Real Estate § 19:7, Other Interests Distin-
guished--Eviction of a Guest or Lodger.
Miller and Starr California Real Estate § 19:30, Periodic Tenancy.
Miller and Starr California Real Estate § 19:33, Contract Term Provided
in the Lease.
Miller and Starr California Real Estate § 19:91, Property Subject to
Control; Exceptions and Exemptions--State Exemption of Specified
Residential Rental Properties.
Miller and Starr California Real Estate § 19:139, Summary of Causes for
Termination.
Miller and Starr California Real Estate § 19:188, Notice Required by
Statute.
Miller and Starr California Real Estate § 19:190, Lease Provisions
Regarding Notice.
Miller and Starr California Real Estate § 19:192, Timing and Service of a
Notice of Termination.
Miller and Starr California Real Estate § 19:193, When a Notice is
Effective.
Miller and Starr California Real Estate § 19:201, Landlord's Alternative
Remedies for Tenant's Breach; When Notice is Required.
Miller and Starr California Real Estate § 19:204, Service of the Notice.
Miller and Starr California Real Estate § 19:218, Required Relationship
of the Parties.
19 NO. 1 Miller & Starr, California Real Estate Newsalert 1, The Perata
Foreclosure Bill (SB 1137): New Rights for Defaulting Borrowers
and Tenants; New Complications for Foreclosing Lenders.
6 Witkin Cal. Proc. 5th Proceedings Without Trial § 32, Implied
Limitations.
12 Witkin, California Summary 10th Real Property § 514, Statutory
Rights of Lodger.
12 Witkin, California Summary 10th Real Property § 680, Periodic
Tenancy.
12 Witkin, California Summary 10th Real Property § 706, Nature of
Defense.
1 Witkin Cal. Summ. 10th Contracts § 525, Disposition of Security.
7 Witkin, California Summary 10th Constitutional Law § 620, Government Assisted Housing Projects.

§ 1946.1.　Renewal and termination with respect to hiring of residential real property for a term not specified by the parties; notice

(a) Notwithstanding Section 1946, a hiring of residential real property for a term not specified by the parties, is deemed to be renewed as stated in Section 1945, at the end of the term implied by law unless one of the parties gives written notice to the other of his or her intention to terminate the tenancy, as provided in this section.

(b) An owner of a residential dwelling giving notice pursuant to this section shall give notice at least 60 days prior to the proposed date of termination. A tenant giving notice pursuant to this section shall give notice for a period at least as long as the term of the periodic tenancy prior to the proposed date of termination.

(c) Notwithstanding subdivision (b), an owner of a residential dwelling giving notice pursuant to this section shall give notice at least 30 days prior to the proposed date of termination if any tenant or resident has resided in the dwelling for less than one year.

(d) Notwithstanding subdivision (b), an owner of a residential dwelling giving notice pursuant to this section shall give notice at least 30 days prior to the proposed date of termination if all of the following apply:

(1) The dwelling or unit is alienable separate from the title to any other dwelling unit.

(2) The owner has contracted to sell the dwelling or unit to a bona fide purchaser for value, and has established an escrow with a title insurer or an underwritten title company, as defined in Sections 12340.4 and 12340.5 of the Insurance Code, respectively, a licensed escrow agent, as defined in Sections 17004 and 17200 of the Financial Code, or a licensed real estate broker, as defined in Section 10131 of the Business and Professions Code.

(3) The purchaser is a natural person or persons.

(4) The notice is given no more than 120 days after the escrow has been established.

(5) Notice was not previously given to the tenant pursuant to this section.

(6) The purchaser in good faith intends to reside in the property for at least one full year after the termination of the tenancy.

(e) After an owner has given notice of his or her intention to terminate the tenancy pursuant to this section, a tenant may also give notice of his or her intention to terminate the tenancy pursuant to this section, provided that the tenant's notice is for a period at least as long as the term of the periodic tenancy and the proposed date of termination occurs before the owner's proposed date of termination.

(f) The notices required by this section shall be given in the manner prescribed in Section 1162 of the Code of Civil Procedure or by sending a copy by certified or registered mail.

(g) This section may not be construed to affect the authority of a public entity that otherwise exists to regulate or monitor the basis for eviction.

(h) Any notice given by an owner pursuant to this section shall contain, in substantially the same form, the following:

"State law permits former tenants to reclaim abandoned personal property left at the former address of the tenant, subject to certain conditions. You may or may not be able to reclaim property without incurring additional costs, depending on the cost of storing the property and the length of time before it is reclaimed. In general, these costs will be lower the sooner you contact your former landlord after being notified that property belonging to you was left behind after you moved out."

(Added by Stats.2006, c. 842 (A.B.1169), § 1. Amended by Stats.2009, c. 347 (S.B.290), § 1; Stats.2012, c. 560 (A.B.2521), § 2; Stats.2012, c. 786 (A.B.2303), § 2.5.)

Research References

Rutter, Cal. Practice Guide: Landlord-Tenant Form 2:A, Residential Rental Agreement.

Rutter, Cal. Practice Guide: Landlord-Tenant Form 7:C, Thirty/Sixty-Day Notice to Terminate.

Miller and Starr California Real Estate § 19:188, Notice Required by Statute.

Miller and Starr California Real Estate § 19:192, Timing and Service of a Notice of Termination.

Miller and Starr California Real Estate § 19:193, When a Notice is Effective.

Miller and Starr California Real Estate § 19:208, Termination of the Lease; Landlord's Recovery of Rent or Damages--Recovery in an Unlawful Detainer Proceeding.

13 NO. 4 Miller & Starr, California Real Estate Newsalert 14, Landlord and Tenant.

17 NO. 4 Miller & Starr, California Real Estate Newsalert 2, Statutory Update:.

17 NO. 6 Miller & Starr, California Real Estate Newsalert 20, Table of Statutes (Newsalert Vol 17).

19 NO. 1 Miller & Starr, California Real Estate Newsalert 1, The Perata Foreclosure Bill (SB 1137): New Rights for Defaulting Borrowers and Tenants; New Complications for Foreclosing Lenders.

20 NO. 4 Miller & Starr, California Real Estate Newsalert 13, Landlord and Tenant.

23 NO. 2 Miller & Starr, California Real Estate Newsalert 1, Housing: Safety Net or Tangled Web? an Overview of Section 8 Tenancy Termination and Related Due Process Issues.

12 Witkin, California Summary 10th Real Property § 680, Periodic Tenancy.

1 Witkin Cal. Summ. 10th Contracts § 525, Disposition of Security.

§ 1946.5. Room by single lodger on periodic basis within dwelling unit occupied by owner; termination; written notice; removal from premises

(a) The hiring of a room by a lodger on a periodic basis within a dwelling unit occupied by the owner may be terminated by either party giving written notice to the other of his or her intention to terminate the hiring, at least as long before the expiration of the term of the hiring as specified in Section 1946. The notice shall be given in a manner prescribed in Section 1162 of the Code of Civil Procedure or by certified or registered mail, restricted delivery, to the other party, with a return receipt requested.

(b) Upon expiration of the notice period provided in the notice of termination given pursuant to subdivision (a), any right of the lodger to remain in the dwelling unit or any part thereof is terminated by operation of law. The lodger's removal from the premises may thereafter be effected pursuant to the provisions of Section 602.3 of the Penal Code or other applicable provisions of law.

(c) As used in this section, "lodger" means a person contracting with the owner of a dwelling unit for a room or room and board within the dwelling unit personally occupied by the owner, where the owner retains a right of access to all areas of the dwelling unit occupied by the lodger and has overall control of the dwelling unit.

(d) This section applies only to owner-occupied dwellings where a single lodger resides. Nothing in this section shall be construed to determine or affect in any way the rights of persons residing as lodgers in an owner-occupied dwelling where more than one lodger resides. *(Added by Stats.1986, c. 1010, § 1.)*

Research References

Miller and Starr California Real Estate § 19:7, Other Interests Distinguished--Eviction of a Guest or Lodger.

12 Witkin, California Summary 10th Real Property § 514, Statutory Rights of Lodger.

12 Witkin, California Summary 10th Real Property § 680, Periodic Tenancy.

§ 1946.7. Victims of domestic violence, sexual assault, stalking, human trafficking, or abuse of elder or dependent adult; written notice to terminate tenancy; requirements of notice; landlord disclosure to third party

Section operative until Jan. 1, 2016. See, also, section operative Jan. 1, 2016.

(a) A tenant may notify the landlord that he or she or a household member was a victim of an act that constitutes an act of domestic violence as defined in Section 6211 of the Family Code, sexual assault as defined in Section 261, 261.5, 262, 286, 288a, or 289 of the Penal Code, stalking as defined in Section 1708.7, human trafficking as defined in Section 236.1 of the Penal Code, or abuse of an elder or a dependent adult as defined in Section 15610.07 of the Welfare and Institutions Code, and that the tenant intends to terminate the tenancy.

(b) A notice to terminate a tenancy under this section shall be in writing, with one of the following attached to the notice:

(1) A copy of a temporary restraining order, emergency protective order, or protective order lawfully issued pursuant to Part 3 (commencing with Section 6240) or Part 4 (commencing with Section 6300) of Division 10 of the Family Code, Section 136.2 of the Penal Code, Section 527.6 of the Code of Civil Procedure, or Section 213.5 or 15657.03 of the Welfare and Institutions Code that protects the tenant or household member from further domestic violence, sexual assault, stalking, human trafficking, or abuse of an elder or a dependent adult.

(2) A copy of a written report by a peace officer employed by a state or local law enforcement agency acting in his or her official capacity * * * stating that the tenant or household member has filed a report alleging that he or she or the household member is a victim of domestic violence, sexual assault, * * * stalking, human trafficking, or abuse of an elder or a dependent adult.

(3)(A) Documentation from a qualified third party based on information received by that third party while acting in his or her professional capacity to indicate that the tenant or household member is seeking assistance for physical or mental injuries or abuse resulting from an act of domestic violence, sexual assault, stalking, human trafficking, elder abuse, or dependent adult abuse.

(B) The documentation shall contain, in substantially the same form, the following:

Tenant Statement and Qualified Third Party Statement under Civil Code Section 1946.7
Part I. Statement By Tenant

I, [insert name of tenant], state as follows:

I, or a member of my household, have been a victim of:
[insert one or more of the following: domestic violence, sexual assault, stalking, human trafficking, elder abuse, or dependent adult abuse.]

The most recent incident(s) happened on or about:
[insert date or dates.]

The incident(s) was/were committed by the following person(s), with these physical description(s), if known and safe to provide:
[if known and safe to provide, insert name(s) and physical description(s).]

_____   _____
(signature of tenant)   (date)

Part II. Qualified Third Party Statement

I, [insert name of qualified third party], state as follows:

My business address and phone number are:
[insert business address and phone number.]

Check and complete one of the following:
____I meet the requirements for a sexual assault counselor provided in Section 1035.2 of the Evidence Code and I am either engaged in an office, hospital, institution, or center commonly known as a rape crisis center described in that section or employed by an organization providing the programs specified in Section 13835.2 of the Penal Code.
____I meet the requirements for a domestic violence counselor provided in Section 1037.1 of the Evidence Code and I am employed, whether financially compensated or not, by a domestic violence victim service organization, as defined in that section.
____I meet the requirements for a human trafficking caseworker provided in Section 1038.2 of the Evidence Code and I am employed, whether financially compensated or not, by an organization that provides programs specified in Section 18294 of the Welfare and Institutions Code or in Section 13835.2 of the Penal Code.
____I am licensed by the State of California as a:
[insert one of the following: physician and surgeon, osteopathic physician and surgeon, registered nurse, psychiatrist, psychologist, licensed clinical social worker, licensed marriage and family therapist, or licensed professional clinical counselor.] and I am licensed by, and my license number is:
[insert name of state licensing entity and license number.]

The person who signed the Statement By Tenant above stated to me that he or she, or a member of his or her household, is a victim of:
[insert one or more of the following: domestic violence, sexual assault, stalking, human trafficking, elder abuse, or dependent adult abuse.]
The person further stated to me the incident(s) occurred on or about the date(s) stated above.

I understand that the person who made the Statement By Tenant may use this document as a basis for terminating a lease with the person's landlord.

_____   _____
(signature of qualified third party)   (date)

(C) The documentation may be signed by a person who meets the requirements for a sexual assault counselor, domestic violence counselor, or a human trafficking caseworker only if the documentation displays the letterhead of the office, hospital, institution, center, or organization, as appropriate, that engages or employs, whether financially compensated or not, this counselor or caseworker.

(c) The notice to terminate the tenancy shall be given within 180 days of the date that any order described in paragraph (1) of subdivision (b) was issued, within 180 days of the date that any written report described in paragraph (2) of subdivision (b) was made, or within the time period described in Section 1946.

(d) If notice to terminate the tenancy is provided to the landlord under this section, the tenant shall be responsible for payment of rent for 30 days following the giving of the notice, or within the appropriate period as described in Section 1946, and thereafter shall be released from any rent payment obligation under the rental agreement without penalty. Existing law governing the security deposit shall apply.

(e) If within the 30 days following the giving of the notice under this section the tenant quits the premises and the premises are rented to another party, the rent due on the premises for that 30–day period shall be prorated. Existing law governing the security deposit shall apply.

(f) Nothing in this section relieves a tenant, other than the tenant who is, or who has a household member who is, a victim of domestic violence, sexual assault, stalking, human trafficking, or abuse of an elder or a dependent adult and members of that tenant's household, from their obligations under the rental agreement.

(g)(1) "Household member," as used in this section, means a member of the tenant's family who lives in the same household as the tenant.

(2) "Qualified third party," as used in this section, means a health practitioner, domestic violence counselor, as defined in Section 1037.1 of the Evidence Code, a sexual assault counselor, as defined in Section 1035.2 of the Evidence Code, or a human trafficking caseworker, as defined in Section 1038.2 of the Evidence Code.

(3) "Health practitioner," as used in this section, means a physician and surgeon, osteopathic physician and surgeon, psychiatrist, psychologist, registered nurse, licensed clinical social worker, licensed marriage and family therapist, or licensed professional clinical counselor.

(h)(1) A landlord shall not disclose any information provided by a tenant under this section to a third party unless the disclosure satisfies any one of the following:

(A) The tenant consents in writing to the disclosure.

(B) The disclosure is required by law or order of the court.

(2) A landlord's communication to a qualified third party who provides documentation under paragraph (3) of subdivision (b) to verify the contents of that documentation is not disclosure for purposes of this subdivision.

(i) This section shall remain in effect only until January 1, 2016, and as of that date is repealed, unless a later enacted statute, that is enacted before January 1, 2016, deletes or extends that date. *(Added by Stats.2008, c. 440 (A.B.2052), § 1, eff. Sept. 27, 2008. Amended by Stats.2011, c. 76 (A.B.588), § 1; Stats. 2012, c. 516 (S.B.1403), § 1; Stats.2013, c. 130 (S.B.612), § 1.)*

Repeal

For repeal of this section, see its terms.

Research References

Miller and Starr California Real Estate § 19:86, Termination of the Obligation to Pay Rent.
19 NO. 4 Miller & Starr, California Real Estate Newsalert 19, Landlord and Tenant.
12 Witkin, California Summary 10th Real Property § 680, Periodic Tenancy.

§ 1946.7. Victims of domestic violence, sexual assault, stalking, human trafficking, or abuse of elder or dependent adult; written notice to terminate tenancy; requirements of notice; landlord disclosure to third party

Section operative Jan. 1, 2016. See, also, section operative until Jan. 1, 2016.

(a) A tenant may notify the landlord that he or she or a household member was a victim of an act that constitutes an act of domestic violence as defined in Section 6211 of the Family Code, sexual assault as defined in Section 261, 261.5, 262, 286, 288a, or 289 of the Penal Code, stalking as defined in Section 1708.7, human trafficking as defined in Section 236.1 of the Penal Code, or abuse of an elder or a dependent adult as defined in Section 15610.07 of the Welfare and Institutions Code, and that the tenant intends to terminate the tenancy.

(b) A notice to terminate a tenancy under this section shall be in writing, with one of the following attached to the notice:

(1) A copy of a temporary restraining order, emergency protective order, or protective order lawfully issued pursuant to Part 3 (commencing with Section 6240) or Part 4 (commencing with Section 6300) of Division 10 of the Family Code, Section 136.2 of the Penal Code, Section 527.6 of the Code of Civil Procedure, or Section 213.5 or 15657.03 of the Welfare and Institutions Code that protects the tenant or household member from further domestic violence, sexual assault, stalking, human trafficking, or abuse of an elder or a dependent adult.

(2) A copy of a written report by a peace officer employed by a state or local law enforcement agency acting in his or her official capacity stating that the tenant or household member has filed a report alleging that he or she or the household member is a victim of domestic violence, sexual assault, stalking, human trafficking, or abuse of an elder or a dependent adult.

(c) The notice to terminate the tenancy shall be given within 180 days of the date that any order described in paragraph (1) of subdivision (b) was issued, within 180 days of the date that any written report described in paragraph (2) of subdivision (b) was made, or within the time period described in Section 1946.

(d) If notice to terminate the tenancy is provided to the landlord under this section, the tenant shall be responsible for payment of rent for 30 days following the giving of the notice, or within the appropriate period as described in Section 1946, and thereafter shall be released from any rent payment obligation under the rental agreement without penalty. Existing law governing the security deposit shall apply.

(e) If within the 30 days following the giving of the notice under this section the tenant quits the premises and the premises are rented to another party, the rent due on the premises for that 30-day period shall be prorated. Existing law governing the security deposit shall apply.

(f) Nothing in this section relieves a tenant, other than the tenant who is, or who has a household member who is, a victim of domestic violence, sexual assault, stalking, human trafficking, or abuse of an elder or a dependent adult and members of that tenant's household, from their obligations under the rental agreement.

(g) "Household member" as used in this section means a member of the tenant's family who lives in the same household as the tenant.

(h) A landlord shall not disclose any information provided by a tenant under this section to a third party unless the disclosure satisfies any one of the following:

(1) The tenant consents in writing to the disclosure.

(2) The disclosure is required by law or order of the court.

(i) This section shall be operative January 1, 2016. *(Added by Stats.2013, c. 130 (S.B.612), § 2, operative Jan. 1, 2016.)*

§ 1947. Rent; time of payment

When there is no usage or contract to the contrary, rents are payable at the termination of the holding, when it does not exceed one year. If the holding is by the day, week, month, quarter, or year, rent is payable at the termination of the respective periods, as it successively becomes due. *(Enacted in 1872.)*

Research References

California Real Estate Forms (Miller & Starr) § 2:21, Retail Lease—15,000 RSF to 30,000 RSF (Tenant Oriented).
California Real Estate Forms (Miller & Starr) § 2:23, Retail Lease—Small Strip-Shopping Center.
California Real Estate Forms (Miller & Starr) § 2:31, Rental Agreement—Self Storage.
California Real Estate Forms (Miller & Starr) § 2:32, Gross Lease—Small Commercial Property.

California Real Estate Forms (Miller & Starr) § 2:65, Residential Lease.

California Real Estate Forms (Miller & Starr) § 2:66, Residential Lease With Purchase Option.

Miller and Starr California Real Estate § 19:78, Time and Place of Payment; Late Charges.

12 Witkin, California Summary 10th Real Property § 503, Statutory Framework.

12 Witkin, California Summary 10th Real Property § 568, (S 568) Nature of Obligation.

§ 1947.3. Cash or electronic funds transfer as exclusive form of payment of rent or security deposit; conditions; right to terminate tenancy; mutual agreement; waiver

(a)(1) Except as provided in paragraph (2), a landlord or a landlord's agent shall allow a tenant to pay rent and deposit of security by at least one form of payment that is neither cash nor electronic funds transfer.

(2) A landlord or a landlord's agent may demand or require cash as the exclusive form of payment of rent or deposit of security if the tenant has previously attempted to pay the landlord or landlord's agent with a check drawn on insufficient funds or the tenant has instructed the drawee to stop payment on a check, draft, or order for the payment of money. The landlord may demand or require cash as the exclusive form of payment only for a period not exceeding three months following an attempt to pay with a check on insufficient funds or following a tenant's instruction to stop payment. If the landlord chooses to demand or require cash payment under these circumstances, the landlord shall give the tenant a written notice stating that the payment instrument was dishonored and informing the tenant that the tenant shall pay in cash for a period determined by the landlord, not to exceed three months, and attach a copy of the dishonored instrument to the notice. The notice shall comply with Section 827 if demanding or requiring payment in cash constitutes a change in the terms of the lease.

(3) Paragraph (2) does not enlarge or diminish a landlord's or landlord's agent's legal right to terminate a tenancy.

(b) For the purposes of this section, the issuance of a money order or a cashier's check is direct evidence only that the instrument was issued.

(c) For purposes of this section, "electronic funds transfer" means any transfer of funds, other than a transaction originated by check, draft, or similar paper instrument, that is initiated through an electronic terminal, telephonic instrument, computer, or magnetic tape so as to order, instruct, or authorize a financial institution to debit or credit an account. "Electronic funds transfer" includes, but is not limited to, point-of-sale transfers, direct deposits or withdrawals of funds, transfers initiated by telephone, transfers via an automated clearinghouse, transfers initiated electronically that deliver a paper instrument, and transfers authorized in advance to recur at substantially regular intervals.

(d) Nothing in this section shall be construed to prohibit the tenant and landlord or agent to mutually agree that rent payments may be made in cash or by electronic funds transfer, so long as another form of payment is also authorized, subject to the requirements of subdivision (a).

(e) A waiver of the provisions of this section is contrary to public policy, and is void and unenforceable. *(Added by Stats.2004, c. 76 (S.B.115), § 1. Amended by Stats.2012, c. 268 (S.B.1055), § 1.)*

Research References

California Real Estate Forms (Miller & Starr) § 2:16, Office Lease— Multistory Office Building.

California Real Estate Forms (Miller & Starr) § 2:17, Office Lease— Mixed Use Building.

California Real Estate Forms (Miller & Starr) § 2:18, Office Lease— Office/Warehouse Building With Four or Fewer Tenants.

California Real Estate Forms (Miller & Starr) § 2:19, Retail Lease— Power Shopping Center.

California Real Estate Forms (Miller & Starr) § 2:20, Retail Lease— Shopping Center With for Profit Parking Garage.

California Real Estate Forms (Miller & Starr) § 2:21, Retail Lease— 15,000 RSF to 30,000 RSF (Tenant Oriented).

California Real Estate Forms (Miller & Starr) § 2:22, Retail Lease— Regional Shopping Center.

California Real Estate Forms (Miller & Starr) § 2:23, Retail Lease— Small Strip-Shopping Center.

California Real Estate Forms (Miller & Starr) § 2:24, Retail Lease— Restaurant.

California Real Estate Forms (Miller & Starr) § 2:25, Industrial Lease.

California Real Estate Forms (Miller & Starr) § 2:26, Triple Net Lease— Industrial Build-To-Suit Lease.

Rutter, Cal. Practice Guide: Landlord-Tenant Form 2:A, Residential Rental Agreement.

Miller and Starr California Real Estate § 19:78, Time and Place of Payment; Late Charges.

15 NO. 4 Miller & Starr, California Real Estate Newsalert 12, Landlord and Tenant.

12 Witkin, California Summary 10th Real Property § 569, (S 569) Form and Determination of Payment.

§ 1947.5. Prohibition by residential dwelling unit landlord of smoking cigarettes or other tobacco products; lease or rental agreement provisions

(a) A landlord of a residential dwelling unit, as defined in Section 1940, or his or her agent, may prohibit the smoking of a cigarette, as defined in Section 104556 of the Health and Safety Code, or other tobacco product on the property or in any building or portion of the building, including any dwelling unit, other interior or exterior area, or the premises on which it is located, in accordance with this article.

(b)(1) Every lease or rental agreement entered into on or after January 1, 2012, for a residential dwelling unit on property on any portion of which the landlord has prohibited the smoking of cigarettes or other tobacco products pursuant to this article shall include a provision that specifies the areas on the property where smoking is prohibited, if the lessee has not previously occupied the dwelling unit.

(2) For a lease or rental agreement entered into before January 1, 2012, a prohibition against the smoking of cigarettes or other tobacco products in any portion of the property in which smoking was previously permitted shall constitute a change of the terms of tenancy, requiring adequate notice in writing, to be provided in the manner prescribed in Section 827.

(c) A landlord who exercises the authority provided in subdivision (a) to prohibit smoking shall be subject to federal, state, and local requirements governing changes to the terms of a lease or rental agreement for tenants with leases or rental agreements that are in existence at the time that the policy limiting or prohibiting smoking is adopted.

(d) This section shall not be construed to preempt any local ordinance in effect on or before January 1, 2012, or any provision of a local ordinance in effect on or after January 1, 2012, that restricts the smoking of cigarettes or other tobacco products.

(e) A limitation or prohibition of the use of any tobacco product shall not affect any other term or condition of the tenancy, nor shall this section be construed to require statutory authority to establish or enforce any other lawful term or condition of the tenancy. *(Added by Stats.2011, c. 264 (S.B.332), § 2.)*

Research References

22 NO. 4 Miller & Starr, California Real Estate Newsalert 15, Landlord and Tenant.

12 Witkin, California Summary 10th Real Property § 632, Nature of Covenant.

§ 1947.7. Local rent stabilization and rent control programs; enforcement; confidential information

(a) The Legislature finds and declares that the operation of local rent stabilization programs can be complex and that disputes often arise with regard to standards of compliance with the regulatory processes of those programs. Therefore, it is the intent of the Legislature to limit the imposition of penalties and sanctions against an owner of residential rental units where that person has attempted in good faith to fully comply with the regulatory processes.

(b) An owner of a residential rental unit who is in substantial compliance with an ordinance or charter that controls or establishes a system of controls on the price at which residential rental units may be offered for rent or lease and which requires the registration of rents, or any regulation adopted pursuant thereto, shall not be assessed a penalty or any other sanction for noncompliance with the ordinance, charter, or regulation.

Restitution to the tenant or recovery of the registration or filing fees due to the local agency shall be the exclusive remedies which may be imposed against an owner of a residential rental unit who is in substantial compliance with the ordinance, charter, or regulation.

"Substantial compliance," as used in this subdivision, means that the owner of a residential rental unit has made a good faith attempt to comply with the ordinance, charter, or regulation sufficient to reasonably carry out the intent and purpose of the ordinance, charter, or regulation, but is not in full compliance, and has, after receiving notice of a deficiency from the local agency, cured the defect in a timely manner, as reasonably determined by the local agency.

"Local agency," as used in this subdivision, means the public entity responsible for the implementation of the ordinance, charter, or regulation.

(c) For any residential unit which has been registered and for which a base rent has been listed or for any residential unit which an owner can show, by a preponderance of the evidence, a good faith attempt to comply with the registration requirements or who was exempt from registration requirements in a previous version of the ordinance or charter and for which the owner of that residential unit has subsequently found not to have been in compliance with the ordinance, charter, or regulation, all annual rent adjustments which may have been denied during the period of the owner's noncompliance shall be restored prospectively once the owner is in compliance with the ordinance, charter, or regulation.

(d) In those jurisdictions where, prior to January 1, 1990, the local ordinance did not allow the restoration of annual rent adjustment, once the owner is in compliance with this section the local agency may phase in any increase in rent caused by the restoration of the annual rent adjustments that is in excess of 20 percent over the rent previously paid by the tenant, in equal installments over three years, if the tenant demonstrates undue financial hardship due to the restoration of the full annual rent adjustments. This subdivision shall remain operative only until January 1, 1993, unless a later enacted statute which is chaptered by January 1, 1993, deletes or extends that date.

(e) For purposes of this subdivision, an owner shall be deemed in compliance with the ordinance, charter, or regulation if he or she is in substantial compliance with the applicable local rental registration requirements and applicable local and state housing code provisions, has paid all fees and penalties owed to the local agency which have not otherwise been barred by the applicable statute of limitations, and has satisfied all claims for refunds of rental overcharges brought by tenants or by the local rent control board on behalf of tenants of the affected unit.

(f) Nothing in this section shall be construed to grant to any public entity any power which it does not possess independent of this section to control or establish a system of control on the price at which accommodations may be offered for rent or lease, or to diminish any power to do so which that public entity may possess, except as specifically provided in this section.

(g) In those jurisdictions where an ordinance or charter controls, or establishes a system of controls on, the price at which residential rental units may be offered for rent or lease and requires the periodic registration of rents, and where, for purposes of compliance with subdivision (e) of Section 1954.53, the local agency requires an owner to provide the name of a present or former tenant, the tenant's name and any additional information provided concerning the tenant, is confidential and shall be treated as confidential information within the meaning of the Information Practices Act of 1977 (Chapter 1 (commencing with Section 1798) of Title 1.8 of this part). A local agency shall, to the extent required by this subdivision, be considered an "agency" as defined in subdivision (b) of Section 1798.3. For purposes of compliance with subdivision (e) of Section 1954.53, a local agency subject to this subdivision may request, but shall not compel, an owner to provide any information regarding a tenant other than the tenant's name. *(Added by Stats.1986, c. 1199, § 1. Amended by Stats.1989, c. 987, § 1; Stats.1996, c. 566 (S.B.1632), § 1.)*

Research References

Miller and Starr California Real Estate § 19:100, Administration; Authority and Duty of the Rent Board.

Miller and Starr California Real Estate § 19:101, Administration; Authority and Duty of the Rent Board--Substantial Compliance; Certificate of Compliance.

Miller and Starr California Real Estate § 19:102, Enforcement and Remedies.

14 NO. 2 Miller & Starr, California Real Estate Newsalert 17, Mobilehomes.

12 Witkin, California Summary 10th Real Property § 573, (S 573) in General.

12 Witkin, California Summary 10th Real Property § 592, Landlord's Good Faith Defense.

§ 1947.8. Local rent controls; establishment and certification of permissible rent levels; appeal; fee; public record

(a) If an ordinance or charter controls or establishes a system of controls on the price at which residential rental units may be offered for rent or lease and requires the registration of rents, the ordinance or charter, or any regulation adopted pursuant thereto, shall provide for the establishment and certification of permissible rent levels for the registered rental units, and any changes thereafter to those rent levels, by the local agency as provided in this section.

(b) If the ordinance, charter, or regulation is in effect on January 1, 1987, the ordinance, charter, or regulation shall provide for the establishment and certification of permissible rent levels on or before January 1, 1988, including completion of all appeals and administrative proceedings connected therewith. After July 1, 1990, no local agency may maintain any action to recover excess rent against any property owner who has registered the unit with the local agency within the time limits set forth in this section if the initial certification of permissible rent levels affecting that particular property has not been completed, unless the delay is willfully and intentionally caused by the property owner or is a result of court proceedings or further administrative proceedings ordered by a court. If the ordinance, charter, or regulation is adopted on or after January 1, 1987, the ordinance, charter, or regulation shall provide for the establishment and certification of permissible rent levels within one year after it is adopted, including completion of all appeals and administrative proceedings connected therewith. Upon the request of the landlord or the tenant, the local agency shall provide the landlord and the tenant with a certificate or other documentation reflecting the permissible rent levels of the rental unit. A landlord may request a certificate of permissible rent levels for rental units which have a base rent established, but which are vacant and not exempt from registration under this section. The landlord or the tenant may appeal the determination of the permissible rent levels reflected in the certificate. The permissible rent levels reflected in the certificate or other documentation shall, in the absence of intentional misrepresentation or fraud, be binding and conclusive upon the local agency unless the determination of the permissible rent levels is being appealed.

(c) After the establishment and certification of permissible rent levels under subdivision (b), the local agency shall, upon the request of the landlord or the tenant, provide the landlord and the tenant with a certificate of the permissible rent levels of the rental unit. The certificate shall be issued within five business days from the date of request by the landlord or the tenant. The permissible rent levels reflected in the certificate shall, in the absence of intentional misrepresentation or fraud, be binding and conclusive upon the local agency unless the determination of the permissible rent levels is being appealed. The landlord or the tenant may appeal the determination of the permissible rent levels reflected in the certificate. Any appeal of a determination of permissible rent levels as reflected in the certificate, other than an appeal made pursuant to subdivision (b), shall be filed with the local agency within 15 days from issuance of the certificate. The local agency shall notify, in writing, the landlord and the tenant of its decision within 60 days following the filing of the appeal.

(d) The local agency may charge the person to whom a certificate is issued a fee in the amount necessary to cover the reasonable costs incurred by the local agency in issuing the certificate.

(e) The absence of a certification of permissible rent levels shall not impair, restrict, abridge, or otherwise interfere with either of the following:

(1) A judicial or administrative hearing.

(2) Any matter in connection with a conveyance of an interest in property.

(f) The record of permissible rent levels is a public record for purposes of the California Public Records Act, Chapter 3.5 (commencing with Section 6250) of Division 7 of Title 1 of the Government Code.

(g) Any notice specifying the rents applicable to residential rental units which is given by an owner to a public entity or tenant in order to comply with Chapter 12.75 (commencing with Section 7060) of Division 7 of Title 1 of the Government Code shall not be considered a registration of rents for purposes of this section.

(h) "Local agency," as used in this section, means the public entity responsible for the implementation of the ordinance, charter, or regulation.

(i) Nothing in this section shall be construed to grant to any public entity any power which it does not possess independent of this section to control or establish a system of control on the price at which accommodations may be offered for rent or lease, or to diminish any such power which that public entity may possess, except as specifically provided in this section. (Added by Stats.1986, c. 1199, § 2. Amended by Stats.1989, c. 987, § 2.)

Research References

Miller and Starr California Real Estate § 19:101, Administration; Authority and Duty of the Rent Board--Substantial Compliance; Certificate of Compliance.

12 Witkin, California Summary 10th Real Property § 573, (S 573) in General.

12 Witkin, California Summary 10th Real Property § 581, Establishing and Certifying Rent Levels.

§ 1947.9. San Francisco rent stabilization ordinance; limitations on compensation for temporary displacement; interpretation of section

(a)(1) Notwithstanding any local law to the contrary, for those units governed by the local rent stabilization ordinance in the City and County of San Francisco, levels of compensation for the temporary displacement of a tenant household for less than 20 days shall be limited to both of the following:

(A) Temporary housing and living expenses, of two hundred seventy-five dollars ($275) per day per tenant household. This limit may be adjusted annually by the city and county in an amount equal to the Consumer Price Index, beginning on January 1, 2014.

(B) Actual moving expenses if it is necessary to move the possessions of the tenant household.

(2) The landlord shall have the option to provide a comparable dwelling unit and pay any actual moving expenses, in lieu of the compensation specified in subparagraph (A) of paragraph (1). The rental housing shall be comparable to the tenant household's existing housing in location, size, number of bedrooms, accessibility, type, and quality of construction, and proximity to services and institutions upon which the displaced tenant household depends.

(b) This section shall not be construed to do any of the following:

(1) To terminate, interrupt, or amend, in any way, a tenancy subject to the lease provisions, or the rights and obligations of either party, including, but not limited to, the payment of rent.

(2) To create or affect any grounds for displacement or requirements of a landlord seeking temporary displacement, except the payment of relocation fees pursuant to subdivision (a) for displacement not exceeding 20 days.

(3) To affect the authority of a public entity that may regulate or monitor the basis for eviction.

(c) If a federal or state law regarding relocation compensation is also applicable to the temporary displacement, the tenant may elect to be compensated under those other provisions, and subdivision (a) shall be inapplicable.

(d) This section shall affect only levels of compensation for a temporary displacement of less than 20 days, and does not affect any other local procedures governing temporary relocation. (Added by Stats.2012, c. 243 (A.B.1925), § 1.)

§ 1947.10. Evictions based on fraudulent intent to occupy; treble damages

(a) After July 1, 1990, in any city, county, or city and county which administers a system of controls on the price at which residential rental units may be offered for rent or lease and which requires the registration of rents, any owner who evicts a tenant based upon the owner's or the owner's immediate relative's intention to occupy the tenant's unit, shall be required to maintain residence in the unit for at least six continuous months. If a court determines that the eviction was based upon fraud by the owner or the owner's immediate relative to not fulfill this six-month requirement, a court may order the owner to pay treble the cost of relocating the tenant from his or her existing unit back into the previous unit and may order the owner to pay treble the amount of any increase in rent which the tenant has paid. If the tenant decides not to relocate back into the previous unit, the court may order the owner to pay treble the amount of one month's rent paid by the tenant for the unit from which he or she was evicted and treble the amount of any costs incurred in relocating to a different unit. The prevailing party shall be awarded attorney's fees and court costs.

(b) The remedy provided by this section shall not be construed to prohibit any other remedies available to a any party affected by this section. *(Added by Stats.1989, c. 987, § 3.)*

Research References

Rutter, Cal. Practice Guide: Insurance Litigation Ch. 7A-C, C. Insuring Clauses-Occurrence vs. Claims-Made Policies.
Miller and Starr California Real Estate § 19:171, Right to Evict for Occupancy by the Landlord.
Miller and Starr California Real Estate § 19:174, Remedies for Wrongful Eviction.
12 Witkin, California Summary 10th Real Property § 591, Where Tenant was Improperly Evicted for Owner Occupancy.

§ 1947.11. Rent charged in excess of certified lawful rent ceiling; refunds

(a) In any city, county, or city and county which administers a system of controls on the price at which residential rental units may be offered for rent or lease and which requires the registration of rents, upon the establishment of a certified rent level, any owner who charges rent to a tenant in excess of the certified lawful rent ceiling shall refund the excess rent to the tenant upon demand. If the owner refuses to refund the excess rent and if a court determines that the owner willfully or intentionally charged the tenant rent in excess of the certified lawful rent ceiling, the court shall award the tenant a judgment for the excess amount of rent and may treble that amount. The prevailing party shall be awarded attorney's fees and court costs.

(b) The remedy provided by this section shall not be construed to prohibit any other remedies available to any party affected by this section.

(c) This section shall not be construed to extend the time within which actions are required to be brought beyond the otherwise applicable limitation set forth in the Code of Civil Procedure. *(Added by Stats.1989, c. 987, § 4. Amended by Stats.1990, c. 216 (S.B.2510), § 7.)*

Research References

Miller and Starr California Real Estate § 19:102, Enforcement and Remedies.
12 Witkin, California Summary 10th Real Property § 590, Where Excess Rent was Charged.

§ 1947.15. Rent control; calculation of fair return to owner; reasonable expenses, fees and costs for professional services

(a) The Legislature declares the purpose of this section is to:

(1) Ensure that owners of residential rental units that are subject to a system of controls on the price at which the units may be offered for rent or lease, or controls on the adjustment of the rent level, are not precluded or discouraged from obtaining a fair return on their properties as guaranteed by the United States Constitution and California Constitution because the professional expenses reasonably required in the course of the administrative proceedings, in order to obtain the rent increases necessary to provide a fair return, are not treated as a legitimate business expense.

(2) Encourage agencies which administer a system of controls on the price at which residential rental units may be offered for rent or lease, or controls the adjustment of the rent level, to enact streamlined administrative procedures governing rent

adjustment petitions which minimize, to the extent possible, the cost and expense of these administrative proceedings.

(3) Ensure that the cost of professional services reasonably incurred and required by owners of residential rental units subject to a system of controls in the price at which the units may be offered for rent or lease, or controls on the adjustments of the rent level in the course of defending rights related to the rent control system, be treated as a legitimate business expense.

(b) Any city, county, or city and county, including a charter city, which administers an ordinance, charter provision, rule, or regulation that controls or establishes a system of controls on the price at which all or any portion of the residential rental units located within the city, county, or city and county, may be offered for rent or lease, or controls the adjustment of the rent level, and which does not include a system of vacancy decontrol, as defined in subdivision (i), shall permit reasonable expenses, fees, and other costs for professional services, including, but not limited to, legal, accounting, appraisal, bookkeeping, consulting, property management, or architectural services, reasonably incurred in the course of successfully pursuing rights under or in relationship to, that ordinance, charter provision, rule, or regulation, or the right to a fair return on an owner's property as protected by the United States Constitution or California Constitution, to be included in any calculation of net operating income and operating expenses used to determine a fair return to the owner of the property. All expenses, fees, and other costs reasonably incurred by an owner of property in relation to administrative proceedings for purposes specified in this subdivision shall be included in the calculation specified in this subdivision.

(c) Reasonable fees that are incurred by the owner in successfully obtaining a judicial reversal of an adverse administrative decision regarding a petition for upward adjustment of rents shall be assessed against the respondent public agency which issued the adverse administrative decision, and shall not be included in the calculations specified in subdivisions (b) and (d).

(d)(1) Notwithstanding subdivision (b), the city, county, or city and county, on the basis of substantial evidence in the record that the expenses reasonably incurred in the underlying proceeding will not reoccur annually, may amortize the expenses for a period not to exceed five years, except that in extraordinary circumstances, the amortization period may be extended to a period of eight years. The extended amortization period shall not apply to vacant units and shall end if the unit becomes vacant during the period that the expense is being amortized. An amortization schedule shall include a reasonable rate of interest.

(2) Any determination of the reasonableness of the expenses claimed, of an appropriate amortization period, or of the award of an upward adjustment of rents to compensate the owner for expenses and costs incurred shall be made as part of, or immediately following, the decision in the underlying administrative proceeding.

(e) Any and all of the following factors shall be considered in the determination of the reasonableness of the expenses, fees, or other costs authorized by this section:

(1) The rate charged for those professional services in the relevant geographic area.

(2) The complexity of the matter.

(3) The degree of administrative burden or judicial burden, or both, imposed upon the property owner.

(4) The amount of adjustment sought or the significance of the rights defended and the results obtained.

(5) The relationship of the result obtained to the expenses, fees, and other costs incurred (that is, whether professional assistance was reasonably related to the result achieved).

(f) This section shall not be applicable to any ordinance, rule, regulation, or charter provision of any city, county, or city and county, including a charter city, to the extent that the ordinance, rule, or regulation, or charter provision places a limit on the amount of rent that an owner may charge a tenant of a mobilehome park.

(g) For purposes of this section, the rights of a property owner shall be deemed to be successfully pursued or defended if the owner obtains an upward adjustment in rents, successfully defends his or her rights in an administrative proceeding brought by the tenant or the local rent board, or prevails in a proceeding, brought pursuant to Section 1947.8 concerning certification of maximum lawful rents.

(h)(1) If it is determined that a landlord petition assisted by attorneys or consultants is wholly without merit, the tenant shall be awarded a reduction in rent to compensate for the reasonable costs of attorneys or consultants retained by the tenant to defend the petition brought by the landlord. The reasonableness of the costs of the tenant's defense of the action brought by the landlord shall be determined pursuant to the same provisions established by this section for determining the reasonableness of the landlord's costs for the professional services. The determination of the reasonableness of the expenses claimed, an appropriate amortization period, and the award of a reduction in rents to compensate the tenant for costs incurred shall be made immediately following the decision in the underlying administrative proceeding.

(2) If it is determined that a landlord's appeal of an adverse administrative decision is frivolous or solely intended to cause unnecessary delay, the public agency which defended the action shall be awarded its reasonably incurred expenses, including attorney's fees, in defending the action. As used in this paragraph, "frivolous" means either (A) totally and completely without merit; or (B) for the sole purpose of harassing an opposing party.

(i) For purposes of this section, the following terms shall have the following meanings:

(1) "Vacancy decontrol" means a system of controls on the price at which residential rental units may be offered for rent or lease which permits the rent to be increased to its market level, without restriction, each time a vacancy occurs. "Vacancy decontrol" includes systems which reimpose controls on the price at which residential rental units may be offered for rent or lease upon renental of the unit.

(2) "Vacancy decontrol" includes circumstances where the tenant vacates the unit of his or her own volition, or where the local jurisdiction permits the rent to be raised to market rate after an eviction for cause, as specified in the ordinance, charter provision, rule, or regulation.

(j) This section shall not be construed to affect in any way the ability of a local agency to set its own fair return standards or to limit other actions under its local rent control program other than those expressly set forth in this section.

(k) This section is not operative unless the Costa-Hawkins Rental Housing Act (Chapter 2.7 (commencing with Section 1954.50) of Title 5 of Part 4 of Division 3) is repealed. *(Added by Stats.1993, c. 843 (A.B.264), § 1. Amended by Stats.1996, c. 566 (S.B.1632), § 2; Stats.2002, c. 301 (S.B.1403), § 2.)*

Operative Effect

By its own terms, this section is not operative unless the Costa-Hawkins Rental Housing Act (Chapter 2.7 (commencing with Section 1954.50) of Title 5 of Part 4 of Division 3) is repealed. See Civil Code § 1954.50 et seq.

Research References

Miller and Starr California Real Estate § 19:99, Vacancy Decontrol and Other Factors.
Miller and Starr California Real Estate § 19:103, Enforcement and Remedies--Recovery of Attorney's Fees.
13 NO. 4 Miller & Starr, California Real Estate Newsalert 14, Landlord and Tenant.
12 Witkin, California Summary 10th Real Property § 597, Expenses, Fees, and Costs.

§ 1948. Attornment to a stranger

The attornment of a tenant to a stranger is void, unless it is made with the consent of the landlord, or in consequence of a judgment of a Court of competent jurisdiction. *(Enacted in 1872.)*

Research References

Miller and Starr California Real Estate § 19:58, Estoppel of Tenant to Deny Landlord's Title--Effect of Attornment of the Tenant to a Stranger.
12 Witkin, California Summary 10th Real Property § 506, Lessor's Transfer and Tenant's Attornment.

§ 1949. Tenant's obligation to deliver certain notices to landlord; damages

Every tenant who receives notice of any proceeding to recover the real property occupied by him or her, or the possession of the real property, shall immediately inform his or her landlord of the proceeding, and also deliver to the landlord the notice, if in writing, and is responsible to the landlord for all damages which he or she may sustain by reason of any omission to inform the landlord of the notice, or to deliver it to him or her if in writing. *(Enacted in 1872. Amended by Code Am.1873–74, c. 612, p. 246, § 207; Stats.1989, c. 1360, § 11.)*

Research References

Miller and Starr California Real Estate § 19:58, Estoppel of Tenant to Deny Landlord's Title--Effect of Attornment of the Tenant to a Stranger.

§ 1950. Letting parts of rooms; double letting of rooms

One who hires part of a room for a dwelling is entitled to the whole of the room, notwithstanding any agreement to the contrary; and if a landlord lets a room as a dwelling for more than one family, the person to whom he first lets any part of it is entitled to the possession of the whole room for the term agreed upon, and every tenant in the building, under the same landlord, is relieved from all obligation to pay rent to him while such double letting of any room continues. *(Enacted in 1872.)*

Research References

California Real Estate Forms (Miller & Starr) § 2:17, Office Lease—Mixed Use Building.
Miller and Starr California Real Estate § 19:153, Landlord's Duty to Deliver Possession to the Tenant.

§ 1950.5. Security for rental agreement for residential property used as dwelling of tenant; amount and disposition; damages

(a) This section applies to security for a rental agreement for residential property that is used as the dwelling of the tenant.

(b) As used in this section, "security" means any payment, fee, deposit, or charge, including, but not limited to, any payment, fee, deposit, or charge, except as provided in Section 1950.6, that is imposed at the beginning of the tenancy to be used to reimburse the landlord for costs associated with processing a new tenant or that is imposed as an advance payment of rent, used or to be used for any purpose, including, but not limited to, any of the following:

(1) The compensation of a landlord for a tenant's default in the payment of rent.

(2) The repair of damages to the premises, exclusive of ordinary wear and tear, caused by the tenant or by a guest or licensee of the tenant.

(3) The cleaning of the premises upon termination of the tenancy necessary to return the unit to the same level of cleanliness it was in at the inception of the tenancy. The amendments to this paragraph enacted by the act adding this sentence shall apply only to tenancies for which the tenant's right to occupy begins after January 1, 2003.

(4) To remedy future defaults by the tenant in any obligation under the rental agreement to restore, replace, or return personal property or appurtenances, exclusive of ordinary wear and tear, if the security deposit is authorized to be applied thereto by the rental agreement.

(c) A landlord may not demand or receive security, however denominated, in an amount or value in excess of an amount equal to two months' rent, in the case of unfurnished residential property, and an amount equal to three months' rent, in the case of furnished residential property, in addition to any rent for the first month paid on or before initial occupancy.

This subdivision does not prohibit an advance payment of not less than six months' rent if the term of the lease is six months or longer.

This subdivision does not preclude a landlord and a tenant from entering into a mutual agreement for the landlord, at the request of the tenant and for a specified fee or charge, to make structural, decorative, furnishing, or other similar alterations, if the alterations are other than cleaning or repairing for which the landlord may charge the previous tenant as provided by subdivision (e).

(d) Any security shall be held by the landlord for the tenant who is party to the lease or agreement. The claim of a tenant to the security shall be prior to the claim of any creditor of the landlord.

(e) The landlord may claim of the security only those amounts as are reasonably necessary for the purposes specified in subdivision (b). The landlord may not assert a claim against the tenant or the security for damages to the premises or any defective conditions that preexisted the tenancy, for ordinary wear and tear or the effects thereof, whether the wear and tear preexisted the tenancy or occurred during the tenancy, or for the cumulative effects of ordinary wear and tear occurring during any one or more tenancies.

(f)(1) Within a reasonable time after notification of either party's intention to terminate the tenancy, or before the end of the lease term, the landlord shall notify the tenant in writing of his or her option to request an initial inspection and of his or her right to be present at the inspection. The requirements of this subdivision do not apply when the tenancy is terminated pursuant to subdivision (2), (3), or (4) of Section 1161 of the Code of Civil Procedure. At a reasonable time, but no earlier than two weeks before the termination or the end of lease date, the landlord, or an agent of the landlord, shall, upon the request of the tenant, make an initial inspection of the premises prior to any final inspection the landlord makes after the tenant has vacated the premises. The purpose of the initial inspection shall be to allow the tenant an opportunity to remedy identified deficiencies, in a manner consistent with the rights and obligations of the parties under the rental agreement, in order to avoid deductions from the security. If a tenant chooses not to request an initial inspection, the duties of the landlord under this subdivision are discharged. If an inspection is requested, the parties shall attempt to schedule the inspection at a mutually acceptable date and time. The landlord shall give at least 48

hours' prior written notice of the date and time of the inspection if either a mutual time is agreed upon, or if a mutually agreed time cannot be scheduled but the tenant still wishes an inspection. The tenant and landlord may agree to forgo the 48–hour prior written notice by both signing a written waiver. The landlord shall proceed with the inspection whether the tenant is present or not, unless the tenant previously withdrew his or her request for the inspection. Written notice by the landlord shall contain, in substantially the same form, the following:

"State law permits former tenants to reclaim abandoned personal property left at the former address of the tenant, subject to certain conditions. You may or may not be able to reclaim property without incurring additional costs, depending on the cost of storing the property and the length of time before it is reclaimed. In general, these costs will be lower the sooner you contact your former landlord after being notified that property belonging to you was left behind after you moved out."

(2) Based on the inspection, the landlord shall give the tenant an itemized statement specifying repairs or cleanings that are proposed to be the basis of any deductions from the security the landlord intends to make pursuant to paragraphs (1) to (4), inclusive, of subdivision (b). This statement shall also include the texts of paragraphs (1) to (4), inclusive, of subdivision (b). The statement shall be given to the tenant, if the tenant is present for the inspection, or shall be left inside the premises.

(3) The tenant shall have the opportunity during the period following the initial inspection until termination of the tenancy to remedy identified deficiencies, in a manner consistent with the rights and obligations of the parties under the rental agreement, in order to avoid deductions from the security.

(4) Nothing in this subdivision shall prevent a landlord from using the security for deductions itemized in the statement provided for in paragraph (2) that were not cured by the tenant so long as the deductions are for damages authorized by this section.

(5) Nothing in this subdivision shall prevent a landlord from using the security for any purpose specified in paragraphs (1) to (4), inclusive, of subdivision (b) that occurs between completion of the initial inspection and termination of the tenancy or was not identified during the initial inspection due to the presence of a tenant's possessions.

(g)(1) No later than 21 calendar days after the tenant has vacated the premises, but not earlier than the time that either the landlord or the tenant provides a notice to terminate the tenancy under Section 1946 and 1946. 1, Section 1161 of the Code of Civil Procedure, or not earlier than 60 calendar days prior to the expiration of a fixed-term lease, the landlord shall furnish the tenant, by personal delivery or by first-class mail, postage prepaid, a copy of an itemized statement indicating the basis for, and the amount of, any security received and the disposition of the security, and shall return any remaining portion of the security to the tenant. After either the landlord or the tenant provides notice to terminate the tenancy, the landlord and tenant may mutually agree to have the landlord deposit any remaining portion of the security deposit electronically to a bank account or other financial institution designated by the tenant. After either the landlord or the tenant provides notice to terminate the tenancy, the landlord and the tenant may also agree to have the landlord provide a copy of the itemized statement along with the copies required by paragraph (2) to an email account provided by the tenant.

(2) Along with the itemized statement, the landlord shall also include copies of documents showing charges incurred and

deducted by the landlord to repair or clean the premises, as follows:

(A) If the landlord or landlord's employee did the work, the itemized statement shall reasonably describe the work performed. The itemized statement shall include the time spent and the reasonable hourly rate charged.

(B) If the landlord or landlord's employee did not do the work, the landlord shall provide the tenant a copy of the bill, invoice, or receipt supplied by the person or entity performing the work. The itemized statement shall provide the tenant with the name, address, and telephone number of the person or entity, if the bill, invoice, or receipt does not include that information.

(C) If a deduction is made for materials or supplies, the landlord shall provide a copy of the bill, invoice, or receipt. If a particular material or supply item is purchased by the landlord on an ongoing basis, the landlord may document the cost of the item by providing a copy of a bill, invoice, receipt, vendor price list, or other vendor document that reasonably documents the cost of the item used in the repair or cleaning of the unit.

(3) If a repair to be done by the landlord or the landlord's employee cannot reasonably be completed within 21 calendar days after the tenant has vacated the premises, or if the documents from a person or entity providing services, materials, or supplies are not in the landlord's possession within 21 calendar days after the tenant has vacated the premises, the landlord may deduct the amount of a good faith estimate of the charges that will be incurred and provide that estimate with the itemized statement. If the reason for the estimate is because the documents from a person or entity providing services, materials, or supplies are not in the landlord's possession, the itemized statement shall include the name, address, and telephone number of the person or entity. Within 14 calendar days of completing the repair or receiving the documentation, the landlord shall complete the requirements in paragraphs (1) and (2) in the manner specified.

(4) The landlord need not comply with paragraph (2) or (3) if either of the following applies:

(A) The deductions for repairs and cleaning together do not exceed one hundred twenty-five dollars ($125).

(B) The tenant waived the rights specified in paragraphs (2) and (3). The waiver shall only be effective if it is signed by the tenant at the same time or after a notice to terminate a tenancy under Section 1946 or 1946.1 has been given, a notice under Section 1161 of the Code of Civil Procedure has been given, or no earlier than 60 calendar days prior to the expiration of a fixed-term lease. The waiver shall substantially include the text of paragraph (2).

(5) Notwithstanding paragraph (4), the landlord shall comply with paragraphs (2) and (3) when a tenant makes a request for documentation within 14 calendar days after receiving the itemized statement specified in paragraph (1). The landlord shall comply within 14 calendar days after receiving the request from the tenant.

(6) Any mailings to the tenant pursuant to this subdivision shall be sent to the address provided by the tenant. If the tenant does not provide an address, mailings pursuant to this subdivision shall be sent to the unit that has been vacated.

(h) Upon termination of the landlord's interest in the premises, whether by sale, assignment, death, appointment of receiver, or otherwise, the landlord or the landlord's agent shall, within a reasonable time, do one of the following acts, either of which shall relieve the landlord of further liability with respect to the security held:

(1) Transfer the portion of the security remaining after any lawful deductions made under subdivision (e) to the landlord's successor in interest. The landlord shall thereafter notify the tenant by personal delivery or by first-class mail, postage prepaid, of the transfer, of any claims made against the security, of the amount of the security deposited, and of the names of the successors in interest, their addresses, and their telephone numbers. If the notice to the tenant is made by personal delivery, the tenant shall acknowledge receipt of the notice and sign his or her name on the landlord's copy of the notice.

(2) Return the portion of the security remaining after any lawful deductions made under subdivision (e) to the tenant, together with an accounting as provided in subdivision (g).

(i) Prior to the voluntary transfer of a landlord's interest in the premises, the landlord shall deliver to the landlord's successor in interest a written statement indicating the following:

(1) The security remaining after any lawful deductions are made.

(2) An itemization of any lawful deductions from any security received.

(3) His or her election under paragraph (1) or (2) of subdivision (h).

This subdivision does not affect the validity of title to the real property transferred in violation of this subdivision.

(j)(1) In the event of noncompliance with subdivision (h), the landlord's successors in interest shall be jointly and severally liable with the landlord for repayment of the security, or that portion thereof to which the tenant is entitled, when and as provided in subdivisions (e) and (g). A successor in interest of a landlord may not require the tenant to post any security to replace that amount not transferred to the tenant or successors in interest as provided in subdivision (h), unless and until the successor in interest first makes restitution of the initial security as provided in paragraph (2) of subdivision (h) or provides the tenant with an accounting as provided in subdivision (g).

(2) This subdivision does not preclude a successor in interest from recovering from the tenant compensatory damages that are in excess of the security received from the landlord previously paid by the tenant to the landlord.

(3) Notwithstanding this subdivision, if, upon inquiry and reasonable investigation, a landlord's successor in interest has a good faith belief that the lawfully remaining security deposit is transferred to him or her or returned to the tenant pursuant to subdivision (h), he or she is not liable for damages as provided in subdivision (l), or any security not transferred pursuant to subdivision (h).

(k) Upon receipt of any portion of the security under paragraph (1) of subdivision (h), the landlord's successors in interest shall have all of the rights and obligations of a landlord holding the security with respect to the security.

(l) The bad faith claim or retention by a landlord or the landlord's successors in interest of the security or any portion thereof in violation of this section, or the bad faith demand of replacement security in violation of subdivision (j), may subject the landlord or the landlord's successors in interest to statutory damages of up to twice the amount of the security, in addition to actual damages. The court may award damages for bad faith whenever the facts warrant that award, regardless of whether the injured party has specifically requested relief. In an action under this section, the landlord or the landlord's successors in interest shall have the burden of proof as to the reasonableness of the amounts claimed or the authority pursuant to this section to demand additional security deposits.

(m) No lease or rental agreement may contain a provision characterizing any security as "nonrefundable."

(n) An action under this section may be maintained in small claims court if the damages claimed, whether actual, statutory, or both, are within the jurisdictional amount allowed by Section 116.220 or 116.221 of the Code of Civil Procedure.

(o) Proof of the existence of and the amount of a security deposit may be established by any credible evidence, including, but not limited to, a canceled check, a receipt, a lease indicating the requirement of a deposit as well as the amount, prior consistent statements or actions of the landlord or tenant, or a statement under penalty of perjury that satisfies the credibility requirements set forth in Section 780 of the Evidence Code.

(p) The amendments to this section made during the 1985 portion of the 1985–86 Regular Session of the Legislature that are set forth in subdivision (e) are declaratory of existing law.

(q) The amendments to this section made during the 2003 portion of the 2003–04 Regular Session of the Legislature that are set forth in paragraph (1) of subdivision (f) are declaratory of existing law. *(Added by Stats.1977, c. 971, p. 2939, § 2. Amended by Stats.1985, c. 1291, § 1; Stats.1985, c. 1555, § 2; Stats.1986, c. 564, § 1; Stats.1993, c. 755 (S.B.444), § 1; Stats. 1994, c. 146 (A.B.3601), § 13; Stats.2002, c. 1061 (A.B.2330), § 1; Stats.2003, c. 335 (S.B.90), § 1; Stats.2003, c. 576 (A.B. 1384), § 1.5; Stats.2004, c. 568 (S.B.1145), § 3; Stats.2006, c. 167 (A.B.2618), § 3; Stats.2012, c. 557 (A.B.1679), § 1; Stats. 2012, c. 560 (A.B.2521), § 3.5; Stats.2013, c. 76 (A.B.383), § 12.)*

Research References

California Real Estate Forms (Miller & Starr) § &, Real Estate Purchase Contract and Receipt for Deposit—Income Property.
California Real Estate Forms (Miller & Starr) § 2:20, Retail Lease—Shopping Center With for Profit Parking Garage.
California Real Estate Forms (Miller & Starr) § 2:22, Retail Lease—Regional Shopping Center.
California Real Estate Forms (Miller & Starr) § 2:23, Retail Lease—Small Strip-Shopping Center.
California Real Estate Forms (Miller & Starr) § 2:24, Retail Lease—Restaurant.
California Real Estate Forms (Miller & Starr) § 2:25, Industrial Lease.
California Real Estate Forms (Miller & Starr) § 2:29, Parking Garage Lease.
California Real Estate Forms (Miller & Starr) § 2:62, Standard Industrial/Commercial Multi-Tenant Lease—Net.
California Real Estate Forms (Miller & Starr) § 2:63, Standard Industrial/Commercial Multi-Tenant Lease—Gross.
California Real Estate Forms (Miller & Starr) § 2:65, Residential Lease.
California Real Estate Forms (Miller & Starr) § 2:66, Residential Lease With Purchase Option.
Rutter, Cal. Practice Guide: Landlord-Tenant Form 2:A, Residential Rental Agreement.
Rutter, Cal. Practice Guide: Landlord-Tenant Form 2:E, Letter to Landlord Demanding Return of Security Deposit.
Rutter, Cal. Practice Guide: Landlord-Tenant Form 2:F, Notice of Vacating Tenant's Right to Request Initial Inspection.
Rutter, Cal. Practice Guide: Landlord-Tenant Form 2:G, Landlord's Itemized Statement of Reparis/Cleaning Identified in Initial Inspection.
Rutter, Cal. Practice Guide: Real Prop. Transactions Ch. 2-A, A. Preliminary Considerations.
Rutter, Cal. Practice Guide: Real Prop. Transactions Ch. 4-E, E. Drafting the Purchase and Sale Agreement-Terms and Conditions.
Rutter, Cal. Practice Guide: Real Prop. Transactions Ch. 10-A, A. General Considerations.
Miller and Starr California Real Estate § 19:140, Type of Tenant's Deposits.
Miller and Starr California Real Estate § 19:141, Landlord's Obligation to Refund Deposits--Residential Premises.
Miller and Starr California Real Estate § 19:143, Landlord's Obligation to Refund Deposits--Obligations Upon Transfer of the Landlord's Reversionary Interest.
13 NO. 4 Miller & Starr, California Real Estate Newsalert 14, Landlord and Tenant.

14 NO. 4 Miller & Starr, California Real Estate Newsalert 10, Landlord and Tenant.
15 NO. 4 Miller & Starr, California Real Estate Newsalert 12, Landlord and Tenant.
2 Witkin Cal. Proc. 5th Courts § 282, (S 282) Particular Actions.
12 Witkin, California Summary 10th Real Property § 567, (S 567) Restrictions on Waivers of Tenants' Rights.
12 Witkin, California Summary 10th Real Property § 573, (S 573) in General.
12 Witkin, California Summary 10th Real Property § 609, (S 609) Landlord's Entry Into Dwelling.
12 Witkin, California Summary 10th Real Property § 701, Liquidated Damages.
12 Witkin, California Summary 10th Real Property § 747, (S 747) Use of Lessee's Deposit.
1 Witkin Cal. Summ. 10th Contracts § 521, (S 521) in General.
1 Witkin Cal. Summ. 10th Contracts § 522, Statutory Regulation: in General.
1 Witkin Cal. Summ. 10th Contracts § 523, Statutory Regulation: Tenant's Right to Initial Inspection by Landlord.
1 Witkin Cal. Summ. 10th Contracts § 524, Statutory Regulation: Termination of Landlord's Interest.
1 Witkin Cal. Summ. 10th Contracts § 525, Disposition of Security.
1 Witkin Cal. Summ. 10th Contracts § 526, What Constitutes Security.
1 Witkin Cal. Summ. 10th Contracts § 527, Landlord Need Not Pay Interest to Tenant.
13 Witkin, California Summary 10th Equity § 127, (S 127) Disgorgement of Unlawful Profits Into Fluid Recovery Fund.

§ 1950.6. Rental application screening fees; amount; receipt; copies of credit reports; construction of section with housing assistance programs

(a) Notwithstanding Section 1950.5, when a landlord or his or her agent receives a request to rent a residential property from an applicant, the landlord or his or her agent may charge that applicant an application screening fee to cover the costs of obtaining information about the applicant. The information requested and obtained by the landlord or his or her agent may include, but is not limited to, personal reference checks and consumer credit reports produced by consumer credit reporting agencies as defined in Section 1785.3. A landlord or his or her agent may, but is not required to, accept and rely upon a consumer credit report presented by an applicant.

(b) The amount of the application screening fee shall not be greater than the actual out-of-pocket costs of gathering information concerning the applicant, including, but not limited to, the cost of using a tenant screening service or a consumer credit reporting service, and the reasonable value of time spent by the landlord or his or her agent in obtaining information on the applicant. In no case shall the amount of the application screening fee charged by the landlord or his or her agent be greater than thirty dollars ($30) per applicant. The thirty dollar ($30) application screening fee may be adjusted annually by the landlord or his or her agent commensurate with an increase in the Consumer Price Index, beginning on January 1, 1998.

(c) Unless the applicant agrees in writing, a landlord or his or her agent may not charge an applicant an application screening fee when he or she knows or should have known that no rental unit is available at that time or will be available within a reasonable period of time.

(d) The landlord or his or her agent shall provide, personally, or by mail, the applicant with a receipt for the fee paid by the applicant, which receipt shall itemize the out-of-pocket expenses and time spent by the landlord or his or her agent to obtain and process the information about the applicant.

(e) If the landlord or his or her agent does not perform a personal reference check or does not obtain a consumer credit report, the landlord or his or her agent shall return any amount of the screening fee that is not used for the purposes authorized by this section to the applicant.

(f) If an application screening fee has been paid by the applicant and if requested by the applicant, the landlord or his or her agent shall provide a copy of the consumer credit report to the applicant who is the subject of that report.

(g) As used in this section, "landlord" means an owner of residential rental property.

(h) As used in this section, "application screening fee" means any nonrefundable payment of money charged by a landlord or his or her agent to an applicant, the purpose of which is to purchase a consumer credit report and to validate, review, or otherwise process an application for the rent or lease of residential rental property.

(i) As used in this section, "applicant" means any entity or individual who makes a request to a landlord or his or her agent to rent a residential housing unit, or an entity or individual who agrees to act as a guarantor or cosignor on a rental agreement.

(j) The application screening fee shall not be considered an "advance fee" as that term is used in Section 10026 of the Business and Professions Code, and shall not be considered "security" as that term is used in Section 1950.5.

(k) This section is not intended to preempt any provisions or regulations that govern the collection of deposits and fees under federal or state housing assistance programs. *(Added by Stats. 1996, c. 525 (A.B.2263), § 1.)*

Research References

Rutter, Cal. Practice Guide: Real Prop. Transactions Ch. 2-A, A. Preliminary Considerations.
Miller and Starr California Real Estate § 19:142, Landlord's Obligation to Refund Deposits--Application or Screening Fees.

§ 1950.7. Payment or deposit of money to secure performance of rental agreement for other than residential property; status of and claims against deposit; duty of landlord on termination of interest

(a) Any payment or deposit of money the primary function of which is to secure the performance of a rental agreement for other than residential property or any part of the agreement, other than a payment or deposit, including an advance payment of rent, made to secure the execution of a rental agreement, shall be governed by the provisions of this section. With respect to residential property, the provisions of Section 1950.5 shall prevail.

(b) The payment or deposit of money shall be held by the landlord for the tenant who is party to the agreement. The claim of a tenant to the payment or deposit shall be prior to the claim of any creditor of the landlord, except a trustee in bankruptcy.

(c) The landlord may claim of the payment or deposit only those amounts as are reasonably necessary to remedy tenant defaults in the payment of rent, to repair damages to the premises caused by the tenant, or to clean the premises upon termination of the tenancy, if the payment or deposit is made for any or all of those specific purposes.

(1) If the claim of the landlord upon the payment or deposit is only for defaults in the payment of rent and the security deposit equals no more than one month's rent plus a deposit amount clearly described as the payment of the last month's rent, then any remaining portion of the payment or deposit shall be returned to the tenant at a time as may be mutually agreed upon by landlord and tenant, but in no event later than 30 days from the date the landlord receives possession of the premises.

(2) If the claim of the landlord upon the payment or deposit is only for defaults in the payment of rent and the security deposit exceeds the amount of one month's rent plus a deposit amount clearly described as the payment of the last month's rent, then any remaining portion of the payment or deposit in excess of an amount equal to one month's rent shall be returned to the tenant no later than two weeks after the date the landlord receives possession of the premises, with the remainder to be returned or accounted for within 30 days from the date the landlord receives possession of the premises.

(3) If the claim of the landlord upon the payment or deposit includes amounts reasonably necessary to repair damages to the premises caused by the tenant or to clean the premises, then any remaining portion of the payment or deposit shall be returned to the tenant at a time as may be mutually agreed upon by landlord and tenant, but in no event later than 30 days from the date the landlord receives possession of the premises.

(d) Upon termination of the landlord's interest in the unit in question, whether by sale, assignment, death, appointment of receiver or otherwise, the landlord or the landlord's agent shall, within a reasonable time, do one of the following acts, either of which shall relieve the landlord of further liability with respect to the payment or deposit:

(1) Transfer the portion of the payment or deposit remaining after any lawful deductions made under subdivision (c) to the landlord's successor in interest, and thereafter notify the tenant by personal delivery or certified mail of the transfer, of any claims made against the payment or deposit, and of the transferee's name and address. If the notice to the tenant is made by personal delivery, the tenant shall acknowledge receipt of the notice and sign his or her name on the landlord's copy of the notice.

(2) Return the portion of the payment or deposit remaining after any lawful deductions made under subdivision (c) to the tenant.

(e) Upon receipt of any portion of the payment or deposit under paragraph (1) of subdivision (d), the transferee shall have all of the rights and obligations of a landlord holding the payment or deposit with respect to the payment or deposit.

(f) The bad faith retention by a landlord or transferee of a payment or deposit or any portion thereof, in violation of this section, may subject the landlord or the transferee to damages not to exceed two hundred dollars ($200), in addition to any actual damages.

(g) This section is declarative of existing law and therefore operative as to all tenancies, leases, or rental agreements for other than residential property created or renewed on or after January 1, 1971. *(Added by Stats.1977, c. 971, p. 2941, § 3. Amended by Stats.1981, c. 259, p. 1336, § 1; Stats.2003, c. 89 (A.B.1361), § 1.)*

Research References

California Real Estate Forms (Miller & Starr) § 1:33, Real Estate Purchase Contract and Receipt for Deposit—Income Property.
California Real Estate Forms (Miller & Starr) § 2:16, Office Lease—Multistory Office Building.
California Real Estate Forms (Miller & Starr) § 2:17, Office Lease—Mixed Use Building.
California Real Estate Forms (Miller & Starr) § 2:18, Office Lease—Office/Warehouse Building With Four or Fewer Tenants.
California Real Estate Forms (Miller & Starr) § 2:19, Retail Lease—Power Shopping Center.
California Real Estate Forms (Miller & Starr) § 2:20, Retail Lease—Shopping Center With for Profit Parking Garage.
California Real Estate Forms (Miller & Starr) § 2:21, Retail Lease—15,000 RSF to 30,000 RSF (Tenant Oriented).
California Real Estate Forms (Miller & Starr) § 2:22, Retail Lease—Regional Shopping Center.
California Real Estate Forms (Miller & Starr) § 2:23, Retail Lease—Small Strip-Shopping Center.
California Real Estate Forms (Miller & Starr) § 2:24, Retail Lease—Restaurant.

California Real Estate Forms (Miller & Starr) § 2:25, Industrial Lease.

California Real Estate Forms (Miller & Starr) § 2:26, Triple Net Lease—Industrial Build-To-Suit Lease.

California Real Estate Forms (Miller & Starr) § 2:28, Triple Net Lease—Stand-Alone Building.

California Real Estate Forms (Miller & Starr) § 2:29, Parking Garage Lease.

California Real Estate Forms (Miller & Starr) § 2:32, Gross Lease—Small Commercial Property.

California Real Estate Forms (Miller & Starr) § 2:33, Sublease5—With Consent of Master Landlord.

California Real Estate Forms (Miller & Starr) § 2:34, Sublease—Shared Office Space.

California Real Estate Forms (Miller & Starr) § 2:62, Standard Industrial/Commercial Multi-Tenant Lease—Net.

California Real Estate Forms (Miller & Starr) § 2:63, Standard Industrial/Commercial Multi-Tenant Lease—Gross.

Rutter, Cal. Practice Guide: Real Prop. Transactions Ch. 7-D, D. Representing the Selling Tenant.

Rutter, Cal. Practice Guide: Real Prop. Transactions Ch. 10-A, A. General Considerations.

Miller and Starr California Real Estate § 19:144, Landlord's Obligation to Refund Deposits--Nonresidential Premises.

14 NO. 4 Miller & Starr, California Real Estate Newsalert 10, Landlord and Tenant.

16 NO. 2 Miller & Starr, California Real Estate Newsalert 14, Landlord and Tenant.

12 Witkin, California Summary 10th Real Property § 701, Liquidated Damages.

12 Witkin, California Summary 10th Real Property § 747, (S 747) Use of Lessee's Deposit.

1 Witkin Cal. Summ. 10th Contracts § 521, (S 521) in General.

1 Witkin Cal. Summ. 10th Contracts § 529, Landlord's Right to Setoff Despite Failure to Comply With Statute.

1 Witkin Cal. Summ. 10th Contracts § 530, (S 530) Other Property.

§ 1950.8. Payment of money, including but not limited to key money, or the lessor's attorney's fees incurred in preparation of lease or rental agreement, as a condition of initiating, continuing, or renewing a lease or rental agreement; statement of payment amount in agreement; penalties

(a) This section applies only to commercial leases and nonresidential tenancies of real property.

(b) It shall be unlawful for any person to require, demand, or cause to make payable any payment of money, including, but not limited to, "key money," however denominated, or the lessor's attorney's fees reasonably incurred in preparing the lease or rental agreement, as a condition of initiating, continuing, or renewing a lease or rental agreement, unless the amount of payment is stated in the written lease or rental agreement.

(c) Any person who requires, demands, or causes to make payable any payment in violation of subdivision (a), shall be subject to civil penalty of three times the amount of actual damages proximately suffered by the person seeking to obtain the lease or rental of real property, and the person so damaged shall be entitled to an award of costs, including reasonable attorney's fees, reasonable incurred in connection with obtaining the civil penalty.

(d) Nothing in this section shall prohibit the advance payment of rent, if the amount and character of the payment are clearly stated in a written lease or rental agreement.

(e) Nothing in this section shall prohibit any person from charging a reasonable amount for the purpose of conducting reasonable business activity in connection with initiating, continuing, or renewing a lease or rental agreement for nonresidential real property, including, but not limited to, verifying creditworthiness or qualifications of any person seeking to initiate, continue, or renew a lease or rental agreement for any use other than residential use, or cleaning fees, reasonably incurred in connection with the hiring of the real property.

(f) Nothing in this section shall prohibit a person from increasing a tenant's rent for nonresidential real property in order to recover building operating costs incurred on behalf of the tenant, if the right to the rent, the method of calculating the increase, and the period of time covered by the increase is stated in the lease or rental agreement. *(Added by Stats.2001, c. 368 (A.B.533), § 1.)*

Research References

Miller and Starr California Real Estate § 19:77, Nature of and Obligation to Pay Rent.

14 NO. 4 Miller & Starr, California Real Estate Newsalert 25, Landlord and Tenant.

1 Witkin Cal. Summ. 10th Contracts § 530, (S 530) Other Property.

§ 1951. "Rent", "lease", defined

As used in Sections 1951.2 to 1952.6, inclusive:

(a) "Rent" includes charges equivalent to rent.

(b) "Lease" includes a sublease. *(Added by Stats.1970, c. 89, p. 104, § 1, operative July 1, 1971.)*

Law Revision Commission Comments

Subdivision (a) makes clear that "rent" includes all charges or expenses to be met or defrayed by the lessee in exchange for use of the leased property. Inclusion of these items in "rent" is necessary to make various subsequent sections apply appropriately. For example, if the defaulting lessee had promised to pay the taxes on the leased property and the lessor could not relet the property under a lease either containing such a provision or providing sufficient additional rental to cover the accruing taxes, the loss of the defaulting lessee's assumption of the tax obligation should be included in the damages the lessor is entitled to recover under Section 1951.2. The same would be true where the lease imposes on the lessee the obligation to provide fire, earthquake, or liability insurance.

Subdivision (b) merely makes clear that the provisions of the statute apply to subleases as well as leases [9 Cal.L.Rev.Comm.Reports 153 (1969)].

Research References

Miller and Starr California Real Estate § 19:19, Lease as a Contract and Conveyance.

Miller and Starr California Real Estate § 19:206, Historical Perspective.

Miller and Starr California Real Estate § 19:207, Termination of the Lease; Landlord's Recovery of Rent or Damages.

12 Witkin, California Summary 10th Real Property § 517, Dual Nature.

12 Witkin, California Summary 10th Real Property § 569, (S 569) Form and Determination of Payment.

12 Witkin, California Summary 10th Real Property § 693, Nature and Scope of Statutes.

1 Witkin Cal. Summ. 10th Contracts § 521, (S 521) in General.

§ 1951.2. Termination of lease; remedy of lessor

(a) Except as otherwise provided in Section 1951.4, if a lessee of real property breaches the lease and abandons the property before the end of the term or if his right to possession is terminated by the lessor because of a breach of the lease, the lease terminates. Upon such termination, the lessor may recover from the lessee:

(1) The worth at the time of award of the unpaid rent which had been earned at the time of termination;

(2) The worth at the time of award of the amount by which the unpaid rent which would have been earned after termination until the time of award exceeds the amount of such rental loss that the lessee proves could have been reasonably avoided;

(3) Subject to subdivision (c), the worth at the time of award of the amount by which the unpaid rent for the balance of the term after the time of award exceeds the amount of such rental loss that the lessee proves could be reasonably avoided; and

(4) Any other amount necessary to compensate the lessor for all the detriment proximately caused by the lessee's failure to

perform his obligations under the lease or which in the ordinary course of things would be likely to result therefrom.

(b) The "worth at the time of award" of the amounts referred to in paragraphs (1) and (2) of subdivision (a) is computed by allowing interest at such lawful rate as may be specified in the lease or, if no such rate is specified in the lease, at the legal rate. The worth at the time of award of the amount referred to in paragraph (3) of subdivision (a) is computed by discounting such amount at the discount rate of the Federal Reserve Bank of San Francisco at the time of award plus 1 percent.

(c) The lessor may recover damages under paragraph (3) of subdivision (a) only if:

(1) The lease provides that the damages he may recover include the worth at the time of award of the amount by which the unpaid rent for the balance of the term after the time of award, or for any shorter period of time specified in the lease, exceeds the amount of such rental loss for the same period that the lessee proves could be reasonably avoided; or

(2) The lessor relet the property prior to the time of award and proves that in reletting the property he acted reasonably and in a good-faith effort to mitigate the damages, but the recovery of damages under this paragraph is subject to any limitations specified in the lease.

(d) Efforts by the lessor to mitigate the damages caused by the lessee's breach of the lease do not waive the lessor's right to recover damages under this section.

(e) Nothing in this section affects the right of the lessor under a lease of real property to indemnification for liability arising prior to the termination of the lease for personal injuries or property damage where the lease provides for such indemnification. (Added by Stats.1970, c. 89, p. 104, § 2, operative July 1, 1971.)

Research References

California Real Estate Forms (Miller & Starr) § 2:16, Office Lease—Multistory Office Building.

California Real Estate Forms (Miller & Starr) § 2:17, Office Lease--Mixed Use Building.

California Real Estate Forms (Miller & Starr) § 2:18, Office Lease--Office/Warehouse Building With Four or Fewer Tenants.

California Real Estate Forms (Miller & Starr) § 2:19, Retail Lease--Power Shopping Center.

California Real Estate Forms (Miller & Starr) § 2:20, Retail Lease--Shopping Center With for Profit Parking Garage.

California Real Estate Forms (Miller & Starr) § 2:21, Retail Lease--15,000 RSF to 30,000 RSF (Tenant Oriented).

California Real Estate Forms (Miller & Starr) § 2:22, Retail Lease--Regional Shopping Center.

California Real Estate Forms (Miller & Starr) § 2:23, Retail Lease--Small Strip-Shopping Center.

California Real Estate Forms (Miller & Starr) § 2:24, Retail Lease--Restaurant.

California Real Estate Forms (Miller & Starr) § 2:25, Industrial Lease.

California Real Estate Forms (Miller & Starr) § 2:26, Triple Net Lease--Industrial Build-To-Suit Lease.

California Real Estate Forms (Miller & Starr) § 2:27, Ground Lease.

California Real Estate Forms (Miller & Starr) § 2:28, Triple Net Lease--Stand-Alone Building.

California Real Estate Forms (Miller & Starr) § 2:29;, Parking Garage Lease.

California Real Estate Forms (Miller & Starr) § 2:30, Storage Lease--Office Building.

California Real Estate Forms (Miller & Starr) § 2:32, Gross Lease--Small Commercial Property.

California Real Estate Forms (Miller & Starr) § 2:62, Standard Industrial/Commercial Multi-Tenant Lease--Net.

California Real Estate Forms (Miller & Starr) § 2:63, Standard Industrial/Commercial Multi-Tenant Lease--Gross.

California Real Estate Forms (Miller & Starr) § 2:65, Residential Lease.

California Real Estate Forms (Miller & Starr) § 2:66, Residential Lease With Purchase Option.

California Real Estate Forms (Miller & Starr) § 2:85, Insurance and Indemnification.

Rutter, Cal. Practice Guide: Landlord-Tenant Ch. 7-E, E. Landlord's Action for Rent and Damages Upon Tenant's Abandonment or Other Premature Termination of Tenancy.

Rutter, Cal. Practice Guide: Landlord-Tenant Form 2:A, Residential Rental Agreement.

Rutter, Cal. Practice Guide: Landlord-Tenant Form 7:B, Three-Day Notice to Cure or Quit (Breach of Covenant).

Rutter, Cal. Practice Guide: Landlord-Tenant Form 7:D, Notice of Belief of Abandonment (CC § 1951.3).

Rutter, Cal. Practice Guide: Landlord-Tenant Form 13:A, Notice of Belief of Abandonment of Floating Home (CC § 800.36(D)).

Rutter, Cal. Practice Guide: Real Prop. Transactions Ch. 7-B, B. Sale of Ground Lease Tenant's Interest-Preliminary Concerns Re Assignment and Subletting.

Rutter, Cal. Practice Guide: Real Prop. Transactions Ch. 7-C, C. Representing the Purchasing Tenant.

Rutter, Cal. Practice Guide: Real Prop. Transactions Ch. 9-F, F. Special Concerns Re Ground Lease Opinions.

Rutter, Cal. Practice Guide: Real Prop. Transactions Ch. 7-C Outline, Outline C.

Miller and Starr California Real Estate § 19:74, Landlord's Remedies for Tenant's Breach of the Restriction.

Miller and Starr California Real Estate § 19:111, Specification or Restriction of Use.

Miller and Starr California Real Estate § 19:196, Surrender.

Miller and Starr California Real Estate § 19:197, Surrender--Surrender by Operation of Law.

Miller and Starr California Real Estate § 19:201, Landlord's Alternative Remedies for Tenant's Breach; When Notice is Required.

Miller and Starr California Real Estate § 19:202, Form and Contents of the Notice; Curable and Noncurable Breaches.

Miller and Starr California Real Estate § 19:207, Termination of the Lease; Landlord's Recovery of Rent or Damages.

Miller and Starr California Real Estate § 19:208, Termination of the Lease; Landlord's Recovery of Rent or Damages--Recovery in an Unlawful Detainer Proceeding.

Miller and Starr California Real Estate § 19:209, Termination of the Lease; Landlord's Recovery of Rent or Damages--Recovery in a Separate Action.

Miller and Starr California Real Estate § 19:210, Continuation of the Lease; Landlord's Recovery of Rent or Damages.

Miller and Starr California Real Estate § 19:211, Landlord's Recovery of Liquidated Damages and Equitable Relief.

14 NO. 6 Miller & Starr, California Real Estate Newsalert 12, Landlord and Tenant.

16 NO. 2 Miller & Starr, California Real Estate Newsalert 14, Landlord and Tenant.

16 NO. 1 Miller & Starr, California Real Estate Newsalert 19, Landlord and Tenant.

21 NO. 5 Miller & Starr, California Real Estate Newsalert 19, Landlord and Tenant.

22 NO. 6 Miller & Starr, California Real Estate Newsalert 11, Deeds of Trust.

22 NO. 4 Miller & Starr, California Real Estate Newsalert 37, Landlord and Tenant.

3 Witkin Cal. Proc. 5th Actions § 508, Action on Written Contract.

12 Witkin, California Summary 10th Real Property § 503, Statutory Framework.

12 Witkin, California Summary 10th Real Property § 552, (S 552) Adoption of Minority Rule.

12 Witkin, California Summary 10th Real Property § 559, (S 559) Remedies for Transfer in Violation of Restriction.

12 Witkin, California Summary 10th Real Property § 564, Effect of Restriction on Remedies for Breach.

12 Witkin, California Summary 10th Real Property § 569, (S 569) Form and Determination of Payment.

12 Witkin, California Summary 10th Real Property § 673, Modern Theory of Dependent Covenants.

12 Witkin, California Summary 10th Real Property § 676, (S 676) Abandonment.

12 Witkin, California Summary 10th Real Property § 693, Nature and Scope of Statutes.

12 Witkin, California Summary 10th Real Property § 694, Right of Action.

12 Witkin, California Summary 10th Real Property § 696, (S 696) Unpaid Rent.

12 Witkin, California Summary 10th Real Property § 697, (S 697) Future Rent.

12 Witkin, California Summary 10th Real Property § 698, (S 698) Other Losses Caused by Breach.

12 Witkin, California Summary 10th Real Property § 699, Mitigating Damages.

12 Witkin, California Summary 10th Real Property § 700, Computation of Damages.

12 Witkin, California Summary 10th Real Property § 733, Governing Law.

12 Witkin, California Summary 10th Real Property § 745, Benefits of Continuation Remedy.

12 Witkin, California Summary 10th Real Property § 746, Termination of Lessee's Right of Possession.

1 Witkin Cal. Summ. 10th Contracts § 861, (S 861) Nature of Anticipatory Breach.

13 Witkin, California Summary 10th Personal Property § 192, Remedies of Lessor.

§ 1951.3. Abandonment by lessee; notice by lessor; form; defenses of lessee

(a) Real property shall be deemed abandoned by the lessee, within the meaning of Section 1951.2, and the lease shall terminate if the lessor gives written notice of his belief of abandonment as provided in this section and the lessee fails to give the lessor written notice, prior to the date of termination specified in the lessor's notice, stating that he does not intend to abandon the real property and stating an address at which the lessee may be served by certified mail in any action for unlawful detainer of the real property.

(b) The lessor may give a notice of belief of abandonment to the lessee pursuant to this section only where the rent on the property has been due and unpaid for at least 14 consecutive days and the lessor reasonably believes that the lessee has abandoned the property. The date of termination of the lease shall be specified in the lessor's notice and shall be not less than 15 days after the notice is served personally or, if mailed, not less than 18 days after the notice is deposited in the mail.

(c) The lessor's notice of belief of abandonment shall be personally delivered to the lessee or sent by first-class mail, postage prepaid, to the lessee at his last known address and, if there is reason to believe that the notice sent to that address will not be received by the lessee, also to such other address, if any, known to the lessor where the lessee may reasonably be expected to receive the notice.

(d) The notice of belief of abandonment shall be in substantially the following form:

Notice of Belief of Abandonment

To: _____
(Name of lessee/tenant)

_____
(Address of lessee/tenant)

This notice is given pursuant to Section 1951.3 of the Civil Code concerning the real property leased by you at _____ (state location of the property by address or other sufficient description). The rent on this property has been due and unpaid for 14 consecutive days and the lessor/landlord believes that you have abandoned the property.

The real property will be deemed abandoned within the meaning of Section 1951.2 of the Civil Code and your lease will terminate on _____ (here insert a date not less than 15 days after this notice is served personally or, if mailed, not less than 18 days after this notice is deposited in the mail) unless before such date the undersigned receives at the address

indicated below a written notice from you stating both of the following:

(1) Your intent not to abandon the real property.

(2) An address at which you may be served by certified mail in any action for unlawful detainer of the real property.

You are required to pay the rent due and unpaid on this real property as required by the lease, and your failure to do so can lead to a court proceeding against you.

Dated: _____

_____
(Signature of lessor/landlord)

_____
(Type or print name of lessor/landlord)

_____
(Address to which lessee/tenant is to send notice)

(e) The real property shall not be deemed to be abandoned pursuant to this section if the lessee proves any of the following:

(1) At the time the notice of belief of abandonment was given, the rent was not due and unpaid for 14 consecutive days.

(2) At the time the notice of belief of abandonment was given, it was not reasonable for the lessor to believe that the lessee had abandoned the real property. The fact that the lessor knew that the lessee left personal property on the real property does not, of itself, justify a finding that the lessor did not reasonably believe that the lessee had abandoned the real property.

(3) Prior to the date specified in the lessor's notice, the lessee gave written notice to the lessor stating his intent not to abandon the real property and stating an address at which he may be served by certified mail in any action for unlawful detainer of the real property.

(4) During the period commencing 14 days before the time the notice of belief of abandonment was given and ending on the date the lease would have terminated pursuant to the notice, the lessee paid to the lessor all or a portion of the rent due and unpaid on the real property.

(f) Nothing in this section precludes the lessor or the lessee from otherwise proving that the real property has been abandoned by the lessee within the meaning of Section 1951.2.

(g) Nothing in this section precludes the lessor from serving a notice requiring the lessee to pay rent or quit as provided in Sections 1161 and 1162 of the Code of Civil Procedure at any time permitted by those sections, or affects the time and manner of giving any other notice required or permitted by law. The giving of the notice provided by this section does not satisfy the requirements of Sections 1161 and 1162 of the Code of Civil Procedure. *(Added by Stats.1974, c. 332, p. 661, § 1.)*

Research References

California Real Estate Forms (Miller & Starr) § 2:23, Retail Lease--Small Strip-Shopping Center.

California Real Estate Forms (Miller & Starr) § 2:32, Gross Lease--Small Commercial Property.

Rutter, Cal. Practice Guide: Landlord-Tenant Form 7:D, Notice of Belief of Abandonment (CC § 1951.3).

Miller and Starr California Real Estate § 19:195, Abandonment.

19 NO. 4 Miller & Starr, California Real Estate Newsalert 19, Landlord and Tenant.

3 Witkin Cal. Proc. 5th Actions § 1022, Unlawful Detainer.

12 Witkin, California Summary 10th Real Property § 695, Proof of Abandonment.

12 Witkin, California Summary 10th Real Property § 698, (S 698) Other Losses Caused by Breach.

12 Witkin, California Summary 10th Real Property § 750, Notice to Claim Property.

12 Witkin, California Summary 10th Real Property § 754B, (New)-Notice.

§ 1951.4. Remedy provided by lease; provisions

(a) The remedy described in this section is available only if the lease provides for this remedy. In addition to any other type of provision used in a lease to provide for the remedy described in this section, a provision in the lease in substantially the following form satisfies this subdivision:

"The lessor has the remedy described in California Civil Code Section 1951.4 (lessor may continue lease in effect after lessee's breach and abandonment and recover rent as it becomes due, if lessee has right to sublet or assign, subject only to reasonable limitations)."

(b) Even though a lessee of real property has breached the lease and abandoned the property, the lease continues in effect for so long as the lessor does not terminate the lessee's right to possession, and the lessor may enforce all the lessor's rights and remedies under the lease, including the right to recover the rent as it becomes due under the lease, if any of the following conditions is satisfied:

(1) The lease permits the lessee, or does not prohibit or otherwise restrict the right of the lessee, to sublet the property, assign the lessee's interest in the lease, or both.

(2) The lease permits the lessee to sublet the property, assign the lessee's interest in the lease, or both, subject to express standards or conditions, provided the standards and conditions are reasonable at the time the lease is executed and the lessor does not require compliance with any standard or condition that has become unreasonable at the time the lessee seeks to sublet or assign. For purposes of this paragraph, an express standard or condition is presumed to be reasonable; this presumption is a presumption affecting the burden of proof.

(3) The lease permits the lessee to sublet the property, assign the lessee's interest in the lease, or both, with the consent of the lessor, and the lease provides that the consent shall not be unreasonably withheld or the lease includes a standard implied by law that consent shall not be unreasonably withheld.

(c) For the purposes of subdivision (b), the following do not constitute a termination of the lessee's right to possession:

(1) Acts of maintenance or preservation or efforts to relet the property.

(2) The appointment of a receiver upon initiative of the lessor to protect the lessor's interest under the lease.

(3) Withholding consent to a subletting or assignment, or terminating a subletting or assignment, if the withholding or termination does not violate the rights of the lessee specified in subdivision (b). *(Added by Stats.1970, c. 89, p. 105, § 3, operative July 1, 1971. Amended by Stats.1989, c. 982, § 1; Stats.1991, c. 67 (S.B.256), § 1.)*

Law Revision Commission Comments

Even though the lessee has breached the lease and abandoned the property, this section permits the lessor to continue to collect the rent as it becomes due under the lease rather than to recover damages based primarily on the loss of future rent under Section 1951.2. This remedy is available only if the lease so provides and contains a provision permitting the lessee to mitigate the damages by subletting or assigning his interest in the property. The lease may give the lessee unlimited discretion in choosing a subtenant or assignee. See subdivision (b)(1). However, generally the lease will impose standards for or conditions on such subletting or assignment or require the consent of the lessor. See subdivision (b)(2), (3). In the latter case, the lessor may not require compliance with an unreasonable standard or condition nor unreasonably withhold his consent. Occasionally, a standard or condition, although reasonable at the time it was included in the lease, is unreasonable under circumstances existing at the time of subletting or assignment. In such a

situation, the lessor may resort to the remedy provided by Section 1951.4 if he does not require compliance with the now unreasonable standard or condition. Common factors that may be considered in determining whether standards or conditions on subletting or assignment are reasonable include: the credit rating of the new tenant; the similarity of the proposed use to the previous use; the nature or character of the new tenant—the use may be similar, but the quality of the tenant quite different; the requirements of the new tenant for services furnished by the lessor; the impact of the new tenant on common facilities.

The right to continue to collect the rent as it becomes due terminates when the lessor evicts the lessee; in such case, the damages are computed under Section 1951.2. The availability of a remedy under this section does not preclude the lessor from terminating the right of a defaulting lessee to possession of the property and then utilizing the remedy provided by Section 1951.2. However, nothing in this section affects the rules of law that determine when the lessor may terminate the lessee's right to possession. See generally 2 WITKIN, SUMMARY OF CALIFORNIA LAW *Real Property* §§ 276–278 (1960). Thus, for example, the lessor's right to terminate the lessee's right to possession may be waived under certain circumstances. *Id.*, at § 278.

Where the lease complies with Section 1951.4, the lessor may recover the rent as it becomes due under the terms of the lease and at the same time has no obligation to retake possession and relet the property in the event the lessee abandons the property. This allocation of the burden of minimizing the loss is most useful where the lessor does not have the desire, facilities, or ability to manage the property and to acquire a suitable tenant and for this reason desires to avoid the burden that Section 1951.2 places on the lessor to mitigate the damages by reletting the property.

The allocation of the duty to minimize damages under Section 1951.4 is important. It permits arrangements for financing the purchase or improvement of real property that might otherwise be seriously jeopardized if the lessor's only right upon breach of the lease and abandonment of the property were the right to recover damages under Section 1951.2. For example, because lease could be enforced under former law, leases were utilized by public entities to finance the construction of public improvements. The lessor constructed the improvement to the specifications of the public entity-lessee, leased the property as improved to the public entity, and at the end of the term of the lease all interest in the property and the improvement vested in the public entity. See, *e.g.*, Dean v. Kuchel, 35 Cal.2d 444, 218 P.2d 521 (1950). Similarly, a lessor could, in reliance on the lessee's rental obligation under a long-term lease, construct an improvement to the specifications of the lessee for the use of the lessee during the lease term. The remedy available under Section 1951.4 retains the substance of the former law and gives the lessor, in effect, security for the repayment of the cost of the improvement in these cases.

Section 1951.4 also facilities assignment by the lessor under a long-term lease of the right to receive the rent under the lease in return for the discounted value of the future rent. The remedy provided by Section 1951.4 makes the right to receive the rental payments an attractive investment since the assignee is assured that the rent will be paid if the tenant is financially responsible.

Subdivision (c) makes clear that certain acts by the lessor do not constitute a termination of the lessee's right to possession. The first paragraph of the subdivision permits the lessor, for example, to show the leased premises to prospective tenants after the lessee has breached the lease and abandoned the property.

The second paragraph of subdivision (c) makes clear that appointment of a receiver to protect the lessor's rights under the lease does not constitute a termination of the lessee's right to possession. For example, an apartment building may be leased under a "master lease" to a lessee who then leases the individual apartments to subtenants. The appointment of a receiver may be appropriate if the lessee under the master lease collects the rent from the subtenants but fails to pay the lessor the rent payable under the master lease. The receiver would collect the rent from the subtenants on behalf of the lessee and pay to the lessor the amount he is entitled to receive under the master lease. This form of relief, would protect the lessor against the lessee's misappropriation of the rent from subtenants and at the same time would preserve the lessee's obligation to pay the rent provided in the master lease.

Under Section 1951.4, in contrast to Section 1951.2, so long as the lessor does not terminate the lease, he is obliged to continue to perform his obligations under the lease. [9 Cal.L.Rev.Comm. Reports 153 (1969)].

Subdivision (a) of Section 1951.4 is amended to provide a "safe harbor" of specific language that satisfies the requirement that the lease provide for the remedy in this section. The amendment should not be construed to imply that no other form of language will satisfy the requirement. Whether any other language will satisfy the requirement depends on the language used and the understanding of the parties.

Subdivision (b)(1) is amended to recognize that a lessee may sublet the property or assign the lessee's interest in the lease whether or not the lease permits it, so long as the lease does not prohibit it. *Cf.* Section 1995.210 (right to transfer commercial lease absent a restriction). Under subdivision (b)(1), a lessor may not include a prohibition against subletting or assignment and thereafter take advantage of the remedy of this section by waiving the prohibition; the lessee must have a legal right to sublet or assign subject only to reasonable limitations from the outset if the lessor is to have the remedy provided in this section.

The parties may agree to express standards and conditions for assignment and sublease. Section 1995.240 (transfer restriction in commercial lease subject to standards and conditions). Subdivision (b)(2) is amended to make clear that an express standard or condition on transfer is presumed reasonable; the presumption is only for the purpose of applying subdivision (b)(2). This is consistent with cases involving the reasonableness standard generally and with the underlying philosophy of this chapter. See Coskran, *Assignment and Sublease Restrictions: The Tribulations of Leasehold Transfers,* 22 Loy. L.A.L.Rev. 405, 474 (1989).

Subdivision (b)(2) also is amended to clarify existing law that the lessor may waive a standard or condition on subletting or assignment that, although originally reasonable, has become unreasonable, and still take advantage of the remedy provided in Section 1951.4. See *Recommendation Relating to Real Property Leases,* 9 Cal.L.Revision Comm'n Reports 153, 168 (1969) ("Occasionally, a standard or condition, although reasonable at the time it was included in the lease, is unreasonable under circumstances existing at the time of the subletting or assignment. In such a situation, the lessor may resort to the remedy provided by Section 1951.4 if he does not require compliance with the now unreasonable standard or condition."). However, subdivision (b)(2) does not permit the lessor to take advantage of the remedy provided in this section by including in the lease a standard or condition that is originally unreasonable and thereafter waive it; the lessee must have a legal right to sublet or assign subject only to reasonable limitations from the outset if the lessor is to have the remedy provided in this section.

Subdivision (b)(3) is amended to recognize that the lessor's consent to an assignment or subletting may not unreasonably be withheld, even though the lease does not require reasonableness, if the lease provides no standard for giving or withholding consent. Section 1995.260 (implied standard for landlord's consent in commercial lease). Under this subdivision a lessor may not take advantage of the remedy provided in this section by including in the lease a clause that subjects the lessor's consent to unreasonable limitations and thereafter waiving the clause; the lessee must have a legal right to sublet or assign subject only to reasonable limitations from the outset if the lessor is to have the remedy provided in this section.

The other changes in Section 1951.4 are technical, intended to render the provision gender-neutral.

The amendments apply to leases executed before, on, or after the operative date of the amendments, except as provided in Section 1952. [20 Cal.L.Rev.Comm.Reports 273 (1990)].

Paragraph (3) is added to Section 1951.4(c) to make clear that the landlord's efforts to preclude or terminate an assignment or sublease that is neither reasonable nor otherwise permitted by the lease are not held to impair the landlord's rights under this section. This clarifies a matter that was unclear under prior law. [20 Cal.L.Rev.Comm.Reports 2405 (1990)].

Research References

California Real Estate Forms (Miller & Starr) § 2:12, Letter of Intent--Restaurant/Food Service (Tenant Oriented).
California Real Estate Forms (Miller & Starr) § 2:16, Office Lease--Multistory Office Building.
California Real Estate Forms (Miller & Starr) § 2:17, Office Lease--Mixed Use Building.
California Real Estate Forms (Miller & Starr) § 2:18, Office Lease--Office/Warehouse Building With Four or Fewer Tenants.
California Real Estate Forms (Miller & Starr) § 2:19, Retail Lease--Power Shopping Center.
California Real Estate Forms (Miller & Starr) § 2:20, Retail Lease--Shopping Center With for Profit Parking Garage.
California Real Estate Forms (Miller & Starr) § 2:21, Retail Lease--15,000 RSF to 30,000 RSF (Tenant Oriented).

California Real Estate Forms (Miller & Starr) § 2:22, Retail Lease--Regional Shopping Center.
California Real Estate Forms (Miller & Starr) § 2:23, Retail Lease--Small Strip-Shopping Center.
California Real Estate Forms (Miller & Starr) § 2:24, Retail Lease--Restaurant.
California Real Estate Forms (Miller & Starr) § 2:25, Industrial Lease.
California Real Estate Forms (Miller & Starr) § 2:26, Triple Net Lease--Industrial Build-To-Suit Lease.
California Real Estate Forms (Miller & Starr) § 2:27, Ground Lease.
California Real Estate Forms (Miller & Starr) § 2:28, Triple Net Lease--Stand-Alone Building.
California Real Estate Forms (Miller & Starr) § 2:29, Parking Garage Lease.
California Real Estate Forms (Miller & Starr) § 2:32, Gross Lease--Small Commercial Property.
California Real Estate Forms (Miller & Starr) § 2:36, Consent to Sublease.
California Real Estate Forms (Miller & Starr) § 2:62, Standard Industrial/Commercial Multi-Tenant Lease--Net.
California Real Estate Forms (Miller & Starr) § 2:63, Standard Industrial/Commercial Multi-Tenant Lease--Gross.
California Real Estate Forms (Miller & Starr) § 2:65, Residential Lease.
California Real Estate Forms (Miller & Starr) § 2:66, Residential Lease With Purchase Option.
Rutter, Cal. Practice Guide: Landlord-Tenant Ch. 7-E, E. Landlord's Action for Rent and Damages Upon Tenant's Abandonment or Other Premature Termination of Tenancy.
Rutter, Cal. Practice Guide: Landlord-Tenant Form 2:A, Residential Rental Agreement.
Rutter, Cal. Practice Guide: Landlord-Tenant Form 2:B, Standard Shopping Center Lease.
Rutter, Cal. Practice Guide: Landlord-Tenant Form 2:C, Office Lease.
Rutter, Cal. Practice Guide: Real Prop. Transactions Ch. 7-B, B. Sale of Ground Lease Tenant's Interest-Preliminary Concerns Re Assignment and Subletting.
Rutter, Cal. Practice Guide: Real Prop. Transactions Ch. 7-C, C. Representing the Purchasing Tenant.
Rutter, Cal. Practice Guide: Real Prop. Transactions Ch. 7-C Outline, Outline C.
Miller and Starr California Real Estate § 19:76, Tenant's Remedies for Landlord's Breach of the Restriction.
Miller and Starr California Real Estate § 33:29, Actions in Which a Receiver May be Appointed--Unlawful Detainer.
Miller and Starr California Real Estate § 19:196, Surrender.
Miller and Starr California Real Estate § 19:201, Landlord's Alternative Remedies for Tenant's Breach; When Notice is Required.
Miller and Starr California Real Estate § 19:202, Form and Contents of the Notice; Curable and Noncurable Breaches.
Miller and Starr California Real Estate § 19:207, Termination of the Lease; Landlord's Recovery of Rent or Damages.
Miller and Starr California Real Estate § 19:210, Continuation of the Lease; Landlord's Recovery of Rent or Damages.
Miller and Starr California Real Estate § 19:227, Prejudgment Remedies; Attachment and Receivership.
22 NO. 6 Miller & Starr, California Real Estate Newsalert 11, Deeds of Trust.
3 Witkin Cal. Proc. 5th Actions § 181, (S 181) Required Election of Rights.
8 Witkin Cal. Proc. 5th Enforcement of Judgment § 56, (S 56) Leasehold Interest in Real Property.
12 Witkin, California Summary 10th Real Property § 552, (S 552) Adoption of Minority Rule.
12 Witkin, California Summary 10th Real Property § 564, Effect of Restriction on Remedies for Breach.
12 Witkin, California Summary 10th Real Property § 694, Right of Action.
12 Witkin, California Summary 10th Real Property § 744, Lessor's Conditional Remedy.
12 Witkin, California Summary 10th Real Property § 745, Benefits of Continuation Remedy.
12 Witkin, California Summary 10th Real Property § 746, Termination of Lessee's Right of Possession.

§ 1951.5. Liquidated damages

Section 1671, relating to liquidated damages, applies to a lease of real property. *(Added by Stats.1970, c. 89, p. 105, § 4, operative July 1, 1971. Amended by Stats.1977, c. 198, p. 720, § 8, operative July 1, 1978.)*

Law Revision Commission Comments

The amount of the lessor's damages may be difficult to determine in some cases since the lessor's right to damages accrues at the time of the breach and abandonment or when the lease is terminated by the lessor. See Section 1951.2. This difficulty may be avoided in appropriate cases by a liquidated damage provision that meets the requirements of Civil Code Sections 1670 and 1671.

Under former law, provisions in real property leases for liquidated damages upon breach by the lessee were held to be void. Jack v. Sinsheimer, 125 Cal. 563, 58 Pac. 130 (1899). However, such holdings were based on the former rule that the lessor's cause of action upon breach of the lease and abandonment of the property or upon termination of the lessee's right to possession was either for the rent as it became due or for the rental deficiency at the end of the lease term.

So far as provisions for liquidated damages upon a lessor's breach are concerned, such provisions were upheld under the preexisting law if reasonable. See Seid Pak Sing v. Barker, 197 Cal. 321, 240 Pac. 765 (1925). Nothing in this section changes this rule. [9 Cal.L.Rev.Comm. Reports 153 (1969)].

Section 1951.5 is amended to reflect the repeal of Section 1670. It should be noted that Section 1671 has been amended to change the rules governing the validity of liquidated damages provisions in certain cases. See Section 1671 and Comment thereto. [13 Cal.L.Rev.Comm. Reports 1735 (1976)].

Research References

Miller and Starr California Real Estate § 19:79, Accelerated Payment.
Miller and Starr California Real Estate § 19:211, Landlord's Recovery of Liquidated Damages and Equitable Relief.
12 Witkin, California Summary 10th Real Property § 701, Liquidated Damages.
1 Witkin Cal. Summ. 10th Contracts § 533, (S 533) Nature and Purpose of Revision.
1 Witkin Cal. Summ. 10th Contracts § 536, (S 536) Deposits.

§ 1951.7. "Advance payment" defined; notice of reletting

(a) As used in this section, "advance payment" means moneys paid to the lessor of real property as prepayment of rent, or as a deposit to secure faithful performance of the terms of the lease, or another payment that is the substantial equivalent of either of these. A payment that is not in excess of the amount of one month's rent is not an advance payment for purposes of this section.

(b) The notice provided by subdivision (c) is required to be given only if all of the following apply:

(1) The lessee has made an advance payment.

(2) The lease is terminated pursuant to Section 1951.2.

(3) The lessee has made a request, in writing, to the lessor that he or she be given notice under subdivision (c).

(c) Upon the initial reletting of the property, the lessor shall send a written notice to the lessee stating that the property has been relet, the name and address of the new lessee, and the length of the new lease and the amount of the rent. The notice shall be delivered to the lessee personally, or be sent by regular mail to the lessee at the address shown on the request, not later than 30 days after the new lessee takes possession of the property. Notice is not required if the amount of the rent due and unpaid at the time of termination exceeds the amount of the advance payment. *(Added by Stats.1970, c. 89, p. 105, § 5, operative July 1, 1971. Amended by Stats.2008, c. 179 (S.B.1498), § 32.)*

Law Revision Commission Comments

Section 1951.7 does not in any way affect the right of the lessor to recover damages nor the right of a lessee to recover prepaid rent, a security deposit, or other payment. The section is included merely to provide a means whereby the lessee whose lease has been terminated

under Section 1951.2 may obtain information concerning the length of the term of the new lease and the rent provided in the new lease. The notice is required only if the lessee so requests and only upon the initial reletting of the property. If the new lease is terminated, the notice, if any, required by this section need be given only to the lessee under the new lease. [9 Cal.L.Rev.Comm. Reports 153 (1969)].

Research References

Miller and Starr California Real Estate § 19:140, Type of Tenant's Deposits.
3 Witkin Cal. Proc. 5th Actions § 216, Landlord's Proceeding Against Tenant.
12 Witkin, California Summary 10th Real Property § 699, Mitigating Damages.

§ 1951.8. Equitable relief

Nothing in Section 1951.2 or 1951.4 affects the right of the lessor under a lease of real property to equitable relief where such relief is appropriate. *(Added by Stats.1970, c. 89, p. 106, § 6, operative July 1, 1971.)*

Law Revision Commission Comments

Generally, where the lessee has breached a lease of real property, the lessor will simply recover damages pursuant to Civil Code Section 1951.2. However, Section 1951.8 makes clear that the lessor remains entitled to equitable relief where such relief is appropriate. For example, even though the lease has terminated pursuant to subdivision (a) of Section 1951.2 and the lessor has recovered damages under that section for loss of rent, he is not precluded from obtaining equitable relief, *e.g.*, an injunction enforcing the lessee's covenant not to compete. [9 Cal.L.Rev.Comm. Reports 153 (1969)].

Research References

Miller and Starr California Real Estate § 19:211, Landlord's Recovery of Liquidated Damages and Equitable Relief.
12 Witkin, California Summary 10th Real Property § 693, Nature and Scope of Statutes.
12 Witkin, California Summary 10th Real Property § 740, (S 740) Res Judicata and Collateral Estoppel.

§ 1952. Actions for unlawful detainer, forcible entry, and forcible detainer; effect

(a) Except as provided in subdivision (c), nothing in Sections 1951 to 1951.8, inclusive, affects the provisions of Chapter 4 (commencing with Section 1159) of Title 3 of Part 3 of the Code of Civil Procedure, relating to actions for unlawful detainer, forcible entry, and forcible detainer.

(b) Unless the lessor amends the complaint as provided in paragraph (1) of subdivision (a) of Section 1952.3 to state a claim for damages not recoverable in the unlawful detainer proceeding, the bringing of an action under the provisions of Chapter 4 (commencing with Section 1159) of Title 3 of Part 3 of the Code of Civil Procedure does not affect the lessor's right to bring a separate action for relief under Sections 1951.2, 1951.5, and 1951.8, but no damages shall be recovered in the subsequent action for any detriment for which a claim for damages was made and determined on the merits in the previous action.

(c) After the lessor obtains possession of the property under a judgment pursuant to Section 1174 of the Code of Civil Procedure, he is no longer entitled to the remedy provided under Section 1951.4 unless the lessee obtains relief under Section 1179 of the Code of Civil Procedure. *(Added by Stats.1970, c. 89, p. 106, § 7, operative July 1, 1971. Amended by Stats.1977, c. 49, p. 426, § 1.)*

Research References

Miller and Starr California Real Estate § 19:19, Lease as a Contract and Conveyance.
Miller and Starr California Real Estate § 19:206, Historical Perspective.
Miller and Starr California Real Estate § 19:207, Termination of the Lease; Landlord's Recovery of Rent or Damages.

Miller and Starr California Real Estate § 19:210, Continuation of the Lease; Landlord's Recovery of Rent or Damages.

Miller and Starr California Real Estate § 19:214, Nature of the Remedy.

Miller and Starr California Real Estate § 19:215, Nature of the Remedy--Effect of Tenant's Abandonment Before Trial.

Miller and Starr California Real Estate § 19:223, Cross-Complaint; Affirmative Defenses.

Miller and Starr California Real Estate § 19:230, Trial; Judgment; Stay of Execution.

Miller and Starr California Real Estate § 19:231, Trial; Judgment; Stay of Execution--Res Judicata Effect of an Unlawful Detainer Judgment.

3 Witkin Cal. Proc. 5th Actions § 181, (S 181) Required Election of Rights.

12 Witkin, California Summary 10th Real Property § 693, Nature and Scope of Statutes.

12 Witkin, California Summary 10th Real Property § 740, (S 740) Res Judicata and Collateral Estoppel.

12 Witkin, California Summary 10th Real Property § 746, Termination of Lessee's Right of Possession.

§ 1952.2. Inapplicability of Sections 1951 to 1952, inclusive, to certain leases

Sections 1951 to 1952, inclusive, do not apply to:

(a) Any lease executed before July 1, 1971.

(b) Any lease executed on or after July 1, 1971, if the terms of the lease were fixed by a lease, option, or other agreement executed before July 1, 1971. *(Added by Stats.1970, c. 89, p. 106, § 8, operative July 1, 1971.)*

Law Revision Commission Comments

This section is included because the contents of the leases therein described may have been determined without reference to the effect of the added sections. [9 Cal.L.Rev.Comm. Reports 153 (1969)].

Research References

12 Witkin, California Summary 10th Real Property § 693, Nature and Scope of Statutes.

§ 1952.3. Unlawful detainer; possession not in issue; conversion to action for damages

(a) Except as provided in subdivisions (b) and (c), if the lessor brings an unlawful detainer proceeding and possession of the property is no longer in issue because possession of the property has been delivered to the lessor before trial or, if there is no trial, before judgment is entered, the case becomes an ordinary civil action in which:

(1) The lessor may obtain any relief to which he is entitled, including, where applicable, relief authorized by Section 1951.2; but, if the lessor seeks to recover damages described in paragraph (3) of subdivision (a) of Section 1951.2 or any other damages not recoverable in the unlawful detainer proceeding, the lessor shall first amend the complaint pursuant to Section 472 or 473 of the Code of Civil Procedure so that possession of the property is no longer in issue and to state a claim for such damages and shall serve a copy of the amended complaint on the defendant in the same manner as a copy of a summons and original complaint is served.

(2) The defendant may, by appropriate pleadings or amendments to pleadings, seek any affirmative relief, and assert all defenses, to which he is entitled, whether or not the lessor has amended the complaint; but subdivision (a) of Section 426.30 of the Code of Civil Procedure does not apply unless, after delivering possession of the property to the lessor, the defendant (i) files a cross-complaint or (ii) files an answer or an amended answer in response to an amended complaint filed pursuant to paragraph (1).

(b) The defendant's time to respond to a complaint for unlawful detainer is not affected by the delivery of possession of the property to the lessor; but, if the complaint is amended as provided in paragraph (1) of subdivision (a), the defendant has the same time to respond to the amended complaint as in an ordinary civil action.

(c) The case shall proceed as an unlawful detainer proceeding if the defendant's default (1) has been entered on the unlawful detainer complaint and (2) has not been opened by an amendment of the complaint or otherwise set aside.

(d) Nothing in this section affects the pleadings that may be filed, relief that may be sought, or defenses that may be asserted in an unlawful detainer proceeding that has not become an ordinary civil action as provided in subdivision (a). *(Added by Stats.1977, c. 49, p. 427, § 2.)*

Research References

Miller and Starr California Real Estate § 19:215, Nature of the Remedy--Effect of Tenant's Abandonment Before Trial.

Miller and Starr California Real Estate § 19:229, Trial Setting and Hearing Preference; Discovery.

Miller and Starr California Real Estate § 19:231, Trial; Judgment; Stay of Execution--Res Judicata Effect of an Unlawful Detainer Judgment.

21 NO. 6 Miller & Starr, California Real Estate Newsalert 14, Judicial Remedies.

12 Witkin, California Summary 10th Real Property § 733, Governing Law.

12 Witkin, California Summary 10th Real Property § 734, Illustrations.

§ 1952.4. Agreement for exploration for or removal of natural resources not lease of real property

An agreement for the exploration for or the removal of natural resources is not a lease of real property within the meaning of Sections 1951 to 1952.2, inclusive. *(Added by Stats.1970, c. 89, p. 106, § 9, operative July 1, 1971.)*

Law Revision Commission Comments

An agreement for the exploration for or the removal of natural resources, such as the so-called oil and gas lease, has been characterized by the California Supreme Court as a *profit a prendre* in gross. See Dabney v. Edwards, 5 Cal.2d 1, 53 P.2d 962 (1935). These agreements are distinguishable from leases generally. The ordinary lease contemplates the use and preservation of the property with compensation for such use, while a natural resources agreement contemplates the extraction of the valuable resources of the property with compensation for such extraction. See 3 LINDLEY, MINES § 861 (3d ed. 1914).

Sections 1951–1952.2 are intended to deal with the ordinary lease of real property, not with agreements for the exploration for or the removal of natural resources. Accordingly, this section limits these sections to their intended purpose. This section does not prohibit application to such agreements of any of the principles expressed in Sections 1951 to 1951.8; it merely provides that nothing in those sections requires such application. [9 Cal.L.Rev.Comm. Reports 153 (1969)].

Research References

Miller and Starr California Real Estate § 19:4, Other Interests Distinguished--Profit à Prendre.

12 Witkin, California Summary 10th Real Property § 693, Nature and Scope of Statutes.

§ 1952.6. Applicability to leases between public entities and nonprofit corporations; substitution of remedies for breach

(a) Sections 1951 to 1952.2, inclusive, shall not apply to any lease or agreement for a lease of real property between any public entity and any nonprofit corporation whose title or interest in the property is subject to reversion to or vesting in a public entity and which issues bonds or other evidences of indebtedness, the interest on which is exempt from federal income taxes for the purpose of acquiring, constructing, or improving the property or a building or other facility thereon, or between any public entity and any other public entity, unless the lease or the agreement shall specifically provide that Sections 1951 to 1952.2, inclusive, or any portions thereof, are applicable to the lease or the agreement.

(b) Except as provided in subdivision (a), a public entity lessee in a contract for a capital lease of real property involving the payment of rents of one million dollars ($1,000,000) or more may elect to waive any of the remedies for a breach of the lease provided in Sections 1951 to 1952.2, inclusive, and contract instead for any other remedy permitted by law. As used in this subdivision, "capital lease" refers to a lease entered into for the purpose of acquiring, constructing, or improving the property or a building or other facility thereon.

(c) As used in this section, "public entity" includes the state, a county, city and county, city, district, public authority, public agency, or any other political subdivision or public corporation. *(Added by Stats.1970, c. 89, p. 106, § 10, operative July 1, 1971. Amended by Stats.1971, c. 732, p. 1457, § 1, eff. Aug. 24, 1971; Stats.1989, c. 613, § 1.)*

Law Revision Commission Comments

Section 1952.6 is included to prevent the application of any provision of Sections 1951 to 1952.2 to lease-purchase agreements by public entities if such application would make the agreement invalid. [9 Cal.L.Rev.Comm. Reports 153 (1969)].

Research References

Miller and Starr California Real Estate § 19:206, Historical Perspective.
12 Witkin, California Summary 10th Real Property § 693, Nature and Scope of Statutes.

§ 1952.8. Gasoline service stations; leases; vapor control system; requirements

On and after the effective date of this section, no owner of a gasoline service station shall enter into a lease with any person for the leasing of the station for the purpose of operating a gasoline service station, unless (a) the station is equipped with a vapor control system for the control of gasoline vapor emissions during gasoline marketing operations, including storage, transport, and transfer operations, if such vapor control system is required by law or by any rule or regulation of the State Air Resources Board or of the air pollution control district in which the station is located or (b) no vapor control system has been certified by the board prior to the date of the lease.

A lease entered into in violation of this section shall be voidable at the option of the lessee. *(Added by Stats.1976, c. 1030, p. 4619, § 1, eff. Sept. 20, 1976.)*

Research References

Miller and Starr California Real Estate § 19:111, Specification or Restriction of Use.

§ 1953. Waiver or modification of lessee's rights; void as contrary to public policy; exception; applicability of section

(a) Any provision of a lease or rental agreement of a dwelling by which the lessee agrees to modify or waive any of the following rights shall be void as contrary to public policy:

(1) His rights or remedies under Section 1950.5 or 1954.

(2) His right to assert a cause of action against the lessor which may arise in the future.

(3) His right to a notice or hearing required by law.

(4) His procedural rights in litigation in any action involving his rights and obligations as a tenant.

(5) His right to have the landlord exercise a duty of care to prevent personal injury or personal property damage where that duty is imposed by law.

(b) Any provision of a lease or rental agreement of a dwelling by which the lessee agrees to modify or waive a statutory right, where the modification or waiver is not void under subdivision (a) or under Section 1942.1, 1942.5, or 1954, shall be void as

contrary to public policy unless the lease or rental agreement is presented to the lessee before he takes actual possession of the premises. This subdivision does not apply to any provisions modifying or waiving a statutory right in agreements renewing leases or rental agreements where the same provision was also contained in the lease or rental agreement which is being renewed.

(c) This section shall apply only to leases and rental agreements executed on or after January 1, 1976. *(Added by Stats.1975, c. 302, p. 749, § 1.)*

Research References

Rutter, Cal. Practice Guide: A.D.R. Ch. 5-C, C. Enforceability of Arbitration Agreements-In General.
Miller and Starr California Real Estate § 19:20, Lease as a Contract and Conveyance--Form, Execution, Delivery, and Recordation.
Miller and Starr California Real Estate § 22:60, Liability for Wrongful or Criminal Conduct of Third Persons--Residential Landlord's Liability for Criminal Conduct.
Miller and Starr California Real Estate § 35:39, Issues Which Cannot be the Subject of Arbitration.
Miller and Starr California Real Estate § 19:119, Tenant's Right to Repair and Deduct.
Miller and Starr California Real Estate § 19:120, Landlord's Common-Law Duty of Maintenance; Implied Warranty of Habitability.
Miller and Starr California Real Estate § 19:154, Landlord's Right of Entry.
Miller and Starr California Real Estate § 19:156, Covenant of Quiet Enjoyment and Possession.
Miller and Starr California Real Estate § 19:167, Defenses.
Miller and Starr California Real Estate § 19:190, Lease Provisions Regarding Notice.
Miller and Starr California Real Estate § 19:201, Landlord's Alternative Remedies for Tenant's Breach; When Notice is Required.
Miller and Starr California Real Estate § 19:202, Form and Contents of the Notice; Curable and Noncurable Breaches.
Miller and Starr California Real Estate § 19:214, Nature of the Remedy.
Miller and Starr California Real Estate § 19:224, Cross-Complaint; Affirmative Defenses--Breach of the Warranty of Habitability.
Miller and Starr California Real Estate § 19:225, Cross-Complaint; Affirmative Defenses--Retaliatory Eviction.
14 NO. 2 Miller & Starr, California Real Estate Newsalert 14, Landlord and Tenant.
22 NO. 3 Miller & Starr, California Real Estate Newsalert 15, Landlord and Tenant.
12 Witkin, California Summary 10th Real Property § 567, (S 567) Restrictions on Waivers of Tenants' Rights.
12 Witkin, California Summary 10th Real Property § 611, General Principles.
1 Witkin Cal. Summ. 10th Contracts § 337, Other Contract or Provision.
1 Witkin Cal. Summ. 10th Contracts § 670, (S 670) Exemption Rejected.
1 Witkin Cal. Summ. 10th Contracts § 683, Waivers by Tenants.
13 Witkin, California Summary 10th Personal Property § 98, Nature of Statute.

§ 1954. Entry of dwelling by landlord; conditions; oral agreement between tenant and landlord

(a) A landlord may enter the dwelling unit only in the following cases:

(1) In case of emergency.

(2) To make necessary or agreed repairs, decorations, alterations or improvements, supply necessary or agreed services, or exhibit the dwelling unit to prospective or actual purchasers, mortgagees, tenants, workers, or contractors or to make an inspection pursuant to subdivision (f) of Section 1950.5.

(3) When the tenant has abandoned or surrendered the premises.

(4) Pursuant to court order.

(b) Except in cases of emergency or when the tenant has abandoned or surrendered the premises, entry may not be made during other than normal business hours unless the tenant consents to an entry during other than normal business hours at the time of entry.

(c) The landlord may not abuse the right of access or use it to harass the tenant.

(d)(1) Except as provided in subdivision (e), or as provided in paragraph (2) or (3), the landlord shall give the tenant reasonable notice in writing of his or her intent to enter and enter only during normal business hours. The notice shall include the date, approximate time, and purpose of the entry. The notice may be personally delivered to the tenant, left with someone of a suitable age and discretion at the premises, or, left on, near, or under the usual entry door of the premises in a manner in which a reasonable person would discover the notice. Twenty-four hours shall be presumed to be reasonable notice in absence of evidence to the contrary. The notice may be mailed to the tenant. Mailing of the notice at least six days prior to an intended entry is presumed reasonable notice in the absence of evidence to the contrary.

(2) If the purpose of the entry is to exhibit the dwelling unit to prospective or actual purchasers, the notice may be given orally, in person or by telephone, if the landlord or his or her agent has notified the tenant in writing within 120 days of the oral notice that the property is for sale and that the landlord or agent may contact the tenant orally for the purpose described above. Twenty-four hours is presumed reasonable notice in the absence of evidence to the contrary. The notice shall include the date, approximate time, and purpose of the entry. At the time of entry, the landlord or agent shall leave written evidence of the entry inside the unit.

(3) The tenant and the landlord may agree orally to an entry to make agreed repairs or supply agreed services. The agreement shall include the date and approximate time of the entry, which shall be within one week of the agreement. In this case, the landlord is not required to provide the tenant a written notice.

(e) No notice of entry is required under this section:

(1) To respond to an emergency.

(2) If the tenant is present and consents to the entry at the time of entry.

(3) After the tenant has abandoned or surrendered the unit. *(Added by Stats.1975, c. 302, p. 750, § 2. Amended by Stats.2002, c. 301 (S.B.1403), § 3; Stats.2002, c. 1061 (A.B.2330), § 2.5; Stats.2003, c. 62 (S.B.600), § 18; Stats.2003, c. 787 (S.B.345), § 1.)*

Research References

California Real Estate Forms (Miller & Starr) § 2:65, Residential Lease.
California Real Estate Forms (Miller & Starr) § 2:66, Residential Lease With Purchase Option.
Rutter, Cal. Practice Guide: Landlord-Tenant Form 2:A, Residential Rental Agreement.
Rutter, Cal. Practice Guide: Landlord-Tenant Form 7:B.2, Three-Day Notice to Cure or Quit (Violation of Statute & Rent Control Ordinance).
Miller and Starr California Real Estate § 19:154, Landlord's Right of Entry.
Miller and Starr California Real Estate § 19:162, Elements of the Offense--Forcible Entry.
Miller and Starr California Real Estate § 19:236, Tenant's Personal Property--Residential Landlord's Lien.
13 NO. 4 Miller & Starr, California Real Estate Newsalert 14, Landlord and Tenant.
14 NO. 4 Miller & Starr, California Real Estate Newsalert 10, Landlord and Tenant.
19 NO. 5 Miller & Starr, California Real Estate Newsalert 22, Landlord and Tenant.
22 NO. 3 Miller & Starr, California Real Estate Newsalert 15, Landlord and Tenant.
12 Witkin, California Summary 10th Real Property § 503, Statutory Framework.
12 Witkin, California Summary 10th Real Property § 567, (S 567) Restrictions on Waivers of Tenants' Rights.
12 Witkin, California Summary 10th Real Property § 609, (S 609) Landlord's Entry Into Dwelling.
12 Witkin, California Summary 10th Real Property § 616, Landlord's Use of Theft, Extortion, or Force.

§ 1954.1. Assignment for the benefit of creditors; right of assignee to occupy business premises; payment of rent; time

In any general assignment for the benefit of creditors, as defined in Section 493.010 of the Code of Civil Procedure, the assignee shall have the right to occupy, for a period of up to 90 days after the date of the assignment, any business premises held under a lease by the assignor upon payment when due of the monthly rental reserved in the lease for the period of such occupancy, notwithstanding any provision in the lease (whether heretofore or hereafter entered into) for the termination thereof upon the making of the assignment or the insolvency of the lessee or other condition relating to the financial condition of the lessee. This section shall be construed as establishing the reasonable rental value of the premises recoverable by a landlord upon a holding-over by the tenant upon the termination of a lease under the circumstances specified herein. *(Added by Stats.1982, c. 35, p. 63, § 1, eff. Feb. 17, 1982.)*

Research References

Miller and Starr California Real Estate § 19:179, Insolvency or Bankruptcy of the Tenant.
1 Witkin Cal. Summ. 10th Contracts § 711, (S 711) Conformity With Federal Statutes.

CHAPTER 2.6. COMMERCIAL RENTAL CONTROL

§ 1954.25. Legislative findings

The Legislature finds that the price charged for commercial real property is a matter of statewide concern. Price controls on commercial rents discourage expansion of commercial development and entrepreneurial enterprise. These controls also discourage competition in the open market by giving artificial price benefits to one enterprise to the disadvantage of another. Because the impact of these controls goes beyond the local boundaries within which the controls are imposed, the adverse economic consequences [1] become statewide.

In order to prevent this statewide economic drain from occurring, the Legislature hereby enacts a uniform system with respect to commercial rents, which shall apply to every local jurisdiction in the state. This legislative action is needed to prevent the imposition of artificial barriers on commercial rents, as well as to define those areas not included within the definition of commercial real property.

In making these findings and in enacting this chapter, the Legislature expressly declares its intent that this chapter shall not apply or be interpreted to apply to local rental controls on residential real property. *(Added by Stats.1987, c. 824, § 2.)*

1 So in chaptered bill.

Research References

12 Witkin, California Summary 10th Real Property § 503, Statutory Framework.
12 Witkin, California Summary 10th Real Property § 573, (S 573) in General.
12 Witkin, California Summary 10th Real Property § 575, (S 575) Commercial Rent Control Prohibited.

§ 1954.26.   Definitions

As used in this chapter, the following terms have the following meanings:

(a) "Owner" includes any person, acting as principal or through an agent, having the right to offer commercial real property for rent, and includes any predecessor in interest to the owner.

(b) "Price" includes any charge or fee, however denominated, for the hiring of commercial real property and includes any security or deposit subject to Section 1950.7.

(c) "Public entity" has the same meaning as defined in Section 811.2 of the Government Code.

(d) "Commercial real property" includes any part, portion, or unit thereof, and any related facilities, space, or services, except the following:

(1) Any dwelling or dwelling unit subject to the provisions of Section 1940.

(2) Any accommodation in any residential hotel, as defined in Section 50519 of the Health and Safety Code, or comparable accommodations which are specifically regulated by a public entity in structures where 20 percent or more of the accommodations are occupied by persons as their primary residence.

(3) Any hotel unit not otherwise specified in paragraph (1) or (2) that is located in a structure with 20 or more units or in which 20 percent or more of the accommodations were occupied as of August 5, 1987, by persons as their primary residence, if, in either circumstance, the unit was subject to rental controls on August 5, 1987, provided that any control exercised thereafter is in accordance with the system of controls in effect on August 5, 1987.

(4) Any space or dwelling unit in any mobilehome park, as defined in Section 18214 of the Health and Safety Code.

(e) "Rent" means to hire real property and includes a lease or sublease.

(f) "Commercial rental control" includes any action of a public entity taken by statute, charter, ordinance, resolution, administrative regulation, or any other governmental enactment to establish, continue, implement, or enforce any control or system of controls, on the price at which, or the term for which, commercial real property may be offered for rent, or control or system of controls which would select, mandate, dictate, or otherwise designate a specific tenant or specific person or entity with whom the owner must negotiate on the formation, extension, or renewal of a tenancy; or any other enactment which has such a purpose.

(g) "Tenant" includes a lessee, subtenant, and sublessee.

(h) "Term" means the period of time for which real property is rented or offered for rent, and includes any provision for a termination or extension of such a period or renewal thereof, except that nothing in this chapter supersedes the specific provisions of this code or of the Code of Civil Procedure which

of themselves establish, prescribe, limit, or define the term for which real property may be rented.

(i) "Impasse notice" means a written notice which states either of the following:

(1) That the owner has not received from the tenant an offer of any terms for an extension or renewal of the lease which are acceptable to the owner, or an acceptance by the tenant of any offer of terms by the owner, and that an impasse with respect to any agreement on a lease extension or renewal has been reached.

(2) That the owner is not willing to extend or renew the lease.

(j) "Negotiation notice" means a written notice by a tenant in privity of estate, and in privity of contract with the owner, stating either of the following:

(1) That the tenant offers to extend or renew the lease on terms set forth in the notice.

(2) That the tenant solicits an offer for the extension or renewal of the lease from the owner.

(k) "Deliver" means to deliver by personal service or by placing a copy of the notice in the mail, postage prepaid, by certified mail, return receipt requested, addressed to the party at the address for the receipt of notices under the lease.

(*l*) "Developer" means any person who enters into an agreement with a redevelopment agency for the purpose of developing specific commercial real property within a redevelopment project area with the intention of acquiring ownership of that property, even if that person does not own that property when the agreement is executed. *(Added by Stats.1987, c. 824, § 2.)*

Research References

Miller and Starr California Real Estate § 19:41, Special Requirements for Renewal of Commercial Leases.
Miller and Starr California Real Estate § 19:90, Property Subject to Control; Exceptions and Exemptions.
Miller and Starr California Real Estate § 19:169, Notice Required on Expiration of a Commercial Lease.
12 Witkin, California Summary 10th Real Property § 575, (S 575) Commercial Rent Control Prohibited.

§ 1954.27.   Rental control enactment or enforcement by public entity; limitations on construction of chapter

(a) No public entity shall enact any measure constituting commercial rental control, nor shall any public entity enforce any commercial rental control, whether enacted prior to or on or after January 1, 1988.

(b) However, nothing in this chapter shall be construed to do any of the following:

(1) Relieve any party to a commercial lease or rental agreement of the duty to perform any obligation thereunder.

(2) Preclude express establishment in a commercial lease or rental agreement of the price at which real property may be offered to a subtenant or sublessee.

(3) Impair any obligation of any contract entered into prior to January 1, 1988.

(4) Affect any provision of, or requirement for mitigation of damages under, Sections 1951 to 1952.6, inclusive.

(5) Limit any adjustment of price required or permitted by law due to constructive eviction.

(6) Enlarge or diminish in any way any power which a public entity may have with respect to regulation of rental rates or the ownership, conveyance, or use of any property specified in paragraph (1), (2), or (3) of subdivision (d) of Section 1954.26.

(7) Relieve any party of any requirement or mandate to arbitrate, or deprive any party of any right to arbitrate or compel

arbitration, which mandate or right exists pursuant to Title 9 (commencing with Section 1280) of Part 3 of the Code of Civil Procedure, titled "Arbitration," Chapter 2.5 (commencing with Section 1141.10) of Title 3 of Part 3 of the Code of Civil Procedure, titled "Judicial Arbitration," Title 1 (commencing with Section 1823) of Part 3 of the Code of Civil Procedure, titled "Pilot Projects," or any other provision of state law.

(8) Affect in any way, or preclude the inclusion of, any provision in a lease creating any lawful option, right of first refusal, or any covenant to renew or extend the lease or sell the real property or any interest therein.

(9) Relieve any person of any duty or deprive any person of any right or cause of action which may exist pursuant to Section 51, 53, or 782. *(Added by Stats.1987, c. 824, § 2.)*

Research References

Miller and Starr California Real Estate § 19:90, Property Subject to Control; Exceptions and Exemptions.
12 Witkin, California Summary 10th Real Property § 575, (S 575) Commercial Rent Control Prohibited.

§ 1954.28. Permissible regulation by or agreements with public entities

Nothing in this chapter limits or affects public entities with respect to any of the following:

(a) The Eminent Domain Law, Title 7 (commencing with Section 1230.10) of Part 3 of the Code of Civil Procedure.

(b) Abatement of nuisances. However, except as to conditions expressly defined as nuisances by statute, authority to abate or bring actions to abate nuisances shall not be used to circumvent the limitations of this chapter with respect to conditions not manifesting the quantum and character of unreasonableness and injuriousness to constitute a nuisance under law.

(c) The Airport Approaches Zoning Law, Article 6.5 (commencing with Section 50485) of Chapter 2 of Part 1 of Division 1 of Title 5 of the Government Code.

(d) Any contract or agreement by which an owner agrees with a public entity to offer any real property for rent at a stipulated or maximum price or under a specified formula for ascertaining a stipulated or maximum price, in consideration for a direct financial contribution; any written contract between a redevelopment agency and an owner or developer of commercial real property within a redevelopment project area; or any written development agreement entered into pursuant to Article 2.5 (commencing with Section 65864) of Chapter 4 of Division 1 of Title 7 of the Government Code. Any contract or agreement specified in this subdivision is not enforceable against an owner who became an owner (1) without actual knowledge of the contract or agreement, and (2) more than 30 days prior to the recording with the county recorder of a written memorandum of the contract or agreement specifically describing its terms and identifying the real property and the owner. The county recorder shall index these memorandums in the grantor-grantee index.

(e) Article 2 (commencing with Section 5020) of Chapter 1 of Division 5 of the Public Resources Code, relating to historical resources.

(f) The Subdivision Map Act, Division 2 (commencing with Section 66410) of Title 7 of the Government Code.

(g) Any contract or agreement entered into by a public entity relating to the transfer, lease, or license of commercial real property owned or leased by that public entity, except any requirement enacted pursuant to Section 1954.31. *(Added by Stats.1987, c. 824, § 2.)*

Research References

Miller and Starr California Real Estate § 19:90, Property Subject to Control; Exceptions and Exemptions.
12 Witkin, California Summary 10th Real Property § 575, (S 575) Commercial Rent Control Prohibited.

§ 1954.29. Zoning and planning and business licenses; effect of chapter on public entity powers

Nothing in this chapter shall, with respect to a public entity:

(a) Grant, enlarge, or diminish any power (1) which it may possess under the provisions of, and for the purposes of, Division 1 (commencing with Section 65000) of Title 7 of the Government Code, (2) with respect to charter cities, planning, or zoning powers granted under Section 5 of Article XI of the California Constitution, or (3) any power which it may possess to mitigate the impact caused by the construction, reconstruction, demolition, or alteration of the size of any commercial real property. However, this subdivision does not apply to any actions taken for the clear or systematic purpose of circumventing this chapter.

(b) Grant, repeal, enlarge, or diminish any authority to require a business license, whether for regulation or revenue. *(Added by Stats.1987, c. 824, § 2.)*

Research References

12 Witkin, California Summary 10th Real Property § 575, (S 575) Commercial Rent Control Prohibited.

§ 1954.30. Effect of chapter on powers of public entity

Nothing in this chapter grants or augments any authority of a public entity which it does not possess independent of this chapter, nor diminish any power of a public entity except as expressly provided in this chapter. *(Added by Stats.1987, c. 824, § 2.)*

Research References

12 Witkin, California Summary 10th Real Property § 575, (S 575) Commercial Rent Control Prohibited.

§ 1954.31. Public entity enactment relating to lease termination upon expiration of its term; contents; construction; application

A public entity may by enactment of a statute, charter or charter amendment, or ordinance, establish a requirement for notice relating to the termination of a lease of commercial real property due to the expiration of its term.

(a) The enactment shall contain provisions dealing with any or all of the following:

(1) The delivery of a negotiation notice by a tenant.

(2) A requirement for an owner to deliver an impasse notice at any time after delivery of the negotiation notice, except that:

(A) The requirement shall be inapplicable unless the tenant has been required to deliver a negotiation notice not less than 270 days before the expiration of the lease, and has done so.

(B) The mandate for delivery of an impasse notice shall not occur earlier than 180 days before expiration of the lease.

(C) No impasse notice shall be required if the parties have executed a renewal or extension of the lease.

(D) Provision shall be made that the notice will include, in a form of type which will distinguish it from the body of the text of the balance of the notice, a disclosure reading, either:

(i) The giving of this notice does not necessarily preclude further dialogue or negotiation on an extension or renewal of the lease if the parties choose to negotiate, but the delivery of this notice discharges all obligations of _____ (the owner) under provisions of _____ (the enactment) and Section 1954.31 of the Civil Code; or

(ii) By giving this notice _____ (the owner) declares that he or she does not intend to negotiate further on any extension or renewal of the lease.

(3) Establish that a bad faith failure to comply with the enactment is subject to a remedy for actual damages.

(4) Any remedy under the enactment or Section 1954.31 shall be available only by an action brought by the owner or the tenant.

(b) The enactment shall contain (or shall be deemed to contain), a provision that:

(1) A tenant may not exercise any right pursuant to the enactment or this chapter, unless the tenant has performed the terms of the lease in such manner as would entitle the tenant to exercise any option he or she might possess under the lease.

(2) No right or cause of action accruing to a tenant pursuant to the enactment or this chapter, may be assigned other than to a person who is a lawful assignee of the lease, is in lawful possession of the premises under the lease, and is in compliance with paragraph (1).

(3) Nothing in the enactment or this chapter creates or imposes, nor shall be construed to create or impose, a duty to extend or renew, or to negotiate on an extension or renewal, of any lease; nor shall the delivery or receipt of any notice provided for by the enactment or by this chapter, constitute a waiver of any rights to continued performance under the covenants under the lease or to actions for possession.

(4) The delivery of any notice pursuant to the enactment or this chapter shall create a rebuttable presumption affecting the burden of proof, that the notice has been properly given.

(c) No enactment shall provide, or be deemed to provide:

(1) For any extension of the term of any lease without the mutual, written consent of the owner and the tenant.

(2) For any requirement on either party to offer to extend or renew or to negotiate an extension or renewal of the lease.

(3) Bar any action brought to recover possession whether by ejectment, unlawful detainer, or other lawful means.

(4) Any remedy under the enactment or this chapter, other than that which may be provided pursuant to paragraph (3) of subdivision (a).

(d) The provisions of any enactment adopted pursuant to this section shall not apply to:

(1) Any lease or rental agreement which is not in writing, which constitutes a tenancy at will, which is for a term of less than one year or for an unspecified term, which is a month-to-month tenancy or a tenancy at sufferance.

(2) Any lease, the term of which expires within 270 days after the effective date of the enactment. *(Added by Stats.1987, c. 824, § 2.)*

Research References

Miller and Starr California Real Estate § 19:41, Special Requirements for Renewal of Commercial Leases.
Miller and Starr California Real Estate § 19:90, Property Subject to Control; Exceptions and Exemptions.
Miller and Starr California Real Estate § 19:169, Notice Required on Expiration of a Commercial Lease.

12 Witkin, California Summary 10th Real Property § 575, (S 575) Commercial Rent Control Prohibited.

CHAPTER 2.7. RESIDENTIAL RENT CONTROL

§ 1954.50. Short title

This chapter shall be known and may be cited as the Costa–Hawkins Rental Housing Act. *(Added by Stats.1995, c. 331 (A.B.1164), § 1.)*

Research References

Miller and Starr California Real Estate § 25:9, Judicial Review.
Miller and Starr California Real Estate § 25:22, Owner's Vested Rights After Map Approval.
Miller and Starr California Real Estate § 25:54, Judicial Review.
13 NO. 5 Miller & Starr, California Real Estate Newsalert 11, Landlord and Tenant.
12 Witkin, California Summary 10th Real Property § 503, Statutory Framework.
12 Witkin, California Summary 10th Real Property § 574, (S 574) Single Family Dwellings, New Construction, and Vacancy Controls.
12 Witkin, California Summary 10th Real Property § 597, Expenses, Fees, and Costs.
8 Witkin, California Summary 10th Constitutional Law § 1006, Commentary and Practice Works.

§ 1954.51. Definitions

As used in this chapter, the following terms have the following meanings:

(a) "Comparable units" means rental units that have approximately the same living space, have the same number of bedrooms, are located in the same or similar neighborhoods, and feature the same, similar, or equal amenities and housing services.

(b) "Owner" includes any person, acting as principal or through an agent, having the right to offer residential real property for rent, and includes a predecessor in interest to the owner, except that this term does not include the owner or operator of a mobilehome park, or the owner of a mobilehome or his or her agent.

(c) "Prevailing market rent" means the rental rate that would be authorized pursuant to 42 U.S.C.A. 1437(f), as calculated by the United States Department of Housing and Urban Development pursuant to Part 888 of Title 24 of the Code of Federal Regulations.

(d) "Public entity" has the same meaning as set forth in Section 811.2 of the Government Code.

(e) "Residential real property" includes any dwelling or unit that is intended for human habitation.

(f) "Tenancy" includes the lawful occupation of property and includes a lease or sublease. *(Added by Stats.1995, c. 331 (A.B.1164), § 1.)*

Research References

Miller and Starr California Real Estate § 19:91, Property Subject to Control; Exceptions and Exemptions--State Exemption of Specified Residential Rental Properties.

§ 1954.52. Rental rates; establishment by owner; conditions

(a) Notwithstanding any other provision of law, an owner of residential real property may establish the initial and all subsequent rental rates for a dwelling or a unit about which any of the following is true:

(1) It has a certificate of occupancy issued after February 1, 1995.

(2) It has already been exempt from the residential rent control ordinance of a public entity on or before February 1, 1995, pursuant to a local exemption for newly constructed units.

(3)(A) It is alienable separate from the title to any other dwelling unit or is a subdivided interest in a subdivision, as specified in subdivision (b), (d), or (f) of Section 11004.5 of the Business and Professions Code.

(B) This paragraph does not apply to either of the following:

(i) A dwelling or unit where the preceding tenancy has been terminated by the owner by notice pursuant to Section 1946.1 or has been terminated upon a change in the terms of the tenancy noticed pursuant to Section 827.

(ii) A condominium dwelling or unit that has not been sold separately by the subdivider to a bona fide purchaser for value. The initial rent amount of the unit for purposes of this chapter shall be the lawful rent in effect on May 7, 2001, unless the rent amount is governed by a different provision of this chapter. However, if a condominium dwelling or unit meets the criteria of paragraph (1) or (2) of subdivision (a), or if all the dwellings or units except one have been sold separately by the subdivider to bona fide purchasers for value, and the subdivider has occupied that remaining unsold condominium dwelling or unit as his or her principal residence for at least one year after the subdivision occurred, then subparagraph (A) of paragraph (3) shall apply to that unsold condominium dwelling or unit.

(C) Where a dwelling or unit in which the initial or subsequent rental rates are controlled by an ordinance or charter provision in effect on January 1, 1995, the following shall apply:

(i) An owner of real property as described in this paragraph may establish the initial and all subsequent rental rates for all existing and new tenancies in effect on or after January 1, 1999, if the tenancy in effect on or after January 1, 1999, was created between January 1, 1996, and December 31, 1998.

(ii) Commencing on January 1, 1999, an owner of real property as described in this paragraph may establish the initial and all subsequent rental rates for all new tenancies if the previous tenancy was in effect on December 31, 1995.

(iii) The initial rental rate for a dwelling or unit as described in this paragraph in which the initial rental rate is controlled by an ordinance or charter provision in effect on January 1, 1995, may not, until January 1, 1999, exceed the amount calculated pursuant to subdivision (c) of Section 1954.53. An owner of residential real property as described in this paragraph may, until January 1, 1999, establish the initial rental rate for a dwelling or unit only where the tenant has voluntarily vacated, abandoned, or been evicted pursuant to paragraph (2) of Section 1161 of the Code of Civil Procedure.

(b) Subdivision (a) does not apply where the owner has otherwise agreed by contract with a public entity in consideration for a direct financial contribution or any other forms of assistance specified in Chapter 4.3 (commencing with Section 65915) of Division 1 of Title 7 of the Government Code.

(c) Nothing in this section shall be construed to affect the authority of a public entity that may otherwise exist to regulate or monitor the basis for eviction.

(d) This section does not apply to any dwelling or unit that contains serious health, safety, fire, or building code violations, excluding those caused by disasters for which a citation has been issued by the appropriate governmental agency and which has remained unabated for six months or longer preceding the vacancy. *(Added by Stats.1995, c. 331 (A.B.1164), § 1. Amended by Stats.2001, c. 729 (S.B.985), § 2; Stats.2004, c. 568 (S.B.1145), § 4.)*

Research References

Miller and Starr California Real Estate § 19:91, Property Subject to Control; Exceptions and Exemptions--State Exemption of Specified Residential Rental Properties.

Miller and Starr California Real Estate § 25:22, Owner's Vested Rights After Map Approval.

Miller and Starr California Real Estate § 25:70, Reliance Upon a Grant of Authority or Permit to Do Specific Work as Described in the Grant or Permit.

Miller and Starr California Real Estate § 19:172, Effect of Withdrawal of the Property from the Market ("Ellis Act").

13 NO. 5 Miller & Starr, California Real Estate Newsalert 11, Landlord and Tenant.

19 NO. 6 Miller & Starr, California Real Estate Newsalert 15, Landlord and Tenant.

12 Witkin, California Summary 10th Real Property § 573, (S 573) in General.

12 Witkin, California Summary 10th Real Property § 574, (S 574) Single Family Dwellings, New Construction, and Vacancy Controls.

12 Witkin, California Summary 10th Real Property § 597, Expenses, Fees, and Costs.

12 Witkin, California Summary 10th Real Property § 601, Demolished Property Later Replaced and Offered for Rent.

§ 1954.53. Initial rental rate; establishment by owner; conditions; exceptions

(a) Notwithstanding any other provision of law, an owner of residential real property may establish the initial rental rate for a dwelling or unit, except where any of the following applies:

(1) The previous tenancy has been terminated by the owner by notice pursuant to Section 1946.1 or has been terminated upon a change in the terms of the tenancy noticed pursuant to Section 827, except a change permitted by law in the amount of rent or fees. For the purpose of this paragraph, the owner's termination or nonrenewal of a contract or recorded agreement with a governmental agency that provides for a rent limitation to a qualified tenant, shall be construed as a change in the terms of the tenancy pursuant to Section 827.

(A) In a jurisdiction that controls by ordinance or charter provision the rental rate for a dwelling or unit, an owner who terminates or fails to renew a contract or recorded agreement with a governmental agency that provides for a rent limitation to a qualified tenant may not set an initial rent for three years following the date of the termination or nonrenewal of the contract or agreement. For any new tenancy established during the three-year period, the rental rate for a new tenancy established in that vacated dwelling or unit shall be at the same rate as the rent under the terminated or nonrenewed contract or recorded agreement with a governmental agency that provided for a rent limitation to a qualified tenant, plus any increases authorized after the termination or cancellation of the contract or recorded agreement.

(B) Subparagraph (A) does not apply to any new tenancy of 12 months or more duration established after January 1, 2000, pursuant to the owner's contract or recorded agreement with a governmental agency that provides for a rent limitation to a qualified tenant, unless the prior vacancy in that dwelling or unit was pursuant to a nonrenewed or canceled contract or recorded agreement with a governmental agency that provides for a rent limitation to a qualified tenant as set forth in that subparagraph.

(2) The owner has otherwise agreed by contract with a public entity in consideration for a direct financial contribution or any

other forms of assistance specified in Chapter 4.3 (commencing with Section 65915) of Division 1 of Title 7 of the Government Code.

(3) The initial rental rate for a dwelling or unit whose initial rental rate is controlled by an ordinance or charter provision in effect on January 1, 1995, may not until January 1, 1999, exceed the amount calculated pursuant to subdivision (c).

(b) Subdivision (a) applies to, and includes, renewal of the initial hiring by the same tenant, lessee, authorized subtenant, or authorized sublessee for the entire period of his or her occupancy at the rental rate established for the initial hiring.

(c) The rental rate of a dwelling or unit whose initial rental rate is controlled by ordinance or charter provision in effect on January 1, 1995, shall, until January 1, 1999, be established in accordance with this subdivision. Where the previous tenant has voluntarily vacated, abandoned, or been evicted pursuant to paragraph (2) of Section 1161 of Code of Civil Procedure, an owner of residential real property may, no more than twice, establish the initial rental rate for a dwelling or unit in an amount that is no greater than 15 percent more than the rental rate in effect for the immediately preceding tenancy or in an amount that is 70 percent of the prevailing market rent for comparable units, whichever amount is greater.

The initial rental rate established pursuant to this subdivision may not substitute for or replace increases in rental rates otherwise authorized pursuant to law.

(d)(1) Nothing in this section or any other provision of law shall be construed to preclude express establishment in a lease or rental agreement of the rental rates to be applicable in the event the rental unit subject thereto is sublet. Nothing in this section shall be construed to impair the obligations of contracts entered into prior to January 1, 1996.

(2) If the original occupant or occupants who took possession of the dwelling or unit pursuant to the rental agreement with the owner no longer permanently reside there, an owner may increase the rent by any amount allowed by this section to a lawful sublessee or assignee who did not reside at the dwelling or unit prior to January 1, 1996.

(3) This subdivision does not apply to partial changes in occupancy of a dwelling or unit where one or more of the occupants of the premises, pursuant to the agreement with the owner provided for above, remains an occupant in lawful possession of the dwelling or unit, or where a lawful sublessee or assignee who resided at the dwelling or unit prior to January 1, 1996, remains in possession of the dwelling or unit. Nothing contained in this section shall be construed to enlarge or diminish an owner's right to withhold consent to a sublease or assignment.

(4) Acceptance of rent by the owner does not operate as a waiver or otherwise prevent enforcement of a covenant prohibiting sublease or assignment or as a waiver of an owner's rights to establish the initial rental rate, unless the owner has received written notice from the tenant that is party to the agreement and thereafter accepted rent.

(e) Nothing in this section shall be construed to affect any authority of a public entity that may otherwise exist to regulate or monitor the grounds for eviction.

(f) This section does not apply to any dwelling or unit if all the following conditions are met:

(1) The dwelling or unit has been cited in an inspection report by the appropriate governmental agency as containing serious health, safety, fire, or building code violations, as defined by Section 17920.3 of the Health and Safety Code, excluding any violation caused by a disaster.

(2) The citation was issued at least 60 days prior to the date of the vacancy.

(3) The cited violation had not been abated when the prior tenant vacated and had remained unabated for 60 days or for a longer period of time. However, the 60–day time period may be extended by the appropriate governmental agency that issued the citation. *(Added by Stats.1995, c. 331 (A.B.1164), § 1. Amended by Stats.1996, c. 1031 (A.B.3244), § 1; Stats.1999, c. 590 (S.B. 1098), § 2; Stats.2004, c. 568 (S.B.1145), § 5.)*

Research References

Miller and Starr California Real Estate § 19:91, Property Subject to Control; Exceptions and Exemptions--State Exemption of Specified Residential Rental Properties.
13 NO. 5 Miller & Starr, California Real Estate Newsalert 11, Landlord and Tenant.
20 NO. 1 Miller & Starr, California Real Estate Newsalert 21, Subdivisions, Land Use Planning, and Approvals.
12 Witkin, California Summary 10th Real Property § 574, (S 574) Single Family Dwellings, New Construction, and Vacancy Controls.
12 Witkin, California Summary 10th Real Property § 597, Expenses, Fees, and Costs.

§ 1954.535. Written notice of termination by owner

Where an owner terminates or fails to renew a contract or recorded agreement with a governmental agency that provides for rent limitations to a qualified tenant, the tenant or tenants who were the beneficiaries of the contract or recorded agreement shall be given at least 90 days' written notice of the effective date of the termination and shall not be obligated to pay more than the tenant's portion of the rent, as calculated under the contract or recorded agreement to be terminated, for 90 days following receipt of the notice of termination of nonrenewal of the contract. *(Added by Stats.1999, c. 590 (S.B.1098), § 3.)*

Research References

Miller and Starr California Real Estate § 25:9, Judicial Review.
Miller and Starr California Real Estate § 19:91, Property Subject to Control; Exceptions and Exemptions--State Exemption of Specified Residential Rental Properties.
Miller and Starr California Real Estate § 25:22, Owner's Vested Rights After Map Approval.
Miller and Starr California Real Estate § 25:54, Judicial Review.
13 NO. 5 Miller & Starr, California Real Estate Newsalert 11, Landlord and Tenant.
13 NO. 3 Miller & Starr, California Real Estate Newsalert 14, Landlord and Tenant.
16 NO. 1 Miller & Starr, California Real Estate Newsalert 19, Landlord and Tenant.
23 NO. 2 Miller & Starr, California Real Estate Newsalert 1, Housing: Safety Net or Tangled Web? an Overview of Section 8 Tenancy Termination and Related Due Process Issues.
12 Witkin, California Summary 10th Real Property § 680, Periodic Tenancy.

CHAPTER 3. HIRING OF PERSONAL PROPERTY

Section
1955. Obligations of lessor.
1956. Expenses.
1957. Expenses of lessee in making good lessor's default.
1958. Return; time and place.
1959. Charter party defined.

§ 1955. Obligations of lessor

Except as otherwise agreed by the lessor and the lessee in lease agreements for a term of more than 20 days, one who leases personal property must deliver it to the lessee, secure his or her quiet enjoyment thereof against all lawful claimants, put it into a condition fit for the purpose for which he or she leases it, and repair all deteriorations thereof not occasioned by the fault of the lessee and not the natural result of its use. *(Enacted in 1872. Amended by Stats.1982, c. 561, p. 2507, § 1.)*

Research References

13 Witkin, California Summary 10th Personal Property § 188, (S 188) in General.

13 Witkin, California Summary 10th Personal Property § 190, (S 190) Warranty and Strict Liability.

6 Witkin, California Summary 10th Torts § 1506, (S 1506) Lessor of Personal Property.

§ 1956. Expenses

Except as otherwise agreed by the lessor and lessee, a lessee of personal property must bear all such expenses concerning it as might naturally be foreseen to attend it during its use by him or her, and all other expenses must be borne by the lessor. *(Enacted in 1872. Amended by Stats.1982, c. 561, p. 2507, § 2.)*

Research References

13 Witkin, California Summary 10th Personal Property § 188, (S 188) in General.

§ 1957. Expenses of lessee in making good lessor's default

If a lessor fails to fulfill his or her obligations, as prescribed by Section 1955, the lessee, after giving him or her notice to do so, if the notice can conveniently be given, may expend any reasonable amount necessary to make good the lessor's default, and may recover such amount from him or her. *(Enacted in 1872. Amended by Stats.1982, c. 561, p. 2507, § 3.)*

Research References

13 Witkin, California Summary 10th Personal Property § 188, (S 188) in General.

13 Witkin, California Summary 10th Personal Property § 190, (S 190) Warranty and Strict Liability.

§ 1958. Return; time and place

At the expiration of the term for which personal property is leased, the lessee must return it to the lessor at the place contemplated by the parties at the time of leasing; or, if no particular place was so contemplated by them, at the place at which it was at that time. *(Enacted in 1872. Amended by Stats.1982, c. 561, p. 2507, § 4.)*

Research References

13 Witkin, California Summary 10th Personal Property § 188, (S 188) in General.

§ 1959. Charter party defined

The contract by which a ship is let is termed a charter party. By it the owner may either let the capacity or burden of the ship, continuing the employment of the owner's master, crew, and equipments, or may surrender the entire ship to the charterer, who then provides them himself. The master or a part owner may be a charterer. *(Enacted in 1872.)*

CHAPTER 4. IDENTIFICATION OF PROPERTY OWNERS

§ 1961. Application of chapter

This chapter shall apply to every dwelling structure containing one or more units offered to the public for rent or for lease for residential purposes. *(Added by Stats.1972, c. 941, p. 1698, § 1, operative July 1, 1973. Amended by Stats.1987, c. 769, § 1.)*

Research References

Rutter, Cal. Practice Guide: Real Prop. Transactions Ch. 10-B, B. Regulation of Real Property Managers and Legal Relationship Between Manager and Owner.

Miller and Starr California Real Estate § 19:12, Apartment House Manager as an Employee--Posted Identification of the Owner.

12 Witkin, California Summary 10th Real Property § 521, Identification of Property Owners or Managers.

§ 1962. Disclosures by owner or rental agent to tenant; agent failing to make disclosure as agent of owner

(a) Any owner of a dwelling structure specified in Section 1961 or a party signing a rental agreement or lease on behalf of the owner shall do all of the following:

(1) Disclose therein the name, telephone number, and usual street address at which personal service may be effected of each person who is:

(A) Authorized to manage the premises.

(B) An owner of the premises or a person who is authorized to act for and on behalf of the owner for the purpose of service of process and for the purpose of receiving and receipting for all notices and demands.

(2) Disclose therein the name, telephone number, and address of the person or entity to whom rent payments shall be made.

(A) If rent payments may be made personally, the usual days and hours that the person will be available to receive the payments shall also be disclosed.

(B) At the owner's option, the rental agreement or lease shall instead disclose the number of either:

(i) The account in a financial institution into which rent payments may be made, and the name and street address of the institution; provided that the institution is located within five miles of the rental property.

(ii) The information necessary to establish an electronic funds transfer procedure for paying the rent.

(3) Disclose therein the form or forms in which rent payments are to be made.

(4) Provide a copy of the rental agreement or lease to the tenant within 15 days of its execution by the tenant. Once each calendar year thereafter, upon request by the tenant, the owner or owner's agent shall provide an additional copy to the tenant within 15 days. If the owner or owner's agent does not possess the rental agreement or lease or a copy of it, the owner or owner's agent shall instead furnish the tenant with a written statement stating that fact and containing the information required by paragraphs (1), (2), and (3).

(b) In the case of an oral rental agreement, the owner, or a person acting on behalf of the owner for the receipt of rent or otherwise, shall furnish the tenant, within 15 days of the agreement, with a written statement containing the information required by paragraphs (1), (2), and (3) of subdivision (a). Once each calendar year thereafter, upon request by the tenant, the owner or owner's agent shall provide an additional copy of the statement to the tenant within 15 days.

(c) The information required by this section shall be kept current and this section shall extend to and be enforceable against any successor owner or manager, who shall comply with this section within 15 days of succeeding the previous owner or manager. A successor owner or manager shall not serve a notice pursuant to paragraph (2) of Section 1161 of the Code of Civil Procedure or otherwise evict a tenant for nonpayment of rent that accrued during the period of noncompliance by a successor owner or manager with this subdivision. Nothing in this subdivision shall relieve the tenant of any liability for unpaid rent.

(d) A party who enters into a rental agreement on behalf of the owner who fails to comply with this section is deemed an agent of each person who is an owner:

(1) For the purpose of service of process and receiving and receipting for notices and demands.

(2) For the purpose of performing the obligations of the owner under law and under the rental agreement.

(3) For the purpose of receiving rental payments, which may be made in cash, by check, by money order, or in any form previously accepted by the owner or owner's agent, unless the form of payment has been specified in the oral or written agreement, or the tenant has been notified by the owner in writing that a particular form of payment is unacceptable.

(e) Nothing in this section limits or excludes the liability of any undisclosed owner.

(f) If the address provided by the owner does not allow for personal delivery, then it shall be conclusively presumed that upon the mailing of any rent or notice to the owner by the tenant to the name and address provided, the notice or rent is deemed receivable by the owner on the date posted, if the tenant can show proof of mailing to the name and address provided by the owner. *(Added by Stats.1972, c. 941, p. 1998, § 1, operative July 1, 1973. Amended by Stats.1987, c. 769, § 2; Stats.2001, c. 729 (S.B.985), § 3; Stats.2012, c. 695 (A.B.1953), § 1.)*

Research References

California Real Estate Forms (Miller & Starr) § 2:65, Residential Lease.
California Real Estate Forms (Miller & Starr) § 2:66, Residential Lease With Purchase Option.
Rutter, Cal. Practice Guide: Real Prop. Transactions Ch. 10-B, B. Regulation of Real Property Managers and Legal Relationship Between Manager and Owner.
Miller and Starr California Real Estate § 19:12, Apartment House Manager as an Employee--Posted Identification of the Owner.
12 Witkin, California Summary 10th Real Property § 521, Identification of Property Owners or Managers.

§ 1962.5. Optional methods of disclosure

(a) Notwithstanding subdivisions (a) and (b) of Section 1962, the information required by paragraph (1) of subdivision (a) of Section 1962 to be disclosed to a tenant may, instead of being disclosed in the manner described in subdivisions (a) and (b) of Section 1962, be disclosed by the following method:

(1) In each dwelling structure containing an elevator a printed or typewritten notice containing the information required by paragraph (1) of subdivision (a) of Section 1962 shall be placed in every elevator and in one other conspicuous place.

(2) In each structure not containing an elevator, a printed or typewritten notice containing the information required by paragraph (1) of subdivision (a) of Section 1962 shall be placed in at least two conspicuous places.

(3) In the case of a single unit dwelling structure, the information to be disclosed under this section may be disclosed by complying with either paragraph (1) or (2).

(b) Except as provided in subdivision (a), all the provisions of Section 1962 shall be applicable. *(Added by Stats.1972, c. 941, p. 1699, § 1, operative July 1, 1973. Amended by Stats.1987, c. 769, § 3; Stats.2001, c. 729 (S.B.985), § 4.)*

Research References

Rutter, Cal. Practice Guide: Real Prop. Transactions Ch. 10-B, B. Regulation of Real Property Managers and Legal Relationship Between Manager and Owner.
Miller and Starr California Real Estate § 19:12, Apartment House Manager as an Employee--Posted Identification of the Owner.
12 Witkin, California Summary 10th Real Property § 521, Identification of Property Owners or Managers.

§ 1962.7. Failure to comply; service of process; mailing to address at which rent is paid

In the event an owner, successor owner, manager, or agent specified in Section 1961 fails to comply with the requirements of this chapter, service of process by a tenant with respect to a dispute arising out of the tenancy may be made by registered or certified mail sent to the address at which rent is paid, in which case the provisions of Section 1013 of the Code of Civil Procedure shall apply. *(Added by Stats.1987, c. 769, § 4. Amended by Stats.2001, c. 729 (S.B.985), § 5.)*

Research References

Rutter, Cal. Practice Guide: Real Prop. Transactions Ch. 10-B, B. Regulation of Real Property Managers and Legal Relationship Between Manager and Owner.
Miller and Starr California Real Estate § 19:12, Apartment House Manager as an Employee--Posted Identification of the Owner.
12 Witkin, California Summary 10th Real Property § 521, Identification of Property Owners or Managers.

CHAPTER 4.5. DISPOSITION OF PERSONAL PROPERTY UPON REQUEST OF TENANT

§ 1965. Surrender of personal property to tenant or representative; costs; exemptions; landlord liability; actions

(a) A residential landlord shall not refuse to surrender, to a residential tenant or to a residential tenant's duly authorized representative, any personal property not owned by the landlord which has been left on the premises after the tenant has vacated the residential premises and the return of which has been requested by the tenant or by the authorized representative of the tenant if all of the following occur:

(1) The tenant requests, in writing, within 18 days of vacating the premises, the surrender of the personal property and the request includes a description of the personal property held by the landlord and specifies the mailing address of the tenant.

(2) The landlord or the landlord's agent has control or possession of the tenant's personal property at the time the request is received.

(3) The tenant, prior to the surrender of the personal property by the landlord and upon written demand by the landlord, tenders payment of all reasonable costs associated with the landlord's removal and storage of the personal property. The landlord's demand for payment of reasonable costs associated with the removal and storage of personal property shall be in writing and shall either be mailed to the tenant at the address provided by the tenant pursuant to paragraph (1) or shall be personally presented to the tenant or to the tenant's authorized representative, within five days after the actual receipt of the tenant's request for surrender of the personal property, unless the property is returned first. The demand shall itemize all charges, specifying the nature and amount of each item of cost.

(4) The tenant agrees to claim and remove the personal property at a reasonable time mutually agreed upon by the landlord and tenant but not later than 72 hours after the tender provided for under paragraph (3).

(b) For the purposes of this chapter, "reasonable costs associated with the landlord's removal and storage of the personal property" shall include, but not be limited to, each of the following:

(1) Reasonable costs actually incurred, or the reasonable value of labor actually provided, or both, in removing the personal property from its original location to the place of storage, including disassembly and transportation.

(2) Reasonable storage costs actually incurred, which shall not exceed the fair rental value of the space reasonably required for the storage of the personal property.

(c) This chapter shall not apply when disposition of the personal property has been initiated or completed pursuant to the procedure set forth in Chapter 5 (commencing with Section 1980) or the occupancy is one defined by subdivision (b) of Section 1940.

(d) A landlord who complies with this chapter shall not be liable to any person with respect to that person's personal property that is given to another person. In the event of conflicting demands, the first timely request for surrender of personal property received by the landlord shall prevail.

(e) Any landlord who retains personal property in violation of this chapter shall be liable to the tenant in a civil action for all the following:

(1) Actual damages not to exceed the value of the personal property, if the personal property is not surrendered by the later of either of the following: (A) within a reasonable time after the tenant's request for surrender of the personal property, or (B) if the landlord has demanded payment of reasonable costs associated with removal and storage and the tenant has complied with the requirements set forth in paragraphs (3) and (4) of subdivision (a), whichever is later. Three days is presumed to be a reasonable time in the absence of evidence to the contrary.

(2) An amount not to exceed two hundred fifty dollars ($250) for each bad faith violation of this section. In determining the amount of the award, the court shall consider proof of matters as justice may require.

(3) The court may award reasonable attorney's fees and cost to the prevailing party.

(f) The remedy provided by this chapter is not exclusive and shall not preclude either the landlord or the tenant from pursuing any other remedy provided by law. *(Added by Stats. 1988, c. 797, § 2.)*

Research References

Rutter, Cal. Practice Guide: Landlord-Tenant Form 2:A, Residential Rental Agreement.

Miller and Starr California Real Estate § 19:233, Tenant's Personal Property.

8 Witkin Cal. Proc. 5th Enforcement of Judgment § 337, (S 337) Disposition of Personal Property.

7 Witkin Cal. Proc. 5th Judgment § 228, (S 228) Landlord and Tenant Actions.

12 Witkin, California Summary 10th Real Property § 503, Statutory Framework.

12 Witkin, California Summary 10th Real Property § 742, (S 742) Storage of Tenant's Property.

12 Witkin, California Summary 10th Real Property § 754, Alternative Procedure on Tenant's Request.

CHAPTER 5. DISPOSITION OF PERSONAL PROPERTY REMAINING ON PREMISES AT TERMINATION OF TENANCY

§ 1980. Definitions

As used in this chapter:

(a) "Landlord" means any operator, keeper, lessor, or sublessor of any furnished or unfurnished premises for hire, or his or her agent or successor in interest.

(b) "Owner" means any person other than the landlord who has any right, title, or interest in personal property.

(c) "Premises" includes any common areas associated therewith.

(d) "Reasonable belief" means the actual knowledge or belief a prudent person would have without making an investigation (including any investigation of public records) except that, where the landlord has specific information indicating that such an investigation would more probably than not reveal pertinent information and the cost of such an investigation would be reasonable in relation to the probable value of the personal property involved, "reasonable belief" includes the actual knowledge or belief a prudent person would have if such an investigation were made.

(e) "Records" means any material, regardless of the physical form, on which information is recorded or preserved by any means, including in written or spoken words, graphically depicted, printed, or electromagnetically transmitted. "Records" does not include publicly available directories containing information an individual has voluntarily consented to have publicly disseminated or listed, such as name, address, or telephone number.

(f) "Tenant" includes any paying guest, lessee, or sublessee of any premises for hire. *(Added by Stats.1974, c. 331, p. 653, § 2. Amended by Stats.2009, c. 134 (A.B.1094), § 4.)*

Law Revision Commission Comments

Section 1980 defines various terms used in this chapter.

Subdivisions (a) and (e) define "landlord" and "tenant" broadly so as to extend coverage of this chapter to all types of rental property whether commercial or residential, furnished or unfurnished. This chapter provides landlords with a general procedure for the disposition of personal property left on the premises after termination of a tenancy. But see Section 1981(b) (relationship to other statutory procedures) and Comment. Former Civil Code Section 1862 provided relief only for those landlords who owned or managed furnished residential facilities. Other landlords had no statutory coverage except in unlawful detainer cases under Code of Civil Procedure Section 1174.

Subdivision (c) makes clear that "premises" includes common areas—such as storage rooms or garages—where personal property may be left when the tenant leaves.

Subdivision (d) establishes a general standard for the landlord's "reasonable belief" as used in Sections 1982 (lost property), 1983 (notice), 1987 (release of property), 1988 (disposition of property), and 1989 (limitation on landlord's liability). This definition has the effect under Sections 1983 and 1989 of requiring an investigation into the ownership of an item of personal property only where the landlord has specific information which would lead him to believe that an investigation would probably reveal another or a different owner and the cost of the investigation would be reasonable in relation to the probable value of the item. Hence, for example, if a valuable item of furniture or a typewriter is left in an office, the landlord is not required to consult public records to determine whether there is a security interest in the property or to call local rental or leasing companies unless, for example, he has specific information indicating that the tenant may not be the owner, such as a prior statement of the tenant that the property is rented or a label on the property indicating a person other than the tenant may be the owner. The mere fact that the property left on the premises is valuable is not sufficient to put a burden of investigation on the landlord. It should be noted, however, that the title taken at a sale of property under Section 1988 is subject to any lien or right preserved by other provisions of law. [11 Cal.L.Rev.Comm. Reports 963 (1973)].

Research References

California Real Estate Forms (Miller & Starr) § 2:16, Office Lease--Multistory Office Building.

California Real Estate Forms (Miller & Starr) § 2:17, Office Lease--Mixed Use Building.

California Real Estate Forms (Miller & Starr) § 2:18, Office Lease--Office/Warehouse Building With Four or Fewer Tenants.

California Real Estate Forms (Miller & Starr) § 2:19, Retail Lease--Power Shopping Center.

California Real Estate Forms (Miller & Starr) § 2:20, Retail Lease--Shopping Center With for Profit Parking Garage.

California Real Estate Forms (Miller & Starr) § 2:21, Retail Lease--15,000 RSF to 30,000 RSF (Tenant Oriented).

California Real Estate Forms (Miller & Starr) § 2:22, Retail Lease--Regional Shopping Center.

California Real Estate Forms (Miller & Starr) § 2:23, Retail Lease--Small Strip-Shopping Center.

California Real Estate Forms (Miller & Starr) § 2:24, Retail Lease--Restaurant.

California Real Estate Forms (Miller & Starr) § 2:25, Industrial Lease.

California Real Estate Forms (Miller & Starr) § 2:26, Triple Net Lease--Industrial Build-To-Suit Lease.

California Real Estate Forms (Miller & Starr) § 2:27, Ground Lease.

California Real Estate Forms (Miller & Starr) § 2:28, Triple Net Lease--Stand-Alone Building.

California Real Estate Forms (Miller & Starr) § 2:29, Parking Garage Lease.

California Real Estate Forms (Miller & Starr) § 2:31, Rental Agreement--Self Storage.

California Real Estate Forms (Miller & Starr) § 2:32, Gross Lease--Small Commercial Property.

California Real Estate Forms (Miller & Starr) § 2:34, Sublease--Shared Office Space.

California Real Estate Forms (Miller & Starr) § 2:59, Landlord Waiver of Rights to Tenant Personal Property.

California Real Estate Forms (Miller & Starr) § 2:65, Residential Lease.

California Real Estate Forms (Miller & Starr) § 2:66, Residential Lease With Purchase Option.

California Real Estate Forms (Miller & Starr) § 2:18.50, Management Office License Agreement.

Rutter, Cal. Practice Guide: Landlord-Tenant Form 2:A, Residential Rental Agreement.

Rutter, Cal. Practice Guide: Landlord-Tenant Form 2:C, Office Lease.

Miller and Starr California Real Estate § 19:233, Tenant's Personal Property.

20 NO. 4 Miller & Starr, California Real Estate Newsalert 13, Landlord and Tenant.

8 Witkin Cal. Proc. 5th Enforcement of Judgment § 337, (S 337) Disposition of Personal Property.

12 Witkin, California Summary 10th Real Property § 503, Statutory Framework.

12 Witkin, California Summary 10th Real Property § 514, Statutory Rights of Lodger.

12 Witkin, California Summary 10th Real Property § 599, Other Acts and Powers of Entity Are Not Affected.

12 Witkin, California Summary 10th Real Property § 615, Expanded Statute.

12 Witkin, California Summary 10th Real Property § 742, (S 742) Storage of Tenant's Property.

12 Witkin, California Summary 10th Real Property § 749, Nature of Statute.

12 Witkin, California Summary 10th Real Property § 750, Notice to Claim Property.

12 Witkin, California Summary 10th Real Property § 753, Limitation of Landlord's Liability.

12 Witkin, California Summary 10th Real Property § 754, Alternative Procedure on Tenant's Request.

12 Witkin, California Summary 10th Real Property § 754A, (New)-Scope of Statute.

13 Witkin, California Summary 10th Personal Property § 224, (S 224) in General.

§ 1980.5. Commercial real property; application of chapter

Except as provided in Section 1993.01, the provisions of this chapter shall not apply to commercial real property, as defined in subdivision (d) of Section 1954.26. For purposes of this section, commercial real property shall not include self-storage units. *(Added by Stats.2008, c. 161 (A.B.2025), § 1.)*

Research References

Miller and Starr California Real Estate § 19:233, Tenant's Personal Property.

12 Witkin, California Summary 10th Real Property § 749, Nature of Statute.

§ 1981. Optional procedure; construction of chapter

(a) This chapter provides an optional procedure for the disposition of personal property that remains on the premises after a tenancy has terminated and the premises have been vacated by the tenant.

(b) This chapter does not apply whenever Section 1862.5, 2080.8, 2080.9, or 2081 to 2081.6, inclusive, applies. This chapter does not apply to property that exists for the purpose of providing utility services and is owned by a public utility, whether or not that property is actually in operation to provide those utility services.

(c) This chapter does not apply to any manufactured home as defined in Section 18007 of the Health and Safety Code, any mobilehome as defined in Section 18008 of the Health and Safety Code, or to any commercial coach as defined in Section 18001.8 of the Health and Safety Code, including attachments thereto or contents thereof, whether or not the manufactured home, mobilehome, or commercial coach is subject to registration under the Health and Safety Code.

(d) This chapter does not apply to the disposition of an animal to which subdivision (d) of Section 1815 or Chapter 7 (commencing with Section 17001) of Part 1 of Division 9 of the Food and Agricultural Code applies, and those animals shall be disposed of in accordance with those provisions.

(e) If the requirements of this chapter are not satisfied, nothing in this chapter affects the rights and liabilities of the landlord, former tenant, or any other person. *(Added by Stats.1974, c. 331, p. 654, § 2. Amended by Stats.1983, c. 1124, § 5, operative Jan. 1, 1984; Stats.1996, c. 653 (A.B.2605), § 1; Stats.2008, c. 265 (A.B.2949), § 3.)*

Law Revision Commission Comments

Section 1981 makes clear that use of the procedures provided by this chapter is optional. A landlord may, but need not, dispose of personal property left on the premises in the manner provided herein. However,

Section 1989 provides limits on the landlord's liability if these procedures are followed.

It should be noted that subdivision (b) provides that the procedures of this chapter may not be used where one of the following statutes applies: Section 1862.5 (property left in a licensed hospital), Section 2080.8 (unclaimed property in possession of the University of California), Section 2080.9 (unclaimed, lost, or abandoned property in possession of a state college), Sections 2081 to 2081.6 (unclaimed property in a warehouse). However, if a motor vehicle is left on the premises, it may be disposed of pursuant either to this chapter or to Chapter 10 (commencing with Section 22650) of Division 11 of the Vehicle Code. This chapter is inapplicable where the landlord seeks a lien on the property. See, e.g., Section 1861a. [11 Cal.L.Rev.Comm. Reports 963 (1973)].

Research References

Miller and Starr California Real Estate § 19:233, Tenant's Personal Property.
12 Witkin, California Summary 10th Real Property § 749, Nature of Statute.

§ 1982. Lost property; disposition

(a) Personal property which the landlord reasonably believes to have been lost shall be disposed of pursuant to Article 1 (commencing with Section 2080) of Chapter 4 of Title 6. The landlord is not liable to the owner of the property if he complies with this subdivision.

(b) If the appropriate police or sheriff's department refuses to accept property pursuant to subdivision (a), the landlord may dispose of the property pursuant to this chapter. *(Added by Stats.1974, c. 331, p. 654, § 2.)*

Law Revision Commission Comments

Section 1982 provides that personal property lost on the premises shall be treated like any other lost property pursuant to the general provisions concerning lost property. All owners who lose property should be able to rely on the lost property laws. See Civil Code §§ 2080–2080.7. See also Section 1980(d) (defining "reasonable belief").

Subdivision (b) is intended to eliminate the uncertainty which would otherwise exist if the police or sheriff's department disagrees with the landlord's belief that property was lost and therefore refuses to accept the property. [11 Cal.L.Rev.Comm. Reports 963 (1973)].

Research References

Miller and Starr California Real Estate § 19:233, Tenant's Personal Property.
12 Witkin, California Summary 10th Real Property § 749, Nature of Statute.

§ 1983. Notice to former tenant and owner of property; description; delivery

(a) Where personal property remains on the premises after a tenancy has terminated and the premises have been vacated by the tenant, the landlord shall give written notice to the tenant and to any other person the landlord reasonably believes to be the owner of the property. If the property consists of records, the tenant shall be presumed to be the owner of the records for the purposes of this chapter.

(b) The notice shall describe the property in a manner reasonably adequate to permit the owner of the property to identify it. The notice may describe all or a portion of the property, but the limitation of liability provided by Section 1989 does not protect the landlord from any liability arising from the disposition of property not described in the notice except that a trunk, valise, box, or other container which is locked, fastened, or tied in a manner which deters immediate access to its contents may be described as such without describing its contents. The notice shall advise the person to be notified that reasonable costs of storage may be charged before the property is returned, where the property may be claimed, and the date before which the claim must be made. The date specified in the notice shall be a date not less than 15 days after the notice is personally delivered or, if mailed, not less than 18 days after the notice is deposited in the mail.

(c) The notice shall be personally delivered to the person to be notified or sent by first-class mail, postage prepaid, to the person to be notified at his or her last known address and, if there is reason to believe that the notice sent to that address will not be received by that person, also to any other address known to the landlord where the person may reasonably be expected to receive the notice. If the notice is sent by mail to the former tenant, one copy shall be sent to the premises vacated by the tenant. If the former tenant provided the landlord with the tenant's email address, the landlord may also send the notice by email. *(Added by Stats.1974, c. 331, p. 654, § 2. Amended by Stats.2009, c. 134 (A.B.1094), § 5; Stats.2012, c. 560 (A.B.2521), § 4.)*

Research References

California Real Estate Forms (Miller & Starr) § 2:16, Office Lease--Multistory Office Building.
California Real Estate Forms (Miller & Starr) § 2:17, Office Lease--Mixed Use Building.
California Real Estate Forms (Miller & Starr) § 2:18, Office Lease--Office/Warehouse Building With Four or Fewer Tenants.
California Real Estate Forms (Miller & Starr) § 2:19, Retail Lease--Power Shopping Center.
California Real Estate Forms (Miller & Starr) § 2:20, Retail Lease--Shopping Center With for Profit Parking Garage.
California Real Estate Forms (Miller & Starr) § 2:21, Retail Lease--15,000 RSF to 30,000 RSF (Tenant Oriented).
California Real Estate Forms (Miller & Starr) § 2:22, Retail Lease--Regional Shopping Center.
California Real Estate Forms (Miller & Starr) § 2:23, Retail Lease--Small Strip-Shopping Center.
California Real Estate Forms (Miller & Starr) § 2:24, Retail Lease--Restaurant.
California Real Estate Forms (Miller & Starr) § 2:25, Industrial Lease.
California Real Estate Forms (Miller & Starr) § 2:26, Triple Net Lease--Industrial Build-To-Suit Lease.
California Real Estate Forms (Miller & Starr) § 2:27, Ground Lease.
California Real Estate Forms (Miller & Starr) § 2:28, Triple Net Lease--Stand-Alone Building.
California Real Estate Forms (Miller & Starr) § 2:29, Parking Garage Lease.
California Real Estate Forms (Miller & Starr) § 2:31, Rental Agreement--Self Storage.
California Real Estate Forms (Miller & Starr) § 2:32, Gross Lease--Small Commercial Property.
California Real Estate Forms (Miller & Starr) § 2:34, Sublease--Shared Office Space.
California Real Estate Forms (Miller & Starr) § 2:18.50, Management Office License Agreement.
Rutter, Cal. Practice Guide: Enforcing Judgments/Debts Ch. 6I-3, Enforcement of Judgment for Possession of Real Property.
Miller and Starr California Real Estate § 34:67, Examples of Actions in Which Fees Cannot be Recovered.
Miller and Starr California Real Estate § 19:233, Tenant's Personal Property.
20 NO. 4 Miller & Starr, California Real Estate Newsalert 13, Landlord and Tenant.
8 Witkin Cal. Proc. 5th Enforcement of Judgment § 337, (S 337) Disposition of Personal Property.
12 Witkin, California Summary 10th Real Property § 742, (S 742) Storage of Tenant's Property.
12 Witkin, California Summary 10th Real Property § 750, Notice to Claim Property.
12 Witkin, California Summary 10th Real Property § 752, Sale or Other Disposition.
12 Witkin, California Summary 10th Real Property § 753, Limitation of Landlord's Liability.

§ 1984. Notice to former tenant; form; contents

(a) A notice given to the former tenant which is in substantially the following form satisfies the requirements of Section 1983:

Notice of Right to Reclaim Abandoned Property

To: _____

(Name of former tenant)

_____

(Address of former tenant)

When you vacated the premises at _____

_____,

(Address of premises, including room or apartment number, if any)

the following personal property remained:

_____

(Insert description of the personal property)

You may claim this property at _____

_____

(Address where property may be claimed).

If you claim this property by ____ (insert date not less than 2 days after the former tenant vacated the premises), you may minimize the costs of storage.If you fail to claim this property by ____ (insert date not less than 2 days after the former tenant vacated the premises), unless you pay the landlord's reasonable cost of storage for all the above-described property, and take possession of the property which you claim, not later than _____ (insert date not less than 15 days after notice is personally delivered or, if mailed, not less than 18 days after notice is deposited in the mail) this property may be disposed of pursuant to Civil Code Section 1988.

(Insert here the statement required by subdivision (b) of this section)

Dated: _____

_____

(Signature of landlord)

_____

(Type or print name of landlord)

_____

(Telephone number)

_____

(Address)

(b) The notice set forth in subdivision (a) shall also contain one of the following statements:

(1) "If you fail to reclaim the property, it will be sold at a public sale after notice of the sale has been given by publication. You have the right to bid on the property at this sale. After the property is sold and the cost of storage, advertising, and sale is deducted, the remaining money will be paid over to the county. You may claim the remaining money at any time within one year after the county receives the money."

(2) "Because this property is believed to be worth less than $700, it may be kept, sold, or destroyed without further notice if you fail to reclaim it within the time indicated above." *(Added by Stats.1974, c. 331, p. 654, § 2. Amended by Stats.1984, c. 1249, § 1; Stats.2012, c. 560 (A.B.2521), § 5.)*

Law Revision Commission Comments

Section 1984 provides a form of notice to the former tenant. See Section 1983 for the requirements of the notice, such as the manner of describing the personal property. [11 Cal.L.Rev.Comm. Reports 963 (1973)].

Research References

Rutter, Cal. Practice Guide: Enforcing Judgments/Debts Ch. 6I-3, Enforcement of Judgment for Possession of Real Property.

Miller and Starr California Real Estate § 19:233, Tenant's Personal Property.

8 Witkin Cal. Proc. 5th Enforcement of Judgment § 337, (S 337) Disposition of Personal Property.

12 Witkin, California Summary 10th Real Property § 750, Notice to Claim Property.

§ 1985. Notice to owner; form

A notice which is in substantially the following form given to a person (other than the former tenant) the landlord reasonably believes to be the owner of personal property satisfies the requirements of Section 1983:

Notice of Right to Reclaim Abandoned Property

To: _____

(Name)

_____

(Address)

When _____ vacated the premises at _____

(name of former tenant)

_____,

(address of premises, including room or apartment number, if any)

the following personal property remained:

_____

(insert description of the personal property)

If you own any of this property, you may claim it at

_____.

(address where property may be claimed).

If you claim this property by ____ (insert date not less than 2 days after the former tenant vacated the premises), you may minimize the costs of storage. If you fail to claim this property by ____ (insert date not less than 2 days after the former tenant vacated the premises), unless you pay the landlord's reasonable cost of storage and take possession of the property to which you are entitled not later than _____ (insert date not less than 15 days after notice is personally delivered or, if mailed, not less than 18 days after notice is deposited in the mail) this property may be disposed of pursuant to Civil Code Section 1988.

Dated: _____

_____

(Signature of landlord)

_____

(Type or print name of land-lord)

_____

(Telephone number)

_____

(Address)

(Added by Stats.1974, c. 331, p. 655, § 2. Amended by Stats.2012, c. 560 (A.B.2521), § 6.)

Law Revision Commission Comments

Section 1985 provides a form for the notice to a person (other than the former tenant) the landlord reasonably believes to be the owner of any personal property remaining on the premises. See Section 1983 for the requirements of the notice, such as the manner of describing the personal property. [11 Cal.L.Rev.Comm. Reports 963 (1973)].

Research References

Miller and Starr California Real Estate § 19:233, Tenant's Personal Property.

12 Witkin, California Summary 10th Real Property § 750, Notice to Claim Property.

§ 1986. Storage of property; place; reasonable care

The personal property described in the notice shall either be left on the vacated premises or be stored by the landlord in a place of safekeeping until the landlord either releases the property pursuant to Section 1987 or disposes of the property pursuant to Section 1988. The landlord shall exercise reasonable care in storing the property, but he is not liable to the tenant or any other owner for any loss not caused by his deliberate or negligent act. *(Added by Stats.1974, c. 331, p. 656, § 2.)*

Research References

Miller and Starr California Real Estate § 35:66, Immunity of Arbitrators and Arbitration Associations.
Miller and Starr California Real Estate § 19:233, Tenant's Personal Property.
12 Witkin, California Summary 10th Real Property § 751, Storage of Property.

§ 1987. Release of property; payment of storage and expenses

(a) The personal property described in the notice shall be released by the landlord to the former tenant or, at the landlord's option, to any person reasonably believed by the landlord to be its owner if that tenant or other person pays the reasonable cost of storage and takes possession of the property not later than the date specified in the notice for taking possession.

(b) Where personal property is not released pursuant to subdivision (a) and the notice stated that the personal property would be sold at a public sale, the landlord shall release the personal property to the former tenant if he or she claims it prior to the time it is sold and pays the reasonable cost of storage, advertising, and sale incurred prior to the time the property is withdrawn from sale.

(c) Notwithstanding subdivision (a), the landlord shall release the personal property described in the notice to the former tenant and shall not require the former tenant to pay the cost of storage if the property remained in the dwelling and the former tenant or other person reasonably believed by the landlord to be its owner reclaims the property within two days of vacating the dwelling. *(Added by Stats.1974, c. 331, p. 656, § 2. Amended by Stats.2012, c. 560 (A.B.2521), § 7.)*

Research References

12 Witkin, California Summary 10th Real Property § 749, Nature of Statute.
12 Witkin, California Summary 10th Real Property § 751, Storage of Property.
12 Witkin, California Summary 10th Real Property § 752, Sale or Other Disposition.
12 Witkin, California Summary 10th Real Property § 753, Limitation of Landlord's Liability.
12 Witkin, California Summary 10th Real Property § 754C, (New)-Storage of Property.
12 Witkin, California Summary 10th Real Property § 754D, (New)-Sale or Other Disposition of Property.
12 Witkin, California Summary 10th Real Property § 754E, (New)-Limitation of Landlord's Liability.

§ 1988. Sale of property; notice; publication; proceeds

(a) If the personal property described in the notice is not released pursuant to Section 1987, it shall be sold at public sale by competitive bidding. However, if the landlord reasonably believes that the total resale value of the property not released is less than seven hundred dollars ($700), the landlord may retain the property for his or her own use or dispose of it in any manner. Nothing in this section shall be construed to preclude

the landlord or tenant from bidding on the property at the public sale.

(b) Notice of the time and place of the public sale shall be given by publication pursuant to Section 6066 of the Government Code in a newspaper of general circulation published in the county where the sale is to be held. The last publication shall be not less than five days before the sale is to be held. The notice of the sale shall not be published before the last of the dates specified for taking possession of the property in any notice given pursuant to Section 1983. The notice of the sale shall describe the property to be sold in a manner reasonably adequate to permit the owner of the property to identify it. The notice may describe all or a portion of the property, but the limitation of liability provided by Section 1989 does not protect the landlord from any liability arising from the disposition of property not described in the notice, except that a trunk, valise, box, or other container which is locked, fastened, or tied in a manner which deters immediate access to its contents may be described as such without describing its contents.

(c) After deduction of the costs of storage, advertising, and sale, any balance of the proceeds of the sale which is not claimed by the former tenant or an owner other than such tenant shall be paid into the treasury of the county in which the sale took place not later than 30 days after the date of sale. The former tenant or other owner may claim the balance within one year from the date of payment to the county by making application to the county treasurer or other official designated by the county. If the county pays the balance or any part thereof to a claimant, neither the county nor any officer or employee thereof is liable to any other claimant as to the amount paid. *(Added by Stats.1974, c. 331, p. 657, § 2. Amended by Stats.1982, c. 811, p. 3099, § 1; Stats.2012, c. 560 (A.B.2521), § 8.)*

Research References

California Real Estate Forms (Miller & Starr) § 2:65, Residential Lease.
California Real Estate Forms (Miller & Starr) § 2:66, Residential Lease With Purchase Option.
Rutter, Cal. Practice Guide: Enforcing Judgments/Debts Ch. 6I-3, Enforcement of Judgment for Possession of Real Property.
Rutter, Cal. Practice Guide: Landlord-Tenant Form 9:N, Statutory Notice to Former Tenant of Right to Reclaim Abandoned Property (CC § 1984).
Rutter, Cal. Practice Guide: Landlord-Tenant Form 9:O, Statutory Notice to Person Other Than Former Tenant of Right to Reclaim Abandoned Property (CC § 1985).
Miller and Starr California Real Estate § 34:67, Examples of Actions in Which Fees Cannot be Recovered.
Miller and Starr California Real Estate § 19:233, Tenant's Personal Property.
3 Witkin Cal. Proc. 5th Actions § 211, in General.
8 Witkin Cal. Proc. 5th Enforcement of Judgment § 337, (S 337) Disposition of Personal Property.
12 Witkin, California Summary 10th Real Property § 742, (S 742) Storage of Tenant's Property.
12 Witkin, California Summary 10th Real Property § 751, Storage of Property.
12 Witkin, California Summary 10th Real Property § 752, Sale or Other Disposition.
12 Witkin, California Summary 10th Real Property § 753, Limitation of Landlord's Liability.

§ 1989. Liability of landlord

(a) Notwithstanding subdivision (c) of Section 1981, where the landlord releases to the former tenant property which remains on the premises after a tenancy is terminated, the landlord is not liable with respect to that property to any person.

(b) Where the landlord releases property pursuant to Section 1987 to a person (other than the former tenant) reasonably believed by the landlord to be the owner of the property, the landlord is not liable with respect to that property to:

(1) Any person to whom notice was given pursuant to Section 1983; or

(2) Any person to whom notice was not given pursuant to Section 1983 unless such person proves that, prior to releasing the property, the landlord believed or reasonably should have believed that such person had an interest in the property and also that the landlord knew or should have known upon reasonable investigation the address of such person.

(c) Where property is disposed of pursuant to Section 1988, the landlord is not liable with respect to that property to:

(1) Any person to whom notice was given pursuant to Section 1983; or

(2) Any person to whom notice was not given pursuant to Section 1983 unless such person proves that, prior to disposing of the property pursuant to Section 1988, the landlord believed or reasonably should have believed that such person had an interest in the property and also that the landlord knew or should have known upon reasonable investigation the address of such person. *(Added by Stats.1974, c. 331, p. 657, § 2.)*

Research References

Rutter, Cal. Practice Guide: Real Prop. Transactions Ch. 11-G, G. Rescission.
Miller and Starr California Real Estate § 19:233, Tenant's Personal Property.
12 Witkin, California Summary 10th Real Property § 753, Limitation of Landlord's Liability.

§ 1990. Costs of storage; assessment

(a) Costs of storage which may be required to be paid under this chapter shall be assessed in the following manner:

(1) Where a former tenant claims property pursuant to Section 1987, he or she may be required to pay the reasonable costs of storage for all the personal property remaining on the premises at the termination of the tenancy which are unpaid at the time the claim is made.

(2) Where an owner other than the former tenant claims property pursuant to Section 1987, he or she may be required to pay the reasonable costs of storage for only the property in which he or she claims an interest.

(b) In determining the costs to be assessed under subdivision (a), the landlord shall not charge more than one person for the same costs.

(c) If the landlord stores the personal property on the premises, the cost of storage shall be the fair rental value of the space reasonably required for that storage for the term of the storage. Costs shall not be assessed if the former tenant reclaims property stored on the premises within two days of having vacated the premises. *(Added by Stats.1974, c. 331, p. 658, § 2. Amended by Stats.2012, c. 560 (A.B.2521), § 9.)*

Law Revision Commission Comments

Section 1990 adopts the principle that the former tenant is primarily responsible and so should pay the reasonable costs incurred in the preservation of all the property left on the premises after the termination of his tenancy. On the other hand, the owner of personal property who is not the tenant should not have to pay the storage costs for any property other than that which he is claiming. Since, insofar as the landlord is concerned, the former tenant is responsible for all property left on the premises, regardless of its ownership, the former tenant may be required to pay the reasonable costs of storage for all the property, even that which is known to belong to another person. Of course, under subdivision (b), the landlord may not charge both the former tenant and another person for the same storage costs. As to the remedy of the former tenant where the landlord demands an excessive amount for storage costs, see the discussion in Gray v. Whitmore, 17 Cal.App.3d 1, 24–25, 94 Cal.Rptr. 904, 917–918 (1971). [11 Cal.L.Rev.Comm. Reports 963 (1973)].

Research References

Miller and Starr California Real Estate § 19:233, Tenant's Personal Property.
8 Witkin Cal. Proc. 5th Enforcement of Judgment § 337, (S 337) Disposition of Personal Property.
12 Witkin, California Summary 10th Real Property § 742, (S 742) Storage of Tenant's Property.
12 Witkin, California Summary 10th Real Property § 749, Nature of Statute.
12 Witkin, California Summary 10th Real Property § 751, Storage of Property.

§ 1991. Notice of belief of abandonment to lessee; notice to former tenant; combined notices

Where a notice of belief of abandonment is given to a lessee pursuant to Section 1951.3, the notice to the former tenant given pursuant to Section 1983 may, but need not, be given at the same time as the notice of belief of abandonment even though the tenancy is not terminated until the end of the period specified in the notice of belief of abandonment. If the notices are so given, the notices may, but need not, be combined in one notice that contains all the information required by the sections under which the notices are given. *(Added by Stats.1974, c. 331, p. 658, § 2.)*

Law Revision Commission Comments

Section 1991 applies where the tenant is in default on the rent and appears to have abandoned the leased real property and the lessor is giving notice of belief of abandonment pursuant to Section 1951.3. In such a case, the notice of the right to reclaim the personal property under this chapter may be given at or after the notice of belief of abandonment under Section 1951.3 is given notwithstanding that the time for the termination of the lease as specified in the notice of belief of abandonment has not arrived. Section 1991 thus is an exception to the requirement of Section 1983 that the notice of right to reclaim abandoned property may be given only where the tenancy has terminated. Section 1991 also authorizes the combination of the notice under Section 1951.3 with the notice under Section 1983. [11 Cal.L.Rev.Comm. Reports 963 (1973)].

Research References

Rutter, Cal. Practice Guide: Landlord-Tenant Form 2:C, Office Lease.
Miller and Starr California Real Estate § 19:233, Tenant's Personal Property.
12 Witkin, California Summary 10th Real Property § 750, Notice to Claim Property.

CHAPTER 5.5. DISPOSITION OF PROPERTY REMAINING ON PREMISES AT TERMINATION OF COMMERCIAL TENANCY

§ 1993. Definitions

This chapter shall only apply to commercial real property. As used in this chapter:

(a) "Commercial real property" has the meaning specified in subdivision (d) of Section 1954.26. For purposes of this chapter, commercial real property shall not include self-storage units.

(b) "Landlord" means any operator, keeper, lessor, or sublessor of any furnished or unfurnished premises for hire, or his or her agent or successor in interest.

(c) "Owner" means any person other than the landlord who has any right, title, or interest in property.

(d) "Premises" includes any common areas associated therewith.

(e) "Reasonable belief" means the actual knowledge or belief a prudent person would have without making an investigation, including any investigation of public records, except that, if the landlord has specific information indicating that an investigation would more probably than not reveal pertinent information and the cost of an investigation would be reasonable in relation to the probable value of the property involved, "reasonable belief" includes the actual knowledge or belief a prudent person would have if an investigation were made.

(f) "Records" means any material, regardless of the physical form, on which information is recorded or preserved by any means, including in written or spoken words, graphically depicted, printed, or electromagnetically transmitted. "Records" does not include publicly available directories containing information an individual has voluntarily consented to have publicly disseminated or listed, such as name, address, or telephone number.

(g) "Tenant" includes any lessee or sublessee of any commercial real property and its premises for hire. *(Added by Stats. 2008, c. 161 (A.B.2025), § 2. Amended by Stats.2009, c. 140 (A.B.1164), § 29; Stats.2009, c. 134 (A.B.1094), § 6.)*

Research References

California Real Estate Forms (Miller & Starr) § 2:16, Office Lease--Multistory Office Building.
California Real Estate Forms (Miller & Starr) § 2:17, Office Lease--Mixed Use Building.
California Real Estate Forms (Miller & Starr) § 2:18, Office Lease--Office/Warehouse Building With Four or Fewer Tenants.
California Real Estate Forms (Miller & Starr) § 2:19, Retail Lease--Power Shopping Center.
California Real Estate Forms (Miller & Starr) § 2:20, Retail Lease--Shopping Center With for Profit Parking Garage.
California Real Estate Forms (Miller & Starr) § 2:21, Retail Lease--15,000 RSF to 30,000 RSF (Tenant Oriented).
California Real Estate Forms (Miller & Starr) § 2:22, Retail Lease--Regional Shopping Center.
California Real Estate Forms (Miller & Starr) § 2:23, Retail Lease--Small Strip-Shopping Center.
California Real Estate Forms (Miller & Starr) § 2:24, Retail Lease--Restaurant.
California Real Estate Forms (Miller & Starr) § 2:25, Industrial Lease.
California Real Estate Forms (Miller & Starr) § 2:26, Triple Net Lease--Industrial Build-To-Suit Lease.
California Real Estate Forms (Miller & Starr) § 2:27, Ground Lease.
California Real Estate Forms (Miller & Starr) § 2:28, Triple Net Lease--Stand-Alone Building.
California Real Estate Forms (Miller & Starr) § 2:29, Parking Garage Lease.
California Real Estate Forms (Miller & Starr) § 2:31, Rental Agreement--Self Storage.
California Real Estate Forms (Miller & Starr) § 2:32, Gross Lease--Small Commercial Property.
California Real Estate Forms (Miller & Starr) § 2:34, Sublease--Shared Office Space.
California Real Estate Forms (Miller & Starr) § 2:18.50, Management Office License Agreement.

Miller and Starr California Real Estate § 19:233, Tenant's Personal Property.
19 NO. 4 Miller & Starr, California Real Estate Newsalert 19, Landlord and Tenant.
20 NO. 4 Miller & Starr, California Real Estate Newsalert 13, Landlord and Tenant.
7 Witkin Cal. Proc. 5th Judgment § 221, (S 221) Actions to Enforce Equitable Servitude.
12 Witkin, California Summary 10th Real Property § 754A, (New)-Scope of Statute.

§ 1993.01. Requirements applicable to this chapter

Notwithstanding Section 1980.5, the requirements of Sections 1982, 1987, and 1990 shall apply to property that is subject to this chapter. *(Added by Stats.2008, c. 161 (A.B.2025), § 2.)*

Research References

12 Witkin, California Summary 10th Real Property § 749, Nature of Statute.

§ 1993.02. Optional procedure for disposition of property; application of chapter

(a) This chapter provides an optional procedure for the disposition of property that remains on the premises after a tenancy of commercial real property has terminated and the premises have been vacated by the tenant.

(b) This chapter does not apply if Section 1862.5, 2080.8, or 2080.9, or Article 2 (commencing with Section 2081) of Chapter 4 of Title 6, apply. This chapter does not apply to property that exists for the purpose of providing utility services and is owned by a public utility, whether or not that property is actually in operation to provide those utility services.

(c) This chapter does not apply to a manufactured home, as defined in Section 18007 of the Health and Safety Code, a mobilehome, as defined in Section 18008 of the Health and Safety Code, or a commercial coach, as defined in Section 18001.8 of the Health and Safety Code, including any attachments or contents, whether or not the manufactured home, mobilehome, or commercial coach is subject to registration under the Health and Safety Code.

(d) This chapter does not apply to the disposition of animals subject to Chapter 7 (commencing with Section 17001) of Part 1 of Division 9 of the Food and Agricultural Code.

(e) This chapter does not apply to residential property or self-storage units.

(f) If the requirements of this chapter are not satisfied, nothing in this chapter affects the rights and liabilities of the landlord, former tenant, or any other person. *(Added by Stats.2008, c. 161 (A.B.2025), § 2. Amended by Stats.2009, c. 140 (A.B.1164), § 30.)*

Research References

12 Witkin, California Summary 10th Real Property § 754A, (New)-Scope of Statute.

§ 1993.03. Written notice provided; contents; delivery

(a) If property remains on the premises after a tenancy has terminated and the premises have been vacated by the tenant, the landlord shall give written notice to the tenant and to any other person the landlord reasonably believes to be the owner of the property. If the property consists of records, the tenant shall be presumed to be the owner of the records for the purposes of this chapter.

(b) The notice shall describe the property in a manner reasonably adequate to permit the owner of the property to identify it. The notice may describe all or a portion of the property, but the limitation of liability provided by Section 1993.08 does not protect the landlord from any liability arising from the disposition of property not described in the notice, except that a trunk, valise, box, safe, vault, or other container that is locked, fastened, or tied in a manner that deters immediate access to its contents may be described as such without describing its contents. The notice shall advise the person to be notified that reasonable costs of storage may be charged before the property is returned, where the property may be claimed, and the date before which the claim must be made. The date specified in the notice shall be a date not less than 15 days after the notice is personally delivered or, if mailed, not less than 18 days after the notice is deposited in the mail.

(c) The notice shall be personally delivered to the person to be notified or sent by first-class mail, postage prepaid, to the person to be notified at his or her last known address and, if there is reason to believe that the notice sent to that address will not be received by that person, also to any other address known to the landlord where the person may reasonably be expected to receive the notice. If the notice is sent by mail to the former tenant, one copy shall be sent to the premises vacated by the tenant. *(Added by Stats.2008, c. 161 (A.B.2025), § 2. Amended by Stats.2009, c. 140 (A.B.1164), § 31; Stats.2009, c. 134 (A.B. 1094), § 7.)*

Research References

California Real Estate Forms (Miller & Starr) § 2:16, Office Lease-- Multistory Office Building.

California Real Estate Forms (Miller & Starr) § 2:17, Office Lease-- Mixed Use Building.

California Real Estate Forms (Miller & Starr) § 2:18, Office Lease-- Office/Warehouse Building With Four or Fewer Tenants.

California Real Estate Forms (Miller & Starr) § 2:19, Retail Lease-- Power Shopping Center.

California Real Estate Forms (Miller & Starr) § 2:20, Retail Lease-- Shopping Center With for Profit Parking Garage.

California Real Estate Forms (Miller & Starr) § 2:21, Retail Lease-- 15,000 RSF to 30,000 RSF (Tenant Oriented).

California Real Estate Forms (Miller & Starr) § 2:22, Retail Lease-- Regional Shopping Center.

California Real Estate Forms (Miller & Starr) § 2:23, Retail Lease--Small Strip-Shopping Center.

California Real Estate Forms (Miller & Starr) § 2:24, Retail Lease-- Restaurant.

California Real Estate Forms (Miller & Starr) § 2:25, Industrial Lease.

California Real Estate Forms (Miller & Starr) § 2:26, Triple Net Lease-- Industrial Build-To-Suit Lease.

California Real Estate Forms (Miller & Starr) § 2:27, Ground Lease.

California Real Estate Forms (Miller & Starr) § 2:28, Triple Net Lease-- Stand-Alone Building.

California Real Estate Forms (Miller & Starr) § 2:29, Parking Garage Lease.

California Real Estate Forms (Miller & Starr) § 2:31, Rental Agreement--Self Storage.

California Real Estate Forms (Miller & Starr) § 2:32, Gross Lease--Small Commercial Property.

California Real Estate Forms (Miller & Starr) § 2:34, Sublease--Shared Office Space.

California Real Estate Forms (Miller & Starr) § 2:18.50, Management Office License Agreement.

Miller and Starr California Real Estate § 19:233, Tenant's Personal Property.

19 NO. 4 Miller & Starr, California Real Estate Newsalert 19, Landlord and Tenant.

20 NO. 4 Miller & Starr, California Real Estate Newsalert 13, Landlord and Tenant.

12 Witkin, California Summary 10th Real Property § 754B, (New)- Notice.

12 Witkin, California Summary 10th Real Property § 754D, (New)-Sale or Other Disposition of Property.

12 Witkin, California Summary 10th Real Property § 754E, (New)- Limitation of Landlord's Liability.

§ 1993.04. Written notice to former tenant by landlord; requirements

(a) A notice given to the former tenant that is in substantially the following form satisfies the requirements of Section 1993.03:

Notice of Right to Reclaim Abandoned Property

To: _____
(Name of former tenant)

_____
(Address of former tenant)

When you vacated the premises at_____,

(Address of premises, including room, if any)
the following personal property remained:

_____
(Insert description of the personal property)
You may claim this property at_____

_____
(Address where property may be claimed)
Unless you pay the reasonable cost of storage for all of the above-described property, and take possession of the property which you claim, not later than _____ (insert date not less than 15 days after notice is personally delivered or, if mailed, not less than 18 days after notice is deposited in the mail) this property may be disposed of pursuant to Section 1993.07 of the Civil Code.

(Insert here the statement required by subdivision (b) of this section)

Dated:_____ _____

_____
(Signature of landlord)

_____
(Type or print name of landlord)

_____
(Telephone number of landlord)

_____
(Address of landlord)

(b) The notice set forth in subdivision (a) shall also contain one of the following statements:

(1) "If you fail to reclaim the property, it will be sold at a public sale after notice of the sale has been given by publication. You have the right to bid on the property at this sale. After the property is sold and the cost of storage, advertising, and sale is deducted, the remaining money will be paid over to the county. You may claim the remaining money at any time within one year after the county receives the money."

(2) "Because you were a commercial tenant and this property is believed to be worth less than the lesser of seven hundred fifty dollars ($750), or one dollar ($1) per square foot of the premises you occupied, it may be kept, sold, or destroyed without further notice if you fail to reclaim it within the time indicated above." *(Added by Stats.2008, c. 161 (A.B.2025), § 2. Amended by Stats.2009, c. 140 (A.B.1164), § 32.)*

Research References

19 NO. 4 Miller & Starr, California Real Estate Newsalert 19, Landlord and Tenant.

12 Witkin, California Summary 10th Real Property § 754B, (New)- Notice.

§ 1993.05. Written notice given owner of personal property; form

A notice in substantially the following form given to a person (other than the former tenant) the landlord reasonably believes to be the owner of personal property satisfies the requirements of Section 1993.03:

Notice of Right to Reclaim Abandoned Property

To: _____
(Name of owner)

_____
(Address of owner)

When _____ vacated the premises at

_____,

(Name of former tenant)

_____

(Address of premises, including room, if any)

the following personal property remained:

_____

(Insert description of the personal property)

You may claim this property at_____

_____

(Address where property may be claimed)

Unless you pay the reasonable cost of storage for all of the above-described property, and take possession of the property that you claim, not later than _____ (insert date not less than 15 days after notice is personally delivered or, if mailed, not less than 18 days after notice is deposited in the mail) this property may be disposed of pursuant to Section 1993.07 of the Civil Code.

   (Insert here the statement required by subdivision (b) of this section)

Dated:_____   _____

(Signature of landlord)

                _____

(Type or print name of landlord)

                _____

(Telephone number of landlord)

                _____

(Address of landlord)

(Added by Stats.2008, c. 161 (A.B.2025), § 2. Amended by Stats.2009, c. 140 (A.B.1164), § 33.)

Research References

19 NO. 4 Miller & Starr, California Real Estate Newsalert 19, Landlord and Tenant.

12 Witkin, California Summary 10th Real Property § 754B, (New)-Notice.

§ 1993.06. Storage of property; place of safekeeping; reasonable care

The personal property described in the notice shall either be left on the vacated premises or be stored by the landlord in a place of safekeeping until the landlord either releases the property pursuant to Section 1987 or disposes of the property pursuant to Section 1993.07. The landlord shall exercise reasonable care in storing the property, but he or she is not liable to the tenant or any other owner for any loss not caused by his or her deliberate or negligent act. *(Added by Stats.2008, c. 161 (A.B.2025), § 2.)*

Research References

19 NO. 4 Miller & Starr, California Real Estate Newsalert 19, Landlord and Tenant.

12 Witkin, California Summary 10th Real Property § 754C, (New)-Storage of Property.

§ 1993.07. Property in notice not released; public sale; publication of time and place; proceeds

(a)(1) The property described in the notice that is not released pursuant to Section 1987 shall be sold at public sale by competitive bidding except that, if the landlord reasonably believes that the total resale value of the property is less than the threshold amount, the landlord may retain the property for his or her own use or dispose of it in any manner.

(2) For the purposes of this section, "threshold amount" means the lesser of seven hundred fifty dollars ($750) or one dollar ($1) per square foot of the premises occupied by the tenant.

(b)(1) Notice of the time and place of the public sale shall be given by publication pursuant to Section 6066 of the Government

Code in a newspaper of general circulation published in the county where the sale is to be held.

(2) The last publication shall be not less than five days before the sale is to be held.

(3) The notice of the sale shall not be published before the last of the dates specified for taking possession of the property in any notice given pursuant to Section 1993.03.

(4) The notice of the sale shall describe the property to be sold in a manner reasonably adequate to permit the owner of the property to identify it.

(5) The notice may describe all or a portion of the property, but the limitation of liability provided by Section 1993.08 does not protect the landlord from any liability arising from the disposition of property not described in the notice, except that a trunk, valise, box, safe, vault, or other container that is locked, fastened, or tied in a manner that deters immediate access to its contents may be described as such without describing its contents.

(c)(1) After deduction of the costs of storage, advertising, and sale, any balance of the proceeds of the sale that is not claimed by the former tenant or an owner other than the tenant shall be paid into the treasury of the county in which the sale took place not later than 30 days after the date of sale.

(2) The former tenant or other owner may claim the balance within one year from the date of payment to the county by making application to the county treasurer or other official designated by the county.

(3) If the county pays the balance or any part thereof to a claimant, neither the county nor any officer or employee thereof shall be liable to any other claimant as to the amount paid.

(d) Nothing in this section precludes a landlord or tenant from bidding on the property at the public sale. *(Added by Stats.2008, c. 161 (A.B.2025), § 2. Amended by Stats.2009, c. 140 (A.B.1164), § 34.)*

Research References

Rutter, Cal. Practice Guide: Landlord-Tenant Form 9:P, Statutory Notice to Former Commercial Tenant of Right to Reclaim Abandoned Property (CC S1993.04).

Rutter, Cal. Practice Guide: Landlord-Tenant Form 9:Q, Statutory Notice to Person Other Than Former Commercial Tenant of Right to Reclaim Abandoned Property (CC S1993.05).

19 NO. 4 Miller & Starr, California Real Estate Newsalert 19, Landlord and Tenant.

12 Witkin, California Summary 10th Real Property § 754C, (New)-Storage of Property.

12 Witkin, California Summary 10th Real Property § 754D, (New)-Sale or Other Disposition of Property.

12 Witkin, California Summary 10th Real Property § 754E, (New)-Limitation of Landlord's Liability.

§ 1993.08. Release of property to former tenant; landlord liability; notice

(a) Notwithstanding subdivision (c) of Section 1993.02, if the landlord releases to the former tenant property that remains on the premises after a tenancy is terminated, the landlord shall not be liable with respect to that property to any person.

(b) If the landlord releases property pursuant to Section 1987 to a person, other than the former tenant, who is reasonably believed by the landlord to be the owner of the property, the landlord shall not be liable with respect to that property to any of the following persons:

(1) A person to whom notice was given pursuant to Section 1993.03.

(2) A person to whom notice was not given pursuant to Section 1993.03, unless the person proves that, prior to releasing

the property, the landlord believed or reasonably should have believed that the person had an interest in the property and also that the landlord knew or should have known upon reasonable investigation the address of the person.

(c) If property is disposed of pursuant to Section 1993.07, the landlord shall not be liable with respect to that property to any of the following persons:

(1) A person to whom notice was given pursuant to Section 1993.03.

(2) A person to whom notice was not given pursuant to Section 1993.03, unless the person proves that, prior to disposing of the property pursuant to Section 1993.07, the landlord believed or reasonably should have believed that the person had an interest in the property and also that the landlord knew or should have known upon reasonable investigation the address of the person. *(Added by Stats.2008, c. 161 (A.B.2025), § 2. Amended by Stats.2009, c. 140 (A.B.1164), § 35.)*

Research References

19 NO. 4 Miller & Starr, California Real Estate Newsalert 19, Landlord and Tenant.
12 Witkin, California Summary 10th Real Property § 754B, (New)-Notice.
12 Witkin, California Summary 10th Real Property § 754D, (New)-Sale or Other Disposition of Property.
12 Witkin, California Summary 10th Real Property § 754E, (New)-Limitation of Landlord's Liability.

§ 1993.09. Notice of belief of abandonment

If a notice of belief of abandonment is given to a lessee pursuant to Section 1951.3, the notice to the former tenant given pursuant to Section 1993.03 may be given at the same time as the notice of belief of abandonment, even though the tenancy is not terminated until the end of the period specified in the notice of belief of abandonment. The notices may be combined in one notice that contains all the information required by the sections under which the notices are given. *(Added by Stats.2008, c. 161 (A.B.2025), § 2. Amended by Stats.2009, c. 140 (A.B.1164), § 36.)*

Research References

19 NO. 4 Miller & Starr, California Real Estate Newsalert 19, Landlord and Tenant.
12 Witkin, California Summary 10th Real Property § 754B, (New)-Notice.

CHAPTER 6. ASSIGNMENT AND SUBLEASE

ARTICLE 1. GENERAL PROVISIONS

§ 1995.010. Application of chapter

This chapter applies to transfer of a tenant's interest in a lease of real property for other than residential purposes. *(Added by Stats.1989, c. 982, § 2.)*

Law Revision Commission Comments

Section 1995.010 limits the scope of this chapter to commercial real property leases. Assignment and sublease issues concerning personal property leases and residential real property leases involve different public policies than commercial real property leases, and therefore are governed by the common law and not by this chapter. [20 Cal.L.Rev.Comm.Reports 263 (1990)].

Research References

California Real Estate Forms (Miller & Starr) § 2:16, Office Lease--Multistory Office Building.
California Real Estate Forms (Miller & Starr) § 2:17, Office Lease--Mixed Use Building.
California Real Estate Forms (Miller & Starr) § 2:18, Office Lease--Office/Warehouse Building With Four or Fewer Tenants.
California Real Estate Forms (Miller & Starr) § 2:19, Retail Lease--Power Shopping Center.
California Real Estate Forms (Miller & Starr) § 2:20, Retail Lease--Shopping Center With for Profit Parking Garage.
California Real Estate Forms (Miller & Starr) § 2:21, Retail Lease--15,000 RSF to 30,000 RSF (Tenant Oriented).
California Real Estate Forms (Miller & Starr) § 2:22, Retail Lease--Regional Shopping Center.
California Real Estate Forms (Miller & Starr) § 2:23, Retail Lease--Small Strip-Shopping Center.
California Real Estate Forms (Miller & Starr) § 2:24, Retail Lease--Restaurant.
California Real Estate Forms (Miller & Starr) § 2:25, Industrial Lease.
California Real Estate Forms (Miller & Starr) § 2:26, Triple Net Lease--Industrial Build-To-Suit Lease.
California Real Estate Forms (Miller & Starr) § 2:28, Triple Net Lease--Stand-Alone Building.
California Real Estate Forms (Miller & Starr) § 2:29, Parking Garage Lease.
California Real Estate Forms (Miller & Starr) § 2:32, Gross Lease--Small Commercial Property.
California Real Estate Forms (Miller & Starr) § 2:36, Consent to Sublease.
California Real Estate Forms (Miller & Starr) § 2:62, Standard Industrial/Commercial Multi-Tenant Lease--Net.
California Real Estate Forms (Miller & Starr) § 2:63, Standard Industrial/Commercial Multi-Tenant Lease--Gross.
California Real Estate Forms (Miller & Starr) § 2:65, Residential Lease.
California Real Estate Forms (Miller & Starr) § 2:66, Residential Lease With Purchase Option.
Rutter, Cal. Practice Guide: Real Prop. Transactions Ch. 7-B, B. Sale of Ground Lease Tenant's Interest-Preliminary Concerns Re Assignment and Subletting.
Rutter, Cal. Practice Guide: Real Prop. Transactions Ch. 8-B, B. Options to Purchase.
Miller and Starr California Real Estate § 19:70, Application of a Covenant or Condition Against Transfer--Restrictions in Commercial Leases.
Miller and Starr California Real Estate § 19:71, Restrictions in Residential Leases.
12 Witkin, California Summary 10th Real Property § 553, (S 553) Codification.
12 Witkin, California Summary 10th Real Property § 555, (S 555) Authorized Restrictions on Right.
12 Witkin, California Summary 10th Real Property § 556, (S 556) Illustration of Permissible Restraint on Right.

§ 1995.020. Definitions

As used in this chapter:

(a) "Landlord" includes a tenant who is a sublandlord under a sublease.

(b) "Lease" means a lease or sublease of real property for other than residential purposes, and includes modifications and other agreements affecting a lease.

(c) "Restriction on transfer" means a provision in a lease that restricts the right of transfer of the tenant's interest in the lease.

(d) "Tenant" includes a subtenant or assignee.

(e) "Transfer" of a tenant's interest in a lease means an assignment, sublease, or other voluntary or involuntary transfer or encumbrance of all or part of a tenant's interest in the lease. *(Added by Stats.1989, c. 982, § 2.)*

Section 1995.020 provides definitions for drafting convenience.

Subdivision (b) is consistent with Section 1995.010 (scope of chapter). A restriction separately agreed to by the parties that affects a lease is part of the lease for purposes of this chapter. The provisions of this chapter apply between parties to a sublease and between parties to an assigned lease, as well as between original parties to a lease.

Under subdivision (c), this chapter does not apply to a restriction on transfer of a lease or on encumbrance of a lease unless the restriction on transfer or the restriction on encumbrance is expressly provided in the lease (as defined in this section).

Subdivision (e) makes clear that statute applies not only to express lease restrictions on assignments and subleases but also to express lease restrictions on encumbrances of the tenant's interest, by way of mortgage, trust deed, assignment for security purposes, or other creation of a security interest, and to express lease restrictions on involuntary transfers of the tenant's interest, including transfer pursuant to execution sale or tax sale. *Cf.* Comment to Section 1995.220 (transfer restriction strictly construed). [20 Cal.L.Rev.Comm.Reports 274 (1990)].

Research References

Miller and Starr California Real Estate § 19:70, Application of a Covenant or Condition Against Transfer--Restrictions in Commercial Leases.
12 Witkin, California Summary 10th Real Property § 553, (S 553) Codification.

§ 1995.030. Further application of chapter

Except as provided in Section 1995.270, this chapter applies to a lease executed before, on, or after January 1, 1990. *(Added by Stats.1989, c. 982, § 2.)*

Section 1995.030 makes clear that this chapter is intended to be applied to existing leases as well as to leases executed after its operative date. An exception is made in the case of the rule of Section 1995.260 (implied standard for landlord's consent), which only applies to leases executed on or after September 23, 1983. See Section 1995.270 (limitation on retroactivity of Section 1995.260). [20 Cal.L.Rev.Comm.Reports 275 (1990)].

Research References

Miller and Starr California Real Estate § 19:70, Application of a Covenant or Condition Against Transfer--Restrictions in Commercial Leases.
12 Witkin, California Summary 10th Real Property § 553, (S 553) Codification.

ARTICLE 2. RESTRICTIONS ON TRANSFER

§ 1995.210. Restrictions on transfer of tenant's interest

(a) Subject to the limitations in this chapter, a lease may include a restriction on transfer of the tenant's interest in the lease.

(b) Unless a lease includes a restriction on transfer, a tenant's rights under the lease include unrestricted transfer of the tenant's interest in the lease. *(Added by Stats.1989, c. 982, § 2.)*

Subdivision (a) of Section 1995.210 is a specific application of general principles of freedom of contract. Subdivision (a) is limited by the provisions of this chapter governing restrictions on transfer. See, e.g.,

Section 1995.260 (implied standard for landlord's consent). Neither the law governing unreasonable restraints on alienation (see, e.g., Civil Code § 711) nor the law governing the implied covenant of good faith and fair dealing (see, e.g., California Lettuce Growers v. Union Sugar Co., 45 Cal.2d 474, 289 P.2d 785 (1955)) prevents the enforcement of a restriction on transfer in accordance with the express terms of the restriction. It should be noted, however, that subdivision (a) remains subject to general principles limiting freedom of contract. See, e.g., 1 B. Witkin, Summary of California Law *Contracts* §§ 23–36 (9th ed. 1987) (adhesion and unconscionable contract doctrines).

Subdivision (b) codifies the common law rule that a tenant may freely assign or sublease unless the right is expressly restricted by the parties. See, e.g., Kassan v. Stout, 9 Cal.3d 39, 507 P.2d 87, 106 Cal.Rptr. 783 (1973) [20 Cal.L.Rev.Comm.Reports. 265 (1990)].

Research References

California Real Estate Forms (Miller & Starr) § 2:12, Letter of Intent--Restaurant/Food Service (Tenant Oriented).
California Real Estate Forms (Miller & Starr) § 2:16, Office Lease--Multistory Office Building.
California Real Estate Forms (Miller & Starr) § 2:17, Office Lease--Mixed Use Building.
California Real Estate Forms (Miller & Starr) § 2:18, Office Lease--Office/Warehouse Building With Four or Fewer Tenants.
California Real Estate Forms (Miller & Starr) § 2:19, Retail Lease--Power Shopping Center.
California Real Estate Forms (Miller & Starr) § 2:20, Retail Lease--Shopping Center With for Profit Parking Garage.
California Real Estate Forms (Miller & Starr) § 2:21, Retail Lease--15,000 RSF to 30,000 RSF (Tenant Oriented).
California Real Estate Forms (Miller & Starr) § 2:22, Retail Lease--Regional Shopping Center.
California Real Estate Forms (Miller & Starr) § 2:23, Retail Lease--Small Strip-Shopping Center.
California Real Estate Forms (Miller & Starr) § 2:24, Retail Lease--Restaurant.
California Real Estate Forms (Miller & Starr) § 2:25, Industrial Lease.
California Real Estate Forms (Miller & Starr) § 2:26, Triple Net Lease--Industrial Build-To-Suit Lease.
California Real Estate Forms (Miller & Starr) § 2:28, Triple Net Lease--Stand-Alone Building.
California Real Estate Forms (Miller & Starr) § 2:29, Parking Garage Lease.
California Real Estate Forms (Miller & Starr) § 2:32, Gross Lease--Small Commercial Property.
California Real Estate Forms (Miller & Starr) § 2:36, Consent to Sublease.
California Real Estate Forms (Miller & Starr) § 2:62, Standard Industrial/Commercial Multi-Tenant Lease--Net.
California Real Estate Forms (Miller & Starr) § 2:63, Standard Industrial/Commercial Multi-Tenant Lease--Gross.
Rutter, Cal. Practice Guide: Real Prop. Transactions Ch. 7-B, B. Sale of Ground Lease Tenant's Interest-Preliminary Concerns Re Assignment and Subletting.
Rutter, Cal. Practice Guide: Real Prop. Transactions Ch. 7-E, E. Representing the Landowner.
Rutter, Cal. Practice Guide: Real Prop. Transactions Ch. 9-F, F. Special Concerns Re Ground Lease Opinions.
Miller and Starr California Real Estate § 19:69, Application of a Covenant or Condition Against Transfer.
Miller and Starr California Real Estate § 19:70, Application of a Covenant or Condition Against Transfer--Restrictions in Commercial Leases.
12 Witkin, California Summary 10th Real Property § 555, (S 555) Authorized Restrictions on Right.
12 Witkin, California Summary 10th Real Property § 556, (S 556) Illustration of Permissible Restraint on Right.

§ 1995.220. Construction in favor of transferability

An ambiguity in a restriction on transfer of a tenant's interest in a lease shall be construed in favor of transferability. *(Added by Stats.1989, c. 982, § 2.)*

Law Revision Commission Comments

Section 1995.220 codifies the common law. See, e.g., Chapman v. Great Western Gypsum Co., 216 Cal. 420, 14 P.2d 758 (1932). This section is also consistent with the common law rule that lease restrictions on involuntary transfer are strictly construed. See discussion in Coskran, *Assignment & Sublease Restrictions: The Tribulations of Leasehold Transfers*, 22 Loy.L.A.L.Rev. 405, 524–31 (1989); *cf.* Section 1995.020(e)("transfer" defined). [20 Cal.L.Rev.Comm. Reports 266 (1990)].

Research References

California Real Estate Forms (Miller & Starr) § 2:12, Letter of Intent--Restaurant/Food Service (Tenant Oriented).

California Real Estate Forms (Miller & Starr) § 2:16, Office Lease--Multistory Office Building.

California Real Estate Forms (Miller & Starr) § 2:17, Office Lease--Mixed Use Building.

California Real Estate Forms (Miller & Starr) § 2:18, Office Lease--Office/Warehouse Building With Four or Fewer Tenants.

California Real Estate Forms (Miller & Starr) § 2:19, Retail Lease--Power Shopping Center.

California Real Estate Forms (Miller & Starr) § 2:20, Retail Lease--Shopping Center With for Profit Parking Garage.

California Real Estate Forms (Miller & Starr) § 2:21, Retail Lease--15,000 RSF to 30,000 RSF (Tenant Oriented).

California Real Estate Forms (Miller & Starr) § 2:22, Retail Lease--Regional Shopping Center.

California Real Estate Forms (Miller & Starr) § 2:23, Retail Lease--Small Strip-Shopping Center.

California Real Estate Forms (Miller & Starr) § 2:24, Retail Lease--Restaurant.

California Real Estate Forms (Miller & Starr) § 2:25, Industrial Lease.

California Real Estate Forms (Miller & Starr) § 2:26, Triple Net Lease--Industrial Build-To-Suit Lease.

California Real Estate Forms (Miller & Starr) § 2:28, Triple Net Lease--Stand-Alone Building.

California Real Estate Forms (Miller & Starr) § 2:29, Parking Garage Lease.

California Real Estate Forms (Miller & Starr) § 2:32, Gross Lease--Small Commercial Property.

California Real Estate Forms (Miller & Starr) § 2:36, Consent to Sublease.

California Real Estate Forms (Miller & Starr) § 2:62, Standard Industrial/Commercial Multi-Tenant Lease--Net.

California Real Estate Forms (Miller & Starr) § 2:63, Standard Industrial/Commercial Multi-Tenant Lease--Gross.

Rutter, Cal. Practice Guide: Real Prop. Transactions Ch. 7-B, B. Sale of Ground Lease Tenant's Interest-Preliminary Concerns Re Assignment and Subletting.

Rutter, Cal. Practice Guide: Real Prop. Transactions Ch. 7-E, E. Representing the Landowner.

Miller and Starr California Real Estate § 19:69, Application of a Covenant or Condition Against Transfer.

Miller and Starr California Real Estate § 19:70, Application of a Covenant or Condition Against Transfer--Restrictions in Commercial Leases.

12 Witkin, California Summary 10th Real Property § 555, (S 555) Authorized Restrictions on Right.

§ 1995.230. Prohibition of transfer

A restriction on transfer of a tenant's interest in a lease may absolutely prohibit transfer. *(Added by Stats.1989, c. 982, § 2.)*

Law Revision Commission Comments

Section 1995.230 settles the question raised in *Kendall v. Ernest Pestana, Inc.*, 40 Cal.3d 488, 220 Cal.Rptr. 818, 709 P.2d 837 (1985), of the validity of a clause absolutely prohibiting assignment or sublease. 40 Cal.3d at 499 n. 14. A lease term absolutely prohibiting transfer of the tenant's interest is not invalid as a restraint on alienation. Such a term is valid subject to general principles governing freedom of contract, including the adhesion contract doctrine, where applicable. See Section 1995.210 and Comment thereto (right to transfer absent a restriction). It should be noted that an absolute prohibition on transfer precludes the landlord's use of the remedy provided in Section 1951.4 (continuation of lease after

breach and abandonment). See Section 1951.4 and Comment thereto. [20 Cal.L.Rev.Comm. Reports 266 (1990)].

Research References

California Real Estate Forms (Miller & Starr) § 2:12, Letter of Intent--Restaurant/Food Service (Tenant Oriented).

California Real Estate Forms (Miller & Starr) § 2:16, Office Lease--Multistory Office Building.

California Real Estate Forms (Miller & Starr) § 2:17, Office Lease--Mixed Use Building.

California Real Estate Forms (Miller & Starr) § 2:18, Office Lease--Office/Warehouse Building With Four or Fewer Tenants.

California Real Estate Forms (Miller & Starr) § 2:19, Retail Lease--Power Shopping Center.

California Real Estate Forms (Miller & Starr) § 2:20, Retail Lease--Shopping Center With for Profit Parking Garage.

California Real Estate Forms (Miller & Starr) § 2:21, Retail Lease--15,000 RSF to 30,000 RSF (Tenant Oriented).

California Real Estate Forms (Miller & Starr) § 2:22, Retail Lease--Regional Shopping Center.

California Real Estate Forms (Miller & Starr) § 2:23, Retail Lease--Small Strip-Shopping Center.

California Real Estate Forms (Miller & Starr) § 2:24, Retail Lease--Restaurant.

California Real Estate Forms (Miller & Starr) § 2:25, Industrial Lease.

California Real Estate Forms (Miller & Starr) § 2:26, Triple Net Lease--Industrial Build-To-Suit Lease

California Real Estate Forms (Miller & Starr) § 2:28, Triple Net Lease--Stand-Alone Building.

California Real Estate Forms (Miller & Starr) § 2:29, Parking Garage Lease.

California Real Estate Forms (Miller & Starr) § 2:32, Gross Lease--Small Commercial Property.

California Real Estate Forms (Miller & Starr) § 2:36, Consent to Sublease.

California Real Estate Forms (Miller & Starr) § 2:62, Standard Industrial/Commercial Multi-Tenant Lease--Net.

California Real Estate Forms (Miller & Starr) § 2:63, Standard Industrial/Commercial Multi-Tenant Lease--Gross.

Rutter, Cal. Practice Guide: Enforcing Judgments/Debts Ch. 5-D, D. Involuntary Bankruptcy.

Rutter, Cal. Practice Guide: Real Prop. Transactions Ch. 7-B, B. Sale of Ground Lease Tenant's Interest-Preliminary Concerns Re Assignment and Subletting.

Rutter, Cal. Practice Guide: Real Prop. Transactions Ch. 7-E, E. Representing the Landowner.

Miller and Starr California Real Estate § 19:70, Application of a Covenant or Condition Against Transfer--Restrictions in Commercial Leases.

Miller and Starr California Real Estate § 19:72, Requirement of Landlord's Consent; Condition to a Transfer.

12 Witkin, California Summary 10th Real Property § 555, (S 555) Authorized Restrictions on Right.

§ 1995.240. Express standards or conditions of transfer

A restriction on transfer of a tenant's interest in a lease may provide that the transfer is subject to any express standard or condition, including, but not limited to, a provision that the landlord is entitled to some or all of any consideration the tenant receives from a transferee in excess of the rent under the lease. *(Added by Stats.1989, c. 982, § 2.)*

Law Revision Commission Comments

Section 1995.240 codifies the statement in *Kendall v. Ernest Pestana, Inc.*, 40 Cal.3d 488, 220 Cal.Rptr. 818, 709 P.2d 837 (1985), that "nothing bars the parties to commercial lease transactions from making their own arrangements respecting the allocation of appreciated rentals if there is a transfer of the leasehold." 40 Cal.3d at 505 n. 17. As used in this section, "consideration" includes "appreciated rentals" or any other term or description used by the parties to define any bonus value of the leasehold interest or any consideration attributable to the value of the leased premises that may be subject to sharing or shifting between the parties pursuant to contract in case of transfer by the tenant. This section does not apply, and Section 1995.250 does apply, to a restriction on transfer of a tenant's interest in a lease that requires the landlord's consent for transfer.

The affirmation stated in this section that the parties may agree to an express lease provision governing allocation of consideration for transfer of the tenant's interest in a lease is not intended to create any presumption that, absent such an express provision, a demand by the landlord for all or part of the consideration as a condition for consenting to the transfer is either reasonable or unreasonable. Whether such a demand would be "unreasonable" within the meaning of Section 1995.250(a) (express standards and conditions for landlord's consent) or 1995.260 (implied standard for landlord's consent) is a question to be governed by the case law on the subject. See also Comments to Sections 1995.250 and 1995.260.

Section 1995.240 is a specific application of subdivision (a) of Section 1995.210 (lease may include transfer restriction). It should be noted that an unreasonable restriction on transfer precludes the landlord's use of the remedy provided in Section 1951.4 (continuation of lease after breach and abandonment). See Section 1951.4 and Comment thereto. Moreover, Section 1995.240 remains subject to general principles limiting freedom of contract. See Section 1995.210 and Comment thereto. [20 Cal.L.Rev. Comm. Reports 275 (1990)].

Research References

California Real Estate Forms (Miller & Starr) § 2:12, Letter of Intent-- Restaurant/Food Service (Tenant Oriented).
California Real Estate Forms (Miller & Starr) § 2:16, Office Lease-- Multistory Office Building.
California Real Estate Forms (Miller & Starr) § 2:17, Office Lease-- Mixed Use Building.
California Real Estate Forms (Miller & Starr) § 2:18, Office Lease-- Office/Warehouse Building With Four or Fewer Tenants.
California Real Estate Forms (Miller & Starr) § 2:19, Retail Lease-- Power Shopping Center.
California Real Estate Forms (Miller & Starr) § 2:20, Retail Lease-- Shopping Center With for Profit Parking Garage.
California Real Estate Forms (Miller & Starr) § 2:21, Retail Lease-- 15,000 RSF to 30,000 RSF (Tenant Oriented).
California Real Estate Forms (Miller & Starr) § 2:22, Retail Lease-- Regional Shopping Center.
California Real Estate Forms (Miller & Starr) § 2:23, Retail Lease--Small Strip-Shopping Center.
California Real Estate Forms (Miller & Starr) § 2:24, Retail Lease-- Restaurant.
California Real Estate Forms (Miller & Starr) § 2:25, Industrial Lease.
California Real Estate Forms (Miller & Starr) § 2:26, Triple Net Lease-- Industrial Build-To-Suit Lease.
California Real Estate Forms (Miller & Starr) § 2:28, Triple Net Lease-- Stand-Alone Building.
California Real Estate Forms (Miller & Starr) § 2:29, Parking Garage Lease.
California Real Estate Forms (Miller & Starr) § 2:32, Gross Lease--Small Commercial Property.
California Real Estate Forms (Miller & Starr) § 2:36, Consent to Sublease.
California Real Estate Forms (Miller & Starr) § 2:62, Standard Industrial/Commercial Multi-Tenant Lease--Net.
California Real Estate Forms (Miller & Starr) § 2:63, Standard Industrial/Commercial Multi-Tenant Lease--Gross.
Rutter, Cal. Practice Guide: Real Prop. Transactions Ch. 7-B, B. Sale of Ground Lease Tenant's Interest-Preliminary Concerns Re Assignment and Subletting.
Rutter, Cal. Practice Guide: Real Prop. Transactions Ch. 7-C, C. Representing the Purchasing Tenant.
Miller and Starr California Real Estate § 19:70, Application of a Covenant or Condition Against Transfer--Restrictions in Commercial Leases.
Miller and Starr California Real Estate § 19:73, Requirement of Landlord's Consent; Condition to a Transfer--Duty of Landlord to Act "Reasonably".
12 Witkin, California Summary 10th Real Property § 555, (S 555) Authorized Restrictions on Right.

12 Witkin, California Summary 10th Real Property § 556, (S 556) Illustration of Permissible Restraint on Right.

§ 1995.250. Consent of landlord; requirements

A restriction on transfer of a tenant's interest in a lease may require the landlord's consent for transfer subject to any express standard or condition for giving or withholding consent, including, but not limited to, either of the following:

(a) The landlord's consent may not be unreasonably withheld.

(b) The landlord's consent may be withheld subject to express standards or conditions. *(Added by Stats.1989, c. 982, § 2.)*

Law Revision Commission Comments

Section 1995.250 is a specific application of the broad latitude provided in this chapter for the parties to a lease to contract for express restrictions on transfer of the tenant's interest in the lease. Such restrictions are valid subject to general principles governing freedom of contract, including the adhesion contract doctrine, where applicable. See Section 1995.210 and Comment thereto (right to transfer absent a restriction). It should be noted that an unreasonable restriction on transfer precludes the landlord's use of the remedy provided in Section 1951.4 (continuation of lease after breach and abandonment). See Section 1951.4 and Comment thereto.

The meaning of "unreasonably withheld" under subdivision (a) is a question of fact that must [be] determined under the circumstances of the particular case, applying an objective standard of commercial reasonableness as developed by case law.

Subdivision (b) makes clear that the lease may condition the landlord's consent in any manner. Standards and conditions for the landlord's consent may include, for example, a provision that, if the lessee receives consideration for the transfer in excess of the rent under the lease, the landlord may recover some or all of the consideration as a condition for consent. *Cf.* Section 1995.240 (transfer restriction subject to standards and conditions). [20 Cal.L.Rev. Comm. Reports 276 (1990)].

Research References

California Real Estate Forms (Miller & Starr) § 2:12, Letter of Intent-- Restaurant/Food Service (Tenant Oriented).
California Real Estate Forms (Miller & Starr) § 2:16, Office Lease-- Multistory Office Building.
California Real Estate Forms (Miller & Starr) § 2:17, Office Lease-- Mixed Use Building.
California Real Estate Forms (Miller & Starr) § 2:18, Office Lease-- Office/Warehouse Building With Four or Fewer Tenants.
California Real Estate Forms (Miller & Starr) § 2:19, Retail Lease-- Power Shopping Center.
California Real Estate Forms (Miller & Starr) § 2:20, Retail Lease-- Shopping Center With for Profit Parking Garage.
California Real Estate Forms (Miller & Starr) § 2:21, Retail Lease-- 15,000 RSF to 30,000 RSF (Tenant Oriented).
California Real Estate Forms (Miller & Starr) § 2:22, Retail Lease-- Regional Shopping Center.
California Real Estate Forms (Miller & Starr) § 2:23, Retail Lease--Small Strip-Shopping Center.
California Real Estate Forms (Miller & Starr) §2:24, Retail Lease-- Restaurant.
California Real Estate Forms (Miller & Starr) § 2:25, Industrial Lease.
California Real Estate Forms (Miller & Starr) § 2:26, Triple Net Lease-- Industrial Build-To-Suit Lease.
California Real Estate Forms (Miller & Starr) § 2:28, Triple Net Lease-- Stand-Alone Building.
California Real Estate Forms (Miller & Starr) § 2:29, Parking Garage Lease.
California Real Estate Forms (Miller & Starr) § 2:32, Gross Lease--Small Commercial Property.
California Real Estate Forms (Miller & Starr) § 2:36, Consent to Sublease.
California Real Estate Forms (Miller & Starr) § 2:62, Standard Industrial/Commercial Multi-Tenant Lease--Net.
California Real Estate Forms (Miller & Starr) § 2:63, Standard Industrial/Commercial Multi-Tenant Lease--Gross.
Rutter, Cal. Practice Guide: Real Prop. Transactions Ch. 7-B, B. Sale of Ground Lease Tenant's Interest-Preliminary Concerns Re Assignment and Subletting.

12 Witkin, California Summary 10th Real Property § 555, (S 555) Authorized Restrictions on Right.
12 Witkin, California Summary 10th Real Property § 558, (S 558) Remedies for Unreasonably Withholding Consent.

§ 1995.260. Unreasonably withheld consent; burden of proof

If a restriction on transfer of the tenant's interest in a lease requires the landlord's consent for transfer but provides no standard for giving or withholding consent, the restriction on transfer shall be construed to include an implied standard that the landlord's consent may not be unreasonably withheld. Whether the landlord's consent has been unreasonably withheld in a particular case is a question of fact on which the tenant has the burden of proof. The tenant may satisfy the burden of proof by showing that, in response to the tenant's written request for a statement of reasons for withholding consent, the landlord has failed, within a reasonable time, to state in writing a reasonable objection to the transfer. *(Added by Stats.1989, c. 982, § 2.)*

Law Revision Commission Comments

Section 1995.260 codifies the rule of *Kendall v. Ernest Pestana, Inc.*, 40 Cal.3d 488, 709 P.2d 837, 220 Cal.Rptr. 818 (1985). The retroactive application of Section 1995.260 is limited by Section 1995.270.

Under Section 1995.260, whether a landlord's consent has been unreasonably withheld may be a question of procedure or substance or both. A landlord may act unreasonably in responding to a request of the tenant for consent to a transfer (for example by delaying or failing to respond or by requiring excessive investigation charges), or the landlord may not have a reasonable objection to the transfer. Either of these circumstances may give rise to a determination that the landlord has unreasonably withheld consent to the transfer within the meaning of this section.

This section provides the tenant a means of satisfying the burden of proof on this matter by making a written request for a statement of reasons. However, this is not the exclusive means of satisfying the burden of proof that the landlord's consent has been unreasonably withheld in a particular case, and proof of unreasonableness may be made by other means.

Although *Kendall* states as a matter of law that denial of consent solely on the basis of personal taste, convenience, or sensibility, and denial of consent in order that the landlord may charge a higher rent than originally contracted for, are not commercially reasonable (40 Cal.3d at 501), Section 1995.260 rejects an absolute approach to the question of commercial reasonableness. Whether a particular objection is reasonable within the meaning of this section is a question of fact that must be determined under the circumstances of the particular case, applying an objective standard of commercial reasonableness as developed by case law. For example, in some circumstances it may be commercially reasonable for the landlord to require, as a condition for consenting to an assignment, that the premium received by the tenant for the assignment be paid to the landlord. See John Hogan Enterprises, Inc. v. Kellogg, 187 Cal.App.3d 589, 231 Cal.Rptr. 711 (1986). [20 Cal.L.Rev. Comm. Reports 269 (1990)].

Research References

California Real Estate Forms (Miller & Starr) § 2:12, Letter of Intent--Restaurant/Food Service (Tenant Oriented).
California Real Estate Forms (Miller & Starr) § 2:16, Office Lease--Multistory Office Building.
California Real Estate Forms (Miller & Starr) § 2:17, Office Lease--Mixed Use Building.
California Real Estate Forms (Miller & Starr) § 2:18, Office Lease--Office/Warehouse Building With Four or Fewer Tenants.
California Real Estate Forms (Miller & Starr) § 2:19, Retail Lease--Power Shopping Center.
California Real Estate Forms (Miller & Starr) § 2:20, Retail Lease--Shopping Center With for Profit Parking Garage.
California Real Estate Forms (Miller & Starr) § 2:21, Retail Lease--15,000 RSF to 30,000 RSF (Tenant Oriented).
California Real Estate Forms (Miller & Starr) § 2:22, Retail Lease--Regional Shopping Center.
California Real Estate Forms (Miller & Starr) § 2:23, Retail Lease--Small Strip-Shopping Center.
California Real Estate Forms (Miller & Starr) § 2:24, Retail Lease--Restaurant.
California Real Estate Forms (Miller & Starr) § 2:25, Industrial Lease.
California Real Estate Forms (Miller & Starr) § 2:26, Triple Net Lease--Industrial Build-To-Suit Lease.
California Real Estate Forms (Miller & Starr) § 2:28, Triple Net Lease--Stand-Alone Building.
California Real Estate Forms (Miller & Starr) § 2:29, Parking Garage Lease.
California Real Estate Forms (Miller & Starr) § 2:32, Gross Lease--Small Commercial Property.
California Real Estate Forms (Miller & Starr) § 2:36, Consent to Sublease.
California Real Estate Forms (Miller & Starr) § 2:62, Standard Industrial/Commercial Multi-Tenant Lease--Net.
California Real Estate Forms (Miller & Starr) § 2:63, Standard Industrial/Commercial Multi-Tenant Lease--Gross.
Rutter, Cal. Practice Guide: Real Prop. Transactions Ch. 7-B, B. Sale of Ground Lease Tenant's Interest-Preliminary Concerns Re Assignment and Subletting.
Rutter, Cal. Practice Guide: Real Prop. Transactions Ch. 7-E, E. Representing the Landowner.
Rutter, Cal. Practice Guide: Real Prop. Transactions Ch. 7-B Outline, Outline B.
Miller and Starr California Real Estate § 19:70, Application of a Covenant or Condition Against Transfer--Restrictions in Commercial Leases.
Miller and Starr California Real Estate § 19:73, Requirement of Landlord's Consent; Condition to a Transfer--Duty of Landlord to Act "Reasonably".
19 NO. 5 Miller & Starr, California Real Estate Newsalert 9, Contracts.
12 Witkin, California Summary 10th Real Property § 555, (S 555) Authorized Restrictions on Right.
12 Witkin, California Summary 10th Real Property § 556, (S 556) Illustration of Permissible Restraint on Right.
12 Witkin, California Summary 10th Real Property § 558, (S 558) Remedies for Unreasonably Withholding Consent.

§ 1995.270. Legislative findings and declarations

(a) The Legislature finds and declares:

(1) It is the public policy of the state and fundamental to the commerce and economic development of the state to enable and facilitate freedom of contract by the parties to commercial real property leases.

(2) The parties to commercial real property leases must be able to negotiate and conduct their affairs in reasonable reliance on the rights and protections given them under the laws of the state.

(3) Until the case of Kendall v. Ernest Pestana, Inc., 40 Cal.3d 488 (1985), and its predecessor, Cohen v. Ratinoff, 147 Cal. App.3d 321 (1983), the parties to commercial real property leases could reasonably rely on the law of the state to provide that if a lease restriction requires the landlord's consent for transfer of the tenant's interest in the lease but provides no standard for giving or withholding consent, the landlord's consent may be unreasonably withheld.

(4) The Kendall and Cohen decisions reversed the law on which parties to commercial real property leases executed before September 23, 1983, the date of the Cohen decision, could reasonably rely, thereby frustrating the expectations of the parties, with the result of impairing commerce and economic development.

(b) Section 1995.260 applies to a restriction on transfer executed on or after September 23, 1983. If a restriction on transfer executed before September 23, 1983, requires the landlord's consent for the tenant's transfer but provides no standard for giving or withholding consent, the landlord's consent may be unreasonably withheld. For purposes of this subdivision, if the terms of a restriction on transfer are fixed by an option or other agreement, the restriction on transfer is deemed to be executed on the date of execution of the option or other agreement. *(Added by Stats.1989, c. 982, § 2.)*

Law Revision Commission Comments

Section 1995.270 limits the retroactive application of Section 1995.260 (implied standard for landlord's consent) and the *Kendall* case which it codifies. Kendall v. Ernest Pestana, Inc., 40 Cal.3d 488, 220 Cal.Rptr. 818, 709 P.2d 837 (1985). The date of applicability of Section 1995.260 is September 23, 1983, the date of *Cohen v. Ratinoff*, 147 Cal.App.3d 321, 195 Cal.Rptr. 84 (1983), which foreshadowed the *Kendall* opinion. If there is a sublease on or after September 23, 1983, under a lease executed before that date, the rights as between the parties to the sublease are governed by Section 1995.260. See Section 1995.020(b) ("lease" means lease or sublease).

Limitation of retroactive operation of Section 1995.260 is supported by the public policy stated in subdivision (a) of Section 1995.270, including the need for foreseeability, reliance, and fairness, and is consistent with case law expressly limiting retroactivity of *Kendall. See Coskran, Assignment and Sublease Restrictions: The Tribulations of Leasehold Transfers*, 22 Loy. L.A.L. Rev. 405, 433–35 (1989); Kendall, *supra*, 40 Cal.3d at 507–11 (dissent); Kreisher v. Mobile Oil Corporation, 198 Cal.App.3d 389, 243 Cal.Rptr. 662 (1988), review denied May 5, 1988.

Nothing in this section is intended to limit the law governing modification or waiver of a lease provision by subsequent conduct or agreement of the parties, including modification or waiver of a restriction on transfer that expressly or impliedly permits the landlord's consent to be unreasonably withheld, whether the lease was executed before or after September 23, 1983. See also Section 1995.020(b) ("lease" includes modifications and other agreements affecting lease). Thus, a tenant may show that the landlord's right to unreasonably withhold consent pursuant to an express or implied lease restriction executed before September 23, 1983, has been modified or waived. [20 Cal.L.Rev. Comm. Reports 276 (1990)].

Research References

California Real Estate Forms (Miller & Starr) § 2:12, Letter of Intent--Restaurant/Food Service (Tenant Oriented).
California Real Estate Forms (Miller & Starr) § 2:16, Office Lease--Multistory Office Building.
California Real Estate Forms (Miller & Starr) § 2:17, Office Lease--Mixed Use Building.
California Real Estate Forms (Miller & Starr) § 2:18, Office Lease--Office/Warehouse Building With Four or Fewer Tenants.
California Real Estate Forms (Miller & Starr) § 2:19, Retail Lease--Power Shopping Center.
California Real Estate Forms (Miller & Starr) § 2:20, Retail Lease--Shopping Center With for Profit Parking Garage.
California Real Estate Forms (Miller & Starr) § 2:21, Retail Lease--15,000 RSF to 30,000 RSF (Tenant Oriented).
California Real Estate Forms (Miller & Starr) § 2:22, Retail Lease--Regional Shopping Center.
California Real Estate Forms (Miller & Starr) § 2:23, Retail Lease--Small Strip-Shopping Center.
California Real Estate Forms (Miller & Starr) § 2:24, Retail Lease--Restaurant.
California Real Estate Forms (Miller & Starr) § 2:25, Industrial Lease.
California Real Estate Forms (Miller & Starr) § 2:26, Triple Net Lease--Industrial Build-To-Suit Lease.
California Real Estate Forms (Miller & Starr) § 2:28, Triple Net Lease--Stand-Alone Building.
California Real Estate Forms (Miller & Starr) § 2:29, Parking Garage Lease.
California Real Estate Forms (Miller & Starr) § 2:32, Gross Lease--Small Commercial Property.
California Real Estate Forms (Miller & Starr) § 2:36, Consent to Sublease.
California Real Estate Forms (Miller & Starr) § 2:62, Standard Industrial/Commercial Multi-Tenant Lease--Net.
California Real Estate Forms (Miller & Starr) § 2:63, Standard Industrial/Commercial Multi-Tenant Lease--Gross.
California Real Estate Forms (Miller & Starr) § 2:65, Residential Lease.
California Real Estate Forms (Miller & Starr) § 2:66, Residential Lease With Purchase Option.
Rutter, Cal. Practice Guide: Real Prop. Transactions Ch. 7-B, B. Sale of Ground Lease Tenant's Interest-Preliminary Concerns Re Assignment and Subletting.

Rutter, Cal. Practice Guide: Real Prop. Transactions Ch. 7-E, E. Representing the Landowner.
Miller and Starr California Real Estate § 19:70, Application of a Covenant or Condition Against Transfer--Restrictions in Commercial Leases.
12 Witkin, California Summary 10th Real Property § 553, (S 553) Codification.
12 Witkin, California Summary 10th Real Property § 555, (S 555) Authorized Restrictions on Right.
12 Witkin, California Summary 10th Real Property § 556, (S 556) Illustration of Permissible Restraint on Right.

ARTICLE 3. BREACH AND REMEDIES

Section

§ 1995.300.   Restrictions on remedies

A remedy provided by law for violation of the rights of the tenant or of the landlord concerning transfer of a tenant's interest in a lease, including a remedy provided in this article, is (a) subject to an express provision in the lease that affects the remedy and (b) subject to any applicable defense, whether legal or equitable, including, but not limited to, waiver and estoppel. *(Added by Stats.1991, c. 67 (S.B.256), § 2.)*

Law Revision Commission Comments

Subdivision (a) of Section 1995.300 codifies the general rule that the parties to a contract may negotiate the remedies to be applied in case of a breach of the contract. This rule is of course subject to general principles limiting freedom of contract. See, e.g., 1 B. Witkin, Summary of California Law *Contracts* §§ 23–36 (9th ed. 1987) (adhesion and unconscionable contract doctrines).

Subdivision (b) codifies the general rule that a party may waive the party's remedies for breach either expressly or by conduct. [21 Cal.L.Rev.Comm.Reports 65 (1991)].

Research References

Rutter, Cal. Practice Guide: Real Prop. Transactions Ch. 7-B, B. Sale of Ground Lease Tenant's Interest-Preliminary Concerns Re Assignment and Subletting.
Miller and Starr California Real Estate § 19:76, Tenant's Remedies for Landlord's Breach of the Restriction.
12 Witkin, California Summary 10th Real Property § 557, (S 557) Adoption of Statute.

§ 1995.310.   Consent of landlord to transfer; unreasonable withholding of consent

If a restriction on transfer of a tenant's interest in a lease requires the landlord's consent for transfer subject to an express or implied standard that the landlord's consent may not be unreasonably withheld, and the landlord unreasonably withholds consent to a transfer in violation of the tenant's rights under the lease, in addition to any other remedies provided by law for breach of a lease, the tenant has all the remedies provided for breach of contract, including, but not limited to, either or both of the following:

(a) The right to contract damages caused by the landlord's breach.

(b) The right to terminate the lease. *(Added by Stats.1991, c. 67 (S.B.256), § 2.)*

Section 1995.310 treats a requirement that the landlord be reasonable in withholding consent as a covenant rather than a condition, violation of which is a breach of the lease. This clarifies California law and is consistent with the majority view in the United States. See Coskran, Assignment and Sublease Restrictions: The Tribulations of Leasehold Transfers, 22 Loy.L.A.L.Rev. 405, 505–07 (1989). Section 1995.310 does not distinguish between breach of an express reasonable consent requirement under Section 1995.250 and an implied reasonable consent requirement under Section 1995.260; a breach of either an express or implied covenant entitles the tenant to the normal remedies for breach of contract.

The remedies available for breach of contract include declaratory relief, specific performance or mandatory injunction, termination of the lease, and contract damages. Under Section 1995.310, the tenant may seek contract damages or exercise the right to terminate the lease or both. See Section 3300 (measure of contract damages).

The landlord's wrongful conduct, such as wrongful withholding of consent, may, in addition to a breach of contract, involve a tort (e.g., interference with contract or prospective economic advantage, or trespass). Other remedies for breach of a lease may include statutory remedies. The tenant may also transfer without the landlord's wrongfully withheld consent. [20 Cal.L.Rev.Comm.Reports 2405 (1990)].

California Real Estate Forms (Miller & Starr) § 2:20, Retail Lease-- Shopping Center With for Profit Parking Garage.
California Real Estate Forms (Miller & Starr) § 2:7, Assignment and Subletting--Tenant Oriented.
Rutter, Cal. Practice Guide: Landlord-Tenant Form 2:B, Standard Shopping Center Lease.
Rutter, Cal. Practice Guide: Landlord-Tenant Form 2:C, Office Lease.
Rutter, Cal. Practice Guide: Real Prop. Transactions Ch. 7-B, B. Sale of Ground Lease Tenant's Interest-Preliminary Concerns Re Assignment and Subletting.
Miller and Starr California Real Estate § 19:76, Tenant's Remedies for Landlord's Breach of the Restriction.
12 Witkin, California Summary 10th Real Property § 558, (S 558) Remedies for Unreasonably Withholding Consent.

§ 1995.320. Transfer by tenant of interest in violation of lease

If a tenant transfers the tenant's interest in a lease in violation of a restriction on transfer of the tenant's interest in the lease, in addition to any other remedies provided by law for breach of a lease, the landlord has all the remedies provided for breach of contract, including, but not limited to, either or both of the following:

(a) The right to contract damages caused by the tenant's breach.

(b) The right to terminate the lease. *(Added by Stats.1991, c. 67 (S.B.256), § 2.)*

Section 1995.320 treats a restriction on transfer as a covenant, violation of which is a breach of the lease. A transfer in violation of the restriction is voidable, not void, and the landlord may waive the landlord's remedies for breach either expressly or by conduct. Section 1995.300 (remedies subject to express provisions in lease and applicable defenses). This principle applies to a sublease as well as an assignment. Section 1995.020(e) ("transfer" defined).

Section 1995.320 makes clear the landlord may seek contract damages caused by the wrongful transfer in addition to termination of the lease. This is a specific application of Section 1951.2 (damages in connection with lease termination).

Section 1995.320 also permits the landlord to waive the termination remedy and still collect contract damages for wrongful transfer. This resolves a matter that was unclear under prior law, consistent with the general principle that a landlord may leave a lease in effect and recover damages for breach of a covenant. See Coskran, *Assignment and Sublease Restrictions: The Tribulations of Leasehold Transfers,* 22 Loy.L.A.L.Rev. 405, 495–98 (1989).

Other remedies available to the landlord for the tenant's breach include unlawful detainer, declaratory relief, and injunctive relief. For remedies against the assignee or subtenant under a wrongful transfer, see Section 1995.330 (application of remedies to assignee or subtenant). [21 Cal.L.Rev.Comm.Reports 65 (1991)].

Rutter, Cal. Practice Guide: Real Prop. Transactions Ch. 7-B, B. Sale of Ground Lease Tenant's Interest-Preliminary Concerns Re Assignment and Subletting.
Miller and Starr California Real Estate § 19:74, Landlord's Remedies for Tenant's Breach of the Restriction.
12 Witkin, California Summary 10th Real Property § 559, (S 559) Remedies for Transfer in Violation of Restriction.

§ 1995.330. Transfers to assignees; joint and several liability for transfers in violation; termination by landlord

(a) An assignee who receives or makes a transfer in violation of a restriction on transfer of a tenant's interest in a lease is jointly and severally liable with the tenant for contract damages under Section 1995.320. For this purpose, the provisions of Section 1951.2 applicable to a lessee apply to an assignee.

(b) The landlord's right to terminate a lease under Section 1995.320 includes the right to terminate a transfer without terminating the lease. If the landlord terminates a transfer without terminating the lease, the assignee or subtenant in possession is guilty of unlawful detainer and the landlord may obtain possession from the assignee or subtenant without terminating the right to possession of the tenant. For this purpose, the landlord may use the procedure provided in Chapter 4 (commencing with Section 1159) of Title 3 of Part 3 of the Code of Civil Procedure, with the changes necessary to make the procedure applicable to this subdivision. *(Added by Stats. 1991, c. 67 (S.B.256), § 2.)*

Subdivision (a) of Section 1995.330 is an application of the general rule that the landlord and assignee are in privity of estate. On the basis of privity of estate an assignee is liable to the landlord for breaches occurring after transfer. Subdivision (a) makes clear that these principles apply to the wrongful transfer itself. An assignee that receives a transfer or makes a subsequent transfer in violation of a transfer restriction is liable to the same extent as a tenant would be.

Subdivision (b) makes clear that the landlord's remedies for breach of a transfer restriction include the right to terminate the transfer without terminating the underlying lease. This right is new in California. See Coskran, Assignment and Sublease Restrictions: The Tribulations of Leasehold Transfers, 22 Loy.L.A.L.Rev. 405, 487–93 (1989). [20 Cal.L.Rev.Comm.Reports 2405 (1990)].

Rutter, Cal. Practice Guide: Real Prop. Transactions Ch. 7-B, B. Sale of Ground Lease Tenant's Interest-Preliminary Concerns Re Assignment and Subletting.
Miller and Starr California Real Estate § 19:74, Landlord's Remedies for Tenant's Breach of the Restriction.
12 Witkin, California Summary 10th Real Property § 559, (S 559) Remedies for Transfer in Violation of Restriction.

§ 1995.340. Subsequent transfers; effect of landlord's consent to or waiver of restrictions for prior transfers

(a) Subject to subdivision (b), a restriction on transfer of a tenant's interest in a lease applies to a subsequent transfer by a tenant, an assignee, or a subtenant notwithstanding the landlord's consent to a prior transfer or the landlord's waiver of a standard or condition for a prior transfer.

(b) Subdivision (a) does not apply if either of the following conditions is satisfied:

(1) The lease provides expressly that the restriction on transfer is limited to the original tenant.

(2) The landlord states expressly in writing that the consent or waiver applies to a subsequent transfer. *(Added by Stats.1991, c. 67 (S.B.256), § 2.)*

Law Revision Commission Comments

Section 1995.340 makes clear that the Rule in Dumpor's Case, 76 Eng.Rep. 1110, 4 Coke 119(b) (K.B. 1578), is not the law in California. This probably codifies existing law. Cf. Coskran, Assignment and Sublease Restrictions: The Tribulations of Leasehold Transfers, 22 Loy.L.A.L.Rev. 405, 560–64 (1989). [20 Cal.L.Rev.Comm.Reports 2405 (1990)].

Research References

California Real Estate Forms (Miller & Starr) § 2:20, Retail Lease--Shopping Center With for Profit Parking Garage.
California Real Estate Forms (Miller & Starr) § 2:22, Retail Lease--Regional Shopping Center.
California Real Estate Forms (Miller & Starr) § 2:24, Retail Lease--Restaurant.
Rutter, Cal. Practice Guide: Real Prop. Transactions Ch. 7-B, B. Sale of Ground Lease Tenant's Interest-Preliminary Concerns Re Assignment and Subletting.
Rutter, Cal. Practice Guide: Real Prop. Transactions Ch. 7-E, E. Representing the Landowner.
Miller and Starr California Real Estate § 19:75, Landlord's Remedies for Tenant's Breach of the Restriction--Enforcement Against Tenant's Successors; Waiver.
12 Witkin, California Summary 10th Real Property § 548, (S 548) Rule in Dumpor's Case.
12 Witkin, California Summary 10th Real Property § 560, (S 560) Rule in Dumpor's Case Abolished.

CHAPTER 7. USE RESTRICTIONS

ARTICLE 1. GENERAL PROVISIONS

§ 1997.010. Application of chapter

This chapter applies to a restriction on use of leased property by a tenant under a lease of real property for other than residential purposes. *(Added by Stats.1991, c. 67 (S.B.256), § 3.)*

Law Revision Commission Comments

Section 1997.010 limits the scope of this chapter to commercial real property leases. Use restriction issues concerning personal property leases and residential real property leases may involve different public policies than commercial real property leases, and therefore are governed by the common law and not by this chapter. [20 Cal.L.Rev.Comm.Reports 2421 (1990)].

Research References

Rutter, Cal. Practice Guide: Real Prop. Transactions Ch. 7-C, C. Representing the Purchasing Tenant.
Rutter, Cal. Practice Guide: Real Prop. Transactions Ch. 9-F, F. Special Concerns Re Ground Lease Opinions.
12 Witkin, California Summary 10th Real Property § 561, Nature and Scope of Statute.
12 Witkin, California Summary 10th Real Property § 562, Lease Provision.

12 Witkin, California Summary 10th Real Property § 563, Change in Use.
12 Witkin, California Summary 10th Real Property § 564, Effect of Restriction on Remedies for Breach.

§ 1997.020. Definitions

As used in this chapter:

(a) "Landlord" includes a tenant who is a sublandlord under a sublease.

(b) "Lease" means a lease or sublease of real property for other than residential purposes, and includes modifications and other agreements affecting a lease.

(c) "Restriction on use" means a provision in a lease that restricts the use of leased property by a tenant, whether by limiting use to a specified purpose, mandating use for a specified purpose, prohibiting use for a specified purpose, limiting or prohibiting a change in use, or otherwise.

(d) "Tenant" includes a subtenant or assignee. *(Added by Stats.1991, c. 67 (S.B.256), § 3.)*

Law Revision Commission Comments

Section 1997.020 provides definitions for drafting convenience.

Subdivision (b) is consistent with Section 1997.010 (scope of chapter). A restriction separately agreed to by the parties that affects a lease is part of the lease for purposes of this chapter. The provisions of this chapter apply between parties to a sublease and between parties to an assigned lease, as well as between original parties to a lease.

Under subdivision (c), this chapter does not apply to a restriction on use unless the restriction is expressly provided in the lease (as defined in this section). [20 Cal.L.Rev.Comm.Reports 2421 (1990)].

Research References

Rutter, Cal. Practice Guide: Real Prop. Transactions Ch. 7-C, C. Representing the Purchasing Tenant.
Miller and Starr California Real Estate § 19:111, Specification or Restriction of Use.
12 Witkin, California Summary 10th Real Property § 561, Nature and Scope of Statute.

§ 1997.030. Restrictions otherwise prohibited by law

Nothing in this chapter authorizes a restriction on use that is otherwise prohibited by law. *(Added by Stats.1991, c. 67 (S.B.256), § 3.)*

Law Revision Commission Comments

Section 1997.030 makes clear that this chapter is not intended to validate a restriction on use that serves an illegal purpose. See, e.g., Civil Code § 53(a) ("every restriction or prohibition as to the use or occupation of real property because of the user's or occupier's sex, race, color, religion, ancestry, national origin, or blindness or other physical disability is void"). However, the chapter is intended to govern a restriction on use notwithstanding any contrary implication in the law governing unreasonable restraints on alienation or the implied covenant of good faith and fair dealing. See Section 1997.210 and its Comment. [20 Cal.L.Rev.Comm.Reports 2421 (1990)].

Research References

Rutter, Cal. Practice Guide: Real Prop. Transactions Ch. 7-C, C. Representing the Purchasing Tenant.
Miller and Starr California Real Estate § 19:111, Specification or Restriction of Use.
12 Witkin, California Summary 10th Real Property § 561, Nature and Scope of Statute.
12 Witkin, California Summary 10th Real Property § 562, Lease Provision.

§ 1997.040. Computation of rental loss; availability of remedy provided by lease

(a) For the purpose of subdivision (a) of Section 1951.2 (damages on termination for breach), the amount of rental loss that could be or could have been reasonably avoided is computed by taking into account any reasonable use of the leased property. However, if the lease contains a restriction on use that is enforceable under this chapter, the computation shall take into account the restricted use of the property except to the extent the tenant proves that under all the circumstances enforcement of the restriction would be unreasonable. The circumstances include, but are not limited to, those involving both the leased property and any building or complex in which it is located.

(b) The remedy described in Section 1951.4 (continuation of lease after breach and abandonment) is available notwithstanding the presence in the lease of a restriction on use of the leased property. The restriction on use applies under Section 1951.4 if it is enforceable under this chapter except to the extent the tenant proves that under all the circumstances enforcement of the restriction would be unreasonable. The circumstances include, but are not limited to, those involving both the leased property and any building or complex in which it is located. *(Added by Stats.1991, c. 67 (S.B.256), § 3.)*

Law Revision Commission Comments

Subdivision (a) of Section 1997.040 makes clear that absent an enforceable use restriction the tenant is entitled to the benefit of mitigation under Section 1951.2 that would be achieved by devoting the leased property to any reasonable use. Thus if the tenant could have changed the use without the landlord's consent, or is limited only by a requirement for the landlord's reasonable consent, the tenant is entitled to have a possible reasonable change in use considered as one of the factors in determining the reasonably avoidable rental loss.

Subdivision (a) also makes clear that an enforceable use restriction may not be ignored in determining the extent of the landlord's obligation to mitigate following termination of the lease for the tenant's breach. Thus, if the tenant could not have changed the use because the terminated lease contained a restriction on use that was absolute, the landlord is not required to give up the bargained-for benefit in order to reduce the damages to the breaching tenant. However, the use restriction is not taken into account in computing mitigation damages to the extent the tenant satisfies the burden of showing that enforcement of the use restriction would be unreasonable. And, if the landlord in fact relets for a purpose that would have violated the use restriction, the reletting is in effect a waiver of the use restriction for that purpose and the tenant is entitled to have that purpose taken into account in the computation of damages regardless of whether enforcement of the use restriction would have been reasonable.

Subdivision (b) makes clear that the landlord's use of the remedy provided in Section 1951.4 does not limit enforceability of a use restriction that is otherwise enforceable. Thus if the lease allows the tenant to change the use without restriction or with the landlord's reasonable consent, the transferee would have the same freedom and limitations. If a use restriction absolutely prohibits change, both the tenant and transferee have to conform to that restraint. However, the landlord's use of the Section 1951.4 remedy precludes the landlord's enforcement of a use restriction to the extent the tenant satisfies the burden of showing that enforcement of the use restriction would be unreasonable.

The circumstances that may be considered in determining the reasonableness of enforcement of a use restriction for purposes of this section include the following and all other relevant circumstances whether of a similar or dissimilar character:

(1) The landlord's desire to preserve or encourage a so-called "tenant mix" in a shopping center.

(2) The landlord's intent to preclude residential uses in a commercial building or complex.

(3) The landlord's intent to preclude medical arts uses in an almost exclusively business-use office building (or vice versa).

(4) The fact that a proposed use by a prospective new tenant would require the landlord to grant the right to engage in that use in the building or complex to the exclusion of other parties or would contravene a preexisting right of exclusive use already possessed by, or promised to, another party.

(5) The fact that a proposed use is already prohibited by an outside party (e.g. a mortgagee or ground lessor or landlord) to whom the landlord is obligated. [20 Cal.L.Rev.Comm.Reports 2421 (1990)].

Research References

Rutter, Cal. Practice Guide: Real Prop. Transactions Ch. 7-C, C. Representing the Purchasing Tenant.

Miller and Starr California Real Estate § 19:111, Specification or Restriction of Use.

Miller and Starr California Real Estate § 19:210, Continuation of the Lease; Landlord's Recovery of Rent or Damages.

12 Witkin, California Summary 10th Real Property § 564, Effect of Restriction on Remedies for Breach.

§ 1997.050. Retrospective and prospective application of chapter to leases

Except as provided in Section 1997.270, this chapter applies to a lease executed before, on, or after January 1, 1992. *(Added by Stats.1991, c. 67 (S.B.256), § 3.)*

Law Revision Commission Comments

Section 1997.050 makes clear that this chapter is intended to be applied to existing leases as well as to leases executed after its operative date. An exception is made in the case of the rule of Section 1997.260 (implied standard for landlord's consent), which only applies to leases executed on or after January 1, 1992. See Section 1997.270 (limitation on retroactivity of Section 1997.260). [20 Cal.L.Rev.Comm.Reports 2421 (1990)].

Research References

12 Witkin, California Summary 10th Real Property § 561, Nature and Scope of Statute.

ARTICLE 2. USE RESTRICTIONS

Section

§ 1997.210. Restrictions included in lease

(a) Subject to the limitations in this chapter, a lease may include a restriction on use of leased property by a tenant.

(b) Unless the lease includes a restriction on use, a tenant's rights under a lease include any reasonable use of leased property. *(Added by Stats.1991, c. 67 (S.B.256), § 3.)*

Law Revision Commission Comments

Subdivision (a) of Section 1997.210 is a specific application of general principles of freedom of contract. Subdivision (a) is limited by the other provisions of this chapter. See, e.g., Sections 1997.030 (use restriction for illegal purpose not authorized), 1997.260 (implied standard for landlord's consent). Neither the law governing unreasonable restraints on alienation nor the law governing the implied covenant of good faith and fair dealing prevents the enforcement of a restriction on use in accordance with the express terms of the restriction. It should be noted, however, that subdivision (a) remains subject to general principles limiting freedom of contract. See, e.g., 1 B. Witkin, Summary of California Law *Contracts* §§ 23–36 (9th ed. 1987) (adhesion and unconscionable contract doctrines).

Subdivision (b) codifies the common law rule that a tenant may make any reasonable use of the leased property unless the right is expressly restricted by the parties. [20 Cal.L.Rev.Comm.Reports 2421 (1990)].

Research References

Rutter, Cal. Practice Guide: Real Prop. Transactions Ch. 7-C, C. Representing the Purchasing Tenant.
Miller and Starr California Real Estate § 19:111, Specification or Restriction of Use.
12 Witkin, California Summary 10th Real Property § 561, Nature and Scope of Statute.
12 Witkin, California Summary 10th Real Property § 562, Lease Provision.

§ 1997.220.   Ambiguities in use restrictions; construction

An ambiguity in a restriction on use of leased property by a tenant shall be construed in favor of unrestricted use. *(Added by Stats.1991, c. 67 (S.B.256), § 3.)*

Law Revision Commission Comments

Section 1997.220 codifies the common law. [20 Cal.L.Rev.Comm.Reports 2421 (1990)].

Research References

Rutter, Cal. Practice Guide: Real Prop. Transactions Ch. 7-C, C. Representing the Purchasing Tenant.
Miller and Starr California Real Estate § 19:111, Specification or Restriction of Use.
12 Witkin, California Summary 10th Real Property § 562, Lease Provision.

§ 1997.230.   Prohibitions on change in use

A restriction on use of leased property by a tenant may absolutely prohibit a change in use. *(Added by Stats.1991, c. 67 (S.B.256), § 3.)*

Law Revision Commission Comments

Section 1997.230 settles the question of the validity of a clause absolutely prohibiting change in use of the leased property by the tenant. Neither the law governing unreasonable restraints on alienation nor the law governing the implied covenant of good faith and fair dealing prevents the enforcement of a restriction that absolutely prohibits a change in use in accordance with the express terms of the restriction. Such a lease clause is valid subject to general principles governing freedom of contract, including the adhesion contract doctrine, where applicable. See Section 1997.210 and its Comment (right of any reasonable use absent a restriction). [20 Cal.L.Rev.Comm.Reports 2421 (1990)].

Research References

Rutter, Cal. Practice Guide: Real Prop. Transactions Ch. 7-C, C. Representing the Purchasing Tenant.
12 Witkin, California Summary 10th Real Property § 563, Change in Use.

§ 1997.240.   Change in use subject to express standards or conditions

A restriction on use of leased property by a tenant may provide that a change in use is subject to any express standard or condition. *(Added by Stats.1991, c. 67 (S.B.256), § 3.)*

Law Revision Commission Comments

Section 1997.240 is a specific application of subdivision (a) of Section 1997.210 (lease may include use restriction). This section does not apply, and Section 1997.250 does apply, to a restriction on use of the leased property by a tenant that requires the landlord's consent for a change in use. Section 1997.240 is subject to general principles limiting freedom of contract. See Section 1997.210 and its Comment. [20 Cal.L.Rev.Comm.Reports 2421 (1990)].

Research References

Rutter, Cal. Practice Guide: Real Prop. Transactions Ch. 7-C, C. Representing the Purchasing Tenant.
Miller and Starr California Real Estate § 19:111, Specification or Restriction of Use.

12 Witkin, California Summary 10th Real Property § 563, Change in Use.

§ 1997.250.   Consent of landlord; standards or conditions for giving or withholding consent

A restriction on use of leased property by a tenant may require the landlord's consent for a change in use subject to any express standard or condition for giving or withholding consent, including, but not limited to, either of the following:

(a) The landlord's consent may not be unreasonably withheld.

(b) The landlord's consent may be withheld subject to express standards or conditions. *(Added by Stats.1991, c. 67 (S.B.256), § 3.)*

Law Revision Commission Comments

Section 1997.250 is a specific application of the broad latitude provided in this chapter for the parties to a lease to contract for express restrictions on use of the leased property by the tenant. Such restrictions on change in use are valid subject to general principles governing freedom of contract, including the adhesion contract doctrine, where applicable. See Section 1997.210 and its Comment (right of any reasonable use absent a restriction).

The meaning of "unreasonably withheld" under subdivision (a) is a question of fact that must be determined under the circumstances of the particular case, applying an objective standard of commercial reasonableness as developed by case law.

Subdivision (b) makes clear that the lease may condition the landlord's consent in any manner. [20 Cal.L.Rev.Comm.Reports 2421 (1990)].

Research References

Rutter, Cal. Practice Guide: Real Prop. Transactions Ch. 7-C, C. Representing the Purchasing Tenant.
Miller and Starr California Real Estate § 19:111, Specification or Restriction of Use.
12 Witkin, California Summary 10th Real Property § 563, Change in Use.

§ 1997.260.   Consent of landlord; absence of standards for giving or withholding consent

If a restriction on use of leased property by a tenant requires the landlord's consent for a change in use but provides no standard for giving or withholding consent, the restriction shall be construed to include an implied standard that the landlord's consent may not be unreasonably withheld. Whether the landlord's consent has been unreasonably withheld in a particular case is a question of fact on which the tenant has the burden of proof. The tenant may satisfy the burden of proof by showing that, in response to the tenant's written request for a statement of reasons for withholding consent, the landlord has failed, within a reasonable time, to state in writing a reasonable objection to the change in use. *(Added by Stats.1991, c. 67 (S.B.256), § 3.)*

Law Revision Commission Comments

Section 1997.260 is new. For an analogous provision, see Section 1995.260 (assignment and sublease). The retroactive application of Section 1997.260 is limited by Section 1997.270.

Under Section 1997.260, whether a landlord's consent has been unreasonably withheld may be a question of procedure or substance or both. A landlord may act unreasonably in responding to a request of the tenant for consent to a change in use (for example by delaying or failing to respond or by requiring excessive investigation charges), or the landlord may not have a reasonable objection to the change in use. Either of these circumstances may give rise to a determination that the landlord has unreasonably withheld consent to the change in use within the meaning of this section.

This section provides the tenant a means of satisfying the burden of proof on this matter by making a written request for a statement of reasons. However, this is not the exclusive means of satisfying the burden of proof that the landlord's consent has been unreasonably withheld in a particular case, and proof of unreasonableness may be made by other means.

Section 1997.260 rejects an absolute approach to the question of commercial reasonableness. Whether a particular objection is reasonable within the meaning of this section is a question of fact that must be determined under the circumstances of the particular case, applying an objective standard of commercial reasonableness as developed by case law. [20 Cal.L.Rev.Comm.Reports 2421 (1990)].

Research References

Rutter, Cal. Practice Guide: Real Prop. Transactions Ch. 7-C, C. Representing the Purchasing Tenant.
Miller and Starr California Real Estate § 19:111, Specification or Restriction of Use.
12 Witkin, California Summary 10th Real Property § 563, Change in Use.

§ 1997.270. Application of § 1997.260; restrictions on use executed prior to Jan. 1, 1992; discretion to give or withhold consent

(a) Section 1997.260 applies to a restriction on use executed on or after January 1, 1992. If a restriction on use executed before January 1, 1992, requires the landlord's consent for a change in use of leased premises by a tenant, but provides no standard for giving or withholding consent, the landlord has sole and absolute discretion to give or withhold consent.

(b) For purposes of this section, if the terms of a restriction on change in use are fixed by an option or other agreement, the restriction on change in use is deemed to be executed on the date of execution of the option or other agreement. (*Added by Stats.1991, c. 67 (S.B.256), § 3.*)

Law Revision Commission Comments

Section 1997.270 limits the retroactive application of Section 1997.260 (implied standard for landlord's consent). The date of applicability of Section 1997.260 is January 1, 1992. Under subdivision (b), if a lease is made on or after January 1, 1992, under an option signed before that date, the rights between the parties to the lease are governed by the second sentence of subdivision (a). If a sublease is made on or after January 1, 1992, under a lease executed before that date, the rights between the parties to the sublease are governed by Section 1997.260. See Section 1997.020(b) ("lease" means lease or sublease).

Limitation of retroactive operation of Section 1997.260 is supported by the public policies of foreseeability, reliance, and fairness.

Nothing in this section is intended to limit the law governing modification or waiver of a lease provision by subsequent conduct or agreement of the parties, including modification or waiver of a restriction on use that expressly or impliedly permits the landlord's consent to be withheld in the landlord's sole and absolute discretion, whether the lease was executed before or after January 1, 1992. See also Section 1995.020(b) ("lease" includes modifications and other agreements affecting lease). Thus, a tenant may show that the landlord's sole and absolute discretion to give or withhold consent pursuant to an express or implied lease restriction executed before January 1, 1992, has been modified or waived. [20 Cal.L.Rev.Comm.Reports 2421 (1990)].

Research References

Rutter, Cal. Practice Guide: Real Prop. Transactions Ch. 7-C, C. Representing the Purchasing Tenant.
Miller and Starr California Real Estate § 19:111, Specification or Restriction of Use.
12 Witkin, California Summary 10th Real Property § 563, Change in Use.

Title 6

SERVICE

CHAPTER 2. PARTICULAR EMPLOYMENTS

ARTICLE 2. AGENTS

§ 2019. Conformity to limits of authority

An agent must not exceed the limits of his actual authority, as defined by the Title on Agency. (*Enacted in 1872.*)

Research References

9 Witkin, California Summary 10th Corporations § 37, in General.

§ 2020. Duty to keep principal informed

An agent must use ordinary diligence to keep his principal informed of his acts in the course of the agency. (*Enacted in 1872.*)

Research References

Miller and Starr California Real Estate § 3:15, Effect of Undisclosed Dual Agency--Effect of the Dual Agency on the Principal.
Miller and Starr California Real Estate § 3:16, Effect of Undisclosed Dual Agency--Duties and Liabilities of the Dual Agent.
Miller and Starr California Real Estate § 6:13, Agency--Duty to Disclose.
Miller and Starr California Real Estate § 6:28, Knowledge of Escrow Holder Imputed to Principal.
Miller and Starr California Real Estate § 11:76, Notice to an Agent; General Rule.
Miller and Starr California Real Estate § 11:79, Notice to a Real Estate Broker.

§ 2021. Duties of collecting agent

An agent employed to collect a negotiable instrument must collect it promptly, and take all measures necessary to charge the parties thereto, in case of its dishonor; and, if it is a bill of exchange, must present it for acceptance with reasonable diligence. (*Enacted in 1872.*)

§ 2022. Responsibility of agent of agent

A mere agent of an agent is not responsible as such to the principal of the latter. (*Enacted in 1872.*)

Research References

Miller and Starr California Real Estate § 3:10, Subagency; Role of the Cooperating Broker.
3 Witkin, California Summary 10th Agency and Employment § 118, (S 118) Acts or Omissions of Subagent.

ARTICLE 3. FACTORS

§ 2026. Factor defined

A factor is an agent who, in the pursuit of an independent calling, is employed by another to sell property for him, and is vested by the latter with the possession or control of the property, or authorized to receive payment therefor from the purchaser. *(Enacted in 1872.)*

Research References

4 Witkin, California Summary 10th Sales § 214, in General.
3 Witkin, California Summary 10th Agency and Employment § 44, Factors.

§ 2027.   Obedience to instructions; exception

A factor must obey the instructions of his principal to the same extent as any other employÉe,[1] notwithstanding any advances he may have made to his principal upon the property consigned to him, except that if the principal forbids him to sell at the market price, he may, nevertheless, sell for his reimbursement, after giving to his principal reasonable notice of his intention to do so, and of the time and place of sale, and proceeding in all respects as a pledgee. *(Enacted in 1872.)*

[1] So in chaptered copy.

Research References

13 Witkin, California Summary 10th Personal Property § 217, (S 217) in General.
3 Witkin, California Summary 10th Agency and Employment § 44, Factors.

§ 2028.   Credit sales

A factor may sell property consigned to him on such credit as is usual; but, having once agreed with the purchaser upon the term of credit, may not extend it. *(Enacted in 1872.)*

§ 2029.   Guaranty commission; liability to pay price

A factor who charges his principal with a guaranty commission upon a sale, thereby assumes absolutely to pay the price when it falls due, as if it were a debt of his own, and not as a mere guarantor for the purchaser; but he does not thereby assume any additional responsibility for the safety of his remittance of the proceeds. *(Enacted in 1872.)*

Research References

3 Witkin, California Summary 10th Agency and Employment § 44, Factors.

§ 2030.   Relief from responsibility to guarantee sales or remittance

A factor who receives property for sale, under a general agreement or usage to guarantee the sales or the remittance of the proceeds, cannot relieve himself from responsibility therefor without the consent of his principal. *(Enacted in 1872.)*

Research References

3 Witkin, California Summary 10th Agency and Employment § 44, Factors.

CHAPTER 3.   SERVICE WITHOUT EMPLOYMENT

ARTICLE 1.   VOLUNTARY INTERFERENCE WITH PROPERTY

§ 2078.   Voluntary interference with property

One who officiously, and without the consent of the real or apparent owner of a thing, takes it into his possession for the purpose of rendering a service about it, must complete such service, and use ordinary care, diligence, and reasonable skill about the same. He is not entitled to any compensation for his service or expenses, except that he may deduct actual and necessary expenses incurred by him about such service from any profits which his service has caused the thing to acquire for its owner, and must account to the owner for the residue. *(Enacted in 1872.)*

Research References

3 Witkin, California Summary 10th Agency and Employment § 117, Gratuitous Agent.

ARTICLE 2.   DUTY TO PROSPECTIVE PURCHASER OF RESIDENTIAL PROPERTY

§ 2079. Real estate brokers and salespersons; inspections and disclosures; standards of professional conduct

(a) It is the duty of a real estate broker or salesperson, licensed under Division 4 (commencing with Section 10000) of the Business and Professions Code, to a prospective purchaser of residential real property comprising one to four dwelling units, or a manufactured home as defined in Section 18007 of the Health and Safety Code, to conduct a reasonably competent and diligent visual inspection of the property offered for sale and to disclose to that prospective purchaser all facts materially affecting the value or desirability of the property that an investigation would reveal, if that broker has a written contract with the seller to find or obtain a buyer or is a broker who acts in cooperation with that broker to find and obtain a buyer.

(b) It is the duty of a real estate broker or salesperson licensed under Division 4 (commencing with Section 10000) of the Business and Professions Code to comply with this section and any regulations imposing standards of professional conduct adopted pursuant to Section 10080 of the Business and Professions Code with reference to Sections 10176 and 10177 of the Business and Professions Code. *(Added by Stats.1985, c. 223, § 2. Amended by Stats.1994, c. 339 (S.B.1509), § 1; Stats.1996, c. 812 (A.B.2221), § 2.)*

Research References

California Real Estate Forms (Miller & Starr) § 1:128, Agent's Visual Inspection Disclosure.

Rutter, Cal. Practice Guide: Real Prop. Transactions Ch. 2-C, C. Broker's Relationship and Obligations to Principal and Third Parties.

Rutter, Cal. Practice Guide: Real Prop. Transactions Ch. 2-C Outline, Outline C.

Miller and Starr California Real Estate § 3:11, Disclosure of Agency Relationships.

Miller and Starr California Real Estate § 3:16, Effect of Undisclosed Dual Agency--Duties and Liabilities of the Dual Agent.

Miller and Starr California Real Estate § 3:25, Fiduciary Duties of an Agent.

Miller and Starr California Real Estate § 3:26, Duty to Exercise Skill, Care, and Diligence; Negligence Liability.

Miller and Starr California Real Estate § 3:27, Duty to Disclose--Generally.

Miller and Starr California Real Estate § 3:30, Fraud or Misrepresentation (Constructive Fraud).

Miller and Starr California Real Estate § 3:34, Statute of Limitations.

Miller and Starr California Real Estate § 3:40, Agent's Duty to Disclose; in General--Statutory Duty to Disclose.

Miller and Starr California Real Estate § 3:43, Negligence Liability.

Miller and Starr California Real Estate § 3:44, Negligence Liability--Duty to Inspect Property Being Sold.

Miller and Starr California Real Estate § 3:45, Duty Owed to Third Persons.

Miller and Starr California Real Estate § 3:46, Statute of Limitations.

Miller and Starr California Real Estate § 4:27, Duty to Disclose--Inspection and Disclosure for Residential Transactions.

Miller and Starr California Real Estate § 1:141, Duty of Seller of Real Property to Disclose--Duty of Other Persons to Disclose.

Miller and Starr California Real Estate § 1:143, Duty of Seller of Real Property to Disclose--Materiality of Facts to be Disclosed.

Miller and Starr California Real Estate § 1:145, Duty of Seller of Real Property to Disclose--Transfer Disclosure Statement in Residential Sales.

Miller and Starr California Real Estate § 1:149, Reliance by Injured Party--Buyer's Duty to Inspect the Property Purchased.

Miller and Starr California Real Estate § 31:47, Authority of Real Estate Brokers.

14 NO. 6 Miller & Starr, California Real Estate Newsalert 2, Agency.

18 NO. 1 Miller & Starr, California Real Estate Newsalert 1, Disclosures in California Residential Real Property Sales.

18 NO. 3 Miller & Starr, California Real Estate Newsalert 2, Agency.

18 NO. 6 Miller & Starr, California Real Estate Newsalert 2, Agency.

18 NO. 3 Miller & Starr, California Real Estate Newsalert 20, Regulation of the Real Estate Industry.

18 NO. 3 Miller & Starr, California Real Estate Newsalert 21, Remedies.

3 Witkin Cal. Proc. 5th Actions § 482, (S 482) Two Years.

3 Witkin Cal. Proc. 5th Actions § 679, (S 679) Delayed Accrual in Action Against Fiduciary.

12 Witkin, California Summary 10th Real Property § 465, (S 465) Statutory Development.

12 Witkin, California Summary 10th Real Property § 470, (S 470) Additional Provisions.

12 Witkin, California Summary 10th Real Property § 471, (S 471) Types of Disclosures.

12 Witkin, California Summary 10th Real Property § 472, Creation of Duty.

12 Witkin, California Summary 10th Real Property § 473, Nature of Duty.

12 Witkin, California Summary 10th Real Property § 474, Scope of Inspection.

12 Witkin, California Summary 10th Real Property § 476, Statute of Limitations.

12 Witkin, California Summary 10th Real Property § 477, Insurance Coverage.

12 Witkin, California Summary 10th Real Property § 478, Broker's Action Against Home Inspection Company.

12 Witkin, California Summary 10th Real Property § 483, (S 483) Content and Intended Use.

12 Witkin, California Summary 10th Real Property § 490, (S 490) Manufactured Home Statement.

12 Witkin, California Summary 10th Real Property § 496, (S 496) Regulation of Inspectors.

3 Witkin, California Summary 10th Agency and Employment § 63, in General.

3 Witkin, California Summary 10th Agency and Employment § 64, Broker's Liability to Vendor.

3 Witkin, California Summary 10th Agency and Employment § 66, (S 66) Legislative Response.

§ 2079.1. Application of article; leases with options; ground leases; real property sales contracts

The provisions of this article relating sale transactions of residential real property comprising one to four dwelling units apply with equal force to leases of that property that include an option to purchase, ground leases of land on which one to four dwelling units have been constructed, or real property sales contracts, as defined in Section 2985, for that property. *(Added by Stats.1985, c. 223, § 2.)*

Research References

Rutter, Cal. Practice Guide: Real Prop. Transactions Ch. 2-C, C. Broker's Relationship and Obligations to Principal and Third Parties.

Miller and Starr California Real Estate § 3:44, Negligence Liability--Duty to Inspect Property Being Sold.

12 Witkin, California Summary 10th Real Property § 472, Creation of Duty.

§ 2079.2. Real estate brokers; standard of care

The standard of care owed by a broker under this article is the degree of care that a reasonably prudent real estate licensee would exercise and is measured by the degree of knowledge through education, experience, and examination, required to obtain a license under Division 4 (commencing with Section 10000) of the Business and Professions Code. *(Added by Stats.1985, c. 223, § 2.)*

Research References

Rutter, Cal. Practice Guide: Real Prop. Transactions Ch. 2-C, C. Broker's Relationship and Obligations to Principal and Third Parties.

Miller and Starr California Real Estate § 3:26, Duty to Exercise Skill, Care, and Diligence; Negligence Liability.

Miller and Starr California Real Estate § 3:39, Agent's Duty to Disclose; in General--Common Law Duty to Disclose Material Facts.

Miller and Starr California Real Estate § 3:43, Negligence Liability.

Miller and Starr California Real Estate § 3:44, Negligence Liability--Duty to Inspect Property Being Sold.

Miller and Starr California Real Estate § 4:27, Duty to Disclose--Inspection and Disclosure for Residential Transactions.

12 Witkin, California Summary 10th Real Property § 473, Nature of Duty.

§ 2079.3. Scope of inspection

The inspection to be performed pursuant to this article does not include or involve an inspection of areas that are reasonably and normally inaccessible to this type of an inspection, nor an affirmative inspection of areas off the site of the subject property or public records or permits concerning the title or use of the property, and, if the property comprises a unit in a planned development as defined in Section 11003 of the Business and Professions Code, a condominium as defined in Section 783, or a stock cooperative as defined in Section 11003.2 of the Business and Professions Code, does not include an inspection of more than the unit offered for sale, if the seller or the broker complies with the provisions of Sections 4525 to 4580, inclusive. *(Added by Stats.1985, c. 223, § 2. Amended by Stats.1994, c. 339 (S.B.1509), § 2; Stats.2012, c. 181 (A.B.806), § 38, operative Jan. 1, 2014.)*

Law Revision Commission Comments

Section 2079.3 is amended to correct a cross-reference to former Section 1368.

The section is also amended to make a stylistic revision. [40 Cal.L.Rev.Comm. Reports 235 (2010)].

§ 2079.4. Breach of duty; limitation of actions

In no event shall the time for commencement of legal action for breach of duty imposed by this article exceed two years from the date of possession, which means the date of recordation, the date of close of escrow, or the date of occupancy, whichever occurs first. *(Added by Stats.1985, c. 223, § 2.)*

Research References

Rutter, Cal. Practice Guide: Real Prop. Transactions Ch. 2-C, C. Broker's Relationship and Obligations to Principal and Third Parties.

Miller and Starr California Real Estate § 3:16, Effect of Undisclosed Dual Agency--Duties and Liabilities of the Dual Agent.

Miller and Starr California Real Estate § 3:34, Statute of Limitations.

Miller and Starr California Real Estate § 3:46, Statute of Limitations.

Miller and Starr California Real Estate § 1:141, Duty of Seller of Real Property to Disclose--Duty of Other Persons to Disclose.

22 NO. 6 Miller & Starr, California Real Estate Newsalert 4, Agency.

3 Witkin Cal. Proc. 5th Actions § 482, (S 482) Two Years.

3 Witkin Cal. Proc. 5th Actions § 653, (S 653) Form of Action or Relief is Not Controlling.

3 Witkin Cal. Proc. 5th Actions § 679, (S 679) Delayed Accrual in Action Against Fiduciary.

12 Witkin, California Summary 10th Real Property § 476, Statute of Limitations.

12 Witkin, California Summary 10th Real Property § 495, (S 495) Sanctions for Noncompliance.

§ 2079.5. Buyers or prospective buyers; duty of reasonable care

Nothing in this article relieves a buyer or prospective buyer of the duty to exercise reasonable care to protect himself or herself, including those facts which are known to or within the diligent attention and observation of the buyer or prospective buyer. *(Added by Stats.1985, c. 223, § 2.)*

Research References

California Real Estate Forms (Miller & Starr) § 1:94, California Residential Purchase Agreement and Joint Escrow Instructions.

Rutter, Cal. Practice Guide: Real Prop. Transactions Ch. 2-C, C. Broker's Relationship and Obligations to Principal and Third Parties.

Miller and Starr California Real Estate § 3:39, Agent's Duty to Disclose; in General--Common Law Duty to Disclose Material Facts.

Miller and Starr California Real Estate § 3:44, Negligence Liability--Duty to Inspect Property Being Sold.

Miller and Starr California Real Estate § 1:143, Duty of Seller of Real Property to Disclose--Materiality of Facts to be Disclosed.

Miller and Starr California Real Estate § 1:149, Reliance by Injured Party--Buyer's Duty to Inspect the Property Purchased.

12 Witkin, California Summary 10th Real Property § 473, Nature of Duty.

§ 2079.6. Subdivision transfers subject to certain reporting requirements

This article does not apply to transfers which are required to be preceded by the furnishing, to a prospective transferee, of a copy of a public report pursuant to Section 11018.1 of the Business and Professions Code and transfers which can be made without a public report pursuant to Section 11010.4 of the Business and Professions Code, unless the property has been previously occupied. *(Added by Stats.1988, c. 274, § 1.)*

Research References

Rutter, Cal. Practice Guide: Real Prop. Transactions Ch. 2-C, C. Broker's Relationship and Obligations to Principal and Third Parties.

Miller and Starr California Real Estate § 3:11, Disclosure of Agency Relationships.

Miller and Starr California Real Estate § 3:44, Negligence Liability--Duty to Inspect Property Being Sold.

12 Witkin, California Summary 10th Real Property § 472, Creation of Duty.

§ 2079.7. Environmental hazards; duty to disclose

(a) If a consumer information booklet described in Section 10084.1 of the Business and Professions Code is delivered to a transferee in connection with the transfer of real property, including property specified in Section 1102 of the Civil Code, or manufactured housing, as defined in Section 18007 of the Health and Safety Code, a seller or broker is not required to provide additional information concerning, and the information shall be deemed to be adequate to inform the transferee regarding, common environmental hazards, as described in the booklet, that can affect real property.

(b) Notwithstanding subdivision (a), nothing in this section either increases or decreases the duties, if any, of sellers or brokers, including but not limited to, the duties of a seller or broker under this article, Article 1.5 (commencing with Section 1102) of Chapter 2 of Title 4 of Part 4 of Division 2, or Section 25359.7 of the Health and Safety Code, or alters the duty of a seller or broker to disclose the existence of known environmental hazards on or affecting the real property. *(Added by Stats.1989, c. 969, § 2.)*

Research References

California Real Estate Forms (Miller & Starr) § 1:5, Non-Residential Statutory Disclosure Checklist.

California Real Estate Forms (Miller & Starr) § 1:94, California Residential Purchase Agreement and Joint Escrow Instructions.

Rutter, Cal. Practice Guide: Real Prop. Transactions Ch. 4-E, E. Drafting the Purchase and Sale Agreement-Terms and Conditions.

Miller and Starr California Real Estate § 3:39, Agent's Duty to Disclose; in General--Common Law Duty to Disclose Material Facts.

Miller and Starr California Real Estate § 3:42, Specific Disclosures Required by Statute.

Miller and Starr California Real Estate § 3:44, Negligence Liability--Duty to Inspect Property Being Sold.

Miller and Starr California Real Estate § 1:144, Duty of Seller of Real Property to Disclose--Statutory Duty of Disclosure.

12 Witkin, California Summary 10th Real Property § 475, Disclosure of Information in Booklets.

§ 2079.8. Delivery of Homeowner's Guide to Earthquake Safety to transferee of real property; effect on duty of sellers or brokers to disclose existence of known hazards

(a) If a Homeowner's Guide to Earthquake Safety described in Section 10149 of the Business and Professions Code is delivered to a transferee in connection with the transfer of real property, including property specified in Section 1102 or under Chapter 7.5 (commencing with Section 2621) of Division 2 of the Public Resources Code, a seller or broker is not required to provide additional information concerning, and the information shall be deemed to be adequate to inform the transferee regarding, geologic and seismic hazards, in general, as described in the guide, that may affect real property and mitigating measures that the transferee or seller might consider.

(b) Notwithstanding subdivision (a), nothing in this section increases or decreases the duties, if any, of sellers or brokers, including, but not limited to, the duties of a seller or broker under this article, Article 1.5 (commencing with Section 1102) of Chapter 2 of Title 4 of Part 4 of Division 2, or under Chapter 7.5 (commencing with Section 2621) of Division 2 of the Public Resources Code, or alters the duty of a seller or broker to disclose the existence of known hazards on or affecting the real property. *(Added by Stats.1990, c. 1499 (A.B.2959), § 2. Amended by Stats.1991, c. 550 (A.B.29), § 2.)*

Research References

California Real Estate Forms (Miller & Starr) § 1:94, California Residential Purchase Agreement and Joint Escrow Instructions.
Rutter, Cal. Practice Guide: Real Prop. Transactions Ch. 2-C, C. Broker's Relationship and Obligations to Principal and Third Parties.
Miller and Starr California Real Estate § 3:42, Specific Disclosures Required by Statute.
Miller and Starr California Real Estate § 1:144, Duty of Seller of Real Property to Disclose--Statutory Duty of Disclosure.
12 Witkin, California Summary 10th Real Property § 475, Disclosure of Information in Booklets.
12 Witkin, California Summary 10th Real Property § 488, (S 488) Homeowner's Guide to Earthquake Safety.

§ 2079.9. Delivery of commercial property owner's guide to earthquake safety to transferee of real property; effect on duty of sellers and brokers to disclose existence of known hazards

(a) If a Commercial Property Owner's Guide to Earthquake Safety described in Section 10147 of the Business and Professions Code is delivered to a transferee in connection with the transfer of real property, including property specified in Section 1102 or under Chapter 7.5 (commencing with Section 2621) of Division 2 of the Public Resources Code, a seller or broker is not required to provide additional information concerning, and the information shall be deemed to be adequate to inform the transferee regarding, geologic and seismic hazards, in general, as described in the guide, that may affect real property and mitigating measures that the transferee or seller might consider.

(b) Notwithstanding subdivision (a), nothing in this section increases or decreases the duties, if any, of sellers, their brokers or agents under this article or under Chapter 7.5 (commencing with Section 2621) or Chapter 7.8 (commencing with Section 2690) of Division 2 of the Public Resources Code, or alters the duty of a seller, agent, or broker to disclose the existence of known hazards on or affecting the real property. *(Added by Stats.1991, c. 859 (A.B.1968), § 2.)*

Research References

California Real Estate Forms (Miller & Starr) § 1:94, California Residential Purchase Agreement and Joint Escrow Instructions.
Miller and Starr California Real Estate § 3:39, Agent's Duty to Disclose; in General--Common Law Duty to Disclose Material Facts.
Miller and Starr California Real Estate § 3:42, Specific Disclosures Required by Statute.
Miller and Starr California Real Estate § 3:44, Negligence Liability--Duty to Inspect Property Being Sold.

Miller and Starr California Real Estate § 1:144, Duty of Seller of Real Property to Disclose--Statutory Duty of Disclosure.

§ 2079.10. Home energy rating program; information booklet

(a) If the informational booklet published pursuant to Section 25402.9 of the Public Resources Code, concerning the statewide home energy rating program adopted pursuant to Section 25942 of the Public Resources Code, is delivered to a transferee in connection with the transfer of real property, including, but not limited to, property specified in Section 1102, manufactured homes as defined in Section 18007 of the Health and Safety Code, and property subject to Chapter 7.5 (commencing with Section 2621) of Division 2 of the Public Resources Code, the seller or broker is not required to provide information additional to that contained in the booklet concerning home energy ratings, and the information in the booklet shall be deemed to be adequate to inform the transferee about the existence of a statewide home energy rating program.

(b) Notwithstanding subdivision (a), nothing in this section alters any existing duty of the seller or broker under any other law including, but not limited to, the duties of a seller or broker under this article, Article 1.5 (commencing with Section 1102) of Chapter 2 of Title 4 of Part 4 of Division 2 of the Civil Code, or Chapter 7.5 (commencing with Section 2621) of Division 2 of the Public Resources Code, to disclose information concerning the existence of a home energy rating program affecting the real property.

(c) If the informational booklet or materials described in Section 375.5 of the Water Code concerning water conservation and water conservation programs are delivered to a transferee in connection with the transfer of real property, including property described in subdivision (a), the seller or broker is not required to provide information concerning water conservation and water conservation programs that is additional to that contained in the booklet or materials, and the information in the booklet or materials shall be deemed to be adequate to inform the transferee about water conservation and water conservation programs. *(Added by Stats.1992, c. 769 (S.B.1207), § 2. Amended by Stats.2004, c. 111 (A.B.2470), § 1.)*

Research References

Miller and Starr California Real Estate § 3:16, Effect of Undisclosed Dual Agency--Duties and Liabilities of the Dual Agent.
Miller and Starr California Real Estate § 3:42, Specific Disclosures Required by Statute.
Miller and Starr California Real Estate § 1:144, Duty of Seller of Real Property to Disclose--Statutory Duty of Disclosure.
18 NO. 1 Miller & Starr, California Real Estate Newsalert 1, Disclosures in California Residential Real Property Sales.
12 Witkin, California Summary 10th Real Property § 475, Disclosure of Information in Booklets.

§ 2079.10.5. Contracts for sale; required notice; gas and hazardous liquid transmission pipelines

(a) Every contract for the sale of residential real property entered into on or after July 1, 2013, shall contain, in not less than 8-point type, a notice as specified below:

NOTICE REGARDING GAS AND HAZARDOUS LIQUID TRANSMISSION PIPELINES

This notice is being provided simply to inform you that information about the general location of gas and hazardous liquid transmission pipelines is available to the public via the National Pipeline Mapping System (NPMS) Internet Web site maintained by the United States Department of Transportation at http://www.npms.phmsa.dot.gov/. To seek further information about possible transmission pipelines near the property, you may contact your local gas utility or other pipeline operators in the area. Contact information for pipeline operators is searchable by ZIP Code and county on the NPMS Internet Web site.

(b) Upon delivery of the notice to the transferee of the real property, the seller or broker is not required to provide information in addition to that contained in the notice regarding gas and hazardous liquid transmission pipelines in subdivision (a). The information in the notice shall be deemed to be adequate to inform the transferee about the existence of a statewide database of the locations of gas and hazardous liquid transmission pipelines and information from the database regarding those locations.

(c) Nothing in this section shall alter any existing duty under any other statute or decisional law imposed upon the seller or broker, including, but not limited to, the duties of a seller or broker under this article, or the duties of a seller or broker under Article 1.5 (commencing with Section 1102) of Chapter 2 of Title 4 of Part 4 of Division 2. *(Added by Stats.2012, c. 91 (A.B.1511), § 1.)*

§ 2079.10a. Lease or rental agreements for residential real property entered into on or after July 1, 1999 and contracts for sale of residential real property comprised of one to four dwelling units entered into on or after that date; contents of notice

(a) Every lease or rental agreement for residential real property entered into on or after July 1, 1999, and every contract for the sale of residential real property comprised of one to four dwelling units entered into on or after that date, shall contain, in not less than 8–point type, a notice as specified in paragraph (1), (2), or (3).

(1) A contract entered into by the parties on or after July 1, 1999, and before September 1, 2005, shall contain the following notice:

Notice: The California Department of Justice, sheriff's departments, police departments serving jurisdictions of 200,000 or more, and many other local law enforcement authorities maintain for public access a database of the locations of persons required to register pursuant to paragraph (1) of subdivision (a) of Section 290.4 of the Penal Code. The database is updated on a quarterly basis and is a source of information about the presence of these individuals in any neighborhood. The Department of Justice also maintains a Sex Offender Identification Line through which inquiries about individuals may be made. This is a "900" telephone service. Callers must have specific information about individuals they are checking. Information regarding neighborhoods is not available through the "900" telephone service.

(2) A contract entered into by the parties on or after September 1, 2005, and before April 1, 2006, shall contain either the notice specified in paragraph (1) or the notice specified in paragraph (3).

(3) A contract entered into by the parties on or after April 1, 2006, shall contain the following notice:

Notice: Pursuant to Section 290.46 of the Penal Code, information about specified registered sex offenders is made available to the public via an Internet Web site maintained by the Department of Justice at www.meganslaw.ca.gov. Depending on an offender's criminal history, this information will include either the address at which the offender resides or the community of residence and ZIP Code in which he or she resides.

(b) Subject to subdivision (c), upon delivery of the notice to the lessee or transferee of the real property, the lessor, seller, or broker is not required to provide information in addition to that contained in the notice regarding the proximity of registered sex offenders. The information in the notice shall be deemed to be adequate to inform the lessee or transferee about the existence of a statewide database of the locations of registered sex offenders and information from the database regarding those locations. The information in the notice shall not give rise to any cause of action against the disclosing party by a registered sex offender.

(c) Notwithstanding subdivisions (a) and (b), nothing in this section shall alter any existing duty of the lessor, seller, or broker under any other statute or decisional law including, but not limited to, the duties of a lessor, seller, or broker under this article, or the duties of a seller or broker under Article 1.5 (commencing with Section 1102) of Chapter 2 of Title 4 of Part 4 of Division 2. *(Added by Stats.1998, c. 645 (S.B.1989), § 1. Amended by Stats.1999, c. 876 (A.B.248), § 4; Stats.2005, c. 722 (A.B.1323), § 1, eff. Oct. 7, 2005.)*

Research References

California Real Estate Forms (Miller & Starr) § 1:94, California Residential Purchase Agreement and Joint Escrow Instructions.

California Real Estate Forms (Miller & Starr) § 1:122, Megan's Law Database Disclosure Regarding Registered Sex Offenders.

Rutter, Cal. Practice Guide: Real Prop. Transactions Ch. 2-C, C. Broker's Relationship and Obligations to Principal and Third Parties.

Rutter, Cal. Practice Guide: Real Prop. Transactions Ch. 4-E, E. Drafting the Purchase and Sale Agreement-Terms and Conditions.

Miller and Starr California Real Estate § 1:144, Duty of Seller of Real Property to Disclose--Statutory Duty of Disclosure.

Miller and Starr California Real Estate § 19:123, Landlord's Duty to Disclose Defects to a Tenant.

16 NO. 4 Miller & Starr, California Real Estate Newsalert 5, Contracts.

16 NO. 4 Miller & Starr, California Real Estate Newsalert 13, Landlord and Tenant.

16 NO. 5 Miller & Starr, California Real Estate Newsalert 26, State Board of Equalization Issues Comprehensive Summary and Qs and As for Transfers of Base Year Values of Principal Residences.

22 NO. 1 Miller & Starr, California Real Estate Newsalert 19, Judicial Remedies.

12 Witkin, California Summary 10th Real Property § 492, (S 492) Location of Sex Offenders.

12 Witkin, California Summary 10th Real Property § 617, (S 617) in General.

§ 2079.11. Consumer information publications; earthquake guide; costs

(a) Except as provided in subdivision (b), to the extent permitted by law, the consumer information publications referred to in this article, including, but not limited to, the information booklets described in Section 10084.1 of the Business and Professions Code and Section 25402.9 of the Public Resources Code, shall be in the public domain and freely available.

(b) Notwithstanding subdivision (a), the Seismic Safety Commission's Homeowner's Guide to Earthquake Safety, published pursuant to Section 10149 of the Business and Professions Code, shall be made available to the public at cost and for reproduction at no cost to any vendor who wishes to publish the guide, provided the vendor agrees to submit the guide to the commission prior to publication for content approval. *(Added by Stats.1994, c. 66 (S.B.1229), § 1. Amended by Stats.1998, c. 65 (A.B.1195), § 4, eff. June 9, 1998, operative June 1, 1998.)*

§ 2079.12. Duty of care for real estate licensees; legislative findings and declarations

(a) The Legislature hereby finds and declares all of the following:

(1) That the imprecision of terms in the opinion rendered in Easton v. Strassburger, 152 Cal.App.3d 90, and the absence of a

comprehensive declaration of duties, standards, and exceptions, has caused insurers to modify professional liability coverage of real estate licensees and has caused confusion among real estate licensees as to the manner of performing the duty ascribed to them by the court.

(2) That it is necessary to resolve and make precise these issues in an expeditious manner.

(3) That it is desirable to facilitate the issuance of professional liability insurance as a resource for aggrieved members of the public.

(4) That Sections 2079 to 2079.6, inclusive, of this article should be construed as a definition of the duty of care found to exist by the holding of Easton v. Strassburger, 152 Cal.App.3d 90, and the manner of its discharge, and is declarative of the common law regarding this duty. However, nothing in this section is intended to affect the court's ability to interpret Sections 2079 to 2079.6, inclusive.

(b) It is the intent of the Legislature to codify and make precise the holding of Easton v. Strassburger, 152 Cal.App.3d 90. It is not the intent of the Legislature to modify or restrict existing duties owed by real estate licensees. *(Added by Stats.1995, c. 428 (S.B.467), § 1. Amended by Stats.1996, c. 124 (A.B.3470), § 7; Stats.1996, c. 476 (A.B.2935), § 1.)*

Research References

Rutter, Cal. Practice Guide: Real Prop. Transactions Ch. 2-C, C. Broker's Relationship and Obligations to Principal and Third Parties.
Rutter, Cal. Practice Guide: Real Prop. Transactions Ch. 4-E, E. Drafting the Purchase and Sale Agreement-Terms and Conditions.
Miller and Starr California Real Estate § 3:25, Fiduciary Duties of an Agent.
Miller and Starr California Real Estate § 3:26, Duty to Exercise Skill, Care, and Diligence; Negligence Liability.
Miller and Starr California Real Estate § 3:40, Agent's Duty to Disclose; in General--Statutory Duty to Disclose.
Miller and Starr California Real Estate § 3:44, Negligence Liability--Duty to Inspect Property Being Sold.
12 Witkin, California Summary 10th Real Property § 472, Creation of Duty.
3 Witkin, California Summary 10th Agency and Employment § 66, (S 66) Legislative Response.

§ 2079.13. Definitions

As used in Sections 2079.14 to 2079.24, inclusive, the following terms have the following meanings:

(a) "Agent" means a person acting under provisions of Title 9 (commencing with Section 2295) in a real property transaction, and includes a person who is licensed as a real estate broker under Chapter 3 (commencing with Section 10130) of Part 1 of Division 4 of the Business and Professions Code, and under whose license a listing is executed or an offer to purchase is obtained.

(b) "Associate licensee" means a person who is licensed as a real estate broker or salesperson under Chapter 3 (commencing with Section 10130) of Part 1 of Division 4 of the Business and Professions Code and who is either licensed under a broker or has entered into a written contract with a broker to act as the broker's agent in connection with acts requiring a real estate license and to function under the broker's supervision in the capacity of an associate licensee.

The agent in the real property transaction bears responsibility for his or her associate licensees who perform as agents of the agent. When an associate licensee owes a duty to any principal, or to any buyer or seller who is not a principal, in a real property transaction, that duty is equivalent to the duty owed to that party by the broker for whom the associate licensee functions.

(c) "Buyer" means a transferee in a real property transaction, and includes a person who executes an offer to purchase real property from a seller through an agent, or who seeks the services of an agent in more than a casual, transitory, or preliminary manner, with the object of entering into a real property transaction. "Buyer" includes vendee or lessee.

(d) "Dual agent" means an agent acting, either directly or through an associate licensee, as agent for both the seller and the buyer in a real property transaction.

(e) "Listing agreement" means a contract between an owner of real property and an agent, by which the agent has been authorized to sell the real property or to find or obtain a buyer.

(f) "Listing agent" means a person who has obtained a listing of real property to act as an agent for compensation.

(g) "Listing price" is the amount expressed in dollars specified in the listing for which the seller is willing to sell the real property through the listing agent.

(h) "Offering price" is the amount expressed in dollars specified in an offer to purchase for which the buyer is willing to buy the real property.

(i) "Offer to purchase" means a written contract executed by a buyer acting through a selling agent which becomes the contract for the sale of the real property upon acceptance by the seller.

(j) "Real property" means any estate specified by subdivision (1) or (2) of Section 761 in property which constitutes or is improved with one to four dwelling units, any leasehold in this type of property exceeding one year's duration, and mobilehomes, when offered for sale or sold through an agent pursuant to the authority contained in Section 10131.6 of the Business and Professions Code.

(k) "Real property transaction" means a transaction for the sale of real property in which an agent is employed by one or more of the principals to act in that transaction, and includes a listing or an offer to purchase.

(*l*) "Sell," "sale," or "sold" refers to a transaction for the transfer of real property from the seller to the buyer, and includes exchanges of real property between the seller and buyer, transactions for the creation of a real property sales contract within the meaning of Section 2985, and transactions for the creation of a leasehold exceeding one year's duration.

(m) "Seller" means the transferor in a real property transaction, and includes an owner who lists real property with an agent, whether or not a transfer results, or who receives an offer to purchase real property of which he or she is the owner from an agent on behalf of another. "Seller" includes both a vendor and a lessor.

(n) "Selling agent" means a listing agent who acts alone, or an agent who acts in cooperation with a listing agent, and who sells or finds and obtains a buyer for the real property, or an agent who locates property for a buyer or who finds a buyer for a property for which no listing exists and presents an offer to purchase to the seller.

(o) "Subagent" means a person to whom an agent delegates agency powers as provided in Article 5 (commencing with Section 2349) of Chapter 1 of Title 9. However, "subagent" does not include an associate licensee who is acting under the supervision of an agent in a real property transaction. *(Added by Stats.1995, c. 428 (S.B.467), § 2.)*

Research References

Rutter, Cal. Practice Guide: Real Prop. Transactions Ch. 2-C, C. Broker's Relationship and Obligations to Principal and Third Parties.
Miller and Starr California Real Estate § 3:5, Creation of an Agency; Identifying the Principal; General Rules.

Miller and Starr California Real Estate § 3:11, Disclosure of Agency Relationships.

Miller and Starr California Real Estate § 3:12, Dual Agency.

Miller and Starr California Real Estate § 3:19, Salesperson as Employee Versus Independent Contractor--Liability of a Broker for Torts of a Salesperson.

12 Witkin, California Summary 10th Real Property § 465, (S 465) Statutory Development.

12 Witkin, California Summary 10th Real Property § 466, (S 466) Definitions.

12 Witkin, California Summary 10th Real Property § 468, (S 468) Contents of Disclosure Form.

3 Witkin, California Summary 10th Agency and Employment § 63, in General.

§ 2079.14. Disclosure form; furnishing to buyer and seller; exceptions

Listing agents and selling agents shall provide the seller and buyer in a real property transaction with a copy of the disclosure form specified in Section 2079.16, and, except as provided in subdivision (c), shall obtain a signed acknowledgment of receipt from that seller or buyer, except as provided in this section or Section 2079.15, as follows:

(a) The listing agent, if any, shall provide the disclosure form to the seller prior to entering into the listing agreement.

(b) The selling agent shall provide the disclosure form to the seller as soon as practicable prior to presenting the seller with an offer to purchase, unless the selling agent previously provided the seller with a copy of the disclosure form pursuant to subdivision (a).

(c) Where the selling agent does not deal on a face-to-face basis with the seller, the disclosure form prepared by the selling agent may be furnished to the seller (and acknowledgment of receipt obtained for the selling agent from the seller) by the listing agent, or the selling agent may deliver the disclosure form by certified mail addressed to the seller at his or her last known address, in which case no signed acknowledgment of receipt is required.

(d) The selling agent shall provide the disclosure form to the buyer as soon as practicable prior to execution of the buyer's offer to purchase, except that if the offer to purchase is not prepared by the selling agent, the selling agent shall present the disclosure form to the buyer not later than the next business day after the selling agent receives the offer to purchase from the buyer. *(Added by Stats.1995, c. 428 (S.B.467), § 3.)*

Research References

California Real Estate Forms (Miller & Starr) § 1:117, Disclosure Regarding Real Estate Agency Relationships.

Rutter, Cal. Practice Guide: Real Prop. Transactions Ch. 2-C, C. Broker's Relationship and Obligations to Principal and Third Parties.

Miller and Starr California Real Estate § 3:11, Disclosure of Agency Relationships.

Miller and Starr California Real Estate § 3:13, Dual Agency--Disclosure of the Dual Agency.

Miller and Starr California Real Estate § 3:25, Fiduciary Duties of an Agent.

Miller and Starr California Real Estate § 4:26, Duty to Disclose--Disclosure of Agency Relationships.

Miller and Starr California Real Estate § 4:27, Duty to Disclose--Inspection and Disclosure for Residential Transactions.

12 Witkin, California Summary 10th Real Property § 466, (S 466) Definitions.

12 Witkin, California Summary 10th Real Property § 467, (S 467) Providing Disclosure Form to Buyer and Seller.

12 Witkin, California Summary 10th Real Property § 469, (S 469) Disclosure of Exclusive or Dual Agency.

12 Witkin, California Summary 10th Real Property § 470, (S 470) Additional Provisions.

§ 2079.15. Acknowledgment of receipt; refusal to sign

In any circumstance in which the seller or buyer refuses to sign an acknowledgment of receipt pursuant to Section 2079.14, the agent, or an associate licensee acting for an agent, shall set forth, sign, and date a written declaration of the facts of the refusal. *(Added by Stats.1995, c. 428 (S.B.467), § 4.)*

Research References

Rutter, Cal. Practice Guide: Real Prop. Transactions Ch. 2-C, C. Broker's Relationship and Obligations to Principal and Third Parties.

Miller and Starr California Real Estate § 3:11, Disclosure of Agency Relationships.

12 Witkin, California Summary 10th Real Property § 467, (S 467) Providing Disclosure Form to Buyer and Seller.

§ 2079.16. Disclosure form

The disclosure form required by Section 2079.14 shall have Sections 2079.13 to 2079.24, inclusive, excluding this section, printed on the back, and on the front of the disclosure form the following shall appear:

DISCLOSURE REGARDING REAL ESTATE AGENCY RELATIONSHIP

(As required by the Civil Code)

When you enter into a discussion with a real estate agent regarding a real estate transaction, you should from the outset understand what type of agency relationship or representation you wish to have with the agent in the transaction.

SELLER'S AGENT

A Seller's agent under a listing agreement with the Seller acts as the agent for the Seller only. A Seller's agent or a subagent of that agent has the following affirmative obligations:

To the Seller:

A fiduciary duty of utmost care, integrity, honesty, and loyalty in dealings with the Seller.

To the Buyer and the Seller:

(a) Diligent exercise of reasonable skill and care in performance of the agent's duties.

(b) A duty of honest and fair dealing and good faith.

(c) A duty to disclose all facts known to the agent materially affecting the value or desirability of the property that are not known to, or within the diligent attention and observation of, the parties.

An agent is not obligated to reveal to either party any confidential information obtained from the other party that does not involve the affirmative duties set forth above.

BUYER'S AGENT

A selling agent can, with a Buyer's consent, agree to act as agent for the Buyer only. In these situations, the agent is not the Seller's agent, even if by agreement the agent may receive compensation for services rendered, either in full or in part from the Seller. An agent acting only for a Buyer has the following affirmative obligations:

To the Buyer:

A fiduciary duty of utmost care, integrity, honesty, and loyalty in dealings with the Buyer.

To the Buyer and the Seller:

(a) Diligent exercise of reasonable skill and care in performance of the agent's duties.

(b) A duty of honest and fair dealing and good faith.

(c) A duty to disclose all facts known to the agent materially affecting the value or desirability of the property that are not known to, or within the diligent attention and observation of, the parties. An agent is not obligated to reveal to either party any confidential information obtained from the other party that does not involve the affirmative duties set forth above.

AGENT REPRESENTING BOTH SELLER AND BUYER

A real estate agent, either acting directly or through one or more associate licensees, can legally be the agent of both the Seller and the Buyer in a transaction, but only with the knowledge and consent of both the Seller and the Buyer.

In a dual agency situation, the agent has the following affirmative obligations to both the Seller and the Buyer:

(a) A fiduciary duty of utmost care, integrity, honesty and loyalty in the dealings with either the Seller or the Buyer.

(b) Other duties to the Seller and the Buyer as stated above in their respective sections.

In representing both Seller and Buyer, the agent may not, without the express permission of the respective party, disclose to the other party that the Seller will accept a price less than the listing price or that the Buyer will pay a price greater than the price offered.

The above duties of the agent in a real estate transaction do not relieve a Seller or Buyer from the responsibility to protect his or her own interests. You should carefully read all agreements to assure that they adequately express your understanding of the transaction. A real estate agent is a person qualified to advise about real estate. If legal or tax advice is desired, consult a competent professional.

Throughout your real property transaction you may receive more than one disclosure form, depending upon the number of agents assisting in the transaction. The law requires each agent with whom you have more than a casual relationship to present you with this disclosure form. You should read its contents each time it is presented to you, considering the relationship between you and the real estate agent in your specific transaction.

This disclosure form includes the provisions of Sections 2079.13 to 2079.24, inclusive, of the Civil Code set forth on the reverse hereof. Read it carefully.

Agent	(date)	Buyer/Seller (Signature)	(date)

Associate Licensee (Signature)	(date)	Buyer/Seller (Signature)	(date)

(Added by Stats.1995, c. 428 (S.B.467), § 5. Amended by Stats.1996, c. 240 (A.B.2383), § 4.)

Research References

California Real Estate Forms (Miller & Starr) § 1:117, Disclosure Regarding Real Estate Agency Relationships.
Rutter, Cal. Practice Guide: Real Prop. Transactions Ch. 2-C, C. Broker's Relationship and Obligations to Principal and Third Parties.
Miller and Starr California Real Estate § 3:11, Disclosure of Agency Relationships.
Miller and Starr California Real Estate § 3:12, Dual Agency.
Miller and Starr California Real Estate § 3:13, Dual Agency--Disclosure of the Dual Agency.
Miller and Starr California Real Estate § 3:16, Effect of Undisclosed Dual Agency--Duties and Liabilities of the Dual Agent.
Miller and Starr California Real Estate § 3:25, Fiduciary Duties of an Agent.

Miller and Starr California Real Estate § 3:27, Duty to Disclose--Generally.
Miller and Starr California Real Estate § 3:39, Agent's Duty to Disclose; in General--Common Law Duty to Disclose Material Facts.
Miller and Starr California Real Estate § 3:40, Agent's Duty to Disclose; in General--Statutory Duty to Disclose.
Miller and Starr California Real Estate § 3:43, Negligence Liability.
Miller and Starr California Real Estate § 3:47, Duties of Buyer's Agent to the Seller.
Miller and Starr California Real Estate § 4:26, Duty to Disclose--Disclosure of Agency Relationships.
Miller and Starr California Real Estate § 4:27, Duty to Disclose--Inspection and Disclosure for Residential Transactions.
21 NO. 3 Miller & Starr, California Real Estate Newsalert 3, Agency.
12 Witkin, California Summary 10th Real Property § 467, (S 467) Providing Disclosure Form to Buyer and Seller.
12 Witkin, California Summary 10th Real Property § 468, (S 468) Contents of Disclosure Form.
3 Witkin, California Summary 10th Agency and Employment § 64, Broker's Liability to Vendor.
3 Witkin, California Summary 10th Agency and Employment § 66, (S 66) Legislative Response.

§ 2079.17. Agency relationship; disclosure and confirmation

(a) As soon as practicable, the selling agent shall disclose to the buyer and seller whether the selling agent is acting in the real property transaction exclusively as the buyer's agent, exclusively as the seller's agent, or as a dual agent representing both the buyer and the seller. This relationship shall be confirmed in the contract to purchase and sell real property or in a separate writing executed or acknowledged by the seller, the buyer, and the selling agent prior to or coincident with execution of that contract by the buyer and the seller, respectively.

(b) As soon as practicable, the listing agent shall disclose to the seller whether the listing agent is acting in the real property transaction exclusively as the seller's agent, or as a dual agent representing both the buyer and seller. This relationship shall be confirmed in the contract to purchase and sell real property or in a separate writing executed or acknowledged by the seller and the listing agent prior to or coincident with the execution of that contract by the seller.

(c) The confirmation required by subdivisions (a) and (b) shall be in the following form:

_____ is the agent of (check one):
(Name of Listing Agent)

[ ] the seller exclusively; or
[ ] both the buyer and seller.

_____
(Name of Selling Agent if not the same as the Listing Agent)

is the agent of (check one):
[ ] the buyer exclusively; or
[ ] the seller exclusively; or
[ ] both the buyer and seller.

(d) The disclosures and confirmation required by this section shall be in addition to the disclosure required by Section 2079.14.
(Added by Stats.1995, c. 428 (S.B.467), § 6.)

Research References

California Real Estate Forms (Miller & Starr) § 1:94, California Residential Purchase Agreement and Joint Escrow Instructions.
Rutter, Cal. Practice Guide: Real Prop. Transactions Ch. 2-C, C. Broker's Relationship and Obligations to Principal and Third Parties.
Miller and Starr California Real Estate § 6:1, Definition of an Escrow.
Miller and Starr California Real Estate § 3:11, Disclosure of Agency Relationships.

12 Witkin, California Summary 10th Real Property § 469, (S 469) Disclosure of Exclusive or Dual Agency.

12 Witkin, California Summary 10th Real Property § 470, (S 470) Additional Provisions.

§ 2079.18. Listing agents; acting as agent for only buyer prohibited

No selling agent in a real property transaction may act as an agent for the buyer only, when the selling agent is also acting as the listing agent in the transaction. *(Added by Stats.1995, c. 428 (S.B.467), § 7.)*

Research References

Miller and Starr California Real Estate § 3:11, Disclosure of Agency Relationships.
Miller and Starr California Real Estate § 3:12, Dual Agency.
12 Witkin, California Summary 10th Real Property § 466, (S 466) Definitions.

§ 2079.19. Payment of compensation; effect on determination of agency relationship

The payment of compensation or the obligation to pay compensation to an agent by the seller or buyer is not necessarily determinative of a particular agency relationship between an agent and the seller or buyer. A listing agent and a selling agent may agree to share any compensation or commission paid, or any right to any compensation or commission for which an obligation arises as the result of a real estate transaction, and the terms of any such agreement shall not necessarily be determinative of a particular relationship. *(Added by Stats.1995, c. 428 (S.B.467), § 8.)*

Research References

Miller and Starr California Real Estate § 3:5, Creation of an Agency; Identifying the Principal; General Rules.
Miller and Starr California Real Estate § 3:11, Disclosure of Agency Relationships.
Miller and Starr California Real Estate § 3:12, Dual Agency.
12 Witkin, California Summary 10th Real Property § 470, (S 470) Additional Provisions.

§ 2079.20. Form of agency relationship; selection; condition of employment

Nothing in this article prevents an agent from selecting, as a condition of the agent's employment, a specific form of agency relationship not specifically prohibited by this article if the requirements of Section 2079.14 and Section 2079.17 are complied with. *(Added by Stats.1995, c. 428 (S.B.467), § 9.)*

Research References

Miller and Starr California Real Estate § 3:11, Disclosure of Agency Relationships.
12 Witkin, California Summary 10th Real Property § 470, (S 470) Additional Provisions.

§ 2079.21. Dual agents; disclosures prohibited

A dual agent shall not disclose to the buyer that the seller is willing to sell the property at a price less than the listing price, without the express written consent of the seller. A dual agent shall not disclose to the seller that the buyer is willing to pay a price greater than the offering price, without the express written consent of the buyer.

This section does not alter in any way the duty or responsibility of a dual agent to any principal with respect to confidential information other than price. *(Added by Stats.1995, c. 428 (S.B.467), § 10.)*

Research References

Rutter, Cal. Practice Guide: Real Prop. Transactions Ch. 2-C, C. Broker's Relationship and Obligations to Principal and Third Parties.

Miller and Starr California Real Estate § 3:11, Disclosure of Agency Relationships.
Miller and Starr California Real Estate § 3:16, Effect of Undisclosed Dual Agency--Duties and Liabilities of the Dual Agent.
Miller and Starr California Real Estate § 3:27, Duty to Disclose-- Generally.
Miller and Starr California Real Estate § 3:40, Agent's Duty to Disclose; in General--Statutory Duty to Disclose.
12 Witkin, California Summary 10th Real Property § 470, (S 470) Additional Provisions.

§ 2079.22. Listing agents; acting as selling agents

Nothing in this article precludes a listing agent from also being a selling agent, and the combination of these functions in one agent does not, of itself, make that agent a dual agent. *(Added by Stats.1995, c. 428 (S.B.467), § 11.)*

Research References

Miller and Starr California Real Estate § 3:11, Disclosure of Agency Relationships.
Miller and Starr California Real Estate § 3:12, Dual Agency.
12 Witkin, California Summary 10th Real Property § 465, (S 465) Statutory Development.
12 Witkin, California Summary 10th Real Property § 466, (S 466) Definitions.

§ 2079.23. Agency contract; modification or alteration

A contract between the principal and agent may be modified or altered to change the agency relationship at any time before the performance of the act which is the object of the agency with the written consent of the parties to the agency relationship. *(Added by Stats.1995, c. 428 (S.B.467), § 12.)*

Research References

Miller and Starr California Real Estate § 3:11, Disclosure of Agency Relationships.
12 Witkin, California Summary 10th Real Property § 470, (S 470) Additional Provisions.

§ 2079.24. Disclosure and fiduciary duties; effect of article

Nothing in this article shall be construed to either diminish the duty of disclosure owed buyers and sellers by agents and their associate licensees, subagents, and employees or to relieve agents and their associate licensees, subagents, and employees from liability for their conduct in connection with acts governed by this article or for any breach of a fiduciary duty or a duty of disclosure. *(Added by Stats.1995, c. 428 (S.B.467), § 13.)*

Research References

Rutter, Cal. Practice Guide: Real Prop. Transactions Ch. 2-C, C. Broker's Relationship and Obligations to Principal and Third Parties.
Rutter, Cal. Practice Guide: Real Prop. Transactions Ch. 4-E, E. Drafting the Purchase and Sale Agreement-Terms and Conditions.
Miller and Starr California Real Estate § 3:11, Disclosure of Agency Relationships.
Miller and Starr California Real Estate § 3:16, Effect of Undisclosed Dual Agency--Duties and Liabilities of the Dual Agent.
Miller and Starr California Real Estate § 3:26, Duty to Exercise Skill, Care, and Diligence; Negligence Liability.
Miller and Starr California Real Estate § 3:27, Duty to Disclose-- Generally.
Miller and Starr California Real Estate § 3:39, Agent's Duty to Disclose; in General--Common Law Duty to Disclose Material Facts.
Miller and Starr California Real Estate § 3:40, Agent's Duty to Disclose; in General--Statutory Duty to Disclose.
Miller and Starr California Real Estate § 3:44, Negligence Liability--Duty to Inspect Property Being Sold.
12 Witkin, California Summary 10th Real Property § 465, (S 465) Statutory Development.
12 Witkin, California Summary 10th Real Property § 468, (S 468) Contents of Disclosure Form.

3 Witkin, California Summary 10th Agency and Employment § 66, (S 66)
Legislative Response.

CHAPTER 4. LOST AND UNCLAIMED PROPERTY

ARTICLE 1. LOST MONEY AND GOODS

§ 2080. Duties of finder

Any person who finds a thing lost is not bound to take charge
of it, unless the person is otherwise required to do so by contract
or law, but when the person does take charge of it he or she is
thenceforward a depositary for the owner, with the rights and
obligations of a depositary for hire. Any person or any public or
private entity that finds and takes possession of any money,
goods, things in action, or other personal property, or saves any
domestic animal from harm, neglect, drowning, or starvation,
shall, within a reasonable time, inform the owner, if known, and
make restitution without compensation, except a reasonable
charge for saving and taking care of the property. Any person
who takes possession of a live domestic animal shall provide for
humane treatment of the animal. (Added by Stats.1967, c. 1512,
p. 3601, § 3.   Amended by Stats.1998, c. 752 (S.B.1785), § 9.)

Research References

Miller and Starr California Real Estate § 19:233, Tenant's Personal
Property.
8 Witkin Cal. Proc. 5th Enforcement of Judgment § 337, (S 337)
Disposition of Personal Property.
12 Witkin, California Summary 10th Real Property § 742, (S 742) Storage
of Tenant's Property.
12 Witkin, California Summary 10th Real Property § 749, Nature of
Statute.
13 Witkin, California Summary 10th Personal Property § 39, (S 39) Other
Statutes Dealing With Unclaimed Property.
13 Witkin, California Summary 10th Personal Property § 118, Former
Law and Revision.
13 Witkin, California Summary 10th Personal Property § 119, Duties and
Rights of Finders.

§ 2080.1. Delivery to police or sheriff; affidavit; charges

(a) If the owner is unknown or has not claimed the property,
the person saving or finding the property shall, if the property is
of the value of one hundred dollars ($100) or more, within a
reasonable time turn the property over to the police department
of the city or city and county, if found therein, or to the sheriff's
department of the county if found outside of city limits, and shall
make an affidavit, stating when and where he or she found or

saved the property, particularly describing it. If the property
was saved, the affidavit shall state:

(1) From what and how it was saved.

(2) Whether the owner of the property is known to the affiant.

(3) That the affiant has not secreted, withheld, or disposed of
any part of the property.

(b) The police department or the sheriff's department shall
notify the owner, if his or her identity is reasonably ascertainable,
that it possesses the property and where it may be claimed. The
police department or sheriff's department may require payment
by the owner of a reasonable charge to defray costs of storage
and care of the property. (Added by Stats.1967, c. 1512, p. 3601,
§ 3.   Amended by Stats.1992, c. 138 (A.B.2457), § 1.)

Research References

13 Witkin, California Summary 10th Personal Property § 119, Duties and
Rights of Finders.

§ 2080.2.   Restoration to owner

If the owner appears within 90 days, after receipt of the
property by the police department or sheriff's department,
proves his ownership of the property, and pays all reasonable
charges, the police department or sheriff's department shall
restore the property to him. (Added by Stats.1967, c. 1512, p.
3601, § 3.)

Research References

13 Witkin, California Summary 10th Personal Property § 119, Duties and
Rights of Finders.

§ 2080.3.   Advertisement; payment of cost; vesting of title in finder

(a) If the reported value of the property is two hundred fifty
dollars ($250) or more and no owner appears and proves his or
her ownership of the property within 90 days, the police
department or sheriff's department shall cause notice of the
property to be published at least once in a newspaper of general
circulation. If, after seven days following the first publication of
the notice, no owner appears and proves his or her ownership of
the property and the person who found or saved the property
pays the cost of the publication, the title shall vest in the person
who found or saved the property unless the property was found
in the course of employment by an employee of any public
agency, in which case the property shall be sold at public auction.
Title to the property shall not vest in the person who found or
saved the property or in the successful bidder at the public
auction unless the cost of publication is first paid to the city,
county, or city and county whose police or sheriff's department
caused the notice to be published.

(b) If the reported value of the property is less than two
hundred fifty dollars ($250) and no owner appears and proves his
or her ownership of the property within 90 days, the title shall
vest in the person who found or saved the property, unless the
property was found in the course of employment by an employee
of any public agency, in which case the property shall be sold at
public auction. (Added by Stats.1967, c. 1512, p. 3601, § 3.
Amended by Stats.1970, c. 260, p. 524, § 1; Stats.1971, c. 1254, p.
2465, § 1; Stats.1977, c. 250, p. 1136, § 1; Stats.1992, c. 138
(A.B.2457), § 2.)

Research References

13 Witkin, California Summary 10th Personal Property § 119, Duties and
Rights of Finders.

13 Witkin, California Summary 10th Personal Property § 120, Exceptions and Special Procedures.

§ 2080.4. Local regulations

Notwithstanding the provisions of Section 2080.3 or Section 2080.6, the legislative body of any city, city and county, or county may provide by ordinance for the care, restitution, sale or destruction of unclaimed property in the possession of the police department of such city or city and county or of the sheriff of such county. Any city, city and county, or county adopting such an ordinance shall provide therein (1) that such unclaimed property shall be held by the police department or sheriff for a period of at least three months, and (2) that thereafter such property will be sold at public auction to the highest bidder, with notice of such sale being given by the chief of police or sheriff at least five days before the time fixed therefor by publication once in a newspaper of general circulation published in the county, or that thereafter such property will be transferred to the local government purchasing and stores agency or other similar agency for sale to the public at public auction. If such property is transferred to a county purchasing agent it may be sold in the manner provided by Article 7 (commencing with Section 25500) of Chapter 5 of Part 2 of Division 2 of Title 3 of the Government Code for the sale of surplus personal property. If property is transferred to the local government purchasing and stores agency or other similar agency pursuant to this section, such property shall not be redeemable by the owner or other person entitled to possession. If the local government purchasing and stores agency or other similar agency determines that any such property transferred to it for sale is needed for a public use, such property may be retained by the agency and need not be sold. *(Added by Stats.1967, c. 1512, p. 3601, § 3. Amended by Stats.1969, c. 857, p. 1689, § 1; Stats.1983, c. 878, § 1.)*

Research References

13 Witkin, California Summary 10th Personal Property § 120, Exceptions and Special Procedures.

§ 2080.5. Authority to sell

The police department or sheriff's department may sell such property by public auction, in the manner and upon the notice of sale of personal property under execution, if it is a thing which is commonly the subject of sale, when the owner cannot, with reasonable diligence, be found, or, being found, refuses upon demand to pay the lawful charges provided by Sections 2080 and 2080.1, in the following cases:

(1) When the thing is in danger of perishing, or of losing the greater part of its value; or,

(2) When the lawful charges provided by Sections 2080 and 2080.1 amount to two-thirds of its value. *(Added by Stats.1967, c. 1512, p. 3601, § 3.)*

Research References

13 Witkin, California Summary 10th Personal Property § 120, Exceptions and Special Procedures.

§ 2080.6. Public agency; adoption of regulations

(a) Any public agency may elect to be governed by the provisions of this article with respect to disposition of personal property found or saved on property subject to its jurisdiction, or may adopt reasonable regulations for the care, restitution, sale or destruction of unclaimed property in its possession. Any public agency adopting such regulations shall provide therein (1) that such unclaimed property shall be held by such agency for a period of at least three months, (2) that thereafter such property will be sold at public auction to the highest bidder, and (3) that notice of such sale shall be given by the chief administrative officer of such agency at least five days before the time fixed

therefor by publication once in a newspaper of general circulation published in the county in which such property was found. Any property remaining unsold after being offered at such public auction may be destroyed or otherwise disposed of by the public agency. In a county having a purchasing agent, the purchasing agent may conduct such sale, in which case the provisions of subdivisions (2) and (3) of this section shall not be applicable. Such sale shall be made by the county purchasing agent in the manner provided by Article 7 (commencing with Section 25500) of Chapter 5 of Part 2 of Division 2 of Title 3 of the Government Code for the sale of surplus personal property. If the public agency determines that any such property transferred to it for sale is needed for a public use, such property may be retained by the agency and need not be sold.

(b) "Public agency" as used in this section means any state agency, including the Department of General Services and the Department of Parks and Recreation, any city, county, city and county, special district, or other political subdivision. *(Added by Stats.1967, c. 1512, p. 3601, § 3. Amended by Stats.1969, c. 857, p. 1690, § 2; Stats.1988, c. 1282, § 1.)*

Research References

13 Witkin, California Summary 10th Personal Property § 120, Exceptions and Special Procedures.

§ 2080.7. Abandoned property

The provisions of this article have no application to things which have been intentionally abandoned by their owner. *(Added by Stats.1967, c. 1512, p. 3601, § 3.)*

Research References

13 Witkin, California Summary 10th Personal Property § 120, Exceptions and Special Procedures.

§ 2080.8. Property in possession of Regents of University of California, University of California Police Department, or any state university

(a) The Regents of the University of California and the Trustees of the California State University, as applicable, may provide by resolution or regulation for the care, restitution, sale, or destruction of unclaimed, lost, or abandoned property in the possession of the Regents of the University of California, the University of California Police Department, or any state university.

(b) Any resolution or regulation adopted pursuant to this section shall provide therein (1) that unclaimed, lost, or abandoned property valued at or above three hundred dollars ($300) shall be held by the Regents of the University of California, the University of California Police Department, or the particular state university for a period of at least three months, (2) that thereafter the property will be sold at public auction to the highest bidder, and (3) that notice of that sale shall be given by the Regents of the University of California, the University of California Police Department, or the Trustees of the California State University at least five days before the time therefor by publication once in a newspaper of general circulation published in the county in which the property is held.

(c) The Regents of the University of California or the Trustees of the California State University may dispose of any of that property upon which no bid is made at any sale. *(Added by Stats.1967, c. 1512, p. 3601, § 3. Amended by Stats.1969, c. 857, p. 1690, § 3; Stats.2010, c. 199 (A.B.1890), § 1.)*

Research References

12 Witkin, California Summary 10th Real Property § 749, Nature of Statute.
12 Witkin, California Summary 10th Real Property § 754A, (New)-Scope of Statute.

13 Witkin, California Summary 10th Personal Property § 120, Exceptions and Special Procedures.

§ 2080.10. Public agency temporarily receiving personalty for safekeeping; duties

(a) When a public agency obtains possession of personal property from a person for temporary safekeeping, the public agency shall do all of the following:

(1) Take responsibility for the storage, documentation, and disposition of the property.

(2) Provide the person from whom the property was taken with a receipt and instructions for the retrieval of the property. The receipt and instructions shall either be given to the person from whom the property was taken at the time the public agency obtains the property or immediately mailed, by first-class mail, to the person from whom the property was taken.

(3) If the public agency has knowledge that the person from whom the property was taken is not the owner, the agency shall make reasonable efforts to identify the owner. If the owner is identified, the public agency shall mail, by first-class mail, a receipt and instructions for the retrieval of the property.

(b) The receipt and instructions shall notify the person from whom the property was taken that the property must be claimed within 60 days after the public agency obtains possession or the property will be disposed of in accordance with the disposal provisions of this article. Within 60 days, the person may do one of the following:

(1) Retrieve the property.

(2) Authorize in writing another person to retrieve the property.

(3) Notify the public agency in writing that he or she is unable to retrieve the property, because he or she is in custody, and request the public agency to hold the property. If a person notifies the public agency that he or she is unable to retrieve the property within 60 days, or have an authorized person retrieve the property, the public agency shall hold the property for not longer than 10 additional months.

(c) The public agency shall not be liable for damages caused by any official action performed with due care regarding the disposition of personal property pursuant to this section and the disposal provisions of this article.

(d) As used in this section, "public agency" means any state agency, any city, county, city and county, special district, or other political subdivision. *(Added by Stats.1998, c. 540 (S.B.1707), § 1.)*

Research References

13 Witkin, California Summary 10th Personal Property § 120, Exceptions and Special Procedures.

ARTICLE 2. UNCLAIMED PROPERTY

§ 2081. Storage by bailee until freight and charges paid

When any goods, merchandise, or other property has been received by any railroad or express company, other common carrier, commission merchant, innkeeper, or warehouseman, for transportation or safekeeping, and is not delivered to the owner, consignee, or other authorized person, the carrier, commission merchant, innkeeper, or warehouseman may hold or store the property with some responsible person until the freight and all just and reasonable charges are paid. *(Added by Stats.1951, c. 656, p. 1867, § 2.)*

Research References

12 Witkin, California Summary 10th Real Property § 749, Nature of Statute.
12 Witkin, California Summary 10th Real Property § 754A, (New)-Scope of Statute.

§ 2081.1. Auction; notice

If within 60 days after its receipt no person calls for the property and pays the freight and charges upon it, the carrier, commission merchant, innkeeper, or warehouseman may sell the property, or so much of it as will pay freight and charges, to the highest bidder at public auction, after first causing such notice of sale to be given as is customary in sales of goods by auction at the place where the goods are held or stored. *(Added by Stats.1951, c. 656, p. 1866, § 2.)*

§ 2081.2. Surplus; disposition

If any surplus remains after paying the freight, storage, expenses of sale, and other reasonable charges, the sum remaining shall be paid over to the owner of the property, upon his demand at any time within 60 days after the sale. *(Added by Stats.1951, c. 656, p. 1867, § 2.)*

§ 2081.3. Surplus; failure of owner to demand; payment to county treasury

If the owner or his agent fails to demand the surplus within 60 days after the sale, it shall be paid into the county treasury, subject to the order of the owner. *(Added by Stats.1951, c. 656, p. 1867, § 2.)*

§ 2081.4. Termination of bailee's responsibility; liability of warehousemen

After the storage of the property the responsibility of the carrier, commission merchant, innkeeper, or warehouseman ceases. The person with whom the property is stored is not liable for loss or damage on its account unless the loss or damage results from his negligence or want of proper care. *(Added by Stats.1951, c. 656, p. 1868, § 2.)*

§ 2081.5. Advances; effect upon sale of unclaimed property

When any commission merchant or warehouseman receives produce, merchandise, or other property on consignment and makes advances upon it, either to the owner or for freight and charges, if the advances are not paid to him within 60 days from the date made, he may cause the produce, merchandise, or property on which the advances were made, to be advertised and sold pursuant to this article. *(Added by Stats.1951, c. 656, p. 1868, § 2.)*

§ 2081.6. Applicable law

All proceedings pursuant to this article are governed entirely by its provisions and are not controlled or affected by Article 2, Chapter 3, Title 7, Part 4, Division 3 of this code.[1] *(Added by Stats.1951, c. 656, p. 1868, § 2.)*

[1] Civil Code § 2114 et seq.

ARTICLE 3. FEES OF OFFICERS

Section
2082. Amount of fees; payment.

§ 2082. Amount of fees; payment

The fees of officers under this chapter are the same allowed by law for similar services, and shall be paid by the taker up or finder and recovered from the owner. *(Added by Stats.1951, c. 656, p. 1868, § 2.)*

Title 7

CARRIAGE

CHAPTER 1. CARRIAGE IN GENERAL

Section
2085. Contract of carriage defined.
2086. Kinds of carriage.
2087. Marine and inland carriers defined.
2088. Marine carriers governed by federal law.
2089. Gratuitous carriers; obligations.
2090. Gratuitous carriers; obligations after commencing to carry.

§ 2085. Contract of carriage defined

The contract of carriage is a contract for the conveyance of property, persons, or messages, from one place to another. *(Enacted in 1872.)*

§ 2086. Kinds of carriage

Carriage is either:

1. Inland; or,

2. Marine. *(Enacted in 1872.)*

§ 2087. Marine and inland carriers defined

Carriers upon the ocean and upon arms of the sea are marine carriers. All others are inland carriers. *(Enacted in 1872.)*

§ 2088. Marine carriers governed by federal law

Rights and duties peculiar to carriers by sea are defined by Acts of Congress. *(Enacted in 1872.)*

§ 2089. Gratuitous carriers; obligations

Carriers without reward are subject to the same rules as employÉ's[1] without reward, except so far as is otherwise provided by this Title. *(Enacted in 1872.)*

   1 So in chaptered copy.

§ 2090. Gratuitous carriers; obligations after commencing to carry

A carrier without reward, who has begun to perform his undertaking, must complete it in like manner as if he had received a reward, unless he restores the person or thing carried to as favorable a position as before he commenced the carriage. *(Enacted in 1872.)*

CHAPTER 2. CARRIAGE OF PERSONS

ARTICLE 1. GRATUITOUS CARRIAGE OF PERSONS

Section
2096. Degree of care.

§ 2096. Degree of care

A carrier of persons without reward must use ordinary care and diligence for their safe carriage. *(Enacted in 1872.)*

Research References

6 Witkin, California Summary 10th Torts § 923, in General.

ARTICLE 2. CARRIAGE FOR REWARD

Section
2100. Care, skill and equipment.
2101. Provision of safe vehicles.
2102. Overcrowding or overloading.
2103. Passengers' accommodations, treatment and attention.
2104. Speed; delays; deviations from route.

§ 2100. Care, skill and equipment

A carrier of persons for reward must use the utmost care and diligence for their safe carriage, must provide everything necessary for that purpose, and must exercise to that end a reasonable degree of skill. *(Enacted in 1872.)*

Research References

6 Witkin, California Summary 10th Torts § 923, in General.
6 Witkin, California Summary 10th Torts § 925, Private Carrier for Hire.
6 Witkin, California Summary 10th Torts § 930, (S 930) Occurrence or Allegation of Prior Assault.
6 Witkin, California Summary 10th Torts § 931, (S 931) No Occurrence or Allegation of Prior Assault.

§ 2101. Provision of safe vehicles

A carrier of persons for reward is bound to provide vehicles safe and fit for the purposes to which they are put, and is not excused for default in this respect by any degree of care. *(Enacted in 1872.)*

§ 2102. Overcrowding or overloading

A carrier of persons for reward must not overcrowd or overload his vehicle. *(Enacted in 1872.)*

§ 2103. Passengers' accommodations, treatment and attention

A carrier of persons for reward must give to passengers all such accommodations as are usual and reasonable, and must treat them with civility, and give them a reasonable degree of attention. *(Enacted in 1872.)*

Research References

7 Witkin, California Summary 10th Constitutional Law § 11, Aviation.

§ 2104. Speed; delays; deviations from route

A carrier of persons for reward must travel at a reasonable rate of speed, and without any unreasonable delay, or deviation from his proper route. *(Enacted in 1872.)*

CHAPTER 3. CARRIAGE OF PROPERTY

ARTICLE 1. GENERAL DEFINITIONS

Section
2110. Freight, freightage, consignor, and consignee defined.

§ 2110. Freight, freightage, consignor, and consignee defined

FREIGHT, CONSIGNOR, ETC., WHAT. Property carried is called freight; the reward, if any, to be paid for its carriage is called freightage; the person who delivers the freight to the carrier is called the consignor; and the person to whom it is to be delivered is called the consignee. *(Enacted in 1872.)*

ARTICLE 2. OBLIGATIONS OF THE CARRIER

Section
2114. Degree of care and diligence required.
2115. Obedience to directions.
2118. Place and manner of delivery.
2119. Place of delivery.
2120. Notice to consignee of arrival.
2121. Consignee's failure to accept and remove freight, storage.

§ 2114. Degree of care and diligence required

A carrier of property for reward must use at least ordinary care and diligence in the performance of all his duties. A carrier without reward must use at least slight care and diligence. *(Enacted in 1872.)*

§ 2115. Obedience to directions

Subject to Section 7303 of the Uniform Commercial Code, a carrier must comply with the directions of the consignor or consignee to the same extent that an employee is bound to comply with those of his employer. *(Enacted in 1872. Amended by Stats.1963, c. 819, p. 1999, § 8, eff. Jan. 1, 1965.)*

Research References

13 Witkin, California Summary 10th Personal Property § 178, California Law.

§ 2118. Place and manner of delivery

Subject to Section 7303 of the Uniform Commercial Code, a carrier of property must deliver it to the consignee, at the place to which it is addressed, in the manner usual at that place. *(Enacted in 1872. Amended by Stats.1963, c. 819, p. 1999, § 10, eff. Jan. 1, 1965.)*

Research References

13 Witkin, California Summary 10th Personal Property § 178, California Law.

§ 2119. Place of delivery

If there is no usage to the contrary at the place of delivery, freight must be delivered as follows:

1. If carried upon a railway owned or managed by the carrier, it may be delivered at the station nearest to the place to which it is addressed;

2. If carried by sea from a foreign country, it may be delivered at the wharf where the ship moors, within a reasonable distance from the place of address; or, if there is no wharf, on board a lighter alongside the ship; or,

3. Subject to Section 7303 of the Uniform Commercial Code, in other cases, it must be delivered to the consignee or his agent, personally, if either can, with reasonable diligence, be found. *(Enacted in 1872. Amended by Stats.1963, c. 819, p. 1999, § 11, eff. Jan. 1, 1965.)*

Research References

13 Witkin, California Summary 10th Personal Property § 178, California Law.

§ 2120. Notice to consignee of arrival

If, for any reason, a carrier does not deliver freight to the consignee or his agent personally, he must give notice to the consignee of its arrival, and keep the same in safety, upon his responsibility as a warehouseman, until the consignee has had a reasonable time to remove it. If the place of residence or business of the consignee be unknown to the carrier, he may give the notice by letter dropped in the nearest Post Office. *(Enacted in 1872. Amended by Code Am.1873–74, c. 612, p. 247, § 213.)*

§ 2121. Consignee's failure to accept and remove freight, storage

If a consignee does not accept and remove freight within a reasonable time after the carrier has fulfilled his obligation to deliver, or duly offered to fulfill the same, the carrier may exonerate himself from further liability by placing the freight in a suitable warehouse, on storage, on account of the consignee, and giving notice thereof to him. *(Enacted in 1872. Amended by Code Am.1873–74, c. 612, p. 248, § 214.)*

ARTICLE 4. FREIGHTAGE

Section
2136. Time for payment.
2137. Liability of consignor.
2138. Liability of consignee.
2139. Natural increase of freight.
2140. Apportionment by bill of lading or other contract.
2141. Apportionment; part of freight not delivered.
2142. Apportionment according to distance.
2143. Freight carried further or more expeditiously than agreed upon; compensation; delivery.
2144. Carrier's lien.

§ 2136. Time for payment

A carrier may require his freightage to be paid upon his receiving the freight; but if he does not demand it then, he cannot until he is ready to deliver the freight to the consignee. *(Enacted in 1872.)*

§ 2137. Liability of consignor

The consignor of freight is presumed to be liable for the freightage, but if the contract between him and the carrier provides that the consignee shall pay it, and the carrier allows the consignee to take the freight, he cannot afterwards recover the freightage from the consignor. *(Enacted in 1872.)*

§ 2138. Liability of consignee

The consignee of freight is liable for the freightage, if he accepts the freight with notice of the intention of the consignor that he should pay it. *(Enacted in 1872.)*

§ 2139. Natural increase of freight

No freightage can be charged upon the natural increase of freight. *(Enacted in 1872.)*

§ 2140. Apportionment by bill of lading or other contract

If freightage is apportioned by a bill of lading or other contract made between a consignor and carrier, the carrier is entitled to payment, according to the apportionment, for so much as he delivers. *(Enacted in 1872.)*

§ 2141. Apportionment; part of freight not delivered

If a part of the freight is accepted by a consignee, without a specific objection that the rest is not delivered, the freightage must be apportioned and paid as to that part, though not apportioned in the original contract. *(Enacted in 1872.)*

§ 2142. Apportionment according to distance

If a consignee voluntarily receives freight at a place short of the one appointed for delivery, the carrier is entitled to a just proportion of the freightage, according to distance. If the carrier, being ready and willing, offers to complete the transit, he is entitled to the full freightage. If he does not thus offer completion, and the consignee receives the freight only from necessity, the carrier is not entitled to any freightage. *(Enacted in 1872.)*

§ 2143. Freight carried further or more expeditiously than agreed upon; compensation; delivery

If freight is carried further, or more expeditiously, than was agreed upon by the parties, the carrier is not entitled to additional compensation, and cannot refuse to deliver it, on the demand of the consignee, at the place and time of its arrival. *(Enacted in 1872.)*

§ 2144. Carrier's lien

A carrier has a lien for (a) freightage and for services rendered at request of shipper or consignee in and about the transportation of the property, (b) care and preservation of the property, (c) money advanced at request of shipper or consignee to discharge a prior lien, and (d), subject to the limitations specified in Section 3051.6, any fines, penalties, costs, expenses, and interest arising from the provision of false or erroneous certifications of gross cargo weight as required by Section 508 of Title 49 of the United States Code. The carrier's rights to this lien are regulated by the title on liens. *(Enacted in 1872. Amended by Stats.1909, c. 663, p. 1000, § 1; Stats.1993, c. 757 (S.B.619), § 1.)*

CHAPTER 4. CARRIAGE OF MESSAGES

Section
2161. Carrier of messages; delivery; toll or ferriage; compensation for messenger.
2162. Care and diligence in transmission and delivery.

§ 2161. Carrier of messages; delivery; toll or ferriage; compensation for messenger

A carrier of messages for reward, other than by telegraph or telephone, must deliver them at the place to which they are addressed, or to the person for whom they are intended. Such carrier, by telegraph or telephone, must deliver them at such place and to such person, *provided* the place of address, or the person for whom they are intended, is within a distance of two miles from the main office of the carrier in the city or town to which the messages are transmitted, and the carrier is not required, in making the delivery, to pay on his route toll or ferriage; but for any distance beyond one mile from such office, compensation may be charged for a messenger employed by the carrier. *(Enacted in 1872. Amended by Code Am.1873–74, c. 612, p. 248, § 216; Stats.1905, c. 469, p. 627, § 1.)*

§ 2162. Care and diligence in transmission and delivery

A carrier of messages for reward, must use great care and diligence in the transmission and delivery of messages. *(Enacted in 1872. Amended by Code Am.1873–74, c. 612, p. 249, § 217.)*

CHAPTER 5. COMMON CARRIERS

ARTICLE 1. COMMON CARRIERS IN GENERAL

§ 2168. Common carrier defined

Every one who offers to the public to carry persons, property, or messages, excepting only telegraphic messages, is a common carrier of whatever he thus offers to carry. *(Enacted in 1872. Amended by Code Am.1873–74, c. 612, p. 249, § 218.)*

Research References

Rutter, Cal. Practice Guide: Personal Injury Ch. 3-D, D. Mitigating Factors in Reduction of Damages.

13 Witkin, California Summary 10th Personal Property § 177, Common and Private Carriers.

8 Witkin, California Summary 10th Constitutional Law § 1094, (S 1094) in General.

§ 2169. Obligation to accept freight

A common carrier must, if able to do so, accept and carry whatever is offered to him, at a reasonable time and place, of a kind that he undertakes or is accustomed to carry. *(Enacted in 1872.)*

§ 2170. Preferences prohibited; schedules of starting times; penalty

A common carrier must not give preference in time, price, or otherwise, to one person over another. Every common carrier of passengers by railroad, or by vessel plying upon waters lying wholly within this State, shall establish a schedule time for the starting of trains or vessel from their respective stations or wharves, of which public notice shall be given, and shall, weather permitting, except in case of accident or detention caused by connecting lines, start their said trains or vessel at or within ten minutes after the schedule time so established and notice given, under a penalty of two hundred and fifty dollars for each neglect so to do, to be recovered by action before any Court of competent jurisdiction, upon complaint filed by the District Attorney of the county in the name of the people, and paid into the Common School Fund of the said county. *(Enacted in 1872. Amended by Code Am.1880, c. 37, p. 1, § 1.)*

Research References

13 Witkin, California Summary 10th Personal Property § 177, Common and Private Carriers.

§ 2171. Preferences to state and United States

A common carrier must always give a preference in time, and may give a preference in price, to the United States and to this State. *(Enacted in 1872.)*

§ 2172. Starting on time; permissible delays

A common carrier must start at such time and place as he announces to the public, unless detained by accident or the elements, or in order to connect with carriers on other lines of travel. *(Enacted in 1872. Amended by Code Am.1873–74, c. 612, p. 249, § 219.)*

§ 2173. Compensation

A common carrier is entitled to a reasonable compensation and no more, which he may require to be paid in advance. If payment thereof is refused, he may refuse to carry. *(Enacted in 1872.)*

§ 2174. Limitation of obligations

The obligations of a common carrier cannot be limited by general notice on his part, but may be limited by special contract. *(Enacted in 1872. Amended by Code Am.1873–74, c. 612, p. 249, § 220.)*

Research References

1 Witkin Cal. Summ. 10th Contracts § 678, Regulated Public Utility.
13 Witkin, California Summary 10th Personal Property § 183, Contractual and Statutory Limitations.

§ 2175. Invalid agreements of exoneration

A common carrier cannot be exonerated, by any agreement made in anticipation thereof, from liability for the gross negligence, fraud, or willful wrong of himself or his servants. *(Enacted in 1872.)*

Research References

13 Witkin, California Summary 10th Personal Property § 180, (S 180) Passenger Using Free Pass.
13 Witkin, California Summary 10th Personal Property § 183, Contractual and Statutory Limitations.

§ 2176. Limitation of liability by contract

A passenger, consignor, or consignee, by accepting a ticket, bill of lading, or written contract for carriage, with a knowledge of its terms, assents to the rate of hire, the time, place, and manner of delivery therein stated; and also to the limitation stated therein upon the amount of the carrier's liability in case property carried in packages, trunks, or boxes, is lost or injured, when the value of such property is not named; and also to the limitation stated therein to the carrier's liability for loss or injury to live animals carried. But his assent to any other modification of the carrier's obligations contained in such instrument can be manifested only by his signature to the same. *(Enacted in 1872. Amended by Code Am.1873–74, c. 612, p. 249, § 221.)*

Research References

1 Witkin Cal. Summ. 10th Contracts § 120, (S 120) Illustrations.
13 Witkin, California Summary 10th Personal Property § 183, Contractual and Statutory Limitations.

§ 2177. Valuable letters; nonliability for loss unless informed of value

A common carrier is not responsible for loss or miscarriage of a letter, or package having the form of a letter, containing money or notes, bills of exchange, or other papers of value, unless he be informed at the time of its receipt of the value of its contents. *(Added by Code Am.1873–74, c. 612, p. 250, § 222.)*

§ 2178. Baggage; limitation of railroad's liability

A common carrier of property by steam or electric railroad which accepts for transportation, storage, handling or safe-keeping, as a part of or in connection with passenger transportation, property carried in trunks, valises, suit cases, traveling bags, boxes, bundles or packages, shall not be liable, in the event of loss of or injury to the same, for more than one hundred dollars for each trunk and contents, nor more than fifty dollars for each valise and contents, or suit case and contents, or traveling bag and contents, nor more than ten dollars for each box, bundle or package and contents, unless the carrier shall have consented in writing to assume a greater liability. The term "common carrier" as used in this section shall include sleeping car companies. *(Added by Stats.1931, c. 614, p. 1323, § 1.)*

Research References

13 Witkin, California Summary 10th Personal Property § 183, Contractual and Statutory Limitations.

ARTICLE 2. COMMON CARRIERS OF PERSONS

Section

§ 2180. Baggage; obligation to carry; charges

A common carrier of persons, unless his vehicle is fitted for the reception of persons exclusively, must receive and carry a reasonable amount of baggage for each passenger without charge, except for an excess of weight over one hundred pounds to a passenger; if such carrier is a proprietor of a stage line, he need not receive and carry for each passenger by such stage line, without charge, more than sixty pounds of baggage. *(Enacted in 1872. Amended by Code Am.1877–78, c. 159, p. 87, § 1; Stats.1905, c. 455, p. 615, § 1.)*

§ 2181. Luggage defined; bicycles

Luggage may consist of whatever the passenger takes with him for his personal use and convenience, according to the habits or wants of the particular class to which he belongs, either with reference to the important necessities or to the ultimate purposes of his journey. Luggage within the meaning of this section shall include the samples, case, wares, appliances and catalogs of commercial travelers or their employers, used by them for the purpose of transacting their business and carried with them solely for that purpose, when securely packed and locked in substantial trunks or sample cases of convenient shape and weight for handling. No crate cover or other protection shall be required for any bicycle carried as luggage, but no passenger shall be entitled to carry as luggage more than one bicycle. *(Enacted in 1872. Amended by Code Am.1897, c. 4, p. 4, § 1; Stats.1911, c. 363, p. 638, § 1.)*

§ 2182. Liability for luggage

The liability of a carrier for luggage received by him with a passenger is the same as that of a common carrier of property. *(Enacted in 1872.)*

§ 2183. Luggage; delivery; checking; risk

A common carrier must deliver every passenger's luggage, whether within the prescribed weight or not, immediately upon the arrival of the passenger at his destination; and, unless the vehicle would be overcrowded or overloaded thereby, must carry it on the same vehicle by which he carries the passenger to whom it belonged, except that where luggage is transported by rail, it must be checked and carried in a regular baggage car; and whenever passengers neglect or refuse to have their luggage so checked and transported, it is carried at their risk. *(Enacted in 1872. Amended by Code Am.1873–74, c. 612, p. 250, § 223.)*

§ 2184. Obligation to provide vehicles; exceptions

A common carrier of persons must provide a sufficient number of vehicles to accommodate all the passengers who can be reasonably expected to require carriage at any one time. This section shall not apply, however, to any passenger stage corporation or street railroad corporation, as defined in Sections 226 and 232, respectively, of the Public Utilities Code, which is subject to the jurisdiction of the Public Utilities Commission. *(Enacted in 1872. Amended by Stats.1957, c. 511, p. 1548, § 1.)*

§ 2185. Obligation to provide seats; exceptions

A common carrier of persons must provide every passenger with a seat. He must not overload his vehicle by receiving and carrying more passengers than its rated capacity allows. This section shall not apply, however, to any city, county, city and county that operates a transportation system, or to any passenger stage corporation or street railroad corporation, as defined in Sections 226 and 232, respectively, of the Public Utilities Code, which is subject to the jurisdiction of the Public Utilities Commission. *(Enacted in 1872. Amended by Stats.1957, c. 511, p. 1549, § 2; Stats.1963, c. 1409, p. 2947, § 1.)*

§ 2186. Rules for conduct of business

A common carrier of persons may make rules for the conduct of his business, and may require passengers to conform to them, if they are lawful, public, uniform in their application, and reasonable. *(Enacted in 1872.)*

§ 2187. Payment of fare

A common carrier may demand the fare of passengers, either at starting or at any subsequent time. *(Enacted in 1872.)*

§ 2188. Ejection of passengers; method; place

A passenger, who refuses to pay his fare, or to conform to any lawful regulation of the carrier, may be ejected from the vehicle by the carrier. But this must be done with as little violence as possible, and within a short distance from some dwelling house. *(Enacted in 1872.)*

§ 2190. Fare not payable after ejection

After having ejected a passenger, a carrier has no right to require the payment of any part of his fare. *(Enacted in 1872.)*

§ 2191. Lien on luggage

A common carrier has a lien upon the luggage of a passenger for the payment of such fare as he is entitled to from him. This lien is regulated by the Title on Liens. *(Enacted in 1872.)*

ARTICLE 3. COMMON CARRIERS OF PROPERTY

§ 2194. Inland carrier's liability for loss; exceptions

Unless the consignor accompanies the freight and retains exclusive control thereof, an inland common carrier of property is liable, from the time that he accepts until he relieves himself from liability pursuant to Sections 2118 to 2122, for the loss or injury thereof from any cause whatever, except:

1. An inherent defect, vice, or weakness, or a spontaneous action, of the property itself;

2. The act of a public enemy of the United States, or of this State;

3. The act of the law; or,

4. Any irresistible superhuman cause. *(Enacted in 1872.)*

Research References

13 Witkin, California Summary 10th Personal Property § 178, California Law.

§ 2195. Inland carrier's liability for negligence

A common carrier is liable, even in the cases excepted by the last section, if his want of ordinary care exposes the property to the cause of the loss. *(Enacted in 1872. Amended by Stats.1905, c. 455, p. 615, § 2.)*

Research References

13 Witkin, California Summary 10th Personal Property § 178, California Law.

§ 2196. Liability for delay

A common carrier is liable for delay only when it is caused by his want of ordinary care and diligence. *(Enacted in 1872. Amended by Code Am.1873–74, c. 612, p. 251, § 224.)*

§ 2197. Liability for storage or equipment rental charges of consignor and consignee causing delay

(a) Liability for storage or equipment rental charges assessed against a motor carrier by a railroad or steamship company shall be as follows if the charges arise out of a delay caused by the consignor or consignee of the freight:

(1) The consignor is liable to the motor carrier for the charges if the consignor caused the delay.

(2) The consignee is liable to the motor carrier for the charges if the consignee caused the delay.

(b) Nothing in this section shall affect the rights, duties, and obligations between a railroad or steamship company and a motor carrier. *(Added by Stats.1988, c. 937, § 1.)*

§ 2197.5. Liability of consignee on prepaid shipments for delay caused by consignor or consignee

(a) In addition to the liability established by Section 2197, the consignee is liable to the motor carrier for the charges if the freight is shipped prepaid and the delay was caused by either the consignor or the consignee.

(b) Nothing in this section shall affect the rights, duties, and obligations between a railroad or steamship company and a motor carrier. *(Added by Stats.1988, c. 937, § 2. Amended by Stats.1992, c. 466 (A.B.2387), § 1.)*

§ 2200. Valuables; limitation of liability; notice of nature of freight; declaration of value

A common carrier of gold, silver, platina, or precious stones, or of imitations thereof, in a manufactured or unmanufactured state; of timepieces of any description; of negotiable paper or other valuable writings; of pictures, glass, or chinaware; of statuary, silk, or laces; or of plated ware of any kind, is not liable for more than fifty dollars upon the loss or injury of any one package of such articles, unless he has notice, upon his receipt thereof, by mark upon the package or otherwise, of the nature of the freight; nor is such carrier liable upon any package carried for more than the value of the articles named in the receipt or the bill of lading. *(Enacted in 1872. Amended by Code Am.1873–74, c. 612, p. 251, § 225.)*

Research References

13 Witkin, California Summary 10th Personal Property § 184, When Limitation is Unenforceable.

§ 2203. Services other than carriage and delivery

In respect to any service rendered by a common carrier about freight, other than its carriage and delivery, his rights and obligations are defined by the Titles on Deposit and Service. *(Enacted in 1872.)*

§ 2204. Perishable property; sale for freightage

If, from any cause other than want of ordinary care and diligence on his part, a common carrier is unable to deliver perishable property transported by him, and collect his charges thereon, he may cause the property to be sold in open market to satisfy his lien for freightage. *(Added Code Am.1873–74, c. 612, p. 251, § 226.)*

§ 2205. Stagelines, etc.; limitation on liability for damage to baggage

The liability of any stageline, transfer company, or other common carriers operating over the public highways for the loss of or for damage to any baggage shall not exceed the sum of five hundred dollars ($500) for each trunk and its contents; two hundred fifty dollars ($250) for each valise, suitcase or traveling bag and its contents; or two hundred fifty dollars ($250) for each box, bundle, or package and its contents, unless a higher valuation is declared at the time of delivery of such baggage to the carrier and assented thereto in writing by such carrier.

All baggage presented to the carrier for checking shall be appropriately tagged by the owner with his name and address. *(Added Stats.1925, c. 146, p. 299, § 1. Amended by Stats.1965, c. 104, p. 1045, § 1; Stats.1969, c. 982, p. 1950, § 1; Stats.1971, c. 1653, p. 3558, § 1.)*

Research References

13 Witkin, California Summary 10th Personal Property § 183, Contractual and Statutory Limitations.

13 Witkin, California Summary 10th Personal Property § 184, When Limitation is Unenforceable.

ARTICLE 4.   COMMON CARRIERS OF MESSAGES

Section
2207.   Telegraphic messages; order of transmission.
2208.   Messages other than telegraphic; order of transmission.
2209.   Damages for refusing or postponing messages.

§ 2207.   Telegraphic messages; order of transmission

A carrier of messages by telegraph must, if it is practicable, transmit every such message immediately upon its receipt. But if this is not practicable, and several messages accumulate upon his hands, he must transmit them in the following order:

1.   Messages from public agents of the United States or of this State, on public business;

2.   Messages intended in good faith for immediate publication in newspapers, and not for any secret use;

3.   Messages giving information relating to the sickness or death of any person;

4.   Other messages in the order in which they were received. *(Enacted in 1872.)*

§ 2208.   Messages other than telegraphic; order of transmission

A common carrier of messages, otherwise than by telegraph, must transmit messages in the order in which he receives them, except messages from agents of the United States or of this State, on public business, to which he must always give priority. But he may fix upon certain times for the simultaneous transmission of messages previously received. *(Enacted in 1872.)*

§ 2209.   Damages for refusing or postponing messages

Every person whose message is refused or postponed, contrary to the provisions of this Chapter, is entitled to recover from the carrier his actual damages, and fifty dollars in addition thereto. *(Enacted in 1872.)*

ARTICLE 5.   SPACE FLIGHT LIABILITY AND IMMUNITY

Section
2210.   Definitions.
2211.   Warning statement; immunity.
2212.   Limitation of liability for injuries arising out of space flight activities; conditions.

§ 2210.   Definitions

For purposes of this article:

(a) "Participant" means a space flight participant as defined in Section 50902 of Title 51 of the United States Code.

(b) "Participant injury" means a bodily injury, including death, emotional injury, or property damage, sustained by the participant.

(c) "Space flight activities" means launch services or reentry services as defined in Section 50902 of Title 51 of the United States Code.

(d) "Space flight entity" means any public or private entity that holds, either directly or through a corporate subsidiary or parent, a license, permit, or other authorization issued by the United States Federal Aviation Administration pursuant to the federal Commercial Space Launch Amendments Act of 2004 (51

U.S.C. Sec. 50905 et seq.), including, but not limited to, a safety approval and a payload determination. *(Added by Stats.2012, c. 416 (A.B.2243), § 2.)*

§ 2211. Warning statement; immunity

(a) A space flight entity providing space flight activities to a participant shall have each participant sign a warning statement that shall contain, at a minimum, and in addition to any language required by federal law, the following notice:

"WARNING AND ACKNOWLEDGMENT: I understand and acknowledge that, under California law, there is limited civil liability for bodily injury, including death, emotional injury, or property damage, sustained by a participant as a result of the inherent risks associated with space flight activities provided by a space flight entity. I have given my informed consent to participate in space flight activities after receiving a description of the inherent risks associated with space flight activities, as required by federal law pursuant to Section 50905 of Title 51 of the United States Code and Section 460.45 of Title 14 of the Code of Federal Regulations. The consent that I have given acknowledges that the inherent risks associated with space flight activities include, but are not limited to, risk of bodily injury, including death, emotional injury, and property damage. I understand and acknowledge that I am participating in space flight activities at my own risk. I have been given the opportunity to consult with an attorney before signing this statement."

(b) Failure to comply with the requirements provided in this section shall prevent a space flight entity from invoking the privileges of immunity provided by Section 2212. *(Added by Stats.2012, c. 416 (A.B.2243), § 2.)*

§ 2212. Limitation of liability for injuries arising out of space flight activities; conditions

(a) Except as provided in subdivision (c), a space flight entity shall not be liable for participant injury arising out of space flight activities if both of the following apply:

(1) The participant has been informed of the risks associated with space flight activities as required by federal law and Section 2211.

(2) The participant has given his or her informed consent that he or she is voluntarily participating in space flight activities after having been informed of the risks associated with those activities, as required by federal law and Section 2211.

(b) If informed consent is given pursuant to subdivision (a), a participant, his or her representative, including the heirs, administrators, executors, assignees, next of kin, and estate of the participant, or any person who attempts to bring a claim on behalf of the participant for a participant injury, shall not be authorized to maintain an action against, or recover from, a space flight entity for a participant injury that resulted from the risks associated with space flight activities, except as provided in subdivision (c).

(c) Nothing in this section shall prevent or limit the liability of a space flight entity that does any of the following:

(1) Commits an act or omission that constitutes gross negligence or willful or wanton disregard for the safety of the participant, and that act or omission proximately causes a participant injury.

(2) Intentionally causes a participant injury.

(3) Has actual knowledge or reasonably should have known of a dangerous condition on the land or in the facilities or equipment used in space flight activities and the dangerous condition proximately causes injury, damage, or death to the participant.

(d) Any limitation on legal liability afforded by this section to a space flight entity is in addition to any other limitations of legal liability otherwise provided by law.

(e) Nothing in this section shall be construed to limit the liability of a manufacturer of a part or component used in space flight activities if a defective part or component proximately causes an injury to the participant. *(Added by Stats.2012, c. 416 (A.B.2243), § 2.)*

Title 8

INVOLUNTARY TRUSTS

§ 2223. Involuntary trustee

One who wrongfully detains a thing is an involuntary trustee thereof, for the benefit of the owner. *(Added by Stats.1986, c. 820, § 8, eff. Sept. 15, 1986, operative July 1, 1987.)*

Law Revision Commission Comments

Section 2223 continues former Section 2223 without change. See also Prob. Code § 15003 (constructive and resulting trusts unaffected by new Trust Law). [18 Cal. L.Rev.Comm. Reports 501 (1986)].

Research References

Miller and Starr California Real Estate § 34:114, Constructive Trusts.
Miller and Starr California Real Estate § 34:115, Requirements to Enforce the Trust.
13 Witkin, California Summary 10th Trusts § 23, Other Provisions Governing Trusts.
13 Witkin, California Summary 10th Trusts § 319, Nature of Constructive Trust.
13 Witkin, California Summary 10th Trusts § 323, (S 323) Where No Benefit is Obtained.

§ 2224. Wrongful act

One who gains a thing by fraud, accident, mistake, undue influence, the violation of a trust, or other wrongful act, is, unless he or she has some other and better right thereto, an involuntary trustee of the thing gained, for the benefit of the person who would otherwise have had it. *(Added by Stats.1986, c. 820, § 8, eff. Sept. 15, 1986, operative July 1, 1987.)*

Law Revision Commission Comments

Section 2224 continues former Section 2224 without change. See also Prob. Code § 15003 (constructive and resulting trusts unaffected by new Trust Law). [18 Cal.L.Rev.Comm. Reports 501 (1986)].

Research References

Rutter, Cal. Practice Guide: Enforcing Judgments/Debts Ch. 3-C, C. Prelawsuit Considerations.
Miller and Starr California Real Estate § 10:31, Other Situations.
Miller and Starr California Real Estate § 34:114, Constructive Trusts.
Miller and Starr California Real Estate § 34:115, Requirements to Enforce the Trust.
13 Witkin, California Summary 10th Trusts § 319, Nature of Constructive Trust.

13 Witkin, California Summary 10th Trusts § 323, (S 323) Where No Benefit is Obtained.

§ 2225. Definitions; proceeds from sale of story of felony; involuntary trust; action to recover proceeds; transfer to Controller; allocation to Restitution Fund; violations; remedies cumulative; limitations of actions

(a) As used in this section:

(1) "Convicted felon" means any person convicted of a felony, or found not guilty by reason of insanity of a felony committed in California, either by a court or jury trial or by entry of a plea in court.

(2) "Felony" means a felony defined by any California or United States statute.

(3)(A) "Representative of the felon" means any person or entity receiving proceeds or profits by designation of that felon, on behalf of that felon, or in the stead of that felon, whether by the felon's designation or by operation of law.

(B) "Profiteer of the felony" means any person who sells or transfers for profit any memorabilia or other property or thing of the felon, the value of which is enhanced by the notoriety gained from the commission of the felony for which the felon was convicted. This subparagraph shall not apply to any media entity reporting on the felon's story or on the sale of the materials, memorabilia, or other property or thing of the felon. Nor shall it apply to the sale of the materials, as the term is defined in paragraph (6), where the seller is exercising his or her first amendment rights. This subparagraph also shall not apply to the sale or transfer by a profiteer of any other expressive work protected by the First Amendment unless the sale or transfer is primarily for a commercial or speculative purpose.

(4)(A) "Beneficiary" means a person who, under applicable law, other than the provisions of this section, has or had a right to recover damages from the convicted felon for physical, mental, or emotional injury, or pecuniary loss proximately caused by the convicted felon as a result of the crime for which the felon was convicted.

(B) If a beneficiary described in subparagraph (A) has died, "beneficiary" also includes a person or estate entitled to recover damages pursuant to Chapter 4 (commencing with Section 377.10) of Title 3 of Part 2 of the Code of Civil Procedure.

(C) If a person has died and the death was proximately caused by the convicted felon as a result of the crime for which the felon was convicted, "beneficiary" also includes a person described in Section 377.60 of the Code of Civil Procedure and any beneficiary of a will of the decedent who had a right under that will to receive more than 25 percent of the value of the estate of the decedent.

(5) "Beneficiary's interest" means that portion of the proceeds or profits necessary to pay the following:

(A) In the case of a beneficiary described in subparagraph (A) or (B) of paragraph (4), those damages that, under applicable law, other than the provisions of this section, the beneficiary has or had a right to recover from the convicted felon for injuries proximately caused by the convicted felon as a result of the crime for which the felon was convicted.

(B) In the case of a beneficiary described in subparagraph (C) of paragraph (4), those damages that, under all the circumstances of the case, may be just.

(C) A beneficiary's interest shall be reduced by the following amount:

(i) Money paid to the beneficiary from the Restitution Fund because of the crime for which the felon was convicted.

(ii) Money paid to the beneficiary by the convicted felon because of a requirement of restitution imposed by a court in connection with the crime for which the felon was convicted.

(iii) Money paid to the beneficiary because of a judgment against the convicted felon based upon the crime for which the felon was convicted.

(D) In the case of an unsatisfied existing judgment or order of restitution against the convicted felon and in favor of a beneficiary, any money paid to the beneficiary pursuant to this section shall be applied to reduce the amount of the unsatisfied judgment or order.

(6) "Materials" means books, magazine or newspaper articles, movies, films, videotapes, sound recordings, interviews or appearances on television and radio stations, and live presentations of any kind.

(7) "Story" means a depiction, portrayal, or reenactment of a felony and shall not be taken to mean a passing mention of the felony, as in a footnote or bibliography.

(8) "Sale" includes lease, license, or any other transfer or alienation taking place in California or elsewhere.

(9) "Proceeds" means all fees, royalties, real property, or other consideration of any and every kind or nature received by or owing to a felon or his or her representatives for the preparation for the purpose of sale of materials, for the sale of the rights to materials, or the sale or distribution by the convicted felon of materials whether earned, accrued, or paid before or after the conviction. It includes any interest, earnings, or accretions upon proceeds, and any property received in exchange for proceeds.

(10) "Profits" means all income from anything sold or transferred by the felon, a representative of the felon, or a profiteer of the felony, including any right, the value of which thing or right is enhanced by the notoriety gained from the commission of a felony for which a convicted felon was convicted. This income may have been accrued, earned, or paid before or after the conviction. However, voluntary donations or contributions to a defendant to assist in the defense of criminal charges shall not be deemed to be "profits," provided the donation or contribution to that defense is not given in exchange for some material of value.

(b)(1) All proceeds from the preparation for the purpose of sale, the sale of the rights to, or the sale of materials that include or are based on the story of a felony for which a convicted felon was convicted, shall be subject to an involuntary trust for the benefit of the beneficiaries set forth in this section. That trust shall continue until five years after the time of payment of the proceeds to the felon or five years after the date of conviction, whichever is later. If an action is filed by a beneficiary to recover his or her interest in a trust within those time limitations, the trust character of the property shall continue until the conclusion of the action. At the end of the five-year trust period, any proceeds that remain in trust that have not been claimed by a beneficiary shall be transferred to the Controller, to be allocated to the Restitution Fund for the payment of claims pursuant to Section 13969 of the Government Code.

(2) All profits shall be subject to an involuntary trust for the benefit of the beneficiaries set forth in this section. That trust shall continue until five years after the time of payment of the profits to the felon or five years after the date of conviction, whichever is later. If an action is filed by a beneficiary to recover his or her interest in a trust within those time limitations, the trust character of the property shall continue until the conclusion of the action. At the end of the five-year trust period, any profits that remain in trust that have not been claimed by a beneficiary shall be transferred to the Controller, to be allocated to the Restitution Fund for the payment of claims pursuant to Section 13969 of the Government Code.

(3) Notwithstanding paragraph (2), in the case of a sale or transfer by a profiteer of the felony, the court in an action under subdivision (c) shall, upon an adequate showing by the profiteer of the felony, exclude from the involuntary trust that portion of the profits that represents the inherent value of the memorabilia, property, or thing sold or transferred and exclusive of the amount of the enhancement to the value due to the notoriety of the convicted felon.

(c)(1) Any beneficiary may bring an action against a convicted felon, representative of the felon, or a profiteer of a felony to recover his or her interest in the trust established by this section.

(2) That action may be brought in the superior court of the county in which the beneficiary resides, or of the county in which the convicted felon resides, or of the county in which proceeds or profits are located.

(3) If the court determines that a beneficiary is entitled to proceeds or profits pursuant to this section, the court shall order the payment from proceeds or profits that have been received, and, if that is insufficient, from proceeds or profits that may be received in the future.

(d) If there are two or more beneficiaries and if the available proceeds or profits are insufficient to pay all beneficiaries, the proceeds or profits shall be equitably apportioned among the beneficiaries taking into account the impact of the crime upon them.

Prior to any distribution of any proceeds to a beneficiary, the court shall determine whether the convicted felon has failed to pay any portion of a restitution fine or penalty fine imposed by a court, or any restitution imposed as a condition of probation. The court shall also determine whether the felon is obligated to reimburse a governmental entity for the costs of his or her defense and whether a portion of the proceeds is needed to cover his or her reasonable attorney's fees incurred in the criminal proceeding related to the felony, or any appeal or other related proceeding, or in the defense of the action brought under this section. The court shall order payment of these obligations prior to any payment to a beneficiary, except that 60 percent of the proceeds or profits shall be reserved for payment to the beneficiaries.

(e)(1) The Attorney General may bring an action to require proceeds or profits received by a convicted felon to be held in an express trust in a bank authorized to act as a trustee.

(2) An action may be brought under this subdivision within one year after the receipt of proceeds or profits by a convicted felon or one year after the date of conviction, whichever is later.

That action may be brought in the superior court of any county in which the Attorney General has an office.

(3) If the Attorney General proves that the proceeds or profits are proceeds or profits from the sale of a story or thing of value that are subject to an involuntary trust pursuant to this section, and that it is more probable than not that there are beneficiaries within the meaning of this section, the court shall order that all proceeds or profits be deposited in a bank and held by the bank as trustee of the trust until an order of disposition is made by a court pursuant to subdivision (d), or until the expiration of the period specified in subdivision (b).

(4) If the Attorney General prevails in an action under this subdivision, the court shall order the payment from the proceeds or profits to the Attorney General of reasonable costs and attorney's fees.

(f)(1) In any action brought pursuant to this section, upon motion of a party the court shall grant a preliminary injunction to prevent any waste of proceeds or profits if it appears that the proceeds or profits are subject to the provisions of this section, and that they may be subject to waste.

(2) Upon motion of the Attorney General or any potential beneficiary, the court shall grant a preliminary injunction against a person against whom an indictment or information for a felony has been filed in superior court to prevent any waste of proceeds or profits if there is probable cause to believe that the proceeds or profits would be subject to an involuntary trust pursuant to this section upon conviction of this person, and that they may be subject to waste.

(g) Any violation of an order of a court made pursuant to this section shall be punishable as contempt.

(h) The remedies provided by this section are in addition to other remedies provided by law.

No period of limitations, except those provided by this section, shall limit the right of recovery under this section. *(Added by Stats.1986, c. 820, § 8, eff. Sept. 15, 1986, operative July 1, 1987. Amended by Stats.1992, c. 178 (S.B.1496), § 2; Stats.1994, c. 556 (S.B.1330), § 1, eff. Sept. 13, 1994; Stats.1995, c. 262 (S.B.287), § 1; Stats.2000, c. 261 (S.B.1565), § 2.)*

Validity

This section was held unconstitutional as a content-based restriction on speech in the case of Keenan v. Superior Court of Los Angeles County (2002) 117 Cal.Rptr.2d 1, 27 Cal.4th 413, 40 P.3d 718, certiorari denied 123 S.Ct. 94, 537 U.S. 818, 154 L.Ed.2d 25.

Law Revision Commission Comments

Section 2225 continues former Section 2224.1 without change. [18 Cal.L.Rev.Comm. Reports 501 (1986)].

Section 2225 is amended to revise section references. These revisions are technical, nonsubstantive changes. [22 Cal.L.Rev.Comm.Reports 895 (1992)].

Research References

Miller and Starr California Real Estate § 8:22, Capacity--In General.
1 Witkin Cal. Summ. 10th Contracts § 58, Persons Deprived of Civil Rights.
7 Witkin, California Summary 10th Constitutional Law § 369, (S 369) Income from Work Describing Crime.
13 Witkin, California Summary 10th Trusts § 258, (S 258) Law Revision Commission Report.
13 Witkin, California Summary 10th Trusts § 321, Crime.

Title 9

AGENCY

CHAPTER 1. AGENCY IN GENERAL

ARTICLE 1. DEFINITION OF AGENCY

Section

2298.   Actual or ostensible agency.
2299.   Actual agency defined.
2300.   Ostensible agency defined.

§ 2295.   Agent defined

AGENCY, WHAT.   An agent is one who represents another, called the principal, in dealings with third persons.   Such representation is called agency.   *(Enacted in 1872.)*

Research References

Rutter, Cal. Practice Guide: Real Prop. Transactions Ch. 2-C, C. Broker's Relationship and Obligations to Principal and Third Parties.
Rutter, Cal. Practice Guide: Real Prop. Transactions Ch. 4-C, C. Parties to the Purchase Agreement.
Miller and Starr California Real Estate § 3:2, "Agency" Defined.
Miller and Starr California Real Estate § 3:11, Disclosure of Agency Relationships.
Miller and Starr California Real Estate § 3:12, Dual Agency.
Miller and Starr California Real Estate § 5:19, Construing a Listing Agreement--In General.
Miller and Starr California Real Estate § 8:31, Scope of Agent's Authority; Power of Attorney.
9 Witkin, California Summary 10th Corporations § 81, Nature and Scope of Statute.
3 Witkin, California Summary 10th Agency and Employment § 2, (S 2) Agent.
3 Witkin, California Summary 10th Agency and Employment § 207, (S 207) Durable Power of Attorney.
14 Witkin, California Summary 10th Wills and Probate § 841, (S 841) in General.

§ 2296.   Capacity to appoint agent; capacity to be agent

WHO MAY APPOINT, AND WHO MAY BE AN AGENT.   Any person having capacity to contract may appoint an agent, and any person may be an agent.   *(Enacted in 1872.)*

Research References

3 Witkin, California Summary 10th Agency and Employment § 89, (S 89) in General.
14 Witkin, California Summary 10th Wills and Probate § 853, in General.

§ 2297.   General and special agents defined

AGENTS, GENERAL OR SPECIAL.   An agent for a particular act or transaction is called a special agent.   All others are general agents.   *(Enacted in 1872.)*

Research References

Rutter, Cal. Practice Guide: Real Prop. Transactions Ch. 2-C, C. Broker's Relationship and Obligations to Principal and Third Parties.
Miller and Starr California Real Estate § 3:2, "Agency" Defined.
Miller and Starr California Real Estate § 3:7, Agent's Authority by Common Law.
Miller and Starr California Real Estate § 10:4, Capacity and Authority of Trustee.
3 Witkin, California Summary 10th Agency and Employment § 2, (S 2) Agent.

§ 2298.   Actual or ostensible agency

AGENCY, ACTUAL OR OSTENSIBLE.   An agency is either actual or ostensible.   *(Enacted in 1872.)*

Research References

Rutter, Cal. Practice Guide: Insurance Litigation Ch. 2-A, A. Agents and Brokers.
Miller and Starr California Real Estate § 3:6, Ostensible Agency.
3 Witkin, California Summary 10th Agency and Employment § 96, Ostensible Agency and Agency by Estoppel.

§ 2299.   Actual agency defined

ACTUAL AGENCY.   An agency is actual when the agent is really employed by the principal.   *(Enacted in 1872.)*

Research References

Rutter, Cal. Practice Guide: A.D.R. Ch. 5-F, F. Arbitration by and Against Nonsignatories.
Rutter, Cal. Practice Guide: Insurance Litigation Ch. 2-A, A. Agents and Brokers.
Rutter, Cal. Practice Guide: Real Prop. Transactions Ch. 2-C, C. Broker's Relationship and Obligations to Principal and Third Parties.
Miller and Starr California Real Estate § 3:6, Ostensible Agency.
3 Witkin, California Summary 10th Agency and Employment § 92, (S 92) Nature and Requisites.

§ 2300.   Ostensible agency defined

OSTENSIBLE AGENCY.   An agency is ostensible when the principal intentionally, or by want of ordinary care, causes a third person to believe another to be his agent who is not really employed by him.   *(Enacted in 1872.)*

Research References

Rutter, Cal. Practice Guide: Insurance Litigation Ch. 2-A, A. Agents and Brokers.
Rutter, Cal. Practice Guide: Real Prop. Transactions Ch. 2-C, C. Broker's Relationship and Obligations to Principal and Third Parties.
Miller and Starr California Real Estate § 3:6, Ostensible Agency.
Miller and Starr California Real Estate § 1:83, Written Authority Required; the Equal Dignities Rule--Exception: Estoppel to Deny Agent's Authority.
3 Witkin, California Summary 10th Agency and Employment § 96, Ostensible Agency and Agency by Estoppel.

ARTICLE 2.   AUTHORITY OF AGENTS

Section

2304.   Authority conferrable; scope.
2305.   Performance of acts required of principal by code.
2306.   Defrauding principal; absence of authority.
2307.   Creation of agency; manner.
2308.   Consideration unnecessary.
2309.   Oral and written authorizations.
2310.   Ratification; manner.
2311.   Ratification; part of indivisible transaction.
2312.   Ratification; invalidity unless principal had power to confer authority.
2313.   Ratification; rights of third persons.
2314.   Ratification; rescission.
2315.   Measure of authority.
2316.   Actual authority defined.
2317.   Ostensible authority defined.
2318.   Authority as to persons having notice of restrictions.
2319.   Necessary authority.
2320.   Power to disobey instructions.
2321.   Authority partly in general and partly in specific terms; construction.
2322.   Authority of agent.
2323.   Sale of personal property; included authority.
2324.   Sale of real estate; included authority.
2325.   General agent; authority to receive price.
2326.   Special agent; authority to receive price.

§ 2304.   Authority conferrable; scope

WHAT AUTHORITY MAY BE CONFERRED.   An agent may be authorized to do any acts which his principal might do, except those to which the latter is bound to give his personal attention.   *(Enacted in 1872.)*

Research References

Rutter, Cal. Practice Guide: Insurance Litigation Ch. 2-A, A. Agents and Brokers.
Miller and Starr California Real Estate § 3:2, "Agency" Defined.
Miller and Starr California Real Estate § 3:7, Agent's Authority by Common Law.

Miller and Starr California Real Estate § 3:17, Real Estate Broker Acting as a Principal.

3 Witkin, California Summary 10th Agency and Employment § 130, (S 130) California Statutes.

3 Witkin, California Summary 10th Agency and Employment § 132, (S 132) Delegation of Authority.

3 Witkin, California Summary 10th Agency and Employment § 135, in General.

§ 2305. Performance of acts required of principal by code

AGENT MAY PERFORM ACTS REQUIRED OF PRINCIPAL BY CODE. Every act which, according to this Code, may be done by or to any person, may be done by or to the agent of such person for that purpose, unless a contrary intention clearly appears. *(Enacted in 1872.)*

Research References

Miller and Starr California Real Estate § 3:7, Agent's Authority by Common Law.

3 Witkin, California Summary 10th Agency and Employment § 130, (S 130) California Statutes.

§ 2306. Defrauding principal; absence of authority

AGENT CANNOT HAVE AUTHORITY TO DEFRAUD PRINCIPAL. An agent can never have authority, either actual or ostensible, to do an act which is, and is known or suspected by the person with whom he deals, to be a fraud upon the principal. *(Enacted in 1872.)*

Research References

Miller and Starr California Real Estate § 3:7, Agent's Authority by Common Law.

Miller and Starr California Real Estate § 3:23, Notice of Termination-- Exception: Agency Coupled With an Interest.

3 Witkin, California Summary 10th Agency and Employment § 135, in General.

§ 2307. Creation of agency; manner

CREATION OF AGENCY. An agency may be created, and an authority may be conferred, by a precedent authorization or a subsequent ratification. *(Enacted in 1872.)*

Research References

Rutter, Cal. Practice Guide: Real Prop. Transactions Ch. 2-C, C. Broker's Relationship and Obligations to Principal and Third Parties.

Miller and Starr California Real Estate § 3:5, Creation of an Agency; Identifying the Principal; General Rules.

Miller and Starr California Real Estate § 3:9, Ratification of the Unauthorized Acts of an Agent.

Miller and Starr California Real Estate § 1:82, Written Authority Required; the Equal Dignities Rule--Exception: Ratification or Waiver by the Principal.

Miller and Starr California Real Estate § 5:39, Authorization for Broker to Accept Deposit.

3 Witkin, California Summary 10th Agency and Employment § 92, (S 92) Nature and Requisites.

3 Witkin, California Summary 10th Agency and Employment § 95, Agency by Ratification.

3 Witkin, California Summary 10th Agency and Employment § 134, (S 134) Authority Given by Principal.

3 Witkin, California Summary 10th Agency and Employment § 139, (S 139) Nature and Effect.

§ 2308. Consideration unnecessary

CONSIDERATION UNNECESSARY. A consideration is not necessary to make an authority, whether precedent or subsequent, binding upon the principal. *(Enacted in 1872.)*

Research References

Rutter, Cal. Practice Guide: Real Prop. Transactions Ch. 2-C, C. Broker's Relationship and Obligations to Principal and Third Parties.

Miller and Starr California Real Estate § 3:5, Creation of an Agency; Identifying the Principal; General Rules.

Miller and Starr California Real Estate § 3:9, Ratification of the Unauthorized Acts of an Agent.

Miller and Starr California Real Estate § 1:82, Written Authority Required; the Equal Dignities Rule--Exception: Ratification or Waiver by the Principal.

§ 2309. Oral and written authorizations

FORM OF AUTHORITY. An oral authorization is sufficient for any purpose, except that an authority to enter into a contract required by law to be in writing can only be given by an instrument in writing. *(Enacted in 1872.)*

Research References

Rutter, Cal. Practice Guide: Real Prop. Transactions Ch. 2-C, C. Broker's Relationship and Obligations to Principal and Third Parties.

Rutter, Cal. Practice Guide: Real Prop. Transactions Ch. 4-C, C. Parties to the Purchase Agreement.

Rutter, Cal. Practice Guide: Real Prop. Transactions Ch. 4-D, D. Selecting the Form of Written Agreement.

Rutter, Cal. Practice Guide: Real Prop. Transactions Ch. 10-C, C. Property Management Agreement.

Rutter, Cal. Practice Guide: Prof. Responsibility Ch. 3-D, D. Authority of Client vs. Authority of Attorney.

Miller and Starr California Real Estate § 3:7, Agent's Authority by Common Law.

Miller and Starr California Real Estate § 1:65, Provisions Applicable to Real Estate Transactions.

Miller and Starr California Real Estate § 1:81, Written Authority Required; the Equal Dignities Rule.

Miller and Starr California Real Estate § 1:82, Written Authority Required; the Equal Dignities Rule--Exception: Ratification or Waiver by the Principal.

Miller and Starr California Real Estate § 5:10, Form of the Memorandum--Signature of the Principal.

Miller and Starr California Real Estate § 5:13, Exception: Agreement Between Brokers to Share a Commission.

Miller and Starr California Real Estate § 5:16, Exception: Estoppel to Raise Statute of Frauds as a Defense.

Miller and Starr California Real Estate § 5:21, Property Management Employment Agreements.

Miller and Starr California Real Estate § 8:28, Insertion of Name After Execution by the Grantor.

Miller and Starr California Real Estate § 8:29, Requirements of Grantor's Signature.

Miller and Starr California Real Estate § 8:30, Execution by an Agent or Attorney-In-Fact.

13 NO. 3 Miller & Starr, California Real Estate Newsalert 6, Deeds.

2 Witkin, California Summary 10th Insurance § 204, Illustrations: Ineffective Waivers.

1 Witkin Cal. Summ. 10th Contracts § 343, California Codes.

1 Witkin Cal. Summ. 10th Contracts § 388, (S 388) Equal Dignities Rule.

1 Witkin Cal. Summ. 10th Contracts § 389, Agent Acting Mechanically.

1 Witkin Cal. Summ. 10th Contracts § 391, Liability of Principal to Agent.

1 Witkin Cal. Summ. 10th Contracts § 396, (S 396) Exception: Agreement to Sell Personal Property.

3 Witkin, California Summary 10th Agency and Employment § 92, (S 92) Nature and Requisites.

3 Witkin, California Summary 10th Agency and Employment § 149, (S 149) Holding Out Agent as Principal.

§ 2310. Ratification; manner

RATIFICATION OF AGENT'S ACT. A ratification can be made only in the manner that would have been necessary to confer an original authority for the act ratified, or where an oral authorization would suffice, by accepting or retaining the benefit of the act, with notice thereof. *(Enacted in 1872.)*

Research References

Rutter, Cal. Practice Guide: Real Prop. Transactions Ch. 4-D, D. Selecting the Form of Written Agreement.

Miller and Starr California Real Estate § 3:9, Ratification of the Unauthorized Acts of an Agent.

Miller and Starr California Real Estate § 1:82, Written Authority Required; the Equal Dignities Rule--Exception: Ratification or Waiver by the Principal.
Miller and Starr California Real Estate § 8:29, Requirements of Grantor's Signature.
13 NO. 3 Miller & Starr, California Real Estate Newsalert 6, Deeds.
1 Witkin Cal. Summ. 10th Contracts § 388, (S 388) Equal Dignities Rule.
1 Witkin Cal. Summ. 10th Contracts § 389, Agent Acting Mechanically.
3 Witkin, California Summary 10th Agency and Employment § 95, Agency by Ratification.
3 Witkin, California Summary 10th Agency and Employment § 140, Formal Ratification: Equal Dignities Rule.
3 Witkin, California Summary 10th Agency and Employment § 141, Voluntary Acceptance of Benefits.
3 Witkin, California Summary 10th Agency and Employment § 146, Ostensible Authority Not Found.
13 Witkin, California Summary 10th Equity § 193, (S 193) Distinctions.

§ 2311. Ratification; part of indivisible transaction

RATIFICATION OF PART OF A TRANSACTION. Ratification of part of an indivisible transaction is a ratification of the whole. *(Enacted in 1872.)*

Research References

Miller and Starr California Real Estate § 3:9, Ratification of the Unauthorized Acts of an Agent.
Miller and Starr California Real Estate § 1:81, Written Authority Required; the Equal Dignities Rule.
Miller and Starr California Real Estate § 1:82, Written Authority Required; the Equal Dignities Rule--Exception: Ratification or Waiver by the Principal.
3 Witkin, California Summary 10th Agency and Employment § 143, (S 143) Limitations on Power to Ratify.

§ 2312. Ratification; invalidity unless principal had power to confer authority

WHEN RATIFICATION VOID. A ratification is not valid unless, at the time of ratifying the act done, the principal has power to confer authority for such an act. *(Enacted in 1872.)*

Research References

Miller and Starr California Real Estate § 3:9, Ratification of the Unauthorized Acts of an Agent.
3 Witkin, California Summary 10th Agency and Employment § 143, (S 143) Limitations on Power to Ratify.

§ 2313. Ratification; rights of third persons

RATIFICATION NOT TO WORK INJURY TO THIRD PERSONS. No unauthorized act can be made valid, retroactively, to the prejudice of third persons, without their consent. *(Enacted in 1872.)*

Research References

Miller and Starr California Real Estate § 3:9, Ratification of the Unauthorized Acts of an Agent.
2 Witkin, California Summary 10th Insurance § 261, (S 261) Assignment of Cause of Action Against Insurer.
3 Witkin, California Summary 10th Agency and Employment § 143, (S 143) Limitations on Power to Ratify.
3 Witkin, California Summary 10th Agency and Employment § 146, Ostensible Authority Not Found.

§ 2314. Ratification; rescission

RESCISSION OF RATIFICATION. A ratification may be rescinded when made without such consent as is required in a contract, or with an imperfect knowledge of the material facts of the transaction ratified, but not otherwise. *(Enacted in 1872.)*

Research References

Miller and Starr California Real Estate § 3:9, Ratification of the Unauthorized Acts of an Agent.

1 Witkin Cal. Summ. 10th Contracts § 935, (S 935) Grounds for Rescission.
3 Witkin, California Summary 10th Agency and Employment § 143, (S 143) Limitations on Power to Ratify.
3 Witkin, California Summary 10th Agency and Employment § 146, Ostensible Authority Not Found.

§ 2315. Measure of authority

MEASURE OF AGENT'S AUTHORITY. An agent has such authority as the principal, actually or ostensibly, confers upon him. *(Enacted in 1872.)*

Research References

Rutter, Cal. Practice Guide: Real Prop. Transactions Ch. 2-C, C. Broker's Relationship and Obligations to Principal and Third Parties.
Miller and Starr California Real Estate § 3:7, Agent's Authority by Common Law.
Miller and Starr California Real Estate § 28:21, Constructive and Imputed Knowledge.
3 Witkin Cal. Proc. 5th Actions § 1047, Ostensible Agent.
3 Witkin, California Summary 10th Agency and Employment § 130, (S 130) California Statutes.

§ 2316. Actual authority defined

ACTUAL AUTHORITY, WHAT. Actual authority is such as a principal intentionally confers upon the agent, or intentionally, or by want of ordinary care, allows the agent to believe himself to possess. *(Enacted in 1872.)*

Research References

Rutter, Cal. Practice Guide: Real Prop. Transactions Ch. 2-C, C. Broker's Relationship and Obligations to Principal and Third Parties.
Miller and Starr California Real Estate § 3:7, Agent's Authority by Common Law.
Miller and Starr California Real Estate § 6:12, Agency--Duty to Comply With Instructions.
14 NO. 4 Miller & Starr, California Real Estate Newsalert 31, Subdivisions.
3 Witkin, California Summary 10th Agency and Employment § 134, (S 134) Authority Given by Principal.

§ 2317. Ostensible authority defined

OSTENSIBLE AUTHORITY, WHAT. Ostensible authority is such as a principal, intentionally or by want of ordinary care, causes or allows a third person to believe the agent to possess. *(Enacted in 1872.)*

Research References

Rutter, Cal. Practice Guide: Insurance Litigation Ch. 2-A, A. Agents and Brokers.
Rutter, Cal. Practice Guide: Real Prop. Transactions Ch. 2-C, C. Broker's Relationship and Obligations to Principal and Third Parties.
Miller and Starr California Real Estate § 3:7, Agent's Authority by Common Law.
Miller and Starr California Real Estate § 1:83, Written Authority Required; the Equal Dignities Rule--Exception: Estoppel to Deny Agent's Authority.
Miller and Starr California Real Estate § 6:12, Agency--Duty to Comply With Instructions.
Miller and Starr California Real Estate § 27:67, Architect's Instructions.
14 NO. 4 Miller & Starr, California Real Estate Newsalert 31, Subdivisions.
3 Witkin Cal. Proc. 5th Actions § 1047, Ostensible Agent.
2 Witkin, California Summary 10th Insurance § 39, Life Insurance Applications.
3 Witkin, California Summary 10th Agency and Employment § 144, (S 144) Nature of Ostensible Authority.

§ 2318. Authority as to persons having notice of restrictions

AGENT'S AUTHORITY AS TO PERSONS HAVING NOTICE OF RESTRICTIONS UPON IT. Every agent has actually such authority as is defined by this Title, unless specially deprived thereof by his principal, and has even then such authority ostensibly, except as to persons who have actual or constructive notice of the restriction upon his authority. *(Enacted in 1872.)*

Research References

Miller and Starr California Real Estate § 3:7, Agent's Authority by Common Law.
3 Witkin, California Summary 10th Agency and Employment § 130, (S 130) California Statutes.
3 Witkin, California Summary 10th Agency and Employment § 135, in General.
3 Witkin, California Summary 10th Agency and Employment § 144, (S 144) Nature of Ostensible Authority.

§ 2319. Necessary authority

AGENT'S NECESSARY AUTHORITY. An agent has authority:

1. To do everything necessary or proper and usual, in the ordinary course of business, for effecting the purpose of his agency; and,

2. To make a representation respecting any matter of fact, not including the terms of his authority, but upon which his right to use his authority depends, and the truth of which cannot be determined by the use of reasonable diligence on the part of the person to whom the representation is made. *(Enacted in 1872.)*

Research References

Rutter, Cal. Practice Guide: Real Prop. Transactions Ch. 2-C, C. Broker's Relationship and Obligations to Principal and Third Parties.
Rutter, Cal. Practice Guide: Real Prop. Transactions Ch. 2-E, E. Listing Agreements.
Rutter, Cal. Practice Guide: Real Prop. Transactions Ch. 4-C, C. Parties to the Purchase Agreement.
Rutter, Cal. Practice Guide: Prof. Responsibility Ch. 5-E, E. Costs Arrangements.
Miller and Starr California Real Estate § 3:7, Agent's Authority by Common Law.
Miller and Starr California Real Estate § 27:67, Architect's Instructions.
3 Witkin, California Summary 10th Agency and Employment § 135, in General.

§ 2320. Power to disobey instructions

AGENT'S POWER TO DISOBEY INSTRUCTIONS. An agent has power to disobey instructions in dealing with the subject of the agency, in cases where it is clearly for the interest of his principal that he should do so, and there is not time to communicate with the principal. *(Enacted in 1872.)*

Research References

Miller and Starr California Real Estate § 3:7, Agent's Authority by Common Law.
3 Witkin, California Summary 10th Agency and Employment § 135, in General.

§ 2321. Authority partly in general and partly in specific terms; construction

AUTHORITY TO BE CONSTRUED BY ITS SPECIFIC, RATHER THAN BY ITS GENERAL TERMS. When an authority is given partly in general and partly in specific terms, the general authority gives no higher powers than those specifically mentioned. *(Enacted in 1872.)*

Research References

Rutter, Cal. Practice Guide: Real Prop. Transactions Ch. 4-C, C. Parties to the Purchase Agreement.
Miller and Starr California Real Estate § 3:7, Agent's Authority by Common Law.
14 Witkin, California Summary 10th Wills and Probate § 836, (S 836) Construction.

§ 2322. Authority of agent

An authority expressed in general terms, however broad, does not authorize an agent to do any of the following:

(a) Act in the agent's own name, unless it is the usual course of business to do so.

(b) Define the scope of the agency.

(c) Violate a duty to which a trustee is subject under Section 16002, 16004, 16005, or 16009 of the Probate Code. *(Enacted in 1872. Amended by Stats.1986, c. 820, § 9, eff. Sept. 15, 1986, operative July 1, 1987; Stats.1988, c. 113, § 5, eff. May 25, 1988.)*

Law Revision Commission Comments

Section 2322 is amended to correct a cross-reference. Although the statutory statement of trustees' duties varies considerably from that in former Civil Code Sections 2228–2240, the amendment of this section is not intended to alter the general rule that agents are subject to the same general standards as trustees. See, e.g., Helbing v. Helbing, 89 Cal. App.2d 224, 227, 200 P.2d 560 (1949); Kinert v. Wright, 81 Cal.App.2d 919, 925, 185 P.2d 364 (1947). [18 Cal.L.Rev.Comm. Reports 501 1986)].

Subdivision (c) of Section 2322 is amended to clarify the application of trustees' duties to agents acting under general authority. See Prob.Code §§ 16002 (duty of loyalty), 16004 (duty to avoid conflict of interest), 16005 (duty not to undertake adverse trust), 16009 (duty to keep property separate and identified). This is a nonsubstantive revision intended to make more specific the technical revision implemented in the 1986 legislation that enacted the Trust Law. See 1986 Cal.Stat. ch. 820, § 9. The purpose of this and the earlier amendment is to provide appropriate cross-references to the law that superseded the repealed sections concerning trustees' duties. Neither amendment is intended to change the law relating to the duties of agents. [19 Cal.L.Rev.Comm.Reports 1033 (1987)].

Research References

Miller and Starr California Real Estate § 3:7, Agent's Authority by Common Law.
Miller and Starr California Real Estate § 3:12, Dual Agency.
Miller and Starr California Real Estate § 3:24, Source of an Agent's Duties to the Principal.
Miller and Starr California Real Estate § 3:25, Fiduciary Duties of an Agent.
Miller and Starr California Real Estate § 3:28, Identity of the Buyer; Agent as a Buyer.
3 Witkin, California Summary 10th Agency and Employment § 97, (S 97) Statement of Rule.
3 Witkin, California Summary 10th Agency and Employment § 135, in General.

§ 2323. Sale of personal property; included authority

WHAT INCLUDED IN AUTHORITY TO SELL PERSONAL PROPERTY. An authority to sell personal property includes authority to warrant the title of the principal, and the quality and quantity of the property. *(Enacted in 1872.)*

Research References

Miller and Starr California Real Estate § 3:7, Agent's Authority by Common Law.
3 Witkin, California Summary 10th Agency and Employment § 43, Auctioneers.
3 Witkin, California Summary 10th Agency and Employment § 136, Authority to Sell.

§ 2324. Sale of real estate; included authority

WHAT INCLUDED IN AUTHORITY TO SELL REAL PROPERTY. An authority to sell and convey real property includes authority to give the usual covenants of warranty. *(Enacted in 1872.)*

Research References

Miller and Starr California Real Estate § 3:7, Agent's Authority by Common Law.
Miller and Starr California Real Estate § 8:31, Scope of Agent's Authority; Power of Attorney.

3 Witkin, California Summary 10th Agency and Employment § 136, Authority to Sell.

§ 2325. General agent; authority to receive price

AUTHORITY OF GENERAL AGENT TO RECEIVE PRICE OF PROPERTY. A general agent to sell, who is intrusted by the principal with the possession of the thing sold, has authority to receive the price. *(Enacted in 1872.)*

Research References

Miller and Starr California Real Estate § 3:7, Agent's Authority by Common Law.
3 Witkin, California Summary 10th Agency and Employment § 137, Authority to Receive or Collect Money.

§ 2326. Special agent; authority to receive price

AUTHORITY OF SPECIAL AGENT TO RECEIVE PRICE. A special agent to sell has authority to receive the price on delivery of the thing sold, but not afterwards. *(Enacted in 1872.)*

Research References

Miller and Starr California Real Estate § 3:7, Agent's Authority by Common Law.
3 Witkin, California Summary 10th Agency and Employment § 137, Authority to Receive or Collect Money.

ARTICLE 3. MUTUAL OBLIGATIONS OF PRINCIPALS AND THIRD PERSONS

Section

§ 2330. Principal's rights and liabilities from acts of agent within scope of authority

PRINCIPAL, HOW AFFECTED BY ACTS OF AGENT WITHIN THE SCOPE OF HIS AUTHORITY. An agent represents his principal for all purposes within the scope of his actual or ostensible authority, and all the rights and liabilities which would accrue to the agent from transactions within such limit, if they had been entered into on his own account, accrue to the principal. *(Enacted in 1872.)*

Research References

Rutter, Cal. Practice Guide: Civil Trials & Evidence Ch. 8D-D, D. Hearsay Exceptions.
Rutter, Cal. Practice Guide: Insurance Litigation Ch. 11-A, A. Background.
Rutter, Cal. Practice Guide: Real Prop. Transactions Ch. 2-C, C. Broker's Relationship and Obligations to Principal and Third Parties.
Rutter, Cal. Practice Guide: Real Prop. Transactions Ch. 10-B, B. Regulation of Real Property Managers and Legal Relationship Between Manager and Owner.
Rutter, Cal. Practice Guide: Prof. Responsibility Ch. 5-E, E. Costs Arrangements.
Miller and Starr California Real Estate § 3:2, "Agency" Defined.
Miller and Starr California Real Estate § 1:32, Termination by Revocation by the Offeror.
Miller and Starr California Real Estate § 3:50, Contractual Liability (Undisclosed Principal).

3 Witkin Cal. Proc. 5th Actions § 1047, Ostensible Agent.
3 Witkin, California Summary 10th Agency and Employment § 130, (S 130) California Statutes.

§ 2331. Incomplete execution of authority

PRINCIPAL, WHEN BOUND BY INCOMPLETE EXECUTION OF AUTHORITY. A principal is bound by an incomplete execution of an authority, when it is consistent with the whole purpose and scope thereof, but not otherwise. *(Enacted in 1872.)*

Research References

Miller and Starr California Real Estate § 3:50, Contractual Liability (Undisclosed Principal).
Miller and Starr California Real Estate § 27:67, Architect's Instructions.

§ 2332. Notice to principal or agent as notice to the other

NOTICE TO AGENT, WHEN NOTICE TO PRINCIPAL. As against a principal, both principal and agent are deemed to have notice of whatever either has notice of, and ought, in good faith and the exercise of ordinary care and diligence, to communicate to the other. *(Enacted in 1872.)*

Research References

Rutter, Cal. Practice Guide: Insurance Litigation Ch. 7A-C, C. Insuring Clauses-Occurrence vs. Claims-Made Policies.
Rutter, Cal. Practice Guide: Insurance Litigation Ch. 7A-L, L. Conditions.
Miller and Starr California Real Estate § 1:32, Termination by Revocation by the Offeror.
Miller and Starr California Real Estate § 3:50, Contractual Liability (Undisclosed Principal).
Miller and Starr California Real Estate § 3:51, Principal's Liability for the Agent's Torts.
Miller and Starr California Real Estate § 6:13, Agency--Duty to Disclose.
Miller and Starr California Real Estate § 6:28, Knowledge of Escrow Holder Imputed to Principal.
Miller and Starr California Real Estate § 1:140, Duty of Seller of Real Property to Disclose.
Miller and Starr California Real Estate § 11:76, Notice to an Agent; General Rule.
Miller and Starr California Real Estate § 11:79, Notice to a Real Estate Broker.
Miller and Starr California Real Estate § 27:67, Architect's Instructions.
Miller and Starr California Real Estate § 29:35, Liability for Negligent Supervision.
15 NO. 6 Miller & Starr, California Real Estate Newsalert 8, Defective Construction.
3 Witkin, California Summary 10th Agency and Employment § 150, (S 150) Theory of Doctrine.

§ 2333. Principal's obligation where authority exceeded

OBLIGATION OF PRINCIPAL WHEN AGENT EXCEEDS HIS AUTHORITY. When an agent exceeds his authority, his principal is bound by his authorized acts so far only as they can be plainly separated from those which are unauthorized. *(Enacted in 1872.)*

Research References

Rutter, Cal. Practice Guide: Real Prop. Transactions Ch. 2-C, C. Broker's Relationship and Obligations to Principal and Third Parties.
Miller and Starr California Real Estate § 3:19, Salesperson as Employee Versus Independent Contractor--Liability of a Broker for Torts of a Salesperson.
Miller and Starr California Real Estate § 3:50, Contractual Liability (Undisclosed Principal).

§ 2334. Principal bound by acts under ostensible authority

A principal is bound by acts of his agent, under a merely ostensible authority, to those persons only who have in good faith, and without want of ordinary care, incurred a liability or parted with value, upon the faith thereof. *(Enacted in 1872. Amended by Stats.1905, c. 457, p. 616, § 1.)*

Research References

Rutter, Cal. Practice Guide: Real Prop. Transactions Ch. 2-C, C. Broker's Relationship and Obligations to Principal and Third Parties.

Miller and Starr California Real Estate § 3:6, Ostensible Agency.

Miller and Starr California Real Estate § 3:19, Salesperson as Employee Versus Independent Contractor--Liability of a Broker for Torts of a Salesperson.

Miller and Starr California Real Estate § 3:50, Contractual Liability (Undisclosed Principal).

Miller and Starr California Real Estate § 27:67, Architect's Instructions.

3 Witkin Cal. Proc. 5th Actions § 1047, Ostensible Agent.

3 Witkin, California Summary 10th Agency and Employment § 144, (S 144) Nature of Ostensible Authority.

§ 2335. Exclusive credit to agent; exoneration of principal

WHEN EXCLUSIVE CREDIT IS GIVEN TO AGENT. If exclusive credit is given to an agent by the person dealing with him, his principal is exonerated by payment or other satisfaction made by him to his agent in good faith, before receiving notice of the creditor's election to hold him responsible. *(Enacted in 1872.)*

Research References

Miller and Starr California Real Estate § 3:50, Contractual Liability (Undisclosed Principal).

§ 2336. Rights of person dealing with agent without knowledge of agency

RIGHTS OF PERSON WHO DEALS WITH AGENT WITHOUT KNOWLEDGE OF AGENCY. One who deals with an agent without knowing or having reason to believe that the agent acts as such in the transaction, may set off against any claim of the principal arising out of the same, all claims which he might have set off against the agent before notice of the agency. *(Enacted in 1872.)*

Research References

Miller and Starr California Real Estate § 3:50, Contractual Liability (Undisclosed Principal).

§ 2337. Instrument within scope of agency intended to bind principal

INSTRUMENT INTENDED TO BIND PRINCIPAL DOES BIND HIM. An instrument within the scope of his authority by which an agent intends to bind his principal, does bind him if such intent is plainly inferable from the instrument itself. *(Enacted in 1872.)*

Research References

Miller and Starr California Real Estate § 3:50, Contractual Liability (Undisclosed Principal).

§ 2338. Responsibility for agent's negligence or omission

PRINCIPAL'S RESPONSIBILITY FOR AGENT'S NEGLIGENCE OR OMISSION. Unless required by or under the authority of law to employ that particular agent, a principal is responsible to third persons for the negligence of his agent in the transaction of the business of the agency, including wrongful acts committed by such agent in and as a part of the transaction of such business, and for his willful omission to fulfill the obligations of the principal. *(Enacted in 1872.)*

Research References

Rutter, Cal. Practice Guide: Real Prop. Transactions Ch. 2-C, C. Broker's Relationship and Obligations to Principal and Third Parties.

Rutter, Cal. Practice Guide: Real Prop. Transactions Ch. 10-B, B. Regulation of Real Property Managers and Legal Relationship Between Manager and Owner.

Rutter, Cal. Practice Guide: Prof. Responsibility Ch. 6-D, D. Professional Liability.

Miller and Starr California Real Estate § 3:19, Salesperson as Employee Versus Independent Contractor--Liability of a Broker for Torts of a Salesperson.

Miller and Starr California Real Estate § 3:51, Principal's Liability for the Agent's Torts.

17 NO. 5 Miller & Starr, California Real Estate Newsalert 4, Construction Contracts.

3 Witkin, California Summary 10th Agency and Employment § 165, (S 165) Statement of Doctrine.

§ 2339. Responsibility for agent's other wrongs

PRINCIPAL'S RESPONSIBILITY FOR WRONGS WILLFULLY COMMITTED BY THE AGENT. A principal is responsible for no other wrongs committed by his agent than those mentioned in the last section, unless he has authorized or ratified them, even though they are committed while the agent is engaged in his service. *(Enacted in 1872.)*

Research References

Rutter, Cal. Practice Guide: Real Prop. Transactions Ch. 2-C, C. Broker's Relationship and Obligations to Principal and Third Parties.

Rutter, Cal. Practice Guide: Real Prop. Transactions Ch. 10-B, B. Regulation of Real Property Managers and Legal Relationship Between Manager and Owner.

Miller and Starr California Real Estate § 3:19, Salesperson as Employee Versus Independent Contractor--Liability of a Broker for Torts of a Salesperson.

Miller and Starr California Real Estate § 3:51, Principal's Liability for the Agent's Torts.

3 Witkin, California Summary 10th Agency and Employment § 163, (S 163) Wrongful Act Directed or Authorized.

3 Witkin, California Summary 10th Agency and Employment § 164, (S 164) Wrongful Act Ratified.

ARTICLE 4. OBLIGATIONS OF AGENTS TO THIRD PERSONS

§ 2342. Warranty of authority

WARRANTY OF AUTHORITY. One who assumes to act as an agent thereby warrants, to all who deal with him in that capacity, that he has the authority which he assumes. *(Enacted in 1872.)*

Research References

Rutter, Cal. Practice Guide: Personal Injury Ch. 4-C, C. Effective Settlement Negotiations.

Rutter, Cal. Practice Guide: Real Prop. Transactions Ch. 2-C, C. Broker's Relationship and Obligations to Principal and Third Parties.

Miller and Starr California Real Estate § 3:8, Warranty of Authority.

Miller and Starr California Real Estate § 5:20, Construing a Listing Agreement--Principles of Interpretation.

3 Witkin, California Summary 10th Agency and Employment § 195, Agent's Warranty of Authority.

§ 2343. Responsibility to third persons

AGENT'S RESPONSIBILITY TO THIRD PERSONS. One who assumes to act as an agent is responsible to third persons as a principal for his acts in the course of his agency, in any of the following cases, and in no others:

1. When, with his consent, credit is given to him personally in a transaction;

2. When he enters into a written contract in the name of his principal, without believing, in good faith, that he has authority to do so; or,

3. When his acts are wrongful in their nature. *(Enacted in 1872.)*

Research References

Rutter, Cal. Practice Guide: Personal Injury Ch. 4-C, C. Effective Settlement Negotiations.
Rutter, Cal. Practice Guide: Real Prop. Transactions Ch. 2-C, C. Broker's Relationship and Obligations to Principal and Third Parties.
Rutter, Cal. Practice Guide: Real Prop. Transactions Ch. 10-B, B. Regulation of Real Property Managers and Legal Relationship Between Manager and Owner.
Miller and Starr California Real Estate § 3:8, Warranty of Authority.
Miller and Starr California Real Estate § 3:36, Tort Liability and Vicarious Liability; Generally.
Miller and Starr California Real Estate § 3:45, Duty Owed to Third Persons.
Miller and Starr California Real Estate § 25B:46, Liability of Officers and Directors; Immunity.
16 NO. 1 Miller & Starr, California Real Estate Newsalert 20, Landowners' Liability.
12 Witkin, California Summary 10th Real Property § 615, Expanded Statute.
5 Witkin, California Summary 10th Torts § 30, (S 30) Agents and Employees.
3 Witkin, California Summary 10th Agency and Employment § 196, (S 196) Contract in Name of Principal.
3 Witkin, California Summary 10th Agency and Employment § 199, in General.

§ 2344. Surrender of property to third persons

OBLIGATION OF AGENT TO SURRENDER PROPERTY TO THIRD PERSON. If an agent receives anything for the benefit of his principal, to the possession of which another person is entitled, he must, on demand, surrender it to such person, or so much of it as he has under his control at the time of demand, on being indemnified for any advance which he has made to his principal, in good faith, on account of the same; and is responsible therefor, if, after notice from the owner, he delivers it to his principal. *(Enacted in 1872.)*

Research References

Miller and Starr California Real Estate § 2:3, Deposit Receipt as a Contract of Sale--Deposit; Duties of Broker Receiving Deposit; Risk of Loss.
Miller and Starr California Real Estate § 6:18, Liability to Third Persons.

§ 2345. Applicability of law of persons

AGENT NOT HAVING CAPACITY TO CONTRACT. The provisions of this Article are subject to the provisions of Part 1, Division First, of this Code. *(Enacted in 1872.)*

ARTICLE 5. DELEGATION OF AGENCY

Section
2349. Authority to delegate powers.
2350. Unauthorized sub-agent; relationship of parties.
2351. Authorized sub-agent; relationship of parties.

§ 2349. Authority to delegate powers

AGENT'S DELEGATION OF HIS POWERS. An agent, unless specially forbidden by his principal to do so, can delegate his powers to another person in any of the following cases, and in no others:

1. When the act to be done is purely mechanical;

2. When it is such as the agent cannot himself, and the sub-agent can lawfully perform;

3. When it is the usage of the place to delegate such powers; or,

4. When such delegation is specially authorized by the principal. *(Enacted in 1872.)*

Research References

Rutter, Cal. Practice Guide: Real Prop. Transactions Ch. 2-C, C. Broker's Relationship and Obligations to Principal and Third Parties.
Miller and Starr California Real Estate § 1:84, Written Authority Required; the Equal Dignities Rule--Exception: Nondiscretionary Acts of the Agent.
Miller and Starr California Real Estate § 3:10, Subagency; Role of the Cooperating Broker.
Miller and Starr California Real Estate § 29:35, Liability for Negligent Supervision.
3 Witkin, California Summary 10th Agency and Employment § 132, (S 132) Delegation of Authority.

§ 2350. Unauthorized sub-agent; relationship of parties

AGENT'S UNAUTHORIZED EMPLOYMENT OF SUB-AGENT. If an agent employs a sub-agent without authority, the former is a principal and the latter his agent, and the principal of the former has no connection with the latter. *(Enacted in 1872.)*

Research References

Rutter, Cal. Practice Guide: Real Prop. Transactions Ch. 2-C, C. Broker's Relationship and Obligations to Principal and Third Parties.
Miller and Starr California Real Estate § 3:10, Subagency; Role of the Cooperating Broker.
3 Witkin, California Summary 10th Agency and Employment § 118, (S 118) Acts or Omissions of Subagent.

§ 2351. Authorized sub-agent; relationship of parties

SUB-AGENT RIGHTFULLY APPOINTED, REPRESENTS PRINCIPAL. A sub-agent, lawfully appointed, represents the principal in like manner with the original agent; and the original agent is not responsible to third persons for the acts of the sub-agent. *(Enacted in 1872.)*

Research References

Rutter, Cal. Practice Guide: Insurance Litigation Ch. 11-J, J. Other Torts Not Necessarily Related to Insurer "Bad Faith".
Rutter, Cal. Practice Guide: Real Prop. Transactions Ch. 2-C, C. Broker's Relationship and Obligations to Principal and Third Parties.
Miller and Starr California Real Estate § 3:10, Subagency; Role of the Cooperating Broker.
Miller and Starr California Real Estate § 3:17, Real Estate Broker Acting as a Principal.
Miller and Starr California Real Estate § 29:35, Liability for Negligent Supervision.
3 Witkin, California Summary 10th Agency and Employment § 174, Subagents and Substitutes.

ARTICLE 6. TERMINATION OF AGENCY

Section
2355. Means of termination.
2356. Agency not coupled with an interest; bona fide transaction; proxies.
2357. Absentee principal; knowledge.

§ 2355. Means of termination

An agency is terminated, as to every person having notice thereof, by any of the following:

(a) The expiration of its term.

(b) The extinction of its subject.

(c) The death of the agent.

(d) The agent's renunciation of the agency.

(e) The incapacity of the agent to act as such. *(Enacted in 1872. Amended by Stats.1972, c. 988, p. 1799, § 1, eff. Aug. 16, 1972; Stats.1980, c. 246, p. 491, § 1; Stats.1983, c. 99, § 5; Stats.1994, c. 307 (S.B.1907), § 1.)*

Law Revision Commission Comments

Section 2355 is amended to delete subdivision (f) relating to the effect of divorce, dissolution, annulment, or separation of principal and agent under a power of attorney, or commencement of an action for these purposes by the agent, in cases involving "absentees." This provision is restated in Probate Code Sections 3722 (effect of legal separation or petition for dissolution, nullity, or legal separation in case of federal absentee) and 4154 (effect of dissolution or nullity). The rules concerning powers of attorney are provided in Probate Code Section 4000 et seq. See also Prob. Code §§ 4022 ("power of attorney" defined), 4050 (types of powers of attorney governed by Probate Code), 4051 (relation to general agency law), 4152 (termination of attorney-in-fact's authority), 4155 (termination of authority under nondurable power of attorney). [24 Cal.L.Rev.Comm.Reports 323 (1994)]..

Research References

Rutter, Cal. Practice Guide: Prof. Responsibility Ch. 10-C, C. Termination by Operation of Law.

Miller and Starr California Real Estate § 1:91, Nonstatutory Form of Agent's Written Authority.

Miller and Starr California Real Estate § 1:92, Statutory Provisions for Powers of Attorney.

Miller and Starr California Real Estate § 3:22, Notice of Termination.

Miller and Starr California Real Estate § 5:53, Termination of the Listing; Owner's Right to Revoke.

Miller and Starr California Real Estate § 5:71, Broker's Contract Rights to a Commission; Probate Listings.

Miller and Starr California Real Estate § 8:31, Scope of Agent's Authority; Power of Attorney.

3 Witkin, California Summary 10th Agency and Employment § 204, (S 204) Acts of Parties.

3 Witkin, California Summary 10th Agency and Employment § 205, (S 205) Operation of Law.

3 Witkin, California Summary 10th Agency and Employment § 213, (S 213) in General.

14 Witkin, California Summary 10th Wills and Probate § 839, (S 839) Enactment of Revised Law.

14 Witkin, California Summary 10th Wills and Probate § 851, Termination of Authority of Attorney-In-Fact.

§ 2356. Agency not coupled with an interest; bona fide transaction; proxies

(a) Unless the power of an agent is coupled with an interest in the subject of the agency, it is terminated by any of the following:

(1) Its revocation by the principal.

(2) The death of the principal.

(3) The incapacity of the principal to contract.

(b) Notwithstanding subdivision (a), any bona fide transaction entered into with an agent by any person acting without actual knowledge of the revocation, death, or incapacity shall be binding upon the principal, his or her heirs, devisees, legatees, and other successors in interest.

(c) Nothing in this section shall affect the provisions of Section 1216.

(d) With respect to a proxy given by a person to another person relating to the exercise of voting rights, to the extent the provisions of this section conflict with or contravene any other provisions of the statutes of California pertaining to the proxy, the latter provisions shall prevail. *(Enacted in 1872. Amended by Stats.1943, c. 413, p. 1951, § 1; Stats.1972, c. 988, p. 1799, § 2, eff. Aug. 16, 1972; Stats.1979, c. 234, p. 488, § 2; Stats.1980, c. 246, p. 491, § 2; Stats.1981, c. 511, p. 1867, § 2; Stats.1983, c. 1204, § 1; Stats.1994, c. 307 (S.B.1907), § 2.)*

Law Revision Commission Comments

Section 2356 is amended to delete the former reference to Section 2307.1 which has been repealed, to make the rules relating to termination of an agency provided by this section subject to the special rules provided by Sections 2400-2407 applicable to a power of attorney, and to make nonsubstantive technical revisions. The substance of the former provision of subdivision (b) relating to a principal who is an "absentee" is continued in Section 2357.

Subdivision (d) is a new provision that makes clear that the provisions of the Uniform Durable Power of Attorney Act (Sections 2400-2407) prevail over the provisions of subdivisions (a) and (b) of Section 2356. Under Sections 2400-2407, a durable power of attorney may be created that remains effective notwithstanding the subsequent disability or incapacity of the principal. In addition, Section 2403 protects the attorney in fact and third persons who rely on a power of attorney in good faith and without actual knowledge of the principal's death, disability, or incapacity, and Section 2404 provides protection to a person acting in good faith in reliance on an affidavit of the attorney in fact that a power of attorney has not been revoked or terminated by the principal's death, disability, or incapacity. [15 Cal.L.Rev. Comm. Reports 351 (1980)].

Subdivision (d) of Section 2356 is amended to add a reference to Article 5 pertaining to powers of attorney for health care decisions. [17 Cal.L.Rev.Comm.Reports 101 (1983)].

Subdivision (d) of Section 2356, concerning powers of attorney, is deleted. The rules concerning powers of attorney are provided in Probate Code Section 4000 et seq. See also Prob. Code §§ 4022 ("power of attorney" defined), 4050(b)(1) (power coupled with an interest), 4051 (relation to general agency law), 4152 (termination of attorney-in-fact's authority), 4155 (termination of authority under nondurable power of attorney), 4304 (effect of death or incapacity of principal). [24 Cal.L.Rev.Comm.Reports 323 (1994)]..

Research References

Rutter, Cal. Practice Guide: Prof. Responsibility Ch. 10-C, C. Termination by Operation of Law.

Miller and Starr California Real Estate § 1:91, Nonstatutory Form of Agent's Written Authority.

Miller and Starr California Real Estate § 1:92, Statutory Provisions for Powers of Attorney.

Miller and Starr California Real Estate § 3:21, Power of Revocation.

Miller and Starr California Real Estate § 3:23, Notice of Termination-- Exception: Agency Coupled With an Interest.

Miller and Starr California Real Estate § 5:53, Termination of the Listing; Owner's Right to Revoke.

Miller and Starr California Real Estate § 8:31, Scope of Agent's Authority; Power of Attorney.

3 Witkin, California Summary 10th Agency and Employment § 204, (S 204) Acts of Parties.

3 Witkin, California Summary 10th Agency and Employment § 205, (S 205) Operation of Law.

3 Witkin, California Summary 10th Agency and Employment § 213, (S 213) in General.

3 Witkin, California Summary 10th Agency and Employment § 215, (S 215) Revocation, Death, or Incapacity of Principal.

3 Witkin, California Summary 10th Agency and Employment § 217, (S 217) Theory of Irrevocable Power.

3 Witkin, California Summary 10th Agency and Employment § 220, in General.

3 Witkin, California Summary 10th Agency and Employment § 221, Hotel Management Contracts.

14 Witkin, California Summary 10th Wills and Probate § 839, (S 839) Enactment of Revised Law.

14 Witkin, California Summary 10th Wills and Probate § 851, Termination of Authority of Attorney-In-Fact.

§ 2357. Absentee principal; knowledge

For the purposes of subdivision (b) of Section 2356, in the case of a principal who is an absentee as defined in Section 1403 of the Probate Code, a person shall be deemed to be without actual knowledge of:

(a) The principal's death or incapacity while the absentee continues in missing status and until the person receives notice of the determination of the death of the absentee by the secretary concerned or the head of the department or agency concerned or the delegate of the secretary or head.

(b) Revocation by the principal during the period described in subdivision (a). *(Added by Stats.1981, c. 511, p. 1867, § 3. Amended by Stats.1994, c. 307 (S.B.1907), § 3.)*

Section 2357 continues the substance of a provision formerly found in Section 2356 but extends the application of the provision to Sections 2403 and 2404. The language of Section 2357 is drawn in part from language found in Section 3708 of the Probate Code (personal property of absentees). [15 Cal.L.Rev. Comm. Reports 351 (1980)].

The references to former Sections 2403 and 2404 (durable powers of attorney) are deleted from Section 2357. The rules concerning powers of attorney are provided in Probate Code Section 4000 et seq. See also Prob. Code §§ 4022 ("power of attorney" defined), 4051 (relation to general agency law). For a similar provision drawn from Section 2357, see Prob. Code § 3721 (knowledge where principal is "absentee"). [24 Cal.L.Rev.Comm.Reports 323 (1994)]..

Research References

Miller and Starr California Real Estate § 1:91, Nonstatutory Form of Agent's Written Authority.
Miller and Starr California Real Estate § 1:92, Statutory Provisions for Powers of Attorney.
Miller and Starr California Real Estate § 8:31, Scope of Agent's Authority; Power of Attorney.
3 Witkin, California Summary 10th Agency and Employment § 215, (S 215) Revocation, Death, or Incapacity of Principal.
14 Witkin, California Summary 10th Wills and Probate § 839, (S 839) Enactment of Revised Law.

CHAPTER 2.   PARTICULAR AGENCIES

ARTICLE 1.   AUCTIONEERS

§ 2362.   Authority from seller

AUCTIONEER'S AUTHORITY FROM THE SELLER. An auctioneer, in the absence of special authorization or usage to the contrary, has authority from the seller, only as follows:

1. To sell by public auction to the highest bidder;

2. To sell for cash only, except such articles as are usually sold on credit at auction;

3. To warrant, in like manner with other agents to sell, according to Section 2323;

4. To prescribe reasonable rules and terms of sale;

5. To deliver the thing sold, upon payment of the price;

6. To collect the price; and,

7. To do whatever else is necessary, or proper and usual, in the ordinary course of business, for effecting these purposes. (Enacted in 1872.)

Research References

3 Witkin, California Summary 10th Agency and Employment § 43, Auctioneers.

§ 2363.   Authority from bidder

AUCTIONEER'S AUTHORITY FROM THE BIDDER. An auctioneer has authority from a bidder at the auction, as well as from the seller, to bind both by a memorandum of the contract, as prescribed in the Title on Sale. (Enacted in 1872.)

Research References

3 Witkin, California Summary 10th Agency and Employment § 43, Auctioneers.

ARTICLE 2.   FACTORS

§ 2367.   Factor defined

FACTOR, WHAT. A factor is an agent, as defined by Section 2026. (Enacted in 1872.)

§ 2368.   Actual authority

ACTUAL AUTHORITY OF FACTOR. In addition to the authority of agents in general, a factor has actual authority from his principal, unless specially restricted:

1. To insure property consigned to him uninsured;

2. To sell, on credit, anything intrusted to him for sale, except such things as it is contrary to usage to sell on credit; but not to pledge, mortgage, or barter the same; and,

3. To delegate his authority to his partner or servant, but not to any person in an independent employment. (Enacted in 1872.)

Research References

3 Witkin, California Summary 10th Agency and Employment § 44, Factors.

§ 2369.   Ostensible authority

OSTENSIBLE AUTHORITY. A factor has ostensible authority to deal with the property of his principal as his own, in transactions with persons not having notice of the actual ownership. (Enacted in 1872.)

Research References

4 Witkin, California Summary 10th Sales § 230, Sale of Motor Vehicle.
3 Witkin, California Summary 10th Agency and Employment § 44, Factors.

ARTICLE 3.   POWERS OF ATTORNEY UNDER PROBATE CODE

§ 2400.   Powers of attorney; applicable law

Powers of attorney are governed by the Power of Attorney Law (Division 4.5 (commencing with Section 4000) of the Probate Code) to the extent provided in that law. (Added by Stats.1994, c. 307 (S.B.1907), § 5.)

Section 2400 provides a cross-reference to the Power of Attorney Law in the Probate Code which supersedes the various power of attorney statutes formerly located at Civil Code Section 2400 et seq. See Prob. Code §§ 4022 ("power of attorney" defined), 4050 (types of powers of attorney governed by Power of Attorney Law). [24 Cal.L.Rev.Comm.Reports 323 (1994)].

Former Section 2400 is restated without substantive change in Probate Code Section 4124 (requirements for durable power of attorney). See Prob. Code § 4124 Comment. [24 Cal.L.Rev.Comm.Reports 323 (1994)].

Research References

Miller and Starr California Real Estate § 8:31, Scope of Agent's Authority; Power of Attorney.
11 Witkin, California Summary 10th Husband and Wife § 146, Proceedings.
3 Witkin, California Summary 10th Agency and Employment § 207, (S 207) Durable Power of Attorney.
14 Witkin, California Summary 10th Wills and Probate § 837, (S 837) Original Statutes.
14 Witkin, California Summary 10th Wills and Probate § 839, (S 839) Enactment of Revised Law.
14 Witkin, California Summary 10th Wills and Probate § 841, (S 841) in General.

Title 10

RECORDING ARTIST CONTRACTS

Section
2500. Definitions.
2501. Audit of books and records of royalty reporting party; conditions.

§ 2500. Definitions

As used in this title:

(a) "Royalty recipient" means a party to a contract for the furnishing of services in the production of sound recordings, as defined in Section 101 of Title 17 of the United States Code, who has the right to receive royalties under that contract.

(b) A "royalty reporting party" is the party obligated to pay royalties to the royalty recipient under the contract described in subdivision (a). *(Added by Stats.2004, c. 150 (S.B.1034), § 2.)*

Research References

13 Witkin, California Summary 10th Personal Property § 56, Audit Rights of Sound Recording Royalty Recipient.
14 Witkin, California Summary 10th Wills and Probate § 876, (S 876) Former Law.

§ 2501. Audit of books and records of royalty reporting party; conditions

Notwithstanding any provision of a contract described in Section 2500:

(a) A royalty recipient may audit the books and records of the royalty reporting party to determine if the royalty recipient earned all of the royalties due the royalty recipient pursuant to the contract, subject to the following:

(1) A royalty recipient may conduct an audit not more than once per year.

(2) A royalty recipient shall request an audit within three years after the end of a royalty earnings period under the contract.

(3) A royalty recipient may not audit a particular royalty earnings period more than once.

(b) The royalty recipient shall retain a qualified royalty auditor of the royalty recipient's choice to conduct an audit described in this section.

(c) The royalty recipient may enter into a contingency fee agreement with the auditor described in subdivision (b).

(d) A qualified royalty auditor may conduct individual audits of the books and records of a royalty reporting party on behalf of different royalty recipients simultaneously.

(e) Except as required by law, a qualified royalty auditor shall not disclose any confidential information obtained solely during an audit without the express consent of the party or parties to whom that information is confidential. This subdivision shall not prohibit the auditor from disclosing to the royalty recipient, or an agent of the recipient, on behalf of whom the auditor is conducting the audit information directly pertaining to that royalty recipient's contract, as described in Section 2500.

(f) The provisions of subdivisions (a), (b), (c), (d), and (e) are in addition to any other rights provided by a contract, as described in Section 2500, between a royalty recipient and a royalty reporting party.

(g) Nothing in subdivision (a), (b), (c), (d), or (e) shall be deemed to extend any limitations period applicable to royalty accounting or payments not specifically addressed in this section.

(h) Nothing in subdivision (a), (b), (c), (d), or (e) shall be deemed to limit any rights provided by collective bargaining agreement or by applicable state or federal law. *(Added by Stats.2004, c. 150 (S.B.1034), § 2.)*

Research References

13 Witkin, California Summary 10th Personal Property § 56, Audit Rights of Sound Recording Royalty Recipient.

Title 11

PHARMACEUTICAL SERVICES

Section
2527. Prescription drug claims processors; requirements; fee studies.
2528. Violations; civil remedy; damages; attorney's fees and costs; standing; notice.

§ 2527. Prescription drug claims processors; requirements; fee studies

(a) On or after January 1, 1984, no prescription drug claims processor, as defined in subdivision (b), shall enter into or perform any provision of any new contract, or perform any provision of any existing contract, with a licensed California pharmacy, or process or assist in the processing of any prescription drug claim submitted by or otherwise involving a service of a licensed California pharmacy unless the processor is in compliance with subdivisions (c) and (d).

(b) A "prescription drug claims processor," as used in this part, means any nongovernmental entity which has a contractual relationship with purchasers of prepaid or insured prescription drug benefits, and which processes, consults, advises on, or otherwise assists in the processing of prepaid or insured prescription drug benefit claims submitted by a licensed California pharmacy or patron thereof. A "prescription drug claims processor" shall not include insurers (as defined in Section 23 of the Insurance Code), health care service plans (as defined in subdivision (f) of Section 1345 of the Health and Safety Code), nonprofit hospital service plans (pursuant to Chapter 11A, (commencing with Section 11491) of Part 2 of Division 2 of the Insurance Code), pharmacy permitholders (pursuant to Section 4080 of the Business and Professions Code), employers, trusts, and other entities which assume the risks of pharmaceutical services for designated beneficiaries. Also, a "prescription drug claims processor" shall not include insurers, health care service plans, and nonprofit hospital service plans which process claims on a nonrisk basis for self-insured clients.

(c) On or before January 1, 1984, every prescription drug claims processor shall have conducted or obtained the results of a study or studies which identifies the fees, separate from ingredient costs, of all, or of a statistically significant sample, of California pharmacies, for pharmaceutical dispensing services to private consumers. The study or studies shall meet reasonable professional standards of the statistical profession. The determination of the pharmacy's fee made for purposes of the study or studies shall be computed by reviewing a sample of the pharmacy's usual charges for a random or other representative sample of commonly prescribed drug products, subtracting the average wholesale price of drug ingredients, and averaging the resulting fees by dividing the aggregate of the fees by the number of prescriptions reviewed. A study report shall include a preface, an explanatory summary of the results and findings including a comparison of the fees of California pharmacies by setting forth the mean fee and standard deviation, the range of fees and fee percentiles (10th, 20th, 30th, 40th, 50th, 60th, 70th, 80th, 90th). This study or these studies shall be conducted or obtained no less often than every 24 months.

(d) The study report or reports obtained pursuant to subdivision (c) shall be transmitted by certified mail by each prescription drug claims processor to the chief executive officer or designee, of each client for whom it performs claims processing services. Consistent with subdivision (c), the processor shall transmit the study or studies to clients no less often than every 24 months.

Nothing in this section shall be construed to require a prescription drug claims processor to transmit to its clients more than two studies meeting the requirements of subdivision (c) during any such 24-month period.

Effective January 1, 1986, a claims processor may comply with subdivision (c) and this subdivision, in the event that no new study or studies meeting the criteria of subdivision (c) have been conducted or obtained subsequent to January 1, 1984, by transmitting the same study or studies previously transmitted, with notice of cost-of-living changes as measured by the Consumer Price Index (CPI) of the United States Department of Labor. *(Added by Stats.1982, c. 296, p. 937, § 1.)*

Validity

This statute was held unconstitutional as a restriction on freedom of speech, in the decision of ARP Pharmacy Services, Inc. v. Gallagher Bassett Services, Inc. (App. 2 Dist. 2006) 42 Cal.Rptr.3d 256, 138 Cal.App.4th 1307.

§ 2528. Violations; civil remedy; damages; attorney's fees and costs; standing; notice

A violation of Section 2527 may result only in imposition of a civil remedy, which includes, but is not limited to, imposition of statutory damages of not less than one thousand dollars ($1,000) or more than ten thousand dollars ($10,000) depending on the severity or gravity of the violation, plus reasonable attorney's fees and costs, declaratory and injunctive relief, and any other relief which the court deems proper. Any owner of a licensed California pharmacy shall have standing to bring an action seeking a civil remedy pursuant to this section so long as his or her pharmacy has a contractual relationship with, or renders pharmaceutical services to, a beneficiary of a client of the prescription drug claims processor, against whom the action is brought provided that no such action may be commenced by the owner unless he or she has notified the processor in writing as to the nature of the alleged violation and the processor fails to remedy the violation within 30 days from the receipt of the notice or fails to undertake steps to remedy the violation within that period and complete the steps promptly thereafter. *(Added by Stats.1982, c. 296, p. 938, § 1.)*

Validity

This statute was held unconstitutional in the decision of ARP Pharmacy Services, Inc. v. Gallagher Bassett Services, Inc. (App. 2 Dist. 2006) 42 Cal.Rptr.3d 256, 138 Cal.App.4th 1307.

Title 12
INDEMNITY

§ 2772. Definitions

Indemnity is a contract by which one engages to save another from a legal consequence of the conduct of one of the parties, or of some other person. *(Enacted in 1872.)*

Research References

Rutter, Cal. Practice Guide: Insurance Litigation Ch. 6I-A, A. Introduction.

Rutter, Cal. Practice Guide: Real Prop. Transactions Ch. 4-E, E. Drafting the Purchase and Sale Agreement-Terms and Conditions.

Miller and Starr California Real Estate § 27:46, Indemnity Provisions; Wrap-Up Insurance.

Miller and Starr California Real Estate § 29:17, Express and Implied Indemnity.

2 Witkin, California Summary 10th Insurance § 4, (S 4) Insurer's Rights of Subrogation, Contribution, and Indemnity.

13 Witkin, California Summary 10th Equity § 178, Equitable Indemnity: Reimbursement from Principal.

§ 2773. Future wrongful act; invalidity

An agreement to indemnify a person against an act thereafter to be done, is void, if the act be known by such person at the time of doing it to be unlawful. *(Enacted in 1872. Amended by Code Am. 1873–74, c. 612, p. 259, § 253.)*

Research References

Rutter, Cal. Practice Guide: Insurance Litigation Ch. 1-A, A. Insurance-In General.
Rutter, Cal. Practice Guide: Insurance Litigation Ch. 3-A, A. Statutory Requirements Re Policy Contents.
Rutter, Cal. Practice Guide: Insurance Litigation Ch. 7A-H, H. Other Exclusions.
Rutter, Cal. Practice Guide: Insurance Litigation Ch. 7A-H, Outline H.
Miller and Starr California Real Estate § 27:46, Indemnity Provisions; Wrap-Up Insurance.
2 Witkin, California Summary 10th Insurance § 100, in General.
5 Witkin, California Summary 10th Torts § 121, (S 121) Void Clauses.

§ 2774. Past wrongful act; validity

An agreement to indemnify a person against an act already done, is valid, even though the act was known to be wrongful, unless it was a felony. *(Enacted in 1872.)*

Research References

Miller and Starr California Real Estate § 27:46, Indemnity Provisions; Wrap-Up Insurance.
5 Witkin, California Summary 10th Torts § 121, (S 121) Void Clauses.

§ 2775. Extension to acts of agents

An agreement to indemnify against the acts of a certain person, applies not only to his acts and their consequences, but also to those of his agents. *(Enacted in 1872.)*

§ 2776. Agreement to indemnify several persons; application

An agreement to indemnify several persons applies to each, unless a contrary intention appears. *(Enacted in 1872.)*

§ 2777. Joint or separate liability

One who indemnifies another against an act to be done by the latter, is liable jointly with the person indemnified, and separately, to every person injured by such act. *(Enacted in 1872.)*

§ 2778. Rules of interpretation

In the interpretation of a contract of indemnity, the following rules are to be applied, unless a contrary intention appears:

1. Upon an indemnity against liability, expressly, or in other equivalent terms, the person indemnified is entitled to recover upon becoming liable;

2. Upon an indemnity against claims, or demands, or damages, or costs, expressly, or in other equivalent terms, the person indemnified is not entitled to recover without payment thereof;

3. An indemnity against claims, or demands, or liability, expressly, or in other equivalent terms, embraces the costs of defense against such claims, demands, or liability incurred in good faith, and in the exercise of a reasonable discretion;

4. The person indemnifying is bound, on request of the person indemnified, to defend actions or proceedings brought against the latter in respect to the matters embraced by the indemnity, but the person indemnified has the right to conduct such defenses, if he chooses to do so;

5. If, after request, the person indemnifying neglects to defend the person indemnified, a recovery against the latter suffered by him in good faith, is conclusive in his favor against the former;

6. If the person indemnifying, whether he is a principal or a surety in the agreement, has not reasonable notice of the action or proceeding against the person indemnified, or is not allowed to control its defense, judgment against the latter is only presumptive evidence against the former;

7. A stipulation that a judgment against the person indemnified shall be conclusive upon the person indemnifying, is inapplicable if he had a good defense upon the merits, which by want of ordinary care he failed to establish in the action. *(Enacted in 1872.)*

Research References

Rutter, Cal. Practice Guide: Civ. Pro. Before Trial Ch. 1-A, A. Accepting a New Case.
Rutter, Cal. Practice Guide: Civil Trials & Evidence Ch. 8D-D, D. Hearsay Exceptions.
California Practice Guide: Employment Litigation Ch. 3-A, A. Employer's Obligation to Indemnify Employees.
Rutter, Cal. Practice Guide: Insurance Litigation Ch. 9-E, E. Requirements for Equitable Subrogation.
Rutter, Cal. Practice Guide: Insurance Litigation Ch. 6I-A, A. Introduction.
Rutter, Cal. Practice Guide: Insurance Litigation Ch. 7A-A, A. Liability Insurance-In General.
Rutter, Cal. Practice Guide: Insurance Litigation Ch. 7B-C, C. Determining Existence of Duty to Defend.
Rutter, Cal. Practice Guide: Insurance Litigation Ch. 7E-A, A. General Considerations.
Rutter, Cal. Practice Guide: Insurance Litigation Ch. 7E-B, B. Commercial General Liability (CGL) Policies.
Rutter, Cal. Practice Guide: Insurance Litigation Ch. 12B-D, D. Refusal to Defend Cases.
Rutter, Cal. Practice Guide: Real Prop. Transactions Ch. 4-E, E. Drafting the Purchase and Sale Agreement-Terms and Conditions.
Miller and Starr California Real Estate § 27:46, Indemnity Provisions; Wrap-Up Insurance.
Miller and Starr California Real Estate § 29:12, Insurance Coverage Applicable to Contractors and Developers.
Miller and Starr California Real Estate § 29:17, Express and Implied Indemnity.
Miller and Starr California Real Estate § 7:196, Scope of Every Insurer's Duty to Defend.
19 NO. 2 Miller & Starr, California Real Estate Newsalert 12, Defective Construction.
20 NO. 4 Miller & Starr, California Real Estate Newsalert 27, Defective Construction.
21 NO. 4 Miller & Starr, California Real Estate Newsalert 22, Construction Law and Contracting.
22 NO. 2 Miller & Starr, California Real Estate Newsalert 15, Judicial Remedies.
7 Witkin Cal. Proc. 5th Judgment § 153, Action Based on Failure to Defend.
7 Witkin Cal. Proc. 5th Judgment § 381, Nonsuit in Jury Trial.
2 Witkin, California Summary 10th Insurance § 300, (S 300) Assignment of Cause of Action Against Insurer.
5 Witkin, California Summary 10th Torts § 120, (S 120) Interpretation of Clauses.
5 Witkin, California Summary 10th Torts § 124, (S 124) Effect of Indemnitee's Settlement of Underlying Claim.
13 Witkin, California Summary 10th Equity § 178, Equitable Indemnity: Reimbursement from Principal.
14 Witkin, California Summary 10th Wills and Probate § 613, Estoppel and Waiver.

§ 2779. Reimbursement of person indemnifying; manner

Where one, at the request of another, engages to answer in damages, whether liquidated or unliquidated, for any violation of duty on the part of the latter, he is entitled to be reimbursed in the same manner as a surety, for whatever he may pay. *(Enacted in 1872.)*

Research References

Rutter, Cal. Practice Guide: Insurance Litigation Ch. 6I-E, E. Surety's Rights Upon Payment of Bond.

§ 2782. Construction contracts; void and unenforceable indemnification provisions; agreements between subcontractors, builders, or general contractors

(a) Except as provided in Sections 2782.1, 2782.2, 2782.5, and 2782.6, provisions, clauses, covenants, or agreements contained in, collateral to, or affecting any construction contract and that purport to indemnify the promisee against liability for damages for death or bodily injury to persons, injury to property, or any other loss, damage or expense arising from the sole negligence or willful misconduct of the promisee or the promisee's agents, servants, or independent contractors who are directly responsible to the promisee, or for defects in design furnished by those persons, are against public policy and are void and unenforceable; provided, however, that this section shall not affect the validity of any insurance contract, workers' compensation, or agreement issued by an admitted insurer as defined by the Insurance Code.

(b)(1) Except as provided in Sections 2782.1, 2782.2, and 2782.5, provisions, clauses, covenants, or agreements contained in, collateral to, or affecting any construction contract with a public agency entered into before January 1, 2013, that purport to impose on the contractor, or relieve the public agency from, liability for the active negligence of the public agency are void and unenforceable.

(2) Except as provided in Sections 2782.1, 2782.2, and 2782.5, provisions, clauses, covenants, or agreements contained in, collateral to, or affecting any construction contract with a public agency entered into on or after January 1, 2013, that purport to impose on any contractor, subcontractor, or supplier of goods or services, or relieve the public agency from, liability for the active negligence of the public agency are void and unenforceable.

(c)(1) Except as provided in subdivision (d) and Sections 2782.1, 2782.2, and 2782.5, provisions, clauses, covenants, or agreements contained in, collateral to, or affecting any construction contract entered into on or after January 1, 2013, with the owner of privately owned real property to be improved and as to which the owner is not acting as a contractor or supplier of materials or equipment to the work, that purport to impose on any contractor, subcontractor, or supplier of goods or services, or relieve the owner from, liability are unenforceable to the extent of the active negligence of the owner, including that of its employees.

(2) For purposes of this subdivision, an owner of privately owned real property to be improved includes the owner of any interest therein, other than a mortgage or other interest that is held solely as security for performance of an obligation.

(3) This subdivision shall not apply to a homeowner performing a home improvement project on his or her own single family dwelling.

(d) For all construction contracts, and amendments thereto, entered into after January 1, 2009, for residential construction, as used in Title 7 (commencing with Section 895) of Part 2 of Division 2, all provisions, clauses, covenants, and agreements contained in, collateral to, or affecting any construction contract, and amendments thereto, that purport to insure or indemnify, including the cost to defend, the builder, as defined in Section 911, or the general contractor or contractor not affiliated with the builder, as described in subdivision (b) of Section 911, by a subcontractor against liability for claims of construction defects are unenforceable to the extent the claims arise out of, pertain to, or relate to the negligence of the builder or contractor or the builder's or contractor's other agents, other servants, or other independent contractors who are directly responsible to the builder, or for defects in design furnished by those persons, or to the extent the claims do not arise out of, pertain to, or relate to the scope of work in the written agreement between the parties. This section shall not be waived or modified by contractual agreement, act, or omission of the parties. Contractual provisions, clauses, covenants, or agreements not expressly prohibited herein are reserved to the agreement of the parties. Nothing in this subdivision shall prevent any party from exercising its rights under subdivision (a) of Section 910. This subdivision shall not

affect the obligations of an insurance carrier under the holding of Presley Homes, Inc. v. American States Insurance Company (2001) 90 Cal.App.4th 571. Nor shall this subdivision affect the obligations of a builder or subcontractor pursuant to Title 7 (commencing with Section 895) of Part 2 of Division 2.

(e) Subdivision (d) does not prohibit a subcontractor and builder or general contractor from mutually agreeing to the timing or immediacy of the defense and provisions for reimbursement of defense fees and costs, so long as that agreement does not waive or modify the provisions of subdivision (d) subject, however, to paragraphs (1) and (2). A subcontractor shall owe no defense or indemnity obligation to a builder or general contractor for a construction defect claim unless and until the builder or general contractor provides a written tender of the claim, or portion thereof, to the subcontractor which includes all of the information provided to the builder or general contractor by the claimant or claimants, including, but not limited to, information provided pursuant to subdivision (a) of Section 910, relating to claims caused by that subcontractor's scope of work. This written tender shall have the same force and effect as a notice of commencement of a legal proceeding. If a builder or general contractor tenders a claim for construction defects, or a portion thereof, to a subcontractor in the manner specified by this provision, the subcontractor shall elect to perform either of the following, the performance of which shall be deemed to satisfy the subcontractor's defense obligation to the builder or general contractor:

(1) Defend the claim with counsel of its choice, and the subcontractor shall maintain control of the defense for any claim or portion of claim to which the defense obligation applies. If a subcontractor elects to defend under this paragraph, the subcontractor shall provide written notice of the election to the builder or general contractor within a reasonable time period following receipt of the written tender, and in no event later than 90 days following that receipt. Consistent with subdivision (d), the defense by the subcontractor shall be a complete defense of the builder or general contractor of all claims or portions thereof to the extent alleged to be caused by the subcontractor, including any vicarious liability claims against the builder or general contractor resulting from the subcontractor's scope of work, but not including claims resulting from the scope of work, actions, or omissions of the builder, general contractor, or any other party. Any vicarious liability imposed upon a builder or general contractor for claims caused by the subcontractor electing to defend under this paragraph shall be directly enforceable against the subcontractor by the builder, general contractor, or claimant.

(2) Pay, within 30 days of receipt of an invoice from the builder or general contractor, no more than a reasonable allocated share of the builder's or general contractor's defense fees and costs, on an ongoing basis during the pendency of the claim, subject to reallocation consistent with subdivision (d), and including any amounts reallocated upon final resolution of the claim, either by settlement or judgment. The builder or general contractor shall allocate a share to itself to the extent a claim or claims are alleged to be caused by its work, actions, or omissions, and a share to each subcontractor to the extent a claim or claims are alleged to be caused by the subcontractor's work, actions, or omissions, regardless of whether the builder or general contractor actually tenders the claim to any particular subcontractor, and regardless of whether that subcontractor is participating in the defense. Any amounts not collected from any particular subcontractor may not be collected from any other subcontractor.

(f) Notwithstanding any other provision of law, if a subcontractor fails to timely and adequately perform its obligations under paragraph (1) of subdivision (e), the builder or general contractor shall have the right to pursue a claim against the subcontractor for any resulting compensatory damages, consequential damages, and reasonable attorney's fees. If a subcontractor fails to timely perform its obligations under paragraph (2) of subdivision (e), the builder or general contractor shall have the right to pursue a claim against the subcontractor for any resulting compensatory and consequential damages, as well as for interest on defense and indemnity costs, from the date incurred, at the rate set forth in subdivision (g) of Section 3260, and for the builder's or general contractor's reasonable attorney's fees incurred to recover these amounts. The builder or general contractor shall bear the burden of proof to establish both the subcontractor's failure to perform under either paragraph (1) or (2) of subdivision (e) and any resulting damages. If, upon request by a subcontractor, a builder or general contractor does not reallocate defense fees to subcontractors within 30 days following final resolution of the claim as described above, the subcontractor shall have the right to pursue a claim against the builder or general contractor for any resulting compensatory and consequential damages, as well as for interest on the fees, from the date of final resolution of the claim, at the rate set forth in subdivision (g) of Section 3260, and the subcontractor's reasonable attorney's fees incurred in connection therewith. The subcontractor shall bear the burden of proof to establish both the failure to reallocate the fees and any resulting damages. Nothing in this section shall prohibit the parties from mutually agreeing to reasonable contractual provisions for damages if any party fails to elect for or perform its obligations as stated in this section.

(g) A builder, general contractor, or subcontractor shall have the right to seek equitable indemnity for any claim governed by this section.

(h) Nothing in this section limits, restricts, or prohibits the right of a builder, general contractor, or subcontractor to seek equitable indemnity against any supplier, design professional, or product manufacturer.

(i) As used in this section, "construction defect" means a violation of the standards set forth in Sections 896 and 897. *(Added by Stats.1967, c. 1327, p. 3158, § 1. Amended by Stats.1980, c. 211, p. 442, § 1; Stats.1982, c. 386, p. 1717, § 1; Stats.1985, c. 567, § 1; Stats.1990, c. 814 (S.B.1922), § 1; Stats.2005, c. 394 (A.B.758), § 1; Stats.2007, c. 32 (S.B.138), § 1; Stats.2008, c. 467 (A.B.2738), § 1; Stats.2011, c. 707 (S.B.474), § 2.)*

Research References

California Real Estate Forms (Miller & Starr) § 4:4, Construction Contract--Cost Plus a Fixed Fee With a Guaranteed Maximum Price.

California Real Estate Forms (Miller & Starr) § 4:6, Construction Contract--Fixed Price--Commercial Project.

California Real Estate Forms (Miller & Starr) § 5:4, Owner--Architect Agreement (Owner-Oriented).

California Real Estate Forms (Miller & Starr) § 5:7, General Conditions to Consultant Agreement.

California Real Estate Forms (Miller & Starr) § 1:23, Purchase and Sale Agreement--Residential Project.

California Real Estate Forms (Miller & Starr) § 1:24, Combination Purchase and Option Agreement--Residential Lots Being Acquired from a Bankrupt Seller.

California Real Estate Forms (Miller & Starr) § 4:14, Construction Agreement-- Master Agreement for Construction Services.

California Real Estate Forms (Miller & Starr) § 4:15, Development Agreement.

California Real Estate Forms (Miller & Starr) § 4:16, Restaurant Development and Construction Agreement.

California Real Estate Forms (Miller & Starr) § 4:20, Service Contract--Elevators.

California Real Estate Forms (Miller & Starr) § 4:21, Environmental Surveying--General Conditions.

California Real Estate Forms (Miller & Starr) § 5:19, Indemnity.

California Real Estate Forms (Miller & Starr) § 5:186, Construction Manager to Indemnify Owner; Owner to Indemnify Construction Manager--Construction Management Agreement.

California Real Estate Forms (Miller & Starr) § 5:196, Detailed Subcontract With General Conditions and General Provisions.

California Real Estate Forms (Miller & Starr) § 5:197, Subcontract Providing for Work to Stop If Hazardous Material Found.

California Real Estate Forms (Miller & Starr) § 5:198, Subcontract (With Progress Payments).

California Real Estate Forms (Miller & Starr) § 5:199, Subcontract (For Use With Union Labor).

California Real Estate Forms (Miller & Starr) § 5:201, Subcontract--Long Form.

California Real Estate Forms (Miller & Starr) § 5:202, Subcontract--Commercial Project.

California Real Estate Forms (Miller & Starr) § 5:205, Subcontract--Glazing.

California Real Estate Forms (Miller & Starr) § 5:405, Subcontractor to Indemnify General Contractor; General Contractor to Indemnify Subcontractor--Subcontract.

California Real Estate Forms (Miller & Starr) § 5:406, Subcontractor to Indemnify General Contractor and Owner Against Claims for Injuries--Subcontract.

Rutter, Cal. Practice Guide: Insurance Litigation Ch. 8-B, B. Contribution Between Insurers.

Rutter, Cal. Practice Guide: Insurance Litigation Ch. 9-E, E. Requirements for Equitable Subrogation.

Rutter, Cal. Practice Guide: Insurance Litigation Ch. 7E-A, A. General Considerations.

Rutter, Cal. Practice Guide: Real Prop. Transactions Ch. 4-E, E. Drafting the Purchase and Sale Agreement-Terms and Conditions.

Miller and Starr California Real Estate § 23:5, Environmental Investigation (Due Diligence).

Miller and Starr California Real Estate § 29:2, Statutory Liability Under "SB800" for Residential Units Sold New After January 1, 2003.

Miller and Starr California Real Estate § 27:46, Indemnity Provisions; Wrap-Up Insurance.

Miller and Starr California Real Estate § 27:85, Contractor's Remedies--"No Damages for Delay" Clauses.

Miller and Starr California Real Estate § 29:11, Owner's Insurance Coverage.

Miller and Starr California Real Estate § 29:17, Express and Implied Indemnity.

Miller and Starr California Real Estate § 29:31, Liability for Defective Plans and Specifications; to the Owner.

16 NO. 4 Miller & Starr, California Real Estate Newsalert 4, Construction Contracts.

16 NO. 5 Miller & Starr, California Real Estate Newsalert 26, State Board of Equalization Issues Comprehensive Summary and Qs and As for Transfers of Base Year Values of Principal Residences.

18 NO. 4 Miller & Starr, California Real Estate Newsalert 5, Construction Contracts.

18 NO. 4 Miller & Starr, California Real Estate Newsalert 45, Table of Statutes (Newsalert Vol 18).

19 NO. 4 Miller & Starr, California Real Estate Newsalert 7, Construction Contracts.

22 NO. 4 Miller & Starr, California Real Estate Newsalert 8, Construction Law and Contracting.

1 Witkin Cal. Summ. 10th Contracts § 666, (S 666) Statutory Prohibitions.

1 Witkin Cal. Summ. 10th Contracts § 667, (S 667) Exceptions.

1 Witkin Cal. Summ. 10th Contracts § 677, in General.

5 Witkin, California Summary 10th Torts § 120, (S 120) Interpretation of Clauses.

5 Witkin, California Summary 10th Torts § 121, (S 121) Void Clauses.

§ 2782.05. Construction contracts; void and unenforceable indemnification provisions; agreements between general contractors, construction managers, or subcontractors

(a) Except as provided in subdivision (b), provisions, clauses, covenants, and agreements contained in, collateral to, or affecting any construction contract and amendments thereto entered into on or after January 1, 2013, that purport to insure or indemnify, including the cost to defend, a general contractor, construction manager, or other subcontractor, by a subcontractor against liability for claims of death or bodily injury to persons, injury to property, or any other loss, damage, or expense are void and unenforceable to the extent the claims arise out of, pertain to, or relate to the active negligence or willful misconduct of that general contractor, construction manager, or other subcontractor, or their other agents, other servants, or other independent contractors who are responsible to the general contractor, construction manager, or other subcontractor, or for defects in design furnished by those persons, or to the extent the claims do not arise out of the scope of work of the subcontractor pursuant to the construction contract. This section shall not be waived or modified by contractual agreement, act, or omission of the parties. Contractual provisions, clauses, covenants, or agreements not expressly prohibited herein are reserved to the agreement of the parties. This section shall not affect the obligations of an insurance carrier under the holding of Presley Homes, Inc. v. American States Insurance Company (2001) 90 Cal.App.4th 571, nor the rights of an insurance carrier under the holding of Buss v. Superior Court (1997) 16 Cal.4th 35.

(b) This section does not apply to:

(1) Contracts for residential construction that are subject to any part of Title 7 (commencing with Section 895) of Part 2 of Division 2.

(2) Direct contracts with a public agency that are governed by subdivision (b) of Section 2782.

(3) Direct contracts with the owner of privately owned real property to be improved that are governed by subdivision (c) of Section 2782.

(4) Any wrap-up insurance policy or program.

(5) A cause of action for breach of contract or warranty that exists independently of an indemnity obligation.

(6) A provision in a construction contract that requires the promisor to purchase or maintain insurance covering the acts or omissions of the promisor, including additional insurance endorsements covering the acts or omissions of the promisor during ongoing and completed operations.

(7) Indemnity provisions contained in loan and financing documents, other than construction contracts to which the contractor and a contracting project owner's lender are parties.

(8) General agreements of indemnity required by sureties as a condition of execution of bonds for construction contracts.

(9) The benefits and protections provided by the workers' compensation laws.

(10) The benefits or protections provided by the governmental immunity laws.

(11) Provisions that require the purchase of any of the following:

(A) Owners and contractors protective liability insurance.

(B) Railroad protective liability insurance.

(C) Contractors all-risk insurance.

(D) Builders all-risk or named perils property insurance.

(12) Contracts with design professionals.

(13) Any agreement between a promisor and an admitted surety insurer regarding the promisor's obligations as a principal or indemnitor on a bond.

(c) Notwithstanding any choice-of-law rules that would apply the laws of another jurisdiction, the law of California shall apply to every contract to which this section applies.

(d) Any waiver of the provisions of this section is contrary to public policy and is void and unenforceable.

(e) Subdivision (a) does not prohibit a subcontractor and a general contractor or construction manager from mutually agreeing to the timing or immediacy of the defense and provisions for reimbursement of defense fees and costs, so long as that agreement does not waive or modify the provisions of subdivision (a) subject, however, to paragraphs (1) and (2). A subcontractor shall owe no defense or indemnity obligation to a general contractor or construction manager for a claim unless and until the general contractor or construction manager provides a written tender of the claim, or portion thereof, to the subcontractor that includes the information provided by the claimant or claimants relating to claims caused by that subcontractor's scope of work. In addition, the general contractor or construction manager shall provide a written statement regarding how the reasonable allocated share of fees and costs was determined. The written tender shall have the same force and effect as a notice of commencement of a legal proceeding. If a general contractor or construction manager tenders a claim, or portion thereof, to a subcontractor in the manner specified by this subdivision, the subcontractor shall elect to perform either of the following, the performance of which shall be deemed to satisfy the subcontractor's defense obligation to the general contractor or construction manager:

(1) Defend the claim with counsel of its choice, and the subcontractor shall maintain control of the defense for any claim or portion of claim to which the defense obligation applies. If a subcontractor elects to defend under this paragraph, the subcontractor shall provide written notice of the election to the general contractor or construction manager within a reasonable time period following receipt of the written tender, and in no event later than 30 days following that receipt. Consistent with subdivision (a), the defense by the subcontractor shall be a complete defense of the general contractor or construction manager of all claims or portions thereof to the extent alleged to be caused by the subcontractor, including any vicarious liability claims against the general contractor or construction manager resulting from the subcontractor's scope of work, but not including claims resulting from the scope of work, actions, or omissions of the general contractor or construction manager, or any other party. Any vicarious liability imposed upon a general contractor or construction manager for claims caused by the subcontractor electing to defend under this paragraph shall be directly enforceable against the subcontractor by the general contractor, construction manager, or claimant. All information, documentation, or evidence, if any, relating to a subcontractor's assertion that another party is responsible for the claim shall be provided by that subcontractor to the general contractor or construction manager that tendered the claim.

(2) Pay, within 30 days of receipt of an invoice from the general contractor or construction manager, no more than a reasonable allocated share of the general contractor's or construction manager's defense fees and costs, on an ongoing basis during the pendency of the claim, subject to reallocation consistent with subdivision (a), and including any amounts reallocated upon final resolution of the claim, either by settlement or judgment. The general contractor or construction manager shall allocate a share to itself to the extent a claim or claims are alleged to be caused by its work, actions, or omissions, and a share to each subcontractor to the extent a claim or claims are alleged to be caused by the subcontractor's work, actions, or omissions, regardless of whether the general contractor or construction manager actually tenders the claim to any particular subcontractor, and regardless of whether that subcontractor is participating in the defense. Any amounts not collected from any particular subcontractor may not be collected from any other subcontractor.

(f) Notwithstanding any other provision of law, if a subcontractor fails to timely and adequately perform its obligations under paragraph (1) of subdivision (e), the general contractor or construction manager shall have the right to pursue a claim against the subcontractor for any resulting compensatory damages, consequential damages, and reasonable attorney's fees. If a subcontractor fails to timely perform its obligations under paragraph (2) of subdivision (e), the general contractor or construction manager shall have the right to pursue a claim against the subcontractor for any resulting compensatory damages, interest on defense and indemnity costs, from the date incurred, at the rate set forth in subdivision (g) of Section 3260, consequential damages, and reasonable attorney's fees incurred to recover these amounts. The general contractor or construction manager shall bear the burden of proof to establish both the subcontractor's failure to perform under either paragraph (1) or (2) of subdivision (e) and any resulting damages. If, upon request by a subcontractor, a general contractor or construction manager does not reallocate defense fees to subcontractors within 30 days following final resolution of the claim, the subcontractor shall have the right to pursue a claim against the general contractor or construction manager for any resulting compensatory damages with interest, from the date of final resolution of the claim, at the rate set forth in subdivision (g) of Section 3260. The subcontractor shall bear the burden of proof to establish both the failure to reallocate the fees and any resulting damages. Nothing in this section shall prohibit the parties from mutually agreeing to reasonable contractual provisions for damages if any party fails to elect for or perform its obligations as stated in this section.

(g) For purposes of this section, "construction manager" means a person or entity, other than a public agency or owner of privately owned real property to be improved, who is contracted by a public agency or the owner of privately owned real property to be improved to direct, schedule, or coordinate the work of contractors for a work of improvement, but does not itself perform the work.

(h) For purposes of this section, "general contractor," in relation to a given subcontractor, means a person who has entered into a construction contract and who has entered into a subcontract with that subcontractor under which the subcontractor agrees to perform a portion of that scope of work. Where a subcontractor has itself subcontracted a portion of its work, that subcontractor, along with its general contractor, shall be considered a general contractor as to its subcontractors.

(i) For purposes of this section, "subcontractor" means a person who has entered into a construction contract either with a contractor to perform a portion of that contractor's work under a construction contract or with any person to perform a construction contract subject to the direction or control of a general contractor or construction manager.

(j) A general contractor, construction manager, or subcontractor shall have the right to seek equitable indemnity for any claim governed by this section.

(k) Nothing in this section limits, restricts, or prohibits the right of a general contractor, construction manager, or subcontractor to seek equitable indemnity against any supplier, design professional, product manufacturer, or other independent contractor or subcontractor.

(l) This section shall not affect the validity of any existing insurance contract or agreement, including, but not limited to, a contract or agreement for workers' compensation or an agreement issued on or before January 1, 2012, by an admitted insurer, as defined in the Insurance Code.

(m) Nothing in this section shall be construed to affect the obligation, if any, of either a contractor or construction manager to indemnify, including defending or paying the costs to defend, a public agency against any claim arising from the alleged active negligence of the public agency under subdivision (b) of Section 2782 or to indemnify, including defending or paying the costs to defend, an owner of privately owned real property to be

improved against any claim arising from the alleged active negligence of the owner under subdivision (c) of Section 2782.

(n) Nothing in this section shall be construed to affect the obligation, if any, of either a contractor or construction manager to provide or maintain insurance covering the acts or omissions of the promisor, including additional insurance endorsements covering the acts or omissions of the promisor during ongoing and completed operations pursuant to a construction contract with a public agency under subdivision (b) of Section 2782 or an owner of privately owned real property to be improved under subdivision (c) of Section 2782. (Added by Stats.2011, c. 707 (S.B.474), § 3.)

Research References

Miller and Starr California Real Estate § 27:46, Indemnity Provisions; Wrap-Up Insurance.
Miller and Starr California Real Estate § 29:17, Express and Implied Indemnity.
22 NO. 4 Miller & Starr, California Real Estate Newsalert 8, Construction Law and Contracting.
2 Witkin, California Summary 10th Insurance § 292, Duty of Insurer.
2 Witkin, California Summary 10th Insurance § 293, Reimbursement for Defense of Uncovered Claims.
5 Witkin, California Summary 10th Torts § 121, (S 121) Void Clauses.

§ 2782.1. Agreement to enter adjacent property; indemnification

Nothing contained in Section 2782 shall prevent a contractor responsible for the performance of a construction contract, as defined in Section 2783, from indemnifying fully a person, firm, corporation, state or other agency for whose account the construction contract is not being performed but who, as an accommodation, enters into an agreement with the contractor permitting such contractor to enter upon or adjacent to its property for the purpose of performing such construction contract for others. (Added by Stats.1968, c. 466, p. 1097, § 1.)

Research References

Rutter, Cal. Practice Guide: Insurance Litigation Ch. 7E-A, A. General Considerations.
Miller and Starr California Real Estate § 27:46, Indemnity Provisions; Wrap-Up Insurance.
Miller and Starr California Real Estate § 29:17, Express and Implied Indemnity.
1 Witkin Cal. Summ. 10th Contracts § 667, (S 667) Exceptions.
5 Witkin, California Summary 10th Torts § 121, (S 121) Void Clauses.

§ 2782.2. Agreement to indemnify professional engineers or agents or employees of engineers; liability for negligence in providing inspection services; requirements

(a) Nothing contained in subdivision (a) of Section 2782 prevents an agreement to indemnify a professional engineer against liability for the negligence of the engineer, or the engineer's agents or employees, in providing inspection services to plants or other facilities if all the following criteria are satisfied:

(1) The promisor is the owner of the plants or facilities inspected.

(2) The promisor is audited annually by an independent certified public accountant, public accountant, or accounting licentiate of another state authorized by the laws of that state to perform the audit.

(3) The net worth of the promisor exceeds ten million dollars ($10,000,000), as determined by the promisor's most recent annual independent audit. The requirement of this paragraph shall be satisfied at the time the contract for indemnification is entered, and a subsequent reduction of the promisor's net worth shall not void the obligation to indemnify.

(4) The promisor is self-insured with respect to liability arising from ownership of the plant or facility.

(5) The indemnification shall not be applicable to the first two hundred fifty thousand dollars ($250,000) of liability.

(b) Subdivision (a) does not authorize contracts for indemnification of liability arising from willful misconduct. *(Added by Stats.1985, c. 567, § 2.)*

Research References

Miller and Starr California Real Estate § 27:46, Indemnity Provisions; Wrap-Up Insurance.
Miller and Starr California Real Estate § 29:17, Express and Implied Indemnity.
1 Witkin Cal. Summ. 10th Contracts § 667, (S 667) Exceptions.

§ 2782.5. Agreements as to allocation or limitation of liability for design defects or of promisee to promisor

Nothing contained in Section 2782 shall prevent a party to a construction contract and the owner or other party for whose account the construction contract is being performed from negotiating and expressly agreeing with respect to the allocation, release, liquidation, exclusion, or limitation as between the parties of any liability (a) for design defects, or (b) of the promisee to the promisor arising out of or relating to the construction contract. *(Added by Stats.1967, c. 1327, p. 3159, § 2. Amended by Stats.1980, c. 211, p. 442, § 2.)*

Research References

California Real Estate Forms (Miller & Starr) § 4:4, Construction Contract--Cost Plus a Fixed Fee With a Guaranteed Maximum Price.
California Real Estate Forms (Miller & Starr) § 4:15, Development Agreement.
California Real Estate Forms (Miller & Starr) § 4:16, Restaurant Development and Construction Agreement.
California Real Estate Forms (Miller & Starr) § 4:20, Service Contract--Elevators.
California Real Estate Forms (Miller & Starr) § 4:21, Environmental Surveying--General Conditions.
Rutter, Cal. Practice Guide: Insurance Litigation Ch. 7E-A, A. General Considerations.
Miller and Starr California Real Estate § 27:46, Indemnity Provisions; Wrap-Up Insurance.
Miller and Starr California Real Estate § 29:17, Express and Implied Indemnity.
Miller and Starr California Real Estate § 29:31, Liability for Defective Plans and Specifications; to the Owner.
1 Witkin Cal. Summ. 10th Contracts § 667, (S 667) Exceptions.
1 Witkin Cal. Summ. 10th Contracts § 677, in General.

§ 2782.6. Professional engineers or geologists; agreements indemnifying work with hazardous materials; criteria; gross negligence or willful misconduct excepted

(a) Nothing in subdivision (a) of Section 2782 prevents an agreement to indemnify a professional engineer or geologist or the agents, servants, independent contractors, subsidiaries, or employees of that engineer or geologist from liability as described in Section 2782 in providing hazardous materials identification, evaluation, preliminary assessment, design, remediation services, or other services of the types described in Sections 25322 and 25323 of the Health and Safety Code or the federal National Oil and Hazardous Substances Pollution Contingency Plan (40 C.F.R. Sec. 300.1 et seq.), if all of the following criteria are satisfied:

(1) The services in whole or in part address subterranean contamination or other concealed conditions caused by the hazardous materials.

(2) The promisor is responsible, or potentially responsible, for all or part of the contamination.

(b) The indemnification described in this section is valid only for damages arising from, or related to, subterranean contamination or concealed conditions, and is not applicable to the first two hundred fifty thousand dollars ($250,000) of liability or such greater amount as is agreed by the parties.

(c) This section does not authorize contracts for indemnification, by promisors specified in paragraph (2) of subdivision (a), of any liability of a promisee arising from the gross negligence or willful misconduct of the promisee.

(d) "Hazardous materials," as used in this section, means any hazardous or toxic substance, material, or waste which is or becomes subject to regulation as such by any agency of the state, any municipality or political subdivision of the state, or the United States. "Hazardous materials" includes, but is not limited to, any material or substance that is any of the following:

(1) A hazardous substance, as defined in Section 25316 of the Health and Safety Code.

(2) Hazardous material, as defined in subdivision (j) of Section 25501 of the Health and Safety Code.[1]

(3) Acutely hazardous material, as defined in subdivision (a) of Section 25532 of the Health and Safety Code.

(4) Hazardous waste, as defined in Section 25117 of the Health and Safety Code.

(5) Extremely hazardous waste, as defined in Section 25115 of the Health and Safety Code.

(6) Petroleum.

(7) Asbestos.

(8) Designated as a hazardous substance for purposes of Section 311 of the Federal Water Pollution Control Act, as amended (33 U.S.C. Sec. 1321).

(9) Hazardous waste, as defined by subsection (5) of Section 1004 of the federal Resource Conservation and Recovery Act of 1976, as amended (42 U.S.C. Sec. 6903).

(10) A hazardous substance, as defined by subsection (14) of Section 101 of the federal Comprehensive Environmental Response, Compensation, and Liability Act of 1980, as amended (42 U.S.C. Sec. 9601).

(11) A regulated substance, as defined by subsection (2) of Section 9001 of the federal Solid Waste Disposal Act, as amended (42 U.S.C. Sec. 6991).

(e) Nothing in this section shall be construed to alter, modify, or otherwise affect the liability of the promisor or promisee, under an indemnity agreement meeting the criteria of this section, to third parties for damages for death or bodily injury to persons, injury to property, or any other loss, damage, or expense.

(f) This section does not apply to public entities, as defined by Section 811.2 of the Government Code. *(Added by Stats.1990, c. 814 (S.B.1922), § 2.)*

1 See Health and Safety Code § 25501(p).

Research References

Rutter, Cal. Practice Guide: Insurance Litigation Ch. 7E-A, A. General Considerations.
Miller and Starr California Real Estate § 23:5, Environmental Investigation (Due Diligence).
Miller and Starr California Real Estate § 27:46, Indemnity Provisions; Wrap-Up Insurance.
Miller and Starr California Real Estate § 29:17, Express and Implied Indemnity.

1 Witkin Cal. Summ. 10th Contracts § 667, (S 667) Exceptions.

§ 2782.8. Public agency contracts for design professional services; indemnification provisions

(a) For all contracts, and amendments thereto, entered into on or after January 1, 2007, with a public agency for design professional services, all provisions, clauses, covenants, and agreements contained in, collateral to, or affecting any such contract, and amendments thereto, that purport to indemnify, including the duty and the cost to defend, the public agency by a design professional against liability for claims against the public agency, are unenforceable, except for claims that arise out of, pertain to, or relate to the negligence, recklessness, or willful misconduct of the design professional. The duty to indemnify, including the duty and the cost to defend, is limited as provided in this section. This section shall not be waived or modified by contractual agreement, act, or omission of the parties. Contractual provisions, clauses, covenants, or agreements not expressly prohibited herein are reserved to the agreement of the parties.

(b) All contracts and all solicitation documents, including requests for proposal, invitations for bid, and other solicitation documents, between a public agency and a design professional, are deemed to incorporate by reference the provisions of this section.

(c) For purposes of this section, the following definitions apply:

(1) "Public agency" includes any county, city, city and county, district, school district, public authority, municipal corporation, or other political subdivision, joint powers authority, or public corporation in the state. Public agency does not include the State of California.

(2) "Design professional" includes all of the following:

(A) An individual licensed as an architect pursuant to Chapter 3 (commencing with Section 5500) of Division 3 of the Business and Professions Code, and a business entity offering architectural services in accordance with that chapter.

(B) An individual licensed as a landscape architect pursuant to Chapter 3. 5 (commencing with Section 5615) of Division 3 of the Business and Professions Code, and a business entity offering landscape architectural services in accordance with that chapter.

(C) An individual registered as a professional engineer pursuant to Chapter 7 (commencing with Section 6700) of Division 3 of the Business and Professions Code, and a business entity offering professional engineering services in accordance with that chapter.

(D) An individual licensed as a professional land surveyor pursuant to Chapter 15 (commencing with Section 8700) of Division 3 of the Business and Professions Code, and a business entity offering professional land surveying services in accordance with that chapter.

(d) This section shall only apply to a professional service contract, or any amendment thereto, entered into on or after January 1, 2007.

(e) The amendments made to this section by the act [1] adding this subdivision shall apply to services offered pursuant to a design professional contract, or any amendment thereto, entered into on or after January 1, 2011.

(f) Nothing in this section shall abrogate the provisions of Section 1104 of the Public Contract Code. *(Added by Stats.2006, c. 455 (A.B.573), § 1. Amended by Stats.2010, c. 510 (S.B.972), § 1.)*

1 Stats.2010, c. 510 (S.B.972).

Research References

Miller and Starr California Real Estate § 27:46, Indemnity Provisions; Wrap-Up Insurance.

Miller and Starr California Real Estate § 29:17, Express and Implied Indemnity.

Miller and Starr California Real Estate § 29:31, Liability for Defective Plans and Specifications; to the Owner.

17 NO. 4 Miller & Starr, California Real Estate Newsalert 2, Statutory Update:.

17 NO. 6 Miller & Starr, California Real Estate Newsalert 20, Table of Statutes (Newsalert Vol 17).

21 NO. 4 Miller & Starr, California Real Estate Newsalert 12, Defective Construction.

1 Witkin Cal. Summ. 10th Contracts § 666, (S 666) Statutory Prohibitions.

5 Witkin, California Summary 10th Torts § 121, (S 121) Void Clauses.

§ 2782.9. Residential construction projects; unenforceable indemnity agreements

(a) All contracts, provisions, clauses, amendments, or agreements contained therein entered into after January 1, 2009, for a residential construction project on which a wrap-up insurance policy, as defined in subdivision (b) of Section 11751.82 of the Insurance Code, or other consolidated insurance program, is applicable, that require an enrolled and participating subcontractor or other participant to indemnify, hold harmless, or defend another for any claim or action covered by that program, arising out of that project are unenforceable.

(b) To the extent any contractual provision is deemed unenforceable pursuant to this section, any party may pursue an equitable indemnity claim against another party for a claim or action unless there is coverage for the claim or action under the wrap-up policy or policies. Nothing in this section shall prohibit a builder or general contractor from requiring a reasonably allocated contribution from a subcontractor or other participant to the self-insured retention or deductible required under the wrap-up policy or other consolidated insurance program, if the maximum amount and method of collection of the participant's contribution is disclosed in the contract with the participant and the contribution is reasonably limited so that each participant may have some financial obligation in the event of a claim alleged to be caused by that participant's scope of work. The contribution shall only be collected when and as any such self-insured retention or deductible is incurred by the builder or general contractor and in an amount that bears a reasonable and proportionate relationship to the alleged liability arising from the claim or claims alleged to be caused by the participant's scope of work, when viewed in the context of the entirety of the alleged claim or claims. Any contribution shall only be collected from a participant after written notice to the participant of the amount of and basis for the contribution. In no event shall the total amount of contributions collected from participants exceed the amount of any self-insured retention or deductible due and payable by the builder or general contractor for the claim or claims. However, this requirement does not prohibit any legally permissible recovery of costs and legal fees to collect a participant's contribution if the contribution satisfies the requirements of this subdivision and is not paid by the participant when due.

(c) This section shall not be waived or modified by contractual agreement, act, or omission of the parties. *(Added by Stats.2008, c. 467 (A.B.2738), § 2.)*

Research References

Miller and Starr California Real Estate § 27:46, Indemnity Provisions; Wrap-Up Insurance.

Miller and Starr California Real Estate § 29:17, Express and Implied Indemnity.

19 NO. 4 Miller & Starr, California Real Estate Newsalert 7, Construction Contracts.

1 Witkin Cal. Summ. 10th Contracts § 658B, (S 658B) (New)-Subcontractor Enrolled in Wrap-Up Insurance Policy.

5 Witkin, California Summary 10th Torts § 121, (S 121) Void Clauses.

§ 2782.95. Residential improvements; wrap-up insurance policies or other consolidated insurance programs; disclosures

For any wrap-up insurance policy or other consolidated insurance program that insures a private residential (as that term is used in Title 7 (commencing with Section 895) of Part 2 of Division 2) work of improvement that first commences construction after January 1, 2009, the following shall apply:

(a) The owner, builder, or general contractor obtaining the wrap-up insurance policy or other consolidated insurance program shall disclose the total amount or method of calculation of any credit or compensation for premium required from a subcontractor or other participant for that wrap-up policy in the contract documents.

(b) The contract documents shall disclose, if and to the extent known:

(1) The policy limits.

(2) The scope of policy coverage.

(3) The policy term.

(4) The basis upon which the deductible or occurrence is triggered by the insurance carrier.

(5) If the policy covers more than one work of improvement, the number of units, if any, indicated on the application for the insurance policy.

(6) A good faith estimate of the amount of available limits remaining under the policy as of a date indicated in the disclosure obtained from the insurer.

(7) Disclosures made pursuant to paragraphs (5) and (6) are recognized to be based upon information at a given moment in time and may not accurately reflect the actual number of units covered by the policy nor the amount of insurance available, if any, when a later claim is made. These disclosures are presumptively made in good faith if the disclosure pursuant to paragraph (5) is the same as that contained in the application to the wrap-up insurer and the disclosure pursuant to paragraph (6) was obtained from the wrap-up insurer or broker. The presumptions stated above shall be overcome only by a showing that the insurer, broker, builder, or general contractor intentionally misrepresented the facts identified in paragraphs (5) or (6).

(c) Upon the written request of any participant, a copy of the insurance policy shall be provided, if available, that shows the coverage terms and items in paragraphs (1) to (4), inclusive, of subdivision (b) above. If the policy is not available at the time of the request, a copy of the insurance binder or declaration of coverage may be provided in lieu of the actual policy. Paragraphs (1) to (4), inclusive, of subdivision (b) may be satisfied by providing the participant with a copy of the binder or declaration. Any party receiving a copy of the policy, binder, or declaration shall not disclose it to third parties other than the participant's insurance broker or attorney unless required to do so by law. The participant's insurance broker or attorney may not disclose the policy, binder, or declaration to any third party unless required to do so by law.

(d) If the owner, builder, or general contractor obtaining the wrap-up insurance policy or other consolidated insurance program does not disclose the total amount or method of calculation of the premium credit or compensation to be charged to the participant prior to the time the participant submits its bid, the participant shall not be legally bound by the bid unless that participant has the right to increase the bid up to the amount equal to the difference between the amount the participant included, if any, for insurance in the original bid and the amount of the actual bid credit required by the owner, builder, or general contractor obtaining the wrap-up insurance policy or other consolidated insurance program. This subdivision shall not apply if the owner, builder, or general contractor obtaining the wrap-up insurance policy or other consolidated insurance program did not require the subcontractor to offset the original bid amount with a deduction for the wrap-up insurance policy or program. *(Added by Stats.2008, c. 467 (A.B.2738), § 3.)*

Research References

Miller and Starr California Real Estate § 27:46, Indemnity Provisions; Wrap-Up Insurance.

Miller and Starr California Real Estate § 29:17, Express and Implied Indemnity.

19 NO. 4 Miller & Starr, California Real Estate Newsalert 7, Construction Contracts.

5 Witkin, California Summary 10th Torts § 121, (S 121) Void Clauses.

§ 2782.96. Public works; wrap-up insurance policy or other consolidated insurance programs; disclosures

If an owner, builder, or general contractor obtains a wrap-up insurance policy or other consolidated insurance program for a public work as defined in Section 1720 of the Labor Code or any other project other than residential construction, as that term is used in Title 7 (commencing with Section 895) of Part 2 of Division 2, that is put out for bid after January 1, 2009, the following shall apply:

(a) The total amount or method of calculation of any credit or compensation for premium required from a subcontractor or other participant for that policy shall be clearly delineated in the bid documents.

(b) The named insured, to the extent known, shall disclose to the subcontractor or other participant in the contract documents the policy limits, known exclusions, and the length of time the policy is intended to remain in effect. In addition, upon written request, once available, the named insured shall provide copies of insurance policies to all those who are covered by the policy. Until such time as the policies are available, the named insured may also satisfy the disclosure requirements of this subdivision by providing the subcontractor or other participant with a copy of the insurance binder or declaration of coverage. Any party receiving a copy of the policy, binder, or declaration shall not disclose it to third parties other than the participant's insurance broker or attorney unless required to do so by law. The participant's insurance broker or attorney may not disclose the policy, binder, or declaration to any third party unless required to do so by law.

(c) The disclosure requirements in subdivisions (a) and (b) do not apply to an insurance policy purchased by an owner, builder, or general contractor that provides additional coverage beyond what was contained in the original wrap-up policy or other consolidated insurance program if no credit or compensation for premium is required of the subcontractor for the additional insurance policy. *(Added by Stats.2008, c. 467 (A.B.2738), § 4. Amended by Stats.2009, c. 140 (A.B.1164), § 37.)*

Research References

Miller and Starr California Real Estate § 27:31, Public Works Competitive Bidding--Procedures.

Miller and Starr California Real Estate § 29:17, Express and Implied Indemnity.

19 NO. 4 Miller & Starr, California Real Estate Newsalert 7, Construction Contracts.

§ 2783. "Construction contract" defined

As used in Sections 2782 and 2782.5, "construction contract" is defined as any agreement or understanding, written or oral, respecting the construction, surveying, design, specifications, alteration, repair, improvement, renovation, maintenance, removal of or demolition of any building, highway, road, parking facility, bridge, water line, sewer line, oil line, gas line, electric utility transmission or distribution line, railroad, airport, pier or dock, excavation or other structure, appurtenance, development or other improvement to real or personal property, or an agreement to perform any portion thereof or any act collateral thereto, or to perform any service reasonably related thereto, including, but not limited to, the erection of all structures or performance of work in connection therewith, electrical power line clearing, tree trimming, vegetation maintenance, the rental of all equipment, all incidental transportation, moving, lifting, crane and rigging service and other goods and services furnished in connection therewith. *(Added by Stats.1967, c. 1327, p. 3159, § 3. Amended by Stats.2011, c. 707 (S.B.474), § 4.)*

Research References

Miller and Starr California Real Estate § 27:46, Indemnity Provisions; Wrap-Up Insurance.
Miller and Starr California Real Estate § 29:17, Express and Implied Indemnity.
Miller and Starr California Real Estate § 29:31, Liability for Defective Plans and Specifications; to the Owner.
22 NO. 4 Miller & Starr, California Real Estate Newsalert 8, Construction Law and Contracting.
5 Witkin, California Summary 10th Torts § 121, (S 121) Void Clauses.

§ 2784. "Design defect" defined

As used in Sections 2782 and 2782.5, a "design defect" is defined as a condition arising out of its design which renders a structure, item of equipment or machinery or any other similar object, movable or immovable, when constructed substantially in accordance with its design, inherently unfit, either wholly or in part, for its intended use or which impairs or renders the use of such structure, equipment, machinery or property dangerous. *(Added by Stats.1967, c. 1327, p. 3159, § 4.)*

Research References

Miller and Starr California Real Estate § 29:17, Express and Implied Indemnity.
1 Witkin Cal. Summ. 10th Contracts § 666, (S 666) Statutory Prohibitions.

§ 2784.5. Hauling, trucking, or cartage contracts; provisions indemnifying against liability for negligence void; exception

Any provision, promise, agreement, clause, or covenant contained in, collateral to, or affecting any hauling, trucking, or cartage contract or agreement is against public policy, void and unenforceable if it purports to indemnify the promisee against liability for any of the following damages which are caused by the sole negligence or willful misconduct of the promisee, agents, servants, or the independent contractors directly responsible to the promisee, except when such agents, servants, or independent contractors are under the direct supervision and control of the promisor:

(a) Damages arising out of bodily injury or death to persons.

(b) Damage to property.

(c) Any other damage or expense arising under either (a) or (b).

This section shall not affect the validity of any insurance contract, workmen's compensation insurance contract, or agreement issued by an admitted insurer as defined by Sections 23 and 24 of the Insurance Code or insurance effected by surplus line brokers under Sections 1760 through 1780 of the Insurance Code. *(Added by Stats.1967, c. 1314, p. 3138, § 1.)*

Research References

Miller and Starr California Real Estate § 29:17, Express and Implied Indemnity.
1 Witkin Cal. Summ. 10th Contracts § 666, (S 666) Statutory Prohibitions.

5 Witkin, California Summary 10th Torts § 121, (S 121) Void Clauses.

Title 13

SURETYSHIP

ARTICLE 1. DEFINITION OF SURETYSHIP

Section
2787. Sureties and guarantors; distinction abolished; definitions; letters of credit.
2788. Surety without knowledge or consent of principal.

§ 2787. Sureties and guarantors; distinction abolished; definitions; letters of credit

The distinction between sureties and guarantors is hereby abolished. The terms and their derivatives, wherever used in this code or in any other statute or law of this state now in force or hereafter enacted, shall have the same meaning as defined in this section. A surety or guarantor is one who promises to answer for the debt, default, or miscarriage of another, or hypothecates property as security therefor. Guaranties of collection and continuing guaranties are forms of suretyship obligations, and except in so far as necessary in order to give effect to provisions specially relating thereto, shall be subject to all provisions of law relating to suretyships in general. A letter of credit is not a form of suretyship obligation. For purposes of this section, the term "letter of credit" means a "letter of credit" as defined in paragraph (10) of subdivision (a) of Section 5102 of the Commercial Code whether or not the engagement is governed by Division 5 (commencing with Section 5101) of the Commercial Code. *(Enacted in 1872. Amended by Stats.1939, c. 453, p. 1796, § 10; Stats.1994, c. 611 (S.B.1612), § 1, eff. Sept. 16, 1994; Stats.1996, c. 176 (S.B.1599), § 1.)*

Research References

California Real Estate Forms (Miller & Starr) § 3:29, Exceptions to Non-Recourse Guaranty--Conduit Loan.
Rutter, Cal. Practice Guide: Enforcing Judgments/Debts Ch. 3-A, A. Evaluating the Claim.
Rutter, Cal. Practice Guide: Insurance Litigation Ch. 9-C, C. Source of Subrogation Right.
Rutter, Cal. Practice Guide: Insurance Litigation Ch. 6I-A, A. Introduction.
Rutter, Cal. Practice Guide: Insurance Litigation Ch. 6I-B, B. Particular Surety Bond Coverages.
Rutter, Cal. Practice Guide: Insurance Litigation Ch. 6I-D, D. Surety's Defenses to Payment of Bond.
Rutter, Cal. Practice Guide: Real Prop. Transactions Ch. 4-E, E. Drafting the Purchase and Sale Agreement-Terms and Conditions.
Rutter, Cal. Practice Guide: Real Prop. Transactions Ch. 6-J, J. Guaranty of the Obligation.
Miller and Starr California Real Estate § 10:10, Requirement of Some Debt or Obligation.
Miller and Starr California Real Estate § 21:31, Who Can Raise the Defense of Usury--Third Parties.
Miller and Starr California Real Estate § 28:93, Suretyship Terminology and Definitions.
Miller and Starr California Real Estate § 10:155, Who May Enforce the One-Action Rule.

Miller and Starr California Real Estate § 10:173, Debt Secured by Deed of Trust and Letter of Credit.
Miller and Starr California Real Estate § 10:263, Definitions; Guarantor, Surety.
Miller and Starr California Real Estate § 10:264, Definitions; Comaker, Accommodation.
Miller and Starr California Real Estate § 10:265, Waiver of Guarantor's Defenses.
Miller and Starr California Real Estate § 10:266, Application of "Exhaustion of the Security" Requirement.
3 Witkin Cal. Proc. 5th Actions § 544, (S 544) Former Rule Refusing to Discharge Sureties.
6 Witkin Cal. Proc. 5th Provisional Remedies § 12, Other Definitions.
6 Witkin Cal. Proc. 5th Provisional Remedies § 72, Exhaustion of Security.
2 Witkin, California Summary 10th Insurance § 133, in General.
1 Witkin Cal. Summ. 10th Contracts § 372, (S 372) Scope of Statute.
1 Witkin Cal. Summ. 10th Contracts § 1002, in General.
4 Witkin, California Summary 10th Security Transactions in Real Property § 109, Release of Part of Property.
4 Witkin, California Summary 10th Security Transactions in Real Property § 204, (S 204) Waiver of Defenses.
4 Witkin, California Summary 10th Secured Transactions in Personal Property § 5, (S 5) Termination of Pledge.
7 Witkin, California Summary 10th Constitutional Law § 624, Clarification of Existing Law.
13 Witkin, California Summary 10th Equity § 178, Equitable Indemnity: Reimbursement from Principal.

§ 2788. Surety without knowledge or consent of principal

A person may become surety even without the knowledge or consent of the principal. *(Enacted in 1872. Amended by Stats.1939, c. 453, p. 1797, § 11.)*

Research References

Rutter, Cal. Practice Guide: Insurance Litigation Ch. 6I-A, A. Introduction.
1 Witkin Cal. Summ. 10th Contracts § 1002, in General.

ARTICLE 2.   CREATION OF SURETYSHIP

Section
2792. Consideration.
2793. Writing; signature.
2794. Original obligations not requiring a writing.
2795. Acceptance of offer; notice.

§ 2792. Consideration

Where a suretyship obligation is entered into at the same time with the original obligation, or with the acceptance of the latter by the creditor, and forms with that obligation a part of the consideration to him, no other consideration need exist. In all other cases there must be a consideration distinct from that of the original obligation. *(Enacted in 1872. Amended by Stats. 1939, c. 453, p. 1797, § 12.)*

Research References

Rutter, Cal. Practice Guide: Enforcing Judgments/Debts Ch. 3-A, A. Evaluating the Claim.
Rutter, Cal. Practice Guide: Insurance Litigation Ch. 6I-A, A. Introduction.
Miller and Starr California Real Estate § 28:94, General Form of the Bond.
Miller and Starr California Real Estate § 10:263, Definitions; Guarantor, Surety.
1 Witkin Cal. Summ. 10th Contracts § 1002, in General.

§ 2793. Writing; signature

Except as prescribed by the next section, a suretyship obligation must be in writing, and signed by the surety; but the writing need not express a consideration. *(Enacted in 1872. Amended by Stats.1939, c. 453, p. 1797, § 13.)*

Research References

California Real Estate Forms (Miller & Starr) § 3:37, Continuing Guaranty.
California Real Estate Forms (Miller & Starr) § 3:38, Completion Guaranty.
Rutter, Cal. Practice Guide: Enforcing Judgments/Debts Ch. 3-A, A. Evaluating the Claim.
Rutter, Cal. Practice Guide: Insurance Litigation Ch. 6I-A, A. Introduction.
Rutter, Cal. Practice Guide: Real Prop. Transactions Ch. 6-J, J. Guaranty of the Obligation.
Miller and Starr California Real Estate § 1:65, Provisions Applicable to Real Estate Transactions.
Miller and Starr California Real Estate § 28:94, General Form of the Bond.
Miller and Starr California Real Estate § 10:263, Definitions; Guarantor, Surety.
1 Witkin Cal. Summ. 10th Contracts § 343, California Codes.
1 Witkin Cal. Summ. 10th Contracts § 1002, in General.

§ 2794. Original obligations not requiring a writing

A promise to answer for the obligation of another, in any of the following cases, is deemed an original obligation of the promisor, and need not be in writing:

(1) Where the promise is made by one who has received property of another upon an undertaking to apply it pursuant to such promise; or by one who has received a discharge from an obligation in whole or in part, in consideration of such promise;

(2) Where the creditor parts with value, or enters into an obligation, in consideration of the obligation in respect to which the promise is made, in terms or under circumstances such as to render the party making the promise the principal debtor and the person in whose behalf it is made, his surety;

(3) Where the promise, being for an antecedent obligation of another, is made upon the consideration that the party receiving it cancels the antecedent obligation, accepting the new promise as a substitute therefor; or upon the consideration that the party receiving it releases the property of another from a levy, or his person from imprisonment under an execution on a judgment obtained upon the antecedent obligation;

(4) Where the promise is upon a consideration beneficial to the promisor, whether moving from either party to the antecedent obligation, or from another person;

(5) Where a factor undertakes, for a commission, to sell merchandise and act as surety in connection with the sale;

(6) Where the holder of an instrument for the payment of money, upon which a third person is or may become liable to him, transfers it in payment of a precedent debt of his own, or for a new consideration, and in connection with such transfer enters into a promise respecting such instrument. *(Enacted in 1872. Amended by Stats.1939, c. 453, p. 1797, § 14.)*

Research References

Rutter, Cal. Practice Guide: Enforcing Judgments/Debts Ch. 3-A, A. Evaluating the Claim.
Rutter, Cal. Practice Guide: Insurance Litigation Ch. 6I-A, A. Introduction.
Rutter, Cal. Practice Guide: Real Prop. Transactions Ch. 6-J, J. Guaranty of the Obligation.
Miller and Starr California Real Estate § 1:65, Provisions Applicable to Real Estate Transactions.
Miller and Starr California Real Estate § 1:68, Agreement to Answer for the Debt of Another; Buyer's Agreement to Pay Seller's Obligations.
Miller and Starr California Real Estate § 10:263, Definitions; Guarantor, Surety.
1 Witkin Cal. Summ. 10th Contracts § 372, (S 372) Scope of Statute.
1 Witkin Cal. Summ. 10th Contracts § 375, in General.
1 Witkin Cal. Summ. 10th Contracts § 376, Main Purpose or Leading Object Rule.

1 Witkin Cal. Summ. 10th Contracts § 1002, in General.

§ 2795. Acceptance of offer; notice

Unless notice of acceptance is expressly required, an offer to become a surety may be accepted by acting upon it, or by acceptance upon other consideration. An absolute suretyship obligation is binding upon the surety without notice of acceptance. *(Enacted in 1872. Amended by Stats.1939, c. 453, p. 1798, § 15.)*

Research References

Rutter, Cal. Practice Guide: Insurance Litigation Ch. 6I-A, A. Introduction.
1 Witkin Cal. Summ. 10th Contracts § 199, Notification to Offeror.
1 Witkin Cal. Summ. 10th Contracts § 1002, in General.

ARTICLE 3. INTERPRETATION OF SURETYSHIP

Section
2799. Incomplete contract; implied terms.
2800. Guaranty that obligation is good or collectible.
2801. Guaranty that obligation is good or collectible; recovery.
2802. Guaranty that obligation is good or collectible; surety's liability.

§ 2799. Incomplete contract; implied terms

In an assumption of liability as surety in connection with a contract, the terms of which are not then settled, it is implied that its terms shall be such as will not expose the surety to greater risks than he would incur under those terms which are most common in similar contracts at the place where the principal contract is to be performed. *(Enacted in 1872. Amended by Stats.1939, c. 453, p. 1798, § 16.)*

Research References

1 Witkin Cal. Summ. 10th Contracts § 1002, in General.

§ 2800. Guaranty that obligation is good or collectible

A guaranty to the effect that an obligation is good, or is collectible, imports that the debtor is solvent, and that the demand is collectible by the usual legal proceedings, if taken with reasonable diligence. *(Enacted in 1872.)*

Research References

Rutter, Cal. Practice Guide: Enforcing Judgments/Debts Ch. 3-A, A. Evaluating the Claim.
Miller and Starr California Real Estate § 10:263, Definitions; Guarantor, Surety.
1 Witkin Cal. Summ. 10th Contracts § 1002, in General.

§ 2801. Guaranty that obligation is good or collectible; recovery

A guaranty, such as is mentioned in the last section, is not discharged by an omission to take proceedings upon the principal debt, or upon any collateral security for its payment, if no part of the debt could have been collected thereby. *(Enacted in 1872.)*

Research References

Rutter, Cal. Practice Guide: Enforcing Judgments/Debts Ch. 3-A, A. Evaluating the Claim.
Miller and Starr California Real Estate § 10:266, Application of "Exhaustion of the Security" Requirement.

Miller and Starr California Real Estate § 28:101, Exoneration of the Surety--In General.

§ 2802. Guaranty that obligation is good or collectible; surety's liability

In the cases mentioned in Section 2800, the removal of the principal from the state, leaving no property therein from which the obligation might be satisfied, is equivalent to the insolvency of the principal in its effect upon the rights and obligations of the guarantor. *(Enacted in 1872.)*

Research References

Rutter, Cal. Practice Guide: Enforcing Judgments/Debts Ch. 3-A, A. Evaluating the Claim.

ARTICLE 4. LIABILITY OF SURETIES

Section
2806. Conditional and unconditional obligations.
2807. Surety for payment or performance; liability without demand or notice.
2808. Surety upon conditional obligation; notice of default.
2809. Surety's obligation commensurate with principal obligation.
2810. Surety's obligation; principal's personal disability.
2811. Bonded principal; agreement with surety, deposit of money and assets, withdrawals.

§ 2806. Conditional and unconditional obligations

A suretyship obligation is to be deemed unconditional unless its terms import some condition precedent to the liability of the surety. *(Enacted in 1872. Amended by Stats.1939, c. 453, p. 1798, § 17.)*

Research References

Rutter, Cal. Practice Guide: Enforcing Judgments/Debts Ch. 3-A, A. Evaluating the Claim.
Rutter, Cal. Practice Guide: Real Prop. Transactions Ch. 6-J, J. Guaranty of the Obligation.
Miller and Starr California Real Estate § 28:95, General Conditions of the Bond.
Miller and Starr California Real Estate § 10:263, Definitions; Guarantor, Surety.
1 Witkin Cal. Summ. 10th Contracts § 1004, Liability of Sureties.

§ 2807. Surety for payment or performance; liability without demand or notice

A surety who has assumed liability for payment or performance is liable to the creditor immediately upon the default of the principal, and without demand or notice. *(Enacted in 1872. Amended by Stats.1939, c. 453, p. 1798, § 18.)*

Research References

California Real Estate Forms (Miller & Starr) § 3:38, Completion Guaranty.
Rutter, Cal. Practice Guide: Enforcing Judgments/Debts Ch. 3-A, A. Evaluating the Claim.
Rutter, Cal. Practice Guide: Insurance Litigation Ch. 6I-A, A. Introduction.
Rutter, Cal. Practice Guide: Insurance Litigation Ch. 6I-C, C. Surety's Obligations and Rights Upon Default by Principal.
Rutter, Cal. Practice Guide: Real Prop. Transactions Ch. 6-J, J. Guaranty of the Obligation.
Miller and Starr California Real Estate § 19:85, Persons Liable for Payment of Rent.
Miller and Starr California Real Estate § 28:97, Measure of Surety's Liability.
Miller and Starr California Real Estate § 10:269, Limitation of Liability.
Miller and Starr California Real Estate § 28:100, Conditions of a Performance Bond--Notice to the Surety of the Contractor's Default.

Miller and Starr California Real Estate § 28:112, Proper Parties in Suit Against Surety; Necessity of Suit Against or Joinder of the Principal.

7 Witkin Cal. Proc. 5th Judgment § 220, (S 220) Actions Against Surety on Government Construction Bond.

6 Witkin Cal. Proc. 5th Provisional Remedies § 224, in General.

1 Witkin Cal. Summ. 10th Contracts § 1004, Liability of Sureties.

§ 2808. Surety upon conditional obligation; notice of default

Where one assumes liability as surety upon a conditional obligation, his liability is commensurate with that of the principal, and he is not entitled to notice of the default of the principal, unless he is unable, by the exercise of reasonable diligence, to acquire information of such default, and the creditor has actual notice thereof. *(Enacted in 1872. Amended by Stats.1939, c. 453, p. 1798, § 19.)*

Research References

Rutter, Cal. Practice Guide: Insurance Litigation Ch. 6I-C, C. Surety's Obligations and Rights Upon Default by Principal.

Rutter, Cal. Practice Guide: Real Prop. Transactions Ch. 6-J, J. Guaranty of the Obligation.

Miller and Starr California Real Estate § 19:85, Persons Liable for Payment of Rent.

Miller and Starr California Real Estate § 28:97, Measure of Surety's Liability.

Miller and Starr California Real Estate § 28:100, Conditions of a Performance Bond—Notice to the Surety of the Contractor's Default.

Miller and Starr California Real Estate § 28:117, Attorney's Fees.

19 NO. 6 Miller & Starr, California Real Estate Newsalert 17, Mechanics' Liens.

7 Witkin Cal. Proc. 5th Judgment § 166, Building Contracts.

7 Witkin Cal. Proc. 5th Judgment § 220, (S 220) Actions Against Surety on Government Construction Bond.

1 Witkin Cal. Summ. 10th Contracts § 1004, Liability of Sureties.

§ 2809. Surety's obligation commensurate with principal obligation

The obligation of a surety must be neither larger in amount nor in other respects more burdensome than that of the principal; and if in its terms it exceeds it, it is reducible in proportion to the principal obligation. *(Enacted in 1872. Amended by Stats.1939, c. 453, p. 1798, § 20.)*

Research References

California Real Estate Forms (Miller & Starr) § 3:37, Continuing Guaranty.

California Real Estate Forms (Miller & Starr) § 3:38, Completion Guaranty.

Rutter, Cal. Practice Guide: Insurance Litigation Ch. 6I-C, C. Surety's Obligations and Rights Upon Default by Principal.

Rutter, Cal. Practice Guide: Insurance Litigation Ch. 6I-D, D. Surety's Defenses to Payment of Bond.

Rutter, Cal. Practice Guide: Landlord-Tenant Form 2:D, Guaranty of Lease.

Rutter, Cal. Practice Guide: Real Prop. Transactions Ch. 6-J, J. Guaranty of the Obligation.

Rutter, Cal. Practice Guide: Real Prop. Transactions Form 6:L, Guaranty.

Miller and Starr California Real Estate § 21:31, Who Can Raise the Defense of Usury—Third Parties.

Miller and Starr California Real Estate § 28:96, Interpretation of the Bond.

Miller and Starr California Real Estate § 28:97, Measure of Surety's Liability.

Miller and Starr California Real Estate § 10:263, Definitions; Guarantor, Surety.

Miller and Starr California Real Estate § 10:265, Waiver of Guarantor's Defenses.

Miller and Starr California Real Estate § 10:267, Guaranty of Purchase-Money Obligation.

18 NO. 2 Miller & Starr, California Real Estate Newsalert 25, Usury.

19 NO. 1 Miller & Starr, California Real Estate Newsalert 9, Deeds of Trust.

7 Witkin Cal. Proc. 5th Judgment § 220, (S 220) Actions Against Surety on Government Construction Bond.

1 Witkin Cal. Summ. 10th Contracts § 680, Other Rights.

1 Witkin Cal. Summ. 10th Contracts § 1002, in General.

4 Witkin, California Summary 10th Security Transactions in Real Property § 202, (S 202) in General.

§ 2810. Surety's obligation; principal's personal disability

A surety is liable, notwithstanding any mere personal disability of the principal, though the disability be such as to make the contract void against the principal; but he is not liable if for any other reason there is no liability upon the part of the principal at the time of the execution of the contract, or the liability of the principal thereafter ceases, unless the surety has assumed liability with knowledge of the existence of the defense. Where the principal is not liable because of mere personal disability, recovery back by the creditor of any res which formed all or part of the consideration for the contract shall have the effect upon the liability of the surety which is attributed to the recovery back of such a res under the law of sales generally. *(Enacted in 1872. Amended by Stats.1939, c. 453, p. 1798, § 21.)*

Research References

California Real Estate Forms (Miller & Starr) § 3:37, Continuing Guaranty.

California Real Estate Forms (Miller & Starr) § 3:38;;0286592591;SA;;0126426;, Completion Guaranty.

Rutter, Cal. Practice Guide: Enforcing Judgments/Debts Ch. 3-A, A. Evaluating the Claim.

Rutter, Cal. Practice Guide: Insurance Litigation Ch. 6I-D, D. Surety's Defenses to Payment of Bond.

Rutter, Cal. Practice Guide: Landlord-Tenant Form 2:D, Guaranty of Lease.

Rutter, Cal. Practice Guide: Real Prop. Transactions Ch. 6-J, J. Guaranty of the Obligation.

Rutter, Cal. Practice Guide: Real Prop. Transactions Form 6:L, Guaranty.

Miller and Starr California Real Estate § 21:31, Who Can Raise the Defense of Usury—Third Parties.

Miller and Starr California Real Estate § 28:90, Release of the Stop Payment Notice.

Miller and Starr California Real Estate § 28:97, Measure of Surety's Liability.

Miller and Starr California Real Estate § 10:267, Guaranty of Purchase-Money Obligation.

Miller and Starr California Real Estate § 28:107, Exoneration of the Surety—Release or Discharge of the Debtor or Principal.

Miller and Starr California Real Estate § 28:108, Exoneration of the Surety—Disability or Death of the Principal.

Miller and Starr California Real Estate § 28:114, Other Defenses Available to the Surety.

1 Witkin Cal. Summ. 10th Contracts § 1004, Liability of Sureties.

4 Witkin, California Summary 10th Security Transactions in Real Property § 194, (S 194) True Guaranty.

4 Witkin, California Summary 10th Security Transactions in Real Property § 202, (S 202) in General.

§ 2811. Bonded principal; agreement with surety, deposit of money and assets, withdrawals

Any party required to give a bond undertaking or other obligation may agree with his surety for the deposit of any money and assets for which the surety is responsible with a bank, savings bank, safe deposit, or trust company authorized by law to do business as such, or other depository approved by the court or a judge thereof, if such deposit is otherwise proper, for the safekeeping of such money and assets and in such manner as to prevent the withdrawal of any or all such money and assets without the written consent of the surety, or an order of court or a judge thereof, made on such notice to the surety as the court or judge may direct. Such agreement shall not in any manner release, or change the liability of, the principal or surety as established by the terms of the bond. *(Added by Stats.1953, c. 37, p. 675, § 4.)*

Research References

1 Witkin Cal. Summ. 10th Contracts § 1004, Liability of Sureties.

ARTICLE 5.   CONTINUING GUARANTY

Section
2814.   Definition.
2815.   Revocation.

§ 2814.   Definition

A guaranty relating to a future liability of the principal, under successive transactions, which either continue his liability or from time to time renew it after it has been satisfied, is called a continuing guaranty. *(Enacted in 1872.)*

Research References

Rutter, Cal. Practice Guide: Enforcing Judgments/Debts Ch. 3-A, A. Evaluating the Claim.
Rutter, Cal. Practice Guide: Real Prop. Transactions Ch. 6-J, J. Guaranty of the Obligation.
Miller and Starr California Real Estate § 11:129, Priority of the Title of an Execution Sale Purchaser.
22 NO. 4 Miller & Starr, California Real Estate Newsalert 29, Deeds of Trust.
1 Witkin Cal. Summ. 10th Contracts § 1002, in General.

§ 2815.   Revocation

A continuing guaranty may be revoked at any time by the guarantor, in respect to future transactions, unless there is a continuing consideration as to such transactions which he does not renounce. *(Enacted in 1872.)*

Research References

Rutter, Cal. Practice Guide: Enforcing Judgments/Debts Ch. 3-A, A. Evaluating the Claim.
Rutter, Cal. Practice Guide: Real Prop. Transactions Ch. 6-J, J. Guaranty of the Obligation.
Miller and Starr California Real Estate § 19:85, Persons Liable for Payment of Rent.
Miller and Starr California Real Estate § 10:269, Limitation of Liability.
15 NO. 6 Miller & Starr, California Real Estate Newsalert 15, Landlord and Tenant.
1 Witkin Cal. Summ. 10th Contracts § 296, Creditor's Duty to Guarantor.
1 Witkin Cal. Summ. 10th Contracts § 1002, in General.
4 Witkin, California Summary 10th Secured Transactions in Personal Property § 5, (S 5) Termination of Pledge.

ARTICLE 6.   EXONERATION OF SURETIES

Section
2819.   Alteration of original obligation; suspension or impairment of remedies or rights against principal.
2820.   Suspension or impairment of remedy; creditor's void promise.
2821.   Rescission of agreement altering obligation or impairing remedy.
2822.   Partial satisfaction of obligation; effect on obligation of surety.
2823.   Delay in proceeding by creditor.
2824.   Indemnified surety; liability notwithstanding modification or release.
2825.   Discharge of principal.

§ 2819.   Alteration of original obligation; suspension or impairment of remedies or rights against principal

A surety is exonerated, except so far as he or she may be indemnified by the principal, if by any act of the creditor, without the consent of the surety the original obligation of the principal is altered in any respect, or the remedies or rights of the creditor

against the principal, in respect thereto, in any way impaired or suspended. However, nothing in this section shall be construed to supersede subdivision (b) of Section 2822. *(Enacted in 1872. Amended by Stats.1939, c. 453, p. 1799, § 22; Stats.1993, c. 149 (A.B.1402), § 1, eff. July 19, 1993.)*

Research References

California Real Estate Forms (Miller & Starr) § 3:29, Exceptions to Non-Recourse Guaranty--Conduit Loan.
California Real Estate Forms (Miller & Starr) § 3:30, Environmental Indemnity--Conduit Loan.
California Real Estate Forms (Miller & Starr) § 3:37, Continuing Guaranty.
California Real Estate Forms (Miller & Starr) § 3:38, Completion Guaranty.
California Real Estate Forms (Miller & Starr) § 3:40, Assignment of Membership Interest.
Rutter, Cal. Practice Guide: Enforcing Judgments/Debts Ch. 3-A, A. Evaluating the Claim.
Rutter, Cal. Practice Guide: Insurance Litigation Ch. 6I-D, D. Surety's Defenses to Payment of Bond.
Rutter, Cal. Practice Guide: Landlord-Tenant Form 2:D, Guaranty of Lease.
Rutter, Cal. Practice Guide: Real Prop. Transactions Ch. 6-J, J. Guaranty of the Obligation.
Rutter, Cal. Practice Guide: Real Prop. Transactions Form 6:L, Guaranty.
Miller and Starr California Real Estate § 10:37, Trustor as a Surety.
Miller and Starr California Real Estate § 19:66, Liability of the Parties--Between Landlord and Tenant-Sublessor.
Miller and Starr California Real Estate § 27:66, Changes in the Work--Exceptions to the Prior Written Consent Requirement.
Miller and Starr California Real Estate § 28:93, Suretyship Terminology and Definitions.
Miller and Starr California Real Estate § 10:256, Liability of the Parties on Negotiation of the Note.
Miller and Starr California Real Estate § 10:266, Application of "Exhaustion of the Security" Requirement.
Miller and Starr California Real Estate § 10:269, Limitation of Liability.
Miller and Starr California Real Estate § 28:101, Exoneration of the Surety--In General.
Miller and Starr California Real Estate § 28:103, Exoneration of the Surety--Modification of the Terms of the Construction Contract.
Miller and Starr California Real Estate § 28:107, Exoneration of the Surety--Release or Discharge of the Debtor or Principal.
Miller and Starr California Real Estate § 28:110, No Exoneration of the Surety Under Bonds in Favor of Claimants.
Miller and Starr California Real Estate § 28:120, Payment and Performance Bonds as to Public Projects.
1 Witkin Cal. Proc. 5th Attorneys § 276, Judgment.
1 Witkin Cal. Summ. 10th Contracts § 1006, Exoneration of Sureties.
4 Witkin, California Summary 10th Security Transactions in Real Property § 202, (S 202) in General.

§ 2820.   Suspension or impairment of remedy; creditor's void promise

That a promise by a creditor is for any cause void, or voidable by him at his option, shall not prevent it from altering the obligation or suspending or impairing the remedy within the meaning of the last section. *(Enacted in 1872. Amended by Stats.1939, c. 453, p. 1795, § 34.)*

Research References

Rutter, Cal. Practice Guide: Landlord-Tenant Form 2:D, Guaranty of Lease.
Miller and Starr California Real Estate § 28:97, Measure of Surety's Liability.
1 Witkin Cal. Summ. 10th Contracts § 1006, Exoneration of Sureties.
4 Witkin, California Summary 10th Security Transactions in Real Property § 110, Extension of Time to Grantee.

§ 2821.   Rescission of agreement altering obligation or impairing remedy

The rescission of an agreement altering the original obligation of a debtor, or impairing the remedy of a creditor, does not restore the liability of a surety who has been exonerated by such agreement. *(Enacted in 1872. Amended by Stats.1939, c. 453, p. 1799, § 23.)*

Research References

Rutter, Cal. Practice Guide: Enforcing Judgments/Debts Ch. 3-A, A. Evaluating the Claim.
Rutter, Cal. Practice Guide: Real Prop. Transactions Ch. 6-J, J. Guaranty of the Obligation.
Miller and Starr California Real Estate § 10:37, Trustor as a Surety.
Miller and Starr California Real Estate § 28:105, Exoneration of the Surety--Rescission or Revocation of the Contract.
1 Witkin Cal. Summ. 10th Contracts § 1006, Exoneration of Sureties.

§ 2822. Partial satisfaction of obligation; effect on obligation of surety

(a) The acceptance, by a creditor, of anything in partial satisfaction of an obligation, reduces the obligation of a surety thereof, in the same measure as that of the principal, but does not otherwise affect it. However, if the surety is liable upon only a portion of an obligation and the principal provides partial satisfaction of the obligation, the principal may designate the portion of the obligation that is to be satisfied.

(b) For purposes of this section and Section 2819, an agreement by a creditor to accept from the principal debtor a sum less than the balance owed on the original obligation, without the prior consent of the surety and without any other change to the underlying agreement between the creditor and principal debtor, shall not exonerate the surety for the lesser sum agreed upon by the creditor and principal debtor. *(Enacted in 1872. Amended by Stats.1939, c. 453, p. 1799, § 24; Stats.1993, c. 149 (A.B.1402), § 2, eff. July 19, 1993.)*

Research References

Rutter, Cal. Practice Guide: Enforcing Judgments/Debts Ch. 3-A, A. Evaluating the Claim.
Rutter, Cal. Practice Guide: Insurance Litigation Ch. 6I-D, D. Surety's Defenses to Payment of Bond.
Rutter, Cal. Practice Guide: Landlord-Tenant Form 2:D, Guaranty of Lease.
Rutter, Cal. Practice Guide: Real Prop. Transactions Ch. 6-J, J. Guaranty of the Obligation.
Miller and Starr California Real Estate § 10:37, Trustor as a Surety.
Miller and Starr California Real Estate § 19:82, Modification of the Rent.
Miller and Starr California Real Estate § 28:101, Exoneration of the Surety--In General.
Miller and Starr California Real Estate § 28:103, Exoneration of the Surety--Modification of the Terms of the Construction Contract.
1 Witkin Cal. Summ. 10th Contracts § 767, (S 767) Election of Alternative Modes of Performance.
1 Witkin Cal. Summ. 10th Contracts § 1006, Exoneration of Sureties.
4 Witkin, California Summary 10th Negotiable Instruments § 69, Applicable Suretyship Defenses.

§ 2823. Delay in proceeding by creditor

Mere delay on the part of a creditor to proceed against the principal, or to enforce any other remedy, does not exonerate a surety. *(Enacted in 1872. Amended by Stats.1939, c. 453, p. 1799, § 25.)*

Research References

Rutter, Cal. Practice Guide: Enforcing Judgments/Debts Ch. 3-A, A. Evaluating the Claim.
Rutter, Cal. Practice Guide: Insurance Litigation Ch. 6I-D, D. Surety's Defenses to Payment of Bond.
Rutter, Cal. Practice Guide: Real Prop. Transactions Ch. 6-J, J. Guaranty of the Obligation.
Miller and Starr California Real Estate § 10:37, Trustor as a Surety.
Miller and Starr California Real Estate § 10:266, Application of "Exhaustion of the Security" Requirement.
Miller and Starr California Real Estate § 28:101, Exoneration of the Surety--In General.

1 Witkin Cal. Summ. 10th Contracts § 1006, Exoneration of Sureties.

§ 2824. Indemnified surety; liability notwithstanding modification or release

A surety, who has been indemnified by the principal, is liable to the creditor to the extent of the indemnity, notwithstanding that the creditor, without the assent of the surety, may have modified the contract or released the principal. *(Enacted in 1872. Amended by Stats.1939, c. 453, p. 1799, § 26.)*

Research References

Rutter, Cal. Practice Guide: Enforcing Judgments/Debts Ch. 3-A, A. Evaluating the Claim.
Rutter, Cal. Practice Guide: Real Prop. Transactions Ch. 6-I, I. Real Property Foreclosures and Antideficiency Laws.
Rutter, Cal. Practice Guide: Real Prop. Transactions Ch. 6-J, J. Guaranty of the Obligation.
Miller and Starr California Real Estate § 28:103, Exoneration of the Surety--Modification of the Terms of the Construction Contract.
Miller and Starr California Real Estate § 28:107, Exoneration of the Surety--Release or Discharge of the Debtor or Principal.
1 Witkin Cal. Summ. 10th Contracts § 1006, Exoneration of Sureties.

§ 2825. Discharge of principal

A surety is not exonerated by the discharge of his principal by operation of law, without the intervention or omission of the creditor. *(Enacted in 1872. Amended by Stats.1939, c. 453, p. 1799, § 27.)*

Research References

Rutter, Cal. Practice Guide: Enforcing Judgments/Debts Ch. 3-A, A. Evaluating the Claim.
Rutter, Cal. Practice Guide: Insurance Litigation Ch. 6I-D, D. Surety's Defenses to Payment of Bond.
Rutter, Cal. Practice Guide: Landlord-Tenant Form 2:D, Guaranty of Lease.
Rutter, Cal. Practice Guide: Real Prop. Transactions Ch. 6-J, J. Guaranty of the Obligation.
Miller and Starr California Real Estate § 10:267, Guaranty of Purchase-Money Obligation.
Miller and Starr California Real Estate § 10:270, Right of Reimbursement from the Trustor-Debtor.
Miller and Starr California Real Estate § 28:101, Exoneration of the Surety--In General.
Miller and Starr California Real Estate § 28:107, Exoneration of the Surety--Release or Discharge of the Debtor or Principal.
1 Witkin Cal. Summ. 10th Contracts § 1006, Exoneration of Sureties.
4 Witkin, California Summary 10th Security Transactions in Real Property § 194, (S 194) True Guaranty.

ARTICLE 7. POSITION OF SURETIES

Section

2855. Arbitration award against principal alone; effect on surety.

2856. Waiver of suretyship rights and defenses; contract language; effectiveness; applicability; validity of waivers executed prior to January 1, 1997.

§ 2832. Ostensible principal may show suretyship

One who appears to be a principal, whether by the terms of a written instrument or otherwise, may show that he is in fact a surety, except as against persons who have acted on the faith of his apparent character of principal. It is not necessary for him to show that the creditor accepted him as surety. *(Enacted in 1872. Amended by Stats.1939, c. 453, p. 1799, § 28.)*

Research References

Rutter, Cal. Practice Guide: Real Prop. Transactions Ch. 4-E, E. Drafting the Purchase and Sale Agreement-Terms and Conditions.
Miller and Starr California Real Estate § 10:10, Requirement of Some Debt or Obligation.
Miller and Starr California Real Estate § 10:263, Definitions; Guarantor, Surety.
1 Witkin Cal. Summ. 10th Contracts § 1002, in General.

§ 2837. Rules of interpretation

In interpreting the terms of a contract of suretyship, the same rules are to be observed as in the case of other contracts. Except as provided in section 2794, the position of a surety to whom consideration moves is the same as that of one who is gratuitous. *(Enacted in 1872. Amended by Stats.1939, c. 453, p. 1799, § 29.)*

Research References

Rutter, Cal. Practice Guide: Insurance Litigation Ch. 6I-A, A. Introduction.
Miller and Starr California Real Estate § 27:81, Owner's Remedies for Late Performance--Liquidated Damages.
Miller and Starr California Real Estate § 28:96, Interpretation of the Bond.
1 Witkin Cal. Summ. 10th Contracts § 1002, in General.

§ 2838. Judgment against surety; effect on relationship of parties

Notwithstanding the recovery of judgment by a creditor against a surety, the latter still occupies the relation of surety. *(Enacted in 1872.)*

Research References

Rutter, Cal. Practice Guide: Enforcing Judgments/Debts Ch. 3-A, A. Evaluating the Claim.
Rutter, Cal. Practice Guide: Insurance Litigation Ch. 6I-C, C. Surety's Obligations and Rights Upon Default by Principal.
Miller and Starr California Real Estate § 33:4, Standards for Appointment.
1 Witkin Cal. Summ. 10th Contracts § 1002, in General.

§ 2839. Exoneration by performance or offer of performance

Performance of the principal obligation, or an offer of such performance, duly made as provided in this code, exonerates a surety. *(Enacted in 1872. Amended by Code Am.1873–74, c. 612, p. 260, § 254.)*

Research References

California Real Estate Forms (Miller & Starr) § 3:37, Continuing Guaranty.
California Real Estate Forms (Miller & Starr) § 3:38, Completion Guaranty.
Rutter, Cal. Practice Guide: Enforcing Judgments/Debts Ch. 3-A, A. Evaluating the Claim.
Rutter, Cal. Practice Guide: Insurance Litigation Ch. 6I-C, C. Surety's Obligations and Rights Upon Default by Principal.

7 Witkin Cal. Proc. 5th Judgment § 220, (S 220) Actions Against Surety on Government Construction Bond.
1 Witkin Cal. Summ. 10th Contracts § 767, (S 767) Election of Alternative Modes of Performance.
1 Witkin Cal. Summ. 10th Contracts § 1006, Exoneration of Sureties.

§ 2845. Requiring creditor to pursue certain remedies; exoneration of surety by creditor's neglect to proceed

A surety may require the creditor, subject to Section 996.440 of the Code of Civil Procedure, to proceed against the principal, or to pursue any other remedy in the creditor's power which the surety cannot pursue, and which would lighten the surety's burden; and if the creditor neglects to do so, the surety is exonerated to the extent to which the surety is thereby prejudiced. *(Enacted in 1872. Amended by Stats.1939, c. 453, p. 1800, § 30; Stats.1972, c. 391, p. 714, § 1; Stats.1982, c. 517, p. 2300, § 73.)*

Law Revision Commission Comments

Section 2845 is amended to correct a section reference and make other technical changes. [16 Cal.L.Rev.Comm. Reports 501 (1981)].

Research References

California Real Estate Forms (Miller & Starr) § 3:29, Exceptions to Non-Recourse Guaranty--Conduit Loan.
California Real Estate Forms (Miller & Starr) § 3:30, Environmental Indemnity--Conduit Loan.
California Real Estate Forms (Miller & Starr) § 3:37, Continuing Guaranty.
California Real Estate Forms (Miller & Starr) § 3:38, Completion Guaranty.
Rutter, Cal. Practice Guide: Enforcing Judgments/Debts Ch. 3-A, A. Evaluating the Claim.
Rutter, Cal. Practice Guide: Enforcing Judgments/Debts Ch. 4-A, A. Attachment.
Rutter, Cal. Practice Guide: Insurance Litigation Ch. 6I-A, A. Introduction.
Rutter, Cal. Practice Guide: Insurance Litigation Ch. 6I-C, C. Surety's Obligations and Rights Upon Default by Principal.
Rutter, Cal. Practice Guide: Landlord-Tenant Form 2:D, Guaranty of Lease.
Rutter, Cal. Practice Guide: Real Prop. Transactions Form 6:L, Guaranty.
Miller and Starr California Real Estate § 28:2, Alternative (Cumulative) Remedies of the Claimant.
Miller and Starr California Real Estate § 10:37, Trustor as a Surety.
Miller and Starr California Real Estate § 28:99, Conditions of a Performance Bond--In General.
Miller and Starr California Real Estate § 10:155, Who May Enforce the One-Action Rule.
Miller and Starr California Real Estate § 10:263, Definitions; Guarantor, Surety.
Miller and Starr California Real Estate § 10:266, Application of "Exhaustion of the Security" Requirement.
Miller and Starr California Real Estate § 28:101, Exoneration of the Surety--In General.
Miller and Starr California Real Estate § 28:112, Proper Parties in Suit Against Surety; Necessity of Suit Against or Joinder of the Principal.
3 Witkin Cal. Proc. 5th Actions § 208, (S 208) Exhaustion of Security or Pursuit of Principal Debtor.
6 Witkin Cal. Proc. 5th Provisional Remedies § 41, (S 41) Judgment.
1 Witkin Cal. Summ. 10th Contracts § 1003, Rights of Sureties.
4 Witkin, California Summary 10th Security Transactions in Real Property § 127, Action is Not Against Mortgagor.
4 Witkin, California Summary 10th Security Transactions in Real Property § 202, (S 202) in General.

§ 2846. Compelling principal to perform

A surety may compel his principal to perform the obligation when due. *(Enacted in 1872.)*

Research References

California Real Estate Forms (Miller & Starr) § 3:29, Exceptions to Non-Recourse Guaranty--Conduit Loan.

Rutter, Cal. Practice Guide: Insurance Litigation Ch. 6I-C, C. Surety's Obligations and Rights Upon Default by Principal.
Miller and Starr California Real Estate § 28:101, Exoneration of the Surety--In General.
1 Witkin Cal. Summ. 10th Contracts § 1003, Rights of Sureties.
13 Witkin, California Summary 10th Equity § 178, Equitable Indemnity: Reimbursement from Principal.

§ 2847. Reimbursement of surety by principal

If a surety satisfies the principal obligation, or any part thereof, whether with or without legal proceedings, the principal is bound to reimburse what he has disbursed, including necessary costs and expenses; but the surety has no claim for reimbursement against other persons, though they may have been benefited by his act, except as prescribed by the next section. *(Enacted in 1872.)*

Research References

California Real Estate Forms (Miller & Starr) § 3:29, Exceptions to Non-Recourse Guaranty--Conduit Loan.
Rutter, Cal. Practice Guide: Insurance Litigation Ch. 6I-A, A. Introduction.
Rutter, Cal. Practice Guide: Insurance Litigation Ch. 6I-E, E. Surety's Rights Upon Payment of Bond.
Miller and Starr California Real Estate § 10:37, Trustor as a Surety.
Miller and Starr California Real Estate § 10:268, Liability for Deficiency After Nonjudicial Foreclosure.
Miller and Starr California Real Estate § 10:270, Right of Reimbursement from the Trustor-Debtor.
Miller and Starr California Real Estate § 28:128, Surety's Right of Subrogation.
3 Witkin Cal. Proc. 5th Actions § 544, (S 544) Former Rule Refusing to Discharge Sureties.
1 Witkin Cal. Summ. 10th Contracts § 1003, Rights of Sureties.
4 Witkin, California Summary 10th Security Transactions in Real Property § 194, (S 194) True Guaranty.
13 Witkin, California Summary 10th Equity § 178, Equitable Indemnity: Reimbursement from Principal.

§ 2848. Enforcement of creditor's remedies against principal; contribution by co-sureties

A surety, upon satisfying the obligation of the principal, is entitled to enforce every remedy which the creditor then has against the principal to the extent of reimbursing what he has expended, and also to require all his co-sureties to contribute thereto, without regard to the order of time in which they became such. *(Enacted in 1872.)*

Research References

California Real Estate Forms (Miller & Starr) § 3:29, Exceptions to Non-Recourse Guaranty--Conduit Loan.
California Real Estate Forms (Miller & Starr) § 3:30, Environmental Indemnity--Conduit Loan.
California Real Estate Forms (Miller & Starr) § 3:37, Continuing Guaranty.
California Real Estate Forms (Miller & Starr) § 3:38, Completion Guaranty.
California Real Estate Forms (Miller & Starr) § 3:40, Assignment of Membership Interest.
Rutter, Cal. Practice Guide: Insurance Litigation Ch. 9-C, C. Source of Subrogation Right.
Rutter, Cal. Practice Guide: Insurance Litigation Ch. 6I-E, E. Surety's Rights Upon Payment of Bond.
Rutter, Cal. Practice Guide: Landlord-Tenant Form 2:D, Guaranty of Lease.
Miller and Starr California Real Estate § 10:73, Performance by a Third Person.
Miller and Starr California Real Estate § 10:270, Right of Reimbursement from the Trustor-Debtor.
Miller and Starr California Real Estate § 11:113, Priority by Equitable Subrogation--In General.
Miller and Starr California Real Estate § 11:115, Priority by Equitable Subrogation--Party Paying Off or Refinancing Senior Lien.

3 Witkin Cal. Proc. 5th Actions § 544, (S 544) Former Rule Refusing to Discharge Sureties.
4 Witkin Cal. Proc. 5th Pleading § 132, Right of Subrogee to Sue.
1 Witkin Cal. Summ. 10th Contracts § 1003, Rights of Sureties.
13 Witkin, California Summary 10th Equity § 183, (S 183) Nature of Doctrine.

§ 2849. Surety entitled to benefits of securities for performance

A surety is entitled to the benefit of every security for the performance of the principal obligation held by the creditor, or by a co-surety at the time of entering into the contract of suretyship, or acquired by him afterwards, whether the surety was aware of the security or not. *(Enacted in 1872.)*

Research References

California Real Estate Forms (Miller & Starr) § 3:29, Exceptions to Non-Recourse Guaranty--Conduit Loan.
California Real Estate Forms (Miller & Starr) § 3:30, Environmental Indemnity--Conduit Loan.
California Real Estate Forms (Miller & Starr) § 3:37, Continuing Guaranty.
California Real Estate Forms (Miller & Starr) § 3:38, Completion Guaranty.
Rutter, Cal. Practice Guide: Enforcing Judgments/Debts Ch. 3-A, A. Evaluating the Claim.
Rutter, Cal. Practice Guide: Insurance Litigation Ch. 6I-E, E. Surety's Rights Upon Payment of Bond.
Rutter, Cal. Practice Guide: Landlord-Tenant Form 2:D, Guaranty of Lease.
Rutter, Cal. Practice Guide: Real Prop. Transactions Form 6:L, Guaranty.
Miller and Starr California Real Estate § 10:73, Performance by a Third Person.
Miller and Starr California Real Estate § 28:99, Conditions of a Performance Bond--In General.
Miller and Starr California Real Estate § 10:266, Application of "Exhaustion of the Security" Requirement.
Miller and Starr California Real Estate § 10:270, Right of Reimbursement from the Trustor-Debtor.
Miller and Starr California Real Estate § 11:113, Priority by Equitable Subrogation--In General.
Miller and Starr California Real Estate § 11:115, Priority by Equitable Subrogation--Party Paying Off or Refinancing Senior Lien.
Miller and Starr California Real Estate § 28:100, Conditions of a Performance Bond--Notice to the Surety of the Contractor's Default.
21 NO. 1 Miller & Starr, California Real Estate Newsalert 9, Deeds of Trust.
3 Witkin Cal. Proc. 5th Actions § 208, (S 208) Exhaustion of Security or Pursuit of Principal Debtor.
6 Witkin Cal. Proc. 5th Provisional Remedies § 72, Exhaustion of Security.
1 Witkin Cal. Summ. 10th Contracts § 1005, Right to Benefit of Securities.
13 Witkin, California Summary 10th Equity § 183, (S 183) Nature of Doctrine.

§ 2850. Property of principal first applied to discharge of obligation

Whenever property of a surety is hypothecated with property of the principal, the surety is entitled to have the property of the principal first applied to the discharge of the obligation. *(Enacted in 1872.)*

Research References

California Real Estate Forms (Miller & Starr) § 3:29, Exceptions to Non-Recourse Guaranty--Conduit Loan.
California Real Estate Forms (Miller & Starr) § 3:30, Environmental Indemnity--Conduit Loan.
California Real Estate Forms (Miller & Starr) § 3:37, Continuing Guaranty.
California Real Estate Forms (Miller & Starr) § 3:38;;0286592591;SA;;0126426;, Completion Guaranty.
Rutter, Cal. Practice Guide: Enforcing Judgments/Debts Ch. 3-A, A. Evaluating the Claim.

Rutter, Cal. Practice Guide: Insurance Litigation Ch. 6I-C, C. Surety's Obligations and Rights Upon Default by Principal.

Rutter, Cal. Practice Guide: Landlord-Tenant Form 2:D, Guaranty of Lease.

Rutter, Cal. Practice Guide: Real Prop. Transactions Form 6:L, Guaranty.

Miller and Starr California Real Estate § 10:266, Application of "Exhaustion of the Security" Requirement.

Miller and Starr California Real Estate § 28:128, Surety's Right of Subrogation.

3 Witkin Cal. Proc. 5th Actions § 208, (S 208) Exhaustion of Security or Pursuit of Principal Debtor.

1 Witkin Cal. Summ. 10th Contracts § 1003, Rights of Sureties.

§ 2854. Creditor entitled to benefits of securities for performance held by surety

A creditor is entitled to the benefit of everything which a surety has received from the debtor by way of security for the performance of the obligation, and may, upon the maturity of the obligation, compel the application of such security to its satisfaction. *(Enacted in 1872.)*

Research References

Miller and Starr California Real Estate § 10:266, Application of "Exhaustion of the Security" Requirement.

1 Witkin Cal. Summ. 10th Contracts § 1005, Right to Benefit of Securities.

§ 2855. Arbitration award against principal alone; effect on surety

An arbitration award rendered against a principal alone shall not be, be deemed to be, or be utilized as, an award against his surety.

The intent of this legislation is to apply existing law to arbitration awards. *(Added by Stats.1979, c. 346, p. 1211, § 1.)*

Research References

California Real Estate Forms (Miller & Starr) § 3:29, Exceptions to Non-Recourse Guaranty--Conduit Loan.

Rutter, Cal. Practice Guide: Insurance Litigation Ch. 6I-A, A. Introduction.

Rutter, Cal. Practice Guide: Insurance Litigation Ch. 6I-D, D. Surety's Defenses to Payment of Bond.

Rutter, Cal. Practice Guide: Landlord-Tenant Form 2:D, Guaranty of Lease.

Rutter, Cal. Practice Guide: Real Prop. Transactions Ch. 6-J, J. Guaranty of the Obligation.

Rutter, Cal. Practice Guide: Real Prop. Transactions Form 6:L, Guaranty.

Miller and Starr California Real Estate § 27:12, Disciplinary Action, Citation, and Fines for Violations of the Contractors License Law.

Miller and Starr California Real Estate § 10:265, Waiver of Guarantor's Defenses.

Miller and Starr California Real Estate § 27:103, Contractor's Obligation of Substantial Performance.

7 Witkin Cal. Proc. 5th Judgment § 220, (S 220) Actions Against Surety on Government Construction Bond.

1 Witkin Cal. Summ. 10th Contracts § 1002, in General.

§ 2856. Waiver of suretyship rights and defenses; contract language; effectiveness; applicability; validity of waivers executed prior to January 1, 1997

(a) Any guarantor or other surety, including a guarantor of a note or other obligation secured by real property or an estate for years, may waive any or all of the following:

(1) The guarantor or other surety's rights of subrogation, reimbursement, indemnification, and contribution and any other rights and defenses that are or may become available to the guarantor or other surety by reason of Sections 2787 to 2855, inclusive.

(2) Any rights or defenses the guarantor or other surety may have in respect of his or her obligations as a guarantor or other surety by reason of any election of remedies by the creditor.

(3) Any rights or defenses the guarantor or other surety may have because the principal's note or other obligation is secured by real property or an estate for years. These rights or defenses include, but are not limited to, any rights or defenses that are based upon, directly or indirectly, the application of Section 580a, 580b, 580d, or 726 of the Code of Civil Procedure to the principal's note or other obligation.

(b) A contractual provision that expresses an intent to waive any or all of the rights and defenses described in subdivision (a) shall be effective to waive these rights and defenses without regard to the inclusion of any particular language or phrases in the contract to waive any rights and defenses or any references to statutory provisions or judicial decisions.

(c) Without limiting any rights of the creditor or any guarantor or other surety to use any other language to express an intent to waive any or all of the rights and defenses described in paragraphs (2) and (3) of subdivision (a), the following provisions in a contract shall effectively waive all rights and defenses described in paragraphs (2) and (3) of subdivision (a):

The guarantor waives all rights and defenses that the guarantor may have because the debtor's debt is secured by real property. This means, among other things:

(1) The creditor may collect from the guarantor without first foreclosing on any real or personal property collateral pledged by the debtor.

(2) If the creditor forecloses on any real property collateral pledged by the debtor:

(A) The amount of the debt may be reduced only by the price for which that collateral is sold at the foreclosure sale, even if the collateral is worth more than the sale price.

(B) The creditor may collect from the guarantor even if the creditor, by foreclosing on the real property collateral, has destroyed any right the guarantor may have to collect from the debtor.

This is an unconditional and irrevocable waiver of any rights and defenses the guarantor may have because the debtor's debt is secured by real property. These rights and defenses include, but are not limited to, any rights or defenses based upon Section 580a, 580b, 580d, or 726 of the Code of Civil Procedure.

(d) Without limiting any rights of the creditor or any guarantor or other surety to use any other language to express an intent to waive all rights and defenses of the surety by reason of any election of remedies by the creditor, the following provision shall be effective to waive all rights and defenses the guarantor or other surety may have in respect of his or her obligations as a surety by reason of an election of remedies by the creditor:

The guarantor waives all rights and defenses arising out of an election of remedies by the creditor, even though that election of remedies, such as a nonjudicial foreclosure with respect to security for a guaranteed obligation, has destroyed the guarantor's rights of subrogation and reimbursement against the principal by the operation of Section 580d of the Code of Civil Procedure or otherwise.

(e) Subdivisions (b), (c), and (d) shall not apply to a guaranty or other type of suretyship obligation made in respect of a loan secured by a deed of trust or mortgage on a dwelling for not more than four families when the dwelling is occupied, entirely or in part, by the borrower and that loan was in fact used to pay all or part of the purchase price of that dwelling.

(f) The validity of a waiver executed before January 1, 1997, shall be determined by the application of the law that existed on the date that the waiver was executed. *(Added by Stats.1996, c. 1013 (A.B.2585), § 2.)*

Research References

California Real Estate Forms (Miller & Starr) § 3:29, Exceptions to Non-Recourse Guaranty--Conduit Loan.

California Real Estate Forms (Miller & Starr) § 3:30, Environmental Indemnity--Conduit Loan.

California Real Estate Forms (Miller & Starr) § 3:37, Continuing Guaranty.

California Real Estate Forms (Miller & Starr) § 3:38, Completion Guaranty.

California Real Estate Forms (Miller & Starr) § 3:40, Assignment of Membership Interest.

Rutter, Cal. Practice Guide: Enforcing Judgments/Debts Ch. 3-A, A. Evaluating the Claim.

Rutter, Cal. Practice Guide: Insurance Litigation Ch. 6I-F, F. Defenses Assertable Against Surety.

Rutter, Cal. Practice Guide: Real Prop. Transactions Ch. 6-J, J. Guaranty of the Obligation.

Rutter, Cal. Practice Guide: Real Prop. Transactions Form 6:L, Guaranty.

Rutter, Cal. Practice Guide: Real Prop. Transactions Ch. 6-J Outline, Outline J.

Miller and Starr California Real Estate § 21:31, Who Can Raise the Defense of Usury--Third Parties.

Miller and Starr California Real Estate § 10:127, Conflict of Laws.

Miller and Starr California Real Estate § 10:265, Waiver of Guarantor's Defenses.

Miller and Starr California Real Estate § 10:266, Application of "Exhaustion of the Security" Requirement.

Miller and Starr California Real Estate § 10:268, Liability for Deficiency After Nonjudicial Foreclosure.

Miller and Starr California Real Estate § 10:269, Limitation of Liability.

Miller and Starr California Real Estate § 28:128, Surety's Right of Subrogation.

22 NO. 2 Miller & Starr, California Real Estate Newsalert 9, Deeds of Trust.

22 NO. 4 Miller & Starr, California Real Estate Newsalert 29, Deeds of Trust.

1 Witkin Cal. Summ. 10th Contracts § 1003, Rights of Sureties.

4 Witkin, California Summary 10th Security Transactions in Real Property § 194, (S 194) True Guaranty.

4 Witkin, California Summary 10th Security Transactions in Real Property § 204, (S 204) Waiver of Defenses.

Title 13.5

OBLIGATION TO DEFEND ACTION

Section

2860.   Conflict of interest; duty to provide independent counsel; waiver; qualifications of independent counsel; fees; disclosure of information.

§ 2860. Conflict of interest; duty to provide independent counsel; waiver; qualifications of independent counsel; fees; disclosure of information

(a) If the provisions of a policy of insurance impose a duty to defend upon an insurer and a conflict of interest arises which creates a duty on the part of the insurer to provide independent counsel to the insured, the insurer shall provide independent counsel to represent the insured unless, at the time the insured is informed that a possible conflict may arise or does exist, the insured expressly waives, in writing, the right to independent counsel. An insurance contract may contain a provision which sets forth the method of selecting that counsel consistent with this section.

(b) For purposes of this section, a conflict of interest does not exist as to allegations or facts in the litigation for which the insurer denies coverage; however, when an insurer reserves its rights on a given issue and the outcome of that coverage issue can be controlled by counsel first retained by the insurer for the defense of the claim, a conflict of interest may exist. No conflict of interest shall be deemed to exist as to allegations of punitive damages or be deemed to exist solely because an insured is sued for an amount in excess of the insurance policy limits.

(c) When the insured has selected independent counsel to represent him or her, the insurer may exercise its right to require that the counsel selected by the insured possess certain minimum qualifications which may include that the selected counsel have (1) at least five years of civil litigation practice which includes substantial defense experience in the subject at issue in the litigation, and (2) errors and omissions coverage. The insurer's obligation to pay fees to the independent counsel selected by the insured is limited to the rates which are actually paid by the insurer to attorneys retained by it in the ordinary course of business in the defense of similar actions in the community where the claim arose or is being defended. This subdivision does not invalidate other different or additional policy provisions pertaining to attorney's fees or providing for methods of settlement of disputes concerning those fees. Any dispute concerning attorney's fees not resolved by these methods shall be resolved by final and binding arbitration by a single neutral arbitrator selected by the parties to the dispute.

(d) When independent counsel has been selected by the insured, it shall be the duty of that counsel and the insured to disclose to the insurer all information concerning the action except privileged materials relevant to coverage disputes, and timely to inform and consult with the insurer on all matters relating to the action. Any claim of privilege asserted is subject to in camera review in the appropriate law and motion department of the superior court. Any information disclosed by the insured or by independent counsel is not a waiver of the privilege as to any other party.

(e) The insured may waive its right to select independent counsel by signing the following statement: "I have been advised and informed of my right to select independent counsel to represent me in this lawsuit. I have considered this matter fully and freely waive my right to select independent counsel at this time. I authorize my insurer to select a defense attorney to represent me in this lawsuit."

(f) Where the insured selects independent counsel pursuant to the provisions of this section, both the counsel provided by the insurer and independent counsel selected by the insured shall be allowed to participate in all aspects of the litigation. Counsel shall cooperate fully in the exchange of information that is consistent with each counsel's ethical and legal obligation to the insured. Nothing in this section shall relieve the insured of his or her duty to cooperate with the insurer under the terms of the insurance contract. (Added by Stats.1987, c. 1498, § 4. Amended by Stats.1988, c. 1114, § 1.)

Research References

Rutter, Cal. Practice Guide: A.D.R. App. A, Selected Statutes Providing for ADR.

Rutter, Cal. Practice Guide: A.D.R. Ch. 5-A, A. General Considerations.

Rutter, Cal. Practice Guide: A.D.R. Ch. 5-J, J. Challenging and Enforcing Arbitrator's Award in Court.

Rutter, Cal. Practice Guide: A.D.R. Ch. 7-B, B. Arbitrators.

California Practice Guide: Employment Litigation Ch. 3-K, K. Right to Independent (Cumis) Counsel.

Rutter, Cal. Practice Guide: Insurance Litigation Ch. 9-E, E. Requirements for Equitable Subrogation.

Rutter, Cal. Practice Guide: Insurance Litigation Ch. 15-C, C. Arbitration/Appraisal/Mediation.

Rutter, Cal. Practice Guide: Insurance Litigation Ch. 15-G, G. Discovery.

Rutter, Cal. Practice Guide: Insurance Litigation Ch. 7B-J, J. Defense Under Reservation of Rights.

Rutter, Cal. Practice Guide: Insurance Litigation Ch. 7B-K, K. Insurer's Duty to Provide Independent Counsel When Conflict of Interest Arises.

Rutter, Cal. Practice Guide: Insurance Litigation Ch. 7B-L, L. Defense Counsel's Obligations-Professional Responsibility Considerations.

Rutter, Cal. Practice Guide: Insurance Litigation Ch. 7K-D, D. Policy Provisions.

Rutter, Cal. Practice Guide: Insurance Litigation Form 7:D, Fee Engagement Letter for Use by Cumis Counsel.

Rutter, Cal. Practice Guide: Insurance Litigation Ch. 12B-D, D. Refusal to Defend Cases.

Rutter, Cal. Practice Guide: Insurance Litigation Gen. Matls., Highlights.

Rutter, Cal. Practice Guide: Personal Injury Ch. 1-B, B. Initial Evaluation of Case: Decision to Accept or Reject Employment or Undertake Further Evaluation of Claim.

Rutter, Cal. Practice Guide: Personal Injury Ch. 4-A, A. General Considerations.

Rutter, Cal. Practice Guide: Personal Injury Ch. 4-C, C. Effective Settlement Negotiations.

Rutter, Cal. Practice Guide: Real Prop. Transactions Ch. 3-G, G. Title Policy Claims and Liability.

Rutter, Cal. Practice Guide: Prof. Responsibility Ch. 3-C, C. Identifying "Client".

Rutter, Cal. Practice Guide: Prof. Responsibility Ch. 4-B, B. Concurrent Representation of Clients With Conflicting Interests (Conflicts Between Present Clients).

Rutter, Cal. Practice Guide: Prof. Responsibility Ch. 5-C, C. Other Statutory Limits on Fees and Fee Agreements.

Rutter, Cal. Practice Guide: Prof. Responsibility Ch. 5-K, K. Fee Recovery/Enforcing Fee Agreements.

Rutter, Cal. Practice Guide: Prof. Responsibility Ch. 7-C, C. Attorney-Client Privilege.

Miller and Starr California Real Estate § 35:50, Defenses to Petition to Compel Arbitration--In General.

Miller and Starr California Real Estate § 35:56, Stay of Litigation Pending Arbitration.

Miller and Starr California Real Estate § 7:196, Scope of Every Insurer's Duty to Defend.

Miller and Starr California Real Estate § 7:201, Insured's Right to Independent (Cumis) Counsel.

Miller and Starr California Real Estate § 7:202, Fees of Independent Counsel.

Miller and Starr California Real Estate § 7:235, Arbitration.

19 NO. 4 Miller & Starr, California Real Estate Newsalert 51, Title Insurance.

21 NO. 5 Miller & Starr, California Real Estate Newsalert 3, Alternative Dispute Resolution.

1 Witkin Cal. Proc. 5th Attorneys § 122, Insured's Right to Independent Counsel.

1 Witkin Cal. Proc. 5th Attorneys § 123, Scope of Right.

2 Witkin Cal. Proc. 5th Jurisdiction § 436, (S 436) Discretion to Stay.

6 Witkin Cal. Proc. 5th Proceedings Without Trial § 503, (S 503) in General.

7 Witkin Cal. Proc. 5th Trial § 84, Actions Classified as Legal.

2 Witkin, California Summary 10th Insurance § 287, in General.

2 Witkin, California Summary 10th Insurance § 288, Existence of Conflict of Interest.

2 Witkin, California Summary 10th Insurance § 290, Selection and Payment.

2 Witkin, California Summary 10th Insurance § 291, Rights and Duties in Course of Litigation.

2 Witkin, California Summary 10th Insurance § 294, (S 294) Courtesy Defense of Uninsured Defendant.

Title 14

LIEN

CHAPTER 1. LIENS IN GENERAL

ARTICLE 1. DEFINITION OF LIENS

§ 2872. Definition

A lien is a charge imposed in some mode other than by a transfer in trust upon specific property by which it is made security for the performance of an act. *(Enacted in 1872. Amended by Code Am.1877–78, c. 74, p. 88, § 1.)*

Research References

Miller and Starr California Real Estate § 10:2, Lien Versus Title Theories.

Miller and Starr California Real Estate § 2:23, Liens and Encumbrances.

Miller and Starr California Real Estate § 7:48, Indemnity for Defects, Liens, and Encumbrances.

Miller and Starr California Real Estate § 10:10, Requirement of Some Debt or Obligation.

22 NO. 1 Miller & Starr, California Real Estate Newsalert 6, Common Interest Developments.

13 Witkin, California Summary 10th Personal Property § 216, Nature and Kinds of Liens.

4 Witkin, California Summary 10th Security Transactions in Real Property § 39, (S 39) in General.

§ 2873. Classification of liens

Liens are either general or special. *(Enacted in 1872.)*

Research References

13 Witkin, California Summary 10th Personal Property § 217, (S 217) in General.

§ 2874. "General lien" defined

A general lien is one which the holder thereof is entitled to enforce as a security for the performance of all the obligations, or all of a particular class of obligations, which exist in his favor against the owner of the property. *(Enacted in 1872.)*

Research References

13 Witkin, California Summary 10th Personal Property § 217, (S 217) in General.

§ 2875. "Special lien" defined

A special lien is one which the holder thereof can enforce only as security for the performance of a particular act or obligation, and of such obligations as may be incidental thereto. *(Enacted in 1872.)*

Research References

Miller and Starr California Real Estate § 10:187, Who Can Reinstate.
Miller and Starr California Real Estate § 11:114, Priority by Equitable Subrogation--Optional Advances to Protect Security.
13 Witkin, California Summary 10th Personal Property § 217, (S 217) in General.

§ 2876. Prior lien satisfied by holder of special lien

Where the holder of a special lien is compelled to satisfy a prior lien for his own protection, he may enforce payment of the amount so paid by him, as a part of the claim for which his own lien exists. *(Enacted in 1872.)*

Research References

Miller and Starr California Real Estate § 10:11, Future Advances Secured.
Miller and Starr California Real Estate § 10:39, Rights of the Parties.
Miller and Starr California Real Estate § 10:137, Failure to Pay Insurance Premiums.
Miller and Starr California Real Estate § 10:138, Failure to Pay Prior Encumbrances.
Miller and Starr California Real Estate § 10:139, Failure to Pay Taxes.
Miller and Starr California Real Estate § 10:187, Who Can Reinstate.
Miller and Starr California Real Estate § 10:189, Amounts that Must be Paid to Reinstate.
Miller and Starr California Real Estate § 10:197, Mode of Redemption.
Miller and Starr California Real Estate § 11:113, Priority by Equitable Subrogation--In General.
Miller and Starr California Real Estate § 11:114, Priority by Equitable Subrogation--Optional Advances to Protect Security.
4 Witkin, California Summary 10th Security Transactions in Real Property § 76, in General.
4 Witkin, California Summary 10th Security Transactions in Real Property § 78, (S 78) Clearing Liens.

§ 2877. Contracts governed by chapter

Contracts of mortgage, pledge, bottomry, or respondentia * * * are subject to all of the provisions of this chapter. *(Enacted in 1872. Amended by Stats.2013, c. 76 (A.B.383), § 13.)*

ARTICLE 2. CREATION OF LIENS

§ 2881. Creation

A lien is created:

1. By contract of the parties; or,

2. By operation of law. *(Enacted in 1872.)*

Research References

Rutter, Cal. Practice Guide: Civ. Pro. Before Trial Ch. 12(II)-H, H. Professional Responsibility Considerations Re Settlements.
Rutter, Cal. Practice Guide: Enforcing Judgments/Debts Ch. 4-A, A. Attachment.
Rutter, Cal. Practice Guide: Prof. Responsibility Ch. 5-F, F. Formalizing Fee Agreements.
Miller and Starr California Real Estate § 28:4, Requirement of a Contract.
2 Witkin, California Summary 10th Insurance § 13, (S 13) Liability for Subrogation Claims.

13 Witkin, California Summary 10th Personal Property § 216, Nature and Kinds of Liens.

§ 2882. Claim not due; no lien by operation of law

No lien arises by mere operation of law until the time at which the act to be secured thereby ought to be performed. *(Enacted in 1872.)*

Research References

Miller and Starr California Real Estate § 10:19, "After-Acquired" Title.
2 Witkin, California Summary 10th Insurance § 13, (S 13) Liability for Subrogation Claims.

§ 2883. Agreement to create a lien; property not yet acquired; undistributed real property of an estate

(a) An agreement may be made to create a lien upon property not yet acquired by the party agreeing to give the lien, or not yet in existence. In that case the lien agreed for attaches from the time when the party agreeing to give it acquires an interest in the thing, to the extent of such interest.

(b) For purposes of subdivision (a), an agreement by a beneficiary of an estate that is subject to administration, as provided in Division 7 (commencing with Section 7000) of the Probate Code, to create a lien upon real property in the estate that is undistributed at the time the agreement is entered into, shall create no lien upon the real property unless and until the real property is distributed to that beneficiary. Upon recordation of an order confirming the sale of the real property pursuant to Section 10313 of the Probate Code and the recording of a duly executed deed in accordance therewith, any expectancy of a lien in the real property under the agreement shall be extinguished. *(Enacted in 1872. Amended by Stats.1993, c. 382 (S.B.848), § 1; Stats.1993, c. 527 (A.B.908), § 1.)*

Research References

Miller and Starr California Real Estate § 10:19, "After-Acquired" Title.
1 Witkin Cal. Proc. 5th Attorneys § 168, Express Contract.
1 Witkin Cal. Summ. 10th Contracts § 726, (S 726) Scope and Waiver of Restrictions.
4 Witkin, California Summary 10th Security Transactions in Real Property § 34, What Property Can be Mortgaged.
14 Witkin, California Summary 10th Wills and Probate § 725, (S 725) No Lien on Real Property Before Distribution.

§ 2884. Obligations not in existence at time of creating lien

A lien may be created by contract, to take immediate effect, as security for the performance of obligations not then in existence. *(Enacted in 1872.)*

Research References

Rutter, Cal. Practice Guide: Enforcing Judgments/Debts Ch. 4-A, A. Attachment.
Rutter, Cal. Practice Guide: Real Prop. Transactions Ch. 6-H, H. Security for Promissory Note.
Miller and Starr California Real Estate § 10:10, Requirement of Some Debt or Obligation.
Miller and Starr California Real Estate § 10:11, Future Advances Secured.
Miller and Starr California Real Estate § 11:106, Liens for Future Advances--In General.
1 Witkin Cal. Proc. 5th Attorneys § 168, Express Contract.

§ 2885. Recordation of state tax liens; notice to tax debtor

Any state agency, upon recording a state tax lien against real property, shall mail written notice of the recordation to the tax debtor, unless previous correspondence mailed to the address of record was returned undelivered with no forwarding address. Failure to notify the tax debtor shall not affect the constructive notice otherwise imparted by recordation, nor shall it affect the force, effect, or priority otherwise accorded such tax lien.

(Added by Stats.1980, c. 1281, p. 4326, § 1. Amended by Stats.1983, c. 643, § 1, eff. Sept. 1, 1983.)

Research References

Miller and Starr California Real Estate § 11:10, Required Form and Contents--In General.
Miller and Starr California Real Estate § 11:157, State and Local Tax Liens; in General.
Miller and Starr California Real Estate § 11:164, Personal Property Tax Liens.
Miller and Starr California Real Estate § 11:165, State Tax Liens--In General.
Miller and Starr California Real Estate § 11:166, State Tax Liens--Sales and Use Tax Liens.
Miller and Starr California Real Estate § 11:167, State Tax Liens--Unemployment Insurance Contribution Liens.
Miller and Starr California Real Estate § 11:168, State Tax Liens--Personal Income and Corporate Franchise Tax Liens.
9 Witkin, California Summary 10th Taxation § 116, State Tax Liens.

ARTICLE 3. EFFECT OF LIENS

Section
2888.   Title not transferred.
2889.   Forfeitures and restraints upon redemption; validity.
2890.   Personal obligation not implied.
2891.   Security of other obligations.
2892.   Compensation of lien holder.

§ 2888.   Title not transferred

Notwithstanding an agreement to the contrary, a lien, or a contract for a lien, transfers no title to the property subject to the lien. *(Enacted in 1872.)*

Research References

Miller and Starr California Real Estate § 10:2, Lien Versus Title Theories.
Miller and Starr California Real Estate § 10:26, Evidence of the Parties' Intentions.
Miller and Starr California Real Estate § 10:27, Enforcement Against a Purchaser from the Creditor or Other Third Person.
9 Witkin Cal. Proc. 5th Appeal § 519, Decision Overlooking Existing Statute.
4 Witkin, California Summary 10th Security Transactions in Real Property § 3, Mortgage.
4 Witkin, California Summary 10th Security Transactions in Real Property § 10, (S 10) Intention to Create Security Interest.

§ 2889.   Forfeitures and restraints upon redemption; validity

All contracts for the forfeiture of property subject to a lien, in satisfaction of the obligation secured thereby, and all contracts in restraint of the right of redemption from a lien, are void. *(Enacted in 1872.)*

Research References

Rutter, Cal. Practice Guide: Real Prop. Transactions Ch. 6-H, H. Security for Promissory Note.
Miller and Starr California Real Estate § 10:26, Evidence of the Parties' Intentions.
Miller and Starr California Real Estate § 10:27, Enforcement Against a Purchaser from the Creditor or Other Third Person.
Miller and Starr California Real Estate § 10:43, Deed in Lieu of Foreclosure.
Miller and Starr California Real Estate § 10:123, Nature of Foreclosure; Termination of Redemption.
Miller and Starr California Real Estate § 10:195, Equity of Redemption (Redemption Prior to Sale).
Miller and Starr California Real Estate § 10:227, Statutory Redemption; Who Can Redeem.
4 Witkin, California Summary 10th Security Transactions in Real Property § 236, Waiver or Sale of Right of Redemption.

§ 2890.   Personal obligation not implied

The creation of a lien does not of itself imply that any person is bound to perform the act for which the lien is a security. *(Enacted in 1872.)*

Research References

Miller and Starr California Real Estate § 10:35, Grantee Takes "Subject To".

§ 2891.   Security of other obligations

The existence of a lien upon property does not of itself entitle the person in whose favor it exists to a lien upon the same property for the performance of any other obligation than that which the lien originally secured. *(Enacted in 1872.)*

Research References

Miller and Starr California Real Estate § 10:12, The "Dragnet" Clause.

§ 2892.   Compensation of lien holder

One who holds property by virtue of a lien thereon, is not entitled to compensation from the owner thereof for any trouble or expense which he incurs respecting it, except to the same extent as a borrower, under sections 1892 and 1893. *(Enacted in 1872.)*

ARTICLE 4. PRIORITY OF LIENS

Section
2897.   Time of creation; exception.
2898.   Mortgages or deeds of trust.
2899.   Marshaling liens.

§ 2897.   Time of creation; exception

Other things being equal, different liens upon the same property have priority according to the time of their creation, except in cases of bottomry and respondentia. *(Enacted in 1872.)*

Research References

Rutter, Cal. Practice Guide: Civ. Pro. Before Trial Ch. 1-A, A. Accepting a New Case.
Rutter, Cal. Practice Guide: Enforcing Judgments/Debts Ch. 4-A, A. Attachment.
Rutter, Cal. Practice Guide: Enforcing Judgments/Debts Ch. 6G-7, Charging Orders Against Debtor Partnership/LLC Interests.
Rutter, Cal. Practice Guide: Enforcing Judgments/Debts Ch. 6G-8, Lien in Pending Action.
Rutter, Cal. Practice Guide: Enforcing Judgments/Debts Ch. 6A-13, Creating an Enforcement of Judgment Plan.
Rutter, Cal. Practice Guide: Family Law Ch. 6-A, A. Child Support.
Rutter, Cal. Practice Guide: Personal Injury Ch. 1-C, C. Formation of Attorney-Client Relationship: the Employment Agreement.
Rutter, Cal. Practice Guide: Real Prop. Transactions Ch. 6-H, H. Security for Promissory Note.
Rutter, Cal. Practice Guide: Prof. Responsibility Ch. 5-F, F. Formalizing Fee Agreements.
Miller and Starr California Real Estate § 11:1, Rules Governing Priorities; Relation to Notice and Recording.
Miller and Starr California Real Estate § 11:130, in General; Off-Record Priority.
Miller and Starr California Real Estate § 11:140, Effect of Cessation of Work on Mechanic's Lien Priorities.
Miller and Starr California Real Estate § 11:164, Personal Property Tax Liens.
23 NO. 3 Miller & Starr, California Real Estate Newsalert 16, Recording and Priorities.
1 Witkin Cal. Proc. 5th Attorneys § 172, (S 172) Priority.

8 Witkin Cal. Proc. 5th Enforcement of Judgment § 68, (S 68) Relation Back and Priorities.

8 Witkin Cal. Proc. 5th Enforcement of Judgment § 299, Equitable Offset.

6 Witkin Cal. Proc. 5th Provisional Remedies § 179, Securities.

6 Witkin Cal. Proc. 5th Provisional Remedies § 185, (S 185) Priority in Time.

13 Witkin, California Summary 10th Personal Property § 216, Nature and Kinds of Liens.

4 Witkin, California Summary 10th Security Transactions in Real Property § 48, (S 48) Priority in Time.

§ 2898. Mortgages or deeds of trust

(a) A mortgage or deed of trust given for the price of real property, at the time of its conveyance, has priority over all other liens created against the purchaser, subject to the operation of the recording laws.

(b) The priority of the lien of a mortgage or deed of trust on an estate for years in real property shall be determined in the same manner as for determining the priority of a lien of a mortgage or deed of trust on real property. *(Enacted in 1872. Amended by Stats.1939, c. 520, p. 1905, § 1; Stats.1989, c. 698, § 3.)*

Research References

Rutter, Cal. Practice Guide: Enforcing Judgments/Debts Ch. 6B-8, Priorities Among Real Property Judgment Liens.

Rutter, Cal. Practice Guide: Real Prop. Transactions Ch. 6-H, H. Security for Promissory Note.

Miller and Starr California Real Estate § 11:1, Rules Governing Priorities; Relation to Notice and Recording.

Miller and Starr California Real Estate § 8:74, Reattaching Liens.

Miller and Starr California Real Estate § 32:53, Subsequently Acquired Property.

Miller and Starr California Real Estate § 32:55, Duration of the Judgment Lien.

Miller and Starr California Real Estate § 11:103, Priority of Purchase Money Liens--In General.

Miller and Starr California Real Estate § 11:104, Priority of Purchase Money Liens--Purchase Money Lien Vis-á-Vis Liens Created Before Title Passes.

Miller and Starr California Real Estate § 11:120, Vendor's Lien.

Miller and Starr California Real Estate § 11:134, Effect of Commencement of Work Before the Grantee Receives Title.

Miller and Starr California Real Estate § 11:182, Priority of Federal Tax Liens--Property to Which the Lien Attaches.

Miller and Starr California Real Estate § 11:184, Priority of Federal Tax Liens--Relation to Liens of Deeds of Trust and Mortgages.

Miller and Starr California Real Estate § 11:192, Personal Property and Fixtures; General Rules of Priority.

Miller and Starr California Real Estate § 11:201, Subordination Agreements; in General.

Miller and Starr California Real Estate § 11:204, Subordination of Seller's Lien to Lien of an Institutional Lender.

Miller and Starr California Real Estate § 11:206, Subordination of Seller's Lien to Lien of a Construction Lender--Types of Agreements; Description of the Issues.

Miller and Starr California Real Estate § 11:212, Executed Seller Subordination Agreements--Distinction Based Upon the Order of Recordation.

4 Witkin, California Summary 10th Security Transactions in Real Property § 48, (S 48) Priority in Time.

4 Witkin, California Summary 10th Security Transactions in Real Property § 74, (S 74) in General.

4 Witkin, California Summary 10th Security Transactions in Real Property § 75, (S 75) Priority Over Vendor's Lien.

§ 2899. Marshaling liens

Where one has a lien upon several things, and other persons have subordinate liens upon, or interests in, some but not all of the same things, the person having the prior lien, if he can do so without risk of loss to himself, or of injustice to other persons, must resort to the property in the following order, on the demand of any party interested:

1. To the things upon which he has an exclusive lien;

2. To the things which are subject to the fewest subordinate liens;

3. In like manner inversely to the number of subordinate liens upon the same thing; and,

4. When several things are within one of the foregoing classes, and subject to the same number of liens, resort must be had—

(1.) To the things which have not been transferred since the prior lien was created;

(2.) To the things which have been so transferred without a valuable consideration; and,

(3.) To the things which have been so transferred for a valuable consideration in the inverse order of the transfer. *(Enacted in 1872.)*

Research References

California Real Estate Forms (Miller & Starr) § 3:8, Deed of Trust, Security Agreement, and Fixture Filing With Assignment of Rents and Agreements.

California Real Estate Forms (Miller & Starr) § 3:14, Construction Deed of Trust, Security Agreement, and Fixture Filing With Assignment of Rents and Agreements.

California Real Estate Forms (Miller & Starr) § 3:29, Exceptions to Non-Recourse Guaranty--Conduit Loan.

California Real Estate Forms (Miller & Starr) § 3:37, Continuing Guaranty.

California Real Estate Forms (Miller & Starr) § 3:38, Completion Guaranty.

California Real Estate Forms (Miller & Starr) § 3:40, Assignment of Membership Interest.

Rutter, Cal. Practice Guide: Enforcing Judgments/Debts Ch. 5-D, D. Involuntary Bankruptcy.

Miller and Starr California Real Estate § 11:1, Rules Governing Priorities; Relation to Notice and Recording.

Miller and Starr California Real Estate § 15:5, Definition and Nature of an Easement.

Miller and Starr California Real Estate § 10:205, Sale When Several Parcels of Real Property Are Encumbered.

Miller and Starr California Real Estate § 11:215, Definition.

Miller and Starr California Real Estate § 11:217, The "Inverse Order of Alienation" Rule.

Miller and Starr California Real Estate § 11:218, Equitable Restrictions.

Miller and Starr California Real Estate § 11:220, Waiver of Marshalling.

13 Witkin, California Summary 10th Personal Property § 216, Nature and Kinds of Liens.

4 Witkin, California Summary 10th Security Transactions in Real Property § 143, Manner of Sale.

13 Witkin, California Summary 10th Equity § 23, Marshaling Assets.

ARTICLE 5. REDEMPTION FROM LIEN

Section

2903. Right of redemption; subrogation.
2904. Rights of inferior lien holder.
2905. Redemption; procedure.
2906. Secured party; option to acquire interest in real property collateral; priority; validity.

§ 2903. Right of redemption; subrogation

Every person, having an interest in property subject to a lien, has a right to redeem it from the lien, at any time after the claim is due, and before his right of redemption is foreclosed, and, by such redemption, becomes subrogated to all the benefits of the lien, as against all owners of other interests in the property, except in so far as he was bound to make such redemption for their benefit. *(Enacted in 1872. Amended by Stats.1905, c. 459, p. 617, § 1.)*

Research References

Rutter, Cal. Practice Guide: Enforcing Judgments/Debts Ch. 6D-4, Levy on Specific Property.
Miller and Starr California Real Estate § 10:1, Historical Perspective.
Miller and Starr California Real Estate § 9:32, Remainders--Rights of Remainder Holders.
Miller and Starr California Real Estate § 10:73, Performance by a Third Person.
Miller and Starr California Real Estate § 12:12, Acquisition of an Adverse Interest.
Miller and Starr California Real Estate § 28:61, Trial and Judgment.
Miller and Starr California Real Estate § 10:123, Nature of Foreclosure; Termination of Redemption.
Miller and Starr California Real Estate § 10:195, Equity of Redemption (Redemption Prior to Sale).
Miller and Starr California Real Estate § 10:196, Who Can Redeem.
Miller and Starr California Real Estate § 10:197, Mode of Redemption.
Miller and Starr California Real Estate § 10:221, Comparison With Nonjudicial Foreclosure.
Miller and Starr California Real Estate § 11:100, Priority of the Purchaser's Title from a Foreclosure Sale.
Miller and Starr California Real Estate § 11:113, Priority by Equitable Subrogation--In General.
Miller and Starr California Real Estate § 11:114, Priority by Equitable Subrogation--Optional Advances to Protect Security.
4 Witkin, California Summary 10th Security Transactions in Real Property § 213, Equity of Redemption.

§ 2904. Rights of inferior lien holder

One who has a lien inferior to another, upon the same property, has a right:

1. To redeem the property in the same manner as its owner might, from the superior lien; and,

2. To be subrogated to all the benefits of the superior lien, when necessary for the protection of his interests, upon satisfying the claim secured thereby. *(Enacted in 1872.)*

Research References

Miller and Starr California Real Estate § 10:39, Rights of the Parties.
Miller and Starr California Real Estate § 10:73, Performance by a Third Person.
Miller and Starr California Real Estate § 10:138, Failure to Pay Prior Encumbrances.
Miller and Starr California Real Estate § 10:139, Failure to Pay Taxes.
Miller and Starr California Real Estate § 10:187, Who Can Reinstate.
Miller and Starr California Real Estate § 10:196, Who Can Redeem.
Miller and Starr California Real Estate § 10:197, Mode of Redemption.
Miller and Starr California Real Estate § 11:100, Priority of the Purchaser's Title from a Foreclosure Sale.
Miller and Starr California Real Estate § 11:113, Priority by Equitable Subrogation--In General.
Miller and Starr California Real Estate § 11:114, Priority by Equitable Subrogation--Optional Advances to Protect Security.

§ 2905. Redemption; procedure

Redemption from a lien is made by performing, or offering to perform, the act for the performance of which it is a security, and paying, or offering to pay, the damages, if any, to which the holder of the lien is entitled for delay. *(Enacted in 1872.)*

Research References

Miller and Starr California Real Estate § 10:123, Nature of Foreclosure; Termination of Redemption.
Miller and Starr California Real Estate § 10:188, Method of Reinstatement.
Miller and Starr California Real Estate § 10:195, Equity of Redemption (Redemption Prior to Sale).
Miller and Starr California Real Estate § 10:197, Mode of Redemption.
Miller and Starr California Real Estate § 10:221, Comparison With Nonjudicial Foreclosure.

Miller and Starr California Real Estate § 11:100, Priority of the Purchaser's Title from a Foreclosure Sale.

§ 2906. Secured party; option to acquire interest in real property collateral; priority; validity

An option granted to a secured party by a debtor to acquire an interest in real property collateral takes priority as of its recording and is effective according to its terms if the right to exercise the option is not dependent upon the occurrence of a default with respect to the security agreement and, where the real property which is the subject of the option is other than residential real property containing four or fewer units, shall not be deemed invalid or ineffective on the basis that the secured party has impaired the debtor's equity of redemption in violation of common law or Section 2889. This section shall not be construed to make valid or effective an otherwise unlawful option nor shall any inference be drawn from this section as to the validity or application of common law with respect to residential real property containing four or fewer units. *(Added by Stats.1984, c. 565, § 1.)*

Research References

Rutter, Cal. Practice Guide: Real Prop. Transactions Ch. 6-H, H. Security for Promissory Note.
Rutter, Cal. Practice Guide: Real Prop. Transactions Ch. 8-B, B. Options to Purchase.
Miller and Starr California Real Estate § 11:6, Instruments Subject to Recording--List of Recordable Documents.
Miller and Starr California Real Estate § 10:194, Waiver of Right to Reinstate.
Miller and Starr California Real Estate § 10:195, Equity of Redemption (Redemption Prior to Sale).
Miller and Starr California Real Estate § 10:236, Policy Objectives; the "Standard" Transaction.
17 NO. 4 Miller & Starr, California Real Estate Newsalert 16, Recording and Priorities.
4 Witkin, California Summary 10th Security Transactions in Real Property § 236, Waiver or Sale of Right of Redemption.

ARTICLE 6. EXTINCTION OF LIENS

Section
2909. Extinction as accessory obligation.
2910. Sale or conversion.
2911. Lapse of time; presumption as to public improvement liens.
2912. Partial performance.
2913. Lien dependent upon possession; restoration of property.
2914. Transactions and security interests governed by Commercial Code.

§ 2909. Extinction as accessory obligation

A lien is to be deemed accessory to the act for the performance of which it is a security, whether any person is bound for such performance or not, and is extinguishable in like manner with any other accessory obligation. *(Enacted in 1872.)*

Research References

4 Witkin, California Summary 10th Security Transactions in Real Property § 47, Lien is Incident of Debt.

§ 2910. Sale or conversion

The sale of any property on which there is a lien, in satisfaction of the claim secured thereby, or in case of personal property, its wrongful conversion by the person holding the lien, extinguishes the lien thereon. *(Enacted in 1872.)*

Research References

Miller and Starr California Real Estate § 10:4, Capacity and Authority of Trustee.
Miller and Starr California Real Estate § 10:42, Transfer of Title to the Beneficiary.
Miller and Starr California Real Estate § 10:218, Measure of Tort Damages.
8 Witkin Cal. Proc. 5th Enforcement of Judgment § 156, (S 156) Effect of Sale.
4 Witkin, California Summary 10th Security Transactions in Real Property § 175, in General.

§ 2911. Lapse of time; presumption as to public improvement liens

A lien is extinguished by the lapse of time within which, under the provisions of the Code of Civil Procedure, either:

1. An action can be brought upon the principal obligation, or

2. A treasurer, street superintendent or other public official may sell any real property to satisfy a public improvement assessment or any bond issued to represent such assessment and which assessment is secured by a lien upon said real property; whichever is later.

Anything to the contrary notwithstanding, any lien heretofore existing or which may hereafter exist upon real property to secure the payment of a public improvement assessment shall be presumed to have been extinguished at the expiration of four years after the due date of such assessment or the last installment thereof, or four years after the date the lien attaches, or on January 1, 1947, whichever is later, or in the event bonds were or shall be issued to represent such assessment, the lien shall then be presumed to have been extinguished at the expiration of four years after the due date of said bonds or of the last installment thereof or of the last principal coupon attached thereto, or on January 1, 1947, whichever is later. The presumptions mentioned in this paragraph shall be conclusive in favor of a bona fide purchaser for value of said property after such dates. *(Enacted in 1872. Amended by Stats.1945, c. 361, p. 821, § 1.)*

Research References

Rutter, Cal. Practice Guide: Real Prop. Transactions Ch. 3-F, F. Alternatives to Endorsements.
Miller and Starr California Real Estate § 10:90, Extension and Renewal.
Miller and Starr California Real Estate § 10:128, Statute of Limitations.
Miller and Starr California Real Estate § 10:131, Debt Secured by a Deed of Trust.
Miller and Starr California Real Estate § 10:132, Ancient Mortgages; Debt Secured by a Deed of Trust.
Miller and Starr California Real Estate § 11:172, Assessment and Bond Liens--Special Tax Liens Under the Mello-Roos Community Facilities Act.
Miller and Starr California Real Estate § 11:173, Assessment and Bond Liens--Statute of Limitations for Enforcement of the Lien.
Miller and Starr California Real Estate § 11:174, Assessment and Bond Liens--Action to Remove the Cloud of an Expired Lien.
Miller and Starr California Real Estate § 11:176, Priorities Among State and Local Tax and Assessment Liens--Priority Between Ad Valorem Tax Liens and Assessment Liens.
Miller and Starr California Real Estate § 11:177, Priorities Among State and Local Tax and Assessment Liens--Priority Between Assessment Liens.
13 NO. 5 Miller & Starr, California Real Estate Newsalert 5, Deeds of Trust.
16 NO. 4 Miller & Starr, California Real Estate Newsalert 26, Deeds of Trust.
18 NO. 2 Miller & Starr, California Real Estate Newsalert 1, The Marketable Record Title Act- Is Private Foreclosure Barred Ten Years After Maturity, or Not?
3 Witkin Cal. Proc. 5th Actions § 430, (S 430) Types of Limitation Statutes.
3 Witkin Cal. Proc. 5th Actions § 484, (S 484) Four Years.
3 Witkin Cal. Proc. 5th Actions § 667, Duration of Tax Lien.

12 Witkin, California Summary 10th Real Property § 328, What Constitutes Bona Fide Purchase.
12 Witkin, California Summary 10th Real Property § 338, Ancient Mortgages and Deeds of Trust.
13 Witkin, California Summary 10th Personal Property § 219, in General.
4 Witkin, California Summary 10th Security Transactions in Real Property § 62, Statute of Limitations.
4 Witkin, California Summary 10th Security Transactions in Real Property § 104, Possession After Statute of Limitations Runs.
4 Witkin, California Summary 10th Security Transactions in Real Property § 121, Mortgage.
4 Witkin, California Summary 10th Security Transactions in Real Property § 122, Deed of Trust.

§ 2912. Partial performance

The partial performance of an act secured by a lien does not extinguish the lien upon any part of the property subject thereto, even if it is divisible. *(Enacted in 1872.)*

Research References

Rutter, Cal. Practice Guide: Real Prop. Transactions Ch. 6-H, H. Security for Promissory Note.
Miller and Starr California Real Estate § 1:112, Accord and Satisfaction--Acceptance of Satisfaction by a Creditor.
Miller and Starr California Real Estate § 10:74, Partial Performance.
Miller and Starr California Real Estate § 10:119, Partial Releases; Definition; Procedure.
Miller and Starr California Real Estate § 10:193, Effect of Receipt of Partial Payments.

§ 2913. Lien dependent upon possession; restoration of property

The voluntary restoration of property to its owner by the holder of a lien thereon dependent upon possession extinguishes the lien as to such property, unless otherwise agreed by the parties, and extinguishes it, notwithstanding any such agreement, as to creditors of the owner and persons, subsequently acquiring a title to the property, or a lien thereon, in good faith, and for value. *(Enacted in 1872. Amended by Code Am.1873–74, c. 612, p. 260, § 255; Stats.1905, c. 459, p. 617, § 2.)*

Research References

Rutter, Cal. Practice Guide: Personal Injury Ch. 1-C, C. Formation of Attorney-Client Relationship: the Employment Agreement.
Rutter, Cal. Practice Guide: Prof. Responsibility Ch. 5-F, F. Formalizing Fee Agreements.
Rutter, Cal. Practice Guide: Prof. Responsibility Ch. 9-E, E. Duty to Deliver Funds or Property Upon Demand.
13 Witkin, California Summary 10th Personal Property § 220, Relinquishment of Possession.

§ 2914. Transactions and security interests governed by Commercial Code

None of the provisions of this chapter apply to any transaction or security interest governed by the Uniform Commercial Code. *(Added by Stats.1963, c. 819, p. 1999, § 14, eff. Jan. 1, 1965.)*

Research References

13 Witkin, California Summary 10th Personal Property § 216, Nature and Kinds of Liens.
4 Witkin, California Summary 10th Security Transactions in Real Property § 34, What Property Can be Mortgaged.

CHAPTER 2. MORTGAGE

§ 2920.   "Mortgage" defined

(a) A mortgage is a contract by which specific property, including an estate for years in real property, is hypothecated for the performance of an act, without the necessity of a change of possession.

(b) For purposes of Sections 2924 to 2924h, inclusive, "mortgage" also means any security device or instrument, other than a deed of trust, that confers a power of sale affecting real property or an estate for years therein, to be exercised after breach of the obligation so secured, including a real property sales contract, as defined in Section 2985, which contains such a provision. *(Enacted in 1872. Amended by Stats.1986, c. 1385, § 1; Stats. 1989, c. 698, § 4.)*

Research References

California Real Estate Forms (Miller & Starr) § 1:34, Installment Land Sale Contract With Power of Sale.

Rutter, Cal. Practice Guide: Enforcing Judgments/Debts Ch. 1-A, A. Lawyer's Role in Debt Collection Process.

Rutter, Cal. Practice Guide: Enforcing Judgments/Debts Ch. 2-B, B. Statutory Liability and Procedures.

Rutter, Cal. Practice Guide: Enforcing Judgments/Debts Ch. 3-A, A. Evaluating the Claim.

Rutter, Cal. Practice Guide: Enforcing Judgments/Debts Ch. 5-A, A. Introduction.

Rutter, Cal. Practice Guide: Real Prop. Transactions Ch. 2-B, B. Licensing and Regulatory Requirements.

Rutter, Cal. Practice Guide: Real Prop. Transactions Ch. 6-H, H. Security for Promissory Note.

Miller and Starr California Real Estate § 9:1, "Estate" Defined.

Miller and Starr California Real Estate § 9:2, Classification, Generally.

Miller and Starr California Real Estate § 10:2, Lien Versus Title Theories.

Miller and Starr California Real Estate § 17:7, UCC Provisions, Generally.

Miller and Starr California Real Estate § 19:2, Lease as Personal Property or Real Property.

Miller and Starr California Real Estate § 4:38, Grounds for Discipline--In General.

Miller and Starr California Real Estate § 10:10, Requirement of Some Debt or Obligation.

Miller and Starr California Real Estate § 10:16, Property Interests that Are Lienable.

Miller and Starr California Real Estate § 10:19, "After-Acquired" Title.

Miller and Starr California Real Estate § 10:180, Power of Sale; Constitutionality.

Miller and Starr California Real Estate § 10:219, Redemption After Trustee's Sale.

Miller and Starr California Real Estate § 10:181.10, Prior Notification and Consultation for Residential Loans Originated Between January 1, 2003 and December 31, 2007.

Miller and Starr California Real Estate § 10:181.20, Prior Notification, Consultation and Modification Requirements for Owner-Occupied First Lien Mortgage Loans Effective January 1, 2013.

22 NO. 3 Miller & Starr, California Real Estate Newsalert 1, Show Me Your Papers: Sales and Assignments of Secured Real Estate Loans and the California Foreclosure Process.

22 NO. 4 Miller & Starr, California Real Estate Newsalert 1, Show Me Your Papers: Sales and Assignments of Secured Real Estate Loans and the California Foreclosure Process (Part II).

4 Witkin Cal. Proc. 5th Pleading § 137, in General.

4 Witkin, California Summary 10th Security Transactions in Real Property § 3, Mortgage.

4 Witkin, California Summary 10th Security Transactions in Real Property § 24, (S 24) in General.

4 Witkin, California Summary 10th Security Transactions in Real Property § 39, (S 39) in General.

4 Witkin, California Summary 10th Security Transactions in Real Property § 95, in General.

4 Witkin, California Summary 10th Security Transactions in Real Property § 144, in General.

3 Witkin, California Summary 10th Agency and Employment § 58, (S 58) in General.

4 Witkin, California Summary 10th Secured Transactions in Personal Property § 13, (S 13) Nature of Mortgage.

2 Witkin Cal. Summ. 10th Workers' Compensation § 155, Recovery from Employer.

§ 2920.5.   Definitions

Section added by Stats.2012, c. 86 (A.B.278), § 2. See, also, another section of the same number added by Stats.2012, c. 87 (S.B.900), § 2.

For purposes of this article, the following definitions apply:

(a) "Mortgage servicer" means a person or entity who directly services a loan, or who is responsible for interacting with the borrower, managing the loan account on a daily basis including collecting and crediting periodic loan payments, managing any escrow account, or enforcing the note and security instrument, either as the current owner of the promissory note or as the current owner's authorized agent. "Mortgage servicer" also means a subservicing agent to a master servicer by contract. "Mortgage servicer" shall not include a trustee, or a trustee's authorized agent, acting under a power of sale pursuant to a deed of trust.

(b) "Foreclosure prevention alternative" means a first lien loan modification or another available loss mitigation option.

(c)(1) Unless otherwise provided and for purposes of Sections 2923.4, 2923.5, 2923.55, 2923.6, 2923.7, 2924.9, 2924.10, 2924.11, 2924.18, and 2924.19, "borrower" means any natural person who is a mortgagor or trustor and who is potentially eligible for any federal, state, or proprietary foreclosure prevention alternative program offered by, or through, his or her mortgage servicer.

(2) For purposes of the sections listed in paragraph (1), "borrower" shall not include any of the following:

(A) An individual who has surrendered the secured property as evidenced by either a letter confirming the surrender or delivery of the keys to the property to the mortgagee, trustee, beneficiary, or authorized agent.

(B) An individual who has contracted with an organization, person, or entity whose primary business is advising people who have decided to leave their homes on how to extend the foreclosure process and avoid their contractual obligations to mortgagees or beneficiaries.

(C) An individual who has filed a case under Chapter 7, 11, 12, or 13 of Title 11 of the United States Code and the bankruptcy court has not entered an order closing or dismissing the bankruptcy case, or granting relief from a stay of foreclosure.

(d) "First lien" means the most senior mortgage or deed of trust on the property that is the subject of the notice of default or notice of sale. *(Added by Stats.2012, c. 86 (A.B.278), § 2.)*

Research References

Rutter, Cal. Practice Guide: Real Prop. Transactions Ch. 6-I, I. Real Property Foreclosures and Antideficiency Laws.
Miller and Starr California Real Estate § 4:12, Mortgage Loan Origination, Brokerage, and Servicing.
Miller and Starr California Real Estate § 4:78, Federal and State Regulation of Residential Mortgage Loan Origination and Servicing--In General.
Miller and Starr California Real Estate § 10:181.20, Prior Notification, Consultation and Modification Requirements for Owner-Occupied First Lien Mortgage Loans Effective January 1, 2013.

§ 2920.5. Definitions

Section added by Stats.2012, c. 87 (S.B.900), § 2. See, also, another section of the same number added by Stats.2012, c. 86 (A.B.278), § 2.

For purposes of this article, the following definitions apply:

(a) "Mortgage servicer" means a person or entity who directly services a loan, or who is responsible for interacting with the borrower, managing the loan account on a daily basis including collecting and crediting periodic loan payments, managing any escrow account, or enforcing the note and security instrument, either as the current owner of the promissory note or as the current owner's authorized agent. "Mortgage servicer" also means a subservicing agent to a master servicer by contract. "Mortgage servicer" shall not include a trustee, or a trustee's

authorized agent, acting under a power of sale pursuant to a deed of trust.

(b) "Foreclosure prevention alternative" means a first lien loan modification or another available loss mitigation option.

(c)(1) Unless otherwise provided and for purposes of Sections 2923.4, 2923.5, 2923.55, 2923.6, 2923.7, 2924.9, 2924.10, 2924.11, 2924.18, and 2924.19, "borrower" means any natural person who is a mortgagor or trustor and who is potentially eligible for any federal, state, or proprietary foreclosure prevention alternative program offered by, or through, his or her mortgage servicer.

(2) For purposes of the sections listed in paragraph (1), "borrower" shall not include any of the following:

(A) An individual who has surrendered the secured property as evidenced by either a letter confirming the surrender or delivery of the keys to the property to the mortgagee, trustee, beneficiary, or authorized agent.

(B) An individual who has contracted with an organization, person, or entity whose primary business is advising people who have decided to leave their homes on how to extend the foreclosure process and avoid their contractual obligations to mortgagees or beneficiaries.

(C) An individual who has filed a case under Chapter 7, 11, 12, or 13 of Title 11 of the United States Code and the bankruptcy court has not entered an order closing or dismissing the bankruptcy case, or granting relief from a stay of foreclosure.

(d) "First lien" means the most senior mortgage or deed of trust on the property that is the subject of the notice of default or notice of sale. *(Added by Stats.2012, c. 87 (S.B.900), § 2.)*

Research References

Rutter, Cal. Practice Guide: Real Prop. Transactions Ch. 6-I, I. Real Property Foreclosures and Antideficiency Laws.
Miller and Starr California Real Estate § 4:12, Mortgage Loan Origination, Brokerage, and Servicing.
Miller and Starr California Real Estate § 4:78, Federal and State Regulation of Residential Mortgage Loan Origination and Servicing--In General.
Miller and Starr California Real Estate § 10:181.20, Prior Notification, Consultation and Modification Requirements for Owner-Occupied First Lien Mortgage Loans Effective January 1, 2013.

§ 2921. Property adversely held

A mortgage may be created upon property held adversely to the mortgagor. *(Enacted in 1872.)*

Research References

Miller and Starr California Real Estate § 16:29, Mortgagor and Mortgagee; Trustor and Beneficiary.

§ 2922. Writing; formalities

A mortgage can be created, renewed, or extended, only by writing, executed with the formalities required in the case of a grant of real property. *(Enacted in 1872.)*

Research References

Rutter, Cal. Practice Guide: Real Prop. Transactions Ch. 6-H, H. Security for Promissory Note.
Miller and Starr California Real Estate § 1:69, Contract for the Sale, Gift, or Financing of Real Property.
Miller and Starr California Real Estate § 10:5, Form and Interpretation.
Miller and Starr California Real Estate § 10:7, Execution and Delivery.
Miller and Starr California Real Estate § 10:10, Requirement of Some Debt or Obligation.
Miller and Starr California Real Estate § 10:90, Extension and Renewal.
Miller and Starr California Real Estate § 10:123, Nature of Foreclosure; Termination of Redemption.
19 NO. 3 Miller & Starr, California Real Estate Newsalert 11, Deeds of Trust.

22 NO. 3 Miller & Starr, California Real Estate Newsalert 1, Show Me Your Papers: Sales and Assignments of Secured Real Estate Loans and the California Foreclosure Process.

22 NO. 2 Miller & Starr, California Real Estate Newsalert 1, Did Someone Say Estoppel?-Courts Show Greater Acceptance of Applying Equitable Principles to Enforce Oral Forbearance Agreements.

4 Witkin, California Summary 10th Security Transactions in Real Property § 40, (S 40) Mortgage.

4 Witkin, California Summary 10th Security Transactions in Real Property § 113, (S 113) as Between Parties.

4 Witkin, California Summary 10th Security Transactions in Real Property § 121, Mortgage.

§ 2923. Special lien independent of possession

The lien of a mortgage is special, unless otherwise expressly agreed, and is independent of possession. *(Enacted in 1872.)*

Research References

Miller and Starr California Real Estate § 10:2, Lien Versus Title Theories.

Miller and Starr California Real Estate § 2:23, Liens and Encumbrances.

Miller and Starr California Real Estate § 10:19, "After-Acquired" Title.

Miller and Starr California Real Estate § 10:210, Attack on Validity of the Sale.

Miller and Starr California Real Estate § 36:1.20, Liability for Negligent Underwriting or Improvident Lending.

Miller and Starr California Real Estate § 10:181.10, Prior Notification and Consultation for Residential Loans Originated Between January 1, 2003 and December 31, 2007.

4 Witkin, California Summary 10th Security Transactions in Real Property § 95, in General.

§ 2923.1. Fiduciary of borrower; violation; duty

(a) A mortgage broker providing mortgage brokerage services to a borrower is the fiduciary of the borrower, and any violation of the broker's fiduciary duties shall be a violation of the mortgage broker's license law. This fiduciary duty includes a requirement that the mortgage broker place the economic interest of the borrower ahead of his or her own economic interest. A mortgage broker who provides mortgage brokerage services to the borrower owes this fiduciary duty to the borrower regardless of whether the mortgage broker is acting as an agent for any other party in connection with the residential mortgage loan transaction.

(b) For purposes of this section, the following definitions apply:

(1) "Licensed person" means a real estate broker licensed under the Real Estate Law (Part 1 (commencing with Section 10000) of Division 4 of the Business and Professions Code), a finance lender or broker licensed under the California Finance Lenders Law (Division 9 (commencing with Section 22000) of the Financial Code), a residential mortgage lender licensed under the California Residential Mortgage Lending Act (Division 20 (commencing with Section 50000) of the Financial Code), a commercial or industrial bank organized under the Banking Law (Division 1 (commencing with Section 99) of the Financial Code), a savings association organized under the Savings Association Law (Division 2 (commencing with Section 5000) of the Financial Code), and a credit union organized under the California Credit Union Law (Division 5 (commencing with Section 14000) of the Financial Code).

(2) "Mortgage broker" means a licensed person who provides mortgage brokerage services. For purposes of this section, a licensed person who makes a residential mortgage loan is a "mortgage broker," and subject to the requirements of this section applicable to mortgage brokers, only with respect to transactions in which the licensed person provides mortgage brokerage services.

(3) "Mortgage brokerage services" means arranging or attempting to arrange, as exclusive agent for the borrower or as dual agent for the borrower and lender, for compensation or in expectation of compensation, paid directly or indirectly, a residential mortgage loan made by an unaffiliated third party.

(4) "Residential mortgage loan" means a consumer credit transaction that is secured by residential real property that is improved by four or fewer residential units.

(c) The duties set forth in this section shall not be construed to limit or narrow any other fiduciary duty of a mortgage broker. *(Added by Stats.2009, c. 629 (A.B.260), § 2.)*

Research References

Miller and Starr California Real Estate § 36:1, Applicable Theories of Liability.

Miller and Starr California Real Estate § 4:58, Requirements in Making or Arranging a Loan--In General.

Miller and Starr California Real Estate § 4:69, Servicing of Secured Obligations--In General.

Miller and Starr California Real Estate § 36:29, Predatory Lending Act.

Miller and Starr California Real Estate § 36:1.20, Liability for Negligent Underwriting or Improvident Lending.

§ 2923.3. Notice of default; summary of key information; delivery requirements; translations

(a) With respect to residential real property containing no more than four dwelling units, a mortgagee, trustee, beneficiary, or authorized agent shall provide to the mortgagor or trustor a copy of the recorded notice of default with an attached separate summary document of the notice of default in English and the languages described in Section 1632, as set forth in subdivision (c), and a copy of the recorded notice of sale with an attached separate summary document of the information required to be contained in the notice of sale in English and the languages described in Section 1632, as set forth in subdivision (d). These summaries are not required to be recorded or published. This subdivision shall become operative on April 1, 2013, or 90 days following the issuance of the translations by the Department of Corporations, pursuant to subdivision (b), whichever is later.

(b)(1) The Department of Corporations shall provide a standard translation of the statement in paragraph (1) of subdivision (c), and of the summary of the notice of default, as set forth in paragraph (2) of subdivision (c) in the languages described in Section 1632.

(2) The Department of Corporations shall provide a standard translation of the statement in paragraph (1) of subdivision (d), and of the summary of the notice of sale, as set forth in paragraph (2) of subdivision (d).

(3) The department shall make the translations described in paragraphs (1) and (2) available without charge on its Internet Web site. Any mortgagee, trustee, beneficiary, or authorized agent who provides the department's translations in the manner prescribed by this section shall be in compliance with this section.

(c)(1) The following statement shall appear in the languages described in Section 1632 at the beginning of the notice of default:

NOTE: THERE IS A SUMMARY OF THE INFORMATION IN THIS DOCUMENT ATTACHED.

(2) The following summary of key information shall be attached to the copy of the notice of default provided to the mortgagor or trustor:

SUMMARY OF KEY INFORMATION

The attached notice of default was sent to [name of the trustor], in relation to [description of the property that secures the mortgage or deed of trust in default]. This property may be sold to satisfy your obligation and any other obligation secured by the deed of trust or mortgage that is in default. [Trustor] has, as described in the notice of default, breached the mortgage or deed of trust on the property described above.

IMPORTANT NOTICE: IF YOUR PROPERTY IS IN FORECLOSURE BECAUSE YOU ARE BEHIND IN YOUR PAYMENTS, IT MAY BE SOLD WITHOUT ANY COURT ACTION, and you may have the legal right to bring your account in good standing by paying all of your past due payments plus permitted costs and expenses within the time permitted by law for reinstatement of your account, which is normally five business days prior to the date set for the sale of your property. No sale date may be set until approximately 90 days from the date the attached notice of default may be recorded (which date of recordation appears on the notice).

This amount is _____ as of ____(date)_____and will increase until your account becomes current.

While your property is in foreclosure, you still must pay other obligations (such as insurance and taxes) required by your note and deed of trust or mortgage. If you fail to make future payments on the loan, pay taxes on the property, provide insurance on the property, or pay other obligations as required in the note and deed of trust or mortgage, the beneficiary or mortgagee may insist that you do so in order to reinstate your account in good standing. In addition, the beneficiary or mortgagee may require as a condition to reinstatement that you provide reliable written evidence that you paid all senior liens, property taxes, and hazard insurance premiums.

Upon your written request, the beneficiary or mortgagee will give you a written itemization of the entire amount you must pay. You may not have to pay the entire unpaid portion of your account, even though full payment was demanded, but you must pay all amounts in default at the time payment is made. However, you and your beneficiary or mortgagee may mutually agree in writing prior to the time the notice of sale is posted (which may not be earlier than three months after this notice of default is recorded) to, among other things, (1) provide additional time in which to cure the default by transfer of the property or otherwise; or (2) establish a schedule of payments in order to cure your default; or both (1) and (2).

Following the expiration of the time period referred to in the first paragraph of this notice, unless the obligation being foreclosed upon or a separate written agreement between you and your creditor permits a longer period, you have only the legal right to stop the sale of your property by paying the entire amount demanded by your creditor.

To find out the amount you must pay, or to arrange for payment to stop the foreclosure, or if your property is in foreclosure for any other reason, contact:

_____

(Name of beneficiary or mortgagee)

_____

(Mailing address)

_____

(Telephone)

If you have any questions, you should contact a lawyer or the governmental agency which may have insured your loan.

Notwithstanding the fact that your property is in foreclosure, you may offer your property for sale, provided the sale is concluded prior to the conclusion of the foreclosure.

Remember, YOU MAY LOSE LEGAL RIGHTS IF YOU DO NOT TAKE PROMPT ACTION.

If you would like additional copies of this summary, you may obtain them by calling [insert telephone number].

(d)(1) The following statement shall appear in the languages described in Section 1632 at the beginning of the notice of sale:

NOTE: THERE IS A SUMMARY OF THE INFORMATION IN THIS DOCUMENT ATTACHED.

(2) The following summary of key information shall be attached to the copy of the notice of sale provided to the mortgagor or trustor:

SUMMARY OF KEY INFORMATION

The attached notice of sale was sent to [trustor], in relation to [description of the property that secures the mortgage or deed of trust in default].

YOU ARE IN DEFAULT UNDER A (Deed of trust or mortgage) DATED _____. UNLESS YOU TAKE ACTION TO PROTECT YOUR PROPERTY, IT MAY BE SOLD AT A PUBLIC SALE.

IF YOU NEED AN EXPLANATION OF THE NATURE OF THE PROCEEDING AGAINST YOU, YOU SHOULD CONTACT A LAWYER.

The total amount due in the notice of sale is _____.

Your property is scheduled to be sold on [insert date and time of sale] at [insert location of sale].

However, the sale date shown on the attached notice of sale may be postponed one or more times by the mortgagee, beneficiary, trustee, or a court, pursuant to Section 2924g of the California Civil Code. The law requires that information about trustee sale postponements be made available to you and to the public, as a courtesy to those not present at the sale. If you wish to learn whether your sale date has been postponed, and, if applicable, the rescheduled time and date for the sale of this property, you may call [telephone number for information regarding the trustee's sale] or visit this Internet Web site [Internet Web site address for information regarding the sale of this property], using the file number assigned to this case [case file number]. Information about postponements that are very short in duration or that occur close in time to the scheduled sale may not immediately be reflected in the telephone information or on the Internet Web site. The best way to verify postponement information is to attend the scheduled sale.

If you would like additional copies of this summary, you may obtain them by calling [insert telephone number].

(e) Failure to provide these summaries to the mortgagor or trustor shall have the same effect as if the notice of default or notice of sale were incomplete or not provided.

(f) This section sets forth a requirement for translation in languages other than English, and a document complying with the provisions of this section may be recorded pursuant to subdivision (b) of Section 27293 of the Government Code. A document that complies with this section shall not be rejected for recordation on the ground that some part of the document is in a language other than English.

(Added by Stats.2012, c. 556 (A.B.1599), § 1.)

§ 2923.4. Purpose of act; availability of loss mitigation options in nonjudicial foreclosure process; effect on consent judgment

> Section added by Stats.2012, c. 86 (A.B.278), § 3.
> See, also, another section of the same number added by Stats.2012, c. 87 (S.B.900), § 3.

(a) The purpose of the act that added this section is to ensure that, as part of the nonjudicial foreclosure process, borrowers are considered for, and have a meaningful opportunity to obtain, available loss mitigation options, if any, offered by or through the borrower's mortgage servicer, such as loan modifications or other alternatives to foreclosure. Nothing in the act that added this section, however, shall be interpreted to require a particular result of that process.

(b) Nothing in this article obviates or supersedes the obligations of the signatories to the consent judgment entered in the case entitled United States of America et al. v. Bank of America Corporation et al., filed in the United States District Court for the District of Columbia, case number 1:12–cv–00361 RMC. (Added by Stats.2012, c. 86 (A.B.278), § 3.)

Research References

Rutter, Cal. Practice Guide: Real Prop. Transactions Ch. 6-I, I. Real Property Foreclosures and Antideficiency Laws.

Miller and Starr California Real Estate § 4:12, Mortgage Loan Origination, Brokerage, and Servicing.

Miller and Starr California Real Estate § 4:78, Federal and State Regulation of Residential Mortgage Loan Origination and Servicing--In General.

Miller and Starr California Real Estate § 10:181.10, Prior Notification and Consultation for Residential Loans Originated Between January 1, 2003 and December 31, 2007.

Miller and Starr California Real Estate § 10:181.20, Prior Notification, Consultation and Modification Requirements for Owner-Occupied First Lien Mortgage Loans Effective January 1, 2013.

§ 2923.4. Purpose of act; availability of loss mitigation options in nonjudicial foreclosure process; effect on consent judgment

> Section added by Stats.2012, c. 87 (S.B.900), § 3.
> See, also, another section of the same number added by Stats.2012, c. 86 (A.B.278), § 3.

(a) The purpose of the act that added this section is to ensure that, as part of the nonjudicial foreclosure process, borrowers are considered for, and have a meaningful opportunity to obtain, available loss mitigation options, if any, offered by or through the borrower's mortgage servicer, such as loan modifications or other alternatives to foreclosure. Nothing in the act that added this section, however, shall be interpreted to require a particular result of that process.

(b) Nothing in this article obviates or supersedes the obligations of the signatories to the consent judgment entered in the case entitled United States of America et al. v. Bank of America Corporation et al., filed in the United States District Court for the District of Columbia, case number 1:12–cv–00361 RMC. (Added by Stats.2012, c. 87 (S.B.900), § 3.)

Research References

Rutter, Cal. Practice Guide: Real Prop. Transactions Ch. 6-I, I. Real Property Foreclosures and Antideficiency Laws.

Miller and Starr California Real Estate § 4:12, Mortgage Loan Origination, Brokerage, and Servicing.

Miller and Starr California Real Estate § 4:78, Federal and State Regulation of Residential Mortgage Loan Origination and Servicing--In General.

Miller and Starr California Real Estate § 10:181.10, Prior Notification and Consultation for Residential Loans Originated Between January 1, 2003 and December 31, 2007.

Miller and Starr California Real Estate § 10:181.20, Prior Notification, Consultation and Modification Requirements for Owner-Occupied First Lien Mortgage Loans Effective January 1, 2013.

§ 2923.5. Notice of default; recording; contact of borrower by mortgage servicer; application to entities described in subd. (b) of Section 2924.18

Section operative until Jan. 1, 2018. See, also, section added by Stats.2012, c. 86 (A.B.278), § 5, operative Jan. 1, 2018, and section added by Stats.2012, c. 87 (S.B.900), § 5, operative Jan. 1, 2018.

(a)(1) A mortgage servicer, mortgagee, trustee, beneficiary, or authorized agent may not record a notice of default pursuant to Section 2924 until both of the following:

(A) Either 30 days after initial contact is made as required by paragraph (2) or 30 days after satisfying the due diligence requirements as described in subdivision (e).

(B) The mortgage servicer complies with paragraph (1) of subdivision (a) of Section 2924.18, if the borrower has provided a complete application as defined in subdivision (d) of Section 2924.18.

(2) A mortgage servicer shall contact the borrower in person or by telephone in order to assess the borrower's financial situation and explore options for the borrower to avoid foreclosure. During the initial contact, the mortgage servicer shall advise the borrower that he or she has the right to request a subsequent meeting and, if requested, the mortgage servicer shall schedule the meeting to occur within 14 days. The assessment of the borrower's financial situation and discussion of options may occur during the first contact, or at the subsequent meeting scheduled for that purpose. In either case, the borrower shall be provided the toll-free telephone number made available by the United States Department of Housing and Urban Development (HUD) to find a HUD–certified housing counseling agency. Any meeting may occur telephonically.

(b) A notice of default recorded pursuant to Section 2924 shall include a declaration that the mortgage servicer has contacted the borrower, has tried with due diligence to contact the borrower as required by this section, or that no contact was required because the individual did not meet the definition of "borrower" pursuant to subdivision (c) of Section 2920.5.

(c) A mortgage servicer's loss mitigation personnel may participate by telephone during any contact required by this section.

(d) A borrower may designate, with consent given in writing, a HUD–certified housing counseling agency, attorney, or other advisor to discuss with the mortgage servicer, on the borrower's behalf, the borrower's financial situation and options for the borrower to avoid foreclosure. That contact made at the direction of the borrower shall satisfy the contact requirements of paragraph (2) of subdivision (a). Any loan modification or workout plan offered at the meeting by the mortgage servicer is subject to approval by the borrower.

(e) A notice of default may be recorded pursuant to Section 2924 when a mortgage servicer has not contacted a borrower as required by paragraph (2) of subdivision (a) provided that the failure to contact the borrower occurred despite the due diligence of the mortgage servicer. For purposes of this section, "due diligence" shall require and mean all of the following:

(1) A mortgage servicer shall first attempt to contact a borrower by sending a first-class letter that includes the toll-free telephone number made available by HUD to find a HUD–certified housing counseling agency.

(2)(A) After the letter has been sent, the mortgage servicer shall attempt to contact the borrower by telephone at least three times at different hours and on different days. Telephone calls shall be made to the primary telephone number on file.

(B) A mortgage servicer may attempt to contact a borrower using an automated system to dial borrowers, provided that, if the telephone call is answered, the call is connected to a live representative of the mortgage servicer.

(C) A mortgage servicer satisfies the telephone contact requirements of this paragraph if it determines, after attempting contact pursuant to this paragraph, that the borrower's primary telephone number and secondary telephone number or numbers on file, if any, have been disconnected.

(3) If the borrower does not respond within two weeks after the telephone call requirements of paragraph (2) have been satisfied, the mortgage servicer shall then send a certified letter, with return receipt requested.

(4) The mortgage servicer shall provide a means for the borrower to contact it in a timely manner, including a toll-free telephone number that will provide access to a live representative during business hours.

(5) The mortgage servicer has posted a prominent link on the homepage of its Internet Web site, if any, to the following information:

(A) Options that may be available to borrowers who are unable to afford their mortgage payments and who wish to avoid foreclosure, and instructions to borrowers advising them on steps to take to explore those options.

(B) A list of financial documents borrowers should collect and be prepared to present to the mortgage servicer when discussing options for avoiding foreclosure.

(C) A toll-free telephone number for borrowers who wish to discuss options for avoiding foreclosure with their mortgage servicer.

(D) The toll-free telephone number made available by HUD to find a HUD–certified housing counseling agency.

(f) This section shall apply only to mortgages or deeds of trust described in Section 2924.15.

(g) This section shall apply only to entities described in subdivision (b) of Section 2924.18.

(h) This section shall remain in effect only until January 1, 2018, and as of that date is repealed, unless a later enacted statute, that is enacted before January 1, 2018, deletes or extends that date. *(Added by Stats.2008, c. 69 (S.B.1137), § 2, eff. July 8, 2008, operative Sept. 6, 2008. Amended by Stats.2009, c. 43 (S.B.306), § 1; Stats.2012, c. 86 (A.B.278), § 4; Stats.2012, c. 87 (S.B.900), § 4.)*

Validity

This section has been held preempted in the case of Rodriguez v. JP Morgan Chase & Co., S.D.Cal.2011, 809 F.Supp.2d 1291.

Repeal

For repeal of this section, see its terms.

Research References

Rutter, Cal. Practice Guide: Real Prop. Transactions Ch. 6-I, I. Real Property Foreclosures and Antideficiency Laws.

Miller and Starr California Real Estate § 36:1, Applicable Theories of Liability.

Miller and Starr California Real Estate § 10:181, Notice of Default--In General.

Miller and Starr California Real Estate § 10:182, Form and Contents.

Miller and Starr California Real Estate § 10:210, Attack on Validity of the Sale.

Miller and Starr California Real Estate § 10:212, Requirement of Tender.

Miller and Starr California Real Estate § 10:221, Comparison With Nonjudicial Foreclosure.

Miller and Starr California Real Estate § 10:181.10, Prior Notification and Consultation for Residential Loans Originated Between January 1, 2003 and December 31, 2007.

Miller and Starr California Real Estate § 10:181.20, Prior Notification, Consultation and Modification Requirements for Owner-Occupied First Lien Mortgage Loans Effective January 1, 2013.

19 NO. 1 Miller & Starr, California Real Estate Newsalert 1, The Perata Foreclosure Bill (SB 1137): New Rights for Defaulting Borrowers and Tenants; New Complications for Foreclosing Lenders.

19 NO. 4 Miller & Starr, California Real Estate Newsalert 10, Deeds of Trust.

20 NO. 4 Miller & Starr, California Real Estate Newsalert 6, Deeds of Trust.

21 NO. 1 Miller & Starr, California Real Estate Newsalert 9, Deeds of Trust.

21 NO. 3 Miller & Starr, California Real Estate Newsalert 10, Deeds of Trust.

22 NO. 6 Miller & Starr, California Real Estate Newsalert 11, Deeds of Trust.

22 NO. 1 Miller & Starr, California Real Estate Newsalert 11, Deeds of Trust.

22 NO. 4 Miller & Starr, California Real Estate Newsalert 29, Deeds of Trust.

23 NO. 1 Miller & Starr, California Real Estate Newsalert 9, Deeds of Trust.

4 Witkin, California Summary 10th Security Transactions in Real Property § 145, in General.

4 Witkin, California Summary 10th Security Transactions in Real Property § 150, Content and Time of Notice.

4 Witkin, California Summary 10th Security Transactions in Real Property § 212, in General.

§ 2923.5. Notice of default; recording; contact of borrower by mortgage servicer

Section added by Stats.2012, c. 86 (A.B.278), § 5, operative Jan. 1, 2018. See, also, section operative until Jan. 1, 2018, and another section of the same number, added by Stats.2012, c. 87 (S.B.900), § 5, operative Jan. 1, 2018.

(a)(1) A mortgage servicer, mortgagee, trustee, beneficiary, or authorized agent may not record a notice of default pursuant to Section 2924 until both of the following:

(A) Either 30 days after initial contact is made as required by paragraph (2) or 30 days after satisfying the due diligence requirements as described in subdivision (e).

(B) The mortgage servicer complies with subdivision (a) of Section 2924.11, if the borrower has provided a complete application as defined in subdivision (f) of Section 2924.11.

(2) A mortgage servicer shall contact the borrower in person or by telephone in order to assess the borrower's financial situation and explore options for the borrower to avoid foreclosure. During the initial contact, the mortgage servicer shall advise the borrower that he or she has the right to request a subsequent meeting and, if requested, the mortgage servicer shall schedule the meeting to occur within 14 days. The assessment of the borrower's financial situation and discussion of options may occur during the first contact, or at the subsequent meeting scheduled for that purpose. In either case, the borrower shall be provided the toll-free telephone number made available by the United States Department of Housing and Urban Development (HUD) to find a HUD–certified housing counseling agency. Any meeting may occur telephonically.

(b) A notice of default recorded pursuant to Section 2924 shall include a declaration that the mortgage servicer has contacted the borrower, has tried with due diligence to contact the borrower as required by this section, or that no contact was required because the individual did not meet the definition of "borrower" pursuant to subdivision (c) of Section 2920.5.

(c) A mortgage servicer's loss mitigation personnel may participate by telephone during any contact required by this section.

(d) A borrower may designate, with consent given in writing, a HUD–certified housing counseling agency, attorney, or other adviser to discuss with the mortgage servicer, on the borrower's behalf, the borrower's financial situation and options for the borrower to avoid foreclosure. That contact made at the direction of the borrower shall satisfy the contact requirements of paragraph (2) of subdivision (a). Any loan modification or workout plan offered at the meeting by the mortgage servicer is subject to approval by the borrower.

(e) A notice of default may be recorded pursuant to Section 2924 when a mortgage servicer has not contacted a borrower as required by paragraph (2) of subdivision (a) provided that the failure to contact the borrower occurred despite the due diligence of the mortgage servicer. For purposes of this section, "due diligence" shall require and mean all of the following:

(1) A mortgage servicer shall first attempt to contact a borrower by sending a first-class letter that includes the toll-free telephone number made available by HUD to find a HUD–certified housing counseling agency.

(2)(A) After the letter has been sent, the mortgage servicer shall attempt to contact the borrower by telephone at least three times at different hours and on different days. Telephone calls shall be made to the primary telephone number on file.

(B) A mortgage servicer may attempt to contact a borrower using an automated system to dial borrowers, provided that, if the telephone call is answered, the call is connected to a live representative of the mortgage servicer.

(C) A mortgage servicer satisfies the telephone contact requirements of this paragraph if it determines, after attempting contact pursuant to this paragraph, that the borrower's primary telephone number and secondary telephone number or numbers on file, if any, have been disconnected.

(3) If the borrower does not respond within two weeks after the telephone call requirements of paragraph (2) have been satisfied, the mortgage servicer shall then send a certified letter, with return receipt requested.

(4) The mortgage servicer shall provide a means for the borrower to contact it in a timely manner, including a toll-free telephone number that will provide access to a live representative during business hours.

(5) The mortgage servicer has posted a prominent link on the homepage of its Internet Web site, if any, to the following information:

(A) Options that may be available to borrowers who are unable to afford their mortgage payments and who wish to avoid foreclosure, and instructions to borrowers advising them on steps to take to explore those options.

(B) A list of financial documents borrowers should collect and be prepared to present to the mortgage servicer when discussing options for avoiding foreclosure.

(C) A toll-free telephone number for borrowers who wish to discuss options for avoiding foreclosure with their mortgage servicer.

(D) The toll-free telephone number made available by HUD to find a HUD–certified housing counseling agency.

(f) This section shall apply only to mortgages or deeds of trust described in Section 2924.15.

(g) This section shall become operative on January 1, 2018. *(Added by Stats.2012, c. 86 (A.B.278), § 5, operative Jan. 1, 2018.)*

Research References

Rutter, Cal. Practice Guide: Real Prop. Transactions Ch. 6-I, I. Real Property Foreclosures and Antideficiency Laws.

Miller and Starr California Real Estate § 36:1, Applicable Theories of Liability.

Miller and Starr California Real Estate § 10:181, Notice of Default--In General.

Miller and Starr California Real Estate § 10:182, Form and Contents.

Miller and Starr California Real Estate § 10:210, Attack on Validity of the Sale.

Miller and Starr California Real Estate § 10:212, Requirement of Tender.

Miller and Starr California Real Estate § 10:221, Comparison With Nonjudicial Foreclosure.

Miller and Starr California Real Estate § 10:181.10, Prior Notification and Consultation for Residential Loans Originated Between January 1, 2003 and December 31, 2007.

Miller and Starr California Real Estate § 10:181.20, Prior Notification, Consultation and Modification Requirements for Owner-Occupied First Lien Mortgage Loans Effective January 1, 2013.

19 NO. 1 Miller & Starr, California Real Estate Newsalert 1, The Perata Foreclosure Bill (SB 1137): New Rights for Defaulting Borrowers and Tenants; New Complications for Foreclosing Lenders.

19 NO. 4 Miller & Starr, California Real Estate Newsalert 10, Deeds of Trust.

20 NO. 4 Miller & Starr, California Real Estate Newsalert 6, Deeds of Trust.

21 NO. 1 Miller & Starr, California Real Estate Newsalert 9, Deeds of Trust.

21 NO. 3 Miller & Starr, California Real Estate Newsalert 10, Deeds of Trust.

22 NO. 6 Miller & Starr, California Real Estate Newsalert 11, Deeds of Trust.

22 NO. 1 Miller & Starr, California Real Estate Newsalert 11, Deeds of Trust.

22 NO. 4 Miller & Starr, California Real Estate Newsalert 29, Deeds of Trust.

23 NO. 1 Miller & Starr, California Real Estate Newsalert 9, Deeds of Trust.

4 Witkin, California Summary 10th Security Transactions in Real Property § 145, in General.

4 Witkin, California Summary 10th Security Transactions in Real Property § 150, Content and Time of Notice.

4 Witkin, California Summary 10th Security Transactions in Real Property § 212, in General.

§ 2923.5. Notice of default; recording; contact of borrower by mortgage servicer

Section added by Stats.2012, c. 87 (S.B.900), § 5, operative Jan. 1, 2018. See, also, section operative until Jan. 1, 2018, and another section of the same number, added by Stats.2012, c. 86 (A.B.278), § 5, operative Jan. 1, 2018.

(a)(1) A mortgage servicer, mortgagee, trustee, beneficiary, or authorized agent may not record a notice of default pursuant to Section 2924 until both of the following:

(A) Either 30 days after initial contact is made as required by paragraph (2) or 30 days after satisfying the due diligence requirements as described in subdivision (e).

(B) The mortgage servicer complies with subdivision (a) of Section 2924.11, if the borrower has provided a complete application as defined in subdivision (f) of Section 2924.11.

(2) A mortgage servicer shall contact the borrower in person or by telephone in order to assess the borrower's financial situation and explore options for the borrower to avoid foreclosure. During the initial contact, the mortgage servicer shall advise the borrower that he or she has the right to request a subsequent meeting and, if requested, the mortgage servicer shall schedule the meeting to occur within 14 days. The assessment of the borrower's financial situation and discussion of options may occur during the first contact, or at the subsequent meeting scheduled for that purpose. In either case, the borrower shall be provided the toll-free telephone number made available by the United States Department of Housing and

Urban Development (HUD) to find a HUD–certified housing counseling agency. Any meeting may occur telephonically.

(b) A notice of default recorded pursuant to Section 2924 shall include a declaration that the mortgage servicer has contacted the borrower, has tried with due diligence to contact the borrower as required by this section, or that no contact was required because the individual did not meet the definition of "borrower" pursuant to subdivision (c) of Section 2920.5.

(c) A mortgage servicer's loss mitigation personnel may participate by telephone during any contact required by this section.

(d) A borrower may designate, with consent given in writing, a HUD–certified housing counseling agency, attorney, or other advisor to discuss with the mortgage servicer, on the borrower's behalf, the borrower's financial situation and options for the borrower to avoid foreclosure. That contact made at the direction of the borrower shall satisfy the contact requirements of paragraph (2) of subdivision (a). Any loan modification or workout plan offered at the meeting by the mortgage servicer is subject to approval by the borrower.

(e) A notice of default may be recorded pursuant to Section 2924 when a mortgage servicer has not contacted a borrower as required by paragraph (2) of subdivision (a) provided that the failure to contact the borrower occurred despite the due diligence of the mortgage servicer. For purposes of this section, "due diligence" shall require and mean all of the following:

(1) A mortgage servicer shall first attempt to contact a borrower by sending a first-class letter that includes the toll-free telephone number made available by HUD to find a HUD–certified housing counseling agency.

(2)(A) After the letter has been sent, the mortgage servicer shall attempt to contact the borrower by telephone at least three times at different hours and on different days. Telephone calls shall be made to the primary telephone number on file.

(B) A mortgage servicer may attempt to contact a borrower using an automated system to dial borrowers, provided that, if the telephone call is answered, the call is connected to a live representative of the mortgage servicer.

(C) A mortgage servicer satisfies the telephone contact requirements of this paragraph if it determines, after attempting contact pursuant to this paragraph, that the borrower's primary telephone number and secondary telephone number or numbers on file, if any, have been disconnected.

(3) If the borrower does not respond within two weeks after the telephone call requirements of paragraph (2) have been satisfied, the mortgage servicer shall then send a certified letter, with return receipt requested.

(4) The mortgage servicer shall provide a means for the borrower to contact it in a timely manner, including a toll-free telephone number that will provide access to a live representative during business hours.

(5) The mortgage servicer has posted a prominent link on the homepage of its Internet Web site, if any, to the following information:

(A) Options that may be available to borrowers who are unable to afford their mortgage payments and who wish to avoid foreclosure, and instructions to borrowers advising them on steps to take to explore those options.

(B) A list of financial documents borrowers should collect and be prepared to present to the mortgage servicer when discussing options for avoiding foreclosure.

(C) A toll-free telephone number for borrowers who wish to discuss options for avoiding foreclosure with their mortgage servicer.

(D) The toll-free telephone number made available by HUD to find a HUD–certified housing counseling agency.

(f) This section shall apply only to mortgages or deeds of trust described in Section 2924.15.

(g) This section shall become operative on January 1, 2018. *(Added by Stats.2012, c. 87 (S.B.900), § 5, operative Jan. 1, 2018.)*

Research References

Rutter, Cal. Practice Guide: Real Prop. Transactions Ch. 6-I, I. Real Property Foreclosures and Antideficiency Laws.

Miller and Starr California Real Estate § 36:1, Applicable Theories of Liability.

Miller and Starr California Real Estate § 10:181, Notice of Default--In General.

Miller and Starr California Real Estate § 10:182, Form and Contents.

Miller and Starr California Real Estate § 10:210, Attack on Validity of the Sale.

Miller and Starr California Real Estate § 10:212, Requirement of Tender.

Miller and Starr California Real Estate § 10:221, Comparison With Nonjudicial Foreclosure.

Miller and Starr California Real Estate § 10:181.10, Prior Notification and Consultation for Residential Loans Originated Between January 1, 2003 and December 31, 2007.

Miller and Starr California Real Estate § 10:181.20, Prior Notification, Consultation and Modification Requirements for Owner-Occupied First Lien Mortgage Loans Effective January 1, 2013.

19 NO. 1 Miller & Starr, California Real Estate Newsalert 1, The Perata Foreclosure Bill (SB 1137): New Rights for Defaulting Borrowers and Tenants; New Complications for Foreclosing Lenders.

19 NO. 4 Miller & Starr, California Real Estate Newsalert 10, Deeds of Trust.

20 NO. 4 Miller & Starr, California Real Estate Newsalert 6, Deeds of Trust.

21 NO. 1 Miller & Starr, California Real Estate Newsalert 9, Deeds of Trust.

21 NO. 3 Miller & Starr, California Real Estate Newsalert 10, Deeds of Trust.

22 NO. 6 Miller & Starr, California Real Estate Newsalert 11, Deeds of Trust.

22 NO. 1 Miller & Starr, California Real Estate Newsalert 11, Deeds of Trust.

22 NO. 4 Miller & Starr, California Real Estate Newsalert 29, Deeds of Trust.

23 NO. 1 Miller & Starr, California Real Estate Newsalert 9, Deeds of Trust.

4 Witkin, California Summary 10th Security Transactions in Real Property § 145, in General.

4 Witkin, California Summary 10th Security Transactions in Real Property § 150, Content and Time of Notice.

4 Witkin, California Summary 10th Security Transactions in Real Property § 212, in General.

§ 2923.55. Notice of default; recording; sending of written information to borrower by mortgage servicer

Section added by Stats.2012, c. 86 (A.B.278), § 6. See, also, another section of the same number added by Stats.2012, c. 87 (S.B.900), § 6

(a) A mortgage servicer, mortgagee, trustee, beneficiary, or authorized agent may not record a notice of default pursuant to Section 2924 until all of the following:

(1) The mortgage servicer has satisfied the requirements of paragraph (1) of subdivision (b).

(2) Either 30 days after initial contact is made as required by paragraph (2) of subdivision (b) or 30 days after satisfying the due diligence requirements as described in subdivision (f).

(3) The mortgage servicer complies with subdivision (c) of Section 2923.6, if the borrower has provided a complete application as defined in subdivision (h) of Section 2923.6.

(b)(1) As specified in subdivision (a), a mortgage servicer shall send the following information in writing to the borrower:

(A) A statement that if the borrower is a servicemember or a dependent of a servicemember, he or she may be entitled to certain protections under the federal Servicemembers Civil Relief Act (50 U.S.C. Appen. Sec. 501 et seq.) regarding the servicemember's interest rate and the risk of foreclosure, and counseling for covered servicemembers that is available at agencies such as Military OneSource and Armed Forces Legal Assistance.

(B) A statement that the borrower may request the following:

(i) A copy of the borrower's promissory note or other evidence of indebtedness.

(ii) A copy of the borrower's deed of trust or mortgage.

(iii) A copy of any assignment, if applicable, of the borrower's mortgage or deed of trust required to demonstrate the right of the mortgage servicer to foreclose.

(iv) A copy of the borrower's payment history since the borrower was last less than 60 days past due.

(2) A mortgage servicer shall contact the borrower in person or by telephone in order to assess the borrower's financial situation and explore options for the borrower to avoid foreclosure. During the initial contact, the mortgage servicer shall advise the borrower that he or she has the right to request a subsequent meeting and, if requested, the mortgage servicer shall schedule the meeting to occur within 14 days. The assessment of the borrower's financial situation and discussion of options may occur during the first contact, or at the subsequent meeting scheduled for that purpose. In either case, the borrower shall be provided the toll-free telephone number made available by the United States Department of Housing and Urban Development (HUD) to find a HUD–certified housing counseling agency. Any meeting may occur telephonically.

(c) A notice of default recorded pursuant to Section 2924 shall include a declaration that the mortgage servicer has contacted the borrower, has tried with due diligence to contact the borrower as required by this section, or that no contact was required because the individual did not meet the definition of "borrower" pursuant to subdivision (c) of Section 2920.5.

(d) A mortgage servicer's loss mitigation personnel may participate by telephone during any contact required by this section.

(e) A borrower may designate, with consent given in writing, a HUD–certified housing counseling agency, attorney, or other adviser to discuss with the mortgage servicer, on the borrower's behalf, the borrower's financial situation and options for the borrower to avoid foreclosure. That contact made at the direction of the borrower shall satisfy the contact requirements of paragraph (2) of subdivision (b). Any foreclosure prevention alternative offered at the meeting by the mortgage servicer is subject to approval by the borrower.

(f) A notice of default may be recorded pursuant to Section 2924 when a mortgage servicer has not contacted a borrower as required by paragraph (2) of subdivision (b), provided that the failure to contact the borrower occurred despite the due diligence of the mortgage servicer. For purposes of this section, "due diligence" shall require and mean all of the following:

(1) A mortgage servicer shall first attempt to contact a borrower by sending a first-class letter that includes the toll-free telephone number made available by HUD to find a HUD–certified housing counseling agency.

(2)(A) After the letter has been sent, the mortgage servicer shall attempt to contact the borrower by telephone at least three times at different hours and on different days. Telephone calls shall be made to the primary telephone number on file.

(B) A mortgage servicer may attempt to contact a borrower using an automated system to dial borrowers, provided that, if the telephone call is answered, the call is connected to a live representative of the mortgage servicer.

(C) A mortgage servicer satisfies the telephone contact requirements of this paragraph if it determines, after attempting contact pursuant to this paragraph, that the borrower's primary telephone number and secondary telephone number or numbers on file, if any, have been disconnected.

(3) If the borrower does not respond within two weeks after the telephone call requirements of paragraph (2) have been satisfied, the mortgage servicer shall then send a certified letter, with return receipt requested, that includes the toll-free telephone number made available by HUD to find a HUD–certified housing counseling agency.

(4) The mortgage servicer shall provide a means for the borrower to contact it in a timely manner, including a toll-free telephone number that will provide access to a live representative during business hours.

(5) The mortgage servicer has posted a prominent link on the homepage of its Internet Web site, if any, to the following information:

(A) Options that may be available to borrowers who are unable to afford their mortgage payments and who wish to avoid foreclosure, and instructions to borrowers advising them on steps to take to explore those options.

(B) A list of financial documents borrowers should collect and be prepared to present to the mortgage servicer when discussing options for avoiding foreclosure.

(C) A toll-free telephone number for borrowers who wish to discuss options for avoiding foreclosure with their mortgage servicer.

(D) The toll-free telephone number made available by HUD to find a HUD–certified housing counseling agency.

(g) This section shall not apply to entities described in subdivision (b) of Section 2924.18.

(h) This section shall apply only to mortgages or deeds of trust described in Section 2924.15.

(i) This section shall remain in effect only until January 1, 2018, and as of that date is repealed, unless a later enacted statute, that is enacted before January 1, 2018, deletes or extends that date. *(Added by Stats.2012, c. 86 (A.B.278), § 6. Amended by Stats.2013, c. 76 (A.B.383), § 14.)*

Repeal

For repeal of this section, see its terms.

Research References

Rutter, Cal. Practice Guide: Real Prop. Transactions Ch. 6-I, I. Real Property Foreclosures and Antideficiency Laws.

Rutter, Cal. Practice Guide: Real Prop. Transactions Gen. Matls., Highlights.

Miller and Starr California Real Estate § 4:12, Mortgage Loan Origination, Brokerage, and Servicing.

Miller and Starr California Real Estate § 4:78, Federal and State Regulation of Residential Mortgage Loan Origination and Servicing--In General.

Miller and Starr California Real Estate § 10:181.10, Prior Notification and Consultation for Residential Loans Originated Between January 1, 2003 and December 31, 2007.

Miller and Starr California Real Estate § 10:181.20, Prior Notification, Consultation and Modification Requirements for Owner-Occupied First Lien Mortgage Loans Effective January 1, 2013.

19 NO. 5 Miller & Starr, California Real Estate Newsalert 2, Deeds of Trust.

20 NO. 4 Miller & Starr, California Real Estate Newsalert 6, Deeds of Trust.

4 Witkin, California Summary 10th Security Transactions in Real Property § 150, Content and Time of Notice.

§ 2923.55. Notice of default; recording; sending of written information to borrower by mortgage servicer

Section added by Stats.2012, c. 87 (S.B.900), § 6. See, also, another section of the same number added by Stats.2012, c. 86 (A.B.278), § 6.

(a) A mortgage servicer, mortgagee, trustee, beneficiary, or authorized agent may not record a notice of default pursuant to Section 2924 until all of the following:

(1) The mortgage servicer has satisfied the requirements of paragraph (1) of subdivision (b).

(2) Either 30 days after initial contact is made as required by paragraph (2) of subdivision (b) or 30 days after satisfying the due diligence requirements as described in subdivision (f).

(3) The mortgage servicer complies with subdivision (c) of Section 2923.6, if the borrower has provided a complete application as defined in subdivision (h) of Section 2923.6.

(b)(1) As specified in subdivision (a), a mortgage servicer shall send the following information in writing to the borrower:

(A) A statement that if the borrower is a servicemember or a dependent of a servicemember, he or she may be entitled to certain protections under the federal Servicemembers Civil Relief Act (50 U.S.C. Appen. Sec. 501 et seq.) regarding the servicemember's interest rate and the risk of foreclosure, and counseling for covered servicemembers that is available at agencies such as Military OneSource and Armed Forces Legal Assistance.

(B) A statement that the borrower may request the following:

(i) A copy of the borrower's promissory note or other evidence of indebtedness.

(ii) A copy of the borrower's deed of trust or mortgage.

(iii) A copy of any assignment, if applicable, of the borrower's mortgage or deed of trust required to demonstrate the right of the mortgage servicer to foreclose.

(iv) A copy of the borrower's payment history since the borrower was last less than 60 days past due.

(2) A mortgage servicer shall contact the borrower in person or by telephone in order to assess the borrower's financial situation and explore options for the borrower to avoid foreclosure. During the initial contact, the mortgage servicer shall advise the borrower that he or she has the right to request a subsequent meeting and, if requested, the mortgage servicer shall schedule the meeting to occur within 14 days. The assessment of the borrower's financial situation and discussion of options may occur during the first contact, or at the subsequent meeting scheduled for that purpose. In either case, the borrower shall be provided the toll-free telephone number made available by the United States Department of Housing and Urban Development (HUD) to find a HUD–certified housing counseling agency. Any meeting may occur telephonically.

(c) A notice of default recorded pursuant to Section 2924 shall include a declaration that the mortgage servicer has contacted the borrower, has tried with due diligence to contact the borrower as required by this section, or that no contact was required because the individual did not meet the definition of "borrower" pursuant to subdivision (c) of Section 2920.5.

(d) A mortgage servicer's loss mitigation personnel may participate by telephone during any contact required by this section.

(e) A borrower may designate, with consent given in writing, a HUD–certified housing counseling agency, attorney, or other adviser to discuss with the mortgage servicer, on the borrower's behalf, the borrower's financial situation and options for the borrower to avoid foreclosure. That contact made at the direction of the borrower shall satisfy the contact requirements of paragraph (2) of subdivision (b). Any foreclosure prevention alternative offered at the meeting by the mortgage servicer is subject to approval by the borrower.

(f) A notice of default may be recorded pursuant to Section 2924 when a mortgage servicer has not contacted a borrower as required by paragraph (2) of subdivision (b), provided that the failure to contact the borrower occurred despite the due diligence of the mortgage servicer. For purposes of this section, "due diligence" shall require and mean all of the following:

(1) A mortgage servicer shall first attempt to contact a borrower by sending a first-class letter that includes the toll-free telephone number made available by HUD to find a HUD–certified housing counseling agency.

(2)(A) After the letter has been sent, the mortgage servicer shall attempt to contact the borrower by telephone at least three times at different hours and on different days. Telephone calls shall be made to the primary telephone number on file.

(B) A mortgage servicer may attempt to contact a borrower using an automated system to dial borrowers, provided that, if the telephone call is answered, the call is connected to a live representative of the mortgage servicer.

(C) A mortgage servicer satisfies the telephone contact requirements of this paragraph if it determines, after attempting contact pursuant to this paragraph, that the borrower's primary telephone number and secondary telephone number or numbers on file, if any, have been disconnected.

(3) If the borrower does not respond within two weeks after the telephone call requirements of paragraph (2) have been satisfied, the mortgage servicer shall then send a certified letter, with return receipt requested, that includes the toll-free telephone number made available by HUD to find a HUD–certified housing counseling agency.

(4) The mortgage servicer shall provide a means for the borrower to contact it in a timely manner, including a toll-free telephone number that will provide access to a live representative during business hours.

(5) The mortgage servicer has posted a prominent link on the homepage of its Internet Web site, if any, to the following information:

(A) Options that may be available to borrowers who are unable to afford their mortgage payments and who wish to avoid foreclosure, and instructions to borrowers advising them on steps to take to explore those options.

(B) A list of financial documents borrowers should collect and be prepared to present to the mortgage servicer when discussing options for avoiding foreclosure.

(C) A toll-free telephone number for borrowers who wish to discuss options for avoiding foreclosure with their mortgage servicer.

(D) The toll-free telephone number made available by HUD to find a HUD–certified housing counseling agency.

(g) This section shall not apply to entities described in subdivision (b) of Section 2924.18.

(h) This section shall apply only to mortgages or deeds of trust described in Section 2924.15.

(i) This section shall remain in effect only until January 1, 2018, and as of that date is repealed, unless a later enacted statute, that is enacted before January 1, 2018, deletes or extends that date. *(Added by Stats.2012, c. 87 (S.B.900), § 6. Amended by Stats.2013, c. 76 (A.B.383), § 15.)*

Research References

Rutter, Cal. Practice Guide: Real Prop. Transactions Ch. 6-I, I. Real Property Foreclosures and Antideficiency Laws.

Rutter, Cal. Practice Guide: Real Prop. Transactions Gen. Matls., Highlights.

Miller and Starr California Real Estate § 4:12, Mortgage Loan Origination, Brokerage, and Servicing.

Miller and Starr California Real Estate § 4:78, Federal and State Regulation of Residential Mortgage Loan Origination and Servicing--In General.

Miller and Starr California Real Estate § 10:181.10, Prior Notification and Consultation for Residential Loans Originated Between January 1, 2003 and December 31, 2007.

Miller and Starr California Real Estate § 10:181.20, Prior Notification, Consultation and Modification Requirements for Owner-Occupied First Lien Mortgage Loans Effective January 1, 2013.

19 NO. 5 Miller & Starr, California Real Estate Newsalert 2, Deeds of Trust.

20 NO. 4 Miller & Starr, California Real Estate Newsalert 6, Deeds of Trust.

4 Witkin, California Summary 10th Security Transactions in Real Property § 150, Content and Time of Notice.

§ 2923.6. Legislative findings and declarations; pooling and servicing agreements; loan modification or workout plan; first lien loan modification applications

Section operative until Jan. 1, 2018. See, also, section added by Stats.2012, c. 86 (A.B.278), § 8, operative Jan. 1, 2018, and section added by Stats.2012, c. 87 (S.B.900), § 8, operative Jan. 1, 2018.

(a) The Legislature finds and declares that any duty that mortgage servicers may have to maximize net present value under their pooling and servicing agreements is owed to all parties in a loan pool, or to all investors under a pooling and servicing agreement, not to any particular party in the loan pool or investor under a pooling and servicing agreement, and that a mortgage servicer acts in the best interests of all parties to the loan pool or investors in the pooling and servicing agreement if it agrees to or implements a loan modification or workout plan for which both of the following apply:

(1) The loan is in payment default, or payment default is reasonably foreseeable.

(2) Anticipated recovery under the loan modification or workout plan exceeds the anticipated recovery through foreclosure on a net present value basis.

(b) It is the intent of the Legislature that the mortgage servicer offer the borrower a loan modification or workout plan if such a modification or plan is consistent with its contractual or other authority.

(c) If a borrower submits a complete application for a first lien loan modification offered by, or through, the borrower's mortgage servicer, a mortgage servicer, mortgagee, trustee, beneficiary, or authorized agent shall not record a notice of default or notice of sale, or conduct a trustee's sale, while the complete first lien loan modification application is pending. A mortgage servicer, mortgagee, trustee, beneficiary, or authorized agent shall not record a notice of default or notice of sale or conduct a trustee's sale until any of the following occurs:

(1) The mortgage servicer makes a written determination that the borrower is not eligible for a first lien loan modification, and any appeal period pursuant to subdivision (d) has expired.

(2) The borrower does not accept an offered first lien loan modification within 14 days of the offer.

(3) The borrower accepts a written first lien loan modification, but defaults on, or otherwise breaches the borrower's obligations under, the first lien loan modification.

(d) If the borrower's application for a first lien loan modification is denied, the borrower shall have at least 30 days from the date of the written denial to appeal the denial and to provide evidence that the mortgage servicer's determination was in error.

(e) If the borrower's application for a first lien loan modification is denied, the mortgage servicer, mortgagee, trustee, beneficiary, or authorized agent shall not record a notice of default or, if a notice of default has already been recorded, record a notice of sale or conduct a trustee's sale until the later of:

(1) Thirty-one days after the borrower is notified in writing of the denial.

(2) If the borrower appeals the denial pursuant to subdivision (d), the later of 15 days after the denial of the appeal or 14 days after a first lien loan modification is offered after appeal but declined by the borrower, or, if a first lien loan modification is offered and accepted after appeal, the date on which the borrower fails to timely submit the first payment or otherwise breaches the terms of the offer.

(f) Following the denial of a first lien loan modification application, the mortgage servicer shall send a written notice to the borrower identifying the reasons for denial, including the following:

(1) The amount of time from the date of the denial letter in which the borrower may request an appeal of the denial of the first lien loan modification and instructions regarding how to appeal the denial.

(2) If the denial was based on investor disallowance, the specific reasons for the investor disallowance.

(3) If the denial is the result of a net present value calculation, the monthly gross income and property value used to calculate the net present value and a statement that the borrower may obtain all of the inputs used in the net present value calculation upon written request to the mortgage servicer.

(4) If applicable, a finding that the borrower was previously offered a first lien loan modification and failed to successfully make payments under the terms of the modified loan.

(5) If applicable, a description of other foreclosure prevention alternatives for which the borrower may be eligible, and a list of the steps the borrower must take in order to be considered for those options. If the mortgage servicer has already approved the borrower for another foreclosure prevention alternative, information necessary to complete the foreclosure prevention alternative.

(g) In order to minimize the risk of borrowers submitting multiple applications for first lien loan modifications for the purpose of delay, the mortgage servicer shall not be obligated to evaluate applications from borrowers who have already been evaluated or afforded a fair opportunity to be evaluated for a first lien loan modification prior to January 1, 2013, or who have been evaluated or afforded a fair opportunity to be evaluated consistent with the requirements of this section, unless there has been a material change in the borrower's financial circumstances since the date of the borrower's previous application and that change is documented by the borrower and submitted to the mortgage servicer.

(h) For purposes of this section, an application shall be deemed "complete" when a borrower has supplied the mortgage servicer with all documents required by the mortgage servicer within the reasonable timeframes specified by the mortgage servicer.

(i) Subdivisions (c) to (h), inclusive, shall not apply to entities described in subdivision (b) of Section 2924.18.

(j) This section shall apply only to mortgages or deeds of trust described in Section 2924.15.

(k) This section shall remain in effect only until January 1, 2018, and as of that date is repealed, unless a later enacted statute, that is enacted before January 1, 2018, deletes or extends that date. *(Added by Stats.2008, c. 69 (S.B.1137), § 3, eff. July 8, 2008. Amended by Stats.2009, c. 43 (S.B.306), § 2; Stats.2012, c. 86 (A.B.278), § 7; Stats.2012, c. 87 (S.B.900), § 7.)*

Repeal

For repeal of this section, see its terms.

Research References

Rutter, Cal. Practice Guide: Real Prop. Transactions Ch. 6-I, I. Real Property Foreclosures and Antideficiency Laws.
Miller and Starr California Real Estate § 4:69, Servicing of Secured Obligations--In General.
Miller and Starr California Real Estate § 10:181.10, Prior Notification and Consultation for Residential Loans Originated Between January 1, 2003 and December 31, 2007.
Miller and Starr California Real Estate § 10:181.20, Prior Notification, Consultation and Modification Requirements for Owner-Occupied First Lien Mortgage Loans Effective January 1, 2013.
19 NO. 1 Miller & Starr, California Real Estate Newsalert 1, The Perata Foreclosure Bill (SB 1137): New Rights for Defaulting Borrowers and Tenants; New Complications for Foreclosing Lenders.
19 NO. 4 Miller & Starr, California Real Estate Newsalert 10, Deeds of Trust.
20 NO. 4 Miller & Starr, California Real Estate Newsalert 6, Deeds of Trust.
4 Witkin, California Summary 10th Security Transactions in Real Property § 212, in General.

§ 2923.6. Legislative findings and declarations; pooling and servicing agreements; loan modification or workout plan

Section added by Stats.2012, c. 86 (A.B.278), § 8, operative Jan. 1, 2018. See, also, section operative until Jan. 1, 2018, and another section of the same number, added by Stats.2012, c. 87 (S.B.900), § 8, operative Jan. 1, 2018.

(a) The Legislature finds and declares that any duty mortgage servicers may have to maximize net present value under their pooling and servicing agreements is owed to all parties in a loan pool, or to all investors under a pooling and servicing agreement, not to any particular party in the loan pool or investor under a pooling and servicing agreement, and that a mortgage servicer acts in the best interests of all parties to the loan pool or investors in the pooling and servicing agreement if it agrees to or implements a loan modification or workout plan for which both of the following apply:

(1) The loan is in payment default, or payment default is reasonably foreseeable.

(2) Anticipated recovery under the loan modification or workout plan exceeds the anticipated recovery through foreclosure on a net present value basis.

(b) It is the intent of the Legislature that the mortgage servicer offer the borrower a loan modification or workout plan if such a modification or plan is consistent with its contractual or other authority.

(c) This section shall become operative on January 1, 2018. *(Added by Stats.2012, c. 86 (A.B.278), § 8, operative Jan. 1, 2018.)*

Research References

Rutter, Cal. Practice Guide: Real Prop. Transactions Ch. 6-I, I. Real Property Foreclosures and Antideficiency Laws.
Miller and Starr California Real Estate § 4:69, Servicing of Secured Obligations--In General.
Miller and Starr California Real Estate § 10:181.10, Prior Notification and Consultation for Residential Loans Originated Between January 1, 2003 and December 31, 2007.
Miller and Starr California Real Estate § 10:181.20, Prior Notification, Consultation and Modification Requirements for Owner-Occupied First Lien Mortgage Loans Effective January 1, 2013.
19 NO. 1 Miller & Starr, California Real Estate Newsalert 1, The Perata Foreclosure Bill (SB 1137): New Rights for Defaulting Borrowers and Tenants; New Complications for Foreclosing Lenders.
19 NO. 4 Miller & Starr, California Real Estate Newsalert 10, Deeds of Trust.
20 NO. 4 Miller & Starr, California Real Estate Newsalert 6, Deeds of Trust.
4 Witkin, California Summary 10th Security Transactions in Real Property § 212, in General.

§ 2923.6. Legislative findings and declarations; pooling and servicing agreements; loan modification or workout plan

Section added by Stats.2012, c. 87 (S.B.900), § 8, operative Jan. 1, 2018. See, also, section operative until Jan. 1, 2018, and another section of the same number, added by Stats.2012, c. 86 (A.B.278), § 8, operative Jan. 1, 2018.

(a) The Legislature finds and declares that any duty mortgage servicers may have to maximize net present value under their pooling and servicing agreements is owed to all parties in a loan pool, or to all investors under a pooling and servicing agreement, not to any particular party in the loan pool or investor under a pooling and servicing agreement, and that a mortgage servicer acts in the best interests of all parties to the loan pool or investors in the pooling and servicing agreement if it agrees to or implements a loan modification or workout plan for which both of the following apply:

(1) The loan is in payment default, or payment default is reasonably foreseeable.

(2) Anticipated recovery under the loan modification or workout plan exceeds the anticipated recovery through foreclosure on a net present value basis.

(b) It is the intent of the Legislature that the mortgage servicer offer the borrower a loan modification or workout plan if such a modification or plan is consistent with its contractual or other authority.

(c) This section shall become operative on January 1, 2018. *(Added by Stats.2012, c. 87 (S.B.900), § 8, operative Jan. 1, 2018.)*

Research References

Rutter, Cal. Practice Guide: Real Prop. Transactions Ch. 6-I, I. Real Property Foreclosures and Antideficiency Laws.
Miller and Starr California Real Estate § 4:69, Servicing of Secured Obligations--In General.
Miller and Starr California Real Estate § 10:181.10, Prior Notification and Consultation for Residential Loans Originated Between January 1, 2003 and December 31, 2007.
Miller and Starr California Real Estate § 10:181.20, Prior Notification, Consultation and Modification Requirements for Owner-Occupied First Lien Mortgage Loans Effective January 1, 2013.
19 NO. 1 Miller & Starr, California Real Estate Newsalert 1, The Perata Foreclosure Bill (SB 1137): New Rights for Defaulting Borrowers and Tenants; New Complications for Foreclosing Lenders.
19 NO. 4 Miller & Starr, California Real Estate Newsalert 10, Deeds of Trust.
20 NO. 4 Miller & Starr, California Real Estate Newsalert 6, Deeds of Trust.

4 Witkin, California Summary 10th Security Transactions in Real Property § 212, in General.

§ 2923.7. Receipt of borrower request for foreclosure prevention alternative; establishment of single point of contact; application

> *Section added by Stats.2012, c. 86 (A.B.278), § 9. See, also, another section of the same number added by Stats.2012, c. 87 (S.B.900), § 9.*

(a) Upon request from a borrower who requests a foreclosure prevention alternative, the mortgage servicer shall promptly establish a single point of contact and provide to the borrower one or more direct means of communication with the single point of contact.

(b) The single point of contact shall be responsible for doing all of the following:

(1) Communicating the process by which a borrower may apply for an available foreclosure prevention alternative and the deadline for any required submissions to be considered for these options.

(2) Coordinating receipt of all documents associated with available foreclosure prevention alternatives and notifying the borrower of any missing documents necessary to complete the application.

(3) Having access to current information and personnel sufficient to timely, accurately, and adequately inform the borrower of the current status of the foreclosure prevention alternative.

(4) Ensuring that a borrower is considered for all foreclosure prevention alternatives offered by, or through, the mortgage servicer, if any.

(5) Having access to individuals with the ability and authority to stop foreclosure proceedings when necessary.

(c) The single point of contact shall remain assigned to the borrower's account until the mortgage servicer determines that all loss mitigation options offered by, or through, the mortgage servicer have been exhausted or the borrower's account becomes current.

(d) The mortgage servicer shall ensure that a single point of contact refers and transfers a borrower to an appropriate supervisor upon request of the borrower, if the single point of contact has a supervisor.

(e) For purposes of this section, "single point of contact" means an individual or team of personnel each of whom has the ability and authority to perform the responsibilities described in subdivisions (b) to (d), inclusive. The mortgage servicer shall ensure that each member of the team is knowledgeable about the borrower's situation and current status in the alternatives to foreclosure process.

(f) This section shall apply only to mortgages or deeds of trust described in Section 2924.15.

(g)(1) This section shall not apply to a depository institution chartered under state or federal law, a person licensed pursuant to Division 9 (commencing with Section 22000) or Division 20 (commencing with Section 50000) of the Financial Code, or a person licensed pursuant to Part 1 (commencing with Section 10000) of Division 4 of the Business and Professions Code, that, during its immediately preceding annual reporting period, as established with its primary regulator, foreclosed on 175 or fewer residential real properties, containing no more than four dwelling units, that are located in California.

(2) Within three months after the close of any calendar year or annual reporting period as established with its primary regulator during which an entity or person described in para-graph (1) exceeds the threshold of 175 specified in paragraph (1), that entity shall notify its primary regulator, in a manner acceptable to its primary regulator, and any mortgagor or trustor who is delinquent on a residential mortgage loan serviced by that entity of the date on which that entity will be subject to this section, which date shall be the first day of the first month that is six months after the close of the calendar year or annual reporting period during which that entity exceeded the threshold. *(Added by Stats.2012, c. 86 (A.B.278), § 9.)*

Research References

Rutter, Cal. Practice Guide: Real Prop. Transactions Ch. 6-I, I. Real Property Foreclosures and Antideficiency Laws.

Miller and Starr California Real Estate § 10:181.10, Prior Notification and Consultation for Residential Loans Originated Between January 1, 2003 and December 31, 2007.

Miller and Starr California Real Estate § 10:181.20, Prior Notification, Consultation and Modification Requirements for Owner-Occupied First Lien Mortgage Loans Effective January 1, 2013.

§ 2923.7. Receipt of borrower request for foreclosure prevention alternative; establishment of single point of contact; application

> *Section added by Stats.2012, c. 87 (S.B.900), § 9. See, also, another section of the same number added by Stats.2012, c. 86 (A.B.278), § 9.*

(a) Upon request from a borrower who requests a foreclosure prevention alternative, the mortgage servicer shall promptly establish a single point of contact and provide to the borrower one or more direct means of communication with the single point of contact.

(b) The single point of contact shall be responsible for doing all of the following:

(1) Communicating the process by which a borrower may apply for an available foreclosure prevention alternative and the deadline for any required submissions to be considered for these options.

(2) Coordinating receipt of all documents associated with available foreclosure prevention alternatives and notifying the borrower of any missing documents necessary to complete the application.

(3) Having access to current information and personnel sufficient to timely, accurately, and adequately inform the borrower of the current status of the foreclosure prevention alternative.

(4) Ensuring that a borrower is considered for all foreclosure prevention alternatives offered by, or through, the mortgage servicer, if any.

(5) Having access to individuals with the ability and authority to stop foreclosure proceedings when necessary.

(c) The single point of contact shall remain assigned to the borrower's account until the mortgage servicer determines that all loss mitigation options offered by, or through, the mortgage servicer have been exhausted or the borrower's account becomes current.

(d) The mortgage servicer shall ensure that a single point of contact refers and transfers a borrower to an appropriate supervisor upon request of the borrower, if the single point of contact has a supervisor.

(e) For purposes of this section, "single point of contact" means an individual or team of personnel each of whom has the ability and authority to perform the responsibilities described in subdivisions (b) to (d), inclusive. The mortgage servicer shall ensure that each member of the team is knowledgeable about the borrower's situation and current status in the alternatives to foreclosure process.

(f) This section shall apply only to mortgages or deeds of trust described in Section 2924.15.

(g)(1) This section shall not apply to a depository institution chartered under state or federal law, a person licensed pursuant to Division 9 (commencing with Section 22000) or Division 20 (commencing with Section 50000) of the Financial Code, or a person licensed pursuant to Part 1 (commencing with Section 10000) of Division 4 of the Business and Professions Code, that, during its immediately preceding annual reporting period, as established with its primary regulator, foreclosed on 175 or fewer residential real properties, containing no more than four dwelling units, that are located in California.

(2) Within three months after the close of any calendar year or annual reporting period as established with its primary regulator during which an entity or person described in paragraph (1) exceeds the threshold of 175 specified in paragraph (1), that entity shall notify its primary regulator, in a manner acceptable to its primary regulator, and any mortgagor or trustor who is delinquent on a residential mortgage loan serviced by that entity of the date on which that entity will be subject to this section, which date shall be the first day of the first month that is six months after the close of the calendar year or annual reporting period during which that entity exceeded the threshold. *(Added by Stats.2012, c. 87 (S.B.900), § 9.)*

Research References

Rutter, Cal. Practice Guide: Real Prop. Transactions Ch. 6-I, I. Real Property Foreclosures and Antideficiency Laws.
Miller and Starr California Real Estate § 10:181.10, Prior Notification and Consultation for Residential Loans Originated Between January 1, 2003 and December 31, 2007.
Miller and Starr California Real Estate § 10:181.20, Prior Notification, Consultation and Modification Requirements for Owner-Occupied First Lien Mortgage Loans Effective January 1, 2013.

§ 2924. Transfer as security deemed mortgage or pledge; power of sale; requirements prior to sale; trustee liability; evidence of compliance; privileged communications; rebuttable presumption

(a) Every transfer of an interest in property, other than in trust, made only as a security for the performance of another act, is to be deemed a mortgage, except when in the case of personal property it is accompanied by actual change of possession, in which case it is to be deemed a pledge. Where, by a mortgage created after July 27, 1917, of any estate in real property, other than an estate at will or for years, less than two, or in any transfer in trust made after July 27, 1917, of a like estate to secure the performance of an obligation, a power of sale is conferred upon the mortgagee, trustee, or any other person, to be exercised after a breach of the obligation for which that mortgage or transfer is a security, the power shall not be exercised except where the mortgage or transfer is made pursuant to an order, judgment, or decree of a court of record, or to secure the payment of bonds or other evidences of indebtedness authorized or permitted to be issued by the Commissioner of Corporations, or is made by a public utility subject to the provisions of the Public Utilities Act, until all of the following apply:

(1) The trustee, mortgagee, or beneficiary, or any of their authorized agents shall first file for record, in the office of the recorder of each county wherein the mortgaged or trust property or some part or parcel thereof is situated, a notice of default. That notice of default shall include all of the following:

(A) A statement identifying the mortgage or deed of trust by stating the name or names of the trustor or trustors and giving the book and page, or instrument number, if applicable, where the mortgage or deed of trust is recorded or a description of the mortgaged or trust property.

(B) A statement that a breach of the obligation for which the mortgage or transfer in trust is security has occurred.

(C) A statement setting forth the nature of each breach actually known to the beneficiary and of his or her election to sell or cause to be sold the property to satisfy that obligation and any other obligation secured by the deed of trust or mortgage that is in default.

(D) If the default is curable pursuant to Section 2924c, the statement specified in paragraph (1) of subdivision (b) of Section 2924c.

(2) Not less than three months shall elapse from the filing of the notice of default.

(3) Except as provided in paragraph (4), after the lapse of the three months described in paragraph (2), the mortgagee, trustee, or other person authorized to take the sale shall give notice of sale, stating the time and place thereof, in the manner and for a time not less than that set forth in Section 2924f.

(4) Notwithstanding paragraph (3), the mortgagee, trustee, or other person authorized to take sale may record a notice of sale pursuant to Section 2924f up to five days before the lapse of the three-month period described in paragraph (2), provided that the date of sale is no earlier than three months and 20 days after the recording of the notice of default.

(5) Until January 1, 2018, whenever a sale is postponed for a period of at least 10 business days pursuant to Section 2924g, a mortgagee, beneficiary, or authorized agent shall provide written notice to a borrower regarding the new sale date and time, within five business days following the postponement. Information provided pursuant to this paragraph shall not constitute the public declaration required by subdivision (d) of Section 2924g. Failure to comply with this paragraph shall not invalidate any sale that would otherwise be valid under Section 2924f. This paragraph shall be inoperative on January 1, 2018.

(6) No entity shall record or cause a notice of default to be recorded or otherwise initiate the foreclosure process unless it is the holder of the beneficial interest under the mortgage or deed of trust, the original trustee or the substituted trustee under the deed of trust, or the designated agent of the holder of the beneficial interest. No agent of the holder of the beneficial interest under the mortgage or deed of trust, original trustee or substituted trustee under the deed of trust may record a notice of default or otherwise commence the foreclosure process except when acting within the scope of authority designated by the holder of the beneficial interest.

(b) In performing acts required by this article, the trustee shall incur no liability for any good faith error resulting from reliance on information provided in good faith by the beneficiary regarding the nature and the amount of the default under the secured obligation, deed of trust, or mortgage. In performing the acts required by this article, a trustee shall not be subject to Title 1.6c (commencing with Section 1788) of Part 4.

(c) A recital in the deed executed pursuant to the power of sale of compliance with all requirements of law regarding the mailing of copies of notices or the publication of a copy of the notice of default or the personal delivery of the copy of the notice of default or the posting of copies of the notice of sale or the publication of a copy thereof shall constitute prima facie evidence of compliance with these requirements and conclusive evidence thereof in favor of bona fide purchasers and encumbrancers for value and without notice.

(d) All of the following shall constitute privileged communications pursuant to Section 47:

(1) The mailing, publication, and delivery of notices as required by this section.

(2) Performance of the procedures set forth in this article.

(3) Performance of the functions and procedures set forth in this article if those functions and procedures are necessary to carry out the duties described in Sections 729.040, 729.050, and 729.080 of the Code of Civil Procedure.

(e) There is a rebuttable presumption that the beneficiary actually knew of all unpaid loan payments on the obligation owed to the beneficiary and secured by the deed of trust or mortgage subject to the notice of default. However, the failure to include an actually known default shall not invalidate the notice of sale and the beneficiary shall not be precluded from asserting a claim to this omitted default or defaults in a separate notice of default.

(f) With respect to residential real property containing no more than four dwelling units, a separate document containing a summary of the notice of default information in English and the languages described in Section 1632 shall be attached to the notice of default provided to the mortgagor or trustor pursuant to Section 2923.3. *(Added by Stats.2009–2010, 2nd Ex.Sess., c. 4 (S.B.7), § 8, eff. May 21, 2009, operative Jan. 1, 2011. Amended by Stats.2010, c. 180 (S.B.1221), § 1; Stats.2012, c. 86 (A.B.278), § 10; Stats.2012, c. 87 (S.B.900), § 10; Stats.2012, c. 556 (A.B.1599), § 2.5.)*

Research References

California Real Estate Forms (Miller & Starr) § 3:8, Deed of Trust, Security Agreement, and Fixture Filing With Assignment of Rents and Agreements.

California Real Estate Forms (Miller & Starr) § 1:34, Installment Land Sale Contract With Power of Sale.

California Real Estate Forms (Miller & Starr) § 3:14, Construction Deed of Trust, Security Agreement, and Fixture Filing With Assignment of Rents and Agreements.

California Real Estate Forms (Miller & Starr) § 3:20, Promissory Note--Conduit Loan.

California Real Estate Forms (Miller & Starr) § 3:21, Deed of Trust, Assignment of Rents, Security Agreement and Fixture Filing--Conduit Loan.

Rutter, Cal. Practice Guide: Civ. Pro. Before Trial Ch. 9(II)-B, B. Receiverships.

Rutter, Cal. Practice Guide: Civil Trials & Evidence Ch. 8G-C, C. Presumptions.

Rutter, Cal. Practice Guide: Enforcing Judgments/Debts Ch. 2-B, B. Statutory Liability and Procedures.

Rutter, Cal. Practice Guide: Personal Injury Ch. 1-C, C. Formation of Attorney-Client Relationship: the Employment Agreement.

Rutter, Cal. Practice Guide: Real Prop. Transactions Ch. 1-C, C. Attorney Fees and Costs Agreements.

Rutter, Cal. Practice Guide: Real Prop. Transactions Ch. 6-I, I. Real Property Foreclosures and Antideficiency Laws.

Rutter, Cal. Practice Guide: Real Prop. Transactions Gen. Matls., Highlights.

Miller and Starr California Real Estate § 10:2, Lien Versus Title Theories.

Miller and Starr California Real Estate § 10:3, Parties.

Miller and Starr California Real Estate § 10:4, Capacity and Authority of Trustee.

Miller and Starr California Real Estate § 11:6, Instruments Subject to Recording--List of Recordable Documents.

Miller and Starr California Real Estate § 11:7, Presumption of Record Title.

Miller and Starr California Real Estate § 19:2, Lease as Personal Property or Real Property.

Miller and Starr California Real Estate § 4:12, Mortgage Loan Origination, Brokerage, and Servicing.

Miller and Starr California Real Estate § 4:67, Requirements in Making or Arranging a Loan--Small Loan Regulations.

Miller and Starr California Real Estate § 4:78, Federal and State Regulation of Residential Mortgage Loan Origination and Servicing--In General.

Miller and Starr California Real Estate § 10:16, Property Interests that Are Lienable.

Miller and Starr California Real Estate § 10:25, Between Debtor and Creditor (Types of Transactions).

Miller and Starr California Real Estate § 10:31, Other Situations.

Miller and Starr California Real Estate § 10:38, What is Assignable; Procedure.

Miller and Starr California Real Estate § 10:39, Rights of the Parties.

Miller and Starr California Real Estate § 11:10, Required Form and Contents--In General.

Miller and Starr California Real Estate § 11:23, Purpose and Effect; Required for Recordation.

Miller and Starr California Real Estate § 11:46, Privileged Publication.

Miller and Starr California Real Estate § 11:48, Pecuniary Loss.

Miller and Starr California Real Estate § 34:57, Buyer's Default; Seller's Remedies.

Miller and Starr California Real Estate § 10:112, Procedure for Reconveyance.

Miller and Starr California Real Estate § 10:130, Ancient Mortgages; Debt Secured by a Mortgage.

Miller and Starr California Real Estate § 10:131, Debt Secured by a Deed of Trust.

Miller and Starr California Real Estate § 10:132, Ancient Mortgages; Debt Secured by a Deed of Trust.

Miller and Starr California Real Estate § 10:150, Effect of the Automatic Stay.

Miller and Starr California Real Estate § 10:179, Nature and Basis of Power of Sale.

Miller and Starr California Real Estate § 10:181, Notice of Default--In General.

Miller and Starr California Real Estate § 10:182, Form and Contents.

Miller and Starr California Real Estate § 10:183, Identification of the Default.

Miller and Starr California Real Estate § 10:184, Execution of the Notice of Default.

Miller and Starr California Real Estate § 10:185, Recording and Mailing.

Miller and Starr California Real Estate § 10:186, Reinstatement--In General.

Miller and Starr California Real Estate § 10:189, Amounts that Must be Paid to Reinstate.

Miller and Starr California Real Estate § 10:194, Waiver of Right to Reinstate.

Miller and Starr California Real Estate § 10:198, Notice of Sale--Contents of the Notice.

Miller and Starr California Real Estate § 10:199, Publication, Mailing, and Recording the Notice.

Miller and Starr California Real Estate § 10:201, Postponement of the Sale.

Miller and Starr California Real Estate § 10:203, Trustee's Liability for Wrongful Conduct of the Sale.

Miller and Starr California Real Estate § 10:208, Purchaser's Title.

Miller and Starr California Real Estate § 10:210, Attack on Validity of the Sale.

Miller and Starr California Real Estate § 10:211, Presumption of Validity.

Miller and Starr California Real Estate § 10:213, Disposition of Sales Proceeds.

Miller and Starr California Real Estate § 10:221, Comparison With Nonjudicial Foreclosure.

Miller and Starr California Real Estate § 10:237, Waiver of Purchase-Money Protection.

Miller and Starr California Real Estate § 25B:125, Governance Under the Time-Share Act--Penalties; Loss of Time-Share Interests.

Miller and Starr California Real Estate § 10:39.10, Assignments Under Mortgage Electronic Registration System (Mers).

Miller and Starr California Real Estate § 10:181.10, Prior Notification and Consultation for Residential Loans Originated Between January 1, 2003 and December 31, 2007.

Miller and Starr California Real Estate § 10:181.20, Prior Notification, Consultation and Modification Requirements for Owner-Occupied First Lien Mortgage Loans Effective January 1, 2013.

15 NO. 3 Miller & Starr, California Real Estate Newsalert 4, Deeds of Trust.

15 NO. 6 Miller & Starr, California Real Estate Newsalert 7, Deeds of Trust.

16 NO. 2 Miller & Starr, California Real Estate Newsalert 1, Trustee Sales: the "Terminator' of Debtors' Equities.

16 NO. 3 Miller & Starr, California Real Estate Newsalert 1, Assessment Liens and Foreclosure in Common Interest Developments.

16 NO. 5 Miller & Starr, California Real Estate Newsalert 1, Traveling in Time: The New California Time-Share Act.

16 NO. 1 Miller & Starr, California Real Estate Newsalert 12, Deeds of Trust.

16 NO. 4 Miller & Starr, California Real Estate Newsalert 26, Deeds of Trust.

17 NO. 4 Miller & Starr, California Real Estate Newsalert 2, Statutory Update:.

17 NO. 6 Miller & Starr, California Real Estate Newsalert 20, Table of Statutes (Newsalert Vol 17).

18 NO. 2 Miller & Starr, California Real Estate Newsalert 1, The Marketable Record Title Act- Is Private Foreclosure Barred Ten Years After Maturity, or Not?

18 NO. 4 Miller & Starr, California Real Estate Newsalert 31, Deeds of Trust.

19 NO. 1 Miller & Starr, California Real Estate Newsalert 1, The Perata Foreclosure Bill (SB 1137): New Rights for Defaulting Borrowers and Tenants; New Complications for Foreclosing Lenders.

19 NO. 4 Miller & Starr, California Real Estate Newsalert 10, Deeds of Trust.

19 NO. 4 Miller & Starr, California Real Estate Newsalert 34, Deeds of Trust.

19 NO. 4 Miller & Starr, California Real Estate Newsalert 43, Judicial Remedies.

19 NO. 4 Miller & Starr, California Real Estate Newsalert 48, Recording and Priorities.

20 NO. 6 Miller & Starr, California Real Estate Newsalert 6, Deeds of Trust.

20 NO. 4 Miller & Starr, California Real Estate Newsalert 26, Deeds of Trust.

21 NO. 3 Miller & Starr, California Real Estate Newsalert 10, Deeds of Trust.

21 NO. 4 Miller & Starr, California Real Estate Newsalert 11, Deeds of Trust.

22 NO. 3 Miller & Starr, California Real Estate Newsalert 1, Show Me Your Papers: Sales and Assignments of Secured Real Estate Loans and the California Foreclosure Process.

22 NO. 4 Miller & Starr, California Real Estate Newsalert 1, Show Me Your Papers: Sales and Assignments of Secured Real Estate Loans and the California Foreclosure Process (Part II).

22 NO. 5 Miller & Starr, California Real Estate Newsalert 6, Deeds of Trust.

22 NO. 2 Miller & Starr, California Real Estate Newsalert 9, Deeds of Trust.

22 NO. 4 Miller & Starr, California Real Estate Newsalert 10, Deeds of Trust.

22 NO. 6 Miller & Starr, California Real Estate Newsalert 11, Deeds of Trust.

23 NO. 2 Miller & Starr, California Real Estate Newsalert 8, Deeds of Trust.

23 NO. 1 Miller & Starr, California Real Estate Newsalert 9, Deeds of Trust.

5 Witkin Cal. Proc. 5th Pleading § 1019, (S 1019) in General.

12 Witkin, California Summary 10th Real Property § 112, (S 112) Liens.

12 Witkin, California Summary 10th Real Property § 146, (S 146) Statutory Development.

12 Witkin, California Summary 10th Real Property § 329, Bona Fide Encumbrancer.

1 Witkin Cal. Summ. 10th Contracts § 681, Waivers by Mortgagors.

4 Witkin, California Summary 10th Security Transactions in Real Property § 10, (S 10) Intention to Create Security Interest.

4 Witkin, California Summary 10th Security Transactions in Real Property § 24, (S 24) in General.

4 Witkin, California Summary 10th Security Transactions in Real Property § 144, in General.

4 Witkin, California Summary 10th Security Transactions in Real Property § 145, in General.

4 Witkin, California Summary 10th Security Transactions in Real Property § 146, Statement of Breach.

4 Witkin, California Summary 10th Security Transactions in Real Property § 150, Content and Time of Notice.

4 Witkin, California Summary 10th Security Transactions in Real Property § 152, Effect of Noncompliance.

4 Witkin, California Summary 10th Security Transactions in Real Property § 164, Effect of Recitals in Trustee's Deed.

4 Witkin, California Summary 10th Security Transactions in Real Property § 165, (S 165) Grounds.

4 Witkin, California Summary 10th Security Transactions in Real Property § 168, Damages for Wrongful Sale.

4 Witkin, California Summary 10th Security Transactions in Real Property § 219, (S 219) Payment or Tender.

4 Witkin, California Summary 10th Security Transactions in Real Property § 227, (S 227) Nature and Purpose of Legislation.

5 Witkin, California Summary 10th Torts § 563, Scope of Privilege.

7 Witkin, California Summary 10th Constitutional Law § 621, Nonjudicial Foreclosure.

§ 2924.1. Transfers of property in common interest developments; recording; validity of sale not affected by failure

(a) Notwithstanding any other law, the transfer, following the sale, of property in a common interest development, as defined by Section 1351, executed under the power of sale contained in any deed of trust or mortgage, shall be recorded within 30 days after the date of sale in the office of the county recorder where the property or a portion of the property is located.

(b) Any failure to comply with the provisions of this section shall not affect the validity of a trustee's sale or a sale in favor of a bona fide purchaser. *(Added by Stats.2012, c. 255 (A.B.2273), § 1.)*

§ 2924.3. Persons undertaking loan collections; notice of default and sale; exemptions

(a) Except as provided in subdivisions (b) and (c), a person who has undertaken as an agent of a mortgagee, beneficiary, or owner of a promissory note secured directly or collaterally by a mortgage or deed of trust on real property or an estate for years therein, to make collections of payments from an obligor under the note, shall mail the following notices, postage prepaid, to each mortgagee, beneficiary or owner for whom the agent has agreed to make collections from the obligor under the note:

(1) A copy of the notice of default filed in the office of the county recorder pursuant to Section 2924 on account of a breach of obligation under the promissory note on which the agent has agreed to make collections of payments, within 15 days after recordation.

(2) Notice that a notice of default has been recorded pursuant to Section 2924 on account of a breach of an obligation secured by a mortgage or deed of trust against the same property or estate for years therein having priority over the mortgage or deed of trust securing the obligation described in paragraph (1), within 15 days after recordation or within three business days after the agent receives the information, whichever is later.

(3) Notice of the time and place scheduled for the sale of the real property or estate for years therein pursuant to Section 2924f under a power of sale in a mortgage or deed of trust securing an obligation described in paragraphs (1) or (2), not less than 15 days before the scheduled date of the sale or not later than the next business day after the agent receives the information, whichever is later.

(b) An agent who has undertaken to make collections on behalf of mortgagees, beneficiaries or owners of promissory notes secured by mortgages or deeds of trust on real property or an estate for years therein shall not be required to comply with the provisions of subdivision (a) with respect to a mortgagee, beneficiary or owner who is entitled to receive notice pursuant to subdivision (c) of Section 2924b or for whom a request for notice has been recorded pursuant to subdivision (b) of Section 2924b if the agent reasonably believes that the address of the mortgagee, beneficiary, or owner described in Section 2924b is the current business or residence address of that person.

(c) An agent who has undertaken to make collections on behalf of mortgagees, beneficiaries or owners of promissory notes secured by mortgages or deeds of trust on real property or an estate for years therein shall not be required to comply with the provisions of paragraph (1) or (2) of subdivision (a) if the agent knows or reasonably believes that the default has already been cured by or on behalf of the obligor.

(d) Any failure to comply with the provisions of this section shall not affect the validity of a sale in favor of a bona fide purchaser or the rights of an encumbrancer for value and without notice. *(Added by Stats.1982, c. 711, p. 2874, § 4. Amended by Stats.1989, c. 698, § 7; Stats.1998, c. 932 (A.B.1094), § 10.)*

Research References

Miller and Starr California Real Estate § 1:79, Form of the Memorandum.

Miller and Starr California Real Estate § 4:69, Servicing of Secured Obligations--In General.

Miller and Starr California Real Estate § 10:185, Recording and Mailing.

Miller and Starr California Real Estate § 10:199, Publication, Mailing, and Recording the Notice.

§ 2924.5. Acceleration clause in deed of trust or mortgage on property containing four or fewer residential units

No clause in any deed of trust or mortgage on property containing four or fewer residential units or on which four or fewer residential units are to be constructed or in any obligation secured by any deed of trust or mortgage on property containing four or fewer residential units or on which four or fewer residential units are to be constructed that provides for the acceleration of the due date of the obligation upon the sale, conveyance, alienation, lease, succession, assignment or other transfer of the property subject to the deed of trust or mortgage shall be valid unless the clause is set forth, in its entirety in both the body of the deed of trust or mortgage and the promissory note or other document evidencing the secured obligation. This section shall apply to all such deeds of trust, mortgages, and obligations secured thereby executed on or after July 1, 1972. *(Added by Stats.1971, c. 429, p. 830, § 1. Amended by Stats.1972, c. 216, p. 451, § 1, eff. June 30, 1972.)*

Research References

Rutter, Cal. Practice Guide: Real Prop. Transactions Ch. 6-F, F. Promissory Note.

Rutter, Cal. Practice Guide: Real Prop. Transactions Ch. 6-H, H. Security for Promissory Note.

Miller and Starr California Real Estate § 10:106, Acceleration on Transfer; "Due-On-Sale" Clause.

Miller and Starr California Real Estate § 10:181.20, Prior Notification, Consultation and Modification Requirements for Owner-Occupied First Lien Mortgage Loans Effective January 1, 2013.

4 Witkin, California Summary 10th Security Transactions in Real Property § 45, Construction of Note and Security Instrument.

4 Witkin, California Summary 10th Security Transactions in Real Property § 88, in General.

§ 2924.6. Acceleration clauses; inapplicability to certain transfers; prohibition of waiver; date of application

(a) An obligee may not accelerate the maturity date of the principal and accrued interest on any loan secured by a mortgage or deed of trust on residential real property solely by reason of any one or more of the following transfers in the title to the real property:

(1) A transfer resulting from the death of an obligor where the transfer is to the spouse who is also an obligor.

(2) A transfer by an obligor where the spouse becomes a coowner of the property.

(3) A transfer resulting from a decree of dissolution of the marriage or legal separation or from a property settlement agreement incidental to such a decree which requires the obligor to continue to make the loan payments by which a spouse who is an obligor becomes the sole owner of the property.

(4) A transfer by an obligor or obligors into an inter vivos trust in which the obligor or obligors are beneficiaries.

(5) Such real property or any portion thereof is made subject to a junior encumbrance or lien.

(b) Any waiver of the provisions of this section by an obligor is void and unenforceable and is contrary to public policy.

(c) For the purposes of this section, "residential real property" means any real property which contains at least one but not more than four housing units.

(d) This act applies only to loans executed or refinanced on or after January 1, 1976. *(Added by Stats.1975, c. 850, p. 1916, § 1.)*

Research References

Rutter, Cal. Practice Guide: Real Prop. Transactions Ch. 6-H, H. Security for Promissory Note.

Miller and Starr California Real Estate § 10:108, Enforceability of the "Due-On-Sale" Clause (The Garn Act).

Miller and Starr California Real Estate § 10:109, Acceleration on Further Encumbrance; "Due on Encumbrance" Clause.

§ 2924.7. Acceleration clause for nonpayment of taxes, rents, assessments, insurance premiums, advances; provision for payment of hazard insurance proceeds to beneficiary, trustee, mortgagee or agent; enforcement of clauses despite impairment of security interest

(a) The provisions of any deed of trust or mortgage on real property which authorize any beneficiary, trustee, mortgagee, or his or her agent or successor in interest, to accelerate the maturity date of the principal and interest on any loan secured thereby or to exercise any power of sale or other remedy contained therein upon the failure of the trustor or mortgagor to pay, at the times provided for under the terms of the deed of trust or mortgage, any taxes, rents, assessments, or insurance premiums with respect to the property or the loan, or any advances made by the beneficiary, mortgagee, or his or her agent or successor in interest shall be enforceable whether or not impairment of the security interest in the property has resulted from the failure of the trustor or mortgagor to pay the taxes, rents, assessments, insurance premiums, or advances.

(b) The provisions of any deed of trust or mortgage on real property which authorize any beneficiary, trustee, mortgagee, or his or her agent or successor in interest, to receive and control the disbursement of the proceeds of any policy of fire, flood, or other hazard insurance respecting the property shall be enforceable whether or not impairment of the security interest in the property has resulted from the event that caused the proceeds of the insurance policy to become payable. *(Added by Stats.1988, c. 179, § 2.)*

Research References

Rutter, Cal. Practice Guide: Real Prop. Transactions Ch. 6-H, H. Security for Promissory Note.

Miller and Starr California Real Estate § 10:60, Payment of Insurance Premiums.

Miller and Starr California Real Estate § 10:61, Rights of the Parties to Insurance Proceeds.

Miller and Starr California Real Estate § 10:134, Nature of Default.

Miller and Starr California Real Estate § 10:135, Curable Versus Noncurable Defaults.

Miller and Starr California Real Estate § 10:137, Failure to Pay Insurance Premiums.

Miller and Starr California Real Estate § 10:138, Failure to Pay Prior Encumbrances.

Miller and Starr California Real Estate § 10:139, Failure to Pay Taxes.

4 Witkin, California Summary 10th Security Transactions in Real Property § 79, (S 79) Payment of Insurance Premiums.

4 Witkin, California Summary 10th Security Transactions in Real Property § 84, (S 84) Security Need Not be Impaired.

§ 2924.8   Required notice for residents of property subject to foreclosure sale

(a)(1) Upon posting a notice of sale pursuant to Section 2924f, a trustee or authorized agent shall also post the following notice, in the manner required for posting the notice of sale on the property to be sold, and a mortgagee, trustee, beneficiary, or authorized agent, concurrently with the mailing of the notice of sale pursuant to Section 2924b, shall send by first-class mail in an envelope addressed to the "Resident of property subject to foreclosure sale" the following notice in English and the languages described in Section 1632:

Foreclosure process has begun on this property, which may affect your right to continue to live in this property. Twenty days or more after the date of this notice, this property may be sold at foreclosure. If you are renting this property, the new property owner may either give you a new lease or rental agreement or provide you with a 90–day eviction notice. You may have a right to stay in your home for longer than 90 days. If you have a fixed-term lease, the new owner must honor the lease unless the new owner will occupy the property as a primary residence or in other limited circumstances. Also, in some cases and in some cities with a "just cause for eviction" law, you may not have to move at all. All rights and obligations under your lease or tenancy, including your obligation to pay rent, will continue after the foreclosure sale. You may wish to contact a lawyer or your local legal aid office or housing counseling agency to discuss any rights you may have.

(2) The amendments to the notice in this subdivision made by the act that added this paragraph [1] shall become operative on March 1, 2013, or 60 days following posting of a dated notice incorporating those amendments on the Department of Consumer Affairs Internet Web site, whichever date is later.

(b) It is an infraction to tear down the notice described in subdivision (a) within 72 hours of posting. Violators shall be subject to a fine of one hundred dollars ($100).

(c) The Department of Consumer Affairs shall make available translations of the notice described in subdivision (a) which may be used by a mortgagee, trustee, beneficiary, or authorized agent to satisfy the requirements of this section.

(d) This section shall only apply to loans secured by residential real property, and if the billing address for the mortgage note is different than the property address.

(e) This section shall remain in effect only until December 31, 2019, and as of that date is repealed, unless a later enacted statute, that is enacted before December 31, 2019, deletes or extends that date. *(Added by Stats.2008, c. 69 (S.B.1137), § 4, eff. July 8, 2008, operative Sept. 6, 2008. Amended by Stats.2009, c. 43 (S.B.306), § 3; Stats.2012, c. 562 (A.B.2610), § 1; Stats. 2013, c. 76 (A.B.383), § 16.)*

[1] Stats.2012, c. 562 (A.B.2610) § 1.

Repeal

For repeal of this section, see its terms.

Research References

Miller and Starr California Real Estate § 10:199, Publication, Mailing, and Recording the Notice.

Miller and Starr California Real Estate § 19:59.10, Termination of Residential Tenancy Following Foreclosure of Landlord's Interest.

19 NO. 1 Miller & Starr, California Real Estate Newsalert 1, The Perata Foreclosure Bill (SB 1137): New Rights for Defaulting Borrowers and Tenants; New Complications for Foreclosing Lenders.

19 NO. 4 Miller & Starr, California Real Estate Newsalert 10, Deeds of Trust.

20 NO. 4 Miller & Starr, California Real Estate Newsalert 6, Deeds of Trust.

4 Witkin, California Summary 10th Security Transactions in Real Property § 151, Posting, Publication, and Recording.

§ 2924.85.   Landlords receiving notice of default on mortgage or deed of trust; notice to prospective tenants; form; violations; remedies; immunity of property managers from liability

(a) Every landlord who offers for rent a single-family dwelling, or a multifamily dwelling not exceeding four units, and who has received a notice of default that has not been rescinded with respect to a mortgage or deed of trust secured by that property shall disclose the notice of default in writing to any prospective tenant prior to executing a lease agreement for the property subject to the notice.

(b) A violation of subdivision (a) shall void the lease at the election of the tenant and shall entitle the tenant to recovery of one month's rent or twice the actual damages, whichever is greater, and all prepaid rent from the landlord who received the notice of default, in addition to any other remedy that the law may provide.

(c) In lieu of the remedies in subdivision (b), if the tenant elects not to terminate the lease and the foreclosure sale has not occurred, the tenant may elect to deduct a total amount equal to one month's rent from future rent obligations owed the landlord who received the notice of default.

(d) The written disclosure notice required by subdivision (a) shall be provided in English and the languages described in Section 1632 substantially in the following form:

The foreclosure process has begun on this property, and this property may be sold at foreclosure. If you rent this property, and a foreclosure sale occurs, the sale may affect your right to continue to live in this property in the future. Your tenancy may continue after the sale. The new owner must honor the lease unless the new owner will occupy the property as a primary residence, or in other limited circumstances. Also, in some cases and in some cities with a "just cause for eviction" law, you may not have to move at all. In order for the new owner to evict you, the new owner must provide you with at least 90 days' written eviction notice in most cases.

(e) A property manager shall not be liable under this section for failure to provide the written disclosure notice in subdivision (d) unless the landlord has notified the property manager of the notice of default and directed him or her in writing to deliver the written disclosure, in which case the property manager shall be liable to the extent specified in subdivision (b). This subdivision shall not preclude a landlord from being held liable when a tenant does not receive the written disclosure notice in subdivision (d).

(f) The rights and remedies provided by this section are in addition to and independent of any other rights and remedies under any other law. Nothing in this section shall be construed to alter, limit, or negate any other rights and remedies.

(g) This section shall remain in effect only until January 1, 2018, and as of that date is repealed, unless a later enacted statute, that is enacted before January 1, 2018, deletes or extends that date. *(Added by Stats.2012, c. 566 (S.B.1191), § 1.)*

§ 2924.9. Mortgage service providers offering one or more foreclosure prevention alternatives; sending of written communication to borrower

Section added by Stats.2012, c. 86 (A.B.278), § 12. See, also, another section of the same number added by Stats.2012, c. 87 (S.B.900), § 12.

(a) Unless a borrower has previously exhausted the first lien loan modification process offered by, or through, his or her mortgage servicer described in Section 2923.6, within five business days after recording a notice of default pursuant to Section 2924, a mortgage servicer that offers one or more foreclosure prevention alternatives shall send a written communication to the borrower that includes all of the following information:

(1) That the borrower may be evaluated for a foreclosure prevention alternative or, if applicable, foreclosure prevention alternatives.

(2) Whether an application is required to be submitted by the borrower in order to be considered for a foreclosure prevention alternative.

(3) The means and process by which a borrower may obtain an application for a foreclosure prevention alternative.

(b) This section shall not apply to entities described in subdivision (b) of Section 2924.18.

(c) This section shall apply only to mortgages or deeds of trust described in Section 2924.15.

(d) This section shall remain in effect only until January 1, 2018, and as of that date is repealed, unless a later enacted statute, that is enacted before January 1, 2018, deletes or extends that date. *(Added by Stats.2012, c. 86 (A.B.278), § 12.)*

Research References

Rutter, Cal. Practice Guide: Real Prop. Transactions Ch. 6-I, I. Real Property Foreclosures and Antideficiency Laws.
Miller and Starr California Real Estate § 4:12, Mortgage Loan Origination, Brokerage, and Servicing.
Miller and Starr California Real Estate § 4:78, Federal and State Regulation of Residential Mortgage Loan Origination and Servicing--In General.
Miller and Starr California Real Estate § 10:181.10, Prior Notification and Consultation for Residential Loans Originated Between January 1, 2003 and December 31, 2007.
Miller and Starr California Real Estate § 10:181.20, Prior Notification, Consultation and Modification Requirements for Owner-Occupied First Lien Mortgage Loans Effective January 1, 2013.

§ 2924.9. Mortgage service providers offering one or more foreclosure prevention alternatives; sending of written communication to borrower

Section added by Stats.2012, c. 87 (S.B.900), § 12. See, also, another section of the same number added by Stats.2012, c. 86 (A.B.278), § 12.

(a) Unless a borrower has previously exhausted the first lien loan modification process offered by, or through, his or her mortgage servicer described in Section 2923.6, within five business days after recording a notice of default pursuant to Section 2924, a mortgage servicer that offers one or more foreclosure prevention alternatives shall send a written communication to the borrower that includes all of the following information:

(1) That the borrower may be evaluated for a foreclosure prevention alternative or, if applicable, foreclosure prevention alternatives.

(2) Whether an application is required to be submitted by the borrower in order to be considered for a foreclosure prevention alternative.

(3) The means and process by which a borrower may obtain an application for a foreclosure prevention alternative.

(b) This section shall not apply to entities described in subdivision (b) of Section 2924.18.

(c) This section shall apply only to mortgages or deeds of trust described in Section 2924.15.

(d) This section shall remain in effect only until January 1, 2018, and as of that date is repealed, unless a later enacted statute, that is enacted before January 1, 2018, deletes or extends that date. *(Added by Stats.2012, c. 87 (S.B.900), § 12.)*

Research References

Rutter, Cal. Practice Guide: Real Prop. Transactions Ch. 6-I, I. Real Property Foreclosures and Antideficiency Laws.
Miller and Starr California Real Estate § 4:12, Mortgage Loan Origination, Brokerage, and Servicing.
Miller and Starr California Real Estate § 4:78, Federal and State Regulation of Residential Mortgage Loan Origination and Servicing--In General.
Miller and Starr California Real Estate § 10:181.10, Prior Notification and Consultation for Residential Loans Originated Between January 1, 2003 and December 31, 2007.
Miller and Starr California Real Estate § 10:181.20, Prior Notification, Consultation and Modification Requirements for Owner-Occupied First Lien Mortgage Loans Effective January 1, 2013.

§ 2924.10. Submission of first lien modification application document; written acknowledgment of receipt

Section added by Stats.2012, c. 86 (A.B.278), § 13. See, also, another section of the same number added by Stats.2012, c. 87 (S.B.900), § 13.

(a) When a borrower submits a complete first lien modification application or any document in connection with a first lien modification application, the mortgage servicer shall provide written acknowledgment of the receipt of the documentation within five business days of receipt. In its initial acknowledgment of receipt of the loan modification application, the mortgage servicer shall include the following information:

(1) A description of the loan modification process, including an estimate of when a decision on the loan modification will be made after a complete application has been submitted by the borrower and the length of time the borrower will have to consider an offer of a loan modification or other foreclosure prevention alternative.

(2) Any deadlines, including deadlines to submit missing documentation, that would affect the processing of a first lien loan modification application.

(3) Any expiration dates for submitted documents.

(4) Any deficiency in the borrower's first lien loan modification application.

(b) For purposes of this section, a borrower's first lien loan modification application shall be deemed to be "complete" when a borrower has supplied the mortgage servicer with all documents required by the mortgage servicer within the reasonable timeframes specified by the mortgage servicer.

(c) This section shall not apply to entities described in subdivision (b) of Section 2924.18.

(d) This section shall apply only to mortgages or deeds of trust described in Section 2924.15.

(e) This section shall remain in effect only until January 1, 2018, and as of that date is repealed, unless a later enacted statute, that is enacted before January 1, 2018, deletes or extends that date. *(Added by Stats.2012, c. 86 (A.B.278), § 13.)*

Repeal

For repeal of this section, see its terms.

Research References

Rutter, Cal. Practice Guide: Real Prop. Transactions Ch. 6-I, I. Real Property Foreclosures and Antideficiency Laws.
Miller and Starr California Real Estate § 4:12, Mortgage Loan Origination, Brokerage, and Servicing.
Miller and Starr California Real Estate § 4:78, Federal and State Regulation of Residential Mortgage Loan Origination and Servicing--In General.
Miller and Starr California Real Estate § 10:181.10, Prior Notification and Consultation for Residential Loans Originated Between January 1, 2003 and December 31, 2007.
Miller and Starr California Real Estate § 10:181.20, Prior Notification, Consultation and Modification Requirements for Owner-Occupied First Lien Mortgage Loans Effective January 1, 2013.

§ 2924.10. Submission of first lien modification application document; written acknowledgment of receipt

Section added by Stats.2012, c. 87 (S.B.900), § 13. See, also, another section of the same number added by Stats.2012, c. 86 (A.B.278), § 13.

(a) When a borrower submits a complete first lien modification application or any document in connection with a first lien modification application, the mortgage servicer shall provide written acknowledgment of the receipt of the documentation within five business days of receipt. In its initial acknowledgment of receipt of the loan modification application, the mortgage servicer shall include the following information:

(1) A description of the loan modification process, including an estimate of when a decision on the loan modification will be made after a complete application has been submitted by the borrower and the length of time the borrower will have to consider an offer of a loan modification or other foreclosure prevention alternative.

(2) Any deadlines, including deadlines to submit missing documentation, that would affect the processing of a first lien loan modification application.

(3) Any expiration dates for submitted documents.

(4) Any deficiency in the borrower's first lien loan modification application.

(b) For purposes of this section, a borrower's first lien loan modification application shall be deemed to be "complete" when a borrower has supplied the mortgage servicer with all documents required by the mortgage servicer within the reasonable timeframes specified by the mortgage servicer.

(c) This section shall not apply to entities described in subdivision (b) of Section 2924.18.

(d) This section shall apply only to mortgages or deeds of trust described in Section 2924.15.

(e) This section shall remain in effect only until January 1, 2018, and as of that date is repealed, unless a later enacted statute, that is enacted before January 1, 2018, deletes or extends that date. *(Added by Stats.2012, c. 87 (S.B.900), § 13.)*

Repeal

For repeal of this section, see its terms.

Research References

Rutter, Cal. Practice Guide: Real Prop. Transactions Ch. 6-I, I. Real Property Foreclosures and Antideficiency Laws.
Miller and Starr California Real Estate § 4:12, Mortgage Loan Origination, Brokerage, and Servicing.
Miller and Starr California Real Estate § 4:78, Federal and State Regulation of Residential Mortgage Loan Origination and Servicing--In General.
Miller and Starr California Real Estate § 10:181.10, Prior Notification and Consultation for Residential Loans Originated Between January 1, 2003 and December 31, 2007.
Miller and Starr California Real Estate § 10:181.20, Prior Notification, Consultation and Modification Requirements for Owner-Occupied First Lien Mortgage Loans Effective January 1, 2013.

§ 2924.11. Approval of foreclosure prevention alternative in writing; circumstances prohibiting recordation of notice of default, recording of notice of sale, or conducting trustee's sale; copy of agreement; recording of rescission of notice of default or cancellation of pending trustee's sale; fees; transfer of loan

Section added by Stats.2012, c. 86 (A.B.278), § 14, operative until Jan. 1, 2018. See, also, section added by Stats.2012, c. 86 (A.B.278), § 15, operative Jan. 1, 2018, another section of the same number added by Stats.2012, c. 87 (S.B.900), § 14, operative until Jan. 1, 2018, and another section of the same number added by Stats.2012, c. 87 (S.B.900), § 15, operative Jan. 1, 2018.

(a) If a foreclosure prevention alternative is approved in writing prior to the recordation of a notice of default, a mortgage servicer, mortgagee, trustee, beneficiary, or authorized agent shall not record a notice of default under either of the following circumstances:

(1) The borrower is in compliance with the terms of a written trial or permanent loan modification, forbearance, or repayment plan.

(2) A foreclosure prevention alternative has been approved in writing by all parties, including, for example, the first lien investor, junior lienholder, and mortgage insurer, as applicable, and proof of funds or financing has been provided to the servicer.

(b) If a foreclosure prevention alternative is approved in writing after the recordation of a notice of default, a mortgage servicer, mortgagee, trustee, beneficiary, or authorized agent shall not record a notice of sale or conduct a trustee's sale under either of the following circumstances:

(1) The borrower is in compliance with the terms of a written trial or permanent loan modification, forbearance, or repayment plan.

(2) A foreclosure prevention alternative has been approved in writing by all parties, including, for example, the first lien investor, junior lienholder, and mortgage insurer, as applicable, and proof of funds or financing has been provided to the servicer.

(c) When a borrower accepts an offered first lien loan modification or other foreclosure prevention alternative, the mortgage servicer shall provide the borrower with a copy of the fully executed loan modification agreement or agreement evidencing the foreclosure prevention alternative following receipt of the executed copy from the borrower.

(d) A mortgagee, beneficiary, or authorized agent shall record a rescission of a notice of default or cancel a pending trustee's sale, if applicable, upon the borrower executing a permanent foreclosure prevention alternative. In the case of a short sale, the rescission or cancellation of the pending trustee's sale shall occur when the short sale has been approved by all parties and proof of funds or financing has been provided to the mortgagee, beneficiary, or authorized agent.

(e) The mortgage servicer shall not charge any application, processing, or other fee for a first lien loan modification or other foreclosure prevention alternative.

(f) The mortgage servicer shall not collect any late fees for periods during which a complete first lien loan modification application is under consideration or a denial is being appealed, the borrower is making timely modification payments, or a foreclosure prevention alternative is being evaluated or exercised.

(g) If a borrower has been approved in writing for a first lien loan modification or other foreclosure prevention alternative, and the servicing of that borrower's loan is transferred or sold to another mortgage servicer, the subsequent mortgage servicer shall continue to honor any previously approved first lien loan modification or other foreclosure prevention alternative, in accordance with the provisions of the act that added this section.

(h) This section shall apply only to mortgages or deeds of trust described in Section 2924.15.

(i) This section shall not apply to entities described in subdivision (b) of Section 2924.18.

(j) This section shall remain in effect only until January 1, 2018, and as of that date is repealed, unless a later enacted statute, that is enacted before January 1, 2018, deletes or extends that date. *(Added by Stats.2012, c. 86 (A.B.278), § 14.)*

Repeal

For repeal of this section, see its terms.

Research References

Rutter, Cal. Practice Guide: Real Prop. Transactions Ch. 6-I, I. Real Property Foreclosures and Antideficiency Laws.

Miller and Starr California Real Estate § 4:12, Mortgage Loan Origination, Brokerage, and Servicing.

Miller and Starr California Real Estate § 4:78, Federal and State Regulation of Residential Mortgage Loan Origination and Servicing--In General.

Miller and Starr California Real Estate § 10:181.10, Prior Notification and Consultation for Residential Loans Originated Between January 1, 2003 and December 31, 2007.

Miller and Starr California Real Estate § 10:181.20, Prior Notification, Consultation and Modification Requirements for Owner-Occupied First Lien Mortgage Loans Effective January 1, 2013.

§ 2924.11. Approval of foreclosure prevention alternative in writing; circumstances prohibiting recordation of notice of default, recording of notice of sale, or conducting trustee's sale; copy of agreement; recording of rescission of notice of default or cancellation of pending trustee's sale; fees; transfer of loan

Section added by Stats.2012, c. 87 (S.B.900), § 14, operative until Jan. 1, 2018. See, also, section added by Stats.2012, c. 87 (S.B.900), § 15, operative Jan. 1, 2018, another section of the same number added by Stats.2012, c. 86 (A.B.278), § 14, operative until Jan. 1, 2018, and another section of the same number added by Stats.2012, c. 86 (A.B.278), § 15, operative Jan. 1, 2018.

(a) If a foreclosure prevention alternative is approved in writing prior to the recordation of a notice of default, a mortgage servicer, mortgagee, trustee, beneficiary, or authorized agent shall not record a notice of default under either of the following circumstances:

(1) The borrower is in compliance with the terms of a written trial or permanent loan modification, forbearance, or repayment plan.

(2) A foreclosure prevention alternative has been approved in writing by all parties, including, for example, the first lien investor, junior lienholder, and mortgage insurer, as applicable, and proof of funds or financing has been provided to the servicer.

(b) If a foreclosure prevention alternative is approved in writing after the recordation of a notice of default, a mortgage servicer, mortgagee, trustee, beneficiary, or authorized agent shall not record a notice of sale or conduct a trustee's sale under either of the following circumstances:

(1) The borrower is in compliance with the terms of a written trial or permanent loan modification, forbearance, or repayment plan.

(2) A foreclosure prevention alternative has been approved in writing by all parties, including, for example, the first lien investor, junior lienholder, and mortgage insurer, as applicable, and proof of funds or financing has been provided to the servicer.

(c) When a borrower accepts an offered first lien loan modification or other foreclosure prevention alternative, the mortgage servicer shall provide the borrower with a copy of the fully executed loan modification agreement or agreement evidencing the foreclosure prevention alternative following receipt of the executed copy from the borrower.

(d) A mortgagee, beneficiary, or authorized agent shall record a rescission of a notice of default or cancel a pending trustee's sale, if applicable, upon the borrower executing a permanent foreclosure prevention alternative. In the case of a short sale, the rescission or cancellation of the pending trustee's sale shall occur when the short sale has been approved by all parties and proof of funds or financing has been provided to the mortgagee, beneficiary, or authorized agent.

(e) The mortgage servicer shall not charge any application, processing, or other fee for a first lien loan modification or other foreclosure prevention alternative.

(f) The mortgage servicer shall not collect any late fees for periods during which a complete first lien loan modification application is under consideration or a denial is being appealed, the borrower is making timely modification payments, or a foreclosure prevention alternative is being evaluated or exercised.

(g) If a borrower has been approved in writing for a first lien loan modification or other foreclosure prevention alternative, and the servicing of that borrower's loan is transferred or sold to another mortgage servicer, the subsequent mortgage servicer shall continue to honor any previously approved first lien loan modification or other foreclosure prevention alternative, in accordance with the provisions of the act that added this section.

(h) This section shall apply only to mortgages or deeds of trust described in Section 2924.15.

(i) This section shall not apply to entities described in subdivision (b) of Section 2924.18.

(j) This section shall remain in effect only until January 1, 2018, and as of that date is repealed, unless a later enacted statute, that is enacted before January 1, 2018, deletes or extends that date. *(Added by Stats.2012, c. 87 (S.B.900), § 14.)*

Repeal

For repeal of this section, see its terms.

Research References

Rutter, Cal. Practice Guide: Real Prop. Transactions Ch. 6-I, I. Real Property Foreclosures and Antideficiency Laws.

Miller and Starr California Real Estate § 4:12, Mortgage Loan Origination, Brokerage, and Servicing.

Miller and Starr California Real Estate § 4:78, Federal and State Regulation of Residential Mortgage Loan Origination and Servicing--In General.

Miller and Starr California Real Estate § 10:181.10, Prior Notification and Consultation for Residential Loans Originated Between January 1, 2003 and December 31, 2007.

Miller and Starr California Real Estate § 10:181.20, Prior Notification, Consultation and Modification Requirements for Owner-Occupied First Lien Mortgage Loans Effective January 1, 2013.

§ 2924.11. Submission of complete foreclosure prevention alternative application; prohibition on recording notice of sale or conducting trustee's sale while application is pending; written notice of denial; approval of foreclosure prevention alternative in writing; circumstances prohibiting recordation of notice of default, recording of notice of sale, or conducting trustee's sale

Section added by Stats.2012, c. 86 (A.B.278), § 15, operative Jan. 1, 2018. See, also, section added by Stats.2012, c. 86 (A.B.278), § 14, operative until Jan. 1, 2018, another section of the same number added by Stats.2012, c. 87 (S.B.900), § 14, operative until Jan. 1, 2018, and another section of the same number added by Stats.2012, c. 87 (S.B.900), § 15, operative Jan. 1, 2018.

(a) If a borrower submits a complete application for a foreclosure prevention alternative offered by, or through, the borrower's mortgage servicer, a mortgage servicer, trustee, mortgagee, beneficiary, or authorized agent shall not record a notice of sale or conduct a trustee's sale while the complete foreclosure prevention alternative application is pending, and until the borrower has been provided with a written determination by the mortgage servicer regarding that borrower's eligibility for the requested foreclosure prevention alternative.

(b) Following the denial of a first lien loan modification application, the mortgage servicer shall send a written notice to the borrower identifying with specificity the reasons for the denial and shall include a statement that the borrower may obtain additional documentation supporting the denial decision upon written request to the mortgage servicer.

(c) If a foreclosure prevention alternative is approved in writing prior to the recordation of a notice of default, a mortgage servicer, mortgagee, trustee, beneficiary, or authorized agent shall not record a notice of default under either of the following circumstances:

(1) The borrower is in compliance with the terms of a written trial or permanent loan modification, forbearance, or repayment plan.

(2) A foreclosure prevention alternative has been approved in writing by all parties, including, for example, the first lien investor, junior lienholder, and mortgage insurer, as applicable, and proof of funds or financing has been provided to the servicer.

(d) If a foreclosure prevention alternative is approved in writing after the recordation of a notice of default, a mortgage servicer, mortgagee, trustee, beneficiary, or authorized agent shall not record a notice of sale or conduct a trustee's sale under either of the following circumstances:

(1) The borrower is in compliance with the terms of a written trial or permanent loan modification, forbearance, or repayment plan.

(2) A foreclosure prevention alternative has been approved in writing by all parties, including, for example, the first lien

investor, junior lienholder, and mortgage insurer, as applicable, and proof of funds or financing has been provided to the servicer.

(e) This section applies only to mortgages or deeds of trust as described in Section 2924.15.

(f) For purposes of this section, an application shall be deemed "complete" when a borrower has supplied the mortgage servicer with all documents required by the mortgage servicer within the reasonable timeframes specified by the mortgage servicer.

(g) This section shall become operative on January 1, 2018. *(Added by Stats.2012, c. 86 (A.B.278), § 15, operative Jan. 1, 2018.)*

Research References

Rutter, Cal. Practice Guide: Real Prop. Transactions Ch. 6-I, I. Real Property Foreclosures and Antideficiency Laws.

Miller and Starr California Real Estate § 4:12, Mortgage Loan Origination, Brokerage, and Servicing.

Miller and Starr California Real Estate § 4:78, Federal and State Regulation of Residential Mortgage Loan Origination and Servicing--In General.

Miller and Starr California Real Estate § 10:181.10, Prior Notification and Consultation for Residential Loans Originated Between January 1, 2003 and December 31, 2007.

Miller and Starr California Real Estate § 10:181.20, Prior Notification, Consultation and Modification Requirements for Owner-Occupied First Lien Mortgage Loans Effective January 1, 2013.

§ 2924.11. Submission of complete foreclosure prevention alternative application; prohibition on recording notice of sale or conducting trustee's sale while application is pending; written notice of denial; approval of foreclosure prevention alternative in writing; circumstances prohibiting recordation of notice of default, recording of notice of sale, or conducting trustee's sale

Section added by Stats.2012, c. 87 (S.B.900), § 15, operative Jan. 1, 2018. See, also, section added by Stats.2012, c. 87 (S.B.900), § 14, operative until Jan. 1, 2018, another section of the same number added by Stats.2012, c. 86 (A.B.278), § 14, operative until Jan. 1, 2018, and another section of the same number added by Stats.2012, c. 86 (A.B.278), § 15, operative Jan. 1, 2018.

(a) If a borrower submits a complete application for a foreclosure prevention alternative offered by, or through, the borrower's mortgage servicer, a mortgage servicer, trustee, mortgagee, beneficiary, or authorized agent shall not record a notice of sale or conduct a trustee's sale while the complete foreclosure prevention alternative application is pending, and until the borrower has been provided with a written determination by the mortgage servicer regarding that borrower's eligibility for the requested foreclosure prevention alternative.

(b) Following the denial of a first lien loan modification application, the mortgage servicer shall send a written notice to the borrower identifying with specificity the reasons for the denial and shall include a statement that the borrower may obtain additional documentation supporting the denial decision upon written request to the mortgage servicer.

(c) If a foreclosure prevention alternative is approved in writing prior to the recordation of a notice of default, a mortgage servicer, mortgagee, trustee, beneficiary, or authorized agent shall not record a notice of default under either of the following circumstances:

(1) The borrower is in compliance with the terms of a written trial or permanent loan modification, forbearance, or repayment plan.

(2) A foreclosure prevention alternative has been approved in writing by all parties, including, for example, the first lien investor, junior lienholder, and mortgage insurer, as applicable, and proof of funds or financing has been provided to the servicer.

(d) If a foreclosure prevention alternative is approved in writing after the recordation of a notice of default, a mortgage servicer, mortgagee, trustee, beneficiary, or authorized agent shall not record a notice of sale or conduct a trustee's sale under either of the following circumstances:

(1) The borrower is in compliance with the terms of a written trial or permanent loan modification, forbearance, or repayment plan.

(2) A foreclosure prevention alternative has been approved in writing by all parties, including, for example, the first lien investor, junior lienholder, and mortgage insurer, as applicable, and proof of funds or financing has been provided to the servicer.

(e) This section applies only to mortgages or deeds of trust as described in Section 2924.15.

(f) For purposes of this section, an application shall be deemed "complete" when a borrower has supplied the mortgage servicer with all documents required by the mortgage servicer within the reasonable timeframes specified by the mortgage servicer.

(g) This section shall become operative on January 1, 2018. *(Added by Stats.2012, c. 87 (S.B.900), § 15, operative Jan. 1, 2018.)*

Research References

Rutter, Cal. Practice Guide: Real Prop. Transactions Ch. 6-I, I. Real Property Foreclosures and Antideficiency Laws.

Miller and Starr California Real Estate § 4:12, Mortgage Loan Origination, Brokerage, and Servicing.

Miller and Starr California Real Estate § 4:78, Federal and State Regulation of Residential Mortgage Loan Origination and Servicing--In General.

Miller and Starr California Real Estate § 10:181.10, Prior Notification and Consultation for Residential Loans Originated Between January 1, 2003 and December 31, 2007.

Miller and Starr California Real Estate § 10:181.20, Prior Notification, Consultation and Modification Requirements for Owner-Occupied First Lien Mortgage Loans Effective January 1, 2013.

§ 2924.12. Material violations of specified foreclosure provisions; action for injunctive relief by borrower prior to recording of trustee's deed upon sale; liability to borrower after recording of trustee's deed upon sale; effect of violation on validity of sale; third-party encumbrancer; signatory to specified consent judgment; attorney's fees and costs

Section added by Stats.2012, c. 86 (A.B.278), § 16, operative until Jan. 1, 2018. See, also, section added by Stats.2012, c. 86 (A.B.278), § 17, operative Jan. 1, 2018, another section of the same number added by Stats.2012, c. 87 (S.B.900), § 16, operative until Jan. 1, 2018, and another section of the same number added by Stats.2012, c. 87 (S.B.900), § 17, operative Jan. 1, 2018.

(a)(1) If a trustee's deed upon sale has not been recorded, a borrower may bring an action for injunctive relief to enjoin a material violation of Section 2923.55, 2923.6, 2923.7, 2924.9, 2924.10, 2924.11, or 2924.17.

(2) Any injunction shall remain in place and any trustee's sale shall be enjoined until the court determines that the mortgage servicer, mortgagee, trustee, beneficiary, or authorized agent has corrected and remedied the violation or violations giving rise to the action for injunctive relief. An enjoined entity may move to dissolve an injunction based on a showing that the material violation has been corrected and remedied.

(b) After a trustee's deed upon sale has been recorded, a mortgage servicer, mortgagee, trustee, beneficiary, or authorized agent shall be liable to a borrower for actual economic damages pursuant to Section 3281, resulting from a material violation of Section 2923.55, 2923.6, 2923.7, 2924.9, 2924.10, 2924.11, or 2924.17 by that mortgage servicer, mortgagee, trustee, beneficiary, or authorized agent where the violation was not corrected and remedied prior to the recordation of the trustee's deed upon sale. If the court finds that the material violation was intentional or reckless, or resulted from willful misconduct by a mortgage servicer, mortgagee, trustee, beneficiary, or authorized agent, the court may award the borrower the greater of treble actual damages or statutory damages of fifty thousand dollars ($50,000).

(c) A mortgage servicer, mortgagee, trustee, beneficiary, or authorized agent shall not be liable for any violation that it has corrected and remedied prior to the recordation of a trustee's deed upon sale, or that has been corrected and remedied by third parties working on its behalf prior to the recordation of a trustee's deed upon sale.

(d) A violation of Section 2923.55, 2923.6, 2923.7, 2924.9, 2924.10, 2924.11, or 2924.17 by a person licensed by the Department of Corporations, Department of Financial Institutions, or Department of Real Estate shall be deemed to be a violation of that person's licensing law.

(e) No violation of this article shall affect the validity of a sale in favor of a bona fide purchaser and any of its encumbrancers for value without notice.

(f) A third-party encumbrancer shall not be relieved of liability resulting from violations of Section 2923.55, 2923.6, 2923.7, 2924.9, 2924.10, 2924.11, or 2924.17 committed by that third-party encumbrancer, that occurred prior to the sale of the subject property to the bona fide purchaser.

(g) A signatory to a consent judgment entered in the case entitled United States of America et al. v. Bank of America Corporation et al., filed in the United States District Court for the District of Columbia, case number 1:12–cv–00361 RMC, that is in compliance with the relevant terms of the Settlement Term Sheet of that consent judgment with respect to the borrower who brought an action pursuant to this section while the consent judgment is in effect shall have no liability for a violation of Section 2923.55, 2923.6, 2923.7, 2924.9, 2924.10, 2924.11, or 2924.17.

(h) The rights, remedies, and procedures provided by this section are in addition to and independent of any other rights, remedies, or procedures under any other law. Nothing in this section shall be construed to alter, limit, or negate any other rights, remedies, or procedures provided by law.

(i) A court may award a prevailing borrower reasonable attorney's fees and costs in an action brought pursuant to this section. A borrower shall be deemed to have prevailed for purposes of this subdivision if the borrower obtained injunctive relief or was awarded damages pursuant to this section.

(j) This section shall not apply to entities described in subdivision (b) of Section 2924.18.

(k) This section shall remain in effect only until January 1, 2018, and as of that date is repealed, unless a later enacted statute, that is enacted before January 1, 2018, deletes or extends that date. *(Added by Stats.2012, c. 86 (A.B.278), § 16.)*

Repeal

For repeal of this section, see its terms.

Research References

Rutter, Cal. Practice Guide: Real Prop. Transactions Ch. 6-I, I. Real Property Foreclosures and Antideficiency Laws.

Miller and Starr California Real Estate § 10:181.10, Prior Notification and Consultation for Residential Loans Originated Between January 1, 2003 and December 31, 2007.

Miller and Starr California Real Estate § 10:181.20, Prior Notification, Consultation and Modification Requirements for Owner-Occupied First Lien Mortgage Loans Effective January 1, 2013.

§ 2924.12. Material violations of specified foreclosure provisions; action for injunctive relief by borrower prior to recording of trustee's deed upon sale; liability to borrower after recording of trustee's deed upon sale; effect of violation on validity of sale; third-party encumbrancer; signatory to specified consent judgment; attorney's fees and costs

Section added by Stats.2012, c. 87 (S.B.900), § 16, operative until Jan. 1, 2018. See, also, section added by Stats.2012, c. 87 (S.B.900), § 17, operative Jan. 1, 2018, another section of the same number added by Stats.2012, c. 86 (A.B.278), § 16, operative until Jan. 1, 2018, and another section of the same number added by Stats.2012, c. 86 (A.B.278), § 17, operative Jan. 1, 2018.

(a)(1) If a trustee's deed upon sale has not been recorded, a borrower may bring an action for injunctive relief to enjoin a material violation of Section 2923.55, 2923.6, 2923.7, 2924.9, 2924.10, 2924.11, or 2924.17.

(2) Any injunction shall remain in place and any trustee's sale shall be enjoined until the court determines that the mortgage servicer, mortgagee, trustee, beneficiary, or authorized agent has corrected and remedied the violation or violations giving rise to the action for injunctive relief. An enjoined entity may move to dissolve an injunction based on a showing that the material violation has been corrected and remedied.

(b) After a trustee's deed upon sale has been recorded, a mortgage servicer, mortgagee, trustee, beneficiary, or authorized agent shall be liable to a borrower for actual economic damages pursuant to Section 3281, resulting from a material violation of Section 2923.55, 2923.6, 2923.7, 2924. 9, 2924.10, 2924.11, or 2924.17 by that mortgage servicer, mortgagee, trustee, beneficiary, or authorized agent where the violation was not corrected and remedied prior to the recordation of the trustee's deed upon sale. If the court finds that the material violation was intentional or reckless, or resulted from willful misconduct by a mortgage servicer, mortgagee, trustee, beneficiary, or authorized agent, the court may award the borrower the greater of treble actual damages or statutory damages of fifty thousand dollars ($50,-000).

(c) A mortgage servicer, mortgagee, trustee, beneficiary, or authorized agent shall not be liable for any violation that it has corrected and remedied prior to the recordation of a trustee's deed upon sale, or that has been corrected and remedied by third parties working on its behalf prior to the recordation of a trustee's deed upon sale.

(d) A violation of Section 2923.55, 2923.6, 2923.7, 2924.9, 2924.10, 2924.11, or 2924.17 by a person licensed by the Department of Corporations, Department of Financial Institutions, or Department of Real Estate shall be deemed to be a violation of that person's licensing law.

(e) No violation of this article shall affect the validity of a sale in favor of a bona fide purchaser and any of its encumbrancers for value without notice.

(f) A third-party encumbrancer shall not be relieved of liability resulting from violations of Section 2923.55, 2923.6, 2923.7, 2924.9, 2924.10, 2924.11, or 2924.17 committed by that third-party encumbrancer, that occurred prior to the sale of the subject property to the bona fide purchaser.

(g) A signatory to a consent judgment entered in the case entitled United States of America et al. v. Bank of America Corporation et al., filed in the United States District Court for the District of Columbia, case number 1:12–cv–00361 RMC, that is in compliance with the relevant terms of the Settlement Term Sheet of that consent judgment with respect to the borrower who brought an action pursuant to this section while the consent judgment is in effect shall have no liability for a violation of Section 2923.55, 2923.6, 2923.7, 2924.9, 2924.10, 2924.11, or 2924.17.

(h) The rights, remedies, and procedures provided by this section are in addition to and independent of any other rights, remedies, or procedures under any other law. Nothing in this section shall be construed to alter, limit, or negate any other rights, remedies, or procedures provided by law.

(i) A court may award a prevailing borrower reasonable attorney's fees and costs in an action brought pursuant to this section. A borrower shall be deemed to have prevailed for purposes of this subdivision if the borrower obtained injunctive relief or was awarded damages pursuant to this section.

(j) This section shall not apply to entities described in subdivision (b) of Section 2924.18.

(k) This section shall remain in effect only until January 1, 2018, and as of that date is repealed, unless a later enacted statute, that is enacted before January 1, 2018, deletes or extends that date. *(Added by Stats.2012, c. 87 (S.B.900), § 16.)*

Repeal

For repeal of this section, see its terms.

Research References

Rutter, Cal. Practice Guide: Real Prop. Transactions Ch. 6-I, I. Real Property Foreclosures and Antideficiency Laws.

Miller and Starr California Real Estate § 10:181.10, Prior Notification and Consultation for Residential Loans Originated Between January 1, 2003 and December 31, 2007.

Miller and Starr California Real Estate § 10:181.20, Prior Notification, Consultation and Modification Requirements for Owner-Occupied First Lien Mortgage Loans Effective January 1, 2013.

§ 2924.12. Material violations of specified foreclosure provisions; action for injunctive relief by borrower prior to recording of trustee's deed upon sale; liability to borrower after recording of trustee's deed upon sale; effect of violation on validity of sale; third-party encumbrancer; attorney's fees and costs

Section added by Stats.2012, c. 86 (A.B.278), § 17, operative Jan. 1, 2018. See, also, section added by Stats.2012, c. 86 (A.B.278), § 16, operative until Jan. 1, 2018, another section of the same number added by Stats.2012, c. 87 (S.B.900), § 16, operative until Jan. 1, 2018, and another section of the same number added by Stats.2012, c. 87 (S.B.900), § 17, operative Jan. 1, 2018.

(a)(1) If a trustee's deed upon sale has not been recorded, a borrower may bring an action for injunctive relief to enjoin a material violation of Section 2923.5, 2923.7, 2924.11, or 2924.17.

(2) Any injunction shall remain in place and any trustee's sale shall be enjoined until the court determines that the mortgage servicer, mortgagee, trustee, beneficiary, or authorized agent has corrected and remedied the violation or violations giving rise to the action for injunctive relief. An enjoined entity may move to dissolve an injunction based on a showing that the material violation has been corrected and remedied.

(b) After a trustee's deed upon sale has been recorded, a mortgage servicer, mortgagee, trustee, beneficiary, or authorized agent shall be liable to a borrower for actual economic damages pursuant to Section 3281, resulting from a material violation of Section 2923.5, 2923.7, 2924.11, or 2924.17 by that mortgage servicer, mortgagee, trustee, beneficiary, or authorized agent where the violation was not corrected and remedied prior to the recordation of the trustee's deed upon sale. If the court finds that the material violation was intentional or reckless, or resulted from willful misconduct by a mortgage servicer, mortgagee, trustee, beneficiary, or authorized agent, the court may award the borrower the greater of treble actual damages or statutory damages of fifty thousand dollars ($50,000).

(c) A mortgage servicer, mortgagee, trustee, beneficiary, or authorized agent shall not be liable for any violation that it has corrected and remedied prior to the recordation of the trustee's deed upon sale, or that has been corrected and remedied by third parties working on its behalf prior to the recordation of the trustee's deed upon sale.

(d) A violation of Section 2923.5, 2923.7, 2924.11, or 2924.17 by a person licensed by the Department of Corporations, Department of Financial Institutions, or Department of Real Estate shall be deemed to be a violation of that person's licensing law.

(e) No violation of this article shall affect the validity of a sale in favor of a bona fide purchaser and any of its encumbrancers for value without notice.

(f) A third-party encumbrancer shall not be relieved of liability resulting from violations of Section 2923.5, 2923.7, 2924.11, or 2924.17 committed by that third-party encumbrancer, that occurred prior to the sale of the subject property to the bona fide purchaser.

(g) The rights, remedies, and procedures provided by this section are in addition to and independent of any other rights, remedies, or procedures under any other law. Nothing in this section shall be construed to alter, limit, or negate any other rights, remedies, or procedures provided by law.

(h) A court may award a prevailing borrower reasonable attorney's fees and costs in an action brought pursuant to this section. A borrower shall be deemed to have prevailed for purposes of this subdivision if the borrower obtained injunctive relief or was awarded damages pursuant to this section.

(i) This section shall become operative on January 1, 2018. (Added by Stats.2012, c. 86 (A.B.278), § 17, operative Jan. 1, 2018.)

Research References

Rutter, Cal. Practice Guide: Real Prop. Transactions Ch. 6-I, I. Real Property Foreclosures and Antideficiency Laws.

Miller and Starr California Real Estate § 10:181.10, Prior Notification and Consultation for Residential Loans Originated Between January 1, 2003 and December 31, 2007.

Miller and Starr California Real Estate § 10:181.20, Prior Notification, Consultation and Modification Requirements for Owner-Occupied First Lien Mortgage Loans Effective January 1, 2013.

§ 2924.12. Material violations of specified foreclosure provisions; action for injunctive relief by borrower prior to recording of trustee's deed upon sale; liability to borrower after recording of trustee's deed upon sale; effect of violation on validity of sale; third-party encumbrancer; attorney's fees and costs

Section added by Stats.2012, c. 87 (S.B.900), § 17, operative Jan. 1, 2018. See, also, section added by Stats.2012, c. 87 (S.B.900), § 16, operative until Jan. 1, 2018, another section of the same number added by Stats.2012, c. 86 (A.B.278), § 16, operative until Jan. 1, 2018, and another section of the same number added by Stats.2012, c. 86 (A.B.278), § 17, operative Jan. 1, 2018.

(a)(1) If a trustee's deed upon sale has not been recorded, a borrower may bring an action for injunctive relief to enjoin a material violation of Section 2923.5, 2923.7, 2924.11, or 2924.17.

(2) Any injunction shall remain in place and any trustee's sale shall be enjoined until the court determines that the mortgage servicer, mortgagee, trustee, beneficiary, or authorized agent has corrected and remedied the violation or violations giving rise to the action for injunctive relief. An enjoined entity may move to dissolve an injunction based on a showing that the material violation has been corrected and remedied.

(b) After a trustee's deed upon sale has been recorded, a mortgage servicer, mortgagee, trustee, beneficiary, or authorized agent shall be liable to a borrower for actual economic damages pursuant to Section 3281, resulting from a material violation of Section 2923.5, 2923.7, 2924.11, or 2924.17 by that mortgage servicer, mortgagee, trustee, beneficiary, or authorized agent where the violation was not corrected and remedied prior to the recordation of the trustee's deed upon sale. If the court finds that the material violation was intentional or reckless, or resulted from willful misconduct by a mortgage servicer, mortgagee, trustee, beneficiary, or authorized agent, the court may award the borrower the greater of treble actual damages or statutory damages of fifty thousand dollars ($50,000).

(c) A mortgage servicer, mortgagee, trustee, beneficiary, or authorized agent shall not be liable for any violation that it has corrected and remedied prior to the recordation of the trustee's deed upon sale, or that has been corrected and remedied by third parties working on its behalf prior to the recordation of the trustee's deed upon sale.

(d) A violation of Section 2923.5, 2923.7, 2924.11, or 2924.17 by a person licensed by the Department of Corporations, Department of Financial Institutions, or Department of Real Estate shall be deemed to be a violation of that person's licensing law.

(e) No violation of this article shall affect the validity of a sale in favor of a bona fide purchaser and any of its encumbrancers for value without notice.

(f) A third-party encumbrancer shall not be relieved of liability resulting from violations of Section 2923.5, 2923.7, 2924.11, or 2924.17 committed by that third-party encumbrancer, that occurred prior to the sale of the subject property to the bona fide purchaser.

(g) The rights, remedies, and procedures provided by this section are in addition to and independent of any other rights, remedies, or procedures under any other law. Nothing in this section shall be construed to alter, limit, or negate any other rights, remedies, or procedures provided by law.

(h) A court may award a prevailing borrower reasonable attorney's fees and costs in an action brought pursuant to this section. A borrower shall be deemed to have prevailed for purposes of this subdivision if the borrower obtained injunctive relief or was awarded damages pursuant to this section.

(i) This section shall become operative on January 1, 2018. (Added by Stats.2012, c. 87 (S.B.900), § 17, operative Jan. 1, 2018.)

Research References

Rutter, Cal. Practice Guide: Real Prop. Transactions Ch. 6-I, I. Real Property Foreclosures and Antideficiency Laws.

Miller and Starr California Real Estate § 10:181.10, Prior Notification and Consultation for Residential Loans Originated Between January 1, 2003 and December 31, 2007.

Miller and Starr California Real Estate § 10:181.20, Prior Notification, Consultation and Modification Requirements for Owner-Occupied First Lien Mortgage Loans Effective January 1, 2013.

§ 2924.15. Application of specified provisions only to first lien mortgages or deeds of trust secured by owner-occupied residential real property containing no more than four dwelling units

Section added by Stats.2012, c. 86 (A.B.278), § 18, operative until Jan. 1, 2018. See, also, section added by Stats.2012, c. 86 (A.B.278), § 19, operative Jan. 1, 2018, another section of the same number added by Stats.2012, c. 87 (S.B.900), § 18, operative until Jan. 1, 2018, and another section of the same number added by Stats.2012, c. 87 (S.B.900), § 19, operative Jan. 1, 2018.

(a) Unless otherwise provided, paragraph (5) of subdivision (a) of Section 2924, and Sections 2923.5, 2923.55, 2923.6, 2923.7, 2924.9, 2924.10, 2924.11, and 2924.18 shall apply only to first lien mortgages or deeds of trust that are secured by owner-occupied residential real property containing no more than four dwelling units. For these purposes, "owner-occupied" means that the property is the principal residence of the borrower and is security for a loan made for personal, family, or household purposes.

(b) This section shall remain in effect only until January 1, 2018, and as of that date is repealed, unless a later enacted statute, that is enacted before January 1, 2018, deletes or extends that date. *(Added by Stats.2012, c. 86 (A.B.278), § 18.)*

Repeal

For repeal of this section, see its terms.

Research References

Miller and Starr California Real Estate § 4:12, Mortgage Loan Origination, Brokerage, and Servicing.

Miller and Starr California Real Estate § 4:78, Federal and State Regulation of Residential Mortgage Loan Origination and Servicing--In General.

Miller and Starr California Real Estate § 10:181, Notice of Default--In General.

Miller and Starr California Real Estate § 10:221, Comparison With Nonjudicial Foreclosure.

Miller and Starr California Real Estate § 10:181.10, Prior Notification and Consultation for Residential Loans Originated Between January 1, 2003 and December 31, 2007.

Miller and Starr California Real Estate § 10:181.20, Prior Notification, Consultation and Modification Requirements for Owner-Occupied First Lien Mortgage Loans Effective January 1, 2013.

§ 2924.15. Application of specified provisions only to first lien mortgages or deeds of trust secured by owner-occupied residential real property containing no more than four dwelling units

Section added by Stats.2012, c. 87 (S.B.900), § 18, operative until Jan. 1, 2018. See, also, section added by Stats.2012, c. 87 (S.B.900), § 19, operative Jan. 1, 2018, another section of the same number added by Stats.2012, c. 86 (A.B.278), § 18, operative until Jan. 1, 2018, and another section of the same number added by Stats.2012, c. 86 (A.B.278), § 19, operative Jan. 1, 2018.

(a) Unless otherwise provided, paragraph (5) of subdivision (a) of Section 2924, and Sections 2923.5, 2923.55, 2923.6, 2923.7, 2924.9, 2924.10, 2924.11, and 2924.18 shall apply only to first lien mortgages or deeds of trust that are secured by owner-occupied residential real property containing no more than four dwelling units. For these purposes, "owner-occupied" means that the property is the principal residence of the borrower and is security for a loan made for personal, family, or household purposes.

(b) This section shall remain in effect only until January 1, 2018, and as of that date is repealed, unless a later enacted statute, that is enacted before January 1, 2018, deletes or extends that date. *(Added by Stats.2012, c. 87 (S.B.900), § 18.)*

Repeal

For repeal of this section, see its terms.

Research References

Miller and Starr California Real Estate § 4:12, Mortgage Loan Origination, Brokerage, and Servicing.

Miller and Starr California Real Estate § 4:78, Federal and State Regulation of Residential Mortgage Loan Origination and Servicing--In General.

Miller and Starr California Real Estate § 10:181, Notice of Default--In General.

Miller and Starr California Real Estate § 10:221, Comparison With Nonjudicial Foreclosure.

Miller and Starr California Real Estate § 10:181.10, Prior Notification and Consultation for Residential Loans Originated Between January 1, 2003 and December 31, 2007.

Miller and Starr California Real Estate § 10:181.20, Prior Notification, Consultation and Modification Requirements for Owner-Occupied First Lien Mortgage Loans Effective January 1, 2013.

§ 2924.15. Application of specified provisions only to first lien mortgages or deeds of trust secured by owner-occupied residential real property containing no more than four dwelling units

Section added by Stats.2012, c. 86 (A.B.278), § 19, operative Jan. 1, 2018. See, also, section added by Stats.2012, c. 86 (A.B.278), § 18, operative until Jan. 1, 2018, another section of the same number added by Stats.2012, c. 87 (S.B.900), § 18, operative until Jan. 1, 2018, and another section of the same number added by Stats.2012, c. 87 (S.B.900), § 19, operative Jan. 1, 2018.

(a) Unless otherwise provided, Sections 2923.5, 2923.7, and 2924.11 shall apply only to first lien mortgages or deeds of trust that are secured by owner-occupied residential real property containing no more than four dwelling units. For these purposes, "owner-occupied" means that the property is the principal residence of the borrower and is security for a loan made for personal, family, or household purposes.

(b) This section shall become operative on January 1, 2018. *(Added by Stats.2012, c. 86 (A.B.278), § 19, operative Jan. 1, 2018.)*

Research References

Miller and Starr California Real Estate § 4:12, Mortgage Loan Origination, Brokerage, and Servicing.

Miller and Starr California Real Estate § 4:78, Federal and State Regulation of Residential Mortgage Loan Origination and Servicing--In General.

Miller and Starr California Real Estate § 10:181, Notice of Default--In General.

Miller and Starr California Real Estate § 10:221, Comparison With Nonjudicial Foreclosure.

Miller and Starr California Real Estate § 10:181.10, Prior Notification and Consultation for Residential Loans Originated Between January 1, 2003 and December 31, 2007.

Miller and Starr California Real Estate § 10:181.20, Prior Notification, Consultation and Modification Requirements for Owner-Occupied First Lien Mortgage Loans Effective January 1, 2013.

§ 2924.15. Application of specified provisions only to first lien mortgages or deeds of trust secured by owner-occupied residential real property containing no more than four dwelling units

Section added by Stats.2012, c. 87 (S.B.900), § 19, operative Jan. 1, 2018. See, also, section added by

Stats.2012, c. 87 (S.B.900), § 18, operative until Jan. 1, 2018, another section of the same number added by Stats.2012, c. 86 (A.B.278), § 18, operative until Jan. 1, 2018, and another section of the same number added by Stats.2012, c. 86 (A.B.278), § 19, operative Jan. 1, 2018.

(a) Unless otherwise provided, Sections 2923.5, 2923.7, and 2924.11 shall apply only to first lien mortgages or deeds of trust that are secured by owner-occupied residential real property containing no more than four dwelling units. For these purposes, "owner-occupied" means that the property is the principal residence of the borrower and is security for a loan made for personal, family, or household purposes.

(b) This section shall become operative on January 1, 2018. *(Added by Stats.2012, c. 87 (S.B.900), § 19, operative Jan. 1, 2018.)*

Research References

Miller and Starr California Real Estate § 4:12, Mortgage Loan Origination, Brokerage, and Servicing.

Miller and Starr California Real Estate § 4:78, Federal and State Regulation of Residential Mortgage Loan Origination and Servicing--In General.

Miller and Starr California Real Estate § 10:181, Notice of Default--In General.

Miller and Starr California Real Estate § 10:221, Comparison With Nonjudicial Foreclosure.

Miller and Starr California Real Estate § 10:181.10, Prior Notification and Consultation for Residential Loans Originated Between January 1, 2003 and December 31, 2007.

Miller and Starr California Real Estate § 10:181.20, Prior Notification, Consultation and Modification Requirements for Owner-Occupied First Lien Mortgage Loans Effective January 1, 2013.

§ 2924.17. Requirement that specified declarations or affidavits be accurate and complete and supported by competent and reliable evidence; review by mortgage servicer; liability for multiple and repeated uncorrected recording or filing violations

Section added by Stats.2012, c. 86 (A.B.278), § 20. See, also, another section of the same number added by Stats.2012, c. 87 (S.B.900), § 20.

(a) A declaration recorded pursuant to Section 2923.5 or, until January 1, 2018, pursuant to Section 2923.55, a notice of default, notice of sale, assignment of a deed of trust, or substitution of trustee recorded by or on behalf of a mortgage servicer in connection with a foreclosure subject to the requirements of Section 2924, or a declaration or affidavit filed in any court relative to a foreclosure proceeding shall be accurate and complete and supported by competent and reliable evidence.

(b) Before recording or filing any of the documents described in subdivision (a), a mortgage servicer shall ensure that it has reviewed competent and reliable evidence to substantiate the borrower's default and the right to foreclose, including the borrower's loan status and loan information.

(c) Until January 1, 2018, any mortgage servicer that engages in multiple and repeated uncorrected violations of subdivision (b) in recording documents or filing documents in any court relative to a foreclosure proceeding shall be liable for a civil penalty of up to seven thousand five hundred dollars ($7,500) per mortgage or deed of trust in an action brought by a government entity identified in Section 17204 of the Business and Professions Code, or in an administrative proceeding brought by the Department of Corporations, the Department of Real Estate, or the Department of Financial Institutions against a respective licensee, in addition to any other remedies available to these entities. This subdivision shall be inoperative on January 1, 2018. *(Added by Stats.2012, c. 86 (A.B.278), § 20.)*

Research References

Rutter, Cal. Practice Guide: Real Prop. Transactions Ch. 6-I, I. Real Property Foreclosures and Antideficiency Laws.

Rutter, Cal. Practice Guide: Real Prop. Transactions Gen. Matls., Highlights.

Miller and Starr California Real Estate § 10:184, Execution of the Notice of Default.

Miller and Starr California Real Estate § 10:185, Recording and Mailing.

Miller and Starr California Real Estate § 10:199, Publication, Mailing, and Recording the Notice.

Miller and Starr California Real Estate § 10:181.10, Prior Notification and Consultation for Residential Loans Originated Between January 1, 2003 and December 31, 2007.

Miller and Starr California Real Estate § 10:181.20, Prior Notification, Consultation and Modification Requirements for Owner-Occupied First Lien Mortgage Loans Effective January 1, 2013.

§ 2924.17. Requirement that specified declarations or affidavits be accurate and complete and supported by competent and reliable evidence; review by mortgage servicer; liability for multiple and repeated uncorrected recording or filing violations

Section added by Stats.2012, c. 87 (S.B.900), § 20. See, also, another section of the same number added by Stats.2012, c. 86 (A.B.278), § 20.

(a) A declaration recorded pursuant to Section 2923.5 or, until January 1, 2018, pursuant to Section 2923.55, a notice of default, notice of sale, assignment of a deed of trust, or substitution of trustee recorded by or on behalf of a mortgage servicer in connection with a foreclosure subject to the requirements of Section 2924, or a declaration or affidavit filed in any court relative to a foreclosure proceeding shall be accurate and complete and supported by competent and reliable evidence.

(b) Before recording or filing any of the documents described in subdivision (a), a mortgage servicer shall ensure that it has reviewed competent and reliable evidence to substantiate the borrower's default and the right to foreclose, including the borrower's loan status and loan information.

(c) Until January 1, 2018, any mortgage servicer that engages in multiple and repeated uncorrected violations of subdivision (b) in recording documents or filing documents in any court relative to a foreclosure proceeding shall be liable for a civil penalty of up to seven thousand five hundred dollars ($7,500) per mortgage or deed of trust in an action brought by a government entity identified in Section 17204 of the Business and Professions Code, or in an administrative proceeding brought by the Department of Corporations, the Department of Real Estate, or the Department of Financial Institutions against a respective licensee, in addition to any other remedies available to these entities. This subdivision shall be inoperative on January 1, 2018. *(Added by Stats.2012, c. 87 (S.B.900), § 20.)*

Research References

Rutter, Cal. Practice Guide: Real Prop. Transactions Ch. 6-I, I. Real Property Foreclosures and Antideficiency Laws.

Rutter, Cal. Practice Guide: Real Prop. Transactions Gen. Matls., Highlights.

Miller and Starr California Real Estate § 10:184, Execution of the Notice of Default.

Miller and Starr California Real Estate § 10:185, Recording and Mailing.

Miller and Starr California Real Estate § 10:199, Publication, Mailing, and Recording the Notice.

Miller and Starr California Real Estate § 10:181.10, Prior Notification and Consultation for Residential Loans Originated Between January 1, 2003 and December 31, 2007.

Miller and Starr California Real Estate § 10:181.20, Prior Notification, Consultation and Modification Requirements for Owner-Occupied First Lien Mortgage Loans Effective January 1, 2013.

§ 2924.18. Submission of complete first lien loan modification application; prohibition on recording notice of default, notice of sale, or conducting trustee's sale while application is pending; approval of foreclosure prevention alternative in writing; circumstances prohibiting recordation of notice of default, recording of notice of sale, or conducting trustee's sale; application to specified entities meeting foreclosure threshold; notification to primary regulator when threshold is exceeded; transfer of loan

Section added by Stats.2012, c. 86 (A.B.278), § 21. See, also, another section of the same number added by Stats.2012, c. 87 (S.B.900), § 21.

(a)(1) If a borrower submits a complete application for a first lien loan modification offered by, or through, the borrower's mortgage servicer, a mortgage servicer, trustee, mortgagee, beneficiary, or authorized agent shall not record a notice of default, notice of sale, or conduct a trustee's sale while the complete first lien loan modification application is pending, and until the borrower has been provided with a written determination by the mortgage servicer regarding that borrower's eligibility for the requested loan modification.

(2) If a foreclosure prevention alternative has been approved in writing prior to the recordation of a notice of default, a mortgage servicer, mortgagee, trustee, beneficiary, or authorized agent shall not record a notice of default under either of the following circumstances:

(A) The borrower is in compliance with the terms of a written trial or permanent loan modification, forbearance, or repayment plan.

(B) A foreclosure prevention alternative has been approved in writing by all parties, including, for example, the first lien investor, junior lienholder, and mortgage insurer, as applicable, and proof of funds or financing has been provided to the servicer.

(3) If a foreclosure prevention alternative is approved in writing after the recordation of a notice of default, a mortgage servicer, mortgagee, trustee, beneficiary, or authorized agent shall not record a notice of sale or conduct a trustee's sale under either of the following circumstances:

(A) The borrower is in compliance with the terms of a written trial or permanent loan modification, forbearance, or repayment plan.

(B) A foreclosure prevention alternative has been approved in writing by all parties, including, for example, the first lien investor, junior lienholder, and mortgage insurer, as applicable, and proof of funds or financing has been provided to the servicer.

(b) This section shall apply only to a depository institution chartered under state or federal law, a person licensed pursuant to Division 9 (commencing with Section 22000) or Division 20 (commencing with Section 50000) of the Financial Code, or a person licensed pursuant to Part 1 (commencing with Section 10000) of Division 4 of the Business and Professions Code, that, during its immediately preceding annual reporting period, as established with its primary regulator, foreclosed on 175 or fewer residential real properties, containing no more than four dwelling units, that are located in California.

(c) Within three months after the close of any calendar year or annual reporting period as established with its primary regulator during which an entity or person described in subdivision (b) exceeds the threshold of 175 specified in subdivision (b), that entity shall notify its primary regulator, in a manner acceptable to its primary regulator, and any mortgagor or trustor who is delinquent on a residential mortgage loan serviced by that entity of the date on which that entity will be subject to Sections 2923.55, 2923.6, 2923.7, 2924.9, 2924.10, 2924.11, and 2924.12, which date shall be the first day of the first month that is six months after the close of the calendar year or annual reporting period during which that entity exceeded the threshold.

(d) For purposes of this section, an application shall be deemed "complete" when a borrower has supplied the mortgage servicer with all documents required by the mortgage servicer within the reasonable timeframes specified by the mortgage servicer.

(e) If a borrower has been approved in writing for a first lien loan modification or other foreclosure prevention alternative, and the servicing of the borrower's loan is transferred or sold to another mortgage servicer, the subsequent mortgage servicer shall continue to honor any previously approved first lien loan modification or other foreclosure prevention alternative, in accordance with the provisions of the act that added this section.

(f) This section shall apply only to mortgages or deeds of trust described in Section 2924.15.

(g) This section shall remain in effect only until January 1, 2018, and as of that date is repealed, unless a later enacted statute, that is enacted before January 1, 2018, deletes or extends that date. *(Added by Stats.2012, c. 86 (A.B.278), § 21.)*

Repeal

For repeal of this section, see its terms.

Research References

Rutter, Cal. Practice Guide: Real Prop. Transactions Ch. 6-I, I. Real Property Foreclosures and Antideficiency Laws.
Miller and Starr California Real Estate § 4:12, Mortgage Loan Origination, Brokerage, and Servicing.
Miller and Starr California Real Estate § 4:78, Federal and State Regulation of Residential Mortgage Loan Origination and Servicing--In General.
Miller and Starr California Real Estate § 10:181.10, Prior Notification and Consultation for Residential Loans Originated Between January 1, 2003 and December 31, 2007.
Miller and Starr California Real Estate § 10:181.20, Prior Notification, Consultation and Modification Requirements for Owner-Occupied First Lien Mortgage Loans Effective January 1, 2013.

§ 2924.18. Submission of complete first lien loan modification application; prohibition on recording notice of default, notice of sale, or conducting trustee's sale while application is pending; approval of foreclosure prevention alternative in writing; circumstances prohibiting recordation of notice of default, recording of notice of sale, or conducting trustee's sale; application to specified entities meeting foreclosure threshold; notification to primary regulator when threshold is exceeded; transfer of loan

Section added by Stats.2012, c. 87 (S.B.900), § 21. See, also, another section of the same number added by Stats.2012, c. 86 (A.B.278), § 21.

(a)(1) If a borrower submits a complete application for a first lien loan modification offered by, or through, the borrower's mortgage servicer, a mortgage servicer, trustee, mortgagee, beneficiary, or authorized agent shall not record a notice of default, notice of sale, or conduct a trustee's sale while the complete first lien loan modification application is pending, and until the borrower has been provided with a written determination by the mortgage servicer regarding that borrower's eligibility for the requested loan modification.

(2) If a foreclosure prevention alternative has been approved in writing prior to the recordation of a notice of default, a mortgage servicer, mortgagee, trustee, beneficiary, or authorized agent shall not record a notice of default under either of the following circumstances:

(A) The borrower is in compliance with the terms of a written trial or permanent loan modification, forbearance, or repayment plan.

(B) A foreclosure prevention alternative has been approved in writing by all parties, including, for example, the first lien investor, junior lienholder, and mortgage insurer, as applicable, and proof of funds or financing has been provided to the servicer.

(3) If a foreclosure prevention alternative is approved in writing after the recordation of a notice of default, a mortgage servicer, mortgagee, trustee, beneficiary, or authorized agent shall not record a notice of sale or conduct a trustee's sale under either of the following circumstances:

(A) The borrower is in compliance with the terms of a written trial or permanent loan modification, forbearance, or repayment plan.

(B) A foreclosure prevention alternative has been approved in writing by all parties, including, for example, the first lien investor, junior lienholder, and mortgage insurer, as applicable, and proof of funds or financing has been provided to the servicer.

(b) This section shall apply only to a depository institution chartered under state or federal law, a person licensed pursuant to Division 9 (commencing with Section 22000) or Division 20 (commencing with Section 50000) of the Financial Code, or a person licensed pursuant to Part 1 (commencing with Section 10000) of Division 4 of the Business and Professions Code, that, during its immediately preceding annual reporting period, as established with its primary regulator, foreclosed on 175 or fewer residential real properties, containing no more than four dwelling units, that are located in California.

(c) Within three months after the close of any calendar year or annual reporting period as established with its primary regulator during which an entity or person described in subdivision (b) exceeds the threshold of 175 specified in subdivision (b), that entity shall notify its primary regulator, in a manner acceptable to its primary regulator, and any mortgagor or trustor who is delinquent on a residential mortgage loan serviced by that entity of the date on which that entity will be subject to Sections 2923.55, 2923.6, 2923.7, 2924.9, 2924.10, 2924.11, and 2924.12, which date shall be the first day of the first month that is six months after the close of the calendar year or annual reporting period during which that entity exceeded the threshold.

(d) For purposes of this section, an application shall be deemed "complete" when a borrower has supplied the mortgage servicer with all documents required by the mortgage servicer within the reasonable timeframes specified by the mortgage servicer.

(e) If a borrower has been approved in writing for a first lien loan modification or other foreclosure prevention alternative, and the servicing of the borrower's loan is transferred or sold to another mortgage servicer, the subsequent mortgage servicer shall continue to honor any previously approved first lien loan modification or other foreclosure prevention alternative, in accordance with the provisions of the act that added this section.

(f) This section shall apply only to mortgages or deeds of trust described in Section 2924.15.

(g) This section shall remain in effect only until January 1, 2018, and as of that date is repealed, unless a later enacted statute, that is enacted before January 1, 2018, deletes or extends that date. *(Added by Stats.2012, c. 87 (S.B.900), § 21.)*

Repeal

For repeal of this section, see its terms.

Research References

Rutter, Cal. Practice Guide: Real Prop. Transactions Ch. 6-I, I. Real Property Foreclosures and Antideficiency Laws.

Miller and Starr California Real Estate § 4:12, Mortgage Loan Origination, Brokerage, and Servicing.

Miller and Starr California Real Estate § 4:78, Federal and State Regulation of Residential Mortgage Loan Origination and Servicing--In General.

Miller and Starr California Real Estate § 10:181.10, Prior Notification and Consultation for Residential Loans Originated Between January 1, 2003 and December 31, 2007.

Miller and Starr California Real Estate § 10:181.20, Prior Notification, Consultation and Modification Requirements for Owner-Occupied First Lien Mortgage Loans Effective January 1, 2013.

§ 2924.19. Material violations of specified foreclosure provisions; action for injunctive relief by borrower prior to recording of trustee's deed upon sale; liability to borrower after recording of trustee's deed upon sale; effect of violation on validity of sale; third-party encumbrancer; attorney's fees and costs; application to entities described in subdivision (b) of Section 2924.18

Section added by Stats.2012, c. 86 (A.B.278), § 22. See, also, another section of the same number added by Stats.2012, c. 87 (S.B.900), § 22

(a)(1) If a trustee's deed upon sale has not been recorded, a borrower may bring an action for injunctive relief to enjoin a material violation of Section 2923.5, 2924.17, or 2924.18.

(2) An injunction shall remain in place and any trustee's sale shall be enjoined until the court determines that the mortgage servicer, mortgagee, beneficiary, or authorized agent has corrected and remedied the violation or violations giving rise to the action for injunctive relief. An enjoined entity may move to dissolve an injunction based on a showing that the material violation has been corrected and remedied.

(b) After a trustee's deed upon sale has been recorded, a mortgage servicer, mortgagee, beneficiary, or authorized agent shall be liable to a borrower for actual economic damages pursuant to Section 3281, resulting from a material violation of Section 2923.5, 2924.17, or 2924.18 by that mortgage servicer, mortgagee, beneficiary, or authorized agent where the violation was not corrected and remedied prior to the recordation of the trustee's deed upon sale. If the court finds that the material violation was intentional or reckless, or resulted from willful misconduct by a mortgage servicer, mortgagee, beneficiary, or authorized agent, the court may award the borrower the greater of treble actual damages or statutory damages of fifty thousand dollars ($50,000).

(c) A mortgage servicer, mortgagee, beneficiary, or authorized agent shall not be liable for any violation that it has corrected and remedied prior to the recordation of the trustee's deed upon sale, or that has been corrected and remedied by third parties working on its behalf prior to the recordation of the trustee's deed upon sale.

(d) A violation of Section 2923.5, 2924.17, or 2924.18 by a person licensed by the Department of Corporations, the Department of Financial Institutions, or the Department of Real Estate shall be deemed to be a violation of that person's licensing law.

(e) A violation of this article shall not affect the validity of a sale in favor of a bona fide purchaser and any of its encumbrancers for value without notice.

(f) A third-party encumbrancer shall not be relieved of liability resulting from violations of Section 2923.5, 2924.17, or 2924.18, committed by that third-party encumbrancer, that occurred prior to the sale of the subject property to the bona fide purchaser.

(g) The rights, remedies, and procedures provided by this section are in addition to and independent of any other rights, remedies, or procedures under any other law. Nothing in this section shall be construed to alter, limit, or negate any other rights, remedies, or procedures provided by law.

(h) A court may award a prevailing borrower reasonable attorney's fees and costs in an action brought pursuant to this section. A borrower shall be deemed to have prevailed for purposes of this subdivision if the borrower obtained injunctive relief or damages pursuant to this section.

(i) This section shall apply only to entities described in subdivision (b) of Section 2924.18.

(j) This section shall remain in effect only until January 1, 2018, and as of that date is repealed, unless a later enacted statute, that is enacted before January 1, 2018, deletes or extends that date. *(Added by Stats.2012, c. 86 (A.B.278), § 22. Amended by Stats.2013, c. 76 (A.B.383), § 17.)*

Repeal

For repeal of this section, see its terms.

Research References

Rutter, Cal. Practice Guide: Real Prop. Transactions Ch. 6-I, I. Real Property Foreclosures and Antideficiency Laws.

Miller and Starr California Real Estate § 4:12, Mortgage Loan Origination, Brokerage, and Servicing.

Miller and Starr California Real Estate § 4:78, Federal and State Regulation of Residential Mortgage Loan Origination and Servicing--In General.

§ 2924.19. Material violations of specified foreclosure provisions; action for injunctive relief by borrower prior to recording of trustee's deed upon sale; liability to borrower after recording of trustee's deed upon sale; effect of violation on validity of sale; third-party encumbrancer; attorney's fees and costs; application to entities described in subdivision (b) of Section 2924.18

Section added by Stats.2012, c. 87 (S.B.900), § 22. See, also, another section of the same number added by Stats.2012, c. 86 (A.B.278), § 22.

(a)(1) If a trustee's deed upon sale has not been recorded, a borrower may bring an action for injunctive relief to enjoin a material violation of Section 2923.5, 2924.17, or 2924.18.

(2) An injunction shall remain in place and any trustee's sale shall be enjoined until the court determines that the mortgage servicer, mortgagee, beneficiary, or authorized agent has corrected and remedied the violation or violations giving rise to the action for injunctive relief. An enjoined entity may move to dissolve an injunction based on a showing that the material violation has been corrected and remedied.

(b) After a trustee's deed upon sale has been recorded, a mortgage servicer, mortgagee, beneficiary, or authorized agent shall be liable to a borrower for actual economic damages pursuant to Section 3281, resulting from a material violation of Section 2923.5, 2924.17, or 2924.18 by that mortgage servicer, mortgagee, beneficiary, or authorized agent where the violation was not corrected and remedied prior to the recordation of the trustee's deed upon sale. If the court finds that the material violation was intentional or reckless, or resulted from willful misconduct by a mortgage servicer, mortgagee, beneficiary, or authorized agent, the court may award the borrower the greater of treble actual damages or statutory damages of fifty thousand dollars ($50,000).

(c) A mortgage servicer, mortgagee, beneficiary, or authorized agent shall not be liable for any violation that it has corrected and remedied prior to the recordation of the trustee's

deed upon sale, or that has been corrected and remedied by third parties working on its behalf prior to the recordation of the trustee's deed upon sale.

(d) A violation of Section 2923.5, 2924.17, or 2924.18 by a person licensed by the Department of Corporations, the Department of Financial Institutions, or the Department of Real Estate shall be deemed to be a violation of that person's licensing law.

(e) A violation of this article shall not affect the validity of a sale in favor of a bona fide purchaser and any of its encumbrancers for value without notice.

(f) A third-party encumbrancer shall not be relieved of liability resulting from violations of Section 2923.5, 2924.17, or 2924.18, committed by that third-party encumbrancer, that occurred prior to the sale of the subject property to the bona fide purchaser.

(g) The rights, remedies, and procedures provided by this section are in addition to and independent of any other rights, remedies, or procedures under any other law. Nothing in this section shall be construed to alter, limit, or negate any other rights, remedies, or procedures provided by law.

(h) A court may award a prevailing borrower reasonable attorney's fees and costs in an action brought pursuant to this section. A borrower shall be deemed to have prevailed for purposes of this subdivision if the borrower obtained injunctive relief or damages pursuant to this section.

(i) This section shall apply only to entities described in subdivision (b) of Section 2924.18.

(j) This section shall remain in effect only until January 1, 2018, and as of that date is repealed, unless a later enacted statute, that is enacted before January 1, 2018, deletes or extends that date. *(Added by Stats.2012, c. 87 (S.B.900), § 22. Amended by Stats.2013, c. 76 (A.B.383), § 18.)*

Repeal

For repeal of this section, see its terms.

Research References

Rutter, Cal. Practice Guide: Real Prop. Transactions Ch. 6-I, I. Real Property Foreclosures and Antideficiency Laws.

Miller and Starr California Real Estate § 4:12, Mortgage Loan Origination, Brokerage, and Servicing.

Miller and Starr California Real Estate § 4:78, Federal and State Regulation of Residential Mortgage Loan Origination and Servicing--In General.

§ 2924.20. Regulations; adoption by Department of Corporations, the Department of Financial Institutions, and the Department of Real Estate; enforcement

Section added by Stats.2012, c. 86 (A.B.278), § 23. See, also, another section of the same number added by Stats.2012, c. 87 (S.B.900), § 23.

Consistent with their general regulatory authority, and notwithstanding subdivisions (b) and (c) of Section 2924.18, the Department of Corporations, the Department of Financial Institutions, and the Department of Real Estate may adopt regulations applicable to any entity or person under their respective jurisdictions that are necessary to carry out the purposes of the act that added this section. A violation of the regulations adopted pursuant to this section shall only be enforceable by the regulatory agency. *(Added by Stats.2012, c. 86 (A.B.278), § 23.)*

Research References

Miller and Starr California Real Estate § 4:12, Mortgage Loan Origination, Brokerage, and Servicing.

Miller and Starr California Real Estate § 4:78, Federal and State Regulation of Residential Mortgage Loan Origination and Servicing--In General.

Miller and Starr California Real Estate § 10:181.10, Prior Notification and Consultation for Residential Loans Originated Between January 1, 2003 and December 31, 2007.

Miller and Starr California Real Estate § 10:181.20, Prior Notification, Consultation and Modification Requirements for Owner-Occupied First Lien Mortgage Loans Effective January 1, 2013.

§ 2924.20. Regulations; adoption by Department of Corporations, the Department of Financial Institutions, and the Department of Real Estate; enforcement

Section added by Stats.2012, c. 87 (S.B.900), § 23. See, also, another section of the same number added by Stats.2012, c. 86 (A.B.278), § 23.

Consistent with their general regulatory authority, and notwithstanding subdivisions (b) and (c) of Section 2924.18, the Department of Corporations, the Department of Financial Institutions, and the Department of Real Estate may adopt regulations applicable to any entity or person under their respective jurisdictions that are necessary to carry out the purposes of the act that added this section. A violation of the regulations adopted pursuant to this section shall only be enforceable by the regulatory agency. *(Added by Stats.2012, c. 87 (S.B.900), § 23.)*

Research References

Miller and Starr California Real Estate § 4:12, Mortgage Loan Origination, Brokerage, and Servicing.

Miller and Starr California Real Estate § 4:78, Federal and State Regulation of Residential Mortgage Loan Origination and Servicing--In General.

Miller and Starr California Real Estate § 10:181.10, Prior Notification and Consultation for Residential Loans Originated Between January 1, 2003 and December 31, 2007.

Miller and Starr California Real Estate § 10:181.20, Prior Notification, Consultation and Modification Requirements for Owner-Occupied First Lien Mortgage Loans Effective January 1, 2013.

§ 2924.25. Licensed title company or underwritten title company; liability; exemption

(a) Unless acting in the capacity of a trustee, a licensed title company or underwritten title company shall not be liable for a violation of Section 2923.5, 2923.55, 2923.6, 2924.11, 2924.18, or 2924.19 if it records or causes to record a notice of default or notice of sale at the request of a trustee, substitute trustee, or beneficiary, in good faith and in the normal course of its business activities.

(b) This section shall remain in effect only until January 1, 2018, and as of that date is repealed, unless a later enacted statute, that is enacted before January 1, 2018, deletes or extends that date. *(Added by Stats.2013, c. 251 (S.B.310), § 1.)*

Repeal

For repeal of this section, see its terms.

§ 2924.26. Licensed title company or underwritten title company; violation of Section 2923.5; exemption

Section operative Jan. 1, 2018.

(a) Unless acting in the capacity of a trustee, a licensed title company or underwritten title company shall not be liable for a violation of Section 2923.5 or 2924.11 if it records or causes to record a notice of default or notice of sale at the request of a trustee, substitute trustee, or beneficiary, in good faith and in the normal course of its business activities.

(b) This section shall become operative on January 1, 2018. *(Added by Stats.2013, c. 251 (S.B.310), § 2, operative Jan. 1, 2018.)*

§ 2924a. Attorney's and authorized agent's authority to conduct trustee's sale

If, by the terms of any trust or deed of trust a power of sale is conferred upon the trustee, the attorney for the trustee, or any duly authorized agent, may conduct the sale and act in the sale as the auctioneer for the trustee. *(Added by Stats.1929, c. 610, p. 1019, § 1. Amended by Stats.2006, c. 575 (A.B.2624), § 5.)*

Research References

Rutter, Cal. Practice Guide: Real Prop. Transactions Ch. 6-I, I. Real Property Foreclosures and Antideficiency Laws.

Miller and Starr California Real Estate § 10:202, Conduct of the Sale.

17 NO. 4 Miller & Starr, California Real Estate Newsalert 2, Statutory Update:.

17 NO. 6 Miller & Starr, California Real Estate Newsalert 20, Table of Statutes (Newsalert Vol 17).

22 NO. 3 Miller & Starr, California Real Estate Newsalert 1, Show Me Your Papers: Sales and Assignments of Secured Real Estate Loans and the California Foreclosure Process.

4 Witkin, California Summary 10th Security Transactions in Real Property § 155, (S 155) in General.

§ 2924b. Notices of default and of sale; mailing upon request for copies and to certain interested persons

(a) Any person desiring a copy of any notice of default and of any notice of sale under any deed of trust or mortgage with power of sale upon real property or an estate for years therein, as to which deed of trust or mortgage the power of sale cannot be exercised until these notices are given for the time and in the manner provided in Section 2924 may, at any time subsequent to recordation of the deed of trust or mortgage and prior to recordation of notice of default thereunder, cause to be filed for record in the office of the recorder of any county in which any part or parcel of the real property is situated, a duly acknowledged request for a copy of the notice of default and of sale. This request shall be signed and acknowledged by the person making the request, specifying the name and address of the person to whom the notice is to be mailed, shall identify the deed of trust or mortgage by stating the names of the parties thereto, the date of recordation thereof, and the book and page where the deed of trust or mortgage is recorded or the recorder's number, and shall be in substantially the following form:

"In accordance with Section 2924b, Civil Code, request is hereby made that a copy of any notice of default and a copy of any notice of sale under the deed of trust (or mortgage) recorded _____, ____, in Book ____ page ____ records of _____ County, (or filed for record with recorder's serial number ____, _____ County) California, executed by _____ as trustor (or mortgagor) in which _____ is named as beneficiary (or mortgagee) and _____ as trustee be mailed to

_____ at _____.
      Name   Address

NOTICE: A copy of any notice of default and of any notice of sale will be sent only to the address contained in this recorded request. If your address changes, a new request must be recorded.

                    Signature _____"

Upon the filing for record of the request, the recorder shall index in the general index of grantors the names of the trustors (or mortgagors) recited therein and the names of persons requesting copies.

(b) The mortgagee, trustee, or other person authorized to record the notice of default or the notice of sale shall do each of the following:

(1) Within 10 business days following recordation of the notice of default, deposit or cause to be deposited in the United States mail an envelope, sent by registered or certified mail with postage prepaid, containing a copy of the notice with the recording date shown thereon, addressed to each person whose name and address are set forth in a duly recorded request therefor, directed to the address designated in the request and to each trustor or mortgagor at his or her last known address if different than the address specified in the deed of trust or mortgage with power of sale.

(2) At least 20 days before the date of sale, deposit or cause to be deposited in the United States mail an envelope, sent by registered or certified mail with postage prepaid, containing a copy of the notice of the time and place of sale, addressed to each person whose name and address are set forth in a duly recorded request therefor, directed to the address designated in the request and to each trustor or mortgagor at his or her last known address if different than the address specified in the deed of trust or mortgage with power of sale.

(3) As used in paragraphs (1) and (2), the "last known address" of each trustor or mortgagor means the last business or residence physical address actually known by the mortgagee, beneficiary, trustee, or other person authorized to record the notice of default. For the purposes of this subdivision, an address is "actually known" if it is contained in the original deed of trust or mortgage, or in any subsequent written notification of a change of physical address from the trustor or mortgagor pursuant to the deed of trust or mortgage. For the purposes of this subdivision, "physical address" does not include an email or any form of electronic address for a trustor or mortgagor. The beneficiary shall inform the trustee of the trustor's last address actually known by the beneficiary. However, the trustee shall incur no liability for failing to send any notice to the last address unless the trustee has actual knowledge of it.

(4) A "person authorized to record the notice of default or the notice of sale" shall include an agent for the mortgagee or beneficiary, an agent of the named trustee, any person designated in an executed substitution of trustee, or an agent of that substituted trustee.

(c) The mortgagee, trustee, or other person authorized to record the notice of default or the notice of sale shall do the following:

(1) Within one month following recordation of the notice of default, deposit or cause to be deposited in the United States mail an envelope, sent by registered or certified mail with postage prepaid, containing a copy of the notice with the recording date shown thereon, addressed to each person set forth in paragraph (2), provided that the estate or interest of any person entitled to receive notice under this subdivision is acquired by an instrument sufficient to impart constructive notice of the estate or interest in the land or portion thereof that is subject to the deed of trust or mortgage being foreclosed, and provided the instrument is recorded in the office of the county recorder so as to impart that constructive notice prior to the recording date of the notice of default and provided the instrument as so recorded sets forth a mailing address that the county recorder shall use, as instructed within the instrument, for the return of the instrument after recording, and which address shall be the address used for the purposes of mailing notices herein.

(2) The persons to whom notice shall be mailed under this subdivision are:

(A) The successor in interest, as of the recording date of the notice of default, of the estate or interest or any portion thereof of the trustor or mortgagor of the deed of trust or mortgage being foreclosed.

(B) The beneficiary or mortgagee of any deed of trust or mortgage recorded subsequent to the deed of trust or mortgage being foreclosed, or recorded prior to or concurrently with the deed of trust or mortgage being foreclosed but subject to a recorded agreement or a recorded statement of subordination to the deed of trust or mortgage being foreclosed.

(C) The assignee of any interest of the beneficiary or mortgagee described in subparagraph (B), as of the recording date of the notice of default.

(D) The vendee of any contract of sale, or the lessee of any lease, of the estate or interest being foreclosed that is recorded subsequent to the deed of trust or mortgage being foreclosed, or recorded prior to or concurrently with the deed of trust or mortgage being foreclosed but subject to a recorded agreement or statement of subordination to the deed of trust or mortgage being foreclosed.

(E) The successor in interest to the vendee or lessee described in subparagraph (D), as of the recording date of the notice of default.

(F) The office of the Controller, Sacramento, California, where, as of the recording date of the notice of default, a "Notice of Lien for Postponed Property Taxes" has been recorded against the real property to which the notice of default applies.

(3) At least 20 days before the date of sale, deposit or cause to be deposited in the United States mail an envelope, sent by registered or certified mail with postage prepaid, containing a copy of the notice of the time and place of sale addressed to each person to whom a copy of the notice of default is to be mailed as provided in paragraphs (1) and (2), and addressed to the office of any state taxing agency, Sacramento, California, that has recorded, subsequent to the deed of trust or mortgage being foreclosed, a notice of tax lien prior to the recording date of the notice of default against the real property to which the notice of default applies.

(4) Provide a copy of the notice of sale to the Internal Revenue Service, in accordance with Section 7425 of the Internal Revenue Code [1] and any applicable federal regulation, if a "Notice of Federal Tax Lien under Internal Revenue Laws" has been recorded, subsequent to the deed of trust or mortgage being foreclosed, against the real property to which the notice of sale applies. The failure to provide the Internal Revenue Service with a copy of the notice of sale pursuant to this paragraph shall be sufficient cause to rescind the trustee's sale and invalidate the trustee's deed, at the option of either the successful bidder at the trustee's sale or the trustee, and in either case with the consent of the beneficiary. Any option to rescind the trustee's sale pursuant to this paragraph shall be exercised prior to any transfer of the property by the successful bidder to a bona fide purchaser for value. A rescission of the trustee's sale pursuant to this paragraph may be recorded in a notice of rescission pursuant to Section 1058.5.

(5) The mailing of notices in the manner set forth in paragraph (1) shall not impose upon any licensed attorney, agent, or employee of any person entitled to receive notices as herein set forth any duty to communicate the notice to the entitled person from the fact that the mailing address used by the county recorder is the address of the attorney, agent, or employee.

(d) Any deed of trust or mortgage with power of sale hereafter executed upon real property or an estate for years therein may contain a request that a copy of any notice of default and a copy of any notice of sale thereunder shall be mailed to any person or party thereto at the address of the person given therein, and a copy of any notice of default and of any notice of sale shall be mailed to each of these at the same time and in the same manner required as though a separate request therefor had been filed by each of these persons as herein authorized. If any deed of trust or mortgage with power of sale executed after September 19, 1939, except a deed of trust or mortgage of any of the classes excepted from the provisions of Section 2924, does not contain a mailing address of the trustor or mortgagor therein named, and if no request for special notice by the trustor or mortgagor in substantially the form set forth in this section has subsequently been recorded, a copy of the notice of default shall be published once a week for at least four weeks in a newspaper of general circulation in the county in which the property is situated, the publication to commence within 10 business days after the filing of the notice of default. In lieu of publication, a copy of the notice of default may be delivered personally to the trustor or mortgagor within the 10 business days or at any time before publication is completed, or by posting the notice of default in a conspicuous place on the property and mailing the notice to the last known address of the trustor or mortgagor.

(e) Any person required to mail a copy of a notice of default or notice of sale to each trustor or mortgagor pursuant to subdivision (b) or (c) by registered or certified mail shall simultaneously cause to be deposited in the United States mail, with postage prepaid and mailed by first-class mail, an envelope containing an additional copy of the required notice addressed to each trustor or mortgagor at the same address to which the notice is sent by registered or certified mail pursuant to subdivision (b) or (c). The person shall execute and retain an affidavit identifying the notice mailed, showing the name and residence or business address of that person, that he or she is over * * * 18 years of age, the date of deposit in the mail, the name and address of the trustor or mortgagor to whom sent, and that the envelope was sealed and deposited in the mail with postage fully prepaid. In the absence of fraud, the affidavit required by this subdivision shall establish a conclusive presumption of mailing.

(f)(1) Notwithstanding subdivision (a), with respect to separate interests governed by an association, as defined in * * * Section 4080 or 6528, the association may cause to be filed in the office of the recorder in the county in which the separate interests are situated a request that a mortgagee, trustee, or other person authorized to record a notice of default regarding any of those separate interests mail to the association a copy of any trustee's deed upon sale concerning a separate interest. The request shall include a legal description or the assessor's parcel number of all the separate interests. A request recorded pursuant to this subdivision shall include the name and address of the association and a statement that it is * * * an association as defined in Section 4080 or 6528. Subsequent requests of an association shall supersede prior requests. A request pursuant to this subdivision shall be recorded before the filing of a notice of default. The mortgagee, trustee, or other authorized person shall mail the requested information to the association within 15 business days following the date of the trustee's sale. Failure to mail the request, pursuant to this subdivision, shall not affect the title to real property.

(2) A request filed pursuant to paragraph (1) does not, for purposes of Section 27288.1 of the Government Code, constitute a document that either effects or evidences a transfer or encumbrance of an interest in real property or that releases or terminates any interest, right, or encumbrance of an interest in real property.

(g) No request for a copy of any notice filed for record pursuant to this section, no statement or allegation in the request, and no record thereof shall affect the title to real property or be deemed notice to any person that any person requesting copies of notice has or claims any right, title, or interest in, or lien or charge upon the property described in the deed of trust or mortgage referred to therein.

(h) "Business day," as used in this section, has the meaning specified in Section 9. *(Added by Stats.1933, c. 642, p. 1670, § 2. Re-enacted by Stats.1935, c. 650, p. 1803, § 2. Amended by Stats.1939, c. 983, p. 2737, § 2; Stats.1951, c. 417, p. 1392, § 2; Stats.1957, c. 1865, p. 3269, § 11; Stats.1959, c. 425, p. 2362, § 1; Stats.1959, c. 1890, p. 4456, § 2; Stats.1961, c. 2218, p. 4567, § 1; Stats.1976, c. 1149, p. 5206, § 1, operative July 1, 1977; Stats.1977, c. 1242, p. 4187, § 2, eff. Oct. 1, 1977; Stats.1978, c. 43, p. 127, § 1, eff. March 16, 1978; Stats.1979, c. 1015, p. 3464, § 1; Stats.1980, c. 925, p. 2933, § 1, eff. Aug. 18, 1980; Stats.1985, c. 154, § 1; Stats.1985, c. 1206, § 1; Stats.1986, c. 1361, § 3; Stats.1986, c. 1385, § 2.5; Stats.1989, c. 698, § 5; Stats.1992, c. 351 (A.B.2981), § 1; Stats.1993, c. 686 (A.B.1219), § 3; Stats. 2001, c. 438 (S.B.958), § 2, eff. Oct. 2, 2001; Stats.2002, c. 809 (S.B.1504), § 1; Stats.2004, c. 177 (S.B.1277), § 1; Stats.2005, c. 224 (A.B.885), § 1; Stats.2008, c. 527 (S.B.1511), § 1; Stats. 2010, c. 133 (A.B.2016), § 1; Stats.2012, c. 181 (A.B.806), § 39, operative Jan. 1, 2014; Stats.2012, c. 255 (A.B.2273), § 2; Stats.2013, c. 183 (S.B.745), § 6; Stats.2013, c. 605 (S.B.752), § 17.)*

1 Internal Revenue Code sections are in Title 26 of the U.S.C.A.

Law Revision Commission Comments

Subdivision (f) of Section 2924b is amended to add a cross-reference to Section 6528, and to make a conforming terminological change, reflecting the enactment of the Commercial and Industrial Common Interest Development Act (Civ. Code §§ 6500–6876). [42 Cal.L.Rev.Comm. Reports 1 (2012)].

Subdivision (f) of Section 2924b is amended to correct a cross-reference to former Section 1351(a). [42 Cal.L.Rev.Comm. Reports 311 (2012)].

Research References

California Real Estate Forms (Miller & Starr) § 3:8, Deed of Trust, Security Agreement, and Fixture Filing With Assignment of Rents and Agreements.

California Real Estate Forms (Miller & Starr) § 1:34, Installment Land Sale Contract With Power of Sale.

California Real Estate Forms (Miller & Starr) § 3:14, Construction Deed of Trust, Security Agreement, and Fixture Filing With Assignment of Rents and Agreements.

California Real Estate Forms (Miller & Starr) § 3:69, Note and Deed of Trust Assumption Agreement.

Rutter, Cal. Practice Guide: Real Prop. Transactions Ch. 6-B, B. Sources and Kinds of Financing.

Rutter, Cal. Practice Guide: Real Prop. Transactions Ch. 6-H, H. Security for Promissory Note.

Rutter, Cal. Practice Guide: Real Prop. Transactions Ch. 6-I, I. Real Property Foreclosures and Antideficiency Laws.

Miller and Starr California Real Estate § 1:79, Form of the Memorandum.

Miller and Starr California Real Estate § 10:5, Form and Interpretation.

Miller and Starr California Real Estate § 11:6, Instruments Subject to Recording--List of Recordable Documents.

Miller and Starr California Real Estate § 4:68, Real Property Credit Sales Transactions (Seller Carry-Back Financing) Negotiated by Licensees.

Miller and Starr California Real Estate § 6:17, Liability and Measure of Damages to the Parties.

Miller and Starr California Real Estate § 25B:4, Overall Powers and Obligations of the Association.

Miller and Starr California Real Estate § 7:166, Trustee's Sale Guarantee.

Miller and Starr California Real Estate § 10:181, Notice of Default--In General.

Miller and Starr California Real Estate § 10:184, Execution of the Notice of Default.

Miller and Starr California Real Estate § 10:185, Recording and Mailing.

Miller and Starr California Real Estate § 10:199, Publication, Mailing, and Recording the Notice.

Miller and Starr California Real Estate § 10:200, Special Notice to the Internal Revenue Service.

Miller and Starr California Real Estate § 10:213, Disposition of Sales Proceeds.

Miller and Starr California Real Estate § 10:237, Waiver of Purchase-Money Protection.

Miller and Starr California Real Estate § 11:100, Priority of the Purchaser's Title from a Foreclosure Sale.

Miller and Starr California Real Estate § 11:112, Liens for Future Advances--Optional Advances; Intervening Interests Not Known to the Lender.

13 NO. 4 Miller & Starr, California Real Estate Newsalert 16, Mortgages and Deeds of Trust.

15 NO. 3 Miller & Starr, California Real Estate Newsalert 4, Deeds of Trust.

15 NO. 4 Miller & Starr, California Real Estate Newsalert 7, Deeds.

16 NO. 2 Miller & Starr, California Real Estate Newsalert 1, Trustee Sales: the "Terminator" of Debtors' Equities.

16 NO. 3 Miller & Starr, California Real Estate Newsalert 1, Assessment Liens and Foreclosure in Common Interest Developments.

16 NO. 4 Miller & Starr, California Real Estate Newsalert 8, Deeds of Trust.

16 NO. 5 Miller & Starr, California Real Estate Newsalert 26, State Board of Equalization Issues Comprehensive Summary and Qs and As for Transfers of Base Year Values of Principal Residences.

19 NO. 1 Miller & Starr, California Real Estate Newsalert 1, The Perata Foreclosure Bill (SB 1137): New Rights for Defaulting Borrowers and Tenants; New Complications for Foreclosing Lenders.

20 NO. 4 Miller & Starr, California Real Estate Newsalert 26, Deeds of Trust.

21 NO. 4 Miller & Starr, California Real Estate Newsalert 5, Common Interest Developments.

12 Witkin, California Summary 10th Real Property § 112, (S 112) Liens.

9 Witkin, California Summary 10th Taxation § 308, Security and Enforcement.

1 Witkin Cal. Summ. 10th Contracts § 681, Waivers by Mortgagors.

4 Witkin, California Summary 10th Security Transactions in Real Property § 46, Recordation.

4 Witkin, California Summary 10th Security Transactions in Real Property § 151, Posting, Publication, and Recording.

4 Witkin, California Summary 10th Security Transactions in Real Property § 152, Effect of Noncompliance.

4 Witkin, California Summary 10th Security Transactions in Real Property § 153, (S 153) Personal Notice on Request.

4 Witkin, California Summary 10th Security Transactions in Real Property § 154, (S 154) Personal Notice to Others.

4 Witkin, California Summary 10th Security Transactions in Real Property § 163, (S 163) Conflicting Claims.

§ 2924c. Cure of default; payment of arrearages, costs and fees; effect on acceleration; notice of default; trustee's or attorney's fees; reinstatement period

(a)(1) Whenever all or a portion of the principal sum of any obligation secured by deed of trust or mortgage on real property or an estate for years therein hereafter executed has, prior to the maturity date fixed in that obligation, become due or been declared due by reason of default in payment of interest or of any installment of principal, or by reason of failure of trustor or mortgagor to pay, in accordance with the terms of that obligation or of the deed of trust or mortgage, taxes, assessments, premiums for insurance, or advances made by beneficiary or mortgagee in accordance with the terms of that obligation or of the deed of trust or mortgage, the trustor or mortgagor or his or her successor in interest in the mortgaged or trust property or any part thereof, or any beneficiary under a subordinate deed of trust or any other person having a subordinate lien or encumbrance of record thereon, at any time within the period specified in subdivision (e), if the power of sale therein is to be exercised, or, otherwise at any time prior to entry of the decree of foreclosure, may pay to the beneficiary or the mortgagee or their successors in interest, respectively, the entire amount due, at the time payment is tendered, with respect to (A) all amounts of principal, interest, taxes, assessments, insurance premiums, or advances actually known by the beneficiary to be, and that are, in

default and shown in the notice of default, under the terms of the deed of trust or mortgage and the obligation secured thereby, (B) all amounts in default on recurring obligations not shown in the notice of default, and (C) all reasonable costs and expenses, subject to subdivision (c), which are actually incurred in enforcing the terms of the obligation, deed of trust, or mortgage, and trustee's or attorney's fees, subject to subdivision (d), other than the portion of principal as would not then be due had no default occurred, and thereby cure the default theretofore existing, and thereupon, all proceedings theretofore had or instituted shall be dismissed or discontinued and the obligation and deed of trust or mortgage shall be reinstated and shall be and remain in force and effect, the same as if the acceleration had not occurred. This section does not apply to bonds or other evidences of indebtedness authorized or permitted to be issued by the Commissioner of Corporations or made by a public utility subject to the Public Utilities Code. For the purposes of this subdivision, the term "recurring obligation" means all amounts of principal and interest on the loan, or rents, subject to the deed of trust or mortgage in default due after the notice of default is recorded; all amounts of principal and interest or rents advanced on senior liens or leaseholds which are advanced after the recordation of the notice of default; and payments of taxes, assessments, and hazard insurance advanced after recordation of the notice of default. If the beneficiary or mortgagee has made no advances on defaults which would constitute recurring obligations, the beneficiary or mortgagee may require the trustor or mortgagor to provide reliable written evidence that the amounts have been paid prior to reinstatement.

(2) If the trustor, mortgagor, or other person authorized to cure the default pursuant to this subdivision does cure the default, the beneficiary or mortgagee or the agent for the beneficiary or mortgagee shall, within 21 days following the reinstatement, execute and deliver to the trustee a notice of rescission which rescinds the declaration of default and demand for sale and advises the trustee of the date of reinstatement. The trustee shall cause the notice of rescission to be recorded within 30 days of receipt of the notice of rescission and of all allowable fees and costs.

No charge, except for the recording fee, shall be made against the trustor or mortgagor for the execution and recordation of the notice which rescinds the declaration of default and demand for sale.

(b)(1) The notice, of any default described in this section, recorded pursuant to Section 2924, and mailed to any person pursuant to Section 2924b, shall begin with the following statement, printed or typed thereon:

"IMPORTANT NOTICE [14–point boldface type if printed or in capital letters if typed]

IF YOUR PROPERTY IS IN FORECLOSURE BECAUSE YOU ARE BEHIND IN YOUR PAYMENTS, IT MAY BE SOLD WITHOUT ANY COURT ACTION, [14–point boldface type if printed or in capital letters if typed] and you may have the legal right to bring your account in good standing by paying all of your past due payments plus permitted costs and expenses within the time permitted by law for reinstatement of your account, which is normally five business days prior to the date set for the sale of your property. No sale date may be set until approximately 90 days from the date this notice of default may be recorded (which date of recordation appears on this notice).

This amount is _____ as of _____

                               (Date)

and will increase until your account becomes current.

While your property is in foreclosure, you still must pay other obligations (such as insurance and taxes) required by your note and deed of trust or mortgage. If you fail to make future payments on the loan, pay taxes on the property, provide insurance on the property, or pay other obligations as required in the note and deed of trust or mortgage, the beneficiary or mortgagee may insist that you do so in order to reinstate your account in good standing. In addition, the beneficiary or mortgagee may require as a condition to reinstatement that you provide reliable written evidence that you paid all senior liens, property taxes, and hazard insurance premiums.

Upon your written request, the beneficiary or mortgagee will give you a written itemization of the entire amount you must pay. You may not have to pay the entire unpaid portion of your account, even though full payment was demanded, but you must pay all amounts in default at the time payment is made. However, you and your beneficiary or mortgagee may mutually agree in writing prior to the time the notice of sale is posted (which may not be earlier than three months after this notice of default is recorded) to, among other things, (1) provide additional time in which to cure the default by transfer of the property or otherwise; or (2) establish a schedule of payments in order to cure your default; or both (1) and (2).

Following the expiration of the time period referred to in the first paragraph of this notice, unless the obligation being foreclosed upon or a separate written agreement between you and your creditor permits a longer period, you have only the legal right to stop the sale of your property by paying the entire amount demanded by your creditor.

To find out the amount you must pay, or to arrange for payment to stop the foreclosure, or if your property is in foreclosure for any other reason, contact:

_____
(Name of beneficiary or mortgagee)

_____
(Mailing address)

_____
(Telephone)

If you have any questions, you should contact a lawyer or the governmental agency which may have insured your loan.

Notwithstanding the fact that your property is in foreclosure, you may offer your property for sale, provided the sale is concluded prior to the conclusion of the foreclosure.

Remember, YOU MAY LOSE LEGAL RIGHTS IF YOU DO NOT TAKE PROMPT ACTION. [14–point boldface type if printed or in capital letters if typed]"

Unless otherwise specified, the notice, if printed, shall appear in at least 12–point boldface type.

If the obligation secured by the deed of trust or mortgage is a contract or agreement described in paragraph (1) or (4) of subdivision (a) of Section 1632, the notice required herein shall be in Spanish if the trustor requested a Spanish language translation of the contract or agreement pursuant to Section 1632. If the obligation secured by the deed of trust or mortgage is contained in a home improvement contract, as defined in Sections 7151.2 and 7159 of the Business and Professions Code, which is subject to Title 2 (commencing with Section 1801), the seller shall specify on the contract whether or not the contract was principally negotiated in Spanish and if the contract was principally negotiated in Spanish, the notice required herein shall be in Spanish. No assignee of the contract or person authorized to record the notice of default shall incur any obligation or liability for failing to mail a notice in Spanish unless

Spanish is specified in the contract or the assignee or person has actual knowledge that the secured obligation was principally negotiated in Spanish. Unless specified in writing to the contrary, a copy of the notice required by subdivision (c) of Section 2924b shall be in English.

(2) Any failure to comply with the provisions of this subdivision shall not affect the validity of a sale in favor of a bona fide purchaser or the rights of an encumbrancer for value and without notice.

(c) Costs and expenses which may be charged pursuant to Sections 2924 to 2924i, inclusive, shall be limited to the costs incurred for recording, mailing, including certified and express mail charges, publishing, and posting notices required by Sections 2924 to 2924i, inclusive, postponement pursuant to Section 2924g not to exceed fifty dollars ($50) per postponement and a fee for a trustee's sale guarantee or, in the event of judicial foreclosure, a litigation guarantee. For purposes of this subdivision, a trustee or beneficiary may purchase a trustee's sale guarantee at a rate meeting the standards contained in Sections 12401.1 and 12401.3 of the Insurance Code.

(d) Trustee's or attorney's fees which may be charged pursuant to subdivision (a), or until the notice of sale is deposited in the mail to the trustor as provided in Section 2924b, if the sale is by power of sale contained in the deed of trust or mortgage, or, otherwise at any time prior to the decree of foreclosure, are hereby authorized to be in a base amount that does not exceed three hundred dollars ($300) if the unpaid principal sum secured is one hundred fifty thousand dollars ($150,000) or less, or two hundred fifty dollars ($250) if the unpaid principal sum secured exceeds one hundred fifty thousand dollars ($150,000), plus one-half of 1 percent of the unpaid principal sum secured exceeding fifty thousand dollars ($50,000) up to and including one hundred fifty thousand dollars ($150,000), plus one-quarter of 1 percent of any portion of the unpaid principal sum secured exceeding one hundred fifty thousand dollars ($150,000) up to and including five hundred thousand dollars ($500,000), plus one-eighth of 1 percent of any portion of the unpaid principal sum secured exceeding five hundred thousand dollars ($500,000). Any charge for trustee's or attorney's fees authorized by this subdivision shall be conclusively presumed to be lawful and valid where the charge does not exceed the amounts authorized herein. For purposes of this subdivision, the unpaid principal sum secured shall be determined as of the date the notice of default is recorded.

(e) Reinstatement of a monetary default under the terms of an obligation secured by a deed of trust, or mortgage may be made at any time within the period commencing with the date of recordation of the notice of default until five business days prior to the date of sale set forth in the initial recorded notice of sale.

In the event the sale does not take place on the date set forth in the initial recorded notice of sale or a subsequent recorded notice of sale is required to be given, the right of reinstatement shall be revived as of the date of recordation of the subsequent notice of sale, and shall continue from that date until five business days prior to the date of sale set forth in the subsequently recorded notice of sale.

In the event the date of sale is postponed on the date of sale set forth in either an initial or any subsequent notice of sale, or is postponed on the date declared for sale at an immediately preceding postponement of sale, and, the postponement is for a period which exceeds five business days from the date set forth in the notice of sale, or declared at the time of postponement, then the right of reinstatement is revived as of the date of postponement and shall continue from that date until five business days prior to the date of sale declared at the time of the postponement.

Nothing contained herein shall give rise to a right of reinstatement during the period of five business days prior to the date of sale, whether the date of sale is noticed in a notice of sale or declared at a postponement of sale.

Pursuant to the terms of this subdivision, no beneficiary, trustee, mortgagee, or their agents or successors shall be liable in any manner to a trustor, mortgagor, their agents or successors or any beneficiary under a subordinate deed of trust or mortgage or any other person having a subordinate lien or encumbrance of record thereon for the failure to allow a reinstatement of the obligation secured by a deed of trust or mortgage during the period of five business days prior to the sale of the security property, and no such right of reinstatement during this period is created by this section. Any right of reinstatement created by this section is terminated five business days prior to the date of sale set forth in the initial date of sale, and is revived only as prescribed herein and only as of the date set forth herein.

As used in this subdivision, the term "business day" has the same meaning as specified in Section 9. *(Added by Stats.1933, c. 642, p. 1671, § 3. Re-enacted by Stats.1935, c. 650, p. 1807, § 3. Amended by Stats.1949, c. 1437, p. 2501, § 1; Stats.1951, c. 417, p. 1392, § 1; Stats.1957, c. 40, p. 599, § 1; Stats.1957, c. 362, p. 1176, § 1; Stats.1973, c. 817, § 2, operative July 1, 1974; Stats.1974, c. 308, § 1, eff. May 31, 1974, operative July 1, 1974; Stats.1979, c. 655, p. 2019, § 4, eff. Sept. 14, 1979, operative Jan. 1, 1980; Stats.1979, c. 1015, p. 3468, § 2; Stats.1980, c. 423, p. 839, § 12, eff. July 11, 1980; Stats.1980, c. 1380, p. 5017, § 18.5, eff. Oct. 1, 1980, operative Jan. 1, 1981; Stats.1981, c. 427, p. 1657, § 2; Stats.1983, c. 112, § 1; Stats.1983, c. 1217, § 1; Stats.1984, c. 919, § 1, operative July 1, 1985; Stats.1984, c. 1730, § 1; Stats.1984, c. 1730, § 1.5, operative July 1, 1985; Stats.1985, c. 1206, § 2; Stats.1986, c. 1385, § 3; Stats.1989, c. 698, § 6; Stats.1990, c. 657 (S.B.2339), § 2; Stats.1992, c. 351 (A.B.2981), § 2; Stats.1993, c. 686 (A.B.1219), § 4; Stats.1996, c. 483 (S.B.1488), § 2; Stats.1997, c. 74 (S.B.665), § 2; Stats.1998, c. 485 (A.B.2803), § 39; Stats.1998, c. 932 (A.B.1094), § 8; Stats. 1999, c. 974 (A.B.431), § 9; Stats.2000, c. 135 (A.B.2539), § 13; Stats.2001, c. 438 (S.B.958), § 3, eff. Oct. 2, 2001, operative Jan. 1, 2002; Stats.2010, c. 180 (S.B.1221), § 3.)*

Research References

California Real Estate Forms (Miller & Starr) § 3:7, Promissory Note.
California Real Estate Forms (Miller & Starr) § 1:34, Installment Land Sale Contract With Power of Sale.
California Real Estate Forms (Miller & Starr) § 3:13, Promissory Note Secured by Construction Deed of Trust.
California Real Estate Forms (Miller & Starr) § 3:20, Promissory Note--Conduit Loan.
Rutter, Cal. Practice Guide: Real Prop. Transactions Ch. 6-F, F. Promissory Note.
Rutter, Cal. Practice Guide: Real Prop. Transactions Ch. 6-I, I. Real Property Foreclosures and Antideficiency Laws.
Rutter, Cal. Practice Guide: Real Prop. Transactions Form 9:A, Sample Opinion Letter (By Borrower's Counsel).
Miller and Starr California Real Estate § 1:79, Form of the Memorandum.
Miller and Starr California Real Estate § 19:2, Lease as Personal Property or Real Property.
Miller and Starr California Real Estate § 4:67, Requirements in Making or Arranging a Loan--Small Loan Regulations.
Miller and Starr California Real Estate § 10:16, Property Interests that Are Lienable.
Miller and Starr California Real Estate § 33:36, Secured Creditor Actions--To Apply Rents and Profits Collected.
Miller and Starr California Real Estate § 10:104, Exercise of the Option.
Miller and Starr California Real Estate § 10:135, Curable Versus Noncurable Defaults.
Miller and Starr California Real Estate § 10:137, Failure to Pay Insurance Premiums.
Miller and Starr California Real Estate § 10:138, Failure to Pay Prior Encumbrances.

Miller and Starr California Real Estate § 10:171, Requirements for a Unified Sale.
Miller and Starr California Real Estate § 10:172, Beneficiary's Alternative Remedies.
Miller and Starr California Real Estate § 10:181, Notice of Default--In General.
Miller and Starr California Real Estate § 10:182, Form and Contents.
Miller and Starr California Real Estate § 10:183, Identification of the Default.
Miller and Starr California Real Estate § 10:185, Recording and Mailing.
Miller and Starr California Real Estate § 10:186, Reinstatement--In General.
Miller and Starr California Real Estate § 10:187, Who Can Reinstate.
Miller and Starr California Real Estate § 10:188, Method of Reinstatement.
Miller and Starr California Real Estate § 10:189, Amounts that Must be Paid to Reinstate.
Miller and Starr California Real Estate § 10:190, Payment of Costs and Charges.
Miller and Starr California Real Estate § 10:191, Attorney's or Trustee's Fees.
Miller and Starr California Real Estate § 10:194, Waiver of Right to Reinstate.
Miller and Starr California Real Estate § 10:198, Notice of Sale--Contents of the Notice.
Miller and Starr California Real Estate § 10:199, Publication, Mailing, and Recording the Notice.
Miller and Starr California Real Estate § 10:201, Postponement of the Sale.
Miller and Starr California Real Estate § 10:221, Comparison With Nonjudicial Foreclosure.
Miller and Starr California Real Estate § 10:237, Waiver of Purchase-Money Protection.
15 NO. 5 Miller & Starr, California Real Estate Newsalert 5, Deeds of Trust.
16 NO. 2 Miller & Starr, California Real Estate Newsalert 1, Trustee Sales: the "Terminator' of Debtors' Equities.
16 NO. 3 Miller & Starr, California Real Estate Newsalert 1, Assessment Liens and Foreclosure in Common Interest Developments.
21 NO. 4 Miller & Starr, California Real Estate Newsalert 11, Deeds of Trust.
12 Witkin, California Summary 10th Real Property § 112, (S 112) Liens.
1 Witkin Cal. Summ. 10th Contracts § 681, Waivers by Mortgagors.
4 Witkin, California Summary 10th Security Transactions in Real Property § 100, Distinction Abolished.
4 Witkin, California Summary 10th Security Transactions in Real Property § 136, Mixed Collateral: Real and Personal Property.
4 Witkin, California Summary 10th Security Transactions in Real Property § 145, in General.
4 Witkin, California Summary 10th Security Transactions in Real Property § 146, Statement of Breach.
4 Witkin, California Summary 10th Security Transactions in Real Property § 147, Warning and Notice of Borrower's Rights.
4 Witkin, California Summary 10th Security Transactions in Real Property § 160, (S 160) Bidding and Payment.
4 Witkin, California Summary 10th Security Transactions in Real Property § 161, (S 161) Costs and Fees.
4 Witkin, California Summary 10th Security Transactions in Real Property § 168, Damages for Wrongful Sale.
4 Witkin, California Summary 10th Security Transactions in Real Property § 216, (S 216) in General.
4 Witkin, California Summary 10th Security Transactions in Real Property § 217, (S 217) Time Limits.
4 Witkin, California Summary 10th Security Transactions in Real Property § 218, (S 218) Costs and Attorneys' Fees.
4 Witkin, California Summary 10th Security Transactions in Real Property § 219, (S 219) Payment or Tender.
4 Witkin, California Summary 10th Security Transactions in Real Property § 220, (S 220) in General.
4 Witkin, California Summary 10th Security Transactions in Real Property § 228, (S 228) Foreclosure Consultant.
13 Witkin, California Summary 10th Equity § 122, Lending Practices.

§ 2924d. Costs and expenses of enforcement; trustee's or attorney's fees; rebates and kickbacks

(a) Commencing with the date that the notice of sale is deposited in the mail, as provided in Section 2924b, and until the property is sold pursuant to the power of sale contained in the mortgage or deed of trust, a beneficiary, trustee, mortgagee, or his or her agent or successor in interest, may demand and receive from a trustor, mortgagor, or his or her agent or successor in interest, or any beneficiary under a subordinate deed of trust, or any other person having a subordinate lien or encumbrance of record those reasonable costs and expenses, to the extent allowed by subdivision (c) of Section 2924c, which are actually incurred in enforcing the terms of the obligation and trustee's or attorney's fees which are hereby authorized to be in a base amount which does not exceed four hundred twenty-five dollars ($425) if the unpaid principal sum secured is one hundred fifty thousand dollars ($150,000) or less, or three hundred sixty dollars ($360) if the unpaid principal sum secured exceeds one hundred fifty thousand dollars ($150,000), plus 1 percent of any portion of the unpaid principal sum secured exceeding fifty thousand dollars ($50,000) up to and including one hundred fifty thousand dollars ($150,000), plus one-half of 1 percent of any portion of the unpaid principal sum secured exceeding one hundred fifty thousand dollars ($150,000) up to and including five hundred thousand dollars ($500,000), plus one-quarter of 1 percent of any portion of the unpaid principal sum secured exceeding five hundred thousand dollars ($500,000). For purposes of this subdivision, the unpaid principal sum secured shall be determined as of the date the notice of default is recorded. Any charge for trustee's or attorney's fees authorized by this subdivision shall be conclusively presumed to be lawful and valid where that charge does not exceed the amounts authorized herein. Any charge for trustee's or attorney's fees made pursuant to this subdivision shall be in lieu of and not in addition to those charges authorized by subdivision (d) of Section 2924c.

(b) Upon the sale of property pursuant to a power of sale, a trustee, or his or her agent or successor in interest, may demand and receive from a beneficiary, or his or her agent or successor in interest, or may deduct from the proceeds of the sale, those reasonable costs and expenses, to the extent allowed by subdivision (c) of Section 2924c, which are actually incurred in enforcing the terms of the obligation and trustee's or attorney's fees which are hereby authorized to be in an amount which does not exceed four hundred twenty-five dollars ($425) or one percent of the unpaid principal sum secured, whichever is greater. For purposes of this subdivision, the unpaid principal sum secured shall be determined as of the date the notice of default is recorded. Any charge for trustee's or attorney's fees authorized by this subdivision shall be conclusively presumed to be lawful and valid where that charge does not exceed the amount authorized herein. Any charges for trustee's or attorney's fees made pursuant to this subdivision shall be in lieu of and not in addition to those charges authorized by subdivision (a) of this section and subdivision (d) of Section 2924c.

(c)(1) No person shall pay or offer to pay or collect any rebate or kickback for the referral of business involving the performance of any act required by this article.

(2) Any person who violates this subdivision shall be liable to the trustor for three times the amount of any rebate or kickback, plus reasonable attorney's fees and costs, in addition to any other remedies provided by law.

(3) No violation of this subdivision shall affect the validity of a sale in favor of a bona fide purchaser or the rights of an encumbrancer for value without notice.

(d) It shall not be unlawful for a trustee to pay or offer to pay a fee to an agent or subagent of the trustee for work performed by the agent or subagent in discharging the trustee's obligations under the terms of the deed of trust. Any payment of a fee by a trustee to an agent or subagent of the trustee for work performed by the agent or subagent in discharging the trustee's obligations under the terms of the deed of trust shall be

conclusively presumed to be lawful and valid if the fee, when combined with other fees of the trustee, does not exceed in the aggregate the trustee's fee authorized by subdivision (d) of Section 2924c or subdivision (a) or (b) of this section.

(e) When a court issues a decree of foreclosure, it shall have discretion to award attorney's fees, costs, and expenses as are reasonable, if provided for in the note, deed of trust, or mortgage, pursuant to Section 580c of the Code of Civil Procedure. *(Added by Stats.1983, c. 1217, § 2. Amended by Stats.1984, c. 1730, § 2; Stats.1985, c. 560, § 1; Stats.1985, c. 1206, § 4; Stats.1993, c. 686 (A.B.1219), § 5; Stats.1997, c. 74 (S.B.665), § 3; Stats.2001, c. 438 (S.B.958), § 4, eff. Oct. 2, 2001, operative Jan. 1, 2002.)*

Research References

Rutter, Cal. Practice Guide: Real Prop. Transactions Ch. 6-F, F. Promissory Note.

Rutter, Cal. Practice Guide: Real Prop. Transactions Ch. 6-I, I. Real Property Foreclosures and Antideficiency Laws.

Miller and Starr California Real Estate § 10:123, Nature of Foreclosure; Termination of Redemption.

Miller and Starr California Real Estate § 10:181, Notice of Default--In General.

Miller and Starr California Real Estate § 10:191, Attorney's or Trustee's Fees.

15 NO. 5 Miller & Starr, California Real Estate Newsalert 5, Deeds of Trust.

19 NO. 2 Miller & Starr, California Real Estate Newsalert 1, Anti-SLAPP Motions in Real Estate Litigation: an Update.

4 Witkin, California Summary 10th Security Transactions in Real Property § 161, (S 161) Costs and Fees.

13 Witkin, California Summary 10th Equity § 122, Lending Practices.

§ 2924e. Junior lienholder requests for written notice of delinquencies; duration; liability for failure to give notice; satisfaction of obligations secured by junior liens

(a) The beneficiary or mortgagee of any deed of trust or mortgage on real property either containing one to four residential units or given to secure an original obligation not to exceed three hundred thousand dollars ($300,000) may, with the written consent of the trustor or mortgagor that is either effected through a signed and dated agreement which shall be separate from other loan and security documents or disclosed to the trustor or mortgagor in at least 10-point type, submit a written request by certified mail to the beneficiary or mortgagee of any lien which is senior to the lien of the requester, for written notice of any or all delinquencies of four months or more, in payments of principal or interest on any obligation secured by that senior lien notwithstanding that the loan secured by the lien of the requester is not then in default as to payments of principal or interest.

The request shall be sent to the beneficiary or mortgagee, or agent which it might designate for the purpose of receiving loan payments, at the address specified for the receipt of these payments, if known, or, if not known, at the address shown on the recorded deed of trust or mortgage.

(b) The request for notice shall identify the ownership or security interest of the requester, the date on which the interest of the requester will terminate as evidenced by the maturity date of the note of the trustor or mortgagor in favor of the requester, the name of the trustor or mortgagor and the name of the current owner of the security property if different from the trustor or mortgagor, the street address or other description of the security property, the loan number (if available to the requester) of the loan secured by the senior lien, the name and address to which notice is to be sent, and shall include or be accompanied by the signed written consent of the trustor or mortgagor, and a fee of forty dollars ($40). For obligations secured by residential properties, the request shall remain valid until withdrawn in writing and shall be applicable to all delinquencies as provided in this section, which occur prior to the date on which the interest of the requester will terminate as specified in the request or the expiration date, as appropriate. For obligations secured by nonresidential properties, the request shall remain valid until withdrawn in writing and shall be applicable to all delinquencies as provided in this section, which occur prior to the date on which the interest of the requester will terminate as specified in the request or the expiration date, as appropriate. The beneficiary or mortgagee of obligations secured by nonresidential properties that have sent five or more notices prior to the expiration of the effective period of the request may charge a fee up to fifteen dollars ($15) for each subsequent notice. A request for notice shall be effective for five years from the mailing of the request or the recording of that request, whichever occurs later, and may be renewed within six months prior to its expiration date by sending the beneficiary or mortgagee, or agent, as the case may be, at the address to which original requests for notice are to be sent, a copy of the earlier request for notice together with a signed statement that the request is renewed and a renewal fee of fifteen dollars ($15). Upon timely submittal of a renewal request for notice, the effectiveness of the original request is continued for five years from the time when it would otherwise have lapsed. Succeeding renewal requests may be submitted in the same manner. The request for notice and renewals thereof shall be recorded in the office of the county recorder of the county in which the security real property is situated. The rights and obligations specified in this section shall inure to the benefit of, or pass to, as the case may be, successors in interest of parties specified in this section. Any successor in interest of a party entitled to notice under this section shall file a request for that notice with any beneficiary or mortgagee of the senior lien and shall pay a processing fee of fifteen dollars ($15). No new written consent shall be required from the trustor or mortgagor.

(c) Unless the delinquency has been cured, within 15 days following the end of four months from any delinquency in payments of principal or interest on any obligation secured by the senior lien which delinquency exists or occurs on or after 10 days from the mailing of the request for notice or the recording of that request, whichever occurs later, the beneficiary or mortgagee shall give written notice to the requester of the fact of any delinquency and the amount thereof.

The notice shall be given by personal service, or by deposit in the mail, first-class postage paid. Following the recording of any notice of default pursuant to Section 2924 with respect to the same delinquency, no notice or further notice shall be required pursuant to this section.

(d) If the beneficiary or mortgagee of any such senior lien fails to give notice to the requester as required in subdivision (c), and a subsequent foreclosure or trustee's sale of the security property occurs, the beneficiary or mortgagee shall be liable to the requester for any monetary damage due to the failure to provide notice within the time period specified in subdivision (c) which the requester has sustained from the date on which notice should have been given to the earlier of the date on which the notice is given or the date of the recording of the notice of default under Section 2924, and shall also forfeit to the requester the sum of three hundred dollars ($300). A showing by the beneficiary or mortgagee by a preponderance of the evidence that the failure to provide timely notice as required by subdivision (c) resulted from a bona fide error notwithstanding the maintenance of procedures reasonably adapted to avoid any such error shall be a defense to any liability for that failure.

(e) If any beneficiary or mortgagee, or agent which it had designated for the purpose of receiving loan payments, has been succeeded in interest by any other person, any request for notice received pursuant to this section shall be transmitted promptly to that person.

(f) Any failure to comply with the provisions of this section shall not affect the validity of a sale in favor of a bona fide purchaser or the rights of an encumbrancer for value and without notice.

(g) Upon satisfaction of an obligation secured by a junior lien with respect to which a notice request was made pursuant to this section, the beneficiary or mortgagee that made the request shall communicate that fact in writing to the senior lienholder to whom the request was made. The communication shall specify that provision of notice pursuant to the prior request under this section is no longer required. *(Added by Stats.1984, c. 1331, § 1, operative July 1, 1985. Amended by Stats.1986, c. 618, § 1; Stats.1988, c. 510, § 1; Stats.1990, c. 788 (S.B.2042), § 1.)*

Research References

Rutter, Cal. Practice Guide: Real Prop. Transactions Ch. 6-B, B. Sources and Kinds of Financing.
Miller and Starr California Real Estate § 4:68, Real Property Credit Sales Transactions (Seller Carry-Back Financing) Negotiated by Licensees.
Miller and Starr California Real Estate § 10:67, Notice of Delinquency.
Miller and Starr California Real Estate § 10:136, Failure to Pay Principal or Interest When Due.
Miller and Starr California Real Estate § 10:185, Recording and Mailing.
4 Witkin, California Summary 10th Security Transactions in Real Property § 149, (S 149) Notice to Junior Lienor of Uncured Default.

§ 2924f. Sale or resale of property where there is a default on the obligation secured by the property; notice; contents; posting and publication

(a) As used in this section and Sections 2924g and 2924h, "property" means real property or a leasehold estate therein, and "calendar week" means Monday through Saturday, inclusive.

(b)(1) Except as provided in subdivision (c), before any sale of property can be made under the power of sale contained in any deed of trust or mortgage, or any resale resulting from a rescission for a failure of consideration pursuant to subdivision (c) of Section 2924h, notice of the sale thereof shall be given by posting a written notice of the time of sale and of the street address and the specific place at the street address where the sale will be held, and describing the property to be sold, at least 20 days before the date of sale in one public place in the city where the property is to be sold, if the property is to be sold in a city, or, if not, then in one public place in the judicial district in which the property is to be sold, and publishing a copy once a week for three consecutive calendar weeks.

(2) The first publication to be at least 20 days before the date of sale, in a newspaper of general circulation published in the city in which the property or some part thereof is situated, if any part thereof is situated in a city, if not, then in a newspaper of general circulation published in the judicial district in which the property or some part thereof is situated, or in case no newspaper of general circulation is published in the city or judicial district, as the case may be, in a newspaper of general circulation published in the county in which the property or some part thereof is situated, or in case no newspaper of general circulation is published in the city or judicial district or county, as the case may be, in a newspaper of general circulation published in the county in this state that is contiguous to the county in which the property or some part thereof is situated and has, by comparison with all similarly contiguous counties, the highest population based upon total county population as determined by the most recent federal decennial census published by the Bureau of the Census.

(3) A copy of the notice of sale shall also be posted in a conspicuous place on the property to be sold at least 20 days

before the date of sale, where possible and where not restricted for any reason. If the property is a single-family residence the posting shall be on a door of the residence, but, if not possible or restricted, then the notice shall be posted in a conspicuous place on the property; however, if access is denied because a common entrance to the property is restricted by a guard gate or similar impediment, the property may be posted at that guard gate or similar impediment to any development community.

(4) The notice of sale shall conform to the minimum requirements of Section 6043 of the Government Code and be recorded with the county recorder of the county in which the property or some part thereof is situated at least 20 days prior to the date of sale.

(5) The notice of sale shall contain the name, street address in this state, which may reflect an agent of the trustee, and either a toll-free telephone number or telephone number in this state of the trustee, and the name of the original trustor, and also shall contain the statement required by paragraph (3) of subdivision (c). In addition to any other description of the property, the notice shall describe the property by giving its street address, if any, or other common designation, if any, and a county assessor's parcel number; but if the property has no street address or other common designation, the notice shall contain a legal description of the property, the name and address of the beneficiary at whose request the sale is to be conducted, and a statement that directions may be obtained pursuant to a written request submitted to the beneficiary within 10 days from the first publication of the notice. Directions shall be deemed reasonably sufficient to locate the property if information as to the location of the property is given by reference to the direction and approximate distance from the nearest crossroads, frontage road, or access road. If a legal description or a county assessor's parcel number and either a street address or another common designation of the property is given, the validity of the notice and the validity of the sale shall not be affected by the fact that the street address, other common designation, name and address of the beneficiary, or the directions obtained therefrom are erroneous or that the street address, other common designation, name and address of the beneficiary, or directions obtained therefrom are omitted.

(6) The term "newspaper of general circulation," as used in this section, has the same meaning as defined in Article 1 (commencing with Section 6000) of Chapter 1 of Division 7 of Title 1 of the Government Code.

(7) The notice of sale shall contain a statement of the total amount of the unpaid balance of the obligation secured by the property to be sold and reasonably estimated costs, expenses, advances at the time of the initial publication of the notice of sale, and, if republished pursuant to a cancellation of a cash equivalent pursuant to subdivision (d) of Section 2924h, a reference of that fact; provided, that the trustee shall incur no liability for any good faith error in stating the proper amount, including any amount provided in good faith by or on behalf of the beneficiary. An inaccurate statement of this amount shall not affect the validity of any sale to a bona fide purchaser for value, nor shall the failure to post the notice of sale on a door as provided by this subdivision affect the validity of any sale to a bona fide purchaser for value.

(8)(A) On and after April 1, 2012, if the deed of trust or mortgage containing a power of sale is secured by real property containing from one to four single-family residences, the notice of sale shall contain substantially the following language, in addition to the language required pursuant to paragraphs (1) to (7), inclusive:

NOTICE TO POTENTIAL BIDDERS: If you are considering bidding on this property lien, you should understand that there are risks involved in bidding at a trustee auction. You will be bidding on a lien, not on a property itself. Placing the highest bid at a trustee auction does not automatically entitle you to free and clear ownership of the property. You should also be aware that the lien being auctioned off may be a junior lien. If you are the highest bidder at the auction, you are or may be responsible for paying off all liens senior to the lien being auctioned off, before you can receive clear title to the property. You are encouraged to investigate the existence, priority, and size of outstanding liens that may exist on this property by contacting the county recorder's office or a title insurance company, either of which may charge you a fee for this information. If you consult either of these resources, you should be aware that the same lender may hold more than one mortgage or deed of trust on the property.

NOTICE TO PROPERTY OWNER: The sale date shown on this notice of sale may be postponed one or more times by the mortgagee, beneficiary, trustee, or a court, pursuant to Section 2924g of the California Civil Code. The law requires that information about trustee sale postponements be made available to you and to the public, as a courtesy to those not present at the sale. If you wish to learn whether your sale date has been postponed, and, if applicable, the rescheduled time and date for the sale of this property, you may call [telephone number for information regarding the trustee's sale] or visit this Internet Web site [Internet Web site address for information regarding the sale of this property], using the file number assigned to this case [case file number]. Information about postponements that are very short in duration or that occur close in time to the scheduled sale may not immediately be reflected in the telephone information or on the Internet Web site. The best way to verify postponement information is to attend the scheduled sale.

(B) A mortgagee, beneficiary, trustee, or authorized agent shall make a good faith effort to provide up-to-date information regarding sale dates and postponements to persons who wish this information. This information shall be made available free of charge. It may be made available via an Internet Web site, a telephone recording that is accessible 24 hours a day, seven days a week, or through any other means that allows 24 hours a day, seven days a week, no-cost access to updated information. A disruption of any of these methods of providing sale date and postponement information to allow for reasonable maintenance or due to a service outage shall not be deemed to be a violation of the good faith standard.

(C) Except as provided in subparagraph (B), nothing in the wording of the notices required by subparagraph (A) is intended to modify or create any substantive rights or obligations for any person providing, or specified in, either of the required notices. Failure to comply with subparagraph (A) or (B) shall not invalidate any sale that would otherwise be valid under Section 2924f.

(D) Information provided pursuant to subparagraph (A) does not constitute the public declaration required by subdivision (d) of Section 2924g.

(9) If the sale of the property is to be a unified sale as provided in subparagraph (B) of paragraph (1) of subdivision (a) of Section 9604 of the Commercial Code, the notice of sale shall also contain a description of the personal property or fixtures to be sold. In the case where it is contemplated that all of the personal property or fixtures are to be sold, the description in the notice of the personal property or fixtures shall be sufficient if it is the same as the description of the personal property or fixtures contained in the agreement creating the security interest in or encumbrance on the personal property or fixtures or the filed

financing statement relating to the personal property or fixtures. In all other cases, the description in the notice shall be sufficient if it would be a sufficient description of the personal property or fixtures under Section 9108 of the Commercial Code. Inclusion of a reference to or a description of personal property or fixtures in a notice of sale hereunder shall not constitute an election by the secured party to conduct a unified sale pursuant to subparagraph (B) of paragraph (1) of subdivision (a) of Section 9604 of the Commercial Code, shall not obligate the secured party to conduct a unified sale pursuant to subparagraph (B) of paragraph (1) of subdivision (a) of Section 9604 of the Commercial Code, and in no way shall render defective or noncomplying either that notice or a sale pursuant to that notice by reason of the fact that the sale includes none or less than all of the personal property or fixtures referred to or described in the notice. This paragraph shall not otherwise affect the obligations or duties of a secured party under the Commercial Code.

(c)(1) This subdivision applies only to deeds of trust or mortgages which contain a power of sale and which are secured by real property containing a single-family, owner-occupied residence, where the obligation secured by the deed of trust or mortgage is contained in a contract for goods or services subject to the provisions of the Unruh Act (Chapter 1 (commencing with Section 1801) of Title 2 of Part 4 of Division 3).

(2) Except as otherwise expressly set forth in this subdivision, all other provisions of law relating to the exercise of a power of sale shall govern the exercise of a power of sale contained in a deed of trust or mortgage described in paragraph (1).

(3) If any default of the obligation secured by a deed of trust or mortgage described in paragraph (1) has not been cured within 30 days after the recordation of the notice of default, the trustee or mortgagee shall mail to the trustor or mortgagor, at his or her last known address, a copy of the following statement:

YOU ARE IN DEFAULT UNDER A

_____ ,
(Deed of trust or mortgage)
DATED _____. UNLESS YOU TAKE ACTION TO PROTECT YOUR PROPERTY, IT MAY BE SOLD AT A PUBLIC SALE. IF YOU NEED AN EXPLANATION OF THE NATURE OF THE PROCEEDING AGAINST YOU, YOU SHOULD CONTACT A LAWYER.

(4) All sales of real property pursuant to a power of sale contained in any deed of trust or mortgage described in paragraph (1) shall be held in the county where the residence is located and shall be made to the person making the highest offer. The trustee may receive offers during the 10–day period immediately prior to the date of sale and if any offer is accepted in writing by both the trustor or mortgagor and the beneficiary or mortgagee prior to the time set for sale, the sale shall be postponed to a date certain and prior to which the property may be conveyed by the trustor to the person making the offer according to its terms. The offer is revocable until accepted. The performance of the offer, following acceptance, according to its terms, by a conveyance of the property to the offeror, shall operate to terminate any further proceeding under the notice of sale and it shall be deemed revoked.

(5) In addition to the trustee fee pursuant to Section 2924c, the trustee or mortgagee pursuant to a deed of trust or mortgage subject to this subdivision shall be entitled to charge an additional fee of fifty dollars ($50).

(6) This subdivision applies only to property on which notices of default were filed on or after the effective date of this subdivision.

(d) With respect to residential real property containing no more than four dwelling units, a separate document containing a summary of the notice of sale information in English and the languages described in Section 1632 shall be attached to the notice of sale provided to the mortgagor or trustor pursuant to Section 2923.3. *(Added by Stats.2010, c. 597 (A.B.2347), § 2, operative Jan. 1, 2013. Amended by Stats.2011, c. 229 (S.B.4), § 2, operative Jan. 1, 2013; Stats.2012, c. 556 (A.B.1599), § 4.)*

Research References

Rutter, Cal. Practice Guide: Real Prop. Transactions Ch. 6-I, I. Real Property Foreclosures and Antideficiency Laws.
Rutter, Cal. Practice Guide: Real Prop. Transactions Gen. Matls., Highlights.
Miller and Starr California Real Estate § 1:79, Form of the Memorandum.
Miller and Starr California Real Estate § 11:6, Instruments Subject to Recording--List of Recordable Documents.
Miller and Starr California Real Estate § 10:16, Property Interests that Are Lienable.
Miller and Starr California Real Estate § 11:23, Purpose and Effect; Required for Recordation.
Miller and Starr California Real Estate § 10:181, Notice of Default--In General.
Miller and Starr California Real Estate § 10:182, Form and Contents.
Miller and Starr California Real Estate § 10:185, Recording and Mailing.
Miller and Starr California Real Estate § 10:198, Notice of Sale--Contents of the Notice.
Miller and Starr California Real Estate § 10:199, Publication, Mailing, and Recording the Notice.
Miller and Starr California Real Estate § 10:201, Postponement of the Sale.
Miller and Starr California Real Estate § 10:207, Default or Breach by the Buyer.
16 NO. 2 Miller & Starr, California Real Estate Newsalert 1, Trustee Sales: the "Terminator' of Debtors' Equities.
16 NO. 3 Miller & Starr, California Real Estate Newsalert 1, Assessment Liens and Foreclosure in Common Interest Developments.
19 NO. 4 Miller & Starr, California Real Estate Newsalert 34, Deeds of Trust.
20 NO. 4 Miller & Starr, California Real Estate Newsalert 6, Deeds of Trust.
21 NO. 4 Miller & Starr, California Real Estate Newsalert 11, Deeds of Trust.
22 NO. 4 Miller & Starr, California Real Estate Newsalert 10, Deeds of Trust.
12 Witkin, California Summary 10th Real Property § 112B, (New)-Higher Value or Longer Delinquency.
4 Witkin, California Summary 10th Security Transactions in Real Property § 8, (S 8) Substitution of Trustee.
4 Witkin, California Summary 10th Security Transactions in Real Property § 148, (S 148) Special Notice for Unruh Act Mortgages.
4 Witkin, California Summary 10th Security Transactions in Real Property § 150, Content and Time of Notice.
4 Witkin, California Summary 10th Security Transactions in Real Property § 151, Posting, Publication, and Recording.
4 Witkin, California Summary 10th Security Transactions in Real Property § 152, Effect of Noncompliance.
4 Witkin, California Summary 10th Security Transactions in Real Property § 155, (S 155) in General.
4 Witkin, California Summary 10th Security Transactions in Real Property § 156, in General.
4 Witkin, California Summary 10th Security Transactions in Real Property § 160, (S 160) Bidding and Payment.
4 Witkin, California Summary 10th Security Transactions in Real Property § 161, (S 161) Costs and Fees.

§ 2924g. Conduct of sale; time; place; interested parties; postponement; order of sale

(a) All sales of property under the power of sale contained in any deed of trust or mortgage shall be held in the county where the property or some part thereof is situated, and shall be made at auction, to the highest bidder, between the hours of 9 a.m. and 5 p.m. on any business day, Monday through Friday.

The sale shall commence at the time and location specified in the notice of sale. Any postponement shall be announced at the time and location specified in the notice of sale for commencement of the sale or pursuant to paragraph (1) of subdivision (c).

If the sale of more than one parcel of real property has been scheduled for the same time and location by the same trustee, (1) any postponement of any of the sales shall be announced at the time published in the notice of sale, (2) the first sale shall commence at the time published in the notice of sale or immediately after the announcement of any postponement, and (3) each subsequent sale shall take place as soon as possible after the preceding sale has been completed.

(b) When the property consists of several known lots or parcels, they shall be sold separately unless the deed of trust or mortgage provides otherwise. When a portion of the property is claimed by a third person, who requires it to be sold separately, the portion subject to the claim may be thus sold. The trustor, if present at the sale, may also, unless the deed of trust or mortgage otherwise provides, direct the order in which property shall be sold, when the property consists of several known lots or parcels which may be sold to advantage separately, and the trustee shall follow that direction. After sufficient property has been sold to satisfy the indebtedness, no more can be sold.

If the property under power of sale is in two or more counties, the public auction sale of all of the property under the power of sale may take place in any one of the counties where the property or a portion thereof is located.

(c)(1) There may be a postponement or postponements of the sale proceedings, including a postponement upon instruction by the beneficiary to the trustee that the sale proceedings be postponed, at any time prior to the completion of the sale for any period of time not to exceed a total of 365 days from the date set forth in the notice of sale. The trustee shall postpone the sale in accordance with any of the following:

(A) Upon the order of any court of competent jurisdiction.

(B) If stayed by operation of law.

(C) By mutual agreement, whether oral or in writing, of any trustor and any beneficiary or any mortgagor and any mortgagee.

(D) At the discretion of the trustee.

(2) In the event that the sale proceedings are postponed for a period or periods totaling more than 365 days, the scheduling of any further sale proceedings shall be preceded by giving a new notice of sale in the manner prescribed in Section 2924f. New fees incurred for the new notice of sale shall not exceed the amounts specified in Sections 2924c and 2924d, and shall not exceed reasonable costs that are necessary to comply with this paragraph.

(d) The notice of each postponement and the reason therefor shall be given by public declaration by the trustee at the time and place last appointed for sale. A public declaration of postponement shall also set forth the new date, time, and place of sale and the place of sale shall be the same place as originally fixed by the trustee for the sale. No other notice of postponement need be given. However, the sale shall be conducted no sooner than on the seventh day after the earlier of (1) dismissal of the action or (2) expiration or termination of the injunction, restraining order, or stay that required postponement of the sale, whether by entry of an order by a court of competent jurisdiction, operation of law, or otherwise, unless the injunction, restraining order, or subsequent order expressly directs the conduct of the sale within that seven- day period. For purposes of this subdivision, the seven-day period shall not include the day on which the action is dismissed, or the day on which the injunction, restraining order, or stay expires or is terminated. If the sale had been scheduled to occur, but this subdivision precludes its conduct during that seven-day period, a new notice of postponement shall be given if the sale had been scheduled to occur during that seven-day period. The trustee shall maintain records of each postponement and the reason therefor.

(e) Notwithstanding the time periods established under subdivision (d), if postponement of a sale is based on a stay imposed by Title 11 of the United States Code (bankruptcy), the sale shall be conducted no sooner than the expiration of the stay imposed by that title and the seven-day provision of subdivision (d) shall not apply. *(Added by Stats.1972, c. 1056, p. 1943, § 4. Amended by Stats.1979, c. 1015, p. 3474, § 4; Stats.1980, c. 423, p. 844, § 14, eff. July 11, 1980; Stats.1984, c. 1730, § 4; Stats.1985, c. 1206, § 5; Stats.1986, c. 1385, § 4; Stats.1992, c. 351 (A.B.2981), § 4; Stats.1993, c. 686 (A.B.1219), § 7; Stats.1994, c. 587 (A.B.3600), § 1.2; Stats.1997, c. 74 (S.B.665), § 5; Stats.2000, c. 636 (A.B.2284), § 7; Stats.2001, c. 438 (S.B.958), § 5, eff. Oct. 2, 2001, operative Jan. 1, 2002; Stats.2005, c. 224 (A.B.885), § 2.)*

Research References

Rutter, Cal. Practice Guide: Real Prop. Transactions Ch. 6-I, I. Real Property Foreclosures and Antideficiency Laws.

Miller and Starr California Real Estate § 4:67, Requirements in Making or Arranging a Loan--Small Loan Regulations.

Miller and Starr California Real Estate § 10:150, Effect of the Automatic Stay.

Miller and Starr California Real Estate § 10:181, Notice of Default--In General.

Miller and Starr California Real Estate § 10:186, Reinstatement--In General.

Miller and Starr California Real Estate § 10:201, Postponement of the Sale.

Miller and Starr California Real Estate § 10:202, Conduct of the Sale.

Miller and Starr California Real Estate § 10:205, Sale When Several Parcels of Real Property Are Encumbered.

15 NO. 3 Miller & Starr, California Real Estate Newsalert 4, Deeds of Trust.

16 NO. 4 Miller & Starr, California Real Estate Newsalert 8, Deeds of Trust.

16 NO. 5 Miller & Starr, California Real Estate Newsalert 26, State Board of Equalization Issues Comprehensive Summary and Qs and As for Transfers of Base Year Values of Principal Residences.

23 NO. 2 Miller & Starr, California Real Estate Newsalert 8, Deeds of Trust.

4 Witkin, California Summary 10th Security Transactions in Real Property § 150, Content and Time of Notice.

4 Witkin, California Summary 10th Security Transactions in Real Property § 155, (S 155) in General.

4 Witkin, California Summary 10th Security Transactions in Real Property § 156, in General.

4 Witkin, California Summary 10th Security Transactions in Real Property § 157, Announcements and Notices.

4 Witkin, California Summary 10th Security Transactions in Real Property § 158, (S 158) Multiple Parcels.

§ 2924h. Bidders at sale; bid as irrevocable offer; security deposit; finality of sale; rescission for failure of consideration; delivery of payment; restraint of bidding; remedies

(a) Each and every bid made by a bidder at a trustee's sale under a power of sale contained in a deed of trust or mortgage shall be deemed to be an irrevocable offer by that bidder to purchase the property being sold by the trustee under the power of sale for the amount of the bid. Any second or subsequent bid by the same bidder or any other bidder for a higher amount shall be a cancellation of the prior bid.

(b) At the trustee's sale the trustee shall have the right (1) to require every bidder to show evidence of the bidder's ability to deposit with the trustee the full amount of his or her final bid in cash, a cashier's check drawn on a state or national bank, a check drawn by a state or federal credit union, or a check drawn by a state or federal savings and loan association, savings association, or savings bank specified in Section 5102 of the Financial Code and authorized to do business in this state, or a cash equivalent which has been designated in the notice of sale as acceptable to the trustee prior to, and as a condition to, the recognizing of the bid, and to conditionally accept and hold these amounts for the duration of the sale, and (2) to require the last and highest bidder to deposit, if not deposited previously, the full amount of the bidder's final bid in cash, a cashier's check drawn on a state or national bank, a check drawn by a state or federal credit union, or a check drawn by a state or federal savings and loan association, savings association, or savings bank specified in Section 5102 of the Financial Code and authorized to do business in this state, or a cash equivalent which has been designated in the notice of sale as acceptable to the trustee, immediately prior to the completion of the sale, the completion of the sale being so announced by the fall of the hammer or in another customary manner. The present beneficiary of the deed of trust under foreclosure shall have the right to offset his or her bid or bids only to the extent of the total amount due the beneficiary including the trustee's fees and expenses.

(c) In the event the trustee accepts a check drawn by a credit union or a savings and loan association pursuant to this subdivision or a cash equivalent designated in the notice of sale, the trustee may withhold the issuance of the trustee's deed to the successful bidder submitting the check drawn by a state or federal credit union or savings and loan association or the cash equivalent until funds become available to the payee or endorsee as a matter of right.

For the purposes of this subdivision, the trustee's sale shall be deemed final upon the acceptance of the last and highest bid, and shall be deemed perfected as of 8 a.m. on the actual date of sale if the trustee's deed is recorded within 15 calendar days after the sale, or the next business day following the 15th day if the county recorder in which the property is located is closed on the 15th day. However, the sale is subject to an automatic rescission for a failure of consideration in the event the funds are not "available for withdrawal" as defined in Section 12413.1 of the Insurance Code. The trustee shall send a notice of rescission for a failure of consideration to the last and highest bidder submitting the check or alternative instrument, if the address of the last and highest bidder is known to the trustee.

If a sale results in an automatic right of rescission for failure of consideration pursuant to this subdivision, the interest of any lienholder shall be reinstated in the same priority as if the previous sale had not occurred.

(d) If the trustee has not required the last and highest bidder to deposit the cash, a cashier's check drawn on a state or national bank, a check drawn by a state or federal credit union, or a check drawn by a state or federal savings and loan association, savings association, or savings bank specified in Section 5102 of the Financial Code and authorized to do business in this state, or a cash equivalent which has been designated in the notice of sale as acceptable to the trustee in the manner set forth in paragraph (2) of subdivision (b), the trustee shall complete the sale. If the last and highest bidder then fails to deliver to the trustee, when demanded, the amount of his or her final bid in cash, a cashier's check drawn on a state or national bank, a check drawn by a state or federal credit union, or a check drawn by a state or federal savings and loan association, savings association, or savings bank specified in Section 5102 of the Financial Code and authorized to do business in this state, or a cash equivalent which has been designated in the notice of sale as acceptable to the trustee, that bidder shall be liable to the trustee for all damages which the trustee may sustain by the refusal to deliver to the

trustee the amount of the final bid, including any court costs and reasonable attorneys' fees.

If the last and highest bidder willfully fails to deliver to the trustee the amount of his or her final bid in cash, a cashier's check drawn on a state or national bank, a check drawn by a state or federal credit union, or a check drawn by a state or federal savings and loan association, savings association, or savings bank specified in Section 5102 of the Financial Code and authorized to do business in this state, or a cash equivalent which has been designated in the notice of sale as acceptable to the trustee, or if the last and highest bidder cancels a cashiers check drawn on a state or national bank, a check drawn by a state or federal credit union, or a check drawn by a state or federal savings and loan association, savings association, or savings bank specified in Section 5102 of the Financial Code and authorized to do business in this state, or a cash equivalent that has been designated in the notice of sale as acceptable to the trustee, that bidder shall be guilty of a misdemeanor punishable by a fine of not more than two thousand five hundred dollars ($2,500).

In the event the last and highest bidder cancels an instrument submitted to the trustee as a cash equivalent, the trustee shall provide a new notice of sale in the manner set forth in Section 2924f and shall be entitled to recover the costs of the new notice of sale as provided in Section 2924c.

(e) Any postponement or discontinuance of the sale proceedings shall be a cancellation of the last bid.

(f) In the event that this section conflicts with any other statute, then this section shall prevail.

(g) It shall be unlawful for any person, acting alone or in concert with others, (1) to offer to accept or accept from another, any consideration of any type not to bid, or (2) to fix or restrain bidding in any manner, at a sale of property conducted pursuant to a power of sale in a deed of trust or mortgage. However, it shall not be unlawful for any person, including a trustee, to state that a property subject to a recorded notice of default or subject to a sale conducted pursuant to this chapter is being sold in an "as-is" condition.

In addition to any other remedies, any person committing any act declared unlawful by this subdivision or any act which would operate as a fraud or deceit upon any beneficiary, trustor, or junior lienor shall, upon conviction, be fined not more than ten thousand dollars ($10,000) or imprisoned in the county jail for not more than one year, or be punished by both that fine and imprisonment. *(Added by Stats.1972, c. 1056, p. 1943, § 5. Amended by Stats.1979, c. 1015, p. 3476, § 5; Stats.1981, c. 427, p. 1660, § 3; Stats.1986, c. 1385, § 6; Stats.1987, c. 725, § 2; Stats.1992, c. 351 (A.B.2981), § 5; Stats.1993, c. 724 (A.B.1196), § 3; Stats.1995, c. 752 (A.B.1695), § 3; Stats.2004, c. 177 (S.B.1277), § 2.)*

Research References

California Real Estate Forms (Miller & Starr) § 3:8, Deed of Trust, Security Agreement, and Fixture Filing With Assignment of Rents and Agreements.

California Real Estate Forms (Miller & Starr) § 1:34, Installment Land Sale Contract With Power of Sale.

California Real Estate Forms (Miller & Starr) § 3:14, Construction Deed of Trust, Security Agreement, and Fixture Filing With Assignment of Rents and Agreements.

California Real Estate Forms (Miller & Starr) § 3:21, Deed of Trust, Assignment of Rents, Security Agreement and Fixture Filing--Conduit Loan.

Rutter, Cal. Practice Guide: Real Prop. Transactions Ch. 6-I, I. Real Property Foreclosures and Antideficiency Laws.

Miller and Starr California Real Estate § 4:67, Requirements in Making or Arranging a Loan--Small Loan Regulations.

Miller and Starr California Real Estate § 10:16, Property Interests that Are Lienable.

Miller and Starr California Real Estate § 10:39, Rights of the Parties.

Miller and Starr California Real Estate § 11:50, Definitions; Rules of Priority.

Miller and Starr California Real Estate § 10:149, Effect of Foreclosure Sale Before or After a Bankruptcy Petition.

Miller and Starr California Real Estate § 10:199, Publication, Mailing, and Recording the Notice.

Miller and Starr California Real Estate § 10:202, Conduct of the Sale.

Miller and Starr California Real Estate § 10:203, Trustee's Liability for Wrongful Conduct of the Sale.

Miller and Starr California Real Estate § 10:204, Who Can Bid at the Sale.

Miller and Starr California Real Estate § 10:206, When the Sale Becomes Final; Reformation.

Miller and Starr California Real Estate § 10:207, Default or Breach by the Buyer.

Miller and Starr California Real Estate § 10:209, Liability for the Defective Condition of the Property.

Miller and Starr California Real Estate § 10:210, Attack on Validity of the Sale.

Miller and Starr California Real Estate § 10:218, Measure of Tort Damages.

Miller and Starr California Real Estate § 10:234, Determination of "Fair Value".

15 NO. 3 Miller & Starr, California Real Estate Newsalert 4, Deeds of Trust.

15 NO. 4 Miller & Starr, California Real Estate Newsalert 7, Deeds.

4 Witkin, California Summary 10th Security Transactions in Real Property § 159, (S 159) Terms of Sale and Creditors' Offsets.

4 Witkin, California Summary 10th Security Transactions in Real Property § 160, (S 160) Bidding and Payment.

4 Witkin, California Summary 10th Security Transactions in Real Property § 165, (S 165) Grounds.

§ 2924i. Balloon payment loans; final payment due date; notice; effect; validity of documents; date of application

(a) This section applies to loans secured by a deed of trust or mortgage on real property containing one to four residential units at least one of which at the time the loan is made is or is to be occupied by the borrower if the loan is for a period in excess of one year and is a balloon payment loan.

(b) This section shall not apply to (1) open end credit as defined in Regulation Z, whether or not the transaction is otherwise subject to Regulation Z, (2) transactions subject to Section 2956, or (3) loans made for the principal purpose of financing the construction of one or more residential units.

(c) At least 90 days but not more than 150 days prior to the due date of the final payment on a loan that is subject to this section, the holder of the loan shall deliver or mail by first-class mail, with a certificate of mailing obtained from the United States Postal Service, to the trustor, or his or her successor in interest, at the last known address of that person, a written notice which shall include all of the following:

(1) A statement of the name and address of the person to whom the final payment is required to be paid.

(2) The date on or before which the final payment is required to be paid.

(3) The amount of the final payment, or if the exact amount is unknown, a good faith estimate of the amount thereof, including unpaid principal, interest and any other charges, such amount to be determined assuming timely payment in full of all scheduled installments coming due between the date the notice is prepared and the date when the final payment is due.

(4) If the borrower has a contractual right to refinance the final payment, a statement to that effect.

If the due date of the final payment of a loan subject to this section is extended prior to the time notice is otherwise required under this subdivision, this notice requirement shall apply only to the due date as extended (or as subsequently extended).

(d) For purposes of this section:

(1) A "balloon payment loan" is a loan which provides for a final payment as originally scheduled which is more than twice the amount of any of the immediately preceding six regularly scheduled payments or which contains a call provision; provided, however, that if the call provision is not exercised by the holder of the loan, the existence of the unexercised call provision shall not cause the loan to be deemed to be a balloon payment loan.

(2) "Call provision" means a loan contract term that provides the holder of the loan with the right to call the loan due and payable either after a specified period has elapsed following closing or after a specified date.

(3) "Regulation Z" means any rule, regulation, or interpretation promulgated by the Board of Governors of the Federal Reserve System under the Federal Truth in Lending Act, as amended (15 U.S.C. Sec. 1601 et seq.), and any interpretation or approval thereof issued by an official or employee of the Federal Reserve System duly authorized by the board under the Truth in Lending Act, as amended, to issue such interpretations or approvals.

(e) Failure to provide notice as required by subdivision (a) does not extinguish any obligation of payment by the borrower, except that the due date for any balloon payment shall be the date specified in the balloon payment note, or 90 days from the date of delivery or mailing of the notice required by subdivision (a), or the due date specified in the notice required by subdivision (a), whichever date is later. If the operation of this section acts to extend the term of any note, interest shall continue to accrue for the extended term at the contract rate and payments shall continue to be due at any periodic interval and on any payment schedule specified in the note and shall be credited to principal or interest under the terms of the note. Default in any extended periodic payment shall be considered a default under terms of the note or security instrument.

(f)(1) The validity of any credit document or of any security document subject to the provisions of this section shall not be invalidated solely because of the failure of any person to comply with this section. However, any person who willfully violates any provision of this section shall be liable in the amount of actual damages suffered by the debtor as the proximate result of the violation, and, if the debtor prevails in any suit to recover that amount, for reasonable attorney's fees.

(2) No person may be held liable in any action under this section if it is shown by a preponderance of the evidence that the violation was not intentional and resulted from a bona fide error notwithstanding the maintenance of procedures reasonably adopted to avoid any such error.

(g) The provisions of this section shall apply to any note executed on or after January 1, 1984. *(Added by Stats.1983, c. 1094, § 1. Amended by Stats.1986, c. 1360, § 1.)*

Research References

Rutter, Cal. Practice Guide: Real Prop. Transactions Ch. 6-F, F. Promissory Note.

Miller and Starr California Real Estate § 1:79, Form of the Memorandum.

Miller and Starr California Real Estate § 4:66, Requirements in Making or Arranging a Loan--Balloon Payment Notes.

Miller and Starr California Real Estate § 10:89, Balloon Payment Loans.

Miller and Starr California Real Estate § 10:181, Notice of Default--In General.

Miller and Starr California Real Estate § 10:185, Recording and Mailing.

Miller and Starr California Real Estate § 10:213, Disposition of Sales Proceeds.

Miller and Starr California Real Estate § 10:236, Policy Objectives; the "Standard" Transaction.

Miller and Starr California Real Estate § 11:100, Priority of the Purchaser's Title from a Foreclosure Sale.

4 Witkin, California Summary 10th Security Transactions in Real Property § 42, (S 42) Alternative Mortgage Transactions for Residential Loans.

§ 2924j. Execution of trustee's deed resulting from surplus proceeds of trustee's sale; notice; priority of claims; due diligence; declaration of unresolved claims; deposit of funds

(a) Unless an interpleader action has been filed, within 30 days of the execution of the trustee's deed resulting from a sale in which there are proceeds remaining after payment of the amounts required by paragraphs (1) and (2) of subdivision (a) of Section 2924k, the trustee shall send written notice to all persons with recorded interests in the real property as of the date immediately prior to the trustee's sale who would be entitled to notice pursuant to subdivisions (b) and (c) of Section 2924b. The notice shall be sent by first-class mail in the manner provided in paragraph (1) of subdivision (c) of Section 2924b and inform each entitled person of each of the following:

(1) That there has been a trustee's sale of the described real property.

(2) That the noticed person may have a claim to all or a portion of the sale proceeds remaining after payment of the amounts required by paragraphs (1) and (2) of subdivision (a) of Section 2924k.

(3) The noticed person may contact the trustee at the address provided in the notice to pursue any potential claim.

(4) That before the trustee can act, the noticed person may be required to present proof that the person holds the beneficial interest in the obligation and the security interest therefor. In the case of a promissory note secured by a deed of trust, proof that the person holds the beneficial interest may include the original promissory note and assignment of beneficial interests related thereto. The noticed person shall also submit a written claim to the trustee, executed under penalty of perjury, stating the following:

(A) The amount of the claim to the date of trustee's sale.

(B) An itemized statement of the principal, interest, and other charges.

(C) That claims must be received by the trustee at the address stated in the notice no later than 30 days after the date the trustee sends notice to the potential claimant.

(b) The trustee shall exercise due diligence to determine the priority of the written claims received by the trustee to the trustee's sale surplus proceeds from those persons to whom notice was sent pursuant to subdivision (a). In the event there is no dispute as to the priority of the written claims submitted to the trustee, proceeds shall be paid within 30 days after the conclusion of the notice period. If the trustee has failed to determine the priority of written claims within 90 days following the 30–day notice period, then within 10 days thereafter the trustee shall deposit the funds with the clerk of the court pursuant to subdivision (c) or file an interpleader action pursuant to subdivision (e). Nothing in this section shall preclude any person from pursuing other remedies or claims as to surplus proceeds.

(c) If, after due diligence, the trustee is unable to determine the priority of the written claims received by the trustee to the trustee's sale surplus of multiple persons or if the trustee determines there is a conflict between potential claimants, the trustee may file a declaration of the unresolved claims and deposit with the clerk of the superior court of the county in which the sale occurred, that portion of the sales proceeds that cannot be distributed, less any fees charged by the clerk pursuant to this subdivision. The declaration shall specify the date of the trustee's sale, a description of the property, the names and addresses of all persons sent notice pursuant to subdivision (a), a statement that the trustee exercised due diligence pursuant to subdivision (b), that the trustee provided written notice as required by subdivisions (a) and (d) and the amount of the sales proceeds deposited by the trustee with the court. Further, the trustee shall submit a copy of the trustee's sales guarantee and any information relevant to the identity, location, and priority of the potential claimants with the court and shall file proof of service of the notice required by subdivision (d) on all persons described in subdivision (a).

The clerk shall deposit the amount with the county treasurer or, if a bank account has been established for moneys held in trust under paragraph (2) of subdivision (a) of Section 77009 of the Government Code, in that account, subject to order of the court upon the application of any interested party. The clerk may charge a reasonable fee for the performance of activities pursuant to this subdivision equal to the fee for filing an interpleader action pursuant to Chapter 5.8 (commencing with Section 70600) of Title 8 of the Government Code. Upon deposit of that portion of the sale proceeds that cannot be distributed by due diligence, the trustee shall be discharged of further responsibility for the disbursement of sale proceeds. A deposit with the clerk of the court pursuant to this subdivision may be either for the total proceeds of the trustee's sale, less any fees charged by the clerk, if a conflict or conflicts exist with respect to the total proceeds, or that portion that cannot be distributed after due diligence, less any fees charged by the clerk.

(d) Before the trustee deposits the funds with the clerk of the court pursuant to subdivision (c), the trustee shall send written notice by first-class mail, postage prepaid, to all persons described in subdivision (a) informing them that the trustee intends to deposit the funds with the clerk of the court and that a claim for the funds must be filed with the court within 30 days from the date of the notice, providing the address of the court in which the funds were deposited, and a telephone number for obtaining further information.

Within 90 days after deposit with the clerk, the court shall consider all claims filed at least 15 days before the date on which the hearing is scheduled by the court, the clerk shall serve written notice of the hearing by first-class mail on all claimants identified in the trustee's declaration at the addresses specified therein. Where the amount of the deposit is twenty-five thousand dollars ($25,000) or less, a proceeding pursuant to this section is a limited civil case. The court shall distribute the deposited funds to any and all claimants entitled thereto.

(e) Nothing in this section restricts the ability of a trustee to file an interpleader action in order to resolve a dispute about the proceeds of a trustee's sale. Once an interpleader action has been filed, thereafter the provisions of this section do not apply.

(f) "Due diligence," for the purposes of this section means that the trustee researched the written claims submitted or other evidence of conflicts and determined that a conflict of priorities exists between two or more claimants which the trustee is unable to resolve.

(g) To the extent required by the Unclaimed Property Law, a trustee in possession of surplus proceeds not required to be deposited with the court pursuant to subdivision (b) shall comply with the Unclaimed Property Law (Chapter 7 (commencing with Section 1500) of Title 10 of Part 3 of the Code of Civil Procedure).

(h) The trustee, beneficiary, or counsel to the trustee or beneficiary, is not liable for providing to any person who is entitled to notice pursuant to this section, information set forth in, or a copy of, subdivision (h) of Section 2945.3. (*Added by*

Stats.1989, c. 849, § 1. Amended by Stats.1990, c. 287 (A.B. 3078), § 1; Stats.1992, c. 351 (A.B.2981), § 6; Stats.1998, c. 932 (A.B.1094), § 9; Stats.1999, c. 974 (A.B.431), § 11; Stats.2002, c. 784 (S.B.1316), § 20; Stats.2003, c. 62 (S.B.600), § 19; Stats. 2004, c. 177 (S.B.1277), § 3; Stats.2005, c. 75 (A.B.145), § 15, eff. July 19, 2005, operative Jan. 1, 2006.)

Law Revision Commission Comments

Subdivisions (c) and (d) of Section 2924j are amended to reflect unification of the municipal and superior courts pursuant to Article VI, Section 5(e), of the California Constitution.

Subdivision (d) is also amended to clarify the jurisdictional classification of a proceeding to distribute excess sale proceeds. This is declaratory of existing law. See Code Civ. Proc. § 85 (limited civil cases) & Comment. See also Code Civ. Proc. § 88 (unlimited civil cases). [32 Cal.L.Rev. Comm. Reports 86 (2002)].

Research References

Rutter, Cal. Practice Guide: Real Prop. Transactions Ch. 6-I, I. Real Property Foreclosures and Antideficiency Laws.
Miller and Starr California Real Estate § 1:79, Form of the Memorandum.
Miller and Starr California Real Estate § 10:200, Special Notice to the Internal Revenue Service.
Miller and Starr California Real Estate § 10:213, Disposition of Sales Proceeds.
Miller and Starr California Real Estate § 11:180, Priority of Federal Tax Liens--In General.
15 NO. 4 Miller & Starr, California Real Estate Newsalert 7, Deeds.
20 NO. 4 Miller & Starr, California Real Estate Newsalert 26, Deeds of Trust.
4 Witkin, California Summary 10th Security Transactions in Real Property § 162, (S 162) Order of Priority.
4 Witkin, California Summary 10th Security Transactions in Real Property § 163, (S 163) Conflicting Claims.

§ 2924k.   Distribution of proceeds of trustee's sale; priority

(a) The trustee, or the clerk of the court upon order to the clerk pursuant to subdivision (d) of Section 2924j, shall distribute the proceeds, or a portion of the proceeds, as the case may be, of the trustee's sale conducted pursuant to Section 2924h in the following order of priority:

(1) To the costs and expenses of exercising the power of sale and of sale, including the payment of the trustee's fees and attorney's fees permitted pursuant to subdivision (b) of Section 2924d and subdivision (b) of this section.

(2) To the payment of the obligations secured by the deed of trust or mortgage which is the subject of the trustee's sale.

(3) To satisfy the outstanding balance of obligations secured by any junior liens or encumbrances in the order of their priority.

(4) To the trustor or the trustor's successor in interest. In the event the property is sold or transferred to another, to the vested owner of record at the time of the trustee's sale.

(b) A trustee may charge costs and expenses incurred for such items as mailing and a reasonable fee for services rendered in connection with the distribution of the proceeds from a trustee's sale, including, but not limited to, the investigation of priority and validity of claims and the disbursement of funds. If the fee charged for services rendered pursuant to this subdivision does not exceed one hundred dollars ($100), or one hundred twenty-five dollars ($125) where there are obligations specified in paragraph (3) of subdivision (a), the fee is conclusively presumed to be reasonable. *(Added by Stats.1990, c. 287 (A.B.3078), § 2. Amended by Stats.1999, c. 974 (A.B.431), § 12.)*

Research References

Rutter, Cal. Practice Guide: Real Prop. Transactions Ch. 6-I, I. Real Property Foreclosures and Antideficiency Laws.

Miller and Starr California Real Estate § 13:5, Voluntary or Involuntary Sale of Homestead; Reinvestment of Proceeds.
Miller and Starr California Real Estate § 10:179, Nature and Basis of Power of Sale.
Miller and Starr California Real Estate § 10:181, Notice of Default--In General.
Miller and Starr California Real Estate § 10:213, Disposition of Sales Proceeds.
Miller and Starr California Real Estate § 11:100, Priority of the Purchaser's Title from a Foreclosure Sale.
17 NO. 1 Miller & Starr, California Real Estate Newsalert 4, Deeds of Trust.
20 NO. 4 Miller & Starr, California Real Estate Newsalert 26, Deeds of Trust.
22 NO. 3 Miller & Starr, California Real Estate Newsalert 1, Show Me Your Papers: Sales and Assignments of Secured Real Estate Loans and the California Foreclosure Process.
22 NO. 2 Miller & Starr, California Real Estate Newsalert 9, Deeds of Trust.
22 NO. 6 Miller & Starr, California Real Estate Newsalert 11, Deeds of Trust.
8 Witkin Cal. Proc. 5th Enforcement of Judgment § 235, (S 235) Attachment of Judgment Lien.
4 Witkin, California Summary 10th Security Transactions in Real Property § 162, (S 162) Order of Priority.
4 Witkin, California Summary 10th Security Transactions in Real Property § 163, (S 163) Conflicting Claims.

§ 2924l.   Declaration of nonmonetary status; trustee named in action or proceeding in trustee capacity; objections

(a) In the event that a trustee under a deed of trust is named in an action or proceeding in which that deed of trust is the subject, and in the event that the trustee maintains a reasonable belief that it has been named in the action or proceeding solely in its capacity as trustee, and not arising out of any wrongful acts or omissions on its part in the performance of its duties as trustee, then, at any time, the trustee may file a declaration of nonmonetary status. The declaration shall be served on the parties in the manner set forth in Chapter 5 (commencing with Section 1010) of Title 14 of the Code of Civil Procedure.

(b) The declaration of nonmonetary status shall set forth the status of the trustee as trustee under the deed of trust that is the subject of the action or proceeding, that the trustee knows or maintains a reasonable belief that it has been named as a defendant in the proceeding solely in its capacity as a trustee under the deed of trust, its reasonable belief that it has not been named as a defendant due to any acts or omissions on its part in the performance of its duties as trustee, the basis for that knowledge or reasonable belief, and that it agrees to be bound by whatever order or judgment is issued by the court regarding the subject deed of trust.

(c) The parties who have appeared in the action or proceeding shall have 15 days from the service of the declaration by the trustee in which to object to the nonmonetary judgment status of the trustee. Any objection shall set forth the factual basis on which the objection is based and shall be served on the trustee.

(d) In the event that no objection is served within the 15-day objection period, the trustee shall not be required to participate any further in the action or proceeding, shall not be subject to any monetary awards as and for damages, attorneys' fees or costs, shall be required to respond to any discovery requests as a nonparty, and shall be bound by any court order relating to the subject deed of trust that is the subject of the action or proceeding.

(e) In the event of a timely objection to the declaration of nonmonetary status, the trustee shall thereafter be required to participate in the action or proceeding.

Additionally, in the event that the parties elect not to, or fail to, timely object to the declaration of nonmonetary status, but later through discovery, or otherwise, determine that the trustee should participate in the action because of the performance of its duties as a trustee, the parties may file and serve on all parties and the trustee a motion pursuant to Section 473 of the Code of Civil Procedure that specifies the factual basis for the demand. Upon the court's granting of the motion, the trustee shall thereafter be required to participate in the action or proceeding, and the court shall provide sufficient time prior to trial for the trustee to be able to respond to the complaint, to conduct discovery, and to bring other pretrial motions in accordance with the Code of Civil Procedure.

(f) Upon the filing of the declaration of nonmonetary status, the time within which the trustee is required to file an answer or other responsive pleading shall be tolled for the period of time within which the opposing parties may respond to the declaration. Upon the timely service of an objection to the declaration on nonmonetary status, the trustee shall have 30 days from the date of service within which to file an answer or other responsive pleading to the complaint or cross-complaint.

(g) For purposes of this section, "trustee" includes any agent or employee of the trustee who performs some or all of the duties of a trustee under this article, and includes substituted trustees and agents of the beneficiary or trustee. *(Added by Stats.1995, c. 752 (A.B.1695), § 4. Amended by Stats.1997, c. 74 (S.B.665), § 6; Stats.1999, c. 974 (A.B.431), § 13; Stats.2004, c. 177 (S.B.1277), § 4.)*

§ 2925. Transfer subject to defeasance on a condition; proof

The fact that a transfer was made subject to defeasance on a condition, may, for the purpose of showing such transfer to be a mortgage, be proved (except as against a subsequent purchaser or incumbrancer for value and without notice), though the fact does not appear by the terms of the instrument. *(Enacted in 1872.)*

Research References

Miller and Starr California Real Estate § 10:26, Evidence of the Parties' Intentions.
Miller and Starr California Real Estate § 10:27, Enforcement Against a Purchaser from the Creditor or Other Third Person.
Miller and Starr California Real Estate § 25C:34, Restrictions on the Receipt and Disbursement of the Buyer's Funds; When No Blanket Encumbrance.

§ 2926. Scope of mortgage lien

A mortgage is a lien upon everything that would pass by a grant of the property. *(Enacted in 1872.)*

Research References

Miller and Starr California Real Estate § 10:2, Lien Versus Title Theories.
Miller and Starr California Real Estate § 10:16, Property Interests that Are Lienable.
Miller and Starr California Real Estate § 11:194, Priority Between a Deed of Trust and a Security Interest in Fixtures.

§ 2927. Possession of mortgaged property

A mortgage does not entitle the mortgagee to the possession of the property, unless authorized by the express terms of the mortgage; but after the execution of the mortgage the mortgagor may agree to such change of possession without a new consideration. *(Enacted in 1872.)*

Research References

Miller and Starr California Real Estate § 10:2, Lien Versus Title Theories.
Miller and Starr California Real Estate § 10:46, Possession and Rents; Mortgagee in Possession.

4 Witkin, California Summary 10th Security Transactions in Real Property § 95, in General.

§ 2928. Personal obligation

A mortgage does not bind the mortgagor personally to perform the act for the performance of which it is a security, unless there is an express covenant therein to that effect. *(Enacted in 1872.)*

§ 2929. Waste

No person whose interest is subject to the lien of a mortgage may do any act which will substantially impair the mortgagee's security. *(Enacted in 1872.)*

Research References

Rutter, Cal. Practice Guide: Real Prop. Transactions Ch. 6-H, H. Security for Promissory Note.
Miller and Starr California Real Estate § 2:19, Right to Possession; Waste.
Miller and Starr California Real Estate § 26:2, Capacity to Dedicate Property; Co-Ownership.
Miller and Starr California Real Estate § 10:53, Waste by the Trustor or a Successor.
Miller and Starr California Real Estate § 10:135, Curable Versus Noncurable Defaults.
Miller and Starr California Real Estate § 19:126, Waste.
4 Witkin, California Summary 10th Security Transactions in Real Property § 85, (S 85) Against Mortgagor.
4 Witkin, California Summary 10th Security Transactions in Real Property § 176, Negligence Claims.

§ 2929.3 Maintenance of vacant residential property purchased at foreclosure sale; violation; fines and penalties

(a)(1) A legal owner shall maintain vacant residential property purchased by that owner at a foreclosure sale, or acquired by that owner through foreclosure under a mortgage or deed of trust. A governmental entity may impose a civil fine of up to one thousand dollars ($1,000) per day for a violation. If the governmental entity chooses to impose a fine pursuant to this section, it shall give notice of the alleged violation, including a description of the conditions that gave rise to the allegation, and notice of the entity's intent to assess a civil fine if action to correct the violation is not commenced within a period of not less than 14 days and completed within a period of not less than 30 days. The notice shall be mailed to the address provided in the deed or other instrument as specified in subdivision (a) of Section 27321.5 of the Government Code, or, if none, to the return address provided on the deed or other instrument.

(2) The governmental entity shall provide a period of not less than 30 days for the legal owner to remedy the violation prior to imposing a civil fine and shall allow for a hearing and opportunity to contest any fine imposed. In determining the amount of the fine, the governmental entity shall take into consideration any timely and good faith efforts by the legal owner to remedy the violation. The maximum civil fine authorized by this section is one thousand dollars ($1,000) for each day that the owner fails to maintain the property, commencing on the day following the expiration of the period to remedy the violation established by the governmental entity.

(3) Subject to the provisions of this section, a governmental entity may establish different compliance periods for different conditions on the same property in the notice of alleged violation mailed to the legal owner.

(b) For purposes of this section, "failure to maintain" means failure to care for the exterior of the property, including, but not limited to, permitting excessive foliage growth that diminishes the value of surrounding properties, failing to take action to prevent trespassers or squatters from remaining on the property, or failing to take action to prevent mosquito larvae from growing in standing water or other conditions that create a public nuisance.

(c) Notwithstanding subdivisions (a) and (b), a governmental entity may provide less than 30 days' notice to remedy a condition before imposing a civil fine if the entity determines that a specific condition of the property threatens public health or safety and provided that notice of that determination and time for compliance is given.

(d) Fines and penalties collected pursuant to this section shall be directed to local nuisance abatement programs, including, but not limited to, legal abatement proceedings.

(e) A governmental entity may not impose fines on a legal owner under both this section and a local ordinance.

(f) These provisions shall not preempt any local ordinance.

(g) This section shall only apply to residential real property.

(h) The rights and remedies provided in this section are cumulative and in addition to any other rights and remedies provided by law. *(Added by Stats.2008, c. 69 (S.B.1137), § 5, eff. July 8, 2008. Amended by Stats.2012, c. 201 (A.B.2314), § 1.)*

Research References

Rutter, Cal. Practice Guide: Real Prop. Transactions Ch. 6-I, I. Real Property Foreclosures and Antideficiency Laws.
Miller and Starr California Real Estate § 22:29, Residential Buildings Which Do Not Comply With Code.
Miller and Starr California Real Estate § 10:208, Purchaser's Title.
19 NO. 1 Miller & Starr, California Real Estate Newsalert 1, The Perata Foreclosure Bill (SB 1137): New Rights for Defaulting Borrowers and Tenants; New Complications for Foreclosing Lenders.
19 NO. 4 Miller & Starr, California Real Estate Newsalert 10, Deeds of Trust.
21 NO. 4 Miller & Starr, California Real Estate Newsalert 11, Deeds of Trust.
4 Witkin, California Summary 10th Security Transactions in Real Property § 102, Duties of Mortgagee in Possession.

§ 2929.4. Failure to maintain vacant property subject to notice of default, purchased at foreclosure sale, or acquired through foreclosure; notice of violation prior to imposition of fine or penalty; opportunity to correct; exception for public health or safety

(a) Prior to imposing a fine or penalty for failure to maintain a vacant property that is subject to a notice of default, that is purchased at a foreclosure sale, or that is acquired through foreclosure under a mortgage or deed of trust, a governmental entity shall provide the owner of that property with a notice of the violation and an opportunity to correct that violation.

(b) This section shall not apply if the governmental entity determines that a specific condition of the property threatens public health or safety. *(Added by Stats.2010, c. 527 (S.B.1427), § 1.)*

Research References

Miller and Starr California Real Estate § 22:29, Residential Buildings Which Do Not Comply With Code.
Miller and Starr California Real Estate § 10:208, Purchaser's Title.
21 NO. 4 Miller & Starr, California Real Estate Newsalert 11, Deeds of Trust.
4 Witkin, California Summary 10th Security Transactions in Real Property § 102, Duties of Mortgagee in Possession.

§ 2929.45. Limit upon nuisance abatement costs recoverable against property subject to notice of default, purchased at foreclosure sale, or acquired through foreclosure; costs adopted by elected officials

(a) An assessment or lien to recover the costs of nuisance abatement measures taken by a governmental entity with regard to property that is subject to a notice of default, that is purchased at a foreclosure sale, or that is acquired through foreclosure under a mortgage or deed of trust, shall not exceed the actual and reasonable costs of nuisance abatement.

(b) A governmental entity shall not impose an assessment or lien unless the costs that constitute the assessment or lien have been adopted by the elected officials of that governmental entity at a public hearing. *(Added by Stats.2010, c. 527 (S.B.1427), § 2.)*

Research References

Miller and Starr California Real Estate § 22:29, Residential Buildings Which Do Not Comply With Code.
Miller and Starr California Real Estate § 10:208, Purchaser's Title.
21 NO. 4 Miller & Starr, California Real Estate Newsalert 11, Deeds of Trust.
4 Witkin, California Summary 10th Security Transactions in Real Property § 102, Duties of Mortgagee in Possession.

§ 2929.5. Hazardous substances; inspection by secured lender

(a) A secured lender may enter and inspect the real property security for the purpose of determining the existence, location, nature, and magnitude of any past or present release or threatened release of any hazardous substance into, onto, beneath, or from the real property security on either of the following:

(1) Upon reasonable belief of the existence of a past or present release or threatened release of any hazardous substance into, onto, beneath, or from the real property security not previously disclosed in writing to the secured lender in conjunction with the making, renewal, or modification of a loan, extension of credit, guaranty, or other obligation involving the borrower.

(2) After the commencement of nonjudicial or judicial foreclosure proceedings against the real property security.

(b) The secured lender shall not abuse the right of entry and inspection or use it to harass the borrower or tenant of the property. Except in case of an emergency, when the borrower or tenant of the property has abandoned the premises, or if it is impracticable to do so, the secured lender shall give the borrower or tenant of the property reasonable notice of the secured lender's intent to enter, and enter only during the borrower's or tenant's normal business hours. Twenty-four hours' notice shall be presumed to be reasonable notice in the absence of evidence to the contrary.

(c) The secured lender shall reimburse the borrower for the cost of repair of any physical injury to the real property security caused by the entry and inspection.

(d) If a secured lender is refused the right of entry and inspection by the borrower or tenant of the property, or is otherwise unable to enter and inspect the property without a breach of the peace, the secured lender may, upon petition, obtain an order from a court of competent jurisdiction to exercise the secured lender's rights under subdivision (a), and that action shall not constitute an action within the meaning of subdivision (a) of Section 726 of the Code of Civil Procedure.

(e) For purposes of this section:

(1) "Borrower" means the trustor under a deed of trust, or a mortgagor under a mortgage, where the deed of trust or mortgage encumbers real property security and secures the performance of the trustor or mortgagor under a loan, extension of credit, guaranty, or other obligation. The term includes any successor-in-interest of the trustor or mortgagor to the real property security before the deed of trust or mortgage has been discharged, reconveyed, or foreclosed upon.

(2) "Hazardous substance" includes all of the following:

(A) Any "hazardous substance" as defined in subdivision (h) of Section 25281 of the Health and Safety Code.

(B) Any "waste" as defined in subdivision (d) of Section 13050 of the Water Code.

(C) Petroleum, including crude oil or any fraction thereof, natural gas, natural gas liquids, liquefied natural gas, or synthetic gas usable for fuel, or any mixture thereof.

(3) "Real property security" means any real property and improvements, other than a separate interest and any related interest in the common area of a residential common interest development, as the terms "separate interest," "common area," and "common interest development" are defined in Sections 4095, 4100, and 4185, or real property consisting of one acre or less which contains 1 to 15 dwelling units.

(4) "Release" means any spilling, leaking, pumping, pouring, emitting, emptying, discharging, injecting, escaping, leaching, dumping, or disposing into the environment, including continuing migration, of hazardous substances into, onto, or through soil, surface water, or groundwater.

(5) "Secured lender" means the beneficiary under a deed of trust against the real property security, or the mortgagee under a mortgage against the real property security, and any successor-in-interest of the beneficiary or mortgagee to the deed of trust or mortgage. *(Added by Stats.1991, c. 1167 (A.B.1735), § 1. Amended by Stats.1992, c. 167 (A.B.2750), § 1; Stats.2002, c. 999 (A.B.2481), § 2; Stats.2012, c. 181 (A.B.806), § 40, operative Jan. 1, 2014.)*

Law Revision Commission Comments

Section 2929.5 is amended to correct cross-references to former Section 1351(a), (b), and (*l*). [40 Cal.L.Rev.Comm. Reports 235 (2010)].

Research References

California Real Estate Forms (Miller & Starr) § 3:8, Deed of Trust, Security Agreement, and Fixture Filing With Assignment of Rents and Agreements.
California Real Estate Forms (Miller & Starr) § 3:10, Environmental Certification, Agreement, and Indemnity of Borrower.
California Real Estate Forms (Miller & Starr) § 3:14, Construction Deed of Trust, Security Agreement, and Fixture Filing With Assignment of Rents and Agreements.
California Real Estate Forms (Miller & Starr) § 3:21, Deed of Trust, Assignment of Rents, Security Agreement and Fixture Filing--Conduit Loan.
California Real Estate Forms (Miller & Starr) § 3:30, Environmental Indemnity--Conduit Loan.
Rutter, Cal. Practice Guide: Enforcing Judgments/Debts Ch. 4-C, C. Receiverships.
Rutter, Cal. Practice Guide: Real Prop. Transactions Ch. 6-I, I. Real Property Foreclosures and Antideficiency Laws.
Rutter, Cal. Practice Guide: Real Prop. Transactions Ch. 6-K, K. Environmental Indemnities.
Rutter, Cal. Practice Guide: Real Prop. Transactions Form 6:I, Deed of Trust (Complex).
Miller and Starr California Real Estate § 33:33, Secured Creditor Actions--In General.
Miller and Starr California Real Estate § 33:39, Secured Creditor Actions--Inspection for Hazardous Substances.
Miller and Starr California Real Estate § 10:157, Exception; Environmentally Impaired Property.
16 NO. 2 Miller & Starr, California Real Estate Newsalert 1, Trustee Sales: the "Terminator' of Debtors' Equities.
6 Witkin Cal. Proc. 5th Provisional Remedies § 426, (S 426) Action by Secured Lender.
4 Witkin, California Summary 10th Security Transactions in Real Property § 128, Remedy is Not Action.
4 Witkin, California Summary 10th Security Transactions in Real Property § 208, (S 208) Nature and Scope of Legislation.

4 Witkin, California Summary 10th Security Transactions in Real Property § 209, (S 209) Inspection of Property.

§ 2930. Title subsequently acquired by mortgagor

Title acquired by the mortgagor subsequent to the execution of the mortgage, inures to the mortgagee as security for the debt in like manner as if acquired before the execution. *(Enacted in 1872. Amended by Code Am. 1873–74, c. 612, p. 260, § 257.)*

Research References

Miller and Starr California Real Estate § 8:73, After-Acquired Title.
Miller and Starr California Real Estate § 10:19, "After-Acquired" Title.
Miller and Starr California Real Estate § 11:100, Priority of the Purchaser's Title from a Foreclosure Sale.
12 Witkin, California Summary 10th Real Property § 334, in General.
4 Witkin, California Summary 10th Security Transactions in Real Property § 34, What Property Can be Mortgaged.

§ 2931. Foreclosure

A mortgagee may foreclose the right of redemption of the mortgagor in the manner prescribed by the Code of Civil Procedure. *(Enacted in 1872.)*

Research References

Miller and Starr California Real Estate § 10:123, Nature of Foreclosure; Termination of Redemption.
Miller and Starr California Real Estate § 10:124, Choice of Remedies.
Miller and Starr California Real Estate § 10:221, Comparison With Nonjudicial Foreclosure.

§ 2931a. Actions relating to real property; tax lien; state agency as party; jurisdiction; contents of complaint or petition; service of process; duties of Attorney General

In any action brought to determine conflicting claims to real property, or for partition of real property or an estate for years therein, or to foreclose a deed of trust, mortgage, or other lien upon real property, or in all eminent domain proceedings under Section 1250.110 et seq., of the Code of Civil Procedure against real property upon which exists a lien to secure the payment of taxes or other obligations to an agency of the State of California, other than ad valorem taxes upon the real property, the state agency charged with the collection of the tax obligation may be made a party. In such an action, the court shall have jurisdiction to determine the priority and effect of the liens described in the complaint in or upon the real property or estate for years therein, but the jurisdiction of the court in the action shall not include a determination of the validity of the tax giving rise to the lien or claim of lien. The complaint or petition in the action shall contain a description of the lien sufficient to enable the tax or other obligation, payment of which it secures, to be identified with certainty, and shall include the name and address of the person owing the tax or other obligation, the name of the state agency that recorded the lien, and the date and place where the lien was recorded. Services of process in the action shall be made upon the agency, officer, board, commission, department, division, or other body charged with the collection of the tax or obligation. It shall be the duty of the Attorney General to represent the state agency in the action. *(Added by Stats.1935, c. 464, p. 1521, § 1. Amended by Stats.1941, c. 1193, p. 2966, § 1; Stats.1980, c. 44, p. 108, § 2; Stats.1986, c. 81, § 1; Stats.1989, c. 698, § 8.)*

Law Revision Commission Comments

Section 2931a is amended to reflect the relocation of the partition provisions. Quiet title provisions now occupy Chapter 4 (commencing with Section 760.010) of Title 10 of Part 2 of the Code of Civil Procedure.

Research References

Miller and Starr California Real Estate § 10:223, Joinder of Parties.

Civil

4 Witkin, California Summary 10th Security Transactions in Real Property § 139, (S 139) Who Should be Joined.

§ 2931b. Tax sale; purchase by state

In all actions in which the State of California is named a party pursuant to the provisions of Section 2931a and in which real property or an estate for years therein is sought to be sold, the Attorney General may, with the consent of the Department of Finance, bid upon and purchase that real property or estate for years. *(Added by Stats.1953, c. 1675, p. 3408, § 1. Amended by Stats.1989, c. 698, § 9.)*

§ 2931c. Action by Attorney General to enforce lien to secure payment of taxes or other obligations to state

The Attorney General may bring an action in the courts of this or any other state or of the United States to enforce any lien to secure the payment of taxes or other obligations to the State of California under the Unemployment Insurance Code, the Revenue and Taxation Code, or Chapter 6 (commencing with Section 16180) of Part 1 of Division 4 of Title 2 of the Government Code or to subject to payment of the liability giving rise to the lien any property in which the debtor has any right, title, or interest. In any action brought under this section the court shall have jurisdiction to determine the priority and effect of the lien in or upon the property, but the jurisdiction of the court in such action shall not extend to a determination of the validity of the liability giving rise to the lien. *(Added by Stats.1963, c. 1308, p. 2832, § 1. Amended by Stats.1977, c. 1242, p. 4190, § 3, eff. Oct. 1, 1977.)*

Research References

4 Witkin Cal. Proc. 5th Pleading § 155, in General.
9 Witkin, California Summary 10th Taxation § 308, Security and Enforcement.
4 Witkin, California Summary 10th Security Transactions in Real Property § 59, (S 59) Priority of Tax Lien Over Mortgage.

§ 2932. Power of sale

A power of sale may be conferred by a mortgage upon the mortgagee or any other person, to be exercised after a breach of the obligation for which the mortgage is a security. *(Enacted in 1872.)*

Research References

Rutter, Cal. Practice Guide: Real Prop. Transactions Ch. 6-H, H. Security for Promissory Note.
Miller and Starr California Real Estate § 10:1, Historical Perspective.
Miller and Starr California Real Estate § 10:124, Choice of Remedies.
Miller and Starr California Real Estate § 10:179, Nature and Basis of Power of Sale.
Miller and Starr California Real Estate § 10:180, Power of Sale; Constitutionality.
Miller and Starr California Real Estate § 10:202, Conduct of the Sale.
Miller and Starr California Real Estate § 10:263, Definitions; Guarantor, Surety.
22 NO. 3 Miller & Starr, California Real Estate Newsalert 1, Show Me Your Papers: Sales and Assignments of Secured Real Estate Loans and the California Foreclosure Process.

§ 2932.5. Power of sale; vesting in assignee

Where a power to sell real property is given to a mortgagee, or other encumbrancer, in an instrument intended to secure the payment of money, the power is part of the security and vests in any person who by assignment becomes entitled to payment of the money secured by the instrument. The power of sale may be exercised by the assignee if the assignment is duly acknowledged and recorded. *(Added by Stats.1986, c. 820, § 11, operative July 1, 1987.)*

Law Revision Commission Comments

Section 2932.5 continues former Section 858 without substantive change. [18 Cal.L.Rev.Comm. Reports 501 (1986)].

Research References

Miller and Starr California Real Estate § 10:3, Parties.
Miller and Starr California Real Estate § 11:6, Instruments Subject to Recording--List of Recordable Documents.
Miller and Starr California Real Estate § 11:8, Evidentiary Effect of Recording.
Miller and Starr California Real Estate § 10:38, What is Assignable; Procedure.
Miller and Starr California Real Estate § 10:39, Rights of the Parties.
Miller and Starr California Real Estate § 10:184, Execution of the Notice of Default.
Miller and Starr California Real Estate § 10:199, Publication, Mailing, and Recording the Notice.
22 NO. 3 Miller & Starr, California Real Estate Newsalert 1, Show Me Your Papers: Sales and Assignments of Secured Real Estate Loans and the California Foreclosure Process.
22 NO. 2 Miller & Starr, California Real Estate Newsalert 9, Deeds of Trust.
22 NO. 6 Miller & Starr, California Real Estate Newsalert 11, Deeds of Trust.
14 Witkin, California Summary 10th Wills and Probate § 803, (S 803) Obligation Secured by Lien on Real Property.

§ 2932.6. Financial institution repair of property acquired through foreclosure

(a) Notwithstanding any other provision of law, a financial institution may undertake to repair any property acquired through foreclosure under a mortgage or deed of trust.

(b) As used in this section, the term "financial institution" includes, but is not limited to, banks, savings associations, credit unions, and industrial loan companies.

(c) The rights granted to a financial institution by this section are in addition to, and not in derogation of, the rights of a financial institution which otherwise exist. *(Added by Stats.1987, c. 187, § 1. Amended by Stats.1988, c. 125, § 1.)*

Research References

Miller and Starr California Real Estate § 10:220, Possession and Rents After Trustee's Sale.

§ 2933. Power of attorney; formalities

A power of attorney to execute a mortgage must be in writing, subscribed, acknowledged, or proved, certified, and recorded in like manner as powers of attorney for grants of real property. *(Enacted in 1872.)*

Research References

Rutter, Cal. Practice Guide: Real Prop. Transactions Ch. 4-C, C. Parties to the Purchase Agreement.
Miller and Starr California Real Estate § 1:91, Nonstatutory Form of Agent's Written Authority.
Miller and Starr California Real Estate § 1:92, Statutory Provisions for Powers of Attorney.
Miller and Starr California Real Estate § 10:7, Execution and Delivery.
Miller and Starr California Real Estate § 11:2, Enforceability of Unrecorded Instruments.
Miller and Starr California Real Estate § 11:6, Instruments Subject to Recording--List of Recordable Documents.
Miller and Starr California Real Estate § 8:30, Execution by an Agent or Attorney-In-Fact.
Miller and Starr California Real Estate § 11:23, Purpose and Effect; Required for Recordation.

Miller and Starr California Real Estate § 10:179, Nature and Basis of Power of Sale.

§ 2934. Assignments; instruments subordinating or waiving priority; recording; effect

Any assignment of a mortgage and any assignment of the beneficial interest under a deed of trust may be recorded, and from the time the same is filed for record operates as constructive notice of the contents thereof to all persons; and any instrument by which any mortgage or deed of trust of, lien upon or interest in real property, (or by which any mortgage of, lien upon or interest in personal property a document evidencing or creating which is required or permitted by law to be recorded), is subordinated or waived as to priority may be recorded, and from the time the same is filed for record operates as constructive notice of the contents thereof, to all persons. *(Enacted in 1872. Amended by Code Am.1873–74, c. 612, p. 261, § 258; Stats.1931, c. 80, p. 101, § 1; Stats.1935, c. 818, p. 2229, § 1.)*

Research References

California Real Estate Forms (Miller & Starr) § 3:8, Deed of Trust, Security Agreement, and Fixture Filing With Assignment of Rents and Agreements.

California Real Estate Forms (Miller & Starr) § 3:14, Construction Deed of Trust, Security Agreement, and Fixture Filing With Assignment of Rents and Agreements.

California Real Estate Forms (Miller & Starr) § 3:21, Deed of Trust, Assignment of Rents, Security Agreement and Fixture Filing--Conduit Loan.

California Real Estate Forms (Miller & Starr) § 3:56, Subordination Agreement (Deed of Trust to Deed of Trust).

Miller and Starr California Real Estate § 11:3, Effect of Recording Statutes on Priority.

Miller and Starr California Real Estate § 11:6, Instruments Subject to Recording--List of Recordable Documents.

Miller and Starr California Real Estate § 10:39, Rights of the Parties.

Miller and Starr California Real Estate § 11:60, Recordation as Constructive Notice.

Miller and Starr California Real Estate § 11:65. Recorded Documents that Do Not Give Constructive Notice--Documents Not Specifically Stated to Impart Constructive Notice by Statute or Which Are Specifically Stated Not to Impart Constructive...

Miller and Starr California Real Estate § 11:201, Subordination Agreements; in General.

22 NO. 3 Miller & Starr, California Real Estate Newsalert 1, Show Me Your Papers: Sales and Assignments of Secured Real Estate Loans and the California Foreclosure Process.

4 Witkin, California Summary 10th Security Transactions in Real Property § 51, (S 51) in General.

4 Witkin, California Summary 10th Security Transactions in Real Property § 106, (S 106) Assignment of Mortgage.

14 Witkin, California Summary 10th Wills and Probate § 803, (S 803) Obligation Secured by Lien on Real Property.

§ 2934a. Substitution of trustees; mailing; recording; contents of substitution; effect; new notice of sale

Text of section in effect until January 1, 1998. See, also, text of section operative Jan. 1, 1998.

(a)(1) The trustee under a trust deed upon real property or an estate for years therein given to secure an obligation to pay money and conferring no other duties upon the trustee than those which are incidental to the exercise of the power of sale therein conferred, may be substituted by the recording in the county in which the property is located of a substitution executed and acknowledged by: (A) all of the beneficiaries under the trust deed, or their successors in interest, and the substitution shall be effective notwithstanding any contrary provision in any trust deed executed on or after January 1, 1968; or (B) the holders of more than 50 percent of the record beneficial interest of a series of notes secured by the same real property or of undivided interests in a note secured by real property equivalent to a series transaction, exclusive of any notes or interests of a licensed real

estate broker that is the issuer or servicer of the notes or interests or of any affiliate of that licensed real estate broker.

(2) A substitution executed pursuant to subparagraph (B) of paragraph (1) is not effective unless all the parties signing the substitution sign, under penalty of perjury, a separate written document stating the following:

(A) The substitution has been signed pursuant to subparagraph (B) of paragraph (1).

(B) None of the undersigned is a licensed real estate broker or an affiliate of the broker that is the issuer or servicer of the obligation secured by the deed of trust.

(C) The undersigned together hold more than 50 percent of the record beneficial interest of a series of notes secured by the same real property or of undivided interests in a note secured by real property equivalent to a series transaction.

(D) Notice of the substitution was sent by certified mail, postage prepaid, with return receipt requested to each holder of an interest in the obligation secured by the deed of trust who has not joined in the execution of the substitution or the separate document.

The separate document shall be attached to the substitution and be recorded in the office of the county recorder of each county in which the real property described in the deed of trust is located. Once the document required by this paragraph is recorded, it shall constitute conclusive evidence of compliance with the requirements of this paragraph in favor of substituted trustees acting pursuant to this section, subsequent assignees of the obligation secured by the deed of trust, and subsequent bona fide purchasers or encumbrancers for value of the real property described therein.

(3) For purposes of this section, "affiliate of the licensed real estate broker" includes any person as defined in Section 25013 of the Corporations Code that is controlled by, or is under common control with, or who controls, a licensed real estate broker. "Control" means the possession, direct or indirect, of the power to direct or cause the direction of management and policies.

(4) The substitution shall contain the date of recordation of the trust deed, the name of the trustor, the book and page or instrument number where the trust deed is recorded, and the name of the new trustee. From the time the substitution is filed for record, the new trustee shall succeed to all the powers, duties, authority, and title granted and delegated to the trustee named in the deed of trust. A substitution may be accomplished, with respect to multiple deeds of trust which are recorded in the same county in which the substitution is being recorded and which all have the same trustee and beneficiary or beneficiaries, by recording a single document, complying with the requirements of this section, substituting trustees for all those deeds of trust.

(b) If the substitution is effected after a notice of default has been recorded but prior to the recording of the notice of sale, the beneficiary or beneficiaries shall cause a copy of the substitution to be mailed, prior to the recording thereof, in the manner provided in Section 2924b, to the trustee then of record and to all persons to whom a copy of the notice of default would be required to be mailed by the provisions of Section 2924b. An affidavit shall be attached to the substitution that notice has been given to those persons and in the manner required by this subdivision.

(c) Notwithstanding any provision of this section or any provision in any deed of trust, unless a new notice of sale containing the name, street address, and telephone number of the substituted trustee is given pursuant to Section 2924f, any sale conducted by the substituted trustee shall be void.

(d) This section shall remain in effect only until January 1, 1998, and shall have no force or effect after that date, unless a later enacted statute, which is enacted before January 1, 1998, deletes or extends that date. *(Added by Stats.1935, c. 609, p. 1720, § 1. Amended by Stats.1957, c. 914, p. 2122, § 1; Stats.1959, c. 727, p. 2714, § 1; Stats.1967, c. 1163, p. 2849, § 1; Stats.1979, c. 1015, p. 3477, § 6; Stats.1982, c. 521, p. 2448, § 1; Stats.1984, c. 1730, § 5; Stats.1989, c. 698, § 10; Stats.1993, c. 686 (A.B.1219), § 8; Stats.1993, c. 754 (S.B.313), § 1, eff. Oct. 4, 1993; Stats.1993, c. 754 (S.B.313), § 1.5, eff. Oct. 4, 1993, operative Jan. 1, 1994; Stats.1996, c. 839 (S.B.1638), § 1.)*

Operative Effect

This section was in effect until January 1, 1998, and by its own terms has no force or effect after that date.

Research References

California Real Estate Forms (Miller & Starr) § 3:8, Deed of Trust, Security Agreement, and Fixture Filing With Assignment of Rents and Agreements.

California Real Estate Forms (Miller & Starr) § 1:34, Installment Land Sale Contract With Power of Sale.

California Real Estate Forms (Miller & Starr) § 3:14, Construction Deed of Trust, Security Agreement, and Fixture Filing With Assignment of Rents and Agreements.

Rutter, Cal. Practice Guide: Real Prop. Transactions Ch. 6-H, H. Security for Promissory Note.

Miller and Starr California Real Estate § 10:8, Substitution of Trustee-- Statutory Procedure.

Miller and Starr California Real Estate § 10:9, Substitution of Trustee-- Contractual Procedure.

Miller and Starr California Real Estate § 11:6, Instruments Subject to Recording--List of Recordable Documents.

Miller and Starr California Real Estate § 10:39, Rights of the Parties.

Miller and Starr California Real Estate § 10:184, Execution of the Notice of Default.

Miller and Starr California Real Estate § 10:198, Notice of Sale-- Contents of the Notice.

13 NO. 6 Miller & Starr, California Real Estate Newsalert 4, Deeds of Trust.

15 NO. 4 Miller & Starr, California Real Estate Newsalert 7, Deeds.

22 NO. 3 Miller & Starr, California Real Estate Newsalert 1, Show Me Your Papers: Sales and Assignments of Secured Real Estate Loans and the California Foreclosure Process.

22 NO. 2 Miller & Starr, California Real Estate Newsalert 9, Deeds of Trust.

22 NO. 1 Miller & Starr, California Real Estate Newsalert 11, Deeds of Trust.

12 Witkin, California Summary 10th Real Property § 112, (S 112) Liens.

4 Witkin, California Summary 10th Security Transactions in Real Property § 8, (S 8) Substitution of Trustee.

§ 2934a. Substitution of trustee; mailing; recording; contents of substitution; substitution after notice of default; authorization of trustee to act; new notice of sale

Text of section operative Jan. 1, 1998. See, also, text of section in effect until Jan. 1, 1998.

(a)(1) The trustee under a trust deed upon real property or an estate for years therein given to secure an obligation to pay money and conferring no other duties upon the trustee than those which are incidental to the exercise of the power of sale therein conferred, may be substituted by the recording in the county in which the property is located of a substitution executed and acknowledged by: (A) all of the beneficiaries under the trust deed, or their successors in interest, and the substitution shall be effective notwithstanding any contrary provision in any trust deed executed on or after January 1, 1968; or (B) the holders of more than 50 percent of the record beneficial interest of a series of notes secured by the same real property or of undivided interests in a note secured by real property equivalent to a series transaction, exclusive of any notes or interests of a licensed real estate broker that is the issuer or servicer of the notes or interests or of any affiliate of that licensed real estate broker.

(2) A substitution executed pursuant to subparagraph (B) of paragraph (1) is not effective unless all the parties signing the substitution sign, under penalty of perjury, a separate written document stating the following:

(A) The substitution has been signed pursuant to subparagraph (B) of paragraph (1).

(B) None of the undersigned is a licensed real estate broker or an affiliate of the broker that is the issuer or servicer of the obligation secured by the deed of trust.

(C) The undersigned together hold more than 50 percent of the record beneficial interest of a series of notes secured by the same real property or of undivided interests in a note secured by real property equivalent to a series transaction.

(D) Notice of the substitution was sent by certified mail, postage prepaid, with return receipt requested to each holder of an interest in the obligation secured by the deed of trust who has not joined in the execution of the substitution or the separate document.

The separate document shall be attached to the substitution and be recorded in the office of the county recorder of each county in which the real property described in the deed of trust is located. Once the document required by this paragraph is recorded, it shall constitute conclusive evidence of compliance with the requirements of this paragraph in favor of substituted trustees acting pursuant to this section, subsequent assignees of the obligation secured by the deed of trust and subsequent bona fide purchasers or encumbrancers for value of the real property described therein.

(3) For purposes of this section, "affiliate of the licensed real estate broker" includes any person as defined in Section 25013 of the Corporations Code that is controlled by, or is under common control with, or who controls, a licensed real estate broker. "Control" means the possession, direct or indirect, of the power to direct or cause the direction of management and policies.

(4) The substitution shall contain the date of recordation of the trust deed, the name of the trustor, the book and page or instrument number where the trust deed is recorded, and the name of the new trustee. From the time the substitution is filed for record, the new trustee shall succeed to all the powers, duties, authority, and title granted and delegated to the trustee named in the deed of trust. A substitution may be accomplished, with respect to multiple deeds of trust which are recorded in the same county in which the substitution is being recorded and which all have the same trustee and beneficiary or beneficiaries, by recording a single document, complying with the requirements of this section, substituting trustees for all those deeds of trust.

(b) If the substitution is executed, but not recorded, prior to or concurrently with the recording of the notice of default, the beneficiary or beneficiaries or their authorized agents shall cause notice of the substitution to be mailed prior to or concurrently with the recording thereof, in the manner provided in Section 2924b, to all persons to whom a copy of the notice of default would be required to be mailed by the provisions of Section 2924b. An affidavit shall be attached to the substitution that notice has been given to those persons and in the manner required by this subdivision.

(c) If the substitution is effected after a notice of default has been recorded but prior to the recording of the notice of sale, the beneficiary or beneficiaries or their authorized agents shall cause a copy of the substitution to be mailed, prior to, or concurrently with, the recording thereof, in the manner provided in Section 2924b, to the trustee then of record and to all persons to whom a copy of the notice of default would be required to be mailed by the provisions of Section 2924b. An affidavit shall be attached to the substitution that notice has been given to those persons and in the manner required by this subdivision.

(d) A trustee named in a recorded substitution of trustee shall be deemed to be authorized to act as the trustee under the mortgage or deed of trust for all purposes from the date the substitution is executed by the mortgagee, beneficiaries, or by their authorized agents. Nothing herein requires that a trustee under a recorded substitution accept the substitution. Once recorded, the substitution shall constitute conclusive evidence of the authority of the substituted trustee or his or her agents to act pursuant to this section.

(e) Notwithstanding any provision of this section or any provision in any deed of trust, unless a new notice of sale containing the name, street address, and telephone number of the substituted trustee is given pursuant to Section 2924f after execution of the substitution, any sale conducted by the substituted trustee shall be void.

(f) This section shall become operative on January 1, 1998. *(Added by Stats.1993, c. 754 (S.B.313), § 2.5, eff. Oct. 4, 1993, operative Jan. 1, 1998. Amended by Stats.1996, c. 839 (S.B.1638), § 2, operative Jan. 1, 1998; Stats.1999, c. 974 (A.B.431), § 14; Stats.2004, c. 177 (S.B.1277), § 5.)*

Research References

California Real Estate Forms (Miller & Starr) § 3:8, Deed of Trust, Security Agreement, and Fixture Filing With Assignment of Rents and Agreements.

California Real Estate Forms (Miller & Starr) § 1:34, Installment Land Sale Contract With Power of Sale.

California Real Estate Forms (Miller & Starr) § 3:14, Construction Deed of Trust, Security Agreement, and Fixture Filing With Assignment of Rents and Agreements.

Rutter, Cal. Practice Guide: Real Prop. Transactions Ch. 6-H, H. Security for Promissory Note.

Miller and Starr California Real Estate § 10:8, Substitution of Trustee--Statutory Procedure.

Miller and Starr California Real Estate § 10:9, Substitution of Trustee--Contractual Procedure.

Miller and Starr California Real Estate § 11:6, Instruments Subject to Recording--List of Recordable Documents.

Miller and Starr California Real Estate § 10:39, Rights of the Parties.

Miller and Starr California Real Estate § 10:184, Execution of the Notice of Default.

Miller and Starr California Real Estate § 10:198, Notice of Sale--Contents of the Notice.

13 NO. 6 Miller & Starr, California Real Estate Newsalert 4, Deeds of Trust.

15 NO. 4 Miller & Starr, California Real Estate Newsalert 7, Deeds.

22 NO. 3 Miller & Starr, California Real Estate Newsalert 1, Show Me Your Papers: Sales and Assignments of Secured Real Estate Loans and the California Foreclosure Process.

22 NO. 2 Miller & Starr, California Real Estate Newsalert 9, Deeds of Trust.

22 NO. 1 Miller & Starr, California Real Estate Newsalert 11, Deeds of Trust.

12 Witkin, California Summary 10th Real Property § 112, (S 112) Liens.

4 Witkin, California Summary 10th Security Transactions in Real Property § 8, (S 8) Substitution of Trustee.

§ 2934b. Application of probate provisions

Sections 15643 and 18102 of the Probate Code apply to trustees under deeds of trust given to secure obligations. *(Added by Stats.1986, c. 820, § 12, operative July 1, 1987.)*

Law Revision Commission Comments

Section 2934b restates the last paragraph of former Civil Code Section 2281 without substantive change. See Prob. Code §§ 15643 (vacancy in office of trustee), 18102 (protection of third person dealing with former trustee). [18 Cal.L.Rev.Comm. Reports 501 (1986)].

Research References

Miller and Starr California Real Estate § 10:8, Substitution of Trustee--Statutory Procedure.

4 Witkin, California Summary 10th Security Transactions in Real Property § 7, (S 7) Strict Trust Compared and Distinguished.

13 Witkin, California Summary 10th Trusts § 3, (S 3) Debt, Security Device, or Impound Account.

§ 2935. Record of assignment not notice to debtor; validity of payments

When a mortgage or deed of trust is executed as security for money due or to become due, on a promissory note, bond, or other instrument, designated in the mortgage or deed of trust, the record of the assignment of the mortgage or of the assignment of the beneficial interest under the deed of trust, is not of itself notice to the debtor, his heirs, or personal representatives, so as to invalidate any payment made by them, or any of them, to the person holding such note, bond, or other instrument. *(Enacted in 1872. Amended by Code Am.1873–74, c. 612, p. 261, § 259; Stats.1931, c. 80, p. 101, § 2.)*

Research References

Miller and Starr California Real Estate § 10:39, Rights of the Parties.

22 NO. 3 Miller & Starr, California Real Estate Newsalert 1, Show Me Your Papers: Sales and Assignments of Secured Real Estate Loans and the California Foreclosure Process.

4 Witkin, California Summary 10th Security Transactions in Real Property § 106, (S 106) Assignment of Mortgage.

14 Witkin, California Summary 10th Wills and Probate § 803, (S 803) Obligation Secured by Lien on Real Property.

§ 2936. Assignment of debt carries security

The assignment of a debt secured by mortgage carries with it the security. *(Enacted in 1872.)*

Research References

Miller and Starr California Real Estate § 10:38, What is Assignable; Procedure.

22 NO. 3 Miller & Starr, California Real Estate Newsalert 1, Show Me Your Papers: Sales and Assignments of Secured Real Estate Loans and the California Foreclosure Process.

1 Witkin Cal. Summ. 10th Contracts § 734, (S 734) Incidental Rights Pass With Assignment.

4 Witkin, California Summary 10th Security Transactions in Real Property § 105, (S 105) Assignment of Debt.

14 Witkin, California Summary 10th Wills and Probate § 803, (S 803) Obligation Secured by Lien on Real Property.

§ 2937. Notices to borrower of transfer of service by existing and new servicing agent of mortgage or deed of trust on single family residential real property

(a) The Legislature hereby finds and declares that borrowers or subsequent obligors have the right to know when a person holding a promissory note, bond, or other instrument transfers servicing of the indebtedness secured by a mortgage or deed of trust on real property containing one to four residential units located in this state. The Legislature also finds that notification to the borrower or subsequent obligor of the transfer may protect the borrower or subsequent obligor from fraudulent business practices and may ensure timely payments.

It is the intent of the Legislature in enacting this section to mandate that a borrower or subsequent obligor be given written notice when a person transfers the servicing of the indebtedness on notes, bonds, or other instruments secured by a mortgage or deed of trust on real property containing one to four residential units and located in this state.

(b) Any person transferring the servicing of indebtedness as provided in subdivision (a) to a different servicing agent and any person assuming from another responsibility for servicing the instrument evidencing indebtedness, shall give written notice to the borrower or subsequent obligor before the borrower or subsequent obligor becomes obligated to make payments to a new servicing agent.

(c) In the event a notice of default has been recorded or a judicial foreclosure proceeding has been commenced, the person transferring the servicing of the indebtedness and the person assuming from another the duty of servicing the indebtedness shall give written notice to the trustee or attorney named in the notice of default or judicial foreclosure of the transfer. A notice of default, notice of sale, or judicial foreclosure shall not be invalidated solely because the servicing agent is changed during the foreclosure process.

(d) Any person transferring the servicing of indebtedness as provided in subdivision (a) to a different servicing agent shall provide to the new servicing agent all existing insurance policy information that the person is responsible for maintaining, including, but not limited to, flood and hazard insurance policy information.

(e) The notices required by subdivision (b) shall be sent by first- class mail, postage prepaid, to the borrower's or subsequent obligor's address designated for loan payment billings, or if escrow is pending, as provided in the escrow, and shall contain each of the following:

(1) The name and address of the person to which the transfer of the servicing of the indebtedness is made.

(2) The date the transfer was or will be completed.

(3) The address where all payments pursuant to the transfer are to be made.

(f) Any person assuming from another responsibility for servicing the instrument evidencing indebtedness shall include in the notice required by subdivision (b) a statement of the due date of the next payment.

(g) The borrower or subsequent obligor shall not be liable to the holder of the note, bond, or other instrument or to any servicing agent for payments made to the previous servicing agent or for late charges if these payments were made prior to the borrower or subsequent obligor receiving written notice of the transfer as provided by subdivision (e) and the payments were otherwise on time.

(h) For purposes of this section, the term servicing agent shall not include a trustee exercising a power of sale pursuant to a deed of trust. *(Added by Stats.1988, c. 1190, § 1. Amended by Stats.1989, c. 96, § 1, eff. July 7, 1989; Stats.2002, c. 70 (S.B.1370), § 1.)*

Research References

Miller and Starr California Real Estate § 1:79, Form of the Memorandum.
Miller and Starr California Real Estate § 4:70, Servicing of Secured Obligations--Additional Requirements for Residential Loan Servicing.
Miller and Starr California Real Estate § 10:39, Rights of the Parties.
Miller and Starr California Real Estate § 10:101, Reasonableness of Amount.
22 NO. 3 Miller & Starr, California Real Estate Newsalert 1, Show Me Your Papers: Sales and Assignments of Secured Real Estate Loans and the California Foreclosure Process.
4 Witkin, California Summary 10th Security Transactions in Real Property § 106, (S 106) Assignment of Mortgage.

§ 2937.7. Service of process on trustee under deed of trust or mortgage; effect on trustor

In any action affecting the interest of any trustor or beneficiary under a deed of trust or mortgage, service of process to the trustee does not constitute service to the trustor or beneficiary and does not impose any obligation on the trustee to notify the trustor or beneficiary of the action. *(Added by Stats.1988, c. 530, § 1.)*

Research References

Miller and Starr California Real Estate § 10:4, Capacity and Authority of Trustee.
22 NO. 4 Miller & Starr, California Real Estate Newsalert 1, Show Me Your Papers: Sales and Assignments of Secured Real Estate Loans and the California Foreclosure Process (Part II).
4 Witkin, California Summary 10th Security Transactions in Real Property § 7, (S 7) Strict Trust Compared and Distinguished.

§ 2938. Assignment of rents; recordation; enforcement; demand; cash proceeds; application of section

(a) A written assignment of an interest in leases, rents, issues, or profits of real property made in connection with an obligation secured by real property, irrespective of whether the assignment is denoted as absolute, absolute conditioned upon default, additional security for an obligation, or otherwise, shall, upon execution and delivery by the assignor, be effective to create a present security interest in existing and future leases, rents, issues, or profits of that real property. As used in this section, "leases, rents, issues, and profits of real property" includes the cash proceeds thereof. "Cash proceeds" means cash, checks, deposit accounts, and the like.

(b) An assignment of an interest in leases, rents, issues, or profits of real property may be recorded in the records of the county recorder in the county in which the underlying real property is located in the same manner as any other conveyance of an interest in real property, whether the assignment is in a separate document or part of a mortgage or deed of trust, and when so duly recorded in accordance with the methods, procedures, and requirements for recordation of conveyances of other interests in real property, (1) the assignment shall be deemed to give constructive notice of the content of the assignment with the same force and effect as any other duly recorded conveyance of an interest in real property and (2) the interest granted by the assignment shall be deemed fully perfected as of the time of recordation with the same force and effect as any other duly recorded conveyance of an interest in real property, notwithstanding a provision of the assignment or a provision of law that would otherwise preclude or defer enforcement of the rights granted the assignee under the assignment until the occurrence of a subsequent event, including, but not limited to, a subsequent default of the assignor, or the assignee's obtaining possession of the real property or the appointment of a receiver.

(c) Upon default of the assignor under the obligation secured by the assignment of leases, rents, issues, and profits, the assignee shall be entitled to enforce the assignment in accordance with this section. On and after the date the assignee takes one or more of the enforcement steps described in this subdivision, the assignee shall be entitled to collect and receive all rents, issues, and profits that have accrued but remain unpaid and uncollected by the assignor or its agent or for the assignor's benefit on that date, and all rents, issues, and profits that accrue on or after the date. The assignment shall be enforced by one or more of the following:

(1) The appointment of a receiver.

(2) Obtaining possession of the rents, issues, or profits.

(3) Delivery to any one or more of the tenants of a written demand for turnover of rents, issues, and profits in the form specified in subdivision (k), a copy of which demand shall also be delivered to the assignor; and a copy of which shall be mailed to all other assignees of record of the leases, rents, issues, and profits of the real property at the address for notices provided in the assignment or, if none, to the address to which the recorded assignment was to be mailed after recording.

(4) Delivery to the assignor of a written demand for the rents, issues, or profits, a copy of which shall be mailed to all other assignees of record of the leases, rents, issues, and profits of the

real property at the address for notices provided in the assignment or, if none, to the address to which the recorded assignment was to be mailed after recording.

Moneys received by the assignee pursuant to this subdivision, net of amounts paid pursuant to subdivision (g), if any, shall be applied by the assignee to the debt or otherwise in accordance with the assignment or the promissory note, deed of trust, or other instrument evidencing the obligation, provided, however, that neither the application nor the failure to so apply the rents, issues, or profits shall result in a loss of any lien or security interest that the assignee may have in the underlying real property or any other collateral, render the obligation unenforceable, constitute a violation of Section 726 of the Code of Civil Procedure, or otherwise limit a right available to the assignee with respect to its security.

(d) If an assignee elects to take the action provided for under paragraph (3) of subdivision (c), the demand provided for therein shall be signed under penalty of perjury by the assignee or an authorized agent of the assignee and shall be effective as against the tenant when actually received by the tenant at the address for notices provided under the lease or other contractual agreement under which the tenant occupies the property or, if no address for notices is so provided, at the property. Upon receipt of this demand, the tenant shall be obligated to pay to the assignee all rents, issues, and profits that are past due and payable on the date of receipt of the demand, and all rents, issues, and profits coming due under the lease following the date of receipt of the demand, unless either of the following occurs:

(1) The tenant has previously received a demand that is valid on its face from another assignee of the leases, issues, rents, and profits sent by the other assignee in accordance with this subdivision and subdivision (c).

(2) The tenant, in good faith and in a manner that is not inconsistent with the lease, has previously paid, or within 10 days following receipt of the demand notice pays, the rent to the assignor.

Payment of rent to an assignee following a demand under an assignment of leases, rents, issues, and profits shall satisfy the tenant's obligation to pay the amounts under the lease. If a tenant pays rent to the assignor after receipt of a demand other than under the circumstances described in this subdivision, the tenant shall not be discharged of the obligation to pay rent to the assignee, unless the tenant occupies the property for residential purposes. The obligation of a tenant to pay rent pursuant to this subdivision and subdivision (c) shall continue until receipt by the tenant of a written notice from a court directing the tenant to pay the rent in a different manner or receipt by the tenant of a written notice from the assignee from whom the demand was received canceling the demand, whichever occurs first. This subdivision does not affect the entitlement to rents, issues, or profits as between assignees as set forth in subdivision (h).

(e) An enforcement action of the type authorized by subdivision (c), and a collection, distribution, or application of rents, issues, or profits by the assignee following an enforcement action of the type authorized by subdivision (c), shall not do any of the following:

(1) Make the assignee a mortgagee in possession of the property, except if the assignee obtains actual possession of the real property, or an agent of the assignor.

(2) Constitute an action, render the obligation unenforceable, violate Section 726 of the Code of Civil Procedure, or, other than with respect to marshaling requirements, otherwise limit any rights available to the assignee with respect to its security.

(3) Be deemed to create a bar to a deficiency judgment pursuant to a provision of law governing or relating to deficiency judgments following the enforcement of any encumbrance, lien,

or security interest, notwithstanding that the action, collection, distribution, or application may reduce the indebtedness secured by the assignment or by a deed of trust or other security instrument.

The application of rents, issues, or profits to the secured obligation shall satisfy the secured obligation to the extent of those rents, issues, or profits, and, notwithstanding any provisions of the assignment or other loan documents to the contrary, shall be credited against any amounts necessary to cure any monetary default for purposes of reinstatement under Section 2924c.

(f) If cash proceeds of rents, issues, or profits to which the assignee is entitled following enforcement as set forth in subdivision (c) are received by the assignor or its agent for collection or by another person who has collected such rents, issues, or profits for the assignor's benefit, or for the benefit of a subsequent assignee under the circumstances described in subdivision (h), following the taking by the assignee of either of the enforcement actions authorized in paragraph (3) or (4) of subdivision (c), and the assignee has not authorized the assignor's disposition of the cash proceeds in a writing signed by the assignee, the rights to the cash proceeds and to the recovery of the cash proceeds shall be determined by the following:

(1) The assignee shall be entitled to an immediate turnover of the cash proceeds received by the assignor or its agent for collection or any other person who has collected the rents, issues, or profits for the assignor's benefit, or for the benefit of a subsequent assignee under the circumstances described in subdivision (h), and the assignor or other described party in possession of those cash proceeds shall turn over the full amount of cash proceeds to the assignee, less any amount representing payment of expenses authorized by the assignee in writing. The assignee shall have a right to bring an action for recovery of the cash proceeds, and to recover the cash proceeds, without the necessity of bringing an action to foreclose a security interest that it may have in the real property. This action shall not violate Section 726 of the Code of Civil Procedure or otherwise limit a right available to the assignee with respect to its security.

(2) As between an assignee with an interest in cash proceeds perfected in the manner set forth in subdivision (b) and enforced in accordance with paragraph (3) or (4) of subdivision (c) and another person claiming an interest in the cash proceeds, other than the assignor or its agent for collection or one collecting rents, issues, and profits for the benefit of the assignor, and subject to subdivision (h), the assignee shall have a continuously perfected security interest in the cash proceeds to the extent that the cash proceeds are identifiable. For purposes hereof, cash proceeds are identifiable if they are either (A) segregated or (B) if commingled with other funds of the assignor or its agent or one acting on its behalf, can be traced using the lowest intermediate balance principle, unless the assignor or other party claiming an interest in proceeds shows that some other method of tracing would better serve the interests of justice and equity under the circumstances of the case. The provisions of this paragraph are subject to any generally applicable law with respect to payments made in the operation of the assignor's business.

(g)(1) If the assignee enforces the assignment under subdivision (c) by means other than the appointment of a receiver and receives rents, issues, or profits pursuant to this enforcement, the assignor or another assignee of the affected real property may make written demand upon the assignee to pay the reasonable costs of protecting and preserving the property, including payment of taxes and insurance and compliance with building and housing codes, if any.

(2) On and after the date of receipt of the demand, the assignee shall pay for the reasonable costs of protecting and

preserving the real property to the extent of any rents, issues, or profits actually received by the assignee, provided, however, that no such acts by the assignee shall cause the assignee to become a mortgagee in possession and the assignee's duties under this subdivision, upon receipt of a demand from the assignor or any other assignee of the leases, rents, issues, and profits pursuant to paragraph (1), shall not be construed to require the assignee to operate or manage the property, which obligation shall remain that of the assignor.

(3) The obligation of the assignee hereunder shall continue until the earlier of (A) the date on which the assignee obtains the appointment of a receiver for the real property pursuant to application to a court of competent jurisdiction, or (B) the date on which the assignee ceases to enforce the assignment.

(4) This subdivision does not supersede or diminish the right of the assignee to the appointment of a receiver.

(h) The lien priorities, rights, and interests among creditors concerning rents, issues, or profits collected before the enforcement by the assignee shall be governed by subdivisions (a) and (b). Without limiting the generality of the foregoing, if an assignee who has recorded its interest in leases, rents, issues, and profits prior to the recordation of that interest by a subsequent assignee seeks to enforce its interest in those rents, issues, or profits in accordance with this section after any enforcement action has been taken by a subsequent assignee, the prior assignee shall be entitled only to the rents, issues, and profits that are accrued and unpaid as of the date of its enforcement action and unpaid rents, issues, and profits accruing thereafter. The prior assignee shall have no right to rents, issues, or profits paid prior to the date of the enforcement action, whether in the hands of the assignor or any subsequent assignee. Upon receipt of notice that the prior assignee has enforced its interest in the rents, issues, and profits, the subsequent assignee shall immediately send a notice to any tenant to whom it has given notice under subdivision (c). The notice shall inform the tenant that the subsequent assignee cancels its demand that the tenant pay rent to the subsequent assignee.

(i)(1) This section shall apply to contracts entered into on or after January 1, 1997.

(2) Sections 2938 and 2938.1, as these sections were in effect prior to January 1, 1997, shall govern contracts entered into prior to January 1, 1997, and shall govern actions and proceedings initiated on the basis of these contracts.

(j) "Real property," as used in this section, means real property or any estate or interest therein.

(k) The demand required by paragraph (3) of subdivision (c) shall be in the following form:

DEMAND TO PAY RENT TO

PARTY OTHER THAN LANDLORD

(SECTION 2938 OF THE CIVIL CODE)

Tenant: [Name of Tenant]

Property Occupied by Tenant: [Address]

Landlord: [Name of Landlord]

Secured Party: [Name of Secured Party]

Address: [Address for Payment of Rent to Secured Party and for Further Information]:

The secured party named above is the assignee of leases, rents, issues, and profits under [name of document] dated ___, and recorded at [recording information] in the official records of ___ County, California. You may request a copy of the assignment from the secured party at ___ (address).

THIS NOTICE AFFECTS YOUR LEASE OR RENTAL AGREEMENT RIGHTS AND OBLIGATIONS. YOU ARE THEREFORE ADVISED TO CONSULT AN ATTORNEY CONCERNING THOSE RIGHTS AND OBLIGATIONS IF YOU HAVE ANY QUESTIONS REGARDING YOUR RIGHTS AND OBLIGATIONS UNDER THIS NOTICE.

IN ACCORDANCE WITH SUBDIVISION (C) OF SECTION 2938 OF THE CIVIL CODE, YOU ARE HEREBY DIRECTED TO PAY TO THE SECURED PARTY, ___ (NAME OF SECURED PARTY) AT ___ (ADDRESS), ALL RENTS UNDER YOUR LEASE OR OTHER RENTAL AGREEMENT WITH THE LANDLORD OR PREDECESSOR IN INTEREST OF LANDLORD, FOR THE OCCUPANCY OF THE PROPERTY AT ___ (ADDRESS OF RENTAL PREMISES) WHICH ARE PAST DUE AND PAYABLE ON THE DATE YOU RECEIVE THIS DEMAND, AND ALL RENTS COMING DUE UNDER THE LEASE OR OTHER RENTAL AGREEMENT FOLLOWING THE DATE YOU RECEIVE THIS DEMAND UNLESS YOU HAVE ALREADY PAID THIS RENT TO THE LANDLORD IN GOOD FAITH AND IN A MANNER NOT INCONSISTENT WITH THE AGREEMENT BETWEEN YOU AND THE LANDLORD. IN THIS CASE, THIS DEMAND NOTICE SHALL REQUIRE YOU TO PAY TO THE SECURED PARTY, ___ (NAME OF THE SECURED PARTY), ALL RENTS THAT COME DUE FOLLOWING THE DATE OF THE PAYMENT TO THE LANDLORD.

IF YOU PAY THE RENT TO THE UNDERSIGNED SECURED PARTY, ___ (NAME OF SECURED PARTY), IN ACCORDANCE WITH THIS NOTICE, YOU DO NOT HAVE TO PAY THE RENT TO THE LANDLORD. YOU WILL NOT BE SUBJECT TO DAMAGES OR OBLIGATED TO PAY RENT TO THE SECURED PARTY IF YOU HAVE PREVIOUSLY RECEIVED A DEMAND OF THIS TYPE FROM A DIFFERENT SECURED PARTY.

[For other than residential tenants] IF YOU PAY RENT TO THE LANDLORD THAT BY THE TERMS OF THIS DEMAND YOU ARE REQUIRED TO PAY TO THE SECURED PARTY, YOU MAY BE SUBJECT TO DAMAGES INCURRED BY THE SECURED PARTY BY REASON OF YOUR FAILURE TO COMPLY WITH THIS DEMAND, AND YOU MAY NOT BE DISCHARGED FROM YOUR OBLIGATION TO PAY THAT RENT TO THE SECURED PARTY. YOU WILL NOT BE SUBJECT TO THOSE DAMAGES OR OBLIGATED TO PAY THAT RENT TO THE SECURED PARTY IF YOU HAVE PREVIOUSLY RECEIVED A DEMAND OF THIS TYPE FROM A DIFFERENT ASSIGNEE.

Your obligation to pay rent under this demand shall continue until you receive either (1) a written notice from a court directing you to pay the rent in a manner provided therein, or (2) a written notice from the secured party named above canceling this demand.

The undersigned hereby certifies, under penalty of perjury, that the undersigned is an authorized officer or agent of the secured party and that the secured party is the assignee, or the current successor to the assignee, under an assignment of leases, rents, issues, or profits executed by the landlord, or a predecessor in interest, that is being enforced pursuant to and in accordance with Section 2938 of the Civil Code.

Executed at _____, California, this ___ day of _____, ___.

[Secured Party]
Name: _____

Title: _____

(Added by Stats.1996, c. 49 (S.B.947), § 2. Amended by Stats. 1997, c. 8 (S.B.23), § 1, eff. April 15, 1997; Stats.2008, c. 179 (S.B.1498), § 33.)

Research References

California Real Estate Forms (Miller & Starr) § 3:8, Deed of Trust, Security Agreement, and Fixture Filing With Assignment of Rents and Agreements.

California Real Estate Forms (Miller & Starr) § 3:9, Assignment of Lessor's Interest in Leases and Seller's Interest in Contracts for Sale.

California Real Estate Forms (Miller & Starr) § 2:23, Retail Lease--Small Strip-Shopping Center.

California Real Estate Forms (Miller & Starr) § 2:24, Retail Lease--Restaurant.

California Real Estate Forms (Miller & Starr) § 2:36, Consent to Sublease.

California Real Estate Forms (Miller & Starr) § 3:14;, Construction Deed of Trust, Security Agreement, and Fixture Filing With Assignment of Rents and Agreements.

California Real Estate Forms (Miller & Starr) § 3:22, Assignment of Leases and Rents--Conduit Loans.

Rutter, Cal. Practice Guide: Enforcing Judgments/Debts Ch. 4-C, C. Receiverships.

Rutter, Cal. Practice Guide: Real Prop. Transactions Ch. 6-H, H. Security for Promissory Note.

Rutter, Cal. Practice Guide: Real Prop. Transactions Ch. 6-I, I. Real Property Foreclosures and Antideficiency Laws.

Rutter, Cal. Practice Guide: Real Prop. Transactions Ch. 9-B, B. Bar Association Reports.

Miller and Starr California Real Estate § 11:6, Instruments Subject to Recording--List of Recordable Documents.

Miller and Starr California Real Estate § 33:4, Standards for Appointment.

Miller and Starr California Real Estate § 10:47, Conditional Assignment of Rents Under Former Law.

Miller and Starr California Real Estate § 10:48, Recorded Assignment of Rents Creates a Present Security Interest.

Miller and Starr California Real Estate § 10:49, Perfection and Priority of Rent Assignments.

Miller and Starr California Real Estate § 10:50, Enforcement of the Assignment Required.

Miller and Starr California Real Estate § 10:51, Rights to Disburse Rents After Receipt.

Miller and Starr California Real Estate § 10:52, Receiver to Collect Rents.

Miller and Starr California Real Estate § 33:11, Preservation and Management--Power of Possession and Control; Rights of Others.

Miller and Starr California Real Estate § 33:33, Secured Creditor Actions--In General.

Miller and Starr California Real Estate § 33:35, Secured Creditor Actions--To Specifically Enforce Possessory Rights or Assignments of Rents and Profits.

Miller and Starr California Real Estate § 33:36, Secured Creditor Actions--To Apply Rents and Profits Collected.

Miller and Starr California Real Estate § 33:37, Secured Creditor Actions--To Preserve Priorities Involving Multiple Securities.

6 Witkin Cal. Proc. 5th Provisional Remedies § 432, (S 432) Action by Assignee Under Assignment of Rents, Issues, or Profits.

4 Witkin, California Summary 10th Security Transactions in Real Property § 98, (S 98) Absolute Assignment.

4 Witkin, California Summary 10th Security Transactions in Real Property § 99, (S 99) Assignment as Additional Security.

4 Witkin, California Summary 10th Security Transactions in Real Property § 100, Distinction Abolished.

4 Witkin, California Summary 10th Security Transactions in Real Property § 101, Receiver.

4 Witkin, California Summary 10th Security Transactions in Real Property § 128, Remedy is Not Action.

4 Witkin, California Summary 10th Security Transactions in Real Property § 200, (S 200) Where Additional Security is Given.

4 Witkin, California Summary 10th Security Transactions in Real Property § 216, (S 216) in General.

§ 2939. Discharge; recording certificate of payment, satisfaction, or discharge

A recorded mortgage must be discharged by a certificate signed by the mortgagee, his personal representatives or assigns, acknowledged or proved and certified as prescribed by the chapter on "recording transfers," stating that the mortgage has been paid, satisfied, or discharged. Reference shall be made in said certificate to the book and page where the mortgage is recorded. *(Enacted in 1872. Amended by Stats.1945, c. 1074, p. 2073, § 1; Stats.1957, c. 297, p. 939, § 1; Stats.1957, c. 1865, p. 3271, § 12.)*

Research References

Miller and Starr California Real Estate § 11:6, Instruments Subject to Recording--List of Recordable Documents.

Miller and Starr California Real Estate § 11:23, Purpose and Effect; Required for Recordation.

Miller and Starr California Real Estate § 10:111, Reconveyance; Definition.

Miller and Starr California Real Estate § 10:112, Procedure for Reconveyance.

Miller and Starr California Real Estate § 10:113, Reconveyance When Trustee Fails to Reconvey.

4 Witkin, California Summary 10th Security Transactions in Real Property § 117, in General.

§ 2939.5. Satisfaction; foreign executors, administrators and guardians

Foreign executors, administrators and guardians may satisfy mortgages upon the records of any county in this state, upon producing and recording in the office of the county recorder of the county in which such mortgage is recorded, a duly certified and authenticated copy of their letters testamentary, or of administration or of guardianship, and which certificate or authentication shall also recite that said letters have not been revoked. For the purposes of this section, "guardian" includes a foreign conservator, committee, or comparable fiduciary. *(Formerly § 2939½, added by Stats.1895, c. 22, p. 29, § 1. Amended by Stats.1913, c. 128, p. 216, § 1. Renumbered § 2939.5 and amended by Stats.1979, c. 730, p. 2469, § 10, operative Jan. 1, 1981.)*

Law Revision Commission Comments

Section 2939½ is renumbered as Section 2939.5 and is amended to add the last sentence since foreign jurisdictions may have conservators, committees, or comparable fiduciaries that serve the function of guardian of minors or adults.

§ 2940. Certificate of discharge; recording

A certificate of the discharge of a mortgage, and the proof or acknowledgment thereof, must be recorded in the office of the county recorder in which the mortgage is recorded. *(Enacted in 1872. Amended by Stats.1945, c. 1074, p. 2073, § 2; Stats.1957, c. 1865, p. 3271, § 13.)*

§ 2941. Satisfaction; obligation to issue discharge certificate or reconvey; failure to execute or record reconveyance; damages; fee; reproduced "original" instruments

(a) Within 30 days after any mortgage has been satisfied, the mortgagee or the assignee of the mortgagee shall execute a certificate of the discharge thereof, as provided in Section 2939, and shall record or cause to be recorded in the office of the county recorder in which the mortgage is recorded. The mortgagee shall then deliver, upon the written request of the mortgagor or the mortgagor's heirs, successors, or assignees, as the case may be, the original note and mortgage to the person making the request.

(b)(1) Within 30 calendar days after the obligation secured by any deed of trust has been satisfied, the beneficiary or the assignee of the beneficiary shall execute and deliver to the trustee the original note, deed of trust, request for a full reconveyance, and other documents as may be necessary to reconvey, or cause to be reconveyed, the deed of trust.

(A) The trustee shall execute the full reconveyance and shall record or cause it to be recorded in the office of the county recorder in which the deed of trust is recorded within 21 calendar days after receipt by the trustee of the original note, deed of trust, request for a full reconveyance, the fee that may be charged pursuant to subdivision (e), recorder's fees, and other documents as may be necessary to reconvey, or cause to be reconveyed, the deed of trust.

(B) The trustee shall deliver a copy of the reconveyance to the beneficiary, its successor in interest, or its servicing agent, if known. The reconveyance instrument shall specify one of the following options for delivery of the instrument, the addresses of which the recorder has no duty to validate:

(i) The trustor or successor in interest, and that person's last known address, as the person to whom the recorder will deliver the recorded instrument pursuant to Section 27321 of the Government Code.

(ii) That the recorder shall deliver the recorded instrument to the trustee's address. If the trustee's address is specified for delivery, the trustee shall mail the recorded instrument to the trustor or the successor in interest to the last known address for that party.

(C) Following execution and recordation of the full reconveyance, upon receipt of a written request by the trustor or the trustor's heirs, successors, or assignees, the trustee shall then deliver, or caused to be delivered, the original note and deed of trust to the person making that request.

(D) If the note or deed of trust, or any copy of the note or deed of trust, is electronic, upon satisfaction of an obligation secured by a deed of trust, any electronic original, or electronic copy which has not been previously marked solely for use as a copy, of the note and deed of trust, shall be altered to indicate that the obligation is paid in full.

(2) If the trustee has failed to execute and record, or cause to be recorded, the full reconveyance within 60 calendar days of satisfaction of the obligation, the beneficiary, upon receipt of a written request by the trustor or trustor's heirs, successor in interest, agent, or assignee, shall execute and acknowledge a document pursuant to Section 2934a substituting itself or another as trustee and issue a full reconveyance.

(3) If a full reconveyance has not been executed and recorded pursuant to either paragraph (1) or paragraph (2) within 75 calendar days of satisfaction of the obligation, then a title insurance company may prepare and record a release of the obligation. However, at least 10 days prior to the issuance and recording of a full release pursuant to this paragraph, the title insurance company shall mail by first-class mail with postage prepaid, the intention to release the obligation to the trustee, trustor, and beneficiary of record, or their successor in interest of record, at the last known address.

(A) The release shall set forth:

(i) The name of the beneficiary.

(ii) The name of the trustor.

(iii) The recording reference to the deed of trust.

(iv) A recital that the obligation secured by the deed of trust has been paid in full.

(v) The date and amount of payment.

(B) The release issued pursuant to this subdivision shall be entitled to recordation and, when recorded, shall be deemed to be the equivalent of a reconveyance of a deed of trust.

(4) Where an obligation secured by a deed of trust was paid in full prior to July 1, 1989, and no reconveyance has been issued and recorded by October 1, 1989, then a release of obligation as provided for in paragraph (3) may be issued.

(5) Paragraphs (2) and (3) do not excuse the beneficiary or the trustee from compliance with paragraph (1). Paragraph (3) does not excuse the beneficiary from compliance with paragraph (2).

(6) In addition to any other remedy provided by law, a title insurance company preparing or recording the release of the obligation shall be liable to any party for damages, including attorney's fees, which any person may sustain by reason of the issuance and recording of the release, pursuant to paragraphs (3) and (4).

(7) A beneficiary may, at its discretion, in accordance with the requirements and procedures of Section 2934a, substitute the title company conducting the escrow through which the obligation is satisfied for the trustee of record, in which case the title company assumes the obligation of a trustee under this subdivision, and may collect the fee authorized by subdivision (e).

(8) In lieu of delivering the original note and deed of trust to the trustee within 30 days of loan satisfaction, as required by paragraph (1) of subdivision (b), a beneficiary who executes and delivers to the trustee a request for a full reconveyance within 30 days of loan satisfaction may, within 120 days of loan satisfaction, deliver the original note and deed of trust to either the trustee or trustor. If the note and deed of trust are delivered as provided in this paragraph, upon satisfaction of the note and deed of trust, the note and deed of trust shall be altered to indicate that the obligation is paid in full. Nothing in this paragraph alters the requirements and obligations set forth in paragraphs (2) and (3).

(c) For the purposes of this section, the phrases "cause to be recorded" and "cause it to be recorded" include, but are not limited to, sending by certified mail with the United States Postal Service or by an independent courier service using its tracking service that provides documentation of receipt and delivery, including the signature of the recipient, the full reconveyance or certificate of discharge in a recordable form, together with payment for all required fees, in an envelope addressed to the county recorder's office of the county in which the deed of trust or mortgage is recorded. Within two business days from the day of receipt, if received in recordable form together with all required fees, the county recorder shall stamp and record the full reconveyance or certificate of discharge. Compliance with this subdivision shall entitle the trustee to the benefit of the presumption found in Section 641 of the Evidence Code.

(d) The violation of this section shall make the violator liable to the person affected by the violation for all damages which that person may sustain by reason of the violation, and shall require that the violator forfeit to that person the sum of five hundred dollars ($500).

(e)(1) The trustee, beneficiary, or mortgagee may charge a reasonable fee to the trustor or mortgagor, or the owner of the land, as the case may be, for all services involved in the preparation, execution, and recordation of the full reconveyance, including, but not limited to, document preparation and forwarding services rendered to effect the full reconveyance, and, in addition, may collect official fees. This fee may be made payable no earlier than the opening of a bona fide escrow or no more than 60 days prior to the full satisfaction of the obligation secured by the deed of trust or mortgage.

(2) If the fee charged pursuant to this subdivision does not exceed forty-five dollars ($45), the fee is conclusively presumed to be reasonable.

(3) The fee described in paragraph (1) may not be charged unless demand for the fee was included in the payoff demand statement described in Section 2943.

(f) For purposes of this section, "original" may include an optically imaged reproduction when the following requirements are met:

(1) The trustee receiving the request for reconveyance and executing the reconveyance as provided in subdivision (b) is an affiliate or subsidiary of the beneficiary or an affiliate or subsidiary of the assignee of the beneficiary, respectively.

(2) The optical image storage media used to store the document shall be nonerasable write once, read many (WORM) optical image media that does not allow changes to the stored document.

(3) The optical image reproduction shall be made consistent with the minimum standards of quality approved by either the National Institute of Standards and Technology or the Association for Information and Image Management.

(4) Written authentication identifying the optical image reproduction as an unaltered copy of the note, deed of trust, or mortgage shall be stamped or printed on the optical image reproduction.

(g) No fee or charge may be imposed on the trustor in connection with, or relating to, any act described in this section except as expressly authorized by this section.

(h) The amendments to this section enacted at the 1999–2000 Regular Session shall apply only to a mortgage or an obligation secured by a deed of trust that is satisfied on or after January 1, 2001.

(i)(1) In any action filed before January 1, 2002, that is dismissed as a result of the amendments to this section enacted at the 2001–02 Regular Session, the plaintiff shall not be required to pay the defendant's costs.

(2) Any claimant, including a claimant in a class action lawsuit, whose claim is dismissed or barred as a result of the amendments to this section enacted at the 2001–02 Regular Session, may, within 6 months of the dismissal or barring of the action or claim, file or refile a claim for actual damages occurring before January 1, 2002, that were proximately caused by a time lapse between loan satisfaction and the completion of the beneficiary's obligations as required under paragraph (1) of subdivision (b). In any action brought under this section, the

defendant may be found liable for actual damages, but may not be found liable for any civil penalty authorized by Section 2941.

(j) Notwithstanding any other penalties, if a beneficiary collects a fee for reconveyance and thereafter has knowledge, or should have knowledge, that no reconveyance has been recorded, the beneficiary shall cause to be recorded the reconveyance, or in the event a release of obligation is earlier and timely recorded, the beneficiary shall refund to the trustor the fee charged to perform the reconveyance. Evidence of knowledge includes, but is not limited to, notice of a release of obligation pursuant to paragraph (3) of subdivision (b). *(Enacted in 1872. Amended by Code Am.1873–74, c. 612, p. 261, § 261; Code Am.1880, c. 81, p. 10, § 1; Stats.1946, 1st Ex.Sess., c. 58, p. 82, § 1, eff. Feb. 25, 1946; Stats.1947, c. 1411, p. 2972, § 1; Stats.1974, c. 267, § 1; Stats.1978, c. 509, p. 1657, § 1; Stats. 1988, c. 1006, § 1, operative July 1, 1989; Stats.1991, c. 1155 (A.B.2146), § 2; Stats.1993, c. 754 (S.B.313), § 3, eff. Oct. 4, 1993; Stats.1994, c. 374 (A.B.3397), § 1; Stats.1996, c. 230 (A.B.372), § 1; Stats.1997, c. 74 (S.B.665), § 7; Stats.2000, c. 1013 (A.B.996), § 1; Stats.2001, c. 560 (A.B.1090), § 1; Stats. 2002, c. 809 (S.B.1504), § 2; Stats.2003, c. 62 (S.B.600), § 20.)*

Research References

Rutter, Cal. Practice Guide: Enforcing Judgments/Debts Ch. 2-C, C. Tort Liability.

Rutter, Cal. Practice Guide: Personal Injury Ch. 3-C, C. Specific Items of Compensatory Damages.

Rutter, Cal. Practice Guide: Real Prop. Transactions Ch. 6-H, H. Security for Promissory Note.

Rutter, Cal. Practice Guide: Real Prop. Transactions Ch. 6-I, I. Real Property Foreclosures and Antideficiency Laws.

Miller and Starr California Real Estate § 10:4, Capacity and Authority of Trustee.

Miller and Starr California Real Estate § 11:6, Instruments Subject to Recording--List of Recordable Documents.

Miller and Starr California Real Estate § 4:83, Residential Mortgage Lenders or Servicers; Licensing and Regulation by Department of Corporations.

Miller and Starr California Real Estate § 10:39, Rights of the Parties.

Miller and Starr California Real Estate § 10:95, Trustor's Right of Prepayment; "Locked-In" Loans.

Miller and Starr California Real Estate § 11:20, Recorder's Liability for Erroneous Recording or Indexing.

Miller and Starr California Real Estate § 11:22, When Recording is Complete--For Constructive Notice.

Miller and Starr California Real Estate § 10:111, Reconveyance; Definition.

Miller and Starr California Real Estate § 10:112, Procedure for Reconveyance.

Miller and Starr California Real Estate § 10:113, Reconveyance When Trustee Fails to Reconvey.

Miller and Starr California Real Estate § 10:115, Remedy for Failure to Reconvey.

Miller and Starr California Real Estate § 10:206, When the Sale Becomes Final; Reformation.

13 NO. 4 Miller & Starr, California Real Estate Newsalert 16, Mortgages and Deeds of Trust.

15 NO. 5 Miller & Starr, California Real Estate Newsalert 5, Deeds of Trust.

17 NO. 2 Miller & Starr, California Real Estate Newsalert 13, Escrows.

20 NO. 2 Miller & Starr, California Real Estate Newsalert 11, Deeds of Trust.

3 Witkin Cal. Proc. 5th Actions § 146, in General.

3 Witkin Cal. Proc. 5th Actions § 497, (S 497) in General.

3 Witkin Cal. Proc. 5th Actions § 664, (S 664) in General.

3 Witkin Cal. Proc. 5th Actions § 668, (S 668) Exceptions.

4 Witkin Cal. Proc. 5th Pleading § 282, (S 282) Sufficient Showing.

4 Witkin, California Summary 10th Security Transactions in Real Property § 36, (S 36) Federal Preemption.

4 Witkin, California Summary 10th Security Transactions in Real Property § 118, Mortgagee's Duty.

4 Witkin, California Summary 10th Security Transactions in Real Property § 214, (S 214) in General.

6 Witkin, California Summary 10th Torts § 1748, (S 1748) Other Cases.

13 Witkin, California Summary 10th Equity § 122, Lending Practices.
14 Witkin, California Summary 10th Wills and Probate § 803, (S 803)
   Obligation Secured by Lien on Real Property.

§ 2941.1. Charging a reconveyance fee where no payoff demand statement is issued

Notwithstanding any other provision of law, if no payoff demand statement is issued pursuant to Section 2943, nothing in Section 2941 shall be construed to prohibit the charging of a reconveyance fee. *(Added by Stats.2001, c. 438 (S.B.958), § 6, eff. Oct. 2, 2001, operative Jan. 1, 2002.)*

Research References

Miller and Starr California Real Estate § 10:181, Notice of Default--In General.
4 Witkin, California Summary 10th Security Transactions in Real Property § 214, (S 214) in General.

§ 2941.5. Obligation to execute certificate of discharge, satisfaction, or request for reconveyance; penalty

Every person who willfully violates Section 2941 is guilty of a misdemeanor punishable by fine of not less than fifty dollars ($50) nor more than four hundred dollars ($400), or by imprisonment in the county jail for not to exceed six months, or by both such fine and imprisonment.

For purposes of this section, "willfully" means simply a purpose or willingness to commit the act, or make the omission referred to. It does not require an intent to violate the law, to injure another, or to acquire any advantage. *(Added by Stats. 1946, 1st Ex.Sess., c. 58, p. 82, § 2, eff. Feb. 25, 1946. Amended by Stats.1983, c. 1092, § 67, eff. Sept. 27, 1983, operative Jan. 1, 1984; Stats.1988, c. 1006, § 2, operative July 1, 1989.)*

Research References

Rutter, Cal. Practice Guide: Real Prop. Transactions Ch. 6-H, H. Security for Promissory Note.
Miller and Starr California Real Estate § 10:111, Reconveyance; Definition.
Miller and Starr California Real Estate § 10:112, Procedure for Reconveyance.
Miller and Starr California Real Estate § 10:115, Remedy for Failure to Reconvey.
4 Witkin, California Summary 10th Security Transactions in Real Property § 118, Mortgagee's Duty.

§ 2941.7. Satisfaction of mortgage or deed of trust; release of lien when mortgagee or beneficiary cannot be found or refuses to issue certificate of discharge or to reconvey

Whenever the obligation secured by a mortgage or deed of trust has been fully satisfied and the present mortgagee or beneficiary of record cannot be located after diligent search, or refuses to execute and deliver a proper certificate of discharge or request for reconveyance, or whenever a specified balance, including principal and interest, remains due and the mortgagor or trustor or the mortgagor's or trustor's successor in interest cannot, after diligent search, locate the then mortgagee or beneficiary of record, the lien of any mortgage or deed of trust shall be released when the mortgagor or trustor or the mortgagor's or trustor's successor in interest records or causes to be recorded, in the office of the county recorder of the county in which the encumbered property is located, a corporate bond accompanied by a declaration, as specified in subdivision (b), and with respect to a deed of trust, a reconveyance as hereinafter provided.

(a) The bond shall be acceptable to the trustee and shall be issued by a corporation lawfully authorized to issue surety bonds in the State of California in a sum equal to the greater of either (1) two times the amount of the original obligation secured by the mortgage or deed of trust and any additional principal amounts, including advances, shown in any recorded amendment thereto, or (2) one-half of the total amount computed pursuant to (1) and any accrued interest on such amount, and shall be conditioned for payment of any sum which the mortgagee or beneficiary may recover in an action on the obligation secured by the mortgage or deed of trust, with costs of suit and reasonable attorneys' fees. The obligees under the bond shall be the mortgagee or mortgagee's successor in interest or the trustee who executes a reconveyance under this section and the beneficiary or beneficiary's successor in interest.

The bond recorded by the mortgagor or trustor or mortgagor's or trustor's successor in interest shall contain the following information describing the mortgage or deed of trust:

(1) Recording date and instrument number or book and page number of the recorded instrument.

(2) Names of original mortgagor and mortgagee or trustor and beneficiary.

(3) Amount shown as original principal sum secured thereby.

(4) The recording information and new principal amount shown in any recorded amendment thereto.

(b) The declaration accompanying the corporate bond recorded by the mortgagor or trustor or the mortgagor's or trustor's successor in interest shall state:

(1) That it is recorded pursuant to this section.

(2) The name of the original mortgagor or trustor and mortgagee or beneficiary.

(3) The name and address of the person making the declaration.

(4) That either the obligation secured by the mortgage or deed of trust has been fully satisfied and the present mortgagee or beneficiary of record cannot be located after diligent search, or refuses to execute and deliver a proper certificate of discharge or request for reconveyance as required under Section 2941; or that a specified balance, including principal and interest, remains due and the mortgagor or trustor or mortgagor's or trustor's successor in interest cannot, after diligent search, locate the then mortgagee or beneficiary.

(5) That the declarant has mailed by certified mail, return receipt requested, to the last address of the person to whom payments under the mortgage or deed of trust were made and to the last mortgagee or beneficiary of record at the address for such mortgagee or beneficiary shown on the instrument creating, assigning, or conveying the interest, a notice of recording a declaration and bond under this section and informing the recipient of the name and address of the mortgagor or trustee, if any, and of the right to record a written objection with respect to the release of the lien of the mortgage or, with respect to a deed of trust, notify the trustee in writing of any objection to the reconveyance of the deed of trust. The declaration shall state the date any notices were mailed pursuant to this section and the names and addresses of all persons to whom mailed.

The declaration provided for in this section shall be signed by the mortgagor or trustor under penalty of perjury.

(c) With respect to a deed of trust, after the expiration of 30 days following the recording of the corporate bond and accompanying declaration provided in subdivisions (a) and (b), and delivery to the trustee of the usual reconveyance fees plus costs and a demand for reconveyance under this section, the trustee shall execute and record, or otherwise deliver as provided in Section 2941, a reconveyance in the same form as if the beneficiary had delivered to the trustee a proper request for reconveyance, provided that the trustee has not received a written objection to the reconveyance from the beneficiary of record. No trustee shall have any liability to any person by reason of its execution of a reconveyance in reliance upon a trustor's or trustor's successor's in interest substantial compliance with this section. The sole remedy of any person damaged by reason of the reconveyance shall be against the trustor, the affiant, or the bond. With respect to a mortgage, a mortgage shall be satisfied of record when 30 days have expired following recordation of the corporate bond and accompanying declaration, provided no objection to satisfaction has been recorded by the mortgagee within that period. A bona fide purchaser or encumbrancer for value shall take the interest conveyed free of such mortgage, provided there has been compliance with subdivisions (a) and (b) and the deed to the purchaser recites that no objections by the mortgagee have been recorded.

Upon recording of a reconveyance under this section, or, in the case of a mortgage the expiration of 30 days following recordation of the corporate bond and accompanying declaration without objection thereto having been recorded, interest shall no longer accrue as to any balance remaining due to the extent the balance due has been alleged in the declaration recorded under subdivision (b).

The sum of any specified balance, including principal and interest, which remains due and which is remitted to any issuer of a corporate bond in conjunction with the issuance of a bond pursuant to this section shall, if unclaimed, escheat to the state after three years pursuant to the Unclaimed Property Law. From the date of escheat the issuer of the bond shall be relieved of any liability to pay to the beneficiary or his or her heirs or other successors in interest the escheated funds and the sole remedy shall be a claim for property paid or delivered to the Controller pursuant to the Unclaimed Property Law.

(d) The term "diligent search," as used in this section, shall mean all of the following:

(1) The mailing of notices as provided in paragraph (5) of subdivision (b), and to any other address that the declarant has used to correspond with or contact the mortgagee or beneficiary.

(2) A check of the telephone directory in the city where the mortgagee or beneficiary maintained the mortgagee's or beneficiary's last known address or place of business.

(3) In the event the mortgagee or beneficiary or the mortgagee's or beneficiary's successor in interest is a corporation, a check of the records of the California Secretary of State and the secretary of state in the state of incorporation, if known.

(4) In the event the mortgagee or beneficiary is a state or national bank or a state or federal savings and loan association, an inquiry of the regulatory authority of such bank or savings and loan association.

(e) This section shall not be deemed to create an exclusive procedure for the issuance of reconveyances and the issuance of bonds and declarations to release the lien of a mortgage and shall not affect any other procedures, whether or not such procedures are set forth in statute, for the issuance of reconveyances and the issuance of bonds and declarations to release the lien of a mortgage.

(f) For purposes of this section, the trustor or trustor's successor in interest may substitute the present trustee of record without conferring any duties upon the trustee other than those that are incidental to the execution of a reconveyance pursuant to this section if all of the following requirements are met:

(1) The present trustee of record and the present mortgagee or beneficiary of record cannot be located after diligent search.

(2) The declaration filed pursuant to subdivision (b) shall state in addition that it is filed pursuant to this subdivision, and shall, in lieu of the provisions of paragraph (4) of subdivision (b), state that the obligation secured by the mortgage or deed of trust has been fully satisfied and the present trustee of record and

present mortgagee or beneficiary of record cannot be located after diligent search.

(3) The substitute trustee is a title insurance company that agrees to accept the substitution. This subdivision shall not impose a duty upon a title insurance company to accept the substitution.

(4) The corporate bond required in subdivision (a) is for a period of five or more years. *(Added by Stats.1980, c. 529, p. 1470, § 1. Amended by Stats.1995, c. 244 (S.B.784), § 1; Stats.1996, c. 762 (S.B.2014), § 2.)*

Research References

Miller and Starr California Real Estate § 18:7, The Unclaimed Property Law--Property Unclaimed or Abandoned.
Miller and Starr California Real Estate § 10:111, Reconveyance; Definition.
Miller and Starr California Real Estate § 10:114, Reconveyance When Beneficiary Cannot be Located.
4 Witkin, California Summary 10th Security Transactions in Real Property § 119, Release When Mortgagee Cannot be Found or Refuses to Act.

§ 2941.9. Trust deed beneficiaries; agreements to be governed by beneficiaries holding more than 50 percent of the record beneficial interest

(a) The purpose of this section is to establish a process through which all of the beneficiaries under a trust deed may agree to be governed by beneficiaries holding more than 50 percent of the record beneficial interest of a series of notes secured by the same real property or of undivided interests in a note secured by real property equivalent to a series transaction, exclusive of any notes or interests of a licensed real estate broker that is the issuer or servicer of the notes or interests or any affiliate of that licensed real estate broker.

(b) All holders of notes secured by the same real property or a series of undivided interests in notes secured by real property equivalent to a series transaction may agree in writing to be governed by the desires of the holders of more than 50 percent of the record beneficial interest of those notes or interests, exclusive of any notes or interests of a licensed real estate broker that is the issuer or servicer of the notes or interests of any affiliate of the licensed real estate broker, with respect to actions to be taken on behalf of all holders in the event of default or foreclosure for matters that require direction or approval of the holders, including designation of the broker, servicing agent, or other person acting on their behalf, and the sale, encumbrance, or lease of real property owned by the holders resulting from foreclosure or receipt of a deed in lieu of foreclosure.

(c) A description of the agreement authorized in subdivision (b) of this section shall be disclosed pursuant to Section 10232.5 of the Business and Professions Code and shall be included in a recorded document such as the deed of trust or the assignment of interests.

(d) Any action taken pursuant to the authority granted in this section is not effective unless all the parties agreeing to the action sign, under penalty of perjury, a separate written document entitled "Majority Action Affidavit" stating the following:

(1) The action has been authorized pursuant to this section.

(2) None of the undersigned is a licensed real estate broker or an affiliate of the broker that is the issuer or servicer of the obligation secured by the deed of trust.

(3) The undersigned together hold more than 50 percent of the record beneficial interest of a series of notes secured by the same real property or of undivided interests in a note secured by real property equivalent to a series transaction.

(4) Notice of the action was sent by certified mail, postage prepaid, with return receipt requested, to each holder of an interest in the obligation secured by the deed of trust who has not joined in the execution of the substitution or this document.

This document shall be recorded in the office of the county recorder of each county in which the real property described in the deed of trust is located. Once the document in this subdivision is recorded, it shall constitute conclusive evidence of compliance with the requirements of this subdivision in favor of trustees acting pursuant to this section, substituted trustees acting pursuant to Section 2934a, subsequent assignees of the obligation secured by the deed of trust, and subsequent bona fide purchasers or encumbrancers for value of the real property described therein.

(e) For purposes of this section, "affiliate of the licensed real estate broker" includes any person as defined in Section 25013 of the Corporations Code who is controlled by, or is under common control with, or who controls, a licensed real estate broker. "Control" means the possession, direct or indirect, of the power to direct or cause the direction of management and policies. *(Added by Stats.1996, c. 839 (S.B.1638), § 3.)*

Research References

Rutter, Cal. Practice Guide: Real Prop. Transactions Ch. 6-H, H. Security for Promissory Note.
Miller and Starr California Real Estate § 4:69, Servicing of Secured Obligations--In General.
Miller and Starr California Real Estate § 5:22, Loan Brokerage and Servicing Agreements.
Miller and Starr California Real Estate § 10:184, Execution of the Notice of Default.

§ 2942. Bottomry and respondentia excluded from chapter

Contracts of bottomry or respondentia, although in the nature of mortgages, are not affected by any of the provisions of this Chapter. *(Enacted in 1872.)*

§ 2943. Definitions; copy of note and modifications; payoff demand statement; reliance by entitled person on beneficiary statement or payoff demand statement

(a) As used in this section:

(1) "Beneficiary" means a mortgagee or beneficiary of a mortgage or deed of trust, or his or her assignees.

(2) "Beneficiary statement" means a written statement showing:

(A) The amount of the unpaid balance of the obligation secured by the mortgage or deed of trust and the interest rate, together with the total amounts, if any, of all overdue installments of either principal or interest, or both.

(B) The amounts of periodic payments, if any.

(C) The date on which the obligation is due in whole or in part.

(D) The date to which real estate taxes and special assessments have been paid to the extent the information is known to the beneficiary.

(E) The amount of hazard insurance in effect and the term and premium of that insurance to the extent the information is known to the beneficiary.

(F) The amount in an account, if any, maintained for the accumulation of funds with which to pay taxes and insurance premiums.

(G) The nature and, if known, the amount of any additional charges, costs, or expenses paid or incurred by the beneficiary which have become a lien on the real property involved.

(H) Whether the obligation secured by the mortgage or deed of trust can or may be transferred to a new borrower.

(3) "Delivery" means depositing or causing to be deposited in the United States mail an envelope with postage prepaid, containing a copy of the document to be delivered, addressed to the person whose name and address is set forth in the demand therefor. The document may also be transmitted by facsimile machine to the person whose name and address is set forth in the demand therefor.

(4) "Entitled person" means the trustor or mortgagor of, or his or her successor in interest in, the mortgaged or trust property or any part thereof, any beneficiary under a deed of trust, any person having a subordinate lien or encumbrance of record thereon, the escrowholder licensed as an agent pursuant to Division 6 (commencing with Section 17000) of the Financial Code, or the party exempt by virtue of Section 17006 of the Financial Code who is acting as the escrowholder.

(5) "Payoff demand statement" means a written statement, prepared in response to a written demand made by an entitled person or authorized agent, setting forth the amounts required as of the date of preparation by the beneficiary, to fully satisfy all obligations secured by the loan that is the subject of the payoff demand statement. The written statement shall include information reasonably necessary to calculate the payoff amount on a per diem basis for the period of time, not to exceed 30 days, during which the per diem amount is not changed by the terms of the note.

(b)(1) A beneficiary, or his or her authorized agent, shall, within 21 days of the receipt of a written demand by an entitled person or his or her authorized agent, prepare and deliver to the person demanding it a true, correct, and complete copy of the note or other evidence of indebtedness with any modification thereto, and a beneficiary statement.

(2) A request pursuant to this subdivision may be made by an entitled person or his or her authorized agent at any time before, or within two months after, the recording of a notice of default under a mortgage or deed of trust, or may otherwise be made more than 30 days prior to the entry of the decree of foreclosure.

(c) A beneficiary, or his or her authorized agent, shall, on the written demand of an entitled person, or his or her authorized agent, prepare and deliver a payoff demand statement to the person demanding it within 21 days of the receipt of the demand. However, if the loan is subject to a recorded notice of default or a filed complaint commencing a judicial foreclosure, the beneficiary shall have no obligation to prepare and deliver this statement as prescribed unless the written demand is received prior to the first publication of a notice of sale or the notice of the first date of sale established by a court.

(d)(1) A beneficiary statement or payoff demand statement may be relied upon by the entitled person or his or her authorized agent in accordance with its terms, including with respect to the payoff demand statement reliance for the purpose of establishing the amount necessary to pay the obligation in full. If the beneficiary notifies the entitled person or his or her authorized agent of any amendment to the statement, then the amended statement may be relied upon by the entitled person or his or her authorized agent as provided in this subdivision.

(2) If notification of any amendment to the statement is not given in writing, then a written amendment to the statement shall be delivered to the entitled person or his or her authorized agent no later than the next business day after notification.

(3) Upon the dates specified in subparagraphs (A) and (B) any sums that were due and for any reason not included in the statement or amended statement shall continue to be recoverable by the beneficiary as an unsecured obligation of the obligor pursuant to the terms of the note and existing provisions of law.

(A) If the transaction is voluntary, the entitled party or his or her authorized agent may rely upon the statement or amended statement upon the earlier of (i) the close of escrow, (ii) transfer of title, or (iii) recordation of a lien.

(B) If the loan is subject to a recorded notice of default or a filed complaint commencing a judicial foreclosure, the entitled party or his or her authorized agent may rely upon the statement or amended statement upon the acceptance of the last and highest bid at a trustee's sale or a court supervised sale.

(e) The following provisions apply to a demand for either a beneficiary statement or a payoff demand statement:

(1) If an entitled person or his or her authorized agent requests a statement pursuant to this section and does not specify a beneficiary statement or a payoff demand statement the beneficiary shall treat the request as a request for a payoff demand statement.

(2) If the entitled person or the entitled person's authorized agent includes in the written demand a specific request for a copy of the deed of trust or mortgage, it shall be furnished with the written statement at no additional charge.

(3) The beneficiary may, before delivering a statement, require reasonable proof that the person making the demand is, in fact, an entitled person or an authorized agent of an entitled person, in which event the beneficiary shall not be subject to the penalties of this section until 21 days after receipt of the proof herein provided for. A statement in writing signed by the entitled person appointing an authorized agent when delivered personally to the beneficiary or delivered by registered return receipt mail shall constitute reasonable proof as to the identity of an agent. Similar delivery of a policy of title insurance, preliminary report issued by a title company, original or photographic copy of a grant deed or certified copy of letters testamentary, guardianship, or conservatorship shall constitute reasonable proof as to the identity of a successor in interest, provided the person demanding a statement is named as successor in interest in the document.

(4) If a beneficiary for a period of 21 days after receipt of the written demand willfully fails to prepare and deliver the statement, he or she is liable to the entitled person for all damages which he or she may sustain by reason of the refusal and, whether or not actual damages are sustained, he or she shall forfeit to the entitled person the sum of three hundred dollars ($300). Each failure to prepare and deliver the statement, occurring at a time when, pursuant to this section, the beneficiary is required to prepare and deliver the statement, creates a separate cause of action, but a judgment awarding an entitled person a forfeiture, or damages and forfeiture, for any failure to prepare and deliver a statement bars recovery of damages and forfeiture for any other failure to prepare and deliver a statement, with respect to the same obligation, in compliance with a demand therefor made within six months before or after the demand as to which the award was made. For the purposes of this subdivision, "willfully" means an intentional failure to comply with the requirements of this section without just cause or excuse.

(5) If the beneficiary has more than one branch, office, or other place of business, then the demand shall be made to the branch or office address set forth in the payment billing notice or payment book, and the statement, unless it specifies otherwise, shall be deemed to apply only to the unpaid balance of the single obligation named in the request and secured by the mortgage or deed of trust which is payable at the branch or office whose address appears on the aforesaid billing notice or payment book.

(6) The beneficiary may make a charge not to exceed thirty dollars ($30) for furnishing each required statement. The provisions of this paragraph shall not apply to mortgages or deeds of trust insured by the Federal Housing Administrator or guaranteed by the Administrator of Veterans Affairs.

(f) The preparation and delivery of a beneficiary statement or a payoff demand statement pursuant to this section shall not change a date of sale established pursuant to Section 2924g.

(g) This section shall become operative on January 1, 2014. *(Added by Stats.2009, c. 43 (S.B.306), § 6, operative Jan. 1, 2014.)*

Research References

California Real Estate Forms (Miller & Starr) § 3:8, Deed of Trust, Security Agreement, and Fixture Filing With Assignment of Rents and Agreements.

California Real Estate Forms (Miller & Starr) § 1:34, Installment Land Sale Contract With Power of Sale.

California Real Estate Forms (Miller & Starr) § 3:14, Construction Deed of Trust, Security Agreement, and Fixture Filing With Assignment of Rents and Agreements.

Rutter, Cal. Practice Guide: Enforcing Judgments/Debts Ch. 4-A, A. Attachment.

Rutter, Cal. Practice Guide: Enforcing Judgments/Debts Ch. 6D-8, Special Requirements for Sale of Real Property Dwellings.

Rutter, Cal. Practice Guide: Real Prop. Transactions Ch. 4-E, E. Drafting the Purchase and Sale Agreement-Terms and Conditions.

Rutter, Cal. Practice Guide: Real Prop. Transactions Ch. 4-F, F. Use of an Escrow.

Rutter, Cal. Practice Guide: Real Prop. Transactions Ch. 6-H, H. Security for Promissory Note.

Rutter, Cal. Practice Guide: Real Prop. Transactions Ch. 6-I, I. Real Property Foreclosures and Antideficiency Laws.

Miller and Starr California Real Estate § 10:4, Capacity and Authority of Trustee.

Miller and Starr California Real Estate § 36:1, Applicable Theories of Liability.

Miller and Starr California Real Estate § 6:12, Agency--Duty to Comply With Instructions.

Miller and Starr California Real Estate § 10:65, Beneficiary Statement After Default.

Miller and Starr California Real Estate § 10:66, Payoff Demand Statement.

Miller and Starr California Real Estate § 10:118, Recovery of Amount Omitted from Demand; Effect of Antideficiency Limitations.

Miller and Starr California Real Estate § 10:189, Amounts that Must be Paid to Reinstate.

Miller and Starr California Real Estate § 10:260, Exception; Erroneous Reconveyance.

Miller and Starr California Real Estate § 10:66.10, Short Sales; Short-Pay Demand Statement.

13 NO. 4 Miller & Starr, California Real Estate Newsalert 21, Deeds of Trust.

15 NO. 3 Miller & Starr, California Real Estate Newsalert 4, Deeds of Trust.

15 NO. 3 Miller & Starr, California Real Estate Newsalert 8, Escrows.

20 NO. 4 Miller & Starr, California Real Estate Newsalert 6, Deeds of Trust.

22 NO. 3 Miller & Starr, California Real Estate Newsalert 1, Show Me Your Papers: Sales and Assignments of Secured Real Estate Loans and the California Foreclosure Process.

4 Witkin, California Summary 10th Security Transactions in Real Property § 214, (S 214) in General.

4 Witkin, California Summary 10th Security Transactions in Real Property § 215, (S 215) Erroneous Payoff Statement.

§ 2944. Transactions and security interests governed by Commercial Code

None of the provisions of this chapter applies to any transaction or security interest governed by the Commercial Code, except to the extent made applicable by reason of an election made by the secured party pursuant to subparagraph (B) of paragraph (1) of subdivision (a) of Section 9604 of the Commercial Code. *(Added by Stats.1963, c. 819, p. 2000, § 15, eff. Jan. 1, 1965. Amended by Stats.1992, c. 1095 (A.B.2734), § 3; Stats. 1999, c. 991 (S.B.45), § 7, operative July 1, 2001.)*

Research References

Miller and Starr California Real Estate § 17:7, UCC Provisions, Generally,

§ 2944.5. Insurance policies; acceptance; lender, mortgagee, or third party with interest in real or personal property

No lender, mortgagee, or any third party having an interest in real or personal property shall refuse to accept a policy issued by an admitted insurer solely because the policy is issued for a continuous period without a fixed expiration date even though the policy premium is due and payable every six months, provided the lender, mortgagee, or third party is entitled to receive (a) notice of renewal from the insurer within 15 days of receipt of payment on the policy by the insured or (b) notice of cancellation or nonrenewal under the terms and conditions set forth in Sections 678 and 2074.8 of the Insurance Code, whichever is applicable. *(Added by Stats.1993, c. 522 (A.B.421), § 1.)*

Research References

Miller and Starr California Real Estate § 17:7, UCC Provisions, Generally.
Miller and Starr California Real Estate § 10:60, Payment of Insurance Premiums.
4 Witkin, California Summary 10th Security Transactions in Real Property § 38, (S 38) Other Legislation.

§ 2944.6. Person who negotiates or offers to perform mortgage loan modifications for fee; violations

(a) Notwithstanding any other provision of law, any person who negotiates, attempts to negotiate, arranges, attempts to arrange, or otherwise offers to perform a mortgage loan modification or other form of mortgage loan forbearance for a fee or other compensation paid by the borrower, shall provide the following to the borrower, as a separate statement, in not less than 14–point bold type, prior to entering into any fee agreement with the borrower:

It is not necessary to pay a third party to arrange for a loan modification or other form of forbearance from your mortgage lender or servicer. You may call your lender directly to ask for a change in your loan terms. Nonprofit housing counseling agencies also offer these and other forms of borrower assistance free of charge. A list of nonprofit housing counseling agencies approved by the United States Department of Housing and Urban Development (HUD) is available from your local HUD office or by visiting www.hud.gov.

(b) If loan modification or other mortgage loan forbearance services are offered or negotiated in one of the languages set forth in Section 1632, a translated copy of the statement in subdivision (a) shall be provided to the borrower in that foreign language.

(c) A violation of this section by a natural person is a public offense punishable by a fine not exceeding ten thousand dollars ($10,000), by imprisonment in the county jail for a term not to exceed one year, or by both that fine and imprisonment, or if by a business entity, the violation is punishable by a fine not exceeding fifty thousand dollars ($50,000). These penalties are cumulative to any other remedies or penalties provided by law.

(d) This section does not apply to a person, or an agent acting on that person's behalf, offering loan modification or other loan forbearance services for a loan owned or serviced by that person.

(e) This section shall apply only to mortgages and deeds of trust secured by residential real property containing four or fewer dwelling units. *(Added by Stats.2009, c. 630 (S.B.94), § 9, eff. Oct. 11, 2009.)*

Research References

Rutter, Cal. Practice Guide: Real Prop. Transactions Ch. 1-C, C. Attorney Fees and Costs Agreements.
Rutter, Cal. Practice Guide: Real Prop. Transactions Ch. 2-B, B. Licensing and Regulatory Requirements.
Rutter, Cal. Practice Guide: Real Prop. Transactions Ch. 6-B, B. Sources and Kinds of Financing.
Rutter, Cal. Practice Guide: Prof. Responsibility Ch. 5-B, B. Types of Fees and Fee Arrangements.
Miller and Starr California Real Estate § 10:145, Regulation of Foreclosure Consultants.
Miller and Starr California Real Estate § 10:145.10, Regulation of Compensation and Advance Fees for Residential Loan Modifications and Forbearances (Which May Include "Short Sales" and Refinancings).
20 NO. 3 Miller & Starr, California Real Estate Newsalert 3, Deeds of Trust.
20 NO. 4 Miller & Starr, California Real Estate Newsalert 6, Deeds of Trust.
1 Witkin Cal. Proc. 5th Attorneys § 480, Statutory Framework.
4 Witkin, California Summary 10th Security Transactions in Real Property § 237, (New)-Mortgage Loan Modification.

§ 2944.7. Person negotiating or offering to perform mortgage loan modification for compensation paid by borrower; unlawful acts; violations

(a) Notwithstanding any other provision of law, it shall be unlawful for any person who negotiates, attempts to negotiate, arranges, attempts to arrange, or otherwise offers to perform a mortgage loan modification or other form of mortgage loan forbearance for a fee or other compensation paid by the borrower, to do any of the following:

(1) Claim, demand, charge, collect, or receive any compensation until after the person has fully performed each and every service the person contracted to perform or represented that he or she would perform.

(2) Take any wage assignment, any lien of any type on real or personal property, or other security to secure the payment of compensation.

(3) Take any power of attorney from the borrower for any purpose.

(b) A violation of this section by a natural person is a public offense punishable by a fine not exceeding ten thousand dollars ($10,000), by imprisonment in the county jail for a term not to exceed one year, or by both that fine and imprisonment, or if by a business entity, the violation is punishable by a fine not exceeding fifty thousand dollars ($50,000). These penalties are cumulative to any other remedies or penalties provided by law.

(c) Nothing in this section precludes a person, or an agent acting on that person's behalf, who offers loan modification or other loan forbearance services for a loan owned or serviced by that person, from doing any of the following:

(1) Collecting principal, interest, or other charges under the terms of a loan, before the loan is modified, including charges to establish a new payment schedule for a nondelinquent loan, after the borrower reduces the unpaid principal balance of that loan for the express purpose of lowering the monthly payment due under the terms of the loan.

(2) Collecting principal, interest, or other charges under the terms of a loan, after the loan is modified.

(3) Accepting payment from a federal agency in connection with the federal Making Home Affordable Plan or other federal plan intended to help borrowers refinance or modify their loans or otherwise avoid foreclosures.

(d) This section shall apply only to mortgages and deeds of trust secured by residential real property containing four or fewer dwelling units. *(Added by Stats.2009, c. 630 (S.B.94), § 10, eff. Oct. 11, 2009.   Amended by Stats.2012, c. 563 (S.B.980), § 4; Stats.2012, c. 569 (A.B.1950), § 3.)*

Research References

Rutter, Cal. Practice Guide: Real Prop. Transactions Ch. 1-C, C. Attorney Fees and Costs Agreements.

Rutter, Cal. Practice Guide: Real Prop. Transactions Ch. 2-B, B. Licensing and Regulatory Requirements.

Rutter, Cal. Practice Guide: Real Prop. Transactions Ch. 6-B, B. Sources and Kinds of Financing.

Rutter, Cal. Practice Guide: Prof. Responsibility Ch. 5-B, B. Types of Fees and Fee Arrangements.

Rutter, Cal. Practice Guide: Prof. Responsibility Ch. 5-F, F. Formalizing Fee Agreements.

Miller and Starr California Real Estate § 4:35, Advance Fees--In General.

Miller and Starr California Real Estate § 10:145, Regulation of Foreclosure Consultants.

Miller and Starr California Real Estate § 10:145.10, Regulation of Compensation and Advance Fees for Residential Loan Modifications and Forbearances (Which May Include "Short Sales" and Refinancings).

20 NO. 3 Miller & Starr, California Real Estate Newsalert 3, Deeds of Trust.

20 NO. 4 Miller & Starr, California Real Estate Newsalert 6, Deeds of Trust.

1 Witkin Cal. Proc. 5th Attorneys § 480, Statutory Framework.

4 Witkin, California Summary 10th Security Transactions in Real Property § 237, (New)-Mortgage Loan Modification.

ARTICLE 1.5.   MORTGAGE FORECLOSURE CONSULTANTS

Section

2945.   Legislative findings and declarations.

2945.1.   Definitions.

2945.2.   Owner's right to cancel contract with consultant; time and manner of cancellation.

2945.3.   Written contract; contents; language, date, and signature; notice of cancellation; form.

2945.4.   Prohibited practices.

2945.45.   Foreclosure consultants; registration and certification; requirements; Foreclosure Consultant Regulation Fund; refusal or revocation of registration; fines and penalties for violation.

2945.5.   Waiver.

2945.6.   Action against consultant; judgment; cumulative remedies; limitation of actions.

2945.7.   Violations; punishment; cumulative remedies.

2945.8.   Severability.

2945.9.   Liability of consultant for statements or acts committed by representative.

2945.10.   Limitation of liability under section 2945.9; voiding provision or contract; arbitration.

2945.11.   Representative of consultant; statements to be provided to owner; remedies.

§ 2945.   Legislative findings and declarations

(a) The Legislature finds and declares that homeowners whose residences are in foreclosure are subject to fraud, deception, harassment, and unfair dealing by foreclosure consultants from the time a Notice of Default is recorded pursuant to Section 2924 until the time surplus funds from any foreclosure sale are distributed to the homeowner or his or her successor. Foreclosure consultants represent that they can assist homeowners who have defaulted on obligations secured by their residences.   These foreclosure consultants, however, often charge high fees, the payment of which is often secured by a deed of trust on the residence to be saved, and perform no service or essentially a worthless service.   Homeowners, relying on the foreclosure consultants' promises of help, take no other

action, are diverted from lawful businesses which could render beneficial services, and often lose their homes, sometimes to the foreclosure consultants who purchase homes at a fraction of their value before the sale.   Vulnerable homeowners are increasingly relying on the services of foreclosure consultants who advise the homeowner that the foreclosure consultant can obtain the remaining funds from the foreclosure sale if the homeowner executes an assignment of the surplus, a deed, or a power of attorney in favor of the foreclosure consultant.   This results in the homeowner paying an exorbitant fee for a service when the homeowner could have obtained the remaining funds from the trustee's sale from the trustee directly for minimal cost if the homeowner had consulted legal counsel or had sufficient time to receive notices from the trustee pursuant to Section 2924j regarding how and where to make a claim for excess proceeds.

(b) The Legislature further finds and declares that foreclosure consultants have a significant impact on the economy of this state and on the welfare of its citizens.

(c) The intent and purposes of this article are the following:

(1) To require that foreclosure consultant service agreements be expressed in writing; to safeguard the public against deceit and financial hardship; to permit rescission of foreclosure consultation contracts; to prohibit representations that tend to mislead; and to encourage fair dealing in the rendition of foreclosure services.

(2) The provisions of this article shall be liberally construed to effectuate this intent and to achieve these purposes. *(Added by Stats.1979, c. 1029, p. 3541, § 2.   Amended by Stats.1980, c. 676, p. 1896, § 51;   Stats.2004, c. 177 (S.B.1277), § 6.)*

Research References

Rutter, Cal. Practice Guide: Real Prop. Transactions Ch. 6-I, I. Real Property Foreclosures and Antideficiency Laws.

Miller and Starr California Real Estate § 10:145, Regulation of Foreclosure Consultants.

13 NO. 6 Miller & Starr, California Real Estate Newsalert 4, Deeds of Trust.

15 NO. 4 Miller & Starr, California Real Estate Newsalert 7, Deeds.

20 NO. 3 Miller & Starr, California Real Estate Newsalert 3, Deeds of Trust.

20 NO. 4 Miller & Starr, California Real Estate Newsalert 6, Deeds of Trust.

4 Witkin, California Summary 10th Security Transactions in Real Property § 227, (S 227) Nature and Purpose of Legislation.

4 Witkin, California Summary 10th Security Transactions in Real Property § 228, (S 228) Foreclosure Consultant.

4 Witkin, California Summary 10th Security Transactions in Real Property § 229, (S 229) Rights of Owner and Obligations of Consultant.

§ 2945.1.   Definitions

The following definitions apply to this chapter:

(a) "Foreclosure consultant" means any person who makes any solicitation, representation, or offer to any owner to perform for compensation or who, for compensation, performs any service which the person in any manner represents will in any manner do any of the following:

(1) Stop or postpone the foreclosure sale.

(2) Obtain any forbearance from any beneficiary or mortgagee.

(3) Assist the owner to exercise the right of reinstatement provided in Section 2924c.

(4) Obtain any extension of the period within which the owner may reinstate his or her obligation.

(5) Obtain any waiver of an acceleration clause contained in any promissory note or contract secured by a deed of trust or

mortgage on a residence in foreclosure or contained that deed of trust or mortgage.

(6) Assist the owner to obtain a loan or advance of funds.

(7) Avoid or ameliorate the impairment of the owner's credit resulting from the recording of a notice of default or the conduct of a foreclosure sale.

(8) Save the owner's residence from foreclosure.

(9) Assist the owner in obtaining from the beneficiary, mortgagee, trustee under a power of sale, or counsel for the beneficiary, mortgagee, or trustee, the remaining proceeds from the foreclosure sale of the owner's residence.

(b) A foreclosure consultant does not include any of the following:

(1) A person licensed to practice law in this state when the person renders service in the course of his or her practice as an attorney at law.

(2) A person licensed under Division 3 (commencing with Section 12000) of the Financial Code when the person is acting as a prorater as defined therein.

(3) A person licensed under Part 1 (commencing with Section 10000) of Division 4 of the Business and Professions Code when the person is acting under the authority of that license, as described in Section 10131 or 10131.1 of the Business and Professions Code.

(4) A person licensed under Chapter 1 (commencing with Section 5000) of Division 3 of the Business and Professions Code when the person is acting in any capacity for which the person is licensed under those provisions.

(5) A person or his or her authorized agent acting under the express authority or written approval of the Department of Housing and Urban Development or other department or agency of the United States or this state to provide services.

(6) A person who holds or is owed an obligation secured by a lien on any residence in foreclosure when the person performs services in connection with this obligation or lien.

(7) Any person licensed to make loans pursuant to Division 9 (commencing with Section 22000) of the Financial Code when the person is acting under the authority of that license.

(8) Any person or entity doing business under any law of this state, or of the United States relating to banks, trust companies, savings and loan associations, industrial loan companies, pension trusts, credit unions, insurance companies, or any person or entity authorized under the laws of this state to conduct a title or escrow business, or a mortgagee which is a United States Department of Housing and Urban Development approved mortgagee and any subsidiary or affiliate of the above, and any agent or employee of the above while engaged in the business of these persons or entities.

(9) A person licensed as a residential mortgage lender or servicer pursuant to Division 20 (commencing with Section 50000) of the Financial Code, when acting under the authority of that license.

(c) Notwithstanding subdivision (b), any person who provides services pursuant to paragraph (9) of subdivision (a) is a foreclosure consultant unless he or she is the owner's attorney.

(d) "Person" means any individual, partnership, corporation, limited liability company, association or other group, however organized.

(e) "Service" means and includes, but is not limited to, any of the following:

(1) Debt, budget, or financial counseling of any type.

(2) Receiving money for the purpose of distributing it to creditors in payment or partial payment of any obligation secured by a lien on a residence in foreclosure.

(3) Contacting creditors on behalf of an owner of a residence in foreclosure.

(4) Arranging or attempting to arrange for an extension of the period within which the owner of a residence in foreclosure may cure his or her default and reinstate his or her obligation pursuant to Section 2924c.

(5) Arranging or attempting to arrange for any delay or postponement of the time of sale of the residence in foreclosure.

(6) Advising the filing of any document or assisting in any manner in the preparation of any document for filing with any bankruptcy court.

(7) Giving any advice, explanation, or instruction to an owner of a residence in foreclosure which in any manner relates to the cure of a default or the reinstatement of an obligation secured by a lien on the residence in foreclosure, the full satisfaction of that obligation, or the postponement or avoidance of a sale of a residence in foreclosure pursuant to a power of sale contained in any deed of trust.

(8) Arranging or attempting to arrange for the payment by the beneficiary, mortgagee, trustee under a power of sale, or counsel for the beneficiary, mortgagee, or trustee, of the remaining proceeds to which the owner is entitled from a foreclosure sale of the owner's residence in foreclosure. Arranging or attempting to arrange for the payment shall include any arrangement where the owner transfers or assigns the right to the remaining proceeds of a foreclosure sale to the foreclosure consultant or any person designated by the foreclosure consultant, whether that transfer is effected by agreement, assignment, deed, power of attorney, or assignment of claim.

(9) Arranging or attempting to arrange an audit of any obligation secured by a lien on a residence in foreclosure.

(f) "Residence in foreclosure" means a residence in foreclosure as defined in Section 1695.1.

(g) "Owner" means a property owner as defined in Section 1695.1.

(h) "Contract" means any agreement, or any term thereof, between a foreclosure consultant and an owner for the rendition of any service as defined in subdivision (e). *(Added by Stats. 1979, c. 1029, p. 3541, § 2. Amended by Stats.1980, c. 108, p. 252, § 3, eff. May 20, 1980; Stats.1980, c. 423, p. 845, § 15, eff. July 11, 1980; Stats.1980, c. 676, p. 1897, § 52; Stats.1980, c. 706, p. 2115, § 2; Stats.1981, c. 724, p. 2835, § 4; Stats.1982, c. 1082, p. 3920, § 3; Stats.1986, c. 248, § 17; Stats.1994, c. 1010 (S.B.2053), § 49; Stats.1995, c. 564 (S.B.946), § 4; Stats.2004, c. 177 (S.B.1277), § 7; Stats.2009, c. 630 (S.B.94), § 11, eff. Oct. 11, 2009; Stats.2010, c. 596 (A.B.2325), § 1.)*

Research References

Rutter, Cal. Practice Guide: Real Prop. Transactions Ch. 6-I, I. Real Property Foreclosures and Antideficiency Laws.

Rutter, Cal. Practice Guide: Prof. Responsibility Ch. 5-B, B. Types of Fees and Fee Arrangements.

Miller and Starr California Real Estate § 4:83, Residential Mortgage Lenders or Servicers; Licensing and Regulation by Department of Corporations.

Miller and Starr California Real Estate § 10:145, Regulation of Foreclosure Consultants.

Miller and Starr California Real Estate § 10:236, Policy Objectives; the "Standard" Transaction.

15 NO. 4 Miller & Starr, California Real Estate Newsalert 7, Deeds.

20 NO. 3 Miller & Starr, California Real Estate Newsalert 3, Deeds of Trust.

20 NO. 4 Miller & Starr, California Real Estate Newsalert 6, Deeds of Trust.

21 NO. 4 Miller & Starr, California Real Estate Newsalert 11, Deeds of Trust.

4 Witkin, California Summary 10th Security Transactions in Real Property § 227, (S 227) Nature and Purpose of Legislation.

4 Witkin, California Summary 10th Security Transactions in Real Property § 228, (S 228) Foreclosure Consultant.

4 Witkin, California Summary 10th Security Transactions in Real Property § 230, (S 230) Consultant's Representative.

§ 2945.2. Owner's right to cancel contract with consultant; time and manner of cancellation

(a) In addition to any other right under law to rescind a contract, an owner has the right to cancel such a contract until midnight of the fifth business day, as defined in subdivision (e) of Section 1689.5, after the day on which the owner signs a contract that complies with Section 2945.3.

(b) Cancellation occurs when the owner gives written notice of cancellation to the foreclosure consultant by mail at the address specified in the contract, or by facsimile or electronic mail at the number or address identified in the contract.

(c) Notice of cancellation, if given by mail, is effective when deposited in the mail properly addressed with postage prepaid. If given by facsimile or electronic mail, notice of cancellation is effective when successfully transmitted.

(d) Notice of cancellation given by the owner need not take the particular form as provided with the contract and, however expressed, is effective if it indicates the intention of the owner not to be bound by the contract. *(Added by Stats.1979, c. 1029, p. 3541, § 2. Amended by Stats.2008, c. 278 (A.B.180), § 2, operative July 1, 2009.)*

Research References

Rutter, Cal. Practice Guide: Real Prop. Transactions Ch. 6-I, I. Real Property Foreclosures and Antideficiency Laws.

Miller and Starr California Real Estate § 10:145, Regulation of Foreclosure Consultants.

19 NO. 4 Miller & Starr, California Real Estate Newsalert 10, Deeds of Trust.

4 Witkin, California Summary 10th Security Transactions in Real Property § 229, (S 229) Rights of Owner and Obligations of Consultant.

§ 2945.3. Written contract; contents; language, date, and signature; notice of cancellation; form

(a) Every contract shall be in writing and shall fully disclose the exact nature of the foreclosure consultant's services and the total amount and terms of compensation.

(b) The following notice, printed in at least 14–point boldface type and completed with the name of the foreclosure consultant, shall be printed immediately above the statement required by subdivision (d):

"NOTICE REQUIRED BY CALIFORNIA LAW

_____ or anyone working
          (Name)

for him or her CANNOT:

(1) Take any money from you or ask you for money

until _____ has
          (Name)
completely finished doing everything he or she said he or she would do; and

(2) Ask you to sign or have you sign any lien, deed of trust, or deed."

(c) The contract shall be written in the same language as principally used by the foreclosure consultant to describe his or her services or to negotiate the contract. In addition, the foreclosure consultant shall provide the owner, before the owner signs the contract, with a copy of a completed contract written in any other language used in any communication between the foreclosure consultant and the owner and in any language described in subdivision (b) of Section 1632 and requested by the owner. If English is the language principally used by the foreclosure consultant to describe the foreclosure consultant's services or to negotiate the contract, the foreclosure consultant shall notify the owner orally and in writing before the owner signs the contract that the owner has the right to ask for a completed copy of the contract in a language described in subdivision (b) of Section 1632.

(d) The contract shall be dated and signed by the owner and shall contain in immediate proximity to the space reserved for the owner's signature a conspicuous statement in a size equal to at least 10–point boldface type, as follows: "You, the owner, may cancel this transaction at any time prior to midnight of the fifth business day after the date of this transaction. See the attached notice of cancellation form for an explanation of this right."

(e) The contract shall contain on the first page, in a type size no smaller than that generally used in the body of the document, each of the following:

(1) The name, mailing address, electronic mail address, and facsimile number of the foreclosure consultant to which the notice of cancellation is to be mailed.

(2) The date the owner signed the contract.

(f) The contract shall be accompanied by a completed form in duplicate, captioned "notice of cancellation," which shall be attached to the contract, shall be easily detachable, and shall contain in type of at least 10–point the following statement written in the same language as used in the contract:

"NOTICE OF CANCELLATION

_____
(Enter date of transaction)   (Date)

You may cancel this transaction, without any penalty or obligation, within five business days from the above date.

To cancel this transaction, mail or deliver a signed and dated copy of this cancellation notice, or any other written notice, or send a telegram,

to _____
        (Name of foreclosure consultant)

at _____
      (Address of foreclosure consultant's place of business)
You may also cancel by sending a facsimile (fax) of signed and dated copy of this cancellation notice, or any other written notice, to the following number:

_____
(Facsimile telephone number of foreclosure consultant's place of business)
You may also cancel by sending an e-mail canceling this transaction to the following e-mail address:

_____
(E-mail address of foreclosure consultant's business)

I hereby cancel this transaction
_____
                (Date)

_____"
         (Owner's signature)

(g) The foreclosure consultant shall provide the owner with a copy of the contract and the attached notice of cancellation.

(h) Until the foreclosure consultant has complied with this section, the owner may cancel the contract. *(Added by Stats. 1979, c. 1029, p. 3541, § 2. Amended by Stats.1980, c. 423, p. 850, § 16, eff. July 11, 1980; Stats.1997, c. 50 (A.B.669), § 4; Stats.2004, c. 183 (A.B.3082), § 39; Stats.2004, c. 177 (S.B.1277), § 8; Stats.2006, c. 538 (S.B.1852), § 54; Stats.2008, c. 278 (A.B.180), § 3, operative July 1, 2009.)*

Research References

Rutter, Cal. Practice Guide: Real Prop. Transactions Ch. 6-I, I. Real Property Foreclosures and Antideficiency Laws.
Miller and Starr California Real Estate § 10:145, Regulation of Foreclosure Consultants.
13 NO. 6 Miller & Starr, California Real Estate Newsalert 4, Deeds of Trust.
15 NO. 4 Miller & Starr, California Real Estate Newsalert 7, Deeds.
19 NO. 4 Miller & Starr, California Real Estate Newsalert 10, Deeds of Trust.
4 Witkin, California Summary 10th Security Transactions in Real Property § 229, (S 229) Rights of Owner and Obligations of Consultant.

§ 2945.4. Prohibited practices

It shall be a violation for a foreclosure consultant to:

(a) Claim, demand, charge, collect, or receive any compensation until after the foreclosure consultant has fully performed each and every service the foreclosure consultant contracted to perform or represented that he or she would perform.

(b) Claim, demand, charge, collect, or receive any fee, interest, or any other compensation for any reason which exceeds 10 percent per annum of the amount of any loan which the foreclosure consultant may make to the owner.

(c) Take any wage assignment, any lien of any type on real or personal property, or other security to secure the payment of compensation. That security shall be void and unenforceable.

(d) Receive any consideration from any third party in connection with services rendered to an owner unless that consideration is fully disclosed to the owner.

(e) Acquire any interest in a residence in foreclosure from an owner with whom the foreclosure consultant has contracted. Any interest acquired in violation of this subdivision shall be voidable, provided that nothing herein shall affect or defeat the title of a bona fide purchaser or encumbrancer for value and without notice of a violation of this article. Knowledge that the property was "residential real property in foreclosure," does not constitute notice of a violation of this article. This subdivision may not be deemed to abrogate any duty of inquiry which exists as to rights or interests of persons in possession of residential real property in foreclosure.

(f) Take any power of attorney from an owner for any purpose.

(g) Induce or attempt to induce any owner to enter into a contract which does not comply in all respects with Sections 2945.2 and 2945.3.

(h) Enter into an agreement at any time to assist the owner in arranging, or arrange for the owner, the release of surplus funds after the trustee's sale is conducted, whether the agreement involves direct payment, assignment, deed, power of attorney, assignment of claim from an owner to the foreclosure consultant or any person designated by the foreclosure consultant, or any other compensation. *(Added by Stats.1979, c. 1029, p. 3541, § 2. Amended by Stats.1980, c. 423, p. 851, § 17, eff. July 11, 1980; Stats.2004, c. 177 (S.B.1277), § 9; Stats.2008, c. 278 (A.B.180), § 4, operative July 1, 2009.)*

Research References

Rutter, Cal. Practice Guide: Real Prop. Transactions Ch. 6-I, I. Real Property Foreclosures and Antideficiency Laws.
Miller and Starr California Real Estate § 4:35, Advance Fees--In General.
Miller and Starr California Real Estate § 10:145, Regulation of Foreclosure Consultants.
13 NO. 6 Miller & Starr, California Real Estate Newsalert 4, Deeds of Trust.
15 NO. 4 Miller & Starr, California Real Estate Newsalert 7, Deeds.
19 NO. 4 Miller & Starr, California Real Estate Newsalert 10, Deeds of Trust.
4 Witkin, California Summary 10th Security Transactions in Real Property § 229, (S 229) Rights of Owner and Obligations of Consultant.
4 Witkin, California Summary 10th Security Transactions in Real Property § 231, (S 231) Penalties and Owner's Remedies.

§ 2945.45. Foreclosure consultants; registration and certification; requirements; Foreclosure Consultant Regulation Fund; refusal or revocation of registration; fines and penalties for violation

(a) Except as provided in subdivision (b) of Section 2945.1, a person shall not take any action specified in subdivision (a) of Section 2945.1 unless the person satisfies the following requirements:

(1) The person registers with, and is issued and maintains a certificate of registration from, the Department of Justice in accordance with the following requirements:

(A) The person shall submit a completed registration form, along with applicable fees, to the department. The registration form shall include the name, address, and telephone number of the foreclosure consultant, all of the names, addresses, telephone numbers, Internet Web sites, and e-mail addresses used or proposed to be used in connection with acting as a foreclosure consultant, a statement that the person has not been convicted of, or pled nolo contendere to, any crime involving fraud, misrepresentation, dishonesty, or a violation of this article, a statement that the person has not been liable under any civil judgment for fraud, misrepresentation, or violations of this article or of Section 17200 or 17500 of the Business and Professions Code, and any additional information required by the department.

(B) The registration form shall be accompanied by a copy of all print or electronic advertising and other promotional material, and scripts of all telephonic or broadcast advertising and other statements used or proposed to be used in connection with acting as a foreclosure consultant.

(C) The registration form shall be accompanied by a copy of the bond required pursuant to paragraph (2).

(D) The person shall file an update of any material change in the information required by subparagraphs (A) and (B) with the department.

(E) The person shall pay any fee set by the department to defray reasonable costs incurred in connection with the department's responsibilities under this article.

(2) The person obtains and maintains in force a surety bond in the amount of one hundred thousand dollars ($100,000). The bond shall be executed by a corporate surety admitted to do business in this state. The bond shall be made in favor of the State of California for the benefit of homeowners for damages caused by the foreclosure consultant's violation of this article or any other provision of law. A copy of the bond shall be filed with the Secretary of State, with a copy provided to the department pursuant to subparagraph (C) of paragraph (1).

(b) The Foreclosure Consultant Regulation Fund is hereby created in the State Treasury for the deposit of fees submitted to the Department of Justice pursuant to subparagraph (A) of paragraph (1) of subdivision (a) for registration as a foreclosure consultant. Moneys in the fund shall be available, upon appropriation by the Legislature, for the costs of the department incurred in connection with the administration of the registration program.

(c) The Department of Justice may refuse to issue, or may revoke, a certificate of registration because of any misstatement in the registration form, because the foreclosure consultant has been held liable for the violation of any law described in subparagraph (A) of paragraph (1) of subdivision (a), because the foreclosure consultant has failed to maintain the bond required under paragraph (2) of subdivision (a), or because of any violation of this chapter.

(d) A person who violates subdivision (a) shall be punished, for each violation, by a fine of not less than one thousand dollars ($1,000) and not more than twenty-five thousand dollars ($25,-000), by imprisonment in the county jail for not more than one year, or by both that fine and imprisonment. The imposition of a penalty pursuant to this subdivision shall not be affected by the availability of any other relief, remedy, or penalty provided by law, and shall not affect the availability of any such relief, remedy, or penalty. *(Added by Stats.2008, c. 278 (A.B.180), § 5, operative July 1, 2009.)*

Research References

Miller and Starr California Real Estate § 4:35, Advance Fees--In General.
Miller and Starr California Real Estate § 10:145, Regulation of Foreclosure Consultants.
19 NO. 4 Miller & Starr, California Real Estate Newsalert 10, Deeds of Trust.
4 Witkin, California Summary 10th Security Transactions in Real Property § 227, (S 227) Nature and Purpose of Legislation.

§ 2945.5. Waiver

Any waiver by an owner of the provisions of this article shall be deemed void and unenforceable as contrary to public policy. Any attempt by a foreclosure consultant to induce an owner to waive his rights shall be deemed a violation of this article. *(Added by Stats.1979, c. 1029, p. 3541, § 2. Amended by Stats.1980, c. 676, p. 1899, § 53.)*

Research References

Rutter, Cal. Practice Guide: Real Prop. Transactions Ch. 6-I, I. Real Property Foreclosures and Antideficiency Laws.
Miller and Starr California Real Estate § 10:145, Regulation of Foreclosure Consultants.
4 Witkin, California Summary 10th Security Transactions in Real Property § 227, (S 227) Nature and Purpose of Legislation.

§ 2945.6. Action against consultant; judgment; cumulative remedies; limitation of actions

(a) An owner may bring an action against a foreclosure consultant for any violation of this chapter. Judgment shall be entered for actual damages, reasonable attorneys' fees and costs, and appropriate equitable relief. The court also may, in its discretion, award exemplary damages and shall award exemplary damages equivalent to at least three times the compensation received by the foreclosure consultant in violation of subdivision (a), (b), or (d) of Section 2945.4, and three times the owner's actual damages for any violation of subdivision (c), (e), or (g) of Section 2945.4, in addition to any other award of actual or exemplary damages.

(b) The rights and remedies provided in subdivision (a) are cumulative to, and not a limitation of, any other rights and remedies provided by law. Any action brought pursuant to this section shall be commenced within four years from the date of the alleged violation. *(Added by Stats.1979, c. 1029, p. 3541, § 2.*

Amended by Stats.1980, c. 676, p. 1899, § 54; Stats.1980, c. 423, p. 852, § 18, eff. July 11, 1980; Stats.1997, c. 50 (A.B.669), § 5.)

Research References

Rutter, Cal. Practice Guide: Real Prop. Transactions Ch. 6-I, I. Real Property Foreclosures and Antideficiency Laws.
Miller and Starr California Real Estate § 10:145, Regulation of Foreclosure Consultants.
4 Witkin, California Summary 10th Security Transactions in Real Property § 231, (S 231) Penalties and Owner's Remedies.

§ 2945.7. Violations; punishment; cumulative remedies

Any person who commits any violation described in Section 2945.4 shall be punished by a fine of not more than ten thousand dollars ($10,000), by imprisonment in the county jail for not more than one year, or pursuant to subdivision (h) of Section 1170 of the Penal Code, or by both that fine and imprisonment for each violation. These penalties are cumulative to any other remedies or penalties provided by law. *(Added by Stats.1979, c. 1029, p. 3541, § 2. Amended by Stats.1980, c. 423, p. 852, § 19, eff. July 11, 1980; Stats.1985, c. 270, § 2; Stats.2011, c. 15 (A.B.109), § 35, eff. April 4, 2011, operative Oct. 1, 2011.)*

Research References

Rutter, Cal. Practice Guide: Real Prop. Transactions Ch. 6-I, I. Real Property Foreclosures and Antideficiency Laws.
Miller and Starr California Real Estate § 10:145, Regulation of Foreclosure Consultants.
4 Witkin, California Summary 10th Security Transactions in Real Property § 231, (S 231) Penalties and Owner's Remedies.

§ 2945.8. Severability

If any provision of this article or the application thereof to any person or circumstance is held to be unconstitutional, the remainder of the article and the application of such provision to other persons and circumstances shall not be affected thereby. *(Added by Stats.1979, c. 1029, p. 3541, § 2.)*

§ 2945.9. Liability of consultant for statements or acts committed by representative

(a) A foreclosure consultant is liable for all damages resulting from any statement made or act committed by the foreclosure consultant's representative in any manner connected with the foreclosure consultant's (1) performance, offer to perform, or contract to perform any of the services described in subdivision (a) of Section 2945.1, (2) receipt of any consideration or property from or on behalf of an owner, or (3) performance of any act prohibited by this article.

(b) "Representative" for the purposes of this section means a person who in any manner solicits, induces, or causes (1) any owner to contract with a foreclosure consultant, (2) any owner to pay any consideration or transfer title to the residence in foreclosure to the foreclosure consultant, or (3) any member of the owner's family or household to induce or cause any owner to pay any consideration or transfer title to the residence in foreclosure to the foreclosure consultant. *(Added by Stats.1990, c. 1537 (S.B.2641), § 4. Amended by Stats.2006, c. 538 (S.B. 1852), § 55.)*

Research References

Miller and Starr California Real Estate § 10:145, Regulation of Foreclosure Consultants.
4 Witkin, California Summary 10th Security Transactions in Real Property § 230, (S 230) Consultant's Representative.

4 Witkin, California Summary 10th Security Transactions in Real Property § 231, (S 231) Penalties and Owner's Remedies.

§ 2945.10. Limitation of liability under section 2945.9; voiding provision or contract; arbitration

(a) Any provision in a contract which attempts or purports to limit the liability of the foreclosure consultant under Section 2945.9 shall be void and shall at the option of the owner render the contract void. The foreclosure consultant shall be liable to the owner for all damages proximately caused by that provision. Any provision in a contract which attempts or purports to require arbitration of any dispute arising under this chapter shall be void at the option of the owner only upon grounds as exist for the revocation of any contract.

(b) This section shall apply to any contract entered into on or after January 1, 1991. *(Added by Stats.1990, c. 1537 (S.B.2641), § 5.)*

Research References

Miller and Starr California Real Estate § 10:145, Regulation of Foreclosure Consultants.
4 Witkin, California Summary 10th Security Transactions in Real Property § 230, (S 230) Consultant's Representative.

§ 2945.11. Representative of consultant; statements to be provided to owner; remedies

(a) Any representative, as defined in subdivision (b) of Section 2945.9, deemed to be the agent or employee or both the agent and the employee of the foreclosure consultant shall be required to provide both of the following:

(1) Written proof to the owner that the representative has a valid current California Real Estate Sales License and that the representative is bonded by an admitted surety insurer in an amount equal to at least twice the fair market value of the real property that is the subject of the contract.

(2) A statement in writing, under penalty of perjury, that the representative has a valid current California Real Estate Sales License, that the representative is bonded by an admitted surety insurer in an amount equal to at least twice the value of the real property that is the subject of the contract and has complied with paragraph (1). The written statement required by this paragraph shall be provided to all parties to the contract prior to the transfer of any interest in the real property that is the subject of the contract.

(b) The failure to comply with subdivision (a) shall, at the option of the owner, render the contract void and the foreclosure consultant shall be liable to the owner for all damages proximately caused by the failure to comply. *(Added by Stats.1990, c. 1537 (S.B.2641), § 6. Amended by Stats.1996, c. 124 (A.B.3470), § 8.)*

Research References

Miller and Starr California Real Estate § 10:145, Regulation of Foreclosure Consultants.
4 Witkin, California Summary 10th Security Transactions in Real Property § 230, (S 230) Consultant's Representative.
4 Witkin, California Summary 10th Security Transactions in Real Property § 231, (S 231) Penalties and Owner's Remedies.

ARTICLE 2. MORTGAGE OF REAL PROPERTY

§ 2947. Property subject to mortgage

Any interest in real property which is capable of being transferred may be mortgaged. *(Enacted in 1872.)*

Research References

Rutter, Cal. Practice Guide: Real Prop. Transactions Ch. 6-H, H. Security for Promissory Note.
Miller and Starr California Real Estate § 2:17, Encumbrance and Homestead.

Miller and Starr California Real Estate § 10:16, Property Interests that Are Lienable.
4 Witkin, California Summary 10th Security Transactions in Real Property § 34, What Property Can be Mortgaged.

§ 2948. Form

A mortgage of real property may be made in substantially the following form:

This mortgage, made the _____ day of _____, in the year _____, by A. B., of _____, mortgagor, to C. D., of _____, mortgagee, witnesseth:

That the mortgagor mortgages to the mortgagee [here describe the property], as security for the payment to him of _____ dollars, on [or before] the _____ day of _____, in the year _____, with interest thereon [or as security for the payment of an obligation, describing it, etc.] A.B. *(Enacted in 1872.)*

Research References

Miller and Starr California Real Estate § 10:2, Lien Versus Title Theories.
Miller and Starr California Real Estate § 10:5, Form and Interpretation.
Miller and Starr California Real Estate § 10:10, Requirement of Some Debt or Obligation.
4 Witkin, California Summary 10th Security Transactions in Real Property § 40, (S 40) Mortgage.

§ 2948.5. Interest on principal obligation under promissory note secured by mortgage or deed of trust on real property improved with residential dwelling units; conditions; accrual of interest; conditions; applicability

(a) A borrower shall not be required to pay interest on a principal obligation under a promissory note secured by a mortgage or deed of trust on real property improved with between one to four residential dwelling units for any period that meets any of the following requirements:

(1) Is more than one day prior to the date that the loan proceeds are disbursed from escrow.

(2) In the event of no escrow, if a request for recording is made in connection with the disbursement, is more than one day prior to the date the loan proceeds are disbursed to the borrower, to a third party on behalf of the borrower, or to the lender to satisfy an existing obligation of the borrower.

(3) In all other circumstances where there is no escrow and no request for recording, is prior to the date funds are disbursed to the borrower, to a third party on behalf of the borrower, or to the lender to satisfy an existing obligation of the borrower.

(b) Interest may commence to accrue on the business day immediately preceding the day of disbursement, for obligations described in paragraphs (1) and (2) of subdivision (a) if both of the following occur:

(1) The borrower affirmatively requests, and the lender agrees, that the disbursement will occur on Monday, or a day immediately following a bank holiday.

(2) The following information is disclosed to the borrower in writing: (A) the amount of additional per diem interest charged to facilitate disbursement on Monday or the day following a holiday, as the case may be, and (B) that it may be possible to avoid the additional per diem interest charge by disbursing the loan proceeds on a day immediately following a business day. This disclosure shall be provided to the borrower and acknowledged by the borrower by signing a copy of the disclosure document prior to placing funds in escrow.

(c) This section does not apply to a loan that is subject to subdivision (c) of Section 10242 of the Business and Professions Code. *(Added by Stats.1985, c. 1393, § 1. Amended by Stats.*

1990, c. 872 (A.B.4267), § 1; Stats.2001, c. 302 (S.B.364), § 1; Stats.2003, c. 554 (A.B.313), § 1.)

Research References

Rutter, Cal. Practice Guide: Real Prop. Transactions Ch. 6-F, F. Promissory Note.
Miller and Starr California Real Estate § 4:83, Residential Mortgage Lenders or Servicers; Licensing and Regulation by Department of Corporations.
Miller and Starr California Real Estate § 6:23, Funding the Escrow.
Miller and Starr California Real Estate § 10:71, Payment or Performance of the Secured Obligation.
Miller and Starr California Real Estate § 21:15, Interest Defined; Method of Calculation.
13 NO. 5 Miller & Starr, California Real Estate Newsalert 13, Lenders' Liability.
14 NO. 4 Miller & Starr, California Real Estate Newsalert 3, Deeds of Trust.
14 NO. 4 Miller & Starr, California Real Estate Newsalert 6, Escrows.
14 NO. 4 Miller & Starr, California Real Estate Newsalert 18, Usury.
16 NO. 2 Miller & Starr, California Real Estate Newsalert 7, Deeds of Trust.
17 NO. 1 Miller & Starr, California Real Estate Newsalert 4, Deeds of Trust.
4 Witkin, California Summary 10th Security Transactions in Real Property § 37, (S 37) Aspects Regulated.

§ 2949. Single-family, owner-occupied dwelling; addition of junior encumbrance by owner; no default or acceleration of maturity

(a) No mortgage or deed of trust on real property containing only a single-family, owner-occupied dwelling may be declared in default, nor may the maturity date of the indebtedness secured thereby be accelerated, solely by reason of the owner further encumbering the real property or any portion thereof, with a junior mortgage or junior deed of trust.

(b) As used in this section, "single-family, owner-occupied dwelling" means a dwelling which will be owned and occupied by a signatory to the mortgage or deed of trust secured by such dwelling within 90 days of the execution of such mortgage or deed of trust. *(Added by Stats.1972, c. 698, p. 1278, § 1.)*

Research References

Rutter, Cal. Practice Guide: Real Prop. Transactions Ch. 6-H, H. Security for Promissory Note.
Miller and Starr California Real Estate § 10:109, Acceleration on Further Encumbrance; "Due on Encumbrance" Clause.
Miller and Starr California Real Estate § 10:236, Policy Objectives; the "Standard" Transaction.
4 Witkin, California Summary 10th Security Transactions in Real Property § 91, (S 91) "Due on Encumbrance" Clause.

§ 2950. Instrument of defeasance affecting grant in absolute form; necessity of recording

When a grant of real property purports to be an absolute conveyance, but is intended to be defeasible on the performance of certain conditions, such grant is not defeated or affected as against any person other than the grantee or his or her heirs or devisees, or persons having actual notice, unless an instrument of defeasance, duly executed and acknowledged, shall have been recorded in the office of the county recorder of the county where the property is situated. *(Enacted in 1872. Amended by Stats.2013, c. 76 (A.B.383), § 19.)*

Research References

Miller and Starr California Real Estate § 11:6, Instruments Subject to Recording--List of Recordable Documents.
Miller and Starr California Real Estate § 10:25, Between Debtor and Creditor (Types of Transactions).
Miller and Starr California Real Estate § 10:27, Enforcement Against a Purchaser from the Creditor or Other Third Person.

Miller and Starr California Real Estate § 11:64, Recorded Documents that Do Not Give Constructive Notice--Documents Not Affecting Title to Real Property and Not Otherwise Authorized for Recordation.

12 Witkin, California Summary 10th Real Property § 326, Recordation Outside Chain of Title.

§ 2952. Recording and acknowledgment; fictitious mortgages and deeds of trust; indexing; incorporation of terms by reference; constructive notice; designation of items not to be recorded

Mortgages and deeds of trust of real property may be acknowledged or proved, certified and recorded, in like manner and with like effect, as grants thereof; provided, however, that a mortgage or deed of trust of real property may be recorded and constructive notice of the same and the contents thereof given in the following manner:

Any person may record in the office of the county recorder of any county fictitious mortgages and deeds of trust of real property. Those fictitious mortgages and deeds of trust need not be acknowledged, or proved or certified to be recorded or entitled to record. Those mortgages and deeds of trust shall have noted upon the face thereof that they are fictitious. The county recorder shall index and record fictitious mortgages and deeds of trust in the same manner as other mortgages and deeds of trust are recorded, and shall note on all indices and records of the same that they are fictitious. Thereafter, any of the provisions of any recorded fictitious mortgage or deed of trust may be included for any and all purposes in any mortgage or deed of trust by reference therein to any of those provisions, without setting the same forth in full; provided, the fictitious mortgage or deed of trust is of record in the county in which the mortgage or deed of trust adopting or including by reference any of the provisions thereof is recorded. The reference shall contain a statement, as to each county in which the mortgage or deed of trust containing such a reference is recorded, of the date the fictitious mortgage or deed of trust was recorded, the county recorder's office wherein it is recorded, and the book or volume and the first page of the records in the recorder's office wherein and at which the fictitious mortgage or deed of trust was recorded, and a statement by paragraph numbers or any other method that will definitely identify the same, of the specific provisions of the fictitious mortgage or deed of trust that are being so adopted and included therein. The recording of any mortgage or deed of trust which has included therein any of those provisions by reference as aforesaid shall operate as constructive notice of the whole thereof including the terms, as a part of the written contents of the mortgage or deed of trust, of those provisions so included by reference as though the same were written in full therein. The parties bound or to be bound by provisions so adopted and included by reference shall be bound thereby in the same manner and with like effect for all purposes as though those provisions had been and were set forth in full in any mortgage or deed of trust.

The amendment to this section enacted by the 1957 Regular Session of the Legislature does not constitute a change in, but is declaratory of, the preexisting law. *(Enacted in 1872. Amended by Code Am.1873–74, c. 612, p. 262, § 263; Stats.1947, c. 1497, p. 3098, § 5; Stats.1949, c. 443, p. 788, § 1; Stats.1957, c. 1220, p. 2503, § 1; Stats.1969, c. 287, p. 638, § 1, operative July 1, 1970; Stats.2000, c. 924 (A.B.2935), § 1.)*

Research References

Miller and Starr California Real Estate § 10:6, "Fictitious" Mortgage or Trust Deed.

Miller and Starr California Real Estate § 10:7, Execution and Delivery.

Miller and Starr California Real Estate § 11:3, Effect of Recording Statutes on Priority.

Miller and Starr California Real Estate § 11:6, Instruments Subject to Recording--List of Recordable Documents.

Miller and Starr California Real Estate § 11:12, Required Form and Contents--Signature of the Property Owner.

Miller and Starr California Real Estate § 11:20, Recorder's Liability for Erroneous Recording or Indexing.

Miller and Starr California Real Estate § 11:23, Purpose and Effect; Required for Recordation.

Miller and Starr California Real Estate § 11:60, Recordation as Constructive Notice.

22 NO. 3 Miller & Starr, California Real Estate Newsalert 1, Show Me Your Papers: Sales and Assignments of Secured Real Estate Loans and the California Foreclosure Process.

12 Witkin, California Summary 10th Real Property § 283, Nature of Requirement.

4 Witkin, California Summary 10th Security Transactions in Real Property § 46, Recordation.

§ 2953. Waiver by borrower of statutory rights; validity; exceptions

Any express agreement made or entered into by a borrower at the time of or in connection with the making of or renewing of any loan secured by a deed of trust, mortgage or other instrument creating a lien on real property, whereby the borrower agrees to waive the rights, or privileges conferred upon him by Sections 2924, 2924b, 2924c of the Civil Code or by Sections 580a or 726 of the Code of Civil Procedure, shall be void and of no effect. The provisions of this section shall not apply to any deed of trust, mortgage or other liens given to secure the payment of bonds or other evidences of indebtedness authorized or permitted to be issued by the Commissioner of Corporations, or is made by a public utility subject to the provisions of the Public Utilities Act. *(Added by Stats.1937, c. 564, p. 1605, § 1. Amended by Stats.1939, c. 585, p. 1991, § 1; Stats.1941, c. 599, p. 1983, § 1.)*

Research References

Rutter, Cal. Practice Guide: Real Prop. Transactions Ch. 6-I, I. Real Property Foreclosures and Antideficiency Laws.

Miller and Starr California Real Estate § 10:1, Historical Perspective.

Miller and Starr California Real Estate § 10:26, Evidence of the Parties' Intentions.

Miller and Starr California Real Estate § 10:27, Enforcement Against a Purchaser from the Creditor or Other Third Person.

Miller and Starr California Real Estate § 10:75, Application and Allocation of Payments.

Miller and Starr California Real Estate § 10:76, Payment by Setoff; General Rules.

Miller and Starr California Real Estate § 10:123, Nature of Foreclosure; Termination of Redemption.

Miller and Starr California Real Estate § 10:156, Waiver; Trustor's Election.

Miller and Starr California Real Estate § 10:167, Offset (Setoff) by the Beneficiary.

Miller and Starr California Real Estate § 10:179, Nature and Basis of Power of Sale.

Miller and Starr California Real Estate § 10:181, Notice of Default--In General.

Miller and Starr California Real Estate § 10:194, Waiver of Right to Reinstate.

Miller and Starr California Real Estate § 10:211, Presumption of Validity.

Miller and Starr California Real Estate § 10:234, Determination of "Fair Value".

Miller and Starr California Real Estate § 10:237, Waiver of Purchase-Money Protection.

15 NO. 4 Miller & Starr, California Real Estate Newsalert 1, California's "One Form of Action" and "Security First" Rules: Have They Cleared the Minefields Yet?

22 NO. 3 Miller & Starr, California Real Estate Newsalert 8, Deeds of Trust.

1 Witkin Cal. Summ. 10th Contracts § 681, Waivers by Mortgagors.

4 Witkin, California Summary 10th Security Transactions in Real Property § 131, (S 131) Advance Waiver is Invalid.

4 Witkin, California Summary 10th Security Transactions in Real Property § 164, Effect of Recitals in Trustee's Deed.

4 Witkin, California Summary 10th Security Transactions in Real Property § 179, (S 179) Nature and Scope of Statutes.

4 Witkin, California Summary 10th Security Transactions in Real Property § 216, (S 216) in General.

§ 2953.1. Real property security instrument; subordination clause; subordination agreement

As used in this section:

(a) "Real property security instrument" shall include any mortgage or trust deed or land contract in or on real property.

(b) "Subordination clause" shall mean a clause in a real property security instrument whereby the holder of the security interest under such instrument agrees that upon the occurrence of conditions or circumstances specified therein his security interest will become subordinate to or he will execute an agreement subordinating his interest to the lien of another real property security instrument which would otherwise be of lower priority than his lien or security interest.

(c) "Subordination agreement" shall mean a separate agreement or instrument whereby the holder of the security interest under a real property security instrument agrees that (1) his existing security interest is subordinate to, or (2) upon the occurrence of conditions or circumstances specified in such separate agreement his security interest will become subordinate to, or (3) he will execute an agreement subordinating his interest to, the lien of another real property security instrument which would otherwise be of lower priority than his lien or security interest. *(Added by Stats.1963, c. 1861, p. 3841, § 1, operative Jan. 2, 1964.)*

Research References

California Real Estate Forms (Miller & Starr) § 3:56, Subordination Agreement (Deed of Trust to Deed of Trust).

Rutter, Cal. Practice Guide: Real Prop. Transactions Ch. 6-H, H. Security for Promissory Note.

Miller and Starr California Real Estate § 11:6, Instruments Subject to Recording--List of Recordable Documents.

Miller and Starr California Real Estate § 11:203, Subordination Agreements; Statutory Requirements.

§ 2953.2. Real property security instrument containing subordination clause; contents

Every real property security instrument which contains or has attached a subordination clause shall contain:

(a) At the top of the real property security instrument there shall appear in at least 10-point bold type, or, if typewritten, in capital letters and underlined, the word "SUBORDINATED" followed by a description of the type of security instrument.

(b) A notice in at least eight-point bold type, or, if typewritten, in capital letters, shall appear immediately below the legend required by subdivision (a) of this section reading as follows: "NOTICE: This (insert description of real property security instrument) contains a subordination clause which may result in your security interest in the property becoming subject to and of lower priority than the lien of some other or later security instrument."

(c) If the terms of the subordination clause allow the obligor on the debt secured by the real property security instrument to obtain a loan, secured by another real property security instrument covering all or any part of the same parcel of real property, the proceeds of which may be used for any purpose or purposes other than defraying the costs for improvement of the land covered by the real property security instrument containing the subordination clause, a notice in at least eight-point bold type, or, if typewritten, in capital letters shall appear directly above the space reserved for the signature of the person whose security interest is to be subordinated, reading as follows: "NOTICE: This (insert description of real property security instrument) contains a subordination clause which allows the person obligated on your real property security instrument to obtain a loan a portion of which may be expended for other purposes than improvement of the land." *(Added by Stats.1963, c. 1861, p. 3842, § 2, operative Jan. 2, 1964.)*

Research References

Rutter, Cal. Practice Guide: Real Prop. Transactions Ch. 6-H, H. Security for Promissory Note.

Miller and Starr California Real Estate § 11:203, Subordination Agreements; Statutory Requirements.

4 Witkin, California Summary 10th Security Transactions in Real Property § 54, (S 54) Notice Requirements.

§ 2953.3. Subordination agreements; contents

Every subordination agreement shall contain:

(a) At the top of the subordination agreement there shall appear in at least 10-point bold type, or, if typewritten, in capital letters and underlined, the words "SUBORDINATION AGREEMENT."

(b) A notice in at least eight-point bold type, or, if typewritten, in capital letters, shall appear immediately below the legend required by subdivision (a) of this section reading as follows:

"NOTICE: This subordination agreement ("may result" or "results" as appropriate) in your security interest in the property becoming subject to and of lower priority than the lien of some other or later security instrument."

(c) If the terms of the subordination agreement provide that the obligor on the debt secured by the real property security instrument may either obtain a loan, or obtain an agreement from the holder of the real property security which will allow him to obtain a loan, the proceeds of which may be used for any purpose or purposes other than defraying the actual contract costs for improvement of the land, covered by the real property security instrument which is, or is to become subordinated, a notice in at least eight-point bold type or, if typewritten, in capital letters shall appear directly above the space reserved for the signature of the person whose security interest is to be subordinated, reading as follows: "NOTICE: This subordination agreement contains a provision which ("allows" or "may allow" as appropriate) the person obligated on your real property security to obtain a loan a portion of which may be expended for other purposes than improvement of the land." *(Added by Stats.1963, c. 1861, p. 3842, § 3, operative Jan. 2, 1964.)*

Research References

California Real Estate Forms (Miller & Starr) § 3:56, Subordination Agreement (Deed of Trust to Deed of Trust).

Rutter, Cal. Practice Guide: Real Prop. Transactions Ch. 6-H, H. Security for Promissory Note.

Miller and Starr California Real Estate § 11:203, Subordination Agreements; Statutory Requirements.

4 Witkin, California Summary 10th Security Transactions in Real Property § 54, (S 54) Notice Requirements.

§ 2953.4. Voidability of subordination clause or agreement; election; waiver

(a) Any subordination clause and any subordination agreement which is executed after the effective date of this act and which does not substantially comply with the provisions of Section 2953.2 or Section 2953.3 shall be voidable upon the election of the person whose security interest is to be subordinated or his successor-in-interest exercised within two years of the date on which the instrument to which his security interest is subordinated is executed; provided that such power of avoidance shall not be exercisable by any person having actual knowledge of the existence and terms of the subordination clause or agreement.

(b) The person whose security interest was to be subordinated or his successor-in-interest shall exercise his election to void the subordination clause or subordination agreement provided by subdivision (a) of this section by recording a notice stating that the provisions of Civil Code Section 2953.2 or Civil Code Section 2953.3 have not been complied with, and that he is the holder of the security instrument which is or was to become subordinated and that he elects to avoid the effect of the subordination clause or subordination agreement.

(c) The provisions of this section may be waived by the subsequent execution and recordation by the holder of the security interest which is or may become subordinated, of a statement that he knows of the existence of the subordination clause or agreement and of its terms and that he waives the provisions of this section and the requirements of Sections 2953.1, 2953.2, and 2953.3. *(Added by Stats.1963, c. 1861, p. 3843, § 4, operative Jan. 2, 1964.)*

Research References

Rutter, Cal. Practice Guide: Real Prop. Transactions Ch. 6-H, H. Security for Promissory Note.

Miller and Starr California Real Estate § 11:203, Subordination Agreements; Statutory Requirements.

4 Witkin, California Summary 10th Security Transactions in Real Property § 54, (S 54) Notice Requirements.

§ 2953.5. Application of §§ 2953.1 through 2953.4 to specified loans

(a) Sections 2953.1 through 2953.4 shall not apply to any subordination clause or subordination agreement which expressly states that the subordinating loan shall exceed twenty-five thousand dollars ($25,000).

(b) Sections 2953.1 through 2953.4 shall not apply to any subordination clause or subordination agreement which is executed in connection with a loan which exceeds twenty-five thousand dollars ($25,000). *(Added by Stats.1963, c. 1861, p. 3843, § 5, operative Jan. 2, 1964.)*

Research References

California Real Estate Forms (Miller & Starr) § 3:56, Subordination Agreement (Deed of Trust to Deed of Trust).

Rutter, Cal. Practice Guide: Real Prop. Transactions Ch. 6-H, H. Security for Promissory Note.

Miller and Starr California Real Estate § 11:6, Instruments Subject to Recording--List of Recordable Documents.

Miller and Starr California Real Estate § 11:203, Subordination Agreements; Statutory Requirements.

4 Witkin, California Summary 10th Security Transactions in Real Property § 54, (S 54) Notice Requirements.

§ 2954. Impound, trust, or other account for payment of taxes, insurance, or other purposes; conditions; accounting

(a)(1) No impound, trust, or other type of account for payment of taxes on the property, insurance premiums, or other purposes relating to the property shall be required as a condition of a real property sale contract or a loan secured by a deed of trust or mortgage on real property containing only a single-family, owner-occupied dwelling, except: (A) where required by a state or federal regulatory authority, (B) where a loan is made, guaranteed, or insured by a state or federal governmental lending or insuring agency, (C) upon a failure of the purchaser or borrower to pay two consecutive tax installments on the property prior to the delinquency date for such payments, (D) where the original principal amount of such a loan is (i) 90 percent or more of the sale price, if the property involved is sold, or is (ii) 90 percent or more of the appraised value of the property securing the loan, (E) whenever the combined principal amount of all loans secured by the real property exceeds 80 percent of the appraised value of the property securing the loans, (F) where a loan is made in compliance with the requirements for higher priced mortgage loans established in Regulation Z, whether or not the loan is a higher priced mortgage loan, or (G) where a loan is refinanced or modified in connection with a lender's homeownership preservation program or a lender's participation in such a program sponsored by a federal, state, or local government authority or a nonprofit organization. Nothing contained in this section shall preclude establishment of such an account on terms mutually agreeable to the parties to the loan, if, prior to the execution of the loan or sale agreement, the seller or lender has furnished to the purchaser or borrower a statement in writing, which may be set forth in the loan application, to the effect that the establishment of such an account shall not be required as a condition to the execution of the loan or sale agreement, and further, stating whether or not interest will be paid on the funds in such an account.

An impound, trust, or other type of account for the payment of taxes, insurance premiums, or other purposes relating to property established in violation of this subdivision is voidable, at the option of the purchaser or borrower, at any time, but shall not otherwise affect the validity of the loan or sale.

(2) For the purposes of this subdivision, "Regulation Z" means any rule, regulation, or interpretation promulgated by the Board of Governors of the Federal Reserve System and any interpretation or approval issued by an official or employee duly authorized by the board to issue interpretations or approvals dealing with, respectively, consumer leasing or consumer lending, pursuant to the federal Truth in Lending Act, as amended (15 U.S.C. Sec. 1601 et seq.).

(b) Every mortgagee of real property, beneficiary under a deed of trust on real property, or vendor on a real property sale contract upon the written request of the mortgagor, trustor, or vendee shall furnish to the mortgagor, trustor, or vendee for each calendar year within 60 days after the end of the year an itemized accounting of moneys received for interest and principal repayment and received and held in or disbursed from an impound or trust account, if any, for payment of taxes on the property, insurance premiums, or other purposes relating to the property subject to the mortgage, deed of trust, or real property sale contract. The mortgagor, trustor, or vendee shall be entitled to receive one such accounting for each calendar year without charge and shall be entitled to additional similar accountings for one or more months upon written request and on payment in advance of fees as follows:

(1) Fifty cents ($0.50) per statement when requested in advance on a monthly basis for one or more years.

(2) One dollar ($1) per statement when requested for only one month.

(3) Five dollars ($5) if requested for a single cumulative statement giving all the information described above back to the last statement rendered.

If the mortgagee, beneficiary, or vendor transmits to the mortgagor, trustor, or vendee a monthly statement or passbook showing moneys received for interest and principal repayment and received and held in and disbursed from an impound or trust account, if any, the mortgagee, beneficiary, or vendor shall be deemed to have complied with this section.

No increase in the monthly rate of payment of a mortgagor, trustor, or vendee on a real property sale contract for impound or trust accounts shall be effective until after the mortgagee, beneficiary, or vendor has furnished the mortgagor, trustor, or vendee with an itemized accounting of the moneys presently held by it in the accounts, and a statement of the new monthly rate of payment, and an explanation of the factors necessitating the increase.

The provisions of this section shall be in addition to the obligations of the parties as stated by Section 2943.

Every person who willfully or repeatedly violates this subdivision shall be subject to punishment by a fine of not less than fifty dollars ($50) nor more than two hundred dollars ($200).

(c) As used in this section, "single-family, owner-occupied dwelling" means a dwelling that will be owned and occupied by a signatory to the mortgage or deed of trust secured by that dwelling within 90 days of the execution of the mortgage or deed of trust. *(Added by Stats.1961, c. 1452, p. 3298, § 1. Amended by Stats.1963, c. 1543, p. 3125, § 1; Stats.1971, c. 117, p. 151, § 1; Stats.1973, c. 975, § 1; Stats.1974, c. 389, § 1; Stats.1982, c. 1196, p. 4265, § 1; Stats.1983, c. 1092, § 68, eff. Sept. 27, 1983, operative Jan. 1. 1984; Stats.2009, c. 57 (S.B.633), § 1; Stats. 2010, c. 328 (S.B.1330), § 30.)*

Research References

Rutter, Cal. Practice Guide: Real Prop. Transactions Ch. 6-H, H. Security for Promissory Note.
Miller and Starr California Real Estate § 4:70, Servicing of Secured Obligations--Additional Requirements for Residential Loan Servicing.
Miller and Starr California Real Estate § 10:63, Impound (Trust Fund) Account.
Miller and Starr California Real Estate § 10:64, Annual Loan Statement by the Beneficiary.
Miller and Starr California Real Estate § 10:251, Third-Party Loan to Purchase Real Property.
20 NO. 4 Miller & Starr, California Real Estate Newsalert 6, Deeds of Trust.
9 Witkin, California Summary 10th Taxation § 307, Payment.
4 Witkin, California Summary 10th Security Transactions in Real Property § 80, (S 80) Impound Accounts.
4 Witkin, California Summary 10th Security Transactions in Real Property § 214, (S 214) in General.

§ 2954.1. Impound, trust, or other accounts maintained for property-related payments; restrictions

No lender or person who purchases obligations secured by real property, or any agent of such lender or person, who maintains an impound, trust, or other type of account for the payment of taxes and assessments on real property, insurance premiums, or other purposes relating to such property shall do any of the following:

(a) Require the borrower or vendee to deposit in such account in any month an amount in excess of that which would be permitted in connection with a federally related mortgage loan pursuant to Section 10 of the Real Estate Settlement Procedures Act of 1974 (12 U.S.C. 2609), as amended.

(b) Require the sums maintained in such account to exceed at any time the amount or amounts reasonably necessary to pay such obligations as they become due. Any sum held in excess of the reasonable amount shall be refunded within 30 days unless the parties mutually agree to the contrary. Such an agreement may be rescinded at any time by any party.

(c) Make payments from the account in a manner so as to cause any policy of insurance to be canceled or so as to cause property taxes or other similar payments to become delinquent.

Nothing contained herein shall prohibit requiring additional amounts to be paid into an impound account in order to recover any deficiency which may exist in the account.

Any person harmed by a violation of this section shall be entitled to sue to recover his or her damages or for injunctive relief; but such violation shall not otherwise affect the validity of the loan or sale.

This section applies to all such accounts maintained after the effective date of this act. *(Added by Stats.1979, c. 257, p. 574, § 1, eff. July 11, 1979. Amended by Stats.1983, c. 74, § 1.)*

Research References

Miller and Starr California Real Estate § 4:70, Servicing of Secured Obligations--Additional Requirements for Residential Loan Servicing.
Miller and Starr California Real Estate § 10:63, Impound (Trust Fund) Account.
4 Witkin, California Summary 10th Security Transactions in Real Property § 80, (S 80) Impound Accounts.

§ 2954.2. One- to four-family residences; written statement by mortgagee; moneys received and disbursed; additional accountings; charges; operative effect

(a) Every mortgagee of record of real property containing only a one- to four-family residence, when the mortgage is given to secure payment of the balance of the purchase price of the property or to refinance such a mortgage, shall furnish to the mortgagor within 60 days after the end of each calendar year a written statement showing the amount of moneys received for interest and principal repayment, late charges, moneys received and held in or disbursed from an impound account, if any, for the payment of taxes on the property, insurance premiums, bond assessments, or other purposes relating to the property, and interest credited to the account, if any. The written statement required to be furnished by this section shall be deemed furnished if the mortgagee of record transmits to the mortgagor of record cumulative statements or receipts which, for each calendar year, provide in one of the statements or receipts the information required by this section. The mortgagor, trustor or vendee shall be entitled to receive one such statement for each calendar year without charge and without request. Such statement shall include a notification in 10-point type that additional accountings can be requested by the mortgagor, trustor, or vendee, pursuant to Section 2954.

(b) For the purposes of this section:

(1) "Mortgagee" includes a beneficiary under a deed of trust, a vendor under a real property sale contract, and an organization which services a mortgage or deed of trust by receiving and disbursing payments for the mortgagee or beneficiary.

(2) "Mortgage" includes a first or second mortgage, a first or second deed of trust, and a real property sale contract.

(3) "Impound account" includes a trust or other type of account established for the purposes described in subdivision (a).

(c) The requirements of this section shall be in addition to the requirements of Section 2954.

(d) This section shall become operative on December 31, 1978, and apply to moneys received by a mortgagee on and after January 1, 1978. *(Added by Stats.1976, c. 774, p. 1815, § 1, operative Dec. 31, 1978.)*

Research References

Miller and Starr California Real Estate § 10:64, Annual Loan Statement by the Beneficiary.
Miller and Starr California Real Estate § 10:236, Policy Objectives; the "Standard" Transaction.
4 Witkin, California Summary 10th Security Transactions in Real Property § 214, (S 214) in General.

§ 2954.4. Single-family, owner occupied dwellings late payment charge; maximum; tender; inapplicable loans

(a) A charge that may be imposed for late payment of an installment due on a loan secured by a mortgage or a deed of trust on real property containing only a single-family, owner-occupied dwelling, shall not exceed either (1) the equivalent of 6 percent of the installment due that is applicable to payment of principal and interest on the loan, or (2) five dollars ($5), whichever is greater. A charge may not be imposed more than once for the late payment of the same installment. However, the imposition of a late charge on any late payment does not eliminate or supersede late charges imposed on prior late payments. A payment is not a "late payment" for the purposes of this section until at least 10 days following the due date of the installment.

(b) A late charge may not be imposed on any installment which is paid or tendered in full on or before its due date, or within 10 days thereafter, even though an earlier installment or installments, or any late charge thereon, may not have been paid in full when due. For the purposes of determining whether late charges may be imposed, any payment tendered by the borrower shall be applied by the lender to the most recent installment due.

(c) A late payment charge described in subdivision (a) is valid if it satisfies the requirements of this section and Section 2954.5.

(d) Nothing in this section shall be construed to alter in any way the duty of the borrower to pay any installment then due or to alter the rights of the lender to enforce the payment of the installments.

(e) This section is not applicable to loans made by a credit union subject to Division 5 (commencing with Section 14000) of the Financial Code, by an industrial loan company subject to Division 7 (commencing with Section 18000) of the Financial Code, or by a finance lender subject to Division 9 (commencing with Section 22000) of the Financial Code, and is not applicable to loans made or negotiated by a real estate broker subject to Article 7 (commencing with Section 10240) of Chapter 3 of Part 1 of Division 4 of the Business and Professions Code.

(f) As used in this section, "single-family, owner-occupied dwelling" means a dwelling that will be owned and occupied by a signatory to the mortgage or deed of trust secured by the dwelling within 90 days of the execution of the mortgage or deed of trust.

(g) This section applies to loans executed on and after January 1, 1976. *(Added by Stats.1975, c. 736, p. 1729, § 1. Amended by Stats.1984, c. 890, § 2; Stats.2001, c. 159 (S.B.662), § 35.)*

Research References

Rutter, Cal. Practice Guide: Enforcing Judgments/Debts Ch. 3-C, C. Prelawsuit Considerations.
Rutter, Cal. Practice Guide: Real Prop. Transactions Ch. 6-F, F. Promissory Note.
Miller and Starr California Real Estate § 10:80, Late Charges.
Miller and Starr California Real Estate § 10:236, Policy Objectives; the "Standard" Transaction.
13 Witkin, California Summary 10th Equity § 122, Lending Practices.

§ 2954.5. Delinquent payment charge; prerequisites to imposition

(a) Before the first default, delinquency, or late payment charge may be assessed by any lender on a delinquent payment of a loan, other than a loan made pursuant to Division 9 (commencing with Section 22000) of the Financial Code, secured by real property, and before the borrower becomes obligated to pay this charge, the borrower shall either (1) be notified in writing and given at least 10 days from mailing of the notice in which to cure the delinquency, or (2) be informed, by a billing or notice sent for each payment due on the loan, of the date after which this charge will be assessed.

The notice provided in either paragraph (1) or (2) shall contain the amount of the charge or the method by which it is calculated.

(b) If a subsequent payment becomes delinquent the borrower shall be notified in writing, before the late charge is to be imposed, that the charge will be imposed if payment is not received, or the borrower shall be notified at least semiannually of the total amount of late charges imposed during the period covered by the notice.

(c) Notice provided by this section shall be sent to the address specified by the borrower, or, if no address is specified, to the borrower's address as shown in the lender's records.

(d) In case of multiple borrowers obligated on the same loan, a notice mailed to one shall be deemed to comply with this section.

(e) The failure of the lender to comply with the requirements of this section does not excuse or defer the borrower's performance of any obligation incurred in the loan transaction, other than his or her obligation to pay a late payment charge, nor does it impair or defer the right of the lender to enforce any other obligation including the costs and expenses incurred in any enforcement authorized by law.

(f) The provisions of this section as added by Chapter 1430 of the Statutes of 1970 shall only affect loans made on and after January 1, 1971.

The amendments to this section made at the 1975–76 Regular Session of the Legislature shall only apply to loans executed on and after January 1, 1976. *(Added by Stats.1970, c. 1430, p. 2773, § 1. Amended by Stats.1971, c. 813, p. 1571, § 1, eff. Sept. 29, 1971; Stats.1975, c. 736, p. 1730, § 2; Stats.1984, c. 890, § 3; Stats.2001, c. 159 (S.B.662), § 36.)*

Research References

Rutter, Cal. Practice Guide: Enforcing Judgments/Debts Ch. 3-C, C. Prelawsuit Considerations.
Rutter, Cal. Practice Guide: Real Prop. Transactions Ch. 6-F, F. Promissory Note.
Miller and Starr California Real Estate § 4:70, Servicing of Secured Obligations--Additional Requirements for Residential Loan Servicing.
Miller and Starr California Real Estate § 10:80, Late Charges.
4 Witkin, California Summary 10th Security Transactions in Real Property § 214, (S 214) in General.

§ 2954.6. Private mortgage insurance or mortgage guaranty insurance; cancellation rights; notification

(a) If private mortgage insurance or mortgage guaranty insurance, as defined in subdivision (a) of Section 12640.02 of the Insurance Code, is required as a condition of a loan secured by a deed of trust or mortgage on real property, the lender or person making or arranging the loan shall notify the borrower whether or not the borrower has the right to cancel the insurance. If the borrower has the right to cancel, then the lender or person making or arranging the loan shall notify the borrower in writing of the following:

(1) Any identifying loan or insurance information necessary to permit the borrower to communicate with the insurer or the lender concerning the insurance.

(2) The conditions that are required to be satisfied before the private mortgage insurance or mortgage guaranty insurance may be subject to cancellation, which shall include, but is not limited to, both of the following:

(A) If the condition is a minimum ratio between the remaining principal balance of the loan and the original or current value of the property, that ratio shall be stated.

(B) Information concerning whether or not an appraisal may be necessary.

(3) The procedure the borrower is required to follow to cancel the private mortgage insurance or mortgage guaranty insurance.

(b) The notice required in subdivision (a) shall be given to the borrower no later than 30 days after the close of escrow. The notice shall be set forth in at least 10–point bold type.

(c) With respect to any loan specified in subdivision (a) for which private mortgage insurance or mortgage guaranty insurance is still maintained, the lender or person making, arranging, or servicing the loan shall provide the borrower with a notice containing the same information as specified in subdivision (a) or a clear and conspicuous written statement indicating that (1) the borrower may be able to cancel the private mortgage insurance or mortgage guaranty insurance based upon various factors, including appreciation of the value of the property derived from a current appraisal performed by an appraiser selected by the lender or servicer, and paid for by the borrower, and (2) the borrower may contact the lender or person making, arranging, or servicing the loan at a designated address and telephone number to determine whether the borrower has a right of cancellation and, if so, the conditions and procedure to effect cancellation. The notice or statement required by this subdivision shall be provided in or with each written statement required by Section 2954.2.

(d) The notice required under this section shall be provided without cost to the borrower.

(e) Any person harmed by a violation of this section may obtain injunctive relief and may recover treble damages and reasonable attorney's fees and costs.

(f) This section shall not apply to any mortgage funded with bond proceeds issued under an indenture requiring mortgage insurance for the life of the loan nor to any insurance issued pursuant to Part 4 (commencing with Section 51600) of Division 31 of the Health and Safety Code, or loans insured by the Federal Housing Administration or Veterans Administration. *(Added by Stats.1988, c. 569, § 1. Amended by Stats.1990, c. 1099 (A.B.3746), § 1; Stats.2001, c. 137 (S.B.270), § 1, operative July 1, 2002.)*

Research References

Miller and Starr California Real Estate § 4:58, Requirements in Making or Arranging a Loan--In General.
Miller and Starr California Real Estate § 10:68, Private Mortgage Insurance.
4 Witkin, California Summary 10th Security Transactions in Real Property § 214, (S 214) in General.

§ 2954.65. Refund of unused premiums

Within 30 days after notice of cancellation from the insured, a private mortgage insurer or mortgage guaranty insurer shall, if the policy is cancellable, refund the remaining portion of the unused premium to the person or persons designated by the insured. *(Added by Stats.1990, c. 1099 (A.B.3746), § 2.)*

Research References

Miller and Starr California Real Estate § 10:68, Private Mortgage Insurance.
4 Witkin, California Summary 10th Security Transactions in Real Property § 214, (S 214) in General.

§ 2954.7. Termination of mortgage insurance payments; conditions; exclusion of specified instruments

Except when a statute, regulation, rule, or written guideline promulgated by an institutional third party applicable to notes or evidence of indebtedness secured by a deed of trust or mortgage purchased in whole or in part by an institutional third party specifically prohibits cancellation during the term of the indebtedness, if a borrower so requests and the conditions established by paragraphs (1) to (5), inclusive, of subdivision (a) are met, a borrower may terminate future payments for private mortgage insurance, or mortgage guaranty insurance as defined in subdivision (a) of Section 12640.02 of the Insurance Code, issued as a condition to the extension of credit in the form of a loan evidenced by a note or other evidence of indebtedness that is secured by a deed of trust or mortgage on the subject real property.

(a) The following conditions shall be satisfied in order for a borrower to be entitled to terminate payments for private mortgage insurance or mortgage guaranty insurance:

(1) The request to terminate future payments for private mortgage insurance or mortgage guaranty insurance shall be in writing.

(2) The origination date of the note or evidence of indebtedness shall be at least two years prior to the date of the request.

(3) The note or evidence of indebtedness shall be for personal, family, household, or purchase money purposes, secured by a deed of trust or mortgage on owner-occupied, one- to four-unit, residential real property.

(4) The unpaid principal balance owed on the secured obligation that is the subject of the private mortgage insurance or mortgage guaranty insurance shall not be more than 75 percent, unless the borrower and lender or servicer of the loan agree in writing upon a higher loan-to-value ratio, of either of the following:

(A) The sale price of the property at the origination date of the note or evidence of indebtedness, provided that the current fair market value of the property is equal to or greater than the original appraised value used at the origination date.

(B) The current fair market value of the property as determined by an appraisal, the cost of which shall be paid for by the borrower. The appraisal shall be ordered and the appraiser shall be selected by the lender or servicer of the loan.

(5) The borrower's monthly installments of principal, interest, and escrow obligations on the encumbrance or encumbrances secured by the real property shall be current at the time the request is made and those installments shall not have been more than 30 days past due over the 24–month period immediately preceding the request, provided further, that no notice of default has been recorded against the security real property pursuant to Section 2924, as a result of a nonmonetary default by the borrower (trustor) during the 24–month period immediately preceding the request.

(b) This section does not apply to any of the following:

(1) A note or evidence of indebtedness secured by a deed of trust or mortgage, or mortgage insurance, executed under the authority of Part 3 (commencing with Section 50900) or Part 4 (commencing with Section 51600) of Division 31 of the Health and Safety Code.

(2) Any note or evidence of indebtedness secured by a deed of trust or mortgage that is funded in whole or in part pursuant to authority granted by statute, regulation, or rule that, as a condition of that funding, prohibits or limits termination of payments for private mortgage insurance or mortgage guaranty insurance during the term of the indebtedness.

(3) Notes or evidence of indebtedness that require private mortgage insurance and were executed prior to January 1, 1991.

(c) If the note secured by the deed of trust or mortgage will be or has been sold in whole or in part to an institutional third party, adherence to the institutional third party's standards for termination of future payments for private mortgage insurance or mortgage guaranty insurance shall be deemed in compliance with the requirements of this section.

(d) For the purposes of this section, "institutional third party" means the Federal National Mortgage Association, the Federal Home Loan Mortgage Corporation, the Government National

Mortgage Association, and other substantially similar institutions, whether public or private, provided the institutions establish and adhere to rules applicable to the right of cancellation of private mortgage insurance or mortgage guaranty insurance, which are the same or substantially the same as those utilized by the above-named institutions. *(Added by Stats.1990, c. 1098 (A.B.3610), § 1. Amended by Stats.1994, c. 356 (A.B.2481), § 1; Stats.2006, c. 538 (S.B.1852), § 56.)*

Research References

Miller and Starr California Real Estate § 10:68, Private Mortgage Insurance.
4 Witkin, California Summary 10th Security Transactions in Real Property § 214, (S 214) in General.

§ 2954.8. Impound accounts; payment of interest; restrictions; exceptions; application

(a) Every financial institution that makes loans upon the security of real property containing only a one- to four-family residence and located in this state or purchases obligations secured by such property and that receives money in advance for payment of taxes and assessments on the property, for insurance, or for other purposes relating to the property, shall pay interest on the amount so held to the borrower. The interest on such amounts shall be at the rate of at least 2 percent simple interest per annum. Such interest shall be credited to the borrower's account annually or upon termination of such account, whichever is earlier.

(b) No financial institution subject to the provisions of this section shall impose any fee or charge in connection with the maintenance or disbursement of money received in advance for the payment of taxes and assessments on real property securing loans made by such financial institution, or for the payment of insurance, or for other purposes relating to such real property, that will result in an interest rate of less than 2 percent per annum being paid on the moneys so received.

(c) For the purposes of this section, "financial institution" means a bank, savings and loan association or credit union chartered under the laws of this state or the United States, or any other person or organization making loans upon the security of real property containing only a one- to four-family residence.

(d) The provisions of this section do not apply to any of the following:

(1) Loans executed prior to the effective date of this section.

(2) Moneys which are required by a state or federal regulatory authority to be placed by a financial institution other than a bank in a non-interest-bearing demand trust fund account of a bank.

The amendment of this section made by the 1979–80 Regular Session of the Legislature shall only apply to loans executed on or after January 1, 1980. *(Added by Stats.1976, c. 25, p. 40, § 1. Amended by Stats.1979, c. 803, p. 2765, § 1.)*

Research References

Rutter, Cal. Practice Guide: Real Prop. Transactions Ch. 6-H, H. Security for Promissory Note.
Miller and Starr California Real Estate § 4:33, Handling of Trust Funds.
Miller and Starr California Real Estate § 4:70, Servicing of Secured Obligations--Additional Requirements for Residential Loan Servicing.
Miller and Starr California Real Estate § 10:63, Impound (Trust Fund) Account.
Miller and Starr California Real Estate § 10:236, Policy Objectives; the "Standard" Transaction.
4 Witkin, California Summary 10th Security Transactions in Real Property § 80, (S 80) Impound Accounts.

13 Witkin, California Summary 10th Trusts § 3, (S 3) Debt, Security Device, or Impound Account.

§ 2954.9. Loans for residential property of four units or less; right to prepayment

(a) (1) Except as otherwise provided by statute, where the original principal obligation is a loan for residential property of four units or less, the borrower under any note or evidence of indebtedness secured by a deed of trust or mortgage or any other lien on real property shall be entitled to prepay the whole or any part of the balance due, together with accrued interest, at any time.

(2) Nothing in this subdivision shall prevent a borrower from obligating himself, by an agreement in writing, to pay a prepayment charge.

(3) This subdivision does not apply during any calendar year to a bona fide loan secured by a deed of trust or mortgage given back during such calendar year to the seller by the purchaser on account of the purchase price if the seller does not take back four or more such deeds of trust or mortgages during such calendar year. Nothing in this subdivision shall be construed to prohibit a borrower from making a prepayment by an agreement in writing with the lender.

(b) Except as otherwise provided in Section 10242.6 of the Business and Professions Code, the principal and accrued interest on any loan secured by a mortgage or deed of trust on owner-occupied residential real property containing only four units or less may be prepaid in whole or in part at any time but only a prepayment made within five years of the date of execution of such mortgage or deed of trust may be subject to a prepayment charge and then solely as herein set forth. An amount not exceeding 20 percent of the original principal amount may be prepaid in any 12-month period without penalty. A prepayment charge may be imposed on any amount prepaid in any 12-month period in excess of 20 percent of the original principal amount of the loan which charge shall not exceed an amount equal to the payment of six months' advance interest on the amount prepaid in excess of 20 percent of the original principal amount.

(c) Notwithstanding subdivisions (a) and (b), there shall be no prepayment penalty charged to a borrower under a loan subject to this section if the residential structure securing the loan has been damaged to such an extent by a natural disaster for which a state of emergency is declared by the Governor, pursuant to Chapter 7 (commencing with Section 8550) of Division 1 of Title 2 of the Government Code, that the residential structure cannot be occupied and the prepayment is causally related thereto. *(Added by Stats.1974, c. 1059, p. 2280, § 1. Amended by Stats.1975, c. 763, p. 1775, § 2; Stats.1977, c. 579, p. 1825, § 32; Stats.1979, c. 391, p. 1458, § 1; Stats.1990, c. 663 (A.B.3660), § 2.)*

Research References

Rutter, Cal. Practice Guide: Real Prop. Transactions Ch. 6-F, F. Promissory Note.
Miller and Starr California Real Estate § 4:67, Requirements in Making or Arranging a Loan--Small Loan Regulations.
Miller and Starr California Real Estate § 4:82, Finance Lenders; Licensing and Regulation by Department of Corporations.
Miller and Starr California Real Estate § 10:96, Statutory Prohibitions Against Restricting Prepayment.
Miller and Starr California Real Estate § 10:97, Prepayment Fee--Obligation for Payment.
Miller and Starr California Real Estate § 10:99, Prepayment Fee Upon Acceleration.
Miller and Starr California Real Estate § 10:101, Reasonableness of Amount.
Miller and Starr California Real Estate § 10:236, Policy Objectives; the "Standard" Transaction.

4 Witkin, California Summary 10th Security Transactions in Real Property § 94, (S 94) Restrictive Legislation.

§ 2954.10. Acceleration of maturity date; penalty for prepayment

An obligee which accelerates the maturity date of the principal and accrued interest, pursuant to contract, on any loan secured by a mortgage or deed of trust on real property or an estate for years therein, upon the conveyance of any right, title, or interest in that property, may not claim, exact, or collect any charge, fee, or penalty for any prepayment resulting from that acceleration.

The provisions of this section shall not apply to a loan other than a loan secured by residential real property or any interest therein containing four units or less, in which the obligor has expressly waived, in writing, the right to repay in whole or part without penalty, or has expressly agreed, in writing, to the payment of a penalty for prepayment upon acceleration. For any loan executed on or after January 1, 1984, this waiver or agreement shall be separately signed or initialed by the obligor and its enforcement shall be supported by evidence of a course of conduct by the obligee of individual weight to the consideration in that transaction for the waiver or agreement. *(Added by Stats.1983, c. 1115, § 1, eff. Sept. 28, 1983. Amended by Stats.1989, c. 698, § 11.)*

Research References

California Real Estate Forms (Miller & Starr) § 3:20, Promissory Note--Conduit Loan.
Rutter, Cal. Practice Guide: Real Prop. Transactions Ch. 6-F, F. Promissory Note.
Rutter, Cal. Practice Guide: Real Prop. Transactions Form 6:G, Promissory Note Secured by Deed of Trust (Complex).
Miller and Starr California Real Estate § 10:99, Prepayment Fee Upon Acceleration.
Miller and Starr California Real Estate § 10:236, Policy Objectives; the "Standard" Transaction.
4 Witkin, California Summary 10th Security Transactions in Real Property § 94, (S 94) Restrictive Legislation.

§ 2954.11. Installment loans; definitions; right to prepay and prepayment charges; disclosure; application of section

(a) As used in this section:

(1) "Open–end credit plan" has the meaning set forth in Regulation Z of the Federal Reserve System (12 C.F.R. 226.2(a)(20)).

(2) "Installment loan" means any loan specified in subdivision (h) extended under an installment loan feature.

(3) "Installment loan feature" means a feature of an open-end credit plan which provides for a separate subaccount of the open-end credit plan pursuant to which the principal of, and interest on, the loan associated with that subaccount are to be repaid in substantially equal installments over a specified period without regard to the amount outstanding under any other feature of the open-end credit plan or the payment schedule with respect to the other feature.

(b)(1) Except as otherwise provided by statute, the borrower under any installment loan shall be entitled to prepay the whole or any part of the installment loan, together with any accrued interest, at any time.

(2) With respect to any installment loan, nothing in this section shall preclude a borrower from becoming obligated, by an agreement in writing, to pay a prepayment charge; but only a prepayment made within five years of the date the installment loan is made may be subject to a prepayment charge and then solely as herein set forth. An amount not exceeding 20 percent of the original principal amount of the installment loan may be prepaid in any one 12–month period without incurring a prepayment charge. A prepayment charge may be imposed on any amount prepaid in any 12–month period in excess of 20 percent of the original principal amount of the installment loan, which charge shall not exceed an amount equal to the payment of six months' advance interest on the amount prepaid in excess of 20 percent of the original principal amount of the installment loan.

(c) For purposes of subdivision (b):

(1) If the deed of trust or mortgage secures repayment of more than one installment loan, each of the installment loans shall be deemed to have been separately made on the date that the proceeds of the installment loan are advanced.

(2) If the outstanding balance of a loan advanced pursuant to an open-end credit plan thereafter becomes subject to an installment loan feature of the credit plan, the loan shall be deemed to have been made when the loan becomes subject to the installment loan feature, whether the feature was available at the borrower's option under original terms of the open-end credit plan or the feature thereafter became available upon modification of the original terms of the open-end credit plan.

(d) Notwithstanding subdivision (b), no prepayment charge may be imposed with respect to an installment loan subject to this section if any of the following apply:

(1) The residential structure securing the installment loan has been damaged to such an extent by a natural disaster for which a state of emergency is declared by the Governor, pursuant to Chapter 7 (commencing with Section 8550) of Division 1 of Title 2 of the Government Code, that the residential structure cannot be occupied and the prepayment is causally related thereto.

(2) The prepayment is made in conjunction with a bona fide sale of the real property securing the installment loan.

(3) The lender does not comply with subdivision (e).

(4) The term of the installment loan is for not more than five years and the original principal amount of the installment loan is less than five thousand dollars ($5,000).

(e)(1) The lender receiving a borrower's obligation to pay a prepayment charge authorized by subdivision (b) shall furnish the borrower with a written disclosure describing the existence of the prepayment charge obligation, the conditions under which the prepayment charge shall be payable, and the method by which the amount of the prepayment charge shall be determined. If subdivision (f) provides the borrower with a right to rescind the installment loan and the related obligation to pay a prepayment charge, the disclosure required by this subdivision shall also inform the borrower of this right to rescind, how and when to exercise the right, and where to mail or deliver a notice of rescission.

(2) The amount of, or the method for determining the amount of, the prepayment charge for an installment loan shall be set forth in the agreement governing the open-end credit plan.

(f)(1) The disclosure required by paragraph (1) of subdivision (e) shall be furnished when or up to 30 days before the borrower signs the agreement or other documents required by the lender for the installment loan, or no earlier than 30 days before nor later than 10 days following the making of the installment loan, if made without the borrower having to sign an agreement or other documentation, such as may be the case if the installment loan may be made on the basis of telephone or other discussions between the lender and the borrower not taking place in person. If the installment loan is made before the borrower has been furnished with the disclosure required by paragraph (1) of subdivision (e), the borrower shall have the right to rescind the installment loan and the related obligation to pay a prepayment charge by personally delivering or mailing notice to that effect to the lender, by first-class mail with postage prepaid, at the lender's location stated in its disclosure concerning the right to rescind within 10 days following the furnishing of the disclosure.

(2) If the disclosure required by paragraph (1) of subdivision (e) is included in the agreement or other document signed by the borrower for the installment loan, the disclosure shall be deemed given at that time. In other cases, the disclosure shall be deemed furnished when personally delivered to the borrower or three days after it is mailed to the borrower, first-class mail with postage prepaid, at the address to which billing statements for the open-end credit plan are being sent.

(3) The disclosure required by paragraph (1) of subdivision (e) may be separately furnished or may be included in the agreement or other document for the installment loan, provided that a copy of the disclosure that the borrower may retain is furnished to the borrower.

(4) If there is more than one borrower with respect to the open-end credit plan, a disclosure to any one of them pursuant to subdivision (e) shall satisfy the requirements of that subdivision with respect to all of them.

(g) If after an installment loan is made the lender receives the borrower's timely notice of the rescission of the installment loan in accordance with subdivision (f), the balance of the installment loan shall be transferred to the open-end subaccount of the open-end credit plan and the borrower shall be obligated to repay the amount under the same terms and conditions, and subject to the same fees and other charges, as would be applicable had the loan initially been extended pursuant to the open-end credit plan or had the installment loan never been made.

(h) This section applies to any installment loan secured by a deed of trust or mortgage or any other lien on residential property of four units or less and Section 2954.9 does not apply to such installment loans. This section shall not apply to any loan that is subject to Section 10242.6 of the Business and Professions Code. *(Added by Stats.1996, c. 32 (S.B.1106), § 1.)*

Research References

Rutter, Cal. Practice Guide: Real Prop. Transactions Ch. 6-F, F. Promissory Note.
Miller and Starr California Real Estate § 4:82, Finance Lenders; Licensing and Regulation by Department of Corporations.
Miller and Starr California Real Estate § 10:98, Prepayment of Consumer Installment Loans.
4 Witkin, California Summary 10th Security Transactions in Real Property § 94, (S 94) Restrictive Legislation.

§ 2954.12. Private mortgage insurance or mortgage guaranty insurance; collection of future payments

(a) Notwithstanding Section 2954.7, and except when a statute, regulation, rule, or written guideline promulgated by an institutional third party applicable to notes or evidence of indebtedness secured by a deed of trust or mortgage purchased in whole or in part by an institutional third party specifically prohibits cancellation during the term of the indebtedness, the lender or servicer of a loan evidenced by a note or other evidence of indebtedness that is secured by a deed of trust or mortgage on the subject property may not charge or collect future payments from a borrower for private mortgage insurance or mortgage guaranty insurance as defined in subdivision (a) of Section 12640.02 of the Insurance Code, if all of the following conditions are satisfied:

(1) The loan is for personal, family, household, or purchase money purposes, the subject property is owner-occupied, one-to-four unit residential real property, and the outstanding principal balance of the note or evidence of indebtedness secured by the senior deed of trust or mortgage on the subject property is equal to or less than 75 percent of the lesser of (A) if the loan was

made for purchase of the property, the sales price of the property under such purchase; or (B) the appraised value of the property, as determined by the appraisal conducted in connection with the making of the loan.

(2) The borrower's scheduled payment of monthly installments of principal, interest, and escrow obligations is current at the time the right to cancellation of mortgage insurance accrues.

(3) During the 12 months prior to the date upon which the right to cancellation accrues, the borrower has not been assessed more than one late penalty for any scheduled payment and has not made any scheduled payment more than 30 days late.

(4) The loan evidenced by a note or evidence of indebtedness was made or executed on or after January 1, 1998.

(5) No notice of default has been recorded against the real property pursuant to Section 2924, as a result of a nonmonetary default on the extension of credit by the borrower during the last 12 months prior to the accrual of the borrower's right to cancellation.

(b) This section does not apply to any of the following:

(1) A note or evidence of indebtedness secured by a deed of trust or mortgage, or mortgage insurance, executed under the authority of Part 3 (commencing with Section 50900) or Part 4 (commencing with Section 51600) of Division 31 of the Health and Safety Code.

(2) Any note or evidence of indebtedness secured by a deed of trust or mortgage that is funded in whole or in part pursuant to authority granted by statute, regulation, or rule that, as a condition of that funding, prohibits or limits termination of payments for private mortgage insurance or mortgage guaranty insurance during the term of the indebtedness.

(c) If the note secured by the deed of trust or mortgage will be or has been sold in whole or in part to an institutional third party, adherence to the institutional third party's standards for termination of future payments for private mortgage insurance or mortgage guaranty insurance shall be deemed in compliance with the requirements of this section.

(d) For the purposes of this section, "institutional third party" means the Federal National Mortgage Association, the Federal Home Loan Mortgage Corporation, the Government National Mortgage Association and other substantially similar institutions, whether public or private, provided the institutions establish and adhere to rules applicable to the right of cancellation of private mortgage insurance or mortgage guaranty insurance, which are the same or substantially the same as those utilized by the above-named institutions. *(Added by Stats.1997, c. 62 (A.B.1160), § 1.)*

Research References

Rutter, Cal. Practice Guide: Real Prop. Transactions Ch. 6-L, L. Real Estate Appraisals.
4 Witkin, California Summary 10th Security Transactions in Real Property § 214, (S 214) in General.

§ 2955. Impound account funds; investments; deposits; injunction for violations

(a) Money held by a mortgagee or a beneficiary of a deed of trust on real property in this state, or held by a vendor on a contract of sale of real property in this state, in an impound account for the payment of taxes and assessments or insurance premiums or other purposes on or relating to the property, shall be retained in this state and, if invested, shall be invested only with residents of this state in the case of individuals, or with partnerships, corporations, or other persons, or the branches or subsidiaries thereof, which are engaged in business within this state.

(b) Notwithstanding subdivision (a), a mortgagee or beneficiary of a deed of trust, secured by a first lien on real property, may deposit money held for the payment of taxes and assessments or insurance premiums or other purposes in an impound account in an out-of-state depository institution insured by the Federal Deposit Insurance Corporation if the mortgagee or beneficiary is any one of the following:

(1) The Federal National Mortgage Association, the Government National Mortgage Association, the Federal Home Loan Mortgage Corporation, the Federal Housing Administration, or the Veteran's Administration.

(2) A bank or subsidiary thereof, bank holding company or subsidiary thereof, trust company, savings bank or savings and loan association or subsidiary thereof, savings bank or savings association holding company or subsidiary thereof, credit union, industrial bank or industrial loan company, commercial finance lender, personal property broker, consumer finance lender, or insurer doing business under the authority of and in accordance with the laws of this state, any other state, or of the United States relating to banks, trust companies, savings banks or savings associations, credit unions, industrial banks or industrial loan companies, commercial finance lenders, personal property brokers, consumer finance lenders, or insurers, as evidenced by a license, certificate, or charter issued by the United States or a state, district, territory, or commonwealth of the United States.

(3) Trustees of a pension, profit-sharing, or welfare fund, if the pension, profit-sharing, or welfare fund has a net worth of not less than fifteen million dollars ($15,000,000).

(4) A corporation with outstanding securities registered under Section 12 of the Securities Exchange Act of 1934,[1] or a wholly owned subsidiary of that corporation.

(5) A syndication or other combination of any of the entities specified in paragraphs (1) to (4), inclusive, that is organized to purchase the promissory note.

(6) The California Housing Finance Agency or a local housing finance agency organized under the Health and Safety Code.

(7) A licensed real estate broker selling all or part of the loan, note, or contract to a lender or purchaser described in paragraphs (1) to (6), inclusive, of this subdivision.

(8) A licensed residential mortgage lender or servicer when acting under the authority of that license.

(c) A mortgagee or beneficiary of a deed of trust who deposits funds held in trust in an out-of-state depository institution in accordance with subdivision (b) shall make available, in this state, the books, records, and files pertaining to those trust accounts to the appropriate state regulatory department or agency, or pay the reasonable expenses for travel and lodging incurred by the regulatory department or agency in order to conduct an examination at an out-of-state location.

(d) The Attorney General may bring an action on behalf of the people of California to enjoin a violation of subdivision (a) or subdivision (b). *(Added by Stats.1970, c. 1212, p. 2130, § 1. Amended by Stats.1992, c. 1055 (A.B.3342), § 3; Stats.1995, c. 564 (S.B.946), § 5.)*

[1] 15 U.S.C.A. § 78l.

Research References

Rutter, Cal. Practice Guide: Real Prop. Transactions Ch. 6-H, H. Security for Promissory Note.
Miller and Starr California Real Estate § 4:33, Handling of Trust Funds.
Miller and Starr California Real Estate § 4:70, Servicing of Secured Obligations--Additional Requirements for Residential Loan Servicing.
Miller and Starr California Real Estate § 10:63, Impound (Trust Fund) Account.

4 Witkin, California Summary 10th Security Transactions in Real Property § 80, (S 80) Impound Accounts.

§ 2955.1. Condominium loans; underwriting requirements for earthquake insurance or fees; disclosures

(a) Any lender originating a loan secured by the borrower's separate interest in a condominium project, as defined in Section 4125 or 6542, which requires earthquake insurance or imposes a fee or any other condition in lieu thereof pursuant to an underwriting requirement imposed by an institutional third-party purchaser shall disclose all of the following to the potential borrower:

(1) That the lender or the institutional third party in question requires earthquake insurance or imposes a fee or any other condition in lieu thereof pursuant to an underwriting requirement imposed by an institutional third-party purchaser.

(2) That not all lenders or institutional third parties require earthquake insurance or impose a fee or any other condition in lieu thereof pursuant to an underwriting requirement imposed by an institutional third-party purchaser.

(3) Earthquake insurance may be required on the entire condominium project.

(4) That lenders or institutional third parties may also require that a condominium project maintain, or demonstrate an ability to maintain, financial reserves in the amount of the earthquake insurance deductible.

(b) For the purposes of this section, "institutional third party" means the Federal Home Loan Mortgage Corporation, the Federal National Mortgage Association, the Government National Mortgage Association, and other substantially similar institutions, whether public or private.

(c) The disclosure required by this section shall be made in writing by the lender as soon as reasonably practicable. *(Added by Stats.1995, c. 925 (S.B.1326), § 1, eff. Oct. 16, 1995. Amended by Stats.2012, c. 181 (A.B.806), § 41, operative Jan. 1, 2014; Stats.2013, c. 605 (S.B.752), § 18.)*

Law Revision Commission Comments

Section 2955.1 is amended to correct a cross-reference to former Section 1351(f). [40 Cal.L.Rev.Comm. Reports 235 (2010)].

Section 2955.1 is amended to add a cross-reference to Section 6542, reflecting the enactment of the Commercial and Industrial Common Interest Development Act (Civ. Code §§ 6500–6876). [42 Cal.L.Rev. Comm. Reports 1 (2012)].

Research References

Miller and Starr California Real Estate § 25B:5, Condominiums--Definition and Description.
Miller and Starr California Real Estate § 25B:59, Earthquake Insurance; Lender Notice Requirement.
4 Witkin, California Summary 10th Security Transactions in Real Property § 37, (S 37) Aspects Regulated.

§ 2955.5. Hazard insurance; lender requiring amount exceeding replacement value; disclosure; relief

(a) No lender shall require a borrower, as a condition of receiving or maintaining a loan secured by real property, to provide hazard insurance coverage against risks to the improvements on that real property in an amount exceeding the replacement value of the improvements on the property.

(b) A lender shall disclose to a borrower, in writing, the contents of subdivision (a), as soon as practicable, but before execution of any note or security documents.

(c) Any person harmed by a violation of this section shall be entitled to obtain injunctive relief and may recover damages and reasonable attorney's fees and costs.

(d) A violation of this section does not affect the validity of the loan, note secured by a deed of trust, mortgage, or deed of trust.

(e) For purposes of this section:

(1) "Hazard insurance coverage" means insurance against losses caused by perils which are commonly covered in policies described as a "Homeowner's Policy," "General Property Form," "Guaranteed Replacement Cost Insurance," "Special Building Form," "Standard Fire," "Standard Fire with Extended Coverage," "Standard Fire with Special Form Endorsement," or comparable insurance coverage to protect the real property against loss or damage from fire and other perils covered within the scope of a standard extended coverage endorsement.

(2) "Improvements" means buildings or structures attached to the real property. *(Added by Stats.1987, c. 715, § 1. Amended by Stats.1988, c. 276, § 1, eff. July 6, 1988; Stats.1999, c. 412 (A.B.1454), § 1, operative July 1, 2000.)*

Research References

California Real Estate Forms (Miller & Starr) § 3:8, Deed of Trust, Security Agreement, and Fixture Filing With Assignment of Rents and Agreements.

California Real Estate Forms (Miller & Starr) § 3:14, Construction Deed of Trust, Security Agreement, and Fixture Filing With Assignment of Rents and Agreements.

California Real Estate Forms (Miller & Starr) § 3:21, Deed of Trust, Assignment of Rents, Security Agreement and Fixture Filing--Conduit Loan.

Rutter, Cal. Practice Guide: Real Prop. Transactions Ch. 6-H, H. Security for Promissory Note.

Miller and Starr California Real Estate § 10:60, Payment of Insurance Premiums.

4 Witkin, California Summary 10th Security Transactions in Real Property § 38, (S 38) Other Legislation.

ARTICLE 3. DISCLOSURES ON PURCHASE MONEY LIENS ON RESIDENTIAL PROPERTY

Section

§ 2956. Form and contents of disclosure; multiple arrangers

In a transaction for the purchase of a dwelling for not more than four families in which there is an arranger of credit, which purchase includes an extension of credit by the vendor, a written disclosure with respect to that credit transaction shall be made, as required by this article:

(a) To the purchaser, by the arranger of credit and the vendor (with respect to information within the knowledge of the vendor).

(b) To the vendor, by the arranger of credit and the purchaser (with respect to information within the knowledge of the purchaser).

If there is more than one arranger of credit and one of those arrangers has obtained the offer by the purchaser to purchase the property, that arranger shall make the disclosure, unless the parties designate another person in writing. *(Added by Stats. 1982, c. 968, p. 3475, § 1, operative July 1, 1983.)*

Research References

California Real Estate Forms (Miller & Starr) § 1:100, Seller Financing Addendum and Disclosure.

Rutter, Cal. Practice Guide: Real Prop. Transactions Ch. 6-D, D. Mortgage Loan Brokers and Mortgage Loan Broker Agreements.

Miller and Starr California Real Estate § 4:66, Requirements in Making or Arranging a Loan--Balloon Payment Notes.

Miller and Starr California Real Estate § 4:68, Real Property Credit Sales Transactions (Seller Carry-Back Financing) Negotiated by Licensees.

Miller and Starr California Real Estate § 4:74, Regulations Applicable to Brokers Who Conduct a High Annual Volume of Mortgage Related Transactions.

Miller and Starr California Real Estate § 10:101, Reasonableness of Amount.

Miller and Starr California Real Estate § 10:236, Policy Objectives; the "Standard" Transaction.

4 Witkin, California Summary 10th Security Transactions in Real Property § 37, (S 37) Aspects Regulated.

§ 2957. Definitions

The following definitions shall apply for the purposes of this article:

(a) "Arranger of credit" means:

(1) A person, other than a party to the credit transaction (except as provided in paragraph (2)), who is involved in developing or negotiating credit terms, participates in the completion of the credit documents, and directly or indirectly receives compensation for arrangement of the credit or from any transaction or transfer of the real property which is facilitated by that extension of credit. As used in this paragraph, "arranger of credit" does not apply to an attorney who is representing one of the parties to the credit transaction.

(2) A party to the transaction who is either a real estate licensee, licensed under provisions of Part 1 (commencing with Section 10000) of Division 4 of the Business and Professions Code, or is an attorney licensed under Chapter 4 (commencing with Section 6000) of Division 3 of the Business and Professions Code if neither party to the transaction is represented by an agent who is a real estate licensee. In any transaction in which disclosure is required solely by the provisions of this paragraph, the obligations of this article shall apply only to a real estate licensee or attorney who is a party to the transaction, and not to any other party.

(3) An arranger of credit does not include a person acting in the capacity as an escrow in the transaction.

(4) Persons described in paragraph (2) who are acting in the capacity as an escrowholder in the transaction shall nevertheless be deemed arrangers of credit where such persons act on behalf of a party to the transaction or an agent of such party in the development or negotiation of credit terms. Neither the completion of credit documents in accordance with instructions of a party or his or her agent nor the furnishing of information regarding credit terms to a party or his or her agent shall be considered to be the development or negotiation of credit terms.

(b) "Balloon payment note" means a note which provides for a final payment as originally scheduled which is more than twice the amount of any of the immediately preceding six regularly scheduled payments or which contains a call provision; provided, however, that if the call provision is not exercised by the holder of the note, the existence of the unexercised call provision shall not cause the note to be deemed to be a balloon payment note.

(c) "Call provision" means a note contract term that provides the holder of the note with the right to call the note due and payable either after a specified period has elapsed following closing or after a specified date.

(d) "Credit" means the right granted by a vendor to a purchaser to purchase property and to defer payment therefore.

The credit involved must be subject to a finance charge or payable by written agreement in more than four installments, whether providing for payment of principal and interest, or interest only, not including a downpayment.

(e) "Credit documents" are those documents which contain the binding credit terms, and include a note or a contract of sale if the contract spells out terms upon which a vendor agrees to provide financing for a purchaser.

(f) "Purchase" includes acquisition of equitable title by a real property sales contract as defined in Section 2985, or lease with an option to purchase, where the facts demonstrate intent to transfer equitable title.

(g) "Security documents" include a mortgage, deed of trust, real property sales contract as defined in Section 2985, or lease with an option to purchase, where the facts demonstrate an intent to transfer equitable title.

(h) "All inclusive trust deed" is an instrument which secures indebtedness owed by the trustor to the beneficiary, which indebtedness includes a debt or debts owed by that beneficiary to the beneficiary of another security document secured by the same property which is senior in priority. *(Added by Stats.1982, c. 968, p. 3475, § 1, operative July 1, 1983. Amended by Stats.1983, c. 1217, § 3; Stats.1986, c. 1360, § 2.)*

Research References

Miller and Starr California Real Estate § 4:68, Real Property Credit Sales Transactions (Seller Carry-Back Financing) Negotiated by Licensees.
Miller and Starr California Real Estate § 10:236, Policy Objectives; the "Standard" Transaction.
4 Witkin, California Summary 10th Security Transactions in Real Property § 37, (S 37) Aspects Regulated.
4 Witkin, California Summary 10th Security Transactions in Real Property § 43, (S 43) Wrap-Around Mortgage.
8 Witkin, California Summary 10th Constitutional Law § 1287, (S 1287) Valid Changes in Remedy or Procedure.

§ 2958. Transactions exempt from disclosure requirements

A disclosure is not required under this article, to a purchaser when that purchaser is entitled to receive, a disclosure pursuant to the Federal Truth-In-Lending Act (15 U.S. Code 1604, as amended), the Real Estate Settlement Procedures Act (12 U.S. Code 2601, as amended), or Section 10240 of the Business and Professions Code; or to a vendor if the vendor is entitled to receive, a disclosure pursuant to Sections 10232.4 and 10232.5 of the Business and Professions Code, or disclosure pursuant to a qualification under Section 25110 of the Corporations Code or disclosure pursuant to regulations of the Department of Corporations granting an exemption from Section 25110 of the Corporations Code. *(Added by Stats.1982, c. 968, p. 3476, § 1, operative July 1, 1983.)*

Research References

Miller and Starr California Real Estate § 4:68, Real Property Credit Sales Transactions (Seller Carry-Back Financing) Negotiated by Licensees.

§ 2959. Timeliness and effect of disclosures; disclosure statement; receipt; signature; copies

The disclosures required by this article shall be made as soon as practicable, but before execution of any note or security documents. If any disclosure is made after the execution of credit documents by the purchaser, such documents shall be contingent on the purchaser's approval of the disclosures prior to execution of the security documents. The disclosure statement shall be receipted for by the purchaser and the vendor. The disclosure shall be signed by the arranger of credit and a copy shall be delivered respectively to the purchaser and the vendor and the arranger shall retain a true copy of the executed statements for three years.

The provisions of this section do not apply to the disclosures required by Section 2966. *(Added by Stats.1982, c. 968, p. 3476, § 1, operative July 1, 1983.)*

Research References

Miller and Starr California Real Estate § 4:68, Real Property Credit Sales Transactions (Seller Carry-Back Financing) Negotiated by Licensees.

§ 2960. Information disclosed, subsequently rendered inaccurate; approximations

If information disclosed in accordance with this article is subsequently rendered inaccurate as a result of any act, occurrence, or agreement between the parties to the transaction subsequent to the delivery of the required disclosures, the inaccuracy resulting therefrom shall not constitute a violation of this article. If, at the time disclosure is to be made, an item of information required to be disclosed is unknown or not available to the vendor, purchaser, or arranger of credit, and the arranger of credit has made a reasonable effort to ascertain it, the disclosure may employ an approximation of the information, provided the approximation is clearly identified as such, is reasonable, is based on the best information available to the arranger, and is not used for the purpose of circumventing or evading the provisions of this article. *(Added by Stats.1982, c. 968, p. 3477, § 1, operative July 1, 1983.)*

Research References

Miller and Starr California Real Estate § 4:68, Real Property Credit Sales Transactions (Seller Carry-Back Financing) Negotiated by Licensees.

§ 2961. Good faith; definition; requirement

Every disclosure required by this article and every act which is to be performed in making that disclosure shall be made in good faith. For the purposes of this article, "good faith" means honesty in fact in the conduct of the transaction. *(Added by Stats.1982, c. 968, p. 3477, § 1, operative July 1, 1983.)*

Research References

Miller and Starr California Real Estate § 4:68, Real Property Credit Sales Transactions (Seller Carry-Back Financing) Negotiated by Licensees.

§ 2962. Amendment of disclosure

Any disclosure made pursuant to this article may be amended in writing by the person making the disclosure, provided that any amendment shall be subject to the provisions of Section 2959. *(Added by Stats.1982, c. 968, p. 3477, § 1, operative July 1, 1983.)*

Research References

Miller and Starr California Real Estate § 4:68, Real Property Credit Sales Transactions (Seller Carry-Back Financing) Negotiated by Licensees.

§ 2963. Disclosures required

The disclosures required to both purchaser and vendor by this article are:

(a) An identification of the note or other credit documents or security documents and of the property which is the security for the transaction.

(b) A description of the terms of the promissory note or other credit documents or a copy of the note or other credit documents.

(c) Insofar as available, the principal terms and conditions of each recorded encumbrance which constitutes a lien upon the property which is or will be senior to the financing being arranged, including the original balance, the current balance, the periodic payment, any balloon payment, the interest rate (and any provisions with respect to variations in the interest rate), the maturity date, and whether or not there is any current default in payment on that encumbrance.

(d) A warning that, if refinancing would be required as a result of lack of full amortization under the terms of any existing or proposed loans, such refinancing might be difficult or impossible in the conventional mortgage marketplace.

(e) If negative amortization is possible as a result of any variable or adjustable rate financing being arranged, a clear disclosure of this fact and an explanation of its potential effect.

(f) In the event that the financing involves an all inclusive trust deed, the disclosure shall indicate whether the credit or security documents specify who is liable for payment or responsible for defense in the case of an attempted acceleration by a lender or other obligee under a prior encumbrance, and whether or not the credit or security documents specify the responsibilities and rights of the parties in the event of a loan prepayment respecting a prior encumbrance which may result in a requirement for refinancing, a prepayment penalty, or a prepayment discount and, if such specification occurs, a recital of the provisions which apply.

(g) If the financing being arranged or any of the financing represented by a prior encumbrance could result in a balloon payment, or in a right in the lender or other obligee under such financing to require a prepayment of the principal balance at or after a stipulated date, or upon the occurrence of a stipulated event, a disclosure of the date and amount of any balloon payment or the amount which would be due upon the exercise of such right by the lender or obligee, and a statement that there is no assurance that new financing or loan extension will be available at the time of such occurrence.

(h) If the financing being arranged involves an all inclusive trust deed or real property sales contract, a disclosure of the party to whom payments will be made and who will be responsible for remitting these funds to payees under prior encumbrances and vendors under this transaction and a warning that, if that person is not a neutral third party, the parties may wish to agree to have a neutral third party designated for these purposes.

(i) A disclosure on the identity, occupation, employment, income, and credit data about the prospective purchaser, as represented to the arranger by the prospective purchaser; or, specifically, that no representation as to the credit-worthiness of the specific prospective purchaser is made by the arranger. A warning should also be expressed that Section 580b of the Code of Civil Procedure may limit any recovery by the vendor to the net proceeds of the sale of the security property in the event of foreclosure.

(j) A statement that loss payee clauses have been added to property insurance protecting the vendor, or that instructions have been or will be directed to the escrowholder, if any, in the transaction or the appropriate insurance carriers for addition of such loss payee clauses, or a statement that, if such provisions have not been made, that the vendor should consider protecting himself or herself by securing such clauses.

(k) A statement that a request for notice of default under Section 2924b has been recorded, or that, if it has not been recorded, the vendor should consider recording a request for notice of default.

(l) That a policy of title insurance has been obtained or will be obtained and be furnished to the vendor and purchaser, insuring the respective interests of the vendor and purchaser, or that the vendor and purchaser individually should consider obtaining a policy of title insurance.

(m) That a tax service has been arranged to report to the vendor whether property taxes have been paid on the property, and who will be responsible for the continued retention and compensation of tax service; or that the vendor should otherwise assure for himself or herself that the taxes on the property have been paid.

(n) A disclosure whether the security documents on the financing being arranged have been or will be recorded pursuant to Section 27280 of the Government Code, or a statement that the security of the vendor may be subject to intervening liens or judgments which may occur after the note is executed and before any resort to security occurs if the security documents are not recorded.

(o) If the purchaser is to receive any cash from the proceeds of the transaction, a statement of that fact, the amount, the source of the funds, and the purpose of the disbursement as represented by the purchaser.

(p) A statement that a request for notice of delinquency under Section 2924e has been made, or that, if it has not been made, the vendor should consider making a request for a notice of delinquency. *(Added by Stats.1982, c. 968, p. 3477, § 1, operative July 1, 1983. Amended by Stats.1983, c. 1217, § 4; Stats.1984, c. 1331, § 4, operative July 1, 1985; Stats.1990, c. 788 (S.B.2042), § 2.)*

Research References

Miller and Starr California Real Estate § 4:68, Real Property Credit Sales Transactions (Seller Carry-Back Financing) Negotiated by Licensees.
Miller and Starr California Real Estate § 11:12, Required Form and Contents--Signature of the Property Owner.

§ 2964. Disclosure obligations arising outside this article

The specification of items for disclosure in this article does not limit or abridge any obligation for disclosure created by any other provision of law or which may exist in order to avoid fraud, misrepresentation, or deceit in the transaction. *(Added by Stats.1982, c. 968, p. 3479, § 1, operative July 1, 1983.)*

Research References

Miller and Starr California Real Estate § 4:68, Real Property Credit Sales Transactions (Seller Carry-Back Financing) Negotiated by Licensees.

§ 2965. Noncompliance with this article; effect on credit or security documents; damages; bona fide errors

The validity of any credit document or of any security document subject to the provisions of this article shall not be invalidated solely because of the failure of any person to comply with this article. However, any person who willfully violates any provision of this article shall be liable in the amount of actual damages suffered by the vendor or purchaser as the proximate result of the violation.

No person may be held liable in any action under this article if it is shown by a preponderance of the evidence that the violation was not intentional and resulted from a bona fide error notwithstanding the maintenance of procedures reasonably adopted to avoid any such error. *(Added by Stats.1982, c. 968, p. 3479, § 1, operative July 1, 1983.)*

Research References

Miller and Starr California Real Estate § 4:68, Real Property Credit Sales Transactions (Seller Carry-Back Financing) Negotiated by Licensees.

§ 2966. Balloon payment note containing term exceeding one year

(a) In a transaction regulated by this article, which includes a balloon payment note when the term for repayment is for a period in excess of one year, the holder of the note shall, not less than 90 nor more than 150 days before the balloon payment is due, deliver or mail by first-class mail, with a certificate of mailing obtained from the United States Postal Service, to the trustor, or his or her successor in interest, at the last known address of such person a written notice, to include:

(1) A statement of the name and address of the person to whom the balloon payment is required to be paid.

(2) The date on or before which the balloon payment was or is required to be paid.

(3) The amount of the balloon payment, or if its exact amount is unknown a good faith estimate of the amount thereof, including unpaid principal, interest, and any other charges (assuming payment in full of all scheduled installments coming due between the date of the notice and the date when the balloon payment is due).

(4) A description of the trustor's right, if any, to refinance the balloon payment, including a summary of the actual terms of the refinancing or an estimate or approximation thereof, to the extent known.

If the due date of the balloon payment of a note subject to this subdivision is extended prior to the time notice is otherwise required under this subdivision, this notice requirement shall apply only to the due date as extended (or as subsequently extended).

(b) Failure to provide notice as required by subdivision (a) does not extinguish any obligation of payment by the trustor, except that the due date for any balloon payment shall be the date specified in the note, or 90 days from the date the delivery or mailing of the notice, or the date specified in the notice, whichever date is later. If the operation of this section acts to extend the term of any such note, interest shall continue to accrue for the extended term at the contract rate and payments shall continue to be due at any periodic interval and on any scheduled payment schedule specified in the note and shall be credited to principal or interest under terms of the note. Default in any extended periodic payment shall be considered a default under terms of the note or security instrument.

(c) Any failure to comply with the provisions of this section shall not affect the validity of a sale in favor of a bona fide purchaser or the rights of an encumbrancer for value and without notice.

(d) Every note subject to the provisions of this section shall include the following statement:

"This note is subject to Section 2966 of the Civil Code, which provides that the holder of this note shall give written notice to the trustor, or his successor in interest, of prescribed information at least 90 and not more than 150 days before any balloon payment is due."

Failure to include this notice shall not invalidate the note.

(e) The provisions of this section shall apply to any note executed on or after July 1, 1983. *(Added by Stats.1982, c. 968, p. 3479, § 1, operative July 1, 1983. Amended by Stats.1986, c. 1360, § 3.)*

Research References

Miller and Starr California Real Estate § 4:66, Requirements in Making or Arranging a Loan--Balloon Payment Notes.
Miller and Starr California Real Estate § 4:68, Real Property Credit Sales Transactions (Seller Carry-Back Financing) Negotiated by Licensees.
Miller and Starr California Real Estate § 10:236, Policy Objectives; the "Standard" Transaction.
19 NO. 1 Miller & Starr, California Real Estate Newsalert 1, The Perata Foreclosure Bill (SB 1137): New Rights for Defaulting Borrowers and Tenants; New Complications for Foreclosing Lenders.

§ 2967. Limitation of actions

Any action arising under this article may be brought within two years from the date on which the liability arises, except that where any material disclosure under this article has been materially and willfully misrepresented, the action may be brought within two years of discovery of the misrepresentation. *(Added by Stats.1982, c. 968, p. 3480, § 1, operative July 1, 1983.)*

Research References

California Real Estate Forms (Miller & Starr) § 1:100, Seller Financing Addendum and Disclosure.
Rutter, Cal. Practice Guide: Real Prop. Transactions Ch. 6-D, D. Mortgage Loan Brokers and Mortgage Loan Broker Agreements.
Miller and Starr California Real Estate § 4:66, Requirements in Making or Arranging a Loan--Balloon Payment Notes.

CHAPTER 2A. HOME EQUITY LOAN DISCLOSURE ACT

Section
2970. "Home equity loan" defined.
2971. Disclosure to customer by creditor at time of initial application.

§ 2970. "Home equity loan" defined

For purposes of this chapter "home equity loan" means any open end consumer credit plan in which a consensual security interest is created or retained against the consumer's dwelling. *(Added by Stats.1988, c. 1315, § 1.)*

Research References

Miller and Starr California Real Estate § 4:64, Requirements in Making or Arranging a Loan--Special Notice for Home Equity Loans.

§ 2971. Disclosure to customer by creditor at time of initial application

(a) At the time that a customer makes an initial application to a creditor for a home equity loan in person, or within three business days if the customer applies by mail or telephone, the creditor shall provide the applicant with a disclosure in either of the following forms:

(1) The statement: "This home equity loan that you are applying for will be secured by your home and your failure to repay the loan for any reason could cause you to lose your home!"

(2) A statement to the effect that a home equity loan is secured by a lien against the home of the consumer and in the event of any default the consumer risks the loss of the home.

(b) The disclosure required in subdivision (a) shall be made by either of the following means:

(1) A separate and specific document attached to or accompanying the application.

(2) A clear and conspicuous statement on the application.

(c) If a creditor is required by federal statute or regulation to make a substantially similar disclosure to that required by subdivision (a), and the creditor complies with that federal statute or regulation, the creditor shall be deemed to have complied with the requirements of this chapter. *(Added by Stats.1988, c. 1315, § 1.)*

Research References

Miller and Starr California Real Estate § 4:64, Requirements in Making or Arranging a Loan--Special Notice for Home Equity Loans.

CHAPTER 2B. AUTOMOBILE
SALES FINANCE ACT

§ 2981. Definitions

As used in this chapter, unless the context otherwise requires:

(a) "Conditional sale contract" means:

(1) A contract for the sale of a motor vehicle between a buyer and a seller, with or without accessories, under which possession is delivered to the buyer and either of the following:

(A) The title vests in the buyer thereafter only upon the payment of all or a part of the price, or the performance of any other condition.

(B) A lien on the property is to vest in the seller as security for the payment of part or all of the price, or for the performance of any other condition.

(2) A contract for the bailment of a motor vehicle between a buyer and a seller, with or without accessories, by which the bailee or lessee agrees to pay as compensation for use a sum substantially equivalent to or in excess of the aggregate value of the vehicle and its accessories, if any, at the time the contract is executed, and by which it is agreed that the bailee or lessee will become, or for no other or for a nominal consideration has the option of becoming, the owner of the vehicle upon full compliance with the terms of the contract.

(b) "Seller" means a person engaged in the business of selling or leasing motor vehicles under conditional sale contracts.

(c) "Buyer" means the person who buys or hires a motor vehicle under a conditional sale contract.

(d) "Person" includes an individual, company, firm, association, partnership, trust, corporation, limited liability company, or other legal entity.

(e) "Cash price" means the amount for which the seller would sell and transfer to the buyer unqualified title to the motor vehicle described in the conditional sale contract, if the property were sold for cash at the seller's place of business on the date the contract is executed, and shall include taxes to the extent imposed on the cash sale and the cash price of accessories or services related to the sale, including, but not limited to, delivery, installation, alterations, modifications, improvements, document preparation fees, a service contract, a vehicle contract cancellation option agreement, and payment of a prior credit or lease balance remaining on property being traded in.

(f) "Downpayment" means a payment that the buyer pays or agrees to pay to the seller in cash or property value or money's worth at or prior to delivery by the seller to the buyer of the motor vehicle described in the conditional sale contract. The term shall also include the amount of any portion of the downpayment the payment of which is deferred until not later than the due date of the second otherwise scheduled payment, if the amount of the deferred downpayment is not subject to a finance charge. The term does not include any administrative finance charge charged, received or collected by the seller as provided in this chapter.

(g) "Amount financed" means the amount required to be disclosed pursuant to paragraph (8) of subdivision (a) of Section 2982.

(h) "Unpaid balance" means the difference between subdivision (e) and subdivision (f), plus all insurance premiums (except for credit life or disability insurance when the amount thereof is included in the finance charge), which are included in the contract balance, and the total amount paid or to be paid as follows:

(1) To a public officer in connection with the transaction.

(2) For license, certificate of title, and registration fees imposed by law, and the amount of the state fee for issuance of a certificate of compliance or certificate of waiver pursuant to Section 9889.56 of the Business and Professions Code.

(i) "Finance charge" has the meaning set forth for that term in Section 226.4 of Regulation Z. The term shall not include delinquency charges or collection costs and fees as provided by subdivision (k) of Section 2982, extension or deferral agreement charges as provided by Section 2982.3, or amounts for insurance, repairs to or preservation of the motor vehicle, or preservation of the security interest therein advanced by the holder under the terms of the contract.

(j) "Total of payments" means the amount required to be disclosed pursuant to subdivision (h) of Section 226.18 of Regulation Z. The term includes any portion of the downpayment that is deferred until not later than the second otherwise scheduled payment and that is not subject to a finance charge. The term shall not include amounts for which the buyer may later become obligated under the terms of the contract in connection with insurance, repairs to or preservation of the motor vehicle, preservation of the security interest therein, or otherwise.

(k) "Motor vehicle" means a vehicle required to be registered under the Vehicle Code that is bought for use primarily for personal or family purposes, and does not mean any vehicle that is bought for use primarily for business or commercial purposes or a mobilehome, as defined in Section 18008 of the Health and Safety Code that is sold on or after July 1, 1981. "Motor vehicle" does not include any trailer that is sold in conjunction with a vessel and that comes within the definition of "goods" under Section 1802.1.

(*l*) "Purchase order" means a sales order, car reservation, statement of transaction or any other such instrument used in the conditional sale of a motor vehicle pending execution of a conditional sale contract. The purchase order shall conform to the disclosure requirements of subdivision (a) of Section 2982 and Section 2984.1, and subdivision (m) of Section 2982 shall apply.

(m) "Regulation Z" means a rule, regulation or interpretation promulgated by the Board of Governors of the Federal Reserve System ("Board") under the federal Truth in Lending Act, as amended (15 U.S.C. 1601, et seq.), and an interpretation or approval issued by an official or employee of the Federal Reserve System duly authorized by the board under the Truth in Lending Act, as amended, to issue the interpretations or approvals.

(n) "Simple-interest basis" means the determination of a finance charge, other than an administrative finance charge, by applying a constant rate to the unpaid balance as it changes from time to time either:

(1) Calculated on the basis of a 365-day year and actual days elapsed (although the seller may, but need not, adjust its calculations to account for leap years); reference in this chapter to the "365-day basis" shall mean this method of determining the finance charge, or

(2) For contracts entered into prior to January 1, 1988, calculated on the basis of a 360-day year consisting of 12 months of 30 days each and on the assumption that all payments will be received by the seller on their respective due dates; reference in this chapter to the "360-day basis" shall mean this method of determining the finance charge.

(o) "Precomputed basis" means the determination of a finance charge by multiplying the original unpaid balance of the contract by a rate and multiplying that product by the number of payment periods elapsing between the date of the contract and the date of the last scheduled payment.

(p) "Service contract" means "vehicle service contract" as defined in subdivision (c) of Section 12800 of the Insurance Code.

(q) "Surface protection product" means the following products installed by the seller after the motor vehicle is sold:

(1) Undercoating.

(2) Rustproofing.

(3) Chemical or film paint sealant or protectant.

(4) Chemical sealant or stain inhibitor for carpet and fabric.

(r) "Theft deterrent device" means the following devices installed by the seller after the motor vehicle is sold:

(1) A vehicle alarm system.

(2) A window etch product.

(3) A body part marking product.

(4) A steering lock.

(5) A pedal or ignition lock.

(6) A fuel or ignition kill switch. *(Added by Stats.1961, c. 1626, p. 3534, § 4, eff. Jan. 1, 1962. Amended by Stats.1968, c. 1338, p. 2556, § 1; Stats.1970, c. 1003, p. 1800, § 1; Stats.1973, c. 696, § 1; Stats.1976, c. 1285, p. 5722, § 1; Stats.1979, c. 805, p. 2781, § 18; Stats.1980, c. 1149, p. 3722, § 7; Stats.1980, c. 1380, p. 5019, § 19, eff. Oct. 1, 1980; Stats.1981, c. 134, p. 892, § 1, eff. July 1, 1981, operative July 1, 1981; Stats.1981, c. 1075, p. 4122, § 12, operative Oct. 1, 1982; Stats.1985, c. 1186, § 2; Stats.1994, c. 1010 (S.B.2053), § 50; Stats.1999, c. 212 (S.B.1092), § 1; Stats.2005, c. 128 (A.B.68), § 2, operative July 1, 2006.)*

Research References

Rutter, Cal. Practice Guide: Civ. Pro. Before Trial Ch. 11-A, A. Voluntary Dismissals.

Rutter, Cal. Practice Guide: Civil Trials & Evidence Ch. 17-E, E. Attorney Fees as Costs.

Rutter, Cal. Practice Guide: Enforcing Judgments/Debts Ch. 3-A, A. Evaluating the Claim.

Rutter, Cal. Practice Guide: Enforcing Judgments/Debts Ch. 3-B, B. Collection Without Suit.

Rutter, Cal. Practice Guide: Enforcing Judgments/Debts Ch. 4-B, B. Claim and Delivery.

Miller and Starr California Real Estate § 10:14, Liens Securing Illegal Obligations.

Miller and Starr California Real Estate § 31:47, Authority of Real Estate Brokers.

Miller and Starr California Real Estate § 34:74, Effect of Dismissal of Action Before Judgment.

2 Witkin Cal. Proc. 5th Courts § 275, Exceptions.

1 Witkin Cal. Summ. 10th Contracts § 123, (S 123) in General.

1 Witkin Cal. Summ. 10th Contracts § 124, (S 124) of Translation.

1 Witkin Cal. Summ. 10th Contracts § 484, (S 484) California Law.

13 Witkin, California Summary 10th Personal Property § 193, (S 193) Nature of Act.

4 Witkin, California Summary 10th Sales § 132, (S 132) Pre-Code Case Law.

4 Witkin, California Summary 10th Sales § 239, Nature and Purpose of Statute.

4 Witkin, California Summary 10th Sales § 240, Scope and Exclusions.

4 Witkin, California Summary 10th Sales § 242, Disclosure of Cost Items.

4 Witkin, California Summary 10th Sales § 245, (S 245) Limitation of Charges.

4 Witkin, California Summary 10th Sales § 253, Exceptions: Mobilehome or Motor Vehicle.

4 Witkin, California Summary 10th Sales § 260, (S 260) Venue, Attorneys' Fees, and Costs.

4 Witkin, California Summary 10th Secured Transactions in Personal Property § 49, Effectiveness of Security Agreement.

§ 2981.5.   Bailments or leases not considered conditional sale contracts

A contract for the bailment or leasing of a motor vehicle, with or without accessories, which establishes the maximum for which a bailee or lessee could be held liable at the end of the lease or bailment period, or upon an earlier termination, by reference to the value of the vehicle at such time, is not a contract by which the bailee or lessee will become or for no other or for a nominal consideration has the option of becoming the owner of the vehicle, for the purposes of paragraph (2) of subdivision (a) of Section 2981 or any other provision of this chapter. *(Added by Stats.1973, c. 696, § 2.)*

Research References

4 Witkin, California Summary 10th Sales § 240, Scope and Exclusions.

§ 2981.7.   Finance charge; calculation on or after January 1, 1983

All contracts entered into between a buyer and a seller on or after January 1, 1983, shall provide for the calculation of the finance charge contemplated by item (A) of paragraph (1) of subdivision (j) of Section 2982 on the simple-interest basis, if the date on which the final installment is due, according to the original terms of the contract, is more than 62 months after the date of the contract. *(Added by Stats.1979, c. 805, p. 2783, § 19. Amended by Stats.1983, c. 142, § 3.)*

Research References

4 Witkin, California Summary 10th Sales § 245, (S 245) Limitation of Charges.

§ 2981.8.   Finance charge; determination on precomputed basis and simple interest basis; exception

No contract shall provide for a finance charge which is determined in part by the precomputed basis and in part by the simple-interest basis except for any finance charge permitted by subdivisions (a) and (c) of Section 2982.8. *(Added by Stats.1979, c. 805, p. 2783, § 19.5. Amended by Stats.1980, c. 1380, p. 5021, § 20, eff. Oct. 1, 1980.)*

Research References

4 Witkin, California Summary 10th Sales § 245, (S 245) Limitation of Charges.

§ 2981.9.   Requirements of conditional sale contracts

Every conditional sale contract subject to this chapter shall be in writing and, if printed, shall be printed in type no smaller than 6-point, and shall contain in a single document all of the agreements of the buyer and seller with respect to the total cost and the terms of payment for the motor vehicle, including any promissory notes or any other evidences of indebtedness. The conditional sale contract or a purchase order shall be signed by the buyer or his or her authorized representative and by the seller or its authorized representative. An exact copy of the contract or purchase order shall be furnished to the buyer by the seller at the time the buyer and the seller have signed it. No motor vehicle shall be delivered pursuant to a contract subject to this chapter until the seller delivers to the buyer a fully executed copy of the conditional sale contract or purchase order and any vehicle purchase proposal and any credit statement which the seller has required or requested the buyer to sign and which he or she has signed during the contract negotiations. The seller shall not obtain the signature of the buyer to a contract when it contains blank spaces to be filled in after it has been signed.

(Added by Stats.1981, c. 1075, p. 4124, § 13, operative Oct. 1, 1982.)

Research References

13 Witkin, California Summary 10th Personal Property § 194, (S 194) Regulatory Provisions.

4 Witkin, California Summary 10th Sales § 241, Written and Signed.

4 Witkin, California Summary 10th Sales § 244, (S 244) Copy to Buyer and Retention by Seller.

4 Witkin, California Summary 10th Sales § 256, (S 256) Violation of Contractual Requirements or Finance Provisions.

§ 2982.   Formalities of conditional sale contracts

A conditional sale contract subject to this chapter shall contain the disclosures required by Regulation Z, whether or not Regulation Z applies to the transaction. In addition, to the extent applicable, the contract shall contain the other disclosures and notices required by, and shall satisfy the requirements and limitations of, this section. The disclosures required by subdivision (a) may be itemized or subtotaled to a greater extent than as required by that subdivision and shall be made together and in the sequence set forth in that subdivision. All other disclosures and notices may appear in the contract in any location or sequence and may be combined or interspersed with other provisions of the contract.

(a) The contract shall contain the following disclosures, as applicable, which shall be labeled "itemization of the amount financed":

(1)(A) The cash price, exclusive of document processing charges, charges to electronically register or transfer the vehicle, taxes imposed on the sale, pollution control certification fees, prior credit or lease balance on property being traded in, the amount charged for a service contract, the amount charged for a theft deterrent system, the amount charged for a surface protection product, the amount charged for an optional debt cancellation agreement, and the amount charged for a contract cancellation option agreement.

(B) The charge to be retained by the seller for document processing authorized pursuant to Section 4456.5 of the Vehicle Code.

(C) The fee charged by the seller for certifying that the motor vehicle complies with applicable pollution control requirements.

(D) A charge for a theft deterrent device.

(E) A charge for a surface protection product.

(F) The total amount charged by the seller for an electric vehicle charging station, which may include only the charges for the electric vehicle charging station device, any materials and wiring, and any installation services. The total amount shall be labeled "EV Charging Station."

(G) Taxes imposed on the sale.

(H) The charge to electronically register or transfer the vehicle authorized pursuant to Section 4456.5 of the Vehicle Code.

(I) The amount charged for a service contract.

(J) The prior credit or lease balance remaining on property being traded in, as required by paragraph (6). The disclosure required by this subparagraph shall be labeled "prior credit or lease balance (see downpayment and trade-in calculation)."

(K) Any charge for an optional debt cancellation agreement.

(L) Any charge for a used vehicle contract cancellation option agreement.

(M) The total cash price, which is the sum of subparagraphs (A) to (L), inclusive.

(N) The disclosures described in subparagraphs (D), (E), and (L) are not required on contracts involving the sale of a motorcycle, as defined in Section 400 of the Vehicle Code, or on contracts involving the sale of an off-highway motor vehicle that is subject to identification under Section 38010 of the Vehicle Code, and the amounts of those charges, if any, are not required to be reflected in the total price under subparagraph (M).

(2) Amounts paid to public officials for the following:

(A) Vehicle license fees.

(B) Registration, transfer, and titling fees.

(C) California tire fees imposed pursuant to Section 42885 of the Public Resources Code.

(3) The aggregate amount of premiums agreed, upon execution of the contract, to be paid for policies of insurance included in the contract, excluding the amount of any insurance premium included in the finance charge.

(4) The amount of the state fee for issuance of a certificate of compliance, noncompliance, exemption, or waiver pursuant to any applicable pollution control statute.

(5) A subtotal representing the sum of the amounts described in paragraphs (1) to (4), inclusive.

(6) The amount of the buyer's downpayment itemized to show the following:

(A) The agreed value of the property being traded in.

(B) The prior credit or lease balance, if any, owing on the property being traded in.

(C) The net agreed value of the property being traded in, which is the difference between the amounts disclosed in subparagraphs (A) and (B). If the prior credit or lease balance of the property being traded in exceeds the agreed value of the property, a negative number shall be stated.

(D) The amount of any portion of the downpayment to be deferred until not later than the due date of the second regularly scheduled installment under the contract and that is not subject to a finance charge.

(E) The amount of any manufacturer's rebate applied or to be applied to the downpayment.

(F) The remaining amount paid or to be paid by the buyer as a downpayment.

(G) The total downpayment. If the sum of subparagraphs (C) to (F), inclusive, is zero or more, that sum shall be stated as the total downpayment, and no amount shall be stated as the prior credit or lease balance under subparagraph (I) of paragraph (1). If the sum of subparagraphs (C) to (F), inclusive, is less than zero, then that sum, expressed as a positive number, shall be stated as the prior credit or lease balance under subparagraph (I) of paragraph (1), and zero shall be stated as the total downpayment. The disclosure required by this subparagraph shall be labeled "total downpayment" and shall contain a descriptor indicating that if the total downpayment is a negative number, a zero shall be disclosed as the total downpayment and a reference made that the remainder shall be included in the disclosure required pursuant to subparagraph (I) of paragraph (1).

(7) The amount of any administrative finance charge, labeled "prepaid finance charge."

(8) The difference between the amount described in paragraph (5) and the sum of the amounts described in paragraphs (6) and (7), labeled "amount financed."

(b) No particular terminology is required to disclose the items set forth in subdivision (a) except as expressly provided in that subdivision.

(c) If payment of all or a portion of the downpayment is to be deferred, the deferred payment shall be reflected in the payment schedule disclosed pursuant to Regulation Z.

(d) If the downpayment includes property being traded in, the contract shall contain a brief description of that property.

(e) The contract shall contain the names and addresses of all persons to whom the notice required pursuant to Section 2983.2 and permitted pursuant to Sections 2983.5 and 2984 is to be sent.

(f)(1) If the contract includes a finance charge determined on the precomputed basis, the contract shall identify the method of computing the unearned portion of the finance charge in the event of prepayment in full of the buyer's obligation and contain a statement of the amount or method of computation of any charge that may be deducted from the amount of any unearned finance charge in computing the amount that will be credited to the obligation or refunded to the buyer. The method of computing the unearned portion of the finance charge shall be sufficiently identified with a reference to the actuarial method if the computation will be under that method. The method of computing the unearned portion of the finance charge shall be sufficiently identified with a reference to the Rule of 78's, the sum of the digits, or the sum of the periodic time balances method in all other cases, and those references shall be deemed to be equivalent for disclosure purposes.

(2) If the contract includes a finance charge that is determined on the simple-interest basis but provides for a minimum finance charge in the event of prepayment in full, the contract shall contain a statement of that fact and the amount of the minimum finance charge or its method of calculation.

(g)(1) If the contract includes a finance charge that is determined on the precomputed basis and provides that the unearned portion of the finance charge to be refunded upon full prepayment of the contract is to be determined by a method other than actuarial, the contract shall contain a notice, in at least 10–point boldface type if the contract is printed, reading as follows: "Notice to buyer: (1) Do not sign this agreement before you read it or if it contains any blank spaces to be filled in. (2) You are entitled to a completely filled-in copy of this agreement. (3) You can prepay the full amount due under this agreement at any time and obtain a partial refund of the finance charge if it is $1 or more. Because of the way the amount of this refund will be figured, the time when you prepay could increase the ultimate cost of credit under this agreement. (4) If you default in the performance of your obligations under this agreement, the vehicle may be repossessed and you may be subject to suit and liability for the unpaid indebtedness evidenced by this agreement."

(2) If the contract includes a finance charge that is determined on the precomputed basis and provides for the actuarial method for computing the unearned portion of the finance charge upon prepayment in full, the contract shall contain a notice, in at least 10–point boldface type if the contract is printed, reading as follows: "Notice to buyer: (1) Do not sign this agreement before you read it or if it contains any blank spaces to be filled in. (2) You are entitled to a completely filled-in copy of this agreement. (3) You can prepay the full amount due under this agreement at any time and obtain a partial refund of the finance charge if it is $1 or more. (4) If you default in the performance of your obligations under this agreement, the vehicle may be repossessed and you may be subject to suit and liability for the unpaid indebtedness evidenced by this agreement."

(3) If the contract includes a finance charge that is determined on the simple-interest basis, the contract shall contain a notice, in at least 10–point boldface type if the contract is printed, reading as follows: "Notice to buyer: (1) Do not sign

this agreement before you read it or if it contains any blank spaces to be filled in. (2) You are entitled to a completely filled-in copy of this agreement. (3) You can prepay the full amount due under this agreement at any time. (4) If you default in the performance of your obligations under this agreement, the vehicle may be repossessed and you may be subject to suit and liability for the unpaid indebtedness evidenced by this agreement."

(h) The contract shall contain a notice in at least 8–point boldface type, acknowledged by the buyer, that reads as follows:

"If you have a complaint concerning this sale, you should try to resolve it with the seller.

Complaints concerning unfair or deceptive practices or methods by the seller may be referred to the city attorney, the district attorney, or an investigator for the Department of Motor Vehicles, or any combination thereof.

After this contract is signed, the seller may not change the financing or payment terms unless you agree in writing to the change. You do not have to agree to any change, and it is an unfair or deceptive practice for the seller to make a unilateral change.

_____
         Buyer's Signature"

(i)(1) The contract shall contain an itemization of any insurance included as part of the amount financed disclosed pursuant to paragraph (3) of subdivision (a) and of any insurance included as part of the finance charge. The itemization shall identify the type of insurance coverage and the premium charged therefor, and, if the insurance expires before the date of the last scheduled installment included in the repayment schedule, the term of the insurance shall be stated.

(2) If any charge for insurance, other than for credit life or disability, is included in the contract balance and disbursement of any part thereof is to be made more than one year after the date of the conditional sale contract, any finance charge on the amount to be disbursed after one year shall be computed from the month the disbursement is to be made to the due date of the last installment under the conditional sale contract.

(j)(1) Except for contracts in which the finance charge or a portion of the finance charge is determined by the simple-interest basis and the amount financed disclosed pursuant to paragraph (8) of subdivision (a) is more than two thousand five hundred dollars ($2,500), the dollar amount of the disclosed finance charge may not exceed the greater of:

(A)(i) One and one-half percent on so much of the unpaid balance as does not exceed two hundred twenty-five dollars ($225), 1 ⅙ percent on so much of the unpaid balance in excess of two hundred twenty-five dollars ($225) as does not exceed nine hundred dollars ($900) and five-sixths of 1 percent on so much of the unpaid balance in excess of nine hundred dollars ($900) as does not exceed two thousand five hundred dollars ($2,500).

(ii) One percent of the entire unpaid balance; multiplied in either case by the number of months (computed on the basis of a full month for any fractional month period in excess of 15 days) elapsing between the date of the contract and the due date of the last installment.

(B) If the finance charge is determined by the precomputed basis, twenty-five dollars ($25).

(C) If the finance charge or a portion thereof is determined by the simple-interest basis:

(i) Twenty–five dollars ($25) if the unpaid balance does not exceed one thousand dollars ($1,000).

(ii) Fifty dollars ($50) if the unpaid balance exceeds one thousand dollars ($1,000) but does not exceed two thousand dollars ($2,000).

(iii) Seventy–five dollars ($75) if the unpaid balance exceeds two thousand dollars ($2,000).

(2) The holder of the contract shall not charge, collect, or receive a finance charge that exceeds the disclosed finance charge, except to the extent (A) caused by the holder's receipt of one or more payments under a contract that provides for determination of the finance charge or a portion thereof on the 365–day basis at a time or times other than as originally scheduled whether or not the parties enter into an agreement pursuant to Section 2982.3, (B) permitted by paragraph (2), (3), or (4) of subdivision (c) of Section 226.17 of Regulation Z, or (C) permitted by subdivisions (a) and (c) of Section 2982.8.

(3) If the finance charge or a portion thereof is determined by the simple-interest basis and the amount of the unpaid balance exceeds five thousand dollars ($5,000), the holder of the contract may, in lieu of its right to a minimum finance charge under subparagraph (C) of paragraph (1), charge, receive, or collect on the date of the contract an administrative finance charge not to exceed seventy-five dollars ($75), provided that the sum of the administrative finance charge and the portion of the finance charge determined by the simple-interest basis shall not exceed the maximum total finance charge permitted by subparagraph (A) of paragraph (1). Any administrative finance charge that is charged, received, or collected by a holder shall be deemed a finance charge earned on the date of the contract.

(4) If a contract provides for unequal or irregular payments, or payments on other than a monthly basis, the maximum finance charge shall be at the effective rate provided for in paragraph (1), having due regard for the schedule of installments.

(k) The contract may provide that for each installment in default for a period of not less than 10 days the buyer shall pay a delinquency charge in an amount not to exceed in the aggregate 5 percent of the delinquent installment, which amount may be collected only once on any installment regardless of the period during which it remains in default. Payments timely received by the seller under an extension or deferral agreement may not be subject to a delinquency charge unless the charge is permitted by Section 2982.3. The contract may provide for reasonable collection costs and fees in the event of delinquency.

(*l*) Notwithstanding any provision of a contract to the contrary, the buyer may pay at any time before maturity the entire indebtedness evidenced by the contract without penalty. In the event of prepayment in full:

(1) If the finance charge was determined on the precomputed basis, the amount required to prepay the contract shall be the outstanding contract balance as of that date, provided, however, that the buyer shall be entitled to a refund credit in the amount of the unearned portion of the finance charge, except as provided in paragraphs (3) and (4). The amount of the unearned portion of the finance charge shall be at least as great a proportion of the finance charge, including any additional finance charge imposed pursuant to Section 2982.8 or other additional charge imposed because the contract has been extended, deferred, or refinanced, as the sum of the periodic monthly time balances payable more than 15 days after the date of prepayment bears to the sum of all the periodic monthly time balances under the schedule of installments in the contract or, if the contract has been extended, deferred, or refinanced, as so extended, deferred, or refinanced. If the amount of the refund credit is less than one dollar ($1), no refund credit need be made by the holder. Any refund credit may be made in cash or

credited to the outstanding obligations of the buyer under the contract.

(2) If the finance charge or a portion of the finance charge was determined on the simple-interest basis, the amount required to prepay the contract shall be the outstanding contract balance as of that date, including any earned finance charges that are unpaid as of that date and, if applicable, the amount provided in paragraph (3), and provided further that in cases where a finance charge is determined on the 360–day basis, the payments received under the contract shall be assumed to have been received on their respective due dates regardless of the actual dates on which the payments were received.

(3) If the minimum finance charge provided by subparagraph (B) or subparagraph (C) of paragraph (1) of subdivision (j), if either is applicable, is greater than the earned finance charge as of the date of prepayment, the holder shall be additionally entitled to the difference.

(4) This subdivision shall not impair the right of the seller or the seller's assignee to receive delinquency charges on delinquent installments and reasonable costs and fees as provided in subdivision (k) or extension or deferral agreement charges as provided in Section 2982.3.

(5) Notwithstanding any provision of a contract to the contrary, if the indebtedness created by any contract is satisfied prior to its maturity through surrender of the motor vehicle, repossession of the motor vehicle, redemption of the motor vehicle after repossession, or any judgment, the outstanding obligation of the buyer shall be determined as provided in paragraph (1) or (2). Notwithstanding, the buyer's outstanding obligation shall be computed by the holder as of the date the holder recovers the value of the motor vehicle through disposition thereof or judgment is entered or, if the holder elects to keep the motor vehicle in satisfaction of the buyer's indebtedness, as of the date the holder takes possession of the motor vehicle.

(m) Notwithstanding any other provision of this chapter to the contrary, any information required to be disclosed in a conditional sale contract under this chapter may be disclosed in any manner, method, or terminology required or permitted under Regulation Z, as in effect at the time that disclosure is made, except that permitted by paragraph (2) of subdivision (c) of Section 226.18 of Regulation Z, if all of the requirements and limitations set forth in subdivision (a) are satisfied. This chapter does not prohibit the disclosure in that contract of additional information required or permitted under Regulation Z, as in effect at the time that disclosure is made.

(n) If the seller imposes a charge for document processing or to electronically register or transfer the vehicle, the contract shall contain a disclosure that the charge is not a governmental fee.

(o) A seller shall not impose an application fee for a transaction governed by this chapter.

(p) The seller or holder may charge and collect a fee not to exceed fifteen dollars ($15) for the return by a depository institution of a dishonored check, negotiated order of withdrawal, or share draft issued in connection with the contract if the contract so provides or if the contract contains a generalized statement that the buyer may be liable for collection costs incurred in connection with the contract.

(q) The contract shall disclose on its face, by printing the word "new" or "used" within a box outlined in red, that is not smaller than one-half inch high and one-half inch wide, whether the vehicle is sold as a new vehicle, as defined in Section 430 of the Vehicle Code, or as a used vehicle, as defined in Section 665 of the Vehicle Code.

(r) The contract shall contain a notice with a heading in at least 12–point bold type and the text in at least 10–point bold type, circumscribed by a line, immediately above the contract signature line, that reads as follows:

THERE IS NO COOLING–OFF PERIOD UNLESS YOU OBTAIN A CONTRACT CANCELLATION OPTION

California law does not provide for a "cooling-off" or other cancellation period for vehicle sales. Therefore, you cannot later cancel this contract simply because you change your mind, decide the vehicle costs too much, or wish you had acquired a different vehicle. After you sign below, you may only cancel this contract with the agreement of the seller or for legal cause, such as fraud.

However, California law does require a seller to offer a two-day contract cancellation option on used vehicles with a purchase price of less than forty thousand dollars ($40,000), subject to certain statutory conditions. This contract cancellation option requirement does not apply to the sale of a recreational vehicle, a motorcycle, or an off-highway motor vehicle subject to identification under California law. See the vehicle contract cancellation option agreement for details.

(s) This section shall become operative on July 1, 2013. *(Added by Stats.2012, c. 675 (A.B.2502), § 2, eff. Sept. 27, 2012, operative July 1, 2013.)*

Research References

Rutter, Cal. Practice Guide: Enforcing Judgments/Debts Ch. 3-A, A. Evaluating the Claim.

Rutter, Cal. Practice Guide: Enforcing Judgments/Debts Gen. Matls., Highlights.

Miller and Starr California Real Estate § 31:49, Advertising and Other Representations; Place of Business.

1 Witkin Cal. Summ. 10th Contracts § 439, (S 439) Sales Contract.

1 Witkin Cal. Summ. 10th Contracts § 484, (S 484) California Law.

13 Witkin, California Summary 10th Personal Property § 194, (S 194) Regulatory Provisions.

4 Witkin, California Summary 10th Sales § 242, Disclosure of Cost Items.

4 Witkin, California Summary 10th Sales § 243, Warning Notices to Buyers.

4 Witkin, California Summary 10th Sales § 245, (S 245) Limitation of Charges.

4 Witkin, California Summary 10th Sales § 249, (S 249) Right to Pay Before Maturity.

4 Witkin, California Summary 10th Sales § 255, (S 255) in General.

4 Witkin, California Summary 10th Sales § 256, (S 256) Violation of Contractual Requirements or Finance Provisions.

4 Witkin, California Summary 10th Sales § 257, (S 257) Violation of Provisions for Prepayment of Balance.

4 Witkin, California Summary 10th Sales § 264, Retail Installment Contract.

13 Witkin, California Summary 10th Equity § 123, Other Practices.

§ 2982.1. Rebates, discounts, commissions, etc.

It shall be unlawful for any seller to induce or attempt to induce any person to enter into a contract subject to this chapter by offering a rebate, discount, commission, or other consideration, contingent upon the happening of a future event, on the condition that the buyer either sells, or gives information or assistance for the purpose of leading to a sale by the seller of, the same or related goods. *(Added by Stats.1968, c. 452, p. 1075, § 3.)*

Research References

13 Witkin, California Summary 10th Personal Property § 194, (S 194) Regulatory Provisions.

4 Witkin, California Summary 10th Sales § 254, Prohibited Terms or Acts.

§ 2982.2. Disclosures required for conditional sale contracts

(a) Prior to the execution of a conditional sale contract, the seller shall provide to a buyer, and obtain the buyer's signature on, a written disclosure that sets forth the following information:

(1)(A) A description and the price of each item sold if the contract includes a charge for the item.

(B) Subparagraph (A) applies to each item in the following categories:

(i) A service contract.

(ii) An insurance product.

(iii) A debt cancellation agreement.

(iv) A theft deterrent device.

(v) A surface protection product.

(vi) A vehicle contract cancellation option agreement.

(2) The sum of all of the charges disclosed under subdivision (a), labeled "total."

(3) The amount that would be calculated under the contract as the regular installment payment if charges for the items disclosed pursuant to subdivision (a) are not included in the contract. The amount disclosed pursuant to this subdivision shall be labeled "Installment Payment EXCLUDING Listed Items."

(4) The amount that would be calculated under the contract as the regular installment payment if charges for the items disclosed under subdivision (a) are included in the contract. The amount disclosed pursuant to this subdivision shall be labeled "Installment Payment INCLUDING Listed Items."

(b) The disclosures required under this section shall be in at least 10–point type and shall be contained in a document that is separate from the conditional sale contract and a purchase order.

(c) This section does not apply to the sale of a motorcycle as defined in Section 400 of the Vehicle Code or an off-highway vehicle subject to identification under Section 38010 of the Vehicle Code. *(Added by Stats.2005, c. 128 (A.B.68), § 4, operative July 1, 2006. Amended by Stats.2006, c. 567 (A.B.2303), § 3.5.)*

Research References

4 Witkin, California Summary 10th Sales § 242A, (S 242A) (New)-Disclosures Separate from Contract.

§ 2982.3. Extension of due date; deferment of payment; charges

(a) The holder of a conditional sale contract may, upon agreement with the buyer, extend the scheduled due date or defer the scheduled payment of all or of any part of any installment or installments payable thereunder. No charge shall be made for any such extension or deferment unless the agreement for such extension or deferment is in writing and signed by the parties thereto. However, the seller or holder may, as an adjunct to or to assist in efforts to collect one or more delinquent installments on the contract, advise one or more obligors on the contract, either in writing or orally, that the due date for one or more installments under the contract shall be extended, with no charge being made for such extension other than any applicable late charge provided for in the contract.

(b) Where the contract includes a finance charge determined on the precomputed basis, the holder may charge and contract for the payment of an extension or deferral agreement charge by the buyer and collect and receive the same, but such charge may not exceed an amount equal to 1 percent per month simple interest on the amount of the installment or installments, or part thereof, extended or deferred for the period of extension or deferral. Such period shall not exceed the period from the date when such extended or deferred installment or installments, or part thereof, would have been payable in the absence of such extension or deferral to the date when such installment or installments, or part thereof, are made payable under the

agreement of extension or deferment; except that a minimum charge of one dollar ($1) for the period of extension or deferral may be made in any case where the extension or deferral agreement charge, when computed at such rate, amounts to less than one dollar ($1).

(c) Where the contract includes a finance charge determined on the simple-interest basis, the holder may charge and contract for the payment of an extension or deferral agreement charge by the buyer and collect and receive the same, but the charge for the extension or deferral agreement may not exceed the lesser of twenty-five dollars ($25) or 10 percent of the then outstanding principal balance of the contract. Such charge shall be in addition to any finance charges which accrue because such extended or deferred payments are received at a time other than as originally scheduled. *(Added by Stats.1980, c. 1380, p. 5039, § 23, eff. Oct. 1, 1980. Amended by Stats.1981, c. 1075, p. 4130, § 15, operative Oct. 1, 1982; Stats.1987, c. 448, § 2.)*

Research References

4 Witkin, California Summary 10th Sales § 245, (S 245) Limitation of Charges.

§ 2982.5. Exemptions from chapter; conditions; proceeds of loan

(a) This chapter may not be deemed to affect a loan, or the security therefor, between a purchaser of a motor vehicle and a supervised financial organization, other than the seller of the motor vehicle, all or a portion of which loan is used in connection with the purchase of a motor vehicle. As used in this chapter, "supervised financial organization" means a person organized, chartered, or holding a license or authorization certificate under a law of this state or the United States to make loans and subject to supervision by an official or agency of this state or the United States.

(b) This chapter may not be deemed to prohibit the seller's assisting the buyer in obtaining a loan upon any security from any third party to be used as a part or all of the downpayment or any other payment on a conditional sale contract or purchase order; provided that the conditional sale contract sets forth on its face the amount of the loan, the finance charge, the total thereof, the number of installments scheduled to repay the loan and the amount of each installment, that the buyer may be required to pledge security for the loan, which security shall be mutually agreed to by the buyer and the lender and notice to the buyer in at least 8–point type that he or she is obligated for the installment payments on both the conditional sale contract and the loan. The seller may not provide any security or other guarantee of payment on the loan, nor shall the seller receive any commission or other remuneration for assisting the buyer to obtain the loan. If the buyer obligates himself or herself to purchase, or receives possession of, the motor vehicle prior to securing the loan, and if the buyer upon appropriate application for the loan is unable to secure the loan, on the conditions stated in the conditional sale contract, the conditional sale contract or purchase order shall be deemed rescinded and all consideration thereupon shall be returned by the respective parties without demand.

(c) The proceeds of any loan payable to the seller after the date of the contract but prior to the due date of the second payment otherwise scheduled thereunder may not be subject to a finance charge and the amount thereof shall be disclosed pursuant to subparagraph (D) of paragraph (6) of subdivision (a) of Section 2982.

(d) This chapter may not be deemed to prohibit the seller's assisting the buyer in obtaining a loan from any third party to be used to pay for the full purchase price, or any part thereof, of a motor vehicle, if each of the following provisions applies:

(1) The loan may be upon any security, but except as provided in paragraph (2), the loan may not be secured in whole or in part by a lien on real property. Any lien on real property taken in violation of this section shall be void and unenforceable.

(2) A lien on real property may be taken to secure a loan of seven thousand five hundred dollars ($7,500) or more used to pay the full purchase price, or any part thereof, of a recreational vehicle, as defined in Section 18010 of the Health and Safety Code, which is not less than 20 feet in length.

(3) The provisions of Sections 2983.2, 2983.3, and 2984.4 shall apply to the loan, but may not authorize the lender or the lender's successor in interest to charge for any costs, fees, or expenses or to obtain any other benefit which the lender is prohibited from charging or obtaining under any regulatory law applicable to the lender. Notwithstanding this paragraph, the provisions of Sections 2983.2 and 2983.3 may not apply to a loan made by a lender licensed under Division 9 (commencing with Section 22000) or Division 10 (commencing with Section 24000) of the Financial Code.

(4) The lender or the lender's successor in interest shall be subject to all claims and defenses which the buyer could assert against the seller, but liability may not exceed the amount of the loan.

(5) If the buyer becomes obligated to purchase, or receives possession of, the motor vehicle prior to obtaining the loan, the agreement between the buyer and the seller shall set forth on its face the amount of the loan, the finance charge, the total thereof, the number of installments scheduled to repay the loan and the amount of each installment, that the buyer may be required to pledge security for the loan, which security must be mutually agreed to by the buyer and the lender, and notice to the buyer in at least 8–point type that the buyer is obligated for the installment payments on the loan and for any payments which may be due on the agreement between the buyer and the seller. The seller may not provide any security or other guarantee of payment on the loan, and the seller may not receive any commission or other remuneration for assisting the buyer to obtain the loan. If the buyer upon proper application for the loan is unable to obtain the loan, on the condition stated in the agreement between the buyer and the seller, the agreement shall be deemed rescinded and all consideration thereupon shall be returned by the respective parties without demand.

(6) Any waiver by the buyer of the provisions of this section shall be void and unenforceable.

This subdivision does not apply to state or federally chartered banks and savings and loan associations and may not be construed to affect existing law regarding a seller's assisting a buyer to obtain a loan from a bank or savings and loan association or any loan obtained by the buyer from those lenders. *(Added by Stats.1968, c. 979, p. 1866, § 1. Amended by Stats.1970, c. 1003, p. 1804, § 3; Stats.1979, c. 805, p. 2793, § 21; Stats.1981, c. 1075, p. 4131, § 16, operative Oct. 1, 1982; Stats.1983, c. 405, § 1; Stats.1985, c. 226, § 1; Stats.2003, c. 37 (A.B.964), § 2.)*

Research References

Miller and Starr California Real Estate § 31:47, Authority of Real Estate Brokers.
4 Witkin, California Summary 10th Sales § 240, Scope and Exclusions.
4 Witkin, California Summary 10th Sales § 251, (S 251) Notice to Cosigner.
4 Witkin, California Summary 10th Sales § 254, Prohibited Terms or Acts.

§ 2982.7. Refund of down payment; breach after leaving motor vehicle as down payment; recovery by buyer

(a) Any payment made by a buyer to a seller pending execution of a conditional sale contract shall be refunded to the buyer in the event the conditional sale contract is not executed.

(b) In the event of breach by the seller of a conditional sale contract or purchase order where the buyer leaves his motor vehicle with the seller as downpayment and such motor vehicle is not returned by the seller to the buyer for whatever reason, the buyer may recover from the seller either the fair market value of the motor vehicle left as a downpayment or its value as stated in the contract or purchase order, whichever is greater. The recovery shall be tendered to the buyer within five business days after the breach.

(c) The remedies of the buyer provided for in subdivision (b) are nonexclusive and cumulative and shall not preclude the buyer from pursuing any other remedy which he may have under any other provision of law. *(Added by Stats.1968, c. 1338, p. 2558, § 2. Amended by Stats.1970, c. 1003, p. 1805, § 4; Stats.1976, c. 1285, p. 5735, § 4.)*

Research References

13 Witkin, California Summary 10th Personal Property § 194, (S 194) Regulatory Provisions.
4 Witkin, California Summary 10th Sales § 248, (S 248) Refund of Payment or Insurance.

§ 2982.8. Amounts advanced by holder to procure insurance; repayment options for buyer; security; notice to buyer

(a) If a buyer is obligated under the terms of the conditional sale contract to maintain insurance on the vehicle and subsequent to the execution of the contract the buyer either fails to maintain or requests the holder to procure the insurance, any amounts advanced by the holder to procure the insurance may be the subject of finance charges from the date of advance as provided in subdivision (e).

(b) These amounts shall be secured as provided in the contract and permitted by Section 2984.2 if the holder notifies the buyer in writing of his or her option to repay those amounts in any one of the following ways:

(1) Full payment within 10 days from the date of giving or mailing the notice.

(2) Full amortization during the term of the insurance.

(3) If offered by the holder, full amortization after the term of the conditional sale contract, to be payable in installments which do not exceed the average payment allocable to a monthly period under the contract.

(4) If offered by the holder, a combination of the methods described in paragraphs (2) and (3), so that there is some amortization during the term of the insurance, with the remainder of the amortization being accomplished after the term of the conditional sale contract, to be payable in installments which do not exceed the average payment allocable to a monthly period under the original terms of the contract.

(5) If offered by the holder, any other amortization plan.

If the buyer neither pays in full the amounts advanced nor notifies the holder in writing of his or her choice regarding amortization options before the expiration of 10 days from the date of giving or mailing the notice by the holder, the holder may amortize the amounts advanced on a secured basis pursuant to paragraph (2) or, if offered by the holder as an option to the buyer, paragraph (3) or (4).

(c) The written notification described in subdivision (b) shall also set forth the amounts advanced by the holder and, with respect to each amortization plan the amount of the additional finance charge, the sum of the amounts advanced and the additional finance charge, the number of installments required, the amount of each installment and the date for payment of the installments.

In addition, the notice shall contain a statement in contrasting red print in at least 8–point bold type, which reads as follows:

"WARNING—IT IS YOUR RESPONSIBILITY UNDER CALIFORNIA LAW TO OBTAIN LIABILITY INSURANCE OR BE SUBJECT TO PENALTIES FOR VIOLATING SECTION 16020 OF THE VEHICLE CODE, WHICH MAY INCLUDE LOSS OF LICENSE OR A FINE. THE INSURANCE ACQUIRED BY THE LIENHOLDER DOES NOT PROVIDE LIABILITY COVERAGE AND DOES NOT SATISFY YOUR RESPONSIBILITY UNDER CALIFORNIA LAW."

(d) If subsequent to the execution of the contract the holder advances amounts for repairs to or preservation of the motor vehicle or preservation of the holder's security interest therein and such advances are occasioned by the buyer's default under the contract, such advances may be the subject of finance charges from the date of advance as provided in subdivision (e) and shall be secured as provided in the contract and permitted by Section 2984.2.

(e) The maximum rate of finance charge which may be imposed on amounts advanced by the holder subsequent to the execution of the contract for insurance, repairs to or preservation of the motor vehicle, or preservation of the holder's security interest therein, shall not exceed the annual percentage rate disclosed pursuant to Section 2982. *(Added by Stats.1976, c. 1265, p. 5601, § 2. Amended by Stats.1977, c. 777, p. 2411, § 1, eff. Sept. 13, 1977; Stats.1978, c. 1057, p. 3264, § 1; Stats.1979, c. 805, p. 2793, § 22; Stats.1980, c. 1149, p. 3736, § 9; Stats.1980, c. 1380, p. 5040, § 24, eff. Oct. 1, 1980; Stats.1981, c. 134, p. 911, § 5, eff. July 1, 1981; Stats.1981, c. 1075, p. 4131, § 17, operative Oct. 1, 1982; Stats.1983, c. 33, § 1; Stats.1985, c. 1292, § 1; Stats.1986, c. 412, § 1; Stats.1987, c. 448, § 3; Stats.1988, c. 1092, § 2.)*

Research References

4 Witkin, California Summary 10th Sales § 245, (S 245) Limitation of Charges.

§ 2982.9. Inability of buyer to obtain financing through third party; rescission of contract

In the event a buyer obligates himself to purchase, or receive possession of, a motor vehicle pursuant to a contract or purchase order, and the seller knows that the buyer intends to obtain financing from a third party without the assistance of the seller, and the buyer is unable to obtain such financing, the contract or purchase order shall be deemed rescinded and all consideration thereupon shall be returned by the respective parties without demand. *(Added by Stats.1976, c. 1285, p. 5736, § 4.5.)*

Research References

4 Witkin, California Summary 10th Sales § 246, (S 246) Right to Rescind If Financing Unavailable.

§ 2982.10. Consideration for assignment of conditional sale contract

(a) In consideration of the assignment of a conditional sale contract, the seller shall not receive or accept from the assignee any payment or credit based upon any amount collected or received, or to be collected or received, under the contract as a finance charge except to the extent the payment or credit does not exceed the amount that would be calculated in accordance with Regulation Z, whether or not Regulation Z applies to the contract, as the contract's finance charge using, for the purposes of the calculation, an annual percentage rate equal to 2.5 percent for a contract having an original scheduled term of 60 monthly payments or less or 2 percent for a contract having an original scheduled term of more than 60 monthly payments.

(b) Subdivision (a) does not apply in the following circumstances:

(1) An assignment that is with full recourse or under other terms requiring the seller to bear the entire risk of financial performance of the buyer.

(2) An assignment that is more than six months following the date of the conditional sale contract.

(3) Isolated instances resulting from bona fide errors that would otherwise constitute a violation of subdivision (a) if the seller maintains reasonable procedures to guard against any errors and promptly, upon notice of the error, remits to the assignee any consideration received in excess of that permitted by subdivision (a).

(4) The assignment of a conditional sale contract involving the sale of a motorcycle, as defined in Section 400 of the Vehicle Code.

(5) The assignment of a conditional sale contract involving the sale of an off-highway motor vehicle that is subject to identification under Section 38010 of the Vehicle Code. *(Added by Stats.2005, c. 128 (A.B.68), § 5, operative July 1, 2006.)*

Research References

4 Witkin, California Summary 10th Sales § 247, (S 247) Assignment by Seller.

§ 2982.11. Conditional sale contract including charge for electric vehicle charging station; written disclosure

(a) Prior to the execution of a conditional sale contract that includes a charge for an electric vehicle charging station, the seller shall provide the buyer with, and obtain the buyer's signature on, a written disclosure that includes a description and price of each of the following:

(1) The electric vehicle charging station device.

(2) Any materials and wiring.

(3) Any installation services included in the total charge.

(b) The disclosures required under this section shall be in at least 12–point type and shall be contained in a document that is separate from the conditional sale contract or purchase order.

(c) This section shall become operative July 1, 2013. *(Added by Stats.2012, c. 675 (A.B.2502), § 3, eff. Sept. 27, 2012, operative July 1, 2013.)*

§ 2983. Enforceability of contract; violation of specified provisions by seller; correction; recovery by buyer; disclosure violations relating to payment of state fees

(a) Except as provided in subdivision (b), if the seller, except as the result of an accidental or bona fide error in computation, violates any provision of Section 2981.9, or of subdivision (a), (j), or (k) of Section 2982, the conditional sale contract shall not be enforceable, except by a bona fide purchaser, assignee, or pledgee for value, or until after the violation is corrected as provided in Section 2984, and, if the violation is not corrected, the buyer may recover from the seller the total amount paid, pursuant to the terms of the contract, by the buyer to the seller or his or her assignee. The amount recoverable for property traded in as all or part of the downpayment shall be equal to the agreed cash value of the property as the value appears on the conditional sale contract or the fair market value of the property as of the time the contract is made, whichever is greater.

(b) A conditional sale contract executed or entered into on or after January 1, 2012, shall not be made unenforceable solely because of a violation by the seller of paragraph (2) or (5) of subdivision (a) of Section 2982. In addition to any other remedies that may be available, the buyer is entitled to any actual damages sustained as a result of a violation of those provisions.

Nothing in this subdivision affects any legal rights, claims, or remedies otherwise available under law. *(Added by Stats.1961, c. 1626, p. 3537, § 4, eff. Jan. 1, 1962. Amended by Stats.1967, c. 815, § 2239, § 1; Stats.1979, c. 805, p. 2794, § 23; Stats.1981, c. 1075, p. 4132, § 18, operative Oct. 1, 1982; Stats.2011, c. 526 (A.B.238), § 2, eff. Oct. 7, 2011; Stats.2012, c. 162 (S.B.1171), § 11.)*

Research References

Rutter, Cal. Practice Guide: Enforcing Judgments/Debts Ch. 3-A, A. Evaluating the Claim.

Rutter, Cal. Practice Guide: Enforcing Judgments/Debts Gen. Matls., Highlights.

4 Witkin, California Summary 10th Sales § 256, (S 256) Violation of Contractual Requirements or Finance Provisions.

§ 2983.1. Enforceability of contract; violation of provisions relating to prepayment, refinancing, or refund of finance charge by seller or holder; recovery by buyer; election to enforce or rescind; disclosure violations relating to payment of state fees

(a) If the seller or holder of a conditional sale contract, except as the result of an accidental or bona fide error of computation, violates any provision of subdivision (*l*) of Section 2982, the buyer may recover from the person three times the amount of any finance charge paid to that person.

(b) Except as provided in subdivision (e), if a holder acquires a conditional sale contract without actual knowledge of the violation by the seller of Section 2981.9, or of subdivision (a), (j), or (k) of Section 2982, the contract shall be valid and enforceable by the holder except the buyer is excused from payment of the unpaid finance charge, unless the violation is corrected as provided in Section 2984.

(c) Except as provided in subdivision (e), if a holder acquires a conditional sale contract with knowledge of a violation of Section 2981.9, or of subdivision (a), (j), or (k) of Section 2982, the conditional sale contract shall not be enforceable except by a bona fide purchaser, assignee, or pledgee for value, or unless the violation is corrected as provided in Section 2984, and, if the violation is not corrected, the buyer may recover the amounts specified in Section 2983 from the person to whom payment was made.

(d) When a conditional sale contract is not enforceable under Section 2983 or this section, the buyer may elect to retain the motor vehicle and continue the contract in force, or may, with reasonable diligence, elect to rescind the contract and return the motor vehicle. The value of the motor vehicle returned shall be credited as restitution by the buyer without any decrease that results from the passage of time in the cash price of the motor vehicle as the price appears on the conditional sale contract.

(e) A conditional sale contract executed or entered into on or after January 1, 2012, shall not be made unenforceable, and the buyer shall not be excused from payment of any finance charge, solely because of a violation by the seller of paragraph (2) or (5) of subdivision (a) of Section 2982. In addition to any other remedies that may be available, the buyer is entitled to any actual damages sustained as a result of a violation of those provisions. Nothing in this subdivision affects any legal rights, claims, or remedies otherwise available under law. *(Added by Stats.1961, c. 1626, p. 3538, § 4, eff. Jan. 1, 1962. Amended by Stats.1979, c. 805, p. 2794, § 24; Stats.1981, c. 1075, p. 4133, § 19, operative Oct. 1, 1982; Stats.2011, c. 526 (A.B.238), § 3, eff. Oct. 7, 2011.)*

Research References

Rutter, Cal. Practice Guide: Enforcing Judgments/Debts Ch. 3-A, A. Evaluating the Claim.

Rutter, Cal. Practice Guide: Enforcing Judgments/Debts Gen. Matls., Highlights.

4 Witkin, California Summary 10th Sales § 256, (S 256) Violation of Contractual Requirements or Finance Provisions.

4 Witkin, California Summary 10th Sales § 257, (S 257) Violation of Provisions for Prepayment of Balance.

§ 2983.2. Disposition after repossession or surrender; notice of intent; service prerequisite to liability for delinquency; contents; accounting of disposition to person liable on contract; surplus; disposition; application of section

(a) Except where the motor vehicle has been seized as described in paragraph (6) of subdivision (b) of Section 2983.3, any provision in any conditional sale contract for the sale of a motor vehicle to the contrary notwithstanding, at least 15 days' written notice of intent to dispose of a repossessed or surrendered motor vehicle shall be given to all persons liable on the contract. The notice shall be personally served or shall be sent by certified mail, return receipt requested, or first-class mail, postage prepaid, directed to the last known address of the persons liable on the contract. If those persons are married to each other, and, according to the most recent records of the seller or holder of the contract, reside at the same address, one notice addressed to both persons at that address is sufficient. Except as otherwise provided in Section 2983.8, those persons shall be liable for any deficiency after disposition of the repossessed or surrendered motor vehicle only if the notice prescribed by this section is given within 60 days of repossession or surrender and does all of the following:

(1) Sets forth that those persons shall have a right to redeem the motor vehicle by paying in full the indebtedness evidenced by the contract until the expiration of 15 days from the date of giving or mailing the notice and provides an itemization of the contract balance and of any delinquency, collection or repossession costs and fees and sets forth the computation or estimate of the amount of any credit for unearned finance charges or canceled insurance as of the date of the notice.

(2) States either that there is a conditional right to reinstate the contract until the expiration of 15 days from the date of giving or mailing the notice and all the conditions precedent thereto or that there is no right of reinstatement and provides a statement of reasons therefor.

(3) States that, upon written request, the seller or holder shall extend for an additional 10 days the redemption period or, if entitled to the conditional right of reinstatement, both the redemption and reinstatement periods. The seller or holder shall provide the proper form for applying for the extensions with the substance of the form being limited to the extension request, spaces for the requesting party to sign and date the form, and instructions that it must be personally served or sent by certified or registered mail, return receipt requested, to a person or office and address designated by the seller or holder and received before the expiration of the initial redemption and reinstatement periods.

(4) Discloses the place at which the motor vehicle will be returned to those persons upon redemption or reinstatement.

(5) Designates the name and address of the person or office to whom payment shall be made.

(6) States the seller's or holder's intent to dispose of the motor vehicle upon the expiration of 15 days from the date of giving or mailing the notice, or if by mail and either the place of deposit in the mail or the place of address is outside of this state, the period shall be 20 days instead of 15 days, and further, that upon written request to extend the redemption period and any applicable reinstatement period for 10 days, the seller or holder shall without further notice extend the period accordingly.

(7) Informs those persons that upon written request, the seller or holder will furnish a written accounting regarding the disposition of the motor vehicle as provided for in subdivision

(b). The seller or holder shall advise them that this request must be personally served or sent first-class mail, postage prepaid, or certified mail, return receipt requested, to a person or office and address designated by the seller or holder.

(8) Includes notice, in at least 10–point bold type if the notice is printed, reading as follows: "NOTICE. YOU MAY BE SUBJECT TO SUIT AND LIABILITY IF THE AMOUNT OBTAINED UPON DISPOSITION OF THE VEHICLE IS INSUFFICIENT TO PAY THE CONTRACT BALANCE AND ANY OTHER AMOUNTS DUE."

(9) Informs those persons that upon the disposition of the motor vehicle, they will be liable for the deficiency balance plus interest at the contract rate, or at the legal rate of interest pursuant to Section 3289 if there is no contract rate of interest, from the date of disposition of the motor vehicle to the date of entry of judgment.

The notice prescribed by this section shall not affect the discretion of the court to strike out an unconscionable interest rate in the contract for which the notice is required, nor affect the court in its determination of whether the rate is unconscionable.

(b) Unless automatically provided to the buyer within 45 days after the disposition of the motor vehicle, the seller or holder shall provide to any person liable on the contract within 45 days after their written request, if the request is made within one year after the disposition, a written accounting regarding the disposition. The accounting shall itemize:

(1) The gross proceeds of the disposition.

(2) The reasonable and necessary expenses incurred for retaking, holding, preparing for and conducting the sale and to the extent provided for in the agreement and not prohibited by law, reasonable attorney fees and legal expenses incurred by the seller or holder in retaking the motor vehicle from any person not a party to the contract.

(3) The satisfaction of indebtedness secured by any subordinate lien or encumbrance on the motor vehicle if written notification of demand therefor is received before distribution of the proceeds is completed. If requested by the seller or holder, the holder of a subordinate lien or encumbrance must seasonably furnish reasonable proof of its interest, and unless it does so, the seller or holder need not comply with its demand.

(c) In all sales which result in a surplus, the seller or holder shall furnish an accounting as provided in subdivision (b) whether or not requested by the buyer. Any surplus shall be returned to the buyer within 45 days after the sale is conducted.

(d) This section shall not apply to a loan made by a lender licensed under Division 9 (commencing with Section 22000) or Division 10 (commencing with Section 24000) of the Financial Code. *(Added by Stats.1977, c. 777, p. 2413, § 3, eff. Sept. 13, 1977, operative Jan. 1, 1978. Amended by Stats.1985, c. 226, § 2; Stats.1987, c. 448, § 4; Stats.1988, c. 1092, § 3; Stats.1996, c. 124 (A.B.3470), § 9; Stats.1996, c. 313 (S.B.1639), § 1.)*

Research References

Rutter, Cal. Practice Guide: Enforcing Judgments/Debts Ch. 3-A, A. Evaluating the Claim.
Rutter, Cal. Practice Guide: Enforcing Judgments/Debts Ch. 3-B, B. Collection Without Suit.
1 Witkin Cal. Summ. 10th Contracts § 124, (S 124) of Translation.
13 Witkin, California Summary 10th Personal Property § 194, (S 194) Regulatory Provisions.
4 Witkin, California Summary 10th Sales § 250, (S 250) Notice of Intent to Sell.
4 Witkin, California Summary 10th Sales § 252, in General.

4 Witkin, California Summary 10th Sales § 253, Exceptions: Mobilehome or Motor Vehicle.

§ 2983.3. Default; prerequisite to acceleration of maturity; repossession or surrender; right of reinstatement by person liable on contract; exceptions; methods; right to deficiency; abrogation; application of section

(a) In the absence of default in the performance of any of the buyer's obligations under the contract, the seller or holder may not accelerate the maturity of any part or all of the amount due thereunder or repossess the motor vehicle.

(b) If after default by the buyer, the seller or holder repossesses or voluntarily accepts surrender of the motor vehicle, any person liable on the contract shall have a right to reinstate the contract and the seller or holder shall not accelerate the maturity of any part or all of the contract prior to expiration of the right to reinstate, unless the seller or holder reasonably and in good faith determines that any of the following has occurred:

(1) The buyer or any other person liable on the contract by omission or commission intentionally provided false or misleading information of material importance on his or her credit application.

(2) The buyer, any other person liable on the contract, or any permissive user in possession of the motor vehicle, in order to avoid repossession has concealed the motor vehicle or removed it from the state.

(3) The buyer, any other person liable on the contract, or any permissive user in possession of the motor vehicle, has committed or threatens to commit acts of destruction, or has failed to take care of the motor vehicle in a reasonable manner, so that the motor vehicle has become substantially impaired in value, or the buyer, any other person liable on the contract, or any nonoccasional permissive user in possession of the motor vehicle has failed to take care of the motor vehicle in a reasonable manner, so that the motor vehicle may become substantially impaired in value.

(4) The buyer or any other person liable on the contract has committed, attempted to commit, or threatened to commit criminal acts of violence or bodily harm against an agent, employee, or officer of the seller or holder in connection with the seller's or holder's repossession of or attempt to repossess the motor vehicle.

(5) The buyer has knowingly used the motor vehicle, or has knowingly permitted it to be used, in connection with the commission of a criminal offense, other than an infraction, as a consequence of which the motor vehicle has been seized by a federal, state, or local agency or authority pursuant to federal, state, or local law.

(6) The motor vehicle has been seized by a federal, state, or local public agency or authority pursuant to (A) Section 1324 of Title 8 of the United States Code or Part 274 of Title 8 of the Code of Federal Regulations, (B) Section 881 of Title 21 of the United States Code or Part 9 of Title 28 of the Code of Federal Regulations, or (C) other federal, state, or local law, including regulations, and, pursuant to that other law, the seizing authority, as a precondition to the return of the motor vehicle to the seller or holder, prohibits the return of the motor vehicle to the buyer or other person liable on the contract or any third person claiming the motor vehicle by or through them or otherwise effects or requires the termination of the property rights in the motor vehicle of the buyer or other person liable on the contract or claimants by or through them.

(c) Exercise of the right to reinstate the contract shall be limited to once in any 12–month period and twice during the term of the contract.

(d) The provisions of this subdivision cover the method by which a contract shall be reinstated with respect to curing events of default which were a ground for repossession or occurred subsequent to repossession:

(1) Where the default is the result of the buyer's failure to make any payment due under the contract, the buyer or any other person liable on the contract shall make the defaulted payments and pay any applicable delinquency charges.

(2) Where the default is the result of the buyer's failure to keep and maintain the motor vehicle free from all encumbrances and liens of every kind, the buyer or any other person liable on the contract shall either satisfy all encumbrances and liens or, in the event the seller or holder satisfies the encumbrances and liens, the buyer or any other person liable on the contract shall reimburse the seller or holder for all reasonable costs and expenses incurred therefor.

(3) Where the default is the result of the buyer's failure to keep and maintain insurance on the motor vehicle, the buyer or any other person liable on the contract shall either obtain the insurance or, in the event the seller or holder has obtained the insurance, the buyer or any other person liable on the contract shall reimburse the seller or holder for premiums paid and all reasonable costs and expenses, including, but not limited to, any finance charge in connection with the premiums permitted by Section 2982.8, incurred therefor.

(4) Where the default is the result of the buyer's failure to perform any other obligation under the contract, unless the seller or holder has made a good faith determination that the default is so substantial as to be incurable, the buyer or any other person liable on the contract shall either cure the default or, if the seller or holder has performed the obligation, reimburse the seller or holder for all reasonable costs and expenses incurred in connection therewith.

(5) Additionally, the buyer or any other person liable on the contract shall, in all cases, reimburse the seller or holder for all reasonable and necessary collection and repossession costs and fees incurred, including attorney's fees and legal expenses expended in retaking and holding the vehicle.

(e) If the seller or holder denies the right to reinstatement under subdivision (b) or paragraph (4) of subdivision (d), the seller or holder shall have the burden of proof that the denial was justified in that it was reasonable and made in good faith. If the seller or holder fails to sustain the burden of proof, the seller or holder shall not be entitled to a deficiency, but it shall not be presumed that the buyer is entitled to damages by reason of the failure of the seller or holder to sustain the burden of proof.

(f) This section shall not apply to a loan made by a lender licensed under Division 9 (commencing with Section 22000) or Division 10 (commencing with Section 24000) of the Financial Code. *(Added by Stats.1961, c. 1626, p. 3539, § 4, eff. Jan. 1, 1962. Amended by Stats.1976, c. 1265, p. 5603, § 4; Stats.1985, c. 226, § 3; Stats.1986, c. 1236, § 1; Stats.1987, c. 448, § 5.)*

Research References

4 Witkin, California Summary 10th Sales § 252, in General.
4 Witkin, California Summary 10th Sales § 254, Prohibited Terms or Acts.

§ 2983.35. Cosigners; notice of delinquency; service; application of section

(a) If a creditor has requested a cosigner as a condition of granting credit to any person for the purpose of acquisition of a motor vehicle, the creditor or holder shall give the cosigner a written notice of delinquency prior to the repossession of the motor vehicle if the motor vehicle is to be repossessed pursuant to the motor vehicle credit agreement. The written notice of delinquency shall be personally served or shall be sent by certified mail, return receipt requested, or first-class mail, postage prepaid, directed to the last known address of the cosigner. If the last known address of the buyer and the cosigner are the same, a single written notice of delinquency given to both the borrower and cosigner prior to repossession satisfies the cosigner notice requirement of this section.

(b) A creditor or holder who fails to comply with this section may not recover any costs associated with the repossession of the vehicle from the cosigner.

(c) This section applies to any motor vehicle credit agreement, notwithstanding Section 2982.5.

(d) The following definitions govern the construction of this section.

(1) "Cosigner" means a buyer who executes a motor vehicle credit agreement but does not in fact receive possession of the motor vehicle that is the subject of the agreement.

(2) "Creditor" means a seller or lender described in paragraph (4).

(3) "Holder" means any other person who is entitled to enforce the motor vehicle credit agreement.

(4) "Motor vehicle credit agreement" means any conditional sales contract as defined in Section 2981 and any contract or agreement in which a lender gives value to enable a purchaser to acquire a motor vehicle and in which the lender obtains a security interest in the motor vehicle. *(Added by Stats.1996, c. 313 (S.B.1639), § 2.)*

Research References

Rutter, Cal. Practice Guide: Enforcing Judgments/Debts Ch. 3-A, A. Evaluating the Claim.
4 Witkin, California Summary 10th Sales § 251, (S 251) Notice to Cosigner.

§ 2983.37. Buy-here-pay-here dealer; prohibited actions after sale of vehicle; violations

(a) After a sale of a vehicle under this chapter, a buy-here-pay-here dealer, as defined in Section 241 of the Vehicle Code, shall not do any of the following:

(1) Utilize electronic tracking technology to obtain or record the location of the vehicle, unless the buyer is expressly made aware of the existence and use of the tracking technology by the buy-here-pay-here dealer, the buyer's written consent is obtained, and either subparagraph (A) or (B), or both, apply:

(A) The electronic tracking technology is used solely to verify and maintain the operational status of the tracking technology, to repossess the vehicle, or to locate the vehicle to service the loan or keep the loan current.

(B) The electronic tracking technology is used solely for any optional service to the buyer and both of the following conditions are met:

(i) The agreement to utilize electronic tracking technology for the optional service is separate from the purchase and sale agreement, is not a condition of the purchase or sale agreement for the vehicle, and is executed after the completion of the purchase or sale agreement for the vehicle.

(ii) The buyer is permitted to cancel the optional service at any point in the future without affecting the sale of the vehicle, and is informed of his or her ability to do so.

(2) Disable the vehicle by using starter interrupt technology, unless the buy-here-pay-here dealer complies with all of the following provisions:

(A) Notifies the buyer in writing at the time of the sale that the vehicle is equipped with starter interrupt technology, which the buy-here-pay-here dealer can use to shut down the vehicle remotely.

(B) The written disclosure provided to the buyer at the time of sale informs the buyer that a warning will be provided no less than 48 hours before the use of the starter interrupt technology to shut down the vehicle remotely and discloses the manner and method in which that warning will occur. The dealer shall offer the buyer a choice of warning methods, including warning from the device, telephone call, email, or text message, if available, provided that the warning method does not violate applicable state or federal law.

(C) In the event of an emergency, the buyer will be provided with the ability to start a dealer-disabled vehicle for no less than 24 hours after the vehicle's initial disablement.

(b) A buy-here-pay-here dealer shall not require the buyer to make payments to the seller in person. For purposes of this subdivision, "payments" does not include the downpayment. If the buyer tenders timely payment of a deferred downpayment, the dealer shall not repossess the vehicle or impose any other charge or penalty on the grounds that the payment was not made in person.

(c) A violation of this section is a misdemeanor punishable by a fine not exceeding one thousand dollars ($1,000). *(Added by Stats.2012, c. 740 (A.B.1447), § 3.)*

§ 2983.4. Prevailing party's right to attorney's fees and costs

Reasonable attorney's fees and costs shall be awarded to the prevailing party in any action on a contract or purchase order subject to the provisions of this chapter regardless of whether the action is instituted by the seller, holder or buyer. Where the defendant alleges in his answer that he tendered to the plaintiff the full amount to which he was entitled, and thereupon deposits in court, for the plaintiff, the amount so tendered, and the allegation is found to be true, then the defendant is deemed to be a prevailing party within the meaning of this section. *(Added by Stats.1961, c. 1626, p. 3539, § 4, eff. Jan. 1, 1962. Amended by Stats.1976, c. 1285, p. 5736, § 5.)*

Research References

Rutter, Cal. Practice Guide: Enforcing Judgments/Debts Ch. 3-C, C. Prelawsuit Considerations.
7 Witkin Cal. Proc. 5th Judgment § 180, Action Where No Contract was Formed.
7 Witkin Cal. Proc. 5th Judgment § 204, (S 204) Distinction: Where Prevailing Party's Right to Fees Arises Under Another Statute.
7 Witkin Cal. Proc. 5th Judgment § 224, (S 224) Consumer Protection Actions.
4 Witkin, California Summary 10th Sales § 260, (S 260) Venue, Attorneys' Fees, and Costs.

§ 2983.5. Assignment of sellers rights; recourse

(a) An assignee of the seller's right is subject to all equities and defenses of the buyer against the seller, notwithstanding an agreement to the contrary, but the assignee's liability may not exceed the amount of the debt owing to the assignee at the time of the assignment.

(b) The assignee shall have recourse against the seller to the extent of any liability incurred by the assignee pursuant to this section regardless of whether the assignment was with or without recourse. *(Added by Stats.1961, c. 1626, p. 3539, § 4, eff. Jan. 1, 1962. Amended by Stats.1965, c. 327, p. 1436, § 1; Stats.1971, c. 999, p. 1917, § 2; Stats.1975, c. 66, p. 129, § 2.)*

Research References

Rutter, Cal. Practice Guide: Enforcing Judgments/Debts Ch. 3-A, A. Evaluating the Claim.
13 Witkin, California Summary 10th Personal Property § 194, (S 194) Regulatory Provisions.

4 Witkin, California Summary 10th Sales § 247, (S 247) Assignment by Seller.
4 Witkin, California Summary 10th Sales § 281, (S 281) Assignment by Seller.

§ 2983.6. Violations; offense

Any person who shall willfully violate any provision of this chapter shall be guilty of a misdemeanor. *(Added by Stats.1968, c. 1338, p. 2558, § 3.)*

Research References

Rutter, Cal. Practice Guide: Enforcing Judgments/Debts Ch. 3-A, A. Evaluating the Claim.
4 Witkin, California Summary 10th Sales § 256, (S 256) Violation of Contractual Requirements or Finance Provisions.
4 Witkin, California Summary 10th Sales § 257, (S 257) Violation of Provisions for Prepayment of Balance.

§ 2983.7. Prohibition of certain provisions

No conditional sale contract shall contain any provision by which:

(a) The buyer agrees not to assert against the seller a claim or defense arising out of the sale or agrees not to assert against an assignee such a claim or defense.

(b) A power of attorney is given to confess judgment in this state, or an assignment of wages is given; provided, that nothing herein contained shall prohibit the giving of an assignment of wages contained in a separate instrument pursuant to Section 300 of the Labor Code.

(c) The buyer waives any right of action against the seller or holder of the contract or other person acting on his behalf, for any illegal act committed in the collection of payments under the contract or in the repossession of the motor vehicle.

(d) The buyer executes a power of attorney appointing the seller or holder of the contract, or other person acting on his behalf, as the buyer's agent in the collection of payments under the contract or in the repossession of the motor vehicle.

(e) The buyer relieves the seller from liability for any legal remedies which the buyer may have against the seller under the contract or any separate instrument executed in connection therewith.

(f) The seller or holder of the contract is given the right to commence action on a contract under the provisions of this chapter in a county other than the county in which the contract was in fact signed by the buyer, the county in which the buyer resides at the commencement of the action, the county in which the buyer resided at the time the contract was entered into, or in the county in which the motor vehicle purchased pursuant to such contract is permanently garaged. *(Added by Stats.1968, c. 1288, p. 2428, § 1.)*

Research References

3 Witkin Cal. Proc. 5th Actions § 786, (S 786) Distinctions and Exceptions.
3 Witkin Cal. Proc. 5th Actions § 845, Actions on Installment Contracts.
4 Witkin, California Summary 10th Sales § 254, Prohibited Terms or Acts.
4 Witkin, California Summary 10th Sales § 260, (S 260) Venue, Attorneys' Fees, and Costs.

§ 2983.8. Deficiency judgment on conditional sale contract for mobilehome or motor vehicle

Notwithstanding Section 2983.2 or any other provision of law, no deficiency judgment shall lie in any event in any of the following instances:

(a) After any sale of any mobilehome for which a permit is required pursuant to Section 35780 or 35790 of the Vehicle Code for failure of the purchaser to complete his or her conditional sale contract given to the seller to secure payment of the balance of the purchase price of such mobilehome. The provisions of this subdivision shall not apply in the event there is substantial damage to the mobilehome other than wear and tear from normal usage. This subdivision shall apply only to contracts entered into on or after the effective date of the act that enacted this subdivision and before July 1, 1981.

(b) After any sale or other disposition of a motor vehicle unless the court has determined that the sale or other disposition was in conformity with the provisions of this chapter and the relevant provisions of Division 9 (commencing with Section 9101) of the Commercial Code, including Sections 9610, 9611, 9612, 9613, 9614, 9615, and 9626. The determination may be made upon an affidavit unless the court requires a hearing in the particular case. *(Added by Stats.1972, c. 1001, p. 1829, § 3. Amended by Stats.1980, c. 1149, p. 3738, § 10; Stats.1984, c. 1376, § 1; Stats.1999, c. 991 (S.B.45), § 8, operative July 1, 2001.)*

Research References

Rutter, Cal. Practice Guide: Enforcing Judgments/Debts Ch. 3-A, A. Evaluating the Claim.

Miller and Starr California Real Estate § 31:68, Default; Nonjudicial Remedies.

4 Witkin, California Summary 10th Sales § 253, Exceptions: Mobilehome or Motor Vehicle.

§ 2984.   Correction of contract to comply with chapter

Any failure to comply with any provision of this chapter (commencing with Section 2981) may be corrected by the holder, provided, however, that a willful violation may not be corrected unless it is a violation appearing on the face of the contract and is corrected within 30 days of the execution of the contract or within 20 days of its sale, assignment or pledge, whichever is later, provided that the 20-day period shall commence with the initial sale, assignment or pledge of the contract, and provided that any other violation appearing on the face of the contract may be corrected only within such time periods. A correction which will increase the amount of the contract balance or the amount of any installment as such amounts appear on the conditional sale contract shall not be effective unless the buyer concurs in writing to the correction. If notified in writing by the buyer of such a failure to comply with any provision of this chapter, the correction shall be made within 10 days of notice. Where any provision of a conditional sale contract fails to comply with any provision of this chapter, the correction shall be made by mailing or delivering a corrected copy of the contract to the buyer. Any amount improperly collected by the holder from the buyer shall be credited against the indebtedness evidenced by the contract or returned to the buyer. A violation corrected as provided in this section shall not be the basis of any recovery by the buyer or affect the enforceability of the contract by the holder and shall not be deemed to be a substantive change in the agreement of the parties. *(Added by Stats.1961, c. 1626, p. 3539, § 4, eff. Jan. 1, 1962. Amended by Stats.1963, c. 838, p. 2037, § 1.)*

Research References

Rutter, Cal. Practice Guide: Enforcing Judgments/Debts Ch. 3-A, A. Evaluating the Claim.

4 Witkin, California Summary 10th Sales § 256, (S 256) Violation of Contractual Requirements or Finance Provisions.

4 Witkin, California Summary 10th Sales § 259, (S 259) Correction.

§ 2984.1.   Contract provision regarding insurance coverage

Every conditional sale contract shall contain a statement in contrasting red print in at least 8–point bold type which shall satisfy the requirements of Section 5604 of the Vehicle Code and be signed or initialed by the buyer, as follows:

THE MINIMUM PUBLIC LIABILITY INSURANCE LIMITS PROVIDED IN LAW MUST BE MET BY EVERY PERSON WHO PURCHASES A VEHICLE. IF YOU ARE UNSURE WHETHER OR NOT YOUR CURRENT INSURANCE POLICY WILL COVER YOUR NEWLY ACQUIRED VEHICLE IN THE EVENT OF AN ACCIDENT, YOU SHOULD CONTACT YOUR INSURANCE AGENT.

WARNING:

YOUR PRESENT POLICY MAY NOT COVER COLLISION DAMAGE OR MAY NOT PROVIDE FOR FULL REPLACEMENT COSTS FOR THE VEHICLE BEING PURCHASED. IF YOU DO NOT HAVE FULL COVERAGE, SUPPLEMENTAL COVERAGE FOR COLLISION DAMAGE MAY BE AVAILABLE TO YOU THROUGH YOUR INSURANCE AGENT OR THROUGH THE SELLING DEALER. HOWEVER, UNLESS OTHERWISE SPECIFIED, THE COVERAGE YOU OBTAIN THROUGH THE DEALER PROTECTS ONLY THE DEALER, USUALLY UP TO THE AMOUNT OF THE UNPAID BALANCE REMAINING AFTER THE VEHICLE HAS BEEN REPOSSESSED AND SOLD.

FOR ADVICE ON FULL COVERAGE THAT WILL PROTECT YOU IN THE EVENT OF LOSS OR DAMAGE TO YOUR VEHICLE, YOU SHOULD CONTACT YOUR INSURANCE AGENT.

THE BUYER SHALL SIGN TO ACKNOWLEDGE THAT HE/SHE UNDERSTANDS THESE PUBLIC LIABILITY TERMS AND CONDITIONS.

S/S _____.

No person shall print for use as a sales contract form, any form which does not comply with this section. *(Added by Stats.1961, c. 1626, p. 3540, § 4, eff. Jan. 1, 1962. Amended by Stats.1965, c. 666, p. 2042, § 1; Stats.1974, c. 577, p. 1396, § 1; Stats.1988, c. 177, § 1.)*

Research References

1 Witkin Cal. Summ. 10th Contracts § 545, (S 545) Residential Property: in General.

13 Witkin, California Summary 10th Personal Property § 194, (S 194) Regulatory Provisions.

4 Witkin, California Summary 10th Sales § 243, Warning Notices to Buyers.

§ 2984.2.   Provision for title to or lien upon other property prohibited; exceptions

(a) No conditional sale contract, and no agreement between a seller and a buyer made in connection with a conditional sale contract, may provide for the inclusion of title to or a lien upon any property other than the following:

(1) The motor vehicle which is the subject matter of the sale, including any replacement of that motor vehicle, or accessories, accessions, or replacement of those accessories or accessions, or proceeds thereof.

(2) The proceeds of any insurance policies covering the motor vehicle which are required by the seller or the returned premiums of any such policies if the premiums for such policies are included in the amount financed.

(3) The proceeds of any credit insurance policies which the buyer purchases in connection with the motor vehicle conditional sale contract or the returned premiums of any such policies if the premiums for such policies are included in the amount financed.

(4) The proceeds and returned price of any service contract if the cost of such contract is included in the amount financed.

(b) Subdivision (a) shall not apply to any agreement which meets the requirements of subdivision (b) of Section 2982.5 and otherwise complies with this chapter, nor, with respect to a mobilehome sold prior to July 1, 1981, to any agreement whereby a security interest is taken in real property on which the mobilehome is installed on a foundation system pursuant to Section 18551 of the Health and Safety Code.

(c) A provision in violation of this section shall be void. *(Added by Stats.1980, c. 1380, p. 5040, § 26, eff. Oct. 1, 1980. Amended by Stats.1981, c. 134, p. 912, § 6, eff. July 1, 1981, operative July 1, 1981; Stats.1981, c. 1075, p. 4133, § 20, operative Oct. 1, 1982; Stats.1987, c. 1043, § 1.)*

Research References

Miller and Starr California Real Estate § 10:14, Liens Securing Illegal Obligations.

13 Witkin, California Summary 10th Personal Property § 194, (S 194) Regulatory Provisions.

4 Witkin, California Summary 10th Sales § 254, Prohibited Terms or Acts.

§ 2984.3. Buyer's acknowledgment of delivery of copy of contract; presumptions

Any acknowledgment by the buyer of delivery of a copy of a conditional sale contract or purchase order and any vehicle purchase proposal and any credit statement that the seller has required or requested the buyer to sign, and that he or she has signed, during the contract negotiations, shall be printed or written in size equal to at least 10-point boldface type and, if contained in the contract, shall appear directly above the space reserved for the buyer's signature or adjacent to any other notices required by law to be placed immediately above the signature space. The buyer's written acknowledgment, conforming to the requirements of this section, of delivery of a completely filled-in copy of the contract, and a copy of the other documents shall be a rebuttable presumption of delivery in any action or proceeding by or against a third party without knowledge to the contrary when he or she acquired his or her interest in the contract. If the third party furnishes the buyer a copy of the documents, or a notice containing the disclosures identified in subdivision (a) of Section 2982, and stating that the buyer shall notify the third party in writing within 30 days if a copy of the documents was not furnished, and that notification is not given, it shall be conclusively presumed in favor of the third party that copies of the documents were furnished as required by this chapter. *(Added by Stats.1961, c. 1626, p. 3540, § 4, eff. Jan. 1, 1962. Amended by Stats.1970, c. 1003, p. 1805, § 5; Stats. 1979, c. 805, p. 2795, § 25; Stats.1980, c. 1149, p. 3739, § 12; Stats.1993, c. 1092 (A.B.431), § 3, operative July 1, 1994; Stats. 1994, c. 146 (A.B.3601), § 15.)*

Research References

1 Witkin Cal. Summ. 10th Contracts § 545, (S 545) Residential Property: in General.

13 Witkin, California Summary 10th Personal Property § 194, (S 194) Regulatory Provisions.

4 Witkin, California Summary 10th Sales § 244, (S 244) Copy to Buyer and Retention by Seller.

§ 2984.4. Actions on contract or purchase order; venue

(a) An action on a contract or purchase order under this chapter shall be tried in the superior court in the county where the contract or purchase order was in fact signed by the buyer, where the buyer resided at the time the contract or purchase order was entered into, where the buyer resides at the commencement of the action, or where the motor vehicle purchased pursuant to the contract or purchase order is permanently garaged.

In any action involving multiple claims, or causes of action, venue shall lie in those courts if there is at least one claim or cause of action arising from a contract subject to this chapter.

(b) In the superior court designated as the proper court in subdivision (a), the proper court location for trial of an action under this chapter is the location where the court tries that type of action that is nearest or most accessible to where the contract, conditional sale contract, or purchase order was in fact signed by the buyer, where the buyer resided at the time the contract, conditional sale contract, or purchase order was entered into, where the buyer resides at the commencement of the action, or where the motor vehicle purchased pursuant to the contract is permanently garaged. Otherwise, any location of the superior court designated as the proper superior court in subdivision (a) is the proper court location for the trial of the action. The court may specify by local rule the nearest or most accessible court location where the court tries that type of case.

(c) In any action subject to this section, concurrently with the filing of the complaint, the plaintiff shall file an affidavit stating facts showing that the action has been commenced in a superior court and court location described in this section as a proper place for the trial of the action. Those facts may be stated in a verified complaint and shall not be stated on information or belief. When that affidavit is filed with the complaint, a copy shall be served with the summons. If a plaintiff fails to file the affidavit or state facts in a verified complaint required by this section, no further proceedings may occur, but the court shall, upon its own motion or upon motion of any party, dismiss the action without prejudice. The court may, on terms that are just, permit the affidavit to be filed subsequent to the filing of the complaint and a copy of the affidavit shall be served on the defendant. The time to answer or otherwise plead shall date from that service. *(Added by Stats.1969, c. 724, p. 1455, § 1. Amended by Stats.1970, c. 725, p. 1325, § 2; Stats.1971, c. 1529, p. 3021, § 2; Stats.1974, c. 1516, p. 3335, § 3, operative Jan. 1, 1977; Stats.1976, c. 1285, p. 5736, § 6; Stats.1998, c. 931 (S.B.2139), § 17, eff. Sept. 28, 1998; Stats.2002, c. 806 (A.B. 3027), § 2.)*

Law Revision Commission Comments

The last two paragraphs of Section 2984.4 are deleted. This section is applicable to actions arising out of consumer transactions. See Civil Code § 2981. The changes made in the attachment title have made these special provisions unnecessary since the remedy of prejudgment attachment is no longer available in such actions. See Code Civ.Proc. § 483.010. See also Comment to Section 1812. [11 Cal.L.Rev.Comm. Reports 701 (1973)].

Section 2984.4 is amended to reflect elimination of the justice court. Cal. Const. art. VI, §§ 1, 5(b). In a county in which there is no municipal court, the superior court has jurisdiction of matters that would be within the subject matter jurisdiction of the municipal court. Cal. Const. art. VI, 10 (superior court jurisdiction); Code Civ. Proc. §§ 85, 85.1 (limited civil cases). [28 Cal.L.Rev.Comm. Reports 51 (1998)].

Research References

Rutter, Cal. Practice Guide: Civ. Pro. Before Trial Ch. 3-D, D. Venue.

Rutter, Cal. Practice Guide: Civ. Pro. Before Trial Ch. 5-G, G. Relief from Default.

Rutter, Cal. Practice Guide: Civ. Pro. Before Trial Ch. 6-B, B. Complaints.

Rutter, Cal. Practice Guide: Enforcing Judgments/Debts Ch. 3-C, C. Prelawsuit Considerations.

Rutter, Cal. Practice Guide: Enforcing Judgments/Debts Ch. 4-B, B. Claim and Delivery.

3 Witkin Cal. Proc. 5th Actions § 845, Actions on Installment Contracts.

4 Witkin Cal. Proc. 5th Pleading § 472, Limited Civil Cases.

6 Witkin Cal. Proc. 5th Proceedings Without Trial § 161, (S 161) Application and Affidavit.

4 Witkin, California Summary 10th Sales § 260, (S 260) Venue, Attorneys' Fees, and Costs.

§ 2984.5. Conditional sales contracts; maintenance of documents by seller

(a) A seller shall maintain the following documents for at least seven years or the length of the conditional sales contract, whichever is longer:

(1) A copy of each buyer's conditional sales contract.

(2) Any documents relied upon by the seller to determine a buyer's creditworthiness, including, but not limited to, any consumer credit report, as defined in Section 1785.3, or any other document containing a buyer's credit score, as defined in Section 1785.15.1.

(3) If the conditional sales contract is sold, assigned, or otherwise transferred, a copy of the terms of that sale, assignment, or transfer.

(b) A seller that unlawfully fails to comply with a court order to produce the documents described in subdivision (a) shall be liable in an action brought by the Attorney General for a civil penalty of five thousand dollars ($5,000) per violation. The penalties provided by this section are in addition to all rights and remedies that are otherwise available under law. *(Added by Stats.2003, c. 59 (S.B.508), § 1.)*

Research References

4 Witkin, California Summary 10th Sales § 244, (S 244) Copy to Buyer and Retention by Seller.

§ 2984.6. Repossession of vehicle connected with incident of violence notice; notice to subsequent assignee

A holder of a conditional sales contract, purchase order, or security interest, or the agent of a holder, who has received a notice pursuant to Section 7507.6 of the Business and Professions Code, shall not make a subsequent assignment to skip trace, locate, or repossess the vehicle without simultaneously, and in the same manner by which the assignment is given, advising the assignee of the assignment of the information contained in the notice. As used in this section, "assignment" has the same meaning set forth in Section 7500.1 of the Business and Professions Code. *(Added by Stats.2007, c. 192 (S.B.659), § 4, eff. Sept. 7, 2007.)*

CHAPTER 2C. REAL PROPERTY SALES CONTRACTS

§ 2985. Definition

(a) A real property sales contract is an agreement in which one party agrees to convey title to real property to another party upon the satisfaction of specified conditions set forth in the contract and that does not require conveyance of title within one year from the date of formation of the contract.

(b) For purposes of this chapter only, a real property sales contract does not include a contract for purchase of an attached residential condominium unit entered into pursuant to a conditional public report issued by the Bureau of Real Estate pursuant to Section 11018.12 of the Business and Professions Code. *(Added by Stats.1961, c. 886, p. 2343, § 30. Amended by Stats.1963, c. 560, p. 1442, § 6; Stats.2006, c. 51 (S.B.504), § 1, eff. June 30, 2006; Stats.2013, c. 352 (A.B.1317), § 53, eff. Sept. 26, 2013, operative July 1, 2013.)*

Research References

California Real Estate Forms (Miller & Starr) § 1:22, Agreement of Purchase and Sale--Multi-Property.

California Real Estate Forms (Miller & Starr) § 1:30, Planned Development Deposit Receipt and Agreement of Sale.

California Real Estate Forms (Miller & Starr) § 1:31, Condominium Deposit Receipt and Agreement of Sale.

California Real Estate Forms (Miller & Starr) § 1:33, Real Estate Purchase Contract and Receipt for Deposit--Income Property.

California Real Estate Forms (Miller & Starr) § 1:34, Installment Land Sale Contract With Power of Sale.

Rutter, Cal. Practice Guide: A.D.R. App. D Form 64, Real Property-Sale-Deposit Receipts, Escrow Instructions, Listing Agreements.

Rutter, Cal. Practice Guide: Real Prop. Transactions Ch. 4-B, B. Interests to be Conveyed.

Rutter, Cal. Practice Guide: Real Prop. Transactions Ch. 4-E, E. Drafting the Purchase and Sale Agreement-Terms and Conditions.

Miller and Starr California Real Estate § 2:14, Statutory Regulation of Installment Sales Contracts.

Miller and Starr California Real Estate § 4:68, Real Property Credit Sales Transactions (Seller Carry-Back Financing) Negotiated by Licensees.

Miller and Starr California Real Estate § 4:72, Sale or Assignment of Secured Obligations.

Miller and Starr California Real Estate § 1:144, Duty of Seller of Real Property to Disclose--Statutory Duty of Disclosure.

Miller and Starr California Real Estate § 1:145, Duty of Seller of Real Property to Disclose--Transfer Disclosure Statement in Residential Sales.

Miller and Starr California Real Estate § 34:42, Comparison of "Marketing" and "Security" Contracts.

Miller and Starr California Real Estate § 10:223, Joinder of Parties.

Miller and Starr California Real Estate § 25C:24, Conditional Public Reports.

Miller and Starr California Real Estate § 25C:37, Installment Sales Contracts (Real Property Sales Contracts).

13 NO. 6 Miller & Starr, California Real Estate Newsalert 1, Using Basura to Make Construction Defect Claims Arbitrable, or Woodside to Send Them to a Referee.

17 NO. 4 Miller & Starr, California Real Estate Newsalert 2, Statutory Update:.

17 NO. 6 Miller & Starr, California Real Estate Newsalert 20, Table of Statutes (Newsalert Vol 17).

12 Witkin, California Summary 10th Real Property § 316, (S 316) Instruments Affecting Title or Possession.

12 Witkin, California Summary 10th Real Property § 485, (S 485) Delivery of Statement.

1 Witkin Cal. Summ. 10th Contracts § 544, (S 544) Scope of Chapter.

4 Witkin, California Summary 10th Security Transactions in Real Property § 24, (S 24) in General.

4 Witkin, California Summary 10th Security Transactions in Real Property § 25, (S 25) Rights of Defaulting Purchaser.

3 Witkin, California Summary 10th Agency and Employment § 66, (S 66) Legislative Response.

§ 2985.1. Transferability

A real property sales contract may not be transferred by the fee owner of the real property unless accompanied by a transfer of the real property which is the subject of the contract, and real property may not be transferred by the fee owner thereof unless accompanied by an assignment of the contract.

Nothing herein shall be deemed to prohibit the assignment or pledge of a real property sales contract, as security or for the purpose of effecting collection thereon, to the holder of a first lien on the real property which is the subject of the contract without a transfer of the real property or the transfer of a fee title in trust without the concurrent assignment of the sales contract. *(Added by Stats.1961, c. 886, p. 2344, § 30, eff. June 28, 1961. Amended by Stats.1963, c. 71, p. 699, § 1.)*

Research References

Miller and Starr California Real Estate § 2:14, Statutory Regulation of Installment Sales Contracts.

Miller and Starr California Real Estate § 4:72, Sale or Assignment of Secured Obligations.

1 Witkin Cal. Summ. 10th Contracts § 717, (S 717) Statutory Prohibition of Assignment.

4 Witkin, California Summary 10th Security Transactions in Real Property § 24, (S 24) in General.

4 Witkin, California Summary 10th Security Transactions in Real Property § 25, (S 25) Rights of Defaulting Purchaser.

§ 2985.2. Encumbering realty sold under unrecorded sales contract in amount exceeding amount due under contract without consent; misdemeanor

Any person, or the assignee of such person, who sells a parcel of land under a sales contract which is not recorded and who thereafter causes an encumbrance or encumbrances not consented to in writing by the parties upon such property in an amount which, together with existing encumbrances thereon exceeds the amount then due under the contract, or under which the aggregate amount of any periodic payments exceeds the periodic payments due on the contract, excluding any pro rata amount for insurance and taxes, shall be guilty of a public offense punishable by a fine not exceeding ten thousand dollars ($10,000), or by imprisonment pursuant to subdivision (h) of Section 1170 of the Penal Code, or in a county jail not exceeding one year, or by both that fine and imprisonment. *(Added by Stats.1963, c. 560, p. 1441, § 3. Amended by Stats.1976, c. 1139, p. 5064, § 7, operative July 1, 1977; Stats.1983, c. 1092, § 69, eff. Sept. 27, 1983, operative Jan. 1, 1984; Stats.2011, c. 15 (A.B.109), § 36, eff. April 4, 2011, operative Oct. 1, 2011.)*

Research References

Miller and Starr California Real Estate § 2:14, Statutory Regulation of Installment Sales Contracts.

Miller and Starr California Real Estate § 25C:37, Installment Sales Contracts (Real Property Sales Contracts).

4 Witkin, California Summary 10th Security Transactions in Real Property § 24, (S 24) in General.

§ 2985.3. Appropriation by seller of payment by buyer when payment by seller on obligation secured by encumbrance on realty due; misdemeanor

Every seller of improved or unimproved real property under a real property sales contract, or his assignee, who knowingly receives an installment payment from the buyer under a real property sales contract at a time when there is then due any payment by the seller, or his assignee, on an obligation secured by an encumbrance on the property subject to the real property sales contract, and who appropriates such payment received from the buyer to a use other than payment of the amount then due on the seller's or assignee's obligation, except to the extent the payment received from the buyer exceeds the amount due from the seller or assignee, is guilty of a public offense punishable by a fine not exceeding ten thousand dollars ($10,-000), or by imprisonment pursuant to subdivision (h) of Section 1170 of the Penal Code, or in a county jail not exceeding one year, or by both that fine and imprisonment. *(Added by Stats.1963, c. 560, p. 1442, § 4. Amended by Stats.1976, c. 1139, p. 5064, § 8, operative July 1, 1977; Stats.1983, c. 1092, § 70, eff. Sept. 27, 1983, operative Jan. 1, 1984; Stats.2011, c. 15 (A.B.109), § 37, eff. April 4, 2011, operative Oct. 1, 2011.)*

Research References

Miller and Starr California Real Estate § 2:14, Statutory Regulation of Installment Sales Contracts.

Miller and Starr California Real Estate § 25C:37, Installment Sales Contracts (Real Property Sales Contracts).

4 Witkin, California Summary 10th Security Transactions in Real Property § 24, (S 24) in General.

§ 2985.4. Holding pro rata payments for insurance and taxes in trust; applicability of section

Every seller of improved or unimproved real property under a real property sales contract who receives pro rata payments for insurance and taxes shall hold these amounts in trust for the purpose designated. These amounts shall not be disbursed for any other purpose without the consent of the payor and any person or corporation holding an encumbrance on the property.

This section shall not apply to a state- or federal-supervised assignee of a seller who as agent for the seller receives and disburses payments. *(Added by Stats.1963, c. 560, p. 1442, § 5.)*

Research References

Miller and Starr California Real Estate § 2:14, Statutory Regulation of Installment Sales Contracts.

Miller and Starr California Real Estate § 25C:37, Installment Sales Contracts (Real Property Sales Contracts).

4 Witkin, California Summary 10th Security Transactions in Real Property § 24, (S 24) in General.

§ 2985.5. Required contents of sales contracts; number of years required to complete payments; basis for tax estimate

Every real property sales contract entered into after January 1, 1966, shall contain a statement of:

(a) The number of years required to complete payment in accordance with the terms of the contract.

(b) The basis upon which the tax estimate is made. *(Added by Stats.1965, c. 1214, p. 3034, § 1.)*

Research References

California Real Estate Forms (Miller & Starr) § 1:34, Installment Land Sale Contract With Power of Sale.

Miller and Starr California Real Estate § 2:14, Statutory Regulation of Installment Sales Contracts.

4 Witkin, California Summary 10th Security Transactions in Real Property § 24, (S 24) in General.

§ 2985.51. Divisions of real property; statement of compliance with Subdivision Map Act; violations; remedies of vendee; misdemeanor

(a) Every real property sales contract entered into on and after January 1, 1978, where the real property that is the subject of such contract resulted from a division of real property occurring on or after January 1, 1978, shall contain or have attached thereto a statement indicating the fact that the division creating the parcel or parcels to be conveyed:

(1) Was made in compliance with the provisions of the Subdivision Map Act, Division 2 (commencing with Section 66410) of Title 7 of the Government Code and local ordinances adopted pursuant thereto, and in such event the statement shall expressly refer to the location, in the records of the county recorder for the county in which the real property is located, of a previously recorded certificate of compliance or conditional certificate of compliance issued pursuant to Section 66499.35 of the Government Code with respect to the real property being sold, or the statement shall describe the real property to be conveyed as an entire lot or parcel by referencing the recorded final or parcel map creating the parcel or parcels to be conveyed and such description shall constitute a certificate of compliance as set forth in subdivision (d) of Section 66499.35 of the Government Code. Provided, however, where reference is made to a recorded parcel map and the approval of such map was conditioned upon the construction of specified offsite and

onsite improvements as a precondition to the issuance of a permit or grant of approval for the development of such parcel and the construction of the improvements has not been completed as of the date of execution of the real property sales contract, then the statement shall expressly set forth all such required offsite and onsite improvements; or

(2) Was exempt from the provisions of the Subdivision Map Act and local ordinances adopted pursuant thereto, and in such event the statement shall expressly set forth the basis for such exemption; or

(3) Was the subject of a waiver of the provisions of the Subdivision Map Act and local ordinances adopted pursuant thereto, and in such event the contract shall have attached thereto a copy of the document issued by the local agency granting the waiver. Provided, however, where the granting of the waiver was conditioned upon the construction of specified offsite and onsite improvements as a precondition to the issuance of a permit or grant of approval for the development of the parcel and the construction of the improvements has not been completed as of the date of execution of the real property sales contract, then such statement shall expressly set forth all such required offsite and onsite improvements; or

(4) Was not subject to the provisions of the Subdivision Map Act and local ordinances adopted pursuant thereto, and in such event the statement shall expressly set forth the basis for the nonapplicability of the Subdivision Map Act to the division.

(b) Every real property sales contract entered into after January 1, 1978, where the real property that is the subject of such contract resulted from a division of real property occurring prior to January 1, 1978, shall:

(1) Contain or have attached thereto a signed statement by the vendor that the parcel or parcels which are the subject of the contract have been created in compliance with, or a waiver has been granted with respect to, the provisions of the Subdivision Map Act, Division 2 (commencing with Section 66410) of Title 7 of the Government Code and local ordinances adopted pursuant thereto, or any prior law regulating the division of land, or, were exempt from or not otherwise subject to any such law at the time of their creation. Provided, however, where the division creating the parcel or parcels being conveyed was by means of a parcel map, or in the event that a waiver of the provisions of the Subdivision Map Act has been granted, and the approval of the parcel map or the granting of the waiver was conditioned upon the construction of specified offsite and onsite improvements as a precondition to the issuance of a permit or grant of approval for the development of such parcel and the construction of the improvements has not been completed as of the date of execution of the real property sales contract, then such contract shall expressly set forth all such required offsite and onsite improvements.

(2) In lieu of the above, the vendor may include in the real property sales contract a description of the real property being conveyed as an entire lot or parcel by referencing the recorded final or parcel map creating the parcel or parcels being conveyed and such description shall constitute a certificate of compliance as set forth in subdivision (d) of Section 66499.35 of the Government Code. Provided, however, where reference is made to a recorded parcel map, or in the event that a waiver of the provisions of the Subdivision Map Act has been granted, and the approval of the parcel map or the granting of the waiver was conditioned upon the construction of specified offsite and onsite improvements as a precondition to the issuance of a permit or grant of approval for the development of such parcel and the construction of the improvements has not been completed as of the date of execution of the real property sales contract, then such contract shall expressly set forth all such required offsite and onsite improvements.

(3) Notwithstanding paragraphs (1) and (2), in the event that the parcel or parcels which are the subject of the real property sales contract were not created in compliance with the provisions of the Subdivision Map Act, Division 2 (commencing with Section 66410) of Title 7 of the Government Code and local ordinances adopted pursuant thereto, or any other prior law regulating the division of land, and were not exempt from, or were otherwise subject to any such law at the time of their creation, the real property sales contract shall contain a statement signed by the vendor and vendee acknowledging such fact. In addition, the vendor shall attach to the real property sales contract a conditional certificate of compliance issued pursuant to Section 66499.35 of the Government Code.

(c) In the event that the parcel or parcels which are the subject of the real property sales contract are found not to have been created in compliance with, or a waiver has not been granted with respect to, the provisions of the Subdivision Map Act, Division 2 (commencing with Section 66410) of Title 7 of the Government Code, or any other prior law regulating the division of land nor to be exempt from, or otherwise subject to such laws and the vendee has reasonably relied upon the statement of such compliance or exemption made by the vendor, or in the event that the vendor has failed to provide the conditional certificate of compliance as required by paragraph (3) of subdivision (b), and the vendor knew or should have known of the fact of such noncompliance, or lack of exemption, or the failure to provide the conditional certificate of compliance, the vendee, or his successor in interest, shall be entitled to: (1) recover from the vendor or his assigns the amount of all costs incurred by the vendee or his successor in interest in complying with all conditions imposed pursuant to Section 66499.35 of the Government Code; or, (2) the real property sales contract, at the sole option of the vendee, or his successor in interest, shall be voidable and in such event the vendee or his successor in interest shall be entitled to damages from the vendor or his assigns. For purposes of this section, damages shall mean all amounts paid under the real estate sales contract with interest thereon at the rate of 9 percent per annum, and in addition thereto a civil penalty in the amount of five hundred dollars ($500) plus attorney's fees and costs. Any action to enforce the rights of a vendee or his successor in interest shall be commenced within one year of the date of discovery of the failure to comply with the provisions of this section.

(d) Any vendor who willfully violates the provisions of subdivision (a) of this section by knowingly providing a vendee with a false statement of compliance with, exemption from, waiver of, or nonapplicability of, the provisions of the Subdivision Map Act, with respect to the real property that is the subject of the real property sales contract, shall be guilty of a misdemeanor punishable by a fine of not to exceed one thousand dollars ($1,000), or imprisonment for not to exceed six months, or both such fine and imprisonment.

(e) For purposes of this section a real property sales contract is an agreement wherein one party agrees to convey title to unimproved real property to another party upon the satisfaction of specified conditions set forth in the contract and which does not require conveyance of title within one year from the date of formation of the contract. Unimproved real property means real property upon which no permanent structure intended for human occupancy or commercial use is located.

(f) The provisions of this section shall not apply to a real property sales contract which, by its terms, requires either a good faith downpayment and a single payment of the balance of the purchase price or a single payment of the purchase price upon completion of the contract, and the provisions of such contract do not require periodic payment of principal or interest. *(Added by Stats.1977, c. 1228, p. 4125, § 1.)*

Research References

California Real Estate Forms (Miller & Starr) § 1:34, Installment Land Sale Contract With Power of Sale.

Miller and Starr California Real Estate § 2:12, Disclosure of Compliance With the Subdivision Map Act.

Miller and Starr California Real Estate § 25:12, Restrictions on the Sale or Improvement of a Divided Parcel Without Act Compliance.

Miller and Starr California Real Estate § 36:11, Fraud.

Miller and Starr California Real Estate § 25C:37, Installment Sales Contracts (Real Property Sales Contracts).

4 Witkin, California Summary 10th Security Transactions in Real Property § 24, (S 24) in General.

§ 2985.6. Prepayment of balance due on real property sales contracts; effect of waiver of provisions

(a) A buyer shall be entitled to prepay all or any part of the balance due on any real property sales contract with respect to the sale of land which has been subdivided into a residential lot or lots which contain a dwelling for not more than four families entered into on or after January 1, 1969; provided, however, that the seller, by an agreement in writing with the buyer, may prohibit prepayment for up to a 12-month period following the sale.

(b) Any waiver by the buyer of the provisions of this section shall be deemed contrary to public policy and shall be unenforceable and void; provided, however, that any such waiver shall in no way affect the validity of the remainder of the contract. *(Added by Stats.1968, c. 437, p. 1041, § 1. Amended by Stats.1969, c. 399, p. 930, § 1; Stats.1978, c. 565, p. 1739, § 1.)*

Research References

Rutter, Cal. Practice Guide: Real Prop. Transactions Ch. 4-B, B. Interests to be Conveyed.

Miller and Starr California Real Estate § 2:14, Statutory Regulation of Installment Sales Contracts.

Miller and Starr California Real Estate § 10:96, Statutory Prohibitions Against Restricting Prepayment.

Miller and Starr California Real Estate § 10:236, Policy Objectives; the "Standard" Transaction.

Miller and Starr California Real Estate § 25C:37, Installment Sales Contracts (Real Property Sales Contracts).

4 Witkin, California Summary 10th Security Transactions in Real Property § 24, (S 24) in General.

CHAPTER 2D.   VEHICLE LEASING ACT

§ 2985.7.   Definitions

(a) "Motor vehicle" means any vehicle required to be registered under the Vehicle Code. Motor vehicle does not include any trailer which is sold in conjunction with a vessel.

(b) "Lessor" includes "bailor" and is a person who is engaged in the business of leasing, offering to lease or arranging the lease of a motor vehicle under a lease contract.

For the purpose of this subdivision, "person" means an individual, partnership, corporation, limited liability company, estate, trust, cooperative, association or any other legal entity.

(c) "Lessee" includes "bailee" and is a natural person who leases, offers to lease or is offered the lease of a motor vehicle under a lease contract.

(d) "Lease contract" means any contract for or in contemplation of the lease or bailment for the use of a motor vehicle, and the purchase of services incidental thereto, by a natural person for a term exceeding four months, primarily for personal, family or household purposes, whether or not it is agreed that the lessee bear the risk of the motor vehicle's depreciation. Lease contract does not include a lease for agricultural, business or commercial purposes, or to a government or governmental agency or instrumentality.

(e) "Regulation M" means any rule, regulation, or interpretation promulgated by the Board of Governors of the Federal Reserve System under the federal Consumer Leasing Act (15 U.S.C. Secs. 1667–1667e), and any interpretation or approval issued by an official or employee of the Federal Reserve System duly authorized by the board to issue such interpretations or approvals.

(f) "Constant yield method" means the following:

(1) In the case of a periodic payment lease, the method of determining the rent charge portion of each base payment in which the rent charge for each computational period is earned in advance by multiplying the constant rate implicit in the lease

contract times the balance subject to rent charge as it declines during the scheduled lease term. At any time during the scheduled term of a periodic payment lease, the balance subject to rent charge is the difference between the adjusted capitalized cost and the sum of (A) all depreciation and other amortized amounts accrued during the preceding computational periods and (B) the first base periodic payment.

(2) In the case of a single payment lease, the method of determining the periodic earning of rent charges in which the rent charge for each computational period is earned in advance by multiplying the constant rate implicit in the lease contract times the balance subject to rent charge as it increases during the scheduled lease term. At any time during the scheduled term of a single payment lease, the balance subject to rent charge is determined by subtracting from the residual value the total rent charge scheduled to be earned over the term of the lease contract and adding to the difference all rent charges accrued during the preceding computational periods.

(3) Periodic rent charge calculations are based on the assumption that the lessor will receive the lease payments on their exact due dates and that the lease does not end before its scheduled termination date. *(Added by Stats.1976, c. 1284, p. 5700, § 2, operative March 23, 1977. Amended by Stats.1984, c. 1114, § 4; Stats.1994, c. 1010 (S.B.2053), § 51; Stats.1997, c. 800 (S.B. 1291), § 3.)*

Research References

Rutter, Cal. Practice Guide: Civil Trials & Evidence Ch. 17-E, E. Attorney Fees as Costs.
Rutter, Cal. Practice Guide: Enforcing Judgments/Debts Ch. 3-A, A. Evaluating the Claim.
Miller and Starr California Real Estate § 10:182, Form and Contents.
1 Witkin Cal. Summ. 10th Contracts § 124, (S 124) of Translation.
13 Witkin, California Summary 10th Personal Property § 187, Applicable Law.
13 Witkin, California Summary 10th Personal Property § 193, (S 193) Nature of Act.
13 Witkin, California Summary 10th Personal Property § 194, (S 194) Regulatory Provisions.

§ 2985.71. Solicitation including statement concerning payments; contents; restriction; violation; liability

(a) Any solicitation to enter into a lease contract that includes any of the following items shall contain the disclosures described in subdivision (b):

(1) The amount of any payment.

(2) A statement of any capitalized cost reduction or other payment required prior to or at consummation or by delivery, if delivery occurs after consummation.

(3) A statement that no capitalized cost reduction or other payment is required prior to or at consummation or by delivery, if delivery occurs after consummation.

(b) A solicitation to enter into a lease contract that includes any item listed in subdivision (a) shall also clearly and conspicuously state all of the following items:

(1) All of the disclosures prescribed by Regulation M set forth in the manner required or permitted by Regulation M, whether or not Regulation M applies to the transaction.

(2) The mileage limit after which mileage charges may accrue and the charge per mile for mileage in excess of the stated mileage limit.

(3) The statement "Plus tax and license" or a substantially similar statement, if amounts due for use tax, license fees, and registration fees are not included in the payments.

(c) No solicitation to aid, promote, or assist directly or indirectly any lease contract may state that a specific lease of any

motor vehicle at specific amounts or terms is available unless the lessor usually and customarily leases or will lease that motor vehicle at those amounts or terms.

(d) A failure to comply with the provisions of this section shall not affect the validity of the leasing contract. No owner or employee of any entity, other than the lessor, that serves as a medium in which a lease solicitation appears or through which a lease solicitation is disseminated, shall be liable under this section. *(Added by Stats.1997, c. 800 (S.B.1291), § 5.)*

Research References

13 Witkin, California Summary 10th Personal Property § 194, (S 194) Regulatory Provisions.

§ 2985.8. Lease contract; requirements; contents

(a) A lease contract shall be in writing, and the print portion of the contract shall be printed in at least 8–point type and shall contain in a single document all of the agreements of the lessor and lessee with respect to the obligations of each party.

(b) At the top of the lease contract, a title that contains the words "LEASE CONTRACT" or "LEASE AGREEMENT" shall appear in at least 12–point boldface type.

(c) A lease contract shall disclose all of the following:

(1) All of the information prescribed by Regulation M set forth in the manner required or permitted by Regulation M, whether or not Regulation M applies to the transaction.

(2) A separate statement labeled "Itemization of Gross Capitalized Cost" that shall appear immediately following or directly adjacent to the disclosures required to be segregated by Regulation M. The Itemization of Gross Capitalized Cost shall include all of the following and shall be circumscribed by a line:

(A) The agreed-upon value of the vehicle as equipped at the time of signing the lease.

(B) The agreed-upon value and a description of each accessory and item of optional equipment the lessor agrees to add to the vehicle after signing the lease.

(C) The premium for each policy of insurance.

(D) The amount charged for each service contract.

(E) Any charge for an optional debt cancellation agreement.

(F) Any outstanding prior credit or lease balance.

(G) An itemization by type and agreed-upon value of each good or service included in the gross capitalized cost other than those items included in the disclosures required in subparagraphs (A) to (F), inclusive.

(3) The vehicle identification number of the leased vehicle.

(4) A brief description of each vehicle or other property being traded in and the agreed-upon value of the vehicle or property if the amount due at the time of signing the lease or upon delivery is paid in whole or in part with a net trade-in allowance or the "Itemization of Gross Capitalized Cost" includes any portion of the outstanding prior credit or lease balance from the trade-in property.

(5) The charge, if any, to be retained by the lessor for document processing authorized pursuant to Section 4456.5 of the Vehicle Code, which may not be represented as a governmental fee.

(6) The charge, if any, to electronically register or transfer the vehicle authorized pursuant to Section 4456.5 of the Vehicle Code, which shall not be represented as a governmental fee.

(d) A lease contract shall contain, in at least 8–point boldface type, above the space provided for the lessee's signature and circumscribed by a line, the following notice: "(1) Do not sign this lease before you read it or if it contains any blank spaces to be filled in; (2) You are entitled to a completely filled in copy of this lease; (3) Warning—Unless a charge is included in this lease for public liability or property damage insurance, payment for that coverage is not provided by this lease."

(e) A lease contract shall contain, in at least 8–point boldface type, on the first page of the contract and circumscribed by a line, the following notice:

"THERE IS NO COOLING OFF PERIOD

California law does not provide for a "cooling off" or other cancellation period for vehicle leases. Therefore, you cannot later cancel this lease simply because you change your mind, decided the vehicle costs too much, or wish you had acquired a different vehicle. You may cancel this lease only with the agreement of the lessor or for legal cause, such as fraud."

(f) A lease contract shall contain, in at least 8–point boldface type, the following notice: "You have the right to return the vehicle, and receive a refund of any payments made if the credit application is not approved, unless nonapproval results from an incomplete application or from incorrect information provided by you."

(g) The lease contract shall be signed by the lessor and lessee, or their authorized representatives, and an exact copy of the fully executed lease contract shall be provided to the lessee at the time of signing.

(h) A motor vehicle shall not be delivered under a lease contract subject to this chapter until the lessor provides to the lessee a fully executed copy of the lease contract.

(i) The lessor shall not obtain the signature of the lessee to a contract when it contains blank spaces to be filled in after it has been signed.

(j) If the lease contract contains a provision that holds the lessee liable for the difference between (1) the adjusted capitalized cost disclosed in the lease contract reduced by the amounts described in subparagraph (A) of paragraph (5) of subdivision (b) of Section 2987 and (2) the settlement proceeds of the lessee's required insurance and deductible in the event of theft or damage to the vehicle that results in a total loss, the lease contract shall contain the following notice in at least 8–point boldface type on the first page of the contract:

"GAP LIABILITY NOTICE

In the event of theft or damage to the vehicle that results in a total loss, there may be a GAP between the amount due upon early termination and the proceeds of your insurance settlement and deductible. THIS LEASE PROVIDES THAT YOU ARE LIABLE FOR THE GAP AMOUNT. Optional coverage for the GAP amount may be offered for an additional price."

(k) This section shall become operative on July 1, 2012. *(Added by Stats.2011, c. 329 (A.B.1215), § 6, operative July 1, 2012.)*

Research References

13 Witkin, California Summary 10th Personal Property § 194, (S 194) Regulatory Provisions.

§ 2985.9. Documents and agreements not required in a lease contract

The following documents and agreements are not required to be contained in a lease contract:

(a) An "express warranty," as that term is defined in paragraph (1) of subdivision (a) of Section 1791.2, whether it relates to the sale or lease of a consumer good.

(b) Titling and transfer documents utilized to register, title, or transfer ownership of vehicles described in the lease contract with government registration authorities.

(c) Insurance policies, service contracts, and optional debt cancellation agreements.

(d) Documents that memorialize the sale or lease of goods or services, relating to the leased vehicle, between the provider of those goods or services and lessee that are included in the gross capitalized cost of the lease and separately itemized in the "Itemization of Gross Capitalized Cost." *(Added by Stats.2001, c. 287 (S.B.281), § 3.)*

Operative Effect

For operative effect of Stats.2001, c. 287 (S.B.281), see § 5 of that Act.

Research References

13 Witkin, California Summary 10th Personal Property § 194, (S 194) Regulatory Provisions.

§ 2986.3. Prohibited provisions

No lease contract shall contain any provision by which:

(a) A power of attorney is given to confess judgment in this state, or an assignment of wages is given; provided that nothing herein contained shall prohibit the giving of an assignment of wages contained in a separate instrument pursuant to Section 300 of the Labor Code.

(b) The lessee waives any right of action against the lessor or holder of the contract or other person acting on his or her behalf for any illegal act committed in the collection of payments under the contract or in the repossession of the motor vehicle.

(c) The lessee relieves the lessor from liability for any legal remedies which the lessee may have against the lessor under the contract or any separate instruments executed in connection therewith.

(d) The lessor or holder of the contract is given the right to commence action on a contract under the provisions of this chapter in a county other than the county in which the contract was in fact signed by the lessee, the county in which the lessee resides at the commencement of the action, the county in which the lessee resided at the time the contract was entered into or in the county in which the motor vehicle leased pursuant to such contract is permanently garaged. *(Added by Stats.1976, c. 1284, p. 5700, § 2, operative March 23, 1977. Amended by Stats.1997, c. 800 (S.B.1291), § 9.)*

Research References

13 Witkin, California Summary 10th Personal Property § 194, (S 194) Regulatory Provisions.

§ 2986.4. Delivery of copy of lease contract, purchase order, lease proposal and credit statement; acknowledgment; effect; failure to notify third party of nondelivery

Any acknowledgment by the lessee of delivery of a copy of a lease contract or purchase order and any vehicle lease proposal and any credit statement which the lessor has required or requested the lessee to sign, and which the lessee has signed, during the contract negotiations, shall be printed or written in size equal to at least 10–point bold type and, if contained in the contract, shall appear directly above the space reserved for the lessee's signature. The lessee's written acknowledgment, conforming to the requirements of this section, of delivery of a completely filled in copy of the contract, and a copy of such other documents shall be a rebuttable presumption of delivery in any action or proceeding by or against a third party without knowledge to the contrary when he or she acquired his or her interest in the contract. If such third party furnishes the lessee a copy of such documents, or a notice containing items set forth in subdivision (c) of Section 2985.8, and stating that the lessee shall notify such third party in writing within 30 days if he or she was not furnished a copy of such documents, and no such notification is given, it shall be conclusively presumed in favor of such a third party that copies of the documents were furnished as required by this chapter. *(Added by Stats.1976, c. 1284, p. 5700, § 2, operative March 23, 1977. Amended by Stats.1997, c. 800 (S.B.1291), § 10.)*

§ 2986.5. Used motor vehicle; requirements for lease; excess charges for licensing or transfer of title; return to lessee

(a) No person shall lease a used motor vehicle for operation on California highways if such vehicle does not meet all of the equipment requirements of Division 12 (commencing with Section 24000) of the Vehicle Code. This subdivision does not apply to an extension or a subsequent lease of the same motor vehicle to the same lessee.

(b) If a lessee of a vehicle pays to the lessor an amount for the licensing or transfer of title of the vehicle which amount is in excess of the actual fees due for such licensing or transfer, or which amount is in excess of the amount which has been paid, prior to the sale, by the lessor to the state in order to avoid penalties that would have accrued because of late payment of such fees, the lessor shall return such excess amount to the lessee, whether or not such lessee requests the return of the excess amount. *(Added by Stats.1976, c. 1284, p. 5700, § 2, operative March 23, 1977.)*

§ 2986.6. Agreement for inclusion of other property as security; unenforceability

No agreement in connection with a lease contract which provides for the inclusion of title to or a lien upon any personal or real property, other than the motor vehicle which is the subject matter of the lease contract, or accessories therefor, or special and auxiliary equipment used in connection therewith, as security for the payment of the contract obligations, shall be enforceable. This section does not apply to a security deposit, advance payment of rent or other cash prepayment. *(Added by Stats.1976, c. 1284, p. 5700, § 2, operative March 23, 1977.)*

Research References

13 Witkin, California Summary 10th Personal Property § 194, (S 194) Regulatory Provisions.

§ 2986.10. Assignee of lessor; rights and liabilities

(a) An assignee of the lessor's rights is subject to all equities and defenses of the lessee against the lessor, notwithstanding an agreement to the contrary, but the assignee's liability may not exceed the amount of the obligation owing to the assignee at the time of the assignment.

(b) The assignee shall have recourse against the lessor to the extent of any liability incurred by the assignee pursuant to this section regardless of whether the assignment was with or without recourse. *(Added by Stats.1976, c. 1284, p. 5700, § 2, operative March 23, 1977.)*

Research References

13 Witkin, California Summary 10th Personal Property § 194, (S 194) Regulatory Provisions.

§ 2986.12. Rebate, discount, etc. for information or assistance in lease or sale of motor vehicle; prohibition

It shall be unlawful for any lessor to induce or attempt to induce any person to enter into a contract subject to this chapter by offering a rebate, discount, commission or other consideration, on the condition that the lessee gives information or assistance for the purpose of enabling a lessor to either lease or sell a motor vehicle to another. *(Added by Stats.1976, c. 1284, p. 5700, § 2, operative March 23, 1977.)*

Research References

13 Witkin, California Summary 10th Personal Property § 194, (S 194) Regulatory Provisions.

§ 2986.13. Payment pending execution of lease contract; refund upon nonexecution; exceptions; remedies

(a) Any payment made by a lessee to a lessor pending the execution of a lease contract shall be refunded to the lessee in the event the lease contract is not executed.

(b) In the event of breach by the lessor of a lease contract where the lessee leaves his or her motor vehicle with the lessor as a trade-in downpayment and the motor vehicle is not returned by the lessor to the lessee for whatever reason, the lessee may recover from the lessor either the fair market value of the motor vehicle left as a downpayment or its value as stated in the lease contract, whichever is greater. The recovery shall be tendered to the lessee within five business days after the breach.

(c) The remedies of the buyer provided for in subdivision (b) are nonexclusive and cumulative and shall not preclude the lessee from pursuing any other remedy which he or she may have under any other provision of law. *(Added by Stats.1976, c. 1284, p. 5700, § 2, operative March 23, 1977. Amended by Stats.1997, c. 800 (S.B.1291), § 11.)*

Research References

13 Witkin, California Summary 10th Personal Property § 194, (S 194) Regulatory Provisions.

§ 2987. Lessee's right to early termination of lease contract; conditions; notice

(a) A lessee has the right to terminate a lease contract at any time prior to the scheduled expiration date specified in the lease contract. Except as provided in subdivision (f), all of the following subdivisions of this section apply in the event of an early termination.

(b) The lessee's liability shall not exceed the sum of the following:

(1) All unpaid periodic lease payments that have accrued up to the date of termination.

(2) All other amounts due and unpaid by the lessee under the lease contract, other than excess wear and mileage charges and unpaid periodic lease payments.

(3) Any charges, however denominated, that the lessor or holder of the lease contract may assess in connection with termination not to exceed in the aggregate the amount of a reasonable disposition fee, if any, disclosed in the lease contract and assessed upon termination of the lease contract.

(4) In the event of the lessee's default, reasonable fees paid by the lessor or holder for reconditioning of the leased vehicle and reasonable and necessary fees paid by the lessor or holder, if any, in connection with the repossession and storage of the leased vehicle.

(5) The difference, if any, between the adjusted capitalized cost disclosed in the lease contract and the sum of (A) all depreciation and other amortized amounts accrued through the date of early termination, calculated in accordance with the constant yield or other generally accepted actuarial method, and (B) the realized value of the vehicle as provided in subdivision (c).

(c) Subject to subdivision (d), the realized value of the vehicle used to calculate the lessee's liability under paragraph (5) of subdivision (b) shall be (1) if the lessee maintains insurance on the leased vehicle as required in the lease contract and the vehicle is a total loss as a result of theft or damage, the amount of any applicable insurance deductible owed by the lessee and the proceeds of the settlement of the insurance claim, unless a higher amount is agreed to by the holder of the lease contract, (2) if the lessee elects to have an appraisal conducted as provided in Regulation M, the value determined on appraisal, (3) if the holder of the lease contract or lessor elects to retain ownership of the vehicle for use or to lease to a subsequent lessee, the wholesale value of the vehicle as specified in the current edition of a recognized used vehicle value guide customarily used by California motor vehicle dealers to value vehicles in this state, including, but not limited to, the Kelley Blue Book Auto Market Report and the N.A.D.A. Official Used Car Guide, or (4) under all other circumstances, the higher of (A) the price paid for the vehicle upon disposition, or (B) any other amount established by the lessor or the lease contract.

(d)(1) The lessor or holder of the lease contract shall act in good faith and in a commercially reasonable manner in connection with the disposition of the vehicle.

(2) In addition to the requirements of paragraph (1), any disposition of the vehicle shall be preceded by a notice complying with both of the following:

(A) The notice shall be in writing and given by the holder of the contract to each lessee and guarantor at least 10 days in advance of any disposition or the date by which the value of the vehicle will be determined pursuant to paragraph (3) of subdivision (c). The notice shall be personally served or shall be sent by certified mail, return receipt requested, or first-class mail, postage prepaid, directed to the last known address of each lessee and guarantor. One notice is sufficient if those persons are married to each other and the most recent records of the holder of the lease contract indicate that they reside at the same address. The last known address of each lessee and guarantor shall be presumed to be the address stated in the lease contract or guaranty for each lessee and guarantor unless the lessee or guarantor notifies the holder of the lease contract of a change of address.

(B) The notice shall set forth (i) the time and place of any public sale, the time on or after which a private sale or other intended disposition is to be made, or the date by which the value of the vehicle will be determined pursuant to paragraph (3) of subdivision (c), (ii) an itemization of all amounts claimed under paragraphs (1) to (4), inclusive, of subdivision (b), (iii) the amount of the difference between the adjusted capitalized cost and the sum of all depreciation and other amortized amounts paid through the date of early termination as provided in paragraph (5) of subdivision (b), (iv) the total of these amounts identified as the "Gross Early Termination Amount," and (v) one of the following statements, whichever is applicable:

[To be inserted when the realized value will be determined pursuant to paragraph (3) of subdivision (c)]

"The amount you owe for early termination will be no more than the difference between the Gross Early Termination Amount stated above and (1) the appraised value of the vehicle

or (2) if there is no appraisal, the wholesale value specified in a recognized used vehicle value guide.

You have the right to get a professional appraisal to establish the value of the vehicle for the purpose of figuring how much you owe on the lease. If you want an appraisal, you will have to arrange for it to be completed at least three days before the scheduled valuation date. The appraiser has to be an independent person acceptable to the holder of the lease. You will have to pay for the appraiser. The appraised value will be considered final and binding on you and the holder of the lease."

[To be inserted in all other circumstances]

"The amount you owe for early termination will be no more than the difference between the Gross Early Termination Amount stated above and (1) the appraised value of the vehicle or (2) if there is no appraisal, either the price received for the vehicle upon disposition or a greater amount established by the lessor or the lease contract.

You have the right to get a professional appraisal to establish the value of the vehicle for the purpose of figuring how much you owe on the lease. If you want an appraisal, you will have to arrange for it to be completed at least three days before the scheduled sale date of the vehicle. The appraiser has to be an independent person acceptable to the holder of the lease. You will have to pay for the appraiser. The appraised value will be considered final and binding on you and the holder of the lease."

(3) The lessee shall have no liability under subdivision (b) if the lessor or holder of the lease contract does not comply with this subdivision. This paragraph does not apply under all the following conditions:

(A) Noncompliance was the result of a bona fide error in stating an amount required to be disclosed pursuant to clause (ii), (iii), or (iv) of subparagraph (B) of paragraph (2).

(B) The holder of the lease gives the lessee written notice of the error within 30 days after discovering the error and before (i) an action is filed to recover the amount claimed to be owed or (ii) written notice of the error is received by the holder of the lease from the lessee.

(C) The lessee is liable for the lesser of the originally claimed amount or the correct amount.

(D) The holder of the lease refunds any amount collected in excess of the amount described in subparagraph (C) within 10 days after notice of the error is given. "Bona fide error," as used in this paragraph, means an error that was not intentional and occurred notwithstanding the maintenance of procedures reasonably adapted to avoid that error. Examples of a bona fide error include clerical errors, calculation errors, errors due to unintentionally improper computer programming or data entry, and printing errors, but does not include an error of legal judgment with respect to a lessor's or lease contractholder's obligations under this section.

(4) This subdivision does not apply when the lessee maintains insurance on the leased vehicle as required in the lease contract and the vehicle is declared a total loss by the insurer as a result of theft or damage.

(e) The lessor or holder of the lease contract shall credit any security deposit or advance rental payment held by the lessor or holder of the lease contract against the lessee's liability under the lease contract as limited by this section. The portion of a security deposit or advance rental payment, if any, remaining after the lessee's liability under the lease contract as limited by this section has been satisfied shall be returned to the lessee within 30 days of the satisfaction of the obligation.

(f) Subdivisions (b) to (d), inclusive, do not apply if, prior to the scheduled expiration date specified in the lease contract, the lessee terminates the lease and purchases the vehicle or trades in the vehicle in connection with the purchase or lease of another vehicle. In such an event, the selling price of the leased vehicle, exclusive of taxes and other charges incidental to the sale, shall not exceed the sum of the following and shall relieve the lessee of any further liability under the lease contract:

(1) All unpaid periodic lease payments that have accrued up to the date of termination.

(2) All other amounts due and unpaid by the lessee under the lease contract, other than excess wear and mileage charges and unpaid periodic lease payments.

(3) Any charges, however denominated, that the lessor or holder of the lease contract may assess in connection with termination of the lease contract and the acquisition of the vehicle, not to exceed in the aggregate the amount of a reasonable purchase option fee, if any, disclosed in the lease contract and assessed upon the scheduled termination of the lease contract.

(4) The adjusted capitalized cost disclosed in the lease contract less all depreciation and other amortized amounts accrued through the date of early termination, calculated in accordance with the constant yield or other generally accepted actuarial method.

(g) If the lessee terminates a lease contract, voluntarily returns possession of the vehicle to the lessor, and timely pays all sums required under the lease contract as limited by this section, the lessor or holder shall not provide any adverse information concerning the early termination to any consumer credit reporting agency.

(h) The Rule of 78 shall not be used to calculate accrued rent charges.

(i) This section shall only apply to lease contracts entered into on and after January 1, 1998. *(Added by Stats.1997, c. 800 (S.B.1291), § 12.)*

Research References

13 Witkin, California Summary 10th Personal Property § 194, (S 194) Regulatory Provisions.

§ 2988. Legislative findings; liability of lessee on expiration of lease based on estimated residual value; reasonableness; rebuttable presumption

(a) The Legislature finds that it is necessary to provide some protection for consumers who enter into lease contracts in which the lessee will bear the risk of the motor vehicle's depreciation. This section is intended to provide relief to the consumer when an ostensibly inexpensive lease contract establishes an excessively low level of periodic payment which results, conversely, in an excessively high liability being imposed on the lessee at the expiration of the lease term because the lessor has failed to act in good faith in either estimating a residual value of the motor vehicle or establishing a level of periodic payment which bears no reasonable relation to the motor vehicle's reasonably expected depreciation during the lease term. Therefore, the lessor will have the obligation to act in good faith and to come forward with competent evidence showing that the estimated residual value was so determined given the circumstances existing at the inception of the lease contract.

(b) Where the lessee is to bear the risk of the motor vehicle's depreciation and the lessee's liability on expiration of a consumer lease is based on the estimated residual value of the motor vehicle such estimated residual value shall be a reasonable approximation of the anticipated actual fair market value of the motor vehicle on lease expiration. There shall be a rebuttable presumption that the estimated residual value is unreasonable to the extent that the estimated residual value exceeds the actual residual value by more than three times the average payment

allocable to a monthly period under the lease. The presumption stated in the preceding sentence shall not apply to the extent the excess of estimated over actual residual value is due to physical damage to the motor vehicle beyond reasonable wear and use, or to excessive use, and the lease may set standards for such wear and use if such standards are not unreasonable.

(c) For the purposes of this chapter, "fair market value" means the value the motor vehicle would have when sold in a commercially reasonable manner in the customary market for such motor vehicle. *(Added by Stats.1976, c. 1284, p. 5700, § 2, operative March 23, 1977.)*

Research References

13 Witkin, California Summary 10th Personal Property § 194, (S 194) Regulatory Provisions.

§ 2988.5. Failure to comply with requirements of §§ 2985.8, 2988; liability; failure to disclose information required by chapter; multiple offenses; limitation of actions

(a) Except as otherwise provided by this section, any lessor who fails to comply with any requirement imposed under Section 2985.8 or 2988 for which no specific relief is provided with respect to any person shall be liable to such person in an amount equal to the sum of:

(1) Any actual damages sustained by such person as a result of the failure.

(2) In the case of an individual action, 25 percent of the total amount of monthly payments under the lease except that liability under this subparagraph shall not be less than one hundred dollars ($100) nor greater than one thousand dollars ($1,000); or in the case of a class action, such amount as the court may allow, except that as to each member of the class no minimum recovery shall be applicable, and the total recovery in such action shall not be more than the lesser of five hundred thousand dollars ($500,000) or 1 percent of the net worth of the lessor.

(3) The costs of the action, together with a reasonable attorney's fee as determined by the court.

(b) In determining the amount of award in any class action, the court shall consider, among other relevant factors, the amount of any actual damages sustained, the frequency and persistence of failure of compliance by the lessor, the resources of the lessor, the number of persons adversely affected, and the extent to which the lessor's failure of compliance was intentional.

(c) A lessor shall not be liable under this section if within 15 days after discovery of an error, and prior to the institution of an action under this section or the receipt of written notice of the error, the lessor notifies the person concerned of the error and makes whatever adjustments in the appropriate account are necessary to insure that the person will not be required to pay any amount in excess of the amount that should correctly have been disclosed.

(d) A lessor may not be held liable in any action brought under this section for a violation of this chapter if the lessor shows by a preponderance of evidence that the violation was not intentional and resulted from a bona fide error notwithstanding the maintenance of procedures reasonably adopted to avoid any such error.

(e) Except as otherwise specifically provided in this chapter, any civil action for a violation of this chapter which may be brought against the original lessor in any lease transaction may be maintained against any subsequent assignee of the original lessor where the violation from which the alleged liability arose is apparent on the face of the instrument assigned unless the assignment is involuntary.

(f) A person may not take any action to offset any amount for which a lessor is potentially liable to such person under paragraph (2) of subdivision (a) against any amount owing to such lessor by such person, unless the amount of the lessor's liability to such person has been determined by judgment of a court of competent jurisdiction in an action to which such person was a party.

(g) No provision of this section imposing any liability shall apply to any act done or omitted in good faith conformity with any rule, regulation or interpretation of federal law, notwithstanding that after such act or omission has occurred, such rule, regulation or interpretation is amended, rescinded or determined by judicial or other authority to be invalid for any reason.

(h) The multiple failure to disclose any information required under this chapter to be disclosed in connection with a single lease transaction shall entitle the person to a single recovery under this section, but continued failure to disclose after a recovery has been granted shall give rise to rights to additional recoveries.

(i) Actions alleging a failure to disclose or otherwise comply with the requirements of this chapter shall be brought within one year of the termination of the lease contract. *(Added by Stats.1976, c. 1284, p. 5700, § 2, operative March 23, 1977.)*

Research References

13 Witkin, California Summary 10th Personal Property § 194, (S 194) Regulatory Provisions.

§ 2988.7. Failure to comply with § 2985.8; rescission of contract

If the lessor fails to comply with Section 2985.8, as an alternative to an action under Section 2988.5, the lessee may rescind the contract if the failure to comply was willful, or if correction will increase the amount of the contract balance, unless the lessor waives the collection of the increased amount. *(Added by Stats.1976, c. 1284, p. 5700, § 2, operative March 23, 1977.)*

Research References

13 Witkin, California Summary 10th Personal Property § 194, (S 194) Regulatory Provisions.

§ 2988.9. Award of reasonable attorney's fees and costs

Reasonable attorney's fees and costs shall be awarded to the prevailing party in any action on a lease contract subject to the provisions of this chapter regardless of whether the action is instituted by the lessor, assignee, or lessee. Where the defendant alleges in his or her answer that he or she tendered to the plaintiff the full amount to which he or she was entitled, and thereupon deposits in court, for the plaintiff, the amount so tendered, and the allegation is found to be true, then the defendant is deemed to be the prevailing party within the meaning of this section. *(Added by Stats.1976, c. 1284, p. 5700, § 2, operative March 23, 1977. Amended by Stats.2004, c. 183 (A.B.3082), § 42.)*

Research References

Rutter, Cal. Practice Guide: Civil Trials & Evidence Ch. 17-E, E. Attorney Fees as Costs.
13 Witkin, California Summary 10th Personal Property § 194, (S 194) Regulatory Provisions.

§ 2989. Preemption of civil action; federal civil action on same facts

No civil action shall be filed against a lessor under the authority of this chapter if a federal civil action has previously been filed based on facts that give rise to a similar cause of action under this chapter. *(Added by Stats.1976, c. 1284, p. 5700, § 2, operative March 23, 1977.)*

§ 2989.2. Fair market value at expiration of lease; depreciation; method of establishment; notice of intent to sell motor vehicle; service on lessee; exception; contents

Where the lessee is to bear the risk of the motor vehicle's depreciation upon the scheduled expiration of the lease contract, the following applies:

(a) When disposing of a vehicle or obtaining cash bids for the purpose of setting the fair market value of a vehicle, the lessor shall act in a commercially reasonable manner in the customary market for such vehicle.

(b) Any provision in a lease contract to the contrary notwithstanding, at least 10 days written notice of intent to sell such motor vehicle shall be given by the holder of the contract to each lessee and guarantor, unless the lessor and lessee have agreed in writing to the amount of the lessee's liability under the lease contract after the lessee returns the motor vehicle to the lessor, or the lessee has satisfied the lease contract obligations by payment to the lessor. The notice shall be personally served or shall be sent by certified mail, return receipt requested, directed to the address of the lessee shown on the contract, unless the lessee has notified the holder in writing of a different address. The notice shall set forth separately any charges or sums due and state that the lessee will be liable for the difference between the amount of liability imposed on the lessee at the expiration of the lease term and the actual cash value of the motor vehicle when it is sold. The notice shall also state that the lessee has the right to submit a cash bid for the purchase of the vehicle. *(Added by Stats.1976, c. 1284, p. 5700, § 2, operative March 23, 1977. Amended by Stats.1997, c. 800 (S.B.1291), § 13.)*

Research References

13 Witkin, California Summary 10th Personal Property § 194, (S 194) Regulatory Provisions.

§ 2989.4. Lessor; prohibited acts; nonliability for violations

(a) A lessor shall not:

(1) Fail to register the leased vehicle pursuant to the lease contract.

(2) Advertise any specific vehicle in the inventory of the lessor for lease without identifying such vehicle by either its vehicle identification number or license number.

(3) Refuse to lease a vehicle to any creditworthy person at the advertised total price, exclusive of sales tax, vehicle registration fees and finance charges.

(b) Notwithstanding Section 2988.5, a lessor shall not suffer civil liability for a violation of this section. *(Added by Stats.1976, c. 1284, p. 5700, § 2, operative March 23, 1977.)*

Research References

13 Witkin, California Summary 10th Personal Property § 194, (S 194) Regulatory Provisions.

§ 2989.5. Records; availability to Department of Motor Vehicles; affidavit; court order; financial institution; report to supervising agency; report of action taken

(a) Except as provided in subdivision (c), a lessor shall make available to investigators of the Department of Motor Vehicles, upon presentation of an affidavit that the department has a consumer complaint within its jurisdiction, the records relevant to the transaction complained of. If the affidavit states that the department has reasonable cause to believe there is a pattern of conduct or common scheme in similar transactions, the records relevant to all such similar transactions shall be made available.

(b) Except as provided in subdivision (c), on petition of the department alleging the receipt of a consumer complaint within its jurisdiction and alleging that the lessor refuses to make available his records as required, the court shall order the lessor to make available such records or show cause why such records should not be produced. The department shall be awarded reasonable attorney's fees and costs if it prevails in such action.

(c) (1) In the case of a financial institution, or a subsidiary or affiliated corporation of such institution, the Director of Motor Vehicles shall report in writing an apparent violation, or failure to comply with this chapter, evidenced by a consumer complaint, to the agency or department of the state or federal government responsible for supervising the leasing activities of such institution.

(2) Within 20 days, such agency or department shall advise the director of the action taken with respect to such report.

(3) If such agency or department fails to so advise the director, the director may commence an action to compel the agency or department to cause the production of the records relevant to the consumer complaint. *(Added by Stats.1976, c. 1284, p. 5700, § 2, operative March 23, 1977.)*

Research References

13 Witkin, California Summary 10th Personal Property § 194, (S 194) Regulatory Provisions.

§ 2989.6. Rules and regulations

The Director of Motor Vehicles may adopt and enforce rules and regulations as may be necessary to carry out or implement the provisions of this chapter.

Rules and regulations shall be adopted, amended or repealed in accordance with Chapter 4.5 (commencing with Section 11370) of Part 1 of Division 3 of Title 2 of the Government Code. *(Added by Stats.1976, c. 1284, p. 5700, § 2, operative March 23, 1977.)*

Research References

13 Witkin, California Summary 10th Personal Property § 194, (S 194) Regulatory Provisions.

§ 2989.8. Violations; misdemeanor

Any person who shall knowingly and willfully violate any provision of this chapter shall be guilty of a misdemeanor. *(Added by Stats.1976, c. 1284, p. 5700, § 2, operative March 23, 1977.)*

Research References

13 Witkin, California Summary 10th Personal Property § 194, (S 194) Regulatory Provisions.

§ 2990. Inapplicability of chapter to transaction regulated by Automobile Sales Finance Act

This chapter shall not apply to any transaction which is regulated by Chapter 2b (commencing with Section 2981) of this title. *(Added by Stats.1976, c. 1284, p. 5700, § 2, operative March 23, 1977.)*

Research References

13 Witkin, California Summary 10th Personal Property § 193, (S 193) Nature of Act.

§ 2991. Forms; Spanish language translations

Any prospective assignee that provides a lessor under a lease contract with any preprinted form for use as a lease contract shall, upon the request of a lessor, provide the lessor with a Spanish language translation of the preprinted form. *(Added by Stats.1999, c. 235 (A.B.713), § 1, operative Jan. 1, 2001.)*

Research References

13 Witkin, California Summary 10th Personal Property § 194, (S 194) Regulatory Provisions.

§ 2992. Preprinted lease contract; design requirements and contents

A prospective assignee that provides a lessor under a lease contract with a preprinted form for use as a lease contract shall design the form in such a manner so as to provide on its face sufficient space for the lessor to include all disclosures and itemizations required pursuant to Section 2985.8 and shall also contain on its face a separate blank space no smaller than seven and one-half square inches for the lessor and lessee to memorialize trade-in, turn-in, and other individualized agreements. *(Added by Stats.2001, c. 287 (S.B.281), § 4.)*

Operative Effect

For operative effect of Stats.2001, c. 287 (S.B.281), see § 5 of that Act.

Research References

13 Witkin, California Summary 10th Personal Property § 194, (S 194) Regulatory Provisions.

§ 2993. Repossession of vehicle connected with incident of violence notice; notice to subsequent assignee

A holder of a lease contract, or the agent of a holder, who has received a notice pursuant to Section 7507.6 of the Business and Professions Code, shall not make a subsequent assignment to skip trace, locate, or repossess the vehicle without simultaneously, and in the same manner by which the assignment is given, advising the assignee of the assignment of the information contained in the notice. As used in this section, "assignment" has the same meaning set forth in Section 7500.1 of the Business and Professions Code. *(Added by Stats.2007, c. 192 (S.B.659), § 5, eff. Sept. 7, 2007.)*

Research References

Miller and Starr California Real Estate § 8:30, Execution by an Agent or Attorney-In-Fact.

CHAPTER 2E. CONTROLLED ESCROWS

Section

§ 2995. Transfer of single-family residential dwelling; real estate developer; financial interest in escrow entity; damages; waiver

No real estate developer shall require as a condition precedent to the transfer of real property containing a single family residential dwelling that escrow services effectuating such transfer shall be provided by an escrow entity in which the real estate developer has a financial interest.

A real estate developer who violates the provisions of this section shall be liable to the purchaser of the real property in the amount of three times the amount charged for the escrow services, but in no event less than two hundred fifty dollars ($250), plus reasonable attorney's fees and costs.

For purposes of this section "financial interest" means ownership or control of 5 percent or more of an escrow entity.

For purposes of this section "real estate developer" means a person or entity having an ownership interest in real property which is improved by such person or entity with single family residential dwellings which are offered for sale to the public.

For purposes of this section "escrow entity" includes a person, firm or corporation.

Any waiver of the prohibition contained in this section shall be against public policy and void. *(Added by Stats.1978, c. 552, p. 1724, § 1, eff. Aug. 25, 1978.)*

Research References

Miller and Starr California Real Estate § 6:3, Who Can Serve as an Escrow Holder.

Miller and Starr California Real Estate § 25C:34, Restrictions on the Receipt and Disbursement of the Buyer's Funds; When No Blanket Encumbrance.

3 Witkin Cal. Proc. 5th Actions § 664, (S 664) in General.

4 Witkin Cal. Proc. 5th Pleading § 282, (S 282) Sufficient Showing.

12 Witkin, California Summary 10th Real Property § 302, (S 302) Escrow Agents.

CHAPTER 3.5.   HEALTH CARE LIENS

Section

3040. Lien for money paid or payable by insured or enrollee for health care services provided under health care service plan contract or disability insurance policy; limit on account.

§ 3040. Lien for money paid or payable by insured or enrollee for health care services provided under health care service plan contract or disability insurance policy; limit on account

(a) No lien asserted by a licensee of the Department of Managed Care or the Department of Insurance, and no lien of a medical group or an independent practice association, to the extent that it asserts or enforces a lien, for the recovery of money paid or payable to or on behalf of an enrollee or insured for health care services provided under a health care service plan contract or a disability insurance policy, when the right of the licensee, medical group, or independent practice association to assert that lien is granted in a plan contract subject to the Knox–Keene Health Care Service Plan Act of 1975 (Chapter 2.2 (commencing with Section 1340) of Division 2 of the Health and Safety Code) or a disability insurance policy subject to the Insurance Code, may exceed the sum of the reasonable costs actually paid by the licensee, medical group, or independent practice association to perfect the lien and one of the following:

(1) For health care services not provided on a capitated basis, the amount actually paid by the licensee, medical group, or independent practice association pursuant to that contract or policy to any treating medical provider.

(2) For health care services provided on a capitated basis, the amount equal to 80 percent of the usual and customary charge for the same services by medical providers that provide health care services on a noncapitated basis in the geographic region in which the services were rendered.

(b) If an enrollee or insured received health care services on a capitated basis and on a noncapitated basis, and the licensee, medical group, or independent practice association that provided the health care services on the capitated basis paid for the health care services the enrollee received on the noncapitated basis, then a lien that is subject to subdivision (a) may not exceed the sum of the reasonable costs actually paid to perfect the lien, and the amounts determined pursuant to both paragraphs (1) and (2) of subdivision (a).

(c) If the enrollee or insured engaged an attorney, then the lien subject to subdivision (a) may not exceed the lesser of the following amounts:

(1) The maximum amount determined pursuant to subdivision (a) or (b), whichever is applicable.

(2) One–third of the moneys due to the enrollee or insured under any final judgment, compromise, or settlement agreement.

(d) If the enrollee or insured did not engage an attorney, then the lien subject to subdivision (a) may not exceed the lesser of the following amounts:

(1) The maximum amount determined pursuant to subdivision (a) or (b), whichever is applicable.

(2) One–half of the moneys due to the enrollee or insured under any final judgment, compromise, or settlement agreement.

(e) Where a final judgment includes a special finding by a judge, jury, or arbitrator, that the enrollee or insured was partially at fault, the lien subject to subdivision (a) or (b) shall be reduced by the same comparative fault percentage by which the enrollee or insured's recovery was reduced.

(f) A lien subject to subdivision (a) or (b) is subject to pro rata reduction, commensurate with the enrollee's or insured's reasonable attorney's fees and costs, in accordance with the common fund doctrine.

(g) This section is not applicable to any of the following:

(1) A lien made against a workers' compensation claim.

(2) A lien for Medi–Cal benefits pursuant to Article 3.5 (commencing with Section 14124.70) of Chapter 7 of Part 3 of Division 9 of the Welfare and Institutions Code.

(3) A lien for hospital services pursuant to Chapter 4 (commencing with Section 3045.1).

(h) This section does not create any lien right that does not exist at law, and does not make a lien that arises out of an employee benefit plan or fund enforceable if preempted by federal law.

(i) The provisions of this section may not be admitted into evidence nor given in any instruction in any civil action or proceeding between an enrollee or insured and a third party. *(Added by Stats.2000, c. 848 (S.B.1471), § 1.)*

Research References

13 Witkin, California Summary 10th Personal Property § 244, (S 244) Hospital's Lien on Damages.

13 Witkin, California Summary 10th Equity § 120, Health Care Practices.

CHAPTER 4.   HOSPITAL LIENS

Section

3045.1. Lien for emergency and ongoing medical or other services upon damages recovered by person injured by accident or wrongful act.

3045.2. Applicability of lien whether damages recovered by judgment, settlement or compromise.

3045.3. Notice to injured person; contents; delivery of copy to insurance carrier.

3045.4. Liability for payment to injured person after notice without satisfying lien.

3045.5. Enforcement of lien by action; limitation.

3045.6. Inapplicability of chapter to claims against common carriers.

§ 3045.1. Lien for emergency and ongoing medical or other services upon damages recovered by person injured by accident or wrongful act

Every person, partnership, association, corporation, public entity, or other institution or body maintaining a hospital licensed under the laws of this state which furnishes emergency and ongoing medical or other services to any person injured by reason of an accident or negligent or other wrongful act not covered by Division 4 (commencing with Section 3201) or

Division 4.5 (commencing with Section 6100) of the Labor Code, shall, if the person has a claim against another for damages on account of his or her injuries, have a lien upon the damages recovered, or to be recovered, by the person, or by his or her heirs or personal representative in case of his or her death to the extent of the amount of the reasonable and necessary charges of the hospital and any hospital affiliated health facility, as defined in Section 1250 of the Health and Safety Code, in which services are provided for the treatment, care, and maintenance of the person in the hospital or health facility affiliated with the hospital resulting from that accident or negligent or other wrongful act. *(Added by Stats.1961, c. 2080, p. 4340, § 1. Amended by Stats.1992, c. 302 (A.B.2733), § 1.)*

Research References

Rutter, Cal. Practice Guide: Civ. Pro. Before Trial Ch. 12(II)-H, H. Professional Responsibility Considerations Re Settlements.
Rutter, Cal. Practice Guide: Enforcing Judgments/Debts Ch. 5-A, A. Introduction.
Rutter, Cal. Practice Guide: Personal Injury Ch. 1-B, B. Initial Evaluation of Case: Decision to Accept or Reject Employment or Undertake Further Evaluation of Claim.
Rutter, Cal. Practice Guide: Prof. Responsibility Ch. 9-F, F. Duties Re Nonclient Funds.
7 Witkin Cal. Proc. 5th Judgment § 251, Fees Denied.
13 Witkin, California Summary 10th Personal Property § 216, Nature and Kinds of Liens.
13 Witkin, California Summary 10th Personal Property § 244, (S 244) Hospital's Lien on Damages.
13 Witkin, California Summary 10th Equity § 120, Health Care Practices.

§ 3045.2. Applicability of lien whether damages recovered by judgment, settlement or compromise

The lien shall apply whether the damages are recovered, or are to be recovered, by judgment, settlement, or compromise. *(Added by Stats.1961, c. 2080, p. 4340, § 1.)*

Research References

Rutter, Cal. Practice Guide: Personal Injury Ch. 1-B, B. Initial Evaluation of Case: Decision to Accept or Reject Employment or Undertake Further Evaluation of Claim.
13 Witkin, California Summary 10th Personal Property § 244, (S 244) Hospital's Lien on Damages.

§ 3045.3. Notice to injured person; contents; delivery of copy to insurance carrier

A lien shall not be effective, however, unless a written notice containing the name and address of the injured person, the date of the accident, the name and location of the hospital, the amount claimed as reasonable and necessary charges, and the name of each person, firm, or corporation known to the hospital and alleged to be liable to the injured person for the injuries received, is delivered or is mailed by registered mail, return receipt requested, postage prepaid, to each person, firm, or corporation known to the hospital and alleged to be liable to the injured person for the injuries sustained prior to the payment of any moneys to the injured person, his attorney, or legal representative as compensation for the injuries.

The hospital shall, also, deliver or mail by registered mail, return receipt requested, postage prepaid, a copy of the notice to any insurance carrier known to the hospital which has insured the person, firm, or corporation alleged to be liable to the injured person against the liability. The person, firm, or corporation alleged to be liable to the injured person shall, upon request of the hospital, disclose to the hospital the name of the insurance carrier which has insured it against the liability. *(Added by Stats.1961, c. 2080, p. 4340, § 1. Amended by Stats.1992, c. 302 (A.B.2733), § 2.)*

Research References

Rutter, Cal. Practice Guide: Personal Injury Ch. 1-B, B. Initial Evaluation of Case: Decision to Accept or Reject Employment or Undertake Further Evaluation of Claim.
13 Witkin, California Summary 10th Personal Property § 244, (S 244) Hospital's Lien on Damages.

§ 3045.4. Liability for payment to injured person after notice without satisfying lien

Any person, firm, or corporation, including, but not limited to, an insurance carrier, making any payment to the injured person, or to his or her attorney, heirs, or legal representative, for the injuries he or she sustained, after the receipt of the notice as provided by Section 3045.3, without paying to the association, corporation, public entity, or other institution or body maintaining the hospital the amount of its lien claimed in the notice, or so much thereof as can be satisfied out of 50 percent of the moneys due under any final judgment, compromise, or settlement agreement after paying any prior liens shall be liable to the person, partnership, association, corporation, public entity, or other institution or body maintaining the hospital for the amount of its lien claimed in the notice which the hospital was entitled to receive as payment for the medical care and services rendered to the injured person. *(Added by Stats.1961, c. 2080, p. 4341, § 1. Amended by Stats.1992, c. 302 (A.B.2733), § 3.)*

Research References

Rutter, Cal. Practice Guide: Personal Injury Ch. 1-B, B. Initial Evaluation of Case: Decision to Accept or Reject Employment or Undertake Further Evaluation of Claim.
13 Witkin, California Summary 10th Personal Property § 244, (S 244) Hospital's Lien on Damages.

§ 3045.5. Enforcement of lien by action; limitation

The person, partnership, association, corporation or other institution or body maintaining the hospital may, at any time within one year after the date of the payment to the injured person, or to his heirs, attorney, or legal representative, enforce its lien by filing an action at law against the person, firm, or corporation making the payment and to whom such notice was given as herein provided. *(Added by Stats.1961, c. 2080, p. 4341, § 1.)*

Research References

13 Witkin, California Summary 10th Personal Property § 244, (S 244) Hospital's Lien on Damages.

§ 3045.6. Inapplicability of chapter to claims against common carriers

The provisions of this chapter shall not apply to any claim or cause of action against a common carrier subject to the jurisdiction of the Public Utilities Commission or the Interstate Commerce Commission. *(Added by Stats.1961, c. 2080, p. 4341, § 1.)*

Research References

Rutter, Cal. Practice Guide: Personal Injury Ch. 1-B, B. Initial Evaluation of Case: Decision to Accept or Reject Employment or Undertake Further Evaluation of Claim.
Rutter, Cal. Practice Guide: Prof. Responsibility Ch. 9-F, F. Duties Re Nonclient Funds.
13 Witkin, California Summary 10th Personal Property § 244, (S 244) Hospital's Lien on Damages.

CHAPTER 6. OTHER LIENS

§ 3046. Vendor's lien

One who sells real property has a vendor's lien thereon, independent of possession, for so much of the price as remains unpaid and unsecured otherwise than by the personal obligation of the buyer. *(Enacted in 1872.)*

Research References

Rutter, Cal. Practice Guide: Real Prop. Transactions Ch. 11-H, H. Other Remedies.

Miller and Starr California Real Estate § 10:33, Vendor's Lien.

Miller and Starr California Real Estate § 11:133, Relation to Prior Interests--Mechanic's Knowledge of a Prior Unrecorded Interest.

4 Witkin, California Summary 10th Security Transactions in Real Property § 19, (S 19) Vendor's Lien.

§ 3047. Vendor's lien; waiver

Where a buyer of real property gives to the seller a written contract for payment of all or part of the price, an absolute transfer of such contract by the seller waives his lien to the extent of the sum payable under the contract, but a transfer of such contract in trust to pay debts, and return the surplus, is not a waiver of the lien. *(Enacted in 1872.)*

Research References

Miller and Starr California Real Estate § 10:33, Vendor's Lien.

4 Witkin, California Summary 10th Security Transactions in Real Property § 19, (S 19) Vendor's Lien.

§ 3048. Vendor's lien; priority

The liens defined in sections 3046 and 3050 are valid against every one claiming under the debtor, except a purchaser or incumbrancer in good faith and for value. *(Enacted in 1872.)*

Research References

Rutter, Cal. Practice Guide: Real Prop. Transactions Ch. 11-H, H. Other Remedies.

Miller and Starr California Real Estate § 11:3, Effect of Recording Statutes on Priority.

Miller and Starr California Real Estate § 11:50, Definitions; Rules of Priority.

Miller and Starr California Real Estate § 11:103, Priority of Purchase Money Liens--In General.

Miller and Starr California Real Estate § 11:120, Vendor's Lien.

4 Witkin, California Summary 10th Security Transactions in Real Property § 75, (S 75) Priority Over Vendor's Lien.

§ 3050. Purchaser's lien

One who pays to the owner any part of the price of real property, under an agreement for the sale thereof, has a special lien upon the property, independent of possession, for such part of the amount paid as he may be entitled to recover back, in case of a failure of consideration. *(Enacted in 1872.)*

Research References

Rutter, Cal. Practice Guide: Real Prop. Transactions Ch. 11-H, H. Other Remedies.

Miller and Starr California Real Estate § 10:34, Vendee's Lien.

Miller and Starr California Real Estate § 34:56, Seller's Default; Buyer's Remedies.

4 Witkin, California Summary 10th Security Transactions in Real Property § 18, (S 18) in General.

§ 3051. Possessory liens for services, repairs, etc.; exceptions

Every person who, while lawfully in possession of an article of personal property, renders any service to the owner thereof, by labor or skill, employed for the protection, improvement, safekeeping, or carriage thereof, has a special lien thereon, dependent on possession, for the compensation, if any, which is due to him from the owner for such service; a person who makes, alters, or repairs any article of personal property, at the request of the owner, or legal possessor of the property, has a lien on the same for his reasonable charges for the balance due for such work done and materials furnished, and may retain possession of the same until the charges are paid; and foundry proprietors and persons conducting a foundry business, have a lien, dependent on possession, upon all patterns in their hands belonging to a customer, for the balance due them from such customers for foundry work; and plastic fabricators and persons conducting a plastic fabricating business, have a lien, dependent on possession, upon all patterns and molds in their hands belonging to a customer, for the balance due them from such customer for plastic fabrication work; and laundry proprietors and persons conducting a laundry business, and drycleaning establishment proprietors and persons conducting a drycleaning establishment, have a general lien, dependent on possession, upon all personal property in their hands belonging to a customer, for the balance due them from such customer for laundry work, and for the balance due them from such customers

Civil

for drycleaning work, but nothing in this section shall be construed to confer a lien in favor of a wholesale drycleaner on materials received from a drycleaning establishment proprietor or a person conducting a drycleaning establishment; and veterinary proprietors and veterinary surgeons shall have a lien dependent on possession, for their compensation in caring for, boarding, feeding, and medical treatment of animals.

This section shall have no application to any vessel, as defined in Section 21 of the Harbors and Navigation Code, to any vehicle, as defined in Section 670 of the Vehicle Code, which is subject to registration pursuant to that code, to any manufactured home, as defined in Section 18007 of the Health and Safety Code, to any mobilehome, as defined in Section 18008 of the Health and Safety Code, or to any commercial coach, as defined in Section 18001.8 of the Health and Safety Code, whether or not the manufactured home, mobilehome, or commercial coach is subject to registration under the Health and Safety Code. *(Enacted in 1872. Amended by Code Am. 1877–78, c. 451, p. 89; Stats.1901, c. 108, p. 270, § 1; Stats.1907, c. 66, p. 85, § 1; Stats.1911, c. 435, p. 887, § 1; Stats.1929, c. 868, p. 1923, § 1; Stats.1935, c. 381, p. 1332, § 1; Stats.1945, c. 861, p. 1619, § 1; Stats.1949, c. 1436, p. 2499, § 4; Stats.1970, c. 1341, p. 2491, § 1; Stats.1976, c. 839, p. 1908, § 1; Stats.1978, c. 1005, p. 3083, § 1; Stats.1979, c. 600, p. 1863, § 1; Stats.1981, c. 202, p. 1125, § 1; Stats.1983, c. 1124, § 6, operative Jan. 1, 1984.)*

Research References

Rutter, Cal. Practice Guide: Enforcing Judgments/Debts Ch. 4-B, B. Claim and Delivery.
Miller and Starr California Real Estate § 31:37, Tax and Possessory Liens.
13 Witkin, California Summary 10th Personal Property § 217, (S 217) in General.
13 Witkin, California Summary 10th Personal Property § 218, (S 218) Requisites of Lien.
13 Witkin, California Summary 10th Personal Property § 233, (S 233) Statutory List.
13 Witkin, California Summary 10th Personal Property § 234, (S 234) Nature and Effect.
13 Witkin, California Summary 10th Personal Property § 235, (S 235) Enforcement.
13 Witkin, California Summary 10th Personal Property § 236, (S 236) Where Charges Do Not Exceed $150.
13 Witkin, California Summary 10th Personal Property § 243, Aircraft Keeper's or Repairer's Lien.

§ 3051a. Possessory liens; services over $300 and safekeeping over $200 requested by nonowners; notice to holder of legal title

That portion of any lien, as provided for in the next preceding section, in excess of three hundred dollars ($300) for any work, services, or care, or in excess of two hundred dollars ($200) for any safekeeping, rendered or performed at the request of any person other than the holder of the legal title, shall be invalid, unless prior to commencing any such work, service, care, or safekeeping, the person claiming such lien shall give actual notice in writing either by personal service or by registered letter addressed to the holder of the legal title to such property, if known. *(Added by Stats.1923, c. 338, p. 695, § 1. Amended by Stats.1931, c. 1048, p. 2202, § 1; Stats.1949, c. 1436, p. 2500, § 5; Stats.1959, c. 197, p. 2089, § 1; Stats.1968, c. 830, p. 1602, § 1; Stats.1978, c. 1005, p. 3084, § 2.)*

Research References

13 Witkin, California Summary 10th Personal Property § 235, (S 235) Enforcement.

§ 3051.5. Possessory lien; carriers; freightage; charges for services and advances; conditions; notice; sale; priority; application of sale proceeds; liability of shipper

(a) A carrier has a lien on freight in its possession for the total amount owed the carrier by the shipper for freightage, charges for services and advances due on freight previously delivered upon the promise of the shipper to pay freightage, charges and advances, as provided in this section.

(b) The lien provided by this section shall not arise:

(1) Unless the carrier has notified the shipper, in writing, that failure to pay billed charges may result in a lien on future shipments, including the cost of storage and appropriate security for the subsequent shipment held pursuant to this section.

(2) As to any freight which consists of perishable goods.

(c) Except as otherwise provided in this section, the notice and sale provisions of Section 3052 shall apply to the sale of property subject to a lien provided by this section.

(d) No sale of property subject to a lien provided by this section may take place for at least 35 days from the date that possession of the property is delivered to the carrier but the notice period set forth in Section 3052 may run concurrently with the 35-day period provided by this subdivision. In addition to the notices required by Section 3052, the lienholder, at least 10 days prior to any sale of the property, shall notify the shipper and the consignee of the property, and each secured party having a perfected security interest in the property, of the date, time and place of the intended sale. This notice shall include the names of both the shipper and the consignee and shall describe the property to be sold.

(e) Any perfected security interest in the property is prior to the lien provided by this section. No sale of the property may be concluded if the amount bid at the sale is not at least equal to the total amount of all outstanding obligations secured by a perfected security interest in the property. If the minimum bid required for the sale of property pursuant to this subdivision is not received, the lienholder shall promptly release the property to the legal owner upon payment of the current amount for freightage, charges for services and advances due for shipment of that property, not including amounts due on freight previously delivered.

The proceeds of the sale shall be applied as follows:

(1) First, to secured parties having a perfected security interest, in the amounts to which they are respectively entitled.

(2) Second, to the discharge of the lien provided by this section and the costs of storage, appropriate security, and of the sale.

(3) The remainder, if any, to the legal owner of the property.

In the event of any violation by the lienholder of any provision of this subdivision the lienholder shall be liable to any secured party for all damages sustained by the secured party as a result thereof plus all expenses reasonably and necessarily incurred in the enforcement of the secured party's rights, including reasonable attorney's fees and costs of suit.

(f) The shipper shall be liable to the consignee for any damage which results from the failure of the property to reach the consignee as scheduled due to the carrier's proper exercise of its lien rights pursuant to this section. The measure of damages shall be determined as set forth in Section 2713 of the Commercial Code. *(Added by Stats.1984, c. 1375, § 1.)*

Research References

13 Witkin, California Summary 10th Personal Property § 231, (S 231) Carrier's Lien.

§ 3051.6. Carrier's lien for fines, penalties, costs, expenses, or interest incurred for false or erroneous certification of gross cargo weight

(a) Except as provided in subdivision (b), a carrier has a lien on freight in its possession for the total amount owed to the carrier by the owner or beneficial owner of the cargo being shipped for the aggregate amount of any fines, penalties, costs, expenses, or interest incurred by the carrier resulting from the inclusion of false or erroneous information as to gross cargo weight in a written or electronic certification provided by the owner, beneficial owner, or person responsible for making the certification pursuant to Section 508 of Title 49 of the United States Code.

(b) This section does not apply to any of the following freight:

(1) Perishable goods.

(2) Freight shipped by a means involving other than intermodal transportation, as that term is defined by Section 508 of Title 49 of the United States Code.

(3) Freight shipped by loaded containers or trailers having a gross projected cargo weight, including packing material and pallets, of less than 10,000 pounds.

(c) Any sale to foreclose a lien specified in this section shall be conducted in accordance with Section 3052, except that (1) the lien sale shall not take place for at least 35 days from the date that possession of the property is delivered to the carrier, but the notice period specified in Section 3052 may run concurrently with this 35-day period and (2), in addition to the notices required by Section 3052, at least 10 days prior to the sale of the property the lienholder shall notify the shipper and consignee of the property of the date, time, and place of the intended sale. This notice shall contain the names of the shipper and consignee and shall generally describe the property to be sold. *(Added by Stats.1993, c. 757 (S.B.619), § 2.)*

§ 3052. Sale by lien holder at auction; notice of sale; redemption; application of proceeds

If the person entitled to the lien provided in Section 3051 is not paid the amount due, and for which such lien is given, within 10 days after the same shall have become due, then such lienholder may proceed to sell such property, or so much thereof as may be necessary to satisfy such lien and costs of sale at public auction, and by giving at least 10 days' but not more than 20 days' previous notice of such sale by advertising in some newspaper published in the county in which such property is situated; or if there be no newspaper printed in such county, then by posting notice of sale in three of the most public places in the town and at the place where such property is to be sold, for 10 days previous to the date of the sale; provided, however, that within 20 days after such sale, the legal owner may redeem any such property so sold to satisfy such lien upon the payment of the amount thereof, all costs and expenses of such sale, together with interest on such sum at the rate of 12 percent per annum from the due date thereof or the date when the same were advanced until the repayment. The proceeds of the sale must be applied to the discharge of the lien and the cost of keeping and selling the property; the remainder, if any, must be paid over to the legal owner thereof. *(Enacted in 1872. Amended by Stats.1907, c. 66, § 2; Stats.1927, c. 368, p. 604, § 1; Stats.1949, c. 1436, p. 2500, § 6; Stats.1959, c. 781, p. 2775, § 1; Stats.1974, c. 1262, p. 2736, § 1, eff. Sept. 23, 1974, operative Nov. 1, 1974; Stats.1977, c. 579, p. 1840, § 34; Stats.1978, c. 1005, p. 3084, § 3.)*

Research References

13 Witkin, California Summary 10th Personal Property § 235, (S 235) Enforcement.
13 Witkin, California Summary 10th Personal Property § 236, (S 236) Where Charges Do Not Exceed $150.

§ 3052a. Jeweler's lien; notice and sale

Every person, firm, or corporation, engaged in performing work upon any watch, clock or jewelry, for a price, shall have a lien upon the watch, clock, or jewelry for the amount of any account that may be due for the work done thereon. The lien shall also include the value or agreed price, if any, of all materials furnished by the lienholder in connection with the work. If any account for work done or materials furnished shall remain unpaid for one year after completing the work, the lienholder may, upon 30 days notice in writing to the owner, specifying the amount due, and informing him that the payment of the amount due within 30 days will entitle him to redeem the property, sell any such article or articles at public or bona fide private sale to satisfy the account. The proceeds of the sale, after paying the expenses thereof, shall first be applied to liquidate the indebtedness secured by the lien and the balance, if any, shall be paid over to the owner.

The notice may be served by registered mail with return receipt demanded, directed to the owner's last known address, or, if the owner or his address be unknown, it may be posted in two public places in the town or city where the property is located. Nothing herein contained shall be construed as preventing the lienholder from waiving the lien herein provided for suing upon the amount if he elects to do so. *(Added by Stats.1937, c. 279, p. 614, § 1.)*

Research References

13 Witkin, California Summary 10th Personal Property § 233, (S 233) Statutory List.
13 Witkin, California Summary 10th Personal Property § 235, (S 235) Enforcement.

§ 3052b. Alternative lien-sale procedure; liens for charges under $150; conditions; notice of sale; redemption; disposition of proceeds

(a) The procedure in this section shall be an alternative to the lien-sale procedure provided in Section 3052, but applies only to liens under Section 3051 for charges not exceeding one hundred fifty dollars ($150), exclusive of additional charges and interest authorized by this section. As a condition precedent to using the procedure specified in this section, the lienholder shall have done all of the following:

(1) Provided the property owner with an accurate written summary of the lien provisions of this section.

(2) Obtained the property owner's address and telephone number, together with a written declaration signed by the property owner stating that the property owner has read and understands the summary provided pursuant to paragraph (1), at the time of entering into the transaction from which the lien arose.

(3) Posted, at the time of the transaction from which the lien arose, a notice which fully and fairly informs the public of the substance of this section. The notice shall be posted in a location clearly visible to the public in the lienholder's business premises.

(b) Any lienholder proceeding under this section shall notify the owner of the property subject to the lien upon completion of the work for which the lien is claimed. This notice shall be by first-class mail.

(c) If a property owner who has actually received notice pursuant to subdivision (b) fails to pay the charges for which the lien is claimed for 30 days following receipt of the notice, the lienholder may thereafter charge two dollars ($2) per day for storing the property subject to the lien and these charges shall also be secured by the lien.

(d) Not less than 30 days following the notice specified in subdivision (b), the lienholder shall notify the property owner by first-class mail that the property will be sold to satisfy the lien, unless the charges are paid within 30 days following the mailing of the notice.

(e) If the lienholder has complied with the notice requirements of subdivisions (b) and (d), not less than 30 days have elapsed since the mailing of the notice required by subdivision (d), and the property owner has not fully paid the original charges for which the lien is claimed plus any additional charges authorized by subdivision (c), the lienholder may sell the property subject to the lien at a public or bona fide private sale to satisfy the sum of those obligations, all costs and expenses of the sale, and interest at the rate of 12 percent per annum from 30 days following receipt of the notice specified in subdivision (b) or the date the same were advanced until repayment.

(f) However, the owner of the property sold pursuant to subdivision (e) may redeem the property sold to satisfy the lien, within 20 days following the sale, upon payment of all charges, costs and expenses, and interest specified in subdivision (e).

(g) The proceeds of the sale shall first be applied to the discharge of the lien, the costs of sale, and interest specified in subdivision (e). The remainder, if any, shall be paid to the former owner of the property so sold. *(Added by Stats.1991, c. 606 (A.B.1939), § 1.)*

Research References

13 Witkin, California Summary 10th Personal Property § 235, (S 235) Enforcement.

13 Witkin, California Summary 10th Personal Property § 236, (S 236) Where Charges Do Not Exceed $150.

§ 3052.5. Service dealers registered with Bureau of Repair Services; lien; notice; disposition of products of nominal value; alternative methods

(a) Sections 3052 and 3052b shall not apply to any service dealer registered with the Bureau of Repair Services pursuant to Chapter 20 (commencing with Section 9800) of Division 3 of the Business and Professions Code if the dealer reasonably believes that the serviced product is of nominal value. For purposes of this section, nominal value shall be ascertained as follows: the product is not readily salable for more than the legitimate charges against it, and either the original retail value of the product was under two hundred dollars ($200) and the product is over three years old, or the original retail value is over two hundred dollars ($200) and the product is over six years old.

Service dealers may use any available materials or information, including, but not limited to, industry publications, code dates, sales records, or receipts to assist in determining value and age of the serviced product.

(b) A service dealer may select one of the following alternative methods for the disposal of unclaimed serviced products determined to have a value as specified in subdivision (a):

(1) The service dealer may provide the owner of the product with the following written notice to be mailed following completion of work on the serviced product:

DATE BROUGHT IN _____

DATE MAILED _____

DATE PRODUCT TO BE SOLD IF NOT CLAIMED ____

NOTICE: YOUR PRODUCT HAS BEEN DETERMINED BY THIS SERVICE DEALER TO BE ONE WHICH WAS EITHER ORIGINALLY SOLD FOR LESS THAN $200 AND IS NOW OVER THREE YEARS OLD OR ONE WHICH WAS ORIGINALLY SOLD FOR MORE THAN $200 AND WHICH IS NOW OVER SIX YEARS OLD AND THE CHARGES FOR SERVICING YOUR PRODUCT WILL EXCEED ITS CURRENT VALUE. UNDER CALIFORNIA CIVIL CODE SECTION 3052.5(a) IF YOU OR YOUR AGENT FAIL TO CLAIM YOUR PRODUCT WITHIN 90 DAYS AFTER THE DEALER MAILS A COPY OF THIS NOTICE TO YOU IT MAY BE SOLD OR OTHERWISE DISPOSED OF BY HIM OR HER.

The notice shall be sent by certified mail, return receipt requested. A serviced product may be disposed of 90 days after the date of deliverance evidenced by the signature in the returned receipt.

(2) The service dealer may publish public notice of the intended sale in a newspaper of general circulation. The notice shall contain a description of the serviced product, the name of the serviced product owner, and the time by which and place where the product may be redeemed. The notice shall be published for a minimum of five times. A serviced product may be disposed of 90 days after the last date of publication.

(3) A service dealer may, upon receipt of any product to be serviced by him or her, provide the owner of the product with the following notice, written in at least 10-point boldface type:

DATE BROUGHT IN _____

DATE MAILED _____

DATE PRODUCT TO BE SOLD IF NOT CLAIMED ____

NOTICE: YOUR PRODUCT HAS BEEN DETERMINED BY THIS SERVICE DEALER TO BE ONE WHICH WAS EITHER ORIGINALLY SOLD FOR LESS THAN $200 AND IS NOW OVER THREE YEARS OLD OR ONE WHICH WAS ORIGINALLY SOLD FOR MORE THAN $200 AND WHICH IS NOW OVER SIX YEARS OLD AND THE CHARGES FOR SERVICING YOUR PRODUCT WILL EXCEED ITS CURRENT VALUE. UNDER CALIFORNIA CIVIL CODE SECTION 3052.5(a) IF YOU OR YOUR AGENT FAIL TO CLAIM YOUR PRODUCT WITHIN 90 DAYS AFTER THE DEALER MAILS A COPY OF THIS NOTICE TO YOU IT MAY BE SOLD OR OTHERWISE DISPOSED OF BY HIM OR HER.

PRINT YOUR NAME AND MAILING ADDRESS WHERE NOTICE MAY BE SENT TO YOU IN THE SPACE PROVIDED BELOW AND SIGN WHERE INDICATED TO SHOW THAT YOU HAVE READ THIS NOTICE.

_____
(Print Name)

_____
(Street Address)

_____
(City, State and ZIP Code)

IF YOU DO NOT AGREE WITH THE ABOVE DETERMINED VALUE OF YOUR ITEM, DO NOT SIGN THIS DOCUMENT.

Signature: _____
(Owner or Agent)

This notice shall be signed, addressed, and dated by the owner, with a copy to be retained by both the owner and the service dealer. At the completion of service, the service dealer shall by first-class mail, mail a completed copy of the notice to the owner of the serviced product at the address given on the notice form. A serviced product may be disposed of 90 days after the date of mailing.

(c) For purposes of this section, an owner is the person or agent who authorizes the original service or repair, or delivers the product to the service dealer. *(Added by Stats.1977, c. 988, p. 2971, § 1. Amended by Stats.1991, c. 606 (A.B.1939), § 2; Stats.2006, c. 538 (S.B.1852), § 57.)*

Research References

13 Witkin, California Summary 10th Personal Property § 235, (S 235) Enforcement.

§ 3053. Factor's lien

A factor has a general lien, dependent on possession, for all that is due to him as such, upon all articles of commercial value that are intrusted to him by the same principal. *(Enacted in 1872.)*

Research References

13 Witkin, California Summary 10th Personal Property § 217, (S 217) in General.

§ 3054. Banker's or savings and loan association's lien; deposit accounts

(a) A banker, or a savings and loan association, has a general lien, dependent on possession, upon all property in his or her hands belonging to a customer, for the balance due to the banker or savings and loan association from the customer in the course of the business.

(b) The exercise of this lien with respect to deposit accounts shall be subject to the limitations and procedures set forth in Section 864 or 6660 of the Financial Code. *(Enacted in 1872. Amended by Stats.1975, c. 948, p. 2121, § 1; Stats.1980, c. 1288, p. 4367, § 1; Stats.1987, c. 56, § 21.)*

Research References

Miller and Starr California Real Estate § 10:167, Offset (Setoff) by the Beneficiary.
13 Witkin, California Summary 10th Personal Property § 217, (S 217) in General.
4 Witkin, California Summary 10th Negotiable Instruments § 81, (S 81) Lien on Securities.

§ 3059. Mechanic's lien

The liens of mechanics, for materials and services upon real property, are regulated by Chapter 4 (commencing with Section 8400) of Title 2 of Part 6 of Division 4. *(Enacted in 1872. Amended by Stats.1975, c. 678, p. 1474, § 4; Stats.2010, c. 697 (S.B.189), § 13, operative July 1, 2012.)*

Law Revision Commission Comments

Section 3059 is amended to correct a cross-reference. [37 Cal.L.Rev. Comm. Reports 527 (2007)].

§ 3060. Mining liens

(a) As used in this section, "mine" means a mining claim or real property worked on as a mine including, but not limited to, any quarry or pit, from which rock, gravel, sand, or any other mineral-containing property is extracted by any mining, or surface-mining, operation.

(b) Any person who performs labor in a mine, either in its development or in working on it by the subtractive process, or furnishes materials to be used or consumed in it, has a lien upon the mine and the works owned and used by the owners for milling or reducing the ores from the mine, for the value of the work or labor done or materials furnished by each, whether done or furnished at the instance of the owner of the mine, or the owner's agent, and every contractor, subcontractor, superintendent, or other person having charge of any mining or work or labor performed in and about the mine, either as lessee or under a working bond or contract thereon, shall be held to be the agent of the owner for the purposes of this section. The liens provided for by this section shall be enforced in the same manner as those provided for by Part 6 (commencing with Section 8000) of Division 4.

(c) This section shall become operative on July 1, 2012. *(Added by Stats.1951, c. 1159, p. 2957, § 2. Amended by Stats.1969, c. 1362, p. 2752, § 1, operative Jan. 1, 1971; Stats. 2010, c. 697 (S.B.189), § 14, operative July 1, 2012; Stats.2012, c. 263 (A.B.2654), § 2, eff. Sept. 7, 2012.)*

Law Revision Commission Comments

Section 3060 is amended to correct a cross-reference. The other changes are technical. [37 Cal.L.Rev.Comm. Reports 527 (2007)].

Research References

23 NO. 2 Miller & Starr, California Real Estate Newsalert 2, Mechanics Liens.
13 Witkin, California Summary 10th Personal Property § 221, Nonpossessory Liens.

§ 3061. Threshermen's liens

Every person performing work or labor in, with, about, or upon any barley crusher, threshing machine or engine, horsepower, wagon, or other appliance thereof, while engaged in crushing or threshing, has a lien thereon to the extent of the value of his services. Such lien extends for ten days after any such person ceases such work or labor; provided, within that time, an action is brought to recover the amount of the claim. If judgment is given in favor of the plaintiff in any such action, and it is further found that he is entitled to a lien under the provisions of this section, property subject thereto, or so much thereof as may be necessary, may be sold to satisfy such judgment; but if several judgment[1] have been recovered against the same property for the enforcement of such liens, the proceeds of the sale must be divided pro rata among the judgment creditors. *(Added by Stats.1905, c. 461, p. 618, § 1.)*

[1] So in enrolled bill.

Research References

Miller and Starr California Real Estate § 11:198, Priority Between Deeds of Trust and Security Interests in Growing Crops.
13 Witkin, California Summary 10th Personal Property § 221, Nonpossessory Liens.

§ 3061.5. Agricultural laborer's lien; liability of severed crops or farm products or proceeds from sale; limitations; exceptions; rights of buyer in ordinary course of business

(a) Except as provided in subdivision (d), any person who as an employee shall, by his or her own labor, do or perform any work harvesting or transporting harvested crops or farm products as defined in Section 55403 of the Food and Agricultural Code which are owned and grown or produced by a limited partnership as defined in Section 15501 of the Corporations Code, has a lien upon any and all of the severed crops or severed farm products or proceeds from their sale for the value of the labor done up to a maximum of earnings for two weeks. The liens attach whether the work was done at the instance of the owner who is the grower or producer of severed crops or severed farm products or of any other person acting by or under the owner's authority, directly or indirectly, as contractor or otherwise; and every contractor, subcontractor, or other person having charge of the harvesting or transporting of the severed crops or severed farm products shall be held to be the agent of the owner for the purposes of this section.

(b) The liens provided for in this section attach from the date of the commencement of the work or labor, and are preferred liens, prior in dignity to all other liens, claims, or encumbrances. Except as provided in subdivisions (a) and (c) they shall not be limited as to amount by any contract price agreed upon between the owner who is the grower or producer of the severed crops or severed farm products and any contractor, but the several liens shall not in any case exceed in amount the reasonable value of the labor done, nor the price agreed upon for the labor between the claimant and his or her employer. In no event, where the claimant was employed by a contractor, or subcontractor, shall the lien extend to any labor not contemplated by, covered by, or reasonably necessary to the execution of, the original contract between the contractor and the owner who is the grower or producer of severed crops or severed farm products and of which contract, or modification thereof, the claimant had actual notice before the performance of the labor.

(c) The maximum liability of severed crops, severed farm products or the proceeds from their sale subject to liens under this section is limited to the lesser of actual proved claims or 25 percent of the fair market value of the severed crops, severed farm products, or 25 percent of the proceeds after their sale.

(d) No person has a lien if the owner who is the grower or producer of the severed crops, severed farm products, or their proceeds, who otherwise would be subject to a lien pursuant to subdivision (a), either gives directly, or requires a person or entity hired or used to furnish labor in connection with harvesting or transporting the severed crops, to give to the Labor Commissioner prior to the harvest and for 45 days after its completion, a bond executed by an admitted surety insurer in an amount and form acceptable to the Labor Commissioner, which is conditioned upon the payment of all wages found to be due and unpaid in connection with such operations under any provision of this code.

(e) A buyer in the ordinary course of business, as defined in paragraph (9) of subdivision (b) of Section 1201 of the Commercial Code, shall take free of any security interest created by this section, notwithstanding the fact that the lien is perfected and the buyer knows of its existence. *(Added by Stats.1976, c. 1059, p. 4688, § 1, operative July 1, 1977. Amended by Stats.1982, c. 517, p. 2327, § 76; Stats.2006, c. 254 (S.B.1481), § 3.)*

Law Revision Commission Comments

Section 3061.5 is amended to delete a provision duplicated in the Bond and Undertaking Law. See Section 995.710 (deposit in lieu of bond). The other changes in Section 3061.5 are technical. [16 Cal.L.Rev.Comm. Reports 501 (1982)].

Research References

Miller and Starr California Real Estate § 11:198, Priority Between Deeds of Trust and Security Interests in Growing Crops.

§ 3061.6. Agricultural laborer's lien

(a) The lien created by Section 3061.5 shall continue in force for a period of 45 days from the time the person claiming such lien shall have ceased to do or perform the work for which such lien is claimed, and such lien shall cease at the expiration of the 45 days unless the claimant, his or her assignee or successor in interest, files a claim with the Labor Commissioner or brings suit to foreclose the lien in which case the lien continues in force until the claim filed with the Labor Commissioner or the lien foreclosure suit is finally determined and closed. If a claim is filed with the Labor Commissioner, the Labor Commissioner shall act upon and finally determine such claim within 180 days after filing. In case such proceedings are not prosecuted to trial within two years after the commencement thereof, the court may in its discretion dismiss the same for want of prosecution.

(b) Upon filing a claim with the Labor Commissioner, the Labor Commissioner, if the owner who is the grower or producer has failed to satisfy the conditions of subdivision (d) of Section 3061.5, shall determine whether or not such owner of the severed crops, severed farm products, or their proceeds is capable financially of satisfying such claim. For purposes of this determination, it shall be proper for the Labor Commissioner after investigation to take into account the potential liability faced by such owner of such severed crops, severed farm products, or their proceeds. If the Labor Commissioner deter-

mines that a lien is necessary to protect the interest of claimants, the Labor Commissioner shall file such lien on the crop, the severed farm product, or their proceeds and notify, in writing, the owner and notify, in writing, all persons who have filed financing statements on the crop, the farm product, or their proceeds pursuant to the provisions of the Commercial Code.

(c) The plaintiff in any such lien foreclosure suit, at the time of issuing the summons or at any time afterwards, may have the severed crops or severed farm products or proceeds from their sale upon which such lien subsists attached, as provided in this code and Title 6.5 (commencing with Section 488.010) of Part 2 of the Code of Civil Procedure, upon delivering to the clerk an affidavit, by or on behalf of the plaintiff, showing that: (1) the plaintiff, or his assignor or predecessor in interest, performed labor in harvesting or transporting the severed crops or severed farm products or both; (2) that such labor has not been paid for; (3) that the sum for which the attachment is asked does not exceed the lesser of the reasonable value of the services rendered or if earnings, does not exceed the lesser of two weeks unpaid earnings or reasonable value of actual services rendered, or 25 percent of the fair market value of the severed crop or severed farm product; and (4) that the attachment is not sought and the action is not brought to hinder, delay or defraud any creditor or creditors of any defendant.

(d) Any number of persons claiming liens under this section and Section 3061.5 may join in the same action and when separate actions are commenced, the court may consolidate them. If after sale of the property subject to the liens provided for in this section and Section 3061.5, under the judgment or decree of foreclosure of such lien or liens, there is a deficiency of proceeds, the proceeds shall be divided pro rata among the lien claimants whose liens are established, regardless of the order in which the liens were created or the order in which the suits to foreclose same were commenced. Judgment for the deficiency may be docketed against the party personally liable therefor and his sureties.

(e) Nothing contained in this section or Section 3061.5 shall be construed to impair or affect the right of any person to whom any debt may be due for work done, to maintain a personal action to recover such debt against the person liable therefor, or his sureties, either in connection with the lien suit or in a separate action. The person bringing such personal action may take out a separate attachment therefor, notwithstanding his or her lien, and in his or her affidavit to procure an attachment need not state that his or her demand is not secured by a lien, and the judgment, if any, obtained by the plaintiff in such personal action shall not be construed to impair or merge any lien held by the plaintiff under this section or Section 3061.5; provided that any money collected on the judgment shall be credited on the amount of such lien in any action brought to enforce the same, in accordance with the provisions of this section.

(f) If the lien has attached to perishable goods, the lienholder may, during the period for which the lien is in effect and prior to the filing of a foreclosure suit, obtain a court order for the sale of such perishable goods pursuant to the provisions of Section 488.530 of the Code of Civil Procedure; provided, however, that in the event that such perishable crop is subject in whole or in part to a valid marketing agreement which is in force between the owner who is the grower or producer and an agricultural marketing cooperative organized under the Food and Agricultural Code or similar laws of other states, the agricultural marketing cooperative may purchase or otherwise take possession or custody of such crop or portion thereof according to the terms of the marketing agreement. Any moneys due and payable to such owner who is the grower or producer in return for such crop shall be paid by the agricultural marketing cooperative to the court. *(Added by Stats.1976, c. 1059, p. 4689, § 2, operative July 1, 1977.)*

§ 3062. Lien for service of stallion, jack, or bull

Every owner or person having in charge any stallion, jack, or bull, used for propagating purposes, has a lien for the agreed price of its service upon any mare or cow and upon the offspring of such service, unless some willfully false representation concerning the breeding or pedigree of such stallion, jack, or bull has been made or published by the owner or person in charge thereof, or by some other person, at the request or instigation of such owner or person in charge. *(Added by Stats.1905, c. 461, p. 618, § 2.)*

§ 3063. Lien for service of stallion, jack, or bull; verified claims; recording; contents; notice

Every claimant of a lien provided for in the preceding section must, within 90 days after the service on account of which the lien is claimed, record in the office of the county recorder of the county where the mare or cow subject thereto is kept, a verified claim containing a particular description of the mare or cow, the date and place of service, the name of the owner or reputed owner of such mare or cow, a description by name, or otherwise, of the stallion, jack, or bull performing the service, the name of the owner or person in charge thereof, and the amount of the lien claimed. Such claim, so recorded, is notice to subsequent purchasers and encumbrancers of such mare or cow and of the offspring of such service for one year after such recording. *(Added by Stats.1905, c. 461, p. 618, § 3. Amended by Stats.1957, c. 815, p. 2031, § 1.)*

§ 3064. Lien for service of stallion, jack, or bull; enforcement action; remedies

An action to enforce any lien created under Section 3062 may be brought in any county wherein any of the property subject thereto may be found, and the plaintiff is entitled to the remedies provided in Section 3065 upon complying with such section, which is hereby made applicable to the proceedings in such action. *(Added by Stats.1905, c. 461, p. 619, § 4. Amended by Stats.1968 c. 48, p. 189, § 4.)*

§ 3064.1. Forfeiture of right to pay for services of breeding animals

Every person who wilfully advertises any cattle, horse, sheep, swine, or other domestic animal for purposes of copulation or profit as having a pedigree other than the true pedigree of such animal shall forfeit all right by law to collect pay for the services of such animal. *(Added by Stats.1955, c. 60, p. 501, § 1.)*

§ 3065. Loggers' and lumbermen's lien

Any person who shall, by his own labor, or by using his livestock, machinery or appliances, or both, do or perform any work or render any service in connection with felling, preparing or transporting any logs, or in manufacturing lumber or other timber products from such logs, including the production of tanbark, shall have a lien upon any and all of such logs and upon any and all of the lumber and other timber products manufactured therefrom, whether said work was done or service was rendered on the logs themselves, or any of them, or in manufacturing the lumber or other timber products from them, for the value of such labor done and for the value of the use of such livestock, machinery and appliances, or both, whether said work was done or service was rendered at the instance of the owner of such logs or timber products manufactured therefrom, or of any other person acting by his authority or under him, directly or indirectly, as contractor or otherwise; and every contractor, subcontractor or other person having charge of the felling, preparing or transporting of the said logs or of their manufacture into timber products shall be held to be the agent of the said owner for the purposes of this section.

The liens provided for in this section shall attach from the date of the commencement of such work or labor, or the date of the commencement of the use of such livestock, machinery or appliances, as the case may be, and shall be preferred liens, prior in dignity to all other liens, claims or encumbrances, except the landowner's claim for a reasonable stumpage in cases where the landowner himself is not the direct employer or contractor, as the case may be. They shall not be limited as to amount by any contract price agreed upon between the owner of said logs or timber products manufactured therefrom and any contractor, except as hereinafter provided, but said several liens shall not in any case exceed in amount the reasonable value of the labor done, or the reasonable value of the use of the livestock, machinery or appliances for which the lien is claimed, nor the price agreed upon for the same between the claimant and the person by whom he was employed or with whom the agreement to use livestock, machinery or appliances was made, nor in any case, where the claimant was employed by a contractor, or subcontractor, shall the lien extend to any labor or the use of any livestock, machinery or appliances not embraced within, contemplated by, covered by, or reasonably necessary to the execution of, the original contract between the contractor and the owner of such logs or timber products manufactured therefrom, or any modification thereof made by or with the consent of such owner, and of which said contract, or modification thereof, the claimant shall have had actual notice before the performance of such labor or the use of such livestock, machinery or appliances.

The recording of such original contract, or modification thereof, in the office of the county recorder of the county in which the timberland on which the work is to be done is situated or in which the logs are to be manufactured into timber products, as the case may be, before the commencement of the work, shall be equivalent to the giving of such actual notice by the owner to all persons performing work or using livestock, machinery or appliances thereunder. In case said original contract shall, before the work is commenced, be so recorded, together with a bond of the contractor with good and sufficient sureties in an amount not less than fifty (50) percent of the contract price named in said contract, which bond shall in addition to any conditions for the performance of the contract, be also conditioned for the payment in full of the claims of all persons performing labor, or using livestock, machinery or appliances, in the execution of such contract and shall also by its terms be made to inure to the benefit of any and all persons who perform labor or use livestock, machinery or appliances in the execution of the work to be done under the contract so as to give such persons, and their assigns or successors in interest, a right of action to recover upon said bond in any suit brought to enforce the liens provided for in this section, or in a separate suit brought on said bond, then the court must, where it would be equitable so to do, restrict the recovery under such liens to an aggregate amount equal to the amount found to be due from the owner of the said logs or timber products manufactured therefrom to the contractor, and render judgment against the contractor and his sureties on said bond for any deficiency or difference there may remain between said amount so found to be due to the claimants for such labor and for the use of such livestock, machinery and appliances. It is the intent and purpose of this section to limit the owner's liability, in all cases, to the measure of the contract price where he shall have filed or cause to be filed, in good faith, with his original contract a valid bond with good and sufficient sureties in the amount and upon the conditions herein provided. It shall be lawful for the owner of such logs and timber products to protect himself against any failure of the contractor to perform his contract and make full payment for all work done thereunder by exacting such bond or other security as he may deem satisfactory. *(Added by Stats.1905, c. 461, p. 619, § 5. Amended by Stats.1927, c. 505, p. 847, § 1; Stats.1973, c. 665, § 2.)*

Research References

Miller and Starr California Real Estate § 17:31, Timber.
13 Witkin, California Summary 10th Personal Property § 221, Nonpossessory Liens.
9 Witkin, California Summary 10th Corporations § 1, (S 1) Nature of Corporation.

§ 3065a. Loggers' and lumbermen's lien; duration; remedies

The lien created by the last preceding section shall continue in force for a period of 30 days from the time the person claiming such lien shall have ceased to do or perform the work or render the service for which said lien is claimed, while such logs, lumber or other manufactured timber products are in the county in which such labor was performed or service rendered, and said lien shall cease at the expiration of the said 30 days unless the claimant thereof, or his assignee or successor in interest, brings suit to foreclose the same, in which case the lien continues in force until the said lien foreclosure suit is finally determined and closed, and in case such proceeding be not prosecuted to trial within two years after the commencement thereof, the court may in its discretion dismiss the same for want of prosecution. If any part of the property on which the lien existed is removed from the said county, the lien continues on the balance remaining in the county to the full extent of the claim.

The plaintiff in any such lien foreclosure suit may have the logs, lumber and other manufactured timber products upon which such lien subsists attached, as provided in this code and the Code of Civil Procedure.

Any number of persons claiming liens under this and the next preceding section may join in the same action and when separate actions are commenced, the court may consolidate them. Whenever upon the sale of the property subject to the liens provided for in this and the next preceding section, under the judgment or decree of foreclosure of such lien or liens, there is a deficiency of proceeds, the proceeds shall be divided pro rata among the lien claimants whose liens are established, regardless of the order in which the liens were created or the order in which the suits to foreclose same were commenced, and judgment for the deficiency may be docketed against the party personally liable therefor and his sureties, in like manner and with like effect as in actions for the foreclosure of mortgages.

Nothing contained in this or the next preceding section shall be construed to impair or affect the right of any person to whom any debt may be due for work done, or for the use of livestock, machinery or appliances, to maintain a personal action to recover said debt against the person liable therefor, or his sureties, either in connection with the lien suit or in a separate action, and the person bringing such personal action may take out a separate attachment therefor, notwithstanding his lien or the amount of his debt, and in his affidavit to procure an attachment he shall state that the attachment is made pursuant to this section, and the judgment, if any, obtained by the plaintiff in such personal action shall not be construed to impair or merge any lien held by said plaintiff under this or the next preceding section; provided, only, that any money collected on said judgment shall be credited on the amount of such lien in any action brought to enforce the same, in accordance with the provisions of this section. *(Added by Stats.1927, c. 505, p. 849, § 2. Amended by Stats.1974, c. 1516, p. 3335, § 4, operative Jan. 1, 1977.)*

Law Revision Commission Comments

Section 3065a is amended to make clear that, although an attachment may issue pursuant to the authority granted by this section, the procedures for issuance are those provided by Title 6.5 (commencing with Section 481.010) of Part 2 of the Code of Civil Procedure. To secure the ex parte issuance of a writ of attachment, the plaintiff must satisfy the requirements of Chapter 5 (commencing with Section 485.010) of Title 6.5. It should be noted, however, that the plaintiff is not bound by the $500 limitation nor the unsecured debt requirement of Section 483.010 of the Code of Civil Procedure. [11 Cal.L.Rev.Comm.Reports 701 (1973)].

Research References

Rutter, Cal. Practice Guide: Enforcing Judgments/Debts Ch. 4-A, A. Attachment.
Miller and Starr California Real Estate § 17:31, Timber.
6 Witkin Cal. Proc. 5th Provisional Remedies § 57, (S 57) in General.

§ 3065b. Loggers' and lumbermen's lien; cessation of work defined

As used in the next preceding section the words "the time the person claiming such lien shall have ceased to do or perform the work or render the service for which said lien is claimed" shall be construed to mean the final date work was done or services were rendered on any of the logs, lumber or other manufactured timber products on which the lien is claimed, so as to give the lien claimant, or his assignee or successor in interest, a full thirty days after final cessation of labor to bring suit to foreclose his lien on any or all of the logs, lumber or other manufactured timber products in question. *(Added by Stats.1929, c. 157, p. 301, § 1.)*

Research References

Miller and Starr California Real Estate § 17:31, Timber.

§ 3065c. Loggers' and lumbermen's lien; affidavit showing wages owed by contractor; filing; stop notice to mill operator; withholding funds due contractor

Whenever any faller, bucker, or millhand has a lien pursuant to Section 3065 and has not been paid for his labor by the contractor employing him, and money is owing to such contractor by a mill operator, any such faller, bucker, or millhand, or several of them acting jointly, may file with the Labor Commissioner an affidavit stating the amount of wages unpaid to him or them and describing the labor for which wages are owed and the period in which such labor was performed. If the Labor Commissioner finds the affidavit in order, he shall send to such mill operator a stop notice directing such mill operator to withhold funds in the amount of the unpaid wages from the contractor. The mill operator shall withhold such funds pursuant to the stop notice for 15 days from the date of service of the notice, subject to garnishment within that period by the faller, bucker, or millhand or any assignee thereof. *(Added by Stats. 1957, c. 338, p. 977, § 1.)*

Research References

Miller and Starr California Real Estate § 17:31, Timber.

§ 3066. Cleaners' and launderers' liens; service and storage; sale; notice; proceeds; posted notices in receiving office

(a) Any garment, clothing, wearing apparel or household goods remaining in the possession of a person, firm, partnership or corporation, on which cleaning, pressing, glazing or washing has been done or upon which alterations or repairs have been made, or on which materials or supplies have been used or furnished, for a period of 90 days or more after the completion of such work may be sold to pay the reasonable or agreed charges and the costs of notifying the owner or owners. Provided, however, that the person, firm, partnership, or corporation to whom such charges are payable and owing shall first notify the owner or owners of the time and place of such sale. Provided further, that property that is to be placed in storage after any of the services or labors mentioned herein, shall not be affected by the provisions of this section.

(b) All garments, clothing, wearing apparel or household goods placed in storage, or on which any of the services or labors mentioned in the preceding section of this act have been performed and then placed in storage by agreement and remaining in the possession of a person, firm, partnership or corporation without the reasonable or agreed charges having been paid for a period of 12 months, may be sold to pay said charges. Provided that the person, firm, partnership or corporation to whom the charges are payable, shall first notify the owner or owners thereof of the time and place of sale. Provided, however, that the persons, firms, partnerships, or corporations operating as warehouses or warehousemen shall not be affected by this section.

(c) The posting or mailing of a registered letter, with a return address marked thereon, addressed to the owner or owners, at their address given at the time of delivery of the article or articles to a person, firm, partnership or corporation to render any of the services or labors set out in this act, stating the time and place of sale, shall constitute notice. Said notice shall be posted or mailed at least 30 days before the date of sale. The cost of posting or mailing said letter shall be added to the charges.

Where the address of an owner is unknown, a posting of notice, for a period of 30 days, at a prominent place in the receiving office of the person, firm, partnership or corporation required to give the notice is sufficient.

(d) The person, firm, partnership or corporation to whom the charges are payable, shall, from the proceeds of the sale, deduct the charges due plus the costs of notifying the owner and shall hold the overplus, if any, subject to the order of the owner and shall immediately thereafter mail to the owner thereof at his address, if known, a notice of the sale, the amount of the overplus, if any, due him, and at any time within 12 months, upon demand by the owner, pay to the owner said sums or overplus in his hands.

(e) All persons, firms, partnerships or corporations taking advantage of this act must keep posted in a prominent place in their receiving office or offices at all times one notice which shall read as follows:

"All articles cleaned, pressed, glazed, laundered, washed, altered or repaired and not called for in 90 days shall be sold to pay charges." "All articles stored by agreement and charges not having been paid for 12 months will be sold to pay charges." *(Added by Stats.1945, c. 910, p. 1695, § 1. Amended by Stats.1955, c. 665, p. 1158, § 1.)*

Research References

13 Witkin, California Summary 10th Personal Property § 235, (S 235) Enforcement.

CHAPTER 6.5. LIENS ON VEHICLES

§ 3067. Definitions

Words used in this chapter which are defined in Division 1 of the Vehicle Code [1] shall have the same meaning as in the Vehicle Code. *(Added by Stats.1959, c. 3, p. 1791, § 3.)*

[1] Vehicle Code, § 100 et seq.

Research References

13 Witkin, California Summary 10th Personal Property § 237, (S 237) in General.
13 Witkin, California Summary 10th Personal Property § 241, Vehicle Removed by Public Agency.

§ 3067.1. Forms

All forms required pursuant to the provisions of this chapter shall be prescribed by the Department of Motor Vehicles. The language used in the notices and declarations shall be simple and nontechnical. *(Added by Stats.1980, c. 1111, p. 3562, § 1.)*

Research References

13 Witkin, California Summary 10th Personal Property § 237, (S 237) in General.

§ 3067.2. Manufactured homes, mobilehomes, or commercial coaches; application of chapter

This chapter shall not apply to any manufactured home, as defined in Section 18007 of the Health and Safety Code, to any mobilehome, as defined in Section 18008 of the Health and Safety Code, or to any commercial coach, as defined in Section 18001.8 of the Health and Safety Code, whether or not the manufactured home, mobilehome, or commercial coach is subject to registration under the Health and Safety Code. *(Added by Stats.1983, c. 1124, § 7, operative Jan. 1, 1984.)*

Research References

Miller and Starr California Real Estate § 31:37, Tax and Possessory Liens.

13 Witkin, California Summary 10th Personal Property § 237, (S 237) in General.

§ 3068. Service lien

(a) Every person has a lien dependent upon possession for the compensation to which the person is legally entitled for making repairs or performing labor upon, and furnishing supplies or materials for, and for the storage, repair, or safekeeping of, and for the rental of parking space for, any vehicle of a type subject to registration under the Vehicle Code, subject to the limitations set forth in this chapter. The lien shall be deemed to arise at the time a written statement of charges for completed work or services is presented to the registered owner or 15 days after the work or services are completed, whichever occurs first. Upon completion of the work or services, the lienholder shall not dismantle, disengage, remove, or strip from the vehicle the parts used to complete the work or services.

(b)(1) Any lien under this section that arises because work or services have been performed on a vehicle with the consent of the registered owner shall be extinguished and no lien sale shall be conducted unless either of the following occurs:

(A) The lienholder applies for an authorization to conduct a lien sale within 30 days after the lien has arisen.

(B) An action in court is filed within 30 days after the lien has arisen.

(2) A person whose lien for work or services on a vehicle has been extinguished shall turn over possession of the vehicle, at the place where the work or services were performed, to the legal owner or the lessor upon demand of the legal owner or lessor, and upon tender by the legal owner or lessor, by cashier's check or in cash, of only the amount for storage, safekeeping, or parking space rental for the vehicle to which the person is entitled by subdivision (c).

(3) Any lien under this section that arises because work or services have been performed on a vehicle with the consent of the registered owner shall be extinguished, and no lien sale shall be conducted, if the lienholder, after written demand made by either personal service or certified mail with return receipt requested by the legal owner or the lessor to inspect the vehicle, fails to permit that inspection by the legal owner or lessor, or his or her agent, within a period of time not sooner than 24 hours nor later than 72 hours after the receipt of that written demand, during the normal business hours of the lienholder.

(4) Any lien under this section that arises because work or services have been performed on a vehicle with the consent of the registered owner shall be extinguished, and no lien sale shall be conducted, if the lienholder, after written demand made by either personal service or certified mail with return receipt requested by the legal owner or the lessor to receive a written copy of the work order or invoice reflecting the services or repairs performed on the vehicle and the authorization from the registered owner requesting the lienholder to perform the services or repairs, fails to provide that copy to the legal owner or lessor, or his or her agent, within 10 days after the receipt of that written demand.

(c) The lienholder shall not charge the legal owner or lessor any amount for release of the vehicle in excess of the amounts authorized by this subdivision.

(1) That portion of the lien in excess of one thousand five hundred dollars ($1,500) for any work or services, or that amount, subject to the limitations contained in Section 10652.5 of the Vehicle Code, in excess of one thousand twenty-five dollars ($1,025) for any storage, safekeeping, or rental of parking space or, if an application for an authorization to conduct a lien sale has been filed pursuant to Section 3071 within 30 days after the commencement of the storage or safekeeping, in excess of

one thousand two hundred fifty dollars ($1,250) for any storage or safekeeping, rendered or performed at the request of any person other than the legal owner or lessor, is invalid, unless prior to commencing any work, services, storage, safekeeping, or rental of parking space, the person claiming the lien gives actual notice in writing either by personal service or by registered letter addressed to the legal owner named in the registration certificate, and the written consent of that legal owner is obtained before any work, services, storage, safekeeping, or rental of parking space are performed.

(2) Subject to the limitations contained in Section 10652.5 of the Vehicle Code, if any portion of a lien includes charges for the care, storage, or safekeeping of, or for the rental of parking space for, a vehicle for a period in excess of 60 days, the portion of the lien that accrued after the expiration of that period is invalid unless Sections 10650 and 10652 of the Vehicle Code have been complied with by the holder of the lien.

(3) The charge for the care, storage, or safekeeping of a vehicle which may be charged to the legal owner or lessor shall not exceed that for one day of storage if, 24 hours or less after the vehicle is placed in storage, a request is made for the release of the vehicle. If the request is made more than 24 hours after the vehicle is placed in storage, charges may be imposed on a full, calendar-day basis for each day, or part thereof, that the vehicle is in storage.

(d) In any action brought by or on behalf of the legal owner or lessor to recover a vehicle alleged to be wrongfully withheld by the person claiming a lien pursuant to this section, the prevailing party shall be entitled to reasonable attorney's fees and costs, not to exceed one thousand seven hundred fifty dollars ($1,750). *(Added by Stats.1959, c. 3, p. 1791, § 3. Amended by Stats.1959, c. 197, p. 2089, § 2; Stats.1965, c. 1135, p. 2786, § 1; Stats.1968, c. 830, p. 1603, § 2; Stats.1974, c. 1262, p. 2736, § 2, eff. Sept. 23, 1974, operative Nov. 1, 1974; Stats.1978, c. 1005, p. 3084, § 4; Stats.1980, c. 1111, p. 3562, § 2; Stats.1983, c. 764, § 1; Stats.1988, c. 1092, § 4; Stats.1991, c. 727 (A.B.1882), § 1; Stats.1994, c. 799 (A.B.3164), § 1; Stats.2007, c. 121 (A.B.1575), § 1.)*

Research References

13 Witkin, California Summary 10th Personal Property § 237, (S 237) in General.

13 Witkin, California Summary 10th Personal Property § 239, Vehicle Valued Over Specified Amount.

13 Witkin, California Summary 10th Personal Property § 240, Vehicle Not Over Specified Value.

§ 3068.1. Towing, storage, or labor lien; storage charges; lien satisfaction; lienholder not liable

(a)(1) Every person has a lien dependent upon possession for the compensation to which the person is legally entitled for towing, storage, or labor associated with recovery or load salvage of any vehicle subject to registration that has been authorized to be removed by a public agency, a private property owner pursuant to Section 22658 of the Vehicle Code, or a lessee, operator, or registered owner of the vehicle. The lien is deemed to arise on the date of possession of the vehicle. Possession is deemed to arise when the vehicle is removed and is in transit, or when vehicle recovery operations or load salvage operations have begun. A person seeking to enforce a lien for the storage and safekeeping of a vehicle shall impose no charge exceeding that for one day of storage if, 24 hours or less after the vehicle is placed in storage, the vehicle is released. If the release is made more than 24 hours after the vehicle is placed in storage, charges may be imposed on a full-calendar-day basis for each day, or part thereof, that the vehicle is in storage. If a request to release the vehicle is made and the appropriate fees are tendered and documentation establishing that the person requesting release is entitled to possession of the vehicle, or is the owner's insurance representative, is presented within the initial 24 hours of storage, and the storage facility fails to comply with the request to release the vehicle or is not open for business during normal business hours, then only one day's charge may be required to be paid until after the first business day. A "business day" is any day in which the lienholder is open for business to the public for at least eight hours. If the request is made more than 24 hours after the vehicle is placed in storage, charges may be imposed on a full-calendar-day basis for each day, or part thereof, that the vehicle is in storage.

(2) "Documentation" that would entitle a person to possession of the vehicle includes, but is not limited to, a certificate of ownership, vehicle registration, information in the possession of the lienholder including ownership information obtained from the Department of Motor Vehicles or a facially valid registration found within the vehicle, or a notarized letter or statement from the legal or registered owner providing authorization to release to a particular person with a government-issued photographic identification card. Documentation that establishes that a person is the owner's insurance representative includes, but is not limited to, a faxed letter or other letter from the owner's insurance company. A lienholder is not responsible for determining the authenticity of documentation specifically described in this subdivision that establishes either a person's entitlement to possession or that a person is the owner's insurance representative.

(b) If the vehicle has been determined to have a value not exceeding four thousand dollars ($4,000), the lien shall be satisfied pursuant to Section 3072. Lien sale proceedings pursuant to Section 3072 shall commence within 15 days of the date the lien arises. No storage shall accrue beyond the 15-day period unless lien sale proceedings pursuant to Section 3072 have commenced. The storage lien may be for a period not exceeding 60 days if a completed notice of a pending lien sale form has been filed pursuant to Section 3072 within 15 days after the lien arises. Notwithstanding this 60-day limitation, the storage lien may be for a period not exceeding 120 days if any one of the following occurs:

(1) A Declaration of Opposition form is filed with the department pursuant to Section 3072.

(2) The vehicle has an out-of-state registration.

(3) The vehicle identification number was altered or removed.

(4) A person who has an interest in the vehicle becomes known to the lienholder after the lienholder has complied with subdivision (b) of Section 3072.

(c) If the vehicle has been determined to have a value exceeding four thousand dollars ($4,000) pursuant to Section 22670 of the Vehicle Code, the lien shall be satisfied pursuant to Section 3071. The storage lien may be for a period not exceeding 120 days if an application for an authorization to conduct a lien sale has been filed pursuant to Section 3071.

(d)(1) Any lien under this section shall be extinguished, and a lien sale shall not be conducted, if any one of the following occurs:

(A) The lienholder, after written demand to inspect the vehicle made by either personal service or certified mail with return receipt requested by the legal owner or the lessor, fails to permit the inspection by the legal owner or lessor, or his or her agent, within a period of time of at least 24 hours, but not to exceed 72 hours, after the receipt of that written demand, during the normal business hours of the lienholder. The legal owner or lessor shall comply with inspection and vehicle release policies of the impounding public agency.

(B) The amount claimed for storage exceeds the posted rates.

(2) "Agent" includes, but is not limited to, any person designated to inspect the vehicle by the request of the legal owner or lessor, in writing or by telephone, to the lienholder. A lienholder is not responsible for determining the authenticity of documentation establishing a person's agency for the purposes of inspection of a vehicle.

(e) A lienholder shall not be liable for any claim or dispute directly arising out of the reliance on documentation specifically described in paragraph (2) of subdivision (a) for purposes of releasing a vehicle. *(Added by Stats.1980, c. 1111, p. 3563, § 3. Amended by Stats.1984, c. 73, § 1; Stats.1987, c. 1091 § 1; Stats.1989, c. 457, § 1; Stats.1991, c. 727 (A.B.1882), § 2; Stats.1991, c. 1004 (S.B.887), § 1; Stats.1992, c. 1220 (A.B.3424), § 1; Stats.1994, c. 799 (A.B.3164), § 2; Stats.1995, c. 404 (S.B.240), § 1; Stats.1996, c. 267 (S.B.223), § 1; Stats.1998, c. 203 (S.B.1650), § 1; Stats.2010, c. 566 (A.B.519), § 1.)*

Research References

13 Witkin, California Summary 10th Personal Property § 242, Towing and Storage Lien.

§ 3068.2. Tow truck operator; deficiency claim; towing and storage charges; lien sale processing fee; persons liable

(a) A tow truck operator who has a lien on a vehicle pursuant to Section 3068.1 has a deficiency claim against the registered owner of the vehicle if the vehicle is not leased or leased with a driver for an amount equal to the towing and storage charges, not to exceed 120 days of storage, and the lien sale processing fee pursuant to Section 3074, less the amount received from the sale of the vehicle.

(b) A tow truck operator who has a lien on a vehicle pursuant to Section 3068.1 has a deficiency claim against the lessee of the vehicle if the vehicle is leased without a driver for an amount equal to the towing and storage charge, not to exceed 120 days of storage, and the lien sale processing fee described in Section 3074, less the amount received from the sale of the vehicle.

(c) Storage costs incurred after the sale shall not be included in calculating the amount received from the sale of the vehicle.

(d) A registered owner who has sold or transferred his or her vehicle prior to the vehicle's removal and who was not responsible for creating the circumstances leading to the removal of the vehicle is not liable for any deficiency under this section if that registered owner executes a notice pursuant to Section 5900 of the Vehicle Code and submits the notice to the Department of Motor Vehicles. The person identified as the transferee in the notice submitted to the Department of Motor Vehicles shall be liable for the amount of any deficiency only if that person received notice of the transfer and is responsible for the event leading to abandonment of the vehicle or requested the removal.

(e) Except as provided in Section 22524.5 of the Vehicle Code, if the transferee is an insurer and the transferor is its insured or his or her agent or representative, the insurer shall not be liable for any deficiency, unless the insurer agrees at the time of the transfer, to assume liability for the deficiency. *(Added by Stats.1994, c. 1220 (A.B.3132), § 2.5, eff. Sept. 30, 1994.)*

Research References

13 Witkin, California Summary 10th Personal Property § 242, Towing and Storage Lien.

§ 3069. Assignment of lien; notice to owner

Any lien provided for in this chapter for labor or materials, or for storage or safekeeping of a vehicle when abandoned on private property may be assigned by written instrument accompanied by delivery of possession of the vehicle, subject to the lien, and the assignee may exercise the rights of a lienholder as provided in this chapter. Any lienholder assigning a lien as authorized herein shall at the time of assigning the lien give written notice either by personal delivery or by registered or certified mail, to the registered and legal owner of the assignment, including the name and address of the person to whom the lien is assigned. *(Added by Stats.1959, c. 3, p. 1791, § 3. Amended by Stats.1969, c. 125, p. 272, § 1.)*

Research References

13 Witkin, California Summary 10th Personal Property § 237, (S 237) in General.

§ 3070. Loss of lien through trick, fraud or device; revival of lien; improperly causing vehicle to be towed or removed to create or acquire lien; forfeiture of claims and liability to owner or lessee

(a) Whenever the possessory lien upon any vehicle is lost through trick, fraud, or device, the repossession of the vehicle by the lienholder revives the possessory lien but any lien so revived is subordinate to any right, title, or interest of any person under any sale, transfer, encumbrance, lien, or other interest acquired or secured in good faith and for value between the time of the loss of possession and the time of repossession.

(b) It is a misdemeanor for any person to obtain possession of any vehicle or any part thereof subject to a lien pursuant to this chapter by trick, fraud, or device.

(c) It is a misdemeanor for any person claiming a lien on a vehicle to knowingly violate this chapter.

(d)(1) Any person who improperly causes a vehicle to be towed or removed in order to create or acquire a lienhold interest enforceable under this chapter, or who violates subdivision (c), shall forfeit all claims for towing, removal, or storage, and shall be liable to the owner or lessee of the vehicle for the cost of removal, transportation, and storage, damages resulting from the towing, removal, transportation, or storage of the vehicle, attorneys' fees, and court costs.

(2) For purposes of this subdivision, "improperly causes a vehicle to be towed or removed" includes, but is not limited to, engaging in any of the following acts, the consequence of which is the towing or removal of a vehicle:

(A) Failure to comply with Section 10650, 10652.5, or 10655 of the Vehicle Code.

(B) Misrepresentation of information described in subdivision (b) of Section 10650 of the Vehicle Code.

(C) Failure to comply with Section 22658 of the Vehicle Code.

(D) Failure, when obtaining authorization for the removal of a vehicle from a vehicle owner or operator where a law enforcement officer is not present at the scene of an accident, to present a form for signature that plainly identifies all applicable towing and storage fees and charges by type and amount, and identifies the name and address of the storage facility unless a different storage facility is specified by the vehicle owner or operator, and to furnish a copy of the signed form to the owner or operator.

(E) Failure by the owner or operator of a facility used for the storage of towed vehicles to display, in plain view at all cashiers' stations, a sign not less than 17 by 22 inches in size with lettering not less than one inch in height, disclosing all storage fees and charges in force, including the maximum daily storage rate.

(F) Undertaking repairs or service on a vehicle which is being stored at a facility used for the storage of towed vehicles without first providing a written estimate to, and obtaining the express written consent of, the owner of the vehicle.

(G) The promise to pay or the payment of money or other valuable consideration by any owner or operator of a towing service to the owner or operator of the premises from which the vehicle is towed or removed, for the privilege of towing or removing the vehicle. *(Added by Stats.1980, c. 1111, p. 3564, § 5. Amended by Stats.1991, c. 1004 (S.B.887), § 2; Stats.1993, c. 479 (A.B.1113), § 1; Stats.1994, c. 799 (A.B.3164), § 3.)*

Research References

13 Witkin, California Summary 10th Personal Property § 237, (S 237) in General.

§ 3071. Lien sale

(a) A lienholder shall apply to the department for the issuance of an authorization to conduct a lien sale pursuant to this section for any vehicle with a value determined to be over four thousand dollars ($4,000). A filing fee shall be charged by the department and may be recovered by the lienholder if a lien sale is conducted or if the vehicle is redeemed. The application shall be executed under penalty of perjury and shall include all of the following information:

(1) A description of the vehicle, including make, year model, identification number, license number, and state of registration. For motorcycles, the engine number also shall be included. If the vehicle identification number is not available, the department shall request an inspection of the vehicle by a peace officer, licensed vehicle verifier, or departmental employee before accepting the application.

(2) The names and addresses of the registered and legal owners of the vehicle, if ascertainable from the registration certificates within the vehicle, and the name and address of any person whom the lienholder knows, or reasonably should know, claims an interest in the vehicle.

(3) A statement of the amount of the lien and the facts that give rise to the lien.

(b) Upon receipt of an application made pursuant to subdivision (a), the department shall do all of the following:

(1) Notify the vehicle registry agency of a foreign state of the pending lien sale, if the vehicle bears indicia of registration in that state.

(2) By certified mail, send a notice, a copy of the application, and a return envelope preaddressed to the department to the registered and legal owners at their addresses of record with the department, and to any other person whose name and address is listed in the application.

(c) The notice required pursuant to subdivision (b) shall include all of the following statements and information:

(1) An application has been made with the department for authorization to conduct a lien sale.

(2) The person has a right to a hearing in court.

(3) If a hearing in court is desired, a Declaration of Opposition form, signed under penalty of perjury, shall be signed and returned to the department within 10 days of the date that the notice required pursuant to subdivision (b) was mailed.

(4) If the Declaration of Opposition form is signed and returned to the department, the lienholder shall be allowed to sell the vehicle only if he or she obtains a court judgment, if he or she obtains a subsequent release from the declarant or if the declarant, cannot be served as described in subdivision (e).

(5) If a court action is filed, the declarant shall be notified of the lawsuit at the address shown on the Declaration of Opposition form and may appear to contest the claim.

(6) The person may be liable for court costs if a judgment is entered in favor of the lienholder.

(d) If the department receives the Declaration of Opposition form in the time specified, the department shall notify the lienholder within 16 days of the receipt of the form that a lien sale shall not be conducted unless the lienholder files an action in court within 30 days of the department's notice under this subdivision. A lien sale of the vehicle shall not be conducted unless judgment is subsequently entered in favor of the lienholder or the declarant subsequently releases his or her interest in the vehicle. If a money judgment is entered in favor of the lienholder and the judgment is not paid within five days after becoming final, then the judgment may be enforced by lien sale proceedings conducted pursuant to subdivision (f).

(e) Service on the declarant in person or by certified mail with return receipt requested, signed by the declarant or an authorized agent of the declarant at the address shown on the Declaration of Opposition form, shall be effective for the serving of process. If the lienholder has served the declarant by certified mail at the address shown on the Declaration of Opposition form and the mail has been returned unclaimed, or if the lienholder has attempted to effect service on the declarant in person with a marshal, sheriff, or licensed process server and the marshal, sheriff, or licensed process server has been unable to effect service on the declarant, the lienholder may proceed with the judicial proceeding or proceed with the lien sale without a judicial proceeding. The lienholder shall notify the department of the inability to effect service on the declarant and shall provide the department with a copy of the documents with which service on the declarant was attempted. Upon receipt of the notification of unsuccessful service, the department shall send authorization of the sale to the lienholder and send notification of the authorization to the declarant.

(f) Upon receipt of authorization to conduct the lien sale from the department, the lienholder shall immediately do all of the following:

(1) At least five days, but not more than 20 days, prior to the lien sale, not counting the day of the sale, give notice of the sale by advertising once in a newspaper of general circulation published in the county in which the vehicle is located. If there is no newspaper published in the county, notice shall be given by posting a Notice of Sale form in three of the most public places in the town in which the vehicle is located and at the place where the vehicle is to be sold for 10 consecutive days prior to and including the day of the sale.

(2) Send a Notice of Pending Lien Sale form 20 days prior to the sale but not counting the day of sale, by certified mail with return receipt requested, to each of the following:

(A) The registered and legal owners of the vehicle, if registered in this state.

(B) All persons known to have an interest in the vehicle.

(C) The department.

(g) All notices required by this section, including the notice forms prescribed by the department, shall specify the make, year model, vehicle identification number, license number, and state of registration, if available, and the specific date, exact time, and place of sale. For motorcycles, the engine number shall also be included.

(h) Following the sale of a vehicle, the person who conducts the sale shall do both of the following:

(1) Remove and destroy the vehicle's license plates.

(2) Within five days of the sale, submit a completed "Notice of Release of Liability" form to the Department of Motor Vehicles.

(i) The Department of Motor Vehicles shall retain all submitted forms described in paragraph (2) of subdivision (h) for two years.

(j) No lien sale shall be undertaken pursuant to this section unless the vehicle has been available for inspection at a location easily accessible to the public for at least one hour before the sale and is at the place of sale at the time and date specified on the notice of sale. Sealed bids shall not be accepted. The lienholder shall conduct the sale in a commercially reasonable manner.

(k) Within 10 days after the sale of any vehicle pursuant to this section, the legal or registered owner may redeem the vehicle upon the payment of the amount of the sale, all costs and expenses of the sale, together with interest on the sum at the rate of 12 percent per annum from the due date thereof or the date when that sum was advanced until the repayment. If the vehicle is not redeemed, all lien sale documents required by the department shall then be completed and delivered to the buyer.

(*l*) Any lien sale pursuant to this section shall be void if the lienholder does not comply with this chapter. Any lien for fees or storage charges for parking and storage of a motor vehicle shall be subject to Section 10652.5 of the Vehicle Code. (*Added by Stats.1980, c. 1111, p. 3564, § 7. Amended by Stats.1984, c. 73, § 2; Stats.1987, c. 1091, § 2; Stats.1990, c. 1284 (A.B.3049), § 1; Stats.1992, c. 1220 (A.B.3424), § 2; Stats.1994, c. 799 (A.B.3164), § 4; Stats.1998, c. 203 (S.B.1650), § 2; Stats.1999, c. 376 (A.B.327), § 1; Stats.2001, c. 127 (S.B.46), § 1, eff. July 30, 2001.*)

Research References

13 Witkin, California Summary 10th Personal Property § 239, Vehicle Valued Over Specified Amount.

13 Witkin, California Summary 10th Personal Property § 241, Vehicle Removed by Public Agency.

13 Witkin, California Summary 10th Personal Property § 242, Towing and Storage Lien.

§ 3071.5. Vehicle in possession of lienor; release by registered or legal owner of interest

(a) A registered or legal owner of a vehicle in the possession of a person holding a lien under this chapter may release any interest in the vehicle after the lien has arisen. The release shall be dated when signed and a copy shall be given at the time the release is signed to the person releasing the interest.

(b) The release shall be in at least 12-point type and shall contain all of the following information in simple, nontechnical language:

(1) A description of the vehicle, including the year and make, the engine or vehicle identification number, and the license number, if available.

(2) The names and addresses of the registered and legal owners of record with the Department of Motor Vehicles, if available.

(3) A statement of the amount of the lien and the facts concerning the claim which gives rise to the lien.

(4) A statement that the person releasing the interest understands that (i) he has a legal right to a hearing in court prior to any sale of the vehicle to satisfy the lien and (ii) he is giving up the right to appear to contest the claim of the lienholder.

(5) A statement that (i) the person releasing the interest gives up any interest he may have in the vehicle and (ii) he is giving the lienholder permission to sell the vehicle.

(c) The release required by this section shall not be filed with the department in connection with any transfer of interest in a vehicle. (*Added by Stats.1974, c. 1262, p. 2739, § 4, eff. Sept. 23, 1974, operative Nov. 1, 1974. Amended by Stats.1978, c. 1005, p. 3089, § 7.*)

Research References

13 Witkin, California Summary 10th Personal Property § 238, in General.

§ 3072. Lien sales; valuation of $4,000 or less

(a) For vehicles with a value determined to be four thousand dollars ($4,000) or less, the lienholder shall apply to the department for the names and addresses of the registered and legal owners of record. The request shall include a description of the vehicle, including make, year, model, identification number, license number, and state of registration. If the vehicle identification number is not available, the Department of Motor Vehicles shall request an inspection of the vehicle by a peace officer, licensed vehicle verifier, or departmental employee before releasing the names and addresses of the registered and legal owners and interested parties.

(b) The lienholder shall, immediately upon receipt of the names and addresses, send, by certified mail with return receipt requested or by United States Postal Service Certificate of Mailing, a completed Notice of Pending Lien Sale form, a blank Declaration of Opposition form, and a return envelope pread-dressed to the department, to the registered owner and legal owner at their addresses of record with the department, and to any other person known to have an interest in the vehicle. The lienholder shall additionally send a copy of the completed Notice of Pending Lien Sale form to the department by certified mail on the same day that the other notices are mailed pursuant to this subdivision.

(c) All notices to persons having an interest in the vehicle shall be signed under penalty of perjury and shall include all of the following information and statements:

(1) A description of the vehicle, including make, year model, identification number, license number, and state of registration. For motorcycles, the engine number shall also be included.

(2) The specific date, exact time, and place of sale, which shall be set not less than 31 days, but not more than 41 days, from the date of mailing.

(3) The names and addresses of the registered and legal owners of the vehicle and any other person known to have an interest in the vehicle.

(4) All of the following statements:

(A) The amount of the lien and the facts concerning the claim which gives rise to the lien.

(B) The person has a right to a hearing in court.

(C) If a court hearing is desired, a Declaration of Opposition form, signed under penalty of perjury, shall be signed and returned to the department within 10 days of the date the Notice of Pending Lien Sale form was mailed.

(D) If the Declaration of Opposition form is signed and returned, the lienholder shall be allowed to sell the vehicle only if he or she obtains a court judgment or if he or she obtains a subsequent release from the declarant or if the declarant cannot be served as described in subdivision (e).

(E) If a court action is filed, the declarant shall be notified of the lawsuit at the address shown on the Declaration of Opposition form and may appear to contest the claim.

(F) The person may be liable for court costs if a judgment is entered in favor of the lienholder.

(d) If the department receives the completed Declaration of Opposition form within the time specified, the department shall notify the lienholder within 16 days that a lien sale shall not be conducted unless the lienholder files an action in court within 30 days of the notice and judgment is subsequently entered in favor of the lienholder or the declarant subsequently releases his or her interest in the vehicle. If a money judgment is entered in

favor of the lienholder and the judgment is not paid within five days after becoming final, then the judgment may be enforced by lien sale proceedings conducted pursuant to subdivision (f).

(e) Service on the declarant in person or by certified mail with return receipt requested, signed by the declarant or an author-ized agent of the declarant at the address shown on the Declaration of Opposition form, shall be effective for the serving of process. If the lienholder has served the declarant by certified mail at the address shown on the Declaration of Opposition form and the mail has been returned unclaimed, or if the lienholder has attempted to effect service on the declarant in person with a marshal, sheriff, or licensed process server and the marshal, sheriff, or licensed process server has been unable to effect service on the declarant, the lienholder may proceed with the judicial proceeding or proceed with the lien sale without a judicial proceeding. The lienholder shall notify the Department of Motor Vehicles of the inability to effect service on the declarant and shall provide the Department of Motor Vehicles with a copy of the documents with which service on the declarant was attempted. Upon receipt of the notification of unsuccessful service, the Department of Motor Vehicles shall send authoriza-tion of the sale to the lienholder and shall send notification of the authorization to the declarant.

(f) At least 10 consecutive days prior to and including the day of the sale, the lienholder shall post a Notice of Pending Lien Sale form in a conspicuous place on the premises of the business office of the lienholder and if the pending lien sale is scheduled to occur at a place other than the premises of the business office of the lienholder, at the site of the forthcoming sale. The Notice of Pending Lien Sale form shall state the specific date and exact time of the sale and description of the vehicle, including the make, year model, identification number, license number, and state of registration. For motorcycles, the engine number shall also be included. The notice of sale shall remain posted until the sale is completed.

(g) Following the sale of a vehicle, the person who conducts the sale shall do both of the following:

(1) Remove and destroy the vehicle's license plates.

(2) Within five days of the sale, submit a completed "Notice of Release of Liability" form with the Department of Motor Vehicles.

(h) The Department of Motor Vehicles shall retain all submitted forms described in paragraph (2) of subdivision (g) for two years.

(i) No lien sale shall be undertaken pursuant to this section unless the vehicle has been available for inspection at a location easily accessible to the public at least one hour before the sale and is at the place of sale at the time and date specified on the notice of sale. Sealed bids shall not be accepted. The lienholder shall conduct the sale in a commercially reasonable manner. All lien sale documents required by the department shall be completed and delivered to the buyer immediately following the sale.

(j) Any lien sale pursuant to this section shall be void if the lienholder does not comply with this chapter. Any lien for fees or storage charges for parking and storage of a motor vehicle shall be subject to Section 10652.5 of the Vehicle Code. *(Added by Stats.1980, c. 1111, p. 3566, § 10. Amended by Stats.1984, c. 73, § 3; Stats.1987, c. 1091, § 3; Stats.1990, c. 1284 (A.B.3049), § 2; Stats.1992, c. 1220 (A.B.3424), § 3; Stats.1994, c. 799 (A.B.3164), § 5; Stats.1998, c. 203 (S.B.1650), § 3; Stats.1999, c. 376 (A.B.327), § 2; Stats.2001, c. 127 (S.B.46), § 2, eff. July 30, 2001.)*

Research References

13 Witkin, California Summary 10th Personal Property § 240, Vehicle Not Over Specified Value.

13 Witkin, California Summary 10th Personal Property § 241, Vehicle Removed by Public Agency.

13 Witkin, California Summary 10th Personal Property § 242, Towing and Storage Lien.

§ 3073. Proceeds of sale; disposition; claims; limitation of actions

The proceeds of a vehicle lien sale under this article shall be disposed of as follows:

(a) The amount necessary to discharge the lien and the cost of processing the vehicle shall be paid to the lienholder. The cost of processing shall not exceed seventy dollars ($70) for each vehicle valued at four thousand dollars ($4,000) or less, or one hundred dollars ($100) for each vehicle valued over four thousand dollars ($4,000).

(b) The balance, if any, shall be forwarded to the Department of Motor Vehicles within 15 days of any sale conducted pursuant to Section 3071 or within five days of any sale conducted pursuant to Section 3072 and deposited in the Motor Vehicle Account in the State Transportation Fund, unless federal law requires these funds to be disposed in a different manner.

(c) Any person claiming an interest in the vehicle may file a claim with the Department of Motor Vehicles for any portion of the funds from the lien sale that were forwarded to the department pursuant to subdivision (b). Upon a determination of the Department of Motor Vehicles that the claimant is entitled to an amount from the balance deposited with the department, the department shall pay that amount determined by the department, which amount shall not exceed the amount forwarded to the department pursuant to subdivision (b) in connection with the sale of the vehicle in which the claimant claims an interest. The department shall not honor any claim unless the claim has been filed within three years of the date the funds were deposited in the Motor Vehicle Account. *(Added by Stats.1980, c. 1111, p. 3567, § 13. Amended by Stats.1988, c. 511, § 1; Stats.1990, c. 1284 (A.B.3049), § 3; Stats.1992, c. 1220 (A.B.3424), § 4; Stats.1994, c. 799 (A.B.3164), § 6; Stats.1998, c. 203 (S.B.1650), § 4.)*

§ 3074. Lien sale preparations; fees

The lienholder may charge a fee for lien sale preparations not to exceed seventy dollars ($70) in the case of a vehicle having a value determined to be four thousand dollars ($4,000) or less and not to exceed one hundred dollars ($100) in the case of a vehicle having a value determined to be greater than four thousand dollars ($4,000), from any person who redeems the vehicle prior to disposal or is paid through a lien sale pursuant to this chapter. These charges may commence and become part of the possessory lien when the lienholder requests the names and addresses of all persons having an interest in the vehicle from the Department of Motor Vehicles. Not more than 50 percent of the allowable fee may be charged until the lien sale notifications are mailed to all interested parties and the lienholder or registration service agent has possession of the required lien processing documents. This charge shall not be made in the case of any vehicle redeemed prior to 72 hours from the initial storage. *(Added by Stats.1995, c. 404 (S.B.240), § 3. Amended by Stats.1996, c. 676 (S.B.1111), § 1; Stats.1998, c. 203 (S.B. 1650), § 5.)*

Research References

13 Witkin, California Summary 10th Personal Property § 238, in General.

CHAPTER 6.7. LIVESTOCK SERVICE LIEN

§ 3080. Definitions

As used in this chapter, the following definitions shall apply:

(a) "Livestock" means any cattle, sheep, swine, goat, or horse, mule, or other equine.

(b) "Livestock servicer" means any individual, corporation, partnership, joint venture, cooperative, association or any other organization or entity which provides livestock services.

(c) "Livestock services" means any and all grazing, feeding, boarding, general care, which includes animal health services, obtained or provided by the livestock servicer, or his employee, transportation or other services rendered by a person to livestock for the owner of livestock, or for any person acting by or under the owner's authority. *(Added by Stats.1979, c. 600, p. 1863, § 2.)*

Research References

Rutter, Cal. Practice Guide: Enforcing Judgments/Debts Ch. 5-A, A. Introduction.

13 Witkin, California Summary 10th Personal Property § 233, (S 233) Statutory List.

§ 3080.01. Livestock services to which lien applicable; priority; amount

A livestock servicer shall have a general lien upon the livestock in its possession to secure the performance of all obligations of the owner of the livestock to the livestock servicer for both of the following:

(a) The provision of livestock services to the livestock in possession of the livestock servicer.

(b) The provision of livestock services to other livestock for which livestock services were provided in connection with or as part of the same livestock service transaction, if such livestock services were provided within the immediately preceding 12 months prior to the date upon which the lien arose. The lien shall have priority over all other liens upon and security interests in the livestock, shall arise as the charges for livestock services become due, and shall be dependent upon possession. The lien shall secure the owner's contractual obligations to the lienholder for the provision of livestock services, the lienholder's reasonable charges for the provision of livestock services after the lien has arisen as set forth in Section 3080.02, and the lienholder's costs of lien enforcement, including attorney's fees. *(Added by Stats.1979, c. 600, p. 1863, § 2.)*

§ 3080.02. Additional rights and remedies of lienholder

In addition to any other rights and remedies provided by law, a lienholder may:

(a) Retain possession of the livestock and charge the owner for the reasonable value of providing livestock services to the livestock until the owner's obligations secured by the lien have been satisfied.

(b) Proceed to sell all or any portion of the livestock pursuant to Section 3080.16 if:

(1) A judicial order authorizing sale has been entered pursuant to Section 3080.06;

(2) A judgment authorizing sale has been entered in favor of the lienholder on the claim which gives rise to the lien; or

(3) The owner of the livestock has released, after the lien has arisen, its interest in the livestock in the form prescribed by Section 3080.20.

(c) A lienholder may commence a legal action on its claim against the owner of the livestock or any other person indebted to the lienholder for services to the livestock and reduce the claim to judgment. When the lienholder has reduced the claim to judgment, any lien or levy or other form of enforcement which may be made upon the livestock by virtue of any execution based upon the judgment shall relate back to the attachment of and have the same priority as the livestock service lien. The lienholder may purchase at a judicial sale held pursuant to the execution on the judgment and thereafter hold the livestock free of any liens upon or security interests in the livestock. *(Added by Stats.1979, c. 600, p. 1863, § 2.)*

§ 3080.03. Order for sale; application; contents; hearing; service on defendant

Upon the filing of the complaint, or at any time thereafter prior to judgment, the lienholder may apply to the court in which the action was commenced for an order authorizing sale of livestock.

(a) The application shall include all of the following:

(1) A statement showing that the sale is sought pursuant to this chapter to enforce a livestock service lien;

(2) A statement of the amount the lienholder seeks to recover from the defendant and the date that amount became due;

(3) A statement setting forth the reasons why a sale should be held prior to judgment;

(4) A description of the livestock to be sold and an estimate of the fair market value thereof; and

(5) A statement of the manner in which the lienholder intends to sell the livestock. The statement shall include, but not be limited to, whether the sale will be public or private, the amount of proceeds expected from the sale, and, why the sale, if authorized, would conform to the standard of commercial reasonableness set forth in Section 3080.16.

(b) The application shall be supported by an affidavit or affidavits showing that on the facts presented therein the lienholder would be entitled to a judgment on the claim upon which the action is brought.

(c) A hearing shall be held in the court in which the lienholder has brought the action before an order authorizing sale is issued under this chapter. Except as provided in Section 3080.15, or as ordered by the court upon good cause shown, the defendant shall be served with a copy of all of the following at least 10 days prior to the date set for hearing:

(1) A summons and complaint;

(2) A notice of application and hearing; and

(3) An application and all affidavits filed in support thereof. *(Added by Stats.1979, c. 600, p. 1863, § 2.)*

§ 3080.04. Notice of application and hearing

The notice of application and hearing shall inform the defendant of all of the following:

(a) The date, time and place of the hearing on the application;

(b) That the order will issue if the court finds, after hearing, that the lienholder has established the probable validity of the claim and has satisfied the other requirements set forth in this chapter;

(c) The hearing is not held for the purpose of determining the actual validity of the claim which determination will be made in other proceedings in the action and will not be affected by the findings made at the hearing on the application for the order;

(d) If the order authorizing sale is issued, the lienholder may proceed to sell the livestock in the manner set forth in the order, and the sale proceeds will be deposited with the court pending judgment on the lienholder's claim;

(e) If the defendant desires to oppose the issuance of the order, the defendant must file with the court and serve on the lienholder a notice of opposition and supporting affidavit as required by Section 3080.05 no later than three days prior to the date set for hearing;

(f) At the hearing, the court may deny the lienholder's application if the defendant files an undertaking as set forth in Section 3080.11; and

(g) The notice shall contain the following statement: "You may seek the advice of an attorney as to any matters concerning the lienholder's complaint and application. If an attorney is to assist you, he or she should be consulted promptly. You or your attorney or both of you may be present at the hearing." *(Added by Stats.1979, c. 600, p. 1863, § 2.)*

§ 3080.05. Notice of opposition; contents; necessity of filing

(a) If a defendant desires to oppose the issuance of an order authorizing sale the defendant shall file and serve upon the lienholder a notice of opposition no later than three days prior to the date set for hearing. The notice shall:

(1) State the grounds upon which the defendant opposes the order;

(2) Be accompanied by an affidavit or affidavits supporting any factual issues raised;

(3) State whether the defendant is prepared to file an undertaking as provided in Section 3080.11; and

(4) If the defendant is prepared to file an undertaking, include an estimate of the amount of such undertaking as set forth in Section 3080.09 and the defendant's basis for the estimate.

(b) Except when the lienholder has made an ex parte application for an order as set forth in Section 3080.15, or for good cause shown, a defendant shall not be permitted to oppose the issuance of an order if it has failed to file a notice of opposition within the time prescribed. *(Added by Stats.1979, c. 600, p. 1863, § 2.)*

§ 3080.06. Order authorizing sale; findings; contents; disposition of proceeds

(a) At the hearing, the court shall consider the showing made by the parties and shall issue an order authorizing the sale of the livestock if it finds all of the following:

(1) The claim upon which the lienholder's action is based is a claim giving rise to a lien upon which an order authorizing sale may be issued under this chapter;

(2) The lienholder has established the probable validity of the claim upon which the action is based;

(3) The lienholder has established the probable validity of the lien sought to be enforced by sale;

(4) The sale is necessary to prevent a possible decline in the value or condition of the livestock or that the sale should be held in the interest of equity;

(5) The sale is not sought for a purpose other than the recovery on the claim upon which the lien is based; and

(6) The sale, if conducted in the manner set forth in the application, would be conducted in a commercially reasonable manner.

(b) The order authorizing sale shall:

(1) Identify the livestock for which sale is authorized;

(2) Specify the manner of sale including the date, time, place, necessary publication or other notice; and

(3) Except as may be ordered pursuant to subdivision (c), direct the lienholder to deposit the proceeds of sale with the clerk of the court pending final judgment in the action.

(c) The court may in its discretion do either of the following:

(1) Authorize the lienholder to deduct and retain funds from the sale proceeds in an amount sufficient to compensate the lienholder for services provided to the livestock from the date that the lien arose until the date of sale.

(2) Determine the amount of sale proceeds reasonably necessary to satisfy the indebtedness secured by the livestock service lien and order any portion or all of the remaining sale proceeds distributed and applied as set forth in paragraph (3) of subdivision (c) of Section 3080.16.

The balance of sale proceeds, if any, remaining after any deductions authorized in this section shall be deposited with the clerk of the court pursuant to this section. *(Added by Stats.1979, c. 600, p. 1863, § 2.)*

§ 3080.07. Denial of order; grounds; return to defendant of livestock

(a) After hearing, the court may issue an order denying the lienholder's application if it finds that:

(1) A sale is not necessary prior to judgment; and

(2) The defendant has filed an undertaking pursuant to Section 3080.11.

(b) If the defendant has filed an undertaking pursuant to Section 3080.11, the order shall direct the lienholder to assemble and make the livestock available to defendant, or to defendant's agent, at a specified date, time and place. *(Added by Stats.1979, c. 600, p. 1863, § 2.)*

§ 3080.08. Findings at hearing; basis; effect; waiver of defenses or of rights on admissibility of evidence

(a) The court's findings at the hearing shall be made upon the basis of the pleadings and other papers in the record. Upon cause shown, the court may receive and consider additional oral or documentary evidence or points and authorities at the hearing, or it may continue the hearing to allow the production of such additional evidence or points and authorities.

(b) The court's findings at the hearing shall have no effect on the determination of any issues in the action other than issues relevant to the proceedings authorized by this chapter, nor shall they affect the rights of the defendant in any other action arising out of the same claim. The court's determinations at the hearing shall neither be admissible as evidence nor referred to at the trial of any such action.

(c) Neither the failure of the defendant to oppose the issuance of an order authorizing sale, nor the defendant's failure to rebut any evidence produced by the lienholder at the hearing held for the issuance of such order, shall constitute a waiver of any defense to the lienholder's claim in the action or in any other action or have any effect on the right of the defendant to produce or exclude evidence at the trial of such action. *(Added by Stats.1979, c. 600, p. 1863, § 2.)*

§ 3080.09. Application for order for substitution of undertaking for livestock

(a) At any time after the lienholder has filed a complaint and claimed a lien under this chapter, or at any time after the owner of the livestock has commenced an action to recover possession of the livestock, the owner of the livestock may apply to the court in which the action was brought for an order for substitution of an undertaking which meets the requirements of Section 3080.11 for the livestock held by the lienholder.

(b) The application for such order shall be executed under oath and, unless included within a notice of opposition to sale as set forth in Section 3080.05, or except for good cause shown, shall be made upon noticed motion. Unless the parties otherwise agree, a hearing shall be held on the motion not less than five nor more than 10 days after service of notice of motion. The application shall contain all of the following:

(1) A description of the livestock to be recovered;

(2) An estimate and the basis for the estimate of the fair market value of the livestock;

(3) A statement identifying and describing the sureties for the undertaking. *(Added by Stats.1979, c. 600, p. 1863, § 2.)*

§ 3080.10. Order for release of livestock to owner; conditions

After hearing, the court may enter an order directing the lienholder to release all or a portion of the livestock to the owner, or to the owner's agent. The order shall be conditioned upon the filing by the owner of an undertaking as set forth in Section 3080.11, and shall include all of the following:

(1) The amount of the undertaking required.

(2) The basis for the court's finding as to the fair market value of the livestock.

(3) A statement that the lienholder has the right to object to the undertaking pursuant to Section 995.910 of the Code of Civil Procedure.

(4) A description of the livestock to be substituted.

(5) A statement of the date, time, place and manner in which the lienholder is to turn over the livestock to the owner. *(Added by Stats.1979, c. 600, p. 1863, § 2. Amended by Stats.1982, c. 517, p. 2328, § 77.)*

Law Revision Commission Comments

Section 3080.10 is amended for consistency with the Bond and Undertaking Law. See Code Civ.Proc. § 995.910 (objections to undertakings). [16 Cal.L.Rev.Comm. Reports 501 (1982)].

§ 3080.11. Undertaking; contents

The undertaking to be substituted for livestock shall be by the owner to pay to the lienholder an amount equal to the sum of (1) the fair market value of the livestock sought to be recovered, and (2) the costs to be incurred by the lienholder in order to assemble and turn over the livestock.   *(Added by Stats.1979, c. 600, p. 1863, § 2. Amended by Stats.1982, c. 517, p. 2329, § 78.)*

Law Revision Commission Comments

Section 3808.11 is amended to delete a provision duplicated in the Bond and Undertaking Law and for consistency with the Bond and Undertaking Law. See Code Civ.Proc. §§ 995.310 (sureties on undertaking) and 995.910 (objections to undertakings). [16 Cal.L.Rev.Comm. Reports 501 (1982)].

§ 3080.15. Order authorizing sale or order for substitution of undertaking without noticed hearing

(a) Except as otherwise provided by statute, or upon noticed hearing as provided in this chapter, no order authorizing sale or order for substitution of undertaking for livestock may issue unless it appears from facts shown by affidavit that great or irreparable injury would result to the party seeking the order if the issuance of the order were delayed until the matter could be heard upon noticed hearing.

(b) In addition to a specific statement of the facts showing great or irreparable injury, any application made under this section for either an order authorizing sale or an order substituting undertaking for livestock shall include the substantive requirements of an application made under Section 3080.03 or Section 3080.09, respectively.

(c) The court shall examine the ex parte application, supporting affidavits and other papers on record and may issue the order sought if it finds all of the following:

(1) The party seeking the order is entitled to the order under the substantive provisions of this chapter;

(2) The party seeking the order will suffer great and irreparable injury if the order is not issued; and

(3) If the ex parte application is made for an order authorizing sale, the court determines that the condition of the livestock will greatly deteriorate or the value of the livestock will greatly depreciate before an order authorizing sale could be obtained pursuant to noticed hearing.

(d) An order issued under this section shall contain such provisions as the court determines to be in the interests of justice and equity to the parties, taking into account the effects on all parties under the circumstances of the particular case. If an order authorizing sale issues under this section, the court may authorize the lienholder to take any action necessary to preserve the value of the livestock so long as the court has determined that such action would be commercially reasonable under the circumstances.

(e) Upon ex parte application of any party affected by an order issued under this section or, if the court so orders, after a noticed hearing, the court may modify or vacate the order if it determines that such action would be proper under the circumstances. *(Added by Stats.1979, c. 600, p. 1863, § 2.)*

§ 3080.16. Sales of livestock; method; disposition of proceeds

(a) Except as otherwise specified by the order authorizing sale or as agreed to by the parties after the lien has arisen, a sale of livestock under this chapter may be held in bulk or in parcels, at wholesale or retail, and at any time and place and on any terms, provided the lienholder acts in good faith and in a commercially reasonable manner. The livestock may be sold in its existing condition or following any commercially reasonable preparation or processing. The fact that a better price could have been

obtained by a sale at a different time or in a different manner from that selected by the lienholder is not of itself sufficient to establish that the sale was not made in a commercially reasonable manner. If the lienholder either sells the livestock in the usual manner in any recognized market therefor or sells at the price current in such market at the time of the sale or, if it has otherwise sold in conformity with reasonable commercial sales practices for the type of livestock sold, it has sold in a commercially reasonable manner.

(b) Except as otherwise specified by order of the court, or as agreed to by all interested parties after the lien has arisen, the proceeds of sale shall be deposited with the clerk of the court in an interest-bearing account to abide the judgment in the action.

(c) Except as otherwise specified in the judgment in the action, the proceeds of sale shall be applied in the following order:

(1) For reasonable expenses incurred by the lienholder in enforcing the lien, including, but not limited to, the charges for livestock services from the date the lien arose to the date of sale; the costs of transporting and preparing the livestock for sale and of conducting the sale; and, the reasonable attorneys' fees and legal costs and expenses incurred by the lienholder;

(2) For satisfaction of the contractual indebtedness secured by the lien; and

(3) For satisfaction of indebtedness secured by any subordinate lien or security interest in the livestock if written notification or demand therefor is received by the court or the lienholder before the proceeds have been distributed. If requested by the lienholder, the holder of a subordinate lien or security interest must seasonably furnish reasonable proof to the court of its subordinate interest before the lienholder need comply with the demand.

(d) The lienholder must account to the owner of the livestock for any surplus and, unless otherwise provided in the judgment in the action, the owner shall be liable for any deficiency. *(Added by Stats.1979, c. 600, p. 1863, § 2.)*

§ 3080.17. Notice of sale

Except as otherwise agreed or specified by order of court, notice of sale shall be given as follows:

(a) A notice in writing of the date, time and place of sale shall be delivered personally or be deposited in the United States mail, postage prepaid, addressed to the owner of the livestock, at his last known address, and to any other person claiming a lien upon or security interest in the livestock, who had on file with the California Secretary of State on the date the lien arose a financing statement covering the livestock for which livestock services secured by the lien were provided at least five days before the date fixed for any public sale or before the day on or after which any private sale or other disposition is to be made.

(b) Notice of the time and place of a public sale shall also be given at least five days before the date of sale by publication once in a newspaper of general circulation published in the county in which the sale is to be held. If there is no such newspaper, notice shall be given by posting, for five days prior to sale, a notice of sale where the sale is to be conducted. *(Added by Stats.1979, c. 600, p. 1863, § 2.)*

§ 3080.18. Public sale; defined; postponement; purchase by lienholder

(a) Any sale of which notice is delivered or mailed and published as provided in this chapter and which is held as provided in this chapter is a public sale.

(b) Any public sale may be postponed from time to time by public announcement at the time and place last scheduled for sale.

(c) The lienholder may purchase the livestock at a public sale. *(Added by Stats.1979, c. 600, p. 1863, § 2.)*

§ 3080.19. Effect of sale; rights of purchaser

(a) A sale of livestock held pursuant to this chapter shall:

(1) Transfer to a purchaser for value all of the owner's rights in the livestock; and

(2) Discharge the lien under which the sale is made and any lien or security interest subordinate thereto.

(b) The purchaser shall take free of all such subordinate rights and interests even though the lienholder fails to comply with the requirements of this chapter or of any judicial proceeding if:

(1) In the case of a public sale, the purchaser has no knowledge of any defects in the sale and does not buy in collusion with the lienholder, other bidders or the person conducting the sale; or

(2) In any other case, the purchaser acts in good faith. *(Added by Stats.1979, c. 600, p. 1863, § 2.)*

§ 3080.20. Release of interest by owner or other person

(a) The owner of livestock or any other person claiming an interest in livestock may release its interest in the livestock at any time after the lien has arisen. The release shall be in writing and dated when signed. A copy of the release shall be given to the person releasing the interest at the time the release is signed.

(b) The release shall contain all of the following information in simple, nontechnical language:

(1) A description of the livestock covered by the release and the releasing party's interest in the livestock;

(2) A statement of the amount of the lien to which the livestock is subject;

(3) A statement that the releasing party has a legal right to a hearing in court prior to any sale of the livestock to satisfy the lien;

(4) A statement by the releasing party that it is giving the lienholder permission to sell the livestock;

(5) A statement of the extent to which the releasing party gives up any interest it may have in the livestock or in the sale proceeds of the livestock; and,

(6) To the extent that the release is not given in full satisfaction of the lienholder's claim or claims against the releasing party, a statement by the releasing party that it is aware that the lienholder may still have a claim against it after the release has been executed. *(Added by Stats.1979, c. 600, p. 1863, § 2.)*

§ 3080.21. Retention of livestock to satisfy claim; proposal; notice; releases; sale after objection

At any time after a lien has arisen, the lienholder may propose to retain any portion or all of the livestock in satisfaction of any portion or all of the claim against the owner or other person indebted to the lienholder for livestock services. The proposal shall be made in writing to the owner and written notice thereof shall be given to any person entitled to receive notice under subdivision (a) of Section 3080.17. If, within 21 days after the notice was sent, the lienholder receives objection in writing from a person entitled to receive notification, the lienholder must proceed to sell the livestock and account for the proceeds pursuant to this chapter. In the absence of such written objection, the lienholder may retain the livestock, or so much thereof as proposed, in satisfaction of all or a portion of the claim against the owner and other person indebted to the lienholder for livestock services, upon the owner's and such other person's execution of a release conforming to Section 3080.20. *(Added by Stats.1979, c. 600, p. 1863, § 2.)*

§ 3080.22. Assignment of lien

Any lien provided for in this chapter may be assigned by written instrument accompanied by delivery of possession of the livestock, subject to the lien, and the assignee may exercise the rights of a lienholder as provided in this chapter. Any lienholder assigning a lien as authorized herein shall at the time of assigning the lien give written notice of the assignment either by personal delivery or by registered or certified mail, to the legal owner and any other person entitled to receive notice under subdivision (a) of Section 3080.17, including the name and address of the person to whom the lien has been assigned. *(Added by Stats.1979, c. 600, p. 1863, § 2.)*

CHAPTER 7. STOPPAGE IN TRANSIT

Section
3081. Safe deposit corporations; disposal of unclaimed contents of boxes.

§ 3081. Safe deposit corporations; disposal of unclaimed contents of boxes

Any corporation engaged in the business of renting to the public safe deposit boxes may dispose of the unclaimed contents of the safe deposit boxes in the manner set forth in Sections 1660 to 1679, inclusive, of the Financial Code. *(Added by Stats.1943, c. 846, p. 2659, § 19. Amended by Stats.1968, c. 48, p. 189, § 5.)*

Title 16

GENERAL PROVISIONS

Section
3268. Waiver of code provisions.

§ 3268. Waiver of code provisions

Except where it is otherwise declared, the provisions of the foregoing titles of this part, in respect to the rights and obligations of parties to contracts, are subordinate to the intention of the parties, when ascertained in the manner prescribed by the chapter on the interpretation of contracts; and the benefit thereof may be waived by any party entitled thereto, unless such waiver would be against public policy. *(Enacted in 1872. Amended by Stats.1963, c. 819, p. 2001, § 20, eff. Jan. 1, 1965.)*

Research References

Rutter, Cal. Practice Guide: Enforcing Judgments/Debts Ch. 3-A, A. Evaluating the Claim.
Miller and Starr California Real Estate § 28:96, Interpretation of the Bond.
Miller and Starr California Real Estate § 10:266, Application of "Exhaustion of the Security" Requirement.
Miller and Starr California Real Estate § 10:268, Liability for Deficiency After Nonjudicial Foreclosure.
Miller and Starr California Real Estate § 19:156, Covenant of Quiet Enjoyment and Possession.
Miller and Starr California Real Estate § 28:110, No Exoneration of the Surety Under Bonds in Favor of Claimants.

Title 17

YEAR 2000 INFORMATION DISCLOSURES

Section
3269. Definitions.

Section

3270. Disclosure of Year 2000 Problem or solutions thereto; liability in tort.

3271. Disclosure of Year 2000 Problem or solutions thereto; liability in tort; exclusion.

Explanatory Note

For another Title 17, "Year 2000 Problem Liability", added by Stats.1999, c. 698 (A.B.1476), § 2, inoperative after July 1, 2001, see Civil Code § 3272 et seq.

§ 3269. Definitions

For purposes of this title, the following definitions apply:

(a) "Year 2000 Problem" means any expected or actual computing, physical, enterprise, or distribution system complications that may occur in any computer system, computer program, software application, embedded systems, embedded chip calculations, or other computing application as a result of the year change from 1999 to 2000. These complications are often associated with the common programming practice of using a two-digit field to represent a year, resulting in erroneous date calculations, an ambiguous interpretation of the term "00," the failure to recognize the year 2000 as a leap year, the use of algorithms that use the year "99" or "00" as a flag for another function, or the use of applications, software, or hardware that are date sensitive.

(b) "Information" means any assessment, projection, estimate, planning document, objective, timetable, test plan, test date, or test result related to the implementation or verification of Year 2000 Problem processing capabilities of a computer system, computer program, software application, embedded systems, embedded chip calculations, or other computing application and intended to solve a Year 2000 Problem.

(c) "Disclosure" and "discloses" mean any dissemination or provision of information without any expectation or right to remuneration or fee therefor.

(d) "Person" means any individual, corporation, partnership, business entity, joint venture, association, the State of California or any of its subdivisions, or any other organization, or any combination thereof. *(Added by Stats.1998, c. 860 (S.B.1173), § 3, eff. Sept. 25, 1998. Amended by Stats.1999, c. 83 (S.B.966), § 23.)*

§ 3270. Disclosure of Year 2000 Problem or solutions thereto; liability in tort

(a) Notwithstanding any other law, any person that discloses information regarding the Year 2000 Problem or any potential solutions to the problem, including, but not limited to, those persons described in subdivision (b), shall not be liable for damages in any tort action brought against that person regarding the Year 2000 Problem for any injury caused by, arising out of, or relating to, the use of the information disclosed, except as provided in Section 3271.

(b) This section shall apply to any person that, when making the disclosures described in subdivision (a), specifically disclaims the universal applicability of the potential solutions disclosed, and expresses a unique experience with any Year 2000 information.

(c) This section does not apply to prospective solutions sold or exchanged for profit or provided for profit by a person or entity holding itself out as a provider of Year 2000 solutions. *(Added by Stats.1998, c. 860 (S.B.1173), § 3, eff. Sept. 25, 1998.)*

§ 3271. Disclosure of Year 2000 Problem or solutions thereto; liability in tort; exclusion

(a) Section 3270 shall not apply if the claimant in an action described in that section establishes that the Year 2000 Problem information disclosure was all of the following:

(1) Material.

(2) False, inaccurate, or misleading.

(3) Either (A) made with the knowledge that the statement was false, inaccurate, or misleading, (B) if the information disclosed was a republication of or otherwise a repetition of information from another person, made without a disclosure that the information was based on information supplied by another person or made with the knowledge that the statement was false, inaccurate, or misleading, or (C) made with gross negligence in the determination of the truth or accuracy of the disclosure or in the determination of whether the disclosure was misleading.

(b) Nothing in this title shall be deemed to affect any other remedy available at law, including, but not limited to, temporary or permanent injunctive relief, against a public or private entity or individual with respect to Year 2000 Problem information disclosures. *(Added by Stats.1998, c. 860 (S.B.1173), § 3, eff. Sept. 25, 1998.)*

Research References

Miller and Starr California Real Estate § 11:130, in General; Off-Record Priority.

Miller and Starr California Real Estate § 11:131, Date Liens Attach; Relation to Subsequent Interests.

Miller and Starr California Real Estate § 11:132, Relation to Prior Interests--In General.

Miller and Starr California Real Estate § 11:133, Relation to Prior Interests--Mechanic's Knowledge of a Prior Unrecorded Interest.

Miller and Starr California Real Estate § 11:134, Effect of Commencement of Work Before the Grantee Receives Title.

Miller and Starr California Real Estate § 11:135, When Construction Commences--Effect on Priority of Mechanics' and Design Professionals' Liens.

Miller and Starr California Real Estate § 11:136, When Construction Commences--Phasing of the Project; in General.

Miller and Starr California Real Estate § 11:137, Phasing of a Project by Separate Direct Contracts With the Owner.

Miller and Starr California Real Estate § 11:138, Site Improvements; Priority of Liens as Distinguished from Liens for Structures or Buildings.

Miller and Starr California Real Estate § 11:139, Priority as Affected by Separate Works of Improvement on Separate Parcels.

Miller and Starr California Real Estate § 11:140, Effect of Cessation of Work on Mechanic's Lien Priorities.

Miller and Starr California Real Estate § 11:141, Priority of the Construction Loan Deed of Trust--In General.

Miller and Starr California Real Estate § 11:142, Priority of the Construction Loan Deed of Trust--Relation to Obligatory Advances.

Miller and Starr California Real Estate § 11:143, Priority of the Construction Loan Deed of Trust--Relation to Optional Advances.

Miller and Starr California Real Estate § 11:144, Priority of the Construction Loan Deed of Trust--Premature Advances as Optional.

Miller and Starr California Real Estate § 11:145, Priority of the Construction Loan Deed of Trust--Advances to Complete Construction.

Miller and Starr California Real Estate § 11:146, Priority of the Construction Loan Deed of Trust--Effect of a Bond Recorded by the Construction Lender.

Division 4

GENERAL PROVISIONS

Part 1

RELIEF

Title 1

RELIEF IN GENERAL

Section
3274. Species of relief.
3275. Relief in case of forfeiture.

§ 3274. Species of relief

SPECIES OF RELIEF. As a general rule, compensation is the relief or remedy provided by the law of this State for the violation of private rights, and the means of securing their observance; and specific and preventive relief may be given in no other cases than those specified in this Part of the Civil Code. *(Enacted in 1872.)*

§ 3275. Relief in case of forfeiture

RELIEF IN CASE OF FORFEITURE. Whenever, by the terms of an obligation, a party thereto incurs a forfeiture, or a loss in the nature of a forfeiture, by reason of his failure to comply with its provisions, he may be relieved therefrom, upon making full compensation to the other party, except in case of a grossly negligent, willful, or fraudulent breach of duty. *(Enacted in 1872.)*

Research References

California Real Estate Forms (Miller & Starr) § 1:17, Purchase and Sale Agreement--Unimproved Real Property--With Escrow Instructions.
California Real Estate Forms (Miller & Starr) § 2:20, Retail Lease--Shopping Center With for Profit Parking Garage.
California Real Estate Forms (Miller & Starr) § 1:166, Liquidated Damages.
Rutter, Cal. Practice Guide: Insurance Litigation Ch. 7A-C, C. Insuring Clauses-Occurrence vs. Claims-Made Policies.
Rutter, Cal. Practice Guide: Real Prop. Transactions Ch. 8-B, B. Options to Purchase.

Miller and Starr California Real Estate § 2:9, Mode and Manner of Exercise.
Miller and Starr California Real Estate § 29:9, General Principles Concerning Owner's Damages.
Miller and Starr California Real Estate § 9:12, Defenses to Enforcement--Equitable Relief.
Miller and Starr California Real Estate § 1:161, Conditions Concurrent.
Miller and Starr California Real Estate § 1:162, Conditions Concurrent--Performance; When "Time is of the Essence" in a Contract.
Miller and Starr California Real Estate § 10:71, Payment or Performance of the Secured Obligation.
Miller and Starr California Real Estate § 19:37, Option to Extend or Renew Lease Term--Requirements for Exercise of the Option.
Miller and Starr California Real Estate § 19:48, Covenants and Conditions Distinguished.
Miller and Starr California Real Estate § 34:59, Buyer's Right of Reinstatement or Redemption.
Miller and Starr California Real Estate § 10:135, Curable Versus Noncurable Defaults.
Miller and Starr California Real Estate § 10:210, Attack on Validity of the Sale.
Miller and Starr California Real Estate § 19:200, Termination for Cause or Default.
Miller and Starr California Real Estate § 19:240, Relief from Forfeiture.
8 Witkin Cal. Proc. 5th Attack Judgment Trial Court § 107, (S 107) Other Issues.
5 Witkin Cal. Proc. 5th Pleading § 1109, (S 1109) Form.
12 Witkin, California Summary 10th Real Property § 531, (S 531) Manner of Exercise.
12 Witkin, California Summary 10th Real Property § 670, Relief from Forfeiture.
1 Witkin Cal. Summ. 10th Contracts § 503, (S 503) in General.
1 Witkin Cal. Summ. 10th Contracts § 505, (S 505) Late-Charge Interest.
1 Witkin Cal. Summ. 10th Contracts § 533, (S 533) Nature and Purpose of Revision.
1 Witkin Cal. Summ. 10th Contracts § 827, (S 827) Excuse of Condition or Equitable Relief.
13 Witkin, California Summary 10th Equity § 20, Equitable Doctrine Codified.
13 Witkin, California Summary 10th Equity § 21, Illustrations.
13 Witkin, California Summary 10th Equity § 60, (S 60) in General.
13 Witkin, California Summary 10th Equity § 62, (S 62) Purchaser Free from Serious Fault.
13 Witkin, California Summary 10th Equity § 63, in General.
13 Witkin, California Summary 10th Equity § 64, Extent of Relief.
13 Witkin, California Summary 10th Equity § 67, Restitution Analogy.
13 Witkin, California Summary 10th Equity § 69, (S 69) Relief to Optionee.
13 Witkin, California Summary 10th Equity § 70, (S 70) No Relief Where Contract is Executed.

Title 2

COMPENSATORY RELIEF

CHAPTER 1. DAMAGES IN GENERAL

ARTICLE 1. GENERAL PRINCIPLES

Section
3281.   Damages; person suffering detriment.
3282.   Detriment defined.
3283.   Damages for detriment after commencement of action;
            future damages.

§ 3281. Damages; person suffering detriment

PERSON SUFFERING DETRIMENT MAY RECOVER DAMAGES. Every person who suffers detriment from the unlawful act or omission of another, may recover from the person in fault a compensation therefor in money, which is called damages. *(Enacted in 1872.)*

Research References

Rutter, Cal. Practice Guide: Insurance Litigation Ch. 4-B, B. "Plain Meaning" vs. Ambiguity.
Rutter, Cal. Practice Guide: Personal Injury Ch. 3-A, A. Introduction.
Rutter, Cal. Practice Guide: Personal Injury Ch. 3-C, C. Specific Items of Compensatory Damages.
Miller and Starr California Real Estate § 27:80, Owner's Remedies for Late Performance--Compensatory Damages.
6 Witkin Cal. Proc. 5th Proceedings Without Trial § 500, Public Policy Considerations.
2 Witkin, California Summary 10th Insurance § 93, "Damages.".
6 Witkin, California Summary 10th Torts § 980, (S 980) Cause of Action Recognized.
6 Witkin, California Summary 10th Torts § 1607, Nature of Requirement.
6 Witkin, California Summary 10th Torts § 1670, (S 1670) Medical Care and Related Expense.

§ 3282. Detriment defined

DETRIMENT, WHAT. Detriment is a loss or harm suffered in person or property. *(Enacted in 1872.)*

Research References

Rutter, Cal. Practice Guide: Personal Injury Ch. 3-C, C. Specific Items of Compensatory Damages.
6 Witkin, California Summary 10th Torts § 980, (S 980) Cause of Action Recognized.
6 Witkin, California Summary 10th Torts § 1555, Anticipated Punitive Damages in Malpractice Action.
6 Witkin, California Summary 10th Torts § 1670, (S 1670) Medical Care and Related Expense.

§ 3283. Damages for detriment after commencement of action; future damages

INJURIES RESULTING OR PROBABLE AFTER SUIT BROUGHT. Damages may be awarded, in a judicial proceeding, for detriment resulting after the commencement thereof, or certain to result in the future. *(Enacted in 1872.)*

Research References

Rutter, Cal. Practice Guide: Personal Injury Ch. 3-A, A. Introduction.
Rutter, Cal. Practice Guide: Personal Injury Ch. 3-C, C. Specific Items of Compensatory Damages.
Rutter, Cal. Practice Guide: Personal Injury Ch. 3-G, G. Independent Damages Claims.
Miller and Starr California Real Estate § 29:10, Measure of Owner's Damages for Defective Construction.
Miller and Starr California Real Estate § 29:35, Liability for Negligent Supervision.
Miller and Starr California Real Estate § 29:38, Measure of Damages.
2 Witkin Cal. Proc. 5th Jurisdiction § 420, (S 420) Express Reservation.
7 Witkin Cal. Proc. 5th Trial § 268, (S 268) Language of Statute.
12 Witkin, California Summary 10th Real Property § 612, Wrongful Notice of Termination.
6 Witkin, California Summary 10th Torts § 1036, Fear of Contracting Disease.
6 Witkin, California Summary 10th Torts § 1552, Prospective Damages.

13 Witkin, California Summary 10th Equity § 153, (S 153) Against Private Nuisance.

ARTICLE 2. INTEREST AS DAMAGES

Section
3287.   Interest on damages; right to recover; time from
            which interest runs; interest rate.
3288.   Interest on damages; noncontractual obligation; discretion of jury.
3289.   Rate of interest chargeable after breach of contract.
3289.5. Retail installment contract; finance charges; prejudgment interest.
3290.   Waiver of interest by acceptance of principal.
3291.   Actions to recover damages for personal injury; claim of interest in complaint; offers to compromise; public entities and public employees.

§ 3287. Interest on damages; right to recover; time from which interest runs; interest rate

(a) A person who is entitled to recover damages certain, or capable of being made certain by calculation, and the right to recover which is vested in * * * the person upon a particular day, is entitled also to recover interest thereon from that day, except * * * when the debtor is prevented by law, or by the act of the creditor from paying the debt. This section is applicable to recovery of damages and interest from any * * * debtor, including the state or any county, city, city and county, municipal corporation, public district, public agency, or any political subdivision of the state.

(b) Every person who is entitled under any judgment to receive damages based upon a cause of action in contract where the claim was unliquidated, may also recover interest thereon from a date prior to the entry of judgment as the court may, in its discretion, fix, but in no event earlier than the date the action was filed.

(c) Unless another statute provides a different interest rate, in a tax or fee claim against a public entity that results in a judgment against the public entity, interest shall accrue at a rate equal to the weekly average one year constant maturity United States Treasury yield, but shall not exceed 7 percent per annum. That rate shall control until the judgment becomes enforceable under Section 965.5 or 970.1 of the Government Code, at which time interest shall accrue at an annual rate equal to the weekly average one year constant maturity United States Treasury yield at the time of the judgment plus 2 percent, but shall not exceed 7 percent per annum. *(Enacted in 1872. Amended by Stats.1955, c. 1477, p. 2689, § 1; Stats.1959, c. 1735, p. 4186, § 1; Stats.1967, c. 1230, p. 2997, § 1; Stats.2013, c. 424 (A.B.748), § 1.)*

Research References

Rutter, Cal. Practice Guide: A.D.R. Ch. 5-I, I. Arbitrator's Award.
Rutter, Cal. Practice Guide: Civil Appeals & Writs Ch. 8-D, D. Limits on Assertion of Issues on Appeal.
Rutter, Cal. Practice Guide: Civ. Pro. Before Trial Ch. 6-B, B. Complaints.
Rutter, Cal. Practice Guide: Civil Trials & Evidence Ch. 13-D, D. Preparing for Closing Argument.
Rutter, Cal. Practice Guide: Civil Trials & Evidence Ch. 17-D, D. Costs.
Rutter, Cal. Practice Guide: Civil Trials & Evidence Ch. 17-F, F. Prejudgment Interest.
California Practice Guide: Employment Litigation Ch. 7-A, A. Title VII and the California Fair Employment and Housing Act.
California Practice Guide: Employment Litigation Ch. 11-J, J. Enforcing California Laws Regulating Employee Compensation.
California Practice Guide: Employment Litigation Ch. 17-I, I. Interest.
Rutter, Cal. Practice Guide: Enforcing Judgments/Debts Ch. 3-C, C. Prelawsuit Considerations.

Rutter, Cal. Practice Guide: Enforcing Judgments/Debts Ch. 4-A, A. Attachment.

Rutter, Cal. Practice Guide: Enforcing Judgments/Debts Ch. 6A-5, Amount Recoverable Under Judgment.

Rutter, Cal. Practice Guide: Insurance Litigation Ch. 8-B, B. Contribution Between Insurers.

Rutter, Cal. Practice Guide: Insurance Litigation Ch. 9-F, F. Amount Recoverable by Insurer Under Subrogation.

Rutter, Cal. Practice Guide: Insurance Litigation Ch. 13-A, A. Contract Damages.

Rutter, Cal. Practice Guide: Insurance Litigation Ch. 13-B, B. Extracontractual Compensatory Damages.

Rutter, Cal. Practice Guide: Insurance Litigation Ch. 13-C, C. Punitive Damages.

Rutter, Cal. Practice Guide: Insurance Litigation Ch. 13-B, Outline B.

Rutter, Cal. Practice Guide: Personal Injury Ch. 3-A, A. Introduction.

Rutter, Cal. Practice Guide: Personal Injury Ch. 4-D, D. Techniques Where Settlement Not Forthcoming.

Rutter, Cal. Practice Guide: Personal Injury Ch. 3-A, Outline a.

Rutter, Cal. Practice Guide: Personal Injury Ch. 4-D, Outline D.

Rutter, Cal. Practice Guide: Real Prop. Transactions Ch. 11-C, C. Seller's Remedies Upon Buyer's Breach-Damages and Specific Performance.

Rutter, Cal. Practice Guide: Real Prop. Transactions Ch. 11-D, D. Buyer's Remedies Upon Seller's Breach-Damages and Specific Performance.

Rutter, Cal. Practice Guide: Real Prop. Transactions Ch. 11-E, E. Damages for Fraud.

Rutter, Cal. Practice Guide: Real Prop. Transactions Ch. 11-G, G. Rescission.

Rutter, Cal. Practice Guide: Real Prop. Transactions Gen. Matls., Highlights.

Rutter, Cal. Practice Guide: Real Prop. Transactions Ch. 11-C Outline, Outline C.

Rutter, Cal. Practice Guide: Real Prop. Transactions Ch. 11-D Outline, Outline D.

Rutter, Cal. Practice Guide: Real Prop. Transactions Ch. 11-E Outline, Outline E.

Miller and Starr California Real Estate § 27:69, Recovery for Extra Work.

Miller and Starr California Real Estate § 27:85, Contractor's Remedies-- "No Damages for Delay" Clauses.

Miller and Starr California Real Estate § 28:62, Prejudgment Interest.

Miller and Starr California Real Estate § 34:32, Prejudgment Interest Recoverable as Damages--Contract Actions.

Miller and Starr California Real Estate § 34:33, Recovery of Pre-Judgment Interest in Tort Actions; Breach of Fiduciary Duty.

Miller and Starr California Real Estate § 34:34, When Interest Commences to Accrue and Cessation.

Miller and Starr California Real Estate § 34:35, Rate of Interest; Compound Interest.

Miller and Starr California Real Estate § 34:54, Prejudgment Interest on Buyer's or Seller's Damages.

Miller and Starr California Real Estate § 10:189, Amounts that Must be Paid to Reinstate.

Miller and Starr California Real Estate § 10:218, Measure of Tort Damages.

Miller and Starr California Real Estate § 19:208, Termination of the Lease; Landlord's Recovery of Rent or Damages--Recovery in an Unlawful Detainer Proceeding.

Miller and Starr California Real Estate § 28:124, Action by Claimants and Others on Public Works Payment Bond--Amount of Recovery; Prejudgment Interest.

19 NO. 1 Miller & Starr, California Real Estate Newsalert 15, Holding Title.

19 NO. 5 Miller & Starr, California Real Estate Newsalert 21, Judicial Remedies.

19 NO. 2 Miller & Starr, California Real Estate Newsalert 23, Remedies.

19 NO. 5 Miller & Starr, California Real Estate Newsalert 30, Usury.

20 NO. 5 Miller & Starr, California Real Estate Newsalert 20, Mechanics' Liens.

9 Witkin Cal. Proc. 5th Administrative Proceedings § 61, Interest Not Recoverable.

9 Witkin Cal. Proc. 5th Administrative Proceedings § 62, Interest Recoverable.

8 Witkin Cal. Proc. 5th Extraordinary Writs § 214, (S 214) Interest in Mandamus Proceeding.

8 Witkin Cal. Proc. 5th Extraordinary Writs § 332, Declaratory Relief.

7 Witkin Cal. Proc. 5th Judgment § 139, (S 139) in General.

7 Witkin Cal. Proc. 5th Judgment § 324, Interest on Obligation or as Damages.

7 Witkin Cal. Proc. 5th Judgment § 325, Interest on Verdict or Decision.

7 Witkin Cal. Proc. 5th Judgment § 332, Other Judgments.

6 Witkin Cal. Proc. 5th Proceedings Without Trial § 107, Prejudgment Interest.

6 Witkin Cal. Proc. 5th Proceedings Without Trial § 566, Confirmation of Award.

1 Witkin Cal. Summ. 10th Contracts § 888, (S 888) General Rule.

1 Witkin Cal. Summ. 10th Contracts § 889, (S 889) Liquidated Sum Due.

1 Witkin Cal. Summ. 10th Contracts § 890, (S 890) Damages Ascertainable by Calculation.

1 Witkin Cal. Summ. 10th Contracts § 892, (S 892) Traditional Rule of Denial.

1 Witkin Cal. Summ. 10th Contracts § 893, in General.

1 Witkin Cal. Summ. 10th Contracts § 895, Debtor Prevented by Law.

1 Witkin Cal. Summ. 10th Contracts § 899, Revised Statutes.

1 Witkin Cal. Summ. 10th Contracts § 1014, (S 1014) Practical Distinctions.

4 Witkin, California Summary 10th Sales § 321, (S 321) in General.

9 Witkin, California Summary 10th Corporations § 294, (S 294) in General.

6 Witkin, California Summary 10th Torts § 1643, in General.

6 Witkin, California Summary 10th Torts § 1647, (S 1647) Interest on Award of Punitive Damages.

3 Witkin, California Summary 10th Agency and Employment § 321, (S 321) Judgment.

4 Witkin, California Summary 10th Negotiable Instruments § 47, (S 47) Additional Liability to Payee or Payee's Assignee.

13 Witkin, California Summary 10th Trusts § 134, Damages.

13 Witkin, California Summary 10th Trusts § 135, Interest.

2 Witkin Cal. Summ. 10th Workers' Compensation § 18, (S 18) Sanctions for Violation.

§ 3288. Interest on damages; noncontractual obligation; discretion of jury

IN ACTIONS OTHER THAN CONTRACT. In an action for the breach of an obligation not arising from contract, and in every case of oppression, fraud, or malice, interest may be given, in the discretion of the jury. *(Enacted in 1872.)*

Research References

Rutter, Cal. Practice Guide: Civil Appeals & Writs Ch. 8-D, D. Limits on Assertion of Issues on Appeal.

Rutter, Cal. Practice Guide: Civ. Pro. Before Trial Ch. 6-B, B. Complaints.

Rutter, Cal. Practice Guide: Civil Trials & Evidence Ch. 13-D, D. Preparing for Closing Argument.

Rutter, Cal. Practice Guide: Civil Trials & Evidence Ch. 17-F, F. Prejudgment Interest.

California Practice Guide: Employment Litigation Ch. 17-I, I. Interest.

Rutter, Cal. Practice Guide: Enforcing Judgments/Debts Ch. 3-C, C. Prelawsuit Considerations.

Rutter, Cal. Practice Guide: Insurance Litigation Ch. 13-A, A. Contract Damages.

Rutter, Cal. Practice Guide: Insurance Litigation Ch. 13-B, B. Extracontractual Compensatory Damages.

Rutter, Cal. Practice Guide: Insurance Litigation Ch. 13-B, Outline B.

Rutter, Cal. Practice Guide: Personal Injury Ch. 3-A, A. Introduction.

Rutter, Cal. Practice Guide: Personal Injury Ch. 4-D, D. Techniques Where Settlement Not Forthcoming.

Rutter, Cal. Practice Guide: Personal Injury Ch. 3-A, Outline a.

Rutter, Cal. Practice Guide: Personal Injury Ch. 4-D, Outline D.

Rutter, Cal. Practice Guide: Real Prop. Transactions Ch. 11-E, E. Damages for Fraud.

Rutter, Cal. Practice Guide: Real Prop. Transactions Ch. 11-G, G. Rescission.

Rutter, Cal. Practice Guide: Real Prop. Transactions Ch. 11-E Outline, Outline E.

Miller and Starr California Real Estate § 3:33, Damages Recoverable by the Principal.

Miller and Starr California Real Estate § 34:32, Prejudgment Interest Recoverable as Damages--Contract Actions.

Miller and Starr California Real Estate § 34:33, Recovery of Pre-Judgment Interest in Tort Actions; Breach of Fiduciary Duty.

3 Witkin Cal. Proc. 5th Actions § 49, (S 49) in General.

7 Witkin Cal. Proc. 5th Judgment § 324, Interest on Obligation or as Damages.
7 Witkin Cal. Proc. 5th Judgment § 329, No Compounding of Post-judgment Interest.
7 Witkin Cal. Proc. 5th Judgment § 332, Other Judgments.
9 Witkin, California Summary 10th Corporations § 294, (S 294) in General.
6 Witkin, California Summary 10th Torts § 1643, in General.
6 Witkin, California Summary 10th Torts § 1644, Obligation Not Arising from Contract.
6 Witkin, California Summary 10th Torts § 1645, General Rule Against Interest.

§ 3289. Rate of interest chargeable after breach of contract

(a) Any legal rate of interest stipulated by a contract remains chargeable after a breach thereof, as before, until the contract is superseded by a verdict or other new obligation.

(b) If a contract entered into after January 1, 1986, does not stipulate a legal rate of interest, the obligation shall bear interest at a rate of 10 percent per annum after a breach.

For the purposes of this subdivision, the term contract shall not include a note secured by a deed of trust on real property. *(Enacted in 1872. Amended by Stats.1985, c. 663, § 1; Stats. 1986, c. 176, § 1, eff. June 23, 1986.)*

Research References
Rutter, Cal. Practice Guide: Civil Trials & Evidence Ch. 17-F, F. Prejudgment Interest.
California Practice Guide: Employment Litigation Ch. 11-J, J. Enforcing California Laws Regulating Employee Compensation.
California Practice Guide: Employment Litigation Ch. 17-I, I. Interest.
Rutter, Cal. Practice Guide: Enforcing Judgments/Debts Ch. 3-C, C. Prelawsuit Considerations.
Rutter, Cal. Practice Guide: Enforcing Judgments/Debts Ch. 4-A, A. Attachment.
Rutter, Cal. Practice Guide: Enforcing Judgments/Debts Ch. 6A-5, Amount Recoverable Under Judgment.
Rutter, Cal. Practice Guide: Insurance Litigation Ch. 8-B, B. Contribution Between Insurers.
Rutter, Cal. Practice Guide: Insurance Litigation Ch. 13-A, A. Contract Damages.
Rutter, Cal. Practice Guide: Insurance Litigation Ch. 6I-B, B. Particular Surety Bond Coverages.
Rutter, Cal. Practice Guide: Real Prop. Transactions Ch. 11-C, C. Seller's Remedies Upon Buyer's Breach-Damages and Specific Performance.
Rutter, Cal. Practice Guide: Real Prop. Transactions Ch. 11-D, D. Buyer's Remedies Upon Seller's Breach-Damages and Specific Performance.
Miller and Starr California Real Estate § 21:1, Policy and Validity of the Usury Law.
Miller and Starr California Real Estate § 34:35, Rate of Interest; Compound Interest.
Miller and Starr California Real Estate § 10:189, Amounts that Must be Paid to Reinstate.
Miller and Starr California Real Estate § 10:203, Trustee's Liability for Wrongful Conduct of the Sale.
Miller and Starr California Real Estate § 10:218, Measure of Tort Damages.
19 NO. 5 Miller & Starr, California Real Estate Newsalert 12, Deeds of Trust.
7 Witkin Cal. Proc. 5th Judgment § 324, Interest on Obligation or as Damages.
1 Witkin Cal. Summ. 10th Contracts § 541, (S 541) Fees Against Credit Card Customers.
1 Witkin Cal. Summ. 10th Contracts § 896, Rate of Interest.
4 Witkin, California Summary 10th Sales § 252, in General.
9 Witkin, California Summary 10th Partnership § 21, (S 21) Governing Law.
14 Witkin, California Summary 10th Wills and Probate § 651, Interest.

§ 3289.5. Retail installment contract; finance charges; pre-judgment interest

For purposes of Section 3289, the rate of the contracted finance charge shall be the legal rate of interest stipulated by a retail installment contract subject to Chapter 1 (commencing with Section 1801) of Title 2 of Part 4 of Division 3. *(Added by Stats.1985, c. 224, § 1.)*

Research References
1 Witkin Cal. Summ. 10th Contracts § 896, Rate of Interest.

§ 3290. Waiver of interest by acceptance of principal

ACCEPTANCE OF PRINCIPAL WAIVES CLAIM TO INTEREST. Accepting payment of the whole principal, as such, waives all claim to interest. *(Enacted in 1872.)*

§ 3291. Actions to recover damages for personal injury; claim of interest in complaint; offers to compromise; public entities and public employees

In any action brought to recover damages for personal injury sustained by any person resulting from or occasioned by the tort of any other person, corporation, association, or partnership, whether by negligence or by willful intent of the other person, corporation, association, or partnership, and whether the injury was fatal or otherwise, it is lawful for the plaintiff in the complaint to claim interest on the damages alleged as provided in this section.

If the plaintiff makes an offer pursuant to Section 998 of the Code of Civil Procedure which the defendant does not accept prior to trial or within 30 days, whichever occurs first, and the plaintiff obtains a more favorable judgment, the judgment shall bear interest at the legal rate of 10 percent per annum calculated from the date of the plaintiff's first offer pursuant to Section 998 of the Code of Civil Procedure which is exceeded by the judgment, and interest shall accrue until the satisfaction of judgment.

This section shall not apply to a public entity, or to a public employee for an act or omission within the scope of employment, and neither the public entity nor the public employee shall be liable, directly or indirectly, to any person for any interest imposed by this section. *(Added by Stats.1982, c. 150, p. 493, § 1.)*

Research References
Rutter, Cal. Practice Guide: A.D.R. Ch. 4-B, B. Judicial Arbitration.
Rutter, Cal. Practice Guide: A.D.R. Ch. 5-H, H. Conduct of Arbitration Proceedings.
Rutter, Cal. Practice Guide: Civil Appeals & Writs Ch. 13-A, A. General Considerations.
Rutter, Cal. Practice Guide: Civ. Pro. Before Trial Ch. 6-B, B. Complaints.
Rutter, Cal. Practice Guide: Civ. Pro. Before Trial Ch. 13-B, B. Judicial Arbitration Distinguished from Contract Arbitration.
Rutter, Cal. Practice Guide: Civ. Pro. Before Trial Ch. 13-F, F. Arbitration Award.
Rutter, Cal. Practice Guide: Civ. Pro. Before Trial Ch. 12(II)-C, C. Statutory Offer to Compromise (CCP § 998).
Rutter, Cal. Practice Guide: Civil Trials & Evidence Ch. 17-D, D. Costs.
Rutter, Cal. Practice Guide: Civil Trials & Evidence Ch. 17-F, F. Prejudgment Interest.
California Practice Guide: Employment Litigation Ch. 17-I, I. Interest.
California Practice Guide: Employment Litigation Ch. 19-H, H. Other Pretrial Procedures.
Rutter, Cal. Practice Guide: Enforcing Judgments/Debts Ch. 3-C, C. Prelawsuit Considerations.
Rutter, Cal. Practice Guide: Enforcing Judgments/Debts Ch. 6A-5, Amount Recoverable Under Judgment.
Rutter, Cal. Practice Guide: Fed.Civ.Pro. Before Trial Ch. 1-D, D. Choosing Between State and Federal Courts.
Rutter, Cal. Practice Guide: Insurance Litigation Ch. 13-A, A. Contract Damages.
Rutter, Cal. Practice Guide: Insurance Litigation Ch. 13-B, B. Extracontractual Compensatory Damages.
Rutter, Cal. Practice Guide: Insurance Litigation Ch. 6G-D, D. Uninsured and Underinsured Motorist Coverages.
Rutter, Cal. Practice Guide: Insurance Litigation Ch. 13-B, Outline B.

Rutter, Cal. Practice Guide: Insurance Litigation Ch. 6G-D, Outline D.

Rutter, Cal. Practice Guide: Personal Injury Ch. 3-A, A. Introduction.

Rutter, Cal. Practice Guide: Personal Injury Ch. 3-F, F. MICRA Provisions Affecting Damages.

Rutter, Cal. Practice Guide: Personal Injury Ch. 4-D, D. Techniques Where Settlement Not Forthcoming.

Rutter, Cal. Practice Guide: Personal Injury Ch. 7-H, H. Arbitration Award and Judgment.

Rutter, Cal. Practice Guide: Personal Injury Ch. 3-A, Outline a.

Rutter, Cal. Practice Guide: Personal Injury Ch. 4-D, Outline D.

Miller and Starr California Real Estate § 11:41, Slander of Title Defined.

Miller and Starr California Real Estate § 34:33, Recovery of Pre-Judgment Interest in Tort Actions; Breach of Fiduciary Duty.

Miller and Starr California Real Estate § 34:35, Rate of Interest; Compound Interest.

Miller and Starr California Real Estate § 34:36, Recovery of Interest After Rejected Settlement Offer.

Miller and Starr California Real Estate § 35:84, Ancillary Remedies.

7 Witkin Cal. Proc. 5th Judgment § 327, Rate of Interest.

7 Witkin Cal. Proc. 5th Judgment § 332, Other Judgments.

6 Witkin Cal. Proc. 5th Proceedings Without Trial § 82, (S 82) in General.

6 Witkin Cal. Proc. 5th Proceedings Without Trial § 90, Offers to Multiple Defendants.

6 Witkin Cal. Proc. 5th Proceedings Without Trial § 96, (L)--Effect of Second Offer.

6 Witkin Cal. Proc. 5th Proceedings Without Trial § 111, Offer by Plaintiff.

6 Witkin Cal. Proc. 5th Proceedings Without Trial § 607, (S 607) Award of Costs.

6 Witkin Cal. Proc. 5th Proceedings Without Trial § 611, Appealability.

2 Witkin, California Summary 10th Insurance § 214, (S 214) Award and Review.

6 Witkin, California Summary 10th Torts § 1643, in General.

6 Witkin, California Summary 10th Torts § 1646, (S 1646) Nature and Scope of Statute.

6 Witkin, California Summary 10th Torts § 1647, (S 1647) Interest on Award of Punitive Damages.

6 Witkin, California Summary 10th Torts § 1648, (S 1648) Verdict for Personal Injury and Other Damages.

6 Witkin, California Summary 10th Torts § 1650, (S 1650) Prejudgment Interest is Not Element of Damages.

6 Witkin, California Summary 10th Torts § 1651, (S 1651) Scope of Personal Injury.

6 Witkin, California Summary 10th Torts § 1652, (S 1652) Actions Excluded.

6 Witkin, California Summary 10th Torts § 1653, (S 1653) Insurer's Settlement Offer as Abrogating Obligation to Pay Prejudgment Interest.

6 Witkin, California Summary 10th Torts § 1654, (S 1654) Arbitration Proceedings.

ARTICLE 3. EXEMPLARY DAMAGES

Section

3294. Exemplary damages; when allowable; definitions.

3295. Protective order; prima facie case of liability prerequisite to certain evidence; discovery limitations; evidence of profits or financial condition.

3296. Insurers and health care service plans; punitive damage judgments; copies to commissioners; sanctions.

§ 3294. Exemplary damages; when allowable; definitions

(a) In an action for the breach of an obligation not arising from contract, where it is proven by clear and convincing evidence that the defendant has been guilty of oppression, fraud, or malice, the plaintiff, in addition to the actual damages, may recover damages for the sake of example and by way of punishing the defendant.

(b) An employer shall not be liable for damages pursuant to subdivision (a), based upon acts of an employee of the employer, unless the employer had advance knowledge of the unfitness of the employee and employed him or her with a conscious disregard of the rights or safety of others or authorized or ratified the wrongful conduct for which the damages are awarded or was personally guilty of oppression, fraud, or malice. With respect to a corporate employer, the advance knowledge and conscious disregard, authorization, ratification or act of oppression, fraud, or malice must be on the part of an officer, director, or managing agent of the corporation.

(c) As used in this section, the following definitions shall apply:

(1) "Malice" means conduct which is intended by the defendant to cause injury to the plaintiff or despicable conduct which is carried on by the defendant with a willful and conscious disregard of the rights or safety of others.

(2) "Oppression" means despicable conduct that subjects a person to cruel and unjust hardship in conscious disregard of that person's rights.

(3) "Fraud" means an intentional misrepresentation, deceit, or concealment of a material fact known to the defendant with the intention on the part of the defendant of thereby depriving a person of property or legal rights or otherwise causing injury.

(d) Damages may be recovered pursuant to this section in an action pursuant to Chapter 4 (commencing with Section 377.10) of Title 3 of Part 2 of the Code of Civil Procedure based upon a death which resulted from a homicide for which the defendant has been convicted of a felony, whether or not the decedent died instantly or survived the fatal injury for some period of time. The procedures for joinder and consolidation contained in Section 377.62 of the Code of Civil Procedure shall apply to prevent multiple recoveries of punitive or exemplary damages based upon the same wrongful act.

(e) The amendments to this section made by Chapter 1498 of the Statutes of 1987 apply to all actions in which the initial trial has not commenced prior to January 1, 1988. *(Enacted in 1872. Amended by Stats.1905, c. 463, p. 621, § 1; Stats.1980, c. 1242, p. 4217, § 1; Stats.1982, c. 174, § 1; Stats.1983, c. 408, § 1; Stats.1987, c. 1498, § 5; Stats.1988, c. 160, § 17; Stats.1992, c. 178 (S.B.1496), § 5.)*

Law Revision Commission Comments

Section 3294 is amended to revise section references. These revisions are technical, nonsubstantive changes. [22 Cal.L.Rev.Comm.Reports 895 (1992)].

Research References

Rutter, Cal. Practice Guide: Civil Appeals & Writs Ch. 8-C, C. Standards of Appellate Review.

Rutter, Cal. Practice Guide: Civil Appeals & Writs Ch. 14-C, C. Trial Court Proceedings After Reversal.

Rutter, Cal. Practice Guide: Civil Appeals & Writs Form 5:E, Application for Permission to File Brief Exceeding Authorized Length Limit (Appellant).

Rutter, Cal. Practice Guide: Civ. Pro. Before Trial Ch. 6-B, B. Complaints.

Rutter, Cal. Practice Guide: Civ. Pro. Before Trial Ch. 10-A, A. Introduction.

Rutter, Cal. Practice Guide: Civ. Pro. Before Trial Ch. 10-F, F. Burden of Proof on Motion.

Rutter, Cal. Practice Guide: Civ. Pro. Before Trial Ch. 8C-5, Privacy Protection.

Rutter, Cal. Practice Guide: Civ. Pro. Before Trial Ch. 7(I)-B, B. Motions to Strike.

Rutter, Cal. Practice Guide: Civ. Pro. Before Trial Ch. 12(I)-E, E. Consolidation, Coordination and Bifurcation.

Rutter, Cal. Practice Guide: Civil Trials & Evidence Ch. 4-F, F. Motions in Limine.

Rutter, Cal. Practice Guide: Civil Trials & Evidence Ch. 12-B, B. Motion for Nonsuit.

Rutter, Cal. Practice Guide: Civil Trials & Evidence Ch. 13-B, B. Proper vs. Improper Closing Argument.

Rutter, Cal. Practice Guide: Civil Trials & Evidence Ch. 13-D, D. Preparing for Closing Argument.

Rutter, Cal. Practice Guide: Civil Trials & Evidence Ch. 8B-A, A. General Considerations.

Rutter, Cal. Practice Guide: Civil Trials & Evidence Ch. 8D-D, D. Hearsay Exceptions.

Rutter, Cal. Practice Guide: Civil Trials & Evidence Ch. 8E-C, C. Right of Privacy.

Rutter, Cal. Practice Guide: Civil Trials & Evidence Ch. 8G-D, D. Burdens and Standards of Proof.

California Practice Guide: Employment Litigation Ch. 3-B, B. Liability Insurance-General Considerations.

California Practice Guide: Employment Litigation Ch. 7-A, A. Title VII and the California Fair Employment and Housing Act.

California Practice Guide: Employment Litigation Ch. 10-D, D. Employer Liability for Workplace Harassment.

California Practice Guide: Employment Litigation Ch. 14-B, B. Breach of Fiduciary Duty (Corporate Officers, Directors).

California Practice Guide: Employment Litigation Ch. 17-B, B. Contract Damages.

California Practice Guide: Employment Litigation Ch. 17-D, D. Punitive Damages.

California Practice Guide: Employment Litigation Ch. 19-N, N. Evidence Issues.

California Practice Guide: Employment Litigation Ch. 19-O, O. Burdens and Standards of Proof.

Rutter, Cal. Practice Guide: Enforcing Judgments/Debts Ch. 2-C, C. Tort Liability.

Rutter, Cal. Practice Guide: Family Law Ch. 7-G, G. Removal of Child from Jurisdiction; Wrongful Taking or Withholding of Child.

Rutter, Cal. Practice Guide: Fed.Civ.Pro. Before Trial Ch. 1-B, B. Federal vs. State Law.

Rutter, Cal. Practice Guide: Fed.Civ.Pro. Before Trial Ch. 1-D, D. Choosing Between State and Federal Courts.

Rutter, Cal. Practice Guide: Insurance Litigation Ch. 11-A, A. Background.

Rutter, Cal. Practice Guide: Insurance Litigation Ch. 11-C, C. Fraud.

Rutter, Cal. Practice Guide: Insurance Litigation Ch. 11-D, D. Negligent Misrepresentation.

Rutter, Cal. Practice Guide: Insurance Litigation Ch. 11-E, E. Intentional Infliction of Emotional Distress.

Rutter, Cal. Practice Guide: Insurance Litigation Ch. 11-F, F. Negligent Infliction of Emotional Distress.

Rutter, Cal. Practice Guide: Insurance Litigation Ch. 11-J, J. Other Torts Not Necessarily Related to Insurer "Bad Faith".

Rutter, Cal. Practice Guide: Insurance Litigation Ch. 13-A, A. Contract Damages.

Rutter, Cal. Practice Guide: Insurance Litigation Ch. 13-B, B. Extracontractual Compensatory Damages.

Rutter, Cal. Practice Guide: Insurance Litigation Ch. 13-C, C. Punitive Damages.

Rutter, Cal. Practice Guide: Insurance Litigation Ch. 15-A, A. Actions Against Insurers.

Rutter, Cal. Practice Guide: Insurance Litigation Ch. 15-F, F. Pretrial Motions.

Rutter, Cal. Practice Guide: Insurance Litigation Ch. 15-I, I. Trial.

Rutter, Cal. Practice Guide: Insurance Litigation Ch. 6E-D, D. Managed Care Plans.

Rutter, Cal. Practice Guide: Insurance Litigation Ch. 7A-I, I. Indemnifications Prohibited by Law.

Rutter, Cal. Practice Guide: Insurance Litigation Ch. 12A-B, B. Capsule History of Insurance "Bad Faith" Cases.

Rutter, Cal. Practice Guide: Insurance Litigation Ch. 12A-C, C. Theory of Recovery-Breach of Implied Covenant of Good Faith and Fair Dealing ("Bad Faith").

Rutter, Cal. Practice Guide: Insurance Litigation Ch. 12B-A, A. Introduction.

Rutter, Cal. Practice Guide: Insurance Litigation Ch. 12B-D, D. Refusal to Defend Cases.

Rutter, Cal. Practice Guide: Insurance Litigation Ch. 12C-A, A. Introduction.

Rutter, Cal. Practice Guide: Insurance Litigation Ch. 12D-B, B. Statute of Limitations.

Rutter, Cal. Practice Guide: Insurance Litigation Ch. 12D-G, G. Insurer's Reliance on Advice of Counsel.

Rutter, Cal. Practice Guide: Personal Injury Ch. 3-A, A. Introduction.

Rutter, Cal. Practice Guide: Personal Injury Ch. 3-E, E. Punitive Damages.

Rutter, Cal. Practice Guide: Personal Injury Ch. 3-G, G. Independent Damages Claims.

Rutter, Cal. Practice Guide: Personal Injury Ch. 5-E, E. Selected Pleading Issues.

Rutter, Cal. Practice Guide: Personal Injury Ch. 6-A, A. Scope of Discovery and Limitations.

Rutter, Cal. Practice Guide: Personal Injury Ch. 9-L, L. Motions to Terminate Trial Before Verdict.

Rutter, Cal. Practice Guide: Real Prop. Transactions Ch. 6-L, L. Real Estate Appraisals.

Rutter, Cal. Practice Guide: Real Prop. Transactions Ch. 11-C, C. Seller's Remedies Upon Buyer's Breach-Damages and Specific Performance.

Rutter, Cal. Practice Guide: Real Prop. Transactions Ch. 11-D, D. Buyer's Remedies Upon Seller's Breach-Damages and Specific Performance.

Rutter, Cal. Practice Guide: Real Prop. Transactions Ch. 11-E, E. Damages for Fraud.

Rutter, Cal. Practice Guide: Real Prop. Transactions Ch. 11-G, G. Rescission.

Rutter, Cal. Practice Guide: Prof. Responsibility Ch. 1-D, D. Unauthorized Practice of Law.

Rutter, Cal. Practice Guide: Prof. Responsibility Ch. 6-C, C. Sexual Relations With Client Affecting Competence.

Rutter, Cal. Practice Guide: Prof. Responsibility Ch. 6-D, D. Professional Liability.

Miller and Starr California Real Estate § 1:61, The Implied Covenant of Good Faith and Fair Dealing.

Miller and Starr California Real Estate § 1:63, The Implied Covenant of Good Faith and Fair Dealing--Tortious Breach of the Implied Covenant in Insurance Contracts.

Miller and Starr California Real Estate § 14:5, Remedies--Injunction.

Miller and Starr California Real Estate § 3:33, Damages Recoverable by the Principal.

Miller and Starr California Real Estate § 3:51, Principal's Liability for the Agent's Torts.

Miller and Starr California Real Estate § 31:9, Abatement of Nuisances.

Miller and Starr California Real Estate § 6:17, Liability and Measure of Damages to the Parties.

Miller and Starr California Real Estate § 1:137, False Promise (Promissory Fraud).

Miller and Starr California Real Estate § 11:48, Pecuniary Loss.

Miller and Starr California Real Estate § 22:25, Exemplary Damages.

Miller and Starr California Real Estate § 22:71, Exception to Exemption; Willful or Malicious Acts of the Owner.

Miller and Starr California Real Estate § 29:10, Measure of Owner's Damages for Defective Construction.

Miller and Starr California Real Estate § 31:29, Duties Regarding Common Areas.

Miller and Starr California Real Estate § 31:36, Notice of Litigation by a Tenant; Attorney's Fees; Penalties.

Miller and Starr California Real Estate § 34:40, Punitive Damages.

Miller and Starr California Real Estate § 34:91, Emotional Distress.

Miller and Starr California Real Estate § 34:92, Punitive Damages--Constitutional Validity and Limits.

Miller and Starr California Real Estate § 34:93, Punitive Damages--Basis of the Award; Burden of Proof.

Miller and Starr California Real Estate § 34:98, Punitive Damages--Employer Liability for Employee's Acts.

Miller and Starr California Real Estate § 7:210, Punitive Damages.

Miller and Starr California Real Estate § 7:219, Special Damages for Breach of the Implied Covenant.

Miller and Starr California Real Estate § 34:131, Exposure to Toxic Contamination.

15 NO. 1 Miller & Starr, California Real Estate Newsalert 1, a New Era: Punitive Damages Reined in by the United States Constitution.

20 NO. 5 Miller & Starr, California Real Estate Newsalert 16, Judicial Remedies.

22 NO. 6 Miller & Starr, California Real Estate Newsalert 18, Landlord and Tenant.

3 Witkin Cal. Proc. 5th Actions § 16, (S 16) Statutory Rules and Exceptions.

3 Witkin Cal. Proc. 5th Actions § 160, Insurer's Refusal to Settle.

3 Witkin Cal. Proc. 5th Actions § 164, (S 164) Waiver of Tort and Suit in Quasi-Contract.

4 Witkin Cal. Proc. 5th Pleading § 514, Statement Preserving Right to Seek Punitive Damages.

5 Witkin Cal. Proc. 5th Pleading § 935, (S 935) Pleading Punitive or Exemplary Damages.

6 Witkin Cal. Proc. 5th Proceedings Without Trial § 267, (S 267) Nature of Remedy.

6 Witkin Cal. Proc. 5th Proceedings Without Trial § 269, in General.

6 Witkin Cal. Proc. 5th Proceedings Without Trial § 273, Compensatory Damage Claim Not Dispositive of Cause of Action.

2 Witkin, California Summary 10th Insurance § 240, (S 240) in General.

2 Witkin, California Summary 10th Insurance § 242, (S 242) Punitive Damages.

2 Witkin, California Summary 10th Insurance § 254, Abrogation of Royal Globe in Moradi-Shalal.

12 Witkin, California Summary 10th Real Property § 715, Tenant's Remedies.

12 Witkin, California Summary 10th Real Property § 789, Actions and Penalties.

1 Witkin Cal. Summ. 10th Contracts § 876, No Award in Contract Case.

11 Witkin, California Summary 10th Community Property § 134, Action for Breach of Duty.

5 Witkin, California Summary 10th Torts § 164, Report Regarding Threat of Violence on School Grounds.

5 Witkin, California Summary 10th Torts § 230, (S 230) No Punitive Damages.

5 Witkin, California Summary 10th Torts § 663, (S 663) Capturing Impression of Personal or Familial Activity.

6 Witkin, California Summary 10th Torts § 952, Punitive Damages.

6 Witkin, California Summary 10th Torts § 1031, Financial Injury.

6 Witkin, California Summary 10th Torts § 1036, Fear of Contracting Disease.

6 Witkin, California Summary 10th Torts § 1550, No Double Recovery.

6 Witkin, California Summary 10th Torts § 1559, Nature and Purpose of Award.

6 Witkin, California Summary 10th Torts § 1571, Recovery of Both Penalty and Punitive Damages.

6 Witkin, California Summary 10th Torts § 1572, Requirement of Actual Malice.

6 Witkin, California Summary 10th Torts § 1574, (S 1574) Nature of Problem and Earlier Cases.

6 Witkin, California Summary 10th Torts § 1576, (S 1576) Rule is Retroactive.

6 Witkin, California Summary 10th Torts § 1578, in General.

6 Witkin, California Summary 10th Torts § 1579, Recovery by Public Entities.

6 Witkin, California Summary 10th Torts § 1581, (S 1581) General Rule of Nonliability.

6 Witkin, California Summary 10th Torts § 1582, (S 1582) Act Authorized or Ratified.

6 Witkin, California Summary 10th Torts § 1585, (S 1585) Codification of Rules.

6 Witkin, California Summary 10th Torts § 1586, (S 1586) Personal Torts.

6 Witkin, California Summary 10th Torts § 1592, Breach by Surety.

6 Witkin, California Summary 10th Torts § 1593, in General.

6 Witkin, California Summary 10th Torts § 1596, (S 1596) Job Discrimination Action.

6 Witkin, California Summary 10th Torts § 1599, Alternative Contract or Tort Actions.

6 Witkin, California Summary 10th Torts § 1600, (S 1600) in General.

6 Witkin, California Summary 10th Torts § 1602, (S 1602) Substantial Probability that Plaintiff Will Prevail.

6 Witkin, California Summary 10th Torts § 1605, Action Against Religious Corporation.

6 Witkin, California Summary 10th Torts § 1607, Nature of Requirement.

6 Witkin, California Summary 10th Torts § 1615, in General.

6 Witkin, California Summary 10th Torts § 1618, (S 1618) Discovery of Financial Condition.

6 Witkin, California Summary 10th Torts § 1686, Statutory Remedies.

6 Witkin, California Summary 10th Torts § 1713, Quasi-Contractual Recovery.

8 Witkin, California Summary 10th Constitutional Law § 950, Damages and Penalties.

13 Witkin, California Summary 10th Equity § 63, in General.

§ 3295. Protective order; prima facie case of liability prerequisite to certain evidence; discovery limitations; evidence of profits or financial condition

(a) The court may, for good cause, grant any defendant a protective order requiring the plaintiff to produce evidence of a prima facie case of liability for damages pursuant to Section 3294, prior to the introduction of evidence of:

(1) The profits the defendant has gained by virtue of the wrongful course of conduct of the nature and type shown by the evidence.

(2) The financial condition of the defendant.

(b) Nothing in this section shall prohibit the introduction of prima facie evidence to establish a case for damages pursuant to Section 3294.

(c) No pretrial discovery by the plaintiff shall be permitted with respect to the evidence referred to in paragraphs (1) and (2) of subdivision (a) unless the court enters an order permitting such discovery pursuant to this subdivision. However, the plaintiff may subpoena documents or witnesses to be available at the trial for the purpose of establishing the profits or financial condition referred to in subdivision (a), and the defendant may be required to identify documents in the defendant's possession which are relevant and admissible for that purpose and the witnesses employed by or related to the defendant who would be most competent to testify to those facts. Upon motion by the plaintiff supported by appropriate affidavits and after a hearing, if the court deems a hearing to be necessary, the court may at any time enter an order permitting the discovery otherwise prohibited by this subdivision if the court finds, on the basis of the supporting and opposing affidavits presented, that the plaintiff has established that there is a substantial probability that the plaintiff will prevail on the claim pursuant to Section 3294. Such order shall not be considered to be a determination on the merits of the claim or any defense thereto and shall not be given in evidence or referred to at the trial.

(d) The court shall, on application of any defendant, preclude the admission of evidence of that defendant's profits or financial condition until after the trier of fact returns a verdict for plaintiff awarding actual damages and finds that a defendant is guilty of malice, oppression, or fraud in accordance with Section 3294. Evidence of profit and financial condition shall be admissible only as to the defendant or defendants found to be liable to the plaintiff and to be guilty of malice, oppression, or fraud. Evidence of profit and financial condition shall be presented to the same trier of fact that found for the plaintiff and found one or more defendants guilty of malice, oppression, or fraud.

(e) No claim for exemplary damages shall state an amount or amounts.

(f) The amendments to this section made by Senate Bill No. 241 of the 1987–88 Regular Session apply to all actions in which the initial trial has not commenced prior to January 1, 1988. *(Added by Stats.1979, c. 778, p. 2662, § 1. Amended by Stats.1980, c. 1242, p. 4218, § 2; Stats.1987, c. 1498, § 6.)*

Research References

Rutter, Cal. Practice Guide: A.D.R. Ch. 4-B, B. Judicial Arbitration.

Rutter, Cal. Practice Guide: Civ. Pro. Before Trial Ch. 3-A, A. Subject Matter Jurisdiction (Competency).

Rutter, Cal. Practice Guide: Civ. Pro. Before Trial Ch. 5-B, B. Entry of Default.

Rutter, Cal. Practice Guide: Civ. Pro. Before Trial Ch. 5-E, E. Limitations on Default Judgments.

Rutter, Cal. Practice Guide: Civ. Pro. Before Trial Ch. 6-B, B. Complaints.

Rutter, Cal. Practice Guide: Civ. Pro. Before Trial Ch. 13-E, E. the Arbitration Hearing.

Rutter, Cal. Practice Guide: Civ. Pro. Before Trial Ch. 8B-1, Leave of Court Generally Not Required.

Rutter, Cal. Practice Guide: Civ. Pro. Before Trial Ch. 8C-5, Privacy Protection.

Rutter, Cal. Practice Guide: Civ. Pro. Before Trial Ch. 7(I)-B, B. Motions to Strike.

Rutter, Cal. Practice Guide: Civ. Pro. Before Trial Ch. 9(I)-D, D. Hearing.

Rutter, Cal. Practice Guide: Civ. Pro. Before Trial Ch. 12(I)-E, E. Consolidation, Coordination and Bifurcation.

Rutter, Cal. Practice Guide: Civil Trials & Evidence Ch. 2-B, B. What Constitutes Jury Trial.

Rutter, Cal. Practice Guide: Civil Trials & Evidence Ch. 3-B, B. Peremptory Challenge of Judge (CCP § 170.6).

Rutter, Cal. Practice Guide: Civil Trials & Evidence Ch. 4-F, F. Motions in Limine.

Rutter, Cal. Practice Guide: Civil Trials & Evidence Ch. 4-G, G. Motion to Sever or Bifurcate.

Rutter, Cal. Practice Guide: Civil Trials & Evidence Ch. 4-H, H. Motions to Consolidate or Coordinate Separate Cases.

Rutter, Cal. Practice Guide: Civil Trials & Evidence Ch. 13-D, D. Preparing for Closing Argument.

Rutter, Cal. Practice Guide: Civil Trials & Evidence Ch. 18-B, B. Motion for New Trial.

Rutter, Cal. Practice Guide: Civil Trials & Evidence Ch. 8E-C, C. Right of Privacy.

Rutter, Cal. Practice Guide: Civil Trials & Evidence Ch. 4-G, Outline G.

California Practice Guide: Employment Litigation Ch. 19-F, F. Discovery.

Rutter, Cal. Practice Guide: Fed.Civ.Pro. Before Trial Ch. 1-B, B. Federal vs. State Law.

Rutter, Cal. Practice Guide: Fed.Civ.Pro. Before Trial Ch. 1-D, D. Choosing Between State and Federal Courts.

Rutter, Cal. Practice Guide: Fed.Civ.Pro. Before Trial Ch. 11(III)-A, A. Limitations on Right to Discovery.

Rutter, Cal. Practice Guide: Fed.Civ.Pro. Before Trial Ch. 11(III)-B, B. Scope of Discovery.

Rutter, Cal. Practice Guide: Insurance Litigation Ch. 13-C, C. Punitive Damages.

Rutter, Cal. Practice Guide: Insurance Litigation Ch. 15-A, A. Actions Against Insurers.

Rutter, Cal. Practice Guide: Insurance Litigation Ch. 15-F, F. Pretrial Motions.

Rutter, Cal. Practice Guide: Insurance Litigation Ch. 15-G, G. Discovery.

Rutter, Cal. Practice Guide: Personal Injury Ch. 3-E, E. Punitive Damages.

Rutter, Cal. Practice Guide: Personal Injury Ch. 5-E, E. Selected Pleading Issues.

Rutter, Cal. Practice Guide: Personal Injury Ch. 6-A, A. Scope of Discovery and Limitations.

Rutter, Cal. Practice Guide: Personal Injury Ch. 9-B, B. In-Chambers Conference Before Commencement of Trial.

Rutter, Cal. Practice Guide: Personal Injury Ch. 9-E, E. Order of Trial and Proof and Related Matters.

Rutter, Cal. Practice Guide: Personal Injury Ch. 9-J, J. Final Arguments Upon Close of Evidence.

Rutter, Cal. Practice Guide: Personal Injury Ch. 9-M, M. Verdicts and Judgment.

Rutter, Cal. Practice Guide: Personal Injury Ch. 10-A, A. Motion for New Trial.

Miller and Starr California Real Estate § 34:92, Punitive Damages-- Constitutional Validity and Limits.

Miller and Starr California Real Estate § 34:93, Punitive Damages--Basis of the Award; Burden of Proof.

Miller and Starr California Real Estate § 34:96, Punitive Damages-- Bifurcated Trial of Liability and Damage.

Rutter Practice Guide: Fed.Civ.Pro. Bef.Trial(5th Cir) Ch. 11(III)-A, A. Limitations on Right to Discovery.

9 Witkin Cal. Proc. 5th Appeal § 891, Whether Complete Retrial is Required.

2 Witkin Cal. Proc. 5th Courts § 156, (S 156) Distinction: Prior Action Not on Merits.

4 Witkin Cal. Proc. 5th Pleading § 496, Form.

4 Witkin Cal. Proc. 5th Pleading § 514, Statement Preserving Right to Seek Punitive Damages.

6 Witkin Cal. Proc. 5th Proceedings Without Trial § 158, (S 158) Requirement of Notice of Amount Sought.

6 Witkin Cal. Proc. 5th Proceedings Without Trial § 600, (S 600) in General.

7 Witkin Cal. Proc. 5th Trial § 146, (S 146) Substitution After Deliberations Have Begun.

7 Witkin Cal. Proc. 5th Trial § 154, in General.

6 Witkin, California Summary 10th Torts § 1559, Nature and Purpose of Award.

6 Witkin, California Summary 10th Torts § 1615, in General.

6 Witkin, California Summary 10th Torts § 1616, Same Trier of Fact.

6 Witkin, California Summary 10th Torts § 1617, Time of Application.

6 Witkin, California Summary 10th Torts § 1618, (S 1618) Discovery of Financial Condition.

§ 3296. Insurers and health care service plans; punitive damage judgments; copies to commissioners; sanctions

(a) Whenever a judgment for punitive damages is entered against an insurer or health care service plan licensed pursuant to Chapter 2.2 (commencing with Section 1340) of Division 2 of the Health and Safety Code, the plaintiff in the action shall, within 10 days of entry of judgment, provide all of the following to the Commissioner of the Department of Insurance or the Director of the Department of Managed Health Care, whichever commissioner has regulatory jurisdiction over the insurer or health care service plan:

(1) A copy of the judgment.

(2) A brief recitation of the facts of the case.

(3) Copies of relevant pleadings, as determined by the plaintiff.

(b) The willful failure to comply with this section may, at the discretion of the trial court, result in the imposition of sanctions against the plaintiff or his or her attorney.

(c) This section shall apply to all judgments entered on or after January 1, 1995.

(d) "Insurer," for purposes of this section, means any person or entity transacting any of the classes of insurance described in Chapter 1 (commencing with Section 100) of Part 1 of Division 1 of the Insurance Code. *(Added by Stats.1994, c. 1061 (A.B. 3570), § 1. Amended by Stats.1999, c. 525 (A.B.78), § 7; Stats.2000, c. 857 (A.B.2903), § 5.)*

Research References

Rutter, Cal. Practice Guide: Insurance Litigation Ch. 13-C, C. Punitive Damages.

Rutter, Cal. Practice Guide: Personal Injury Ch. 3-E, E. Punitive Damages.

Miller and Starr California Real Estate § 1:137, False Promise (Promissory Fraud).

Miller and Starr California Real Estate § 34:93, Punitive Damages--Basis of the Award; Burden of Proof.

Miller and Starr California Real Estate § 7:210, Punitive Damages.

Miller and Starr California Real Estate § 7:219, Special Damages for Breach of the Implied Covenant.

CHAPTER 2. MEASURE OF DAMAGES

ARTICLE 1. DAMAGES FOR BREACH OF CONTRACT

Section

3308.   Lease terminated for breach by lessee; measure of lessor's damages.

3315.   Breach of carrier's obligation to receive goods, etc.

3316.   Breach of carrier's obligation to deliver.

3317.   Carrier's delay in delivery.

3318.   Breach of warranty of agent's authority.

3319.   Contract for private works of improvement; late payment penalty; terms; nature and application.

3320.   Contracts for public works of improvement; progress and final retention payments to prime design professionals; dispute; penalty; nature and application.

3321.   Contracts for public works of improvement; payment to subconsultant design professional; dispute; penalty; nature and application.

3322.   Payment by broker of construction trucking services of transportation charges submitted by motor carrier of property in dump truck equipment; conditions; violations.

§ 3300. Measure

For the breach of an obligation arising from contract, the measure of damages, except where otherwise expressly provided by this code, is the amount which will compensate the party aggrieved for all the detriment proximately caused thereby, or which, in the ordinary course of things, would be likely to result therefrom. *(Enacted in 1872. Amended by Code Am.1873–74, c. 612, p. 265, § 276.)*

Research References

California Practice Guide: Employment Litigation Ch. 17-B, B. Contract Damages.

California Practice Guide: Employment Litigation Ch. 17-C, C. Extracontractual Compensatory Damages (Tort and Statutory).

Rutter, Cal. Practice Guide: Enforcing Judgments/Debts Ch. 2-B, B. Statutory Liability and Procedures.

Rutter, Cal. Practice Guide: Insurance Litigation Ch. 11-A, A. Background.

Rutter, Cal. Practice Guide: Insurance Litigation Ch. 13-A, A. Contract Damages.

Rutter, Cal. Practice Guide: Insurance Litigation Ch. 15-A, A. Actions Against Insurers.

Rutter, Cal. Practice Guide: Insurance Litigation Ch. 6I-C, C. Surety's Obligations and Rights Upon Default by Principal.

Rutter, Cal. Practice Guide: Insurance Litigation Ch. 7E-A, A. General Considerations.

Rutter, Cal. Practice Guide: Insurance Litigation Ch. 12B-D, D. Refusal to Defend Cases.

Rutter, Cal. Practice Guide: Insurance Litigation Ch. 12D-B, B. Statute of Limitations.

Rutter, Cal. Practice Guide: Real Prop. Transactions Ch. 4-E, E. Drafting the Purchase and Sale Agreement-Terms and Conditions.

Rutter, Cal. Practice Guide: Real Prop. Transactions Ch. 11-D, D. Buyer's Remedies Upon Seller's Breach-Damages and Specific Performance.

Rutter, Cal. Practice Guide: Real Prop. Transactions Ch. 11-E, E. Damages for Fraud.

Rutter, Cal. Practice Guide: Real Prop. Transactions Gen. Matls., Highlights.

Rutter, Cal. Practice Guide: Real Prop. Transactions Ch. 11-D Outline, Outline D.

Miller and Starr California Real Estate § 29:9, General Principles Concerning Owner's Damages.

Miller and Starr California Real Estate § 34:2, What Constitutes a Breach of Contract.

Miller and Starr California Real Estate § 36:4, Liability for Breach of Commitment.

Miller and Starr California Real Estate § 6:17, Liability and Measure of Damages to the Parties.

Miller and Starr California Real Estate § 1:137, False Promise (Promissory Fraud).

Miller and Starr California Real Estate § 19:17, Breach of the Agreement to Lease; Damages.

Miller and Starr California Real Estate § 24:26, Rights of Enforcement--Remedies for Breach.

Miller and Starr California Real Estate § 27:80, Owner's Remedies for Late Performance--Compensatory Damages.

Miller and Starr California Real Estate § 29:10, Measure of Owner's Damages for Defective Construction.

Miller and Starr California Real Estate § 29:35, Liability for Negligent Supervision.

Miller and Starr California Real Estate § 34:29, Compensatory Damages.

Miller and Starr California Real Estate § 34:45, Consequential Damages Recoverable by a Buyer.

Miller and Starr California Real Estate § 34:46, Damages to Buyer for Delay of Conveyance.

Miller and Starr California Real Estate § 7:206, Contract Damages for Breach of the Duty to Defend.

Miller and Starr California Real Estate § 7:217, Compensatory Damages; Failure to Settle Third-Party Claim.

Miller and Starr California Real Estate § 7:230, Insured's Measure of Compensatory Damages.

Miller and Starr California Real Estate § 10:269, Limitation of Liability.

Miller and Starr California Real Estate § 19:130, Landlord's Remedies.

Miller and Starr California Real Estate § 19:160, Covenant of Quiet Enjoyment and Possession--Tenant's Remedies for Breach of the Covenant.

Miller and Starr California Real Estate § 19:209, Termination of the Lease; Landlord's Recovery of Rent or Damages--Recovery in a Separate Action.

Miller and Starr California Real Estate § 27:107, Remedies for Failure to Complete.

18 NO. 1 Miller & Starr, California Real Estate Newsalert 1, Disclosures in California Residential Real Property Sales.

22 NO. 5 Miller & Starr, California Real Estate Newsalert 8, Easements.

7 Witkin Cal. Proc. 5th Judgment § 421, (S 421) in General.

2 Witkin, California Summary 10th Insurance § 257, (S 257) Nature of Duty.

12 Witkin, California Summary 10th Real Property § 612, Wrongful Notice of Termination.

12 Witkin, California Summary 10th Real Property § 692, Purpose of Revision.

12 Witkin, California Summary 10th Real Property § 698, (S 698) Other Losses Caused by Breach.

1 Witkin Cal. Summ. 10th Contracts § 246, (S 246) Damages.

1 Witkin Cal. Summ. 10th Contracts § 869, (S 869) Nature of Remedy.

1 Witkin Cal. Summ. 10th Contracts § 870, (S 870) Causation.

1 Witkin Cal. Summ. 10th Contracts § 871, Rule of Hadley v. Baxendale.

1 Witkin Cal. Summ. 10th Contracts § 888, (S 888) General Rule.

1 Witkin Cal. Summ. 10th Contracts § 900, Delay in Conveyance.

1 Witkin Cal. Summ. 10th Contracts § 905, (S 905) Credit for Higher Resale Price.

1 Witkin Cal. Summ. 10th Contracts § 909, Breach by Contractor.

4 Witkin, California Summary 10th Sales § 191, (S 191) Lost Profits.

4 Witkin, California Summary 10th Sales § 203, Statutory Rules.

6 Witkin, California Summary 10th Torts § 1716, Illustrations.

6 Witkin, California Summary 10th Torts § 1717, (S 1717) Breach of Fiduciary Duty.

3 Witkin, California Summary 10th Agency and Employment § 267, in General.

3 Witkin, California Summary 10th Agency and Employment § 269, Contracts Terminable on Conditions.

§ 3301. Certainty

DAMAGES MUST BE CERTAIN. No damages can be recovered for a breach of contract which are not clearly ascertainable in both their nature and origin. *(Enacted in 1872.)*

Research References

California Practice Guide: Employment Litigation Ch. 17-B, B. Contract Damages.

Rutter, Cal. Practice Guide: Real Prop. Transactions Ch. 11-D, D. Buyer's Remedies Upon Seller's Breach-Damages and Specific Performance.

Miller and Starr California Real Estate § 34:31, Loss of Profits.

1 Witkin Cal. Summ. 10th Contracts § 879, Requirement of Certainty.

§ 3302. Breach of obligation to pay money only

BREACH OF CONTRACT TO PAY LIQUIDATED SUM. The detriment caused by the breach of an obligation to pay money only, is deemed to be the amount due by the terms of the obligation, with interest thereon. *(Enacted in 1872.)*

Research References

Rutter, Cal. Practice Guide: Civ. Pro. Before Trial Ch. 6-B, B. Complaints.
Rutter, Cal. Practice Guide: Enforcing Judgments/Debts Ch. 2-B, B. Statutory Liability and Procedures.
Rutter, Cal. Practice Guide: Enforcing Judgments/Debts Ch. 3-C, C. Prelawsuit Considerations.
Rutter, Cal. Practice Guide: Insurance Litigation Ch. 13-A, A. Contract Damages.
Miller and Starr California Real Estate § 10:80, Late Charges.
Miller and Starr California Real Estate § 27:69, Recovery for Extra Work.
Miller and Starr California Real Estate § 10:218, Measure of Tort Damages.
7 Witkin Cal. Proc. 5th Judgment § 324, Interest on Obligation or as Damages.
1 Witkin Cal. Summ. 10th Contracts § 908, (S 908) Agreement to Pay Money.

§ 3304. Breach of covenant of seizin, of right to convey, of warranty, or of quiet enjoyment

DETRIMENT CAUSED BY BREACH OF COVENANT OF SEIZIN, ETC.; WHAT IS. The detriment caused by the breach of a covenant of "seizin," of "right to convey," of "warranty," or of "quiet enjoyment," in a grant of an estate in real property, is deemed to be:

1. The price paid to the grantor; or, if the breach is partial only, such proportion of the price as the value of the property affected by the breach bore at the time of the grant to the value of the whole property;

2. Interest thereon for the time during which the grantee derived no benefit from the property, not exceeding five years;

3. Any expenses properly incurred by the covenantee in defending his possession. *(Enacted in 1872.)*

Research References

Miller and Starr California Real Estate § 8:1, Definitions and Terminology.
Miller and Starr California Real Estate § 8:11, Grantee's Remedies.
Miller and Starr California Real Estate § 34:45, Consequential Damages Recoverable by a Buyer.
12 Witkin, California Summary 10th Real Property § 258, Warranty Deed.

§ 3305. Breach of covenant against incumbrances

DETRIMENT CAUSED BY BREACH OF COVENANT AGAINST INCUMBRANCES, IS WHAT. The detriment caused by the breach of a covenant against incumbrances in a grant of an estate in real property is deemed to be the amount which has been actually expended by the covenantee in extinguishing either the principal or interest thereof, not exceeding in the former case a proportion of the price paid to the grantor equivalent to the relative value at the time of the grant of the property affected by the breach, as compared with the whole, or, in the latter case, interest on a like amount. *(Enacted in 1872.)*

Research References

Miller and Starr California Real Estate § 2:23, Liens and Encumbrances.
Miller and Starr California Real Estate § 8:11, Grantee's Remedies.
Miller and Starr California Real Estate § 34:45, Consequential Damages Recoverable by a Buyer.

§ 3306. Breach of agreement to convey real estate

The detriment caused by the breach of an agreement to convey an estate in real property, is deemed to be the price paid, and the expenses properly incurred in examining the title and preparing the necessary papers, the difference between the price agreed to be paid and the value of the estate agreed to be conveyed at the time of the breach, the expenses properly incurred in preparing to enter upon the land, consequential damages according to proof, and interest. *(Enacted in 1872. Amended by Stats.1983, c. 262, § 1.)*

Research References

California Real Estate Forms (Miller & Starr) § 1:14, Right of First Offer Agreement..
California Real Estate Forms (Miller & Starr) § 1:15, Option Agreement--Long Form.
California Real Estate Forms (Miller & Starr) § 1:16, Option Agreement--Short Form.
California Real Estate Forms (Miller & Starr) § 1:17, Purchase and Sale Agreement--Unimproved Real Property--With Escrow Instructions.
California Real Estate Forms (Miller & Starr) § 1:18, Purchase and Sale Agreement--Raw Land.
California Real Estate Forms (Miller & Starr) § 1:19, Agreement for Purchase and Sale of Realty--Build-To-Suit.
California Real Estate Forms (Miller & Starr) § 1:20, Purchase and Sale Agreement--Small Commercial Properties Subject to Tenant Leases.
California Real Estate Forms (Miller & Starr) § 1:21, Purchase and Sale Agreement--Commercial Property Subject to Tenant Leases.
California Real Estate Forms (Miller & Starr) § 1:22, Agreement of Purchase and Sale--Multi-Property.
California Real Estate Forms (Miller & Starr) § 1:23, Purchase and Sale Agreement--Residential Project.
California Real Estate Forms (Miller & Starr) § 1:24, Combination Purchase and Option Agreement--Residential Lots Being Acquired from a Bankrupt Seller.
California Real Estate Forms (Miller & Starr) § 1:25, Purchase and Sale Agreement--Multi-Tenant Residential Property (With Lease-Back).
California Real Estate Forms (Miller & Starr) § 1:26, Purchase and Sale Agreement--Seller-Oriented Short Form.
California Real Estate Forms (Miller & Starr) § 1:27, Purchase and Sale Agreement--Multitenant Residential Property.
California Real Estate Forms (Miller & Starr) § 1:28, Purchase and Sale Agreement--Hotel.
California Real Estate Forms (Miller & Starr) § 1:29, Purchase and Sale Agreement--Seller Oriented With Seller Financing.
California Real Estate Forms (Miller & Starr) § 1:30, Planned Development Deposit Receipt and Agreement of Sale.
California Real Estate Forms (Miller & Starr) § 1:31, Condominium Deposit Receipt and Agreement of Sale.
California Real Estate Forms (Miller & Starr) § 1:32, Hotel Purchase and Sale Agreement With Escrow Instructions.
California Real Estate Forms (Miller & Starr) § 1:33, Real Estate Purchase Contract and Receipt for Deposit--Income Property.

California Real Estate Forms (Miller & Starr) § 1:34, Installment Land Sale Contract With Power of Sale.

California Real Estate Forms (Miller & Starr) § 1:35, Purchase and Sale Agreement--Partially Constructed Project.

California Real Estate Forms (Miller & Starr) § 1:49, Bill of Sale--Warranty.

California Real Estate Forms (Miller & Starr) § 1:51, Assignment of Leases and Security Deposits.

California Real Estate Forms (Miller & Starr) § 1:52, Assignment of Trade Name.

California Real Estate Forms (Miller & Starr) § 1:76, Standard Offer, Agreement and Escrow Instructions for Purchase of Real Estate.

California Real Estate Forms (Miller & Starr) § 2:18, Office Lease--Office/Warehouse Building With Four or Fewer Tenants.

California Real Estate Forms (Miller & Starr) § 2:20, Retail Lease--Shopping Center With for Profit Parking Garage.

California Real Estate Forms (Miller & Starr) § 2:22, Retail Lease--Regional Shopping Center.

California Real Estate Forms (Miller & Starr) § 2:23, Retail Lease--Small Strip-Shopping Center.

California Real Estate Forms (Miller & Starr) § 2:25, Industrial Lease.

California Real Estate Forms (Miller & Starr) § 2:27, Ground Lease.

California Real Estate Forms (Miller & Starr) § 2:28, Triple Net Lease--Stand-Alone Building.

California Real Estate Forms (Miller & Starr) § 2:32, Gross Lease--Small Commercial Property.

California Real Estate Forms (Miller & Starr) § 2:33, Sublease-- With Consent of Master Landlord.

California Real Estate Forms (Miller & Starr) § 2:34, Sublease--Shared Office Space.

California Real Estate Forms (Miller & Starr) § 2:52, Option to Lease.

California Real Estate Forms (Miller & Starr) § 2:65;, Residential Lease.

California Real Estate Forms (Miller & Starr) § 2:66, Residential Lease With Purchase Option.

California Real Estate Forms (Miller & Starr) § 3:57, Loan Purchase and Sale Agreement.

California Real Estate Forms (Miller & Starr) § 3:66, Deed in Lieu of Foreclosure--Transfer Agreement.

California Real Estate Forms (Miller & Starr) § 4:15, Development Agreement.

Rutter, Cal. Practice Guide: Real Prop. Transactions Ch. 11-D, D. Buyer's Remedies Upon Seller's Breach-Damages and Specific Performance.

Rutter, Cal. Practice Guide: Real Prop. Transactions Ch. 11-D Outline, Outline D.

Miller and Starr California Real Estate § 6:26, Return of Deposit.

Miller and Starr California Real Estate § 19:17, Breach of the Agreement to Lease; Damages.

Miller and Starr California Real Estate § 33:24, Actions in Which a Receiver May be Appointed--By Vendor to Vacate Fraudulent Purchase.

Miller and Starr California Real Estate § 34:29, Compensatory Damages.

Miller and Starr California Real Estate § 34:44, Buyer's Compensatory Damages for Breach of the Marketing Contract.

Miller and Starr California Real Estate § 34:45, Consequential Damages Recoverable by a Buyer.

Miller and Starr California Real Estate § 34:46, Damages to Buyer for Delay of Conveyance.

Miller and Starr California Real Estate § 34:54, Prejudgment Interest on Buyer's or Seller's Damages.

Miller and Starr California Real Estate § 10:203, Trustee's Liability for Wrongful Conduct of the Sale.

16 NO. 1 Miller & Starr, California Real Estate Newsalert 4, Agency.

21 NO. 4 Miller & Starr, California Real Estate Newsalert 34, Judicial Remedies.

3 Witkin Cal. Proc. 5th Actions § 405, (S 405) Amount and Nature of Undertaking.

12 Witkin, California Summary 10th Real Property § 755, (S 755) in General.

1 Witkin Cal. Summ. 10th Contracts § 898, Former Limited Rule.

1 Witkin Cal. Summ. 10th Contracts § 899, Revised Statutes.

1 Witkin Cal. Summ. 10th Contracts § 900, Delay in Conveyance.

3 Witkin, California Summary 10th Agency and Employment § 155, (S 155) Distinction: Good Faith of Principal.

§ 3306a. Breach of agreement to deliver quitclaim; minimum detriment

The minimum detriment caused by the breach of an agreement to execute and deliver a quitclaim deed to real property is deemed to be the expenses incurred by the promisee in quieting title to such property, and the expenses incidental to the entry upon such property. Such expenses which shall include reasonable attorneys' fees shall be fixed by the court in the quiet title action. *(Added by Stats.1935, c. 661, p. 1825, § 1.)*

Research References

Miller and Starr California Real Estate § 34:45, Consequential Damages Recoverable by a Buyer.

1 Witkin Cal. Summ. 10th Contracts § 900, Delay in Conveyance.

1 Witkin Cal. Summ. 10th Contracts § 907, (S 907) Agreement to Give Quitclaim Deed.

§ 3307. Breach of agreement to purchase real estate

The detriment caused by the breach of an agreement to purchase an estate in real property is deemed to be the excess, if any, of the amount which would have been due to the seller under the contract over the value of the property to him or her, consequential damages according to proof, and interest. *(Enacted in 1872. Amended by Stats.1983, c. 262, § 2.)*

Research References

Rutter, Cal. Practice Guide: Real Prop. Transactions Ch. 4-E, E. Drafting the Purchase and Sale Agreement-Terms and Conditions.

Rutter, Cal. Practice Guide: Real Prop. Transactions Ch. 11-C, C. Seller's Remedies Upon Buyer's Breach-Damages and Specific Performance.

Rutter, Cal. Practice Guide: Real Prop. Transactions Ch. 11-D, D. Buyer's Remedies Upon Seller's Breach-Damages and Specific Performance.

Miller and Starr California Real Estate § 34:27, Specific Performance by a Seller Under a Real Property Contract.

Miller and Starr California Real Estate § 34:29, Compensatory Damages.

Miller and Starr California Real Estate § 34:45, Consequential Damages Recoverable by a Buyer.

Miller and Starr California Real Estate § 34:49, Seller's Damages for the Buyer's Breach of the Marketing Contract--In General.

Miller and Starr California Real Estate § 34:50, Determining "Value of the Property"; Comparison of the Terms of Sale.

Miller and Starr California Real Estate § 34:51, Seller's Consequential ("Special") Damages.

Miller and Starr California Real Estate § 34:52, Seller's Damages for Period Between Breach and Resale.

Miller and Starr California Real Estate § 34:54, Prejudgment Interest on Buyer's or Seller's Damages.

Miller and Starr California Real Estate § 34:60, Buyer's Right to Restitution.

20 NO. 5 Miller & Starr, California Real Estate Newsalert 16, Judicial Remedies.

1 Witkin Cal. Summ. 10th Contracts § 899, Revised Statutes.

1 Witkin Cal. Summ. 10th Contracts § 900, Delay in Conveyance.

1 Witkin Cal. Summ. 10th Contracts § 901, (S 901) Measure of Damages.

1 Witkin Cal. Summ. 10th Contracts § 903, (S 903) in General.

1 Witkin Cal. Summ. 10th Contracts § 905, (S 905) Credit for Higher Resale Price.

§ 3308. Lease terminated for breach by lessee; measure of lessor's damages

The parties to any lease of real or personal property may agree therein that if the lease shall be terminated by the lessor by reason of any breach thereof by the lessee, the lessor shall thereupon be entitled to recover from the lessee the worth at the time of the termination, of the excess, if any, of the amount of rent and charges equivalent to rent reserved in the lease for the balance of the stated term or any shorter period of time over the then reasonable rental value of the property for the same period.

The rights of the lessor under the agreement shall be cumulative to all other rights or remedies now or hereafter given to the lessor by law or by the terms of the lease; provided, however, that the election of the lessor to exercise the remedy hereinabove permitted shall be binding upon him or her and exclude recourse thereafter to any other remedy for rental or charges equivalent to rental or damages for breach of the covenant to pay the rent or charges accruing subsequent to the time of the termination. The parties to the lease may further agree therein that unless the remedy provided by this section is exercised by the lessor within a specified time the right thereto shall be barred.

This section does not apply to a lease of real property unless (a) the lease was executed before July 1, 1971, or (b) the terms of the lease were fixed by a lease, option, or other agreement executed before July 1, 1971.

This section does not apply to leases subject to Division 10 (commencing with Section 10101) of the Commercial Code. *(Added by Stats.1937, c. 504, p. 1494, § 1. Amended by Stats.1970, c. 89, p. 107, § 11, operative July 1, 1971; Stats.1988, c. 1368, § 2, operative Jan. 1, 1990.)*

Law Revision Commission Comments

This section has been amended to exclude reference to leases of real property; insofar as the section related to real property, it has been superseded by Sections 1951–1952.6. Neither deletion of real property leases from this section nor enactment of Sections 1951–1952.6 affects any remedy or benefit available to a lessor or a lessee of personal property under this section, under Section 3300, or under the rules applicable to contracts generally. [9 Cal.L.Rev.Comm.Reports 153 (1969)].

Research References

12 Witkin, California Summary 10th Real Property § 691, Special Lease Provisions.
13 Witkin, California Summary 10th Personal Property § 192, Remedies of Lessor.

§ 3315. Breach of carrier's obligation to receive goods, etc.

BREACH OF CARRIER'S OBLIGATION TO RECEIVE GOODS, ETC. The detriment caused by the breach of a carrier's obligation to accept freight, messages, or passengers, is deemed to be the difference between the amount which he had a right to charge for the carriage and the amount which it would be necessary to pay for the same service when it ought to be performed. *(Enacted in 1872.)*

§ 3316. Breach of carrier's obligation to deliver

BREACH OF CARRIER'S OBLIGATION TO DELIVER. The detriment caused by the breach of a carrier's obligation to deliver freight, where he has not converted it to his own use, is deemed to be the value thereof at the place and on the day at which it should have been delivered, deducting the freightage to which he would have been entitled if he had completed the delivery. *(Enacted in 1872.)*

§ 3317. Carrier's delay in delivery

CARRIER'S DELAY. The detriment caused by a carrier's delay in the delivery of freight, is deemed to be the depreciation in the intrinsic value of the freight during the delay, and also the depreciation, if any, in the market value thereof, otherwise than by reason of a depreciation in its intrinsic value, at the place where it ought to have been delivered, and between the day at which it ought to have been delivered, and the day of its actual delivery. *(Enacted in 1872.)*

§ 3318. Breach of warranty of agent's authority

BREACH OF WARRANTY OF AUTHORITY. The detriment caused by the breach of a warranty of an agent's authority, is deemed to be the amount which could have been recovered and collected from his principal if the warranty had been complied with, and the reasonable expenses of legal proceedings taken, in good faith, to enforce the act of the agent against his principal. *(Enacted in 1872.)*

Research References

Rutter, Cal. Practice Guide: Personal Injury Ch. 4-C, C. Effective Settlement Negotiations.
Miller and Starr California Real Estate § 3:8, Warranty of Authority.
Miller and Starr California Real Estate § 5:20, Construing a Listing Agreement--Principles of Interpretation.
7 Witkin Cal. Proc. 5th Judgment § 175, No Judicially Established Bilateral Fee-Shifting.
3 Witkin, California Summary 10th Agency and Employment § 195, Agent's Warranty of Authority.

§ 3319. Contract for private works of improvement; late payment penalty; terms; nature and application

(a) In each written contract for private works of improvement entered into on or after January 1, 1996, the contracting party and the design professional may agree to contractual provisions that include a late payment penalty, in lieu of any interest otherwise due. The terms of the late payment penalty shall be specifically set forth in the written contract.

(b) The penalty authorized pursuant to subdivision (a) shall be separate from, and in addition to, the design professionals liens provided by Chapter 3 (commencing with Section 8300) of Title 2 of Part 6 of Division 4, mechanics liens provided by Chapter 4 (commencing with Section 8400) of Title 2 of Part 6 of Division 4, and stop payment notices provided by Chapter 5 (commencing with Section 8500) of Title 2 of Part 6 of Division 4.

(c) None of the rights or obligations created or permitted by this section between design professionals and contracting parties shall apply to construction loan funds held by a lender pursuant to a construction loan agreement.

(d) For purposes of this section, the following definitions apply:

(1) "Contracting party" means any person or entity entering into a written contract with a design professional for professional design services for a private work of improvement.

(2) "Design professional" means a person licensed as an architect pursuant to Chapter 3 (commencing with Section 5500) of Division 3 of the Business and Professions Code, registered as a professional engineer pursuant to Chapter 7 (commencing with Section 6700) of Division 3 of the Business and Professions Code, or licensed as a land surveyor pursuant to Chapter 15 (commencing with Section 8700) of Division 3 of the Business and Professions Code. *(Added by Stats.1995, c. 429 (S.B.1286), § 1. Amended by Stats.1996, c. 124 (A.B.3470), § 10; Stats.2010, c. 697 (S.B.189), § 17, operative July 1, 2012.)*

Law Revision Commission Comments

Section 3319 is amended to correct cross-references and make stylistic revisions. [37 Cal.L.Rev.Comm. Reports 527 (2007)].

Research References

Miller and Starr California Real Estate § 27:91, Prompt Payment of Progress Payments and Contract Retention.
Miller and Starr California Real Estate § 27:114, Amount of Compensation.
1 Witkin Cal. Summ. 10th Contracts § 911, (S 911) Works of Improvement Contracts.

§ 3320. Contracts for public works of improvement; progress and final retention payments to prime design professionals; dispute; penalty; nature and application

(a) In each contract for public works of improvement, entered into on or after January 1, 1996, the public agency shall pay to the prime design professional any progress payment within 30 days of receipt of a written demand for payment in accordance with the contract, and the final retention payment within 45 days of receipt of a written demand for payment in accordance with the contract. If the public agency disputes in good faith any portion of the amount due, it may withhold from the payment an amount not to exceed 150 percent of the disputed amount. The disputed amount withheld is not subject to any penalty authorized by this section.

(b) If any amount is wrongfully withheld or is not timely paid in violation of this section, the prime design professional shall be entitled to a penalty of 1 ½ percent for the improperly withheld amount, in lieu of any interest otherwise due, per month for every month that payment is not made. In any action for the collection of amounts withheld in violation of this section, the prevailing party is entitled to his or her reasonable attorney's fees and costs.

(c) The penalty described in subdivision (b) is separate from, and in addition to, the design professionals liens provided by Chapter 3 (commencing with Section 8300) of Title 2 of Part 6 of Division 4, mechanics liens provided by Chapter 4 (commencing with Section 8400) of Title 2 of Part 6 of Division 4, and stop payment notices on public works provided by Chapter 4 (commencing with Section 9350) of Title 3 of Part 6 of Division 4.

(d) This section does not apply to state agency contracts subject to Section 927.6 of the Government Code.

(e) None of the rights or obligations created by this section between prime design professionals and public agencies apply to construction loan funds held by a lender pursuant to a construction loan agreement.

(f) For purposes of this section:

(1) "Public agency" means the state, any county, any city, any city and county, any district, any public authority, any public agency, any municipal corporation, or other political subdivision or political corporation of the state.

(2) "Design professional" means a person licensed as an architect pursuant to Chapter 3 (commencing with Section 5500) of Division 3 of the Business and Professions Code, registered as a professional engineer pursuant to Chapter 7 (commencing with Section 6700) of Division 3 of the Business and Professions Code, or licensed as a land surveyor pursuant to Chapter 15 (commencing with Section 8700) of Division 3 of the Business and Professions Code.

(3) "Prime design professional" means a design professional with a written contract directly with the public agency. *(Added by Stats.1995, c. 429 (S.B.1286), § 2. Amended by Stats.1996, c. 124 (A.B.3470), § 11; Stats.2000, c. 776 (A.B.2890), § 1, eff. Sept. 27, 2000; Stats.2010, c. 697 (S.B.189), § 18, operative July 1, 2012.)*

Law Revision Commission Comments

Section 3320 is amended to correct a cross-reference. The references to liens are not continued; the lien remedy is unavailable on a public works contract. [37 Cal.L.Rev.Comm. Reports 527 (2007)].

Research References

Miller and Starr California Real Estate § 27:91, Prompt Payment of Progress Payments and Contract Retention.
Miller and Starr California Real Estate § 27:114, Amount of Compensation.
1 Witkin Cal. Summ. 10th Contracts § 911, (S 911) Works of Improvement Contracts.

§ 3321. Contracts for public works of improvement; payment to subconsultant design professional; dispute; penalty; nature and application

(a) In each contract for public works of improvement, a prime design professional shall pay to each subconsultant design professional the amount due him or her from the payment received, not later than 15 days after receipt of each progress payment or final retention payment. If the prime design professional disputes in good faith any portion of the amount due, he or she may withhold from the payment an amount not to exceed 150 percent of the disputed amount. The disputed amount withheld shall not be subject to any penalty authorized by this section.

(b) If any amount is wrongfully withheld or is not timely paid in violation of this section, the subconsultant design professional shall be entitled to a penalty of 1 ½ percent of the improperly withheld amount, in lieu of any interest otherwise due, per month, for each month that payment is not made. In any action for the collection of amounts withheld in violation of this section, the prevailing party shall be entitled to his or her reasonable attorney's fees and costs.

(c) The penalty described in subdivision (b) shall be separate from, and in addition to, the design professionals liens provided by Chapter 3 (commencing with Section 8300) of Title 2 of Part 6 of Division 4, mechanics liens provided by Chapter 4 (commencing with Section 8400) of Title 2 of Part 6 of Division 4, and stop payment notices on public works provided by Chapter 4 (commencing with Section 9350) of Title 3 of Part 6 of Division 4.

(d) None of the rights or obligations created by this section between prime design professionals and subconsultant design professionals shall apply to construction loan funds held by a lender pursuant to a construction loan agreement.

(e) For purposes of this section:

(1) "Public agency" means the state, any county, any city, any city and county, any district, any public authority, any public agency, any municipal corporation, or other political subdivision or political corporation of the state.

(2) "Design professional" means a person licensed as an architect pursuant to Chapter 3 (commencing with Section 5500) of Division 3 of the Business and Professions Code, registered as a professional engineer pursuant to Chapter 7 (commencing with Section 6700) of Division 3 of the Business and Professions Code, or licensed as a land surveyor pursuant to Chapter 15 (commencing with Section 8700) of Division 3 of the Business and Professions Code.

(3) "Prime design professional" means a design professional having a written contract directly with the public agency.

(4) "Subconsultant design professional" means a design professional having a written contract with a prime design professional. *(Added by Stats.1995, c. 429 (S.B.1286), § 3. Amended by Stats.1996, c. 124 (A.B.3470), § 12; Stats.2010, c. 697 (S.B.189), § 19, operative July 1, 2012.)*

Civil

Section 3321 is amended to correct a cross-reference. The references to liens are not continued; the lien remedy is unavailable on a public works contract. [37 Cal.L.Rev.Comm. Reports 527 (2007)].

Research References

Miller and Starr California Real Estate § 27:91, Prompt Payment of Progress Payments and Contract Retention.
Miller and Starr California Real Estate § 27:114, Amount of Compensation.
1 Witkin Cal. Summ. 10th Contracts § 911, (S 911) Works of Improvement Contracts.

§ 3322. Payment by broker of construction trucking services of transportation charges submitted by motor carrier of property in dump truck equipment; conditions; violations

(a)(1) A broker of construction trucking services shall pay all transportation charges submitted by a motor carrier of property in dump truck equipment by the 25th day following the last day of the calendar month in which the transportation was performed, if the charges, including all necessary documentation, are submitted by the fifth day following the last day of the calendar month in which the transportation was performed. If there is a good faith dispute over a portion of the charges claimed, the broker may withhold payment of an amount not to exceed 150 percent of the estimated cost of the disputed amount.

(2) A broker who violates paragraph (1) shall pay to the motor carrier of property in dump truck equipment a penalty of 2 percent per month on the improperly withheld amount.

(3) In an action for the collection of moneys not paid in accordance with paragraph (1), the prevailing party shall be entitled to his or her attorney's fees and costs.

(b) For purposes of subdivision (a), the following definitions apply:

(1) A "broker of construction trucking services" means any person, excluding a licensed contractor, that, as a principal or agent, arranges for transportation services to be provided by an independent contractor motor carrier of property in dump truck equipment and who is responsible for paying the transportation charges of the motor carrier.

(2) A "motor carrier of property in dump truck equipment" means a motor carrier of property permitted by the Department of Motor Vehicles that hauls any type of construction commodity or material in dump truck equipment.

(c) Subdivision (a) only applies if a motor carrier of property is in compliance with Division 14.85 (commencing with Section 36000) of the Vehicle Code at the time the dump truck transportation work is performed. (Added by Stats.2004, c. 518 (A.B.2201), § 1.)

Research References

Miller and Starr California Real Estate § 27:91, Prompt Payment of Progress Payments and Contract Retention.

ARTICLE 2. DAMAGES FOR WRONGS

§ 3333. Torts in general

BREACH OF OBLIGATION OTHER THAN CONTRACT. For the breach of an obligation not arising from contract, the measure of damages, except where otherwise expressly provided by this code, is the amount which will compensate for all the detriment proximately caused thereby, whether it could have been anticipated or not. (Enacted in 1872.)

Research References

Rutter, Cal. Practice Guide: Civ. Pro. Before Trial Ch. 6-B, B. Complaints.
California Practice Guide: Employment Litigation Ch. 17-C, C. Extracontractual Compensatory Damages (Tort and Statutory).
Rutter, Cal. Practice Guide: Insurance Litigation Ch. 9-F, F. Amount Recoverable by Insurer Under Subrogation.
Rutter, Cal. Practice Guide: Insurance Litigation Ch. 11-A, A. Background.
Rutter, Cal. Practice Guide: Insurance Litigation Ch. 11-C, C. Fraud.
Rutter, Cal. Practice Guide: Insurance Litigation Ch. 11-D, D. Negligent Misrepresentation.
Rutter, Cal. Practice Guide: Insurance Litigation Ch. 11-E, E. Intentional Infliction of Emotional Distress.
Rutter, Cal. Practice Guide: Insurance Litigation Ch. 13-A, A. Contract Damages.

Rutter, Cal. Practice Guide: Insurance Litigation Ch. 13-B, B. Extracontractual Compensatory Damages.

Rutter, Cal. Practice Guide: Insurance Litigation Ch. 6D-E, E. Recovery for Future Disability.

Rutter, Cal. Practice Guide: Insurance Litigation Ch. 6E-D, D. Managed Care Plans.

Rutter, Cal. Practice Guide: Insurance Litigation Ch. 6G-B, B. Property Loss Coverages.

Rutter, Cal. Practice Guide: Insurance Litigation Ch. 6H-F, F. Damages Recoverable Against Title Insurer.

Rutter, Cal. Practice Guide: Insurance Litigation Ch. 12A-C, C. Theory of Recovery-Breach of Implied Covenant of Good Faith and Fair Dealing ("Bad Faith").

Rutter, Cal. Practice Guide: Insurance Litigation Ch. 12B-D, D. Refusal to Defend Cases.

Rutter, Cal. Practice Guide: Personal Injury Ch. 3-A, A. Introduction.

Rutter, Cal. Practice Guide: Personal Injury Ch. 3-B, B. Potential Claimants in a Personal Injury Case.

Rutter, Cal. Practice Guide: Personal Injury Ch. 3-C, C. Specific Items of Compensatory Damages.

Rutter, Cal. Practice Guide: Real Prop. Transactions Ch. 4-E, E. Drafting the Purchase and Sale Agreement-Terms and Conditions.

Rutter, Cal. Practice Guide: Real Prop. Transactions Ch. 6-L, L. Real Estate Appraisals.

Rutter, Cal. Practice Guide: Real Prop. Transactions Ch. 11-C, C. Seller's Remedies Upon Buyer's Breach-Damages and Specific Performance.

Rutter, Cal. Practice Guide: Real Prop. Transactions Ch. 11-E, E. Damages for Fraud.

Rutter, Cal. Practice Guide: Prof. Responsibility Ch. 6-D, D. Professional Liability.

Miller and Starr California Real Estate § 1:63, The Implied Covenant of Good Faith and Fair Dealing--Tortious Breach of the Implied Covenant in Insurance Contracts.

Miller and Starr California Real Estate § 29:9, General Principles Concerning Owner's Damages.

Miller and Starr California Real Estate § 3:33, Damages Recoverable by the Principal.

Miller and Starr California Real Estate § 6:17, Liability and Measure of Damages to the Parties.

Miller and Starr California Real Estate § 1:137, False Promise (Promissory Fraud).

Miller and Starr California Real Estate § 10:15, Loans Obtained by Fraud.

Miller and Starr California Real Estate § 11:48, Pecuniary Loss.

Miller and Starr California Real Estate § 14:26, Damages.

Miller and Starr California Real Estate § 22:22, Measure of Damages.

Miller and Starr California Real Estate § 29:10, Measure of Owner's Damages for Defective Construction.

Miller and Starr California Real Estate § 29:16, Liability to Third Persons.

Miller and Starr California Real Estate § 29:30, Measure of Damages Applicable to Developers.

Miller and Starr California Real Estate § 29:34, Liability to the General Contractor.

Miller and Starr California Real Estate § 29:38, Measure of Damages.

Miller and Starr California Real Estate § 29:41, Negligence.

Miller and Starr California Real Estate § 34:29, Compensatory Damages.

Miller and Starr California Real Estate § 34:83, General Principles; Election of Remedies.

Miller and Starr California Real Estate § 34:88, Expenditures in Reliance on the Fraud.

Miller and Starr California Real Estate § 7:207, Tort Damages for Breach of the Duty to Defend.

Miller and Starr California Real Estate § 7:210, Punitive Damages.

Miller and Starr California Real Estate § 7:217, Compensatory Damages; Failure to Settle Third-Party Claim.

Miller and Starr California Real Estate § 7:218, Compensatory Damages; Failure to Pay Claims of the Insured.

Miller and Starr California Real Estate § 7:219, Special Damages for Breach of the Implied Covenant.

Miller and Starr California Real Estate § 10:218, Measure of Tort Damages.

Miller and Starr California Real Estate § 34:132, Measure of Damages.

14 NO. 2 Miller & Starr, California Real Estate Newsalert 2, Agency.

16 NO. 4 Miller & Starr, California Real Estate Newsalert 37, Remedies.

18 NO. 1 Miller & Starr, California Real Estate Newsalert 1, Disclosures in California Residential Real Property Sales.

20 NO. 4 Miller & Starr, California Real Estate Newsalert 34, Judicial Remedies.

4 Witkin, California Summary 10th Security Transactions in Real Property § 177, Claims Against Third Parties.

5 Witkin, California Summary 10th Torts § 17, State Constitution.

5 Witkin, California Summary 10th Torts § 398, Causation of Injury.

6 Witkin, California Summary 10th Torts § 1031, Financial Injury.

6 Witkin, California Summary 10th Torts § 1548, Theory and Distinctions.

6 Witkin, California Summary 10th Torts § 1553, Nature of Requirement.

6 Witkin, California Summary 10th Torts § 1655, (S 1655) General Rule: Fees Are Not Recoverable.

6 Witkin, California Summary 10th Torts § 1665, (S 1665) in General.

6 Witkin, California Summary 10th Torts § 1670, (S 1670) Medical Care and Related Expense.

6 Witkin, California Summary 10th Torts § 1700, (S 1700) Abuse of Process.

6 Witkin, California Summary 10th Torts § 1714, Elements of Damage.

6 Witkin, California Summary 10th Torts § 1716, Illustrations.

6 Witkin, California Summary 10th Torts § 1717, (S 1717) Breach of Fiduciary Duty.

6 Witkin, California Summary 10th Torts § 1722, Alternative Measures.

6 Witkin, California Summary 10th Torts § 1727, Diminution in Value.

§ 3333.1. Negligence of health care provider; evidence of benefits and premiums paid; subrogation

(a) In the event the defendant so elects, in an action for personal injury against a health care provider based upon professional negligence, he may introduce evidence of any amount payable as a benefit to the plaintiff as a result of the personal injury pursuant to the United States Social Security Act,[1] any state or federal income disability or worker's compensation act, any health, sickness or income-disability insurance, accident insurance that provides health benefits or income-disability coverage, and any contract or agreement of any group, organization, partnership, or corporation to provide, pay for, or reimburse the cost of medical, hospital, dental, or other health care services. Where the defendant elects to introduce such evidence, the plaintiff may introduce evidence of any amount which the plaintiff has paid or contributed to secure his right to any insurance benefits concerning which the defendant has introduced evidence.

(b) No source of collateral benefits introduced pursuant to subdivision (a) shall recover any amount against the plaintiff nor shall it be subrogated to the rights of the plaintiff against a defendant.

(c) For the purposes of this section:

(1) "Health care provider" means any person licensed or certified pursuant to Division 2 (commencing with Section 500) of the Business and Professions Code, or licensed pursuant to the Osteopathic Initiative Act, or the Chiropractic Initiative Act, or licensed pursuant to Chapter 2.5 (commencing with Section 1440) of Division 2 of the Health and Safety Code; and any clinic, health dispensary, or health facility, licensed pursuant to Division 2 (commencing with Section 1200) of the Health and Safety Code. "Health care provider" includes the legal representatives of a health care provider;

(2) "Professional negligence" means a negligent act or omission to act by a health care provider in the rendering of professional services, which act or omission is the proximate cause of a personal injury or wrongful death, provided that such services are within the scope of services for which the provider is licensed and which are not within any restriction imposed by the licensing agency or licensed hospital. *(Added by Stats.1975, 2nd Ex.Sess., c. 1, p. 3968, § 24.5. Amended by Stats.1975, 2nd Ex.Sess., c. 2, p. 3990, § 1.19, eff. Sept. 24, 1975, operative Dec. 12, 1975; Stats.1976, c. 1079, p. 4852, § 4.)*

1 42 U.S.C.A. § 301 et seq.

Research References

Rutter, Cal. Practice Guide: Civ. Pro. Before Trial Ch. 8C-2, "Reasonably Calculated to Lead to Discovery of Admissible Evidence".

Rutter, Cal. Practice Guide: Civil Trials & Evidence Ch. 5-G, G. Scope of Permissible Voir Dire-Proper vs. Improper Questions.

Rutter, Cal. Practice Guide: Civil Trials & Evidence Ch. 13-B, B. Proper vs. Improper Closing Argument.

Rutter, Cal. Practice Guide: Civil Trials & Evidence Ch. 8E-D, D. Other Public Policy Exclusions.

Rutter, Cal. Practice Guide: Insurance Litigation Ch. 9-E, E. Requirements for Equitable Subrogation.

Rutter, Cal. Practice Guide: Insurance Litigation Ch. 6E-C, C. Health Insurance Policies.

Rutter, Cal. Practice Guide: Personal Injury Ch. 1-A, A. Initial Client Interview.

Rutter, Cal. Practice Guide: Personal Injury Ch. 1-B, B. Initial Evaluation of Case: Decision to Accept or Reject Employment or Undertake Further Evaluation of Claim.

Rutter, Cal. Practice Guide: Personal Injury Ch. 3-C, C. Specific Items of Compensatory Damages.

Rutter, Cal. Practice Guide: Personal Injury Ch. 3-F, F. MICRA Provisions Affecting Damages.

Rutter, Cal. Practice Guide: Personal Injury Ch. 10-D, D. Government Entity Defendant Post-Trial Elections, Requests, Motions and Hearings.

Rutter, Cal. Practice Guide: Personal Injury Ch. 3-F, Outline F.

6 Witkin, California Summary 10th Torts § 956, in General.

6 Witkin, California Summary 10th Torts § 957, Constitutionality and Construction.

6 Witkin, California Summary 10th Torts § 1631, Nature of Rule.

6 Witkin, California Summary 10th Torts § 1637, Nature of Statute.

2 Witkin Cal. Summ. 10th Workers' Compensation § 74, (S 74) No Credit in MICRA Action.

§ 3333.2. Negligence of health care provider; noneconomic losses; limitation

(a) In any action for injury against a health care provider based on professional negligence, the injured plaintiff shall be entitled to recover noneconomic losses to compensate for pain, suffering, inconvenience, physical impairment, disfigurement and other nonpecuniary damage.

(b) In no action shall the amount of damages for noneconomic losses exceed two hundred fifty thousand dollars ($250,000).

(c) For the purposes of this section:

(1) "Health care provider" means any person licensed or certified pursuant to Division 2 (commencing with Section 500) of the Business and Professions Code, or licensed pursuant to the Osteopathic Initiative Act, or the Chiropractic Initiative Act, or licensed pursuant to Chapter 2.5 (commencing with Section 1440) of Division 2 of the Health and Safety Code; and any clinic, health dispensary, or health facility, licensed pursuant to Division 2 (commencing with Section 1200) of the Health and Safety Code. "Health care provider" includes the legal representatives of a health care provider;

(2) "Professional negligence" means a negligent act or omission to act by a health care provider in the rendering of professional services, which act or omission is the proximate cause of a personal injury or wrongful death, provided that such services are within the scope of services for which the provider is licensed and which are not within any restriction imposed by the licensing agency or licensed hospital. *(Added by Stats.1975, 2nd Ex.Sess., c. 1, p. 3969, § 24.6. Amended by Stats.1975, 2nd Ex.Sess., c. 2, p. 3991, § 1.191, eff. Sept. 24, 1975, operative Dec. 12, 1975.)*

Research References

Rutter, Cal. Practice Guide: Civ. Pro. Before Trial Ch. 12(II)-E, E. Motion to Determine "Good Faith" of "Piecemeal" Settlement (CCP § 877.6).

Rutter, Cal. Practice Guide: Personal Injury Ch. 3-A, A. Introduction.

Rutter, Cal. Practice Guide: Personal Injury Ch. 3-B, B. Potential Claimants in a Personal Injury Case.

Rutter, Cal. Practice Guide: Personal Injury Ch. 3-C, C. Specific Items of Compensatory Damages.

Rutter, Cal. Practice Guide: Personal Injury Ch. 3-D, D. Mitigating Factors in Reduction of Damages.

Rutter, Cal. Practice Guide: Personal Injury Ch. 3-F, F. MICRA Provisions Affecting Damages.

Rutter, Cal. Practice Guide: Personal Injury Ch. 4-D, D. Techniques Where Settlement Not Forthcoming.

Rutter, Cal. Practice Guide: Personal Injury Ch. 9-M, M. Verdicts and Judgment.

Rutter, Cal. Practice Guide: Personal Injury Ch. 3-F, Outline F.

Rutter, Cal. Practice Guide: Personal Injury Ch. 4-D, Outline D.

Miller and Starr California Real Estate § 3:35, Elder Abuse and Dependent Adult Care Civil Protection Act.

6 Witkin Cal. Proc. 5th Proceedings Without Trial § 89, Offers to Multiple Plaintiffs.

6 Witkin, California Summary 10th Torts § 945, Computation of Fee.

6 Witkin, California Summary 10th Torts § 946, in General.

6 Witkin, California Summary 10th Torts § 952, Punitive Damages.

6 Witkin, California Summary 10th Torts § 958, in General.

6 Witkin, California Summary 10th Torts § 959, Constitutionality.

6 Witkin, California Summary 10th Torts § 960, Comparative Negligence.

6 Witkin, California Summary 10th Torts § 962, Action for Equitable Indemnity.

6 Witkin, California Summary 10th Torts § 963, Action Under Federal Patient-Dumping Statute.

6 Witkin, California Summary 10th Torts § 964, Periodic Payments.

6 Witkin, California Summary 10th Torts § 965, Intentional Torts.

6 Witkin, California Summary 10th Torts § 969, No Interest on Periodic Payments.

6 Witkin, California Summary 10th Torts § 1660, Punitive Damages.

6 Witkin, California Summary 10th Torts § 1686, Statutory Remedies.

§ 3333.3. Negligence of plaintiff; injuries of plaintiff proximately caused by plaintiff's commission of any felony, or immediate flight therefrom; limitation

In any action for damages based on negligence, a person may not recover any damages if the plaintiff's injuries were in any way proximately caused by the plaintiff's commission of any felony, or immediate flight therefrom, and the plaintiff has been duly convicted of that felony. *(Added by Initiative Measure (Prop. 213, § 3, approved Nov. 5, 1996, eff. Nov. 5, 1996).)*

Research References

Rutter, Cal. Practice Guide: Personal Injury Ch. 3-D, D. Mitigating Factors in Reduction of Damages.

6 Witkin, California Summary 10th Torts § 1657, (S 1657) in General.

6 Witkin, California Summary 10th Torts § 1660, Punitive Damages.

7 Witkin, California Summary 10th Constitutional Law § 634, Initiative Measure.

§ 3333.4. Operation or use of motor vehicles; noneconomic losses; limitation

(a) Except as provided in subdivision (c), in any action to recover damages arising out of the operation or use of a motor vehicle, a person shall not recover non-economic losses to compensate for pain, suffering, inconvenience, physical impairment, disfigurement, and other nonpecuniary damages if any of the following applies:

(1) The injured person was at the time of the accident operating the vehicle in violation of Section 23152 or 23153 of the Vehicle Code, and was convicted of that offense.

(2) The injured person was the owner of a vehicle involved in the accident and the vehicle was not insured as required by the financial responsibility laws of this state.

(3) The injured person was the operator of a vehicle involved in the accident and the operator can not establish his or her financial responsibility as required by the financial responsibility laws of this state.

(b) Except as provided in subdivision (c), an insurer shall not be liable, directly or indirectly, under a policy of liability or uninsured motorist insurance to indemnify for non-economic losses of a person injured as described in subdivision (a).

(c) In the event a person described in paragraph (2) of subdivision (a) was injured by a motorist who at the time of the accident was operating his or her vehicle in violation of Section 23152 or 23153 of the Vehicle Code, and was convicted of that offense, the injured person shall not be barred from recovering non-economic losses to compensate for pain, suffering, inconvenience, physical impairment, disfigurement, and other nonpecuniary damages. *(Added by Initiative Measure (Prop. 213, § 3, approved Nov. 5, 1996, eff. Nov. 5, 1996).)*

Research References

Rutter, Cal. Practice Guide: Civil Appeals & Writs Form 15:B.1, Sample Reply to Opposition to Writ Petition.
Rutter, Cal. Practice Guide: Civ. Pro. Before Trial Ch. 12(II)-E, E. Motion to Determine "Good Faith" of "Piecemeal" Settlement (CCP § 877.6).
Rutter, Cal. Practice Guide: Insurance Litigation Ch. 6G-D, D. Uninsured and Underinsured Motorist Coverages.
Rutter, Cal. Practice Guide: Insurance Litigation Ch. 7D-A, A. Statutory Requirements.
Rutter, Cal. Practice Guide: Personal Injury Ch. 3-D, D. Mitigating Factors in Reduction of Damages.
Rutter, Cal. Practice Guide: Personal Injury Gen. Matls., Highlights.
Miller and Starr California Real Estate § 22:18, Governmental Agencies.
2 Witkin, California Summary 10th Insurance § 14, Financial Responsibility Law.
2 Witkin, California Summary 10th Insurance § 180, (S 180) Nature and Purpose.
2 Witkin, California Summary 10th Insurance § 309, (S 309) in General.
6 Witkin, California Summary 10th Torts § 883, Driving in Wrong Location or Manner.
6 Witkin, California Summary 10th Torts § 1657, (S 1657) in General.
6 Witkin, California Summary 10th Torts § 1658, in General.
6 Witkin, California Summary 10th Torts § 1659, Products Liability.
6 Witkin, California Summary 10th Torts § 1660, Punitive Damages.
6 Witkin, California Summary 10th Torts § 1661, Wrongful Death.
6 Witkin, California Summary 10th Torts § 1662, Action Against Public Entity.
6 Witkin, California Summary 10th Torts § 1663, Causal Connection.
6 Witkin, California Summary 10th Torts § 1664, Insured Vehicle.
7 Witkin, California Summary 10th Constitutional Law § 634, Initiative Measure.
8 Witkin, California Summary 10th Constitutional Law § 799, Valid Classifications.

§ 3333.5. Pipeline corporations; oil spills; liability; costs; attorneys' fees; clean-up responsibility; application of section; definitions

(a) Each pipeline corporation that qualifies as a public utility within Section 216 of the Public Utilities Code that transports any crude oil or fraction thereof in a public utility oil pipeline system that meets the requirements of subdivision (h) shall be absolutely liable without regard to fault for any damages incurred by any injured party that arise out of, or are caused by, the discharge or leaking of crude oil or fraction thereof from the public utility pipeline.

(b) A pipeline corporation is not liable to an injured party under this section for any of the following:

(1) Damages, other than costs of removal incurred by the state or a local government caused solely by an act of war, hostilities, civil war, or insurrection or by an unanticipated grave natural disaster or other act of God of an exceptional, inevitable, and irresistible character, other than an earthquake, which damages could not have been prevented or avoided by the exercise of due care or foresight.

(2) Damages in the proportion caused by the negligence, intentional malfeasance, or criminal act of the landowner, or an agent, employee, or contractor of the landowner, upon whose property the pipeline system is located.

(3) Except as provided by paragraph (2), damages caused solely by the negligence or intentional malfeasance of the injured person.

(4) Except as provided by paragraph (2), damages caused solely by the criminal act of a third party other than the pipeline corporation or an agent or employee of the pipeline corporation.

(5) Natural seepage from sources other than the public utility oil pipeline.

(6) Damages that arise out of, or are caused by, a discharge that is authorized by a state or federal permit.

(c) Damages for which a pipeline corporation is liable under this section are the following:

(1) All costs of response, containment, cleanup, removal, and treatment, including, but not limited to, monitoring and administration costs.

(2) Injury to, or economic losses resulting from destruction of or injury to, real or personal property.

(3) Injury to, destruction of, or loss of, natural resources, including, but not limited to, the reasonable cost of rehabilitating wildlife, habitat, and other resources and the reasonable cost of assessing that injury, destruction, or loss, in any action brought by the state, a county, city, or district.

(4) Loss of taxes, royalties, rents, use, or profit shares caused by the injury, destruction, loss, or impairment of use of real property, personal property, or natural resources.

(5) Loss of use and enjoyment of natural resources and other public resources or facilities in any action brought by the state, county, city, or district.

(d) The court may award reasonable costs of the suit, attorneys' fees, and the cost of any necessary expert witnesses to any prevailing plaintiff. The court may award reasonable costs of the suit, attorneys' fees, and the cost of any necessary expert witnesses to any prevailing defendant if the court finds that the plaintiff commenced or prosecuted the suit under this section in bad faith or solely for purposes of harassing the defendant.

(e)(1) A pipeline corporation shall immediately clean up all crude oil, or any fraction thereof, that leaks or is discharged from a pipeline subject to this section. Additionally, the pipeline corporation shall abate immediately, or as soon as practical, the effects of the leak or discharge and take all other necessary remedial action.

(2) A pipeline corporation may recover the costs of the activities specified in this section for which it is not at fault by means of any otherwise available cause of action, including, but not limited to, indemnification or subrogation.

(f) This section shall not apply to claims, or causes of action, for damages for personal injury or wrongful death.

(g) This section shall not prohibit any party from bringing any action for damages under any other provision or principle of law, including but not limited to, common law. However, damages shall not be awarded pursuant to this section to an injured party to the extent the same party is or has been awarded damages for the same injury under any other provision or principle of law.

(h) This section shall only apply to all of the following:

(1) The pipeline system proposed to be constructed by Pacific Pipeline System, Inc., identified in Public Utilities Commission Application No. 91–10–013, for which the maximum requirement of one hundred million dollars ($100,000,000) set forth in paragraph (1) of subdivision (j) shall apply.

(2) Any other public utility pipeline system for which construction is completed on or after January 1, 1996, other than a

pipeline system the entire length of which is subject to the Lempert–Keene–Seastrand Oil Spill Prevention and Response Act, (Division 7.8 (commencing with Section 8750) of the Public Resources Code). If part, but not all, of a pipeline system is subject to the Lempert–Keene–Seastrand Oil Spill Prevention and Response Act, any evidence of financial responsibility that satisfies that act, and that meets the conditions of this section, shall be credited toward the requirements of this section.

(3) Any major relocation of three miles or greater of a portion of a pipeline system along substantially new alignments accomplished through the exercise of eminent domain. This section shall not apply to the portions of the pipeline not relocated.

(i) This section shall not apply to the following:

(1) A pipeline system in existence prior to January 1, 1996, that is converted to a public utility prior or subsequent to January 1, 1996.

(2) A public utility pipeline system not otherwise subject to this section, that is the object of repair, replacement or maintenance, unless that activity constitutes relocation as described in paragraph (3) of subdivision (h).

(j)(1) No pipeline system subject to this section shall be permitted to operate unless the State Fire Marshal certifies that the pipeline corporation demonstrates sufficient financial responsibility to respond to the liability imposed by this section. The minimum financial responsibility required by the State Fire Marshal shall be seven hundred fifty dollars ($750) times the maximum capacity of the pipeline in the number of barrels per day up to a maximum of one hundred million dollars ($100,000,-000) per pipeline system, or a maximum of two hundred million dollars ($200,000,000) per multiple pipeline systems.

(2) For the purposes of this section, financial responsibility shall be demonstrated by evidence that is substantially equivalent to that required by regulations issued under Section 8670.37.54 of the Government Code, including insurance, surety bond, letter of credit, guaranty, qualification as a self-insurer, or combination thereof or any other evidence of financial responsibility. The State Fire Marshal shall require the documentation evidencing financial responsibility to be placed on file with that office, and shall administer the documentation in a manner substantially equivalent to that provided by regulations issued under Section 8670.37.54 of the Government Code. Financial responsibility shall be available for payment of claims for damages described in subdivision (c) of any party, including, but not limited to, the State of California, local governments, special districts, and private parties, that obtains a final judgment therefor against the pipeline corporation.

(k) The State Fire Marshal shall require evidence of financial responsibility to fund postclosure cleanup costs. The evidence of financial responsibility shall be 15 percent of the amount of financial responsibility required under subdivision (j) and shall be maintained by the pipeline corporation for four years from the date the pipeline is fully idled pursuant to a closure plan approved by the State Fire Marshal.

(*l*) "Fraction" of crude oil means a group of compounds collected by fractional distillation that condenses within the same temperature band, or a material that consists primarily of that group of compounds or of a mixture of those groups of compounds.

(m)(1) Notwithstanding Section 228 of the Public Utilities Code, for purposes of this section, "pipeline corporation" means every corporation or person directly operating, managing or owning any pipeline system that qualifies as a public utility within Section 216 of the Public Utilities Code and for compensation within this state.

(2) For purposes of this section, "owning" refers to the legal entity owning the pipeline system itself and does not include legal entities having an ownership interest, in whole or in part, in the entity owning the pipeline system or multiple pipeline systems.

(3) "Pipeline system" means a collective assemblage of intrastate line pipe, valves, and other appurtenances connected to line pipe, pumping units, fabricated assemblies associated with pumping units, metering and delivery station, and fabricated assemblies constructed for the same purpose at substantially the same time that form a facility through which crude oil or a fraction thereof moves in transportation. *(Formerly § 3333.4, added by Stats.1995, c. 979, § 2. Renumbered § 3333.5 and amended by Stats.1998, c. 485 (A.B.2803), § 40.)*

§ 3333.7. Recovery of treble damages by injured person from employer of driver of commercial motor vehicle who was driving under the influence of alcohol or a controlled substance

(a) Notwithstanding any other provision of law, any person who suffers injury that is proximately caused by the driver of a commercial motor vehicle shall be entitled to recover treble damages from the driver's employer where it is shown both that the driver of a commercial motor vehicle was under the influence of alcohol or a controlled substance at the time that the injury was caused and that the driver's employer willfully failed at the time of the injury to comply with any of the requirements of federal law described in subdivision (a) of Section 34520 of the Vehicle Code in regard to the involved driver.

(b) For the purposes of subdivision (a), "willfully failed" has the same meaning as "willful failure" as defined in paragraph (3) of subdivision (c) of Section 34623 of the Vehicle Code.

(c) For purposes of subdivision (a), an "employer" is a person or entity who employs the driver or who contracts with an owner-operator, who meets the requirements set forth in subdivision (b) of Section 34624 of the Vehicle Code, to provide transportation services, and who is required to engage in mandatory substance abuse testing pursuant to subdivision (a) of Section 34520 of the Vehicle Code. This subdivision shall not be construed to change the definition of "employer," "employee," or "independent contractor" for any purpose.

(d) Nothing in this section is intended to preclude or affect existing rights. *(Added by Stats.2001, c. 298 (S.B.871), § 1.)*

Research References

Rutter, Cal. Practice Guide: Personal Injury Ch. 3-E, E. Punitive Damages.
6 Witkin, California Summary 10th Torts § 1570, Treble Damages.

§ 3334. Real estate; wrongful occupation; value of the use of property

(a) The detriment caused by the wrongful occupation of real property, in cases not embraced in Section 3335 of this code, the Eminent Domain Law (Title 7 (commencing with Section 1230.010) of Part 3 of the Code of Civil Procedure), or Section 1174 of the Code of Civil Procedure, is deemed to include the value of the use of the property for the time of that wrongful occupation, not exceeding five years next preceding the commencement of the action or proceeding to enforce the right to damages, the reasonable cost of repair or restoration of the property to its original condition, and the costs, if any, of recovering the possession.

(b) (1) Except as provided in paragraph (2), for purposes of subdivision (a), the value of the use of the property shall be the greater of the reasonable rental value of that property or the benefits obtained by the person wrongfully occupying the property by reason of that wrongful occupation.

(2) If a wrongful occupation of real property subject to this section is the result of a mistake of fact of the wrongful occupier, the value of the use of the property, for purposes of subdivision (a), shall be the reasonable rental value of the property. *(Enacted in 1872. Amended by Stats.1979, c. 373, p. 1264, § 47; Stats.1992, c. 469 (A.B.2663), § 1.)*

Research References

Rutter, Cal. Practice Guide: Real Prop. Transactions Ch. 5-D, D. Common Law Environmental Hazards Liability.
Miller and Starr California Real Estate § 17:24, Minerals--Oil and Gas Leases.
Miller and Starr California Real Estate § 19:30, Periodic Tenancy.
Miller and Starr California Real Estate § 19:46, Liability of Holdover Tenant.
Miller and Starr California Real Estate § 19:85, Persons Liable for Payment of Rent.
Miller and Starr California Real Estate § 23:69, Trespass.
Miller and Starr California Real Estate § 19:208, Termination of the Lease; Landlord's Recovery of Rent or Damages--Recovery in an Unlawful Detainer Proceeding.
Miller and Starr California Real Estate § 19:213, Damages.
Miller and Starr California Real Estate § 34:104, Who Can Bring the Action.
16 NO. 1 Miller & Starr, California Real Estate Newsalert 16, Hazardous Substances.
18 NO. 3 Miller & Starr, California Real Estate Newsalert 21, Remedies.
6 Witkin, California Summary 10th Torts § 1726, (S 1726) Wrongful Occupancy.

§ 3335. Real estate; willful holding over

WILLFUL HOLDING OVER. For willfully holding over real property, by a person who entered upon the same, as guardian or trustee for an infant, or by right of an estate terminable with any life or lives, after the termination of the trust or particular estate, without the consent of the party immediately entitled after such termination, the measure of damages is the value of the profits received during such holding over. *(Enacted in 1872.)*

Research References

Rutter, Cal. Practice Guide: Personal Injury Ch. 3-C, C. Specific Items of Compensatory Damages.
Miller and Starr California Real Estate § 9:24, Termination; Merger; Partition.
Miller and Starr California Real Estate § 19:46, Liability of Holdover Tenant.
Miller and Starr California Real Estate § 19:213, Damages.
Miller and Starr California Real Estate § 34:104, Who Can Bring the Action.

§ 3336. Personal property; conversion; presumption

The detriment caused by the wrongful conversion of personal property is presumed to be:

First—The value of the property at the time of the conversion, with the interest from that time, or, an amount sufficient to indemnify the party injured for the loss which is the natural, reasonable and proximate result of the wrongful act complained of and which a proper degree of prudence on his part would not have averted; and

Second—A fair compensation for the time and money properly expended in pursuit of the property. *(Enacted in 1872. Amended by Code Am.1873–74, c. 612, p. 266, § 277; Code Am.1877–78, c. 20, p. 89, § 1; Stats.1931, c. 633, p. 1358, § 1.)*

Research References

Rutter, Cal. Practice Guide: Civil Trials & Evidence Ch. 17-F, F. Prejudgment Interest.
Rutter, Cal. Practice Guide: Enforcing Judgments/Debts Ch. 3-C, C. Prelawsuit Considerations.
Miller and Starr California Real Estate § 10:18, Personal Property Located on the Realty.

Miller and Starr California Real Estate § 33:11, Preservation and Management--Power of Possession and Control; Rights of Others.
Miller and Starr California Real Estate § 19:233, Tenant's Personal Property.
6 Witkin, California Summary 10th Torts § 1643, in General.
6 Witkin, California Summary 10th Torts § 1722, Alternative Measures.
4 Witkin, California Summary 10th Negotiable Instruments § 58, (S 58) Conversion.

§ 3336.5. Junk dealers or recyclers; possession of fire hydrants, fire department connections, manhole covers, or backflow devices; agency certification required; liability for wrongful possession; unknowing possession and notification after discovery; legislative intent regarding liability to third parties

(a)(1) Any junk dealer or recycler who possesses a fire hydrant, fire department connection, including, but not limited to, brass fittings and parts, manhole cover or lid or part of that cover or lid, or backflow device or connection to that device or part of that device without a written certification from the agency or utility owning or previously owning the material shall be liable to the agency or utility for the wrongful possession of that material as provided in subdivision (b).

(2) A written certification under this subdivision shall be on the agency's or utility's letterhead and shall certify both that the agency or utility has sold the material described or is offering the material for sale, salvage, or recycling, and that the person possessing the certification or identified in the certification is authorized to negotiate the sale of that material.

(b) Except as provided in subdivision (c), a junk dealer or recycler in violation of this section shall be liable to the agency or utility owning or previously owning the prohibited material as described in subdivision (a) for the actual damages incurred by the agency or utility, including the value of the material, the cost of replacing the material, labor costs, and the costs of repairing any damage caused by the removal of the material. The court shall also award exemplary damages of three times the actual damages incurred by the agency or utility, unless the court decides that extenuating circumstances do not justify awarding these exemplary damages.

(c)(1) A junk dealer or recycler who unknowingly takes possession of one or more of the materials described in subdivision (a) as part of a load of otherwise nonprohibited materials without the written certification described in subdivision (a) shall notify the appropriate law enforcement agency by the end of the next business day upon discovery of the prohibited materials. Written confirmation of that notice shall relieve the junk dealer or recycler of liability to the agency or utility for the possession of those materials.

(2) The following definitions shall apply for purposes of this subdivision:

(A) "Appropriate law enforcement agency" means, in the case of any material described in subdivision (a) that is located within the territorial limits of an incorporated city, the police chief of the city or his or her designee, or, in the case of any material described in subdivision (a) that is located outside the territorial limits of an incorporated city, the sheriff of the county or his or her designee.

(B) "Written confirmation" means any confirmation received from the law enforcement agency as electronic mail, facsimile, or other written correspondence, including, but not limited to, a letter delivered in person or by certified mail.

(d) Nothing in this section is intended to create a basis for liability on the part of the junk dealers and recyclers to third parties for damages or injuries related to or arising from the theft of the materials described in this section. *(Added by Stats.2012, c. 393 (S.B.1045), § 2.)*

§ 3337. Personal property; conversion; subsequent application of property to benefit of owner

SAME. The presumption declared by the last section cannot be repelled, in favor of one whose possession was wrongful from the beginning, by his subsequent application of the property to the benefit of the owner, without his consent. *(Enacted in 1872.)*

§ 3338. Personal property; conversion; lienor's damages

DAMAGES OF LIENOR. One having a mere lien on personal property, cannot recover greater damages for its conversion, from one having a right thereto superior to his, after his lien is discharged, than the amount secured by the lien, and the compensation allowed by section three thousand three hundred and thirty-six for loss of time and expenses. *(Enacted in 1872.)*

Research References

Miller and Starr California Real Estate § 19:233, Tenant's Personal Property.

§ 3339. Legislative findings, declarations and intent; immigration status; severability

The Legislature finds and declares the following:

(a) All protections, rights, and remedies available under state law, except any reinstatement remedy prohibited by federal law, are available to all individuals regardless of immigration status who have applied for employment, or who are or who have been employed, in this state.

(b) For purposes of enforcing state labor, employment, civil rights, and employee housing laws, a person's immigration status is irrelevant to the issue of liability, and in proceedings or discovery undertaken to enforce those state laws no inquiry shall be permitted into a person's immigration status except where the person seeking to make this inquiry has shown by clear and convincing evidence that this inquiry is necessary in order to comply with federal immigration law.

(c) The provisions of this section are declaratory of existing law.

(d) The provisions of this section are severable. If any provision of this section or its application is held invalid, that invalidity shall not affect other provisions or applications that can be given effect without the invalid provision or application. *(Added by Stats.2002, c. 1071 (S.B.1818), § 1.)*

Research References

Rutter, Cal. Practice Guide: Civ. Pro. Before Trial Ch. 8C-2, "Reasonably Calculated to Lead to Discovery of Admissible Evidence".
California Practice Guide: Employment Litigation Ch. 11-I, I. Enforcing Federal Laws Regulating Employee Compensation.
California Practice Guide: Employment Litigation Ch. 19-F, F. Discovery.
California Practice Guide: Employment Litigation Ch. 19-O, O. Burdens and Standards of Proof.
8 Witkin, California Summary 10th Constitutional Law § 897, Other Discrimination Statutes.
8 Witkin, California Summary 10th Constitutional Law § 914, Enforcement.
8 Witkin, California Summary 10th Constitutional Law § 951, Judicial Enforcement.

§ 3340. Injuries to animals; exemplary damages

INJURIES TO ANIMALS. For wrongful injuries to animals being subjects of property, committed willfully or by gross negligence, in disregard of humanity, exemplary damages may be given. *(Enacted in 1872.)*

Research References

Rutter, Cal. Practice Guide: Personal Injury Ch. 3-E, E. Punitive Damages.

§ 3341. Liability of owner, possessor, or harborer of animal killing or injuring other animals; scienter; right to kill animal found committing injury; accidental killing or injury

The owner, possessor, or harborer of any dog or other animal, that shall, on the premises of any person other than the owner, possessor, or harborer of such dog or other animal, kill, worry, or wound any bovine animal, swine, horse, mule, burro, sheep, angora goat, or cashmere goat, or poultry, shall be liable to the owner of the same for the damages and costs of suit, to be recovered in any court of competent jurisdiction:

1. In the prosecution of actions under the provisions of this chapter, it shall not be necessary for the plaintiff to show that the owner, possessor, or harborer of such dog or other animal, had knowledge of the fact that such dog or other animal would kill, wound or worry bovine animals, swine, horses, mules, burros, sheep, goats, or poultry.

2. Any person on finding any dog or dogs, or other animal, not on the premises of the owner or possessor of such dog or dogs, or other animal, worrying, wounding, or killing any bovine animals, swine, horses, mules, burros, sheep, angora or cashmere goats, may, at the time of finding such dog or dogs, or other animal, kill the same, and the owner or owners thereof shall sustain no action for damages against any person so killing such dog or dogs, or other animal.

Nothing in this section shall render an owner, possessor, or harborer of a dog liable for the accidental or unavoidable killing or injury of any bovine animal, swine, horse, mule, burro, sheep, angora goat, cashmere goat, or poultry which occurs in connection with or as an incident to the driving or herding the same from the premises of the owner, possessor, or harborer of the dog, whether such killing or injury occurs upon such premises or off of such premises. *(Added by Stats.1883, c. 55, p. 283, § 1. Amended by Stats.1903, c. 51, p. 54, § 1; Stats.1945, c. 1327, p. 2500, § 1.)*

Research References

4 Witkin Cal. Proc. 5th Pleading § 625, (S 625) Injuries from Animals.
5 Witkin, California Summary 10th Torts § 157, (L)--Protection of Property Against Dog.
5 Witkin, California Summary 10th Torts § 423, Defense Against Animal.
6 Witkin, California Summary 10th Torts § 1407, Statutory Liability.

§ 3342. Dog bites; liability of owner; military or police work excluded; limitations

(a) The owner of any dog is liable for the damages suffered by any person who is bitten by the dog while in a public place or lawfully in a private place, including the property of the owner of the dog, regardless of the former viciousness of the dog or the owner's knowledge of such viciousness. A person is lawfully upon the private property of such owner within the meaning of this section when he is on such property in the performance of any duty imposed upon him by the laws of this state or by the laws or postal regulations of the United States, or when he is on such property upon the invitation, express or implied, of the owner.

(b) Nothing in this section shall authorize the bringing of an action pursuant to subdivision (a) against any governmental agency using a dog in military or police work if the bite or bites occurred while the dog was defending itself from an annoying, harassing, or provoking act, or assisting an employee of the agency in any of the following:

(1) In the apprehension or holding of a suspect where the employee has a reasonable suspicion of the suspect's involvement in criminal activity.

(2) In the investigation of a crime or possible crime.

(3) In the execution of a warrant.

(4) In the defense of a peace officer or another person.

(c) Subdivision (b) shall not apply in any case where the victim of the bite or bites was not a party to, nor a participant in, nor suspected to be a party to or a participant in, the act or acts that prompted the use of the dog in the military or police work.

(d) Subdivision (b) shall apply only where a governmental agency using a dog in military or police work has adopted a written policy on the necessary and appropriate use of a dog for the police or military work enumerated in subdivision (b). (Added by Stats.1953, c. 37, p. 675, § 6. Amended by Stats.1988, c. 298, § 1.)

Research References

Rutter, Cal. Practice Guide: Personal Injury Ch. 3-D, D. Mitigating Factors in Reduction of Damages.
Rutter, Cal. Practice Guide: Personal Injury Ch. 5-B, B. When to Sue-Statute of Limitations.
Miller and Starr California Real Estate § 22:46, Liability for Injury Caused by Animals or Insects.
4 Witkin Cal. Proc. 5th Pleading § 625, (S 625) Injuries from Animals.
6 Witkin, California Summary 10th Torts § 1077, Statutory Duty.
6 Witkin, California Summary 10th Torts § 1356, Miscellaneous Activities.
6 Witkin, California Summary 10th Torts § 1407, Statutory Liability.
6 Witkin, California Summary 10th Torts § 1408, (S 1408) in General.
6 Witkin, California Summary 10th Torts § 1409, (S 1409) Private Place.
6 Witkin, California Summary 10th Torts § 1411, (S 1411) Immunity for Military and Police Dogs.
6 Witkin, California Summary 10th Torts § 1412, Liability Independent of Statute.

§ 3342.5. Duty of owner; action; dogs trained to fight, attack, or kill; legislation by city and county

(a) The owner of any dog that has bitten a human being shall have the duty to take such reasonable steps as are necessary to remove any danger presented to other persons from bites by the animal.

(b) Whenever a dog has bitten a human being on at least two separate occasions, any person, the district attorney, or city attorney may bring an action against the owner of the animal to determine whether conditions of the treatment or confinement of the dog or other circumstances existing at the time of the bites have been changed so as to remove the danger to other persons presented by the animal. This action shall be brought in the county where a bite occurred. The court, after hearing, may make any order it deems appropriate to prevent the recurrence of such an incident, including, but not limited to, the removal of the animal from the area or its destruction if necessary.

(c) Whenever a dog trained to fight, attack, or kill has bitten a human being, causing substantial physical injury, any person, including the district attorney, or city attorney may bring an action against the owner of the animal to determine whether conditions of the treatment or confinement of the dog or other circumstances existing at the time of the bites have been changed so as to remove the danger to other persons presented by the animal. This action shall be brought in the county where a bite occurred. The court, after hearing, may make any order it deems appropriate to prevent the recurrence of such an incident, including, but not limited to, the removal of the animal from the area or its destruction if necessary.

(d) Nothing in this section shall authorize the bringing of an action pursuant to subdivision (b) based on a bite or bites inflicted upon a trespasser, or by a dog used in military or police work if the bite or bites occurred while the dog was actually performing in that capacity.

(e) Nothing in this section shall be construed to prevent legislation in the field of dog control by any city, county, or city and county.

(f) Nothing in this section shall be construed to affect the liability of the owner of a dog under Section 3342 or any other provision of the law.

(g) A proceeding under this section is a limited civil case. (Added by Stats.1968, c. 1274, p. 2400, § 1. Amended by Stats.1976, c. 470, p. 1216, § 1; Stats.1984, c. 655, § 1; Stats. 1998, c. 931 (S.B.2139), § 18, eff. Sept. 28, 1998.)

Law Revision Commission Comments

Section 3342.5 is amended to accommodate unification of the municipal and superior courts in a county. Cal. Const. art. VI, § 5(e).

A limited civil case is within the original jurisdiction of the municipal court or of the superior court in a county in which there is no municipal court. Cal. Const. art. VI, 10 (superior court jurisdiction); Code Civ. Proc. §§ 85, 85.1 (limited civil cases). See also Code Civ. Proc. §§ 91, 904.2, 1085 (trial procedures and writ and appellate jurisdiction for limited civil cases). [28 Cal.L.Rev.Comm. Reports 51 (1998)].

Research References

Miller and Starr California Real Estate § 22:46, Liability for Injury Caused by Animals or Insects.
6 Witkin, California Summary 10th Torts § 1077, Statutory Duty.

§ 3343. Fraud in purchase, sale or exchange of property; additional damages

(a) One defrauded in the purchase, sale or exchange of property is entitled to recover the difference between the actual value of that with which the defrauded person parted and the actual value of that which he received, together with any additional damage arising from the particular transaction, including any of the following:

(1) Amounts actually and reasonably expended in reliance upon the fraud.

(2) An amount which would compensate the defrauded party for loss of use and enjoyment of the property to the extent that any such loss was proximately caused by the fraud.

(3) Where the defrauded party has been induced by reason of the fraud to sell or otherwise part with the property in question, an amount which will compensate him for profits or other gains which might reasonably have been earned by use of the property had he retained it.

(4) Where the defrauded party has been induced by reason of the fraud to purchase or otherwise acquire the property in question, an amount which will compensate him for any loss of profits or other gains which were reasonably anticipated and would have been earned by him from the use or sale of the property had it possessed the characteristics fraudulently attributed to it by the party committing the fraud, provided that lost profits from the use or sale of the property shall be recoverable only if and only to the extent that all of the following apply:

(i) The defrauded party acquired the property for the purpose of using or reselling it for a profit.

(ii) The defrauded party reasonably relied on the fraud in entering into the transaction and in anticipating profits from the subsequent use or sale of the property.

(iii) Any loss of profits for which damages are sought under this paragraph have been proximately caused by the fraud and the defrauded party's reliance on it.

(b) Nothing in this section shall do either of the following:

(1) Permit the defrauded person to recover any amount measured by the difference between the value of property as represented and the actual value thereof.

(2) Deny to any person having a cause of action for fraud or deceit any legal or equitable remedies to which such person may be entitled. *(Added by Stats.1935, c. 536, p. 1612, § 1. Amended by Stats.1971, c. 943, p. 1850, § 1.)*

Research References

Rutter, Cal. Practice Guide: Real Prop. Transactions Ch. 11-E, E. Damages for Fraud.

Miller and Starr California Real Estate § 3:33, Damages Recoverable by the Principal.

Miller and Starr California Real Estate § 34:9, "Reimbursement" or "Consequential Damages".

Miller and Starr California Real Estate § 27:87, Quantum Meruit Recovery.

Miller and Starr California Real Estate § 29:10, Measure of Owner's Damages for Defective Construction.

Miller and Starr California Real Estate § 29:30, Measure of Damages Applicable to Developers.

Miller and Starr California Real Estate § 29:38, Measure of Damages.

Miller and Starr California Real Estate § 34:39, Damages for Pain and Suffering.

Miller and Starr California Real Estate § 34:46, Damages to Buyer for Delay of Conveyance.

Miller and Starr California Real Estate § 34:83, General Principles; Election of Remedies.

Miller and Starr California Real Estate § 34:85, Measure of Damages.

Miller and Starr California Real Estate § 34:86, Compensatory Damages.

Miller and Starr California Real Estate § 34:87, Consequential Damages.

Miller and Starr California Real Estate § 34:88, Expenditures in Reliance on the Fraud.

Miller and Starr California Real Estate § 34:89, Compensation for the Loss of Use and Enjoyment.

Miller and Starr California Real Estate § 34:90, Loss of Profits.

Miller and Starr California Real Estate § 34:91, Emotional Distress.

Miller and Starr California Real Estate § 34:128, When Conduct is Also Fraudulent.

14 NO. 2 Miller & Starr, California Real Estate Newsalert 2, Agency.

16 NO. 4 Miller & Starr, California Real Estate Newsalert 37, Remedies.

18 NO. 1 Miller & Starr, California Real Estate Newsalert 1, Disclosures in California Residential Real Property Sales.

3 Witkin Cal. Proc. 5th Actions § 164, (S 164) Waiver of Tort and Suit in Quasi-Contract.

5 Witkin Cal. Proc. 5th Pleading § 941, Fraud.

1 Witkin Cal. Summ. 10th Contracts § 317, (S 317) Effect of Undue Influence.

4 Witkin, California Summary 10th Security Transactions in Real Property § 177, Claims Against Third Parties.

5 Witkin, California Summary 10th Torts § 811, (S 811) Securities Cases.

6 Witkin, California Summary 10th Torts § 1031, Financial Injury.

6 Witkin, California Summary 10th Torts § 1635, (S 1635) Illustrations.

6 Witkin, California Summary 10th Torts § 1710, Nature of Rule.

6 Witkin, California Summary 10th Torts § 1711, Value of Property.

6 Witkin, California Summary 10th Torts § 1713, Quasi-Contractual Recovery.

6 Witkin, California Summary 10th Torts § 1714, Elements of Damage.

6 Witkin, California Summary 10th Torts § 1715, Fraud on Purchaser.

6 Witkin, California Summary 10th Torts § 1716, Illustrations.

6 Witkin, California Summary 10th Torts § 1717, (S 1717) Breach of Fiduciary Duty.

6 Witkin, California Summary 10th Torts § 1623A, (New)-Uncompensated or Potential Harm as Affecting Amount.

§ 3343.5. Unlawful motor vehicle subleasing; persons entitled to bring action; relief granted by court; definitions

Section operative until July 1, 2014. See, also, section operative July 1, 2014.

(a) Any one or more of the following who suffers any damage proximately resulting from one or more acts of unlawful motor vehicle subleasing, as described in Chapter 12.7 (commencing with Section 570) of Title 13 of Part 1 of the Penal Code, may bring an action against the person who has engaged in those acts:

(1) A seller or other secured party under a conditional sale contract or a security agreement.

(2) A lender under a direct loan agreement.

(3) A lessor under a lease contract.

(4) A buyer under a conditional sale contract.

(5) A purchaser under a direct loan agreement, an agreement which provides for a security interest, or an agreement which is equivalent to these types of agreements.

(6) A lessee under a lease contract.

(7) An actual or purported transferee or assignee of any right or interest of a buyer, a purchaser, or a lessee.

(b) The court in an action under subdivision (a) may award actual damages; equitable relief, including, but not limited to, an injunction and restitution of money and property; punitive damages; reasonable attorney's fees and costs; and any other relief which the court deems proper.

(c) As used in this section, the following terms have the following meanings:

(1) "Buyer" has the meaning set forth in subdivision (c) of Section 2981.

(2) "Conditional sale contract" has the meaning set forth in subdivision (a) of Section 2981. Notwithstanding subdivision (k) of Section 2981, "conditional sale contract" includes any contract for the sale or bailment of a motor vehicle between a buyer and a seller primarily for business or commercial purposes.

(3) "Direct loan agreement" means an agreement between a lender and a purchaser whereby the lender has advanced funds pursuant to a loan secured by the motor vehicle which the purchaser has purchased.

(4) "Lease contract" means a lease contract between a lessor and lessee as this term and these parties are defined in Section 2985.7. Notwithstanding subdivision (d) of Section 2985.7, "lease contract" includes a lease for business or commercial purposes.

(5) "Motor vehicle" means any vehicle required to be registered under the Vehicle Code.

(6) "Person" means an individual, company, firm, association, partnership, trust, corporation, limited liability company, or other legal entity.

(7) "Purchaser" has the meaning set forth in paragraph (30) of subdivision (b) of Section 1201 of the Commercial Code.

(8) "Security agreement" and "secured party" have the meanings set forth, respectively, in paragraphs (73) and (72) of subdivision (a) of Section 9102 of the Commercial Code. "Security interest" has the meaning set forth in paragraph (35) of subdivision (b) of Section 1201 of the Commercial Code.

(9) "Seller" has the meaning set forth in subdivision (b) of Section 2981, and includes the present holder of the conditional sale contract.

(d) The rights and remedies provided in this section are in addition to any other rights and remedies provided by law. *(Added by Stats.1987, c. 1072, § 1. Amended by Stats.1994, c. 1010 (S.B.2053), § 52; Stats.1999, c. 991 (S.B.45), § 8.5, operative July 1, 2001; Stats.2006, c. 254 (S.B.1481), § 4.)*

§ 3343.5. Unlawful motor vehicle subleasing; persons entitled to bring action; relief granted by court; definitions

Section operative July 1, 2014. See, also, section operative until July 1, 2014.

(a) Any one or more of the following who suffers any damage proximately resulting from one or more acts of unlawful motor vehicle subleasing, as described in Chapter 12.7 (commencing with Section 570) of Title 13 of Part 1 of the Penal Code, may bring an action against the person who has engaged in those acts:

(1) A seller or other secured party under a conditional sale contract or a security agreement.

(2) A lender under a direct loan agreement.

(3) A lessor under a lease contract.

(4) A buyer under a conditional sale contract.

(5) A purchaser under a direct loan agreement, an agreement which provides for a security interest, or an agreement which is equivalent to these types of agreements.

(6) A lessee under a lease contract.

(7) An actual or purported transferee or assignee of any right or interest of a buyer, a purchaser, or a lessee.

(b) The court in an action under subdivision (a) may award actual damages; equitable relief, including, but not limited to, an injunction and restitution of money and property; punitive damages; reasonable attorney's fees and costs; and any other relief which the court deems proper.

(c) As used in this section, the following terms have the following meanings:

(1) "Buyer" has the meaning set forth in subdivision (c) of Section 2981.

(2) "Conditional sale contract" has the meaning set forth in subdivision (a) of Section 2981. Notwithstanding subdivision (k) of Section 2981, "conditional sale contract" includes any contract for the sale or bailment of a motor vehicle between a buyer and a seller primarily for business or commercial purposes.

(3) "Direct loan agreement" means an agreement between a lender and a purchaser whereby the lender has advanced funds pursuant to a loan secured by the motor vehicle which the purchaser has purchased.

(4) "Lease contract" means a lease contract between a lessor and lessee as this term and these parties are defined in Section 2985.7. Notwithstanding subdivision (d) of Section 2985.7, "lease contract" includes a lease for business or commercial purposes.

(5) "Motor vehicle" means any vehicle required to be registered under the Vehicle Code.

(6) "Person" means an individual, company, firm, association, partnership, trust, corporation, limited liability company, or other legal entity.

(7) "Purchaser" has the meaning set forth in paragraph (30) of subdivision (b) of Section 1201 of the Commercial Code.

(8) "Security agreement" and "secured party" have the meanings set forth, respectively, in paragraphs (74) and (73) * * * of subdivision (a) of Section 9102 of the Commercial Code. "Security interest" has the meaning set forth in paragraph (35) of subdivision (b) of Section 1201 of the Commercial Code.

(9) "Seller" has the meaning set forth in subdivision (b) of Section 2981, and includes the present holder of the conditional sale contract.

(d) The rights and remedies provided in this section are in addition to any other rights and remedies provided by law. *(Added by Stats.1987, c. 1072, § 1. Amended by Stats.1994, c. 1010 (S.B.2053), § 52; Stats.1999, c. 991 (S.B.45), § 8.5, operative July 1, 2001; Stats.2006, c. 254 (S.B.1481), § 4; Stats.2013, c. 531 (A.B.502), § 1, operative July 1, 2014.)*

Research References

13 Witkin, California Summary 10th Personal Property § 195, (S 195) Unlawful Subleasing.

§ 3343.7. Fraudulent inducement to join a nonprofit organization operated on cooperative basis by and for independent retailers; action for rescission of contract or damages

An action may be brought against any nonprofit organization operated on a cooperative basis by and for independent retailers which wholesales goods and services primarily to its member retailers as described in paragraph (3) of subdivision (d) of Section 20001 of the Business and Professions Code or subdivision (c) of Section 31005 of the Corporations Code, for rescission of a membership contract entered into, or for any damages sustained, as a consequence of being fraudulently induced to join the organization. For purposes of this section, "fraudulently induced" means the misrepresentation of a material fact, or the omission of a material fact, including the failure of the organization to disclose all information required under subparagraph (H) of paragraph (3) of subdivision (d) of Section 20001 of the Business and Professions Code or paragraph (8) of subdivision (c) of Section 31005 of the Corporations Code, unless the defendant proves that the plaintiff knew the facts concerning the untruth or omission or that the defendant exercised reasonable care and did not know (or if the defendant had exercised reasonable care would not have known) of the untruth or omission. *(Added by Stats.1989, c. 1380, § 2.)*

Research References

3 Witkin, California Summary 10th Agency and Employment § 7, in General.

ARTICLE 3. PENAL DAMAGES

§ 3344. Use of another's name, voice, signature, photograph, or likeness for advertising or selling or soliciting purposes

(a) Any person who knowingly uses another's name, signature, photograph, or likeness, in any manner, on or in products, merchandise, or goods, or for purposes of advertising or selling, or soliciting purchases of, products, merchandise, goods or services, without such person's prior consent, or, in the case of a minor, the prior consent of his parent or legal guardian, shall be liable for any damages sustained by the person or persons injured as a result thereof. In addition, in any action brought under this section, the person who violated the section shall be liable to the injured party or parties in an amount equal to the greater of seven hundred fifty dollars ($750) or the actual damages suffered by him or her as a result of the unauthorized use, and any profits from the unauthorized use that are attributable to the use and are not taken into account in computing the actual damages. In establishing such profits, the injured party or parties are required to present proof only of the gross revenue attributable to such use, and the person who violated this section is required to prove his or her deductible expenses. Punitive damages may also be awarded to the injured party or parties. The prevailing party in any action under this section shall also be entitled to attorney's fees and costs.

(b) As used in this section, "photograph" means any photograph or photographic reproduction, still or moving, or any videotape or live television transmission, of any person, such that the person is readily identifiable.

(1) A person shall be deemed to be readily identifiable from a photograph when one who views the photograph with the naked eye can reasonably determine that the person depicted in the photograph is the same person who is complaining of its unauthorized use.

(2) If the photograph includes more than one person so identifiable, then the person or persons complaining of the use shall be represented as individuals rather than solely as members of a definable group represented in the photograph. A definable group includes, but is not limited to, the following examples: a crowd at any sporting event, a crowd in any street or public building, the audience at any theatrical or stage production, a glee club, or a baseball team.

(3) A person or persons shall be considered to be represented as members of a definable group if they are represented in the photograph solely as a result of being present at the time the photograph was taken and have not been singled out as individuals in any manner.

(c) Where a photograph or likeness of an employee of the person using the photograph or likeness appearing in the advertisement or other publication prepared by or in behalf of the user is only incidental, and not essential, to the purpose of the publication in which it appears, there shall arise a rebuttable presumption affecting the burden of producing evidence that the failure to obtain the consent of the employee was not a knowing use of the employee's photograph or likeness.

(d) For purposes of this section, a use of a name, voice, signature, photograph, or likeness in connection with any news, public affairs, or sports broadcast or account, or any political campaign, shall not constitute a use for which consent is required under subdivision (a).

(e) The use of a name, voice, signature, photograph, or likeness in a commercial medium shall not constitute a use for which consent is required under subdivision (a) solely because the material containing such use is commercially sponsored or contains paid advertising. Rather it shall be a question of fact whether or not the use of the person's name, voice, signature, photograph, or likeness was so directly connected with the commercial sponsorship or with the paid advertising as to constitute a use for which consent is required under subdivision (a).

(f) Nothing in this section shall apply to the owners or employees of any medium used for advertising, including, but not limited to, newspapers, magazines, radio and television networks and stations, cable television systems, billboards, and transit ads, by whom any advertisement or solicitation in violation of this section is published or disseminated, unless it is established that such owners or employees had knowledge of the unauthorized use of the person's name, voice, signature, photograph, or likeness as prohibited by this section.

(g) The remedies provided for in this section are cumulative and shall be in addition to any others provided for by law. *(Added by Stats.1971, c. 1595, p. 3426, § 1. Amended by Stats.1984, c. 1704, § 2.)*

Validity

In the of case of Laws v. Sony Music Entertainment, Inc., C.A.9 (Cal.)2006, 448 F.3d 1134, 78 U.S.P.Q.2d 1910, certiorari denied 127 S.Ct. 1371, 549 U.S. 1252, 167 L.Ed.2d 159., federal copyright law preempted the plaintiff's claim under this section.

Research References

Rutter, Cal. Practice Guide: Civ. Pro. Before Trial Ch. 6-B, B. Complaints.

California Practice Guide: Employment Litigation Ch. 5-K, K. Invasion of Privacy.

Rutter, Cal. Practice Guide: Enforcing Judgments/Debts Ch. 3-C, C. Prelawsuit Considerations.

Miller and Starr California Real Estate § 34:74, Effect of Dismissal of Action Before Judgment.

7 Witkin Cal. Proc. 5th Judgment § 89, Determining Who is Prevailing Party.

7 Witkin Cal. Proc. 5th Judgment § 229, (S 229) Actions Involving Personal Injury or Intentional Torts.

5 Witkin Cal. Proc. 5th Pleading § 747, Complaint Sufficient.

1 Witkin Cal. Summ. 10th Contracts § 912, (S 912) Actor's Contract for Publicity.

13 Witkin, California Summary 10th Personal Property § 59, in General.

13 Witkin, California Summary 10th Personal Property § 60, Preemption Confined to State Copyright Laws.

5 Witkin, California Summary 10th Torts § 655, Oral Disclosure.

5 Witkin, California Summary 10th Torts § 676, (S 676) in General.

5 Witkin, California Summary 10th Torts § 681, (S 681) in General.

5 Witkin, California Summary 10th Torts § 682, (S 682) Conditions of Recovery.

5 Witkin, California Summary 10th Torts § 683, (S 683) Exemptions.

5 Witkin, California Summary 10th Torts § 685, (S 685) Statutory Right.

§ 3344.1. Deceased personality's name, voice, signature, photograph, or likeness; unauthorized use; damages and profits from use; protected uses; persons entitled to exercise rights; successors in interest or licensees; registration of claim

(a)(1) Any person who uses a deceased personality's name, voice, signature, photograph, or likeness, in any manner, on or in products, merchandise, or goods, or for purposes of advertising or selling, or soliciting purchases of, products, merchandise, goods, or services, without prior consent from the person or persons specified in subdivision (c), shall be liable for any damages sustained by the person or persons injured as a result thereof. In addition, in any action brought under this section, the person who violated the section shall be liable to the injured party or parties in an amount equal to the greater of seven hundred fifty dollars ($750) or the actual damages suffered by the injured party or parties, as a result of the unauthorized use, and any profits from the unauthorized use that are attributable to the use and are not taken into account in computing the actual damages. In establishing these profits, the injured party or parties shall be required to present proof only of the gross revenue attributable to the use, and the person who violated the section is required to prove his or her deductible expenses. Punitive damages may also be awarded to the injured party or parties. The prevailing party or parties in any action under this section shall also be entitled to attorney's fees and costs.

(2) For purposes of this subdivision, a play, book, magazine, newspaper, musical composition, audiovisual work, radio or television program, single and original work of art, work of political or newsworthy value, or an advertisement or commercial announcement for any of these works, shall not be considered a product, article of merchandise, good, or service if it is fictional or nonfictional entertainment, or a dramatic, literary, or musical work.

(3) If a work that is protected under paragraph (2) includes within it a use in connection with a product, article of merchandise, good, or service, this use shall not be exempt under this

subdivision, notwithstanding the unprotected use's inclusion in a work otherwise exempt under this subdivision, if the claimant proves that this use is so directly connected with a product, article of merchandise, good, or service as to constitute an act of advertising, selling, or soliciting purchases of that product, article of merchandise, good, or service by the deceased personality without prior consent from the person or persons specified in subdivision (c).

(b) The rights recognized under this section are property rights, freely transferable or descendible, in whole or in part, by contract or by means of any trust or any other testamentary instrument, executed before or after January 1, 1985. The rights recognized under this section shall be deemed to have existed at the time of death of any deceased personality who died prior to January 1, 1985, and, except as provided in subdivision (*o*), shall vest in the persons entitled to these property rights under the testamentary instrument of the deceased personality effective as of the date of his or her death. In the absence of an express transfer in a testamentary instrument of the deceased personality's rights in his or her name, voice, signature, photograph, or likeness, a provision in the testamentary instrument that provides for the disposition of the residue of the deceased personality's assets shall be effective to transfer the rights recognized under this section in accordance with the terms of that provision. The rights established by this section shall also be freely transferable or descendible by contract, trust, or any other testamentary instrument by any subsequent owner of the deceased personality's rights as recognized by this section. Nothing in this section shall be construed to render invalid or unenforceable any contract entered into by a deceased personality during his or her lifetime by which the deceased personality assigned the rights, in whole or in part, to use his or her name, voice, signature, photograph, or likeness, regardless of whether the contract was entered into before or after January 1, 1985.

(c) The consent required by this section shall be exercisable by the person or persons to whom the right of consent, or portion thereof, has been transferred in accordance with subdivision (b), or if no transfer has occurred, then by the person or persons to whom the right of consent, or portion thereof, has passed in accordance with subdivision (d).

(d) Subject to subdivisions (b) and (c), after the death of any person, the rights under this section shall belong to the following person or persons and may be exercised, on behalf of and for the benefit of all of those persons, by those persons who, in the aggregate, are entitled to more than a one-half interest in the rights:

(1) The entire interest in those rights belongs to the surviving spouse of the deceased personality unless there are any surviving children or grandchildren of the deceased personality, in which case one-half of the entire interest in those rights belongs to the surviving spouse.

(2) The entire interest in those rights belongs to the surviving children of the deceased personality and to the surviving children of any dead child of the deceased personality unless the deceased personality has a surviving spouse, in which case the ownership of a one-half interest in rights is divided among the surviving children and grandchildren.

(3) If there is no surviving spouse, and no surviving children or grandchildren, then the entire interest in those rights belongs to the surviving parent or parents of the deceased personality.

(4) The rights of the deceased personality's children and grandchildren are in all cases divided among them and exercisable in the manner provided in Section 240 of the Probate Code according to the number of the deceased personality's children represented. The share of the children of a dead child of a

deceased personality can be exercised only by the action of a majority of them.

(e) If any deceased personality does not transfer his or her rights under this section by contract, or by means of a trust or testamentary instrument, and there are no surviving persons as described in subdivision (d), then the rights set forth in subdivision (a) shall terminate.

(f)(1) A successor in interest to the rights of a deceased personality under this section or a licensee thereof shall not recover damages for a use prohibited by this section that occurs before the successor in interest or licensee registers a claim of the rights under paragraph (2).

(2) Any person claiming to be a successor in interest to the rights of a deceased personality under this section or a licensee thereof may register that claim with the Secretary of State on a form prescribed by the Secretary of State and upon payment of a fee as set forth in subdivision (d) of Section 12195 of the Government Code. The form shall be verified and shall include the name and date of death of the deceased personality, the name and address of the claimant, the basis of the claim, and the rights claimed.

(3) Upon receipt and after filing of any document under this section, the Secretary of State shall post the document along with the entire registry of persons claiming to be a successor in interest to the rights of a deceased personality or a registered licensee under this section upon the Secretary of State's Internet Web site. The Secretary of State may microfilm or reproduce by other techniques any of the filings or documents and destroy the original filing or document. The microfilm or other reproduction of any document under this section shall be admissible in any court of law. The microfilm or other reproduction of any document may be destroyed by the Secretary of State 70 years after the death of the personality named therein.

(4) Claims registered under this subdivision shall be public records.

(g) An action shall not be brought under this section by reason of any use of a deceased personality's name, voice, signature, photograph, or likeness occurring after the expiration of 70 years after the death of the deceased personality.

(h) As used in this section, "deceased personality" means any natural person whose name, voice, signature, photograph, or likeness has commercial value at the time of his or her death, or because of his or her death, whether or not during the lifetime of that natural person the person used his or her name, voice, signature, photograph, or likeness on or in products, merchandise, or goods, or for purposes of advertising or selling, or solicitation of purchase of, products, merchandise, goods, or services. A "deceased personality" shall include, without limitation, any such natural person who has died within 70 years prior to January 1, 1985.

(i) As used in this section, "photograph" means any photograph or photographic reproduction, still or moving, or any videotape or live television transmission, of any person, such that the deceased personality is readily identifiable. A deceased personality shall be deemed to be readily identifiable from a photograph if one who views the photograph with the naked eye can reasonably determine who the person depicted in the photograph is.

(j) For purposes of this section, the use of a name, voice, signature, photograph, or likeness in connection with any news, public affairs, or sports broadcast or account, or any political campaign, shall not constitute a use for which consent is required under subdivision (a).

(k) The use of a name, voice, signature, photograph, or likeness in a commercial medium shall not constitute a use for which consent is required under subdivision (a) solely because the material containing the use is commercially sponsored or contains paid advertising. Rather, it shall be a question of fact whether or not the use of the deceased personality's name, voice, signature, photograph, or likeness was so directly connected with the commercial sponsorship or with the paid advertising as to constitute a use for which consent is required under subdivision (a).

(*l*) Nothing in this section shall apply to the owners or employees of any medium used for advertising, including, but not limited to, newspapers, magazines, radio and television networks and stations, cable television systems, billboards, and transit advertisements, by whom any advertisement or solicitation in violation of this section is published or disseminated, unless it is established that the owners or employees had knowledge of the unauthorized use of the deceased personality's name, voice, signature, photograph, or likeness as prohibited by this section.

(m) The remedies provided for in this section are cumulative and shall be in addition to any others provided for by law.

(n) This section shall apply to the adjudication of liability and the imposition of any damages or other remedies in cases in which the liability, damages, and other remedies arise from acts occurring directly in this state. For purposes of this section, acts giving rise to liability shall be limited to the use, on or in products, merchandise, goods, or services, or the advertising or selling, or soliciting purchases of, products, merchandise, goods, or services prohibited by this section.

(*o*) Notwithstanding any provision of this section to the contrary, if an action was taken prior to May 1, 2007, to exercise rights recognized under this section relating to a deceased personality who died prior to January 1, 1985, by a person described in subdivision (d), other than a person who was disinherited by the deceased personality in a testamentary instrument, and the exercise of those rights was not challenged successfully in a court action by a person described in subdivision (b), that exercise shall not be affected by subdivision (b). In that case, the rights that would otherwise vest in one or more persons described in subdivision (b) shall vest solely in the person or persons described in subdivision (d), other than a person disinherited by the deceased personality in a testamentary instrument, for all future purposes.

(p) The rights recognized by this section are expressly made retroactive, including to those deceased personalities who died before January 1, 1985. *(Formerly § 990, added by Stats.1984, c. 1704, § 1. Amended by Stats.1988, c. 113, § 2, eff. May 25, 1988, operative July 1, 1988. Renumbered § 3344.1 and amended by Stats.1999, c. 998 (S.B.209), § 1. Amended by Stats.1999, c. 1000 (S.B.284), § 9.5; Stats.2007, c. 439 (S.B.771), § 1; Stats.2009, c. 88 (A.B.176), § 15; Stats.2010, c. 20 (A.B.585), § 1; Stats.2011, c. 296 (A.B.1023), § 35.)*

Law Revision Commission Comments

Section 990 is amended to conform terminology. [19 Cal.L.Rev.Comm.Reports 1033 (1987)].

Subdivision (i) of Section 3344.1 is amended to reflect advances in recording technology and for consistency of terminology. For a similar reform, see 2002 Cal. Stat. ch. 1068 (replacing numerous references to "audiotape" in Civil Discovery Act with either "audio technology," "audio recording," or "audio record," as context required). [37 Cal. L. Revision Comm'n Reports 211 (2007)].

Research References

5 Witkin, California Summary 10th Torts § 653, No Relational Right.
5 Witkin, California Summary 10th Torts § 676, (S 676) in General.
5 Witkin, California Summary 10th Torts § 680, (S 680) Transformative Matters.
5 Witkin, California Summary 10th Torts § 681, (S 681) in General.
5 Witkin, California Summary 10th Torts § 684, (S 684) Background.

5 Witkin, California Summary 10th Torts § 685, (S 685) Statutory Right.

§ 3344.5. Campaign advertisement with unauthorized signature; cause of action

(a) Any person whose signature is used in violation of, and any candidate for elective office whose election or defeat is expressly advocated in any campaign advertisement that violates, subdivision (b) of Section 115.1 of the Penal Code, shall have a civil cause of action against any person committing the violation.

(b) If a mass mailing or other printed matter that violates subdivision (b) of Section 115.1 of the Penal Code expressly advocates the election or defeat of more than one candidate only a person whose signature is used and the candidate or candidates to whom the unauthorized signature directly relates shall have a civil cause of action pursuant to this section.

(c) Any person bringing a cause of action pursuant to this section may recover damages in an amount of two times the cost of the communication, but not to exceed fifty thousand dollars ($50,000), with regard to which the unauthorized signature was used.

(d) As used in this section, "signature" means either of the following:

(1) A handwritten or mechanical signature, or a copy thereof.

(2) Any representation of a person's name, including, but not limited to, a printed or typewritten representation, that serves the same purpose as a handwritten or mechanical signature. *(Added by Stats.1990, c. 1590 (S.B.1865), § 1, eff. Sept. 30, 1990. Amended by Stats.1993, c. 334 (A.B.1117), § 1.)*

Research References

5 Witkin, California Summary 10th Torts § 681, (S 681) in General.

§ 3344.6. Campaign advertisement falsely representing official public documents; cause of action for damages

(a) Any candidate for elective office whose election or defeat is expressly advocated in any campaign advertisement which violates subdivision (a) of Section 115.2 of the Penal Code shall have a civil cause of action against any person committing the violation.

(b) If a mass mailing or other printed matter which violates subdivision (a) of Section 115.2 of the Penal Code expressly advocates the election or defeat of more than one candidate, only the candidate or candidates to whom the misstatement or misrepresentation directly relates shall have a civil cause of action pursuant to this section.

(c) Any person bringing a cause of action pursuant to this section may recover damages in an amount of two times the cost of the communication, but not to exceed fifty thousand dollars ($50,000). *(Added by Stats.1991, c. 1051 (S.B.209), § 1.)*

§ 3345. Unfair or deceptive practices against senior citizens or disabled persons; treble damages

(a) This section shall apply only in actions brought by, on behalf of, or for the benefit of senior citizens or disabled persons, as those terms are defined in subdivisions (f) and (g) of Section 1761, to redress unfair or deceptive acts or practices or unfair methods of competition.

(b) Whenever a trier of fact is authorized by a statute to impose either a fine, or a civil penalty or other penalty, or any other remedy the purpose or effect of which is to punish or deter, and the amount of the fine, penalty, or other remedy is subject to the trier of fact's discretion, the trier of fact shall consider all of the following factors, in addition to other appropriate factors, in determining the amount of fine, civil penalty or other penalty, or other remedy to impose. Whenever the trier of fact makes an affirmative finding in regard to one or more of the following factors, it may impose a fine, civil penalty or other penalty, or other remedy in an amount up to three times greater than authorized by the statute, or, where the statute does not authorize a specific amount, up to three times greater than the amount the trier of fact would impose in the absence of that affirmative finding:

(1) Whether the defendant knew or should have known that his or her conduct was directed to one or more senior citizens or disabled persons.

(2) Whether the defendant's conduct caused one or more senior citizens or disabled persons to suffer: loss or encumbrance of a primary residence, principal employment, or source of income; substantial loss of property set aside for retirement, or for personal or family care and maintenance; or substantial loss of payments received under a pension or retirement plan or a government benefits program, or assets essential to the health or welfare of the senior citizen or disabled person.

(3) Whether one or more senior citizens or disabled persons are substantially more vulnerable than other members of the public to the defendant's conduct because of age, poor health or infirmity, impaired understanding, restricted mobility, or disability, and actually suffered substantial physical, emotional, or economic damage resulting from the defendant's conduct. *(Added by Stats.1988, c. 823, § 4.)*

Research References

Rutter, Cal. Practice Guide: Insurance Litigation Ch. 11-K, K. Statutory Liability.
Rutter, Cal. Practice Guide: Insurance Litigation Ch. 13-C, C. Punitive Damages.
Rutter, Cal. Practice Guide: Prof. Responsibility Ch. 1-E, E. Regulation of Form of Practice.
1 Witkin Cal. Proc. 5th Attorneys § 100, Sale of Financial Products to Client.
13 Witkin, California Summary 10th Equity § 125, (S 125) in General.
13 Witkin, California Summary 10th Equity § 126, (S 126) Civil Penalties.

§ 3346. Injuries to timber, trees, or underwood; treble damages; double damages; actual detriment

(a) For wrongful injuries to timber, trees, or underwood upon the land of another, or removal thereof, the measure of damages is three times such sum as would compensate for the actual detriment, except that where the trespass was casual or involuntary, or that the defendant in any action brought under this section had probable cause to believe that the land on which the trespass was committed was his own or the land of the person in whose service or by whose direction the act was done, the measure of damages shall be twice the sum as would compensate for the actual detriment, and excepting further that where the wood was taken by the authority of highway officers for the purpose of repairing a public highway or bridge upon the land or adjoining it, in which case judgment shall only be given in a sum equal to the actual detriment.

(b) The measure of damages to be assessed against a defendant for any trespass committed while acting in reliance upon a survey of boundary lines which improperly fixes the location of a boundary line, shall be the actual detriment incurred if both of the following conditions exist:

1. The trespass was committed by a defendant who either himself procured, or whose principal, lessor, or immediate predecessor in title procured the survey to be made; and

2. The survey was made by a person licensed under the laws of this State to practice land surveying.

(c) Any action for the damages specified by subdivisions (a) and (b) of this section must be commenced within five years from the date of the trespass. *(Added by Stats.1957, c. 2346, p. 4076, § 2.)*

Research References

Rutter, Cal. Practice Guide: Civ. Pro. Before Trial Ch. 5-E, E. Limitations on Default Judgments.
Rutter, Cal. Practice Guide: Personal Injury Ch. 3-E, E. Punitive Damages.
Miller and Starr California Real Estate § 14:9, Self-Help for Encroaching Trees.
Miller and Starr California Real Estate § 14:11, Damages.
Miller and Starr California Real Estate § 14:12, Trees Located on Common Boundary.
Miller and Starr California Real Estate § 17:31, Timber.
Miller and Starr California Real Estate § 34:99, Punitive Damages--Judicial Review.
20 NO. 4 Miller & Starr, California Real Estate Newsalert 34, Judicial Remedies.
23 NO. 2 Miller & Starr, California Real Estate Newsalert 3, Adjoining Landowners.
3 Witkin Cal. Proc. 5th Actions § 458, (S 458) Period Extended.
3 Witkin Cal. Proc. 5th Actions § 483, (S 483) Three Years.
3 Witkin Cal. Proc. 5th Actions § 485, (S 485) Five Years.
6 Witkin Cal. Proc. 5th Proceedings Without Trial § 158, (S 158) Requirement of Notice of Amount Sought.
6 Witkin, California Summary 10th Torts § 1570, Treble Damages.
6 Witkin, California Summary 10th Torts § 1732, Ordinary Injury or Taking: Actual Damages.
6 Witkin, California Summary 10th Torts § 1733, Trespass Under Mistake: Double Damages.
6 Witkin, California Summary 10th Torts § 1734, Wilful and Malicious Trespass: Treble Damages.

ARTICLE 4. GENERAL PROVISIONS

§ 3353. Estimating damages; value to seller

VALUE, HOW ESTIMATED IN FAVOR OF SELLER. In estimating damages, the value of property to a seller thereof is deemed to be the price which he could have obtained therefor in the market nearest to the place at which it should have been accepted by the buyer, and at such time after the breach of the contract as would have sufficed, with reasonable diligence, for the seller to effect a resale. *(Enacted in 1872.)*

Research References

Miller and Starr California Real Estate § 34:50, Determining "Value of the Property"; Comparison of the Terms of Sale.
1 Witkin Cal. Summ. 10th Contracts § 902, (S 902) Resale Price as Evidence.

§ 3354. Estimating damages; value to buyer

VALUE, HOW ESTIMATED IN FAVOR OF BUYER. In estimating damages, except as provided by Sections 3355 and 3356, the value of property, to a buyer or owner thereof, deprived of its possession, is deemed to be the price at which he might have bought an equivalent thing in the market nearest to the place where the property ought to have been put into his possession, and at such time after the breach of duty upon which his right to damages is founded as would suffice, with reasonable diligence, for him to make such a purchase. *(Enacted in 1872.)*

Miller and Starr California Real Estate § 34:50, Determining "Value of the Property"; Comparison of the Terms of Sale.
4 Witkin, California Summary 10th Sales § 196, (S 196) Lost Profits.

§ 3355. Property of peculiar value

PROPERTY OF PECULIAR VALUE. Where certain property has a peculiar value to a person recovering damages for deprivation thereof, or injury thereto, that may be deemed to be its value against one who had notice thereof before incurring a liability to damages in respect thereof, or against a willful wrongdoer. *(Enacted in 1872.)*

Rutter, Cal. Practice Guide: Personal Injury Ch. 3-C, C. Specific Items of Compensatory Damages.
Rutter, Cal. Practice Guide: Real Prop. Transactions Ch. 11-D, D. Buyer's Remedies Upon Seller's Breach-Damages and Specific Performance.
Rutter, Cal. Practice Guide: Real Prop. Transactions Gen. Matls., Highlights.
Miller and Starr California Real Estate § 34:29, Compensatory Damages.
22 NO. 5 Miller & Starr, California Real Estate Newsalert 8, Easements.
5 Witkin, California Summary 10th Torts § 68, Instructions.

§ 3356. Estimating damages; value of instrument in writing

For the purpose of estimating damages, the value of an instrument in writing is presumed to be equal to that of the property to which it entitles its owner. *(Enacted in 1872. Amended by Code Am.1873–74, c. 612, p. 266, § 278.)*

Miller and Starr California Real Estate § 10:218, Measure of Tort Damages.
6 Witkin, California Summary 10th Torts § 1723, Conversion of Secured Note.

§ 3357. Damages prescribed by chapter exclusive of exemplary damages and interest

DAMAGES ALLOWED IN THIS CHAPTER, EXCLUSIVE OF OTHERS. The damages prescribed by this Chapter are exclusive of exemplary damages and interest, except where those are expressly mentioned. *(Enacted in 1872.)*

Miller and Starr California Real Estate § 34:92, Punitive Damages--Constitutional Validity and Limits.
1 Witkin Cal. Summ. 10th Contracts § 888, (S 888) General Rule.

§ 3358. Limitation of damages; exception

Except as expressly provided by statute, no person can recover a greater amount in damages for the breach of an obligation, than he could have gained by the full performance thereof on both sides. *(Enacted in 1872. Amended by Stats.1977, c. 198, p. 720, § 9, operative July 1, 1978.)*

Law Revision Commission Comments

Section 3358 is amended to replace the former listing of specific provisions with a general reference to statutes that constitute an exception to the rule stated. The former listing of specific provisions was incomplete. See the Comment to Section 1671. See also Sections 3294, 3339, 3340, 3346–3348. [13 Cal.L.Rev.Comm. Reports 1735 (1976)].

Rutter, Cal. Practice Guide: Real Prop. Transactions Ch. 11-C, C. Seller's Remedies Upon Buyer's Breach-Damages and Specific Performance.
Miller and Starr California Real Estate § 34:29, Compensatory Damages.
Miller and Starr California Real Estate § 34:50, Determining "Value of the Property"; Comparison of the Terms of Sale.
Miller and Starr California Real Estate § 34:51, Seller's Consequential ("Special") Damages.

22 NO. 4 Miller & Starr, California Real Estate Newsalert 37, Landlord and Tenant.
2 Witkin, California Summary 10th Insurance § 265, (S 265) Breach by Insurer that Does Not Defend.
12 Witkin, California Summary 10th Real Property § 698, (S 698) Other Losses Caused by Breach.
1 Witkin Cal. Summ. 10th Contracts § 533, (S 533) Nature and Purpose of Revision.
1 Witkin Cal. Summ. 10th Contracts § 875, Damages Exceeding Value of Performance.
1 Witkin Cal. Summ. 10th Contracts § 903, (S 903) in General.
1 Witkin Cal. Summ. 10th Contracts § 905, (S 905) Credit for Higher Resale Price.

§ 3359. Reasonableness of damages

DAMAGES TO BE REASONABLE. Damages must, in all cases, be reasonable, and where an obligation of any kind appears to create a right to unconscionable and grossly oppressive damages, contrary to substantial justice, no more than reasonable damages can be recovered. *(Enacted in 1872.)*

California Practice Guide: Employment Litigation Ch. 17-B, B. Contract Damages.
California Practice Guide: Employment Litigation Ch. 17-F, F. Mitigation of Damages (Avoidable Consequences Doctrine).
Rutter, Cal. Practice Guide: Personal Injury Ch. 3-A, A. Introduction.
Rutter, Cal. Practice Guide: Personal Injury Ch. 3-C, C. Specific Items of Compensatory Damages.
Miller and Starr California Real Estate § 34:29, Compensatory Damages.
Miller and Starr California Real Estate § 34:50, Determining "Value of the Property"; Comparison of the Terms of Sale.
1 Witkin Cal. Summ. 10th Contracts § 874, Unconscionable or Oppressive Damages.
1 Witkin Cal. Summ. 10th Contracts § 913, (S 913) Franchise Agreement.
6 Witkin, California Summary 10th Torts § 1725, Use Value in Excess of Value of Property.

§ 3360. Nominal damages

NOMINAL DAMAGES. When a breach of duty has caused no appreciable detriment to the party affected, he may yet recover nominal damages. *(Enacted in 1872.)*

1 Witkin Cal. Summ. 10th Contracts § 878, (S 878) Nominal Damages.
1 Witkin Cal. Summ. 10th Contracts § 888, (S 888) General Rule.
5 Witkin, California Summary 10th Torts § 430, Necessity for Awareness or Harm.
6 Witkin, California Summary 10th Torts § 1545, (S 1545) Right to Nominal Damages.
6 Witkin, California Summary 10th Torts § 1546, (S 1546) Where Award is Proper.

Title 3

SPECIFIC AND PREVENTIVE RELIEF

CHAPTER 1. GENERAL PRINCIPLES

§ 3366. Allowance of specific or preventive relief

Specific or preventive relief may be given as provided by the laws of this state. *(Enacted in 1872. Amended by Stats.1905, c. 465, p. 622, § 1.)*

§ 3367. Specific relief; method of giving

SPECIFIC RELIEF, HOW GIVEN. Specific relief is given:

1. By taking possession of a thing, and delivering it to a claimant;

2. By compelling a party himself to do that which ought to be done; or,

3. By declaring and determining the rights of parties, otherwise than by an award of damages. *(Enacted in 1872.)*

§ 3368. Preventive relief; method of giving

PREVENTIVE RELIEF, HOW GIVEN. Preventive relief is given by prohibiting a party from doing that which ought not to be done. *(Enacted in 1872.)*

§ 3369. Penalties or forfeitures; availability of specific or preventive relief

Neither specific nor preventive relief can be granted to enforce a penalty or forfeiture in any case, nor to enforce a penal law, except in a case of nuisance or as otherwise provided by law. *(Enacted in 1872. Amended by Stats.1933, c. 953, p. 2482, § 1; Stats.1963, c. 1606, p. 3184, § 1; Stats.1972, c. 1084, p. 2020, § 1; Stats.1974, c. 746, p. 1654, § 1; Stats.1976, c. 1005, p. 2378, § 1; Stats.1977, c. 299, p. 1203, § 2.)*

Research References

California Real Estate Forms (Miller & Starr) § 1:17, Purchase and Sale Agreement--Unimproved Real Property--With Escrow Instructions.
California Real Estate Forms (Miller & Starr) § 1:166, Liquidated Damages.
Miller and Starr California Real Estate § 10:135, Curable Versus Noncurable Defaults.
Miller and Starr California Real Estate § 19:200, Termination for Cause or Default.
6 Witkin Cal. Proc. 5th Provisional Remedies § 335, Crime that is Enjoinable Tort.
1 Witkin Cal. Summ. 10th Contracts § 827, (S 827) Excuse of Condition or Equitable Relief.
13 Witkin, California Summary 10th Equity § 20, Equitable Doctrine Codified.
13 Witkin, California Summary 10th Equity § 47, (S 47) Contract is Illegal or Impossible.
13 Witkin, California Summary 10th Equity § 63, in General.
13 Witkin, California Summary 10th Equity § 105, (S 105) in General.
13 Witkin, California Summary 10th Equity § 106, in General.
13 Witkin, California Summary 10th Equity § 125, (S 125) in General.
14 Witkin, California Summary 10th Wills and Probate § 564, Strict Construction.

CHAPTER 1.5. INVESTMENT ADVISERS

Section
3372. Liability; exclusions.

§ 3372. Liability; exclusions

(a) Any person engaged in the business of advising others for compensation as to the advisability of purchasing, holding or selling property for investment and who represents himself or herself to be an expert with respect to investment decisions in such property, or any class of such property, shall be liable to any person to whom such advisory services are furnished for compensation and who is damaged by reason of such person's reliance upon such services, for the amount of such compensation and for such damages, unless the person rendering such services proves that such services were performed with the due care and skill reasonably to be expected of a person who is such an expert.

(b) For the purposes of this section, the following apply:

(1) A person represents that such person is an "expert" within the meaning of this section if such person represents that he or she is a "financial planner," "financial adviser," "financial counselor," "financial consultant" or an "investment adviser," "investment counselor" or "investment consultant" or that such person renders "financial planning services," "financial advisory services," "financial counseling services," "financial consulting services" or "investment advisory services," "investment counseling services" or "investment consulting services" or makes substantially equivalent representations with respect to such person's business or qualifications.

(2) "Person" includes an individual, corporation, partnership, limited liability company, joint venture, an association, joint stock company, a trust or unincorporated association.

(c) The following persons are not liable under the provisions of this section:

(1) Any person, when engaged in the purchase or sale of tangible personal property for his or her own account, and the agents and employees of such persons.

(2) Any person, and the agents and employees of such person, licensed under, exempted from licensing under, or not subject to licensing under by reason of an express exclusion from a definition contained in, the Commodity Exchange Act, the Investment Advisers Act of 1940, the California Commodity Law, the Corporate Securities Law of 1968, the Insurance Code, the Real Estate Law, or any state or federal law for the licensing and regulation of banks or savings and loan associations. *(Added by Stats.1978, c. 1380, p. 4573, § 1. Amended by Stats.1986, c. 698, § 1; Stats.1994, c. 1010 (S.B.2053), § 53.)*

Research References

6 Witkin, California Summary 10th Torts § 997, Miscellaneous Professionals.

CHAPTER 2. SPECIFIC RELIEF

ARTICLE 1. POSSESSION OF REAL PROPERTY

Section
3375. Judgment for possession or requiring perfection of title.

§ 3375. Judgment for possession or requiring perfection of title

JUDGMENT FOR POSSESSION OR TITLE. A person entitled to specific real property, by reason either of a perfected title, or of a claim to title which ought to be perfected, may recover the same in the manner prescribed by the Code of Civil Procedure, either by a judgment for its possession, to be executed by the sheriff, or by a judgment requiring the other party to perfect the title, and to deliver possession of the property. *(Enacted in 1872.)*

Research References

Miller and Starr California Real Estate § 34:104, Who Can Bring the Action.

ARTICLE 2. POSSESSION OF PERSONAL PROPERTY

Section
3379. Recovery of possession.
3380. Specific delivery.

§ 3379. Recovery of possession

JUDGMENT FOR DELIVERY. A person entitled to the immediate possession of specific personal property may recover the same in the manner provided by the Code of Civil Procedure. *(Enacted in 1872.)*

Research References

5 Witkin, California Summary 10th Torts § 700, Remedies.

§ 3380. Specific delivery

Any person having the possession or control of a particular article of personal property, of which he is not the owner, may be compelled specifically to deliver it to the person entitled to its immediate possession. *(Enacted in 1872. Amended by Code Am.1873–74, c. 612, p. 266, § 279.)*

Research References

Miller and Starr California Real Estate § 6:14, Agency--Duty to Hold Contents of Escrow Until Conditions Are Satisfied.
Miller and Starr California Real Estate § 6:26, Return of Deposit.

ARTICLE 3. SPECIFIC PERFORMANCE OF OBLIGATIONS

Section
3384. Compelling specific performance.
3386. Mutuality of remedy.
3387. Breach of agreement to transfer real estate; presumption of inadequacy of damages.
3388. Enforcement of contract signed by one party only.
3389. Enforcement of contract imposing penalty or liquidated damages.
3390. Obligations not specifically enforceable.
3391. Parties who cannot be compelled to perform.
3392. Parties who cannot have specific performance.
3394. Agreement for sale; seller without good title.
3395. Relief against parties claiming under person bound to perform.

§ 3384. Compelling specific performance

Except as otherwise provided in this article, the specific performance of an obligation may be compelled. *(Enacted in 1872. Amended by Code Am.1873–74, c. 612, p. 266, § 280.)*

Research References

Rutter, Cal. Practice Guide: Real Prop. Transactions Ch. 11-C, C. Seller's Remedies Upon Buyer's Breach-Damages and Specific Performance.
Rutter, Cal. Practice Guide: Real Prop. Transactions Ch. 11-D, D. Buyer's Remedies Upon Seller's Breach-Damages and Specific Performance.
Rutter, Cal. Practice Guide: Real Prop. Transactions Form 4:H, (Attorney-Drafted) Purchase and Sale Agreement and Joint Escrow Instructions.
Miller and Starr California Real Estate § 34:17, When Specific Performance is Available; Prerequisites.
Miller and Starr California Real Estate § 34:27, Specific Performance by a Seller Under a Real Property Contract.

13 Witkin, California Summary 10th Equity § 24, (S 24) Adequacy of Legal Remedy.

§ 3386. Mutuality of remedy

Notwithstanding that the agreed counterperformance is not or would not have been specifically enforceable, specific performance may be compelled if:

(a) Specific performance would otherwise be an appropriate remedy; and

(b) The agreed counterperformance has been substantially performed or its concurrent or future performance is assured or, if the court deems necessary, can be secured to the satisfaction of the court. *(Enacted in 1872. Amended by Stats.1969, c. 156, p. 410, § 1.)*

Law Revision Commission Comments

This section is amended to eliminate the requirement that, to obtain specific performance, the plaintiff be "compellable specifically to perform, everything to which the [defendant] is entitled under the same obligation." The amendment substitutes the rules of the Restatement of Contracts that (1) specific enforcement should not be denied in an appropriate case solely because of a lack of "mutuality of remedies" and (2) that such enforcement may be denied if the defendant's receipt of the counterperformance is not assured and cannot be secured to the satisfaction of the court. The introductory portion of the section as amended is based on subdivision (1) of Section 372 of the Restatement of Contracts, and subdivision (b) is based on Section 373 of that Restatement. With respect to subdivision (b), the assurance or security that the defendant will receive the agreed counterperformance may be provided by the plaintiff's past conduct, by his economic interest in performing, or by granting a conditional decree or requiring the plaintiff to give security for his performance. For further pertinent discussion, see the comments and illustrations to Sections 372 and 373 of the Restatement of Contracts.

The section as amended achieves the only reasonable objective of the mutuality of remedies rule formerly stated by the section and developed in the case law: It assures that the defendant will not be forced to perform without receiving the agreed counterperformance from the plaintiff. See Ellis v. Mihelis, 60 Cal.2d 206, 215, 32 Cal.Rptr. 415, 420, 384 P.2d 7, 12 (1963) ("[T]he only important consideration is whether a court of equity which is asked to specifically enforce a contract against the defendant is able to assure that he will receive the agreed performance from the plaintiff."). See also Recommendation and A Study Relating to Mutuality of Remedies in Suits for Specific Performance, 9 Cal. L. Revision Comm'n Reports 201 (1969); 4 Witkin, Summary of California Law Equity §§ 39–43 at 2818–2821 (7th ed. 1960).

Deletion of the former language concerning partial performance "together with full compensation for any want of entire performance" makes no substantive change in existing law. The requirement of substantial performance of all conditions precedent, the dispensation for an insubstantial failure to perform, and the requirement of compensation for partial default are all more fully covered by Section 3392. [9 Cal.L.Rev.Comm. Reports 201 (1969)].

Research References

Rutter, Cal. Practice Guide: Real Prop. Transactions Ch. 4-E, E. Drafting the Purchase and Sale Agreement-Terms and Conditions.
Rutter, Cal. Practice Guide: Real Prop. Transactions Ch. 11-D, D. Buyer's Remedies Upon Seller's Breach-Damages and Specific Performance.
Miller and Starr California Real Estate § 1:82, Written Authority Required; the Equal Dignities Rule--Exception: Ratification or Waiver by the Principal.
Miller and Starr California Real Estate § 19:18, Specific Performance.
Miller and Starr California Real Estate § 34:19, Buyer's Performance or Tender of Performance.
Miller and Starr California Real Estate § 34:20, Satisfaction of Conditions.
Miller and Starr California Real Estate § 34:24, Mutuality of Remedy; Seller's Defective Title.
5 Witkin Cal. Proc. 5th Pleading § 802, (S 802) Certainty of Counterperformance.
13 Witkin, California Summary 10th Equity § 24, (S 24) Adequacy of Legal Remedy.
13 Witkin, California Summary 10th Equity § 53, Former Defense of Lack of Mutuality.

13 Witkin, California Summary 10th Equity § 54, Requirement of Security.

§ 3387. Breach of agreement to transfer real estate; presumption of inadequacy of damages

It is to be presumed that the breach of an agreement to transfer real property cannot be adequately relieved by pecuniary compensation. In the case of a single-family dwelling which the party seeking performance intends to occupy, this presumption is conclusive. In all other cases, this presumption is a presumption affecting the burden of proof. *(Enacted in 1872. Amended by Stats.1931, c. 1070, p. 2261, § 11; Stats.1984, c. 937, § 1.)*

Research References

Rutter, Cal. Practice Guide: Civ. Pro. Before Trial Ch. 9(I)-J, J. Motion to Expunge Lis Pendens.

Rutter, Cal. Practice Guide: Civ. Pro. Before Trial Ch. 9(II)-A, A. Injunctions.

Rutter, Cal. Practice Guide: Civil Trials & Evidence Ch. 8G-C, C. Presumptions.

Rutter, Cal. Practice Guide: Real Prop. Transactions Ch. 4-E, E. Drafting the Purchase and Sale Agreement-Terms and Conditions.

Rutter, Cal. Practice Guide: Real Prop. Transactions Ch. 11-C, C. Seller's Remedies Upon Buyer's Breach-Damages and Specific Performance.

Rutter, Cal. Practice Guide: Real Prop. Transactions Ch. 11-D, D. Buyer's Remedies Upon Seller's Breach-Damages and Specific Performance.

Rutter, Cal. Practice Guide: Real Prop. Transactions Ch. 11-I, I. Lis Pendens.

Rutter, Cal. Practice Guide: Real Prop. Transactions Ch. 11-I Outline, Outline I.

Miller and Starr California Real Estate § 34:18, Specific Performance by a Buyer Under a Real Property Contract.

Miller and Starr California Real Estate § 34:27, Specific Performance by a Seller Under a Real Property Contract.

Miller and Starr California Real Estate § 11:153, Expungement of a Lis Pendens--Policy.

Miller and Starr California Real Estate § 11:154, Expungement of a Lis Pendens--Procedure and Grounds for Expungement.

18 NO. 5 Miller & Starr, California Real Estate Newsalert 20, Remedies.

3 Witkin Cal. Proc. 5th Actions § 404, (S 404) in General.

13 Witkin, California Summary 10th Equity § 24, (S 24) Adequacy of Legal Remedy.

13 Witkin, California Summary 10th Equity § 28, Action by Purchaser.

13 Witkin, California Summary 10th Equity § 30, (S 30) Contract Concerning Personal Property.

§ 3388. Enforcement of contract signed by one party only

CONTRACT SIGNED BY ONE PARTY ONLY, MAY BE ENFORCED BY OTHER. A party who has signed a written contract may be compelled specifically to perform it, though the other party has not signed it, if the latter has performed, or offers to perform it on his part, and the case is otherwise proper for enforcing specific performance. *(Enacted in 1872.)*

Research References

Rutter, Cal. Practice Guide: Real Prop. Transactions Ch. 11-D, D. Buyer's Remedies Upon Seller's Breach-Damages and Specific Performance.

Miller and Starr California Real Estate § 1:72, Effect When Statute of Frauds Not Satisfied.

Miller and Starr California Real Estate § 1:78, Signature Required.

Miller and Starr California Real Estate § 1:82, Written Authority Required; the Equal Dignities Rule--Exception: Ratification or Waiver by the Principal.

Miller and Starr California Real Estate § 6:30, Requirement of a Contract.

Miller and Starr California Real Estate § 34:25, Parties by Whom and Against Whom Decree Can be Rendered.

13 Witkin, California Summary 10th Equity § 24, (S 24) Adequacy of Legal Remedy.

13 Witkin, California Summary 10th Equity § 55, Offer of Performance by Nonsigner.

§ 3389. Enforcement of contract imposing penalty or liquidated damages

LIQUIDATION OF DAMAGES NOT A BAR TO SPECIFIC PERFORMANCE. A contract otherwise proper to be specifically enforced, may be thus enforced, though a penalty is imposed, or the damages are liquidated for its breach, and the party in default is willing to pay the same. *(Enacted in 1872.)*

Research References

California Real Estate Forms (Miller & Starr) § 1:166, Liquidated Damages.

Rutter, Cal. Practice Guide: Real Prop. Transactions Ch. 4-E, E. Drafting the Purchase and Sale Agreement-Terms and Conditions.

Rutter, Cal. Practice Guide: Real Prop. Transactions Ch. 11-D, D. Buyer's Remedies Upon Seller's Breach-Damages and Specific Performance.

Miller and Starr California Real Estate § 34:18, Specific Performance by a Buyer Under a Real Property Contract.

1 Witkin Cal. Summ. 10th Contracts § 544, (S 544) Scope of Chapter.

13 Witkin, California Summary 10th Equity § 20, Equitable Doctrine Codified.

13 Witkin, California Summary 10th Equity § 24, (S 24) Adequacy of Legal Remedy.

§ 3390. Obligations not specifically enforceable

The following obligations cannot be specifically enforced:

1. An obligation to render personal service;

2. An obligation to employ another in personal service;

3. An agreement to perform an act which the party has not power lawfully to perform when required to do so;

4. An agreement to procure the act or consent of the wife of the contracting party, or of any other third person; or,

5. An agreement, the terms of which are not sufficiently certain to make the precise act which is to be done clearly ascertainable. *(Enacted in 1872. Amended by Stats.1961, c. 461, p. 1551, § 5.)*

Research References

Rutter, Cal. Practice Guide: Civ. Pro. Before Trial Ch. 9(II)-A, A. Injunctions.

California Practice Guide: Employment Litigation Ch. 17-A, A. Equitable Relief.

Rutter, Cal. Practice Guide: Real Prop. Transactions Ch. 4-D, D. Selecting the Form of Written Agreement.

Rutter, Cal. Practice Guide: Real Prop. Transactions Ch. 8-B, B. Options to Purchase.

Rutter, Cal. Practice Guide: Real Prop. Transactions Ch. 11-D, D. Buyer's Remedies Upon Seller's Breach-Damages and Specific Performance.

Miller and Starr California Real Estate § 1:157, Condition Distinguished from a Covenant.

Miller and Starr California Real Estate § 1:160, Duty to Make Good-Faith Attempt to Satisfy a Condition--Condition Based on Approval or Satisfaction.

Miller and Starr California Real Estate § 34:17, When Specific Performance is Available; Prerequisites.

Miller and Starr California Real Estate § 34:22, Certainty of Contract Terms.

Miller and Starr California Real Estate § 34:25, Parties by Whom and Against Whom Decree Can be Rendered.

18 NO. 2 Miller & Starr, California Real Estate Newsalert 7, Contracts.

19 NO. 4 Miller & Starr, California Real Estate Newsalert 1, California Supreme Court Reduces Terms Required to Specifically Enforce a Real Property Sales Contract to Three P's: Parties, Price, and Property Description.

6 Witkin Cal. Proc. 5th Proceedings Without Trial § 512, Agreement is Enforceable.

13 Witkin, California Summary 10th Equity § 24, (S 24) Adequacy of Legal Remedy.

13 Witkin, California Summary 10th Equity § 36, (S 36) Arbitration Agreement.

13 Witkin, California Summary 10th Equity § 42, in General.
13 Witkin, California Summary 10th Equity § 47, (S 47) Contract is Illegal or Impossible.
13 Witkin, California Summary 10th Equity § 48, General Rule Against Specific Performance.
13 Witkin, California Summary 10th Equity § 59, (S 59) Time for Removing Defect.

§ 3391. Parties who cannot be compelled to perform

WHAT PARTIES CANNOT BE COMPELLED TO PERFORM. Specific performance cannot be enforced against a party to a contract in any of the following cases:

1. If he has not received an adequate consideration for the contract;

2. If it is not, as to him, just and reasonable;

3. If his assent was obtained by the misrepresentation, concealment, circumvention, or unfair practices of any party to whom performance would become due under the contract, or by any promise of such party which has not been substantially fulfilled; or,

4. If his assent was given under the influence of mistake, misapprehension, or surprise, except that where the contract provides for compensation in case of mistake, a mistake within the scope of such provision may be compensated for, and the contract specifically enforced in other respects, if proper to be so enforced. *(Enacted in 1872.)*

Research References

Rutter, Cal. Practice Guide: Real Prop. Transactions Ch. 6-H, H. Security for Promissory Note.
Rutter, Cal. Practice Guide: Real Prop. Transactions Ch. 11-D, D. Buyer's Remedies Upon Seller's Breach-Damages and Specific Performance.
Miller and Starr California Real Estate § 1:57, to Support an Action for Specific Performance.
Miller and Starr California Real Estate § 34:17, When Specific Performance is Available; Prerequisites.
Miller and Starr California Real Estate § 34:21, Adequacy of Consideration.
Miller and Starr California Real Estate § 34:27, Specific Performance by a Seller Under a Real Property Contract.
Miller and Starr California Real Estate § 35:44, Petition to Compel Arbitration.
21 NO. 6 Miller & Starr, California Real Estate Newsalert 15, Landlord and Tenant.
22 NO. 1 Miller & Starr, California Real Estate Newsalert 20, Landlord and Tenant.
5 Witkin Cal. Proc. 5th Pleading § 791, (S 791) Rule and Theory.
5 Witkin Cal. Proc. 5th Pleading § 796, Deviations of Form.
6 Witkin Cal. Proc. 5th Proceedings Without Trial § 123, Agreement Made in Mediation.
6 Witkin Cal. Proc. 5th Proceedings Without Trial § 540, Unjust or Unreasonable Provision.
4 Witkin, California Summary 10th Security Transactions in Real Property § 55, Reasonableness of Agreement.
13 Witkin, California Summary 10th Equity § 24, (S 24) Adequacy of Legal Remedy.
13 Witkin, California Summary 10th Equity § 38, (S 38) Consideration is Inadequate.
13 Witkin, California Summary 10th Equity § 39, in General.
13 Witkin, California Summary 10th Equity § 41, (S 41) Fraud, Unfair Practices, or Mistake.
13 Witkin, California Summary 10th Equity § 56, (S 56) in General.

§ 3392. Parties who cannot have specific performance

WHAT PARTIES CANNOT HAVE SPECIFIC PERFORMANCE IN THEIR FAVOR. Specific performance cannot be enforced in favor of a party who has not fully and fairly performed all the conditions precedent on his part to the obligation of the other party, except where his failure to perform is only partial, and either entirely immaterial, or capable of being fully compensated, in which case specific performance may be compelled, upon full compensation being made for the default. *(Enacted in 1872.)*

Research References

Rutter, Cal. Practice Guide: Real Prop. Transactions Ch. 11-C, C. Seller's Remedies Upon Buyer's Breach-Damages and Specific Performance.
Rutter, Cal. Practice Guide: Real Prop. Transactions Ch. 11-D, D. Buyer's Remedies Upon Seller's Breach-Damages and Specific Performance.
Miller and Starr California Real Estate § 6:25, Right to Terminate Escrow for Failure to Perform.
Miller and Starr California Real Estate § 1:161, Conditions Concurrent.
Miller and Starr California Real Estate § 1:162, Conditions Concurrent--Performance; When "Time is of the Essence" in a Contract.
Miller and Starr California Real Estate § 34:17, When Specific Performance is Available; Prerequisites.
Miller and Starr California Real Estate § 34:19, Buyer's Performance or Tender of Performance.
Miller and Starr California Real Estate § 34:20, Satisfaction of Conditions.
Miller and Starr California Real Estate § 34:27, Specific Performance by a Seller Under a Real Property Contract.
13 Witkin, California Summary 10th Equity § 24, (S 24) Adequacy of Legal Remedy.
13 Witkin, California Summary 10th Equity § 56, (S 56) in General.
13 Witkin, California Summary 10th Equity § 57, (S 57) Specific Performance With Compensation.
13 Witkin, California Summary 10th Equity § 64, Extent of Relief.

§ 3394. Agreement for sale; seller without good title

AGREEMENT TO SELL PROPERTY BY ONE WHO HAS NO TITLE. An agreement for the sale of property cannot be specifically enforced in favor of a seller who cannot give to the buyer a title free from reasonable doubt. *(Enacted in 1872.)*

Research References

Miller and Starr California Real Estate § 2:22, Marketable or Merchantable Title.
Miller and Starr California Real Estate § 34:27, Specific Performance by a Seller Under a Real Property Contract.
13 Witkin, California Summary 10th Equity § 24, (S 24) Adequacy of Legal Remedy.
13 Witkin, California Summary 10th Equity § 56, (S 56) in General.

§ 3395. Relief against parties claiming under person bound to perform

RELIEF AGAINST PARTIES CLAIMING UNDER PERSON BOUND TO PERFORM. Whenever an obligation in respect to real property would be specifically enforced against a particular person, it may be in like manner enforced against any other person claiming under him by a title created subsequently to the obligation, except a purchaser or encumbrancer in good faith and for value, and except, also, that any such person may exonerate himself by conveying all his estate to the person entitled to enforce the obligation. *(Enacted in 1872.)*

Research References

Rutter, Cal. Practice Guide: Real Prop. Transactions Ch. 11-C, C. Seller's Remedies Upon Buyer's Breach-Damages and Specific Performance.
Rutter, Cal. Practice Guide: Real Prop. Transactions Ch. 11-D, D. Buyer's Remedies Upon Seller's Breach-Damages and Specific Performance.
Miller and Starr California Real Estate § 11:2, Enforceability of Unrecorded Instruments.
Miller and Starr California Real Estate § 11:3, Effect of Recording Statutes on Priority.
Miller and Starr California Real Estate § 11:50, Definitions; Rules of Priority.
Miller and Starr California Real Estate § 34:17, When Specific Performance is Available; Prerequisites.
Miller and Starr California Real Estate § 34:25, Parties by Whom and Against Whom Decree Can be Rendered.
7 Witkin Cal. Proc. 5th Judgment § 208, (S 208) Fees Denied.

13 Witkin, California Summary 10th Equity § 24, (S 24) Adequacy of Legal Remedy.

ARTICLE 4. REVISION OF CONTRACTS

Section
3399. When contract may be revised.
3400. Presumption of intent to make an equitable and conscientious agreement.
3401. Principles of revision.
3402. Enforcement of revised contract.

§ 3399. When contract may be revised

WHEN CONTRACT MAY BE REVISED. When, through fraud or a mutual mistake of the parties, or a mistake of one party, which the other at the time knew or suspected, a written contract does not truly express the intention of the parties, it may be revised on the application of a party aggrieved, so as to express that intention, so far as it can be done without prejudice to rights acquired by third persons, in good faith and for value. *(Enacted in 1872.)*

Research References

Rutter, Cal. Practice Guide: Insurance Litigation Ch. 5-E, E. Reformation.
Rutter, Cal. Practice Guide: Real Prop. Transactions Ch. 4-D, D. Selecting the Form of Written Agreement.
Rutter, Cal. Practice Guide: Real Prop. Transactions Ch. 11-F, F. Reformation.
Miller and Starr California Real Estate § 8:57, Conveyance in Violation of Public Policy or Statute.
Miller and Starr California Real Estate § 1:118, Unilateral Mistake.
Miller and Starr California Real Estate § 1:123, Remedies for Mistake.
Miller and Starr California Real Estate § 11:70, Defects in the Record Title Enforceable Against a Bona Fide Purchaser--In General.
Miller and Starr California Real Estate § 11:73, Defects in the Record Title Enforceable Against a Bona Fide Purchaser--Fraud on Obtaining an Instrument.
Miller and Starr California Real Estate § 11:74, Defects in the Record Title Enforceable Against a Bona Fide Purchaser--Error in Recorded Description.
Miller and Starr California Real Estate § 34:11, Nature of the Remedy; Requirement of a Prior Agreement.
Miller and Starr California Real Estate § 34:12, Fraud as Basis for Reformation.
Miller and Starr California Real Estate § 34:14, Equitable Remedy.
13 NO. 6 Miller & Starr, California Real Estate Newsalert 4, Deeds of Trust.
5 Witkin Cal. Proc. 5th Pleading § 806, (S 806) Nature of Action.
5 Witkin Cal. Proc. 5th Pleading § 809, (S 809) Plaintiff's Interest.
2 Witkin, California Summary 10th Insurance § 216, (S 216) in General.
2 Witkin, California Summary 10th Insurance § 217, (S 217) Mistake as Ground.
1 Witkin Cal. Summ. 10th Contracts § 276, (S 276) Nature of Remedy.
1 Witkin Cal. Summ. 10th Contracts § 279, (S 279) in General.
1 Witkin Cal. Summ. 10th Contracts § 281, Types of Mistake.
1 Witkin Cal. Summ. 10th Contracts § 283, Intervening Rights of Third Persons.
1 Witkin Cal. Summ. 10th Contracts § 285, (S 285) in General.

§ 3400. Presumption of intent to make an equitable and conscientious agreement

PRESUMPTION AS TO INTENT OF PARTIES. For the purpose of revising a contract, it must be presumed that all the parties thereto intended to make an equitable and conscientious agreement. *(Enacted in 1872.)*

Research References

Miller and Starr California Real Estate § 34:11, Nature of the Remedy; Requirement of a Prior Agreement.
5 Witkin Cal. Proc. 5th Pleading § 818, When Reformation is Unavailable.

1 Witkin Cal. Summ. 10th Contracts § 279, (S 279) in General.

§ 3401. Principles of revision

PRINCIPLES OF REVISION. In revising a written instrument, the court may inquire what the instrument was intended to mean, and what were intended to be its legal consequences, and is not confined to the inquiry what the language of the instrument was intended to be. *(Enacted in 1872.)*

Research References

Rutter, Cal. Practice Guide: Real Prop. Transactions Ch. 11-F, F. Reformation.
Miller and Starr California Real Estate § 8:57, Conveyance in Violation of Public Policy or Statute.
Miller and Starr California Real Estate § 34:11, Nature of the Remedy; Requirement of a Prior Agreement.
Miller and Starr California Real Estate § 34:14, Equitable Remedy.
1 Witkin Cal. Summ. 10th Contracts § 276, (S 276) Nature of Remedy.
1 Witkin Cal. Summ. 10th Contracts § 279, (S 279) in General.

§ 3402. Enforcement of revised contract

ENFORCEMENT OF REVISED CONTRACT. A contract may be first revised and then specifically enforced. *(Enacted in 1872.)*

Research References

Rutter, Cal. Practice Guide: Real Prop. Transactions Ch. 11-F, F. Reformation.
Miller and Starr California Real Estate § 1:123, Remedies for Mistake.
Miller and Starr California Real Estate § 34:14, Equitable Remedy.
Miller and Starr California Real Estate § 34:22, Certainty of Contract Terms.
1 Witkin Cal. Summ. 10th Contracts § 276, (S 276) Nature of Remedy.
1 Witkin Cal. Summ. 10th Contracts § 279, (S 279) in General.

ARTICLE 6. CANCELLATION OF INSTRUMENTS

Section
3412. Grounds for cancellation.
3413. Instrument obviously void.
3414. Cancellation in part.
3415. Lost or destroyed documents; establishment; issuance of duplicate; security.

§ 3412. Grounds for cancellation

WHEN CANCELLATION MAY BE ORDERED. A written instrument, in respect to which there is a reasonable apprehension that if left outstanding it may cause serious injury to a person against whom it is void or voidable, may, upon his application, be so adjudged, and ordered to be delivered up or canceled. *(Enacted in 1872.)*

Research References

Rutter, Cal. Practice Guide: Real Prop. Transactions Ch. 11-H, H. Other Remedies.
Miller and Starr California Real Estate § 11:4, Instruments Subject to Recording--Requirements.
Miller and Starr California Real Estate § 8:23, Mental Incapacity to Convey.
Miller and Starr California Real Estate § 8:57, Conveyance in Violation of Public Policy or Statute.
Miller and Starr California Real Estate § 11:63, Recorded Documents that Do Not Give Constructive Notice--Defectively or Improperly Recorded Instruments.
Miller and Starr California Real Estate § 34:108, Types of Actions for Quiet Title.
Miller and Starr California Real Estate § 34:112, Cancellation of Instruments: Nature of the Remedy.
Miller and Starr California Real Estate § 34:113, Grounds for Cancellation.
18 NO. 1 Miller & Starr, California Real Estate Newsalert 22, Subdivisions.
22 NO. 6 Miller & Starr, California Real Estate Newsalert 11, Deeds of Trust.

3 Witkin Cal. Proc. 5th Actions § 129, Miscellaneous Actions.
3 Witkin Cal. Proc. 5th Actions § 491, Cancellation of Void Instrument.
4 Witkin Cal. Proc. 5th Pleading § 543, (S 543) Other Actions Distinguished.
5 Witkin Cal. Proc. 5th Pleading § 655, (S 655) Other Actions Distinguished.
5 Witkin Cal. Proc. 5th Pleading § 668, General Pleading.
5 Witkin Cal. Proc. 5th Pleading § 671, in General.
5 Witkin Cal. Proc. 5th Pleading § 673, Defendant's Instrument.

§ 3413. Instrument obviously void

INSTRUMENT OBVIOUSLY VOID. An instrument, the invalidity of which is apparent upon its face, or upon the face of another instrument which is necessary to the use of the former in evidence, is not to be deemed capable of causing injury, within the provisions of the last section. *(Enacted in 1872.)*

Research References

Rutter, Cal. Practice Guide: Real Prop. Transactions Ch. 11-H, H. Other Remedies.
Miller and Starr California Real Estate § 8:57, Conveyance in Violation of Public Policy or Statute.
Miller and Starr California Real Estate § 11:63, Recorded Documents that Do Not Give Constructive Notice--Defectively or Improperly Recorded Instruments.
Miller and Starr California Real Estate § 34:112, Cancellation of Instruments: Nature of the Remedy.
23 NO. 1 Miller & Starr, California Real Estate Newsalert 14, Judicial Remedies.
5 Witkin Cal. Proc. 5th Pleading § 673, Defendant's Instrument.

§ 3414. Cancellation in part

CANCELLATION IN PART. Where an instrument is evidence of different rights or obligations, it may be canceled in part, and allowed to stand for the residue. *(Enacted in 1872.)*

Research References

Rutter, Cal. Practice Guide: Real Prop. Transactions Ch. 11-H, H. Other Remedies.
Miller and Starr California Real Estate § 34:112, Cancellation of Instruments: Nature of the Remedy.

§ 3415. Lost or destroyed documents; establishment; issuance of duplicate; security

(a) An action may be maintained by any person interested in any private document or instrument in writing, which has been lost or destroyed, to prove or establish the document or instrument or to compel the issuance, execution, and acknowledgment of a duplicate of the document or instrument.

(b) If the document or instrument is a negotiable instrument, the court shall compel the owner of the negotiable instrument to give an indemnity bond to the person reissuing, reexecuting, or reacknowledging the same, against loss, damage, expense, or other liability that may be suffered by the person by reason of the issuance of the duplicate instrument or by the original instrument still remaining outstanding. *(Added by Stats.Ex.Sess.1906, c. 64, p. 86, § 1. Amended by Stats.1947, c. 313, p. 869, § 1; Stats.1982, c. 517, p. 2329, § 85; Stats.2006, c. 538 (S.B.1852), § 59.)*

Law Revision Commission Comments

Section 3415 is amended for consistency with the Bond and Undertaking Law. See Code Civ.Proc. § 995.910 (objections to bond). [16 Cal.L.Rev.Comm. Reports 501].

CHAPTER 3. PREVENTIVE RELIEF

§ 3420. Preventive relief; injunction

PREVENTIVE RELIEF, HOW GRANTED. Preventive relief is granted by injunction, provisional or final. *(Enacted in 1872.)*

Research References

9 Witkin Cal. Proc. 5th Administrative Proceedings § 138, (S 138) in General.
6 Witkin Cal. Proc. 5th Provisional Remedies § 274, in General.
6 Witkin Cal. Proc. 5th Provisional Remedies § 289, (S 289) Conditions.
11 Witkin, California Summary 10th Husband and Wife § 371, (S 371) Civil Remedies.

§ 3421. Provisional injunctions

PROVISIONAL INJUNCTIONS. Provisional injunctions are regulated by the Code of Civil Procedure. *(Enacted in 1872.)*

Research References

6 Witkin Cal. Proc. 5th Provisional Remedies § 289, (S 289) Conditions.

§ 3422. Final injunction; grounds

INJUNCTION, WHEN ALLOWED. Except where otherwise provided by this title, a final injunction may be granted to prevent the breach of an obligation existing in favor of the applicant:

1. Where pecuniary compensation would not afford adequate relief;

2. Where it would be extremely difficult to ascertain the amount of compensation which would afford adequate relief;

3. Where the restraint is necessary to prevent a multiplicity of judicial proceedings; or,

4. Where the obligation arises from a trust. *(Enacted in 1872.)*

Research References

6 Witkin Cal. Proc. 5th Provisional Remedies § 289, (S 289) Conditions.
6 Witkin Cal. Proc. 5th Provisional Remedies § 294, Inadequacy of Other Remedies.
6 Witkin Cal. Proc. 5th Provisional Remedies § 295, Irreparable Injury.
6 Witkin Cal. Proc. 5th Provisional Remedies § 296, Multiplicity of Actions.
6 Witkin Cal. Proc. 5th Provisional Remedies § 309, Business and Personal Property Interests.
13 Witkin, California Summary 10th Trusts § 232, (S 232) Orders and Appeal.

§ 3423. Injunction; circumstances requiring denial

An injunction may not be granted:

(a) To stay a judicial proceeding pending at the commencement of the action in which the injunction is demanded, unless this restraint is necessary to prevent a multiplicity of proceedings.

(b) To stay proceedings in a court of the United States.

(c) To stay proceedings in another state upon a judgment of a court of that state.

(d) To prevent the execution of a public statute, by officers of the law, for the public benefit.

(e) To prevent the breach of a contract the performance of which would not be specifically enforced, other than a contract in writing for the rendition of personal services from one to another where the promised service is of a special, unique, unusual, extraordinary, or intellectual character, which gives it peculiar value, the loss of which cannot be reasonably or adequately compensated in damages in an action at law, and where the compensation for the personal services is as follows:

(1) As to contracts entered into on or before December 31, 1993, the minimum compensation provided in the contract for the personal services shall be at the rate of six thousand dollars ($6,000) per annum.

(2) As to contracts entered into on or after January 1, 1994, the criteria of subparagraph (A) or (B), as follows, are satisfied:

(A) The compensation is as follows:

(i) The minimum compensation provided in the contract shall be at the rate of nine thousand dollars ($9,000) per annum for the first year of the contract, twelve thousand dollars ($12,000) per annum for the second year of the contract, and fifteen thousand dollars ($15,000) per annum for the third to seventh years, inclusive, of the contract.

(ii) In addition, after the third year of the contract, there shall actually have been paid for the services through and including the contract year during which the injunctive relief is sought, over and above the minimum contractual compensation specified in clause (i), the amount of fifteen thousand dollars ($15,000) per annum during the fourth and fifth years of the contract, and thirty thousand dollars ($30,000) per annum during the sixth and seventh years of the contract. As a condition to petitioning for an injunction, amounts payable under this clause may be paid at any time prior to seeking injunctive relief.

(B) The aggregate compensation actually received for the services provided under a contract that does not meet the criteria of subparagraph (A), is at least 10 times the applicable aggregate minimum amount specified in clauses (i) and (ii) of subparagraph (A) through and including the contract year during which the injunctive relief is sought. As a condition to petitioning for an injunction, amounts payable under this subparagraph may be paid at any time prior to seeking injunctive relief.

(3) Compensation paid in any contract year in excess of the minimums specified in subparagraphs (A) and (B) of paragraph (2) shall apply to reduce the compensation otherwise required to be paid under those provisions in any subsequent contract years.

However, an injunction may be granted to prevent the breach of a contract entered into between any nonprofit cooperative corporation or association and a member or stockholder thereof in respect to any provision regarding the sale or delivery to the corporation or association of the products produced or acquired by the member or stockholder.

(f) To prevent the exercise of a public or private office, in a lawful manner, by the person in possession.

(g) To prevent a legislative act by a municipal corporation. *(Enacted in 1872. Amended by Code Am.1873–74, c. 612, p. 267, § 282; Stats.1919, c. 226, p. 328; § 1; Stats.1925, c. 409, p. 829, § 1; Stats.1992, c. 177 (S.B.1459), § 1; Stats.1993, c. 5 (S.B.32), § 1, eff. April 3, 1993; Stats.1993, c. 836 (S.B.487), § 1.)*

Research References

Rutter, Cal. Practice Guide: Civ. Pro. Before Trial Ch. 9(II)-A, A. Injunctions.
California Practice Guide: Employment Litigation Ch. 14-E, E. Breach of Covenant Not to Compete.
California Practice Guide: Employment Litigation Ch. 17-A, A. Equitable Relief.
Miller and Starr California Real Estate § 34:23, Availability of Injunction.
9 Witkin Cal. Proc. 5th Administrative Proceedings § 146, (S 146) Injunction.
9 Witkin Cal. Proc. 5th Appeal § 760, Illustrations.
2 Witkin Cal. Proc. 5th Jurisdiction § 320, (S 320) Granting of Relief as Excess of Jurisdiction.
6 Witkin Cal. Proc. 5th Provisional Remedies § 305, (S 305) in General.
6 Witkin Cal. Proc. 5th Provisional Remedies § 306, (S 306) Unique Personal Services.
6 Witkin Cal. Proc. 5th Provisional Remedies § 308, (S 308) Other Contracts.
6 Witkin Cal. Proc. 5th Provisional Remedies § 331, (S 331) Injunction Against Enforcement.
6 Witkin Cal. Proc. 5th Provisional Remedies § 332, (S 332) Injunction Against Enactment.
6 Witkin Cal. Proc. 5th Provisional Remedies § 333, Judicial Proceeding.
6 Witkin Cal. Proc. 5th Provisional Remedies § 338, (S 338) Judicial Remedy.
7 Witkin, California Summary 10th Constitutional Law § 98, (S 98) in General.
13 Witkin, California Summary 10th Equity § 25, (S 25) Negative Covenants.
13 Witkin, California Summary 10th Equity § 37, (S 37) Other Contracts.
13 Witkin, California Summary 10th Equity § 51, (S 51) Nature and Purpose of Statute.
13 Witkin, California Summary 10th Equity § 52, (S 52) Option to Pay is Insufficient.

§ 3424. Modification or dissolution of final injunction; notice and motion; service

(a) Upon notice and motion, the court may modify or dissolve a final injunction upon a showing that there has been a material change in the facts upon which the injunction was granted, that the law upon which the injunction was granted has changed, or that the ends of justice would be served by the modification or dissolution of the injunction.

(b) Service of this motion to modify or dissolve a final injunction shall be made upon the nonmoving party by one of the following methods:

(1) If the party has not appeared in the action, the motion shall be served in the same manner as a summons pursuant to Article 3 (commencing with Section 415.10) of Chapter 4 of Title 5 of Part 2 of the Code of Civil Procedure.

(2) If the party has appeared in the action, the motion shall be served either upon the party or his or her attorney, or upon the party if he or she has appeared without an attorney, either in the same manner as a summons pursuant to Article 3 (commencing with Section 415.10) of Chapter 4 of Title 5 of the Code of Civil Procedure or in the manner provided by Chapter 5 (commencing with Section 1010) of Title 14 of Part 2 of the Code of Civil Procedure.

(c) This section does not apply to a final injunction issued pursuant to the Family Code. *(Added by Stats.1995, c. 796 (S.B.45), § 1.5.)*

Research References

6 Witkin Cal. Proc. 5th Proceedings Without Trial § 577, (S 577) Review of Remedies Granted by Arbitrator.
6 Witkin Cal. Proc. 5th Provisional Remedies § 399, (S 399) Statutory Authority and Inherent Power.
6 Witkin Cal. Proc. 5th Provisional Remedies § 401, (S 401) Service of Motion to Modify Permanent Injunction.
6 Witkin Cal. Proc. 5th Provisional Remedies § 406, in General.
6 Witkin Cal. Proc. 5th Provisional Remedies § 407, Service of Motion to Dissolve Permanent Injunction.

Title 4

UNIFORM SINGLE PUBLICATION ACT

Section

§ 3425.1. Citation

This title may be cited as the Uniform Single Publication Act. *(Added by Stats.1955, c. 867, p. 1481, § 1.)*

Research References

4 Witkin Cal. Proc. 5th Pleading § 53, Uniform Single Publication Act.
5 Witkin, California Summary 10th Torts § 538, Single Publication Rule.

§ 3425.2. Interpretation

This act shall be so interpreted as to effectuate its purpose to make uniform the law of those states or jurisdictions which enact it. *(Added by Stats.1955, c. 867, p. 1481, § 1.)*

§ 3425.3. One cause of action; recovery

No person shall have more than one cause of action for damages for libel or slander or invasion of privacy or any other tort founded upon any single publication or exhibition or utterance, such as any one issue of a newspaper or book or magazine or any one presentation to an audience or any one broadcast over radio or television or any one exhibition of a motion picture. Recovery in any action shall include all damages for any such tort suffered by the plaintiff in all jurisdictions. *(Added by Stats.1955, c. 867, p. 1481, § 1.)*

Research References

California Practice Guide: Employment Litigation Ch. 5-D, D. Defamation.
Rutter, Cal. Practice Guide: Personal Injury Ch. 5-B, B. When to Sue-Statute of Limitations.
3 Witkin Cal. Proc. 5th Actions § 551, Single Publication Rule.
4 Witkin Cal. Proc. 5th Pleading § 53, Uniform Single Publication Act.
5 Witkin, California Summary 10th Torts § 538, Single Publication Rule.
5 Witkin, California Summary 10th Torts § 676, (S 676) in General.

§ 3425.4. Judgment as bar

A judgment in any jurisdiction for or against the plaintiff upon the substantive merits of any action for damages founded upon a single publication or exhibition or utterance as described in Section 3425.3 shall bar any other action for damages by the same plaintiff against the same defendant founded upon the same publication or exhibition or utterance. *(Added by Stats. 1955, c. 867, p. 1481, § 1.)*

Research References

4 Witkin Cal. Proc. 5th Pleading § 53, Uniform Single Publication Act.

§ 3425.5. Existing causes of action

This title shall not be retroactive as to causes of action existing on its effective date. *(Added by Stats.1955, c. 867, p. 1481, § 1.)*

Title 5

UNIFORM TRADE SECRETS ACT

§ 3426. Short title

This title may be cited as the Uniform Trade Secrets Act. *(Added by Stats.1984, c. 1724, § 1.)*

Research References

Rutter, Cal. Practice Guide: Civ. Pro. Before Trial Ch. 8B-4, Status of Pleadings Affecting Right to Discovery.
Rutter, Cal. Practice Guide: Civ. Pro. Before Trial Ch. 9(II)-A, A. Injunctions.
Rutter, Cal. Practice Guide: Civil Trials & Evidence Ch. 8G-D, D. Burdens and Standards of Proof.
California Practice Guide: Employment Litigation Ch. 5-E, E. Intentional Interference With Contract or Prospective Economic Advantage.
California Practice Guide: Employment Litigation Ch. 14-C, C. Misappropriation of Employer's Trade Secrets.
9 Witkin Cal. Proc. 5th Appeal § 15, (S 15) Illustrations.
5 Witkin Cal. Proc. 5th Pleading § 778, Misappropriation of Trade Secrets.
13 Witkin, California Summary 10th Equity § 81, (S 81) Theory of Protection.
13 Witkin, California Summary 10th Equity § 85, (S 85) Inevitable Disclosure Doctrine Rejected.
13 Witkin, California Summary 10th Equity § 86, (S 86) in General.
13 Witkin, California Summary 10th Equity § 89, (S 89) Injunction.

§ 3426.1. Definitions

As used in this title, unless the context requires otherwise:

(a) "Improper means" includes theft, bribery, misrepresentation, breach or inducement of a breach of a duty to maintain secrecy, or espionage through electronic or other means. Reverse engineering or independent derivation alone shall not be considered improper means.

(b) "Misappropriation" means:

(1) Acquisition of a trade secret of another by a person who knows or has reason to know that the trade secret was acquired by improper means; or

(2) Disclosure or use of a trade secret of another without express or implied consent by a person who:

(A) Used improper means to acquire knowledge of the trade secret; or

(B) At the time of disclosure or use, knew or had reason to know that his or her knowledge of the trade secret was:

(i) Derived from or through a person who had utilized improper means to acquire it;

(ii) Acquired under circumstances giving rise to a duty to maintain its secrecy or limit its use; or

(iii) Derived from or through a person who owed a duty to the person seeking relief to maintain its secrecy or limit its use; or

(C) Before a material change of his or her position, knew or had reason to know that it was a trade secret and that knowledge of it had been acquired by accident or mistake.

(c) "Person" means a natural person, corporation, business trust, estate, trust, partnership, limited liability company, association, joint venture, government, governmental subdivision or agency, or any other legal or commercial entity.

(d) "Trade secret" means information, including a formula, pattern, compilation, program, device, method, technique, or process, that:

(1) Derives independent economic value, actual or potential, from not being generally known to the public or to other persons who can obtain economic value from its disclosure or use; and

(2) Is the subject of efforts that are reasonable under the circumstances to maintain its secrecy. *(Added by Stats.1984, c. 1724, § 1.   Amended by Stats.1994, c. 1010 (S.B.2053), § 54.)*

Research References

Rutter, Cal. Practice Guide: Civ. Pro. Before Trial Ch. 9(II)-A, A. Injunctions.
Rutter, Cal. Practice Guide: Civil Trials & Evidence Ch. 8E-A, A. Privileges.
California Practice Guide: Employment Litigation Ch. 14-C, C. Misappropriation of Employer's Trade Secrets.
Rutter, Cal. Practice Guide: Personal Injury Ch. 6-A, A. Scope of Discovery and Limitations.
5 Witkin Cal. Proc. 5th Pleading § 778, Misappropriation of Trade Secrets.
13 Witkin, California Summary 10th Equity § 82, (S 82) What Constitutes Trade Secret.
13 Witkin, California Summary 10th Equity § 86, (S 86) in General.
13 Witkin, California Summary 10th Equity § 87, (S 87) Definitions.
13 Witkin, California Summary 10th Equity § 88, (S 88) When Claim Arises.
13 Witkin, California Summary 10th Equity § 93, Confidential List of Customers.

§ 3426.2.   Injunctions

(a) Actual or threatened misappropriation may be enjoined. Upon application to the court, an injunction shall be terminated when the trade secret has ceased to exist, but the injunction may be continued for an additional period of time in order to eliminate commercial advantage that otherwise would be derived from the misappropriation.

(b) If the court determines that it would be unreasonable to prohibit future use, an injunction may condition future use upon payment of a reasonable royalty for no longer than the period of time the use could have been prohibited.

(c) In appropriate circumstances, affirmative acts to protect a trade secret may be compelled by court order. *(Added by Stats.1984, c. 1724, § 1.)*

Research References

Rutter, Cal. Practice Guide: Civ. Pro. Before Trial Ch. 9(II)-A, A. Injunctions.
California Practice Guide: Employment Litigation Ch. 14-C, C. Misappropriation of Employer's Trade Secrets.
5 Witkin Cal. Proc. 5th Pleading § 778, Misappropriation of Trade Secrets.
13 Witkin, California Summary 10th Equity § 89, (S 89) Injunction.

§ 3426.3.   Damages; royalties; exemplary damages

(a) A complainant may recover damages for the actual loss caused by misappropriation. A complainant also may recover for the unjust enrichment caused by misappropriation that is not taken into account in computing damages for actual loss.

(b) If neither damages nor unjust enrichment caused by misappropriation are provable, the court may order payment of a reasonable royalty for no longer than the period of time the use could have been prohibited.

(c) If willful and malicious misappropriation exists, the court may award exemplary damages in an amount not exceeding twice any award made under subdivision (a) or (b). *(Added by Stats.1984, c. 1724, § 1.)*

Research References

California Practice Guide: Employment Litigation Ch. 14-C, C. Misappropriation of Employer's Trade Secrets.
13 Witkin, California Summary 10th Equity § 90, (S 90) Damages.

§ 3426.4.   Awarding attorney's fees and costs

If a claim of misappropriation is made in bad faith, a motion to terminate an injunction is made or resisted in bad faith, or

willful and malicious misappropriation exists, the court may award reasonable attorney's fees and costs to the prevailing party.   Recoverable costs hereunder shall include a reasonable sum to cover the services of expert witnesses, who are not regular employees of any party, actually incurred and reasonably necessary in either, or both, preparation for trial or arbitration, or during trial or arbitration, of the case by the prevailing party. *(Added by Stats.1984, c. 1724, § 1.   Amended by Stats.2006, c. 62 (S.B.1636), § 1.)*

Research References

Rutter, Cal. Practice Guide: Civ. Pro. Before Trial Ch. 9(II)-A, A. Injunctions.
California Practice Guide: Employment Litigation Ch. 14-C, C. Misappropriation of Employer's Trade Secrets.
California Practice Guide: Employment Litigation Gen. Matls, Highlights.
13 Witkin, California Summary 10th Equity § 86, (S 86) in General.
13 Witkin, California Summary 10th Equity § 91, (S 91) Attorneys' Fees.

§ 3426.5.   Preservation of secrecy in judicial proceeding

In an action under this title, a court shall preserve the secrecy of an alleged trade secret by reasonable means, which may include granting protective orders in connection with discovery proceedings, holding in-camera hearings, sealing the records of the action, and ordering any person involved in the litigation not to disclose an alleged trade secret without prior court approval. *(Added by Stats.1984, c. 1724, § 1.)*

Research References

Rutter, Cal. Practice Guide: A.D.R. App. D Form 143, Order Appointing Referee for the Purpose of Discovery.
Rutter, Cal. Practice Guide: Civ. Pro. Before Trial Ch. 8B-4, Status of Pleadings Affecting Right to Discovery.
Rutter, Cal. Practice Guide: Civ. Pro. Before Trial Ch. 8C-5, Privacy Protection.
Rutter, Cal. Practice Guide: Civil Trials & Evidence Ch. 8E-A, A. Privileges.
13 Witkin, California Summary 10th Equity § 92, (S 92) Orders to Preserve Secrecy.

§ 3426.6.   Time for bringing action

An action for misappropriation must be brought within three years after the misappropriation is discovered or by the exercise of reasonable diligence should have been discovered.   For the purposes of this section, a continuing misappropriation constitutes a single claim. *(Added by Stats.1984, c. 1724, § 1.)*

Research References

3 Witkin Cal. Proc. 5th Actions § 483, (S 483) Three Years.
13 Witkin, California Summary 10th Equity § 88, (S 88) When Claim Arises.

§ 3426.7.   Construction with other statutes;   other remedies;   disclosure of public records

(a) Except as otherwise expressly provided, this title does not supersede any statute relating to misappropriation of a trade secret, or any statute otherwise regulating trade secrets.

(b) This title does not affect (1) contractual remedies, whether or not based upon misappropriation of a trade secret, (2) other civil remedies that are not based upon misappropriation of a trade secret, or (3) criminal remedies, whether or not based upon misappropriation of a trade secret.

(c) This title does not affect the disclosure of a record by a state or local agency under the California Public Records Act (Chapter 3.5 (commencing with Section 6250) of Division 7 of Title 1 of the Government Code).   Any determination as to whether the disclosure of a record under the California Public Records Act constitutes a misappropriation of a trade secret and the rights and remedies with respect thereto shall be made pursuant to the law in effect before the operative date of this title. *(Added by Stats.1984, c. 1724, § 1.)*

Research References

California Practice Guide: Employment Litigation Ch. 14-C, C. Misappropriation of Employer's Trade Secrets.
13 Witkin, California Summary 10th Equity § 86, (S 86) in General.

§ 3426.8. Application and construction of title

This title shall be applied and construed to effectuate its general purpose to make uniform the law with respect to the subject of this title among states enacting it. *(Added by Stats.1984, c. 1724, § 1.)*

Research References

13 Witkin, California Summary 10th Equity § 86, (S 86) in General.

§ 3426.9. Severability of provisions

If any provision of this title or its application to any person or circumstances is held invalid, the invalidity does not affect other provisions or applications of the title which can be given effect without the invalid provision or application, and to this end the provisions of this title are severable. *(Added by Stats.1984, c. 1724, § 1.)*

Research References

13 Witkin, California Summary 10th Equity § 86, (S 86) in General.

§ 3426.10. Misappropriations occurring prior to January 1, 1985; application of title

This title does not apply to misappropriation occurring prior to January 1, 1985. If a continuing misappropriation otherwise covered by this title began before January 1, 1985, this title does not apply to the part of the misappropriation occurring before that date. This title does apply to the part of the misappropriation occurring on or after that date unless the appropriation was not a misappropriation under the law in effect before the operative date of this title. *(Added by Stats.1984, c. 1724, § 1.)*

Research References

California Practice Guide: Employment Litigation Ch. 14-C, C. Misappropriation of Employer's Trade Secrets.

§ 3426.11. Privileged communications; trade secrets disclosed in official proceedings

Notwithstanding subdivision (b) of Section 47, in any legislative or judicial proceeding, or in any other official proceeding authorized by law, or in the initiation or course of any other proceeding authorized by law and reviewable pursuant to Chapter 2 (commencing with Section 1084) of Title 1 of Part 3 of the Code of Civil Procedure, the voluntary, intentional disclosure of trade secret information, unauthorized by its owner, to a competitor or potential competitor of the owner of the trade secret information or the agent or representative of such a competitor or potential competitor is not privileged and is not a privileged communication for purposes of Part 2 (commencing with Section 43) of Division 1.

This section does not in any manner limit, restrict, impair, or otherwise modify either the application of the other subdivisions of Section 47 to the conduct to which this section applies or the court's authority to control, order, or permit access to evidence in any case before it.

Nothing in this section shall be construed to limit, restrict, or otherwise impair, the capacity of persons employed by public entities to report improper government activity, as defined in Section 10542 of the Government Code, or the capacity of private persons to report improper activities of a private business. *(Added by Stats.1992, c. 165 (A.B.1445), § 1.)*

Research References

Rutter, Cal. Practice Guide: Civ. Pro. Before Trial Ch. 1-C, C. Prelawsuit Notices, Claims and Demands.
5 Witkin, California Summary 10th Torts § 563, Scope of Privilege.
13 Witkin, California Summary 10th Equity § 81, (S 81) Theory of Protection.

Title 6

INTERFERENCE WITH ACCESS TO HEALTH CARE

Section

§ 3427. Definitions

As used in this title:

(a) "Aggrieved" means and refers to any of the following persons or entities:

(1) A person physically present at a health care facility when a commercial blockade occurs whose access is obstructed or impeded.

(2) A person physically present at a health care facility when a commercial blockade occurs whose health care is disrupted.

(3) A health care facility where a commercial blockade occurs, its employees, contractors, or volunteers.

(4) The owner of a health care facility where a commercial blockade occurs or of the building or property upon which the health care facility is located.

(b) "Commercial blockade" means acts constituting the tort of commercial blockade, as defined in Section 3427.1.

(c) "Disrupting the normal functioning of a health care facility" means intentionally rendering or attempting to render a health care facility temporarily or permanently unavailable or unusable by a licensed health practitioner, the facility's staff, or patients. "Disrupting the normal functioning of a health care facility" does not include acts of the owner of the facility, an agent acting on behalf of the owner, or officers or employees of a governmental entity acting to protect the public health or safety.

(d) "Health care facility" means a facility that provides health care services directly to patients, including, but not limited to, a hospital, clinic, licensed health practitioner's office, health maintenance organization, diagnostic or treatment center, neuropsychiatric or mental health facility, hospice, or nursing home. *(Added by Stats.1994, c. 1193 (A.B.600), § 1.)*

Research References

5 Witkin, California Summary 10th Torts § 462, (S 462) Commercial Blockade.

§ 3427.1. Commercial blockade

It is unlawful, and constitutes the tort of commercial blockade for a person, alone or in concert with others, to intentionally prevent an individual from entering or exiting a health care facility by physically obstructing the individual's passage or by disrupting the normal functioning of a health care facility. *(Added by Stats.1994, c. 1193 (A.B.600), § 1.)*

Research References

5 Witkin, California Summary 10th Torts § 462, (S 462) Commercial Blockade.

§ 3427.2. Civil damages; parties to action

A person or health care facility aggrieved by the actions prohibited by this title may seek civil damages from those who committed the prohibited acts and those acting in concert with them. *(Added by Stats.1994, c. 1193 (A.B.600), § 1. Amended by Stats.1995, c. 91 (S.B.975), § 19.)*

Research References

5 Witkin, California Summary 10th Torts § 462, (S 462) Commercial Blockade.

§ 3427.3. Safeguarding individual privacy and prevention of harassment in civil proceeding

The court having jurisdiction over a civil proceeding under this title shall take all steps reasonably necessary to safeguard the individual privacy and prevent harassment of a health care patient, licensed health practitioner, or employee, client, or customer of a health care facility who is a party or witness in the proceeding, including granting protective orders. Health care patients, licensed health practitioners, and employees, clients, and customers of the health care facility may use pseudonyms to protect their privacy. *(Added by Stats.1994, c. 1193 (A.B.600), § 1.)*

Research References

5 Witkin, California Summary 10th Torts § 462, (S 462) Commercial Blockade.

§ 3427.4. Construction

This title shall not be construed to impair any constitutionally protected activity or any activities protected by the labor laws of this state or the United States of America. *(Added by Stats.1994, c. 1193 (A.B.600), § 1.)*

Research References

5 Witkin, California Summary 10th Torts § 462, (S 462) Commercial Blockade.

Title 7

DUTY OF HEALTH CARE SERVICE PLANS AND MANAGED CARE ENTITIES

Section

3428. Duty of ordinary care; indemnity; liability; waiver; damages; exhaustion of procedures under medical review system.

§ 3428. Duty of ordinary care; indemnity; liability; waiver; damages; exhaustion of procedures under medical review system

(a) For services rendered on or after January 1, 2001, a health care service plan or managed care entity, as described in subdivision (f) of Section 1345 of the Health and Safety Code, shall have a duty of ordinary care to arrange for the provision of medically necessary health care service to its subscribers and enrollees, where the health care service is a benefit provided under the plan, and shall be liable for any and all harm legally caused by its failure to exercise that ordinary care when both of the following apply:

(1) The failure to exercise ordinary care resulted in the denial, delay, or modification of the health care service recommended for, or furnished to, a subscriber or enrollee.

(2) The subscriber or enrollee suffered substantial harm.

(b) For purposes of this section: (1) substantial harm means loss of life, loss or significant impairment of limb or bodily function, significant disfigurement, severe and chronic physical pain, or significant financial loss; (2) health care services need not be recommended or furnished by an in-plan provider, but may be recommended or furnished by any health care provider practicing within the scope of his or her practice; and (3) health care services shall be recommended or furnished at any time prior to the inception of the action, and the recommendation need not be made prior to the occurrence of substantial harm.

(c) Health care service plans and managed care entities are not health care providers under any provision of law, including, but not limited to, Section 6146 of the Business and Professions Code, Sections 3333.1 or 3333.2 of this code, or Sections 340.5, 364, 425.13, 667.7, or 1295 of the Code of Civil Procedure.

(d) A health care service plan or managed care entity shall not seek indemnity, whether contractual or equitable, from a provider for liability imposed under subdivision (a). Any provision to the contrary in a contract with providers is void and unenforceable.

(e) This section shall not create any liability on the part of an employer or an employer group purchasing organization that purchases coverage or assumes risk on behalf of its employees or on behalf of self-funded employee benefit plans.

(f) Any waiver by a subscriber or enrollee of the provisions of this section is contrary to public policy and shall be unenforceable and void.

(g) This section does not create any new or additional liability on the part of a health care service plan or managed care entity for harm caused that is attributable to the medical negligence of a treating physician or other treating health care provider.

(h) This section does not abrogate or limit any other theory of liability otherwise available at law.

(i) This section shall not apply in instances where subscribers or enrollees receive treatment by prayer, consistent with the provisions of subdivision (a) of Section 1270 of the Health and Safety Code, in lieu of medical treatment.

(j) Damages recoverable for a violation of this section include, but are not limited to, those set forth in Section 3333.

(k)(1) A person may not maintain a cause of action pursuant to this section against any entity required to comply with any independent medical review system or independent review system required by law unless the person or his or her representative has exhausted the procedures provided by the applicable independent review system.

(2) Compliance with paragraph (1) is not required in a case where either of the following applies:

(A) Substantial harm, as defined in subdivision (b), has occurred prior to the completion of the applicable review.

(B) Substantial harm, as defined, in subdivision (b), will imminently occur prior to the completion of the applicable review.

(3) This subdivision shall become operative only if Senate Bill 189 and Assembly Bill 55 of the 1999–2000 Regular Session are also enacted and enforceable.

(*l*) If any provision of this section or the application thereof to any person or circumstance is held to be unconstitutional or otherwise invalid or unenforceable, the remainder of the section and the application of those provisions to other persons or circumstances shall not be affected thereby. *(Added by Stats. 1999, c. 536 (S.B.21), § 3.)*

Research References

Rutter, Cal. Practice Guide: Insurance Litigation Ch. 11-K, K. Statutory Liability.

Rutter, Cal. Practice Guide: Insurance Litigation Ch. 6E-D, D. Managed Care Plans.

Rutter, Cal. Practice Guide: Insurance Litigation Ch. 6E-H, H. Preemption Defenses.

Rutter, Cal. Practice Guide: Insurance Litigation Ch. 6E-D, Outline D.

Rutter, Cal. Practice Guide: Personal Injury Ch. 3-E, E. Punitive Damages.

Rutter, Cal. Practice Guide: Personal Injury Ch. 3-F, F. MICRA Provisions Affecting Damages.

6 Witkin, California Summary 10th Torts § 936, (S 936) Health Care Provider.

6 Witkin, California Summary 10th Torts § 937, (S 937) Hmo.

Part 2

SPECIAL RELATIONS OF DEBTOR AND CREDITOR

Title 1

GENERAL PRINCIPLES

§ 3429. Debtor defined

WHO IS A DEBTOR. A debtor, within the meaning of this title, is one who, by reason of an existing obligation, is or may become liable to pay money to another, whether such liability is certain or contingent. *(Enacted in 1872.)*

§ 3430. Creditor defined

WHO IS A CREDITOR. A creditor, within the meaning of this title, is one in whose favor an obligation exists, by reason of which he is, or may become, entitled to the payment of money. *(Enacted in 1872.)*

§ 3431. Validity of debtor's contracts

CONTRACTS OF DEBTOR ARE VALID. In the absence of fraud, every contract of a debtor is valid against all his creditors, existing or subsequent, who have not acquired a lien on the property affected by such contract. *(Enacted in 1872.)*

§ 3432. Payments or security in preference

PAYMENTS IN PREFERENCE. A debtor may pay one creditor in preference to another, or may give to one creditor security for the payment of his demand in preference to another. *(Enacted in 1872.)*

Research References

Rutter, Cal. Practice Guide: Enforcing Judgments/Debts Ch. 3-C, C. Prelawsuit Considerations.

8 Witkin Cal. Proc. 5th Enforcement of Judgment § 480, (S 480) Distinctions.

8 Witkin Cal. Proc. 5th Enforcement of Judgment § 495, Transfer With Intent to Defraud.

1 Witkin Cal. Summ. 10th Contracts § 710, (S 710) in General.

§ 3433. Marshaling assets

RELATIVE RIGHTS OF DIFFERENT CREDITORS. Where a creditor is entitled to resort to each of several funds for the satisfaction of his claim, and another person has an interest in, or is entitled as a creditor to resort to some, but not all of them, the latter may require the former to seek satisfaction from those funds to which the latter has no such claim, so far as it can be done without impairing the right of the former to complete satisfaction, and without doing injustice to third persons. *(Enacted in 1872.)*

Research References

California Real Estate Forms (Miller & Starr) § 3:29, Exceptions to Non-Recourse Guaranty--Conduit Loan.

California Real Estate Forms (Miller & Starr) § 3:37, Continuing Guaranty.

California Real Estate Forms (Miller & Starr) § 3:38, Completion Guaranty.

California Real Estate Forms (Miller & Starr) § 3:40, Assignment of Membership Interest.

Rutter, Cal. Practice Guide: Enforcing Judgments/Debts Ch. 5-D, D. Involuntary Bankruptcy.

Miller and Starr California Real Estate § 11:215, Definition.

Miller and Starr California Real Estate § 11:216, The "Two-Fund" Rule.

Miller and Starr California Real Estate § 11:218, Equitable Restrictions.

Miller and Starr California Real Estate § 11:220, Waiver of Marshalling.

4 Witkin, California Summary 10th Security Transactions in Real Property § 143, Manner of Sale.

13 Witkin, California Summary 10th Equity § 23, Marshaling Assets.

§ 3434. Liability of lender financing design, manufacture, construction, repair, modification or improvement of real or personal property

A lender who makes a loan of money, the proceeds of which are used or may be used by the borrower to finance the design, manufacture, construction, repair, modification or improvement of real or personal property for sale or lease to others, shall not be held liable to third persons for any loss or damage occasioned by any defect in the real or personal property so designed, manufactured, constructed, repaired, modified or improved or for any loss or damage resulting from the failure of the borrower to use due care in the design, manufacture, construction, repair, modification or improvement of such real or personal property, unless such loss or damage is a result of an act of the lender outside the scope of the activities of a lender of money or unless the lender has been a party to misrepresentations with respect to such real or personal property. *(Added by Stats.1969, c. 1584, p. 3222, § 1.)*

Research References

Miller and Starr California Real Estate § 29:1, General Observations; Theories of Liability.

Miller and Starr California Real Estate § 36:5, Breach of a Construction Loan Agreement.

Miller and Starr California Real Estate § 36:7, Liability to Third Persons.

Miller and Starr California Real Estate § 36:8, Liability for Defective Construction--In General.

Miller and Starr California Real Estate § 36:10, Negligence.

Miller and Starr California Real Estate § 36:15, Liability for Fraud.

6 Witkin, California Summary 10th Torts § 1279, Distinction: Financing Agency is Not Liable.

Title 2

FRAUDULENT INSTRUMENTS AND TRANSFERS

CHAPTER 1. UNIFORM FRAUDULENT TRANSFER ACT

§ 3439. Short title

This chapter may be cited as the Uniform Fraudulent Transfer Act. *(Added by Stats.1986, c. 383, § 2.)*

Research References

Rutter, Cal. Practice Guide: Enforcing Judgments/Debts Ch. 3-A, A. Evaluating the Claim.
Rutter, Cal. Practice Guide: Enforcing Judgments/Debts Ch. 4-A, A. Attachment.
Rutter, Cal. Practice Guide: Enforcing Judgments/Debts Ch. 5-B, B. Overview of Substantive Bankruptcy Law.
Rutter, Cal. Practice Guide: Enforcing Judgments/Debts Ch. 5-D, D. Involuntary Bankruptcy.
Rutter, Cal. Practice Guide: Enforcing Judgments/Debts Ch. 6A-11, Property Subject to Enforcement Procedures.
Rutter, Cal. Practice Guide: Enforcing Judgments/Debts Ch. 6A-13, Creating an Enforcement of Judgment Plan.
Miller and Starr California Real Estate § 8:54, Fraud.
Miller and Starr California Real Estate § 11:70, Defects in the Record Title Enforceable Against a Bona Fide Purchaser--In General.
Miller and Starr California Real Estate § 32:52, Previously Conveyed Property.
Miller and Starr California Real Estate § 11:124, Relation to Prior Interests.
Miller and Starr California Real Estate § 11:127, Relation to Prior Interests.
Miller and Starr California Real Estate § 1:58.10, Sufficiency of Consideration Under Uniform Fraudulent Conveyance Act.
15 NO. 1 Miller & Starr, California Real Estate Newsalert 14, Recording and Priorities.
3 Witkin Cal. Proc. 5th Actions § 400, (S 400) Action to Set Aside Fraudulent Conveyance.
8 Witkin Cal. Proc. 5th Enforcement of Judgment § 2, (S 2) in General.
8 Witkin Cal. Proc. 5th Enforcement of Judgment § 134, (S 134) Deposit Accounts and Boxes in Third Person's Name.
8 Witkin Cal. Proc. 5th Enforcement of Judgment § 483, (S 483) Adoption of Act.
8 Witkin Cal. Proc. 5th Enforcement of Judgment § 488, (S 488) Adoption of Act.
8 Witkin Cal. Proc. 5th Enforcement of Judgment § 504, (S 504) Bulk Sales.
6 Witkin Cal. Proc. 5th Provisional Remedies § 81, Fraudulently Transferred Property.
6 Witkin Cal. Proc. 5th Provisional Remedies § 144, in General.
12 Witkin, California Summary 10th Real Property § 2, Uniform Laws and Model Acts.
4 Witkin, California Summary 10th Sales § 214, in General.
4 Witkin, California Summary 10th Sales § 228, (S 228) Applicability of Fraudulent Transfer Act.
9 Witkin, California Summary 10th Corporations § 184, (S 184) Unlawful Dividends or Purchases of Shares.
9 Witkin, California Summary 10th Corporations § 289, Distributions to Members Prohibited.
6 Witkin, California Summary 10th Torts § 1607, Nature of Requirement.
9 Witkin, California Summary 10th Partnership § 1, Statutes Affecting Partnerships.
9 Witkin, California Summary 10th Partnership § 87, (S 87) Capital Account and Contributions.
9 Witkin, California Summary 10th Partnership § 120, Rights and Privileges of Dissenting Limited Partners.
9 Witkin, California Summary 10th Partnership § 156, (S 156) Capital Contributions.
9 Witkin, California Summary 10th Partnership § 121AAA, (New)-Rights and Privileges of Dissenting Limited Partners.
14 Witkin, California Summary 10th Wills and Probate § 333, (S 333) Right to Disclaim and Waiver.
14 Witkin, California Summary 10th Wills and Probate § 478, Duty to Recover Property.

§ 3439.01. Definitions

As used in this chapter the following definitions are applicable:

(a) "Asset" means property of a debtor, but the term does not include, the following:

(1) Property to the extent it is encumbered by a valid lien.

(2) Property to the extent it is generally exempt under nonbankruptcy law.

(3) An interest in property held in tenancy by the entireties to the extent it is not subject to process by a creditor holding a claim against only one tenant.

(b) "Claim" means a right to payment, whether or not the right is reduced to judgment, liquidated, unliquidated, fixed, contingent, matured, unmatured, disputed, undisputed, legal, equitable, secured, or unsecured.

(c) "Creditor" means a person who has a claim, and includes an assignee of a general assignment for the benefit of creditors, as defined in Section 493.010 of the Code of Civil Procedure, of a debtor.

(d) "Debt" means liability on a claim.

(e) "Debtor" means a person who is liable on a claim.

(f) "Lien" means a charge against or an interest in property to secure payment of a debt or performance of an obligation, and includes a security interest created by agreement, a judicial lien obtained by legal or equitable process or proceedings, a common-law lien, or a statutory lien.

(g) "Person" means an individual, partnership, corporation, limited liability company, association, organization, government or governmental subdivision or agency, business trust, estate, trust, or any other legal or commercial entity.

(h) "Property" means anything that may be the subject of ownership.

(i) "Transfer" means every mode, direct or indirect, absolute or conditional, voluntary or involuntary, of disposing of or parting with an asset or an interest in an asset, and includes payment of money, release, lease, and creation of a lien or other encumbrance.

(j) "Valid lien" means a lien that is effective against the holder of a judicial lien subsequently obtained by legal or equitable process or proceedings. *(Added by Stats.1986, c. 383, § 2. Amended by Stats.1994, c. 1010 (S.B.2053), § 55.)*

Research References

California Real Estate Forms (Miller & Starr) § 3:37, Continuing Guaranty.

California Real Estate Forms (Miller & Starr) § 3:38, Completion Guaranty.

Rutter, Cal. Practice Guide: Enforcing Judgments/Debts Ch. 3-C, C. Prelawsuit Considerations.

Miller and Starr California Real Estate § 1:58.10, Sufficiency of Consideration Under Uniform Fraudulent Conveyance Act.

20 NO. 4 Miller & Starr, California Real Estate Newsalert 25, Contracts.

8 Witkin Cal. Proc. 5th Enforcement of Judgment § 479, (S 479) Nature and Classes of Fraudulent Transfers.

8 Witkin Cal. Proc. 5th Enforcement of Judgment § 480, (S 480) Distinctions.

8 Witkin Cal. Proc. 5th Enforcement of Judgment § 484, Actual Intent to Defraud.

8 Witkin Cal. Proc. 5th Enforcement of Judgment § 489, in General.

8 Witkin Cal. Proc. 5th Enforcement of Judgment § 490, Insolvency.

8 Witkin Cal. Proc. 5th Enforcement of Judgment § 502, Undertaking by Transferee.

§ 3439.02. Insolvency

(a) A debtor is insolvent if, at fair valuations, the sum of the debtor's debts is greater than all of the debtor's assets.

(b) A debtor which is a partnership is insolvent if, at fair valuations, the sum of the partnership's debts is greater than the aggregate of all of the partnership's assets and the sum of the excess of the value of each general partner's nonpartnership assets over the partner's nonpartnership debts.

(c) A debtor who is generally not paying his or her debts as they become due is presumed to be insolvent.

(d) Assets under this section do not include property that has been transferred, concealed, or removed with intent to hinder, delay, or defraud creditors or that has been transferred in a manner making the transfer voidable under this chapter.

(e) Debts under this section do not include an obligation to the extent it is secured by a valid lien on property of the debtor not included as an asset. *(Added by Stats.1986, c. 383, § 2.)*

Research References

Rutter, Cal. Practice Guide: Enforcing Judgments/Debts Ch. 3-C, C. Prelawsuit Considerations.

Miller and Starr California Real Estate § 1:58.10, Sufficiency of Consideration Under Uniform Fraudulent Conveyance Act.

8 Witkin Cal. Proc. 5th Enforcement of Judgment § 485, Transfer by Insolvent Person Without Fair Consideration.

8 Witkin Cal. Proc. 5th Enforcement of Judgment § 490, Insolvency.

8 Witkin Cal. Proc. 5th Enforcement of Judgment § 496, Transfer Without Receipt of Reasonably Equivalent Value.

§ 3439.03. Value

Value is given for a transfer or an obligation if, in exchange for the transfer or obligation, property is transferred or an antecedent debt is secured or satisfied, but value does not include an unperformed promise made otherwise than in the ordinary course of the promisor's business to furnish support to the debtor or another person. *(Added by Stats.1986, c. 383, § 2.)*

Research References

Rutter, Cal. Practice Guide: Enforcing Judgments/Debts Ch. 3-C, C. Prelawsuit Considerations.

Rutter, Cal. Practice Guide: Enforcing Judgments/Debts Ch. 5-B, B. Overview of Substantive Bankruptcy Law.

8 Witkin Cal. Proc. 5th Enforcement of Judgment § 485, Transfer by Insolvent Person Without Fair Consideration.

8 Witkin Cal. Proc. 5th Enforcement of Judgment § 491, Value for Transfer or Obligation.

8 Witkin Cal. Proc. 5th Enforcement of Judgment § 496, Transfer Without Receipt of Reasonably Equivalent Value.

§ 3439.04. Transfers fraudulent as to present and future creditors; factors to determining intent

(a) A transfer made or obligation incurred by a debtor is fraudulent as to a creditor, whether the creditor's claim arose before or after the transfer was made or the obligation was incurred, if the debtor made the transfer or incurred the obligation as follows:

(1) With actual intent to hinder, delay, or defraud any creditor of the debtor.

(2) Without receiving a reasonably equivalent value in exchange for the transfer or obligation, and the debtor either:

(A) Was engaged or was about to engage in a business or a transaction for which the remaining assets of the debtor were unreasonably small in relation to the business or transaction.

(B) Intended to incur, or believed or reasonably should have believed that he or she would incur, debts beyond his or her ability to pay as they became due.

(b) In determining actual intent under paragraph (1) of subdivision (a), consideration may be given, among other factors, to any or all of the following:

(1) Whether the transfer or obligation was to an insider.

(2) Whether the debtor retained possession or control of the property transferred after the transfer.

(3) Whether the transfer or obligation was disclosed or concealed.

(4) Whether before the transfer was made or obligation was incurred, the debtor had been sued or threatened with suit.

(5) Whether the transfer was of substantially all the debtor's assets.

(6) Whether the debtor absconded.

(7) Whether the debtor removed or concealed assets.

(8) Whether the value of the consideration received by the debtor was reasonably equivalent to the value of the asset transferred or the amount of the obligation incurred.

(9) Whether the debtor was insolvent or became insolvent shortly after the transfer was made or the obligation was incurred.

(10) Whether the transfer occurred shortly before or shortly after a substantial debt was incurred.

(11) Whether the debtor transferred the essential assets of the business to a lienholder who transferred the assets to an insider of the debtor.

(c) The amendment to this section made during the 2004 portion of the 2003–04 Regular Session of the Legislature, set forth in subdivision (b), does not constitute a change in, but is declaratory of, existing law, and is not intended to affect any judicial decisions that have interpreted this chapter. *(Added by Stats.1986, c. 383, § 2. Amended by Stats.2004, c. 50 (S.B.1408), § 1.)*

Research References

Rutter, Cal. Practice Guide: Enforcing Judgments/Debts Ch. 3-C, C. Prelawsuit Considerations.

Miller and Starr California Real Estate § 11:70, Defects in the Record Title Enforceable Against a Bona Fide Purchaser--In General.

Miller and Starr California Real Estate § 12:63, Liability for Debts and Judgments.

Miller and Starr California Real Estate § 10:263, Definitions; Guarantor, Surety.

Miller and Starr California Real Estate § 1:58.10, Sufficiency of Consideration Under Uniform Fraudulent Conveyance Act.

14 NO. 2 Miller & Starr, California Real Estate Newsalert 6, Deeds.
15 NO. 4 Miller & Starr, California Real Estate Newsalert 7, Deeds.
8 Witkin Cal. Proc. 5th Enforcement of Judgment § 485, Transfer by
   Insolvent Person Without Fair Consideration.
8 Witkin Cal. Proc. 5th Enforcement of Judgment § 495, Transfer With
   Intent to Defraud.
8 Witkin Cal. Proc. 5th Enforcement of Judgment § 496, Transfer
   Without Receipt of Reasonably Equivalent Value.
8 Witkin Cal. Proc. 5th Enforcement of Judgment § 497, Requirement of
   Injury to Creditor.
8 Witkin Cal. Proc. 5th Enforcement of Judgment § 499, Transfers that
   Are Not Voidable.
4 Witkin Cal. Proc. 5th Pleading § 416, (S 416) Other Examples.
11 Witkin, California Summary 10th Community Property § 153, (S 153)
   Authority to Transmute.

§ 3439.05.   Transfers fraudulent as to present creditors

A transfer made or obligation incurred by a debtor is fraudulent as to a creditor whose claim arose before the transfer was made or the obligation was incurred if the debtor made the transfer or incurred the obligation without receiving a reasonably equivalent value in exchange for the transfer or obligation and the debtor was insolvent at that time or the debtor became insolvent as a result of the transfer or obligation. *(Added by Stats.1986, c. 383, § 2.)*

Research References

Rutter, Cal. Practice Guide: Enforcing Judgments/Debts Ch. 3-C, C.
   Prelawsuit Considerations.
Miller and Starr California Real Estate § 1:58.10, Sufficiency of Consideration Under Uniform Fraudulent Conveyance Act.
8 Witkin Cal. Proc. 5th Enforcement of Judgment § 486, Other Types.
8 Witkin Cal. Proc. 5th Enforcement of Judgment § 496, Transfer
   Without Receipt of Reasonably Equivalent Value.
8 Witkin Cal. Proc. 5th Enforcement of Judgment § 497, Requirement of
   Injury to Creditor.
8 Witkin Cal. Proc. 5th Enforcement of Judgment § 499, Transfers that
   Are Not Voidable.

§ 3439.06.   When transfer is made or obligation is incurred

For the purposes of this chapter:

(a) A transfer is made:

(1) With respect to an asset that is real property other than a fixture, but including the interest of a seller or purchaser under a contract for the sale of the asset, when the transfer is so far perfected that a good faith purchaser of the asset from the debtor against whom applicable law permits the transfer to be perfected cannot acquire an interest in the asset that is superior to the interest of the transferee; and

(2) With respect to an asset that is not real property or that is a fixture, when the transfer is so far perfected that a creditor on a simple contract cannot acquire a judicial lien otherwise than under this chapter that is superior to the interest of the transferee.

(b) If applicable law permits the transfer to be perfected as provided in subdivision (a) and the transfer is not so perfected before the commencement of an action for relief under this chapter, the transfer is deemed made immediately before the commencement of the action.

(c) If applicable law does not permit the transfer to be perfected as provided in subdivision (a), the transfer is made when it becomes effective between the debtor and the transferee.

(d) A transfer is not made until the debtor has acquired rights in the asset transferred.

(e) An obligation is incurred:

(1) If oral, when it becomes effective between the parties; or

(2) If evidenced by a writing, when the writing executed by the obligor is delivered to or for the benefit of the obligee. *(Added by Stats.1986, c. 383, § 2.)*

Research References

Rutter, Cal. Practice Guide: Enforcing Judgments/Debts Ch. 3-C, C.
   Prelawsuit Considerations.
8 Witkin Cal. Proc. 5th Enforcement of Judgment § 492, in General.
8 Witkin Cal. Proc. 5th Enforcement of Judgment § 493, When Transfer
   is Made or Obligation is Incurred.
11 Witkin, California Summary 10th Community Property § 153, (S 153)
   Authority to Transmute.

§ 3439.07.   Remedies of creditors

(a) In an action for relief against a transfer or obligation under this chapter, a creditor, subject to the limitations in Section 3439.08, may obtain:

(1) Avoidance of the transfer or obligation to the extent necessary to satisfy the creditor's claim.

(2) An attachment or other provisional remedy against the asset transferred or its proceeds in accordance with the procedures described in Title 6.5 (commencing with Section 481.010) of Part 2 of the Code of Civil Procedure.

(3) Subject to applicable principles of equity and in accordance with applicable rules of civil procedure, the following:

(A) An injunction against further disposition by the debtor or a transferee, or both, of the asset transferred or its proceeds.

(B) Appointment of a receiver to take charge of the asset transferred or its proceeds.

(C) Any other relief the circumstances may require.

(b) If a creditor has commenced an action on a claim against the debtor, the creditor may attach the asset transferred or its proceeds if the remedy of attachment is available in the action under applicable law and the property is subject to attachment in the hands of the transferee under applicable law.

(c) If a creditor has obtained a judgment on a claim against the debtor, the creditor may levy execution on the asset transferred or its proceeds.

(d) A creditor who is an assignee of a general assignment for the benefit of creditors, as defined in Section 493.010 of the Code of Civil Procedure, may exercise any and all of the rights and remedies specified in this section if they are available to any one or more creditors of the assignor who are beneficiaries of the assignment, and, in that event (1) only to the extent the rights or remedies are so available and (2) only for the benefit of those creditors whose rights are asserted by the assignee. *(Added by Stats.1986, c. 383, § 2.)*

Research References

Rutter, Cal. Practice Guide: Enforcing Judgments/Debts Ch. 3-C, C.
   Prelawsuit Considerations.
Rutter, Cal. Practice Guide: Enforcing Judgments/Debts Ch. 4-C, C.
   Receiverships.
Rutter, Cal. Practice Guide: Enforcing Judgments/Debts Ch. 5-D, D.
   Involuntary Bankruptcy.
Rutter, Cal. Practice Guide: Enforcing Judgments/Debts Ch. 6B-2,
   Interests Subject to Judgment Lien.
Miller and Starr California Real Estate § 11:124, Relation to Prior
   Interests.
Miller and Starr California Real Estate § 11:150, Actions in Which a Lis
   Pendens May or Must be Recorded.
Miller and Starr California Real Estate § 1:58.10, Sufficiency of Consider-
   ation Under Uniform Fraudulent Conveyance Act.
14 NO. 2 Miller & Starr, California Real Estate Newsalert 6, Deeds.
15 NO. 1 Miller & Starr, California Real Estate Newsalert 14, Recording
   and Priorities.
21 NO. 2 Miller & Starr, California Real Estate Newsalert 7, Contracts.

8 Witkin Cal. Proc. 5th Enforcement of Judgment § 484, Actual Intent to Defraud.

8 Witkin Cal. Proc. 5th Enforcement of Judgment § 498, (S 498) Remedies of Creditors.

8 Witkin Cal. Proc. 5th Enforcement of Judgment § 500, Restrictions on Creditor's Judgment.

6 Witkin Cal. Proc. 5th Provisional Remedies § 81, Fraudulently Transferred Property.

6 Witkin Cal. Proc. 5th Provisional Remedies § 178, Deposit Accounts and Boxes in Third Person's Name.

6 Witkin Cal. Proc. 5th Provisional Remedies § 423, Specific Statutory Enumeration.

6 Witkin Cal. Proc. 5th Provisional Remedies § 425, (S 425) Action by Vendor or Creditor.

1 Witkin Cal. Summ. 10th Contracts § 711, (S 711) Conformity With Federal Statutes.

§ 3439.08. Defenses, liability, and protection of transferee

(a) A transfer or an obligation is not voidable under paragraph (1) of subdivision (a) of Section 3439.04, against a person who took in good faith and for a reasonably equivalent value or against any subsequent transferee or obligee.

(b) Except as otherwise provided in this section, to the extent a transfer is voidable in an action by a creditor under paragraph (1) of subdivision (a) of Section 3439.07, the creditor may recover judgment for the value of the asset transferred, as adjusted under subdivision (c), or the amount necessary to satisfy the creditor's claim, whichever is less. The judgment may be entered against the following:

(1) The first transferee of the asset or the person for whose benefit the transfer was made.

(2) Any subsequent transferee other than a good faith transferee who took for value or from any subsequent transferee.

(c) If the judgment under subdivision (b) is based upon the value of the asset transferred, the judgment shall be for an amount equal to the value of the asset at the time of the transfer, subject to adjustment as the equities may require.

(d) Notwithstanding voidability of a transfer or an obligation under this chapter, a good faith transferee or obligee is entitled, to the extent of the value given the debtor for the transfer or obligation, to the following:

(1) A lien on or a right to retain any interest in the asset transferred.

(2) Enforcement of any obligation incurred.

(3) A reduction in the amount of the liability on the judgment.

(e) A transfer is not voidable under paragraph (2) of subdivision (a) of Section 3439.04 or Section 3439.05 if the transfer results from the following:

(1) Termination of a lease upon default by the debtor when the termination is pursuant to the lease and applicable law.

(2) Enforcement of a lien in a noncollusive manner and in compliance with applicable law, including Division 9 (commencing with Section 9101) of the Commercial Code, other than a retention of collateral under Sections 9620 and 9621 of the Commercial Code and other than a voluntary transfer of the collateral by the debtor to the lienor in satisfaction of all or part of the secured obligation. *(Added by Stats.1986, c. 383, § 2. Amended by Stats.1987, c. 40, § 1, eff. June 8, 1987; Stats.1999, c. 991 (S.B.45), § 9, operative July 1, 2001; Stats.2005, c. 34 (A.B.248), § 1, eff. July 7, 2005.)*

Research References

Rutter, Cal. Practice Guide: Enforcing Judgments/Debts Ch. 3-C, C. Prelawsuit Considerations.

Rutter, Cal. Practice Guide: Enforcing Judgments/Debts Ch. 5-B, B. Overview of Substantive Bankruptcy Law.

Rutter, Cal. Practice Guide: Enforcing Judgments/Debts Ch. 6B-2, Interests Subject to Judgment Lien.

Miller and Starr California Real Estate § 11:70, Defects in the Record Title Enforceable Against a Bona Fide Purchaser--In General.

Miller and Starr California Real Estate § 11:127, Relation to Prior Interests.

Miller and Starr California Real Estate § 1:58.10, Sufficiency of Consideration Under Uniform Fraudulent Conveyance Act.

16 NO. 4 Miller & Starr, California Real Estate Newsalert 7, Deeds.

16 NO. 5 Miller & Starr, California Real Estate Newsalert 26, State Board of Equalization Issues Comprehensive Summary and Qs and As for Transfers of Base Year Values of Principal Residences.

18 NO. 2 Miller & Starr, California Real Estate Newsalert 9, Deeds.

21 NO. 2 Miller & Starr, California Real Estate Newsalert 7, Contracts.

8 Witkin Cal. Proc. 5th Enforcement of Judgment § 496, Transfer Without Receipt of Reasonably Equivalent Value.

8 Witkin Cal. Proc. 5th Enforcement of Judgment § 498, (S 498) Remedies of Creditors.

8 Witkin Cal. Proc. 5th Enforcement of Judgment § 499, Transfers that Are Not Voidable.

8 Witkin Cal. Proc. 5th Enforcement of Judgment § 500, Restrictions on Creditor's Judgment.

8 Witkin Cal. Proc. 5th Enforcement of Judgment § 501, Rights Where Value is Given in Good Faith.

6 Witkin Cal. Proc. 5th Provisional Remedies § 81, Fraudulently Transferred Property.

§ 3439.09. Extinguishment of cause of action

A cause of action with respect to a fraudulent transfer or obligation under this chapter is extinguished unless action is brought pursuant to subdivision (a) of Section 3439.07 or levy made as provided in subdivision (b) or (c) of Section 3439.07:

(a) Under paragraph (1) of subdivision (a) of Section 3439.04, within four years after the transfer was made or the obligation was incurred or, if later, within one year after the transfer or obligation was or could reasonably have been discovered by the claimant.

(b) Under paragraph (2) of subdivision (a) of Section 3439.04 or Section 3439.05, within four years after the transfer was made or the obligation was incurred.

(c) Notwithstanding any other provision of law, a cause of action with respect to a fraudulent transfer or obligation is extinguished if no action is brought or levy made within seven years after the transfer was made or the obligation was incurred. *(Added by Stats.1986, c. 383, § 2. Amended by Stats.2005, c. 34 (A.B.248), § 2, eff. July 7, 2005.)*

Research References

Rutter, Cal. Practice Guide: Enforcing Judgments/Debts Ch. 3-C, C. Prelawsuit Considerations.

Miller and Starr California Real Estate § 13:11, Effect of a Fraudulent Conveyance.

Miller and Starr California Real Estate § 1:58.10, Sufficiency of Consideration Under Uniform Fraudulent Conveyance Act.

16 NO. 4 Miller & Starr, California Real Estate Newsalert 7, Deeds.

16 NO. 5 Miller & Starr, California Real Estate Newsalert 26, State Board of Equalization Issues Comprehensive Summary and Qs and As for Transfers of Base Year Values of Principal Residences.

21 NO. 4 Miller & Starr, California Real Estate Newsalert 25, Deeds of Trust.

8 Witkin Cal. Proc. 5th Enforcement of Judgment § 55, (S 55) in General.

8 Witkin Cal. Proc. 5th Enforcement of Judgment § 487, (S 487) Remedies of Creditors.

8 Witkin Cal. Proc. 5th Enforcement of Judgment § 492, in General.

8 Witkin Cal. Proc. 5th Enforcement of Judgment § 494, Statute Runs from Date of Judgment on Underlying Debt.

1 Witkin Cal. Summ. 10th Contracts § 711, (S 711) Conformity With Federal Statutes.

§ 3439.10. Supplementary provisions

Unless displaced by the provisions of this chapter, the principles of law and equity, including the law merchant and the law relating to principal and agent, estoppel, laches, fraud, misrepresentation, duress, coercion, mistake, insolvency, or other validating or invalidating cause, supplement its provisions. *(Added by Stats.1986, c. 383, § 2.)*

Research References

Rutter, Cal. Practice Guide: Civ. Pro. Before Trial Ch. 9(II)-B, B. Receiverships.

Rutter, Cal. Practice Guide: Enforcing Judgments/Debts Ch. 3-C, C. Prelawsuit Considerations.

Miller and Starr California Real Estate § 1:58.10, Sufficiency of Consideration Under Uniform Fraudulent Conveyance Act.

8 Witkin Cal. Proc. 5th Enforcement of Judgment § 488, (S 488) Adoption of Act.

8 Witkin Cal. Proc. 5th Enforcement of Judgment § 498, (S 498) Remedies of Creditors.

§ 3439.11. Uniformity of application and construction

This chapter shall be applied and construed to effectuate its general purpose to make uniform the law with respect to the subject of this chapter among states enacting it. *(Added by Stats.1986, c. 383, § 2.)*

Research References

California Real Estate Forms (Miller & Starr) § 3:37, Continuing Guaranty.

California Real Estate Forms (Miller & Starr) § 3:38, Completion Guaranty.

8 Witkin Cal. Proc. 5th Enforcement of Judgment § 483, (S 483) Adoption of Act.

8 Witkin Cal. Proc. 5th Enforcement of Judgment § 488, (S 488) Adoption of Act.

§ 3439.12. Application; prior provisions; construction

This chapter, and the other changes in the law made by Chapter 383 of the Statutes of 1986, apply only to transfers made or obligations incurred on or after January 1, 1987; and, as to transfers made or obligations incurred prior to that date, the law in effect at the time the transfer was made or the obligation was incurred shall apply. The provisions of this chapter, insofar as they are substantially the same as the provisions of Chapter 1 (commencing with Section 3439) of Title 2 of Part 2 of Division 4, which was repealed by Chapter 383 of the Statutes of 1986, shall be construed as restatements and continuations, and not as new enactments. *(Added by Stats.1987, c. 40, § 2, eff. June 8, 1987.)*

Research References

Rutter, Cal. Practice Guide: Enforcing Judgments/Debts Ch. 3-A, A. Evaluating the Claim.

Rutter, Cal. Practice Guide: Enforcing Judgments/Debts Ch. 4-A, A. Attachment.

Rutter, Cal. Practice Guide: Enforcing Judgments/Debts Ch. 5-B, B. Overview of Substantive Bankruptcy Law.

Rutter, Cal. Practice Guide: Enforcing Judgments/Debts Ch. 6A-13, Creating an Enforcement of Judgment Plan.

Miller and Starr California Real Estate § 11:70, Defects in the Record Title Enforceable Against a Bona Fide Purchaser--In General.

Miller and Starr California Real Estate § 1:58.10, Sufficiency of Consideration Under Uniform Fraudulent Conveyance Act.

8 Witkin Cal. Proc. 5th Enforcement of Judgment § 483, (S 483) Adoption of Act.

8 Witkin Cal. Proc. 5th Enforcement of Judgment § 488, (S 488) Adoption of Act.

CHAPTER 2. CONVEYANCE OF PERSONAL PROPERTY WITHOUT DELIVERY

Section

3440.   Transfers without delivery and actual and continued change of possession; invalidity; creditors.

Section

3440.1.   Exceptions; application of chapter.

3440.2.   Invalidity of transfer; exception.

3440.3.   Transfers satisfying specified provisions; invalidity.

3440.4.   Buyers purchasing transferred personal property from transferees or successors in interest; rights of buyers; effect of chapter.

3440.5.   Rights of secured party acquiring security interest from transferee or successor.

3440.6.   Actions; limitations.

3440.9.   Application of chapter to Commercial Code provisions.

Law Revision Commission Comments

A chapter heading is added to Sections 3440–3443 for organizational purposes. [16 Cal.L.Rev.Comm. Reports 501].

§ 3440. Transfers without delivery and actual and continued change of possession; invalidity; creditors

(a) Except as otherwise provided in this chapter, every transfer of personal property made by a person having at the time the possession of the property, and not accompanied by an immediate delivery followed by an actual and continued change of possession of the property, is void as against the transferor's creditors (secured or unsecured) at the time of the transfer and those who become creditors while the transferor remains in possession and the successors in interest of those creditors, and as against buyers from the transferor for value in good faith subsequent to the transfer.

(b) As used in this chapter, "creditor" means a person who has a claim, as defined in Section 3439.01, and includes an assignee of a general assignment for the benefit of creditors, as defined in Section 493.010 of the Code of Civil Procedure, of a debtor. "Creditor" also includes any person to whom the transferor's estate devolves in trust for the benefit of persons other than the transferor. Any such assignee or trustee may exercise any and all the rights and remedies specified in this chapter, if they are available to any one or more creditors of the assignor or transferor who are beneficiaries of the assignment or trust, and, in that event (1) only to the extent the rights or remedies are so available and (2) only for the benefit of those creditors whose rights are asserted by the assignee or trustee. *(Added by Stats.1951, c. 1687, p. 3884, § 2. Amended by Stats.1953, c. 1775, p. 3547, § 1; Stats.1959, c. 1794, p. 4274, § 1; Stats.1959, c. 1795, p. 4276, § 2; Stats.1963, c. 819, p. 2001, § 22, eff. Jan. 1, 1965; Stats.1967, c. 799, p. 2200, § 1; Stats.1982, c. 517, p. 2330, § 89; Stats.1985, c. 1368, § 1; Stats.1987, c. 40, § 3, eff. June 8, 1987.)*

Law Revision Commission Comments

Former Section 3440 is divided into several sections for organizational purposes. See Sections 3440–3443. The other changes in Sections 3440–3443 are technical. [16 Cal.L.Rev.Comm. Reports 501].

Research References

Rutter, Cal. Practice Guide: Enforcing Judgments/Debts Ch. 3-C, C. Prelawsuit Considerations.

Rutter, Cal. Practice Guide: Enforcing Judgments/Debts Ch. 5-D, D. Involuntary Bankruptcy.

Rutter, Cal. Practice Guide: Enforcing Judgments/Debts Ch. 3-C, Outline C.

8 Witkin Cal. Proc. 5th Enforcement of Judgment § 503, (S 503) Transfer of Personal Property Without Change of Possession.

4 Witkin, California Summary 10th Sales § 215, (S 215) Requirement of Immediate Change of Possession.

4 Witkin, California Summary 10th Sales § 216, (S 216) Exceptions.

4 Witkin, California Summary 10th Sales § 218, Insufficient Change.

4 Witkin, California Summary 10th Sales § 228, (S 228) Applicability of Fraudulent Transfer Act.

4 Witkin, California Summary 10th Secured Transactions in Personal Property § 3, Necessity of Delivery.

§ 3440.1. Exceptions; application of chapter

This chapter does not apply to any of the following:

(a) Things in action.

(b) Ships or cargoes if either are at sea or in a foreign port.

(c) The sale of accounts, chattel paper, payment intangibles, or promissory notes governed by the Uniform Commercial Code, security interests, and contracts of bottomry or respondentia.

(d) Wines or brandies in the wineries, distilleries, or wine cellars of the makers or owners of the wines or brandies, or other persons having possession, care, and control of the wines or brandies, and the pipes, casks, and tanks in which the wines or brandies are contained, if the transfers are made in writing and executed and acknowledged, and if the transfers are recorded in the book of official records in the office of the county recorder of the county in which the wines, brandies, pipes, casks, and tanks are situated.

(e) A transfer or assignment made for the benefit of creditors generally or by any assignee acting under an assignment for the benefit of creditors generally.

(f) Property exempt from enforcement of a money judgment.

(g) Standing timber.

(h) Subject to the limitations in Section 3440.3, a transfer of personal property if all of the following conditions are satisfied:

(1) Prior to the date of the intended transfer, the transferor or the transferee files a financing statement, with respect to the property transferred, authorized in an authenticated record by the transferor. The financing statement shall be filed in the office of the Secretary of State in accordance with Chapter 5 (commencing with Section 9501) of Division 9 of the Commercial Code, but may use the terms " transferor" in lieu of "debtor" and "transferee" in lieu of "secured party." The provisions of Chapter 5 (commencing with Section 9501) of Division 9 of the Commercial Code shall apply as appropriate to the financing statement.

(2) The transferor or the transferee publishes a notice of the intended transfer one time in a newspaper of general circulation published in the judicial district in which the personal property is located, if there is one, and if there is none in the judicial district, then in a newspaper of general circulation in the county embracing the judicial district. The publication shall be completed not less than 10 days before the date the transfer occurs. The notice shall contain the name and address of the transferor and transferee and a general statement of the character of the personal property intended to be transferred, and shall indicate the place where the personal property is located and a date on or after which the transfer is to be made.

(i) Personal property not located within this state at the time of the transfer or attachment of the lien if the provisions of this subdivision are not used for the purpose of evading this chapter.

(j) A transfer of property that (1) is subject to a statute or treaty of the United States or a statute of this state that provides for the registration of transfers of title or issuance of certificates of title and (2) is so far perfected under that statute or treaty that a bona fide purchaser cannot acquire an interest in the property transferred that is superior to the interest of the transferee.

(k) A transfer of personal property in connection with a transaction in which the property is immediately thereafter leased by the transferor from the transferee provided the transferee purchased the property for value and in good faith (subdivision (c) of Section 10308 of the Commercial Code).

(*l*) Transition property, as defined in Section 840 of the Public Utilities Code, or recovery property, as defined in Section 848 of the Public Utilities Code.

(m) A transfer of property by any governmental entity. *(Formerly § 3441, added by Stats.1982, c. 517, p. 2330, § 90. Renumbered § 3440.1 and amended by Stats.1985, c. 1368, § 6. Amended by Stats.1988, c. 1368, § 3, operative Jan. 1, 1990; Stats.1994, c. 668 (S.B.1405), § 3; Stats.1996, c. 854 (A.B.1890), § 3, eff. Sept. 24, 1996; Stats.1999, c. 991 (S.B.45), § 10, operative July 1, 2001; Stats.2004, c. 46 (S.B.772), § 3, eff. June 7, 2004; Stats.2005, c. 43 (A.B.238), § 1; Stats.2012, c. 60 (A.B.2667), § 1.)*

Research References

Rutter, Cal. Practice Guide: Enforcing Judgments/Debts Ch. 3-C, C. Prelawsuit Considerations.

8 Witkin Cal. Proc. 5th Enforcement of Judgment § 503, (S 503) Transfer of Personal Property Without Change of Possession.

4 Witkin, California Summary 10th Sales § 215, (S 215) Requirement of Immediate Change of Possession.

4 Witkin, California Summary 10th Sales § 216, (S 216) Exceptions.

4 Witkin, California Summary 10th Sales § 222, (S 222) Exceptions.

§ 3440.2. Invalidity of transfer; exception

Subject to Section 3440.3, a transfer of personal property shall not be void under Section 3440 as against a creditor of the transferor or as against a buyer from the transferor, if the creditor's or buyer's claim or right against the transferor arises after the date all of the requirements of subdivision (h) of Section 3440.1 have been met, other than the requirement that filing of the financing statement and publication of the notice referred to therein be completed prior to the transfer. *(Added by Stats.1985, c. 1368, § 2.)*

Research References

8 Witkin Cal. Proc. 5th Enforcement of Judgment § 503, (S 503) Transfer of Personal Property Without Change of Possession.

4 Witkin, California Summary 10th Sales § 216, (S 216) Exceptions.

§ 3440.3. Transfers satisfying specified provisions; invalidity

A transfer of personal property, as to which the conditions set forth in subdivision (h) of Section 3440.1, Section 3440.2, or subdivision (b) of Section 3440.5 are satisfied, shall, nevertheless, be void under Section 3440 as against a person who has purchased the personal property from the transferor and who is a "buyer in the ordinary course of business," as defined in paragraph (9) of subdivision (b) of Section 1201 of the Commercial Code. *(Added by Stats.1985, c. 1368, § 3. Amended by Stats.2006, c. 254 (S.B.1481), § 5.)*

Research References

Rutter, Cal. Practice Guide: Enforcing Judgments/Debts Ch. 3-C, C. Prelawsuit Considerations.

8 Witkin Cal. Proc. 5th Enforcement of Judgment § 503, (S 503) Transfer of Personal Property Without Change of Possession.

4 Witkin, California Summary 10th Sales § 215, (S 215) Requirement of Immediate Change of Possession.

4 Witkin, California Summary 10th Sales § 216, (S 216) Exceptions.

§ 3440.4. Buyers purchasing transferred personal property from transferees or successors in interest; rights of buyers; effect of chapter

This chapter does not affect the rights of a buyer for value in good faith who purchases the transferred personal property from the transferee or from a successor in interest of the transferee, provided the transferor is no longer in possession of the personal property at the time of the purchase by that buyer. *(Added by Stats.1985, c. 1368, § 4.)*

§ 3440.5. Rights of secured party acquiring security interest from transferee or successor

(a) This chapter does not affect the rights of a secured party who, for value and in good faith, acquires a security interest in the transferred personal property from the transferee, or from the transferee's successor in interest, if the transferor is no longer in possession of the personal property at the time the security interest attaches.

(b) Additionally, except as provided in Section 3440.3, this chapter does not affect the rights of a secured party who acquires a security interest from the transferee, or from the transferee's successor in interest, in the personal property, if all of the following conditions are satisfied:

(1) On or before the date the security agreement is executed, the intended debtor or secured party files a financing statement with respect to the property transferred, signed by the intended debtor. The financing statement shall be filed in the office of the Secretary of State in accordance with Chapter 5 (commencing with Section 9501) of Division 9 of the Commercial Code, but shall use the terms "transferor" in lieu of "debtor," "transferee" in lieu of "secured party," and "secured party" in lieu of "assignee of secured party." The provisions of Chapter 5 (commencing with Section 9501) of Division 9 of the Commercial Code shall apply as appropriate to such a statement. For the purpose of indexing, and in any certification of search, the Secretary of State may refer to any financing statement filed pursuant to this paragraph as a financing statement under the Commercial Code and may describe the transferor as a debtor and the transferee as a secured party.

Compliance with this paragraph shall, however, not perfect the security interest of the secured party. Perfection of such a security interest shall be governed by Division 9 (commencing with Section 9101) of the Commercial Code.

(2) The intended debtor or secured party publishes a notice of the transfer one time in a newspaper of general circulation published in the judicial district in which the personal property is located, if there is one, and if there is none in the judicial district, then in a newspaper of general circulation in the county embracing the judicial district. The publication shall be completed not less than 10 days before the date of execution by the intended debtor of the intended security agreement. The notice shall contain the names and addresses of the transferor and transferee and of the intended debtor and secured party, a general statement of the character of the personal property transferred and intended to be subject to the security interest, the location of the personal property, and the date on or after which the security agreement is to be executed by the intended debtor. *(Formerly § 3442, added by Stats.1982, c. 517, p. 2331, § 91. Renumbered § 3440.5 and amended by Stats.1985, c. 1368, § 9. Amended by Stats.1999, c. 991 (S.B.45), § 11, operative July 1, 2001; Stats.2000, c. 1003 (S.B.2002), § 2, operative July 1, 2001.)*

§ 3440.6. Actions; limitations

No action shall be brought or levy made under this chapter more than one year after the earliest of the following dates:

(a) The date the person bringing the action or making the levy should have discovered the transfer in the exercise of reasonable diligence.

(b) The date the person bringing the action or making the levy obtained actual knowledge of the transfer.

(c) The date the delivery of, and actual and continued change of possession of, the property transferred occurred.

(d) If the financing statement filed pursuant to subdivision (h) of Section 3440.1 has not lapsed, the date the filing and publication requirements of subdivision (h) of Section 3440.1 were met, other than the requirement that the filing of the financing statement and publication of the notice referred to therein be completed prior to the transfer. *(Added by Stats.1985, c. 1368, § 5.)*

§ 3440.9. Application of chapter to Commercial Code provisions

Subdivision (2) of Section 2402 and subdivision (a) of Section 10308 of the Commercial Code are not restricted by the provisions of this chapter. *(Formerly § 3443, added by Stats. 1982, c. 517, p. 2331, § 92. Renumbered § 3440.9 and amended by Stats.1985, c. 1368, § 10. Amended by Stats.1988, c. 1368, § 4, operative Jan. 1, 1990; Stats.1994, c. 668 (S.B.1405), § 4.)*

CHAPTER 3. UNDERTAKING IN FRAUDULENT TRANSFER ACTION

Section

§ 3445. Definitions

As used in this chapter:

(a) "Transfer" means "transfer" as defined in Section 3439.01.

(b) "Creditor" means "creditor" as defined in Section 3439.01.

(c) "Transferee" means the person to whom property was transferred or an obligation was incurred, or the successors or assigns of the person. *(Added by Stats.1982, c. 517, p. 2332, § 93. Amended by Stats.1986, c. 383, § 4.)*

Law Revision Commission Comments

Section 3445 is intended to simplify drafting. [16 Cal.L.Rev.Comm. Reports 501].

Research References

8 Witkin Cal. Proc. 5th Enforcement of Judgment § 502, Undertaking by Transferee.

§ 3446. Transferee; rights of disposition of property or obligation

(a) In an action by a creditor for relief against a transfer or obligation under Chapter 1 (commencing with Section 3439) of Title 2 of Part 2 of Division 4 on the ground that the transfer or obligation is fraudulent as to the creditor, the transferee may give an undertaking as provided in this chapter.

(b) If an undertaking is given as provided in this chapter, the transferee may sell, encumber, transfer, convey, mortgage, pledge, or otherwise dispose of the property or obligation, or a part thereof, and the purchaser, encumbrancer, transferee, mortgagee, grantee, or pledgee of the property or obligation takes, owns, holds, and possesses the property or obligation unaffected by the action and any judgment that is rendered in the action. *(Added by Stats.1982, c. 517, p. 2332, § 93. Amended by Stats.1986, c. 383, § 5.)*

Law Revision Commission Comments

Section 3446 continues the substance of former Code of Civil Procedure Section 676. [16 Cal.L.Rev.Comm. Reports 501].

Research References

Rutter, Cal. Practice Guide: Enforcing Judgments/Debts Ch. 3-C, C. Prelawsuit Considerations.
8 Witkin Cal. Proc. 5th Enforcement of Judgment § 502, Undertaking by Transferee.

§ 3447. Condition; payment to creditor

The undertaking shall be conditioned that, if it is determined in the action that the transfer or obligation was fraudulent as to the creditor, the transferee will pay to the creditor the lesser of the following amounts:

(a) The value of the property or obligation as estimated in the undertaking.

(b) The amount determined in the action to be due and owing to the creditor by the person who transferred the property or incurred the obligation. *(Added by Stats.1982, c. 517, p. 2332, § 93. Amended by Stats.1986, c. 383, § 6.)*

Law Revision Commission Comments

Section 3447 continues the substance of the third sentence of former Code of Civil Procedure Section 677. [16 Cal.L.Rev.Comm. Reports 501].

Research References

Rutter, Cal. Practice Guide: Enforcing Judgments/Debts Ch. 3-C, C. Prelawsuit Considerations.

§ 3448. Amount

The undertaking shall be in the lesser of the following amounts:

(a) Double the value of the property or obligation.

(b) Double the amount of the creditor's claim in the action. *(Added by Stats.1982, c. 517, p. 2332, § 93.)*

Law Revision Commission Comments

Section 3448 continues the substance of a portion of the first sentence of former Code of Civil Procedure Section 677. [16 Cal.L.Rev.Comm. Reports 501].

Research References

Rutter, Cal. Practice Guide: Enforcing Judgments/Debts Ch. 3-C, C. Prelawsuit Considerations.
8 Witkin Cal. Proc. 5th Enforcement of Judgment § 502, Undertaking by Transferee.
1 Witkin Cal. Summ. 10th Contracts § 710, (S 710) in General.

§ 3449. Effective date of undertaking

The undertaking becomes effective 10 days after service of the undertaking on the creditor. *(Added by Stats.1982, c. 517, p. 2332, § 93.)*

Law Revision Commission Comments

Section 3449 continues the substance of the first portion of former Code of Civil Procedure Section 680. For additional provisions governing the effective time of the undertaking, see Code of Civil Procedure Section 995.420 (time undertaking becomes effective). [16 Cal.L.Rev.Comm. Reports 501].

Research References

Rutter, Cal. Practice Guide: Enforcing Judgments/Debts Ch. 3-C, C. Prelawsuit Considerations.
8 Witkin Cal. Proc. 5th Enforcement of Judgment § 502, Undertaking by Transferee.

Part 3

NUISANCE

Title 1

GENERAL PRINCIPLES

§ 3479. Nuisance; what constitutes

Anything which is injurious to health, including, but not limited to, the illegal sale of controlled substances, or is indecent or offensive to the senses, or an obstruction to the free use of property, so as to interfere with the comfortable enjoyment of life or property, or unlawfully obstructs the free passage or use, in the customary manner, of any navigable lake, or river, bay, stream, canal, or basin, or any public park, square, street, or highway, is a nuisance. *(Enacted in 1872. Amended by Code Am.1873–74, c. 612, p. 268, § 284; Stats.1996, c. 658 (A.B.2970), § 1.)*

Research References

Rutter, Cal. Practice Guide: Insurance Litigation Ch. 7H-B, B. Underlying Claims-Theories of Liability.

Rutter, Cal. Practice Guide: Real Prop. Transactions Ch. 5-D, D. Common Law Environmental Hazards Liability.

Miller and Starr California Real Estate § 14:2, in General; Nature and Extent.

Miller and Starr California Real Estate § 22:2, "Nuisance" Defined and Compared With Other Causes of Action.

Miller and Starr California Real Estate § 22:3, Nuisance Per Se.

Miller and Starr California Real Estate § 22:5, Public or Private Nuisance.

Miller and Starr California Real Estate § 22:8, Conditions Dangerous to Health and Safety; Noise and Emissions.

Miller and Starr California Real Estate § 22:9, Sale of Alcohol or Drugs.

Miller and Starr California Real Estate § 17:28, Airspace.

Miller and Starr California Real Estate § 22:10, Indecent or Offensive Acts.

Miller and Starr California Real Estate § 22:28, Actions by Public Entities.

Miller and Starr California Real Estate § 22:47, Liability to Persons Injured Due to Dangerous Conditions Off the Premises.

Miller and Starr California Real Estate § 23:68, Nuisance.

Miller and Starr California Real Estate § 19:200, Termination for Cause or Default.

19 NO. 2 Miller & Starr, California Real Estate Newsalert 24, Subdivisions, Land Use Planning, and Approvals.

22 NO. 5 Miller & Starr, California Real Estate Newsalert 15, Landowners' Liability.

22 NO. 6 Miller & Starr, California Real Estate Newsalert 19, Landowners' Liability.

3 Witkin Cal. Proc. 5th Actions § 237, (S 237) Tort Claims.

5 Witkin, California Summary 10th Torts § 224, (S 224) Liability Under Statutes and Constitution.

5 Witkin, California Summary 10th Torts § 229, (S 229) Tort Claims Act Immunities Extend to Liabilities Imposed by Other Statutes.

5 Witkin, California Summary 10th Torts § 339, (S 339) Nuisances.

7 Witkin, California Summary 10th Constitutional Law § 455, Civil Proceedings Against Obscene Matter.

13 Witkin, California Summary 10th Equity § 73, Exception: Public Nuisance.

13 Witkin, California Summary 10th Equity § 133, (S 133) Statutory Framework.

13 Witkin, California Summary 10th Equity § 144, (S 144) Exhibition of Obscene Matter.

§ 3480. Public nuisance

A public nuisance is one which affects at the same time an entire community or neighborhood, or any considerable number of persons, although the extent of the annoyance or damage inflicted upon individuals may be unequal. *(Enacted in 1872. Amended by Code Am.1873–74, c. 612, p. 268, § 285.)*

Research References

Rutter, Cal. Practice Guide: Real Prop. Transactions Ch. 5-D, D. Common Law Environmental Hazards Liability.

Miller and Starr California Real Estate § 22:5, Public or Private Nuisance.

19 NO. 3 Miller & Starr, California Real Estate Newsalert 1, The Solar Shade Control Act- from Trees Versus Solar to Trees and Solar?

22 NO. 5 Miller & Starr, California Real Estate Newsalert 15, Landowners' Liability.

6 Witkin Cal. Proc. 5th Provisional Remedies § 335, Crime that is Enjoinable Tort.

7 Witkin, California Summary 10th Constitutional Law § 455, Civil Proceedings Against Obscene Matter.

13 Witkin, California Summary 10th Equity § 73, Exception: Public Nuisance.

13 Witkin, California Summary 10th Equity § 133, (S 133) Statutory Framework.

13 Witkin, California Summary 10th Equity § 135, (S 135) Public and Private Nuisances.

13 Witkin, California Summary 10th Equity § 144, (S 144) Exhibition of Obscene Matter.

§ 3481. Private nuisance

Every nuisance not included in the definition of the last section is private. *(Enacted in 1872.)*

Research References

Rutter, Cal. Practice Guide: Real Prop. Transactions Ch. 5-D, D. Common Law Environmental Hazards Liability.

Miller and Starr California Real Estate § 22:5, Public or Private Nuisance.

Miller and Starr California Real Estate § 14:38, Rights to Protection and Siting of Solar Energy Facilities.

13 Witkin, California Summary 10th Equity § 133, (S 133) Statutory Framework.

13 Witkin, California Summary 10th Equity § 135, (S 135) Public and Private Nuisances.

§ 3482. Acts under statutory authority not a nuisance

Nothing which is done or maintained under the express authority of a statute can be deemed a nuisance. *(Enacted in 1872.)*

Research References

Rutter, Cal. Practice Guide: Real Prop. Transactions Ch. 5-D, D. Common Law Environmental Hazards Liability.

Miller and Starr California Real Estate § 17:28, Airspace.

Miller and Starr California Real Estate § 22:12, Obstruction of Light and Air.

Miller and Starr California Real Estate § 22:18, Governmental Agencies.

Miller and Starr California Real Estate § 22:22, Measure of Damages.

Miller and Starr California Real Estate § 22:37, Acts Permitted by Statute.

13 NO. 3 Miller & Starr, California Real Estate Newsalert 11, Hazardous Substances.

18 NO. 1 Miller & Starr, California Real Estate Newsalert 17, Inverse Condemnation.

19 NO. 2 Miller & Starr, California Real Estate Newsalert 18, Landlord and Tenant.

21 NO. 1 Miller & Starr, California Real Estate Newsalert 19, Landowners' Liability.

21 NO. 4 Miller & Starr, California Real Estate Newsalert 35, Landowners' Liability.

22 NO. 5 Miller & Starr, California Real Estate Newsalert 15, Landowners' Liability.

13 Witkin, California Summary 10th Equity § 133, (S 133) Statutory Framework.

13 Witkin, California Summary 10th Equity § 160, in General.

13 Witkin, California Summary 10th Equity § 161, Illustrations: No Express Authority.

§ 3482.1. Operation or use of sport shooting ranges; civil liability or criminal prosecution; noise or noise pollution nuisance

(a) As used in this section:

(1) "Person" means an individual, proprietorship, partnership, corporation, club, or other legal entity.

(2) "Sport shooting range" or "range" means an area designed and operated for the use of rifles, shotguns, pistols, silhouettes, skeet, trap, black powder, or any other similar sport or law enforcement training purpose.

(3) "Indoor shooting range" means a totally enclosed facility designed to offer a totally controlled shooting environment that includes impenetrable walls, floor and ceiling, adequate ventilation and lighting systems, and acoustical treatment for sound attenuation suitable for the range's approved use.

(4) "Nighttime" means between the hours of 10 p.m. and 7 a.m.

(b)(1) Except as provided in subdivision (f), a person who operates or uses a sport shooting range in this state shall not be subject to civil liability or criminal prosecution in any matter relating to noise or noise pollution resulting from the operation or use of the range if the range is in compliance with any noise control laws or ordinances that applied to the range and its operation at the time construction or operation of the range was approved by a local public entity having jurisdiction in the matter, or if there were no such laws or ordinances that applied to the range and its operation at that time.

(2) Except as provided in subdivision (f), a person who operates or uses a sport shooting range or law enforcement training range is not subject to an action for nuisance, and a court shall not enjoin the use or operation of a range, on the basis of noise or noise pollution if the range is in compliance with any noise control laws or ordinances that applied to the range and its operation at the time construction or operation of the range was approved by a local public entity having jurisdiction in the matter, or if there were no such laws or ordinances that applied to the range and its operation at that time.

(3) Rules or regulations adopted by any state department or agency for limiting levels of noise in terms of decibel level which may occur in the outdoor atmosphere shall not apply to a sport shooting range exempted from liability under this section.

(c) A person who acquires title to or who owns real property adversely affected by the use of property with a permanently located and improved sport shooting range may not maintain a nuisance action with respect to noise or noise pollution against the person who owns the range to restrain, enjoin, or impede the use of the range where there has been no substantial change in the nature or use of the range. This section does not prohibit actions for negligence or recklessness in the operation of the range or by a person using the range.

(d) A sport shooting range that is in operation and not in violation of existing law at the time of the enactment of an ordinance described in subdivision (b) shall be permitted to continue in operation even if the operation of the sport shooting range at a later date does not conform to a new ordinance or an amendment to an existing ordinance if there has been no substantial change in the nature or use of the range. Nothing in this section shall be construed to limit the authority of a local agency to enforce any term of a conditional use permit.

(e) Except as otherwise provided in this section, this section does not prohibit a local public entity having jurisdiction in the matter from regulating the location and construction of a sport shooting range after the effective date of this section.

(f) This section does not prohibit a local public entity having jurisdiction in the matter from requiring that noise levels at the nearest residential property line to a range not exceed the level of normal city street noise which shall not be more than 60 decibels for nighttime shooting. The subdivision does not abrogate any existing local standards for nighttime shooting. The operator of a sport shooting range shall not unreasonably refuse to use trees, shrubs, or barriers, when appropriate, to mitigate the noise generated by nighttime shooting. For the purpose of this section, a reasonable effort to mitigate is an action that can be accomplished in a manner and at a cost that does not impose an unreasonable financial burden upon the operator of the range.

(g) This section does not apply to indoor shooting ranges.

(h) This section does not apply to a range in existence prior to January 1, 1998, that is operated for law enforcement training purposes by a county of the sixth class if the range is located without the boundaries of that county and within the boundaries of another county. This subdivision shall become operative on July 1, 1999. *(Added by Stats.1997, c. 880 (S.B.517), § 1. Amended by Stats.1998, c. 141 (S.B.1620), § 1, eff. July 13, 1998.)*

Research References

13 Witkin, California Summary 10th Equity § 162, Properly Conducted Shooting Range.

§ 3482.5. Agricultural activity not a nuisance; exceptions; construction with other laws

(a)(1) No agricultural activity, operation, or facility, or appurtenances thereof, conducted or maintained for commercial purposes, and in a manner consistent with proper and accepted customs and standards, as established and followed by similar agricultural operations in the same locality, shall be or become a nuisance, private or public, due to any changed condition in or about the locality, after it has been in operation for more than three years if it was not a nuisance at the time it began.

(2) No activity of a district agricultural association that is operated in compliance with Division 3 (commencing with Section 3001) of the Food and Agricultural Code, shall be or become a private or public nuisance due to any changed condition in or about the locality, after it has been in operation for more than three years if it was not a nuisance at the time it began. This paragraph shall not apply to any activities of the 52nd District Agricultural Association that are conducted on the grounds of the California Exposition and State Fair, nor to any public nuisance action brought by a city, county, or city and county alleging that the activities, operations, or conditions of a district agricultural association have substantially changed after more than three years from the time that the activities, operations, or conditions began.

(b) Paragraph (1) of subdivision (a) shall not apply if the agricultural activity, operation, or facility, or appurtenances thereof obstruct the free passage or use, in the customary manner, of any navigable lake, river, bay, stream, canal, or basin, or any public park, square, street, or highway.

(c) Paragraph (1) of subdivision (a) shall not invalidate any provision contained in the Health and Safety Code, Fish and Game Code, Food and Agricultural Code, or Division 7 (commencing with Section 13000) of the Water Code, if the agricultural activity, operation, or facility, or appurtenances thereof constitute a nuisance, public or private, as specifically defined or described in any of those provisions.

(d) This section shall prevail over any contrary provision of any ordinance or regulation of any city, county, city and county, or other political subdivision of the state. However, nothing in this section shall preclude a city, county, city and county, or other political subdivision of this state, acting within its constitutional or statutory authority and not in conflict with other provisions of state law, from adopting an ordinance that allows notification to a prospective homeowner that the dwelling is in close proximity to an agricultural activity, operation, facility, or appurtenances thereof and is subject to the provisions of this section consistent with Section 1102.6a.

(e) For purposes of this section, the term "agricultural activity, operation, or facility, or appurtenances thereof" shall include, but not be limited to, the cultivation and tillage of the soil, dairying, the production, cultivation, growing, and harvesting of any agricultural commodity including timber, viticulture, apiculture, or horticulture, the raising of livestock, fur bearing animals, fish, or poultry, and any practices performed by a farmer or on a farm as incident to or in conjunction with those farming operations, including preparation for market, delivery to storage or to market, or delivery to carriers for transportation to market. *(Added by Stats.1981, c. 545, p. 2192, § 1. Amended by*

Stats.1991, c. 828 (S.B.1093), § 1; Stats.1992, c. 97 (A.B.1190), § 1.)

Research References

Miller and Starr California Real Estate § 1:144, Duty of Seller of Real Property to Disclose--Statutory Duty of Disclosure.
Miller and Starr California Real Estate § 14:15, Flood Waters.
Miller and Starr California Real Estate § 22:33, in General; Coming to the Nuisance.
Miller and Starr California Real Estate § 25C:17, Notice of Intention; Requirements.
13 Witkin, California Summary 10th Equity § 163, Properly Conducted Agricultural Enterprise.

§ 3482.6. Agricultural processing activity not a nuisance; increase in activity; construction with other laws

(a) No agricultural processing activity, operation, facility, or appurtenances thereof, conducted or maintained for commercial purposes, and in a manner consistent with proper and accepted customs and standards, shall be or become a nuisance, private or public, due to any changed condition in or about the locality, after it has been in continuous operation for more than three years if it was not a nuisance at the time it began.

(b) If an agricultural processing activity, operation, facility, or appurtenances thereof substantially increases its activities or operations after January 1, 1993, then a public or private nuisance action may be brought with respect to those increases in activities or operations that have a significant effect on the environment. For increases in activities or operations that have been in effect more than three years, there is a rebuttable presumption affecting the burden of producing evidence that the increase was not substantial.

(c) This section does not supersede any other provision of law, except other provisions of this part, if the agricultural processing activity, operation, facility, or appurtenances thereof, constitute a nuisance, public or private, as specifically defined or described in the provision.

(d) This section prevails over any contrary provision of any ordinance or regulation of any city, county, city and county, or other political subdivision of the state, except regulations adopted pursuant to Section 41700 of the Health and Safety Code as applied to agricultural processing activities, operations, facilities, or appurtenances thereof that are surrounded by housing or commercial development on January 1, 1993. However, nothing in this section precludes a city, county, city and county, or other political subdivision of this state, acting within its constitutional or statutory authority and not in conflict with other provisions of state law, from adopting an ordinance that allows notification to a prospective homeowner that the dwelling is in close proximity to an agricultural processing activity, operation, facility, or appurtenances thereof and is subject to provisions of this section consistent with Section 1102.6a.

(e) For the purposes of this section, the following definitions apply:

(1) "Agricultural processing activity, operation, facility, or appurtenances thereof" includes, but is not limited to rendering plants licensed pursuant to Section 19300 of the Food and Agricultural Code and collection centers licensed pursuant to Section 19300.5 of the Food and Agricultural Code, the canning or freezing of agricultural products, the processing of dairy products, the production and bottling of beer and wine, the processing of meat and egg products, the drying of fruits and grains, the packing and cooling of fruits and vegetables, and the storage or warehousing of any agricultural products, and includes processing for wholesale or retail markets of agricultural products.

(2) "Continuous operation" means at least 30 days of agricultural processing operations per year.

(3) "Proper and accepted customs and standards" means the compliance with all applicable state and federal statutes and regulations governing the operation of the agricultural processing activity, operation, facility, or appurtenances thereof with respect to the condition or effect alleged to be a nuisance.

(f) This section does not apply to any litigation pending or cause of action accruing prior to January 1, 1993. *(Added by Stats.1992, c. 97 (A.B.1190), § 2. Amended by Stats.1993, c. 99 (A.B.258), § 1; Stats.1994, c. 146 (A.B.3601), § 17; Stats.1999, c. 329 (S.B.1274), § 1.)*

Research References

Miller and Starr California Real Estate § 22:33, in General; Coming to the Nuisance.
Miller and Starr California Real Estate § 30:10, Interference by Low-Flying Aircraft.
13 Witkin, California Summary 10th Equity § 163, Properly Conducted Agricultural Enterprise.

§ 3482.8. Use of building or property for dogfighting or cockfighting; public nuisance

Any building or property used for the purpose of willfully conducting dogfighting in violation of Section 597.5 of the Penal Code or cockfighting in violation of subdivision (b) of Section 597b of the Penal Code is a public nuisance. *(Added by Stats.2011, c. 128 (S.B.426), § 1.)*

Research References

Miller and Starr California Real Estate § 22:17, Landlord and Tenant.
Miller and Starr California Real Estate § 19:200, Termination for Cause or Default.
22 NO. 4 Miller & Starr, California Real Estate Newsalert 15, Landlord and Tenant.
5 Witkin Cal. Proc. 5th Pleading § 644, Lessee's Default or Breach.
12 Witkin, California Summary 10th Real Property § 674, (S 674) Illegal Use of Premises.
13 Witkin, California Summary 10th Equity § 150, Other Statutes.

§ 3483. Continuing nuisance; liability of successive owners for failure to abate

Every successive owner of property who neglects to abate a continuing nuisance upon, or in the use of, such property, created by a former owner, is liable therefor in the same manner as the one who first created it. *(Enacted in 1872.)*

Research References

Rutter, Cal. Practice Guide: Real Prop. Transactions Ch. 5-D, D. Common Law Environmental Hazards Liability.
Rutter, Cal. Practice Guide: Real Prop. Transactions Form 6:I, Deed of Trust (Complex).
Rutter, Cal. Practice Guide: Real Prop. Transactions Ch. 5-D Outline, Outline D.
Miller and Starr California Real Estate § 22:16, Successors in Interest.
Miller and Starr California Real Estate § 23:68, Nuisance.

§ 3484. Damages recoverable notwithstanding abatement

The abatement of a nuisance does not prejudice the right of any person to recover damages for its past existence. *(Enacted in 1872.)*

Research References

Miller and Starr California Real Estate § 22:21, Damages; Continuing Versus Permanent Nuisance.

§ 3486. Illegal conduct involving controlled substance purpose; unlawful detainer action by city prosecutor or city attorney to abate nuisance; notice; waiver of testimony costs; information provided to California Research Bureau

Section operative Jan. 1, 2014, contingent upon specified reporting requirements.

(a) To abate the nuisance caused by illegal conduct involving a controlled substance purpose on real property, the city prosecutor or city attorney may file, in the name of the people, an action for unlawful detainer against any person who is in violation of the nuisance or illegal purpose provisions of subdivision 4 of Section 1161 of the Code of Civil Procedure, with respect to that controlled substance purpose. In filing this action, which shall be based upon an arrest report or other report by a law enforcement agency, reporting an offense committed on the property and documented by the observations of a police officer, the city prosecutor or city attorney shall use the procedures set forth in Chapter 4 (commencing with Section 1159) of Title 3 of Part 3 of the Code of Civil Procedure, except that in cases filed under this section, the following also shall apply:

(1)(A) Prior to filing an action pursuant to this section, the city prosecutor or city attorney shall give 30 calendar days' written notice to the owner, requiring the owner to file an action for the removal of the person who is in violation of the nuisance or illegal purpose provisions of subdivision 4 of Section 1161 of the Code of Civil Procedure with respect to a controlled substance purpose.

(B) This notice shall include sufficient documentation establishing a violation of the nuisance or illegal purpose provisions of subdivision 4 of Section 1161 of the Code of Civil Procedure and an advisement to the owner of the assignment provision contained in subparagraph (D). The notice shall be served upon the owner and the tenant in accordance with subdivision (e).

(C) The notice to the tenant shall, in at least 14–point bold type, meet the following requirements:

(i) The notice shall contain the following language:

"(Date)

(Name of tenant)

(Address of tenant)

Re: Civil Code Section 3486

Dear (name of tenant):

This letter is to inform you that an eviction action may soon be filed in court against you for suspected drug activity. According to state law, Civil Code Section 3486 provides for eviction of persons engaging in such conduct, as described below.

(Name of police department) records indicate that you, (name of arrestee), were arrested on (date) for violations of (list violations) on (address of property).

A letter has been sent to the property owner(s) advising of your arrest and the requirements of state law, as well as the landlord's option to assign the unlawful detainer action to the (name of city attorney or prosecutor's office).

A list of legal assistance providers is provided below. Please note, this list is not exclusive and is provided for your information only; the (name of city attorney or prosecutor's office) does not endorse or recommend any of the listed agencies.

Sincerely,

(Name of deputy city attorney or city prosecutor)

Deputy City (Attorney or Prosecutor)

Notice to Tenant: This notice is not a notice of eviction. You should call (name of the city attorney or prosecutor pursuing the action) at (telephone number) or a legal assistance provider to stop the eviction action if any of the following is applicable:

(1) You are not the person named in this notice.

(2) The person named in the notice does not live with you.

(3) The person named in the notice has permanently moved.

(4) You do not know the person named in the notice.

(5) You want to request that only the person involved in the nuisance be evicted, allowing the other residents to stay.

(6) You have any other legal defense or legal reason to stop the eviction action.

A list of legal assistance providers is attached to this notice. Some provide free legal assistance if you are eligible."

(ii) The notice shall be provided to the tenant in English and, as translated, in all of the languages identified in subdivision (a) of Section 1632 of the Civil Code.

(D) The owner shall, within 30 calendar days of the mailing of the written notice, either provide the city prosecutor or city attorney with all relevant information pertaining to the unlawful detainer case, or provide a written explanation setting forth any safety-related reasons for noncompliance, and an assignment to the city prosecutor or city attorney of the right to bring an unlawful detainer action against the tenant.

(E) The assignment shall be on a form provided by the city prosecutor or city attorney and may contain a provision for costs of investigation, discovery, and reasonable attorney's fees, in an amount not to exceed six hundred dollars ($600).

(F) If the city prosecutor or city attorney accepts the assignment of the right of the owner to bring the unlawful detainer action, the owner shall retain all other rights and duties, including the handling of the tenant's personal property, following issuance of the writ of possession and its delivery to and execution by the appropriate agency.

(2) Upon the failure of the owner to file an action pursuant to this section, or to respond to the city prosecutor or city attorney as provided in paragraph (1), or having filed an action, if the owner fails to prosecute it diligently and in good faith, the city prosecutor or city attorney may file and prosecute the action, and join the owner as a defendant in the action. This action shall have precedence over any similar proceeding thereafter brought by the owner, or to one previously brought by the owner and not prosecuted diligently and in good faith. Service of the summons and complaint upon the defendant owner shall be in accordance with Sections 415.10, 415.20, 415.30, 415.40, and 415.50 of the Code of Civil Procedure.

(3) If a jury or court finds the defendant tenant guilty of unlawful detainer in a case filed pursuant to paragraph (2), the city prosecutor or city attorney may be awarded costs, including the costs of investigation and discovery and reasonable attorney's fees. These costs shall be assessed against the defendant owner, to whom notice was directed pursuant to paragraph (1), and once an abstract of judgment is recorded, it shall constitute a lien on the subject real property.

(4) Nothing in this section shall prevent a local governing body from adopting and enforcing laws, consistent with this article, relating to drug abatement. Where local laws duplicate or supplement this section, this section shall be construed as providing alternative remedies and not preempting the field.

(5) Nothing in this section shall prevent a tenant from receiving relief against a forfeiture of a lease pursuant to Section 1179 of the Code of Civil Procedure.

(b) In any proceeding brought under this section, the court may, upon a showing of good cause, issue a partial eviction ordering the removal of any person, including, but not limited to, members of the tenant's household if the court finds that the person has engaged in the activities described in subdivision (a). Persons removed pursuant to this section may be permanently barred from returning to or reentering any portion of the entire premises. The court may further order as an express condition of the tenancy that the remaining tenants shall not give permission to or invite any person who has been removed pursuant to this subdivision to return to or reenter any portion of the entire premises.

(c) For the purposes of this section, "controlled substance purpose" means the manufacture, cultivation, importation into the state, transportation, possession, possession for sale, sale, furnishing, administering, or giving away, or providing a place to use or fortification of a place involving, cocaine, phencyclidine, heroin, methamphetamine, or any other controlled substance, in a violation of subdivision (a) of Section 11350, Section 11351, 11351.5, 11352, or 11359, subdivision (a) of Section 11360, or Section 11366, 11366.6, 11377, 11378, 11378.5, 11379, 11379.5, 11379.6, or 11383 of the Health and Safety Code.

(d) Notwithstanding subdivision (b) of Section 68097.2 of the Government Code, a public entity may waive all or part of the costs incurred in furnishing the testimony of a peace officer in an unlawful detainer action brought pursuant to this section.

(e) The notice and documentation described in paragraph (1) of subdivision (a) shall be given in writing and may be given either by personal delivery or by deposit in the United States mail in a sealed envelope, postage prepaid, addressed to the owner at the address known to the public entity giving the notice, or as shown on the last equalized assessment roll, if not known. Separate notice of not less than 30 calendar days and documentation shall be provided to the tenant in accordance with this subdivision. Service by mail shall be deemed to be completed at the time of deposit in the United States mail. Proof of giving the notice may be made by a declaration signed under penalty of perjury by any employee of the public entity which shows service in conformity with this section.

(f) This section shall apply only in the County of Los Angeles to any court having jurisdiction over unlawful detainer cases involving real property situated in the City of Los Angeles.

(g) This section shall become operative on January 1, 2014, only if the City of Los Angeles has regularly reported to the California Research Bureau as required by this section, as it read during the period from January 1, 2010, to January 1, 2014, inclusive. For purposes of this section, the City of Los Angeles shall be deemed to have complied with this reporting requirement if the 2013 report to the Legislature by the California Research Bureau indicates that the City of Los Angeles has regularly reported to the bureau. *(Added by Stats.2009, c. 244 (A.B.530), § 3, operative contingent.)*

Research References

Miller and Starr California Real Estate § 19:218, Required Relationship of the Parties.
5 Witkin Cal. Proc. 5th Pleading § 644, Lessee's Default or Breach.
13 Witkin, California Summary 10th Equity § 150, Other Statutes.

Title 2

PUBLIC NUISANCES

§ 3490. Lapse of time cannot legalize public nuisance

No lapse of time can legalize a public nuisance, amounting to an actual obstruction of public right. *(Enacted in 1872.)*

Research References

Miller and Starr California Real Estate § 22:5, Public or Private Nuisance.
Miller and Starr California Real Estate § 22:38, Lapse of Time for Injunction; Public Nuisances.
Miller and Starr California Real Estate § 22:39, Lapse of Time for Injunction; Private Nuisances.
19 NO. 2 Miller & Starr, California Real Estate Newsalert 18, Landlord and Tenant.
3 Witkin Cal. Proc. 5th Actions § 489, Express Statutory Provisions.
13 Witkin, California Summary 10th Equity § 135, (S 135) Public and Private Nuisances.

§ 3491. Remedies; public

The remedies against a public nuisance are:

1. Indictment or information;

2. A civil action; or,

3. Abatement. *(Enacted in 1872. Amended by Code Am.1880, c. 11, p. 1, § 1.)*

Research References

Rutter, Cal. Practice Guide: Civ. Pro. Before Trial Ch. 9(II)-A, A. Injunctions.
Miller and Starr California Real Estate § 31:7, Management.
Miller and Starr California Real Estate § 22:28, Actions by Public Entities.
13 Witkin, California Summary 10th Equity § 73, Exception: Public Nuisance.
13 Witkin, California Summary 10th Equity § 133, (S 133) Statutory Framework.
13 Witkin, California Summary 10th Equity § 157, Criminal Proceedings.

§ 3492. Remedies; indictment or information; regulation

The remedy by indictment or information is regulated by the Penal Code. *(Enacted in 1872. Amended by Code Am.1880, c. 11, p. 1, § 2.)*

§ 3493. Remedies; private person

A private person may maintain an action for a public nuisance, if it is specially injurious to himself, but not otherwise. *(Enacted in 1872.)*

Research References

Rutter, Cal. Practice Guide: Real Prop. Transactions Ch. 5-D, D. Common Law Environmental Hazards Liability.
Miller and Starr California Real Estate § 22:5, Public or Private Nuisance.
Miller and Starr California Real Estate § 15:10, Easements for Light, Air, or View.
Miller and Starr California Real Estate § 22:12, Obstruction of Light and Air.
Miller and Starr California Real Estate § 22:26, Damages; Attorney's Fees.
Miller and Starr California Real Estate § 22:27, Actions by Private Persons for Public Nuisance.
19 NO. 4 Miller & Starr, California Real Estate Newsalert 45, Landowners' Liability.
13 Witkin, California Summary 10th Equity § 158, No Private Remedy.

§ 3494. Abatement; parties authorized

A public nuisance may be abated by any public body or officer authorized thereto by law. *(Enacted in 1872.)*

Research References

Miller and Starr California Real Estate § 22:28, Actions by Public Entities.
Miller and Starr California Real Estate § 22:31, Summary Abatement.

7 Witkin Cal. Proc. 5th Judgment § 95, (S 95) Prevailing Party in Specified Actions.

§ 3495. Abatement; private person; method

Any person may abate a public nuisance which is specially injurious to him by removing, or, if necessary, destroying the thing which constitutes the same, without committing a breach of the peace, or doing unnecessary injury. *(Enacted in 1872.)*

Research References

Miller and Starr California Real Estate § 22:27, Actions by Private Persons for Public Nuisance.
13 Witkin, California Summary 10th Equity § 158, No Private Remedy.

§ 3496. Award of costs and attorney fees; cases where authorized

In any of the following described cases, the court may award costs, including the costs of investigation and discovery, and reasonable attorney's fees, which are not compensated for pursuant to some other provision of law, to the prevailing party:

(a) In any case in which a governmental agency seeks to enjoin the sale, distribution, or public exhibition, for commercial consideration, of obscene matter, as defined in Section 311 of the Penal Code.

(b) In any case in which a governmental agency seeks to enjoin the use of a building or place for the purpose of illegal gambling, lewdness, assignation, human trafficking, or prostitution; or any case in which a governmental agency seeks to enjoin acts of illegal gambling, lewdness, assignation, human trafficking, or prostitution in or upon a building or place, as authorized in Article 2 (commencing with Section 11225) of Chapter 3 of Title 1 of Part 4 of the Penal Code.

(c) In any case in which a governmental agency seeks to enjoin the use of a building or place, or seeks to enjoin in or upon any building or place the unlawful sale, manufacture, service, storage, or keeping or giving away of any controlled substance, as authorized in Article 3 (commencing with Section 11570) of Chapter 10 of Division 10 of the Health and Safety Code.

(d) In any case in which a governmental agency seeks to enjoin the unlawful sale, service, storage, or keeping or giving away of alcoholic liquor, as authorized in Article 1 (commencing with Section 11200) of Chapter 3 of Title 1 of Part 4 of the Penal Code. *(Added by Stats.1982, c. 1267, p. 4671, § 1. Amended by Stats.1983, c. 1178, p. 4671, § 1; Stats.1987, c. 1076, § 1; Stats.2012, c. 254 (A.B.2212), § 1.)*

Research References

Rutter, Cal. Practice Guide: Civil Trials & Evidence Ch. 17-E, E. Attorney Fees as Costs.
Miller and Starr California Real Estate § 22:11, Indecent or Offensive Acts--Adult Entertainment; First Amendment Protection.
Miller and Starr California Real Estate § 22:26, Damages; Attorney's Fees.
Miller and Starr California Real Estate § 22:27, Actions by Private Persons for Public Nuisance.
Miller and Starr California Real Estate § 22:28, Actions by Public Entities.
Miller and Starr California Real Estate § 22:32, Recovery of Abatement Costs.
Miller and Starr California Real Estate § 34:66, Examples of Actions in Which Fees Can be Recovered.
Miller and Starr California Real Estate § 34:67, Examples of Actions in Which Fees Cannot be Recovered.
21 NO. 4 Miller & Starr, California Real Estate Newsalert 35, Landowners' Liability.
7 Witkin Cal. Proc. 5th Judgment § 224, (S 224) Consumer Protection Actions.
7 Witkin Cal. Proc. 5th Judgment § 311, in General.
7 Witkin Cal. Proc. 5th Judgment § 312, Use of Lodestar Approach.

13 Witkin, California Summary 10th Equity § 149, (S 149) Decision and Order.

Title 3

PRIVATE NUISANCES

Section
3501. Remedies.
3502. Abatement; method.
3503. Abatement; notice.

§ 3501. Remedies

The remedies against a private nuisance are:

1. A civil action; or,

2. Abatement. *(Enacted in 1872.)*

Research References

Miller and Starr California Real Estate § 22:19, Alternative Remedies.
13 Witkin, California Summary 10th Equity § 133, (S 133) Statutory Framework.
13 Witkin, California Summary 10th Equity § 153, (S 153) Against Private Nuisance.

§ 3502. Abatement; method

A person injured by a private nuisance may abate it by removing, or, if necessary, destroying the thing which constitutes the nuisance, without committing a breach of the peace, or doing unnecessary injury. *(Enacted in 1872.)*

Research References

Miller and Starr California Real Estate § 22:19, Alternative Remedies.
13 Witkin, California Summary 10th Equity § 158, No Private Remedy.

§ 3503. Abatement; notice

Where a private nuisance results from a mere omission of the wrongdoer, and cannot be abated without entering upon his land, reasonable notice must be given to him before entering to abate it. *(Enacted in 1872.)*

Research References

Miller and Starr California Real Estate § 22:19, Alternative Remedies.
5 Witkin, California Summary 10th Torts § 697, Other Privileged Entries.

Title 4

MOTION PICTURES

Section
3504. Definitions.
3505. Exhibition of intentional killing or cruelty; nuisance.
3506. Commencement of actions; proper showing.
3507. Adversary trial; permanent injunctions; appeals; stay.
3507.1. Admissibility of evidence; burden of proof.
3507.2. Time for bringing actions; precedence over other actions; speedy and expeditious adjudication.
3507.3. Violations or disobedience of injunctions or orders; punishment.
3507.4. Distributors and producers; joint and several liability.
3508. Application of title; exceptions; federal supremacy.
3508.1. Misstatements by producers; misdemeanor.
3508.2. Severability.

§ 3504. Definitions

As used in this title:

(a) "Animal" means any amphibian, bird, mammal or reptile. It does not include any fish or insect.

(b) "Motion picture" means any motion picture, regardless of length or content, which is exhibited in a motion picture theater to paying customers, or is exhibited on television to paying customers or under the sponsorship of a paying advertiser. It shall not include motion pictures made for scientific, research, or educational purposes, or motion pictures exhibited as home movies, or amateur films, which are shown free or at cost to friends, neighbors or civic groups.

(c) "Person" means individuals, corporations, associations, partnerships, limited liability companies, trustees, lessees, agents and assignees. (Added by Stats.1978, c. 1152, p. 3535, § 1. Amended by Stats.1994, c. 1010 (S.B.2053), § 56.)

§ 3505. Exhibition of intentional killing or cruelty; nuisance

(a) The exhibition of any motion picture, if any intentional killing of, or cruelty to, a human being or an animal is shown in the motion picture and such intentional killing of, or cruelty to, a human being or an animal actually occurred in the production of the motion picture for the purpose of such production, is a nuisance, which shall be enjoined, abated, and prevented.

(b) As used in this section, "killing" and "cruelty" mean conduct which both (1) results in the death or the infliction of any physical injury or wound, including, but not limited to, any temporary or permanent physical harm resulting from the administration of any drug or chemical, and (2) is patently offensive to the average person, applying contemporary state-wide community standards. It does not include conduct committed against a human being to which the human being has given his or her consent. In determining whether conduct is patently offensive, the trier of fact may consider any or all of the following: (i) the degree or extent of the physical injury inflicted, (ii) the manner in which the injury is inflicted, (iii) the extent to which the injuring or wounding or acts resulting therein are depicted on the screen, (iv) the number of instances of infliction of injury, wound or harm occurring in the making of the motion picture, and (v) whether such conduct is lawful or unlawful under any provision of law other than this title.

(c) For the purposes of this section, it shall not be a requirement that the entire motion picture and all of the conduct resulting therein be taken into account in determining whether a nuisance exists, and to this end, the Legislature finds and declares that any specific conduct which intentionally results in the killing of, or cruelty to, an animal or a human being in the making of a motion picture is unnecessary and is a nuisance, and that if a motion picture cannot be completed in the absence of such conduct, it is, therefore, a nuisance in its entirety. (Added by Stats.1978, c. 1152, p. 3535, § 1.)

Research References
13 Witkin, California Summary 10th Equity § 150, Other Statutes.

§ 3506. Commencement of actions; proper showing

Whenever there is reasonable cause to believe that a nuisance as defined in this title is kept, maintained or is in existence in any county, the district attorney or the Attorney General, in the name of the people of the State of California, shall, on a proper showing, commence an action in equity to abate and prevent the nuisance and to perpetually enjoin the person conducting or maintaining it, and the owner, lessee or agent of the building, or place, in or upon which the nuisance exists, from maintaining or permitting it. As used herein, a proper showing to commence an action under this title must be based upon evidence independent of the motion picture itself that intentional killing of, or cruelty to, a human being or an animal actually occurred in the

production of the motion picture for the purpose of such production. (Added by Stats.1978, c. 1152, p. 3535, § 1.)

§ 3507. Adversary trial; permanent injunctions; appeals; stay

Whenever an action is initiated under this title to abate an alleged nuisance, an adversary trial on the merits shall be held pursuant to Section 3507.2. If the court finds that the exhibition of the particular motion picture constitutes a nuisance, it shall issue a permanent injunction to abate and prevent the continuance or recurrence of such nuisance. No temporary restraining order or preliminary injunction shall be granted in such an action. An appeal may be taken from an order issuing a permanent injunction, and any injunction issued pursuant to this title by the trial court may be stayed by such court pending the outcome of such appeal. No appeal may be taken from a ruling by the trial court denying an injunction requested under this title. (Added by Stats.1978, c. 1152, p. 3535, § 1.)

§ 3507.1. Admissibility of evidence; burden of proof

In actions brought under this title, the motion picture shall be admissible into evidence. The burden of proof that the exhibition of the particular motion picture constitutes a nuisance shall be met by the district attorney or Attorney General only when clear and convincing evidence, independent of the motion picture itself, is provided that the acts alleged actually occurred in the production of the motion picture. (Added by Stats.1978, c. 1152, p. 3535, § 1.)

§ 3507.2. Time for bringing actions; precedence over other actions; speedy and expeditious adjudication

Actions brought under this title shall be brought as promptly as possible. Such actions shall have precedence over all actions, excepting criminal proceedings and election contests. It is also the intent of the Legislature that actions commenced under this title be adjudicated in the most speedy and expeditious manner. (Added by Stats.1978, c. 1152, p. 3535, § 1.)

§ 3507.3. Violations or disobedience of injunctions or orders; punishment

Any violation or disobedience of an injunction or order expressly provided for by this title is punishable as a contempt of court by a fine of not less than two hundred dollars ($200) nor more than one thousand dollars ($1,000). (Added by Stats.1978, c. 1152, p. 3535, § 1.)

§ 3507.4. Distributors and producers; joint and several liability

The distributor who furnished a motion picture to a person who is made a defendant in an action under this title, and the producer of a motion picture which is the subject of this title shall be jointly and severally liable, upon proof and after an opportunity to appear and interpose any appropriate defenses, to such person and the exhibitor for damages, including loss of profits, attorney's fees, and other costs of defending such action. Such distributor and such producer shall actively assist in such defense to the extent that such person possesses information necessary to such defense concerning the production of the motion picture which is not otherwise available to the defendant. The exhibitor shall not be liable upon any portion of any contract made on or after January 1, 1979, which requires the exhibition or advertisement of a motion picture subject to this title on or after the date of the filing of any action under this title, if the motion picture by final decision of a court is determined to be a nuisance under this title. (Added by Stats.1978, c. 1152, p. 3535, § 1.)

§ 3508. Application of title; exceptions; federal supremacy

(a) This title shall not apply to any of the following:

(1) The exhibition of any motion picture, such as a newsreel or documentary, involving acts of killing or cruelty which were not intentionally committed for the purpose of producing the motion picture.

(2) Any motion picture made, in whole or in part, prior to January 1, 1979.

(3) Any motion picture all or part of which has been edited or remade so that any previous conduct which constituted a nuisance under this title no longer appears.

(4) The taking of any animal as permitted by any provision of the Fish and Game Code or pursuant thereto in accordance with regulations adopted by the Fish and Game Commission unless the time, place, or manner of such taking violates any provision of law except this title. This title shall apply to any other animal whether or not the time, place, or manner of the taking is prohibited by any laws other than this title, however, this title shall not apply to the taking of any animal authorized by law in any other jurisdiction unless the time, place or manner of such taking is prohibited by law or regulation.

(5) A motion picture which includes scenes of killing or cruelty to animals if the acts constituting the killing or cruelty were authorized by the laws governing such acts in the jurisdiction where the scenes were filmed.

(6) Any motion picture which bears within its contents a statement from the producer of the motion picture that all scenes depicting animals were filmed without the intentional killing of, or cruelty to an animal or that any killing or cruelty to an animal was authorized by the laws of the jurisdiction where the scenes were filmed or that the film is otherwise exempt under this title.

(7) Any motion picture if the exhibitor thereof has a written signed statement, or a copy thereof, from the producer of the motion picture that all scenes depicting animals were filmed without the intentional killing of, or cruelty to an animal or that any killing or cruelty to an animal was authorized by the laws of the jurisdiction where the scenes were filmed or that the film is otherwise exempt under this title.

(b) This title shall not apply in any case in which it would conflict with federal supremacy in the field of television broadcasting. *(Added by Stats.1978, c. 1152, p. 3535, § 1.)*

§ 3508.1. Misstatements by producers; misdemeanor

Any producer who willfully misstates or causes to be misstated any fact contained in a statement under paragraph (6) or (7) of Section 3508 is guilty of a misdemeanor. *(Added by Stats.1978, c. 1152, p. 3535, § 1.)*

§ 3508.2. Severability

If any provision of this title or the application thereof to any person or circumstances is held invalid, such invalidity shall not affect other provisions or applications of this title which can be given effect without the invalid provision or application, and to this end the provisions of this title are severable. *(Added by Stats.1978, c. 1152, p. 3535, § 1.)*

Part 4

MAXIMS OF JURISPRUDENCE

§ 3509. Intent and effect of maxims

The maxims of jurisprudence hereinafter set forth are intended not to qualify any of the foregoing provisions of this code, but to aid in their just application. *(Enacted in 1872. Amended by Stats.2013, c. 76 (A.B.383), § 20.)*

Research References

Rutter, Cal. Practice Guide: Civil Trials & Evidence Ch. 13-D, D. Preparing for Closing Argument.

6 Witkin, California Summary 10th Torts § 1426, Excavation and Earth Moving.

§ 3510. Reason for rule ceasing

When the reason of a rule ceases, so should the rule itself. *(Enacted in 1872.)*

§ 3511. Reason same

Where the reason is the same, the rule should be the same. *(Enacted in 1872.)*

§ 3512. Change of purpose

One must not change his purpose to the injury of another. *(Enacted in 1872.)*

§ 3513. Waiver of advantage; law established for public reason

Any one may waive the advantage of a law intended solely for his benefit. But a law established for a public reason cannot be contravened by a private agreement. *(Enacted in 1872.)*

Research References

Rutter, Cal. Practice Guide: Civ. Pro. Before Trial Ch. 9(II)-A, A. Injunctions.

Miller and Starr California Real Estate § 25:9, Judicial Review.

Miller and Starr California Real Estate § 13:12, Waiver of the Homestead Exemption.

Miller and Starr California Real Estate § 25:54, Judicial Review.

Miller and Starr California Real Estate § 35:39, Issues Which Cannot be the Subject of Arbitration.

Miller and Starr California Real Estate § 10:156, Waiver; Trustor's Election.

Miller and Starr California Real Estate § 10:214, Deficiency Judgment.

Miller and Starr California Real Estate § 10:234, Determination of "Fair Value".

Miller and Starr California Real Estate § 10:237, Waiver of Purchase-Money Protection.

Miller and Starr California Real Estate § 25A:23, Type of Action; Time to File; Preparation of Administrative Record.

13 NO. 6 Miller & Starr, California Real Estate Newsalert 4, Deeds of Trust.

15 NO. 2 Miller & Starr, California Real Estate Newsalert 3, Commercial Arbitration.

22 NO. 6 Miller & Starr, California Real Estate Newsalert 6, CEQA.

6 Witkin Cal. Proc. 5th Proceedings Without Trial § 514, (S 514) Oral Agreement.

6 Witkin Cal. Proc. 5th Proceedings Without Trial § 518, Discrimination Claims.

6 Witkin Cal. Proc. 5th Provisional Remedies § 383A, (S 383A) (New)-Waiver or Forfeiture.

12 Witkin, California Summary 10th Real Property § 482, (S 482) No Waiver of Disclosure Requirements.

1 Witkin Cal. Summ. 10th Contracts § 679, Procedural Provisions.

1 Witkin Cal. Summ. 10th Contracts § 682, Waivers by Employees.

10 Witkin, California Summary 10th Parent and Child § 76, Nature and Effect of Adoption.

4 Witkin, California Summary 10th Security Transactions in Real Property § 56, Waiver of Invalid Clause.

4 Witkin, California Summary 10th Security Transactions in Real Property § 131, (S 131) Advance Waiver is Invalid.

§ 3514. Use of rights

One must so use his own rights as not to infringe upon the rights of another. *(Enacted in 1872.)*

Research References

Miller and Starr California Real Estate § 14:9, Self-Help for Encroaching Trees.

Miller and Starr California Real Estate § 17:2, Property as "Bundle of Rights".

Miller and Starr California Real Estate § 36:6, Liability to the Borrower for Negligent Disbursement of Loan Funds.

Miller and Starr California Real Estate § 22:53, Liability for Condition Arising After the Tenant Takes Possession.

6 Witkin, California Summary 10th Torts § 1415, Earlier Cases.

6 Witkin, California Summary 10th Torts § 1426, Excavation and Earth Moving.

§ 3515. Consent; effect

He who consents to an act is not wronged by it. *(Enacted in 1872.)*

Research References

Miller and Starr California Real Estate § 22:36, Consent.

5 Witkin, California Summary 10th Torts § 126, in General.

§ 3516. Acquiescence in error

Acquiescence in error takes away the right of objecting to it. *(Enacted in 1872.)*

Research References

Miller and Starr California Real Estate § 1:82, Written Authority Required; the Equal Dignities Rule--Exception: Ratification or Waiver by the Principal.

Miller and Starr California Real Estate § 1:123, Remedies for Mistake.

§ 3517. Advantage of own wrong

No one can take advantage of his own wrong. *(Enacted in 1872.)*

Research References

Rutter, Cal. Practice Guide: Civil Trials & Evidence Ch. 13-D, D. Preparing for Closing Argument.

Rutter, Cal. Practice Guide: Real Prop. Transactions Ch. 2-C, C. Broker's Relationship and Obligations to Principal and Third Parties.

Miller and Starr California Real Estate § 3:48, Secret Profits.

Miller and Starr California Real Estate § 1:166, Excuse or Waiver of Conditions.

Miller and Starr California Real Estate § 21:38, Remedies for Usury--Treble Damages; Punitive Damages.

Miller and Starr California Real Estate § 19:120, Landlord's Common-Law Duty of Maintenance; Implied Warranty of Habitability.

Miller and Starr California Real Estate § 19:160, Covenant of Quiet Enjoyment and Possession--Tenant's Remedies for Breach of the Covenant.

Miller and Starr California Real Estate § 34:114, Constructive Trusts.

23 NO. 2 Miller & Starr, California Real Estate Newsalert 8, Deeds of Trust.

1 Witkin Cal. Summ. 10th Contracts § 470, Recovery of Interest.

13 Witkin, California Summary 10th Equity § 7, (S 7) Taking Advantage of One's Own Wrong.

14 Witkin, California Summary 10th Wills and Probate § 791, (S 791) Murder of Decedent.

2 Witkin Cal. Summ. 10th Workers' Compensation § 99, (S 99) Where Employer's Negligence is Not Judicially Determined.

§ 3518. Fraudulent conveyances

He who has fraudulently dispossessed himself of a thing may be treated as if he still had possession. *(Enacted in 1872.)*

§ 3519. Presumptive agency

He who can and does not forbid that which is done on his behalf, is deemed to have bidden it. *(Enacted in 1872.)*

Research References

Miller and Starr California Real Estate § 27:67, Architect's Instructions.

§ 3520. Suffering from act of another

No one should suffer by the act of another. *(Enacted in 1872.)*

Research References

Rutter, Cal. Practice Guide: Civil Trials & Evidence Ch. 13-D, D. Preparing for Closing Argument.

§ 3521. Benefit and burden

He who takes the benefit must bear the burden. *(Enacted in 1872.)*

Research References

Miller and Starr California Real Estate § 10:235, Potentially Liable Persons.

4 Witkin, California Summary 10th Security Transactions in Real Property § 134, Distinction: No Waiver of Underlying Debt.

§ 3522. Essentials to use of thing granted

One who grants a thing is presumed to grant also whatever is essential to its use. *(Enacted in 1872.)*

Research References

Miller and Starr California Real Estate § 15:20, Sale of Property or Division of Title.

Miller and Starr California Real Estate § 15:24, Sale of Property or Division of Title--Implied Reservation to the Grantor.

Miller and Starr California Real Estate § 19:27, Description of the Premises--Appurtenances; Implied Easements.

§ 3523. Remedy for wrong

For every wrong there is a remedy. *(Enacted in 1872.)*

Research References

Rutter, Cal. Practice Guide: Civil Trials & Evidence Ch. 13-D, D. Preparing for Closing Argument.
California Practice Guide: Employment Litigation Ch. 5-K, K. Invasion of Privacy.
California Practice Guide: Employment Litigation Ch. 17-A, A. Equitable Relief.
3 Witkin Cal. Proc. 5th Actions § 2, (S 2) Nature of Judicial Remedy.
3 Witkin Cal. Proc. 5th Actions § 3, Statutory Declarations.
3 Witkin Cal. Proc. 5th Actions § 4, Obligation May be Enforced.
3 Witkin Cal. Proc. 5th Actions § 5, Remedy for Every Wrong.
5 Witkin, California Summary 10th Torts § 19, in General.
5 Witkin, California Summary 10th Torts § 729, Abduction of Child.
6 Witkin, California Summary 10th Torts § 980, (S 980) Cause of Action Recognized.
13 Witkin, California Summary 10th Equity § 3, (S 3) Adequacy of Legal Remedy.

§ 3524. Equally in right or in wrong

Between those who are equally in the right, or equally in the wrong, the law does not interpose. *(Enacted in 1872.)*

Research References

Rutter, Cal. Practice Guide: Insurance Litigation Ch. 8-B, B. Contribution Between Insurers.
Rutter, Cal. Practice Guide: Prof. Responsibility Ch. 6-D, D. Professional Liability.
Miller and Starr California Real Estate § 11:83, Effect of Fraudulent Representations by the Seller.

§ 3525. Preference of earliest right

Between rights otherwise equal, the earliest is preferred. *(Enacted in 1872.)*

Research References

13 Witkin, California Summary 10th Equity § 8, (S 8) Equal Equities and Bona Fide Purchase.

§ 3526. Responsibility for unavoidable occurrences

No man is responsible for that which no man can control. *(Enacted in 1872.)*

Research References

Rutter, Cal. Practice Guide: Civil Trials & Evidence Ch. 13-D, D. Preparing for Closing Argument.
Miller and Starr California Real Estate § 22:41, General Rule of Landowner's or Occupier's Duty to Third Persons.
Miller and Starr California Real Estate § 22:53, Liability for Condition Arising After the Tenant Takes Possession.

§ 3527. Vigilance and delay

The law helps the vigilant, before those who sleep on their rights. *(Enacted in 1872.)*

Research References

13 Witkin, California Summary 10th Equity § 16, Nature of Defense.

§ 3528. Form and substance

The law respects form less than substance. *(Enacted in 1872.)*

Research References

13 Witkin, California Summary 10th Equity § 4, (S 4) Substance Rather Than Form.

§ 3529. Presumption of performance

That which ought to have been done is to be regarded as done, in favor of him to whom, and against him from whom, performance is due. *(Enacted in 1872.)*

Research References

Miller and Starr California Real Estate § 10:19, "After-Acquired" Title.
Miller and Starr California Real Estate § 25A:15, Procedures for Preparing an Environmental Impact Report.
13 Witkin, California Summary 10th Equity § 5, (S 5) Equity Regards that Which Ought to be Done as Done.

§ 3530. Nonexistence

That which does not appear to exist is to be regarded as if it did not exist. *(Enacted in 1872.)*

§ 3531. Impossibilities

The law never requires impossibilities. *(Enacted in 1872.)*

Research References

23 NO. 3 Miller & Starr, California Real Estate Newsalert 18, Subdivisions, Land Use, Planning and Approvals.

§ 3532. Idle acts

The law neither does nor requires idle acts. *(Enacted in 1872.)*

Research References

8 Witkin Cal. Proc. 5th Enforcement of Judgment § 497, Requirement of Injury to Creditor.

§ 3533. Trifles

The law disregards trifles. *(Enacted in 1872.)*

Research References

Miller and Starr California Real Estate § 22:20, Injunctive Relief; Balancing of Hardships or Equities.
Miller and Starr California Real Estate § 19:120, Landlord's Common-Law Duty of Maintenance; Implied Warranty of Habitability.

§ 3534. Particular and general expressions

Particular expressions qualify those which are general. *(Enacted in 1872.)*

Research References

Rutter, Cal. Practice Guide: Enforcing Judgments/Debts Ch. 6E-5, Specific Exempt Property.
Rutter, Cal. Practice Guide: Insurance Litigation Ch. 4-B, B. "Plain Meaning" vs. Ambiguity.
2 Witkin, California Summary 10th Insurance § 48, Governing Rules and Principles.

§ 3535. Contemporaneous exposition

Contemporaneous exposition is in general the best. *(Enacted in 1872.)*

§ 3536. Greater contains the less

The greater contains the less. *(Enacted in 1872.)*

§ 3537. Superfluity

Superfluity does not vitiate. *(Enacted in 1872.)*

§ 3538. Certainty

That is certain which can be made certain. *(Enacted in 1872.)*

§ 3539. Time; void act

Time does not confirm a void act. *(Enacted in 1872.)*

§ 3540. Incident follows principal

The incident follows the principal, and not the principal the incident. *(Enacted in 1872.)*

§ 3541. Interpretation; preference

An interpretation which gives effect is preferred to one which makes void. *(Enacted in 1872.)*

Research References

Miller and Starr California Real Estate § 1:59, Rules of Contract Interpretation.
1 Witkin Cal. Summ. 10th Contracts § 750, General Rule.

§ 3542. Interpretation; reasonableness

Interpretation must be reasonable. *(Enacted in 1872.)*

Research References

Miller and Starr California Real Estate § 1:59, Rules of Contract Interpretation.
Miller and Starr California Real Estate § 19:47, Rules of Interpretation.
18 NO. 6 Miller & Starr, California Real Estate Newsalert 1, Does the Density Bonus Law (Gov. Code § 65915) Require Local Government to Approve Mixed Use and Housing Projects Where Local Zoning Does Not Allow Housing at All?

§ 3543. Which of two innocent persons must suffer

Where one of two innocent persons must suffer by the act of a third, he, by whose negligence it happened, must be the sufferer. *(Enacted in 1872.)*

Research References

Miller and Starr California Real Estate § 3:51, Principal's Liability for the Agent's Torts.
Miller and Starr California Real Estate § 8:28, Insertion of Name After Execution by the Grantor.
Miller and Starr California Real Estate § 8:41, "Delivery" Defined.
Miller and Starr California Real Estate § 8:52, Forgery.
Miller and Starr California Real Estate § 1:118, Unilateral Mistake.
Miller and Starr California Real Estate § 1:153, Contractual Provision Against Fraud Liability.
Miller and Starr California Real Estate § 11:83, Effect of Fraudulent Representations by the Seller.
22 NO. 6 Miller & Starr, California Real Estate Newsalert 10, Deeds.
7 Witkin Cal. Proc. 5th Trial § 394, (S 394) Announcement of Tentative Decision.
4 Witkin, California Summary 10th Sales § 229, General Principles.
4 Witkin, California Summary 10th Sales § 230, Sale of Motor Vehicle.
4 Witkin, California Summary 10th Secured Transactions in Personal Property § 12, (S 12) Entruster and Third Parties.

§ 3545. Private transactions

Private transactions are fair and regular. *(Added by Stats. 1965, c. 299, p. 1357, § 11, operative Jan. 1, 1967.)*

Law Revision Commission Comments

Sections 3545–3548 are new sections added to the Civil Code. They recast the presumptions declared by subdivisions 19, 28, 32, and 33 of Code of Civil Procedure Section 1963 as maxims of jurisprudence and supersede those subdivisions.

These superseded subdivisions of Section 1963 of the Code of Civil Procedure are not continued in the Evidence Code as presumptions for a variety of reasons. Some do not fit the definition of a presumption contained in Evidence Code Section 600 in that they do not arise upon the proof of a preliminary fact. Others seem to be little more than truisms. They are cited most frequently in the appellate cases to uphold lower court decisions that could be sustained anyway either on the ground that the party with the burden of proof failed to persuade the trier of fact or one the ground that the evidence would support the inference drawn by the trier of fact.

Accordingly, these propositions are continued as maxims of jurisprudence, not as presumptions. As maxims, they are not intended to qualify any substantive provisions of law but merely to aid in their just application. Civil Code § 3509. [7 Cal.L.Rev.Comm. Reports 1 (1965)].

Research References

Rutter, Cal. Practice Guide: A.D.R. Ch. 5-D, D. Defenses to Enforcement.

§ 3546. Ordinary course of nature

Things happen according to the ordinary course of nature and the ordinary habits of life. *(Added by Stats. 1965, c. 299, p. 1357, § 12, operative Jan. 1, 1967.)*

Law Revision Commission Comments

See the Comment to Civil Code Section 3545. [7 Cal.L.Rev.Comm. Reports 1 (1965)].

Research References

Rutter, Cal. Practice Guide: Civil Trials & Evidence Ch. 13-D, ·D. Preparing for Closing Argument.

§ 3547. Existence of things

A thing continues to exist as long as is usual with things of that nature. *(Added by Stats. 1965, c. 299, p. 1357, § 13, operative Jan. 1, 1967.)*

Law Revision Commission Comments

See the Comment to Civil Code Section 3545. [7 Cal.L.Rev.Comm. Reports 1 (1965)].

§ 3548. Law obeyed

The law has been obeyed. *(Added by Stats. 1965, c. 299, p. 1357, § 14, operative Jan. 1, 1967.)*

Law Revision Commission Comments

See the Comment to Civil Code Section 3545. [7 Cal.L.Rev.Comm. Reports 1 (1965)].

Research References

Miller and Starr California Real Estate § 25A:15, Procedures for Preparing an Environmental Impact Report.

Part 5

COMMON INTEREST DEVELOPMENTS

Publisher's Note

The following table was provided by the California Law Revision Commission, and is reproduced with minor modifications. The original table was published in the California Law Revision Commission recommendation titled "Statutory Clarification and Simplification of CID Law" [40 Cal.L.Rev.Comm. Reports 235 (2010)].

DISPOSITION OF FORMER LAW

The table below shows the relationship between each provision of the existing Davis–Stirling Common Interest Development Act and the corresponding provision of the proposed law.

Existing Provision	New Provision(s)
1350	4000
1350.5	4005
1350.7	omitted, but see 4040, 4045, 4050
1351 (intro.)	4075
1351(a)	4080
1351(b)	4095
1351(c)	4100
1351(d)	4105
1351(e)(1)-(2)	4285
1351(e)(3) (except last ¶)	4285, 4290
1351(e)(last ¶)	4295
1351(f)	4125
1351(g)	4130
1351(h)	4135
1351(i)	4145
1351(j)	4150
1351(k)	4175
1351(l)	4185
1351(m)	4190
1352	4200
1352.5	4225(a)-(b), (d)
1353(a)(1) (1st & 2d sent.)	4250(a)
1353(a)(1)-(4) (except 1st & 2d sent.)	4255
1353(b)	4250(b)
1353.5	4705
1353.6	4710
1353.7	4720
1353.8	4735
1353.9	4745
1354	5975
1355(a)	4270(a)
1355(b) (1st sent.)	4260
1355(b)(1)	5115(e)
1355(b)(2)	4270(b)
1355(b)(3)	4270(a)(3)
1355.5	4230
1356	4275
1357(a)	4265(a)
1357(b) (except part of 1st sent.)	omitted
1357(b) (part of 1st sent.)	4265(b)
1357(c)	omitted
1357(d)	4265(c)
1357.100(a)	4340(a)
1357.100(b)	4340(b)
1357.110	4350
1357.120	4355
1357.130	4360
1357.140	4365
1357.150	4370
1358(a)	4625
1358(b)	4630
1358(c)	4635
1358(d)	4640
1358 (last ¶)	4650
1358 (next to last ¶)	4645
1359	4610

Existing Provision	New Provision(s)
1360	4760
1360.2	4740
1360.5	4715
1361	4505
1361.5	4510
1362	4500
1363(a)	4800
1363(b)	omitted
1363(c)	4805
1363(d)	5000(a)
1363(e) (1st sent.)	5240(b)
1363(e) (2d sent.)	omitted
1363(f) (1st sent.)	5850(a)
1363(f) (2d sent.)	omitted
1363(g)	5855
1363(h)	4820
1363(i)	5865
1363.001	5400
1363.005	omitted
1363.03(a)	5105(a)
1363.03(b) (1st sent.)	5100(a)
1363.03(b) (2d & 3d sents.)	5115(b)
1363.03(b) (4th sent.)	5115(c)
1363.03(c)	5110
1363.03(d)	5130
1363.03(e)	5115(a)
1363.03(f)	5120(a)
1363.03(g)	5120(b)
1363.03(h)	5125(a)
1363.03(i)	5125(b)
1363.03(j)	5105(b)
1363.03(k)	5115(d)
1363.03(l)	5100(c)
1363.03(m)	5100(d)
1363.03(n)	5100(e)
1363.03(o)	omitted
1363.04	5135
1363.05(a)	4900
1363.05(b) (1st part of 1st sent.)	4925(a)
1363.05(b) (2d part of 1st sent.)	4935(a)
1363.05(b) (2d sent.)	4935(b)
1363.05(b) (3d sent.)	4925(a)
1363.05(c)	4935(e)
1363.05(d)	4950(a)
1363.05(e)	4950(b)
1363.05(f)	4920
1363.05(g)	4923
1363.05(h)	4925(b), 5000(b)
1363.05(i)	4930
1363.05(j)	4910
1363.05(k)(1)	4155
1363.05(k)(2)	4090
1363.07 (except (a)(3)(F))	4600
1363.07(a)(3)(F)	4202(a)(4)
1363.09 (re elections)	5145
1363.09(a)-(b) (re exclusive use grant)	4605
1363.09(a)-(b) (re open meetings)	4955
1363.1(a)	5375
1363.1(b) (except ¶ (1))	4158
1363.1(b)(1)	5385
1363.2(a)-(e)	5380(a)-(e)

CHAPTER 1.   GENERAL PROVISIONS

ARTICLE 1.   PRELIMINARY PROVISIONS

§ 4000.   Short title

This part shall be known and may be cited as the Davis–Stirling Common Interest Development Act. In a provision of this part, the part may be referred to as the act. *(Added by Stats.2012, c. 180 (A.B.805), § 2, operative Jan. 1, 2014.)*

Law Revision Commission Comments

The first sentence of Section 4000 continues former Section 1350 without change. The second sentence is added for drafting convenience. [40 Cal.L.Rev.Comm. Reports 235 (2010)].

Research References

5 Witkin Cal. Proc. 5th Pleading § 884, Family Law Act Changes.

11 Witkin, California Summary 10th Husband and Wife § 1, (S 1) Family Law Act.

11 Witkin, California Summary 10th Husband and Wife § 42, (S 42) in General.

11 Witkin, California Summary 10th Husband and Wife § 46, (S 46) Certificate of Registry.

§ 4005.   Effect of headings on scope, meaning, or intent of act

Division, part, title, chapter, * * * article, and section headings do not in any manner affect the scope, meaning, or intent of this act. *(Added by Stats.2012, c. 180 (A.B.805), § 2, operative Jan. 1, 2014.   Amended by Stats.2013, c. 183 (S.B.745), § 7.)*

Law Revision Commission Comments

Section 4005 continues former Section 1350.5 without change, except as indicated below.

The following nonsubstantive changes are made:

● "Article" is added to the list of headings.

● The last word of the sentence is replaced with "act."

Section 4005 is a standard provision found in many codes. See, e.g., Evid. Code § 5; Fam. Code § 5; Prob. Code § 4. [40 Cal.L.Rev.Comm. Reports 235 (2010)].

Section 4005 is amended to correct a drafting error. [42 Cal.L.Rev. Comm. Reports 311 (2012)].

§ 4010.   Continuation of prior law

Nothing in the act that added this part shall be construed to invalidate a document prepared or action taken before January 1, 2014, if the document or action was proper under the law governing common interest developments at the time that the document was prepared or the action was taken. For the purposes of this section, "document" does not include a governing document. *(Added by Stats.2012, c. 180 (A.B.805), § 2, operative Jan. 1, 2014.)*

Law Revision Commission Comments

Section 4010 is new. It makes clear that any changes to former law made by enactment of this act shall not be construed to retroactively invalidate documents prepared or actions taken prior to the operative date of the act.

The term "documents" is used to describe notices, forms, and other procedural or transactional instruments. It is not meant to include the governing documents of the association. Governing documents must conform to the law. See Section 4205.

See also Section 4100 ("common interest development"), 4150 ("governing documents"). [40 Cal.L.Rev.Comm. Reports 235 (2010)].

§ 4020.   Construction of zoning ordinances

Unless a contrary intent is clearly expressed, a local zoning ordinance is construed to treat like structures, lots, parcels, areas, or spaces in like manner regardless of the form of the common interest development. *(Added by Stats.2012, c. 180 (A.B.805), § 2, operative Jan. 1, 2014.)*

Law Revision Commission Comments

Section 4020 continues former Section 1372 without change, except as indicated below.

The following nonsubstantive change is made:

● A list of all of the types of common interest developments is replaced with general language.

See also Section 4100 ("common interest development"). [40 Cal. L.Rev.Comm. Reports 235 (2010)].

§ 4035.   Delivery of document to association

(a) If a provision of this act requires that a document be delivered to an association, the document shall be delivered to the person designated in the annual policy statement, prepared pursuant to Section 5310, to receive documents on behalf of the association. If no person has been designated to receive documents, the document shall be delivered to the president or secretary of the association.

(b) A document delivered pursuant to this section may be delivered by any of the following methods:

(1) By _email_, facsimile, or other electronic means, if the association has assented to that method of delivery.

(2) By personal delivery, if the association has assented to that method of delivery. If the association accepts a document by personal delivery it shall provide a written receipt acknowledging delivery of the document.

(3) By first-class mail, postage prepaid, registered or certified mail, express mail, or overnight delivery by an express service center. *(Added by Stats.2012, c. 180 (A.B.805), § 2, operative Jan. 1, 2014. Amended by Stats.2013, c. 183 (S.B.745), § 8.)*

Law Revision Commission Comments

Section 4035 is new. It provides a standard rule for delivery of a document to the association.

See also Sections 4078 ("annual policy statement"), 4080 ("association"), 4170 ("person"). [40 Cal.L.Rev.Comm. Reports 235 (2010)].

Section 4035 is amended to correct a drafting error. [42 Cal.L.Rev. Comm. Reports 311 (2012)].

§ 4040. Individual delivery or individual notice

(a) If a provision of this act requires that an association deliver a document by "individual delivery" or "individual notice," the document shall be delivered by one of the following methods:

(1) First-class mail, postage prepaid, registered or certified mail, express mail, or overnight delivery by an express service carrier. The document shall be addressed to the recipient at the address last shown on the books of the association.

(2) E-mail, facsimile, or other electronic means, if the recipient has consented, in writing, to that method of delivery. The consent may be revoked, in writing, by the recipient.

(b) Upon receipt of a request by a member, pursuant to Section 5260, identifying a secondary address for delivery of notices of the following types, the association shall deliver an additional copy of those notices to the secondary address identified in the request:

(1) The documents to be delivered to the member pursuant to Article 7 (commencing with Section 5300) of Chapter 6.

(2) The documents to be delivered to the member pursuant to Article 2 (commencing with Section 5650) of Chapter 8, and Section 5710.

(c) For the purposes of this section, an unrecorded provision of the governing documents providing for a particular method of delivery does not constitute agreement by a member to that method of delivery. *(Added by Stats.2012, c. 180 (A.B.805), § 2, operative Jan. 1, 2014.)*

Law Revision Commission Comments

Section 4040 is new. It specifies acceptable methods for delivery of a notice to an individual member, as distinguished from a notice that is to be delivered to every member. See Section 4045 (general notice). The methods listed in subdivision (a) are drawn from former Section 1350.7(b)(2)-(3).

Subdivision (b) continues part of the substance of former Sections 1365.1(c) and 1367.1(k). See also Section 5260.

Subdivision (c) continues former Section 1350.7(d). It precludes use of electronic delivery methods when the recipient has not consented to use of those methods or has withdrawn such consent.

See also Sections 4080 ("association"), 4150 ("governing documents"), 4160 ("member"). [40 Cal.L.Rev.Comm. Reports 235 (2010)].

§ 4045. General delivery or general notice

(a) If a provision of this act requires "general delivery" or "general notice," the document shall be provided by one or more of the following methods:

(1) Any method provided for delivery of an individual notice pursuant to Section 4040.

(2) Inclusion in a billing statement, newsletter, or other document that is delivered by one of the methods provided in this section.

(3) Posting the printed document in a prominent location that is accessible to all members, if the location has been designated for the posting of general notices by the association in the annual policy statement, prepared pursuant to Section 5310.

(4) If the association broadcasts television programming for the purpose of distributing information on association business to its members, by inclusion in the programming.

(b) Notwithstanding subdivision (a), if a member requests to receive general notices by individual delivery, all general notices to that member, given under this section, shall be delivered pursuant to Section 4040. The option provided in this subdivision shall be described in the annual policy statement, prepared pursuant to Section 5310. *(Added by Stats.2012, c. 180 (A.B. 805), § 2, operative Jan. 1, 2014.)*

Law Revision Commission Comments

Section 4045 is new. It specifies acceptable methods for delivery of a notice to the membership generally, as distinguished from a notice that is to be delivered to a specific member. See Section 4040 (individual notice). Nothing in this section prevents an association from using supplemental notice methods, such as posting on an Internet website, so long as a method authorized by this section is also used.

Subdivision (b) reserves the right of any member, on request, to receive general notices by the delivery methods provided for delivery of an individual notice. Thus, in an association that posts general notices on a notice board in a prominent location pursuant to subdivision (a)(3), individual members would still have the right, on request, to receive those notices by mail.

See also Sections 4078 ("annual policy statement"), 4080 ("association"), 4160 ("member"). [40 Cal.L.Rev.Comm. Reports 235 (2010)].

§ 4050. Time of delivery

(a) This section governs the delivery of a document pursuant to this act.

(b) If a document is delivered by mail, delivery is deemed to be complete on deposit into the United States mail.

(c) If a document is delivered by electronic means, delivery is complete at the time of transmission. *(Added by Stats.2012, c. 180 (A.B.805), § 2, operative Jan. 1, 2014.)*

Law Revision Commission Comments

Section 4050 is new. Subdivision (b) generalizes the second sentence of former Section 1350.7(b)(2).

Subdivision (c) generalizes the second sentence of former Section 1350.7(b)(3). [40 Cal.L.Rev.Comm. Reports 235 (2010)].

§ 4055. Electronic delivery; satisfaction of written information requirement

If the association or a member has consented to receive information by electronic delivery, and a provision of this act requires that the information be in writing, that requirement is satisfied if the information is provided in an electronic record capable of retention by the recipient at the time of receipt. An electronic record is not capable of retention by the recipient if the sender or its information processing system inhibits the ability of the recipient to print or store the electronic record. *(Added by Stats.2012, c. 180 (A.B.805), § 2, operative Jan. 1, 2014.)*

§ 4065.   Approval by majority

If a provision of this act requires that an action be approved by a majority of all members, the action shall be approved or ratified by an affirmative vote of a majority of the votes entitled to be cast.   *(Added by Stats.2012, c. 180 (A.B.805), § 2, operative Jan. 1, 2014.)*

Law Revision Commission Comments

Section 4065 is new. It is added for drafting convenience. This section only governs an election conducted pursuant to a provision of this act (i.e., the Davis–Stirling Common Interest Development Act). An election that is not required by this act would be governed by the association's governing documents.

See also Section 4160 ("member").   [40 Cal.L.Rev.Comm. Reports 235 (2010)].

§ 4070.   Approval by majority of quorum

If a provision of this act requires that an action be approved by a majority of a quorum of the members, the action shall be approved or ratified by an affirmative vote of a majority of the votes represented and voting in a duly held * * * election in which a quorum is represented, which affirmative votes also constitute a majority of the required quorum.   *(Added by Stats.2012, c. 180 (A.B.805), § 2, operative Jan. 1, 2014. Amended by Stats.2013, c. 183 (S.B.745), § 9.)*

Law Revision Commission Comments

Section 4070 is new. It is added for drafting convenience. This section only governs an election conducted pursuant to a provision of this act (i.e., the Davis–Stirling Common Interest Development Act). An election that is not required by this act would be governed by the association's governing documents.

See also Section 4160 ("member").   [40 Cal.L.Rev.Comm. Reports 235 (2010)].

Section 4070 is amended to make clear that it applies to any lawfully conducted member election, whether conducted at a meeting, by mailed ballot pursuant to Sections 5100–5145, or by any other lawful means.   [43 Cal.L.Rev.Comm. Reports 23 (2013)].

ARTICLE 2.   DEFINITIONS

§ 4075.   Construction of act

The definitions in this article govern the construction of this act.   *(Added by Stats.2012, c. 180 (A.B.805), § 2, operative Jan. 1, 2014.)*

Law Revision Commission Comments

Section 4075 continues the substance of the introductory clause of former Section 1351.   [40 Cal.L.Rev.Comm. Reports 235 (2010)].

§ 4076.   "Annual budget report" defined

"Annual budget report" means the report described in Section 5300.   *(Added by Stats.2012, c. 180 (A.B.805), § 2, operative Jan. 1, 2014.)*

Law Revision Commission Comments

Section 4076 is new. It is added for drafting convenience.   [40 Cal.L.Rev.Comm. Reports 235 (2010)].

§ 4078.   "Annual policy statement" defined

"Annual policy statement" means the statement described in Section 5310.   *(Added by Stats.2012, c. 180 (A.B.805), § 2, operative Jan. 1, 2014.)*

Law Revision Commission Comments

Section 4078 is new. It is added for drafting convenience.   [40 Cal.L.Rev.Comm. Reports 235 (2010)].

§ 4080.   "Association" defined

"Association" means a nonprofit corporation or unincorporated association created for the purpose of managing a common interest development.   *(Added by Stats.2012, c. 180 (A.B.805), § 2, operative Jan. 1, 2014.)*

Law Revision Commission Comments

Section 4080 continues former Section 1351(a) without change.

See also Section 4100 ("common interest development").   [40 Cal.L.Rev.Comm. Reports 235 (2010)].

§ 4085.   "Board" defined

"Board" means the board of directors of the association.   *(Added by Stats.2012, c. 180 (A.B.805), § 2, operative Jan. 1, 2014.)*

Law Revision Commission Comments

Section 4085 is new.

See also Sections 4080 ("association"), 4140 ("director").   [40 Cal.L.Rev.Comm. Reports 235 (2010)].

§ 4090.   "Board meeting" defined

"Board meeting" means either of the following:

(a) A congregation, at the same time and place, of a sufficient number of directors to establish a quorum of the board, to hear, discuss, or deliberate upon any item of business that is within the authority of the board.

(b) A teleconference, where a sufficient number of directors to establish a quorum of the board, in different locations, are connected by electronic means, through audio or video, or both. A teleconference meeting shall be conducted in a manner that protects the rights of members of the association and otherwise complies with the requirements of this act.   Except for a meeting that will be held solely in executive session, the notice of the teleconference meeting shall identify at least one physical location so that members of the association may attend, and at least one director or a person designated by the board shall be present at that location. Participation by directors in a teleconference meeting constitutes presence at that meeting as long as all directors participating are able to hear one another, as well as members of the association speaking on matters before the board. *(Added by Stats.2012, c. 180 (A.B.805), § 2, operative Jan. 1, 2014. Amended by Stats.2013, c. 183 (S.B.745), § 10.)*

Law Revision Commission Comments

Section 4090 continues former Section 1363.05(k)(2) without change, except as indicated below.

The following substantive change is made:

• The number of directors required to establish a board meeting is changed from a majority of the members to a number constituting a quorum.

• The definition is generalized so that it applies to the entire act.

The following nonsubstantive changes are made:

• The word "meeting" is replaced with "board meeting," to distinguish between a board meeting and a member meeting. See Section 4090 ("board meeting").

• The words "board member" are replaced with "director." See Section 4140 ("director").

• The provision in subdivision (a) is restated for clarity.

• The word "title" is replaced with "act."

See also Section 4085 ("board"), 4155 ("item of business"). [40 Cal.L.Rev.Comm. Reports 235 (2010)].

Subdivision (b) of Section 4090 is amended to continue, without substantive change, a revision to former Section 1363.05(k)(2) made in 2012 by AB 2697 (Assembly Committee on Housing and Community Development). See 2012 Cal. Stat. ch. 770, § 3. This is a technical revision. [42 Cal.L.Rev.Comm. Reports 311 (2012)].

§ 4095. "Common area" defined

(a) "Common area" means the entire common interest development except the separate interests therein. The estate in the common area may be a fee, a life estate, an estate for years, or any combination of the foregoing.

(b) Notwithstanding subdivision (a), in a planned development described in subdivision (b) of Section 4175, the common area may consist of mutual or reciprocal easement rights appurtenant to the separate interests. *(Added by Stats.2012, c. 180 (A.B.805), § 2, operative Jan. 1, 2014.)*

Law Revision Commission Comments

Subdivision (a) of Section 4095 continues the first two sentences of former Section 1351(b) without change.

Subdivision (b) continues the substance of the third sentence of former Section 1351(b), but restates it for clarity.

See also Sections 4100 ("common interest development"), 4175 ("planned development"), 4185 ("separate interest"). [40 Cal.L.Rev. Comm. Reports 235 (2010)].

§ 4100. "Common interest development" defined

"Common interest development" means any of the following:

(a) A community apartment project.

(b) A condominium project.

(c) A planned development.

(d) A stock cooperative. *(Added by Stats.2012, c. 180 (A.B. 805), § 2, operative Jan. 1, 2014.)*

Law Revision Commission Comments

Section 4100 continues former Section 1351(c) without change.

See also Sections 4105 ("community apartment project"), 4125 ("condominium project"), 4175 ("planned development"), 4190 ("stock cooperative"). [40 Cal.L.Rev.Comm. Reports 235 (2010)].

Research References

8 Witkin, California Summary 10th Constitutional Law § 910, (S 910) Classification Based on Marital Status.

§ 4105. "Community apartment project" defined

"Community apartment project" means a development in which an undivided interest in land is coupled with the right of exclusive occupancy of any apartment located thereon. *(Added by Stats.2012, c. 180 (A.B.805), § 2, operative Jan. 1, 2014.)*

Law Revision Commission Comments

Section 4105 continues former Section 1351(d) without change. [40 Cal.L.Rev.Comm. Reports 235 (2010)].

§ 4110. "Community service organization or similar entity" defined

(a) "Community service organization or similar entity" means a nonprofit entity, other than an association, that is organized to provide services to residents of the common interest development or to the public in addition to the residents, to the extent community common area or facilities are available to the public.

(b) "Community service organization or similar entity" does not include an entity that has been organized solely to raise moneys and contribute to other nonprofit organizations that are qualified as tax exempt under Section 501(c)(3) of the Internal Revenue Code [1] and that provide housing or housing assistance. *(Added by Stats.2012, c. 180 (A.B.805), § 2, operative Jan. 1, 2014.)*

[1] Internal Revenue Code sections are in Title 26 of the U.S.C.A.

Law Revision Commission Comments

Section 4110 continues former Section 1368(c)(3) without change, except as indicated below.

The following nonsubstantive changes are made:

• The former section is divided into subdivisions.

• The phrase "common areas" is singularized.

See also Sections 4080 ("association"), 4095 ("common area"), 4100 ("common interest development"). [40 Cal.L.Rev.Comm. Reports 235 (2010)].

§ 4120. "Condominium plan" defined

"Condominium plan" means a plan described in Section 4285. *(Added by Stats.2012, c. 180 (A.B.805), § 2, operative Jan. 1, 2014.)*

Law Revision Commission Comments

Section 4120 is new. It is added for drafting convenience. [40 Cal.L.Rev.Comm. Reports 235 (2010)].

§ 4125. "Condominium project" defined

(a) A "condominium project" means a real property development consisting of condominiums.

(b) A condominium consists of an undivided interest in common in a portion of real property coupled with a separate interest in space called a unit, the boundaries of which are described on a recorded final map, parcel map, or condominium plan in sufficient detail to locate all boundaries thereof. The area within these boundaries may be filled with air, earth, water, or fixtures, or any combination thereof, and need not be physically attached to land except by easements for access and, if necessary, support. The description of the unit may refer to (1) boundaries described in the recorded final map, parcel map, or condominium plan, (2) physical boundaries, either in existence, or to be constructed, such as walls, floors, and ceilings of a structure or any portion thereof, (3) an entire structure containing one or more units, or (4) any combination thereof.

(c) The portion or portions of the real property held in undivided interest may be all of the real property, except for the separate interests, or may include a particular three-dimensional portion thereof, the boundaries of which are described on a recorded final map, parcel map, or condominium plan. The area within these boundaries may be filled with air, earth, water, or fixtures, or any combination thereof, and need not be physically attached to land except by easements for access and, if necessary, support.

(d) An individual condominium within a condominium project may include, in addition, a separate interest in other portions of the real property. *(Added by Stats.2012, c. 180 (A.B.805), § 2, operative Jan. 1, 2014.)*

Law Revision Commission Comments

Section 4125 continues former Section 1351(f), without change, except as indicated below.

The following nonsubstantive changes are made:

- The section is organized into subdivisions for ease of reference.
- In subdivision (a), the word "development" is replaced with "real property development."
- Subdivisions (b) and (c) make clear that the contents of the area within the boundaries of a condominium may include "fixtures."

See also Sections 4120 ("condominium plan"), 4185 ("separate interest"). [40 Cal.L.Rev.Comm. Reports 235 (2010)].

§ 4130. "Declarant" defined

"Declarant" means the person or group of persons designated in the declaration as declarant, or if no declarant is designated, the person or group of persons who sign the original declaration or who succeed to special rights, preferences, or privileges designated in the declaration as belonging to the signator of the original declaration. *(Added by Stats.2012, c. 180 (A.B.805), § 2, operative Jan. 1, 2014.)*

Law Revision Commission Comments

Section 4130 continues former Section 1351(g) without change.

See also Sections 4135 ("declaration"), 4170 ("person"). [40 Cal. L.Rev.Comm. Reports 235 (2010)].

§ 4135. "Declaration" defined

"Declaration" means the document, however denominated, that contains the information required by Sections 4250 and 4255. *(Added by Stats.2012, c. 180 (A.B.805), § 2, operative Jan. 1, 2014.)*

Law Revision Commission Comments

Section 4135 continues former Section 1351(h) without change, except as indicated below.

The following nonsubstantive changes are made:

- The word "which" is replaced with "that."
- The statutory cross-reference is updated to reflect the new location of the referenced provision. [40 Cal.L.Rev.Comm. Reports 235 (2010)].

§ 4140. "Director" defined

"Director" means a natural person who serves on the board. *(Added by Stats.2012, c. 180 (A.B.805), § 2, operative Jan. 1, 2014.)*

Law Revision Commission Comments

Section 4140 is new. It is added for drafting convenience.

See also Section 4085 ("board"). [40 Cal.L.Rev.Comm. Reports 235 (2010)].

§ 4145. "Exclusive use common area" defined

(a) "Exclusive use common area" means a portion of the common area designated by the declaration for the exclusive use of one or more, but fewer than all, of the owners of the separate interests and which is or will be appurtenant to the separate interest or interests.

(b) Unless the declaration otherwise provides, any shutters, awnings, window boxes, doorsteps, stoops, porches, balconies, patios, exterior doors, doorframes, and hardware incident thereto, screens and windows or other fixtures designed to serve a single separate interest, but located outside the boundaries of the separate interest, are exclusive use common area allocated exclusively to that separate interest.

(c) Notwithstanding the provisions of the declaration, internal and external telephone wiring designed to serve a single separate interest, but located outside the boundaries of the separate interest, is exclusive use common area allocated exclusively to that separate interest. *(Added by Stats.2012, c. 180 (A.B.805), § 2, operative Jan. 1, 2014.)*

Law Revision Commission Comments

Section 4145 continues former Section 1351(i) without change, except as indicated below.

The following nonsubstantive change is made:

- The phrase "common areas" is singularized.

See also Sections 4095 ("common area"), 4135 ("declaration"), 4185 ("separate interest"). [40 Cal.L.Rev.Comm. Reports 235 (2010)].

§ 4148. "General notice" defined

"General notice" means the delivery of a document pursuant to Section 4045. *(Added by Stats.2012, c. 180 (A.B.805), § 2, operative Jan. 1, 2014.)*

Law Revision Commission Comments

Section 4148 is new. It is added for drafting convenience. [40 Cal.L.Rev.Comm. Reports 235 (2010)].

§ 4150. "Governing documents" defined

"Governing documents" means the declaration and any other documents, such as bylaws, operating rules, articles of incorporation, or articles of association, which govern the operation of the common interest development or association. *(Added by Stats.2012, c. 180 (A.B.805), § 2, operative Jan. 1, 2014.)*

Law Revision Commission Comments

Section 4150 continues former Section 1351(j) without change, except as indicated below.

The following nonsubstantive change is made:

- The superfluous words "of the association" are not continued.

See also Sections 4080 ("association"), 4100 ("common interest development"), 4135 ("declaration"). [40 Cal.L.Rev.Comm. Reports 235 (2010)].

§ 4153. "Individual notice" defined

"Individual notice" means the delivery of a document pursuant to Section 4040. *(Added by Stats.2012, c. 180 (A.B.805), § 2, operative Jan. 1, 2014.)*

Law Revision Commission Comments

Section 4153 is new. It is added for drafting convenience. [40 Cal.L.Rev.Comm. Reports 235 (2010)].

§ 4155. "Item of business" defined

"Item of business" means any action within the authority of the board, except those actions that the board has validly delegated to any other person or persons, managing agent, officer of the association, or committee of the board comprising less than a quorum of the board. *(Added by Stats.2012, c. 180 (A.B.805), § 2, operative Jan. 1, 2014.)*

Law Revision Commission Comments

Section 4155 continues former Section 1363.05(k)(1) without change, except as indicated below.

The following substantive change is made:

• The number of directors required to establish a board meeting is changed from a majority of the members to a number constituting a quorum.

See also Sections 4080 ("association"), 4085 ("board"), 4158 ("managing agent"), 4170 ("person"). [40 Cal.L.Rev.Comm. Reports 235 (2010)].

§ 4158. "Managing agent" defined

(a) A "managing agent" is a person who, for compensation or in expectation of compensation, exercises control over the assets of a common interest development.

(b) A "managing agent" does not include any of the following:

(1) A regulated financial institution operating within the normal course of its regulated business practice.

(2) An attorney at law acting within the scope of the attorney's license. *(Added by Stats.2012, c. 180 (A.B.805), § 2, operative Jan. 1, 2014.)*

Law Revision Commission Comments

Section 4158 continues former Sections 1363.1(b) and 1363.2(f) without change, except as indicated below.

The following substantive change is made:

• The definition is generalized so that it applies to the entire act.

The following nonsubstantive changes are made:

• The words "or entity" are not continued. See Section 4170 ("person").

• An exception for a full-time employee of the association is not continued in the generalized definition. That exception is continued without change in Section 5385.

See also Sections 4080 ("association"), 4100 ("common interest development"), 4170 ("person"). [40 Cal.L.Rev.Comm. Reports 235 (2010)].

§ 4160. "Member" defined

"Member" means an owner of a separate interest. *(Added by Stats.2012, c. 180 (A.B.805), § 2, operative Jan. 1, 2014.)*

Law Revision Commission Comments

Section 4160 is new. It is added for drafting convenience.

See also Section 4185 ("separate interest"). [40 Cal.L.Rev.Comm. Reports 235 (2010)].

§ 4170. "Person" defined

"Person" means a natural person, corporation, government or governmental subdivision or agency, business trust, estate, trust, partnership, limited liability company, association, or other entity. *(Added by Stats.2012, c. 180 (A.B.805), § 2, operative Jan. 1, 2014.)*

Law Revision Commission Comments

Section 4170 is new. It is added for drafting convenience. [40 Cal.L.Rev.Comm. Reports 235 (2010)].

§ 4175. "Planned development" defined

"Planned development" means a real property development other than a community apartment project, a condominium project, or a stock cooperative, having either or both of the following features:

(a) Common area that is owned either by an association or in common by the owners of the separate interests who possess appurtenant rights to the beneficial use and enjoyment of the common area.

(b) Common area and an association that maintains the common area with the power to levy assessments that may become a lien upon the separate interests in accordance with

Article 2 (commencing with Section 5650) of Chapter 8. *(Added by Stats.2012, c. 180 (A.B.805), § 2, operative Jan. 1, 2014.)*

Law Revision Commission Comments

Section 4175 continues the substance of former Section 1351(k), except as indicated below.

The following nonsubstantive changes are made:

• In the introductory clause, the word "development" is replaced with "real property development."

• Subdivision (a) is restated for clarity.

• Subdivision (b) is restated for clarity and to update a cross-reference.

See also Sections 4080 ("association"), 4095 ("common area"), 4105 ("community apartment project"), 4125 ("condominium project"), 4185 ("separate interest"), 4190 ("stock cooperative"). [40 Cal.L.Rev.Comm. Reports 235 (2010)].

§ 4177. "Reserve accounts" defined

"Reserve accounts" means both of the following:

(a) Moneys that the board has identified for use to defray the future repair or replacement of, or additions to, those major components that the association is obligated to maintain.

(b) The funds received, and not yet expended or disposed of, from either a compensatory damage award or settlement to an association from any person for injuries to property, real or personal, arising from any construction or design defects. These funds shall be separately itemized from funds described in subdivision (a). *(Added by Stats.2012, c. 180 (A.B.805), § 2, operative Jan. 1, 2014.)*

Law Revision Commission Comments

Section 4177 continues former Section 1365.5(f) without change, except as indicated below.

The following substantive change is made:

• The definition is generalized so that it applies to the entire act.

The following nonsubstantive changes are made:

• A cross-reference is updated to reflect the new location of the referenced provisions.

• The words "association's board of directors" are replaced with "board." See Section 4085 ("board").

• The words "or entity" are not continued. See Section 4170 ("person").

See also Sections 4080 ("association"), 4085 ("board"). [40 Cal.L.Rev.Comm. Reports 235 (2010)].

§ 4178. "Reserve account requirements" defined

"Reserve account requirements" means the estimated funds that the board has determined are required to be available at a specified point in time to repair, replace, or restore those major components that the association is obligated to maintain. *(Added by Stats.2012, c. 180 (A.B.805), § 2, operative Jan. 1, 2014.)*

Law Revision Commission Comments

Section 4178 continues former Section 1365.5(g) without change, except as indicated below.

The following substantive change is made:

• The definition is generalized so that it applies to the entire act.

The following nonsubstantive change is made:

• The words "association's board of directors" are replaced with "board." See Section 4085 ("board").

See also Section 4080 ("association"). [40 Cal.L.Rev.Comm. Reports 235 (2010)].

§ 4185. "Separate interest" defined

(a) "Separate interest" has the following meanings:

(1) In a community apartment project, "separate interest" means the exclusive right to occupy an apartment, as specified in Section 4105.

(2) In a condominium project, "separate interest" means a separately owned unit, as specified in Section 4125.

(3) In a planned development, "separate interest" means a separately owned lot, parcel, area, or space.

(4) In a stock cooperative, "separate interest" means the exclusive right to occupy a portion of the real property, as specified in Section 4190.

(b) Unless the declaration or condominium plan, if any exists, otherwise provides, if walls, floors, or ceilings are designated as boundaries of a separate interest, the interior surfaces of the perimeter walls, floors, ceilings, windows, doors, and outlets located within the separate interest are part of the separate interest and any other portions of the walls, floors, or ceilings are part of the common area.

(c) The estate in a separate interest may be a fee, a life estate, an estate for years, or any combination of the foregoing. *(Added by Stats.2012, c. 180 (A.B.805), § 2, operative Jan. 1, 2014.)*

Law Revision Commission Comments

Section 4185 continues former Section 1351(*l*) without change, except as indicated below.

The following nonsubstantive changes are made:

• In subdivision (a)(2), the words "individual unit" are replaced with "separately owned unit."

• The last two unnumbered paragraphs of former Section 1351(*l*) are designated as subdivisions (b) and (c).

• Cross-references are updated to reflect the new locations of referenced provisions.

• The phrase "common areas" is singularized.

See also Sections 4095 ("common area"), 4105 ("community apartment project"), 4120 ("condominium plan"), 4125 ("condominium project"), 4135 ("declaration"), 4175 ("planned development"), 4190 ("stock cooperative"). [40 Cal.L.Rev.Comm. Reports 235 (2010)].

§ 4190. "Stock cooperative" defined

(a) "Stock cooperative" means a development in which a corporation is formed or availed of, primarily for the purpose of holding title to, either in fee simple or for a term of years, improved real property, and all or substantially all of the shareholders of the corporation receive a right of exclusive occupancy in a portion of the real property, title to which is held by the corporation. The owners' interest in the corporation, whether evidenced by a share of stock, a certificate of membership, or otherwise, shall be deemed to be an interest in a common interest development and a real estate development for purposes of subdivision (f) of Section 25100 of the Corporations Code.

(b) A "stock cooperative" includes a limited equity housing cooperative which is a stock cooperative that meets the criteria of Section 817. *(Added by Stats.2012, c. 180 (A.B.805), § 2, operative Jan. 1, 2014.)*

Law Revision Commission Comments

Section 4190 continues former Section 1351(m) without change, except as indicated below.

The following nonsubstantive change is made:

• The unnumbered paragraphs are designated as subdivisions.

See also Section 4100 ("common interest development"). [40 Cal. L.Rev.Comm. Reports 235 (2010)].

CHAPTER 2. APPLICATION OF ACT

Section

4200. Creation of common interest development; application of act.

4201. Development not containing common area; application of act.

§ 4200. Creation of common interest development; application of act

This act applies and a common interest development is created whenever a separate interest coupled with an interest in the common area or membership in the association is, or has been, conveyed, provided all of the following are recorded:

(a) A declaration.

(b) A condominium plan, if any exists.

(c) A final map or parcel map, if Division 2 (commencing with Section 66410) of Title 7 of the Government Code requires the recording of either a final map or parcel map for the common interest development. *(Added by Stats.2012, c. 180 (A.B.805), § 2, operative Jan. 1, 2014.)*

Law Revision Commission Comments

Section 4200 continues former Section 1352 without change, except as indicated below.

The following nonsubstantive change is made:

• The word "title" is replaced with "act."

See also Sections 4080 ("association"), 4095 ("common area"), 4100 ("common interest development"), 4120 ("condominium plan"), 4135 ("declaration"), 4185 ("separate interest"). [40 Cal.L.Rev.Comm. Reports 235 (2010)].

§ 4201. Development not containing common area; application of act

Nothing in this act may be construed to apply to a real property development that does not contain common area. This section is declaratory of existing law. *(Added by Stats.2012, c. 180 (A.B.805), § 2, operative Jan. 1, 2014.)*

Law Revision Commission Comments

Section 4201 continues the substance of former Section 1374 without change, except as indicated below.

The following nonsubstantive changes are made:

• The word "title" is replaced with "act."

• The phrase "wherein there does not exist" is restated for clarity.

See also Section 4095 ("common area"). [40 Cal.L.Rev.Comm. Reports 235 (2010)].

§ 4202. Commercial or industrial common interest developments

* * * This part does not apply to a commercial or industrial common interest development * * *, as defined in Section 6531.

* * * *(Added by Stats.2012, c. 180 (A.B.805), § 2, operative Jan. 1, 2014. Amended by Stats.2013, c. 605 (S.B.752), § 19.)*

Law Revision Commission Comments

Section 4202 continues former Section 1373 without change, except as indicated below.

The following nonsubstantive changes are made:

• Former Section 1373(a)(3) is superfluous and is not continued.

• Cross-references are updated to reflect the new locations of the referenced provisions.

• Subdivision (a)(4) is added to continue the substance of former Section 1363.07(a)(3)(F).

• Subdivision (a)(10) refers only to Section 5605(b). It does not refer to the emergency exception provisions of Section 5610, which were also part of former Section 1366(b).

See also Sections 4100 ("common interest development"), 4135 ("declaration"). [40 Cal.L.Rev.Comm. Reports 235 (2010)].

Section 4202 is amended to make the provisions of the Davis–Stirling Common Interest Development Act inapplicable to an exclusively commercial or industrial common interest development, as defined in Section

6531. Many provisions of that act are continued and made applicable to exclusively commercial or industrial common interest developments by the Commercial and Industrial Common Interest Development Act, Part 5.3 (commencing with Section 6500) of Division 4. To determine whether that act continues a particular provision of the Davis–Stirling Common Interest Development Act, see *Commercial and Industrial Common Interest Developments*, 42 Cal. L. Revision Comm'n Reports 1 (2012). [42 Cal.L.Rev.Comm. Reports 1 (2012)].

CHAPTER 3.   GOVERNING DOCUMENTS

ARTICLE 1.   GENERAL PROVISIONS

§ 4205.   Authority of documents

(a) To the extent of any <u>conflict</u> between the governing documents and the law, the law * * * <u>shall prevail</u>.

(b) To the extent of any <u>conflict</u> between the articles of incorporation and the declaration, the declaration * * * <u>shall prevail</u>.

(c) To the extent of any <u>conflict</u> between the bylaws and the articles of incorporation or declaration, the articles of incorporation or declaration * * * <u>shall prevail</u>.

(d) To the extent of any <u>conflict</u> between the operating rules and the bylaws, articles of incorporation, or declaration, the bylaws, articles of incorporation, or declaration * * * <u>shall prevail</u>. *(Added by Stats.2012, c. 180 (A.B.805), § 2, operative Jan. 1, 2014. Amended by Stats.2013, c. 183 (S.B.745), § 11.)*

Law Revision Commission Comments

Section 4205 is added to clarify the relationship between the law and the most common types of governing documents. Nothing in the section is intended to create an affirmative duty to amend a governing document to delete superseded material.

Subdivisions (a) and (b) of Section 4205 are new.

Subdivision (c) is consistent with Corporations Code Section 7151(c), providing that the bylaws shall be consistent with the articles of incorporation.

Subdivision (d) is consistent with Section 4350(c), providing that an operating rule may not be inconsistent with the declaration, articles of incorporation, or bylaws of the association.

See also Sections 4135 ("declaration"), 4150 ("governing documents"). [42 Cal.L.Rev.Comm. Reports 409 (2012)].

Section 4205 is amended to clarify its meaning. The section is intended to provide guidance on how to resolve a conflict between the specified authorities. It is not intended to state a rule for determining when such a conflict exists.

The amendment would conform the terminology used in Section 4205 to that used in numerous other statutory provisions that establish a rule of

supremacy between authority without exhaustively specifying the circumstances in which the rule is to be applied. See, e.g., Civ. Code §§ 799.10, 2924h, 5100(e); Educ. Code §§ 24953(h), 69522; Fish & Game Code § 7090(h); Food & Agric. Code § 13169; Health & Safety Code §§ 1568.065, 1787; Ins. Code § 11580.2; Pub. Res. Code §§ 2770.6, 2772.5, 71530; Pub. Util. Code § 5142; Veh. Code § 15200. [43 Cal.L.Rev.Comm. Reports 23 (2013)].

§ 4210.   Statements for collection of regular and special assessments, transfer fees, and other charges

In order to facilitate the collection of regular assessments, special assessments, transfer fees as authorized by Sections 4530, 4575, and 4580, and similar charges, the board is authorized to record a statement or amended statement identifying relevant information for the association. This statement may include any or all of the following information:

(a) The name of the association as shown in the declaration or the current name of the association, if different.

(b) The name and address of a managing agent or treasurer of the association or other individual or entity authorized to receive assessments and fees imposed by the association.

(c) A daytime telephone number of the authorized party identified in subdivision (b) if a telephone number is available.

(d) A list of separate interests subject to assessment by the association, showing the assessor's parcel number or legal description, or both, of the separate interests.

(e) The recording information identifying the declaration governing the association.

(f) If an amended statement is being recorded, the recording information identifying the prior statement or statements which the amendment is superseding. *(Added by Stats.2012, c. 180 (A.B.805), § 2, operative Jan. 1, 2014.)*

Law Revision Commission Comments

Section 4210 continues former Section 1366.2(a) without change, except as indicated below.

The following nonsubstantive changes are made:

• The words "of any association" are not continued.

• The words "board of directors" are replaced with "board." See Section 4085 ("board").

• In subdivisions (a) and (e), the words "conditions, covenants, and restrictions" are replaced with "declaration." See Section 4135 ("declaration").

See also Sections 4080 ("association"), 4158 ("managing agent"), 4185 ("separate interest"). [40 Cal.L.Rev.Comm. Reports 235 (2010)].

§ 4215.   Liberal construction of instruments

Any deed, declaration, or condominium plan for a common interest development shall be liberally construed to facilitate the operation of the common interest development, and its provisions shall be presumed to be independent and severable. Nothing in Article 3 (commencing with Section 715) of Chapter 2 of Title 2 of Part 1 of Division 2 shall operate to invalidate any provisions of the governing documents. *(Added by Stats.2012, c. 180 (A.B.805), § 2, operative Jan. 1, 2014.)*

Law Revision Commission Comments

Section 4215 continues former Section 1370 without change, except as indicated below.

The following nonsubstantive changes are made:

• "This division" is replaced with "Division 2."

• The words "of a common interest development" are not continued.

See also Sections 4100 ("common interest development"), 4120 ("condominium plan"), 4135 ("declaration"), 4150 ("governing documents"). [40 Cal.L.Rev.Comm. Reports 235 (2010)].

§ 4220. Boundaries of units; presumptions

In interpreting deeds and condominium plans, the existing physical boundaries of a unit in a condominium project, when the boundaries of the unit are contained within a building, or of a unit reconstructed in substantial accordance with the original plans thereof, shall be conclusively presumed to be its boundaries rather than the metes and bounds expressed in the deed or condominium plan, if any exists, regardless of settling or lateral movement of the building and regardless of minor variance between boundaries shown on the plan or in the deed and those of the building. *(Added by Stats.2012, c. 180 (A.B.805), § 2, operative Jan. 1, 2014.)*

Law Revision Commission Comments

Section 4220 continues former Section 1371 without change.

See also Sections 4120 ("condominium plan"), 4125 ("condominium project"). [40 Cal.L.Rev.Comm. Reports 235 (2010)].

§ 4225. Restrictive covenants; deletion from declaration or other governing document; recording or filing of amended document

(a) No declaration or other governing document shall include a restrictive covenant in violation of Section 12955 of the Government Code.

(b) Notwithstanding any other provision of law or provision of the governing documents, the board, without approval of the members, shall amend any declaration or other governing document that includes a restrictive covenant prohibited by this section to delete the restrictive covenant, and shall restate the declaration or other governing document without the restrictive covenant but with no other change to the declaration or governing document.

(c) If the declaration is amended under this section, the board shall record the restated declaration in each county in which the common interest development is located. If the articles of incorporation are amended under this section, the board shall file a certificate of amendment with the Secretary of State pursuant to Section 7814 of the Corporations Code.

(d) If after providing written notice to an association, pursuant to Section 4035, requesting that the association delete a restrictive covenant that violates subdivision (a), and the association fails to delete the restrictive covenant within 30 days of receiving the notice, the Department of Fair Employment and Housing, a city or county in which a common interest development is located, or any person may bring an action against the association for injunctive relief to enforce subdivision (a). The court may award attorney's fees to the prevailing party. *(Added by Stats.2012, c. 180 (A.B.805), § 2, operative Jan. 1, 2014.)*

Law Revision Commission Comments

Section 4225 continues former Section 1352.5 without change, except as indicated below.

The following nonsubstantive changes are made:

• In subdivision (b), the words "board of directors of an association" are replaced with "board." See Section 4085 ("board").

• In subdivision (b), the word "owners" is replaced with "members." See Section 4160 ("member").

• Subdivision (c) is added.

• Subdivision (d) is revised to include a reference to the provision governing notice to an association (Section 4035).

See also Sections 4080 ("association"), 4085 ("board"), 4100 ("common interest development"), 4135 ("declaration"), 4150 ("governing documents"), 4170 ("person"). [40 Cal.L.Rev.Comm. Reports 235 (2010)].

§ 4230. Amendment of governing documents to delete construction or marketing provisions after completion by developer; requirements

(a) Notwithstanding any provision of the governing documents to the contrary, the board may, after the developer has completed construction of the development, has terminated construction activities, and has terminated marketing activities for the sale, lease, or other disposition of separate interests within the development, adopt an amendment deleting from any of the governing documents any provision which is unequivocally designed and intended, or which by its nature can only have been designed or intended, to facilitate the developer in completing the construction or marketing of the development. However, provisions of the governing documents relative to a particular construction or marketing phase of the development may not be deleted under the authorization of this subdivision until that construction or marketing phase has been completed.

(b) The provisions which may be deleted by action of the board shall be limited to those which provide for access by the developer over or across the common area for the purposes of (1) completion of construction of the development, and (2) the erection, construction, or maintenance of structures or other facilities designed to facilitate the completion of construction or marketing of separate interests.

(c) At least 30 days prior to taking action pursuant to subdivision (a), the board shall deliver to all members, by individual delivery, pursuant to Section 4040, (1) a copy of all amendments to the governing documents proposed to be adopted under subdivision (a), and (2) a notice of the time, date, and place the board will consider adoption of the amendments. The board may consider adoption of amendments to the governing documents pursuant to subdivision (a) only at a meeting that is open to all members, who shall be given opportunity to make comments thereon. All deliberations of the board on any action proposed under subdivision (a) shall only be conducted in an open meeting.

(d) The board may not amend the governing documents pursuant to this section without the approval of a majority of a quorum of the members, pursuant to Section 4070. For the purposes of this section, "quorum" means more than 50 percent of the members who own no more than two separate interests in the development. *(Added by Stats.2012, c. 180 (A.B.805), § 2, operative Jan. 1, 2014.)*

Law Revision Commission Comments

Section 4230 continues former Section 1355.5 without change, except as indicated below.

The following substantive change is made:

• Subdivision (c) is revised to provide for individual delivery of the specified notice. See Section 4040.

The following nonsubstantive changes are made:

• The words "his or her" are not continued in subdivision (a).

• The words "of a common interest development" are not continued in subdivision (a).

• The words "board of directors" and "board of directors of the association" are replaced throughout with "board." See Section 4085 ("board").

• Subdivision (b) is revised to use numerals to number the listed items, rather than letters.

• Subdivisions (c) and (d) are revised to use "member." See Section 4160 ("member").

• Subdivision (c) is revised to delete the unnecessary word "such."

• Subdivision (c) is revised to replace the word "which" with "that."

• Subdivision (d) is revised to use the standard term "approval of a majority of a quorum of the members." See Section 4070.

See also Sections 4095 ("common area"), 4150 ("governing documents"), 4185 ("separate interest"). [40 Cal.L.Rev.Comm. Reports 235 (2010)].

§ 4235. Correction of statutory references in documents

(a) Notwithstanding any other provision of law or provision of the governing documents, if the governing documents include a reference to a provision of the Davis–Stirling Common Interest Development Act that was repealed and continued in a new provision by the act that added this section, the board may amend the governing documents, solely to correct the cross-reference, by adopting a board resolution that shows the correction. Member approval is not required in order to adopt a resolution pursuant to this section.

(b) A declaration that is corrected under this section may be restated in corrected form and recorded, provided that a copy of the board resolution authorizing the corrections is recorded along with the restated declaration. *(Added by Stats.2012, c. 180 (A.B.805), § 2, operative Jan. 1, 2014.)*

Law Revision Commission Comments

Section 4235 is new. It is intended to provide a simplified method to correct statutory cross-references in an association's governing documents that are required as a result of the enactment of the act that added this section. No other amendment can be made under this section.

See also Sections 4085 ("board"), 4135 ("declaration"), 4150 ("governing documents"). [40 Cal.L.Rev.Comm. Reports 235 (2010)].

ARTICLE 2. DECLARATION

Section
4250. Contents of declaration.
4255. Notice of airport in vicinity; notice of San Francisco Bay Conservation and Development Commission jurisdiction.
4260. Amendment of declaration; authorization.
4265. Extension of term of declaration.
4270. Amendment of declaration; procedure.
4275. Amendment of declaration; petition; contents; filing; findings by court; power of court to approve amendment; recording amendment; delivery.

§ 4250. Contents of declaration

(a) A declaration, recorded on or after January 1, 1986, shall contain a legal description of the common interest development, and a statement that the common interest development is a community apartment project, condominium project, planned development, stock cooperative, or combination thereof. The declaration shall additionally set forth the name of the association and the restrictions on the use or enjoyment of any portion of the common interest development that are intended to be enforceable equitable servitudes.

(b) The declaration may contain any other matters the declarant or the members consider appropriate. *(Added by Stats.2012, c. 180 (A.B.805), § 2, operative Jan. 1, 2014.)*

Law Revision Commission Comments

Subdivision (a) of Section 4250 continues the first two sentences of former Section 1353(a)(1) without change.

Subdivision (b) continues former Section 1353(b) without change, except as indicated below.

The following nonsubstantive changes are made:

• The word "owners" is replaced with "members." See Section 4160 ("member").

• The words "original signator of the declaration" are replaced with "declarant." See Section 4130 ("declarant").

See also Sections 4080 ("association"), 4100 ("common interest development"), 4105 ("community apartment project"), 4125 ("condominium project"), 4135 ("declaration"), 4175 ("planned development"), 4190 ("stock cooperative"). [40 Cal.L.Rev.Comm. Reports 235 (2010)].

§ 4255. Notice of airport in vicinity; notice of San Francisco Bay Conservation and Development Commission jurisdiction

(a) If a common interest development is located within an airport influence area, a declaration, recorded after January 1, 2004, shall contain the following statement:

"NOTICE OF AIRPORT IN VICINITY

This property is presently located in the vicinity of an airport, within what is known as an airport influence area. For that reason, the property may be subject to some of the annoyances or inconveniences associated with proximity to airport operations (for example: noise, vibration, or odors). Individual sensitivities to those annoyances can vary from person to person. You may wish to consider what airport annoyances, if any, are associated with the property before you complete your purchase and determine whether they are acceptable to you."

(b) For purposes of this section, an "airport influence area," also known as an "airport referral area," is the area in which current or future airport-related noise, overflight, safety, or airspace protection factors may significantly affect land uses or necessitate restrictions on those uses as determined by an airport land use commission.

(c) If a common interest development is within the San Francisco Bay Conservation and Development Commission jurisdiction, as described in Section 66610 of the Government Code, a declaration recorded on or after January 1, 2006, shall contain the following notice:

"NOTICE OF SAN FRANCISCO BAY CONSERVATION AND DEVELOPMENT COMMISSION JURISDICTION

This property is located within the jurisdiction of the San Francisco Bay Conservation and Development Commission. Use and development of property within the commission's jurisdiction may be subject to special regulations, restrictions, and permit requirements. You may wish to investigate and determine whether they are acceptable to you and your intended use of the property before you complete your transaction."

(d) The statement in a declaration acknowledging that a property is located in an airport influence area or within the jurisdiction of the San Francisco Bay Conservation and Development Commission does not constitute a title defect, lien, or encumbrance. *(Added by Stats.2012, c. 180 (A.B.805), § 2, operative Jan. 1, 2014.)*

Law Revision Commission Comments

Section 4255 continues all but the first two sentences of former Section 1353(a)(1)-(4) without change, except as indicated below.

The following nonsubstantive change is made:

• The words "the property" are replaced with "a common interest development" to improve clarity. See also Bus. & Prof. Code § 11010 (disclosure of property within airport influence area); Pub. Util. Code § 21675 (designation of "airport influence area" by county airport land use commission).

See also Sections 4100 ("common interest development"), 4135 ("declaration"). [40 Cal.L.Rev.Comm. Reports 235 (2010)].

§ 4260. Amendment of declaration; authorization

Except to the extent that a declaration provides by its express terms that it is not amendable, in whole or in part, a declaration that fails to include provisions permitting its amendment at all times during its existence may be amended at any time. *(Added by Stats.2012, c. 180 (A.B.805), § 2, operative Jan. 1, 2014.)*

Law Revision Commission Comments

Section 4260 continues the first sentence of former Section 1355(b) without change, except as indicated below.

The following nonsubstantive change is made:

• The word "which" is replaced with "that."

See also Section 4135 ("declaration"). [40 Cal.L.Rev.Comm. Reports 235 (2010)].

§ 4265. Extension of term of declaration

(a) The Legislature finds that there are common interest developments that have been created with deed restrictions that do not provide a means for the members to extend the term of the declaration. The Legislature further finds that covenants and restrictions contained in the declaration, are an appropriate method for protecting the common plan of developments and to provide for a mechanism for financial support for the upkeep of common area including, but not limited to, roofs, roads, heating systems, and recreational facilities. If declarations terminate prematurely, common interest developments may deteriorate and the housing supply of affordable units could be impacted adversely. The Legislature further finds and declares that it is in the public interest to provide a vehicle for extending the term of the declaration if the extension is approved by a majority of all members, pursuant to Section 4065.

(b) A declaration that specifies a termination date, but that contains no provision for extension of the termination date, may be extended, before its termination date, by the approval of members pursuant to Section 4270.

(c) No single extension of the terms of the declaration made pursuant to this section shall exceed the initial term of the declaration or 20 years, whichever is less. However, more than one extension may occur pursuant to this section. *(Added by Stats.2012, c. 180 (A.B.805), § 2, operative Jan. 1, 2014.)*

Law Revision Commission Comments

Subdivision (a) of Section 4265 continues former Section 1357(a) without change, except as indicated below.

The following nonsubstantive changes are made:

• The defined term "member" is used. See Section 4160 ("member").

• The phrase "common areas" is singularized.

• The word "which" is replaced with "that."

• A reference to approval by "members having more than 50 percent of the votes in the association" is replaced with standard terminology.

Subdivision (b) continues part of the substance of former Section 1357(b), authorizing extension of the termination date of a declaration that does not provide for extension of the termination date, except as indicated below.

The following nonsubstantive change is made:

• Language is added to make clear that the extension must occur before the termination date.

The procedure for extension of the termination date provided in former Section 1357(b)-(c) is not continued. An extension would instead be made pursuant to the general procedure for amendment of a declaration. See Section 4270.

Subdivision (c) continues former Section 1357(d) without change.

See also Sections 4095 ("common area"), 4100 ("common interest development"), 4135 ("declaration"). [40 Cal.L.Rev.Comm. Reports 235 (2010)].

§ 4270. Amendment of declaration; procedure

(a) A declaration may be amended pursuant to the declaration or this act. Except as provided in Section 4275, an amendment is effective after all of the following requirements have been met:

(1) The amendment has been approved by the percentage of members required by the declaration and any other person whose approval is required by the declaration.

(2) That fact has been certified in a writing executed and acknowledged by the officer designated in the declaration or by the association for that purpose, or if no one is designated, by the president of the association.

(3) The amendment has been recorded in each county in which a portion of the common interest development is located.

(b) If the declaration does not specify the percentage of members who must approve an amendment of the declaration, an amendment may be approved by a majority of all members, pursuant to Section 4065. *(Added by Stats.2012, c. 180 (A.B. 805), § 2, operative Jan. 1, 2014.)*

Law Revision Commission Comments

Subdivision (a) of Section 4270 continues former Section 1355(a) without change, except as indicated below.

The following substantive changes are made:

• The term "governing documents" is replaced with the term "declaration." See Section 4135 ("declaration").

• Paragraph (a)(1) is revised to recognize that a declaration may require that an amendment be approved by a non-member.

The following nonsubstantive changes are made:

• The first word is replaced with "A."

• The word "title" is replaced with "act."

• The defined term "member" is used. See Section 4160 ("member").

• The subdivision is divided into paragraphs, with conforming technical adjustments to the language.

Subdivision (b) generalizes a rule stated in former Sections 1355(b) and 1357.

See also Sections 4080 ("association"), 4100 ("common interest development"), 4170 ("person"). [40 Cal.L.Rev.Comm. Reports 235 (2010)].

§ 4275. Amendment of declaration; petition; contents; filing; findings by court; power of court to approve amendment; recording amendment; delivery

(a) If in order to amend a declaration, the declaration requires members having more than 50 percent of the votes in the association, in a single class voting structure, or members having more than 50 percent of the votes in more than one class in a voting structure with more than one class, to vote in favor of the amendment, the association, or any member, may petition the superior court of the county in which the common interest development is located for an order reducing the percentage of the affirmative votes necessary for such an amendment. The petition shall describe the effort that has been made to solicit approval of the association members in the manner provided in the declaration, the number of affirmative and negative votes actually received, the number or percentage of affirmative votes required to effect the amendment in accordance with the existing declaration, and other matters the petitioner considers relevant to the court's determination. The petition shall also contain, as exhibits thereto, copies of all of the following:

(1) The governing documents.

(2) A complete text of the amendment.

(3) Copies of any notice and solicitation materials utilized in the solicitation of member approvals.

(4) A short explanation of the reason for the amendment.

(5) Any other documentation relevant to the court's determination.

(b) Upon filing the petition, the court shall set the matter for hearing and issue an ex parte order setting forth the manner in which notice shall be given.

(c) The court may, but shall not be required to, grant the petition if it finds all of the following:

(1) The petitioner has given not less than 15 days written notice of the court hearing to all members of the association, to any mortgagee of a mortgage or beneficiary of a deed of trust

who is entitled to notice under the terms of the declaration, and to the city, county, or city and county in which the common interest development is located that is entitled to notice under the terms of the declaration.

(2) Balloting on the proposed amendment was conducted in accordance with the governing documents, this act, and any other applicable law.

(3) A reasonably diligent effort was made to permit all eligible members to vote on the proposed amendment.

(4) Members having more than 50 percent of the votes, in a single class voting structure, voted in favor of the amendment. In a voting structure with more than one class, where the declaration requires a majority of more than one class to vote in favor of the amendment, members having more than 50 percent of the votes of each class required by the declaration to vote in favor of the amendment voted in favor of the amendment.

(5) The amendment is reasonable.

(6) Granting the petition is not improper for any reason stated in subdivision (e).

(d) If the court makes the findings required by subdivision (c), any order issued pursuant to this section may confirm the amendment as being validly approved on the basis of the affirmative votes actually received during the balloting period or the order may dispense with any requirement relating to quorums or to the number or percentage of votes needed for approval of the amendment that would otherwise exist under the governing documents.

(e) Subdivisions (a) to (d), inclusive, notwithstanding, the court shall not be empowered by this section to approve any amendment to the declaration that:

(1) Would change provisions in the declaration requiring the approval of members having more than 50 percent of the votes in more than one class to vote in favor of an amendment, unless members having more than 50 percent of the votes in each affected class approved the amendment.

(2) Would eliminate any special rights, preferences, or privileges designated in the declaration as belonging to the declarant, without the consent of the declarant.

(3) Would impair the security interest of a mortgagee of a mortgage or the beneficiary of a deed of trust without the approval of the percentage of the mortgagees and beneficiaries specified in the declaration, if the declaration requires the approval of a specified percentage of the mortgagees and beneficiaries.

(f) An amendment is not effective pursuant to this section until the court order and amendment have been recorded in every county in which a portion of the common interest development is located. The amendment may be acknowledged by, and the court order and amendment may be recorded by, any person designated in the declaration or by the association for that purpose, or if no one is designated for that purpose, by the president of the association. Upon recordation of the amendment and court order, the declaration, as amended in accordance with this section, shall have the same force and effect as if the amendment were adopted in compliance with every requirement imposed by the governing documents.

(g) Within a reasonable time after the amendment is recorded the association shall deliver to each member, by individual delivery, pursuant to Section 4040, a copy of the amendment, together with a statement that the amendment has been recorded. *(Added by Stats.2012, c. 180 (A.B.805), § 2, operative Jan. 1, 2014.)*

Law Revision Commission Comments

Section 4275 continues former Section 1356 without change, except as indicated below.

The following substantive change is made:

● Language is added to paragraph (c)(2) to require a finding that a vote is held in accordance with "this act, and any other applicable law."

The following nonsubstantive changes are made:

● Subdivision (g) is revised to specify the procedure for individual delivery of notice and to use "member." See Section 4160 ("member").

An incorporated association may also petition the court under Corporations Code Section 7515 with respect to actions governed by that provision.

See also Sections 4080 ("association"), 4100 ("common interest development"), 4130 ("declarant"), 4135 ("declaration"), 4150 ("governing documents"), 4170 ("person"). [40 Cal.L.Rev.Comm. Reports 235 (2010)].

ARTICLE 3. ARTICLES OF INCORPORATION

Section
4280. Association articles of incorporation; required statements.

§ 4280. Association articles of incorporation; required statements

(a) The articles of incorporation of an association filed with the Secretary of State shall include a statement, which shall be in addition to the statement of purposes of the corporation, that does all of the following:

(1) Identifies the corporation as an association formed to manage a common interest development under the Davis–Stirling Common Interest Development Act.

(2) States the business or corporate office of the association, if any, and, if the office is not on the site of the common interest development, states the front street and nearest cross street for the physical location of the common interest development.

(3) States the name and address of the association's managing agent, if any.

(b) The statement filed by an incorporated association with the Secretary of State pursuant to Section 8210 of the Corporations Code shall also contain a statement identifying the corporation as an association formed to manage a common interest development under the Davis–Stirling Common Interest Development Act.

(c) Documents filed prior to January 1, 2014, in compliance with former Section 1363.5, as it read on January 1, 2013, are deemed to be in compliance with this section. *(Added by Stats.2012, c. 180 (A.B.805), § 2, operative Jan. 1, 2014. Amended by Stats.2013, c. 605 (S.B.752), § 20.)*

Law Revision Commission Comments

Section 4280 continues former Section 1363.5 without change, except as indicated below.

The following nonsubstantive changes are made:

● A cross-reference to the definition of "managing agent" is not continued. See Section 4158 ("managing agent").

● References to "common interest development association" have been standardized.

See also Corp. Code §§ 1502 (annual statement), 7130–7135 (content of articles of incorporation), 7810–7820 (amendment of articles of incorporation), 7150–7153 (content and amendment of bylaws).

See also Sections 4080 ("association"), 4100 ("common interest development"). [40 Cal.L.Rev.Comm. Reports 235 (2010)].

Subdivision (c) is new. It makes clear that the section does not invalidate documents that were filed in compliance with former law. [43 Cal.L.Rev.Comm. Reports ___-(Appendix 5) (2012)].

ARTICLE 4. CONDOMINIUM PLAN

§ 4285. Contents of condominium plan

A condominium plan shall contain all of the following:

(a) A description or survey map of a condominium project, which shall refer to or show monumentation on the ground.

(b) A three-dimensional description of a condominium project, one or more dimensions of which may extend for an indefinite distance upwards or downwards, in sufficient detail to identify the common area and each separate interest.

(c) A certificate consenting to the recordation of the condominium plan pursuant to this act that is signed and acknowledged as provided in Section 4290. *(Added by Stats.2012, c. 180 (A.B.805), § 2, operative Jan. 1, 2014.)*

Law Revision Commission Comments

Section 4285 continues the introduction of former Section 1351(e) without change, except as indicated below.

The following nonsubstantive changes are made:

• The enumerated items are set out as subdivisions.

• The word "title" is replaced with "act."

• The list of persons who must sign and acknowledge the certificate consenting to recordation of the condominium plan is replaced with a reference to the section governing the creation and recordation of a condominium plan.

See also Sections 4095 ("common area"), 4125 ("condominium project"), 4185 ("separate interest"). [40 Cal.L.Rev.Comm. Reports 235 (2010)].

§ 4290. Certificate consenting to recordation of condominium plan; signatures and acknowledgements

(a) The certificate consenting to the recordation of a condominium plan that is required by subdivision (c) of Section 4285 shall be signed and acknowledged by all of the following persons:

(1) The record owner of fee title to that property included in the condominium project.

(2) In the case of a condominium project that will terminate upon the termination of an estate for years, by all lessors and lessees of the estate for years.

(3) In the case of a condominium project subject to a life estate, by all life tenants and remainder interests.

(4) The trustee or the beneficiary of each recorded deed of trust, and the mortgagee of each recorded mortgage encumbering the property.

(b) Owners of mineral rights, easements, rights-of-way, and other nonpossessory interests do not need to sign the certificate.

(c) In the event a conversion to condominiums of a community apartment project or stock cooperative has been approved by the required number of owners, trustees, beneficiaries, and mortgagees pursuant to Section 66452.10 of the Government Code, the certificate need only be signed by those owners, trustees, beneficiaries, and mortgagees approving the conversion. *(Added by Stats.2012, c. 180 (A.B.805), § 2, operative Jan. 1, 2014. Amended by Stats.2013, c. 183 (S.B.745), § 12.)*

Law Revision Commission Comments

Section 4290 continues the substance of former Section 1351(e)(3), except as indicated below.

The following nonsubstantive changes are made:

• The last paragraph of former Section 1351(e) is not continued in this section.

• A cross-reference to Section 4120(c) is added to the first paragraph.

• Subdivision (b) is revised to make clear that it states an exception to who must sign the certificate of consent to recordation, rather than the condominium plan itself.

See also Sections 4105 ("community apartment project"), 4120 ("condominium plan"), 4125 ("condominium project"), 4170 ("person"), 4190 ("stock cooperative"). [40 Cal.L.Rev.Comm. Reports 235 (2010)].

Subdivision (a) of Section 4290 is amended to correct a reference error. [42 Cal.L.Rev.Comm. Reports 311 (2012)].

§ 4295. Amendment or revocation of condominium plan

A condominium plan may be amended or revoked by a recorded instrument that is acknowledged and signed by all the persons who, at the time of amendment or revocation, are persons whose signatures are required under Section 4290. *(Added by Stats.2012, c. 180 (A.B.805), § 2, operative Jan. 1, 2014.)*

Law Revision Commission Comments

Section 4295 continues the last paragraph of former Section 1351(e) without change, except as indicated below.

The following nonsubstantive change is made:

• Language is added to make clear that the persons whose signatures are required for amendment or revocation of a condominium plan are the persons who fall within the groups described in Section 4290 at the time of amendment or revocation.

See also Sections 4120 ("condominium plan"), 4170 ("person"). [40 Cal.L.Rev.Comm. Reports 235 (2010)].

ARTICLE 5. OPERATING RULES

§ 4340. Definitions

For the purposes of this article:

(a) "Operating rule" means a regulation adopted by the board that applies generally to the management and operation of the common interest development or the conduct of the business and affairs of the association.

(b) "Rule change" means the adoption, amendment, or repeal of an operating rule by the board. *(Added by Stats.2012, c. 180 (A.B.805), § 2, operative Jan. 1, 2014.)*

Law Revision Commission Comments

Section 4340 continues former Section 1357.100 without change, except as indicated below.

The following nonsubstantive change is made:

• The words "board of directors of the association" are replaced with "board." See Section 4085 ("board").

See also Sections 4080 ("association"), 4100 ("common interest development"). [40 Cal.L.Rev.Comm. Reports 235 (2010)].

§ 4350. Requirements for validity and enforceability

An operating rule is valid and enforceable only if all of the following requirements are satisfied:

(a) The rule is in writing.

(b) The rule is within the authority of the board conferred by law or by the declaration, articles of incorporation or association, or bylaws of the association.

(c) The rule is not * * * in conflict with governing law and the declaration, articles of incorporation or association, or bylaws of the association.

(d) The rule is adopted, amended, or repealed in good faith and in substantial compliance with the requirements of this article.

(e) The rule is reasonable. *(Added by Stats.2012, c. 180 (A.B.805), § 2, operative Jan. 1, 2014. Amended by Stats.2013, c. 183 (S.B.745), § 13.)*

Law Revision Commission Comments

Section 4350 continues former Section 1357.110 without change, except as indicated below.

The following nonsubstantive change is made:

• The words "board of directors of the association" are replaced with "board." See Section 4085 ("board"). .

See also Sections 4080 ("association"), 4135 ("declaration"), 4340(a) ("operating rule"). [40 Cal.L.Rev.Comm. Reports 235 (2010)].

Section 4350 is amended to conform the terminology used in subdivision (c) to that used in Section 4205. [43 Cal.L.Rev.Comm. Reports 23 (2013)].

§ 4355. Approved subject matters; board action to propose rule change; special meetings of members to reverse rule change

(a) Sections 4360 and 4365 only apply to an operating rule that relates to one or more of the following subjects:

(1) Use of the common area or of an exclusive use common area.

(2) Use of a separate interest, including any aesthetic or architectural standards that govern alteration of a separate interest.

(3) Member discipline, including any schedule of monetary penalties for violation of the governing documents and any procedure for the imposition of penalties.

(4) Any standards for delinquent assessment payment plans.

(5) Any procedures adopted by the association for resolution of disputes.

(6) Any procedures for reviewing and approving or disapproving a proposed physical change to a member's separate interest or to the common area.

(7) Procedures for elections.

(b) Sections 4360 and 4365 do not apply to the following actions by the board:

(1) A decision regarding maintenance of the common area.

(2) A decision on a specific matter that is not intended to apply generally.

(3) A decision setting the amount of a regular or special assessment.

(4) A rule change that is required by law, if the board has no discretion as to the substantive effect of the rule change.

(5) Issuance of a document that merely repeats existing law or the governing documents. *(Added by Stats.2012, c. 180 (A.B. 805), § 2, operative Jan. 1, 2014.)*

Law Revision Commission Comments

Section 4355 continues former Section 1357.120 without change, except as indicated below.

The following nonsubstantive change is made:

• The words "board of directors" and "board of directors of the association" are replaced with "board." See Section 4085 ("board").

See also Sections 4080 ("association"), 4095 ("common area"), 4145 ("exclusive use common area"), 4150 ("governing documents"), 4160 ("member"), 4340(a) ("operating rule"), 4340(b) ("rule change"), 4185 ("separate interest"). [40 Cal.L.Rev.Comm. Reports 235 (2010)].

§ 4360. Proposed rule change by board action; notice; meeting

(a) The board shall provide general notice pursuant to Section 4045 of a proposed rule change at least 30 days before making the rule change. The notice shall include the text of the proposed rule change and a description of the purpose and effect of the proposed rule change. Notice is not required under this subdivision if the board determines that an immediate rule change is necessary to address an imminent threat to public health or safety or imminent risk of substantial economic loss to the association.

(b) A decision on a proposed rule change shall be made at a board meeting, after consideration of any comments made by association members.

(c) As soon as possible after making a rule change, but not more than 15 days after making the rule change, the board shall deliver general notice pursuant to Section 4045 of the rule change. If the rule change was an emergency rule change made under subdivision (d), the notice shall include the text of the rule change, a description of the purpose and effect of the rule change, and the date that the rule change expires.

(d) If the board determines that an immediate rule change is required to address an imminent threat to public health or safety, or an imminent risk of substantial economic loss to the association, it may make an emergency rule change, and no notice is required, as specified in subdivision (a). An emergency rule change is effective for 120 days, unless the rule change provides for a shorter effective period. A rule change made under this subdivision may not be readopted under this subdivision. *(Added by Stats.2012, c. 180 (A.B.805), § 2, operative Jan. 1, 2014.)*

Law Revision Commission Comments

Section 4360 continues former Section 1357.130 without change, except as indicated below.

The following substantive changes are made:

• A reference to former Section 1350.7 is replaced with references to the provision governing general notice. Delivery of "general notice" under Section 4045 preserves most of the substance of former law governing delivery of notice under this section, except that Section 4045 permits the posting of notices and requires that individual notice delivery methods be used for a member who has requested that form of delivery. *Cf.* former Section 1350.7. See Sections 4085 ("board"), 4090 ("board meeting").

The following nonsubstantive changes are made:

• The words "to the members" are not continued in subdivision (a).

• The words "board of directors" are replaced throughout with the "board." See Section 4085 ("board").

• The words "meeting of the board of directors" are replaced with "board meeting." See Section 4090 ("board meeting").

• In subdivision (d), a semi-colon is replaced with a comma, for grammatical reasons.

See also Sections 4080 ("association"), 4160 ("member"), 4340(b) ("rule change"). [40 Cal.L.Rev.Comm. Reports 235 (2010)].

§ 4365. Special meeting of members to reverse rule change; notice; voting requirements; effect of approved reversal

(a) Members of an association owning 5 percent or more of the separate interests may call a special vote of the members to reverse a rule change.

(b) A special vote of the members may be called by delivering a written request to the association. Not less than 35 days nor more than 90 days after receipt of a proper request, the association shall hold a vote of the members on whether to reverse the rule change, pursuant to Article 4 (commencing with Section 5100) of Chapter 6. The written request may not be delivered more than 30 days after the association gives general notice of the rule change, pursuant to Section 4045.

(c) For the purposes of Section 5225 of this code and Section 8330 of the Corporations Code, collection of signatures to call a special vote under this section is a purpose reasonably related to the interests of the members of the association. A member request to copy or inspect the membership list solely for that purpose may not be denied on the grounds that the purpose is not reasonably related to the member's interests as a member.

(d) The rule change may be reversed by the affirmative vote of a majority of a quorum of the members, pursuant to Section 4070, or if the declaration or bylaws require a greater percentage, by the affirmative vote of the percentage required.

(e) Unless otherwise provided in the declaration or bylaws, for the purposes of this section, a member may cast one vote per separate interest owned.

(f) A rule change reversed under this section may not be readopted for one year after the date of the vote reversing the rule change. Nothing in this section precludes the board from adopting a different rule on the same subject as the rule change that has been reversed.

(g) As soon as possible after the close of voting, but not more than 15 days after the close of voting, the board shall provide general notice pursuant to Section 4045 of the results of the member vote.

(h) This section does not apply to an emergency rule change made under subdivision (d) of Section 4360. (Added by Stats. 2012, c. 180 (A.B.805), § 2, operative Jan. 1, 2014.)

Law Revision Commission Comments

Section 4365 continues former Section 1357.140 without change, except as indicated below.

The following substantive changes are made:

• A reference to former Section 1350.7 is replaced with references to the provision governing general notice pursuant to Section 4045.

• A reference to voting pursuant to Corporations Code Section 7513 is replaced with a reference to the voting provisions of this act.

The following nonsubstantive changes are made:

• Cross-references are updated to reflect the new locations of referenced provisions.

• The words "board of directors" are replaced with "board." See Section 4085 ("board").

See also Sections 4080 ("association"), 4135 ("declaration"), 4340(b) ("rule change"), 4185 ("separate interest"). [40 Cal.L.Rev.Comm. Reports 235 (2010)].

Research References

Rutter, Cal. Practice Guide: Civil Appeals & Writs Ch. 3-E, E. Filing Steps.
Rutter, Cal. Practice Guide: Civil Appeals & Writs Ch. 3-E, Outline E.

§ 4370. Applicability of article to changes commenced before and after January 1, 2004

(a) This article applies to a rule change commenced on or after January 1, 2004.

(b) Nothing in this article affects the validity of a rule change commenced before January 1, 2004.

(c) For the purposes of this section, a rule change is commenced when the board takes its first official action leading to adoption of the rule change. (Added by Stats.2012, c. 180 (A.B.805), § 2, operative Jan. 1, 2014.)

Law Revision Commission Comments

Section 4370 continues former Section 1357.150 without change, except as indicated below.

The following nonsubstantive change is made:

• The words "board of directors of the association" are replaced with "board." See Section 4085 ("board").

See also Section 4340(b) ("rule change"). [40 Cal.L.Rev.Comm. Reports 235 (2010)].

Research References

9 Witkin Cal. Proc. 5th Appeal § 38, (S 38) Former Attorney Requesting Fees.
11 Witkin, California Summary 10th Husband and Wife § 175, (S 175) Development of Law.
11 Witkin, California Summary 10th Husband and Wife § 180, (S 180) in General.

CHAPTER 4. OWNERSHIP AND TRANSFER OF INTERESTS

ARTICLE 1. OWNERSHIP RIGHTS AND INTERESTS

§ 4500. Ownership of common areas

Unless the declaration otherwise provides, in a condominium project, or in a planned development in which the common area is owned by the owners of the separate interests, the common area is owned as tenants in common, in equal shares, one for each separate interest. (Added by Stats.2012, c. 180 (A.B.805), § 2, operative Jan. 1, 2014.)

Law Revision Commission Comments

Section 4500 continues former Section 1362 without change, except as indicated below.

The following nonsubstantive changes are made:

• The phrase "common areas" is singularized.

• The words "unit or lot" are replaced with "separate interest."

See also Sections 4095 ("common area"), 4125 ("condominium project"), 4135 ("declaration"), 4175 ("planned development"), 4185 ("separate interest"). [40 Cal.L.Rev.Comm. Reports 235 (2010)].

§ 4505. Rights and easements of ingress, egress, and support

Unless the declaration otherwise provides:

(a) In a community apartment project and condominium project, and in those planned developments with common area owned in common by the owners of the separate interests, there are appurtenant to each separate interest nonexclusive rights of ingress, egress, and support, if necessary, through the common area. The common area is subject to these rights.

(b) In a stock cooperative, and in a planned development with common area owned by the association, there is an easement for ingress, egress, and support, if necessary, appurtenant to each separate interest. The common area is subject to these easements. (Added by Stats.2012, c. 180 (A.B.805), § 2, operative Jan. 1, 2014.)

Law Revision Commission Comments

Section 4505 continues former Section 1361 without change, except as indicated below.

The following nonsubstantive change is made:

● The phrase "common areas" is singularized.

See also Sections 4080 ("association"), 4095 ("common area"), 4105 ("community apartment project"), 4125 ("condominium project"), 4135 ("declaration"), 4175 ("planned development"), 4185 ("separate interest"), 4190 ("stock cooperative"). [40 Cal.L.Rev.Comm. Reports 235 (2010)].

§ 4510. Physical access to owner or occupant's separate interest

Except as otherwise provided in law, an order of the court, or an order pursuant to a final and binding arbitration decision, an association may not deny a member or occupant physical access to the member's or occupant's separate interest, either by restricting access through the common area to the separate interest, or by restricting access solely to the separate interest. *(Added by Stats.2012, c. 180 (A.B.805), § 2, operative Jan. 1, 2014.)*

Law Revision Commission Comments

Section 4510 continues former Section 1361.5 without change, except as indicated below.

The following nonsubstantive changes are made:

● The words "his or her" are replaced with "the member's or occupant's."

● References to the "owner's" separate interest are revised to omit the word "owner's." This will help to avoid any implication that the reference does not also apply to an "occupant" of a separate interest.

● The word "owner" is replaced with "member" throughout. See Section 4160 ("member").

● The phrase "common areas" is singularized.

See also Sections 4080 ("association"), 4095 ("common area"), 4185 ("separate interest"). [40 Cal.L.Rev.Comm. Reports 235 (2010)].

Research References

11 Witkin, California Summary 10th Husband and Wife § 63, Nature of Ground.

ARTICLE 2. TRANSFER DISCLOSURE

Section

§ 4525. Sale or title transfer; provision of specified items to prospective purchasers

(a) The owner of a separate interest shall provide the following documents to a prospective purchaser of the separate interest, as soon as practicable before the transfer of title or the execution of a real property sales contract, as defined in Section 2985:

(1) A copy of all governing documents. If the association is not incorporated, this shall include a statement in writing from an authorized representative of the association that the association is not incorporated.

(2) If there is a restriction in the governing documents limiting the occupancy, residency, or use of a separate interest on the basis of age in a manner different from that provided in Section 51.3, a statement that the restriction is only enforceable to the extent permitted by Section 51.3 and a statement specifying the applicable provisions of Section 51.3.

(3) A copy of the most recent documents distributed pursuant to Article 7 (commencing with Section 5300) of Chapter 6.

(4) A true statement in writing obtained from an authorized representative of the association as to the amount of the association's current regular and special assessments and fees, any assessments levied upon the owner's interest in the common interest development that are unpaid on the date of the statement, and any monetary fines or penalties levied upon the owner's interest and unpaid on the date of the statement. The statement obtained from an authorized representative shall also include true information on late charges, interest, and costs of collection which, as of the date of the statement, are or may be made a lien upon the owner's interest in a common interest development pursuant to Article 2 (commencing with Section 5650) of Chapter 8.

(5) A copy or a summary of any notice previously sent to the owner pursuant to Section 5855 that sets forth any alleged violation of the governing documents that remains unresolved at the time of the request. The notice shall not be deemed a waiver of the association's right to enforce the governing documents against the owner or the prospective purchaser of the separate interest with respect to any violation. This paragraph shall not be construed to require an association to inspect an owner's separate interest.

(6) A copy of the initial list of defects provided to each member pursuant to Section 6000, unless the association and the builder subsequently enter into a settlement agreement or otherwise resolve the matter and the association complies with Section 6100. Disclosure of the initial list of defects pursuant to this paragraph does not waive any privilege attached to the document. The initial list of defects shall also include a statement that a final determination as to whether the list of defects is accurate and complete has not been made.

(7) A copy of the latest information provided for in Section 6100.

(8) Any change in the association's current regular and special assessments and fees which have been approved by the board, but have not become due and payable as of the date disclosure is provided pursuant to this subdivision.

(9) If there is a provision in the governing documents that prohibits the rental or leasing of any of the separate interests in the common interest development to a renter, lessee, or tenant, a statement describing the prohibition * * *.

(10) If requested by the prospective purchaser, a copy of the minutes of board meetings, excluding meetings held in executive session, conducted over the previous 12 months, that were approved by the board.

(b) This section does not apply to an owner that is subject to * * * Section 11018.6 of the Business and Professions Code. *(Added by Stats.2012, c. 180 (A.B.805), § 2, operative Jan. 1, 2014. Amended by Stats.2013, c. 183 (S.B.745), § 14.)*

Law Revision Commission Comments

Section 4525 continues the substance of subdivision (a) of former Section 1368 without change, except as indicated below.

The following nonsubstantive changes are made:

● Cross-references are updated to reflect the new locations of the referenced provisions.

● The words "association's board of directors" are replaced with "board." See Section 4085 ("board").

● Subdivision (a)(1) is revised to make clear that all governing documents must be provided. See Section 4150 ("governing documents").

● The words "member of the association" are replaced with "member." See Section 4160 ("member").

- The words "meetings ... of the association's board of directors" are replaced with "board meetings." See Section 4090 ("board meeting").

See also Sections 4080 ("association"), 4100 ("common interest development"), 4185 ("separate interest"). [40 Cal.L.Rev.Comm. Reports 235 (2010)].

Paragraph (9) of subdivision (a) of Section 4525 is amended to continue, without substantive change, a revision to former Section 1368 made in 2012 by AB 2697 (Assembly Committee on Housing and Community Development). See 2012 Cal. Stat. ch. 770, § 4.5. This is a technical revision. [42 Cal.L.Rev.Comm. Reports 311 (2012)].

§ 4528. Billing disclosures; form

The form for billing disclosures required by Section 4530 shall be in <u>at least 10–point type and</u> substantially the following form:

CHARGES FOR DOCUMENTS PROVIDED AS REQUIRED BY SECTION 4525*
Property Address
Owner of Property
Owner's Mailing Address (If known or different from property address.)
Provider of the Section 4525 Items:
Print Name _____ Position or Title
_____ Association or Agent
Date Form Completed
Check or Complete Applicable Column or Columns Below

Document	Civil Code Section Included	Not Available (N/A) or Not Applicable (N/App)
Articles of Incorporation or statement that not incorporated	Section 4525(a)(1)	
CC&Rs	Section 4525(a)(1)	
Bylaws	Section 4525(a)(1)	
Operating Rules	Section 4525(a)(1)	
Age restrictions, if any	Section 4525(a)(2)	
Rental restrictions, if any	Section 4525(a)(9)	
Annual budget report or summary, including reserve study	Sections 5300 and 4525(a)(3)	
Assessment and reserve funding disclosure summary	Sections 5300 and 4525(a)(4)	
Financial statement review	Sections 5305 and 4525(a)(3)	
Assessment enforcement policy	Sections 5310 and 4525(a)(4)	
Insurance summary	Sections 5300 and 4525(a)(3)	
Regular assessment	Section 4525(a)(4)	
Special assessment	Section 4525(a)(4)	
Emergency assessment	Section 4525(a)(4)	
Other unpaid obligations of seller	Sections 5675 and 4525(a)(4)	
Approved changes to assessments	Sections 5300 and 4525(a)(4), (8)	
Settlement notice regarding common area defects	Sections 4525(a)(6), (7), and 6100	
Preliminary list of defects	Sections 4525(a)(6), 6000, and 6100	
Notice(s) of violation	Sections 5855 and 4525(a)(5)	
Required statement of fees	Section 4525	
Minutes of regular board meetings conducted over the previous 12 months, if requested	Section 4525(a)(10)	
Total fees for these documents:		

* The information provided by this form may not include all fees that may be imposed before the close of escrow. Additional fees that are not related to the requirements of Section 4525 may be charged separately.

(Added by Stats.2012, c. 180 (A.B.805), § 2, operative Jan. 1, 2014. Amended by Stats.2013, c. 183 (S.B.745), § 15.)

Law Revision Commission Comments

Section 4528 continues former Section 1368.2 without change, except as indicated below.

The following nonsubstantive changes are made:

- Cross-references are updated to reflect the new locations of the referenced provisions.
- The words "meetings of the board of directors" are replaced with "board meetings." See Section 4090 ("board meeting").
- The words "pro forma operating budget" are replaced with "annual budget report." See Section 4076 ("annual budget report").
- An erroneous statutory reference in the form to former Section 1368(a)(9), which should have referred to former Section 1368(a)(10), is corrected.

See also Sections 4080 ("association"), 4340(a) ("operating rule"). [40 Cal.L.Rev.Comm. Reports 235 (2010)].

Section 4528 is amended to continue, without substantive change, a revision to former Section 1368.2 made in 2012 by AB 1838 (Calderon). See 2012 Cal. Stat. ch. 475, § 2. This is a technical revision. [42 Cal.L.Rev.Comm. Reports 311 (2012)].

§ 4530. Copies of requested documents; fees

(a)<u>(1)</u> Upon written request, the association shall, within 10 days of the mailing or delivery of the request, provide the owner of a separate interest, or any other recipient authorized by the owner, with a copy of the requested documents specified in Section 4525.

* * * <u>(2)</u> The documents required to be made available pursuant to this section may be maintained in electronic form, and may be posted on the association's Internet Web site. Requesting parties shall have the option of receiving the documents by electronic transmission if the association maintains the documents in electronic form.

<u>(3) Delivery of the documents required by this section shall not be withheld for any reason nor subject to any condition except the payment of the fee authorized pursuant to subdivision (b).</u>

(b)<u>(1)</u> The association may collect a reasonable fee based upon the association's actual cost for the procurement, preparation, reproduction, and delivery of the documents requested pursuant to * * * <u>this section. Additional fees shall not be charged by the association for the electronic delivery of the documents requested.</u>

<u>(2) Upon receipt of a written request, the association shall provide, on the form described in Section 4528, a written or</u>

electronic estimate of the fees that will be assessed for providing the requested documents.

(3)(A) A cancellation fee for documents specified in subdivision (a) shall not be collected if either of the following applies:

(i) The request was canceled in writing by the same party that placed the order and work had not yet been performed on the order.

(ii) The request was canceled in writing and any work that had been performed on the order was compensated.

(B) The association shall refund all fees collected pursuant to paragraph (1) if the request was canceled in writing and work had not yet been performed on the order.

(C) If the request was canceled in writing, the association shall refund the share of fees collected pursuant to paragraph (1) that represents the portion of the work not performed on the order.

(4) Fees for any documents required by this section shall be distinguished from other fees, fines, or assessments billed as part of the transfer or sales transaction. * * *

(c) An association may contract with any person or entity to facilitate compliance with * * * this section on behalf of the association.

(d) The association shall also provide a recipient authorized by the owner of a separate interest with a copy of the completed form specified in Section 4528 at the time the required documents are delivered. *(Added by Stats.2012, c. 180 (A.B.805), § 2, operative Jan. 1, 2014. Amended by Stats.2013, c. 183 (S.B.745), § 16.)*

Law Revision Commission Comments

Section 4530 continues former Section 1368(b) without change, except as indicated below.

The following nonsubstantive change is made:

● Cross-references are updated to reflect the new locations of the referenced provisions.

See also Sections 4080 ("association"), 4185 ("separate interest"). [40 Cal.L.Rev.Comm. Reports 235 (2010)].

Subdivisions (a) and (b) of Section 4530 are amended to continue, without substantive change, a revision to former Section 1368 made in 2012 by AB 2697 (Assembly Committee on Housing and Community Development). See 2012 Cal. Stat. ch. 770, § 4.5. This is a technical revision.

Subdivision (c) of Section 4530 is amended to correct an erroneous cross-reference. [43 Cal.L.Rev.Comm. Reports ___-(Appendix 4) (2013)].

Research References

2 Witkin Cal. Proc. 5th Jurisdiction § 271, (S 271) Domicile as Basis.
11 Witkin, California Summary 10th Husband and Wife § 138, (S 138) Exception for "Unique Circumstances.".

§ 4535. Additional requirements

In addition to the requirements of this article, an owner transferring title to a separate interest shall comply with applicable requirements of Sections 1133 and 1134. *(Added by Stats.2012, c. 180 (A.B.805), § 2, operative Jan. 1, 2014.)*

Law Revision Commission Comments

Section 4535 continues former Section 1368(f) without change, except as indicated below.

The following nonsubstantive change is made:

● "Section" is replaced with "article" to reflect that former Section 1368 is continued in this article.

See also Section 4185 ("separate interest"). [40 Cal.L.Rev.Comm. Reports 235 (2010)].

§ 4540. Violations; penalties; attorney fees

Any person who willfully violates this article is liable to the purchaser of a separate interest that is subject to this section for actual damages occasioned thereby and, in addition, shall pay a civil penalty in an amount not to exceed five hundred dollars ($500). In an action to enforce this liability, the prevailing party shall be awarded reasonable attorney's fees. *(Added by Stats. 2012, c. 180 (A.B.805), § 2, operative Jan. 1, 2014.)*

Law Revision Commission Comments

Section 4540 continues former Section 1368(d) without change, except as indicated below.

The following nonsubstantive changes are made:

● "Section" is replaced with "article."

● The words "or entity" are not continued. See Section 4170 ("person").

See also Section 4185 ("separate interest"). [40 Cal.L.Rev.Comm. Reports 235 (2010)].

§ 4545. Validity of title transferred in violation of article

Nothing in this article affects the validity of title to real property transferred in violation of this article. *(Added by Stats.2012, c. 180 (A.B.805), § 2, operative Jan. 1, 2014.)*

Law Revision Commission Comments

Section 4545 continues former Section 1368(e) without change, except as indicated below.

The following nonsubstantive change is made:

● "Section" is replaced with "article." [40 Cal.L.Rev.Comm. Reports 235 (2010)].

ARTICLE 3. TRANSFER FEE

Section
4575. Transfer fees prohibited; exceptions.
4580. Application of transfer fee prohibition.

§ 4575. Transfer fees prohibited; exceptions

Except as provided in Section 4580, neither an association nor a community service organization or similar entity may impose or collect any assessment, penalty, or fee in connection with a transfer of title or any other interest except for the following:

(a) An amount not to exceed the association's actual costs to change its records.

(b) An amount authorized by Section 4530. *(Added by Stats.2012, c. 180 (A.B.805), § 2, operative Jan. 1, 2014.)*

Law Revision Commission Comments

Section 4575 continues former Section 1368(c)(1) without change, except as indicated below.

The following nonsubstantive change is made:

● Cross-references are updated to reflect the new locations of the referenced provisions.

See also Sections 4080 ("association"), 4110 ("community service organization or similar entity"). [40 Cal.L.Rev.Comm. Reports 235 (2010)].

§ 4580. Application of transfer fee prohibition

The prohibition in Section 4575 does not apply to a community service organization or similar entity, or to a nonprofit entity that provides services to a common interest development under a declaration of trust, of either of the following types:

(a) An organization or entity that satisfies both of the following conditions:

(1) It was established before February 20, 2003.

(2) It exists and operates, in whole or in part, to fund or perform environmental mitigation or to restore or maintain

wetlands or native habitat, as required by the state or local government as an express written condition of development.

(b) An organization or entity that satisfies all of the following conditions:

(1) It is not an organization or entity described by subdivision (a).

(2) It was established and received a transfer fee before January 1, 2004.

(3) On and after January 1, 2006, it offers a purchaser the following payment options for the fee or charge it collects at time of transfer:

(A) Paying the fee or charge at the time of transfer.

(B) Paying the fee or charge pursuant to an installment payment plan for a period of not less than seven years. If the purchaser elects to pay the fee or charge in installment payments, the organization or entity may also collect additional amounts that do not exceed the actual costs for billing and financing on the amount owed. If the purchaser sells the separate interest before the end of the installment payment plan period, the purchaser shall pay the remaining balance before the transfer. *(Added by Stats.2012, c. 180 (A.B.805), § 2, operative Jan. 1, 2014.)*

Law Revision Commission Comments

Section 4580 continues the substance of former Section 1368(c)(2).

See also Sections 4100 ("common interest development"), 4110 ("community service organization or similar entity"), 4185 ("separate interest"). [40 Cal.L.Rev.Comm. Reports 235 (2010)].

ARTICLE 4.　RESTRICTIONS ON TRANSFER

Section
4600.　Exclusive use of common area; affirmative vote required; exceptions; contents of proposed measure.
4605.　Remedies.
4610.　Restrictions on partition.
4615.　Liens for labor and materials.

§ 4600.　Exclusive use of common area; affirmative vote required; exceptions; contents of proposed measure

(a) Unless the governing documents specify a different percentage, the affirmative vote of members owning at least 67 percent of the separate interests in the common interest development shall be required before the board may grant exclusive use of any portion of the common area to a member.

(b) Subdivision (a) does not apply to the following actions:

(1) A reconveyance of all or any portion of that common area to the subdivider to enable the continuation of development that is in substantial conformance with a detailed plan of phased development submitted to the Real Estate Commissioner with the application for a public report.

(2) Any grant of exclusive use that is in substantial conformance with a detailed plan of phased development submitted to the Real Estate Commissioner with the application for a public report or in accordance with the governing documents approved by the Real Estate Commissioner.

(3) Any grant of exclusive use that is for any of the following reasons:

(A) To eliminate or correct engineering errors in documents recorded with the county recorder or on file with a public agency or utility company.

(B) To eliminate or correct encroachments due to errors in construction of any improvements.

(C) To permit changes in the plan of development submitted to the Real Estate Commissioner in circumstances where the changes are the result of topography, obstruction, hardship, aesthetic considerations, or environmental conditions.

(D) To fulfill the requirement of a public agency.

(E) To transfer the burden of management and maintenance of any common area that is generally inaccessible and not of general use to the membership at large of the association.

(F) To accommodate a disability.

(G) To assign a parking space, storage unit, or other amenity, that is designated in the declaration for assignment, but is not assigned by the declaration to a specific separate interest.

(H) To install and use an electric vehicle charging station in an owner's garage or a designated parking space that meets the requirements of Section 4745, where the installation or use of the charging station requires reasonable access through, or across, the common area for utility lines or meters.

(I) To install and use an electric vehicle charging station through a license granted by an association under Section 4745.

(J) To comply with governing law.

(c) Any measure placed before the members requesting that the board grant exclusive use of any portion of the common area shall specify whether the association will receive any monetary consideration for the grant and whether the association or the transferee will be responsible for providing any insurance coverage for exclusive use of the common area. *(Added by Stats.2012, c. 180 (A.B.805), § 2, operative Jan. 1, 2014.)*

Law Revision Commission Comments

Section 4600 continues former Section 1363.07 without change, except as indicated below.

The following substantive changes are made:

- The section is no longer limited in its application to a common area that the association owns or in which the association has an easement right. It now also applies to common area that is owned by the members as tenants in common.

- Paragraphs (b)(3)(F), (G), and (J) are new.

The following nonsubstantive changes are made:

- An introductory clause is added in subdivision (b), to introduce the list of exceptions.

- The substance of former subdivision (a)(3)(F) is continued in Section 4202.

- The words "board of directors" are replaced throughout with "board." See Section 4085 ("board").

See also Sections 4080 ("association"), 4095 ("common area"), 4100 ("common interest development"), 4135 ("declaration"), 4145 ("exclusive use common area"), 4150 ("governing documents"), 4160 ("member"), 4185 ("separate interest"). [42 Cal.L.Rev.Comm. Reports 409 (2012)].

Research References

10 Witkin, California Summary 10th Parent and Child § 2, The Family Code.
10 Witkin, California Summary 10th Parent and Child § 65, (S 65) Former Law.
10 Witkin, California Summary 10th Parent and Child § 68, (S 68) Constitutional Rights of Natural Father.
10 Witkin, California Summary 10th Parent and Child § 218, (S 218) Statutory Rule.
10 Witkin, California Summary 10th Parent and Child § 232, Statutory Authorization.
10 Witkin, California Summary 10th Parent and Child § 233, in General.
10 Witkin, California Summary 10th Parent and Child § 320, (S 320) Statutory Ground.
10 Witkin, California Summary 10th Parent and Child § 322, (S 322) Insufficient Showing.
10 Witkin, California Summary 10th Parent and Child § 632, Standard of Proof.

14 Witkin, California Summary 10th Wills and Probate § 928, (S 928) Illustrations.

§ 4605. Remedies

(a) A member of an association may bring a civil action for declaratory or equitable relief for a violation of Section 4600 by the association, including, but not limited to, injunctive relief, restitution, or a combination thereof, within one year of the date the cause of action accrues.

(b) A member who prevails in a civil action to enforce the member's rights pursuant to Section 4600 shall be entitled to reasonable attorney's fees and court costs, and the court may impose a civil penalty of up to five hundred dollars ($500) for each violation, except that each identical violation shall be subject to only one penalty if the violation affects each member equally. A prevailing association shall not recover any costs, unless the court finds the action to be frivolous, unreasonable, or without foundation. *(Added by Stats.2012, c. 180 (A.B.805), § 2, operative Jan. 1, 2014.)*

Law Revision Commission Comments

Section 4605 continues former Section 1363.09(a)-(b) without change, except as indicated below.

The following nonsubstantive changes are made:

● The words "an association of which he or she is a member" are replaced with "the association."

● The words "this article" are replaced with "Section 4600."

● The words "his or her" are replaced with "the member's."

● The second sentence of former Section 1363.09(a) is not continued because it is irrelevant to judicial enforcement of this article.

● The words "member of the association" are replaced with "member." See Section 4160 ("member").

See also Section 4080 ("association"). [40 Cal.L.Rev.Comm. Reports 235 (2010)].

§ 4610. Restrictions on partition

(a) Except as provided in this section, the common area in a condominium project shall remain undivided, and there shall be no judicial partition thereof. Nothing in this section shall be deemed to prohibit partition of a cotenancy in a condominium.

(b) The owner of a separate interest in a condominium project may maintain a partition action as to the entire project as if the owners of all of the separate interests in the project were tenants in common in the entire project in the same proportion as their interests in the common area. The court shall order partition under this subdivision only by sale of the entire condominium project and only upon a showing of one of the following:

(1) More than three years before the filing of the action, the condominium project was damaged or destroyed, so that a material part was rendered unfit for its prior use, and the condominium project has not been rebuilt or repaired substantially to its state prior to the damage or destruction.

(2) Three-fourths or more of the project is destroyed or substantially damaged and owners of separate interests holding in the aggregate more than a 50–percent interest in the common area oppose repair or restoration of the project.

(3) The project has been in existence more than 50 years, is obsolete and uneconomic, and owners of separate interests holding in the aggregate more than a 50–percent interest in the common area oppose repair or restoration of the project.

(4) Any conditions in the declaration for sale under the circumstances described in this subdivision have been met. *(Added by Stats.2012, c. 180 (A.B.805), § 2, operative Jan. 1, 2014.)*

Law Revision Commission Comments

Section 4610 continues former Section 1359 without change, except as indicated below.

The following nonsubstantive changes are made:

● The phrase "common areas" is singularized.

● Subdivision (b)(4) is rephrased to avoid use of "such."

See also Sections 4095 ("common area"), 4125 ("condominium project"), 4135 ("declaration"), 4185 ("separate interest"). [40 Cal.L.Rev. Comm. Reports 235 (2010)].

§ 4615. Liens for labor and materials

(a) In a condominium project, no labor performed or services or materials furnished with the consent of, or at the request of, an owner in the condominium project or the owners' agent or contractor shall be the basis for the filing of a lien against any other property of any other owner in the condominium project unless that other owner has expressly consented to or requested the performance of the labor or furnishing of the materials or services. However, express consent shall be deemed to have been given by the owner of any condominium in the case of emergency repairs thereto.

(b) Labor performed or services or materials furnished for the common area, if duly authorized by the association, shall be deemed to be performed or furnished with the express consent of each condominium owner.

(c) The owner of any condominium may remove that owner's condominium from a lien against two or more condominiums or any part thereof by payment to the holder of the lien of the fraction of the total sum secured by the lien that is attributable to the owner's condominium. *(Added by Stats.2012, c. 180 (A.B. 805), § 2, operative Jan. 1, 2014.)*

Law Revision Commission Comments

Section 4615 continues former Section 1369 without change, except as indicated below.

The following nonsubstantive changes are made:

● The section is divided into subdivisions for ease of reference.

● The words "his or her" are replaced with "owner" throughout.

● The phrase "common areas" is singularized.

● The word "which" is replaced with "that" in subdivision (c).

See also Sections 4080 ("association"), 4095 ("common area"), 4125 ("condominium project"). [40 Cal.L.Rev.Comm. Reports 235 (2010)].

ARTICLE 5.   TRANSFER OF SEPARATE INTEREST

§ 4625. Community apartment project; interests included in conveyance, judicial sale or transfer of separate interests

In a community apartment project, any conveyance, judicial sale, or other voluntary or involuntary transfer of the separate interest includes the undivided interest in the community apartment project. Any conveyance, judicial sale, or other voluntary or involuntary transfer of the owner's entire estate also includes the owner's membership interest in the association. *(Added by Stats.2012, c. 180 (A.B.805), § 2, operative Jan. 1, 2014.)*

Section 4625 continues former Section 1358(a) without change.

See also Sections 4080 ("association"), 4105 ("community apartment project"), 4185 ("separate interest"). [40 Cal.L.Rev.Comm. Reports 235 (2010)].

§ 4630. Condominium project; interests included in conveyance, judicial sale or transfer of separate interests

In a condominium project the common area is not subject to partition, except as provided in Section 4610. Any conveyance, judicial sale, or other voluntary or involuntary transfer of the separate interest includes the undivided interest in the common area. Any conveyance, judicial sale, or other voluntary or involuntary transfer of the owner's entire estate also includes the owner's membership interest in the association. *(Added by Stats.2012, c. 180 (A.B.805), § 2, operative Jan. 1, 2014.)*

Section 4630 continues former Section 1358(b) without change, except as indicated below.

The following nonsubstantive changes are made:

• A cross-reference is updated to reflect the new location of the referenced provision.

• The phrase "common areas" is singularized.

See also Sections 4080 ("association"), 4095 ("common area"), 4125 ("condominium project"), 4185 ("separate interest"). [40 Cal.L.Rev. Comm. Reports 235 (2010)].

§ 4635. Planned development; interests included in conveyance, judicial sale or transfer of separate interests

In a planned development, any conveyance, judicial sale, or other voluntary or involuntary transfer of the separate interest includes the undivided interest in the common area, if any exists. Any conveyance, judicial sale, or other voluntary or involuntary transfer of the owner's entire estate also includes the owner's membership interest in the association. *(Added by Stats.2012, c. 180 (A.B.805), § 2, operative Jan. 1, 2014.)*

Section 4635 continues former Section 1358(c) without change, except as indicated below.

The following nonsubstantive change is made:

• The phrase "common areas" is singularized.

See also Sections 4080 ("association"), 4095 ("common area"), 4175 ("planned development"), 4185 ("separate interest"). [40 Cal.L.Rev. Comm. Reports 235 (2010)].

§ 4640. Stock cooperative; interests included in conveyance, judicial sale or transfer of separate interests

In a stock cooperative, any conveyance, judicial sale, or other voluntary or involuntary transfer of the separate interest includes the ownership interest in the corporation, however evidenced. Any conveyance, judicial sale, or other voluntary or involuntary transfer of the owner's entire estate also includes the owner's membership interest in the association. *(Added by Stats.2012, c. 180 (A.B.805), § 2, operative Jan. 1, 2014.)*

Section 4640 continues former Section 1358(d) without change.

See also Sections 4080 ("association"), 4185 ("separate interest"), 4190 ("stock cooperative"). [40 Cal.L.Rev.Comm. Reports 235 (2010)].

§ 4645. Transfer of exclusive use areas

Nothing in this article prohibits the transfer of exclusive use areas, independent of any other interest in a common interest subdivision, if authorization to separately transfer exclusive use areas is expressly stated in the declaration and the transfer occurs in accordance with the terms of the declaration. *(Added by Stats.2012, c. 180 (A.B.805), § 2, operative Jan. 1, 2014.)*

Section 4645 continues the next to last paragraph of former Section 1358 without change, except as indicated below.

The following nonsubstantive change is made:

• "Section" is replaced with "article."

See also Section 4135 ("declaration"). [40 Cal.L.Rev.Comm. Reports 235 (2010)].

§ 4650. Restrictions upon severability of component interests

Any restrictions upon the severability of the component interests in real property which are contained in the declaration shall not be deemed conditions repugnant to the interest created within the meaning of Section 711. However, these restrictions shall not extend beyond the period in which the right to partition a project is suspended under Section 4610. *(Added by Stats. 2012, c. 180 (A.B.805), § 2, operative Jan. 1, 2014.)*

Section 4650 continues the last paragraph of former Section 1358 without change, except as indicated below.

The following nonsubstantive changes are made:

• A superfluous reference to the "Civil Code" is not continued.

• The cross-reference is updated to reflect the new location of the referenced provision.

See also Section 4135 ("declaration"). [40 Cal.L.Rev.Comm. Reports 235 (2010)].

CHAPTER 5. PROPERTY USE AND MAINTENANCE

ARTICLE 1. PROTECTED USES

§ 4700. Scope of article; related provisions

This article includes provisions that limit the authority of an association or the governing documents to regulate the use of a member's separate interest. Nothing in this article is intended to affect the application of any other provision that limits the authority of an association to regulate the use of a member's separate interest, including, but not limited to, the following provisions:

(a) Sections 712 and 713, relating to the display of signs.

(b) Sections 714 and 714.1, relating to solar energy systems.

(c) Section 714.5, relating to structures that are constructed offsite and moved to the property in sections or modules.

(d) Sections 782, 782.5, and 6150 of this code and Section 12956.1 of the Government Code, relating to racial restrictions.

(e) Section 12927 of the Government Code, relating to the modification of property to accommodate a disability.

(f) Section 1597.40 of the Health and Safety Code, relating to the operation of a family day care home. *(Added by Stats.2012, c. 180 (A.B.805), § 2, operative Jan. 1, 2014.)*

Law Revision Commission Comments

Section 4700 is new. It provides a non-exclusive list of provisions outside of this act that limit the authority of an association to regulate separate interest property use.

See also Sections 4080 ("association"), 4150 ("governing documents"), 4160 ("member"), 4185 ("separate interest"). [40 Cal.L.Rev.Comm. Reports 235 (2010)].

Research References

6 Witkin Cal. Proc. 5th Proceedings Without Trial § 152, Prayer on Dissolution Petition Form.

10 Witkin, California Summary 10th Parent and Child § 2, The Family Code.

10 Witkin, California Summary 10th Parent and Child § 378, (S 378) Former Law.

§ 4705. Display of United States flag by owner on or in owner's separate interest or within exclusive use common area

(a) Except as required for the protection of the public health or safety, no governing document shall limit or prohibit, or be construed to limit or prohibit, the display of the flag of the United States by a member on or in the member's separate interest or within the member's exclusive use common area.

(b) For purposes of this section, "display of the flag of the United States" means a flag of the United States made of fabric, cloth, or paper displayed from a staff or pole or in a window, and does not mean a depiction or emblem of the flag of the United States made of lights, paint, roofing, siding, paving materials, flora, or balloons, or any other similar building, landscaping, or decorative component.

(c) In any action to enforce this section, the prevailing party shall be awarded reasonable attorney's fees and costs. *(Added by Stats.2012, c. 180 (A.B.805), § 2, operative Jan. 1, 2014.)*

Law Revision Commission Comments

Section 4705 continues former Section 1353.5 without change, except as indicated below.

The following nonsubstantive changes are made:

• A superfluous cross-reference to governing definitions is not continued.

• A superfluous reference to a declaration is not continued.

• The word "owner" is replaced with "member." See Section 4160 ("member").

See also Sections 4095 ("common area"), 4145 ("exclusive use common area"), 4150 ("governing documents"), 4185 ("separate interest"). [40 Cal.L.Rev.Comm. Reports 235 (2010)].

§ 4710. Prohibition of posting or displaying noncommercial signs, posters, flags, or banners; permitted placement of posting or displaying; exceptions

(a) The governing documents may not prohibit posting or displaying of noncommercial signs, posters, flags, or banners on or in a member's separate interest, except as required for the protection of public health or safety or if the posting or display would violate a local, state, or federal law.

(b) For purposes of this section, a noncommercial sign, poster, flag, or banner may be made of paper, cardboard, cloth, plastic, or fabric, and may be posted or displayed from the yard, window, door, balcony, or outside wall of the separate interest, but may not be made of lights, roofing, siding, paving materials, flora, or balloons, or any other similar building, landscaping, or decorative component, or include the painting of architectural surfaces.

(c) An association may prohibit noncommercial signs and posters that are more than nine square feet in size and noncommercial flags or banners that are more than 15 square feet in size. *(Added by Stats.2012, c. 180 (A.B.805), § 2, operative Jan. 1, 2014.)*

Law Revision Commission Comments

Section 4710 continues former Section 1353.6 without change, except as indicated below.

The following nonsubstantive changes are made:

• The words "including the operating rules" are not continued.

• The word "owner" is replaced with "member." See Section 4160 ("member").

• In subdivision (c), the numeral "9" is replaced with "nine" for stylistic reasons.

See also Sections 4080 ("association"), 4150 ("governing documents"), 4185 ("separate interest"). [40 Cal.L.Rev.Comm. Reports 235 (2010)].

§ 4715. Pets within common interest developments

(a) No governing documents shall prohibit the owner of a separate interest within a common interest development from keeping at least one pet within the common interest development, subject to reasonable rules and regulations of the association. This section may not be construed to affect any other rights provided by law to an owner of a separate interest to keep a pet within the development.

(b) For purposes of this section, "pet" means any domesticated bird, cat, dog, aquatic animal kept within an aquarium, or other animal as agreed to between the association and the homeowner.

(c) If the association implements a rule or regulation restricting the number of pets an owner may keep, the new rule or regulation shall not apply to prohibit an owner from continuing to keep any pet that the owner currently keeps in the owner's separate interest if the pet otherwise conforms with the previous rules or regulations relating to pets.

(d) For the purposes of this section, "governing documents" shall include, but are not limited to, the conditions, covenants, and restrictions of the common interest development, and the bylaws, rules, and regulations of the association.

(e) This section shall become operative on January 1, 2001 [1], and shall only apply to governing documents entered into, amended, or otherwise modified on or after that date. *(Added by Stats.2012, c. 180 (A.B.805), § 2, operative Jan. 1, 2014.)*

1 See former Civil Code § 1360.5, operative Jan. 1, 2001, from which this section is derived.

Law Revision Commission Comments

Section 4715 continues former Section 1360.5 without change, except as indicated below.

The following nonsubstantive change is made:

• The words "his or her" are replaced with "the owner's" in subdivision (c).

See also Sections 4080 ("association"), 4100 ("common interest development"), 4150 ("governing documents"), 4185 ("separate interest"). [40 Cal.L.Rev.Comm. Reports 235 (2010)].

§ 4720. Roof installation or repair; roofing materials

(a) No association may require a homeowner to install or repair a roof in a manner that is in violation of Section 13132.7 of the Health and Safety Code.

(b) Governing documents of a common interest development located within a very high fire severity zone, as designated by the Director of Forestry and Fire Protection pursuant to Article 9 (commencing with Section 4201) of Chapter 1 of Part 2 of Division 4 of the Public Resources Code or by a local agency pursuant to Chapter 6.8 (commencing with Section 51175) of Part 1 of Division 1 of Title 5 of the Government Code, shall allow for at least one type of fire retardant roof covering material that meets the requirements of Section 13132.7 of the Health and Safety Code. *(Added by Stats.2012, c. 180 (A.B.805), § 2, operative Jan. 1, 2014.)*

Law Revision Commission Comments

Section 4720 continues former Section 1353.7 without change, except as indicated below.

The following nonsubstantive change is made:

• In subdivision (a), the words "common interest development" are replaced with "association."

See also Section 4765(a)(3) ("Notwithstanding a contrary provision of the governing documents, a decision on a proposed change may not violate any governing provision of law, including, but not limited to, the Fair Employment and Housing Act (Part 2.8 (commencing with Section 12900) of Division 3 of Title 2 of the Government Code), or a building code or other applicable law governing land use or public safety."). See also Sections 4100 ("common interest development"), 4150 ("governing documents"). [40 Cal.L.Rev.Comm. Reports 235 (2010)].

Research References

10 Witkin, California Summary 10th Parent and Child § 391, Former Law.

10 Witkin, California Summary 10th Parent and Child § 394, in General.

§ 4725. Restrictions on installation or use of video or television antenna; enforceability based on size; reasonable restrictions; application approval; attorney's fees

(a) Any covenant, condition, or restriction contained in any deed, contract, security instrument, or other instrument affecting the transfer or sale of, or any interest in, a common interest development that effectively prohibits or restricts the installation or use of a video or television antenna, including a satellite dish, or that effectively prohibits or restricts the attachment of that antenna to a structure within that development where the antenna is not visible from any street or common area, except as otherwise prohibited or restricted by law, is void and unenforceable as to its application to the installation or use of a video or television antenna that has a diameter or diagonal measurement of 36 inches or less.

(b) This section shall not apply to any covenant, condition, or restriction, as described in subdivision (a), that imposes reasonable restrictions on the installation or use of a video or television antenna, including a satellite dish, that has a diameter or diagonal measurement of 36 inches or less. For purposes of this section, "reasonable restrictions" means those restrictions that do not significantly increase the cost of the video or television antenna system, including all related equipment, or significantly decrease its efficiency or performance and include all of the following:

(1) Requirements for application and notice to the association prior to the installation.

(2) Requirement of a member to obtain the approval of the association for the installation of a video or television antenna that has a diameter or diagonal measurement of 36 inches or less on a separate interest owned by another.

(3) Provision for the maintenance, repair, or replacement of roofs or other building components.

(4) Requirements for installers of a video or television antenna to indemnify or reimburse the association or its members for loss or damage caused by the installation, maintenance, or use of a video or television antenna that has a diameter or diagonal measurement of 36 inches or less.

(c) Whenever approval is required for the installation or use of a video or television antenna, including a satellite dish, the application for approval shall be processed by the appropriate approving entity for the common interest development in the same manner as an application for approval of an architectural modification to the property, and the issuance of a decision on the application shall not be willfully delayed.

(d) In any action to enforce compliance with this section, the prevailing party shall be awarded reasonable attorney's fees. *(Added by Stats.2012, c. 180 (A.B.805), § 2, operative Jan. 1, 2014.)*

Law Revision Commission Comments

Section 4725 continues former Section 1376 without change, except as indicated below.

The following nonsubstantive change is made:

• The word "owner" is replaced with "member." See Section 4160 ("member").

See also 47 C.F.R. § 1.4000.

See also Sections 4080 ("association"), 4095 ("common area"), 4100 ("common interest development"), 4185 ("separate interest"). [40 Cal. L.Rev.Comm. Reports 235 (2010)].

§ 4730. Prohibition against association rule or regulation that arbitrarily or unreasonably restricts owner's ability to market his or her interest in common development; other enumerated restrictions

(a) Any provision of a governing document that arbitrarily or unreasonably restricts an owner's ability to market the owner's interest in a common interest development is void.

(b) No association may adopt, enforce, or otherwise impose any governing document that does either of the following:

(1) Imposes an assessment or fee in connection with the marketing of an owner's interest in an amount that exceeds the association's actual or direct costs. That assessment or fee shall be deemed to violate the limitation set forth in subdivision (b) of Section 5600.

(2) Establishes an exclusive relationship with a real estate broker through which the sale or marketing of interests in the development is required to occur. The limitation set forth in this paragraph does not apply to the sale or marketing of separate interests owned by the association or to the sale or marketing of common area by the association.

(c) For purposes of this section, "market" and "marketing" mean listing, advertising, or obtaining or providing access to show the owner's interest in the development.

(d) This section does not apply to rules or regulations made pursuant to Section 712 or 713 regarding real estate signs. *(Added by Stats.2012, c. 180 (A.B.805), § 2, operative Jan. 1, 2014.)*

Law Revision Commission Comments

Section 4730 continues former Section 1368.1 without change, except as indicated below.

The following substantive changes are made:

• The introductory clause is revised to make clear that a void provision does not void the entire governing document that contains it.

• The words "rule or regulation" are replaced with "governing document." See Section 4150 ("governing documents"). This broadens the application of the section so that it governs any provision in the governing documents and not just an operating rule.

The following nonsubstantive changes are made:

● The words "his or her" are replaced with "the owner's" in subdivision (a).

● The phrase "common areas" is singularized.

● The words "of an association" are not continued.

See also Sections 4080 ("association"), 4095 ("common area"), 4100 ("common interest development"), 4185 ("separate interest"). [42 Cal. L.Rev.Comm. Reports 409 (2012)].

§ 4735. Governing documents; void and unenforceable provisions

(a) Notwithstanding any other law, a provision of the governing documents shall be void and unenforceable if it does any of the following:

(1) Prohibits, or includes conditions that have the effect of prohibiting, the use of low water-using plants as a group.

(2) Has the effect of prohibiting or restricting compliance with either of the following:

(A) A water-efficient landscape ordinance adopted or in effect pursuant to subdivision (c) of Section 65595 of the Government Code.

(B) Any regulation or restriction on the use of water adopted pursuant to Section 353 or 375 of the Water Code.

(b) This section shall not prohibit an association from applying landscaping rules established in the governing documents, to the extent the rules fully conform with the requirements of subdivision (a). (Added by Stats.2012, c. 180 (A.B.805), § 2, operative Jan. 1, 2014.)

Law Revision Commission Comments

Section 4735 continues former Section 1353.8 without change, except as indicated below.

The following nonsubstantive change is made:

● Surplus language is not continued (i.e., the phrases "of any," "of a common interest development," and "and regulations"). The term "governing documents" includes all governing documents of a common interest development. See Section 4150 ("governing documents").

See also Section 4080 ("association"). [40 Cal.L.Rev.Comm. Reports 235 (2010)].

§ 4740. Rental or leasing of separate interests; provisions in governing documents

(a) An owner of a separate interest in a common interest development shall not be subject to a provision in a governing document or an amendment to a governing document that prohibits the rental or leasing of any of the separate interests in that common interest development to a renter, lessee, or tenant unless that governing document, or amendment thereto, was effective prior to the date the owner acquired title to his or her separate interest.

(b) Notwithstanding the provisions of this section, an owner of a separate interest in a common interest development may expressly consent to be subject to a governing document or an amendment to a governing document that prohibits the rental or leasing of any of the separate interests in the common interest development to a renter, lessee, or tenant.

(c) For purposes of this section, the right to rent or lease the separate interest of an owner shall not be deemed to have terminated if the transfer by the owner of all or part of the separate interest meets at least one of the following conditions:

(1) Pursuant to Section 62 or 480.3 of the Revenue and Taxation Code, the transfer is exempt, for purposes of reassessment by the county tax assessor.

(2) Pursuant to subdivision (b) of, solely with respect to probate transfers, or subdivision (e), (f), or (g) of, Section 1102.2, the transfer is exempt from the requirements to prepare and deliver a Real Estate Transfer Disclosure Statement, as set forth in Section 1102.6.

(d) Prior to renting or leasing his or her separate interest as provided by this section, an owner shall provide the association verification of the date the owner acquired title to the separate interest and the name and contact information of the prospective tenant or lessee or the prospective tenant's or lessee's representative.

(e) Nothing in this section shall be deemed to revise, alter, or otherwise affect the voting process by which a common interest development adopts or amends its governing documents.

(f) This section shall apply only to a provision in a governing document or a provision in an amendment to a governing document that becomes effective on or after January 1, 2012. (Added by Stats.2012, c. 180 (A.B.805), § 2, operative Jan. 1, 2014.)

Law Revision Commission Comments

Section 4740 continues former Section 1360.2 without change.

See also Sections 4080 ("association"), 4100 (common interest development), 4150 (governing documents), 4185 ("separate interest). [40 Cal.L.Rev.Comm. Reports 235 (2010)].

§ 4745. Electric vehicle charging stations

(a) Any covenant, restriction, or condition contained in any deed, contract, security instrument, or other instrument affecting the transfer or sale of any interest in a common interest development, and any provision of a governing document, as defined in Section 4150, that either effectively prohibits or unreasonably restricts the installation or use of an electric vehicle charging station in an owner's designated parking space, including, but not limited to, a deeded parking space, a parking space in an owner's exclusive use common area, or a parking space that is specifically designated for use by a particular owner, or is in conflict with the provisions of this section is void and unenforceable.

(b)(1) This section does not apply to provisions that impose reasonable restrictions on electric vehicle charging stations. However, it is the policy of the state to promote, encourage, and remove obstacles to the use of electric vehicle charging stations.

(2) For purposes of this section, "reasonable restrictions" are restrictions that do not significantly increase the cost of the station or significantly decrease its efficiency or specified performance.

(c) An electric vehicle charging station shall meet applicable health and safety standards and requirements imposed by state and local authorities, and all other applicable zoning, land use, or other ordinances, or land use permits.

(d) For purposes of this section, "electric vehicle charging station" means a station that is designed in compliance with the California Building Standards Code and delivers electricity from a source outside an electric vehicle into one or more electric vehicles. An electric vehicle charging station may include several charge points simultaneously connecting several electric vehicles to the station and any related equipment needed to facilitate charging plug-in electric vehicles.

(e) If approval is required for the installation or use of an electric vehicle charging station, the application for approval shall be processed and approved by the association in the same manner as an application for approval of an architectural modification to the property, and shall not be willfully avoided or delayed. The approval or denial of an application shall be in writing. If an application is not denied in writing within 60 days from the date of receipt of the application, the application shall be deemed approved, unless that delay is the result of a reasonable request for additional information.

(f) If the electric vehicle charging station is to be placed in a common area or an exclusive use common area, as designated in the common interest development's declaration, the following provisions apply:

(1) The owner first shall obtain approval from the association to install the electric vehicle charging station and the association shall approve the installation if the owner agrees in writing to do all of the following:

(A) Comply with the association's architectural standards for the installation of the charging station.

(B) Engage a licensed contractor to install the charging station.

(C) Within 14 days of approval, provide a certificate of insurance that names the association as an additional insured under the owner's insurance policy in the amount set forth in paragraph (3).

(D) Pay for the electricity usage associated with the charging station.

(2) The owner and each successive owner of the charging station shall be responsible for all of the following:

(A) Costs for damage to the charging station, common area, exclusive use common area, or separate interests resulting from the installation, maintenance, repair, removal, or replacement of the charging station.

(B) Costs for the maintenance, repair, and replacement of the charging station until it has been removed and for the restoration of the common area after removal.

(C) The cost of electricity associated with the charging station.

(D) Disclosing to prospective buyers the existence of any charging station of the owner and the related responsibilities of the owner under this section.

(3) The owner and each successive owner of the charging station, at all times, shall maintain a homeowner liability coverage policy in the amount of one million dollars ($1,000,000) and shall name the association as a named additional insured under the policy with a right to notice of cancellation.

(4) A homeowner shall not be required to maintain a homeowner liability coverage policy for an existing National Electrical Manufacturers Association standard alternating current power plug.

(g) Except as provided in subdivision (h), installation of an electric vehicle charging station for the exclusive use of an owner in a common area, that is not an exclusive use common area, shall be authorized by the association only if installation in the owner's designated parking space is impossible or unreasonably expensive. In such cases, the association shall enter into a license agreement with the owner for the use of the space in a common area, and the owner shall comply with all of the requirements in subdivision (f).

(h) The association or owners may install an electric vehicle charging station in the common area for the use of all members of the association and, in that case, the association shall develop appropriate terms of use for the charging station.

(i) An association may create a new parking space where one did not previously exist to facilitate the installation of an electric vehicle charging station.

(j) An association that willfully violates this section shall be liable to the applicant or other party for actual damages, and shall pay a civil penalty to the applicant or other party in an amount not to exceed one thousand dollars ($1,000).

(k) In any action to enforce compliance with this section, the prevailing plaintiff shall be awarded reasonable attorney's fees. *(Added by Stats.2012, c. 180 (A.B.805), § 2, operative Jan. 1, 2014.)*

Law Revision Commission Comments

Section 4745 continues former Section 1353.9 without change, except as indicated below.

The following nonsubstantive change is made:

● A cross-reference in subdivision (a) is updated to reflect the new location of the referenced provision.

See also Section 4080 ("association"), 4095 ("common area"), 4100 ("common interest development"), 4135 ("declaration"), 4145 ("exclusive use common area"), 4150 ("governing documents"). [40 Cal.L.Rev. Comm. Reports 235 (2010)].

ARTICLE 2. MODIFICATION OF SEPARATE INTEREST

Section
4760. Modification of member's separate interest; facilitation of access for handicapped; approval by project association.
4765. Physical change to member's separate interest or common area; requirements to approve or disapprove proposed changes; notice of requirements.

§ 4760. Modification of member's separate interest; facilitation of access for handicapped; approval by project association

(a) Subject to the governing documents and applicable law, a member may do the following:

(1) Make any improvement or alteration within the boundaries of the member's separate interest that does not impair the structural integrity or mechanical systems or lessen the support of any portions of the common interest development.

(2) Modify the member's separate interest, at the member's expense, to facilitate access for persons who are blind, visually handicapped, deaf, or physically disabled, or to alter conditions which could be hazardous to these persons. These modifications may also include modifications of the route from the public way to the door of the separate interest for the purposes of this paragraph if the separate interest is on the ground floor or already accessible by an existing ramp or elevator. The right granted by this paragraph is subject to the following conditions:

(A) The modifications shall be consistent with applicable building code requirements.

(B) The modifications shall be consistent with the intent of otherwise applicable provisions of the governing documents pertaining to safety or aesthetics.

(C) Modifications external to the dwelling shall not prevent reasonable passage by other residents, and shall be removed by the member when the separate interest is no longer occupied by persons requiring those modifications who are blind, visually handicapped, deaf, or physically disabled.

(D) Any member who intends to modify a separate interest pursuant to this paragraph shall submit plans and specifications to the association for review to determine whether the modifications will comply with the provisions of this paragraph. The association shall not deny approval of the proposed modifications under this paragraph without good cause.

(b) Any change in the exterior appearance of a separate interest shall be in accordance with the governing documents and applicable provisions of law. *(Added by Stats.2012, c. 180 (A.B.805), § 2, operative Jan. 1, 2014.)*

Law Revision Commission Comments

Section 4760 continues former Section 1360 without change, except as indicated below.

The following substantive change is made:

● The scope of the provision is broadened to apply to any separate interest, and not just a unit in a condominium project.

The following nonsubstantive changes are made:

● The words "his or her" are not continued in subdivision (a)(2)(D).

● The word "owner" is replaced with "member" throughout. See Section 4160 ("member").

See also Section 4765 (association decision on modification of separate interest must comply with Fair Employment and Housing Act); Gov't Code § 12927 (accommodation of disability under Fair Employment and Housing Act).

See also Sections 4080 ("association"), 4100 ("common interest development"), 4150 ("governing documents"), 4185 ("separate interest"). [40 Cal.L.Rev.Comm. Reports 235 (2010)].

§ 4765. Physical change to member's separate interest or common area; requirements to approve or disapprove proposed changes; notice of requirements

(a) This section applies if the governing documents require association approval before a member may make a physical change to the member's separate interest or to the common area. In reviewing and approving or disapproving a proposed change, the association shall satisfy the following requirements:

(1) The association shall provide a fair, reasonable, and expeditious procedure for making its decision. The procedure shall be included in the association's governing documents. The procedure shall provide for prompt deadlines. The procedure shall state the maximum time for response to an application or a request for reconsideration by the board.

(2) A decision on a proposed change shall be made in good faith and may not be unreasonable, arbitrary, or capricious.

(3) Notwithstanding a contrary provision of the governing documents, a decision on a proposed change may not violate any governing provision of law, including, but not limited to, the Fair Employment and Housing Act (Part 2.8 (commencing with Section 12900) of Division 3 of Title 2 of the Government Code), or a building code or other applicable law governing land use or public safety.

(4) A decision on a proposed change shall be in writing. If a proposed change is disapproved, the written decision shall include both an explanation of why the proposed change is disapproved and a description of the procedure for reconsideration of the decision by the board.

(5) If a proposed change is disapproved, the applicant is entitled to reconsideration by the board, at an open meeting of the board. This paragraph does not require reconsideration of a decision that is made by the board or a body that has the same membership as the board, at a meeting that satisfies the requirements of Article 2 (commencing with Section 4900) of Chapter 6. Reconsideration by the board does not constitute dispute resolution within the meaning of Section 5905.

(b) Nothing in this section authorizes a physical change to the common area in a manner that is inconsistent with an association's governing documents, unless the change is required by law.

(c) An association shall annually provide its members with notice of any requirements for association approval of physical changes to property. The notice shall describe the types of changes that require association approval and shall include a copy of the procedure used to review and approve or disapprove a proposed change. *(Added by Stats.2012, c. 180 (A.B.805), § 2, operative Jan. 1, 2014.)*

Law Revision Commission Comments

Section 4765 continues former Section 1378 without change, except as indicated below.

The following nonsubstantive changes are made:

● The words "board of directors" and "board of directors of the association" are replaced with "board." See Sections 4085 ("board").

● A reference to the "association's" governing documents is not continued. See Section 4150 ("governing documents").

● The word "owner" is replaced with "member." See Section 4160 ("member").

See also Sections 4080 ("association"), 4095 ("common area"), 4185 ("separate interest"). [40 Cal.L.Rev.Comm. Reports 235 (2010)].

ARTICLE 3. MAINTENANCE

Section
4775. Responsibility for repair, replacement, or maintenance.
4780. Damage by wood-destroying pests or organisms.
4785. Temporary removal of occupant for treatment of wood-destroying pests or organisms.
4790. Access for maintenance of telephone wiring.

§ 4775. Responsibility for repair, replacement, or maintenance

(a) Unless otherwise provided in the declaration of a common interest development, the association is responsible for repairing, replacing, or maintaining the common area, other than exclusive use common area, and the owner of each separate interest is responsible for maintaining that separate interest and any exclusive use common area appurtenant to the separate interest.

(b) The costs of temporary relocation during the repair and maintenance of the areas within the responsibility of the association shall be borne by the owner of the separate interest affected. *(Added by Stats.2012, c. 180 (A.B.805), § 2, operative Jan. 1, 2014.)*

Law Revision Commission Comments

Subdivision (a) of Section 4775 continues former Section 1364(a) without change, except as indicated below.

The following nonsubstantive change is made:

● The phrase "common areas" is singularized.

Subdivision (b) continues former Section 1364(c) without change.

See also Sections 4080 ("association"), 4095 ("common area"), 4100 ("common interest development"), 4135 ("declaration"), 4145 ("exclusive use common area"), 4185 ("separate interest"). [40 Cal.L.Rev.Comm. Reports 235 (2010)].

§ 4780. Damage by wood-destroying pests or organisms

(a) In a community apartment project, condominium project, or stock cooperative, unless otherwise provided in the declaration, the association is responsible for the repair and maintenance of the common area occasioned by the presence of wood-destroying pests or organisms.

(b) In a planned development, unless a different maintenance scheme is provided in the declaration, each owner of a separate interest is responsible for the repair and maintenance of that separate interest as may be occasioned by the presence of wood-destroying pests or organisms. Upon approval of the majority of all members of the association, pursuant to Section 4065, that responsibility may be delegated to the association, which shall be entitled to recover the cost thereof as a special assessment. *(Added by Stats.2012, c. 180 (A.B.805), § 2, operative Jan. 1, 2014.)*

Law Revision Commission Comments

Subdivision (a) of Section 4780 continues former Section 1364(b)(1) without change, except as indicated below.

The following nonsubstantive change is made:

• A superfluous cross-reference to governing definitions is not continued.

Subdivision (b) continues former Section 1364(b)(2) without change, except as indicated below.

The following nonsubstantive changes are made:

• A superfluous cross-reference to a governing definition is not continued.

• A cross-reference to Section 4065 is added.

• The last sentence is revised to avoid use of the word "such."

See also Sections 4080 ("association"), 4095 ("common area"), 4105 ("community apartment project"), 4125 ("condominium project"), 4135 ("declaration"), 4160 ("member"), 4175 ("planned development"), 4185 ("separate interest"), 4190 ("stock cooperative"). [40 Cal.L.Rev.Comm. Reports 235 (2010)].

§ 4785. Temporary removal of occupant for treatment of wood-destroying pests or organisms

(a) The association may cause the temporary, summary removal of any occupant of a common interest development for such periods and at such times as may be necessary for prompt, effective treatment of wood-destroying pests or organisms.

(b) The association shall give notice of the need to temporarily vacate a separate interest to the occupants and to the owners, not less than 15 days nor more than 30 days prior to the date of the temporary relocation. The notice shall state the reason for the temporary relocation, the date and time of the beginning of treatment, the anticipated date and time of termination of treatment, and that the occupants will be responsible for their own accommodations during the temporary relocation.

(c) Notice by the association shall be deemed complete upon either:

(1) Personal delivery of a copy of the notice to the occupants, and if an occupant is not the owner, individual delivery pursuant to Section 4040, of a copy of the notice to the owner.

(2) Individual delivery pursuant to Section 4040 to the occupant at the address of the separate interest, and if the occupant is not the owner, individual delivery pursuant to Section 4040, of a copy of the notice to the owner.

(d) For purposes of this section, "occupant" means an owner, resident, guest, invitee, tenant, lessee, sublessee, or other person in possession of the separate interest. *(Added by Stats.2012, c. 180 (A.B.805), § 2, operative Jan. 1, 2014.)*

Law Revision Commission Comments

Section 4785 continues former Section 1364(d)-(e) without change, except as indicated below.

The following substantive change is made:

• The provision is revised to incorporate the "individual delivery" notice procedure.

The following nonsubstantive changes are made:

• Subdivision (c) is revised to improve its clarity.

• A typographical error is corrected in subdivision (d).

See also Sections 4080 ("association"), 4100 ("common interest development"), 4185 ("separate interest"). [40 Cal.L.Rev.Comm. Reports 235 (2010)].

§ 4790. Access for maintenance of telephone wiring

Notwithstanding the provisions of the declaration, a member is entitled to reasonable access to the common area for the purpose of maintaining the internal and external telephone wiring made part of the exclusive use common area of the member's separate interest pursuant to subdivision (c) of Section 4145. The access shall be subject to the consent of the association, whose approval shall not be unreasonably withheld, and which may include the association's approval of telephone wiring upon the exterior of the common area, and other conditions as the association determines reasonable. *(Added by Stats.2012, c. 180 (A.B.805), § 2, operative Jan. 1, 2014.)*

Law Revision Commission Comments

Section 4790 continues former Section 1364(f) without change, except as indicated below.

The following nonsubstantive changes are made:

• A cross-reference is updated to reflect the new location of the referenced provision.

• The word "owner" is replaced with "member." See Section 4160 ("member").

• The phrase "common areas" is singularized.

See also Sections 4080 ("association"), 4095 ("common area"), 4135 ("declaration"), 4145 ("exclusive use common area"), 4185 ("separate interest"). [40 Cal.L.Rev.Comm. Reports 235 (2010)].

CHAPTER 6. ASSOCIATION GOVERNANCE

ARTICLE 1. ASSOCIATION EXISTENCE AND POWERS

§ 4800. Management by association

A common interest development shall be managed by an association that may be incorporated or unincorporated. The association may be referred to as an owners' association or a community association. *(Added by Stats.2012, c. 180 (A.B.805), § 2, operative Jan. 1, 2014.)*

Law Revision Commission Comments

Section 4800 continues former Section 1363(a) without change, except as indicated below.

The following nonsubstantive change is made:

• Use of the term "owners' association" to describe the association is expressly authorized.

See also Sections 4080 ("association"), 4100 ("common interest development"). [40 Cal.L.Rev.Comm. Reports 235 (2010)].

Research References

9 Witkin Cal. Proc. 5th Appeal § 60, (S 60) Case Law Background.
2 Witkin, California Summary 10th Insurance § 181, Personal Injury Coverage: Uninsured Motorists.
11 Witkin, California Summary 10th Community Property § 45, (S 45) Proceeds of Personal Injury Damages.
11 Witkin, California Summary 10th Community Property § 76, (S 76) Award to Employee Spouse With Offset.
11 Witkin, California Summary 10th Community Property § 106, Date of Valuation of Law Practice.
11 Witkin, California Summary 10th Community Property § 185, (S 185) Illustrations.
11 Witkin, California Summary 10th Community Property § 189, (S 189) Current Law Eliminating Fault.
11 Witkin, California Summary 10th Community Property § 193, in General.
11 Witkin, California Summary 10th Community Property § 200, (S 200) Division by Agreement.
11 Witkin, California Summary 10th Community Property § 210, (S 210) Publicly Traded Stock.

11 Witkin, California Summary 10th Community Property § 216, (S 216) Reservation of Jurisdiction to Divide.

11 Witkin, California Summary 10th Community Property § 217, (S 217) Nonjudicial Division.

11 Witkin, California Summary 10th Community Property § 225, Postseparation Payments.

§ 4805. Powers of association

(a) Unless the governing documents provide otherwise, and regardless of whether the association is incorporated or unincorporated, the association may exercise the powers granted to a nonprofit mutual benefit corporation, as enumerated in Section 7140 of the Corporations Code, except that an unincorporated association may not adopt or use a corporate seal or issue membership certificates in accordance with Section 7313 of the Corporations Code.

(b) The association, whether incorporated or unincorporated, may exercise the powers granted to an association in this act. *(Added by Stats.2012, c. 180 (A.B.805), § 2, operative Jan. 1, 2014.)*

Law Revision Commission Comments

Section 4805 continues former Section 1363(c) without change, except as indicated below.

The following nonsubstantive changes are made:

● The provision is divided into subdivisions for ease of reference.

● The word "title" is replaced with "act."

See also Sections 4080 ("association"), 4150 ("governing documents"). [40 Cal.L.Rev.Comm. Reports 235 (2010)].

§ 4820. Consolidation of associations

Whenever two or more associations have consolidated any of their functions under a joint neighborhood association or similar organization, members of each participating association shall be (a) entitled to attend all meetings of the joint association other than executive sessions, (b) given reasonable opportunity for participation in those meetings, and (c) entitled to the same access to the joint association's records as they are to the participating association's records. *(Added by Stats.2012, c. 180 (A.B.805), § 2, operative Jan. 1, 2014.)*

Law Revision Commission Comments

Section 4820 continues former Section 1363(h) without change.

See also Sections 4080 ("association"), 4160 ("member"). [40 Cal. L.Rev.Comm. Reports 235 (2010)].

ARTICLE 2. BOARD MEETING

§ 4900. Short title

This article shall be known and may be cited as the Common Interest Development Open Meeting Act. *(Added by Stats.2012, c. 180 (A.B.805), § 2, operative Jan. 1, 2014.)*

Law Revision Commission Comments

Section 4900 continues former Section 1363.05(a) without change, except as indicated below.

The following nonsubstantive change is made:

● The word "section" is replaced with "article." [40 Cal.L.Rev. Comm. Reports 235 (2010)].

§ 4910. Action on items outside of meeting prohibited; electronic transmissions as method of conducting meeting

(a) The board shall not take action on any item of business outside of a board meeting.

(b)(1) Notwithstanding Section 7211 of the Corporations Code, the board shall not conduct a meeting via a series of electronic transmissions, including, but not limited to, electronic mail, except as specified in paragraph (2).

(2) Electronic transmissions may be used as a method of conducting an emergency board meeting if all directors, individually or collectively, consent in writing to that action, and if the written consent or consents are filed with the minutes of the board meeting. These written consents may be transmitted electronically. *(Added by Stats.2012, c. 180 (A.B.805), § 2, operative Jan. 1, 2014.)*

Law Revision Commission Comments

Section 4910 continues former Section 1363.05(j) without change, except as indicated below.

The following nonsubstantive changes are made:

● The words "board of directors" are replaced with "board." See Section 4085 ("board").

● The words "members of the board" are replaced with "directors." See Section 4140 ("director").

● The words "meeting" and "meeting of the board" are replaced with "board meeting." See Section 4090 ("board meeting").

See also Section 4155 ("item of business"). [40 Cal.L.Rev.Comm. Reports 235 (2010)].

§ 4920. Notice

(a) Except as provided in subdivision (b), the association shall give notice of the time and place of a board meeting at least four days before the meeting.

(b)(1) If a board meeting is an emergency meeting held pursuant to Section 4923, the association is not required to give notice of the time and place of the meeting.

(2) If a nonemergency board meeting is held solely in executive session, the association shall give notice of the time and place of the meeting at least two days prior to the meeting.

(3) If the association's governing documents require a longer period of notice than is required by this section, the association shall comply with the period stated in its governing documents. For the purposes of this paragraph, a governing document provision does not apply to a notice of an emergency meeting or a meeting held solely in executive session unless it specifically states that it applies to those types of meetings.

(c) Notice of a board meeting shall be given by general delivery pursuant to Section 4045.

(d) Notice of a board meeting shall contain the agenda for the meeting. *(Added by Stats.2012, c. 180 (A.B.805), § 2, operative Jan. 1, 2014. Amended by Stats.2013, c. 183 (S.B.745), § 17.)*

Law Revision Commission Comments

Section 4920 continues the substance of former Section 1363.05(f), except as indicated below.

The following substantive changes are made:

● The word "bylaws" is replaced with "governing documents," to broaden the scope of the provision.

• Specific rules on delivery of notice are replaced with a functionally equivalent requirement that notice be given by "general delivery," pursuant to Section 4045.

The following nonsubstantive change is made:

• The subdivision is restated for clarity.

See also Sections 4080 ("association"), 4090 ("board meeting"), 4150 ("governing documents"), 4160 ("member"). [40 Cal.L.Rev.Comm. Reports 235 (2010)].

Section 4920(b)(3) is amended to provide that a governing document addressing the period of notice for a board meeting does not affect an emergency meeting or a meeting conducted solely in executive session, unless it expressly states such application. That preserves part of the effect of the first sentence of former Section 1363.05(f). [43 Cal.L.Rev. Comm. Reports 23 (2013)].

§ 4923. Emergency board meeting

An emergency board meeting may be called by the president of the association, or by any two directors other than the president, if there are circumstances that could not have been reasonably foreseen which require immediate attention and possible action by the board, and which of necessity make it impracticable to provide notice as required by Section 4920. *(Added by Stats.2012, c. 180 (A.B.805), § 2, operative Jan. 1, 2014.)*

Law Revision Commission Comments

Section 4923 continues the substance of former Section 1363.05(g), except as indicated below.

The following nonsubstantive changes are made:

• The words "members of the governing body" are replaced with "directors." See Section 4140 ("director").

• The words "meeting of the board" are replaced with "board meeting." See Section 4090 ("board meeting").

• A reference to "this section" is updated to reflect the new location of the referenced provision.

See also Sections 4080 ("association"), 4085 ("board"). [40 Cal.L.Rev. Comm. Reports 235 (2010)].

§ 4925. Open meeting; executive session exception

(a) Any member may attend board meetings, except when the board adjourns to, or meets solely in, executive session. As specified in subdivision (b) of Section 4090, a member of the association shall be entitled to attend a teleconference meeting or the portion of a teleconference meeting that is open to members, and that meeting or portion of the meeting shall be audible to the members in a location specified in the notice of the meeting.

(b) The board shall permit any member to speak at any meeting of the association or the board, except for meetings of the board held in executive session. A reasonable time limit for all members of the association to speak to the board or before a meeting of the association shall be established by the board. *(Added by Stats.2012, c. 180 (A.B.805), § 2, operative Jan. 1, 2014.)*

Law Revision Commission Comments

Subdivision (a) of Section 4925 continues the substance of part of the first sentence of former Section 1363.05(b), and the third sentence of former Section 1363.05(b), except as indicated below.

The following nonsubstantive changes are made:

• The words "member of the association" are replaced with "member." See Section 4160 ("member").

• The words "meetings of the board of directors of the association" are replaced with "board meetings." See Section 4090 ("board meeting").

• Subdivision (a) does not continue language specifying when a board may meet in executive session. The substance of that language is continued in Section 4935.

• A cross-reference is updated to reflect the new location of the referenced provision.

Subdivision (b) continues former Section 1363.05(h) without change, except as indicated below.

The following nonsubstantive change is made:

• The words "board of directors" and "board of directors of the association" are replaced with "board." See Section 4085 ("board").

• The words "member of the association" are replaced with "member." See Section 4160 ("member").

See also Section 4080 ("association"). [40 Cal.L.Rev.Comm. Reports 235 (2010)].

§ 4930. Subjects of meeting; issues not on agenda

(a) Except as described in subdivisions (b) to (e), inclusive, the board may not discuss or take action on any item at a nonemergency meeting unless the item was placed on the agenda included in the notice that was distributed pursuant to subdivision (a) of Section 4920. This subdivision does not prohibit a member or resident who is not a director from speaking on issues not on the agenda.

(b) Notwithstanding subdivision (a), a director, a managing agent or other agent of the board, or a member of the staff of the board, may do any of the following:

(1) Briefly respond to statements made or questions posed by a person speaking at a meeting as described in subdivision (b) of Section 4925.

(2) Ask a question for clarification, make a brief announcement, or make a brief report on the person's own activities, whether in response to questions posed by a member or based upon the person's own initiative.

(c) Notwithstanding subdivision (a), the board or a director, subject to rules or procedures of the board, may do any of the following:

(1) Provide a reference to, or provide other resources for factual information to, its managing agent or other agents or staff.

(2) Request its managing agent or other agents or staff to report back to the board at a subsequent meeting concerning any matter, or take action to direct its managing agent or other agents or staff to place a matter of business on a future agenda.

(3) Direct its managing agent or other agents or staff to perform administrative tasks that are necessary to carry out this section.

(d) Notwithstanding subdivision (a), the board may take action on any item of business not appearing on the agenda distributed pursuant to subdivision (a) of Section 4920 under any of the following conditions:

(1) Upon a determination made by a majority of the board present at the meeting that an emergency situation exists. An emergency situation exists if there are circumstances that could not have been reasonably foreseen by the board, that require immediate attention and possible action by the board, and that, of necessity, make it impracticable to provide notice.

(2) Upon a determination made by the board by a vote of two-thirds of the directors present at the meeting, or, if less than two-thirds of total membership of the board is present at the meeting, by a unanimous vote of the directors present, that there is a need to take immediate action and that the need for action came to the attention of the board after the agenda was distributed pursuant to subdivision (a) of Section 4920.

(3) The item appeared on an agenda that was distributed pursuant to subdivision (a) of Section 4920 for a prior meeting of the board that occurred not more than 30 calendar days before the date that action is taken on the item and, at the prior meeting, action on the item was continued to the meeting at which the action is taken.

(e) Before discussing any item pursuant to subdivision (d), the board shall openly identify the item to the members in attendance at the meeting. *(Added by Stats.2012, c. 180 (A.B.805), § 2, operative Jan. 1, 2014.)*

Law Revision Commission Comments

Section 4930 continues former Section 1363.05(i) without change, except as indicated below.

The following nonsubstantive changes are made:

• References to "posting" of notice are not continued. Section 4920 does not require that notice be "posted."

• The numbering of the paragraphs of the former provision is simplified.

• Statutory references are updated to reflect the new locations of the referenced provisions.

• In subdivision (b)(2), the words "his or her" are replaced with "the person's."

• Subdivision (d)(2) is revised to make clear that the "members" referenced in that paragraph are members of the board.

• The words "board of directors" are replaced throughout with "board." See Section 4085 ("board").

• The words "board member" are replaced with "director" throughout. See Section 4140 ("director").

• The word "member" is added to the second sentence of subdivision (a) to make clear that the section applies to nonresident members. See Section 4160 ("member").

See also Sections 4155 ("item of business"), 4158 ("managing agent"). [40 Cal.L.Rev.Comm. Reports 235 (2010)].

§ 4935. Executive session

(a) The board may adjourn to, or meet solely in, executive session to consider litigation, matters relating to the formation of contracts with third parties, member discipline, personnel matters, or to meet with a member, upon the member's request, regarding the member's payment of assessments, as specified in Section 5665.

(b) The board shall adjourn to, or meet solely in, executive session to discuss member discipline, if requested by the member who is the subject of the discussion. That member shall be entitled to attend the executive session.

(c) The board shall adjourn to, or meet solely in, executive session to discuss a payment plan pursuant to Section 5665.

(d) The board shall adjourn to, or meet solely in, executive session to decide whether to foreclose on a lien pursuant to subdivision (b) of Section 5705.

(e) Any matter discussed in executive session shall be generally noted in the minutes of the immediately following meeting that is open to the entire membership. *(Added by Stats.2012, c. 180 (A.B.805), § 2, operative Jan. 1, 2014.)*

Law Revision Commission Comments

Subdivision (a) of Section 4935 continues the substance of part of the first sentence of former Section 1363.05(b). The substance of the remainder of the former sentence is continued in Section 4925(a).

Subdivision (b) continues the substance of the second sentence of former Section 1363.05(b).

Subdivision (c) is new. It provides a cross-reference to a provision requiring that the board meet in executive session when discussing a proposed payment plan.

Subdivision (d) is new. It provides a cross-reference to a provision requiring that the board meet in executive session when deciding whether to foreclose on a lien for overdue assessments.

Subdivision (e) continues former Section 1363.05(c) without change. See also Sections 4085 ("board"), 4160 ("member"). [40 Cal.L.Rev. Comm. Reports 235 (2010)].

§ 4950. Meeting minutes

(a) The minutes, minutes proposed for adoption that are marked to indicate draft status, or a summary of the minutes, of

any board meeting, other than an executive session, shall be available to members within 30 days of the meeting. The minutes, proposed minutes, or summary minutes shall be distributed to any member upon request and upon reimbursement of the association's costs for making that distribution.

(b) The annual policy statement, prepared pursuant to Section 5310, shall inform the members of their right to obtain copies of board meeting minutes and of how and where to do so. *(Added by Stats.2012, c. 180 (A.B.805), § 2, operative Jan. 1, 2014.)*

Law Revision Commission Comments

Subdivision (a) of Section 4950 continues former Section 1363.05(d) without change, except as indicated below.

The following nonsubstantive changes are made:

• The words "any meeting of the board of directors of the association" are replaced with "board meeting." See Section 4090 ("board meeting").

• The words "member of the association" are replaced with "member." See Section 4160 ("member").

Subdivision (b) is consistent with the substance of former Section 1363.05(e), but recasts it to be consistent with the annual distribution of the policy statement pursuant to Section 5310.

See also Sections 4078 ("annual policy statement"), 4080 ("association"). [40 Cal.L.Rev.Comm. Reports 235 (2010)].

§ 4955. Civil action for violation of article; costs and attorney's fees

(a) A member of an association may bring a civil action for declaratory or equitable relief for a violation of this article by the association, including, but not limited to, injunctive relief, restitution, or a combination thereof, within one year of the date the cause of action accrues.

(b) A member who prevails in a civil action to enforce the member's rights pursuant to this article shall be entitled to reasonable attorney's fees and court costs, and the court may impose a civil penalty of up to five hundred dollars ($500) for each violation, except that each identical violation shall be subject to only one penalty if the violation affects each member equally. A prevailing association shall not recover any costs, unless the court finds the action to be frivolous, unreasonable, or without foundation. *(Added by Stats.2012, c. 180 (A.B.805), § 2, operative Jan. 1, 2014.)*

Law Revision Commission Comments

Section 4955 continues former Section 1363.09(a)-(b) without change, except as indicated below.

The following nonsubstantive changes are made:

• The words "an association of which he or she is a member" are replaced with "the association."

• The second sentence of former Section 1363.09(a) is not continued because it is irrelevant to judicial enforcement of this article.

• The words "his or her" are replaced with "the member's."

• The words "member of the association" are replaced with "member." See Section 4160 ("member").

See also Section 4080 ("association"). [40 Cal.L.Rev.Comm. Reports 235 (2010)].

ARTICLE 3. MEMBER MEETING

Section
5000. Use of parliamentary procedure.

§ 5000. Use of parliamentary procedure

(a) Meetings of the membership of the association shall be conducted in accordance with a recognized system of parliamentary procedure or any parliamentary procedures the association may adopt.

(b) The board shall permit any member to speak at any meeting of the membership of the association. A reasonable time limit for all members to speak at a meeting of the association shall be established by the board. *(Added by Stats.2012, c. 180 (A.B.805), § 2, operative Jan. 1, 2014.)*

Law Revision Commission Comments

Subdivision (a) of Section 5000 continues former Section 1363(d) without change.

Subdivision (b) continues the substance of former Section 1363.05(h), as that provision applied to member meetings.

See also Sections 4080 ("association"), 4085 ("board"), 4160 ("member"). [40 Cal.L.Rev.Comm. Reports 235 (2010)].

ARTICLE 4. MEMBER ELECTION

Section
5100. Scope of article.
5105. Rules.
5110. Inspector of elections.
5115. Ballots; quorum; cumulative voting; election by mail; inclusion of text of proposed amendment of governing documents.
5120. Counting and tabulation of votes; reporting of tabulated results.
5125. Custody of ballots.
5130. Proxies; definitions.
5135. Campaign funding.
5145. Civil action for violation of article; attorney's fees and costs; small claims court.

§ 5100. Scope of article

(a) Notwithstanding any other law or provision of the governing documents, elections regarding assessments legally requiring a vote, election and removal of directors, amendments to the governing documents, or the grant of exclusive use of common area pursuant to Section 4600 shall be held by secret ballot in accordance with the procedures set forth in this article.

(b) This article also governs an election on any topic that is expressly identified in the operating rules as being governed by this article.

(c) The provisions of this article apply to both incorporated and unincorporated associations, notwithstanding any contrary provision of the governing documents.

(d) The procedures set forth in this article shall apply to votes cast directly by the membership, but do not apply to votes cast by delegates or other elected representatives.

(e) In the event of a conflict between this article and the provisions of the Nonprofit Mutual Benefit Corporation Law (Part 3 (commencing with Section 7110) of Division 2 of Title 1 of the Corporations Code) relating to elections, the provisions of this article shall prevail. *(Added by Stats.2012, c. 180 (A.B.805), § 2, operative Jan. 1, 2014.)*

Law Revision Commission Comments

Subdivision (a) of Section 5100 continues the first sentence of former Section 1363.03(b) without change, except as indicated below.

The following nonsubstantive changes are made:

• "Section" is replaced with "article."

• A cross-reference is updated to reflect the new location of the referenced provision.

• "Association board of directors" is replaced with "board." See Section 4085 ("board").

• The words "board member" are replaced with "director." See Section 4140 ("director").

• The words "common area property" are replaced with "common area."

Subdivision (b) is new. It permits an association to adopt an operating rule applying the requirements of this article to an election that would not otherwise be governed by this article.

Subdivisions (c)-(e) continue former Section 1363.03(*l*)-(n), respectively, without change, except as indicated below.

The following nonsubstantive change is made:

• The word "section" is replaced with "article" throughout.

Former Section 1363.03(*o*), stating the operative date of the former section, is obsolete and is not continued.

See also Sections 4080 ("association"), 4095 ("common area"), 4150 ("governing documents"). [40 Cal.L.Rev.Comm. Reports 235 (2010)].

Research References

11 Witkin, California Summary 10th Community Property § 2, (S 2) Development of Modern California Law.

§ 5105. Rules

(a) An association shall adopt rules, in accordance with the procedures prescribed by Article 5 (commencing with Section 4340) of Chapter 3, that do all of the following:

(1) Ensure that if any candidate or member advocating a point of view is provided access to association media, newsletters, or Internet Web sites during a campaign, for purposes that are reasonably related to that election, equal access shall be provided to all candidates and members advocating a point of view, including those not endorsed by the board, for purposes that are reasonably related to the election. The association shall not edit or redact any content from these communications, but may include a statement specifying that the candidate or member, and not the association, is responsible for that content.

(2) Ensure access to the common area meeting space, if any exists, during a campaign, at no cost, to all candidates, including those who are not incumbents, and to all members advocating a point of view, including those not endorsed by the board, for purposes reasonably related to the election.

(3) Specify the qualifications for candidates for the board and any other elected position, and procedures for the nomination of candidates, consistent with the governing documents. A nomination or election procedure shall not be deemed reasonable if it disallows any member from nominating himself or herself for election to the board.

(4) Specify the qualifications for voting, the voting power of each membership, the authenticity, validity, and effect of proxies, and the voting period for elections, including the times at which polls will open and close, consistent with the governing documents.

(5) Specify a method of selecting one or three independent third parties as inspector or inspectors of elections utilizing one of the following methods:

(A) Appointment of the inspector or inspectors by the board.

(B) Election of the inspector or inspectors by the members of the association.

(C) Any other method for selecting the inspector or inspectors.

(6) Allow the inspector or inspectors to appoint and oversee additional persons to verify signatures and to count and tabulate votes as the inspector or inspectors deem appropriate, provided that the persons are independent third parties.

(b) Notwithstanding any other provision of law, the rules adopted pursuant to this section may provide for the nomination of candidates from the floor of membership meetings or nomination by any other manner. Those rules may permit write-in candidates for ballots. *(Added by Stats.2012, c. 180 (A.B.805), § 2, operative Jan. 1, 2014.)*

Law Revision Commission Comments

Subdivision (a) of Section 5105 continues former Section 1363.03(a) without change, except as indicated below.

The following nonsubstantive changes are made:

• The words "board of directors" are replaced with "board." See Section 4085 ("board").

• The words "member of the association" are replaced with "member." See Section 4160 ("member").

Subdivision (b) continues former Section 1363.03(j) without change.

See also Sections 4080 ("association"), 4095 ("common area"), 4150 ("governing documents"). [40 Cal.L.Rev.Comm. Reports 235 (2010)].

Research References

11 Witkin, California Summary 10th Community Property § 130, (S 130) Present, Existing, and Equal Interest.

§ 5110. Inspector of elections

(a) The association shall select an independent third party or parties as an inspector of elections. The number of inspectors of elections shall be one or three.

(b) For the purposes of this section, an independent third party includes, but is not limited to, a volunteer poll worker with the county registrar of voters, a licensee of the California Board of Accountancy, or a notary public. An independent third party may be a member, but may not be a director or a candidate for director or be related to a director or to a candidate for director. An independent third party may not be a person, business entity, or subdivision of a business entity who is currently employed or under contract to the association for any compensable services unless expressly authorized by rules of the association adopted pursuant to paragraph (5) of subdivision (a) of Section 5105.

(c) The inspector or inspectors of elections shall do all of the following:

(1) Determine the number of memberships entitled to vote and the voting power of each.

(2) Determine the authenticity, validity, and effect of proxies, if any.

(3) Receive ballots.

(4) Hear and determine all challenges and questions in any way arising out of or in connection with the right to vote.

(5) Count and tabulate all votes.

(6) Determine when the polls shall close, consistent with the governing documents.

(7) Determine the tabulated results of the election.

(8) Perform any acts as may be proper to conduct the election with fairness to all members in accordance with this article, the Corporations Code, and all applicable rules of the association regarding the conduct of the election that are not in conflict with this article.

(d) An inspector of elections shall perform all duties impartially, in good faith, to the best of the inspector of election's ability, and as expeditiously as is practical. If there are three inspectors of elections, the decision or act of a majority shall be effective in all respects as the decision or act of all. Any report made by the inspector or inspectors of elections is prima facie evidence of the facts stated in the report. *(Added by Stats.2012, c. 180 (A.B.805), § 2, operative Jan. 1, 2014.)*

Law Revision Commission Comments

Section 5110 continues former Section 1363.03(c) without change, except as indicated below.

The following nonsubstantive changes are made:

• "Section" is replaced with "article" throughout.

• A cross-reference is updated to reflect the new location of the referenced provision.

• The words "his or her" are replaced in subdivision (d).

• The second sentence of subdivision (b) is reworded to clarify its meaning.

• The words "board of directors" are replaced with "board." See Section 4085 ("board").

• The words "board member" are replaced with "director." See Section 4140 ("director").

• The words "member of the association" are replaced with "member." See Section 4160 ("member").

See also Sections 4080 ("association"), 4150 ("governing documents"). [40 Cal.L.Rev.Comm. Reports 235 (2010)].

Research References

7 Witkin Cal. Proc. 5th Judgment § 462, (S 462) General Rule.

11 Witkin, California Summary 10th Community Property § 4, (S 4) Community Property.

11 Witkin, California Summary 10th Community Property § 22, (S 22) Community Property.

§ 5115. Ballots; quorum; cumulative voting; election by mail; inclusion of text of proposed amendment of governing documents

(a) Ballots and two preaddressed envelopes with instructions on how to return ballots shall be mailed by first-class mail or delivered by the association to every member not less than 30 days prior to the deadline for voting. In order to preserve confidentiality, a voter may not be identified by name, address, or lot, parcel, or unit number on the ballot. The association shall use as a model those procedures used by California counties for ensuring confidentiality of vote by mail ballots, including all of the following:

(1) The ballot itself is not signed by the voter, but is inserted into an envelope that is sealed. This envelope is inserted into a second envelope that is sealed. In the upper left hand corner of the second envelope, the voter shall sign the voter's name, indicate the voter's name, and indicate the address or separate interest identifier that entitles the voter to vote.

(2) The second envelope is addressed to the inspector or inspectors of elections, who will be tallying the votes. The envelope may be mailed or delivered by hand to a location specified by the inspector or inspectors of elections. The member may request a receipt for delivery.

(b) A quorum shall be required only if so stated in the governing documents or other provisions of law. If a quorum is required by the governing documents, each ballot received by the inspector of elections shall be treated as a member present at a meeting for purposes of establishing a quorum.

(c) An association shall allow for cumulative voting using the secret ballot procedures provided in this section, if cumulative voting is provided for in the governing documents.

(d) Except for the meeting to count the votes required in subdivision (a) of Section 5120, an election may be conducted entirely by mail unless otherwise specified in the governing documents.

(e) In an election to approve an amendment of the governing documents, the text of the proposed amendment shall be delivered to the members with the ballot. *(Added by Stats.2012, c. 180 (A.B.805), § 2, operative Jan. 1, 2014.)*

Law Revision Commission Comments

Subdivision (a) of Section 5115 continues former Section 1363.03(e) without change, except as indicated below.

The following nonsubstantive change is made:

• The words "his or her" are replaced throughout.

Subdivision (b) continues the second and third sentences of former Section 1363.03(b) without change, except as indicated below.

The following nonsubstantive change is made:

• The words "of the association" are not continued.

Subdivision (c) continues the fourth sentence of former Section 1363.03(b) without change.

Subdivision (d) continues former Section 1363.03(k) without change, except as indicated below.

The following nonsubstantive change is made:

• A cross-reference is updated to reflect the new location of the referenced provision.

Subdivision (e) is new. It generalizes part of former Section 1355(b)(1), which required distribution of the text of a proposed amendment when amending the declaration.

See also Sections 4080 ("association"), 4150 ("governing documents"), 4160 ("member"), 4185 ("separate interest").　[40 Cal.L.Rev.Comm. Reports 235 (2010)].

§ 5120.　Counting and tabulation of votes; reporting of tabulated results

(a) All votes shall be counted and tabulated by the inspector or inspectors of elections, or the designee of the inspector of elections, in public at a properly noticed open meeting of the board or members.　Any candidate or other member of the association may witness the counting and tabulation of the votes. No person, including a member of the association or an employee of the management company, shall open or otherwise review any ballot prior to the time and place at which the ballots are counted and tabulated.　The inspector of elections, or the designee of the inspector of elections, may verify the member's information and signature on the outer envelope prior to the meeting at which ballots are tabulated.　Once a secret ballot is received by the inspector of elections, it shall be irrevocable.

(b) The tabulated results of the election shall be promptly reported to the board and shall be recorded in the minutes of the next meeting of the board and shall be available for review by members of the association.　Within 15 days of the election, the board shall give general notice pursuant to Section 4045 of the tabulated results of the election.　*(Added by Stats.2012, c. 180 (A.B.805), § 2, operative Jan. 1, 2014.)*

Law Revision Commission Comments

Section 5120 continues former Section 1363.03(f)-(g) without change, except as indicated below.

The following substantive change is made:

• Ambiguous language requiring that election results be "publicized" is replaced with a reference to the requirements for giving general notice pursuant to Section 4045.

The following nonsubstantive changes are made:

• The words "his or her designee" are replaced with "the designee of the inspector of elections" throughout.

• The words "board of directors" and "board of directors of the association" are replaced with "board." See Section 4085 ("board").

See also Sections 4080 ("association"), 4160 ("member").　[40 Cal. L.Rev.Comm. Reports 235 (2010)].

Research References

11 Witkin, California Summary 10th Community Property § 172, (S 172) Liability of Separate Property for Debts.

11 Witkin, California Summary 10th Community Property § 173, (S 173) Liability of Community Property for Debts.

§ 5125.　Custody of ballots

The sealed ballots at all times shall be in the custody of the inspector or inspectors of elections or at a location designated by the inspector or inspectors until after the tabulation of the vote, and until the time allowed by Section 5145 for challenging the election has expired, at which time custody shall be transferred to the association.　If there is a recount or other challenge to the election process, the inspector or inspectors of elections shall, upon written request, make the ballots available for inspection and review by an association member or the member's authorized representative.　Any recount shall be conducted in a manner that preserves the confidentiality of the vote.　*(Added by Stats.2012, c. 180 (A.B.805), § 2, operative Jan. 1, 2014.)*

Law Revision Commission Comments

Section 5125 continues former Section 1363.03(h)-(i) without change, except as indicated below.

The following substantive change is made:

• The reference to the time for filing an action under Corporations Code Section 7527 is replaced with a reference to the time for filing an action under Section 5145.

The following nonsubstantive change is made:

• The words "his or her" are replaced with "the members" in subdivision (a).

See also Sections 4080 ("association"), 4160 ("member").　[40 Cal. L.Rev.Comm. Reports 235 (2010)].

Research References

13 Witkin, California Summary 10th Personal Property § 146, (S 146) Effect of Transfer.

11 Witkin, California Summary 10th Community Property § 132, (S 132) Current Law: Control by Either Spouse.

11 Witkin, California Summary 10th Community Property § 209, (S 209) Family Business.

§ 5130.　Proxies; definitions

(a) For purposes of this article, the following definitions shall apply:

(1) "Proxy" means a written authorization signed by a member or the authorized representative of the member that gives another member or members the power to vote on behalf of that member.

(2) "Signed" means the placing of the member's name on the proxy (whether by manual signature, typewriting, telegraphic transmission, or otherwise) by the member or authorized representative of the member.

(b) Proxies shall not be construed or used in lieu of a ballot. An association may use proxies if permitted or required by the bylaws of the association and if those proxies meet the requirements of this article, other laws, and the governing documents, but the association shall not be required to prepare or distribute proxies pursuant to this article.

(c) Any instruction given in a proxy issued for an election that directs the manner in which the proxyholder is to cast the vote shall be set forth on a separate page of the proxy that can be detached and given to the proxyholder to retain.　The proxyholder shall cast the member's vote by secret ballot.　The proxy may be revoked by the member prior to the receipt of the ballot by the inspector of elections as described in Section 7613 of the Corporations Code.　*(Added by Stats.2012, c. 180 (A.B.805), § 2, operative Jan. 1, 2014.)*

Law Revision Commission Comments

Section 5130 continues former Section 1363.03(d) without change, except as indicated below.

The following nonsubstantive changes are made:

• "Section" is replaced with "article" throughout.

• A reference to the "association's" governing documents is not continued.

See also Sections 4080 ("association"), 4150 ("governing documents"), 4160 ("member").　[40 Cal.L.Rev.Comm. Reports 235 (2010)].

§ 5135.　Campaign funding

(a) Association funds shall not be used for campaign purposes in connection with any association board election.　Funds of the association shall not be used for campaign purposes in connection with any other association election except to the extent necessary to comply with duties of the association imposed by law.

(b) For the purposes of this section, "campaign purposes" includes, but is not limited to, the following:

(1) Expressly advocating the election or defeat of any candidate that is on the association election ballot.

(2) Including the photograph or prominently featuring the name of any candidate on a communication from the association or its board, excepting the ballot, ballot materials, or a communication that is legally required, within 30 days of an election. This is not a campaign purpose if the communication is one for which subdivision (a) of Section 5105 requires that equal access be provided to another candidate or advocate. *(Added by Stats.2012, c. 180 (A.B.805), § 2, operative Jan. 1, 2014.)*

Law Revision Commission Comments

Section 5135 continues former Section 1363.04 without change, except as indicated below.

The following substantive change is made:

• An exception is added to the definition of "campaign purposes" for the inclusion of a candidate's name or photograph in a communication that is legally required. For example, preparation of meeting minutes would not be barred merely because the minutes include the name of a candidate in a pending election. See Section 4950 (board meeting minutes).

The following nonsubstantive change is made:

• A cross-reference in former Section 1363.04(b)(2) is updated to reflect the new location of the referenced provision.

See also Sections 4080 ("association"), 4085 ("board"). [40 Cal.L.Rev. Comm. Reports 235 (2010)].

§ 5145. Civil action for violation of article; attorney's fees and costs; small claims court

(a) A member of an association may bring a civil action for declaratory or equitable relief for a violation of this article by the association, including, but not limited to, injunctive relief, restitution, or a combination thereof, within one year of the date the cause of action accrues. Upon a finding that the election procedures of this article, or the adoption of and adherence to rules provided by Article 5 (commencing with Section 4340) of Chapter 3, were not followed, a court may void any results of the election.

(b) A member who prevails in a civil action to enforce the member's rights pursuant to this article shall be entitled to reasonable attorney's fees and court costs, and the court may impose a civil penalty of up to five hundred dollars ($500) for each violation, except that each identical violation shall be subject to only one penalty if the violation affects each member of the association equally. A prevailing association shall not recover any costs, unless the court finds the action to be frivolous, unreasonable, or without foundation.

(c) A cause of action under Sections 5100 to 5130, inclusive, with respect to access to association resources by a candidate or member advocating a point of view, the receipt of a ballot by a member, or the counting, tabulation, or reporting of, or access to, ballots for inspection and review after tabulation may be brought in small claims court if the amount of the demand does not exceed the jurisdiction of that court. *(Added by Stats.2012, c. 180 (A.B.805), § 2, operative Jan. 1, 2014.)*

Law Revision Commission Comments

Subdivision (a) of Section 5145 continues former Section 1363.09(a) without change, except as indicated below.

The following nonsubstantive changes are made:

• A cross-reference is updated to reflect the new location of the referenced provision.

• The words "an association of which he or she is a member" are replaced with "the association."

Subdivision (b) continues former Section 1363.09(b) without change, except as indicated below.

The following nonsubstantive change is made:

• The words "his or her" are replaced with "the member's."

Subdivision (c) continues former Section 1363.09(c) without change, except as indicated below.

The following nonsubstantive change is made:

• A cross-reference is updated to reflect the new location of the referenced provision.

See also Sections 4080 ("association"), 4160 ("member"). [40 Cal. L.Rev.Comm. Reports 235 (2010)].

ARTICLE 5. RECORD INSPECTION

§ 5200. Definitions

For the purposes of this article, the following definitions shall apply:

(a) "Association records" means all of the following:

(1) Any financial document required to be provided to a member in Article 7 (commencing with Section 5300) or in Sections 5565 and 5810.

(2) Any financial document or statement required to be provided in Article 2 (commencing with Section 4525) of Chapter 4.

(3) Interim financial statements, periodic or as compiled, containing any of the following:

(A) Balance sheet.

(B) Income and expense statement.

(C) Budget comparison.

(D) General ledger. A "general ledger" is a report that shows all transactions that occurred in an association account over a specified period of time.

The records described in this paragraph shall be prepared in accordance with an accrual or modified accrual basis of accounting.

(4) Executed contracts not otherwise privileged under law.

(5) Written board approval of vendor or contractor proposals or invoices.

(6) State and federal tax returns.

(7) Reserve account balances and records of payments made from reserve accounts.

(8) Agendas and minutes of meetings of the members, the board, and any committees appointed by the board pursuant to Section 7212 of the Corporations Code; excluding, however, minutes and other information from executive sessions of the board as described in Article 2 (commencing with Section 4900).

(9) Membership lists, including name, property address, and mailing address, but not including information for members who have opted out pursuant to Section 5220.

(10) Check registers.

(11) The governing documents.

(12) An accounting prepared pursuant to subdivision (b) of Section 5520.

(13) An "enhanced association record" as defined in subdivision (b).

(b) "Enhanced association records" means invoices, receipts and canceled checks for payments made by the association, purchase orders approved by the association, credit card statements for credit cards issued in the name of the association, statements for services rendered, and reimbursement requests submitted to the association. *(Added by Stats.2012, c. 180 (A.B.805), § 2, operative Jan. 1, 2014.)*

Law Revision Commission Comments

Subdivision (a) of Section 5200 continues former Section 1365.2(a)(1) without change, except as indicated below.

The following substantive change is made:

• Paragraphs (a)(11)-(13) are new.

The following nonsubstantive changes are made:

• "Section" is replaced with "article" in the introductory clause.

• Cross-references are updated to reflect the new locations of the referenced provisions.

• Substantive limitations on access to the membership list are not appropriate for inclusion in a definition and are relocated, without substantive change, to Sections 5220 and 5225. A cross-reference to Section 5220 is added.

• The words "board of directors" are replaced throughout with "board." See Section 4085 ("board").

Subdivision (b) continues former Section 1365.2(a)(2) without change, except as indicated below.

The following nonsubstantive change is made:

• A substantive rule providing that a person submitting a reimbursement request is "solely responsible for removing all personal identification information from the request" is not appropriate for inclusion in a definition and is relocated, without substantive change, to Section 5205(g). For more information about the significance of the term "enhanced association records," see Section 5205(g) generally.

See also Sections 4080 ("association"), 4150 ("governing documents"), 4160 ("member"), 4177 ("reserve accounts"). [40 Cal.L.Rev.Comm. Reports 235 (2010)].

§ 5205. Availability to members

(a) The association shall make available association records for the time periods and within the timeframes provided in Section 5210 for inspection and copying by a member of the association, or the member's designated representative.

(b) A member of the association may designate another person to inspect and copy the specified association records on the member's behalf. The member shall make this designation in writing.

(c) The association shall make the specified association records available for inspection and copying in the association's business office within the common interest development.

(d) If the association does not have a business office within the development, the association shall make the specified association records available for inspection and copying at a place agreed to by the requesting member and the association.

(e) If the association and the requesting member cannot agree upon a place for inspection and copying pursuant to subdivision (d) or if the requesting member submits a written request directly to the association for copies of specifically identified records, the association may satisfy the requirement to make the association records available for inspection and copying by delivering copies of the specifically identified records to the member by individual delivery pursuant to Section 4040 within the timeframes set forth in subdivision (b) of Section 5210.

(f) The association may bill the requesting member for the direct and actual cost of copying and mailing requested documents. The association shall inform the member of the amount of the copying and mailing costs, and the member shall agree to pay those costs, before copying and sending the requested documents.

(g) In addition to the direct and actual costs of copying and mailing, the association may bill the requesting member an amount not in excess of ten dollars ($10) per hour, and not to exceed two hundred dollars ($200) total per written request, for the time actually and reasonably involved in redacting an enhanced association record. If the enhanced association record includes a reimbursement request, the person submitting the reimbursement request shall be solely responsible for removing all personal identification information from the request. The association shall inform the member of the estimated costs, and the member shall agree to pay those costs, before retrieving the requested documents.

(h) Requesting parties shall have the option of receiving specifically identified records by electronic transmission or machine-readable storage media as long as those records can be transmitted in a redacted format that does not allow the records to be altered. The cost of duplication shall be limited to the direct cost of producing the copy of a record in that electronic format. The association may deliver specifically identified records by electronic transmission or machine-readable storage media as long as those records can be transmitted in a redacted format that prevents the records from being altered. *(Added by Stats.2012, c. 180 (A.B.805), § 2, operative Jan. 1, 2014.)*

Law Revision Commission Comments

Subdivisions (a) through (g) of Section 5205 continue former Section 1365.2(b)-(c) without change, except as indicated below.

The following substantive change is made:

• Language is added to provide for "individual delivery" of records, rather than mailing. See Section 4040.

The following nonsubstantive changes are made:

• Cross-references are updated to reflect the new locations of the referenced provisions.

• The words "member of the association" are replaced with "member." See Section 4160 ("member").

• A superfluous reference to "enhanced association records" is not continued in subdivision (a). See Section 5200(a)(12) ("association records" includes "enhanced association records").

• Subdivision (d) is rephrased to avoid ending the sentence with a preposition.

• The second sentence of subdivision (g) is added to continue the substance of the last clause of former Section 1365.2(a)(2).

Subdivision (h) continues former Section 1365.2(h) without change.

See also Sections 4080 ("association"), 4100 ("common interest development"). [40 Cal.L.Rev.Comm. Reports 235 (2010)].

§ 5210. Time periods of required availability

(a) Association records are subject to member inspection for the following time periods:

(1) For the current fiscal year and for each of the previous two fiscal years.

(2) Notwithstanding paragraph (1), minutes of member and board meetings are subject to inspection permanently. If a committee has decisionmaking authority, minutes of the meetings of that committee shall be made available commencing January 1, 2007, and shall thereafter be permanently subject to inspection.

(b) When a member properly requests access to association records, access to the requested records shall be granted within the following time periods:

(1) Association records prepared during the current fiscal year, within 10 business days following the association's receipt of the request.

(2) Association records prepared during the previous two fiscal years, within 30 calendar days following the association's receipt of the request.

(3) Any record or statement available pursuant to Article 2 (commencing with Section 4525) of Chapter 4, Article 7 (commencing with Section 5300), Section 5565, or Section 5810, within the timeframe specified therein.

(4) Minutes of member and board meetings, within the timeframe specified in subdivision (a) of Section 4950.

(5) Minutes of meetings of committees with decisionmaking authority for meetings commencing on or after January 1, 2007, within 15 calendar days following approval.

(6) Membership list, within the timeframe specified in Section 8330 of the Corporations Code.

(c) There shall be no liability pursuant to this article for an association that fails to retain records for the periods specified in subdivision (a) that were created prior to January 1, 2006. *(Added by Stats.2012, c. 180 (A.B.805), § 2, operative Jan. 1, 2014.)*

Law Revision Commission Comments

Subdivisions (a) and (b) of Section 5210 continue the substance of former Section 1365.2(i)-(j).

Subdivision (c) continues former Section 1365.2(k) without change, except as indicated below.

The following nonsubstantive changes are made:

• The word "section" is replaced with "article."

• A cross-reference is updated to reflect the new location of the referenced provision.

See also Sections 4080 ("association"), 4090 ("board meeting"), 4160 ("member"). [40 Cal.L.Rev.Comm. Reports 235 (2010)].

§ 5215. Redaction

(a) Except as provided in subdivision (b), the association may withhold or redact information from the association records if any of the following are true:

(1) The release of the information is reasonably likely to lead to identity theft. For the purposes of this section, "identity theft" means the unauthorized use of another person's personal identifying information to obtain credit, goods, services, money, or property. Examples of information that may be withheld or redacted pursuant to this paragraph include bank account numbers of members or vendors, social security or tax identification numbers, and check, stock, and credit card numbers.

(2) The release of the information is reasonably likely to lead to fraud in connection with the association.

(3) The information is privileged under law. Examples include documents subject to attorney-client privilege or relating to litigation in which the association is or may become involved, and confidential settlement agreements.

(4) The release of the information is reasonably likely to compromise the privacy of an individual member of the association.

(5) The information contains any of the following:

(A) Records of goods or services provided a la carte to individual members of the association for which the association received monetary consideration other than assessments.

(B) Records of disciplinary actions, collection activities, or payment plans of members other than the member requesting the records.

(C) Any person's personal identification information, including, without limitation, social security number, tax identification number, driver's license number, credit card account numbers, bank account number, and bank routing number.

(D) Minutes and other information from executive sessions of the board as described in Article 2 (commencing with Section 4900), except for executed contracts not otherwise privileged. Privileged contracts shall not include contracts for maintenance, management, or legal services.

(E) Personnel records other than the payroll records required to be provided under subdivision (b).

(F) Interior architectural plans, including security features, for individual homes.

(b) Except as provided by the attorney-client privilege, the association may not withhold or redact information concerning the compensation paid to employees, vendors, or contractors. Compensation information for individual employees shall be set forth by job classification or title, not by the employee's name, social security number, or other personal information.

(c) No association, officer, director, employee, agent, or volunteer of an association shall be liable for damages to a member of the association or any third party as the result of identity theft or other breach of privacy because of the failure to withhold or redact that member's information under this section unless the failure to withhold or redact the information was intentional, willful, or negligent.

(d) If requested by the requesting member, an association that denies or redacts records shall provide a written explanation specifying the legal basis for withholding or redacting the requested records. *(Added by Stats.2012, c. 180 (A.B.805), § 2, operative Jan. 1, 2014.)*

Law Revision Commission Comments

Section 5215 continues former Section 1365.2(d) without change, except as indicated below.

The following nonsubstantive changes are made:

• A cross-reference is updated to reflect the new location of the referenced provision.

• The words "board of directors" are replaced with "board." See Section 4085 ("board").

See also Sections 4080 ("association"), 4140 ("director"), 4160 ("member"). [40 Cal.L.Rev.Comm. Reports 235 (2010)].

§ 5220. Information sharing; member opt out

A member of the association may opt out of the sharing of that member's name, property address, and mailing address by notifying the association in writing that the member prefers to be contacted via the alternative process described in subdivision (c) of Section 8330 of the Corporations Code. This opt out shall remain in effect until changed by the member. *(Added by Stats.2012, c. 180 (A.B.805), § 2, operative Jan. 1, 2014.)*

Law Revision Commission Comments

Section 5220 continues former Section 1365.2(a)(1)(I)(iii) without change, except as indicated below.

The following nonsubstantive changes are made:

• The words "his or her" are replaced with "member" throughout.

• "Opt-out" is replaced with "opt out" to reflect modern usage.

See also Sections 4080 ("association"), 4160 ("member"). [40 Cal. L.Rev.Comm. Reports 235 (2010)].

§ 5225. Request for membership list

A member requesting the membership list shall state the purpose for which the list is requested which purpose shall be reasonably related to the requester's interest as a member. If the association reasonably believes that the information in the list will be used for another purpose, it may deny the member access to the list. If the request is denied, in any subsequent action brought by the member under Section 5235, the association shall have the burden to prove that the member would have allowed use of the information for purposes unrelated to the member's interest as a member. *(Added by Stats.2012, c. 180 (A.B.805), § 2, operative Jan. 1, 2014.)*

Law Revision Commission Comments

Section 5225 continues former Section 1365.2(a)(1)(I)(ii) without change, except as indicated below.

The following nonsubstantive changes are made:

- A comma is added in the first sentence.
- "The member requesting the list" is replaced with "a member requesting the membership list," to improve clarity.
- A cross-reference is updated to reflect the new location of the referenced provision.
- "His or her" is replaced with "the member's."

See also Sections 4080 ("association"), 4160 ("member"). [40 Cal. L.Rev.Comm. Reports 235 (2010)].

§ 5230. Prohibited use of list

(a) The association records, and any information from them, may not be sold, used for a commercial purpose, or used for any other purpose not reasonably related to a member's interest as a member. An association may bring an action against any person who violates this article for injunctive relief and for actual damages to the association caused by the violation.

(b) This article may not be construed to limit the right of an association to damages for misuse of information obtained from the association records pursuant to this article or to limit the right of an association to injunctive relief to stop the misuse of this information.

(c) An association shall be entitled to recover reasonable costs and expenses, including reasonable attorney's fees, in a successful action to enforce its rights under this article. *(Added by Stats.2012, c. 180 (A.B.805), § 2, operative Jan. 1, 2014.)*

Law Revision Commission Comments

Section 5230 continues former Section 1365.2(e) without change, except as indicated below.

The following nonsubstantive change is made:

- "This section" is replaced with "this article" throughout.

See also Sections 4080 ("association"), 4160 ("member"), 4170 ("person"). [40 Cal.L.Rev.Comm. Reports 235 (2010)].

§ 5235. Remedies

(a) A member may bring an action to enforce that member's right to inspect and copy the association records. If a court finds that the association unreasonably withheld access to the association records, the court shall award the member reasonable costs and expenses, including reasonable attorney's fees, and may assess a civil penalty of up to five hundred dollars ($500) for the denial of each separate written request.

(b) A cause of action under this section may be brought in small claims court if the amount of the demand does not exceed the jurisdiction of that court.

(c) A prevailing association may recover any costs if the court finds the action to be frivolous, unreasonable, or without foundation. *(Added by Stats.2012, c. 180 (A.B.805), § 2, operative Jan. 1, 2014.)*

Law Revision Commission Comments

Section 5235 continues former Section 1365.2(f) without change, except as indicated below.

The following nonsubstantive changes are made:

- The provision is divided into subdivisions for ease of reference.
- The words "member of an association" are replaced with "member." See Section 4160 ("member").

See also Section 4080 ("association"). [40 Cal.L.Rev.Comm. Reports 235 (2010)].

§ 5240. Construction with Corporations Code

(a) As applied to an association and its members, the provisions of this article are intended to supersede the provisions of Sections 8330 and 8333 of the Corporations Code to the extent those sections are inconsistent.

(b) Except as provided in subdivision (a), members of the association shall have access to association records, including accounting books and records and membership lists, in accordance with Article 3 (commencing with Section 8330) of Chapter 13 of Part 3 of Division 2 of Title 1 of the Corporations Code.

(c) * * * This article applies to any community service organization or similar entity that is related to the association, and to any nonprofit entity that provides services to a common interest development under a declaration of trust. This article shall operate to give a member of the organization or entity a right to inspect and copy the records of that organization or entity equivalent to that granted to association members by this article.

(d) * * * This article shall not apply to any common interest development in which separate interests are being offered for sale by a subdivider under the authority of a public report issued by the Bureau of Real Estate so long as the subdivider or all subdividers offering those separate interests for sale, or any employees of those subdividers or any other person who receives direct or indirect compensation from any of those subdividers, comprise a majority of the directors. Notwithstanding the foregoing, this article shall apply to that common interest development no later than 10 years after the close of escrow for the first sale of a separate interest to a member of the general public pursuant to the public report issued for the first phase of the development. *(Added by Stats.2012, c. 180 (A.B.805), § 2, operative Jan. 1, 2014. Amended by Stats.2013, c. 352 (A.B.1317), § 54, eff. Sept. 26, 2013, operative Jan. 1, 2014.)*

Law Revision Commission Comments

Subdivision (a) of Section 5240 continues former Section 1365.2(*l*) without change, except as indicated below.

The following nonsubstantive change is made:

- The word "section" is replaced with "article."

Subdivision (b) continues the first sentence of former Section 1363(e) without change, except as indicated below.

The following nonsubstantive change is made:

- The introductory clause is added to clarify the relationship between this provision and subdivision (a). The second sentence of former Section 1363(e) is not continued. That provision is unnecessary because its substance is subsumed within Section 5200(a)(11), which guarantees access to all governing documents, and not just the operating rules.

Subdivision (c) continues former Section 1365.2(g) without change, except as indicated below.

The following nonsubstantive changes are made:

- "Section" is replaced with "article" throughout.
- A superfluous reference to the definition of "community service organization" is not continued. See Section 4110 ("community service organization or similar entity").

Subdivision (d) continues former Section 1365.2(m) without change, except as indicated below.

The following nonsubstantive changes are made:

- "Section" is replaced with "article" throughout.
- The words "board of directors of the association" are replaced with "board." See Section 4085 ("board").
- The words "board member" are replaced with "director." See Section 4140 ("director").

See also Sections 4080 ("association"), 4100 ("common interest development"), 4110 ("community service organization or similar entity"), 4160 ("member"), 4185 ("separate interest"). [40 Cal.L.Rev.Comm. Reports 235 (2010)].

ARTICLE 6. RECORDKEEPING

Section
5260.   Requests to be delivered in writing.

§ 5260. Requests to be delivered in writing

To be effective, any of the following requests shall be delivered in writing to the association, pursuant to Section 4035:

(a) A request to change the member's information in the association membership list.

(b) A request to add or remove a second address for delivery of individual notices to the member, pursuant to subdivision (b) of Section 4040.

(c) A request for individual delivery of general notices to the member, pursuant to subdivision (b) of Section 4045, or a request to cancel a prior request for individual delivery of general notices.

(d) A request to opt out of the membership list pursuant to Section 5220, or a request to cancel a prior request to opt out of the membership list.

(e) A request to receive a full copy of a specified annual budget report or annual policy statement pursuant to Section 5320.

(f) A request to receive all reports in full, pursuant to subdivision (b) of Section 5320, or a request to cancel a prior request to receive all reports in full. *(Added by Stats.2012, c. 180 (A.B.805), § 2, operative Jan. 1, 2014.)*

Law Revision Commission Comments

Section 5260 is new. It requires that the specified requests be written and delivered to the association pursuant to Section 4035.

See also Sections 4076 ("annual budget report"), 4078 ("annual policy statement"), 4080 ("association"), 4160 ("member"). [40 Cal.L.Rev. Comm. Reports 235 (2010)].

ARTICLE 7. ANNUAL REPORTS

Section
5300.   Annual budget report.
5305.   Standards for preparation of review of financial statement of association.
5310.   Annual policy statement; contents.
5320.   Delivery of reports.

§ 5300. Annual budget report

(a) Notwithstanding a contrary provision in the governing documents, an association shall distribute an annual budget report 30 to 90 days before the end of its fiscal year.

(b) Unless the governing documents impose more stringent standards, the annual budget report shall include all of the following information:

(1) A pro forma operating budget, showing the estimated revenue and expenses on an accrual basis.

(2) A summary of the association's reserves, prepared pursuant to Section 5565.

(3) A summary of the reserve funding plan adopted by the board, as specified in paragraph (5) of subdivision (b) of Section 5550. The summary shall include notice to members that the full reserve study plan is available upon request, and the association shall provide the full reserve plan to any member upon request.

(4) A statement as to whether the board has determined to defer or not undertake repairs or replacement of any major component with a remaining life of 30 years or less, including a justification for the deferral or decision not to undertake the repairs or replacement.

(5) A statement as to whether the board, consistent with the reserve funding plan adopted pursuant to Section 5560, has determined or anticipates that the levy of one or more special assessments will be required to repair, replace, or restore any major component or to provide adequate reserves therefor. If so, the statement shall also set out the estimated amount, commencement date, and duration of the assessment.

(6) A statement as to the mechanism or mechanisms by which the board will fund reserves to repair or replace major components, including assessments, borrowing, use of other assets, deferral of selected replacements or repairs, or alternative mechanisms.

(7) A general statement addressing the procedures used for the calculation and establishment of those reserves to defray the future repair, replacement, or additions to those major components that the association is obligated to maintain. The statement shall include, but need not be limited to, reserve calculations made using the formula described in paragraph (4) of subdivision (b) of Section 5570, and may not assume a rate of return on cash reserves in excess of 2 percent above the discount rate published by the Federal Reserve Bank of San Francisco at the time the calculation was made.

(8) A statement as to whether the association has any outstanding loans with an original term of more than one year, including the payee, interest rate, amount outstanding, annual payment, and when the loan is scheduled to be retired.

(9) A summary of the association's property, general liability, earthquake, flood, and fidelity insurance policies. For each policy, the summary shall include the name of the insurer, the type of insurance, the policy limit, and the amount of the deductible, if any. To the extent that any of the required information is specified in the insurance policy declaration page, the association may meet its obligation to disclose that information by making copies of that page and distributing it with the annual budget report. The summary distributed pursuant to this paragraph shall contain, in at least 10–point boldface type, the following statement:

"This summary of the association's policies of insurance provides only certain information, as required by Section 5300 of the Civil Code, and should not be considered a substitute for the complete policy terms and conditions contained in the actual policies of insurance. Any association member may, upon request and provision of reasonable notice, review the association's insurance policies and, upon request and payment of reasonable duplication charges, obtain copies of those policies. Although the association maintains the policies of insurance specified in this summary, the association's policies of insurance may not cover your property, including personal property or real property improvements to or around your dwelling, or personal injuries or other losses that occur within or around your dwelling. Even if a loss is covered, you may nevertheless be responsible for paying all or a portion of any deductible that applies. Association members should consult with their individual insurance broker or agent for appropriate additional coverage."

(c) The annual budget report shall be made available to the members pursuant to Section 5320.

(d) The summary of the association's reserves disclosed pursuant to paragraph (2) of subdivision (b) shall not be admissible in evidence to show improper financial management of an association, provided that other relevant and competent evidence of the financial condition of the association is not made inadmissible by this provision.

Civil

(e) The Assessment and Reserve Funding Disclosure Summary form, prepared pursuant to Section 5570, shall accompany each annual budget report or summary of the annual budget report that is delivered pursuant to this article. *(Added by Stats.2012, c. 180 (A.B.805), § 2, operative Jan. 1, 2014.)*

Law Revision Commission Comments

Subdivision (a) of Section 5300 continues the substance of the last paragraph of former Section 1365(a).

Subdivision (b)(1) continues the substance of former Section 1365(a)(1).

Subdivision (b)(2) continues the substance of the introduction of former Section 1365(a)(2). The substance of the remainder of former Section 1365(a)(2) is continued in Section 5565.

Subdivision (b)(3) continues former Section 1365(b) without change, except as indicated below.

The following nonsubstantive changes are made:

• The commencement date of that provision (January 1, 2009) is not continued.

• An erroneous cross-reference to former Section 1365.5(e)(4) is revised to refer to Section 5560(b)(5), which continues former Section 1365.5(e)(5).

• The words "board of directors of the association" are replaced with "board." See Section 4085 ("board").

Subdivision (b)(4) continues former Section 1365(a)(3)(A) without change, except as indicated below.

The following nonsubstantive changes are made:

• The introductory clause is added.

• The words "board of directors of the association" are replaced with "board." See Section 4085 ("board").

Subdivision (b)(5) continues former Section 1365(a)(3)(B) without change, except as indicated below.

The following nonsubstantive changes are made:

• The introductory clause is added.

• The words "board of directors of the association" are replaced with "board." See Section 4085 ("board").

Subdivision (b)(6) continues former Section 1365(a)(3)(C) without change, except as indicated below.

The following nonsubstantive changes are made:

• The introductory clause is added.

• The words "board of directors of the association" are replaced with "board." See Section 4085 ("board").

Subdivision (b)(7) continues the first paragraph of former Section 1365(a)(4) without change, except as indicated below.

The following nonsubstantive changes are made:

• A cross-reference is updated to reflect the new location of the referenced provision.

• The word "report" is replaced with "statement," for terminological consistency.

Subdivision (b)(8) continues former Section 1365(a)(3)(D) without change, except as indicated below.

The following nonsubstantive change is made:

• The introductory clause is added.

Subdivision (b)(9) continues former Section 1365(f)(1), (3)-(4) without change, except as indicated below.

The following nonsubstantive changes are made:

• The redundant word "any" is replaced with "the."

• An extraneous comma is deleted from the statutory notice text.

• The substance of the second clause of the first sentence of former Section 1365(f)(1) is subsumed within subdivision (a) of Section 5300.

Subdivision (c) is consistent with former Section 1365(d).

Subdivision (d) continues the second paragraph of former Section 1365(a)(4) without change, except as indicated below.

The following nonsubstantive change is made:

• A cross-reference is updated to reflect the new location of the referenced provision.

Subdivision (e) continues the substance of former Section 1365.2.5(b)(3).

See also Sections 4080 ("association"), 4135 ("declaration"), 4150 ("governing documents"), 4160 ("member"). [40 Cal.L.Rev.Comm. Reports 235 (2010)].

Research References

1 Witkin Cal. Summ. 10th Contracts § 399, (S 399) Marital and Premarital Agreements.

14 Witkin, California Summary 10th Wills and Probate § 324, Enforcement.

§ 5305. Standards for preparation of review of financial statement of association

Unless the governing documents impose more stringent standards, a review of the financial statement of the association shall be prepared in accordance with generally accepted accounting principles by a licensee of the California Board of Accountancy for any fiscal year in which the gross income to the association exceeds seventy-five thousand dollars ($75,000). A copy of the review of the financial statement shall be distributed to the members within 120 days after the close of each fiscal year, by individual delivery pursuant to Section 4040. *(Added by Stats. 2012, c. 180 (A.B.805), § 2, operative Jan. 1, 2014.)*

Law Revision Commission Comments

Section 5305 continues former Section 1365(c) without change, except as indicated below.

The following substantive change is made:

• Language is added to specify the method of delivery.

The following nonsubstantive change is made:

• An introductory clause is added, consistent with the introduction of former Section 1365.

See also Sections 4080 ("association"), 4150 ("governing documents"). [40 Cal.L.Rev.Comm. Reports 235 (2010)].

§ 5310. Annual policy statement; contents

(a) Within 30 to 90 days before the end of its fiscal year, the board shall distribute an annual policy statement that provides the members with information about association policies. The annual policy statement shall include all of the following information:

(1) The name and address of the person designated to receive official communications to the association, pursuant to Section 4035.

(2) A statement explaining that a member may submit a request to have notices sent to up to two different specified addresses, pursuant to subdivision (b) of Section 4040.

(3) The location, if any, designated for posting of a general notice, pursuant to paragraph (3) of subdivision (a) of Section 4045.

(4) Notice of a member's option to receive general notices by individual delivery, pursuant to subdivision (b) of Section 4045.

(5) Notice of a member's right to receive copies of meeting minutes, pursuant to subdivision (b) of Section 4950.

(6) The statement of assessment collection policies required by Section 5730.

(7) A statement describing the association's policies and practices in enforcing lien rights or other legal remedies for default in the payment of assessments.

(8) A statement describing the association's discipline policy, if any, including any schedule of penalties for violations of the governing documents pursuant to Section 5850.

(9) A summary of dispute resolution procedures, pursuant to Sections 5920 and 5965.

(10) A summary of any requirements for association approval of a physical change to property, pursuant to Section 4765.

(11) The mailing address for overnight payment of assessments, pursuant to Section 5655.

(12) Any other information that is required by law or the governing documents or that the board determines to be appropriate for inclusion.

(b) The annual policy statement shall be made available to the members pursuant to Section 5320. *(Added by Stats.2012, c. 180 (A.B.805), § 2, operative Jan. 1, 2014.)*

§ 5320. Delivery of reports

(a) When a report is prepared pursuant to Section 5300 or 5310, the association shall deliver one of the following documents to all members, by individual delivery pursuant to Section 4040:

(1) The full report.

(2) A summary of the report. The summary shall include a general description of the content of the report. Instructions on how to request a complete copy of the report at no cost to the member shall be printed in at least 10–point boldface type on the first page of the summary.

(b) Notwithstanding subdivision (a), if a member has requested to receive all reports in full, the association shall deliver the full report to that member, rather than a summary of the report. *(Added by Stats.2012, c. 180 (A.B.805), § 2, operative Jan. 1, 2014.)*

ARTICLE 8. CONFLICT OF INTEREST

Section
5350. Applicability of Corporations Code provisions; prohibited actions.

§ 5350. Applicability of Corporations Code provisions; prohibited actions

(a) Notwithstanding any other law, and regardless of whether an association is incorporated or unincorporated, the provisions of Sections 7233 and 7234 of the Corporations Code shall apply to any contract or other transaction authorized, approved, or ratified by the board or a committee of the board.

(b) A director or member of a committee shall not vote on any of the following matters:

(1) Discipline of the director or committee member.

(2) An assessment against the director or committee member for damage to the common area or facilities.

(3) A request, by the director or committee member, for a payment plan for overdue assessments.

(4) A decision whether to foreclose on a lien on the separate interest of the director or committee member.

(5) Review of a proposed physical change to the separate interest of the director or committee member.

(6) A grant of exclusive use common area to the director or committee member.

(c) Nothing in this section limits any other provision of law or the governing documents that govern a decision in which a director may have an interest. *(Added by Stats.2012, c. 180 (A.B.805), § 2, operative Jan. 1, 2014.)*

ARTICLE 9. MANAGING AGENT

Section
5375. Prospective managing agent; written disclosures.
5380. Managing agent; deposit of funds received; requirements; separate record; commingling of funds.
5385. "Managing agent" does not include full-time employee of association.

§ 5375. Prospective managing agent; written disclosures

A prospective managing agent of a common interest development shall provide a written statement to the board as soon as practicable, but in no event more than 90 days, before entering into a management agreement which shall contain all of the following information concerning the managing agent:

(a) The names and business addresses of the owners or general partners of the managing agent. If the managing agent is a corporation, the written statement shall include the names and business addresses of the directors and officers and shareholders holding greater than 10 percent of the shares of the corporation.

(b) Whether or not any relevant licenses such as architectural design, construction, engineering, real estate, or accounting have been issued by this state and are currently held by the persons specified in subdivision (a). If a license is currently held by any of those persons, the statement shall contain the following information:

(1) What license is held.

(2) The dates the license is valid.

(3) The name of the licensee appearing on that license.

(c) Whether or not any relevant professional certifications or designations such as architectural design, construction, engineering, real property management, or accounting are currently held by any of the persons specified in subdivision (a), including, but not limited to, a professional common interest development manager. If any certification or designation is held, the statement shall include the following information:

(1) What the certification or designation is and what entity issued it.

(2) The dates the certification or designation is valid.

(3) The names in which the certification or designation is held. *(Added by Stats.2012, c. 180 (A.B.805), § 2, operative Jan. 1, 2014.)*

Law Revision Commission Comments

Section 5375 continues former Section 1363.1(a) without change, except as indicated below.

The following nonsubstantive changes are made:

• The words "of a common interest development" are not continued.

• The words "board of directors of the association" are replaced with "board." See Section 4085 ("board").

See also Sections 4100 ("common interest development"), 4140 ("director"), 4158 ("managing agent"). [40 Cal.L.Rev.Comm. Reports 235 (2010)].

§ 5380. Managing agent; deposit of funds received; requirements; separate record; commingling of funds

(a) A managing agent of a common interest development who accepts or receives funds belonging to the association shall deposit those funds that are not placed into an escrow account with a bank, savings association, or credit union or into an account under the control of the association, into a trust fund account maintained by the managing agent in a bank, savings association, or credit union in this state. All funds deposited by the managing agent in the trust fund account shall be kept in this state in a financial institution, as defined in Section 31041 of the Financial Code, which is insured by the federal government, and shall be maintained there until disbursed in accordance with written instructions from the association entitled to the funds.

(b) At the written request of the board, the funds the managing agent accepts or receives on behalf of the association shall be deposited into an interest-bearing account in a bank, savings association, or credit union in this state, provided all of the following requirements are met:

(1) The account is in the name of the managing agent as trustee for the association or in the name of the association.

(2) All of the funds in the account are covered by insurance provided by an agency of the federal government.

(3) The funds in the account are kept separate, distinct, and apart from the funds belonging to the managing agent or to any other person for whom the managing agent holds funds in trust except that the funds of various associations may be commingled as permitted pursuant to subdivision (d).

(4) The managing agent discloses to the board the nature of the account, how interest will be calculated and paid, whether service charges will be paid to the depository and by whom, and any notice requirements or penalties for withdrawal of funds from the account.

(5) No interest earned on funds in the account shall inure directly or indirectly to the benefit of the managing agent or the managing agent's employees.

(c) The managing agent shall maintain a separate record of the receipt and disposition of all funds described in this section, including any interest earned on the funds.

(d) The managing agent shall not commingle the funds of the association with the managing agent's own money or with the money of others that the managing agent receives or accepts, unless all of the following requirements are met:

(1) The managing agent commingled the funds of various associations on or before February 26, 1990, and has obtained a written agreement with the board of each association that the managing agent will maintain a fidelity and surety bond in an amount that provides adequate protection to the associations as agreed upon by the managing agent and the board of each association.

(2) The managing agent discloses in the written agreement whether the managing agent is deriving benefits from the commingled account or the bank, credit union, or savings institution where the moneys will be on deposit.

(3) The written agreement provided pursuant to this subdivision includes, but is not limited to, the name and address of the bonding companies, the amount of the bonds, and the expiration dates of the bonds.

(4) If there are any changes in the bond coverage or the companies providing the coverage, the managing agent discloses that fact to the board of each affected association as soon as practical, but in no event more than 10 days after the change.

(5) The bonds assure the protection of the association and provide the association at least 10 days' notice prior to cancellation.

(6) Completed payments on the behalf of the association are deposited within 24 hours or the next business day and do not remain commingled for more than 10 calendar days.

(e) The prevailing party in an action to enforce this section shall be entitled to recover reasonable legal fees and court costs.

(f) As used in this section, "completed payment" means funds received that clearly identify the account to which the funds are to be credited. (Added by Stats.2012, c. 180 (A.B.805), § 2, operative Jan. 1, 2014.)

Law Revision Commission Comments

Subdivision (a) of Section 5380 continues former Section 1363.2(a) without change, except for the following nonsubstantive change: "All such" is replaced with "those" to conform to standard legislative drafting practice.

Subdivisions (b) and (c) continue former Section 1363.2(b)-(c) without change, except as indicated below.

The following nonsubstantive changes are made:

• The words "his or her" are replaced with "the managing agent's."

• The words "or entity" are not continued. See Section 4170 ("person").

• The words "board of directors" are replaced with "board." See Section 4085 ("board").

Subdivision (d) continues former Section 1363.2(d) without change, except as indicated below.

The following nonsubstantive changes are made:

• The words "he or she" and "his or her" are replaced with "the managing agent" or "the managing agent's" throughout.

• The words "board of directors" are replaced with "board." See Section 4085 ("board").

Subdivision (e) continues former Section 1363.2(e) without change.

Subdivision (f) continues former Section 1363.2(g) without change, except as indicated below.

The following nonsubstantive changes are made:

• The word "which" is replaced with "that."

See also Sections 4080 ("association"), 4100 ("common interest development"), 4158 ("managing agent"). [40 Cal.L.Rev.Comm. Reports 235 (2010)].

§ 5385. "Managing agent" does not include full-time employee of association

For the purposes of this article, "managing agent" does not include a full-time employee of the association. (Added by Stats.2012, c. 180 (A.B.805), § 2, operative Jan. 1, 2014.)

Law Revision Commission Comments

Section 5385 continues the substance of former Section 1363.1(b)(1) and the first clause of the second sentence of former Section 1363.2(f).

See also Sections 4080 ("association"), 4158 ("managing agent"). [40 Cal.L.Rev.Comm. Reports 235 (2010)].

ARTICLE 10. GOVERNMENT ASSISTANCE

Section

Section

tive board directors and nonjudicial foreclosure process.

5405.   Assistance with identification of common interest developments; submission of information by each association; time; notice of change of address; penalty for violation of filing requirements; availability of information.

§ 5400.   Online education course regarding role, duties, laws and responsibilities of board directors and prospective board directors and nonjudicial foreclosure process

To the extent existing funds are available, the Department of Consumer Affairs and the Bureau of Real Estate shall develop an online education course for the board regarding the role, duties, laws, and responsibilities of directors and prospective directors, and the nonjudicial foreclosure process. (*Added by Stats.2012, c. 180 (A.B.805), § 2, operative Jan. 1, 2014. Amended by Stats.2013, c. 352 (A.B.1317), § 55, eff. Sept. 26, 2013, operative Jan. 1, 2014.*)

Law Revision Commission Comments

Section 5400 continues the substance of former Section 1363.001, except as indicated below.

The following nonsubstantive changes are made:

• The words "board of directors" are replaced with "board." See Section 4085 ("board").

• The words "board member" are replaced with "director." See Section 4140 ("director").

• The word "on-line" is replaced with "online." [40 Cal.L.Rev. Comm. Reports 235 (2010)].

§ 5405.   Assistance with identification of common interest developments; submission of information by each association; time; notice of change of address; penalty for violation of filing requirements; availability of information

(a) To assist with the identification of common interest developments, each association, whether incorporated or unincorporated, shall submit to the Secretary of State, on a form and for a fee not to exceed thirty dollars ($30) that the Secretary of State shall prescribe, the following information concerning the association and the development that it manages:

(1) A statement that the association is formed to manage a common interest development under the Davis–Stirling Common Interest Development Act.

(2) The name of the association.

(3) The street address of the business or corporate office of the association, if any.

(4) The street address of the association's onsite office, if different from the street address of the business or corporate office, or if there is no onsite office, the street address of the responsible officer or managing agent of the association.

(5) The name, address, and either the daytime telephone number or email address of the president of the association, other than the address, telephone number, or email address of the association's onsite office or managing agent.

(6) The name, street address, and daytime telephone number of the association's managing agent, if any.

(7) The county, and, if in an incorporated area, the city in which the development is physically located. If the boundaries of the development are physically located in more than one county, each of the counties in which it is located.

(8) If the development is in an unincorporated area, the city closest in proximity to the development.

(9) The front street and nearest cross street of the physical location of the development.

(10) The type of common interest development managed by the association.

(11) The number of separate interests in the development.

(b) The association shall submit the information required by this section as follows:

(1) By incorporated associations, within 90 days after the filing of its original articles of incorporation, and thereafter at the time the association files its statement of principal business activity with the Secretary of State pursuant to Section 8210 of the Corporations Code.

(2) By unincorporated associations, in July 2003, and in that same month biennially thereafter. Upon changing its status to that of a corporation, the association shall comply with the filing deadlines in paragraph (1).

(c) The association shall notify the Secretary of State of any change in the street address of the association's onsite office or of the responsible officer or managing agent of the association in the form and for a fee prescribed by the Secretary of State, within 60 days of the change.

(d) The penalty for an incorporated association's noncompliance with the initial or biennial filing requirements of this section shall be suspension of the association's rights, privileges, and powers as a corporation and monetary penalties, to the same extent and in the same manner as suspension and monetary penalties imposed pursuant to Section 8810 of the Corporations Code.

(e) The statement required by this section may be filed, notwithstanding suspension of the corporate powers, rights, and privileges under this section or under provisions of the Revenue and Taxation Code. Upon the filing of a statement under this section by a corporation that has suffered suspension under this section, the Secretary of State shall certify that fact to the Franchise Tax Board and the corporation may thereupon be relieved from suspension, unless the corporation is held in suspension by the Franchise Tax Board by reason of Section 23301, 23301.5, or 23775 of the Revenue and Taxation Code.

(f) The Secretary of State shall make the information submitted pursuant to paragraph (5) of subdivision (a) available only for governmental purposes and only to Members of the Legislature and the Business, * * * Consumer Services, and Housing Agency, upon written request. All other information submitted pursuant to this section shall be subject to public inspection pursuant to the California Public Records Act (Chapter 3.5 (commencing with Section 6250) of Division 7 of Title 1 of the Government Code). The information submitted pursuant to this section shall be made available for governmental or public inspection.

(g) Whenever any form is filed pursuant to this section, it supersedes any previously filed form.

(h) The Secretary of State may destroy or otherwise dispose of any form filed pursuant to this section after it has been superseded by the filing of a new form. (*Added by Stats.2012, c. 180 (A.B.805), § 2, operative Jan. 1, 2014. Amended by Stats. 2013, c. 353 (S.B.820), § 12, eff. Sept. 26, 2013, operative Jan. 1, 2014.*)

Law Revision Commission Comments

Section 5405 continues former Section 1363.6 without change, except as indicated below.

The following nonsubstantive changes are made:

• The words "of the association" at the end of Section 1363.6(a)(5) are not continued.

• Superfluous references to definition sections are not continued.

• Obsolete transitional dates are not continued in subdivisions (d) and (f).

● The words "as the case may be" are not continued in subdivision (f).

See also Sections 4080 ("association"), 4100 ("common interest development"), 4158 ("managing agent"). [40 Cal.L.Rev.Comm. Reports 235 (2010)].

CHAPTER 7. FINANCES

ARTICLE 1. ACCOUNTING

§ 5500. Duties of board

Unless the governing documents impose more stringent standards, the board shall do all of the following:

(a) Review a current reconciliation of the association's operating accounts on at least a quarterly basis.

(b) Review a current reconciliation of the association's reserve accounts on at least a quarterly basis.

(c) Review, on at least a quarterly basis, the current year's actual reserve revenues and expenses compared to the current year's budget.

(d) Review the latest account statements prepared by the financial institutions where the association has its operating and reserve accounts.

(e) Review an income and expense statement for the association's operating and reserve accounts on at least a quarterly basis. *(Added by Stats.2012, c. 180 (A.B.805), § 2, operative Jan. 1, 2014.)*

Law Revision Commission Comments

Section 5500 continues former Section 1365.5(a) without change, except as indicated below.

The following nonsubstantive change is made:

● The words "board of directors of the association" are replaced with "board." See Section 4085 ("board").

See also Sections 4080 ("association"), 4150 ("governing documents"), 4177 ("reserve accounts"). [40 Cal.L.Rev.Comm. Reports 235 (2010)].

ARTICLE 2. USE OF RESERVE FUNDS

§ 5510. Signatures required for withdrawals; purpose of expenditure

(a) The signatures of at least two persons, who shall be directors, or one officer who is not a director and one who is a director, shall be required for the withdrawal of moneys from the association's reserve accounts.

(b) The board shall not expend funds designated as reserve funds for any purpose other than the repair, restoration, replacement, or maintenance of, or litigation involving the repair, restoration, replacement, or maintenance of, major components that the association is obligated to repair, restore, replace, or maintain and for which the reserve fund was established. *(Added by Stats.2012, c. 180 (A.B.805), § 2, operative Jan. 1, 2014.)*

Law Revision Commission Comments

Subdivision (a) of Section 5510 continues former Section 1365.5(b) without change, except as indicated below.

The following nonsubstantive changes are made:

● The words "board of directors" are replaced with "board." See Section 4085 ("board").

● The words "one who is" are added to the sentence to make its meaning clearer.

● The words "board member" are replaced with "director." See Section 4140 ("director").

Subdivision (b) continues former Section 1365.5(c)(1) without change, except as indicated below.

The following nonsubstantive change is made:

● The words "board of directors" are replaced with "board." See Section 4085 ("board").

See also Sections 4080 ("association"), 4177 ("reserve accounts"). [40 Cal.L.Rev.Comm. Reports 235 (2010)].

§ 5515. Temporary transfers to general operating fund

(a) Notwithstanding Section 5510, the board may authorize the temporary transfer of moneys from a reserve fund to the association's general operating fund to meet short-term cashflow requirements or other expenses, if the board has provided notice of the intent to consider the transfer in a board meeting notice provided pursuant to Section 4920.

(b) The notice shall include the reasons the transfer is needed, some of the options for repayment, and whether a special assessment may be considered.

(c) If the board authorizes the transfer, the board shall issue a written finding, recorded in the board's minutes, explaining the reasons that the transfer is needed, and describing when and how the moneys will be repaid to the reserve fund.

(d) The transferred funds shall be restored to the reserve fund within one year of the date of the initial transfer, except that the board may, after giving the same notice required for considering a transfer, and, upon making a finding supported by documentation that a temporary delay would be in the best interests of the common interest development, temporarily delay the restoration.

(e) The board shall exercise prudent fiscal management in maintaining the integrity of the reserve account, and shall, if necessary, levy a special assessment to recover the full amount of the expended funds within the time limits required by this section. This special assessment is subject to the limitation imposed by Section 5605. The board may, at its discretion, extend the date the payment on the special assessment is due. Any extension shall not prevent the board from pursuing any legal remedy to enforce the collection of an unpaid special assessment. *(Added by Stats.2012, c. 180 (A.B.805), § 2, operative Jan. 1, 2014.)*

Law Revision Commission Comments

Section 5515 continues former Section 1365.5(c)(2) without change, except as indicated below.

The following nonsubstantive changes are made:

● The provision is divided into subdivisions for ease of reference.

● Cross-references are updated to reflect the new locations of the referenced provisions.

● The introductory word "However" is replaced with "Notwithstanding Section 5510."

● The last clause of subdivision (a) is rephrased for clarity.

See also Sections 4080 ("association"), 4085 ("board"), 4090 ("board meeting"), 4100 ("common interest development"), 4177 ("reserve accounts"). [40 Cal.L.Rev.Comm. Reports 235 (2010)].

§ 5520. Notice of action; accounting of expenses

(a) When the decision is made to use reserve funds or to temporarily transfer moneys from the reserve fund to pay for litigation pursuant to subdivision (b) of Section 5510, the association shall provide general notice pursuant to Section 4045 of that decision, and of the availability of an accounting of those expenses.

(b) Unless the governing documents impose more stringent standards, the association shall make an accounting of expenses related to the litigation on at least a quarterly basis. The accounting shall be made available for inspection by members of the association at the association's office. *(Added by Stats.2012, c. 180 (A.B.805), § 2, operative Jan. 1, 2014.)*

Law Revision Commission Comments

Section 5520 continues former Section 1365.5(d) without change, except as indicated below.

The following substantive change is made:

● A reference to notice pursuant to Corporations Code Section 5016 is replaced with a requirement of general notice pursuant to Section 4045.

The following nonsubstantive changes are made:

● The provision is divided into subdivisions for ease of reference.

● A cross-reference to Section 5510(b) is added for clarity.

● The words "members of the association" are replaced with "members." See Section 4160 ("member").

See also Sections 4080 ("association"), 4085 ("board"), 4150 ("governing documents"). [40 Cal.L.Rev.Comm. Reports 235 (2010)].

ARTICLE 3. RESERVE PLANNING

Section
5550. Inspection of components; study minimum requirements.
5560. Reserve funding plan; inclusion of schedule of change in assessments; adoption by board; separate approval of assessment increase.
5565. Summary of association's reserves; contents.
5570. Form for disclosure of fiscal matters.
5580. Community service organization reports; information on components to complete disclosures or reserve reports; reliance upon and access to information.

§ 5550. Inspection of components; study minimum requirements

(a) At least once every three years, the board shall cause to be conducted a reasonably competent and diligent visual inspection of the accessible areas of the major components that the association is obligated to repair, replace, restore, or maintain as part of a study of the reserve account requirements of the common interest development, if the current replacement value of the major components is equal to or greater than one-half of the gross budget of the association, excluding the association's reserve account for that period. The board shall review this study, or cause it to be reviewed, annually and shall consider and implement necessary adjustments to the board's analysis of the reserve account requirements as a result of that review.

(b) The study required by this section shall at a minimum include:

(1) Identification of the major components that the association is obligated to repair, replace, restore, or maintain that, as of the date of the study, have a remaining useful life of less than 30 years.

(2) Identification of the probable remaining useful life of the components identified in paragraph (1) as of the date of the study.

(3) An estimate of the cost of repair, replacement, restoration, or maintenance of the components identified in paragraph (1).

(4) An estimate of the total annual contribution necessary to defray the cost to repair, replace, restore, or maintain the components identified in paragraph (1) during and at the end of their useful life, after subtracting total reserve funds as of the date of the study.

(5) A reserve funding plan that indicates how the association plans to fund the contribution identified in paragraph (4) to meet the association's obligation for the repair and replacement of all major components with an expected remaining life of 30 years or less, not including those components that the board has determined will not be replaced or repaired. *(Added by Stats.2012, c. 180 (A.B.805), § 2, operative Jan. 1, 2014.)*

Law Revision Commission Comments

Section 5550 continues former Section 1365.5(e)(1)-(4) and the first sentence of (e)(5) without change, except as indicated below.

The following nonsubstantive change is made:

● The words "board of directors" are replaced with "board." See Section 4085 ("board").

See also Sections 4080 ("association"), 4100 ("common interest development"), 4177 ("reserve accounts"), 4177 ("reserve account requirements"). [40 Cal.L.Rev.Comm. Reports 235 (2010)].

§ 5560. Reserve funding plan; inclusion of schedule of change in assessments; adoption by board; separate approval of assessment increase

(a) The reserve funding plan required by Section 5550 shall include a schedule of the date and amount of any change in regular or special assessments that would be needed to sufficiently fund the reserve funding plan.

(b) The plan shall be adopted by the board at an open meeting before the membership of the association as described in Article 2 (commencing with Section 4900) of Chapter 6.

(c) If the board determines that an assessment increase is necessary to fund the reserve funding plan, any increase shall be approved in a separate action of the board that is consistent with the procedure described in Section 5605. *(Added by Stats.2012, c. 180 (A.B.805), § 2, operative Jan. 1, 2014.)*

Law Revision Commission Comments

Section 5560 continues the second, third, and fourth sentences of former Section 1365.5(e)(5) without change, except as indicated below.

The following nonsubstantive changes are made:

● The introductory clause is restated, without substantive change.

● Cross-references are updated to reflect the new locations of the referenced provisions.

● The words "board of directors" are replaced with "board." See Section 4085 ("board").

See also Section 4080 ("association"). [40 Cal.L.Rev.Comm. Reports 235 (2010)].

§ 5565. Summary of association's reserves; contents

The summary of the association's reserves required by paragraph (2) of subdivision (b) of Section 5300 shall be based on the most recent review or study conducted pursuant to Section 5550, shall be based only on assets held in cash or cash equivalents, shall be printed in boldface type, and shall include all of the following:

(a) The current estimated replacement cost, estimated remaining life, and estimated useful life of each major component.

(b) As of the end of the fiscal year for which the study is prepared:

(1) The current estimate of the amount of cash reserves necessary to repair, replace, restore, or maintain the major components.

(2) The current amount of accumulated cash reserves actually set aside to repair, replace, restore, or maintain major components.

(3) If applicable, the amount of funds received from either a compensatory damage award or settlement to an association from any person for injuries to property, real or personal, arising out of any construction or design defects, and the expenditure or disposition of funds, including the amounts expended for the direct and indirect costs of repair of construction or design defects. These amounts shall be reported at the end of the fiscal year for which the study is prepared as separate line items under cash reserves pursuant to paragraph (2). Instead of complying with the requirements set forth in this paragraph, an association that is obligated to issue a review of its financial statement pursuant to Section 5305 may include in the review a statement containing all of the information required by this paragraph.

(c) The percentage that the amount determined for purposes of paragraph (2) of subdivision (b) equals the amount determined for purposes of paragraph (1) of subdivision (b).

(d) The current deficiency in reserve funding expressed on a per unit basis. The figure shall be calculated by subtracting the amount determined for purposes of paragraph (2) of subdivision (b) from the amount determined for purposes of paragraph (1) of subdivision (b) and then dividing the result by the number of separate interests within the association, except that if assessments vary by the size or type of ownership interest, then the association shall calculate the current deficiency in a manner that reflects the variation. *(Added by Stats.2012, c. 180 (A.B.805), § 2, operative Jan. 1, 2014.)*

Law Revision Commission Comments

Section 5565 continues former Section 1365(a)(2) without change, except as indicated below.

The following nonsubstantive changes are made:

• The introductory clause is revised to reflect the organization of this provision as a separate section and to make minor grammatical improvements.

• Subdivision (b)(3) corrects an erroneous cross-reference (to the financial statement required under Section 5305).

• In subdivision (b)(3), the words "or entity" are not continued. See Section 4170 ("person").

• In subdivision (b)(3), the word "their" is replaced with "its" for grammatical reasons.

• Cross-references are updated to reflect the new locations of the referenced provisions.

See also Sections 4080 ("association"), 4185 ("separate interest"). [40 Cal.L.Rev.Comm. Reports 235 (2010)].

§ 5570. Form for disclosure of fiscal matters

(a) The disclosures required by this article with regard to an association or a property shall be summarized on the following form:

Assessment and Reserve Funding Disclosure Summary
For the Fiscal Year Ending _____

(1) The regular assessment per ownership interest is $_____ per _____. Note: If assessments vary by the size or type of ownership interest, the assessment applicable to this ownership interest may be found on page _____ of the attached summary.

(2) Additional regular or special assessments that have already been scheduled to be imposed or charged, regardless of the purpose, if they have been approved by the board and/or members:

Date assessment will be due:	(If assessments are variable, see note immediately below):	Purpose of the assessment:
Total:		

Note: If assessments vary by the size or type of ownership interest, the assessment applicable to this ownership interest may be found on page _____ of the attached report.

(3) Based upon the most recent reserve study and other information available to the board of directors, will currently projected reserve account balances be sufficient at the end of each year to meet the association's obligation for repair and/or replacement of major components during the next 30 years?

Yes _____   No _____

(4) If the answer to (3) is no, what additional assessments or other contributions to reserves would be necessary to ensure that sufficient reserve funds will be available each year during the next 30 years that have not yet been approved by the board or the members?

Approximate date assessment will be due:	Amount per ownership interest per month or year:
Total:	

(5) All major components are included in the reserve study and are included in its calculations.

(6) Based on the method of calculation in paragraph (4) of subdivision (b) of Section 5570, the estimated amount required in the reserve fund at the end of the current fiscal year is $_____, based in whole or in part on the last reserve study or update prepared by _____ as of _____ (month), _____ (year). The projected reserve fund cash balance at the end of the current fiscal year is $_____, resulting in reserves being _____ percent funded at this date.

If an alternate, but generally accepted, method of calculation is also used, the required reserve amount is $_____. (See attached explanation)

(7) Based on the method of calculation in paragraph (4) of subdivision (b) of Section 5570 of the Civil Code, the estimated amount required in the reserve fund at the end of each of the next five budget years is $_____, and the projected reserve fund cash balance in each of those years, taking into account only assessments already approved and other known revenues, is $_____, leaving the reserve at _____ percent funding. If the reserve funding plan approved by the association is implemented, the projected reserve fund cash balance in each of those years will be $_____, leaving the reserve at _____ percent funding.

Note: The financial representations set forth in this summary are based on the best estimates of the preparer at that time. The estimates are subject to change. At the time this summary

(The bottom left table, under paragraph (2):)

	Amount per ownership interest per month or year

was prepared, the assumed long-term before-tax interest rate earned on reserve funds was ___ percent per year, and the assumed long-term inflation rate to be applied to major component repair and replacement costs was ___ percent per year.

(b) For the purposes of preparing a summary pursuant to this section:

(1) "Estimated remaining useful life" means the time reasonably calculated to remain before a major component will require replacement.

(2) "Major component" has the meaning used in Section 55530. Components with an estimated remaining useful life of more than 30 years may be included in a study as a capital asset or disregarded from the reserve calculation, so long as the decision is revealed in the reserve study report and reported in the Assessment and Reserve Funding Disclosure Summary.

(3) The form set out in subdivision (a) shall accompany each annual budget report or summary thereof that is delivered pursuant to Section 5300. The form may be supplemented or modified to clarify the information delivered, so long as the minimum information set out in subdivision (a) is provided.

(4) For the purpose of the report and summary, the amount of reserves needed to be accumulated for a component at a given time shall be computed as the current cost of replacement or repair multiplied by the number of years the component has been in service divided by the useful life of the component. This shall not be construed to require the board to fund reserves in accordance with this calculation. *(Added by Stats.2012, c. 180 (A.B.805), § 2, operative Jan. 1, 2014.)*

§ 5580. Community service organization reports; information on components to complete disclosures or reserve reports; reliance upon and access to information

(a) Unless the governing documents impose more stringent standards, any community service organization whose funding from the association or its members exceeds 10 percent of the organization's annual budget shall prepare and distribute to the association a report that meets the requirements of Section 5012 of the Corporations Code, and that describes in detail administrative costs and identifies the payees of those costs in a manner consistent with the provisions of Article 5 (commencing with Section 5200) of Chapter 6.

(b) If the community service organization does not comply with the standards, the report shall disclose the noncompliance in detail. If a community service organization is responsible for the maintenance of major components for which an association would otherwise be responsible, the community service organization shall supply to the association the information regarding those components that the association would use to complete disclosures and reserve reports required under this article and Section 5300. An association may rely upon information received from a community service organization, and shall provide access to the information pursuant to the provisions of

Article 5 (commencing with Section 5200) of Chapter 6. *(Added by Stats.2012, c. 180 (A.B.805), § 2, operative Jan. 1, 2014.)*

CHAPTER 8. ASSESSMENTS AND ASSESSMENT COLLECTION

ARTICLE 1. ESTABLISHMENT AND IMPOSITION OF ASSESSMENTS

§ 5600. Levy of assessments; limit on amount

(a) Except as provided in Section 5605, the association shall levy regular and special assessments sufficient to perform its obligations under the governing documents and this act.

(b) An association shall not impose or collect an assessment or fee that exceeds the amount necessary to defray the costs for which it is levied. *(Added by Stats.2012, c. 180 (A.B.805), § 2, operative Jan. 1, 2014.)*

§ 5605. Limitation on increases

(a) Annual increases in regular assessments for any fiscal year shall not be imposed unless the board has complied with paragraphs (1), (2), (4), (5), (6), (7), and (8) of subdivision (b) of Section 5300 with respect to that fiscal year, or has obtained the approval of a majority of a quorum of members, pursuant to Section 4070, at a member meeting or election.

(b) Notwithstanding more restrictive limitations placed on the board by the governing documents, the board may not impose a regular assessment that is more than 20 percent greater than the regular assessment for the association's preceding fiscal year or impose special assessments which in the aggregate exceed 5 percent of the budgeted gross expenses of the association for that fiscal year without the approval of a majority of a quorum of members, pursuant to Section 4070, at a member meeting or election.

(c) For the purposes of this section, "quorum" means more than 50 percent of the members. *(Added by Stats.2012, c. 180 (A.B.805), § 2, operative Jan. 1, 2014.)*

Law Revision Commission Comments

Subdivision (a) of Section 5605 continues the second sentence of former Section 1366(a) without change, except as indicated below.

The following nonsubstantive changes are made:

• Language requiring approval of a majority of members casting a vote at a meeting at which a quorum is established is replaced with a reference to the standard provision on approval by a majority of a quorum of members (Section 4070).

• A reference to an assessment increase "as authorized by subdivision (b)" is superfluous and potentially confusing, and is not continued.

• Language requiring that a meeting or election be conducted pursuant to the Corporations Code is inconsistent with former Section 1363.03 and is not continued.

• A cross-reference to former Section 1365(a) is replaced with a cross-reference to Section 5300(b)(1)-(2), (4)-(8).

Subdivision (b) continues the first sentence of former Section 1366(b) without change, except as indicated below.

The following nonsubstantive changes are made:

• Language requiring approval of a majority of members casting a vote at a meeting at which a quorum is established is replaced with a reference to the standard provision on approval by a majority of a quorum of members (Section 4070).

• Language requiring that a meeting or election be conducted pursuant to the Corporations Code is inconsistent with former Section 1363.03 and is not continued.

• The words "board of directors" are replaced with "board." See Section 4085 ("board").

Subdivision (c) continues the substance of the last sentence of former Section 1366(a) and the second sentence of former Section 1366(b).

See also Sections 4080 ("association"), 4150 ("governing documents"), 4160 ("member"). [40 Cal.L.Rev.Comm. Reports 235 (2010)].

§ 5610. Increases for emergency situations

Section 5605 does not limit assessment increases necessary for emergency situations. For purposes of this section, an emergency situation is any one of the following:

(a) An extraordinary expense required by an order of a court.

(b) An extraordinary expense necessary to repair or maintain the common interest development or any part of it for which the association is responsible where a threat to personal safety on the property is discovered.

(c) An extraordinary expense necessary to repair or maintain the common interest development or any part of it for which the association is responsible that could not have been reasonably foreseen by the board in preparing and distributing the annual budget report under Section 5300. However, prior to the imposition or collection of an assessment under this subdivision, the board shall pass a resolution containing written findings as to the necessity of the extraordinary expense involved and why the expense was not or could not have been reasonably foreseen in the budgeting process, and the resolution shall be distributed to the members with the notice of assessment. *(Added by Stats. 2012, c. 180 (A.B.805), § 2, operative Jan. 1, 2014.)*

Law Revision Commission Comments

Section 5610 continues the third and fourth sentences and paragraphs (1) to (3), inclusive, of former Section 1366(b), without change, except as indicated below.

The following nonsubstantive changes are made:

• The words "pro forma operating budget" are replaced with "annual budget report." See Section 4076 ("annual budget report").

• Cross-references are updated to reflect the new locations of the referenced provisions.

See also Sections 4080 ("association"), 4085 ("board"), 4100 ("common interest development"), 4160 ("member"). [40 Cal.L.Rev.Comm. Reports 235 (2010)].

§ 5615. Individual notice of increases

The association shall provide individual notice pursuant to Section 4040 to the members of any increase in the regular or special assessments of the association, not less than 30 nor more than 60 days prior to the increased assessment becoming due. *(Added by Stats.2012, c. 180 (A.B.805), § 2, operative Jan. 1, 2014.)*

Law Revision Commission Comments

Section 5615 continues former Section 1366(d) without change, except as indicated below.

The following nonsubstantive changes are made:

• A requirement of delivery by first class mail is replaced with a requirement of "individual notice."

• The word "owner" is replaced with "member." See Section 4160 ("member").

See also Section 4080 ("association"). [40 Cal.L.Rev.Comm. Reports 235 (2010)].

§ 5620. Exemption from execution by judgment creditor of association

(a) Regular assessments imposed or collected to perform the obligations of an association under the governing documents or this act shall be exempt from execution by a judgment creditor of the association only to the extent necessary for the association to perform essential services, such as paying for utilities and insurance. In determining the appropriateness of an exemption, a court shall ensure that only essential services are protected under this subdivision.

(b) This exemption shall not apply to any consensual pledges, liens, or encumbrances that have been approved by a majority of a quorum of members, pursuant to Section 4070, at a member meeting or election, or to any state tax lien, or to any lien for labor or materials supplied to the common area. *(Added by Stats.2012, c. 180 (A.B.805), § 2, operative Jan. 1, 2014.)*

Law Revision Commission Comments

Section 5620 continues former Section 1366(c) without change, except as indicated below.

The following nonsubstantive changes are made:

• The provision is divided into subdivisions for ease of reference.

• A reference to approval of a majority of members casting a vote at a meeting at which a quorum is established is replaced with a reference to the standard provision on approval by a majority of a quorum of members (Section 4070).

• Quorum-related language from former Section 1366(b)-(c) is not continued.

• The word "title" is replaced with "act."

See also Sections 4080 ("association"), 4095 ("common area"), 4150 ("governing documents"), 4160 ("member"). [40 Cal.L.Rev.Comm. Reports 235 (2010)].

§ 5625. Levies on separate interests

(a) Except as provided in subdivision (b), notwithstanding any provision of this act or the governing documents to the contrary, an association shall not levy assessments on separate interests within the common interest development based on the taxable value of the separate interests unless the association, on or before December 31, 2009, in accordance with its governing documents, levied assessments on those separate interests based on their taxable value, as determined by the tax assessor of the county in which the separate interests are located.

(b) An association that is responsible for paying taxes on the separate interests within the common interest development may levy that portion of assessments on separate interests that is related to the payment of taxes based on the taxable value of the separate interest, as determined by the tax assessor. *(Added by Stats.2012, c. 180 (A.B.805), § 2, operative Jan. 1, 2014.)*

Law Revision Commission Comments

Section 5625 continues former Section 1366.4 without change, except as indicated below.

The following nonsubstantive change is made:
- The word "title" is replaced with "act."

See also Sections 4080 ("association"), 4100 ("common interest development"), 4150 ("governing documents"), 4185 ("separate interest"). [40 Cal.L.Rev.Comm. Reports 235 (2010)].

ARTICLE 2. ASSESSMENT PAYMENT AND DELINQUENCY

Section

§ 5650. Debt of owner of separate interest; time of delinquency; interest

(a) A regular or special assessment and any late charges, reasonable fees and costs of collection, reasonable attorney's fees, if any, and interest, if any, as determined in accordance with subdivision (b), shall be a debt of the owner of the separate interest at the time the assessment or other sums are levied.

(b) Regular and special assessments levied pursuant to the governing documents are delinquent 15 days after they become due, unless the declaration provides a longer time period, in which case the longer time period shall apply. If an assessment is delinquent, the association may recover all of the following:

(1) Reasonable costs incurred in collecting the delinquent assessment, including reasonable attorney's fees.

(2) A late charge not exceeding 10 percent of the delinquent assessment or ten dollars ($10), whichever is greater, unless the declaration specifies a late charge in a smaller amount, in which case any late charge imposed shall not exceed the amount specified in the declaration.

(3) Interest on all sums imposed in accordance with this section, including the delinquent assessments, reasonable fees and costs of collection, and reasonable attorney's fees, at an annual interest rate not to exceed 12 percent, commencing 30 days after the assessment becomes due, unless the declaration specifies the recovery of interest at a rate of a lesser amount, in which case the lesser rate of interest shall apply.

(c) Associations are hereby exempted from interest-rate limitations imposed by Article XV of the California Constitution, subject to the limitations of this section. *(Added by Stats.2012, c. 180 (A.B.805), § 2, operative Jan. 1, 2014.)*

Law Revision Commission Comments

Subdivision (a) of Section 5650 continues the first sentence of former Section 1367.1(a) without change, except as indicated below.

The following nonsubstantive change is made:
- A cross-reference is updated to reflect the new location of the referenced provision.

Subdivision (b) continues former Section 1366(e) without change.

Subdivision (c) continues former Section 1366(f) without change.

See also Sections 4080 ("association"), 4135 ("declaration"), 4150 ("governing documents"), 4185 ("separate interest"). [40 Cal.L.Rev. Comm. Reports 235 (2010)].

§ 5655. Application of payment; receipt; mailing address for overnight payment

(a) Any payments made by the owner of a separate interest toward a debt described in subdivision (a) of Section 5650 shall first be applied to the assessments owed, and, only after the assessments owed are paid in full shall the payments be applied to the fees and costs of collection, attorney's fees, late charges, or interest.

(b) When an owner makes a payment, the owner may request a receipt and the association shall provide it. The receipt shall indicate the date of payment and the person who received it.

(c) The association shall provide a mailing address for overnight payment of assessments. The address shall be provided in the annual policy statement. *(Added by Stats.2012, c. 180 (A.B.805), § 2, operative Jan. 1, 2014.)*

Law Revision Commission Comments

Section 5655 continues the substance of former Section 1367.1(b), except as indicated below.

The following nonsubstantive changes are made:
- A superfluous comma is deleted in the first sentence.
- A superfluous reference to assessment debt "set forth, as required in subdivision (a)" is deleted to make the meaning of the provision clearer.
- The provision is divided into subdivisions for ease of reference.
- The second sentence of subdivision (c) is added to refer to the requirement of Section 5310(a)(11).

See also Sections 4078 ("annual policy statement"), 4080 ("association"), 4185 ("separate interest"). [40 Cal.L.Rev.Comm. Reports 235 (2010)].

§ 5658. Disputed charge or sum levied by association; payment under protest; action in small claims court

(a) If a dispute exists between the owner of a separate interest and the association regarding any disputed charge or sum levied by the association, including, but not limited to, an assessment, fine, penalty, late fee, collection cost, or monetary penalty imposed as a disciplinary measure, and the amount in dispute does not exceed the jurisdictional limits of the small claims court stated in Sections 116.220 and 116.221 of the Code of Civil Procedure, the owner of the separate interest may, in addition to pursuing dispute resolution pursuant to Article 3 (commencing with Section 5925) of Chapter 10, pay under protest the disputed amount and all other amounts levied, including any fees and reasonable costs of collection, reasonable attorney's fees, late charges, and interest, if any, pursuant to subdivision (b) of Section 5650, and commence an action in small claims court pursuant to Chapter 5.5 (commencing with Section 116.110) of Title 1 of the Code of Civil Procedure.

(b) Nothing in this section shall impede an association's ability to collect delinquent assessments as provided in this article or Article 3 (commencing with Section 5700). *(Added by Stats.2012, c. 180 (A.B.805), § 2, operative Jan. 1, 2014.)*

Law Revision Commission Comments

Section 5658 continues former Section 1367.6 without change, except as indicated below.

The following nonsubstantive changes are made:

• Cross-references are updated to reflect the new locations of the referenced provisions.

• A reference to the "small claims court" is added for clarity.

See also Sections 4080 ("association"), 4185 ("separate interest"). [40 Cal.L.Rev.Comm. Reports 235 (2010)].

§ 5660. Notice; contents

At least 30 days prior to recording a lien upon the separate interest of the owner of record to collect a debt that is past due under Section 5650, the association shall notify the owner of record in writing by certified mail of the following:

(a) A general description of the collection and lien enforcement procedures of the association and the method of calculation of the amount, a statement that the owner of the separate interest has the right to inspect the association records pursuant to Section 5205, and the following statement in 14–point boldface type, if printed, or in capital letters, if typed:

"IMPORTANT NOTICE: IF YOUR SEPARATE INTEREST IS PLACED IN FORECLOSURE BECAUSE YOU ARE BEHIND IN YOUR ASSESSMENTS, IT MAY BE SOLD WITHOUT COURT ACTION."

(b) An itemized statement of the charges owed by the owner, including items on the statement which indicate the amount of any delinquent assessments, the fees and reasonable costs of collection, reasonable attorney's fees, any late charges, and interest, if any.

(c) A statement that the owner shall not be liable to pay the charges, interest, and costs of collection, if it is determined the assessment was paid on time to the association.

(d) The right to request a meeting with the board as provided in Section 5665.

(e) The right to dispute the assessment debt by submitting a written request for dispute resolution to the association pursuant to the association's "meet and confer" program required in Article 2 (commencing with Section 5900) of Chapter 10.

(f) The right to request alternative dispute resolution with a neutral third party pursuant to Article 3 (commencing with Section 5925) of Chapter 10 before the association may initiate foreclosure against the owner's separate interest, except that binding arbitration shall not be available if the association intends to initiate a judicial foreclosure. *(Added by Stats.2012, c. 180 (A.B.805), § 2, operative Jan. 1, 2014.)*

Law Revision Commission Comments

Section 5660 continues the second sentence of former Section 1367.1(a), and paragraphs (1) to (6) of that provision, inclusive, without change, except as indicated below.

The following nonsubstantive changes are made:

• The reference to inspection of records under Corporations Code Section 8333 is replaced with a reference to inspection of records under Section 5205.

• Cross-references are updated to reflect the new locations of the referenced provisions.

See also Sections 4080 ("association"), 4085 ("board"), 4185 ("separate interest"). [40 Cal.L.Rev.Comm. Reports 235 (2010)].

§ 5665. Payment plans; request; meeting; contents; default

(a) An owner, other than an owner of any interest that is described in Section 11212 of the Business and Professions Code that is not otherwise exempt from this section pursuant to subdivision (a) of Section 11211.7 of the Business and Professions Code, may submit a written request to meet with the board to discuss a payment plan for the debt noticed pursuant to Section 5660. The association shall provide the owners the standards for payment plans, if any exists.

(b) The board shall meet with the owner in executive session within 45 days of the postmark of the request, if the request is mailed within 15 days of the date of the postmark of the notice, unless there is no regularly scheduled board meeting within that period, in which case the board may designate a committee of one or more directors to meet with the owner.

(c) Payment plans may incorporate any assessments that accrue during the payment plan period. Additional late fees shall not accrue during the payment plan period if the owner is in compliance with the terms of the payment plan.

(d) Payment plans shall not impede an association's ability to record a lien on the owner's separate interest to secure payment of delinquent assessments.

(e) In the event of a default on any payment plan, the association may resume its efforts to collect the delinquent assessments from the time prior to entering into the payment plan. *(Added by Stats.2012, c. 180 (A.B.805), § 2, operative Jan. 1, 2014.)*

Law Revision Commission Comments

Section 5665 continues former Section 1367.1(c)(3) without change, except as indicated below.

The following nonsubstantive changes are made:

• Cross-references are updated to reflect the new locations of the referenced provisions.

• The provision is divided into subdivisions for ease of reference.

• The words "board member" are replaced with "director." See Section 4140 ("director").

• In subdivision (a), the cross-reference is revised to refer to the Business and Professions Code.

See also Sections 4080 ("association"), 4085 ("board"), 4090 ("board meeting"), 4185 ("separate interest"). [40 Cal.L.Rev.Comm. Reports 235 (2010)].

§ 5670. Dispute resolution

Prior to recording a lien for delinquent assessments, an association shall offer the owner and, if so requested by the owner, participate in dispute resolution pursuant to the association's "meet and confer" program required in Article 2 (commencing with Section 5900) of Chapter 10. *(Added by Stats. 2012, c. 180 (A.B.805), § 2, operative Jan. 1, 2014.)*

Law Revision Commission Comments

Section 5670 continues former Section 1367.1(c)(1)(A) without change, except as indicated below.

The following nonsubstantive change is made:

• A cross-reference is updated to reflect the new location of the referenced provision.

See also Section 4080 ("association"). [40 Cal.L.Rev.Comm. Reports 235 (2010)].

§ 5673. Recording lien; decision made by board

For liens recorded on or after January 1, 2006, the decision to record a lien for delinquent assessments shall be made only by the board and may not be delegated to an agent of the association. The board shall approve the decision by a majority vote of the directors in an open meeting. The board shall record the vote in the minutes of that meeting. *(Added by Stats.2012, c. 180 (A.B.805), § 2, operative Jan. 1, 2014.)*

Law Revision Commission Comments

Section 5673 continues former Section 1367.1(c)(2) without change, except as indicated below.

The following nonsubstantive changes are made:

• The words "board of directors of the association" are replaced with "board." See Section 4085 ("board").

• The words "board member" are replaced with "director." See Section 4140 ("director").

See also Section 4080 ("association"). [40 Cal.L.Rev.Comm. Reports 235 (2010)].

§ 5675. Lien on separate interest; notice of delinquent assessment

(a) The amount of the assessment, plus any costs of collection, late charges, and interest assessed in accordance with subdivision (b) of Section 5650, shall be a lien on the owner's separate interest in the common interest development from and after the time the association causes to be recorded with the county recorder of the county in which the separate interest is located, a notice of delinquent assessment, which shall state the amount of the assessment and other sums imposed in accordance with subdivision (b) of Section 5650, a legal description of the owner's separate interest in the common interest development against which the assessment and other sums are levied, and the name of the record owner of the separate interest in the common interest development against which the lien is imposed.

(b) The itemized statement of the charges owed by the owner described in subdivision (b) of Section 5660 shall be recorded together with the notice of delinquent assessment.

(c) In order for the lien to be enforced by nonjudicial foreclosure as provided in Sections 5700 to 5710, inclusive, the notice of delinquent assessment shall state the name and address of the trustee authorized by the association to enforce the lien by sale.

(d) The notice of delinquent assessment shall be signed by the person designated in the declaration or by the association for that purpose, or if no one is designated, by the president of the association.

(e) A copy of the recorded notice of delinquent assessment shall be mailed by certified mail to every person whose name is shown as an owner of the separate interest in the association's records, and the notice shall be mailed no later than 10 calendar days after recordation. *(Added by Stats.2012, c. 180 (A.B.805), § 2, operative Jan. 1, 2014.)*

Law Revision Commission Comments

Section 5675 continues the first five sentences of former Section 1367.1(d) without change, except as indicated below.

The following nonsubstantive change is made:

• Cross-references are updated to reflect the new locations of the referenced provisions.

See also Sections 4080 ("association"), 4100 ("common interest development"), 4135 ("declaration"), 4170 ("person"), 4185 ("separate interest"). [40 Cal.L.Rev.Comm. Reports 235 (2010)].

§ 5680. Priority

A lien created pursuant to Section 5675 shall be prior to all other liens recorded subsequent to the notice of delinquent assessment, except that the declaration may provide for the subordination thereof to any other liens and encumbrances. *(Added by Stats.2012, c. 180 (A.B.805), § 2, operative Jan. 1, 2014.)*

Law Revision Commission Comments

Section 5680 continues former Section 1367.1(f) without change, except as indicated below.

The following nonsubstantive changes are made:

• The words "notice of assessment" are replaced with the more specific "notice of delinquent assessment."

• A cross-reference is updated to reflect the new location of the referenced provision.

See also Section 4135 ("declaration"). [40 Cal.L.Rev.Comm. Reports 235 (2010)].

§ 5685. Recording of lien

(a) Within 21 days of the payment of the sums specified in the notice of delinquent assessment, the association shall record or cause to be recorded in the office of the county recorder in which the notice of delinquent assessment is recorded a lien release or notice of rescission and provide the owner of the separate interest a copy of the lien release or notice that the delinquent assessment has been satisfied.

(b) If it is determined that a lien previously recorded against the separate interest was recorded in error, the party who recorded the lien shall, within 21 calendar days, record or cause to be recorded in the office of the county recorder in which the notice of delinquent assessment is recorded a lien release or notice of rescission and provide the owner of the separate interest with a declaration that the lien filing or recording was in error and a copy of the lien release or notice of rescission.

(c) If it is determined that an association has recorded a lien for a delinquent assessment in error, the association shall promptly reverse all late charges, fees, interest, attorney's fees, costs of collection, costs imposed for the notice prescribed in Section 5660, and costs of recordation and release of the lien authorized under subdivision (b) of Section 5720, and pay all costs related to any related dispute resolution or alternative dispute resolution. *(Added by Stats.2012, c. 180 (A.B.805), § 2, operative Jan. 1, 2014.)*

Law Revision Commission Comments

Subdivision (a) of Section 5685 continues the sixth sentence of former Section 1367.1(d) without change.

Subdivision (b) continues former Section 1367.1(i) without change.

Subdivision (c) continues former Section 1367.5 without change, except as indicated below.

The following substantive change is made:

• The requirement that the error be discovered as a result of alternative dispute resolution is not continued.

The following nonsubstantive change is made:

• Cross-references are updated to reflect the new locations of the referenced provisions.

See also Sections 4080 ("association"), 4185 ("separate interest"). [40 Cal.L.Rev.Comm. Reports 235 (2010)].

§ 5690. Recommencement of notice process for failure to comply with procedures

An association that fails to comply with the procedures set forth in this article shall, prior to recording a lien, recommence the required notice process. Any costs associated with recommencing the notice process shall be borne by the association and not by the owner of a separate interest. *(Added by Stats.2012, c. 180 (A.B.805), § 2, operative Jan. 1, 2014.)*

Law Revision Commission Comments

Section 5690 continues former Section 1367.1(*l*) without change, except as indicated below.

The following nonsubstantive change is made:

• The word "section" is replaced with "article."

See also Section 4080 ("association"), 4185 ("separate interest"). [40 Cal.L.Rev.Comm. Reports 235 (2010)].

ARTICLE 3. ASSESSMENT COLLECTION

Section

5720.   Debts for assessments that arise on and after Jan. 1, 2006; collection of delinquent assessments; application of limitation on foreclosure of assessment liens.

5725.   Monetary charge for repair of damage to common area and facilities; monetary penalties.

5730.   Inclusion of notice in annual policy statement.

5735.   Assignment or pledge prohibited; exception.

5740.   Application of article to liens.

§ 5700.   Enforcement of lien

(a) Except as otherwise provided in this article, after the expiration of 30 days following the recording of a lien created pursuant to Section 5675, the lien may be enforced in any manner permitted by law, including sale by the court, sale by the trustee designated in the notice of delinquent assessment, or sale by a trustee substituted pursuant to Section 2934a.

(b) Nothing in Article 2 (commencing with Section 5650) or in subdivision (a) of Section 726 of the Code of Civil Procedure prohibits actions against the owner of a separate interest to recover sums for which a lien is created pursuant to Article 2 (commencing with Section 5650) or prohibits an association from taking a deed in lieu of foreclosure. *(Added by Stats.2012, c. 180 (A.B.805), § 2, operative Jan. 1, 2014.)*

Law Revision Commission Comments

Subdivision (a) of Section 5700 continues the substance of the second sentence of former Section 1367.1(g), except as indicated below.

The following nonsubstantive changes are made:

• The introductory clause is broadened to recognize the application of all restrictions on collection that are provided in this article. See, e.g., Sections 5720 (limitation on foreclosure), 5735 (limitation on assignment).

• Cross-references are updated to reflect the new locations of the referenced provisions.

Subdivision (b) continues former Section 1367.1(h) without change, except as indicated below.

The following nonsubstantive change is made:

• Cross-references are updated to reflect the new locations of the referenced provisions.

See also Sections 4080 ("association"), 4185 ("separate interest"). [40 Cal.L.Rev.Comm. Reports 235 (2010)].

§ 5705.   Debts for assessments that arise on and after Jan. 1, 2006; dispute resolution; board to make decision to initiate foreclosure of lien; notice

(a) Notwithstanding any law or any provisions of the governing documents to the contrary, this section shall apply to debts for assessments that arise on and after January 1, 2006.

(b) Prior to initiating a foreclosure on an owner's separate interest, the association shall offer the owner and, if so requested by the owner, participate in dispute resolution pursuant to the association's "meet and confer" program required in Article 2 (commencing with Section 5900) of Chapter 10 or alternative dispute resolution as set forth in Article 3 (commencing with Section 5925) of Chapter 10. The decision to pursue dispute resolution or a particular type of alternative dispute resolution shall be the choice of the owner, except that binding arbitration shall not be available if the association intends to initiate a judicial foreclosure.

(c) The decision to initiate foreclosure of a lien for delinquent assessments that has been validly recorded shall be made only by the board and may not be delegated to an agent of the association. The board shall approve the decision by a majority vote of the directors in an executive session. The board shall record the vote in the minutes of the next meeting of the board open to all members. The board shall maintain the confidentiality of the owner or owners of the separate interest by identifying the matter in the minutes by the parcel number of the property,

rather than the name of the owner or owners. A board vote to approve foreclosure of a lien shall take place at least 30 days prior to any public sale.

(d) The board shall provide notice by personal service in accordance with the manner of service of summons in Article 3 (commencing with Section 415.10) of Chapter 4 of Title 5 of Part 2 of the Code of Civil Procedure to an owner of a separate interest who occupies the separate interest or to the owner's legal representative, if the board votes to foreclose upon the separate interest. The board shall provide written notice to an owner of a separate interest who does not occupy the separate interest by first-class mail, postage prepaid, at the most current address shown on the books of the association. In the absence of written notification by the owner to the association, the address of the owner's separate interest may be treated as the owner's mailing address. *(Added by Stats.2012, c. 180 (A.B.805), § 2, operative Jan. 1, 2014.)*

Law Revision Commission Comments

Subdivision (a) of Section 5705 continues former Section 1367.4(a), as it related to the substance of this section, without change.

Subdivision (b) continues former Section 1367.4(c)(1) without change, except as indicated below.

The following nonsubstantive change is made:

• Cross-references are updated to reflect the new locations of the referenced provisions.

Subdivision (b) is also consistent with former Section 1367.1(c)(1)(B).

Subdivision (c) continues former Section 1367.4(c)(2) without change, except as indicated below.

The following nonsubstantive changes are made:

• The words "board of directors of the association" are replaced with "board." See Section 4085 ("board").

• The words "board member" are replaced with "director." See Section 4140 ("director").

Subdivision (d) continues former Section 1367.4(c)(3) without change.

See also Sections 4080 ("association"), 4150 ("governing documents"), 4160 ("member"), 4185 ("separate interest"). [40 Cal.L.Rev.Comm. Reports 235 (2010)].

§ 5710.   Trustee sale; procedure; notice; trustee fees

(a) Any sale by the trustee shall be conducted in accordance with Sections 2924, 2924b, and 2924c applicable to the exercise of powers of sale in mortgages and deeds of trust.

(b) In addition to the requirements of Section 2924, the association shall serve a notice of default on the person named as the owner of the separate interest in the association's records or, if that person has designated a legal representative pursuant to this subdivision, on that legal representative. Service shall be in accordance with the manner of service of summons in Article 3 (commencing with Section 415.10) of Chapter 4 of Title 5 of Part 2 of the Code of Civil Procedure. An owner may designate a legal representative in a writing that is mailed to the association in a manner that indicates that the association has received it.

(c) The fees of a trustee may not exceed the amounts prescribed in Sections 2924c and 2924d, plus the cost of service for either of the following:

(1) The notice of default pursuant to subdivision (b).

(2) The decision of the board to foreclose upon the separate interest of an owner as described in subdivision (d) of Section 5705. *(Added by Stats.2012, c. 180 (A.B.805), § 2, operative Jan. 1, 2014.)*

Law Revision Commission Comments

Subdivision (a) of Section 5710 continues the third sentence of former Section 1367.1(g) without change.

Subdivision (b) continues the substance of former Section 1367.1(j).

Subdivision (c) continues the fourth sentence, and paragraphs (1) and (2), of former Section 1367.1(g) without change, except as indicated below.

The following nonsubstantive change is made:

• Cross-references are updated to reflect the new locations of the referenced provisions.

See also Sections 4080 ("association"), 4085 ("board"), 4170 ("person"), 4185 ("separate interest"). [40 Cal.L.Rev.Comm. Reports 235 (2010)].

§ 5715. Debts for assessments that arise on and after Jan. 1, 2006; nonjudicial foreclosure

(a) Notwithstanding any law or any provisions of the governing documents to the contrary, this section shall apply to debts for assessments that arise on and after January 1, 2006.

(b) A nonjudicial foreclosure by an association to collect upon a debt for delinquent assessments shall be subject to a right of redemption. The redemption period within which the separate interest may be redeemed from a foreclosure sale under this paragraph ends 90 days after the sale. In addition to the requirements of Section 2924f, a notice of sale in connection with an association's foreclosure of a separate interest in a common interest development shall include a statement that the property is being sold subject to the right of redemption created in this section. *(Added by Stats.2012, c. 180 (A.B.805), § 2, operative Jan. 1, 2014.)*

Law Revision Commission Comments

Subdivision (a) of Section 5715 continues former Section 1367.4(a), as it related to the substance of this section, without change.

Subdivision (b) continues former Section 1367.4(c)(4) without change, except as indicated below.

The following nonsubstantive change is made:

• "This paragraph" is replaced with "this section."

See also Sections 4080 ("association"), 4100 ("common interest development"), 4150 ("governing documents"), 4185 ("separate interest"). [40 Cal.L.Rev.Comm. Reports 235 (2010)].

§ 5720. Debts for assessments that arise on and after Jan. 1, 2006; collection of delinquent assessments; application of limitation on foreclosure of assessment liens

(a) Notwithstanding any law or any provisions of the governing documents to the contrary, this section shall apply to debts for assessments that arise on and after January 1, 2006.

(b) An association that seeks to collect delinquent regular or special assessments of an amount less than one thousand eight hundred dollars ($1,800), not including any accelerated assessments, late charges, fees and costs of collection, attorney's fees, or interest, may not collect that debt through judicial or nonjudicial foreclosure, but may attempt to collect or secure that debt in any of the following ways:

(1) By a civil action in small claims court, pursuant to Chapter 5.5 (commencing with Section 116.110) of Title 1 of Part 1 of the Code of Civil Procedure. An association that chooses to proceed by an action in small claims court, and prevails, may enforce the judgment as permitted under Article 8 (commencing with Section 116.810) of Chapter 5.5 of Title 1 of Part 1 of the Code of Civil Procedure. The amount that may be recovered in small claims court to collect upon a debt for delinquent assessments may not exceed the jurisdictional limits of the small claims court and shall be the sum of the following:

(A) The amount owed as of the date of filing the complaint in the small claims court proceeding.

(B) In the discretion of the court, an additional amount to that described in subparagraph (A) equal to the amount owed for the period from the date the complaint is filed until satisfaction of the judgment, which total amount may include accruing unpaid assessments and any reasonable late charges,

fees and costs of collection, attorney's fees, and interest, up to the jurisdictional limits of the small claims court.

(2) By recording a lien on the owner's separate interest upon which the association may not foreclose until the amount of the delinquent assessments secured by the lien, exclusive of any accelerated assessments, late charges, fees and costs of collection, attorney's fees, or interest, equals or exceeds one thousand eight hundred dollars ($1,800) or the assessments secured by the lien are more than 12 months delinquent. An association that chooses to record a lien under these provisions, prior to recording the lien, shall offer the owner and, if so requested by the owner, participate in dispute resolution as set forth in Article 2 (commencing with Section 5900) of Chapter 10.

(3) Any other manner provided by law, except for judicial or nonjudicial foreclosure.

(c) The limitation on foreclosure of assessment liens for amounts under the stated minimum in this section does not apply to any of the following:

(1) Assessments secured by a lien that are more than 12 months delinquent.

(2) Assessments owed by owners of separate interests in time-share estates, as defined in subdivision (x) of Section 11212 of the Business and Professions Code.

(3) Assessments owed by the developer. *(Added by Stats. 2012, c. 180 (A.B.805), § 2, operative Jan. 1, 2014.)*

Law Revision Commission Comments

Subdivision (a) of Section 5720 continues former Section 1367.4(a), as it related to the substance of this section, without change.

Subdivision (b) continues former Section 1367.4(b) without change, except as indicated below.

The following nonsubstantive changes are made:

• A cross-reference is updated to reflect the new location of the referenced provision.

• Incomplete cross-references in paragraph (1) are corrected.

Subdivision (c) continues former Section 1367.4(d) without change, except as indicated below.

The following nonsubstantive changes are made:

• The first paragraph is added to reflect the rule in former Section 1367.4(c).

• The second paragraph replaces an erroneous cross-reference to Business and Professions Code Section 11112(x) with a cross-reference to Business and Professions Code Section 11212(x).

See also Sections 4080 ("association"), 4150 ("governing documents"), 4185 ("separate interest"). [40 Cal.L.Rev.Comm. Reports 235 (2010)].

§ 5725. Monetary charge for repair of damage to common area and facilities; monetary penalties

(a) A monetary charge imposed by the association as a means of reimbursing the association for costs incurred by the association in the repair of damage to common area and facilities caused by a member or the member's guest or tenant may become a lien against the member's separate interest enforceable by the sale of the interest under Sections 2924, 2924b, and 2924c, provided the authority to impose a lien is set forth in the governing documents. It is the intent of the Legislature not to contravene Section 2792.26 of Title 10 of the California Code of Regulations, as that section appeared on January 1, 1996, for associations of subdivisions that are being sold under authority of a subdivision public report, pursuant to Part 2 (commencing with Section 11000) of Division 4 of the Business and Professions Code.

(b) A monetary penalty imposed by the association as a disciplinary measure for failure of a member to comply with the governing documents, except for the late payments, may not be characterized nor treated in the governing documents as an assessment that may become a lien against the member's separate interest enforceable by the sale of the interest under Sections 2924, 2924b, and 2924c. *(Added by Stats.2012, c. 180 (A.B.805), § 2, operative Jan. 1, 2014.)*

Law Revision Commission Comments

Subdivision (a) of Section 5725 continues the seventh and eighth sentences of former Section 1367.1(d) without change, except as indicated below.

The following nonsubstantive change is made:

• The phrase "common areas" is singularized.

Subdivision (b) continues former Section 1367.1(e) without change, except as indicated below.

The following nonsubstantive changes are made:

• The introductory clause "except as indicated in subdivision (d)" is not continued.

• The words "governing instruments" are replaced with "governing documents." See Section 4150 ("governing documents").

• The words "subdivision separate interest" are replaced with "separate interest." See Section 4185 ("separate interest").

See also Sections 4080 ("association"), 4095 ("common area"), 4160 ("member"). [40 Cal.L.Rev.Comm. Reports 235 (2010)].

§ 5730. Inclusion of notice in annual policy statement

(a) The annual policy statement, prepared pursuant to Section 5310, shall include the following notice, in at least 12–point type:

"NOTICE ASSESSMENTS AND FORECLOSURE

This notice outlines some of the rights and responsibilities of owners of property in common interest developments and the associations that manage them. Please refer to the sections of the Civil Code indicated for further information. A portion of the information in this notice applies only to liens recorded on or after January 1, 2003. You may wish to consult a lawyer if you dispute an assessment.

ASSESSMENTS AND FORECLOSURE

Assessments become delinquent 15 days after they are due, unless the governing documents provide for a longer time. The failure to pay association assessments may result in the loss of an owner's property through foreclosure. Foreclosure may occur either as a result of a court action, known as judicial foreclosure, or without court action, often referred to as nonjudicial foreclosure. For liens recorded on and after January 1, 2006, an association may not use judicial or nonjudicial foreclosure to enforce that lien if the amount of the delinquent assessments or dues, exclusive of any accelerated assessments, late charges, fees, attorney's fees, interest, and costs of collection, is less than one thousand eight hundred dollars ($1,800). For delinquent assessments or dues in excess of one thousand eight hundred dollars ($1,800) or more than 12 months delinquent, an association may use judicial or nonjudicial foreclosure subject to the conditions set forth in Article 3 (commencing with Section 5700) of Chapter 8 of Part 5 of Division 4 of the Civil Code. When using judicial or nonjudicial foreclosure, the association records a lien on the owner's property. The owner's property may be sold to satisfy the lien if the amounts secured by the lien are not paid. (Sections 5700 through 5720 of the Civil Code, inclusive)

In a judicial or nonjudicial foreclosure, the association may recover assessments, reasonable costs of collection, reasonable attorney's fees, late charges, and interest. The association may not use nonjudicial foreclosure to collect fines or penalties, except for costs to repair common area damaged by a member or a member's guests, if the governing documents provide for this. (Section 5725 of the Civil Code)

The association must comply with the requirements of Article 2 (commencing with Section 5650) of Chapter 8 of Part 5 of Division 4 of the Civil Code when collecting delinquent assessments. If the association fails to follow these requirements, it may not record a lien on the owner's property until it has satisfied those requirements. Any additional costs that result from satisfying the requirements are the responsibility of the association. (Section 5675 of the Civil Code)

At least 30 days prior to recording a lien on an owner's separate interest, the association must provide the owner of record with certain documents by certified mail, including a description of its collection and lien enforcement procedures and the method of calculating the amount. It must also provide an itemized statement of the charges owed by the owner. An owner has a right to review the association's records to verify the debt. (Section 5660 of the Civil Code)

If a lien is recorded against an owner's property in error, the person who recorded the lien is required to record a lien release within 21 days, and to provide an owner certain documents in this regard. (Section 5685 of the Civil Code)

The collection practices of the association may be governed by state and federal laws regarding fair debt collection. Penalties can be imposed for debt collection practices that violate these laws.

PAYMENTS

When an owner makes a payment, the owner may request a receipt, and the association is required to provide it. On the receipt, the association must indicate the date of payment and the person who received it. The association must inform owners of a mailing address for overnight payments. (Section 5655 of the Civil Code)

An owner may, but is not obligated to, pay under protest any disputed charge or sum levied by the association, including, but not limited to, an assessment, fine, penalty, late fee, collection cost, or monetary penalty imposed as a disciplinary measure, and by so doing, specifically reserve the right to contest the disputed charge or sum in court or otherwise.

An owner may dispute an assessment debt by submitting a written request for dispute resolution to the association as set forth in Article 2 (commencing with Section 5900) of Chapter 10 of Part 5 of Division 4 of the Civil Code. In addition, an association may not initiate a foreclosure without participating in alternative dispute resolution with a neutral third party as set forth in Article 3 (commencing with Section 5925) of Chapter 10 of Part 5 of Division 4 of the Civil Code, if so requested by the owner. Binding arbitration shall not be available if the association intends to initiate a judicial foreclosure.

An owner is not liable for charges, interest, and costs of collection, if it is established that the assessment was paid properly on time. (Section 5685 of the Civil Code)

MEETINGS AND PAYMENT PLANS

An owner of a separate interest that is not a time-share interest may request the association to consider a payment plan to satisfy a delinquent assessment. The association must inform owners of the standards for payment plans, if any exists. (Section 5665 of the Civil Code)

The board must meet with an owner who makes a proper written request for a meeting to discuss a payment plan when the owner has received a notice of a delinquent assessment. These payment plans must conform with the payment plan standards of the association, if they exist. (Section 5665 of the Civil Code)"

(b) An association distributing the notice required by this section to an owner of an interest that is described in Section 11212 of the Business and Professions Code that is not otherwise exempt from this section pursuant to subdivision (a) of Section 11211.7 of the Business and Professions Code may delete from the notice described in subdivision (a) the portion regarding meetings and payment plans. *(Added by Stats.2012, c. 180 (A.B.805), § 2, operative Jan. 1, 2014.)*

Law Revision Commission Comments

Section 5730 continues former Section 1365.1 without change, except as indicated below.

The following nonsubstantive changes are made:

• The introductory clause is revised to reflect distribution of this notice as part of the annual policy statement.

• A limited exception for units in time shares is moved to subdivision (b), without any substantive change.

• The substance of former Section 1365.1(c) is generalized in Section 4040(b).

• Erroneous references to "Division 2 of the Civil Code" are corrected. The references should have been to "Part 2 of Division 2 of the Civil Code."

• An erroneous reference to former Section 1368.810 is corrected. It should have referred to former Section 1363.810.

• An erroneous reference to former Section 1367.1 in the last paragraph under the heading "Payments" is corrected. The reference should have been to former Section 1367.5.

• Cross-references are updated throughout to reflect the new locations of the referenced provisions.

• The words "board of directors" are replaced with "board." See Section 4085 ("board").

• The phrase "common areas" is singularized.

• The words "he or she" are replaced with "owner."

See also Sections 4078 ("annual policy statement"), 4080 ("association"), 4095 ("common area"), Section 4100 ("common interest development"), 4150 ("governing documents"), 4160 ("member"), 4170 ("person"), 4185 ("separate interest"). [40 Cal.L.Rev.Comm. Reports 235 (2010)].

§ 5735. Assignment or pledge prohibited; exception

(a) An association may not voluntarily assign or pledge the association's right to collect payments or assessments, or to enforce or foreclose a lien to a third party, except when the assignment or pledge is made to a financial institution or lender chartered or licensed under federal or state law, when acting within the scope of that charter or license, as security for a loan obtained by the association.

(b) Nothing in subdivision (a) restricts the right or ability of an association to assign any unpaid obligations of a former member to a third party for purposes of collection. *(Added by Stats.2012, c. 180 (A.B.805), § 2, operative Jan. 1, 2014.)*

Law Revision Commission Comments

Section 5735 continues the first sentence of former Section 1367.1(g) without change, except as indicated below.

The following nonsubstantive changes are made:

• The provision is divided into subdivisions for ease of reference.

• An introductory clause is added in subdivision (b) to make the relationship between the two provisions clearer.

See also Sections 4080 ("association"), 4160 ("member"). [40 Cal. L.Rev.Comm. Reports 235 (2010)].

§ 5740. Application of article to liens

(a) Except as otherwise provided, this article applies to a lien created on or after January 1, 2003.

(b) A lien created before January 1, 2003, is governed by the law in existence at the time the lien was created. *(Added by Stats.2012, c. 180 (A.B.805), § 2, operative Jan. 1, 2014.)*

Law Revision Commission Comments

Section 5740 is new. A lien created on or after January 1, 1986, and before January 1, 2003, is governed by former Section 1367. See 2002 Cal. Stat. ch. 111, § 7. [40 Cal.L.Rev.Comm. Reports 235 (2010)].

CHAPTER 9. INSURANCE AND LIABILITY

Section

5800. Tortious act or omission of volunteer officer or director of association managing residential development; liability; criteria; limitations.

5805. Tort actions against owner of separate interest; tenant-in-common in common area; association liability; insurance requirements.

5810. Individual notice to members of changes in insurance coverage.

§ 5800. Tortious act or omission of volunteer officer or director of association managing residential development; liability; criteria; limitations

(a) A volunteer officer or volunteer director of an association that manages a common interest development that is exclusively residential, shall not be personally liable in excess of the coverage of insurance specified in paragraph (4) to any person who suffers injury, including, but not limited to, bodily injury, emotional distress, wrongful death, or property damage or loss as a result of the tortious act or omission of the volunteer officer or volunteer director if all of the following criteria are met:

(1) The act or omission was performed within the scope of the officer's or director's association duties.

(2) The act or omission was performed in good faith.

(3) The act or omission was not willful, wanton, or grossly negligent.

(4) The association maintained and had in effect at the time the act or omission occurred and at the time a claim is made one or more policies of insurance that shall include coverage for (A) general liability of the association and (B) individual liability of officers and directors of the association for negligent acts or omissions in that capacity; provided that both types of coverage are in the following minimum amounts:

(A) At least five hundred thousand dollars ($500,000) if the common interest development consists of 100 or fewer separate interests.

(B) At least one million dollars ($1,000,000) if the common interest development consists of more than 100 separate interests.

(b) The payment of actual expenses incurred by a director or officer in the execution of the duties of that position does not affect the director's or officer's status as a volunteer within the meaning of this section.

(c) An officer or director who at the time of the act or omission was a declarant, or who received either direct or indirect compensation as an employee from the declarant, or from a financial institution that purchased a separate interest at a judicial or nonjudicial foreclosure of a mortgage or deed of trust on real property, is not a volunteer for the purposes of this section.

(d) Nothing in this section shall be construed to limit the liability of the association for its negligent act or omission or for any negligent act or omission of an officer or director of the association.

(e) This section shall only apply to a volunteer officer or director who is a tenant of a separate interest in the common interest development or is an owner of no more than two separate interests in the common interest development.

(f)(1) For purposes of paragraph (1) of subdivision (a), the scope of the officer's or director's association duties shall include, but shall not be limited to, both of the following decisions:

(A) Whether to conduct an investigation of the common interest development for latent deficiencies prior to the expiration of the applicable statute of limitations.

(B) Whether to commence a civil action against the builder for defects in design or construction.

(2) It is the intent of the Legislature that this section clarify the scope of association duties to which the protections against personal liability in this section apply. It is not the intent of the Legislature that these clarifications be construed to expand, or limit, the fiduciary duties owed by the directors or officers. *(Added by Stats.2012, c. 180 (A.B.805), § 2, operative Jan. 1, 2014.)*

Law Revision Commission Comments

Section 5800 continues former Section 1365.7 without change, except as indicated below.

The following nonsubstantive changes are made:

• Superfluous cross-references to governing definitions are not continued.

• Subdivision (a) is revised in two places to replace "which" with "that."

See also Corp. Code § 7231 (standard of care and liability of director of nonprofit mutual benefit corporation).

See also Sections 4080 ("association"), 4100 ("common interest development"), 4130 ("declarant"), 4140 ("director"), 4170 ("person"), 4185 ("separate interest"). [40 Cal.L.Rev.Comm. Reports 235 (2010)].

§ 5805. Tort actions against owner of separate interest; tenant-in-common in common area; association liability; insurance requirements

(a) It is the intent of the Legislature to offer civil liability protection to owners of the separate interests in a common interest development that have common area owned in tenancy-in-common if the association carries a certain level of prescribed insurance that covers a cause of action in tort.

(b) Any cause of action in tort against any owner of a separate interest arising solely by reason of an ownership interest as a tenant-in-common in the common area of a common interest development shall be brought only against the association and not against the individual owners of the separate interests, if both of the insurance requirements in paragraphs (1) and (2) are met:

(1) The association maintained and has in effect for this cause of action, one or more policies of insurance that include coverage for general liability of the association.

(2) The coverage described in paragraph (1) is in the following minimum amounts:

(A) At least two million dollars ($2,000,000) if the common interest development consists of 100 or fewer separate interests.

(B) At least three million dollars ($3,000,000) if the common interest development consists of more than 100 separate interests. *(Added by Stats.2012, c. 180 (A.B.805), § 2, operative Jan. 1, 2014.)*

Law Revision Commission Comments

Section 5805 continues former Section 1365.9 without change, except as indicated below.

The following nonsubstantive changes are made:

• A superfluous cross-reference to a governing definition is not continued.

• The phrase "common areas" is singularized.

• In subdivision (b)(1), the word "which" is replaced with "that."

See also Sections 4080 ("association"), 4095 ("common area"), 4100 ("common interest development"), 4185 ("separate interest"). [40 Cal. L.Rev.Comm. Reports 235 (2010)].

§ 5810. Individual notice to members of changes in insurance coverage

The association shall, as soon as reasonably practicable, provide individual notice pursuant to Section 4040 to all members if any of the policies described in the annual budget report pursuant to Section 5300 have lapsed, been canceled, and are not immediately renewed, restored, or replaced, or if there is a significant change, such as a reduction in coverage or limits or an increase in the deductible, as to any of those policies. If the association receives any notice of nonrenewal of a policy described in the annual budget report pursuant to Section 5300, the association shall immediately notify its members if replacement coverage will not be in effect by the date the existing coverage will lapse. *(Added by Stats.2012, c. 180 (A.B.805), § 2, operative Jan. 1, 2014.)*

Law Revision Commission Comments

Section 5810 continues former Section 1365(f)(2) without change, except as indicated below.

The following substantive change is made:

• The reference to delivery by first-class mail is replaced with a reference to individual delivery pursuant to Section 4040.

The following nonsubstantive change is made:

• Cross-references are updated to reflect the new locations of the referenced provisions.

See also Sections 4076 ("annual budget report"), 4080 ("association"), 4160 ("member"). [40 Cal.L.Rev.Comm. Reports 235 (2010)].

CHAPTER 10. DISPUTE RESOLUTION AND ENFORCEMENT

ARTICLE 1. DISCIPLINE AND COST REIMBURSEMENT

§ 5850. Monetary penalties; provision of information to members

(a) If an association adopts or has adopted a policy imposing any monetary penalty, including any fee, on any association member for a violation of the governing documents, including any monetary penalty relating to the activities of a guest or tenant of the member, the board shall adopt and distribute to each member, in the annual policy statement prepared pursuant to Section 5310, a schedule of the monetary penalties that may be assessed for those violations, which shall be in accordance with authorization for member discipline contained in the governing documents.

(b) Any new or revised monetary penalty that is adopted after complying with subdivision (a) may be included in a supplement that is delivered to the members individually, pursuant to Section 4040.

(c) A monetary penalty for a violation of the governing documents shall not exceed the monetary penalty stated in the schedule of monetary penalties or supplement that is in effect at the time of the violation.

(d) An association shall provide a copy of the most recently distributed schedule of monetary penalties, along with any applicable supplements to that schedule, to any member upon request. *(Added by Stats.2012, c. 180 (A.B.805), § 2, operative Jan. 1, 2014.)*

Law Revision Commission Comments

Subdivision (a) of Section 5850 continues the first sentence of former Section 1363(f) without change, except as indicated below.

The following substantive changes are made:

● A reference to delivery by personal delivery or first class mail is changed to refer to delivery by inclusion in the annual policy statement prepared pursuant to Section 5310.

● The word "invitee" is replaced with "tenant," to make clear that the provision applies to tenants.

The following nonsubstantive changes are made:

● A reference to the "rules of the association" is superfluous and is not continued. The term "governing documents" encompasses rules. See Section 4150 ("governing documents").

● The words "board of directors" are replaced with "board." See Section 4085 ("board").

Subdivisions (b)-(d) are new.

See also Sections 4078 ("annual policy statement"), 4080 ("association"), 4160 ("member"). [40 Cal.L.Rev.Comm. Reports 235 (2010)].

§ 5855. Board disciplinary proceedings; notice to member

(a) When the board is to meet to consider or impose discipline upon a member, or to impose a monetary charge as a means of reimbursing the association for costs incurred by the association in the repair of damage to common area and facilities caused by a member or the member's guest or tenant, the board shall notify the member in writing, by either personal delivery or individual delivery pursuant to Section 4040, at least 10 days prior to the meeting.

(b) The notification shall contain, at a minimum, the date, time, and place of the meeting, the nature of the alleged violation for which a member may be disciplined or the nature of the damage to the common area and facilities for which a monetary charge may be imposed, and a statement that the member has a right to attend and may address the board at the meeting. The board shall meet in executive session if requested by the member.

(c) If the board imposes discipline on a member or imposes a monetary charge on the member for damage to the common area and facilities, the board shall provide the member a written notification of the decision, by either personal delivery or individual delivery pursuant to Section 4040, within 15 days following the action.

(d) A disciplinary action or the imposition of a monetary charge for damage to the common area shall not be effective against a member unless the board fulfills the requirements of this section. *(Added by Stats.2012, c. 180 (A.B.805), § 2, operative Jan. 1, 2014.)*

Law Revision Commission Comments

Section 5855 continues former Section 1363(g) without change, except as indicated below.

The following substantive changes are made:

● The scope of the provision is expanded to include an action to impose a monetary charge on a member for damage to the common area.

● "Individual delivery" is substituted for first class mailing. See Section 4040.

The following nonsubstantive changes are made:

● The provision is divided into subdivisions for ease of reference.

● The word "subdivision" is replaced with "section."

● The words "board of directors" and "board of directors of the association" are replaced with "board." See Section 4085 ("board").

See also Sections 4080 ("association"), 4095 ("common area"), 4160 ("member"). [40 Cal.L.Rev.Comm. Reports 235 (2010)].

§ 5865. Authority of board to impose monetary penalties

Nothing in Section 5850 or 5855 shall be construed to create, expand, or reduce the authority of the board to impose monetary penalties on a member for a violation of the governing documents. *(Added by Stats.2012, c. 180 (A.B.805), § 2, operative Jan. 1, 2014.)*

Law Revision Commission Comments

Section 5865 continues the substance of former Section 1363(i), except as indicated below.

The following nonsubstantive changes are made:

● The words "board of directors of the association" are replaced with "board." See Section 4085 ("board").

● The words "or rules of the association" are not continued.

● The words "an association member" are replaced with "member." See Section 4160 ("member").

● The reference to Sections 5850 and 5855 is narrower than the reference in former Section 1363(i), which encompassed the entirety of former Section 1363.

See also Section 4150 ("governing documents" includes the operating rules of the association). [40 Cal.L.Rev.Comm. Reports 235 (2010)].

ARTICLE 2. INTERNAL DISPUTE RESOLUTION

§ 5900. Application of article

(a) This article applies to a dispute between an association and a member involving their rights, duties, or liabilities under this act, under the Nonprofit Mutual Benefit Corporation Law (Part 3 (commencing with Section 7110) of Division 2 of Title 1 of the Corporations Code), or under the governing documents of the common interest development or association.

(b) This article supplements, and does not replace, Article 3 (commencing with Section 5925), relating to alternative dispute resolution as a prerequisite to an enforcement action. *(Added by Stats.2012, c. 180 (A.B.805), § 2, operative Jan. 1, 2014.)*

Law Revision Commission Comments

Section 5900 continues former Section 1363.810 without change, except as indicated below.

The following nonsubstantive change is made:

● Cross-references are updated to reflect the new locations of the referenced provisions.

See also Sections 4080 ("association"), 4100 ("common interest development"), 4150 ("governing documents"), 4160 ("member"). [40 Cal. L.Rev.Comm. Reports 235 (2010)].

§ 5905. Fair, reasonable, and expeditious procedure to resolve disputes; use of local dispute resolution programs

(a) An association shall provide a fair, reasonable, and expeditious procedure for resolving a dispute within the scope of this article.

(b) In developing a procedure pursuant to this article, an association shall make maximum, reasonable use of available local dispute resolution programs involving a neutral third party, including low-cost mediation programs such as those listed on the Internet Web sites of the Department of Consumer Affairs and the United States Department of Housing and Urban Development.

(c) If an association does not provide a fair, reasonable, and expeditious procedure for resolving a dispute within the scope of this article, the procedure provided in Section 5915 applies and satisfies the requirement of subdivision (a). *(Added by Stats. 2012, c. 180 (A.B.805), § 2, operative Jan. 1, 2014.)*

Law Revision Commission Comments

Section 5905 continues former Section 1363.820 without change, except as indicated below.

The following nonsubstantive change is made:

• A cross-reference is updated to reflect the new location of the referenced provision.

See also Section 4080 ("association"). [40 Cal.L.Rev.Comm. Reports 235 (2010)].

§ 5910. Requirements of fair, reasonable, and expeditious dispute resolution program

A fair, reasonable, and expeditious dispute resolution procedure shall at a minimum satisfy all of the following requirements:

(a) The procedure may be invoked by either party to the dispute. A request invoking the procedure shall be in writing.

(b) The procedure shall provide for prompt deadlines. The procedure shall state the maximum time for the association to act on a request invoking the procedure.

(c) If the procedure is invoked by a member, the association shall participate in the procedure.

(d) If the procedure is invoked by the association, the member may elect not to participate in the procedure. If the member participates but the dispute is resolved other than by agreement of the member, the member shall have a right of appeal to the board.

(e) A resolution of a dispute pursuant to the procedure, which is not in conflict with the law or the governing documents, binds the association and is judicially enforceable. An agreement reached pursuant to the procedure, which is not in conflict with the law or the governing documents, binds the parties and is judicially enforceable.

(f) The procedure shall provide a means by which the member and the association may explain their positions.

(g) A member of the association shall not be charged a fee to participate in the process. *(Added by Stats.2012, c. 180 (A.B. 805), § 2, operative Jan. 1, 2014.)*

Law Revision Commission Comments

Section 5910 continues former Section 1363.830 without change, except as indicated below.

The following nonsubstantive changes are made:

• Subdivision (e) is revised to replace "that" with "which."

• The words "association's board of directors" are replaced with "board." See Section 4085 ("board").

See also Sections 4080 ("association"), 4150 ("governing documents"), 4160 ("member"). [40 Cal.L.Rev.Comm. Reports 235 (2010)].

§ 5915. Application of section; use of procedures; dispute resolution agreements; conditions; fees

(a) This section applies to an association that does not otherwise provide a fair, reasonable, and expeditious dispute resolution procedure. The procedure provided in this section is fair, reasonable, and expeditious, within the meaning of this article.

(b) Either party to a dispute within the scope of this article may invoke the following procedure:

(1) The party may request the other party to meet and confer in an effort to resolve the dispute. The request shall be in writing.

(2) A member of an association may refuse a request to meet and confer. The association may not refuse a request to meet and confer.

(3) The board shall designate a director to meet and confer.

(4) The parties shall meet promptly at a mutually convenient time and place, explain their positions to each other, and confer in good faith in an effort to resolve the dispute.

(5) A resolution of the dispute agreed to by the parties shall be memorialized in writing and signed by the parties, including the board designee on behalf of the association.

(c) An agreement reached under this section binds the parties and is judicially enforceable if both of the following conditions are satisfied:

(1) The agreement is not in conflict with law or the governing documents of the common interest development or association.

(2) The agreement is either consistent with the authority granted by the board to its designee or the agreement is ratified by the board.

(d) A member may not be charged a fee to participate in the process. *(Added by Stats.2012, c. 180 (A.B.805), § 2, operative Jan. 1, 2014.)*

Law Revision Commission Comments

Section 5915 continues former Section 1363.840 without change, except as indicated below.

The following nonsubstantive changes are made:

• The words "in an association" are replaced with "to an association."

• The words "association's board of directors" are replaced with "board."

• The words "of the association" and "of the common interest development or association" are not continued.

• The words "board member" are replaced with "director." See Section 4140 ("director").

See also Sections 4080 ("association"), 4085 ("board"), 4100 ("common interest development"), 4160 ("member"), 4150 ("governing documents"). [40 Cal.L.Rev.Comm. Reports 235 (2010)].

§ 5920. Annual policy statement; description of internal dispute resolution process

The annual policy statement prepared pursuant to Section 5310 shall include a description of the internal dispute resolution process provided pursuant to this article. *(Added by Stats.2012, c. 180 (A.B.805), § 2, operative Jan. 1, 2014.)*

Law Revision Commission Comments

Section 5920 continues former Section 1363.850 without change, except as indicated below.

The following nonsubstantive change is made:

• A reference to a notice delivered pursuant to former Section 1369.590 is changed to refer to distribution as part of the annual policy statement prepared pursuant to Section 5310.

See also Section 4078 ("annual policy statement"). [40 Cal.L.Rev. Comm. Reports 235 (2010)].

ARTICLE 3. ALTERNATIVE DISPUTE RESOLUTION PREREQUISITE TO CIVIL ACTION

Section

5945. Tolling of statute of limitations.

5950. Certificates filed with initial pleading; grounds for demurrer or motion to strike.

5955. Referral of actions to alternative dispute resolution; stay of referred action; costs.

5960. Award of fees and costs.

5965. Annual summary of provisions of article; contents of summary; inclusion in annual policy statement.

§ 5925. Definitions

As used in this article:

(a) "Alternative dispute resolution" means mediation, arbitration, conciliation, or other nonjudicial procedure that involves a neutral party in the decisionmaking process. The form of alternative dispute resolution chosen pursuant to this article may be binding or nonbinding, with the voluntary consent of the parties.

(b) "Enforcement action" means a civil action or proceeding, other than a cross-complaint, for any of the following purposes:

(1) Enforcement of this act.

(2) Enforcement of the Nonprofit Mutual Benefit Corporation Law (Part 3 (commencing with Section 7110) of Division 2 of Title 1 of the Corporations Code).

(3) Enforcement of the governing documents. *(Added by Stats.2012, c. 180 (A.B.805), § 2, operative Jan. 1, 2014.)*

§ 5930. Filing enforcement actions; application of section

(a) An association or a member may not file an enforcement action in the superior court unless the parties have endeavored to submit their dispute to alternative dispute resolution pursuant to this article.

(b) This section applies only to an enforcement action that is solely for declaratory, injunctive, or writ relief, or for that relief in conjunction with a claim for monetary damages not in excess of the jurisdictional limits stated in Sections 116.220 and 116.221 of the Code of Civil Procedure.

(c) This section does not apply to a small claims action.

(d) Except as otherwise provided by law, this section does not apply to an assessment dispute. *(Added by Stats.2012, c. 180 (A.B.805), § 2, operative Jan. 1, 2014.)*

§ 5935. Initiation of process; serving a Request for Resolution; personal delivery; acceptance or rejection of request

(a) Any party to a dispute may initiate the process required by Section 5930 by serving on all other parties to the dispute a Request for Resolution. The Request for Resolution shall include all of the following:

(1) A brief description of the dispute between the parties.

(2) A request for alternative dispute resolution.

(3) A notice that the party receiving the Request for Resolution is required to respond within 30 days of receipt or the request will be deemed rejected.

(4) If the party on whom the request is served is the member, a copy of this article.

(b) Service of the Request for Resolution shall be by personal delivery, first-class mail, express mail, facsimile transmission, or other means reasonably calculated to provide the party on whom the request is served actual notice of the request.

(c) A party on whom a Request for Resolution is served has 30 days following service to accept or reject the request. If a party does not accept the request within that period, the request is deemed rejected by the party. *(Added by Stats.2012, c. 180 (A.B.805), § 2, operative Jan. 1, 2014.)*

§ 5940. Timeline for completion of alternative dispute resolution; application of Evidence Code; costs

(a) If the party on whom a Request for Resolution is served accepts the request, the parties shall complete the alternative dispute resolution within 90 days after the party initiating the request receives the acceptance, unless this period is extended by written stipulation signed by both parties.

(b) Chapter 2 (commencing with Section 1115) of Division 9 of the Evidence Code applies to any form of alternative dispute resolution initiated by a Request for Resolution under this article, other than arbitration.

(c) The costs of the alternative dispute resolution shall be borne by the parties. *(Added by Stats.2012, c. 180 (A.B.805), § 2, operative Jan. 1, 2014.)*

§ 5945. Tolling of statute of limitations

If a Request for Resolution is served before the end of the applicable time limitation for commencing an enforcement action, the time limitation is tolled during the following periods:

(a) The period provided in Section 5935 for response to a Request for Resolution.

(b) If the Request for Resolution is accepted, the period provided by Section 5940 for completion of alternative dispute resolution, including any extension of time stipulated to by the parties pursuant to Section 5940. *(Added by Stats.2012, c. 180 (A.B.805), § 2, operative Jan. 1, 2014.)*

§ 5950. Certificates filed with initial pleading; grounds for demurrer or motion to strike

(a) At the time of commencement of an enforcement action, the party commencing the action shall file with the initial pleading a certificate stating that one or more of the following conditions are satisfied:

(1) Alternative dispute resolution has been completed in compliance with this article.

(2) One of the other parties to the dispute did not accept the terms offered for alternative dispute resolution.

(3) Preliminary or temporary injunctive relief is necessary.

(b) Failure to file a certificate pursuant to subdivision (a) is grounds for a demurrer or a motion to strike unless the court finds that dismissal of the action for failure to comply with this article would result in substantial prejudice to one of the parties. *(Added by Stats.2012, c. 180 (A.B.805), § 2, operative Jan. 1, 2014.)*

Law Revision Commission Comments

Section 5950 continues former Section 1369.560 without change. [40 Cal.L.Rev.Comm. Reports 235 (2010)].

§ 5955. Referral of actions to alternative dispute resolution; stay of referred action; costs

(a) After an enforcement action is commenced, on written stipulation of the parties, the matter may be referred to alternative dispute resolution. The referred action is stayed. During the stay, the action is not subject to the rules implementing subdivision (c) of Section 68603 of the Government Code.

(b) The costs of the alternative dispute resolution shall be borne by the parties. *(Added by Stats.2012, c. 180 (A.B.805), § 2, operative Jan. 1, 2014.)*

Law Revision Commission Comments

Section 5955 continues former Section 1369.570 without change. [40 Cal.L.Rev.Comm. Reports 235 (2010)].

§ 5960. Award of fees and costs

In an enforcement action in which attorney's fees and costs may be awarded, the court, in determining the amount of the award, may consider whether a party's refusal to participate in alternative dispute resolution before commencement of the action was reasonable. *(Added by Stats.2012, c. 180 (A.B.805), § 2, operative Jan. 1, 2014.)*

Law Revision Commission Comments

Section 5960 generalizes former Section 1369.580 so that it applies to any enforcement action in which fees and costs may be awarded and not just to an action to enforce the governing documents. [40 Cal.L.Rev. Comm. Reports 235 (2010)].

§ 5965. Annual summary of provisions of article; contents of summary; inclusion in annual policy statement

(a) An association shall annually provide its members a summary of the provisions of this article that specifically references this article. The summary shall include the following language:

"Failure of a member of the association to comply with the alternative dispute resolution requirements of Section 5930 of the Civil Code may result in the loss of the member's right to sue the association or another member of the association regarding enforcement of the governing documents or the applicable law."

(b) The summary shall be included in the annual policy statement prepared pursuant to Section 5310. *(Added by Stats.2012, c. 180 (A.B.805), § 2, operative Jan. 1, 2014.)*

Law Revision Commission Comments

Subdivision (a) of Section 5965 continues former Section 1369.590(a), except as indicated below.

The following nonsubstantive changes are made:

• A cross-reference is updated to reflect the new location of the referenced provision.

• The pronoun "your" is replaced with "the member's" to improve the clarity of the notice.

Subdivision (b) is similar to the first sentence of former Section 1369.590(b).

See also Sections 4078 ("annual policy statement"), 4080 ("association"), 4150 ("governing documents"), 4160 ("member"). [40 Cal.L.Rev. Comm. Reports 235 (2010)].

ARTICLE 4. CIVIL ACTION

Section
5975. Covenants and restrictions in declaration as equitable servitudes; enforcement; alternative dispute resolution.
5980. Standing.
5985. Reduction of damages awarded; comparative fault of association.

§ 5975. Covenants and restrictions in declaration as equitable servitudes; enforcement; alternative dispute resolution

(a) The covenants and restrictions in the declaration shall be enforceable equitable servitudes, unless unreasonable, and shall inure to the benefit of and bind all owners of separate interests in the development. Unless the declaration states otherwise, these servitudes may be enforced by any owner of a separate interest or by the association, or by both.

(b) A governing document other than the declaration may be enforced by the association against an owner of a separate interest or by an owner of a separate interest against the association.

(c) In an action to enforce the governing documents, the prevailing party shall be awarded reasonable attorney's fees and costs. *(Added by Stats.2012, c. 180 (A.B.805), § 2, operative Jan. 1, 2014.)*

Law Revision Commission Comments

Section 5975 continues former Section 1354 without change.

See also Sections 4080 ("association"), 4135 ("declaration"), 4150 ("governing documents"), 4185 ("separate interest"). [40 Cal.L.Rev. Comm. Reports 235 (2010)].

§ 5980. Standing

An association has standing to institute, defend, settle, or intervene in litigation, arbitration, mediation, or administrative proceedings in its own name as the real party in interest and without joining with it the members, in matters pertaining to the following:

(a) Enforcement of the governing documents.

(b) Damage to the common area.

(c) Damage to a separate interest that the association is obligated to maintain or repair.

(d) Damage to a separate interest that arises out of, or is integrally related to, damage to the common area or a separate interest that the association is obligated to maintain or repair. *(Added by Stats.2012, c. 180 (A.B.805), § 2, operative Jan. 1, 2014.)*

Law Revision Commission Comments

Section 5980 continues former Section 1368.3 without change, except as indicated below.

The following nonsubstantive changes are made:

● The word "owner" is replaced with "member." See Section 4160 ("member").

● The words "established to manage a common interest development" are not continued.

See also Sections 4080 ("association"), 4095 ("common area"), 4150 ("governing documents"), 4185 ("separate interest"). [40 Cal.L.Rev. Comm. Reports 235 (2010)].

§ 5985. Reduction of damages awarded; comparative fault of association

(a) In an action maintained by an association pursuant to subdivision (b), (c), or (d) of Section 5980, the amount of damages recovered by the association shall be reduced by the amount of damages allocated to the association or its managing agents in direct proportion to their percentage of fault based upon principles of comparative fault. The comparative fault of the association or its managing agents may be raised by way of defense, but shall not be the basis for a cross-action or separate action against the association or its managing agents for contribution or implied indemnity, where the only damage was sustained by the association or its members. It is the intent of the Legislature in enacting this subdivision to require that comparative fault be pleaded as an affirmative defense, rather than a separate cause of action, where the only damage was sustained by the association or its members.

(b) In an action involving damages described in subdivision (b), (c), or (d) of Section 5980, the defendant or cross-defendant may allege and prove the comparative fault of the association or its managing agents as a setoff to the liability of the defendant or cross-defendant even if the association is not a party to the litigation or is no longer a party whether by reason of settlement, dismissal, or otherwise.

(c) Subdivisions (a) and (b) apply to actions commenced on or after January 1, 1993.

(d) Nothing in this section affects a person's liability under Section 1431, or the liability of the association or its managing agent for an act or omission that causes damages to another. *(Added by Stats.2012, c. 180 (A.B.805), § 2, operative Jan. 1, 2014.)*

Law Revision Commission Comments

Section 5985 continues former Section 1368.4 without change.

See also Sections 4080 ("association"), 4158 ("managing agent"), 4160 ("member"), 4170 ("person"). [40 Cal.L.Rev.Comm. Reports 235 (2010)].

CHAPTER 11. CONSTRUCTION DEFECT LITIGATION

§ 6000. Actions for damages against common interest development builders, developers, or general contractors

(a) Before an association files a complaint for damages against a builder, developer, or general contractor (respondent) of a common interest development based upon a claim for defects in the design or construction of the common interest development, all of the requirements of this section shall be satisfied with respect to the builder, developer, or general contractor.

(b) The association shall serve upon the respondent a "Notice of Commencement of Legal Proceedings." The notice shall be served by certified mail to the registered agent of the respondent, or if there is no registered agent, then to any officer of the respondent. If there are no current officers of the respondent, service shall be upon the person or entity otherwise authorized by law to receive service of process. Service upon the general contractor shall be sufficient to initiate the process set forth in this section with regard to any builder or developer, if the builder or developer is not amenable to service of process by the foregoing methods. This notice shall toll all applicable statutes of limitation and repose, whether contractual or statutory, by and against all potentially responsible parties, regardless of whether they were named in the notice, including claims for indemnity applicable to the claim for the period set forth in subdivision (c). The notice shall include all of the following:

(1) The name and location of the project.

(2) An initial list of defects sufficient to apprise the respondent of the general nature of the defects at issue.

(3) A description of the results of the defects, if known.

(4) A summary of the results of a survey or questionnaire distributed to homeowners to determine the nature and extent of defects, if a survey has been conducted or a questionnaire has been distributed.

(5) Either a summary of the results of testing conducted to determine the nature and extent of defects or the actual test results, if that testing has been conducted.

(c) Service of the notice shall commence a period, not to exceed 180 days, during which the association, the respondent, and all other participating parties shall try to resolve the dispute through the processes set forth in this section. This 180–day period may be extended for one additional period, not to exceed 180 days, only upon the mutual agreement of the association, the respondent, and any parties not deemed peripheral pursuant to paragraph (3) of subdivision (e). Any extensions beyond the first extension shall require the agreement of all participating parties. Unless extended, the dispute resolution process prescribed by this section shall be deemed completed. All extensions shall continue the tolling period described in subdivision (b).

(d) Within 25 days of the date the association serves the Notice of Commencement of Legal Proceedings, the respondent may request in writing to meet and confer with the board. Unless the respondent and the association otherwise agree, there shall be not more than one meeting, which shall take place no later than 10 days from the date of the respondent's written request, at a mutually agreeable time and place. The meeting shall be subject to subdivision (a) of Section 4925 and subdivisions (a) and (b) of Section 4935. The discussions at the meeting are privileged communications and are not admissible in evidence in any civil action, unless the association and the respondent consent in writing to their admission.

(e) Upon receipt of the notice, the respondent shall, within 60 days, comply with the following:

(1) The respondent shall provide the association with access to, for inspection and copying of, all plans and specifications, subcontracts, and other construction files for the project that are reasonably calculated to lead to the discovery of admissible evidence regarding the defects claimed. The association shall provide the respondent with access to, for inspection and copying of, all files reasonably calculated to lead to the discovery of admissible evidence regarding the defects claimed, including all reserve studies, maintenance records and any survey questionnaires, or results of testing to determine the nature and extent of defects. To the extent any of the above documents are withheld based on privilege, a privilege log shall be prepared and

submitted to all other parties. All other potentially responsible parties shall have the same rights as the respondent regarding the production of documents upon receipt of written notice of the claim, and shall produce all relevant documents within 60 days of receipt of the notice of the claim.

(2) The respondent shall provide written notice by certified mail to all subcontractors, design professionals, their insurers, and the insurers of any additional insured whose identities are known to the respondent or readily ascertainable by review of the project files or other similar sources and whose potential responsibility appears on the face of the notice. This notice to subcontractors, design professionals, and insurers shall include a copy of the Notice of Commencement of Legal Proceedings, and shall specify the date and manner by which the parties shall meet and confer to select a dispute resolution facilitator pursuant to paragraph (1) of subdivision (f), advise the recipient of its obligation to participate in the meet and confer or serve a written acknowledgment of receipt regarding this notice, advise the recipient that it will waive any challenge to selection of the dispute resolution facilitator if it elects not to participate in the meet and confer, advise the recipient that it may seek the assistance of an attorney, and advise the recipient that it should contact its insurer, if any. Any subcontractor or design professional, or insurer for that subcontractor, design professional, or additional insured, who receives written notice from the respondent regarding the meet and confer shall, prior to the meet and confer, serve on the respondent a written acknowledgment of receipt. That subcontractor or design professional shall, within 10 days of service of the written acknowledgment of receipt, provide to the association and the respondent a Statement of Insurance that includes both of the following:

(A) The names, addresses, and contact persons, if known, of all insurance carriers, whether primary or excess and regardless of whether a deductible or self-insured retention applies, whose policies were in effect from the commencement of construction of the subject project to the present and which potentially cover the subject claims.

(B) The applicable policy numbers for each policy of insurance provided.

(3) Any subcontractor or design professional, or insurer for that subcontractor, design professional, or additional insured, who so chooses, may, at any time, make a written request to the dispute resolution facilitator for designation as a peripheral party. That request shall be served contemporaneously on the association and the respondent. If no objection to that designation is received within 15 days, or upon rejection of that objection, the dispute resolution facilitator shall designate that subcontractor or design professional as a peripheral party, and shall thereafter seek to limit the attendance of that subcontractor or design professional only to those dispute resolution sessions deemed peripheral party sessions or to those sessions during which the dispute resolution facilitator believes settlement as to peripheral parties may be finalized. Nothing in this subdivision shall preclude a party who has been designated a peripheral party from being reclassified as a nonperipheral party, nor shall this subdivision preclude a party designated as a nonperipheral party from being reclassified as a peripheral party after notice to all parties and an opportunity to object. For purposes of this subdivision, a peripheral party is a party having total claimed exposure of less than twenty-five thousand dollars ($25,000).

(f)(1) Within 20 days of sending the notice set forth in paragraph (2) of subdivision (e), the association, respondent, subcontractors, design professionals, and their insurers who have been sent a notice as described in paragraph (2) of subdivision (e) shall meet and confer in an effort to select a dispute resolution facilitator to preside over the mandatory dispute resolution process prescribed by this section. Any subcontractor

or design professional who has been given timely notice of this meeting but who does not participate, waives any challenge he or she may have as to the selection of the dispute resolution facilitator. The role of the dispute resolution facilitator is to attempt to resolve the conflict in a fair manner. The dispute resolution facilitator shall be sufficiently knowledgeable in the subject matter and be able to devote sufficient time to the case. The dispute resolution facilitator shall not be required to reside in or have an office in the county in which the project is located. The dispute resolution facilitator and the participating parties shall agree to a date, time, and location to hold a case management meeting of all parties and the dispute resolution facilitator, to discuss the claims being asserted and the scheduling of events under this section. The case management meeting with the dispute resolution facilitator shall be held within 100 days of service of the Notice of Commencement of Legal Proceedings at a location in the county where the project is located. Written notice of the case management meeting with the dispute resolution facilitator shall be sent by the respondent to the association, subcontractors and design professionals, and their insurers who are known to the respondent to be on notice of the claim, no later than 10 days prior to the case management meeting, and shall specify its date, time, and location. The dispute resolution facilitator in consultation with the respondent shall maintain a contact list of the participating parties.

(2) No later than 10 days prior to the case management meeting, the dispute resolution facilitator shall disclose to the parties all matters that could cause a person aware of the facts to reasonably entertain a doubt that the proposed dispute resolution facilitator would be able to resolve the conflict in a fair manner. The facilitator's disclosure shall include the existence of any ground specified in Section 170.1 of the Code of Civil Procedure for disqualification of a judge, any attorney-client relationship the facilitator has or had with any party or lawyer for a party to the dispute resolution process, and any professional or significant personal relationship the facilitator or his or her spouse or minor child living in the household has or had with any party to the dispute resolution process. The disclosure shall also be provided to any subsequently noticed subcontractor or design professional within 10 days of the notice.

(3) A dispute resolution facilitator shall be disqualified by the court if he or she fails to comply with this subdivision and any party to the dispute resolution process serves a notice of disqualification prior to the case management meeting. If the dispute resolution facilitator complies with this subdivision, he or she shall be disqualified by the court on the basis of the disclosure if any party to the dispute resolution process serves a notice of disqualification prior to the case management meeting.

(4) If the parties cannot mutually agree to a dispute resolution facilitator, then each party shall submit a list of three dispute resolution facilitators. Each party may then strike one nominee from the other parties' list, and petition the court, pursuant to the procedure described in subdivisions (n) and (o), for final selection of the dispute resolution facilitator. The court may issue an order for final selection of the dispute resolution facilitator pursuant to this paragraph.

(5) Any subcontractor or design professional who receives notice of the association's claim without having previously received timely notice of the meet and confer to select the dispute resolution facilitator shall be notified by the respondent regarding the name, address, and telephone number of the dispute resolution facilitator. Any such subcontractor or design professional may serve upon the parties and the dispute resolution facilitator a written objection to the dispute resolution facilitator within 15 days of receiving notice of the claim. Within seven days after service of this objection, the subcontractor or design professional may petition the superior court to replace

the dispute resolution facilitator. The court may replace the dispute resolution facilitator only upon a showing of good cause, liberally construed. Failure to satisfy the deadlines set forth in this subdivision shall constitute a waiver of the right to challenge the dispute resolution facilitator.

(6) The costs of the dispute resolution facilitator shall be apportioned in the following manner: one-third to be paid by the association; one-third to be paid by the respondent; and one-third to be paid by the subcontractors and design professionals, as allocated among them by the dispute resolution facilitator. The costs of the dispute resolution facilitator shall be recoverable by the prevailing party in any subsequent litigation pursuant to Section 1032 of the Code of Civil Procedure, provided however that any nonsettling party may, prior to the filing of the complaint, petition the facilitator to reallocate the costs of the dispute resolution facilitator as they apply to any nonsettling party. The determination of the dispute resolution facilitator with respect to the allocation of these costs shall be binding in any subsequent litigation. The dispute resolution facilitator shall take into account all relevant factors and equities between all parties in the dispute resolution process when reallocating costs.

(7) In the event the dispute resolution facilitator is replaced at any time, the case management statement created pursuant to subdivision (h) shall remain in full force and effect.

(8) The dispute resolution facilitator shall be empowered to enforce all provisions of this section.

(g)(1) No later than the case management meeting, the parties shall begin to generate a data compilation showing the following information regarding the alleged defects at issue:

(A) The scope of the work performed by each potentially responsible subcontractor.

(B) The tract or phase number in which each subcontractor provided goods or services, or both.

(C) The units, either by address, unit number, or lot number, at which each subcontractor provided goods or services, or both.

(2) This data compilation shall be updated as needed to reflect additional information. Each party attending the case management meeting, and any subsequent meeting pursuant to this section, shall provide all information available to that party relevant to this data compilation.

(h) At the case management meeting, the parties shall, with the assistance of the dispute resolution facilitator, reach agreement on a case management statement, which shall set forth all of the elements set forth in paragraphs (1) to (8), inclusive, except that the parties may dispense with one or more of these elements if they agree that it is appropriate to do so. The case management statement shall provide that the following elements shall take place in the following order:

(1) Establishment of a document depository, located in the county where the project is located, for deposit of documents, defect lists, demands, and other information provided for under this section. All documents exchanged by the parties and all documents created pursuant to this subdivision shall be deposited in the document depository, which shall be available to all parties throughout the prefiling dispute resolution process and in any subsequent litigation. When any document is deposited in the document depository, the party depositing the document shall provide written notice identifying the document to all other parties. The costs of maintaining the document depository shall be apportioned among the parties in the same manner as the costs of the dispute resolution facilitator.

(2) Provision of a more detailed list of defects by the association to the respondent after the association completes a visual inspection of the project. This list of defects shall provide sufficient detail for the respondent to ensure that all potentially responsible subcontractors and design professionals are provided with notice of the dispute resolution process. If not already completed prior to the case management meeting, the Notice of Commencement of Legal Proceedings shall be served by the respondent on all additional subcontractors and design professionals whose potential responsibility appears on the face of the more detailed list of defects within seven days of receipt of the more detailed list. The respondent shall serve a copy of the case management statement, including the name, address, and telephone number of the dispute resolution facilitator, to all the potentially responsible subcontractors and design professionals at the same time.

(3) Nonintrusive visual inspection of the project by the respondent, subcontractors, and design professionals.

(4) Invasive testing conducted by the association, if the association deems appropriate. All parties may observe and photograph any testing conducted by the association pursuant to this paragraph, but may not take samples or direct testing unless, by mutual agreement, costs of testing are shared by the parties.

(5) Provision by the association of a comprehensive demand which provides sufficient detail for the parties to engage in meaningful dispute resolution as contemplated under this section.

(6) Invasive testing conducted by the respondent, subcontractors, and design professionals, if they deem appropriate.

(7) Allowance for modification of the demand by the association if new issues arise during the testing conducted by the respondent, subcontractor, or design professionals.

(8) Facilitated dispute resolution of the claim, with all parties, including peripheral parties, as appropriate, and insurers, if any, present and having settlement authority. The dispute resolution facilitators shall endeavor to set specific times for the attendance of specific parties at dispute resolution sessions. If the dispute resolution facilitator does not set specific times for the attendance of parties at dispute resolution sessions, the dispute resolution facilitator shall permit those parties to participate in dispute resolution sessions by telephone.

(i) In addition to the foregoing elements of the case management statement described in subdivision (h), upon mutual agreement of the parties, the dispute resolution facilitator may include any or all of the following elements in a case management statement: the exchange of consultant or expert photographs; expert presentations; expert meetings; or any other mechanism deemed appropriate by the parties in the interest of resolving the dispute.

(j) The dispute resolution facilitator, with the guidance of the parties, shall at the time the case management statement is established, set deadlines for the occurrence of each event set forth in the case management statement, taking into account such factors as the size and complexity of the case, and the requirement of this section that this dispute resolution process not exceed 180 days absent agreement of the parties to an extension of time.

(k)(1)(A) At a time to be determined by the dispute resolution facilitator, the respondent may submit to the association all of the following:

(i) A request to meet with the board to discuss a written settlement offer.

(ii) A written settlement offer, and a concise explanation of the reasons for the terms of the offer.

(iii) A statement that the respondent has access to sufficient funds to satisfy the conditions of the settlement offer.

(iv) A summary of the results of testing conducted for the purposes of determining the nature and extent of defects, if this testing has been conducted, unless the association provided the respondent with actual test results.

(B) If the respondent does not timely submit the items required by this subdivision, the association shall be relieved of any further obligation to satisfy the requirements of this subdivision only.

(C) No less than 10 days after the respondent submits the items required by this paragraph, the respondent and the board shall meet and confer about the respondent's settlement offer.

(D) If the board rejects a settlement offer presented at the meeting held pursuant to this subdivision, the board shall hold a meeting open to each member of the association. The meeting shall be held no less than 15 days before the association commences an action for damages against the respondent.

(E) No less than 15 days before this meeting is held, a written notice shall be sent to each member of the association specifying all of the following:

(i) That a meeting will take place to discuss problems that may lead to the filing of a civil action, and the time and place of this meeting.

(ii) The options that are available to address the problems, including the filing of a civil action and a statement of the various alternatives that are reasonably foreseeable by the association to pay for those options and whether these payments are expected to be made from the use of reserve account funds or the imposition of regular or special assessments, or emergency assessment increases.

(iii) The complete text of any written settlement offer, and a concise explanation of the specific reasons for the terms of the offer submitted to the board at the meeting held pursuant to subdivision (d) that was received from the respondent.

(F) The respondent shall pay all expenses attributable to sending the settlement offer to all members of the association. The respondent shall also pay the expense of holding the meeting, not to exceed three dollars ($3) per association member.

(G) The discussions at the meeting and the contents of the notice and the items required to be specified in the notice pursuant to subparagraph (E) are privileged communications and are not admissible in evidence in any civil action, unless the association consents to their admission.

(H) No more than one request to meet and discuss a written settlement offer may be made by the respondent pursuant to this subdivision.

(*l*) All defect lists and demands, communications, negotiations, and settlement offers made in the course of the prelitigation dispute resolution process provided by this section shall be inadmissible pursuant to Sections 1119 to 1124, inclusive, of the Evidence Code and all applicable decisional law. This inadmissibility shall not be extended to any other documents or communications which would not otherwise be deemed inadmissible.

(m) Any subcontractor or design professional may, at any time, petition the dispute resolution facilitator to release that party from the dispute resolution process upon a showing that the subcontractor or design professional is not potentially responsible for the defect claims at issue. The petition shall be served contemporaneously on all other parties, who shall have 15 days from the date of service to object. If a subcontractor or design professional is released, and it later appears to the dispute resolution facilitator that it may be a responsible party in light of the current defect list or demand, the respondent shall renotice the party as provided by paragraph (2) of subdivision (e), provide a copy of the current defect list or demand, and direct the party to attend a dispute resolution session at a stated time and location. A party who subsequently appears after having been released by the dispute resolution facilitator shall not be prejudiced by its absence from the dispute resolution process as the result of having been previously released by the dispute resolution facilitator.

(n) Any party may, at any time, petition the superior court in the county where the project is located, upon a showing of good cause, and the court may issue an order, for any of the following, or for appointment of a referee to resolve a dispute regarding any of the following:

(1) To take a deposition of any party to the process, or subpoena a third party for deposition or production of documents, which is necessary to further prelitigation resolution of the dispute.

(2) To resolve any disputes concerning inspection, testing, production of documents, or exchange of information provided for under this section.

(3) To resolve any disagreements relative to the timing or contents of the case management statement.

(4) To authorize internal extensions of timeframes set forth in the case management statement.

(5) To seek a determination that a settlement is a good faith settlement pursuant to Section 877.6 of the Code of Civil Procedure and all related authorities. The page limitations and meet and confer requirements specified in this section shall not apply to these motions, which may be made on shortened notice. Instead, these motions shall be subject to other applicable state law, rules of court, and local rules. A determination made by the court pursuant to this motion shall have the same force and effect as the determination of a postfiling application or motion for good faith settlement.

(6) To ensure compliance, on shortened notice, with the obligation to provide a Statement of Insurance pursuant to paragraph (2) of subdivision (e).

(7) For any other relief appropriate to the enforcement of the provisions of this section, including the ordering of parties, and insurers, if any, to the dispute resolution process with settlement authority.

(*o*)(1) A petition filed pursuant to subdivision (n) shall be filed in the superior court in the county in which the project is located. The court shall hear and decide the petition within 10 days after filing. The petitioning party shall serve the petition on all parties, including the date, time, and location of the hearing no later than five business days prior to the hearing. Any responsive papers shall be filed and served no later than three business days prior to the hearing. Any petition or response filed under this section shall be no more than three pages in length.

(2) All parties shall meet with the dispute resolution facilitator, if one has been appointed and confer in person or by telephone prior to the filing of that petition to attempt to resolve the matter without requiring court intervention.

(p) As used in this section:

(1) "Association" shall have the same meaning as defined in Section 4080.

(2) "Builder" means the declarant, as defined in Section 4130.

(3) "Common interest development" shall have the same meaning as in Section 4100, except that it shall not include developments or projects with less than 20 units.

(q) The alternative dispute resolution process and procedures described in this section shall have no application or legal effect other than as described in this section.

(r) This section shall become operative on July 1, 2002, however it shall not apply to any pending suit or claim for which notice has previously been given.

(s) This section shall become inoperative on July 1, 2017, and, as of January 1, 2018, is repealed, unless a later enacted statute, that becomes operative on or before January 1, 2018, deletes or extends the dates on which it becomes inoperative and is repealed. *(Added by Stats.2012, c. 180 (A.B.805), § 2, operative Jan. 1, 2014.)*

Inoperative Date and Repeal

For inoperative date and repeal of this section, see its terms.

Law Revision Commission Comments

Section 6000 continues former Section 1375 without change, except as indicated below.

The following nonsubstantive changes are made:

• Cross-references are updated to reflect the new locations of the referenced provisions.

• The words "board of directors" and "board of directors of the association" are replaced throughout with "board." See Section 4085 ("board").

• Subdivision (e)(2) is revised to delete references to former Section 1375.05, which was repealed by its own terms on January 1, 2011.

• Subdivision (f)(3) is revised to correct erroneous references to "this paragraph." The revised provision refers to "this subdivision."

• Subdivision (*l*) is revised to delete a reference to former Section 1375.05, which was repealed by its own terms on January 1, 2011.

See also Sections 4080 ("association"), 4100 ("common interest development"), 4160 ("member"), 4170 ("person"), 4177 ("reserve accounts"). [40 Cal.L.Rev.Comm. Reports 235 (2010)].

§ 6100. Settlement agreements regarding alleged defects; notice of resolution to members on record; disclosures

(a) As soon as is reasonably practicable after the association and the builder have entered into a settlement agreement or the matter has otherwise been resolved regarding alleged defects in the common areas, alleged defects in the separate interests that the association is obligated to maintain or repair, or alleged defects in the separate interests that arise out of, or are integrally related to, defects in the common areas or separate interests that the association is obligated to maintain or repair, where the defects giving rise to the dispute have not been corrected, the association shall, in writing, inform only the members of the association whose names appear on the records of the association that the matter has been resolved, by settlement agreement or other means, and disclose all of the following:

(1) A general description of the defects that the association reasonably believes, as of the date of the disclosure, will be corrected or replaced.

(2) A good faith estimate, as of the date of the disclosure, of when the association believes that the defects identified in paragraph (1) will be corrected or replaced. The association may state that the estimate may be modified.

(3) The status of the claims for defects in the design or construction of the common interest development that were not identified in paragraph (1) whether expressed in a preliminary list of defects sent to each member of the association or otherwise claimed and disclosed to the members of the association.

(b) Nothing in this section shall preclude an association from amending the disclosures required pursuant to subdivision (a), and any amendments shall supersede any prior conflicting information disclosed to the members of the association and shall retain any privilege attached to the original disclosures.

(c) Disclosure of the information required pursuant to subdivision (a) or authorized by subdivision (b) shall not waive any privilege attached to the information.

(d) For the purposes of the disclosures required pursuant to this section, the term "defects" shall be defined to include any damage resulting from defects. *(Added by Stats.2012, c. 180 (A.B.805), § 2, operative Jan. 1, 2014.)*

Law Revision Commission Comments

Section 6100 continues former Section 1375.1 without change.

See also Sections 4080 ("association"), 4095 ("common area"), 4100 ("common interest development"), 4160 ("member"), 4185 ("separate interest"). [40 Cal.L.Rev.Comm. Reports 235 (2010)].

§ 6150. Written notice to members prior to filing civil action; contents

(a) Not later than 30 days prior to the filing of any civil action by the association against the declarant or other developer of a common interest development for alleged damage to the common areas, alleged damage to the separate interests that the association is obligated to maintain or repair, or alleged damage to the separate interests that arises out of, or is integrally related to, damage to the common areas or separate interests that the association is obligated to maintain or repair, the board shall provide a written notice to each member of the association who appears on the records of the association when the notice is provided. This notice shall specify all of the following:

(1) That a meeting will take place to discuss problems that may lead to the filing of a civil action.

(2) The options, including civil actions, that are available to address the problems.

(3) The time and place of this meeting.

(b) Notwithstanding subdivision (a), if the association has reason to believe that the applicable statute of limitations will expire before the association files the civil action, the association may give the notice, as described above, within 30 days after the filing of the action. *(Added by Stats.2012, c. 180 (A.B.805), § 2, operative Jan. 1, 2014.)*

Law Revision Commission Comments

Section 6150 continues former Section 1368.5 without change, except as indicated below.

The following nonsubstantive change is made:

• The words "board of directors of the association" are replaced with "board." See Section 4085 ("board").

See also Sections 4080 ("association"), 4095 ("common area"), 4100 ("common interest development"), 4130 ("declarant"), 4160 ("member"), 4185 ("separate interest"). [40 Cal.L.Rev.Comm. Reports 235 (2010)].

Part 5.3

COMMERCIAL AND INDUSTRIAL COMMON INTEREST DEVELOPMENTS

CHAPTER 1. GENERAL PROVISIONS

ARTICLE 1. PRELIMINARY PROVISIONS

§ 6500.   Short title

This part shall be known, and may be cited, as the Commercial and Industrial Common Interest Development Act. In a provision of this part, the part may be referred to as the act. *(Added by Stats.2013, c. 605 (S.B.752), § 21.)*

Law Revision Commission Comments

Section 6500 is new.

Common interest developments in general are governed by the Davis–Stirling Common Interest Development Act. See Sections 4000-6150. However, common interest developments that are exclusively commercial or industrial are exempted from the provisions of that act by Section 4202.

This part (Sections 6500-6876) establishes a separate body of law, largely based on provisions of the Davis–Stirling Common Interest Development Act, that applies to and governs exclusively commercial or industrial common interest developments.

The Comments to the sections of this act identify sections of the Davis–Stirling Common Interest Development Act that are sources of the provisions of this act, and describe how each provision in this act compares with its source. [42 Cal.L.Rev.Comm. Reports 1 (2012)].

§ 6502.   Effect of headings on scope, meaning, or intent of act

Division, part, title, chapter, article, and section headings do not in any manner affect the scope, meaning, or intent of this act. *(Added by Stats.2013, c. 605 (S.B.752), § 21.)*

Law Revision Commission Comments

With respect to a commercial or industrial common interest development, Section 6502 continues Section 1350.5 without change, except as indicated below.

The following nonsubstantive changes are made:

● "Article" is added to the list of headings.

● The last word of the sentence is replaced with "act."

For further information, see Section 6500 Comment.

Section 6502 is a standard provision found in many codes. See, e.g., Evid. Code § 5; Fam. Code § 5; Prob. Code § 4.

For a similar provision in the Davis–Stirling Common Interest Development Act, see Section 4005. [42 Cal.L.Rev.Comm. Reports 1 (2012)].

§ 6505.   Continuation of prior law

Nothing in the act that added this part shall be construed to invalidate a document prepared or action taken before January 1, 2014, if the document or action was proper under the law governing common interest developments at the time that the document was prepared or the action was taken. For the purposes of this section, "document" does not include a governing document. *(Added by Stats.2013, c. 605 (S.B.752), § 21.)*

Law Revision Commission Comments

Section 6505 is new. It makes clear that any changes to law made by enactment of this act shall not be construed to retroactively invalidate documents prepared or actions taken prior to the operative date of the act.

The term "documents" is used to describe notices, forms, and other procedural or transactional instruments. It is not meant to include the governing documents of the association. Governing documents must conform to the law. See Section 6600.

See also Sections 6534 ("common interest development"), 6552 ("governing documents"). For a similar provision in the Davis–Stirling Common Interest Development Act, see Section 4010. [42 Cal.L.Rev.Comm. Reports 1 (2012)].

§ 6510.   Construction of zoning ordinances

Unless a contrary intent is clearly expressed, a local zoning ordinance is construed to treat like structures, lots, parcels, areas, or spaces in like manner regardless of the form of the common interest development. *(Added by Stats.2013, c. 605 (S.B.752), § 21.)*

Law Revision Commission Comments

With respect to a commercial or industrial common interest development, Section 6510 continues Section 1372 without change, except as indicated below.

The following nonsubstantive change is made:

● A list of all of the types of common interest developments is replaced with general language.

For further information, see Section 6500 Comment.

See also Section 6534 ("common interest development").

For a similar provision in the Davis–Stirling Common Interest Development Act, see Section 4020. [42 Cal.L.Rev.Comm. Reports 1 (2012)].

§ 6512.   Delivery of document to association

(a) If a provision of this act requires that a document be delivered to an association, the document shall be delivered to the person designated to receive documents on behalf of the association, in a written notice delivered by the association to members by individual delivery. If notice of this designation has not been given, the document shall be delivered to the president or secretary of the association.

(b) A document delivered pursuant to this section may be delivered by any of the following methods:

(1) First-class mail, postage prepaid, registered or certified mail, express mail, or overnight delivery by an express service carrier.

(2) By email, facsimile, or other electronic means, if the association has assented to that method of delivery.

(3) By personal delivery, if the association has assented to that method of delivery. If the association accepts a document by personal delivery it shall provide a written receipt acknowledging delivery of the document. *(Added by Stats.2013, c. 605 (S.B. 752), § 21.)*

Law Revision Commission Comments

Section 6512 is new. It provides a standard rule for delivery of a document to the association.

See also Sections 6514 (individual delivery), 6520 (electronic delivery).

See also Section 6528 ("association").

For a similar provision in the Davis–Stirling Common Interest Development Act, see Section 4035. [43 Cal.L.Rev.Comm. Reports ___ (Appendix 5) (2013)].

§ 6514.   Individual delivery or individual notice

(a) If a provision of this act requires that an association deliver a document by "individual delivery" or "individual notice," the document shall be delivered by one of the following methods:

(1) First-class mail, postage prepaid, registered or certified mail, express mail, or overnight delivery by an express service carrier. The document shall be addressed to the recipient at the address last shown on the books of the association.

(2) Email, facsimile, or other electronic means, if the recipient has consented, in writing, to that method of delivery. The consent may be revoked, in writing, by the recipient.

(b) For the purposes of this section, an unrecorded provision of the governing documents providing for a particular method of delivery does not constitute agreement by a member to that method of delivery. (*Added by Stats.2013, c. 605 (S.B.752), § 21.*)

Law Revision Commission Comments

Section 6514 is new. It specifies acceptable methods for delivery of a notice to an individual member. The methods listed in subdivision (a) are drawn from Section 1350.7(b)(2)-(3).

Subdivision (b) is drawn from Section 1350.7(d). It precludes use of electronic delivery methods when the recipient has not consented to use of those methods or has withdrawn such consent.

See also Section 6520 (electronic delivery).

See also Sections 6528 ("association"), 6552 ("governing documents"), 6554 ("member").

For a similar provision in the Davis–Stirling Common Interest Development Act, see Section 4040. [42 Cal.L.Rev.Comm. Reports 1 (2012)].

§ 6518. Time of delivery

(a) This section governs the delivery of a document pursuant to this act.

(b) If a document is delivered by mail, delivery is deemed to be complete on deposit into the United States mail.

(c) If a document is delivered by electronic means, delivery is complete at the time of transmission. (*Added by Stats.2013, c. 605 (S.B.752), § 21.*)

Law Revision Commission Comments

Section 6518 is new. Subdivision (b) is drawn from the second sentence of Section 1350.7(b)(2).

Subdivision (c) is drawn from the second sentence of Section 1350.7(b)(3).

For a similar provision in the Davis–Stirling Common Interest Development Act, see Section 4050. [42 Cal.L.Rev.Comm. Reports 1 (2012)].

§ 6520. Electronic delivery; satisfaction of written information requirement

If the association or a member has consented to receive information by electronic delivery, and a provision of this act requires that the information be in writing, that requirement is satisfied if the information is provided in an electronic record capable of retention by the recipient at the time of receipt. An electronic record is not capable of retention by the recipient if the sender or its information processing system inhibits the ability of the recipient to print or store the electronic record. (*Added by Stats.2013, c. 605 (S.B.752), § 21.*)

Law Revision Commission Comments

Section 6520 is new. It is drawn from and is similar to the substance of Section 1633.8(a), which is part of the Uniform Electronic Transactions Act ("UETA").

See also Sections 6528 ("association"), 6554 ("member").

For a similar provision in the Davis–Stirling Common Interest Development Act, see Section 4055. [42 Cal.L.Rev.Comm. Reports 1 (2012)].

§ 6522. Approval by majority

If a provision of this act requires that an action be approved by a majority of all members, the action shall be approved or ratified by an affirmative vote of a majority of the votes entitled to be cast. (*Added by Stats.2013, c. 605 (S.B.752), § 21.*)

Law Revision Commission Comments

Section 6522 is new. It is added for drafting convenience. This section only governs an election conducted pursuant to a provision of this act (i.e., the Commercial and Industrial Common Interest Development Act). An election that is not required by this act would be governed by the association's governing documents.

See also Section 6554 ("member").

For a similar provision in the Davis–Stirling Common Interest Development Act, see Section 4065. [42 Cal.L.Rev.Comm. Reports 1 (2012)].

§ 6524. Approval by majority of quorum

If a provision of this act requires that an action be approved by a majority of a quorum of the members, the action shall be approved or ratified by an affirmative vote of a majority of the votes represented and voting in a duly held election in which a quorum is represented, which affirmative votes also constitute a majority of the required quorum. (*Added by Stats.2013, c. 605 (S.B.752), § 21.*)

Law Revision Commission Comments

Section 6524 is new. It is added for drafting convenience. This section only applies to any member election conducted pursuant to a provision of this act (i.e., the Commercial and Industrial Common Interest Development Act), whether conducted at a meeting, by mailed ballot, or by any other lawful means. An election that is not required by this act would be governed by the association's governing documents.

See also Section 6554 ("member").

For a similar provision in the Davis–Stirling Common Interest Development Act, see Section 4070. [43 Cal.L.Rev.Comm. Reports ___ (Appendix 5) (2013)].

ARTICLE 2. DEFINITIONS

§ 6526. Construction of act

The definitions in this article govern the construction of this act. (*Added by Stats.2013, c. 605 (S.B.752), § 21.*)

Law Revision Commission Comments

With respect to a commercial or industrial common interest development, Section 6526 continues the substance of the introductory clause of Section 1351.

For further information, see Section 6500 Comment.

For a similar provision in the Davis–Stirling Common Interest Development Act, see Section 4075. [42 Cal.L.Rev.Comm. Reports 1 (2012)].

§ 6528. "Association" defined

"Association" means a nonprofit corporation or unincorporated association created for the purpose of managing a common interest development. *(Added by Stats.2013, c. 605 (S.B.752), § 21.)*

Law Revision Commission Comments

With respect to a commercial or industrial common interest development, Section 6528 continues Section 1351(a) without change.

For further information, see Section 6500 Comment.

See also Section 6534 ("common interest development").

For a similar provision in the Davis–Stirling Common Interest Development Act, see Section 4080. [42 Cal.L.Rev.Comm. Reports 1 (2012)].

§ 6530. "Board" defined

"Board" means the board of directors of the association. *(Added by Stats.2013, c. 605 (S.B.752), § 21.)*

Law Revision Commission Comments

Section 6530 is new.

See also Section 6528 ("association").

For a similar provision in the Davis–Stirling Common Interest Development Act, see Section 4085. [42 Cal.L.Rev.Comm. Reports 1 (2012)].

§ 6531. "Commercial or industrial common interest development" defined

A "commercial or industrial common interest development" means a common interest development that is limited to industrial or commercial uses by law or by a declaration of covenants, conditions, and restrictions that has been recorded in the official records of each county in which the common interest development is located. For the purposes of this section, "commercial use" includes, but is not limited to, the operation of a business that provides facilities for the overnight stay of its customers, employees, or agents. *(Added by Stats.2013, c. 605 (S.B.752), § 21.)*

Law Revision Commission Comments

Section 6531 is drawn from Section 1373(a). However, Section 6531 makes clear that it applies when any law, not just a zoning law, limits a subdivision to commercial or industrial uses. See, e.g., Health & Safety Code § 25232(b) (restricting residential use of property that is on the "border-zone" of hazardous contamination). See also Health & Safety Code § 25117.4 ("border-zone property" defined).

The last sentence of Section 6531 is new. It is added to make clear that the operation of a business that provides facilities for overnight stays by its customers, employees, or agents is a commercial use. For example, under this provision the operation of a hotel, inpatient medical facility, or apartment complex is a commercial use. Similarly, the operation of a business that provides overnight living space to its employees and agents is a commercial use.

See also Section 6534 ("common interest development").

For a similar provision in the Davis–Stirling Common Interest Development Act, see Section 4202. [43 Cal.L.Rev.Comm. Reports ___ (Appendix 5) (2013)].

§ 6532. "Common area" defined

(a) "Common area" means the entire common interest development except the separate interests therein. The estate in the common area may be a fee, a life estate, an estate for years, or any combination of the foregoing.

(b) Notwithstanding subdivision (a), in a planned development described in subdivision (b) of Section 6562, the common area may consist of mutual or reciprocal easement rights appurtenant to the separate interests. *(Added by Stats.2013, c. 605 (S.B.752), § 21.)*

Law Revision Commission Comments

With respect to a commercial or industrial common interest development, subdivision (a) of Section 6532 continues the first two sentences of Section 1351(b) without change.

With respect to a commercial or industrial common interest development, subdivision (b) continues the substance of the third sentence of Section 1351(b), but restates it for clarity.

For further information, see Section 6500 Comment.

See also Sections 6534 ("common interest development"), 6562 ("planned development"), 6564 ("separate interest").

For a similar provision in the Davis–Stirling Common Interest Development Act, see Section 4090. [42 Cal.L.Rev.Comm. Reports 1 (2012)].

§ 6534. "Common interest development" defined

"Common interest development" means any of the following:

(a) A condominium project.

(b) A planned development.

(c) A stock cooperative. *(Added by Stats.2013, c. 605 (S.B. 752), § 21.)*

Law Revision Commission Comments

With respect to a commercial or industrial common interest development, Section 6534 continues Section 1351(c) without change, except as indicated below.

The following nonsubstantive change is made:

● The reference to a "community apartment project" is not continued.

For further information, see Section 6500 Comment.

See also Sections 6542 ("condominium project"), 6562 ("planned development"), 6566 ("stock cooperative").

For a similar provision in the Davis–Stirling Common Interest Development Act, see Section 4100. [42 Cal.L.Rev.Comm. Reports 1 (2012)].

§ 6540. "Condominium plan" defined

"Condominium plan" means a plan described in Section 6624. *(Added by Stats.2013, c. 605 (S.B.752), § 21.)*

Law Revision Commission Comments

Section 6540 is new. It is included for drafting convenience.

For a similar provision in the Davis–Stirling Common Interest Development Act, see Section 4120. [42 Cal.L.Rev.Comm. Reports 1 (2012)].

§ 6542. "Condominium project" defined

(a) A "condominium project" means a real property development consisting of condominiums.

(b) A condominium consists of an undivided interest in common in a portion of real property coupled with a separate interest in space called a unit, the boundaries of which are described on a recorded final map, parcel map, or condominium plan in sufficient detail to locate all boundaries thereof. The area within these boundaries may be filled with air, earth, water, or fixtures, or any combination thereof, and need not be physically attached to land except by easements for access and, if necessary, support. The description of the unit may refer to (1) boundaries described in the recorded final map, parcel map, or condominium plan, (2) physical boundaries, either in existence, or to be constructed, such as walls, floors, and ceilings of a structure or any portion thereof, (3) an entire structure containing one or more units, or (4) any combination thereof.

(c) The portion or portions of the real property held in undivided interest may be all of the real property, except for the separate interests, or may include a particular three-dimensional portion thereof, the boundaries of which are described on a recorded final map, parcel map, or condominium plan. The area within these boundaries may be filled with air, earth, water, or fixtures, or any combination thereof, and need not be physically attached to land except by easements for access and, if necessary, support.

(d) An individual condominium within a condominium project may include, in addition, a separate interest in other portions of the real property. *(Added by Stats.2013, c. 605 (S.B.752), § 21.)*

Law Revision Commission Comments

With respect to a commercial or industrial common interest development, Section 6542 continues Section 1351(f) without change, except as indicated below.

The following nonsubstantive changes are made:

● The section is organized into subdivisions for ease of reference.

● In subdivision (a), the word "development" is replaced with "real property development."

● Subdivisions (b) and (c) make clear that the contents of the area within the boundaries of a condominium may include "fixtures."

For further information, see Section 6500 Comment.

See also Sections 6540 ("condominium plan"), 6564 ("separate interest").

For a similar provision in the Davis–Stirling Common Interest Development Act, see Section 4125. [42 Cal.L.Rev.Comm. Reports 1 (2012)].

§ 6544. "Declarant" defined

"Declarant" means the person or group of persons designated in the declaration as declarant, or if no declarant is designated, the person or group of persons who sign the original declaration or who succeed to special rights, preferences, or privileges designated in the declaration as belonging to the signator of the original declaration. *(Added by Stats.2013, c. 605 (S.B.752), § 21.)*

Law Revision Commission Comments

With respect to a commercial or industrial common interest development, Section 6544 continues Section 1351(g) without change.

For further information, see Section 6500 Comment.

See also Sections 6546 ("declaration"), 6560 ("person").

For a similar provision in the Davis–Stirling Common Interest Development Act, see Section 4130. [42 Cal.L.Rev.Comm. Reports 1 (2012)].

§ 6546. "Declaration" defined

"Declaration" means the document, however denominated, that contains the information required by Section 6614. *(Added by Stats.2013, c. 605 (S.B.752), § 21.)*

Law Revision Commission Comments

With respect to a commercial or industrial common interest development, Section 6546 continues Section 1351(h) without change, except as indicated below.

The following nonsubstantive changes are made:

● The word "which" is replaced with "that."

● The statutory cross-reference is updated to reflect the new location of the referenced provision.

For further information, see Section 6500 Comment.

For a similar provision in the Davis–Stirling Common Interest Development Act, see Section 4135. [42 Cal.L.Rev.Comm. Reports 1 (2012)].

§ 6548. "Director" defined

"Director" means a natural person who serves on the board. *(Added by Stats.2013, c. 605 (S.B.752), § 21.)*

Law Revision Commission Comments

Section 6548 is new. It is added for drafting convenience.

See also Section 6530 ("board").

For a similar provision in the Davis–Stirling Common Interest Development Act, see Section 4140. [42 Cal.L.Rev.Comm. Reports 1 (2012)].

§ 6550. "Exclusive use common area" defined

(a) "Exclusive use common area" means a portion of the common area designated by the declaration for the exclusive use of one or more, but fewer than all, of the owners of the separate interests and which is or will be appurtenant to the separate interest or interests.

(b) Unless the declaration otherwise provides, any shutters, awnings, window boxes, doorsteps, stoops, porches, balconies, patios, exterior doors, doorframes, and hardware incident thereto, screens and windows or other fixtures designed to serve a single separate interest, but located outside the boundaries of the separate interest, are exclusive use common area allocated exclusively to that separate interest.

(c) Notwithstanding the provisions of the declaration, internal and external telephone wiring designed to serve a single separate interest, but located outside the boundaries of the separate interest, is exclusive use common area allocated exclusively to that separate interest. *(Added by Stats.2013, c. 605 (S.B.752), § 21.)*

Law Revision Commission Comments

With respect to a commercial or industrial common interest development, Section 6550 continues Section 1351(i) without change, except as indicated below.

The following nonsubstantive changes are made:

● The phrase "common areas" is singularized.

● Subdivision (c) is revised to correct a drafting error.

For further information, see Section 6500 Comment.

See also Sections 6532 ("common area"), 6546 ("declaration"), 6564 ("separate interest").

For a similar provision in the Davis–Stirling Common Interest Development Act, see Section 4145. [42 Cal.L.Rev.Comm. Reports 1 (2012)].

§ 6552. "Governing documents" defined

"Governing documents" means the declaration and any other documents, such as bylaws, operating rules, articles of incorporation, or articles of association, which govern the operation of the common interest development or association. *(Added by Stats.2013, c. 605 (S.B.752), § 21.)*

Law Revision Commission Comments

With respect to a commercial or industrial common interest development, Section 6552 continues Section 1351(j) without change, except as indicated below.

The following nonsubstantive change is made:

● The superfluous words "of the association" are not continued.

For further information, see Section 6500 Comment.

See also Sections 6528 ("association"), 6534 ("common interest development"), 6546 ("declaration").

For a similar provision in the Davis–Stirling Common Interest Development Act, see Section 4150. [42 Cal.L.Rev.Comm. Reports 1 (2012)].

§ 6553. "Individual notice" defined

"Individual notice" means the delivery of a document pursuant to Section 6514. *(Added by Stats.2013, c. 605 (S.B.752), § 21.)*

Law Revision Commission Comments

Section 6553 is new. It is added for drafting convenience.

For a similar provision in the Davis–Stirling Common Interest Development Act, see Section 4153. [42 Cal.L.Rev.Comm. Reports 1 (2012)].

§ 6554. "Member" defined

"Member" means an owner of a separate interest. *(Added by Stats.2013, c. 605 (S.B.752), § 21.)*

Law Revision Commission Comments

Section 6554 is new. It is added for drafting convenience.

See also Section 6564 ("separate interest").

For a similar provision in the Davis–Stirling Common Interest Development Act, see Section 4160. [42 Cal.L.Rev.Comm. Reports 1 (2012)].

§ 6560. "Person" defined

"Person" means a natural person, corporation, government or governmental subdivision or agency, business trust, estate, trust, partnership, limited liability company, association, or other entity. *(Added by Stats.2013, c. 605 (S.B.752), § 21.)*

Law Revision Commission Comments

Section 6560 is new. It is added for drafting convenience.

For a similar provision in the Davis–Stirling Common Interest Development Act, see Section 4170. [42 Cal.L.Rev.Comm. Reports 1 (2012)].

§ 6562. "Planned development" defined

"Planned development" means a real property development other than a condominium project, or a stock cooperative, having either or both of the following features:

(a) Common area that is owned either by an association or in common by the owners of the separate interests who possess appurtenant rights to the beneficial use and enjoyment of the common area.

(b) Common area and an association that maintains the common area with the power to levy assessments that may become a lien upon the separate interests in accordance with Article 2 (commencing with Section 6808) of Chapter 7. *(Added by Stats.2013, c. 605 (S.B.752), § 21.)*

Law Revision Commission Comments

With respect to a commercial or industrial common interest development, Section 6562 continues the substance of Section 1351(k), except as indicated below.

The following nonsubstantive changes are made:

● In the introductory clause, the word "development" is replaced with "real property development."

● Parentheses in the introductory clause are deleted, and are replaced with a comma following the term "stock cooperative."

● A reference to a "community apartment project" is not continued.

● Subdivision (a) is restated for clarity.

● Subdivision (b) is restated for clarity and to update a cross-reference.

For further information, see Section 6500 Comment.

See also Sections 6528 ("association"), 6532 ("common area"), 6542 ("condominium project"), 6564 ("separate interest"), 6566 ("stock cooperative").

For a similar provision in the Davis–Stirling Common Interest Development Act, see Section 4175. [42 Cal.L.Rev.Comm. Reports 1 (2012)].

§ 6564. "Separate interest" defined

(a) "Separate interest" has the following meanings:

(1) In a condominium project, "separate interest" means a separately owned unit, as specified in Section 6542.

(2) In a planned development, "separate interest" means a separately owned lot, parcel, area, or space.

(3) In a stock cooperative, "separate interest" means the exclusive right to occupy a portion of the real property, as specified in Section 6566.

(b) Unless the declaration or condominium plan, if any exists, otherwise provides, if walls, floors, or ceilings are designated as boundaries of a separate interest, the interior surfaces of the perimeter walls, floors, ceilings, windows, doors, and outlets located within the separate interest are part of the separate interest and any other portions of the walls, floors, or ceilings are part of the common area.

(c) The estate in a separate interest may be a fee, a life estate, an estate for years, or any combination of the foregoing. *(Added by Stats.2013, c. 605 (S.B.752), § 21.)*

Law Revision Commission Comments

With respect to a commercial or industrial common interest development, Section 6564 continues Section 1351(*l*) without change, except as indicated below.

The following nonsubstantive changes are made:

● In subdivision (a)(2), the words "individual unit" are replaced with "separately owned unit."

● The last two unnumbered paragraphs of Section 1351(*l*) are designated as subdivisions (b) and (c).

● Cross-references are updated to reflect the new locations of referenced provisions.

● The phrase "common areas" is singularized.

● Section 1351(*l*)(1), which states the meaning of "separate interest" in a community apartment project, is not continued.

For further information, see Section 6500 Comment.

See also Sections 6532 ("common area"), 6540 ("condominium plan"), 6542 ("condominium project"), 6546 ("declaration"), 6562 ("planned development"), 6566 ("stock cooperative").

For a similar provision in the Davis–Stirling Common Interest Development Act, see Section 4185. [42 Cal.L.Rev.Comm. Reports 1 (2012)].

§ 6566. "Stock cooperative" defined

"Stock cooperative" means a development in which a corporation is formed or availed of, primarily for the purpose of holding title to, either in fee simple or for a term of years, improved real property, and all or substantially all of the shareholders of the corporation receive a right of exclusive occupancy in a portion of the real property, title to which is held by the corporation. The owners' interest in the corporation, whether evidenced by a share of stock, a certificate of membership, or otherwise, shall be deemed to be an interest in a common interest development and a real estate development for purposes of subdivision (f) of Section 25100 of the Corporations Code. *(Added by Stats.2013, c. 605 (S.B.752), § 21.)*

Law Revision Commission Comments

With respect to a commercial or industrial common interest development, Section 6566 continues the first paragraph of Section 1351(m) without change.

For further information, see Section 6500 Comment.

See also Section 6534 ("common interest development").

For a similar provision in the Davis–Stirling Common Interest Development Act, see Section 4190. [42 Cal.L.Rev.Comm. Reports 1 (2012)].

CHAPTER 2. APPLICATION OF ACT

Section
6580. Creation of common interest development; application of act.
6582. Act applicable only to commercial or industrial common interest developments.

§ 6580. Creation of common interest development; application of act

Subject to Section 6582, this act applies and a common interest development is created whenever a separate interest coupled with an interest in the common area or membership in the association is, or has been, conveyed, provided all of the following are recorded:

(a) A declaration.

(b) A condominium plan, if any exists.

(c) A final map or parcel map, if Division 2 (commencing with Section 66410) of Title 7 of the Government Code requires the recording of either a final map or parcel map for the common interest development. *(Added by Stats.2013, c. 605 (S.B.752), § 21.)*

Law Revision Commission Comments

With respect to a commercial or industrial common interest development, Section 6580 continues Section 1352 without change, except as indicated below.

The following nonsubstantive changes are made:

● The term "title" is replaced with "act."

● A cross-reference is added to refer to Section 6582.

For further information, see Section 6500 Comment.

See also Sections 6528 ("association"), 6532 ("common area"), 6534 ("common interest development"), 6540 ("condominium plan"), 6546 ("declaration"), 6564 ("separate interest").

For a similar provision in the Davis–Stirling Common Interest Development Act, see Section 4200. [42 Cal.L.Rev.Comm. Reports 1 (2012)].

§ 6582. Act applicable only to commercial or industrial common interest developments

(a) This act applies only to a commercial or industrial common interest development.

(b) Nothing in this act may be construed to apply to a real property development that does not contain common area. This subdivision is declaratory of existing law. *(Added by Stats.2013, c. 605 (S.B.752), § 21.)*

Law Revision Commission Comments

Subdivision (a) of Section 6582 is consistent with Section 1373 as that section provided prior to the enactment of 2012 Cal. Stat. ch. 180, except that the act that added this section makes the following provisions of the Davis–Stirling Common Interest Development Act inapplicable to a commercial or industrial common interest development: Section 1350.7, Section 1351(d), the provisions of Section 1353 that require notice if a development is within an airport influence area or within the jurisdiction of the San Francisco Bay Conservation and Development Commission, Section 1353.7, Section 1354(c), a portion of Section 1355(b), a portion of Section 1357(b)-(c), Section 1363(d), (e), (g), and (h), Section 1363.001, Section 1363.005, Section 1363.03, Section 1363.04, Section 1363.05, Section 1363.07, Section 1363.09, Section 1363.1, Section 1363.2, Sections 1363.810 through 1363.850, Section 1365.1, Section 1365.2, Section 1365.2.5, Section 1365.3, Section 1365.7, the last two sentences of Section 1366(a), Section 1366(d)-(f), Section 1366.2, Section 1366.3, Section 1366.4, Section 1367.1(c), (k), and (n), Section 1367.4, Section 1367.5, Section 1367.6, Section 1368.2, and Sections 1369.510 through 1369.590.

A common interest development is created as provided in Section 6580.

With respect to a commercial or industrial common interest development, subdivision (b) continues Section 1374 without change, except as indicated below.

The following nonsubstantive changes are made:

● The word "title" is replaced with "act."

● The phrase "wherein there does not exist" is restated for clarity.

For further information, see Section 6500 Comment.

See also Sections 6531 ("commercial or industrial common interest development"), 6532 ("common area").

For a similar provision in the Davis–Stirling Common Interest Development Act, see Section 4201. [43 Cal.L.Rev.Comm. Reports ___ (Appendix 5) (2013)].

CHAPTER 3.   GOVERNING DOCUMENTS

ARTICLE 1.   GENERAL PROVISIONS

§ 6600.   Authority of documents

(a) To the extent of any conflict between the governing documents and the law, the law shall prevail.

(b) To the extent of any conflict between the articles of incorporation and the declaration, the declaration shall prevail.

(c) To the extent of any conflict between the bylaws and the articles of incorporation or declaration, the articles of incorporation or declaration shall prevail.

(d) To the extent of any conflict between the operating rules and the bylaws, articles of incorporation, or declaration, the bylaws, articles of incorporation, or declaration shall prevail. *(Added by Stats.2013, c. 605 (S.B.752), § 21.)*

Law Revision Commission Comments

Section 6600 is added to clarify the relationship between the law and the most common types of governing documents. The section is intended to provide guidance on how to resolve a conflict between the specified authorities. It is not intended to state a rule for determining when such a conflict exists.

The terminology used is consistent with that used in numerous other statutory provisions that establish a rule of supremacy between authority without exhaustively specifying the circumstances in which the rule is to be applied. See, e.g., Civ. Code §§ 799.10, 2924h, 5100(e); Educ. Code §§ 24953(h), 69522; Fish & Game Code § 7090(h); Food & Agric. Code § 13169; Health & Safety Code §§ 1568.065, 1787; Ins. Code § 11580.2; Pub. Res. Code §§ 2770.6, 2772.5, 71530; Pub. Util. Code § 5142; Veh. Code § 15200.

Nothing in the section is intended to create an affirmative duty to amend a governing document to delete superseded material.

Subdivisions (a) and (b) of Section 6600 are new.

Subdivision (c) is consistent with Corporations Code Section 7151(c), providing that the bylaws shall be consistent with the articles of incorporation.

Subdivision (d) is drawn from Section 1357.110, providing that an operating rule may not be inconsistent with the declaration, articles of incorporation, or bylaws of the association.

See also Sections 6546 ("declaration"), 6552 ("governing documents").

For a similar provision in the Davis–Stirling Common Interest Development Act, see Section 4205. [43 Cal.L.Rev.Comm. Reports ___ (Appendix 5) (2013)].

§ 6602.   Liberal construction of instruments

Any deed, declaration, or condominium plan for a common interest development shall be liberally construed to facilitate the operation of the common interest development, and its provisions shall be presumed to be independent and severable. Nothing in Article 3 (commencing with Section 715) of Chapter 2 of Title 2 of Part 1 of Division 2 shall operate to invalidate any provisions of the governing documents. *(Added by Stats.2013, c. 605 (S.B.752), § 21.)*

Law Revision Commission Comments

With respect to a commercial or industrial common interest development, Section 6602 continues Section 1370 without change, except as indicated below.

The following nonsubstantive changes are made:

● "This division" is replaced with "Division 2."

● The words "of a common interest development" are not continued.

For further information, see Section 6500 Comment. See also Sections 6534 ("common interest development"), 6540 ("condominium plan"), 6546 ("declaration"), 6552 ("governing documents").

For a similar provision in the Davis–Stirling Common Interest Development Act, see Section 4215. [42 Cal.L.Rev.Comm. Reports 1 (2012)].

§ 6604. Boundaries of units; presumptions

In interpreting deeds and condominium plans, the existing physical boundaries of a unit in a condominium project, when the boundaries of the unit are contained within a building, or of a unit reconstructed in substantial accordance with the original plans thereof, shall be conclusively presumed to be its boundaries rather than the metes and bounds expressed in the deed or condominium plan, if any exists, regardless of settling or lateral movement of the building and regardless of minor variance between boundaries shown on the plan or in the deed and those of the building. *(Added by Stats.2013, c. 605 (S.B.752), § 21.)*

Law Revision Commission Comments

With respect to a commercial or industrial common interest development, Section 6604 continues Section 1371 without change.

For further information, see Section 6500 Comment.

See also Sections 6540 ("condominium plan"), 6542 ("condominium project").

For a similar provision in the Davis–Stirling Common Interest Development Act, see Section 4220. [42 Cal.L.Rev.Comm. Reports 1 (2012)].

§ 6606. Restrictive covenants; deletion from declaration or other governing document; recording or filing of amended document

(a) No declaration or other governing document shall include a restrictive covenant in violation of Section 12955 of the Government Code.

(b) Notwithstanding any other provision of law or provision of the governing documents, the board, without approval of the members, shall amend any declaration or other governing document that includes a restrictive covenant prohibited by this section to delete the restrictive covenant, and shall restate the declaration or other governing document without the restrictive covenant but with no other change to the declaration or governing document.

(c) If the declaration is amended under this section, the board shall record the restated declaration in each county in which the common interest development is located. If the articles of incorporation are amended under this section, the board shall file a certificate of amendment with the Secretary of State pursuant to Section 7814 of the Corporations Code.

(d) If after providing written notice to an association, pursuant to Section 6512, requesting that the association delete a restrictive covenant that violates subdivision (a), and the association fails to delete the restrictive covenant within 30 days of receiving the notice, the Department of Fair Employment and Housing, a city or county in which a common interest development is located, or any person may bring an action against the association for injunctive relief to enforce subdivision (a). The court may award attorney's fees to the prevailing party. *(Added by Stats.2013, c. 605 (S.B.752), § 21.)*

Law Revision Commission Comments

With respect to a commercial or industrial common interest development, Section 6606 continues Section 1352.5 without change, except as indicated below.

The following nonsubstantive changes are made:

● In subdivision (b), the words "board of directors of an association" are replaced with "board." See Section 6530 ("board").

● In subdivision (b), the word "owners" is replaced with "members." See Section 6554 ("member").

● Subdivision (c) is added.

● Subdivision (d) is revised to include a reference to the provision governing notice to an association (Section 6512).

For further information, see Section 6500 Comment.

See also Sections 6528 ("association"), 6530 ("board"), 6534 ("common interest development"), 6546 ("declaration"), 6552 ("governing documents"), 6560 ("person").

For a similar provision in the Davis–Stirling Common Interest Development Act, see Section 4225. [42 Cal.L.Rev.Comm. Reports 1 (2012)].

§ 6608. Amendment of governing documents to delete construction or marketing provisions after completion by developer; requirements

(a) Notwithstanding any provision of the governing documents to the contrary, the board may, after the developer has completed construction of the development, has terminated construction activities, and has terminated marketing activities for the sale, lease, or other disposition of separate interests within the development, adopt an amendment deleting from any of the governing documents any provision which is unequivocally designed and intended, or which by its nature can only have been designed or intended, to facilitate the developer in completing the construction or marketing of the development. However, provisions of the governing documents relative to a particular construction or marketing phase of the development may not be deleted under the authorization of this subdivision until that construction or marketing phase has been completed.

(b) The provisions which may be deleted by action of the board shall be limited to those which provide for access by the developer over or across the common area for the purposes of (1) completion of construction of the development, and (2) the erection, construction, or maintenance of structures or other facilities designed to facilitate the completion of construction or marketing of separate interests.

(c) At least 30 days prior to taking action pursuant to subdivision (a), the board shall deliver to all members, by individual delivery pursuant to Section 6514, (1) a copy of all amendments to the governing documents proposed to be adopted under subdivision (a), and (2) a notice of the time, date, and place the board will consider adoption of the amendments.

The board may consider adoption of amendments to the governing documents pursuant to subdivision (a) only at a meeting that is open to all members, who shall be given opportunity to make comments thereon. All deliberations of the board on any action proposed under subdivision (a) shall only be conducted in an open meeting.

(d) The board may not amend the governing documents pursuant to this section without the approval of a majority of a quorum of the members, pursuant to Section 6524. For the purposes of this section, "quorum" means more than 50 percent of the members who own no more than two separate interests in the development. *(Added by Stats.2013, c. 605 (S.B.752), § 21.)*

Law Revision Commission Comments

With respect to a commercial or industrial common interest development, Section 6608 continues Section 1355.5 without change, except as indicated below.

The following substantive change is made:

● Subdivision (c) is revised to provide for individual delivery of the specified notice. See Section 6514.

The following nonsubstantive changes are made:

● The words "his or her" are not continued in subdivision (a).

● The words "of a common interest development" are not continued in subdivision (a).

● The words "board of directors" and "board of directors of the association" are replaced throughout with "board." See Section 6530 ("board").

● Subdivision (b) are revised to use numerals to number the listed items, rather than letters.

• Subdivisions (c) and (d) are revised to use "member." See Section 6554 ("member").

• Subdivision (c) is revised to delete the unnecessary word "such."

• Subdivision (c) is revised to replace the word "which" with "that."

• Subdivision (d) is revised to use the standard term "approval of a majority of a quorum of the members." See Section 6524.

For further information, see Section 6500 Comment.

See also Sections 6530 ("board"), 6532 ("common area"), 6552 ("governing documents"), 6564 ("separate interest").

For a similar provision in the Davis–Stirling Common Interest Development Act, see Section 4230. [42 Cal.L.Rev.Comm. Reports 1 (2012)].

§ 6610. References to provisions of Davis–Stirling Common Interest Development Act; corrections

(a) Notwithstanding any other law or provision of the governing documents, if the governing documents include a reference to a provision of the Davis–Stirling Common Interest Development Act that was continued in a new provision by the act that added this section, the board may amend the governing documents, solely to correct the cross-reference, by adopting a board resolution that shows the correction. Member approval is not required in order to adopt a resolution pursuant to this section.

(b) A declaration that is corrected under this section may be restated in corrected form and recorded, provided that a copy of the board resolution authorizing the corrections is recorded along with the restated declaration. *(Added by Stats.2013, c. 605 (S.B.752), § 21.)*

Law Revision Commission Comments

Section 6610 is new. It is intended to provide a simplified method to correct statutory cross-references in an association's governing documents that are required as a result of the enactment of the act that added this section. No other amendment can be made under this section.

See also Sections 6530 ("board"), 6546 ("declaration"), 6552 ("governing documents").

For a similar provision in the Davis–Stirling Common Interest Development Act, see Section 4235. [42 Cal.L.Rev.Comm. Reports 1 (2012)].

ARTICLE 2. DECLARATION

Section
6614. Contents of declaration.
6616. Amendment of declaration; authorization.
6618. Extension of term of declaration.
6620. Amendment of declaration; procedure.

§ 6614. Contents of declaration

(a) A declaration, recorded on or after January 1, 1986, shall contain a legal description of the common interest development, and a statement that the common interest development is a condominium project, planned development, stock cooperative, or combination thereof. The declaration shall additionally set forth the name of the association and the restrictions on the use or enjoyment of any portion of the common interest development that are intended to be enforceable equitable servitudes.

(b) The declaration may contain any other matters the declarant or the members consider appropriate. *(Added by Stats.2013, c. 605 (S.B.752), § 21.)*

Law Revision Commission Comments

With respect to a commercial or industrial common interest development, subdivision (a) of Section 6614 continues the first two sentences of Section 1353(a)(1) without change, except as indicated below.

The following nonsubstantive change is made:

• A reference to a "community apartment project" is not continued.

With respect to a commercial or industrial common interest development, subdivision (b) continues Section 1353(b) without change, except as indicated below.

The following nonsubstantive changes are made:

• The word "owners" is replaced with "members." See Section 6554 ("member").

• The words "original signator of the declaration" are replaced with "declarant." See Section 6544 ("declarant").

For further information, see Section 6500 Comment.

See also Sections 6528 ("association"), 6534 ("common interest development"), 6542 ("condominium project"), 6546 ("declaration"), 6562 ("planned development"), 6566 ("stock cooperative").

For a similar provision in the Davis–Stirling Common Interest Development Act, see Section 4250. [42 Cal.L.Rev.Comm. Reports 1 (2012)].

§ 6616. Amendment of declaration; authorization

Except to the extent that a declaration provides by its express terms that it is not amendable, in whole or in part, a declaration that fails to include provisions permitting its amendment at all times during its existence may be amended at any time. *(Added by Stats.2013, c. 605 (S.B.752), § 21.)*

Law Revision Commission Comments

With respect to a commercial or industrial common interest development, Section 6616 continues the first sentence of Section 1355(b) without change, except as indicated below.

The following nonsubstantive change is made:

• The word "which" is replaced with "that."

For the procedure to amend a declaration, see Section 6620.

For further information, see Section 6500 Comment.

See also Section 6546 ("declaration").

For a similar provision in the Davis–Stirling Common Interest Development Act, see Section 4260. [42 Cal.L.Rev.Comm. Reports 1 (2012)].

§ 6618. Extension of term of declaration

(a) The Legislature finds that there are common interest developments that have been created with deed restrictions that do not provide a means for the members to extend the term of the declaration. The Legislature further finds that covenants and restrictions, contained in the declaration, are an appropriate method for protecting the common plan of developments and to provide for a mechanism for financial support for the upkeep of common area including, but not limited to, roofs, roads, heating systems, and recreational facilities. If declarations terminate prematurely, common interest developments may deteriorate and the supply of affordable units could be impacted adversely. The Legislature further finds and declares that it is in the public interest to provide a vehicle for extending the term of the declaration if the extension is approved by a majority of all members, pursuant to Section 6522.

(b) A declaration that specifies a termination date, but that contains no provision for extension of the termination date, may be extended, before its termination date, by the approval of members pursuant to Section 6620.

(c) No single extension of the terms of the declaration made pursuant to this section shall exceed the initial term of the declaration or 20 years, whichever is less. However, more than one extension may occur pursuant to this section. *(Added by Stats.2013, c. 605 (S.B.752), § 21.)*

Law Revision Commission Comments

With respect to a commercial or industrial common interest development, subdivision (a) of Section 6618 continues Section 1357(a) without change, except as indicated below.

The following nonsubstantive changes are made:

• The defined term "member" is used. See Section 6554 ("member").

• The phrase "common areas" is singularized.

• The word "which" is replaced with "that."

• A reference to approval by "members having more than 50 percent of the votes in the association" is replaced with standard terminology.

• A reference to "housing" is deleted.

• A comma is added after the word "restrictions" in the second sentence.

With respect to a commercial or industrial common interest development, subdivision (b) continues part of the substance of Section 1357(b), authorizing extension of the termination date of a declaration that does not provide for extension of the termination date, except as indicated below.

The following nonsubstantive change is made:

• Language is added to make clear that the extension must occur before the termination date.

The procedure for extension of the termination date provided in Section 1357(b)-(c) is not continued. An extension would instead be made pursuant to the general procedure for amendment of a declaration. See Section 6620.

With respect to a commercial or industrial common interest development, subdivision (c) continues Section 1357(d) without change.

For further information, see Section 6500 Comment.

See also Sections 6532 ("common area"), 6534 ("common interest development"), 6546 ("declaration").

For a similar provision in the Davis–Stirling Common Interest Development Act, see Section 4265. [42 Cal.L.Rev.Comm. Reports 1 (2012)].

§ 6620. Amendment of declaration; procedure

(a) A declaration may be amended pursuant to the declaration or this act. An amendment is effective after all of the following requirements have been met:

(1) The proposed amendment has been delivered by individual notice to all members not less than 15 days and not more than 60 days prior to any approval being solicited.

(2) The amendment has been approved by the percentage of members required by the declaration and any other person whose approval is required by the declaration.

(3) That fact has been certified in a writing executed and acknowledged by the officer designated in the declaration or by the association for that purpose, or if no one is designated, by the president of the association.

(4) The amendment has been recorded in each county in which a portion of the common interest development is located.

(b) If the declaration does not specify the percentage of members who must approve an amendment of the declaration, an amendment may be approved by a majority of all members, pursuant to Section 6522. *(Added by Stats.2013, c. 605 (S.B.752), § 21.)*

Law Revision Commission Comments

With respect to a commercial or industrial common interest development, subdivision (a) of Section 6620 continues Section 1355(a) without change, except as indicated below.

The following substantive changes are made:

• A notice requirement drawn from Section 1355(b) is added.

• The term "governing documents" is replaced with the term "declaration." See Section 6546 ("declaration").

• Paragraph (a)(2) is revised to recognize that a declaration may require that an amendment be approved by a non-member.

The following nonsubstantive changes are made:

• The first word is replaced with "A."

• The word "title" is replaced with "act."

• A reference to a statutory exception that is not continued in this act is deleted.

• The defined term "member" is used. See Section 6554 ("member").

• The subdivision is divided into paragraphs, with conforming technical adjustments to the language.

Subdivision (b) generalizes a rule stated in Sections 1355(b) and 1357.

For further information, see Section 6500 Comment.

See also Sections 6528 ("association"), 6534 ("common interest development"), 6553 ("individual notice"), 6560 ("person").

For a similar provision in the Davis–Stirling Common Interest Development Act, see Section 4270. [42 Cal.L.Rev.Comm. Reports 1 (2012)].

ARTICLE 3. ARTICLES OF INCORPORATION

Section

6622. Association articles of incorporation; required statements.

§ 6622. Association articles of incorporation; required statements

(a) The articles of incorporation of an association filed with the Secretary of State shall include a statement, which shall be in addition to the statement of purposes of the corporation, that does all of the following:

(1) Identifies the corporation as an association formed to manage a common interest development under the Commercial and Industrial Common Interest Development Act.

(2) States the business or corporate office of the association, if any, and, if the office is not on the site of the common interest development, states the front street and nearest cross street for the physical location of the common interest development.

(3) States the name and address of the association's managing agent, if any.

(b) The statement filed by an incorporated association with the Secretary of State pursuant to Section 8210 of the Corporations Code shall also contain a statement identifying the corporation as an association formed to manage a common interest development under the Commercial and Industrial Common Interest Development Act.

(c) Documents filed prior to January 1, 2014, in compliance with former Section 1363.5, as it read on January 1, 2013, are deemed to be in compliance with this section. *(Added by Stats.2013, c. 605 (S.B.752), § 21.)*

Law Revision Commission Comments

With respect to a commercial or industrial common interest development, Section 6622 continues Section 1363.5 without change, except as indicated below.

The following substantive changes are made:

• A cross-reference to the definition of "managing agent" is not continued.

• A reference to this act is substituted for a reference to the Davis Stirling Common Interest Development Act.

The following nonsubstantive changes are made:

• References to "common interest development association" have been standardized.

• Subdivision (c) is added to make clear that the section does not invalidate documents that were filed in compliance with former law.

Nothing in paragraph (a)(3) precludes an owner of a separate interest from serving as the association's managing agent.

See also Corp. Code §§ 1502 (annual statement), 7130-7135 (content of articles of incorporation), 7810-7820 (amendment of articles of incorporation), 7150-7153 (content and amendment of bylaws).

See also Sections 6528 ("association"), 6534 ("common interest development").

For a similar provision in the Davis–Stirling Common Interest Development Act, see Section 4280. [43 Cal.L.Rev.Comm. Reports ___ (Appendix 5) (2013)].

ARTICLE 4. CONDOMINIUM PLAN

Section

6624. Contents of condominium plan.

6626. Certificate consenting to recordation of condominium plan; signatures and acknowledgements.

6628. Amendment or revocation of condominium plan.

§ 6624. Contents of condominium plan

A condominium plan shall contain all of the following:

(a) A description or survey map of a condominium project, which shall refer to or show monumentation on the ground.

(b) A three-dimensional description of a condominium project, one or more dimensions of which may extend for an indefinite distance upwards or downwards, in sufficient detail to identify the common area and each separate interest.

(c) A certificate consenting to the recordation of the condominium plan pursuant to this act that is signed and acknowledged as provided in Section 6626. *(Added by Stats.2013, c. 605 (S.B.752), § 21.)*

Law Revision Commission Comments

With respect to a commercial or industrial common interest development, Section 6624 continues Section 1351(e)(1)-(2) and a part of Section 1351(e)(3) without change, except as indicated below.

The following nonsubstantive changes are made:

● The enumerated items are set out as subdivisions.

● The word "title" is replaced with "act."

● The list of persons who must sign and acknowledge the certificate consenting to recordation of the condominium plan is replaced with a reference to the section governing the creation and recordation of a condominium plan.

For further information, see Section 6500 Comment.

See also Sections 6532 ("common area"), 6542 ("condominium project"), 6564 ("separate interest").

For a similar provision in the Davis–Stirling Common Interest Development Act, see Section 4285. [42 Cal.L.Rev.Comm. Reports 1 (2012)].

§ 6626. Certificate consenting to recordation of condominium plan; signatures and acknowledgements

(a) The certificate consenting to the recordation of a condominium plan that is required by subdivision (c) of Section 6624 shall be signed and acknowledged by all of the following persons:

(1) The record owner of fee title to that property included in the condominium project.

(2) In the case of a condominium project that will terminate upon the termination of an estate for years, by all lessors and lessees of the estate for years.

(3) In the case of a condominium project subject to a life estate, by all life tenants and remainder interests.

(4) The trustee or the beneficiary of each recorded deed of trust, and the mortgagee of each recorded mortgage encumbering the property.

(b) Owners of mineral rights, easements, rights-of-way, and other nonpossessory interests do not need to sign the certificate.

(c) In the event a conversion to condominiums of a stock cooperative has been approved by the required number of owners, trustees, beneficiaries, and mortgagees pursuant to Section 66452.10 of the Government Code, the certificate need only be signed by those owners, trustees, beneficiaries, and mortgagees approving the conversion. *(Added by Stats.2013, c. 605 (S.B.752), § 21.)*

Law Revision Commission Comments

With respect to a commercial or industrial common interest development, Section 6626 continues the substance of Section 1351(e)(3), except as indicated below.

The following nonsubstantive changes are made:

● A reference to a conversion of a community apartment project is not continued.

● The last paragraph of Section 1351(e) is not continued in this section.

● A cross-reference to Section 6624(c) is added to the first paragraph.

● Subdivision (b) is revised to make clear that it states an exception to who must sign the certificate of consent to recordation, rather than the condominium plan itself.

For further information, see Section 6500 Comment.

See also Sections 6540 ("condominium plan"), 6542 ("condominium project"), 6560 ("person"), 6566 ("stock cooperative").

For a similar provision in the Davis–Stirling Common Interest Development Act, see Section 4290. [42 Cal.L.Rev.Comm. Reports 1 (2012)].

§ 6628. Amendment or revocation of condominium plan

A condominium plan may be amended or revoked by a recorded instrument that is acknowledged and signed by all the persons who, at the time of amendment or revocation, are persons whose signatures are required under Section 6626. *(Added by Stats.2013, c. 605 (S.B.752), § 21.)*

Law Revision Commission Comments

With respect to a commercial or industrial common interest development, Section 6628 continues the last paragraph of Section 1351(e) without change, except as indicated below.

The following nonsubstantive change is made:

● Language is added to make clear that the persons whose signatures are required for amendment or revocation of a condominium plan are the persons who fall within the groups described in Section 6626 at the time of amendment or revocation.

For further information, see Section 6500 Comment.

See also Sections 6540 ("condominium plan"), 6560 ("person").

For a similar provision in the Davis–Stirling Common Interest Development Act, see Section 4295. [42 Cal.L.Rev.Comm. Reports 1 (2012)].

ARTICLE 5. OPERATING RULES

Section
6630. "Operating rule" defined.
6632. Requirements for validity and enforceability.

§ 6630. "Operating rule" defined

For the purposes of this article, "operating rule" means a regulation adopted by the board that applies generally to the management and operation of the common interest development or the conduct of the business and affairs of the association. *(Added by Stats.2013, c. 605 (S.B.752), § 21.)*

Law Revision Commission Comments

With respect to a commercial or industrial common interest development, Section 6630 continues Section 1357.100(a) without change.

See also Sections 6528 ("association"), 6534 ("common interest development").

For a similar provision in the Davis–Stirling Common Interest Development Act, see Section 4340. [42 Cal.L.Rev.Comm. Reports 1 (2012)].

§ 6632. Requirements for validity and enforceability

An operating rule is valid and enforceable only if all of the following requirements are satisfied:

(a) The rule is in writing.

(b) The rule is within the authority of the board conferred by law or by the declaration, articles of incorporation or association, or bylaws of the association.

(c) The rule is not in conflict with governing law and the declaration, articles of incorporation or association, or bylaws of the association.

(d) The rule is reasonable, and is adopted, amended, or repealed in good faith. *(Added by Stats.2013, c. 605 (S.B.752), § 21.)*

Law Revision Commission Comments

With respect to a commercial or industrial common interest development, Section 6632 continues Section 1357.110(a)-(c), the first part of (d), and (e), without change, except as indicated below.

The following nonsubstantive changes are made:

● The words "board of directors of the association" are replaced with "board." See Section 6530 ("board").

• Terminology used in subdivision (c) is conformed to that used in Section 6600.

See also Sections 6528 ("association"), 6546 ("declaration"), 6630 ("operating rule").

For a similar provision in the Davis–Stirling Common Interest Development Act, see Section 4350. [43 Cal.L.Rev.Comm. Reports ___ (Appendix 5) (2013)].

CHAPTER 4. OWNERSHIP AND TRANSFER OF INTERESTS

ARTICLE 1. OWNERSHIP RIGHTS AND INTERESTS

§ 6650. Ownership of common areas

Unless the declaration otherwise provides, in a condominium project, or in a planned development in which the common area is owned by the owners of the separate interests, the common area is owned as tenants in common, in equal shares, one for each separate interest. *(Added by Stats.2013, c. 605 (S.B.752), § 21.)*

Law Revision Commission Comments

With respect to a commercial or industrial common interest development, Section 6650 continues Section 1362 without change, except as indicated below.

The following nonsubstantive changes are made:

• The phrase "common areas" is singularized.

• The words "unit or lot" are replaced with "separate interest."

For further information, see Section 6500 Comment.

See also Sections 6532 ("common area"), 6542 ("condominium project"), 6546 ("declaration"), 6562 ("planned development"), 6564 ("separate interest").

For a similar provision in the Davis–Stirling Common Interest Development Act, see Section 4500. [42 Cal.L.Rev.Comm. Reports 1 (2012)].

§ 6652. Rights and easements of ingress, egress, and support

Unless the declaration otherwise provides:

(a) In a condominium project, and in those planned developments with common area owned in common by the owners of the separate interests, there are appurtenant to each separate interest nonexclusive rights of ingress, egress, and support, if necessary, through the common area. The common area is subject to these rights.

(b) In a stock cooperative, and in a planned development with common area owned by the association, there is an easement for ingress, egress, and support, if necessary, appurtenant to each separate interest. The common area is subject to these easements. *(Added by Stats.2013, c. 605 (S.B.752), § 21.)*

Law Revision Commission Comments

With respect to a commercial or industrial common interest development, Section 6652 continues Section 1361 without change, except as indicated below.

The following nonsubstantive changes are made:

• A reference to a "community apartment project" is not continued.

• The phrase "common areas" is singularized.

For further information, see Section 6500 Comment.

See also Sections 6528 ("association"), 6532 ("common area"), 6542 ("condominium project"), 6546 ("declaration"), 6562 ("planned development"), 6564 ("separate interest"), 6566 ("stock cooperative").

For a similar provision in the Davis–Stirling Common Interest Development Act, see Section 4505. [42 Cal.L.Rev.Comm. Reports 1 (2012)].

§ 6654. Physical access to owner or occupant's separate interest

Except as otherwise provided in law, an order of the court, or an order pursuant to a final and binding arbitration decision, an association may not deny a member or occupant physical access to the member's or occupant's separate interest, either by restricting access through the common area to the separate interest, or by restricting access solely to the separate interest. *(Added by Stats.2013, c. 605 (S.B.752), § 21.)*

Law Revision Commission Comments

With respect to a commercial or industrial common interest development, Section 6654 continues Section 1361.5 without change, except as indicated below.

The following nonsubstantive changes are made:

• The words "his or her" are replaced with "the member's or occupant's."

• References to the "owner's" separate interest are revised to omit the word "owner's." This will help to avoid any implication that the reference does not also apply to an "occupant" of a separate interest.

• The word "owner" is replaced with "member" throughout. See Section 6554 ("member").

• The phrase "common areas" is singularized.

For further information, see Section 6500 Comment.

See also Sections 6528 ("association"), 6532 ("common area"), 6564 ("separate interest").

For a similar provision in the Davis–Stirling Common Interest Development Act, see Section 4510. [42 Cal.L.Rev.Comm. Reports 1 (2012)].

ARTICLE 2. RESTRICTIONS ON TRANSFERS

§ 6656. Restrictions on partition

(a) Except as provided in this section, the common area in a condominium project shall remain undivided, and there shall be no judicial partition thereof. Nothing in this section shall be deemed to prohibit partition of a cotenancy in a condominium.

(b) The owner of a separate interest in a condominium project may maintain a partition action as to the entire project as if the owners of all of the separate interests in the project were tenants in common in the entire project in the same proportion as their interests in the common area. The court shall order partition under this subdivision only by sale of the entire condominium project and only upon a showing of one of the following:

(1) More than three years before the filing of the action, the condominium project was damaged or destroyed, so that a material part was rendered unfit for its prior use, and the condominium project has not been rebuilt or repaired substantially to its state prior to the damage or destruction.

(2) Three-fourths or more of the project is destroyed or substantially damaged and owners of separate interests holding in the aggregate more than a 50–percent interest in the common area oppose repair or restoration of the project.

(3) The project has been in existence more than 50 years, is obsolete and uneconomic, and owners of separate interests holding in the aggregate more than a 50–percent interest in the common area oppose repair or restoration of the project.

(4) Any conditions in the declaration for sale under the circumstances described in this subdivision have been met. *(Added by Stats.2013, c. 605 (S.B.752), § 21.)*

Law Revision Commission Comments

With respect to a commercial or industrial common interest development, Section 6656 continues Section 1359 without change, except as indicated below.

The following nonsubstantive changes are made:

• The phrase "common areas" is singularized.

• Subdivision (b)(4) is rephrased to avoid use of "such."

For further information, see Section 6500 Comment.

See also Sections 6532 ("common area"), 6542 ("condominium project"), 6546 ("declaration"), 6564 ("separate interest").

For a similar provision in the Davis–Stirling Common Interest Development Act, see Section 4610. [42 Cal.L.Rev.Comm. Reports 1 (2012)].

§ 6658. Liens for labor and materials

(a) In a condominium project, no labor performed or services or materials furnished with the consent of, or at the request of, an owner in the condominium project or the owners' agent or contractor shall be the basis for the filing of a lien against any other property of any other owner in the condominium project unless that other owner has expressly consented to or requested the performance of the labor or furnishing of the materials or services. However, express consent shall be deemed to have been given by the owner of any condominium in the case of emergency repairs thereto.

(b) Labor performed or services or materials furnished for the common area, if duly authorized by the association, shall be deemed to be performed or furnished with the express consent of each condominium owner.

(c) The owner of any condominium may remove that owner's condominium from a lien against two or more condominiums or any part thereof by payment to the holder of the lien of the fraction of the total sum secured by the lien that is attributable to the owner's condominium. *(Added by Stats.2013, c. 605 (S.B. 752), § 21.)*

Law Revision Commission Comments

With respect to a commercial or industrial common interest development, Section 6658 continues Section 1369 without change, except as indicated below.

The following nonsubstantive changes are made:

• The section is divided into subdivisions for ease of reference.

• The words "his or her" are replaced with "owner" throughout.

• The phrase "common areas" is singularized.

• The word "which" is replaced with "that" in subdivision (c).

For further information, see Section 6500 Comment.

See also Sections 6528 ("association"), 6532 ("common area"), 6542 ("condominium project").

For a similar provision in the Davis–Stirling Common Interest Development Act, see Section 4615. [42 Cal.L.Rev.Comm. Reports 1 (2012)].

ARTICLE 3. TRANSFER OF SEPARATE INTEREST

Section

§ 6662. Condominium project; interests included in conveyance, judicial sale or transfer of separate interests

In a condominium project the common area is not subject to partition, except as provided in Section 6656. Any conveyance, judicial sale, or other voluntary or involuntary transfer of the separate interest includes the undivided interest in the common area. Any conveyance, judicial sale, or other voluntary or involuntary transfer of the owner's entire estate also includes the owner's membership interest in the association. *(Added by Stats.2013, c. 605 (S.B.752), § 21.)*

Law Revision Commission Comments

With respect to a commercial or industrial common interest development, Section 6662 continues Section 1358(b) without change, except as indicated below.

The following nonsubstantive changes are made:

• A cross-reference is updated to reflect the new location of the referenced provision.

• The phrase "common areas" is singularized.

For further information, see Section 6500 Comment.

See also Sections 6528 ("association"), 6532 ("common area"), 6542 ("condominium project"), 6564 ("separate interest").

For a similar provision in the Davis–Stirling Common Interest Development Act, see Section 4630. [42 Cal.L.Rev.Comm. Reports 1 (2012)].

§ 6664. Planned development; interests included in conveyance, judicial sale or transfer of separate interests

In a planned development, any conveyance, judicial sale, or other voluntary or involuntary transfer of the separate interest includes the undivided interest in the common area, if any exists. Any conveyance, judicial sale, or other voluntary or involuntary transfer of the owner's entire estate also includes the owner's membership interest in the association. *(Added by Stats.2013, c. 605 (S.B.752), § 21.)*

Law Revision Commission Comments

With respect to a commercial or industrial common interest development, Section 6664 continues Section 1358(c) without change, except as indicated below.

The following nonsubstantive change is made:

• The phrase "common areas" is singularized.

For further information, see Section 6500 Comment.

See also Sections 6528 ("association"), 6532 ("common area"), 6562 ("planned development"), 6564 ("separate interest").

For a similar provision in the Davis–Stirling Common Interest Development Act, see Section 4635. [42 Cal.L.Rev.Comm. Reports 1 (2012)].

§ 6666. Stock cooperative; interests included in conveyance, judicial sale or transfer of separate interests

In a stock cooperative, any conveyance, judicial sale, or other voluntary or involuntary transfer of the separate interest includes the ownership interest in the corporation, however evidenced. Any conveyance, judicial sale, or other voluntary or involuntary transfer of the owner's entire estate also includes the owner's membership interest in the association. *(Added by Stats.2013, c. 605 (S.B.752), § 21.)*

Law Revision Commission Comments

With respect to a commercial or industrial common interest development, Section 6666 continues Section 1358(d) without change.

For further information, see Section 6500 Comment.

See also Sections 6528 ("association"), 6564 ("separate interest"), 6566 ("stock cooperative").

For a similar provision in the Davis–Stirling Common Interest Development Act, see Section 4640. [42 Cal.L.Rev.Comm. Reports 1 (2012)].

§ 6668. Transfer of exclusive use areas

Nothing in this article prohibits the transfer of exclusive use areas, independent of any other interest in a common interest subdivision, if authorization to separately transfer exclusive use areas is expressly stated in the declaration and the transfer occurs in accordance with the terms of the declaration. *(Added by Stats.2013, c. 605 (S.B.752), § 21.)*

Law Revision Commission Comments

With respect to a commercial or industrial common interest development, Section 6668 continues the next to last paragraph of Section 1358 without change, except as indicated below.

The following nonsubstantive change is made:
- "Section" is replaced with "article."

For further information, see Section 6500 Comment.

See also Section 6546 ("declaration").

For a similar provision in the Davis–Stirling Common Interest Development Act, see Section 4645. [42 Cal.L.Rev.Comm. Reports 1 (2012)].

§ 6670. Restrictions upon severability of component interests

Any restrictions upon the severability of the component interests in real property which are contained in the declaration shall not be deemed conditions repugnant to the interest created within the meaning of Section 711. However, these restrictions shall not extend beyond the period in which the right to partition a project is suspended under Section 6656. *(Added by Stats. 2013, c. 605 (S.B.752), § 21.)*

Law Revision Commission Comments

With respect to a commercial or industrial common interest development, Section 6670 continues the last paragraph of Section 1358 without change, except as indicated below.

The following nonsubstantive changes are made:
- A superfluous reference to the "Civil Code" is not continued.
- The cross-reference is updated to reflect the new location of the referenced provision.

For further information, see Section 6500 Comment.

See also Section 6546 ("declaration").

For a similar provision in the Davis–Stirling Common Interest Development Act, see Section 4650. [42 Cal.L.Rev.Comm. Reports 1 (2012)].

CHAPTER 5. PROPERTY USE AND MAINTENANCE

ARTICLE 1. PROTECTED USES

§ 6700. Scope of article; related provisions

This article includes provisions that limit the authority of an association or the governing documents to regulate the use of a member's separate interest. Nothing in this article is intended to affect the application of any other provision that limits the authority of an association to regulate the use of a member's separate interest, including, but not limited to, the following provisions:

(a) Sections 712 and 713, relating to the display of signs.

(b) Sections 714 and 714.1, relating to solar energy systems.

(c) Section 714.5, relating to structures that are constructed offsite and moved to the property in sections or modules.

(d) Sections 782, 782.5, and 6150 of this code and Section 12956.1 of the Government Code, relating to racial restrictions. *(Added by Stats.2013, c. 605 (S.B.752), § 21.)*

Law Revision Commission Comments

Section 6700 is new. It provides a non-exclusive list of provisions outside of this act that limit the authority of an association to regulate separate interest property use.

See also Sections 6528 ("association"), 6552 ("governing documents"), 6554 ("member"), 6564 ("separate interest").

For a similar provision in the Davis–Stirling Common Interest Development Act, see Section 4700. [42 Cal.L.Rev.Comm. Reports 1 (2012)].

§ 6702. Display of United States flag by owner on or in owner's separate interest or within exclusive use common area

(a) Except as required for the protection of the public health or safety, no governing document shall limit or prohibit, or be construed to limit or prohibit, the display of the flag of the United States by a member on or in the member's separate interest or within the member's exclusive use common area.

(b) For purposes of this section, "display of the flag of the United States" means a flag of the United States made of fabric, cloth, or paper displayed from a staff or pole or in a window, and does not mean a depiction or emblem of the flag of the United States made of lights, paint, roofing, siding, paving materials, flora, or balloons, or any other similar building, landscaping, or decorative component.

(c) In any action to enforce this section, the prevailing party shall be awarded reasonable attorney's fees and costs. *(Added by Stats.2013, c. 605 (S.B.752), § 21.)*

Law Revision Commission Comments

With respect to a commercial or industrial common interest development, Section 6702 continues Section 1353.5 without change, except as indicated below.

The following nonsubstantive changes are made:
- A superfluous cross-reference to governing definitions is not continued.
- A superfluous reference to a declaration is not continued.
- The word "owner" is replaced with "member." See Section 6554 ("member").

For further information, see Section 6500 Comment.

See also Sections 6532 ("common area"), 6546 ("declaration"), 6550 ("exclusive use common area"), 6552 ("governing documents"), 6564 ("separate interest").

For a similar provision in the Davis–Stirling Common Interest Development Act, see Section 4705. [42 Cal.L.Rev.Comm. Reports 1 (2012)].

§ 6704. Prohibition of posting or displaying noncommercial signs, posters, flags, or banners; permitted placement; exceptions

(a) The governing documents may not prohibit posting or displaying of noncommercial signs, posters, flags, or banners on or in a member's separate interest, except as required for the protection of public health or safety or if the posting or display would violate a local, state, or federal law.

(b) For purposes of this section, a noncommercial sign, poster, flag, or banner may be made of paper, cardboard, cloth, plastic, or fabric, and may be posted or displayed from the yard, window, door, balcony, or outside wall of the separate interest, but may not be made of lights, roofing, siding, paving materials, flora, or balloons, or any other similar building, landscaping, or decorative component, or include the painting of architectural surfaces.

(c) An association may prohibit noncommercial signs and posters that are more than nine square feet in size and noncommercial flags or banners that are more than 15 square feet in size. *(Added by Stats.2013, c. 605 (S.B.752), § 21.)*

Law Revision Commission Comments

With respect to a commercial or industrial common interest development, Section 6704 continues Section 1353.6 without change, except as indicated below.

The following nonsubstantive changes are made:

• The words "including the operating rules" are not continued.

• The word "owner" is replaced with "member." See Section 6554 ("member").

• In subdivision (c), the numeral "9" is replaced with "nine" for stylistic reasons.

For further information, see Section 6500 Comment.

See also Sections 6528 ("association"), 6552 ("governing documents"), 6564 ("separate interest").

For a similar provision in the Davis–Stirling Common Interest Development Act, see Section 4710. [42 Cal.L.Rev.Comm. Reports 1 (2012)].

§ 6706. Pets within common interest developments

Notwithstanding Section 4202, Section 4715 applies to an owner of a separate interest in a common interest development who kept a pet in that common interest development before January 1, 2014. *(Added by Stats.2013, c. 605 (S.B.752), § 21.)*

Law Revision Commission Comments

Section 6706 is new. It provides that Section 4715 governs an owner who kept a pet in a commercial or industrial common interest development prior to January 1, 2014.

See also Sections 6534 ("common interest development"), 6564 ("separate interest"). [43 Cal.L.Rev.Comm. Reports ___ (Appendix 5) (2013)].

§ 6708. Restrictions on installation or use of video or television antenna; enforceability based on size; reasonable restrictions; application approval; attorney's fees

(a) Any covenant, condition, or restriction contained in any deed, contract, security instrument, or other instrument affecting the transfer or sale of, or any interest in, a common interest development that effectively prohibits or restricts the installation or use of a video or television antenna, including a satellite dish, or that effectively prohibits or restricts the attachment of that antenna to a structure within that development where the antenna is not visible from any street or common area, except as otherwise prohibited or restricted by law, is void and unenforceable as to its application to the installation or use of a video or television antenna that has a diameter or diagonal measurement of 36 inches or less.

(b) This section shall not apply to any covenant, condition, or restriction, as described in subdivision (a), that imposes reasonable restrictions on the installation or use of a video or television antenna, including a satellite dish, that has a diameter or diagonal measurement of 36 inches or less. For purposes of this section, "reasonable restrictions" means those restrictions that do not significantly increase the cost of the video or television antenna system, including all related equipment, or significantly decrease its efficiency or performance and include all of the following:

(1) Requirements for application and notice to the association prior to the installation.

(2) Requirement of a member to obtain the approval of the association for the installation of a video or television antenna that has a diameter or diagonal measurement of 36 inches or less on a separate interest owned by another.

(3) Provision for the maintenance, repair, or replacement of roofs or other building components.

(4) Requirements for installers of a video or television antenna to indemnify or reimburse the association or its members for loss or damage caused by the installation, maintenance, or use of a video or television antenna that has a diameter or diagonal measurement of 36 inches or less.

(c) Whenever approval is required for the installation or use of a video or television antenna, including a satellite dish, the application for approval shall be processed by the appropriate approving entity for the common interest development in the same manner as an application for approval of an architectural modification to the property, and the issuance of a decision on the application shall not be willfully delayed.

(d) In any action to enforce compliance with this section, the prevailing party shall be awarded reasonable attorney's fees. *(Added by Stats.2013, c. 605 (S.B.752), § 21.)*

Law Revision Commission Comments

With respect to a commercial or industrial common interest development, Section 6708 continues Section 1376 without change, except as indicated below.

The following nonsubstantive change is made:

• The word "owner" is replaced with "member." See Section 6554 ("member").

For further information, see Section 6500 Comment.

See also 47 C.F.R. § 1.4000.

See also Sections 6528 ("association"), 6532 ("common area"), 6534 ("common interest development"), 6564 ("separate interest").

For a similar provision in the Davis–Stirling Common Interest Development Act, see Section 4725. [42 Cal.L.Rev.Comm. Reports 1 (2012)].

§ 6710. Prohibition against association rule or regulation that arbitrarily or unreasonably restricts owner's ability to market his or her interest in common development; other enumerated restrictions

(a) Any provision of a governing document that arbitrarily or unreasonably restricts an owner's ability to market the owner's interest in a common interest development is void.

(b) No association may adopt, enforce, or otherwise impose any governing document that does either of the following:

(1) Imposes an assessment or fee in connection with the marketing of an owner's interest in an amount that exceeds the association's actual or direct costs.

(2) Establishes an exclusive relationship with a real estate broker through which the sale or marketing of interests in the development is required to occur. The limitation set forth in this paragraph does not apply to the sale or marketing of separate interests owned by the association or to the sale or marketing of common area by the association.

(c) For purposes of this section, "market" and "marketing" mean listing, advertising, or obtaining or providing access to show the owner's interest in the development.

(d) This section does not apply to rules or regulations made pursuant to Section 712 or 713 regarding real estate signs. *(Added by Stats.2013, c. 605 (S.B.752), § 21.)*

With respect to a commercial or industrial common interest development, Section 6710 continues Section 1368.1 without change, except as indicated below.

The following substantive changes are made:

• The introductory clause is revised to make clear that a void provision does not void the entire governing document that contains it.

• The words "rule or regulation" are replaced with "governing document." See Section 6552 ("governing documents"). This broadens the application of the section so that it governs any provision in the governing documents and not just an operating rule.

The following nonsubstantive changes are made:

• The words "his or her" are replaced with "the owner's" in subdivision (a).

• The phrase "common areas" is singularized.

• The words "of an association" are not continued.

• A reference to a statutory limitation set forth in Section 1366.1, a provision that is not continued in this act, is deleted.

For further information, see Section 6500 Comment.

See also Sections 6528 ("association"), 6532 ("common area"), 6534 ("common interest development"), 6552 ("governing documents"), 6564 ("separate interest").

For a similar provision in the Davis–Stirling Common Interest Development Act, see Section 4730. [42 Cal.L.Rev.Comm. Reports 1 (2012)].

§ 6712. Governing documents; void and unenforceable provisions

(a) Notwithstanding any other law, a provision of the governing documents shall be void and unenforceable if it does any of the following:

(1) Prohibits, or includes conditions that have the effect of prohibiting, the use of low water-using plants as a group.

(2) Has the effect of prohibiting or restricting compliance with either of the following:

(A) A water-efficient landscape ordinance adopted or in effect pursuant to subdivision (c) of Section 65595 of the Government Code.

(B) Any regulation or restriction on the use of water adopted pursuant to Section 353 or 375 of the Water Code.

(b) This section shall not prohibit an association from applying landscaping rules established in the governing documents, to the extent the rules fully conform with the requirements of subdivision (a). *(Added by Stats.2013, c. 605 (S.B.752), § 21.)*

With respect to a commercial or industrial common interest development, Section 6712 continues Section 1353.8 without change, except as indicated below.

The following nonsubstantive change is made:

• Surplus language is not continued (i.e., the phrases "of any," "of a common interest development," and "and regulations"). The term "governing documents" includes all governing documents of a common interest development. See Section 6552 ("governing documents").

For further information, see Section 6500 Comment.

See also Sections 6528 ("association"), 6552 ("governing documents").

For a similar provision in the Davis–Stirling Common Interest Development Act, see Section 4735. [42 Cal.L.Rev.Comm. Reports 1 (2012)].

§ 6713. Restrictions on electric vehicle charging stations

(a) Any covenant, restriction, or condition contained in any deed, contract, security instrument, or other instrument affecting the transfer or sale of any interest in a common interest development, and any provision of a governing document, as defined in Section 6552, that either effectively prohibits or unreasonably restricts the installation or use of an electric vehicle charging station in an owner's designated parking space, including, but not limited to, a deeded parking space, a parking space in an owner's exclusive use common area, or a parking space that is specifically designated for use by a particular owner, or is in conflict with the provisions of this section is void and unenforceable.

(b)(1) This section does not apply to provisions that impose reasonable restrictions on electric vehicle charging stations. However, it is the policy of the state to promote, encourage, and remove obstacles to the use of electric vehicle charging stations.

(2) For purposes of this section, "reasonable restrictions" are restrictions that do not significantly increase the cost of the station or significantly decrease its efficiency or specified performance.

(c) An electric vehicle charging station shall meet applicable health and safety standards and requirements imposed by state and local authorities, and all other applicable zoning, land use or other ordinances, or land use permits.

(d) For purposes of this section, "electric vehicle charging station" means a station that is designed in compliance with the California Building Standards Code and delivers electricity from a source outside an electric vehicle into one or more electric vehicles. An electric vehicle charging station may include several charge points simultaneously connecting several electric vehicles to the station and any related equipment needed to facilitate charging plug-in electric vehicles.

(e) If approval is required for the installation or use of an electric vehicle charging station, the application for approval shall be processed and approved by the association in the same manner as an application for approval of an architectural modification to the property, and shall not be willfully avoided or delayed. The approval or denial of an application shall be in writing. If an application is not denied in writing within 60 days from the date of receipt of the application, the application shall be deemed approved, unless that delay is the result of a reasonable request for additional information.

(f) If the electric vehicle charging station is to be placed in a common area or an exclusive use common area, as designated in the common interest development's declaration, the following provisions apply:

(1) The owner first shall obtain approval from the association to install the electric vehicle charging station and the association shall approve the installation if the owner agrees in writing to do all of the following:

(A) Comply with the association's architectural standards for the installation of the charging station.

(B) Engage a licensed contractor to install the charging station.

(C) Within 14 days of approval, provide a certificate of insurance that names the association as an additional insured under the owner's insurance policy in the amount set forth in paragraph (3).

(D) Pay for the electricity usage associated with the charging station.

(2) The owner and each successive owner of the charging station shall be responsible for all of the following:

(A) Costs for damage to the charging station, common area, exclusive use common area, or separate interests resulting from the installation, maintenance, repair, removal, or replacement of the charging station.

(B) Costs for the maintenance, repair, and replacement of the charging station until it has been removed and for the restoration of the common area after removal.

(C) The cost of electricity associated with the charging station.

(D) Disclosing to prospective buyers the existence of any charging station of the owner and the related responsibilities of the owner under this section.

(3) The owner and each successive owner of the charging station, at all times, shall maintain a liability coverage policy in the amount of one million dollars ($1,000,000), and shall name the association as a named additional insured under the policy with a right to notice of cancellation.

(4) An owner shall not be required to maintain a liability coverage policy for an existing National Electrical Manufacturers Association standard alternating current power plug.

(g) Except as provided in subdivision (h), installation of an electric vehicle charging station for the exclusive use of an owner in a common area, that is not an exclusive use common area, shall be authorized by the association only if installation in the owner's designated parking space is impossible or unreasonably expensive. In such cases, the association shall enter into a license agreement with the owner for the use of the space in a common area, and the owner shall comply with all of the requirements in subdivision (f).

(h) The association or owners may install an electric vehicle charging station in the common area for the use of all members of the association and, in that case, the association shall develop appropriate terms of use for the charging station.

(i) An association may create a new parking space where one did not previously exist to facilitate the installation of an electric vehicle charging station.

(j) An association that willfully violates this section shall be liable to the applicant or other party for actual damages, and shall pay a civil penalty to the applicant or other party in an amount not to exceed one thousand dollars ($1,000).

(k) In any action to enforce compliance with this section, the prevailing plaintiff shall be awarded reasonable attorney's fees. *(Added by Stats.2013, c. 605 (S.B.752), § 21.)*

Law Revision Commission Comments

With respect to a commercial or industrial common interest development, Section 6713 continues Section 1353.9 without change, except as indicated below.

The following substantive changes are made:

● In paragraphs (f)(3) and (4), the word "homeowner" is deleted or replaced with "owner."

The following nonsubstantive changes are made:

● A cross-reference in subdivision (a) is updated to reflect the new location of the referenced provision.

● In subdivision (c), the words "as well as" are replaced with ", and."

For further information, see Section 6500 Comment.

See also Sections 6528 ("association"), 6532 ("common area"), 6534 ("common interest development"), 6546 ("declaration"), 6550 ("exclusive use common area"), 6552 ("governing documents"), 6564 ("separate interest").

For a similar provision in the Davis–Stirling Common Interest Development Act, see Section 4745. [42 Cal.L.Rev.Comm. Reports 1 (2012)].

ARTICLE 2. MODIFICATION OF SEPARATE INTEREST

Section
6714. Modification of member's separate interest; facilitation of access for handicapped; approval by association.

§ 6714. Modification of member's separate interest; facilitation of access for handicapped; approval by association

(a) Subject to the governing documents and applicable law, a member may do the following:

(1) Make any improvement or alteration within the boundaries of the member's separate interest that does not impair the structural integrity or mechanical systems or lessen the support of any portions of the common interest development.

(2) Modify the member's separate interest, at the member's expense, to facilitate access for persons who are blind, visually handicapped, deaf, or physically disabled, or to alter conditions which could be hazardous to these persons. These modifications may also include modifications of the route from the public way to the door of the separate interest for the purposes of this paragraph if the separate interest is on the ground floor or already accessible by an existing ramp or elevator. The right granted by this paragraph is subject to the following conditions:

(A) The modifications shall be consistent with applicable building code requirements.

(B) The modifications shall be consistent with the intent of otherwise applicable provisions of the governing documents pertaining to safety or aesthetics.

(C) Modifications external to the separate interest shall not prevent reasonable passage by other residents, and shall be removed by the member when the separate interest is no longer occupied by persons requiring those modifications who are blind, visually handicapped, deaf, or physically disabled.

(D) Any member who intends to modify a separate interest pursuant to this paragraph shall submit plans and specifications to the association for review to determine whether the modifications will comply with the provisions of this paragraph. The association shall not deny approval of the proposed modifications under this paragraph without good cause.

(b) Any change in the exterior appearance of a separate interest shall be in accordance with the governing documents and applicable provisions of law. *(Added by Stats.2013, c. 605 (S.B.752), § 21.)*

Law Revision Commission Comments

With respect to a commercial or industrial common interest development, Section 6714 continues Section 1360 without change, except as indicated below.

The following substantive change is made:

● The scope of the provision is broadened to apply to any separate interest, and not just a unit in a condominium project.

The following nonsubstantive changes are made:

● The word "dwelling" is replaced with "separate interest" in subdivision (a)(2)(C). See Section 6564 ("separate interest").

● The words "his or her" are not continued in subdivision (a)(2)(D).

● The word "owner" is replaced with "member" throughout. See Section 6554 ("member").

For further information, see Section 6500 Comment.

See also Sections 6528 ("association"), 6534 ("common interest development"), 6552 ("governing documents").

For a similar provision in the Davis–Stirling Common Interest Development Act, see Section 4760. [42 Cal.L.Rev.Comm. Reports 1 (2012)].

ARTICLE 3. MAINTENANCE

Section
6716. Responsibility for repair, replacement, or maintenance.
6718. Damage by wood-destroying pests or organisms.
6720. Temporary removal of occupant for treatment of wood-destroying pests or organisms.
6722. Access for maintenance of telephone wiring.

§ 6716. Responsibility for repair, replacement, or maintenance

(a) Unless otherwise provided in the declaration of a common interest development, the association is responsible for repairing, replacing, or maintaining the common area, other than exclusive use common area, and the owner of each separate interest is responsible for maintaining that separate interest and any exclusive use common area appurtenant to the separate interest.

(b) The costs of temporary relocation during the repair and maintenance of the areas within the responsibility of the association shall be borne by the owner of the separate interest affected. *(Added by Stats.2013, c. 605 (S.B.752), § 21.)*

Law Revision Commission Comments

With respect to a commercial or industrial common interest development, subdivision (a) of Section 6716 continues Section 1364(a) without change, except as indicated below.

The following nonsubstantive change is made:

• The phrase "common areas" is singularized.

With respect to a commercial or industrial common interest development, subdivision (b) continues Section 1364(c) without change.

For further information, see Section 6500 Comment.

See also Sections 6528 ("association"), 6532 ("common area"), 6534 ("common interest development"), 6546 ("declaration"), 6550 ("exclusive use common area"), 6564 ("separate interest").

For a similar provision in the Davis–Stirling Common Interest Development Act, see Section 4775. [42 Cal.L.Rev.Comm. Reports 1 (2012)].

§ 6718. Damage by wood-destroying pests or organisms

(a) In a condominium project or stock cooperative, unless otherwise provided in the declaration, the association is responsible for the repair and maintenance of the common area occasioned by the presence of wood-destroying pests or organisms.

(b) In a planned development, unless a different maintenance scheme is provided in the declaration, each owner of a separate interest is responsible for the repair and maintenance of that separate interest as may be occasioned by the presence of wood-destroying pests or organisms. Upon approval of the majority of all members of the association, pursuant to Section 6522, that responsibility may be delegated to the association, which shall be entitled to recover the cost thereof as a special assessment. *(Added by Stats.2013, c. 605 (S.B.752), § 21.)*

Law Revision Commission Comments

With respect to a commercial or industrial common interest development, subdivision (a) of Section 6718 continues Section 1364(b)(1) without change, except as indicated below.

The following nonsubstantive changes are made:

• A reference to a "community apartment project" is not continued.

• A superfluous cross-reference to governing definitions is not continued.

With respect to a commercial or industrial common interest development, subdivision (b) continues Section 1364(b)(2) without change, except as indicated below.

The following nonsubstantive changes are made:

• A superfluous cross-reference to a governing definition is not continued.

• A cross-reference to Section 6522 is added.

• The last sentence is revised to avoid use of the word "such."

For further information, see Section 6500 Comment.

See also Sections 6528 ("association"), 6532 ("common area"), 6542 ("condominium project"), 6546 ("declaration"), 6554 ("member"), 6562 ("planned development"), 6564 ("separate interest"), 6566 ("stock cooperative").

For a similar provision in the Davis–Stirling Common Interest Development Act, see Section 4780. [42 Cal.L.Rev.Comm. Reports 1 (2012)].

§ 6720. Temporary removal of occupant for treatment of wood-destroying pests or organisms

(a) The association may cause the temporary, summary removal of any occupant of a common interest development for such periods and at such times as may be necessary for prompt, effective treatment of wood-destroying pests or organisms.

(b) The association shall give notice of the need to temporarily vacate a separate interest to the occupants and to the owners, not less than 15 days nor more than 30 days prior to the date of the temporary relocation. The notice shall state the reason for the temporary relocation, the date and time of the beginning of treatment, the anticipated date and time of termination of treatment, and that the occupants will be responsible for their own accommodations during the temporary relocation.

(c) Notice by the association shall be deemed complete upon either:

(1) Personal delivery of a copy of the notice to the occupants, and, if an occupant is not the owner, individual delivery pursuant to Section 6514 of a copy of the notice to the owner.

(2) Individual delivery pursuant to Section 6514 to the occupant at the address of the separate interest, and, if the occupant is not the owner, individual delivery pursuant to Section 6514 of a copy of the notice to the owner.

(d) For purposes of this section, "occupant" means an owner, resident, guest, invitee, tenant, lessee, sublessee, or other person in possession of the separate interest. *(Added by Stats.2013, c. 605 (S.B.752), § 21.)*

Law Revision Commission Comments

With respect to a commercial or industrial common interest development, Section 6720 continues Section 1364(d)-(e) without change, except as indicated below.

The following substantive change is made:

• The provision is revised to incorporate the "individual delivery" notice procedure.

The following nonsubstantive changes are made:

• Subdivision (c) is revised to improve its clarity.

• A typographical error is corrected in subdivision (d).

For further information, see Section 6500 Comment.

See also Sections 6528 ("association"), 6534 ("common interest development"), 6564 ("separate interest").

For a similar provision in the Davis–Stirling Common Interest Development Act, see Section 4785. [42 Cal.L.Rev.Comm. Reports 1 (2012)].

§ 6722. Access for maintenance of telephone wiring

Notwithstanding the provisions of the declaration, a member is entitled to reasonable access to the common area for the purpose of maintaining the internal and external telephone wiring made part of the exclusive use common area of the member's separate interest pursuant to subdivision (c) of Section 6550. The access shall be subject to the consent of the association, whose approval shall not be unreasonably withheld, and which may include the association's approval of telephone wiring upon the exterior of the common area, and other conditions as the association determines reasonable. *(Added by Stats.2013, c. 605 (S.B.752), § 21.)*

Law Revision Commission Comments

With respect to a commercial or industrial common interest development, Section 6722 continues Section 1364(f) without change, except as indicated below.

The following nonsubstantive changes are made:

• A cross-reference is updated to reflect the new location of the referenced provision.

• The word "owner" is replaced with "member." See Section 6554 ("member").

• The phrase "common areas" is singularized.

For further information, see Section 6500 Comment.

See also Sections 6528 ("association"), 6532 ("common area"), 6546 ("declaration"), 6550 ("exclusive use common area"), 6564 ("separate interest").

For a similar provision in the Davis–Stirling Common Interest Development Act, see Section 4790. [42 Cal.L.Rev.Comm. Reports 1 (2012)].

CHAPTER 6. ASSOCIATION GOVERNANCE

ARTICLE 1. ASSOCIATION EXISTENCE AND POWERS

Section
6750. Management by association.
6752. Powers of association.

§ 6750. Management by association

A common interest development shall be managed by an association that may be incorporated or unincorporated. The association may be referred to as an owners' association or a community association. *(Added by Stats.2013, c. 605 (S.B.752), § 21.)*

Law Revision Commission Comments

With respect to a commercial or industrial common interest development, Section 6750 continues Section 1363(a) without change, except as indicated below.

The following nonsubstantive change is made:

● Use of the term "owners' association" to describe the association is expressly authorized.

For further information, see Section 6500 Comment.

See also Sections 6528 ("association"), 6534 ("common interest development").

For a similar provision in the Davis–Stirling Common Interest Development Act, see Section 4800. [42 Cal.L.Rev.Comm. Reports 1 (2012)].

§ 6752. Powers of association

(a) Unless the governing documents provide otherwise, and regardless of whether the association is incorporated or unincorporated, the association may exercise the powers granted to a nonprofit mutual benefit corporation, as enumerated in Section 7140 of the Corporations Code, except that an unincorporated association may not adopt or use a corporate seal or issue membership certificates in accordance with Section 7313 of the Corporations Code.

(b) The association, whether incorporated or unincorporated, may exercise the powers granted to an association in this act. *(Added by Stats.2013, c. 605 (S.B.752), § 21.)*

Law Revision Commission Comments

With respect to a commercial or industrial common interest development, Section 6752 continues Section 1363(c) without change, except as indicated below.

The following nonsubstantive changes are made:

● The provision is divided into subdivisions for ease of reference.

● The word "title" is replaced with "act."

For further information, see Section 6500 Comment.

See also Sections 6528 ("association"), 6552 ("governing documents").

For a similar provision in the Davis–Stirling Common Interest Development Act, see Section 4805. [42 Cal.L.Rev.Comm. Reports 1 (2012)].

ARTICLE 2. RECORD KEEPING

Section
6756. Request to change member's information; delivery in writing.

§ 6756. Request to change member's information; delivery in writing

To be effective, a request to change the member's information in the association membership list shall be delivered in writing to the association, pursuant to Section 6512. *(Added by Stats.2013, c. 605 (S.B.752), § 21.)*

Law Revision Commission Comments

Section 6756 is new. It requires that a request to change a member's information in an association membership list be written and delivered to the association pursuant to Section 6512.

See also Sections 6528 ("association"), 6554 ("member").

For a similar provision in the Davis–Stirling Common Interest Development Act, see Section 5260. [43 Cal.L.Rev.Comm. Reports ___ (Appendix 5) (2013)].

ARTICLE 3. CONFLICT OF INTEREST

Section
6758. Applicability of Corporations Code provisions; prohibited actions.

§ 6758. Applicability of Corporations Code provisions; prohibited actions

(a) Notwithstanding any other law, and regardless of whether an association is incorporated or unincorporated, the provisions of Sections 7233 and 7234 of the Corporations Code shall apply to any contract or other transaction authorized, approved, or ratified by the board or a committee of the board.

(b) A director or member of a committee shall not vote on any of the following matters:

(1) Discipline of the director or committee member.

(2) An assessment against the director or committee member for damage to the common area or facilities.

(3) A request, by the director or committee member, for a payment plan for overdue assessments.

(4) A decision whether to foreclose on a lien on the separate interest of the director or committee member.

(5) Review of a proposed physical change to the separate interest of the director or committee member.

(6) A grant of exclusive use common area to the director or committee member.

(c) Nothing in this section limits any other provision of law or the governing documents that govern a decision in which a director may have an interest. *(Added by Stats.2013, c. 605 (S.B.752), § 21.)*

Law Revision Commission Comments

With respect to a commercial or industrial common interest development, subdivision (a) of Section 6758 continues the substance of Section 1365.6, except as indicated below.

The following nonsubstantive change is made:

● The reference to Corporations Code Section 310, which governs the General Corporation Law, is replaced with a reference to Corporations Code Sections 7233 and 7234, which state equivalent rules for nonprofit mutual benefit corporations.

Subdivisions (b) and (c) are new. The "discipline" referenced in subdivision (b)(1) may include discipline for a violation of the governing documents, this act, or a fiduciary duty.

For further information, see Section 6500 Comment.

See also Sections 6528 ("association"), 6530 ("board"), 6532 ("common area"), 6548 ("director"), 6550 ("exclusive use common area"), 6552 ("governing documents"), 6564 ("separate interest").

For a similar provision in the Davis–Stirling Common Interest Development Act, see Section 5350. [42 Cal.L.Rev.Comm. Reports 1 (2012)].

ARTICLE 4.   GOVERNMENT ASSISTANCE

Section
6760.   Assistance with identification of commercial or industrial common interest developments; submission of
information by each association; time; notice of
change of address; penalty for violation of filing
requirements; availability of information.

§ 6760.   **Assistance with identification of commercial or industrial common interest developments; submission of information by each association; time; notice of change of
address; penalty for violation of filing requirements; availability of information**

(a) To assist with the identification of commercial or industrial common interest developments, each association, whether
incorporated or unincorporated, shall submit to the Secretary of
State, on a form and for a fee, to cover the reasonable cost to the
Secretary of State of processing the form, not to exceed thirty
dollars ($30), that the Secretary of State shall prescribe, the
following information concerning the association and the development that it manages:

(1) A statement that the association is formed to manage a
common interest development under the Commercial and Industrial Common Interest Development Act.

(2) The name of the association.

(3) The street address of the business or corporate office of
the association, if any.

(4) The street address of the association's onsite office, if
different from the street address of the business or corporate
office, or if there is no onsite office, the street address of the
responsible officer or managing agent of the association.

(5) The name, address, and either the daytime telephone
number or email address of the association's onsite office or
managing agent.

(6) The name, street address, and daytime telephone number
of the association's managing agent, if any.

(7) The county, and, if in an incorporated area, the city in
which the development is physically located. If the boundaries
of the development are physically located in more than one
county, each of the counties in which it is located.

(8) If the development is in an unincorporated area, the city
closest in proximity to the development.

(9) The front street and nearest cross street of the physical
location of the development.

(10) The type of common interest development managed by
the association.

(11) The number of separate interests in the development.

(b) The association shall submit the information required by
this section as follows:

(1) By incorporated associations, within 90 days after the
filing of its original articles of incorporation, and thereafter at
the time the association files its statement of principal business
activity with the Secretary of State pursuant to Section 8210 of
the Corporations Code.

(2) By unincorporated associations, in July of 2003, and in
that same month biennially thereafter. Upon changing its status
to that of a corporation, the association shall comply with the
filing deadlines in paragraph (1).

(c) The association shall notify the Secretary of State of any
change in the street address of the association's onsite office or
of the responsible officer or managing agent of the association in
the form and for a fee, to cover the reasonable cost to the

Secretary of State of processing the form, prescribed by the
Secretary of State, within 60 days of the change.

(d) The penalty for an incorporated association's noncompliance with the initial or biennial filing requirements of this section
shall be suspension of the association's rights, privileges, and
powers as a corporation and monetary penalties, to the same
extent and in the same manner as suspension and monetary
penalties imposed pursuant to Section 8810 of the Corporations
Code.

(e) The statement required by this section may be filed,
notwithstanding suspension of the corporate powers, rights, and
privileges under this section or under provisions of the Revenue
and Taxation Code. Upon the filing of a statement under this
section by a corporation that has suffered suspension under this
section, the Secretary of State shall certify that fact to the
Franchise Tax Board and the corporation may thereupon be
relieved from suspension, unless the corporation is held in
suspension by the Franchise Tax Board by reason of Section
23301, 23301.5, or 23775 of the Revenue and Taxation Code.

(f) The Secretary of State shall make the information submitted pursuant to paragraph (5) of subdivision (a) available only
for governmental purposes and only to Members of the Legislature and the Business, Consumer Services, and Housing Agency,
upon written request. All other information submitted pursuant
to this section shall be subject to public inspection pursuant to
the California Public Records Act (Chapter 3.5 (commencing
with Section 6250) of Division 7 of Title 1 of the Government
Code). The information submitted pursuant to this section shall
be made available for governmental or public inspection.

(g) Whenever any form is filed pursuant to this section, it
supersedes any previously filed form.

(h) The Secretary of State may destroy or otherwise dispose
of any form filed pursuant to this section after it has been
superseded by the filing of a new form. *(Added by Stats.2013, c.
605 (S.B.752), § 21.)*

Law Revision Commission Comments

With respect to a commercial or industrial common interest development, Section 6760 continues Section 1363.6 without change, except as
indicated below.

The following substantive change is made:

● A reference to this act is substituted for a reference to the Davis–
Stirling Common Interest Development Act.

The following nonsubstantive changes are made:

● The words "of the association" at the end of Section 1363.6(a)(5) are
not continued.

● Superfluous references to definition sections are not continued.

● In paragraph (a)(7), a comma is added after the word "and."

● Obsolete transitional dates are not continued in subdivisions (d) and
(f).

● The words "as the case may be" are not continued in subdivision (f).

● In subdivision (f), a comma is deleted after "California Public
Records Act" and parentheses are added around the following statutory
reference to that act.

For further information, see Section 6500 Comment.

See also Sections 6528 ("association"), 6534 ("common interest development").

For a similar provision in the Davis–Stirling Common Interest Development Act, see Section 5405. [42 Cal.L.Rev.Comm. Reports 1 (2012)].

CHAPTER 7.   ASSESSMENTS AND
ASSESSMENT COLLECTION

ARTICLE 1. ESTABLISHMENT AND IMPOSITION OF ASSESSMENTS

§ 6800. Levy of assessments

The association shall levy regular and special assessments sufficient to perform its obligations under the governing documents and this act. *(Added by Stats.2013, c. 605 (S.B.752), § 21.)*

Law Revision Commission Comments

With respect to a commercial or industrial common interest development, Section 6800 continues the first sentence of Section 1366(a) without change, except as indicated below.

The following nonsubstantive changes are made:

● The word "title" is replaced with "act."

● A superfluous reference to the remainder of Section 1366 is deleted.

For further information, see Section 6500 Comment.

See also Sections 6528 ("association"), 6552 ("governing documents").

For a similar provision in the Davis–Stirling Common Interest Development Act, see Section 5600. [42 Cal.L.Rev.Comm. Reports 1 (2012)].

§ 6804. Exemption from execution by judgment creditor of association

(a) Regular assessments imposed or collected to perform the obligations of an association under the governing documents or this act shall be exempt from execution by a judgment creditor of the association only to the extent necessary for the association to perform essential services, such as paying for utilities and insurance. In determining the appropriateness of an exemption, a court shall ensure that only essential services are protected under this subdivision.

(b) This exemption shall not apply to any consensual pledges, liens, or encumbrances that have been approved by a majority of a quorum of members, pursuant to Section 6524, at a member meeting or election, or to any state tax lien, or to any lien for labor or materials supplied to the common area. *(Added by Stats.2013, c. 605 (S.B.752), § 21.)*

Law Revision Commission Comments

With respect to a commercial or industrial common interest development, Section 6804 continues Section 1366(c) without change, except as indicated below.

The following nonsubstantive changes are made:

● The provision is divided into subdivisions for ease of reference.

● A reference to approval of a majority of members casting a vote at a meeting at which a quorum is established is replaced with a reference to the standard provision on approval by a majority of a quorum of members (Section 6524).

● Quorum-related language from Section 1366(b)-(c) is not continued.

● The word "title" is replaced with "act."

For further information, see Section 6500 Comment.

See also Sections 6528 ("association"), 6532 ("common area"), 6552 ("governing documents"), 6554 ("member").

For a similar provision in the Davis–Stirling Common Interest Development Act, see Section 5620. [42 Cal.L.Rev.Comm. Reports 1 (2012)].

ARTICLE 2. ASSESSMENT PAYMENT AND DELINQUENCY

§ 6808. Debt of owner of separate interest

A regular or special assessment and any late charges, reasonable fees and costs of collection, reasonable attorney's fees, if any, and interest, if any, shall be a debt of the owner of the separate interest at the time the assessment or other sums are levied. *(Added by Stats.2013, c. 605 (S.B.752), § 21.)*

Law Revision Commission Comments

With respect to a commercial or industrial common interest development, Section 6808 continues the first sentence of Section 1367.1(a) without change, except as indicated below.

The following nonsubstantive change is made:

● A cross-reference to Section 1366 is deleted.

For further information, see Section 6500 Comment. See also Section 6564 ("separate interest").

For a similar provision in the Davis–Stirling Common Interest Development Act, see Section 5650. [43 Cal.L.Rev.Comm. Reports __ (Appendix 5) (2013)].

§ 6810. Payment toward assessment; receipt; mailing address for overnight payment

(a) When an owner of a separate interest makes a payment toward an assessment, the owner may request a receipt and the association shall provide it. The receipt shall indicate the date of payment and the person who received it.

(b) The association shall provide a mailing address for overnight payment of assessments.

(c) An owner shall not be liable for any charges, interest, or costs of collection for an assessment payment that is asserted to be delinquent, if it is determined the assessment was paid on time to the association. *(Added by Stats.2013, c. 605 (S.B.752), § 21.)*

Law Revision Commission Comments

With respect to a commercial or industrial common interest development, subdivisions (a) and (b) of Section 6810 continue the substance of Section 1367.1(b), except as indicated below.

The following substantive change is made:

● The first sentence of Section 1367.1(b) is not continued.

The following nonsubstantive change is made:

● The provision is divided into subdivisions for ease of reference.

Subdivision (c) of Section 6810 is new. *Cf.* Section 1366(e).

For further information, see Section 6500 Comment.

See also Sections 6528 ("association"), 6564 ("separate interest").

For a similar provision in the Davis–Stirling Common Interest Development Act, see Section 5655. [43 Cal.L.Rev.Comm. Reports __ (Appendix 5) (2013)].

§ 6812. Notice prior to recording lien upon separate interest; contents

At least 30 days prior to recording a lien upon the separate interest of the owner of record to collect a debt that is past due under Section 6808, the association shall notify the owner of record in writing by certified mail of the following:

(a) A general description of the collection and lien enforcement procedures of the association and the method of calculation of the amount, a statement that the owner of the separate interest has the right to inspect the association records pursuant to Section 8333 of the Corporations Code, and the following statement in 14–point boldface type, if printed, or in capital letters, if typed:

"IMPORTANT NOTICE: IF YOUR SEPARATE INTEREST IS PLACED IN FORECLOSURE BECAUSE YOU ARE BEHIND IN YOUR ASSESSMENTS, IT MAY BE SOLD WITHOUT COURT ACTION."

(b) An itemized statement of the charges owed by the owner, including items on the statement which indicate the amount of any delinquent assessments, the fees and reasonable costs of collection, reasonable attorney's fees, any late charges, and interest, if any.

(c) A statement that the owner shall not be liable to pay the charges, interest, and costs of collection, if it is determined the assessment was paid on time to the association. *(Added by Stats.2013, c. 605 (S.B.752), § 21.)*

Law Revision Commission Comments

With respect to a commercial or industrial common interest development, Section 6812 continues the second sentence of Section 1367.1(a), and paragraphs (1) to (3) of that provision, inclusive, without change, except as indicated below.

The following nonsubstantive change is made:

• A cross-reference is updated to reflect the new location of the referenced provision.

For further information, see Section 6500 Comment.

See also Sections 6528 ("association"), 6564 ("separate interest").

For a similar provision in the Davis–Stirling Common Interest Development Act, see Section 5660. [42 Cal.L.Rev.Comm. Reports 1 (2012)].

§ 6814. Lien on separate interest; notice of delinquent assessment

(a) The amount of the assessment, plus any costs of collection, late charges, and interest assessed in accordance with Section 6808, shall be a lien on the owner's separate interest in the common interest development from and after the time the association causes to be recorded with the county recorder of the county in which the separate interest is located, a notice of delinquent assessment, which shall state the amount of the assessment and other sums imposed in accordance with Section 6808, a legal description of the owner's separate interest in the common interest development against which the assessment and other sums are levied, and the name of the record owner of the separate interest in the common interest development against which the lien is imposed.

(b) The itemized statement of the charges owed by the owner described in subdivision (b) of Section 6812 shall be recorded together with the notice of delinquent assessment.

(c) In order for the lien to be enforced by nonjudicial foreclosure as provided in Sections 6820 and 6822, the notice of delinquent assessment shall state the name and address of the trustee authorized by the association to enforce the lien by sale.

(d) The notice of delinquent assessment shall be signed by the person designated in the declaration or by the association for that purpose, or if no one is designated, by the president of the association.

(e) A copy of the recorded notice of delinquent assessment shall be mailed by certified mail to every person whose name is shown as an owner of the separate interest in the association's records, and the notice shall be mailed no later than 10 calendar days after recordation. *(Added by Stats.2013, c. 605 (S.B.752), § 21.)*

Law Revision Commission Comments

With respect to a commercial or industrial common interest development, Section 6814 continues the first five sentences of Section 1367.1(d) without change, except as indicated below.

The following nonsubstantive change is made:

• Cross-references are updated to reflect the new locations of the referenced provisions.

For further information, see Section 6500 Comment.

See also Sections 6528 ("association"), 6534 ("common interest development"), 6546 ("declaration"), 6560 ("person"), 6564 ("separate interest").

For a similar provision in the Davis–Stirling Common Interest Development Act, see Section 5675. [42 Cal.L.Rev.Comm. Reports 1 (2012)].

§ 6816. Priority of lien

A lien created pursuant to Section 6814 shall be prior to all other liens recorded subsequent to the notice of delinquent assessment, except that the declaration may provide for the subordination thereof to any other liens and encumbrances. *(Added by Stats.2013, c. 605 (S.B.752), § 21.)*

Law Revision Commission Comments

With respect to a commercial or industrial common interest development, Section 6816 continues Section 1367.1(f) without change, except as indicated below.

The following nonsubstantive changes are made:

• The words "notice of assessment" are replaced with the more specific "notice of delinquent assessment."

• A cross-reference is updated to reflect the new location of the referenced provision.

For further information, see Section 6500 Comment.

See also Section 6546 ("declaration").

For a similar provision in the Davis–Stirling Common Interest Development Act, see Section 5680. [42 Cal.L.Rev.Comm. Reports 1 (2012)].

§ 6818. Recording of lien

(a) Within 21 days of the payment of the sums specified in the notice of delinquent assessment, the association shall record or cause to be recorded in the office of the county recorder in which the notice of delinquent assessment is recorded a lien release or notice of rescission and provide the owner of the separate interest a copy of the lien release or notice that the delinquent assessment has been satisfied.

(b) If it is determined that a lien previously recorded against the separate interest was recorded in error, the party who recorded the lien shall, within 21 calendar days, record or cause to be recorded in the office of the county recorder in which the notice of delinquent assessment is recorded a lien release or notice of rescission and provide the owner of the separate interest with a declaration that the lien filing or recording was in error and a copy of the lien release or notice of rescission. *(Added by Stats.2013, c. 605 (S.B.752), § 21.)*

Law Revision Commission Comments

With respect to a commercial or industrial common interest development, subdivision (a) of Section 6818 continues the sixth sentence of Section 1367.1(d) without change.

With respect to a commercial or industrial common interest development, subdivision (b) continues Section 1367.1(i) without change.

For further information, see Section 6500 Comment.

See also Sections 6528 ("association"), 6564 ("separate interest").

For a similar provision in the Davis–Stirling Common Interest Development Act, see Section 5685. [42 Cal.L.Rev.Comm. Reports 1 (2012)].

§ 6819. Recommencement of notice process for failure to comply with procedures

An association that fails to comply with the procedures set forth in this section shall, prior to recording a lien, recommence the required notice process. Any costs associated with recommencing the notice process shall be borne by the association and not by the owner of a separate interest. *(Added by Stats.2013, c. 605 (S.B.752), § 21.)*

With respect to a commercial or industrial common interest development, Section 6819 continues Section 1367.1(*l*) without change, except as indicated below.

The following nonsubstantive change is made:

● The word "section" is replaced with "article."

For further information, see Section 6500 Comment.

See also Sections 6528 ("association"), 6564 ("separate interest").

For a similar provision in the Davis–Stirling Common Interest Development Act, see Section 5690. [42 Cal.L.Rev.Comm. Reports 1 (2012)].

ARTICLE 3.   ASSESSMENT COLLECTION

Section
6820.   Enforcement of lien.
6822.   Trustee sale; procedure; notice; trustee fees.
6824.   Monetary charge for repair of damage to common area
             and facilities; monetary penalties.
6826.   Assignment or pledge prohibited; exception.
6828.   Application of article to liens.

§ 6820.   Enforcement of lien

(a) Except as otherwise provided in this article, after the expiration of 30 days following the recording of a lien created pursuant to Section 6814, the lien may be enforced in any manner permitted by law, including sale by the court, sale by the trustee designated in the notice of delinquent assessment, or sale by a trustee substituted pursuant to Section 2934a.

(b) Nothing in Article 2 (commencing with Section 6808) or in subdivision (a) of Section 726 of the Code of Civil Procedure prohibits actions against the owner of a separate interest to recover sums for which a lien is created pursuant to Article 2 (commencing with Section 6808) or prohibits an association from taking a deed in lieu of foreclosure. *(Added by Stats.2013, c. 605 (S.B.752), § 21.)*

With respect to a commercial or industrial common interest development, subdivision (a) of Section 6820 continues the substance of the second sentence of Section 1367.1(g), except as indicated below.

The following nonsubstantive changes are made:

● The introductory clause is broadened to recognize the application of all restrictions on collection that are provided in this article. See, e.g., Section 6826 (limitation on assignment).

● Cross-references are updated to reflect the new locations of the referenced provisions.

With respect to a commercial or industrial common interest development, subdivision (b) continues Section 1367.1(h) without change, except as indicated below.

The following nonsubstantive change is made:

● Cross-references are updated to reflect the new locations of the referenced provisions.

For further information, see Section 6500 Comment.

See also Sections 6528 ("association"), 6564 ("separate interest").

For a similar provision in the Davis–Stirling Common Interest Development Act, see Section 5700. [42 Cal.L.Rev.Comm. Reports 1 (2012)].

§ 6822.   Trustee sale; procedure; notice; trustee fees

(a) Any sale by the trustee shall be conducted in accordance with Sections 2924, 2924b, and 2924c applicable to the exercise of powers of sale in mortgages and deeds of trust.

(b) In addition to the requirements of Section 2924, the association shall serve a notice of default on the person named as the owner of the separate interest in the association's records or, if that person has designated a legal representative pursuant to this subdivision, on that legal representative. Service shall be in accordance with the manner of service of summons in Article 3 (commencing with Section 415.10) of Chapter 4 of Title 5 of Part 2 of the Code of Civil Procedure.   An owner may designate a

legal representative in a writing that is mailed to the association in a manner that indicates that the association has received it.

(c) The fees of a trustee may not exceed the amounts prescribed in Sections 2924c and 2924d, plus the cost of service for the notice of default pursuant to subdivision (b).   *(Added by Stats.2013, c. 605 (S.B.752), § 21.)*

With respect to a commercial or industrial common interest development, subdivision (a) of Section 6822 continues the third sentence of Section 1367.1(g) without change.

With respect to a commercial or industrial common interest development, subdivision (b) continues the substance of Section 1367.1(j).

With respect to a commercial or industrial common interest development, subdivision (c) continues the fourth sentence and paragraph (1) of Section 1367.1(g), without change.

For further information, see Section 6500 Comment.

See also Sections 6528 ("association"), 6564 ("separate interest").

For a similar provision in the Davis–Stirling Common Interest Development Act, see Section 5710. [42 Cal.L.Rev.Comm. Reports 1 (2012)].

§ 6824.   Monetary charge for repair of damage to common area and facilities;   monetary penalties

(a) A monetary charge imposed by the association as a means of reimbursing the association for costs incurred by the association in the repair of damage to common areas and facilities caused by a member or the member's guest or tenant may become a lien against the member's separate interest enforceable by the sale of the interest under Sections 2924, 2924b, and 2924c, provided the authority to impose a lien is set forth in the governing documents.

(b) A monetary penalty imposed by the association as a disciplinary measure for failure of a member to comply with the governing documents, except for the late payments, may not be characterized nor treated in the governing documents as an assessment that may become a lien against the member's separate interest enforceable by the sale of the interest under Sections 2924, 2924b, and 2924c. *(Added by Stats.2013, c. 605 (S.B.752), § 21.)*

With respect to a commercial or industrial common interest development, subdivision (a) of Section 6824 continues the seventh sentence of Section 1367.1(d) without change, except as indicated below.

The following nonsubstantive change is made:

● The phrase "common areas" is singularized.

With respect to a commercial or industrial common interest development, subdivision (b) continues Section 1367.1(e) without change, except as indicated below.

The following nonsubstantive changes are made:

● The introductory clause "except as indicated in subdivision (d)" is not continued.

● The words "governing instruments" are replaced with "governing documents." See Section 6552 ("governing documents").

● The words "subdivision separate interest" are replaced with "separate interest." See Section 6564 ("separate interest").

For further information, see Section 6500 Comment.

See also Sections 6528 ("association"), 6532 ("common area"), 6552 ("governing documents"), 6554 ("member").

For a similar provision in the Davis–Stirling Common Interest Development Act, see Section 5725. [42 Cal.L.Rev.Comm. Reports 1 (2012)].

§ 6826.   Assignment or pledge prohibited; exception

(a) An association may not voluntarily assign or pledge the association's right to collect payments or assessments, or to enforce or foreclose a lien to a third party, except when the assignment or pledge is made to a financial institution or lender chartered or licensed under federal or state law, when acting within the scope of that charter or license, as security for a loan obtained by the association.

(b) Nothing in subdivision (a) restricts the right or ability of an association to assign any unpaid obligations of a former member to a third party for purposes of collection. *(Added by Stats.2013, c. 605 (S.B.752), § 21.)*

Law Revision Commission Comments

With respect to a commercial or industrial common interest development, Section 6826 continues the first sentence of Section 1367.1(g) without change, except as indicated below.

The following nonsubstantive changes are made:

• The provision is divided into subdivisions for ease of reference.

• An introductory clause is added in subdivision (b) to make the relationship between the two provisions clearer.

For further information, see Section 6500 Comment.

See also Sections 6528 ("association"), 6554 ("member").

For a similar provision in the Davis–Stirling Common Interest Development Act, see Section 5735. [42 Cal.L.Rev.Comm. Reports 1 (2012)].

§ 6828. Application of article to liens

(a) Except as otherwise provided, this article applies to a lien created on or after January 1, 2014.

(b) A lien created before January 1, 2014, is governed by the law in existence at the time the lien was created. *(Added by Stats.2013, c. 605 (S.B.752), § 21.)*

Law Revision Commission Comments

Section 6828 is new. A lien created on or after January 1, 1986, and before January 1, 2003, is governed by Section 1367. See 2002 Cal. Stat. ch. 111, § 7. A lien created on or after January 1, 2003 and before the operative date of the act that added this section, is governed by Section 1367.1 and Section 1367.4.

For a similar provision in the Davis–Stirling Common Interest Development Act, see Section 5740. [42 Cal.L.Rev.Comm. Reports 1 (2012)].

CHAPTER 8. INSURANCE AND LIABILITY

Section
6840. Tort actions against owner of separate interest; tenant in common in common area; association liability; insurance requirements.

§ 6840. Tort actions against owner of separate interest; tenant in common in common area; association liability; insurance requirements

(a) It is the intent of the Legislature to offer civil liability protection to owners of the separate interests in a common interest development that have common area owned in tenancy in common if the association carries a certain level of prescribed insurance that covers a cause of action in tort.

(b) Any cause of action in tort against any owner of a separate interest arising solely by reason of an ownership interest as a tenant in common in the common area of a common interest development shall be brought only against the association and not against the individual owners of the separate interests, if both of the insurance requirements in paragraphs (1) and (2) are met:

(1) The association maintained and has in effect for this cause of action, one or more policies of insurance that include coverage for general liability of the association.

(2) The coverage described in paragraph (1) is in the following minimum amounts:

(A) At least two million dollars ($2,000,000) if the common interest development consists of 100 or fewer separate interests.

(B) At least three million dollars ($3,000,000) if the common interest development consists of more than 100 separate interests. *(Added by Stats.2013, c. 605 (S.B.752), § 21.)*

Law Revision Commission Comments

With respect to a commercial or industrial common interest development, Section 6840 continues Section 1365.9 without change, except as indicated below.

The following nonsubstantive changes are made:

• A superfluous cross-reference to a governing definition is not continued.

• The phrase "common areas" is singularized.

• In subdivision (b)(1), the word "which" is replaced with "that."

For further information, see Section 6500 Comment.

See also Sections 6528 ("association"), 6532 ("common area"), 6534 ("common interest development"), 6564 ("separate interest").

For a similar provision in the Davis–Stirling Common Interest Development Act, see Section 5805. [42 Cal.L.Rev.Comm. Reports 1 (2012)].

CHAPTER 9. DISPUTE RESOLUTION AND ENFORCEMENT

ARTICLE 1. DISCIPLINARY ACTION

Section
6850. Monetary penalties; provision of information to members.
6854. Authority of board to impose monetary penalties.

§ 6850. Monetary penalties; provision of information to members

(a) If an association adopts or has adopted a policy imposing any monetary penalty, including any fee, on any association member for a violation of the governing documents, including any monetary penalty relating to the activities of a guest or tenant of the member, the board shall adopt and distribute to each member, by individual notice, a schedule of the monetary penalties that may be assessed for those violations, which shall be in accordance with authorization for member discipline contained in the governing documents.

(b) Any new or revised monetary penalty that is adopted after complying with subdivision (a) may be included in a supplement that is delivered to the members individually, pursuant to Section 6553.

(c) A monetary penalty for a violation of the governing documents shall not exceed the monetary penalty stated in the schedule of monetary penalties or supplement that is in effect at the time of the violation.

(d) An association shall provide a copy of the most recently distributed schedule of monetary penalties, along with any applicable supplements to that schedule, to any member on request. *(Added by Stats.2013, c. 605 (S.B.752), § 21.)*

Law Revision Commission Comments

With respect to a commercial or industrial common interest development, subdivision (a) of Section 6850 continues the first sentence of Section 1363(f) without change, except as indicated below.

The following substantive changes are made:

• A reference to delivery by personal delivery or first class mail is changed to incorporate the "individual notice" procedure.

• The word "invitee" is replaced with "tenant," to make clear that the provision applies to tenants.

The following nonsubstantive changes are made:

• A reference to the "rules of the association" is superfluous and is not continued. The term "governing documents" encompasses rules. See Section 6552 ("governing documents").

• The words "board of directors" are replaced with "board." See Section 6530 ("board").

Subdivisions (b)-(d) are new.

For further information, see Section 6500 Comment.

See also Sections 6528 ("association"), 6553 ("individual notice"), 6554 ("member").

For a similar provision in the Davis–Stirling Common Interest Development Act, see Section 5850. [42 Cal.L.Rev.Comm. Reports 1 (2012)].

§ 6854. Authority of board to impose monetary penalties

Nothing in Section 6850 shall be construed to create, expand, or reduce the authority of the board to impose monetary penalties on a member for a violation of the governing documents. *(Added by Stats.2013, c. 605 (S.B.752), § 21.)*

Law Revision Commission Comments

With respect to a commercial or industrial common interest development, Section 6854 continues the substance of Section 1363(i) without substantive change, except as indicated below.

The following nonsubstantive changes are made:

• The words "board of directors of the association" are replaced with "board." See Section 6530 ("board").

• The words "or rules of the association" are not continued.

• The words "an association member" are replaced with "member." See Section 6554 ("member").

• The reference to Section 6850 is narrower than the reference in Section 1363(i), which encompasses the entirety of Section 1363.

For further information, see Section 6500 Comment.

See also Section 6552 ("governing documents" includes the operating rules of the association).

For a similar provision in the Davis–Stirling Common Interest Development Act, see Section 5865. [42 Cal.L.Rev.Comm. Reports 1 (2012)].

ARTICLE 2. CIVIL ACTIONS

Section
6856. Covenants and restrictions in declaration as equitable servitudes; enforcement.
6858. Standing.
6860. Reduction of damages awarded; comparative fault of association.

§ 6856. Covenants and restrictions in declaration as equitable servitudes; enforcement

(a) The covenants and restrictions in the declaration shall be enforceable equitable servitudes, unless unreasonable, and shall inure to the benefit of and bind all owners of separate interests in the development. Unless the declaration states otherwise, these servitudes may be enforced by any owner of a separate interest or by the association, or by both.

(b) A governing document other than the declaration may be enforced by the association against an owner of a separate interest or by an owner of a separate interest against the association. *(Added by Stats.2013, c. 605 (S.B.752), § 21.)*

Law Revision Commission Comments

With respect to a commercial or industrial common interest development, Section 6856 continues Section 1354(a) and (b) without change.

For further information, see Section 6500 Comment.

See also Sections 6528 ("association"), 6546 ("declaration"), 6552 ("governing documents"), 6564 ("separate interest").

For a similar provision in the Davis–Stirling Common Interest Development Act, see Section 5975. [42 Cal.L.Rev.Comm. Reports 1 (2012)].

§ 6858. Standing

An association has standing to institute, defend, settle, or intervene in litigation, arbitration, mediation, or administrative proceedings in its own name as the real party in interest and without joining with it, the members, in matters pertaining to the following:

(a) Enforcement of the governing documents.

(b) Damage to the common area.

(c) Damage to a separate interest that the association is obligated to maintain or repair.

(d) Damage to a separate interest that arises out of, or is integrally related to, damage to the common area or a separate interest that the association is obligated to maintain or repair. *(Added by Stats.2013, c. 605 (S.B.752), § 21.)*

Law Revision Commission Comments

With respect to a commercial or industrial common interest development, Section 6858 continues Section 1368.3 without change, except as indicated below.

The following nonsubstantive changes are made:

• The word "owner" is replaced with "member." See Section 6554 ("member").

• The words "established to manage a common interest development" are not continued. For further information, see Section 6500 Comment. See also Sections 6528 ("association"), 6532 ("common area"), 6552 ("governing documents"), 6564 ("separate interest").

For a similar provision in the Davis–Stirling Common Interest Development Act, see Section 5980. [42 Cal.L.Rev.Comm. Reports 1 (2012)].

§ 6860. Reduction of damages awarded; comparative fault of association

(a) In an action maintained by an association pursuant to subdivision (b), (c), or (d) of Section 6858, the amount of damages recovered by the association shall be reduced by the amount of damages allocated to the association or its managing agents in direct proportion to their percentage of fault based upon principles of comparative fault. The comparative fault of the association or its managing agents may be raised by way of defense, but shall not be the basis for a cross-action or separate action against the association or its managing agents for contribution or implied indemnity, where the only damage was sustained by the association or its members. It is the intent of the Legislature in enacting this subdivision to require that comparative fault be pleaded as an affirmative defense, rather than a separate cause of action, where the only damage was sustained by the association or its members.

(b) In an action involving damages described in subdivision (b), (c), or (d) of Section 6858, the defendant or cross-defendant may allege and prove the comparative fault of the association or its managing agents as a setoff to the liability of the defendant or cross-defendant even if the association is not a party to the litigation or is no longer a party whether by reason of settlement, dismissal, or otherwise.

(c) Subdivisions (a) and (b) apply to actions commenced on or after January 1, 1993.

(d) Nothing in this section affects a person's liability under Section 1431, or the liability of the association or its managing agent for an act or omission that causes damages to another. *(Added by Stats.2013, c. 605 (S.B.752), § 21.)*

Law Revision Commission Comments

With respect to a commercial or industrial common interest development, Section 6860 continues Section 1368.4 without change.

For further information, see Section 6500 Comment.

See also Sections 6528 ("association"), 6554 ("member"), 6560 ("person").

For a similar provision in the Davis–Stirling Common Interest Development Act, see Section 5985. [42 Cal.L.Rev.Comm. Reports 1 (2012)].

CHAPTER 10. CONSTRUCTION DEFECT LITIGATION

Section
6870.   Actions for damages against common interest development builders, developers, or general contractors.
6874.   Settlement agreements regarding alleged defects; notice of resolution to members on record; disclosures.
6876.   Written notice to members prior to filing civil action; contents.

§ 6870. Actions for damages against common interest development builders, developers, or general contractors

(a) Before an association files a complaint for damages against a builder, developer, or general contractor (respondent) of a common interest development based upon a claim for defects in the design or construction of the common interest development, all of the requirements of this section shall be satisfied with respect to the builder, developer, or general contractor.

(b) The association shall serve upon the respondent a "Notice of Commencement of Legal Proceedings." The notice shall be served by certified mail to the registered agent of the respondent, or if there is no registered agent, then to any officer of the respondent. If there are no current officers of the respondent, service shall be upon the person or entity otherwise authorized by law to receive service of process. Service upon the general contractor shall be sufficient to initiate the process set forth in this section with regard to any builder or developer, if the builder or developer is not amenable to service of process by the foregoing methods. This notice shall toll all applicable statutes of limitation and repose, whether contractual or statutory, by and against all potentially responsible parties, regardless of whether they were named in the notice, including claims for indemnity applicable to the claim for the period set forth in subdivision (c). The notice shall include all of the following:

(1) The name and location of the project.

(2) An initial list of defects sufficient to apprise the respondent of the general nature of the defects at issue.

(3) A description of the results of the defects, if known.

(4) A summary of the results of a survey or questionnaire distributed to owners to determine the nature and extent of defects, if a survey has been conducted or a questionnaire has been distributed.

(5) Either a summary of the results of testing conducted to determine the nature and extent of defects or the actual test results, if that testing has been conducted.

(c) Service of the notice shall commence a period, not to exceed 180 days, during which the association, the respondent, and all other participating parties shall try to resolve the dispute through the processes set forth in this section. This 180-day period may be extended for one additional period, not to exceed 180 days, only upon the mutual agreement of the association, the respondent, and any parties not deemed peripheral pursuant to paragraph (3) of subdivision (e). Any extensions beyond the first extension shall require the agreement of all participating parties. Unless extended, the dispute resolution process prescribed by this section shall be deemed completed. All extensions shall continue the tolling period described in subdivision (b).

(d) Within 25 days of the date the association serves the Notice of Commencement of Legal Proceedings, the respondent may request in writing to meet and confer with the board. Unless the respondent and the association otherwise agree, there shall be not more than one meeting, which shall take place no later than 10 days from the date of the respondent's written request, at a mutually agreeable time and place. The meeting may be conducted in executive session, excluding the association's members. The discussions at the meeting are privileged communications and are not admissible in evidence in any civil action, unless the association and the respondent consent in writing to their admission.

(e) Upon receipt of the notice, the respondent shall, within 60 days, comply with the following:

(1) The respondent shall provide the association with access to, for inspection and copying of, all plans and specifications, subcontracts, and other construction files for the project that are reasonably calculated to lead to the discovery of admissible evidence regarding the defects claimed. The association shall provide the respondent with access to, for inspection and copying of, all files reasonably calculated to lead to the discovery of admissible evidence regarding the defects claimed, including all reserve studies, maintenance records and any survey questionnaires, or results of testing to determine the nature and extent of defects. To the extent any of the above documents are withheld based on privilege, a privilege log shall be prepared and submitted to all other parties. All other potentially responsible parties shall have the same rights as the respondent regarding the production of documents upon receipt of written notice of the claim, and shall produce all relevant documents within 60 days of receipt of the notice of the claim.

(2) The respondent shall provide written notice by certified mail to all subcontractors, design professionals, their insurers, and the insurers of any additional insured whose identities are known to the respondent or readily ascertainable by review of the project files or other similar sources and whose potential responsibility appears on the face of the notice. This notice to subcontractors, design professionals, and insurers shall include a copy of the Notice of Commencement of Legal Proceedings, and shall specify the date and manner by which the parties shall meet and confer to select a dispute resolution facilitator pursuant to paragraph (1) of subdivision (f), advise the recipient of its obligation to participate in the meet and confer or serve a written acknowledgment of receipt regarding this notice, advise the recipient that it will waive any challenge to selection of the dispute resolution facilitator if it elects not to participate in the meet and confer, advise the recipient that it may seek the assistance of an attorney, and advise the recipient that it should contact its insurer, if any. Any subcontractor or design professional, or insurer for that subcontractor, design professional, or additional insured, who receives written notice from the respondent regarding the meet and confer shall, prior to the meet and confer, serve on the respondent a written acknowledgment of receipt. That subcontractor or design professional shall, within 10 days of service of the written acknowledgment of receipt, provide to the association and the respondent a Statement of Insurance that includes both of the following:

(A) The names, addresses, and contact persons, if known, of all insurance carriers, whether primary or excess and regardless of whether a deductible or self-insured retention applies, whose policies were in effect from the commencement of construction of the subject project to the present and which potentially cover the subject claims.

(B) The applicable policy numbers for each policy of insurance provided.

(3) Any subcontractor or design professional, or insurer for that subcontractor, design professional, or additional insured, who so chooses, may, at any time, make a written request to the dispute resolution facilitator for designation as a peripheral

party. That request shall be served contemporaneously on the association and the respondent. If no objection to that designation is received within 15 days, or upon rejection of that objection, the dispute resolution facilitator shall designate that subcontractor or design professional as a peripheral party, and shall thereafter seek to limit the attendance of that subcontractor or design professional only to those dispute resolution sessions deemed peripheral party sessions or to those sessions during which the dispute resolution facilitator believes settlement as to peripheral parties may be finalized. Nothing in this subdivision shall preclude a party who has been designated a peripheral party from being reclassified as a nonperipheral party, nor shall this subdivision preclude a party designated as a nonperipheral party from being reclassified as a peripheral party after notice to all parties and an opportunity to object. For purposes of this subdivision, a peripheral party is a party having total claimed exposure of less than twenty-five thousand dollars ($25,000).

(f)(1) Within 20 days of sending the notice set forth in paragraph (2) of subdivision (e), the association, respondent, subcontractors, design professionals, and their insurers who have been sent a notice as described in paragraph (2) of subdivision (e) shall meet and confer in an effort to select a dispute resolution facilitator to preside over the mandatory dispute resolution process prescribed by this section. Any subcontractor or design professional who has been given timely notice of this meeting but who does not participate, waives any challenge he or she may have as to the selection of the dispute resolution facilitator. The role of the dispute resolution facilitator is to attempt to resolve the conflict in a fair manner. The dispute resolution facilitator shall be sufficiently knowledgeable in the subject matter and be able to devote sufficient time to the case. The dispute resolution facilitator shall not be required to reside in or have an office in the county in which the project is located. The dispute resolution facilitator and the participating parties shall agree to a date, time, and location to hold a case management meeting of all parties and the dispute resolution facilitator, to discuss the claims being asserted and the scheduling of events under this section. The case management meeting with the dispute resolution facilitator shall be held within 100 days of service of the Notice of Commencement of Legal Proceedings at a location in the county where the project is located. Written notice of the case management meeting with the dispute resolution facilitator shall be sent by the respondent to the association, subcontractors and design professionals, and their insurers who are known to the respondent to be on notice of the claim, no later than 10 days prior to the case management meeting, and shall specify its date, time, and location. The dispute resolution facilitator in consultation with the respondent shall maintain a contact list of the participating parties.

(2) No later than 10 days prior to the case management meeting, the dispute resolution facilitator shall disclose to the parties all matters that could cause a person aware of the facts to reasonably entertain a doubt that the proposed dispute resolution facilitator would be able to resolve the conflict in a fair manner. The facilitator's disclosure shall include the existence of any ground specified in Section 170.1 of the Code of Civil Procedure for disqualification of a judge, any attorney-client relationship the facilitator has or had with any party or lawyer for a party to the dispute resolution process, and any professional or significant personal relationship the facilitator or his or her spouse or minor child living in the household has or had with any party to the dispute resolution process. The disclosure shall also be provided to any subsequently noticed subcontractor or design professional within 10 days of the notice.

(3) A dispute resolution facilitator shall be disqualified by the court if he or she fails to comply with this subdivision and any party to the dispute resolution process serves a notice of disqualification prior to the case management meeting. If the dispute resolution facilitator complies with this subdivision, he or she shall be disqualified by the court on the basis of the disclosure if any party to the dispute resolution process serves a notice of disqualification prior to the case management meeting.

(4) If the parties cannot mutually agree to a dispute resolution facilitator, then each party shall submit a list of three dispute resolution facilitators. Each party may then strike one nominee from the other parties' list, and petition the court, pursuant to the procedure described in subdivisions (n) and (o), for final selection of the dispute resolution facilitator. The court may issue an order for final selection of the dispute resolution facilitator pursuant to this paragraph.

(5) Any subcontractor or design professional who receives notice of the association's claim without having previously received timely notice of the meet and confer to select the dispute resolution facilitator shall be notified by the respondent regarding the name, address, and telephone number of the dispute resolution facilitator. Any such subcontractor or design professional may serve upon the parties and the dispute resolution facilitator a written objection to the dispute resolution facilitator within 15 days of receiving notice of the claim. Within seven days after service of this objection, the subcontractor or design professional may petition the superior court to replace the dispute resolution facilitator. The court may replace the dispute resolution facilitator only upon a showing of good cause, liberally construed. Failure to satisfy the deadlines set forth in this subdivision shall constitute a waiver of the right to challenge the dispute resolution facilitator.

(6) The costs of the dispute resolution facilitator shall be apportioned in the following manner: one-third to be paid by the association; one-third to be paid by the respondent; and one-third to be paid by the subcontractors and design professionals, as allocated among them by the dispute resolution facilitator. The costs of the dispute resolution facilitator shall be recoverable by the prevailing party in any subsequent litigation pursuant to Section 1032 of the Code of Civil Procedure, provided however that any nonsettling party may, prior to the filing of the complaint, petition the facilitator to reallocate the costs of the dispute resolution facilitator as they apply to any nonsettling party. The determination of the dispute resolution facilitator with respect to the allocation of these costs shall be binding in any subsequent litigation. The dispute resolution facilitator shall take into account all relevant factors and equities between all parties in the dispute resolution process when reallocating costs.

(7) In the event the dispute resolution facilitator is replaced at any time, the case management statement created pursuant to subdivision (h) shall remain in full force and effect.

(8) The dispute resolution facilitator shall be empowered to enforce all provisions of this section.

(g)(1) No later than the case management meeting, the parties shall begin to generate a data compilation showing the following information regarding the alleged defects at issue:

(A) The scope of the work performed by each potentially responsible subcontractor.

(B) The tract or phase number in which each subcontractor provided goods or services, or both.

(C) The units, either by address, unit number, or lot number, at which each subcontractor provided goods or services, or both.

(2) This data compilation shall be updated as needed to reflect additional information. Each party attending the case management meeting, and any subsequent meeting pursuant to this section, shall provide all information available to that party relevant to this data compilation.

(h) At the case management meeting, the parties shall, with the assistance of the dispute resolution facilitator, reach agreement on a case management statement, which shall set forth all of the elements set forth in paragraphs (1) to (8), inclusive, except that the parties may dispense with one or more of these elements if they agree that it is appropriate to do so. The case management statement shall provide that the following elements shall take place in the following order:

(1) Establishment of a document depository, located in the county where the project is located, for deposit of documents, defect lists, demands, and other information provided for under this section. All documents exchanged by the parties and all documents created pursuant to this subdivision shall be deposited in the document depository, which shall be available to all parties throughout the prefiling dispute resolution process and in any subsequent litigation. When any document is deposited in the document depository, the party depositing the document shall provide written notice identifying the document to all other parties. The costs of maintaining the document depository shall be apportioned among the parties in the same manner as the costs of the dispute resolution facilitator.

(2) Provision of a more detailed list of defects by the association to the respondent after the association completes a visual inspection of the project. This list of defects shall provide sufficient detail for the respondent to ensure that all potentially responsible subcontractors and design professionals are provided with notice of the dispute resolution process. If not already completed prior to the case management meeting, the Notice of Commencement of Legal Proceedings shall be served by the respondent on all additional subcontractors and design professionals whose potential responsibility appears on the face of the more detailed list of defects within seven days of receipt of the more detailed list. The respondent shall serve a copy of the case management statement, including the name, address, and telephone number of the dispute resolution facilitator, to all the potentially responsible subcontractors and design professionals at the same time.

(3) Nonintrusive visual inspection of the project by the respondent, subcontractors, and design professionals.

(4) Invasive testing conducted by the association, if the association deems appropriate. All parties may observe and photograph any testing conducted by the association pursuant to this paragraph, but may not take samples or direct testing unless, by mutual agreement, costs of testing are shared by the parties.

(5) Provision by the association of a comprehensive demand which provides sufficient detail for the parties to engage in meaningful dispute resolution as contemplated under this section.

(6) Invasive testing conducted by the respondent, subcontractors, and design professionals, if they deem appropriate.

(7) Allowance for modification of the demand by the association if new issues arise during the testing conducted by the respondent, subcontractors, or design professionals.

(8) Facilitated dispute resolution of the claim, with all parties, including peripheral parties, as appropriate, and insurers, if any, present and having settlement authority. The dispute resolution facilitators shall endeavor to set specific times for the attendance of specific parties at dispute resolution sessions. If the dispute resolution facilitator does not set specific times for the attendance of parties at dispute resolution sessions, the dispute resolution facilitator shall permit those parties to participate in dispute resolution sessions by telephone.

(i) In addition to the foregoing elements of the case management statement described in subdivision (h), upon mutual agreement of the parties, the dispute resolution facilitator may include any or all of the following elements in a case management statement: the exchange of consultant or expert photographs; expert presentations; expert meetings; or any other mechanism deemed appropriate by the parties in the interest of resolving the dispute.

(j) The dispute resolution facilitator, with the guidance of the parties, shall at the time the case management statement is established, set deadlines for the occurrence of each event set forth in the case management statement, taking into account such factors as the size and complexity of the case, and the requirement of this section that this dispute resolution process not exceed 180 days absent agreement of the parties to an extension of time.

(k)(1) At a time to be determined by the dispute resolution facilitator, the respondent may submit to the association all of the following:

(A) A request to meet with the board to discuss a written settlement offer.

(B) A written settlement offer and a concise explanation of the reasons for the terms of the offer.

(C) A statement that the respondent has access to sufficient funds to satisfy the conditions of the settlement offer.

(D) A summary of the results of testing conducted for the purposes of determining the nature and extent of defects, if this testing has been conducted, unless the association provided the respondent with actual test results.

(2) If the respondent does not timely submit the items required by this subdivision, the association shall be relieved of any further obligation to satisfy the requirements of this subdivision only.

(3) No less than 10 days after the respondent submits the items required by this paragraph, the respondent and the board shall meet and confer about the respondent's settlement offer.

(4) If the board rejects a settlement offer presented at the meeting held pursuant to this subdivision, the board shall hold a meeting open to each member of the association. The meeting shall be held no less than 15 days before the association commences an action for damages against the respondent.

(5) No less than 15 days before this meeting is held, a written notice shall be sent to each member of the association specifying all of the following:

(A) That a meeting will take place to discuss problems that may lead to the filing of a civil action, and the time and place of this meeting.

(B) The options that are available to address the problems, including the filing of a civil action and a statement of the various alternatives that are reasonably foreseeable by the association to pay for those options and whether these payments are expected to be made from the use of reserve account funds or the imposition of regular or special assessments, or emergency assessment increases.

(C) The complete text of any written settlement offer and a concise explanation of the specific reasons for the terms of the offer submitted to the board at the meeting held pursuant to subdivision (d) that was received from the respondent.

(6) The respondent shall pay all expenses attributable to sending the settlement offer to all members of the association. The respondent shall also pay the expense of holding the meeting, not to exceed three dollars ($3) per association member.

(7) The discussions at the meeting and the contents of the notice and the items required to be specified in the notice pursuant to paragraph (5) are privileged communications and are not admissible in evidence in any civil action, unless the association consents to their admission.

(8) No more than one request to meet and discuss a written settlement offer may be made by the respondent pursuant to this subdivision.

(*l*) All defect lists and demands, communications, negotiations, and settlement offers made in the course of the prelitigation dispute resolution process provided by this section shall be inadmissible pursuant to Sections 1119 to 1124, inclusive, of the Evidence Code and all applicable decisional law. This inadmissibility shall not be extended to any other documents or communications which would not otherwise be deemed inadmissible.

(m) Any subcontractor or design professional may, at any time, petition the dispute resolution facilitator to release that party from the dispute resolution process upon a showing that the subcontractor or design professional is not potentially responsible for the defect claims at issue. The petition shall be served contemporaneously on all other parties, who shall have 15 days from the date of service to object. If a subcontractor or design professional is released, and it later appears to the dispute resolution facilitator that it may be a responsible party in light of the current defect list or demand, the respondent shall renotice the party as provided by paragraph (2) of subdivision (e), provide a copy of the current defect list or demand, and direct the party to attend a dispute resolution session at a stated time and location. A party who subsequently appears after having been released by the dispute resolution facilitator shall not be prejudiced by its absence from the dispute resolution process as the result of having been previously released by the dispute resolution facilitator.

(n) Any party may, at any time, petition the superior court in the county where the project is located, upon a showing of good cause, and the court may issue an order, for any of the following, or for appointment of a referee to resolve a dispute regarding any of the following:

(1) To take a deposition of any party to the process, or subpoena a third party for deposition or production of documents, which is necessary to further prelitigation resolution of the dispute.

(2) To resolve any disputes concerning inspection, testing, production of documents, or exchange of information provided for under this section.

(3) To resolve any disagreements relative to the timing or contents of the case management statement.

(4) To authorize internal extensions of timeframes set forth in the case management statement.

(5) To seek a determination that a settlement is a good faith settlement pursuant to Section 877.6 of the Code of Civil Procedure and all related authorities. The page limitations and meet and confer requirements specified in this section shall not apply to these motions, which may be made on shortened notice. Instead, these motions shall be subject to other applicable state law, rules of court, and local rules. A determination made by the court pursuant to this motion shall have the same force and effect as the determination of a postfiling application or motion for good faith settlement.

(6) To ensure compliance, on shortened notice, with the obligation to provide a Statement of Insurance pursuant to paragraph (2) of subdivision (e).

(7) For any other relief appropriate to the enforcement of the provisions of this section, including the ordering of parties, and insurers, if any, to the dispute resolution process with settlement authority.

(*o*)(1) A petition filed pursuant to subdivision (n) shall be filed in the superior court in the county in which the project is located. The court shall hear and decide the petition within 10 days after filing. The petitioning party shall serve the petition on all parties, including the date, time, and location of the hearing no later than five business days prior to the hearing. Any responsive papers shall be filed and served no later than three business days prior to the hearing. Any petition or response filed under this section shall be no more than three pages in length.

(2) All parties shall meet with the dispute resolution facilitator, if one has been appointed and confer in person or by the telephone prior to the filing of that petition to attempt to resolve the matter without requiring court intervention.

(p) As used in this section:

(1) "Association" shall have the same meaning as defined in Section 6528.

(2) "Builder" means the declarant, as defined in Section 6544.

(3) "Common interest development" shall have the same meaning as in Section 6534, except that it shall not include developments or projects with less than 20 units.

(q) The alternative dispute resolution process and procedures described in this section shall have no application or legal effect other than as described in this section.

(r) This section shall become operative on July 1, 2002, however it shall not apply to any pending suit or claim for which notice has previously been given.

(s) This section shall become inoperative on July 1, 2017, and, as of January 1, 2018, is repealed, unless a later enacted statute, that becomes operative on or before January 1, 2018, deletes or extends the dates on which it becomes inoperative and is repealed. *(Added by Stats.2013, c. 605 (S.B.752), § 21.)*

Law Revision Commission Comments

With respect to a commercial or industrial common interest development, Section 6870 continues Section 1375 without change, except as indicated below.

The following substantive change is made:

● A reference in Section 1375(d) to a meeting subject to Section 1363.05(b) is replaced with the relevant substance of Section 1363.05(b). Section 1363.05 is not continued in this act.

The following nonsubstantive changes are made:

● Cross-references are updated to reflect the new location of the referenced provisions.

● In subdivision (a), quotation marks are removed before and after the word "respondent."

● A reference to "homeowner" in paragraph (4) of subdivision (b) is changed to "owner."

● The words "board of directors" and "board of directors of the association" are replaced throughout with "board." See Section 6530 ("board").

● Subdivision (e)(2) is revised to delete references to former Section 1375.05, which was repealed by its own terms on January 1, 2011.

● Subdivision (f)(3) is revised to correct erroneous references to "this paragraph." The revised provision refers to "this subdivision."

● In subparagraph (k)(1)(G), the word "paragraph" is replaced with "subparagraph."

● Subdivision (*l*) is revised to delete a reference to former Section 1375.05, which was repealed by its own terms on January 1, 2011.

For further information, see Section 6500 Comment.

See also Sections 6528 ("association"), 6534 ("common interest development"), 6554 ("member"), 6560 ("person").

For a similar provision in the Davis–Stirling Common Interest Development Act, see Section 6000. [42 Cal.L.Rev.Comm. Reports 1 (2012)].

Inoperative Date and Repeal

For inoperative date and repeal of this section, see its terms.

§ 6874. Settlement agreements regarding alleged defects; notice of resolution to members on record; disclosures

(a) As soon as is reasonably practicable after the association and the builder have entered into a settlement agreement or the matter has otherwise been resolved regarding alleged defects in the common areas, alleged defects in the separate interests that the association is obligated to maintain or repair, or alleged defects in the separate interests that arise out of, or are integrally related to, defects in the common areas or separate interests that the association is obligated to maintain or repair, where the defects giving rise to the dispute have not been corrected, the association shall, in writing, inform only the members of the association whose names appear on the records of the association that the matter has been resolved, by settlement agreement or other means, and disclose all of the following:

(1) A general description of the defects that the association reasonably believes, as of the date of the disclosure, will be corrected or replaced.

(2) A good faith estimate, as of the date of the disclosure, of when the association believes that the defects identified in paragraph (1) will be corrected or replaced. The association may state that the estimate may be modified.

(3) The status of the claims for defects in the design or construction of the common interest development that were not identified in paragraph (1) whether expressed in a preliminary list of defects sent to each member of the association or otherwise claimed and disclosed to the members of the association.

(b) Nothing in this section shall preclude an association from amending the disclosures required pursuant to subdivision (a), and any amendments shall supersede any prior conflicting information disclosed to the members of the association and shall retain any privilege attached to the original disclosures.

(c) Disclosure of the information required pursuant to subdivision (a) or authorized by subdivision (b) shall not waive any privilege attached to the information.

(d) For the purposes of the disclosures required pursuant to this section, the term "defects" shall be defined to include any damage resulting from defects. *(Added by Stats.2013, c. 605 (S.B.752), § 21.)*

Law Revision Commission Comments

With respect to a commercial or industrial common interest development, Section 6874 continues Section 1375.1 without change.

For further information, see Section 6500 Comment.

See also Sections 6528 ("association"), 6532 ("common area"), 6534 ("common interest development"), 6554 ("member"), 6564 ("separate interest").

For a similar provision in the Davis–Stirling Common Interest Development Act, see Section 6100. [42 Cal.L.Rev.Comm. Reports 1 (2012)].

§ 6876. Written notice to members prior to filing civil action; contents

(a) Not later than 30 days prior to the filing of any civil action by the association against the declarant or other developer of a common interest development for alleged damage to the common areas, alleged damage to the separate interests that the association is obligated to maintain or repair, or alleged damage to the separate interests that arises out of, or is integrally related to, damage to the common areas or separate interests that the association is obligated to maintain or repair, the board shall provide a written notice to each member of the association who appears on the records of the association when the notice is provided. This notice shall specify all of the following:

(1) That a meeting will take place to discuss problems that may lead to the filing of a civil action.

(2) The options, including civil actions, that are available to address the problems.

(3) The time and place of this meeting.

(b) Notwithstanding subdivision (a), if the association has reason to believe that the applicable statute of limitations will expire before the association files the civil action, the association may give the notice, as described above, within 30 days after the filing of the action. *(Added by Stats.2013, c. 605 (S.B.752), § 21.)*

Law Revision Commission Comments

With respect to a commercial or industrial common interest development, Section 6876 continues Section 1368.5 without change, except as indicated below.

The following nonsubstantive change is made:

● The words "board of directors of the association" are replaced with "board." See Section 6530 ("board").

For further information, see Section 6500 Comment.

See also Sections 6528 ("association"), 6532 ("common area"), 6534 ("common interest development"), 6544 ("declarant"), 6554 ("member"), 6564 ("separate interest").

For a similar provision in the Davis–Stirling Common Interest Development Act, see Section 6150. [42 Cal.L.Rev.Comm. Reports 1 (2012)].

Part 5.5

AUTOMATIC CHECKOUT SYSTEM

Law Revision Commission Comments

The heading of Part 8 (Sections 7100–7106) is amended to renumber the part as Part 5.5. The section numbers and text of the part remain unchanged. [40 Cal.L.Rev.Comm. Reports 49 (2010)].

§ 7100. Readable prices on packaged consumer commodities; exemptions; listing and posting; definitions

(a) Every retail grocery store or grocery department within a general retail merchandise store which uses a point-of-sale system shall cause to have a clearly readable price indicated on 85 percent of the total number of packaged consumer commodities offered for sale which are not exempt pursuant to subdivision (b).

The management of any such retail grocery store or grocery department shall determine the number of consumer commodities normally offered for sale on a daily basis, shall determine the consumer commodities to be exempted pursuant to this subdivision, and shall maintain a list of those consumer commodities exempt pursuant to this subdivision. The list shall be made available to a designated representative of the appropriate local union, the members of which are responsible for item pricing, in those stores or departments that have collective bargaining agreements, seven days prior to an item or items being exempted pursuant to this subdivision. In addition, the list shall be available and posted in a prominent place in the store seven days prior to an item or items being exempted pursuant to this subdivision.

(b) The provisions of this section shall not apply to any of the following:

(1) Any consumer commodity which was not generally item-priced on January 1, 1977, as determined by the Department of Food and Agriculture pursuant to subdivision (c) of Section 12604.5 of the Business and Professions Code, as in effect July 8, 1977.

(2) Any unpackaged fresh food produce, or to consumer commodities which are under three cubic inches in size, weigh less than three ounces, and are priced under forty cents ($0.40).

(3) Any consumer commodity offered as a sale item or as a special.

(4) Any business which has as its only regular employees the owner thereof, or the parent, spouse, or child of such owner, or, in addition thereto, not more than two other regular employees.

(5) Identical items within a multi-item package.

(6) Items sold through a vending machine.

(c) For the purposes of this section:

(1) "Point-of-sale system" means any computer or electronic system used by a retail establishment such as, but not limited to, Universal Product Code scanners, price lookup codes, or an electronic price lookup system as a means for determining the price of the item being purchased by a consumer.

(2) "Consumer commodity" includes:

(A) Food, including all material whether solid, liquid, or mixed, and whether simple or compound, which is used or intended for consumption by human beings or domestic animals normally kept as household pets, and all substances or ingredients added to any such material for any purpose. This definition shall not apply to individual packages of cigarettes or individual cigars.

(B) Napkins, facial tissues, toilet tissues, foil wrapping, plastic wrapping, paper toweling, and disposable plates and cups.

(C) Detergents, soaps, and other cleaning agents.

(D) Pharmaceuticals, including nonprescription drugs, bandages, female hygiene products, and toiletries.

(3) "Grocery department" means an area within a general retail merchandise store which is engaged primarily in the retail sale of packaged food, rather than food prepared for immediate consumption on or off the premises.

(4) "Grocery store" means a store engaged primarily in the retail sale of packaged food, rather than food prepared for consumption on the premises.

(5) "Sale item or special" means any consumer commodity offered in good faith for a period of 14 days or less, on sale at a price below the normal price that item is usually sold for in that store. The Department of Food and Agriculture shall determine the normal length of a sale held for consumer commodities generally item priced on January 1, 1977, in stores regulated pursuant to this chapter, and that period shall be used for the purposes of this subdivision. The department's determination as to the normal length of a sale shall be binding for the purposes of this section, but each such determination shall not exceed seven days. *(Added by Stats.1981, c. 224, § 2. Amended by Stats.2006, c. 566 (A.B.2285), § 6.)*

Research References

4 Witkin, California Summary 10th Sales § 361, (S 361) Groceries Commodities Pricing.

§ 7101. Violations; civil fines; injunctions

(a) The intentional violation of Section 7100 is punishable by a civil penalty of not less than twenty-five dollars ($25) nor more than five hundred dollars ($500).

(b) Failure to have a clearly readable price indicated on 12 units of the same item required to be item-priced of the same commodity shall constitute a presumption of intent to violate Section 7100.

(c) Every additional 12 units of the same item required to be item-priced that fail to have a price indicated on them shall constitute a presumption of intent to violate Section 7100.

(d) Each day that a violation continues shall also constitute a separate violation after notification thereof to the manager or assistant manager of the retail grocery store or the grocery department of the general retail merchandise store and shall constitute a presumption of intent to violate Section 7100.

(e) Notwithstanding any other provision of law, any person may bring an action to enjoin a violation of Section 7100. *(Added by Stats.1981, c. 224, § 2.)*

Research References

4 Witkin, California Summary 10th Sales § 361, (S 361) Groceries Commodities Pricing.

§ 7102. Liability for losses and expenses; additional penalty; applicability

Any person, firm, corporation, or association who violates Sections 7100 and 7101 shall be liable to any person injured for any losses and expenses thereby incurred, and for the sum of fifty dollars ($50) in addition thereto. The remedy set forth herein is applicable only to actions brought in the name of, and on behalf of, a single plaintiff and shall not be applicable in multiple plaintiff or class actions. *(Added by Stats.1981, c. 224, § 2.)*

§ 7103. Unintentional error

Improper pricing on the shelf or on the item due to unintentional error shall not constitute a violation of this division. *(Added by Stats.1981, c. 224, § 2.)*

§ 7104. Exclusive remedies

The remedies set forth in Sections 7101 and 7102 are the exclusive remedies available to any person, state or local agency or law enforcement official. *(Added by Stats.1981, c. 224, § 2.)*

§ 7105. Short title

This part shall be known and may be cited as the Rosenthal–Roberti Item Pricing Act. *(Added by Stats.1981, c. 224, § 2.)*

§ 7106. State preemption of item pricing

It is the intention of the Legislature that this part shall occupy the field with regard to item pricing and shall preempt all local ordinances, rules, or regulations concerning item pricing. *(Added by Stats.1981, c. 224, § 2.)*

Part 6

WORKS OF IMPROVEMENT

Operative Effect

For operative effect of Part 6, see Civil Code § 8052 and Stats.2010, c. 697 (S.B.189), § 105.

Civil

Title 1

WORKS OF IMPROVEMENT GENERALLY

Operative Effect

For operative effect of Part 6, see Civil Code § 8052 and Stats.2010, c. 697 (S.B.189), § 105.

CHAPTER 1. GENERAL PROVISIONS

Operative Effect

For operative effect of Part 6, see Civil Code § 8052 and Stats.2010, c. 697 (S.B.189), § 105.

ARTICLE 1. DEFINITIONS

Operative Effect

For operative effect of Part 6, see Civil Code § 8052 and Stats.2010, c. 697 (S.B.189), § 105.

§ 8000. Construction of part

Unless the provision or context otherwise requires, the definitions in this article govern the construction of this part. *(Added by Stats.2010, c. 697 (S.B.189), § 20, operative July 1, 2012.)*

Operative Effect

For operative effect of Part 6, see Civil Code § 8052 and Stats.2010, c. 697 (S.B.189), § 105.

Law Revision Commission Comments

Section 8000 continues former Section 3082 without substantive change. [37 Cal.L.Rev.Comm. Reports 527 (2007)].

Research References

California Real Estate Forms (Miller & Starr) § 3:15, Construction Loan Agreement.

Rutter, Cal. Practice Guide: Insurance Litigation Ch. 6I-A, A. Introduction.

Rutter, Cal. Practice Guide: Insurance Litigation Ch. 6I-B, B. Particular Surety Bond Coverages.

Rutter, Cal. Practice Guide: Insurance Litigation Gen. Matls., Highlights.

Miller and Starr California Real Estate § 28:1, Introduction.

Miller and Starr California Real Estate § 28:3, Source and Purpose of the Mechanics Lien.

Miller and Starr California Real Estate § 11:130, in General; Off-Record Priority.

Miller and Starr California Real Estate § 11:131, Date Liens Attach; Relation to Subsequent Interests.

Miller and Starr California Real Estate § 11:132, Relation to Prior Interests--In General.

Miller and Starr California Real Estate § 11:133, Relation to Prior Interests--Mechanic's Knowledge of a Prior Unrecorded Interest.

Miller and Starr California Real Estate § 11:134, Effect of Commencement of Work Before the Grantee Receives Title.

Miller and Starr California Real Estate § 11:135, When Construction Commences--Effect on Priority of Mechanics' and Design Professionals' Liens.

Miller and Starr California Real Estate § 11:136, When Construction Commences--Phasing of the Project; in General.

Miller and Starr California Real Estate § 11:137, Phasing of a Project by Separate Direct Contracts With the Owner.

Miller and Starr California Real Estate § 11:138, Site Improvements; Priority of Liens as Distinguished from Liens for Structures or Buildings.

Miller and Starr California Real Estate § 11:139, Priority as Affected by Separate Works of Improvement on Separate Parcels.

Miller and Starr California Real Estate § 11:140, Effect of Cessation of Work on Mechanic's Lien Priorities.

Miller and Starr California Real Estate § 11:141, Priority of the Construction Loan Deed of Trust--In General.

Miller and Starr California Real Estate § 11:142, Priority of the Construction Loan Deed of Trust--Relation to Obligatory Advances.

Miller and Starr California Real Estate § 11:143, Priority of the Construction Loan Deed of Trust--Relation to Optional Advances.

Miller and Starr California Real Estate § 11:144, Priority of the Construction Loan Deed of Trust--Premature Advances as Optional.

Miller and Starr California Real Estate § 11:145, Priority of the Construction Loan Deed of Trust--Advances to Complete Construction.

Miller and Starr California Real Estate § 11:146, Priority of the Construction Loan Deed of Trust--Effect of a Bond Recorded by the Construction Lender.

Miller and Starr California Real Estate § 28:103, Exoneration of the Surety--Modification of the Terms of the Construction Contract.

21 NO. 4 Miller & Starr, California Real Estate Newsalert 1, Everything Old is New Again: Impact of SB 189 on Mechanics' Lien Law.

3 Witkin Cal. Proc. 5th Actions § 65, (S 65) Statutory Classes.

3 Witkin Cal. Proc. 5th Actions § 217, in General.

3 Witkin Cal. Proc. 5th Actions § 218, Preliminary Notice.

3 Witkin Cal. Proc. 5th Actions § 219, (S 219) Private Property: Stop Notice.

3 Witkin Cal. Proc. 5th Actions § 220, (S 220) Public Property: Stop Notice.

3 Witkin Cal. Proc. 5th Actions § 221, (S 221) Constitutionality of Statutes.

3 Witkin Cal. Proc. 5th Actions § 243, (S 243) Mechanics' Liens.

3 Witkin Cal. Proc. 5th Actions § 380, (S 380) Specific Permissive Statutes.

3 Witkin Cal. Proc. 5th Actions § 442, Limitation Affecting Property Right.

3 Witkin Cal. Proc. 5th Actions § 477, (S 477) Ninety Days or Three Months.

3 Witkin Cal. Proc. 5th Actions § 480, (S 480) One Hundred Eighty Days or Six Months.

3 Witkin Cal. Proc. 5th Actions § 481, (S 481) One Year.

3 Witkin Cal. Proc. 5th Actions § 221A, (S 221A) (New)-In General.

3 Witkin Cal. Proc. 5th Actions § 221C, (S 221C) (New)-Private Property: Preliminary Notice.

4 Witkin, California Summary 10th Security Transactions in Real Property § 26, (S 26) in General.

4 Witkin, California Summary 10th Security Transactions in Real Property § 27, (S 27) Right to Lien.

4 Witkin, California Summary 10th Security Transactions in Real Property § 28, (S 28) Amount of Lien.

4 Witkin, California Summary 10th Security Transactions in Real Property § 29, (S 29) Enforcing or Protecting Against Lien.

4 Witkin, California Summary 10th Security Transactions in Real Property § 30, in General.

4 Witkin, California Summary 10th Security Transactions in Real Property § 31, Conditional Waiver of Release.

4 Witkin, California Summary 10th Security Transactions in Real Property § 31A, (S 31A) (New)-Nature and Purpose of Revision.

3 Witkin, California Summary 10th Agency and Employment § 5, (S 5) Labor and Laborer.

3 Witkin, California Summary 10th Agency and Employment § 410, (S 410) State Law Preempted.

3 Witkin, California Summary 10th Agency and Employment § 411, (S 411) State Law Not Preempted.

§ 8002. "Admitted surety insurer" defined

"Admitted surety insurer" has the meaning provided in Section 995.120 of the Code of Civil Procedure. *(Added by Stats.2010, c. 697 (S.B.189), § 20, operative July 1, 2012.)*

Operative Effect

For operative effect of Part 6, see Civil Code § 8052 and Stats.2010, c. 697 (S.B.189), § 105.

Law Revision Commission Comments

Section 8002 is new. It is included for drafting convenience. "Admitted surety insurer" replaces references in former law to a corporate surety authorized to write or issue surety bonds in the State of California.

See Sections 8424 (lien claim release bond), 8510 (stop payment notice release bond), 8534 (construction lender objection to bonded stop payment notice), 8604 (lending institution objection to surety on payment bond), 8606 (payment bond). [40 Cal.L.Rev.Comm. Reports 49 [AR:apx5] (2010)].

Research References

Rutter, Cal. Practice Guide: Insurance Litigation Ch. 6I-A, A. Introduction.

Miller and Starr California Real Estate § 28:27, Limiting Owner's Liability by Recording Direct Contract and Bond.

Miller and Starr California Real Estate § 28:74, Duty of Lender to Withhold Funds; Effect of a Bond.

Miller and Starr California Real Estate § 28:81, Release, Bond and Waiver of Stop Payment Notice.

Miller and Starr California Real Estate § 28:93, Suretyship Terminology and Definitions.

21 NO. 4 Miller & Starr, California Real Estate Newsalert 1, Everything Old is New Again: Impact of SB 189 on Mechanics' Lien Law.

§ 8004. "Claimant" defined

"Claimant" means a person that has a right under this part to record a claim of lien, give a stop payment notice, or assert a claim against a payment bond, or do any combination of the foregoing. *(Added by Stats.2010, c. 697 (S.B.189), § 20, operative July 1, 2012.)*

Operative Effect

For operative effect of Part 6, see Civil Code § 8052 and Stats.2010, c. 697 (S.B.189), § 105.

Law Revision Commission Comments

Section 8004 restates former Section 3085 without substantive change.

See also Sections 8026 ("lien"), 8030 ("payment bond"), 8032 ("person"), 8044 ("stop payment notice"). [40 Cal.L.Rev.Comm. Reports 49 [AR:apx5] (2010)].

Research References

Rutter, Cal. Practice Guide: Insurance Litigation Ch. 6I-A, A. Introduction.

Miller and Starr California Real Estate § 28:2, Alternative (Cumulative) Remedies of the Claimant.

Miller and Starr California Real Estate § 28:27, Limiting Owner's Liability by Recording Direct Contract and Bond.

Miller and Starr California Real Estate § 28:118, Action by Claimant to Recover on a Bond as to Private Projects--In General.

3 Witkin Cal. Proc. 5th Actions § 221C, (S 221C) (New)-Private Property: Preliminary Notice.

3 Witkin Cal. Proc. 5th Actions § 221E, (S 221E) (New)-Public Property: Stop Notice.

§ 8006. "Construction lender" defined

"Construction lender" means either of the following:

(a) A mortgagee or beneficiary under a deed of trust lending funds with which the cost of all or part of a work of improvement is to be paid, or the assignee or successor in interest of the mortgagee or beneficiary.

(b) An escrow holder or other person holding funds provided by an owner, lender, or another person as a fund for with which the cost of all or part of a work of improvement is to be paid. *(Added by Stats.2010, c. 697 (S.B.189), § 20, operative July 1, 2012.)*

Operative Effect

For operative effect of Part 6, see Civil Code § 8052 and Stats.2010, c. 697 (S.B.189), § 105.

Law Revision Commission Comments

Section 8006 restates former Section 3087 without substantive change.

See also Section 14 (present includes future).

See also Sections 8032 ("person"), 8050 ("work of improvement"). [40 Cal.L.Rev.Comm. Reports 49 [AR:apx5] (2010)].

Research References

Rutter, Cal. Practice Guide: Insurance Litigation Ch. 6I-B, B. Particular Surety Bond Coverages.

Miller and Starr California Real Estate § 28:68, Nature and Validity of the Stop Payment Notice.

Miller and Starr California Real Estate § 28:118, Action by Claimant to Recover on a Bond as to Private Projects--In General.

3 Witkin Cal. Proc. 5th Actions § 221C, (S 221C) (New)-Private Property: Preliminary Notice.

§ 8008. "Contract" defined

"Contract" means an agreement that provides for all or part of a work of improvement. *(Added by Stats.2010, c. 697 (S.B.189), § 20, operative July 1, 2012.)*

Operative Effect

For operative effect of Part 6, see Civil Code § 8052 and Stats.2010, c. 697 (S.B.189), § 105.

Law Revision Commission Comments

Section 8008 broadens the definition of contract in former Section 3088.

There are instances in this part where the term is not used in its defined sense. See, e.g., Section 8444(d)(2). See also Section 8000 (application of definitions).

An agreement between an owner and a direct contractor that provides for all or part of a work of improvement is a "direct contract". See Section 8016.

See also Section 8050 ("work of improvement"). [40 Cal.L.Rev.Comm. Reports 49 [AR:apx5] (2010)].

Research References

Miller and Starr California Real Estate § 28:9, Contractors.

§ 8010. "Contract price" defined

"Contract price" means the price agreed to in a direct contract for a work of improvement. *(Added by Stats.2010, c. 697 (S.B.189), § 20, operative July 1, 2012.)*

Operative Effect

For operative effect of Part 6, see Civil Code § 8052 and Stats.2010, c. 697 (S.B.189), § 105.

Law Revision Commission Comments

Section 8010 is new. It is included for drafting convenience.

See also Sections 8016 ("direct contract"), 8050 ("work of improvement"). [40 Cal.L.Rev.Comm. Reports 49 [AR:apx5] (2010)].

§ 8012. "Contractor" defined

"Contractor" includes a direct contractor, subcontractor, or both. This section does not apply to Sections 8018 and 8046. *(Added by Stats.2010, c. 697 (S.B.189), § 20, operative July 1, 2012.)*

Operative Effect

For operative effect of Part 6, see Civil Code § 8052 and Stats.2010, c. 697 (S.B.189), § 105.

Law Revision Commission Comments

Section 8012 is new. It is included for drafting convenience.

See also Sections 8018 ("direct contractor"), 8046 ("subcontractor"). [40 Cal.L.Rev.Comm. Reports 49 [AR:apx5] (2010)].

Research References

Miller and Starr California Real Estate § 28:9, Contractors.
Miller and Starr California Real Estate § 28:38, Time to File.

§ 8014. "Design professional" defined

"Design professional" means a person licensed as an architect pursuant to Chapter 3 (commencing with Section 5500) of Division 3 of the Business and Professions Code, licensed as a landscape architect pursuant to Chapter 3.5 (commencing with Section 5615) of Division 3 of the Business and Professions Code, registered as a professional engineer pursuant to Chapter 7 (commencing with Section 6700) of Division 3 of the Business and Professions Code, or licensed as a land surveyor pursuant to Chapter 15 (commencing with Section 8700) of Division 3 of the Business and Professions Code. *(Added by Stats.2010, c. 697 (S.B.189), § 20, operative July 1, 2012.)*

Operative Effect

For operative effect of Part 6, see Civil Code § 8052 and Stats.2010, c. 697 (S.B.189), § 105.

Law Revision Commission Comments

Section 8014 generalizes the first paragraph of former Section 3081.1, and adds a licensed landscape architect to the persons included within the definition of "design professional."

See also Sections 8032 ("person"), 8050 ("work of improvement"). [40 Cal.L.Rev.Comm. Reports 49 [AR:apx5] (2010)].

Research References

Miller and Starr California Real Estate § 28:8, "Claimant" Defined.
Miller and Starr California Real Estate § 28:16, Design Professionals Liens; Rights to Mechanics Liens.
Miller and Starr California Real Estate § 11:131, Date Liens Attach; Relation to Subsequent Interests.

Miller and Starr California Real Estate § 11:135, When Construction Commences--Effect on Priority of Mechanics' and Design Professionals' Liens.
4 Witkin, California Summary 10th Security Transactions in Real Property § 32, Design Professional's Lien.

§ 8016. "Direct contract" defined

"Direct contract" means a contract between an owner and a direct contractor that provides for all or part of a work of improvement. *(Added by Stats.2010, c. 697 (S.B.189), § 20, operative July 1, 2012.)*

Operative Effect

For operative effect of Part 6, see Civil Code § 8052 and Stats.2010, c. 697 (S.B.189), § 105.

Law Revision Commission Comments

Section 8016 restates former Section 3088 without substantive change.

See also Sections 8008 ("contract"), 8018 ("direct contractor"), 8050 ("work of improvement"). [40 Cal.L.Rev.Comm. Reports 49 [AR:apx5] (2010)].

Research References

3 Witkin Cal. Proc. 5th Actions § 221C, (S 221C) (New)-Private Property: Preliminary Notice.

§ 8018. "Direct contractor" defined

"Direct contractor" means a contractor that has a direct contractual relationship with an owner. A reference in another statute to a "prime contractor" in connection with the provisions in this part means a "direct contractor." *(Added by Stats.2010, c. 697 (S.B.189), § 20, operative July 1, 2012.)*

Operative Effect

For operative effect of Part 6, see Civil Code § 8052 and Stats.2010, c. 697 (S.B.189), § 105.

Law Revision Commission Comments

Section 8018 supersedes former Section 3095 ("original contractor"). A direct contractor within the meaning of this section is one that contracts directly with the owner, as opposed to one that contracts with another contractor (i.e., a subcontractor).

A direct contractor is at times referred to in other code sections as a "prime contractor." See e.g., Pub. Cont. Code § 4113. [40 Cal.L.Rev. Comm. Reports 49 [AR:apx5] (2010)].

Research References

Rutter, Cal. Practice Guide: Insurance Litigation Ch. 6I-B, B. Particular Surety Bond Coverages.
Rutter, Cal. Practice Guide: Insurance Litigation Gen. Matls., Highlights.
Miller and Starr California Real Estate § 28:4, Requirement of a Contract.
Miller and Starr California Real Estate § 28:8, "Claimant" Defined.
Miller and Starr California Real Estate § 28:9, Contractors.
Miller and Starr California Real Estate § 28:36, Time and Method for Service of the Preliminary Notice.
Miller and Starr California Real Estate § 28:38, Time to File.
Miller and Starr California Real Estate § 28:40, When Notice of Cessation Recorded.
3 Witkin Cal. Proc. 5th Actions § 221B, (S 221B) (New)-Principal Changes.
3 Witkin Cal. Proc. 5th Actions § 221C, (S 221C) (New)-Private Property: Preliminary Notice.
4 Witkin, California Summary 10th Security Transactions in Real Property § 31B, (S 31B) (New)-Principal Changes.

§ 8020. "Funds" defined

For the purposes of Title 3 (commencing with Section 9000), "funds" means warrant, check, money, or bonds (if bonds are to be issued in payment of the public works contract). *(Added by Stats.2010, c. 697 (S.B.189), § 20, operative July 1, 2012.)*

For operative effect of Part 6, see Civil Code § 8052 and Stats.2010, c. 697 (S.B.189), § 105.

Law Revision Commission Comments

Section 8020 is new. It is included for drafting convenience. It generalizes provisions of former Sections 3186, 3187, and 3196.

See also Section 8038 ("public works contract"). [40 Cal.L.Rev.Comm. Reports 49 [AR:apx5] (2010)].

§ 8022. "Labor, service, equipment, or material" defined

"Labor, service, equipment, or material" includes, but is not limited to, labor, skills, services, material, supplies, equipment, appliances, power, and surveying, provided for a work of improvement. *(Added by Stats.2010, c. 697 (S.B.189), § 20, operative July 1, 2012.)*

For operative effect of Part 6, see Civil Code § 8052 and Stats.2010, c. 697 (S.B.189), § 105.

Law Revision Commission Comments

Section 8022 is new. It is included for drafting convenience. The phrase is intended to replace various phrases used throughout the former law, including "labor or material," "labor, services, equipment, or materials," "appliances, teams, or power," and the like, and is not intended to effect any change in the law. The definition applies to variant grammatical forms of the phrase used in this part, such as "labor, service, equipment, *and* material."

See also Section 8050 ("work of improvement"). [40 Cal.L.Rev.Comm. Reports 49 [AR:apx5] (2010)].

Research References

Rutter, Cal. Practice Guide: Insurance Litigation Ch. 6I-B, B. Particular Surety Bond Coverages.

§ 8024. "Laborer" defined

(a) "Laborer" means a person who, acting as an employee, performs labor upon, or bestows skill or other necessary services on, a work of improvement.

(b) "Laborer" includes a person or entity to which a portion of a laborer's compensation for a work of improvement, including, but not limited to, employer payments described in Section 1773.1 of the Labor Code and implementing regulations, is paid by agreement with that laborer or the collective bargaining agent of that laborer.

(c) A person or entity described in subdivision (b) that has standing under applicable law to maintain a direct legal action, in its own name or as an assignee, to collect any portion of compensation owed for a laborer for a work of improvement, shall have standing to enforce any rights or claims of the laborer under this part, to the extent of the compensation agreed to be paid to the person or entity for labor on that improvement. This subdivision is intended to give effect to the longstanding public policy of this state to protect the entire compensation of a laborer on a work of improvement, regardless of the form in which that compensation is to be paid. *(Added by Stats.2010, c. 697 (S.B.189), § 20, operative July 1, 2012.)*

For operative effect of Part 6, see Civil Code § 8052 and Stats.2010, c. 697 (S.B.189), § 105.

Law Revision Commission Comments

Subdivision (a) of Section 8024 continues former Section 3089(a) without substantive change.

Subdivision (b) restates the first sentence of former Section 3089(b) and a part of former Section 3111 without substantive change.

Subdivision (c) restates the second and third sentences of former Section 3089(b) and a part of former Section 3111 without substantive change.

See also Sections 8032 ("person"), 8050 ("work of improvement"). [40 Cal.L.Rev.Comm. Reports 49 [AR:apx5] (2010)].

Research References

Miller and Starr California Real Estate § 28:8, "Claimant" Defined.
Miller and Starr California Real Estate § 28:9, Contractors.
Miller and Starr California Real Estate § 28:13, Laborers Defined.
Miller and Starr California Real Estate § 28:15, Entities Entitled to a Portion of Employee Compensation.
Miller and Starr California Real Estate § 28:29, Preliminary Notice-- Purpose and Validity.
Miller and Starr California Real Estate § 28:34, Express Trust Fund; Former Exemption.
Miller and Starr California Real Estate § 28:70, Who May File a Stop Payment Notice.
Miller and Starr California Real Estate § 28:71, Requirement of a Preliminary Notice.
3 Witkin Cal. Proc. 5th Actions § 221C, (S 221C) (New)-Private Property: Preliminary Notice.
3 Witkin Cal. Proc. 5th Actions § 222A, (S 222A) (New)-Revised Law for Action on Payment Bond for Work of Improvement.

§ 8026. "Lien" defined

"Lien" means a lien under Title 2 (commencing with Section 8160) and includes a lien of a design professional under Section 8302, a lien for a work of improvement under Section 8400, and a lien for a site improvement under Section 8402. *(Added by Stats.2010, c. 697 (S.B.189), § 20, operative July 1, 2012.)*

For operative effect of Part 6, see Civil Code § 8052 and Stats.2010, c. 697 (S.B.189), § 105.

Law Revision Commission Comments

Section 8026 is new. It is included for drafting convenience. There are instances in this part where the term is not used in its defined sense. See Section 8000 (application of definitions).

Note that the application of this part to a design professionals lien is limited. See Section 8308 (application of part).

See also Sections 8014 ("design professional"), 8042 ("site improvement"), 8050 ("work of improvement"). [40 Cal.L.Rev.Comm. Reports 49 [AR:apx5] (2010)].

§ 8028. "Material supplier" defined

"Material supplier" means a person that provides material or supplies to be used or consumed in a work of improvement. *(Added by Stats.2010, c. 697 (S.B.189), § 20, operative July 1, 2012.)*

For operative effect of Part 6, see Civil Code § 8052 and Stats.2010, c. 697 (S.B.189), § 105.

Law Revision Commission Comments

Section 8028 continues former Section 3090 without substantive change. It replaces the term "materialman" with the term "material supplier" to conform to contemporary usage under this part.

See also Sections 8032 ("person"), 8050 ("work of improvement"). [40 Cal.L.Rev.Comm. Reports 49 [AR:apx5] (2010)].

Research References

Miller and Starr California Real Estate § 28:8, "Claimant" Defined.
Miller and Starr California Real Estate § 28:9, Contractors.
3 Witkin Cal. Proc. 5th Actions § 221B, (S 221B) (New)-Principal Changes.

Civil

4 Witkin, California Summary 10th Security Transactions in Real Property § 31B, (S 31B) (New)-Principal Changes.

§ 8030. "Payment bond" defined

(a) For the purposes of Title 2 (commencing with Section 8160), "payment bond" means a bond given under Section 8600.

(b) For the purposes of Title 3 (commencing with Section 9000), "payment bond" means a bond required by Section 9550. *(Added by Stats.2010, c. 697 (S.B.189), § 20, operative July 1, 2012.)*

Operative Effect

For operative effect of Part 6, see Civil Code § 8052 and Stats.2010, c. 697 (S.B.189), § 105.

Law Revision Commission Comments

Section 8030 supersedes former Section 3096. There are instances in this part where the term is not used in its defined sense. See, e.g., Sections 8452 (payment bond obtained by holder of mortgage or deed of trust), 8720–8722 (payment bond as security for large project). See also Section 8000 (application of definitions). [37 Cal.L.Rev.Comm. Reports 527 (2007)].

Research References

Miller and Starr California Real Estate § 28:74, Duty of Lender to Withhold Funds; Effect of a Bond.
Miller and Starr California Real Estate § 28:92, Construction-Related Bonds; in General.

§ 8032. "Person" defined

"Person" means an individual, corporation, public entity, business trust, estate, trust, partnership, limited liability company, association, or other entity. *(Added by Stats.2010, c. 697 (S.B.189), § 20, operative July 1, 2012.)*

Operative Effect

For operative effect of Part 6, see Civil Code § 8052 and Stats.2010, c. 697 (S.B.189), § 105.

Law Revision Commission Comments

Section 8032 is a new definition. It is included for drafting convenience. It supplements Section 14 ("person" includes corporation as well as natural person).

See also Section 8036 ("public entity"). [37 Cal.L.Rev.Comm. Reports 527 (2007)].

§ 8034. "Preliminary notice" defined

(a) For the purposes of Title 2 (commencing with Section 8160), "preliminary notice" means the notice provided for in Chapter 2 (commencing with Section 8200) of Title 2.

(b) For the purposes of Title 3 (commencing with Section 9000), "preliminary notice" means the notice provided for in Chapter 3 (commencing with Section 9300) of Title 3. *(Added by Stats.2010, c. 697 (S.B.189), § 20, operative July 1, 2012.)*

Operative Effect

For operative effect of Part 6, see Civil Code § 8052 and Stats.2010, c. 697 (S.B.189), § 105.

Law Revision Commission Comments

Section 8034 supersedes parts of former Sections 3097 and 3098. The substantive requirements for preliminary notice on a private work are relocated to Section 8200 *et seq.* The substantive requirements for preliminary notice on a public work are relocated to Section 9300 *et seq.* [40 Cal.L.Rev.Comm. Reports 49 [AR:apx5] (2010)].

Research References

California Real Estate Forms (Miller & Starr) § 4:13, Construction Agreement--Tenant Improvements.
Rutter, Cal. Practice Guide: Insurance Litigation Ch. 6I-B, B. Particular Surety Bond Coverages.
Rutter, Cal. Practice Guide: Insurance Litigation Gen. Matls., Highlights.
Miller and Starr California Real Estate § 28:15, Entities Entitled to a Portion of Employee Compensation.
Miller and Starr California Real Estate § 28:24, Amount of Lien Claims; Extent of Owner's Liability.
Miller and Starr California Real Estate § 28:98, Notice as Condition Precedent to Surety's Liability on Payment Bond.
Miller and Starr California Real Estate § 11:137, Phasing of a Project by Separate Direct Contracts With the Owner.
Miller and Starr California Real Estate § 28:122, Action by Claimants and Others on Public Works Payment Bond--Procedure and Notice.
Miller and Starr California Real Estate § 28:124, Action by Claimants and Others on Public Works Payment Bond--Amount of Recovery; Prejudgment Interest.
21 NO. 4 Miller & Starr, California Real Estate Newsalert 1, Everything Old is New Again: Impact of SB 189 on Mechanics' Lien Law.
3 Witkin Cal. Proc. 5th Actions § 221C, (S 221C) (New)-Private Property: Preliminary Notice.
3 Witkin Cal. Proc. 5th Actions § 221D, (S 221D) (New)-Private Property: Stop Notice.
3 Witkin Cal. Proc. 5th Actions § 221E, (S 221E) (New)-Public Property: Stop Notice.
3 Witkin Cal. Proc. 5th Actions § 222A, (S 222A) (New)-Revised Law for Action on Payment Bond for Work of Improvement.

§ 8036. "Public entity" defined

"Public entity" means the state, Regents of the University of California, a county, city, district, public authority, public agency, and any other political subdivision or public corporation in the state. *(Added by Stats.2010, c. 697 (S.B.189), § 20, operative July 1, 2012.)*

Operative Effect

For operative effect of Part 6, see Civil Code § 8052 and Stats.2010, c. 697 (S.B.189), § 105.

Law Revision Commission Comments

Section 8036 continues former Section 3099 without change.
See also Section 14 ("county" includes city and county). [40 Cal.L.Rev. Comm. Reports 49 [AR:apx5] (2010)].

Research References

Miller and Starr California Real Estate § 28:85, Nature of Public Works Stop Payment Notice.
Miller and Starr California Real Estate § 28:120, Payment and Performance Bonds as to Public Projects.

§ 8038. "Public works contract" defined

"Public works contract" has the meaning provided in Section 1101 of the Public Contract Code. *(Added by Stats.2010, c. 697 (S.B.189), § 20, operative July 1, 2012.)*

Operative Effect

For operative effect of Part 6, see Civil Code § 8052 and Stats.2010, c. 697 (S.B.189), § 105.

Law Revision Commission Comments

Section 8038 supersedes former Section 3100 ("public work"). Under Public Contract Code Section 1101, "public works contract" means an agreement for the erection, construction, alteration, repair, or improvement of any public structure, building, road, or other public improvement of any kind. [40 Cal.L.Rev.Comm. Reports 49 [AR:apx5] (2010)].

Research References

Rutter, Cal. Practice Guide: Insurance Litigation Ch. 6I-B, B. Particular Surety Bond Coverages.

Miller and Starr California Real Estate § 28:45, Public Works.

Miller and Starr California Real Estate § 28:86, Who Can File the Stop Payment Notice.

Miller and Starr California Real Estate § 28:120, Payment and Performance Bonds as to Public Projects.

§ 8040. "Site" defined

"Site" means the real property on which a work of improvement is situated or planned. *(Added by Stats.2010, c. 697 (S.B.189), § 20, operative July 1, 2012.)*

Operative Effect

For operative effect of Part 6, see Civil Code § 8052 and Stats.2010, c. 697 (S.B.189), § 105.

Law Revision Commission Comments

Section 8040 continues former Section 3101 without substantive change, except to add a reference to a planned work of improvement. See Section 8302 (design professionals lien).

See also Section 8050 ("work of improvement"). [37 Cal.L.Rev.Comm. Reports 527 (2007)].

Research References

Miller and Starr California Real Estate § 11:130, in General; Off-Record Priority.

§ 8042. "Site improvement" defined

"Site improvement" means any of the following work on real property:

(a) Demolition or removal of improvements, trees, or other vegetation.

(b) Drilling test holes.

(c) Grading, filling, or otherwise improving the real property or a street, highway, or sidewalk in front of or adjoining the real property.

(d) Construction or installation of sewers or other public utilities.

(e) Construction of areas, vaults, cellars, or rooms under sidewalks.

(f) Any other work or improvements in preparation of the site for a work of improvement. *(Added by Stats.2010, c. 697 (S.B.189), § 20, operative July 1, 2012.)*

Operative Effect

For operative effect of Part 6, see Civil Code § 8052 and Stats.2010, c. 697 (S.B.189), § 105.

Law Revision Commission Comments

Section 8042 continues former Section 3102 without substantive change, except that subdivision (f) makes clear that the reference in former law to "making any improvements" means preparatory work, and does not include construction of a structure.

See also Sections 8040 ("site"), 8048 ("work"), 8050 ("work of improvement"). [40 Cal.L.Rev.Comm. Reports 49 [AR:apx5] (2010)].

Research References

Rutter, Cal. Practice Guide: Insurance Litigation Ch. 6I-B, B. Particular Surety Bond Coverages.

Miller and Starr California Real Estate § 28:16, Design Professionals Liens; Rights to Mechanics Liens.

Miller and Starr California Real Estate § 28:17, "Work of Improvement".

Miller and Starr California Real Estate § 28:22, Time for Posting and Recording Notice.

Miller and Starr California Real Estate § 28:44, Public Improvements Under Private Contract.

Miller and Starr California Real Estate § 11:138, Site Improvements; Priority of Liens as Distinguished from Liens for Structures or Buildings.

4 Witkin, California Summary 10th Security Transactions in Real Property § 31C, (New)-Right to Lien and Property Affected.

§ 8044. "Stop payment notice" defined

(a)(1) For the purposes of Title 2 (commencing with Section 8160), "stop payment notice" means the notice given by a claimant under Chapter 5 (commencing with Section 8500) of Title 2.

(2) A stop payment notice given under Title 2 (commencing with Section 8160) may be bonded or unbonded. A "bonded stop payment notice" is a notice given with a bond under Section 8532. An "unbonded stop payment notice" is a notice not given with a bond under Section 8532.

(3) Except to the extent Title 2 (commencing with Section 8160) distinguishes between a bonded and an unbonded stop payment notice, a reference in that title to a stop payment notice includes both a bonded and an unbonded notice.

(b) For the purposes of Title 3 (commencing with Section 9000), "stop payment notice" means the notice given by a claimant under Chapter 4 (commencing with Section 9350) of Title 3.

(c) A reference in another statute to a "stop notice" in connection with the remedies provided in this part means a stop payment notice. *(Added by Stats.2010, c. 697 (S.B.189), § 20, operative July 1, 2012.)*

Operative Effect

For operative effect of Part 6, see Civil Code § 8052 and Stats.2010, c. 697 (S.B.189), § 105.

Law Revision Commission Comments

Section 8044 supersedes former Section 3103. The term "stop payment notice" replaces the term "stop notice" used in former law.

See also Section 8004 ("claimant"). [40 Cal.L.Rev.Comm. Reports 49 [AR:apx5] (2010)].

Research References

Rutter, Cal. Practice Guide: Insurance Litigation Ch. 6I-B, B. Particular Surety Bond Coverages.

Rutter, Cal. Practice Guide: Insurance Litigation Gen. Matls., Highlights.

§ 8046. "Subcontractor" defined

"Subcontractor" means a contractor that does not have a direct contractual relationship with an owner. The term includes a contractor that has a contractual relationship with a direct contractor or with another subcontractor. *(Added by Stats.2010, c. 697 (S.B.189), § 20, operative July 1, 2012.)*

Operative Effect

For operative effect of Part 6, see Civil Code § 8052 and Stats.2010, c. 697 (S.B.189), § 105.

Law Revision Commission Comments

The first sentence of Section 8046 continues former Section 3104 without substantive change. The second sentence is new; it makes clear that the term "subcontractor" includes a subcontractor of a subcontractor.

See also Section 8018 ("direct contractor"). [40 Cal.L.Rev.Comm. Reports 49 [AR:apx5] (2010)].

Research References

Miller and Starr California Real Estate § 28:8, "Claimant" Defined.

Miller and Starr California Real Estate § 28:9, Contractors.

Miller and Starr California Real Estate § 28:10, Subcontractors.

Miller and Starr California Real Estate § 28:38, Time to File.

Miller and Starr California Real Estate § 28:86, Who Can File the Stop Payment Notice.

Miller and Starr California Real Estate § 28:121, Action by Claimants and Others on Public Works Payment Bond--In General.

§ 8048. "Work" defined

"Work" means labor, service, equipment, or material provided to a work of improvement. *(Added by Stats.2010, c. 697 (S.B.189), § 20, operative July 1, 2012.)*

Operative Effect

For operative effect of Part 6, see Civil Code § 8052 and Stats.2010, c. 697 (S.B.189), § 105.

Law Revision Commission Comments

Section 8048 is new. It is included for drafting convenience.

See also Sections 8022 ("labor, service, equipment, or material"), 8050 ("work of improvement").   [40 Cal.L.Rev.Comm. Reports 49 [AR:apx5] (2010)].

Research References

Rutter, Cal. Practice Guide: Insurance Litigation Ch. 6I-B, B. Particular Surety Bond Coverages.
Miller and Starr California Real Estate § 28:86, Who Can File the Stop Payment Notice.

§ 8050. "Work of improvement" defined

(a) "Work of improvement" includes, but is not limited to:

(1) Construction, alteration, repair, demolition, or removal, in whole or in part, of, or addition to, a building, wharf, bridge, ditch, flume, aqueduct, well, tunnel, fence, machinery, railroad, or road.

(2) Seeding, sodding, or planting of real property for landscaping purposes.

(3) Filling, leveling, or grading of real property.

(b) Except as otherwise provided in this part, "work of improvement" means the entire structure or scheme of improvement as a whole, and includes site improvement. *(Added by Stats.2010, c. 697 (S.B.189), § 20, operative July 1, 2012.)*

Operative Effect

For operative effect of Part 6, see Civil Code § 8052 and Stats.2010, c. 697 (S.B.189), § 105.

Law Revision Commission Comments

Section 8050 restates former Section 3106. The section is revised to reorganize and tabulate the different types of work falling within the definition, to expand the coverage of the definition, and to make various technical, nonsubstantive revisions. The term "real property" replaces "lot or tract of land".

A site improvement is treated under this part in the same manner as a work of improvement, except as specifically provided in this part. See e.g., Sections 8450 (priority of lien), 8458 (priority of site improvement lien).

See also Section 8042 ("site improvement").   [40 Cal.L.Rev.Comm. Reports 49 [AR:apx5] (2010)].

Research References

Miller and Starr California Real Estate § 28:11, Material Suppliers Defined; Distinction Between Material Supplier and Subcontractor.
Miller and Starr California Real Estate § 28:17, "Work of Improvement".
Miller and Starr California Real Estate § 11:131, Date Liens Attach; Relation to Subsequent Interests.
Miller and Starr California Real Estate § 11:136, When Construction Commences--Phasing of the Project; in General.
Miller and Starr California Real Estate § 11:137, Phasing of a Project by Separate Direct Contracts With the Owner.
Miller and Starr California Real Estate § 11:138, Site Improvements; Priority of Liens as Distinguished from Liens for Structures or Buildings.

21 NO. 4 Miller & Starr, California Real Estate Newsalert 1, Everything Old is New Again: Impact of SB 189 on Mechanics' Lien Law.
3 Witkin Cal. Proc. 5th Actions § 221C, (S 221C) (New)-Private Property: Preliminary Notice.
2 Witkin Cal. Proc. 5th Jurisdiction § 359, Subcontractor's Contract.
4 Witkin, California Summary 10th Security Transactions in Real Property § 31C, (New)-Right to Lien and Property Affected.

ARTICLE 2. MISCELLANEOUS PROVISIONS

Section
8052.   Operative date and effect.
8054.   Transactions excluded from application of part.
8056.   Application of Code of Civil Procedure.
8058.   "Day" defined.
8060.   Filing or recording with county recorder; satisfaction of provisions; procedure; charge and collection of fees.
8062.   Construction of good faith and compliant acts.
8064.   Acts on behalf of co-owner.
8066.   Acts by agents.

Operative Effect

For operative effect of Part 6, see Civil Code § 8052 and Stats.2010, c. 697 (S.B.189), § 105.

§ 8052. Operative date and effect

(a) This part is operative on July 1, 2012.

(b) Notwithstanding subdivision (a), the effectiveness of a notice given or other action taken on a work of improvement before July 1, 2012, is governed by the applicable law in effect before July 1, 2012, and not by this part.

(c) A provision of this part, insofar as it is substantially the same as a previously existing provision relating to the same subject matter, shall be construed as a restatement and continuation thereof and not as a new enactment. *(Added by Stats.2010, c. 697 (S.B.189), § 20, operative July 1, 2012.)*

Operative Effect

For operative effect of Part 6, see the terms of this section and Stats.2010, c. 697 (S.B.189), § 105.

Law Revision Commission Comments

Section 8052 is new. Although this part applies generally to all works of improvement on or after July 1, 2012, it does not govern notices given or actions taken prior to July 1, 2012, on a work of improvement. Such notices or actions are governed by former law.

Subdivision (c) states the relationship between a provision of this part and a provision of former law that the provision of this part continues or restates. See also Section 107 of Chapter 697 of the Statutes of 2010.

See also Section 8050 (work of improvement).   [40 Cal.L.Rev.Comm. Reports 49 [AR:apx5] (2010)].

Research References

California Real Estate Forms (Miller & Starr) § 4:13, Construction Agreement--Tenant Improvements.
Miller and Starr California Real Estate § 28:1, Introduction.
21 NO. 4 Miller & Starr, California Real Estate Newsalert 1, Everything Old is New Again: Impact of SB 189 on Mechanics' Lien Law.
3 Witkin Cal. Proc. 5th Actions § 221A, (S 221A) (New)-In General.
3 Witkin Cal. Proc. 5th Actions § 222A, (S 222A) (New)-Revised Law for Action on Payment Bond for Work of Improvement.

4 Witkin, California Summary 10th Security Transactions in Real Property § 31A, (S 31A) (New)-Nature and Purpose of Revision.

§ 8054.   Transactions excluded from application of part

(a) This part does not apply to a transaction governed by the Oil and Gas Lien Act (Chapter 2.5 (commencing with Section 1203.50) of Title 4 of Part 3 of the Code of Civil Procedure).

(b) This part does not apply to or change improvement security under the Subdivision Map Act (Division 2 (commencing with Section 66410) of Title 7 of the Government Code).

(c) This part does not apply to a transaction governed by Sections 20457 to 20464, inclusive, of the Public Contract Code. *(Added by Stats.2010, c. 697 (S.B.189), § 20, operative July 1, 2012.)*

Operative Effect

For operative effect of Part 6, see Civil Code § 8052 and Stats.2010, c. 697 (S.B.189), § 105.

Law Revision Commission Comments

Subdivision (a) of Section 8054 restates former Section 3266(a).

Subdivision (b) is new. It clarifies the interrelation between this part and the Subdivision Map Act. For relevant provisions of that act, see Government Code Sections 66499–66499.10 (improvement security).

Subdivision (c) restates former Section 3266(b). This provision updates the former cross-reference to Streets and Highways Code Sections 5290–5297, which were repealed in 1982 when the Public Contract Code was created. See 1982 Cal. Stat. ch. 465, § 56. The repealed sections were superseded by Public Contract Code Sections 20457–20464. See 1982 Cal. Stat. ch. 465, § 11. The new sections apply to bonds in street work projects under Division 2 (commencing with Section 1600) of the Public Contract Code. See Pub. Cont. Code § 20457.   [40 Cal.L.Rev.Comm. Reports 49 [AR:apx5] (2010)].

§ 8056.   Application of Code of Civil Procedure

Except as otherwise provided in this part, Part 2 (commencing with Section 307) of the Code of Civil Procedure provides the rules of practice in proceedings under this part.   *(Added by Stats.2010, c. 697 (S.B.189), § 20, operative July 1, 2012.)*

Operative Effect

For operative effect of Part 6, see Civil Code § 8052 and Stats.2010, c. 697 (S.B.189), § 105.

Law Revision Commission Comments

Section 8056 continues the first sentence of former Section 3259 without substantive change. The second sentence of former Section 3259 is not continued; this part does not include special provisions relating to new trials or appeals.

Section 8056 makes former Section 3149, relating to joinder and consolidation of actions, unnecessary. Part 2 of the Code of Civil Procedure enables persons claiming liens on the same property to join in the same action to enforce their liens. See Code Civ. Proc. § 378 (permissive joinder). If separate actions are commenced, the court may consolidate them. See Code Civ. Proc. § 1048 (consolidation of actions). [40 Cal.L.Rev.Comm. Reports 49 [AR:apx5] (2010)].

Research References

3 Witkin Cal. Proc. 5th Actions § 66, (S 66) General Policy of Uniformity in Procedure.
8 Witkin Cal. Proc. 5th Attack Judgment Trial Court § 22, in General.

§ 8058.   "Day" defined

For purposes of this part, "day" means a calendar day. *(Added by Stats.2010, c. 697 (S.B.189), § 20, operative July 1, 2012.)*

Operative Effect

For operative effect of Part 6, see Civil Code § 8052 and Stats.2010, c. 697 (S.B.189), § 105.

Law Revision Commission Comments

Section 8058 is new. A reference to the term "day" in a statute typically means a calendar day, unless otherwise specifically indicated. Iverson v. Superior Court, 167 Cal.App.3d 544, 548, 213 Cal.Rptr. 399 (1985).)

See also Sections 10 (computing time), 11 (holidays).   [40 Cal.L.Rev. Comm. Reports 49 [AR:apx5] (2010)].

Research References

California Real Estate Forms (Miller & Starr) § 4:6, Construction Contract--Fixed Price--Commercial Project.
California Real Estate Forms (Miller & Starr) § 4:14, Construction Agreement-- Master Agreement for Construction Services.

§ 8060.   Filing or recording with county recorder; satisfaction of provisions; procedure; charge and collection of fees

(a) If this part provides for filing a contract, plan, or other paper with the county recorder, the provision is satisfied by filing the paper in the office of the county recorder of the county in which the work of improvement or part of it is situated.

(b) If this part provides for recording a notice, claim of lien, release of lien, payment bond, or other paper, the provision is satisfied by filing the paper for record in the office of the county recorder of the county in which the work of improvement or part of it is situated.

(c) The county recorder shall number, index, and preserve a contract, plan, or other paper presented for filing under this part, and shall number, index, and transcribe into the official records, in the same manner as a conveyance of real property, a notice, claim of lien, payment bond, or other paper recorded under this part.

(d) The county recorder shall charge and collect the fees provided in Article 5 (commencing with Section 27360) of Chapter 6 of Part 3 of Division 2 of Title 3 of the Government Code for performing duties under this section.   *(Added by Stats.2010, c. 697 (S.B.189), § 20, operative July 1, 2012.)*

Operative Effect

For operative effect of Part 6, see Civil Code § 8052 and Stats.2010, c. 697 (S.B.189), § 105.

Law Revision Commission Comments

Subdivisions (a) and (b) of Section 8060 are new. They generalize a number of provisions of former law. See also Section 1170 (recordation), Gov't Code §§ 27280, 27287 (recordation of documents).

Subdivisions (c) and (d) continue former Section 3258 without substantive change.

See also Sections 8008 ("contract"), 8024 ("lien"), 8030 ("payment bond"), 8050 ("work of improvement").   [40 Cal.L.Rev.Comm. Reports 49 [AR:apx5] (2010)].

Research References

Miller and Starr California Real Estate § 11:4, Instruments Subject to Recording--Requirements.
Miller and Starr California Real Estate § 11:5, Instruments Subject to Recording--Recorder's Refusal to Record.
Miller and Starr California Real Estate § 11:6, Instruments Subject to Recording--List of Recordable Documents.
Miller and Starr California Real Estate § 11:10, Required Form and Contents--In General.
Miller and Starr California Real Estate § 11:18, Reproduction of Documents.

Miller and Starr California Real Estate § 11:68, Constructive Notice of Interests Barred by the Statute of Limitations--"Ancient Documents" and the Marketable Record Title Act.

Miller and Starr California Real Estate § 28:27, Limiting Owner's Liability by Recording Direct Contract and Bond.

Miller and Starr California Real Estate § 28:37, Claim of Lien--Necessity, Purpose, and Effect.

Miller and Starr California Real Estate § 28:39, When Notice of Completion Recorded.

Miller and Starr California Real Estate § 28:40, When Notice of Cessation Recorded.

Miller and Starr California Real Estate § 11:130, in General; Off-Record Priority.

Miller and Starr California Real Estate § 11:146, Priority of the Construction Loan Deed of Trust--Effect of a Bond Recorded by the Construction Lender.

§ 8062. Construction of good faith and compliant acts

No act of an owner in good faith and in compliance with a provision of this part shall be construed to prevent a direct contractor's performance of the contract, or exonerate a surety on a performance or payment bond. *(Added by Stats.2010, c. 697 (S.B.189), § 20, operative July 1, 2012.)*

Operative Effect

For operative effect of Part 6, see Civil Code § 8052 and Stats.2010, c. 697 (S.B.189), § 105.

Law Revision Commission Comments

Section 8062 restates former Section 3263 without substantive change.

See also Section 8152 (no release of surety from liability).

See also Sections 8008 ("contract"), 8018 ("direct contractor"), 8030 ("payment bond"). [40 Cal.L.Rev.Comm. Reports 49 [AR:apx5] (2010)].

Research References

California Real Estate Forms (Miller & Starr) § 4:6, Construction Contract--Fixed Price--Commercial Project.

California Real Estate Forms (Miller & Starr) § 4:14, Construction Agreement-- Master Agreement for Construction Services.

Miller and Starr California Real Estate § 28:110, No Exoneration of the Surety Under Bonds in Favor of Claimants.

§ 8064. Acts on behalf of co-owner

An owner may give a notice or execute or file a document under this part on behalf of a co-owner if the owner acts on the co-owner's behalf and includes in the notice or document the name and address of the co-owner on whose behalf the owner acts. *(Added by Stats.2010, c. 697 (S.B.189), § 20, operative July 1, 2012.)*

Operative Effect

For operative effect of Part 6, see Civil Code § 8052 and Stats.2010, c. 697 (S.B.189), § 105.

Law Revision Commission Comments

Section 8064 is new. It generalizes provisions found in former Sections 3092 (notice of cessation) and 3093 (notice of completion). [40 Cal. L.Rev.Comm. Reports 49 [AR:apx5] (2010)].

Research References

Miller and Starr California Real Estate § 28:39, When Notice of Completion Recorded.

Miller and Starr California Real Estate § 28:40, When Notice of Cessation Recorded.

§ 8066. Acts by agents

An act that may be done by or to a person under this part may be done by or to the person's agent to the extent the act is within the scope of the agent's authority. *(Added by Stats.2010, c. 697 (S.B.189), § 20, operative July 1, 2012.)*

Operative Effect

For operative effect of Part 6, see Civil Code § 8052 and Stats.2010, c. 697 (S.B.189), § 105.

Law Revision Commission Comments

Section 8066 is a specific application of Section 2305. This section makes clear that an agent's authority is limited to the scope of the agency. Thus, to the extent a direct contractor is deemed to be the agent of an owner for the purpose of engaging a subcontractor, the scope of the agency does not include other acts, such as compromise of litigation.

For provisions relating to the agency authority of co-owners, see Section 8064 (co-owners).

See also Section 8032 ("person"). [40 Cal.L.Rev.Comm. Reports 49 [AR:apx5] (2010)].

Research References

Miller and Starr California Real Estate § 28:39, When Notice of Completion Recorded.

Miller and Starr California Real Estate § 28:40, When Notice of Cessation Recorded.

Miller and Starr California Real Estate § 28:46, Contents of the Claim of Lien; Purpose.

Miller and Starr California Real Estate § 28:72, Contents of the Stop Payment Notice.

21 NO. 4 Miller & Starr, California Real Estate Newsalert 1, Everything Old is New Again: Impact of SB 189 on Mechanics' Lien Law.

3 Witkin Cal. Proc. 5th Actions § 221A, (S 221A) (New)-In General.

4 Witkin, California Summary 10th Security Transactions in Real Property § 31A, (S 31A) (New)-Nature and Purpose of Revision.

CHAPTER 2. NOTICE

Section

8100.	Written notice.
8102.	Information to be included in notice.
8104.	Failure to pay laborer full compensation; additional information required.
8106.	Manner of giving notice.
8108.	Location for giving notice.
8110.	Notice by mail.
8114.	Posting of notice; conspicuous location.
8116.	Completion of notice; time deemed given.
8118.	Proof of notice; declaration.

Operative Effect

For operative effect of Part 6, see Civil Code § 8052 and Stats.2010, c. 697 (S.B.189), § 105.

§ 8100. Written notice

Notice under this part shall be in writing. Writing includes printing and typewriting. *(Added by Stats.2010, c. 697 (S.B.189), § 20, operative July 1, 2012.)*

Operative Effect

For operative effect of Part 6, see Civil Code § 8052 and Stats.2010, c. 697 (S.B.189), § 105.

Law Revision Commission Comments

Section 8100 generalizes various provisions of former law. See, e.g., former Sections 3092 (notice of cessation), 3093 (notice of completion), 3094 (notice of nonresponsibility), 3097 (preliminary notice (private work)), 3103 (stop notice).

See also Evid. Code § 250 (writing). [40 Cal.L.Rev.Comm. Reports 49 [AR:apx5] (2010)].

Research References

California Real Estate Forms (Miller & Starr) § 4:6, Construction Contract--Fixed Price--Commercial Project.

California Real Estate Forms (Miller & Starr) § 4:13, Construction Agreement--Tenant Improvements.

California Real Estate Forms (Miller & Starr) § 4:14, Construction Agreement-- Master Agreement for Construction Services.

Rutter, Cal. Practice Guide: Insurance Litigation Ch. 6I-B, B. Particular Surety Bond Coverages.

Miller and Starr California Real Estate § 28:16, Design Professionals Liens; Rights to Mechanics Liens.

Miller and Starr California Real Estate § 28:28, Statutory Provisions Governing Notice.

Miller and Starr California Real Estate § 28:35, Contents of the Preliminary Notice.

Miller and Starr California Real Estate § 28:67, Payment, Release, and Waiver of the Lien.

Miller and Starr California Real Estate § 28:76, Duty of Owner to Withhold Funds; Effect of a Bond.

Miller and Starr California Real Estate § 28:88, Contents and Service of the Stop Payment Notice.

Miller and Starr California Real Estate § 28:90, Release of the Stop Payment Notice.

Miller and Starr California Real Estate § 11:137, Phasing of a Project by Separate Direct Contracts With the Owner.

21 NO. 4 Miller & Starr, California Real Estate Newsalert 1, Everything Old is New Again: Impact of SB 189 on Mechanics' Lien Law.

3 Witkin Cal. Proc. 5th Actions § 221A, (S 221A) (New)-In General.

3 Witkin Cal. Proc. 5th Actions § 221C, (S 221C) (New)-Private Property: Preliminary Notice.

3 Witkin Cal. Proc. 5th Actions § 221E, (S 221E) (New)-Public Property: Stop Notice.

3 Witkin Cal. Proc. 5th Actions § 222A, (S 222A) (New)-Revised Law for Action on Payment Bond for Work of Improvement.

4 Witkin, California Summary 10th Security Transactions in Real Property § 31A, (S 31A) (New)-Nature and Purpose of Revision.

4 Witkin, California Summary 10th Security Transactions in Real Property § 31E, (New)-Preliminary Notice.

4 Witkin, California Summary 10th Security Transactions in Real Property § 31H, (New)-Protecting Against Lien.

4 Witkin, California Summary 10th Security Transactions in Real Property § 31-I, (New)-Release of Lien.

§ 8102. Information to be included in notice

(a) Notice under this part shall, in addition to any other information required by statute for that type of notice, include all of the following information to the extent known to the person giving the notice:

(1) The name and address of the owner or reputed owner.

(2) The name and address of the direct contractor.

(3) The name and address of the construction lender, if any.

(4) A description of the site sufficient for identification, including the street address of the site, if any. If a sufficient legal description of the site is given, the effectiveness of the notice is not affected by the fact that the street address is erroneous or is omitted.

(5) The name, address, and relationship to the parties of the person giving the notice.

(6) If the person giving the notice is a claimant:

(A) A general statement of the work provided.

(B) The name of the person to or for whom the work is provided.

(C) A statement or estimate of the claimant's demand, if any, after deducting all just credits and offsets.

(b) Notice is not invalid by reason of any variance from the requirements of this section if the notice is sufficient to substantially inform the person given notice of the information required by this section and other information required in the notice. *(Added by Stats.2010, c. 697 (S.B.189), § 20, operative July 1, 2012.)*

Operative Effect

For operative effect of Part 6, see Civil Code § 8052 and Stats.2010, c. 697 (S.B.189), § 105.

Law Revision Commission Comments

Section 8102 is new. It generalizes and standardizes provisions found throughout former law. See, e.g., former Sections 3092 (notice of cessation), 3093 (notice of completion), 3097 (preliminary notice), 3103 (stop notice).

See also Sections 8004 ("claimant"), 8006 ("construction lender"), 8018 ("direct contractor"), 8032 ("person"), 8040 ("site"), 8048 ("work"). [40 Cal.L.Rev.Comm. Reports 49 [AR:apx5] (2010)].

Research References

California Real Estate Forms (Miller & Starr) § 4:6, Construction Contract--Fixed Price--Commercial Project.

California Real Estate Forms (Miller & Starr) § 4:13, Construction Agreement--Tenant Improvements.

California Real Estate Forms (Miller & Starr) § 4:14, Construction Agreement-- Master Agreement for Construction Services.

Miller and Starr California Real Estate § 28:15, Entities Entitled to a Portion of Employee Compensation.

Miller and Starr California Real Estate § 28:23, Form and Procedural Requirements.

Miller and Starr California Real Estate § 28:28, Statutory Provisions Governing Notice.

Miller and Starr California Real Estate § 28:33, Laborers.

Miller and Starr California Real Estate § 28:35, Contents of the Preliminary Notice.

Miller and Starr California Real Estate § 28:39, When Notice of Completion Recorded.

Miller and Starr California Real Estate § 28:40, When Notice of Cessation Recorded.

Miller and Starr California Real Estate § 28:71, Requirement of a Preliminary Notice.

Miller and Starr California Real Estate § 28:72, Contents of the Stop Payment Notice.

Miller and Starr California Real Estate § 28:83, Suit to Enforce the Stop Payment Notice.

Miller and Starr California Real Estate § 28:87, Requirement for and Contents of a Preliminary Notice.

Miller and Starr California Real Estate § 28:88, Contents and Service of the Stop Payment Notice.

Miller and Starr California Real Estate § 28:89, Duty of Public Agency After Receipt of Stop Payment Notice.

Miller and Starr California Real Estate § 28:122, Action by Claimants and Others on Public Works Payment Bond--Procedure and Notice.

3 Witkin Cal. Proc. 5th Actions § 221C, (S 221C) (New)-Private Property: Preliminary Notice.

3 Witkin Cal. Proc. 5th Actions § 221E, (S 221E) (New)-Public Property: Stop Notice.

4 Witkin, California Summary 10th Security Transactions in Real Property § 31E, (New)-Preliminary Notice.

§ 8104. Failure to pay laborer full compensation; additional information required

(a) A direct contractor or subcontractor on a work of improvement governed by this part that employs a laborer and fails to pay the full compensation due the laborer, including any employer payments described in Section 1773.1 of the Labor Code and implementing regulations, shall not later than the date the compensation became delinquent, give the laborer, the laborer's bargaining representative, if any, the construction lender or reputed construction lender, if any, and the owner or reputed owner, notice that includes all of the following information, in addition to the information required by Section 8102:

(1) The name and address of the laborer, and of any person or entity described in subdivision (b) of Section 8024 to which employer payments are due.

(2) The total number of straight time and overtime hours worked by the laborer on each job.

(3) The amount then past due and owing.

(b) Failure to give the notice required by subdivision (a) constitutes grounds for disciplinary action under the Contractors' State License Law, Chapter 9 (commencing with Section 7000) of Division 3 of the Business and Professions Code. *(Added by Stats.2010, c. 697 (S.B.189), § 20, operative July 1, 2012.)*

Operative Effect

For operative effect of Part 6, see Civil Code § 8052 and Stats.2010, c. 697 (S.B.189), § 105.

Law Revision Commission Comments

Section 8104 restates former Section 3097(k), with the additional requirement that the information provided be given to the owner or reputed owner, and include the name and address of the unpaid laborer. See also Sections 8100–8118 (notice).

The reference to the Registrar of Contractors in the final sentence of former Section 3097(k) is revised to refer to the Contractors' State License Law. This is a technical, nonsubstantive change.

The information required in this notice is in addition to the information required by Section 8102 (contents of notice).

Compliance with this section does not excuse compliance with Section 8202(b), if applicable. See Section 8202 (contents of preliminary notice).

See also Sections 8006 ("construction lender"), 8018 ("direct contractor"), 8024 ("laborer"), 8032 ("person"), 8046 ("subcontractor"), 8050 ("work of improvement"). [40 Cal.L.Rev.Comm. Reports 49 [AR:apx5] (2010)].

Research References

Miller and Starr California Real Estate § 28:15, Entities Entitled to a Portion of Employee Compensation.
Miller and Starr California Real Estate § 28:33, Laborers.
Miller and Starr California Real Estate § 28:70, Who May File a Stop Payment Notice.
3 Witkin Cal. Proc. 5th Actions § 221C, (S 221C) (New)-Private Property: Preliminary Notice.

§ 8106. Manner of giving notice

Except as otherwise provided by statute, notice under this part shall be given by any of the following means:

(a) Personal delivery.

(b) Mail in the manner provided in Section 8110.

(c) Leaving the notice and mailing a copy in the manner provided in Section 415.20 of the Code of Civil Procedure for service of summons and complaint in a civil action. *(Added by Stats.2010, c. 697 (S.B.189), § 20, operative July 1, 2012.)*

Operative Effect

For operative effect of Part 6, see Civil Code § 8052 and Stats.2010, c. 697 (S.B.189), § 105.

Law Revision Commission Comments

Section 8106 is new. It generalizes and standardizes provisions found throughout former law. See, e.g., former Sections 3097 (preliminary notice), 3103 (stop notice), 3144.5 (notice of release bond), 3227 (notice to principal and surety), 3259.5 (notice of recordation of notice of completion), 3260.2 (stop work notice).

Under subdivision (c), when notice is given in the manner provided in Code of Civil Procedure Section 415.20 for service of summons and complaint, the notice is complete five days after mailing the notice. See Section 8116 (when notice complete). The 10 day delay provided in the Code of Civil Procedure for completion of service under that code is inapplicable.

This part may prescribe a different or more limited manner of giving a particular notice. See, e.g., Section 8486 (service of petition for order releasing lien). [37 Cal.L.Rev.Comm. Reports 527 (2007)].

Research References

California Real Estate Forms (Miller & Starr) § 4:13, Construction Agreement--Tenant Improvements.
Rutter, Cal. Practice Guide: Insurance Litigation Ch. 6I-B, B. Particular Surety Bond Coverages.
Miller and Starr California Real Estate § 28:28, Statutory Provisions Governing Notice.
Miller and Starr California Real Estate § 28:36, Time and Method for Service of the Preliminary Notice.
Miller and Starr California Real Estate § 28:71, Requirement of a Preliminary Notice.
Miller and Starr California Real Estate § 28:83, Suit to Enforce the Stop Payment Notice.
Miller and Starr California Real Estate § 28:87, Requirement for and Contents of a Preliminary Notice.
Miller and Starr California Real Estate § 28:89, Duty of Public Agency After Receipt of Stop Payment Notice.
Miller and Starr California Real Estate § 28:90, Release of the Stop Payment Notice.
Miller and Starr California Real Estate § 28:122, Action by Claimants and Others on Public Works Payment Bond--Procedure and Notice.
3 Witkin Cal. Proc. 5th Actions § 221C, (S 221C) (New)-Private Property: Preliminary Notice.
3 Witkin Cal. Proc. 5th Actions § 221E, (S 221E) (New)-Public Property: Stop Notice.
4 Witkin, California Summary 10th Security Transactions in Real Property § 31E, (New)-Preliminary Notice.

§ 8108. Location for giving notice

Except as otherwise provided by this part, notice under this part shall be given to the person to be notified at the person's residence, the person's place of business, or at any of the following addresses:

(a) If the person to be notified is an owner other than a public entity, the owner's address shown on the direct contract, the building permit, or a construction trust deed.

(b) If the person to be notified is a public entity, the office of the public entity or another address specified by the public entity in the contract or elsewhere for service of notices, papers, and other documents.

(c) If the person to be notified is a construction lender, the construction lender's address shown on the construction loan agreement or construction trust deed.

(d) If the person to be notified is a direct contractor or a subcontractor, the contractor's address shown on the building permit, on the contractor's contract, or on the records of the Contractors' State License Board.

(e) If the person to be notified is a claimant, the claimant's address shown on the claimant's contract, preliminary notice, claim of lien, stop payment notice, or claim against a payment bond, or on the records of the Contractors' State License Board.

(f) If the person to be notified is a surety on a bond, the surety's address shown on the bond for service of notices, papers, and other documents, or on the records of the Department of Insurance. *(Added by Stats.2010, c. 697 (S.B.189), § 20, operative July 1, 2012.)*

Operative Effect

For operative effect of Part 6, see Civil Code § 8052 and Stats.2010, c. 697 (S.B.189), § 105.

Law Revision Commission Comments

Section 8108 is new. It generalizes and standardizes provisions found throughout former law. For an example of a more particularized notice provision, see Section 8506.

Subdivision (f) does not continue the unique provisions found in former Section 3227 for notice to alternate persons in the case of a personal surety or admitted surety insurer. The bond and undertaking law requires every bond to include the address at which the principal and sureties may be served with notices, papers, and other documents. See Code Civ. Proc. § 995.320.

See also Sections 8004 ("claimant"), 8006 ("construction lender"), 8008 ("contract"), 8012 ("contractor"), 8016 ("direct contract"), 8018 ("direct contractor"), 8026 ("lien"), 8030 ("payment bond"), 8032 ("person"), 8034 ("preliminary notice"), 8036 ("public entity"), 8044 ("stop payment notice"), 8046 ("subcontractor"). [40 Cal.L.Rev.Comm. Reports 49 [AR:apx5] (2010)].

Research References

Miller and Starr California Real Estate § 28:28, Statutory Provisions Governing Notice.
Miller and Starr California Real Estate § 28:71, Requirement of a Preliminary Notice.
Miller and Starr California Real Estate § 28:87, Requirement for and Contents of a Preliminary Notice.
Miller and Starr California Real Estate § 28:88, Contents and Service of the Stop Payment Notice.
Miller and Starr California Real Estate § 28:122, Action by Claimants and Others on Public Works Payment Bond--Procedure and Notice.

§ 8110. Notice by mail

Except as otherwise provided by this part, notice by mail under this part shall be given by registered or certified mail, express mail, or overnight delivery by an express service carrier. *(Added by Stats.2010, c. 697 (S.B.189), § 20, operative July 1, 2012.)*

Operative Effect

For operative effect of Part 6, see Civil Code § 8052 and Stats.2010, c. 697 (S.B.189), § 105.

Law Revision Commission Comments

Section 8110 is a new provision included for drafting convenience. It generalizes a number of provisions of former law, and expands the methods of giving notice to include delivery by express service carrier.

For an example of a more particularized notice provision, see Section 8486. [37 Cal.L.Rev.Comm. Reports 527 (2007)].

Research References

Rutter, Cal. Practice Guide: Insurance Litigation Ch. 6I-B, B. Particular Surety Bond Coverages.
Miller and Starr California Real Estate § 28:28, Statutory Provisions Governing Notice.
Miller and Starr California Real Estate § 28:36, Time and Method for Service of the Preliminary Notice.
Miller and Starr California Real Estate § 28:71, Requirement of a Preliminary Notice.
Miller and Starr California Real Estate § 28:73, Service of the Stop Payment Notice.
Miller and Starr California Real Estate § 28:83, Suit to Enforce the Stop Payment Notice.
Miller and Starr California Real Estate § 28:87, Requirement for and Contents of a Preliminary Notice.
Miller and Starr California Real Estate § 28:89, Duty of Public Agency After Receipt of Stop Payment Notice.
Miller and Starr California Real Estate § 28:90, Release of the Stop Payment Notice.
3 Witkin Cal. Proc. 5th Actions § 221C, (S 221C) (New)-Private Property: Preliminary Notice.

4 Witkin, California Summary 10th Security Transactions in Real Property § 31E, (New)-Preliminary Notice.

§ 8114. Posting of notice; conspicuous location

A notice required by this part to be posted shall be displayed in a conspicuous location at the site. *(Added by Stats.2010, c. 697 (S.B.189), § 20, operative July 1, 2012.)*

Operative Effect

For operative effect of Part 6, see Civil Code § 8052 and Stats.2010, c. 697 (S.B.189), § 105.

Law Revision Commission Comments

Section 8114 is new. It generalizes provisions found in former law. See, e.g., former Sections 3094 (notice of nonresponsibility), 3260.2 (stop work notice).

See also Section 8040 ("site"). [40 Cal.L.Rev.Comm. Reports 49 [AR:apx5] (2010)].

Research References

Miller and Starr California Real Estate § 28:23, Form and Procedural Requirements.
Miller and Starr California Real Estate § 28:28, Statutory Provisions Governing Notice.

§ 8116. Completion of notice; time deemed given

Notice under this part is complete and deemed to have been given at the following times:

(a) If given by personal delivery, when delivered.

(b) If given by mail, when deposited in the mail or with an express service carrier in the manner provided in Section 1013 of the Code of Civil Procedure.

(c) If given by leaving the notice and mailing a copy in the manner provided in Section 415.20 of the Code of Civil Procedure for service of summons in a civil action, five days after mailing.

(d) If given by posting, when displayed.

(e) If given by recording, when recorded in the office of the county recorder. *(Added by Stats.2010, c. 697 (S.B.189), § 20, operative July 1, 2012.)*

Operative Effect

For operative effect of Part 6, see Civil Code § 8052 and Stats.2010, c. 697 (S.B.189), § 105.

Law Revision Commission Comments

Section 8116 is new. It generalizes and standardizes provisions found in former law. See, e.g., former Section 3097(f)(3) (service of preliminary notice).

Under subdivision (b), when notice is given in the manner provided in Code of Civil Procedure Section 1013, the notice is complete when deposited in the mail or with an express service carrier. The 10 and 20 day delays provided in the Code of Civil Procedure for completion of service under that code are inapplicable. For an exception to this rule, see Section 8486 (notice of hearing on lien release petition).

Under subdivision (c), when notice is given in the manner provided in Code of Civil Procedure Section 415.20 for service of summons and complaint, the notice is complete five days after mailing of the notice. The 10 day delay provided in the Code of Civil Procedure for completion of service under that code is inapplicable.

See also Sections 1170 (recordation), 8058 (calculation of time), 8060 (filing and recordation of papers), 8110 (mailed notice), 8114 (posting of notice). [40 Cal.L.Rev.Comm. Reports 49 [AR:apx5] (2010)].

Research References

Miller and Starr California Real Estate § 28:28, Statutory Provisions Governing Notice.
Miller and Starr California Real Estate § 28:36, Time and Method for Service of the Preliminary Notice.

Miller and Starr California Real Estate § 28:71, Requirement of a
   Preliminary Notice.
Miller and Starr California Real Estate § 28:73, Service of the Stop
   Payment Notice.

§ 8118.   Proof of notice; declaration

(a) Proof that notice was given to a person in the manner
required by this part shall be made by a proof of notice
declaration that states all of the following:

(1) The type or description of the notice given.

(2) The date, place, and manner of notice, and facts showing
that notice was given in the manner required by statute.

(3) The name and address of the person to which notice was
given, and, if appropriate, the title or capacity in which the
person was given notice.

(b) If the notice is given by mail, the declaration shall be
accompanied by one of the following:

(1) Documentation provided by the United States Postal
Service showing that payment was made to mail the notice using
registered or certified mail, or express mail.

(2) Documentation provided by an express service carrier
showing that payment was made to send the notice using an
overnight delivery service.

(3) A return receipt, delivery confirmation, signature confirmation, tracking record, or other proof of delivery or attempted
delivery provided by the United States Postal Service, or a
photocopy of the record of delivery and receipt maintained by
the United States Postal Service, showing the date of delivery
and to whom delivered, or in the event of nondelivery, by the
returned envelope itself.

(4) A tracking record or other documentation provided by an
express service carrier showing delivery or attempted delivery of
the notice. *(Added by Stats.2010, c. 697 (S.B.189), § 20,
operative July 1, 2012.)*

Operative Effect

*For operative effect of Part 6, see Civil Code § 8052
and Stats.2010, c. 697 (S.B.189), § 105.*

Law Revision Commission Comments

Section 8118 is new. It generalizes and standardizes provisions found
throughout former law, and expands the methods of proof to include
documentation of the mailing provided by the United States Postal
Service or an express service carrier. See, e.g., former Sections 3097
(preliminary notice), 3260.2 (stop work notice).

Subdivision (b) specifies the documentation that must be attached to a
proof of notice declaration when notice is given by mail. Documentation
establishing proof of delivery or attempted delivery of the notice as
specified in subdivision (b)(3)-(4) is sufficient, but not necessary, to satisfy
the requirement of the subdivision. Proof that payment was made to the
United States Postal Service or an express service carrier for an approved
method of delivery is also sufficient. See subdivision (b)(1)-(2).

See also Section 8110 (mailed notice).

See also Section 8032 ("person"). [40 Cal.L.Rev.Comm. Reports 49
[AR:apx5] (2010)].

Research References

California Real Estate Forms (Miller & Starr) § 4:13, Construction
   Agreement--Tenant Improvements.
Miller and Starr California Real Estate § 28:16, Design Professionals
   Liens; Rights to Mechanics Liens.
Miller and Starr California Real Estate § 28:28, Statutory Provisions
   Governing Notice.
Miller and Starr California Real Estate § 28:36, Time and Method for
   Service of the Preliminary Notice.
Miller and Starr California Real Estate § 28:67, Payment, Release, and
   Waiver of the Lien.

Miller and Starr California Real Estate § 28:71, Requirement of a
   Preliminary Notice.
Miller and Starr California Real Estate § 28:90, Release of the Stop
   Payment Notice.
21 NO. 4 Miller & Starr, California Real Estate Newsalert 1, Everything
   Old is New Again: Impact of SB 189 on Mechanics' Lien Law.
3 Witkin Cal. Proc. 5th Actions § 221A, (S 221A) (New)-In General.
4 Witkin, California Summary 10th Security Transactions in Real Property
   § 31A, (S 31A) (New)-Nature and Purpose of Revision.
4 Witkin, California Summary 10th Security Transactions in Real Property
   § 31F, (S 31F) (New)-Requirements of Claim.

CHAPTER 3.   WAIVER AND RELEASE

Operative Effect

*For operative effect of Part 6, see Civil Code § 8052
and Stats.2010, c. 697 (S.B.189), § 105.*

§ 8120.   Application of chapter

The provisions of this chapter apply to a work of improvement
governed by this part. *(Added by Stats.2010, c. 697 (S.B.189),
§ 20, operative July 1, 2012.)*

Operative Effect

*For operative effect of Part 6, see Civil Code § 8052
and Stats.2010, c. 697 (S.B.189), § 105.*

Law Revision Commission Comments

Section 8120 is new. It provides the scope of applicability of the
provisions of Chapter 3 of Title 1.

See also Section 8050 ("work of improvement"). [40 Cal.L.Rev.Comm.
Reports 49 [AR:apx5] (2010)].

Research References

21 NO. 4 Miller & Starr, California Real Estate Newsalert 1, Everything
   Old is New Again: Impact of SB 189 on Mechanics' Lien Law.
3 Witkin Cal. Proc. 5th Actions § 221A, (S 221A) (New)-In General.
4 Witkin, California Summary 10th Security Transactions in Real Property
   § 31A, (S 31A) (New)-Nature and Purpose of Revision.

§ 8122.   Waiver or impairment of rights prohibited; exception

An owner, direct contractor, or subcontractor may not, by
contract or otherwise, waive, affect, or impair any other claimant's rights under this part, whether with or without notice, and
any term of a contract that purports to do so is void and
unenforceable unless and until the claimant executes and
delivers a waiver and release under this article. *(Added by
Stats.2010, c. 697 (S.B.189), § 20, operative July 1, 2012.)*

Operative Effect

*For operative effect of Part 6, see Civil Code § 8052
and Stats.2010, c. 697 (S.B.189), § 105.*

Section 8122 continues the first and second sentences of former Section 3262(a) without substantive change, except to add a reference to a subcontractor.

See also Sections 8004 ("claimant"), 8008 ("contract"), 8018 ("direct contractor"), 8046 ("subcontractor"). [40 Cal.L.Rev.Comm. Reports 49 [AR:apx5] (2010)].

Research References

Rutter, Cal. Practice Guide: Insurance Litigation Ch. 6I-D, D. Surety's Defenses to Payment of Bond.
Miller and Starr California Real Estate § 28:67, Payment, Release, and Waiver of the Lien.
Miller and Starr California Real Estate § 28:110, No Exoneration of the Surety Under Bonds in Favor of Claimants.
Miller and Starr California Real Estate § 28:112, Proper Parties in Suit Against Surety; Necessity of Suit Against or Joinder of the Principal.
Miller and Starr California Real Estate § 28:118, Action by Claimant to Recover on a Bond as to Private Projects--In General.
1 Witkin Cal. Summ. 10th Contracts § 684, Miscellaneous Substantive Rights.
1 Witkin Cal. Summ. 10th Contracts § 1000, (S 1000) Abandonment Theory Not Applicable Against Public Entity.

§ 8124. Release from lien or claim; conditions

A claimant's waiver and release does not release the owner, construction lender, or surety on a payment bond from a lien or claim unless both of the following conditions are satisfied:

(a) The waiver and release is in substantially the form provided in this article and is signed by the claimant.

(b) If the release is a conditional release, there is evidence of payment to the claimant. Evidence of payment may be either of the following:

(1) The claimant's endorsement on a single or joint payee check that has been paid by the financial institution on which it was drawn.

(2) Written acknowledgment of payment by the claimant. *(Added by Stats.2010, c. 697 (S.B.189), § 20, operative July 1, 2012.)*

Operative Effect

For operative effect of Part 6, see Civil Code § 8052 and Stats.2010, c. 697 (S.B.189), § 105.

Law Revision Commission Comments

Section 8124 continues the third and fourth sentences of former Section 3262(a) without substantive change. The term "financial institution" replaces "bank" in subdivision (b) and in the forms provided in this article.

The waiver and release may be signed by the claimant's agent. See Section 8066 (agency).

See also Sections 8004 ("claimant"), 8006 ("construction lender"), 8026 ("lien"), 8030 ("payment bond"). [40 Cal.L.Rev.Comm. Reports 49 [AR:apx5] (2010)].

Research References

Miller and Starr California Real Estate § 28:67, Payment, Release, and Waiver of the Lien.
Miller and Starr California Real Estate § 28:110, No Exoneration of the Surety Under Bonds in Favor of Claimants.

§ 8126. Estoppel or impairment of lien or claim; conditions

An oral or written statement purporting to waive, release, impair or otherwise adversely affect a lien or claim is void and unenforceable and does not create an estoppel or impairment of the lien or claim unless either of the following conditions is satisfied:

(a) The statement is pursuant to a waiver and release under this article.

(b) The claimant has actually received payment in full for the claim. *(Added by Stats.2010, c. 697 (S.B.189), § 20, operative July 1, 2012.)*

Operative Effect

For operative effect of Part 6, see Civil Code § 8052 and Stats.2010, c. 697 (S.B.189), § 105.

Law Revision Commission Comments

Section 8126 continues former Section 3262(b)(1) without substantive change.

See also Section 8004 ("claimant"), 8026 ("lien"). [40 Cal.L.Rev. Comm. Reports 49 [AR:apx5] (2010)].

Research References

Miller and Starr California Real Estate § 28:61, Trial and Judgment.
Miller and Starr California Real Estate § 28:67, Payment, Release, and Waiver of the Lien.
Miller and Starr California Real Estate § 28:83, Suit to Enforce the Stop Payment Notice.
Miller and Starr California Real Estate § 28:118, Action by Claimant to Recover on a Bond as to Private Projects--In General.

§ 8128. Stop payment notice; reduction or release

(a) A claimant may reduce the amount of, or release in its entirety, a stop payment notice. The reduction or release shall be in writing and may be given in a form other than a waiver and release form provided in this article.

(b) The writing shall identify whether it is a reduction of the amount of the stop payment notice, or a release of the notice in its entirety. If the writing is a reduction, it shall state the amount of the reduction, and the amount to remain withheld after the reduction.

(c) A claimant's reduction or release of a stop payment notice has the following effect:

(1) The reduction or release releases the claimant's right to enforce payment of the claim stated in the notice to the extent of the reduction or release.

(2) The reduction or release releases the person given the notice from the obligation to withhold funds pursuant to the notice to the extent of the reduction or release.

(3) The reduction or release does not preclude the claimant from giving a subsequent stop payment notice that is timely and proper.

(4) The reduction or release does not release any right of the claimant other than the right to enforce payment of the claim stated in the stop payment notice to the extent of the reduction or release. *(Added by Stats.2010, c. 697 (S.B.189), § 20, operative July 1, 2012.)*

Operative Effect

For operative effect of Part 6, see Civil Code § 8052 and Stats.2010, c. 697 (S.B.189), § 105.

Law Revision Commission Comments

Subdivisions (a) and (c) of Section 8128 generalize former Section 3262(b)(2), so as to apply to a stop payment notice given to a construction lender as well as to a stop payment notice given to an owner.

Subdivision (b) is new.

See also Sections 8004 ("claimant"), 8032 ("person"), 8044 ("stop payment notice"). [40 Cal.L.Rev.Comm. Reports 49 [AR:apx5] (2010)].

Research References

Miller and Starr California Real Estate § 28:67, Payment, Release, and Waiver of the Lien.
Miller and Starr California Real Estate § 28:81, Release, Bond and Waiver of Stop Payment Notice.

1 Witkin Cal. Summ. 10th Contracts § 684, Miscellaneous Substantive Rights.

§ 8130. Accord and satisfaction; effect of article

This article does not affect the enforceability of either an accord and satisfaction concerning a good faith dispute or an agreement made in settlement of an action pending in court if the accord and satisfaction or agreement and settlement make specific reference to the lien or claim. *(Added by Stats.2010, c. 697 (S.B.189), § 20, operative July 1, 2012.)*

Operative Effect

For operative effect of Part 6, see Civil Code § 8052 and Stats.2010, c. 697 (S.B.189), § 105.

Law Revision Commission Comments

Section 8130 continues former Section 3262(c) without substantive change.

See also Section 8026 ("lien"). [40 Cal.L.Rev.Comm. Reports 49 [AR:apx5] (2010)].

Research References

Miller and Starr California Real Estate § 28:67, Payment, Release, and Waiver of the Lien.

§ 8132. Conditional waiver and release on progress payment; form

If a claimant is required to execute a waiver and release in exchange for, or in order to induce payment of, a progress payment and the claimant is not, in fact, paid in exchange for the waiver and release or a single payee check or joint payee check is given in exchange for the waiver and release, the waiver and release shall be null, void, and unenforceable unless it is in substantially the following form:

CONDITIONAL WAIVER AND RELEASE ON PROGRESS PAYMENT

NOTICE: THIS DOCUMENT WAIVES THE CLAIMANT'S LIEN, STOP PAYMENT NOTICE, AND PAYMENT BOND RIGHTS EFFECTIVE ON RECEIPT OF PAYMENT. A PERSON SHOULD NOT RELY ON THIS DOCUMENT UNLESS SATISFIED THAT THE CLAIMANT HAS RECEIVED PAYMENT.

Identifying Information

Name of Claimant: _____
Name of Customer: _____
Job Location: _____
Owner: _____
Through Date: _____

Conditional Waiver and Release

This document waives and releases lien, stop payment notice, and payment bond rights the claimant has for labor and service provided, and equipment and material delivered, to the customer on this job through the Through Date of this document. Rights based upon labor or service provided, or equipment or material delivered, pursuant to a written change order that has been fully executed by the parties prior to the date that this document is signed by the claimant, are waived and released by this document, unless listed as an Exception below. This document is effective only on the claimant's receipt of payment

from the financial institution on which the following check is drawn:

Maker of Check: _____
Amount of Check: $ _____
Check Payable to: _____

Exceptions

This document does not affect any of the following:
(1) Retentions.
(2) Extras for which the claimant has not received payment.
(3) The following progress payments for which the claimant has previously given a conditional waiver and release but has not received payment:
Date(s) of waiver and release: _____
Amount(s) of unpaid progress payment(s): $ _____
(4) Contract rights, including (A) a right based on rescission, abandonment, or breach of contract, and (B) the right to recover compensation for work not compensated by the payment.

Signature

Claimant's Signature: _____
Claimant's Title: _____
Date of Signature: _____

(Added by Stats.2010, c. 697 (S.B.189), § 20, operative July 1, 2012.)

Operative Effect

For operative effect of Part 6, see Civil Code § 8052 and Stats.2010, c. 697 (S.B.189), § 105.

Law Revision Commission Comments

Section 8132 restates former Section 3262(d)(1) without substantive change, except to add language relating to progress payments covered by previous releases that have not been paid. The statutory form is recast for clarity.

See also Sections 8004 ("claimant"), 8008 ("contract"), 8026 ("lien"), 8030 ("payment bond"), 8032 ("person"), 8044 ("stop payment notice"), 8048 ("work"). [40 Cal.L.Rev.Comm. Reports 49 [AR:apx5] (2010)].

Research References

Rutter, Cal. Practice Guide: Insurance Litigation Ch. 6I-D, D. Surety's Defenses to Payment of Bond.

Miller and Starr California Real Estate § 28:67, Payment, Release, and Waiver of the Lien.

21 NO. 4 Miller & Starr, California Real Estate Newsalert 1, Everything Old is New Again: Impact of SB 189 on Mechanics' Lien Law.

4 Witkin, California Summary 10th Security Transactions in Real Property § 31-I, (New)-Release of Lien.

§ 8134. Unconditional waiver and release on progress payment; form

If the claimant is required to execute a waiver and release in exchange for, or in order to induce payment of, a progress payment and the claimant asserts in the waiver that the claimant has, in fact, been paid the progress payment, the waiver and release shall be null, void, and unenforceable unless it is in substantially the following form, with the text of the "Notice to Claimant" in at least as large a type as the largest type otherwise in the form:

UNCONDITIONAL WAIVER AND RELEASE ON PROGRESS PAYMENT

NOTICE TO CLAIMANT: THIS DOCUMENT WAIVES AND RELEASES LIEN, STOP PAYMENT NOTICE, AND PAYMENT BOND RIGHTS UNCONDITIONALLY AND STATES THAT YOU HAVE BEEN PAID FOR GIVING UP THOSE RIGHTS. THIS DOCUMENT IS ENFORCEABLE AGAINST YOU IF YOU SIGN IT, EVEN IF YOU HAVE NOT BEEN PAID. IF YOU HAVE NOT BEEN PAID, USE A CONDITIONAL WAIVER AND RELEASE FORM.

Identifying Information

Name of Claimant: _____
Name of Customer: _____
Job Location: _____
Owner: _____
Through Date: _____

Unconditional Waiver and Release

This document waives and releases lien, stop payment notice, and payment bond rights the claimant has for labor and service provided, and equipment and material delivered, to the customer on this job through the Through Date of this document. Rights based upon labor or service provided, or equipment or material delivered, pursuant to a written change order that has been fully executed by the parties prior to the date that this document is signed by the claimant, are waived and released by this document, unless listed as an Exception below. The claimant has received the following progress payment: $ _

Exceptions

This document does not affect any of the following:
(1) Retentions.
(2) Extras for which the claimant has not received payment.
(3) Contract rights, including (A) a right based on rescission, abandonment, or breach of contract, and (B) the right to recover compensation for work not compensated by the payment.

Signature

Claimant's Signature: _____
Claimant's Title: _____
Date of Signature: _____

(Added by Stats.2010, c. 697 (S.B.189), § 20, operative July 1, 2012.)

Operative Effect

For operative effect of Part 6, see Civil Code § 8052 and Stats.2010, c. 697 (S.B.189), § 105.

Law Revision Commission Comments

Section 8134 restates former Section 3262(d)(2) without substantive change. The statutory form is recast for clarity.

See also Sections 8004 ("claimant"), 8008 ("contract"), 8026 ("lien"), 8030 ("payment bond"), 8044 ("stop payment notice"), 8048 ("work"). [40 Cal.L.Rev.Comm. Reports 49 [AR:apx5] (2010)].

Research References

California Real Estate Forms (Miller & Starr) § 3:8, Deed of Trust, Security Agreement, and Fixture Filing With Assignment of Rents and Agreements.

California Real Estate Forms (Miller & Starr) § 3:14, Construction Deed of Trust, Security Agreement, and Fixture Filing With Assignment of Rents and Agreements.

California Real Estate Forms (Miller & Starr) § 3:21, Deed of Trust, Assignment of Rents, Security Agreement and Fixture Filing-- Conduit Loan.

California Real Estate Forms (Miller & Starr) § 3:35, Long Form DEed of Trust and Assignment of Rents.

Miller and Starr California Real Estate § 28:67, Payment, Release, and Waiver of the Lien.

4 Witkin, California Summary 10th Security Transactions in Real Property § 31-I, (New)-Release of Lien.

§ 8136. Conditional waiver and release on final payment; form

If the claimant is required to execute a waiver and release in exchange for, or in order to induce payment of, a final payment and the claimant is not, in fact, paid in exchange for the waiver and release or a single payee check or joint payee check is given in exchange for the waiver and release, the waiver and release shall be null, void, and unenforceable unless it is in substantially the following form:

CONDITIONAL WAIVER AND RELEASE ON FINAL PAYMENT

NOTICE: THIS DOCUMENT WAIVES THE CLAIMANT'S LIEN, STOP PAYMENT NOTICE, AND PAYMENT BOND RIGHTS EFFECTIVE ON RECEIPT OF PAYMENT. A PERSON SHOULD NOT RELY ON THIS DOCUMENT UNLESS SATISFIED THAT THE CLAIMANT HAS RECEIVED PAYMENT.

Identifying Information

Name of Claimant: _____
Name of Customer: _____
Job Location: _____
Owner: _____

Conditional Waiver and Release

This document waives and releases lien, stop payment notice, and payment bond rights the claimant has for labor and service provided, and equipment and material delivered, to the customer on this job. Rights based upon labor or service provided, or equipment or material delivered, pursuant to a written change order that has been fully executed by the parties prior to the date that this document is signed by the claimant, are waived and released by this document, unless listed as an Exception below. This document is effective only on the claimant's receipt of payment from the financial institution on which the following check is drawn:

Maker of Check: _____
Amount of Check: $ _____
Check Payable to: _____

Exceptions

This document does not affect any of the following: Disputed claims for extras in the amount of: $ ___

Signature

Claimant's Signature: _____
Claimant's Title: _____
Date of Signature: _____

(Added by Stats.2010, c. 697 (S.B.189), § 20, operative July 1, 2012.)

Operative Effect

For operative effect of Part 6, see Civil Code § 8052 and Stats.2010, c. 697 (S.B.189), § 105.

Law Revision Commission Comments

Section 8136 restates former Section 3262(d)(3) without substantive change, except to add a line for identification of the waivant's customer. The statutory form is recast for clarity.

See also Sections 8004 ("claimant"), 8026 ("lien"), 8030 ("payment bond"), 8032 ("person"), 8044 ("stop payment notice"). [40 Cal.L.Rev. Comm. Reports 49 [AR:apx5] (2010)].

Research References

Miller and Starr California Real Estate § 28:67, Payment, Release, and Waiver of the Lien.

§ 8138. Unconditional waiver and release on final payment; form

If the claimant is required to execute a waiver and release in exchange for, or in order to induce payment of, a final payment and the claimant asserts in the waiver that the claimant has, in fact, been paid the final payment, the waiver and release shall be null, void, and unenforceable unless it is in substantially the following form, with the text of the "Notice to Claimant" in at least as large a type as the largest type otherwise in the form:

UNCONDITIONAL WAIVER AND RELEASE ON
FINAL PAYMENT

NOTICE TO CLAIMANT: THIS DOCUMENT WAIVES AND RELEASES LIEN, STOP PAYMENT NOTICE, AND PAYMENT BOND RIGHTS UNCONDITIONALLY AND STATES THAT YOU HAVE BEEN PAID FOR GIVING UP THOSE RIGHTS. THIS DOCUMENT IS ENFORCEABLE AGAINST YOU IF YOU SIGN IT, EVEN IF YOU HAVE NOT BEEN PAID. IF YOU HAVE NOT BEEN PAID, USE A CONDITIONAL WAIVER AND RELEASE FORM.

Identifying Information

Name of Claimant: _____
Name of Customer: _____
Job Location: _____
Owner: _____

Unconditional Waiver and Release

This document waives and releases lien, stop payment notice, and payment bond rights the claimant has for all labor and service provided, and equipment and material delivered, to the customer on this job. Rights based upon labor or service provided, or equipment or material delivered, pursuant to a written change order that has been fully executed by the parties prior to the date that this document is signed by the claimant, are waived and released by this document, unless listed as an Exception below. The claimant has been paid in full.

Exceptions

This document does not affect the following:
Disputed claims for extras in the amount of: $ ___

Signature

Claimant's Signature: _____
Claimant's Title: _____
Date of Signature: _____

(Added by Stats.2010, c. 697 (S.B.189), § 20, operative July 1, 2012.)

Operative Effect

For operative effect of Part 6, see Civil Code § 8052 and Stats.2010, c. 697 (S.B.189), § 105.

Law Revision Commission Comments

Section 8138 restates former Section 3262(d)(4) without substantive change. The statutory form is recast for clarity.

See also Sections 8004 ("claimant"), 8026 ("lien"), 8030 ("payment bond"), 8044 ("stop payment notice"). [40 Cal.L.Rev.Comm. Reports 49 [AR:apx5] (2010)].

Research References

Miller and Starr California Real Estate § 28:67, Payment, Release, and Waiver of the Lien.
21 NO. 4 Miller & Starr, California Real Estate Newsalert 1, Everything Old is New Again: Impact of SB 189 on Mechanics' Lien Law.
3 Witkin Cal. Proc. 5th Actions § 221A, (S 221A) (New)-In General.
4 Witkin, California Summary 10th Security Transactions in Real Property § 31A, (S 31A) (New)-Nature and Purpose of Revision.

CHAPTER 4.   BONDS

Section
8150.   Application of Bond and Undertaking Law.
8152.   Acts not releasing surety from liability on bond given under this part.
8154.   Construction of bond; liability of surety; condition for recovery on bond.

Operative Effect

For operative effect of Part 6, see Civil Code § 8052 and Stats.2010, c. 697 (S.B.189), § 105.

§ 8150.   Application of Bond and Undertaking Law

The Bond and Undertaking Law (Chapter 2 (commencing with Section 995.010) of Title 14 of Part 2 of the Code of Civil Procedure) applies to a bond given under this part, except to the extent this part prescribes a different rule or is inconsistent. *(Added by Stats.2010, c. 697 (S.B.189), § 20, operative July 1, 2012.)*

Operative Effect

For operative effect of Part 6, see Civil Code § 8052 and Stats.2010, c. 697 (S.B.189), § 105.

Law Revision Commission Comments

Section 8150 is new. It is a specific application of Code of Civil Procedure Section 995.020 (application of Bond and Undertaking Law).

Former Section 3227, relating to notice to principal and surety, is not continued. Its substance is superseded by Sections 8100–8118 (notice). [40 Cal.L.Rev.Comm. Reports 49 [AR:apx5] (2010)].

Research References

Rutter, Cal. Practice Guide: Insurance Litigation Ch. 6I-B, B. Particular Surety Bond Coverages.
Miller and Starr California Real Estate § 28:93, Suretyship Terminology and Definitions.

21 NO. 4 Miller & Starr, California Real Estate Newsalert 1, Everything Old is New Again: Impact of SB 189 on Mechanics' Lien Law.
3 Witkin Cal. Proc. 5th Actions § 221A, (S 221A) (New)-In General.
4 Witkin, California Summary 10th Security Transactions in Real Property § 31A, (S 31A) (New)-Nature and Purpose of Revision.

§ 8152. Acts not releasing surety from liability on bond given under this part

None of the following releases a surety from liability on a bond given under this part:

(a) A change, alteration, or modification to a contract, plan, specification, or agreement for a work of improvement or for work provided for a work of improvement.

(b) A change or modification to the terms of payment or an extension of the time for payment for a work of improvement.

(c) A rescission or attempted rescission of a contract, agreement, or bond.

(d) A condition precedent or subsequent in the bond purporting to limit the right of recovery of a claimant otherwise entitled to recover pursuant to a contract, agreement, or bond.

(e) In the case of a bond given for the benefit of claimants, the fraud of a person other than the claimant seeking to recover on the bond. *(Added by Stats.2010, c. 697 (S.B.189), § 20, operative July 1, 2012.)*

Operative Effect

For operative effect of Part 6, see Civil Code § 8052 and Stats.2010, c. 697 (S.B.189), § 105.

Law Revision Commission Comments

Section 8152 restates former Section 3225 without substantive change. See also Section 8062 (effect of act by owner).

See also Sections 8004 ("claimant"), 8008 ("contract"), 8032 ("person"), 8048 ("work"), 8050 ("work of improvement"). [40 Cal.L.Rev. Comm. Reports 49 [AR:apx5] (2010)].

Research References

California Real Estate Forms (Miller & Starr) § 4:14, Construction Agreement-- Master Agreement for Construction Services.
Rutter, Cal. Practice Guide: Insurance Litigation Ch. 6I-D, D. Surety's Defenses to Payment of Bond.
Miller and Starr California Real Estate § 28:103, Exoneration of the Surety--Modification of the Terms of the Construction Contract.
Miller and Starr California Real Estate § 28:105, Exoneration of the Surety--Rescission or Revocation of the Contract.
Miller and Starr California Real Estate § 28:107, Exoneration of the Surety--Release or Discharge of the Debtor or Principal.
Miller and Starr California Real Estate § 28:110, No Exoneration of the Surety Under Bonds in Favor of Claimants.
Miller and Starr California Real Estate § 28:112, Proper Parties in Suit Against Surety; Necessity of Suit Against or Joinder of the Principal.
Miller and Starr California Real Estate § 28:114, Other Defenses Available to the Surety.
Miller and Starr California Real Estate § 28:120, Payment and Performance Bonds as to Public Projects.

§ 8154. Construction of bond; liability of surety; condition for recovery on bond

(a) A bond given under this part shall be construed most strongly against the surety and in favor of all persons for whose benefit the bond is given.

(b) A surety is not released from liability to those for whose benefit the bond has been given by reason of a breach of the direct contract or on the part of any obligee named in the bond.

(c) Except as otherwise provided by statute, the sole conditions of recovery on the bond are that the claimant is a person described in Article 1 (commencing with Section 8400) of Chapter 4 of Title 2, or in Section 9100, and has not been paid

the full amount of the claim. *(Added by Stats.2010, c. 697 (S.B.189), § 20, operative July 1, 2012.)*

Operative Effect

For operative effect of Part 6, see Civil Code § 8052 and Stats.2010, c. 697 (S.B.189), § 105.

Law Revision Commission Comments

Section 8154 restates former Section 3226 without substantive change. See also Sections 8400–8404 (who is entitled to lien).

See also Sections 8004 ("claimant"), 8016 ("direct contract"), 8032 ("person"). [40 Cal.L.Rev.Comm. Reports 49 [AR:apx5] (2010)].

Research References

Rutter, Cal. Practice Guide: Insurance Litigation Ch. 6I-A, A. Introduction.
Rutter, Cal. Practice Guide: Insurance Litigation Ch. 6I-B, B. Particular Surety Bond Coverages.
Rutter, Cal. Practice Guide: Insurance Litigation Gen. Matls., Highlights.
Miller and Starr California Real Estate § 28:8, "Claimant" Defined.
Miller and Starr California Real Estate § 28:96, Interpretation of the Bond.
Miller and Starr California Real Estate § 28:97, Measure of Surety's Liability.
Miller and Starr California Real Estate § 28:103, Exoneration of the Surety--Modification of the Terms of the Construction Contract.
Miller and Starr California Real Estate § 28:110, No Exoneration of the Surety Under Bonds in Favor of Claimants.
Miller and Starr California Real Estate § 28:120, Payment and Performance Bonds as to Public Projects.
21 NO. 4 Miller & Starr, California Real Estate Newsalert 1, Everything Old is New Again: Impact of SB 189 on Mechanics' Lien Law.
3 Witkin Cal. Proc. 5th Actions § 221A, (S 221A) (New)-In General.
4 Witkin, California Summary 10th Security Transactions in Real Property § 31A, (S 31A) (New)-Nature and Purpose of Revision.

Title 2

PRIVATE WORKS OF IMPROVEMENT

Operative Effect

For operative effect of Part 6, see Civil Code § 8052 and Stats.2010, c. 697 (S.B.189), § 105.

CHAPTER 1. GENERAL PROVISIONS

Operative Effect

For operative effect of Part 6, see Civil Code § 8052 and Stats.2010, c. 697 (S.B.189), § 105.

ARTICLE 1. APPLICATION OF TITLE

Section
8160. Application of title.

Operative Effect

*For operative effect of Part 6, see Civil Code § 8052
and Stats.2010, c. 697 (S.B.189), § 105.*

§ 8160. Application of title

This title applies to a work of improvement that is not
governed by Title 3 (commencing with Section 9000) of this part.
*(Added by Stats.2010, c. 697 (S.B.189), § 20, operative July 1,
2012.)*

Operative Effect

*For operative effect of Part 6, see Civil Code § 8052
and Stats.2010, c. 697 (S.B.189), § 105.*

Law Revision Commission Comments

Section 8160 is new. It provides the scope of applicability of the
provisions of this title. Title 3 (commencing with Section 9000) of this part
governs a work of improvement contracted for by a public entity. See
Section 9000.

See also Section 8050 (work of improvement). [40 Cal.L.Rev.Comm.
Reports 49 [AR:apx5] (2010)].

Research References

Rutter, Cal. Practice Guide: Insurance Litigation Ch. 6I-B, B. Particular
   Surety Bond Coverages.
Rutter, Cal. Practice Guide: Insurance Litigation Gen. Matls., Highlights.
Miller and Starr California Real Estate § 28:85, Nature of Public Works
   Stop Payment Notice.
21 NO. 4 Miller & Starr, California Real Estate Newsalert 1, Everything
   Old is New Again: Impact of SB 189 on Mechanics' Lien Law.
3 Witkin Cal. Proc. 5th Actions § 65, (S 65) Statutory Classes.
3 Witkin Cal. Proc. 5th Actions § 477, (S 477) Ninety Days or Three
   Months.
3 Witkin Cal. Proc. 5th Actions § 221A, (S 221A) (New)-In General.
3 Witkin Cal. Proc. 5th Actions § 221C, (S 221C) (New)-Private Property:
   Preliminary Notice.
3 Witkin Cal. Proc. 5th Actions § 221E, (S 221E) (New)-Public Property:
   Stop Notice.
2 Witkin Cal. Proc. 5th Jurisdiction § 359, Subcontractor's Contract.
4 Witkin, California Summary 10th Security Transactions in Real Property
   § 21, (S 21) No Subcontractor's Lien on Loan Fund.
4 Witkin, California Summary 10th Security Transactions in Real Property
   § 31A, (S 31A) (New)-Nature and Purpose of Revision.

ARTICLE 2.   CONSTRUCTION DOCUMENTS

Operative Effect

*For operative effect of Part 6, see Civil Code § 8052
and Stats.2010, c. 697 (S.B.189), § 105.*

§ 8170.   Written direct contracts; contents

(a) A written direct contract shall provide a space for the
owner to enter the following information:

(1) The owner's name, address, and place of business, if any.

(2) The name and address of the construction lender, if any.
This paragraph does not apply to a home improvement contract
or swimming pool contract subject to Article 10 (commencing
with Section 7150) of Chapter 9 of Division 3 of the Business and
Professions Code.

(b) A written contract entered into between a direct contractor and subcontractor, or between subcontractors, shall provide a
space for the name and address of the owner, direct contractor,
and construction lender, if any. *(Added by Stats.2010, c. 697
(S.B.189), § 20, operative July 1, 2012.)*

Operative Effect

*For operative effect of Part 6, see Civil Code § 8052
and Stats.2010, c. 697 (S.B.189), § 105.*

Law Revision Commission Comments

Section 8170 restates the parts of former Section 3097(*l*) and (m)
relating to the contents of contracts, deleting the limitation to the owner's
residence address.

The reference to "written" contract is added to subdivision (b) for
consistency with subdivision (a). The reference to "lender or lenders" in
subdivision (a) is shortened to "lender" for consistency with subdivision
(b). See Section 14 (singular includes plural, and plural includes singular).
These and other minor wording changes are technical, nonsubstantive
revisions.

For the direct contractor's duty to provide information to persons
seeking to serve a preliminary notice, see Section 8208.

This section does not require that all contracts between an owner and a
direct contractor be in writing.

See also Sections 8006 ("construction lender"), 8008 ("contract"), 8016
("direct contract"), 8018 ("direct contractor"), 8046 ("subcontractor").
[40 Cal.L.Rev.Comm. Reports 49 [AR:apx5] (2010)].

Research References

Miller and Starr California Real Estate § 28:31, Who Must Give, and
   Who Must Receive, The Preliminary Notice.

§ 8172.   Building permits; application form; information re-
garding construction lenders

(a) A public entity that issues building permits shall, in its
application form for a building permit, provide space and a
designation for the applicant to enter the name, branch designation, if any, and address of the construction lender and shall keep
the information on file open for public inspection during the
regular business hours of the public entity.

(b) If there is no known construction lender, the applicant
shall note that fact in the designated space.

(c) Failure of the applicant to indicate the name and address
of the construction lender on the application does not relieve a
person required to give the construction lender preliminary
notice from that duty. *(Added by Stats.2010, c. 697 (S.B.189),
§ 20, operative July 1, 2012.)*

Operative Effect

*For operative effect of Part 6, see Civil Code § 8052
and Stats.2010, c. 697 (S.B.189), § 105.*

Law Revision Commission Comments

Section 8172 continues former Section 3097(i) without substantive
change.

See also Sections 8006 ("construction lender"), 8032 ("person"), 8034
("preliminary notice"), 8036 ("public entity"). [40 Cal.L.Rev.Comm.
Reports 49 [AR:apx5] (2010)].

Research References

Miller and Starr California Real Estate § 28:31, Who Must Give, and
   Who Must Receive, The Preliminary Notice.
Miller and Starr California Real Estate § 28:71, Requirement of a
   Preliminary Notice.

§ 8174.   Construction trust deed; contents

(a) A mortgage, deed of trust, or other instrument securing a
loan, any of the proceeds of which may be used for a work of
improvement, shall bear the designation "Construction Trust
Deed" prominently on its face and shall state all of the following:

(1) The name and address of the construction lender.

(2) The name and address of the owner of the real property described in the instrument.

(3) A legal description of the real property that secures the loan and, if known, the street address of the property.

(b) Failure to comply with subdivision (a) does not affect the validity of the mortgage, deed of trust, or other instrument.

(c) Failure to comply with subdivision (a) does not relieve a person required to give preliminary notice from that duty.

(d) The county recorder of the county in which the instrument is recorded shall indicate in the general index of the official records of the county that the instrument secures a construction loan. *(Added by Stats.2010, c. 697 (S.B.189), § 20, operative July 1, 2012.)*

Operative Effect

For operative effect of Part 6, see Civil Code § 8052 and Stats.2010, c. 697 (S.B.189), § 105.

Law Revision Commission Comments

Section 8174 continues former Section 3097(j) without substantive change.

See also Section 8060 (filing and recordation of papers).

See also Sections 8006 ("construction lender"), 8032 ("person"), 8034 ("preliminary notice"), 8050 ("work of improvement"). [40 Cal.L.Rev. Comm. Reports 49 [AR:apx5] (2010)].

Research References

Miller and Starr California Real Estate § 11:6, Instruments Subject to Recording--List of Recordable Documents.
Miller and Starr California Real Estate § 28:31, Who Must Give, and Who Must Receive, The Preliminary Notice.
Miller and Starr California Real Estate § 28:71, Requirement of a Preliminary Notice.

ARTICLE 3.   COMPLETION

Section
8180.   Acts signifying completion.
8182.   Notice of completion; recording; contents.
8184.   Acceptance and recording of notice of completion.
8186.   Multiple contracts; notice of completion for portion of work of improvement.
8188.   Notice of cessation; recording; contents.
8190.   Notice of completion or cessation; copies to be provided.

Operative Effect

For operative effect of Part 6, see Civil Code § 8052 and Stats.2010, c. 697 (S.B.189), § 105.

§ 8180.   Acts signifying completion

(a) For the purpose of this title, completion of a work of improvement occurs upon the occurrence of any of the following events:

(1) Actual completion of the work of improvement.

(2) Occupation or use by the owner accompanied by cessation of labor.

(3) Cessation of labor for a continuous period of 60 days.

(4) Recordation of a notice of cessation after cessation of labor for a continuous period of 30 days.

(b) Notwithstanding subdivision (a), if a work of improvement is subject to acceptance by a public entity, completion occurs on acceptance. *(Added by Stats.2010, c. 697 (S.B.189), § 20, operative July 1, 2012.)*

Operative Effect

For operative effect of Part 6, see Civil Code § 8052 and Stats.2010, c. 697 (S.B.189), § 105.

Law Revision Commission Comments

Section 8180 restates former Section 3086, to the extent it applied to a private work.

References to occupation or use by an owner may include occupation or use by the owner's agent. See Section 8066 (agency).

"Acceptance by the owner" is not continued as a form of completion.

The provision in subdivision (b) for acceptance by a public entity refers to acceptance pursuant to a legislative enactment of the public entity and not to inspection and approval or issuance of a certificate of occupancy under building regulations.

Subdivision (b) applies only to a private work of improvement. See Section 8160 (application of title).

See also Sections 1170 (recordation), 8058 (calculation of time), 8060 (filing and recordation of papers), 8188 (notice of cessation).

See also Sections 8036 ("public entity"), 8050 ("work of improvement"). [40 Cal.L.Rev.Comm. Reports 49 [AR:apx5] (2010)].

Research References

Rutter, Cal. Practice Guide: Insurance Litigation Ch. 6I-B, B. Particular Surety Bond Coverages.
Miller and Starr California Real Estate § 27:91, Prompt Payment of Progress Payments and Contract Retention.
Miller and Starr California Real Estate § 28:40, When Notice of Cessation Recorded.
Miller and Starr California Real Estate § 28:41, When No Notice of Completion or Cessation Recorded.
Miller and Starr California Real Estate § 28:44, Public Improvements Under Private Contract.
Miller and Starr California Real Estate § 11:140, Effect of Cessation of Work on Mechanic's Lien Priorities.
21 NO. 4 Miller & Starr, California Real Estate Newsalert 1, Everything Old is New Again: Impact of SB 189 on Mechanics' Lien Law.
3 Witkin Cal. Proc. 5th Actions § 221A, (S 221A) (New)-In General.
3 Witkin Cal. Proc. 5th Actions § 222A, (S 222A) (New)-Revised Law for Action on Payment Bond for Work of Improvement.
4 Witkin, California Summary 10th Security Transactions in Real Property § 31A, (S 31A) (New)-Nature and Purpose of Revision.
4 Witkin, California Summary 10th Security Transactions in Real Property § 31F, (S 31F) (New)-Requirements of Claim.

§ 8182.   Notice of completion;   recording;   contents

(a) An owner may record a notice of completion on or within 15 days after the date of completion of a work of improvement.

(b) The notice of completion shall be signed and verified by the owner.

(c) The notice shall comply with the requirements of Chapter 2 (commencing with Section 8100) of Title 1, and shall also include all of the following information:

(1) If the notice is given only of completion of a contract for a particular portion of the work of improvement as provided in Section 8186, the name of the direct contractor under that contract and a general statement of the work provided pursuant to the contract.

(2) If signed by the owner's successor in interest, the name and address of the successor's transferor.

(3) The nature of the interest or estate of the owner.

(4) The date of completion. An erroneous statement of the date of completion does not affect the effectiveness of the notice if the true date of completion is 15 days or less before the date of recordation of the notice.

(d) A notice of completion that does not comply with the provisions of this section is not effective.

(e) For the purpose of this section, "owner" means the owner who causes a building, improvement, or structure to be constructed, altered, or repaired, or that person's successor in interest at the date a notice of completion is recorded, whether the interest or estate of the owner be in fee, as vendee under a contract of purchase, as lessee, or other interest or estate less than the fee. Where the interest or estate is held by two or more persons as joint tenants or tenants in common, any one or more of the cotenants may be deemed to be the "owner" within the meaning of this section. *(Added by Stats.2010, c. 697 (S.B.189), § 20, operative July 1, 2012.)*

Operative Effect

For operative effect of Part 6, see Civil Code § 8052 and Stats.2010, c. 697 (S.B.189), § 105.

Law Revision Commission Comments

Section 8182 restates former Section 3093 without substantive change, except that the 10 day period for recording a notice of completion is extended to 15 days. For the date of completion of a work of improvement, see Section 8180.

A notice of completion may be signed and verified or recorded by an agent of the owner, to the extent the act is within the scope of the agent's authority. See Section 8066 (agency).

For the effect of a recordation of a notice of completion, see Sections 8412 and 8414 (time for claim of lien), 8612 (notice of payment bond claim).

A claim of lien must be filed within 30 or 60 days after recordation of a notice of completion (depending on the nature of the claimant), subject to a maximum of 90 days after actual completion. See Sections 8412 and 8414 (recordation of claim of lien). However, an owner that records a notice of completion that states an incorrect date of completion may be estopped from asserting the running of the filing period. See Doherty v. Carruthers, 171 Cal.App.2d 214, 340 P.2d 58 (1959).

A notice of completion is ineffective to shorten the time for a claim of lien unless notice of recordation is given to the person whose claim of lien is affected. See Section 8190 (notice of recordation by owner).

A notice of completion is recorded in the office of the county recorder of the county in which the work of improvement or part of it is situated. See Section 8060(a) (filing and recordation of papers). A notice of completion is recorded when it is filed for record. See Sections 1170 (recordation), 8060(b) (filing and recordation of papers).

The reference to a successor's "transferors" is omitted from subdivision (c)(2). See Section 14 (singular includes plural).

See also Sections 8058 (calculation of time), 8064 (co-owners).

See also Sections 8008 ("contract"), 8018 ("direct contractor"), 8032 ("person"), 8040 ("site"), 8048 ("work"), 8050 ("work of improvement"). [40 Cal.L.Rev.Comm. Reports 49 [AR:apx5] (2010)].

Research References

Rutter, Cal. Practice Guide: Insurance Litigation Ch. 6I-B, B. Particular Surety Bond Coverages.

Miller and Starr California Real Estate § 11:6, Instruments Subject to Recording--List of Recordable Documents.

Miller and Starr California Real Estate § 11:12, Required Form and Contents--Signature of the Property Owner.

Miller and Starr California Real Estate § 28:28, Statutory Provisions Governing Notice.

Miller and Starr California Real Estate § 28:39, When Notice of Completion Recorded.

Miller and Starr California Real Estate § 28:41, When No Notice of Completion or Cessation Recorded.

Miller and Starr California Real Estate § 28:42, When There Are Two or More Contracts With the Owner.

13 Witkin, California Summary 10th Personal Property § 2, Special Meanings.

4 Witkin, California Summary 10th Security Transactions in Real Property § 31F, (S 31F) (New)-Requirements of Claim.

§ 8184. Acceptance and recording of notice of completion

A notice of completion in otherwise proper form, verified and containing the information required by this title, shall be accepted by the recorder for recording and is deemed duly recorded without acknowledgment. *(Added by Stats.2010, c. 697 (S.B.189), § 20, operative July 1, 2012.)*

Operative Effect

For operative effect of Part 6, see Civil Code § 8052 and Stats.2010, c. 697 (S.B.189), § 105.

Law Revision Commission Comments

Section 8184 continues a portion of former Section 3093 without substantive change.

See also Sections 1170 (recordation), 8058 (filing and recordation of papers), 8182 (notice of completion), 8186 (notice of completion of contract for portion of work of improvement), 8190 (notice of recordation by owner); Gov't Code §§ 27280, 27287 (recordation of documents). [40 Cal.L.Rev.Comm. Reports 49 [AR:apx5] (2010)].

Research References

Miller and Starr California Real Estate § 11:6, Instruments Subject to Recording--List of Recordable Documents.

Miller and Starr California Real Estate § 11:12, Required Form and Contents--Signature of the Property Owner.

Miller and Starr California Real Estate § 28:39, When Notice of Completion Recorded.

Miller and Starr California Real Estate § 28:40, When Notice of Cessation Recorded.

Miller and Starr California Real Estate § 28:42, When There Are Two or More Contracts With the Owner.

§ 8186. Multiple contracts; notice of completion for portion of work of improvement

If a work of improvement is made pursuant to two or more direct contracts, each covering a portion of the work of improvement:

(a) The owner may record a notice of completion of a direct contract for a portion of the work of improvement. On recordation of the notice of completion, for the purpose of Sections 8412 and 8414, a direct contractor is deemed to have completed the contract for which the notice of completion is recorded and a claimant other than a direct contractor is deemed to have ceased providing work.

(b) If the owner does not record a notice of completion under this section, the period for recording a claim of lien is that provided in Sections 8412 and 8414. *(Added by Stats.2010, c. 697 (S.B.189), § 20, operative July 1, 2012.)*

Operative Effect

For operative effect of Part 6, see Civil Code § 8052 and Stats.2010, c. 697 (S.B.189), § 105.

Law Revision Commission Comments

Section 8186 continues the substance of former Section 3117, but eliminates the 10 day period for recordation of a notice of completion of a contract for a portion of a work of improvement.

This section omits the rules found in former law governing the time for recordation of a lien claim after a notice of completion for a portion of a work of improvement. The general rules governing the time for recordation do not distinguish among types of notice of completion, and appear to be satisfactory for purposes of this section, with the clarification set out in subdivision (a). A claim of lien must be recorded within 30 or 60 days after recordation of notice of completion (depending on the nature of the claimant), subject to a maximum of 90 days after actual completion. See Sections 8412 and 8414 (recordation of claim of lien).

For the effect of a recordation of a notice of completion, see Sections 8412 and 8414 (time for recordation of lien claim), 8612 (notice of payment bond claim).

The recordation of a notice of completion of a contract for a portion of a work of improvement does not affect the rights of a claimant with respect to work provided pursuant to another contract.

See also Sections 8064 (co-owners), 8182 (notice of completion).

See also Sections 8004 ("claimant"), 8008 ("contract"), 8016 ("direct contract"), 8018 ("direct contractor"), 8026 ("lien"), 8048 ("work"), 8050 ("work of improvement"). [40 Cal.L.Rev.Comm. Reports 49 [AR:apx5] (2010)].

Research References

Miller and Starr California Real Estate § 28:9, Contractors.

Miller and Starr California Real Estate § 28:37, Claim of Lien--Necessity, Purpose, and Effect.

Miller and Starr California Real Estate § 28:38, Time to File.

Miller and Starr California Real Estate § 28:40, When Notice of Cessation Recorded.

Miller and Starr California Real Estate § 28:42, When There Are Two or More Contracts With the Owner.

Miller and Starr California Real Estate § 11:137, Phasing of a Project by Separate Direct Contracts With the Owner.

Miller and Starr California Real Estate § 11:140, Effect of Cessation of Work on Mechanic's Lien Priorities.

§ 8188. Notice of cessation; recording; contents

(a) An owner may record a notice of cessation if there has been a continuous cessation of labor on a work of improvement for at least 30 days prior to the recordation that continues through the date of the recordation.

(b) The notice shall be signed and verified by the owner.

(c) The notice shall comply with the requirements of Chapter 2 (commencing with Section 8100) of Title 1, and shall also include all of the following information:

(1) The date on or about which labor ceased.

(2) A statement that the cessation has continued until the recordation of the notice.

(d) For the purpose of this section, "owner" means the owner who causes a building, improvement, or structure to be constructed, altered, or repaired, or that person's successor in interest at the date a notice of cessation is recorded, whether the interest or estate of the owner be in fee, as vendee under a contract of purchase, as lessee, or other interest or estate less than the fee. Where the interest or estate is held by two or more persons as joint tenants or tenants in common, any one or more of the cotenants may be deemed to be the "owner" within the meaning of this section. (Added by Stats.2010, c. 697 (S.B.189), § 20, operative July 1, 2012.)

Operative Effect

For operative effect of Part 6, see Civil Code § 8052 and Stats.2010, c. 697 (S.B.189), § 105.

Law Revision Commission Comments

Section 8188 restates former Section 3092 without substantive change.

The notice of cessation may be signed, verified, and recorded by an agent of the owner to the extent the act is within the scope of the agent's authority. See Section 8066 (agency).

For the effect of a recordation of a notice of cessation, see Sections 8412 and 8414 (time for recordation of lien claim).

A notice of cessation is recorded in the office of the county recorder of the county in which the work of improvement or part of it is performed. See Section 8060(a) (filing and recordation of papers). The notice is recorded when it is filed for record. See Sections 1170 (recordation), 8060(b) (filing and recordation of papers).

A notice of cessation is ineffective to shorten the time for a claim of lien unless notice of recordation is given to the person whose claim of lien is affected. See Section 8190 (notice of recordation by owner).

See also Sections 8058 (calculation of time), 8064 (co-owners).

See also Sections 8032 ("person"), 8050 ("work of improvement"). [40 Cal.L.Rev.Comm. Reports 49 [AR:apx5] (2010)].

Research References

Rutter, Cal. Practice Guide: Insurance Litigation Ch. 6I-B, B. Particular Surety Bond Coverages.

Miller and Starr California Real Estate § 11:6, Instruments Subject to Recording--List of Recordable Documents.

Miller and Starr California Real Estate § 28:40, When Notice of Cessation Recorded.

Miller and Starr California Real Estate § 11:140, Effect of Cessation of Work on Mechanic's Lien Priorities.

13 Witkin, California Summary 10th Personal Property § 2, Special Meanings.

4 Witkin, California Summary 10th Security Transactions in Real Property § 31F, (S 31F) (New)-Requirements of Claim.

§ 8190. Notice of completion or cessation; copies to be provided

(a) An owner that records a notice of completion or cessation shall, within 10 days of the date the notice of completion or cessation is filed for record, give a copy of the notice to all of the following persons:

(1) A direct contractor.

(2) A claimant that has given the owner preliminary notice.

(b) The copy of the notice shall be given in compliance with the requirements of Chapter 2 (commencing with Section 8100) of Title 1.

(c) If the owner fails to give notice to a person as required by subdivision (a), the notice is ineffective to shorten the time within which that person may record a claim of lien under Sections 8412 and 8414. The ineffectiveness of the notice is the sole liability of the owner for failure to give notice to a person under subdivision (a).

(d) For the purpose of this section, "owner" means a person who has an interest in real property, or the person's successor in interest on the date a notice of completion or notice of cessation is recorded, who causes a building, improvement, or structure, to be constructed, altered, or repaired on the property. If the property is owned by two or more persons as joint tenants or tenants in common, any one or more of the cotenants may be deemed to be the "owner" within the meaning of this section. However, this section does not apply to any of the following owners:

(1) A person that occupies the real property as a personal residence, if the dwelling contains four or fewer residential units.

(2) A person that has a security interest in the property.

(3) A person that obtains an interest in the property pursuant to a transfer described in subdivision (b), (c), or (d) of Section 1102.2. (Added by Stats.2010, c. 697 (S.B.189), § 20, operative July 1, 2012.)

Operative Effect

For operative effect of Part 6, see Civil Code § 8052 and Stats.2010, c. 697 (S.B.189), § 105.

Law Revision Commission Comments

Section 8190 restates former Section 3259.5, replacing the notice of recordation with a copy of the notice that the owner files for recordation, and expanding the manner of notice. The notice may no longer be given by regular mail. See Sections 8106 (manner of giving notice), 8110 (mailed notice).

Subdivision (c) is recast in terms of the ineffectiveness of the notice of completion or cessation, in place of the former references to extension of time.

A notice is recorded when it is filed for record. See Sections 1170 (recordation), 8060 (filing and recordation of papers).

See also Sections 8058 (calculation of time), 8064 (co-owners), 8180 (completion), 8182 (notice of completion), 8186 (notice of completion of contract for portion of work of improvement), 8188 (notice of cessation).

See also Sections 8004 ("claimant"), 8018 ("direct contractor"), 8026 ("lien"), 8032 ("person"), 8034 ("preliminary notice"). [40 Cal.L.Rev. Comm. Reports 49 [AR:apx5] (2010)].

Research References

Rutter, Cal. Practice Guide: Insurance Litigation Ch. 6I-B, B. Particular Surety Bond Coverages.

Miller and Starr California Real Estate § 28:39, When Notice of Completion Recorded.

Miller and Starr California Real Estate § 28:40, When Notice of Cessation Recorded.

21 NO. 4 Miller & Starr, California Real Estate Newsalert 1, Everything Old is New Again: Impact of SB 189 on Mechanics' Lien Law.

3 Witkin Cal. Proc. 5th Actions § 221A, (S 221A) (New)-In General.

4 Witkin, California Summary 10th Security Transactions in Real Property § 31A, (S 31A) (New)-Nature and Purpose of Revision.

CHAPTER 2. PRELIMINARY NOTICE

Section

8200. Preliminary notice; persons to receive; necessity of compliance with this section; exceptions.

8202. Notice to property owner.

8204. Time for giving preliminary notice.

8206. Single or multiple preliminary notice.

8208. Information to be provided by direct contractor.

8210. Additional construction loans; information to be provided to persons giving preliminary notice.

8212. Waiver of rights void and unenforceable.

8214. Filing of preliminary notice; mailing of notification; destruction of documents; purpose of filing pursuant to this section.

8216. Subcontractors; failure to give notice as grounds for disciplinary action.

Operative Effect

For operative effect of Part 6, see Civil Code § 8052 and Stats.2010, c. 697 (S.B.189), § 105.

§ 8200. Preliminary notice; persons to receive; necessity of compliance with this section; exceptions

(a) Except as otherwise provided by statute, before recording a lien claim, giving a stop payment notice, or asserting a claim against a payment bond, a claimant shall give preliminary notice to the following persons:

(1) The owner or reputed owner.

(2) The direct contractor or reputed direct contractor to which the claimant provides work, either directly or through one or more subcontractors.

(3) The construction lender or reputed construction lender, if any.

(b) The notice shall comply with the requirements of Chapter 2 (commencing with Section 8100) of Title 1.

(c) Compliance with this section is a necessary prerequisite to the validity of a lien claim or stop payment notice under this title.

(d) Compliance with this section or with Section 8612 is a necessary prerequisite to the validity of a claim against a payment bond under this title.

(e) Notwithstanding the foregoing subdivisions:

(1) A laborer is not required to give preliminary notice.

(2) A claimant with a direct contractual relationship with an owner or reputed owner is required to give preliminary notice only to the construction lender or reputed construction lender, if any. *(Added by Stats.2010, c. 697 (S.B.189), § 20, operative July 1, 2012.)*

Operative Effect

For operative effect of Part 6, see Civil Code § 8052 and Stats.2010, c. 697 (S.B.189), § 105.

Law Revision Commission Comments

Section 8200 restates the introductory clause and parts of subdivisions (a) and (b) of former Section 3097. Some repetitive detail is omitted in reliance on defined terms and other substantive provisions.

Subdivision (e)(2) makes clear that all direct contractors must give preliminary notice to the construction lender or reputed construction lender, if any. This resolves a possible ambiguity in former Section 3097(b).

For an exception to the requirement that preliminary notice must be given before asserting a claim against a payment bond, see Section 8612.

The substance of former Sections 3097(f) and 3097.1 are continued in the general notice provisions of this part. See Sections 8100–8118 (notice).

The transitional provisions of former Section 3097(p) are obsolete and not continued.

See also Sections 8004 ("claimant"), 8006 ("construction lender"), 8018 ("direct contractor"), 8024 ("laborer"), 8026 ("lien"), 8030 ("payment bond"), 8032 ("person"), 8034 ("preliminary notice"), 8044 ("stop payment notice"), 8046 ("subcontractor"), 8048 ("work"). [40 Cal.L.Rev. Comm. Reports 49 [AR:apx5] (2010)].

Research References

California Real Estate Forms (Miller & Starr) § 4:13, Construction Agreement--Tenant Improvements.

Rutter, Cal. Practice Guide: Insurance Litigation Ch. 6I-B, B. Particular Surety Bond Coverages.

Miller and Starr California Real Estate § 28:29, Preliminary Notice-- Purpose and Validity.

Miller and Starr California Real Estate § 28:30, Result of a Failure to Draft and Serve the Notice Properly.

Miller and Starr California Real Estate § 28:31, Who Must Give, and Who Must Receive, The Preliminary Notice.

Miller and Starr California Real Estate § 28:32, Persons in Direct Contract With the Owner.

Miller and Starr California Real Estate § 28:33, Laborers.

Miller and Starr California Real Estate § 28:34, Express Trust Fund; Former Exemption.

Miller and Starr California Real Estate § 28:71, Requirement of a Preliminary Notice.

Miller and Starr California Real Estate § 28:98, Notice as Condition Precedent to Surety's Liability on Payment Bond.

21 NO. 4 Miller & Starr, California Real Estate Newsalert 1, Everything Old is New Again: Impact of SB 189 on Mechanics' Lien Law.

22 NO. 6 Miller & Starr, California Real Estate Newsalert 21, Mechanics' Liens.

3 Witkin Cal. Proc. 5th Actions § 218, Preliminary Notice.

3 Witkin Cal. Proc. 5th Actions § 221A, (S 221A) (New)-In General.

3 Witkin Cal. Proc. 5th Actions § 221C, (S 221C) (New)-Private Property: Preliminary Notice.

3 Witkin Cal. Proc. 5th Actions § 221D, (S 221D) (New)-Private Property: Stop Notice.

3 Witkin Cal. Proc. 5th Actions § 221E, (S 221E) (New)-Public Property: Stop Notice.

3 Witkin Cal. Proc. 5th Actions § 222A, (S 222A) (New)-Revised Law for Action on Payment Bond for Work of Improvement.

4 Witkin, California Summary 10th Security Transactions in Real Property § 31A, (S 31A) (New)-Nature and Purpose of Revision.

4 Witkin, California Summary 10th Security Transactions in Real Property § 31E, (New)-Preliminary Notice.

§ 8202. Notice to property owner

(a) The preliminary notice shall comply with the requirements of Section 8102, and shall also include:

(1) A general description of the work to be provided.

(2) An estimate of the total price of the work provided and to be provided.

(3) The following statement in boldface type:

NOTICE TO PROPERTY OWNER

EVEN THOUGH YOU HAVE PAID YOUR CONTRACTOR IN FULL, if the person or firm that has given you this notice is not paid in full for labor, service, equipment, or material provided or to be provided to your construction project, a lien may be placed on your property. Foreclosure of the lien may lead to loss of all or part of your property. You may wish to protect yourself against this by (1) requiring your contractor to provide a signed release by the person or firm that has given you this notice before making payment to your contractor, or (2) any other method that is appropriate under the circumstances.

This notice is required by law to be served by the undersigned as a statement of your legal rights. This notice is not intended to reflect upon the financial condition of the contractor or the person employed by you on the construction project.

If you record a notice of cessation or completion of your construction project, you must within 10 days after recording, send a copy of the notice of completion to your contractor and the person or firm that has given you this notice. The notice must be sent by registered or certified mail. Failure to send the notice will extend the deadline to record a claim of lien. You are not required to send the notice if you are a residential homeowner of a dwelling containing four or fewer units.

(b) If preliminary notice is given by a subcontractor that has not paid all compensation due to a laborer, the notice shall include the name and address of the laborer and any person or entity described in subdivision (b) of Section 8024 to which payments are due.

(c) If an invoice for material or certified payroll contains the information required by this section and Section 8102, a copy of the invoice or payroll, given in compliance with the requirements of Chapter 2 (commencing with Section 8100) of Title 1, is sufficient. *(Added by Stats.2010, c. 697 (S.B.189), § 20, operative July 1, 2012.)*

Operative Effect

For operative effect of Part 6, see Civil Code § 8052 and Stats.2010, c. 697 (S.B.189), § 105.

Law Revision Commission Comments

Section 8202 continues the substance of former Section 3097(c)(1)-(6), the unnumbered paragraph following paragraph (6), and the requirement of former Section 3097(a) that the preliminary notice be written. See also Sections 8100–8118 (notice). The reference to an "express trust fund" is replaced by a reference to a generalized category of persons or entities included within the definition of "laborer." See Section 8024 ("laborer").

The continuation of the provision in subdivision (c) is not intended to make any change with respect to otherwise applicable privacy rights.

The information required in this notice is in addition to the information required by Section 8102 (contents of notice).

See also Sections 1170 (recordation), 8058 (calculation of time), 8060 (filing and recordation of papers), 8182 (notice of completion), 8186 (notice of completion of contract for portion of work of improvement), 8188 (notice of cessation).

See also Sections 8012 ("contractor"), 8022 ("labor, service, equipment, or material"), 8024 ("laborer"), 8026 ("lien"), 8032 ("person"), 8034 ("preliminary notice"), 8046 ("subcontractor"), 8048 ("work"). [40 Cal.L.Rev.Comm. Reports 49 [AR:apx5] (2010)].

Research References

California Real Estate Forms (Miller & Starr) § 4:13, Construction Agreement--Tenant Improvements.
Miller and Starr California Real Estate § 28:28, Statutory Provisions Governing Notice.
Miller and Starr California Real Estate § 28:29, Preliminary Notice--Purpose and Validity.

Miller and Starr California Real Estate § 28:35, Contents of the Preliminary Notice.
Miller and Starr California Real Estate § 28:71, Requirement of a Preliminary Notice.
3 Witkin Cal. Proc. 5th Actions § 221C, (S 221C) (New)-Private Property: Preliminary Notice.
4 Witkin, California Summary 10th Security Transactions in Real Property § 31E, (New)-Preliminary Notice.

§ 8204. Time for giving preliminary notice

(a) A preliminary notice shall be given not later than 20 days after the claimant has first furnished work on the work of improvement. If work has been provided by a claimant who did not give a preliminary notice, that claimant shall not be precluded from giving a preliminary notice at any time thereafter. The claimant shall, however, be entitled to record a lien, give a stop payment notice, and assert a claim against a payment bond only for work performed within 20 days prior to the service of the preliminary notice, and at any time thereafter.

(b) A design professional who has furnished services for the design of the work of improvement and who gives a preliminary notice not later than 20 days after the work of improvement has commenced shall be deemed to have complied with Section 8200 with respect to the design services furnished, or to be furnished. *(Added by Stats.2010, c. 697 (S.B.189), § 20, operative July 1, 2012.)*

Operative Effect

For operative effect of Part 6, see Civil Code § 8052 and Stats.2010, c. 697 (S.B.189), § 105.

Law Revision Commission Comments

Subdivision (a) of Section 8204 continues former Section 3097(d) without substantive change.

Subdivision (b) continues the unnumbered paragraph preceding former Section 3097(d) without substantive change, except to add a licensed landscape architect to the group of design professionals to which the provision is applicable.

See also Section 8058 (calculation of time).

See also Sections 8004 ("claimant"), 8014 ("design professional"), 8026 ("lien"), 8030 ("payment bond"), 8034 ("preliminary notice"), 8044 ("stop payment notice"), 8048 ("work"), 8050 ("work of improvement"). [40 Cal.L.Rev.Comm. Reports 49 [AR:apx5] (2010)].

Research References

Rutter, Cal. Practice Guide: Insurance Litigation Ch. 6I-B, B. Particular Surety Bond Coverages.
Miller and Starr California Real Estate § 28:36, Time and Method for Service of the Preliminary Notice.
21 NO. 4 Miller & Starr, California Real Estate Newsalert 1, Everything Old is New Again: Impact of SB 189 on Mechanics' Lien Law.
3 Witkin Cal. Proc. 5th Actions § 221C, (S 221C) (New)-Private Property: Preliminary Notice.
3 Witkin Cal. Proc. 5th Actions § 221D, (S 221D) (New)-Private Property: Stop Notice.
4 Witkin, California Summary 10th Security Transactions in Real Property § 31E, (New)-Preliminary Notice.

§ 8206. Single or multiple preliminary notice

(a) Except as provided in subdivision (b), a claimant need give only one preliminary notice to each person to which notice must be given under this chapter with respect to all work provided by the claimant for a work of improvement.

(b) If a claimant provides work pursuant to contracts with more than one subcontractor, the claimant shall give a separate preliminary notice with respect to work provided pursuant to each contract.

(c) A preliminary notice that contains a general description of work provided by the claimant through the date of the notice also covers work provided by the claimant after the date of the notice whether or not they are within the scope of the general description contained in the notice. *(Added by Stats.2010, c. 697 (S.B.189), § 20, operative July 1, 2012.)*

Operative Effect

For operative effect of Part 6, see Civil Code § 8052 and Stats.2010, c. 697 (S.B.189), § 105.

Law Revision Commission Comments

Section 8206 restates former Section 3097(g) without substantive change.

See also Sections 8004 ("claimant"), 8008 ("contract"), 8032 ("person"), 8034 ("preliminary notice"), 8046 ("subcontractor"), 8048 ("work"), 8050 ("work of improvement"). [40 Cal.L.Rev.Comm. Reports 49 [AR:apx5] (2010)].

Research References

Miller and Starr California Real Estate § 28:36, Time and Method for Service of the Preliminary Notice.
3 Witkin Cal. Proc. 5th Actions § 221C, (S 221C) (New)-Private Property: Preliminary Notice.
4 Witkin, California Summary 10th Security Transactions in Real Property § 31E, (New)-Preliminary Notice.

§ 8208. Information to be provided by direct contractor

A direct contractor shall make available to any person seeking to give preliminary notice the following information:

(a) The name and address of the owner.

(b) The name and address of the construction lender, if any. *(Added by Stats.2010, c. 697 (S.B.189), § 20, operative July 1, 2012.)*

Operative Effect

For operative effect of Part 6, see Civil Code § 8052 and Stats.2010, c. 697 (S.B.189), § 105.

Law Revision Commission Comments

Section 8208 restates the parts of former Section 3097(*l*) and (m) relating to a direct contractor's duty to provide information, deleting the limitation to the owner's residence address.

See also Sections 8006 ("construction lender"), 8018 ("direct contractor"), 8032 ("person"), 8034 ("preliminary notice"). [40 Cal.L.Rev. Comm. Reports 49 [AR:apx5] (2010)].

Research References

Miller and Starr California Real Estate § 28:31, Who Must Give, and Who Must Receive, The Preliminary Notice.
3 Witkin Cal. Proc. 5th Actions § 221C, (S 221C) (New)-Private Property: Preliminary Notice.

§ 8210. Additional construction loans; information to be provided to persons giving preliminary notice

If one or more construction loans are obtained after commencement of a work of improvement, the owner shall give notice of the name and address of the construction lender or lenders to each person that has given the owner preliminary notice. *(Added by Stats.2010, c. 697 (S.B.189), § 20, operative July 1, 2012.)*

Operative Effect

For operative effect of Part 6, see Civil Code § 8052 and Stats.2010, c. 697 (S.B.189), § 105.

Law Revision Commission Comments

Section 8210 continues former Section 3097(n) without substantive change. The reference to commencement of construction is changed to commencement of a work of improvement for consistency with the remainder of this part.

See also Sections 8006 ("construction lender"), 8032 ("person"), 8034 ("preliminary notice"), 8050 ("work of improvement"). [40 Cal.L.Rev. Comm. Reports 49 [AR:apx5] (2010)].

Research References

Miller and Starr California Real Estate § 28:31, Who Must Give, and Who Must Receive, The Preliminary Notice.

§ 8212. Waiver of rights void and unenforceable

An agreement made or entered into by an owner whereby the owner agrees to waive the rights conferred on the owner by this chapter is void and unenforceable. *(Added by Stats.2010, c. 697 (S.B.189), § 20, operative July 1, 2012.)*

Operative Effect

For operative effect of Part 6, see Civil Code § 8052 and Stats.2010, c. 697 (S.B.189), § 105.

Law Revision Commission Comments

Section 8212 continues former Section 3097(e) without substantive change. [40 Cal.L.Rev.Comm. Reports 49 [AR:apx5] (2010)].

Research References

Miller and Starr California Real Estate § 28:29, Preliminary Notice-- Purpose and Validity.
3 Witkin Cal. Proc. 5th Actions § 221C, (S 221C) (New)-Private Property: Preliminary Notice.

§ 8214. Filing of preliminary notice; mailing of notification; destruction of documents; purpose of filing pursuant to this section

(a) Each person who has served a preliminary notice may file the preliminary notice with the county recorder. A preliminary notice filed pursuant to this section shall comply with the requirements of Section 8102.

(b) Upon the acceptance for recording of a notice of completion or notice of cessation the county recorder shall mail to those persons who have filed a preliminary notice, notification that a notice of completion or notice of cessation has been recorded on the property, and shall affix the date that the notice of completion or notice of cessation was recorded with the county recorder. The notification given by the county recorder under this section is not governed by the requirements of Chapter 2 (commencing with Section 8100) of Title 1.

(c) The failure of the county recorder to mail the notification to the person who filed a preliminary notice, or the failure of those persons to receive the notification or to receive complete notification, shall not affect the period within which a claim of lien is required to be recorded. However, the county recorder shall make a good faith effort to mail notification to those persons who have filed the preliminary notice under this section and to do so within five days after the recording of a notice of completion or notice of cessation.

(d) The county recorder may cause to be destroyed all documents filed pursuant to this section, two years after the date of filing.

(e) The preliminary notice that a person may file pursuant to this section is for the limited purpose of facilitating the mailing of notice by the county recorder of recorded notices of completion and notices of cessation. The notice that is filed is not a recordable document and shall not be entered into those official records of the county which by law impart constructive notice. Notwithstanding any other provision of law, the index maintained by the recorder of filed preliminary notices shall be separate and distinct from those indexes maintained by the county recorder of those official records of the county which by law impart constructive notice. The filing of a preliminary notice with the county recorder does not give rise to any actual or constructive notice with respect to any party of the existence or contents of a filed preliminary notice nor to any duty of inquiry on the part of any party as to the existence or contents of that notice. *(Added by Stats.2010, c. 697 (S.B.189), § 20, operative July 1, 2012.)*

Operative Effect

For operative effect of Part 6, see Civil Code § 8052 and Stats.2010, c. 697 (S.B.189), § 105.

Law Revision Commission Comments

Section 8214 continues former Section 3097(*o*) without substantive change.

The former reference to the date after which the county recorder is authorized to act is deleted as a transitional provision that is now obsolete.

See also Sections 8060(a) (filing with county recorder), 8102 (contents of notice), 8182 (notice of completion), 8186 (notice of completion of contract for portion of work of improvement), 8188 (notice of cessation), 8412 (time for claim of lien by direct contractor), 8414 (time for claim of lien by claimant other than direct contractor).

See also Sections 8026 ("lien"), 8032 ("person"), 8034 ("preliminary notice"). [40 Cal.L.Rev.Comm. Reports 49 [AR:apx5] (2010)].

Research References

California Real Estate Forms (Miller & Starr) § 4:4, Construction Contract--Cost Plus a Fixed Fee With a Guaranteed Maximum Price.
California Real Estate Forms (Miller & Starr) § 4:5, Construction Agreement--Cost Plus a Percentage Fee With a Guaranteed Maximum Price.
California Real Estate Forms (Miller & Starr) § 4:6, Construction Contract--Fixed Price--Commercial Project.
California Real Estate Forms (Miller & Starr) § 4:8, Construction Contract--Turnkey Industrial Project (Cost-Plus)--Letter Form.
California Real Estate Forms (Miller & Starr) § 4:14, Construction Agreement-- Master Agreement for Construction Services.
California Real Estate Forms (Miller & Starr) § 4:16, Restaurant Development and Construction Agreement.
California Real Estate Forms (Miller & Starr) § 4:14.50, Construction Agreement--Cost Plus a Percentage Fee With a Control Estimate.
Miller and Starr California Real Estate § 11:6, Instruments Subject to Recording--List of Recordable Documents.
Miller and Starr California Real Estate § 28:36, Time and Method for Service of the Preliminary Notice.
Miller and Starr California Real Estate § 11:137, Phasing of a Project by Separate Direct Contracts With the Owner.

§ 8216. Subcontractors; failure to give notice as grounds for disciplinary action

If the contract of any subcontractor on a particular work of improvement provides for payment to the subcontractor of more than four hundred dollars ($400), the failure of that subcontractor, licensed under the Contractors' State License Law (Chapter 9 (commencing with Section 7000) of Division 3 of the Business and Professions Code), to give the notice provided for in this chapter, constitutes grounds for disciplinary action under the Contractors' State License Law. *(Added by Stats.2010, c. 697 (S.B.189), § 20, operative July 1, 2012.)*

Operative Effect

For operative effect of Part 6, see Civil Code § 8052 and Stats.2010, c. 697 (S.B.189), § 105.

Law Revision Commission Comments

Section 8216 continues the first paragraph of former Section 3097(h) without substantive change.

See also Sections 8008 ("contract"), 8046 ("subcontractor"), 8050 ("work of improvement"). [40 Cal.L.Rev.Comm. Reports 49 [AR:apx5] (2010)].

Research References

Miller and Starr California Real Estate § 28:15, Entities Entitled to a Portion of Employee Compensation.
Miller and Starr California Real Estate § 28:30, Result of a Failure to Draft and Serve the Notice Properly.
Miller and Starr California Real Estate § 28:35, Contents of the Preliminary Notice.
21 NO. 4 Miller & Starr, California Real Estate Newsalert 1, Everything Old is New Again: Impact of SB 189 on Mechanics' Lien Law.
3 Witkin Cal. Proc. 5th Actions § 221A, (S 221A) (New)-In General.
3 Witkin Cal. Proc. 5th Actions § 221C, (S 221C) (New)-Private Property: Preliminary Notice.
4 Witkin, California Summary 10th Security Transactions in Real Property § 31A, (S 31A) (New)-Nature and Purpose of Revision.

CHAPTER 3.   DESIGN PROFESSIONALS LIEN

Operative Effect

For operative effect of Part 6, see Civil Code § 8052 and Stats.2010, c. 697 (S.B.189), § 105.

§ 8300.   "Design professional" defined

For purposes of this chapter, a "design professional" is a person described in Section 8014 who provides services pursuant to a written contract with a landowner for the design, engineering, or planning of a work of improvement. *(Added by Stats.2010, c. 697 (S.B.189), § 20, operative July 1, 2012.)*

Operative Effect

For operative effect of Part 6, see Civil Code § 8052 and Stats.2010, c. 697 (S.B.189), § 105.

Law Revision Commission Comments

Section 8300 restates former Section 3081.1, adding a licensed landscape architect to the design professionals who may claim a lien under this chapter. See Section 8014 ("design professional").

The introductory clause and the second paragraph of former Section 3081.1 are not continued because they are surplus. See Section 8000 (application of definitions).

See also Sections 8032 ("person"), 8050 ("work of improvement"). [40 Cal.L.Rev.Comm. Reports 49 [AR:apx5] (2010)].

Research References

Miller and Starr California Real Estate § 28:16, Design Professionals Liens; Rights to Mechanics Liens.
Miller and Starr California Real Estate § 11:131, Date Liens Attach; Relation to Subsequent Interests.
Miller and Starr California Real Estate § 11:135, When Construction Commences--Effect on Priority of Mechanics' and Design Professionals' Liens.
21 NO. 4 Miller & Starr, California Real Estate Newsalert 1, Everything Old is New Again: Impact of SB 189 on Mechanics' Lien Law.

3 Witkin Cal. Proc. 5th Actions § 221A, (S 221A) (New)-In General.
1 Witkin Cal. Summ. 10th Contracts § 911, (S 911) Works of Improvement Contracts.
4 Witkin, California Summary 10th Security Transactions in Real Property § 32, Design Professional's Lien.
4 Witkin, California Summary 10th Security Transactions in Real Property § 31A, (S 31A) (New)-Nature and Purpose of Revision.

§ 8302. Circumstances giving rise to lien; amount

(a) A design professional has, from the date of recordation of a claim of lien under this chapter, a lien on the site notwithstanding the absence of commencement of the planned work of improvement, if the landowner who contracted for the design professional's services is also the owner of the site at the time of recordation of the claim of lien.

(b) The lien of the design professional is for the amount of the design professional's fee for services provided under the contract or the reasonable value of those services, whichever is less. The amount of the lien is reduced by the amount of any deposit or prior payment under the contract.

(c) A design professional may not record a claim of lien, and a lien may not be created, under this chapter unless a building permit or other governmental approval in furtherance of the work of improvement has been obtained in connection with or utilizing the services provided by the design professional. (Added by Stats.2010, c. 697 (S.B.189), § 20, operative July 1, 2012.)

Operative Effect

For operative effect of Part 6, see Civil Code § 8052 and Stats.2010, c. 697 (S.B.189), § 105.

Law Revision Commission Comments

Section 8302 restates former Section 3081.2. The amount of the lien is limited to the fee for services provided under the contract rather than the fee for services provided before commencement of the work of improvement, since the lien provided by this section is only available prior to commencement of the work of improvement. See also Section 8306 (lien terminates on commencement of work).

See also Sections 1170 (recordation), 8060 (filing and recordation of papers), 8300 (design professional lien claimant).

See also Sections 8014 ("design professional"), 8026 ("lien"), 8040 ("site"), 8050 ("work of improvement"). [40 Cal.L.Rev.Comm. Reports 49 [AR:apx5] (2010)].

Research References

Miller and Starr California Real Estate § 28:16, Design Professionals Liens; Rights to Mechanics Liens.
4 Witkin, California Summary 10th Security Transactions in Real Property § 32, Design Professional's Lien.

§ 8304. Entitlement to lien; conditions

A design professional is not entitled to a lien under this chapter unless all of the following conditions are satisfied:

(a) The work of improvement for which the design professional provided services has not commenced.

(b) The landowner defaults in a payment required under the contract or refuses to pay the demand of the design professional made under the contract.

(c) Not less than 10 days before recording a claim of lien, the design professional gives the landowner notice making a demand for payment, and stating that a default has occurred under the contract and the amount of the default.

(d) The design professional records a claim of lien. The claim of lien shall include all of the following information:

(1) The name of the design professional.

(2) The amount of the claim.

(3) The current owner of record of the site.

(4) A legal description of the site.

(5) Identification of the building permit or other governmental approval for the work of improvement. (Added by Stats.2010, c. 697 (S.B.189), § 20, operative July 1, 2012.)

Operative Effect

For operative effect of Part 6, see Civil Code § 8052 and Stats.2010, c. 697 (S.B.189), § 105.

Law Revision Commission Comments

Section 8304 restates former Section 3081.3, with the clarification that a lien under this chapter is unavailable if construction has commenced. See subdivision (a).

A building permit or other governmental approval for the work of improvement obtained in connection with or utilizing the services provided by the design professional is required as a condition of recordation of a lien claim under Section 8302 (lien).

See also Sections 1170 (recordation), 8058 (calculation of time), 8060 (filing and recordation of papers), 8300 (design professional lien claimant).

See also Sections 8014 ("design professional"), 8026 ("lien"), 8040 ("site"), 8050 ("work of improvement"). [40 Cal.L.Rev.Comm. Reports 49 [AR:apx5] (2010)].

Research References

Miller and Starr California Real Estate § 28:16, Design Professionals Liens; Rights to Mechanics Liens.
4 Witkin, California Summary 10th Security Transactions in Real Property § 32, Design Professional's Lien.

§ 8306. Creation of lien; expiration; satisfaction

(a) On recordation of the claim of lien, a lien is created in favor of the named design professional.

(b) The lien automatically expires and is null and void and of no further force or effect on the occurrence of either of the following events:

(1) The commencement of the work of improvement for which the design professional provided services.

(2) The expiration of 90 days after recording the claim of lien, unless the design professional commences an action to enforce the lien within that time.

(c) If the landowner partially or fully satisfies the lien, the design professional shall execute and record a document that evidences a partial or full satisfaction and release of the lien, as applicable. (Added by Stats.2010, c. 697 (S.B.189), § 20, operative July 1, 2012.)

Operative Effect

For operative effect of Part 6, see Civil Code § 8052 and Stats.2010, c. 697 (S.B.189), § 105.

Law Revision Commission Comments

Section 8306 restates former Section 3081.4. On expiration of the lien as a result of commencement of the work of improvement, the design professional may obtain a lien under Section 8400 (mechanics lien). See Section 8310 (mechanics lien right not affected).

See also Sections 1170 (recordation), 8058 (calculation of time), 8060 (filing and recordation of papers), 8300 (design professional lien claimant).

See also Sections 8014 ("design professional"), 8026 ("lien"), 8050 ("work of improvement"). [40 Cal.L.Rev.Comm. Reports 49 [AR:apx5] (2010)].

Research References

Miller and Starr California Real Estate § 11:6, Instruments Subject to Recording--List of Recordable Documents.
Miller and Starr California Real Estate § 28:16, Design Professionals Liens; Rights to Mechanics Liens.

4 Witkin, California Summary 10th Security Transactions in Real Property § 32, Design Professional's Lien.

§ 8308. Application of part

(a) Except as provided in subdivision (b), no provision of this part applies to a lien created under this chapter.

(b) The following provisions of this part apply to a lien created under this chapter:

(1) This chapter.

(2) Article 1 (commencing with Section 8000) of Chapter 1 of Title 1.

(3) Section 8424.

(4) Article 6 (commencing with Section 8460) of Chapter 4.

(5) Article 7 (commencing with Section 8480) of Chapter 4.

(6) Article 8 (commencing with Section 8490) of Chapter 4. *(Added by Stats.2010, c. 697 (S.B.189), § 20, operative July 1, 2012.)*

Operative Effect

For operative effect of Part 6, see Civil Code § 8052 and Stats.2010, c. 697 (S.B.189), § 105.

Law Revision Commission Comments

Section 8308 continues the substance of former Section 3081.5, and provides for the application of the definitional provisions of this part.

See also Section 8026 ("lien"). [40 Cal.L.Rev.Comm. Reports 49 [AR:apx5] (2010)].

Research References

Miller and Starr California Real Estate § 28:16, Design Professionals Liens; Rights to Mechanics Liens.
4 Witkin, California Summary 10th Security Transactions in Real Property § 32, Design Professional's Lien.

§ 8310. Availability of mechanics lien

This chapter does not affect the ability of a design professional to obtain a lien for a work of improvement under Section 8400. *(Added by Stats.2010, c. 697 (S.B.189), § 20, operative July 1, 2012.)*

Operative Effect

For operative effect of Part 6, see Civil Code § 8052 and Stats.2010, c. 697 (S.B.189), § 105.

Law Revision Commission Comments

Section 8310 restates former Section 3081.6.
See Section 8300 (design professional lien claimant).
See also Sections 8014 ("design professional"), 8026 ("lien"), 8050 ("work of improvement"). [40 Cal.L.Rev.Comm. Reports 49 [AR:apx5] (2010)].

Research References

Miller and Starr California Real Estate § 28:16, Design Professionals Liens; Rights to Mechanics Liens.
4 Witkin, California Summary 10th Security Transactions in Real Property § 32, Design Professional's Lien.

§ 8312. Time for recording claim of lien

A design professional shall record a claim of lien under this chapter no later than 90 days after the design professional knows or has reason to know that the work of improvement will not be commenced. *(Added by Stats.2010, c. 697 (S.B.189), § 20, operative July 1, 2012.)*

Operative Effect

For operative effect of Part 6, see Civil Code § 8052 and Stats.2010, c. 697 (S.B.189), § 105.

Law Revision Commission Comments

Section 8312 restates former Section 3081.7.
See also Sections 1170 (recordation), 8058 (calculation of time), 8060 (filing and recordation of papers), 8300 (design professional lien claimant).
See also Sections 8014 ("design professional"), 8026 ("lien"), 8050 ("work of improvement"). [40 Cal.L.Rev.Comm. Reports 49 [AR:apx5] (2010)].

Research References

Miller and Starr California Real Estate § 28:16, Design Professionals Liens; Rights to Mechanics Liens.
4 Witkin, California Summary 10th Security Transactions in Real Property § 32, Design Professional's Lien.

§ 8314. Additional remedies

The creation of a lien under this chapter does not affect the ability of the design professional to pursue other remedies. *(Added by Stats.2010, c. 697 (S.B.189), § 20, operative July 1, 2012.)*

Operative Effect

For operative effect of Part 6, see Civil Code § 8052 and Stats.2010, c. 697 (S.B.189), § 105.

Law Revision Commission Comments

Section 8314 restates former Section 3081.8.
See also Section 8300 (design professional lien claimant).
See also Sections 8014 ("design professional"), 8026 ("lien"). [40 Cal.L.Rev.Comm. Reports 49 [AR:apx5] (2010)].

Research References

Miller and Starr California Real Estate § 28:16, Design Professionals Liens; Rights to Mechanics Liens.
4 Witkin, California Summary 10th Security Transactions in Real Property § 32, Design Professional's Lien.

§ 8316. Priority of lien

(a) No lien created under this chapter affects or takes priority over the interest of record of a purchaser, lessee, or encumbrancer, if the interest of the purchaser, lessee, or encumbrancer in the real property was duly recorded before recordation of the claim of lien.

(b) No lien created under this chapter affects or takes priority over an encumbrance of a construction lender that funds the loan for the work of improvement for which the design professional provided services. *(Added by Stats.2010, c. 697 (S.B.189), § 20, operative July 1, 2012.)*

Operative Effect

For operative effect of Part 6, see Civil Code § 8052 and Stats.2010, c. 697 (S.B.189), § 105.

Law Revision Commission Comments

Section 8316 restates former Section 3081.9.
See also Sections 1170 (recordation), 8058 (calculation of time), 8060 (filing and recordation of papers), 8300 (design professional lien claimant).
See also Sections 8006 ("construction lender"), 8014 ("design professional"), 8026 ("lien"), 8050 ("work of improvement"). [40 Cal.L.Rev.Comm. Reports 49 [AR:apx5] (2010)].

Research References

Miller and Starr California Real Estate § 28:6, Priority of the Lien.

Miller and Starr California Real Estate § 28:16, Design Professionals Liens; Rights to Mechanics Liens.

4 Witkin, California Summary 10th Security Transactions in Real Property § 71, Real Mortgage and Design Professional's Lien.

§ 8318. Exemptions

A design professional may not obtain a lien under this chapter for services provided for a work of improvement relating to a single-family, owner-occupied residence for which the expected construction cost is less than one hundred thousand dollars ($100,000). *(Added by Stats.2010, c. 697 (S.B.189), § 20, operative July 1, 2012.)*

Operative Effect

For operative effect of Part 6, see Civil Code § 8052 and Stats.2010, c. 697 (S.B.189), § 105.

Law Revision Commission Comments

Section 8318 restates former Section 3081.10. The exemption is based on expected construction cost, since the lien is only available if the work of improvement is not constructed. See Section 8306 (creation, expiration, and release of lien).

See also Section 8300 (design professional lien claimant).

See also Sections 8014 ("design professional"), 8026 ("lien"), 8050 ("work of improvement"). [40 Cal.L.Rev.Comm. Reports 49 [AR:apx5] (2010)].

Research References

Miller and Starr California Real Estate § 28:16, Design Professionals Liens; Rights to Mechanics Liens.

Miller and Starr California Real Estate § 11:131, Date Liens Attach; Relation to Subsequent Interests.

Miller and Starr California Real Estate § 11:135, When Construction Commences--Effect on Priority of Mechanics' and Design Professionals' Liens.

21 NO. 4 Miller & Starr, California Real Estate Newsalert 1, Everything Old is New Again: Impact of SB 189 on Mechanics' Lien Law.

3 Witkin Cal. Proc. 5th Actions § 221A, (S 221A) (New)-In General.

4 Witkin, California Summary 10th Security Transactions in Real Property § 32, Design Professional's Lien.

4 Witkin, California Summary 10th Security Transactions in Real Property § 31A, (S 31A) (New)-Nature and Purpose of Revision.

§ 8319. Conversion of design professional lien to mechanics lien

(a) A design professional may convert a recorded design professional lien to a mechanics lien if all of the following requirements are met:

(1) The design professional lien expires pursuant to paragraph (1) of subdivision (b) of Section 8306.

(2) The design professional lien remains fully or partially unpaid.

(3) Within 30 days of the expiration of the design professional lien pursuant to paragraph (1) of subdivision (b) of Section 8306, the design professional records a mechanics lien for the amount of the unpaid design professional lien.

(4) The recorded mechanics lien states that it is a converted design professional lien but shall be recorded and enforced as a mechanics lien, except the design professional need not provide a preliminary notice to enforce this mechanics lien. This mechanics lien shall be effective as of the date of recordation of this mechanics lien and shall be given priority pursuant to the provisions of Section 8450.

(b) This section shall not apply if a design professional lien expires pursuant to paragraph (2) of subdivision (b) of Section 8306. *(Added by Stats.2011, c. 127 (S.B.424), § 1, operative July 1, 2012.)*

Operative Effect

For operative effect of Stats.2011, c. 127 (S.B.424), see § 2 of that Act.

Research References

Miller and Starr California Real Estate § 28:16, Design Professionals Liens; Rights to Mechanics Liens.

22 NO. 4 Miller & Starr, California Real Estate Newsalert 17, Mechanics' Liens.

4 Witkin, California Summary 10th Security Transactions in Real Property § 32, Design Professional's Lien.

CHAPTER 4. MECHANICS LIEN

Operative Effect

For operative effect of Part 6, see Civil Code § 8052 and Stats.2010, c. 697 (S.B.189), § 105.

ARTICLE 1. WHO IS ENTITLED TO LIEN

Operative Effect

For operative effect of Part 6, see Civil Code § 8052 and Stats.2010, c. 697 (S.B.189), § 105.

§ 8400. Persons providing work authorized for work of improvement

A person that provides work authorized for a work of improvement, including, but not limited to, the following persons, has a lien right under this chapter:

(a) Direct contractor.

(b) Subcontractor.

(c) Material supplier.

(d) Equipment lessor.

(e) Laborer.

(f) Design professional. *(Added by Stats.2010, c. 697 (S.B. 189), § 20, operative July 1, 2012.)*

Operative Effect

For operative effect of Part 6, see Civil Code § 8052 and Stats.2010, c. 697 (S.B.189), § 105.

Law Revision Commission Comments

Section 8400 restates the part of former Section 3110 providing a lien for contributions to a work of improvement. It implements the directive of Article XIV, Section 3, of the California Constitution that, "Mechanics, persons furnishing materials, artisans, and laborers of every class, shall have a lien upon the property upon which they have bestowed labor or furnished material for the value of such labor done and material furnished; and the Legislature shall provide, by law, for the speedy and efficient enforcement of such liens."

The reference in the introductory portion of Section 8400 to work "authorized" replaces the references in former Section 3110 to the "instance or request of the owner or any other person acting by his authority or under him, as contractor or otherwise." See Section 8404 (who may authorize work).

The type of contribution to the work of improvement that qualifies for a lien right is described in the introductory portion of Section 8400 as provision of "work." Elimination of the former references to "bestowing skill or other necessary services" or "furnishing appliances, teams, or power" or "work done or materials furnished" is not a substantive change. See Section 8048 ("work").

The listing of classes of persons with lien rights in subdivisions (a)-(f) restates without substantive change the comparable part of former Section 3110. This provision does not continue the former listing of types of contractors, subcontractors, laborers, and design professionals, such as mechanics, artisans, machinists, builders, teamsters, draymen, architects, registered engineers, and licensed land surveyors. This is not a substantive change; these classes are included in the defined terms used in this section.

A person or entity described in Section 8024(b) has the same lien right as the laborer in subdivision (e), to the extent of the laborer's compensation agreed to be paid to the person or entity for labor on the improvement. See Section 8024 ("laborer").

See also Sections 8014 ("design professional"), 8018 ("direct contractor"), 8026 ("lien"), 8028 ("material supplier"), 8032 ("person"), 8046 ("subcontractor"), 8050 ("work of improvement"). [40 Cal.L.Rev.Comm. Reports 49 [AR:apx5] (2010)].

Research References

Rutter, Cal. Practice Guide: Insurance Litigation Ch. 6I-B, B. Particular Surety Bond Coverages.
Miller and Starr California Real Estate § 28:3, Source and Purpose of the Mechanics Lien.
Miller and Starr California Real Estate § 28:4, Requirement of a Contract.
Miller and Starr California Real Estate § 28:8, "Claimant" Defined.
Miller and Starr California Real Estate § 28:12, Supplier of Labor or Equipment.
Miller and Starr California Real Estate § 28:13, Laborers Defined.
Miller and Starr California Real Estate § 28:15, Entities Entitled to a Portion of Employee Compensation.
Miller and Starr California Real Estate § 28:16, Design Professionals Liens; Rights to Mechanics Liens.
Miller and Starr California Real Estate § 28:17, "Work of Improvement".
Miller and Starr California Real Estate § 28:70, Who May File a Stop Payment Notice.
Miller and Starr California Real Estate § 28:72, Contents of the Stop Payment Notice.
Miller and Starr California Real Estate § 11:130, in General; Off-Record Priority.
Miller and Starr California Real Estate § 11:136, When Construction Commences--Phasing of the Project; in General.
21 NO. 4 Miller & Starr, California Real Estate Newsalert 1, Everything Old is New Again: Impact of SB 189 on Mechanics' Lien Law.
3 Witkin Cal. Proc. 5th Actions § 221A, (S 221A) (New)-In General.
2 Witkin Cal. Proc. 5th Courts § 246, (S 246) Particular Equitable Actions.
2 Witkin Cal. Proc. 5th Jurisdiction § 359, Subcontractor's Contract.
6 Witkin Cal. Proc. 5th Proceedings Without Trial § 547, No Waiver by Mere Filing or Limited Participation.
1 Witkin Cal. Summ. 10th Contracts § 911, (S 911) Works of Improvement Contracts.
4 Witkin, California Summary 10th Security Transactions in Real Property § 32, Design Professional's Lien.
4 Witkin, California Summary 10th Security Transactions in Real Property § 31A, (S 31A) (New)-Nature and Purpose of Revision.
4 Witkin, California Summary 10th Security Transactions in Real Property § 31C, (New)-Right to Lien and Property Affected.
3 Witkin, California Summary 10th Agency and Employment § 5, (S 5) Labor and Laborer.
3 Witkin, California Summary 10th Agency and Employment § 410, (S 410) State Law Preempted.

3 Witkin, California Summary 10th Agency and Employment § 411, (S 411) State Law Not Preempted.

§ 8402. Persons providing work authorized for site improvement

A person that provides work authorized for a site improvement has a lien right under this chapter. *(Added by Stats.2010, c. 697 (S.B.189), § 20, operative July 1, 2012.)*

Operative Effect

For operative effect of Part 6, see Civil Code § 8052 and Stats.2010, c. 697 (S.B.189), § 105.

Law Revision Commission Comments

Section 8402 restates former Section 3112. The reference to work done or material furnished is superseded by the reference to work. See Section 8048 (work). The reference to work at the instance or request of the owner or any person acting by or under authority of the owner as contractor or otherwise is replaced by the reference to work authorized. See Section 8404 (who may authorize work).

A site improvement is treated in the same manner as a work of improvement, except as provided in Sections 8448 (claim against separate residential units), 8450 (priority of lien), 8454 (separate contract for site improvement), 8458 (priority of site improvement lien). See Section 8050 (work of improvement).

See also Sections 8026 (lien), 8032 (person), 8042 (site improvement). [40 Cal.L.Rev.Comm. Reports 49 [AR:apx5] (2010)].

Research References

Rutter, Cal. Practice Guide: Insurance Litigation Ch. 6I-B, B. Particular Surety Bond Coverages.
Miller and Starr California Real Estate § 28:17, "Work of Improvement".
Miller and Starr California Real Estate § 28:22, Time for Posting and Recording Notice.
4 Witkin, California Summary 10th Security Transactions in Real Property § 31C, (New)-Right to Lien and Property Affected.

§ 8404. Work authorized for work of improvement or site improvement

Work is authorized for a work of improvement or for a site improvement in any of the following circumstances:

(a) It is provided at the request of or agreed to by the owner.

(b) It is provided or authorized by a direct contractor, subcontractor, architect, project manager, or other person having charge of all or part of the work of improvement or site improvement. *(Added by Stats.2010, c. 697 (S.B.189), § 20, operative July 1, 2012.)*

Operative Effect

For operative effect of Part 6, see Civil Code § 8052 and Stats.2010, c. 697 (S.B.189), § 105.

Law Revision Commission Comments

Section 8404 restates parts of former Sections 3110 and 3112.

The reference in subdivision (a) to work provided at the request of an owner includes work provided at the instance of the owner, or of a person acting by or under the owner's authority. See Section 8066 (agency).

The inclusion in subdivision (b) of project managers is new.

The references in former law to sub-subcontractors and builders are omitted as surplus. A contractor either has a contract with the owner (and is a direct contractor) or does not (and is a subcontractor). This part does not distinguish among levels of subcontractor. The term builder was not defined in former law and was used only in former Section 3110.

A work of improvement includes a site improvement. See Section 8050 ("work of improvement").

See also Sections 8018 ("direct contractor"), 8032 ("person"), 8042 ("site improvement"), 8046 ("subcontractor"), 8048 ("work"). [40 Cal. L.Rev.Comm. Reports 49 [AR:apx5] (2010)].

Research References

Rutter, Cal. Practice Guide: Insurance Litigation Ch. 6I-B, B. Particular Surety Bond Coverages.
Miller and Starr California Real Estate § 28:3, Source and Purpose of the Mechanics Lien.
Miller and Starr California Real Estate § 28:4, Requirement of a Contract.
Miller and Starr California Real Estate § 28:11, Material Suppliers Defined; Distinction Between Material Supplier and Subcontractor.
Miller and Starr California Real Estate § 28:12, Supplier of Labor or Equipment.
Miller and Starr California Real Estate § 11:130, in General; Off-Record Priority.
Miller and Starr California Real Estate § 11:136, When Construction Commences--Phasing of the Project; in General.
21 NO. 4 Miller & Starr, California Real Estate Newsalert 1, Everything Old is New Again: Impact of SB 189 on Mechanics' Lien Law.
2 Witkin Cal. Proc. 5th Jurisdiction § 359, Subcontractor's Contract.
4 Witkin, California Summary 10th Security Transactions in Real Property § 31C, (New)-Right to Lien and Property Affected.

ARTICLE 2.   CONDITIONS TO ENFORCING A LIEN

Section
8410.   Preliminary notice; proof of notice.
8412.   Direct contractors; time for recording claim.
8414.   Persons other than direct contractors; time for recording claim.
8416.   Written statement; contents; form; recording; service.
8422.   Erroneous information.
8424.   Lien release bond.

Operative Effect

For operative effect of Part 6, see Civil Code § 8052 and Stats.2010, c. 697 (S.B.189), § 105.

§ 8410.   Preliminary notice; proof of notice

A claimant may enforce a lien only if the claimant has given preliminary notice to the extent required by Chapter 2 (commencing with Section 8200) and made proof of notice. *(Added by Stats.2010, c. 697 (S.B.189), § 20, operative July 1, 2012.)*

Operative Effect

For operative effect of Part 6, see Civil Code § 8052 and Stats.2010, c. 697 (S.B.189), § 105.

Law Revision Commission Comments

Section 8410 restates former Section 3114 without substantive change. A claimant must give preliminary notice to the extent provided in the preliminary notice provisions of this part. See Section 8200 *et seq*.

See also Section 8118 (proof of notice).

See also Sections 8004 ("claimant"), 8026 ("lien"), 8034 ("preliminary notice"). [40 Cal.L.Rev.Comm. Reports 49 [AR:apx5] (2010)].

Research References

Miller and Starr California Real Estate § 28:30, Result of a Failure to Draft and Serve the Notice Properly.
Miller and Starr California Real Estate § 11:140, Effect of Cessation of Work on Mechanic's Lien Priorities.
3 Witkin Cal. Proc. 5th Actions § 221C, (S 221C) (New)-Private Property: Preliminary Notice.
4 Witkin, California Summary 10th Security Transactions in Real Property § 21, (S 21) No Subcontractor's Lien on Loan Fund.

4 Witkin, California Summary 10th Security Transactions in Real Property § 31F, (S 31F) (New)-Requirements of Claim.

§ 8412.   Direct contractors; time for recording claim

A direct contractor may not enforce a lien unless the contractor records a claim of lien after the contractor completes the direct contract, and before the earlier of the following times:

(a) Ninety days after completion of the work of improvement.

(b) Sixty days after the owner records a notice of completion or cessation. *(Added by Stats.2010, c. 697 (S.B.189), § 20, operative July 1, 2012.)*

Operative Effect

For operative effect of Part 6, see Civil Code § 8052 and Stats.2010, c. 697 (S.B.189), § 105.

Law Revision Commission Comments

Section 8412 restates former Section 3115 without substantive change. A contract is complete within the meaning of this section when the contractor's obligations under it are substantially performed, excused, or otherwise discharged. See Howard S. Wright Construction Co. v. BBIC Investors, LLC, 136 Cal.App.4th 228, 38 Cal.Rptr.3d 769 (2006).

For completion of a work of improvement, see Section 8180. For recordation of a notice of completion, see Sections 8182 (notice of completion), 8186 (notice of completion of contract for portion of work of improvement). For recordation of a notice of cessation, see Section 8188 (notice of cessation).

See also Sections 1170 (recordation), 8058 (calculation of time), 8060 (filing and recordation of papers).

See also Sections 8016 ("direct contract"), 8018 ("direct contractor"), 8026 ("lien"), 8050 ("work of improvement"). [40 Cal.L.Rev.Comm. Reports 49 [AR:apx5] (2010)].

Research References

Rutter, Cal. Practice Guide: Insurance Litigation Ch. 6I-B, B. Particular Surety Bond Coverages.
Miller and Starr California Real Estate § 28:9, Contractors.
Miller and Starr California Real Estate § 28:37, Claim of Lien--Necessity, Purpose, and Effect.
Miller and Starr California Real Estate § 28:38, Time to File.
Miller and Starr California Real Estate § 28:39, When Notice of Completion Recorded.
Miller and Starr California Real Estate § 28:40, When Notice of Cessation Recorded.
Miller and Starr California Real Estate § 28:41, When No Notice of Completion or Cessation Recorded.
Miller and Starr California Real Estate § 28:42, When There Are Two or More Contracts With the Owner.
Miller and Starr California Real Estate § 28:44, Public Improvements Under Private Contract.
Miller and Starr California Real Estate § 11:140, Effect of Cessation of Work on Mechanic's Lien Priorities.
3 Witkin Cal. Proc. 5th Actions § 221C, (S 221C) (New)-Private Property: Preliminary Notice.
3 Witkin Cal. Proc. 5th Actions § 221D, (S 221D) (New)-Private Property: Stop Notice.
4 Witkin, California Summary 10th Security Transactions in Real Property § 31F, (S 31F) (New)-Requirements of Claim.

§ 8414.   Persons other than direct contractors; time for recording claim

A claimant other than a direct contractor may not enforce a lien unless the claimant records a claim of lien within the following times:

(a) After the claimant ceases to provide work.

(b) Before the earlier of the following times:

(1) Ninety days after completion of the work of improvement.

(2) Thirty days after the owner records a notice of completion or cessation. *(Added by Stats.2010, c. 697 (S.B.189), § 20, operative July 1, 2012.)*

Operative Effect

For operative effect of Part 6, see Civil Code § 8052 and Stats.2010, c. 697 (S.B.189), § 105.

Law Revision Commission Comments

Section 8414 restates former Section 3116 without substantive change.

For completion of a work of improvement, see Section 8180. For recordation of a notice of completion, see Sections 8182 (notice of completion), 8186 (notice of completion of contract for portion of work of improvement). For recordation of a notice of cessation, see Section 8188 (notice of cessation).

See also Sections 1170 (recordation), 8058 (calculation of time), 8060 (filing and recordation of papers).

See also Sections 8004 ("claimant"), 8018 ("direct contractor"), 8026 ("lien"), 8048 ("work"), 8050 ("work of improvement"). [40 Cal.L.Rev. Comm. Reports 49 [AR:apx5] (2010)].

Research References

California Real Estate Forms (Miller & Starr) § 4:4, Construction Contract--Cost Plus a Fixed Fee With a Guaranteed Maximum Price.

California Real Estate Forms (Miller & Starr) § 4:5, Construction Agreement--Cost Plus a Percentage Fee With a Guaranteed Maximum Price.

California Real Estate Forms (Miller & Starr) § 4:6, Construction Contract--Fixed Price--Commercial Project.

California Real Estate Forms (Miller & Starr) § 4:8, Construction Contract--Turnkey Industrial Project (Cost-Plus)--Letter Form.

California Real Estate Forms (Miller & Starr) § 4:14, Construction Agreement-- Master Agreement for Construction Services.

California Real Estate Forms (Miller & Starr) § 4:16, Restaurant Development and Construction Agreement.

California Real Estate Forms (Miller & Starr) § 4:14.50, Construction Agreement--Cost Plus a Percentage Fee With a Control Estimate.

Rutter, Cal. Practice Guide: Insurance Litigation Ch. 6I-B, B. Particular Surety Bond Coverages.

Miller and Starr California Real Estate § 28:37, Claim of Lien--Necessity, Purpose, and Effect.

Miller and Starr California Real Estate § 28:38, Time to File.

Miller and Starr California Real Estate § 28:39, When Notice of Completion Recorded.

Miller and Starr California Real Estate § 28:40, When Notice of Cessation Recorded.

Miller and Starr California Real Estate § 28:41, When No Notice of Completion or Cessation Recorded.

Miller and Starr California Real Estate § 28:42, When There Are Two or More Contracts With the Owner.

Miller and Starr California Real Estate § 28:44, Public Improvements Under Private Contract.

Miller and Starr California Real Estate § 11:140, Effect of Cessation of Work on Mechanic's Lien Priorities.

4 Witkin, California Summary 10th Security Transactions in Real Property § 31F, (S 31F) (New)-Requirements of Claim.

§ 8416. Written statement; contents; form; recording; service

(a) A claim of mechanics lien shall be a written statement, signed and verified by the claimant, containing all of the following:

(1) A statement of the claimant's demand after deducting all just credits and offsets.

(2) The name of the owner or reputed owner, if known.

(3) A general statement of the kind of work furnished by the claimant.

(4) The name of the person by whom the claimant was employed or to whom the claimant furnished work.

(5) A description of the site sufficient for identification.

(6) The claimant's address.

(7) A proof of service affidavit completed and signed by the person serving a copy of the claim of mechanics lien pursuant to subdivision (c). The affidavit shall show the date, place, and manner of service, and facts showing that the service was made in accordance with this section. The affidavit shall show the name and address of the owner or reputed owner upon whom the copy of the claim of mechanics lien was served pursuant to paragraphs (1) or (2) of subdivision (c), and the title or capacity in which the person or entity was served.

(8) The following statement, printed in at least 10–point boldface type. The letters of the last sentence shall be printed in uppercase type, excepting the Internet Web site address of the Contractors' State License Board, which shall be printed in lowercase type:

"NOTICE OF MECHANICS LIEN
ATTENTION!

Upon the recording of the enclosed MECHANICS LIEN with the county recorder's office of the county where the property is located, your property is subject to the filing of a legal action seeking a court-ordered foreclosure sale of the real property on which the lien has been recorded. That legal action must be filed with the court no later than 90 days after the date the mechanics lien is recorded.

The party identified in the enclosed mechanics lien may have provided labor or materials for improvements to your property and may not have been paid for these items. You are receiving this notice because it is a required step in filing a mechanics lien foreclosure action against your property. The foreclosure action will seek a sale of your property in order to pay for unpaid labor, materials, or improvements provided to your property. This may affect your ability to borrow against, refinance, or sell the property until the mechanics lien is released.

BECAUSE THE LIEN AFFECTS YOUR PROPERTY, YOU MAY WISH TO SPEAK WITH YOUR CONTRACTOR IMMEDIATELY, OR CONTACT AN ATTORNEY, OR FOR MORE INFORMATION ON MECHANICS LIENS GO TO THE CONTRACTORS' STATE LICENSE BOARD WEB SITE AT www.cslb.ca.gov."

(b) A claim of mechanics lien in otherwise proper form, verified and containing the information required in subdivision (a), shall be accepted by the recorder for recording and shall be deemed duly recorded without acknowledgment.

(c) A copy of the claim of mechanics lien, which includes the Notice of Mechanics Lien required by paragraph (8) of subdivision (a), shall be served on the owner or reputed owner. Service shall be made as follows:

(1) For an owner or reputed owner to be notified who resides in or outside this state, by registered mail, certified mail, or first-class mail, evidenced by a certificate of mailing, postage prepaid, addressed to the owner or reputed owner at the owner's or reputed owner's residence or place of business address or at the address shown by the building permit on file with the authority issuing a building permit for the work, or as otherwise provided in Section 8174.

(2) If the owner or reputed owner cannot be served by this method, then the copy of the claim of mechanics lien may be given by registered mail, certified mail, or first-class mail, evidenced by a certificate of mailing, postage prepaid, addressed to the construction lender or to the original contractor.

(d) Service of the copy of the claim of mechanics lien by registered mail, certified mail, or first-class mail, evidenced by a certificate of mailing, postage prepaid, is complete at the time of the deposit of that first-class, certified, or registered mail.

(e) Failure to serve the copy of the claim of mechanics lien as prescribed by this section, including the Notice of Mechanics Lien required by paragraph (8) of subdivision (a), shall cause the claim of mechanics lien to be unenforceable as a matter of law. *(Added by Stats.2010, c. 697 (S.B.189), § 20, operative July 1, 2012. Amended by Stats.2011, c. 673 (A.B.456), § 2, operative July 1, 2012.)*

Operative Effect

For operative effect of Part 6, see Civil Code § 8052 and Stats.2010, c. 697 (S.B.189), § 105.

Law Revision Commission Comments

Paragraphs (1)-(5), (7), and (8) of subdivision (a) of Section 8416 restate former Section 3084(a) without substantive change.

Subdivision (b) restates former Section 3084(b) without substantive change.

Subdivision (a)(6) is new. It implements other provisions that invoke a claimant's address. *Cf.* Sections 8424 (release bond), 8486 (time of hearing).

Subdivision (c) restates former Section 3084(c)(1) without substantive change.

Subdivision (d) restates former Section 3084(c)(2) without substantive change.

Subdivision (e) restates former Section 3084(d) without substantive change.

The claim of lien may be executed by the claimant's authorized agent. See Section 8066 (agency).

See also Sections 1170 (recordation); 8058 (filing and recordation of papers); Gov't Code §§ 27280, 27287 (recordation of documents).

See also Sections 8004 (claimant), 8006 (construction lender), 8032 (person), 8040 (site), 8048 (work). [40 Cal.L.Rev.Comm. Reports 49 [AR:apx5] (2010)].

Research References

Rutter, Cal. Practice Guide: Insurance Litigation Ch. 6I-B, B. Particular Surety Bond Coverages.

Miller and Starr California Real Estate § 11:6, Instruments Subject to Recording--List of Recordable Documents.

Miller and Starr California Real Estate § 11:12, Required Form and Contents--Signature of the Property Owner.

Miller and Starr California Real Estate § 28:46, Contents of the Claim of Lien; Purpose.

Miller and Starr California Real Estate § 28:48, Mistake in the Amount Claimed.

Miller and Starr California Real Estate § 28:49, Mistake in the Name of the Owner.

Miller and Starr California Real Estate § 28:50, Mistake in the Description of the Labor And/Or Materials Furnished.

Miller and Starr California Real Estate § 28:51, Mistake in Name of Person to Whom Labor or Materials Furnished.

Miller and Starr California Real Estate § 28:52, Mistake in the Property Description.

21 NO. 4 Miller & Starr, California Real Estate Newsalert 1, Everything Old is New Again: Impact of SB 189 on Mechanics' Lien Law.

4 Witkin, California Summary 10th Security Transactions in Real Property § 31F, (S 31F) (New)-Requirements of Claim.

§ 8422. Erroneous information

(a) Except as provided in subdivisions (b) and (c), erroneous information contained in a claim of lien relating to the claimant's demand, credits and offsets deducted, the work provided, or the description of the site, does not invalidate the claim of lien.

(b) Erroneous information contained in a claim of lien relating to the claimant's demand, credits and offsets deducted, or the work provided, invalidates the claim of lien if the court determines either of the following:

(1) The claim of lien was made with intent to defraud.

(2) An innocent third party, without notice, actual or constructive, became the bona fide owner of the property after recordation of the claim of lien, and the claim of lien was so deficient that it did not put the party on further inquiry in any manner.

(c) Any person who shall willfully include in a claim of lien labor, services, equipment, or materials not furnished for the property described in the claim, shall thereby forfeit the person's lien. *(Added by Stats.2010, c. 697 (S.B.189), § 20, operative July 1, 2012. Amended by Stats.2011, c. 44 (S.B.190), § 5, operative July 1, 2012.)*

Operative Effect

For operative effect of Part 6, see Civil Code § 8052 and Stats.2010, c. 697 (S.B.189), § 105.

Law Revision Commission Comments

Section 8422 combines the substance of former Sections 3118 and 3261. The terminology of the combined provision is conformed to Section 8416 (contents of claim of lien).

Subdivision (b)(1) expands the bases for invalidity to include intent to slander title.

See also Sections 8004 (claimant), 8048 (work), 8026 (lien), 8040 (site). [40 Cal.L.Rev.Comm. Reports 49 [AR:apx5] (2010)].

Section 8422 is amended to avoid any misunderstanding that might result from the reference to slander of title. Subdivision (c) continues former Section 3118 without substantive change. [41 Cal.L.Rev.Comm. Reports ___ (2011)].

Research References

Rutter, Cal. Practice Guide: Insurance Litigation Ch. 6I-B, B. Particular Surety Bond Coverages.

Miller and Starr California Real Estate § 28:47, Substantial Compliance.

Miller and Starr California Real Estate § 28:48, Mistake in the Amount Claimed.

Miller and Starr California Real Estate § 28:50, Mistake in the Description of the Labor And/Or Materials Furnished.

Miller and Starr California Real Estate § 28:52, Mistake in the Property Description.

Miller and Starr California Real Estate § 28:53, When Claimant Furnished Labor or Materials to Two or More Works of Improvement.

22 NO. 4 Miller & Starr, California Real Estate Newsalert 17, Mechanics' Liens.

4 Witkin, California Summary 10th Security Transactions in Real Property § 31F, (S 31F) (New)-Requirements of Claim.

§ 8424. Lien release bond

(a) An owner of real property or an owner of any interest in real property subject to a recorded claim of lien, or a direct contractor or subcontractor affected by the claim of lien, that disputes the correctness or validity of the claim may obtain release of the real property from the claim of lien by recording a lien release bond. The principal on the bond may be the owner of the property, the direct contractor, or the subcontractor.

(b) The bond shall be conditioned on payment of any judgment and costs the claimant recovers on the lien. The bond shall be in an amount equal to 125 percent of the amount of the claim of lien or 125 percent of the amount allocated in the claim of lien to the real property to be released. The bond shall be executed by an admitted surety insurer.

(c) The bond may be recorded either before or after commencement of an action to enforce the lien. On recordation of the bond, the real property is released from the claim of lien and from any action to enforce the lien.

(d) A person that obtains and records a lien release bond shall give notice to the claimant. The notice shall comply with the requirements of Chapter 2 (commencing with Section 8100) of Title 1 and shall include a copy of the bond. Failure to give the notice required by this section does not affect the validity of the bond, but the statute of limitations for an action on the bond is tolled until notice is given. The claimant shall commence an action on the bond within six months after notice is given. *(Added by Stats.2010, c. 697 (S.B.189), § 20, operative July 1, 2012.)*

Operative Effect

For operative effect of Part 6, see Civil Code § 8052 and Stats.2010, c. 697 (S.B.189), § 105.

Law Revision Commission Comments

Subdivisions (a)-(c) of Section 8424 restate former Section 3143, reducing the required amount of the lien release bond to 125% of the amount of the recorded claim of lien applicable to the liened property. This harmonizes the required amount of a lien release bond with the required amount of a stop payment notice release bond. See Section 8510. The language of the section is harmonized with the Bond and Undertaking Law, Chapter 2 (commencing with Section 995.010) of Title 14 of Part 2 of the Code of Civil Procedure.

Subdivision (d) restates former Section 3144.5 without substantive change, except to broaden the notice provisions.

The reference to recordation of the bond in the county in which the claim of lien is recorded is omitted as unnecessary. Both the claim of lien and the bond are recorded in the office of the county recorder of the county in which the work of improvement or part of it is situated. See Sections 1170 (recordation), 8060 (filing and recordation of papers).

If an action to enforce a lien has been timely commenced before a release bond is recorded, the claimant may name the surety as a defendant and seek recovery against the bond in the enforcement action; the claimant is not required to commence a new action on the bond. See Hutnick v. United States Fidelity & Guaranty Co., 47 Cal.3d 456, 763 P.2d 1326, 253 Cal.Rptr. 236 (1988).

See also Sections 8002 (admitted surety insurer), 8004 (claimant), 8018 (direct contractor), 8026 (lien), 8032 (person), 8046 (subcontractor). [40 Cal.L.Rev.Comm. Reports 49 [AR:apx5] (2010)].

Research References

Rutter, Cal. Practice Guide: Insurance Litigation Ch. 6I-B, B. Particular Surety Bond Coverages.
Miller and Starr California Real Estate § 28:47, Substantial Compliance.
Miller and Starr California Real Estate § 28:66, Bond to Release the Lien.
Miller and Starr California Real Estate § 28:92, Construction-Related Bonds; in General.
3 Witkin Cal. Proc. 5th Actions § 480, (S 480) One Hundred Eighty Days or Six Months.
3 Witkin Cal. Proc. 5th Actions § 221A, (S 221A) (New)-In General.
4 Witkin, California Summary 10th Security Transactions in Real Property § 31A, (S 31A) (New)-Nature and Purpose of Revision.
4 Witkin, California Summary 10th Security Transactions in Real Property § 31H, (New)-Protecting Against Lien.

ARTICLE 3.   AMOUNT OF LIEN

Section
8430.   Direct liens; amount.
8432.   Work included in claim; filing of contract or modification as constructive notice.
8434.   Recovery by direct contractor or subcontractor.

Operative Effect

For operative effect of Part 6, see Civil Code § 8052 and Stats.2010, c. 697 (S.B.189), § 105.

§ 8430.   Direct liens; amount

(a) The lien is a direct lien for the lesser of the following amounts:

(1) The reasonable value of the work provided by the claimant.

(2) The price agreed to by the claimant and the person that contracted for the work.

(b) The lien is not limited in amount by the contract price for the work of improvement except as provided in Section 8600.

(c) This section does not preclude the claimant from including in a claim of lien work performed based on a written modification of the contract, or as a result of rescission, abandonment, or breach of the contract. If there is a rescission, abandonment, or breach of the contract, the amount of the lien may not exceed the reasonable value of the work provided by the claimant. *(Added by Stats.2010, c. 697 (S.B.189), § 20, operative July 1, 2012.)*

Operative Effect

For operative effect of Part 6, see Civil Code § 8052 and Stats.2010, c. 697 (S.B.189), § 105.

Law Revision Commission Comments

Section 8430 restates former Section 3123(a)-(b) and a part of former Section 3110. The provision of former Section 3123(c) that required an owner to give notice of a change of 5 percent or more is not continued.

As used in this section, the reasonable value of work includes the reasonable use value of appliances, equipment, teams, and power.

See also Sections 8416 (contents of claim of lien), 8600 (payment bond).

See also Sections 8004 ("claimant"), 8008 ("contract"), 8010 ("contract price"), 8026 ("lien"), 8032 ("person"), 8048 ("work"), 8050 ("work of improvement"). [40 Cal.L.Rev.Comm. Reports 49 [AR:apx5] (2010)].

Research References

Rutter, Cal. Practice Guide: Insurance Litigation Ch. 6I-B, B. Particular Surety Bond Coverages.
Miller and Starr California Real Estate § 28:3, Source and Purpose of the Mechanics Lien.
Miller and Starr California Real Estate § 28:4, Requirement of a Contract.
Miller and Starr California Real Estate § 28:5, Nature of the Lien; Owner's Personal Liability.
Miller and Starr California Real Estate § 28:24, Amount of Lien Claims; Extent of Owner's Liability.
Miller and Starr California Real Estate § 28:26, Lien of a Subcontractor.
Miller and Starr California Real Estate § 28:62, Prejudgment Interest.
Miller and Starr California Real Estate § 28:63, Costs and Attorney's Fees.
Miller and Starr California Real Estate § 11:130, in General; Off-Record Priority.
Miller and Starr California Real Estate § 11:136, When Construction Commences--Phasing of the Project; in General.
2 Witkin Cal. Proc. 5th Jurisdiction § 359, Subcontractor's Contract.
4 Witkin, California Summary 10th Security Transactions in Real Property § 31D, (New)-Amount of Lien.

§ 8432.   Work included in claim; filing of contract or modification as constructive notice

(a) A lien does not extend to work, whether or not the work is authorized by a direct contractor or subcontractor, if the work is not included in a direct contract or a modification of that contract, and the claimant had actual knowledge or constructive notice of the provisions of that contract or modification before providing the work.

(b) The filing of a contract or modification of that contract with the county recorder, before the commencement of a work of improvement, is constructive notice of the provisions of the contract or modification to a person providing work on that work of improvement. *(Added by Stats.2010, c. 697 (S.B.189), § 20, operative July 1, 2012.)*

Operative Effect

For operative effect of Part 6, see Civil Code § 8052 and Stats.2010, c. 697 (S.B.189), § 105.

Law Revision Commission Comments

Section 8432 restates former Section 3124 without substantive change.

In subdivision (a), "direct contractor" is substituted for the undefined "contractor." The concept of "authorized" is substituted for "employed." See Section 8404 (who may authorize work). See also Sections 1170 (recordation), 8060 (filing and recordation of papers).

See also Sections 8004 ("claimant"), 8008 ("contract"), 8016 ("direct contract"), 8018 ("direct contractor"), 8026 ("lien"), 8032 ("person"), 8046 ("subcontractor"), 8048 ("work"), 8050 ("work of improvement"). [40 Cal.L.Rev.Comm. Reports 49 [AR:apx5] (2010)].

Research References

Miller and Starr California Real Estate § 11:6, Instruments Subject to Recording--List of Recordable Documents.
Miller and Starr California Real Estate § 11:68, Constructive Notice of Interests Barred by the Statute of Limitations--"Ancient Documents" and the Marketable Record Title Act.
Miller and Starr California Real Estate § 28:26, Lien of a Subcontractor.
Miller and Starr California Real Estate § 28:27, Limiting Owner's Liability by Recording Direct Contract and Bond.
4 Witkin, California Summary 10th Security Transactions in Real Property § 31D, (New)-Amount of Lien.

§ 8434. Recovery by direct contractor or subcontractor

A direct contractor or a subcontractor may enforce a lien only for the amount due pursuant to that contractor's contract after deducting all lien claims of other claimants for work provided and embraced within that contract. *(Added by Stats.2010, c. 697 (S.B.189), § 20, operative July 1, 2012.)*

Operative Effect

For operative effect of Part 6, see Civil Code § 8052 and Stats.2010, c. 697 (S.B.189), § 105.

Law Revision Commission Comments

Section 8434 continues former Section 3140 without substantive change.
See also Sections 8004 ("claimant"), 8008 ("contract"), 8012 ("contractor"), 8018 ("direct contractor"), 8026 ("lien"), 8046 ("subcontractor"), 8048 ("work"). [40 Cal.L.Rev.Comm. Reports 49 [AR:apx5] (2010)].

Research References

Miller and Starr California Real Estate § 28:24, Amount of Lien Claims; Extent of Owner's Liability.
Miller and Starr California Real Estate § 28:25, Lien of a Direct Contractor.
Miller and Starr California Real Estate § 28:26, Lien of a Subcontractor.
Miller and Starr California Real Estate § 28:67, Payment, Release, and Waiver of the Lien.
4 Witkin, California Summary 10th Security Transactions in Real Property § 31D, (New)-Amount of Lien.

ARTICLE 4. PROPERTY SUBJECT TO LIEN

Section
8440. Attachment to work and real property.
8442. Interests in real property.
8444. Notice of nonresponsibility.
8446. One claim on two or more works of improvement; conditions.
8448. Separate residential units.

Operative Effect

For operative effect of Part 6, see Civil Code § 8052 and Stats.2010, c. 697 (S.B.189), § 105.

§ 8440. Attachment to work and real property

Subject to Section 8442, a lien attaches to the work of improvement and to the real property on which the work of improvement is situated, including as much space about the work of improvement as is required for the convenient use and occupation of the work of improvement. *(Added by Stats.2010, c. 697 (S.B.189), § 20, operative July 1, 2012.)*

Operative Effect

For operative effect of Part 6, see Civil Code § 8052 and Stats.2010, c. 697 (S.B.189), § 105.

Law Revision Commission Comments

Section 8440 restates the parts of former Sections 3128 and 3112 that described property subject to the lien, without substantive change. A reference to "real property" is substituted for references to "land."

See also Sections 8026 ("lien"), 8050 ("work of improvement"). [40 Cal.L.Rev.Comm. Reports 49 [AR:apx5] (2010)].

Research References

Miller and Starr California Real Estate § 28:12, Supplier of Labor or Equipment.
Miller and Starr California Real Estate § 28:18, Property Included Within the Lien.
Miller and Starr California Real Estate § 11:130, in General; Off-Record Priority.
Miller and Starr California Real Estate § 11:134, Effect of Commencement of Work Before the Grantee Receives Title.
Miller and Starr California Real Estate § 11:139, Priority as Affected by Separate Works of Improvement on Separate Parcels.
4 Witkin, California Summary 10th Security Transactions in Real Property § 31C, (New)-Right to Lien and Property Affected.

§ 8442. Interests in real property

The following interests in real property to which a lien attaches are subject to the lien:

(a) The interest of a person that contracted for the work of improvement.

(b) The interest of a person that did not contract for the work of improvement, if work for which the lien is claimed was provided with the knowledge of that person, unless that person gives notice of nonresponsibility under Section 8444. *(Added by Stats.2010, c. 697 (S.B.189), § 20, operative July 1, 2012.)*

Operative Effect

For operative effect of Part 6, see Civil Code § 8052 and Stats.2010, c. 697 (S.B.189), § 105.

Law Revision Commission Comments

Section 8442 restates the last part of former Section 3128, and former Section 3129, without substantive change. A reference to "work" is substituted for the former reference to "commencement of the work or of the furnishing of the materials." See Section 8048 ("work").

It should be noted that under this section, the interest of a person that contracts for a work of improvement indirectly, for example through a provision in a lease that requires a tenant to make the work of improvement, may be subject to the lien. Likewise, the interest of a person that did not contract for a work of improvement might in some circumstances be subject to the lien if the person is a "participating owner." See, e.g., Los Banos Gravel Co. v. Freeman, 58 Cal.App.3d 785, 130 Cal.Rptr. 180 (1976).

See also Sections 8026 ("lien"), 8032 ("person"), 8050 ("work of improvement"). [40 Cal.L.Rev.Comm. Reports 49 [AR:apx5] (2010)].

Research References

California Real Estate Forms (Miller & Starr) § 2:18, Office Lease--Office/Warehouse Building With Four or Fewer Tenants.
California Real Estate Forms (Miller & Starr) § 2:22, Retail Lease--Regional Shopping Center.
California Real Estate Forms (Miller & Starr) § 2:23, Retail Lease--Small Strip-Shopping Center.
California Real Estate Forms (Miller & Starr) § 2:24, Retail Lease--Restaurant.

California Real Estate Forms (Miller & Starr) § 2:26, Triple Net Lease--Industrial Build-To-Suit Lease.

California Real Estate Forms (Miller & Starr) § 2:27, Ground Lease.

California Real Estate Forms (Miller & Starr) § 2:28, Triple Net Lease--Stand-Alone Building.

California Real Estate Forms (Miller & Starr) § 2:49, Work Letter--Industrial Build-To-Suit Lease.

California Real Estate Forms (Miller & Starr) § 2:62, Standard Industrial/Commercial Multi-Tenant Lease--Net.

California Real Estate Forms (Miller & Starr) § 2:63, Standard Industrial/Commercial Multi-Tenant Lease--Gross.

Miller and Starr California Real Estate § 28:12, Supplier of Labor or Equipment.

Miller and Starr California Real Estate § 28:19, When Person Authorizing the Work Owns Less Than a Fee Title.

Miller and Starr California Real Estate § 28:20, Notice of Nonresponsibility--In General.

Miller and Starr California Real Estate § 28:32, Persons in Direct Contract With the Owner.

Miller and Starr California Real Estate § 11:130, in General; Off-Record Priority.

Miller and Starr California Real Estate § 11:134, Effect of Commencement of Work Before the Grantee Receives Title.

Miller and Starr California Real Estate § 11:139, Priority as Affected by Separate Works of Improvement on Separate Parcels.

1 Witkin Cal. Summ. 10th Contracts § 29, Contract Relating to Real Property.

4 Witkin, California Summary 10th Security Transactions in Real Property § 31C, (New)-Right to Lien and Property Affected.

§ 8444. Notice of nonresponsibility

(a) An owner of real property or a person claiming an interest in real property on which a work of improvement is situated that did not contract for the work of improvement may give notice of nonresponsibility.

(b) A notice of nonresponsibility shall be signed and verified by the owner.

(c) The notice shall comply with the requirements of Chapter 2 (commencing with Section 8100) of Title 1.

(d) The notice shall also include all of the following information:

(1) The nature of the owner's title or interest.

(2) The name of a purchaser under contract, if any, or lessee, if known.

(3) A statement that the person giving the notice is not responsible for claims arising from the work of improvement.

(e) A notice of nonresponsibility is not effective unless, within 10 days after the person giving notice has knowledge of the work of improvement, the person both posts and records the notice. *(Added by Stats.2010, c. 697 (S.B.189), § 20, operative July 1, 2012.)*

Operative Effect

For operative effect of Part 6, see Civil Code § 8052 and Stats.2010, c. 697 (S.B.189), § 105.

Law Revision Commission Comments

Section 8444 restates former Section 3094.

The information required in this notice is in addition to the information required by Section 8102 (contents of notice).

The notice of nonresponsibility may be signed and verified by the owner or person owning or claiming an interest in the property, or by the owner's or other person's agent. See Section 8066 (agency).

A notice of nonresponsibility is recorded in the office of the county recorder of the county in which the work of improvement or part of it is situated. See Section 8060 (filing and recordation of papers).

See also Sections 1170 (recordation), 8058 (calculation of time), 8064 (co-owners), 8114 (posting of notice).

See also Sections 8032 ("person"), 8050 ("work of improvement"). [40 Cal.L.Rev.Comm. Reports 49 [AR:apx5] (2010)].

Research References

California Real Estate Forms (Miller & Starr) § 2:18, Office Lease--Office/Warehouse Building With Four or Fewer Tenants.

California Real Estate Forms (Miller & Starr) § 2:22, Retail Lease--Regional Shopping Center.

California Real Estate Forms (Miller & Starr) § 2:23, Retail Lease--Small Strip-Shopping Center.

California Real Estate Forms (Miller & Starr) § 2:24, Retail Lease--Restaurant.

California Real Estate Forms (Miller & Starr) § 2:26, Triple Net Lease--Industrial Build-To-Suit Lease.

California Real Estate Forms (Miller & Starr) § 2:27, Ground Lease.

California Real Estate Forms (Miller & Starr) § 2:28, Triple Net Lease--Stand-Alone Building.

California Real Estate Forms (Miller & Starr) § 2:49, Work Letter--Industrial Build-To-Suit Lease.

California Real Estate Forms (Miller & Starr) § 2:62, Standard Industrial/Commercial Multi-Tenant Lease--Net.

California Real Estate Forms (Miller & Starr) § 2:63, Standard Industrial/Commercial Multi-Tenant Lease--Gross.

Miller and Starr California Real Estate § 11:6, Instruments Subject to Recording--List of Recordable Documents.

Miller and Starr California Real Estate § 28:19, When Person Authorizing the Work Owns Less Than a Fee Title.

Miller and Starr California Real Estate § 28:20, Notice of Nonresponsibility--In General.

Miller and Starr California Real Estate § 28:21, Constructive and Imputed Knowledge.

Miller and Starr California Real Estate § 28:22, Time for Posting and Recording Notice.

Miller and Starr California Real Estate § 28:23, Form and Procedural Requirements.

Miller and Starr California Real Estate § 11:139, Priority as Affected by Separate Works of Improvement on Separate Parcels.

4 Witkin, California Summary 10th Security Transactions in Real Property § 31C, (New)-Right to Lien and Property Affected.

4 Witkin, California Summary 10th Security Transactions in Real Property § 31H, (New)-Protecting Against Lien.

§ 8446. One claim on two or more works of improvement; conditions

A claimant may record one claim of lien on two or more works of improvement, subject to the following conditions:

(a) The works of improvement have or are reputed to have the same owner, or the work was contracted for by the same person for the works of improvement whether or not they have the same owner.

(b) The claimant in the claim of lien designates the amount due for each work of improvement. If the claimant contracted for a lump sum payment for work provided for the works of improvement and the contract does not segregate the amount due for each work of improvement separately, the claimant may estimate an equitable distribution of the amount due for each work of improvement based on the proportionate amount of work provided for each. If the claimant does not designate the amount due for each work of improvement, the lien is subordinate to other liens.

(c) If there is a single structure on real property of different owners, the claimant need not segregate the proportion of work provided for the portion of the structure situated on real property of each owner. In the lien enforcement action the court may, if it determines it equitable to do so, designate an equitable distribution of the lien among the real property of the owners.

(d) The lien does not extend beyond the amount designated as against other creditors having liens, by judgment, mortgage, or otherwise, on either the works of improvement or the real property on which the works of improvement are situated. *(Added by Stats.2010, c. 697 (S.B.189), § 20, operative July 1, 2012.)*

Operative Effect

For operative effect of Part 6, see Civil Code § 8052 and Stats.2010, c. 697 (S.B.189), § 105.

Law Revision Commission Comments

Section 8446 restates former Section 3130 without substantive change. The concept of "contracted for" is substituted for employed in subdivisions (a) and (b). See Section 8404 (who may authorize work).

Subdivision (c) is intended to apply to a single work of improvement situated on two or more parcels of land that have distinct owners.

See also Sections 1170 (recordation), 8060 (filing and recordation of papers).

See also Sections 8004 ("claimant"), 8008 ("contract"), 8026 ("lien"), 8032 ("person"), 8048 ("work"), 8050 ("work of improvement"). [40 Cal.L.Rev.Comm. Reports 49 [AR:apx5] (2010)].

Research References

Rutter, Cal. Practice Guide: Insurance Litigation Ch. 6I-B, B. Particular Surety Bond Coverages.
Miller and Starr California Real Estate § 28:53, When Claimant Furnished Labor or Materials to Two or More Works of Improvement.
Miller and Starr California Real Estate § 11:130, in General; Off-Record Priority.
Miller and Starr California Real Estate § 11:139, Priority as Affected by Separate Works of Improvement on Separate Parcels.

§ 8448.   Separate residential units

(a) As used in this section, "separate residential unit" means one residential structure, including a residential structure containing multiple condominium units, together with any common area, garage, or other appurtenant improvements.

(b) If a work of improvement consists of the construction of two or more separate residential units:

(1) Each unit is deemed a separate work of improvement, and completion of each unit is determined separately for purposes of the time for recording a claim of lien on that unit. This paragraph does not affect any lien right under Section 8402 or 8446.

(2) Material provided for the work of improvement is deemed to be provided for use or consumption in each separate residential unit in which the material is actually used or consumed; but if the claimant is unable to segregate the amounts used or consumed in separate residential units, the claimant has the right to all the benefits of Section 8446. *(Added by Stats.2010, c. 697 (S.B.189), § 20, operative July 1, 2012.)*

Operative Effect

For operative effect of Part 6, see Civil Code § 8052 and Stats.2010, c. 697 (S.B.189), § 105.

Law Revision Commission Comments

Section 8448 restates the first paragraph of former Section 3131 without substantive change. The reference to "filing" a claim of lien is changed to recording. See Sections 1170 (recordation), 8060 (filing and recordation of papers), 8412 and 8414 (recordation of claim of lien).

The second paragraph of former Section 3131 is not continued.

See also Sections 8180 (completion), 8402 (site improvement lien), 8416 (contents of claim of lien), 8446 (multiple works of improvement).

See also Sections 8004 ("claimant"), 8026 ("lien"), 8050 ("work of improvement"). [40 Cal.L.Rev.Comm. Reports 49 [AR:apx5] (2010)].

Research References

Miller and Starr California Real Estate § 28:43, When Project Consists of Two or More Residential Units.
Miller and Starr California Real Estate § 28:53, When Claimant Furnished Labor or Materials to Two or More Works of Improvement.
Miller and Starr California Real Estate § 11:130, in General; Off-Record Priority.
Miller and Starr California Real Estate § 11:139, Priority as Affected by Separate Works of Improvement on Separate Parcels.

ARTICLE 5.   PRIORITIES

Operative Effect

For operative effect of Part 6, see Civil Code § 8052 and Stats.2010, c. 697 (S.B.189), § 105.

§ 8450.   Priority of lien under this chapter

(a) A lien under this chapter, other than a lien provided for in Section 8402, has priority over a lien, mortgage, deed of trust, or other encumbrance on the work of improvement or the real property on which the work of improvement is situated, that (1) attaches after commencement of the work of improvement or (2) was unrecorded at the commencement of the work of improvement and of which the claimant had no notice.

(b) Subdivision (a) is subject to the exception provided for in Section 8452. *(Added by Stats.2010, c. 697 (S.B.189), § 20, operative July 1, 2012.)*

Operative Effect

For operative effect of Part 6, see Civil Code § 8052 and Stats.2010, c. 697 (S.B.189), § 105.

Law Revision Commission Comments

Section 8450 restates former Section 3134 without substantive change. For the priority of a site improvement lien, see Section 8458 (priority of site improvement lien).

See also Sections 1170 (recordation), 8060 (filing and recordation of papers), 8402 (site improvement lien), 8452 (payment bond obtained by holder of mortgage or deed of trust).

See also Sections 8004 ("claimant"), 8026 ("lien"), 8050 ("work of improvement"). [40 Cal.L.Rev.Comm. Reports 49 [AR:apx5] (2010)].

Research References

Rutter, Cal. Practice Guide: Insurance Litigation Ch. 6H-B, B. Types of Policies and Services Provided by Title Insurers.
Rutter, Cal. Practice Guide: Insurance Litigation Ch. 6I-B, B. Particular Surety Bond Coverages.
Miller and Starr California Real Estate § 28:6, Priority of the Lien.

Miller and Starr California Real Estate § 28:79, Effect of Assignment of Loan Funds or Inadequate Funds.

Miller and Starr California Real Estate § 11:104, Priority of Purchase Money Liens--Purchase Money Lien Vis-á-Vis Liens Created Before Title Passes.

Miller and Starr California Real Estate § 11:131, Date Liens Attach; Relation to Subsequent Interests.

Miller and Starr California Real Estate § 11:132, Relation to Prior Interests--In General.

Miller and Starr California Real Estate § 11:133, Relation to Prior Interests--Mechanic's Knowledge of a Prior Unrecorded Interest.

Miller and Starr California Real Estate § 11:135, When Construction Commences--Effect on Priority of Mechanics' and Design Professionals' Liens.

Miller and Starr California Real Estate § 11:138, Site Improvements; Priority of Liens as Distinguished from Liens for Structures or Buildings.

Miller and Starr California Real Estate § 11:140, Effect of Cessation of Work on Mechanic's Lien Priorities.

Miller and Starr California Real Estate § 11:141, Priority of the Construction Loan Deed of Trust--In General.

Miller and Starr California Real Estate § 11:145, Priority of the Construction Loan Deed of Trust--Advances to Complete Construction.

4 Witkin, California Summary 10th Security Transactions in Real Property § 32, Design Professional's Lien.

4 Witkin, California Summary 10th Security Transactions in Real Property § 69, (S 69) Basic Rule.

4 Witkin, California Summary 10th Security Transactions in Real Property § 70, (S 70) Commencement of Work.

§ 8452. Mortgage or deed of trust; recordation of payment bond; requirements

A mortgage or deed of trust, otherwise subordinate to a lien under Section 8450, has priority over a lien for work provided after recordation of a payment bond that satisfies all of the following requirements:

(a) The bond refers to the mortgage or deed of trust.

(b) The bond is in an amount not less than 75 percent of the principal amount of the mortgage or deed of trust. *(Added by Stats.2010, c. 697 (S.B.189), § 20, operative July 1, 2012.)*

Operative Effect

For operative effect of Part 6, see Civil Code § 8052 and Stats.2010, c. 697 (S.B.189), § 105.

Law Revision Commission Comments

Section 8452 restates former Section 3138 without substantive change. See also Sections 1170 (recordation), 8060 (filing and recordation of papers).

See also Sections 8026 ("lien"), 8030 ("payment bond"), 8048 ("work"). [40 Cal.L.Rev.Comm. Reports 49 [AR:apx5] (2010)].

Research References

Rutter, Cal. Practice Guide: Insurance Litigation Ch. 6I-B, B. Particular Surety Bond Coverages.

Miller and Starr California Real Estate § 28:6, Priority of the Lien.

Miller and Starr California Real Estate § 11:139, Priority as Affected by Separate Works of Improvement on Separate Parcels.

Miller and Starr California Real Estate § 11:146, Priority of the Construction Loan Deed of Trust--Effect of a Bond Recorded by the Construction Lender.

§ 8454. Site improvements as separate direct contract

If a site improvement is provided for in a direct contract separate from the direct contract for the remainder of the work of improvement, the site improvement is deemed a separate work of improvement and commencement of the site improvement is not commencement of the remainder of the work of improvement. *(Added by Stats.2010, c. 697 (S.B.189), § 20, operative July 1, 2012.)*

Operative Effect

For operative effect of Part 6, see Civil Code § 8052 and Stats.2010, c. 697 (S.B.189), § 105.

Law Revision Commission Comments

Section 8454 restates former Section 3135 without substantive change.

See also Sections 8016 ("direct contract"), 8042 ("site improvement"), 8050 ("work of improvement"). [40 Cal.L.Rev.Comm. Reports 49 [AR:apx5] (2010)].

Research References

Miller and Starr California Real Estate § 28:6, Priority of the Lien.

Miller and Starr California Real Estate § 28:17, "Work of Improvement".

Miller and Starr California Real Estate § 28:22, Time for Posting and Recording Notice.

Miller and Starr California Real Estate § 28:44, Public Improvements Under Private Contract.

Miller and Starr California Real Estate § 28:79, Effect of Assignment of Loan Funds or Inadequate Funds.

Miller and Starr California Real Estate § 11:138, Site Improvements; Priority of Liens as Distinguished from Liens for Structures or Buildings.

4 Witkin, California Summary 10th Security Transactions in Real Property § 70, (S 70) Commencement of Work.

§ 8456. Construction loan secured by mortgage or deed of trust; optional advance of funds

(a) This section applies to a construction loan secured by a mortgage or deed of trust that has priority over a lien under this chapter.

(b) An optional advance of funds by the construction lender that is used for construction costs has the same priority as a mandatory advance of funds by the construction lender, provided that the total of all advances does not exceed the amount of the original construction loan. *(Added by Stats.2010, c. 697 (S.B. 189), § 20, operative July 1, 2012.)*

Operative Effect

For operative effect of Part 6, see Civil Code § 8052 and Stats.2010, c. 697 (S.B.189), § 105.

Law Revision Commission Comments

Section 8456 restates former Section 3136.

See also Sections 8006 ("construction lender"), 8026 ("lien"). [40 Cal.L.Rev.Comm. Reports 49 [AR:apx5] (2010)].

Research References

Miller and Starr California Real Estate § 28:6, Priority of the Lien.

Miller and Starr California Real Estate § 28:79, Effect of Assignment of Loan Funds or Inadequate Funds.

Miller and Starr California Real Estate § 11:111, Liens for Future Advances--Construction Loans.

Miller and Starr California Real Estate § 11:141, Priority of the Construction Loan Deed of Trust--In General.

Miller and Starr California Real Estate § 11:143, Priority of the Construction Loan Deed of Trust--Relation to Optional Advances.

Miller and Starr California Real Estate § 11:145, Priority of the Construction Loan Deed of Trust--Advances to Complete Construction.

Miller and Starr California Real Estate § 11:146, Priority of the Construction Loan Deed of Trust--Effect of a Bond Recorded by the Construction Lender.

4 Witkin, California Summary 10th Security Transactions in Real Property § 73, (S 73) Optional Advances.

§ 8458. Liens for site improvements

(a) Except as provided in subdivision (b), a lien provided for in Section 8402 has priority over:

(1) A mortgage, deed of trust, or other encumbrance that attaches after commencement of the site improvement.

(2) A mortgage, deed of trust, or other encumbrance that was unrecorded at the commencement of the site improvement and of which the claimant had no notice.

(3) A mortgage, deed of trust, or other encumbrance that was recorded before commencement of the site improvement, if given for the sole or primary purpose of financing the site improvement. This subdivision does not apply if the loan proceeds are, in good faith, placed in the control of the lender pursuant to a binding agreement with the borrower to the effect that (A) the proceeds are to be applied to the payment of claimants and (B) no portion of the proceeds will be paid to the borrower in the absence of satisfactory evidence that all claims have been paid or that the time for recording a claim of lien has expired and no claim of lien has been recorded.

(b) A mortgage or deed of trust, otherwise subordinate under subdivision (a), has priority over a lien provided for in Section 8402 if a payment bond in an amount not less than 50 percent of the principal amount of the mortgage or deed of trust is recorded before completion of the work of improvement. *(Added by Stats.2010, c. 697 (S.B.189), § 20, operative July 1, 2012.)*

Operative Effect

For operative effect of Part 6, see Civil Code § 8052 and Stats.2010, c. 697 (S.B.189), § 105.

Law Revision Commission Comments

Subdivision (a) of Section 8458 restates former Section 3137 without substantive change.

Subdivision (b) restates former Section 3139 without substantive change.

See also Sections 1170 (recordation), 8060 (filing and recordation of papers), 8180 (completion), 8402 (site improvement lien).

See also Sections 8004 ("claimant"), 8026 ("lien"), 8030 ("payment bond"), 8042 ("site improvement"), 8050 ("work of improvement"). [40 Cal.L.Rev.Comm. Reports 49 [AR:apx5] (2010)].

Research References

Rutter, Cal. Practice Guide: Insurance Litigation Ch. 6I-B, B. Particular Surety Bond Coverages.
Miller and Starr California Real Estate § 28:6, Priority of the Lien.
Miller and Starr California Real Estate § 28:79, Effect of Assignment of Loan Funds or Inadequate Funds.
Miller and Starr California Real Estate § 11:132, Relation to Prior Interests--In General.
Miller and Starr California Real Estate § 11:138, Site Improvements; Priority of Liens as Distinguished from Liens for Structures or Buildings.
Miller and Starr California Real Estate § 11:146, Priority of the Construction Loan Deed of Trust--Effect of a Bond Recorded by the Construction Lender.
4 Witkin, California Summary 10th Security Transactions in Real Property § 69, (S 69) Basic Rule.

ARTICLE 6. ENFORCEMENT OF LIEN

Operative Effect

For operative effect of Part 6, see Civil Code § 8052 and Stats.2010, c. 697 (S.B.189), § 105.

§ 8460. Time for commencement of action; exception for extension of credit

(a) The claimant shall commence an action to enforce a lien within 90 days after recordation of the claim of lien. If the claimant does not commence an action to enforce the lien within that time, the claim of lien expires and is unenforceable.

(b) Subdivision (a) does not apply if the claimant and owner agree to extend credit, and notice of the fact and terms of the extension of credit is recorded (1) within 90 days after recordation of the claim of lien or (2) more than 90 days after recordation of the claim of lien but before a purchaser or encumbrancer for value and in good faith acquires rights in the property. In that event the claimant shall commence an action to enforce the lien within 90 days after the expiration of the credit, but in no case later than one year after completion of the work of improvement. If the claimant does not commence an action to enforce the lien within that time, the claim of lien expires and is unenforceable. *(Added by Stats.2010, c. 697 (S.B.189), § 20, operative July 1, 2012.)*

Operative Effect

For operative effect of Part 6, see Civil Code § 8052 and Stats.2010, c. 697 (S.B.189), § 105.

Law Revision Commission Comments

Section 8460 restates former Sections 3144 and 3145.

Subdivision (b) makes clear that the owner must be a party to the extension of credit, and allows for late recording of the extension of credit. This codifies the rule in *Richards v. Hillside Development Co.*, 177 Cal.App.2d 776, 2 Cal.Rptr. 693 (1960), and overrules *Dorer v. McKinsey*, 188 Cal.App.2d 199, 10 Cal.Rptr. 287 (1961).

See also Sections 1170 (recordation), 8058 (calculation of time), 8060 (filing and recordation of papers), 8180 (completion).

See also Sections 8004 ("claimant"), 8026 ("lien"), 8050 ("work of improvement"). [40 Cal.L.Rev.Comm. Reports 49 [AR:apx5] (2010)].

Research References

Rutter, Cal. Practice Guide: Insurance Litigation Ch. 6I-B, B. Particular Surety Bond Coverages.
Miller and Starr California Real Estate § 28:37, Claim of Lien--Necessity, Purpose, and Effect.
Miller and Starr California Real Estate § 28:54, Enforcement by Foreclosure.
Miller and Starr California Real Estate § 28:56, Statute of Limitations; Time to File a Complaint.
Miller and Starr California Real Estate § 28:57, Extension of Time to File Complaint.
Miller and Starr California Real Estate § 11:131, Date Liens Attach; Relation to Subsequent Interests.
21 NO. 4 Miller & Starr, California Real Estate Newsalert 1, Everything Old is New Again: Impact of SB 189 on Mechanics' Lien Law.
3 Witkin Cal. Proc. 5th Actions § 442, Limitation Affecting Property Right.
3 Witkin Cal. Proc. 5th Actions § 477, (S 477) Ninety Days or Three Months.
3 Witkin Cal. Proc. 5th Actions § 481, (S 481) One Year.
4 Witkin Cal. Proc. 5th Pleading § 481, (S 481) Actual Ignorance.
4 Witkin Cal. Proc. 5th Pleading § 490, Delay in Seeking Amendment.
4 Witkin, California Summary 10th Security Transactions in Real Property § 32, Design Professional's Lien.
4 Witkin, California Summary 10th Security Transactions in Real Property § 31G, (S 31G) (New)-Action to Foreclose Lien.

4 Witkin, California Summary 10th Security Transactions in Real Property § 31-I, (New)-Release of Lien.

§ 8461. Recording of notice of pendency of action

After commencement of an action to enforce a lien, the plaintiff shall record in the office of the county recorder of the county, or of the several counties in which the property is situated, a notice of the pendency of the action, as provided in Title 4.5 (commencing with Section 405) of Part 2 of the Code of Civil Procedure, on or before 20 days after the commencement of the action. Only from the time of recording that notice shall a purchaser or encumbrancer of the property affected thereby be deemed to have constructive notice of the pendency of the action, and in that event only of its pendency against parties designated by their real names. *(Added by Stats.2010, c. 697 (S.B.189), § 20, operative July 1, 2012.)*

Operative Effect

For operative effect of Part 6, see Civil Code § 8052 and Stats.2010, c. 697 (S.B.189), § 105.

Law Revision Commission Comments

Section 8461 restates former Section 3146 without substantive change. See also Sections 1170 (recordation), 8058 (calculation of time), 8060 (filing and recordation of papers).

See also Section 8026 ("lien"). [40 Cal.L.Rev.Comm. Reports 49 [AR:apx5] (2010)].

Research References

Rutter, Cal. Practice Guide: Insurance Litigation Ch. 6I-B, B. Particular Surety Bond Coverages.
Miller and Starr California Real Estate § 11:63, Recorded Documents that Do Not Give Constructive Notice--Defectively or Improperly Recorded Instruments.
Miller and Starr California Real Estate § 28:59, Recording a Lis Pendens.
21 NO. 4 Miller & Starr, California Real Estate Newsalert 1, Everything Old is New Again: Impact of SB 189 on Mechanics' Lien Law.
3 Witkin Cal. Proc. 5th Actions § 380, (S 380) Specific Permissive Statutes.
4 Witkin, California Summary 10th Security Transactions in Real Property § 31G, (S 31G) (New)-Action to Foreclose Lien.

§ 8462. Dismissal

Notwithstanding Section 583.420 of the Code of Civil Procedure, if an action to enforce a lien is not brought to trial within two years after commencement of the action, the court may in its discretion dismiss the action for want of prosecution. *(Added by Stats.2010, c. 697 (S.B.189), § 20, operative July 1, 2012.)*

Operative Effect

For operative effect of Part 6, see Civil Code § 8052 and Stats.2010, c. 697 (S.B.189), § 105.

Law Revision Commission Comments

Section 8462 restates former Section 3147 without substantive change. The cross-reference to the Code of Civil Procedure is added to make clear that this section modifies the general three-year period for discretionary dismissal. See also Section 8056 (rules of practice).

See also Section 8026 ("lien"). [40 Cal.L.Rev.Comm. Reports 49 [AR:apx5] (2010)].

Research References

Miller and Starr California Real Estate § 28:61, Trial and Judgment.
4 Witkin, California Summary 10th Security Transactions in Real Property § 31G, (S 31G) (New)-Action to Foreclose Lien.

§ 8464. Costs

In addition to any other costs allowed by law, the court in an action to enforce a lien shall allow as costs to each claimant whose lien is established the amount paid to verify and record

the claim of lien, whether the claimant is a plaintiff or defendant. *(Added by Stats.2010, c. 697 (S.B.189), § 20, operative July 1, 2012.)*

Operative Effect

For operative effect of Part 6, see Civil Code § 8052 and Stats.2010, c. 697 (S.B.189), § 105.

Law Revision Commission Comments

Section 8464 continues former Section 3150 without substantive change. See also Sections 8004 ("claimant"), 8026 ("lien"). [40 Cal.L.Rev. Comm. Reports 49 [AR:apx5] (2010)].

Research References

Miller and Starr California Real Estate § 28:63, Costs and Attorney's Fees.

§ 8466. Deficiency judgment

If there is a deficiency of proceeds from the sale of property on a judgment for enforcement of a lien, a deficiency judgment may be entered against a party personally liable for the deficiency in the same manner and with the same effect as in an action to foreclose a mortgage. *(Added by Stats.2010, c. 697 (S.B.189), § 20, operative July 1, 2012.)*

Operative Effect

For operative effect of Part 6, see Civil Code § 8052 and Stats.2010, c. 697 (S.B.189), § 105.

Law Revision Commission Comments

Section 8466 restates former Section 3151 without substantive change. See also Section 8026 ("lien"). [40 Cal.L.Rev.Comm. Reports 49 [AR:apx5] (2010)].

Research References

Miller and Starr California Real Estate § 28:61, Trial and Judgment.
4 Witkin, California Summary 10th Security Transactions in Real Property § 31G, (S 31G) (New)-Action to Foreclose Lien.

§ 8468. Personal actions; application for writ of attachment; judgment; credit for money collected

(a) This chapter does not affect any of the following rights of a claimant:

(1) The right to maintain a personal action to recover a debt against the person liable, either in a separate action or in an action to enforce a lien.

(2) The right to a writ of attachment. In an application for a writ of attachment, the claimant shall refer to this section. The claimant's recording of a claim of lien does not affect the right to a writ of attachment.

(3) The right to enforce a judgment.

(b) A judgment obtained by the claimant in a personal action described in subdivision (a) does not impair or merge the claim of lien, but any amount collected on the judgment shall be credited on the amount of the lien. *(Added by Stats.2010, c. 697 (S.B.189), § 20, operative July 1, 2012.)*

Operative Effect

For operative effect of Part 6, see Civil Code § 8052 and Stats.2010, c. 697 (S.B.189), § 105.

Law Revision Commission Comments

Section 8468 restates former Section 3152 without substantive change. The reference in the introductory portion of the section to "this title" is changed to "this chapter" consistent with the scope of the chapter.

For provisions relating to attachment, see Code Civ. Proc. § 481.010 *et seq.* For provisions relating to enforcement of a money judgment, see Code Civ. Proc. § 681.010 *et seq.*

See also Sections 8004 ("claimant"), 8026 ("lien"), 8032 ("person"). [40 Cal.L.Rev.Comm. Reports 49 [AR:apx5] (2010)].

Research References

Miller and Starr California Real Estate § 28:2, Alternative (Cumulative) Remedies of the Claimant.
Miller and Starr California Real Estate § 28:26, Lien of a Subcontractor.
Miller and Starr California Real Estate § 28:65, Assignment of the Lien.
7 Witkin Cal. Proc. 5th Judgment § 402, Single Cause of Action.

§ 8470. Defense by contractor at own expense; withholding and deducting funds due contractor; recovery of judgment and costs by owner

In an action to enforce a lien for work provided to a contractor:

(a) The contractor shall defend the action at the contractor's own expense. During the pendency of the action the owner may withhold from the direct contractor the amount of the lien claim.

(b) If the judgment in the action is against the owner or the owner's property, the owner may deduct the amount of the judgment and costs from any amount owed to the direct contractor. If the amount of the judgment and costs exceeds the amount owed to the direct contractor, or if the owner has settled with the direct contractor in full, the owner may recover from the direct contractor, or the sureties on a bond given by the direct contractor for faithful performance of the direct contract, the amount of the judgment and costs that exceed the contract price and for which the direct contractor was originally liable. *(Added by Stats.2010, c. 697 (S.B.189), § 20, operative July 1, 2012.)*

Operative Effect

For operative effect of Part 6, see Civil Code § 8052 and Stats.2010, c. 697 (S.B.189), § 105.

Law Revision Commission Comments

Section 8470 restates former Section 3153 without substantive change. This section does not apply to an action to enforce a lien brought by a direct contractor.

See also Sections 8010 ("contract price"), 8012 ("contractor"), 8016 ("direct contract"), 8026 ("lien"), 8018 ("direct contractor"), 8048 ("work"). [40 Cal.L.Rev.Comm. Reports 49 [AR:apx5] (2010)].

Research References

California Real Estate Forms (Miller & Starr) § 4:3, Construction Contract--Small Project (Owner-Oriented).
California Real Estate Forms (Miller & Starr) § 4:6, Construction Contract--Fixed Price--Commercial Project.
California Real Estate Forms (Miller & Starr) § 4:11, Construction Contract--Construction Manager Representing Owner's Interests.
California Real Estate Forms (Miller & Starr) § 4:13, Construction Agreement--Tenant Improvements.
California Real Estate Forms (Miller & Starr) § 4:14, Construction Agreement-- Master Agreement for Construction Services.
California Real Estate Forms (Miller & Starr) § 4:15, Development Agreement.
California Real Estate Forms (Miller & Starr) § 4:20, Service Contract-- Elevators.
Miller and Starr California Real Estate § 28:25, Lien of a Direct Contractor.
Miller and Starr California Real Estate § 28:26, Lien of a Subcontractor.
21 NO. 4 Miller & Starr, California Real Estate Newsalert 1, Everything Old is New Again: Impact of SB 189 on Mechanics' Lien Law.

4 Witkin, California Summary 10th Security Transactions in Real Property § 31G, (S 31G) (New)-Action to Foreclose Lien.

ARTICLE 7. RELEASE ORDER

Section
8480. Release order; other actions or claims; joinder of claims.
8482. Time for petition; notice.
8484. Verified petition; contents.
8486. Hearing date; service.
8488. Hearing; burden of production; burden of proof; effect of judgment; attorney fees.

Operative Effect

For operative effect of Part 6, see Civil Code § 8052 and Stats.2010, c. 697 (S.B.189), § 105.

§ 8480. Release order; other actions or claims; joinder of claims

(a) The owner of property or the owner of any interest in property subject to a claim of lien may petition the court for an order to release the property from the claim of lien if the claimant has not commenced an action to enforce the lien within the time provided in Section 8460.

(b) This article does not bar any other cause of action or claim for relief by the owner of the property. A release order does not bar any other cause of action or claim for relief by the claimant, other than an action to enforce the claim of lien that is the subject of the release order.

(c) A petition for a release order under this article may be joined with a pending action to enforce the claim of lien that is the subject of the petition. No other action or claim for relief may be joined with a petition under this article.

(d) Notwithstanding Section 8056, Chapter 2.5 (commencing with Section 1141.10) of Title 3 of Part 3 of the Code of Civil Procedure does not apply to a proceeding under this article. *(Added by Stats.2010, c. 697 (S.B.189), § 20, operative July 1, 2012.)*

Operative Effect

For operative effect of Part 6, see Civil Code § 8052 and Stats.2010, c. 697 (S.B.189), § 105.

Law Revision Commission Comments

Subdivision (a) of Section 8480 restates former Section 3154(a) without substantive change.

Subdivision (b) restates the first sentence of former Section 3154(h) without substantive change. In *Solit v. Tokai Bank, Ltd. New York Branch,* 68 Cal.App.4th 1435, 81 Cal.Rptr.2d 243 (1999), the court held that an order releasing a lien because a lien had not been timely enforced may not bar the recordation of a new claim for the same work, if the time for recordation of a new claim of lien had not yet expired.

Subdivision (c) provides a limited exception to the last sentence of former Section 3154(h), allowing the petition to be joined with a pending action to enforce the claim of lien that is the subject of the petition.

Subdivision (d) continues former Section 3154(i) without substantive change.

See also Sections 8004 ("claimant"), 8026 ("lien"). [40 Cal.L.Rev. Comm. Reports 49 [AR:apx5] (2010)].

Research References

Miller and Starr California Real Estate § 28:37, Claim of Lien--Necessity, Purpose, and Effect.
Miller and Starr California Real Estate § 28:38, Time to File.
Miller and Starr California Real Estate § 28:67, Payment, Release, and Waiver of the Lien.

4 Witkin, California Summary 10th Security Transactions in Real Property § 31-I, (New)-Release of Lien.

§ 8482. Time for petition; notice

An owner of property may not petition the court for a release order under this article unless at least 10 days before filing the petition the owner gives the claimant notice demanding that the claimant execute and record a release of the claim of lien. The notice shall comply with the requirements of Chapter 2 (commencing with Section 8100) of Title 1, and shall state the grounds for the demand. *(Added by Stats.2010, c. 697 (S.B.189), § 20, operative July 1, 2012.)*

Operative Effect

For operative effect of Part 6, see Civil Code § 8052 and Stats.2010, c. 697 (S.B.189), § 105.

Law Revision Commission Comments

Section 8482 is new. If the lien claimant complies with the demand, a release proceeding is unnecessary.

See also Section 8058 (calculation of time).

See also Sections 8004 ("claimant"), 8026 ("lien"). [40 Cal.L.Rev. Comm. Reports 49 [AR:apx5] (2010)].

Research References

Miller and Starr California Real Estate § 28:67, Payment, Release, and Waiver of the Lien.
4 Witkin, California Summary 10th Security Transactions in Real Property § 31-I, (New)-Release of Lien.

§ 8484. Verified petition; contents

A petition for a release order shall be verified and shall allege all of the following:

(a) The date of recordation of the claim of lien. A certified copy of the claim of lien shall be attached to the petition.

(b) The county in which the claim of lien is recorded.

(c) The book and page or series number of the place in the official records where the claim of lien is recorded.

(d) The legal description of the property subject to the claim of lien.

(e) Whether an extension of credit has been granted under Section 8460, if so to what date, and that the time for commencement of an action to enforce the lien has expired.

(f) That the owner has given the claimant notice under Section 8482 demanding that the claimant execute and record a release of the lien and that the claimant is unable or unwilling to do so or cannot with reasonable diligence be found.

(g) Whether an action to enforce the lien is pending.

(h) Whether the owner of the property or interest in the property has filed for relief in bankruptcy or there is another restraint that prevents the claimant from commencing an action to enforce the lien. *(Added by Stats.2010, c. 697 (S.B.189), § 20, operative July 1, 2012.)*

Operative Effect

For operative effect of Part 6, see Civil Code § 8052 and Stats.2010, c. 697 (S.B.189), § 105.

Law Revision Commission Comments

Section 8484 restates former Section 3154(b).

The information included in the petition is intended to facilitate the court's order under Section 8488 (hearing and order). The reference to series number is added to cover a county in which the recorder uses a sequence number for record location.

See also Sections 1170 (recordation), 8060 (filing and recordation of papers).

See also Sections 8004 ("claimant"), 8026 ("lien"). [40 Cal.L.Rev. Comm. Reports 49 [AR:apx5] (2010)].

Research References

Miller and Starr California Real Estate § 28:67, Payment, Release, and Waiver of the Lien.
4 Witkin, California Summary 10th Security Transactions in Real Property § 31-I, (New)-Release of Lien.

§ 8486. Hearing date; service

(a) On the filing of a petition for a release order, the clerk shall set a hearing date. The date shall be not more than 30 days after the filing of the petition. The court may continue the hearing only on a showing of good cause, but in any event the court shall rule and make any necessary orders on the petition not later than 60 days after the filing of the petition.

(b) The petitioner shall serve a copy of the petition and a notice of hearing on the claimant at least 15 days before the hearing. Service shall be made in the same manner as service of summons, or by certified or registered mail, postage prepaid, return receipt requested, addressed to the claimant as provided in Section 8108.

(c) Notwithstanding Section 8116, when service is made by mail, service is complete on the fifth day following deposit of the petition and notice in the mail. *(Added by Stats.2010, c. 697 (S.B.189), § 20, operative July 1, 2012.)*

Operative Effect

For operative effect of Part 6, see Civil Code § 8052 and Stats.2010, c. 697 (S.B.189), § 105.

Law Revision Commission Comments

Section 8486 restates former Section 3154(c)-(d), and the first sentence of Section 3154(e), increasing the time for serving a copy of the petition and notice of hearing to 15 days, and adding a requirement that the court act no later than 60 days after the petition is filed. See also Section 8058 (calculation of time).

The specific notice provisions in subdivisions (b) and (c) supersede the general notice provisions in Sections 8100–8118, to the extent inconsistent.

See also Section 8004 ("claimant"). [40 Cal.L.Rev.Comm. Reports 49 [AR:apx5] (2010)].

Research References

Miller and Starr California Real Estate § 28:67, Payment, Release, and Waiver of the Lien.
4 Witkin, California Summary 10th Security Transactions in Real Property § 31-I, (New)-Release of Lien.

§ 8488. Hearing; burden of production; burden of proof; effect of judgment; attorney fees

(a) At the hearing both (1) the petition and (2) the issue of compliance with the service and date for hearing requirements of this article are deemed controverted by the claimant. The petitioner has the initial burden of producing evidence on those matters. The petitioner has the burden of proof as to the issue of compliance with the service and date for hearing requirements of this article. The claimant has the burden of proof as to the validity of the lien.

(b) If judgment is in favor of the petitioner, the court shall order the property released from the claim of lien.

(c) The prevailing party is entitled to reasonable attorney's fees. *(Added by Stats.2010, c. 697 (S.B.189), § 20, operative July 1, 2012.)*

Operative Effect

For operative effect of Part 6, see Civil Code § 8052 and Stats.2010, c. 697 (S.B.189), § 105.

Subdivision (a) of Section 8488 restates the last sentence of former Section 3154(b)(5) and the last two sentences of former Section 3154(e) without substantive change, except that language is added to clarify the burden of production and the burden of proof.

Subdivision (b) restates a part of former Section 3154(f); the remainder of the former provision is continued in Article 8 (commencing with Section 8490) (removal of claim of lien from record).

Subdivision (c) restates former Section 3154(g), deleting the $2,000 limitation.

See also Section 8056 (rules of practice), Evid. Code §§ 500 (burden of proof), 550 (burden of producing evidence).

See also Sections 8004 ("claimant"), 8026 ("lien"). [40 Cal.L.Rev. Comm. Reports 49 [AR:apx5] (2010)].

Research References

Miller and Starr California Real Estate § 28:67, Payment, Release, and Waiver of the Lien.
4 Witkin, California Summary 10th Security Transactions in Real Property § 31-I, (New)-Release of Lien.

ARTICLE 8. REMOVAL OF CLAIM OF LIEN FROM RECORD

Section
8490. Order dismissing cause of action or judgment that no lien exists; contents; effect of order or judgment; recordable instrument; application.
8494. Expiration or recordation of order or judgment; actual or constructive notice.

Operative Effect

For operative effect of Part 6, see Civil Code § 8052 and Stats.2010, c. 697 (S.B.189), § 105.

§ 8490. Order dismissing cause of action or judgment that no lien exists; contents; effect of order or judgment; recordable instrument; application

(a) A court order dismissing a cause of action to enforce a lien or releasing property from a claim of lien, or a judgment that no lien exists, shall include all of the following information:

(1) The date of recordation of the claim of lien.

(2) The county in which the claim of lien is recorded.

(3) The book and page or series number of the place in the official records where the claim of lien is recorded.

(4) The legal description of the property.

(b) A court order or judgment under this section is equivalent to cancellation of the claim of lien and its removal from the record.

(c) A court order or judgment under this section is a recordable instrument. On recordation of a certified copy of the court order or judgment, the property described in the order or judgment is released from the claim of lien.

(d) This section does not apply to a court order dismissing an action to enforce a lien that is expressly stated to be without prejudice. *(Added by Stats.2010, c. 697 (S.B.189), § 20, operative July 1, 2012.)*

Operative Effect

For operative effect of Part 6, see Civil Code § 8052 and Stats.2010, c. 697 (S.B.189), § 105.

Subdivision (a) of Section 8490 generalizes a part of former Section 3154(f). The reference to sequence number is added to cover a county in which the recorder uses a series number for record location. The reference to the city where the claim of lien is recorded is omitted as superfluous.

Subdivisions (b) and (d) generalize former Section 3148.

Subdivision (c) generalizes the second sentence of former Section 3154(f)(4).

See also Sections 1170 (recordation), 8058 (calculation of time), 8060 (filing and recordation of papers).

See also Section 8026 ("lien"). [40 Cal.L.Rev.Comm. Reports 49 [AR:apx5] (2010)].

Research References

Miller and Starr California Real Estate § 28:37, Claim of Lien--Necessity, Purpose, and Effect.
Miller and Starr California Real Estate § 28:38, Time to File.
Miller and Starr California Real Estate § 28:61, Trial and Judgment.
Miller and Starr California Real Estate § 28:67, Payment, Release, and Waiver of the Lien.
4 Witkin, California Summary 10th Security Transactions in Real Property § 31G, (S 31G) (New)-Action to Foreclose Lien.

§ 8494. Expiration or recordation of order or judgment; actual or constructive notice

If a claim of lien expires and is unenforceable under Section 8460, or if a court order or judgment is recorded under Section 8490, the claim of lien does not constitute actual or constructive notice of any of the matters contained, claimed, alleged, or contended in the claim of lien, or create a duty of inquiry in any person thereafter dealing with the affected property. *(Added by Stats.2010, c. 697 (S.B.189), § 20, operative July 1, 2012.)*

Operative Effect

For operative effect of Part 6, see Civil Code § 8052 and Stats.2010, c. 697 (S.B.189), § 105.

Section 8494 is drawn from Code of Civil Procedure Section 405.60 (lis pendens).

See also Sections 8026 ("lien"), 8032 ("person"). [40 Cal.L.Rev. Comm. Reports 49 [AR:apx5] (2010)].

Research References

3 Witkin Cal. Proc. 5th Actions § 221A, (S 221A) (New)-In General.
4 Witkin, California Summary 10th Security Transactions in Real Property § 31A, (S 31A) (New)-Nature and Purpose of Revision.

CHAPTER 5. STOP PAYMENT NOTICE

Operative Effect

For operative effect of Part 6, see Civil Code § 8052 and Stats.2010, c. 697 (S.B.189), § 105.

ARTICLE 1. GENERAL PROVISIONS

Section
8500. Exclusive remedy.
8502. Requirements; contents; amount claimed.
8504. False stop payment notice or willful inclusion of demand to withhold for work not provided.
8506. Notice.
8508. Validity of notice; conditions.
8510. Release bond.

Operative Effect

For operative effect of Part 6, see Civil Code § 8052 and Stats.2010, c. 697 (S.B.189), § 105.

§ 8500. Exclusive remedy

The rights of all persons furnishing work for any work of improvement, with respect to any fund for payment of construction costs, are governed exclusively by this chapter, and no person may assert any legal or equitable right with respect to the fund, other than a right created by a written contract between that person and the person holding the fund, except pursuant to the provisions of this chapter. *(Added by Stats.2010, c. 697 (S.B.189), § 20, operative July 1, 2012.)*

Operative Effect

For operative effect of Part 6, see Civil Code § 8052 and Stats.2010, c. 697 (S.B.189), § 105.

Law Revision Commission Comments

Section 8500 continues Section 3264 without substantive change, except that it is limited to a private work. See Section 8160 (application of title). For a comparable provision applicable to a public work, see Section 9350 (stop payment notice exclusive remedy to reach construction funds).

The reference to a "direct" written contract has been revised to avoid confusion with the term "direct contract." See Section 8016 ("direct contract"). The revision is non-substantive.

This section is not intended to either ratify or abrogate the holding of *Nibbi Brothers, Inc. v. Home Fed. Sav. & Loan Ass'n*, 205 Cal.App.3d 1415, 253 Cal.Rptr. 289 (1988), that in an appropriate case a person providing labor or materials may recover from a construction lender on a theory of unjust enrichment.

See also Sections 8032 ("person"), 8048 ("work"), 8050 ("work of improvement"). [40 Cal.L.Rev.Comm. Reports 49 [AR:apx5] (2010)].

Research References

Rutter, Cal. Practice Guide: Insurance Litigation Ch. 6I-B, B. Particular Surety Bond Coverages.

Miller and Starr California Real Estate § 28:75, Other Claims Against Construction Loan Funds; Demise of the Equitable Lien.

Miller and Starr California Real Estate § 28:77, Priority of Stop Payment Notices; Liability of Fund Holder.

Miller and Starr California Real Estate § 28:89, Duty of Public Agency After Receipt of Stop Payment Notice.

21 NO. 4 Miller & Starr, California Real Estate Newsalert 1, Everything Old is New Again: Impact of SB 189 on Mechanics' Lien Law.

3 Witkin Cal. Proc. 5th Actions § 219, (S 219) Private Property: Stop Notice.

3 Witkin Cal. Proc. 5th Actions § 221A, (S 221A) (New)-In General.

3 Witkin Cal. Proc. 5th Actions § 221D, (S 221D) (New)-Private Property: Stop Notice.

1 Witkin Cal. Summ. 10th Contracts § 911, (S 911) Works of Improvement Contracts.

4 Witkin, California Summary 10th Security Transactions in Real Property § 21, (S 21) No Subcontractor's Lien on Loan Fund.

4 Witkin, California Summary 10th Security Transactions in Real Property § 22, (S 22) No Contractor's Lien on Loan Fund.

4 Witkin, California Summary 10th Security Transactions in Real Property § 31A, (S 31A) (New)-Nature and Purpose of Revision.

§ 8502. Requirements; contents; amount claimed

(a) A stop payment notice shall comply with the requirements of Chapter 2 (commencing with Section 8100) of Title 1, and shall be signed and verified by the claimant.

(b) The notice shall include a general description of work to be provided, and an estimate of the total amount in value of the work to be provided.

(c) The amount claimed in the notice may include only the amount due the claimant for work provided through the date of the notice. *(Added by Stats.2010, c. 697 (S.B.189), § 20, operative July 1, 2012.)*

Operative Effect

For operative effect of Part 6, see Civil Code § 8052 and Stats.2010, c. 697 (S.B.189), § 105.

Law Revision Commission Comments

Section 8502 supersedes subdivisions (a) through (d) of former Section 3103. A stop payment notice may be executed by the claimant's agent. See Section 8066 (agency).

Subdivision (c) is drawn from the last sentence of former Section 3159(a)(3), and provides a special rule that supplements the requirement of Section 8102(a)(6)(C) (demand of claimant).

See also Sections 8100–8118 (notice).

See also Sections 8004 ("claimant"), 8044 ("stop payment notice"), 8048 ("work"). [40 Cal.L.Rev.Comm. Reports 49 [AR:apx5] (2010)].

Research References

Rutter, Cal. Practice Guide: Insurance Litigation Ch. 6I-B, B. Particular Surety Bond Coverages.

Miller and Starr California Real Estate § 28:28, Statutory Provisions Governing Notice.

Miller and Starr California Real Estate § 28:72, Contents of the Stop Payment Notice.

§ 8504. False stop payment notice or willful inclusion of demand to withhold for work not provided

A claimant that willfully gives a false stop payment notice or that willfully includes in the notice a demand to withhold for work that has not been provided forfeits all right to participate in the distribution of the funds withheld and all right to a lien under Chapter 4 (commencing with Section 8400). *(Added by Stats. 2010, c. 697 (S.B.189), § 20, operative July 1, 2012.)*

Operative Effect

For operative effect of Part 6, see Civil Code § 8052 and Stats.2010, c. 697 (S.B.189), § 105.

Law Revision Commission Comments

Section 8504 restates former Section 3168 without substantive change.

See also Sections 8004 ("claimant"), 8026 ("lien"), 8044 ("stop payment notice"), 8048 ("work"). [40 Cal.L.Rev.Comm. Reports 49 [AR:apx5] (2010)].

Research References

Miller and Starr California Real Estate § 28:72, Contents of the Stop Payment Notice.

Miller and Starr California Real Estate § 28:77, Priority of Stop Payment Notices; Liability of Fund Holder.

§ 8506. Notice

(a) A stop payment notice to an owner shall be given to the owner or to the owner's architect, if any.

(b) A stop payment notice to a construction lender holding construction funds shall not be effective unless given to the manager or other responsible officer or person at the office or branch of the lender administering or holding the construction funds.

(c) A stop payment notice shall comply with the requirements of Chapter 2 (commencing with Section 8100) of Title 1. *(Added by Stats.2010, c. 697 (S.B.189), § 20, operative July 1, 2012.)*

Operative Effect

For operative effect of Part 6, see Civil Code § 8052 and Stats.2010, c. 697 (S.B.189), § 105.

Subdivisions (a) and (b) of Section 8506 restate a part of the last two sentences of former Section 3083, and a part of the second paragraph of former Section 3103, without substantive change.

Subdivision (c) supersedes the last paragraph of former Section 3103.

See also Sections 8006 ("construction lender"), 8032 ("person"), 8044 ("stop payment notice"). [40 Cal.L.Rev.Comm. Reports 49 (2010)].

Miller and Starr California Real Estate § 28:73, Service of the Stop Payment Notice.

§ 8508. Validity of notice; conditions

A stop payment notice is not valid unless both of the following conditions are satisfied:

(a) The claimant gave preliminary notice to the extent required by Chapter 2 (commencing with Section 8200).

(b) The claimant gave the stop payment notice before expiration of the time within which a claim of lien must be recorded under Chapter 4 (commencing with Section 8400). *(Added by Stats.2010, c. 697 (S.B.189), § 20, operative July 1, 2012.)*

Operative Effect

For operative effect of Part 6, see Civil Code § 8052 and Stats.2010, c. 697 (S.B.189), § 105.

Section 8508 restates a part of the first sentence of former Section 3159 and former Section 3160 without substantive change. For the time within which a claim of lien must be recorded, see Sections 8412 and 8414 (time for claim of lien); see also Section 8186 (notice of completion of contract for portion of work of improvement). For the person to which the notice must be given, see Section 8506.

See also Sections 8004 ("claimant"), 8026 ("lien"), 8034 ("preliminary notice"), 8044 ("stop payment notice"). [40 Cal.L.Rev.Comm. Reports 49 [AR:apx5] (2010)].

Rutter, Cal. Practice Guide: Insurance Litigation Ch. 6I-B, B. Particular Surety Bond Coverages.
Miller and Starr California Real Estate § 28:30, Result of a Failure to Draft and Serve the Notice Properly.
Miller and Starr California Real Estate § 28:71, Requirement of a Preliminary Notice.
Miller and Starr California Real Estate § 28:73, Service of the Stop Payment Notice.
3 Witkin Cal. Proc. 5th Actions § 221D, (S 221D) (New)-Private Property: Stop Notice.

§ 8510. Release bond

(a) A person may obtain release of funds withheld pursuant to a stop payment notice by giving the person withholding the funds a release bond.

(b) A release bond shall be given by an admitted surety insurer and shall be conditioned for payment of any amount not exceeding the penal obligation of the bond that the claimant recovers on the claim, together with costs of suit awarded in the action. The bond shall be in an amount equal to 125 percent of the amount claimed in the stop payment notice.

(c) On receipt of a release bond, the person withholding funds pursuant to the stop payment notice shall release them. *(Added by Stats.2010, c. 697 (S.B.189), § 20, operative July 1, 2012.)*

Operative Effect

For operative effect of Part 6, see Civil Code § 8052 and Stats.2010, c. 697 (S.B.189), § 105.

Section 8510 restates former Section 3171, eliminating the restrictions on the persons and the conditions under which a release bond may be given, and requiring the bond to be given by an admitted surety insurer. See Sections 8002 ("admitted surety insurer"), 8150 (application of Bond and Undertaking Law).

See also Sections 8004 ("claimant"), 8032 ("person"), 8044 ("stop payment notice"). [40 Cal.L.Rev.Comm. Reports 49 [AR:apx5] (2010)].

Rutter, Cal. Practice Guide: Insurance Litigation Ch. 6I-B, B. Particular Surety Bond Coverages.
Rutter, Cal. Practice Guide: Insurance Litigation Ch. 6I-C, C. Surety's Obligations and Rights Upon Default by Principal.
Miller and Starr California Real Estate § 28:81, Release, Bond and Waiver of Stop Payment Notice.
Miller and Starr California Real Estate § 28:92, Construction-Related Bonds; in General.
21 NO. 4 Miller & Starr, California Real Estate Newsalert 1, Everything Old is New Again: Impact of SB 189 on Mechanics' Lien Law.
3 Witkin Cal. Proc. 5th Actions § 221A, (S 221A) (New)-In General.
4 Witkin, California Summary 10th Security Transactions in Real Property § 31A, (S 31A) (New)-Nature and Purpose of Revision.

ARTICLE 2. STOP PAYMENT NOTICE TO OWNER

Operative Effect

For operative effect of Part 6, see Civil Code § 8052 and Stats.2010, c. 697 (S.B.189), § 105.

§ 8520. Persons who may give notice

(a) A person that has a lien right under Chapter 4 (commencing with Section 8400), other than a direct contractor, may give the owner a stop payment notice.

(b) The owner may give notice, in compliance with the requirements of Chapter 2 (commencing with Section 8100) of Title 1, demanding that a person that has a lien right under Chapter 4 (commencing with Section 8400) give the owner a stop payment notice. If the person fails to give the owner a bonded or unbonded stop payment notice, the person forfeits the right to a lien under Chapter 4 (commencing with Section 8400). *(Added by Stats.2010, c. 697 (S.B.189), § 20, operative July 1, 2012.)*

Operative Effect

For operative effect of Part 6, see Civil Code § 8052 and Stats.2010, c. 697 (S.B.189), § 105.

Section 8520 restates former Section 3158. It makes clear that the owner's demand under subdivision (b) requires either a bonded or an unbonded stop payment notice.

See also Sections 8018 ("direct contractor"), 8026 ("lien"), 8032 ("person"), 8044 ("stop payment"). [40 Cal.L.Rev.Comm. Reports 49 [AR:apx5] (2010)].

Rutter, Cal. Practice Guide: Insurance Litigation Ch. 6I-B, B. Particular Surety Bond Coverages.
Miller and Starr California Real Estate § 28:8, "Claimant" Defined.
Miller and Starr California Real Estate § 28:68, Nature and Validity of the Stop Payment Notice.
Miller and Starr California Real Estate § 28:69, Owner's Right to Prevent, or to Require, Filing of Stop Payment Notice.

Miller and Starr California Real Estate § 28:70, Who May File a Stop
     Payment Notice.
Miller and Starr California Real Estate § 28:72, Contents of the Stop
     Payment Notice.
3 Witkin Cal. Proc. 5th Actions § 221D, (S 221D) (New)-Private
     Property: Stop Notice.

§ 8522. Withholding of sufficient amount to pay claim; exception

(a) Except as provided in subdivision (b), on receipt of a stop payment notice an owner shall withhold from the direct contractor or from any person acting under authority of a direct contractor a sufficient amount due or to become due to the direct contractor to pay the claim stated in the notice.

(b) The owner may, but is not required to, withhold funds if the owner has previously recorded a payment bond under Section 8600. If the owner does not withhold funds, the owner shall, within 30 days after receipt of the stop payment notice, give notice to the claimant that a payment bond has been recorded and provide the claimant a copy of the bond. The notice shall comply with the requirements of Chapter 2 (commencing with Section 8100) of Title 1. *(Added by Stats.2010, c. 697 (S.B.189), § 20, operative July 1, 2012.)*

Operative Effect

*For operative effect of Part 6, see Civil Code § 8052
and Stats.2010, c. 697 (S.B.189), § 105.*

Law Revision Commission Comments

Section 8522 restates former Section 3161.
     See also Sections 1170 (recordation), 8058 (calculation of time), 8060 (filing and recordation of papers).
     See also Sections 8004 ("claimant"), 8018 ("direct contractor"), 8030 ("payment bond"), 8032 ("person"), 8044 ("stop payment notice"). [40 Cal.L.Rev.Comm. Reports 49 [AR:apx5] (2010)].

Research References

Rutter, Cal. Practice Guide: Insurance Litigation Ch. 6I-B, B. Particular
     Surety Bond Coverages.
Miller and Starr California Real Estate § 28:76, Duty of Owner to
     Withhold Funds; Effect of a Bond.
Miller and Starr California Real Estate § 28:77, Priority of Stop Payment
     Notices; Liability of Fund Holder.
Miller and Starr California Real Estate § 28:81, Release, Bond and
     Waiver of Stop Payment Notice.

ARTICLE 3. STOP PAYMENT NOTICE TO CONSTRUCTION LENDER

Section
8530. Person who may give notice.
8532. Bond.
8534. Notice of objection to sufficiency of sureties; substitution.
8536. Withholding of sufficient funds; exception.
8538. Request for notice of election; requirements of notice; conditions for nonliability for failure to include copy of bond.

Operative Effect

*For operative effect of Part 6, see Civil Code § 8052
and Stats.2010, c. 697 (S.B.189), § 105.*

§ 8530. Person who may give notice

A person that has a lien right under Chapter 4 (commencing with Section 8400) may give a construction lender a stop payment notice. *(Added by Stats.2010, c. 697 (S.B.189), § 20, operative July 1, 2012.)*

Operative Effect

*For operative effect of Part 6, see Civil Code § 8052
and Stats.2010, c. 697 (S.B.189), § 105.*

Law Revision Commission Comments

Section 8530 restates a part of the first sentence of former Section 3159 without substantive change. See also Section 8508 (requirements for valid stop payment notice).

For provisions governing the amount withheld where the person giving a stop payment notice is a direct contractor or subcontractor and there is a claim of another subcontractor or material supplier, see Section 8542 (amount withheld).

See also Sections 8006 ("construction lender"), 8026 ("lien"), 8032 ("person"), 8044 ("stop payment notice"). [40 Cal.L.Rev.Comm. Reports 49 [AR:apx5] (2010)].

Research References

Rutter, Cal. Practice Guide: Insurance Litigation Ch. 6I-B, B. Particular
     Surety Bond Coverages.
Miller and Starr California Real Estate § 28:8, "Claimant" Defined.
Miller and Starr California Real Estate § 28:68, Nature and Validity of
     the Stop Payment Notice.
Miller and Starr California Real Estate § 28:70, Who May File a Stop
     Payment Notice.
Miller and Starr California Real Estate § 28:72, Contents of the Stop
     Payment Notice.
3 Witkin Cal. Proc. 5th Actions § 221D, (S 221D) (New)-Private
     Property: Stop Notice.

§ 8532. Bond

A claimant may give a construction lender a stop payment notice accompanied by a bond in an amount equal to 125 percent of the amount of the claim. The bond shall be conditioned that if the defendant recovers judgment in an action to enforce payment of the claim stated in the stop payment notice or to enforce a claim of lien recorded by the claimant, the claimant will pay all costs that are awarded the owner, direct contractor, or construction lender, and all damages to the owner, direct contractor, or construction lender that result from the stop payment notice or recordation of the claim of lien, not exceeding the amount of the bond. *(Added by Stats.2010, c. 697 (S.B.189), § 20, operative July 1, 2012.)*

Operative Effect

*For operative effect of Part 6, see Civil Code § 8052
and Stats.2010, c. 697 (S.B.189), § 105.*

Law Revision Commission Comments

Section 8532 restates the first sentence of former Section 3083 without substantive change. The former reference to "good and sufficient sureties" on the bond is omitted as unnecessary. See Code Civ. Proc. § 995.310 (sufficient sureties on bond required). The second two sentences of former Section 3083 are continued in Section 8506(b) (manner of giving stop payment notice).

See also Sections 8004 ("claimant"), 8006 ("construction lender"), 8018 ("direct contractor"), 8026 ("lien"), 8044 ("stop payment notice"). [40 Cal.L.Rev.Comm. Reports 49 [AR:apx5] (2010)].

Research References

Rutter, Cal. Practice Guide: Insurance Litigation Ch. 6I-B, B. Particular
     Surety Bond Coverages.
Miller and Starr California Real Estate § 28:74, Duty of Lender to
     Withhold Funds; Effect of a Bond.
Miller and Starr California Real Estate § 28:82, Damages for Wrongful
     Stop Payment Notice.
Miller and Starr California Real Estate § 28:92, Construction-Related
     Bonds; in General.

3 Witkin Cal. Proc. 5th Actions § 221D, (S 221D) (New)-Private Property: Stop Notice.

§ 8534. Notice of objection to sufficiency of sureties; substitution

(a) A construction lender that objects to the sufficiency of sureties on the bond given with a bonded stop payment notice shall give notice to the claimant of the objection, within 20 days after the bonded stop payment notice is given. The notice shall comply with the requirements of Chapter 2 (commencing with Section 8100) of Title 1.

(b) The claimant may within 10 days after notice of the objection is given substitute for the initial bond a bond executed by an admitted surety insurer. If the claimant does not substitute a bond executed by an admitted surety insurer, the construction lender may disregard the bonded stop payment notice and release all funds withheld in response to that notice. *(Added by Stats.2010, c. 697 (S.B.189), § 20, operative July 1, 2012.)*

Operative Effect

*For operative effect of Part 6, see Civil Code § 8052
and Stats.2010, c. 697 (S.B.189), § 105.*

Law Revision Commission Comments

Section 8534 restates former Section 3163 without substantive change. See also Section 8058 (calculation of time).

See also Sections 8002 ("admitted surety insurer"), 8004 ("claimant"), 8006 ("construction lender"), 8044 (("stop payment notice"). [40 Cal.L.Rev.Comm. Reports 49 [AR:apx5] (2010)].

Research References

Miller and Starr California Real Estate § 28:74, Duty of Lender to Withhold Funds; Effect of a Bond.

§ 8536. Withholding of sufficient funds; exception

(a) Except as provided in subdivision (b), on receipt of a stop payment notice a construction lender shall withhold from the borrower or other person to whom the lender or the owner is obligated to make payments or advancement out of the construction fund sufficient funds to pay the claim stated in the notice.

(b) The construction lender may, at its option, elect not to withhold funds in any of the following circumstances:

(1) The stop payment notice is unbonded.

(2) The stop payment notice is given by a claimant other than a direct contractor, and a payment bond is recorded before the lender is given any stop payment notice. *(Added by Stats.2010, c. 697 (S.B.189), § 20, operative July 1, 2012.)*

Operative Effect

*For operative effect of Part 6, see Civil Code § 8052
and Stats.2010, c. 697 (S.B.189), § 105.*

Law Revision Commission Comments

Section 8536 restates former Sections 3159(a)(1)-(2) and 3162(a)(1)-(2). The requirement in former Section 3162(a) that the lender withhold sufficient funds to pay any claim of lien that may be recorded therefor is omitted; any amount paid pursuant to a stop payment notice reduces the claim of lien. The reference to recordation of a payment bond "in the office of the county recorder where the site is located" is omitted from subdivision (b)(2) as unnecessary.

If a bonded stop payment notice is given by a direct contractor, the construction lender must withhold funds regardless of whether a payment bond has previously been recorded under Section 8600.

For provisions governing the amount withheld where the person giving a stop payment notice is a direct contractor or subcontractor and there is a claim of another subcontractor or material supplier, see Section 8542 (amount withheld).

See also Sections 1170 (recordation), 8060 (filing and recordation of papers).

See also Sections 8004 ("claimant"), 8006 ("construction lender"), 8018 ("direct contractor"), 8030 ("payment bond"), 8032 ("person"), 8044 ("stop payment notice"). [40 Cal.L.Rev.Comm. Reports 49 [AR:apx5] (2010)].

Research References

Rutter, Cal. Practice Guide: Insurance Litigation Ch. 6I-B, B. Particular Surety Bond Coverages.
Miller and Starr California Real Estate § 28:69, Owner's Right to Prevent, or to Require, Filing of Stop Payment Notice.
Miller and Starr California Real Estate § 28:74, Duty of Lender to Withhold Funds; Effect of a Bond.
Miller and Starr California Real Estate § 28:77, Priority of Stop Payment Notices; Liability of Fund Holder.
Miller and Starr California Real Estate § 28:81, Release, Bond and Waiver of Stop Payment Notice.

§ 8538. Request for notice of election; requirements of notice; conditions for nonliability for failure to include copy of bond

(a) The claimant may make a written request for notice of an election by the construction lender under Section 8536 not to withhold funds. The request shall be made at the time the claimant gives the construction lender the stop payment notice and shall be accompanied by a preaddressed, stamped envelope.

(b) If the construction lender elects not to withhold funds under Section 8536, the lender shall, within 30 days after making the election, give notice of that fact to a claimant who has requested notice of the election under subdivision (a). The notice shall comply with the requirements of Chapter 2 (commencing with Section 8100) of Title 1. If the basis of the election is the recordation of a payment bond under Section 8600, the construction lender shall include a copy of the bond with the notice.

(c) A construction lender is not liable for failure to include a copy of the bond with the notice under this section if all of the following conditions are satisfied:

(1) The failure was not intentional and resulted from a bona fide error.

(2) The lender maintains reasonable procedures to avoid an error of that type.

(3) The lender corrected the error not later than 20 days after the date the lender discovered the violation. *(Added by Stats. 2010, c. 697 (S.B.189), § 20, operative July 1, 2012.)*

Operative Effect

*For operative effect of Part 6, see Civil Code § 8052
and Stats.2010, c. 697 (S.B.189), § 105.*

Law Revision Commission Comments

Section 8538 restates former Sections 3159(a)(3) and 3162(a)(3) without substantive change, except that the last sentence of former Section 3159(a)(3) is continued in Section 8502(c) (contents of stop payment notice).

See also Section 8058 (calculation of time).

See also Sections 8004 ("claimant"), 8006 ("construction lender"), 8030 ("payment bond"), 8044 ("stop payment notice"). [40 Cal.L.Rev.Comm. Reports 49 [AR:apx5] (2010)].

Research References

Rutter, Cal. Practice Guide: Insurance Litigation Ch. 6I-B, B. Particular Surety Bond Coverages.
Miller and Starr California Real Estate § 28:74, Duty of Lender to Withhold Funds; Effect of a Bond.

Miller and Starr California Real Estate § 28:92, Construction-Related Bonds; in General.

ARTICLE 4. PRIORITIES

Section

8540. Order of priority; pro rata distribution.

8542. Recovery of net amount due only; maximum amount required to be withheld.

8544. Assignment of construction loan funds; rights of claimant not affected.

Operative Effect

For operative effect of Part 6, see Civil Code § 8052 and Stats.2010, c. 697 (S.B.189), § 105.

§ 8540. Order of priority; pro rata distribution

(a) Funds withheld pursuant to a stop payment notice shall be distributed in the following order of priority:

(1) First, to pay claims of persons that have given a bonded stop payment notice. If funds are insufficient to pay the claims of those persons in full, the funds shall be distributed pro rata among the claimants in the ratio that the claim of each bears to the aggregate of all claims for which a bonded stop payment notice is given.

(2) Second, to pay claims of persons that have given an unbonded stop payment notice. If funds are insufficient to pay the claims of those persons in full, the funds shall be distributed among the claimants in the ratio that the claim of each bears to the aggregate of all claims for which an unbonded stop payment notice is given.

(b) Pro rata distribution under this section shall be made among the persons entitled to share in the distribution without regard to the order in which the person has given a stop payment notice or commenced an enforcement action. *(Added by Stats.2010, c. 697 (S.B.189), § 20, operative July 1, 2012.)*

Operative Effect

For operative effect of Part 6, see Civil Code § 8052 and Stats.2010, c. 697 (S.B.189), § 105.

Law Revision Commission Comments

Section 8540 restates former Section 3167 without substantive change. Only valid claims, as determined in an enforcement action, are entitled to participate in the distribution. *Cf.* Idaho Lumber Co. v. Northwestern S. & L. Ass'n, 265 Cal.App.2d 490, 71 Cal.Rptr. 422 (1968).

The amount of the claim of a contractor is governed by Section 8542.

See also Sections 8004 ("claimant"), 8032 ("person"), 8044 ("stop payment notice"). [40 Cal.L.Rev.Comm. Reports 49 [AR:apx5] (2010)].

Research References

Miller and Starr California Real Estate § 28:77, Priority of Stop Payment Notices; Liability of Fund Holder.

§ 8542. Recovery of net amount due only; maximum amount required to be withheld

Notwithstanding Section 8540:

(a) If funds are withheld pursuant to a stop payment notice given to a construction lender by a direct contractor or subcontractor, the direct contractor or subcontractor may recover only the net amount due the direct contractor or subcontractor after deducting any funds that are withheld by the construction lender pursuant to the claims of subcontractors and material suppliers that have given a stop payment notice for work done on behalf of the direct contractor or subcontractor.

(b) In no event is the construction lender required to withhold, pursuant to a stop payment notice, more than the net amount provided in subdivision (a). Notwithstanding any other provision of this chapter, a construction lender is not liable for failure to withhold more than that net amount on receipt of a stop payment notice. *(Added by Stats.2010, c. 697 (S.B.189), § 20, operative July 1, 2012.)*

Operative Effect

For operative effect of Part 6, see Civil Code § 8052 and Stats.2010, c. 697 (S.B.189), § 105.

Law Revision Commission Comments

Section 8542 restates former Sections 3159(b)-(c) and 3162(b)-(c), except that the rules governing a bonded notice are generalized to also apply to funds that a construction lender actually withholds pursuant to an unbonded notice.

See also Sections 8006 ("construction lender"), 8018 ("direct contractor"), 8028 ("material supplier"), 8044 ("stop payment notice"), 8046 ("subcontractor"), 8048 ("work"). [40 Cal.L.Rev.Comm. Reports 49 [AR:apx5] (2010)].

Research References

Miller and Starr California Real Estate § 28:77, Priority of Stop Payment Notices; Liability of Fund Holder.

Miller and Starr California Real Estate § 28:78, Amount that Must be Withheld.

§ 8544. Assignment of construction loan funds; rights of claimant not affected

The rights of a claimant who gives a construction lender a stop payment notice are not affected by an assignment of construction loan funds made by the owner or direct contractor, and the stop payment notice has priority over the assignment, whether the assignment is made before or after the stop payment notice is given. *(Added by Stats.2010, c. 697 (S.B.189), § 20, operative July 1, 2012.)*

Operative Effect

For operative effect of Part 6, see Civil Code § 8052 and Stats.2010, c. 697 (S.B.189), § 105.

Law Revision Commission Comments

Section 8544 restates former Section 3166 without substantive change.

See also Sections 8004 ("claimant"), 8006 ("construction lender"), 8018 ("direct contractor"), 8044 ("stop payment notice"). [40 Cal.L.Rev. Comm. Reports 49 [AR:apx5] (2010)].

Research References

Rutter, Cal. Practice Guide: Insurance Litigation Ch. 6I-B, B. Particular Surety Bond Coverages.

Miller and Starr California Real Estate § 28:77, Priority of Stop Payment Notices; Liability of Fund Holder.

Miller and Starr California Real Estate § 28:79, Effect of Assignment of Loan Funds or Inadequate Funds.

Miller and Starr California Real Estate § 28:80, Effect of Inadequate Funds to Pay Claimants and to Complete Construction.

Miller and Starr California Real Estate § 11:111, Liens for Future Advances--Construction Loans.

ARTICLE 5. ENFORCEMENT OF CLAIM STATED IN STOP PAYMENT NOTICE

Section

8550. Time for commencement of action; notice.

8552. Multiple claimants.

8554. Dismissal for want of prosecution.

8556. Dismissal or judgment; effect.

8558. Attorney fees; prevailing party.

8560. Interest.

Operative Effect

*For operative effect of Part 6, see Civil Code § 8052
and Stats.2010, c. 697 (S.B.189), § 105.*

§ 8550. Time for commencement of action; notice

(a) A claimant shall commence an action to enforce payment of the claim stated in a stop payment notice at any time after 10 days from the date the claimant gives the stop payment notice.

(b) A claimant shall commence an action to enforce payment of the claim stated in a stop payment notice not later than 90 days after expiration of the time within which a stop payment notice must be given.

(c) An action under this section may not be brought to trial or judgment entered before expiration of the time provided in subdivision (b).

(d) If a claimant does not commence an action to enforce payment of the claim stated in a stop payment notice within the time prescribed in subdivision (b), the notice ceases to be effective and the person withholding funds pursuant to the notice shall release them.

(e) Within five days after commencement of an action to enforce payment of the claim stated in a stop payment notice, the claimant shall give notice of commencement of the action to the persons to whom the stop payment notice was given. The notice shall comply with the requirements of Chapter 2 (commencing with Section 8100) of Title 1. *(Added by Stats.2010, c. 697 (S.B.189), § 20, operative July 1, 2012.)*

Operative Effect

*For operative effect of Part 6, see Civil Code § 8052
and Stats.2010, c. 697 (S.B.189), § 105.*

Law Revision Commission Comments

Section 8550 restates former Section 3172 without substantive change.

A stop payment notice must be given before expiration of the time within which a claim of lien must be recorded under Chapter 4 (commencing with Section 8400). See Section 8508 (requirements for valid stop payment notice).

For the manner in which notice of commencement of an enforcement action is to be given, see Section 8506 (manner of giving stop payment notice).

Funds released for failure to timely commence an enforcement action must be paid or delivered to the person to which they are due. See also Section 8058 (calculation of time).

See also Sections 8004 ("claimant"), 8032 ("person"), 8044 ("stop payment notice"). [40 Cal.L.Rev.Comm. Reports 49 [AR:apx5] (2010)].

Research References

Rutter, Cal. Practice Guide: Insurance Litigation Ch. 6I-B, B. Particular Surety Bond Coverages.

Miller and Starr California Real Estate § 28:83, Suit to Enforce the Stop Payment Notice.

3 Witkin Cal. Proc. 5th Actions § 477, (S 477) Ninety Days or Three Months.

§ 8552. Multiple claimants

If more than one claimant has given a stop payment notice:

(a) Any number of claimants may join in the same enforcement action.

(b) If claimants commence separate actions, the court first acquiring jurisdiction may order the actions consolidated.

(c) On motion of the owner or construction lender the court shall require all claimants to be impleaded in one action, to the end that the rights of all parties may be adjudicated in the action. *(Added by Stats.2010, c. 697 (S.B.189), § 20, operative July 1, 2012.)*

Operative Effect

*For operative effect of Part 6, see Civil Code § 8052
and Stats.2010, c. 697 (S.B.189), § 105.*

Law Revision Commission Comments

Section 8552 restates former Section 3175 without substantive change. Subdivision (a) is a specific application of the general rule stated in Section 8056 (rules of practice).

See also Sections 8004 ("claimant"), 8006 ("construction lender"), 8044 ("stop payment notice"). [40 Cal.L.Rev.Comm. Reports 49 [AR:apx5] (2010)].

Research References

Rutter, Cal. Practice Guide: Civil Trials & Evidence Ch. 4-H, H. Motions to Consolidate or Coordinate Separate Cases.

Miller and Starr California Real Estate § 28:83, Suit to Enforce the Stop Payment Notice.

4 Witkin Cal. Proc. 5th Pleading § 342, Statutory Basis.

§ 8554. Dismissal for want of prosecution

Notwithstanding Section 583.420 of the Code of Civil Procedure, if an action to enforce payment of the claim stated in a stop payment notice is not brought to trial within two years after commencement of the action, the court may in its discretion dismiss the action for want of prosecution. *(Added by Stats.2010, c. 697 (S.B.189), § 20, operative July 1, 2012.)*

Operative Effect

*For operative effect of Part 6, see Civil Code § 8052
and Stats.2010, c. 697 (S.B.189), § 105.*

Law Revision Commission Comments

Section 8554 restates former Section 3173 without substantive change. The cross-reference to the Code of Civil Procedure is added to make clear that this section modifies the general three-year period for discretionary dismissal. *Cf.* Section 8056 (rules of practice).

See also Section 8044 ("stop payment notice"). [40 Cal.L.Rev.Comm. Reports 49 [AR:apx5] (2010)].

Research References

Miller and Starr California Real Estate § 28:83, Suit to Enforce the Stop Payment Notice.

§ 8556. Dismissal or judgment; effect

A stop payment notice ceases to be effective, and a person withholding funds pursuant to the notice shall release them, in either of the following circumstances:

(a) An action to enforce payment of the claim stated in the stop payment notice is dismissed, unless expressly stated to be without prejudice.

(b) Judgment in an action to enforce payment of the claim stated in the stop payment notice is against the claimant. *(Added by Stats.2010, c. 697 (S.B.189), § 20, operative July 1, 2012.)*

Operative Effect

*For operative effect of Part 6, see Civil Code § 8052
and Stats.2010, c. 697 (S.B.189), § 105.*

Law Revision Commission Comments

Section 8556 restates former Section 3174 without substantive change. Funds released as a result of dismissal of the action or judgment against the claimant must be paid or delivered to the person to which they are due.

See also Sections 8004 ("claimant"), 8032 ("person"), 8044 ("stop payment notice"). [40 Cal.L.Rev.Comm. Reports 49 [AR:apx5] (2010)].

Research References

Miller and Starr California Real Estate § 28:83, Suit to Enforce the Stop Payment Notice.

§ 8558. Attorney fees; prevailing party

(a) In an action to enforce payment of the claim stated in a bonded stop payment notice, the prevailing party is entitled to a reasonable attorney's fee in addition to costs and damages.

(b) The court, on notice and motion by a party, shall determine who is the prevailing party or that there is no prevailing party for the purpose of this section, regardless of whether the action proceeds to final judgment. The prevailing party is the party that recovers greater relief in the action, subject to the following limitations:

(1) If the action is voluntarily dismissed or dismissed pursuant to a settlement, there is no prevailing party.

(2) If the defendant tenders to the claimant the full amount to which the claimant is entitled, and deposits in court for the claimant the amount so tendered, and alleges those facts in the answer and the allegation is determined to be true, the defendant is deemed to be the prevailing party. *(Added by Stats.2010, c. 697 (S.B.189), § 20, operative July 1, 2012.)*

Operative Effect

For operative effect of Part 6, see Civil Code § 8052 and Stats.2010, c. 697 (S.B.189), § 105.

Law Revision Commission Comments

Section 8558 restates former Section 3176 without substantive change.

See also Sections 8004 ("claimant"), 8044 ("stop payment notice"). [40 Cal.L.Rev.Comm. Reports 49 [AR:apx5] (2010)].

Research References

Rutter, Cal. Practice Guide: Insurance Litigation Ch. 6I-B, B. Particular Surety Bond Coverages.

Rutter, Cal. Practice Guide: Insurance Litigation Ch. 6I-C, C. Surety's Obligations and Rights Upon Default by Principal.

Miller and Starr California Real Estate § 28:78, Amount that Must be Withheld.

Miller and Starr California Real Estate § 28:81, Release, Bond and Waiver of Stop Payment Notice.

Miller and Starr California Real Estate § 28:82, Damages for Wrongful Stop Payment Notice.

Miller and Starr California Real Estate § 28:84, Recovery of Attorney's Fees.

7 Witkin Cal. Proc. 5th Judgment § 230, (S 230) Actions Involving Real Property or Environmental Issues.

§ 8560. Interest

If the claimant is the prevailing party in an action to enforce payment of the claim stated in a bonded stop payment notice, any amount awarded on the claim shall include interest at the legal rate calculated from the date the stop payment notice is given. *(Added by Stats.2010, c. 697 (S.B.189), § 20, operative July 1, 2012.)*

Operative Effect

For operative effect of Part 6, see Civil Code § 8052 and Stats.2010, c. 697 (S.B.189), § 105.

Law Revision Commission Comments

Section 8560 continues former Section 3176.5 without substantive change.

See also Sections 8004 ("claimant"), 8044 ("stop payment notice"). [40 Cal.L.Rev.Comm. Reports 49 [AR:apx5] (2010)].

Research References

Rutter, Cal. Practice Guide: Insurance Litigation Ch. 6I-B, B. Particular Surety Bond Coverages.

Rutter, Cal. Practice Guide: Insurance Litigation Ch. 6I-C, C. Surety's Obligations and Rights Upon Default by Principal.

Miller and Starr California Real Estate § 28:78, Amount that Must be Withheld.

Miller and Starr California Real Estate § 28:81, Release, Bond and Waiver of Stop Payment Notice.

Miller and Starr California Real Estate § 28:83, Suit to Enforce the Stop Payment Notice.

Miller and Starr California Real Estate § 28:89, Duty of Public Agency After Receipt of Stop Payment Notice.

3 Witkin Cal. Proc. 5th Actions § 221A, (S 221A) (New)-In General.

4 Witkin, California Summary 10th Security Transactions in Real Property § 31A, (S 31A) (New)-Nature and Purpose of Revision.

CHAPTER 6. PAYMENT BOND

Operative Effect

For operative effect of Part 6, see Civil Code § 8052 and Stats.2010, c. 697 (S.B.189), § 105.

§ 8600. Application; restriction of lien enforcement

(a) This section applies if, before the commencement of work, the owner in good faith files a direct contract with the county recorder, and records a payment bond of the direct contractor in an amount not less than 50 percent of the price stated in the direct contract.

(b) If the conditions of subdivision (a) are satisfied, the court shall, where equitable to do so, restrict lien enforcement under this title to the aggregate amount due from the owner to the direct contractor and shall enter judgment against the direct contractor and surety on the bond for any deficiency that remains between the amount due to the direct contractor and the whole amount due to claimants. *(Added by Stats.2010, c. 697 (S.B.189), § 20, operative July 1, 2012.)*

Operative Effect

For operative effect of Part 6, see Civil Code § 8052 and Stats.2010, c. 697 (S.B.189), § 105.

Law Revision Commission Comments

Subdivision (a) of Section 8600 restates the first part of former Section 3235 and the first sentence of former Section 3236 without substantive change. It makes clear that the bond, as well as the contract, must be recorded before the commencement of work. See also Sections 1170 (recordation), 8060 (filing and recordation of papers).

Subdivision (b) restates the last part of former Section 3235 without substantive change.

See also Sections 8004 ("claimant"), 8016 ("direct contract"), 8018 ("direct contractor"), 8026 ("lien"), 8030 ("payment bond"), 8048 ("work"). [40 Cal.L.Rev.Comm. Reports 49 [AR:apx5] (2010)].

Research References

Rutter, Cal. Practice Guide: Insurance Litigation Ch. 6I-B, B. Particular Surety Bond Coverages.

Miller and Starr California Real Estate § 11:6, Instruments Subject to Recording--List of Recordable Documents.

Miller and Starr California Real Estate § 11:68, Constructive Notice of Interests Barred by the Statute of Limitations--"Ancient Documents" and the Marketable Record Title Act.

Miller and Starr California Real Estate § 28:27, Limiting Owner's Liability by Recording Direct Contract and Bond.

Miller and Starr California Real Estate § 28:74, Duty of Lender to Withhold Funds; Effect of a Bond.

Miller and Starr California Real Estate § 28:92, Construction-Related Bonds; in General.

Miller and Starr California Real Estate § 28:110, No Exoneration of the Surety Under Bonds in Favor of Claimants.

Miller and Starr California Real Estate § 28:118, Action by Claimant to Recover on a Bond as to Private Projects--In General.

21 NO. 4 Miller & Starr, California Real Estate Newsalert 1, Everything Old is New Again: Impact of SB 189 on Mechanics' Lien Law.

3 Witkin Cal. Proc. 5th Actions § 222, Action on Payment Bond for Work of Improvement.

3 Witkin Cal. Proc. 5th Actions § 221A, (S 221A) (New)-In General.

3 Witkin Cal. Proc. 5th Actions § 222A, (S 222A) (New)-Revised Law for Action on Payment Bond for Work of Improvement.

4 Witkin, California Summary 10th Security Transactions in Real Property § 31A, (S 31A) (New)-Nature and Purpose of Revision.

4 Witkin, California Summary 10th Security Transactions in Real Property § 31D, (New)-Amount of Lien.

§ 8602. Bond or other security

Section 8600 does not preclude an owner from requiring a performance bond, payment bond, or other security as protection against a direct contractor's failure to perform the direct contract or to make full payment for all work provided pursuant to the contract. *(Added by Stats.2010, c. 697 (S.B.189), § 20, operative July 1, 2012.)*

Operative Effect

For operative effect of Part 6, see Civil Code § 8052 and Stats.2010, c. 697 (S.B.189), § 105.

Law Revision Commission Comments

Section 8602 restates the second sentence of former Section 3236 without substantive change.

See also Sections 8016 ("direct contract"), 8018 ("direct contractor"), 8030 ("payment bond"), 8048 ("work"). [40 Cal.L.Rev.Comm. Reports 49 [AR:apx5] (2010)].

Research References

Miller and Starr California Real Estate § 11:6, Instruments Subject to Recording--List of Recordable Documents.

Miller and Starr California Real Estate § 11:68, Constructive Notice of Interests Barred by the Statute of Limitations--"Ancient Documents" and the Marketable Record Title Act.

Miller and Starr California Real Estate § 28:110, No Exoneration of the Surety Under Bonds in Favor of Claimants.

§ 8604. Lending institutions; objections to bond

(a) If a lending institution requires that a payment bond be given as a condition of lending money to finance a work of improvement, and accepts in writing as sufficient a bond given in fulfillment of the requirement, the lending institution may not thereafter object to the borrower as to the validity of the bond or refuse to make the loan based on an objection to the bond if the bond is given by an admitted surety insurer.

(b) For purposes of this section, a "lending institution" includes a commercial bank, savings and loan institution, credit union, or other organization or person engaged in the business of financing loans. *(Added by Stats.2010, c. 697 (S.B.189), § 20, operative July 1, 2012.)*

Operative Effect

For operative effect of Part 6, see Civil Code § 8052 and Stats.2010, c. 697 (S.B.189), § 105.

Law Revision Commission Comments

Section 8604 supersedes former Section 3237. It makes clear that the lender may not object to the bond if given by an admitted surety insurer.

This section is not intended to either ratify or abrogate the holding of *Azusa Western, Inc. v. City of West Covina*, 45 Cal.App.3d 259, 119 Cal.Rptr. 434 (1975), requiring a public entity in an appropriate case to ensure that the surety on a stop payment notice release bond is not the surety that issued a payment bond on the project.

See also Sections 8002 ("admitted surety insurer"), 8030 ("payment bond"), 8032 ("person"), 8050 ("work of improvement"). [40 Cal.L.Rev. Comm. Reports 49 [AR:apx5] (2010)].

§ 8606. Nature of bond; principal; enforcement

(a) A payment bond under this title shall be conditioned for the payment in full of the claims of all claimants and shall by its terms inure to the benefit of all claimants so as to give a claimant a right of action to enforce the liability on the bond. The bond shall be given by an admitted surety insurer.

(b) An owner, direct contractor, or subcontractor may be the principal on the bond.

(c) A claimant may enforce the liability on the bond in an action to enforce a lien under this part or in a separate action on the bond. *(Added by Stats.2010, c. 697 (S.B.189), § 20, operative July 1, 2012.)*

Operative Effect

For operative effect of Part 6, see Civil Code § 8052 and Stats.2010, c. 697 (S.B.189), § 105.

Law Revision Commission Comments

Section 8606 restates former Section 3096 without substantive change, except to add a requirement that the bond be given by an admitted surety insurer. See also Section 8150 (application of Bond and Undertaking Law).

See also Sections 8002 ("admitted surety insurer"), 8004 ("claimant"), 8018 ("direct contractor"), 8026 ("lien"), 8030 ("payment bond"), 8046 ("subcontractor"). [40 Cal.L.Rev.Comm. Reports 49 [AR:apx5] (2010)].

Research References

Rutter, Cal. Practice Guide: Insurance Litigation Ch. 6I-B, B. Particular Surety Bond Coverages.

Miller and Starr California Real Estate § 28:2, Alternative (Cumulative) Remedies of the Claimant.

Miller and Starr California Real Estate § 28:27, Limiting Owner's Liability by Recording Direct Contract and Bond.

Miller and Starr California Real Estate § 28:92, Construction-Related Bonds; in General.

Miller and Starr California Real Estate § 11:146, Priority of the Construction Loan Deed of Trust--Effect of a Bond Recorded by the Construction Lender.

Miller and Starr California Real Estate § 28:118, Action by Claimant to Recover on a Bond as to Private Projects--In General.

§ 8608. Work done for direct contractor on bond; claim

(a) This title does not give a claimant a right to recover on a direct contractor's payment bond given under this chapter unless the claimant provided work to the direct contractor either directly or through one or more subcontractors, pursuant to a direct contract.

(b) Nothing in this section affects the stop payment notice right of, and relative priorities among, design professionals and holders of secured interests in the real property. *(Added by Stats.2010, c. 697 (S.B.189), § 20, operative July 1, 2012.)*

Operative Effect

For operative effect of Part 6, see Civil Code § 8052 and Stats.2010, c. 697 (S.B.189), § 105.

Law Revision Commission Comments

Section 8608 restates former Section 3267 without substantive change, clarifying that claimants providing work to subcontractors at every level have a right to recover against a direct contractor's payment bond as provided in this section. See Union Asphalt, Inc. v. Planet Ins. Co., 21 Cal.App.4th 1762, 27 Cal.Rptr.2d 371 (1994).

Note that design professional includes a licensed landscape architect. See Section 8014.

See also Sections 8004 ("claimant"), 8016 ("direct contract"), 8018 ("direct contractor"), 8030 ("payment bond"), 8044 ("stop payment notice"), 8046 ("subcontractor"), 8048 ("work"). [40 Cal.L.Rev.Comm. Reports 49 [AR:apx5] (2010)].

Research References

Rutter, Cal. Practice Guide: Insurance Litigation Ch. 6I-B, B. Particular Surety Bond Coverages.
Miller and Starr California Real Estate § 28:118, Action by Claimant to Recover on a Bond as to Private Projects--In General.
Miller and Starr California Real Estate § 28:121, Action by Claimants and Others on Public Works Payment Bond--In General.
1 Witkin Cal. Summ. 10th Contracts § 1001, Miscellaneous Provisions.

§ 8609. Invalidity of provisions limiting actions

Any provision in a payment bond attempting by contract to shorten the period prescribed in Section 337 of the Code of Civil Procedure for the commencement of an action on the bond shall not be valid under either of the following circumstances:

(a) If the provision attempts to limit the time for commencement of an action on the bond to a shorter period than six months from the completion of any work of improvement.

(b) As applied to any action brought by a claimant, unless the bond is recorded before the work of improvement is commenced. *(Added by Stats.2010, c. 697 (S.B.189), § 20, operative July 1, 2012.)*

Operative Effect

For operative effect of Part 6, see Civil Code § 8052 and Stats.2010, c. 697 (S.B.189), § 105.

Law Revision Commission Comments

Section 8609 continues former Section 3239 without substantive change. See also Sections 1170 (recordation), 8060 (filing and recordation of papers), 8180 (completion).

See also Sections 8004 ("claimant"), 8030 ("payment bond"), 8050 ("work of improvement"). [40 Cal.L.Rev.Comm. Reports 49 [AR:apx5] (2010)].

Research References

Rutter, Cal. Practice Guide: Insurance Litigation Ch. 6I-B, B. Particular Surety Bond Coverages.
Miller and Starr California Real Estate § 28:113, Statute of Limitations--Action by Owner or Obligee.
Miller and Starr California Real Estate § 28:119, Statute of Limitations--Action by Claimant.
3 Witkin Cal. Proc. 5th Actions § 469, (S 469) General Rule: Shorter Period is Valid If Reasonable.

§ 8610. Bonds recorded before improvements completed; actions against sureties

Notwithstanding Section 8609, if a payment bond under this title is recorded before completion of a work of improvement, an action to enforce the liability on the bond may not be commenced later than six months after completion of the work of improvement. *(Added by Stats.2010, c. 697 (S.B.189), § 20, operative July 1, 2012.)*

Operative Effect

For operative effect of Part 6, see Civil Code § 8052 and Stats.2010, c. 697 (S.B.189), § 105.

Law Revision Commission Comments

Section 8610 restates former Section 3240, broadening it to cover enforcement of any liability on the bond, not limited to the liability of the surety. *Cf.* Code Civ. Proc. § 996.440 (judgment on bond against principal and sureties).

See also Sections 1170 (recordation), 8060 (filing and recordation of papers), 8180 (completion).

See also Sections 8030 ("payment bond"), 8050 ("work of improvement"). [40 Cal.L.Rev.Comm. Reports 49 [AR:apx5] (2010)].

Research References

Rutter, Cal. Practice Guide: Insurance Litigation Ch. 6I-B, B. Particular Surety Bond Coverages.
Miller and Starr California Real Estate § 28:113, Statute of Limitations--Action by Owner or Obligee.
Miller and Starr California Real Estate § 28:118, Action by Claimant to Recover on a Bond as to Private Projects--In General.
Miller and Starr California Real Estate § 28:119, Statute of Limitations--Action by Claimant.

§ 8612. Preliminary notice required; notice to surety and bond principal; extension; exceptions

(a) In order to enforce a claim against a payment bond under this title, a claimant shall give the preliminary notice provided in Chapter 2 (commencing with Section 8200).

(b) If preliminary notice was not given as provided in Chapter 2 (commencing with Section 8200), a claimant may enforce a claim by giving written notice to the surety and the bond principal within 15 days after recordation of a notice of completion. If no notice of completion has been recorded, the time for giving written notice to the surety and the bond principal is extended to 75 days after completion of the work of improvement.

(c) Commencing July 1, 2012, and except as provided in subdivision (b), if the preliminary notice was required to be given by a person who has no direct contractual relationship with the contractor, and who has not given notice as provided in Chapter 2 (commencing with Section 8200), that person may enforce a claim by giving written notice to the surety and the bond principal, as provided in Section 8614, within 15 days after recordation of a notice of completion. If no notice of completion has been recorded, the time for giving written notice to the surety and the bond principal is extended to 75 days after completion of the work of improvement.

(d) Subdivision (c) shall not apply in either of the following circumstances:

(1) All progress payments, except for those disputed in good faith, have been made to a subcontractor who has a direct contractual relationship with the general contractor to whom the claimant has provided materials or services.

(2) The subcontractor who has a direct contractual relationship with the general contractor to whom the claimant has provided materials or services has been terminated from the project pursuant to the contract, and all progress payments, except those disputed in good faith, have been made as of the termination date.

(e) Pursuant to Section 8200, this section shall not apply to a laborer, as defined under Section 8024.

(f) This section shall become operative on July 1, 2012. *(Added by Stats.2010, c. 697 (S.B.189), § 20, operative July 1, 2012. Amended by Stats.2011, c. 700 (S.B.293), § 3, operative July 1, 2012.)*

Operative Effect

For operative effect of Part 6, see Civil Code § 8052 and Stats.2010, c. 697 (S.B.189), § 105.

Law Revision Commission Comments

Section 8612 restates former Section 3242 without substantive change. The former limitation to a contract entered into on or after January 1, 1995, is omitted due to lapse of time.

See also Sections 1170 (recordation), 8100–8118 (notice), 8058 (calculation of time), 8060 (filing and recordation of papers), 8180 (completion), 8182 (notice of completion), 8184 (notice of completion of contract for portion of work of improvement).

See also Sections 8004 ("claimant"), 8030 ("payment bond"), 8034 ("preliminary notice"), 8050 ("work of improvement"). [40 Cal.L.Rev. Comm. Reports 49 [AR:apx5] (2010)].

Research References

Rutter, Cal. Practice Guide: Insurance Litigation Ch. 6I-B, B. Particular Surety Bond Coverages.

Miller and Starr California Real Estate § 28:31, Who Must Give, and Who Must Receive, The Preliminary Notice.

Miller and Starr California Real Estate § 28:98, Notice as Condition Precedent to Surety's Liability on Payment Bond.

Miller and Starr California Real Estate § 28:118, Action by Claimant to Recover on a Bond as to Private Projects--In General.

22 NO. 4 Miller & Starr, California Real Estate Newsalert 8, Construction Law and Contracting.

3 Witkin Cal. Proc. 5th Actions § 222A, (S 222A) (New)-Revised Law for Action on Payment Bond for Work of Improvement.

§ 8614. Notice requirements

Notice to the principal and surety under Section 8612 shall comply with the requirements of Chapter 2 (commencing with Section 8100) of Title 1. *(Added by Stats.2010, c. 697 (S.B.189), § 20, operative July 1, 2012.)*

Operative Effect

For operative effect of Part 6, see Civil Code § 8052 and Stats.2010, c. 697 (S.B.189), § 105.

Law Revision Commission Comments

Section 8614 restates former Section 3227.

Cf. Code Civ. Proc. §§ 995.170 ("principal"), 995.185 ("surety"). [40 Cal.L.Rev.Comm. Reports 49 [AR:apx5] (2010)].

Research References

Miller and Starr California Real Estate § 28:31, Who Must Give, and Who Must Receive, The Preliminary Notice.

Miller and Starr California Real Estate § 28:98, Notice as Condition Precedent to Surety's Liability on Payment Bond.

Miller and Starr California Real Estate § 28:118, Action by Claimant to Recover on a Bond as to Private Projects--In General.

21 NO. 4 Miller & Starr, California Real Estate Newsalert 1, Everything Old is New Again: Impact of SB 189 on Mechanics' Lien Law.

3 Witkin Cal. Proc. 5th Actions § 221A, (S 221A) (New)-In General.

3 Witkin Cal. Proc. 5th Actions § 222A, (S 222A) (New)-Revised Law for Action on Payment Bond for Work of Improvement.

4 Witkin, California Summary 10th Security Transactions in Real Property § 31A, (S 31A) (New)-Nature and Purpose of Revision.

CHAPTER 7. SECURITY FOR LARGE PROJECT

Operative Effect

For operative effect of Part 6, see Civil Code § 8052 and Stats.2010, c. 697 (S.B.189), § 105.

ARTICLE 1. APPLICATION OF CHAPTER

Operative Effect

For operative effect of Part 6, see Civil Code § 8052 and Stats.2010, c. 697 (S.B.189), § 105.

§ 8700. Conditions for application of chapter

(a) This chapter applies if any of the following conditions is satisfied:

(1) The owner of the fee interest in property contracts for a work of improvement on the property with a contract price greater than five million dollars ($5,000,000).

(2) The owner of a less than fee interest in property, including a leasehold interest, contracts for a work of improvement on the property with a contract price greater than one million dollars ($1,000,000).

(b) For the purpose of this section:

(1) The owner of the fee interest in property is not deemed to be the owner of a less than fee interest by reason of a mortgage, deed of trust, ground lease, or other lien or encumbrance or right of occupancy that encumbers the fee interest.

(2) A lessee of real property is deemed to be the owner of a fee interest in the real property if all of the following conditions are satisfied:

(A) The initial term of the lease is at least 35 years.

(B) The lease covers one or more lawful parcels under the Subdivision Map Act, Division 2 (commencing with Section 66410) of Title 7 of the Government Code, and any applicable local ordinance adopted under that act, in their entirety, including, but not limited to, a parcel approved pursuant to a certificate of compliance proceeding. *(Added by Stats.2010, c. 697 (S.B.189), § 20, operative July 1, 2012.)*

Operative Effect

For operative effect of Part 6, see Civil Code § 8052 and Stats.2010, c. 697 (S.B.189), § 105.

Law Revision Commission Comments

Subdivision (a) of Section 8700 restates former Section 3110.5(a)(2) without substantive change.

Subdivision (b) restates former Section 3110.5(a)(1) without substantive change.

Under this section, if the owner that contracts for the work of improvement owns the fee interest in the property, the owner of a less than fee interest that does not contract for the work of improvement is not required to provide security or to comply with any other obligation of an owner under this chapter.

If the owner that contracts for a work of improvement owns a less than fee interest in the property, the owner of the fee interest that does not contract for the work of improvement is not required to provide security or to comply with any other obligation of an owner under this chapter.

See also Sections 8010 ("contract price"), 8050 ("work of improvement"). [40 Cal.L.Rev.Comm. Reports 49 [AR:apx5] (2010)].

Research References

Rutter, Cal. Practice Guide: Insurance Litigation Ch. 6I-B, B. Particular Surety Bond Coverages.

Miller and Starr California Real Estate § 27:52, Owner Security Obligations for Private Work.

Miller and Starr California Real Estate § 27:90, Procedure and Method of Payment; in General.

Miller and Starr California Real Estate § 28:92, Construction-Related
　　Bonds; in General.
21 NO. 4 Miller & Starr, California Real Estate Newsalert 1, Everything
　　Old is New Again: Impact of SB 189 on Mechanics' Lien Law.
3 Witkin Cal. Proc. 5th Actions § 221A, (S 221A) (New)-In General.
4 Witkin, California Summary 10th Security Transactions in Real Property
　　§ 31A, (S 31A) (New)-Nature and Purpose of Revision.

§ 8702. Chapter not applicable to specified works of improvement

This chapter does not apply to any of the following works of improvement:

(a) A single-family residence, including a single-family residence located within a subdivision, and any associated fixed work that requires the services of a general engineering contractor as defined in Section 7056 of the Business and Professions Code. As used in this subdivision, "single-family residence" means a real property improvement used or intended to be used as a dwelling unit for one family.

(b) A housing development eligible for a density bonus under Section 65915 of the Government Code. *(Added by Stats.2010, c. 697 (S.B.189), § 20, operative July 1, 2012.)*

Operative Effect

*For operative effect of Part 6, see Civil Code § 8052
and Stats.2010, c. 697 (S.B.189), § 105.*

Law Revision Commission Comments

Section 8702 restates former Section 3110.5(e) without substantive change, except to omit reference to a public work. This part does not apply to a public work. See Section 8160 (application of title).

See also Section 8050 ("work of improvement"). [40 Cal.L.Rev.Comm. Reports 49 [AR:apx5] (2010)].

Research References

Rutter, Cal. Practice Guide: Insurance Litigation Ch. 6I-B, B. Particular
　　Surety Bond Coverages.

§ 8704. Chapter not applicable to specified owners

This chapter does not apply to any of the following owners:

(a) A qualified publicly traded company or a wholly owned subsidiary of a qualified publicly traded company, if the obligations of the subsidiary pursuant to the contract for the work of improvement are guaranteed by the parent. As used in this subdivision, "qualified publicly traded company" means a company having a class of equity securities listed for trading on the New York Stock Exchange, the American Stock Exchange, or the NASDAQ stock market, and the nonsubordinated debt securities of which are rated as "investment grade" by either Fitch ICBA, Inc., Moody's Investor Services, Inc., Standard & Poor's Ratings Services, or a similar statistical rating organization that is nationally recognized for rating the creditworthiness of a publicly traded company. If at any time before final payment of all amounts due pursuant to the contract the nonsubordinated debt securities of the qualified publicly traded company are downgraded to below " investment grade" by any of those rating organizations, the owner is no longer exempt from this chapter.

(b) A qualified private company or a wholly owned subsidiary of a qualified private company, if the obligations of the subsidiary pursuant to the contract for the work of improvement are guaranteed by the parent. As used in this subdivision, "qualified private company" means a company that has no equity securities listed for trading on the New York Stock Exchange, the American Stock Exchange, or the NASDAQ stock market, and that has a net worth determined in accordance with generally accepted accounting principles in excess of fifty million dollars ($50,000,000). If at any time before final payment of all amounts due pursuant to the contract the net worth of the qualified private company is reduced below that level, the owner is no longer exempt from this chapter. *(Added by Stats.2010, c. 697 (S.B.189), § 20, operative July 1, 2012.)*

Operative Effect

*For operative effect of Part 6, see Civil Code § 8052
and Stats.2010, c. 697 (S.B.189), § 105.*

Law Revision Commission Comments

Section 8704 restates former Section 3110.5(f) without substantive change.

See also Sections 8008 ("contract"), 8050 ("work of improvement"). [40 Cal.L.Rev.Comm. Reports 49 [AR:apx5] (2010)].

Research References

Rutter, Cal. Practice Guide: Insurance Litigation Ch. 6I-B, B. Particular
　　Surety Bond Coverages.
21 NO. 4 Miller & Starr, California Real Estate Newsalert 1, Everything
　　Old is New Again: Impact of SB 189 on Mechanics' Lien Law.

ARTICLE 2.　SECURITY REQUIREMENT

Section
8710.　Security and copy of recorded construction mortgage or
　　　　deed of trust disclosing the amount of the construction loan to be provided to direct contractor.
8712.　Failure to provide or maintain security.
8714.　Waiver against public policy.
8716.　Affect on rights of subcontractor.

Operative Effect

*For operative effect of Part 6, see Civil Code § 8052
and Stats.2010, c. 697 (S.B.189), § 105.*

§ 8710. Security and copy of recorded construction mortgage or deed of trust disclosing the amount of the construction loan to be provided to direct contractor

An owner described in subdivision (a) of Section 8700 shall provide the direct contractor all of the following:

(a) Security for the owner's payment obligation pursuant to the contract. The security shall be used only if the owner defaults on the payment obligation to the direct contractor. This subdivision does not apply to an owner that is the majority owner of the direct contractor.

(b) A copy, certified by the county recorder, of any recorded mortgage or deed of trust that secures the construction loan of a lending institution for the work of improvement, disclosing the amount of the loan. *(Added by Stats.2010, c. 697 (S.B.189), § 20, operative July 1, 2012.)*

Operative Effect

*For operative effect of Part 6, see Civil Code § 8052
and Stats.2010, c. 697 (S.B.189), § 105.*

Law Revision Commission Comments

Section 8710 restates the first part of former Section 3110.5(b) without substantive change. As used in this section, owner includes the "owner" of the fee simple absolute interest or any lesser interest in the property. See Section 8700 (application of chapter).

See also Sections 8060 (filing and recordation of papers), 8100–8118 (notice), 8174 (construction trust deed).

See also Sections 8008 ("contract"), 8018 ("direct contractor"), 8022 ("lending institution"), 8050 ("work of improvement"). [40 Cal.L.Rev. Comm. Reports 49 [AR:apx5] (2010)].

Rutter, Cal. Practice Guide: Insurance Litigation Ch. 6I-B, B. Particular Surety Bond Coverages.

§ 8712. Failure to provide or maintain security

If an owner fails to provide or maintain the security required by this chapter, the direct contractor may give the owner notice demanding security. The notice shall comply with the requirements of Chapter 2 (commencing with Section 8100) of Title 1. If the owner does not provide or maintain the security within 10 days after notice demanding security is given, the direct contractor may suspend work until the owner provides or maintains the security. *(Added by Stats.2010, c. 697 (S.B.189), § 20, operative July 1, 2012.)*

Operative Effect

For operative effect of Part 6, see Civil Code § 8052 and Stats.2010, c. 697 (S.B.189), § 105.

Law Revision Commission Comments

Section 8712 restates the second sentence of former Section 3110.5(c) without substantive change.

See also Section 8058 (calculation of time).

See also Sections 8018 ("direct contractor"), 8048 ("work"). [40 Cal.L.Rev.Comm. Reports 49 [AR:apx5] (2010)].

Rutter, Cal. Practice Guide: Insurance Litigation Ch. 6I-B, B. Particular Surety Bond Coverages.

§ 8714. Waiver against public policy

It is against public policy to waive the provisions of this chapter by contract. *(Added by Stats.2010, c. 697 (S.B.189), § 20, operative July 1, 2012.)*

Operative Effect

For operative effect of Part 6, see Civil Code § 8052 and Stats.2010, c. 697 (S.B.189), § 105.

Law Revision Commission Comments

Section 8714 restates former Section 3110.5(g) without substantive change. This title does not apply to a public work. See Section 8160 (application of title). [40 Cal.L.Rev.Comm. Reports 49 [AR:apx5] (2010)].

§ 8716. Affect on rights of subcontractor

This chapter does not affect any statute providing for mechanics liens, stop payment notices, bond remedies, or prompt payment rights of a subcontractor, including the direct contractor's payment responsibilities under Section 7108.5 of the Business and Professions Code. *(Added by Stats.2010, c. 697 (S.B.189), § 20, operative July 1, 2012.)*

Operative Effect

For operative effect of Part 6, see Civil Code § 8052 and Stats.2010, c. 697 (S.B.189), § 105.

Law Revision Commission Comments

Section 8716 restates former Section 3110.5(d) without substantive change, except to omit the reference to Public Contract Code Section 10262. This title does not apply to a public work. See Section 8160 (application of title).

See also Sections 8018 ("direct contractor"), 8030 ("payment bond"), 8044 ("stop payment notice"), 8046 ("subcontractor"). [40 Cal.L.Rev. Comm. Reports 49 [AR:apx5] (2010)].

ARTICLE 3. FORM OF SECURITY

Operative Effect

For operative effect of Part 6, see Civil Code § 8052 and Stats.2010, c. 697 (S.B.189), § 105.

§ 8720. Means of providing security

An owner shall provide security by any of the following means:

(a) A bond that satisfies Section 8722.

(b) An irrevocable letter of credit that satisfies Section 8724.

(c) An escrow account that satisfies Section 8726. *(Added by Stats.2010, c. 697 (S.B.189), § 20, operative July 1, 2012.)*

Operative Effect

For operative effect of Part 6, see Civil Code § 8052 and Stats.2010, c. 697 (S.B.189), § 105.

Law Revision Commission Comments

Section 8720 restates a part of former Section 3110.5(b) without substantive change. [40 Cal.L.Rev.Comm. Reports 49 [AR:apx5] (2010)].

Rutter, Cal. Practice Guide: Insurance Litigation Ch. 6I-B, B. Particular Surety Bond Coverages.

§ 8722. Bond; requirements

A bond under this chapter shall satisfy all of the following requirements:

(a) The bond shall be executed by an admitted surety insurer that is either listed in the Department of the Treasury's Listing of Approved Sureties (Department Circular 570) or that has an A.M. Best rating of A or better and has an underwriting limitation, under Section 12090 of the Insurance Code, greater than the amount of the bond.

(b) The bond shall be in an amount not less than 15 percent of the contract price for the work of improvement or, if the work of improvement is to be substantially completed within six months after the commencement of work, not less than 25 percent of the contract price.

(c) The bond shall be conditioned for payment on default by the owner of any undisputed amount pursuant to the contract that is due and payable for more than 30 days. *(Added by Stats.2010, c. 697 (S.B.189), § 20, operative July 1, 2012.)*

Operative Effect

For operative effect of Part 6, see Civil Code § 8052 and Stats.2010, c. 697 (S.B.189), § 105.

Law Revision Commission Comments

Section 8722 restates former Section 3110.5(b)(1) without substantive change.

See also Section 8058 (calculation of time).

See also Sections 8002 ("admitted surety insurer"), 8008 ("contract"), 8010 ("contract price"), 8048 ("work"), 8050 ("work of improvement"). [40 Cal.L.Rev.Comm. Reports 49 [AR:apx5] (2010)].

§ 8724. Irrevocable letter of credit; requirements

An irrevocable letter of credit under this chapter shall satisfy all of the following requirements:

(a) The letter of credit shall be issued by a financial institution, as defined in Section 5107 of the Financial Code, inuring to the benefit of the direct contractor.

(b) The letter of credit shall be in an amount not less than 15 percent of the contract price for the work of improvement or, if the work of improvement is to be substantially completed within six months after the commencement of work, not less than 25 percent of the contract price.

(c) The maturity date and other terms of the letter of credit shall be determined by agreement between the owner, the direct contractor, and the financial institution, except that the owner shall maintain the letter of credit in effect until the owner has satisfied its payment obligation to the direct contractor. *(Added by Stats.2010, c. 697 (S.B.189), § 20, operative July 1, 2012.)*

Operative Effect

For operative effect of Part 6, see Civil Code § 8052 and Stats.2010, c. 697 (S.B.189), § 105.

Law Revision Commission Comments

Section 8724 restates former Section 3110.5(b)(2) without substantive change.

See also Sections 8010 ("contract price"), 8018 ("direct contractor"), 8048 ("work"), 8050 ("work of improvement"). [40 Cal.L.Rev.Comm. Reports 49 [AR:apx5] (2010)].

§ 8726. Escrow account; requirements

An escrow account under this chapter shall satisfy all of the following requirements:

(a) The account shall be designated as a "construction security escrow account."

(b) The account shall be located in this state and maintained with an escrow agent licensed under the Escrow Law, Division 6 (commencing with Section 17000) of the Financial Code, or with any person exempt from the Escrow Law under paragraph (1) or (3) of subdivision (a) of Section 17006 of the Financial Code.

(c) The owner shall deposit funds in the account in the amount provided in Section 8728. This chapter does not require a construction lender to agree to deposit proceeds of a construction loan in the account.

(d) The owner shall grant the direct contractor a perfected, first priority security interest in the account and in all funds deposited by the owner in the account and in their proceeds, established to the reasonable satisfaction of the direct contractor, which may be by a written opinion of legal counsel for the owner.

(e) The funds on deposit in the account shall be the sole property of the owner, subject to the security interest of the direct contractor. The owner and the direct contractor shall instruct the escrow holder to hold the funds on deposit in the account for the purpose of perfecting the direct contractor's security interest in the account and to disburse those funds only on joint authorization of the owner and the direct contractor, or pursuant to a court order that is binding on both of them. *(Added by Stats.2010, c. 697 (S.B.189), § 20, operative July 1, 2012.)*

Operative Effect

For operative effect of Part 6, see Civil Code § 8052 and Stats.2010, c. 697 (S.B.189), § 105.

Law Revision Commission Comments

Section 8726 restates parts of former Section 3110.5(b)(3) without substantive change.

See also Sections 8006 ("construction lender"), 8018 ("direct contractor"), 8032 ("person"). [40 Cal.L.Rev.Comm. Reports 49 [AR:apx5] (2010)].

§ 8728. Construction security escrow account; deposit or disbursement

The following provisions govern a deposit to or disbursement from a construction security escrow account under this chapter:

(a) Before the commencement of work the owner shall make an initial deposit to the account in an amount not less than 15 percent of the contract price for the work of improvement or, if the work of improvement is to be substantially completed within six months after the commencement of work, not less than 25 percent of the contract price.

(b) If the contract provides for a retention to be withheld from a periodic payment to the direct contractor, the owner shall deposit to the account the amount withheld as retention at the time the owner makes the corresponding payment to the direct contractor from which the retention is withheld.

(c) The amount required to be maintained on deposit shall not exceed the total amount remaining to be paid to the direct contractor pursuant to the contract or as adjusted by agreement between the owner and the direct contractor. If the amount on deposit equals or exceeds the total amount remaining to be paid to the direct contractor, the owner and the direct contractor shall authorize disbursement to the direct contractor for progress payments then due the direct contractor, but a party is not obligated to authorize disbursement that would cause the amount remaining on deposit following the disbursement to be less than the total amount remaining to be paid to the direct contractor.

(d) The owner and the direct contractor shall authorize the disbursement to the owner of any funds remaining on deposit after the direct contractor has been paid all amounts due pursuant to the contract. The owner and the direct contractor shall authorize the disbursement of funds on deposit pursuant to a court order that is binding on both of them. The owner and the direct contractor may agree in the contract to additional conditions for the disbursement of funds on deposit, except that the conditions may not cause the amount remaining on deposit to be less than the amount required under this section. *(Added by Stats.2010, c. 697 (S.B.189), § 20, operative July 1, 2012.)*

Operative Effect

For operative effect of Part 6, see Civil Code § 8052 and Stats.2010, c. 697 (S.B.189), § 105.

Law Revision Commission Comments

Section 8728 restates parts of former Section 3110.5(b)(3) without substantive change.

See also Sections 8008 ("contract"), 8010 ("contract price"), 8018 ("direct contractor"), 8048 ("work"), 8050 ("work of improvement"). [40 Cal.L.Rev.Comm. Reports 49 [AR:apx5] (2010)].

§ 8730. Contract price not fixed price; amount of security

If the contract price for a work of improvement is not a fixed price, the amount of security provided under this chapter shall be the guaranteed maximum price or, if there is no guaranteed maximum price, the owner's and direct contractor's good faith estimate of the reasonable value of the work to be provided pursuant to the contract. *(Added by Stats.2010, c. 697 (S.B.189), § 20, operative July 1, 2012.)*

Operative Effect

For operative effect of Part 6, see Civil Code § 8052 and Stats.2010, c. 697 (S.B.189), § 105.

Law Revision Commission Comments

Section 8730 restates the first sentence of former Section 3110.5(c) without substantive change.

See also Sections 8008 ("contract"), 8010 ("contract price"), 8018 ("direct contractor"), 8048 ("work"), 8050 ("work of improvement"). [40 Cal.L.Rev.Comm. Reports 49 [AR:apx5] (2010)].

Research References

Miller and Starr California Real Estate § 27:52, Owner Security Obligations for Private Work.

Miller and Starr California Real Estate § 27:90, Procedure and Method of Payment; in General.

Miller and Starr California Real Estate § 28:92, Construction-Related Bonds; in General.

3 Witkin Cal. Proc. 5th Actions § 221A, (S 221A) (New)-In General.

4 Witkin, California Summary 10th Security Transactions in Real Property § 31A, (S 31A) (New)-Nature and Purpose of Revision.

CHAPTER 8. PROMPT PAYMENT

Operative Effect

For operative effect of Part 6, see Civil Code § 8052 and Stats.2010, c. 697 (S.B.189), § 105.

ARTICLE 1. PROGRESS PAYMENT

Operative Effect

For operative effect of Part 6, see Civil Code § 8052 and Stats.2010, c. 697 (S.B.189), § 105.

§ 8800. Progress payments; good faith disputes; liability of owner

(a) Except as otherwise agreed in writing by the owner and direct contractor, the owner shall pay the direct contractor, within 30 days after notice demanding payment pursuant to the contract is given, any progress payment due as to which there is no good faith dispute between them. The notice given shall comply with the requirements of Chapter 2 (commencing with Section 8100) of Title 1.

(b) If there is a good faith dispute between the owner and direct contractor as to a progress payment due, the owner may withhold from the progress payment an amount not in excess of 150 percent of the disputed amount.

(c) An owner that violates this section is liable to the direct contractor for a penalty of 2 percent per month on the amount wrongfully withheld, in place of any interest otherwise due. In an action for collection of the amount wrongfully withheld, the prevailing party is entitled to costs and a reasonable attorney's fee.

(d) This section does not supersede any requirement of Article 2 (commencing with Section 8810) relating to the withholding of a retention. *(Added by Stats.2010, c. 697 (S.B.189), § 20, operative July 1, 2012.)*

Operative Effect

For operative effect of Part 6, see Civil Code § 8052 and Stats.2010, c. 697 (S.B.189), § 105.

Law Revision Commission Comments

Section 8800 restates former Section 3260.1, adding a reasonableness limitation on an attorney's fee. This title is limited to a private work. See Section 8160 (application of title).

The owner's duty runs from the time notice is complete, rather than the time of "receipt." See Section 8116 (when notice is complete).

The operative date provision of former Section 3260.1 is omitted due to lapse of time.

See also Section 8058 (calculation of time).

See also Sections 8008 ("contract"), 8018 ("direct contractor"). [40 Cal.L.Rev.Comm. Reports 49 [AR:apx5] (2010)].

Research References

Miller and Starr California Real Estate § 27:91, Prompt Payment of Progress Payments and Contract Retention.

Miller and Starr California Real Estate § 28:64, Prompt Payment Penalties.

21 NO. 4 Miller & Starr, California Real Estate Newsalert 1, Everything Old is New Again: Impact of SB 189 on Mechanics' Lien Law.

3 Witkin Cal. Proc. 5th Actions § 221A, (S 221A) (New)-In General.

7 Witkin Cal. Proc. 5th Judgment § 230, (S 230) Actions Involving Real Property or Environmental Issues.

4 Witkin, California Summary 10th Security Transactions in Real Property § 31A, (S 31A) (New)-Nature and Purpose of Revision.

4 Witkin, California Summary 10th Security Transactions in Real Property § 31-I, (New)-Release of Lien.

§ 8802. Payments to subcontractors; liability of direct contractor; additional remedies

(a) This section applies to a contract between a public utility and a direct contractor for all or part of a work of improvement.

(b) Unless the direct contractor and a subcontractor otherwise agree in writing, within 21 days after receipt of a progress payment from the public utility the direct contractor shall pay the subcontractor the amount allowed the direct contractor on account of the work performed by the subcontractor to the extent of the subcontractor's interest in the work. If there is a good faith dispute over all or part of the amount due on a progress payment from the direct contractor to a subcontractor, the direct contractor may withhold an amount not in excess of 150 percent of the disputed amount.

(c) A direct contractor that violates this section is liable to the subcontractor for a penalty of 2 percent of the disputed amount due per month for every month that payment is not made. In an action for collection of the amount wrongfully withheld, the prevailing party is entitled to costs and a reasonable attorney's fee.

(d) This section does not limit or impair a contractual, administrative, or judicial remedy otherwise available to a contractor or subcontractor in a dispute involving late payment or nonpayment by the contractor or deficient performance or nonperformance by the subcontractor. *(Added by Stats.2010, c. 697 (S.B.189), § 20, operative July 1, 2012.)*

Operative Effect

For operative effect of Part 6, see Civil Code § 8052 and Stats.2010, c. 697 (S.B.189), § 105.

Law Revision Commission Comments

Section 8802 restates former Section 3262.5, adding a reasonableness limitation on an attorney's fee.

The reference to 15 "working days" is converted to 21 "days," consistent with the remainder of the mechanics lien law. See Section 8058 (calculation of time).

See also Sections 8008 ("contract"), 8012 ("contractor"), 8018 ("direct contractor"), 8046 ("subcontractor"), 8048 ("work"), 8050 ("work of improvement"). [40 Cal.L.Rev.Comm. Reports 49 [AR:apx5] (2010)].

Research References

Miller and Starr California Real Estate § 27:91, Prompt Payment of Progress Payments and Contract Retention.
Miller and Starr California Real Estate § 28:64, Prompt Payment Penalties.
21 NO. 4 Miller & Starr, California Real Estate Newsalert 1, Everything Old is New Again: Impact of SB 189 on Mechanics' Lien Law.

ARTICLE 2. RETENTION PAYMENT

Section

8810. Scope of article.
8812. Time for payment of retention to direct contractor; conditional payment; good faith disputes.
8814. Time for payment of retention to subcontractor; specifically designated payments; good faith disputes.
8816. Notice that disputed work has been completed in accordance with contract; time for notice of acceptance or rejection; payment of retention relating to disputed work.
8818. Failure to make payment within required time; liability.
8820. Waiver against public policy.
8822. Retention payments withheld by lender pursuant to construction loan agreement.

Operative Effect

For operative effect of Part 6, see Civil Code § 8052 and Stats.2010, c. 697 (S.B.189), § 105.

§ 8810. Scope of article

This article governs a retention payment withheld by an owner from a direct contractor or by a direct contractor from a subcontractor. *(Added by Stats.2010, c. 697 (S.B.189), § 20, operative July 1, 2012.)*

Operative Effect

For operative effect of Part 6, see Civil Code § 8052 and Stats.2010, c. 697 (S.B.189), § 105.

Law Revision Commission Comments

Section 8810 restates former Section 3260(b) without substantive change. This title is limited to a private work. See Section 8160 (application of title).

The transitional provision found in former Section 3260(a), relating to contracts entered into before 1991, 1993, and 1994, is omitted due to lapse of time.

See also Sections 8018 ("direct contractor"), 8046 ("subcontractor"). [40 Cal.L.Rev.Comm. Reports 49 [AR:apx5] (2010)].

Research References

Miller and Starr California Real Estate § 27:91, Prompt Payment of Progress Payments and Contract Retention.

§ 8812. Time for payment of retention to direct contractor; conditional payment; good faith disputes

(a) If an owner withholds a retention from a direct contractor, the owner shall, within 45 days after completion of the work of improvement, pay the retention to the contractor.

(b) If part of a work of improvement ultimately will become the property of a public entity, the owner may condition payment of a retention allocable to that part on acceptance of the part by the public entity.

(c) If there is a good faith dispute between the owner and direct contractor as to a retention payment due, the owner may withhold from final payment an amount not in excess of 150 percent of the disputed amount. *(Added by Stats.2010, c. 697 (S.B.189), § 20, operative July 1, 2012.)*

Operative Effect

For operative effect of Part 6, see Civil Code § 8052 and Stats.2010, c. 697 (S.B.189), § 105.

Law Revision Commission Comments

Section 8812 restates former Section 3260(c) without substantive change, except that detailed provisions defining the date of completion are eliminated in reliance on the general provisions of this part governing completion. See Section 8180 (completion).

The right of the owner to withhold disputed amounts is made subject to a condition of good faith, consistent with other provisions of this part.

See also Section 8058 (calculation of time).

See also Sections 8018 ("direct contractor"), 8036 ("public entity"), 8050 ("work of improvement"). [40 Cal.L.Rev.Comm. Reports 49 [AR:apx5] (2010)].

Research References

California Real Estate Forms (Miller & Starr) § 4:4, Construction Contract--Cost Plus a Fixed Fee With a Guaranteed Maximum Price.
California Real Estate Forms (Miller & Starr) § 4:5, Construction Agreement--Cost Plus a Percentage Fee With a Guaranteed Maximum Price.
California Real Estate Forms (Miller & Starr) § 4:6, Construction Contract--Fixed Price--Commercial Project.
California Real Estate Forms (Miller & Starr) § 4:8, Construction Contract--Turnkey Industrial Project (Cost-Plus)--Letter Form.
California Real Estate Forms (Miller & Starr) § 4:14, Construction Agreement-- Master Agreement for Construction Services.
California Real Estate Forms (Miller & Starr) § 4:16, Restaurant Development and Construction Agreement.
California Real Estate Forms (Miller & Starr) § 4:14.50, Construction Agreement--Cost Plus a Percentage Fee With a Control Estimate.
Miller and Starr California Real Estate § 27:91, Prompt Payment of Progress Payments and Contract Retention.
Miller and Starr California Real Estate § 28:64, Prompt Payment Penalties.

§ 8814. Time for payment of retention to subcontractor; specifically designated payments; good faith disputes

(a) If a direct contractor has withheld a retention from one or more subcontractors, the direct contractor shall, within 10 days after receiving all or part of a retention payment, pay to each subcontractor from whom retention has been withheld that subcontractor's share of the payment.

(b) If a retention received by the direct contractor is specifically designated for a particular subcontractor, the direct contractor shall pay the retention payment to the designated subcontractor, if consistent with the terms of the subcontract.

(c) If a good faith dispute exists between the direct contractor and a subcontractor, the direct contractor may withhold from the retention to the subcontractor an amount not in excess of 150 percent of the estimated value of the disputed amount. *(Added by Stats.2010, c. 697 (S.B.189), § 20, operative July 1, 2012.)*

Operative Effect

*For operative effect of Part 6, see Civil Code § 8052
and Stats.2010, c. 697 (S.B.189), § 105.*

Law Revision Commission Comments

Section 8814 restates former Section 3260(d)-(e) without substantive change.

See also Section 8058 (calculation of time).

See also Sections 8018 ("direct contractor"), 8046 ("subcontractor"). [40 Cal.L.Rev.Comm. Reports 49 [AR:apx5] (2010)].

Research References

California Real Estate Forms (Miller & Starr) § 4:4, Construction Contract--Cost Plus a Fixed Fee With a Guaranteed Maximum Price..
California Real Estate Forms (Miller & Starr) § 4:5, Construction Agreement--Cost Plus a Percentage Fee With a Guaranteed Maximum Price.
California Real Estate Forms (Miller & Starr) § 4:6, Construction Contract--Fixed Price--Commercial Project.
California Real Estate Forms (Miller & Starr) § 4:8, Construction Contract--Turnkey Industrial Project (Cost-Plus)--Letter Form.
California Real Estate Forms (Miller & Starr) § 4:14, Construction Agreement-- Master Agreement for Construction Services.
California Real Estate Forms (Miller & Starr) § 4:16, Restaurant Development and Construction Agreement.
California Real Estate Forms (Miller & Starr) § 4:14.50, Construction Agreement--Cost Plus a Percentage Fee With a Control Estimate.
Miller and Starr California Real Estate § 27:91, Prompt Payment of Progress Payments and Contract Retention.
Miller and Starr California Real Estate § 28:64, Prompt Payment Penalties.

§ 8816. Notice that disputed work has been completed in accordance with contract; time for notice of acceptance or rejection; payment of retention relating to disputed work

(a) If the direct contractor gives the owner, or a subcontractor gives the direct contractor, notice that work in dispute has been completed in accordance with the contract, the owner or direct contractor shall within 10 days give notice advising the notifying party of the acceptance or rejection of the disputed work. Both notices shall comply with the requirements of Chapter 2 (commencing with Section 8100) of Title 1.

(b) Within 10 days after acceptance of disputed work, the owner or direct contractor shall pay the portion of the retention relating to the disputed work. *(Added by Stats.2010, c. 697 (S.B.189), § 20, operative July 1, 2012.)*

Operative Effect

*For operative effect of Part 6, see Civil Code § 8052
and Stats.2010, c. 697 (S.B.189), § 105.*

Law Revision Commission Comments

Section 8816 restates former Section 3260(f) without substantive change.

See also Section 8058 (calculation of time).

See also Sections 8008 ("contract"), 8018 ("direct contractor"), 8046 ("subcontractor"), 8048 ("work"). [40 Cal.L.Rev.Comm. Reports 49 [AR:apx5] (2010)].

Research References

Miller and Starr California Real Estate § 27:91, Prompt Payment of Progress Payments and Contract Retention.

Miller and Starr California Real Estate § 28:64, Prompt Payment Penalties.

§ 8818. Failure to make payment within required time; liability

If an owner or direct contractor does not make a retention payment within the time required by this article:

(a) The owner or direct contractor is liable to the person to which payment is owed for a penalty of 2 percent per month on the amount wrongfully withheld, in place of any interest otherwise due.

(b) In an action for collection of the amount wrongfully withheld, the prevailing party is entitled to costs and reasonable attorney's fees. *(Added by Stats.2010, c. 697 (S.B.189), § 20, operative July 1, 2012.)*

Operative Effect

*For operative effect of Part 6, see Civil Code § 8052
and Stats.2010, c. 697 (S.B.189), § 105.*

Law Revision Commission Comments

Section 8818 restates former Section 3260(g) without substantive change, except to add a reasonableness limitation on an attorney's fee.
See also Sections 8018 ("direct contractor"), 8032 ("person"). [40 Cal.L.Rev.Comm. Reports 49 [AR:apx5] (2010)].

Research References

Miller and Starr California Real Estate § 27:91, Prompt Payment of Progress Payments and Contract Retention.
Miller and Starr California Real Estate § 28:64, Prompt Payment Penalties.
7 Witkin Cal. Proc. 5th Judgment § 230, (S 230) Actions Involving Real Property or Environmental Issues.

§ 8820. Waiver against public policy

It is against public policy to waive the provisions of this article by contract. *(Added by Stats.2010, c. 697 (S.B.189), § 20, operative July 1, 2012.)*

Operative Effect

*For operative effect of Part 6, see Civil Code § 8052
and Stats.2010, c. 697 (S.B.189), § 105.*

Law Revision Commission Comments

Section 8820 restates former Section 3260(h) without substantive change. [37 Cal.L.Rev.Comm. Reports 527 (2007)].

Research References

Miller and Starr California Real Estate § 28:64, Prompt Payment Penalties.

§ 8822. Retention payments withheld by lender pursuant to construction loan agreement

This article does not apply to a retention payment withheld by a lender pursuant to a construction loan agreement. *(Added by Stats.2010, c. 697 (S.B.189), § 20, operative July 1, 2012.)*

Operative Effect

*For operative effect of Part 6, see Civil Code § 8052
and Stats.2010, c. 697 (S.B.189), § 105.*

Law Revision Commission Comments

Section 8822 restates former Section 3260(i) without substantive change. [37 Cal.L.Rev.Comm. Reports 527 (2007)].

Research References

Miller and Starr California Real Estate § 27:91, Prompt Payment of Progress Payments and Contract Retention.

Miller and Starr California Real Estate § 28:64, Prompt Payment Penalties.

ARTICLE 3. STOP WORK NOTICE

Section
8830. "Stop work notice" defined.
8832. Conditions for stop work notice.
8834. Additional notice with stop work notice.
8836. Copy of notice to be given to construction lender.
8838. Liability for delay or damage; limitations on liability.
8840. Resolution of claim or cancellation of stop work notice; posting of notice.
8842. Other remedies.
8844. Expedited proceeding.
8846. Waiver against public policy.
8848. Application of article.

Operative Effect

For operative effect of Part 6, see Civil Code § 8052 and Stats.2010, c. 697 (S.B.189), § 105.

§ 8830. "Stop work notice" defined

"Stop work notice" means notice given under this article by a direct contractor to an owner that the contractor will stop work if the amount owed the contractor is not paid within 10 days after notice is given. *(Added by Stats.2010, c. 697 (S.B.189), § 20, operative July 1, 2012.)*

Operative Effect

For operative effect of Part 6, see Civil Code § 8052 and Stats.2010, c. 697 (S.B.189), § 105.

Law Revision Commission Comments

Section 8830 restates a part of the first sentence of former Section 3260.2(a) without substantive change. The term "stop work notice" replaces the term "10–day stop work order" used in former law.

This article is limited to a private work of improvement. See Section 8160 (application of title).

Former Section 3260.2(g), relating to the mechanics of the notice, is superseded by Sections 8100–8118 (notice).

See also Section 8058 (calculation of time).

See also Sections 8018 ("direct contractor"), 8048 ("work"). [40 Cal.L.Rev.Comm. Reports 49 [AR:apx5] (2010)].

Research References

Rutter, Cal. Practice Guide: Insurance Litigation Ch. 6I-B, B. Particular Surety Bond Coverages.
Rutter, Cal. Practice Guide: Insurance Litigation Ch. 6I-D, D. Surety's Defenses to Payment of Bond.
3 Witkin Cal. Proc. 5th Actions § 221D, (S 221D) (New)-Private Property: Stop Notice.

§ 8832. Conditions for stop work notice

If a direct contractor is not paid the amount due pursuant to a written contract within 35 days after the date payment is due under the contract, and there is no dispute as to the satisfactory performance of the contractor, the contractor may give the owner a stop work notice. The notice shall comply with the requirements of Chapter 2 (commencing with Section 8100) of Title 1. *(Added by Stats.2010, c. 697 (S.B.189), § 20, operative July 1, 2012.)*

Operative Effect

For operative effect of Part 6, see Civil Code § 8052 and Stats.2010, c. 697 (S.B.189), § 105.

Law Revision Commission Comments

Section 8832 restates a part of the first sentence of former Section 3260.2(a) without substantive change.

See also Section 8058 (calculation of time).

See also Sections 8008 ("contract"), 8018 ("direct contractor"), 8830 ("stop work notice"). [40 Cal.L.Rev.Comm. Reports 49 [AR:apx5] (2010)].

Research References

California Real Estate Forms (Miller & Starr) § 4:4, Construction Contract--Cost Plus a Fixed Fee With a Guaranteed Maximum Price.
California Real Estate Forms (Miller & Starr) § 4:5, Construction Agreement--Cost Plus a Percentage Fee With a Guaranteed Maximum Price.
California Real Estate Forms (Miller & Starr) § 4:6, Construction Contract--Fixed Price--Commercial Project.
California Real Estate Forms (Miller & Starr) § 4:8, Construction Contract--Turnkey Industrial Project (Cost-Plus)--Letter Form.
California Real Estate Forms (Miller & Starr) § 4:14, Construction Agreement-- Master Agreement for Construction Services.
California Real Estate Forms (Miller & Starr) § 4:16, Restaurant Development and Construction Agreement.
California Real Estate Forms (Miller & Starr) § 4:14.50, Construction Agreement--Cost Plus a Percentage Fee With a Control Estimate.
Rutter, Cal. Practice Guide: Insurance Litigation Ch. 6I-B, B. Particular Surety Bond Coverages.

§ 8834. Additional notice with stop work notice

A direct contractor that gives an owner a stop work notice shall give the following additional notice:

(a) At least five days before giving the stop work notice, the contractor shall post notice of intent to give a stop work notice. The notice shall comply with the requirements of Chapter 2 (commencing with Section 8100) of Title 1. In addition to posting the notice pursuant to Section 8114, the notice shall also be posted at the main office of the site, if one exists.

(b) At the same time the contractor gives the stop work notice, the contractor shall give a copy of the stop work notice to all subcontractors with whom the contractor has a direct contractual relationship on the work of improvement. *(Added by Stats.2010, c. 697 (S.B.189), § 20, operative July 1, 2012.)*

Operative Effect

For operative effect of Part 6, see Civil Code § 8052 and Stats.2010, c. 697 (S.B.189), § 105.

Law Revision Commission Comments

Section 8834 restates the second and third sentences of former Section 3260.2(a), and requires that the contractor give a copy of the stop work notice to the contractor's subcontractors.

See also Sections 8058 (calculation of time), 8114 (posting of notice).

See also Sections 8018 ("direct contractor"), 8040 ("site"), 8046 ("subcontractor"), 8050 ("work of improvement"), 8830 ("stop work notice"). [40 Cal.L.Rev.Comm. Reports 49 [AR:apx5] (2010)].

Research References

Rutter, Cal. Practice Guide: Insurance Litigation Ch. 6I-B, B. Particular Surety Bond Coverages.

§ 8836. Copy of notice to be given to construction lender

Within five days after receipt of a stop work notice from a direct contractor, the owner shall give a copy of the notice to the construction lender, if any. The copy of the notice shall be given in compliance with the requirements of Chapter 2 (commencing with Section 8100) of Title 1. *(Added by Stats.2010, c. 697 (S.B.189), § 20, operative July 1, 2012.)*

Operative Effect

For operative effect of Part 6, see Civil Code § 8052 and Stats.2010, c. 697 (S.B.189), § 105.

Law Revision Commission Comments

Section 8836 restates the fourth sentence of former Section 3260.2(a).

See also Section 8058 (calculation of time).

See also Sections 8006 ("construction lender"), 8018 ("direct contractor"), 8830 ("stop work notice"). [40 Cal.L.Rev.Comm. Reports 49 [AR:apx5] (2010)].

§ 8838. Liability for delay or damage; limitations on liability

(a) The direct contractor or the direct contractor's surety, or a subcontractor or a subcontractor's surety, is not liable for delay or damage that the owner or a contractor of a subcontractor may suffer as a result of the direct contractor giving a stop work notice and subsequently stopping work for nonpayment, if the notice and posting requirements of this article are satisfied.

(b) A direct contractor's or original subcontractor's liability to a subcontractor or material supplier after the direct contractor stops work under this article is limited to the amount the subcontractor or material supplier could otherwise recover under this title for work provided up to the date the subcontractor or material supplier ceases work, subject to the following exceptions:

(1) The direct contractor's or original subcontractor's liability continues for work provided up to and including the 10–day notice period and not beyond.

(2) This subdivision does not limit liability for custom work, including materials that have been fabricated, manufactured, or ordered to specifications that are unique to the job. *(Added by Stats.2010, c. 697 (S.B.189), § 20, operative July 1, 2012.)*

Operative Effect

For operative effect of Part 6, see Civil Code § 8052 and Stats.2010, c. 697 (S.B.189), § 105.

Law Revision Commission Comments

Section 8838 restates former Section 3260.2(c), correcting two inadvertent drafting errors in former law.

See also Sections 8018 ("direct contractor"), 8028 ("material supplier"), 8046 ("subcontractor"), 8048 ("work"), 8830 ("stop work notice"). [40 Cal.L.Rev.Comm. Reports 49 [AR:apx5] (2010)].

Research References

Rutter, Cal. Practice Guide: Insurance Litigation Ch. 6I-B, B. Particular Surety Bond Coverages.
Rutter, Cal. Practice Guide: Insurance Litigation Ch. 6I-D, D. Surety's Defenses to Payment of Bond.

§ 8840. Resolution of claim or cancellation of stop work notice; posting of notice

On resolution of the claim in the stop work notice or the direct contractor's cancellation of the stop work notice, the contractor shall post, and give subcontractors with whom the contractor has a direct contractual relationship on the work of improvement, notice of the resolution or cancellation. The notice shall comply with the requirements of Chapter 2 (commencing with Section 8100) of Title 1. In addition to posting the notice pursuant to Section 8114, the notice shall also be posted at the main office of the site, if one exists. *(Added by Stats.2010, c. 697 (S.B.189), § 20, operative July 1, 2012.)*

Operative Effect

For operative effect of Part 6, see Civil Code § 8052 and Stats.2010, c. 697 (S.B.189), § 105.

Law Revision Commission Comments

Section 8840 restates the second paragraph of former Section 3260.2(a) without substantive change.

See also Section 8114 (posting of notice).

See also Sections 8018 ("direct contractor"), 8040 ("site"), 8046 ("subcontractor"), 8050 ("work of improvement"), 8830 ("stop work notice"). [40 Cal.L.Rev.Comm. Reports 49 [AR:apx5] (2010)].

Research References

Rutter, Cal. Practice Guide: Insurance Litigation Ch. 6I-B, B. Particular Surety Bond Coverages.
21 NO. 4 Miller & Starr, California Real Estate Newsalert 1, Everything Old is New Again: Impact of SB 189 on Mechanics' Lien Law.

§ 8842. Other remedies

A direct contractor's right to stop work under this article is in addition to other rights the direct contractor may have under the law. *(Added by Stats.2010, c. 697 (S.B.189), § 20, operative July 1, 2012.)*

Operative Effect

For operative effect of Part 6, see Civil Code § 8052 and Stats.2010, c. 697 (S.B.189), § 105.

Law Revision Commission Comments

Section 8842 restates former Section 3260.2(b) without substantive change.

See also Sections 8018 ("direct contractor"), 8048 ("work"). [40 Cal.L.Rev.Comm. Reports 49 [AR:apx5] (2010)].

§ 8844. Expedited proceeding

(a) If payment of the amount claimed is not made within 10 days after a stop work notice is given, the direct contractor, the direct contractor's surety, or an owner may in an expedited proceeding in the superior court in the county in which the private work of improvement is located, seek a judicial determination of liability for the amount due.

(b) The expedited proceeding shall be set for hearing or trial at the earliest possible date in order that it shall be quickly heard and determined, and shall take precedence over all other cases except older matter of the same character and other matters to which special precedence has been given. *(Added by Stats.2010, c. 697 (S.B.189), § 20, operative July 1, 2012.)*

Operative Effect

For operative effect of Part 6, see Civil Code § 8052 and Stats.2010, c. 697 (S.B.189), § 105.

Law Revision Commission Comments

Subdivision (a) of Section 8844 restates former Section 3260.2(d) without substantive change, except to additionally allow an owner to seek a judicial determination of liability for the amount due in an expedited proceeding.

Subdivision (b) is comparable to Code of Civil Procedure Sections 1062.3 and 1260.010.

See also Section 8058 (calculation of time).

See also Sections 8018 ("direct contractor"), 8050 ("work of improvement"), 8830 ("stop work notice"). [40 Cal.L.Rev.Comm. Reports 49 [AR:apx5] (2010)].

Research References

Rutter, Cal. Practice Guide: Insurance Litigation Ch. 6I-B, B. Particular
   Surety Bond Coverages.

§ 8846. Waiver against public policy

It is against public policy to waive the provisions of this article
by contract. *(Added by Stats.2010, c. 697 (S.B.189), § 20,
operative July 1, 2012.)*

Operative Effect

*For operative effect of Part 6, see Civil Code § 8052
and Stats.2010, c. 697 (S.B.189), § 105.*

Law Revision Commission Comments

Section 8846 restates former Section 3260.2(e) without substantive
change. [37 Cal.L.Rev.Comm. Reports 527 (2007)].

§ 8848. Application of article

(a) This article applies to a contract entered into on or after
January 1, 1999.

(b) This article does not apply to a retention withheld by a
lender pursuant to a construction loan agreement. *(Added by
Stats.2010, c. 697 (S.B.189), § 20, operative July 1, 2012.)*

Operative Effect

*For operative effect of Part 6, see Civil Code § 8052
and Stats.2010, c. 697 (S.B.189), § 105.*

Law Revision Commission Comments

Section 8848 restates former Section 3260.2(f) without substantive
change.
  See also Section 8008 ("contract"). [37 Cal.L.Rev.Comm. Reports 527
(2007)].

Research References

Rutter, Cal. Practice Guide: Insurance Litigation Ch. 6I-B, B. Particular
   Surety Bond Coverages.
Rutter, Cal. Practice Guide: Insurance Litigation Gen. Matls., Highlights.
3 Witkin Cal. Proc. 5th Actions § 221A, (S 221A) (New)-In General.
4 Witkin, California Summary 10th Security Transactions in Real Property
   § 31A, (S 31A) (New)-Nature and Purpose of Revision.

Title 3

PUBLIC WORK OF IMPROVEMENT

Operative Effect

*For operative effect of Part 6, see Civil Code § 8052
and Stats.2010, c. 697 (S.B.189), § 105.*

CHAPTER 1. GENERAL PROVISIONS

Operative Effect

*For operative effect of Part 6, see Civil Code § 8052
and Stats.2010, c. 697 (S.B.189), § 105.*

ARTICLE 1. APPLICATION OF TITLE

Section
9000. Application of title.

Operative Effect

*For operative effect of Part 6, see Civil Code § 8052
and Stats.2010, c. 697 (S.B.189), § 105.*

§ 9000. Application of title

This title applies to a work of improvement contracted for by a
public entity. *(Added by Stats.2010, c. 697 (S.B.189), § 20,
operative July 1, 2012.)*

Operative Effect

*For operative effect of Part 6, see Civil Code § 8052
and Stats.2010, c. 697 (S.B.189), § 105.*

Law Revision Commission Comments

Section 9000 restates former Sections 3100 and 3179.
  See also Sections 8036 ("public entity"), 8050 ("work of improvement"). [40 Cal.L.Rev.Comm. Reports 49 [AR:apx5] (2010)].

Research References

Rutter, Cal. Practice Guide: Insurance Litigation Ch. 6I-B, B. Particular
   Surety Bond Coverages.
Rutter, Cal. Practice Guide: Insurance Litigation Gen. Matls., Highlights.
21 NO. 4 Miller & Starr, California Real Estate Newsalert 1, Everything
   Old is New Again: Impact of SB 189 on Mechanics' Lien Law.
3 Witkin Cal. Proc. 5th Actions § 220, (S 220) Public Property: Stop
   Notice.
3 Witkin Cal. Proc. 5th Actions § 221A, (S 221A) (New)-In General.
3 Witkin Cal. Proc. 5th Actions § 221E, (S 221E) (New)-Public Property:
   Stop Notice.
4 Witkin, California Summary 10th Security Transactions in Real Property
   § 21, (S 21) No Subcontractor's Lien on Loan Fund.
4 Witkin, California Summary 10th Security Transactions in Real Property
   § 31A, (S 31A) (New)-Nature and Purpose of Revision.

ARTICLE 2. CLAIMANTS

Section
9100. Persons who may give stop payment notice or assert
      claim against payment bond.

Operative Effect

*For operative effect of Part 6, see Civil Code § 8052
and Stats.2010, c. 697 (S.B.189), § 105.*

§ 9100. Persons who may give stop payment notice or assert claim against payment bond

(a) Except as provided in subdivision (b), any of the following
persons that have not been paid in full may give a stop payment
notice to the public entity or assert a claim against a payment
bond:

(1) A person that provides work for a public works contract, if
the work is authorized by a direct contractor, subcontractor,
architect, project manager, or other person having charge of all
or part of the public works contract.

(2) A laborer.

(3) A person described in Section 4107.7 of the Public
Contract Code.

(b) A direct contractor may not give a stop payment notice or
assert a claim against a payment bond under this title. *(Added
by Stats.2010, c. 697 (S.B.189), § 20, operative July 1, 2012.)*

Operative Effect

For operative effect of Part 6, see Civil Code § 8052 and Stats.2010, c. 697 (S.B.189), § 105.

Law Revision Commission Comments

Section 9100 restates former Section 3181, and parts of former Sections 3110, 3111, and 3112. The former references to site improvement work and to provisions, provender, or other supplies are included within the meaning of subdivision (a). See Section 8048 ("work").

The reference to an "express trust fund" in former Section 3111 is replaced by a reference to a generalized category of persons or entities included within the definition of "laborer." See Section 8024 ("laborer").

See also Sections 8018 ("direct contractor"), 8024 ("laborer"), 8030 ("payment bond"), 8032 ("person"), 8036 ("public entity"), 8038 ("public works contract"), 8044 ("stop payment notice"), 8046 ("subcontractor"), 8048 ("work"). [40 Cal.L.Rev.Comm. Reports 49 [AR:apx5] (2010)].

Research References

Rutter, Cal. Practice Guide: Insurance Litigation Ch. 6I-B, B. Particular Surety Bond Coverages.
Miller and Starr California Real Estate § 28:3, Source and Purpose of the Mechanics Lien.
Miller and Starr California Real Estate § 28:4, Requirement of a Contract.
Miller and Starr California Real Estate § 28:8, "Claimant" Defined.
Miller and Starr California Real Estate § 28:45, Public Works.
Miller and Starr California Real Estate § 28:85, Nature of Public Works Stop Payment Notice.
Miller and Starr California Real Estate § 28:86, Who Can File the Stop Payment Notice.
Miller and Starr California Real Estate § 28:121, Action by Claimants and Others on Public Works Payment Bond--In General.
3 Witkin Cal. Proc. 5th Actions § 243, (S 243) Mechanics' Liens.
3 Witkin Cal. Proc. 5th Actions § 221A, (S 221A) (New)-In General.
8 Witkin Cal. Proc. 5th Enforcement of Judgment § 319, Debt Owed Under Public Works Contract.
2 Witkin Cal. Proc. 5th Jurisdiction § 359, Subcontractor's Contract.
4 Witkin, California Summary 10th Security Transactions in Real Property § 31A, (S 31A) (New)-Nature and Purpose of Revision.

CHAPTER 2.   COMPLETION

Operative Effect

For operative effect of Part 6, see Civil Code § 8052 and Stats.2010, c. 697 (S.B.189), § 105.

§ 9200.   Time of completion

For the purpose of this title, completion of a work of improvement occurs at the earliest of the following times:

(a) Acceptance of the work of improvement by the public entity.

(b) Cessation of labor on the work of improvement for a continuous period of 60 days. This subdivision does not apply to a contract awarded under the State Contract Act, Part 2 (commencing with Section 10100) of Division 2 of the Public Contract Code. *(Added by Stats.2010, c. 697 (S.B.189), § 20, operative July 1, 2012.)*

Operative Effect

For operative effect of Part 6, see Civil Code § 8052 and Stats.2010, c. 697 (S.B.189), § 105.

Law Revision Commission Comments

Section 9200 restates former Section 3086 to the extent it applied to a public work of improvement, but extends the period of continuous cessation of labor necessary to constitute completion from 30 days to 60 days.

See also Section 8058 (calculation of time).

See also Sections 8008 ("contract"), 8036 ("public entity"), 8050 ("work of improvement"). [40 Cal.L.Rev.Comm. Reports 49 [AR:apx5] (2010)].

Research References

Rutter, Cal. Practice Guide: Insurance Litigation Ch. 6I-B, B. Particular Surety Bond Coverages.
Miller and Starr California Real Estate § 28:41, When No Notice of Completion or Cessation Recorded.
Miller and Starr California Real Estate § 28:45, Public Works.
Miller and Starr California Real Estate § 28:88, Contents and Service of the Stop Payment Notice.
3 Witkin Cal. Proc. 5th Actions § 221A, (S 221A) (New)-In General.
4 Witkin, California Summary 10th Security Transactions in Real Property § 31A, (S 31A) (New)-Nature and Purpose of Revision.

§ 9202.   Notice of cessation;   recording;   requirements and contents

(a) A public entity may record a notice of cessation if there has been a continuous cessation of labor for at least 30 days prior to the recordation that continues through the date of the recordation.

(b) The notice shall be signed and verified by the public entity or its agent.

(c) The notice shall comply with the requirements of Chapter 2 (commencing with Section 8100) of Title 1, and shall also include all of the following information:

(1) The date on or about which the labor ceased.

(2) A statement that the cessation has continued until the recordation of the notice. *(Added by Stats.2010, c. 697 (S.B.189), § 20, operative July 1, 2012.)*

Operative Effect

For operative effect of Part 6, see Civil Code § 8052 and Stats.2010, c. 697 (S.B.189), § 105.

Law Revision Commission Comments

Section 9202 restates former Section 3092, to the extent it applied to a public works contract. For the effect of recordation of a notice of cessation, see Sections 9356 (time for giving stop payment notice), 9558 (time for enforcing payment bond claim).

A notice of cessation is recorded in the office of the county recorder of the county in which the public works contract or part of it is performed. See Section 8060 (recordation of notice). A notice of cessation is recorded when it is filed for record. See Sections 1170 (recordation), 8060 (recordation of notice).

See also Sections 8058 (calculation of time), 8066 (agency).

See also Section 8036 ("public entity"). [40 Cal.L.Rev.Comm. Reports 49 [AR:apx5] (2010)].

Research References

Rutter, Cal. Practice Guide: Insurance Litigation Ch. 6I-B, B. Particular Surety Bond Coverages.
Miller and Starr California Real Estate § 11:6, Instruments Subject to Recording--List of Recordable Documents.

§ 9204.   Notice of completion;   recording;   requirements and contents

(a) A public entity may record a notice of completion on or within 15 days after the date of completion of a work of improvement.

(b) The notice shall be signed and verified by the public entity or its agent.

(c) The notice shall comply with the requirements of Chapter 2 (commencing with Section 8100) of Title 1, and shall also include the date of completion. An erroneous statement of the date of completion does not affect the effectiveness of the notice if the true date of completion is 15 days or less before the date of recordation of the notice. *(Added by Stats.2010, c. 697 (S.B.189), § 20, operative July 1, 2012.)*

Operative Effect

For operative effect of Part 6, see Civil Code § 8052 and Stats.2010, c. 697 (S.B.189), § 105.

Law Revision Commission Comments

Section 9204 restates former Section 3093 to the extent it applied to a public works contract, extending the 10-day period for recordation of a notice of completion under former law to 15 days. For the date of completion of a work of improvement, see Section 9200.

For the effect of recordation of a notice of completion, see Sections 9356 (time for giving stop payment notice), 9558 (time for enforcing payment bond claim), 9560 (notice of payment bond claim).

A notice of completion is recorded in the office of the county recorder of the county in which the public works contract or part of it is performed. See Section 8060 (recordation of notice). A notice of completion is recorded when it is filed for record. See Sections 1170 (recordation), 8060 (recordation of notice).

See also Sections 8058 (calculation of time), 8066 (agency).

See also Sections 8036 ("public entity"), 8050 ("work of improvement"). [40 Cal.L.Rev.Comm. Reports 49 [AR:apx5] (2010)].

Research References

Rutter, Cal. Practice Guide: Insurance Litigation Ch. 6I-B, B. Particular Surety Bond Coverages.

Miller and Starr California Real Estate § 11:6, Instruments Subject to Recording--List of Recordable Documents.

Miller and Starr California Real Estate § 11:12, Required Form and Contents--Signature of the Property Owner.

§ 9208. Acceptance of notice of completion by recorder

A notice of completion in otherwise proper form, verified and containing the information required by this title shall be accepted by the recorder for recording and is deemed duly recorded without acknowledgment. *(Added by Stats.2010, c. 697 (S.B.189), § 20, operative July 1, 2012.)*

Operative Effect

For operative effect of Part 6, see Civil Code § 8052 and Stats.2010, c. 697 (S.B.189), § 105.

Law Revision Commission Comments

Section 9208 continues a portion of former Section 3093 without substantive change. See also Sections 1170 (recordation); 8058 (filing and recordation of papers); Gov't Code §§ 27280, 27287 (recordation of documents).

See also Section 9204 (notice of completion). [40 Cal.L.Rev.Comm. Reports 49 [AR:apx5] (2010)].

Research References

Miller and Starr California Real Estate § 11:6, Instruments Subject to Recording--List of Recordable Documents.

Miller and Starr California Real Estate § 11:12, Required Form and Contents--Signature of the Property Owner.

3 Witkin Cal. Proc. 5th Actions § 221A, (S 221A) (New)-In General.

4 Witkin, California Summary 10th Security Transactions in Real Property § 31A, (S 31A) (New)-Nature and Purpose of Revision.

CHAPTER 3. PRELIMINARY NOTICE

Section
9300. Persons who should receive notice; persons not required to provide notice.

Section
9302. Notice to be in compliance with Chapter 2 of Title 1; exception.
9303. Additional compliance requirements and contents.
9304. Stop payment notice or assertion of claim only for work provided within 20 days before giving preliminary notice.
9306. Failure of subcontractor to give notice; grounds for discipline.

Operative Effect

For operative effect of Part 6, see Civil Code § 8052 and Stats.2010, c. 697 (S.B.189), § 105.

§ 9300. Persons who should receive notice; persons not required to provide notice

(a) Except as otherwise provided by statute, before giving a stop payment notice or asserting a claim against a payment bond, a claimant shall give preliminary notice to the following persons:

(1) The public entity.

(2) The direct contractor to which the claimant provides work.

(b) Notwithstanding subdivision (a):

(1) A laborer is not required to give preliminary notice.

(2) A claimant that has a direct contractual relationship with a direct contractor is not required to give preliminary notice.

(c) Compliance with this section is a necessary prerequisite to the validity of a stop payment notice under this title.

(d) Compliance with this section or with Section 9562 is a necessary prerequisite to the validity of a claim against a payment bond under this title. *(Added by Stats.2010, c. 697 (S.B.189), § 20, operative July 1, 2012.)*

Operative Effect

For operative effect of Part 6, see Civil Code § 8052 and Stats.2010, c. 697 (S.B.189), § 105.

Law Revision Commission Comments

Section 9300 restates part of the introductory clause and subdivisions (a) and (c) of former Section 3098. Repetitive detail is omitted, in reliance on defined terms and other substantive provisions. For a statutory exception to the preliminary notice requirement, see Section 9560 (notice of claim against payment bond).

The transitional provision of former Section 3098(e) is not continued due to lapse of time.

See also Sections 8004 ("claimant"), 8018 ("direct contractor"), 8024 ("laborer"), 8030 ("payment bond"), 8032 ("person"), 8034 ("preliminary notice"), 8036 ("public entity"), 8044 ("stop payment notice"), 8048 ("work"). [40 Cal.L.Rev.Comm. Reports 49 [AR:apx5] (2010)].

Research References

Rutter, Cal. Practice Guide: Insurance Litigation Ch. 6I-B, B. Particular Surety Bond Coverages.

Miller and Starr California Real Estate § 28:15, Entities Entitled to a Portion of Employee Compensation.

Miller and Starr California Real Estate § 28:87, Requirement for and Contents of a Preliminary Notice.

Miller and Starr California Real Estate § 28:121, Action by Claimants and Others on Public Works Payment Bond--In General.

Miller and Starr California Real Estate § 28:122, Action by Claimants and Others on Public Works Payment Bond--Procedure and Notice.

Miller and Starr California Real Estate § 28:124, Action by Claimants and Others on Public Works Payment Bond--Amount of Recovery; Prejudgment Interest.

3 Witkin Cal. Proc. 5th Actions § 221A, (S 221A) (New)-In General.

3 Witkin Cal. Proc. 5th Actions § 221E, (S 221E) (New)-Public Property: Stop Notice.

3 Witkin Cal. Proc. 5th Actions § 222A, (S 222A) (New)-Revised Law for Action on Payment Bond for Work of Improvement.

4 Witkin, California Summary 10th Security Transactions in Real Property § 31A, (S 31A) (New)-Nature and Purpose of Revision.

§ 9302. Notice to be in compliance with Chapter 2 of Title 1; exception

(a) Except as provided in subdivision (b), preliminary notice shall be given in compliance with the requirements of Chapter 2 (commencing with Section 8100) of Title 1.

(b) If the public works contract is for work constructed by the Department of Public Works or the Department of General Services of the state, preliminary notice to the public entity shall be given to the disbursing officer of the department constructing the work. *(Added by Stats.2010, c. 697 (S.B.189), § 20, operative July 1, 2012.)*

Operative Effect

For operative effect of Part 6, see Civil Code § 8052 and Stats.2010, c. 697 (S.B.189), § 105.

Law Revision Commission Comments

Section 9302 restates the second and fourth sentences of former Section 3098(a).

See also Sections 8036 ("public entity"), 8034 ("preliminary notice"), 8038 ("public works contract"), 8048 ("work"). [40 Cal.L.Rev.Comm. Reports 49 [AR:apx5] (2010)].

Research References

Miller and Starr California Real Estate § 28:28, Statutory Provisions Governing Notice.
Miller and Starr California Real Estate § 28:87, Requirement for and Contents of a Preliminary Notice.
3 Witkin Cal. Proc. 5th Actions § 221E, (S 221E) (New)-Public Property: Stop Notice.

§ 9303. Additional compliance requirements and contents

The preliminary notice shall comply with the requirements of Section 8102, and shall also include:

(a) A general description of the work to be provided.

(b) An estimate of the total price of the work provided and to be provided. *(Added by Stats.2010, c. 697 (S.B.189), § 20, operative July 1, 2012.)*

Operative Effect

For operative effect of Part 6, see Civil Code § 8052 and Stats.2010, c. 697 (S.B.189), § 105.

Law Revision Commission Comments

Section 9303 restates a part of former Section 3098(a).
See also Sections 8034 ("preliminary notice"), 8048 ("work"). [40 Cal.L.Rev.Comm. Reports 49 [AR:apx5] (2010)].

Research References

Rutter, Cal. Practice Guide: Insurance Litigation Ch. 6I-B, B. Particular Surety Bond Coverages.
Miller and Starr California Real Estate § 28:87, Requirement for and Contents of a Preliminary Notice.
Miller and Starr California Real Estate § 28:122, Action by Claimants and Others on Public Works Payment Bond--Procedure and Notice.
3 Witkin Cal. Proc. 5th Actions § 221E, (S 221E) (New)-Public Property: Stop Notice.

§ 9304. Stop payment notice or assertion of claim only for work provided within 20 days before giving preliminary notice

A claimant may give a stop payment notice or assert a claim against a payment bond only for work provided within 20 days before giving preliminary notice and at any time thereafter. *(Added by Stats.2010, c. 697 (S.B.189), § 20, operative July 1, 2012.)*

Operative Effect

For operative effect of Part 6, see Civil Code § 8052 and Stats.2010, c. 697 (S.B.189), § 105.

Law Revision Commission Comments

Section 9304 restates parts of former Sections 3098(a) and 3098(d).
See also Section 8058 (calculation of time).
See also Sections 8004 ("claimant"), 8030 ("payment bond"), 8034 ("preliminary notice"), 8044 ("stop payment notice"), 8048 ("work"). [40 Cal.L.Rev.Comm. Reports 49 [AR:apx5] (2010)].

Research References

Rutter, Cal. Practice Guide: Insurance Litigation Ch. 6I-B, B. Particular Surety Bond Coverages.
Miller and Starr California Real Estate § 28:87, Requirement for and Contents of a Preliminary Notice.
Miller and Starr California Real Estate § 28:122, Action by Claimants and Others on Public Works Payment Bond--Procedure and Notice.
3 Witkin Cal. Proc. 5th Actions § 221E, (S 221E) (New)-Public Property: Stop Notice.

§ 9306. Failure of subcontractor to give notice; grounds for discipline

If the contract of any subcontractor on a particular work of improvement provides for payment to the subcontractor of more than four hundred dollars ($400), the failure of that subcontractor, licensed under the Contractors' State License Law (Chapter 9 (commencing with Section 7000) of Division 3 of the Business and Professions Code), to give the notice provided for in this chapter, constitutes grounds for disciplinary action under the Contractors' State License Law. *(Added by Stats.2010, c. 697 (S.B.189), § 20, operative July 1, 2012.)*

Operative Effect

For operative effect of Part 6, see Civil Code § 8052 and Stats.2010, c. 697 (S.B.189), § 105.

Law Revision Commission Comments

Section 9306 continues the first paragraph of former Section 3098(b) without substantive change.

See also Sections 8008 ("contract"), 8046 ("subcontractor"), 8050 ("work of improvement"). [40 Cal.L.Rev.Comm. Reports 49 [AR:apx5] (2010)].

Research References

Miller and Starr California Real Estate § 28:87, Requirement for and Contents of a Preliminary Notice.
3 Witkin Cal. Proc. 5th Actions § 221A, (S 221A) (New)-In General.
4 Witkin, California Summary 10th Security Transactions in Real Property § 31A, (S 31A) (New)-Nature and Purpose of Revision.

CHAPTER 4. STOP PAYMENT NOTICE

Operative Effect

For operative effect of Part 6, see Civil Code § 8052 and Stats.2010, c. 697 (S.B.189), § 105.

ARTICLE 1. GENERAL PROVISIONS

Operative Effect

For operative effect of Part 6, see Civil Code § 8052 and Stats.2010, c. 697 (S.B.189), § 105.

§ 9350. Rights of persons furnishing work pursuant to public works contract

The rights of all persons furnishing work pursuant to a public works contract, with respect to any fund for payment of construction costs, are governed exclusively by this chapter, and no person may assert any legal or equitable right with respect to that fund, other than a right created by direct written contract between the person and the person holding the fund, except pursuant to the provisions of this chapter. *(Added by Stats.2010, c. 697 (S.B.189), § 20, operative July 1, 2012.)*

Operative Effect

For operative effect of Part 6, see Civil Code § 8052 and Stats.2010, c. 697 (S.B.189), § 105.

Law Revision Commission Comments

Section 9350 restates former Section 3264, to the extent it applied to a public works contract. For a comparable provision applicable to a private work, see Section 8500.

There may be specific statutory provisions that authorize payment by a public entity from a fund designated for a public work, notwithstanding the provisions of Section 9350. See, e.g., Code Civ. Proc. § 708.760 (satisfaction of judgment against direct contractor on public work), Labor Code § 1727 (public entity to withhold amounts needed to satisfy prevailing wage violations from funds due direct contractor on public work). This section is not intended to change existing law with respect to such provisions.

The term "fund" has a meaning distinct from the term "funds" as defined in Section 8020. Consistent with former Section 3264, "fund" refers to the source for payment of construction costs, not the form of payment itself.

See also Sections 8032 ("person"), 8038 ("public works contract"), 8048 ("work"). [40 Cal.L.Rev.Comm. Reports 49 [AR:apx5] (2010)].

Research References

Miller and Starr California Real Estate § 28:89, Duty of Public Agency After Receipt of Stop Payment Notice.
Miller and Starr California Real Estate § 28:90, Release of the Stop Payment Notice.
3 Witkin Cal. Proc. 5th Actions § 221A, (S 221A) (New)–In General.
8 Witkin Cal. Proc. 5th Enforcement of Judgment § 319, Debt Owed Under Public Works Contract.
1 Witkin Cal. Summ. 10th Contracts § 911, (S 911) Works of Improvement Contracts.
4 Witkin, California Summary 10th Security Transactions in Real Property § 21, (S 21) No Subcontractor's Lien on Loan Fund.
4 Witkin, California Summary 10th Security Transactions in Real Property § 22, (S 22) No Contractor's Lien on Loan Fund.
4 Witkin, California Summary 10th Security Transactions in Real Property § 31A, (S 31A) (New)–Nature and Purpose of Revision.

§ 9352. Stop payment notice; requirements; contents; amount claimed

(a) A stop payment notice shall comply with the requirements of Chapter 2 (commencing with Section 8100) of Title 1, and shall be signed and verified by the claimant.

(b) The notice shall include a general description of work to be provided, and an estimate of the total amount in value of the work to be provided.

(c) The amount claimed in the notice may include only the amount due the claimant for work provided through the date of the notice. *(Added by Stats.2010, c. 697 (S.B.189), § 20, operative July 1, 2012.)*

Operative Effect

For operative effect of Part 6, see Civil Code § 8052 and Stats.2010, c. 697 (S.B.189), § 105.

Law Revision Commission Comments

Section 9352 supersedes former Section 3103(a)-(d). A stop payment notice may be executed by the claimant's agent. See Section 8066 (agency).

Subdivision (c) provides a special rule that supplements the requirement of Section 8102(a)(5)(C) (demand of claimant).

See also Sections 8100–8118 (notice).

See also Sections 8004 ("claimant"), 8044 ("stop payment notice"), 8048 ("work"). [40 Cal.L.Rev.Comm. Reports 49 [AR:apx5] (2010)].

Research References

Rutter, Cal. Practice Guide: Insurance Litigation Ch. 6I-B, B. Particular Surety Bond Coverages.
Miller and Starr California Real Estate § 28:28, Statutory Provisions Governing Notice.
Miller and Starr California Real Estate § 28:88, Contents and Service of the Stop Payment Notice.

§ 9354. Notice to public entity

(a) Except as provided in subdivision (b), a stop payment notice shall be given in compliance with the requirements of Chapter 2 (commencing with Section 8100) of Title 1.

(b) A stop payment notice shall be given to the public entity by giving the notice to the following person:

(1) In the case of a public works contract of the state, the director of the department that awarded the contract.

(2) In the case of a public works contract of a public entity other than the state, the office of the controller, auditor, or other public disbursing officer whose duty it is to make payment pursuant to the contract, or the commissioners, managers, trustees, officers, board of supervisors, board of trustees, common council, or other body by which the contract was awarded. *(Added by Stats.2010, c. 697 (S.B.189), § 20, operative July 1, 2012.)*

Operative Effect

For operative effect of Part 6, see Civil Code § 8052 and Stats.2010, c. 697 (S.B.189), § 105.

Law Revision Commission Comments

Section 9354 restates the first unnumbered paragraph of former Section 3103.

A claimant wishing to receive return notice of the time within which payment of the claim stated in a stop payment notice must be enforced must pay the public entity ten dollars ($10) at the time of giving the stop payment notice. See Section 9362.

See also Sections 8032 ("person"), 8036 ("public entity"), 8038 ("public works contract"), 8044 ("stop payment notice"). [40 Cal.L.Rev.Comm. Reports 49 [AR:apx5] (2010)].

§ 9356. Time for giving stop payment notice

A stop payment notice is not effective unless given before the expiration of whichever of the following time periods is applicable:

(a) If a notice of completion, acceptance, or cessation is recorded, 30 days after that recordation.

(b) If a notice of completion, acceptance, or cessation is not recorded, 90 days after cessation or completion. *(Added by Stats.2010, c. 697 (S.B.189), § 20, operative July 1, 2012.)*

Operative Effect

For operative effect of Part 6, see Civil Code § 8052 and Stats.2010, c. 697 (S.B.189), § 105.

Law Revision Commission Comments

Section 9356 restates former Section 3184.

See also Sections 1170 (recordation), 8058 (calculation of time), 8060 (recordation of notice), 9200 (completion), 9202 (notice of cessation), 9204 (notice of completion).

See also Section 8044 ("stop payment notice"). [40 Cal.L.Rev.Comm. Reports 49 [AR:apx5] (2010)].

§ 9358. Withholding of sufficient funds

(a) The public entity shall, on receipt of a stop payment notice, withhold from the direct contractor sufficient funds due or to become due to the direct contractor to pay the claim stated in the stop payment notice and to provide for the public entity's reasonable cost of any litigation pursuant to the stop payment notice.

(b) The public entity may satisfy its duty under this section by refusing to release funds held in escrow under Section 10263 or 22300 of the Public Contract Code. *(Added by Stats.2010, c. 697 (S.B.189), § 20, operative July 1, 2012.)*

Operative Effect

For operative effect of Part 6, see Civil Code § 8052 and Stats.2010, c. 697 (S.B.189), § 105.

Law Revision Commission Comments

Section 9358 restates former Section 3186. See also Section 8066 (agency).

See also Sections 8018 ("direct contractor"), 8020 ("funds"), 8036 ("public entity"), 8044 ("stop payment notice"). [40 Cal.L.Rev.Comm. Reports 49 [AR:apx5] (2010)].

§ 9360. Payment of funds before stop payment notice received; payment of amounts in excess of amount necessary to pay claims

(a) This chapter does not prohibit payment of funds to a direct contractor or a direct contractor's assignee if a stop payment notice is not received before the disbursing officer actually surrenders possession of the funds.

(b) This chapter does not prohibit payment of any amount due to a direct contractor or a direct contractor's assignee in excess of the amount necessary to pay the total amount of all claims stated in stop payment notices received by the public entity at the time of payment plus any interest and court costs that might reasonably be anticipated in connection with the claims. *(Added by Stats.2010, c. 697 (S.B.189), § 20, operative July 1, 2012.)*

Operative Effect

For operative effect of Part 6, see Civil Code § 8052 and Stats.2010, c. 697 (S.B.189), § 105.

Law Revision Commission Comments

Section 9360 restates former Section 3187.

See also Sections 8018 ("direct contractor"), 8020 ("funds"), 8036 ("public entity"), 8044 ("stop payment notice"). [40 Cal.L.Rev.Comm. Reports 49 [AR:apx5] (2010)].

§ 9362. Notice of time for commencing action to enforce payment of claim

(a) Not later than 10 days after each of the following events, the public entity shall give notice to a claimant that has given a stop payment notice of the time within which an action to enforce payment of the claim stated in the stop payment notice must be commenced:

(1) Completion of a public works contract, whether by acceptance or cessation.

(2) Recordation of a notice of cessation or completion.

(b) The notice shall comply with the requirements of Chapter 2 (commencing with Section 8100) of Title 1.

(c) A public entity need not give notice under this section unless the claimant has paid the public entity ten dollars ($10) at the time of giving the stop payment notice. *(Added by Stats. 2010, c. 697 (S.B.189), § 20, operative July 1, 2012.)*

Operative Effect

For operative effect of Part 6, see Civil Code § 8052 and Stats.2010, c. 697 (S.B.189), § 105.

Law Revision Commission Comments

Section 9362 restates former Section 3185. The $2 fee is increased to $10 in recognition of the change in the value of the dollar since the fee's enactment.

See also Sections 1170 (recordation), 8058 (calculation of time), 8060 (recordation of notice), 9200 (completion), 9202 (notice of cessation), 9204 (notice of completion), 9502 (time for enforcement of payment of claim stated in stop payment notice).

See also Sections 8004 ("claimant"), 8036 ("public entity"), 8038 ("public works contract"), 8044 ("stop payment notice"). [40 Cal.L.Rev. Comm. Reports 49 [AR:apx5] (2010)].

Research References

Miller and Starr California Real Estate § 28:89, Duty of Public Agency After Receipt of Stop Payment Notice.
3 Witkin Cal. Proc. 5th Actions § 243, (S 243) Mechanics' Liens.

§ 9364. Release bond; procedure

(a) A public entity may, in its discretion, permit the direct contractor to give the public entity a release bond. The bond shall be executed by an admitted surety insurer, in an amount equal to 125 percent of the claim stated in the stop payment notice, conditioned for the payment of any amount the claimant recovers in an action on the claim, together with court costs if the claimant prevails.

(b) On receipt of a release bond, the public entity shall not withhold funds from the direct contractor pursuant to the stop payment notice.

(c) The surety on a release bond is jointly and severally liable to the claimant with the sureties on any payment bond given under Chapter 5 (commencing with Section 9550). *(Added by Stats.2010, c. 697 (S.B.189), § 20, operative July 1, 2012.)*

Operative Effect

For operative effect of Part 6, see Civil Code § 8052 and Stats.2010, c. 697 (S.B.189), § 105.

Law Revision Commission Comments

Section 9364 restates former Section 3196.

See also Sections 8002 ("admitted surety insurer"), 8004 ("claimant"), 8018 ("direct contractor"), 8020 ("funds"), 8030 ("payment bond"), 8036 ("public entity"), 8044 ("stop payment notice"). [40 Cal.L.Rev.Comm. Reports 49 [AR:apx5] (2010)].

Research References

Rutter, Cal. Practice Guide: Insurance Litigation Ch. 6I-B, B. Particular Surety Bond Coverages.
Rutter, Cal. Practice Guide: Insurance Litigation Ch. 6I-C, C. Surety's Obligations and Rights Upon Default by Principal.
Miller and Starr California Real Estate § 28:89, Duty of Public Agency After Receipt of Stop Payment Notice.
Miller and Starr California Real Estate § 28:90, Release of the Stop Payment Notice.
Miller and Starr California Real Estate § 28:92, Construction-Related Bonds; in General.
3 Witkin Cal. Proc. 5th Actions § 243, (S 243) Mechanics' Liens.
3 Witkin Cal. Proc. 5th Actions § 664, (S 664) in General.
3 Witkin Cal. Proc. 5th Actions § 221A, (S 221A) (New)-In General.
9 Witkin Cal. Proc. 5th Appeal § 173, (S 173) Attachment.
4 Witkin, California Summary 10th Security Transactions in Real Property § 31A, (S 31A) (New)-Nature and Purpose of Revision.

ARTICLE 2. SUMMARY PROCEEDING FOR RELEASE OF FUNDS

Section

Section

Operative Effect

For operative effect of Part 6, see Civil Code § 8052 and Stats.2010, c. 697 (S.B.189), § 105.

§ 9400. Release of funds; grounds

A direct contractor may obtain release of funds withheld pursuant to a stop payment notice under the summary proceeding provided in this article on any of the following grounds:

(a) The claim on which the notice is based is not a type for which a stop payment notice is authorized under this chapter.

(b) The claimant is not a person authorized under Section 9100 to give a stop payment notice.

(c) The amount of the claim stated in the stop payment notice is excessive.

(d) There is no basis for the claim stated in the stop payment notice. *(Added by Stats.2010, c. 697 (S.B.189), § 20, operative July 1, 2012.)*

Operative Effect

For operative effect of Part 6, see Civil Code § 8052 and Stats.2010, c. 697 (S.B.189), § 105.

Law Revision Commission Comments

Section 9400 restates former Section 3197.

See also Sections 8004 ("claimant"), 8018 ("direct contractor"), 8020 ("funds"), 8032 ("person"), 8044 ("stop payment notice"). [40 Cal. L.Rev.Comm. Reports 49 [AR:apx5] (2010)].

Research References

Miller and Starr California Real Estate § 28:89, Duty of Public Agency After Receipt of Stop Payment Notice.
Miller and Starr California Real Estate § 28:90, Release of the Stop Payment Notice.
9 Witkin Cal. Proc. 5th Appeal § 173, (S 173) Attachment.

§ 9402. Affidavit; service on public entity; contents

The direct contractor shall serve on the public entity an affidavit, together with a copy of the affidavit, in compliance with the requirements of Chapter 2 (commencing with Section 8100) of Title 1, that includes all of the following information:

(a) An allegation of the grounds for release of the funds and a statement of the facts supporting the allegation.

(b) A demand for the release of all or the portion of the funds that are alleged to be withheld improperly or in an excessive amount.

(c) A statement of the address of the contractor within the state for the purpose of permitting service by mail on the contractor of any notice or document. *(Added by Stats.2010, c. 697 (S.B.189), § 20, operative July 1, 2012.)*

Operative Effect

For operative effect of Part 6, see Civil Code § 8052 and Stats.2010, c. 697 (S.B.189), § 105.

Law Revision Commission Comments

Section 9402 restates former Section 3198. The grounds for release are provided in Section 9400.

See also Sections 8018 ("direct contractor"), 8020 ("funds"), 8036 ("public entity"). [40 Cal.L.Rev.Comm. Reports 49 [AR:apx5] (2010)].

Research References

Miller and Starr California Real Estate § 28:90, Release of the Stop Payment Notice.

§ 9404. Affidavit; service of copy on claimant

The public entity shall serve on the claimant a copy of the direct contractor's affidavit, together with a notice stating that the public entity will release the funds withheld, or the portion of the funds demanded, unless the claimant serves on the public entity a counteraffidavit on or before the time stated in the notice. The time stated in the notice shall be not less than 10 days nor more than 20 days after service on the claimant of the copy of the affidavit. The notice shall comply with the requirements of Chapter 2 (commencing with Section 8100) of Title 1. *(Added by Stats.2010, c. 697 (S.B.189), § 20, operative July 1, 2012.)*

Operative Effect

For operative effect of Part 6, see Civil Code § 8052 and Stats.2010, c. 697 (S.B.189), § 105.

Law Revision Commission Comments

Section 9404 restates former Section 3199.

See also Section 8058 (calculation of time).

See also Sections 8004 ("claimant"), 8018 ("direct contractor"), 8020 ("funds"), 8036 ("public entity"). [40 Cal.L.Rev.Comm. Reports 49 [AR:apx5] (2010)].

Research References

Miller and Starr California Real Estate § 28:90, Release of the Stop Payment Notice.

§ 9406. Counteraffidavit; service on public entity; release of funds if not served within time stated in public entity's notice

(a) A claimant that contests the direct contractor's affidavit shall serve on the public entity a counteraffidavit alleging the details of the claim and describing the specific basis on which the claimant contests or rebuts the allegations of the contractor's affidavit. The counteraffidavit shall be served within the time stated in the public entity's notice, together with proof of service of a copy of the counteraffidavit on the direct contractor. The service of the counteraffidavit on the public entity and the copy of the affidavit on the direct contractor shall comply with the requirements of Chapter 2 (commencing with Section 8100) of Title 1.

(b) If no counteraffidavit with proof of service is served on the public entity within the time stated in the public entity's notice, the public entity shall immediately release the funds, or the portion of the funds demanded by the affidavit, without further notice to the claimant, and the public entity is not liable in any manner for their release.

(c) The public entity is not responsible for the validity of an affidavit or counteraffidavit under this article. *(Added by Stats.2010, c. 697 (S.B.189), § 20, operative July 1, 2012.)*

Operative Effect

For operative effect of Part 6, see Civil Code § 8052 and Stats.2010, c. 697 (S.B.189), § 105.

Law Revision Commission Comments

Section 9406 restates former Section 3200.

See also Section 8058 (calculation of time).

See also Sections 8004 ("claimant"), 8018 ("direct contractor"), 8020 ("funds"), 8036 ("public entity"). [40 Cal.L.Rev.Comm. Reports 49 [AR:apx5] (2010)].

Research References

Miller and Starr California Real Estate § 28:90, Release of the Stop Payment Notice.

§ 9408. Action for declaration of rights of parties; commencement; notice of hearing; time for hearing

(a) If a counteraffidavit, together with proof of service, is served under Section 9406, either the direct contractor or the claimant may commence an action for a declaration of the rights of the parties.

(b) After commencement of the action, either the direct contractor or the claimant may move the court for a determination of rights under the affidavit and counteraffidavit. The party making the motion shall give not less than five days' notice of the hearing to the public entity and to the other party.

(c) The notice of hearing shall comply with the requirements of Chapter 2 (commencing with Section 8100) of Title 1. Notwithstanding Section 8116, when notice of the hearing is made by mail, the notice is complete on the fifth day following deposit of the notice in the mail.

(d) The court shall hear the motion within 15 days after the date of the motion, unless the court continues the hearing for good cause. *(Added by Stats.2010, c. 697 (S.B.189), § 20, operative July 1, 2012.)*

Operative Effect

For operative effect of Part 6, see Civil Code § 8052 and Stats.2010, c. 697 (S.B.189), § 105.

Law Revision Commission Comments

Section 9408 restates former Section 3201, and provides that notice of the hearing by mail is complete five days after mailing.

See also Sections 8056 (rules of practice), 8058 (calculation of time).

See also Sections 8004 ("claimant"), 8018 ("direct contractor"), 8036 ("public entity"). [40 Cal.L.Rev.Comm. Reports 49 [AR:apx5] (2010)].

Research References

Miller and Starr California Real Estate § 28:90, Release of the Stop Payment Notice.

§ 9410. Affidavit and counteraffidavit to constitute pleadings; burden of proof

(a) The affidavit and counteraffidavit shall be filed with the court by the public entity and shall constitute the pleadings, subject to the power of the court to permit an amendment in the interest of justice. The affidavit of the direct contractor shall be deemed controverted by the counteraffidavit of the claimant, and both shall be received in evidence.

(b) At the hearing, the direct contractor has the burden of proof. *(Added by Stats.2010, c. 697 (S.B.189), § 20, operative July 1, 2012.)*

Operative Effect

For operative effect of Part 6, see Civil Code § 8052 and Stats.2010, c. 697 (S.B.189), § 105.

Law Revision Commission Comments

Section 9410 restates former Section 3202.

See also Section 8056 (rules of practice).

See also Sections 8004 ("claimant"), 8018 ("direct contractor"), 8036 ("public entity"). [40 Cal.L.Rev.Comm. Reports 49 [AR:apx5] (2010)].

Research References

Miller and Starr California Real Estate § 28:90, Release of the Stop Payment Notice.

§ 9412. Findings not required; continuance of hearing; order at conclusion of hearing; service of copy of order on public entity

(a) No findings are required in a summary proceeding under this article.

(b) If at the hearing no evidence other than the affidavit and counteraffidavit is offered, the court may, if satisfied that sufficient facts are shown, make a determination on the basis of the affidavit and counteraffidavit. If the court is not satisfied that sufficient facts are shown, the court shall order the hearing continued for production of other evidence, oral or documentary, or the filing of other affidavits and counteraffidavits.

(c) At the conclusion of the hearing, the court shall make an order determining whether the demand for release is allowed. The court's order is determinative of the right of the claimant to have funds further withheld by the public entity.

(d) The direct contractor shall serve a copy of the court's order on the public entity in compliance with the requirements of Chapter 2 (commencing with Section 8100) of Title 1. *(Added by Stats.2010, c. 697 (S.B.189), § 20, operative July 1, 2012.)*

Operative Effect

For operative effect of Part 6, see Civil Code § 8052 and Stats.2010, c. 697 (S.B.189), § 105.

Law Revision Commission Comments

Section 9412 restates former Section 3203. Former Section 3204 relating to jury trial is not continued; proceedings under this article are tried to the judge, not to a jury.

See also Section 8056 (rules of practice).

See also Sections 8004 ("claimant"), 8018 ("direct contractor"), 8020 ("funds"), 8036 ("public entity"). [40 Cal.L.Rev.Comm. Reports 49 [AR:apx5] (2010)].

Research References

Miller and Starr California Real Estate § 28:90, Release of the Stop Payment Notice.

§ 9414. Determination not res judicata

A determination in a summary proceeding under this article is not res judicata with respect to a right of action by the claimant against either the principal or surety on a payment bond or with respect to a right of action against a party personally liable to the claimant. *(Added by Stats.2010, c. 697 (S.B.189), § 20, operative July 1, 2012.)*

Operative Effect

For operative effect of Part 6, see Civil Code § 8052 and Stats.2010, c. 697 (S.B.189), § 105.

Law Revision Commission Comments

Section 9414 restates former Section 3205. The former reference to a "labor and material bond" is replaced by a reference to a payment bond.

See also Sections 8004 ("claimant"), 8030 ("payment bond"). [40 Cal.L.Rev.Comm. Reports 49 [AR:apx5] (2010)].

Research References

Miller and Starr California Real Estate § 28:89, Duty of Public Agency After Receipt of Stop Payment Notice.

Miller and Starr California Real Estate § 28:90, Release of the Stop Payment Notice.

ARTICLE 3. DISTRIBUTION OF FUNDS WITHHELD

Section
9450. Insufficient funds to pay all claims; pro rata distribution.
9452. Unpaid deficit; recovery on payment bond.
9454. False stop payment notice or inclusion of work not provided for in contract.
9456. Priority of stop payment notice.

Operative Effect

For operative effect of Part 6, see Civil Code § 8052 and Stats.2010, c. 697 (S.B.189), § 105.

§ 9450. Insufficient funds to pay all claims; pro rata distribution

If funds withheld pursuant to a stop payment notice are insufficient to pay in full the claims of all persons who have given a stop payment notice, the funds shall be distributed among the claimants in the ratio that the claim of each bears to the aggregate of all claims for which a stop payment notice is given, without regard to the order in which the notices were given or enforcement actions were commenced. *(Added by Stats.2010, c. 697 (S.B.189), § 20, operative July 1, 2012.)*

Operative Effect

For operative effect of Part 6, see Civil Code § 8052 and Stats.2010, c. 697 (S.B.189), § 105.

Law Revision Commission Comments

Section 9450 restates former Section 3190.

Only valid claims, as determined in an enforcement action, are entitled to participate in the distribution. *Cf.* Idaho Lumber Co. v. Northwestern S. & L. Ass'n, 265 Cal.App.2d 490, 71 Cal.Rptr. 422 (1968).

The amount of the claim for which payment is required is determined under Article 4 (commencing with Section 9500) (enforcement of payment of claim stated in stop payment notice).

See also Sections 8004 ("claimant"), 8020 ("funds"), 8032 ("person"), 8044 ("stop payment notice"). [40 Cal.L.Rev.Comm. Reports 49 [AR:apx5] (2010)].

Research References

Miller and Starr California Real Estate § 28:91, Suit to Enforce the Stop Payment Notice.

§ 9452. Unpaid deficit; recovery on payment bond

Nothing in this chapter impairs the right of a claimant to recover from the direct contractor or the contractor's sureties in an action on a payment bond under Chapter 5 (commencing with Section 9550) any deficit that remains unpaid after the distribution under Section 9450. *(Added by Stats.2010, c. 697 (S.B.189), § 20, operative July 1, 2012.)*

Operative Effect

For operative effect of Part 6, see Civil Code § 8052 and Stats.2010, c. 697 (S.B.189), § 105.

Law Revision Commission Comments

Section 9452 restates former Section 3191.

See also Sections 8004 ("claimant"), 8018 ("direct contractor"), 8030 ("payment bond"). [40 Cal.L.Rev.Comm. Reports 49 [AR:apx5] (2010)].

Research References

Miller and Starr California Real Estate § 28:85, Nature of Public Works Stop Payment Notice.

§ 9454. False stop payment notice or inclusion of work not provided for in contract

A person that willfully gives a false stop payment notice to the public entity or that willfully includes in the notice work not provided for the public works contract for which the stop payment notice is given forfeits all right to participate in the distribution under Section 9450. *(Added by Stats.2010, c. 697 (S.B.189), § 20, operative July 1, 2012.)*

Operative Effect

For operative effect of Part 6, see Civil Code § 8052 and Stats.2010, c. 697 (S.B.189), § 105.

Law Revision Commission Comments

Section 9454 restates former Section 3192.

See also Sections 8032 ("person"), 8036 ("public entity"), 8038 ("public works contract"), 8044 ("stop payment notice"), 8048 ("work"). [40 Cal.L.Rev.Comm. Reports 49 [AR:apx5] (2010)].

Research References

Miller and Starr California Real Estate § 28:89, Duty of Public Agency After Receipt of Stop Payment Notice.

§ 9456. Priority of stop payment notice

(a) A stop payment notice takes priority over an assignment by a direct contractor of any amount due or to become due pursuant to a public works contract, including contract changes, whether made before or after the giving of a stop payment notice, and the assignment has no effect on the rights of the claimant.

(b) Any garnishment of an amount due or to become due pursuant to a public works contract by a creditor of a direct contractor under Article 8 (commencing with Section 708.710) of Chapter 6 of Division 2 of Title 9 of Part 2 of the Code of Civil Procedure and any statutory lien on that amount is subordinate to the rights of a claimant. *(Added by Stats.2010, c. 697 (S.B.189), § 20, operative July 1, 2012.)*

Operative Effect

For operative effect of Part 6, see Civil Code § 8052 and Stats.2010, c. 697 (S.B.189), § 105.

Law Revision Commission Comments

Section 9456 restates former Section 3193.

See also Sections 8004 ("claimant"), 8018 ("direct contractor"), 8038 ("public works contract"), 8044 ("stop payment notice"). [40 Cal.L.Rev. Comm. Reports 49 [AR:apx5] (2010)].

Research References

Miller and Starr California Real Estate § 28:89, Duty of Public Agency After Receipt of Stop Payment Notice.
3 Witkin Cal. Proc. 5th Actions § 243, (S 243) Mechanics' Liens.

ARTICLE 4. ENFORCEMENT OF PAYMENT OF CLAIM STATED IN STOP PAYMENT NOTICE

Operative Effect

For operative effect of Part 6, see Civil Code § 8052 and Stats.2010, c. 697 (S.B.189), § 105.

§ 9500. Claim filing procedures for actions against public entities

(a) A claimant may not enforce payment of the claim stated in a stop payment notice unless the claimant has complied with all of the following conditions:

(1) The claimant has given preliminary notice to the extent required by Chapter 3 (commencing with Section 9300).

(2) The claimant has given the stop payment notice within the time provided in Section 9356.

(b) The claim filing procedures of Part 3 (commencing with Section 900) of Division 3.6 of Title 1 of the Government Code do not apply to an action under this article. *(Added by Stats.2010, c. 697 (S.B.189), § 20, operative July 1, 2012.)*

Operative Effect

For operative effect of Part 6, see Civil Code § 8052 and Stats.2010, c. 697 (S.B.189), § 105.

Law Revision Commission Comments

Subdivision (a) of Section 9500 restates former Section 3183.

Subdivision (b) restates former Section 3265.

See also Sections 8004 ("claimant"), 8034 ("preliminary notice"), 8044 ("stop payment notice"). [40 Cal.L.Rev.Comm. Reports 49 [AR:apx5] (2010)].

Research References

Rutter, Cal. Practice Guide: Insurance Litigation Ch. 6I-B, B. Particular Surety Bond Coverages.
Miller and Starr California Real Estate § 28:75, Other Claims Against Construction Loan Funds; Demise of the Equitable Lien.

§ 9502. Commencement of action

(a) The claimant shall commence an action against the public entity and the direct contractor to enforce payment of the claim stated in a stop payment notice at any time after 10 days from the date the claimant gives the stop payment notice.

(b) The claimant shall commence an action against the public entity and the direct contractor to enforce payment of the claim stated in a stop payment notice not later than 90 days after expiration of the time within which a stop payment notice must be given.

(c) An action under this section may not be brought to trial or judgment entered before expiration of the time provided in subdivision (b).

(d) If a claimant does not commence an action to enforce payment of the claim stated in a stop payment notice within the time provided in subdivision (b), the notice ceases to be effective and the public entity shall release funds withheld pursuant to the notice. *(Added by Stats.2010, c. 697 (S.B.189), § 20, operative July 1, 2012.)*

Operative Effect

For operative effect of Part 6, see Civil Code § 8052 and Stats.2010, c. 697 (S.B.189), § 105.

Law Revision Commission Comments

Section 9502 restates former Section 3210.

See also Sections 8058 (calculation of time), 9356 (time within which stop payment notice must be given).

See also Sections 8004 ("claimant"), 8018 ("direct contractor"), 8020 ("funds"), 8036 ("public entity"), 8044 ("stop payment notice"). [40 Cal.L.Rev.Comm. Reports 49 [AR:apx5] (2010)].

Research References

Rutter, Cal. Practice Guide: Insurance Litigation Ch. 6I-B, B. Particular Surety Bond Coverages.
Miller and Starr California Real Estate § 28:89, Duty of Public Agency After Receipt of Stop Payment Notice.
Miller and Starr California Real Estate § 28:91, Suit to Enforce the Stop Payment Notice.
3 Witkin Cal. Proc. 5th Actions § 477, (S 477) Ninety Days or Three Months.

§ 9504. Notice of commencement of action

Within five days after commencement of an action to enforce payment of the claim stated in a stop payment notice, the claimant shall give notice of commencement of the action to the public entity in the same manner that a stop payment notice is given. *(Added by Stats.2010, c. 697 (S.B.189), § 20, operative July 1, 2012.)*

Operative Effect

For operative effect of Part 6, see Civil Code § 8052 and Stats.2010, c. 697 (S.B.189), § 105.

Law Revision Commission Comments

Section 9504 restates former Section 3211. See Sections 8058 (calculation of time), 8100–8118 (notice), 9354 (giving of stop payment notice).

See also Sections 8004 ("claimant"), 8036 ("public entity"), 8044 ("stop payment notice"). [40 Cal.L.Rev.Comm. Reports 49 [AR:apx5] (2010)].

Research References

Rutter, Cal. Practice Guide: Insurance Litigation Ch. 6I-B, B. Particular Surety Bond Coverages.
Miller and Starr California Real Estate § 28:91, Suit to Enforce the Stop Payment Notice.

§ 9506. Multiple claimants

If more than one claimant has given a stop payment notice:

(a) Any number of claimants may join in the same enforcement action.

(b) If claimants commence separate actions, the court that first acquires jurisdiction may order the actions consolidated.

(c) On request of the public entity, the court shall require that all claimants be impleaded in one action and shall adjudicate the rights of all parties in the action. *(Added by Stats.2010, c. 697 (S.B.189), § 20, operative July 1, 2012.)*

Operative Effect

For operative effect of Part 6, see Civil Code § 8052 and Stats.2010, c. 697 (S.B.189), § 105.

Law Revision Commission Comments

Section 9506 restates former Section 3214. See also Section 8056 (rules of practice).

See also Sections 8004 ("claimant"), 8036 ("public entity"), 8044 ("stop payment notice"). [40 Cal.L.Rev.Comm. Reports 49 [AR:apx5] (2010)].

Research References

Rutter, Cal. Practice Guide: Civil Trials & Evidence Ch. 4-H, H. Motions to Consolidate or Coordinate Separate Cases.
Miller and Starr California Real Estate § 28:91, Suit to Enforce the Stop Payment Notice.

4 Witkin Cal. Proc. 5th Pleading § 342, Statutory Basis.

§ 9508. Dismissal

Notwithstanding Section 583.420 of the Code of Civil Procedure, if an action to enforce payment of the claim stated in a stop payment notice is not brought to trial within two years after commencement of the action, the court may in its discretion dismiss the action for want of prosecution. *(Added by Stats.2010, c. 697 (S.B.189), § 20, operative July 1, 2012.)*

Operative Effect

For operative effect of Part 6, see Civil Code § 8052 and Stats.2010, c. 697 (S.B.189), § 105.

Law Revision Commission Comments

Section 9508 restates former Section 3212. The cross-reference to the Code of Civil Procedure is added to make clear that this section modifies the general three-year period for discretionary dismissal. *Cf.* Section 8056 (rules of practice).

See also Section 8044 ("stop payment notice"). [40 Cal.L.Rev.Comm. Reports 49 [AR:apx5] (2010)].

Research References

Miller and Starr California Real Estate § 28:91, Suit to Enforce the Stop Payment Notice.

§ 9510. Effect of dismissal or judgment

A stop payment notice ceases to be effective, and the public entity shall release funds withheld, in either of the following circumstances:

(a) An action to enforce payment of the claim stated in the stop payment notice is dismissed, unless expressly stated to be without prejudice.

(b) Judgment in an action to enforce payment of the claim stated in the stop payment notice is against the claimant. *(Added by Stats.2010, c. 697 (S.B.189), § 20, operative July 1, 2012.)*

Operative Effect

For operative effect of Part 6, see Civil Code § 8052 and Stats.2010, c. 697 (S.B.189), § 105.

Law Revision Commission Comments

Section 9510 restates former Section 3213.

See also Sections 8004 ("claimant"), 8020 ("funds"), 8036 ("public entity"), 8044 ("stop payment notice"). [40 Cal.L.Rev.Comm. Reports 49 [AR:apx5] (2010)].

Research References

Miller and Starr California Real Estate § 28:89, Duty of Public Agency After Receipt of Stop Payment Notice.
Miller and Starr California Real Estate § 28:91, Suit to Enforce the Stop Payment Notice.
3 Witkin Cal. Proc. 5th Actions § 221A, (S 221A) (New)-In General.
4 Witkin, California Summary 10th Security Transactions in Real Property § 31A, (S 31A) (New)-Nature and Purpose of Revision.

CHAPTER 5. PAYMENT BOND

Operative Effect

For operative effect of Part 6, see Civil Code § 8052 and Stats.2010, c. 697 (S.B.189), § 105.

§ 9550. Necessity of bond; inclusion in call for bids; original and supplementary contracts

(a) A direct contractor that is awarded a public works contract involving an expenditure in excess of twenty-five thousand dollars ($25,000) shall, before commencement of work, give a payment bond to and approved by the officer or public entity by whom the contract was awarded.

(b) A public entity shall state in its call for bids that a payment bond is required for a public works contract involving an expenditure in excess of twenty-five thousand dollars ($25,000).

(c) A payment bond given and approved under this section will permit performance of and provide coverage for work pursuant to a public works contract that supplements the contract for which the bond is given, if the requirement of a new bond is waived by the public entity.

(d) For the purpose of this section, a design professional is not deemed a direct contractor and is not required to give a payment bond.

(e) This section does not apply to a public works contract with a "state entity" as defined in subdivision (d) of Section 7103 of the Public Contract Code. *(Added by Stats.2010, c. 697 (S.B. 189), § 20, operative July 1, 2012.)*

Operative Effect

For operative effect of Part 6, see Civil Code § 8052 and Stats.2010, c. 697 (S.B.189), § 105.

Law Revision Commission Comments

Section 9550 restates former Section 3247. The transitional provisions of the former section are omitted due to lapse of time.

Subdivision (c) is an exception to the rule stated in *Electrical Electronic Control, Inc. v. Los Angeles Unified*, 126 Cal.App.4th 601, 24 Cal.Rptr.3d 316 (2005), holding that a payment bond under former Section 3247, unless otherwise stated or agreed upon, provides coverage only for work performed pursuant to the contract for which the bond was given.

Note that "design professional" includes a licensed landscape architect. See Section 8014.

See also Sections 8018 ("direct contractor"), 8036 ("public entity"), 8030 ("payment bond"), 8038 ("public works contract"), 8048 ("work"). [40 Cal.L.Rev.Comm. Reports 49 [AR:apx5] (2010)].

Research References

Rutter, Cal. Practice Guide: Insurance Litigation Ch. 6I-B, B. Particular Surety Bond Coverages.

Miller and Starr California Real Estate § 28:92, Construction-Related Bonds; in General.

Miller and Starr California Real Estate § 28:120, Payment and Performance Bonds as to Public Projects.

3 Witkin Cal. Proc. 5th Actions § 222, Action on Payment Bond for Work of Improvement.

3 Witkin Cal. Proc. 5th Actions § 221A, (S 221A) (New)-In General.

3 Witkin Cal. Proc. 5th Actions § 222A, (S 222A) (New)-Revised Law for Action on Payment Bond for Work of Improvement.

7 Witkin Cal. Proc. 5th Judgment § 220, (S 220) Actions Against Surety on Government Construction Bond.

4 Witkin, California Summary 10th Security Transactions in Real Property § 31A, (S 31A) (New)-Nature and Purpose of Revision.

3 Witkin, California Summary 10th Agency and Employment § 390, (S 390) No Action Against Agency Under Tort Claims Act.

§ 9552. Payment bond not given and approved

If a payment bond is not given and approved as required by Section 9550:

(a) Neither the public entity awarding the public works contract nor any officer of the public entity shall audit, allow, or pay a claim of the direct contractor pursuant to the contract.

(b) A claimant shall receive payment of a claim pursuant to a stop payment notice in the manner provided by Chapter 4 (commencing with Section 9350). *(Added by Stats.2010, c. 697 (S.B.189), § 20, operative July 1, 2012.)*

Operative Effect

For operative effect of Part 6, see Civil Code § 8052 and Stats.2010, c. 697 (S.B.189), § 105.

Law Revision Commission Comments

Section 9552 restates former Section 3251. The former operative date provision is deleted due to lapse of time.

See also Sections 8004 ("claimant"), 8018 ("direct contractor"), 8030 ("payment bond"), 8036 ("public entity"), 8038 ("public works contract"), 8044 ("stop payment notice"). [40 Cal.L.Rev.Comm. Reports 49 [AR:apx5] (2010)].

Research References

Rutter, Cal. Practice Guide: Insurance Litigation Ch. 6I-B, B. Particular Surety Bond Coverages.

Miller and Starr California Real Estate § 28:120, Payment and Performance Bonds as to Public Projects.

§ 9554. Amount of bond; provisions regarding surety's obligation; conditioned for payment in full; subcontractor bond to indemnify contractor

(a) A payment bond shall be in an amount not less than 100 percent of the total amount payable pursuant to the public works contract. The bond shall be in the form of a bond and not a deposit in lieu of a bond. The bond shall be executed by an admitted surety insurer.

(b) The payment bond shall provide that if the direct contractor or a subcontractor fails to pay any of the following, the surety will pay the obligation and, if an action is brought to enforce the liability on the bond, a reasonable attorney's fee, to be fixed by the court:

(1) A person authorized under Section 9100 to assert a claim against a payment bond.

(2) Amounts due under the Unemployment Insurance Code with respect to work or labor performed pursuant to the public works contract.

(3) Amounts required to be deducted, withheld, and paid over to the Employment Development Department from the wages of employees of the contractor and subcontractors under Section 13020 of the Unemployment Insurance Code with respect to the work and labor.

(c) The payment bond shall be conditioned for the payment in full of the claims of all claimants and by its terms inure to the benefit of any person authorized under Section 9100 to assert a claim against a payment bond so as to give a right of action to that person or that person's assigns in an action to enforce the liability on the bond.

(d) The direct contractor may require that a subcontractor give a bond to indemnify the direct contractor for any loss sustained by the direct contractor because of any default of the subcontractor under this section. *(Added by Stats.2010, c. 697 (S.B.189), § 20, operative July 1, 2012.)*

Operative Effect

For operative effect of Part 6, see Civil Code § 8052 and Stats.2010, c. 697 (S.B.189), § 105.

Law Revision Commission Comments

Section 9554 restates former Section 3248, and supersedes former Section 3096.

Subdivision (a) of Section 9554 also restates a part of Code of Civil Procedure Section 995.311(a), which provides that a payment bond required on a public works contract shall be executed by an admitted surety insurer.

See also Sections 8002 ("admitted surety insurer"), 8012 ("contractor"), 8018 ("direct contractor"), 8030 ("payment bond"), 8032 ("person"), 8038 ("public works contract"), 8046 ("subcontractor"), 8048 ("work"). [40 Cal.L.Rev.Comm. Reports 49 [AR:apx5] (2010)].

Research References

Rutter, Cal. Practice Guide: Insurance Litigation Ch. 6I-B, B. Particular Surety Bond Coverages.
Rutter, Cal. Practice Guide: Insurance Litigation Ch. 6I-C, C. Surety's Obligations and Rights Upon Default by Principal.
Miller and Starr California Real Estate § 28:92, Construction-Related Bonds; in General.
Miller and Starr California Real Estate § 28:120, Payment and Performance Bonds as to Public Projects.
Miller and Starr California Real Estate § 28:121, Action by Claimants and Others on Public Works Payment Bond--In General.
Miller and Starr California Real Estate § 28:124, Action by Claimants and Others on Public Works Payment Bond--Amount of Recovery; Prejudgment Interest.
Miller and Starr California Real Estate § 28:125, Action by Claimants and Others on Public Works Payment Bond--Recovery of Attorney's Fees.

§ 9558. Commencement of action to enforce liability on bond; limitations

A claimant may commence an action to enforce the liability on the bond at any time after the claimant ceases to provide work, but not later than six months after the period in which a stop payment notice may be given under Section 9356. *(Added by Stats.2010, c. 697 (S.B.189), § 20, operative July 1, 2012.)*

Operative Effect

For operative effect of Part 6, see Civil Code § 8052 and Stats.2010, c. 697 (S.B.189), § 105.

Law Revision Commission Comments

Section 9558 restates former Section 3249, and broadens it to cover enforcement of any liability on the bond, not limited to the liability of the surety. *Cf.* Code Civ. Proc. § 996.440 (judgment on bond against principal and sureties).

See also Sections 8058 (calculation of time), 8060 (recordation of notice), 9200 (completion), 9202 (notice of cessation), 9204 (notice of completion).

See also Sections 8004 ("claimant"), 8044 ("stop payment notice"), 8048 ("work"). [40 Cal.L.Rev.Comm. Reports 49 [AR:apx5] (2010)].

Research References

Rutter, Cal. Practice Guide: Insurance Litigation Ch. 6I-B, B. Particular Surety Bond Coverages.
Rutter, Cal. Practice Guide: Insurance Litigation Ch. 6I-D, D. Surety's Defenses to Payment of Bond.
Miller and Starr California Real Estate § 28:123, Action by Claimants and Others on Public Works Payment Bond--Time to File Suit on Payment Bond.

§ 9560. Claim against payment bond; preliminary notice required; notice to surety and bond principal; extension; exceptions

(a) In order to enforce a claim against a payment bond, a claimant shall give the preliminary notice provided in Chapter 3 (commencing with Section 9300).

(b) If preliminary notice was not given as provided in Chapter 3 (commencing with Section 9300), a claimant may enforce a claim by giving written notice to the surety and the bond principal within 15 days after recordation of a notice of completion. If no notice of completion has been recorded, the time for giving written notice to the surety and the bond principal is extended to 75 days after completion of the work of improvement.

(c) Commencing July 1, 2012, and except as provided in subdivision (b), if the preliminary notice was required to be given by a person who has no direct contractual relationship with the contractor, and who has not given notice as provided in Chapter 3 (commencing with Section 9300), that person may enforce a claim by giving written notice to the surety and the bond principal, as provided in Section 9562, within 15 days after recordation of a notice of completion. If no notice of completion has been recorded, the time for giving written notice to the surety and the bond principal is extended to 75 days after completion of the work of improvement.

(d) Subdivision (c) shall not apply in either of the following circumstances:

(1) All progress payments, except for those disputed in good faith, have been made to a subcontractor who has a direct contractual relationship with the general contractor to whom the claimant has provided materials or services.

(2) The subcontractor who has a direct contractual relationship with the general contractor to whom the claimant has provided materials or services has been terminated from the project pursuant to the contract, and all progress payments, except those disputed in good faith, have been made as of the termination date.

(e) Pursuant to Section 9300, this section shall not apply to a laborer, as defined under Section 8024.

(f) This section shall become operative on July 1, 2012. *(Added by Stats.2010, c. 697 (S.B.189), § 20.1, operative July 1, 2012. Amended by Stats.2011, c. 700 (S.B.293), § 4, operative July 1, 2012.)*

Operative Effect

For operative effect of Part 6, see Civil Code § 8052 and Stats.2010, c. 697 (S.B.189), § 105.

Law Revision Commission Comments

Section 9560 restates former Section 3252. The former limitation to a contract entered into on or after January 1, 1995, is omitted due to lapse of time.

See also Sections 1170 (recordation), 8058 (calculation of time), 8060 (recordation of notice), 9200 (completion), 9204 (notice of completion).

See also Sections 8004 ("claimant"), 8030 ("payment bond"), 8034 ("preliminary notice"), 8050 ("work of improvement"). [40 Cal.L.Rev. Comm. Reports 49 [AR:apx5] (2010)].

Research References

Rutter, Cal. Practice Guide: Insurance Litigation Ch. 6I-B, B. Particular Surety Bond Coverages.
Miller and Starr California Real Estate § 28:31, Who Must Give, and Who Must Receive, The Preliminary Notice.
Miller and Starr California Real Estate § 28:98, Notice as Condition Precedent to Surety's Liability on Payment Bond.
Miller and Starr California Real Estate § 28:121, Action by Claimants and Others on Public Works Payment Bond--In General.

Civil

Miller and Starr California Real Estate § 28:122, Action by Claimants and Others on Public Works Payment Bond--Procedure and Notice.

Miller and Starr California Real Estate § 28:123, Action by Claimants and Others on Public Works Payment Bond--Time to File Suit on Payment Bond.

22 NO. 4 Miller & Starr, California Real Estate Newsalert 8, Construction Law and Contracting.

3 Witkin Cal. Proc. 5th Actions § 222A, (S 222A) (New)-Revised Law for Action on Payment Bond for Work of Improvement.

§ 9562. Notice to principal and surety; requirements

Notice to the principal and surety under Section 9560 shall comply with the requirements of Chapter 2 (commencing with Section 8100) of Title 1. *(Added by Stats.2010, c. 697 (S.B.189), § 20, operative July 1, 2012.)*

Operative Effect

For operative effect of Part 6, see Civil Code § 8052 and Stats.2010, c. 697 (S.B.189), § 105.

Law Revision Commission Comments

Section 9562 restates former Section 3227.

Cf. Code Civ. Proc. §§ 995.170 ("principal"), 995.185 ("surety"). [40 Cal.L.Rev.Comm. Reports 49 [AR:apx5] (2010)].

Research References

Miller and Starr California Real Estate § 28:31, Who Must Give, and Who Must Receive, The Preliminary Notice.

Miller and Starr California Real Estate § 28:98, Notice as Condition Precedent to Surety's Liability on Payment Bond.

Miller and Starr California Real Estate § 28:122, Action by Claimants and Others on Public Works Payment Bond--Procedure and Notice.

3 Witkin Cal. Proc. 5th Actions § 222A, (S 222A) (New)-Revised Law for Action on Payment Bond for Work of Improvement.

§ 9564. Maintenance of action without filing stop notice or suing public entity or officer; attorney fees

(a) A claimant may maintain an action to enforce the liability of a surety on a payment bond whether or not the claimant has given the public entity a stop payment notice.

(b) A claimant may maintain an action to enforce the liability on the bond separately from and without commencement of an action against the public entity by whom the contract was awarded or against any officer of the public entity.

(c) In an action to enforce the liability on the bond, the court shall award the prevailing party a reasonable attorney's fee. *(Added by Stats.2010, c. 697 (S.B.189), § 20, operative July 1, 2012.)*

Operative Effect

For operative effect of Part 6, see Civil Code § 8052 and Stats.2010, c. 697 (S.B.189), § 105.

Law Revision Commission Comments

Section 9564 restates former Section 3250. The provision that a reasonable attorney's fee is to be taxed as costs is deleted as surplus. See Code Civ. Proc. § 1033.5(a)(10)(B) (attorney's fee allowable as costs). See also Section 8056 (rules of practice).

See also Sections 8004 ("claimant"), 8008 ("contract"), 8030 ("payment bond"), 8036 ("public entity"), 8044 ("stop payment notice").

Research References

Rutter, Cal. Practice Guide: Insurance Litigation Ch. 6I-B, B. Particular Surety Bond Coverages.

Rutter, Cal. Practice Guide: Insurance Litigation Ch. 6I-C, C. Surety's Obligations and Rights Upon Default by Principal.

Miller and Starr California Real Estate § 28:120, Payment and Performance Bonds as to Public Projects.

Miller and Starr California Real Estate § 28:125, Action by Claimants and Others on Public Works Payment Bond--Recovery of Attorney's Fees.

7 Witkin Cal. Proc. 5th Judgment § 220, (S 220) Actions Against Surety on Government Construction Bond.

7 Witkin Cal. Proc. 5th Judgment § 311, in General.

§ 9566. Work done for direct contractor on bond; claim

(a) A claimant does not have a right to recover on a payment bond unless the claimant provided work to the direct contractor either directly or through one or more subcontractors pursuant to a public works contract.

(b) Nothing in this section affects the stop payment notice rights of, and relative priorities among, design professionals. *(Added by Stats.2010, c. 697 (S.B.189), § 20, operative July 1, 2012.)*

Operative Effect

For operative effect of Part 6, see Civil Code § 8052 and Stats.2010, c. 697 (S.B.189), § 105.

Law Revision Commission Comments

Section 9566 restates former Section 3267, clarifying that claimants providing work to subcontractors at every level have a right to recover against a direct contractor's payment bond as provided in this section. See Union Asphalt, Inc. v. Planet Ins. Co., 21 Cal.App.4th 1762, 27 Cal.Rptr.2d 371 (1994).

Note that "design professional" includes a licensed landscape architect. See Section 8014.

This section omits the reference in former law to holders of secured interests in the land; although the relevance of that provision to a public works contract is limited, this section is not intended to affect priorities among those interests to the extent they may exist.

See also Sections 8004 ("claimant"), 8018 ("direct contractor"), 8030 ("payment bond"), 8038 ("public works contract"), 8044 ("stop payment notice"), 8046 ("subcontractor"), 8048 ("work"). [40 Cal.L.Rev.Comm. Reports 49 [AR:apx5] (2010)].

Research References

Rutter, Cal. Practice Guide: Insurance Litigation Ch. 6I-A, A. Introduction.

Rutter, Cal. Practice Guide: Insurance Litigation Ch. 6I-B, B. Particular Surety Bond Coverages.

Rutter, Cal. Practice Guide: Insurance Litigation Gen. Matls., Highlights.

Miller and Starr California Real Estate § 28:1, Introduction.

Miller and Starr California Real Estate § 11:130, in General; Off-Record Priority.

Miller and Starr California Real Estate § 11:131, Date Liens Attach; Relation to Subsequent Interests.

Miller and Starr California Real Estate § 11:132, Relation to Prior Interests--In General.

Miller and Starr California Real Estate § 11:133, Relation to Prior Interests--Mechanic's Knowledge of a Prior Unrecorded Interest.

Miller and Starr California Real Estate § 11:134, Effect of Commencement of Work Before the Grantee Receives Title.

Miller and Starr California Real Estate § 11:135, When Construction Commences--Effect on Priority of Mechanics' and Design Professionals' Liens.

Miller and Starr California Real Estate § 11:136, When Construction Commences--Phasing of the Project; in General.

Miller and Starr California Real Estate § 11:137, Phasing of a Project by Separate Direct Contracts With the Owner.

Miller and Starr California Real Estate § 11:138, Site Improvements; Priority of Liens as Distinguished from Liens for Structures or Buildings.

Miller and Starr California Real Estate § 11:139, Priority as Affected by Separate Works of Improvement on Separate Parcels.

Miller and Starr California Real Estate § 11:140, Effect of Cessation of Work on Mechanic's Lien Priorities.

Miller and Starr California Real Estate § 11:141, Priority of the Construction Loan Deed of Trust--In General.

Miller and Starr California Real Estate § 11:142, Priority of the Construction Loan Deed of Trust--Relation to Obligatory Advances.

Miller and Starr California Real Estate § 11:143, Priority of the Construction Loan Deed of Trust--Relation to Optional Advances.

Miller and Starr California Real Estate § 11:144, Priority of the Construction Loan Deed of Trust--Premature Advances as Optional.

Miller and Starr California Real Estate § 11:145, Priority of the Construction Loan Deed of Trust--Advances to Complete Construction.

Miller and Starr California Real Estate § 11:146, Priority of the Construction Loan Deed of Trust--Effect of a Bond Recorded by the Construction Lender.

Miller and Starr California Real Estate § 28:103, Exoneration of the Surety--Modification of the Terms of the Construction Contract.

Miller and Starr California Real Estate § 28:121, Action by Claimants and Others on Public Works Payment Bond--In General.

21 NO. 4 Miller & Starr, California Real Estate Newsalert 1, Everything Old is New Again: Impact of SB 189 on Mechanics' Lien Law.

3 Witkin Cal. Proc. 5th Actions § 221A, (S 221A) (New)-In General.

1 Witkin Cal. Summ. 10th Contracts § 1001, Miscellaneous Provisions.

4 Witkin, California Summary 10th Security Transactions in Real Property § 31A, (S 31A) (New)-Nature and Purpose of Revision.

CODE OF CIVIL PROCEDURE

TITLE OF ACT

§ 1.   Title and division of code

This act shall be known as the Code of Civil Procedure, and is divided into four parts, as follows:

Part
I.   Of Courts of Justice.
II. Of Civil Actions.
III. Of Special Proceedings of a Civil Nature.
IV. Miscellaneous Provisions.

(Enacted in 1872.   Amended by Stats.1965, c. 299, p. 1357, § 15, operative Jan. 1, 1967.)

Law Revision Commission Comments

The title of Part IV has been changed to reflect the fact that the evidence provisions in Part IV have been placed in the Evidence Code.

Research References

Rutter, Cal. Practice Guide: A.D.R. Ch. 4-B, B. Judicial Arbitration.
Rutter, Cal. Practice Guide: A.D.R. Ch. 7-B, B. Arbitrators.
Rutter, Cal. Practice Guide: Civ. Pro. Before Trial Ch. 1-C, C. Prelawsuit Notices, Claims and Demands.
Rutter, Cal. Practice Guide: Civ. Pro. Before Trial Ch. 9(I)-B, B. Preparing and Filing Motions.
Rutter, Cal. Practice Guide: Personal Injury Ch. 3-A, A. Introduction.
Rutter, Cal. Practice Guide: Personal Injury Ch. 3-F, F. MICRA Provisions Affecting Damages.
Rutter, Cal. Practice Guide: Personal Injury Ch. 5-B, B. When to Sue-Statute of Limitations.
15 NO. 2 Miller & Starr, California Real Estate Newsalert 1, SLAPP Happy: An Analysis of California's Anti-SLAPP (Strategic Lawsuits Against Public Participation) Statute.
3 Witkin Cal. Proc. 5th Actions § 569, (S 569) Definition of Disability.
3 Witkin Cal. Proc. 5th Actions § 585, (S 585) Tolling of One-Year Period.
3 Witkin Cal. Proc. 5th Actions § 635, (S 635) Conflicting Decisions in Courts of Appeal.
3 Witkin Cal. Proc. 5th Actions § 723, Medical Malpractice.
3 Witkin Cal. Proc. 5th Actions § 822, (S 822) Torts to Personal Property Other Than Physical Injury.
9 Witkin Cal. Proc. 5th Appeal § 26, (S 26) Motion to Vacate.
8 Witkin Cal. Proc. 5th Attack Judgment Trial Court § 144, (S 144) Nature of Relief.
8 Witkin Cal. Proc. 5th Enforcement of Judgment § 26, in General.
4 Witkin Cal. Proc. 5th Pleading § 68, (S 68) Party Appearing as Both Plaintiff and Defendant.
6 Witkin Cal. Proc. 5th Proceedings Without Trial § 294, (S 294) Right to Dismiss After Motion for Summary Judgment.
6 Witkin Cal. Proc. 5th Proceedings Without Trial § 477, Demurrer Sustained.
14 Witkin, California Summary 10th Wills and Probate § 517, (S 517) Action Against Decedent.

PRELIMINARY PROVISIONS

§ 2.   Effective date

WHEN THIS CODE TAKES EFFECT. This Code takes effect at twelve o'clock noon, on the first day of January, eighteen hundred and seventy-three. *(Enacted in 1872.)*

Research References

Rutter, Cal. Practice Guide: A.D.R. Ch. 5-G, G. Procedures to Enforce Arbitration.
Rutter, Cal. Practice Guide: Civ. Pro. Before Trial Ch. 9(I)-F, F. Ex Parte Motions.
Rutter, Cal. Practice Guide: Civ. Pro. Before Trial Ch. 9(II)-A, A. Injunctions.

Rutter, Cal. Practice Guide: Civil Trials & Evidence Ch. 16-E, E. Statement of Decision.

California Practice Guide: Employment Litigation Ch. 16-E, E. Statute of Limitations.

Rutter, Cal. Practice Guide: Personal Injury Ch. 5-B, B. When to Sue-Statute of Limitations.

Rutter, Cal. Practice Guide: Personal Injury Ch. 8-A, A. Case Management.

3 Witkin Cal. Proc. 5th Actions § 630, Alternative Periods.

9 Witkin Cal. Proc. 5th Appeal § 20, (S 20) Jurisdiction Over Collateral Matters.

8 Witkin Cal. Proc. 5th Attack Judgment Trial Court § 62, Commencement and Running of Period.

8 Witkin Cal. Proc. 5th Attack Judgment Trial Court § 208, (S 208) No Jurisdiction of Person.

8 Witkin Cal. Proc. 5th Enforcement of Judgment § 23, Enforcement of Particular Judgments.

8 Witkin Cal. Proc. 5th Enforcement of Judgment § 275, Written Interrogatories to Judgment Debtor.

8 Witkin Cal. Proc. 5th Enforcement of Judgment § 398, (S 398) Nature of Remedy.

8 Witkin Cal. Proc. 5th Enforcement of Judgment § 453, (S 453) Jurisdiction and Venue.

7 Witkin Cal. Proc. 5th Judgment § 101, (S 101) Recovery Below Small Claims Maximum.

2 Witkin Cal. Proc. 5th Jurisdiction § 37, (S 37) Single Plaintiff and Single Defendant.

4 Witkin Cal. Proc. 5th Pleading § 26, Additional Fees.

4 Witkin Cal. Proc. 5th Pleading § 460, (S 460) Former Requirement of Denial of Instrument.

6 Witkin Cal. Proc. 5th Proceedings Without Trial § 5, (S 5) Time of Motion.

6 Witkin Cal. Proc. 5th Proceedings Without Trial § 15, (S 15) Required Period Before Hearing.

6 Witkin Cal. Proc. 5th Proceedings Without Trial § 36, (S 36) Nature of Hearing.

6 Witkin Cal. Proc. 5th Proceedings Without Trial § 179, Premature Entry.

6 Witkin Cal. Proc. 5th Proceedings Without Trial § 355, Motion to Dismiss.

6 Witkin Cal. Proc. 5th Proceedings Without Trial § 603, (S 603) Depositions.

7 Witkin Cal. Proc. 5th Trial § 237, Nature and Scope.

2 Witkin, California Summary 10th Insurance § 260, (S 260) Discovery of Policy Limits.

§ 3. Prospective application

NOT RETROACTIVE. No part of it is retroactive, unless expressly so declared. *(Enacted in 1872.)*

Research References

Rutter, Cal. Practice Guide: A.D.R. Ch. 5-G, G. Procedures to Enforce Arbitration.

Rutter, Cal. Practice Guide: Civil Appeals & Writs Ch. 8-D, D. Limits on Assertion of Issues on Appeal.

Rutter, Cal. Practice Guide: Civ. Pro. Before Trial Ch. 1-C, C. Prelawsuit Notices, Claims and Demands.

Rutter, Cal. Practice Guide: Civ. Pro. Before Trial Ch. 9(I)-B, B. Preparing and Filing Motions.

Rutter, Cal. Practice Guide: Civil Trials & Evidence Ch. 16-C, C. Motion for Judgment (CCP § 631.8).

California Practice Guide: Employment Litigation Ch. 18-C, C. Contractual Arbitration.

Rutter, Cal. Practice Guide: Enforcing Judgments/Debts Ch. 3-B, B. Collection Without Suit.

Rutter, Cal. Practice Guide: Personal Injury Ch. 5-A, A. Prelawsuit Filings.

Rutter, Cal. Practice Guide: Personal Injury Ch. 5-B, B. When to Sue-Statute of Limitations.

Rutter, Cal. Practice Guide: Real Prop. Transactions Ch. 6-I, I. Real Property Foreclosures and Antideficiency Laws.

Miller and Starr California Real Estate § 10:236, Policy Objectives; The "Standard" Transaction.

6 Witkin Cal. Proc. 5th Proceedings Without Trial § 603, (S 603) Depositions.

2 Witkin, California Summary 10th Insurance § 12, (S 12) in General.

2 Witkin, California Summary 10th Insurance § 309, (S 309) in General.

5 Witkin, California Summary 10th Torts § 813, (S 813) No General Duty to Investigate.

14 Witkin, California Summary 10th Wills and Probate § 931, (S 931) Vexatious Litigants.

§ 4. Establishment of law; liberal construction

RULE OF CONSTRUCTION OF CODE. The rule of the common law, that statutes in derogation thereof are to be strictly construed, has no application to this Code. The Code establishes the law of this State respecting the subjects to which it relates, and its provisions and all proceedings under it are to be liberally construed, with a view to effect its objects and to promote justice. *(Enacted in 1872.)*

Research References

Rutter, Cal. Practice Guide: Personal Injury Ch. 5-B, B. When to Sue-Statute of Limitations.

Rutter, Cal. Practice Guide: Real Prop. Transactions Ch. 11-H, H. Other Remedies.

Rutter, Cal. Practice Guide: Prof. Responsibility Ch. 5-K, K. Fee Recovery/Enforcing Fee Agreements.

2 Witkin Cal. Proc. 5th Courts § 259, (S 259) Local Standards and Procedure.

8 Witkin Cal. Proc. 5th Enforcement of Judgment § 20, Redemption.

6 Witkin Cal. Proc. 5th Proceedings Without Trial § 531, in General.

§ 5. Construction of certain sections as continuations of existing statutes

PROVISIONS SIMILAR TO EXISTING LAWS, HOW CONSTRUED. The provisions of this Code, so far as they are substantially the same as existing statutes, must be construed as continuations thereof, and not as new enactments. *(Enacted in 1872.)*

Research References

Rutter, Cal. Practice Guide: A.D.R. App. D Form 29, Governing Law Clauses.

Rutter, Cal. Practice Guide: Fed.Civ.Pro. Before Trial Ch. 1-B, B. Federal vs. State Law.

Rutter, Cal. Practice Guide: Personal Injury Ch. 8-A, A. Case Management.

7 Witkin Cal. Proc. 5th Trial § 188, (S 188) Limitations on Punishment.

6 Witkin, California Summary 10th Torts § 1357, Adoption of Doctrine.

§ 6. Preservation of tenure of existing officers

TENURE OF OFFICES PRESERVED. All persons who at the time this Code takes effect hold office under any of the Acts repealed, continue to hold the same according to the tenure thereof, except those offices which are not continued by one of the Codes adopted at this session of the Legislature. *(Enacted in 1872.)*

Research References

3 Witkin Cal. Proc. 5th Actions § 187, (S 187) Attachment.

3 Witkin Cal. Proc. 5th Actions § 371, (S 371) Nature and Purpose.

3 Witkin Cal. Proc. 5th Actions § 403, (S 403) Current Law.

9 Witkin Cal. Proc. 5th Appeal § 257, (S 257) Objections.

8 Witkin Cal. Proc. 5th Attack Judgment Trial Court § 54, (S 54) Late Filing is Void.

8 Witkin Cal. Proc. 5th Attack Judgment Trial Court § 62, Commencement and Running of Period.

8 Witkin Cal. Proc. 5th Attack Judgment Trial Court § 67, in General.

8 Witkin Cal. Proc. 5th Attack Judgment Trial Court § 142, Hearing and Determination.

1 Witkin Cal. Proc. 5th Attorneys § 224, Scope of Jurisdiction.

8 Witkin Cal. Proc. 5th Enforcement of Judgment § 102, (S 102) Preservation of Property.

8 Witkin Cal. Proc. 5th Enforcement of Judgment § 366, (S 366) General Rules Governing Undertakings.

7 Witkin Cal. Proc. 5th Judgment § 46, Minute Order on Motion.

2 Witkin Cal. Proc. 5th Jurisdiction § 91, (S 91) Violation of Jurisdictional Time Limit.

2 Witkin, California Summary 10th Insurance § 133, in General.

2 Witkin, California Summary 10th Insurance § 214, (S 214) Award and Review.

11 Witkin, California Summary 10th Husband and Wife § 371, (S 371) Civil Remedies.

4 Witkin, California Summary 10th Negotiable Instruments § 17, (S 17) Payee.

2 Witkin Cal. Summ. 10th Workers' Compensation § 85, (S 85) Action by Employer: Intervention by Employee.

§ 7. Offices abolished by repeal

CONSTRUCTION OF REPEAL AS TO CERTAIN OFFICES. When any office is abolished by the repeal of any Act, and such Act is not in substance reenacted or continued in either of the Codes, such office ceases at the time the Codes take effect. *(Enacted in 1872.)*

Research References

4 Witkin Cal. Proc. 5th Pleading § 397, (S 397) Pleading Truthfully.

6 Witkin Cal. Proc. 5th Proceedings Without Trial § 18, Extension by Stipulation or Court Order.

6 Witkin Cal. Proc. 5th Proceedings Without Trial § 114, (S 114) Former Motion Procedure.

§ 8. Pending actions and accrued rights; effect of code

ACTIONS, ETC., NOT AFFECTED BY THIS CODE. No action or proceeding commenced before this Code takes effect, and no right accrued, is affected by its provisions, but the proceedings therein must conform to the requirements of this Code as far as applicable. *(Enacted in 1872.)*

Research References

3 Witkin Cal. Proc. 5th Actions § 684, (S 684) Mandamus.

9 Witkin Cal. Proc. 5th Appeal § 185, Orders Dealing With Enforcement.

6 Witkin Cal. Proc. 5th Provisional Remedies § 79, (S 79) Community Property.

6 Witkin Cal. Proc. 5th Provisional Remedies § 86, (S 86) Homestead.

9 Witkin, California Summary 10th Taxation § 369, Enforcement and Collection.

10 Witkin, California Summary 10th Parent and Child § 285, (S 285) in General.

11 Witkin, California Summary 10th Husband and Wife § 335, (S 335) Levy by Agency.

11 Witkin, California Summary 10th Husband and Wife § 362, Integrated Agreement.

5 Witkin, California Summary 10th Torts § 105, Contribution Statute.

13 Witkin, California Summary 10th Equity § 178, Equitable Indemnity: Reimbursement from Principal.

13 Witkin, California Summary 10th Equity § 179, (S 179) Nature of Doctrine.

14 Witkin, California Summary 10th Wills and Probate § 645, Right to Bring Action.

14 Witkin, California Summary 10th Wills and Probate § 651, Interest.

14 Witkin, California Summary 10th Wills and Probate § 772, (S 772) Liability of Property.

§ 9. Running of limitations; effect of code

When a limitation or period of time prescribed in any existing statute for acquiring a right or barring a remedy, or for any other purpose, has begun to run before this Code goes into effect, and the same or any limitation is prescribed in this Code, the time which has already run shall be deemed part of the time prescribed as such limitation by this Code. *(Enacted in 1872. Amended by Code Am.1873–74, c. 383, p. 279, § 1.)*

Research References

Rutter, Cal. Practice Guide: Civil Appeals & Writs Ch. 8-C, C. Standards of Appellate Review.

Rutter, Cal. Practice Guide: Personal Injury Ch. 3-E, E. Punitive Damages.

8 Witkin Cal. Proc. 5th Enforcement of Judgment § 166, (S 166) Restitution After Reversal.

8 Witkin Cal. Proc. 5th Enforcement of Judgment § 362, (S 362) Review by Certiorari or Habeas Corpus.

11 Witkin, California Summary 10th Husband and Wife § 332, (S 332) Appeal.

7 Witkin, California Summary 10th Constitutional Law § 360, Requirement of License or Permit.

§ 10. Holidays

Holidays within the meaning of this code are every Sunday and any other days that are specified or provided for as judicial holidays in Section 135. *(Enacted in 1872. Amended by Code Am.1880, c. 51, p. 59, § 1; Stats.1889, c. 43, p. 46, § 1; Stats.1893, c. 159, p. 186, § 1; Stats.1897, c. 19, p. 15, § 1; Stats.1907, c. 287 p. 561, § 1; Stats.1907, Ex.Sess., c. 7, p. 7, § 1; Stats.1909, c. 29, p. 22, § 1; Stats.1911, c. 597, p. 1122, § 1; Stats.1925, c. 93, p. 225, § 1; Stats.1957, c. 43, p. 602, § 1; Stats.1982, c. 838, p. 3161, § 1, eff. Sept. 10, 1982; Stats.1994, c. 1011 (S.B.1373), § 1; Stats.2001, c. 542 (S.B.1112), § 1.)*

Research References

Rutter, Cal. Practice Guide: Civ. Pro. Before Trial Ch. 8E-2, When Depositions May be Taken.

Rutter, Cal. Practice Guide: Enforcing Judgments/Debts Ch. 6A-5, Amount Recoverable Under Judgment.

Rutter, Cal. Practice Guide: Personal Injury Ch. 5-A, A. Prelawsuit Filings.

Rutter, Cal. Practice Guide: Real Prop. Transactions Ch. 5-D, D. Common Law Environmental Hazards Liability.

Miller and Starr California Real Estate § 13:16, Residency, Ownership and Use.

3 Witkin Cal. Proc. 5th Actions § 741, General Rule.

§ 11. Certified mail; compliance with mailing provisions

Wherever any notice or other communication is required by this code to be mailed by registered mail by or to any person or corporation, the mailing of such notice or other communication by certified mail shall be deemed to be a sufficient compliance with the requirements of law. *(Added by Stats.1959, c. 426, p. 2364, § 2.)*

§ 12. Computation of time

COMPUTATION OF TIME. The time in which any act provided by law is to be done is computed by excluding the first day, and including the last, unless the last day is a holiday, and then it is also excluded. *(Enacted in 1872.)*

Research References

Rutter, Cal. Practice Guide: Civil Appeals & Writs Ch. 3-B, B. Filing Deadlines.

Rutter, Cal. Practice Guide: Civil Appeals & Writs Ch. 13-B, B. Petition for Review Procedures.

Rutter, Cal. Practice Guide: Civ. Pro. Before Trial Ch. 6-C, C. Answer.

Rutter, Cal. Practice Guide: Civ. Pro. Before Trial Ch. 10-C, C. Procedural Requirements-Moving Party.

Rutter, Cal. Practice Guide: Civ. Pro. Before Trial Ch. 9(I)-B, B. Preparing and Filing Motions.

Rutter, Cal. Practice Guide: Civil Trials & Evidence Ch. 18-B, B. Motion for New Trial.

Rutter, Cal. Practice Guide: Enforcing Judgments/Debts Ch. 6E-3, Procedures for Claiming Exemptions.

Rutter, Cal. Practice Guide: Personal Injury Ch. 4-D, D. Techniques Where Settlement Not Forthcoming.

Rutter, Cal. Practice Guide: Personal Injury Ch. 5-B, B. When to Sue-Statute of Limitations.

Rutter, Cal. Practice Guide: Personal Injury Ch. 10-A, A. Motion for New Trial.

Rutter, Cal. Practice Guide: Prof. Responsibility Ch. 11-H, H. Proceedings Before Trial.

Miller and Starr California Real Estate § 6:24, Timeliness of Performance.

Miller and Starr California Real Estate § 28:38, Time to File.

Miller and Starr California Real Estate § 28:56, Statute of Limitations; Time to File a Complaint.

Miller and Starr California Real Estate § 19:205, Service of the Notice--Legal Effect of the Notice; Tenant's Right to Cure a Default.

Miller and Starr California Real Estate § 25A:23, Type of Action; Time to File; Preparation of Administrative Record.

22 NO. 1 Miller & Starr, California Real Estate Newsalert 5, CEQA.

3 Witkin Cal. Proc. 5th Actions § 507, Computing Time.

3 Witkin Cal. Proc. 5th Actions § 719, Limitations Periods.

8 Witkin Cal. Proc. 5th Attack Judgment Trial Court § 62, Commencement and Running of Period.

2 Witkin Cal. Proc. 5th Courts § 50, (S 50) Where Last Day is Holiday.

2 Witkin Cal. Proc. 5th Courts § 142, 10-Day/5-Day Rule.

10 Witkin, California Summary 10th Parent and Child § 770, Time for Filing Welf.C. 602 Petition.

14 Witkin, California Summary 10th Wills and Probate § 517, (S 517) Action Against Decedent.

§ 12a. Computation of time; holidays; application of section

(a) If the last day for the performance of any act provided or required by law to be performed within a specified period of time is a holiday, then that period is hereby extended to and including the next day that is not a holiday. For purposes of this section, "holiday" means all day on Saturdays, all holidays specified in Section 135 and, to the extent provided in Section 12b, all days that by terms of Section 12b are required to be considered as holidays.

(b) This section applies to Sections 659, 659a, and 921, and to all other provisions of law providing or requiring an act to be performed on a particular day or within a specified period of time, whether expressed in this or any other code or statute, ordinance, rule, or regulation. *(Added by Stats.1933, c. 29, p. 304, § 1. Amended by Stats.1951, c. 492, p. 1646, § 2; Stats. 1955, c. 59, p. 498, § 1; Stats.1961, c. 1370, p. 3144, § 1; Stats.1982, c. 838, p. 3162, § 2, eff. Sept. 10, 1982; Stats.1994, c. 1011 (S.B.1373), § 2; Stats.2001, c. 542 (S.B.1112), § 2; Stats. 2007, c. 263 (A.B.310), § 3.)*

Law Revision Commission Comments

Subdivision (b) of Section 12a is amended to correct the cross-reference to former Section 946, which was repealed by 1968 Cal. Stat. ch. 385, § 1. The relevant substance of former Section 946 is continued in Section 921.

Subdivision (b) is further amended to delete the cross-references to former Sections 974 to 982. Those provisions have been repealed. See 1963 Cal. Stat. ch. 871, § 15. Justice and police courts no longer exist, so there are no corresponding new provisions.

Section 12a is also amended to make grammatical corrections and delete surplus language. [37 Cal.L.Rev.Comm. Reports App.4 (2007)].

Research References

California Real Estate Forms (Miller & Starr) § 2:17, Office Lease--Mixed Use Building.

California Real Estate Forms (Miller & Starr) § 2:18, Office Lease--Office/Warehouse Building With Four or Fewer Tenants.

California Real Estate Forms (Miller & Starr) § 2:23, Retail Lease--Small Strip-Shopping Center.

California Real Estate Forms (Miller & Starr) § 2:24, Retail Lease--Restaurant.

California Real Estate Forms (Miller & Starr) § 2:25, Industrial Lease.

California Real Estate Forms (Miller & Starr) § 2:38, Lease Amendment Expansion of Premises.

California Real Estate Forms (Miller & Starr) § 2:52, Option to Lease.

California Real Estate Forms (Miller & Starr) § 2:66, Residential Lease With Purchase Option.

Rutter, Cal. Practice Guide: Civil Appeals & Writs Ch. 3-B, B. Filing Deadlines.

Rutter, Cal. Practice Guide: Civil Appeals & Writs Ch. 13-B, B. Petition for Review Procedures.

Rutter, Cal. Practice Guide: Civ. Pro. Before Trial Ch. 1-C, C. Prelawsuit Notices, Claims and Demands.

Rutter, Cal. Practice Guide: Civ. Pro. Before Trial Ch. 4-D, D. Service of Summons.

Rutter, Cal. Practice Guide: Civ. Pro. Before Trial Ch. 11-B, B. Involuntary Dismissals.

Rutter, Cal. Practice Guide: Civ. Pro. Before Trial Ch. 13-G, G. Trial De Novo.

Rutter, Cal. Practice Guide: Civ. Pro. Before Trial Ch. 9(I)-B, B. Preparing and Filing Motions.

Rutter, Cal. Practice Guide: Civil Trials & Evidence Ch. 1-A, A. Importance of Statewide and Local Rules of Court.

Rutter, Cal. Practice Guide: Civil Trials & Evidence Ch. 18-B, B. Motion for New Trial.

Rutter, Cal. Practice Guide: Enforcing Judgments/Debts Ch. 6E-3, Procedures for Claiming Exemptions.

Rutter, Cal. Practice Guide: Personal Injury Ch. 4-D, D. Techniques Where Settlement Not Forthcoming.

Rutter, Cal. Practice Guide: Personal Injury Ch. 5-A, A. Prelawsuit Filings.

Rutter, Cal. Practice Guide: Personal Injury Ch. 5-B, B. When to Sue-Statute of Limitations.

Rutter, Cal. Practice Guide: Personal Injury Ch. 10-A, A. Motion for New Trial.

Rutter, Cal. Practice Guide: Prof. Responsibility Ch. 5-K, K. Fee Recovery/Enforcing Fee Agreements.

Rutter, Cal. Practice Guide: Prof. Responsibility Ch. 11-H, H. Proceedings Before Trial.

Miller and Starr California Real Estate § 19:37, Option to Extend or Renew Lease Term--Requirements for Exercise of the Option.

Miller and Starr California Real Estate § 28:38, Time to File.

14 NO. 2 Miller & Starr, California Real Estate Newsalert 14, Landlord and Tenant.

3 Witkin Cal. Proc. 5th Actions § 586, Limitations Periods.

3 Witkin Cal. Proc. 5th Actions § 688, (S 688) in General.

3 Witkin Cal. Proc. 5th Actions § 719, Limitations Periods.

9 Witkin Cal. Proc. 5th Appeal § 1019, (S 1019) Rehearing.

8 Witkin Cal. Proc. 5th Attack Judgment Trial Court § 62, Commencement and Running of Period.

8 Witkin Cal. Proc. 5th Attack Judgment Trial Court § 74, (S 74) Extensions.

1 Witkin Cal. Proc. 5th Attorneys § 231, Trial After Arbitration.

2 Witkin Cal. Proc. 5th Courts § 50, (S 50) Where Last Day is Holiday.

2 Witkin Cal. Proc. 5th Courts § 51, (S 51) No Extension by Intervening Holiday.

4 Witkin Cal. Proc. 5th Pleading § 9, (S 9) Computation of Time.

6 Witkin Cal. Proc. 5th Proceedings Without Trial § 322, Service Within 3 Years.

7 Witkin Cal. Proc. 5th Trial § 428, Order by Judge After Jury is Discharged.

12 Witkin, California Summary 10th Real Property § 531, (S 531) Manner of Exercise.

14 Witkin, California Summary 10th Wills and Probate § 517, (S 517) Action Against Decedent.

§ 12b. Computation of time; day on which public office closed considered holiday

If any city, county, state, or public office, other than a branch office, is closed for the whole of any day, insofar as the business of that office is concerned, that day shall be considered as a holiday for the purposes of computing time under Sections 12 and 12a. *(Added by Stats.1951, c. 655, p. 1852, § 25.)*

Research References

Rutter, Cal. Practice Guide: Civil Appeals & Writs Ch. 3-B, B. Filing Deadlines.

Rutter, Cal. Practice Guide: Civil Appeals & Writs Ch. 13-B, B. Petition for Review Procedures.

Rutter, Cal. Practice Guide: Civ. Pro. Before Trial Ch. 9(I)-B, B. Preparing and Filing Motions.

Rutter, Cal. Practice Guide: Civil Trials & Evidence Ch. 18-B, B. Motion for New Trial.

Rutter, Cal. Practice Guide: Enforcing Judgments/Debts Ch. 6E-3, Procedures for Claiming Exemptions.

Rutter, Cal. Practice Guide: Personal Injury Ch. 5-A, A. Prelawsuit Filings.

Rutter, Cal. Practice Guide: Personal Injury Ch. 5-B, B. When to Sue-Statute of Limitations.

Rutter, Cal. Practice Guide: Personal Injury Ch. 10-A, A. Motion for New Trial.

Rutter, Cal. Practice Guide: Prof. Responsibility Ch. 5-K, K. Fee Recovery/Enforcing Fee Agreements.

Rutter, Cal. Practice Guide: Prof. Responsibility Ch. 11-H, H. Proceedings Before Trial.

Miller and Starr California Real Estate § 28:38, Time to File.

3 Witkin Cal. Proc. 5th Actions § 719, Limitations Periods.

2 Witkin Cal. Proc. 5th Courts § 50, (S 50) Where Last Day is Holiday.

14 Witkin, California Summary 10th Wills and Probate § 517, (S 517) Action Against Decedent.

§ 12c. Computation of time; counting backward from hearing date

(a) Where any law requires an act to be performed no later than a specified number of days before a hearing date, the last day to perform that act shall be determined by counting backward from the hearing date, excluding the day of the hearing as provided by Section 12.

(b) Any additional days added to the specified number of days because of a particular method of service shall be computed by counting backward from the day determined in accordance with subdivision (a). *(Added by Stats.2010, c. 41 (A.B.2119), § 1.)*

Research References

Rutter, Cal. Practice Guide: A.D.R. Ch. 4-B, B. Judicial Arbitration.

Rutter, Cal. Practice Guide: Civ. Pro. Before Trial Ch. 10-C, C. Procedural Requirements-Moving Party.

Rutter, Cal. Practice Guide: Civ. Pro. Before Trial Ch. 9(I)-B, B. Preparing and Filing Motions.

Rutter, Cal. Practice Guide: Enforcing Judgments/Debts Ch. 6G-1, Examination of Judgment Debtor and Third Parties.

3 Witkin Cal. Proc. 5th Actions § 507, (S 507) Computing Time.

§ 13. Holidays; postponing performance

CERTAIN ACTS NOT TO BE DONE ON HOLIDAYS. Whenever any act of a secular nature, other than a work of necessity or mercy, is appointed by law or contract to be performed upon a particular day, which day falls upon a holiday, such act may be performed upon the next business day with the same effect as if it had been performed upon the day appointed. *(Enacted in 1872.)*

Research References

Rutter, Cal. Practice Guide: Prof. Responsibility Ch. 11-H, H. Proceedings Before Trial.

§ 13a. Special holidays; optional performance or postponement

Any act required by law to be performed on a particular day or within a specified period of time may be performed (but is not hereby required to be performed) on a special holiday as that term is used in Section 6705 of the Government Code, with like effect as if performed on a day which is not a holiday. *(Added by Stats.1933, c. 29, p. 305, § 2. Amended by Stats.1959, c. 594, p. 2565, § 1.)*

Research References

Rutter, Cal. Practice Guide: Prof. Responsibility Ch. 11-H, H. Proceedings Before Trial.

§ 13b. Saturday; optional performance

Any act required by law to be performed on a particular day or within a specified period may be performed (but is not hereby required to be performed) on a Saturday, with like effect as if performed on a day which is not a holiday. *(Added by Stats.1961, c. 1370, p. 3145, § 2.)*

Research References

Rutter, Cal. Practice Guide: Prof. Responsibility Ch. 11-H, H. Proceedings Before Trial.

Miller and Starr California Real Estate § 6:24, Timeliness of Performance.

2 Witkin Cal. Proc. 5th Courts § 50, (S 50) Where Last Day is Holiday.

§ 14. Seal defined

"SEAL" DEFINED. When the seal of a Court, public officer, or person is required by law to be affixed to any paper, the word "seal" includes an impression of such seal upon the paper alone as well as upon wax or a wafer affixed thereto. *(Enacted in 1872.)*

§ 15. Joint authority; majority control

JOINT AUTHORITY. Words giving a joint authority to three or more public officers or other persons are construed as giving such authority to a majority of them, unless it is otherwise expressed in the Act giving the authority. *(Enacted in 1872.)*

Research References

Rutter, Cal. Practice Guide: Civ. Pro. Before Trial Ch. 9(I)-B, B. Preparing and Filing Motions.

Rutter, Cal. Practice Guide: Enforcing Judgments/Debts Ch. 4-C, C. Receiverships.

Rutter, Cal. Practice Guide: Personal Injury Ch. 8-B, B. After Trial Date Set (Three to Four Months Before Trial).

§ 16. Construction of words and phrases

WORDS AND PHRASES. Words and phrases are construed according to the context and the approved usage of the language; but technical words and phrases, and such others as have acquired a peculiar and appropriate meaning in law, or are defined in the succeeding section, are to be construed according to such peculiar and appropriate meaning or definition. *(Enacted in 1872.)*

Research References

Rutter, Cal. Practice Guide: Enforcing Judgments/Debts Ch. 4-B, B. Claim and Delivery.

§ 17. Words and phrases; included meanings; signature by mark, formalities; interpretations and definitions

(a) Words used in this code in the present tense include the future as well as the present; words used in the masculine gender include the feminine and neuter; the singular number includes the plural and the plural the singular; the word "person" includes a corporation as well as a natural person; the word "county" includes "city and county"; writing includes printing and typewriting; oath includes affirmation or declaration; and every mode of oral statement, under oath or affirmation, is embraced by the term "testify," and every written one in the term "depose"; signature or subscription includes mark, when the person cannot write, his or her name being written near it by a person who writes his or her own name as a witness; provided, that when a signature is by mark it must, in order that the same may be acknowledged or may serve as the signature to any sworn statement, be witnessed by two persons who must subscribe their own names as witness thereto.

(b) The following words have in this code the signification attached to them in this section, unless otherwise apparent from the context:

(1) The word "property" includes both real and personal property.

(2) The words "real property" are coextensive with lands, tenements, and hereditaments.

(3) The words "personal property" include money, goods, chattels, things in action, and evidences of debt.

(4) The word "month" means a calendar month, unless otherwise expressed.

(5) The word "will" includes codicil.

(6) The word "writ" signifies an order or precept in writing, issued in the name of the people, or of a court or judicial officer, and the word "process" signifies a writ or summons issued in the course of judicial proceedings.

(7) The word "state," when applied to the different parts of the United States, includes the District of Columbia and the territories, and the words "United States" may include the district and territories.

(8) The word "section," whenever hereinafter employed, refers to a section of this code, unless some other code or statute is expressly mentioned.

(9) The word "affinity," when applied to the marriage relation, signifies the connection existing in consequence of marriage, between each of the married persons and the blood relatives of the other.

(10) The word "sheriff" shall include "marshal." *(Enacted in 1872. Amended by Code Am.1873–74, c. 383, p. 280, § 3; Stats.1903, c. 123, p. 134, § 1; Stats.1933, c. 742, p. 1804, § 1; Stats.1951, c. 1737, p. 4081, § 1, operative Jan. 1, 1952; Stats. 1996, c. 872 (A.B.3472), § 5; Stats.2002, c. 784 (S.B.1316), § 21; Stats.2003, c. 62 (S.B.600), § 21.)*

Law Revision Commission Comments

Section 17 is amended to reflect unification of the municipal and superior courts pursuant to Article VI, Section 5(e), of the California Constitution. See Section 38 (judicial district). *Cf.* Gov't Code § 71042.5 (preservation of judicial districts for purpose of publication). [32 Cal.L.Rev.Comm. Reports 89 (2002)].

Research References

Rutter, Cal. Practice Guide: Civ. Pro. Before Trial Ch. 4-A, A. Requirements-In General.
Rutter, Cal. Practice Guide: Civil Trials & Evidence Ch. 5-I, I. Challenging Prospective Jurors.
Miller and Starr California Real Estate § 19:2, Lease as Personal Property or Real Property.
Miller and Starr California Real Estate § 32:28, Attachment of Real Property.
3 Witkin Cal. Proc. 5th Actions § 959, Nature of Process.
6 Witkin Cal. Proc. 5th Proceedings Without Trial § 423, Extension Where Less Than 6 Months Remain.
13 Witkin, California Summary 10th Personal Property § 90, Test of Mobility.
14 Witkin, California Summary 10th Wills and Probate § 140, Signature by Mark.
14 Witkin, California Summary 10th Wills and Probate § 142, Typewritten Signature.

§ 18. Repeal of statutes relating to subjects covered by code; protection of vested rights; private statutes unaffected

STATUTES, ETC. INCONSISTENT WITH CODE REPEALED. No statute, law, or rule is continued in force because it is consistent with the provisions of this Code on the same subject; but in all cases provided for by this Code, all statutes, laws, and rules heretofore in force in this State, whether consistent or not with the provisions of this Code, unless expressly continued in force by it, are repealed and abrogated. This repeal or abrogation does not revive any former law heretofore repealed, nor does it affect any right already existing or accrued, or any action or proceeding already taken, except as in this Code provided; nor does it affect any private statute not expressly repealed. *(Enacted in 1872.)*

§ 19. Citation of code

THIS ACT, HOW CITED, ENUMERATED, ETC. This Act, whenever cited, enumerated, referred to, or amended, may be designated simply as "The Code of Civil Procedure," adding, when necessary, the number of the section. *(Enacted in 1872.)*

§ 20. Judicial remedies defined

JUDICIAL REMEDIES DEFINED. Judicial remedies are such as are administered by the Courts of justice, or by judicial officers empowered for that purpose by the Constitution and statutes of this State. *(Enacted in 1872.)*

Research References

Rutter, Cal. Practice Guide: Civil Appeals & Writs Ch. 2-B, B. Appealable Judgments and Orders.
Rutter, Cal. Practice Guide: Civil Appeals & Writs Ch. 15-C, C. Statutory Writs.
Rutter, Cal. Practice Guide: Civ. Pro. Before Trial Ch. 9(I)-J, J. Motion to Expunge Lis Pendens.
Rutter, Cal. Practice Guide: Civ. Pro. Before Trial Gen. Matls., Highlights.
3 Witkin Cal. Proc. 5th Actions § 2, (S 2) Nature of Judicial Remedy.
4 Witkin Cal. Proc. 5th Pleading § 485, (S 485) Illustrations.
6 Witkin Cal. Proc. 5th Provisional Remedies § 203, Nature of Lien.

§ 21. Classes of judicial remedies

DIVISION OF JUDICIAL REMEDIES. These remedies are divided into two classes:

1. Actions; and,

2. Special proceedings. *(Enacted in 1872.)*

Research References

Rutter, Cal. Practice Guide: Civil Appeals & Writs Ch. 7-A, A. Overview.
3 Witkin Cal. Proc. 5th Actions § 2, (S 2) Nature of Judicial Remedy.

§ 22. Action defined

An action is an ordinary proceeding in a court of justice by which one party prosecutes another for the declaration, enforcement, or protection of a right, the redress or prevention of a wrong, or the punishment of a public offense. *(Enacted in 1872. Amended by Stats.1933, c. 742, p. 1805, § 2.)*

Research References

Rutter, Cal. Practice Guide: A.D.R. Ch. 5-D, D. Defenses to Enforcement.
Rutter, Cal. Practice Guide: Real Prop. Transactions Ch. 6-I, I. Real Property Foreclosures and Antideficiency Laws.
Miller and Starr California Real Estate § 11:149, Procedural and Formal Requirements for a Lis Pendens.
15 NO. 4 Miller & Starr, California Real Estate Newsalert 1, California's "One Form of Action" and "Security First" Rules: Have They Cleared the Minefields Yet?
3 Witkin Cal. Proc. 5th Actions § 62, (S 62) Definition and Distinctions.
6 Witkin Cal. Proc. 5th Provisional Remedies § 38, Nature of Motion.
4 Witkin, California Summary 10th Security Transactions in Real Property § 128, Remedy is Not Action.
4 Witkin, California Summary 10th Security Transactions in Real Property § 129, Property or Mortgagor is Outside State.
4 Witkin, California Summary 10th Security Transactions in Real Property § 134, Distinction: No Waiver of Underlying Debt.

§ 23. Special proceeding defined

SPECIAL PROCEEDING DEFINED. Every other remedy is a special proceeding. *(Enacted in 1872.)*

Research References

Rutter, Cal. Practice Guide: A.D.R. Ch. 6-C, C. Referees.
Rutter, Cal. Practice Guide: Civil Appeals & Writs Ch. 7-A, A. Overview.
Rutter, Cal. Practice Guide: Civil Trials & Evidence Ch. 16-G, G. Trial by Reference.
3 Witkin Cal. Proc. 5th Actions § 64, (S 64) Distinguished from Action.
6 Witkin Cal. Proc. 5th Proceedings Without Trial § 440, Premature Dismissal is Improper.

§ 24. Kinds of actions

DIVISION OF ACTIONS. Actions are of two kinds:

1. Civil; and,

2. Criminal. *(Enacted in 1872.)*

§ 25. Civil action; origin

CIVIL ACTIONS ARISE OUT OF OBLIGATIONS OR INJURIES. A civil action arises out of:

1. An obligation;

2. An injury. *(Enacted in 1872.)*

§ 26. Obligation defined

An obligation is a legal duty, by which one person is bound to do or not to do a certain thing, and arises from:

One—Contract; or,

Two—Operation of law. *(Enacted in 1872. Amended by Code Am.1873–74, c. 383, p. 281, § 4.)*

§ 27. Kinds of injuries

DIVISION OF INJURIES. An injury is of two kinds:

1. To the person; and,

2. To property. *(Enacted in 1872.)*

§ 28. Injury to property defined

INJURIES TO PROPERTY. An injury to property consists in depriving its owner of the benefit of it, which is done by taking, withholding, deteriorating, or destroying it. *(Enacted in 1872.)*

§ 29. Injury to person defined

INJURIES TO THE PERSON. Every other injury is an injury to the person. *(Enacted in 1872.)*

§ 30. Civil action defined

A civil action is prosecuted by one party against another for the declaration, enforcement or protection of a right, or the redress or prevention of a wrong. *(Enacted in 1872. Amended by Stats.1933, c. 742, p. 1805, § 3.)*

§ 31. Criminal actions

CRIMINAL ACTIONS. The Penal Code defines and provides for the prosecution of a criminal action. *(Enacted in 1872.)*

§ 32. Separation of civil and criminal remedies

CIVIL AND CRIMINAL REMEDIES NOT MERGED. When the violation of a right admits of both a civil and criminal remedy, the right to prosecute the one is not merged in the other. *(Enacted in 1872.)*

§ 32.5. Jurisdictional classification

The "jurisdictional classification" of a case means its classification as a limited civil case or an unlimited civil case. *(Added by Stats.1998, c. 931 (S.B.2139), § 19, eff. Sept. 28, 1998. Amended by Stats.2002, c. 784 (S.B.1316), § 22.)*

Law Revision Commission Comments

Section 32.5 is added to accommodate unification of the municipal and superior courts in a county. Cal. Const. art. VI, § 5(e). See Section 85 (limited civil cases) & Comment. The term is used in Sections 395.9, 996.430, 1140, 1171, 1206, and 1287.4. [28 Cal.L.Rev.Comm. Reports 51 (1998)].

Section 32.5 is amended to replace the reference to "otherwise" with a reference to an "unlimited civil case." See Section 88 (civil action or proceeding other than limited civil case may be referred to as unlimited civil case). [32 Cal.L.Rev.Comm. Reports 90 (2002)].

Part 1

OF COURTS OF JUSTICE

Title 1

ORGANIZATION AND JURISDICTION

CHAPTER 1. COURTS OF JUSTICE IN GENERAL

Section

§ 33. Crimes against property; civil resolution in lieu of criminal complaint; prosecutor's discretion

A prosecuting attorney, in his or her discretion, may assist in the civil resolution of a violation of an offense described in Title 13 (commencing with Section 450) of Part 1 of the Penal Code in lieu of filing a criminal complaint. *(Added by Stats.1982, c. 1518, p. 5890, § 1.)*

Research References

Rutter, Cal. Practice Guide: Civil Trials & Evidence Ch. 8E-D, D. Other Public Policy Exclusions.

§ 35. Election matters; precedence

Proceedings in cases involving the registration or denial of registration of voters, the certification or denial of certification of candidates, the certification or denial of certification of ballot measures, and election contests shall be placed on the calendar in the order of their date of filing and shall be given precedence. *(Added by Stats.1971, c. 980, p. 1893, § 1.)*

Research References

Rutter, Cal. Practice Guide: Civ. Pro. Before Trial Ch. 12(I)-C, C. Claims for Trial Setting Preference.
7 Witkin Cal. Proc. 5th Trial § 72, (S 72) Miscellaneous Statutes.

§ 36. Motion for preference; party over 70 years of age; party under 14 years of age; medical reasons; interests of justice; time of trial

(a) A party to a civil action who is over 70 years of age may petition the court for a preference, which the court shall grant if the court makes both of the following findings:

(1) The party has a substantial interest in the action as a whole.

(2) The health of the party is such that a preference is necessary to prevent prejudicing the party's interest in the litigation.

(b) A civil action to recover damages for wrongful death or personal injury shall be entitled to preference upon the motion of any party to the action who is under 14 years of age unless the court finds that the party does not have a substantial interest in the case as a whole. A civil action subject to subdivision (a) shall be given preference over a case subject to this subdivision.

(c) Unless the court otherwise orders:

(1) A party may file and serve a motion for preference supported by a declaration of the moving party that all essential parties have been served with process or have appeared.

(2) At any time during the pendency of the action, a party who reaches 70 years of age may file and serve a motion for preference.

(d) In its discretion, the court may also grant a motion for preference that is accompanied by clear and convincing medical documentation that concludes that one of the parties suffers from an illness or condition raising substantial medical doubt of survival of that party beyond six months, and that satisfies the court that the interests of justice will be served by granting the preference.

(e) Notwithstanding any other provision of law, the court may in its discretion grant a motion for preference that is supported by a showing that satisfies the court that the interests of justice will be served by granting this preference.

(f) Upon the granting of such a motion for preference, the court shall set the matter for trial not more than 120 days from that date and there shall be no continuance beyond 120 days from the granting of the motion for preference except for physical disability of a party or a party's attorney, or upon a showing of good cause stated in the record. Any continuance shall be for no more than 15 days and no more than one continuance for physical disability may be granted to any party.

(g) Upon the granting of a motion for preference pursuant to subdivision (b), a party in an action based upon a health provider's alleged professional negligence, as defined in Section 364, shall receive a trial date not sooner than six months and not later than nine months from the date that the motion is granted. *(Added by Stats.1979, c. 151, p. 348, § 2. Amended by Stats.1981, c. 215, § 1; Stats.1988, c. 1237, § 1; Stats.1989, c. 913, § 1; Stats.1990, c. 428 (A.B.3811), § 1; Stats.2008, c. 218 (A.B.1949), § 1.)*

Research References

Rutter, Cal. Practice Guide: A.D.R. Ch. 4-B, B. Judicial Arbitration.
Rutter, Cal. Practice Guide: Civil Appeals & Writs Ch. 5-B, B. Types of Motions, Applications and Requests.
Rutter, Cal. Practice Guide: Civil Appeals & Writs Ch. 15-B, B. Common Law Writs.
Rutter, Cal. Practice Guide: Civ. Pro. Before Trial Ch. 6-B, B. Complaints.
Rutter, Cal. Practice Guide: Civ. Pro. Before Trial Ch. 11-B, B. Involuntary Dismissals.
Rutter, Cal. Practice Guide: Civ. Pro. Before Trial Ch. 13-C, C. Civil Proceedings Subject to Judicial Arbitration.
Rutter, Cal. Practice Guide: Civ. Pro. Before Trial Ch. 8C-5, Privacy Protection.
Rutter, Cal. Practice Guide: Civ. Pro. Before Trial Ch. 12(I)-C, C. Claims for Trial Setting Preference.
Rutter, Cal. Practice Guide: Civ. Pro. Before Trial Ch. 12(I)-F, F. Motions to Continue Trial.
Rutter, Cal. Practice Guide: Civ. Pro. Before Trial Ch. 12(I)-F, Outline F.
Rutter, Cal. Practice Guide: Civil Trials & Evidence Ch. 1-A, A. Importance of Statewide and Local Rules of Court.
Rutter, Cal. Practice Guide: Civil Trials & Evidence Ch. 1-K, K. Continuance Motions.
Rutter, Cal. Practice Guide: Civil Trials & Evidence Ch. 1-K, Outline K.
Rutter, Cal. Practice Guide: Fed.Civ.Pro. Before Trial Ch. 1-D, D. Choosing Between State and Federal Courts.
Rutter, Cal. Practice Guide: Personal Injury Ch. 3-E, E. Punitive Damages.
Rutter, Cal. Practice Guide: Personal Injury Ch. 6-A, A. Scope of Discovery and Limitations.
Rutter, Cal. Practice Guide: Personal Injury Ch. 7-C, C. Actions Subject to Judicial Arbitration.
Rutter, Cal. Practice Guide: Personal Injury Ch. 8-A, A. Case Management.
Rutter, Cal. Practice Guide: Personal Injury Ch. 9-A, A. Assignment to Trial.
Rutter, Cal. Practice Guide: Personal Injury Ch. 6-A, Outline a.
Rutter, Cal. Practice Guide: Personal Injury Ch. 9-A, Outline a.

9 Witkin Cal. Proc. 5th Appeal § 764, Statutory Preferences and Advancement.
1 Witkin Cal. Proc. 5th Attorneys § 324, (S 324) Illustrations.
2 Witkin Cal. Proc. 5th Courts § 173, (S 173) Nature of Inherent Powers.
2 Witkin Cal. Proc. 5th Courts § 257, (S 257) Nature and Scope.
6 Witkin Cal. Proc. 5th Proceedings Without Trial § 425, (S 425) in General.
6 Witkin Cal. Proc. 5th Proceedings Without Trial § 458, Effect of Trial Preference.
6 Witkin Cal. Proc. 5th Proceedings Without Trial § 583, (S 583) Cases Excluded from Arbitration.
7 Witkin Cal. Proc. 5th Trial § 31, (S 31) Particular Actions and Proceedings.
7 Witkin Cal. Proc. 5th Trial § 66, (S 66) in General.
7 Witkin Cal. Proc. 5th Trial § 69, (S 69) Party Over Age 70.
7 Witkin Cal. Proc. 5th Trial § 70, (S 70) Party Under Age 14.
7 Witkin Cal. Proc. 5th Trial § 71, (S 71) Party's Survival in Doubt.
6 Witkin, California Summary 10th Torts § 1603, (S 1603) Time Limits.
7 Witkin, California Summary 10th Constitutional Law § 581, (S 581) Discovery of Medical Patient's Records.
14 Witkin, California Summary 10th Wills and Probate § 578, (S 578) Trial.

§ 36.5. Motion for preference; affidavit

An affidavit submitted in support of a motion for preference under subdivision (a) of Section 36 may be signed by the attorney for the party seeking preference based upon information and belief as to the medical diagnosis and prognosis of any party. The affidavit is not admissible for any purpose other than a motion for preference under subdivision (a) of Section 36. *(Added by Stats.1990, c. 1232 (A.B.3820), § 1.)*

Research References

Rutter, Cal. Practice Guide: Civ. Pro. Before Trial Ch. 12(I)-C, C. Claims for Trial Setting Preference.
Rutter, Cal. Practice Guide: Personal Injury Ch. 8-A, A. Case Management.
7 Witkin Cal. Proc. 5th Trial § 69, (S 69) Party Over Age 70.

§ 37. Preference; action for damages incurred during felony; time

(a) A civil action shall be entitled to preference, if the action is one in which the plaintiff is seeking damages which were alleged to have been caused by the defendant during the commission of a felony offense for which the defendant has been criminally convicted.

(b) The court shall endeavor to try the action within 120 days of the grant of preference. *(Added by Stats.1982, c. 514, p. 2297, § 1. Amended by Stats.1983, c. 938, § 1, eff. Sept. 20, 1983.)*

Research References

Rutter, Cal. Practice Guide: Civil Appeals & Writs Ch. 5-B, B. Types of Motions, Applications and Requests.
Rutter, Cal. Practice Guide: Civ. Pro. Before Trial Ch. 12(I)-C, C. Claims for Trial Setting Preference.
Rutter, Cal. Practice Guide: Personal Injury Ch. 8-A, A. Case Management.
7 Witkin Cal. Proc. 5th Trial § 72, (S 72) Miscellaneous Statutes.

§ 38. Judicial district

Unless the provision or context otherwise requires, a reference in a statute to a judicial district means:

(a) As it relates to a court of appeal, the court of appeal district.

(b) As it relates to a superior court, the county.

(c) As it relates to a municipal court, the municipal court district.

(d) As it relates to a county in which there is no municipal court, the county. *(Added by Stats.1998, c. 931 (S.B.2139), § 20, eff. Sept. 28, 1998.)*

Law Revision Commission Comments

Section 38 is intended for drafting convenience. See also Section 17 ("judicial district" includes city and county). Court of appeal districts and municipal court districts are constitutionally mandated. See Cal. Const. art. VI, §§ 3, 5. Superior court districts do not exist except in Los Angeles County. See Gov't Code §§ 69640–69650.

By operation of this section, in a county in which the superior and municipal courts have unified, a statutory reference to a judicial district means the county rather than a former municipal court district. This general rule is subject to exceptions. See, e.g., Gov't Code 71042.5 (preservation of judicial districts for purpose of publication). [28 Cal.L.Rev.Comm. Reports 51 (1998)].

Research References

Miller and Starr California Real Estate § 10:199, Publication, Mailing, and Recording the Notice.
Miller and Starr California Real Estate § 10:226, The Judicial Sale.
2 Witkin Cal. Proc. 5th Courts § 166, Consolidation of Municipal and Superior Court.

CHAPTER 3. SUPREME COURT [AND COURTS OF APPEAL]

Section
41. Transaction of business.
42. Adjournments construed as recesses.
43. Supreme court and courts of appeal; powers in appealed cases; questions determinable; judgment.
44. Preference in hearing on appeal; probate proceedings; election cases.
45. Appeal from judgment freeing or denying a recommendation to free a minor from parent custody and control; priority; extension of time.

§ 41. Transaction of business

The Supreme Court and the courts of appeal may transact business at any time. *(Formerly § 61.4, added by Stats.1951, c. 655, p. 1839, § 8. Amended by Stats.1953, c. 206, p. 1339, § 2. Renumbered § 41 and amended by Stats.1967, c. 17, p. 827, § 7.)*

Research References

2 Witkin Cal. Proc. 5th Courts § 45, Judicial Days.
2 Witkin Cal. Proc. 5th Courts § 328, (S 328) Sessions and Conferences.
2 Witkin Cal. Proc. 5th Courts § 334, (S 334) Sessions and Conferences.

§ 42. Adjournments construed as recesses

Adjournments from day to day, or from time to time, are to be construed as recesses in the sessions, and shall not prevent the Supreme Court or the courts of appeal from sitting at any time. *(Formerly § 48, added by Code Am.1880, c. 35, p. 25, § 1. Renumbered § 42 and amended by Stats.1967, c. 17, p. 827, § 4.)*

Research References

2 Witkin Cal. Proc. 5th Courts § 45, Judicial Days.

§ 43. Supreme court and courts of appeal; powers in appealed cases; questions determinable; judgment

The Supreme Court, and the courts of appeal, may affirm, reverse, or modify any judgment or order appealed from, and may direct the proper judgment or order to be entered, or direct a new trial or further proceedings to be had. In giving its decision, if a new trial be granted, the court shall pass upon and determine all the questions of law involved in the case, presented upon such appeal, and necessary to the final determination of the case. Its judgment in appealed cases shall be remitted to the court from which the appeal was taken. *(Formerly § 53, added by Code Am.1880, c. 35, p. 25, § 1. Amended by Stats.1933, c. 743, p. 1807, § 6. Renumbered § 43 and amended by Stats.1967, c. 17, p. 827, § 5.)*

Research References

Rutter, Cal. Practice Guide: Civil Appeals & Writs Ch. 8-D, D. Limits on Assertion of Issues on Appeal.

Rutter, Cal. Practice Guide: Civil Appeals & Writs Ch. 11-D, D. Disposition.

Rutter, Cal. Practice Guide: Civil Appeals & Writs Ch. 14-A, A. Remittitur.

Rutter, Cal. Practice Guide: Civil Appeals & Writs Ch. 14-C, C. Trial Court Proceedings After Reversal.

9 Witkin Cal. Proc. 5th Appeal § 343, (S 343) Exception: Guidance of Trial Court or Administrative Body.

9 Witkin Cal. Proc. 5th Appeal § 842, (S 842) Procedure.

9 Witkin Cal. Proc. 5th Appeal § 843, (S 843) Proceedings in Which Remittitur Issues.

9 Witkin Cal. Proc. 5th Appeal § 853, (S 853) Nature and Effect.

9 Witkin Cal. Proc. 5th Appeal § 855, (S 855) Nature of Power.

9 Witkin Cal. Proc. 5th Appeal § 883, in General.

8 Witkin Cal. Proc. 5th Attack Judgment Trial Court § 4, Coram Nobis and Coram Vobis.

§ 44. Preference in hearing on appeal; probate proceedings; election cases

Appeals in probate proceedings, in contested election cases, and in actions for libel or slander by a person who holds any elective public office or a candidate for any such office alleged to have occurred during the course of an election campaign shall be given preference in hearing in the courts of appeal, and in the Supreme Court when transferred thereto. All these cases shall be placed on the calendar in the order of their date of issue, next after cases in which the people of the state are parties. *(Formerly § 57, added by Stats.1887, c. 73, p. 82, § 1. Amended by Stats.1903, c. 62, p. 69, § 1; Stats.1933, c. 743, p. 1807, § 7. Renumbered § 44 and amended by Stats.1967, c. 17, § 6. Amended by Stats.1982, c. 1642, p. 6676, § 1.)*

Research References

Rutter, Cal. Practice Guide: Civil Appeals & Writs Ch. 5-B, B. Types of Motions, Applications and Requests.

Rutter, Cal. Practice Guide: Civil Appeals & Writs Form 5:F.1, Motion for Calendar Preference.

9 Witkin Cal. Proc. 5th Appeal § 764, Statutory Preferences and Advancement.

7 Witkin, California Summary 10th Constitutional Law § 270A, (S 270A) (New)-Election Contests.

§ 45. Appeal from judgment freeing or denying a recommendation to free a minor from parent custody and control; priority; extension of time

An appeal from a judgment freeing a minor who is a dependent child of the juvenile court from parental custody and control, or denying a recommendation to free a minor from parental custody or control, shall have precedence over all cases in the court to which an appeal in the matter is taken. In order to enable the child to be available for adoption as soon as possible and to minimize the anxiety to all parties, the appellate court shall grant an extension of time to a court reporter or to counsel only upon an exceptional showing of good cause. *(Added by Stats.1988, c. 805, § 2, operative Jan. 1, 1993. Amended by Stats.1997, c. 510 (A.B.329), § 1.)*

Research References

Rutter, Cal. Practice Guide: Civil Appeals & Writs Ch. 5-B, B. Types of Motions, Applications and Requests.

9 Witkin Cal. Proc. 5th Appeal § 764, Statutory Preferences and Advancement.

10 Witkin, California Summary 10th Parent and Child § 351, (S 351) in General.

CHAPTER 4. SUPERIOR COURTS

§ 71. Process

The process of superior courts shall extend throughout the state. *(Added by Stats.1967, c. 17, p. 827, § 8.)*

Research References

3 Witkin Cal. Proc. 5th Actions § 965, Necessity and Scope of Service.

2 Witkin Cal. Proc. 5th Courts § 209, (S 209) Court of Particular County.

5 Witkin, California Summary 10th Torts § 95, in General.

§ 73c. Savings and loan associations; place of hearings relating to sale, exchange, or other disposition of property

Notwithstanding anything to the contrary contained in any other law of this state, the judges of the superior court of the county in which is located the principal office in this state of any savings and loan association of whose business, property and assets possession shall have been taken by the Commissioner of Financial Institutions, may, in their discretion, whenever those judges deem it necessary or advisable, hold hearings relating to the sale, exchange or other disposition of any parcel of real property or any item of personal property of the association, regardless of the location of the property, at the county seat of any county in this state or at the places in the county in which the principal office in this state of the association is located at which sessions of the superior court are held. *(Added by Stats.1945, c. 3, p. 310, § 1. Amended by Stats.2003, c. 149 (S.B.79), § 1.)*

Law Revision Commission Comments

Section 73c is amended to reflect enactment of Government Code Section 69740(a) (number and location of trial court sessions).

The section is also amended to delete language referring to "the judge" of the court. Every superior court has at least two judgeships as a result of trial court unification. See Gov't Code § 69580 *et seq.* (number of judges). Where a court has only one judge due to a vacancy or otherwise, a reference to the judges of the court means the sole judge of the court. See Gov't Code § 13 (plural includes singular).

The section is also amended to delete the references to former Sections 73 and 142.

The section is also amended to replace the reference to the former "Building and Loan Commissioner" with a reference to the "Commissioner of Financial Institutions." See 1955 Cal. Stat. ch. 40, § 1; Fin. Code § 210.5(c).

The section is also amended to replace the reference to "building and loan association" with a reference to "savings and loan association." See 1955 Cal. Stat. ch. 40, § 1. [33 Cal.L.Rev.Comm. Reports 185, 186 (2003)].

§ 73d. Savings and loan associations; special hearings; expenses of court officials

Whenever, under Section 73c, it becomes necessary for a judge, clerk, deputy clerk, court reporter or bailiff of or sitting in the superior court of the county in this state in which is located the principal office of any savings and loan association whose business, property and assets are in the possession of the Commissioner of Financial Institutions, to travel to another county, there temporarily to attend hearings relating to the sale, exchange or other disposition of real or personal property of the association, each judge, clerk, deputy clerk, court reporter or bailiff shall be allowed the necessary expenses in going to, returning from and attending upon the business of the court. The expenses shall, upon order of the court, be a charge against the funds of the association and paid out of those funds by the Commissioner of Financial Institutions. *(Added by Stats.1945, c. 3, p. 310, § 2. Amended by Stats.2003, c. 149 (S.B.79), § 2.)*

Law Revision Commission Comments

Section 73d is amended to replace references to the former "Building and Loan Commissioner" with references to the "Commissioner of Financial Institutions." See 1955 Cal. Stat. ch. 40, § 1; Fin. Code § 210.5(c).

The section is also amended to replace the reference to "building and loan association" with a reference to "savings and loan association." See 1955 Cal. Stat. ch. 40, § 1. [33 Cal.L.Rev.Comm. Reports 186 (2003)].

§ 73e. Sessions; judicial districts in which juvenile hall located

Notwithstanding any other provisions of law, in each county wherein the juvenile hall is not located at the county seat of the county, a majority of the judges of the superior court in and for such county may by an order filed with the clerk of the court direct that a session or sessions of the superior court, while sitting for the purpose of hearing and determining cases and proceedings arising under Chapter 2 of Part 1 of Division 2 or Chapter 2 of Part 1 of Division 6 or Chapter 4 of Part 4 of Division 6 of the Welfare and Institutions Code, may be held or continued in any place in the county in which the juvenile hall is located and thereafter such session or sessions of the court may be held or continued in the location designated in such order. In a county having two superior court judges the presiding judge may make the order. *(Added by Stats.1947, c. 1346, p. 2902, § 1. Amended by Stats.1951, c. 1737, p. 4080, 4082, § 2, operative Jan. 1, 1952; Stats.1955, c. 966, p. 1866, § 1; Stats.2002, c. 784 (S.B.1316), § 24.)*

Law Revision Commission Comments

Section 73e is amended to reflect unification of the municipal and superior courts pursuant to Article VI, Section 5(e), of the California Constitution. *Cf.* Section 38 (judicial district).

The section is also amended to reflect elimination of the county clerk's role as ex officio clerk of the superior court. See former Gov't Code § 26800 (county clerk acting as clerk of superior court). The powers, duties, and responsibilities formerly exercised by the county clerk as ex officio clerk of the court are delegated to the court administrative or executive officer, and the county clerk is relieved of those powers, duties, and responsibilities. See Gov't Code §§ 69840 (powers, duties, and responsibilities of clerk of court and deputy clerk of court), 71620 (trial court personnel).

The section is also amended to replace language referring to the senior judge with language referring to the presiding judge. Every superior court has a presiding judge. See Gov't Code §§ 69508, 69508.5. [32 Cal.L.Rev. Comm. Reports 91 (2002)].

Research References

2 Witkin Cal. Proc. 5th Courts § 219, in General.

§ 74. Adjournments construed as recesses

Adjournments from day to day, or from time to time, are to be construed as recesses in the sessions, and shall not prevent the Court from sitting at any time. *(Added by Code Am.1880, c. 35, p. 28, § 1.)*

Research References

2 Witkin Cal. Proc. 5th Courts § 45, Judicial Days.

§ 75. Submission of noncontested matter; statement

The superior court in any county may by rule provide that, whenever all judges are absent from the county, any noncontested matter in which no evidence is required, or which may be submitted upon affidavits, shall be deemed submitted upon the filing with the clerk of a statement of submission by the party or the party's attorney or upon the date set for the hearing. *(Added by Stats.1953, c. 1111, p. 2606, § 1. Amended by Stats.1959, c. 744, p. 2731, § 1; Stats.2002, c. 784 (S.B.1316), § 25.)*

Law Revision Commission Comments

Section 75 is amended to reflect the fact that every superior court has at least two judgeships as a result of trial court unification. See Gov't Code § 69580 *et seq.* (number of judges). [32 Cal.L.Rev.Comm. Reports 92 (2002)].

Research References

Rutter, Cal. Practice Guide: Fed.Civ.Pro. Before Trial Ch. 1-D, D. Choosing Between State and Federal Courts.

§ 77. Appellate division of superior court; composition; designated judges; decisions; transaction of business; jurisdiction and powers; procedure

(a) In every county and city and county, there is an appellate division of the superior court consisting of three judges or, when the Chief Justice finds it necessary, four judges.

The Chief Justice shall assign judges to the appellate division for specified terms pursuant to rules, not inconsistent with statute, adopted by the Judicial Council to promote the independence and quality of each appellate division. Each judge assigned to the appellate division of a superior court shall be a judge of that court, a judge of the superior court of another county, or a judge retired from the superior court or a court of higher jurisdiction in this state.

The Chief Justice shall designate one of the judges of each appellate division as the presiding judge of the division.

(b) In each appellate division, no more than three judges shall participate in a hearing or decision. The presiding judge of the division shall designate the three judges who shall participate.

(c) In addition to their other duties, the judges designated as members of the appellate division of the superior court shall serve for the period specified in the order of designation. Whenever a judge is designated to serve in the appellate division of the superior court of a county other than the county in which that judge was elected or appointed as a superior court judge, or if the judge is retired, in a county other than the county in which the judge resides, the judge shall receive expenses for travel, board, and lodging. If the judge is out of the judge's county overnight or longer, by reason of the designation, that judge shall be paid a per diem allowance in lieu of expenses for board and lodging in the same amounts as are payable for those purposes to justices of the Supreme Court under the rules of the California Victim Compensation and Government Claims Board. In addition, a retired judge shall receive for the time so served, amounts equal to that which the judge would have received if the judge had been assigned to the superior court of the county.

(d) The concurrence of two judges of the appellate division of the superior court shall be necessary to render the decision in every case in, and to transact any other business except business that may be done at chambers by the presiding judge of, the division. The presiding judge shall convene the appellate division when necessary. The presiding judge shall also supervise its business and transact any business that may be done at chambers.

(e) The appellate division of the superior court has jurisdiction on appeal in all cases in which an appeal may be taken to the superior court or the appellate division of the superior court as provided by law, except where the appeal is a retrial in the superior court.

(f) The powers of each appellate division shall be the same as are now or may hereafter be provided by law or rule of the

Judicial Council relating to appeals to the appellate division of the superior courts.

(g) The Judicial Council shall promulgate rules, not inconsistent with law, to promote the independence of, and govern the practice and procedure and the disposition of the business of, the appellate division.

(h) Notwithstanding subdivisions (b) and (d), appeals from convictions of traffic infractions may be heard and decided by one judge of the appellate division of the superior court. *(Added by Stats.1955, c. 527, p. 1000, § 1. Amended by Stats.1961, c. 937, p. 2570, § 1; Stats.1976, c. 1288, p. 5758, § 1; Stats.1984, c. 704, § 1; Stats.1998, c. 931 (S.B.2139), § 21, eff. Sept. 28, 1998; Stats.1998, c. 932 (A.B.1094), § 11.5, operative Jan. 1, 1999; Stats.1999, c. 344 (S.B.210), § 2, eff. Sept. 7, 1999; Stats.1999, c. 853 (S.B.832), § 1.5; Stats.2002, c. 784 (S.B.1316), § 26; Stats.2006, c. 538 (S.B.1852), § 60.)*

Law Revision Commission Comments

Section 77 is amended to accommodate unification of the municipal and superior courts in a county. Cal. Const. art. VI, § 5(e).

Subdivision (a) requires adoption of court rules intended to promote the independence and quality of judges serving in the appellate division. See Cal. Const. art. VI, § 4 (expressly recognizing the goal of promoting the independence of the appellate division). Rules may provide relevant factors to be used in making appointments to the appellate division, such as length of service as a judge, reputation within the unified court, and degree of separateness of the appellate division workload from the judge's regular assignments (e.g., a superior court judge who routinely handles large numbers of misdemeanors might ordinarily not serve in the appellate division). Review by a panel of judges might include judges assigned from another county in appropriate circumstances, or even by a panel of appellate division judges from different superior courts who sit in turn in each of the superior courts in the "circuit."

Subdivision (b) continues the rule that the appellate division sits in panels of three. A judge may not participate in appellate review of any proceeding that the judge tried or heard. Section 170.1(b).

Subdivision (e) is amended to reflect elimination of the justice court. Cal. Const. art. VI, §§ 1, 5(b). It is also amended to specify the jurisdiction of the appellate division in a unified superior court. For guidance on which civil cases are subject to the appellate jurisdiction of the appellate division, see Section 904.2 (taking appeal in limited civil case) and Constitution Article VI, Section 11.

Section 77 is amended throughout to replace references to the appellate department with references to the appellate division, and to replace references to the Chairperson of the Judicial Council with references to the Chief Justice. This is consistent with the terminology used in Constitution Article VI. [28 Cal.L.Rev.Comm. Reports App. 7 (1998)].

Subdivision (h) of Section 77 is amended to refer more precisely to the appellate division. See Cal. Const. art. VI, § 4. [29 Cal.L.Rev.Comm. Reports App. 5 (1999)].

Subdivision (c) of Section 77 is amended to reflect enactment of the Trial Court Funding Act. See Gov't Code §§ 77003 ("court operations" defined), 77200 (state funding of trial court operations).

Subdivisions (e) and (h) are amended to reflect unification of the municipal and superior courts pursuant to Article VI, Section 5(e), of the California Constitution.

Subdivision (i) is deleted as obsolete. [32 Cal.L.Rev.Comm. Reports 92 (2002)].

Research References

Rutter, Cal. Practice Guide: Civil Appeals & Writs Ch. 3-A, A. Necessity of Timely Filing for Appeal.
Rutter, Cal. Practice Guide: Civil Appeals & Writs Ch. 16-A, A. Introduction.
9 Witkin Cal. Proc. 5th Appeal § 1002, in General.
2 Witkin Cal. Proc. 5th Courts § 339, (S 339) Organization.
2 Witkin Cal. Proc. 5th Courts § 340, (S 340) Operation.
2 Witkin Cal. Proc. 5th Courts § 341, (S 341) Jurisdiction.

2 Witkin Cal. Proc. 5th Jurisdiction § 20, in General.

CHAPTER 5.1. LIMITED CIVIL CASES

ARTICLE 1. JURISDICTION IN LIMITED CIVIL CASES

§ 85. Actions treated as limited civil case; conditions

Section operative until Jan. 1, 2016. See, also, section operative Jan. 1, 2016.

An action or special proceeding shall be treated as a limited civil case if all of the following conditions are satisfied, and, notwithstanding any statute that classifies an action or special proceeding as a limited civil case, an action or special proceeding shall not be treated as a limited civil case unless all of the following conditions are satisfied:

(a) The amount in controversy does not exceed twenty-five thousand dollars ($25,000). As used in this section, "amount in controversy" means the amount of the demand, or the recovery sought, or the value of the property, or the amount of the lien, that is in controversy in the action, exclusive of attorneys' fees, interest, and costs.

(b) The relief sought is a type that may be granted in a limited civil case.

(c) The relief sought, whether in the complaint, a cross-complaint, or otherwise, is exclusively of a type described in one or more statutes that classify an action or special proceeding as a limited civil case or that provide that an action or special proceeding is within the original jurisdiction of the municipal court, including, but not limited to, the following provisions:

(1) Section 798.61 or 798.88 of the Civil Code.

(2) Section 1719 of the Civil Code.

(3) Section 3342.5 of the Civil Code.

(4) Section 86.

(5) Section 86.1.

(6) Section 1710.20.

(7) Section 7581 of the Food and Agricultural Code.

(8) Section 12647 of the Food and Agricultural Code.

(9) Section 27601 of the Food and Agricultural Code.

(10) Section 31503 of the Food and Agricultural Code.

(11) Section 31621 of the Food and Agricultural Code.

(12) Section 52514 of the Food and Agricultural Code.

(13) Section 53564 of the Food and Agricultural Code.

(14) Section 53069.4 of the Government Code.

(15) Section 53075.6 of the Government Code.

(16) Section 53075.61 of the Government Code.

(17) Section 5411.5 of the Public Utilities Code.

(18) Section 9872.1 of the Vehicle Code.

(19) Section 10751 of the Vehicle Code.

(20) Section 14607.6 of the Vehicle Code.

(21) Section 40230 of the Vehicle Code.

(22) Section 40256 of the Vehicle Code.

(d) This section shall remain in effect only until January 1, 2016, and as of that date is repealed, unless a later enacted statute, that is enacted before January 1, 2016, deletes or extends that date. *(Added by Stats.1998, c. 931 (S.B.2139), § 28, eff. Sept. 28, 1998. Amended by Stats.2012, c. 99 (A.B.2272), § 3.)*

Repeal

For repeal of this section, see its terms.

Law Revision Commission Comments

Section 85 is added to accommodate unification of the municipal and superior courts in a county. Cal. Const. art. VI, § 5(e). It facilitates differentiation among civil cases for purposes such as determining original jurisdiction in a county in which there is a municipal court (see Section 85.1), applying economic litigation procedures (see Section 91), and defining appellate jurisdiction (see Sections 904.1, 904.2).

The amount in controversy requirement of subdivision (a) derives from the $25,000 jurisdictional limit that applied to the municipal courts. *See, e.g.,* 2 B. Witkin, California Procedure *Courts* 249, at 323–25 (4th ed. 1996). Now, a case is a limited civil case and subject to the procedures for a limited civil case only if the amount in controversy is $25,000 or less. The last sentence of subdivision (a), defining "amount in controversy," continues the former second sentence of Section 91 without change. For discussion of calculating amounts in controversy in cases involving multiple causes, see R. Weil & I. Brown, Jr., California Practice Guide: Civil Procedure Before Trial, *Jurisdiction and Venue* 3:97–3:111, at 3–22 to 3–24 (1997); 2 B. Witkin, California Procedure *Jurisdiction* 38–44, at 582–86 (4th ed. 1996).

Subdivision (b) reflects and preserves limitations on the types of equitable relief awardable in a municipal court. See Section 580 & Comment. Where a money judgment for $25,000 or less would fully resolve a dispute and there is no need for a declaration of future rights, the case is a limited civil case despite a prayer for declaratory relief. See Cardellini v. Casey, 181 Cal.App.3d 389, 396, 226 Cal.Rptr. 659 (1986).

Subdivision (c) continues the effect of former law, under which each county had one or more municipal courts and a superior court. Causes like those now listed in subdivision (c) were within the original jurisdiction of the municipal court and subject to procedures now applicable to a limited civil case. Where a cause within the original jurisdiction of the municipal court was properly joined with one within the original jurisdiction of the superior court, the entire case would be tried in the superior court. *See, e.g.,* Wiggins v. Washington Nat'l Life Ins. Co., 246 Cal.App.2d 840, 848, 55 Cal.Rptr. 129 (1966) ("from the moment defendant filed its cross-complaint for declaratory relief in the instant action the municipal court lost jurisdiction over the cause and was obliged to suspend further proceedings in the action and to transfer it to the superior court"); Armstrong v. Transcontinental Land & Water Co., 134 Cal.App.2d Supp. 889, 285 P.2d 1031 (1955) (joinder of equitable cross-complaint compelled transfer of entire action to superior court). Subdivision (c) continues that policy by requiring that relief in a limited civil case be exclusively of a type described in one or more of the listed provisions, or an unlisted provision if the provision classifies the case as a limited civil case or places the case within the original jurisdiction of the municipal court. See, e.g., Section 688.010 (enforcement of state tax liability pursuant to warrant or notice of levy). If another type of cause is joined, the procedures for a limited civil case do not apply.

See Sections 22 (action defined), 23 (special proceeding defined). [28 Cal.L.Rev.Comm. Reports App. 7 (1998)].

Research References

Rutter, Cal. Practice Guide: A.D.R. Ch. 4-B, B. Judicial Arbitration.

Rutter, Cal. Practice Guide: Civil Appeals & Writs Ch. 16-A, A. Introduction.

Rutter, Cal. Practice Guide: Civ. Pro. Before Trial Ch. 3-A, A. Subject Matter Jurisdiction (Competency).

Rutter, Cal. Practice Guide: Civ. Pro. Before Trial Ch. 13-C, C. Civil Proceedings Subject to Judicial Arbitration.

Rutter, Cal. Practice Guide: Civil Trials & Evidence Ch. 17-E, E. Attorney Fees as Costs.

California Practice Guide: Employment Litigation Ch. 17-G, G. Costs.

California Practice Guide: Employment Litigation Ch. 17-H, H. Attorney Fees.

Rutter, Cal. Practice Guide: Enforcing Judgments/Debts Ch. 6B-5, Amount of Judgment Lien.

Rutter, Cal. Practice Guide: Enforcing Judgments/Debts Ch. 6C-4, Amount of Lien.

Rutter, Cal. Practice Guide: Enforcing Judgments/Debts Ch. 6E-4, Opposing Claim of Exemption.

Rutter, Cal. Practice Guide: Personal Injury Ch. 4-D, D. Techniques Where Settlement Not Forthcoming.

Rutter, Cal. Practice Guide: Personal Injury Ch. 5-D, D. Classification as Limited or Unlimited Civil Case.

Rutter, Cal. Practice Guide: Personal Injury Ch. 9-M, M. Verdicts and Judgment.

3 Witkin Cal. Proc. 5th Actions § 780, Illustrations.

3 Witkin Cal. Proc. 5th Actions § 783, (S 783) Consolidation of Trial Courts.

9 Witkin Cal. Proc. 5th Appeal § 167, Order Dealing With Jurisdictional Reclassification.

8 Witkin Cal. Proc. 5th Attack Judgment Trial Court § 222, in General.

2 Witkin Cal. Proc. 5th Courts § 241, (S 241) Nature and Scope of Classification.

2 Witkin Cal. Proc. 5th Courts § 242, (S 242) Conditions for Limited Civil Cases.

8 Witkin Cal. Proc. 5th Enforcement of Judgment § 51, (S 51) in General.

8 Witkin Cal. Proc. 5th Extraordinary Writs § 4, (S 4) Constitutional Consolidation of Trial Courts.

7 Witkin Cal. Proc. 5th Judgment § 31, Installment Payments.

7 Witkin Cal. Proc. 5th Judgment § 101, (S 101) Recovery Below Small Claims Maximum.

2 Witkin Cal. Proc. 5th Jurisdiction § 6, (S 6) Jurisdictional Classification.

2 Witkin Cal. Proc. 5th Jurisdiction § 25, (S 25) Interest and Costs.

2 Witkin Cal. Proc. 5th Jurisdiction § 26, (S 26) Attorneys' Fees.

2 Witkin Cal. Proc. 5th Jurisdiction § 45, (S 45) in General.

2 Witkin Cal. Proc. 5th Jurisdiction § 54, Cross-Complaint Ousting Jurisdiction.

2 Witkin Cal. Proc. 5th Jurisdiction § 407, Determination of Lack of Jurisdiction.

2 Witkin Cal. Proc. 5th Jurisdiction § 411, (S 411) in General.

6 Witkin Cal. Proc. 5th Proceedings Without Trial § 369, 5-Year Period.

12 Witkin, California Summary 10th Real Property § 459, Nature and Scope of Statute.

§ 85. Actions treated as limited civil case; conditions

Section operative Jan. 1, 2016. See, also, section operative until Jan. 1, 2016.

An action or special proceeding shall be treated as a limited civil case if all of the following conditions are satisfied, and, notwithstanding any statute that classifies an action or special proceeding as a limited civil case, an action or special proceeding shall not be treated as a limited civil case unless all of the following conditions are satisfied:

(a) The amount in controversy does not exceed twenty-five thousand dollars ($25,000). As used in this section, "amount in controversy" means the amount of the demand, or the recovery sought, or the value of the property, or the amount of the lien, that is in controversy in the action, exclusive of attorneys' fees, interest, and costs.

(b) The relief sought is a type that may be granted in a limited civil case.

(c) The relief sought, whether in the complaint, a cross-complaint, or otherwise, is exclusively of a type described in one or more statutes that classify an action or special proceeding as a limited civil case or that provide that an action or special proceeding is within the original jurisdiction of the municipal court, including, but not limited to, the following provisions:

(1) Section 798.61 of the Civil Code.

(2) Section 1719 of the Civil Code.

(3) Section 3342.5 of the Civil Code.

(4) Section 86.

(5) Section 86.1.

(6) Section 1710.20.

(7) Section 7581 of the Food and Agricultural Code.

(8) Section 12647 of the Food and Agricultural Code.

(9) Section 27601 of the Food and Agricultural Code.

(10) Section 31503 of the Food and Agricultural Code.

(11) Section 31621 of the Food and Agricultural Code.

(12) Section 52514 of the Food and Agricultural Code.

(13) Section 53564 of the Food and Agricultural Code.

(14) Section 53069.4 of the Government Code.

(15) Section 53075.6 of the Government Code.

(16) Section 53075.61 of the Government Code.

(17) Section 5411.5 of the Public Utilities Code.

(18) Section 9872.1 of the Vehicle Code.

(19) Section 10751 of the Vehicle Code.

(20) Section 14607.6 of the Vehicle Code.

(21) Section 40230 of the Vehicle Code.

(22) Section 40256 of the Vehicle Code.

(d) This section shall become operative on January 1, 2016. *(Added by Stats.2012, c. 99 (A.B.2272), § 4, operative Jan. 1, 2016.)*

Research References

Rutter, Cal. Practice Guide: A.D.R. Ch. 4-B, B. Judicial Arbitration.

Rutter, Cal. Practice Guide: Civil Appeals & Writs Ch. 16-A, A. Introduction.

Rutter, Cal. Practice Guide: Civ. Pro. Before Trial Ch. 3-A, A. Subject Matter Jurisdiction (Competency).

Rutter, Cal. Practice Guide: Civ. Pro. Before Trial Ch. 13-C, C. Civil Proceedings Subject to Judicial Arbitration.

Rutter, Cal. Practice Guide: Civil Trials & Evidence Ch. 17-E, E. Attorney Fees as Costs.

California Practice Guide: Employment Litigation Ch. 17-G, G. Costs.

California Practice Guide: Employment Litigation Ch. 17-H, H. Attorney Fees.

Rutter, Cal. Practice Guide: Enforcing Judgments/Debts Ch. 6B-5, Amount of Judgment Lien.

Rutter, Cal. Practice Guide: Enforcing Judgments/Debts Ch. 6C-4, Amount of Lien.

Rutter, Cal. Practice Guide: Enforcing Judgments/Debts Ch. 6E-4, Opposing Claim of Exemption.

Rutter, Cal. Practice Guide: Personal Injury Ch. 4-D, D. Techniques Where Settlement Not Forthcoming.

Rutter, Cal. Practice Guide: Personal Injury Ch. 5-D, D. Classification as Limited or Unlimited Civil Case.

Rutter, Cal. Practice Guide: Personal Injury Ch. 9-M, M. Verdicts and Judgment.

3 Witkin Cal. Proc. 5th Actions § 780, Illustrations.

3 Witkin Cal. Proc. 5th Actions § 783, (S 783) Consolidation of Trial Courts.

9 Witkin Cal. Proc. 5th Appeal § 167, Order Dealing With Jurisdictional Reclassification.

8 Witkin Cal. Proc. 5th Attack Judgment Trial Court § 222, in General.

2 Witkin Cal. Proc. 5th Courts § 241, (S 241) Nature and Scope of Classification.

2 Witkin Cal. Proc. 5th Courts § 242, (S 242) Conditions for Limited Civil Cases.

8 Witkin Cal. Proc. 5th Enforcement of Judgment § 51, (S 51) in General.

8 Witkin Cal. Proc. 5th Extraordinary Writs § 4, (S 4) Constitutional Consolidation of Trial Courts.

7 Witkin Cal. Proc. 5th Judgment § 31, Installment Payments.

7 Witkin Cal. Proc. 5th Judgment § 101, (S 101) Recovery Below Small Claims Maximum.

2 Witkin Cal. Proc. 5th Jurisdiction § 6, (S 6) Jurisdictional Classification.

2 Witkin Cal. Proc. 5th Jurisdiction § 25, (S 25) Interest and Costs.

2 Witkin Cal. Proc. 5th Jurisdiction § 26, (S 26) Attorneys' Fees.

2 Witkin Cal. Proc. 5th Jurisdiction § 45, (S 45) in General.

2 Witkin Cal. Proc. 5th Jurisdiction § 54, Cross-Complaint Ousting Jurisdiction.

2 Witkin Cal. Proc. 5th Jurisdiction § 407, Determination of Lack of Jurisdiction.

2 Witkin Cal. Proc. 5th Jurisdiction § 411, (S 411) in General.

6 Witkin Cal. Proc. 5th Proceedings Without Trial § 369, 5-Year Period.

12 Witkin, California Summary 10th Real Property § 459, Nature and Scope of Statute.

§ 86. Jurisdiction

(a) The following civil cases and proceedings are limited civil cases:

(1) A case at law in which the demand, exclusive of interest, or the value of the property in controversy amounts to twenty-five thousand dollars ($25,000) or less. This paragraph does not apply to a case that involves the legality of any tax, impost, assessment, toll, or municipal fine, except an action to enforce payment of delinquent unsecured personal property taxes if the legality of the tax is not contested by the defendant.

(2) An action for dissolution of partnership where the total assets of the partnership do not exceed twenty-five thousand dollars ($25,000); an action of interpleader where the amount of money or the value of the property involved does not exceed twenty-five thousand dollars ($25,000).

(3) An action to cancel or rescind a contract when the relief is sought in connection with an action to recover money not exceeding twenty-five thousand dollars ($25,000) or property of a value not exceeding twenty-five thousand dollars ($25,000), paid or delivered under, or in consideration of, the contract; an action to revise a contract where the relief is sought in an action upon the contract if the action otherwise is a limited civil case.

(4) A proceeding in forcible entry or forcible or unlawful detainer where the whole amount of damages claimed is twenty-five thousand dollars ($25,000) or less.

(5) An action to enforce and foreclose a lien on personal property where the amount of the lien is twenty-five thousand dollars ($25,000) or less.

(6) An action to enforce and foreclose, or a petition to release, a lien arising under * * * Chapter 4 (commencing with Section 8400) of Title 2 of Part 6 of Division 4 of the Civil Code, or to enforce and foreclose an assessment lien on a common interest development as defined in Section 4100 or 6534 of the Civil Code, where the amount of the liens is twenty-five thousand dollars ($25,000) or less. However, if an action to enforce the lien affects property that is also affected by a similar pending action that is not a limited civil case, or if the total amount of liens sought to be foreclosed against the same property aggregates an amount in excess of twenty-five thousand dollars ($25,000), the action is not a limited civil case.

(7) An action for declaratory relief when brought pursuant to either of the following:

(A) By way of cross-complaint as to a right of indemnity with respect to the relief demanded in the complaint or a cross-complaint in an action or proceeding that is otherwise a limited civil case.

(B) To conduct a trial after a nonbinding fee arbitration between an attorney and client, pursuant to Article 13 (commencing with Section 6200) of Chapter 4 of Division 3 of the Business and Professions Code, where the amount in controversy is twenty-five thousand dollars ($25,000) or less.

(8) An action to issue a temporary restraining order or preliminary injunction; to take an account, where necessary to preserve the property or rights of any party to a limited civil case;

to make any order or perform any act, pursuant to Title 9 (commencing with Section 680.010) of Part 2 (enforcement of judgments) in a limited civil case; to appoint a receiver pursuant to Section 564 in a limited civil case; to determine title to personal property seized in a limited civil case.

(9) An action under Article 3 (commencing with Section 708.210) of Chapter 6 of Division 2 of Title 9 of Part 2 for the recovery of an interest in personal property or to enforce the liability of the debtor of a judgment debtor where the interest claimed adversely is of a value not exceeding twenty-five thousand dollars ($25,000) or the debt denied does not exceed twenty-five thousand dollars ($25,000).

(10) An arbitration-related petition filed pursuant to either of the following:

(A) Article 2 (commencing with Section 1292) of Chapter 5 of Title 9 of Part 3, except for uninsured motorist arbitration proceedings in accordance with Section 11580.2 of the Insurance Code, if the petition is filed before the arbitration award becomes final and the matter to be resolved by arbitration is a limited civil case under paragraphs (1) to (9), inclusive, of subdivision (a) or if the petition is filed after the arbitration award becomes final and the amount of the award and all other rulings, pronouncements, and decisions made in the award are within paragraphs (1) to (9), inclusive, of subdivision (a).

(B) To confirm, correct, or vacate a fee arbitration award between an attorney and client that is binding or has become binding, pursuant to Article 13 (commencing with Section 6200) of Chapter 4 of Division 3 of the Business and Professions Code, where the arbitration award is twenty-five thousand dollars ($25,000) or less.

(b) The following cases in equity are limited civil cases:

(1) A case to try title to personal property when the amount involved is not more than twenty-five thousand dollars ($25,000).

(2) A case when equity is pleaded as a defensive matter in any case that is otherwise a limited civil case.

(3) A case to vacate a judgment or order of the court obtained in a limited civil case through extrinsic fraud, mistake, inadvertence, or excusable neglect. *(Added by Stats.1976, c. 1288, p. 5760, § 5. Amended by Stats.1978, c. 146, p. 369, § 1, operative July 1, 1979; Stats.1979, c. 958, p. 3299, § 1; Stats.1981, c. 714, § 57; Stats.1982, c. 466, p. 2006, § 14; Stats.1982, c. 497, p. 2150, § 25, operative July 1, 1983; Stats.1984, c. 538, § 1; Stats.1984, c. 1719, § 1.1; Stats.1985, c. 879, § 1; Stats.1985, c. 1383, § 1; Stats.1986, c. 88, § 1, eff. May 13, 1986; Stats.1986, c. 953, § 1; Stats.1987, c. 104, § 1; Stats.1988, c. 463, § 1; Stats.1993, c. 1261 (S.B.401), § 1; Stats.1993, c. 1262 (A.B.1272), § 4.5; Stats.1997, c. 527 (S.B.150), § 2; Stats.1998, c. 931 (S.B.2139), § 29, eff. Sept. 28, 1998; Stats.2001, c. 44 (S.B.562), § 1; Stats.2010, c. 697 (S.B.189), § 21, operative July 1, 2012; Stats.2012, c. 181 (A.B. 806), § 42, operative Jan. 1, 2014; Stats.2013, c. 605 (S.B.752), § 22.)*

Law Revision Commission Comments

Section 86 is amended to conform to Title 9 (commencing with Section 680.010) of Part 2 (Enforcement of Judgments Law). [15 Cal.L.Rev. Comm. Reports (2001)].

Subdivision (a)(6) of Section 86 is amended to make clear that the municipal and justice courts have jurisdiction over actions to enforce and foreclose condominium assessment liens to the same extent as actions to enforce and foreclose mechanics' and laborers' liens. [17 Cal.L.Rev. Comm. Reports 975 (1984)].

Section 86 is amended to accommodate unification of the municipal and superior courts in a county. Cal. Const. art. VI, § 5(e).

The matters listed in subdivisions (a) and (b) are not limited civil cases if the amount in controversy exceeds $25,000. See Section 85. Formerly, each county had one or more municipal courts and a superior court, and the matters listed in Section 86(a)-(b) were within the original jurisdiction of the municipal court, unless the amount in controversy exceeded $25,000. A limited civil case is equivalent to a matter within the original jurisdiction of the municipal court under former law, so subdivisions (a) and (b) as amended continue the effect of former law. See Section 85 (limited civil cases) & Comment.

Former subdivision (a)(11) is continued in Penal Code Section 1214, with modifications to accommodate trial court unification.

Former subdivision (c) is continued without substantive change in Section 580 (relief awardable in civil causes).

Former subdivision (d) is deleted as obsolete. [28 Cal.L.Rev.Comm. Reports 51 (1998)].

Subdivision (a)(6) of Section 86 is amended to clarify the jurisdictional classification of a petition to release a mechanic's lien. This is declaratory of existing law. See Section 85 (limited civil cases) & Comment. See also Section 88 (unlimited civil case).

Subdivision (a)(6) is also amended to reflect elimination of the municipal courts as a result of unification with the superior courts pursuant to Article VI, Section 5(e), of the California Constitution. For reclassification of an action in a unified superior court, see Sections 403.010–403.090.

Subdivision (a)(8) is amended to delete the language on circumstances for appointment of a receiver in a limited civil case, and insert a cross-reference to Section 564, which now governs appointment of receivers in both limited and unlimited civil cases. The language deleted from the first clause of subdivision (a)(8) is continued in Section 564(b)(8), but broadened to apply to all cases. See Section 564 Comment. The language deleted from the second clause of subdivision (a)(8) is not continued, because it is redundant with Section 564(b)(3) and (b)(4). [31 Cal.L.Rev. Comm. Reports 67 (2001)].

Paragraph (6) of subdivision (a) of Section 86 is amended to correct a cross-reference and eliminate obsolete terminology.

The section is also amended to make stylistic revisions. [37 Cal.L.Rev. Comm. Reports 527 (2007)].

Section 86 is amended to correct a cross-reference to former Civil Code Section 1351(c). [40 Cal.L.Rev.Comm. Reports 235 (2010)].

Paragraph (6) of subdivision (a) of Section 86 is amended to add a cross-reference to Civil Code Section 6534, reflecting the enactment of the Commercial and Industrial Common Interest Development Act (Civ. Code §§ 6500–6876). [42 Cal.L.Rev.Comm. Reports 1 (2012)].

Research References

Rutter, Cal. Practice Guide: A.D.R. Ch. 5-G, G. Procedures to Enforce Arbitration.

Rutter, Cal. Practice Guide: A.D.R. Ch. 5-J, J. Challenging and Enforcing Arbitrator's Award in Court.

Rutter, Cal. Practice Guide: Civil Appeals & Writs Ch. 8-C, C. Standards of Appellate Review.

Rutter, Cal. Practice Guide: Civil Appeals & Writs Ch. 16-A, A. Introduction.

Rutter, Cal. Practice Guide: Civ. Pro. Before Trial Ch. 3-A, A. Subject Matter Jurisdiction (Competency).

Rutter, Cal. Practice Guide: Civ. Pro. Before Trial Ch. 5-E, E. Limitations on Default Judgments.

Rutter, Cal. Practice Guide: Civ. Pro. Before Trial Ch. 5-G, G. Relief from Default.

Rutter, Cal. Practice Guide: Enforcing Judgments/Debts Ch. 4-C, C. Receiverships.

Rutter, Cal. Practice Guide: Enforcing Judgments/Debts Ch. 6B-5, Amount of Judgment Lien.

Rutter, Cal. Practice Guide: Enforcing Judgments/Debts Ch. 6C-4, Amount of Lien.

Rutter, Cal. Practice Guide: Enforcing Judgments/Debts Ch. 6E-4, Opposing Claim of Exemption.

Rutter, Cal. Practice Guide: Insurance Litigation Ch. 15-B, B. Actions by Insurers.

Rutter, Cal. Practice Guide: Personal Injury Ch. 4-D, D. Techniques Where Settlement Not Forthcoming.

Rutter, Cal. Practice Guide: Personal Injury Ch. 5-D, D. Classification as Limited or Unlimited Civil Case.

Rutter, Cal. Practice Guide: Personal Injury Ch. 9-M, M. Verdicts and Judgment.

Miller and Starr California Real Estate § 28:55, Venue.

Miller and Starr California Real Estate § 25B:93, Foreclosure of Lien by Sale; Redemption Rights.

3 Witkin Cal. Proc. 5th Actions § 783, (S 783) Consolidation of Trial Courts.

8 Witkin Cal. Proc. 5th Attack Judgment Trial Court § 222, in General.

2 Witkin Cal. Proc. 5th Courts § 241, (S 241) Nature and Scope of Classification.

2 Witkin Cal. Proc. 5th Courts § 243, (S 243) in General.

2 Witkin Cal. Proc. 5th Courts § 244, (S 244) Forcible Entry and Unlawful Detainer.

2 Witkin Cal. Proc. 5th Courts § 245, (S 245) in General.

2 Witkin Cal. Proc. 5th Courts § 246, (S 246) Particular Equitable Actions.

2 Witkin Cal. Proc. 5th Courts § 247, (S 247) Ancillary Remedies.

2 Witkin Cal. Proc. 5th Courts § 248, (S 248) Equitable Defenses.

2 Witkin Cal. Proc. 5th Courts § 249, (S 249) Declaratory Relief.

8 Witkin Cal. Proc. 5th Extraordinary Writs § 4, (S 4) Constitutional Consolidation of Trial Courts.

2 Witkin Cal. Proc. 5th Jurisdiction § 2, (S 2) Power to Apply Substantive Law Remedies.

2 Witkin Cal. Proc. 5th Jurisdiction § 23, (S 23) Actual Recovery is Not Controlling.

2 Witkin Cal. Proc. 5th Jurisdiction § 25, (S 25) Interest and Costs.

2 Witkin Cal. Proc. 5th Jurisdiction § 34, Forcible Entry and Unlawful Detainer.

2 Witkin Cal. Proc. 5th Jurisdiction § 37, (S 37) Single Plaintiff and Single Defendant.

2 Witkin Cal. Proc. 5th Jurisdiction § 45, (S 45) in General.

2 Witkin Cal. Proc. 5th Jurisdiction § 46, What Constitutes Tax.

2 Witkin Cal. Proc. 5th Jurisdiction § 47, When Legality is Involved.

2 Witkin Cal. Proc. 5th Jurisdiction § 52, (S 52) in General.

2 Witkin Cal. Proc. 5th Jurisdiction § 53, (S 53) Construction of Complaint as One for Declaratory Relief.

5 Witkin Cal. Proc. 5th Pleading § 850, (S 850) Nature of Action.

6 Witkin Cal. Proc. 5th Provisional Remedies § 276, Jurisdiction.

6 Witkin Cal. Proc. 5th Provisional Remedies § 419, (S 419) Nature of Receivership.

12 Witkin, California Summary 10th Real Property § 728, Jurisdiction, Venue, and Process.

§ 86.1. Jurisdiction of proceedings brought pursuant to Long-Term Care, Health, Safety, and Security Act of 1973

An action brought pursuant to the Long–Term Care, Health, Safety, and Security Act of 1973 (Chapter 2.4 (commencing with Section 1417) of Division 2 of the Health and Safety Code) is a limited civil case if civil penalties are not sought or amount to twenty-five thousand dollars ($25,000) or less. *(Added by Stats.1985, c. 11, § 1, eff. March 6, 1985. Amended by Stats.1990, c. 1133 (A.B.3536), § 1; Stats.1990, c. 1134 (A.B.1967), § 1; Stats.1998, c. 931 (S.B.2139), § 30, eff. Sept. 28, 1998; Stats.2002, c. 784 (S.B.1316), § 29.)*

Law Revision Commission Comments

Section 86.1 is amended to accommodate unification of the municipal and superior courts in a county. Cal. Const. art. VI, § 5(e). It is also amended to reflect elimination of the justice court. Cal. Const. art. VI, §§ 1, 5(b).

An action pursuant to the Long–Term Care, Health, Safety, and Security Act of 1973 is not a limited civil case if the amount in controversy exceeds $25,000. See Section 85 (limited civil cases). Formerly, each county had one or more municipal courts and a superior court, and an action pursuant to the Long–Term Care, Health, Safety, and Security Act of 1973 was within the original jurisdiction of the municipal court, unless the amount in controversy exceeded $25,000. A limited civil case is equivalent to a matter within the original jurisdiction of the municipal court under former law, so Section 86.1 as amended continues the effect of former law. See Section 85 & Comment. [28 Cal.L.Rev.Comm. Reports 51 (1998)].

Section 86.1 is amended to reflect unification of the municipal and superior courts pursuant to Article VI, Section 5(e), of the California Constitution. See Section 1048 (consolidation of actions in superior court). [32 Cal.L.Rev.Comm. Reports 95 (2002)].

Research References

3 Witkin Cal. Proc. 5th Actions § 783, (S 783) Consolidation of Trial Courts.

2 Witkin Cal. Proc. 5th Courts § 241, (S 241) Nature and Scope of Classification.

2 Witkin Cal. Proc. 5th Courts § 243, (S 243) in General.

8 Witkin Cal. Proc. 5th Extraordinary Writs § 4, (S 4) Constitutional Consolidation of Trial Courts.

§ 87. Small claims division; conflicts of law

(a) A limited civil case may be brought in the small claims division if the case is within the jurisdiction of the small claims division as otherwise provided by statute. Where a statute or rule applicable to a small claims case conflicts with a statute or rule applicable to a limited civil case, the statute or rule applicable to a small claims case governs the small claims case and the statute or rule applicable to a limited civil case does not.

(b) Nothing in this section affects the jurisdiction of the small claims division as otherwise provided by statute. *(Added by Stats.1999, c. 344 (S.B.210), § 3, eff. Sept. 7, 1999.)*

Law Revision Commission Comments

Section 87 is added to clarify the appropriate treatment of a small claims case. The provision is declarative of existing law. Because a small claims case is a limited civil case, a provision that applies to a case other than a limited civil case (e.g., Sections 564, 1283.05) does not apply to a small claims case. Where, however, there is a conflict between a provision applicable to a limited civil case and a provision applicable to a small claims case, the provision applicable to a small claims case prevails over the more general provision in a small claims case. For example, Section 904.2 governs an appeal in a limited civil case. It is inapplicable to a small claims case because Section 904.5 specifies different procedures for an appeal from the small claims division. This is comparable to the situation that existed before the Constitution was amended to permit unification of the municipal and superior courts in a county: In a small claims case, a provision applicable to a small claims case prevailed over a general provision for a municipal court case. See, e.g., former Sections 904.2 (appeal from municipal or justice court), 904.5 (appeal from small claims division of municipal or justice court).

See Sections 85 (limited civil cases) & Comment, 116.220 (jurisdiction of the small claims division). [29 Cal.L.Rev.Comm. Reports App. 5 (1999)].

Research References

Rutter, Cal. Practice Guide: Civil Appeals & Writs Ch. 16-A, A. Introduction.

Rutter, Cal. Practice Guide: Civ. Pro. Before Trial Ch. 3-A, A. Subject Matter Jurisdiction (Competency).

1 Witkin Cal. Proc. 5th Attorneys § 340, (S 340) Regulation by Court.

2 Witkin Cal. Proc. 5th Courts § 241, (S 241) Nature and Scope of Classification.

2 Witkin Cal. Proc. 5th Courts § 281, (S 281) in General.

2 Witkin Cal. Proc. 5th Courts § 341, (S 341) Jurisdiction.

2 Witkin Cal. Proc. 5th Jurisdiction § 197, (S 197) Corporation.

4 Witkin Cal. Proc. 5th Pleading § 87, in General.

§ 88. Unlimited civil case; reference

A civil action or proceeding other than a limited civil case may be referred to as an unlimited civil case. *(Added by Stats.1999, c. 344 (S.B.210), § 4, eff. Sept. 7, 1999.)*

Law Revision Commission Comments

Section 88 is added to provide a convenient means of referring to a civil case other than a limited civil case. The new term ('unlimited civil case') reflects the broad jurisdiction of the superior court. Cal. Const. art. VI, § 10. A small claims case is a type of limited civil case, not an unlimited civil case. See Sections 85 & 87 & Comments. [29 Cal.L.Rev.Comm. Reports App. 5 (1999)].

Research References

Rutter, Cal. Practice Guide: Civil Appeals & Writs Ch. 16-A, A. Introduction.

Rutter, Cal. Practice Guide: Civ. Pro. Before Trial Ch. 3-A, A. Subject Matter Jurisdiction (Competency).

Rutter, Cal. Practice Guide: Civil Trials & Evidence Ch. 17-E, E. Attorney Fees as Costs.

California Practice Guide: Employment Litigation Ch. 17-G, G. Costs.

California Practice Guide: Employment Litigation Ch. 17-H, H. Attorney Fees.

Rutter, Cal. Practice Guide: Personal Injury Ch. 5-D, D. Classification as Limited or Unlimited Civil Case.

2 Witkin Cal. Proc. 5th Courts § 241, (S 241) Nature and Scope of Classification.

2 Witkin Cal. Proc. 5th Jurisdiction § 45, (S 45) in General.

2 Witkin Cal. Proc. 5th Jurisdiction § 411, (S 411) in General.

6 Witkin Cal. Proc. 5th Proceedings Without Trial § 369, 5-Year Period.

12 Witkin, California Summary 10th Real Property § 728, Jurisdiction, Venue, and Process.

§ 89. Limited and unlimited civil cases; authority of court

(a) The existence of a statute relating to the authority of the court in a limited civil case does not, by itself, imply that the same authority does or does not exist in an unlimited civil case.

(b) The existence of a statute relating to the authority of the court in an unlimited civil case does not, by itself, imply that the same authority does or does not exist in a limited civil case. *(Added by Stats.2001, c. 44 (S.B.562), § 2.)*

Law Revision Commission Comments

Section 89 is added to provide guidance in interpreting statutory provisions that expressly authorize particular conduct in a limited civil case but are silent as to an unlimited civil case, or vice versa. See, e.g., Section 402.5 (transfer of limited civil case). [30 Cal.L.Rev.Comm. Reports 479 (2000)].

Research References

Rutter, Cal. Practice Guide: Civ. Pro. Before Trial Ch. 3-A, A. Subject Matter Jurisdiction (Competency).

2 Witkin Cal. Proc. 5th Courts § 241, (S 241) Nature and Scope of Classification.

ARTICLE 2. ECONOMIC LITIGATION FOR LIMITED CIVIL CASES

Section

90. Application of law applicable to civil actions.
91. Application of article provisions; withdrawal of action from application.
92. Pleadings; answer; motions.
93. Questionnaires.
94. Discovery.
95. Additional discovery.
96. Request for statement of witnesses, and description and copies of evidence; statement of response; effect.
97. Prohibition of call of witness or introduction of evidence not included in statement on objection; exceptions.
98. Prepared testimony in lieu of direct testimony; conditions.
99. Judgment or final order; conclusiveness.
100. Appeals.

§ 90. Application of law applicable to civil actions

Except where changed by the provisions of this article, all provisions of law applicable to civil actions generally apply to actions subject to this article. *(Added by Stats.1982, c. 1581, p. 6226, § 1. Amended by Stats.2003, c. 149 (S.B.79), § 3.)*

Law Revision Commission Comments

Section 90 is amended to reflect the repeal of former Part 3.5 (commencing with Section 1823) of the Code of Civil Procedure, relating to pilot projects. See 1994 Cal. Stat. ch. 146, § 26; 1996 Cal. Stat. ch. 124, § 15. [33 Cal.L.Rev.Comm. Reports 187 (2003)].

Research References

Rutter, Cal. Practice Guide: Civ. Pro. Before Trial Ch. 8L-1, Limitations on Existing Discovery Procedures.

Rutter, Cal. Practice Guide: Civ. Pro. Before Trial Ch. 12(I)-B, B. Case Management ("Fast Track") System.

Rutter, Cal. Practice Guide: Enforcing Judgments/Debts Ch. 6G-2, Written Interrogatories to Judgment Debtor.

Rutter, Cal. Practice Guide: Personal Injury Ch. 6-E, E. Special Discovery Rules and Procedures in Limited Civil Cases.

Rutter, Cal. Practice Guide: Personal Injury Ch. 8-A, A. Case Management.

Rutter, Cal. Practice Guide: Personal Injury Ch. 9-N, N. Special Trial Rules in Limited Civil Cases (CCP § 90 et seq.).

2 Witkin Cal. Proc. 5th Courts § 251, Nature and Scope of Statute.

2 Witkin Cal. Proc. 5th Courts § 254, Disclosure of Witnesses and Evidence.

4 Witkin Cal. Proc. 5th Pleading § 5, (S 5) Small Claims Courts and Limited Civil Cases.

4 Witkin Cal. Proc. 5th Pleading § 467, Answer.

5 Witkin Cal. Proc. 5th Pleading § 1009, Statutory Provisions.

5 Witkin Cal. Proc. 5th Pleading § 1059, Where Complaint is Not Verified.

5 Witkin Cal. Proc. 5th Pleading § 1061, Where Complaint is Verified.

6 Witkin Cal. Proc. 5th Proceedings Without Trial § 594, (S 594) Discovery.

§ 91. Application of article provisions; withdrawal of action from application

(a) Except as otherwise provided in this section, the provisions of this article apply to every limited civil case.

(b) The provisions of this article do not apply to any action under Chapter 5.5 (commencing with Section 116.110) or any proceeding under Chapter 4 (commencing with Section 1159) of Title 3 of Part 3.

(c) Any action may, upon noticed motion, be withdrawn from the provisions of this article, upon a showing that it is impractical to prosecute or defend the action within the limitations of these provisions. *(Added by Stats.1982, c. 1581, p. 6226, § 1. Amended by Stats.1983, c. 102, § 1, eff. June 16, 1983; Stats.1985, c. 1383, § 2; Stats.1998, c. 931 (S.B.2139), § 36, eff. Sept. 28, 1998.)*

Law Revision Commission Comments

Subdivision (a) of Section 91 is amended to accommodate unification of the municipal and superior courts in a county. Cal. Const. art. VI, § 5(e). It is also amended to reflect elimination of the justice court. Cal. Const. art. VI, §§ 1, 5(b).

Formerly, each county had one or more municipal courts and a superior court, and economic litigation procedures applied to cases tried in the municipal courts. Now, the matters formerly triable in those courts are classified as limited civil cases. See Section 85 (limited civil cases) & Comment. By making economic litigation procedures applicable to limited civil cases, Section 91 continues the effect of former law. The former second sentence of subdivision (a), defining "amount in controversy," is continued without substantive change in Section 85.

Subdivision (b) is amended to delete the reference to former Chapter 5A (commencing with Section 116), which has been repealed. Instead, subdivision (b) now refers to Chapter 5.5 (commencing with Section 116.110), which contains the current small claims provisions.

Subdivision (d) is deleted as obsolete. [28 Cal.L.Rev.Comm. Reports 51 (1998)].

Research References

Rutter, Cal. Practice Guide: Civ. Pro. Before Trial Ch. 4-F, F. Procedures for Challenging Service of Summons.

Rutter, Cal. Practice Guide: Civ. Pro. Before Trial Ch. 8L-1, Limitations on Existing Discovery Procedures.

Rutter, Cal. Practice Guide: Civ. Pro. Before Trial Ch. 7(I)-A, A. Demurrers.

Rutter, Cal. Practice Guide: Enforcing Judgments/Debts Ch. 6G-2, Written Interrogatories to Judgment Debtor.

2 Witkin Cal. Proc. 5th Courts § 242, (S 242) Conditions for Limited Civil Cases.

2 Witkin Cal. Proc. 5th Courts § 251, Nature and Scope of Statute.

§ 92. Pleadings; answer; motions

(a) The pleadings allowed are complaints, answers, cross-complaints, answers to cross-complaints and general demurrers.

(b) The answer need not be verified, even if the complaint or cross-complaint is verified.

(c) Special demurrers are not allowed.

(d) Motions to strike are allowed only on the ground that the damages or relief sought are not supported by the allegations of the complaint.

(e) Except as limited by this section, all other motions are permitted. *(Added by Stats.1982, c. 1581, p. 6227, § 1. Amended by Stats.1983, c. 102, § 2, eff. June 16, 1983.)*

Research References

Rutter, Cal. Practice Guide: Civ. Pro. Before Trial Ch. 6-C, C. Answer.
Rutter, Cal. Practice Guide: Civ. Pro. Before Trial Ch. 7(I)-A, A. Demurrers.
Rutter, Cal. Practice Guide: Civ. Pro. Before Trial Ch. 7(I)-B, B. Motions to Strike.
Rutter, Cal. Practice Guide: Insurance Litigation Ch. 15-E, E. Pleadings.
2 Witkin Cal. Proc. 5th Courts § 252, Pleadings and Motions.
4 Witkin Cal. Proc. 5th Pleading § 5, (S 5) Small Claims Courts and Limited Civil Cases.
4 Witkin Cal. Proc. 5th Pleading § 467, Answer.
5 Witkin Cal. Proc. 5th Pleading § 1009, Statutory Provisions.

§ 93. Questionnaires

(a) The plaintiff has the option to serve case questionnaires with the complaint, using forms approved by the Judicial Council. The questionnaires served shall include a completed copy of the plaintiff's completed case questionnaire, and a blank copy of the defendant's case questionnaire.

(b) Any defendant upon whom a case questionnaire is served shall serve a completed defendant's case questionnaire upon the requesting plaintiff with the answer.

(c) The case questionnaire shall be designed to elicit fundamental information about each party's case, including names and addresses of all witnesses with knowledge of any relevant facts, a list of all documents relevant to the case, a statement of the nature and amount of damages, and information covering insurance coverages, injuries and treating physicians. The Judicial Council shall design and develop forms for case questionnaires.

(d) Approved forms shall be made available by the clerk of the court.

(e) If a party on whom a case questionnaire has been served under subdivision (a) or (b) fails to serve a timely or a complete response to that questionnaire, the party serving the questionnaire may move for an order compelling a response or a further response and for a monetary sanction under Chapter 7 (commencing with Section 2023.010) of Title 4 of Part 4. If a party then fails to obey an order compelling a response or a further response, the court may make those orders that are just, including the imposition of an issue sanction, an evidence sanction, or a terminating sanction under Chapter 7 (commencing with Section 2023.010) of Title 4 of Part 4. In lieu of or in addition to that sanction, the court may impose a monetary sanction under Chapter 7 (commencing with Section 2023.010) of Title 4 of Part 4. *(Added by Stats.1982, c. 1581, p. 6227, § 1. Amended by Stats.1987, c. 86, § 1, eff. July 2, 1987, operative July 1, 1987; Stats.2004, c. 182 (A.B.3081), § 5, operative July 1, 2005.)*

Law Revision Commission Comments

Subdivision (e) of Section 93 is amended to reflect nonsubstantive reorganization of the rules governing civil discovery. [33 Cal.L.Rev. Comm. Reports 979 (2004)].

Research References

Rutter, Cal. Practice Guide: Civ. Pro. Before Trial Ch. 8L-2, Special Discovery Procedures Permitted.
Rutter, Cal. Practice Guide: Personal Injury Ch. 6-E, E. Special Discovery Rules and Procedures in Limited Civil Cases.
2 Witkin Cal. Proc. 5th Courts § 252, Pleadings and Motions.

§ 94. Discovery

Discovery is permitted only to the extent provided by this section and Section 95. This discovery shall comply with the notice and format requirements of the particular method of discovery, as provided in Title 4 (commencing with Section 2016.010) of Part 4. As to each adverse party, a party may use the following forms of discovery:

(a) Any combination of 35 of the following:

(1) Interrogatories (with no subparts) under Chapter 13 (commencing with Section 2030.010) of Title 4 of Part 4.

(2) Demands to produce documents or things under Chapter 14 (commencing with Section 2031.010) of Title 4 of Part 4.

(3) Requests for admission (with no subparts) under Chapter 16 (commencing with Section 2033.010) of Title 4 of Part 4.

(b) One oral or written deposition under Chapter 9 (commencing with Section 2025.010), Chapter 10 (commencing with Section 2026.010), or Chapter 11 (commencing with Section 2028.010) of Title 4 of Part 4. For purposes of this subdivision, a deposition of an organization shall be treated as a single deposition even though more than one person may be designated or required to testify pursuant to Section 2025.230.

(c) Any party may serve on any person a deposition subpoena duces tecum requiring the person served to mail copies of documents, books, or records to the party's counsel at a specified address, along with an affidavit complying with Section 1561 of the Evidence Code.

The party who issued the deposition subpoena shall mail a copy of the response to any other party who tenders the reasonable cost of copying it.

(d) Physical and mental examinations under Chapter 15 (commencing with Section 2032.010) of Title 4 of Part 4.

(e) The identity of expert witnesses under Chapter 18 (commencing with Section 2034.010) of Title 4 of Part 4. *(Added by Stats.1982, c. 1581, p. 6227, § 1. Amended by Stats.1987, c. 86, § 1.3, eff. July 2, 1987, operative July 1, 1987; Stats.2004, c. 182 (A.B.3081), § 6, operative July 1, 2005; Stats.2005, c. 294 (A.B.333), § 2; Stats.2006, c. 538 (S.B.1852), § 61.)*

Law Revision Commission Comments

Section 94 is amended to reflect nonsubstantive reorganization of the rules governing civil discovery. [33 Cal.L.Rev.Comm. Reports 980 (2004)].

Subdivision (b) of Section 94 is amended to make clear the proper treatment of a deposition of an organization. Subdivision (b) is also amended to make a stylistic revision. [34 Cal.L.Rev.Comm. Reports 137 (2004)].

Research References

Rutter, Cal. Practice Guide: A.D.R. Ch. 8-E, E. Special Drafting Considerations Re Arbitration Agreements.
Rutter, Cal. Practice Guide: Civ. Pro. Before Trial Ch. 8F-3, Propounding Interrogatories.
Rutter, Cal. Practice Guide: Civ. Pro. Before Trial Ch. 8L-1, Limitations on Existing Discovery Procedures.

Rutter, Cal. Practice Guide: Enforcing Judgments/Debts Ch. 6G-2, Written Interrogatories to Judgment Debtor.

Rutter, Cal. Practice Guide: Personal Injury Ch. 6-E, E. Special Discovery Rules and Procedures in Limited Civil Cases.

2 Witkin Cal. Proc. 5th Courts § 253, Discovery.

§ 95. Additional discovery

(a) The court may, on noticed motion and subject to such terms and conditions as are just, authorize a party to conduct additional discovery, but only upon a showing that the moving party will be unable to prosecute or defend the action effectively without the additional discovery. In making a determination under this section, the court shall take into account whether the moving party has used all applicable discovery in good faith, and whether the party has attempted to secure the additional discovery by stipulation or by means other than formal discovery.

(b) The parties may stipulate to additional discovery. *(Added by Stats.1982, c. 1581, p. 6228, § 1.)*

Research References

Rutter, Cal. Practice Guide: Civ. Pro. Before Trial Ch. 8F-3, Propounding Interrogatories.

Rutter, Cal. Practice Guide: Civ. Pro. Before Trial Ch. 8L-1, Limitations on Existing Discovery Procedures.

Rutter, Cal. Practice Guide: Enforcing Judgments/Debts Ch. 6G-2, Written Interrogatories to Judgment Debtor.

Rutter, Cal. Practice Guide: Personal Injury Ch. 6-E, E. Special Discovery Rules and Procedures in Limited Civil Cases.

2 Witkin Cal. Proc. 5th Courts § 253, Discovery.

§ 96. Request for statement of witnesses, and description and copies of evidence; statement of response; effect

(a) Any party may serve on any other party a request in substantially the following form:

TO: _____,

attorney for _____:

You are requested to serve on the undersigned, within 20 days, a statement of: the names and addresses of witnesses (OTHER THAN A PARTY WHO IS AN INDIVIDUAL) you intend to call at trial; a description of physical evidence you intend to offer; and a description and copies of documentary evidence you intend to offer or, if the documents are not available to you, a description of them. Witnesses and evidence that will be used only for impeachment need not be included. YOU WILL NOT BE PERMITTED TO CALL ANY WITNESS, OR INTRODUCE ANY EVIDENCE, NOT INCLUDED IN THE STATEMENT SERVED IN RESPONSE TO THIS REQUEST, EXCEPT AS OTHERWISE PROVIDED BY LAW.

(b) The request shall be served no more than 45 days or less than 30 days prior to the date first set for trial, unless otherwise ordered.

(c) A statement responding to the request shall be served within 20 days from the service of the request.

(d) No additional, amended or late statement is permitted except by written stipulation or unless ordered for good cause on noticed motion.

(e) No request or statement served under this section shall be filed, unless otherwise ordered.

(f) The clerk shall furnish forms for requests under this rule.

(g) The time for performing acts required under this section shall be computed as provided by law, including Section 1013. *(Added by Stats.1982, c. 1581, p. 6228, § 1.)*

Research References

Rutter, Cal. Practice Guide: Civ. Pro. Before Trial Ch. 8C-2, "Reasonably Calculated to Lead to Discovery of Admissible Evidence".

Rutter, Cal. Practice Guide: Civ. Pro. Before Trial Ch. 8C-4, Attorney Work Product Protection.

Rutter, Cal. Practice Guide: Civ. Pro. Before Trial Ch. 8L-2, Special Discovery Procedures Permitted.

Rutter, Cal. Practice Guide: Civil Trials & Evidence Ch. 1-A, A. Importance of Statewide and Local Rules of Court.

Rutter, Cal. Practice Guide: Civil Trials & Evidence Ch. 4-B, B. Preliminary Matters Discussed in Final Status Conference or In-Chambers Conference.

Rutter, Cal. Practice Guide: Civil Trials & Evidence Ch. 4-F, F. Motions in Limine.

Rutter, Cal. Practice Guide: Personal Injury Ch. 6-A, A. Scope of Discovery and Limitations.

Rutter, Cal. Practice Guide: Personal Injury Ch. 6-E, E. Special Discovery Rules and Procedures in Limited Civil Cases.

Rutter, Cal. Practice Guide: Personal Injury Ch. 9-N, N. Special Trial Rules in Limited Civil Cases (CCP § 90 et seq.).

2 Witkin Cal. Proc. 5th Courts § 254, Disclosure of Witnesses and Evidence.

§ 97. Prohibition of call of witness or introduction of evidence not included in statement on objection; exceptions

(a) Except as provided in this section, upon objection of a party who served a request in compliance with Section 96, no party required to serve a responding statement may call a witness or introduce evidence, except for purposes of impeachment, against the objecting party unless the witness or evidence was included in the statement served.

(b) The exceptions to subdivision (a) are:

(1) A person who, in his or her individual capacity, is a party to the litigation and who calls himself or herself as a witness.

(2) An adverse party.

(3) Witnesses and evidence used solely for purposes of impeachment.

(4) Documents obtained by discovery authorized by this chapter.

(5) The court may, upon such terms as may be just (including, but not limited to, continuing the trial for a reasonable period of time and awarding costs and litigation expenses), permit a party to call a witness or introduce evidence which is required to be, but is not included in such party's statement so long as the court finds that such party has made a good faith effort to comply with subdivision (c) of Section 96 or that the failure to comply was the result of his or her mistake, inadvertence, surprise or excusable neglect as provided in Section 473.

(c) Nothing in this article limits the introduction of evidence in any hearing pursuant to Section 585. *(Added by Stats.1982, c. 1581, p. 6229, § 1. Amended by Stats.1983, c. 102, § 3, eff. June 16, 1983.)*

Research References

Rutter, Cal. Practice Guide: Civ. Pro. Before Trial Ch. 8L-2, Special Discovery Procedures Permitted.

Rutter, Cal. Practice Guide: Civil Trials & Evidence Ch. 1-A, A. Importance of Statewide and Local Rules of Court.

Rutter, Cal. Practice Guide: Civil Trials & Evidence Ch. 4-B, B. Preliminary Matters Discussed in Final Status Conference or In-Chambers Conference.

Rutter, Cal. Practice Guide: Civil Trials & Evidence Ch. 4-F, F. Motions in Limine.

Rutter, Cal. Practice Guide: Personal Injury Ch. 6-E, E. Special Discovery Rules and Procedures in Limited Civil Cases.

Rutter, Cal. Practice Guide: Personal Injury Ch. 9-N, N. Special Trial Rules in Limited Civil Cases (CCP § 90 et seq.).

2 Witkin Cal. Proc. 5th Courts § 254, Disclosure of Witnesses and Evidence.

§ 98. Prepared testimony in lieu of direct testimony; conditions

A party may, in lieu of presenting direct testimony, offer the prepared testimony of revelant [1] witnesses in the form of affidavits or declarations under penalty of perjury. The prepared testimony may include, but need not be limited to, the opinions of expert witnesses, and testimony which authenticates documentary evidence. To the extent the contents of the prepared testimony would have been admissible were the witness to testify orally thereto, the prepared testimony shall be received as evidence in the case, provided that either of the following applies:

(a) A copy has been served on the party against whom it is offered at least 30 days prior to the trial, together with a current address of the affiant that is within 150 miles of the place of trial, and the affiant is available for service of process at that place for a reasonable period of time, during the 20 days immediately prior to trial.

(b) The statement is in the form of all or part of a deposition in the case, and the party against whom it is offered had an opportunity to participate in the deposition.

The court shall determine whether the affidavit or declaration shall be read into the record in lieu of oral testimony or admitted as a documentary exhibit. *(Added by Stats.1982, c. 1581, p. 6229, § 1. Amended by Stats.1983, c. 102, § 4, eff. June 16, 1983.)*

[1] So in chaptered copy.

Research References

Rutter, Cal. Practice Guide: Civ. Pro. Before Trial Ch. 3-A, A. Subject Matter Jurisdiction (Competency).
Rutter, Cal. Practice Guide: Civ. Pro. Before Trial Ch. 8L-1, Limitations on Existing Discovery Procedures.
Rutter, Cal. Practice Guide: Civil Trials & Evidence Ch. 1-C, C. Marshalling the Evidence.
Rutter, Cal. Practice Guide: Civil Trials & Evidence Ch. 9-A, A. Preliminary Considerations.
Rutter, Cal. Practice Guide: Personal Injury Ch. 9-N, N. Special Trial Rules in Limited Civil Cases (CCP § 90 et seq.).
2 Witkin Cal. Proc. 5th Courts § 255, Use of Prepared Testimony.

§ 99. Judgment or final order; conclusiveness

A judgment or final order, in respect to the matter directly adjudged, is conclusive between the parties and their successors in interest but does not operate as collateral estoppel of a party or a successor in interest to a party in other litigation with a person who was not a party or a successor in interest to a party to the action in which the judgment or order is rendered. *(Added by Stats.1982, c. 1581, p. 6229, § 1.)*

Research References

Rutter, Cal. Practice Guide: Civ. Pro. Before Trial Ch. 3-A, A. Subject Matter Jurisdiction (Competency).
2 Witkin Cal. Proc. 5th Courts § 256, Judgment and Appeal.
7 Witkin Cal. Proc. 5th Judgment § 413, (S 413) General Principle.

§ 100. Appeals

Any party shall have the right to appeal any judgment or final order consistent with the law governing appeals. *(Added by Stats.1982, c. 1581, p. 6230, § 1.)*

Research References

2 Witkin Cal. Proc. 5th Courts § 256, Judgment and Appeal.

CHAPTER 5.5. SMALL CLAIMS COURT

ARTICLE 1. GENERAL PROVISIONS

§ 116.110. Short title

This chapter shall be known and may be cited as "The Small Claims Act." *(Added by Stats.1990, c. 1305 (S.B.2627), § 3.)*

Research References

Rutter, Cal. Practice Guide: Civil Appeals & Writs Ch. 16-A, A. Introduction.
Rutter, Cal. Practice Guide: Civ. Pro. Before Trial Ch. 3-A, A. Subject Matter Jurisdiction (Competency).
Rutter, Cal. Practice Guide: Civil Trials & Evidence Ch. 8D-C, C. General Parameters Re Admissibility of Hearsay Evidence.
Rutter, Cal. Practice Guide: Enforcing Judgments/Debts Ch. 3-C, C. Prelawsuit Considerations.
2 Witkin Cal. Proc. 5th Courts § 251, Nature and Scope of Statute.
2 Witkin Cal. Proc. 5th Courts § 268, (S 268) Statutory Framework.
7 Witkin Cal. Proc. 5th Judgment § 352, Small Claims Division.
12 Witkin, California Summary 10th Real Property § 112A, (New)-Lower Value and Shorter Delinquency.

§ 116.120. Legislative findings and declaration

The Legislature hereby finds and declares as follows:

(a) Individual minor civil disputes are of special importance to the parties and of significant social and economic consequence collectively.

(b) In order to resolve minor civil disputes expeditiously, inexpensively, and fairly, it is essential to provide a judicial forum accessible to all parties directly involved in resolving these disputes.

(c) The small claims divisions have been established to provide a forum to resolve minor civil disputes, and for that reason constitute a fundamental element in the administration of justice and the protection of the rights and property of individuals.

(d) The small claims divisions, the provisions of this chapter, and the rules of the Judicial Council regarding small claims actions shall operate to ensure that the convenience of parties and witnesses who are individuals shall prevail, to the extent possible, over the convenience of any other parties or witnesses. *(Added by Stats.1990, c. 1305 (S.B.2627), § 3. Amended by Stats.1998, c. 931 (S.B.2139), § 37, eff. Sept. 28, 1998.)*

Law Revision Commission Comments

Section 116.120 is amended to accommodate unification of the municipal and superior courts in a county. Cal. Const. art. VI, § 5(e). It is also amended to reflect elimination of the justice court. Cal. Const. art. VI, §§ 1, 5(b). [28 Cal.L.Rev.Comm.Reports 51 (1998)].

Civ. Pro.

Research References

2 Witkin Cal. Proc. 5th Courts § 267, (S 267) Nature and Organization.
2 Witkin Cal. Proc. 5th Courts § 283, (S 283) Mass Claims.

§ 116.130. Definitions

In this chapter, unless the context indicates otherwise:

(a) "Plaintiff" means the party who has filed a small claims action. The term includes a defendant who has filed a claim against a plaintiff.

(b) "Defendant" means the party against whom the plaintiff has filed a small claims action. The term includes a plaintiff against whom a defendant has filed a claim.

(c) "Judgment creditor" means the party, whether plaintiff or defendant, in whose favor a money judgment has been rendered.

(d) "Judgment debtor" means the party, whether plaintiff or defendant, against whom a money judgment has been rendered.

(e) "Person" means an individual, corporation, partnership, limited liability partnership, limited liability company, firm, association, or other entity.

(f) "Individual" means a natural person.

(g) "Party" means a plaintiff or defendant.

(h) "Motion" means a party's written request to the court for an order or other action. The term includes an informal written request to the court, such as a letter.

(i) "Declaration" means a written statement signed by an individual which includes the date and place of signing, and a statement under penalty of perjury under the laws of this state that its contents are true and correct.

(j) "Good cause" means circumstances sufficient to justify the requested order or other action, as determined by the judge.

(k) "Mail" means first-class mail with postage fully prepaid, unless stated otherwise. *(Added by Stats.1990, c. 1305 (S.B. 2627), § 3. Amended by Stats.1991, c. 915 (S.B.771), § 1; Stats.1994, c. 1010 (S.B.2053), § 57; Stats.2003, c. 449 (A.B. 1712), § 4.)*

Research References

2 Witkin Cal. Proc. 5th Courts § 268, (S 268) Statutory Framework.

§ 116.140. Time extensions; prejudgment attachments; application to small claims actions

The following do not apply in small claims actions:

(a) Subdivision (a) of Section 1013 and subdivision (b) of Section 1005, on the extension of the time for taking action when notice is given by mail.

(b) Title 6.5 (commencing with Section 481.010) of Part 2, on the issuance of prejudgment attachments. *(Added by Stats.1991, c. 915 (S.B.771), § 2.)*

Research References

Rutter, Cal. Practice Guide: Enforcing Judgments/Debts Ch. 3-C, C. Prelawsuit Considerations.
Rutter, Cal. Practice Guide: Enforcing Judgments/Debts Ch. 4-A, A. Attachment.
2 Witkin Cal. Proc. 5th Courts § 289, (S 289) in General.
6 Witkin Cal. Proc. 5th Proceedings Without Trial § 31, Express Limitations.
6 Witkin Cal. Proc. 5th Provisional Remedies § 93, (S 93) Courts and Court Commissioners.

ARTICLE 2. SMALL CLAIMS COURT

§ 116.210. Small claims division

In each superior court there shall be a small claims division. The small claims division may be known as the small claims court. *(Added by Stats.1990, c. 1305 (S.B.2627), § 3. Amended by Stats.1998, c. 931 (S.B.2139), § 38, eff. Sept. 28, 1998; Stats.2002, c. 784 (S.B.1316), § 30.)*

Law Revision Commission Comments

Section 116.210 is amended to accommodate unification of the municipal and superior courts in a county. Cal. Const. art. VI, § 5(e). It is also amended to reflect elimination of the justice court. Cal. Const. art. VI, §§ 1, 5(b).

Section 116.210 is also amended to expressly authorize continued use of the name "small claims court," even though the small claims division is not a separate court. [28 Cal.L.Rev.Comm. Reports 51 (1998)].

Section 116.210 is amended to reflect unification of the municipal and superior courts pursuant to Article VI, Section 5(e), of the California Constitution. [32 Cal.L.Rev.Comm. Reports 95 (2002)].

Research References

Rutter, Cal. Practice Guide: Enforcing Judgments/Debts Ch. 3-C, C. Prelawsuit Considerations.
9 Witkin Cal. Proc. 5th Appeal § 1003, Distinction: Appeal from Small Claims Court.
2 Witkin Cal. Proc. 5th Courts § 267, (S 267) Nature and Organization.
2 Witkin Cal. Proc. 5th Courts § 268, (S 268) Statutory Framework.

§ 116.220. Jurisdiction

(a) The small claims court has jurisdiction in the following actions:

(1) Except as provided in subdivisions (c), (e), and (f), for recovery of money, if the amount of the demand does not exceed five thousand dollars ($5,000).

(2) Except as provided in subdivisions (c), (e), and (f), to enforce payment of delinquent unsecured personal property taxes in an amount not to exceed five thousand dollars ($5,000), if the legality of the tax is not contested by the defendant.

(3) To issue the writ of possession authorized by Sections 1861.5 and 1861.10 of the Civil Code if the amount of the demand does not exceed five thousand dollars ($5,000).

(4) To confirm, correct, or vacate a fee arbitration award not exceeding five thousand dollars ($5,000) between an attorney and client that is binding or has become binding, or to conduct a hearing de novo between an attorney and client after nonbinding arbitration of a fee dispute involving no more than five thousand

dollars ($5,000) in controversy, pursuant to Article 13 (commencing with Section 6200) of Chapter 4 of Division 3 of the Business and Professions Code.

(5) For an injunction or other equitable relief only when a statute expressly authorizes a small claims court to award that relief.

(b) In any action seeking relief authorized by paragraphs (1) to (4), inclusive, of subdivision (a), the court may grant equitable relief in the form of rescission, restitution, reformation, and specific performance, in lieu of, or in addition to, money damages. The court may issue a conditional judgment. The court shall retain jurisdiction until full payment and performance of any judgment or order.

(c) Notwithstanding subdivision (a), the small claims court has jurisdiction over a defendant guarantor as follows:

(1) For any action brought by a natural person against the Registrar of the Contractors' State License Board as the defendant guarantor, the small claims jurisdictional limit stated in Section 116.221 shall apply.

(2) For any action against a defendant guarantor that does not charge a fee for its guarantor or surety services, if the amount of the demand does not exceed two thousand five hundred dollars ($2,500).

(3) For any action brought by a natural person against a defendant guarantor that charges a fee for its guarantor or surety services, if the amount of the demand does not exceed six thousand five hundred dollars ($6,500).

(4) For any action brought by an entity other than a natural person against a defendant guarantor that charges a fee for its guarantor or surety services or against the Registrar of the Contractors' State License Board as the defendant guarantor, if the amount of the demand does not exceed four thousand dollars ($4,000).

(d) In any case in which the lack of jurisdiction is due solely to an excess in the amount of the demand, the excess may be waived, but any waiver is not operative until judgment.

(e) Notwithstanding subdivision (a), in any action filed by a plaintiff incarcerated in a Department of Corrections and Rehabilitation facility, the small claims court has jurisdiction over a defendant only if the plaintiff has alleged in the complaint that he or she has exhausted his or her administrative remedies against that department, including compliance with Sections 905.2 and 905.4 of the Government Code. The final administrative adjudication or determination of the plaintiff's administrative claim by the department may be attached to the complaint at the time of filing in lieu of that allegation.

(f) In any action governed by subdivision (e), if the plaintiff fails to provide proof of compliance with the requirements of subdivision (e) at the time of trial, the judicial officer shall, at his or her discretion, either dismiss the action or continue the action to give the plaintiff an opportunity to provide that proof.

(g) For purposes of this section, "department" includes an employee of a department against whom a claim has been filed under this chapter arising out of his or her duties as an employee of that department. *(Added by Stats.1990, c. 1305 (S.B.2627), § 3. Amended by Stats.1990, c. 1683 (A.B.3916), § 3; Stats.1991, c. 133 (A.B.1827), § 1; Stats.1991, c. 915 (S.B.771), § 3; Stats.1992, c. 8 (A.B.1551), § 1, eff. Feb. 19, 1992; Stats.1992, c. 142 (S.B.1376), § 2; Stats.1993, c. 1262 (A.B.1272), § 5; Stats. 1993, c. 1264 (S.B.574), § 95; Stats.1994, c. 479 (A.B.3219), § 10; Stats.1995, c. 366 (A.B.725), § 1; Stats.1998, c. 240 (A.B.771), § 2; Stats.1999, c. 982 (A.B.1678), § 6; Stats.2006, c. 150 (A.B.2455), § 1; Stats.2008, c. 157 (S.B.1432), § 4; Stats. 2009, c. 468 (A.B.712), § 1.)*

Research References

Rutter, Cal. Practice Guide: Civ. Pro. Before Trial Ch. 3-A, A. Subject Matter Jurisdiction (Competency).

Rutter, Cal. Practice Guide: Civ. Pro. Before Trial Gen. Matls., Highlights.

Rutter, Cal. Practice Guide: Enforcing Judgments/Debts Ch. 3-C, C. Prelawsuit Considerations.

Rutter, Cal. Practice Guide: Prof. Responsibility Ch. 5-K, K. Fee Recovery/Enforcing Fee Agreements.

Miller and Starr California Real Estate § 32:6, Who Can Attach.

Miller and Starr California Real Estate § 20:11, The Unruh Civil Rights Act--Violations and Enforcement.

Miller and Starr California Real Estate § 19:235, Tenant's Personal Property--Innkeeper's Lien.

19 NO. 4 Miller & Starr, California Real Estate Newsalert 7, Construction Contracts.

2 Witkin Cal. Proc. 5th Courts § 281, (S 281) in General.

2 Witkin Cal. Proc. 5th Courts § 282, (S 282) Particular Actions.

2 Witkin Cal. Proc. 5th Courts § 287, (S 287) Restrictions on Transfer.

2 Witkin Cal. Proc. 5th Courts § 288, (S 288) Action Against Department of Corrections and Rehabilitation.

2 Witkin Cal. Proc. 5th Courts § 295, Claim in Same Action.

2 Witkin Cal. Proc. 5th Courts § 296, Action on Claim in Another Court.

2 Witkin Cal. Proc. 5th Courts § 302, (S 302) in General.

6 Witkin Cal. Proc. 5th Proceedings Without Trial § 482, (S 482) Programs and Legislation.

12 Witkin, California Summary 10th Real Property § 125, (S 125) Alternative Dispute Resolution.

12 Witkin, California Summary 10th Real Property § 728, Jurisdiction, Venue, and Process.

1 Witkin Cal. Summ. 10th Contracts § 522, Statutory Regulation: in General.

13 Witkin, California Summary 10th Personal Property § 226, Application, Writ, and Restraining Order.

§ 116.221. Additional jurisdiction

In addition to the jurisdiction conferred by Section 116.220, the small claims court has jurisdiction in an action brought by a natural person, if the amount of the demand does not exceed ten thousand dollars ($10,000), except for actions specified in Section 116.224, or otherwise prohibited by subdivision (c) of Section 116.220 or subdivision (a) of Section 116.231. *(Added by Stats.2005, c. 600 (S.B.422), § 2. Amended by Stats.2011, c. 64 (S.B.221), § 1.)*

Research References

Rutter, Cal. Practice Guide: Civ. Pro. Before Trial Ch. 3-A, A. Subject Matter Jurisdiction (Competency).

Rutter, Cal. Practice Guide: Civ. Pro. Before Trial Gen. Matls., Highlights.

Rutter, Cal. Practice Guide: Enforcing Judgments/Debts Ch. 3-C, C. Prelawsuit Considerations.

Rutter, Cal. Practice Guide: Enforcing Judgments/Debts Gen. Matls., Highlights.

Rutter, Cal. Practice Guide: Landlord-Tenant Gen. Matls, Highlights.

Rutter, Cal. Practice Guide: Prof. Responsibility Ch. 5-K, K. Fee Recovery/Enforcing Fee Agreements.

Miller and Starr California Real Estate § 20:11, The Unruh Civil Rights Act--Violations and Enforcement.

Miller and Starr California Real Estate § 35:15, Statutory Provisions for Mediations (And Arbitration) of Real Property Disputes.

2 Witkin Cal. Proc. 5th Courts § 281, (S 281) in General.

2 Witkin Cal. Proc. 5th Courts § 282, (S 282) Particular Actions.

2 Witkin Cal. Proc. 5th Courts § 295, Claim in Same Action.

2 Witkin Cal. Proc. 5th Courts § 296, Action on Claim in Another Court.

2 Witkin Cal. Proc. 5th Courts § 302, (S 302) in General.

6 Witkin Cal. Proc. 5th Proceedings Without Trial § 482, (S 482) Programs and Legislation.

12 Witkin, California Summary 10th Real Property § 125, (S 125) Alternative Dispute Resolution.

1 Witkin Cal. Summ. 10th Contracts § 522, Statutory Regulation: in General.

§ 116.222. Actions to enforce payment of debt; statement of calculation of liability; required content

Text of section as added by Stats.2005, c. 600 (S.B. 422), § 3. See, also, another section of the same number as added by Stats.2005, c. 618 (A.B.1459), § 3.

If the action is to enforce the payment of a debt, the statement of calculation of liability shall separately state the original debt, each payment credited to the debt, each fee and charge added to the debt, each payment credited against those fees and charges, all other debits or charges to the account, and an explanation of the nature of those fees, charges, debits, and all other credits to the debt, by source and amount. *(Added by Stats.2005, c. 600 (S.B.422), § 3.)*

Research References

Rutter, Cal. Practice Guide: Civ. Pro. Before Trial Ch. 3-A, A. Subject Matter Jurisdiction (Competency).
2 Witkin Cal. Proc. 5th Courts § 292, in General.

§ 116.222. Actions to enforce payment of debt; statement of calculation of liability; required content

Text of section as added by Stats.2005, c. 618 (A.B. 1459), § 3. See, also, another section of the same number as added by Stats.2005, c. 600 (S.B.422), § 3.

If the action is to enforce the payment of a debt, the statement of calculation of liability shall separately state the original debt, each payment credited to the debt, each fee and charge added to the debt, each payment credited against those fees and charges, all other debits or charges to the account, and an explanation of the nature of those fees, charges, debits, and all other credits to the debt, by source and amount. *(Added by Stats.2005, c. 618 (A.B.1459), § 3.)*

Research References

Rutter, Cal. Practice Guide: Civ. Pro. Before Trial Ch. 3-A, A. Subject Matter Jurisdiction (Competency).
2 Witkin Cal. Proc. 5th Courts § 292, in General.

§ 116.224. Action brought by natural person for damages for bodily injuries from automobile accident

(a) Notwithstanding Section 116.221, the small claims court has jurisdiction in an action brought by a natural person for damages for bodily injuries resulting from an automobile accident if the amount of the demand does not exceed seven thousand five hundred dollars ($7,500).

(b) This section shall apply only if a defendant is covered by an automobile insurance policy that includes a duty to defend.

(c) This section shall remain in effect only until January 1, 2015, and as of that date is repealed, unless a later enacted statute, that is enacted before January 1, 2015, deletes or extends that date. *(Added by Stats.2011, c. 64 (S.B.221), § 3.)*

Repeal

For repeal of this section, see its terms.

Research References

Rutter, Cal. Practice Guide: Civ. Pro. Before Trial Ch. 3-A, A. Subject Matter Jurisdiction (Competency).
Rutter, Cal. Practice Guide: Enforcing Judgments/Debts Ch. 3-C, C. Prelawsuit Considerations.
Rutter, Cal. Practice Guide: Enforcing Judgments/Debts Gen. Matls., Highlights.

2 Witkin Cal. Proc. 5th Courts § 281, (S 281) in General.

§ 116.225. Status of agreements entered or renewed on or after January 1, 2003, to establish a forum outside California for actions within the jurisdiction of a small claims court of California

An agreement entered into or renewed on or after January 1, 2003, establishing a forum outside of California for an action arising from an offer or provision of goods, services, property, or extensions of credit primarily for personal, family, or household purposes that is otherwise within the jurisdiction of a small claims court of this state is contrary to public policy and is void and unenforceable. *(Added by Stats.2002, c. 247 (A.B.2949), § 1.)*

Research References

Rutter, Cal. Practice Guide: Civ. Pro. Before Trial Ch. 3-B, B. Jurisdiction Over Parties-Personal Jurisdiction.
2 Witkin Cal. Proc. 5th Courts § 281, (S 281) in General.
1 Witkin Cal. Summ. 10th Contracts § 484, (S 484) California Law.

§ 116.230. Filing fees

(a) In a small claims case, the clerk of the court shall charge and collect only those fees authorized under this chapter.

(b) If the party filing a claim has filed 12 or fewer small claims in the state within the previous 12 months, the filing fee is the following:

(1) Thirty dollars ($30) if the amount of the demand is one thousand five hundred dollars ($1,500) or less.

(2) Fifty dollars ($50) if the amount of the demand is more than one thousand five hundred dollars ($1,500) but less than or equal to five thousand dollars ($5,000).

(3) Seventy-five dollars ($75) if the amount of the demand is more than five thousand dollars ($5,000).

(c) If the party has filed more than 12 other small claims in the state within the previous 12 months, the filing fee is one hundred dollars ($100).

(d)(1) If, after having filed a claim and paid the required fee under paragraph (1) of subdivision (b), a party files an amended claim or amendment to a claim that raises the amount of the demand so that the filing fee under paragraph (2) of subdivision (b) would be charged, the filing fee for the amended claim or amendment is twenty dollars ($20).

(2) If, after having filed a claim and paid the required fee under paragraph (2) of subdivision (b), a party files an amended claim or amendment to a claim that raises the amount of the demand so that the filing fee under paragraph (3) of subdivision (b) would be charged, the filing fee for the amended claim or amendment is twenty-five dollars ($25).

(3) If, after having filed a claim and paid the required fee under paragraph (1) of subdivision (b), a party files an amended claim or amendment to a claim that raises the amount of the demand so that the filing fee under paragraph (3) of subdivision (b) would be charged, the filing fee for the amended claim or amendment is forty-five dollars ($45).

(4) The additional fees paid under this subdivision are due upon filing. The court shall not reimburse a party if the party's claim is amended to demand a lower amount that falls within the range for a filing fee lower than that originally paid.

(e) Each party filing a claim shall file a declaration with the claim stating whether that party has filed more than 12 other small claims in the state within the last 12 months.

(f) The clerk of the court shall deposit fees collected under this section into a bank account established for this purpose by the Administrative Office of the Courts and maintained under rules adopted by or trial court financial policies and procedures authorized by the Judicial Council under subdivision (a) of Section 77206 of the Government Code. The deposits shall be made as required under Section 68085.1 of the Government Code and trial court financial policies and procedures authorized by the Judicial Council.

(g)(1) The Administrative Office of the Courts shall distribute six dollars ($6) of each thirty-dollar ($30) fee, eight dollars ($ 8) of each fifty-dollar ($50) fee, ten dollars ($10) of each seventy-five- dollar ($75) fee, and fourteen dollars ($14) of each one hundred-dollar ($ 100) fee collected under subdivision (b) or (c) to a special account in the county in which the court is located to be used for the small claims advisory services described in Section 116.940, or, if the small claims advisory services are administered by the court, to the court. The Administrative Office of the Courts shall also distribute two dollars ($2) of each seventy- five-dollar ($75) fee collected under subdivision (b) to the law library fund in the county in which the court is located.

(2) From the fees collected under subdivision (d), the Administrative Office of the Courts shall distribute two dollars ($2) to the law library fund in the county in which the court is located, and three dollars ($3) to the small claims advisory services described in Section 116.940, or, if the small claims advisory services are administered by the court, to the court.

(3) Records of these moneys shall be available from the Administrative Office of the Courts for inspection by the public on request.

(4) Nothing in this section precludes the court or county from contracting with a third party to provide small claims advisory services as described in Section 116.940.

(h) The remainder of the fees collected under subdivisions (b), (c), and (d) shall be transmitted monthly to the Controller for deposit in the Trial Court Trust Fund.

(i) All money distributed under this section to be used for small claims advisory services shall be used only for providing those services as described in Section 116.940. Nothing in this section shall preclude the county or the court from procuring other funding to comply with the requirements of Section 116.940. *(Added by Stats.2005, c. 75 (A.B.145), § 19, eff. July 19, 2005, operative Jan. 1, 2006. Amended by Stats.2005, c. 706 (A.B.1742), § 3; Stats.2007, c. 738 (A.B.1248), § 3.)*

Research References

Rutter, Cal. Practice Guide: Enforcing Judgments/Debts Ch. 3-C, C. Prelawsuit Considerations.
2 Witkin Cal. Proc. 5th Courts § 180, Court Fees.
2 Witkin Cal. Proc. 5th Courts § 290, (S 290) Uniform Fees.
2 Witkin Cal. Proc. 5th Courts § 292, in General.
2 Witkin Cal. Proc. 5th Courts § 295, Claim in Same Action.
2 Witkin Cal. Proc. 5th Courts § 302, (S 302) in General.

§ 116.231. Limitation on number of actions filed each year; demand amount; exceptions

(a) Except as provided in subdivision (d), no person may file more than two small claims actions in which the amount demanded exceeds two thousand five hundred dollars ($2,500), anywhere in the state in any calendar year.

(b) Except as provided in subdivision (d), if the amount demanded in any small claims action exceeds two thousand five hundred dollars ($2,500), the party making the demand shall file a declaration under penalty of perjury attesting to the fact that not more than two small claims actions in which the amount of the demand exceeded two thousand five hundred dollars ($2,500) have been filed by that party in this state within the calendar year.

(c) The Legislature finds and declares that the pilot project conducted under the authority of Chapter 1196 of the Statutes of 1991 demonstrated the efficacy of the removal of the limitation on the number of actions public entities may file in the small claims courts on claims exceeding two thousand five hundred dollars ($2,500).

(d) The limitation on the number of filings exceeding two thousand five hundred dollars ($2,500) does not apply to filings where the claim does not exceed five thousand dollars ($5,000) that are filed by a city, county, city and county, school district, county office of education, community college district, local district, or any other local public entity. If any small claims action is filed by a city, county, city and county, school district, county office of education, community college district, local district, or any other local public entity pursuant to this section, and the defendant informs the court either in advance of the hearing by written notice or at the time of the hearing, that he or she is represented in the action by legal counsel, the action shall be transferred out of the small claims division. A city, county, city and county, school district, county office of education, community college district, local district, or any other local public entity may not file a claim within the small claims division if the amount of the demand exceeds five thousand dollars ($5,000). *(Added by Stats.1990, c. 1683 (A.B.3916), § 4. Amended by Stats.1991, c. 915 (S.B.771), § 5; Stats.1991, c. 1196 (A.B.1755), § 4; Stats.1994, c. 971 (A.B.2937), § 1; Stats.1998, c. 931 (S.B.2139), § 39, eff. Sept. 28, 1998.)*

Law Revision Commission Comments

Section 116.231 is amended to accommodate unification of the municipal and superior courts in a county. Cal. Const. art. VI, § 5(e). [28 Cal.L.Rev.Comm.Reports 51 (1998)].

Research References

Rutter, Cal. Practice Guide: Civ. Pro. Before Trial Ch. 3-A, A. Subject Matter Jurisdiction (Competency).
Rutter, Cal. Practice Guide: Enforcing Judgments/Debts Ch. 3-C, C. Prelawsuit Considerations.
2 Witkin Cal. Proc. 5th Courts § 281, (S 281) In General.
2 Witkin Cal. Proc. 5th Courts § 295, Claim in Same Action.
2 Witkin Cal. Proc. 5th Courts § 296, Action on Claim in Another Court.
2 Witkin Cal. Proc. 5th Courts § 302, (S 302) in General.

§ 116.232. Fee for mailing service of a claim and order on defendant

A fee of fifteen dollars ($15) shall be charged and collected from the plaintiff for each defendant to whom the court clerk mails a copy of the claim under Section 116.340. This fee shall be distributed to the court in which it was collected. *(Added by Stats.2005, c. 75 (A.B.145), § 20, eff. July 19, 2005, operative Jan. 1, 2006. Amended by Stats.2013, c. 31 (S.B.75), § 1, eff. June 27, 2013.)*

Research References

2 Witkin Cal. Proc. 5th Courts § 290, (S 290) Uniform Fees.
2 Witkin Cal. Proc. 5th Courts § 294, (S 294) Notice to Appear.

§ 116.240. Temporary judges; course of study on ethics and substantive law

(a) With the consent of the parties who appear at the hearing, the court may order a case to be heard by a temporary judge who is a member of the State Bar, and who has been sworn and empowered to act until final determination of the case.

(b) Prior to serving as a temporary judge in small claims court, on and after July 1, 2006, and at least every three years thereafter, each temporary judge shall take the course of study offered by the courts on ethics and substantive law under rules adopted by the Judicial Council. The course shall include, but not be limited to, state and federal consumer laws, landlord-tenant law along with any applicable county specific rent deposit law, the state and federal Fair Debt Collection Practices Acts, [1] the federal Truth in Lending Act, [2] the federal Fair Credit Billing Act, [3] the federal Electronic Fund Transfer Act, [4] tort law, and contract law, including defenses to contracts and defenses to debts. On substantive law, the courts may receive assistance from the Department of Consumer Affairs, to the extent that the department is fiscally able to provide that assistance. *(Added by Stats.1990, c. 1305 (S.B.2627), § 3. Amended by Stats.2005, c. 600 (S.B.422), § 4; Stats.2005, c. 618 (A.B.1459), § 4.)*

[1] See Civil Code § 1788 et seq.; 15 U.S.C.A. § 1692 et seq.

[2] See 15 U.S.C.A. § 1601 et seq.

[3] See 15 U.S.C.A. § 1666 et seq.

[4] See 15 U.S.C.A. § 1693 et seq.

Research References

2 Witkin Cal. Proc. 5th Courts § 298, (S 298) Conduct of Hearing.

§ 116.250. Court sessions; schedules

(a) Sessions of the small claims court may be scheduled at any time and on any day, including Saturdays, but excluding other judicial holidays.

(b) Each small claims division of a superior court with seven or more judicial officers shall conduct at least one night session or Saturday session each month for the purpose of hearing small claims cases other than small claims appeals. The term "session" includes, but is not limited to, a proceeding conducted by a member of the State Bar acting as a mediator or referee. *(Added by Stats.1990, c. 1305 (S.B.2627), § 3. Amended by Stats.1998, c. 931 (S.B.2139), § 40, eff. Sept. 28, 1998; Stats.2002, c. 784 (S.B.1316), § 31; Stats.2003, c. 149 (S.B.79), § 4.)*

Law Revision Commission Comments

Section 116.250 is amended to accommodate unification of the municipal and superior courts in a county. Cal. Const. art. VI, § 5(e). For guidance in applying Section 116.250, see Section 38 (judicial districts) & Comment. [28 Cal.L.Rev.Comm. Reports 51 (1998)].

Section 116.250 is amended to reflect unification of the municipal and superior courts pursuant to Article VI, Section 5(e), of the California Constitution. See Section 38 (judicial district). [32 Cal.L.Rev.Comm. Reports 95 (2002)].

Subdivision (a) of Section 116.250 is amended to reflect enactment of Government Code Section 69740(a) (number and location of trial court sessions). [33 Cal.L.Rev.Comm. Reports 187 (2003)].

Research References

2 Witkin Cal. Proc. 5th Courts § 291, (S 291) Venue, Location, and Sessions.

§ 116.260. Advice to litigants

In each county, individual assistance shall be made available to advise small claims litigants and potential litigants without charge as provided in Section 116.940 and by rules adopted by the Judicial Council. *(Added by Stats.1990, c. 1305 (S.B.2627), § 3.)*

Research References

2 Witkin Cal. Proc. 5th Courts § 271, (S 271) Small Claims Legal Advisers.

5 Witkin, California Summary 10th Torts § 494, (S 494) Small Claims Proceeding.

§ 116.270. Law clerks authorized

Any small claims division may use law clerks to assist the judge with legal research of small claims cases. *(Added by Stats.1990, c. 1305 (S.B.2627), § 3.)*

ARTICLE 3. ACTIONS

§ 116.310. Pleadings; discovery

(a) No formal pleading, other than the claim described in Section 116.320 or 116.360, is necessary to initiate a small claims action.

(b) The pretrial discovery procedures described in Section 2019.010 are not permitted in small claims actions. *(Added by Stats.1990, c. 1305 (S.B.2627), § 3. Amended by Stats.1991, c. 915 (S.B.771), § 6; Stats.2003, c. 149 (S.B.79), § 5; Stats.2004, c. 182 (A.B.3081), § 7, operative July 1, 2005.)*

Law Revision Commission Comments

Subdivision (a) of Section 116.310 is amended to correct the cross-reference. See 1991 Cal. Stat. ch. 915, § 11. [33 Cal.L.Rev.Comm. Reports 188 (2003)].

Subdivision (b) of Section 116.310 is amended to reflect nonsubstantive reorganization of the rules governing civil discovery. [33 Cal.L.Rev. Comm. Reports 982 (2004)].

Research References

Rutter, Cal. Practice Guide: Civ. Pro. Before Trial Ch. 3-A, A. Subject Matter Jurisdiction (Competency).

Rutter, Cal. Practice Guide: Civ. Pro. Before Trial Ch. 8B-3, Limitations on Right to Discovery.

Rutter, Cal. Practice Guide: Enforcing Judgments/Debts Ch. 3-C, C. Prelawsuit Considerations.

2 Witkin Cal. Proc. 5th Courts § 268, (S 268) Statutory Framework.

2 Witkin Cal. Proc. 5th Courts § 289, (S 289) in General.

4 Witkin Cal. Proc. 5th Pleading § 5, (S 5) Small Claims Courts and Limited Civil Cases.

§ 116.320. Commencement of action; claim form; necessary information

(a) A plaintiff may commence an action in the small claims court by filing a claim under oath with the clerk of the small claims court in person, by mail, by facsimile transmission if authorized pursuant to Section 1010.5, or by electronic means as authorized by Section 1010.6.

(b) The claim form shall be a simple nontechnical form approved or adopted by the Judicial Council. The claim form shall set forth a place for (1) the name and address of the defendant, if known; (2) the amount and the basis of the claim; (3) that the plaintiff, where possible, has demanded payment and, in applicable cases, possession of the property; (4) that the defendant has failed or refused to pay, and, where applicable, has refused to surrender the property; and (5) that the plaintiff understands that the judgment on his or her claim will be conclusive and without a right of appeal.

(c) The form or accompanying instructions shall include information that the plaintiff (1) may not be represented by an attorney, (2) has no right of appeal, and (3) may ask the court to waive fees for filing and serving the claim on the ground that the plaintiff is unable to pay them, using the forms approved by the Judicial Council for that purpose. *(Added by Stats.1990, c. 1305*

(S.B.2627), § 3. Amended by Stats.1991, c. 915 (S.B.771), § 7; Stats.2007, c. 738 (A.B.1248), § 4.)

Research References

Rutter, Cal. Practice Guide: Enforcing Judgments/Debts Ch. 3-C, C. Prelawsuit Considerations.
2 Witkin Cal. Proc. 5th Courts § 292, in General.
4 Witkin Cal. Proc. 5th Pleading § 5, (S 5) Small Claims Courts and Limited Civil Cases.

§ 116.330. Schedule of hearing on case; order directing parties to appear

(a) When a claim is filed, the clerk shall schedule the case for hearing and shall issue an order directing the parties to appear at the time set for the hearing with witnesses and documents to prove their claim or defense. The case shall be scheduled for hearing no earlier than 20 days but not more than 70 days from the date of the order.

(b) In lieu of the method of setting the case for hearing described in subdivision (a), at the time a claim is filed the clerk may do all of the following:

(1) Cause a copy of the claim to be mailed to the defendant by any form of mail providing for a return receipt.

(2) On receipt of proof that the claim was served as provided in paragraph (1), issue an order scheduling the case for hearing in accordance with subdivision (a) and directing the parties to appear at the time set for the hearing with witnesses and documents to prove their claim or defense.

(3) Cause a copy of the order setting the case for hearing and directing the parties to appear, to be served upon the parties by any form of mail providing for a return receipt. *(Added by Stats.1990, c. 1305 (S.B.2627), § 3. Amended by Stats.2005, c. 706 (A.B.1742), § 4.)*

Research References

3 Witkin Cal. Proc. 5th Actions § 962, (S 962) Notice or Order to Show Cause.
2 Witkin Cal. Proc. 5th Courts § 294, (S 294) Notice to Appear.
2 Witkin Cal. Proc. 5th Courts § 295, Claim in Same Action.
2 Witkin Cal. Proc. 5th Courts § 297, (S 297) Postponement.
2 Witkin Cal. Proc. 5th Courts § 308, (S 308) Motion to Vacate Default Judgment.

§ 116.340. Service of claim and order on defendant

(a) Service of the claim and order on the defendant may be made by any one of the following methods:

(1) The clerk may cause a copy of the claim and order to be mailed to the defendant by any form of mail providing for a return receipt.

(2) The plaintiff may cause a copy of the claim and order to be delivered to the defendant in person.

(3) The plaintiff may cause service of a copy of the claim and order to be made by substituted service as provided in subdivision (a) or (b) of Section 415.20 without the need to attempt personal service on the defendant. For these purposes, substituted service as provided in subdivision (b) of Section 415.20 may be made at the office of the sheriff or marshal who shall deliver a copy of the claim and order to any person authorized by the defendant to receive service, as provided in Section 416.90, who is at least 18 years of age, and thereafter mailing a copy of the claim and order to the defendant's usual mailing address.

(4) The clerk may cause a copy of the claim to be mailed, the order to be issued, and a copy of the order to be mailed as provided in subdivision (b) of Section 116.330.

(b) Service of the claim and order on the defendant shall be completed at least 15 days before the hearing date if the defendant resides within the county in which the action is filed, or at least 20 days before the hearing date if the defendant resides outside the county in which the action is filed.

(c) Proof of service of the claim and order shall be filed with the small claims court at least five days before the hearing.

(d) Service by the methods described in subdivision (a) shall be deemed complete on the date that the defendant signs the mail return receipt, on the date of the personal service, as provided in Section 415.20, or as established by other competent evidence, whichever applies to the method of service used.

(e) Service shall be made within this state, except as provided in subdivisions (f) and (g).

(f) The owner of record of real property in California who resides in another state and who has no lawfully designated agent in California for service of process may be served by any of the methods described in this section if the claim relates to that property.

(g) A nonresident owner or operator of a motor vehicle involved in an accident within this state may be served pursuant to the provisions on constructive service in Sections 17450 to 17461, inclusive, of the Vehicle Code without regard to whether the defendant was a nonresident at the time of the accident or when the claim was filed. Service shall be made by serving both the Director of the California Department of Motor Vehicles and the defendant, and may be made by any of the methods authorized by this chapter or by registered mail as authorized by Section 17454 or 17455 of the Vehicle Code.

(h) If an action is filed against a principal and his or her guaranty or surety pursuant to a guarantor or suretyship agreement, a reasonable attempt shall be made to complete service on the principal. If service is not completed on the principal, the action shall be transferred to the court of appropriate jurisdiction. *(Added by Stats.1990, c. 1305 (S.B. 2627), § 3. Amended by Stats.1991, c. 915 (S.B.771), § 8; Stats.1995, c. 576 (A.B.1225), § 1; Stats.1996, c. 1159 (A.B.3471), § 1; Stats.2002, c. 806 (A.B.3027), § 3; Stats.2005, c. 706 (A.B.1742), § 5.)*

Research References

Rutter, Cal. Practice Guide: Civ. Pro. Before Trial Ch. 4-D, D. Service of Summons.
Rutter, Cal. Practice Guide: Enforcing Judgments/Debts Ch. 3-C, C. Prelawsuit Considerations.
14 NO. 2 Miller & Starr, California Real Estate Newsalert 19, Subdivisions.
3 Witkin Cal. Proc. 5th Actions § 962, (S 962) Notice or Order to Show Cause.
2 Witkin Cal. Proc. 5th Courts § 290, (S 290) Uniform Fees.
2 Witkin Cal. Proc. 5th Courts § 294, (S 294) Notice to Appear.
2 Witkin Cal. Proc. 5th Courts § 295, Claim in Same Action.
2 Witkin Cal. Proc. 5th Courts § 297, (S 297) Postponement.

§ 116.360. Counterclaims

(a) The defendant may file a claim against the plaintiff in the same action in an amount not to exceed the jurisdictional limits stated in Sections 116.220, 116.221, and 116.231. The claim need not relate to the same subject or event as the plaintiff's claim.

(b) The defendant's claim shall be filed and served in the manner provided for filing and serving a claim of the plaintiff under Sections 116.330 and 116.340.

(c) The defendant shall cause a copy of the claim and order to be served on the plaintiff at least five days before the hearing date, unless the defendant was served 10 days or less before the hearing date, in which event the defendant shall cause a copy of the defendant's claim and order to be served on the plaintiff at least one day before the hearing date. *(Formerly § 116.380,* added by Stats.1990, c. 1305 (S.B.2627), § 3. Renumbered § 116.360 and amended by Stats.1991, c. 915 (S.B.771), § 11. Amended by Stats.1996, c. 1159 (A.B.3471), § 2; Stats.2006, c. 167 (A.B.2618), § 4.)

Research References

Rutter, Cal. Practice Guide: Civ. Pro. Before Trial Ch. 3-A, A. Subject Matter Jurisdiction (Competency).

Rutter, Cal. Practice Guide: Enforcing Judgments/Debts Ch. 3-C, C. Prelawsuit Considerations.

2 Witkin Cal. Proc. 5th Courts § 295, Claim in Same Action.

4 Witkin Cal. Proc. 5th Pleading § 5, (S 5) Small Claims Courts and Limited Civil Cases.

§ 116.370. Venue; court location; challenges to venue or court location

(a) Venue and court location requirements in small claims actions shall be the same as in other civil actions. The court may prescribe by local rule the proper court locations for small claims actions.

(b) A defendant may challenge venue or court location by writing to the court and mailing a copy of the challenge to each of the other parties to the action, without personally appearing at the hearing.

(c) In all cases, including those in which the defendant does not either challenge venue or court location or appear at the hearing, the court shall inquire into the facts sufficiently to determine whether venue and court location are proper, and shall make its determination accordingly.

(1) If the court determines that the action was not commenced in the proper venue, the court, on its own motion, shall dismiss the action without prejudice, unless all defendants are present and agree that the action may be heard. If the court determines that the action was not commenced in the proper court location, the court may transfer the action to a proper court location pursuant to local rule.

(2) If the court determines that the action was commenced in the proper venue and court location, the court may hear the case if all parties are present. If the defendant challenged venue or court location and all parties are not present, the court shall postpone the hearing for at least 15 days and shall notify all parties by mail of the court's decision and the new hearing date, time, and place. (Added by Stats.1990, c. 1305 (S.B.2627), § 3. Amended by Stats.1991, c. 133 (A.B.1827), § 2; Stats.1991, c. 915 (S.B.771), § 10.5; Stats.1992, c. 201 (A.B.3653), § 1; Stats.1996, c. 1159 (A.B.3471), § 3; Stats.2002, c. 806 (A.B.3027), § 4.)

Research References

3 Witkin Cal. Proc. 5th Actions § 783, (S 783) Consolidation of Trial Courts.

2 Witkin Cal. Proc. 5th Courts § 291, (S 291) Venue, Location, and Sessions.

2 Witkin Cal. Proc. 5th Courts § 297, (S 297) Postponement.

§ 116.390. Counterclaims in excess of jurisdictional limit; transfer of claims

(a) If a defendant has a claim against a plaintiff that exceeds the jurisdictional limits stated in Sections 116.220, 116.221, and 116.231, and the claim relates to the contract, transaction, matter, or event which is the subject of the plaintiff's claim, the defendant may commence an action against the plaintiff in a court of competent jurisdiction and request the small claims court to transfer the small claims action to that court.

(b) The defendant may make the request by filing with the small claims court in which the plaintiff commenced the action, at or before the time set for the hearing of that action, a declaration stating the facts concerning the defendant's action against the plaintiff with a true copy of the complaint so filed by

the defendant against the plaintiff. The defendant shall cause a copy of the declaration and complaint to be personally delivered to the plaintiff at or before the time set for the hearing of the small claims action.

(c) In ruling on a motion to transfer, the small claims court may do any of the following: (1) render judgment on the small claims case prior to the transfer; (2) not render judgment and transfer the small claims case; (3) refuse to transfer the small claims case on the grounds that the ends of justice would not be served. If the small claims action is transferred prior to judgment, both actions shall be tried together in the transferee court.

(d) When the small claims court orders the action transferred, it shall transmit all files and papers to the transferee court.

(e) The plaintiff in the small claims action shall not be required to pay to the clerk of the transferee court any transmittal, appearance, or filing fee unless the plaintiff appears in the transferee court, in which event the plaintiff shall be required to pay the filing fee and any other fee required of a defendant in the transferee court. However, if the transferee court rules against the plaintiff in the action filed in that court, the court may award to the defendant in that action the costs incurred as a consequence of the transfer, including attorney's fees and filing fees. (Added by Stats.1990, c. 1305 (S.B.2627), § 3. Amended by Stats.1991, c. 915 (S.B.771), § 11.5; Stats. 1996, c. 1159 (A.B.3471), § 4; Stats.2005, c. 75 (A.B.145), § 21, eff. July 19, 2005, operative Jan. 1, 2006; Stats.2006, c. 167 (A.B.2618), § 5.)

Research References

Rutter, Cal. Practice Guide: Civ. Pro. Before Trial Ch. 3-A, A. Subject Matter Jurisdiction (Competency).

Rutter, Cal. Practice Guide: Enforcing Judgments/Debts Ch. 3-C, C. Prelawsuit Considerations.

2 Witkin Cal. Proc. 5th Courts § 296, Action on Claim in Another Court.

2 Witkin Cal. Proc. 5th Courts § 319, No Power to Consolidate or Dismiss Action.

ARTICLE 4. PARTIES

§ 116.410. Competency as party

(a) Any person who is at least 18 years of age, or legally emancipated, and mentally competent may be a party to a small claims action.

(b) A minor or incompetent person may appear by a guardian ad litem appointed by a judge of the court in which the action is filed. (Added by Stats.1990, c. 1305 (S.B.2627), § 3. Amended by Stats.2004, c. 171 (A.B.3078), § 1.)

Research References

2 Witkin Cal. Proc. 5th Courts § 268, (S 268) Statutory Framework.

2 Witkin Cal. Proc. 5th Courts § 273, (S 273) in General.

§ 116.420. Assigned claims

(a) No claim shall be filed or maintained in small claims court by the assignee of the claim.

(b) This section does not prevent the filing or defense of an action in the small claims court by (1) a trustee in bankruptcy in the exercise of the trustee's duties as trustee, or (2) by the holder of a security agreement, retail installment contract, or lien contract subject to the Unruh Act (Chapter 1 (commencing with

Section 1801) of Title 2 of Part 4 of Division 3 of the Civil Code) or the Automobile Sales Finance Act (Chapter 2b (commencing with Section 2981) of Title 14 of Part 4 of Division 3 of the Civil Code), purchased by the holder for the holder's portfolio of investments, provided that the holder is not an assignee for the purpose of collection.

(c) This section does not prevent the filing in small claims court by a local government which is self-insured for purposes of workers' compensation and is seeking subrogation pursuant to Section 3852 of the Labor Code. *(Added by Stats.1990, c. 1305 (S.B.2627), § 3. Amended by Stats.1994, c. 231 (S.B.1771), § 1.)*

Research References

Rutter, Cal. Practice Guide: Civ. Pro. Before Trial Ch. 3-A, A. Subject Matter Jurisdiction (Competency).
Rutter, Cal. Practice Guide: Enforcing Judgments/Debts Ch. 3-C, C. Prelawsuit Considerations.
2 Witkin Cal. Proc. 5th Courts § 274, General Rule.
2 Witkin Cal. Proc. 5th Courts § 275, Exceptions.
4 Witkin Cal. Proc. 5th Pleading § 25, Basic Fees.

§ 116.430. Fictitious business names; compliance with fictitious business name laws

(a) If the plaintiff operates or does business under a fictitious business name and the claim relates to that business, the claim shall be accompanied by the filing of a declaration stating that the plaintiff has complied with the fictitious business name laws by executing, filing, and publishing a fictitious business name statement as required.

(b) A small claims action filed by a person who has not complied with the applicable fictitious business name laws by executing, filing, and publishing a fictitious business name statement as required shall be dismissed without prejudice.

(c) For purposes of this section, "fictitious business name" means the term as defined in Section 17900 of the Business and Professions Code, and "fictitious business name statement" means the statement described in Section 17913 of the Business and Professions Code. *(Added by Stats.1990, c. 1305 (S.B.2627), § 3. Amended by Stats.1991, c. 915 (S.B.771), § 12.)*

Research References

2 Witkin Cal. Proc. 5th Courts § 293, Use of Fictitious Business Name.

ARTICLE 5. HEARING

Section

§ 116.510. Informal hearing

The hearing and disposition of the small claims action shall be informal, the object being to dispense justice promptly, fairly, and inexpensively. *(Added by Stats.1990, c. 1305 (S.B.2627), § 3. Amended by Stats.1991, c. 915 (S.B.771), § 13.)*

Research References

Rutter, Cal. Practice Guide: Civil Trials & Evidence Ch. 2-A, A. Sources of Right to Jury Trial.
2 Witkin Cal. Proc. 5th Courts § 268, (S 268) Statutory Framework.
2 Witkin Cal. Proc. 5th Courts § 298, (S 298) Conduct of Hearing.
2 Witkin Cal. Proc. 5th Courts § 301, (S 301) Admission and Exclusion of Evidence.
2 Witkin Cal. Proc. 5th Courts § 316, in General.

§ 116.520. Evidence; witnesses

(a) The parties have the right to offer evidence by witnesses at the hearing or, with the permission of the court, at another time.

(b) If the defendant fails to appear, the court shall still require the plaintiff to present evidence to prove his or her claim.

(c) The court may consult witnesses informally and otherwise investigate the controversy with or without notice to the parties. *(Added by Stats.1990, c. 1305 (S.B.2627), § 3.)*

Research References

2 Witkin Cal. Proc. 5th Courts § 298, (S 298) Conduct of Hearing.
2 Witkin Cal. Proc. 5th Courts § 301, (S 301) Admission and Exclusion of Evidence.
6 Witkin Cal. Proc. 5th Proceedings Without Trial § 137, (S 137) Restrictions on Default Judgments.

§ 116.530. Appearance by attorney; restrictions

(a) Except as permitted by this section, no attorney may take part in the conduct or defense of a small claims action.

(b) Subdivision (a) does not apply if the attorney is appearing to maintain or defend an action in any of the following capacities:

(1) By or against himself or herself.

(2) By or against a partnership in which he or she is a general partner and in which all the partners are attorneys.

(3) By or against a professional corporation of which he or she is an officer or director and of which all other officers and directors are attorneys.

(c) Nothing in this section shall prevent an attorney from doing any of the following:

(1) Providing advice to a party to a small claims action, either before or after the commencement of the action.

(2) Testifying to facts of which he or she has personal knowledge and about which he or she is competent to testify.

(3) Representing a party in an appeal to the superior court.

(4) Representing a party in connection with the enforcement of a judgment. *(Added by Stats.1990, c. 1305 (S.B.2627), § 3. Amended by Stats.1991, c. 915 (S.B.771), § 14; Stats.2003, c. 449 (A.B.1712), § 5.)*

Research References

Rutter, Cal. Practice Guide: Civ. Pro. Before Trial Ch. 2-B, B. Capacity to Sue or Defend.
Rutter, Cal. Practice Guide: Civ. Pro. Before Trial Ch. 3-A, A. Subject Matter Jurisdiction (Competency).
Rutter, Cal. Practice Guide: Enforcing Judgments/Debts Ch. 3-C, C. Prelawsuit Considerations.
Rutter, Cal. Practice Guide: Prof. Responsibility Ch. 1-D, D. Unauthorized Practice of Law.
2 Witkin Cal. Proc. 5th Courts § 276, General Rule.
2 Witkin Cal. Proc. 5th Courts § 277, When Attorney May Appear.
2 Witkin Cal. Proc. 5th Courts § 278, Distinction: Attorney Adviser.
2 Witkin Cal. Proc. 5th Courts § 299, (S 299) When Personal Appearance is Excused.

§ 116.531. Experts; assistance; testimony

Nothing in this article shall prevent a representative of an insurer or other expert in the matter before the small claims court from rendering assistance to a party in the litigation except during the conduct of the hearing, either before or after the commencement of the action, unless otherwise prohibited by law; nor shall anything in this article prevent those individuals from testifying to facts of which they have personal knowledge and about which they are competent to testify. *(Added by Stats.1990, c. 1683 (A.B.3916), § 5.)*

Research References

Rutter, Cal. Practice Guide: Civ. Pro. Before Trial Ch. 3-A, A. Subject Matter Jurisdiction (Competency).

2 Witkin Cal. Proc. 5th Courts § 279, When Agent May Appear.

§ 116.540. Appearance by person other than plaintiff or defendant; personal appearance by plaintiff or defendant

(a) Except as permitted by this section, no individual other than the plaintiff and the defendant may take part in the conduct or defense of a small claims action.

(b) Except as additionally provided in subdivision (i), a corporation may appear and participate in a small claims action only through a regular employee, or a duly appointed or elected officer or director, who is employed, appointed, or elected for purposes other than solely representing the corporation in small claims court.

(c) A party who is not a corporation or a natural person may appear and participate in a small claims action only through a regular employee, or a duly appointed or elected officer or director, or in the case of a partnership, a partner, engaged for purposes other than solely representing the party in small claims court.

(d) If a party is an individual doing business as a sole proprietorship, the party may appear and participate in a small claims action by a representative and without personally appearing if both of the following conditions are met:

(1) The claim can be proved or disputed by evidence of an account that constitutes a business record as defined in Section 1271 of the Evidence Code, and there is no other issue of fact in the case.

(2) The representative is a regular employee of the party for purposes other than solely representing the party in small claims actions and is qualified to testify to the identity and mode of preparation of the business record.

(e) A plaintiff is not required to personally appear, and may submit declarations to serve as evidence supporting his or her claim or allow another individual to appear and participate on his or her behalf, if (1) the plaintiff is serving on active duty in the United States Armed Forces outside this state, (2) the plaintiff was assigned to his or her duty station after his or her claim arose, (3) the assignment is for more than six months, (4) the representative is serving without compensation, and (5) the representative has appeared in small claims actions on behalf of others no more than four times during the calendar year. The defendant may file a claim in the same action in an amount not to exceed the jurisdictional limits stated in Sections 116.220, 116.221, and 116.231.

(f) A party incarcerated in a county jail, a Department of Corrections and Rehabilitation facility, or a Division of Juvenile Facilities facility is not required to personally appear, and may submit declarations to serve as evidence supporting his or her claim, or may authorize another individual to appear and participate on his or her behalf if that individual is serving without compensation and has appeared in small claims actions on behalf of others no more than four times during the calendar year.

(g) A defendant who is a nonresident owner of real property may defend against a claim relating to that property without

personally appearing by (1) submitting written declarations to serve as evidence supporting his or her defense, (2) allowing another individual to appear and participate on his or her behalf if that individual is serving without compensation and has appeared in small claims actions on behalf of others no more than four times during the calendar year, or (3) taking the action described in both (1) and (2).

(h) A party who is an owner of rental real property may appear and participate in a small claims action through a property agent under contract with the owner to manage the rental of that property, if (1) the owner has retained the property agent principally to manage the rental of that property and not principally to represent the owner in small claims court, and (2) the claim relates to the rental property.

(i) A party that is an association created to manage a common interest development, as defined in Section 4100 or in Sections 6528 and 6534 of the Civil Code, may appear and participate in a small claims action through an agent, a management company representative, or bookkeeper who appears on behalf of that association.

(j) At the hearing of a small claims action, the court shall require any individual who is appearing as a representative of a party under subdivisions (b) to (i), inclusive, to file a declaration stating (1) that the individual is authorized to appear for the party, and (2) the basis for that authorization. If the representative is appearing under subdivision (b), (c), (d), (h), or (i), the declaration also shall state that the individual is not employed solely to represent the party in small claims court. If the representative is appearing under subdivision (e), (f), or (g), the declaration also shall state that the representative is serving without compensation, and has appeared in small claims actions on behalf of others no more than four times during the calendar year.

(k) A husband or wife who sues or who is sued with his or her spouse may appear and participate on behalf of his or her spouse if (1) the claim is a joint claim, (2) the represented spouse has given his or her consent, and (3) the court determines that the interests of justice would be served.

(*l*) If the court determines that a party cannot properly present his or her claim or defense and needs assistance, the court may in its discretion allow another individual to assist that party.

(m) Nothing in this section shall operate or be construed to authorize an attorney to participate in a small claims action except as expressly provided in Section 116.530. *(Added by Stats.1990, c. 1305 (S.B.2627), § 3. Amended by Stats.1991, c. 915 (S.B.771), § 15; Stats.1992, c. 201 (A.B.3653), § 2; Stats. 1996, c. 693 (A.B.2567), § 1; Stats.2005, c. 452 (S.B.137), § 7; Stats.2006, c. 167 (A.B.2618), § 6; Stats.2012, c. 181 (A.B.806), § 43, operative Jan. 1, 2014; Stats.2013, c. 605 (S.B.752), § 23.)*

Law Revision Commission Comments

Subdivision (i) of Section 116.540 is amended to correct a cross-reference to former Civil Code Section 1351(c). [40 Cal.L.Rev.Comm. Reports 235 (2010)].

Subdivision (i) of Section 116.540 is amended to add cross-references to Civil Code Sections 6528 and 6534, reflecting the enactment of the Commercial and Industrial Common Interest Development Act (Civ. Code §§ 6500–6876). [42 Cal.L.Rev.Comm. Reports 1 (2012)].

Research References

Rutter, Cal. Practice Guide: Civ. Pro. Before Trial Ch. 2-B, B. Capacity to Sue or Defend.

Rutter, Cal. Practice Guide: Civ. Pro. Before Trial Ch. 3-A, A. Subject Matter Jurisdiction (Competency).

Rutter, Cal. Practice Guide: Enforcing Judgments/Debts Ch. 3-C, C. Prelawsuit Considerations.

Rutter, Cal. Practice Guide: Prof. Responsibility Ch. 1-D, D. Unauthorized Practice of Law.

Miller and Starr California Real Estate § 19:121, Tenant's Remedies for Landlord's Breach of the Implied Warranty.

16 NO. 5 Miller & Starr, California Real Estate Newsalert 26. State Board of Equalization Issues Comprehensive Summary and Qs and As for Transfers of Base Year Values of Principal Residences State Board of Equalization Issues Comprehensive Summary and Qs and As for Transfers of...

2 Witkin Cal. Proc. 5th Courts § 276, General Rule.

2 Witkin Cal. Proc. 5th Courts § 279, When Agent May Appear.

2 Witkin Cal. Proc. 5th Courts § 280, Agent's Declaration.

2 Witkin Cal. Proc. 5th Courts § 295, Claim in Same Action.

2 Witkin Cal. Proc. 5th Courts § 299, (S 299) When Personal Appearance is Excused.

§ 116.541.　Department of Corrections; Department of the Youth Authority; appearance by regular employees

(a) Notwithstanding Section 116.540 or any other provision of law, the Department of Corrections or the Department of the Youth Authority may appear and participate in a small claims action through a regular employee, who is employed or appointed for purposes other than solely representing that department in small claims court.

(b) Where the Department of Corrections or the Department of the Youth Authority is named as a defendant in small claims court, the representative of the department is not required to personally appear to challenge the plaintiff's compliance with the pleading requirements and may submit pleadings or declarations to assert that challenge.

(c) At the hearing of a small claims action, the court shall require any individual who is appearing as a representative of the Department of Corrections or the Department of the Youth Authority under subdivision (a) to file a declaration stating (1) that the individual is authorized to appear for the party, (2) the basis for that authorization, and (3) that the individual is not employed solely to represent the party in small claims court.

(d) Nothing in this section shall operate or be construed to authorize an attorney to participate in a small claims action except as expressly provided in Section 116.530.

(e) For purposes of this section, all references to the Department of Corrections or the Department of the Youth Authority include an employee thereof, against whom a claim has been filed under this chapter arising out of his or her duties as an employee of that department. *(Added by Stats.1995, c. 366 (A.B.725), § 2.)*

Research References

2 Witkin Cal. Proc. 5th Courts § 279, When Agent May Appear.

2 Witkin Cal. Proc. 5th Courts § 280, Agent's Declaration.

2 Witkin Cal. Proc. 5th Courts § 288, (S 288) Action Against Department of Corrections and Rehabilitation.

§ 116.550.　English language understanding; interpreter list; hearing postponement

(a) If the court determines that a party does not speak or understand English sufficiently to comprehend the proceedings or give testimony, and needs assistance in so doing, the court may permit another individual (other than an attorney) to assist that party.

(b) Each small claims court shall make a reasonable effort to maintain and make available to the parties a list of interpreters who are able and willing to aid parties in small claims actions either for no fee, or for a fee which is reasonable considering the nature and complexity of the claims. The list shall include interpreters for all languages that require interpretation before the court, as determined by the court in its discretion and in view of the court's experience.

(c) Failure to maintain a list of interpreters, or failure to include an interpreter for a particular language, shall not invalidate any proceedings before the court.

(d) If a court interpreter or other competent interpreter is not available to aid a party in a small claims action, at the first hearing of the case the court shall postpone the hearing one time only to allow the party the opportunity to obtain another individual (other than an attorney) to assist that party. Any additional continuances shall be at the discretion of the court. *(Added by Stats.1990, c. 1305 (S.B.2627), § 3. Amended by Stats.1991, c. 915 (S.B.771), § 16; Stats.1993, c. 1191 (S.B.236), § 2.)*

Research References

2 Witkin Cal. Proc. 5th Courts § 279, When Agent May Appear.

2 Witkin Cal. Proc. 5th Courts § 297, (S 297) Postponement.

2 Witkin Cal. Proc. 5th Courts § 300, (S 300) Use of Interpreters.

§ 116.560.　Fictitious business names; legal name of defendant

(a) Whenever a claim that is filed against a person operating or doing business under a fictitious business name relates to the defendant's business, the court shall inquire at the time of the hearing into the defendant's correct legal name and the name or names under which the defendant does business. If the correct legal name of the defendant, or the name actually used by the defendant, is other than the name stated on the claim, the court shall amend the claim to state the correct legal name of the defendant, and the name or names actually used by the defendant.

(b) The plaintiff may request the court at any time, whether before or after judgment, to amend the plaintiff's claim or judgment to include both the correct legal name and the name or names actually used by the defendant. Upon a showing of good cause, the court shall amend the claim or judgment to state the correct legal name of the defendant, and the name or names actually used by the defendant.

(c) For purposes of this section, "fictitious business name" means the term as defined in Section 17900 of the Business and Professions Code. *(Added by Stats.1991, c. 915 (S.B.771), § 17.)*

Research References

2 Witkin Cal. Proc. 5th Courts § 293, Use of Fictitious Business Name.

§ 116.570.　Postponement of hearing

(a) Any party may submit a written request to postpone a hearing date for good cause.

(1) The written request may be made either by letter or on a form adopted or approved by the Judicial Council.

(2) The request shall be filed at least 10 days before the hearing date, unless the court determines that the requesting party has good cause to file the request at a later date.

(3) On the date of making the written request, the requesting party shall mail or personally deliver a copy to each of the other parties to the action.

(4)(A) If the court finds that the interests of justice would be served by postponing the hearing, the court shall postpone the hearing, and shall notify all parties by mail of the new hearing date, time, and place.

(B) On one occasion, upon the written request of a defendant guarantor, the court shall postpone the hearing for at least 30 days, and the court shall take this action without a hearing. This subparagraph does not limit the discretion of the court to grant additional postponements under subparagraph (A).

(5) The court shall provide a prompt response by mail to any person making a written request for postponement of a hearing date under this subdivision.

(b) If service of the claim and order upon the defendant is not completed within the number of days before the hearing date required by subdivision (b) of Section 116.340, and the defendant has not personally appeared and has not requested a postponement, the court shall postpone the hearing for at least 15 days. If a postponement is ordered under this subdivision, the clerk shall promptly notify all parties by mail of the new hearing date, time, and place.

(c) This section does not limit the inherent power of the court to order postponements of hearings in appropriate circumstances.

(d) A fee of ten dollars ($10) shall be charged and collected for the filing of a request for postponement and rescheduling of a hearing date after timely service pursuant to subdivision (b) of Section 116.340 has been made upon the defendant. *(Added by Stats.1991, c. 915 (S.B.771), § 18. Amended by Stats.1992, c. 696 (A.B.1344), § 5, eff. Sept. 15, 1992; Stats.1994, c. 587 (A.B.3600), § 2; Stats.1996, c. 1159 (A.B.3471), § 5; Stats.1998, c. 240 (A.B.771), § 3; Stats.2002, c. 806 (A.B.3027), § 5.)*

Research References

2 Witkin Cal. Proc. 5th Courts § 290, (S 290) Uniform Fees.
2 Witkin Cal. Proc. 5th Courts § 297, (S 297) Postponement.

ARTICLE 6. JUDGMENT

Section
116.610. Damages; equitable relief; several judgment; costs; entry of judgment.
116.620. Payment of judgment; installments.
116.630. Amendment of name of party.

§ 116.610. Damages; equitable relief; several judgment; costs; entry of judgment

(a) The small claims court shall give judgment for damages, or equitable relief, or both damages and equitable relief, within the jurisdictional limits stated in Sections 116.220, 116.221, and 116.231, and may make any orders as to time of payment or otherwise as the court deems just and equitable for the resolution of the dispute.

(b) The court may, at its discretion or on request of any party, continue the matter to a later date in order to permit and encourage the parties to attempt resolution by informal or alternative means.

(c) The judgment shall include a determination whether the judgment resulted from a motor vehicle accident on a California highway caused by the defendant's operation of a motor vehicle, or by the operation by some other individual, of a motor vehicle registered in the defendant's name.

(d) If the defendant has filed a claim against the plaintiff, or if the judgment is against two or more defendants, the judgment, and the statement of decision if one is rendered, shall specify the basis for and the character and amount of the liability of each of the parties, including, in the case of multiple judgment debtors, whether the liability of each is joint or several.

(e) If specific property is referred to in the judgment, whether it be personal or real, tangible or intangible, the property shall be identified with sufficient detail to permit efficient implementation or enforcement of the judgment.

(f) In an action against several defendants, the court may, in its discretion, render judgment against one or more of them, leaving the action to proceed against the others, whenever a several judgment is proper.

(g)(1) The prevailing party is entitled to the costs of the action, including the costs of serving the order for the appearance of the defendant.

(2) Notwithstanding paragraph (1) of this subdivision and subdivision (b) of Section 1032, the amount of the small claims court fee paid by a party pursuant to subdivision (c) of Section 116.230 that exceeds the amount that would have been paid if the party had paid the fee pursuant to subdivision (b) of Section 116.230 shall not be recoverable as costs.

(h) When the court renders judgment, the clerk shall promptly deliver or mail notice of entry of the judgment to the parties, and shall execute a certificate of personal delivery or mailing and place it in the file.

(i) The notice of entry of judgment shall be on a form approved or adopted by the Judicial Council. *(Added by Stats.1990, c. 1305 (S.B.2627), § 3. Amended by Stats.1991, c. 133 (A.B.1827), § 3; Stats.1991, c. 915 (S.B.771), § 19; Stats. 1992, c. 8 (A.B.1551), § 2, eff. Feb. 19, 1992; Stats.1992, c. 142 (S.B.1376), § 3; Stats.1996, c. 1159 (A.B.3471), § 6; Stats.2005, c. 600 (S.B.422), § 5; Stats.2005, c. 618 (A.B.1459), § 5; Stats.2006, c. 167 (A.B.2618), § 7.)*

Research References

2 Witkin Cal. Proc. 5th Courts § 268, (S 268) Statutory Framework.
2 Witkin Cal. Proc. 5th Courts § 302, (S 302) in General.
2 Witkin Cal. Proc. 5th Courts § 320, Judgment.
8 Witkin Cal. Proc. 5th Enforcement of Judgment § 69, in General.
8 Witkin Cal. Proc. 5th Enforcement of Judgment § 75, (S 75) Amount of Lien.
8 Witkin Cal. Proc. 5th Enforcement of Judgment § 85, (S 85) Amount of Lien.

§ 116.620. Payment of judgment; installments

(a) The judgment debtor shall pay the amount of the judgment either immediately or at the time and upon the terms and conditions, including payment by installments, which the court may order.

(b) The court may at any time, for good cause, upon motion by a party and notice by the clerk to all affected parties at their last known address, amend the terms and conditions for payment of the judgment to provide for payment by installment. The determination shall be made without regard to the nature of the underlying debt and without regard to whether the moving party appeared before entry of the judgment.

(c) In determining the terms and conditions of payment, the court may consider any factors which would be relevant to a claim of exemption under Chapter 4 (commencing with Section 703.010) of Division 2 of Title 9 of Part 2. *(Added by Stats.1990, c. 1305 (S.B.2627), § 3.)*

Research References

2 Witkin Cal. Proc. 5th Courts § 304, Terms and Conditions.

§ 116.630. Amendment of name of party

The court may, at any time after judgment, for good cause, upon motion by a party and notice by the clerk to all affected parties at their last known address, amend the name of any party to include both the correct legal name and the actually used name or names of that party. *(Added by Stats.1990, c. 1305 (S.B.2627), § 3.)*

Research References

2 Witkin Cal. Proc. 5th Courts § 293, Use of Fictitious Business Name.

2 Witkin Cal. Proc. 5th Courts § 302, (S 302) in General.

ARTICLE 7.　MOTION TO VACATE, APPEAL, AND RELATED MATTERS

Section

116.710.　Right to appeal.

116.720.　Failure of plaintiff to appear at hearing; motion to vacate judgment; hearing rescheduled.

116.725.　Clerical error; motion to correct.

116.730.　Failure of defendant to appear at hearing; motion to vacate judgment; appeal of denied motion; hearing rescheduled.

116.740.　Defective service on defendant; motion to vacate judgment.

116.745.　Filing; collection of fees.

116.750.　Notice of appeal.

116.760.　Filing fees; distribution.

116.770.　Hearing de novo.

116.780.　Judgment on appeal; effect of judgment; costs and fees.

116.790.　Attorney's fees.

116.795.　Failure to appear or delayed hearing; dismissal of appeal.

116.798.　Petition seeking writ of review, mandamus, or prohibition relating to action of, appeal from, or postjudgment enforcement order of small claims division; judges who may hear; filing fee; procedural rules.

Law Revision Commission Comments

The heading ""Motion to Vacate and Appeal" is amended to broaden its scope and reflect the addition of Section 116.798 (writ petition). [41 Cal.L.Rev.Comm. Reports 313 (2011)].

§ 116.710.　Right to appeal

(a) The plaintiff in a small claims action shall have no right to appeal the judgment on the plaintiff's claim, but a plaintiff who did not appear at the hearing may file a motion to vacate the judgment in accordance with Section 116.720.

(b) The defendant with respect to the plaintiff's claim, and a plaintiff with respect to a claim of the defendant, may appeal the judgment to the superior court in the county in which the action was heard.

(c) With respect to the plaintiff's claim, the insurer of the defendant may appeal the judgment to the superior court in the county in which the matter was heard if the judgment exceeds two thousand five hundred dollars ($2,500) and the insurer stipulates that its policy with the defendant covers the matter to which the judgment applies.

(d) A defendant who did not appear at the hearing has no right to appeal the judgment, but may file a motion to vacate the judgment in accordance with Section 116.730 or 116.740 and also may appeal the denial of that motion. *(Added by Stats.1990, c. 1305 (S.B.2627), § 3.　Amended by Stats.1990, c. 1683 (A.B. 3916), § 6.)*

Research References

Rutter, Cal. Practice Guide: Civ. Pro. Before Trial Ch. 3-A, A. Subject Matter Jurisdiction (Competency).

Rutter, Cal. Practice Guide: Enforcing Judgments/Debts Ch. 3-C, C. Prelawsuit Considerations.

Rutter, Cal. Practice Guide: Enforcing Judgments/Debts Ch. 6E-4, Opposing Claim of Exemption.

9 Witkin Cal. Proc. 5th Appeal § 1003, Distinction: Appeal from Small Claims Court.

2 Witkin Cal. Proc. 5th Courts § 268, (S 268) Statutory Framework.

2 Witkin Cal. Proc. 5th Courts § 308, (S 308) Motion to Vacate Default Judgment.

2 Witkin Cal. Proc. 5th Courts § 309, No Appeal from Adverse Judgment.

2 Witkin Cal. Proc. 5th Courts § 311, Distinction Where Defendant Files Cross-Claim.

2 Witkin Cal. Proc. 5th Courts § 312, (S 312) Nature of Right.

2 Witkin Cal. Proc. 5th Courts § 314, (S 314) Appeal by Defendant Who Defaults.

8 Witkin Cal. Proc. 5th Extraordinary Writs § 34, (S 34) in General.

7 Witkin Cal. Proc. 5th Judgment § 352, Small Claims Division.

§ 116.720.　Failure of plaintiff to appear at hearing; motion to vacate judgment; hearing rescheduled

(a) A plaintiff who did not appear at the hearing in the small claims court may file a motion to vacate the judgment with the clerk of the small claims court. The motion shall be filed within 30 days after the clerk has mailed notice of entry of the judgment to the parties.

(b) The clerk shall schedule the hearing on the motion to vacate for a date no earlier than 10 days after the clerk has mailed written notice of the date, time, and place of the hearing to the parties.

(c) Upon a showing of good cause, the small claims court may grant the motion. If the defendant is not present, the court shall hear the motion in the defendant's absence.

(d) If the motion is granted, and if all parties are present and agree, the court may hear the case without rescheduling it. If the defendant is not present, the judge or clerk shall reschedule the case and give notice in accordance with Section 116.330. *(Added by Stats.1990, c. 1305 (S.B.2627), § 3.　Amended by Stats.1991, c. 915 (S.B.771), § 20.)*

Research References

2 Witkin Cal. Proc. 5th Courts § 308, (S 308) Motion to Vacate Default Judgment.

§ 116.725.　Clerical error; motion to correct

(a) A motion to correct a clerical error in a judgment or to set aside and vacate a judgment on the ground of an incorrect or erroneous legal basis for the decision may be made as follows:

(1) By the court on its own motion at any time.

(2) By a party within 30 days after the clerk mails notice of entry of judgment to the parties.

(b) Each party may file only one motion to correct a clerical error or to set aside and vacate the judgment on the ground of an incorrect or erroneous legal basis for the decision. *(Added by Stats.2005, c. 706 (A.B.1742), § 7.)*

Research References

Rutter, Cal. Practice Guide: Enforcing Judgments/Debts Ch. 3-C, C. Prelawsuit Considerations.

2 Witkin Cal. Proc. 5th Courts § 302, (S 302) in General.

§ 116.730.　Failure of defendant to appear at hearing; motion to vacate judgment; appeal of denied motion; hearing rescheduled

(a) A defendant who did not appear at the hearing in the small claims court may file a motion to vacate the judgment with the clerk of the small claims court. The motion shall be filed within 30 days after the clerk has mailed notice of entry of the judgment to the parties.

(b) The defendant shall appear at any hearing on the motion, or submit written justification for not appearing together with a declaration in support of the motion.

(c) Upon a showing of good cause, the court may grant the motion to vacate the judgment. If the plaintiff is not present, the court shall hear the motion in the plaintiff's absence.

(d) If the motion is granted, and if all parties are present and agree, the court may hear the case without rescheduling it. If the plaintiff is not present, the judge or clerk shall reschedule the case and give notice in accordance with Section 116.330.

(e) If the motion is denied, the defendant may appeal to the superior court only on the denial of the motion to vacate the judgment. The defendant shall file the notice of appeal with the clerk of the small claims court within 10 days after the small claims court has mailed or delivered notice of the court's denial of the motion to vacate the judgment.

(f) If the superior court determines that the defendant's motion to vacate the judgment should have been granted, the superior court may hear the claims of all parties without rescheduling the matter, provided that all parties are present and the defendant has previously complied with this article, or may order the case transferred to the small claims court for a hearing. *(Added by Stats.1990, c. 1305 (S.B.2627), § 3. Amended by Stats.1991, c. 915 (S.B.771), § 21.)*

Research References

Rutter, Cal. Practice Guide: Enforcing Judgments/Debts Ch. 3-C, C. Prelawsuit Considerations.
Rutter, Cal. Practice Guide: Enforcing Judgments/Debts Ch. 6A-7, Period During Which Judgment Enforceable; Renewal Procedures.
Rutter, Cal. Practice Guide: Enforcing Judgments/Debts Ch. 6D-6, Debtor's Recourse Against Execution Levy.
2 Witkin Cal. Proc. 5th Courts § 308, (S 308) Motion to Vacate Default Judgment.

§ 116.740. Defective service on defendant; motion to vacate judgment

(a) If the defendant was not properly served as required by Section 116.330 or 116.340 and did not appear at the hearing in the small claims court, the defendant may file a motion to vacate the judgment with the clerk of the small claims court. The motion shall be accompanied by a supporting declaration, and shall be filed within 180 days after the defendant discovers or should have discovered that judgment was entered against the defendant.

(b) The court may order that the enforcement of the judgment shall be suspended pending a hearing and determination of the motion to vacate the judgment.

(c) Upon a showing of good cause, the court may grant the motion to vacate the judgment. If the plaintiff is not present, the court shall hear the motion in the plaintiff's absence.

(d) Subdivisions (d), (e), and (f) of Section 116.730 apply to any motion to vacate a judgment. *(Added by Stats.1990, c. 1305 (S.B.2627), § 3. Amended by Stats.1991, c. 915 (S.B.771), § 22.)*

Research References

Rutter, Cal. Practice Guide: Enforcing Judgments/Debts Ch. 3-C, C. Prelawsuit Considerations.
Rutter, Cal. Practice Guide: Enforcing Judgments/Debts Ch. 6A-7, Period During Which Judgment Enforceable; Renewal Procedures.
Rutter, Cal. Practice Guide: Enforcing Judgments/Debts Ch. 6D-6, Debtor's Recourse Against Execution Levy.
2 Witkin Cal. Proc. 5th Courts § 303, (S 303) Enforcement and Stay.
2 Witkin Cal. Proc. 5th Courts § 308, (S 308) Motion to Vacate Default Judgment.

§ 116.745. Filing; collection of fees

The clerk shall collect a fee of twenty dollars ($20) for the filing of a motion to vacate. *(Added by Stats.1995, c. 576 (A.B.1225), § 1.5. Amended by Stats.2005, c. 75 (A.B.145), § 22, eff. July 19, 2005, operative Jan. 1, 2006.)*

Research References

2 Witkin Cal. Proc. 5th Courts § 290, (S 290) Uniform Fees.

2 Witkin Cal. Proc. 5th Courts § 308, (S 308) Motion to Vacate Default Judgment.

§ 116.750. Notice of appeal

(a) An appeal from a judgment in a small claims action is taken by filing a notice of appeal with the clerk of the small claims court.

(b) A notice of appeal shall be filed not later than 30 days after the clerk has delivered or mailed notice of entry of the judgment to the parties. A notice of appeal filed after the 30-day period is ineffective for any purpose.

(c) The time for filing a notice of appeal is not extended by the filing of a request to correct a mistake or by virtue of any subsequent proceedings on that request, except that a new period for filing notice of appeal shall begin on the delivery or mailing of notice of entry of any modified judgment. *(Added by Stats.1990, c. 1305 (S.B.2627), § 3. Amended by Stats.1991, c. 915 (S.B.771), § 23.)*

Research References

Rutter, Cal. Practice Guide: Civil Appeals & Writs Ch. 16-A, A. Introduction.
Rutter, Cal. Practice Guide: Enforcing Judgments/Debts Ch. 6E-4, Opposing Claim of Exemption.
2 Witkin Cal. Proc. 5th Courts § 315, (S 315) Notice of Appeal.

§ 116.760. Filing fees; distribution

(a) The appealing party shall pay a fee of seventy-five dollars ($75) for filing a notice of appeal.

(b) A party who does not appeal shall not be charged any fee for filing any document relating to the appeal.

(c) The fee shall be distributed as follows:

(1) To the county law library fund, as provided in Section 6320 of the Business and Professions Code, the amount specified in Section 6321 and 6322.1 of the Business and Professions Code.

(2) To the Trial Court Trust Fund, the remainder of the fee. *(Added by Stats.1990, c. 1305 (S.B.2627), § 3. Amended by Stats.1991, c. 915 (S.B.771), § 24; Stats.1998, c. 931 (S.B.2139), § 41, eff. Sept. 28, 1998; Stats.2000, c. 447 (S.B.1533), § 1; Stats.2005, c. 75 (A.B.145), § 23, eff. July 19, 2005, operative Jan. 1, 2006.)*

Law Revision Commission Comments

Section 116.760 is amended to accommodate unification of the municipal and superior courts in a county. Cal. Const. art. VI, § 5(e). It is also amended to reflect elimination of the justice court. Cal. Const. art. VI, §§ 1, 5(b).

Under subdivision (a), the fee for appealing from a small claims judgment is the same as the fee for an appeal to the appellate division of the superior court, which is specified in Section 26824 of the Government Code.

Subdivision (b) is amended to reflect relocation of the small claims division from the municipal court to the superior court in a county in which the municipal and superior courts unify their operations. Because the small claims division is in the same court that hears small claims appeals, subdivision (b) extends only to documents relating to the appeal, not to all documents filed in superior court. [28 Cal.L.Rev.Comm. Reports 51 (1998)].

Research References

2 Witkin Cal. Proc. 5th Courts § 290, (S 290) Uniform Fees.
2 Witkin Cal. Proc. 5th Courts § 316, in General.

§ 116.770. Hearing de novo

(a) The appeal to the superior court shall consist of a new hearing before a judicial officer other than the judicial officer who heard the action in the small claims division.

(b) The hearing on an appeal to the superior court shall be conducted informally. The pretrial discovery procedures described in Section 2019.010 are not permitted, no party has a right to a trial by jury, and no tentative decision or statement of decision is required.

(c) Article 5 (commencing with Section 116.510) on hearings in the small claims court applies in hearings on appeal in the superior court, except that attorneys may participate.

(d) The scope of the hearing shall include the claims of all parties who were parties to the small claims action at the time the notice of appeal was filed. The hearing shall include the claim of a defendant that was heard in the small claims court.

(e) The clerk of the superior court shall schedule the hearing for the earliest available time and shall mail written notice of the hearing to the parties at least 14 days prior to the time set for the hearing.

(f) The Judicial Council may prescribe by rule the practice and procedure on appeal and the time and manner in which the record on appeal shall be prepared and filed. *(Added by Stats.1990, c. 1305 (S.B.2627), § 3. Amended by Stats.1991, c. 133 (A.B.1827), § 4; Stats.1991, c. 915 (S.B.771), § 25; Stats. 1992, c. 8 (A.B.1551), § 3, eff. Feb. 19, 1992; Stats.1998, c. 931 (S.B.2139), § 42, eff. Sept. 28, 1998; Stats.2004, c. 182 (A.B. 3081), § 8, operative July 1, 2005.)*

Law Revision Commission Comments

Section 116.770 is amended to accommodate unification of the municipal and superior courts in a county. Cal. Const. art. VI, § 5(e). [28 Cal.L.Rev.Comm. Reports 51 (1998)].

Subdivision (b) of Section 116.770 is amended to reflect nonsubstantive reorganization of the rules governing civil discovery. [33 Cal.L.Rev. Comm. Reports 982 (2004)].

Research References

Rutter, Cal. Practice Guide: Civil Appeals & Writs Ch. 16-A, A. Introduction.
Rutter, Cal. Practice Guide: Civ. Pro. Before Trial Ch. 2-B, B, Capacity to Sue or Defend.
Rutter, Cal. Practice Guide: Civ. Pro. Before Trial Ch. 3-A, A. Subject Matter Jurisdiction (Competency).
Rutter, Cal. Practice Guide: Civ. Pro. Before Trial Ch. 8B-3, Limitations on Right to Discovery.
Rutter, Cal. Practice Guide: Civ. Pro. Before Trial Ch. 12(I)-D, D. Demand for Jury Trial and Waiver.
Rutter, Cal. Practice Guide: Civil Trials & Evidence Ch. 2-A, A. Sources of Right to Jury Trial.
Rutter, Cal. Practice Guide: Enforcing Judgments/Debts Ch. 3-C, C. Prelawsuit Considerations.
Rutter, Cal. Practice Guide: Enforcing Judgments/Debts Ch. 6E-4, Opposing Claim of Exemption.
9 Witkin Cal. Proc. 5th Appeal § 1003, Distinction: Appeal from Small Claims Court.
2 Witkin Cal. Proc. 5th Courts § 301, (S 301) Admission and Exclusion of Evidence.
2 Witkin Cal. Proc. 5th Courts § 316, in General.
2 Witkin Cal. Proc. 5th Courts § 317, Affirmative Relief to Losing Defendant.
2 Witkin Cal. Proc. 5th Courts § 318, No Right to Jury Trial.
2 Witkin Cal. Proc. 5th Courts § 341, (S 341) Jurisdiction.
8 Witkin Cal. Proc. 5th Extraordinary Writs § 34, (S 34) in General.
7 Witkin Cal. Proc. 5th Judgment § 352, Small Claims Division.

§ 116.780. Judgment on appeal; effect of judgment; costs and fees

(a) The judgment of the superior court after a hearing on appeal is final and not appealable.

(b) Article 6 (commencing with Section 116.610) on judgments of the small claims court applies to judgments of the superior court after a hearing on appeal, except as provided in subdivision (c).

(c) For good cause and where necessary to achieve substantial justice between the parties, the superior court may award a party to an appeal reimbursement of (1) attorney's fees actually and reasonably incurred in connection with the appeal, not exceeding one hundred fifty dollars ($150), and (2) actual loss of earnings and expenses of transportation and lodging actually and reasonably incurred in connection with the appeal, not exceeding one hundred fifty dollars ($150). *(Added by Stats.1990, c. 1305 (S.B.2627), § 3. Amended by Stats.1991, c. 915 (S.B.771), § 26; Stats.1994, c. 587 (A.B.3600), § 3; Stats.2005, c. 706 (A.B.1742), § 8; Stats.2011, c. 308 (S.B.647), § 1.)*

Law Revision Commission Comments

Section 116.780 is amended to delete an obsolete reference to subdivision (d), which no longer exists. For the legislation that eliminated subdivision (d), see 2005 Cal. Stat. ch. 706, § 8. For the text of that subdivision, see 1994 Cal. Stat. ch. 587, § 3; 1991 Cal. Stat. ch. 915, § 26. [39 Cal.L.Rev.Comm. Reports 223 (2009)].

Research References

Rutter, Cal. Practice Guide: Civil Appeals & Writs Ch. 16-A, A. Introduction.
Rutter, Cal. Practice Guide: Civil Appeals & Writs Ch. 16-B, B. Appealability and Standing.
Rutter, Cal. Practice Guide: Civ. Pro. Before Trial Ch. 3-A, A. Subject Matter Jurisdiction (Competency).
Rutter, Cal. Practice Guide: Enforcing Judgments/Debts Ch. 3-C, C. Prelawsuit Considerations.
2 Witkin Cal. Proc. 5th Courts § 320, Judgment.
2 Witkin Cal. Proc. 5th Courts § 321, No Appeal or Motion Attacking Judgment.
2 Witkin Cal. Proc. 5th Courts § 323, Review of Decision by Mandamus.
2 Witkin Cal. Proc. 5th Courts § 341, (S 341) Jurisdiction.
8 Witkin Cal. Proc. 5th Extraordinary Writs § 34, (S 34) in General.
7 Witkin Cal. Proc. 5th Judgment § 222, (S 222) Actions in Bad Faith.

§ 116.790. Attorney's fees

If the superior court finds that the appeal was without substantial merit and not based on good faith, but was intended to harass or delay the other party, or to encourage the other party to abandon the claim, the court may award the other party (a) attorney's fees actually and reasonably incurred in connection with the appeal, not exceeding one thousand dollars ($1,000), and (b) any actual loss of earnings and any expenses of transportation and lodging actually and reasonably incurred in connection with the appeal, not exceeding one thousand dollars ($1,000), following a hearing on the matter. *(Added by Stats. 1990, c. 1305 (S.B.2627), § 3. Amended by Stats.1990, c. 1683 (A.B.3916), § 7; Stats.1991, c. 915 (S.B.771), § 27.)*

Research References

Rutter, Cal. Practice Guide: Civ. Pro. Before Trial Ch. 3-A, A. Subject Matter Jurisdiction (Competency).
2 Witkin Cal. Proc. 5th Courts § 320, Judgment.
7 Witkin Cal. Proc. 5th Judgment § 222, (S 222) Actions in Bad Faith.

§ 116.795. Failure to appear or delayed hearing; dismissal of appeal

(a) The superior court may dismiss the appeal if the appealing party does not appear at the hearing or if the appeal is not heard within one year from the date of filing the notice of appeal with the clerk of the small claims court.

(b) Upon dismissal of an appeal by the superior court, the small claims court shall thereafter have the same jurisdiction as if no appeal had been filed. *(Added by Stats.1990, c. 1305 (S.B.2627), § 3.)*

Research References

Rutter, Cal. Practice Guide: Enforcing Judgments/Debts Ch. 3-C, C. Prelawsuit Considerations.

2 Witkin Cal. Proc. 5th Courts § 313, (S 313) Abandonment and Dismissal.

§ 116.798. Petition seeking writ of review, mandamus, or prohibition relating to action of, appeal from, or post-judgment enforcement order of small claims division; judges who may hear; filing fee; procedural rules

(a)(1) A petition that seeks a writ of review, a writ of mandate, or a writ of prohibition relating to an act of the small claims division, other than a postjudgment enforcement order, may be heard by a judge who is assigned to the appellate division of the superior court.

(2) A petition described by paragraph (1) may also be heard by the court of appeal or by the Supreme Court.

(3) Where a judge described in paragraph (1) grants a writ directed to the small claims division, the small claims division is an inferior tribunal for purposes of Title 1 (commencing with Section 1067) of Part 3.

(4) The fee for filing a writ petition in the superior court under paragraph (1) is the same as the fee for filing a notice of appeal under Section 116.760.

(5) The Judicial Council shall promulgate procedural rules for a writ proceeding under paragraph (1).

(6) An appeal shall not be taken from a judgment granting or denying a petition under paragraph (1) for issuance of a writ. An appellate court may, in its discretion, upon petition for extraordinary writ, review the judgment.

(b) A petition that seeks a writ of review, a writ of mandate, or a writ of prohibition relating to an act of a superior court in a small claims appeal may be heard by the court of appeal or by the Supreme Court.

(c) A petition that seeks a writ of review, a writ of mandate, or a writ of prohibition relating to a postjudgment enforcement order of the small claims division may be heard by the appellate division of the superior court, by the court of appeal, or by the Supreme Court. *(Added by Stats.2012, c. 470 (A.B.1529), § 3.)*

Law Revision Commission Comments

Section 116.798 is added solely to clarify which tribunal has jurisdiction of a writ petition relating to a small claims case after trial court unification. This provision neither expands nor contracts the circumstances under which a small claims litigant may seek an extraordinary writ. The proper tribunal for seeking such a writ depends on the stage of the case at the time of the act that is challenged in the writ petition.

Subdivision (a) makes clear that a writ petition relating to the initial hearing in the small claims division of the superior court may be heard by a member of the court's appellate division. See Cal. Const. art. VI, § 10 ("The ... superior courts, and their judges have original jurisdiction ... in proceedings for extraordinary relief in the nature of mandamus, certiorari, and prohibition."); see also People v. Konow, 32 Cal. 4th 995, 1019–21, 88 P.3d 36, 12 Cal. Rptr. 3d 301 (2004) (superior court judge who considers order entered by another superior court judge does not unconstitutionally enjoin, restrain, or otherwise interfere with judicial act of another superior court judge if later judge acts under statutory authority). A ruling on such a writ petition is not appealable. For a similar restriction, see Section 904.3.

Under subdivision (a), the court of appeal and the Supreme Court also have jurisdiction to consider a writ petition relating to the initial hearing in the small claims division. See Cal. Const. art. VI, § 10 ("The Supreme Court, courts of appeal, ... and their judges have original jurisdiction ... in proceedings for extraordinary relief in the nature of mandamus certiorari, and prohibition."). In addition to other grounds for denying the writ, however, those courts may deny the writ on the ground that it was not first presented to a lower tribunal pursuant to subdivision (a). See generally In re Ramirez, 89 Cal. App. 4th 1312, 1316, 1320, 108 Cal. Rptr. 229 (2001); In re Hillery, 202 Cal. App. 2d 293, 294, 20 Cal. Rptr. 759 (1962); Cal. R. Ct. 8.486; 2 B. Witkin, California Procedure *Jurisdiction* § 397, p. 1041 (5th ed. 2008).

Subdivision (b) makes clear that a writ petition relating to a small claims appeal may only be heard by the court of appeal or by the Supreme Court. This rule is consistent with historical practice. See, e.g., Crouchman v. Superior Court, 45 Cal. 3d 1167, 755 P.2d 1075, 248 Cal. Rptr. 626 (1988); Universal City Nissan, Inc. v. Superior Court, 65 Cal. App. 4th 203, 75 Cal. Rptr. 2d 910 (1998); Houghtaling v. Superior Court, 17 Cal. App. 4th 1128, 21 Cal. Rptr. 2d 855 (1993); see generally Cal. Const. art. VI, § 11 (Except for death penalty cases, "courts of appeal have appellate jurisdiction when superior courts have original jurisdiction in causes of a type within the appellate jurisdiction of the courts of appeal on June 30, 1995 ...."). For the filing fee for such a writ petition, see Gov't Code §§ 68926, 68926.1. For guidance on the applicable procedures, see Cal. R. Ct. 8.485–8.493.

Subdivision (c) makes clear that a writ petition relating to a postjudgment enforcement order of the small claims division may be heard by the appellate division of the superior court. This codifies *General Electric Capital Auto Financial Services, Inc. v. Appellate Division of the Superior Court*, 88 Cal. App. 4th 136, 105 Cal. Rptr. 2d 552 (2001). For the filing fee for such a writ petition, see Gov't Code § 70621. For guidance on the applicable procedures, see Cal. R. Ct. 8.930–8.936.

Subdivision (c) further makes clear that the court of appeal and the Supreme Court also have jurisdiction to consider a writ petition relating to a postjudgment enforcement order of the small claims division. See Cal. Const. art. VI, § 10. In addition to other grounds for denying the writ, however, those courts may deny the writ on the ground that it was not first presented to the appellate division of the superior court. See sources cited *supra.* [41 Cal.L.Rev.Comm. Reports 313 (2011)]..

ARTICLE 8. SATISFACTION AND ENFORCEMENT OF JUDGMENT

§ 116.810. Suspension of judgment during time for appeal

(a) Enforcement of the judgment of a small claims court, including the issuance or recording of any abstract of the judgment, is automatically suspended, without the filing of a bond by the defendant, until the expiration of the time for appeal.

(b) If an appeal is filed as provided in Article 7 (commencing with Section 116.710), enforcement of the judgment of the small claims court is suspended unless (1) the appeal is dismissed by the superior court pursuant to Section 116.795, or (2) the superior court determines that the small claims court properly denied the defendant's motion to vacate filed under Section 116.730 or 116.740. In either of those events, the judgment of the small claims court may be enforced.

(c) The scope of the suspension of enforcement under this section and, unless otherwise ordered, of any suspension of enforcement ordered by the court, shall include any enforcement procedure described in Title 9 (commencing with Section 680.010) of Part 2 and in Sections 674 and 1174. *(Added by*

Stats.1990, c. 1305 (S.B.2627), § 3. Amended by Stats.1991, c. 915 (S.B.771), § 28.)

Research References

Rutter, Cal. Practice Guide: Civil Appeals & Writs Ch. 7-B, B. Automatic Stay.

Rutter, Cal. Practice Guide: Enforcing Judgments/Debts Ch. 3-C, C. Prelawsuit Considerations.

Rutter, Cal. Practice Guide: Enforcing Judgments/Debts Ch. 6A-7, Period During Which Judgment Enforceable; Renewal Procedures.

Rutter, Cal. Practice Guide: Enforcing Judgments/Debts Ch. 6D-6, Debtor's Recourse Against Execution Levy.

9 Witkin Cal. Proc. 5th Appeal § 269, Theory.

2 Witkin Cal. Proc. 5th Courts § 268, (S 268) Statutory Framework.

2 Witkin Cal. Proc. 5th Courts § 303, (S 303) Enforcement and Stay.

2 Witkin Cal. Proc. 5th Courts § 319, No Power to Consolidate or Dismiss Action.

8 Witkin Cal. Proc. 5th Enforcement of Judgment § 23, Enforcement of Particular Judgments.

12 Witkin, California Summary 10th Real Property § 112A, (New)-Lower Value and Shorter Delinquency.

§ 116.820. Enforcement of judgments; fees; costs and interest to prevailing party

(a) The judgment of a small claims court, or the judgment of the superior court after a hearing on appeal, may be enforced by the small claims court as provided in Title 9 (commencing with Section 680.010) of Part 2 and in Sections 674 and 1174 on the enforcement of judgments of other courts.

(b) The clerk of the court shall charge and collect all fees associated with the enforcement of judgments under Title 9 (commencing with Section 680.010) of Part 2. The clerk shall immediately deposit all the fees collected under this section into a bank account established for this purpose by the Administrative Office of the Courts. The money shall be remitted to the State Treasury under rules adopted by, or trial court financial policies and procedures authorized by, the Judicial Council under subdivision (a) of Section 77206 of the Government Code. The Controller shall distribute the fees to the Trial Court Trust Fund as provided in Section 68085.1 of the Government Code.

(c) The prevailing party in any action subject to this chapter is entitled to the costs of enforcing the judgment and accrued interest. *(Added by Stats.1990, c. 1305 (S.B.2627), § 3. Amended by Stats.1991, c. 915 (S.B.771), § 29; Stats.1993, c. 158 (A.B.392), § 3, eff. July 21, 1993; Stats.1994, c. 926 (A.B.2533), § 2; Stats.1995, c. 576 (A.B.1225), § 2; Stats.1996, c. 1159 (A.B.3471), § 7; Stats.2003, c. 159 (A.B.1759), § 3, eff. Aug. 2, 2003; Stats.2005, c. 75 (A.B.145), § 24, eff. July 19, 2005, operative Jan. 1, 2006; Stats.2009, c. 596 (S.B.556), § 1; Stats. 2011, c. 308 (S.B.647), § 2.)*

Law Revision Commission Comments

Section 116.820 is amended to delete obsolete language referring to a transfer "under subdivision (d) of Section 116.780."

In the past, subdivision (d) of Section 116.780 required a superior court to transfer a small claims appeal to the small claims court for enforcement after the superior court resolved the appeal. See 1994 Cal. Stat. ch. 587, § 3; 1991 Cal. Stat. ch. 915, § 26. Such a transfer was necessary before the municipal and superior courts unified, because the small claims court was a division of the municipal court, not the superior court.

Now that the trial courts have unified, the small claims court is a division of the superior court. See Code Civ. Proc. § 116.210. Upon resolving a small claims appeal, it is no longer necessary to effect a transfer to the municipal court system. Accordingly, Section 116.780 was amended to delete subdivision (d). See 2005 Cal. Stat. ch. 706, § 8. Section 116.820 is now amended to reflect that development. [39 Cal.L.Rev.Comm. Reports 223 (2009)].

Research References

Rutter, Cal. Practice Guide: Enforcing Judgments/Debts Ch. 3-C, C. Prelawsuit Considerations.

Rutter, Cal. Practice Guide: Enforcing Judgments/Debts Ch. 6A-7, Period During Which Judgment Enforceable; Renewal Procedures.

2 Witkin Cal. Proc. 5th Courts § 290, (S 290) Uniform Fees.

2 Witkin Cal. Proc. 5th Courts § 302, (S 302) in General.

2 Witkin Cal. Proc. 5th Courts § 303, (S 303) Enforcement and Stay.

2 Witkin Cal. Proc. 5th Courts § 341, (S 341) Jurisdiction.

§ 116.830. Assets of judgment debtor; information form to be supplied to judgment creditor; punishment for failure to comply

(a) At the time judgment is rendered, or notice of entry of the judgment is mailed to the parties, the clerk shall deliver or mail to the judgment debtor a form containing questions regarding the nature and location of any assets of the judgment debtor.

(b) Within 30 days after the clerk has mailed notice of entry of the judgment, unless the judgment has been satisfied, the judgment debtor shall complete the form and cause it to be delivered to the judgment creditor.

(c) In the event a motion is made to vacate the judgment or a notice of appeal is filed, a judgment debtor shall complete and deliver the form within 30 days after the clerk has delivered or mailed notice of denial of the motion to vacate, or notice of dismissal of or entry of judgment on the appeal, whichever is applicable.

(d) In case of the judgment debtor's willful failure to comply with subdivision (b) or (c), the judgment creditor may request the court to apply the sanctions, including arrest and attorney's fees, as provided in Section 708.170, on contempt of court.

(e) The Judicial Council shall approve or adopt the form to be used for the purpose of this section. *(Added by Stats.1990, c. 1305 (S.B.2627), § 3. Amended by Stats.1991, c. 915 (S.B.771), § 30.)*

Research References

2 Witkin Cal. Proc. 5th Courts § 302, (S 302) in General.

§ 116.840. Payment to judgment creditor or court

(a) At the option of the judgment debtor, payment of the judgment may be made either (1) to the judgment creditor in accordance with Section 116.850, or (2) to the court in which the judgment was entered in accordance with Section 116.860.

(b) The small claims court may order entry of satisfaction of judgment in accordance with subdivisions (c) and (d) of Section 116.850, or subdivision (b) of Section 116.860. *(Added by Stats.1990, c. 1305 (S.B.2627), § 3.)*

Research References

Rutter, Cal. Practice Guide: Enforcing Judgments/Debts Ch. 6K-4, Acknowledgment of Satisfaction of Small Claims Court Judgment.

2 Witkin Cal. Proc. 5th Courts § 304, Terms and Conditions.

2 Witkin Cal. Proc. 5th Courts § 305, Payment to Creditor and Acknowledgement.

2 Witkin Cal. Proc. 5th Courts § 306, Payment to Court.

8 Witkin Cal. Proc. 5th Enforcement of Judgment § 387, (S 387) in General.

§ 116.850. Acknowledgment of satisfaction of judgment; penalty for failure to comply; presumption of payment

(a) If full payment of the judgment is made to the judgment creditor or to the judgment creditor's assignee of record, then immediately upon receipt of payment, the judgment creditor or assignee shall file with the clerk of the court an acknowledgment of satisfaction of the judgment.

(b) Any judgment creditor or assignee of record who, after receiving full payment of the judgment and written demand by the judgment debtor, fails without good cause to execute and file an acknowledgment of satisfaction of the judgment with the clerk of the court in which the judgment is entered within 14 days after receiving the request, is liable to the judgment debtor or the judgment debtor's grantees or heirs for all damages sustained by reason of the failure and, in addition, the sum of fifty dollars ($50).

(c) The clerk of the court shall enter a satisfaction of judgment at the request of the judgment debtor if the judgment debtor either (1) establishes a rebuttable presumption of full payment under subdivision (d), or (2) establishes a rebuttable presumption of partial payment under subdivision (d) and complies with subdivision (c) of Section 116.860.

(d) A rebuttable presumption of full or partial payment of the judgment, whichever is applicable, is created if the judgment debtor files both of the following with the clerk of the court in which the judgment was entered:

(1) Either a canceled check or money order for the full or partial amount of the judgment written by the judgment debtor after judgment and made payable to and endorsed by the judgment creditor, or a cash receipt for the full or partial amount of the judgment written by the judgment debtor after judgment and signed by the judgment creditor.

(2) A declaration stating that (A) the judgment debtor has made full or partial payment of the judgment including accrued interest and costs; (B) the judgment creditor has been requested to file an acknowledgment of satisfaction of the judgment and refuses to do so, or refuses to accept subsequent payments, or the present address of the judgment creditor is unknown; and (C) the documents identified in and accompanying the declaration constitute evidence of the judgment creditor's receipt of full or partial payment. *(Added by Stats.1990, c. 1305 (S.B.2627), § 3. Amended by Stats.1991, c. 915 (S.B.771), § 31.)*

Research References

Rutter, Cal. Practice Guide: Enforcing Judgments/Debts Ch. 6K-1, Acknowledgment of Full Satisfaction of Judgment.
Rutter, Cal. Practice Guide: Enforcing Judgments/Debts Ch. 6K-4, Acknowledgment of Satisfaction of Small Claims Court Judgment.
2 Witkin Cal. Proc. 5th Courts § 304, Terms and Conditions.
2 Witkin Cal. Proc. 5th Courts § 305, Payment to Creditor and Acknowledgement.

§ 116.860.   Payment to court; entry of satisfaction of judgment

(a) A judgment debtor who desires to make payment to the court in which the judgment was entered may file a request to make payment, which shall be made on a form approved or adopted by the Judicial Council.

(b) Upon the filing of the request to make payment and the payment to the clerk of the amount of the judgment and any accrued interest and costs after judgment, plus any required fee authorized by this section, the clerk shall enter satisfaction of the judgment and shall remit payment to the judgment creditor as provided in this section.

(c) If partial payment of the judgment has been made to the judgment creditor, and the judgment debtor files the declaration and evidence of partial payment described in subdivision (d) of Section 116.850, the clerk shall enter satisfaction of the judgment upon receipt by the clerk of the balance owing on the judgment, including any accrued interest and costs after judgment, and the fee required by this section.

(d) If payment is made by means other than money order, certified or cashier's check, or cash, entry of satisfaction of the judgment shall be delayed for 30 days.

(e) The clerk shall notify the judgment creditor, at his or her last known address, that the judgment debtor has satisfied the judgment by making payment to the court. The notification shall explain the procedures which the judgment creditor has to follow to receive payment.

(f) For purposes of this section, "costs after judgment" consist of only those costs itemized in a memorandum of costs filed by the judgment creditor or otherwise authorized by the court.

(g) Payments that remain unclaimed for three years shall go to the superior court pursuant to Section 68084.1 of the Government Code.

(h) A fee of twenty dollars ($20) shall be paid by the judgment debtor for the costs of administering this section. *(Added by Stats.1990, c. 1305 (S.B.2627), § 3. Amended by Stats.1991, c. 915 (S.B.771), § 32; Stats.2005, c. 75 (A.B.145), § 25, eff. July 19, 2005, operative Jan. 1, 2006.)*

Research References

Rutter, Cal. Practice Guide: Enforcing Judgments/Debts Ch. 6K-4, Acknowledgment of Satisfaction of Small Claims Court Judgment.
2 Witkin Cal. Proc. 5th Courts § 290, (S 290) Uniform Fees.
2 Witkin Cal. Proc. 5th Courts § 304, Terms and Conditions.
2 Witkin Cal. Proc. 5th Courts § 305, Payment to Creditor and Acknowledgement.
2 Witkin Cal. Proc. 5th Courts § 306, Payment to Court.

§ 116.870.   Claims for damages resulting from a traffic accident; suspension of privilege to operate motor vehicle upon failure to satisfy judgment

Sections 16250 to 16381, inclusive, of the Vehicle Code, regarding the suspension of the judgment debtor's privilege to operate a motor vehicle for failing to satisfy a judgment, apply if the judgment (1) was for damage to property in excess of seven hundred fifty dollars ($750) or for bodily injury to, or death of, a person in any amount, and (2) resulted from the operation of a motor vehicle upon a California highway by the defendant, or by any other person for whose conduct the defendant was liable, unless the liability resulted from the defendant's signing the application of a minor for a driver's license. *(Added by Stats.1990, c. 1305 (S.B.2627), § 3. Amended by Stats.2003, c. 451 (A.B.1718), § 1.)*

Research References

Rutter, Cal. Practice Guide: Enforcing Judgments/Debts Ch. 6A-13, Creating an Enforcement of Judgment Plan.
2 Witkin Cal. Proc. 5th Courts § 307, (S 307) Motor Vehicle License Suspension.

§ 116.880.   Motor vehicle accident claims; unsatisfied judgments; notice requesting suspension of judgment debtor's driving privilege; liability of public agencies

(a) If the judgment (1) was for seven hundred fifty dollars ($750) or less, (2) resulted from a motor vehicle accident occurring on a California highway caused by the defendant's operation of a motor vehicle, and (3) has remained unsatisfied for more than 90 days after the judgment became final, the judgment creditor may file with the Department of Motor Vehicles a notice requesting a suspension of the judgment debtor's privilege to operate a motor vehicle.

(b) The notice shall state that the judgment has not been satisfied, and shall be accompanied by (1) a fee set by the department, (2) the judgment of the court determining that the judgment resulted from a motor vehicle accident occurring on a California highway caused by the judgment debtor's operation of a motor vehicle, and (3) a declaration that the judgment has not been satisfied. The fee shall be used by the department to finance the costs of administering this section and may not exceed the department's actual costs.

(c) Upon receipt of a notice, the department shall attempt to notify the judgment debtor by telephone, if possible, otherwise by certified mail, that the judgment debtor's privilege to operate a motor vehicle will be suspended for a period of 90 days, beginning 20 days after receipt of notice by the department from the judgment creditor, unless satisfactory proof, as provided in subdivision (e), is provided to the department before that date.

(d) At the time the notice is filed, the department shall give the judgment creditor a copy of the notice that shall indicate the filing fee paid by the judgment creditor, and shall include a space to be signed by the judgment creditor acknowledging payment of the judgment by the judgment debtor. The judgment creditor shall mail or deliver a signed copy of the acknowledgment to the judgment debtor once the judgment is satisfied.

(e) The department shall terminate the suspension, or the suspension proceedings, upon the occurrence of one or more of the following:

(1) Receipt of proof that the judgment has been satisfied, either (A) by a copy of the notice required by this section signed by the judgment creditor acknowledging satisfaction of the judgment, or (B) by a declaration of the judgment debtor stating that the judgment has been satisfied.

(2) Receipt of proof that the judgment debtor is complying with a court-ordered payment schedule.

(3) Proof that the judgment debtor had insurance covering the accident sufficient to satisfy the judgment.

(4) A deposit with the department of the amount of the unsatisfied judgment, if the judgment debtor presents proof, satisfactory to the department, of inability to locate the judgment creditor.

(5) At the end of 90 days.

(f) When the suspension has been terminated under subdivision (e), the action is final and may not be reinstituted. Whenever the suspension is terminated, Section 14904 of the Vehicle Code shall apply. Money deposited with the department under this section shall be handled in the same manner as money deposited under subdivision (d) of Section 16377 of the Vehicle Code.

(g) A public agency is not liable for an injury caused by the suspension, termination of suspension, or the failure to suspend a person's privilege to operate a motor vehicle as authorized by this section. *(Added by Stats.1990, c. 1305 (S.B.2627), § 3. Amended by Stats.1991, c. 915 (S.B.771), § 33; Stats.2003, c. 451 (A.B.1718), § 2.)*

Research References

Rutter, Cal. Practice Guide: Enforcing Judgments/Debts Ch. 6A-13, Creating an Enforcement of Judgment Plan.
2 Witkin Cal. Proc. 5th Courts § 307, (S 307) Motor Vehicle License Suspension.

ARTICLE 9. ADMINISTRATION

§ 116.920. Rules for practice and procedure; forms; information services

(a) The Judicial Council shall provide by rule for the practice and procedure and for the forms and their use in small claims actions. The rules and forms so adopted shall be consistent with this chapter.

(b) The Judicial Council, in consultation with the Department of Consumer Affairs, shall adopt rules to ensure that litigants receive adequate notice of the availability of assistance from small claims advisors, to prescribe other qualifications and the conduct of advisors, to prescribe training standards for advisors and for temporary judges hearing small claims matters, to prescribe, where appropriate, uniform rules and procedures regarding small claims actions and judgments, and to address other matters that are deemed necessary and appropriate. *(Added by Stats.1990, c. 1305 (S.B.2627), § 3. Amended by Stats.1991, c. 915 (S.B.771), § 35.)*

Research References

2 Witkin Cal. Proc. 5th Courts § 269, (S 269) Judicial Council Rules and Forms.
2 Witkin Cal. Proc. 5th Courts § 271, (S 271) Small Claims Legal Advisers.
4 Witkin Cal. Proc. 5th Pleading § 5, (S 5) Small Claims Courts and Limited Civil Cases.

§ 116.930. Informational publications to be available in courtrooms; manuals for litigants, judges and general public

(a) Each small claims division shall provide in each courtroom in which small claims actions are heard a current copy of a publication describing small claims court law and the procedures that are applicable in the small claims courts, including the law and procedures that apply to the enforcement of judgments. The Small Claims Court and Consumer Law California Judge's Bench Book developed by the California Center for Judicial Education and Research is illustrative of a publication that satisfies the requirement of this subdivision.

(b) Each small claims division may formulate and distribute to litigants and the public a manual on small claims court rules and procedures. The manual shall explain how to complete the necessary forms, how to determine the proper court in which small claims actions may be filed, how to present and defend against claims, how to appeal, how to enforce a judgment, how to protect property that is exempt from execution, and such other matters that the court deems necessary or desirable.

(c) If the Department of Consumer Affairs determines there are sufficient private or public funds available in addition to the funds available within the department's current budget, the department, in cooperation with the Judicial Council, shall prepare a manual or information booklet on small claims court rules and procedures. The department shall distribute copies to the general public and to each small claims division.

(d) If funding is available, the Judicial Council, in cooperation with the Department of Consumer Affairs, shall prepare and distribute to each judge who sits in a small claims court a bench book describing all state and federal consumer protection laws reasonably likely to apply in small claims actions. *(Added by Stats.1990, c. 1305 (S.B.2627), § 3.)*

Research References

2 Witkin Cal. Proc. 5th Courts § 270, (S 270) Manuals and Benchbooks.
2 Witkin Cal. Proc. 5th Courts § 396, (S 396) Specialized Programs.

§ 116.940. Advisory services; immunities

(a) Except as otherwise provided in this section or in rules adopted by the Judicial Council, which are consistent with the requirements of this section, the characteristics of the small claims advisory service required by Section 116.260 shall be determined by each county, or by the superior court in a county where the small claims advisory service is administered by the court, in accordance with local needs and conditions.

(b) Each advisory service shall provide the following services:

(1) Individual personal advisory services, in person or by telephone, and by any other means reasonably calculated to provide timely and appropriate assistance. The topics covered

by individual personal advisory services shall include, but not be limited to, preparation of small claims court filings, procedures, including procedures related to the conduct of the hearing, and information on the collection of small claims court judgments.

(2) Recorded telephone messages may be used to supplement the individual personal advisory services, but shall not be the sole means of providing advice available in the county.

(3) Adjacent counties, superior courts in adjacent counties, or any combination thereof, may provide advisory services jointly.

(c) In a county in which the number of small claims actions filed annually is 1,000 or less as averaged over the immediately preceding two fiscal years, the county or the superior court may elect to exempt itself from the requirements set forth in subdivision (b). If the small claims advisory service is administered by the county, this exemption shall be formally noticed through the adoption of a resolution by the board of supervisors. If the small claims advisory service is administered by the superior court, this exemption shall be formally noticed through adoption of a local rule. If a county or court so exempts itself, the county or court shall nevertheless provide the following minimum advisory services in accordance with rules adopted by the Judicial Council:

(1) Recorded telephone messages providing general information relating to small claims actions filed in the county shall be provided during regular business hours.

(2) Small claims information booklets shall be provided in the court clerk's office of each superior court, appropriate county offices, and in any other location that is convenient to prospective small claims litigants in the county.

(d) The advisory service shall operate in conjunction and cooperation with the small claims division, and shall be administered so as to avoid the existence or appearance of a conflict of interest between the individuals providing the advisory services and any party to a particular small claims action or any judicial officer deciding small claims actions.

(e) Advisers may be volunteers, and shall be members of the State Bar, law students, paralegals, or persons experienced in resolving minor disputes, and shall be familiar with small claims court rules and procedures. Advisers may not appear in court as an advocate for any party.

(f) Advisers, including independent contractors, other employees, and volunteers, have the immunity conferred by Section 818.9 of the Government Code with respect to advice provided as a public service on behalf of a court or county to small claims litigants and potential litigants under this chapter.

(g) * * * This section does not preclude a court or county from contracting with a third party to provide small claims advisory services as described in this section. (Added by Stats.1990, c. 1305 (S.B.2627), § 3. Amended by Stats.1998, c. 931 (S.B.2139), § 43, eff. Sept. 28, 1998; Stats.2002, c. 806 (A.B.3027), § 6; Stats.2005, c. 600 (S.B.422), § 6; Stats.2005, c. 618 (A.B.1459), § 6; Stats.2012, c. 470 (A.B.1529), § 4; Stats. 2013, c. 76 (A.B.383), § 21.)

Law Revision Commission Comments

Section 116.940 is amended to accommodate unification of the municipal and superior courts in a county. Cal. Const. art. VI, § 5(e). It is also amended to reflect elimination of the justice court, Cal. Const. art. VI, §§ 1, 5(b). [28 Cal.L.Rev.Comm. Reports 51 (1998)].

Section 116.940 is amended to reflect enactment of the Lockyer–Isenberg Trial Court Funding Act, 1997 Cal. Stat. ch. 850 (see generally Gov't Code §§ 77000–77655). See Gov't Code §§ 77003 ("court operations" defined), 77200 (state funding of "court operations"); see also Cal. R. Ct. 10.810(d), Function 10 ("small claims advisor program costs").

As amended, Section 116.940 makes explicit that a small claims advisory service can be run by the county, by the court, or by a third party who has

contracted with the county or the court to provide small claims advisory services. For a similar provision, see Section 116.230 (filing fees for small claims cases). [39 Cal.L.Rev.Comm. Reports 157 (2009)].

Research References

2 Witkin Cal. Proc. 5th Courts § 271, (S 271) Small Claims Legal Advisers.

5 Witkin, California Summary 10th Torts § 494, (S 494) Small Claims Proceeding.

§ 116.950. Advisory committee; operation of section

(a) This section shall become operative only if the Department of Consumer Affairs determines that sufficient private or public funds are available in addition to the funds available in the department's current budget to cover the costs of implementing this section.

(b) There shall be established an advisory committee, constituted as set forth in this section, to study small claims practice and procedure, with particular attention given to the improvement of procedures for the enforcement of judgments.

(c) The members of the advisory committee shall serve without compensation, but shall be reimbursed for expenses actually and necessarily incurred by them in the performance of their duties.

(d) The advisory committee shall be composed as follows:

(1) The Attorney General or a representative.

(2) Two consumer representatives from consumer groups or agencies, appointed by the Secretary of the State and Consumer Services Agency.

(3) One representative appointed by the Speaker of the Assembly and one representative appointed by the President pro Tempore of the Senate.

(4) Two representatives appointed by the Board of Governors of the State Bar.

(5) Two representatives of the business community, appointed by the Secretary of Technology, Trade, and Commerce.

(6) Six judicial officers who have extensive experience presiding in small claims court, appointed by the Judicial Council. Judicial officers appointed under this subdivision may include judicial officers of the superior court, judges of the appellate courts, retired judicial officers, and temporary judges.

(7) One representative appointed by the Governor.

(8) Two clerks of the court appointed by the Judicial Council.

(e) Staff assistance to the advisory committee shall be provided by the Department of Consumer Affairs, with the assistance of the Judicial Council, as needed. (Added by Stats.1990, c. 1305 (S.B.2627), § 3. Amended by Stats.1993, c. 1153 (A.B.1732), § 1, eff. Oct. 11, 1993; Stats.1998, c. 931 (S.B.2139), § 44, eff. Sept. 28, 1998; Stats.1999, c. 344 (S.B.210), § 5, eff. Sept. 7, 1999; Stats.2001, c. 745 (S.B.1191), § 8, eff. Oct. 12, 2001; Stats.2002, c. 664 (A.B.3034), § 46; Stats.2002, c. 784 (S.B.1316), § 32.)

Contingent Operation

By its own terms, operation of this section is contingent upon availability of funding.

Law Revision Commission Comments

Section 116.950 is amended to accommodate unification of the municipal and superior courts in a county. Cal. Const. art. VI, § 5(e). It is also amended to reflect elimination of the justice court, Cal. Const. art. VI, §§ 1, 5(b). [28 Cal.L.Rev.Comm. Reports 51 (1998)].

Subdivision (d) of Section 116.950 is amended to broaden the range of judicial officers eligible to serve on the Small Claims Advisory Committee. [29 Cal.L.Rev.Comm. Reports App. 5 (1999)].

Civ. Pro.

Subdivision (d)(6) of Section 116.950 is amended to reflect unification of the municipal and superior courts pursuant to Article VI, Section 5(e), of the California Constitution.

CHAPTER 6. GENERAL PROVISIONS RESPECTING COURTS OF JUSTICE

ARTICLE 1. PUBLICITY OF PROCEEDINGS

Section
124. Public sittings; exceptions.

§ 124. Public sittings; exceptions

Except as provided in Section 214 of the Family Code or any other provision of law, the sittings of every court shall be public. *(Enacted in 1872.   Amended by Code Am.1880, c. 35, p. 36, § 1; Stats.1971, c. 762, p. 1510, § 2; Stats.1990, c. 1363 (A.B.3532), § 10, operative July 1, 1991; Stats.1992, c. 163 (A.B.2641), § 12, operative Jan. 1, 1994.)*

Law Revision Commission Comments

Section 124 is amended to substitute a reference to Family Code Section 214 for the former Civil Code references. Family Code Section 214 gives the court general authority to direct that the trial of any issue of fact joined in a proceeding under the Family Code be private and to exclude all persons except the officers of the court, the parties, their witnesses, and counsel. Section 124 also recognizes that other provisions of law may qualify the rule stated in Section 124 or provide a contrary rule.

Other provisions of the Family Code may provide more restrictive rules that prevail over the rule stated in Family Code Section 214 or may provide special rules concerning exclusion of the public from hearings under the Family Code that prevail over the general rule stated in Section 214. See Fam. Code § 214 Comment. [22 Cal.L.Rev.Comm.Reports 1 (1992)].

Research References

Rutter, Cal. Practice Guide: Civ. Pro. Before Trial Ch. 9(I)-D, D. Hearing.
Rutter, Cal. Practice Guide: Civil Trials & Evidence Ch. 4-I, I. Other Motions at Final Status Conference.
2 Witkin Cal. Proc. 5th Courts § 33, General Requirement.
7 Witkin, California Summary 10th Constitutional Law § 423, (S 423) Civil Trial.

ARTICLE 2. INCIDENTAL POWERS AND DUTIES OF COURTS

Section
128.   Powers of courts; contempt orders; execution of sentence; stay pending appeal; orders affecting county government.
128.5. Frivolous actions or delaying tactics; order for payment of expenses; punitive damages.
128.7. Signature requirement for court papers; certification that specified conditions met; violations; sanctions; punitive damages.
129.   Photographs, etc., taken in course of post mortem examination or autopsy; prohibition against reproduction or dissemination; exceptions; personal liability of coroner.

Section
130.   Deceased minor victims of criminal acts; sealing of autopsy report and associated evidence.

§ 128. Powers of courts; contempt orders; execution of sentence; stay pending appeal; orders affecting county government

(a) Every court shall have the power to do all of the following:

(1) To preserve and enforce order in its immediate presence.

(2) To enforce order in the proceedings before it, or before a person or persons empowered to conduct a judicial investigation under its authority.

(3) To provide for the orderly conduct of proceedings before it, or its officers.

(4) To compel obedience to its judgments, orders, and process, and to the orders of a judge out of court, in an action or proceeding pending therein.

(5) To control in furtherance of justice, the conduct of its ministerial officers, and of all other persons in any manner connected with a judicial proceeding before it, in every matter pertaining thereto.

(6) To compel the attendance of persons to testify in an action or proceeding pending therein, in the cases and manner provided in this code.

(7) To administer oaths in an action or proceeding pending therein, and in all other cases where it may be necessary in the exercise of its powers and duties.

(8) To amend and control its process and orders so as to make them conform to law and justice. An appellate court shall not reverse or vacate a duly entered judgment upon an agreement or stipulation of the parties unless the court finds both of the following:

(A) There is no reasonable possibility that the interests of nonparties or the public will be adversely affected by the reversal.

(B) The reasons of the parties for requesting reversal outweigh the erosion of public trust that may result from the nullification of a judgment and the risk that the availability of stipulated reversal will reduce the incentive for pretrial settlement.

(b) Notwithstanding Section 1211 or any other law, if an order of contempt is made affecting an attorney, his or her agent, investigator, or any person acting under the attorney's direction, in the preparation and conduct of any action or proceeding, the execution of any sentence shall be stayed pending the filing within three judicial days of a petition for extraordinary relief testing the lawfulness of the court's order, the violation of which is the basis of the contempt except for the conduct as may be proscribed by subdivision (b) of Section 6068 of the Business and Professions Code, relating to an attorney's duty to maintain respect due to the courts and judicial officers.

(c) Notwithstanding Section 1211 or any other law, if an order of contempt is made affecting a public safety employee acting within the scope of employment for reason of the employee's failure to comply with a duly issued subpoena or subpoena duces tecum, the execution of any sentence shall be stayed pending the filing within three judicial days of a petition for extraordinary relief testing the lawfulness of the court's order, a violation of which is the basis for the contempt.

As used in this subdivision, "public safety employee" includes any peace officer, firefighter, paramedic, or any other employee of a public law enforcement agency whose duty is either to maintain official records or to analyze or present evidence for investigative or prosecutorial purposes.

(d) Notwithstanding Section 1211 or any other law, if an order of contempt is made affecting the victim of a sexual assault, where the contempt consists of refusing to testify concerning that sexual assault, the execution of any sentence shall be stayed pending the filing within three judicial days of a petition for extraordinary relief testing the lawfulness of the court's order, a violation of which is the basis for the contempt.

As used in this subdivision, "sexual assault" means any act made punishable by Section 261, 262, 264.1, 285, 286, 288, 288a, or 289 of the Penal Code.

(e) Notwithstanding Section 1211 or any other law, if an order of contempt is made affecting the victim of domestic violence, where the contempt consists of refusing to testify concerning that domestic violence, the execution of any sentence shall be stayed pending the filing within three judicial days of a petition for extraordinary relief testing the lawfulness of the court's order, a violation of which is the basis for the contempt.

As used in this subdivision, the term "domestic violence" means "domestic violence" as defined in Section 6211 of the Family Code.

(f) Notwithstanding Section 1211 or any other provision of law, no order of contempt shall be made affecting a county government or any member of its governing body acting pursuant to its constitutional or statutory authority unless the court finds, based on a review of evidence presented at a hearing conducted for this purpose, that either of the following conditions exist:

(1) That the county has the resources necessary to comply with the order of the court.

(2) That the county has the authority, without recourse to voter approval or without incurring additional indebtedness, to generate the additional resources necessary to comply with the order of the court, that compliance with the order of the court will not expose the county, any member of its governing body, or any other county officer to liability for failure to perform other constitutional or statutory duties, and that compliance with the order of the court will not deprive the county of resources necessary for its reasonable support and maintenance. *(Added by Stats.1987, c. 3, § 2, eff. March 11, 1987, operative March 11, 1989. Amended by Stats.1991, c. 866 (A.B.363), § 1; Stats.1992, c. 163 (A.B.2641), § 13; Stats.1992, c. 697 (S.B.1559), § 2; Stats.1993, c. 219 (A.B.1500), § 63.3; Stats.1999, c. 508 (A.B. 1676), § 1.)*

Law Revision Commission Comments

Subdivision (e) of Section 128 is amended to substitute a reference to the Family Code provision defining "domestic violence." See Fam. Code § 6211 ("domestic violence" defined) & Comment. [23 Cal.L.Rev. Comm. Reports 1 (1993)].

Research References

Rutter, Cal. Practice Guide: Civil Appeals & Writs Ch. 6-C, C. Practical Considerations Re Settlement.

Rutter, Cal. Practice Guide: Civil Appeals & Writs Ch. 6-E, E. Disposition After Settlement.

Rutter, Cal. Practice Guide: Civil Appeals & Writs Ch. 15-D, D. Writ Review of Contempt Orders.

Rutter, Cal. Practice Guide: Civil Appeals & Writs Form 6:A, Stipulation for Reversal of Judgment.

Rutter, Cal. Practice Guide: Civil Appeals & Writs Ch. 6-C, Outline C.

Rutter, Cal. Practice Guide: Civil Appeals & Writs Gen. Matls., Highlights.

Rutter, Cal. Practice Guide: Civ. Pro. Before Trial Ch. 1-A, A. Accepting a New Case.

Rutter, Cal. Practice Guide: Civ. Pro. Before Trial Ch. 8K-5, Appointment of Referee in Aid of Discovery.

Rutter, Cal. Practice Guide: Civ. Pro. Before Trial Ch. 9(I)-G, G. Motions Regulating Counsel.

Rutter, Cal. Practice Guide: Civ. Pro. Before Trial Ch. 12(I)-B, B. Case Management ("Fast Track") System.

Rutter, Cal. Practice Guide: Civ. Pro. Before Trial Ch. 12(II)-F, F. Motion to Enforce Settlement (CCP §§ 664.6, 664.7).

Rutter, Cal. Practice Guide: Civ. Pro. Before Trial Ch. 9(III)-A, A. Sources of Sanctions Power.

Rutter, Cal. Practice Guide: Civil Trials & Evidence Ch. 4-F, F. Motions in Limine.

Rutter, Cal. Practice Guide: Civil Trials & Evidence Ch. 4-I, I. Other Motions at Final Status Conference.

Rutter, Cal. Practice Guide: Civil Trials & Evidence Ch. 6-A, A. General Considerations.

Rutter, Cal. Practice Guide: Civil Trials & Evidence Ch. 7-A, A. Court's Power to Control Juror Conduct.

Rutter, Cal. Practice Guide: Civil Trials & Evidence Ch. 12-A, A. Motion for Mistrial.

Rutter, Cal. Practice Guide: Civil Trials & Evidence Ch. 12-D, D. Other Motions During Trial.

Rutter, Cal. Practice Guide: Civil Trials & Evidence Ch. 12-E, E. Contempt Proceedings.

Rutter, Cal. Practice Guide: Civil Trials & Evidence Ch. 18-C, C. Other Post-Trial Motions.

California Practice Guide: Employment Litigation Ch. 18-A, A. Settlement Considerations.

Rutter, Cal. Practice Guide: Enforcing Judgments/Debts Ch. 6A-1, Jurisdiction to Enforce Judgments.

Rutter, Cal. Practice Guide: Enforcing Judgments/Debts Ch. 6A-13, Creating an Enforcement of Judgment Plan.

Rutter, Cal. Practice Guide: Family Law Gen. Matls., Highlights.

Rutter, Cal. Practice Guide: Personal Injury Ch. 3-A, A. Introduction.

Rutter, Cal. Practice Guide: Personal Injury Ch. 4-G, G. Concluding and Enforcing Settlement.

Rutter, Cal. Practice Guide: Personal Injury Ch. 8-B, B. After Trial Date Set (Three to Four Months Before Trial).

Rutter, Cal. Practice Guide: Personal Injury Ch. 9-B, B. In-Chambers Conference Before Commencement of Trial.

Rutter, Cal. Practice Guide: Prof. Responsibility Ch. 2-D, D. In-Person Solicitation for Profit.

Rutter, Cal. Practice Guide: Prof. Responsibility Ch. 4-C, C. Conflicts Between Present and Former Clients (Successive Representation).

Rutter, Cal. Practice Guide: Prof. Responsibility Ch. 4-G, G. Procedural Considerations for Disqualification Based on Conflict of Interest.

Rutter, Cal. Practice Guide: Prof. Responsibility Ch. 8-D, D. Restrictions on Speech and Behavior Outside Courtroom.

Rutter, Cal. Practice Guide: Prof. Responsibility Ch. 8-E, E. Consequences of Improper Advocacy.

Miller and Starr California Real Estate § 3:36, Tort Liability and Vicarious Liability; Generally.

Miller and Starr California Real Estate § 35:5, --Voluntary Participation and Self Determination in Mediations.

15 NO. 3 Miller & Starr, California Real Estate Newsalert 18, Subdivisions.

9 Witkin Cal. Proc. 5th Appeal § 738, (S 738) Notice of Settlement.

9 Witkin Cal. Proc. 5th Appeal § 893, (S 893) Presumption in Favor of Stipulation.

9 Witkin Cal. Proc. 5th Appeal § 896, (S 896) Abrogation of Presumption Favoring Stipulation.

9 Witkin Cal. Proc. 5th Appeal § 897, (S 897) Procedure.

9 Witkin Cal. Proc. 5th Appeal § 899, (S 899) Consent to Vacation of Judgment.

1 Witkin Cal. Proc. 5th Attorneys § 104, (S 104) Remedies and Sanctions.

2 Witkin Cal. Proc. 5th Courts § 174, (S 174) What Courts May Exercise Inherent Powers.

2 Witkin Cal. Proc. 5th Courts § 175, (S 175) Illustrations.

2 Witkin Cal. Proc. 5th Courts § 177, (S 177) Imposition of Money Sanctions.

2 Witkin Cal. Proc. 5th Courts § 201, (S 201) Local Policy.

8 Witkin Cal. Proc. 5th Enforcement of Judgment § 340, Nature and Scope of Power.

8 Witkin Cal. Proc. 5th Enforcement of Judgment § 356, (S 356) in General.

7 Witkin Cal. Proc. 5th Trial § 169, Any Judicial Tribunal.

7 Witkin Cal. Proc. 5th Trial § 171, (S 171) Statutory Framework.

7 Witkin Cal. Proc. 5th Trial § 172, (S 172) Legislative Regulation.

7 Witkin Cal. Proc. 5th Trial § 184, (S 184) Order Affecting County Government.

7 Witkin Cal. Proc. 5th Trial § 202, Victim of Sexual Assault.

7 Witkin Cal. Proc. 5th Trial § 203, Victim of Domestic Violence.

7 Witkin Cal. Proc. 5th Trial § 226, (S 226) in General.

11 Witkin, California Summary 10th Husband and Wife § 372, (S 372) Criminal Proceedings.

14 Witkin, California Summary 10th Wills and Probate § 348, (S 348) Current Law: General Jurisdiction.

14 Witkin, California Summary 10th Wills and Probate § 874, (S 874) Petition.

14 Witkin, California Summary 10th Wills and Probate § 898, (S 898) Petition.

§ 128.5. Frivolous actions or delaying tactics; order for payment of expenses; punitive damages

(a) Every trial court may order a party, the party's attorney, or both to pay any reasonable expenses, including attorney's fees, incurred by another party as a result of bad-faith actions or tactics that are frivolous or solely intended to cause unnecessary delay. This section also applies to judicial arbitration proceedings under Chapter 2.5 (commencing with Section 1141.10) of Title 3 of Part 3.

(b) For purposes of this section:

(1) "Actions or tactics" include, but are not limited to, the making or opposing of motions or the filing and service of a complaint or cross-complaint only if the actions or tactics arise from a complaint filed, or a proceeding initiated, on or before December 31, 1994. The mere filing of a complaint without service thereof on an opposing party does not constitute "actions or tactics" for purposes of this section.

(2) "Frivolous" means (A) totally and completely without merit or (B) for the sole purpose of harassing an opposing party.

(c) Expenses pursuant to this section shall not be imposed except on notice contained in a party's moving or responding papers; or the court's own motion, after notice and opportunity to be heard. An order imposing expenses shall be in writing and shall recite in detail the conduct or circumstances justifying the order.

(d) In addition to any award pursuant to this section for conduct described in subdivision (a), the court may assess punitive damages against the plaintiff upon a determination by the court that the plaintiff's action was an action maintained by a person convicted of a felony against the person's victim, or the victim's heirs, relatives, estate, or personal representative, for injuries arising from the acts for which the person was convicted of a felony, and that the plaintiff is guilty of fraud, oppression, or malice in maintaining the action.

(e) The liability imposed by this section is in addition to any other liability imposed by law for acts or omissions within the purview of this section. (Added by Stats.1981, c. 762, § 1. Amended by Stats.1984, c. 355, § 1; Stats.1985, c. 296, § 1; Stats.1990, c. 887 (S.B.2766), § 1; Stats.1994, c. 1062 (A.B.3594), § 1.)

Research References

Rutter, Cal. Practice Guide: A.D.R. Ch. 4-B, B. Judicial Arbitration.

Rutter, Cal. Practice Guide: Civil Appeals & Writs Ch. 2-A, A. Overview.

Rutter, Cal. Practice Guide: Civil Appeals & Writs Ch. 7-C, C. Stay by Posting Security (Bond or Undertaking).

Rutter, Cal. Practice Guide: Civil Appeals & Writs Ch. 11-E, E. Appellate Costs and Sanctions.

Rutter, Cal. Practice Guide: Civil Appeals & Writs Ch. 15-C, C. Statutory Writs.

Rutter, Cal. Practice Guide: Civil Appeals & Writs Ch. 15-D, D. Writ Review of Contempt Orders.

Rutter, Cal. Practice Guide: Civil Appeals & Writs Ch. 7 App., Appendix: Methods of Obtaining Stay for Particular Judgments and Orders.

Rutter, Cal. Practice Guide: Civ. Pro. Before Trial Ch. 1-B, B. Prelawsuit Investigations, Research and Analysis.

Rutter, Cal. Practice Guide: Civ. Pro. Before Trial Ch. 3-D, D. Venue.

Rutter, Cal. Practice Guide: Civ. Pro. Before Trial Ch. 11-A, A. Voluntary Dismissals.

Rutter, Cal. Practice Guide: Civ. Pro. Before Trial Ch. 13-E, E. the Arbitration Hearing.

Rutter, Cal. Practice Guide: Civ. Pro. Before Trial Ch. 8E-16, Sanctions Re Depositions.

Rutter, Cal. Practice Guide: Civ. Pro. Before Trial Ch. 7(II)-F, F. Procedure.

Rutter, Cal. Practice Guide: Civ. Pro. Before Trial Ch. 7(II)-G, G. "SLAPPback" Motions.

Rutter, Cal. Practice Guide: Civ. Pro. Before Trial Ch. 9(III)-A, A. Sources of Sanctions Power.

Rutter, Cal. Practice Guide: Civ. Pro. Before Trial Ch. 9(III)-B, B. Sanctions Under CCP § 128.5 (Pre-1995 and SLAPP Cases).

Rutter, Cal. Practice Guide: Civ. Pro. Before Trial Ch. 9(III)-C, C. Sanctions Under CCP § 128.7.

Rutter, Cal. Practice Guide: Civil Trials & Evidence Ch. 12-A, A. Motion for Mistrial.

Rutter, Cal. Practice Guide: Civil Trials & Evidence Ch. 17-E, E. Attorney Fees as Costs.

Rutter, Cal. Practice Guide: Civil Trials & Evidence Ch. 12-A, Outline a.

Rutter, Cal. Practice Guide: Insurance Litigation Ch. 7A-G, G. Intentional Acts Limitation.

Rutter, Cal. Practice Guide: Insurance Litigation Ch. 7A-G, Outline G.

Rutter, Cal. Practice Guide: Personal Injury Ch. 3-A, A. Introduction.

Rutter, Cal. Practice Guide: Personal Injury Ch. 6-B, B. Overview of Selected Discovery Procedures.

Rutter, Cal. Practice Guide: Prof. Responsibility Ch. 6-D, D. Professional Liability.

Miller and Starr California Real Estate § 32:40, Malicious Prosecution Compared.

Miller and Starr California Real Estate § 34:64, Recovery of Attorney's Fees; Basis for Recovery.

Miller and Starr California Real Estate § 34:66, Examples of Actions in Which Fees Can be Recovered.

Miller and Starr California Real Estate § 34:80, Recovery by Attorney for Self-Representation; House Counsel.

Miller and Starr California Real Estate § 35:74, Hearing Procedures; Control Over Conduct of the Hearing.

Miller and Starr California Real Estate § 11:154, Expungement of a Lis Pendens--Procedure and Grounds for Expungement.

18 NO. 1 Miller & Starr, California Real Estate Newsalert 15, Hazardous Substances.

3 Witkin Cal. Proc. 5th Actions § 394, Burden and Degree of Proof.

3 Witkin Cal. Proc. 5th Actions § 400, (S 400) Action to Set Aside Fraudulent Conveyance.

3 Witkin Cal. Proc. 5th Actions § 410, (S 410) Attorneys' Fees and Costs.

9 Witkin Cal. Proc. 5th Administrative Proceedings § 94, (S 94) Sanctions.

9 Witkin Cal. Proc. 5th Appeal § 182, When Order Affects Judgment or Relates to Enforcement.

9 Witkin Cal. Proc. 5th Appeal § 233, Attorneys' Fees Awarded as Sanction.

9 Witkin Cal. Proc. 5th Appeal § 1000, (S 1000) Sanction Denied.

8 Witkin Cal. Proc. 5th Attack Judgment Trial Court § 185, (S 185) Statement of Reasons.

1 Witkin Cal. Proc. 5th Attorneys § 539, Inadvertently Receiving Privileged Material.

2 Witkin Cal. Proc. 5th Courts § 155, (S 155) Illustrations: Conservatorship.

2 Witkin Cal. Proc. 5th Courts § 177, (S 177) Imposition of Money Sanctions.

8 Witkin Cal. Proc. 5th Enforcement of Judgment § 508, (S 508) Joint Obligor: Contribution.

7 Witkin Cal. Proc. 5th Judgment § 175, No Judicially Established Bilateral Fee-Shifting.

7 Witkin Cal. Proc. 5th Judgment § 217, Standard for Awarding Fees.

7 Witkin Cal. Proc. 5th Judgment § 222, (S 222) Actions in Bad Faith.

7 Witkin Cal. Proc. 5th Judgment § 259, (S 259) Nature and Scope of Statute.

7 Witkin Cal. Proc. 5th Judgment § 416, (S 416) Nature of First Proceeding.

2 Witkin Cal. Proc. 5th Jurisdiction § 343, (S 343) California Rule.

5 Witkin Cal. Proc. 5th Pleading § 1041, (S 1041) Right of Prevailing Plaintiff.

5 Witkin Cal. Proc. 5th Pleading § 1043, in General.

6 Witkin Cal. Proc. 5th Proceedings Without Trial § 7, General Requirement of Notice.

6 Witkin Cal. Proc. 5th Proceedings Without Trial § 55, (S 55) Statutory Authorization.

6 Witkin Cal. Proc. 5th Proceedings Without Trial § 563, Remedies.

6 Witkin Cal. Proc. 5th Proceedings Without Trial § 604, Sanctions for Failure to Participate.

7 Witkin Cal. Proc. 5th Trial § 59, (S 59) Judicial Council Rules.

7 Witkin Cal. Proc. 5th Trial § 64, (S 64) Right to Hearing.

7 Witkin Cal. Proc. 5th Trial § 188, (S 188) Limitations on Punishment.

7 Witkin Cal. Proc. 5th Trial § 226, (S 226) in General.

7 Witkin Cal. Proc. 5th Trial § 227, Scope and Definitions.

7 Witkin Cal. Proc. 5th Trial § 228, Who May Recover Sanctions.

7 Witkin Cal. Proc. 5th Trial § 229, Who May be Sanctioned.

7 Witkin Cal. Proc. 5th Trial § 230, Subjective Bad Faith is Required.

7 Witkin Cal. Proc. 5th Trial § 233, (S 233) Notice.

7 Witkin Cal. Proc. 5th Trial § 234, (S 234) Hearing.

7 Witkin Cal. Proc. 5th Trial § 235, (S 235) Order.

7 Witkin Cal. Proc. 5th Trial § 237, Nature and Scope.

7 Witkin Cal. Proc. 5th Trial § 239, Motion and Order.

2 Witkin, California Summary 10th Insurance § 101, (S 101) Conduct Intended to Harm or Inherently Harmful.

11 Witkin, California Summary 10th Husband and Wife § 8, (S 8) in General.

5 Witkin, California Summary 10th Torts § 471, Action as Disfavored.

5 Witkin, California Summary 10th Torts § 487, (S 487) Public Entity Cannot Sue.

5 Witkin, California Summary 10th Torts § 490, (S 490) Order to Show Cause.

5 Witkin, California Summary 10th Torts § 496, (S 496) Family Law Proceedings.

5 Witkin, California Summary 10th Torts § 508, (S 508) Some, But Not All, Claims or Amounts Supported by Probable Cause.

6 Witkin, California Summary 10th Torts § 1606, Felon's Action Against Victim.

§ 128.7. Signature requirement for court papers; certification that specified conditions met; violations; sanctions; punitive damages

(a) Every pleading, petition, written notice of motion, or other similar paper shall be signed by at least one attorney of record in the attorney's individual name, or, if the party is not represented by an attorney, shall be signed by the party. Each paper shall state the signer's address and telephone number, if any. Except when otherwise provided by law, pleadings need not be verified or accompanied by affidavit. An unsigned paper shall be stricken unless omission of the signature is corrected promptly after being called to the attention of the attorney or party.

(b) By presenting to the court, whether by signing, filing, submitting, or later advocating, a pleading, petition, written notice of motion, or other similar paper, an attorney or unrepresented party is certifying that to the best of the person's knowledge, information, and belief, formed after an inquiry reasonable under the circumstances, all of the following conditions are met:

(1) It is not being presented primarily for an improper purpose, such as to harass or to cause unnecessary delay or needless increase in the cost of litigation.

(2) The claims, defenses, and other legal contentions therein are warranted by existing law or by a nonfrivolous argument for the extension, modification, or reversal of existing law or the establishment of new law.

(3) The allegations and other factual contentions have evidentiary support or, if specifically so identified, are likely to have evidentiary support after a reasonable opportunity for further investigation or discovery.

(4) The denials of factual contentions are warranted on the evidence or, if specifically so identified, are reasonably based on a lack of information or belief.

(c) If, after notice and a reasonable opportunity to respond, the court determines that subdivision (b) has been violated, the court may, subject to the conditions stated below, impose an appropriate sanction upon the attorneys, law firms, or parties that have violated subdivision (b) or are responsible for the violation. In determining what sanctions, if any, should be ordered, the court shall consider whether a party seeking sanctions has exercised due diligence.

(1) A motion for sanctions under this section shall be made separately from other motions or requests and shall describe the specific conduct alleged to violate subdivision (b). Notice of motion shall be served as provided in Section 1010, but shall not be filed with or presented to the court unless, within 21 days after service of the motion, or any other period as the court may prescribe, the challenged paper, claim, defense, contention, allegation, or denial is not withdrawn or appropriately corrected. If warranted, the court may award to the party prevailing on the motion the reasonable expenses and attorney's fees incurred in presenting or opposing the motion. Absent exceptional circumstances, a law firm shall be held jointly responsible for violations committed by its partners, associates, and employees.

(2) On its own motion, the court may enter an order describing the specific conduct that appears to violate subdivision (b) and directing an attorney, law firm, or party to show cause why it has not violated subdivision (b), unless, within 21 days of service of the order to show cause, the challenged paper, claim, defense, contention, allegation, or denial is withdrawn or appropriately corrected.

(d) A sanction imposed for violation of subdivision (b) shall be limited to what is sufficient to deter repetition of this conduct or comparable conduct by others similarly situated. Subject to the limitations in paragraphs (1) and (2), the sanction may consist of, or include, directives of a nonmonetary nature, an order to pay a penalty into court, or, if imposed on motion and warranted for effective deterrence, an order directing payment to the movant of some or all of the reasonable attorney's fees and other expenses incurred as a direct result of the violation.

(1) Monetary sanctions may not be awarded against a represented party for a violation of paragraph (2) of subdivision (b).

(2) Monetary sanctions may not be awarded on the court's motion unless the court issues its order to show cause before a voluntary dismissal or settlement of the claims made by or against the party that is, or whose attorneys are, to be sanctioned.

(e) When imposing sanctions, the court shall describe the conduct determined to constitute a violation of this section and explain the basis for the sanction imposed.

(f) In addition to any award pursuant to this section for conduct described in subdivision (b), the court may assess punitive damages against the plaintiff upon a determination by the court that the plaintiff's action was an action maintained by a person convicted of a felony against the person's victim, or the victim's heirs, relatives, estate, or personal representative, for injuries arising from the acts for which the person was convicted of a felony, and that the plaintiff is guilty of fraud, oppression, or malice in maintaining the action.

(g) This section shall not apply to disclosures and discovery requests, responses, objections, and motions.

(h) A motion for sanctions brought by a party or a party's attorney primarily for an improper purpose, such as to harass or to cause unnecessary delay or needless increase in the cost of litigation, shall itself be subject to a motion for sanctions. It is the intent of the Legislature that courts shall vigorously use its sanctions authority to deter that improper conduct or comparable conduct by others similarly situated.

(i) This section shall apply to a complaint or petition filed on or after January 1, 1995, and any other pleading, written notice of motion, or other similar paper filed in that matter. *(Added by Stats.1994, c. 1062 (A.B.3594), § 3. Amended by Stats.1998, c. 121 (S.B.1511), § 2; Stats.2002, c. 491 (S.B.2009), § 1; Stats. 2005, c. 706 (A.B.1742), § 9.)*

Research References

Rutter, Cal. Practice Guide: A.D.R. Ch. 4-B, B. Judicial Arbitration.

Rutter, Cal. Practice Guide: A.D.R. Ch. 4-C, C. Statutorily-Mandated Court Mediation Programs.

Rutter, Cal. Practice Guide: A.D.R. Ch. 4-D, D. Mandatory Settlement Conferences.

Rutter, Cal. Practice Guide: A.D.R. Ch. 5-D, D. Defenses to Enforcement.

Rutter, Cal. Practice Guide: A.D.R. Ch. 5-J, J. Challenging and Enforcing Arbitrator's Award in Court.

Rutter, Cal. Practice Guide: A.D.R. Ch. 6-B, B. Temporary Judges.

Rutter, Cal. Practice Guide: A.D.R. Ch. 4-D, Outline D.

Rutter, Cal. Practice Guide: Civil Appeals & Writs Ch. 2-B, B. Appealable Judgments and Orders.

Rutter, Cal. Practice Guide: Civil Appeals & Writs Ch. 3-C, C. Extensions of Filing Deadline.

Rutter, Cal. Practice Guide: Civil Appeals & Writs Ch. 7-C, C. Stay by Posting Security (Bond or Undertaking).

Rutter, Cal. Practice Guide: Civil Appeals & Writs Ch. 8-C, C. Standards of Appellate Review.

Rutter, Cal. Practice Guide: Civil Appeals & Writs Ch. 11-E, E. Appellate Costs and Sanctions.

Rutter, Cal. Practice Guide: Civil Appeals & Writs Ch. 7 App., Appendix: Methods of Obtaining Stay for Particular Judgments and Orders.

Rutter, Cal. Practice Guide: Civ. Pro. Before Trial Ch. 1-A, A. Accepting a New Case.

Rutter, Cal. Practice Guide: Civ. Pro. Before Trial Ch. 1-B, B. Prelawsuit Investigations, Research and Analysis.

Rutter, Cal. Practice Guide: Civ. Pro. Before Trial Ch. 1-D, D. Prelawsuit Consultation Requirement in Certain Professional Negligence Actions.

Rutter, Cal. Practice Guide: Civ. Pro. Before Trial Ch. 2-C, C. Joinder of Parties.

Rutter, Cal. Practice Guide: Civ. Pro. Before Trial Ch. 5-B, B. Entry of Default.

Rutter, Cal. Practice Guide: Civ. Pro. Before Trial Ch. 6-B, B. Complaints.

Rutter, Cal. Practice Guide: Civ. Pro. Before Trial Ch. 6-C, C. Answer.

Rutter, Cal. Practice Guide: Civ. Pro. Before Trial Ch. 10-A, A. Introduction.

Rutter, Cal. Practice Guide: Civ. Pro. Before Trial Ch. 10-D, D. Procedural Requirements-Opposing Party.

Rutter, Cal. Practice Guide: Civ. Pro. Before Trial Ch. 10-H, H. Entry of Judgment or Order.

Rutter, Cal. Practice Guide: Civ. Pro. Before Trial Ch. 11-A, A. Voluntary Dismissals.

Rutter, Cal. Practice Guide: Civ. Pro. Before Trial Ch. 13-E, E. the Arbitration Hearing.

Rutter, Cal. Practice Guide: Civ. Pro. Before Trial Ch. 8A-3, Civil Discovery Act.

Rutter, Cal. Practice Guide: Civ. Pro. Before Trial Ch. 8F-8, Sanctions in Enforcing Discovery.

Rutter, Cal. Practice Guide: Civ. Pro. Before Trial Ch. 8G-3, Propounding Requests.

Rutter, Cal. Practice Guide: Civ. Pro. Before Trial Ch. 1-B, Outline B.

Rutter, Cal. Practice Guide: Civ. Pro. Before Trial Ch. 6-B, Outline B.

Rutter, Cal. Practice Guide: Civ. Pro. Before Trial Ch. 6-C, Outline C.

Rutter, Cal. Practice Guide: Civ. Pro. Before Trial Ch. 7(I)-B, B. Motions to Strike.

Rutter, Cal. Practice Guide: Civ. Pro. Before Trial Ch. 7(I)-C, C. Motion for Judgment on the Pleadings.

Rutter, Cal. Practice Guide: Civ. Pro. Before Trial Ch. 9(I)-A, A. Introduction.

Rutter, Cal. Practice Guide: Civ. Pro. Before Trial Ch. 9(I)-B, B. Preparing and Filing Motions.

Rutter, Cal. Practice Guide: Civ. Pro. Before Trial Ch. 9(I)-C, C. Opposing the Motion-And Rebutting the Opposition.

Rutter, Cal. Practice Guide: Civ. Pro. Before Trial Ch. 9(I)-E, E. Posthearing Procedures.

Rutter, Cal. Practice Guide: Civ. Pro. Before Trial Ch. 10-D, Outline D.

Rutter, Cal. Practice Guide: Civ. Pro. Before Trial Ch. 11-A, Outline a.

Rutter, Cal. Practice Guide: Civ. Pro. Before Trial Ch. 8A-3, Outline 3.

Rutter, Cal. Practice Guide: Civ. Pro. Before Trial Gen. Matls., Highlights.

Rutter, Cal. Practice Guide: Civ. Pro. Before Trial Ch. 12(II)-A, A. Mandatory Settlement Conference ("Msc").

Rutter, Cal. Practice Guide: Civ. Pro. Before Trial Ch. 9(III)-A, A. Sources of Sanctions Power.

Rutter, Cal. Practice Guide: Civ. Pro. Before Trial Ch. 9(III)-B, B. Sanctions Under CCP § 128.5 (Pre-1995 and SLAPP Cases).

Rutter, Cal. Practice Guide: Civ. Pro. Before Trial Ch. 9(III)-C, C. Sanctions Under CCP § 128.7.

Rutter, Cal. Practice Guide: Civ. Pro. Before Trial Ch. 12(II)-A, Outline a.

Rutter, Cal. Practice Guide: Civ. Pro. Before Trial Ch. 9(III)-C, Outline C.

Rutter, Cal. Practice Guide: Civil Trials & Evidence Ch. 12-A, A. Motion for Mistrial.

Rutter, Cal. Practice Guide: Civil Trials & Evidence Ch. 16-E, E. Statement of Decision.

Rutter, Cal. Practice Guide: Civil Trials & Evidence Ch. 18-C, C. Other Post-Trial Motions.

California Practice Guide: Employment Litigation Ch. 19-C, C. Plaintiff's Complaint.

Rutter, Cal. Practice Guide: Enforcing Judgments/Debts Ch. 1-B, B. Accepting the Collection Case.

Rutter, Cal. Practice Guide: Enforcing Judgments/Debts Ch. 4-A, A. Attachment.

Rutter, Cal. Practice Guide: Enforcing Judgments/Debts Ch. 6A-5, Amount Recoverable Under Judgment.

Rutter, Cal. Practice Guide: Enforcing Judgments/Debts Ch. 1-B, Outline B.

Rutter, Cal. Practice Guide: Fed.Civ.Pro. Before Trial Ch. 1-D, D. Choosing Between State and Federal Courts.

Rutter, Cal. Practice Guide: Insurance Litigation Ch. 13-B, B. Extracontractual Compensatory Damages.

Rutter, Cal. Practice Guide: Insurance Litigation Ch. 15-E, E. Pleadings.

Rutter, Cal. Practice Guide: Insurance Litigation Ch. 7K-D, D. Policy Provisions.

Rutter, Cal. Practice Guide: Insurance Litigation Ch. 7K-D, Outline D.

Rutter, Cal. Practice Guide: Personal Injury Ch. 1-B, B. Initial Evaluation of Case: Decision to Accept or Reject Employment or Undertake Further Evaluation of Claim.

Rutter, Cal. Practice Guide: Personal Injury Ch. 3-A, A. Introduction.

Rutter, Cal. Practice Guide: Personal Injury Ch. 3-E, E. Punitive Damages.

Rutter, Cal. Practice Guide: Personal Injury Ch. 4-F, F. Court-Conducted Settlement Proceedings.

Rutter, Cal. Practice Guide: Personal Injury Ch. 6-B, B. Overview of Selected Discovery Procedures.

Rutter, Cal. Practice Guide: Personal Injury Ch. 7-F, F. Preparing for Arbitration.

Rutter, Cal. Practice Guide: Personal Injury Ch. 7-J, J. Arbitration of Uninsured Motorist Claims.

Rutter, Cal. Practice Guide: Personal Injury Ch. 8-B, B. After Trial Date Set (Three to Four Months Before Trial).

Rutter, Cal. Practice Guide: Personal Injury Ch. 1-B, Outline B.

Rutter, Cal. Practice Guide: Personal Injury Ch. 3-A, Outline a.

Rutter, Cal. Practice Guide: Personal Injury Ch. 4-F, Outline F.

Rutter, Cal. Practice Guide: Prof. Responsibility Ch. 1-A, A. Sources of Regulation of Practice of Law in California-Overview.

Rutter, Cal. Practice Guide: Prof. Responsibility Ch. 2-D, D. In-Person Solicitation for Profit.

Rutter, Cal. Practice Guide: Prof. Responsibility Ch. 3-D, D. Authority of Client vs. Authority of Attorney.

Rutter, Cal. Practice Guide: Prof. Responsibility Ch. 4-G, G. Procedural Considerations for Disqualification Based on Conflict of Interest.

Rutter, Cal. Practice Guide: Prof. Responsibility Ch. 6-B, B. Elements of Attorney Competence.

Rutter, Cal. Practice Guide: Prof. Responsibility Ch. 8-B, B. Accepting or Rejecting Employment.

Rutter, Cal. Practice Guide: Prof. Responsibility Ch. 8-E, E. Consequences of Improper Advocacy.

Miller and Starr California Real Estate § 11:154, Expungement of a Lis Pendens--Procedure and Grounds for Expungement.

3 Witkin Cal. Proc. 5th Actions § 369, Hearing, Determination, and Security.

9 Witkin Cal. Proc. 5th Appeal § 182, When Order Affects Judgment or Relates to Enforcement.
1 Witkin Cal. Proc. 5th Attorneys § 556, (S 556) Other Measures.
2 Witkin Cal. Proc. 5th Courts § 177, (S 177) Imposition of Money Sanctions.
7 Witkin Cal. Proc. 5th Judgment § 175, No Judicially Established Bilateral Fee-Shifting.
7 Witkin Cal. Proc. 5th Judgment § 217, Standard for Awarding Fees.
7 Witkin Cal. Proc. 5th Judgment § 222, (S 222) Actions in Bad Faith.
4 Witkin Cal. Proc. 5th Pleading § 397, (S 397) Pleading Truthfully.
4 Witkin Cal. Proc. 5th Pleading § 459, (S 459) Nature of Verification.
4 Witkin Cal. Proc. 5th Pleading § 469, Certification of Pleadings.
4 Witkin Cal. Proc. 5th Pleading § 471, Superior Court.
4 Witkin Cal. Proc. 5th Pleading § 630, Exposure to Toxic Materials.
5 Witkin Cal. Proc. 5th Pleading § 1011, (S 1011) Procedural Defects Not Subject to Demurrer.
5 Witkin Cal. Proc. 5th Pleading § 1042, (S 1042) After Dismissal.
6 Witkin Cal. Proc. 5th Proceedings Without Trial § 9, Formal Requisites.
6 Witkin Cal. Proc. 5th Proceedings Without Trial § 54, (S 54) Sanctions.
6 Witkin Cal. Proc. 5th Proceedings Without Trial § 55, (S 55) Statutory Authorization.
6 Witkin Cal. Proc. 5th Proceedings Without Trial § 573, Procedure to Correct or Vacate Award.
7 Witkin Cal. Proc. 5th Trial § 58, (S 58) in General.
7 Witkin Cal. Proc. 5th Trial § 59, (S 59) Judicial Council Rules.
7 Witkin Cal. Proc. 5th Trial § 226, (S 226) in General.
7 Witkin Cal. Proc. 5th Trial § 227, Scope and Definitions.
7 Witkin Cal. Proc. 5th Trial § 233, (S 233) Notice.
7 Witkin Cal. Proc. 5th Trial § 237, Nature and Scope.
7 Witkin Cal. Proc. 5th Trial § 238, Signing and Certification.
7 Witkin Cal. Proc. 5th Trial § 239, Motion and Order.
7 Witkin Cal. Proc. 5th Trial § 240, Safe Harbor Provision.
7 Witkin Cal. Proc. 5th Trial § 241, Improper Use of Sanctions Statute.
10 Witkin, California Summary 10th Parent and Child § 467, (S 467) Power to Hear Cases.
6 Witkin, California Summary 10th Torts § 1606, Felon's Action Against Victim.

§ 129. Photographs, etc., taken in course of post mortem examination or autopsy; prohibition against reproduction or dissemination; exceptions; personal liability of coroner

(a) Notwithstanding any other * * * law, a copy, reproduction, or facsimile of any kind * * * of a photograph, negative, or print, including instant photographs and video recordings, of the body, or any portion of the body, of a deceased person, taken by or for the coroner at the scene of death or in the course of a post mortem examination or autopsy * * *, shall not be made or disseminated except as follows:

(1) For use in a criminal action or proceeding in this state that relates to the death of that person * * *:

(2) As a court of this state permits, by order after good cause has been shown and after written notification of the request for the court order has been served, at least five days before the order is made, upon the district attorney of the county in which the post mortem examination or autopsy has been made or caused to be made.

(b) This section shall not apply to the making * * * or dissemination of a copy, reproduction, or facsimile for use in the field of forensic pathology, * * * in medical or scientific education or research, or * * * by a coroner or any law enforcement agency in * * * the United States for investigative purposes, including identification and identification confirmation.

(c) This section shall apply to * * * a copy, reproduction, or facsimile, and to * * * a photograph, negative, or print, * * * regardless of when it was made.

(d) A coroner is not personally liable for monetary damages in a civil action for any act or omission in compliance with this section. (Added by Stats.1968, c. 6, 1st Ex.Sess., p. 37, § 1, eff. Sept. 25, 1969. Amended by Stats.1985, c. 304, § 1; Stats.2009, c. 88 (A.B.176), § 16; Stats.2013, c. 53 (A.B.957), § 1.)

Law Revision Commission Comments

Section 129 is amended to reflect advances in recording technology and for consistency of terminology. For a similar reform, see 2002 Cal. Stat. ch. 1068 (replacing numerous references to "audiotape" in Civil Discovery Act with either "audio technology," "audio recording," or "audio record," as context required). [37 Cal. L. Revision Comm'n Reports 211 (2007)].

§ 130. Deceased minor victims of criminal acts; sealing of autopsy report and associated evidence

(a) Subject to the provisions of this section, when a child who is under 18 years of age is killed as a result of a criminal act and a person has been convicted and sentenced for the commission of that criminal act, or a person has been found to have committed that offense by the juvenile court and adjudged a ward of the juvenile court, upon the request of a qualifying family member of the deceased child, the autopsy report and evidence associated with the examination of the victim in the possession of a public agency, as defined in Section 6252 of the Government Code, shall be sealed and not disclosed, except that an autopsy report and evidence associated with the examination of the victim which has been sealed pursuant to this section may be disclosed, as follows:

(1) To law enforcement, prosecutorial agencies and experts hired by those agencies, public social service agencies, child death review teams, or the hospital that treated the child immediately prior to death, to be used solely for investigative, prosecutorial, or review purposes, and may not be disseminated further.

(2) To the defendant and the defense team in the course of criminal proceedings or related habeas proceedings, to be used solely for investigative, criminal defense, and review purposes, including review for the purpose of initiating any criminal proceeding or related habeas proceeding, and may not be disseminated further. The "defense team" includes, but is not limited to, all of the following: attorneys, investigators, experts, paralegals, support staff, interns, students, and state and privately funded legal assistance projects hired or consulted for the purposes of investigation, defense, appeal, or writ of habeas corpus on behalf of the person accused of killing the deceased child victim.

(3) To civil litigants in a cause of action related to the victim's death with a court order upon a showing of good cause and proper notice under Section 129, to be used solely to pursue the cause of action, and may not be disseminated further.

(b) Nothing in this section shall prohibit the use of autopsy reports and evidence in relation to court proceedings.

(c) Nothing in this section shall abrogate the rights of victims, their authorized representatives, or insurance carriers to request the release of information pursuant to subdivision (f) of Section 6254 of the Government Code. However, if a seal has been requested, an insurance carrier receiving items pursuant to a request under that subdivision is prohibited from disclosing the requested items except as necessary in the normal course of business. An insurance carrier shall not, under any circumstances, disclose to the general public items received pursuant to subdivision (f) of Section 6254 of the Government Code.

(d) This section may not be invoked by a qualifying family member who has been charged with or convicted of any act in furtherance of the victim's death. Upon the filing of those charges against a qualifying family member, any seal maintained at the request of that qualifying family member under this section shall be removed.

(e) A coroner or medical examiner shall not be liable for damages in a civil action for any reasonable act or omission taken in good faith in compliance with this section.

(f) If sealing of the autopsy report has been requested by a qualifying family member and another qualifying family member opposes sealing, the opposing party may request a hearing in the superior court in the county with jurisdiction over the crime leading to the child's death for a determination of whether the sealing should be maintained. The opposing party shall notify all other qualifying family members, the medical examiner's office that conducted the autopsy, and the district attorney's office with jurisdiction over the crime at least 10 court days in advance of the hearing. At the hearing, the court shall consider the interests of all qualifying family members, the protection of the memory of the deceased child, any evidence that the qualifying family member requesting the seal was involved in the crime that resulted in the death of the child, the public interest in scrutiny of the autopsy report or the performance of the medical examiner, any impact that unsealing would have on pending investigations or pending litigation, and any other relevant factors. Official information in the possession of a public agency necessary to the determination of the hearing shall be received in camera upon a proper showing. In its discretion, the court may, to the extent allowable by law and with good cause shown, restrict the dissemination of an autopsy report or evidence associated with the examination of a victim. This section shall not apply if a public agency has independently determined that the autopsy report may not be disclosed pursuant to subdivision (f) of Section 6254 of the Government Code because it is an investigative file. In that instance, nothing in this section shall preclude the application of Sections 6258 and 6259 of the Government Code.

(g) If a seal has been maintained pursuant to this section, a qualifying family member, or a biological or adoptive aunt, uncle, sibling, first cousin, child, or grandparent of the deceased child may request that the seal be removed. The request to remove the seal shall be adjudicated pursuant to subdivision (f), with the party requesting the removal of the seal being the opposing party.

(h) Nothing in this section shall limit the public access to information contained in the death certificate including: name, age, gender, race, date, time and location of death, the name of a physician reporting a death in a hospital, the name of the certifying pathologist, date of certification, burial information, and cause of death.

(i) When a medical examiner declines a request to provide a copy of an autopsy report that has been sealed pursuant to this section, the examiner shall cite this section as the reason for declining to provide a copy of the report.

(j) For purposes of this section:

(1) A "child who is under 18 years of age" does not include any child who comes within either of the following descriptions:

(A) He or she was a dependent child of the juvenile court pursuant to Section 300 of the Welfare and Institutions Code at the time of his or her death, or, pursuant to subdivision (b) of Section 10850.4 of the Welfare and Institutions Code, abuse or neglect is determined to have led to his or her death.

(B) He or she was residing in a state or county juvenile facility, or a private facility under contract with the state or county for the placement of juveniles, as a ward of the juvenile court pursuant to Section 602 of the Welfare and Institutions Code at the time of his or her death.

(2) "Evidence associated with the examination of a victim" means any object, writing, diagram, recording, computer file, photograph, video, DVD, CD, film, digital device, or other item that was collected during, or serves to document, the autopsy of a deceased child.

(3) "Qualifying family member" means the biological or adoptive parent, spouse, or legal guardian.

(k) Nothing in this section shall limit the discovery provisions set forth in Chapter 10 (commencing with Section 1054) of Title 6 of the Penal Code.

(*l*) Nothing in this section shall be construed to limit the authority of the court to seal records or restrict the dissemination of an autopsy report or evidence associated with the examination of a victim under case law, other statutory law, or the rules of court.

(m) The provisions of this section are severable. If any provision of this section or its application is held invalid, that invalidity shall not affect other provisions or applications that can be given effect without the invalid provision or application. *(Added by Stats.2010, c. 302 (S.B.5), § 3, eff. Sept. 27, 2010.)*

ARTICLE 3.   JUDICIAL HOLIDAYS

Section

§ 133.   Day for transacting judicial business

Courts of justice may be held and judicial business transacted on any day, except as provided in this article. *(Added by Stats.1985, c. 1450, § 2, operative Jan. 1, 1989.)*

Research References

2 Witkin Cal. Proc. 5th Courts § 45, Judicial Days.

§ 134.   Court closure on judicial holidays; exceptions

(a) Except as provided in subdivision (c), the courts shall be closed for the transaction of judicial business on judicial holidays for all but the following purposes:

(1) To give, upon their request, instructions to a jury when deliberating on their verdict.

(2) To receive a verdict or discharge a jury.

(3) For the conduct of arraignments and the exercise of the powers of a magistrate in a criminal action, or in a proceeding of a criminal nature.

(4) For the conduct of Saturday small claims court sessions pursuant to the Small Claims Act set forth in Chapter 5.5 (commencing with Section 116.110).

(b) Injunctions and writs of prohibition may be issued and served on any day.

(c) In any superior court, one or more departments of the court may remain open and in session for the transaction of any business that may come before the department in the exercise of the civil or criminal jurisdiction of the court, or both, on a judicial holiday or at any hours of the day or night, or both, as the judges of the court prescribe.

(d) The fact that a court is open on a judicial holiday shall not make that day a nonholiday for purposes of computing the time required for the conduct of any proceeding nor for the performance of any act. Any paper lodged with the court at a time when the court is open pursuant to subdivision (c), shall be filed by the court on the next day that is not a judicial holiday, if the document meets appropriate criteria for filing. *(Added by Stats.1985, c. 1450, § 2, operative Jan. 1, 1989. Amended by Stats.1986, c. 1398, § 2, operative Jan. 1, 1989; Stats.1990, c. 1305 (S.B.2627), § 4; Stats.1992, c. 460 (S.B.1805), § 2; Stats.1998, c. 931 (S.B.2139), § 45, eff. Sept. 28, 1998; Stats.2002, c. 784 (S.B.1316), § 33.)*

Law Revision Commission Comments

Section 134 is amended to reflect the elimination of the justice court. Cal. Const. art. VI, §§ 1, 5(b). [28 Cal.L.Rev.Comm. Reports 51 (1998)].

Subdivision (c) of Section 134 is amended to reflect unification of the municipal and superior courts pursuant to Article VI, Section 5(e), of the California Constitution. [32 Cal.L.Rev.Comm. Reports 97 (2002)].

Research References

Rutter, Cal. Practice Guide: Civil Appeals & Writs Ch. 3-B, B. Filing Deadlines.

Rutter, Cal. Practice Guide: Civil Trials & Evidence Ch. 15-D, D. Juror Requests for Additional Information During Deliberations.

2 Witkin Cal. Proc. 5th Courts § 45, Judicial Days.

2 Witkin Cal. Proc. 5th Courts § 47, (S 47) General Rule: No Judicial Business.

2 Witkin Cal. Proc. 5th Courts § 48, (S 48) Exceptions.

6 Witkin Cal. Proc. 5th Provisional Remedies § 389, (S 389) Service of Writ.

7 Witkin Cal. Proc. 5th Trial § 332, (S 332) With Judge or Court Officer.

7 Witkin Cal. Proc. 5th Trial § 339, Receipt of Verdict.

§ 135. Judicial holidays; alternate day of observance from Saturday or Sunday

Every full day designated as a holiday by Section 6700 of the Government Code, including that Thursday of November declared by the President to be Thanksgiving Day, is a judicial holiday, except September 9, known as "Admission Day," and any other day appointed by the President, but not by the Governor, for a public fast, thanksgiving, or holiday. If a judicial holiday falls on a Saturday or a Sunday, the Judicial Council may designate an alternative day for observance of the holiday. Every Saturday and the day after Thanksgiving Day is a judicial holiday. Officers and employees of the courts shall observe only the judicial holidays established pursuant to this section. *(Added by Stats.1985, c. 1450, § 2, operative Jan. 1, 1989. Amended by Stats.1986, c. 1398, § 3, operative Jan. 1, 1989; Stats.1992, c. 460 (S.B.1805), § 3; Stats.1994, c. 1011 (S.B.1373), § 3; Stats.2001, c. 542 (S.B.1112), § 3.)*

Research References

Rutter, Cal. Practice Guide: Civil Appeals & Writs Ch. 3-B, B. Filing Deadlines.

2 Witkin Cal. Proc. 5th Courts § 46, (S 46) What Are Holidays.

2 Witkin Cal. Proc. 5th Courts § 47, (S 47) General Rule: No Judicial Business.

§ 136. Postponement of sitting or adjournment; dates falling on judicial holiday

If a day appointed for the holding or sitting of a court, or to which it is adjourned, falls on a judicial holiday, it shall be deemed appointed for or adjourned to the next day. *(Added by Stats.1985, c. 1450, § 2, operative Jan. 1, 1989.)*

Research References

2 Witkin Cal. Proc. 5th Courts § 47, (S 47) General Rule: No Judicial Business.

ARTICLE 4. PROCEEDINGS IN CASE OF ABSENCE OF JUDGE

Section

139. Absence of judge; adjournments from day to day; order adjourning to day certain.

§ 139. Absence of judge; adjournments from day to day; order adjourning to day certain

If no judge attends on the day appointed for the holding or sitting of a court, or on the day to which it may have been adjourned, within one hour after the time appointed, the sheriff, marshal, or clerk shall adjourn the same until the next day, at 10 o'clock a.m., and if no judge attend on that day, before noon, the sheriff, marshal, or clerk shall adjourn the same until the following day at the same hour; and so on, from day to day unless the judge, by written order, directs it to be adjourned to some day certain, fixed in said order, in which case it shall be so adjourned. *(Enacted in 1872. Amended by Code Am.1880, c. 35, p. 38, § 1; Stats.1907, c. 357, p. 681, § 1; Stats.1933, c. 743, p. 1824, § 36; Stats.1951, c. 1737, p. 4090, § 28, operative Jan. 1, 1952; Stats.1996, c. 872 (A.B.3472), § 6.)*

Research References

7 Witkin Cal. Proc. 5th Trial § 21, (S 21) Absence of Judge.

ARTICLE 6.   SEALS OF COURTS

Section

153. Documents to which seal must be or need not be affixed.

§ 153. Documents to which seal must be or need not be affixed

Except as otherwise expressly provided by law, the seal of a court need not be affixed to any proceeding therein, or to any document, except to the following:

(a) A writ.

(b) A summons.

(c) A warrant of arrest. *(Formerly § 152, enacted in 1872. Amended by Code Am.1873–74, c. 383, p. 284, § 12. Renumbered § 153 and amended by Code Am.1880, c. 35, p. 40, § 1. Amended by Stats.1933, c. 743, p. 1826, § 42; Stats.1951, c. 1737, p. 4092, § 35, operative Jan. 1, 1952; Stats.1965, c. 299, p. 1358, § 18, operative Jan. 1, 1967; Stats.1979, c. 730, p. 2472, § 15, operative Jan. 1, 1981; Stats.1988, c. 1199, § 2, operative July 1, 1989.)*

Law Revision Commission Comments

The deleted language, which relates to the authentication of copies of judicial records, is superseded by Evidence Code Section 1530.

Section 153 is amended to add the certificate of appointment of a conservator to the exceptions stated in subdivision 4.

Section 153 is amended to delete the former reference to papers in probate. This provision was unnecessary, since the seal is expressly provided for in the relevant statutes in these cases. See, e.g., Prob.Code §§ 2311 (letters of guardianship or conservatorship), 8405 (letters of personal representative) [19 Cal.L.Rev.Comm.Reports 1034 (1988)].

Research References

Rutter, Cal. Practice Guide: Enforcing Judgments/Debts Ch. 6D-2, Writ of Execution.

3 Witkin Cal. Proc. 5th Actions § 981, (S 981) in General.

Title 2

JUDICIAL OFFICERS

CHAPTER 2. POWER OF JUDGES AT CHAMBERS

Section

165. Justices of supreme court and courts of appeal.

166. Judges of superior and municipal courts.

166.1. Controlling question of law involving substantial grounds for difference of opinion and appellate

Section

    resolution of which may materially advance conclusion of litigation; indication by judge in interlocutory order.

167.   Performance of acts of clerk.

§ 165. Justices of supreme court and courts of appeal

The justices of the Supreme Court and of the courts of appeal, or any of them, may, at chambers, grant all orders and writs which are usually granted in the first instance upon an ex parte application, except writs of mandamus, certiorari, and prohibition; and may, in their discretion, hear applications to discharge such orders and writs. *(Enacted in 1872. Amended by Code Am.1880, c. 35, p. 41, § 1; Stats.1935, c. 74, p. 410, § 3; Stats.1967, c. 17, p. 828, § 10.)*

Research References

2 Witkin Cal. Proc. 5th Courts § 21, (S 21) Distinction Between Court and Judge.
2 Witkin Cal. Proc. 5th Courts § 23, in General.
2 Witkin Cal. Proc. 5th Courts § 326, (S 326) Powers of Individual Judges.

§ 166. Judges of superior and municipal courts

(a) The judges of the superior courts may, in chambers:

(1) Grant all orders and writs that are usually granted in the first instance upon an ex parte application, and hear and dispose of those orders and writs, appoint referees, require and receive inventories and accounts to be filed, order notice of settlement of supplemental accounts, suspend the powers of personal representatives, guardians, or conservators in the cases allowed by law, appoint special administrators, grant letters of temporary guardianship or conservatorship, approve or reject claims, and direct the issuance from the court of all writs and process necessary in the exercise of their powers in matters of probate.

(2) Hear and determine all motions made pursuant to Section 657 or 663.

(3) Hear and determine all uncontested actions, proceedings, demurrers, motions, petitions, applications, and other matters pending before the court other than actions for dissolution of marriage, for legal separation, or for a judgment of nullity of the marriage, and except also applications for confirmation of sale of real property in probate proceedings.

(4) Hear and determine motions to tax costs of enforcing a judgment.

(5) Approve bonds and undertakings.

(b) A judge may, out of court, anywhere in the state, exercise all the powers and perform all the functions and duties conferred upon a judge as contradistinguished from the court, or that a judge may exercise or perform in chambers. *(Enacted in 1872. Amended by Code Am.1880, c. 35, p. 41, § 1; Stats.1929, c. 487, p. 849, § 1; Stats.1933, c. 743, p. 1827, § 47; Stats.1951, c. 1737. p. 4092, § 36, operative Jan. 1, 1952; Stats.1979, c. 730, p. 2472, § 16, operative Jan. 1, 1981; Stats.1982, c. 517, p. 2332, § 94; Stats.1982, c. 497, p. 2153, § 30, operative July 1, 1983; Stats.1983, c. 18, § 6, eff. April 21, 1983; Stats.1988, c. 1199, § 3, operative July 1, 1989; Stats.1998, c. 931 (S.B.2139), § 46, eff. Sept. 28, 1998; Stats.2002, c. 784 (S.B.1316), § 34.)*

Law Revision Commission Comments

Section 166 is amended to add authority for the judge to suspend the powers of a conservator and to issue letters of temporary conservatorship. See Prob.Code §§ 2250–2251, 2258, 2654. Other technical revisions are also made.

Subdivision (a) (4) is added to Section 166 to continue a provision of former Section 1033.7 (15 Cal.L.Rev.Comm. Reports 2001).

Section 166 is amended to authorize judges at chambers to approve bonds and undertakings. Formerly approval of probate bonds only at

chambers was authorized. The other changes in Section 166 are technical. [16 Cal.L.Rev.Comm. Reports 2239 (1982)].

Section 166 is amended to provide additional probate matters that may be heard and determined in chambers. The added provisions restate former provisions of the Probate Code without substantive change. See former Prob. Code §§ 460–464 (appointment of special administrator), 613–615 (citation to account), 703, 710–713, 718 (rejection of claim), 921–922 (citation to account), 1020.5 (notice of settlement of supplementary accounts). Section 166 is also amended to change the phrase "at chambers" to "in chambers" in conformity with modern usage [19 Cal.L.Rev.Comm.Reports 1034 (1988)].

Section 166 is amended to reflect the elimination of the justice court. Cal. Const. art. VI, §§ 1, 5(b). [28 Cal.L.Rev.Comm. Reports 51 (1998)].

Subdivision (a) of Section 166 is amended to reflect unification of the municipal and superior courts pursuant to Article VI, Section 5(e), of the California Constitution. Subdivision (a) is also amended to delete language referring to "the judge" of the court. Every superior court has at least two judgeships as a result of trial court unification. See Gov't Code § 69580 *et seq.* (number of judges). Where a court has only one judge due to a vacancy or otherwise, a reference to the judges of the court means the sole judge of the court. See Gov't Code § 13 (plural includes singular). [32 Cal.L.Rev.Comm. Reports 98 (2002)].

Research References

Rutter, Cal. Practice Guide: Civ. Pro. Before Trial Ch. 9(I)-A, A. Introduction.
Rutter, Cal. Practice Guide: Civil Trials & Evidence Ch. 18-B, B. Motion for New Trial.
8 Witkin Cal. Proc. 5th Attack Judgment Trial Court § 68, Evidence and Argument.
2 Witkin Cal. Proc. 5th Courts § 23, in General.
2 Witkin Cal. Proc. 5th Courts § 24, Direction to Clerk.
2 Witkin Cal. Proc. 5th Courts § 25, Hearing With Consent.
2 Witkin Cal. Proc. 5th Courts § 26, Distinction: Judge at Home.
2 Witkin Cal. Proc. 5th Courts § 27, (S 27) Powers of Judge Out of County.
2 Witkin Cal. Proc. 5th Courts § 220, Sessions Outside Courtroom.
8 Witkin Cal. Proc. 5th Extraordinary Writs § 185, (S 185) Summary Determination.
6 Witkin Cal. Proc. 5th Proceedings Without Trial § 3, (S 3) Main Action of Proceeding.
6 Witkin Cal. Proc. 5th Proceedings Without Trial § 36, (S 36) Nature of Hearing.
14 Witkin, California Summary 10th Wills and Probate § 426, Procedure for Appointment.

§ 166.1. Controlling question of law involving substantial grounds for difference of opinion and appellate resolution of which may materially advance conclusion of litigation; indication by judge in interlocutory order

Upon the written request of any party or his or her counsel, or at the judge's discretion, a judge may indicate in any interlocutory order a belief that there is a controlling question of law as to which there are substantial grounds for difference of opinion, appellate resolution of which may materially advance the conclusion of the litigation. Neither the denial of a request for, nor the objection of another party or counsel to, such a commentary in the interlocutory order, may be grounds for a writ or appeal. *(Added by Stats.2002, c. 708 (A.B.2865), § 1.)*

Research References

Rutter, Cal. Practice Guide: Civil Appeals & Writs Ch. 15-A, A. Overview.
Rutter, Cal. Practice Guide: Civ. Pro. Before Trial Ch. 10-J, J. Appellate Review of Summary Judgment and Adjudication Orders.
Rutter, Cal. Practice Guide: Civ. Pro. Before Trial Ch. 9(I)-E, E. Posthearing Procedures.
9 Witkin Cal. Proc. 5th Appeal § 88, (S 88) Discretionary Appeal.

§ 167. Performance of acts of clerk

Any act required or permitted to be performed by the clerk of a court may be performed by a judge thereof. *(Added by*

Stats.1969, c. 1610, p. 3362, § 1, operative July 1, 1970. Amended by Stats.1989, c. 1417, § 1.)

Research References

Rutter, Cal. Practice Guide: A.D.R. Ch. 6-B, B. Temporary Judges.
2 Witkin Cal. Proc. 5th Courts § 26, Distinction: Judge at Home.

CHAPTER 3. DISQUALIFICATIONS OF JUDGES

§ 170. Duty to decide

A judge has a duty to decide any proceeding in which he or she is not disqualified. *(Added by Stats.1984, c. 1555, § 2.)*

Research References

Rutter, Cal. Practice Guide: Civil Appeals & Writs Ch. 11-A, A. the Decisionmaking Process.
Rutter, Cal. Practice Guide: Civil Trials & Evidence Ch. 3-A, A. Challenges for Cause.
Rutter, Cal. Practice Guide: Civil Trials & Evidence Ch. 3-B, B. Peremptory Challenge of Judge (CCP § 170.6).
3 Witkin Cal. Proc. 5th Actions § 6, Illustrations.
8 Witkin Cal. Proc. 5th Attack Judgment Trial Court § 74, (S 74) Extensions.
2 Witkin Cal. Proc. 5th Courts § 93, (S 93) in General.
2 Witkin Cal. Proc. 5th Courts § 94, Theory that Judgment is Void.
2 Witkin Cal. Proc. 5th Courts § 98, Procedure.
2 Witkin Cal. Proc. 5th Courts § 102, (S 102) What Are Not Grounds.
2 Witkin Cal. Proc. 5th Courts § 108, (S 108) Former Case Law on Financial Interest.
2 Witkin Cal. Proc. 5th Courts § 110, (S 110) Former Case Law on Securities Holdings.
2 Witkin Cal. Proc. 5th Courts § 114, in General.
2 Witkin Cal. Proc. 5th Courts § 140, (S 140) General Rule and Limitations.
2 Witkin Cal. Proc. 5th Jurisdiction § 234, Peremptory Challenge of Judge.
2 Witkin Cal. Proc. 5th Jurisdiction § 354, (S 354) in General.
6 Witkin Cal. Proc. 5th Proceedings Without Trial § 70, (S 70) Objection to Referee.
14 Witkin, California Summary 10th Wills and Probate § 350, (S 350) Disqualification of Judge.

§ 170.1. Grounds for disqualification

(a) A judge shall be disqualified if any one or more of the following are true:

(1)(A) The judge has personal knowledge of disputed evidentiary facts concerning the proceeding.

(B) A judge shall be deemed to have personal knowledge within the meaning of this paragraph if the judge, or the spouse of the judge, or a person within the third degree of relationship to either of them, or the spouse of such a person is to the judge's knowledge likely to be a material witness in the proceeding.

(2)(A) The judge served as a lawyer in the proceeding, or in any other proceeding involving the same issues he or she served as a lawyer for a party in the present proceeding or gave advice to a party in the present proceeding upon a matter involved in the action or proceeding.

(B) A judge shall be deemed to have served as a lawyer in the proceeding if within the past two years:

(i) A party to the proceeding, or an officer, director, or trustee of a party, was a client of the judge when the judge was in the private practice of law or a client of a lawyer with whom the judge was associated in the private practice of law.

(ii) A lawyer in the proceeding was associated in the private practice of law with the judge.

(C) A judge who served as a lawyer for, or officer of, a public agency that is a party to the proceeding shall be deemed to have served as a lawyer in the proceeding if he or she personally advised or in any way represented the public agency concerning the factual or legal issues in the proceeding.

(3)(A) The judge has a financial interest in the subject matter in a proceeding or in a party to the proceeding.

(B) A judge shall be deemed to have a financial interest within the meaning of this paragraph if:

(i) A spouse or minor child living in the household has a financial interest.

(ii) The judge or the spouse of the judge is a fiduciary who has a financial interest.

(C) A judge has a duty to make reasonable efforts to inform himself or herself about his or her personal and fiduciary interests and those of his or her spouse and the personal financial interests of children living in the household.

(4) The judge, or the spouse of the judge, or a person within the third degree of relationship to either of them, or the spouse of such a person is a party to the proceeding or an officer, director, or trustee of a party.

(5) A lawyer or a spouse of a lawyer in the proceeding is the spouse, former spouse, child, sibling, or parent of the judge or the judge's spouse or if such a person is associated in the private practice of law with a lawyer in the proceeding.

(6)(A) For any reason:

(i) The judge believes his or her recusal would further the interests of justice.

(ii) The judge believes there is a substantial doubt as to his or her capacity to be impartial.

(iii) A person aware of the facts might reasonably entertain a doubt that the judge would be able to be impartial.

(B) Bias or prejudice toward a lawyer in the proceeding may be grounds for disqualification.

(7) By reason of permanent or temporary physical impairment, the judge is unable to properly perceive the evidence or is unable to properly conduct the proceeding.

(8)(A) The judge has a current arrangement concerning prospective employment or other compensated service as a dispute resolution neutral or is participating in, or, within the last two years has participated in, discussions regarding prospective employment or service as a dispute resolution neutral, or has been engaged in that employment or service, and any of the following applies:

(i) The arrangement is, or the prior employment or discussion was, with a party to the proceeding.

(ii) The matter before the judge includes issues relating to the enforcement of either an agreement to submit a dispute to an alternative dispute resolution process or an award or other final decision by a dispute resolution neutral.

(iii) The judge directs the parties to participate in an alternative dispute resolution process in which the dispute resolution neutral will be an individual or entity with whom the judge has the arrangement, has previously been employed or served, or is discussing or has discussed the employment or service.

(iv) The judge will select a dispute resolution neutral or entity to conduct an alternative dispute resolution process in the matter before the judge, and among those available for selection is an individual or entity with whom the judge has the arrangement, with whom the judge has previously been employed or served, or with whom the judge is discussing or has discussed the employment or service.

(B) For the purposes of this paragraph, all of the following apply:

(i) "Participating in discussions" or "has participated in discussion" means that the judge solicited or otherwise indicated an interest in accepting or negotiating possible employment or service as an alternative dispute resolution neutral, or responded to an unsolicited statement regarding, or an offer of, that employment or service by expressing an interest in that employment or service, making an inquiry regarding the employment or service, or encouraging the person making the statement or offer to provide additional information about that possible employment or service. If a judge's response to an unsolicited statement regarding, a question about, or offer of, prospective employment or other compensated service as a dispute resolution neutral is limited to responding negatively, declining the offer, or declining to discuss that employment or service, that response does not constitute participating in discussions.

(ii) "Party" includes the parent, subsidiary, or other legal affiliate of any entity that is a party and is involved in the transaction, contract, or facts that gave rise to the issues subject to the proceeding.

(iii) "Dispute resolution neutral" means an arbitrator, mediator, temporary judge appointed under Section 21 of Article VI of the California Constitution, referee appointed under Section 638 or 639, special master, neutral evaluator, settlement officer, or settlement facilitator.

(9)(A) The judge has received a contribution in excess of one thousand five hundred dollars ($1500) from a party or lawyer in the proceeding, and either of the following applies:

(i) The contribution was received in support of the judge's last election, if the last election was within the last six years.

(ii) The contribution was received in anticipation of an upcoming election.

(B) Notwithstanding subparagraph (A), the judge shall be disqualified based on a contribution of a lesser amount if subparagraph (A) of paragraph (6) applies.

(C) The judge shall disclose any contribution from a party or lawyer in a matter that is before the court that is required to be reported under subdivision (f) of Section 84211 of the Government Code, even if the amount would not require disqualification under this paragraph. The manner of disclosure shall be the same as that provided in Canon 3E of the Code of Judicial Ethics.

(D) Notwithstanding paragraph (1) of subdivision (b) of Section 170.3, the disqualification required under this paragraph may be waived by the party that did not make the contribution unless there are other circumstances that would prohibit a waiver pursuant to paragraph (2) of subdivision (b) of Section 170.3.

(b) A judge before whom a proceeding was tried or heard shall be disqualified from participating in any appellate review of that proceeding.

(c) At the request of a party or on its own motion an appellate court shall consider whether in the interests of justice it should direct that further proceedings be heard before a trial judge other than the judge whose judgment or order was reviewed by the appellate court. *(Added by Stats.1984, c. 1555, § 5. Amended by Stats.2002, c. 1094 (A.B.2504), § 1; Stats.2005, c. 332 (A.B.1322), § 1, eff. Sept. 22, 2005; Stats.2010, c. 686 (A.B.2487), § 1.)*

Research References

Rutter, Cal. Practice Guide: A.D.R. Ch. 3-C, C. Confidentiality.

Rutter, Cal. Practice Guide: A.D.R. Ch. 4-B, B. Judicial Arbitration.

Rutter, Cal. Practice Guide: A.D.R. Ch. 5-D, D. Defenses to Enforcement.

Rutter, Cal. Practice Guide: A.D.R. Ch. 5-G, G. Procedures to Enforce Arbitration.

Rutter, Cal. Practice Guide: A.D.R. Ch. 5-J, J. Challenging and Enforcing Arbitrator's Award in Court.

Rutter, Cal. Practice Guide: A.D.R. Ch. 6-B, B. Temporary Judges.

Rutter, Cal. Practice Guide: A.D.R. Ch. 7-A, A. Mediators.

Rutter, Cal. Practice Guide: A.D.R. Ch. 7-B, B. Arbitrators.

Rutter, Cal. Practice Guide: A.D.R. Ch. 7-C, C. Private Judges.

Rutter, Cal. Practice Guide: A.D.R. Ch. 7-D, D. Referees.

Rutter, Cal. Practice Guide: Civil Appeals & Writs Ch. 2-C, C. Nonappealable Orders.

Rutter, Cal. Practice Guide: Civil Appeals & Writs Ch. 14-C, C. Trial Court Proceedings After Reversal.

Rutter, Cal. Practice Guide: Civil Appeals & Writs Ch. 15-C, C. Statutory Writs.

Rutter, Cal. Practice Guide: Civil Appeals & Writs Ch. 16-A, A. Introduction.

Rutter, Cal. Practice Guide: Civ. Pro. Before Trial Ch. 13-A, A. Introduction.

Rutter, Cal. Practice Guide: Civ. Pro. Before Trial Ch. 13-D, D. the Arbitrator.

Rutter, Cal. Practice Guide: Civ. Pro. Before Trial Ch. 13-F, F. Arbitration Award.

Rutter, Cal. Practice Guide: Civ. Pro. Before Trial Ch. 9(I)-D, D. Hearing.

Rutter, Cal. Practice Guide: Civil Trials & Evidence Ch. 3-A, A. Challenges for Cause.

Rutter, Cal. Practice Guide: Civil Trials & Evidence Ch. 3-B, B. Peremptory Challenge of Judge (CCP § 170.6).

Rutter, Cal. Practice Guide: Civil Trials & Evidence Ch. 4-B, B. Preliminary Matters Discussed in Final Status Conference or In-Chambers Conference.

Rutter, Cal. Practice Guide: Civil Trials & Evidence Ch. 5-I, I. Challenging Prospective Jurors.

Rutter, Cal. Practice Guide: Civil Trials & Evidence Ch. 9-A, A. Preliminary Considerations.

Rutter, Cal. Practice Guide: Civil Trials & Evidence Ch. 12-A, A. Motion for Mistrial.

Rutter, Cal. Practice Guide: Civil Trials & Evidence Ch. 18-B, B. Motion for New Trial.

Rutter, Cal. Practice Guide: Civil Trials & Evidence Ch. 8C-A, A. Testimony.

California Practice Guide: Employment Litigation Ch. 18-F, F. Selecting the Neutral.

Rutter, Cal. Practice Guide: Insurance Litigation Ch. 15-C, C. Arbitration/Appraisal/Mediation.

Rutter, Cal. Practice Guide: Personal Injury Ch. 7-A, A. Introduction-Nature and Purpose of "Judicial Arbitration" in General.

Rutter, Cal. Practice Guide: Personal Injury Ch. 7-E, E. the Arbitrator.

Rutter, Cal. Practice Guide: Personal Injury Ch. 7-J, J. Arbitration of Uninsured Motorist Claims.

Rutter, Cal. Practice Guide: Personal Injury Ch. 9-A, A. Assignment to Trial.

Rutter, Cal. Practice Guide: Personal Injury Ch. 9-B, B. In-Chambers Conference Before Commencement of Trial.

Rutter, Cal. Practice Guide: Personal Injury Ch. 10-A, A. Motion for New Trial.

Rutter, Cal. Practice Guide: Prof. Responsibility Ch. 4-B, B. Concurrent Representation of Clients With Conflicting Interests (Conflicts Between Present Clients).

Rutter, Cal. Practice Guide: Prof. Responsibility Ch. 8-D, D. Restrictions on Speech and Behavior Outside Courtroom.

Rutter, Cal. Practice Guide: Prof. Responsibility Ch. 11-I, I. Trial Proceedings.

Miller and Starr California Real Estate § 35:7, --Mediator Impartiality, Conflicts of Interest, Disclosure, and Withdrawal.

Miller and Starr California Real Estate § 35:69, Arbitrator's Duty of Written Disclosure.

Miller and Starr California Real Estate § 35:70, Disqualification of the Arbitrator.

3 Witkin Cal. Proc. 5th Actions § 957, Disqualified Judge.

9 Witkin Cal. Proc. 5th Appeal § 883, in General.

1 Witkin Cal. Proc. 5th Attorneys § 567, (S 567) Disqualification of Judges.

2 Witkin Cal. Proc. 5th Courts § 57, (S 57) Conduct of Judicial Proceedings (Canon 3).

2 Witkin Cal. Proc. 5th Courts § 93, (S 93) in General.

2 Witkin Cal. Proc. 5th Courts § 98, Procedure.

2 Witkin Cal. Proc. 5th Courts § 102, (S 102) What Are Not Grounds.

2 Witkin Cal. Proc. 5th Courts § 103, Party to Proceeding.

2 Witkin Cal. Proc. 5th Courts § 104, Personal Knowledge of Facts.

2 Witkin Cal. Proc. 5th Courts § 105, (S 105) in General.

2 Witkin Cal. Proc. 5th Courts § 111, Relationship to Party or Attorney.

2 Witkin Cal. Proc. 5th Courts § 112, (S 112) in General.

2 Witkin Cal. Proc. 5th Courts § 118, (S 118) Current Statute.

2 Witkin Cal. Proc. 5th Courts § 119, Trial Judge During and After Appeal.

2 Witkin Cal. Proc. 5th Courts § 120, Physical Disability.

2 Witkin Cal. Proc. 5th Courts § 121, Dispute Resolution Conflict.

2 Witkin Cal. Proc. 5th Courts § 124, Judge's Consent or Answer.

2 Witkin Cal. Proc. 5th Courts § 160, (S 160) Statutory Procedure.

2 Witkin Cal. Proc. 5th Courts § 121A, (New)-Campaign Contribution.

6 Witkin Cal. Proc. 5th Proceedings Without Trial § 557, Statutory Requirements.

6 Witkin Cal. Proc. 5th Proceedings Without Trial § 591, Disqualification.

10 Witkin, California Summary 10th Parent and Child § 465, (S 465) Qualifications and Appointment.

§ 170.2. Circumstances not constituting grounds for disqualification

It shall not be grounds for disqualification that the judge:

(a) Is or is not a member of a racial, ethnic, religious, sexual or similar group and the proceeding involves the rights of such a group.

(b) Has in any capacity expressed a view on a legal or factual issue presented in the proceeding, except as provided in paragraph (2) of subdivision (a) of, or subdivision (b) or (c) of, Section 170.1.

(c) Has as a lawyer or public official participated in the drafting of laws or in the effort to pass or defeat laws, the meaning, effect or application of which is in issue in the proceeding unless the judge believes that his or her prior involvement was so well known as to raise a reasonable doubt in the public mind as to his or her capacity to be impartial. (*Added by Stats.1984, c. 1555, § 6.*)

Research References

Rutter, Cal. Practice Guide: Civil Trials & Evidence Ch. 3-A, A. Challenges for Cause.

Rutter, Cal. Practice Guide: Personal Injury Ch. 4-F, F. Court-Conducted Settlement Proceedings.

Miller and Starr California Real Estate § 35:70, Disqualification of the Arbitrator.

2 Witkin Cal. Proc. 5th Courts § 93, (S 93) in General.

2 Witkin Cal. Proc. 5th Courts § 102, (S 102) What Are Not Grounds.

§ 170.3. Proceedings; waiver; failure or refusal to withdraw

(a)(1) If a judge determines himself or herself to be disqualified, the judge shall notify the presiding judge of the court of his or her recusal and shall not further participate in the proceeding, except as provided in Section 170.4, unless his or her disqualification is waived by the parties as provided in subdivision (b).

(2) If the judge disqualifying himself or herself is the only judge or the presiding judge of the court, the notification shall be sent to the person having authority to assign another judge to replace the disqualified judge.

(b)(1) A judge who determines himself or herself to be disqualified after disclosing the basis for his or her disqualification on the record may ask the parties and their attorneys whether they wish to waive the disqualification, except where the basis for disqualification is as provided in paragraph (2). A waiver of disqualification shall recite the basis for the disqualification, and is effective only when signed by all parties and their attorneys and filed in the record.

(2) There shall be no waiver of disqualification if the basis therefor is either of the following:

(A) The judge has a personal bias or prejudice concerning a party.

(B) The judge served as an attorney in the matter in controversy, or the judge has been a material witness concerning that matter.

(3) The judge shall not seek to induce a waiver and shall avoid any effort to discover which lawyers or parties favored or opposed a waiver of disqualification.

(4) If grounds for disqualification are first learned of or arise after the judge has made one or more rulings in a proceeding, but before the judge has completed judicial action in a proceeding, the judge shall, unless the disqualification be waived, disqualify himself or herself, but in the absence of good cause the rulings he or she has made up to that time shall not be set aside by the judge who replaces the disqualified judge.

(c)(1) If a judge who should disqualify himself or herself refuses or fails to do so, any party may file with the clerk a written verified statement objecting to the hearing or trial before the judge and setting forth the facts constituting the grounds for disqualification of the judge. The statement shall be presented at the earliest practicable opportunity after discovery of the facts constituting the ground for disqualification. Copies of the statement shall be served on each party or his or her attorney who has appeared and shall be personally served on the judge alleged to be disqualified, or on his or her clerk, provided that the judge is present in the courthouse or in chambers.

(2) Without conceding his or her disqualification, a judge whose impartiality has been challenged by the filing of a written statement may request any other judge agreed upon by the parties to sit and act in his or her place.

(3) Within 10 days after the filing or service, whichever is later, the judge may file a consent to disqualification in which case the judge shall notify the presiding judge or the person authorized to appoint a replacement of his or her recusal as provided in subdivision (a), or the judge may file a written verified answer admitting or denying any or all of the allegations contained in the party's statement and setting forth any additional facts material or relevant to the question of disqualification. The clerk shall forthwith transmit a copy of the judge's answer to each party or his or her attorney who has appeared in the action.

(4) A judge who fails to file a consent or answer within the time allowed shall be deemed to have consented to his or her disqualification and the clerk shall notify the presiding judge or person authorized to appoint a replacement of the recusal as provided in subdivision (a).

(5) A judge who refuses to recuse himself or herself shall not pass upon his or her own disqualification or upon the sufficiency in law, fact, or otherwise, of the statement of disqualification filed by a party. In that case, the question of disqualification

shall be heard and determined by another judge agreed upon by all the parties who have appeared or, in the event they are unable to agree within five days of notification of the judge's answer, by a judge selected by the chairperson of the Judicial Council, or if the chairperson is unable to act, the vice chairperson. The clerk shall notify the executive officer of the Judicial Council of the need for a selection. The selection shall be made as expeditiously as possible. No challenge pursuant to this subdivision or Section 170.6 may be made against the judge selected to decide the question of disqualification.

(6) The judge deciding the question of disqualification may decide the question on the basis of the statement of disqualification and answer and any written arguments as the judge requests, or the judge may set the matter for hearing as promptly as practicable. If a hearing is ordered, the judge shall permit the parties and the judge alleged to be disqualified to argue the question of disqualification and shall for good cause shown hear evidence on any disputed issue of fact. If the judge deciding the question of disqualification determines that the judge is disqualified, the judge hearing the question shall notify the presiding judge or the person having authority to appoint a replacement of the disqualified judge as provided in subdivision (a).

(d) The determination of the question of the disqualification of a judge is not an appealable order and may be reviewed only by a writ of mandate from the appropriate court of appeal sought only by the parties to the proceeding. The petition for the writ shall be filed and served within 10 days after service of written notice of entry of the court's order determining the question of disqualification. If the notice of entry is served by mail, that time shall be extended as provided in subdivision (a) of Section 1013. *(Added by Stats.1984, c. 1555, § 7. Amended by Stats. 1990, c. 910 (S.B.2316), § 1; Stats.2006, c. 567 (A.B.2303), § 4.)*

Research References

Rutter, Cal. Practice Guide: A.D.R. Ch. 4-B, B. Judicial Arbitration.
Rutter, Cal. Practice Guide: A.D.R. Ch. 7-B, B. Arbitrators.
Rutter, Cal. Practice Guide: A.D.R. Ch. 7-C, C. Private Judges.
Rutter, Cal. Practice Guide: A.D.R. Ch. 7-D, D. Referees.
Rutter, Cal. Practice Guide: Civil Appeals & Writs Ch. 2-C, C. Nonappealable Orders.
Rutter, Cal. Practice Guide: Civil Appeals & Writs Ch. 15-C, C. Statutory Writs.
Rutter, Cal. Practice Guide: Civ. Pro. Before Trial Ch. 13-D, D. the Arbitrator.
Rutter, Cal. Practice Guide: Civ. Pro. Before Trial Ch. 9(I)-D, D. Hearing.
Rutter, Cal. Practice Guide: Civ. Pro. Before Trial Ch. 9(I)-D, Outline D.
Rutter, Cal. Practice Guide: Civil Trials & Evidence Ch. 3-A, A. Challenges for Cause.
Rutter, Cal. Practice Guide: Civil Trials & Evidence Ch. 3-B, B. Peremptory Challenge of Judge (CCP § 170.6).
California Practice Guide: Employment Litigation Ch. 19-T, T. Appeals.
Rutter, Cal. Practice Guide: Personal Injury Ch. 9-A, A. Assignment to Trial.
Rutter, Cal. Practice Guide: Personal Injury Ch. 10-A, A. Motion for New Trial.
Rutter, Cal. Practice Guide: Prof. Responsibility Ch. 4-B, B. Concurrent Representation of Clients With Conflicting Interests (Conflicts Between Present Clients).
9 Witkin Cal. Proc. 5th Appeal § 169, Miscellaneous Orders.
2 Witkin Cal. Proc. 5th Courts § 93, (S 93) in General.
2 Witkin Cal. Proc. 5th Courts § 98, Procedure.
2 Witkin Cal. Proc. 5th Courts § 122, Judge's Voluntary Declaration of Disqualification.
2 Witkin Cal. Proc. 5th Courts § 123, Party's Statement of Disqualification.
2 Witkin Cal. Proc. 5th Courts § 124, Judge's Consent or Answer.
2 Witkin Cal. Proc. 5th Courts § 125, Determination of Question of Disqualification.
2 Witkin Cal. Proc. 5th Courts § 127, (S 127) Powers of Disqualified Judge.
2 Witkin Cal. Proc. 5th Courts § 128, Waiver of Disqualification.

2 Witkin Cal. Proc. 5th Courts § 133, Motion Without Notice.
2 Witkin Cal. Proc. 5th Courts § 137, One Challenge in Any One Action.
2 Witkin Cal. Proc. 5th Courts § 160, (S 160) Statutory Procedure.
2 Witkin Cal. Proc. 5th Courts § 121A, (New)-Campaign Contribution.
8 Witkin Cal. Proc. 5th Extraordinary Writs § 167, Court or Board.
2 Witkin Cal. Proc. 5th Jurisdiction § 234, Peremptory Challenge of Judge.

§ 170.4. Powers of disqualified judges

(a) A disqualified judge, notwithstanding his or her disqualification may do any of the following:

(1) Take any action or issue any order necessary to maintain the jurisdiction of the court pending the assignment of a judge not disqualified.

(2) Request any other judge agreed upon by the parties to sit and act in his or her place.

(3) Hear and determine purely default matters.

(4) Issue an order for possession prior to judgment in eminent domain proceedings.

(5) Set proceedings for trial or hearing.

(6) Conduct settlement conferences.

(b) Notwithstanding paragraph (5) of subdivision (c) of Section 170.3, if a statement of disqualification is untimely filed or if on its face it discloses no legal grounds for disqualification, the trial judge against whom it was filed may order it stricken.

(c)(1) If a statement of disqualification is filed after a trial or hearing has commenced by the start of voir dire, by the swearing of the first witness or by the submission of a motion for decision, the judge whose impartiality has been questioned may order the trial or hearing to continue, notwithstanding the filing of the statement of disqualification. The issue of disqualification shall be referred to another judge for decision as provided in subdivision (a) of Section 170.3, and if it is determined that the judge is disqualified, all orders and rulings of the judge found to be disqualified made after the filing of the statement shall be vacated.

(2) For the purposes of this subdivision, if (A) a proceeding is filed in a single judge court or has been assigned to a single judge for comprehensive disposition, and (B) the proceeding has been set for trial or hearing 30 or more days in advance before a judge whose name was known at the time, the trial or hearing shall be deemed to have commenced 10 days prior to the date scheduled for trial or hearing as to any grounds for disqualification known before that time.

(3) A party may file no more than one statement of disqualification against a judge unless facts suggesting new grounds for disqualification are first learned of or arise after the first statement of disqualification was filed. Repetitive statements of disqualification not alleging facts suggesting new grounds for disqualification shall be stricken by the judge against whom they are filed.

(d) Except as provided in this section, a disqualified judge shall have no power to act in any proceeding after his or her disqualification or after the filing of a statement of disqualification until the question of his or her disqualification has been determined. *(Added by Stats.1984, c. 1555, § 8.)*

Research References

Rutter, Cal. Practice Guide: A.D.R. Ch. 7-C, C. Private Judges.
Rutter, Cal. Practice Guide: Civ. Pro. Before Trial Ch. 9(I)-D, D. Hearing.
Rutter, Cal. Practice Guide: Civil Trials & Evidence Ch. 3-A, A. Challenges for Cause.
Rutter, Cal. Practice Guide: Civil Trials & Evidence Ch. 3-B, B. Peremptory Challenge of Judge (CCP § 170.6).

Rutter, Cal. Practice Guide: Civil Trials & Evidence Ch. 12-A, A. Motion for Mistrial.

2 Witkin Cal. Proc. 5th Courts § 93, (S 93) in General.

2 Witkin Cal. Proc. 5th Courts § 94, Theory that Judgment is Void.

2 Witkin Cal. Proc. 5th Courts § 122, Judge's Voluntary Declaration of Disqualification.

2 Witkin Cal. Proc. 5th Courts § 124, Judge's Consent or Answer.

2 Witkin Cal. Proc. 5th Courts § 126, (S 126) General Rule: Limited Power to Act.

2 Witkin Cal. Proc. 5th Courts § 127, (S 127) Powers of Disqualified Judge.

§ 170.5. Definitions

For the purposes of Sections 170 to 170.5, inclusive, the following definitions apply:

(a) "Judge" means judges of the superior courts, and court commissioners and referees.

(b) "Financial interest" means ownership of more than a 1 percent legal or equitable interest in a party, or a legal or equitable interest in a party of a fair market value in excess of one thousand five hundred dollars ($1,500), or a relationship as director, advisor or other active participant in the affairs of a party, except as follows:

(1) Ownership in a mutual or common investment fund that holds securities is not a "financial interest" in those securities unless the judge participates in the management of the fund.

(2) An office in an educational, religious, charitable, fraternal, or civic organization is not a "financial interest" in securities held by the organization.

(3) The proprietary interest of a policyholder in a mutual insurance company, or a depositor in a mutual savings association, or a similar proprietary interest, is a "financial interest" in the organization only if the outcome of the proceeding could substantially affect the value of the interest.

(c) "Officer of a public agency" does not include a Member of the Legislature or a state or local agency official acting in a legislative capacity.

(d) The third degree of relationship shall be calculated according to the civil law system.

(e) "Private practice of law" includes a fee for service, retainer, or salaried representation of private clients or public agencies, but excludes lawyers as full-time employees of public agencies or lawyers working exclusively for legal aid offices, public defender offices, or similar nonprofit entities whose clientele is by law restricted to the indigent.

(f) "Proceeding" means the action, case, cause, motion, or special proceeding to be tried or heard by the judge.

(g) "Fiduciary" includes any executor, trustee, guardian, or administrator. *(Added by Stats.1984, c. 1555, § 9. Amended by Stats.1998, c. 931 (S.B.2139), § 47, eff. Sept. 28, 1998; Stats.2002, c. 784 (S.B.1316), § 35.)*

Law Revision Commission Comments

Section 170.5 is amended to reflect the elimination of the justice court. Cal. Const. art. VI, §§ 1, 5(b). [28 Cal.L.Rev.Comm. Reports 51 (1998)].

Subdivision (a) of Section 170.5 is amended to reflect unification of the municipal and superior courts pursuant to Article VI, Section 5(e), of the California Constitution. [32 Cal.L.Rev.Comm. Reports 99 (2002)].

Research References

Rutter, Cal. Practice Guide: A.D.R. Ch. 6-B, B. Temporary Judges.

Rutter, Cal. Practice Guide: A.D.R. Ch. 7-B, B. Arbitrators.

Rutter, Cal. Practice Guide: A.D.R. Ch. 7-D, D. Referees.

Rutter, Cal. Practice Guide: Civil Appeals & Writs Ch. 11-A, A. the Decisionmaking Process.

Rutter, Cal. Practice Guide: Civil Trials & Evidence Ch. 3-A, A. Challenges for Cause.

California Practice Guide: Employment Litigation Ch. 18-F, F. Selecting the Neutral.

Rutter, Cal. Practice Guide: Prof. Responsibility Ch. 8-D, D. Restrictions on Speech and Behavior Outside Courtroom.

8 Witkin Cal. Proc. 5th Attack Judgment Trial Court § 74, (S 74) Extensions.

2 Witkin Cal. Proc. 5th Courts § 93, (S 93) in General.

2 Witkin Cal. Proc. 5th Courts § 98, Procedure.

2 Witkin Cal. Proc. 5th Courts § 104, Personal Knowledge of Facts.

2 Witkin Cal. Proc. 5th Courts § 105, (S 105) in General.

2 Witkin Cal. Proc. 5th Courts § 111, Relationship to Party or Attorney.

2 Witkin Cal. Proc. 5th Courts § 112, (S 112) in General.

2 Witkin Cal. Proc. 5th Courts § 113, (S 113) Former Prosecutor or Public Defender.

2 Witkin Cal. Proc. 5th Courts § 129, Original Statute Unconstitutional.

§ 170.6. Prejudice against party, attorney or interest thereof; motion and affidavit; assignment of another judge, court commissioner or referee; number of motions; continuance; cumulative remedy; severability

(a)(1) A judge, court commissioner, or referee of a superior court of the State of California shall not try a civil or criminal action or special proceeding of any kind or character nor hear any matter therein that involves a contested issue of law or fact when it is established as provided in this section that the judge or court commissioner is prejudiced against a party or attorney or the interest of a party or attorney appearing in the action or proceeding.

(2) A party to, or an attorney appearing in, an action or proceeding may establish this prejudice by an oral or written motion without prior notice supported by affidavit or declaration under penalty of perjury, or an oral statement under oath, that the judge, court commissioner, or referee before whom the action or proceeding is pending, or to whom it is assigned, is prejudiced against a party or attorney, or the interest of the party or attorney, so that the party or attorney cannot, or believes that he or she cannot, have a fair and impartial trial or hearing before the judge, court commissioner, or referee. If the judge, other than a judge assigned to the case for all purposes, court commissioner, or referee assigned to, or who is scheduled to try, the cause or hear the matter is known at least 10 days before the date set for trial or hearing, the motion shall be made at least 5 days before that date. If directed to the trial of a cause with a master calendar, the motion shall be made to the judge supervising the master calendar not later than the time the cause is assigned for trial. If directed to the trial of a criminal cause that has been assigned to a judge for all purposes, the motion shall be made to the assigned judge or to the presiding judge by a party within 10 days after notice of the all purpose assignment, or if the party has not yet appeared in the action, then within 10 days after the appearance. If directed to the trial of a civil cause that has been assigned to a judge for all purposes, the motion shall be made to the assigned judge or to the presiding judge by a party within 15 days after notice of the all purpose assignment, or if the party has not yet appeared in the action, then within 15 days after the appearance. If the court in which the action is pending is authorized to have no more than one judge, and the motion claims that the duly elected or appointed judge of that court is prejudiced, the motion shall be made before the expiration of 30 days from the date of the first appearance in the action of the party who is making the motion or whose attorney is making the motion. In no event shall a judge, court commissioner, or referee entertain the motion if it is made after the drawing of the name of the first juror, or if there is no jury, after the making of an opening statement by counsel for plaintiff, or if there is no opening statement by counsel for plaintiff, then after swearing in the first witness or the giving of any evidence or after trial of the cause has otherwise commenced. If the motion is directed to a hearing, other than the trial of a cause, the motion shall be made not later than the commencement of the

hearing. In the case of trials or hearings not specifically provided for in this paragraph, the procedure specified herein shall be followed as nearly as possible. The fact that a judge, court commissioner, or referee has presided at, or acted in connection with, a pretrial conference or other hearing, proceeding, or motion prior to trial, and not involving a determination of contested fact issues relating to the merits, shall not preclude the later making of the motion provided for in this paragraph at the time and in the manner herein provided.

A motion under this paragraph may be made following reversal on appeal of a trial court's decision, or following reversal on appeal of a trial court's final judgment, if the trial judge in the prior proceeding is assigned to conduct a new trial on the matter. Notwithstanding paragraph (4), the party who filed the appeal that resulted in the reversal of a final judgment of a trial court may make a motion under this section regardless of whether that party or side has previously done so. The motion shall be made within 60 days after the party or the party's attorney has been notified of the assignment.

(3) A party to a civil action making that motion under this section shall serve notice on all parties no later than five days after making the motion.

(4) If the motion is duly presented, and the affidavit or declaration under penalty of perjury is duly filed or an oral statement under oath is duly made, thereupon and without any further act or proof, the judge supervising the master calendar, if any, shall assign some other judge, court commissioner, or referee to try the cause or hear the matter. In other cases, the trial of the cause or the hearing of the matter shall be assigned or transferred to another judge, court commissioner, or referee of the court in which the trial or matter is pending or, if there is no other judge, court commissioner, or referee of the court in which the trial or matter is pending, the Chair of the Judicial Council shall assign some other judge, court commissioner, or referee to try the cause or hear the matter as promptly as possible. Except as provided in this section, no party or attorney shall be permitted to make more than one such motion in any one action or special proceeding pursuant to this section. In actions or special proceedings where there may be more than one plaintiff or similar party or more than one defendant or similar party appearing in the action or special proceeding, only one motion for each side may be made in any one action or special proceeding.

(5) Unless required for the convenience of the court or unless good cause is shown, a continuance of the trial or hearing shall not be granted by reason of the making of a motion under this section. If a continuance is granted, the cause or matter shall be continued from day to day or for other limited periods upon the trial or other calendar and shall be reassigned or transferred for trial or hearing as promptly as possible.

(6) Any affidavit filed pursuant to this section shall be in substantially the following form:

(Here set forth court and cause)

State of California,   ss.   PEREMPTORY CHALLENGE
County of _____

_____, being duly sworn, deposes and says: That he or she is a party (or attorney for a party) to the within action (or special proceeding). That ____ the judge, court commissioner, or referee before whom the trial of the (or a hearing in the) action (or special proceeding) is pending (or to whom it is assigned) is prejudiced against the party (or his or her attorney) or the interest of the party (or his or her attorney) so that affiant cannot or believes that he or she cannot have a fair and impartial trial or hearing before the judge, court commissioner, or referee.

Subscribed and sworn to before me this

_____ day of _____, 20____.
(Clerk or notary public or other
officer administering oath)

(7) Any oral statement under oath or declaration under penalty of perjury made pursuant to this section shall include substantially the same contents as the affidavit above.

(b) Nothing in this section shall affect or limit Section 170 or Title 4 (commencing with Section 392) of Part 2, and this section shall be construed as cumulative thereto.

(c) If any provision of this section or the application to any person or circumstance is held invalid, that invalidity shall not affect other provisions or applications of the section that can be given effect without the invalid provision or application and, to this end, the provisions of this section are declared to be severable. *(Added by Stats.1957, c. 1055, p. 2288, § 1. Amended by Stats.1959, c. 640, p. 2620, § 1; Stats.1961, c. 526, p. 1628, § 1; Stats.1965, c. 1442, p. 3375, § 1; Stats.1967, c. 1602, p. 3832, § 2; Stats.1976, c. 1071, p. 4815, § 1; Stats.1981, c. 192, § 1; Stats.1982, c. 1644, p. 6682, § 2; Stats.1985, c. 715, § 1; Stats.1989, c. 537, § 1; Stats.1998, c. 167 (A.B.1199), § 1; Stats.2002, c. 784 (S.B.1316), § 36; Stats.2003, c. 62 (S.B.600), § 22; Stats.2010, c. 131 (A.B.1894), § 1.)*

Law Revision Commission Comments

Subdivision (1) of Section 170.6 is amended to reflect the elimination of the justice court. Cal. Const. art. VI, §§ 1, 5(b). [28 Cal.L.Rev.Comm. Reports 51 (1998)].

Subdivision (1) of Section 170.6 is amended to reflect unification of the municipal and superior courts pursuant to Article VI, Section 5(e), of the California Constitution. [32 Cal.L.Rev.Comm. Reports 100 (2002)].

Research References

Rutter, Cal. Practice Guide: A.D.R. Ch. 4-B, B. Judicial Arbitration.
Rutter, Cal. Practice Guide: A.D.R. Ch. 6-C, C. Referees.
Rutter, Cal. Practice Guide: A.D.R. Ch. 7-C, C. Private Judges.
Rutter, Cal. Practice Guide: A.D.R. Ch. 7-D, D. Referees.
Rutter, Cal. Practice Guide: Civil Appeals & Writs Ch. 2-C, C. Nonappealable Orders.
Rutter, Cal. Practice Guide: Civil Appeals & Writs Ch. 8-C, C. Standards of Appellate Review.
Rutter, Cal. Practice Guide: Civil Appeals & Writs Ch. 14-C, C. Trial Court Proceedings After Reversal.
Rutter, Cal. Practice Guide: Civil Appeals & Writs Ch. 15-C, C. Statutory Writs.
Rutter, Cal. Practice Guide: Civil Appeals & Writs Ch. 15-E, E. Procedures on Writ Review.
Rutter, Cal. Practice Guide: Civil Appeals & Writs Ch. 16-A, A. Introduction.
Rutter, Cal. Practice Guide: Civil Appeals & Writs Ch. 8-C, Outline C.
Rutter, Cal. Practice Guide: Civ. Pro. Before Trial Ch. 3-E, E. Federal vs. State Courts.
Rutter, Cal. Practice Guide: Civ. Pro. Before Trial Ch. 13-D, D. the Arbitrator.
Rutter, Cal. Practice Guide: Civ. Pro. Before Trial Ch. 9(I)-D, D. Hearing.
Rutter, Cal. Practice Guide: Civ. Pro. Before Trial Ch. 13-D, Outline D.
Rutter, Cal. Practice Guide: Civ. Pro. Before Trial Ch. 12(I)-B, B. Case Management ("Fast Track") System.
Rutter, Cal. Practice Guide: Civ. Pro. Before Trial Ch. 12(I)-E, E. Consolidation, Coordination and Bifurcation.
Rutter, Cal. Practice Guide: Civ. Pro. Before Trial Gen. Matls., Highlights.
Rutter, Cal. Practice Guide: Civ. Pro. Before Trial Ch. 12(II)-E, E. Motion to Determine "Good Faith" of "Piecemeal" Settlement (CCP § 877.6).
Rutter, Cal. Practice Guide: Civ. Pro. Before Trial Ch. 9(I)-D, Outline D.
Rutter, Cal. Practice Guide: Civil Trials & Evidence Ch. 1-A, A. Importance of Statewide and Local Rules of Court.
Rutter, Cal. Practice Guide: Civil Trials & Evidence Ch. 1-L, L. Assignment to Trial Department.
Rutter, Cal. Practice Guide: Civil Trials & Evidence Ch. 3-A, A. Challenges for Cause.

Rutter, Cal. Practice Guide: Civil Trials & Evidence Ch. 3-B, B. Peremptory Challenge of Judge (CCP § 170.6).

Rutter, Cal. Practice Guide: Civil Trials & Evidence Ch. 12-A, A. Motion for Mistrial.

Rutter, Cal. Practice Guide: Civil Trials & Evidence Ch. 16-E, E. Statement of Decision.

Rutter, Cal. Practice Guide: Civil Trials & Evidence Ch. 16-G, G. Trial by Reference.

Rutter, Cal. Practice Guide: Civil Trials & Evidence Gen. Matls., Highlights.

California Practice Guide: Employment Litigation Ch. 18-F, F. Selecting the Neutral.

Rutter, Cal. Practice Guide: Family Law Gen. Matls, Highlights.

Rutter, Cal. Practice Guide: Fed.Civ.Pro. Before Trial Ch. 1-D, D. Choosing Between State and Federal Courts.

Rutter, Cal. Practice Guide: Fed.Civ.Pro. Before Trial Ch. 16-D, D. Motion to Disqualify Judge.

Rutter, Cal. Practice Guide: Fed.Civ.Pro. Before Trial Ch. 2D-1, General Considerations.

Rutter, Cal. Practice Guide: Insurance Litigation Ch. 15-F, F. Pretrial Motions.

Rutter, Cal. Practice Guide: Insurance Litigation Ch. 15-F, Outline F.

Rutter, Cal. Practice Guide: Personal Injury Ch. 7-E, E. the Arbitrator.

Rutter, Cal. Practice Guide: Personal Injury Ch. 8-A, A. Case Management.

Rutter, Cal. Practice Guide: Personal Injury Ch. 8-B, B. After Trial Date Set (Three to Four Months Before Trial).

Rutter, Cal. Practice Guide: Personal Injury Ch. 9-A, A. Assignment to Trial.

Rutter, Cal. Practice Guide: Personal Injury Ch. 10-A, A. Motion for New Trial.

Rutter, Cal. Practice Guide: Personal Injury Ch. 10-B, B. Motion for Judgment Notwithstanding the Verdict.

Rutter, Cal. Practice Guide: Personal Injury Ch. 8-B, Outline B.

Rutter, Cal. Practice Guide: Personal Injury Ch. 9-A, Outline a.

Rutter, Cal. Practice Guide: Personal Injury Gen. Matls., Highlights.

Rutter, Cal. Practice Guide: Real Prop. Transactions Form 4:H, (Attorney-Drafted) Purchase and Sale Agreement and Joint Escrow Instructions.

Rutter, Cal. Practice Guide: Prof. Responsibility Ch. 11-I, I. Trial Proceedings.

8 Witkin Cal. Proc. 5th Attack Judgment Trial Court § 74, (S 74) Extensions.

2 Witkin Cal. Proc. 5th Courts § 93, (S 93) in General.

2 Witkin Cal. Proc. 5th Courts § 125, Determination of Question of Disqualification.

2 Witkin Cal. Proc. 5th Courts § 131, Constitutionality Reaffirmed.

2 Witkin Cal. Proc. 5th Courts § 132, (S 132) Scope: Courts and Proceedings.

2 Witkin Cal. Proc. 5th Courts § 133, Motion Without Notice.

2 Witkin Cal. Proc. 5th Courts § 134, Automatic Reassignment.

2 Witkin Cal. Proc. 5th Courts § 135, in General.

2 Witkin Cal. Proc. 5th Courts § 136, Challenge by Cross-Defendant.

2 Witkin Cal. Proc. 5th Courts § 137, One Challenge in Any One Action.

2 Witkin Cal. Proc. 5th Courts § 138, One Challenge for Each Side.

2 Witkin Cal. Proc. 5th Courts § 140, (S 140) General Rule and Limitations.

2 Witkin Cal. Proc. 5th Courts § 141, (S 141) Before Commencement.

2 Witkin Cal. Proc. 5th Courts § 142, 10-Day/5-Day Rule.

2 Witkin Cal. Proc. 5th Courts § 143, Effect of Assignment to Department.

2 Witkin Cal. Proc. 5th Courts § 144, Case Law Development.

2 Witkin Cal. Proc. 5th Courts § 145, Exception: Local Delay Reduction Rule.

2 Witkin Cal. Proc. 5th Courts § 146, Codification.

2 Witkin Cal. Proc. 5th Courts § 147, in General.

2 Witkin Cal. Proc. 5th Courts § 148, What Constitutes All Purpose Assignment.

2 Witkin Cal. Proc. 5th Courts § 149, (S 149) One-Judge Court.

2 Witkin Cal. Proc. 5th Courts § 150, (S 150) Coordination Judge.

2 Witkin Cal. Proc. 5th Courts § 151, (S 151) New Trial After Reversal.

2 Witkin Cal. Proc. 5th Courts § 152, (S 152) General Rule.

2 Witkin Cal. Proc. 5th Courts § 156, (S 156) Distinction: Prior Action Not on Merits.

2 Witkin Cal. Proc. 5th Courts § 159, (S 159) Case Law Development.

2 Witkin Cal. Proc. 5th Courts § 160, (S 160) Statutory Procedure.

2 Witkin Cal. Proc. 5th Courts § 257, (S 257) Nature and Scope.

2 Witkin Cal. Proc. 5th Courts § 262, Minimum Time Standards.

2 Witkin Cal. Proc. 5th Courts § 355, Distinction: Status as Party Litigant is Not Relinquished.

8 Witkin Cal. Proc. 5th Extraordinary Writs § 66, Excess of Jurisdiction.

8 Witkin Cal. Proc. 5th Extraordinary Writs § 244, (S 244) Invalid Injunction.

2 Witkin Cal. Proc. 5th Jurisdiction § 210, Motions.

2 Witkin Cal. Proc. 5th Jurisdiction § 234, Peremptory Challenge of Judge.

4 Witkin Cal. Proc. 5th Pleading § 355, (S 355) Peremptory Challenge of Assigned Judge.

6 Witkin Cal. Proc. 5th Proceedings Without Trial § 53, (S 53) Reconsideration by Different Judge.

6 Witkin Cal. Proc. 5th Proceedings Without Trial § 70, (S 70) Objection to Referee.

6 Witkin Cal. Proc. 5th Proceedings Without Trial § 402, No Courtroom or Judge.

6 Witkin Cal. Proc. 5th Proceedings Without Trial § 591, Disqualification.

10 Witkin, California Summary 10th Parent and Child § 364, Jurisdictional Problems.

10 Witkin, California Summary 10th Parent and Child § 465, (S 465) Qualifications and Appointment.

10 Witkin, California Summary 10th Parent and Child § 773, Form and Content.

10 Witkin, California Summary 10th Parent and Child § 779, Citation.

10 Witkin, California Summary 10th Parent and Child § 815, (S 815) Participation by District Attorney.

10 Witkin, California Summary 10th Parent and Child § 816, (S 816) Impartial Judge or Referee.

10 Witkin, California Summary 10th Parent and Child § 891, Deferred Entry of Judgment.

10 Witkin, California Summary 10th Parent and Child § 907, Nature and Purpose.

§ 170.7. Judge serving on appellate division; application of § 170.6

Section 170.6 does not apply to a judge designated or assigned to serve on the appellate division of a superior court in the judge's capacity as a judge of that division. *(Added by Stats.1963, c. 872, p. 2120, § 1. Amended by Stats.1998, c. 931 (S.B.2139), § 48, eff. Sept. 28, 1998.)*

Law Revision Commission Comments

Section 170.7 is amended to refer more precisely to the appellate division. See Cal. Const. art. VI, § 4. [28 Cal.L.Rev.Comm. Reports 51 (1998)].

Research References

Rutter, Cal. Practice Guide: Civil Appeals & Writs Ch. 16-A, A. Introduction.

2 Witkin Cal. Proc. 5th Courts § 132, (S 132) Scope: Courts and Proceedings.

§ 170.8. No qualified judge; assignment of judge

When there is no judge of a court qualified to hear an action or proceeding, the clerk shall forthwith notify the Chairman of the Judicial Council of that fact. The judge assigned by the Chairman of the Judicial Council shall hear the action or proceeding at the time fixed therefor or, if no time has been fixed or good cause appears for changing the time theretofore fixed, the judge shall fix a time for hearing in accordance with law and rules and hear the action or proceeding at the time so fixed. *(Added by Stats.1963, c. 872, p. 2120, § 2. Amended by Stats.1989, c. 1417, § 2.)*

Research References

2 Witkin Cal. Proc. 5th Courts § 134, Automatic Reassignment.

§ 170.9. Acceptance of gifts; value limit; exceptions; adjustments; travel expenses

(a) A judge shall not accept gifts from a single source in a calendar year with a total value of more than two hundred fifty dollars ($250). This section shall not be construed to authorize the receipt of gifts that would otherwise be prohibited by the Code of Judicial Ethics adopted by the California Supreme Court or any other law.

(b) This section shall not prohibit or limit the following:

(1) Payments, advances, or reimbursements for travel and related lodging and subsistence permitted by subdivision (e).

(2) Wedding gifts and gifts exchanged between individuals on birthdays, holidays, and other similar occasions, if the gifts exchanged are not substantially disproportionate in value.

(3) A gift, bequest, favor, or loan from a person whose preexisting relationship with a judge would prevent the judge from hearing a case involving that person, under the Code of Judicial Ethics adopted by the California Supreme Court.

(c) For purposes of this section, "judge" includes all of the following:

(1) Judges of the superior courts.

(2) Justices of the courts of appeal and the Supreme Court.

(3) Subordinate judicial officers, as defined in Section 71601 of the Government Code.

(d) The gift limitation amounts in this section shall be adjusted biennially by the Commission on Judicial Performance to reflect changes in the Consumer Price Index, rounded to the nearest ten dollars ($10).

(e) Payments, advances, or reimbursements for travel, including actual transportation and related lodging and subsistence that is reasonably related to a judicial or governmental purpose, or to an issue of state, national, or international public policy, are not prohibited or limited by this section if any of the following apply:

(1) The travel is in connection with a speech, practice demonstration, or group or panel discussion given or participated in by the judge, the lodging and subsistence expenses are limited to the day immediately preceding, the day of, and the day immediately following the speech, demonstration, or discussion, and the travel is within the United States.

(2) The travel is provided by a government, a governmental agency or authority, a foreign government, a foreign bar association, an international service organization, a bona fide public or private educational institution, as defined in Section 203 of the Revenue and Taxation Code, or a nonprofit charitable or religious organization that is exempt from taxation under Section 501(c)(3) of the Internal Revenue Code [1], or by a person domiciled outside the United States who substantially satisfies the requirements for tax-exempt status under Section 501(c)(3) of the Internal Revenue Code.

For purposes of this section, "foreign bar association" means an association of attorneys located outside the United States (A) that performs functions substantially equivalent to those performed by state or local bar associations in this state and (B) that permits membership by attorneys in that country representing various legal specialties and does not limit membership to attorneys generally representing one side or another in litigation. "International service organization" means a bona fide international service organization of which the judge is a member. A judge who accepts travel payments from an international service organization pursuant to this subdivision shall not preside over or participate in decisions affecting that organization, its state or local chapters, or its local members.

(3) The travel is provided by a state or local bar association or judges professional association in connection with testimony before a governmental body or attendance at any professional function hosted by the bar association or judges professional association, the lodging and subsistence expenses are limited to the day immediately preceding, the day of, and the day immediately following the professional function.

(f) Payments, advances, and reimbursements for travel not described in subdivision (e) are subject to the limit in subdivision (a).

(g) No judge shall accept any honorarium.

(h) "Honorarium" means a payment made in consideration for any speech given, article published, or attendance at a public or private conference, convention, meeting, social event, meal, or like gathering.

(i) "Honorarium" does not include earned income for personal services that are customarily provided in connection with the practice of a bona fide business, trade, or profession, such as teaching or writing for a publisher, and does not include fees or other things of value received pursuant to Section 94.5 of the Penal Code for performance of a marriage.

For purposes of this section, "teaching" shall include presentations to impart educational information to lawyers in events qualifying for credit under mandatory continuing legal education, to students in bona fide educational institutions, and to associations or groups of judges.

(j) Subdivisions (a) and (e) shall apply to all payments, advances, and reimbursements for travel and related lodging and subsistence.

(k) This section does not apply to any honorarium that is not used and, within 30 days after receipt, is either returned to the donor or delivered to the Controller for deposit in the General Fund without being claimed as a deduction from income for tax purposes.

(l) "Gift" means a payment to the extent that consideration of equal or greater value is not received and includes a rebate or discount in the price of anything of value unless the rebate or discount is made in the regular course of business to members of the public without regard to official status. A person, other than a defendant in a criminal action, who claims that a payment is not a gift by reason of receipt of consideration has the burden of proving that the consideration received is of equal or greater value. However, the term "gift" does not include any of the following:

(1) Informational material such as books, reports, pamphlets, calendars, periodicals, cassettes and discs, or free or reduced-price admission, tuition, or registration, for informational conferences or seminars. No payment for travel or reimbursement for any expenses shall be deemed "informational material."

(2) Gifts that are not used and, within 30 days after receipt, are returned to the donor or delivered to a charitable organization without being claimed as a charitable contribution for tax purposes.

(3) Gifts from a judge's spouse, child, parent, grandparent, grandchild, brother, sister, parent-in-law, brother-in-law, sister-in-law, nephew, niece, aunt, uncle, or first cousin or the spouse of any such person. However, a gift from any of those persons shall be considered a gift if the donor is acting as an agent or intermediary for a person not covered by this paragraph.

(4) Campaign contributions required to be reported under Chapter 4 (commencing with Section 84100) of Title 9 of the Government Code.

(5) Any devise or inheritance.

(6) Personalized plaques and trophies with an individual value of less than two hundred fifty dollars ($250).

(7) Admission to events hosted by state or local bar associations or judges professional associations, and provision of related food and beverages at those events, when attendance does not require "travel," as described in paragraph (3) of subdivision (e).

(m) The Commission on Judicial Performance shall enforce the prohibitions of this section with regard to judges of the superior courts and justices of the courts of appeal and the Supreme Court. With regard to subordinate judicial officers, consistent with Section 18.1 of Article VI of the California Constitution, the court employing the subordinate judicial officer shall exercise initial jurisdiction to enforce the prohibitions of this section, and the Commission on Judicial Performance shall exercise discretionary jurisdiction with respect to the enforcement of the prohibitions of this section. *(Added by Stats.1994, c. 1238 (A.B.3638), § 1. Amended by Stats.1995, c. 378 (S.B.353), § 1; Stats.1996, c. 557 (S.B.1589), § 1; Stats.2002, c. 784 (S.B.1316), § 37; Stats.2010, c. 206 (A.B.2116), § 1; Stats.2011, c. 296 (A.B.1023), § 36.)*

1 Internal Revenue Code sections are in Title 26 of the U.S.C.A.

Law Revision Commission Comments

Subdivision (c) of Section 170.9 is amended to reflect unification of the municipal and superior courts pursuant to Article VI, Section 5(e), of the California Constitution. [32 Cal.L.Rev.Comm. Reports 103 (2002)].

Research References

Rutter, Cal. Practice Guide: A.D.R. Ch. 7-B, B. Arbitrators.
2 Witkin Cal. Proc. 5th Courts § 64, (S 64) Gratuities for Solemnizing Marriages.
2 Witkin Cal. Proc. 5th Courts § 65, (S 65) Gifts, Honoraria, and Travel Expenses.

CHAPTER 4. INCIDENTAL POWERS AND DUTIES OF JUDICIAL OFFICERS

§ 177. Conduct of proceedings

Every judicial officer shall have power:

1. To preserve and enforce order in his immediate presence, and in proceedings before him, when he is engaged in the performance of official duty;

2. To compel obedience to his lawful orders as provided in this Code;

3. To compel the attendance of persons to testify in a proceeding before him, in the cases and manner provided in this Code;

4. To administer oaths to persons in a proceeding pending before him, and in all other cases where it may be necessary in the exercise of his powers and duties. *(Enacted in 1872. Amended by Code Am.1880, c. 35, p. 42, § 1.)*

Research References

Rutter, Cal. Practice Guide: Enforcing Judgments/Debts Ch. 6A-1, Jurisdiction to Enforce Judgments.
Rutter, Cal. Practice Guide: Personal Injury Ch. 9-B, B. In-Chambers Conference Before Commencement of Trial.
2 Witkin Cal. Proc. 5th Courts § 174, (S 174) What Courts May Exercise Inherent Powers.
2 Witkin Cal. Proc. 5th Courts § 175, (S 175) Illustrations.

§ 177.5. Money sanctions

A judicial officer shall have the power to impose reasonable money sanctions, not to exceed fifteen hundred dollars ($1,500), notwithstanding any other provision of law, payable to the court, for any violation of a lawful court order by a person, done

without good cause or substantial justification. This power shall not apply to advocacy of counsel before the court. For the purposes of this section, the term "person" includes a witness, a party, a party's attorney, or both.

Sanctions pursuant to this section shall not be imposed except on notice contained in a party's moving or responding papers; or on the court's own motion, after notice and opportunity to be heard. An order imposing sanctions shall be in writing and shall recite in detail the conduct or circumstances justifying the order. *(Added by Stats.1982, c. 1564, p. 6173, § 1. Amended by Stats.2005, c. 75 (A.B.145), § 27, eff. July 19, 2005, operative Jan. 1, 2006.)*

Research References

Rutter, Cal. Practice Guide: A.D.R. Ch. 4-B, B. Judicial Arbitration.
Rutter, Cal. Practice Guide: A.D.R. Ch. 6-B, B. Temporary Judges.
Rutter, Cal. Practice Guide: Civil Appeals & Writs Ch. 8-C, C. Standards of Appellate Review.
Rutter, Cal. Practice Guide: Civ. Pro. Before Trial Ch. 3-D, D. Venue.
Rutter, Cal. Practice Guide: Civ. Pro. Before Trial Ch. 11-A, A. Voluntary Dismissals.
Rutter, Cal. Practice Guide: Civ. Pro. Before Trial Ch. 13-E, E. the Arbitration Hearing.
Rutter, Cal. Practice Guide: Civ. Pro. Before Trial Ch. 8F-8, Sanctions in Enforcing Discovery.
Rutter, Cal. Practice Guide: Civ. Pro. Before Trial Ch. 8E-16, Sanctions Re Depositions.
Rutter, Cal. Practice Guide: Civ. Pro. Before Trial Ch. 12(I)-B, B. Case Management ("Fast Track") System.
Rutter, Cal. Practice Guide: Civ. Pro. Before Trial Gen. Matls., Highlights.
Rutter, Cal. Practice Guide: Civ. Pro. Before Trial Ch. 9(III)-A, A. Sources of Sanctions Power.
Rutter, Cal. Practice Guide: Civ. Pro. Before Trial Ch. 9(III)-D, D. Other Sanctions Statutes and Rules.
Rutter, Cal. Practice Guide: Civ. Pro. Before Trial Ch. 9(III)-D, Outline D.
Rutter, Cal. Practice Guide: Prof. Responsibility Ch. 1-A, A. Sources of Regulation of Practice of Law in California-Overview.
Rutter, Cal. Practice Guide: Prof. Responsibility Ch. 8-D, D. Restrictions on Speech and Behavior Outside Courtroom.
Rutter, Cal. Practice Guide: Prof. Responsibility Ch. 8-E, E. Consequences of Improper Advocacy.
Miller and Starr California Real Estate § 34:66, Examples of Actions in Which Fees Can be Recovered.
2 Witkin Cal. Proc. 5th Courts § 177, (S 177) Imposition of Money Sanctions.
2 Witkin Cal. Proc. 5th Courts § 264, in General.
6 Witkin Cal. Proc. 5th Proceedings Without Trial § 55, (S 55) Statutory Authorization.
7 Witkin Cal. Proc. 5th Trial § 58, (S 58) in General.
7 Witkin Cal. Proc. 5th Trial § 59, (S 59) Judicial Council Rules.
7 Witkin Cal. Proc. 5th Trial § 226, (S 226) in General.
7 Witkin Cal. Proc. 5th Trial § 228, Who May Recover Sanctions.

§ 178. Punishment for contempt

For the effectual exercise of the powers conferred by the last section, a judicial officer may punish for contempt in the cases provided in this Code. *(Enacted in 1872. Amended by Code Am.1880, c. 35, p. 42, § 1.)*

Research References

2 Witkin Cal. Proc. 5th Courts § 175, (S 175) Illustrations.
7 Witkin Cal. Proc. 5th Trial § 171, (S 171) Statutory Framework.

§ 179. Taking and certifying acknowledgments, affidavits or depositions

Each of the justices of the Supreme Court and of any court of appeal and the judges of the superior courts, shall have power in any part of the state to take and certify:

(a) The proof and acknowledgment of a conveyance of real property, or of any other written instrument.

(b) The acknowledgment of satisfaction of a judgment of any court.

(c) An affidavit or deposition to be used in this state. *(Enacted in 1872. Amended by Code Am.1880, c. 35, p. 42, § 1; Stats.1933, c. 743, p. 1831, § 49; Stats.1953, c. 457, p. 1701, § 4; Stats.1967, c. 17, p. 828, § 11; Stats.1998, c. 931 (S.B.2139), § 49, eff. Sept. 28, 1998; Stats.2002, c. 784 (S.B.1316), § 38; Stats.2003, c. 62 (S.B.600), § 23.)*

Law Revision Commission Comments

Section 179 is amended to reflect the elimination of the justice court. Cal. Const. art. VI, §§ 1, 5(b). [28 Cal.L.Rev.Comm. Reports 51 (1998)].

Section 179 is amended to reflect unification of the municipal and superior courts pursuant to Article VI, Section 5(e), of the California Constitution. [32 Cal.L.Rev.Comm. Reports 107 (2002)].

Research References

Miller and Starr California Real Estate § 11:24, Qualifying Officers.
2 Witkin Cal. Proc. 5th Courts § 175, (S 175) Illustrations.
12 Witkin, California Summary 10th Real Property § 288, (S 288) in General.

CHAPTER 5. MISCELLANEOUS PROVISIONS RESPECTING COURTS OF JUSTICE

Section
182.   Effect of chapter heading.
184.   Vacancies; effect upon proceedings.
185.   Proceedings in English; translations of court orders and court order forms.
186.   Abbreviations and numbers.
187.   Jurisdiction; means to carry into effect; mode of proceeding.

§ 182.   Effect of chapter heading

The heading to this chapter shall not be deemed to govern or limit the scope or meaning of this chapter. *(Added by Stats.1955, c. 59, p. 499, § 4.)*

§ 184.   Vacancies; effect upon proceedings

No proceeding in any court of justice, in an action or special proceeding pending therein, shall be affected by a vacancy in the office of all or any of the judges or justices thereof. *(Enacted in 1872. Amended by Code Am.1880, c. 35, p. 43, § 1; Stats.1933, c. 743, p. 1831, § 51.)*

Research References

2 Witkin Cal. Proc. 5th Courts § 18, What Successor Cannot Do.

§ 185.   Proceedings in English; translations of court orders and court order forms

(a) Every written proceeding in a court of justice in this state shall be in the English language, and judicial proceedings shall be conducted, preserved, and published in no other. Nothing in this section shall prohibit a court from providing an unofficial translation of a court order issued pursuant to Section 527.6 or 527.8 of the Code of Civil Procedure, or Part 1 (commencing with Section 6200) of Division 10 of the Family Code, or Section 136.2 of the Penal Code, in a language other than English.

(b) The Judicial Council shall, by July 1, 2001, make available to all courts, translations of domestic violence protective order forms in languages other than English, as the Judicial Council deems appropriate, for protective orders issued pursuant to Section 527.6 or 527.8 of the Code of Civil Procedure, or Part 1 (commencing with Section 6200) of Division 10 of the Family Code, or Section 136.2 of the Penal Code. *(Enacted in 1872.*

Amended by Code Am.1880, c. 35, p. 43, § 1; Stats.1999, c. 662 (S.B.218), § 1.)

Research References

2 Witkin Cal. Proc. 5th Courts § 29, (S 29) Use of English.

§ 186.   Abbreviations and numbers

Such abbreviations as are in common use may be used, and numbers may be expressed by figures or numerals in the customary manner. *(Enacted in 1872. Amended by Code Am.1880, c. 35, p. 43, § 1.)*

§ 187.   Jurisdiction; means to carry into effect; mode of proceeding

When jurisdiction is, by the Constitution or this Code, or by any other statute, conferred on a Court or judicial officer, all the means necessary to carry it into effect are also given; and in the exercise of this jurisdiction, if the course of proceeding be not specifically pointed out by this Code or the statute, any suitable process or mode of proceeding may be adopted which may appear most conformable to the spirit of this code. *(Enacted in 1872. Amended by Code Am.1880, c. 35, p. 43, § 1.)*

Research References

Rutter, Cal. Practice Guide: Civil Appeals & Writs Ch. 5-B, B. Types of Motions, Applications and Requests.
Rutter, Cal. Practice Guide: Civ. Pro. Before Trial Ch. 6-B, B. Complaints.
Rutter, Cal. Practice Guide: Civ. Pro. Before Trial Ch. 12(I)-B, B. Case Management ("Fast Track") System.
Rutter, Cal. Practice Guide: Civ. Pro. Before Trial Gen. Matls., Highlights.
Rutter, Cal. Practice Guide: Civil Trials & Evidence Ch. 18-C, C. Other Post-Trial Motions.
Rutter, Cal. Practice Guide: Enforcing Judgments/Debts Ch. 6G-7, Charging Orders Against Debtor Partnership/LLC Interests.
Rutter, Cal. Practice Guide: Enforcing Judgments/Debts Ch. 6A-1, Jurisdiction to Enforce Judgments.
Rutter, Cal. Practice Guide: Enforcing Judgments/Debts Ch. 6G-14, Amending Judgment to Change Name of Judgment Debtor.
Rutter, Cal. Practice Guide: Enforcing Judgments/Debts Ch. 6G-15, Amending Judgment to Add Nonparty Alter Egos as Judgment Debtors.
Rutter, Cal. Practice Guide: Enforcing Judgments/Debts Ch. 6G-16, Amending Judgment to Add Third Party (Not Alter Ego).
Rutter, Cal. Practice Guide: Enforcing Judgments/Debts Gen. Matls., Highlights.
Miller and Starr California Real Estate § 35:5, --Voluntary Participation and Self Determination in Mediations.
3 Witkin Cal. Proc. 5th Actions § 3, Statutory Declarations.
3 Witkin Cal. Proc. 5th Actions § 6, Illustrations.
3 Witkin Cal. Proc. 5th Actions § 7, Exceptions.
3 Witkin Cal. Proc. 5th Actions § 1007, (S 1007) Method Devised by Court.
2 Witkin Cal. Proc. 5th Courts § 98, Procedure.
2 Witkin Cal. Proc. 5th Courts § 175, (S 175) Illustrations.
2 Witkin Cal. Proc. 5th Courts § 185, Nature of Power.
2 Witkin Cal. Proc. 5th Courts § 201, (S 201) Local Policy.
2 Witkin Cal. Proc. 5th Courts § 239, in General.
2 Witkin Cal. Proc. 5th Courts § 303, (S 303) Enforcement and Stay.
6 Witkin Cal. Proc. 5th Proceedings Without Trial § 258, (S 258) Amendment.
7 Witkin Cal. Proc. 5th Trial § 58, (S 58) in General.
7 Witkin Cal. Proc. 5th Trial § 226, (S 226) in General.
10 Witkin, California Summary 10th Parent and Child § 839, Determination of Present Competency.

Title 3

PERSONS SPECIALLY INVESTED WITH POWERS OF A JUDICIAL NATURE

CHAPTER 1. TRIAL JURY SELECTION AND MANAGEMENT ACT

§ 190. Citation

This chapter shall be known and may be cited as the Trial Jury Selection and Management Act. *(Added by Stats.1988, c. 1245, § 2.)*

Research References

7 Witkin Cal. Proc. 5th Trial § 116, Adoption of Uniform System.

§ 191. State policy; random selection; opportunity and obligation to serve

The Legislature recognizes that trial by jury is a cherished constitutional right, and that jury service is an obligation of citizenship.

It is the policy of the State of California that all persons selected for jury service shall be selected at random from the population of the area served by the court; that all qualified persons have an equal opportunity, in accordance with this chapter, to be considered for jury service in the state and an obligation to serve as jurors when summoned for that purpose; and that it is the responsibility of jury commissioners to manage all jury systems in an efficient, equitable, and cost-effective manner, in accordance with this chapter. *(Added by Stats.1988, c. 1245, § 2.)*

Research References

Rutter, Cal. Practice Guide: Civil Trials & Evidence Ch. 5-A, A. Obtaining Prospective Jurors.
7 Witkin Cal. Proc. 5th Trial § 116, Adoption of Uniform System.
7 Witkin Cal. Proc. 5th Trial § 118, Selection.

§ 192. Application of chapter

This chapter applies to the selection of jurors, and the formation of trial juries, for both civil and criminal cases, in all trial courts of the state. *(Added by Stats.1988, c. 1245, § 2.)*

Research References

7 Witkin Cal. Proc. 5th Trial § 116, Adoption of Uniform System.

§ 193. Kinds of juries

Juries are of three kinds:

(a) Grand juries established pursuant to Title 4 (commencing with Section 888) of Part 2 of the Penal Code.

(b) Trial juries.

(c) Juries of inquest. *(Added by Stats.1988, c. 1245, § 2.)*

§ 194. Definitions

The following definitions govern the construction of this chapter:

(a) "County" means any county or any coterminous city and county.

(b) "Court" means a superior court of this state, and includes, when the context requires, any judge of the court.

(c) "Deferred jurors" are those prospective jurors whose request to reschedule their service to a more convenient time is granted by the jury commissioner.

(d) "Excused jurors" are those prospective jurors who are excused from service by the jury commissioner for valid reasons based on statute, state or local court rules, and policies.

(e) "Juror pool" means the group of prospective qualified jurors appearing for assignment to trial jury panels.

(f) "Jury of inquest" is a body of persons summoned from the citizens before the sheriff, coroner, or other ministerial officers, to inquire of particular facts.

(g) "Master list" means a list of names randomly selected from the source lists.

(h) "Potential juror" means any person whose name appears on a source list.

(i) "Prospective juror" means a juror whose name appears on the master list.

(j) "Qualified juror" means a person who meets the statutory qualifications for jury service.

(k) "Qualified juror list" means a list of qualified jurors.

(*l*) "Random" means that which occurs by mere chance indicating an unplanned sequence of selection where each juror's name has substantially equal probability of being selected.

(m) "Source list" means a list used as a source of potential jurors.

(n) "Summons list" means a list of prospective or qualified jurors who are summoned to appear or to be available for jury service.

(o) "Trial jurors" are those jurors sworn to try and determine by verdict a question of fact.

(p) "Trial jury" means a body of persons selected from the citizens of the area served by the court and sworn to try and determine by verdict a question of fact.

(q) "Trial jury panel" means a group of prospective jurors assigned to a courtroom for the purpose of voir dire. *(Added by Stats.1988, c. 1245, § 2. Amended by Stats.1998, c. 931 (S.B. 2139), § 50, eff. Sept. 28, 1998; Stats.2002, c. 784 (S.B.1316), § 39.)*

Law Revision Commission Comments

Subdivision (b) of Section 194 is amended to reflect the elimination of the justice court. Cal. Const. art. VI, §§ 1, 5(b). [28 Cal.L.Rev.Comm. Reports 51 (1998)].

Subdivision (b) of Section 194 is amended to reflect unification of the municipal and superior courts pursuant to Article VI, Section 5(e), of the California Constitution. [32 Cal.L.Rev.Comm. Reports 107 (2002)].

Research References

Rutter, Cal. Practice Guide: Civil Trials & Evidence Ch. 2-B, B. What Constitutes Jury Trial.

Rutter, Cal. Practice Guide: Civil Trials & Evidence Ch. 5-A, A. Obtaining Prospective Jurors.

7 Witkin Cal. Proc. 5th Trial § 116, Adoption of Uniform System.

7 Witkin Cal. Proc. 5th Trial § 117, Types of Lists.

7 Witkin Cal. Proc. 5th Trial § 118, Selection.

7 Witkin Cal. Proc. 5th Trial § 120, Ordinary Panel.

§ 195. Jury commissioners; appointment; term; ex officio commissioners; clerk/administrators; salaries; duties

(a) In each county, there shall be one jury commissioner who shall be appointed by, and serve at the pleasure of, a majority of the judges of the superior court. In any county where there is a superior court administrator or executive officer, that person shall serve as ex officio jury commissioner. In any court jurisdiction where any person other than a court administrator or clerk/administrator is serving as jury commissioner on the effective date of this section, that person shall continue to so serve at the pleasure of a majority of the judges of the appointing court.

(b) Any jury commissioner may, whenever the business of court requires, appoint deputy jury commissioners. Salaries and benefits of those deputies shall be fixed in the same manner as salaries and benefits of other court employees.

(c) The jury commissioner shall be primarily responsible for managing the jury system under the general supervision of the court in conformance with the purpose and scope of this act. He or she shall have authority to establish policies and procedures necessary to fulfill this responsibility. *(Added by Stats.1988, c. 1245, § 2. Amended by Stats.1998, c. 931 (S.B.2139), § 51, eff. Sept. 28, 1998; Stats.2002, c. 784 (S.B.1316), § 40.)*

Law Revision Commission Comments

Section 195 is amended to reflect the elimination of the justice court. Cal. Const. art. VI, §§ 1, 5(b). [28 Cal.L.Rev.Comm. Reports 51 (1998)].

Subdivision (a) of Section 195 is amended to reflect unification of the municipal and superior courts pursuant to Article VI, Section 5(e), of the California Constitution.

Subdivision (b) is amended to reflect enactment of the Trial Court Employment Protection and Governance Act. See Gov't Code §§ 71620 (trial court personnel), 71623 (salaries). [32 Cal.L.Rev.Comm. Reports 108 (2002)].

Research References

2 Witkin Cal. Proc. 5th Courts § 343, (S 343) in General.

7 Witkin Cal. Proc. 5th Trial § 116, Adoption of Uniform System.

§ 196. Jury commissioners; inquiry into qualifications; oaths; travel expenses; failure of prospective to respond; summons

(a) The jury commissioner or the court shall inquire as to the qualifications of persons on the master list or source list who are or may be summoned for jury service. The commissioner or the court may require any person to answer, under oath, orally or in written form, all questions as may be addressed to that person, regarding the person's qualifications and ability to serve as a prospective trial juror. The commissioner and his or her assistants shall have power to administer oaths and shall be allowed actual traveling expenses incurred in the performance of their duties.

(b) Response to the jury commissioner or the court concerning an inquiry or summons may be made by any person having knowledge that the prospective juror is unable to respond to such inquiry or summons.

(c) Any person who fails to respond to jury commissioner or court inquiry as instructed, may be summoned to appear before the jury commissioner or the court to answer the inquiry, or may be deemed to be qualified for jury service in the absence of a response to the inquiry. Any information thus acquired by the court or jury commissioner shall be noted in jury commissioner or court records. *(Added by Stats.1988, c. 1245, § 2. Amended by Stats.2003, c. 149 (S.B.79), § 6.)*

Law Revision Commission Comments

Subdivision (a) of Section 196 is amended to reflect enactment of the Trial Court Funding Act. See Gov't Code §§ 77003 ("court operations" defined), 77200 (state funding of trial court operations). *Cf.* Cal. R. Ct. 810(d), Function 2 (jury services). Subdivision (a) is also amended to reflect enactment of Government Code Section 69505 (business-related travel expenses of trial court judges and employees). [33 Cal.L.Rev. Comm. Reports 189 (2003)].

Research References

Rutter, Cal. Practice Guide: Civil Trials & Evidence Ch. 5-A, A. Obtaining Prospective Jurors.
7 Witkin Cal. Proc. 5th Trial § 116, Adoption of Uniform System.

§ 197. Source lists of jurors; contents; data from department of motor vehicles; confidentiality

(a) All persons selected for jury service shall be selected at random, from a source or sources inclusive of a representative cross section of the population of the area served by the court. Sources may include, in addition to other lists, customer mailing lists, telephone directories, or utility company lists.

(b) The list of registered voters and the Department of Motor Vehicles' list of licensed drivers and identification cardholders resident within the area served by the court, are appropriate source lists for selection of jurors. These two source lists, when substantially purged of duplicate names, shall be considered inclusive of a representative cross section of the population, within the meaning of subdivision (a).

(c) The Department of Motor Vehicles shall furnish the jury commissioner of each county with the current list of the names, addresses, and other identifying information of persons residing in the county who are age 18 years or older and who are holders of a current driver's license or identification card issued pursuant to Article 3 (commencing with Section 12800) of, or Article 5 (commencing with Section 13000) of, Chapter 1 of Division 6 of the Vehicle Code. The conditions under which these lists shall be compiled semiannually shall be determined by the director, consistent with any rules which may be adopted by the Judicial Council. This service shall be provided by the Department of Motor Vehicles pursuant to Section 1812 of the Vehicle Code. The jury commissioner shall not disclose the information furnished by the Department of Motor Vehicles pursuant to this section to any person, organization, or agency. *(Added by Stats.1988, c. 1245, § 2.)*

Research References

Rutter, Cal. Practice Guide: Civil Trials & Evidence Ch. 5-A, A. Obtaining Prospective Jurors.
7 Witkin Cal. Proc. 5th Trial § 117, Types of Lists.
7 Witkin Cal. Proc. 5th Trial § 118, Selection.

§ 198. Master and qualified juror lists; random selection; use of lists

(a) Random selection shall be utilized in creating master and qualified juror lists, commencing with selection from source lists, and continuing through selection of prospective jurors for voir dire.

(b) The jury commissioner shall, at least once in each 12–month period, randomly select names of prospective trial jurors from the source list or lists, to create a master list.

(c) The master jury list shall be used by the jury commissioner, as provided by statute and state and local court rules, for the purpose of (1) mailing juror questionnaires and subsequent creation of a qualified juror list, and (2) summoning prospective jurors to respond or appear for qualification and service. *(Added by Stats.1988, c. 1245, § 2.)*

Research References

Rutter, Cal. Practice Guide: Civil Trials & Evidence Ch. 5-A, A. Obtaining Prospective Jurors.
7 Witkin Cal. Proc. 5th Trial § 117, Types of Lists.
7 Witkin Cal. Proc. 5th Trial § 118, Selection.
8 Witkin, California Summary 10th Constitutional Law § 739, (S 739) in General.

§ 198.5. Selection of master jury lists and qualified jury lists to serve in session of superior court from area where session is held pursuant to local superior court rule

If sessions of the superior court are held in a location other than the county seat, the names for master jury lists and qualified jury lists to serve in a session may be selected from the area in which the session is held, pursuant to a local superior court rule that divides the county in a manner that provides all qualified persons in the county an equal opportunity to be considered for jury service. Nothing in this section precludes the court, in its discretion, from ordering a countywide venire in the interest of justice. *(Added by Stats.1988, c. 1245, § 2. Amended by Stats.1998, c. 931 (S.B.2139), § 52, eff. Sept. 28, 1998; Stats.2002, c. 784 (S.B.1316), § 41, operative Jan. 1, 2004; Stats.2003, c. 449 (A.B.1712), § 6.)*

Law Revision Commission Comments

Section 198.5 is amended to accommodate unification of the municipal and superior courts in a county. Cal. Const. art. VI, § 5(e). Subdivision (b) is drawn from Section 191 (policy of state to select jury from population of area served by court; all qualified persons to have an equal opportunity to be considered for jury service). A local rule promulgated pursuant to subdivision (b) may differentiate between misdemeanors and limited civil cases, on the one hand, and felonies and civil cases other than limited civil cases, on the other. See Code Civ. Proc. § 85 (limited civil cases) & Comment; Penal Code § 691 (definitions) & Comment. [28 Cal.L.Rev. Comm. Reports 51 (1998)].

Section 198.5 is amended, effective January 1, 2004, to reflect unification of the municipal and superior courts pursuant to Article VI, Section 5(e), of the California Constitution. It incorporates provisions drawn from Sections 199 (El Dorado County venires), 199.2 (Placer County venires), 199.3 (Nevada County venires), and 199.5 (Santa Barbara County venires). [32 Cal.L.Rev.Comm. Reports 109 (2002)].

Research References

Rutter, Cal. Practice Guide: Civil Trials & Evidence Ch. 5-A, A. Obtaining Prospective Jurors.
7 Witkin Cal. Proc. 5th Trial § 118, Selection.

§ 201. Superior courts; separate trial jury panels; use of jurors from one panel on another

In any superior court, a separate trial jury panel may be drawn, summoned, and impaneled for each judge, or any one panel may be drawn, summoned, and impaneled by any one of the judges, for use in the trial of cases before any of the judges, as occasion may require. In those courts, when a panel of jurors is in attendance for service before one or more of the judges, whether impaneled for common use or not, the whole or any number of the jurors from such panel may be required to attend and serve in the trial of cases, or to complete a panel, or jury, before any other of the judges. *(Added by Stats.1988, c. 1245, § 2. Amended by Stats.2002, c. 784 (S.B.1316), § 47.)*

Law Revision Commission Comments

Section 201 is amended to reflect unification of the municipal and superior courts pursuant to Article VI, Section 5(e), of the California Constitution.

The section is also amended to reflect the fact that every superior court has at least two judgeships as a result of trial court unification. See Gov't Code § 69580 *et seq.* (number of judges). [32 Cal.L.Rev.Comm. Reports 112 (2002)].

Research References

Rutter, Cal. Practice Guide: Civil Trials & Evidence Ch. 5-A, A. Obtaining Prospective Jurors.

7 Witkin Cal. Proc. 5th Trial § 121, Common Panel.

§ 202. Mechanical, electric, or electronic equipment

Mechanical, electric, or electronic equipment, which in the opinion of the jury commissioner is satisfactory therefor, may be used in the performance of any function specified by this chapter for the selection and drawing of jurors. *(Added by Stats.1988, c. 1245, § 2.)*

Research References

Rutter, Cal. Practice Guide: Civil Trials & Evidence Ch. 5-A, A. Obtaining Prospective Jurors.

7 Witkin Cal. Proc. 5th Trial § 120, Ordinary Panel.

§ 203. Persons qualified to be trial jurors; exceptions

(a) All persons are eligible and qualified to be prospective trial jurors, except the following:

(1) Persons who are not citizens of the United States.

(2) Persons who are less than 18 years of age.

(3) Persons who are not domiciliaries of the State of California, as determined pursuant to Article 2 (commencing with Section 2020) of Chapter 1 of Division 2 of the Elections Code.

(4) Persons who are not residents of the jurisdiction wherein they are summoned to serve.

(5) Persons who have been convicted of malfeasance in office or a felony, and whose civil rights have not been restored.

(6) Persons who are not possessed of sufficient knowledge of the English language, provided that no person shall be deemed incompetent solely because of the loss of sight or hearing in any degree or other disability which impedes the person's ability to communicate or which impairs or interferes with the person's mobility.

(7) Persons who are serving as grand or trial jurors in any court of this state.

(8) Persons who are the subject of conservatorship.

(b) No person shall be excluded from eligibility for jury service in the State of California, for any reason other than those reasons provided by this section. *(Added by Stats.1988, c. 1245, § 2. Amended by Stats.1994, c. 923 (S.B.1546), § 1.)*

Research References

Rutter, Cal. Practice Guide: Civil Trials & Evidence Ch. 5-A, A. Obtaining Prospective Jurors.

Rutter, Cal. Practice Guide: Civil Trials & Evidence Ch. 5-B, B. Procedures Before Voir Dire.

Rutter, Cal. Practice Guide: Civil Trials & Evidence Ch. 5-D, D. Examination by Trial Judge.

Rutter, Cal. Practice Guide: Civil Trials & Evidence Ch. 5-I, I. Challenging Prospective Jurors.

Rutter, Cal. Practice Guide: Personal Injury Ch. 9-C, C. Impanelment of Jury.

7 Witkin Cal. Proc. 5th Trial § 111, (S 111) Qualifications of Jurors.

§ 204. Exemptions and excuses from jury service

(a) No eligible person shall be exempt from service as a trial juror by reason of occupation, economic status, or any characteristic listed or defined in Section 11135 of the Government Code, or for any other reason. No person shall be excused from service as a trial juror except as specified in subdivision (b).

(b) An eligible person may be excused from jury service only for undue hardship, upon themselves or upon the public, as defined by the Judicial Council. *(Added by Stats.1988, c. 1245,*

§ 2. Amended by Stats.2000, c. 43 (A.B.2418), § 2; Stats.2007, c. 568 (A.B.14), § 15.)

Research References

Rutter, Cal. Practice Guide: Civil Trials & Evidence Ch. 5-A, A. Obtaining Prospective Jurors.

Rutter, Cal. Practice Guide: Civil Trials & Evidence Ch. 5-B, B. Procedures Before Voir Dire.

Rutter, Cal. Practice Guide: Civil Trials & Evidence Ch. 5-D, D. Examination by Trial Judge.

Rutter, Cal. Practice Guide: Civil Trials & Evidence Ch. 5-I, I. Challenging Prospective Jurors.

California Practice Guide: Employment Litigation Ch. 19-K, K. Jury Selection.

Rutter, Cal. Practice Guide: Personal Injury Ch. 9-C, C. Impanelment of Jury.

7 Witkin Cal. Proc. 5th Trial § 111, (S 111) Qualifications of Jurors.

7 Witkin Cal. Proc. 5th Trial § 112, in General.

7 Witkin Cal. Proc. 5th Trial § 113, Rule of Court.

§ 205. Juror questionnaires; contents; use; additional questionnaires

(a) If a jury commissioner requires a person to complete a questionnaire, the questionnaire shall ask only questions related to juror identification, qualification, and ability to serve as a prospective juror.

(b) Except as ordered by the court, the questionnaire referred to in subdivision (a) shall be used solely for qualifying prospective jurors, and for management of the jury system, and not for assisting in the courtroom voir dire process of selecting trial jurors for specific cases.

(c) The court may require a prospective juror to complete such additional questionnaires as may be deemed relevant and necessary for assisting in the voir dire process or to ascertain whether a fair cross section of the population is represented as required by law, if such procedures are established by local court rule.

(d) The trial judge may direct a prospective juror to complete additional questionnaires as proposed by counsel in a particular case to assist the voir dire process. *(Added by Stats.1988, c. 1245, § 2.)*

Research References

Rutter, Cal. Practice Guide: Civil Trials & Evidence Ch. 5-A, A. Obtaining Prospective Jurors.

Rutter, Cal. Practice Guide: Civil Trials & Evidence Ch. 5-C, C. Voir Dire-General Considerations.

7 Witkin Cal. Proc. 5th Trial § 116, Adoption of Uniform System.

7 Witkin Cal. Proc. 5th Trial § 136, (S 136) in General.

7 Witkin, California Summary 10th Constitutional Law § 421, (S 421) Jury Voir Dire.

§ 206. Criminal actions; discussion of deliberation or verdict after discharge of jury; informing jury; violations

(a) Prior to discharging the jury from the case, the judge in a criminal action shall inform the jurors that they have an absolute right to discuss or not to discuss the deliberation or verdict with anyone. The judge shall also inform the jurors of the provisions set forth in subdivisions (b), (d), and (e).

(b) Following the discharge of the jury in a criminal case, the defendant, or his or her attorney or representative, or the prosecutor, or his or her representative, may discuss the jury deliberation or verdict with a member of the jury, provided that the juror consents to the discussion and that the discussion takes place at a reasonable time and place.

(c) If a discussion of the jury deliberation or verdict with a member of the jury pursuant to subdivision (b) occurs at any time more than 24 hours after the verdict, prior to discussing the jury deliberation or verdict with a member of a jury pursuant to subdivision (b), the defendant or his or her attorney or representative, or the prosecutor or his or her representative, shall inform the juror of the identity of the case, the party in that case which the person represents, the subject of the interview, the absolute right of the juror to discuss or not discuss the deliberations or verdict in the case with the person, and the juror's right to review and have a copy of any declaration filed with the court.

(d) Any unreasonable contact with a juror by the defendant, or his or her attorney or representative, or by the prosecutor, or his or her representative, without the juror's consent shall be immediately reported to the trial judge.

(e) Any violation of this section shall be considered a violation of a lawful court order and shall be subject to reasonable monetary sanctions in accordance with Section 177.5 of the Code of Civil Procedure.

(f) Nothing in the section shall prohibit a peace officer from investigating an allegation of criminal conduct.

(g) Pursuant to Section 237, a defendant or defendant's counsel may, following the recording of a jury's verdict in a criminal proceeding, petition the court for access to personal juror identifying information within the court's records necessary for the defendant to communicate with jurors for the purpose of developing a motion for new trial or any other lawful purpose. This information consists of jurors' names, addresses, and telephone numbers. The court shall consider all requests for personal juror identifying information pursuant to Section 237. *(Added by Stats.1988, c. 1245, § 2. Amended by Stats.1992, c. 971 (S.B.1299), § 2; Stats.1993, c. 632 (A.B.1915), § 1; Stats.1995, c. 964 (S.B.508), § 2; Stats.1996, c. 636 (S.B.2123), § 1, eff. Sept. 19, 1996; Stats.2000, c. 242 (A.B.2567), § 1.)*

Research References

Rutter, Cal. Practice Guide: Civil Trials & Evidence Ch. 18-B, B. Motion for New Trial.
Rutter, Cal. Practice Guide: Prof. Responsibility Ch. 8-D, D. Restrictions on Speech and Behavior Outside Courtroom.

§ 207. Records; maintenance; preservation

(a) The jury commissioner shall maintain records regarding selection, qualification, and assignment of prospective jurors.

(b) The jury commissioner shall maintain records providing a clear audit trail regarding a juror's attendance, jury fees, and mileage.

(c) All records and papers maintained or compiled by the jury commissioner in connection with the selection or service of a juror may be kept on an electronic or microfilm medium and such records shall be preserved for at least three years after the list used in their selection is prepared, or for any longer period ordered by the court or the jury commissioner. *(Added by Stats.1988, c. 1245, § 2.)*

Research References

7 Witkin Cal. Proc. 5th Trial § 116, Adoption of Uniform System.

§ 208. Summoning jurors; methods of serving summons

The jury commissioner shall estimate the number of prospective jurors that may be required to serve the needs of the court, and shall summon prospective jurors for service. Prospective jurors shall be summoned by mailing a summons by first-class mail or by personal service or, in urgency situations, as elsewhere provided by law. The summons, when served by mail, shall be mailed at least 10 days prior to the date of required appearance. Once a prospective juror has been summoned, the date, time, or place of appearance may be modified or further specified by the jury commissioner, by means of written, telegraphic, telephonic, or direct oral communication with the prospective juror. *(Added*

by *Stats.1988, c. 1245, § 2. Amended by Stats.2003, c. 149 (S.B.79), § 7.)*

Law Revision Commission Comments

Section 208 is amended to reflect unification of the municipal and superior courts pursuant to former Section 5(e) of Article VI of the California Constitution. [33 Cal.L.Rev.Comm. Reports 189 (2003)].

Research References

Rutter, Cal. Practice Guide: Civil Trials & Evidence Ch. 5-A, A. Obtaining Prospective Jurors.
7 Witkin Cal. Proc. 5th Trial § 120, Ordinary Panel.

§ 209. Failure to respond to summons; attachment; compelling attendance; contempt

(a) Any prospective trial juror who has been summoned for service, and who fails to attend as directed or to respond to the court or jury commissioner and to be excused from attendance, may be attached and compelled to attend. Following an order to show cause hearing, the court may find the prospective juror in contempt of court, punishable by fine, incarceration, or both, as otherwise provided by law.

(b) In lieu of imposing sanctions for contempt as set forth in subdivision (a), the court may impose reasonable monetary sanctions, as provided in this subdivision, on a prospective juror who has not been excused pursuant to Section 204 after first providing the prospective juror with notice and an opportunity to be heard. If a juror fails to respond to the initial summons the court may issue a second summons indicating that the person failed to appear in response to a previous summons and ordering the person to appear for jury duty. The second summons may be issued no earlier than 90 days after the initial failure to appear. Upon the failure of the juror to appear in response to the second summons, the court may issue a failure to appear notice informing the person that failure to respond may result in the imposition of money sanctions. If the prospective juror does not attend the court within the time period as directed by the failure to appear notice, the court shall issue an order to show cause. Payment of monetary sanctions imposed pursuant to this subdivision does not relieve the person of his or her obligation to perform jury duty.

(c)(1) The court may give notice of its intent to impose sanctions by either of the following means:

(A) Verbally to a prospective juror appearing in person in open court.

(B) The issuance on its own motion of an order to show cause requiring the prospective juror to demonstrate reasons for not imposing sanctions. The court may serve the order to show cause by certified or first-class mail.

(2) The monetary sanctions imposed pursuant to subdivision (b) may not exceed two hundred fifty dollars ($250) for the first violation, seven hundred fifty dollars ($750) for the second violation, and one thousand five hundred dollars ($1,500) for the third and any subsequent violation. Monetary sanctions may not be imposed on a prospective juror more than once during a single juror pool cycle. The prospective juror may be excused from paying sanctions pursuant to subdivision (b) of Section 204 or in the interests of justice. The full amount of any sanction paid shall be deposited in a bank account established for this purpose by the Administrative Office of the Courts and transmitted from that account monthly to the Controller for deposit in the Trial Court Trust Fund, as provided in Section 68085.1 of the Government Code. It is the intent of the Legislature that the funds derived from the monetary sanctions authorized in this section be allocated, to the extent feasible, to the family courts and the civil courts. The Judicial Council shall, by rule, provide for a procedure by which a prospective juror against whom a

sanction has been imposed by default may move to set aside the default. *(Added by Stats.1988, c. 1245, § 2. Amended by Stats.2003, c. 359 (A.B.1180), § 1; Stats.2005, c. 75 (A.B.145), § 28, eff. July 19, 2005, operative Jan. 1, 2006; Stats.2006, c. 567 (A.B.2303), § 5; Stats.2009, c. 44 (S.B.319), § 1.)*

Research References

Rutter, Cal. Practice Guide: Civil Trials & Evidence Ch. 5-A, A. Obtaining Prospective Jurors.
7 Witkin Cal. Proc. 5th Trial § 120, Ordinary Panel.
7 Witkin Cal. Proc. 5th Trial § 171, (S 171) Statutory Framework.

§ 210. Summons; contents

The summons shall contain the date, time, and place of appearance required of the prospective juror or, alternatively, instructions as to the procedure for calling the jury commissioner for telephonic instructions for appearance as well as such additional juror information as deemed appropriate by the jury commissioner. *(Added by Stats.1988, c. 1245, § 2.)*

Research References

Rutter, Cal. Practice Guide: Civil Trials & Evidence Ch. 5-A, A. Obtaining Prospective Jurors.
7 Witkin Cal. Proc. 5th Trial § 120, Ordinary Panel.

§ 210.5. Standardized jury summons

The Judicial Council shall adopt a standardized jury summons for use, with appropriate modifications, around the state, that is understandable and has consumer appeal. The standardized jury summons shall include a specific reference to the rules for breast-feeding mothers. The use of the standardized jury summons shall be voluntary, unless otherwise prescribed by the rules of court. *(Added by Stats.2000, c. 266 (A.B.1814), § 2.)*

Research References

7 Witkin Cal. Proc. 5th Trial § 120, Ordinary Panel.

§ 211. Additional jurors; summoning qualified citizens to complete panel

When a court has no prospective jurors remaining available for voir dire from panels furnished by, or available from, the jury commissioner, and finds that not proceeding with voir dire will place a party's right to a trial by jury in jeopardy, the court may direct the sheriff or marshal to summon, serve, and immediately attach the person of a sufficient number of citizens having the qualifications of jurors, to complete the panel. *(Added by Stats.1988, c. 1245, § 2. Amended by Stats.1996, c. 872 (A.B. 3472), § 7.)*

Research References

Rutter, Cal. Practice Guide: Civil Trials & Evidence Ch. 5-A, A. Obtaining Prospective Jurors.
7 Witkin Cal. Proc. 5th Trial § 122, Special Panel.

§ 213. Availability of jurors on telephone notice

Unless excused by reason of undue hardship, all or any portion of the summoned prospective jurors shall be available on one-hour notice by telephone to appear for service, when the jury commissioner determines that it will efficiently serve the operational requirements of the court.

Jurors available on one-hour telephone notice shall receive credit for each day of such availability towards their jury service obligation, but they shall not be paid unless they are actually required to make an appearance. *(Added by Stats.1988, c. 1245, § 2.)*

Research References

Rutter, Cal. Practice Guide: Civil Trials & Evidence Ch. 5-A, A. Obtaining Prospective Jurors.

7 Witkin Cal. Proc. 5th Trial § 120, Ordinary Panel.

§ 214. Orientation for new jurors; notice of rights under Labor Code

The jury commissioner shall provide orientation for new jurors, which shall include necessary basic information concerning jury service. The jury commissioner shall notify each juror of the provisions of Section 230 of the Labor Code. *(Added by Stats.1988, c. 1245, § 2. Amended by Stats.1989, c. 1416, § 8.)*

Research References

7 Witkin Cal. Proc. 5th Trial § 116, Adoption of Uniform System.
7 Witkin Cal. Proc. 5th Trial § 118, Selection.

§ 215. Fees for jurors; mileage

(a) Except as provided in subdivision (b), on and after July 1, 2000, the fee for jurors in the superior court, in civil and criminal cases, is fifteen dollars ($15) a day for each day's attendance as a juror after the first day.

(b) A juror who is employed by a federal, state, or local government entity, or by any other public entity as defined in Section 481.200, and who receives regular compensation and benefits while performing jury service, may not be paid the fee described in subdivision (a).

(c) All jurors in the superior court, in civil and criminal cases, shall be reimbursed for mileage at the rate of thirty-four cents ($ 0.34) per mile for each mile actually traveled in attending court as a juror after the first day, in going only. *(Added by Stats.1988, c. 1245, § 2. Amended by Stats.1998, c. 931 (S.B. 2139), § 54, eff. Sept. 28, 1998; Stats.2000, c. 127 (A.B.2866), § 1, eff. July 10, 2000; Stats.2002, c. 784 (S.B.1316), § 48; Stats.2002, c. 144 (A.B.2925), § 1; Stats.2004, c. 227 (S.B.1102), § 9, eff. Aug. 16, 2004.)*

Law Revision Commission Comments

Subdivision (a) of Section 215 is amended to reflect the elimination of the justice court. Cal. Const. art. VI, §§ 1, 5(b). [28 Cal.L.Rev.Comm. Reports 51 (1998)].

References to the municipal courts are deleted from subdivisions (a) and (b) of Section 215 to reflect unification of the municipal and superior courts pursuant to Article VI, Section 5(e), of the California Constitution.

Research References

Rutter, Cal. Practice Guide: Civ. Pro. Before Trial Ch. 12(I)-D, D. Demand for Jury Trial and Waiver.
Rutter, Cal. Practice Guide: Civil Trials & Evidence Ch. 2-D, D. Securing Trial by Jury.
Rutter, Cal. Practice Guide: Civil Trials & Evidence Ch. 5-A, A. Obtaining Prospective Jurors.
Rutter, Cal. Practice Guide: Personal Injury Ch. 9-C, C. Impanelment of Jury.
7 Witkin Cal. Proc. 5th Judgment § 136, (S 136) Jury Fees and Expenses.
7 Witkin Cal. Proc. 5th Trial § 99, Advance and Subsequent Deposits.

§ 216. Deliberation rooms; restriction of jury assembly facilities

(a) At each court facility where jury cases are heard, the board of supervisors shall provide a deliberation room or rooms for use of jurors when they have retired for deliberation. The deliberation rooms shall be designed to minimize unwarranted intrusions by other persons in the court facility, shall have suitable furnishings, equipment, and supplies, and shall also have restroom accommodations for male and female jurors.

(b) If the board of supervisors neglects to provide the facilities required by this section, the court may order the sheriff or marshal to do so, and the expenses incurred in carrying the order into effect, when certified by the court, are a county charge.

(c) Unless authorized by the jury commissioner, jury assembly facilities shall be restricted to use by jurors and jury commissioner staff. *(Added by Stats.1988, c. 1245, § 2. Amended by Stats.1996, c. 872 (A.B.3472), § 8.)*

Research References

Rutter, Cal. Practice Guide: Civil Trials & Evidence Ch. 15-A, A. General Considerations.
7 Witkin Cal. Proc. 5th Trial § 318, (S 318) in General.

§ 217. Criminal cases; food, lodging, and necessities for jurors; expenses

In criminal cases only, while the jury is kept together, either during the progress of the trial or after their retirement for deliberation, the court may direct the sheriff or marshal to provide the jury with suitable and sufficient food and lodging, or other reasonable necessities. The expenses incurred under this section shall be charged against the Trial Court Operations Fund of the county in which the court is held. All those expenses shall be paid on the order of the court. *(Added by Stats.1988, c. 1245, § 2. Amended by Stats.1996, c. 872 (A.B.3472), § 9; Stats.1998, c. 931 (S.B.2139), § 55, eff. Sept. 28, 1998; Stats.2002, c. 784 (S.B.1316), § 49.)*

Law Revision Commission Comments

Section 217 is amended to reflect the elimination of the justice court. Cal. Const. art. VI, §§ 1, 5(b). [28 Cal.L.Rev.Comm. Reports 51 (1998)].

Section 217 is amended to reflect unification of the municipal and superior courts pursuant to Article VI, Section 5(e), of the California Constitution.

The section is also amended to reflect enactment of the Trial Court Funding Act. See Gov't Code §§ 77003 ("court operations" defined), 77009 (Trial Court Operations Fund), 77200 (state funding of trial court operations). [32 Cal.L.Rev.Comm. Reports 113 (2002)].

§ 218. Written excuses of jurors; acceptance by commissioner

The jury commissioner shall hear the excuses of jurors summoned, in accordance with the standards prescribed by the Judicial Council. It shall be left to the discretion of the jury commissioner to accept an excuse under subdivision (b) of Section 204 without a personal appearance. All excuses shall be in writing setting forth the basis of the request and shall be signed by the juror. *(Added by Stats.1988, c. 1245, § 2.)*

Research References

Rutter, Cal. Practice Guide: Civil Trials & Evidence Ch. 5-A, A. Obtaining Prospective Jurors.
7 Witkin Cal. Proc. 5th Trial § 120, Ordinary Panel.

§ 219. Selection of jurors for voir dire; exemption of peace officers

(a) Except as provided in subdivision (b), the jury commissioner shall randomly select jurors for jury panels to be sent to courtrooms for voir dire.

(b)(1) Notwithstanding subdivision (a), no peace officer, as defined in Section 830.1, subdivision (a) of Section 830.2, and subdivision (a) of Section 830.33, of the Penal Code, shall be selected for voir dire in civil or criminal matters.

(2) Notwithstanding subdivision (a), no peace officer, as defined in subdivisions (b) and (c) of Section 830.2 of the Penal Code, shall be selected for voir dire in criminal matters. *(Added by Stats.1988, c. 1245, § 2. Amended by Stats.1992, c. 324 (A.B.2577), § 1; Stats.1994, c. 742 (S.B.2066), § 2; Stats.1998, c. 606 (S.B.1880), § 1; Stats.2001, c. 55 (S.B.303), § 1.)*

Research References

Rutter, Cal. Practice Guide: Civil Trials & Evidence Ch. 5-A, A. Obtaining Prospective Jurors.
7 Witkin Cal. Proc. 5th Trial § 112, in General.

7 Witkin Cal. Proc. 5th Trial § 120, Ordinary Panel.

§ 219.5. Adoption by Judicial Council of rule of court requiring trial courts to establish procedures for jury service giving peace officers scheduling accommodations when necessary

The Judicial Council shall adopt a rule of court, on or before January 1, 2005, requiring the trial courts to establish procedures for jury service that gives peace officers, as defined by Section 830.5 of the Penal Code, scheduling accommodations when necessary. *(Added by Stats.2003, c. 353 (A.B.513), § 1.)*

Research References

Rutter, Cal. Practice Guide: Civil Trials & Evidence Ch. 5-A, A. Obtaining Prospective Jurors.
7 Witkin Cal. Proc. 5th Trial § 112, in General.

§ 220. Number of jurors

A trial jury shall consist of 12 persons, except that in civil actions and cases of misdemeanor, it may consist of 12 or any number less than 12, upon which the parties may agree. *(Added by Stats.1988, c. 1245, § 2.)*

Research References

Rutter, Cal. Practice Guide: Civil Trials & Evidence Ch. 2-B, B. What Constitutes Jury Trial.
Rutter, Cal. Practice Guide: Personal Injury Ch. 9-C, C. Impanelment of Jury.
7 Witkin Cal. Proc. 5th Trial § 83, Jury of Fewer Than Twelve Persons.

§ 222. Selection for voir dire; panel list; seating

(a) Except as provided in subdivision (b), when an action is called for trial by jury, the clerk shall randomly select the names of the jurors for voir dire, until the jury is selected or the panel is exhausted.

(b) When the jury commissioner has provided the court with a listing of the trial jury panel in random order, the court shall seat prospective jurors for voir dire in the order provided by the panel list. *(Added by Stats.1988, c. 1245, § 2. Amended by Stats.2007, c. 263 (A.B.310), § 4.)*

Law Revision Commission Comments

Section 222 is amended to delete unnecessary language authorizing the judge to substitute for the clerk if there is no clerk. See Code Civ. Proc. § 167 (judge may perform any act court clerk may perform); Government Code §§ 69840–69848 (duties of clerk of superior court), 71620(b) (executive or administrative officer has authority of clerk of court). [35 Cal.L.Rev.Comm. Reports 219 (2006)].

Research References

Rutter, Cal. Practice Guide: Civil Trials & Evidence Ch. 5-B, B. Procedures Before Voir Dire.
7 Witkin Cal. Proc. 5th Trial § 123, Drawing Names.

§ 222.5. Prospective jurors; examination; opening statements; questionnaires

To select a fair and impartial jury in civil jury trials, the trial judge shall examine the prospective jurors. Upon completion of the judge's initial examination, counsel for each party shall have the right to examine, by oral and direct questioning, any of the prospective jurors in order to enable counsel to intelligently exercise both peremptory challenges and challenges for cause. During any examination conducted by counsel for the parties, the trial judge should permit liberal and probing examination calculated to discover bias or prejudice with regard to the circumstances of the particular case. The fact that a topic has been included in the judge's examination should not preclude additional nonrepetitive or nonduplicative questioning in the same area by counsel.

Civ. Pro.

The trial judge should allow a brief opening statement by counsel for each party prior to the commencement of the oral questioning phase of the voir dire process.

The scope of the examination conducted by counsel shall be within reasonable limits prescribed by the trial judge in the judge's sound discretion. In exercising his or her sound discretion as to the form and subject matter of voir dire questions, the trial judge should consider, among other criteria, any unique or complex elements, legal or factual, in the case and the individual responses or conduct of jurors which may evince attitudes inconsistent with suitability to serve as a fair and impartial juror in the particular case. Specific unreasonable or arbitrary time limits shall not be imposed in any case. The trial judge shall not establish a blanket policy of a time limit for voir dire.

The trial judge should permit counsel to conduct voir dire examination without requiring prior submission of the questions unless a particular counsel engages in improper questioning. For purposes of this section, an "improper question" is any question that, as its dominant purpose, attempts to precondition the prospective jurors to a particular result, indoctrinate the jury, or question the prospective jurors concerning the pleadings or the applicable law. A court shall not arbitrarily or unreasonably refuse to submit reasonable written questionnaires, the contents of which are determined by the court in its sound discretion, when requested by counsel. If a questionnaire is utilized, the parties should be given reasonable time to evaluate the responses to the questionnaires before oral questioning commences. To help facilitate the jury selection process, the judge in civil trials should provide the parties with both the alphabetical list and the list of prospective jurors in the order in which they will be called.

In civil cases, the court may, upon stipulation by counsel for all the parties appearing in the action, permit counsel to examine the prospective jurors outside a judge's presence. *(Added by Stats.1990, c. 1232 (A.B.3820), § 1.5. Amended by Stats.2011, c. 409 (A.B.1403), § 1.)*

Research References

Rutter, Cal. Practice Guide: Civil Trials & Evidence Ch. 4-C, C. Jury Matters.
Rutter, Cal. Practice Guide: Civil Trials & Evidence Ch. 5-B, B. Procedures Before Voir Dire.
Rutter, Cal. Practice Guide: Civil Trials & Evidence Ch. 5-C, C. Voir Dire-General Considerations.
Rutter, Cal. Practice Guide: Civil Trials & Evidence Ch. 5-D, D. Examination by Trial Judge.
Rutter, Cal. Practice Guide: Civil Trials & Evidence Ch. 5-F, F. Questioning Technique-Practice Pointers.
Rutter, Cal. Practice Guide: Civil Trials & Evidence Ch. 5-G, G. Scope of Permissible Voir Dire-Proper vs. Improper Questions.
Rutter, Cal. Practice Guide: Civil Trials & Evidence Gen. Matls., Highlights.
Rutter, Cal. Practice Guide: Civil Trials & Evidence Ch. 5 App. B, Appendix B.
Rutter, Cal. Practice Guide: Personal Injury Ch. 9-B, B. In-Chambers Conference Before Commencement of Trial.
Rutter, Cal. Practice Guide: Personal Injury Ch. 9-C, C. Impanelment of Jury.
Rutter, Cal. Practice Guide: Personal Injury Gen. Matls., Highlights.
7 Witkin Cal. Proc. 5th Trial § 136, (S 136) in General.
7 Witkin Cal. Proc. 5th Trial § 137, (S 137) Voir Dire Procedure.
7 Witkin Cal. Proc. 5th Trial § 143, Improper Questions by Attorneys.

§ 223. Criminal cases; voir dire examination by court and counsel

In a criminal case, the court shall conduct an initial examination of prospective jurors. The court may submit to the prospective jurors additional questions requested by the parties as it deems proper. Upon completion of the court's initial examination, counsel for each party shall have the right to examine, by oral and direct questioning, any or all of the prospective jurors. The court may, in the exercise of its discretion, limit the oral and direct questioning of prospective jurors by counsel. The court may specify the maximum amount of time that counsel for each party may question an individual juror, or may specify an aggregate amount of time for each party, which can then be allocated among the prospective jurors by counsel. Voir dire of any prospective jurors shall, where practicable, occur in the presence of the other jurors in all criminal cases, including death penalty cases. Examination of prospective jurors shall be conducted only in aid of the exercise of challenges for cause.

The trial court's exercise of its discretion in the manner in which voir dire is conducted, including any limitation on the time which will be allowed for direct questioning of prospective jurors by counsel and any determination that a question is not in aid of the exercise of challenges for cause, shall not cause any conviction to be reversed unless the exercise of that discretion has resulted in a miscarriage of justice, as specified in Section 13 of Article VI of the California Constitution. *(Added by Initiative Measure (Prop. 115), approved June 5, 1990, eff. June 6, 1990. Amended by Stats.2000, c. 192 (A.B.2406), § 1.)*

Research References

Rutter, Cal. Practice Guide: Civil Trials & Evidence Ch. 5-C, C. Voir Dire-General Considerations.
Rutter, Cal. Practice Guide: Civil Trials & Evidence Ch. 5-G, G. Scope of Permissible Voir Dire-Proper vs. Improper Questions.

§ 224. Disabled jurors; presence of service providers; instructions; appointment

(a) If a party does not cause the removal by challenge of an individual juror who is deaf, hearing impaired, blind, visually impaired, or speech impaired and who requires auxiliary services to facilitate communication, the party shall (1) stipulate to the presence of a service provider in the jury room during jury deliberations, and (2) prepare and deliver to the court proposed jury instructions to the service provider.

(b) As used in this section, "service provider" includes, but is not limited to, a person who is a sign language interpreter, oral interpreter, deaf-blind interpreter, reader, or speech interpreter. If auxiliary services are required during the course of jury deliberations, the court shall instruct the jury and the service provider that the service provider for the juror with a disability is not to participate in the jury's deliberations in any manner except to facilitate communication between the juror with a disability and other jurors.

(c) The court shall appoint a service provider whose services are needed by a juror with a disability to facilitate communication or participation. A sign language interpreter, oral interpreter, or deaf-blind interpreter appointed pursuant to this section shall be a qualified interpreter, as defined in subdivision (f) of Section 754 of the Evidence Code. Service providers appointed by the court under this subdivision shall be compensated in the same manner as provided in subdivision (i) of Section 754 of the Evidence Code. *(Added by Stats.1988, c. 1245, § 2. Amended by Stats.1992, c. 913 (A.B.1077), § 9; Stats.1993, c. 1214 (A.B.551), § 3.)*

Research References

Rutter, Cal. Practice Guide: Civil Trials & Evidence Ch. 5-B, B. Procedures Before Voir Dire.
Rutter, Cal. Practice Guide: Civil Trials & Evidence Ch. 5-I, I. Challenging Prospective Jurors.
Rutter, Cal. Practice Guide: Civil Trials & Evidence Ch. 15-A, A. General Considerations.
Rutter, Cal. Practice Guide: Personal Injury Ch. 9-C, C. Impanelment of Jury.

Rutter, Cal. Practice Guide: Personal Injury Ch. 9-K, K. Submission of Case to Jury.

7 Witkin Cal. Proc. 5th Trial § 320, (S 320) Secrecy of Deliberations.

7 Witkin Cal. Proc. 5th Trial § 330, (S 330) in General.

§ 225. Challenges; definition; classes and types

A challenge is an objection made to the trial jurors that may be taken by any party to the action, and is of the following classes and types:

(a) A challenge to the trial jury panel for cause.

(1) A challenge to the panel may only be taken before a trial jury is sworn. The challenge shall be reduced to writing, and shall plainly and distinctly state the facts constituting the ground of challenge.

(2) Reasonable notice of the challenge to the jury panel shall be given to all parties and to the jury commissioner, by service of a copy thereof.

(3) The jury commissioner shall be permitted the services of legal counsel in connection with challenges to the jury panel.

(b) A challenge to a prospective juror by either:

(1) A challenge for cause, for one of the following reasons:

(A) General disqualification—that the juror is disqualified from serving in the action on trial.

(B) Implied bias—as, when the existence of the facts as ascertained, in judgment of law disqualifies the juror.

(C) Actual bias—the existence of a state of mind on the part of the juror in reference to the case, or to any of the parties, which will prevent the juror from acting with entire impartiality, and without prejudice to the substantial rights of any party.

(2) A peremptory challenge to a prospective juror. *(Added by Stats.1988, c. 1245, § 2.)*

Research References

Rutter, Cal. Practice Guide: Civil Trials & Evidence Ch. 5-D, D. Examination by Trial Judge.

Rutter, Cal. Practice Guide: Civil Trials & Evidence Ch. 5-I, I. Challenging Prospective Jurors.

California Practice Guide: Employment Litigation Ch. 19-K, K. Jury Selection.

Rutter, Cal. Practice Guide: Personal Injury Ch. 9-C, C. Impanelment of Jury.

6 Witkin Cal. Proc. 5th Proceedings Without Trial § 127, Plaintiff's Duties After Settlement.

7 Witkin Cal. Proc. 5th Trial § 124, (S 124) Nature and Kinds.

7 Witkin Cal. Proc. 5th Trial § 132, (S 132) Nature and Illustrations.

7 Witkin Cal. Proc. 5th Trial § 134, Challenge for Cause.

§ 226. Challenges to individual jurors; time; form; exclusion on peremptory challenge

(a) A challenge to an individual juror may only be made before the jury is sworn.

(b) A challenge to an individual juror may be taken orally or may be made in writing, but no reason need be given for a peremptory challenge, and the court shall exclude any juror challenged peremptorily.

(c) All challenges for cause shall be exercised before any peremptory challenges may be exercised.

(d) All challenges to an individual juror, except a peremptory challenge, shall be taken, first by the defendants, and then by the people or plaintiffs. *(Added by Stats.1988, c. 1245, § 2.)*

Research References

Rutter, Cal. Practice Guide: Civ. Pro. Before Trial Ch. 9(I)-D, D. Hearing.

Rutter, Cal. Practice Guide: Civil Trials & Evidence Ch. 4-C, C. Jury Matters.

Rutter, Cal. Practice Guide: Civil Trials & Evidence Ch. 5-I, I. Challenging Prospective Jurors.

Rutter, Cal. Practice Guide: Personal Injury Ch. 9-C, C. Impanelment of Jury.

7 Witkin Cal. Proc. 5th Trial § 124, (S 124) Nature and Kinds.

7 Witkin Cal. Proc. 5th Trial § 134, Challenge for Cause.

7 Witkin Cal. Proc. 5th Trial § 135, Peremptory Challenge.

§ 227. Challenges for cause; time; order

The challenges of either party for cause need not all be taken at once, but they may be taken separately, in the following order, including in each challenge all the causes of challenge belonging to the same class and type:

(a) To the panel.

(b) To an individual juror, for a general disqualification.

(c) To an individual juror, for an implied bias.

(d) To an individual juror, for an actual bias. *(Added by Stats.1988, c. 1245, § 2.)*

Research References

Rutter, Cal. Practice Guide: Civil Trials & Evidence Ch. 5-I, I. Challenging Prospective Jurors.

California Practice Guide: Employment Litigation Ch. 19-K, K. Jury Selection.

Rutter, Cal. Practice Guide: Personal Injury Ch. 9-C, C. Impanelment of Jury.

7 Witkin Cal. Proc. 5th Trial § 134, Challenge for Cause.

§ 228. Challenges for general disqualification; grounds

Challenges for general disqualification may be taken on one or both of the following grounds, and for no other:

(a) A want of any of the qualifications prescribed by this code to render a person competent as a juror.

(b) The existence of any incapacity which satisfies the court that the challenged person is incapable of performing the duties of a juror in the particular action without prejudice to the substantial rights of the challenging party. *(Added by Stats.1988, c. 1245, § 2. Amended by Stats.2002, c. 1008 (A.B.3028), § 1.)*

Research References

Rutter, Cal. Practice Guide: Civil Trials & Evidence Ch. 5-I, I. Challenging Prospective Jurors.

Rutter, Cal. Practice Guide: Personal Injury Ch. 9-C, C. Impanelment of Jury.

7 Witkin Cal. Proc. 5th Trial § 130, Statutory Grounds.

§ 229. Challenges for implied bias; causes

A challenge for implied bias may be taken for one or more of the following causes, and for no other:

(a) Consanguinity or affinity within the fourth degree to any party, to an officer of a corporation which is a party, or to any alleged witness or victim in the case at bar.

(b) Standing in the relation of, or being the parent, spouse, or child of one who stands in the relation of, guardian and ward, conservator and conservatee, master and servant, employer and clerk, landlord and tenant, principal and agent, or debtor and creditor, to either party or to an officer of a corporation which is a party, or being a member of the family of either party; or a partner in business with either party; or surety on any bond or obligation for either party, or being the holder of bonds or shares of capital stock of a corporation which is a party; or having stood within one year previous to the filing of the complaint in the action in the relation of attorney and client with either party or with the attorney for either party. A depositor of a bank or a holder of a savings account in a savings and loan association shall not be deemed a creditor of that bank or savings and loan association for the purpose of this paragraph solely by reason of his or her being a depositor or account holder.

(c) Having served as a trial or grand juror or on a jury of inquest in a civil or criminal action or been a witness on a previous or pending trial between the same parties, or involving the same specific offense or cause of action; or having served as a trial or grand juror or on a jury within one year previously in any criminal or civil action or proceeding in which either party was the plaintiff or defendant or in a criminal action where either party was the defendant.

(d) Interest on the part of the juror in the event of the action, or in the main question involved in the action, except his or her interest as a member or citizen or taxpayer of a county, city and county, incorporated city or town, or other political subdivision of a county, or municipal water district.

(e) Having an unqualified opinion or belief as to the merits of the action founded upon knowledge of its material facts or of some of them.

(f) The existence of a state of mind in the juror evincing enmity against, or bias towards, either party.

(g) That the juror is party to an action pending in the court for which he or she is drawn and which action is set for trial before the panel of which the juror is a member.

(h) If the offense charged is punishable with death, the entertaining of such conscientious opinions as would preclude the juror finding the defendant guilty; in which case the juror may neither be permitted nor compelled to serve. *(Added by Stats.1988, c. 1245, § 2.)*

Research References

Rutter, Cal. Practice Guide: Civil Trials & Evidence Ch. 5-D, D. Examination by Trial Judge.
Rutter, Cal. Practice Guide: Civil Trials & Evidence Ch. 5-I, I. Challenging Prospective Jurors.
California Practice Guide: Employment Litigation Ch. 19-K, K. Jury Selection.
Rutter, Cal. Practice Guide: Personal Injury Ch. 9-C, C. Impanelment of Jury.
7 Witkin Cal. Proc. 5th Trial § 130, Statutory Grounds.
7 Witkin Cal. Proc. 5th Trial § 131, Membership in Health Plan.
7 Witkin Cal. Proc. 5th Trial § 132, (S 132) Nature and Illustrations.
2 Witkin, California Summary 10th Insurance § 214, (S 214) Award and Review.

§ 230. Challenges for cause; trial; witnesses

Challenges for cause shall be tried by the court. The juror challenged and any other person may be examined as a witness in the trial of the challenge, and shall truthfully answer all questions propounded to them. *(Added by Stats.1988, c. 1245, § 2.)*

Research References

Rutter, Cal. Practice Guide: Civil Trials & Evidence Ch. 5-I, I. Challenging Prospective Jurors.
Rutter, Cal. Practice Guide: Personal Injury Ch. 9-C, C. Impanelment of Jury.
7 Witkin Cal. Proc. 5th Trial § 134, Challenge for Cause.

§ 231. Peremptory challenges; number; joint defendants; passing challenges

(a) In criminal cases, if the offense charged is punishable with death, or with imprisonment in the state prison for life, the defendant is entitled to 20 and the people to 20 peremptory challenges. Except as provided in subdivision (b), in a trial for any other offense, the defendant is entitled to 10 and the state to 10 peremptory challenges. When two or more defendants are jointly tried, their challenges shall be exercised jointly, but each defendant shall also be entitled to five additional challenges which may be exercised separately, and the people shall also be entitled to additional challenges equal to the number of all the additional separate challenges allowed the defendants.

(b) If the offense charged is punishable with a maximum term of imprisonment of 90 days or less, the defendant is entitled to six and the state to six peremptory challenges. When two or more defendants are jointly tried, their challenges shall be exercised jointly, but each defendant shall also be entitled to four additional challenges which may be exercised separately, and the state shall also be entitled to additional challenges equal to the number of all the additional separate challenges allowed the defendants.

(c) In civil cases, each party shall be entitled to six peremptory challenges. If there are more than two parties, the court shall, for the purpose of allotting peremptory challenges, divide the parties into two or more sides according to their respective interests in the issues. Each side shall be entitled to eight peremptory challenges. If there are several parties on a side, the court shall divide the challenges among them as nearly equally as possible. If there are more than two sides, the court shall grant such additional peremptory challenges to a side as the interests of justice may require; provided that the peremptory challenges of one side shall not exceed the aggregate number of peremptory challenges of all other sides. If any party on a side does not use his or her full share of peremptory challenges, the unused challenges may be used by the other party or parties on the same side.

(d) Peremptory challenges shall be taken or passed by the sides alternately, commencing with the plaintiff or people; and each party shall be entitled to have the panel full before exercising any peremptory challenge. When each side passes consecutively, the jury shall then be sworn, unless the court, for good cause, shall otherwise order. The number of peremptory challenges remaining with a side shall not be diminished by any passing of a peremptory challenge.

(e) If all the parties on both sides pass consecutively, the jury shall then be sworn, unless the court, for good cause, shall otherwise order. The number of peremptory challenges remaining with a side shall not be diminished by any passing of a peremptory challenge. *(Added by Stats.1988, c. 1245, § 2. Amended by Stats.1989, c. 1416, § 9.)*

Research References

Rutter, Cal. Practice Guide: Civ. Pro. Before Trial Ch. 3-E, E. Federal vs. State Courts.
Rutter, Cal. Practice Guide: Civ. Pro. Before Trial Ch. 13-D, D. the Arbitrator.
Rutter, Cal. Practice Guide: Civil Trials & Evidence Ch. 4-C, C. Jury Matters.
Rutter, Cal. Practice Guide: Civil Trials & Evidence Ch. 5-B, B. Procedures Before Voir Dire.
Rutter, Cal. Practice Guide: Civil Trials & Evidence Ch. 5-I, I. Challenging Prospective Jurors.
California Practice Guide: Employment Litigation Ch. 19-K, K. Jury Selection.
Rutter, Cal. Practice Guide: Fed.Civ.Pro. Before Trial Ch. 1-D, D. Choosing Between State and Federal Courts.
Rutter, Cal. Practice Guide: Personal Injury Ch. 9-C, C. Impanelment of Jury.
3 Witkin Cal. Proc. 5th Actions § 104, Nature of Right and Procedure.
7 Witkin Cal. Proc. 5th Trial § 126, Number.
7 Witkin Cal. Proc. 5th Trial § 135, Peremptory Challenge.

§ 231.5. Peremptory challenges to remove prospective jurors; bias

A party may not use a peremptory challenge to remove a prospective juror on the basis of an assumption that the prospective juror is biased merely because of his or her race, color, religion, sex, national origin, sexual orientation, or similar grounds. *(Added by Stats.2000, c. 43 (A.B.2418), § 3.)*

Research References

Rutter, Cal. Practice Guide: Civil Trials & Evidence Ch. 5-I, I. Challenging Prospective Jurors.
Rutter, Cal. Practice Guide: Personal Injury Ch. 9-C, C. Impanelment of Jury.
7 Witkin Cal. Proc. 5th Trial § 127, (S 127) in General.
8 Witkin, California Summary 10th Constitutional Law § 745, (S 745) Exclusionary Use of Peremptory Challenge.

§ 232. Perjury acknowledgement and agreement

(a) Prior to the examination of prospective trial jurors in the panel assigned for voir dire, the following perjury acknowledgement and agreement shall be obtained from the panel, which shall be acknowledged by the prospective jurors with the statement "I do":

"Do you, and each of you, understand and agree that you will accurately and truthfully answer, under penalty of perjury, all questions propounded to you concerning your qualifications and competency to serve as a trial juror in the matter pending before this court; and that failure to do so may subject you to criminal prosecution."

(b) As soon as the selection of the trial jury is completed, the following acknowledgment and agreement shall be obtained from the trial jurors, which shall be acknowledged by the statement "I do":

"Do you and each of you understand and agree that you will well and truly try the cause now pending before this court, and a true verdict render according only to the evidence presented to you and to the instructions of the court." *(Added by Stats.1988, c. 1245, § 2. Amended by Stats.1989, c. 1416, § 10.)*

Research References

Rutter, Cal. Practice Guide: Civil Trials & Evidence Ch. 5-B, B. Procedures Before Voir Dire.
Rutter, Cal. Practice Guide: Civil Trials & Evidence Ch. 5-I, I. Challenging Prospective Jurors.
Rutter, Cal. Practice Guide: Civil Trials & Evidence Ch. 8G-C, C. Presumptions.
Rutter, Cal. Practice Guide: Personal Injury Ch. 9-C, C. Impanelment of Jury.
Rutter, Cal. Practice Guide: Prof. Responsibility Ch. 11-A, A. Grounds for Discipline.
7 Witkin Cal. Proc. 5th Trial § 123, Drawing Names.
7 Witkin Cal. Proc. 5th Trial § 144, Completion and Oath.

§ 233. Discharge of juror unable to perform duties; alternate jurors; discharge of jury

If, before the jury has returned its verdict to the court, a juror becomes sick or, upon other good cause shown to the court, is found to be unable to perform his or her duty, the court may order the juror to be discharged. If any alternate jurors have been selected as provided by law, one of them shall then be designated by the court to take the place of the juror so discharged. If after all alternate jurors have been made regular jurors or if there is no alternate juror, a juror becomes sick or otherwise unable to perform the juror's duty and has been discharged by the court as provided in this section, the jury shall be discharged and a new jury then or afterwards impaneled, and the cause may again be tried. Alternatively, with the consent of all parties, the trial may proceed with only the remaining jurors, or another juror may be sworn and the trial begin anew. *(Added by Stats.1988, c. 1245, § 2.)*

Research References

Rutter, Cal. Practice Guide: Civil Trials & Evidence Ch. 5-I, I. Challenging Prospective Jurors.

Rutter, Cal. Practice Guide: Civil Trials & Evidence Ch. 5-J, J. Alternate Jurors.
Rutter, Cal. Practice Guide: Civil Trials & Evidence Ch. 7-F, F. Juror Misconduct During Trial.
Rutter, Cal. Practice Guide: Civil Trials & Evidence Ch. 7-G, G. Replacing Juror Unable to Continue.
Rutter, Cal. Practice Guide: Civil Trials & Evidence Ch. 15-E, E. Replacing Jurors During Deliberations.
Rutter, Cal. Practice Guide: Civil Trials & Evidence Ch. 15-F, F. Juror Misconduct During Deliberations.
Rutter, Cal. Practice Guide: Personal Injury Ch. 10-A, A. Motion for New Trial.
7 Witkin Cal. Proc. 5th Trial § 145, (S 145) in General.
7 Witkin Cal. Proc. 5th Trial § 167, Mistrial.

§ 234. Alternate jurors; drawing and examining; qualifications; attendance; confinement; replacing original juror; fees and expenses

Whenever, in the opinion of a judge of a superior court about to try a civil or criminal action or proceeding, the trial is likely to be a protracted one, or upon stipulation of the parties, the court may cause an entry to that effect to be made in the minutes of the court and thereupon, immediately after the jury is impaneled and sworn, the court may direct the calling of one or more additional jurors, in its discretion, to be known as "alternate jurors."

These alternate jurors shall be drawn from the same source, and in the same manner, and have the same qualifications, as the jurors already sworn, and shall be subject to the same examination and challenges. However, each side, or each defendant, as provided in Section 231, shall be entitled to as many peremptory challenges to the alternate jurors as there are alternate jurors called.

The alternate jurors shall be seated so as to have equal power and facilities for seeing and hearing the proceedings in the case, and shall take the same oath as the jurors already selected, and shall, unless excused by the court, attend at all times upon the trial of the cause in company with the other jurors, but shall not participate in deliberation unless ordered by the court, and for a failure to do so are liable to be punished for contempt.

They shall obey the orders of and be bound by the admonition of the court, upon each adjournment of the court; but if the regular jurors are ordered to be kept in the custody of the sheriff or marshal during the trial of the cause, the alternate jurors shall also be kept in confinement with the other jurors; and upon final submission of the case to the jury, the alternate jurors shall be kept in the custody of the sheriff or marshal who shall not suffer any communication to be made to them except by order of the court, and shall not be discharged until the original jurors are discharged, except as provided in this section.

If at any time, whether before or after the final submission of the case to the jury, a juror dies or becomes ill, or upon other good cause shown to the court is found to be unable to perform his or her duty, or if a juror requests a discharge and good cause appears therefor, the court may order the juror to be discharged and draw the name of an alternate, who shall then take his or her place in the jury box, and be subject to the same rules and regulations as though he or she had been selected as one of the original jurors.

All laws relative to fees, expenses, and mileage or transportation of jurors shall be applicable to alternate jurors, except that in civil cases the sums for fees and mileage or transportation need not be deposited until the judge directs alternate jurors to be impaneled. *(Added by Stats.1988, c. 1245, § 2. Amended by Stats.1996, c. 872 (A.B.3472), § 10; Stats.1998, c. 931 (S.B.2139), § 56, eff. Sept. 28, 1998; Stats.2002, c. 784 (S.B.1316), § 50; Stats.2010, c. 328 (S.B.1330), § 33.)*

Civ. Pro.

Law Revision Commission Comments

Section 234 is amended to reflect the elimination of the justice court. Cal. Const. art. VI, §§ 1, 5(b). [28 Cal.L.Rev.Comm. Reports 51 (1998)].

Section 234 is amended to reflect unification of the municipal and superior courts pursuant to Article VI, Section 5(e), of the California Constitution. [32 Cal.L.Rev.Comm. Reports 114 (2002)].

Research References

Rutter, Cal. Practice Guide: Civil Trials & Evidence Ch. 4-C, C. Jury Matters.
Rutter, Cal. Practice Guide: Civil Trials & Evidence Ch. 5-I, I. Challenging Prospective Jurors.
Rutter, Cal. Practice Guide: Civil Trials & Evidence Ch. 5-J, J. Alternate Jurors.
Rutter, Cal. Practice Guide: Civil Trials & Evidence Ch. 7-G, G. Replacing Juror Unable to Continue.
Rutter, Cal. Practice Guide: Civil Trials & Evidence Ch. 15-A, A. General Considerations.
California Practice Guide: Employment Litigation Ch. 19-K, K. Jury Selection.
Rutter, Cal. Practice Guide: Personal Injury Ch. 9-B, B. In-Chambers Conference Before Commencement of Trial.
Rutter, Cal. Practice Guide: Personal Injury Ch. 9-C, C. Impanelment of Jury.
Rutter, Cal. Practice Guide: Personal Injury Ch. 9-K, K. Submission of Case to Jury.
7 Witkin Cal. Proc. 5th Trial § 145, (S 145) in General.
7 Witkin Cal. Proc. 5th Trial § 146, (S 146) Substitution After Deliberations Have Begun.

§ 235. Juries of inquest; selection; compensation

At the request of the sheriff, coroner, or other ministerial officer, the jury commissioner shall provide such prospective jurors as may be required to form a jury of inquest. Prospective jurors so provided shall be selected, obligated, and compensated in the same manner as other jurors selected under the provisions of this chapter. *(Added by Stats.1988, c. 1245, § 2.)*

§ 236. Juries of inquest; oath; duties

When six or more prospective jurors of inquest attend, they shall be sworn by the coroner to inquire who the person was, and when, where, and by what means the person came to his or her death, to inquire into the circumstances attending the death, and to render a true verdict thereon, according to the evidence offered them or arising from the inspection of the body. *(Added by Stats.1988, c. 1245, § 2.)*

Research References

1 Witkin Cal. Summ. 10th Contracts § 201, (S 201) Waiver of Defect in Acceptance.

§ 237. Access to juror information; sealed records; violations

(a)(1) The names of qualified jurors drawn from the qualified juror list for the superior court shall be made available to the public upon request unless the court determines that a compelling interest, as defined in subdivision (b), requires that this information should be kept confidential or its use limited in whole or in part.

(2) Upon the recording of a jury's verdict in a criminal jury proceeding, the court's record of personal juror identifying information of trial jurors, as defined in Section 194, consisting of names, addresses, and telephone numbers, shall be sealed until further order of the court as provided by this section.

(3) For purposes of this section, "sealed" or "sealing" means extracting or otherwise removing the personal juror identifying information from the court record.

(4) This subdivision applies only to cases in which a jury verdict was returned on or after January 1, 1996.

(b) Any person may petition the court for access to these records. The petition shall be supported by a declaration that includes facts sufficient to establish good cause for the release of the juror's personal identifying information. The court shall set the matter for hearing if the petition and supporting declaration establish a prima facie showing of good cause for the release of the personal juror identifying information, but shall not set the matter for hearing if there is a showing on the record of facts that establish a compelling interest against disclosure. A compelling interest includes, but is not limited to, protecting jurors from threats or danger of physical harm. If the court does not set the matter for hearing, the court shall by minute order set forth the reasons and make express findings either of a lack of a prima facie showing of good cause or the presence of a compelling interest against disclosure.

(c) If a hearing is set pursuant to subdivision (b), the petitioner shall provide notice of the petition and the time and place of the hearing at least 20 days prior to the date of the hearing to the parties in the criminal action. The court shall provide notice to each affected former juror by personal service or by first-class mail, addressed to the last known address of the former juror as shown in the records of the court. In a capital case, the petitioner shall also serve notice on the Attorney General. Any affected former juror may appear in person, in writing, by telephone, or by counsel to protest the granting of the petition. A former juror who wishes to appear at the hearing to oppose the unsealing of the personal juror identifying information may request the court to close the hearing in order to protect the former juror's anonymity.

(d) After the hearing, the records shall be made available as requested in the petition, unless a former juror's protest to the granting of the petition is sustained. The court shall sustain the protest of the former juror if, in the discretion of the court, the petitioner fails to show good cause, the record establishes the presence of a compelling interest against disclosure as defined in subdivision (b), or the juror is unwilling to be contacted by the petitioner. The court shall set forth reasons and make express findings to support the granting or denying of the petition to disclose. The court may require the person to whom disclosure is made, or his or her agent or employee, to agree not to divulge jurors' identities or identifying information to others; the court may otherwise limit disclosure in any manner it deems appropriate.

(e) Any court employee who has legal access to personal juror identifying information sealed under subdivision (a), who discloses the information, knowing it to be a violation of this section or a court order issued under this section, is guilty of a misdemeanor.

(f) Any person who intentionally solicits another to unlawfully access or disclose personal juror identifying information contained in records sealed under subdivision (a), knowing that the records have been sealed, or who, knowing that the information was unlawfully secured, intentionally discloses it to another person is guilty of a misdemeanor. *(Added by Stats.1992, c. 971 (S.B.1299), § 3. Amended by Stats.1993, c. 632 (A.B.1915), § 2; Stats.1995, c. 964 (S.B.508), § 3; Stats.1996, c. 636 (S.B.2123), § 2, eff. Sept. 19, 1996.)*

Research References

Rutter, Cal. Practice Guide: Civil Trials & Evidence Ch. 5-C, C. Voir Dire-General Considerations.
Rutter, Cal. Practice Guide: Civil Trials & Evidence Ch. 18-B, B. Motion for New Trial.

7 Witkin Cal. Proc. 5th Trial § 119, Public Inspection of Juror Lists and Questionnaires.

CHAPTER 2. COURT COMMISSIONERS

Section
259. Powers and duties.

§ 259. Powers and duties

Subject to the supervision of the court, every court commissioner shall have power to do all of the following:

(a) Hear and determine ex parte motions for orders and alternative writs and writs of habeas corpus in the superior court for which the court commissioner is appointed.

(b) Take proof and make and report findings thereon as to any matter of fact upon which information is required by the court. Any party to any contested proceeding may except to the report and the subsequent order of the court made thereon within five days after written notice of the court's action. A copy of the exceptions shall be filed and served upon opposing party or counsel within the five days. The party may argue any exceptions before the court on giving notice of motion for that purpose within 10 days from entry thereof. After a hearing before the court on the exceptions, the court may sustain, or set aside, or modify its order.

(c) Take and approve any bonds and undertakings in actions or proceedings, and determine objections to the bonds and undertakings.

(d) Act as temporary judge when otherwise qualified so to act and when appointed for that purpose, on stipulation of the parties litigant. While acting as temporary judge the commissioner shall receive no compensation therefor other than compensation as commissioner.

(e) Hear and report findings and conclusions to the court for approval, rejection, or change, all preliminary matters including motions or petitions for the custody and support of children, the allowance of temporary spousal support, costs and attorneys' fees, and issues of fact in contempt proceedings in proceedings for support, dissolution of marriage, nullity of marriage, or legal separation.

(f) Hear actions to establish paternity and to establish or enforce child and spousal support pursuant to subdivision (a) of Section 4251 of the Family Code.

(g) Hear, report on, and determine all uncontested actions and proceedings subject to the requirements of subdivision (d). *(Enacted in 1872. Amended by Code Am.1877–78, c. 154, p. 98, § 1; Code Am.1880, c. 35, p. 51, § 1; Stats.1980, c. 229, § 1; Stats.1982, c. 517, p. 2333, § 95; Stats.1989, c. 1105, § 5; Stats.1990, c. 411 (A.B.3973), § 5, eff. July 25, 1990; Stats.1992, c. 163 (A.B.2641), § 14, operative Jan. 1, 1994; Stats.1994, c. 1266 (A.B.3804), § 1; Stats.1996, c. 957 (A.B.1058), § 1; Stats.2004, c. 49 (S.B.1225), § 1.)*

Law Revision Commission Comments

Section 259 is amended for consistency with the Bond and Undertaking Law. See Section 995.910 (objections to bonds and undertakings). The other changes in Section 259 are technical. [16 Cal.L.Rev.Comm. Reports 501].

Subdivision (f) of Section 259 is amended to conform to the language of the Family Code. [22 Cal.L.Rev.Comm.Reports 1 (1992)].

Former subdivisions (d), (i), (j), and (k) of Section 259 are repealed as obsolete. The repeal of these provisions does not preclude a court commissioner from administering an oath or affirmation, or from taking proof or acknowledgment of an instrument. See Code Civ. Proc. § 2093(a) (every officer or person authorized to take testimony in any action or proceeding, or to decide upon evidence, has the power to administer oaths and affirmations); Civ. Code § 1181 (officers authorized to take proof or acknowledgment of instrument include court commissioner).

Former subdivision (e) is amended to replace the provision for appointment of a commissioner as temporary judge on written consent of an appearing party with the constitutional standard for appointment of a temporary judge. See Cal. Const. art. VI, § 21. Under the Constitution, written consent is not required in case of implied consent or tantamount stipulation. See, e.g., *In re Courtney H.*, 38 Cal.App.4th 1221, 1227–28, 45 Cal.Rptr.2d 560, 564 (1995). Under the Constitution, whether the stipulation of a party is required for designation of a temporary judge is determined by the party's status as a litigant, not by whether the party is an appearing party. See, e.g., Sarracino v. Superior Court, 13 Cal.3d 1, 529 P.2d 53, 118 Cal.Rptr. 21 (1974); Barfield v. Superior Court, 216 Cal.App.2d 476, 477, 31 Cal.Rptr. 30 (1963). [33 Cal.L.Rev.Comm. Reports 685 (2004)].

Research References

Rutter, Cal. Practice Guide: A.D.R. Ch. 6-B, B. Temporary Judges.

Rutter, Cal. Practice Guide: A.D.R. Ch. 6-C, C. Referees.

Rutter, Cal. Practice Guide: Civ. Pro. Before Trial Ch. 9(I)-A, A. Introduction.

Rutter, Cal. Practice Guide: Civ. Pro. Before Trial Ch. 9(I)-D, D. Hearing.

Miller and Starr California Real Estate § 33:4, Standards for Appointment.

2 Witkin Cal. Proc. 5th Courts § 344, (S 344) Statutory Duties.

2 Witkin Cal. Proc. 5th Courts § 345, (S 345) Scope of Authority.

2 Witkin Cal. Proc. 5th Courts § 347, (S 347) Court Commissioner as Referee.

2 Witkin Cal. Proc. 5th Courts § 350, (S 350) Temporary Judge Requested by Parties.

6 Witkin Cal. Proc. 5th Proceedings Without Trial § 65, in General.

6 Witkin Cal. Proc. 5th Proceedings Without Trial § 67, Improper Reference.

10 Witkin, California Summary 10th Parent and Child § 477, Court Commissioners.

3 Witkin, California Summary 10th Agency and Employment § 205, (S 205) Operation of Law.

Title 4

MINISTERIAL OFFICERS OF COURTS OF JUSTICE

CHAPTER 1. OF MINISTERIAL OFFICERS, GENERALLY

Section

262.10. Elisor or coroner; execution of process; compensation.

262.11. New counties; execution of process by sheriff of new county.

§ 262. Written instructions excusing sheriff from liability; electronic transmission

The direction or authority of a party or his or her attorney to a sheriff, in respect to the execution of process or return thereof, or to any related act or omission, is not available to discharge or excuse the sheriff from a liability for neglect or misconduct, unless it is contained in written instructions by the attorney of the party, including the signature and name of the attorney of the party, or by the party, if he or she has no attorney. Subject to subdivision (c) of Section 263, the instructions may be transmitted electronically pursuant to Chapter 2 (commencing with Section 263). *(Added by Stats.1951, c. 655, p. 1847, § 14. Amended by Stats.2010, c. 680 (A.B.2394), § 1.)*

Research References

2 Witkin Cal. Proc. 5th Courts § 389, (S 389) Duties in Connection With Process and Notices.

§ 262.1. Process and order; apparent regularity; execution justified

A sheriff or other ministerial officer is justified in the execution of, and shall execute, all process and orders regular on their face and issued by competent authority, whatever may be the defect in the proceedings upon which they were issued. *(Added by Stats.1951, c. 655, p. 1847, § 14.)*

Research References

Rutter, Cal. Practice Guide: Enforcing Judgments/Debts Ch. 6I-3, Enforcement of Judgment for Possession of Real Property.

Miller and Starr California Real Estate § 19:232, Recovery of Possession; Writ of Possession.

2 Witkin Cal. Proc. 5th Courts § 389, (S 389) Duties in Connection With Process and Notices.

8 Witkin Cal. Proc. 5th Enforcement of Judgment § 33, Liability of Officer.

8 Witkin Cal. Proc. 5th Enforcement of Judgment § 167, (S 167) Damages for Improper Sale.

6 Witkin Cal. Proc. 5th Provisional Remedies § 157, Limited Liability of Officer.

5 Witkin, California Summary 10th Torts § 161, Reliance on Court Process or Order.

5 Witkin, California Summary 10th Torts § 348, Nature of Immunities and Defenses.

§ 262.2. Process; duty to exhibit on request; duty to exhibit at office

Except as otherwise provided, the officer executing process shall, so long as he or she retains the original process, show it to any interested person, upon request. The officer shall show the process, with all papers, or electronic copies of all papers, attached, at his or her office whenever the office is open for business. *(Added by Stats.1951, c. 655, p. 1847, § 14. Amended by Stats.1955, c. 1197, p. 2213, § 1; Stats.2010, c. 680 (A.B.2394), § 2.)*

Research References

2 Witkin Cal. Proc. 5th Courts § 389, (S 389) Duties in Connection With Process and Notices.

§ 262.3. Sheriff; unexecuted process; execution by successor in office

When any process remains with the sheriff unexecuted, in whole or in part, at the time of his death, resignation of office, or at the expiration of his term of office, such process shall be executed by his successor or successors in office. *(Added by Stats.1951, c. 655, p. 1847, § 14.)*

§ 262.4. Sheriff; execution sale; delivery and validity of deeds and conveyances; electronic recording

If the sheriff sells real estate, under and by virtue of an execution or order of court, the sheriff, or his or her successors in office, shall execute and deliver to the purchaser or purchasers all deeds and conveyances required by law and necessary for the purpose, and those deeds and conveyances shall be valid in law as if they had been executed by the sheriff who made the sale. The deeds and conveyances may be recorded electronically pursuant to Chapter 2 (commencing with Section 263) if they comply with the Electronic Recording Delivery Act of 2004 (Article 6 (commencing with Section 27390) of Chapter 6 of Part 3 of Division 2 of Title 3 of the Government Code). *(Added by Stats.1951, c. 655, p. 1847, § 14. Amended by Stats.2010, c. 680 (A.B.2394), § 3.)*

Research References

Rutter, Cal. Practice Guide: Enforcing Judgments/Debts Ch. 6D-7, Sale and Collection of Property Levied Upon.

§ 262.5. Sheriff; service of papers other than process

Service of a paper, other than process, upon the sheriff may be made by delivering it to him or to one of his deputies, or to a person in charge of the office during office hours, or, if no such person is there, by leaving it in a conspicuous place in the office. *(Added by Stats.1951, c. 655, p. 1847, § 14.)*

§ 262.6. Sheriff a party; process and orders executed by coroner

When the sheriff is a party to an action or proceeding, the process and orders therein, which it would otherwise be the duty of the sheriff to execute, shall be executed by the coroner of the county. *(Added by Stats.1951, c. 655, p. 1847, § 14.)*

Research References

2 Witkin Cal. Proc. 5th Courts § 389, (S 389) Duties in Connection With Process and Notices.

§ 262.7. Sheriff a defendant; process and orders served by citizen over 18

When any action is begun against the sheriff, all process and orders may be served by any person, a citizen of the United States over the age of 18 years, in the manner provided in this code. *(Added by Stats.1951, c. 655, p. 1847, § 14.)*

Research References

3 Witkin Cal. Proc. 5th Actions § 997, (S 997) Officer or Private Person.

§ 262.8. Elisor; execution of process or orders

Process or orders in an action or proceeding may be executed by a person residing in the county, designated by the court, or the judge thereof, and denominated an elisor, in the following cases:

(a) When the sheriff and coroner are both parties.

(b) When either of these officers is a party, and the process is against the other.

(c) When either of these officers is a party, and there is a vacancy in the office of the other, or where it appears, by affidavit, to the satisfaction of the court in which the proceeding is pending, or the judge thereof, that both of these officers are disqualified, or by reason of any bias, prejudice, or other cause would not act promptly or impartially. *(Added by Stats.1951, c. 655, p. 1848, § 14.)*

Research References

3 Witkin Cal. Proc. 5th Actions § 997, (S 997) Officer or Private Person.
2 Witkin Cal. Proc. 5th Courts § 389, (S 389) Duties in Connection With Process and Notices.

§ 262.9. Elisor; execution of process or order; manner

When process is delivered to an elisor, he shall execute and return it in the same manner as the sheriff is required to execute similar process. *(Added by Stats.1951, c. 655, p. 1848, § 14.)*

§ 262.10. Elisor or coroner; execution of process; compensation

Whenever process is executed, or any act performed by a coroner or elisor, he shall receive a reasonable compensation, to be fixed by the court, to be paid by the plaintiff in case of the summoning of jurors to complete the panel, and by the person or party requiring the service in all other cases in private action. If rendered at the instance of the people, it shall be audited and paid as a county charge. *(Added by Stats.1951, c. 655, p. 1848, § 14.)*

§ 262.11. New counties; execution of process by sheriff of new county

In all cases where new counties have been or may hereafter be created, and executions, orders of sale upon foreclosures of mortgages, or other process affecting specific real estate have been or may hereafter be adjudged by the final judgment or decree of a court of competent jurisdiction, to be executed by the sheriff of the county in which such real estate was originally situated, such process may be executed by the sheriff of the new county in which such real estate is found to be situated, with the like effect as if he were the sheriff of the county designated in the judgment, decree, or order of sale to execute the same. *(Added by Stats.1955, c. 59, p. 499, § 5.)*

CHAPTER 2. LEVYING OFFICER ELECTRONIC TRANSACTIONS ACT

Section
263.   Short title; findings and declarations.
263.1.   Definitions.
263.2.   Information processing system; technical problems.
263.3.   Fax transmissions; cover sheets; requirements; electronic storage.
263.4.   Electronic records; accompanying information; requirements; electronic mail.
263.6.   Return of levying officer's actions in lieu of original writ; record retention; writ directed to another county.
263.7.   Redaction of identifiers; last four digits; writ returns.

§ 263. Short title; findings and declarations

(a) This chapter may be cited as the Levying Officer Electronic Transactions Act.

(b) The Legislature finds and declares that modern technologies offer alternatives to paper-based systems and provide the means to create, store, retrieve, and transmit records and documents in electronic form resulting in increased efficiency, taxpayer savings, and improved public access to levying officers. It is the intent of the Legislature in enacting this act to accommodate current and future technologies based on industry standards.

(c) Nothing in this chapter shall be construed to require a court or levying officer to comply with any of its provisions unless the court and the levying officer have (1) jointly determined that both the court and the sheriff's department have the resources and the technological capacity to do so, and (2) have mutually agreed to electronically act upon documents as provided in this chapter. *(Added by Stats.2010, c. 680 (A.B.2394), § 4.)*

Research References

Rutter, Cal. Practice Guide: Enforcing Judgments/Debts Ch. 6D-3, Levy of Writ of Execution-In General.
8 Witkin Cal. Proc. 5th Enforcement of Judgment § 29, Instructions from Judgment Creditor.
8 Witkin Cal. Proc. 5th Enforcement of Judgment § 106, (S 106) Release of Property.
8 Witkin Cal. Proc. 5th Enforcement of Judgment § 114, (S 114) Return of Writ.
8 Witkin Cal. Proc. 5th Enforcement of Judgment § 140, Garnishee's Memorandum.
8 Witkin Cal. Proc. 5th Enforcement of Judgment § 259, (S 259) Payment of Amounts Withheld.
8 Witkin Cal. Proc. 5th Enforcement of Judgment § 33A, (New)-Electronic Transactions.

§ 263.1. Definitions

As used in this chapter, the following terms have the following definitions:

(a) "Electronic mail" or "e-mail" means an electronic message that is sent to an e-mail address and transmitted between two or more telecommunications devices, computers, or electronic devices capable of receiving electronic messages through a local, regional, or global computer network, whether or not the message is converted to hard copy format after receipt, viewed upon transmission, or stored for later retrieval.

(b) "Electronic record" means a document or record created, generated, sent, communicated, received, or stored by electronic means.

(c) "Electronic signature" means an electronic sound, symbol, or process attached to, or logically associated with, an electronic record and executed or adopted by a person with the intent to sign the electronic record.

(d) "Fax" is an abbreviation for "facsimile" and refers, as indicated by the context, to a facsimile transmission or to a document so transmitted.

(e) "Fax machine" means a machine that can send and receive a facsimile transmission using industry standards and includes a fax modem connected to a computer.

(f) "Fax transmission" means the electronic transmission and reconstruction of a document that prints a duplicate of the original document at the receiving end. "Fax transmission" includes, but is not limited to, the use of a facsimile machine or the process of integrating an electronic fax software application to automate the sending and receiving of a faxed document as an electronic record, in portable data format, by e-mail or similar electronic means.

(g) "Information processing system" means an electronic system for creating, generating, sending, receiving, storing, displaying, retrieving, or processing information, but does not include a fax machine.

(h) "Instructions" and "levying officer instructions" mean a written request to a levying officer to serve process, perform a levy, execute an arrest warrant, or perform some other act.

(i) "Legal entity" means the legal form of an artificial person and includes a corporation, defunct corporation, unincorporated association, partnership, public agency, limited liability company, joint stock company or association, and limited liability partnership.

(j) "Levying officer" means the sheriff or marshal acting as a ministerial officer pursuant to Section 26608 of the Government Code.

(k) "Record" means information that is inscribed on a tangible medium, or that is stored in an electronic or other medium and is retrievable in perceivable form.

(*l*) "Transmission record" means the electronic record or document printed by the sending fax machine, stating the telephone number of the receiving fax machine, the number of pages sent, the transmission time and date, and an indication of any errors in transmission. *(Added by Stats.2010, c. 680 (A.B. 2394), § 4.)*

Research References

Rutter, Cal. Practice Guide: Enforcing Judgments/Debts Ch. 6D-3, Levy of Writ of Execution-In General.
8 Witkin Cal. Proc. 5th Enforcement of Judgment § 33A, (New)-Electronic Transactions.

§ 263.2. Information processing system; technical problems

(a) A levying officer may utilize an information processing system to create, generate, send, receive, store, display, retrieve, or process information, electronic records, and documents when based on industry standards and only to the extent that the levying officer has the resources and technological capacity to do so.

(b) If a technical problem with the levying officer's system prevents the levying officer from receiving an electronic transmission during regular business hours on a particular court day, and the electronic sender demonstrates an attempt to electronically transmit the document on that day, the levying officer shall deem the document or record as filed on that day. *(Added by Stats.2010, c. 680 (A.B.2394), § 4.)*

Research References

Rutter, Cal. Practice Guide: Enforcing Judgments/Debts Ch. 6D-3, Levy of Writ of Execution-In General.
8 Witkin Cal. Proc. 5th Enforcement of Judgment § 33A, (New)-Electronic Transactions.

§ 263.3. Fax transmissions; cover sheets; requirements; electronic storage

Whenever the fax transmission of a document or record to a levying officer is authorized pursuant to this chapter, all of the following shall apply:

(a) A levying officer may act upon an electronic record or document transmitted by a facsimile machine in the same manner as the paper record or document upon which the electronic record or document is based.

(b) A facsimile cover sheet shall accompany the faxed record or document and include all of the following information:

(1) The name of the sender.

(2) The fax number of the sender.

(3) The name of the levying officer.

(4) The fax number of the levying officer.

(5) A description of the record or document, including its name, if any, and the number of pages.

(6) A statement directing the recipient of the faxed document or record to fax to the sender a confirmation, if true, that the fax was properly received.

(c) A person authorized to fax a record or document to the levying officer pursuant to this chapter shall do all of the following:

(1) Retain the paper version of the record or document.

(2) Print or otherwise retain a transmission record of the fax transmission.

(3) Deliver the paper version of the record, document, or transmission record to the levying officer within five days after a request to do so has been mailed to the sender by the levying officer.

(d) The levying officer shall retain the facsimile cover sheet together with the faxed record or document.

(e) The levying officer may electronically copy and store the printed cover sheet, record, or document as an electronic record. *(Added by Stats.2010, c. 680 (A.B.2394), § 4.)*

Research References

Rutter, Cal. Practice Guide: Enforcing Judgments/Debts Ch. 6D-3, Levy of Writ of Execution-In General.
8 Witkin Cal. Proc. 5th Enforcement of Judgment § 33A, (New)-Electronic Transactions.

§ 263.4. Electronic records; accompanying information; requirements; electronic mail

(a) A levying officer may create, store, print, or transmit an electronic record in the place of, and in the same manner as, the paper record or document upon which the electronic record is based.

(b) An electronic record transmitted to a levying officer shall be accompanied by all of the following information:

(1) The name of the sender.

(2) The electronic address of the sender.

(3) The name of the levying officer.

(4) The electronic address or fax number of the levying officer.

(c) The person transmitting the electronic record shall do both of the following:

(1) Retain the paper version of the record or document.

(2) Deliver the paper version of the record or document to the levying officer within five days after a request to do so has been mailed to the sender by the levying officer.

(d) For the purpose of this section, "transmission" of an electronic record includes sending the electronic record included in, or in conjunction with, an electronic mail message, as defined in Section 263.1. *(Added by Stats.2010, c. 680 (A.B.2394), § 4.)*

Research References

Rutter, Cal. Practice Guide: Enforcing Judgments/Debts Ch. 6D-3, Levy of Writ of Execution-In General.
8 Witkin Cal. Proc. 5th Enforcement of Judgment § 33A, (New)-Electronic Transactions.

§ 263.6. Return of levying officer's actions in lieu of original writ; record retention; writ directed to another county

(a) In lieu of returning to court the paper version of an original writ of execution, the levying officer may retain the original writ or an electronic copy of the original writ and file only a return of the levying officer's actions.

(b) If the original writ is not returned to court as provided in subdivision (a), the levying officer shall retain, for not less than two years after the levying officer's return is filed with court, each of the following, as applicable:

(1) The original paper writ or digital image of the writ.

(2) The memorandum of garnishee.

(3) The employer's return.

(4) An inventory of the levied property.

(c) A creditor seeking the issuance of a writ directed to another county may direct the levying officer to file an accounting of the levying officer's actions with the court.

(1) The filing of the accounting described in this subdivision does not constitute a return of the writ.

(2) The accounting shall indicate that the levying officer is in possession of an active writ. *(Added by Stats.2010, c. 680 (A.B.2394), § 4.)*

Research References

Rutter, Cal. Practice Guide: Enforcing Judgments/Debts Ch. 6D-3, Levy of Writ of Execution-In General.

8 Witkin Cal. Proc. 5th Enforcement of Judgment § 114, (S 114) Return of Writ.

8 Witkin Cal. Proc. 5th Enforcement of Judgment § 33A, (New)-Electronic Transactions.

§ 263.7. Redaction of identifiers; last four digits; writ returns

(a) A levying officer shall exclude or redact the following identifiers from any record or document made available to the public:

(1) Social security number.

(2) Financial account number.

(b) If an identifier is redacted, only the last four digits of the number may be used.

(c) A levying officer also shall exclude or redact the identifiers listed in subdivision (a) from any writ return filed with the court.

(d) The term "public" does not include the creditor, debtor, garnishee, or third-party claimant. *(Added by Stats.2010, c. 680 (A.B.2394), § 4.)*

Research References

Rutter, Cal. Practice Guide: Enforcing Judgments/Debts Ch. 6D-3, Levy of Writ of Execution-In General.

8 Witkin Cal. Proc. 5th Enforcement of Judgment § 33A, (New)-Electronic Transactions.

CHAPTER 3. PHONOGRAPHIC REPORTERS

Section

§ 269. Superior courts; duties; preparation of record on appeal from felony conviction

(a) An official reporter or official reporter pro tempore of the superior court shall take down in shorthand all testimony, objections made, rulings of the court, exceptions taken, arraignments, pleas, sentences, arguments of the attorneys to the jury, and statements and remarks made and oral instructions given by the judge or other judicial officer, in the following cases:

(1) In a civil case, on the order of the court or at the request of a party.

(2) In a felony case, on the order of the court or at the request of the prosecution, the defendant, or the attorney for the defendant.

(3) In a misdemeanor or infraction case, on the order of the court.

(b) If a transcript is ordered by the court or requested by a party, or if a nonparty requests a transcript that the nonparty is entitled to receive, regardless of whether the nonparty was permitted to attend the proceeding to be transcribed, the official reporter or official reporter pro tempore shall, within a reasonable time after the trial of the case that the court designates, write the transcripts out, or the specific portions thereof as may be requested, in plain and legible longhand, or by typewriter, or other printing machine, and certify that the transcripts were correctly reported and transcribed, and when directed by the court, file the transcripts with the clerk of the court.

(c) If a defendant is convicted of a felony, after a trial on the merits, the record on appeal shall be prepared immediately after the verdict or finding of guilt is announced unless the court determines that it is likely that no appeal from the decision will be made. The court's determination of a likelihood of appeal shall be based upon standards and rules adopted by the Judicial Council. *(Enacted in 1872. Amended by Code Am.1873–74, c. 383, p. 288, § 24; Code Am.1880, c. 35, p. 53, § 1; Stats.1903, c. 200, p. 234, § 1; Stats.1953, c. 206, p. 1340, § 3; Stats.1990, c. 636 (A.B.2865), § 1; Stats.1993, c. 1016 (A.B.1929), § 1; Stats. 1998, c. 931 (S.B.2139), § 57, eff. Sept. 28, 1998; Stats.2002, c. 71 (S.B.1371), § 1.)*

Law Revision Commission Comments

Section 269 is amended to accommodate unification of the municipal and superior courts in a county. Cal. Const. art. VI, § 5(e). See Section 85 (limited civil cases) & Comment. [28 Cal.L.Rev.Comm. Reports 51 (1998)].

Subdivision (a) of Section 269 is amended to:

(1) Continue former Section 274c without substantive change.

(2) Refer to official reporters pro tempore, as well as official reporters. This is not a substantive change. See Gov't Code § 69941 (appointment of official reporter and official reporter pro tempore).

(3) Substitute "arguments of the attorneys" for "arguments of the prosecuting attorney," consistent with standard practice. See, e.g., Gov't Code § 72194.5 ("arguments of the attorneys").

(4) Substitute "prosecution" for "district attorney," to reflect that the Attorney General sometimes acts as prosecutor in place of the district attorney. See Gov't Code § 12553 (disqualification of district attorney); see also Penal Code § 1424 (motion to disqualify district attorney).

(5) Make clear that it requires shorthand reporting regardless of whether a proceeding is conducted by a judge or by another type of judicial officer (e.g., a commissioner). For an exception to this rule, see Gov't Code § 70141.11 (court reporting for Contra Costa County commissioner).

(6) Make clear that a felony defendant, whether represented by counsel or in pro per, is entitled to a court reporter on request by the defendant personally or by the defendant's attorney (if any). This is not a substantive change. See generally People v. Turner, 67 Cal.App.4th 1258, 1266, 79 Cal.Rptr.2d 740 (1998) ("verbatim record is implicitly among the rights of which a defendant appearing in propria persona must be apprised"); Andrus v. Municipal Court, 143 Cal.App.3d 1041, 1050, 192 Cal.Rptr. 341 (1983) (California confers right to free verbatim record "in felony proceedings by statute (Code Civ. Proc., § 269)."); *In re* Armstrong, 126 Cal.App.3d 565, 572, 178 Cal.Rptr. 902 (1981) (felony defendant "*is*, as a matter of right, entitled to have 'taken down,' all related testimony and oral proceedings") (emphasis in original); People v. Goudeau, 8 Cal. App.3d 275, 279–80, 87 Cal.Rptr. 424 (1970) ("In California felony proceedings a court reporter must be present if requested by the defendant, the district attorney, or on order of the court. (Code Civ. Proc., § 269.)"); People v. Hollander, 194 Cal.App.2d 386, 391–93, 14 Cal.Rptr. 917 (1961) (denial of transcript to pro per indigent defendant was prejudicial error).

Subdivision (b) is amended to make clear that a nonparty is generally entitled to request preparation of a transcript. This is consistent with longstanding practice and conforms to constitutional constraints. See, e.g., Press–Enterprise Co. v. Superior Court, 478 U.S. 1 (1986) (media request for transcript of preliminary hearing); Fisher v. King, 232 F.3d 391, 397 (4th Cir. 2000) (general public and press "enjoy a qualified right of access under the First Amendment to criminal proceedings *and the transcripts thereof*") (emphasis added); United States v. Antar, 38 F.3d 1348, 1360–61

(3d Cir. 1994) ("First Amendment right of access must extend equally to transcripts as to live proceedings"); United States v. Berger, 990 F. Supp. 1054, 1057 (C.D. Ill. 1998) ("There is no question that a written transcript of the Governor's deposition would be made available to the public upon the admission of his testimony before the jury."); State *ex rel.* Scripps Howard Broadcasting Co. v. Cuyahoga County Court of Common Pleas, 73 Ohio St. 3d 19, 21, 652 N.E.2d 179 (1995) (right of access "includes both the live proceedings and the transcripts which document those proceedings"); see also NBC Subsidiary (KNBC–TV), Inc. v. Superior Court, 20 Cal.4th 1178, 980 P.2d 337, 86 Cal.Rptr.2d 778 (1999) (constitutional right of access applies to civil as well as criminal cases). A nonparty is entitled to a transcript of (1) a proceeding that was open to the public, see *Scripps Howard Broadcasting*, 73 Ohio St. 3d at 21; (2) a proceeding that was erroneously closed to the public, see generally *Press-Enterprise*, 478 U.S. at 15; and (3) a proceeding that was properly closed, once "the competing interests precipitating closure are no longer viable," see Phoenix Newspapers, Inc. v. United States Dist. Court, 156 F.3d 940, 947–48 (9th Cir. 1998).

Subdivision (b) is also amended to refer to official reporters pro tempore, as well as official reporters.

Former subdivision (c) is continued in Section 271 without substantive change.

The other revisions in Section 269 are technical, nonsubstantive changes. [31 Cal.L.Rev.Comm. Reports 235 (2002)].

Research References

Rutter, Cal. Practice Guide: Civil Appeals & Writs Ch. 4-A, A. General Considerations.
Rutter, Cal. Practice Guide: Civil Appeals & Writs Ch. 4-C, C. Record Preparation Procedure.
Rutter, Cal. Practice Guide: Civ. Pro. Before Trial Ch. 9(I)-A, A. Introduction.
Rutter, Cal. Practice Guide: Civil Trials & Evidence Ch. 1-A, A. Importance of Statewide and Local Rules of Court.
Rutter, Cal. Practice Guide: Civil Trials & Evidence Ch. 1-L, L. Assignment to Trial Department.
Rutter, Cal. Practice Guide: Civil Trials & Evidence Ch. 15-D, D. Juror Requests for Additional Information During Deliberations.
2 Witkin Cal. Proc. 5th Courts § 380, Reporting and Clerical Assistance.
2 Witkin Cal. Proc. 5th Courts § 381, Transcription.
2 Witkin Cal. Proc. 5th Courts § 383, Electronic Recording.

§ 271. Computer-readable format; time to request copies; standards

(a) Any court, party, or other person entitled to a transcript may request that it be delivered in computer-readable form, except that an original transcript shall be on paper. A copy of the original transcript ordered within 120 days of the filing or delivery of the transcript by the official reporter or official reporter pro tempore shall be delivered in computer-readable form upon request if the proceedings were produced utilizing computer-aided transcription equipment.

(b) Except as modified by standards adopted by the Judicial Council, the computer-readable transcript shall be on disks in standard ASCII code, unless otherwise agreed by the reporter and the court, party, or other person requesting the transcript. Each disk shall be labeled with the case name and court number, the dates of proceedings contained on the disk, and the page and volume numbers of the data contained on the disk. Except where modifications are necessary to reflect corrections of a transcript, each disk as produced by the official reporter shall contain the identical volume divisions, pagination, line numbering, and text of the certified original paper transcript or any portion thereof. Each disk shall be sequentially numbered within the series of disks. *(Added by Stats.2002, c. 71 (S.B.1371), § 2.)*

Law Revision Commission Comments

Section 271 continues former Section 269(c) without change, except to insert subdivisions, refer to official reporters pro tempore as well as official reporters, make clear that a computer-readable version of a transcript is available only where a person is entitled to a hard-copy

version, and clarify how the provision applies where a transcript is corrected. These revisions are nonsubstantive. See Gov't Code § 69941 (appointment of official reporter and official reporter pro tempore). [31 Cal.L.Rev.Comm. Reports 238 (2002)].

Research References

Rutter, Cal. Practice Guide: Civil Appeals & Writs Ch. 4-C, C. Record Preparation Procedure.
Rutter, Cal. Practice Guide: Civil Appeals & Writs Ch. 4-E, E. Filing and Correction of Record.
Rutter, Cal. Practice Guide: Civil Trials & Evidence Ch. 1-L, L. Assignment to Trial Department.
2 Witkin Cal. Proc. 5th Courts § 381, Transcription.

§ 273. Transcribed and certified reports as prima facie evidence; rough draft transcripts; instant visual displays

Section operative until Jan. 1, 2017. See,
also, section operative Jan. 1, 2017.

(a) The report of the official reporter, or official reporter pro tempore, of any court, duly appointed and sworn, when transcribed and certified as being a correct transcript of the testimony and proceedings in the case, is prima facie evidence of that testimony and proceedings.

(b) The report of the official reporter, or official reporter pro tempore, of any court, duly appointed and sworn, when prepared as a rough draft transcript, shall not be certified and cannot be used, cited, distributed, or transcribed as the official certified transcript of the proceedings. A rough draft transcript shall not be cited or used in any way or at any time to rebut or contradict the official certified transcript of the proceedings as provided by the official reporter or official reporter pro tempore. The production of a rough draft transcript shall not be required.

(c) The instant visual display of the testimony or proceedings, or both, shall not be certified and cannot be used, cited, distributed, or transcribed as the official certified transcript of the proceedings. The instant visual display of the testimony or proceedings, or both, shall not be cited or used in any way or at any time to rebut or contradict the official certified transcript of the proceedings as provided by the official reporter or official reporter pro tempore.

(d) This section shall remain in effect only until January 1, 2017, and as of that date is repealed, unless a later enacted statute, that is enacted before January 1, 2017, deletes or extends that date. *(Formerly § 270, enacted in 1872. Amended by Code Am.1873–74, c. 591, p. 400, § 1. Renumbered § 273 and amended by Code Am.1880, c. 35, p. 54, § 1. Amended by Stats.1903, c. 200, p. 234, § 2; Stats.1997, c. 183 (A.B.1372), § 1; Stats.2009, c. 87 (A.B.170), § 1.)*

Repeal

For repeal of this section, see its terms.

Research References

Rutter, Cal. Practice Guide: Civil Trials & Evidence Ch. 1-L, L. Assignment to Trial Department.
Rutter, Cal. Practice Guide: Civil Trials & Evidence Ch. 8G-C, C. Presumptions.
2 Witkin Cal. Proc. 5th Courts § 381, Transcription.
2 Witkin Cal. Proc. 5th Courts § 383, Electronic Recording.

§ 273. Transcribed and certified reports as prima facie evidence; rough draft transcripts

Section operative Jan. 1, 2017. See, also,
section operative until Jan. 1, 2017.

(a) The report of the official reporter, or official reporter pro tempore, of any court, duly appointed and sworn, when transcribed and certified as being a correct transcript of the testimony and proceedings in the case, is prima facie evidence of that testimony and proceedings.

(b) The report of the official reporter, or official reporter pro tempore, of any court, duly appointed and sworn, when prepared as a rough draft transcript, shall not be certified and cannot be used, cited, distributed, or transcribed as the official certified transcript of the proceedings. A rough draft transcript shall not be cited or used in any way or at any time to rebut or contradict the official certified transcript of the proceedings as provided by the official reporter or official reporter pro tempore. The production of a rough draft transcript shall not be required.

(c) This section shall become operative on January 1, 2017. *(Added by Stats.2009, c. 87 (A.B.170), § 2, operative Jan. 1, 2017.)*

Research References

Rutter, Cal. Practice Guide: Civil Trials & Evidence Ch. 1-L, L. Assignment to Trial Department.
Rutter, Cal. Practice Guide: Civil Trials & Evidence Ch. 8G-C, C. Presumptions.
2 Witkin Cal. Proc. 5th Courts § 381, Transcription.
2 Witkin Cal. Proc. 5th Courts § 383, Electronic Recording.

§ 274a. Transcription of matters at request of judge; county charge; exception

Any judge of the superior court may have any opinion given or rendered by the judge in the trial of a felony case or an unlimited civil case, pending in that court, or any necessary order, petition, citation, commitment or judgment in any probate proceeding, proceeding concerning new or additional bonds of county officials or juvenile court proceeding, or the testimony or judgment relating to the custody or support of minor children in any proceeding in which the custody or support of minor children is involved, taken down in shorthand and transcribed together with such copies as the court may deem necessary by the official reporter or an official reporter pro tempore of the court. *(Added by Stats.1907, c. 22, p. 15, § 1. Amended by Stats.1911, c. 308, p. 499, § 1; Stats.1929, c. 720, p. 1310, § 1; Stats.1933, c. 740, p. 1803, § 2; Stats.1947, c. 152, p. 681, § 1; Stats.1963, c. 298, § 1; Stats.1998, c. 931 (S.B.2139), § 58, eff. Sept. 28, 1998; Stats.2002, c. 784 (S.B.1316), § 51.)*

Law Revision Commission Comments

Section 274a is amended to accommodate unification of the municipal and superior courts in a county. Cal. Const. art. VI, § 5(e). See Section 85 (limited civil cases) & Comment. [28 Cal.L.Rev.Comm. Reports 51 (1998)].

Section 274a is amended to reflect enactment of the Trial Court Funding Act. See Gov't Code §§ 77003 ("court operations" defined), 77009 (Trial Court Operations Fund), 77200 (state funding of trial court operations). See also Gov't Code §§ 69941 (appointment of official reporters), 70311 (responsibility for court operations and facilities).

The section is also amended to delete the reference to insanity proceedings or proceedings for the feebleminded. That provision is superseded by Government Code Section 69952(a)(4) (verbatim record in proceedings under Lanterman–Petris–Short Act).

The section is also amended to replace "civil case other than a limited civil case" with a reference to "unlimited civil case." See Section 88 (civil action or proceeding other than limited civil case may be referred to as unlimited civil case). [32 Cal.L.Rev.Comm.Reports 116 (2002)].

Research References

2 Witkin Cal. Proc. 5th Courts § 380, Reporting and Clerical Assistance.

Title 5

PERSONS SPECIALLY INVESTED WITH MINISTERIAL POWERS RELATING TO COURTS OF JUSTICE

CHAPTER 1. ATTORNEYS AND COUNSELORS AT LAW

§ 283. Authority

An attorney and counselor shall have authority:

1. To bind his client in any of the steps of an action or proceeding by his agreement filed with the Clerk, or entered upon the minutes of the Court, and not otherwise;

2. To receive money claimed by his client in an action or proceeding during the pendency thereof, or after judgment, unless a revocation of his authority is filed, and upon the payment thereof, and not otherwise, to discharge the claim or acknowledge satisfaction of the judgment. *(Enacted in 1872. Amended by Code Am.1880, c. 35, p. 57, § 1.)*

Research References

Rutter, Cal. Practice Guide: Civ. Pro. Before Trial Ch. 1-A, A. Accepting a New Case.
Rutter, Cal. Practice Guide: Civil Trials & Evidence Ch. 8C-K, K. Stipulations.
Rutter, Cal. Practice Guide: Civil Trials & Evidence Ch. 8D-D, D. Hearsay Exceptions.
Rutter, Cal. Practice Guide: Enforcing Judgments/Debts Ch. 6K-1, Acknowledgment of Full Satisfaction of Judgment.
Rutter, Cal. Practice Guide: Enforcing Judgments/Debts Ch. 6A-10, Service of Writs, Notices and Other Papers in Enforcement Proceedings.
Rutter, Cal. Practice Guide: Prof. Responsibility Ch. 3-A, A. Nature of Attorney-Client Relationship.
Rutter, Cal. Practice Guide: Prof. Responsibility Ch. 3-D, D. Authority of Client vs. Authority of Attorney.
1 Witkin Cal. Proc. 5th Attorneys § 235, (S 235) General Rules of Agency Apply.
1 Witkin Cal. Proc. 5th Attorneys § 249, (S 249) Ratification.
1 Witkin Cal. Proc. 5th Attorneys § 255, (S 255) in General.
1 Witkin Cal. Proc. 5th Attorneys § 259, Receipt of Money in Settlement.
1 Witkin Cal. Proc. 5th Attorneys § 266, in General.
1 Witkin Cal. Proc. 5th Attorneys § 267, Written Stipulation Filed.
1 Witkin Cal. Proc. 5th Attorneys § 268, Oral Stipulation in Minutes.
1 Witkin Cal. Proc. 5th Attorneys § 269, (S 269) in General.
8 Witkin Cal. Proc. 5th Enforcement of Judgment § 26, in General.
3 Witkin, California Summary 10th Agency and Employment § 143, (S 143) Limitations on Power to Ratify.

§ 284. Change or substitution; consent; order of court

The attorney in an action or special proceeding may be changed at any time before or after judgment or final determination, as follows:

1. Upon the consent of both client and attorney, filed with the clerk, or entered upon the minutes;

2. Upon the order of the court, upon the application of either client or attorney, after notice from one to the other.

(Enacted in 1872. Amended by Code Am.1873–74, c. 383, p. 289, § 26; Code Am.1880, c. 35, p. 57, § 1; Stats.1935, c. 560, p. 1647, § 1; Stats.1967, c. 161, p. 1246, § 1.)

Research References

Rutter, Cal. Practice Guide: Civil Appeals & Writs Ch. 1-E, E. Preappeal Evaluation and "Housekeeping" Steps.

Rutter, Cal. Practice Guide: Civ. Pro. Before Trial Ch. 9(I)-G, G. Motions Regulating Counsel.

Rutter, Cal. Practice Guide: Civil Trials & Evidence Ch. 1-A, A. Importance of Statewide and Local Rules of Court.

Rutter, Cal. Practice Guide: Enforcing Judgments/Debts Ch. 1-B, B. Accepting the Collection Case.

Rutter, Cal. Practice Guide: Personal Injury Ch. 1-C, C. Formation of Attorney-Client Relationship: the Employment Agreement.

Rutter, Cal. Practice Guide: Real Prop. Transactions Ch. 1-C, C. Attorney Fees and Costs Agreements.

Rutter, Cal. Practice Guide: Prof. Responsibility Ch. 1-I, I. Regulation of Sale of Law Practice.

Rutter, Cal. Practice Guide: Prof. Responsibility Ch. 5-F, F. Formalizing Fee Agreements.

Rutter, Cal. Practice Guide: Prof. Responsibility Ch. 5-K, K. Fee Recovery/Enforcing Fee Agreements.

Rutter, Cal. Practice Guide: Prof. Responsibility Ch. 8-B, B. Accepting or Rejecting Employment.

Rutter, Cal. Practice Guide: Prof. Responsibility Ch. 10-B, B. Withdrawal (Termination) by Lawyer.

1 Witkin Cal. Proc. 5th Attorneys § 45, (S 45) Association for Particular Case.

1 Witkin Cal. Proc. 5th Attorneys § 69, (S 69) Motion to Withdraw.

1 Witkin Cal. Proc. 5th Attorneys § 70, (S 70) Discretion of Court.

1 Witkin Cal. Proc. 5th Attorneys § 75, Absolute Right to Discharge.

1 Witkin Cal. Proc. 5th Attorneys § 78, (S 78) Former Attorney's Authority.

1 Witkin Cal. Proc. 5th Attorneys § 80, (S 80) in General.

1 Witkin Cal. Proc. 5th Attorneys § 81, (S 81) Notice of Substitution.

1 Witkin Cal. Proc. 5th Attorneys § 98, Where Fee Agreement Creates Conflict of Interest.

1 Witkin Cal. Proc. 5th Attorneys § 147, (S 147) Enforcement of Collective Bargaining Rights.

1 Witkin Cal. Proc. 5th Attorneys § 423, (S 423) Nature and Scope of Rule.

11 Witkin, California Summary 10th Husband and Wife § 74, (S 74) Limited Scope Legal Representation.

3 Witkin, California Summary 10th Agency and Employment § 579, Attorneys Employed by County Counsel.

2 Witkin Cal. Summ. 10th Workers' Compensation § 353, Appearance and Representation.

§ 285. Change or substitution; notice

When an attorney is changed, as provided in the last section, written notice of the change and of the substitution of a new attorney, or of the appearance of the party in person, must be given to the adverse party. Until then he must recognize the former attorney. *(Enacted in 1872. Amended by Code Am.1880, c. 35, p. 57, § 1.)*

Research References

Rutter, Cal. Practice Guide: Personal Injury Ch. 1-C, C. Formation of Attorney-Client Relationship: the Employment Agreement.

Rutter, Cal. Practice Guide: Prof. Responsibility Ch. 10-B, B. Withdrawal (Termination) by Lawyer.

1 Witkin Cal. Proc. 5th Attorneys § 45, (S 45) Association for Particular Case.

1 Witkin Cal. Proc. 5th Attorneys § 78, (S 78) Former Attorney's Authority.

1 Witkin Cal. Proc. 5th Attorneys § 423, (S 423) Nature and Scope of Rule.

§ 285.1. Withdrawal of attorneys of record in domestic relations proceedings; notice; contents; mailing and service

An attorney of record for any party in any civil action or proceeding for dissolution of marriage, legal separation, or for a declaration of void or voidable marriage, or for the support,

maintenance or custody of minor children may withdraw at any time subsequent to the time when any judgment in such action or proceeding, other than an interlocutory judgment, becomes final, and prior to service upon him of pleadings or motion papers in any proceeding then pending in said cause, by filing a notice of withdrawal. Such notice shall state (a) date of entry of final decree or judgment, (b) the last known address of such party, (c) that such attorney withdraws as attorney for such party. A copy of such notice shall be mailed to such party at his last known address and shall be served upon the adverse party. *(Added by Stats.1963, c. 1333, p. 2856, § 1. Amended by Stats.1969, c. 1608, p. 3344, § 10, operative Jan. 1, 1970.)*

Research References

Rutter, Cal. Practice Guide: Prof. Responsibility Ch. 6-D, D. Professional Liability.

Rutter, Cal. Practice Guide: Prof. Responsibility Ch. 10-B, B. Withdrawal (Termination) by Lawyer.

Rutter, Cal. Practice Guide: Prof. Responsibility Ch. 6-D, Outline D.

3 Witkin Cal. Proc. 5th Actions § 644, Statute Not Tolled.

1 Witkin Cal. Proc. 5th Attorneys § 71, (S 71) Cases Involving Family Law or Minors.

6 Witkin Cal. Proc. 5th Proceedings Without Trial § 14, Exceptions.

§ 285.2. Reduction in public funding; permission to withdraw for material impairment of ability to represent indigent client

If a reduction in public funding for legal service materially impairs a legal service agency attorney's ability to represent an indigent client, the court, on its own motion or on the motion of either the client or attorney, shall permit the withdrawal of such attorney upon a showing that all of the following apply:

(a) There are not adequate public funds to continue the effective representation of the indigent client.

(b) A good faith effort was made to find alternate representation for such client.

(c) All reasonable steps to reduce the legal prejudice to the client have been taken.

A showing of indigency of the client, in and of itself, will not be deemed sufficient cause to deny the application for withdrawal. *(Added by Stats.1983, c. 279, § 1.)*

Research References

Rutter, Cal. Practice Guide: Prof. Responsibility Ch. 8-B, B. Accepting or Rejecting Employment.

Rutter, Cal. Practice Guide: Prof. Responsibility Ch. 10-B, B. Withdrawal (Termination) by Lawyer.

1 Witkin Cal. Proc. 5th Attorneys § 74, Legal Service Agency Attorney.

§ 285.3. Tolling statute of limitations; withdrawal of attorney for reduction in public funding

The court, upon the granting of a motion for withdrawal pursuant to Section 285.2, may toll the running of any statute of limitations, filing requirement, statute providing for mandatory dismissal, notice of appeal, or discovery requirement, for a period not to exceed 90 days, on the court's own motion or on motion of any party or attorney, when the court finds that tolling is required to avoid legal prejudice caused by the withdrawal of the legal service agency attorney. *(Added by Stats.1983, c. 279, § 2.)*

Research References

Rutter, Cal. Practice Guide: Prof. Responsibility Ch. 10-B, B. Withdrawal (Termination) by Lawyer.

1 Witkin Cal. Proc. 5th Attorneys § 74, Legal Service Agency Attorney.

§ 285.4. Withdrawal due to reduction in public funding; appointment of attorney, law firm or law corporation without compensation

The court, upon the granting of a motion for withdrawal pursuant to Section 285.2, may appoint any member of the bar or any law firm or professional law corporation to represent the indigent client without compensation, upon a showing of good cause. Nothing herein shall preclude the appointed attorney from recovering any attorneys' fees and costs to which the client may be entitled by law. In determining the existence of good cause, the court may consider, but is not limited to, the following factors:

(a) The probable merit of the client's claim.

(b) The client's financial ability to pay for legal services.

(c) The availability of alternative legal representation.

(d) The need for legal representation to avoid irreparable legal prejudice to the indigent client.

(e) The ability of appointed counsel to effectively represent the indigent client.

(f) Present and recent pro bono work of the appointed attorney, law firm or private law corporation.

(g) The ability of the indigent client to represent himself.

(h) The workload of the appointed attorney. *(Added by Stats.1983, c. 279, § 3.)*

Research References

Rutter, Cal. Practice Guide: Prof. Responsibility Ch. 8-B, B. Accepting or Rejecting Employment.
Rutter, Cal. Practice Guide: Prof. Responsibility Ch. 10-B, B. Withdrawal (Termination) by Lawyer.
1 Witkin Cal. Proc. 5th Attorneys § 74, Legal Service Agency Attorney.

§ 286. Death, removal, etc.; new appointment or appearance in person

When an attorney dies, or is removed or suspended, or ceases to act as such, a party to an action, for whom he was acting as attorney, must, before any further proceedings are had against him, be required by the adverse party, by written notice, to appoint another attorney, or to appear in person. *(Enacted in 1872. Amended by Code Am.1880, c. 35, p. 57, § 1.)*

Research References

Rutter, Cal. Practice Guide: Civ. Pro. Before Trial Ch. 5-G, G. Relief from Default.
Rutter, Cal. Practice Guide: Civ. Pro. Before Trial Ch. 5-G, Outline G.
Rutter, Cal. Practice Guide: Prof. Responsibility Ch. 10-C, C. Termination by Operation of Law.
1 Witkin Cal. Proc. 5th Attorneys § 66, Death or Incapacity of Attorney.
1 Witkin Cal. Proc. 5th Attorneys § 70, (S 70) Discretion of Court.
2 Witkin Cal. Proc. 5th Jurisdiction § 198, (S 198) in General.
5 Witkin, California Summary 10th Torts § 528, (S 528) Defense of Absolute Privilege.

Part 2

OF CIVIL ACTIONS

Title 1

OF THE FORM OF CIVIL ACTIONS

§ 307. One form only

ONE FORM OF CIVIL ACTION ONLY. There is in this State but one form of civil actions for the enforcement or protection of private rights and the redress or prevention of private wrongs. *(Enacted in 1872.)*

Research References

Rutter, Cal. Practice Guide: Civ. Pro. Before Trial Ch. 6-A, A. Introduction.
4 Witkin Cal. Proc. 5th Pleading § 30, Nature of Reform.
13 Witkin, California Summary 10th Equity § 2, (S 2) Distinctive Features of Equity.

§ 308. Parties; designation

PARTIES TO ACTIONS, HOW DESIGNATED. In such action the party complaining is known as the plaintiff, and the adverse party as the defendant. *(Enacted in 1872.)*

Research References

4 Witkin Cal. Proc. 5th Pleading § 67, (S 67) Designation of Parties.

§ 309. Trial of questions of fact not put in issue by pleadings; order for trial

SPECIAL ISSUES NOT MADE BY PLEADINGS, HOW TRIED. A question of fact not put in issue by the pleadings may be tried by a jury, upon an order for the trial, stating distinctly and plainly the question of fact to be tried; and such order is the only authority necessary for a trial. *(Enacted in 1872.)*

Title 2

OF THE TIME OF COMMENCING CIVIL ACTIONS

CHAPTER 1. THE TIME OF COMMENCING ACTIONS IN GENERAL

§ 312. General limitations; special cases

Civil actions, without exception, can only be commenced within the periods prescribed in this title, after the cause of action shall have accrued, unless where, in special cases, a different limitation is prescribed by statute. *(Enacted in 1872. Amended by Stats.1897, c. 21, p. 16, § 1.)*

Research References

Rutter, Cal. Practice Guide: Fed.Civ.Pro. Before Trial Ch. 5-C, C. Issuance of Summons; Form and Content.
Rutter, Cal. Practice Guide: Personal Injury Ch. 5-B, B. When to Sue-Statute of Limitations.
Miller and Starr California Real Estate § 16:17, In General; Statutory Period.
Miller and Starr California Real Estate § 7:211, Statute of Limitations.
Miller and Starr California Real Estate § 7:221, Statute of Limitations.
3 Witkin Cal. Proc. 5th Actions § 431, (S 431) Statutory Classification.
3 Witkin Cal. Proc. 5th Actions § 447, (S 447) Actions and Special Proceedings.
3 Witkin Cal. Proc. 5th Actions § 493, What Constitutes Accrual.

§ 313. Claims against local public entities

The general procedure for the presentation of claims as a prerequisite to commencement of actions for money or damages against the State of California, counties, cities, cities and counties, districts, local authorities, and other political subdivisions of the State, and against the officers, employees, and servants thereof, is prescribed by Division 3.6 (commencing with Section 810) of Title 1 of the Government Code. *(Added by Stats.1959, c. 1724, p. 4138, § 3. Amended by Stats.1963, c. 1715, p. 3396, § 9.)*

CHAPTER 2. THE TIME OF COMMENCING ACTIONS FOR THE RECOVERY OF REAL PROPERTY

§ 315. Actions by people

WHEN THE PEOPLE WILL NOT SUE. The people of this State will not sue any person for or in respect to any real property, or the issues or profits thereof, by reason of the right or title of the people to the same, unless:

1. Such right or title shall have accrued within ten years before any action or other proceeding for the same is commenced; or,

2. The people, or those from whom they claim, shall have received the rents and profits of such real property, or of some part thereof, within the space of ten years. *(Enacted in 1872.)*

Research References

Miller and Starr California Real Estate § 16:43, Political Entities and Public Agencies--Property Held in a Governmental Capacity.
Miller and Starr California Real Estate § 16:44, Political Entities and Public Agencies--Property Held in a Proprietary Capacity.
23 NO. 2 Miller & Starr, California Real Estate Newsalert 3, Adjoining Landowners.
3 Witkin Cal. Proc. 5th Actions § 456, State or Political Subdivision.
3 Witkin Cal. Proc. 5th Actions § 488, (S 488) Ten Years.
12 Witkin, California Summary 10th Real Property § 233, Showing of Seisin or Possession.

§ 316. Action by grantee from state

WHEN ACTION CANNOT BE BROUGHT BY GRANTEE FROM THE STATE. No action can be brought for or in respect to real property by any person claiming under letters patent or grants from this State, unless the same might have been commenced by the people as herein specified, in case such patent had not been issued or grant made. *(Enacted in 1872.)*

Research References

Miller and Starr California Real Estate § 16:43, Political Entities and Public Agencies--Property Held in a Governmental Capacity.
3 Witkin Cal. Proc. 5th Actions § 488, (S 488) Ten Years.

§ 317. Actions by people or grantees; five year limit

When letters patent or grants of real property issued or made by the people of this State, are declared void by the determination of a competent Court, an action for the recovery of the property so conveyed may be brought, either by the people of the State, or by any subsequent patentee or grantee of the property, his heirs or assigns, within five years after such determination, but not after that period. *(Enacted in 1872. Amended by Code Am.1873–74, c. 383, p. 291, § 30.)*

Research References

3 Witkin Cal. Proc. 5th Actions § 485, (S 485) Five Years.

§ 318. Seizin within five years; necessity

SEIZIN WITHIN FIVE YEARS, WHEN NECESSARY IN ACTION FOR REAL PROPERTY. No action for the recovery of real property, or for the recovery of the possession thereof, can be maintained, unless it appear that the plaintiff, his ancestor, predecessor, or grantor, was seized or possessed of the property in question, within five years before the commencement of the action. *(Enacted in 1872.)*

Research References

Rutter, Cal. Practice Guide: Real Prop. Transactions Ch. 11-H, H. Other Remedies.
Miller and Starr California Real Estate § 14:7, Limitations of Actions.
Miller and Starr California Real Estate § 8:23, Mental Incapacity to Convey.
Miller and Starr California Real Estate § 14:44, Elements of Agreed Boundary Doctrine--Occupancy; Period of Use.
Miller and Starr California Real Estate § 15:31, Public or Private Easement by Prescription.
Miller and Starr California Real Estate § 15:38, Prescriptive Period.
Miller and Starr California Real Estate § 15:84, Easements by Necessity--Termination of the Necessity.
Miller and Starr California Real Estate § 16:17, In General; Statutory Period.
Miller and Starr California Real Estate § 16:21, Interruption of Possession--Suit by the Owner.
Miller and Starr California Real Estate § 16:26, Capacity; Quiet Title Action by an Adverse Possessor.
Miller and Starr California Real Estate § 17:28, Airspace.
Miller and Starr California Real Estate § 25:54, Judicial Review.
Miller and Starr California Real Estate § 30:15, Statute of Limitations; Defenses.
Miller and Starr California Real Estate § 34:106, Statute of Limitations.
Miller and Starr California Real Estate § 34:110, Burden of Proof.
Miller and Starr California Real Estate § 34:112, Cancellation of Instruments: Nature of the Remedy.
Miller and Starr California Real Estate § 34:118, Statute of Limitations.
14 NO. 6 Miller & Starr, California Real Estate Newsalert 1, Too Much of a Good Thing: California Courts Weigh in on Exclusive Prescriptive Easements.
14 NO. 5 Miller & Starr, California Real Estate Newsalert 10, Easements.
19 NO. 5 Miller & Starr, California Real Estate Newsalert 20, Inverse Condemnation.
21 NO. 2 Miller & Starr, California Real Estate Newsalert 16, Inverse Condemnation.
22 NO. 6 Miller & Starr, California Real Estate Newsalert 12, Easements.
3 Witkin Cal. Proc. 5th Actions § 398, (S 398) Action to Impose Constructive Trust.
3 Witkin Cal. Proc. 5th Actions § 485, (S 485) Five Years.
3 Witkin Cal. Proc. 5th Actions § 491, Cancellation of Void Instrument.
3 Witkin Cal. Proc. 5th Actions § 508, Action on Written Contract.
3 Witkin Cal. Proc. 5th Actions § 596, (S 596) Scope of Statute.
3 Witkin Cal. Proc. 5th Actions § 605, (S 605) Distinction: Inverse Condemnation.
3 Witkin Cal. Proc. 5th Actions § 658, (S 658) Recovery of Real Property.
3 Witkin Cal. Proc. 5th Actions § 681, What Statutes Apply.
12 Witkin, California Summary 10th Real Property § 227, (S 227) Continuous Possession.
12 Witkin, California Summary 10th Real Property § 229, (S 229) Laches Does Not Bar Claim of Adverse Possession.
12 Witkin, California Summary 10th Real Property § 233, Showing of Seisin or Possession.
12 Witkin, California Summary 10th Real Property § 398, (S 398) Right to Easement.

8 Witkin, California Summary 10th Constitutional Law § 1166, Statute of Limitations.

§ 319. Seizin within five years; necessity to action or defense; cases involving title, rents or profits

SUCH SEIZIN, WHEN NECESSARY IN ACTION OR DEFENSE ARISING OUT OF TITLE TO OR RENTS OF REAL PROPERTY. No cause of action, or defense to an action, arising out of the title to real property, or to rents or profits out of the same, can be effectual, unless it appear that the person prosecuting the action, or making the defense, or under whose title the action is prosecuted, or the defense is made, or the ancestor, predecessor, or grantor of such person was seized or possessed of the premises in question within five years before the commencement of the act in respect to which such action is prosecuted or defense made. *(Enacted in 1872.)*

Research References

Rutter, Cal. Practice Guide: Real Prop. Transactions Ch. 11-H, H. Other Remedies.
Miller and Starr California Real Estate § 8:23, Mental Incapacity to Convey.
Miller and Starr California Real Estate § 15:38, Prescriptive Period
Miller and Starr California Real Estate § 16:17, In General; Statutory Period.
Miller and Starr California Real Estate § 17:28, Airspace.
Miller and Starr California Real Estate § 25:54, Judicial Review.
Miller and Starr California Real Estate § 30:15, Statute of Limitations; Defenses.
Miller and Starr California Real Estate § 34:106, Statute of Limitations.
Miller and Starr California Real Estate § 34:112, Cancellation of Instruments: Nature of the Remedy.
15 NO. 2 Miller & Starr, California Real Estate Newsalert 11, Subdivisions.
19 NO. 5 Miller & Starr, California Real Estate Newsalert 20, Inverse Condemnation.
21 NO. 2 Miller & Starr, California Real Estate Newsalert 16, Inverse Condemnation.
3 Witkin Cal. Proc. 5th Actions § 462, in General.
3 Witkin Cal. Proc. 5th Actions § 485, (S 485) Five Years.
3 Witkin Cal. Proc. 5th Actions § 491, Cancellation of Void Instrument.
12 Witkin, California Summary 10th Real Property § 227, (S 227) Continuous Possession.
8 Witkin, California Summary 10th Constitutional Law § 1166, Statute of Limitations.

§ 320. Entry; sufficiency; one and five year limitation of actions

ENTRY ON REAL ESTATE. No entry upon real estate is deemed sufficient or valid as a claim, unless an action be commenced thereupon within one year after making such entry, and within five years from the time when the right to make it descended or accrued. *(Enacted in 1872.)*

Research References

Rutter, Cal. Practice Guide: Enforcing Judgments/Debts Form 6:YY.3, Notice of Motion to Charge LLC Member's Interst.
Miller and Starr California Real Estate § 11:68, Constructive Notice of Interests Barred by the Statute of Limitations--"Ancient Documents" and the Marketable Record Title Act.
Miller and Starr California Real Estate § 34:106, Statute of Limitations.
12 Witkin, California Summary 10th Real Property § 343, (S 343) Operative Date of Provisions.

§ 321. Presumption of timely possession; presumption of subordinate occupation; adverse possession for five years

POSSESSION, WHEN PRESUMED. In every action for the recovery of real property, or the possession thereof, the person establishing a legal title to the property is presumed to have been possessed thereof within the time required by law, and the occupation of the property by any other person is deemed to have been under and in subordination to the legal title, unless it appear that the property has been held and possessed adversely to such legal title, for five years before the commencement of the action. *(Enacted in 1872.)*

Research References

Miller and Starr California Real Estate § 14:7, Limitations of Actions.
Miller and Starr California Real Estate § 16:2, Required Facts; Burden of Proof.
Miller and Starr California Real Estate § 15:29, Elements and Requirements.
Miller and Starr California Real Estate § 15:31, Public or Private Easement by Prescription.
Miller and Starr California Real Estate § 15:32, Burden of Proof to Establish a Prescriptive Easement.
Miller and Starr California Real Estate § 15:35, Use Requirements--Hostile, Adverse, and Under Claim of Right.
Miller and Starr California Real Estate § 15:38, Prescriptive Period.
Miller and Starr California Real Estate § 16:17, In General; Statutory Period.
Miller and Starr California Real Estate § 16:27, Grantor and Grantee; Donor and Donee.
Miller and Starr California Real Estate § 34:106, Statute of Limitations.
14 NO. 5 Miller & Starr, California Real Estate Newsalert 10, Easements.
12 Witkin, California Summary 10th Real Property § 218, (S 218) Vendor and Purchaser, Grantor and Grantee.
12 Witkin, California Summary 10th Real Property § 227, (S 227) Continuous Possession.

§ 322. Occupation under claim of title founded upon written instrument or judgment; presumption of adverse possession after five years; tract divided into lots

OCCUPATION UNDER WRITTEN INSTRUMENT OR JUDGMENT, WHEN DEEMED ADVERSE. When it appears that the occupant, or those under whom he claims, entered into the possession of the property under claim of title, exclusive of other right, founding such claim upon a written instrument, as being a conveyance of the property in question, or upon the decree or judgment of a competent Court, and that there has been a continued occupation and possession of the property included in such instrument, decree, or judgment, or of some part of the property, under such claim, for five years, the property so included is deemed to have been held adversely, except that when it consists of a tract divided into lots, the possession of one lot is not deemed a possession of any other lot of the same tract. *(Enacted in 1872.)*

Research References

Miller and Starr California Real Estate § 16:3, Distinction Between Color of Title and Claim of Right.
Miller and Starr California Real Estate § 16:4, "Color of Title" Defined.
Miller and Starr California Real Estate § 15:32, Burden of Proof to Establish a Prescriptive Easement.
Miller and Starr California Real Estate § 15:38, Prescriptive Period.
Miller and Starr California Real Estate § 16:11, Color-Of-Title Situations.
Miller and Starr California Real Estate § 16:17, In General; Statutory Period.
12 Witkin, California Summary 10th Real Property § 224, Sufficiency of Possession.
12 Witkin, California Summary 10th Real Property § 227, (S 227) Continuous Possession.
12 Witkin, California Summary 10th Real Property § 232, (S 232) Constructive Adverse Possession.

§ 323. Adverse possession under claim of title founded upon written instrument or judgment defined

WHAT CONSTITUTES ADVERSE POSSESSION UNDER WRITTEN INSTRUMENT OR JUDGMENT. For the purpose of constituting an adverse possession by any person claiming a title founded upon a written instrument, or a judgment or decree, land is deemed to have been possessed and occupied in the following cases:

1. Where it has been usually cultivated or improved;

2. Where it has been protected by a substantial inclosure;

3. Where, although not inclosed, it has been used for the supply of fuel, or of fencing timber for the purposes of husbandry, or for pasturage, or for the ordinary use of the occupant;

4. Where a known farm or single lot has been partly improved, the portion of such farm or lot that may have been left not cleared, or not inclosed according to the usual course and custom of the adjoining country, shall be deemed to have been occupied for the same length of time as the part improved and cultivated. *(Enacted in 1872.)*

Research References

Miller and Starr California Real Estate § 16:3, Distinction Between Color of Title and Claim of Right.
Miller and Starr California Real Estate § 16:11, Color-Of-Title Situations.
Miller and Starr California Real Estate § 16:12, Color-Of-Title Situations--Use Appropriate to the Property.
12 Witkin, California Summary 10th Real Property § 224, Sufficiency of Possession.

§ 324. Occupation under claim of title; adverse possession of premises actually occupied

PREMISES ACTUALLY OCCUPIED UNDER CLAIM OF TITLE DEEMED TO BE HELD ADVERSELY. Where it appears that there has been an actual continued occupation of land, under a claim of title, exclusive of any other right, but not founded upon a written instrument, judgment, or decree, the land so actually occupied, and no other, is deemed to have been held adversely. *(Enacted in 1872.)*

Research References

Miller and Starr California Real Estate § 16:3, Distinction Between Color of Title and Claim of Right.
Miller and Starr California Real Estate § 15:32, Burden of Proof to Establish a Prescriptive Easement.
12 Witkin, California Summary 10th Real Property § 226, Sufficiency of Possession.

§ 325. Adverse possession; claim of title not founded upon written instrument, judgment, or decree; possession and occupancy of land; payment of taxes

(a) For the purpose of constituting an adverse possession by a person claiming title, not founded upon a written instrument, judgment, or decree, land is deemed to have been possessed and occupied in the following cases only:

(1) Where it has been protected by a substantial enclosure.

(2) Where it has been usually cultivated or improved.

(b) In no case shall adverse possession be considered established under the provision of any section of this code, unless it shall be shown that the land has been occupied and claimed for the period of five years continuously, and the party or persons, their predecessors and grantors, have timely paid all state, county, or municipal taxes that have been levied and assessed upon the land for the period of five years during which the land has been occupied and claimed. Payment of those taxes by the party or persons, their predecessors and grantors shall be established by certified records of the county tax collector. *(Enacted in 1872. Amended by Code Am.1877–78, c. 590, p. 99, § 1; Stats.2010, c. 55 (A.B.1684), § 1.)*

Research References

Rutter, Cal. Practice Guide: Real Prop. Transactions Ch. 4-B, B. Interests to be Conveyed.
Miller and Starr California Real Estate § 16:3, Distinction Between Color of Title and Claim of Right.
Miller and Starr California Real Estate § 16:7, Claim-Of-Right Situations.
Miller and Starr California Real Estate § 16:8, Claim-Of-Right Situations--Substantial Enclosure.
Miller and Starr California Real Estate § 15:32, Burden of Proof to Establish a Prescriptive Easement.

Miller and Starr California Real Estate § 15:38, Prescriptive Period.
Miller and Starr California Real Estate § 15:39, Payment of Taxes.
Miller and Starr California Real Estate § 16:10, Claim-Of-Right Situations--Improvement.
Miller and Starr California Real Estate § 16:17, In General; Statutory Period.
Miller and Starr California Real Estate § 16:23, Requirement that the Claimant Pay Taxes.
Miller and Starr California Real Estate § 19:57, Estoppel of Tenant to Deny Landlord's Title.
14 NO. 6 Miller & Starr, California Real Estate Newsalert 1, Too Much of a Good Thing: California Courts Weigh in on Exclusive Prescriptive Easements.
16 NO. 6 Miller & Starr, California Real Estate Newsalert 1, Ten Years After Silacci, Mehdizadeh and Scruby, Neighbors in California Are Still Behaving Like the "Hatfields and Mccoys".
21 NO. 4 Miller & Starr, California Real Estate Newsalert 3, Adverse Possession.
22 NO. 2 Miller & Starr, California Real Estate Newsalert 2, Adverse Possession.
12 Witkin, California Summary 10th Real Property § 226, Sufficiency of Possession.
12 Witkin, California Summary 10th Real Property § 227, (S 227) Continuous Possession.
12 Witkin, California Summary 10th Real Property § 230, (S 230) in General.
12 Witkin, California Summary 10th Real Property § 402, (S 402) Issues and Proof.

§ 326. Adverse possession; relation of landlord and tenant; effect

RELATION OF LANDLORD AND TENANT AS AFFECTING ADVERSE POSSESSION. When the relation of landlord and tenant has existed between any persons, the possession of the tenant is deemed the possession of the landlord until the expiration of five years from the termination of the tenancy, or, where there has been no written lease, until the expiration of five years from the time of the last payment of rent, notwithstanding that such tenant may have acquired another title, or may have claimed to hold adversely to his landlord. But such presumptions cannot be made after the periods herein limited. *(Enacted in 1872.)*

Research References

Miller and Starr California Real Estate § 15:37, Use Requirements--Effect of Relationship Between the Parties.
Miller and Starr California Real Estate § 15:38, Prescriptive Period.
Miller and Starr California Real Estate § 16:19, Continuity of Possession--Successors in Interest.
Miller and Starr California Real Estate § 16:39, Landlord and Tenant.

§ 327. Right of possession; death of person in possession; effect of descent

RIGHT OF POSSESSION NOT AFFECTED BY DESCENT CAST. The right of a person to the possession of real property is not impaired or affected by a descent cast in consequence of the death of a person in possession of such property. *(Enacted in 1872.)*

Research References

Miller and Starr California Real Estate § 15:33, Use Requirements--Continuous and Exclusive.

§ 328. Computation of time; exclusion of certain disabilities

If a person entitled to commence an action for the recovery of real property, or for the recovery of the possession thereof, or to make any entry or defense founded on the title to real property, or to rents or services out of the property, is at the time title first descends or accrues either under the age of majority or insane, the time, not exceeding 20 years, during which the disability continues is not deemed any portion of the time in this chapter limited for the commencement of the action, or the making of the entry or defense, but the action may be commenced, or entry or defense made, within the period of five years after the disability shall cease, or after the death of the person entitled, who shall die under the disability; but the action shall not be commenced, or entry or defense made, after that period. *(Enacted in 1872. Amended by Code Am.1903, c. 160, p. 177, § 1; Stats.1994, c. 1083 (S.B.1445), § 2.)*

Research References

Rutter, Cal. Practice Guide: Real Prop. Transactions Ch. 11-H, H. Other Remedies.
Miller and Starr California Real Estate § 8:23, Mental Incapacity to Convey.
Miller and Starr California Real Estate § 15:38, Prescriptive Period.
Miller and Starr California Real Estate § 16:41, Minors and Others Under Legal Disability.
Miller and Starr California Real Estate § 34:112, Cancellation of Instruments: Nature of the Remedy.
20 NO. 3 Miller & Starr, California Real Estate Newsalert 5, Adverse Possession.
3 Witkin Cal. Proc. 5th Actions § 491, Cancellation of Void Instrument.
3 Witkin Cal. Proc. 5th Actions § 695, (S 695) In General.
12 Witkin, California Summary 10th Real Property § 235, Disabilities.

§ 328.5. Computation of time; imprisonment

If a person entitled to commence an action for the recovery of real property, or for the recovery of the possession thereof, or to make any entry or defense founded on the title to real property, or to rents or services out of the property, is, at the time the title first descends or accrues, imprisoned on a criminal charge, or in execution upon conviction of a criminal offense, for a term less than life, the time, not exceeding two years, during which imprisonment continues is not deemed any portion of the time in this chapter limited for the commencement of the action, or the making of the entry or defense, but the action may be commenced, or entry or defense made, within the period of five years after the imprisonment ceases, or after the death of the person entitled, who dies while imprisoned; but the action shall not be commenced, or entry or defense made, after that period. *(Added by Stats.1994, c. 1083 (S.B.1445), § 3.)*

Research References

Miller and Starr California Real Estate § 15:38, Prescriptive Period.
Miller and Starr California Real Estate § 16:41, Minors and Others Under Legal Disability.
3 Witkin Cal. Proc. 5th Actions § 695, (S 695) In General.
12 Witkin, California Summary 10th Real Property § 235, Disabilities.

§ 329. Foreclosure of street improvement assessment liens; constructive presumption of payment

The time within which an action for the foreclosure of a lien securing an assessment against real property for street improvements, the proceedings for which are prescribed by legislation of any political unit other than the state, may be commenced, shall be two years from and after the date on which the assessment, or any bond secured thereby, or the last installment of the assessment or bond, shall be due, or, as to existing rights of action not heretofore barred, one year after the effective date hereof, whichever time is later. After that time, if the lien has not been otherwise removed, the lien ceases to exist and the assessment is conclusively presumed to be paid. The official having charge of the records of the assessment shall mark it "Conclusively presumed paid," if, at the expiration of the time within which such action might be brought he has received no written notice of the pendency of the action. *(Added by Stats.1933, c. 883, p. 2291, § 1. Amended by Stats.1945, c. 362, p. 822, § 1; Stats.1981, c. 714, § 68.)*

Research References

Miller and Starr California Real Estate § 11:173, Assessment and Bond Liens--Statute of Limitations for Enforcement of the Lien.

3 Witkin Cal. Proc. 5th Actions § 430, (S 430) Types of Limitation
    Statutes.
3 Witkin Cal. Proc. 5th Actions § 482, (S 482) Two Years.
3 Witkin Cal. Proc. 5th Actions § 667, Duration of Tax Lien.

§ 329.5. Validity of public improvement assessments; appeal

The validity of an assessment or supplemental assessment
against real property for public improvements, the proceedings
for which are prescribed by the legislative body of any chartered
city, shall not be contested in any action or proceeding unless the
action or proceeding is commenced within 30 days after the
assessment is levied, or such longer period as the legislative body
may provide. Any appeal from a final judgment in such an
action or proceeding shall be perfected within 30 days after the
entry of judgment. *(Added by Stats.1959, c. 1007, p. 3028, § 1.)*

Research References

Miller and Starr California Real Estate § 11:169, Assessment and Bond
    Liens--Assessment and Lien.
3 Witkin Cal. Proc. 5th Actions § 475, (S 475) Thirty Days.
9 Witkin Cal. Proc. 5th Appeal § 582, (S 582) Special Statutes.
9 Witkin, California Summary 10th Taxation § 141, (S 141) in General.

§ 330. Public improvement assessment liens; time for sale

In all cases in which there is now vested or there shall
hereafter be vested in a treasurer, street superintendent, or other
public official the power to sell at public auction, after demand
upon him by the holder of any public improvement bond, any lot
or parcel of land upon which exists or which shall hereafter exist
a lien to secure the payment of a public improvement assessment
represented by said bond, and the act or law establishing such
power fails to prescribe the time within which such official may
act, said official may sell at any time prior to the expiration of
four years after the due date of said bond or of the last
installment thereof or of the last principal coupon attached
thereto, or prior to January 1, 1947, whichever is later, but not
thereafter. This section is not intended to extend, enlarge or
revive any power of sale which has heretofore been lost by
reason of lapse of time or otherwise. *(Added by Stats.1945, c.
360, p. 821, § 1.)*

Research References

Miller and Starr California Real Estate § 11:173, Assessment and Bond
    Liens--Statute of Limitations for Enforcement of the Lien.
Miller and Starr California Real Estate § 11:177, Priorities Among State
    and Local Tax and Assessment Liens--Priority Between Assessment
    Liens.
3 Witkin Cal. Proc. 5th Actions § 430, (S 430) Types of Limitation
    Statutes.
3 Witkin Cal. Proc. 5th Actions § 484, (S 484) Four Years.
3 Witkin Cal. Proc. 5th Actions § 667, Duration of Tax Lien.
4 Witkin, California Summary 10th Security Transactions in Real Property
    § 62, Statute of Limitations.

CHAPTER 3. THE TIME OF COMMENCING
ACTIONS OTHER THAN FOR THE
RECOVERY OF REAL PROPERTY

§ 335. Periods of limitation

PERIODS OF LIMITATION PRESCRIBED. The periods prescribed for the commencement of actions other than for the recovery of real property, are as follows: *(Enacted in 1872.)*

§ 335.1. Two years; actions for assault, battery, or injury to, or for death of, individual caused by wrongful act or neglect

Within two years: An action for assault, battery, or injury to, or for the death of, an individual caused by the wrongful act or neglect of another. *(Added by Stats.2002, c. 448 (S.B.688), § 2.)*

Research References

Rutter, Cal. Practice Guide: Civ. Pro. Before Trial Ch. 1-C, C. Prelawsuit Notices, Claims and Demands.

California Practice Guide: Employment Litigation Ch. 5-A, A. Wrongful Discharge in Violation of Public Policy (Tameny Claims).

California Practice Guide: Employment Litigation Ch. 5-B, B. Intentional Infliction of Emotional Distress.

California Practice Guide: Employment Litigation Ch. 10-A, A. Sources of Law Prohibiting Harassment.

California Practice Guide: Employment Litigation Ch. 16-E, E. Statute of Limitations.

California Practice Guide: Employment Litigation Ch. 19-A, A. Plaintiff's Forum Selection.

Rutter, Cal. Practice Guide: Enforcing Judgments/Debts Ch. 2-C, C. Tort Liability.

Rutter, Cal. Practice Guide: Insurance Litigation Ch. 9-C, C. Source of Subrogation Right.

Rutter, Cal. Practice Guide: Insurance Litigation Ch. 9-H, H. Defenses to Subrogation Action by Insurer.

Rutter, Cal. Practice Guide: Insurance Litigation Ch. 15-B, B. Actions by Insurers.

Rutter, Cal. Practice Guide: Insurance Litigation Ch. 12D-B, B. Statute of Limitations.

Rutter, Cal. Practice Guide: Personal Injury Ch. 1-A, A. Initial Client Interview.

Rutter, Cal. Practice Guide: Personal Injury Ch. 3-G, G. Independent Damages Claims.

Rutter, Cal. Practice Guide: Personal Injury Ch. 5-A, A. Prelawsuit Filings.

Rutter, Cal. Practice Guide: Personal Injury Ch. 5-B, B. When to Sue-Statute of Limitations.

Rutter, Cal. Practice Guide: Personal Injury Ch. 7-J, J. Arbitration of Uninsured Motorist Claims.

Rutter, Cal. Practice Guide: Personal Injury Ch. 5-A, Outline a.

Rutter, Cal. Practice Guide: Personal Injury Ch. 5-B, Outline B.

Rutter, Cal. Practice Guide: Personal Injury Gen. Matls., Highlights.

Rutter, Cal. Practice Guide: Prof. Responsibility Ch. 6-D, D. Professional Liability.

Miller and Starr California Real Estate § 22:40, Limitations Period for Recovery of Damages; Permanent and Continuing Nuisance Distinguished.

Miller and Starr California Real Estate § 22:79, Statute of Limitations.

Miller and Starr California Real Estate § 23:73, Statutes of Limitation Applicable to Common Law Theories.

Miller and Starr California Real Estate § 29:64, Negligence.

Miller and Starr California Real Estate § 29:67, Warranty.

Miller and Starr California Real Estate § 29:74, Actions Within and Outside the 10-Year Statute.

Miller and Starr California Real Estate § 34:127, Statute of Limitations.

Miller and Starr California Real Estate § 34:130, Statute of Limitations.

3 Witkin Cal. Proc. 5th Actions § 306, (S 306) Time and Statute of Limitations.

3 Witkin Cal. Proc. 5th Actions § 451, (S 451) Cross-Complaint by Uninsured Motorist.

3 Witkin Cal. Proc. 5th Actions § 458, (S 458) Period Extended.

3 Witkin Cal. Proc. 5th Actions § 461, (S 461) Construction to Avoid Retroactivity.

3 Witkin Cal. Proc. 5th Actions § 463, Sexual Abuse of Minor: 1986 Extension of Period.

3 Witkin Cal. Proc. 5th Actions § 482, (S 482) Two Years.

3 Witkin Cal. Proc. 5th Actions § 552, (S 552) in General.

3 Witkin Cal. Proc. 5th Actions § 553, (S 553) Scope of Statute.

3 Witkin Cal. Proc. 5th Actions § 555, (S 555) Malicious Prosecution and Abuse of Process.

3 Witkin Cal. Proc. 5th Actions § 556, (S 556) Invasion of Privacy.

3 Witkin Cal. Proc. 5th Actions § 558, (S 558) Civil Rights Violations.

3 Witkin Cal. Proc. 5th Actions § 559, (S 559) Personal Injuries.

3 Witkin Cal. Proc. 5th Actions § 560, (S 560) Wrongful Death.

3 Witkin Cal. Proc. 5th Actions § 561, (S 561) Action Based on Imputed Liability.

3 Witkin Cal. Proc. 5th Actions § 562, Personal Injury Action Against Third-Party Tortfeasor.

3 Witkin Cal. Proc. 5th Actions § 563, Action for Termination of Employment in Violation of Public Policy.

3 Witkin Cal. Proc. 5th Actions § 570, (S 570) Cause of Disability.

3 Witkin Cal. Proc. 5th Actions § 572, (S 572) Distinction: Loss of Consortium.

3 Witkin Cal. Proc. 5th Actions § 574, Infliction of Emotional Distress.

3 Witkin Cal. Proc. 5th Actions § 575, (S 575) in General.

3 Witkin Cal. Proc. 5th Actions § 578, (S 578) Statutory Rule: in General.

3 Witkin Cal. Proc. 5th Actions § 596, (S 596) Scope of Statute.

3 Witkin Cal. Proc. 5th Actions § 629, Nature and Scope of Statute.

3 Witkin Cal. Proc. 5th Actions § 649, Intentional Wrongs.

3 Witkin Cal. Proc. 5th Actions § 650, Negligent Wrongs.

3 Witkin Cal. Proc. 5th Actions § 664, (S 664) in General.

3 Witkin Cal. Proc. 5th Actions § 665, (S 665) Federal Civil Rights Action.

3 Witkin Cal. Proc. 5th Actions § 690, Personal Injury Claim Not Involving Medical Malpractice.

3 Witkin Cal. Proc. 5th Actions § 693, Public Employee.

3 Witkin Cal. Proc. 5th Actions § 714, Action in Personam.

3 Witkin Cal. Proc. 5th Actions § 724, Equitable Indemnity.

3 Witkin Cal. Proc. 5th Actions § 741, General Rule.

3 Witkin Cal. Proc. 5th Actions § 760, (S 760) General Rule of Tolling.

3 Witkin Cal. Proc. 5th Actions § 763, (S 763) Promise of Performance.

6 Witkin, California Summary 10th Torts § 1379, Statute of Limitations.

3 Witkin, California Summary 10th Agency and Employment § 243, Nature and Scope of Action.

§ 336. Five years; mesne profits

Within five years:

(a) An action for mesne profits of real property.

(b) An action for violation of a restriction, as defined in Section 784 of the Civil Code. The period prescribed in this subdivision runs from the time the person seeking to enforce the restriction discovered or, through the exercise of reasonable diligence, should have discovered the violation. A failure to commence an action for violation of a restriction within the period prescribed in this subdivision does not waive the right to commence an action for any other violation of the restriction and does not, in itself, create an implication that the restriction is abandoned, obsolete, or otherwise unenforceable. This subdivision shall not bar commencement of an action for violation of a restriction before January 1, 2001, and until January 1, 2001, any other applicable statutory or common law limitation shall continue to apply to that action. *(Enacted in 1872. Amended by Code Am.1873–74, c. 383, p. 291, § 31; Stats.1953, c. 1153, p. 2652, § 1; Stats.1998, c. 14 (A.B.707), § 3.)*

Law Revision Commission Comments

Subdivision (b) is added to Section 336 to make clear that the statutory limitation period applicable to enforcement of a restriction is five years, consistent with the general statutes governing recovery of real property. *Cf.* Section 319 (five years). This ensures a uniform limitation period regardless of whether the restriction is in the form of a covenant, condition, negative easement, or equitable servitude. See Civ. Code § 784 ("restriction" defined); *cf.* 2 A. Bowman, Ogden's Revised California Real Property Law 23.25, at 1155, 23.32, at 1159 (1975) (five years).

For purposes of subdivision (b), the time when a homeowners' association is deemed to have knowledge of a violation of a restriction would be determined under general principles of imputed knowledge. See, e.g., Civ. Code § 2332. Thus an incorporated or unincorporated homeowner's association is deemed to have knowledge of a violation of a restriction when an appropriate officer or agent of the association has knowledge of the violation.

Under subdivision (b), a failure to enforce a violation within the limitation period should not alone be grounds to imply a waiver or abandonment of the restriction. However, such failure may, combined with other circumstances, be grounds for waiver or estoppel or evidence of abandonment or obsolescence. See, e.g., Bryant v. Whitney, 178 Cal. 640, 174 P. 32 (1918) (waiver).

Subdivision (b) provides a two-year grace period to enable action on a violation that would become unenforceable upon enactment of this chapter and a shorter grace period for action on a violation that would become unenforceable within two years after enactment of this chapter. The two-year grace period does not operate to extend the time to act on a violation that would become unenforceable by operation of law apart from this chapter, either pursuant to case law limitations or applicable statutes of limitation. [28 Cal.L.Rev.Comm. Reports App. 4 (1998)].

Research References

Rutter, Cal. Practice Guide: Real Prop. Transactions Ch. 4-A, A. Property to be Sold.
Miller and Starr California Real Estate § 24:1, Types of Enforceable Restrictions.
Miller and Starr California Real Estate § 24:29, Rights of Enforcement--Statute of Limitations.
Miller and Starr California Real Estate § 25B:107, Enforcement of the Restrictions--Statute of Limitations.
18 NO. 5 Miller & Starr, California Real Estate Newsalert 4, Common Interest Developments.
3 Witkin Cal. Proc. 5th Actions § 485, (S 485) Five Years.
5 Witkin Cal. Proc. 5th Pleading § 1119, Pleading Facts.
5 Witkin Cal. Proc. 5th Pleading § 1121, Pleading Subdivision.
12 Witkin, California Summary 10th Real Property § 123, (S 123) Statute of Limitations.
12 Witkin, California Summary 10th Real Property § 451, in General.

§ 336a. Six years; corporate obligations held by public; corporate mortgages, deeds of trust, etc.

Within six years. 1. An action upon any bonds, notes or debentures issued by any corporation or pursuant to permit of the Commissioner of Corporations, or upon any coupons issued with such bonds, notes or debentures, if such bonds, notes or debentures shall have been issued to or held by the public.

2. An action upon any mortgage, trust deed or other agreement pursuant to which such bonds, notes or debentures were issued. Nothing in this section shall apply to bonds or other evidences of indebtedness of a public district or corporation. *(Added by Stats.1935, c. 614, p. 1740, § 1.)*

Research References

Miller and Starr California Real Estate § 3:34, Statute of Limitations.
22 NO. 6 Miller & Starr, California Real Estate Newsalert 4, Agency.
3 Witkin Cal. Proc. 5th Actions § 486, (S 486) Six Years.

§ 337. Four years: written contract; exception; book account; account stated based upon account in writing; balance of mutual, open and current account in writing; rescission of written contract

Within four years. 1. An action upon any contract, obligation or liability founded upon an instrument in writing, except as provided in Section 336a of this code; provided, that the time within which any action for a money judgment for the balance due upon an obligation for the payment of which a deed of trust or mortgage with power of sale upon real property or any interest therein was given as security, following the exercise of the power of sale in such deed of trust or mortgage, may be brought shall not extend beyond three months after the time of sale under such deed of trust or mortgage.

2. An action to recover (1) upon a book account whether consisting of one or more entries; (2) upon an account stated based upon an account in writing, but the acknowledgment of the account stated need not be in writing; (3) a balance due upon a mutual, open and current account, the items of which are in writing; provided, however, that where an account stated is based upon an account of one item, the time shall begin to run from the date of said item, and where an account stated is based upon an account of more than one item, the time shall begin to run from the date of the last item.

3. An action based upon the rescission of a contract in writing. The time begins to run from the date upon which the facts that entitle the aggrieved party to rescind occurred. Where the ground for rescission is fraud or mistake, the time does not begin to run until the discovery by the aggrieved party of the facts constituting the fraud or mistake. Where the ground for rescission is misrepresentation under Section 359 of the Insurance Code, the time does not begin to run until the representation becomes false. *(Enacted in 1872. Amended by Code Am.1873–74, c. 383, p. 291, § 32; Stats.1906, c. 1, p. 5, § 1; Stats.1907, c. 323, p. 599, § 1; Stats.1917, c. 203, p. 299, § 1; Stats.1933, c. 790, p. 2116, § 1; Stats.1935, c. 614, p. 1740, § 2; Stats.1947, c. 809, p. 1923, § 1; Stats.1961, c. 589, p. 1735, § 6.)*

Research References

Rutter, Cal. Practice Guide: A.D.R. Ch. 5-D, D. Defenses to Enforcement.
Rutter, Cal. Practice Guide: Civ. Pro. Before Trial Ch. 6-B, B. Complaints.
Rutter, Cal. Practice Guide: Civ. Pro. Before Trial Ch. 6-D, D. Cross-Complaint.
California Practice Guide: Employment Litigation Ch. 11-D, D. Payment of Wages.
California Practice Guide: Employment Litigation Ch. 11-J, J. Enforcing California Laws Regulating Employee Compensation.
California Practice Guide: Employment Litigation Ch. 16-E, E. Statute of Limitations.
Rutter, Cal. Practice Guide: Enforcing Judgments/Debts Ch. 3-A, A. Evaluating the Claim.
Rutter, Cal. Practice Guide: Enforcing Judgments/Debts Ch. 3-C, C. Prelawsuit Considerations.
Rutter, Cal. Practice Guide: Enforcing Judgments/Debts Ch. 6G-4, Creditor's Suit.
Rutter, Cal. Practice Guide: Insurance Litigation Ch. 5-F, F. Rescission by Insurer.
Rutter, Cal. Practice Guide: Insurance Litigation Ch. 8-B, B. Contribution Between Insurers.

Rutter, Cal. Practice Guide: Insurance Litigation Ch. 9-H, H. Defenses to Subrogation Action by Insurer.

Rutter, Cal. Practice Guide: Insurance Litigation Ch. 15-E, E. Pleadings.

Rutter, Cal. Practice Guide: Insurance Litigation Ch. 15-K, K. Judgment Creditor's Action to Enforce Judgment Debtor's Liability Insurance (INS.C. § 11580(B)(2)).

Rutter, Cal. Practice Guide: Insurance Litigation Ch. 6A-D, D. Conditions Governing Claims.

Rutter, Cal. Practice Guide: Insurance Litigation Ch. 6D-C, C. Policy Conditions.

Rutter, Cal. Practice Guide: Insurance Litigation Ch. 6F-D, D. ERISA Preemption and Remedies.

Rutter, Cal. Practice Guide: Insurance Litigation Ch. 6G-D, D. Uninsured and Underinsured Motorist Coverages.

Rutter, Cal. Practice Guide: Insurance Litigation Ch. 6I-B, B. Particular Surety Bond Coverages.

Rutter, Cal. Practice Guide: Insurance Litigation Ch. 6I-D, D. Surety's Defenses to Payment of Bond.

Rutter, Cal. Practice Guide: Insurance Litigation Ch. 6I-E, E. Surety's Rights Upon Payment of Bond.

Rutter, Cal. Practice Guide: Insurance Litigation Ch. 7B-I, I. Statute of Limitations on Action Against Insurer.

Rutter, Cal. Practice Guide: Insurance Litigation Ch. 12D-B, B. Statute of Limitations.

Rutter, Cal. Practice Guide: Personal Injury Ch. 5-B, B. When to Sue-Statute of Limitations.

Rutter, Cal. Practice Guide: Personal Injury Ch. 7-J, J. Arbitration of Uninsured Motorist Claims.

Rutter, Cal. Practice Guide: Real Prop. Transactions Ch. 8-D, D. Preemptive Purchase Rights-Rights of First Refusal and Rights of First Offer.

Rutter, Cal. Practice Guide: Real Prop. Transactions Ch. 11-B, B. Determining Breach.

Rutter, Cal. Practice Guide: Real Prop. Transactions Ch. 11-H, H. Other Remedies.

Rutter, Cal. Practice Guide: Prof. Responsibility Ch. 5-K, K. Fee Recovery/Enforcing Fee Agreements.

Miller and Starr California Real Estate § 1:61, The Implied Covenant of Good Faith and Fair Dealing.

Miller and Starr California Real Estate § 3:16, Effect of Undisclosed Dual Agency--Duties and Liabilities of the Dual Agent.

Miller and Starr California Real Estate § 3:34, Statute of Limitations.

Miller and Starr California Real Estate § 3:46, Statute of Limitations.

Miller and Starr California Real Estate § 6:17, Liability and Measure of Damages to the Parties.

Miller and Starr California Real Estate § 8:11, Grantee's Remedies.

Miller and Starr California Real Estate § 19:78, Time and Place of Payment; Late Charges.

Miller and Starr California Real Estate § 23:33, Defenses.

Miller and Starr California Real Estate § 24:29, Rights of Enforcement--Statute of Limitations.

Miller and Starr California Real Estate § 29:63, Breach of Contract.

Miller and Starr California Real Estate § 29:67, Warranty.

Miller and Starr California Real Estate § 29:71, Special Maximum Periods; Latent and Patent Defects.

Miller and Starr California Real Estate § 29:73, Maximum 10-Year Period.

Miller and Starr California Real Estate § 7:221, Statute of Limitations.

Miller and Starr California Real Estate § 10:118, Recovery of Amount Omitted from Demand; Effect of Antideficiency Limitations.

Miller and Starr California Real Estate § 10:128, Statute of Limitations.

Miller and Starr California Real Estate § 10:269, Limitation of Liability.

Miller and Starr California Real Estate § 19:144, Landlord's Obligation to Refund Deposits--Nonresidential Premises.

Miller and Starr California Real Estate § 28:113, Statute of Limitations--Action by Owner or Obligee.

Miller and Starr California Real Estate § 28:119, Statute of Limitations--Action by Claimant.

Miller and Starr California Real Estate § 25B:107, Enforcement of the Restrictions--Statute of Limitations.

18 NO. 2 Miller & Starr, California Real Estate Newsalert 1, The Marketable Record Title Act- Is Private Foreclosure Barred Ten Years After Maturity, or Not?

18 NO. 4 Miller & Starr, California Real Estate Newsalert 30, Covenants, Conditions, and Restrictions.

19 NO. 3 Miller & Starr, California Real Estate Newsalert 11, Deeds of Trust.

19 NO. 4 Miller & Starr, California Real Estate Newsalert 40, Hazardous Substances.

20 NO. 2 Miller & Starr, California Real Estate Newsalert 12, Defective Construction.

22 NO. 6 Miller & Starr, California Real Estate Newsalert 4, Agency.

3 Witkin Cal. Proc. 5th Actions § 160, Insurer's Refusal to Settle.

3 Witkin Cal. Proc. 5th Actions § 477, (S 477) Ninety Days or Three Months.

3 Witkin Cal. Proc. 5th Actions § 484, (S 484) Four Years.

3 Witkin Cal. Proc. 5th Actions § 497, (S 497) in General.

3 Witkin Cal. Proc. 5th Actions § 508, Action on Written Contract.

3 Witkin Cal. Proc. 5th Actions § 510, (S 510) Other Implied Promises.

3 Witkin Cal. Proc. 5th Actions § 511, (S 511) Distinctions.

3 Witkin Cal. Proc. 5th Actions § 512, in General.

3 Witkin Cal. Proc. 5th Actions § 513, Oral Express Contracts.

3 Witkin Cal. Proc. 5th Actions § 515, in General.

3 Witkin Cal. Proc. 5th Actions § 520, (S 520) General Rule.

3 Witkin Cal. Proc. 5th Actions § 523, Conflict in Courts of Appeal.

3 Witkin Cal. Proc. 5th Actions § 537, in General.

3 Witkin Cal. Proc. 5th Actions § 540, Mutual, Open, and Current Account.

3 Witkin Cal. Proc. 5th Actions § 542, Account Stated.

3 Witkin Cal. Proc. 5th Actions § 543, Liability Accrues When Principal Obligation Matures.

3 Witkin Cal. Proc. 5th Actions § 544, (S 544) Former Rule Refusing to Discharge Sureties.

3 Witkin Cal. Proc. 5th Actions § 609, (S 609) Retroactive Application of Statute.

3 Witkin Cal. Proc. 5th Actions § 611, (S 611) Delayed Accrual Rules.

3 Witkin Cal. Proc. 5th Actions § 650, Negligent Wrongs.

3 Witkin Cal. Proc. 5th Actions § 681, What Statutes Apply.

3 Witkin Cal. Proc. 5th Actions § 683, (S 683) Accounting.

3 Witkin Cal. Proc. 5th Actions § 684, (S 684) Mandamus.

3 Witkin Cal. Proc. 5th Actions § 686, (S 686) Restitution After Rescission.

3 Witkin Cal. Proc. 5th Actions § 741, General Rule.

3 Witkin Cal. Proc. 5th Actions § 760, (S 760) General Rule of Tolling.

5 Witkin Cal. Proc. 5th Pleading § 1119, Pleading Facts.

5 Witkin Cal. Proc. 5th Pleading § 1120, Pleading Section Where No Subdivision.

5 Witkin Cal. Proc. 5th Pleading § 1121, Pleading Subdivision.

6 Witkin Cal. Proc. 5th Proceedings Without Trial § 531, in General.

6 Witkin Cal. Proc. 5th Provisional Remedies § 40, (S 40) Statute of Limitations.

2 Witkin, California Summary 10th Insurance § 205, (S 205) in General.

2 Witkin, California Summary 10th Insurance § 309, (S 309) in General.

12 Witkin, California Summary 10th Real Property § 123, (S 123) Statute of Limitations.

11 Witkin, California Summary 10th Community Property § 180, (S 180) Personal Liability for Debts for Spouse's Necessaries.

3 Witkin, California Summary 10th Agency and Employment § 418, (S 418) in General.

13 Witkin, California Summary 10th Equity § 33, Defenses.

14 Witkin, California Summary 10th Wills and Probate § 517, (S 517) Action Against Decedent.

14 Witkin, California Summary 10th Wills and Probate § 986, Sureties.

§ 337a. "Book account," defined

The term "book account" means a detailed statement which constitutes the principal record of one or more transactions between a debtor and a creditor arising out of a contract or some fiduciary relation, and shows the debits and credits in connection therewith, and against whom and in favor of whom entries are made, is entered in the regular course of business as conducted by such creditor or fiduciary, and is kept in a reasonably permanent form and manner and is (1) in a bound book, or (2) on a sheet or sheets fastened in a book or to backing but detachable therefrom, or (3) on a card or cards of a permanent character, or is kept in any other reasonably permanent form and manner. *(Added by Stats.1959, c. 1010, p. 3034, § 1.)*

Research References

Rutter, Cal. Practice Guide: Civ. Pro. Before Trial Ch. 6-B, B. Complaints.

Rutter, Cal. Practice Guide: Enforcing Judgments/Debts Ch. 3-C, C. Prelawsuit Considerations.

3 Witkin Cal. Proc. 5th Actions § 517, (S 517) Permanent Record Without Book.

§ 337.1. Four years; actions for damages from persons performing or furnishing design, specifications, surveying, planning, supervision or observation of construction or construction of improvement to realty

(a) Except as otherwise provided in this section, no action shall be brought to recover damages from any person performing or furnishing the design, specifications, surveying, planning, supervision or observation of construction or construction of an improvement to real property more than four years after the substantial completion of such improvement for any of the following:

(1) Any patent deficiency in the design, specifications, surveying, planning, supervision or observation of construction or construction of an improvement to, or survey of, real property;

(2) Injury to property, real or personal, arising out of any such patent deficiency; or

(3) Injury to the person or for wrongful death arising out of any such patent deficiency.

(b) If, by reason of such patent deficiency, an injury to property or the person or an injury causing wrongful death occurs during the fourth year after such substantial completion, an action in tort to recover damages for such an injury or wrongful death may be brought within one year after the date on which such injury occurred, irrespective of the date of death, but in no event may such an action be brought more than five years after the substantial completion of construction of such improvement.

(c) Nothing in this section shall be construed as extending the period prescribed by the laws of this state for the bringing of any action.

(d) The limitation prescribed by this section shall not be asserted by way of defense by any person in actual possession or the control, as owner, tenant or otherwise, of such an improvement at the time any deficiency in such an improvement constitutes the proximate cause of the injury or death for which it is proposed to bring an action.

(e) As used in this section, "patent deficiency" means a deficiency which is apparent by reasonable inspection.

(f) Subdivisions (a) and (b) shall not apply to any owner-occupied single-unit residence. *(Added by Stats.1967, c. 1326, p. 3157, § 1.)*

Research References

Rutter, Cal. Practice Guide: A.D.R. Ch. 5-B, B. Federal vs. State Law Governing.

Rutter, Cal. Practice Guide: A.D.R. Ch. 5-C, C. Enforceability of Arbitration Agreements-In General.

Rutter, Cal. Practice Guide: A.D.R. App. D Form 64, Real Property-Sale-Deposit Receipts, Escrow Instructions, Listing Agreements.

Rutter, Cal. Practice Guide: Personal Injury Ch. 5-B, B. When to Sue-Statute of Limitations.

Miller and Starr California Real Estate § 17:40, Tests for Determining Whether an Item is a Fixture--Means of Annexation; Difficulty of Removal.

Miller and Starr California Real Estate § 22:79, Statute of Limitations.

Miller and Starr California Real Estate § 29:32, Liability to Third Persons.

Miller and Starr California Real Estate § 29:65, Negligent Supervision.

Miller and Starr California Real Estate § 29:71, Special Maximum Periods; Latent and Patent Defects.

Miller and Starr California Real Estate § 29:72, Limitations Period for Patent Defects.

Miller and Starr California Real Estate § 29:73, Maximum 10-Year Period.

Miller and Starr California Real Estate § 29:74, Actions Within and Outside the 10-Year Statute.

Miller and Starr California Real Estate § 29:75, Indemnity and the 10-Year Period of Repose.

Miller and Starr California Real Estate § 35:25, Written Agreement Required.

Miller and Starr California Real Estate § 35:28, Real Estate Contracts and Listing Agreements.

Miller and Starr California Real Estate § 25B:113, Arbitration or Other Resolution of Disputes With the Subdivider.

13 NO. 6 Miller & Starr, California Real Estate Newsalert 1, Using Basura to Make Construction Defect Claims Arbitrable, or Woodside to Send Them to a Referee.

20 NO. 6 Miller & Starr, California Real Estate Newsalert 7, Defective Construction.

20 NO. 2 Miller & Starr, California Real Estate Newsalert 12, Defective Construction.

3 Witkin Cal. Proc. 5th Actions § 484, (S 484) Four Years.

3 Witkin Cal. Proc. 5th Actions § 606, (S 606) Scope of Statute.

3 Witkin Cal. Proc. 5th Actions § 607, (S 607) Distinctions.

3 Witkin Cal. Proc. 5th Actions § 615, Personal Injury or Death.

3 Witkin Cal. Proc. 5th Actions § 617, Defects in Construction of Residential Real Property: Ten Years.

3 Witkin Cal. Proc. 5th Actions § 761, (S 761) Distinction: Latent Defects in Real Property.

1 Witkin Cal. Summ. 10th Contracts § 981, (S 981) Challenged Contract.

6 Witkin, California Summary 10th Torts § 1159, Former Owner's Liability for Improvement.

§ 337.15. Ten years; developer, contractor, architect, etc. of real property; latent deficiency in design, supervision, etc.; injury to property

(a) No action may be brought to recover damages from any person, or the surety of a person, who develops real property or performs or furnishes the design, specifications, surveying, planning, supervision, testing, or observation of construction or construction of an improvement to real property more than 10 years after the substantial completion of the development or improvement for any of the following:

(1) Any latent deficiency in the design, specification, surveying, planning, supervision, or observation of construction or construction of an improvement to, or survey of, real property.

(2) Injury to property, real or personal, arising out of any such latent deficiency.

(b) As used in this section, "latent deficiency" means a deficiency which is not apparent by reasonable inspection.

(c) As used in this section, "action" includes an action for indemnity brought against a person arising out of that person's performance or furnishing of services or materials referred to in this section, except that a cross-complaint for indemnity may be filed pursuant to subdivision (b) of Section 428.10 in an action which has been brought within the time period set forth in subdivision (a) of this section.

(d) Nothing in this section shall be construed as extending the period prescribed by the laws of this state for bringing any action.

(e) The limitation prescribed by this section shall not be asserted by way of defense by any person in actual possession or the control, as owner, tenant or otherwise, of such an improvement, at the time any deficiency in the improvement constitutes the proximate cause for which it is proposed to bring an action.

(f) This section shall not apply to actions based on willful misconduct or fraudulent concealment.

(g) The 10-year period specified in subdivision (a) shall commence upon substantial completion of the improvement, but not later than the date of one of the following, whichever first occurs:

(1) The date of final inspection by the applicable public agency.

(2) The date of recordation of a valid notice of completion.

(3) The date of use or occupation of the improvement.

(4) One year after termination or cessation of work on the improvement.

The date of substantial completion shall relate specifically to the performance or furnishing design, specifications, surveying, planning, supervision, testing, observation of construction or construction services by each profession or trade rendering services to the improvement. *(Added by Stats.1971, c. 1569, p. 3149, § 1. Amended by Stats.1979, c. 373, p. 1265, § 49; Stats.1979, c. 571, p. 1797, § 1; Stats.1980, c. 676, § 63; Stats.1981, c. 88, § 1.)*

Research References

Rutter, Cal. Practice Guide: A.D.R. Ch. 3B-A, A. Introduction.
Rutter, Cal. Practice Guide: A.D.R. App. D Form 64, Real Property-Sale-Deposit Receipts, Escrow Instructions, Listing Agreements.
Rutter, Cal. Practice Guide: Civ. Pro. Before Trial Ch. 6-D, D. Cross-Complaint.
Rutter, Cal. Practice Guide: Insurance Litigation Ch. 9-H, H. Defenses to Subrogation Action by Insurer.
Rutter, Cal. Practice Guide: Insurance Litigation Ch. 6I-D, D. Surety's Defenses to Payment of Bond.
Rutter, Cal. Practice Guide: Personal Injury Ch. 5-B, B. When to Sue-Statute of Limitations.
Rutter, Cal. Practice Guide: Real Prop. Transactions Ch. 5-D, D. Common Law Environmental Hazards Liability.
Miller and Starr California Real Estate § 29:2, Statutory Liability Under "SB800" for Residential Units Sold New After January 1, 2003.
Miller and Starr California Real Estate § 29:6, Contractor's Liability for Fraud.
Miller and Starr California Real Estate § 22:40, Limitations Period for Recovery of Damages; Permanent and Continuing Nuisance Distinguished.
Miller and Starr California Real Estate § 23:33, Defenses.
Miller and Starr California Real Estate § 23:42, Statutes of Limitations.
Miller and Starr California Real Estate § 23:68, Nuisance.
Miller and Starr California Real Estate § 29:64, Negligence.
Miller and Starr California Real Estate § 29:70, Tolling and Extension.
Miller and Starr California Real Estate § 29:71, Special Maximum Periods; Latent and Patent Defects.
Miller and Starr California Real Estate § 29:72, Limitations Period for Patent Defects.
Miller and Starr California Real Estate § 29:73, Maximum 10-Year Period.
Miller and Starr California Real Estate § 29:74, Actions Within and Outside the 10-Year Statute.
Miller and Starr California Real Estate § 29:75, Indemnity and the 10-Year Period of Repose.
Miller and Starr California Real Estate § 30:15, Statute of Limitations; Defenses.
Miller and Starr California Real Estate § 35:25, Written Agreement Required.
Miller and Starr California Real Estate § 35:28, Real Estate Contracts and Listing Agreements.
Miller and Starr California Real Estate § 25B:113, Arbitration or Other Resolution of Disputes With the Subdivider.
13 NO. 3 Miller & Starr, California Real Estate Newsalert 1, Change to Spare: The New California Construction Warranty and Defects Law Under SB 800.
13 NO. 6 Miller & Starr, California Real Estate Newsalert 1, Using Basura to Make Construction Defect Claims Arbitrable, or Woodside to Send Them to a Referee.
14 NO. 2 Miller & Starr, California Real Estate Newsalert 1, "The Outer Limit": The California Supreme Court Reigns in the 10-Year Statute of Repose for Construction Defects.
14 NO. 2 Miller & Starr, California Real Estate Newsalert 7, Defective Construction.
15 NO. 6 Miller & Starr, California Real Estate Newsalert 8, Defective Construction.
15 NO. 4 Miller & Starr, California Real Estate Newsalert 25, Defective Construction.
16 NO. 6 Miller & Starr, California Real Estate Newsalert 7, Defective Construction.
16 NO. 2 Miller & Starr, California Real Estate Newsalert 8, Defective Construction.
19 NO. 5 Miller & Starr, California Real Estate Newsalert 13, Defective Construction.
19 NO. 4 Miller & Starr, California Real Estate Newsalert 35, Defective Construction.
19 NO. 4 Miller & Starr, California Real Estate Newsalert 40, Hazardous Substances.
3 Witkin Cal. Proc. 5th Actions § 488, (S 488) Ten Years.
3 Witkin Cal. Proc. 5th Actions § 498, Awareness of Injury and Its Cause.
3 Witkin Cal. Proc. 5th Actions § 544, (S 544) Former Rule Refusing to Discharge Sureties.
3 Witkin Cal. Proc. 5th Actions § 545, (S 545) Legislative Repudiation of Rule.
3 Witkin Cal. Proc. 5th Actions § 561, (S 561) Action Based on Imputed Liability.
3 Witkin Cal. Proc. 5th Actions § 596, (S 596) Scope of Statute.
3 Witkin Cal. Proc. 5th Actions § 601, in General.
3 Witkin Cal. Proc. 5th Actions § 604, (S 604) Act Causing Consequential Injuries.
3 Witkin Cal. Proc. 5th Actions § 608, (S 608) Scope of Statute.
3 Witkin Cal. Proc. 5th Actions § 609, (S 609) Retroactive Application of Statute.
3 Witkin Cal. Proc. 5th Actions § 610, (S 610) Commencement of Ten-Year Period.
3 Witkin Cal. Proc. 5th Actions § 611, (S 611) Delayed Accrual Rules.
3 Witkin Cal. Proc. 5th Actions § 612, in General.
3 Witkin Cal. Proc. 5th Actions § 613, (S 613) Exception Held Applicable.
3 Witkin Cal. Proc. 5th Actions § 614, (S 614) Exception Held Inapplicable.
3 Witkin Cal. Proc. 5th Actions § 615, Personal Injury or Death.
3 Witkin Cal. Proc. 5th Actions § 616, Action by Homeowner for Defects in Original Construction of Residence.
3 Witkin Cal. Proc. 5th Actions § 617, Defects in Construction of Residential Real Property: Ten Years.
3 Witkin Cal. Proc. 5th Actions § 721, in General.
3 Witkin Cal. Proc. 5th Actions § 761, (S 761) Distinction: Latent Defects in Real Property.
1 Witkin Cal. Summ. 10th Contracts § 720, (S 720) in General.
1 Witkin Cal. Summ. 10th Contracts § 981, (S 981) Challenged Contract.
5 Witkin, California Summary 10th Torts § 192, Comparative Impairment Analysis.
6 Witkin, California Summary 10th Torts § 1159, Former Owner's Liability for Improvement.
6 Witkin, California Summary 10th Torts § 1503, (S 1503) Vendor of Tract Lots.

§ 337.2. Four years; breach of written lease and abandonment of property

Where a lease of real property is in writing, no action shall be brought under Section 1951.2 of the Civil Code more than four years after the breach of the lease and abandonment of the property, or more than four years after the termination of the right of the lessee to possession of the property, whichever is the earlier time. *(Added by Stats.1970, c. 89, p. 107, § 12, operative July 1, 1971.)*

Law Revision Commission Comments

The four-year period provided in Section 337.2 is consistent with the general statute of limitations applicable to written contracts. See Section 337. Although the former law was not clear, it appears that, if the lessor terminated a lease because of the lessee's breach and evicted the lessee, his cause of action for the damages resulting from the loss of the rentals due under the lease did not accrue until the end of the original lease term. See De Hart v. Allen, 26 Cal.2d 829, 161 P.2d 453 (1945); Treff v. Gulko, 214 Cal. 591, 7 P.2d 697 (1932). Under Civil Code Section 1951.2, however, an aggrieved lessor may sue immediately for the damages resulting from the loss of the rentals that would have accrued under the lease. Accordingly, Section 337.2 relates the period of limitations to breach and abandonment or to termination of the right of the lessee to possession.

Research References

Miller and Starr California Real Estate § 19:223, Cross-Complaint; Affirmative Defenses.

3 Witkin Cal. Proc. 5th Actions § 484, (S 484) Four Years.

3 Witkin Cal. Proc. 5th Actions § 508, Action on Written Contract.

§ 337.5. Ten years; municipal general obligation bonds or coupons; judgments or decrees

Within 10 years:

(a) An action upon any general obligation bonds or coupons, not secured in whole or in part by a lien on real property, issued by any county, city and county, municipal corporation, district (including school districts), or other political subdivision of the State of California.

(b) An action upon a judgment or decree of any court of the United States or of any state within the United States. *(Added by Stats.1939, c. 724, p. 2255, § 1. Amended by Stats.1947, c. 626, p. 1634, § 1; Stats.1953, c. 1153, p. 2653, § 2; Stats.2010, c. 719 (S.B.856), § 7, eff. Oct. 19, 2010.)*

Research References

Rutter, Cal. Practice Guide: Enforcing Judgments/Debts Ch. 6A-7, Period During Which Judgment Enforceable; Renewal Procedures.

Rutter, Cal. Practice Guide: Enforcing Judgments/Debts Ch. 6J-2, Enforcing Sister State Judgments in California.

Rutter, Cal. Practice Guide: Insurance Litigation Ch. 15-K, K. Judgment Creditor's Action to Enforce Judgment Debtor's Liability Insurance (INS.C. § 11580(B)(2)).

Miller and Starr California Real Estate § 32:55, Duration of the Judgment Lien.

Miller and Starr California Real Estate § 32:56, Renewal of the Judgment Lien.

14 NO. 5 Miller & Starr, California Real Estate Newsalert 15, Involuntary Liens.

15 NO. 6 Miller & Starr, California Real Estate Newsalert 8, Defective Construction.

3 Witkin Cal. Proc. 5th Actions § 486, (S 486) Six Years.

3 Witkin Cal. Proc. 5th Actions § 488, (S 488) Ten Years.

3 Witkin Cal. Proc. 5th Actions § 489, Express Statutory Provisions.

3 Witkin Cal. Proc. 5th Actions § 675, Action on Judgment: Ten Years.

3 Witkin Cal. Proc. 5th Actions § 741, General Rule.

8 Witkin Cal. Proc. 5th Enforcement of Judgment § 34, in General.

8 Witkin Cal. Proc. 5th Enforcement of Judgment § 35, (S 35) Right to Renew.

8 Witkin Cal. Proc. 5th Enforcement of Judgment § 40, (S 40) Effect of Renewal on Enforcement.

8 Witkin Cal. Proc. 5th Enforcement of Judgment § 432, Enforcement Mechanisms.

8 Witkin Cal. Proc. 5th Enforcement of Judgment § 436, Action on Judgment.

8 Witkin Cal. Proc. 5th Enforcement of Judgment § 455, (S 455) Form and Content.

8 Witkin Cal. Proc. 5th Enforcement of Judgment § 462, Former Law: Uniform Foreign Money Judgments Recognition Act.

§ 337.6. Municipal general obligation bonds or coupons; additional time

Notwithstanding the provisions of Section 337.5 of this code actions may be brought on bonds or coupons as set forth in subsection 2 of said section, against which the statute of limitations ran on or after August 27, 1937; provided, such actions are brought on or before June 30, 1959. Upon presentation for payment they shall be registered and payment shall not be made thereon until the next fiscal year following presentation unless available funds are sufficient to first pay obligations which are due or will become due from the same fund during the fiscal year of presentation and during the next succeeding six months. Interest shall not be paid on bonds or coupons registered for the purpose of this section. *(Added by Stats.1949, c. 1282, p. 2265, § 1. Amended by Stats.1957, c. 719, p. 1925, § 1.)*

§ 338. Three years

Within three years:

(a) An action upon a liability created by statute, other than a penalty or forfeiture.

(b) An action for trespass upon or injury to real property.

(c)(1) An action for taking, detaining, or injuring any goods or chattels, including actions for the specific recovery of personal property.

(2) The cause of action in the case of theft, as described in Section 484 of the Penal Code, of any article of historical, interpretive, scientific, or artistic significance is not deemed to have accrued until the discovery of the whereabouts of the article by the aggrieved party, his or her agent, or the law enforcement agency that originally investigated the theft.

(3)(A) Notwithstanding paragraphs (1) and (2), an action for the specific recovery of a work of fine art brought against a museum, gallery, auctioneer, or dealer, in the case of an unlawful taking or theft, as described in Section 484 of the Penal Code, of a work of fine art, including a taking or theft by means of fraud or duress, shall be commenced within six years of the actual discovery by the claimant or his or her agent, of both of the following:

(i) The identity and the whereabouts of the work of fine art. In the case where there is a possibility of misidentification of the object of fine art in question, the identity can be satisfied by the identification of facts sufficient to determine that the work of fine art is likely to be the work of fine art that was unlawfully taken or stolen.

(ii) Information or facts that are sufficient to indicate that the claimant has a claim for a possessory interest in the work of fine art that was unlawfully taken or stolen.

(B) The provisions of this paragraph shall apply to all pending and future actions commenced on or before December 31, 2017, including any actions dismissed based on the expiration of statutes of limitation in effect prior to the date of enactment of this statute if the judgment in that action is not yet final or if the time for filing an appeal from a decision on that action has not expired, provided that the action concerns a work of fine art that was taken within 100 years prior to the date of enactment of this statute.

(C) For purposes of this paragraph:

(i) "Actual discovery," notwithstanding Section 19 of the Civil Code, does not include any constructive knowledge imputed by law.

(ii) "Auctioneer" means any individual who is engaged in, or who by advertising or otherwise holds himself or herself out as being available to engage in, the calling for, the recognition of, and the acceptance of, offers for the purchase of goods at an auction as defined in subdivision (b) of Section 1812.601 of the Civil Code.

(iii) "Dealer" means a person who holds a valid seller's permit and who is actively and principally engaged in, or conducting the business of, selling works of fine art.

(iv) "Duress" means a threat of force, violence, danger, or retribution against an owner of the work of fine art in question, or his or her family member, sufficient to coerce a reasonable person of ordinary susceptibilities to perform an act that otherwise would not have been performed or to acquiesce to an act to which he or she would otherwise not have acquiesced.

(v) "Fine art" has the same meaning as defined in paragraph (1) of subdivision (d) of Section 982 of the Civil Code.

(vi) "Museum or gallery" shall include any public or private organization or foundation operating as a museum or gallery.

(4) Section 361 shall not apply to an action brought pursuant to paragraph (3).

(5) A party in an action to which paragraph (3) applies may raise all equitable and legal affirmative defenses and doctrines, including, without limitation, laches and unclean hands.

(d) An action for relief on the ground of fraud or mistake. The cause of action in that case is not deemed to have accrued until the discovery, by the aggrieved party, of the facts constituting the fraud or mistake.

(e) An action upon a bond of a public official except any cause of action based on fraud or embezzlement is not deemed to have accrued until the discovery, by the aggrieved party or his or her agent, of the facts constituting the cause of action upon the bond.

(f)(1) An action against a notary public on his or her bond or in his or her official capacity except that any cause of action based on malfeasance or misfeasance is not deemed to have accrued until discovery, by the aggrieved party or his or her agent, of the facts constituting the cause of action.

(2) Notwithstanding paragraph (1), an action based on malfeasance or misfeasance shall be commenced within one year from discovery, by the aggrieved party or his or her agent, of the facts constituting the cause of action or within three years from the performance of the notarial act giving rise to the action, whichever is later.

(3) Notwithstanding paragraph (1), an action against a notary public on his or her bond or in his or her official capacity shall be commenced within six years.

(g) An action for slander of title to real property.

(h) An action commenced under Section 17536 of the Business and Professions Code. The cause of action in that case shall not be deemed to have accrued until the discovery by the aggrieved party, the Attorney General, the district attorney, the county counsel, the city prosecutor, or the city attorney of the facts constituting grounds for commencing the action.

(i) An action commenced under the Porter–Cologne Water Quality Control Act (Division 7 (commencing with Section 13000) of the Water Code). The cause of action in that case shall not be deemed to have accrued until the discovery by the State Water Resources Control Board or a regional water quality control board of the facts constituting grounds for commencing actions under their jurisdiction.

(j) An action to recover for physical damage to private property under Section 19 of Article I of the California Constitution.

(k) An action commenced under Division 26 (commencing with Section 39000) of the Health and Safety Code. These causes of action shall not be deemed to have accrued until the discovery by the State Air Resources Board or by a district, as defined in Section 39025 of the Health and Safety Code, of the facts constituting grounds for commencing the action under its jurisdiction.

(l) An action commenced under Section 1603.1, 1615, or 5650.1 of the Fish and Game Code. These causes of action shall not be deemed to have accrued until discovery by the agency bringing the action of the facts constituting the grounds for commencing the action.

(m) An action challenging the validity of the levy upon a parcel of a special tax levied by a local agency on a per parcel basis.

(n) An action commencing under Section 51.7 of the Civil Code. *(Enacted in 1872. Amended by Stats.1921, c. 183, p. 192, § 1; Stats.1933, c. 306, p. 878, § 1; Stats.1935, c. 581, p. 1673, § 1; Stats.1943, c. 1025, p. 2963, § 1; Stats.1949, c. 1540, p. 2734,* § 1; *Stats.1957, c. 649, p. 1849, § 1; Stats.1972, c. 823, p. 1470, § 2; Stats.1981, c. 247, § 1, eff. July 21, 1981; Stats.1981, c. 494, § 2; Stats.1982, c. 340, p. 1642, § 1; Stats.1987, c. 1200, § 1; Stats.1987, c. 1201, § 1; Stats.1988, c. 1186, § 1; Stats.1989, c. 467, § 1; Stats.1990, c. 669 (A.B.4049), § 1; Stats.1995, c. 238 (A.B.1174), § 1; Stats.1998, c. 342 (A.B.1933), § 1; Stats.2005, c. 123 (A.B.378), § 2; Stats.2005, c. 383 (S.B.1110), § 1.5; Stats. 2006, c. 538 (S.B.1852), § 62; Stats.2010, c. 691 (A.B.2765), § 2.)*

Research References

California Practice Guide: Employment Litigation Ch. 6-D, D. Worker Adjustment and Retraining Notification Act (Warn Act).

California Practice Guide: Employment Litigation Ch. 11-F, F. Payment of Overtime Compensation.

California Practice Guide: Employment Litigation Ch. 11-J, J. Enforcing California Laws Regulating Employee Compensation.

California Practice Guide: Employment Litigation Ch. 16-E, E. Statute of Limitations.

Rutter, Cal. Practice Guide: Enforcing Judgments/Debts Ch. 3-A, A. Evaluating the Claim.

Rutter, Cal. Practice Guide: Enforcing Judgments/Debts Ch. 3-B, B. Collection Without Suit.

Rutter, Cal. Practice Guide: Enforcing Judgments/Debts Ch. 3-C, C. Prelawsuit Considerations.

Rutter, Cal. Practice Guide: Insurance Litigation Ch. 5-E, E. Reformation.

Rutter, Cal. Practice Guide: Insurance Litigation Ch. 9-H, H. Defenses to Subrogation Action by Insurer.

Rutter, Cal. Practice Guide: Insurance Litigation Ch. 10-A, A. Conservatorship and Liquidation Proceedings.

Rutter, Cal. Practice Guide: Insurance Litigation Ch. 15-K, K. Judgment Creditor's Action to Enforce Judgment Debtor's Liability Insurance (INS.C. § 11580(B)(2)).

Rutter, Cal. Practice Guide: Insurance Litigation Ch. 6I-B, B. Particular Surety Bond Coverages.

Rutter, Cal. Practice Guide: Insurance Litigation Ch. 12D-B, B. Statute of Limitations.

Rutter, Cal. Practice Guide: Personal Injury Ch. 1-A, A. Initial Client Interview.

Rutter, Cal. Practice Guide: Personal Injury Ch. 5-B, B. When to Sue-Statute of Limitations.

Rutter, Cal. Practice Guide: Real Prop. Transactions Ch. 5-D, D. Common Law Environmental Hazards Liability.

Rutter, Cal. Practice Guide: Real Prop. Transactions Ch. 11-H, H. Other Remedies.

Rutter, Cal. Practice Guide: Prof. Responsibility Ch. 6-D, D. Professional Liability.

Miller and Starr California Real Estate § 14:7, Limitations of Actions.

Miller and Starr California Real Estate § 25:9, Judicial Review.

Miller and Starr California Real Estate § 3:16, Effect of Undisclosed Dual Agency--Duties and Liabilities of the Dual Agent.

Miller and Starr California Real Estate § 3:34, Statute of Limitations.

Miller and Starr California Real Estate § 3:46, Statute of Limitations.

Miller and Starr California Real Estate § 34:5, Economic Duress as Basis for Rescission.

Miller and Starr California Real Estate § 4:63, Requirements in Making or Arranging a Loan--Special Notice to Cosigners in Consumer Credit Transactions.

Miller and Starr California Real Estate § 1:123, Remedies for Mistake.

Miller and Starr California Real Estate § 1:125, Intentional Misrepresentation.

Miller and Starr California Real Estate § 11:31, Liability of the Notary--Available Defenses; Statute of Limitations.

Miller and Starr California Real Estate § 11:33, Liability of the Notary's Surety.

Miller and Starr California Real Estate § 11:49, Statute of Limitations.

Miller and Starr California Real Estate § 14:17, Statute of Limitations.

Miller and Starr California Real Estate § 14:28, Statute of Limitations.

Miller and Starr California Real Estate § 16:33, Cotenants--Examples of Adverse Occupancy Between Cotenants.

Miller and Starr California Real Estate § 18:10, The Unclaimed Property Law--Duties of the State.

Miller and Starr California Real Estate § 20:11, The Unruh Civil Rights Act--Violations and Enforcement.

Miller and Starr California Real Estate § 22:40, Limitations Period for Recovery of Damages; Permanent and Continuing Nuisance Distinguished.

Miller and Starr California Real Estate § 23:33, Defenses.

Miller and Starr California Real Estate § 23:59, Remedies.

Miller and Starr California Real Estate § 23:68, Nuisance.

Miller and Starr California Real Estate § 23:69, Trespass.

Miller and Starr California Real Estate § 23:73, Statutes of Limitation Applicable to Common Law Theories.

Miller and Starr California Real Estate § 25:54, Judicial Review.

Miller and Starr California Real Estate § 27:91, Prompt Payment of Progress Payments and Contract Retention.

Miller and Starr California Real Estate § 29:15, Terms and Provisions of Excess Policies.

Miller and Starr California Real Estate § 29:64, Negligence.

Miller and Starr California Real Estate § 29:65, Negligent Supervision.

Miller and Starr California Real Estate § 29:66, Fraud.

Miller and Starr California Real Estate § 29:67, Warranty.

Miller and Starr California Real Estate § 29:68, Strict Liability.

Miller and Starr California Real Estate § 29:69, When Statutes Commence to Run.

Miller and Starr California Real Estate § 29:73, Maximum 10-Year Period.

Miller and Starr California Real Estate § 29:74, Actions Within and Outside the 10-Year Statute.

Miller and Starr California Real Estate § 30:15, Statute of Limitations; Defenses.

Miller and Starr California Real Estate § 30:33, Statute of Limitations.

Miller and Starr California Real Estate § 34:16, Statute of Limitations.

Miller and Starr California Real Estate § 10:118, Recovery of Amount Omitted from Demand; Effect of Antideficiency Limitations.

Miller and Starr California Real Estate § 10:210, Attack on Validity of the Sale.

Miller and Starr California Real Estate § 19:102, Enforcement and Remedies.

Miller and Starr California Real Estate § 19:174, Remedies for Wrongful Eviction.

Miller and Starr California Real Estate § 19:235, Tenant's Personal Property--Innkeeper's Lien.

Miller and Starr California Real Estate § 34:102, Punitive Damages--Statute of Limitations.

Miller and Starr California Real Estate § 34:106, Statute of Limitations.

Miller and Starr California Real Estate § 34:118, Statute of Limitations.

13 NO. 6 Miller & Starr, California Real Estate Newsalert 8, Inverse Condemnation.

14 NO. 2 Miller & Starr, California Real Estate Newsalert 1, "The Outer Limit": The California Supreme Court Reigns in the 10-Year Statute of Repose for Construction Defects.

14 NO. 6 Miller & Starr, California Real Estate Newsalert 1, Too Much of a Good Thing: California Courts Weigh in on Exclusive Prescriptive Easements.

14 NO. 5 Miller & Starr, California Real Estate Newsalert 9, Discrimination.

14 NO. 5 Miller & Starr, California Real Estate Newsalert 10, Easements.

15 NO. 2 Miller & Starr, California Real Estate Newsalert 11, Subdivisions.

16 NO. 3 Miller & Starr, California Real Estate Newsalert 4, Contracts.

16 NO. 5 Miller & Starr, California Real Estate Newsalert 20, Remedies.

18 NO. 5 Miller & Starr, California Real Estate Newsalert 20, Remedies.

19 NO. 5 Miller & Starr, California Real Estate Newsalert 10, Covenants, Conditions, and Restrictions.

19 NO. 3 Miller & Starr, California Real Estate Newsalert 11, Deeds of Trust.

19 NO. 2 Miller & Starr, California Real Estate Newsalert 24, Subdivisions, Land Use Planning, and Approvals.

20 NO. 2 Miller & Starr, California Real Estate Newsalert 12, Defective Construction.

21 NO. 2 Miller & Starr, California Real Estate Newsalert 16, Inverse Condemnation.

21 NO. 2 Miller & Starr, California Real Estate Newsalert 21, Recording and Priorities.

21 NO. 4 Miller & Starr, California Real Estate Newsalert 32, Inverse Condemnation.

22 NO. 6 Miller & Starr, California Real Estate Newsalert 4, Agency.

22 NO. 6 Miller & Starr, California Real Estate Newsalert 24, Specific Contracts.

3 Witkin Cal. Proc. 5th Actions § 58, Federal Statute Without Express Limitation.

3 Witkin Cal. Proc. 5th Actions § 437, (S 437) Illustration: Action Alleging Violation of Proposition 62.

3 Witkin Cal. Proc. 5th Actions § 481, (S 481) One Year.

3 Witkin Cal. Proc. 5th Actions § 483, (S 483) Three Years.

3 Witkin Cal. Proc. 5th Actions § 486, (S 486) Six Years.

3 Witkin Cal. Proc. 5th Actions § 497, (S 497) in General.

3 Witkin Cal. Proc. 5th Actions § 498, Awareness of Injury and Its Cause.

3 Witkin Cal. Proc. 5th Actions § 511, (S 511) Distinctions.

3 Witkin Cal. Proc. 5th Actions § 519, (S 519) Contract of Sale: Four Years.

3 Witkin Cal. Proc. 5th Actions § 544, (S 544) Former Rule Refusing to Discharge Sureties.

3 Witkin Cal. Proc. 5th Actions § 558, (S 558) Civil Rights Violations.

3 Witkin Cal. Proc. 5th Actions § 561, (S 561) Action Based on Imputed Liability.

3 Witkin Cal. Proc. 5th Actions § 576, (S 576) Suspicion of Wrongdoing.

3 Witkin Cal. Proc. 5th Actions § 586, Limitations Periods.

3 Witkin Cal. Proc. 5th Actions § 596, (S 596) Scope of Statute.

3 Witkin Cal. Proc. 5th Actions § 598, Buildings Damaged by Hazardous Substances.

3 Witkin Cal. Proc. 5th Actions § 600, Injury Not Abatable at Reasonable Cost.

3 Witkin Cal. Proc. 5th Actions § 601, in General.

3 Witkin Cal. Proc. 5th Actions § 603, Environmental Contamination.

3 Witkin Cal. Proc. 5th Actions § 605, (S 605) Distinction: Inverse Condemnation.

3 Witkin Cal. Proc. 5th Actions § 606, (S 606) Scope of Statute.

3 Witkin Cal. Proc. 5th Actions § 607, (S 607) Distinctions.

3 Witkin Cal. Proc. 5th Actions § 608, (S 608) Scope of Statute.

3 Witkin Cal. Proc. 5th Actions § 611, (S 611) Delayed Accrual Rules.

3 Witkin Cal. Proc. 5th Actions § 618, Slander of Title to Real Property: Three Years.

3 Witkin Cal. Proc. 5th Actions § 619, (S 619) Scope of Statute.

3 Witkin Cal. Proc. 5th Actions § 620, in General.

3 Witkin Cal. Proc. 5th Actions § 621, Action for Recovery or Conversion of Personal Property Left in Hotel and Similar Establishments.

3 Witkin Cal. Proc. 5th Actions § 622, Action for Conversion Based on Underground Trespass on Oil or Gas Well.

3 Witkin Cal. Proc. 5th Actions § 623, Conversion by Original Wrongful Act.

3 Witkin Cal. Proc. 5th Actions § 653, (S 653) Form of Action or Relief is Not Controlling.

3 Witkin Cal. Proc. 5th Actions § 654, (S 654) Tort Action.

3 Witkin Cal. Proc. 5th Actions § 655, (S 655) Equitable Action.

3 Witkin Cal. Proc. 5th Actions § 656, Money Obtained by Fraud or Mistake.

3 Witkin Cal. Proc. 5th Actions § 657, Money Paid Under Duress.

3 Witkin Cal. Proc. 5th Actions § 659, General Rule.

3 Witkin Cal. Proc. 5th Actions § 660, Illustrations: Accrual Postponed.

3 Witkin Cal. Proc. 5th Actions § 664, (S 664) in General.

3 Witkin Cal. Proc. 5th Actions § 665, (S 665) Federal Civil Rights Action.

3 Witkin Cal. Proc. 5th Actions § 666, Action to Collect Taxes.

3 Witkin Cal. Proc. 5th Actions § 668, (S 668) Exceptions.

3 Witkin Cal. Proc. 5th Actions § 669, (S 669) Obligation Payable in Installments.

3 Witkin Cal. Proc. 5th Actions § 670, (S 670) Action Against Surety of Public Officer.

3 Witkin Cal. Proc. 5th Actions § 672, (S 672) Action for Reimbursement for Costs of State-Mandated Programs.

3 Witkin Cal. Proc. 5th Actions § 673, (S 673) Action for Violation of Community Redevelopment Law.

3 Witkin Cal. Proc. 5th Actions § 678, Illustrations.

3 Witkin Cal. Proc. 5th Actions § 680, Analysis of Problem.

3 Witkin Cal. Proc. 5th Actions § 681, What Statutes Apply.

3 Witkin Cal. Proc. 5th Actions § 682, Accrual on Knowledge of Facts.

3 Witkin Cal. Proc. 5th Actions § 683, (S 683) Accounting.

3 Witkin Cal. Proc. 5th Actions § 684, (S 684) Mandamus.

3 Witkin Cal. Proc. 5th Actions § 703, Exceptions and Distinctions.

3 Witkin Cal. Proc. 5th Actions § 760, (S 760) General Rule of Tolling.

3 Witkin Cal. Proc. 5th Actions § 773, (S 773) Fraud Cases Compared.

3 Witkin Cal. Proc. 5th Actions § 777, Estoppel by Duress.

3 Witkin Cal. Proc. 5th Actions § 622A, (New)-Action for Specific Recovery of Unlawfully Taken Fine Art.

9 Witkin Cal. Proc. 5th Administrative Proceedings § 129, (S 129) Statutes of Limitations.

8 Witkin Cal. Proc. 5th Enforcement of Judgment § 494, Statute Runs from Date of Judgment on Underlying Debt.

4 Witkin Cal. Proc. 5th Pleading § 54, (S 54) Injuries to Person and Property from One Act.

2 Witkin, California Summary 10th Insurance § 216, (S 216) in General.

12 Witkin, California Summary 10th Real Property § 476, Statute of Limitations.

12 Witkin, California Summary 10th Real Property § 594, Violation as Defense in Unlawful Detainer Action.

12 Witkin, California Summary 10th Real Property § 899, in General.

9 Witkin, California Summary 10th Taxation § 133, (S 133) Rule.

9 Witkin, California Summary 10th Taxation § 232, (S 232) Time Limits.

13 Witkin, California Summary 10th Personal Property § 42, Procedure in Escheating Property.

13 Witkin, California Summary 10th Personal Property § 123, Adverse Possession.

4 Witkin, California Summary 10th Sales § 213, Statute of Limitations.

11 Witkin, California Summary 10th Husband and Wife § 343, (S 343) CalWORKs Aid.

5 Witkin, California Summary 10th Torts § 702, Intangible Property.

5 Witkin, California Summary 10th Torts § 813, (S 813) No General Duty to Investigate.

3 Witkin, California Summary 10th Agency and Employment § 360, (S 360) in General.

3 Witkin, California Summary 10th Agency and Employment § 399, (S 399) Wilful Failure.

8 Witkin, California Summary 10th Constitutional Law § 1011, (S 1011) Statutes of Limitation on Attack.

8 Witkin, California Summary 10th Constitutional Law § 1166, Statute of Limitations.

2 Witkin Cal. Summ. 10th Workers' Compensation § 83, (S 83) Statute of Limitations.

§ 338.1. Five years; civil penalties or punitive damages for hazardous waste or substance violations

An action for civil penalties or punitive damages authorized under Chapter 6.5 (commencing with Section 25100), Chapter 6.7 (commencing with Section 25280), Chapter 6.8 (commencing with Section 25300), or Chapter 6.95 (commencing with Section 25500) of Division 20 of the Health and Safety Code shall be commenced within five years after the discovery by the agency bringing the action of the facts constituting the grounds for commencing the action. *(Added by Stats.1988, c. 1186, § 2. Amended by Stats.2009, c. 429 (A.B.305), § 1.)*

Research References

Remedies, Miller and Starr California Real Estate § 23:54.

3 Witkin Cal. Proc. 5th Actions § 485, (S 485) Five Years.

§ 339. Two years; oral contract; certificate, abstract or guaranty of title; title insurance policy; sheriff; coroner; rescission of oral contract

Within two years: 1. An action upon a contract, obligation or liability not founded upon an instrument of writing, except as provided in Section 2725 of the Commercial Code or subdivision 2 of Section 337 of this code; or an action founded upon a contract, obligation or liability, evidenced by a certificate, or abstract or guaranty of title of real property, or by a policy of title insurance; provided, that the cause of action upon a contract, obligation or liability evidenced by a certificate, or abstract or guaranty of title of real property or policy of title insurance shall not be deemed to have accrued until the discovery of the loss or damage suffered by the aggrieved party thereunder.

2. An action against a sheriff or coroner upon a liability incurred by the doing of an act in an official capacity and in virtue of office, or by the omission of an official duty including the nonpayment of money collected in the enforcement of a judgment.

3. An action based upon the rescission of a contract not in writing. The time begins to run from the date upon which the

facts that entitle the aggrieved party to rescind occurred. Where the ground for rescission is fraud or mistake, the time does not begin to run until the discovery by the aggrieved party of the facts constituting the fraud or mistake. *(Enacted in 1872. Amended by Code Am.1873–74, c. 383, p. 291, § 33; Stats.1905, c. 258, p. 231, § 1; Stats.1906, c. 1, p. 5, § 2; Stats.1907, c. 323, p. 599, § 2; Stats.1913, c. 187, p. 332, § 1; Stats.1917, c. 203, p. 299, § 2; Stats.1961, c. 589, p. 1736, § 7; Stats.1980, c. 1307, § 1; Stats.1982, c. 497, p. 2154, § 31, operative July 1, 1983; Stats.1996, c. 872 (A.B.3472), § 11.)*

Law Revision Commission Comments

Subdivision 2 of Section 339 is amended to conform to the Enforcement of Judgments Law and to delete the exception to the two-year statute of limitations for an action for an escape. Former subdivision 4 of Section 340 which applied a one-year statute of limitations in this case was repealed by 1973 Cal.Stats. ch. 20, § 1. (15 Cal.L.Rev.Comm. Reports 2001).

Research References

Rutter, Cal. Practice Guide: Civ. Pro. Before Trial Ch. 6-B, B. Complaints.

Rutter, Cal. Practice Guide: Civ. Pro. Before Trial Ch. 6-C, C. Answer.

Rutter, Cal. Practice Guide: Civ. Pro. Before Trial Ch. 6-D, D. Cross-Complaint.

California Practice Guide: Employment Litigation Ch. 11-D, D. Payment of Wages.

California Practice Guide: Employment Litigation Ch. 11-J, J. Enforcing California Laws Regulating Employee Compensation.

California Practice Guide: Employment Litigation Ch. 16-E, E. Statute of Limitations.

California Practice Guide: Employment Litigation Form 19:B, Answer to Complaint for Damages for Sexual Harassment, Retaliation, Breach of Contract, Wrongful Discharge in Violation of Public Policy.

Rutter, Cal. Practice Guide: Enforcing Judgments/Debts Ch. 3-A, A. Evaluating the Claim.

Rutter, Cal. Practice Guide: Enforcing Judgments/Debts Ch. 3-C, C. Prelawsuit Considerations.

Rutter, Cal. Practice Guide: Insurance Litigation Ch. 8-B, B. Contribution Between Insurers.

Rutter, Cal. Practice Guide: Insurance Litigation Ch. 9-H, H. Defenses to Subrogation Action by Insurer.

Rutter, Cal. Practice Guide: Insurance Litigation Ch. 6A-D, D. Conditions Governing Claims.

Rutter, Cal. Practice Guide: Insurance Litigation Ch. 6H-E, E. Statute of Limitations.

Rutter, Cal. Practice Guide: Insurance Litigation Ch. 7B-I, I. Statute of Limitations on Action Against Insurer.

Rutter, Cal. Practice Guide: Insurance Litigation Ch. 12D-B, B. Statute of Limitations.

Rutter, Cal. Practice Guide: Personal Injury Ch. 5-B, B. When to Sue-Statute of Limitations.

Rutter, Cal. Practice Guide: Real Prop. Transactions Ch. 3-G, G. Title Policy Claims and Liability.

Rutter, Cal. Practice Guide: Real Prop. Transactions Ch. 6-L, L. Real Estate Appraisals.

Rutter, Cal. Practice Guide: Prof. Responsibility Ch. 5-K, K. Fee Recovery/Enforcing Fee Agreements.

Miller and Starr California Real Estate § 1:4, Quasi-Contracts ("Implied in Law").

Miller and Starr California Real Estate § 1:61, The Implied Covenant of Good Faith and Fair Dealing.

Miller and Starr California Real Estate § 3:16, Effect of Undisclosed Dual Agency--Duties and Liabilities of the Dual Agent.

Miller and Starr California Real Estate § 3:34, Statute of Limitations.

Miller and Starr California Real Estate § 3:46, Statute of Limitations.

Miller and Starr California Real Estate § 34:5, Economic Duress as Basis for Rescission.

Miller and Starr California Real Estate § 4:98, Appraiser's Liability.

Miller and Starr California Real Estate § 8:11, Grantee's Remedies.

Miller and Starr California Real Estate § 1:125, Intentional Misrepresentation.

Miller and Starr California Real Estate § 11:49, Statute of Limitations.

Miller and Starr California Real Estate § 12:36, Origin; Requirement of Marriage; Domestic Partnerships.

Miller and Starr California Real Estate § 21:37, Remedies for Usury--Cancellation of Interest.

Miller and Starr California Real Estate § 29:63, Breach of Contract.

Miller and Starr California Real Estate § 29:64, Negligence.

Miller and Starr California Real Estate § 29:65, Negligent Supervision.

Miller and Starr California Real Estate § 29:67, Warranty.

Miller and Starr California Real Estate § 32:73, Attack on Validity of Sale.

Miller and Starr California Real Estate § 7:211, Statute of Limitations.

Miller and Starr California Real Estate § 7:221, Statute of Limitations.

Miller and Starr California Real Estate § 7:234, Statute of Limitations for an Action on the Title Policy.

Miller and Starr California Real Estate § 10:210, Attack on Validity of the Sale.

21 NO. 2 Miller & Starr, California Real Estate Newsalert 23, Title Insurance.

22 NO. 6 Miller & Starr, California Real Estate Newsalert 4, Agency.

22 NO. 2 Miller & Starr, California Real Estate Newsalert 15, Judicial Remedies.

22 NO. 6 Miller & Starr, California Real Estate Newsalert 24, Specific Contracts.

3 Witkin Cal. Proc. 5th Actions § 452, (S 452) Cross-Complaint Against Suspended Corporation.

3 Witkin Cal. Proc. 5th Actions § 482, (S 482) Two Years.

3 Witkin Cal. Proc. 5th Actions § 495, Cause Accruing Before Substantial Damage.

3 Witkin Cal. Proc. 5th Actions § 497, (S 497) in General.

3 Witkin Cal. Proc. 5th Actions § 502, (S 502) General Rule: Professional Negligence Cases.

3 Witkin Cal. Proc. 5th Actions § 503, (S 503) Distinction: Remedy Uncertain or Ineffective.

3 Witkin Cal. Proc. 5th Actions § 510, (S 510) Other Implied Promises.

3 Witkin Cal. Proc. 5th Actions § 511, (S 511) Distinctions.

3 Witkin Cal. Proc. 5th Actions § 512, in General.

3 Witkin Cal. Proc. 5th Actions § 513, Oral Express Contracts.

3 Witkin Cal. Proc. 5th Actions § 514, Quasi-Contract Obligations.

3 Witkin Cal. Proc. 5th Actions § 519, (S 519) Contract of Sale: Four Years.

3 Witkin Cal. Proc. 5th Actions § 520, (S 520) General Rule.

3 Witkin Cal. Proc. 5th Actions § 523, Conflict in Courts of Appeal.

3 Witkin Cal. Proc. 5th Actions § 525, Distinction: Insured's Delay in Notifying Insurer of Loss.

3 Witkin Cal. Proc. 5th Actions § 530, (S 530) Distinction: Action on Title Insurance Policy.

3 Witkin Cal. Proc. 5th Actions § 555, (S 555) Malicious Prosecution and Abuse of Process.

3 Witkin Cal. Proc. 5th Actions § 563, Action for Termination of Employment in Violation of Public Policy.

3 Witkin Cal. Proc. 5th Actions § 596, (S 596) Scope of Statute.

3 Witkin Cal. Proc. 5th Actions § 620, in General.

3 Witkin Cal. Proc. 5th Actions § 621, Action for Recovery or Conversion of Personal Property Left in Hotel and Similar Establishments.

3 Witkin Cal. Proc. 5th Actions § 626, (S 626) Former Law.

3 Witkin Cal. Proc. 5th Actions § 648, in General.

3 Witkin Cal. Proc. 5th Actions § 649, Intentional Wrongs.

3 Witkin Cal. Proc. 5th Actions § 650, Negligent Wrongs.

3 Witkin Cal. Proc. 5th Actions § 653, (S 653) Form of Action or Relief is Not Controlling.

3 Witkin Cal. Proc. 5th Actions § 656, Money Obtained by Fraud or Mistake.

3 Witkin Cal. Proc. 5th Actions § 664, (S 664) in General.

3 Witkin Cal. Proc. 5th Actions § 668, (S 668) Exceptions.

3 Witkin Cal. Proc. 5th Actions § 670, (S 670) Action Against Surety of Public Officer.

3 Witkin Cal. Proc. 5th Actions § 680, Analysis of Problem.

3 Witkin Cal. Proc. 5th Actions § 683, (S 683) Accounting.

3 Witkin Cal. Proc. 5th Actions § 686, (S 686) Restitution After Rescission.

3 Witkin Cal. Proc. 5th Actions § 743, Effect of Federal Tolling Statute.

3 Witkin Cal. Proc. 5th Actions § 758, Title Insurance.

3 Witkin Cal. Proc. 5th Actions § 760, (S 760) General Rule of Tolling.

2 Witkin, California Summary 10th Insurance § 309, (S 309) in General.

11 Witkin, California Summary 10th Community Property § 180, (S 180) Personal Liability for Debts for Spouse's Necessaries.

11 Witkin, California Summary 10th Community Property § 276, Illustrations: Recovery Allowed.

3 Witkin, California Summary 10th Agency and Employment § 418, (S 418) in General.

14 Witkin, California Summary 10th Wills and Probate § 358, Conduct of Proceeding.

14 Witkin, California Summary 10th Wills and Probate § 517, (S 517) Action Against Decedent.

§ 339.5. Two years; breach of unwritten lease and abandonment of property

Where a lease of real property is not in writing, no action shall be brought under Section 1951.2 of the Civil Code more than two years after the breach of the lease and abandonment of the property, or more than two years after the termination of the right of the lessee to possession of the property, whichever is the earlier time. (Added by Stats.1970, c. 89, p. 107, § 13, operative July 1, 1971.)

Law Revision Commission Comments

The two-year period provided in Section 339.5 is consistent with the general statute of limitations applicable to contracts not in writing. See Section 339. See also the Comment to Section 337.2.

Research References

Miller and Starr California Real Estate § 19:223, Cross-Complaint; Affirmative Defenses.

3 Witkin Cal. Proc. 5th Actions § 482, (S 482) Two Years.

3 Witkin Cal. Proc. 5th Actions § 512, in General.

§ 340. One year: (a) Statutory penalty or forfeiture to individual and state; (b) Statutory forfeiture or penalty to state; (c) Libel, slander, false imprisonment, seduction, forged or raised checks, injury to animals by feeder or veterinarian; (d) Damages for seizure; (e) Action by good faith buyer

Within one year:

(a) An action upon a statute for a penalty or forfeiture, if the action is given to an individual, or to an individual and the state, except if the statute imposing it prescribes a different limitation.

(b) An action upon a statute for a forfeiture or penalty to the people of this state.

(c) An action for libel, slander, false imprisonment, seduction of a person below the age of legal consent, or by a depositor against a bank for the payment of a forged or raised check, or a check that bears a forged or unauthorized endorsement, or against any person who boards or feeds an animal or fowl or who engages in the practice of veterinary medicine as defined in Section 4826 of the Business and Professions Code, for that person's neglect resulting in injury or death to an animal or fowl in the course of boarding or feeding the animal or fowl or in the course of the practice of veterinary medicine on that animal or fowl.

(d) An action against an officer to recover damages for the seizure of any property for a statutory forfeiture to the state, or for the detention of, or injury to property so seized, or for damages done to any person in making that seizure.

(e) An action by a good faith improver for relief under Chapter 10 (commencing with Section 871.1) of Title 10 of Part 2. The time begins to run from the date upon which the good faith improver discovers that the good faith improver is not the owner of the land upon which the improvements have been made. (Enacted in 1872. Amended by Code Am.1873–74, c. 383, p. 292, § 34; Code Am.1875–76, c. 29, p. 89, § 1; Stats.1905, c. 258, p. 232, § 2; Stats.1929, c. 518, p. 896, § 1; Stats.1939, c. 1103, p. 3036, § 1; Stats.1949, c. 863, p. 1637, § 1; Stats.1953, c. 1382, p. 2959, § 1; Stats.1963, c. 1681, p. 3284, § 2; Stats.1968, c. 150, p. 373, § 1; Stats.1973, c. 20, p. 32, § 1; Stats.1982, c. 517, p. 2334, § 97; Stats.2002, c. 448 (S.B.688), § 3.)

Law Revision Commission Comments

Section 340 is amended to reflect the fact that arrest and imprisonment in a civil action is no longer permitted. See CODE CIV.PROC. § 478 and Comment thereto. See also former GOVT.CODE § 26681 et seq. (liability of sheriff for escape of person held upon civil arrest). Cf. former CODE CIV.PROC. § 501 (liability of officer for escape).

Section 340 is amended to delete the reference to an undertaking in a criminal action. Undertakings of bail are no longer governed by Section 340. See People v. Burton, 146 Cal.App.2d Supp. 878, 305 P.2d 302 (1956). Other undertakings in criminal actions are governed by the same rules that apply to undertakings generally. See Section 337 (four-year statute of limitations). The other changes in Section 340 are technical. [16 Cal.L.Rev.Comm. Reports 501 (1982)].

Research References

Rutter, Cal. Practice Guide: Civ. Pro. Before Trial Ch. 6-C, C. Answer.
California Practice Guide: Employment Litigation Ch. 5-D, D. Defamation.
California Practice Guide: Employment Litigation Ch. 5-J, J. False Imprisonment.
California Practice Guide: Employment Litigation Ch. 11-F, F. Payment of Overtime Compensation.
California Practice Guide: Employment Litigation Ch. 11-J, J. Enforcing California Laws Regulating Employee Compensation.
California Practice Guide: Employment Litigation Ch. 16-E, E. Statute of Limitations.
California Practice Guide: Employment Litigation Form 19:B, Answer to Complaint for Damages for Sexual Harassment, Retaliation, Breach of Contract, Wrongful Discharge in Violation of Public Policy.
Rutter, Cal. Practice Guide: Enforcing Judgments/Debts Ch. 2-C, C. Tort Liability.
Rutter, Cal. Practice Guide: Insurance Litigation Ch. 12D-B, B. Statute of Limitations.
Rutter, Cal. Practice Guide: Personal Injury Ch. 1-A, A. Initial Client Interview.
Rutter, Cal. Practice Guide: Personal Injury Ch. 5-B, B. When to Sue-Statute of Limitations.
Rutter, Cal. Practice Guide: Personal Injury Ch. 5-B, Outline B.
Rutter, Cal. Practice Guide: Real Prop. Transactions Ch. 5-B, B. Governing Legislation.
Rutter, Cal. Practice Guide: Real Prop. Transactions Ch. 6-H, H. Security for Promissory Note.
Miller and Starr California Real Estate § 11:41, Slander of Title Defined.
Miller and Starr California Real Estate § 17:44, Where Improver Believes He or She Owns the Improved Property.
Miller and Starr California Real Estate § 23:18,k Remedies.
Miller and Starr California Real Estate § 23:24, The Safe Drinking Water and Toxic Enforcement Act of 1986.
Miller and Starr California Real Estate § 23:68, Nuisance.
Miller and Starr California Real Estate § 32:40, Malicious Prosecution Compared.
Miller and Starr California Real Estate § 32:41, Abuse of Process Compared.
Miller and Starr California Real Estate § 10:115, Remedy for Failure to Reconvey.
Miller and Starr California Real Estate § 19:102, Enforcement and Remedies.
Miller and Starr California Real Estate § 19:174, Remedies for Wrongful Eviction.
13 NO. 6 Miller & Starr, California Real Estate Newsalert 7, Hazardous Substances.
3 Witkin Cal. Proc. 5th Actions § 451, (S 451) Cross-Complaint by Uninsured Motorist.
3 Witkin Cal. Proc. 5th Actions § 456, State or Political Subdivision.
3 Witkin Cal. Proc. 5th Actions § 458, (S 458) Period Extended.
3 Witkin Cal. Proc. 5th Actions § 461, (S 461) Construction to Avoid Retroactivity.
3 Witkin Cal. Proc. 5th Actions § 463, Sexual Abuse of Minor: 1986 Extension of Period.
3 Witkin Cal. Proc. 5th Actions § 464, Sexual Abuse of Minor: 1990 Extension of Period.
3 Witkin Cal. Proc. 5th Actions § 481, (S 481) One Year.
3 Witkin Cal. Proc. 5th Actions § 483, (S 483) Three Years.
3 Witkin Cal. Proc. 5th Actions § 489, Express Statutory Provisions.
3 Witkin Cal. Proc. 5th Actions § 497, (S 497) in General.

3 Witkin Cal. Proc. 5th Actions § 519, (S 519) Contract of Sale: Four Years.
3 Witkin Cal. Proc. 5th Actions § 549, (S 549) False Imprisonment.
3 Witkin Cal. Proc. 5th Actions § 550, in General.
3 Witkin Cal. Proc. 5th Actions § 552, (S 552) in General.
3 Witkin Cal. Proc. 5th Actions § 553, (S 553) Scope of Statute.
3 Witkin Cal. Proc. 5th Actions § 555, (S 555) Malicious Prosecution and Abuse of Process.
3 Witkin Cal. Proc. 5th Actions § 556, (S 556) Invasion of Privacy.
3 Witkin Cal. Proc. 5th Actions § 558, (S 558) Civil Rights Violations.
3 Witkin Cal. Proc. 5th Actions § 561, (S 561) Action Based on Imputed Liability.
3 Witkin Cal. Proc. 5th Actions § 563, Action for Termination of Employment in Violation of Public Policy.
3 Witkin Cal. Proc. 5th Actions § 570, (S 570) Cause of Disability.
3 Witkin Cal. Proc. 5th Actions § 572, (S 572) Distinction: Loss of Consortium.
3 Witkin Cal. Proc. 5th Actions § 575, (S 575) in General.
3 Witkin Cal. Proc. 5th Actions § 576, (S 576) Suspicion of Wrongdoing.
3 Witkin Cal. Proc. 5th Actions § 578, (S 578) Statutory Rule: in General.
3 Witkin Cal. Proc. 5th Actions § 596, (S 596) Scope of Statute.
3 Witkin Cal. Proc. 5th Actions § 649, Intentional Wrongs.
3 Witkin Cal. Proc. 5th Actions § 650, Negligent Wrongs.
3 Witkin Cal. Proc. 5th Actions § 656, Money Obtained by Fraud or Mistake.
3 Witkin Cal. Proc. 5th Actions § 664, (S 664) in General.
3 Witkin Cal. Proc. 5th Actions § 668, (S 668) Exceptions.
3 Witkin Cal. Proc. 5th Actions § 690, Personal Injury Claim Not Involving Medical Malpractice.
3 Witkin Cal. Proc. 5th Actions § 693, Public Employee.
3 Witkin Cal. Proc. 5th Actions § 714, Action in Personam.
3 Witkin Cal. Proc. 5th Actions § 724, Equitable Indemnity.
3 Witkin Cal. Proc. 5th Actions § 760, (S 760) General Rule of Tolling.
3 Witkin Cal. Proc. 5th Actions § 763, (S 763) Promise of Performance.
3 Witkin Cal. Proc. 5th Actions § 769, (S 769) Current Rule: Statute Tolled.
9 Witkin Cal. Proc. 5th Appeal § 736, Dismissal Sought to Avoid Precedent.
4 Witkin Cal. Proc. 5th Pleading § 54, (S 54) Injuries to Person and Property from One Act.
5 Witkin Cal. Proc. 5th Pleading § 1121, Pleading Subdivision.
12 Witkin, California Summary 10th Real Property § 459, Nature and Scope of Statute.
12 Witkin, California Summary 10th Real Property § 903, Federal Statutes.
3 Witkin, California Summary 10th Agency and Employment § 399, (S 399) Wilful Failure.
4 Witkin, California Summary 10th Negotiable Instruments § 88, Enforcing the Provisions of Division 4.
4 Witkin, California Summary 10th Negotiable Instruments § 130, Preclusion Period and Statute of Limitations.
2 Witkin Cal. Summ. 10th Workers' Compensation § 83, (S 83) Statute of Limitations.
2 Witkin Cal. Summ. 10th Workers' Compensation § 86, (S 86) Action by Employee: Joinder or Intervention by Employer.

§ 340.1. Childhood sexual abuse; certificates of merit executed by attorney; violations; failure to file; name designation of defendant; periods of limitation; legislative intent

(a) In an action for recovery of damages suffered as a result of childhood sexual abuse, the time for commencement of the action shall be within eight years of the date the plaintiff attains the age of majority or within three years of the date the plaintiff discovers or reasonably should have discovered that psychological injury or illness occurring after the age of majority was caused by the sexual abuse, whichever period expires later, for any of the following actions:

(1) An action against any person for committing an act of childhood sexual abuse.

(2) An action for liability against any person or entity who owed a duty of care to the plaintiff, where a wrongful or negligent act by that person or entity was a legal cause of the childhood sexual abuse which resulted in the injury to the plaintiff.

(3) An action for liability against any person or entity where an intentional act by that person or entity was a legal cause of the childhood sexual abuse which resulted in the injury to the plaintiff.

(b)(1) No action described in paragraph (2) or (3) of subdivision (a) may be commenced on or after the plaintiff's 26th birthday.

(2) This subdivision does not apply if the person or entity knew or had reason to know, or was otherwise on notice, of any unlawful sexual conduct by an employee, volunteer, representative, or agent, and failed to take reasonable steps, and to implement reasonable safeguards, to avoid acts of unlawful sexual conduct in the future by that person, including, but not limited to, preventing or avoiding placement of that person in a function or environment in which contact with children is an inherent part of that function or environment. For purposes of this subdivision, providing or requiring counseling is not sufficient, in and of itself, to constitute a reasonable step or reasonable safeguard.

(c) Notwithstanding any other provision of law, any claim for damages described in paragraph (2) or (3) of subdivision (a) that is permitted to be filed pursuant to paragraph (2) of subdivision (b) that would otherwise be barred as of January 1, 2003, solely because the applicable statute of limitations has or had expired, is revived, and, in that case, a cause of action may be commenced within one year of January 1, 2003. Nothing in this subdivision shall be construed to alter the applicable statute of limitations period of an action that is not time barred as of January 1, 2003.

(d) Subdivision (c) does not apply to either of the following:

(1) Any claim that has been litigated to finality on the merits in any court of competent jurisdiction prior to January 1, 2003. Termination of a prior action on the basis of the statute of limitations does not constitute a claim that has been litigated to finality on the merits.

(2) Any written, compromised settlement agreement which has been entered into between a plaintiff and a defendant where the plaintiff was represented by an attorney who was admitted to practice law in this state at the time of the settlement, and the plaintiff signed the agreement.

(e) "Childhood sexual abuse" as used in this section includes any act committed against the plaintiff that occurred when the plaintiff was under the age of 18 years and that would have been proscribed by Section 266j of the Penal Code; Section 285 of the Penal Code; paragraph (1) or (2) of subdivision (b), or of subdivision (c), of Section 286 of the Penal Code; subdivision (a) or (b) of Section 288 of the Penal Code; paragraph (1) or (2) of subdivision (b), or of subdivision (c), of Section 288a of the Penal Code; subdivision (h), (i), or (j) of Section 289 of the Penal Code; Section 647.6 of the Penal Code; or any prior laws of this state of similar effect at the time the act was committed. Nothing in this subdivision limits the availability of causes of action permitted under subdivision (a), including causes of action against persons or entities other than the alleged perpetrator of the abuse.

(f) Nothing in this section shall be construed to alter the otherwise applicable burden of proof, as defined in Section 115 of the Evidence Code, that a plaintiff has in a civil action subject to this section.

(g) Every plaintiff 26 years of age or older at the time the action is filed shall file certificates of merit as specified in subdivision (h).

(h) Certificates of merit shall be executed by the attorney for the plaintiff and by a licensed mental health practitioner selected by the plaintiff declaring, respectively, as follows, setting forth the facts which support the declaration:

(1) That the attorney has reviewed the facts of the case, that the attorney has consulted with at least one mental health practitioner who is licensed to practice and practices in this state and who the attorney reasonably believes is knowledgeable of the relevant facts and issues involved in the particular action, and that the attorney has concluded on the basis of that review and consultation that there is reasonable and meritorious cause for the filing of the action. The person consulted may not be a party to the litigation.

(2) That the mental health practitioner consulted is licensed to practice and practices in this state and is not a party to the action, that the practitioner is not treating and has not treated the plaintiff, and that the practitioner has interviewed the plaintiff and is knowledgeable of the relevant facts and issues involved in the particular action, and has concluded, on the basis of his or her knowledge of the facts and issues, that in his or her professional opinion there is a reasonable basis to believe that the plaintiff had been subject to childhood sexual abuse.

(3) That the attorney was unable to obtain the consultation required by paragraph (1) because a statute of limitations would impair the action and that the certificates required by paragraphs (1) and (2) could not be obtained before the impairment of the action. If a certificate is executed pursuant to this paragraph, the certificates required by paragraphs (1) and (2) shall be filed within 60 days after filing the complaint.

(i) Where certificates are required pursuant to subdivision (g), the attorney for the plaintiff shall execute a separate certificate of merit for each defendant named in the complaint.

(j) In any action subject to subdivision (g), no defendant may be served, and the duty to serve a defendant with process does not attach, until the court has reviewed the certificates of merit filed pursuant to subdivision (h) with respect to that defendant, and has found, in camera, based solely on those certificates of merit, that there is reasonable and meritorious cause for the filing of the action against that defendant. At that time, the duty to serve that defendant with process shall attach.

(k) A violation of this section may constitute unprofessional conduct and may be the grounds for discipline against the attorney.

(*l*) The failure to file certificates in accordance with this section shall be grounds for a demurrer pursuant to Section 430.10 or a motion to strike pursuant to Section 435.

(m) In any action subject to subdivision (g), no defendant may be named except by "Doe" designation in any pleadings or papers filed in the action until there has been a showing of corroborative fact as to the charging allegations against that defendant.

(n) At any time after the action is filed, the plaintiff may apply to the court for permission to amend the complaint to substitute the name of the defendant or defendants for the fictitious designation, as follows:

(1) The application shall be accompanied by a certificate of corroborative fact executed by the attorney for the plaintiff. The certificate shall declare that the attorney has discovered one or more facts corroborative of one or more of the charging allegations against a defendant or defendants, and shall set forth in clear and concise terms the nature and substance of the corroborative fact. If the corroborative fact is evidenced by the statement of a witness or the contents of a document, the certificate shall declare that the attorney has personal knowledge of the statement of the witness or of the contents of the document, and the identity and location of the witness or document shall be included in the certificate. For purposes of this section, a fact is corroborative of an allegation if it confirms or supports the allegation. The opinion of any mental health

practitioner concerning the plaintiff shall not constitute a corroborative fact for purposes of this section.

(2) Where the application to name a defendant is made prior to that defendant's appearance in the action, neither the application nor the certificate of corroborative fact by the attorney shall be served on the defendant or defendants, nor on any other party or their counsel of record.

(3) Where the application to name a defendant is made after that defendant's appearance in the action, the application shall be served on all parties and proof of service provided to the court, but the certificate of corroborative fact by the attorney shall not be served on any party or their counsel of record.

(o) The court shall review the application and the certificate of corroborative fact in camera and, based solely on the certificate and any reasonable inferences to be drawn from the certificate, shall, if one or more facts corroborative of one or more of the charging allegations against a defendant has been shown, order that the complaint may be amended to substitute the name of the defendant or defendants.

(p) The court shall keep under seal and confidential from the public and all parties to the litigation, other than the plaintiff, any and all certificates of corroborative fact filed pursuant to subdivision (n).

(q) Upon the favorable conclusion of the litigation with respect to any defendant for whom a certificate of merit was filed or for whom a certificate of merit should have been filed pursuant to this section, the court may, upon the motion of a party or upon the court's own motion, verify compliance with this section by requiring the attorney for the plaintiff who was required by subdivision (h) to execute the certificate to reveal the name, address, and telephone number of the person or persons consulted with pursuant to subdivision (h) that were relied upon by the attorney in preparation of the certificate of merit. The name, address, and telephone number shall be disclosed to the trial judge in camera and in the absence of the moving party. If the court finds there has been a failure to comply with this section, the court may order a party, a party's attorney, or both, to pay any reasonable expenses, including attorney's fees, incurred by the defendant for whom a certificate of merit should have been filed.

(r) The amendments to this section enacted at the 1990 portion of the 1989–90 Regular Session shall apply to any action commenced on or after January 1, 1991, including any action otherwise barred by the period of limitations in effect prior to January 1, 1991, thereby reviving those causes of action which had lapsed or technically expired under the law existing prior to January 1, 1991.

(s) The Legislature declares that it is the intent of the Legislature, in enacting the amendments to this section enacted at the 1994 portion of the 1993–94 Regular Session, that the express language of revival added to this section by those amendments shall apply to any action commenced on or after January 1, 1991.

(t) Nothing in the amendments to this section enacted at the 1998 portion of the 1997–98 Regular Session is intended to create a new theory of liability.

(u) The amendments to subdivision (a) of this section, enacted at the 1998 portion of the 1997–98 Regular Session, shall apply to any action commenced on or after January 1, 1999, and to any action filed prior to January 1, 1999, and still pending on that date, including any action or causes of action which would have been barred by the laws in effect prior to January 1, 1999. Nothing in this subdivision is intended to revive actions or causes of action as to which there has been a final adjudication prior to January 1, 1999. *(Added by Stats.1986, c. 914, § 1. Amended by Stats.1990, c. 1578 (S.B.108), § 1; Stats.1994, c. 288*

(A.B.2846), § 1; Stats.1998, c. 1032 (A.B.1651), § 1; Stats.1999, c. 120 (S.B.674), § 1; Stats.2002, c. 149 (S.B.1779), § 1.)

Validity

This section was held unconstitutional in the decision of Perez v. Richard Roe 1 (App. 2 Dist. 2006) 52 Cal.Rptr.3d 762, 146 Cal.App.4th 171, as modified, review denied.

Research References

Rutter, Cal. Practice Guide: Civ. Pro. Before Trial Ch. 1-C, C. Prelawsuit Notices, Claims and Demands.

Rutter, Cal. Practice Guide: Civ. Pro. Before Trial Ch. 1-G, G. Prior Court Order Required for Certain Pleadings.

Rutter, Cal. Practice Guide: Civ. Pro. Before Trial Ch. 6-B, B. Complaints.

Rutter, Cal. Practice Guide: Civ. Pro. Before Trial Ch. 6-E, E. Amended and Supplemental Pleadings.

Rutter, Cal. Practice Guide: Civ. Pro. Before Trial Ch. 7(I)-A, A. Demurrers.

Rutter, Cal. Practice Guide: Personal Injury Ch. 3-A, A. Introduction.

Rutter, Cal. Practice Guide: Personal Injury Ch. 3-E, E. Punitive Damages.

Rutter, Cal. Practice Guide: Personal Injury Ch. 5-A, A. Prelawsuit Filings.

Rutter, Cal. Practice Guide: Personal Injury Ch. 5-B, B. When to Sue-Statute of Limitations.

Rutter, Cal. Practice Guide: Personal Injury Ch. 5-E, E. Selected Pleading Issues.

Rutter, Cal. Practice Guide: Personal Injury Ch. 3-A, Outline a.

Rutter, Cal. Practice Guide: Personal Injury Ch. 5-B, Outline B.

Rutter, Cal. Practice Guide: Personal Injury Gen. Matls., Highlights.

3 Witkin Cal. Proc. 5th Actions § 256, Statute of Limitations Rule Governs.

3 Witkin Cal. Proc. 5th Actions § 463, Sexual Abuse of Minor: 1986 Extension of Period.

3 Witkin Cal. Proc. 5th Actions § 464, Sexual Abuse of Minor: 1990 Extension of Period.

3 Witkin Cal. Proc. 5th Actions § 465, Sexual Abuse of Minor: 2002 Extension of Period.

3 Witkin Cal. Proc. 5th Actions § 483, (S 483) Three Years.

3 Witkin Cal. Proc. 5th Actions § 487, (S 487) Eight Years.

3 Witkin Cal. Proc. 5th Actions § 592, (S 592) Postponed Accrual Denied.

3 Witkin Cal. Proc. 5th Actions § 593, (S 593) Statutory Rule.

3 Witkin Cal. Proc. 5th Actions § 594, (S 594) Scope of Statute.

3 Witkin Cal. Proc. 5th Actions § 595, (S 595) Delayed Accrual and Tolling During Minority.

3 Witkin Cal. Proc. 5th Actions § 689, Scope and Accrual.

7 Witkin Cal. Proc. 5th Trial § 305, Errors in Content.

6 Witkin, California Summary 10th Torts § 913, (S 913) False Diagnosis of Recovered Memory.

§ 340.15. Action for damages suffered as result of domestic violence

(a) In any civil action for recovery of damages suffered as a result of domestic violence, the time for commencement of the action shall be the later of the following:

(1) Within three years from the date of the last act of domestic violence by the defendant against the plaintiff.

(2) Within three years from the date the plaintiff discovers or reasonably should have discovered that an injury or illness resulted from an act of domestic violence by the defendant against the plaintiff.

(b) As used in this section, "domestic violence" has the same meaning as defined in Section 6211 of the Family Code. *(Added by Stats.1995, c. 602 (S.B.924), § 1. Amended by Stats.1998, c. 123 (S.B.1939), § 1.)*

Research References

Rutter, Cal. Practice Guide: Personal Injury Ch. 5-B, B. When to Sue-Statute of Limitations.

3 Witkin Cal. Proc. 5th Actions § 483, (S 483) Three Years.

5 Witkin, California Summary 10th Torts § 467, Domestic Violence.

§ 340.2. Exposure to asbestos; actions for injury, illness or wrongful death

(a) In any civil action for injury or illness based upon exposure to asbestos, the time for the commencement of the action shall be the later of the following:

(1) Within one year after the date the plaintiff first suffered disability.

(2) Within one year after the date the plaintiff either knew, or through the exercise of reasonable diligence should have known, that such disability was caused or contributed to by such exposure.

(b) "Disability" as used in subdivision (a) means the loss of time from work as a result of such exposure which precludes the performance of the employee's regular occupation.

(c) In an action for the wrongful death of any plaintiff's decedent, based upon exposure to asbestos, the time for commencement of an action shall be the later of the following:

(1) Within one year from the date of the death of the plaintiff's decedent.

(2) Within one year from the date the plaintiff first knew, or through the exercise of reasonable diligence should have known, that the death was caused or contributed to by such exposure. *(Added by Stats.1979, c. 513, p. 1689, § 1.)*

Research References

Rutter, Cal. Practice Guide: Personal Injury Ch. 5-B, B. When to Sue-Statute of Limitations.
Rutter, Cal. Practice Guide: Personal Injury Gen. Matls., Highlights.
Rutter, Cal. Practice Guide: Real Prop. Transactions Ch. 5-D, D. Common Law Environmental Hazards Liability.
3 Witkin Cal. Proc. 5th Actions § 568, (S 568) Statutory Rule of Postponed Accrual.
3 Witkin Cal. Proc. 5th Actions § 569, (S 569) Definition of Disability.
3 Witkin Cal. Proc. 5th Actions § 570, (S 570) Cause of Disability.
3 Witkin Cal. Proc. 5th Actions § 571, (S 571) Knowledge of Disability.
3 Witkin Cal. Proc. 5th Actions § 572, (S 572) Distinction: Loss of Consortium.
3 Witkin Cal. Proc. 5th Actions § 573, Exposure to Hazardous Material or Toxic Substance.
3 Witkin Cal. Proc. 5th Actions § 639, (S 639) Conflicting Decisions in Courts of Appeal.
5 Witkin, California Summary 10th Torts § 192, Comparative Impairment Analysis.

§ 340.3. Actions for damages against defendant arising from felony offense; limitation of actions; stay of judgment; restitution

(a) Unless a longer period is prescribed for a specific action, in any action for damages against a defendant based upon the defendant's commission of a felony offense for which the defendant has been convicted, the time for commencement of the action shall be within one year after judgment is pronounced.

(b)(1) Notwithstanding subdivision (a), an action for damages against a defendant based upon the defendant's commission of a felony offense for which the defendant has been convicted may be commenced within 10 years of the date on which the defendant is discharged from parole if the conviction was for any offense specified in paragraph (1), except voluntary manslaughter, (2), (3), (4), (5), (6), (7), (9), (16), (17), (20), (22), (25), (34), or (35) of subdivision (c) of Section 1192.7 of the Penal Code.

(2) No civil action may be commenced pursuant to paragraph (1) if any of the following applies:

(A) The defendant has received either a certificate of rehabilitation as provided in Chapter 3.5 (commencing with Section 4852.01) of Title 6 of Part 3 of the Penal Code or a pardon as

provided in Chapter 1 (commencing with Section 4800) or Chapter 3 (commencing with Section 4850) of Title 6 of Part 3 of the Penal Code.

(B) Following a conviction for murder or attempted murder, the defendant has been paroled based in whole or in part upon evidence presented to the Board of Prison Terms that the defendant committed the crime because he or she was the victim of intimate partner battering.

(C) The defendant was convicted of murder or attempted murder in the second degree in a trial at which substantial evidence was presented that the person committed the crime because he or she was a victim of intimate partner battering.

(c) If the sentence or judgment is stayed, the time for the commencement of the action shall be tolled until the stay is lifted. For purposes of this section, a judgment is not stayed if the judgment is appealed or the defendant is placed on probation.

(d)(1) Subdivision (b) shall apply to any action commenced before, on, or after the effective date of this section, including any action otherwise barred by a limitation of time in effect prior to the effective date of this section, thereby reviving those causes of action that had lapsed or expired under the law in effect prior to the effective date of this section.

(2) Paragraph (1) does not apply to either of the following:

(A) Any claim that has been litigated to finality on the merits in any court of competent jurisdiction prior to January 1, 2003. For purposes of this section, termination of a prior action on the basis of the statute of limitations does not constitute a claim that has been litigated to finality on the merits.

(B) Any written, compromised settlement agreement that has been entered into between a plaintiff and a defendant if the plaintiff was represented by an attorney who was admitted to practice law in this state at the time of the settlement, and the plaintiff signed the agreement.

(e) Any restitution paid by the defendant to the victim shall be credited against any judgment, award, or settlement obtained pursuant to this section. Any judgment, award, or settlement obtained pursuant to an action under this section shall be subject to the provisions of Section 13966.01 of the Government Code. *(Added by Stats.1983, c. 938, § 2, eff. Sept. 20, 1983. Amended by Stats.2002, c. 633 (S.B.1887), § 1, eff. Sept. 18, 2002; Stats.2005, c. 215 (A.B.220), § 1.)*

Research References

Rutter, Cal. Practice Guide: Personal Injury Ch. 5-B, B. When to Sue-Statute of Limitations.
3 Witkin Cal. Proc. 5th Actions § 481, (S 481) One Year.
3 Witkin Cal. Proc. 5th Actions § 488, (S 488) Ten Years.

§ 340.35. Causes of action involving sexual abuse of a minor; statutes of limitation

(a) This section shall apply if both of the following conditions are met:

(1) A complaint, information, or indictment was filed in a criminal case initiated pursuant to subdivision (f), (g), or (h) of Section 803 of the Penal Code.

(2) The case was dismissed or overturned pursuant to the United States Supreme Court's decision in Stogner v. California (2003) 156 L.Ed.2d 544.

(b) Unless a longer period is prescribed for a specific action, any action for damages against an individual for committing an act of childhood sexual abuse shall be commenced before January 1, 2006.

(c) This section shall apply to any action commenced before, on, or after the effective date of this section, including any action otherwise barred by a limitation of time in effect prior to the effective date of this section, thereby reviving those causes of action that had lapsed or expired under the law in effect prior to the effective date of this section.

(d) This section shall not apply to any of the following:

(1) Any claim against a person or entity other than the individual against whom a complaint, information, or indictment was filed as described in paragraph (1) of subdivision (a).

(2) Any claim that has been litigated to finality on the merits in any court of competent jurisdiction prior to the effective date of this section. For purposes of this section, termination of a prior action on the basis of the statute of limitations does not constitute a claim that has been "litigated to finality on the merits."

(3) Any written, compromised settlement agreement that has been entered into between a plaintiff and a defendant, if the plaintiff was represented by an attorney who was admitted to practice law in this state at the time of the settlement, and the plaintiff signed the agreement.

(e) Any restitution paid by the defendant to the victim shall be credited against any judgment, award, or settlement obtained pursuant to this section. Any judgment, award, or settlement obtained pursuant to an action under this section shall be subject to Section 13966.01 of the Government Code. *(Added by Stats.2004, c. 741 (S.B.1678), § 1.)*

§ 340.4. Minors; action for personal injuries before or during birth; limitation of actions

An action by or on behalf of a minor for personal injuries sustained before or in the course of his or her birth must be commenced within six years after the date of birth, and the time the minor is under any disability mentioned in Section 352 shall not be excluded in computing the time limited for the commencement of the action. *(Added by Stats.1992, c. 163 (A.B. 2641), § 16, operative Jan. 1, 1994.)*

Law Revision Commission Comments

Section 340.4 continues the last part of former Civil Code Section 29 without substantive change. [22 Cal.L.Rev.Comm.Reports 1 (1992)].

Research References

Rutter, Cal. Practice Guide: Personal Injury Ch. 5-B, B. When to Sue-Statute of Limitations.
Rutter, Cal. Practice Guide: Personal Injury Ch. 5-B, Outline B.
3 Witkin Cal. Proc. 5th Actions § 443, Limitation in Statute Creating Right.
3 Witkin Cal. Proc. 5th Actions § 459, (S 459) Period Shortened.
3 Witkin Cal. Proc. 5th Actions § 486, (S 486) Six Years.
3 Witkin Cal. Proc. 5th Actions § 553, (S 553) Scope of Statute.
3 Witkin Cal. Proc. 5th Actions § 589, (S 589) Prenatal Injuries.
3 Witkin Cal. Proc. 5th Actions § 695, (S 695) in General.
5 Witkin, California Summary 10th Torts § 728, (S 728) Injury to Unborn Child.

§ 340.5. Action against health care provider; three years from injury or one year from discovery; exceptions; minors

In an action for injury or death against a health care provider based upon such person's alleged professional negligence, the time for the commencement of action shall be three years after the date of injury or one year after the plaintiff discovers, or through the use of reasonable diligence should have discovered, the injury, whichever occurs first. In no event shall the time for commencement of legal action exceed three years unless tolled for any of the following: (1) upon proof of fraud, (2) intentional concealment, or (3) the presence of a foreign body, which has no therapeutic or diagnostic purpose or effect, in the person of the injured person. Actions by a minor shall be commenced within three years from the date of the alleged wrongful act except that

actions by a minor under the full age of six years shall be commenced within three years or prior to his eighth birthday whichever provides a longer period. Such time limitation shall be tolled for minors for any period during which parent or guardian and defendant's insurer or health care provider have committed fraud or collusion in the failure to bring an action on behalf of the injured minor for professional negligence.

For the purposes of this section:

(1) "Health care provider" means any person licensed or certified pursuant to Division 2 (commencing with Section 500) of the Business and Professions Code, or licensed pursuant to the Osteopathic Initiative Act, or the Chiropractic Initiative Act, or licensed pursuant to Chapter 2.5 (commencing with Section 1440) of Division 2 of the Health and Safety Code; and any clinic, health dispensary, or health facility, licensed pursuant to Division 2 (commencing with Section 1200) of the Health and Safety Code. "Health care provider" includes the legal representatives of a health care provider;

(2) "Professional negligence" means a negligent act or omission to act by a health care provider in the rendering of professional services, which act or omission is the proximate cause of a personal injury or wrongful death, provided that such services are within the scope of services for which the provider is licensed and which are not within any restriction imposed by the licensing agency or licensed hospital. *(Added by Stats.1970, c. 360, p. 772, § 1. Amended by Stats.1975, 2nd Ex.Sess., c. 1, p. 3969, § 25; Stats.1975, 2nd Ex.Sess., c. 2, p. 3991, § 1.192, eff. Sept. 24, 1975, operative Dec. 15, 1975.)*

Research References

Rutter, Cal. Practice Guide: Civ. Pro. Before Trial Ch. 1-C, C. Prelawsuit Notices, Claims and Demands.
Rutter, Cal. Practice Guide: Civ. Pro. Before Trial Ch. 6-E, E. Amended and Supplemental Pleadings.
Rutter, Cal. Practice Guide: Civil Trials & Evidence Ch. 4-G, G. Motion to Sever or Bifurcate.
Rutter, Cal. Practice Guide: Insurance Litigation Ch. 15-B, B. Actions by Insurers.
Rutter, Cal. Practice Guide: Personal Injury Ch. 3-F, F. MICRA Provisions Affecting Damages.
Rutter, Cal. Practice Guide: Personal Injury Ch. 3-G, G. Independent Damages Claims.
Rutter, Cal. Practice Guide: Personal Injury Ch. 5-A, A. Prelawsuit Filings.
Rutter, Cal. Practice Guide: Personal Injury Ch. 5-B, B. When to Sue-Statute of Limitations.
Rutter, Cal. Practice Guide: Personal Injury Ch. 5-A, Outline a.
Rutter, Cal. Practice Guide: Personal Injury Ch. 5-B, Outline B.
Rutter, Cal. Practice Guide: Real Prop. Transactions Ch. 5-D, D. Common Law Environmental Hazards Liability.
3 Witkin Cal. Proc. 5th Actions § 256, Statute of Limitations Rule Governs.
3 Witkin Cal. Proc. 5th Actions § 481, (S 481) One Year.
3 Witkin Cal. Proc. 5th Actions § 506, (S 506) Alternative Remedy With Longer Period.
3 Witkin Cal. Proc. 5th Actions § 508, Action on Written Contract.
3 Witkin Cal. Proc. 5th Actions § 559, (S 559) Personal Injuries.
3 Witkin Cal. Proc. 5th Actions § 573, Exposure to Hazardous Material or Toxic Substance.
3 Witkin Cal. Proc. 5th Actions § 575, (S 575) in General.
3 Witkin Cal. Proc. 5th Actions § 578, (S 578) Statutory Rule: in General.
3 Witkin Cal. Proc. 5th Actions § 579, in General.
3 Witkin Cal. Proc. 5th Actions § 580, Illustrations.
3 Witkin Cal. Proc. 5th Actions § 581, (S 581) Three Years After Injury.
3 Witkin Cal. Proc. 5th Actions § 582, in General.
3 Witkin Cal. Proc. 5th Actions § 584, Presence of Foreign Body.
3 Witkin Cal. Proc. 5th Actions § 585, (S 585) Tolling of One-Year Period.
3 Witkin Cal. Proc. 5th Actions § 586, Limitations Periods.
3 Witkin Cal. Proc. 5th Actions § 587, Delayed Accrual and Tolling of Period.
3 Witkin Cal. Proc. 5th Actions § 588, Effect of Reaching Majority.

Civ. Pro.

3 Witkin Cal. Proc. 5th Actions § 589, (S 589) Prenatal Injuries.

3 Witkin Cal. Proc. 5th Actions § 590, (S 590) Wrongful Death.

3 Witkin Cal. Proc. 5th Actions § 591, (S 591) Postponed Accrual Allowed.

3 Witkin Cal. Proc. 5th Actions § 647, (S 647) Equitable Tolling and Estoppel Doctrines.

3 Witkin Cal. Proc. 5th Actions § 650, Negligent Wrongs.

3 Witkin Cal. Proc. 5th Actions § 664, (S 664) in General.

3 Witkin Cal. Proc. 5th Actions § 689, Scope and Accrual.

3 Witkin Cal. Proc. 5th Actions § 691, (S 691) Two-Year Period.

3 Witkin Cal. Proc. 5th Actions § 698, Scope of Suspension.

3 Witkin Cal. Proc. 5th Actions § 703, Exceptions and Distinctions.

3 Witkin Cal. Proc. 5th Actions § 710, Absence.

3 Witkin Cal. Proc. 5th Actions § 723, Medical Malpractice.

3 Witkin Cal. Proc. 5th Actions § 724, Equitable Indemnity.

3 Witkin Cal. Proc. 5th Actions § 727, (S 727) Service of Notice.

3 Witkin Cal. Proc. 5th Actions § 728, (S 728) Duration of Tolling.

8 Witkin Cal. Proc. 5th Attack Judgment Trial Court § 147, (S 147) in General.

4 Witkin Cal. Proc. 5th Pleading § 481, (S 481) Actual Ignorance.

6 Witkin, California Summary 10th Torts § 934, (S 934) Ordinary Versus Professional Negligence.

6 Witkin, California Summary 10th Torts § 954, Extension of Applicable Statute of Limitations.

6 Witkin, California Summary 10th Torts § 1379, Statute of Limitations.

6 Witkin, California Summary 10th Torts § 1687, Exception for Professional Negligence by Health Care Provider.

8 Witkin, California Summary 10th Constitutional Law § 779, (S 779) Invalid Classification.

§ 340.6. Attorneys; wrongful professional act or omission; tolling of period

(a) An action against an attorney for a wrongful act or omission, other than for actual fraud, arising in the performance of professional services shall be commenced within one year after the plaintiff discovers, or through the use of reasonable diligence should have discovered, the facts constituting the wrongful act or omission, or four years from the date of the wrongful act or omission, whichever occurs first. If the plaintiff is required to establish his or her factual innocence for an underlying criminal charge as an element of his or her claim, the action shall be commenced within two years after the plaintiff achieves postconviction exoneration in the form of a final judicial disposition of the criminal case. Except for a claim for which the plaintiff is required to establish his or her factual innocence, in no event shall the time for commencement of legal action exceed four years except that the period shall be tolled during the time that any of the following exist:

(1) The plaintiff has not sustained actual injury.

(2) The attorney continues to represent the plaintiff regarding the specific subject matter in which the alleged wrongful act or omission occurred.

(3) The attorney willfully conceals the facts constituting the wrongful act or omission when such facts are known to the attorney, except that this subdivision shall toll only the four-year limitation.

(4) The plaintiff is under a legal or physical disability which restricts the plaintiff's ability to commence legal action.

(b) In an action based upon an instrument in writing, the effective date of which depends upon some act or event of the future, the period of limitations provided for by this section shall commence to run upon the occurrence of that act or event. *(Added by Stats.1977, c. 863, p. 2609, § 1. Amended by Stats.2009, c. 432 (A.B.316), § 2.)*

Research References

Rutter, Cal. Practice Guide: Personal Injury Ch. 5-B, B. When to Sue-Statute of Limitations.

Rutter, Cal. Practice Guide: Prof. Responsibility Ch. 6-D, D. Professional Liability.

Rutter, Cal. Practice Guide: Prof. Responsibility Ch. 6-G, G. Professional Competence in Criminal Cases.

Rutter, Cal. Practice Guide: Prof. Responsibility Gen. Matls., Highlights.

14 NO. 2 Miller & Starr, California Real Estate Newsalert 1, "The Outer Limit": The California Supreme Court Reigns in the 10-Year Statute of Repose for Construction Defects.

3 Witkin Cal. Proc. 5th Actions § 497, (S 497) in General.

3 Witkin Cal. Proc. 5th Actions § 606, (S 606) Scope of Statute.

3 Witkin Cal. Proc. 5th Actions § 629, Nature and Scope of Statute.

3 Witkin Cal. Proc. 5th Actions § 630, Alternative Periods.

3 Witkin Cal. Proc. 5th Actions § 631, Statutory Tolling Provisions.

3 Witkin Cal. Proc. 5th Actions § 633, (S 633) Laird Rule: Adverse Judgment or Dismissal.

3 Witkin Cal. Proc. 5th Actions § 634, (S 634) Distinction: Negligent Advice About Settlement.

3 Witkin Cal. Proc. 5th Actions § 635, (S 635) Conflicting Decisions in Courts of Appeal.

3 Witkin Cal. Proc. 5th Actions § 636, (S 636) Itt Rule: Adverse Judgment, Settlement, or Dismissal.

3 Witkin Cal. Proc. 5th Actions § 637, (S 637) Problems With Itt Rule.

3 Witkin Cal. Proc. 5th Actions § 638, (S 638) Itt Rule Overruled: Malpractice is Question of Fact.

3 Witkin Cal. Proc. 5th Actions § 639, (S 639) Conflicting Decisions in Courts of Appeal.

3 Witkin Cal. Proc. 5th Actions § 640, (S 640) Adams Rule: Question of Fact.

3 Witkin Cal. Proc. 5th Actions § 641, (S 641) Illustrations.

3 Witkin Cal. Proc. 5th Actions § 642, Criminal Case Malpractice.

3 Witkin Cal. Proc. 5th Actions § 643, Statute Tolled.

3 Witkin Cal. Proc. 5th Actions § 644, Statute Not Tolled.

3 Witkin Cal. Proc. 5th Actions § 645, Tolling After Attorney Leaves Law Firm.

3 Witkin Cal. Proc. 5th Actions § 646, (S 646) Tolling While Plaintiff is Under Legal or Physical Disability.

3 Witkin Cal. Proc. 5th Actions § 647, (S 647) Equitable Tolling and Estoppel Doctrines.

3 Witkin Cal. Proc. 5th Actions § 649, Intentional Wrongs.

3 Witkin Cal. Proc. 5th Actions § 650, Negligent Wrongs.

3 Witkin Cal. Proc. 5th Actions § 739, (S 739) Equitable Tolling Doctrine.

3 Witkin Cal. Proc. 5th Actions § 740, (S 740) First Action Outside California.

3 Witkin Cal. Proc. 5th Actions § 762, in General.

1 Witkin Cal. Proc. 5th Attorneys § 69, (S 69) Motion to Withdraw.

1 Witkin Cal. Proc. 5th Attorneys § 315, Exoneration by Postconviction Relief.

6 Witkin Cal. Proc. 5th Proceedings Without Trial § 219, (S 219) Consideration of Other Papers.

§ 340.7. Dalkon Shield Claimants' Trust claims; tolling for bankruptcy of A.H. Robins Co.

(a) Notwithstanding Section 335.1, a civil action brought by, or on behalf of, a Dalkon Shield victim against the Dalkon Shield Claimants' Trust, shall be brought in accordance with the procedures established by A.H. Robins Company, Inc. Plan of Reorganization, and shall be brought within 15 years of the date on which the victim's injury occurred, except that the statute shall be tolled from August 21, 1985, the date on which the A.H. Robins Company filed for Chapter 11 Reorganization in Richmond, Virginia.

(b) This section applies regardless of when the action or claim shall have accrued or been filed and regardless of whether it might have lapsed or otherwise be barred by time under California law. However, this section shall only apply to victims who, prior to January 1, 1990, filed a civil action, a timely claim, or a claim that is declared to be timely under the sixth Amended and Restated Disclosure Statement filed pursuant to Section 1125 of the Federal Bankruptcy Code in re: A.H. Robins Company, Inc., dated March 28, 1988, U.S. Bankruptcy Court, Eastern District of Virginia (case number 85–01307–R). *(Added by Stats.1994, c. 107 (A.B.2855), § 1. Amended by Stats.2007, c. 130 (A.B.299), § 35; Stats.2008, c. 179 (S.B.1498), § 34.)*

Research References

3 Witkin Cal. Proc. 5th Actions § 575, (S 575) in General.

§ 340.8. Exposure to hazardous materials or toxic substances; time for commencement of action; injury or illness; wrongful death actions; definitions

(a) In any civil action for injury or illness based upon exposure to a hazardous material or toxic substance, the time for commencement of the action shall be no later than either two years from the date of injury, or two years after the plaintiff becomes aware of, or reasonably should have become aware of, (1) an injury, (2) the physical cause of the injury, and (3) sufficient facts to put a reasonable person on inquiry notice that the injury was caused or contributed to by the wrongful act of another, whichever occurs later.

(b) In an action for the wrongful death of any plaintiff's decedent, based upon exposure to a hazardous material or toxic substance, the time for commencement of an action shall be no later than either (1) two years from the date of the death of the plaintiff's decedent, or (2) two years from the first date on which the plaintiff is aware of, or reasonably should have become aware of, the physical cause of the death and sufficient facts to put a reasonable person on inquiry notice that the death was caused or contributed to by the wrongful act of another, whichever occurs later.

(c) For purposes of this section:

(1) A "civil action for injury or illness based upon exposure to a hazardous material or toxic substance" does not include an action subject to Section 340.2 or 340.5.

(2) Media reports regarding the hazardous material or toxic substance contamination do not, in and of themselves, constitute sufficient facts to put a reasonable person on inquiry notice that the injury or death was caused or contributed to by the wrongful act of another.

(d) Nothing in this section shall be construed to limit, abrogate, or change the law in effect on the effective date of this section with respect to actions not based upon exposure to a hazardous material or toxic substance. *(Added by Stats.2003, c. 873 (S.B.331), § 1.)*

Research References

Rutter, Cal. Practice Guide: Personal Injury Ch. 5-B, B. When to Sue-Statute of Limitations.

Rutter, Cal. Practice Guide: Real Prop. Transactions Ch. 5-D, D. Common Law Environmental Hazards Liability.

3 Witkin Cal. Proc. 5th Actions § 573, Exposure to Hazardous Material or Toxic Substance.

3 Witkin Cal. Proc. 5th Actions § 661, Illustrations: Accrual Not Postponed.

§ 340.9. Northridge earthquake insurance claims

(a) Notwithstanding any other provision of law or contract, any insurance claim for damages arising out of the Northridge earthquake of 1994 which is barred as of the effective date of this section solely because the applicable statute of limitations has or had expired is hereby revived and a cause of action thereon may be commenced provided that the action is commenced within one year of the effective date of this section. This subdivision shall only apply to cases in which an insured contacted an insurer or an insurer's representative prior to January 1, 2000, regarding potential Northridge earthquake damage.

(b) Any action pursuant to this section commenced prior to, or within one year from, the effective date of this section shall not be barred based upon this limitations period.

(c) Nothing in this section shall be construed to alter the applicable limitations period of an action that is not time barred as of the effective date of this section.

(d) This section shall not apply to either of the following:

(1) Any claim that has been litigated to finality in any court of competent jurisdiction prior to the effective date of this section.

(2) Any written compromised settlement agreement which has been made between an insurer and its insured where the insured was represented by counsel admitted to the practice of law in California at the time of the settlement, and who signed the agreement. *(Added by Stats.2000, c. 1090 (S.B.1899), § 1.)*

Research References

Rutter, Cal. Practice Guide: Insurance Litigation Ch. 10-C, C. Claims Involving Insurance Guarantee Associations.

Rutter, Cal. Practice Guide: Insurance Litigation Ch. 6A-D, D. Conditions Governing Claims.

3 Witkin Cal. Proc. 5th Actions § 466, Action on Northridge Earthquake Insurance Claim.

3 Witkin Cal. Proc. 5th Actions § 757, Liability Insurance.

6 Witkin Cal. Proc. 5th Proceedings Without Trial § 52, Distinction: Court's Authority to Construe as Different Motion.

2 Witkin, California Summary 10th Insurance § 12, (S 12) in General.

2 Witkin, California Summary 10th Insurance § 251, Traditional Tort Actions.

2 Witkin, California Summary 10th Insurance § 309, (S 309) in General.

2 Witkin, California Summary 10th Insurance § 317, Notice and Proof of Loss.

8 Witkin, California Summary 10th Constitutional Law § 1291, Insurance Contracts.

§ 340.10. "Terrorist victim" defined; statute of limitations for actions brought for injury or death to terrorist victim

(a) For purposes of this section, "terrorist victim" means any individual who died or was injured as a consequence of the terrorist-related aircraft crashes of September 11, 2001, including persons who were present at the World Trade Center in New York City, New York, the Pentagon in Arlington, Virginia, or at the site of the crash at Shanksville, Pennsylvania, or in the immediate aftermath of the terrorist-related aircraft crashes of September 11, 2001, including members of the flight crew and passengers on American Airlines Flight 11, American Airlines Flight 77, United Airlines Flight 175, and United Airlines Flight 93, and who suffered physical harm or death as a result of any of the crashes, as defined in Section 40101 of Title 49 of the United States Code and the related, applicable regulations, other than an individual identified by the Attorney General of the United States as a participant or conspirator in the terrorist-related aircraft crashes, or a representative or heir of such an individual.

(b) The statute of limitations for injury or death set forth in Section 335.1 shall apply to any action brought for injury to, or for the death of, any terrorist victim described in subdivision (a) and caused by the wrongful act or neglect of another, regardless of whether that action lapsed or was otherwise barred by time under California law predating the passage of this section and Section 335.1. *(Added by Stats.2002, c. 448 (S.B.688), § 4.)*

Research References

3 Witkin Cal. Proc. 5th Actions § 552, (S 552) in General.

§ 341. Six months; officer for seizure as tax collector; stock sold for delinquent assessment; vacation of act of trustees of dissolved corporation

Within six months:

An action against an officer, or officer de facto:

1. To recover any goods, wares, merchandise, or other property, seized by any such officer in his official capacity as tax collector, or to recover the price or value of any goods, wares, merchandise, or other personal property so seized, or for damages for the seizure, detention, sale of, or injury to any goods, wares, merchandise, or other personal property seized, or

for damages done to any person or property in making any such seizure.

2. To recover stock sold for a delinquent assessment, as provided in section three hundred forty-seven of the Civil Code.[1]

3. To set aside or invalidate any action taken or performed by a majority of the trustees of any corporation heretofore or hereafter dissolved by operation of law, including the revivor of any such corporation. *(Enacted in 1872. Amended by Code Am.1873–74, c. 383, p. 292, § 35; Stats.1917, c. 217, p. 381, § 1.)*

[1] Now Corporations Code § 423.

Research References

Miller and Starr California Real Estate § 19:7, Other Interests Distinguished--Eviction of a Guest or Lodger.
3 Witkin Cal. Proc. 5th Actions § 480, (S 480) One Hundred Eighty Days or Six Months.
3 Witkin Cal. Proc. 5th Actions § 620, in General.

§ 341.5. Actions challenging the constitutionality of state funding for municipalities, school districts, special districts, or local agencies; commencement

Notwithstanding any other provision of law, any action or proceeding in which a county, city, city and county, school district, special district, or any other local agency is a plaintiff or petitioner, that is brought against the State of California challenging the constitutionality of any statute relating to state funding for counties, cities, cities and counties, school districts, special districts, or other local agencies, shall be commenced within 90 days of the effective date of the statute at issue in the action. For purposes of this section, "State of California" means the State of California itself, or any of its agencies, departments, commissions, boards, or public officials. *(Added by Stats.1994, c. 155 (A.B.860), § 1, eff. July 11, 1994. Amended by Stats.1994, c. 156 (S.B.2127), § 1, eff. July 11, 1994.)*

Research References

3 Witkin Cal. Proc. 5th Actions § 477, (S 477) Ninety Days or Three Months.

§ 341a. Ninety days; recovery or conversion of personal property, baggage, etc., left at hotel, hospital, boarding house, etc.

All civil actions for the recovery or conversion of personal property, wearing apparel, trunks, valises or baggage alleged to have been left at a hotel, hospital, rest home, sanitarium, boarding house, lodging house, furnished apartment house, or furnished bungalow court, shall be begun within 90 days from and after the date of the departure of the owner of said personal property, wearing apparel, trunks, valises or baggage from said hotel, hospital, rest home, sanitarium, boarding house, lodging house, furnished apartment house, or furnished bungalow court. *(Added by Stats.1921, c. 152, p. 150, § 1. Amended by Stats.1927, c. 826, p. 1657, § 1; Stats.1943, c. 405, p. 1930, § 1.)*

Research References

Miller and Starr California Real Estate § 19:235, Tenant's Personal Property--Innkeeper's Lien.
3 Witkin Cal. Proc. 5th Actions § 477, (S 477) Ninety Days or Three Months.
3 Witkin Cal. Proc. 5th Actions § 620, in General.
3 Witkin Cal. Proc. 5th Actions § 621, Action for Recovery or Conversion of Personal Property Left in Hotel and Similar Establishments.
13 Witkin, California Summary 10th Personal Property § 168, Liability: in General.

§ 342. Actions against public entities

An action against a public entity upon a cause of action for which a claim is required to be presented in accordance with Chapter 1 (commencing with Section 900) and Chapter 2 (commencing with Section 910) of Part 3 of Division 3.6 of Title 1 of the Government Code must be commenced within the time provided in Section 945.6 of the Government Code. *(Added by Stats.1963, c. 1715, p. 3394, § 4.)*

Law Revision Commission Comments

This section is placed among the limitation of actions provisions of the Code of Civil Procedure so that the statute of limitations applicable to actions upon claims against public entities may be discovered by looking at either this section or the appropriate section of the Government Code.

Research References

3 Witkin Cal. Proc. 5th Actions § 690, Personal Injury Claim Not Involving Medical Malpractice.

§ 343. Four years; relief not otherwise provided for

ACTIONS FOR RELIEF NOT HEREINBEFORE PROVIDED FOR. An action for relief not hereinbefore provided for must be commenced within four years after the cause of action shall have accrued. *(Enacted in 1872.)*

Research References

Rutter, Cal. Practice Guide: Insurance Litigation Ch. 12D-B, B. Statute of Limitations.
Rutter, Cal. Practice Guide: Personal Injury Ch. 5-B, B. When to Sue-Statute of Limitations.
Rutter, Cal. Practice Guide: Prof. Responsibility Ch. 6-D, D. Professional Liability.
Miller and Starr California Real Estate § 3:16, Effect of Undisclosed Dual Agency--Duties and Liabilities of the Dual Agent.
Miller and Starr California Real Estate § 3:34, Statute of Limitations.
Miller and Starr California Real Estate § 3:46, Statute of Limitations.
Miller and Starr California Real Estate § 14:44, Elements of Agreed Boundary Doctrine--Occupancy; Period of Use.
Miller and Starr California Real Estate § 24:39, Amendment to Restrictions--Generally.
Miller and Starr California Real Estate § 19:144, Landlord's Obligation to Refund Deposits--Nonresidential Premises.
Miller and Starr California Real Estate § 34:118, Statute of Limitations.
Miller and Starr California Real Estate § 34:123, Statute of Limitations.
18 NO. 1 Miller & Starr, California Real Estate Newsalert 16, Holding Title.
20 NO. 1 Miller & Starr, California Real Estate Newsalert 6, Covenants, Equitable Servitudes, and Other Restrictions.
22 NO. 6 Miller & Starr, California Real Estate Newsalert 4, Agency.
22 NO. 2 Miller & Starr, California Real Estate Newsalert 15, Judicial Remedies.
23 NO. 2 Miller & Starr, California Real Estate Newsalert 3, Adjoining Landowners.
3 Witkin Cal. Proc. 5th Actions § 431, (S 431) Statutory Classification.
3 Witkin Cal. Proc. 5th Actions § 480, (S 480) One Hundred Eighty Days or Six Months.
3 Witkin Cal. Proc. 5th Actions § 484, (S 484) Four Years.
3 Witkin Cal. Proc. 5th Actions § 491, Cancellation of Void Instrument.
3 Witkin Cal. Proc. 5th Actions § 502, (S 502) General Rule: Professional Negligence Cases.
3 Witkin Cal. Proc. 5th Actions § 563, Action for Termination of Employment in Violation of Public Policy.
3 Witkin Cal. Proc. 5th Actions § 675, Action on Judgment: Ten Years.
3 Witkin Cal. Proc. 5th Actions § 676, Action by Beneficiary Against Trustee: Three Years.
3 Witkin Cal. Proc. 5th Actions § 677, in General.
3 Witkin Cal. Proc. 5th Actions § 678, Illustrations.
3 Witkin Cal. Proc. 5th Actions § 679, (S 679) Delayed Accrual in Action Against Fiduciary.
3 Witkin Cal. Proc. 5th Actions § 680, Analysis of Problem.
3 Witkin Cal. Proc. 5th Actions § 681, What Statutes Apply.
3 Witkin Cal. Proc. 5th Actions § 682, Accrual on Knowledge of Facts.
3 Witkin Cal. Proc. 5th Actions § 683, (S 683) Accounting.
3 Witkin Cal. Proc. 5th Actions § 684, (S 684) Mandamus.
3 Witkin Cal. Proc. 5th Actions § 749, Trial of Insured's Murderer.
9 Witkin Cal. Proc. 5th Administrative Proceedings § 129, (S 129) Statutes of Limitations.
8 Witkin Cal. Proc. 5th Enforcement of Judgment § 462, Former Law: Uniform Foreign Money Judgments Recognition Act.

9 Witkin, California Summary 10th Taxation § 293, Procedure.

11 Witkin, California Summary 10th Community Property § 264, (S 264) Judicially Developed Rules.

11 Witkin, California Summary 10th Community Property § 276, Illustrations: Recovery Allowed.

9 Witkin, California Summary 10th Corporations § 9, Nature of Doctrine.

13 Witkin, California Summary 10th Equity § 33, Defenses.

13 Witkin, California Summary 10th Trusts § 137, Limitations and Laches.

§ 344. Balance upon mutual, open and current account; accrual of cause

WHERE CAUSE OF ACTION ACCRUES ON MUTUAL ACCOUNT. In an action brought to recover a balance due upon a mutual, open, and current account, where there have been reciprocal demands between the parties, the cause of action is deemed to have accrued from the time of the last item proved in the account on either side. *(Enacted in 1872.)*

Research References

3 Witkin Cal. Proc. 5th Actions § 484, (S 484) Four Years.

3 Witkin Cal. Proc. 5th Actions § 540, Mutual, Open, and Current Account.

§ 345. Actions in name of state or county; applicability of chapter; support of patients at state or county hospitals; four year limit

The limitations prescribed in this chapter apply to actions brought in the name of the state or county or for the benefit of the state or county, in the same manner as to actions by private parties. Accounts for the support of patients at state or county hospitals are book accounts as defined in Section 337a, and actions on them may be commenced at any time within four years after the last date of service or the last date of payment. *(Enacted in 1872. Amended by Stats.1905, c. 381, p. 487, § 1; Stats.1921, c. 475, p. 722, § 1; Stats.1943, c. 177, p. 1071, § 1; Stats.1984, c. 797, § 1.)*

Research References

3 Witkin Cal. Proc. 5th Actions § 456, State or Political Subdivision.

3 Witkin Cal. Proc. 5th Actions § 484, (S 484) Four Years.

4 Witkin Cal. Proc. 5th Pleading § 105, as Plaintiffs.

§ 346. Action to redeem mortgage; effect of five years adverse possession

ACTION TO REDEEM A MORTGAGE WITHOUT ACCOUNT OF RENTS AND PROFITS. An action to redeem a mortgage of real property, with or without an account of rents and profits, may be brought by the mortgagor or those claiming under him, against the mortgagee in possession, or those claiming under him, unless he or they have continuously maintained an adverse possession of the mortgaged premises for five years after breach of some condition of the mortgage. *(Enacted in 1872, unpublished Act of 1872.)*

Research References

Miller and Starr California Real Estate § 16:29, Mortgagor and Mortgagee; Trustor and Beneficiary.

Miller and Starr California Real Estate § 10:227, Statutory Redemption; Who Can Redeem.

§ 347. Action to redeem mortgage; multiple mortgagors or persons claiming under mortgagor

SAME, WHEN THERE ARE TWO OR MORE SUCH MORTGAGES. If there is more than one such mortgagor, or more than one person claiming under a mortgagor, some of whom are not entitled to maintain such an action under the provisions of this Chapter, any one of them who is entitled to maintain such an action may redeem therein a divided or undivided part of the mortgaged premises, according as his interest may appear and have an accounting, for a part of the rents and profits proportionate to

his interest in the mortgaged premises, on payment of a part of the mortgage money, bearing the same proportion to the whole of such money as the value of his divided or undivided interest in the premises bears to the whole of such premises. *(Enacted in 1872, unpublished Act of 1872.)*

Research References

Miller and Starr California Real Estate § 12:12, Acquisition of an Adverse Interest.

Miller and Starr California Real Estate § 10:227, Statutory Redemption; Who Can Redeem.

4 Witkin, California Summary 10th Security Transactions in Real Property § 234, (S 234) Pro Tanto Redemption.

§ 348. No limitation; action to recover deposit of money or property; effect of insolvency

To actions brought to recover money or other property deposited with any bank, banker, trust company, building and loan association, or savings and loan society or evidenced by a certificate issued by an industrial loan company or credit union there is no limitation.

This section shall not apply to banks, bankers, trust companies, building and loan associations, industrial loan companies, credit unions, and savings and loan societies which have become insolvent and are in process of liquidation and in such cases the statute of limitations shall be deemed to have commenced to run from the beginning of the process of liquidation; provided, however, nothing herein contained shall be construed so as to relieve any stockholder of any banking corporation or trust company from stockholders' liability as shall at any time, be provided by law. *(Added by Code Am.1873–74, c. 383, p. 293, § 36. Amended by Stats.1915, c. 411, p. 684, § 1; Stats.1917, c. 756, p. 1573, § 1; Stats.1955, c. 208, p. 677, § 1.)*

Research References

Miller and Starr California Real Estate § 18:10, The Unclaimed Property Law--Duties of the State.

3 Witkin Cal. Proc. 5th Actions § 489, Express Statutory Provisions.

§ 348.5. No limitation; action upon bonds or coupons issued by State of California

An action upon any bonds or coupons issued by the State of California shall have no limitation. *(Added by Stats.2010, c. 719 (S.B.856), § 8, eff. Oct. 19, 2010.)*

Research References

3 Witkin Cal. Proc. 5th Actions § 488, (S 488) Ten Years.

3 Witkin Cal. Proc. 5th Actions § 489, Express Statutory Provisions.

§ 349¾. One hundred eighty days; underground trespass, use or occupancy by oil or gas well; conversion, taking or removal of oil, gas or other liquid; time of accrual; single cause of action; measure of damages; applicability to existing causes; definitions; exceptions

Within one hundred eighty days:

(a) An action to enjoin, abate, or for damages on account of, an underground trespass, use or occupancy, by means of a well drilled for oil or gas or both from a surface location on land other than real property in which the aggrieved party has some right, title or interest or in respect to which the aggrieved party has some right, title or interest.

(b) An action for conversion or for the taking or removing of oil, gas or other liquid, or fluids by means of any such well.

When any of said acts is by means of a new well the actual drilling of which is commenced after this section becomes effective, and such act was knowingly committed with actual intent to commit such act, the cause of action in such case shall not be deemed to have accrued until the discovery, by the aggrieved party, of the act or acts complained of; but in all other cases, and as to wells heretofore or hereafter drilled, the cause of action shall be deemed to have accrued ten days after the time when the well which is the subject of the cause of action was first placed on production.

Notwithstanding the continuing character of any such act, there shall be but one cause of action for any such act, and the cause of action shall accrue as aforesaid.

In all cases where oil or gas has been heretofore or is hereafter extracted from any existing or subsequently drilled well in this State, by a person without right but asserting a claim of right in good faith or acting under an honest mistake of law or fact, the measure of damages, if there be any right of recovery under existing law, shall be the value of the oil or gas at the time of extraction, without interest, after deducting all costs of development, operation and production, which costs shall include taxes and interest on all expenditures from the date thereof.

This section shall apply to causes of action existing when this section becomes effective. The time for commencement of existing causes of action which would be barred by this section within the first one hundred eighty days after this section becomes effective, shall be the said first one hundred eighty days.

Whenever the term "oil" is used in this section it shall be taken to include "petroleum," and the term "gas" shall mean natural gas coming from the earth.

The limitations prescribed by this section shall not apply to rights of action or actions to be brought in the name of or for the benefit of the people of this State, or of any county, city and county, city or other political subdivision of this State. *(Added by Stats.1935, c. 852, p. 2285, § 1.)*

Research References

3 Witkin Cal. Proc. 5th Actions § 456, State or Political Subdivision.
3 Witkin Cal. Proc. 5th Actions § 480, (S 480) One Hundred Eighty Days or Six Months.
3 Witkin Cal. Proc. 5th Actions § 620, in General.
3 Witkin Cal. Proc. 5th Actions § 622, Action for Conversion Based on Underground Trespass on Oil or Gas Well.
5 Witkin, California Summary 10th Torts § 694, Invasion On, Above, or Below Surface.

§ 349.1.　Six months; contesting validity of formation, organization, consolidation, etc., of public entities

The validity of any acts or proceedings taken under color of law for the formation, organization, incorporation, dissolution, consolidation, change of organization or reorganization of, or for any change in the territorial boundaries of, any city, county, city and county, special district, public corporation or other public entity, or improvement district within any of the foregoing, shall not be contested in any action unless such action shall have been brought within six months from the date of completion of said acts or proceedings. Unless an action is commenced within said period all said acts or proceedings shall be held valid and in every respect legal and incontestable.

This section shall not amend or repeal any existing statute prescribing a shorter period of limitation than that specified herein. *(Added by Stats.1957, c. 1344, p. 2675, § 1. Amended by Stats.1959, c. 1995, p. 4613, § 1; Stats.1965, c. 2044, p. 4767, § 3.5.)*

Research References

3 Witkin Cal. Proc. 5th Actions § 476, (S 476) Sixty Days or Two Months.

3 Witkin Cal. Proc. 5th Actions § 480, (S 480) One Hundred Eighty Days or Six Months.

§ 349.2.　Six months; contesting validity of authorization, issuance and sale of bonds by public entities

Where any acts or proceedings are taken under color of law by or on behalf of any city, county, city and county, special district, public corporation or other public entity for the authorization, sale or issuance of bonds:

(1) The validity of any such acts or proceedings for the authorization of bonds shall not be contested in any action unless such action shall have been brought within six months from the date of election authorizing said bonds, in cases where said bonds are required by law to be authorized at an election, or within six months from the date of adoption of a resolution or ordinance authorizing such bonds, in cases where bonds are not required by law to be authorized at an election;

(2) The validity of any such acts or proceedings for the sale of bonds (including all acts or proceedings taken prior thereto and providing for the issuance of such bonds) shall not be contested in any action unless such action shall have been brought within six months from the date of sale of said bonds;

(3) The validity of any such acts or proceedings for the issuance and delivery of, or payment for, bonds shall not be contested in any action unless such action shall have been brought within six months from the date of issuance and delivery of, or payment for, said bonds.

Unless an action is commenced within the applicable time hereinabove specified, said acts or proceedings for the authorization, sale or issuance of bonds shall be held valid and in every respect legal and incontestable.

This section shall not amend or repeal any existing statute prescribing a shorter period of limitation than that specified herein.

As used in this section, the term "bonds" means all instruments evidencing indebtedness incurred or to be incurred for any public purpose, all instruments evidencing the borrowing of money in anticipation of taxes, revenues or other income of a public body, all instruments payable from revenues or special funds, and all instruments funding or refunding any thereof or any indebtedness, but shall not include any special assessment bonds, special assessment refunding bonds, or bonds or other instruments issued to represent special assessments which are, directly or indirectly, secured by or payable from specific assessments levied against lands benefited, including bonds or other instruments issued under or pursuant to any statute, charter or ordinance providing for the improvement of streets, the opening and widening of streets, the provision for off-street parking, or the refunding of any of the same. *(Added by Stats.1957, c. 1345, p. 2675, § 1.)*

Research References

3 Witkin Cal. Proc. 5th Actions § 476, (S 476) Sixty Days or Two Months.
3 Witkin Cal. Proc. 5th Actions § 480, (S 480) One Hundred Eighty Days or Six Months.

§ 349.4.　Validation of formation, organization, consolidation, etc., of public entities; notice; effect of failure to file action within specified period

All acts and proceedings heretofore or hereafter taken under color of law for the formation, organization or incorporation of, or for any change in the territorial boundaries of, any city, county, city and county, special district, public corporation or other public entity, or improvement district, annexed area or zone within any of the foregoing, and for the authorization, issuance, sale, or exchange of bonds of the entity or the territory thereof may be confirmed, validated, and declared legally effective in the manner provided in this section.

The legislative body of the entity may instruct its clerk or secretary to mail a notice to all owners of property within the entity, within the improvement district or zone, or within the annexed area, as the case may be, as their names and addresses appear on the last equalized county assessment roll, or as known to the clerk or secretary. Such notice shall include the name of the entity, the date the entity or the zone or improvement district therein was ordered formed or its territory changed by annexation or otherwise, as the case may be, the amount of bonds authorized, if any, and a statement that commencing with the date of mailing of said notice there shall be a 60-calendar-day period during which period any property owner may file an action contesting the validity of the formation of the entity, or of such improvement district or zone, or of such change of boundaries by annexation or otherwise, as the case may be, or the validity of the bond authorization, if any. The clerk or secretary shall make and file with the legislative body of the entity a certificate of mailing of the notices. The legislative body of the entity may order the clerk or secretary to include in such notice such other additional information that it deems pertinent.

If no action is filed during such 60-day period, the formation of the entity or of such improvement district or zone, or the change of boundaries by annexation or otherwise, as the case may be, and the bond authorization, if any, are valid and uncontestable. *(Added by Stats.1977, c. 7, p. 16, § 2, eff. March 4, 1977.)*

Research References

3 Witkin Cal. Proc. 5th Actions § 456, State or Political Subdivision.
3 Witkin Cal. Proc. 5th Actions § 476, (S 476) Sixty Days or Two Months.

CHAPTER 4. GENERAL PROVISIONS AS TO THE TIME OF COMMENCING ACTIONS

§ 350. Action commenced with filing complaint

WHEN AN ACTION IS COMMENCED. An action is commenced, within the meaning of this Title, when the complaint is filed. *(Enacted in 1872.)*

Research References

Rutter, Cal. Practice Guide: Personal Injury Ch. 5-B, B. When to Sue-Statute of Limitations.
3 Witkin Cal. Proc. 5th Actions § 585, (S 585) Tolling of One-Year Period.
3 Witkin Cal. Proc. 5th Actions § 735, (S 735) in General.
4 Witkin Cal. Proc. 5th Pleading § 470, Nature of Pleading.

§ 351. Absence from state; effect on limitation period

EXCEPTION, WHERE DEFENDANT IS OUT OF THE STATE. If, when the cause of action accrues against a person, he is out of the State, the action may be commenced within the term herein limited, after his return to the State, and if, after the cause of action accrues, he departs from the State, the time of his absence is not part of the time limited for the commencement of the action. *(Enacted in 1872.)*

Validity

This section was held unconstitutional, as violative of the commerce clause, with respect to residents who travel in the course of interstate commerce, in the decision of Filet Menu, Inc. v. Cheng (App. 2 Dist. 1999) 84 Cal.Rptr.2d 384, 71 Cal.App.4th 1276.

Research References

Rutter, Cal. Practice Guide: Civ. Pro. Before Trial Ch. 11-B, B. Involuntary Dismissals.
Rutter, Cal. Practice Guide: Enforcing Judgments/Debts Ch. 3-A, A. Evaluating the Claim.
Rutter, Cal. Practice Guide: Enforcing Judgments/Debts Ch. 6A-7, Period During Which Judgment Enforceable; Renewal Procedures.
Rutter, Cal. Practice Guide: Personal Injury Ch. 5-B, B. When to Sue-Statute of Limitations.
Rutter, Cal. Practice Guide: Personal Injury Ch. 5-B, Outline B.
Rutter, Cal. Practice Guide: Prof. Responsibility Ch. 6-D, D. Professional Liability.
3 Witkin Cal. Proc. 5th Actions § 447, (S 447) Actions and Special Proceedings.
3 Witkin Cal. Proc. 5th Actions § 646, (S 646) Tolling While Plaintiff is Under Legal or Physical Disability.
3 Witkin Cal. Proc. 5th Actions § 709, Disability of Attorney.
3 Witkin Cal. Proc. 5th Actions § 710, Absence.
3 Witkin Cal. Proc. 5th Actions § 711, Nonresidence.
3 Witkin Cal. Proc. 5th Actions § 712, Constitutionality.
3 Witkin Cal. Proc. 5th Actions § 714, Action in Personam.
3 Witkin Cal. Proc. 5th Actions § 715, Distinction: No Express Statute.
9 Witkin Cal. Proc. 5th Appeal § 906, New Points Are Not Allowed.
2 Witkin, California Summary 10th Insurance § 205, (S 205) in General.
9 Witkin, California Summary 10th Partnership § 69, (S 69) Nature of Limited Partnership.

Civ. Pro.

8 Witkin, California Summary 10th Constitutional Law § 1300, (S 1300) in General; Dormant Commerce Clause.

§ 352. Disabilities of minority or insanity

(a) If a person entitled to bring an action, mentioned in Chapter 3 (commencing with Section 335) is, at the time the cause of action accrued either under the age of majority or insane, the time of the disability is not part of the time limited for the commencement of the action.

(b) This section does not apply to an action against a public entity or public employee upon a cause of action for which a claim is required to be presented in accordance with Chapter 1 (commencing with Section 900) or Chapter 2 (commencing with Section 910) of Part 3, or Chapter 3 (commencing with Section 950) of Part 4, of Division 3.6 of Title 1 of the Government Code. This subdivision shall not apply to any claim presented to a public entity prior to January 1, 1971. *(Enacted in 1872. Amended by Stats.1959, c. 192, p. 2085, § 1; Stats.1970, c. 104, p. 323, § 1, operative Jan. 1, 1971; Stats.1975, c. 1241, p. 3187, § 1.5; Stats.1986, c. 1161, § 1; Stats.1994, c. 1083 (S.B.1445), § 4.)*

Law Revision Commission Comments

Subdivision (b) has been added so that Section 352, which operates to toll the statute of limitations for minors, insane persons, and prisoners, will not apply to the causes of action against a public entity or public employee described in this subdivision. Such actions are governed by the period of limitations specified in subdivision (a) of Section 945.6 of the Government Code. To safeguard the minor or incompetent from an inadvertent reliance on the tolling provision of Section 352, notice of rejection of his claim in the form provided in Government Code Section 913 is required to be given by the public entity. If notice is not given the claimant has two years from the accrual of his cause of action in which to sue. See Government Code Section 945.6(a).

Special exceptions for prisoners exist in both subdivision (b) of Section 945.6 and subdivision (c) of Section 950.6 of the Government Code, which toll the statute of limitations during the period of their civil disability.

The other general provisions of the Code of Civil Procedure relating to the time within which actions must be commenced—Sections 350, 351, 353–363—are applicable to actions against public entities and public employees. See Williams v. Los Angeles Metropolitan Transit Authority, 68 Cal.2d 599, 68 Cal.Rptr. 297, 440 P.2d 497 (1968). See also Government Code Sections 950.2 and 950.4.

Research References

Rutter, Cal. Practice Guide: Civ. Pro. Before Trial Ch. 1-C, C. Prelawsuit Notices, Claims and Demands.
Rutter, Cal. Practice Guide: Civ. Pro. Before Trial Ch. 2-B, B. Capacity to Sue or Defend.
Rutter, Cal. Practice Guide: Civ. Pro. Before Trial Ch. 11-B, B. Involuntary Dismissals.
Rutter, Cal. Practice Guide: Insurance Litigation Ch. 6G-D, D. Uninsured and Underinsured Motorist Coverages.
Rutter, Cal. Practice Guide: Personal Injury Ch. 5-A, A. Prelawsuit Filings.
Rutter, Cal. Practice Guide: Personal Injury Ch. 5-B, B. When to Sue-Statute of Limitations.
Rutter, Cal. Practice Guide: Prof. Responsibility Ch. 6-D, D. Professional Liability.
Miller and Starr California Real Estate § 12:57, Management and Control--Restriction on Gifts of Community Property.
Miller and Starr California Real Estate § 16:41, Minors and Others Under Legal Disability.
3 Witkin Cal. Proc. 5th Actions § 58, Federal Statute Without Express Limitation.
3 Witkin Cal. Proc. 5th Actions § 215, Creditor's Action Against Estate.
3 Witkin Cal. Proc. 5th Actions § 227, Miscellaneous Statutory Requirements.
3 Witkin Cal. Proc. 5th Actions § 304, Filing and Service of Petition.
3 Witkin Cal. Proc. 5th Actions § 312, Current Law Applying Doctrine.
3 Witkin Cal. Proc. 5th Actions § 443, Limitation in Statute Creating Right.

3 Witkin Cal. Proc. 5th Actions § 463, Sexual Abuse of Minor: 1986 Extension of Period.
3 Witkin Cal. Proc. 5th Actions § 464, Sexual Abuse of Minor: 1990 Extension of Period.
3 Witkin Cal. Proc. 5th Actions § 582, in General.
3 Witkin Cal. Proc. 5th Actions § 585, (S 585) Tolling of One-Year Period.
3 Witkin Cal. Proc. 5th Actions § 587, Delayed Accrual and Tolling of Period.
3 Witkin Cal. Proc. 5th Actions § 589, (S 589) Prenatal Injuries.
3 Witkin Cal. Proc. 5th Actions § 590, (S 590) Wrongful Death.
3 Witkin Cal. Proc. 5th Actions § 595, (S 595) Delayed Accrual and Tolling During Minority.
3 Witkin Cal. Proc. 5th Actions § 646, (S 646) Tolling While Plaintiff is Under Legal or Physical Disability.
3 Witkin Cal. Proc. 5th Actions § 688, (S 688) in General.
3 Witkin Cal. Proc. 5th Actions § 695, (S 695) in General.
3 Witkin Cal. Proc. 5th Actions § 696, Scope of Suspension.
3 Witkin Cal. Proc. 5th Actions § 697, Exceptions and Distinctions.
3 Witkin Cal. Proc. 5th Actions § 698, Scope of Suspension.
3 Witkin Cal. Proc. 5th Actions § 700, Unconsciousness as Insanity.
3 Witkin Cal. Proc. 5th Actions § 702, Scope of Suspension.
3 Witkin Cal. Proc. 5th Actions § 741, General Rule.

§ 352.1. Disability of imprisonment

(a) If a person entitled to bring an action, mentioned in Chapter 3 (commencing with Section 335), is, at the time the cause of action accrued, imprisoned on a criminal charge, or in execution under the sentence of a criminal court for a term less than for life, the time of that disability is not a part of the time limited for the commencement of the action, not to exceed two years.

(b) This section does not apply to an action against a public entity or public employee upon a cause of action for which a claim is required to be presented in accordance with Chapter 1 (commencing with Section 900) or Chapter 2 (commencing with Section 910) of Part 3, or Chapter 3 (commencing with Section 950) of Part 4, of Division 3.6 of Title 1 of the Government Code. This subdivision shall not apply to any claim presented to a public entity prior to January 1, 1971.

(c) This section does not apply to an action, other than an action to recover damages or that portion of an action that is for the recovery of damages, relating to the conditions of confinement, including an action brought by that person pursuant to Section 1983 of Title 42 of the United States Code. *(Added by Stats.1994, c. 1083 (S.B.1445), § 5.)*

Research References

Rutter, Cal. Practice Guide: Personal Injury Ch. 5-B, B. When to Sue-Statute of Limitations.
Rutter, Cal. Practice Guide: Prof. Responsibility Ch. 6-D, D. Professional Liability.
3 Witkin Cal. Proc. 5th Actions § 58, Federal Statute Without Express Limitation.
3 Witkin Cal. Proc. 5th Actions § 459, (S 459) Period Shortened.
3 Witkin Cal. Proc. 5th Actions § 582, in General.
3 Witkin Cal. Proc. 5th Actions § 585, (S 585) Tolling of One-Year Period.
3 Witkin Cal. Proc. 5th Actions § 646, (S 646) Tolling While Plaintiff is Under Legal or Physical Disability.
3 Witkin Cal. Proc. 5th Actions § 695, (S 695) in General.
3 Witkin Cal. Proc. 5th Actions § 702, Scope of Suspension.
3 Witkin Cal. Proc. 5th Actions § 703, Exceptions and Distinctions.

§ 352.5. Action against person under order for restitution as condition of probation; tolling

If, after a cause of action accrues against a person, that person comes under an order for restitution as a condition of probation with respect to the specific act or omission giving rise to such person's liability, the time during which the order is in effect is not a part of the time limited for the commencement of such an action based upon that act or omission. *(Added by Stats.1976, c. 282, p. 589, § 1.)*

Research References

3 Witkin Cal. Proc. 5th Actions § 756, Probation With Order of Restitution.

§ 353.1. Court assuming jurisdiction over attorney's practice; effect on limitation period

If a person entitled to bring an action or other proceeding, which action or other proceeding has not been filed or otherwise instituted, is represented by an attorney over whose practice a court of this state has assumed jurisdiction pursuant to Section 6180 or Section 6190 of the Business and Professions Code, and the application for the court to assume jurisdiction is filed prior to the expiration of the applicable statute of limitation or claim statute, the person shall have six months from the date of entry of the order assuming jurisdiction within which to file or otherwise institute the matter, if the applicable statute of limitation otherwise would have expired. *(Added by Stats.1983, c. 254, § 3.)*

Research References

Rutter, Cal. Practice Guide: Personal Injury Ch. 5-B, B. When to Sue-Statute of Limitations.
Rutter, Cal. Practice Guide: Prof. Responsibility Ch. 1-H, H. Disposition of Solo Law Practice Upon Death, Disability, Incapacity, Discipline, etc.
Rutter, Cal. Practice Guide: Prof. Responsibility Ch. 6-D, D. Professional Liability.
3 Witkin Cal. Proc. 5th Actions § 709, Disability of Attorney.
1 Witkin Cal. Proc. 5th Attorneys § 89, Relief Available to Clients.

§ 354. Disability during war; effect on limitation period

When a person is, by reason of the existence of a state of war, under a disability to commence an action, the time of the continuance of such disability is not part of the period limited for the commencement of the action whether such cause of action shall have accrued prior to or during the period of such disability. *(Enacted in 1872. Amended by Stats.1943, c. 151, p. 1043, § 1.)*

Research References

Rutter, Cal. Practice Guide: Prof. Responsibility Ch. 6-D, D. Professional Liability.
3 Witkin Cal. Proc. 5th Actions § 695, (S 695) in General.
3 Witkin Cal. Proc. 5th Actions § 704, General Suspension Statute.
3 Witkin Cal. Proc. 5th Actions § 706, Statute Already Running.

§ 354.3. Recovery of Holocaust-era artwork from enumerated entities

(a) The following definitions govern the construction of this section:

(1) "Entity" means any museum or gallery that displays, exhibits, or sells any article of historical, interpretive, scientific, or artistic significance.

(2) "Holocaust-era artwork" means any article of artistic significance taken as a result of Nazi persecution during the period of 1929 to 1945, inclusive.

(b) Notwithstanding any other provision of law, any owner, or heir or beneficiary of an owner, of Holocaust-era artwork, may bring an action to recover Holocaust-era artwork from any entity described in paragraph (1) of subdivision (a). Subject to Section 410.10, that action may be brought in a superior court of this state, which court shall have jurisdiction over that action until its completion or resolution. Section 361 does not apply to this section.

(c) Any action brought under this section shall not be dismissed for failure to comply with the applicable statute of limitation, if the action is commenced on or before December 31, 2010. *(Added by Stats.2002, c. 332 (A.B.1758), § 2.)*

Validity

This section was held preempted by the foreign affairs doctrine in the decision of Von Saher v. Norton Simon Museum of Art at Pasadena, C.A.9 (Cal.)2010, 592 F.3d 954, certiorari denied 131 S.Ct. 3055, 180 L.Ed.2d 885, on remand 862 F.Supp.2d 1044.

Research References

3 Witkin Cal. Proc. 5th Actions § 705, Special Suspension Statutes.
2 Witkin Cal. Proc. 5th Jurisdiction § 257, Tangible Personal Property and Documents.

§ 354.4. Armenian Genocide victims; insurance policy claims; waiver of statute of limitations

(a) The following definitions govern the construction of this section:

(1) "Armenian Genocide victim" means any person of Armenian or other ancestry living in the Ottoman Empire during the period of 1915 to 1923, inclusive, who died, was deported, or escaped to avoid persecution during that period.

(2) "Insurer" means an insurance provider doing business in the state, or whose contacts in the state satisfy the constitutional requirements for jurisdiction, that sold life, property, liability, health, annuities, dowry, educational, casualty, or any other insurance covering persons or property to persons in Europe or Asia at any time between 1875 and 1923.

(b) Notwithstanding any other provision of law, any Armenian Genocide victim, or heir or beneficiary of an Armenian Genocide victim, who resides in this state and has a claim arising out of an insurance policy or policies purchased or in effect in Europe or Asia between 1875 and 1923 from an insurer described in paragraph (2) of subdivision (a), may bring a legal action or may continue a pending legal action to recover on that claim in any court of competent jurisdiction in this state, which court shall be deemed the proper forum for that action until its completion or resolution.

(c) Any action, including any pending action brought by an Armenian Genocide victim or the heir or beneficiary of an Armenian Genocide victim, whether a resident or nonresident of this state, seeking benefits under the insurance policies issued or in effect between 1875 and 1923 shall not be dismissed for failure to comply with the applicable statute of limitation, provided the action is filed on or before December 31, 2016.

(d) The provisions of this section are severable. If any provision of this section or its application is held invalid, that invalidity shall not affect other provisions or applications that can be given effect without the invalid provision or application. *(Added by Stats.2000, c. 543 (S.B.1915), § 2, eff. Sept. 20, 2000. Amended by Stats.2011, c. 70 (A.B.173), § 1, eff. July 8, 2011.)*

Validity

For validity of this section, see Movsesian v. Victoria Versicherung AG, C.A.9 (Cal.)2012, 670 F.3d 1067, petition for certiorari filed 2012 WL 2813825, referred to 2012 WL 4475507.

Research References

3 Witkin Cal. Proc. 5th Actions § 705, Special Suspension Statutes.

§ 354.45. Armenian Genocide victims; deposited and looted assets; waiver of statute of limitations

(a) For purposes of this section, the following terms have the following meanings:

(1) "Armenian Genocide victim" means any person of Armenian or other ancestry living in the Ottoman Empire during the period of 1890 to 1923, inclusive, who died, was injured in person or property, was deported, or escaped to avoid persecution during that period.

(2) "Bank" means any banking or financial institution, including any institution that issued bonds, that conducted business in Ottoman Turkey at any time during the period of 1890 to 1923, inclusive.

(3) "Deposited assets" means any and all cash, securities, bonds, gold, jewels or jewelry, or any other tangible or intangible items of personal property, or any documents indicating ownership or possessory interests in real, personal, or intangible property, that were deposited with and held by a bank.

(4) "Looted assets" means any and all personal, commercial, real, and intangible property, including cash, securities, gold, jewelry, businesses, artwork, equipment, and intellectual property, that was taken from the ownership or control of an individual, organization, or entity, by theft, forced transfer, or exploitation, during the period of 1890 to 1923, inclusive, by any person, organization, or entity acting on behalf of, or in furtherance of the acts of, the Turkish Government, that were received by and deposited with a bank.

(b) Notwithstanding any other law, any Armenian Genocide victim, or heir or beneficiary of an Armenian Genocide victim, who resides in this state and has a claim arising out of a failure of a bank to pay or turn over deposited assets, or to turn over looted assets, may bring an action or may continue a pending action, to recover on that claim in any court of competent jurisdiction in this state, which court shall be deemed the proper forum for that action until its completion or resolution.

(c) Any action, including any pending action brought by an Armenian Genocide victim, or the heir or beneficiary of an Armenian Genocide victim, who resides in this state, seeking payment for, or the return of, deposited assets, or the return of looted assets, shall not be dismissed for failure to comply with the applicable statute of limitation, if the action is filed on or before December 31, 2016.

(d) The provisions of this section are severable. If any provision of this section or its application is held invalid, that invalidity shall not affect other provisions or applications that can be given effect without the invalid provision or application. *(Added by Stats.2006, c. 443 (S.B.1524), § 2.)*

Validity

This section was recognized as preempted for conflicting with the federal government's resolution of wartime claims arising out of World War I in the decision of Deirmenjian v. Deutsche Bank, A.G., C.D.Cal.2007, 526 F.Supp.2d 1068.

Research References

3 Witkin Cal. Proc. 5th Actions § 705, Special Suspension Statutes.
2 Witkin Cal. Proc. 5th Jurisdiction § 257, Tangible Personal Property and Documents.

§ 354.5. Holocaust victims; insurance policy claims purchased in Europe; legal action to recover on claims

(a) The following definitions govern the construction of this section:

(1) "Holocaust victim" means any person who was persecuted during the period of 1929 to 1945, inclusive, by Nazi Germany, its allies, or sympathizers.

(2) "Related company" means any parent, subsidiary, reinsurer, successor in interest, managing general agent, or affiliate company of the insurer.

(3) "Insurer" means an insurance provider doing business in the state, or whose contacts in the state satisfy the constitutional requirements for jurisdiction, that sold life, property, liability, health, annuities, dowry, educational, casualty, or any other insurance covering persons or property to persons in Europe at any time before 1945, directly or through a related company, whether the sale of the insurance occurred before or after the insurer and the related company became related.

(b) Notwithstanding any other provision of law, any Holocaust victim, or heir or beneficiary of a Holocaust victim, who resides in this state and has a claim arising out of an insurance policy or policies purchased or in effect in Europe before 1945 from an insurer described in paragraph (3) of subdivision (a), may bring a legal action to recover on that claim in any superior court of the state for the county in which the plaintiff or one of the plaintiffs resides, which court shall be vested with jurisdiction over that action until its completion or resolution.

(c) Any action brought by a Holocaust victim or the heir or beneficiary of a Holocaust victim, whether a resident or nonresident of this state, seeking proceeds of the insurance policies issued or in effect before 1945 shall not be dismissed for failure to comply with the applicable statute of limitation, provided the action is commenced on or before December 31, 2010. *(Added by Stats.1998, c. 43 (A.B.1334), § 2, eff. May 22, 1998. Amended by Stats.1999, c. 827 (A.B.600), § 1, eff. Oct. 10, 1999.)*

Validity

This statute was held preempted by United States foreign policy favoring settlement of such claims by International Commission on Holocaust Era Insurance Claims, in the decision of Steinberg v. International Com'n on Holocaust Era Ins. Claims (App. 2 Dist. 2005) 34 Cal.Rptr.3d 944, 133 Cal.App.4th 689.

Research References

Rutter, Cal. Practice Guide: Civ. Pro. Before Trial Ch. 3-D, D. Venue.
3 Witkin Cal. Proc. 5th Actions § 705, Special Suspension Statutes.

§ 354.6. Second World War slave or forced labor victims; heirs; actions for recovery of compensation; limitations

(a) As used in this section:

(1) "Second World War slave labor victim" means any person taken from a concentration camp or ghetto or diverted from transportation to a concentration camp or from a ghetto to perform labor without pay for any period of time between 1929 and 1945, by the Nazi regime, its allies and sympathizers, or enterprises transacting business in any of the areas occupied by or under control of the Nazi regime or its allies and sympathizers.

(2) 'Second World War forced labor victim" means any person who was a member of the civilian population conquered by the Nazi regime, its allies or sympathizers, or prisoner-of-war of the Nazi regime, its allies or sympathizers, forced to perform labor without pay for any period of time between 1929 and 1945, by the Nazi regime, its allies and sympathizers, or enterprises transacting business in any of the areas occupied by or under control of the Nazi regime or its allies and sympathizers.

(3) "Compensation" means the present value of wages and benefits that individuals should have been paid and damages for injuries sustained in connection with the labor performed. Present value shall be calculated on the basis of the market value of the services at the time they were performed, plus interest from the time the services were performed, compounded annually to date of full payment without diminution for wartime or postwar currency devaluation.

(b) Any Second World War slave labor victim, or heir of a Second World War slave labor victim, Second World War forced labor victim, or heir of a Second World War forced labor victim, may bring an action to recover compensation for labor performed as a Second World War slave labor victim or Second World War forced labor victim from any entity or successor in interest thereof, for whom that labor was performed, either directly or through a subsidiary or affiliate. That action may be brought in a superior court of this state, which court shall have jurisdiction over that action until its completion or resolution.

(c) Any action brought under this section shall not be dismissed for failure to comply with the applicable statute of limitation, if the action is commenced on or before December 31, 2010. *(Added by Stats.1999, c. 216 (S.B.1245), § 4, eff. July 28, 1999.)*

Validity

This statute was recognized as preempted by United States foreign policy favoring settlement of such claims by International Commission on Holocaust Era Insurance Claims, in the decision of Steinberg v. International Com'n on Holocaust Era Ins. Claims (App. 2 Dist. 2005) 34 Cal.Rptr.3d 944, 133 Cal.App.4th 689.

This section was held unconstitutional in the decision of In re World War II Era Japanese Forced Labor Litigation, N.D.Cal.2001, 164 F.Supp.2d 1160, 108 A.L.R.5th 743, affirmed 317 F.3d 1005, amended and superseded on denial of rehearing 324 F.3d 692, 192 A.L.R. Fed. 657, certiorari denied 124 S.Ct. 105, 540 U.S. 820, 157 L.Ed.2d 39, certiorari denied 124 S.Ct. 132, 540 U.S. 820, 157 L.Ed.2d 39, certiorari denied 124 S.Ct. 133, 540 U.S. 821, 157 L.Ed.2d 39.

Research References

3 Witkin Cal. Proc. 5th Actions § 705, Special Suspension Statutes.
8 Witkin, California Summary 10th Constitutional Law § 1340, Supremacy Over State Law.

§ 354.7. Braceros, heirs or beneficiaries of braceros; right of action for recovery of savings fund amounts; limitations; severability of provisions

(a) The following definitions govern the construction of this section:

(1) "Bracero" means any person who participated in the labor importation program known as the Bracero program between January 1, 1942, and January 1, 1950, pursuant to agreements between the United States and Mexico.

(2) "Savings fund" means funds withheld from the wages of braceros as savings to be paid to braceros upon their return to Mexico.

(b) Notwithstanding any other provision of law, any bracero, or heir or beneficiary of a bracero, who has a claim arising out of a failure to pay or turn over savings fund amounts may bring a legal action or may continue a pending legal action to recover on that claim in any court of competent jurisdiction in this state, which court shall be deemed a proper forum for that action until its completion or resolution.

(c) Notwithstanding any other provision of law, any action brought by a bracero, or heir or beneficiary of a bracero, arising out of a failure to pay or turn over savings fund amounts shall not be dismissed for failure to comply with the otherwise applicable statute of limitations, provided the action is filed on or before December 31, 2005.

(d) The provisions of this section are severable. If any provision of this section or its application is held invalid, that invalidity shall not affect other provisions or applications that can be given effect without the invalid provision or application. *(Added by Stats.2002, c. 1070 (A.B.2913), § 2, eff. Sept. 29, 2002.)*

Research References

3 Witkin Cal. Proc. 5th Actions § 705, Special Suspension Statutes.

§ 355. Reversal of judgment; limitation on new action

If an action is commenced within the time prescribed therefor, and a judgment therein for the plaintiff be reversed on appeal other than on the merits, a new action may be commenced within one year after the reversal. *(Enacted in 1872. Amended by Stats.1992, c. 178 (S.B.1496), § 7.)*

Law Revision Commission Comments

Section 355 is amended for conformity with the revised rules concerning litigation after death of a party. See Sections 377.10–377.62. This section is also revised to make clear that it does not apply where the judgment was reversed on the merits. See, e.g., Watterson v. Owens River Canal Co., 190 Cal. 88, 93, 210 P. 625 (1922); Schneider v. Schimmels, 256 Cal.App.2d 366, 370, 64 Cal.Rptr. 273 (1967). [22 Cal.L.Rev.Comm.Reports 895 (1992)].

Research References

Rutter, Cal. Practice Guide: Personal Injury Ch. 5-B, B. When to Sue-Statute of Limitations.
20 NO. 1 Miller & Starr, California Real Estate Newsalert 22, Failure to File a Timely Property Tax Refund Claim is a Jurisdictional Defect Overriding All Other Issues.
3 Witkin Cal. Proc. 5th Actions § 738, (S 738) in General.
3 Witkin Cal. Proc. 5th Actions § 739, (S 739) Equitable Tolling Doctrine.
3 Witkin Cal. Proc. 5th Actions § 740, (S 740) First Action Outside California.

§ 356. Injunction against commencement of action; effect on limitation period

PROVISION WHERE ACTION IS STAYED BY INJUNCTION. When the commencement of an action is stayed by injunction or statutory prohibition, the time of the continuance of the injunction or prohibition is not part of the time limited for the commencement of the action. *(Enacted in 1872.)*

Research References

Rutter, Cal. Practice Guide: Enforcing Judgments/Debts Ch. 3-A, A. Evaluating the Claim.
Rutter, Cal. Practice Guide: Enforcing Judgments/Debts Ch. 6A-7, Period During Which Judgment Enforceable; Renewal Procedures.
Rutter, Cal. Practice Guide: Personal Injury Ch. 5-A, A. Prelawsuit Filings.
Rutter, Cal. Practice Guide: Personal Injury Ch. 5-B, B. When to Sue-Statute of Limitations.
Rutter, Cal. Practice Guide: Prof. Responsibility Ch. 6-D, D. Professional Liability.
Miller and Starr California Real Estate § 29:70, Tolling and Extension.
Miller and Starr California Real Estate § 10:150, Effect of the Automatic Stay.
Miller and Starr California Real Estate § 11:173, Assessment and Bond Liens--Statute of Limitations for Enforcement of the Lien.
16 NO. 2 Miller & Starr, California Real Estate Newsalert 8, Defective Construction.
3 Witkin Cal. Proc. 5th Actions § 720, (S 720) Injunction.
3 Witkin Cal. Proc. 5th Actions § 721, in General.
3 Witkin Cal. Proc. 5th Actions § 728, (S 728) Duration of Tolling.
3 Witkin Cal. Proc. 5th Actions § 729, in General.
3 Witkin Cal. Proc. 5th Actions § 734, Pending Review Proceedings in Related Action.

§ 357. Disability; necessity of existence when right of action accrued

DISABILITY MUST EXIST WHEN RIGHT OF ACTION ACCRUED. No person can avail himself of a disability, unless it existed when his right of action accrued. *(Enacted in 1872.)*

Research References

Rutter, Cal. Practice Guide: Personal Injury Ch. 5-B, B. When to Sue-Statute of Limitations.
3 Witkin Cal. Proc. 5th Actions § 698, Scope of Suspension.
3 Witkin Cal. Proc. 5th Actions § 706, Statute Already Running.
3 Witkin Cal. Proc. 5th Actions § 709, Disability of Attorney.

§ 358. Coexisting disabilities; effect on limitation period

WHEN TWO OR MORE DISABILITIES EXIST, ETC. When two or more disabilities coexist at the time the right of action accrues, the limitation does not attach until they are removed. *(Enacted in 1872.)*

Research References

Rutter, Cal. Practice Guide: Personal Injury Ch. 5-B, B. When to Sue-Statute of Limitations.
3 Witkin Cal. Proc. 5th Actions § 695, (S 695) in General.

§ 359. Corporate directors, stockholders or members; actions to recover penalty or forfeiture or enforce liability; inapplicability of title; limitation period

This title does not affect actions against directors, shareholders, or members of a corporation, to recover a penalty or forfeiture imposed, or to enforce a liability created by law; but such actions must be brought within three years after the discovery by the aggrieved party of the facts upon which the penalty or forfeiture attached, or the liability was created. *(Enacted in 1872. Amended by Stats.1978, c. 1305, p. 4265, § 1, operative Jan. 1, 1980.)*

Research References

3 Witkin Cal. Proc. 5th Actions § 483, (S 483) Three Years.
3 Witkin Cal. Proc. 5th Actions § 497, (S 497) in General.
3 Witkin Cal. Proc. 5th Actions § 671, (S 671) Action Against Shareholders and Directors.
9 Witkin, California Summary 10th Corporations § 9, Nature of Doctrine.
9 Witkin, California Summary 10th Corporations § 102, in General.

§ 359.5. Principal and surety; performance bond; expiration of statute of limitations re obligations of principal; bar to action against principal or surety under bond

If the obligations under a surety bond are conditioned upon performance of the principal, the expiration of the statute of limitations with respect to the obligations of the principal, other than the obligations of the principal under the bond, shall also bar an action against the principal or surety under the bond, unless the terms of the bond provide otherwise. *(Added by Stats.1982, c. 106, § 1.)*

Research References

California Real Estate Forms (Miller & Starr) § 3:37, Continuing Guaranty.
California Real Estate Forms (Miller & Starr) § 3:38, Completion Guaranty.
Rutter, Cal. Practice Guide: Insurance Litigation Ch. 6I-D, D. Surety's Defenses to Payment of Bond.
Rutter, Cal. Practice Guide: Insurance Litigation Ch. 6I-F, F. Defenses Assertable Against Surety.
Miller and Starr California Real Estate § 29:74, Actions Within and Outside the 10-Year Statute.
3 Witkin Cal. Proc. 5th Actions § 545, (S 545) Legislative Repudiation of Rule.

§ 360. Acknowledgment or promise; payment on account; sufficiency to take case out of statute of limitations

No acknowledgment or promise is sufficient evidence of a new or continuing contract, by which to take the case out of the operation of this title, unless the same is contained in some writing, signed by the party to be charged thereby, provided that any payment on account of principal or interest due on a promissory note made by the party to be charged shall be deemed a sufficient acknowledgment or promise of a continuing contract to stop, from time to time as any such payment is made, the running of the time within which an action may be commenced upon the principal sum or upon any installment of principal or interest due on such note, and to start the running of a new period of time, but no such payment of itself shall revive a cause of action once barred. *(Enacted in 1872. Amended by Stats.1947, c. 1108, p. 2547, § 1; Stats.1955, c. 417, p. 874, § 1.)*

Research References

Miller and Starr California Real Estate § 1:65, Provisions Applicable to Real Estate Transactions.
Miller and Starr California Real Estate § 10:90, Extension and Renewal.
Miller and Starr California Real Estate § 10:129, Waiver or Extension of Limitations Period .
3 Witkin Cal. Proc. 5th Actions § 468, Extending Period by Waiver.
3 Witkin Cal. Proc. 5th Actions § 751, (S 751) Formal Requisites.
3 Witkin Cal. Proc. 5th Actions § 755, (S 755) Part Payment of Promissory Note.
1 Witkin Cal. Summ. 10th Contracts § 240, (S 240) Writing.
1 Witkin Cal. Summ. 10th Contracts § 343, California Codes.
1 Witkin Cal. Summ. 10th Contracts § 400, (S 400) Miscellaneous Provisions.

§ 360.5. Waiver of statute of limitations; effective period; renewal

No waiver shall bar a defense to any action that the action was not commenced within the time limited by this title unless the waiver is in writing and signed by the person obligated. No waiver executed prior to the expiration of the time limited for the commencement of the action by this title shall be effective for a period exceeding four years from the date of expiration of the time limited for commencement of the action by this title and no waiver executed after the expiration of such time shall be effective for a period exceeding four years from the date thereof, but any such waiver may be renewed for a further period of not exceeding four years from the expiration of the immediately preceding waiver. Such waivers may be made successively. The provisions of this section shall not be applicable to any acknowledgment, promise or any form of waiver which is in writing and signed by the person obligated and given to any county to secure repayment of indigent aid or the repayment of moneys fraudulently or illegally obtained from the county. *(Added by Stats. 1951, c. 1106, p. 2863, § 1. Amended by Stats.1953, c. 655, p. 1906, § 1.)*

Research References

California Real Estate Forms (Miller & Starr) § 3:8, Deed of Trust, Security Agreement, and Fixture Filing With Assignment of Rents and Agreements.
California Real Estate Forms (Miller & Starr) § 3:14, Construction Deed of Trust, Security Agreement, and Fixture Filing With Assignment of Rents and Agreements.
Rutter, Cal. Practice Guide: Civ. Pro. Before Trial Ch. 12(I)-B, B. Case Management ("Fast Track") System.
California Practice Guide: Employment Litigation Ch. 16-E, E. Statute of Limitations.
California Practice Guide: Employment Litigation Ch. 18-A, A. Settlement Considerations.
Rutter, Cal. Practice Guide: Enforcing Judgments/Debts Ch. 3-A, A. Evaluating the Claim.
Rutter, Cal. Practice Guide: Personal Injury Ch. 5-B, B. When to Sue-Statute of Limitations.
Miller and Starr California Real Estate § 10:90, Extension and Renewal.
Miller and Starr California Real Estate § 29:63, Breach of Contract.
Miller and Starr California Real Estate § 10:129, Waiver or Extension of Limitations Period.
Miller and Starr California Real Estate § 10:130, Ancient Mortgages; Debt Secured by a Mortgage.
Miller and Starr California Real Estate § 10:269, Limitation of Liability.

3 Witkin Cal. Proc. 5th Actions § 468, Extending Period by Waiver.

12 Witkin, California Summary 10th Real Property § 338, Ancient Mortgages and Deeds of Trust.

§ 361. Effect of limitation laws of other states

LIMITATION LAWS OF OTHER STATES, EFFECT OF. When a cause of action has arisen in another State, or in a foreign country, and by the laws thereof an action thereon cannot there be maintained against a person by reason of the lapse of time, an action thereon shall not be maintained against him in this State, except in favor of one who has been a citizen of this State, and who has held the cause of action from the time it accrued. *(Enacted in 1872.)*

Research References

Rutter, Cal. Practice Guide: Enforcing Judgments/Debts Ch. 3-A, A. Evaluating the Claim.

Rutter, Cal. Practice Guide: Enforcing Judgments/Debts Ch. 6J-2, Enforcing Sister State Judgments in California.

Rutter, Cal. Practice Guide: Personal Injury Ch. 5-B, B. When to Sue- Statute of Limitations.

3 Witkin Cal. Proc. 5th Actions § 56, (S 56) the "Borrowing Statute.".

3 Witkin Cal. Proc. 5th Actions § 622A, (New)-Action for Specific Recovery of Unlawfully Taken Fine Art.

5 Witkin, California Summary 10th Torts § 192, Comparative Impairment Analysis.

§ 362. Exemption of existing causes of action

EXISTING CAUSES OF ACTION NOT AFFECTED. This Title does not extend to actions already commenced, nor to cases where the time prescribed in any existing statute for acquiring a right or barring a remedy has fully run, but the laws now in force are applicable to such actions and cases, and are repealed subject to the provisions of this section. *(Enacted in 1872.)*

§ 363. Action defined

The word "action" as used in this Title is to be construed, whenever it is necessary so to do, as including a special proceeding of a civil nature. *(Enacted in 1872, unpublished Act of 1872.)*

Research References

3 Witkin Cal. Proc. 5th Actions § 66, (S 66) General Policy of Uniformity in Procedure.

3 Witkin Cal. Proc. 5th Actions § 447, (S 447) Actions and Special Proceedings.

CHAPTER 5. THE COMMENCEMENT OF ACTIONS BASED UPON PROFESSIONAL NEGLIGENCE

Section

364. Notice of intention; time; law governing; fictitious name; effect of failure to comply.

365. Failure to comply with chapter; effect.

§ 364. Notice of intention; time; law governing; fictitious name; effect of failure to comply

(a) No action based upon the health care provider's professional negligence may be commenced unless the defendant has been given at least 90 days' prior notice of the intention to commence the action.

(b) No particular form of notice is required, but it shall notify the defendant of the legal basis of the claim and the type of loss sustained, including with specificity the nature of the injuries suffered.

(c) The notice may be served in the manner prescribed in Chapter 5 (commencing with Section 1010) of Title 14 of Part 2.

(d) If the notice is served within 90 days of the expiration of the applicable statute of limitations, the time for the commencement of the action shall be extended 90 days from the service of the notice.

(e) The provisions of this section shall not be applicable with respect to any defendant whose name is unknown to the plaintiff at the time of filing the complaint and who is identified therein by a fictitious name, as provided in Section 474.

(f) For the purposes of this section:

(1) "Health care provider" means any person licensed or certified pursuant to Division 2 (commencing with Section 500) of the Business and Professions Code, or licensed pursuant to the Osteopathic Initiative Act, or the Chiropractic Initiative Act, or licensed pursuant to Chapter 2.5 (commencing with Section 1440) of Division 2 of the Health and Safety Code; and any clinic, health dispensary, or health facility, licensed pursuant to Division 2 (commencing with Section 1200) of the Health and Safety Code. "Health care provider" includes the legal representatives of a health care provider;

(2) "Professional negligence" means negligent act or omission to act by a health care provider in the rendering of professional services, which act or omission is the proximate cause of a personal injury or wrongful death, provided that such services are within the scope of services for which the provider is licensed and which are not within any restriction imposed by the licensing agency or licensed hospital. *(Added by Stats.1975, 2nd Ex.Sess., c. 1, p. 3970, § 25.5. Amended by Stats.1975, 2nd Ex.Sess., c. 2, p. 3992, § 1.193, eff. Sept. 24, 1975 operative Dec. 15, 1975.)*

Research References

Rutter, Cal. Practice Guide: A.D.R. Ch. 5-D, D. Defenses to Enforcement.

Rutter, Cal. Practice Guide: Civil Appeals & Writs Ch. 14-D, D. Precedential Effect of Appellate Court Opinions.

Rutter, Cal. Practice Guide: Civ. Pro. Before Trial Ch. 1-C, C. Prelawsuit Notices, Claims and Demands.

Rutter, Cal. Practice Guide: Civ. Pro. Before Trial Ch. 6-B, B. Complaints.

Rutter, Cal. Practice Guide: Fed.Civ.Pro. Before Trial Ch. 1-B, B. Federal vs. State Law.

Rutter, Cal. Practice Guide: Insurance Litigation Ch. 15-B, B. Actions by Insurers.

Rutter, Cal. Practice Guide: Insurance Litigation Ch. 7A-C, C. Insuring Clauses-Occurrence vs. Claims-Made Policies.

Rutter, Cal. Practice Guide: Personal Injury Ch. 5-A, A. Prelawsuit Filings.

Rutter, Cal. Practice Guide: Personal Injury Ch. 5-B, B. When to Sue- Statute of Limitations.

Rutter, Cal. Practice Guide: Personal Injury Ch. 5-B, Outline B.

3 Witkin Cal. Proc. 5th Actions § 224, Malpractice Action Against Health Care Provider.

3 Witkin Cal. Proc. 5th Actions § 284, Illustrations: Defects Waived.

3 Witkin Cal. Proc. 5th Actions § 304, Filing and Service of Petition.

3 Witkin Cal. Proc. 5th Actions § 582, in General.

3 Witkin Cal. Proc. 5th Actions § 585, (S 585) Tolling of One-Year Period.

3 Witkin Cal. Proc. 5th Actions § 587, Delayed Accrual and Tolling of Period.

3 Witkin Cal. Proc. 5th Actions § 722, (S 722) in General.

3 Witkin Cal. Proc. 5th Actions § 723, Medical Malpractice.

3 Witkin Cal. Proc. 5th Actions § 724, Equitable Indemnity.

3 Witkin Cal. Proc. 5th Actions § 725, Distinction: Intentional Torts.

3 Witkin Cal. Proc. 5th Actions § 726, (S 726) Form of Notice.

3 Witkin Cal. Proc. 5th Actions § 727, (S 727) Service of Notice.

3 Witkin Cal. Proc. 5th Actions § 728, (S 728) Duration of Tolling.

8 Witkin Cal. Proc. 5th Attack Judgment Trial Court § 147, (S 147) in General.

2 Witkin Cal. Proc. 5th Jurisdiction § 103, (S 103) Statute of Limitations and Other Time Provisions.

7 Witkin Cal. Proc. 5th Trial § 70, (S 70) Party Under Age 14.

6 Witkin, California Summary 10th Torts § 934, (S 934) Ordinary Versus Professional Negligence.

Civ. Pro.

6 Witkin, California Summary 10th Torts § 953, in General.

6 Witkin, California Summary 10th Torts § 954, Extension of Applicable Statute of Limitations.

6 Witkin, California Summary 10th Torts § 955, Government Tort Claim is Not Notice of Intent to Sue.

6 Witkin, California Summary 10th Torts § 965, Intentional Torts.

§ 365. Failure to comply with chapter; effect

Failure to comply with this chapter shall not invalidate any proceedings of any court of this state, nor shall it affect the jurisdiction of the court to render a judgment therein. However, failure to comply with such provisions by any attorney at law shall be grounds for professional discipline and the State Bar of California shall investigate and take appropriate action in any such cases brought to its attention. *(Added by Stats.1975, 2nd Ex.Sess., c. 1, p. 3970, § 25.5.)*

Research References

Rutter, Cal. Practice Guide: Civ. Pro. Before Trial Ch. 1-C, C. Prelawsuit Notices, Claims and Demands.

Rutter, Cal. Practice Guide: Personal Injury Ch. 5-A, A. Prelawsuit Filings.

3 Witkin Cal. Proc. 5th Actions § 224, Malpractice Action Against Health Care Provider.

3 Witkin Cal. Proc. 5th Actions § 728, (S 728) Duration of Tolling.

6 Witkin, California Summary 10th Torts § 953, in General.

CHAPTER 6. TIME OF COMMENCEMENT OF ACTION AFTER PERSON'S DEATH

Section

366.1. Death of person entitled to bring action; limitation period.

366.2. Death of person against whom action may be brought; limitation period.

366.3. Claims arising from promise or agreement relating to distribution from estate or trust or under other instrument; limitation period.

§ 366.1. Death of person entitled to bring action; limitation period

If a person entitled to bring an action dies before the expiration of the applicable limitations period, and the cause of action survives, an action may be commenced before the expiration of the later of the following times:

(a) Six months after the person's death.

(b) The limitations period that would have been applicable if the person had not died. *(Added by Stats.1992, c. 178 (S.B. 1496), § 8.)*

Law Revision Commission Comments

Section 366.1 restates part of former Section 353(a) without substantive change. This section makes clear that the decedent's death does not shorten the limitations period applicable to the decedent's cause of action, but may extend it for up to six months. As to survival of causes of action, see Section 377.20. For persons entitled to bring the action, see Section 377.30 (commencement of action decedent could have brought). See also Section 355 (one-year limitations period after reversal). [22 Cal.L.Rev.Comm.Reports 895 (1992)].

Research References

Rutter, Cal. Practice Guide: Personal Injury Ch. 5-B, B. When to Sue-Statute of Limitations.

3 Witkin Cal. Proc. 5th Actions § 717, (S 717) Death of Prospective Plaintiff.

14 Witkin, California Summary 10th Wills and Probate § 512, Statutory Framework.

14 Witkin, California Summary 10th Wills and Probate § 516, (S 516) Decedent's Cause of Action.

14 Witkin, California Summary 10th Wills and Probate § 518, (S 518) in General.

14 Witkin, California Summary 10th Wills and Probate § 622, (S 622) Claims Under Specific Statutes.

§ 366.2. Death of person against whom action may be brought; limitation period

(a) If a person against whom an action may be brought on a liability of the person, whether arising in contract, tort, or otherwise, and whether accrued or not accrued, dies before the expiration of the applicable limitations period, and the cause of action survives, an action may be commenced within one year after the date of death, and the limitations period that would have been applicable does not apply.

(b) The limitations period provided in this section for commencement of an action shall not be tolled or extended for any reason except as provided in any of the following, where applicable:

(1) Sections 12, 12a, and 12b of this code.

(2) Part 4 (commencing with Section 9000) of Division 7 of the Probate Code (creditor claims in administration of estates of decedents).

(3) Part 8 (commencing with Section 19000) of Division 9 of the Probate Code (payment of claims, debts, and expenses from revocable trust of deceased settlor).

(4) Former Part 3 (commencing with Section 21300) of Division 11 of the Probate Code (no contest clauses), as that part read prior to its repeal by Chapter 174 of the Statutes of 2008.

(c) This section applies to actions brought on liabilities of persons dying on or after January 1, 1993. *(Added by Stats.1992, c. 178 (S.B.1496), § 8. Amended by Stats.1993, c. 151 (A.B. 1704), § 2, eff. July 19, 1993; Stats.1994, c. 40 (A.B.797), § 1, eff. April 19, 1994, operative Jan. 1, 1995; Stats.1996, c. 862 (A.B. 2751), § 1; Stats.1998, c. 581 (A.B.2801), § 1; Stats.2006, c. 221 (A.B.2864), § 1; Stats.2009, c. 348 (S.B.308), § 2.)*

Law Revision Commission Comments

Section 366.2 restates former Section 353(b) without substantive change. This section applies a one-year statute of limitations on all actions against a decedent on which the statute of limitations otherwise applicable has not run at the time of death. This one-year limitations period applies regardless of whether the statute otherwise applicable would have expired before or after the one-year period.

If a general personal representative is appointed during the one-year period, the personal representative must notify known creditors, and the filing of a claim tolls the statute of limitations. See Prob. Code §§ 9050 (notice required), 9352 (tolling of statute of limitations). If the creditor is concerned that the decedent's beneficiaries may not have a general personal representative appointed during the one-year period, the creditor may petition for appointment during that time. See Prob. Code §§ 8000 (petition), 8461 (priority for appointment); see also Prob. Code § 48 ("interested person" defined).

The reference to the decedent's "representatives" was deleted from former Section 353(b). This section is concerned only with the time within which an action on a liability of the decedent may be brought, not with the proper parties in such a case. See Section 377.40 (assertion of cause of action against decedent). The one-year limitation of Section 366.2 applies in any action on a liability of the decedent, whether against a personal representative under Probate Code Sections 9350–9354 or against another person, such as a distributee under Probate Code Section 9392, a person who takes the decedent's property and is liable for the decedent's debts under Probate Code Sections 13109 (affidavit procedure for collection or transfer of personal property), 13156 (court order determining succession to real property), 13204 (affidavit procedure for real property of small value), or 13554 (passage of property to surviving spouse without administration), or a trustee. For cases where an action may be brought against the estate of the decedent, rather than the personal representative, see Section 377.50 and Probate Code Sections 550–555 (insured claims). See also Prob. Code § 58 ("personal representative" defined). As to survival of causes of action, see Section 377.20.

Subdivision (c) makes clear that this section does not apply to persons who died before January 1, 1993. The rules applicable to cases involving decedents who died before January 1, 1993, are set forth in former Section 353. The repeal of former Section 353 does not have any effect on the application of subdivisions (c) and (d) of former Section 353 in the cases to which they applied. [22 Cal.L.Rev.Comm.Reports 895 (1992)].

Section 366.2 is amended to make clear it is subject to the trust claims procedure as well as the probate claims procedure. This does not change, but clarifies, existing law.

Under these procedures, a creditor's claim may be extinguished before expiration of the one-year limitations period by failure to file a claim. Prob. Code §§ 9002 (probate), 19004 (trust). Conversely, filing of a claim tolls the one-year limitations period. Prob. Code §§ 9352 (probate), 19253 (trust). [23 Cal.L.Rev.Comm. Reports 901 (1993) (Annual Report, App. 5)].

Section 366.2 is amended to reflect the repeal of former Part 3 (commencing with Section 21300) of Division 11 of the Probate Code. See 2008 Cal. Stat. ch. 174. The reference to the former law is retained because the former law continues to apply to the enforcement of a no contest clause in an instrument that became irrevocable prior to January 1, 2001, notwithstanding the repeal of the former law. See Prob. Code §§ 3(g) ("If the new law does not apply to a matter that occurred before the operative date, the old law continues to govern the matter notwithstanding its amendment or repeal by the new law."), 21315(b) (new law does not apply to instrument that became irrevocable prior to January 1, 2001). See also former Prob. Code § 21308 (limitations period tolled during declaratory relief proceedings). [38 Cal. L. Revision Comm'n Reports 203 (2008)].

Research References

Rutter, Cal. Practice Guide: Civ. Pro. Before Trial Ch. 1-C, C. Prelawsuit Notices, Claims and Demands.
Rutter, Cal. Practice Guide: Enforcing Judgments/Debts Ch. 3-A, A. Evaluating the Claim.
Rutter, Cal. Practice Guide: Enforcing Judgments/Debts Ch. 3-B, B. Collection Without Suit.
Rutter, Cal. Practice Guide: Enforcing Judgments/Debts Ch. 6G-23, Enforcement After Judgment Debtor's Death.
Rutter, Cal. Practice Guide: Enforcing Judgments/Debts Gen. Matls., Highlights.
Rutter, Cal. Practice Guide: Personal Injury Ch. 5-A, A. Prelawsuit Filings.
Rutter, Cal. Practice Guide: Personal Injury Ch. 5-B, B. When to Sue-Statute of Limitations.
Rutter, Cal. Practice Guide: Personal Injury Ch. 5-E, E. Selected Pleading Issues.
Rutter, Cal. Practice Guide: Personal Injury Ch. 5-A, Outline a.
18 NO. 1 Miller & Starr, California Real Estate Newsalert 16, Holding Title.
3 Witkin Cal. Proc. 5th Actions § 678, Illustrations.
3 Witkin Cal. Proc. 5th Actions § 719, Limitations Periods.
3 Witkin Cal. Proc. 5th Actions § 762, in General.
11 Witkin, California Summary 10th Community Property § 180, (S 180) Personal Liability for Debts for Spouse's Necessaries.
11 Witkin, California Summary 10th Husband and Wife § 248, in General.
13 Witkin, California Summary 10th Trusts § 248, (S 248) Claims Against Trust.
13 Witkin, California Summary 10th Trusts § 268, (S 268) in General.
13 Witkin, California Summary 10th Trusts § 269, (S 269) Amended and Revised Claims.
13 Witkin, California Summary 10th Trusts § 270, (S 270) Petition to File Late Claim.
13 Witkin, California Summary 10th Trusts § 287, (S 287) in General.
13 Witkin, California Summary 10th Trusts § 288, (S 288) Limitations.
14 Witkin, California Summary 10th Wills and Probate § 39, Major Changes.
14 Witkin, California Summary 10th Wills and Probate § 424, (S 424) Procedure.
14 Witkin, California Summary 10th Wills and Probate § 515, (S 515) Decedent's Liability Covered by Insurance.
14 Witkin, California Summary 10th Wills and Probate § 517, (S 517) Action Against Decedent.
14 Witkin, California Summary 10th Wills and Probate § 518, (S 518) in General.

14 Witkin, California Summary 10th Wills and Probate § 617, Liability of Distributee to Known or Ascertainable Creditors.
14 Witkin, California Summary 10th Wills and Probate § 622, (S 622) Claims Under Specific Statutes.
14 Witkin, California Summary 10th Wills and Probate § 632, Action to Enforce Security Interest.
14 Witkin, California Summary 10th Wills and Probate § 633, Time Period.
14 Witkin, California Summary 10th Wills and Probate § 634, Amended and Revised Claims.
14 Witkin, California Summary 10th Wills and Probate § 635, Petition to File Late Claim.
14 Witkin, California Summary 10th Wills and Probate § 646, Statute of Limitations.
14 Witkin, California Summary 10th Wills and Probate § 785, (S 785) Personal Liability for Unsecured Debts.
14 Witkin, California Summary 10th Wills and Probate § 804, (S 804) Liability for Decedent's Debts.
14 Witkin, California Summary 10th Wills and Probate § 810, (S 810) Liability for Decedent's Debts.
14 Witkin, California Summary 10th Wills and Probate § 816, Liability of Transferee.
14 Witkin, California Summary 10th Wills and Probate § 823, Debts of Deceased Spouse.

§ 366.3. Claims arising from promise or agreement relating to distribution from estate or trust or under other instrument; limitation period

(a) If a person has a claim that arises from a promise or agreement with a decedent to distribution from an estate or trust or under another instrument, whether the promise or agreement was made orally or in writing, an action to enforce the claim to distribution may be commenced within one year after the date of death, and the limitations period that would have been applicable does not apply.

(b) The limitations period provided in this section for commencement of an action shall not be tolled or extended for any reason except as provided in Sections 12, 12a, and 12b of this code, and former Part 3 (commencing with Section 21300) of Division 11 of the Probate Code, as that part read prior to its repeal by Chapter 174 of the Statutes of 2008.

(c) This section applies to actions brought on claims concerning persons dying on or after the effective date of this section. *(Added by Stats.2000, c. 17 (A.B.1491), § 1. Amended by Stats.2006, c. 221 (A.B.2864), § 2; Stats.2009, c. 348 (S.B.308), § 3.)*

Law Revision Commission Comments

Section 366.3 is amended to reflect the repeal of former Part 3 (commencing with Section 21300) of Division 11 of the Probate Code. See 2008 Cal. Stat. ch. 174. The reference to the former law is retained because the former law continues to apply to the enforcement of a no contest clause in an instrument that became irrevocable prior to January 1, 2001, notwithstanding the repeal of the former law. See Prob. Code §§ 3(g) ("If the new law does not apply to a matter that occurred before the operative date, the old law continues to govern the matter notwithstanding its amendment or repeal by the new law."), 21315(b) (new law does not apply to instrument that became irrevocable prior to January 1, 2001). See also former Prob. Code § 21308 (limitations period tolled during declaratory relief proceedings). [38 Cal. L. Revision Comm'n Reports 203 (2008)].

Research References

Rutter, Cal. Practice Guide: Family Law Ch. 6-B, B. Spousal Support.
Miller and Starr California Real Estate § 9:20, Creation.
Miller and Starr California Real Estate § 12:36, Origin; Requirement of Marriage; Domestic Partnerships.
21 NO. 2 Miller & Starr, California Real Estate Newsalert 7, Contracts.
21 NO. 6 Miller & Starr, California Real Estate Newsalert 12, Holding Title.
3 Witkin Cal. Proc. 5th Actions § 719, Limitations Periods.

14 Witkin, California Summary 10th Wills and Probate § 517, (S 517) Action Against Decedent.

Title 3

OF THE PARTIES TO CIVIL ACTIONS

CHAPTER 1.   GENERAL PROVISIONS

§ 367.   Real party in interest; prosecution in party's name

Every action must be prosecuted in the name of the real party in interest, except as otherwise provided by statute. *(Enacted in 1872. Amended by Code Am.1880, c. 68, p. 63, § 1; Stats.1976, c. 595, p. 1439, § 1; Stats.1992, c. 178 (S.B.1496), § 10.)*

Law Revision Commission Comments

Section 367 is amended to eliminate the obsolete listing of statutes that permit prosecution of an action in the name of a person other than the real party in interest. Statutes that permit prosecution in the name of a person other than the real party in interest include Civil Code Section 1363 (association to manage common interest development), Code of Civil Procedure Section 369 (fiduciaries), and Probate Code Sections 550–555 (insured claims). [22 Cal.L.Rev.Comm.Reports 895 (1992)].

Research References

Rutter, Cal. Practice Guide: Civ. Pro. Before Trial Ch. 2-A, A. Standing to Sue-"Real Party in Interest" Requirement.
California Practice Guide: Employment Litigation Ch. 19-C, C. Plaintiff's Complaint.
Rutter, Cal. Practice Guide: Insurance Litigation Ch. 12B-B, B. Bad Faith Refusal to Settle.
Rutter, Cal. Practice Guide: Personal Injury Ch. 5-C, C. Selected Issues Affecting Parties.
Miller and Starr California Real Estate § 1:22, Assignment of Contracts.
Miller and Starr California Real Estate § 19:220, Parties.
Miller and Starr California Real Estate § 28:112, Proper Parties in Suit Against Surety; Necessity of Suit Against or Joinder of the Principal.
22 NO. 4 Miller & Starr, California Real Estate Newsalert 1, Show Me Your Papers: Sales and Assignments of Secured Real Estate Loans and the California Foreclosure Process (Part II).
4 Witkin Cal. Proc. 5th Pleading § 120, Nature of Rule.
4 Witkin Cal. Proc. 5th Pleading § 121, (S 121) Statement of Doctrine.
4 Witkin Cal. Proc. 5th Pleading § 262, (S 262) Transferee's Election.
12 Witkin, California Summary 10th Real Property § 729, Parties.
13 Witkin, California Summary 10th Trusts § 222, Illustrative Cases.

§ 367.5.   Appearance by telephone

(a) It is the intent of this section to promote uniformity in the procedures and practices relating to telephone appearances in civil cases. To improve access to the courts and reduce litigation costs, courts should, to the extent feasible, permit parties to appear by telephone at appropriate conferences, hearings, and proceedings in civil cases.

(b) Except as provided in subdivision (c), in all general civil cases, as defined in the California Rules of Court, a party that has provided notice may appear by telephone at the following conferences, hearings, and proceedings:

(1) A case management conference, provided the party has made a good faith effort to meet and confer before the conference as required by law and has timely served and filed a case management statement.

(2) A trial setting conference.

(3) A hearing on law and motion, except motions in limine.

(4) A hearing on a discovery motion.

(5) A conference to review the status of an arbitration or mediation.

(6) A hearing to review the dismissal of an action.

(7) Any other hearing, conference, or proceeding if the court determines that a telephone appearance is appropriate.

(c) The court may require a party to appear in person at a hearing, conference, or proceeding listed in subdivision (b) if the court determines on a hearing-by-hearing basis that a personal appearance would materially assist in the determination of the proceedings or in the effective management or resolution of the particular case.

(d) Consistent with its constitutional rulemaking authority, the Judicial Council shall adopt rules effectuating the policies and provisions in this section by January 1, 2008, and may adopt rules relating to matters not covered by subdivision (a). The rules may prescribe, but are not limited to prescribing, the notice to be given by a party requesting a telephone appearance under subdivision (a), the manner in which telephone appearances are to be conducted, the conditions required for a party to be permitted to appear by telephone, and provisions relating to the courts' use of private vendors to provide telephone services.

(e) This section does not apply to any types of cases or types of conferences, hearings, and proceedings except those specified in subdivision (b). Consistent with its constitutional rulemaking authority, the Judicial Council may by rule provide for the procedures and practices, and for the administration of, telephone appearances for all types of cases and matters not specified in subdivision (b). For these other cases and matters, the Judicial Council may specify the types of cases and matters in which parties may appear by telephone, the types of cases and matters in which parties shall appear personally, the conditions under which a party may be permitted to appear by telephone, and any other rules governing telephone and personal appearances that are within its rulemaking authority. *(Added by Stats.2007, c. 268 (A.B.500), § 1.)*

Research References

Rutter, Cal. Practice Guide: Civ. Pro. Before Trial Ch. 9(I)-D, D. Hearing.
Rutter, Cal. Practice Guide: Civ. Pro. Before Trial Ch. 12(I)-B, B. Case Management ("Fast Track") System.
Rutter, Cal. Practice Guide: Personal Injury Ch. 8-A, A. Case Management.
3 Witkin Cal. Proc. 5th Actions § 429C, (New)-Costs Excused.
5 Witkin Cal. Proc. 5th Pleading § 981, (S 981) Hearing.
6 Witkin Cal. Proc. 5th Proceedings Without Trial § 39, Appearance by Telephone.

7 Witkin Cal. Proc. 5th Trial § 57, Appearance at Conferences by Telephone.

§ 367.6.   Fees for telephone appearance; waiver

(a) On or before July 1, 2011, the Judicial Council shall establish statewide, uniform fees to be paid by a party for appearing by telephone, which shall supersede any fees paid to vendors and courts under any previously existing agreements and procedures. The fees to be paid for telephone appearances shall include:

(1) A fee for providing the telephone appearance service pursuant to a timely request to the vendor or court.

(2) An additional fee for providing services if the request is made shortly before the hearing, as defined by the Judicial Council.

(3) A fee for canceling a telephone appearance request.

(b) If a party has received a waiver of fees pursuant to Article 6 (commencing with Section 68630) of Chapter 2 of Title 8 of the Government Code, neither a vendor nor a court shall charge that party any of the fees authorized by this section, subject to the following:

(1) The vendor or court that provides the telephone appearance service shall have a lien, as provided by rule of court, on any judgment, including a judgment for costs, that the party may receive, in the amount of the fee that the party would have paid for the telephone appearance.

(2) If the vendor or court later receives a fee or a portion of a fee for appearance by telephone that was previously waived, that fee shall be distributed consistent with Section 72011 of the Government Code.

(c) The fee described in this section shall be a recoverable cost under Section 1033.5 of the Code of Civil Procedure. *(Added by Stats.2010, c. 720 (S.B.857), § 3, eff. Oct. 19, 2010. Amended by Stats.2012, c. 41 (S.B.1021), § 1, eff. June 27, 2012.)*

Research References

Rutter, Cal. Practice Guide: Civ. Pro. Before Trial Ch. 9(I)-D, D. Hearing.
6 Witkin Cal. Proc. 5th Proceedings Without Trial § 39, Appearance by Telephone.
7 Witkin Cal. Proc. 5th Trial § 57, Appearance at Conferences by Telephone.

§ 368.   Defense not prejudiced by assignment; exception

ASSIGNMENT OF THING IN ACTION NOT TO PREJUDICE DEFENSE. In the case of an assignment of a thing in action, the action by the assignee is without prejudice to any set-off, or other defense existing at the time of, or before, notice of the assignment; but this section does not apply to a negotiable promissory note or bill of exchange, transferred in good faith, and upon good consideration, before maturity. *(Enacted in 1872.)*

Research References

Miller and Starr California Real Estate § 1:22, Assignment of Contracts.
22 NO. 4 Miller & Starr, California Real Estate Newsalert 1, Show Me Your Papers: Sales and Assignments of Secured Real Estate Loans and the California Foreclosure Process (Part II).
1 Witkin Cal. Summ. 10th Contracts § 735, in General.

§ 368.5.   Transfer of interest; effect on action

An action or proceeding does not abate by the transfer of an interest in the action or proceeding or by any other transfer of an interest. The action or proceeding may be continued in the name of the original party, or the court may allow the person to whom the transfer is made to be substituted in the action or proceeding. *(Added by Stats.1992, c. 178 (S.B.1496), § 11.)*

Law Revision Commission Comments

Section 368.5 restates part of former Section 385 without substantive change. [22 Cal.L.Rev.Comm.Reports 895 (1992)].

Research References

Rutter, Cal. Practice Guide: Civ. Pro. Before Trial Ch. 2-A, A. Standing to Sue-"Real Party in Interest" Requirement.
Rutter, Cal. Practice Guide: Civ. Pro. Before Trial Ch. 2-G, G. Substitution of Parties.
Rutter, Cal. Practice Guide: Personal Injury Ch. 5-E, E. Selected Pleading Issues.
4 Witkin Cal. Proc. 5th Pleading § 262, (S 262) Transferee's Election.
4 Witkin Cal. Proc. 5th Pleading § 265, (S 265) Procedure.
4 Witkin Cal. Proc. 5th Pleading § 266, Succession of Officer.

§ 369.   Persons authorized to sue without joining beneficiary

(a) The following persons may sue without joining as parties the persons for whose benefit the action is prosecuted:

(1) A personal representative, as defined in subdivision (a) of Section 58 of the Probate Code.

(2) A trustee of an express trust.

(3) Except for a person upon whom a power of sale has been conferred pursuant to a deed of trust or mortgage, a person with whom, or in whose name, a contract is made for the benefit of another.

(4) Any other person expressly authorized by statute.

(b) Notwithstanding subdivision (a), a trustee upon whom a power of sale has been conferred pursuant to a deed of trust or mortgage may sue to exercise the trustee's powers and duties pursuant to Chapter 2 (commencing with Section 2920) of Title 14 of Part 4 of Division 3 of the Civil Code. *(Enacted in 1872. Amended by Stats.1988, c. 530, § 2; Stats.1992, c. 178 (S.B.1496), § 12.)*

Law Revision Commission Comments

Subdivision (a) of Section 369 is reorganized and the terminology clarified. These changes are technical and not substantive. See also Prob. Code §§ 58 ("personal representative" defined), 82 ("trust" defined), 84 ("trustee" defined). [22 Cal.L.Rev.Comm.Reports 895 (1992)].

Research References

Rutter, Cal. Practice Guide: Civ. Pro. Before Trial Ch. 2-A, A. Standing to Sue-"Real Party in Interest" Requirement.
Rutter, Cal. Practice Guide: Civ. Pro. Before Trial Ch. 6-B, B. Complaints.
22 NO. 4 Miller & Starr, California Real Estate Newsalert 1, Show Me Your Papers: Sales and Assignments of Secured Real Estate Loans and the California Foreclosure Process (Part II).
4 Witkin Cal. Proc. 5th Pleading § 120, Nature of Rule.
4 Witkin Cal. Proc. 5th Pleading § 134, Personal Representative as Real Party in Interest.
4 Witkin Cal. Proc. 5th Pleading § 137, in General.
4 Witkin Cal. Proc. 5th Pleading § 141, Action by Agent.
4 Witkin Cal. Proc. 5th Pleading § 142, Action by Promisee.
4 Witkin Cal. Proc. 5th Pleading § 144, Nature of Provision.
4 Witkin Cal. Proc. 5th Pleading § 170, (S 170) Other Examples.
13 Witkin, California Summary 10th Trusts § 115, (L)--Actions and Proceedings.
13 Witkin, California Summary 10th Trusts § 222, Illustrative Cases.
14 Witkin, California Summary 10th Wills and Probate § 513, (S 513) in General.

§ 369.5.   Partnerships, unincorporated associations; joinder of individual members

(a) A partnership or other unincorporated association, whether organized for profit or not, may sue and be sued in the name it has assumed or by which it is known.

(b) A member of the partnership or other unincorporated association may be joined as a party in an action against the unincorporated association. If service of process is made on the

Civ. Pro.

member as an individual, whether or not the member is also served as a person upon whom service is made on behalf of the unincorporated association, a judgment against the member based on the member's personal liability may be obtained in the action, whether the liability is joint, joint and several, or several. *(Added by Stats.1992, c. 178 (S.B.1496), § 13.)*

Law Revision Commission Comments

Section 369.5 restates former Section 388 without substantive change. [22 Cal.L.Rev.Comm.Reports 895 (1992)].

Research References

Rutter, Cal. Practice Guide: Civ. Pro. Before Trial Ch. 2-B, B. Capacity to Sue or Defend.
Rutter, Cal. Practice Guide: Civ. Pro. Before Trial Ch. 6-B, B. Complaints.
Rutter, Cal. Practice Guide: Enforcing Judgments/Debts Ch. 3-A, A. Evaluating the Claim.
Rutter, Cal. Practice Guide: Fed.Civ.Pro. Before Trial Ch. 7-B, B. Capacity to Sue or Defend.
Rutter, Cal. Practice Guide: Fed.Civ.Pro. Before Trial Ch. 2C-3, How "Citizenship" Determined.
3 Witkin Cal. Proc. 5th Actions § 1054, Domestic Association.
2 Witkin Cal. Proc. 5th Jurisdiction § 181, Domestic Partnerships or Associations.
4 Witkin Cal. Proc. 5th Pleading § 94, Reformation of Rule.
4 Witkin Cal. Proc. 5th Pleading § 98, (S 98) Any Association May be Sued.
4 Witkin Cal. Proc. 5th Pleading § 99, (S 99) Joinder of Individual Members.
4 Witkin Cal. Proc. 5th Pleading § 269, (S 269) Scope of Action.
4 Witkin Cal. Proc. 5th Pleading § 474, Corporations and Associations.
5 Witkin Cal. Proc. 5th Pleading § 901, (S 901) Partnership or Other Unincorporated Association.
9 Witkin, California Summary 10th Corporations § 39, Entity Status.
9 Witkin, California Summary 10th Corporations § 50, Liability of Trustees and Trust Estate.
5 Witkin, California Summary 10th Torts § 38, (S 38) in General.
9 Witkin, California Summary 10th Partnership § 1, Statutes Affecting Partnerships.
9 Witkin, California Summary 10th Partnership § 8, (S 8) Effect of Failure to Comply.
9 Witkin, California Summary 10th Partnership § 40, (S 40) Remedies of Creditors.

CHAPTER 2.   MARRIED PERSON

Section
370.   Married persons.
371.   Husband and wife; defense by spouse.

§ 370.   Married persons

A married person may be sued without his or her spouse being joined as a party, and may sue without his or her spouse being joined as a party in all actions. *(Enacted in 1872. Amended by Code Am.1873–74, c. 383, p. 293, § 37; Stats.1913, c. 130, p. 217, § 1; Stats.1921, c. 110, p. 102, § 1; Stats.1975, c. 1241, p. 3187, § 2.)*

Research References

4 Witkin Cal. Proc. 5th Pleading § 86, (S 86) Married Persons.
4 Witkin Cal. Proc. 5th Pleading § 153, (S 153) Husband and Wife.
11 Witkin, California Summary 10th Husband and Wife § 18, (S 18) in General.
5 Witkin, California Summary 10th Torts § 725, Personal Injury to Spouse.

§ 371.   Husband and wife; defense by spouse

If a husband and wife are sued together, each may defend for his or her own right, but if one spouse neglects to defend, the other spouse may defend for that spouse's right also. *(Enacted in 1872. Amended by Stats.1975, c. 1241, p. 3187, § 3.)*

Research References

Rutter, Cal. Practice Guide: Civ. Pro. Before Trial Ch. 2-A, A. Standing to Sue-"Real Party in Interest" Requirement.
Rutter, Cal. Practice Guide: Prof. Responsibility Ch. 1-D, D. Unauthorized Practice of Law.
4 Witkin Cal. Proc. 5th Pleading § 86, (S 86) Married Persons.
11 Witkin, California Summary 10th Husband and Wife § 18, (S 18) in General.

CHAPTER 3.   DISABILITY OF PARTY

Section
372.   Minors, incompetent persons or persons for whom conservator appointed; appearance by guardian, conservator or guardian ad litem; powers; disposition of moneys recovered; waiver of juvenile law rights.
373.   Guardian ad litem; appointment procedure.
373.5.   Guardian ad litem; persons not ascertained, not in being or unknown; powers; expenses.
374.   Minor under age 12; appearance without counsel when accompanied by guardian ad litem; conditions.
374.5.   Orders affecting minors; jurisdiction.
375.   Disability of party; effect on action.
376.   Parents; injuries to child; failure of one parent to join as plaintiff; service on parent not joining; illegitimate child; ward; parties defendant; death of child or ward; damages; consolidation of injury and death action.

§ 372.   Minors, incompetent persons or persons for whom conservator appointed; appearance by guardian, conservator or guardian ad litem; powers; disposition of moneys recovered; waiver of juvenile law rights

(a) When a minor, an incompetent person, or a person for whom a conservator has been appointed is a party, that person shall appear either by a guardian or conservator of the estate or by a guardian ad litem appointed by the court in which the action or proceeding is pending, or by a judge thereof, in each case. A guardian ad litem may be appointed in any case when it is deemed by the court in which the action or proceeding is prosecuted, or by a judge thereof, expedient to appoint a guardian ad litem to represent the minor, incompetent person, or person for whom a conservator has been appointed, notwithstanding that the person may have a guardian or conservator of the estate and may have appeared by the guardian or conservator of the estate. The guardian or conservator of the estate or guardian ad litem so appearing for any minor, incompetent person, or person for whom a conservator has been appointed shall have power, with the approval of the court in which the action or proceeding is pending, to compromise the same, to agree to the order or judgment to be entered therein for or against the ward or conservatee, and to satisfy any judgment or order in favor of the ward or conservatee or release or discharge any claim of the ward or conservatee pursuant to that compromise. Any money or other property to be paid or delivered pursuant to the order or judgment for the benefit of a minor, incompetent person, or person for whom a conservator has been appointed shall be paid and delivered as provided in Chapter 4 (commencing with Section 3600) of Part 8 of Division 4 of the Probate Code.

Where reference is made in this section to "incompetent person," such reference shall be deemed to include "a person for whom a conservator may be appointed."

Nothing in this section, or in any other provision of this code, the Civil Code, the Family Code, or the Probate Code is intended by the Legislature to prohibit a minor from exercising an intelligent and knowing waiver of his or her constitutional rights in any proceedings under the Juvenile Court Law, Chapter 2 (commencing with Section 200) of Part 1 of Division 2 of the Welfare and Institutions Code.

(b)(1) Notwithstanding subdivision (a), a minor 12 years of age or older may appear in court without a guardian, counsel, or guardian ad litem, for the purpose of requesting or opposing a request for any of the following:

(A) An injunction or temporary restraining order or both to prohibit harassment pursuant to Section 527.6.

(B) An injunction or temporary restraining order or both against violence or a credible threat of violence in the workplace pursuant to Section 527.8.

(C) A protective order pursuant to Division 10 (commencing with Section 6200) of the Family Code.

(D) A protective order pursuant to Sections 7710 and 7720 of the Family Code.

The court may, either upon motion or in its own discretion, and after considering reasonable objections by the minor to the appointment of specific individuals, appoint a guardian ad litem to assist the minor in obtaining or opposing the order, provided that the appointment of the guardian ad litem does not delay the issuance or denial of the order being sought. In making the determination concerning the appointment of a particular guardian ad litem, the court shall consider whether the minor and the guardian have divergent interests.

(2) For purposes of this subdivision only, upon the issuance of an order pursuant to paragraph (1), if the minor initially appeared in court seeking an order without a guardian or guardian ad litem, and if the minor is residing with a parent or guardian, the court shall send a copy of the order to at least one parent or guardian designated by the minor, unless, in the discretion of the court, notification of a parent or guardian would be contrary to the best interest of the minor. The court is not required to send the order to more than one parent or guardian.

(3) The Judicial Council shall adopt forms by July 1, 1999, to facilitate the appointment of a guardian ad litem pursuant to this subdivision.

(c)(1) Notwithstanding subdivision (a), a minor may appear in court without a guardian ad litem in the following proceedings if the minor is a parent of the child who is the subject of the proceedings:

(A) Family court proceedings pursuant to Part 3 (commencing with Section 7600) of Division 12 of the Family Code.

(B) Dependency proceedings pursuant to Chapter 2 (commencing with Section 200) of Part 1 of Division 2 of the Welfare and Institutions Code.

(C) Guardianship proceedings for a minor child pursuant to Part 2 (commencing with Section 1500) of Division 4 of the Probate Code.

(D) Any other proceedings concerning child custody, visitation, or support.

(2) If the court finds that the minor parent is unable to understand the nature of the proceedings or to assist counsel in preparing the case, the court shall, upon its own motion or upon a motion by the minor parent or the minor parent's counsel, appoint a guardian ad litem. *(Enacted in 1872. Amended by Code Am.1873–74, c. 383, p. 294, § 38; Code Am.1880, c. 68, p. 63, § 2; Stats.1913, c. 202, p. 350, § 1; Stats.1933, c. 744, p. 1837, § 1; Stats.1939, c. 313, p. 1599, § 1; Stats.1951, c. 1737, p. 4097, § 43; Stats.1953, c. 1315, p. 2873, § 1; Stats.1961, c. 721, p. 1962, § 1; Stats.1963, c. 127, p. 803, § 4; Stats.1967, c. 1259, p. 3046, § 1; Stats.1979, c. 730, p. 2476, § 19, operative Jan. 1, 1981;*

Stats.1994, c. 1269 (A.B.2208), § 2; Stats.1996, c. 727 (A.B.2155), § 2; Stats.1998, c. 706 (S.B.326), § 1, eff. Sept. 22, 1998; Stats.2008, c. 181 (S.B.1612), § 1.)

Law Revision Commission Comments

Recommendations relating to Guardianship-Conservatorship Law 14 Cal.L.Rev.Comm. Reports 501 (1978).

Section 372 is amended to change the reference in Section 372 to former Section 1510 of the Probate Code to reflect the revision and recodification of that provision. Other technical revisions to Section 372 are also made.

Section 372 is amended to add a reference to the Family Code to reflect the fact that provisions concerning the capacity of minors have been moved from the Civil Code to the Family Code. This is a technical, nonsubstantive change. [24 Cal.L.Rev.Comm. Reports 621 (1994)].

Research References

Rutter, Cal. Practice Guide: A.D.R. Ch. 1-E, E. Enforcing ADR Settlements.

Rutter, Cal. Practice Guide: Civil Appeals & Writs Ch. 5-B, B. Types of Motions, Applications and Requests.

Rutter, Cal. Practice Guide: Civ. Pro. Before Trial Ch. 2-B, B. Capacity to Sue or Defend.

Rutter, Cal. Practice Guide: Civ. Pro. Before Trial Ch. 6-B, B. Complaints.

Rutter, Cal. Practice Guide: Civ. Pro. Before Trial Ch. 12(II)-B, B. Settlements on Behalf of Minors or Incompetents.

Rutter, Cal. Practice Guide: Civ. Pro. Before Trial Ch. 12(II)-F, F. Motion to Enforce Settlement (CCP §§ 664.6, 664.7).

Rutter, Cal. Practice Guide: Civil Trials & Evidence Ch. 6-G, G. Preparing Opening Statement.

Rutter, Cal. Practice Guide: Civil Trials & Evidence Ch. 8E-A, A. Privileges.

Rutter, Cal. Practice Guide: Family Law Ch. 7-B, B. Contested Custody Proceedings, Generally.

Rutter, Cal. Practice Guide: Fed.Civ.Pro. Before Trial Ch. 7-B, B. Capacity to Sue or Defend.

Rutter, Cal. Practice Guide: Personal Injury Ch. 3-B, B. Potential Claimants in a Personal Injury Case.

Rutter, Cal. Practice Guide: Personal Injury Ch. 4-G, G. Concluding and Enforcing Settlement.

Rutter, Cal. Practice Guide: Personal Injury Ch. 5-C, C. Selected Issues Affecting Parties.

3 Witkin Cal. Proc. 5th Actions § 213, Steps Relating to Capacity of Parties.

9 Witkin Cal. Proc. 5th Appeal § 737, (S 737) Compromise of Claim of Minor or Incompetent.

4 Witkin Cal. Proc. 5th Pleading § 70, (S 70) in General.

4 Witkin Cal. Proc. 5th Pleading § 73, (S 73) Exception: Injunction or Protective Order.

4 Witkin Cal. Proc. 5th Pleading § 78, (S 78) General Limitations on Power.

4 Witkin Cal. Proc. 5th Pleading § 80, Nature and Scope of Power.

4 Witkin Cal. Proc. 5th Pleading § 81, Petition.

4 Witkin Cal. Proc. 5th Pleading § 82, Hearing and Order.

4 Witkin Cal. Proc. 5th Pleading § 83, (S 83) Judgment is Ordinarily Subject to Disaffirmance.

5 Witkin Cal. Proc. 5th Pleading § 682, Interests of Other Persons.

6 Witkin Cal. Proc. 5th Proceedings Without Trial § 126, (S 126) Other Means of Enforcement.

7 Witkin Cal. Proc. 5th Trial § 158, (S 158) Where Defendant is Incompetent.

12 Witkin, California Summary 10th Real Property § 67, Parties.

10 Witkin, California Summary 10th Parent and Child § 572, (S 572) Appointment of Guardian Ad Litem or Child Advocate.

10 Witkin, California Summary 10th Parent and Child § 577, (S 577) Hearing.

11 Witkin, California Summary 10th Husband and Wife § 77, Standing of Guardian or Conservator.

11 Witkin, California Summary 10th Husband and Wife § 146, Proceedings.

11 Witkin, California Summary 10th Husband and Wife § 379, in General.

14 Witkin, California Summary 10th Wills and Probate § 374, Guardian Ad Litem.

Civ. Pro.

14 Witkin, California Summary 10th Wills and Probate § 1014, (S 1014) Procedure for Court Approval.

§ 373. Guardian ad litem; appointment procedure

When a guardian ad litem is appointed, he or she shall be appointed as follows:

(a) If the minor is the plaintiff the appointment must be made before the summons is issued, upon the application of the minor, if the minor is of the age of 14 years, or if under that age, upon the application of a relative or friend of the minor.

(b) If the minor is the defendant, upon the application of the minor, if the minor is of the age of 14 years, and the minor applies within 10 days after the service of the summons, or if under that age, or if the minor neglects to apply, then upon the application of a relative or friend of the minor, or of any other party to the action, or by the court on its own motion.

(c) If an insane or incompetent person is a party to an action or proceeding, upon the application of a relative or friend of such insane or incompetent person, or of any other party to the action or proceeding, or by the court on its own motion. *(Enacted in 1872. Amended by Code Am.1880, c. 68, p. 63, § 3; Stats.1933, c. 744, p. 1837, § 2; Stats.1971, c. 755, p. 1501, § 1; Stats.1980, c. 676, p. 1905, § 64.)*

Research References

Rutter, Cal. Practice Guide: Civ. Pro. Before Trial Ch. 2-B, B. Capacity to Sue or Defend.
Rutter, Cal. Practice Guide: Family Law Ch. 7-B, B. Contested Custody Proceedings, Generally.
Rutter, Cal. Practice Guide: Personal Injury Ch. 3-B, B. Potential Claimants in a Personal Injury Case.
Rutter, Cal. Practice Guide: Personal Injury Ch. 5-C, C. Selected Issues Affecting Parties.
4 Witkin Cal. Proc. 5th Pleading § 74, (S 74) Who May Apply.
4 Witkin Cal. Proc. 5th Pleading § 75, (S 75) Time of Application.
5 Witkin Cal. Proc. 5th Pleading § 682, Interests of Other Persons.

§ 373.5. Guardian ad litem; persons not ascertained, not in being or unknown; powers; expenses

If under the terms of a written instrument, or otherwise, a person or persons of a designated class who are not ascertained or who are not in being, or a person or persons who are unknown, may be or may become legally or equitably interested in any property, real or personal, the court in which any action, petition or proceeding of any kind relative to or affecting the property is pending, may, upon the representation of any party thereto, or of any person interested, appoint a suitable person to appear and act therein as guardian ad litem of the person or persons not ascertained, not in being, or who are unknown; and the judgment, order or decree in the proceedings, made after the appointment, shall be conclusive upon all persons for whom the guardian ad litem was appointed.

The guardian ad litem shall have power, with the approval of the court in which the action, petition or proceeding is pending, to compromise the same, to agree to the order or judgment to be entered therein for or against the persons for whom the guardian ad litem was appointed, and to satisfy any judgment or order in favor of the persons, or release, or discharge any claim of the persons pursuant to the compromise. The court shall have the same power with respect to the money or other property to be paid or delivered under such order or judgment as is provided in Section 372 of this code.

The reasonable expenses of the guardian ad litem, including compensation and counsel fees, shall be determined by the court and paid as it may order, either out of the property or by plaintiff or petitioner. If the expenses are to be paid by the plaintiff or petitioner, execution therefor may issue in the name of the guardian ad litem. *(Added by Stats.1949, c. 511, p. 869, § 1.*

Amended by Stats.1957, c. 976, p. 2217, § 1; Stats.1961, c. 435, p. 1503, § 1.)

Research References

1 Witkin Cal. Proc. 5th Attorneys § 48, Ordinary Civil Proceedings.
4 Witkin Cal. Proc. 5th Pleading § 70, (S 70) in General.
4 Witkin Cal. Proc. 5th Pleading § 74, (S 74) Who May Apply.
4 Witkin Cal. Proc. 5th Pleading § 80, Nature and Scope of Power.
4 Witkin Cal. Proc. 5th Pleading § 272, Unborn Remainderpersons.
5 Witkin Cal. Proc. 5th Pleading § 682, Interests of Other Persons.
13 Witkin, California Summary 10th Trusts § 205, in General.

§ 374. Minor under age 12; appearance without counsel when accompanied by guardian ad litem; conditions

(a) A minor under 12 years of age, accompanied by a duly appointed and acting guardian ad litem, shall be permitted to appear in court without counsel for the limited purpose of requesting or opposing a request for (1) an injunction or temporary restraining order or both to prohibit harassment pursuant to Section 527.6, (2) an injunction or temporary restraining order or both against violence or a credible threat of violence in the workplace pursuant to Section 527.8, (3) a protective order pursuant to Division 10 (commencing with Section 6200) of the Family Code, or (4) a protective order pursuant to Sections 7710 and 7720 of the Family Code.

(b) In making the determination concerning appointment of a particular guardian ad litem for purposes of this section, the court shall consider whether the minor and the guardian have divergent interests.

(c) The Judicial Council shall adopt forms by July 1, 1999, to implement this section. The forms shall be designed to facilitate the appointment of the guardian ad litem for purposes of this section. *(Added by Stats.1998, c. 706 (S.B.326), § 2, eff. Sept. 22, 1998.)*

Research References

Rutter, Cal. Practice Guide: Civ. Pro. Before Trial Ch. 2-B, B. Capacity to Sue or Defend.
22 NO. 4 Miller & Starr, California Real Estate Newsalert 1, Show Me Your Papers: Sales and Assignments of Secured Real Estate Loans and the California Foreclosure Process (Part II).
3 Witkin Cal. Proc. 5th Actions § 213, Steps Relating to Capacity of Parties.
4 Witkin Cal. Proc. 5th Pleading § 73, (S 73) Exception: Injunction or Protective Order.
4 Witkin Cal. Proc. 5th Pleading § 152, (S 152) Common Interest Development Association.
12 Witkin, California Summary 10th Real Property § 122, (S 122) Parties to Enforcement.
11 Witkin, California Summary 10th Husband and Wife § 373, (S 373) in General.
5 Witkin, California Summary 10th Torts § 723, (S 723) Types of Actions.

§ 374.5. Orders affecting minors; jurisdiction

A proceeding initiated by or brought against a minor for any of the injunctions or orders described in paragraph (1) of subdivision (b) of Section 372 or subdivision (a) of Section 374 shall be heard in the court assigned to hear those matters; except that, if the minor bringing the action or against whom the action is brought has previously been adjudged a dependent child or a ward of the juvenile court, the matter shall be heard in the juvenile court having jurisdiction over the minor. *(Added by Stats.1998, c. 706 (S.B.326), § 3, eff. Sept. 22, 1998.)*

Research References

4 Witkin Cal. Proc. 5th Pleading § 73, (S 73) Exception: Injunction or Protective Order.

§ 375. Disability of party; effect on action

An action or proceeding does not abate by the disability of a party. The court, on motion, shall allow the action or proceeding to be continued by or against the party's representative. *(Added by Stats.1992, c. 178 (S.B.1496), § 17.)*

Law Revision Commission Comments

Section 375 restates part of former Section 385, but makes clear that substitution of the representative of a disabled person is mandatory rather than permissive. [22 Cal.L.Rev.Comm.Reports 895 (1992)].

Research References

Rutter, Cal. Practice Guide: Civ. Pro. Before Trial Ch. 2-B, B. Capacity to Sue or Defend.
Rutter, Cal. Practice Guide: Personal Injury Ch. 5-A, A. Prelawsuit Filings.
4 Witkin Cal. Proc. 5th Pleading § 259, Necessity of Substitution.
4 Witkin Cal. Proc. 5th Pleading § 260, Procedure.
5 Witkin, California Summary 10th Torts § 723, (S 723) Types of Actions.

§ 376. Parents; injuries to child; failure of one parent to join as plaintiff; service on parent not joining; illegitimate child; ward; parties defendant; death of child or ward; damages; consolidation of injury and death action

(a) The parents of a legitimate unmarried minor child, acting jointly, may maintain an action for injury to the child caused by the wrongful act or neglect of another. If either parent fails on demand to join as plaintiff in the action or is dead or cannot be found, then the other parent may maintain the action. The parent, if living, who does not join as plaintiff shall be joined as a defendant and, before trial or hearing of any question of fact, shall be served with summons either in the manner provided by law for the service of a summons in a civil action or by sending a copy of the summons and complaint by registered mail with proper postage prepaid addressed to that parent's last known address with request for a return receipt. If service is made by registered mail, the production of a return receipt purporting to be signed by the addressee creates a rebuttable presumption that the summons and complaint have been duly served. The presumption established by this section is a presumption affecting the burden of producing evidence. The respective rights of the parents to any award shall be determined by the court.

(b) A parent may maintain an action for such an injury to his or her illegitimate unmarried minor child if a guardian has not been appointed. Where a parent who does not have care, custody, or control of the child brings the action, the parent who has care, custody, or control of the child shall be served with the summons either in the manner provided by law for the serving of a summons in a civil action or by sending a copy of the summons and complaint by registered mail, with proper postage prepaid, addressed to the last known address of that parent, with request for a return receipt. If service is made by registered mail, the production of a return receipt purporting to be signed by the addressee creates a rebuttable presumption that the summons and complaint have been duly served. The presumption established by this section is a presumption affecting the burden of producing evidence. The respective rights of the parents to any award shall be determined by the court.

(c) The father of an illegitimate child who maintains an action under this section shall have acknowledged in writing prior to the child's injury, in the presence of a competent witness, that he is the father of the child, or, prior to the child's injury, have been judicially determined to be the father of the child.

(d) A parent of an illegitimate child who does not maintain an action under this section may be joined as a party thereto.

(e) A guardian may maintain an action for such an injury to his or her ward.

(f) An action under this section may be maintained against the person causing the injury. If any other person is responsible for the wrongful act or neglect, the action may also be maintained against the other person. The death of the child or

ward does not abate the parents' or guardian's cause of action for the child's injury as to damages accruing before the child's death.

(g) In an action under this section, damages may be awarded that, under all of the circumstances of the case, may be just, except that:

(1) In an action maintained after the death of the child, the damages recoverable are as provided in Section 377.34.

(2) Where the person causing the injury is deceased, the damages recoverable in an action against the decedent's personal representative are as provided in Section 377.42.

(h) If an action arising out of the same wrongful act or neglect may be maintained pursuant to Section 377.60 for wrongful death of a child described in this section, the action authorized by this section may be consolidated therewith for trial as provided in Section 1048. *(Enacted in 1872. Amended by Code Am.1873–74, c. 383, p. 294, § 39; Stats.1939, 1939, c. 425, p. 1759, § 1; Stats.1949, c. 1380, p. 2400, § 3; Stats.1961, c. 657, p. 1868, § 4; Stats.1969, c. 1611, p. 3378, § 4, operative July 1, 1970; Stats.1975, c. 1241, p. 3187, § 4; Stats.1992, c. 178 (S.B.1496), § 18.)*

Law Revision Commission Comments

Section 376 is revised to correct cross-references, to add subdivision letters to the existing paragraphs, and to improve the wording. The word "ward" in subdivision (g)(1) has been omitted as surplus; this is a technical, nonsubstantive change.

Subdivision (h) is revised for consistency with Section 377.62. [22 Cal.L.Rev.Comm.Reports 895 (1992)].

Research References

Rutter, Cal. Practice Guide: Civ. Pro. Before Trial Ch. 2-A, A. Standing to Sue-"Real Party in Interest" Requirement.
Rutter, Cal. Practice Guide: Civ. Pro. Before Trial Ch. 6-B, B. Complaints.
Rutter, Cal. Practice Guide: Civil Trials & Evidence Ch. 8D-D, D. Hearsay Exceptions.
Rutter, Cal. Practice Guide: Civil Trials & Evidence Ch. 8E-A, A. Privileges.
4 Witkin Cal. Proc. 5th Pleading § 153, (S 153) Husband and Wife.
4 Witkin Cal. Proc. 5th Pleading § 193, (S 193) Joinder Required by Special Statutes.
5 Witkin, California Summary 10th Torts § 23, (S 23) Survival of Tort Liability.
5 Witkin, California Summary 10th Torts § 726, (S 726) Action by Parents.

CHAPTER 4. EFFECT OF DEATH

ARTICLE 1. DEFINITIONS

Section

§ 377.10. Beneficiary of the decedent's estate

For the purposes of this chapter, "beneficiary of the decedent's estate" means:

(a) If the decedent died leaving a will, the sole beneficiary or all of the beneficiaries who succeed to a cause of action, or to a particular item of property that is the subject of a cause of action, under the decedent's will.

(b) If the decedent died without leaving a will, the sole person or all of the persons who succeed to a cause of action, or to a particular item of property that is the subject of a cause of action, under Sections 6401 and 6402 of the Probate Code or, if the law of a sister state or foreign nation governs succession to the cause of action or particular item of property, under the law of the sister state or foreign nation. *(Added by Stats.1992, c. 178 (S.B.1496), § 20.)*

Law Revision Commission Comments

Section 377.10 is a new provision drawn from Probate Code Section 13006. See also Section 377.11 ("decedent's successor in interest" defined). [22 Cal.L.Rev.Comm.Reports 895 (1992)].

Research References

3 Witkin Cal. Proc. 5th Actions § 12, Nature of Topic.
5 Witkin, California Summary 10th Torts § 23, (S 23) Survival of Tort Liability.
6 Witkin, California Summary 10th Torts § 1586, (S 1586) Personal Torts.
14 Witkin, California Summary 10th Wills and Probate § 512, Statutory Framework.
14 Witkin, California Summary 10th Wills and Probate § 518, (S 518) in General.

§ 377.11. Decedent's successor in interest

For the purposes of this chapter, "decedent's successor in interest" means the beneficiary of the decedent's estate or other successor in interest who succeeds to a cause of action or to a particular item of the property that is the subject of a cause of action. *(Added by Stats.1992, c. 178 (S.B.1496), § 20.)*

Law Revision Commission Comments

Section 377.11 is new. The term "successor in interest" is derived from the second sentence of former Section 385. "Beneficiary of the decedent's estate" is defined in Section 377.10, and refers to takers of assets that are or would be subject to probate. Other successors in interest include persons who take property at the decedent's death by operation of law or a contract or account agreement.

The decedent's successor in interest does not include a person to whom the cause of action or property was assigned during the decedent's lifetime. [22 Cal.L.Rev.Comm.Reports 895 (1992)].

Research References

Rutter, Cal. Practice Guide: Civ. Pro. Before Trial Ch. 2-A, A. Standing to Sue-"Real Party in Interest" Requirement.
California Practice Guide: Employment Litigation Ch. 17-C, C. Extracontractual Compensatory Damages (Tort and Statutory).
Rutter, Cal. Practice Guide: Personal Injury Ch. 3-B, B. Potential Claimants in a Personal Injury Case.
14 Witkin, California Summary 10th Wills and Probate § 518, (S 518) in General.

ARTICLE 2. SURVIVAL AND CONTINUATION

Section
377.20. Cause of action survives; limitations; loss or damage simultaneous with death.
377.21. Pending actions.
377.22. Assignment of cause of action.

§ 377.20. Cause of action survives; limitations; loss or damage simultaneous with death

(a) Except as otherwise provided by statute, a cause of action for or against a person is not lost by reason of the person's death, but survives subject to the applicable limitations period.

(b) This section applies even though a loss or damage occurs simultaneously with or after the death of a person who would have been liable if the person's death had not preceded or occurred simultaneously with the loss or damage. *(Added by Stats.1992, c. 178 (S.B.1496), § 20.)*

Law Revision Commission Comments

Subdivision (a) of Section 377.20 restates the first part of former Probate Code Section 573(a) without substantive change. Subdivision (b) restates former Probate Code Section 573(d) without substantive change. The applicable limitations period may be affected by the death of a person. See Sections 366.1–366.2 (time of commencement of action after death of person). [22 Cal.L.Rev.Comm.Reports 895 (1992)].

Research References

Rutter, Cal. Practice Guide: Civil Appeals & Writs Ch. 2-D, D. Standing to Appeal.
Rutter, Cal. Practice Guide: Civ. Pro. Before Trial Ch. 2-G, G. Substitution of Parties.
Rutter, Cal. Practice Guide: Fed.Civ.Pro. Before Trial Ch. 1-B, B. Federal vs. State Law.
Rutter, Cal. Practice Guide: Insurance Litigation Ch. 15-A, A. Actions Against Insurers.
Rutter, Cal. Practice Guide: Personal Injury Ch. 3-G, G. Independent Damages Claims.
Rutter, Cal. Practice Guide: Personal Injury Ch. 5-B, B. When to Sue-Statute of Limitations.
Miller and Starr California Real Estate § 21:30, Who Can Raise the Defense of Usury--Successors in Interest; Grantees.
Miller and Starr California Real Estate § 21:32, Who is Liable for Usury Penalties.
3 Witkin Cal. Proc. 5th Actions § 15, Current Rule of Survivability.
3 Witkin Cal. Proc. 5th Actions § 717, (S 717) Death of Prospective Plaintiff.
3 Witkin Cal. Proc. 5th Actions § 718, Survival of Action.
11 Witkin, California Summary 10th Husband and Wife § 152, Survival of Cause of Action.
5 Witkin, California Summary 10th Torts § 23, (S 23) Survival of Tort Liability.
6 Witkin, California Summary 10th Torts § 1273, Statutory Liability for Operation of Vessel.
6 Witkin, California Summary 10th Torts § 1384, Action Under Federal Civil Rights Act.
6 Witkin, California Summary 10th Torts § 1671, in General.
8 Witkin, California Summary 10th Constitutional Law § 841, (S 841) in General.
14 Witkin, California Summary 10th Wills and Probate § 516, (S 516) Decedent's Cause of Action.
14 Witkin, California Summary 10th Wills and Probate § 518, (S 518) in General.

§ 377.21. Pending actions

A pending action or proceeding does not abate by the death of a party if the cause of action survives. *(Added by Stats.1992, c. 178 (S.B.1496), § 20.)*

Law Revision Commission Comments

Section 377.21 restates part of the first sentence of former Section 385 without substantive change. [22 Cal.L.Rev.Comm.Reports 895 (1992)].

Research References

Rutter, Cal. Practice Guide: Civ. Pro. Before Trial Ch. 2-G, G. Substitution of Parties.
California Practice Guide: Employment Litigation Ch. 17-C, C. Extracontractual Compensatory Damages (Tort and Statutory).
California Practice Guide: Employment Litigation Ch. 19-H, H. Other Pretrial Procedures.
14 Witkin, California Summary 10th Wills and Probate § 518, (S 518) in General.

§ 377.22. Assignment of cause of action

Nothing in this chapter shall be construed as affecting the assignability of causes of action. *(Added by Stats.1992, c. 178 (S.B.1496), § 20.)*

Civ. Pro.

Law Revision Commission Comments

Section 377.22 restates former Probate Code Section 573(e) without substantive change. [22 Cal.L.Rev.Comm.Reports 895 (1992)].

Research References

Rutter, Cal. Practice Guide: Insurance Litigation Ch. 9-E, E. Requirements for Equitable Subrogation.
1 Witkin Cal. Summ. 10th Contracts § 727, (S 727) Claims for Personal Wrongs.
6 Witkin, California Summary 10th Torts § 1273, Statutory Liability for Operation of Vessel.
14 Witkin, California Summary 10th Wills and Probate § 518, (S 518) in General.

ARTICLE 3. DECEDENT'S CAUSE OF ACTION

Section

377.30. Surviving cause of action; person to whom passes; commencement of action.
377.31. Pending action or proceeding; continuance.
377.32. Statement from successor in interest; information required.
377.33. Court orders.
377.34. Damages recoverable.
377.35. Application of article.

§ 377.30. Surviving cause of action; person to whom passes; commencement of action

A cause of action that survives the death of the person entitled to commence an action or proceeding passes to the decedent's successor in interest, subject to Chapter 1 (commencing with Section 7000) of Part 1 of Division 7 of the Probate Code, and an action may be commenced by the decedent's personal representative or, if none, by the decedent's successor in interest. *(Added by Stats.1992, c. 178 (S.B.1496), § 20.)*

Law Revision Commission Comments

Section 377.30 restates the first part of former Code of Civil Procedure Section 353(a) and part of former Probate Code Section 573(a) without substantive change, but adds the reference to the successor in interest drawn from former Code of Civil Procedure Section 385. Under this section, an action or proceeding may be commenced by the decedent's successor in interest only if there is no personal representative. The distributee of the cause of action in probate is the successor in interest or, if there is no distribution, the heir, devisee, trustee, or other successor has the right to proceed under this article. See Section 377.11 ("decedent's successor in interest" defined). See also Prob. Code § 58 ("personal representative" defined). The addition of the reference to the successor in interest makes the rules applicable to commencement of an action consistent with the rules applicable to continuation of a pending action. Thus, the distinction between commencing and continuing the decedent's action drawn in Everett v. Commissioner, T.C.M. (P–H) ¶ 89,124 (Mar. 27, 1989), is not applicable under Sections 377.30 and 377.31. [22 Cal.L.Rev.Comm.Reports 895 (1992)].

Research References

Rutter, Cal. Practice Guide: Civil Appeals & Writs Ch. 2-D, D. Standing to Appeal.
Rutter, Cal. Practice Guide: Civ. Pro. Before Trial Ch. 2-A, A. Standing to Sue-"Real Party in Interest" Requirement.
Rutter, Cal. Practice Guide: Insurance Litigation Ch. 15-A, A. Actions Against Insurers.
Rutter, Cal. Practice Guide: Personal Injury Ch. 3-B, B. Potential Claimants in a Personal Injury Case.
Rutter, Cal. Practice Guide: Personal Injury Ch. 3-G, G. Independent Damages Claims.
Rutter, Cal. Practice Guide: Personal Injury Ch. 5-B, B. When to Sue-Statute of Limitations.
Rutter, Cal. Practice Guide: Personal Injury Ch. 3-G, Outline G.
Miller and Starr California Real Estate § 21:32, Who is Liable for Usury Penalties.
3 Witkin Cal. Proc. 5th Actions § 15, Current Rule of Survivability.

3 Witkin Cal. Proc. 5th Actions § 717, (S 717) Death of Prospective Plaintiff.
4 Witkin Cal. Proc. 5th Pleading § 134, Personal Representative as Real Party in Interest.
6 Witkin, California Summary 10th Torts § 1273, Statutory Liability for Operation of Vessel.
6 Witkin, California Summary 10th Torts § 1378, in General.
14 Witkin, California Summary 10th Wills and Probate § 519, (S 519) Decedent's Cause of Action.
14 Witkin, California Summary 10th Wills and Probate § 521, (S 521) Wrongful Death.
14 Witkin, California Summary 10th Wills and Probate § 801, (S 801) Successor's Entitlement to Property.

§ 377.31. Pending action or proceeding; continuance

On motion after the death of a person who commenced an action or proceeding, the court shall allow a pending action or proceeding that does not abate to be continued by the decedent's personal representative or, if none, by the decedent's successor in interest. *(Added by Stats.1992, c. 178 (S.B.1496), § 20.)*

Law Revision Commission Comments

Section 377.31 restates part of former Section 385, but recognizes that the personal representative or successor in interest has an absolute right to be substituted for the decedent; substitution in this situation is not discretionary with the court. See, e.g., Pepper v. Superior Court, 76 Cal.App.3d 252, 260–61, 142 Cal.Rptr. 759 (1977). See also Section 377.11 ("decedent's successor in interest" defined); Prob.Code § 58 ("personal representative" defined).

This section is consistent with the application of former Section 385 in a federal Tax Court. See Everett v. Commissioner, T.C.M. (P–H) ¶ 89,124 (Mar. 27, 1989) (daughter of decedent petitioner substituted as party under federal rules adopting local law as to proper parties). [22 Cal.L.Rev.Comm.Reports 895 (1992)].

Research References

Rutter, Cal. Practice Guide: Civ. Pro. Before Trial Ch. 2-G, G. Substitution of Parties.
California Practice Guide: Employment Litigation Ch. 19-H, H. Other Pretrial Procedures.
4 Witkin Cal. Proc. 5th Pleading § 259, Necessity of Substitution.
4 Witkin Cal. Proc. 5th Pleading § 260, Procedure.
6 Witkin, California Summary 10th Torts § 1378, in General.
14 Witkin, California Summary 10th Wills and Probate § 519, (S 519) Decedent's Cause of Action.
14 Witkin, California Summary 10th Wills and Probate § 521, (S 521) Wrongful Death.

§ 377.32. Statement from successor in interest; information required

(a) The person who seeks to commence an action or proceeding or to continue a pending action or proceeding as the decedent's successor in interest under this article, shall execute and file an affidavit or a declaration under penalty of perjury under the laws of this state stating all of the following:

(1) The decedent's name.

(2) The date and place of the decedent's death.

(3) "No proceeding is now pending in California for administration of the decedent's estate."

(4) If the decedent's estate was administered, a copy of the final order showing the distribution of the decedent's cause of action to the successor in interest.

(5) Either of the following, as appropriate, with facts in support thereof:

(A) "The affiant or declarant is the decedent's successor in interest (as defined in Section 377.11 of the California Code of Civil Procedure) and succeeds to the decedent's interest in the action or proceeding."

(B) "The affiant or declarant is authorized to act on behalf of the decedent's successor in interest (as defined in Section 377.11

of the California Code of Civil Procedure) with respect to the decedent's interest in the action or proceeding."

(6) "No other person has a superior right to commence the action or proceeding or to be substituted for the decedent in the pending action or proceeding."

(7) "The affiant or declarant affirms or declares under penalty of perjury under the laws of the State of California that the foregoing is true and correct."

(b) Where more than one person executes the affidavit or declaration under this section, the statements required by subdivision (a) shall be modified as appropriate to reflect that fact.

(c) A certified copy of the decedent's death certificate shall be attached to the affidavit or declaration. *(Added by Stats.1992, c. 178 (S.B.1496), § 20.)*

Law Revision Commission Comments

Section 337.330 [sic] is new. The affidavit provided in this section is drawn from the affidavit provided in Probate Code Section 13101. [22 Cal.L.Rev.Comm.Reports 895 (1992)].

Research References

Rutter, Cal. Practice Guide: Civ. Pro. Before Trial Ch. 2-A, A. Standing to Sue-"Real Party in Interest" Requirement.
Rutter, Cal. Practice Guide: Civ. Pro. Before Trial Ch. 2-G, G. Substitution of Parties.
Rutter, Cal. Practice Guide: Personal Injury Ch. 5-B, B. When to Sue-Statute of Limitations.
18 NO. 4 Miller & Starr, California Real Estate Newsalert 40, Remedies.
14 Witkin, California Summary 10th Wills and Probate § 519, (S 519) Decedent's Cause of Action.

§ 377.33.   Court orders

The court in which an action is commenced or continued under this article may make any order concerning parties that is appropriate to ensure proper administration of justice in the case, including appointment of the decedent's successor in interest as a special administrator or guardian ad litem. *(Added by Stats.1992, c. 178 (S.B.1496), § 20.)*

Law Revision Commission Comments

Section 377.33 is new. The court in which the action or proceeding is pending has authority to resolve questions concerning the proper parties to the litigation and to make conclusive and binding orders, including determinations of the right of a successor in interest to commence or continue an action or proceeding. The references to appointment of the successor in interest as a special administrator or guardian ad litem are intended to recognize that there may be a need to impose fiduciary duties on the successor to protect the interests of other potential beneficiaries. See Code Civ.Proc. §§ 372–373.5 (guardian ad litem); Prob. Code §§ 8540–8547 (special administrator). [22 Cal.L.Rev.Comm.Reports 895 (1992)].

Research References

Rutter, Cal. Practice Guide: Civ. Pro. Before Trial Ch. 2-G, G. Substitution of Parties.
Rutter, Cal. Practice Guide: Civ. Pro. Before Trial Ch. 9(I)-F, F. Ex Parte Motions.
California Practice Guide: Employment Litigation Ch. 19-H, H. Other Pretrial Procedures.
14 Witkin, California Summary 10th Wills and Probate § 519, (S 519) Decedent's Cause of Action.

§ 377.34.   Damages recoverable

In an action or proceeding by a decedent's personal representative or successor in interest on the decedent's cause of action, the damages recoverable are limited to the loss or damage that the decedent sustained or incurred before death, including any penalties or punitive or exemplary damages that the decedent would have been entitled to recover had the decedent lived, and do not include damages for pain, suffering, or disfigurement. *(Added by Stats.1992, c. 178 (S.B.1496), § 20.)*

Law Revision Commission Comments

Section 377.34 restates former Probate Code Section 573(c) without substantive change, and adds the reference to the successor in interest. See Section 377.11 ("decedent's successor in interest" defined); Prob. Code § 58 ("personal representative" defined). The limitations in this section apply to the decedent's cause of action and not to a cause of action that others may have for the wrongful death of the decedent. See Sections 377.60–377.62 (wrongful death). [22 Cal.L.Rev.Comm.Reports 895 (1992)].

Research References

Rutter, Cal. Practice Guide: Civ. Pro. Before Trial Ch. 2-A, A. Standing to Sue-"Real Party in Interest" Requirement.
Rutter, Cal. Practice Guide: Civ. Pro. Before Trial Ch. 2-G, G. Substitution of Parties.
Rutter, Cal. Practice Guide: Civil Trials & Evidence Ch. 17-C, C. Entry of Judgment.
Rutter, Cal. Practice Guide: Civil Trials & Evidence Ch. 8G-D, D. Burdens and Standards of Proof.
California Practice Guide: Employment Litigation Ch. 17-C, C. Extracontractual Compensatory Damages (Tort and Statutory).
California Practice Guide: Employment Litigation Ch. 19-H, H. Other Pretrial Procedures.
Rutter, Cal. Practice Guide: Insurance Litigation Ch. 15-A, A. Actions Against Insurers.
Rutter, Cal. Practice Guide: Personal Injury Ch. 3-B, B. Potential Claimants in a Personal Injury Case.
Rutter, Cal. Practice Guide: Personal Injury Ch. 3-E, E. Punitive Damages.
Rutter, Cal. Practice Guide: Personal Injury Ch. 3-F, F. MICRA Provisions Affecting Damages.
Rutter, Cal. Practice Guide: Personal Injury Ch. 3-G, G. Independent Damages Claims.
Miller and Starr California Real Estate § 21:30, Who Can Raise the Defense of Usury--Successors in Interest; Grantees.
Miller and Starr California Real Estate § 34:39, Damages for Pain and Suffering.
Miller and Starr California Real Estate § 34:93, Punitive Damages--Basis of the Award; Burden of Proof.
3 Witkin Cal. Proc. 5th Actions § 16, (S 16) Statutory Rules and Exceptions.
3 Witkin Cal. Proc. 5th Actions § 17, (S 17) Illustrations.
3 Witkin Cal. Proc. 5th Actions § 45, (S 45) Distinction Between Substance and Procedure.
9 Witkin Cal. Proc. 5th Appeal § 406, Exceptions to Requirement.
1 Witkin Cal. Proc. 5th Attorneys § 324, (S 324) Illustrations.
5 Witkin, California Summary 10th Torts § 23, (S 23) Survival of Tort Liability.
5 Witkin, California Summary 10th Torts § 230, (S 230) No Punitive Damages.
6 Witkin, California Summary 10th Torts § 1273, Statutory Liability for Operation of Vessel.
6 Witkin, California Summary 10th Torts § 1671, in General.
6 Witkin, California Summary 10th Torts § 1686, Statutory Remedies.
8 Witkin, California Summary 10th Constitutional Law § 841, (S 841) in General.
14 Witkin, California Summary 10th Wills and Probate § 519, (S 519) Decedent's Cause of Action.
14 Witkin, California Summary 10th Wills and Probate § 521, (S 521) Wrongful Death.

§ 377.35.   Application of article

On or after January 1, 1993, this article applies to the commencement of an action or proceeding the decedent was entitled to commence, and to the continuation of an action or proceeding commenced by the decedent, regardless of whether the decedent died before, on, or after January 1, 1993. *(Added by Stats.1992, c. 178 (S.B.1496), § 20.)*

Law Revision Commission Comments

Section 377.35 makes clear that, as of the operative date, the procedures provided by this article apply regardless of the date of the decedent's death. Thus, for example, if the limitations period provided in Section 366.1 has not run, a successor in interest of a decedent who died before January 1, 1993, may proceed under this article, assuming that a personal representative has not been appointed. See, e.g., Section 377.30 (commencement of action by personal representative or, if none, by successor in interest). However, if the limitations period under Section 366.1 has run before January 1, 1993, this article cannot be applied to revive the cause of action. Similarly, an action commenced by a decedent who died before January 1, 1993, may be continued by a successor in interest or personal representative as provided in this article. [22 Cal.L.Rev.Comm.Reports 895 (1992)].

ARTICLE 4. CAUSE OF ACTION AGAINST DECEDENT

Section
377.40. Persons subject to suit.
377.41. Pending actions; continuance; restrictions.
377.42. Damages recoverable.
377.43. Application of article.

§ 377.40. Persons subject to suit

Subject to Part 4 (commencing with Section 9000) of Division 7 of the Probate Code governing creditor claims, a cause of action against a decedent that survives may be asserted against the decedent's personal representative or, to the extent provided by statute, against the decedent's successor in interest. *(Added by Stats.1992, c. 178 (S.B.1496), § 20.)*

Law Revision Commission Comments

Section 377.40 restates a portion of the first sentence of former Code of Civil Procedure Section 353(b) and part of former Probate Code Section 573(a) without substantive change. For special rules providing direct liability of successors in interest, see, e.g., Prob. Code §§ 13109 (transferee of property by affidavit), 13550 (surviving spouse who takes property without administration).

The introductory portion of Section 377.40, referring to Part 4 (creditor claims) of Division 7 of the Probate Code, is intended for cross-referencing purposes. See Prob. Code §§ 9350–9399 (claims in litigation). For special rules governing liability covered by insurance, see Code Civ.Proc. § 377.50; Prob. Code §§ 550–555.

See also Code Civ.Proc. § 377.11 ("decedent's successor in interest" defined); Prob. Code § 58 ("personal representative" defined). [22 Cal.L.Rev.Comm.Reports 895 (1992)].

Research References

Rutter, Cal. Practice Guide: Insurance Litigation Ch. 15-A, A. Actions Against Insurers.
Rutter, Cal. Practice Guide: Personal Injury Ch. 5-B, B. When to Sue- Statute of Limitations.
Miller and Starr California Real Estate § 21:32, Who is Liable for Usury Penalties.
3 Witkin Cal. Proc. 5th Actions § 15, Current Rule of Survivability.
3 Witkin Cal. Proc. 5th Actions § 718, Survival of Action.
4 Witkin Cal. Proc. 5th Pleading § 134, Personal Representative as Real Party in Interest.
6 Witkin, California Summary 10th Torts § 1273, Statutory Liability for Operation of Vessel.
14 Witkin, California Summary 10th Wills and Probate § 515, (S 515) Decedent's Liability Covered by Insurance.
14 Witkin, California Summary 10th Wills and Probate § 520, (S 520) Cause of Action Against Decedent.

§ 377.41. Pending actions; continuance; restrictions

On motion, the court shall allow a pending action or proceeding against the decedent that does not abate to be continued against the decedent's personal representative or, to the extent provided by statute, against the decedent's successor in interest, except that the court may not permit an action or proceeding to be continued against the personal representative unless proof of compliance with Part 4 (commencing with Section 9000) of Division 7 of the Probate Code governing creditor claims is first made. *(Added by Stats.1992, c. 178 (S.B.1496), § 20.)*

Law Revision Commission Comments

Section 377.41 supersedes part of former Section 385. An action or proceeding may be continued against the decedent's successor in interest only if a statute provides for liability in such cases. For special rules providing direct liability of successors in interest, see, e.g., Prob.Code §§ 13109 (transferee of property by affidavit), 13550 (surviving spouse who takes property without administration), 18201 (trust assets). See also Section 377.11 ("decedent's successor in interest" defined); Prob. Code § 58 ("personal representative" defined); Veh. Code § 17452 (continuation of action against personal representative of nonresident defendant involved in motor vehicle accident). [22 Cal.L.Rev.Comm.Reports 895 (1992)].

Research References

Rutter, Cal. Practice Guide: Civ. Pro. Before Trial Ch. 2-G, G. Substitution of Parties.
4 Witkin Cal. Proc. 5th Pleading § 259, Necessity of Substitution.
4 Witkin Cal. Proc. 5th Pleading § 260, Procedure.
14 Witkin, California Summary 10th Wills and Probate § 432, Service of Process.
14 Witkin, California Summary 10th Wills and Probate § 520, (S 520) Cause of Action Against Decedent.

§ 377.42. Damages recoverable

In an action or proceeding against a decedent's personal representative or, to the extent provided by statute, against the decedent's successor in interest, on a cause of action against the decedent, all damages are recoverable that might have been recovered against the decedent had the decedent lived except damages recoverable under Section 3294 of the Civil Code or other punitive or exemplary damages. *(Added by Stats.1992, c. 178 (S.B.1496), § 20.)*

Law Revision Commission Comments

Section 377.42 restates former Probate Code Section 573(b) without substantive change, and applies the rule to successors in interest, to the extent they are liable. See Comments to Sections 377.40 & 377.41. See also Code Civ.Proc. § 377.11 ("decedent's successor in interest" defined); Prob. Code § 58 ("personal representative" defined). [22 Cal.L.Rev.Comm.Reports 895 (1992)].

Research References

Rutter, Cal. Practice Guide: Civil Appeals & Writs Ch. 2-D, D. Standing to Appeal.
Rutter, Cal. Practice Guide: Civ. Pro. Before Trial Ch. 2-G, G. Substitution of Parties.
Rutter, Cal. Practice Guide: Insurance Litigation Ch. 15-A, A. Actions Against Insurers.
Rutter, Cal. Practice Guide: Personal Injury Ch. 3-B, B. Potential Claimants in a Personal Injury Case.
Rutter, Cal. Practice Guide: Personal Injury Ch. 3-E, E. Punitive Damages.
Rutter, Cal. Practice Guide: Personal Injury Ch. 3-G, G. Independent Damages Claims.
Miller and Starr California Real Estate § 21:32, Who is Liable for Usury Penalties.
Miller and Starr California Real Estate § 34:93, Punitive Damages--Basis of the Award; Burden of Proof.
3 Witkin Cal. Proc. 5th Actions § 16, (S 16) Statutory Rules and Exceptions.
5 Witkin, California Summary 10th Torts § 23, (S 23) Survival of Tort Liability.
6 Witkin, California Summary 10th Torts § 1273, Statutory Liability for Operation of Vessel.
6 Witkin, California Summary 10th Torts § 1580, in General.
14 Witkin, California Summary 10th Wills and Probate § 520, (S 520) Cause of Action Against Decedent.

§ 377.43. Application of article

This article applies to the commencement on or after January 1, 1993, of an action or proceeding against the decedent's personal representative or successor in interest, or to the making of a motion on or after January 1, 1993, to continue a pending action or proceeding against the decedent's personal representative or successor in interest, regardless of whether the decedent died before, on, or after January 1, 1993. *(Added by Stats.1992, c. 178 (S.B.1496), § 20.)*

Law Revision Commission Comments

Section 377.43 makes clear that, as of the operative date, the procedures provided by this article apply to commencing an action, or making a motion to continue an action, against a personal representative or successor in interest regardless of the date of the decedent's death. Thus, for example, if a motion to substitute a successor in interest as a defendant has been made before January 1, 1993, this article would not apply to the case. A motion made after January 1, 1993, would be governed by this article even though the decedent died before that date. See, e.g., Section 377.41 (continuation of pending action against personal representative or successor in interest). [22 Cal.L.Rev.Comm.Reports 895 (1992)].

ARTICLE 5. INSURED CLAIMS

Section
377.50. Commencement or continuance of action.

§ 377.50. Commencement or continuance of action

An action to establish the decedent's liability for which the decedent was protected by insurance may be commenced or continued against the decedent's estate as provided in Chapter 1 (commencing with Section 550) of Part 13 of Division 2 of the Probate Code. *(Added by Stats.1992, c. 178 (S.B.1496), § 20.)*

Law Revision Commission Comments

Section 377.50 is a new provision that provides a cross-reference to the special provisions in the Probate Code concerning insured claims against the decedent. [22 Cal.L.Rev.Comm.Reports 895 (1992)].

Research References

Rutter, Cal. Practice Guide: Civ. Pro. Before Trial Ch. 2-G, G. Substitution of Parties.
3 Witkin Cal. Proc. 5th Actions § 718, Survival of Action.
14 Witkin, California Summary 10th Wills and Probate § 520, (S 520) Cause of Action Against Decedent.

ARTICLE 6. WRONGFUL DEATH

Section
377.60. Persons with standing.
377.61. Damages recoverable.
377.62. Joinder with decedent's cause of action.

§ 377.60. Persons with standing

A cause of action for the death of a person caused by the wrongful act or neglect of another may be asserted by any of the following persons or by the decedent's personal representative on their behalf:

(a) The decedent's surviving spouse, domestic partner, children, and issue of deceased children, or, if there is no surviving issue of the decedent, the persons, including the surviving spouse or domestic partner, who would be entitled to the property of the decedent by intestate succession.

(b) Whether or not qualified under subdivision (a), if they were dependent on the decedent, the putative spouse, children of the putative spouse, stepchildren, or parents. As used in this subdivision, "putative spouse" means the surviving spouse of a void or voidable marriage who is found by the court to have believed in good faith that the marriage to the decedent was valid.

(c) A minor, whether or not qualified under subdivision (a) or (b), if, at the time of the decedent's death, the minor resided for the previous 180 days in the decedent's household and was dependent on the decedent for one-half or more of the minor's support.

(d) This section applies to any cause of action arising on or after January 1, 1993.

(e) The addition of this section by Chapter 178 of the Statutes of 1992 was not intended to adversely affect the standing of any party having standing under prior law, and the standing of parties governed by that version of this section as added by Chapter 178 of the Statutes of 1992 shall be the same as specified herein as amended by Chapter 563 of the Statutes of 1996.

(f)(1) For the purpose of this section, "domestic partner" means a person who, at the time of the decedent's death, was the domestic partner of the decedent in a registered domestic partnership established in accordance with subdivision (b) of Section 297 of the Family Code.

(2) Notwithstanding paragraph (1), for a death occurring prior to January 1, 2002, a person may maintain a cause of action pursuant to this section as a domestic partner of the decedent by establishing the factors listed in paragraphs (1) to (6), inclusive, of subdivision (b) of Section 297 of the Family Code, as it read pursuant to Section 3 of Chapter 893 of the Statutes of 2001, prior to its becoming inoperative on January 1, 2005.

(3) The amendments made to this subdivision during the 2003–04 Regular Session of the Legislature are not intended to revive any cause of action that has been fully and finally adjudicated by the courts, or that has been settled, or as to which the applicable limitations period has run. *(Added by Stats.1992, c. 178 (S.B.1496), § 20. Amended by Stats.1996, c. 563 (S.B.392), § 1; Stats.1997, c. 13 (S.B.449), § 1, eff. May 23, 1997; Stats. 2001, c. 893 (A.B.25), § 2; Stats.2004, c. 947 (A.B.2580), § 1.)*

Law Revision Commission Comments

Section 377.60 restates subdivision (b) and the first part of the first sentence of subdivision (a) of former Section 377 without substantive change, except as discussed below. If the wrongdoer dies before or after the decedent, the cause of action provided in this section may be asserted against the personal representative of the wrongdoer. See Sections 377.20 (survival of cause of action), 377.40 (assertion of cause of action against decedent). See also Prob.Code § 6400 *et seq.* (intestate succession). Unlike other provisions of this chapter that relate to causes of action belonging to the decedent, this article relates to a cause of action for the decedent's wrongful death, which belongs not to the decedent, but to the persons specified in this section. Thus, the cause of action is not property in the estate of the decedent, and the authority of the personal representative to assert the cause of action is for administrative convenience only and is not for the benefit of creditors or other persons interested in the decedent's estate.

Subdivision (a) revises the language of former Section 377(b)(1) to refer specifically to the decedent's surviving spouse, children, and issue of deceased children, as proper parties plaintiff in a wrongful death action. This makes clear that, even if the decedent's estate is entirely community property, the decedent's children and issue of deceased children are proper parties plaintiff, along with the decedent's surviving spouse. This codifies Fiske v. Wilkie, 67 Cal.App.2d 440, 444, 154 P.2d 725 (1945). Under Probate Code Section 258, Section 377.60 is subject to the rules relating to the effect of homicide. This changes the rule of Marks v. Lyerla, 1 Cal.App.4th 556, 2 Cal.Rptr.2d 63 (1991).

For background, see *Standing To Sue for Wrongful Death*, 22 Cal.L.Revision Comm'n Reports 955 (1992). [22 Cal.L.Rev.Comm.Reports 895 (1992)].

Research References

Rutter, Cal. Practice Guide: Civ. Pro. Before Trial Ch. 2-A, A. Standing to Sue-"Real Party in Interest" Requirement.
Rutter, Cal. Practice Guide: Civ. Pro. Before Trial Ch. 2-E, E. Intervention.
Rutter, Cal. Practice Guide: Civ. Pro. Before Trial Gen. Matls., Highlights.

Rutter, Cal. Practice Guide: Civil Trials & Evidence Ch. 8D-D, D. Hearsay Exceptions.

Rutter, Cal. Practice Guide: Civil Trials & Evidence Ch. 8E-A, A. Privileges.

Rutter, Cal. Practice Guide: Family Law Gen. Matls, Highlights.

Rutter, Cal. Practice Guide: Fed.Civ.Pro. Before Trial Ch. 2C-3, How "Citizenship" Determined.

Rutter, Cal. Practice Guide: Personal Injury Ch. 3-B, B. Potential Claimants in a Personal Injury Case.

Rutter, Cal. Practice Guide: Personal Injury Ch. 3-G, G. Independent Damages Claims.

15 NO. 4 Miller & Starr, California Real Estate Newsalert 11, Holding Title.

17 NO. 3 Miller & Starr, California Real Estate Newsalert 1, Always a Bridesmaid? Unveiling California's Domestic Partner Laws, Including Their Impact on Real Property.

3 Witkin Cal. Proc. 5th Actions § 590, (S 590) Wrongful Death.

3 Witkin Cal. Proc. 5th Actions § 707, Representative With Right to Sue.

4 Witkin Cal. Proc. 5th Pleading § 145, (S 145) Wrongful Death.

4 Witkin Cal. Proc. 5th Pleading § 193, (S 193) Joinder Required by Special Statutes.

4 Witkin Cal. Proc. 5th Pleading § 201, (S 201) Wrongful Death.

11 Witkin, California Summary 10th Husband and Wife § 33, Other Rights.

6 Witkin, California Summary 10th Torts § 948, Persons Who Did Not Sign: in General.

6 Witkin, California Summary 10th Torts § 1378, in General.

6 Witkin, California Summary 10th Torts § 1381, Scope of Action.

6 Witkin, California Summary 10th Torts § 1382, No Action for Death of Unborn Child.

6 Witkin, California Summary 10th Torts § 1385, in General.

6 Witkin, California Summary 10th Torts § 1389, Listed Persons Under Current Law.

6 Witkin, California Summary 10th Torts § 1390, Putative Spouse.

6 Witkin, California Summary 10th Torts § 1391, Domestic Partner.

6 Witkin, California Summary 10th Torts § 1393, Child of Presumed Parent.

6 Witkin, California Summary 10th Torts § 1394, Other Persons.

6 Witkin, California Summary 10th Torts § 1397, Other Persons.

6 Witkin, California Summary 10th Torts § 1513, (S 1513) Physical Injury or Wrongful Death.

6 Witkin, California Summary 10th Torts § 1661, Wrongful Death.

6 Witkin, California Summary 10th Torts § 1683, No Recovery by Child.

6 Witkin, California Summary 10th Torts § 1690, Recovery of Loss.

14 Witkin, California Summary 10th Wills and Probate § 521, (S 521) Wrongful Death.

2 Witkin Cal. Summ. 10th Workers' Compensation § 69, (S 69) in General.

§ 377.61. Damages recoverable

In an action under this article, damages may be awarded that, under all the circumstances of the case, may be just, but may not include damages recoverable under Section 377.34. The court shall determine the respective rights in an award of the persons entitled to assert the cause of action. *(Added by Stats.1992, c. 178 (S.B.1496), § 20.)*

Law Revision Commission Comments

Section 377.61 restates the third and fourth sentences of former Section 377(a) without substantive change. [22 Cal.L.Rev.Comm.Reports 895 (1992)].

Research References

Rutter, Cal. Practice Guide: Civ. Pro. Before Trial Ch. 2-C, C. Joinder of Parties.

Rutter, Cal. Practice Guide: Civ. Pro. Before Trial Ch. 12(I)-D, D. Demand for Jury Trial and Waiver.

Rutter, Cal. Practice Guide: Personal Injury Ch. 3-G, G. Independent Damages Claims.

7 Witkin Cal. Proc. 5th Trial § 94, Special Proceedings.

7 Witkin Cal. Proc. 5th Trial § 348, Procedure and Judge's Discretion.

6 Witkin, California Summary 10th Torts § 1380, Lump Sum Verdict.

6 Witkin, California Summary 10th Torts § 1690, Recovery of Loss.

6 Witkin, California Summary 10th Torts § 1691, Value of Society and Companionship.

14 Witkin, California Summary 10th Wills and Probate § 521, (S 521) Wrongful Death.

§ 377.62. Joinder with decedent's cause of action

(a) An action under Section 377.30 may be joined with an action under Section 377.60 arising out of the same wrongful act or neglect.

(b) An action under Section 377.60 and an action under Section 377.31 arising out of the same wrongful act or neglect may be consolidated for trial as provided in Section 1048. *(Added by Stats.1992, c. 178 (S.B.1496), § 20.)*

Law Revision Commission Comments

Subdivision (a) of Section 377.62 restates and generalizes the fifth sentence of former Section 377(a).

Subdivision (b) replaces the last sentence of former Section 377(a). This subdivision incorporates the general provision governing consolidation of actions which recognizes the court's discretion to order consolidation. Former Section 377(a) provided that the court "shall" order consolidation on motion of an interested party. [22 Cal.L.Rev.Comm.Reports 895 (1992)].

Research References

Rutter, Cal. Practice Guide: Civ. Pro. Before Trial Ch. 12(I)-E, E. Consolidation, Coordination and Bifurcation.

Rutter, Cal. Practice Guide: Civil Trials & Evidence Ch. 4-H, H. Motions to Consolidate or Coordinate Separate Cases.

4 Witkin Cal. Proc. 5th Pleading § 342, Statutory Basis.

6 Witkin, California Summary 10th Torts § 1378, in General.

6 Witkin, California Summary 10th Torts § 1586, (S 1586) Personal Torts.

14 Witkin, California Summary 10th Wills and Probate § 521, (S 521) Wrongful Death.

CHAPTER 5.   PERMISSIVE JOINDER

§ 378.   Plaintiffs; joinder; relief granted

(a) All persons may join in one action as plaintiffs if:

(1) They assert any right to relief jointly, severally, or in the alternative, in respect of or arising out of the same transaction, occurrence, or series of transactions or occurrences and if any question of law or fact common to all these persons will arise in the action; or

(2) They have a claim, right, or interest adverse to the defendant in the property or controversy which is the subject of the action.

(b) It is not necessary that each plaintiff be interested as to every cause of action or as to all relief prayed for. Judgment may be given for one or more of the plaintiffs according to their respective right to relief. *(Enacted in 1872. Amended by Stats.1927, c. 386, p. 631, § 1; Stats.1971, c. 244, p. 374, § 4, operative July 1, 1972.)*

Research References

Rutter, Cal. Practice Guide: Civ. Pro. Before Trial Ch. 2-C, C. Joinder of Parties.

Rutter, Cal. Practice Guide: Civ. Pro. Before Trial Ch. 6-D, D. Cross-Complaint.

Rutter, Cal. Practice Guide: Civ. Pro. Before Trial Ch. 7(I)-A, A. Demurrers.

Rutter, Cal. Practice Guide: Civil Trials & Evidence Ch. 4-G, G. Motion to Sever or Bifurcate.
Rutter, Cal. Practice Guide: Fed.Civ.Pro. Before Trial Ch. 1-D, D. Choosing Between State and Federal Courts.
Rutter, Cal. Practice Guide: Personal Injury Ch. 5-C, C. Selected Issues Affecting Parties.
Rutter, Cal. Practice Guide: Personal Injury Ch. 5-E, E. Selected Pleading Issues.
Miller and Starr California Real Estate § 28:112, Proper Parties in Suit Against Surety; Necessity of Suit Against or Joinder of the Principal.
Miller and Starr California Real Estate § 25B:101, Enforcement of the Restrictions.
3 Witkin Cal. Proc. 5th Actions § 872, (S 872) Parties Covered.
7 Witkin Cal. Proc. 5th Judgment § 38, (S 38) in General.
4 Witkin Cal. Proc. 5th Pleading § 69, (S 69) Party Must be an Entity.
4 Witkin Cal. Proc. 5th Pleading § 173, (S 173) Origin and Nature of Joinder Rules.
4 Witkin Cal. Proc. 5th Pleading § 178, Permissive Joinder.
4 Witkin Cal. Proc. 5th Pleading § 179, (S 179) Legislative Revision of 1971.
4 Witkin Cal. Proc. 5th Pleading § 194, in General.
4 Witkin Cal. Proc. 5th Pleading § 195, (S 195) Nature and Scope of Transaction Clause.
4 Witkin Cal. Proc. 5th Pleading § 198, in General.
4 Witkin Cal. Proc. 5th Pleading § 211, (S 211) Separate Trials.
4 Witkin Cal. Proc. 5th Pleading § 223, (S 223) Before or During Trial.
4 Witkin Cal. Proc. 5th Pleading § 334, (S 334) Classes of Causes.
9 Witkin, California Summary 10th Corporations § 173, Joinder.

§ 379. Defendants; joinder

(a) All persons may be joined in one action as defendants if there is asserted against them:

(1) Any right to relief jointly, severally, or in the alternative, in respect of or arising out of the same transaction, occurrence, or series of transactions or occurrences and if any question of law or fact common to all these persons will arise in the action; or

(2) A claim, right, or interest adverse to them in the property or controversy which is the subject of the action.

(b) It is not necessary that each defendant be interested as to every cause of action or as to all relief prayed for. Judgment may be given against one or more defendants according to their respective liabilities.

(c) Where the plaintiff is in doubt as to the person from whom he or she is entitled to redress, he or she may join two or more defendants, with the intent that the question as to which, if any, of the defendants is liable, and to what extent, may be determined between the parties. *(Enacted in 1872. Amended by Stats.1971, c. 244, p. 375, § 5, operative July 1, 1972; Stats.1971, c. 950, p. 1857, § 1, operative July 1, 1972; Stats.1975, c. 1241, p. 3190, § 6.)*

Research References

Rutter, Cal. Practice Guide: Civ. Pro. Before Trial Ch. 2-C, C. Joinder of Parties.
Rutter, Cal. Practice Guide: Civ. Pro. Before Trial Ch. 6-B, B. Complaints.
Rutter, Cal. Practice Guide: Civ. Pro. Before Trial Ch. 6-D, D. Cross-Complaint.
Rutter, Cal. Practice Guide: Civ. Pro. Before Trial Ch. 7(I)-A, A. Demurrers.
California Practice Guide: Employment Litigation Ch. 19-C, C. Plaintiff's Complaint.
Rutter, Cal. Practice Guide: Fed.Civ.Pro. Before Trial Ch. 1-D, D. Choosing Between State and Federal Courts.
Rutter, Cal. Practice Guide: Personal Injury Ch. 5-C, C. Selected Issues Affecting Parties.
Rutter, Cal. Practice Guide: Personal Injury Ch. 5-E, E. Selected Pleading Issues.
Miller and Starr California Real Estate § 28:112, Proper Parties in Suit Against Surety; Necessity of Suit Against or Joinder of the Principal.
Miller and Starr California Real Estate § 34:107, Identification of Defendants.

7 Witkin Cal. Proc. 5th Judgment § 38, (S 38) in General.
4 Witkin Cal. Proc. 5th Pleading § 178, Permissive Joinder.
4 Witkin Cal. Proc. 5th Pleading § 179, (S 179) Legislative Revision of 1971.
4 Witkin Cal. Proc. 5th Pleading § 198, in General.
4 Witkin Cal. Proc. 5th Pleading § 199, (S 199) in General.
4 Witkin Cal. Proc. 5th Pleading § 204, (S 204) Nature of Statute.
4 Witkin Cal. Proc. 5th Pleading § 205, (S 205) Method of Pleading.
4 Witkin Cal. Proc. 5th Pleading § 211, (S 211) Separate Trials.
4 Witkin Cal. Proc. 5th Pleading § 223, (S 223) Before or During Trial.

§ 379.5. Order preventing embarrassment, etc.; separate trials

When parties have been joined under Section 378 or 379, the court may make such orders as may appear just to prevent any party from being embarrassed, delayed, or put to undue expense, and may order separate trials or make such other order as the interests of justice may require. *(Added by Stats.1971, c. 244, p. 375, § 9, operative July 1, 1972.)*

Research References

Rutter, Cal. Practice Guide: Civ. Pro. Before Trial Ch. 2-C, C. Joinder of Parties.
Rutter, Cal. Practice Guide: Civ. Pro. Before Trial Ch. 7(I)-A, A. Demurrers.
Rutter, Cal. Practice Guide: Civ. Pro. Before Trial Ch. 12(I)-E, E. Consolidation, Coordination and Bifurcation.
Rutter, Cal. Practice Guide: Civil Trials & Evidence Ch. 4-G, G. Motion to Sever or Bifurcate.
Rutter, Cal. Practice Guide: Civil Trials & Evidence Ch. 4-G, Outline G.
4 Witkin Cal. Proc. 5th Pleading § 196, (S 196) Tort Transaction.
4 Witkin Cal. Proc. 5th Pleading § 207, Torts to Person.
4 Witkin Cal. Proc. 5th Pleading § 211, (S 211) Separate Trials.

§ 382. Nonconsent to joinder as plaintiff; representative actions

If the consent of any one who should have been joined as plaintiff cannot be obtained, he may be made a defendant, the reason thereof being stated in the complaint; and when the question is one of a common or general interest, of many persons, or when the parties are numerous, and it is impracticable to bring them all before the court, one or more may sue or defend for the benefit of all. *(Enacted in 1872. Amended by Stats.1971, c. 244, p. 375, § 12, operative July 1, 1972.)*

Research References

Rutter, Cal. Practice Guide: Civ. Pro. Before Trial Ch. 2-C, C. Joinder of Parties.
Rutter, Cal. Practice Guide: Civ. Pro. Before Trial Ch. 5-A, A. General.
Rutter, Cal. Practice Guide: Civ. Pro. Before Trial Ch. 14-A, A. General Considerations.
Rutter, Cal. Practice Guide: Civ. Pro. Before Trial Ch. 14-B, B. Class Action Requirements-In General.
Rutter, Cal. Practice Guide: Civ. Pro. Before Trial Ch. 14-C, C. Procedural Issues.
Rutter, Cal. Practice Guide: Civ. Pro. Before Trial Gen. Matls., Highlights.
California Practice Guide: Employment Litigation Ch. 11-J, J. Enforcing California Laws Regulating Employee Compensation.
California Practice Guide: Employment Litigation Ch. 19-C, C. Plaintiff's Complaint.
California Practice Guide: Employment Litigation Ch. 19-H, H. Other Pretrial Procedures.
California Practice Guide: Employment Litigation Ch. 19-H, Outline H.
Rutter, Cal. Practice Guide: Fed.Civ.Pro. Before Trial Ch. 2C-6, Limitation-Party Joinder Requirements.
Rutter, Cal. Practice Guide: Insurance Litigation Ch. 9-F, F. Amount Recoverable by Insurer Under Subrogation.
Rutter, Cal. Practice Guide: Insurance Litigation Ch. 9-G, G. Procedures to Enforce Subrogation Right.
Rutter, Cal. Practice Guide: Insurance Litigation Ch. 11-K, K. Statutory Liability.
Rutter, Cal. Practice Guide: Insurance Litigation Ch. 15-A, A. Actions Against Insurers.

Rutter, Cal. Practice Guide: Personal Injury Ch. 5-C, C. Selected Issues Affecting Parties.

Miller and Starr California Real Estate § 18:12, Distribution of Unclaimed Class Action Judgments.

Miller and Starr California Real Estate § 25B:108, Homeowner's Actions.

Miller and Starr California Real Estate § 25B:110, Actions for Construction Defects.

3 Witkin Cal. Proc. 5th Actions § 898, (S 898) Nominal Defendant.

4 Witkin Cal. Proc. 5th Pleading § 68, (S 68) Party Appearing as Both Plaintiff and Defendant.

4 Witkin Cal. Proc. 5th Pleading § 133, Rights of Partial Subrogee and Subrogor.

4 Witkin Cal. Proc. 5th Pleading § 170, (S 170) Other Examples.

4 Witkin Cal. Proc. 5th Pleading § 176, Compulsory Joinder.

4 Witkin Cal. Proc. 5th Pleading § 209, (S 209) Joinder of Unwilling Party.

4 Witkin Cal. Proc. 5th Pleading § 268, (S 268) California Law and Uniform Act.

4 Witkin Cal. Proc. 5th Pleading § 271, in General.

4 Witkin Cal. Proc. 5th Pleading § 277, (S 277) Superiority of Pending Federal Action.

4 Witkin Cal. Proc. 5th Pleading § 278, (S 278) in General.

4 Witkin Cal. Proc. 5th Pleading § 281, (S 281) in General.

4 Witkin Cal. Proc. 5th Pleading § 297, Illustrations.

4 Witkin Cal. Proc. 5th Pleading § 302, Statutory Authorization.

4 Witkin Cal. Proc. 5th Pleading § 303, Fraud in Sales.

4 Witkin Cal. Proc. 5th Pleading § 311, (S 311) Factors Considered by Court.

4 Witkin Cal. Proc. 5th Pleading § 321, (S 321) Election to be Included.

4 Witkin Cal. Proc. 5th Pleading § 331, (S 331) Distribution of Unpaid Residuals.

7 Witkin Cal. Proc. 5th Trial § 42, (S 42) in General.

6 Witkin, California Summary 10th Torts § 1386, Effect of Settlement by One Plaintiff.

6 Witkin, California Summary 10th Torts § 1387, Action by Omitted Heir.

13 Witkin, California Summary 10th Equity § 124, Parties.

13 Witkin, California Summary 10th Equity § 127, (S 127) Disgorgement of Unlawful Profits Into Fluid Recovery Fund.

13 Witkin, California Summary 10th Equity § 124B, (S 124B) (New)-Standing Established Under Proposition 64.

§ 384. Distribution of unpaid residuals in class action litigation

(a) It is the intent of the Legislature in enacting this section to ensure that the unpaid residuals in class action litigation are distributed, to the extent possible, in a manner designed either to further the purposes of the underlying causes of action, or to promote justice for all Californians. The Legislature finds that the use of funds collected by the State Bar pursuant to this section for these purposes is in the public interest, is a proper use of the funds, and is consistent with essential public and governmental purposes.

(b) Except as provided in subdivision (c), prior to the entry of any judgment in a class action established pursuant to Section 382, the court shall determine the total amount that will be payable to all class members, if all class members are paid the amount to which they are entitled pursuant to the judgment. The court shall also set a date when the parties shall report to the court the total amount that was actually paid to the class members. After the report is received, the court shall amend the judgment to direct the defendant to pay the sum of the unpaid residue, plus interest on that sum at the legal rate of interest from the date of entry of the initial judgment, to nonprofit organizations or foundations to support projects that will benefit the class or similarly situated persons, or that promote the law consistent with the objectives and purposes of the underlying cause of action, to child advocacy programs, or to nonprofit organizations providing civil legal services to the indigent. The court shall ensure that the distribution of any unpaid residual derived from multistate or national cases brought under California law shall provide substantial or commensurate benefit to California consumers.

(c) This section shall not apply to any class action brought against any public entity, as defined in Section 811.2 of the Government Code, or against any public employee, as defined in Section 811.4 of the Government Code. However, this section shall not be construed to abrogate any equitable cy pres remedy which may be available in any class action with regard to all or part of the residue. *(Formerly § 383, added by Stats.1993, c. 863 (S.B.536), § 2. Renumbered § 384 and amended by Stats.1994, c. 146 (A.B.3601), § 19. Amended by Stats.1994, c. 237 (S.B.2105), § 1, eff. July 18, 1994; Stats.2001, c. 96 (S.B.1218), § 2.)*

Research References

Rutter, Cal. Practice Guide: Civ. Pro. Before Trial Ch. 14-C, C. Procedural Issues.

Rutter, Cal. Practice Guide: Civil Trials & Evidence Ch. 18-C, C. Other Post-Trial Motions.

4 Witkin Cal. Proc. 5th Pleading § 176, Compulsory Joinder.

4 Witkin Cal. Proc. 5th Pleading § 178, Permissive Joinder.

4 Witkin Cal. Proc. 5th Pleading § 296, Fluid Class Recovery.

4 Witkin Cal. Proc. 5th Pleading § 331, (S 331) Distribution of Unpaid Residuals.

13 Witkin, California Summary 10th Equity § 127, (S 127) Disgorgement of Unlawful Profits Into Fluid Recovery Fund.

CHAPTER 6. INTERPLEADER

§ 386. Interpleader

(a) **[Defendant in action on contract or for specific personal property; substitution of third party claimant or cross-complaint; deposit in court or delivery; discharge from liability; action against conflicting claimants]** A defendant, against whom an action is pending upon a contract, or for specific personal property, may, at any time before answer, upon affidavit that a person not a party to the action makes against him, and without any collusion with him, a demand upon such contract, or for such property, upon notice to such person and the adverse party, apply to the court for an order to substitute such person in his place, and discharge him from liability to either party, on his depositing in court the amount claimed on the contract, or delivering the property or its value to such person as the court may direct; and the court may, in its discretion, make the order; or such defendant may file a verified cross-complaint in interpleader, admitting that he has no interest in such amount or such property claimed, or in a portion of such amount or such property and alleging that all or such portion of the amount or property is demanded by parties to such action or cross-action and apply to the court upon notice to such parties for an order to deliver such property or portion thereof or its value to such person as the court shall direct. And whenever conflicting claims are or may be made upon a person for or relating to personal property, or the performance of an obligation, or any portion thereof, such person may bring an action against the conflicting claimants to compel them to interplead and litigate their several claims. The order of substitution may be made and the action of interpleader may be maintained, and the applicant or interpleading party be discharged from liability to all or any of the conflicting claimants, although their titles or claims have not a common origin, or are not identical but are adverse to and independent of one another.

(b) **[Entity or person subject to multiple claims which give rise to multiple liability; action against claimants to compel interpleader and litigation of claims]** Any person, firm, corporation, association or other entity against whom double or multiple claims are made, or may be made, by two or more persons which are such that they may give rise to double or multiple liability, may bring an action against the claimants to compel them to interplead and litigate their several claims.

When the person, firm, corporation, association or other entity against whom such claims are made, or may be made, is a defendant in an action brought upon one or more of such claims, it may either file a verified cross-complaint in interpleader, admitting that it has no interest in the money or property claimed, or in only a portion thereof, and alleging that all or such portion is demanded by parties to such action, and apply to the court upon notice to such parties for an order to deliver such money or property or such portion thereof to such person as the court shall direct; or may bring a separate action against the claimants to compel them to interplead and litigate their several claims. The action of interpleader may be maintained although the claims have not a common origin, are not identical but are adverse to and independent of one another, or the claims are unliquidated and no liability on the part of the party bringing the action or filing the cross-complaint has arisen. The applicant or interpleading party may deny liability in whole or in part to any or all of the claimants. The applicant or interpleading party may join as a defendant in such action any other party against whom claims are made by one or more of the claimants or such other party may interplead by cross-complaint; provided, however, that such claims arise out of the same transaction or occurrence.

(c) **[Deposit of amount payable in court; stoppage of interest and damages for detention of property]** Any amount which a plaintiff or cross-complainant admits to be payable may be deposited by him with the clerk of the court at the time of the filing of the complaint or cross-complaint in interpleader without first obtaining an order of the court therefor. Any interest on amounts deposited and any right to damages for detention of property so delivered, or its value, shall cease to accrue after the date of such deposit or delivery.

(d) **[Answer by defendant; allegation of ownership or interest]** A defendant named in a complaint to compel conflicting claimants to interplead and litigate their claims, or a defendant named in a cross-complaint in interpleader, may, in lieu of or in addition to any other pleading, file an answer to the complaint or cross-complaint which shall be served upon all other parties to the action and which shall contain allegations of fact as to his ownership of or other interest in the amount or property and any affirmative defenses and the relief requested. The allegations in such answer shall be deemed denied by all other parties to the action, unless otherwise admitted in the pleadings.

(e) **[Conflicting claims to property on deposit; issue triable by court; deficiency; trial of claim]** Except in cases where by the law a right to a jury trial is now given, conflicting claims to funds or property or the value thereof so deposited or delivered shall be deemed issues triable by the court, and such issues may be first tried. In the event the amount deposited shall be less than the amount claimed to be due by one or more of the conflicting claimants thereto, or in the event the property or the value thereof delivered is less than all of the property or the value thereof claimed by one or more of such conflicting claimants, any issues of fact involved in determining whether there is a deficiency in such deposit or delivery shall be tried by the court or a jury as provided in Title 8 (commencing with Section 577) of Part 2 of this code.

(f) **[Other proceedings; restraining order]** After any such complaint or cross-complaint in interpleader has been filed, the court in which it is filed may enter its order restraining all parties to the action from instituting or further prosecuting any other proceeding in any court in this state affecting the rights and obligations as between the parties to the interpleader until

further order of the court. *(Enacted in 1872. Amended by Stats.1881, c. 23, p. 19, § 1; Stats.1951, c. 1142, p. 2911, § 1; Stats.1970, c. 563, p. 1136, § 1; Stats.1975, c. 670, p. 1462, § 1.)*

Research References

Rutter, Cal. Practice Guide: Civ. Pro. Before Trial Ch. 2-F, F. Interpleader.

Rutter, Cal. Practice Guide: Civ. Pro. Before Trial Ch. 6-D, D. Cross-Complaint.

Rutter, Cal. Practice Guide: Fed.Civ.Pro. Before Trial Ch. 10-B, B. Interpleader.

Rutter, Cal. Practice Guide: Insurance Litigation Ch. 15-B, B. Actions by Insurers.

Rutter, Cal. Practice Guide: Insurance Litigation Ch. 6C-A, A. Life Insurance.

Rutter, Cal. Practice Guide: Insurance Litigation Ch. 12B-B, B. Bad Faith Refusal to Settle.

Rutter, Cal. Practice Guide: Real Prop. Transactions Ch. 4-F, F. Use of an Escrow.

Miller and Starr California Real Estate § 2:3, Deposit Receipt as a Contract of Sale--Deposit; Duties of Broker Receiving Deposit; Risk of Loss.

Miller and Starr California Real Estate § 6:12, Agency--Duty to Comply With Instructions.

Miller and Starr California Real Estate § 6:14, Agency--Duty to Hold Contents of Escrow Until Conditions Are Satisfied.

Miller and Starr California Real Estate § 19:57, Estoppel of Tenant to Deny Landlord's Title.

Miller and Starr California Real Estate § 28:127, Recovery on a Contractor's License Bond.

22 NO. 4 Miller & Starr, California Real Estate Newsalert 25, Construction Law and Contracting.

9 Witkin Cal. Proc. 5th Appeal § 195, Exception: Order Vacating Nonappealable Order.

7 Witkin Cal. Proc. 5th Judgment § 105, Interpleader Proceeding.

4 Witkin Cal. Proc. 5th Pleading § 237, Nature and Early Restrictions.

4 Witkin Cal. Proc. 5th Pleading § 238, Adoption of Federal Rule.

4 Witkin Cal. Proc. 5th Pleading § 242, (S 242) Former Law.

4 Witkin Cal. Proc. 5th Pleading § 243, (S 243) Modern View.

4 Witkin Cal. Proc. 5th Pleading § 244, (S 244) in General.

4 Witkin Cal. Proc. 5th Pleading § 245, (S 245) Application and Affidavit.

4 Witkin Cal. Proc. 5th Pleading § 246, (S 246) Substitution and Discharge.

4 Witkin Cal. Proc. 5th Pleading § 247, (S 247) in General.

4 Witkin Cal. Proc. 5th Pleading § 249, (S 249) Defendants' Pleadings.

4 Witkin Cal. Proc. 5th Pleading § 250, (S 250) Restraining Order.

4 Witkin Cal. Proc. 5th Pleading § 251, (S 251) Hearing and Interlocutory Order.

4 Witkin Cal. Proc. 5th Pleading § 252, (S 252) Discharge of Plaintiff.

4 Witkin Cal. Proc. 5th Pleading § 253, Interpleader by Cross-Complaint.

4 Witkin Cal. Proc. 5th Pleading § 254, Partial Interpleader.

4 Witkin Cal. Proc. 5th Pleading § 256, (S 256) Nature of Trial.

4 Witkin Cal. Proc. 5th Pleading § 257, Costs and Attorneys' Fees.

4 Witkin Cal. Proc. 5th Pleading § 466, Complaint or Petition.

6 Witkin Cal. Proc. 5th Provisional Remedies § 461, Nature of Remedy.

12 Witkin, California Summary 10th Real Property § 607, (S 607) Estoppel to Deny Landlord's Title.

§ 386.1. Investment of deposits; allocation of interest

Where a deposit has been made pursuant to Section 386, the court shall, upon the application of any party to the action, order such deposit to be invested in an insured interest-bearing account. Interest on such amount shall be allocated to the parties in the same proportion as the original funds are allocated. *(Added by Stats.1972, c. 553, § 1. Amended by Stats.1979, c. 173, p. 392, § 1.)*

Research References

Rutter, Cal. Practice Guide: Civ. Pro. Before Trial Ch. 2-F, F. Interpleader.

Rutter, Cal. Practice Guide: Insurance Litigation Ch. 15-B, B. Actions by Insurers.

4 Witkin Cal. Proc. 5th Pleading § 251, (S 251) Hearing and Interlocutory Order.

4 Witkin Cal. Proc. 5th Pleading § 257, Costs and Attorneys' Fees.

§ 386.5. Stakeholder; dismissal from action on deposit with clerk

Where the only relief sought against one of the defendants is the payment of a stated amount of money alleged to be wrongfully withheld, such defendant may, upon affidavit that he is a mere stakeholder with no interest in the amount or any portion thereof and that conflicting demands have been made upon him for the amount by parties to the action, upon notice to such parties, apply to the court for an order discharging him from liability and dismissing him from the action on his depositing with the clerk of the court the amount in dispute and the court may, in its discretion, make such order. *(Added by Stats.1953, c. 328, p. 1598, § 1.)*

Research References

Rutter, Cal. Practice Guide: Civ. Pro. Before Trial Ch. 2-F, F. Interpleader.

Rutter, Cal. Practice Guide: Insurance Litigation Ch. 15-B, B. Actions by Insurers.

Miller and Starr California Real Estate § 2:3, Deposit Receipt as a Contract of Sale--Deposit; Duties of Broker Receiving Deposit; Risk of Loss.

7 Witkin Cal. Proc. 5th Judgment § 105, Interpleader Proceeding.

4 Witkin Cal. Proc. 5th Pleading § 244, (S 244) in General.

4 Witkin Cal. Proc. 5th Pleading § 257, Costs and Attorneys' Fees.

§ 386.6. Costs and attorney fees; attorney pro se

(a) A party to an action who follows the procedure set forth in Section 386 or 386.5 may insert in his motion, petition, complaint, or cross complaint a request for allowance of his costs and reasonable attorney fees incurred in such action. In ordering the discharge of such party, the court may, in its discretion, award such party his costs and reasonable attorney fees from the amount in dispute which has been deposited with the court. At the time of final judgment in the action the court may make such further provision for assumption of such costs and attorney fees by one or more of the adverse claimants as may appear proper.

(b) A party shall not be denied the attorney fees authorized by subdivision (a) for the reason that he is himself an attorney, appeared in pro se, and performed his own legal services. *(Added by Stats.1955, c. 951, p. 1837, § 1. Amended by Stats.1974, c. 273, p. 498, § 1.)*

Research References

Rutter, Cal. Practice Guide: Civ. Pro. Before Trial Ch. 1-A, A. Accepting a New Case.

Rutter, Cal. Practice Guide: Civ. Pro. Before Trial Ch. 2-F, F. Interpleader.

Rutter, Cal. Practice Guide: Civil Trials & Evidence Ch. 17-E, E. Attorney Fees as Costs.

Rutter, Cal. Practice Guide: Insurance Litigation Ch. 15-B, B. Actions by Insurers.

Rutter, Cal. Practice Guide: Insurance Litigation Ch. 12B-B, B. Bad Faith Refusal to Settle.

Miller and Starr California Real Estate § 6:14, Agency--Duty to Hold Contents of Escrow Until Conditions Are Satisfied.

Miller and Starr California Real Estate § 34:66, Examples of Actions in Which Fees Can be Recovered.

Miller and Starr California Real Estate § 28:127, Recovery on a Contractor's License Bond.

22 NO. 5 Miller & Starr, California Real Estate Newsalert 17, Mechanics' Liens.

7 Witkin Cal. Proc. 5th Judgment § 105, Interpleader Proceeding.

7 Witkin Cal. Proc. 5th Judgment § 139, (S 139) in General.

4 Witkin Cal. Proc. 5th Pleading § 248, (S 248) Complaint.

4 Witkin Cal. Proc. 5th Pleading § 251, (S 251) Hearing and Interlocutory Order.

4 Witkin Cal. Proc. 5th Pleading § 257, Costs and Attorneys' Fees.

CHAPTER 7. INTERVENTION

Section
387. Intervention; authorization; procedure.
388. Pleadings alleging environmental damage; copy to Attorney General.

§ 387. Intervention; authorization; procedure

(a) Upon timely application, any person, who has an interest in the matter in litigation, or in the success of either of the parties, or an interest against both, may intervene in the action or proceeding. An intervention takes place when a third person is permitted to become a party to an action or proceeding between other persons, either by joining the plaintiff in claiming what is sought by the complaint, or by uniting with the defendant in resisting the claims of the plaintiff, or by demanding anything adversely to both the plaintiff and the defendant, and is made by complaint, setting forth the grounds upon which the intervention rests, filed by leave of the court and served upon the parties to the action or proceeding who have not appeared in the same manner as upon the commencement of an original action, and upon the attorneys of the parties who have appeared, or upon the party if he has appeared without an attorney, in the manner provided for service of summons or in the manner provided by Chapter 5 (commencing with Section 1010) Title 14 of Part 2. A party served with a complaint in intervention may within 30 days after service move, demur, or otherwise plead to the complaint in the same manner as to an original complaint.

(b) If any provision of law confers an unconditional right to intervene or if the person seeking intervention claims an interest relating to the property or transaction which is the subject of the action and that person is so situated that the disposition of the action may as a practical matter impair or impede that person's ability to protect that interest, unless that person's interest is adequately represented by existing parties, the court shall, upon timely application, permit that person to intervene. *(Enacted in 1872. Amended by Code Am.1873–74, c. 383, p. 296, § 44; Stats.1907, c. 371, p. 703, § 1; Stats.1969, c. 1611, p. 3379, § 5, operative July 1, 1970; Stats.1970, c. 484, p. 961, § 1; Stats.1977, c. 450, p. 1486, § 1.)*

Research References

Rutter, Cal. Practice Guide: Civil Appeals & Writs Ch. 2-D, D. Standing to Appeal.

Rutter, Cal. Practice Guide: Civil Appeals & Writs Ch. 7-A, A. Overview.

Rutter, Cal. Practice Guide: Civil Appeals & Writs Ch. 8-C, C. Standards of Appellate Review.

Rutter, Cal. Practice Guide: Civ. Pro. Before Trial Ch. 2-E, E. Intervention.

Rutter, Cal. Practice Guide: Civil Trials & Evidence Ch. 17-E, E. Attorney Fees as Costs.

California Practice Guide: Employment Litigation Ch. 19-H, H. Other Pretrial Procedures.

Rutter, Cal. Practice Guide: Enforcing Judgments/Debts Ch. 4-A, A. Attachment.

Rutter, Cal. Practice Guide: Enforcing Judgments/Debts Ch. 6G-8, Lien in Pending Action.

Rutter, Cal. Practice Guide: Insurance Litigation Ch. 9-F, F. Amount Recoverable by Insurer Under Subrogation.

Rutter, Cal. Practice Guide: Insurance Litigation Ch. 9-G, G. Procedures to Enforce Subrogation Right.

Rutter, Cal. Practice Guide: Insurance Litigation Ch. 15-A, A. Actions Against Insurers.

Rutter, Cal. Practice Guide: Insurance Litigation Ch. 15-B, B. Actions by Insurers.

Rutter, Cal. Practice Guide: Personal Injury Ch. 3-A, A. Introduction.

Rutter, Cal. Practice Guide: Personal Injury Ch. 4-F, F. Court-Conducted Settlement Proceedings.

4 Witkin Cal. Proc. 5th Pleading § 257, Costs and Attorneys' Fees.

Rutter, Cal. Practice Guide: Personal Injury Ch. 5-C, C. Selected Issues Affecting Parties.
Rutter, Cal. Practice Guide: Prof. Responsibility Ch. 5-B, B. Types of Fees and Fee Arrangements.
Miller and Starr California Real Estate § 29:11, Owner's Insurance Coverage.
Miller and Starr California Real Estate § 27:128, Public Enforcement of the False Claims Act.
16 NO. 1 Miller & Starr, California Real Estate Newsalert 13, Defective Construction.
19 NO. 2 Miller & Starr, California Real Estate Newsalert 12, Defective Construction.
3 Witkin Cal. Proc. 5th Actions § 735, (S 735) in General.
8 Witkin Cal. Proc. 5th Enforcement of Judgment § 297, (S 297) Nature and Scope of Remedy.
7 Witkin Cal. Proc. 5th Judgment § 290, (S 290) Attorney Whose Client Does Not Request Fee Award.
4 Witkin Cal. Proc. 5th Pleading § 191, Application.
4 Witkin Cal. Proc. 5th Pleading § 214, California Rule.
4 Witkin Cal. Proc. 5th Pleading § 215, Special Statutes.
4 Witkin Cal. Proc. 5th Pleading § 216, Other Procedures Compared.
4 Witkin Cal. Proc. 5th Pleading § 218, Test: Interest in Subject Matter or Success of Party.
4 Witkin Cal. Proc. 5th Pleading § 219, (S 219) Complaint in Intervention.
4 Witkin Cal. Proc. 5th Pleading § 220, (S 220) Application and Ex Parte Order.
4 Witkin Cal. Proc. 5th Pleading § 223, (S 223) Before or During Trial.
4 Witkin Cal. Proc. 5th Pleading § 224, (S 224) After Judgment.
4 Witkin Cal. Proc. 5th Pleading § 225, (S 225) Diligence.
4 Witkin Cal. Proc. 5th Pleading § 228, (S 228) No Time Limit on Service.
4 Witkin Cal. Proc. 5th Pleading § 229, Interest in Success of One Party.
4 Witkin Cal. Proc. 5th Pleading § 230, (S 230) in General.
11 Witkin, California Summary 10th Husband and Wife § 317, (S 317) Nature of Proceedings.
4 Witkin, California Summary 10th Security Transactions in Real Property § 141, (S 141) Failure to Join Parties.
14 Witkin, California Summary 10th Wills and Probate § 49, (S 49) Persons and Entities.
2 Witkin Cal. Summ. 10th Workers' Compensation § 69, (S 69) in General.

§ 388. Pleadings alleging environmental damage; copy to Attorney General

In an action brought by a party for relief of any nature other than solely for money damages where a pleading alleges facts or issues concerning alleged pollution or adverse environmental effects which could affect the public generally, the party filing the pleading shall furnish a copy to the Attorney General of the State of California. The copy shall be furnished by the party filing the pleading within 10 days after filing. *(Added by Stats.1992, c. 178 (S.B.1496), § 26.)*

Law Revision Commission Comments
Section 388 restates former Section 389.6 without substantive change. [22 Cal.L.Rev.Comm.Reports 895 (1992)].
Former Section 388 is restated in Section 369.5 without substantive change. [22 Cal.L.Rev.Comm.Reports 895 (1992)].

Research References
4 Witkin Cal. Proc. 5th Pleading § 29, (S 29) Service.
4 Witkin Cal. Proc. 5th Pleading § 98, (S 98) Any Association May be Sued.
4 Witkin Cal. Proc. 5th Pleading § 99, (S 99) Joinder of Individual Members.
4 Witkin Cal. Proc. 5th Pleading § 160, Intervention by Attorney General.
9 Witkin, California Summary 10th Corporations § 50, Liability of Trustees and Trust Estate.
5 Witkin, California Summary 10th Torts § 38, (S 38) in General.

CHAPTER 8. COMPULSORY JOINDER

Section
389. Joinder as party, conditions; indispensable person, factors; statement of reasons for nonjoinder; class actions.
389.5. Application to be made a party.

§ 389. Joinder as party, conditions; indispensable person, factors; statement of reasons for nonjoinder; class actions

(a) A person who is subject to service of process and whose joinder will not deprive the court of jurisdiction over the subject matter of the action shall be joined as a party in the action if (1) in his absence complete relief cannot be accorded among those already parties or (2) he claims an interest relating to the subject of the action and is so situated that the disposition of the action in his absence may (i) as a practical matter impair or impede his ability to protect that interest or (ii) leave any of the persons already parties subject to a substantial risk of incurring double, multiple, or otherwise inconsistent obligations by reason of his claimed interest. If he has not been so joined, the court shall order that he be made a party.

(b) If a person as described in paragraph (1) or (2) of subdivision (a) cannot be made a party, the court shall determine whether in equity and good conscience the action should proceed among the parties before it, or should be dismissed without prejudice, the absent person being thus regarded as indispensable. The factors to be considered by the court include: (1) to what extent a judgment rendered in the person's absence might be prejudicial to him or those already parties; (2) the extent to which, by protective provisions in the judgment, by the shaping of relief, or other measures, the prejudice can be lessened or avoided; (3) whether a judgment rendered in the person's absence will be adequate; (4) whether the plaintiff or cross-complainant will have an adequate remedy if the action is dismissed for nonjoinder.

(c) A complaint or cross-complaint shall state the names, if known to the pleader, of any persons as described in paragraph (1) or (2) of subdivision (a) who are not joined, and the reasons why they are not joined.

(d) Nothing in this section affects the law applicable to class actions. *(Enacted in 1872. Amended by 1897, c. 12, p. 9, § 1; Stats.1907, c. 371, p. 704, § 3; Stats.1957, c. 1498, p. 2824, § 2; Stats.1971, c. 244, p. 376, § 15, operative July 1, 1972.)*

Law Revision Commission Comments
Bringing new parties into civil actions; recommendation and study. Cal.Law Revision Comm. (1957) Vol. 1, p. M–5; Leg.Hist., Vol. 1, p. XII.
Purpose of bill amending this section as explained by the California Law Revision Commission. Report of the Senate Interim Judiciary Committee, 1957, p. 183, Vol. 1 of Appendix to Journal of the Senate, Reg.Sess., 1957.
Recommendation and study relating to counterclaims and cross-complaints, joinder of causes of action, and related provisions. 10 Cal.L.Revision Comm. Reports 501 (1971); Report of Senate Committee on Judiciary on Senate Bill 201, S. Journal, April 1, 1971; Communication From Assembly Committee on Judiciary on Senate Bill 201, A. Journal, June 16, 1971.
Sovereign immunity study, joinder of conditionally necessary parties. Cal.Law Revision Comm. (1963) Vol. 5, p. 373.
Section 389 is revised to substitute practically in its entirety Rule 19 of the Federal Rules of Civil Procedure for former Section 389. The words "without prejudice" have been added to the language of the Federal Rule in subdivision (b) of Section 389 merely to avoid any contrary implication that might be created by the omission of the somewhat similar provision formerly found in Section 389. See Wilson v. Frakes, 178 Cal.App.2d 580, 3 Cal.Rptr. 434 (1960).
Basically, as amended, Section 389 requires joinder of persons materially interested in an action whenever feasible. In certain instances, joinder cannot be accomplished because it would deprive the court of subject matter jurisdiction. For example, the federal courts have exclusive jurisdiction over proceedings against foreign consuls or vice consuls (28 U.S.C.A. § 1351) and, more importantly, over suits against the United States under the Federal Tort Claims Act. See 28 U.S.C.A. §§ 1346(b), 2679(b). In other situations, joinder will be impossible because personal jurisdiction over the party cannot be obtained.
When joinder cannot be accomplished, the circumstances must be examined and a choice made between proceeding with or dismissing the

action. The adequacy of the relief that may be granted in a person's absence and the possibility of prejudice to either such person or the parties before the court are factors to be considered in making this choice. However, a person is regarded as indispensable only in the conclusory sense that in his absence, the court has decided the action should be dismissed. Where the decision is to proceed the court has the power to make a legally binding adjudication between the parties properly before it.

Section 389 formerly attempted not only to avoid prejudice to the parties or absent person but also to promote the general convenience of the courts by preventing a multiplicity of suits. As revised, Section 389 takes a different approach; it limits compulsory joinder to those situations where the absence of a person may result in substantial prejudice to that person or to the parties already before the court. See Recommendation and Study Relating to Counterclaims and Cross-Complaints, Joinder of Causes of Action, and Related Provisions, 10 Cal.L.Revision Comm'n. Reports 501, 515 (1971). Section 389 was widely criticized because it formerly appeared to require joinder of parties merely for the general convenience of the courts by preventing a multiplicity of suits. See Friedenthal, Joinder of Claims, Counterclaims, and Cross-Complaints: Suggested Revision of the California Provisions, 23 Stan. L. Rev. 1 (1970); Comments, Bringing New Parties Into Civil Actions in California, 46 Cal.L.Rev. 100 (1958); Joinder of Parties in Civil Actions in California, 33 So.Cal.Rev. 428 (1960). However, an examination of the appellate cases decided since the convenience of the courts provision was added to Section 389 in 1957 discloses that the provision was not relied upon; instead, the courts continued to apply the principles enunciated in Bank of California v. Superior Court, 16 Cal.2d 516, 106 P.2d 879 (1940).

Under the former law, an indispensable party had to be joined in the action; until and unless he was, the court had no jurisdiction to proceed with the case. See, e.g., Irwin v. City of Manhattan Beach, 227 Cal.App.2d 634, 38 Cal.Rptr. 875 (1964). This absolute rule has been changed; however, practically speaking, the change is perhaps more one of emphasis. The guidelines provided in Section 389 are substantially those that have guided the courts for years. See Bank of California v. Superior Court, 16 Cal.2d 516, 106 P.2d 879 (1940). These guidelines should require dismissal in the same circumstances where formerly a person was characterized as indispensable.

As noted above, Section 389 has been revised to conform substantially to Rule 19 of the Federal Rules of Civil Procedure. Accordingly, the explanatory note prepared by the Advisory Committee in conjunction with the amendment of Rule 19 in 1966 is particularly helpful in describing the nature and effect of Section 389. This explanatory note is set out below with appropriate deletions and additions:

ADVISORY COMMITTEE'S NOTE
1973 Main Volume Advisory Committee's Note
General Considerations

Whenever feasible, the persons materially interested in the subject of an action—see the more detailed description of these persons in the discussion of new subdivision (a) below—should be joined as parties so that they may be heard and a complete disposition made. When this comprehensive joinder cannot be accomplished—a situation which may be encountered . . . because of limitations on service of process [and] subject matter jurisdiction . . .—the case should be examined pragmatically and a choice made between the alternatives of proceeding with the action in the absence of particular interested persons, and dismissing the action.

Even if the court is mistaken in its decision to proceed in the absence of an interested person, it does not by that token deprive itself of the power to adjudicate as between the parties already before it through proper service of process. But the court can make a legally binding adjudication only between the parties actually joined in the action. It is true that an adjudication between the parties before the court may on occasion adversely affect the absent person as a practical matter, or leave a party exposed to a later inconsistent recovery by the absent person. These are factors which should be considered in deciding whether the action should proceed, or should rather be dismissed; but they do not themselves negate the court's power to adjudicate as between the parties who have been joined.

Defects in the Original Rule

The foregoing propositions were well understood in the older equity practice, see Hazard, Indispensable Party: The Historical Origin of a Procedural Phantom, 61 Colum.L.Rev. 1254 (1961), and Rule 19 could be and often was applied in consonance with them. But experience showed that the [original] rule was defective in its phrasing and did not point clearly to the proper basis of decision.

The Amended Rule

New subdivision (a) defines the persons whose joinder in the action is desirable. Clause (1) stresses the desirability of joining those persons in whose absence the court would be obliged to grant partial or "hollow" rather than complete relief to the parties before the court. The interests that are being furthered here are not only those of the parties, but also that of the public in avoiding repeated lawsuits on the same essential subject matter. Clause (2)(i) recognizes the importance of protecting the person whose joinder is in question against the practical prejudice to him which may arise through a disposition of the action in his absence. Clause (2)(ii) recognizes the need for considering whether a party may be left, after the adjudication, in a position where a person not joined can subject him to a double or otherwise inconsistent liability. See [Reed, Compulsory Joinder of Parties in Civil Actions, 55 Mich.L.Rev. 327, 330, 338 (1957); Note, Indispensable Parties in the Federal Courts, 65 Harv.L.Rev. 1050, 1052–57 (1952); Developments in the Law—Multiparty Litigation in the Federal Courts, 71 Harv.L.Rev. 874, 881–85 (1958)].

The subdivision (a) definition of persons to be joined is not couched in terms of the abstract nature of their interests—"joint," "United," "separable," or the like. See . . . Developments in the Law, supra, at 880. It should be noted particularly, however, that the description is not at variance with the settled authorities holding that a tortfeasor with the usual "joint-and-several" liability is merely a permissive party to an action against another with like liability. See 3 Moore's Federal Practice, 2153 (2d ed. 1963); 2 Barron & Holtzoff, Federal Practice & Procedure 513.8 (Wright ed. 1961). Joinder of these tortfeasors continues to be regulated by Rule 20 . . . . [Cal.Code Civ.Proc. 378, 379. Where an indemnity action would lie against a third person, the California rule appears to be that the indemnitor is not an "indispensable," but is a "conditionally necessary" party. See De Stackelberg v. Lamb Transp. Co., 168 Cal.App.2d 174, 335 P.2d 522 (1959). In practice, where advantageous, a defendant-indemnitee will simply join his indemnitor by cross-complaint. See Cal.Code Civ.Proc. 428.10, 428.20.]

If a person as described in subdivision (a)(1)–(2) is amenable to service of process and his joinder would not deprive the court of jurisdiction in the sense of competence over the action, he should be joined as a party; and if he has not been joined, the court should order him to be brought into the action . . . .

Subdivision (b). When a person as described in subdivision (a)(1)–(2) cannot be made a party, the court is to determine whether in equity and good conscience the action should proceed among the parties already before it, or should be dismissed. That this decision is to be made in the light of pragmatic considerations has often been acknowledged by the courts. See Roos v. Texas Co., 23 F.2d 171 (2d Cir. 1927), cert. denied, 277 U.S. 587 (1928); Niles–Bement–Pond Co. v. Iron Moulders' Union, 254 U.S. 77, 80 (1920). The subdivision sets out four relevant considerations drawn from the experience revealed in the decided cases. The factors are to a certain extent overlapping, and they are not intended to exclude other considerations which may be applicable in particular situations.

The first factor brings in a consideration of what a judgment in the action would mean to the absentee. Would the absentee be adversely affected in a practical sense, and if so, would the prejudice be immediate and serious, or remote and minor? The possible collateral consequences of the judgment upon the parties already joined are also to be appraised. Would any party be exposed to a fresh action by the absentee, and if so, how serious is the threat? See the elaborate discussion in Reed, supra; cf. A. L. Smith Iron Co. v. Dickson, 141 F.2d 3 (2d Cir. 1944); Caldwell Mfg. Co. v. Unique Balance Co., 18 F.R.D. 258 (S.D.N.Y.1955).

The second factor calls attention to the measures by which prejudice may be averted or lessened. The "shaping of relief" is a familiar expedient to this end. See, e.g., the award of money damages in lieu of specific relief where the latter might affect an absentee adversely. Ward v. Deavers, 203 F.2d 72 (D.C.Cir.1953); Miller & Lux, Inc. v. Nickel, 141 F.Supp. 41 (N.D.Calif.1956). On the use of "protective provisions," see Roos v. Texas Co., supra; Atwood v. Rhode Island Hosp. Trust Co., 275 Fed. 513, 519 (1st Cir. 1921), cert. denied, 257 U.S. 661 (1922); cf. Stumpf v. Fidelity Gas Co., 294 F.2d 886 (9th Cir. 1961); and the general statement in National Licorice Co. v. Labor Board, 309 U.S. 350, 363 (1940).

Sometimes the party is himself able to take measures to avoid prejudice. Thus a defendant faced with a prospect of a second suit by an absentee may be in a position to bring the latter into the action by defensive interpleader. See [Cal.Code Civ.Proc. 428.10, 428.20;] Hudson v. Newell, 172 F.2d 848, 852, mod., 176 F.2d 546 (5th Cir. 1949); Gauss v. Kirk, 198 F.2d 83, 86 (D.C.Cir.1952); Abel v. Brayton Flying Service, Inc., 248 F.2d 713, 716 (5th Cir. 1957) (suggestion of possibility of counterclaim under

Rule 13(b); cf. Parker Rust–Proof Co. v. Western Union Tel. Co., 105 F.2d 976 (2d Cir. 1939), cert. denied, 308 U.S. 597 (1939). So also the absentee may sometimes be able to avert prejudice to himself by voluntarily appearing in the action or intervening on an ancillary basis. See Developments in the Law, supra, 71 Harv.L.Rev. at 882; Annot., Intervention or Subsequent Joinder of Parties as Affecting Jurisdiction of Federal Court Based on Diversity of Citizenship, 134 A.L.R. 335 (1941); Johnson v. Middleton, 175 F.2d 535 (7th Cir. 1949); Kentucky Nat. Cas Corp. v. Duggins, 165 F.2d 1011 (6th Cir. 1948); McComb v. McCormack, 159 F.2d 219 (5th Cir. 1947). The court should consider whether this, in turn, would impose undue hardship on the absentee. (For the possibility of the court's informing an absentee of the pendency of the action, see comment under subdivision (c) below.)

The third factor—whether an "adequate" judgment can be rendered in the absence of a given person—calls attention to the extent of the relief that can be accorded among the parties joined. It meshes with the other factors, especially the "shaping of relief" mentioned under the second factor. Cf. Kroese v. General Steel Castings Corp., 179 F.2d 760 (3d Cir. 1949), cert. denied, 339 U.S. 983 (1950).

The fourth factor, looking to the practical effects of a dismissal, indicates that the court should consider whether there is any assurance that the plaintiff, if dismissed, could sue effectively in another forum where better joinder would be possible. See Fitzgerald v. Haynes, 241 F.2d 417, 420 (3d Cir. 1957); Fouke v. Schenewerk, 197 F.2d 234, 236 (5th Cir. 1952); cf. Warfield v. Marks, 190 F.2d 178 (5th Cir. 1951).

The subdivision uses the word "indispensable" only in a conclusory sense, that is, a person is "regarded as indispensable" when he cannot be made a party and, upon consideration of the factors above-mentioned, it is determined that in his absence it would be preferable to dismiss the action, rather than to retain it.

A person may be added as a party at any stage of the action on motion or on the court's initiative . . .; and a motion to dismiss, on the ground that a person has not been joined and justice requires that the action should not proceed in his absence, may be made as late as the trial on the merits . . . . However, when the moving party is seeking dismissal in order to protect himself against a later suit by the absent person (subdivision (a)(2)(ii)), and is not seeking vicariously to protect the absent person against a prejudicial judgment (subdivision (a)(2)(i)), his undue delay in making the motion can properly be counted against him as a reason for denying the motion. A joinder question should be decided with reasonable promptness, but decision may properly be deferred if adequate information is not available at the time. Thus the relationship of an absent person to the action, and the practical effects of an adjudication upon him and others, may not be sufficiently revealed at the pleading stage; in such a case it would be appropriate to defer decision until the action was further advanced . . . .

Subdivision (c) parallels the predecessor subdivision (c) of Rule 19. In some situations it may be desirable to advise a person who has not been joined of the fact that the action is pending, and in particular cases the court in its discretion may itself convey this information by directing a letter or other informal notice to the absentee.

Subdivision (d) repeats the exception contained in the first clause of the predecessor subdivision (a).

Research References

Rutter, Cal. Practice Guide: Civil Appeals & Writs Ch. 8-C, C. Standards of Appellate Review.
Rutter, Cal. Practice Guide: Civ. Pro. Before Trial Ch. 2-C, C. Joinder of Parties.
Rutter, Cal. Practice Guide: Civ. Pro. Before Trial Ch. 2-E, E. Intervention.
Rutter, Cal. Practice Guide: Civ. Pro. Before Trial Ch. 7(I)-D, D. Motion to Dismiss.
Rutter, Cal. Practice Guide: Personal Injury Ch. 5-C, C. Selected Issues Affecting Parties.
Miller and Starr California Real Estate § 25A:23, Type of Action; Time to File; Preparation of Administrative Record.
Miller and Starr California Real Estate § 28:112, Proper Parties in Suit Against Surety; Necessity of Suit Against or Joinder of the Principal.
16 NO. 1 Miller & Starr, California Real Estate Newsalert 13, Defective Construction.
18 NO. 1 Miller & Starr, California Real Estate Newsalert 22, Subdivisions.
22 NO. 4 Miller & Starr, California Real Estate Newsalert 1, Show Me Your Papers: Sales and Assignments of Secured Real Estate Loans and the California Foreclosure Process (Part II).

9 Witkin Cal. Proc. 5th Administrative Proceedings § 138, (S 138) in General.
9 Witkin Cal. Proc. 5th Appeal § 946, (S 946) Power to Exercise Discretion After Retransfer.
8 Witkin Cal. Proc. 5th Enforcement of Judgment § 291, (S 291) Nature of Action.
7 Witkin Cal. Proc. 5th Judgment § 379, (S 379) in General.
2 Witkin Cal. Proc. 5th Jurisdiction § 99, (S 99) Defects of Parties.
4 Witkin Cal. Proc. 5th Pleading § 177, Joinder by Order of Court.
4 Witkin Cal. Proc. 5th Pleading § 179, (S 179) Legislative Revision of 1971.
4 Witkin Cal. Proc. 5th Pleading § 180, (S 180) in General.
4 Witkin Cal. Proc. 5th Pleading § 181, (S 181) Test Under Revised Statute.
4 Witkin Cal. Proc. 5th Pleading § 182, in General.
4 Witkin Cal. Proc. 5th Pleading § 185, (S 185) Where Joinder is Possible.
4 Witkin Cal. Proc. 5th Pleading § 186, in General.
4 Witkin Cal. Proc. 5th Pleading § 188, Effect of Sovereign Immunity.
4 Witkin Cal. Proc. 5th Pleading § 189, Standard of Review.
4 Witkin Cal. Proc. 5th Pleading § 190, in General.
4 Witkin Cal. Proc. 5th Pleading § 191, Application.
4 Witkin Cal. Proc. 5th Pleading § 192, Court's Own Motion.
4 Witkin Cal. Proc. 5th Pleading § 200, (S 200) Joint, Concurrent, and Successive Tortfeasors.
4 Witkin Cal. Proc. 5th Pleading § 223, (S 223) Before or During Trial.
5 Witkin Cal. Proc. 5th Pleading § 972, Nonjoinder of Parties.
5 Witkin Cal. Proc. 5th Pleading § 1178, (S 1178) Court Without Jurisdiction.
6 Witkin Cal. Proc. 5th Proceedings Without Trial § 328, (S 328) Joinder of Defendant by Order of Court.
6 Witkin Cal. Proc. 5th Proceedings Without Trial § 474, in General.
12 Witkin, California Summary 10th Real Property § 67, Parties.
1 Witkin Cal. Summ. 10th Contracts § 604, Action for Indirect Injury.
10 Witkin, California Summary 10th Parent and Child § 34, (S 34) Rescinding or Setting Aside Declaration.
10 Witkin, California Summary 10th Parent and Child § 47, (S 47) Where Presumption of Paternity Applies.
10 Witkin, California Summary 10th Parent and Child § 58, (S 58) Grant or Denial.
6 Witkin, California Summary 10th Torts § 1373, (S 1373) Release.

§ 389.5.   Application to be made a party

When, in an action for the recovery of real or personal property, or to determine conflicting claims thereto, a person not a party to the action but having an interest in the subject thereof makes application to the court to be made a party, it may order him to be brought in by the proper amendment. *(Added by Stats.1957, c. 1498, p. 2825, § 3.)*

Research References

4 Witkin Cal. Proc. 5th Pleading § 191, Application.
4 Witkin Cal. Proc. 5th Pleading § 216, Other Procedures Compared.

Title 3A

VEXATIOUS LITIGANTS

§ 391. Definitions

As used in this title, the following terms have the following meanings:

(a) "Litigation" means any civil action or proceeding, commenced, maintained or pending in any state or federal court.

(b) "Vexatious litigant" means a person who does any of the following:

(1) In the immediately preceding seven-year period has commenced, prosecuted, or maintained in propria persona at least five litigations other than in a small claims court that have been (i) finally determined adversely to the person or (ii) unjustifiably permitted to remain pending at least two years without having been brought to trial or hearing.

(2) After a litigation has been finally determined against the person, repeatedly relitigates or attempts to relitigate, in propria persona, either (i) the validity of the determination against the same defendant or defendants as to whom the litigation was finally determined or (ii) the cause of action, claim, controversy, or any of the issues of fact or law, determined or concluded by the final determination against the same defendant or defendants as to whom the litigation was finally determined.

(3) In any litigation while acting in propria persona, repeatedly files unmeritorious motions, pleadings, or other papers, conducts unnecessary discovery, or engages in other tactics that are frivolous or solely intended to cause unnecessary delay.

(4) Has previously been declared to be a vexatious litigant by any state or federal court of record in any action or proceeding based upon the same or substantially similar facts, transaction, or occurrence.

(c) "Security" means an undertaking to assure payment, to the party for whose benefit the undertaking is required to be furnished, of the party's reasonable expenses, including attorney's fees and not limited to taxable costs, incurred in or in connection with a litigation instituted, caused to be instituted, or maintained or caused to be maintained by a vexatious litigant.

(d) "Plaintiff" means the person who commences, institutes or maintains a litigation or causes it to be commenced, instituted or maintained, including an attorney at law acting in propria persona.

(e) "Defendant" means a person (including corporation, association, partnership and firm or governmental entity) against whom a litigation is brought or maintained or sought to be brought or maintained. *(Added by Stats.1963, c. 1471, p. 3088, § 1. Amended by Stats.1982, c. 517, p. 2335, § 98; Stats.1990, c. 621 (S.B.2675), § 1; Stats.1994, c. 587 (A.B.3600), § 3.5.)*

Law Revision Commission Comments

Section 391 is amended to delete a provision duplicated in the Bond and Undertaking Law. See Section 995.710 (deposit in lieu of undertaking). The other changes in Section 391 are technical. [16 Cal.L.Rev. Comm. Reports 501 (1982)].

Research References

Rutter, Cal. Practice Guide: Civil Appeals & Writs Ch. 2-C, C. Nonappealable Orders.
Rutter, Cal. Practice Guide: Civil Appeals & Writs Ch. 5-B, B. Types of Motions, Applications and Requests.
Rutter, Cal. Practice Guide: Civil Appeals & Writs Ch. 11-E, E. Appellate Costs and Sanctions.
Rutter, Cal. Practice Guide: Civil Appeals & Writs Ch. 15-B, B. Common Law Writs.
Rutter, Cal. Practice Guide: Civ. Pro. Before Trial Ch. 1-G, G. Prior Court Order Required for Certain Pleadings.
Rutter, Cal. Practice Guide: Insurance Litigation Ch. 6I-B, B. Particular Surety Bond Coverages.
Rutter, Cal. Practice Guide: Prof. Responsibility Ch. 8-B, B. Accepting or Rejecting Employment.

Miller and Starr California Real Estate § 34:66, Examples of Actions in Which Fees Can be Recovered.
3 Witkin Cal. Proc. 5th Actions § 365, (S 365) in General.
3 Witkin Cal. Proc. 5th Actions § 366, Statutory Definition.
3 Witkin Cal. Proc. 5th Actions § 367, Litigant Acting in Pro. Per.
3 Witkin Cal. Proc. 5th Actions § 369, Hearing, Determination, and Security.
3 Witkin Cal. Proc. 5th Actions § 370, Order Prohibiting Filing of New Litigation.
11 Witkin, California Summary 10th Husband and Wife § 5, Generally Applicable Procedures.
8 Witkin, California Summary 10th Constitutional Law § 792, Vexatious Litigant in Pro. Per.
14 Witkin, California Summary 10th Wills and Probate § 931, (S 931) Vexatious Litigants.
14 Witkin, California Summary 10th Wills and Probate § 959A, (S 959A) (New)-Vexatious Litigants.

§ 391.1. Motion for order requiring security; grounds

In any litigation pending in any court of this state, at any time until final judgment is entered, a defendant may move the court, upon notice and hearing, for an order requiring the plaintiff to furnish security or for an order dismissing the litigation pursuant to subdivision (b) of Section 391.3. The motion for an order requiring the plaintiff to furnish security shall be based upon the ground, and supported by a showing, that the plaintiff is a vexatious litigant and that there is not a reasonable probability that he or she will prevail in the litigation against the moving defendant. *(Added by Stats.1963, c. 1471, p. 3038, § 1. Amended by Stats.1975, c. 381, p. 855, § 1; Stats.1990, c. 621 (S.B.2675), § 2; Stats.2012, c. 417 (A.B.2274), § 1.)*

Research References

Rutter, Cal. Practice Guide: Civ. Pro. Before Trial Ch. 1-G, G. Prior Court Order Required for Certain Pleadings.
Rutter, Cal. Practice Guide: Civ. Pro. Before Trial Gen. Matls., Highlights.
3 Witkin Cal. Proc. 5th Actions § 368, Motion and Grounds.
3 Witkin Cal. Proc. 5th Actions § 370, Order Prohibiting Filing of New Litigation.

§ 391.2. Scope of hearing; ruling not deemed determination of issues

At the hearing upon the motion the court shall consider any evidence, written or oral, by witnesses or affidavit, as may be material to the ground of the motion. Except for an order dismissing the litigation pursuant to subdivision (b) of Section 391.3, no determination made by the court in determining or ruling upon the motion shall be or be deemed to be a determination of any issue in the litigation or of the merits thereof. *(Added by Stats.1963, c. 1471, p. 3038, § 1. Amended by Stats.2012, c. 417 (A.B.2274), § 2.)*

Research References

3 Witkin Cal. Proc. 5th Actions § 369, Hearing, Determination, and Security.
7 Witkin Cal. Proc. 5th Judgment § 433, Issue was Not Properly Triable.

§ 391.3. Order to furnish security; amount; dismissal of litigation

(a) Except as provided in subdivision (b), if, after hearing the evidence upon the motion, the court determines that the plaintiff is a vexatious litigant and that there is no reasonable probability that the plaintiff will prevail in the litigation against the moving defendant, the court shall order the plaintiff to furnish, for the benefit of the moving defendant, security in such amount and within such time as the court shall fix.

(b) If, after hearing evidence on the motion, the court determines that the litigation has no merit and has been filed for the purposes of harassment or delay, the court shall order the litigation dismissed. This subdivision shall only apply to litigation filed in a court of this state by a vexatious litigant subject to a prefiling order pursuant to Section 391.7 who was represented by counsel at the time the litigation was filed and who became in propria persona after the withdrawal of his or her attorney.

(c) A defendant may make a motion for relief in the alternative under either subdivision (a) or (b) and shall combine all grounds for relief in one motion. *(Added by Stats.1963, c. 1471, p. 3038, § 1. Amended by Stats.1982, c. 517, p. 2335, § 99; Stats.2012, c. 417 (A.B.2274), § 3.)*

Law Revision Commission Comments

Section 391.3 is amended to delete a provision duplicated in the Bond and Undertaking Law. See Sections 996.010 (undertaking in action or proceeding) and 996.030 (reduced undertaking). [16 Cal.L.Rev.Comm. Reports 501 (1982)].

Research References

Rutter, Cal. Practice Guide: Civil Appeals & Writs Ch. 2-D, D. Standing to Appeal.
Rutter, Cal. Practice Guide: Civ. Pro. Before Trial Ch. 11-B, B. Involuntary Dismissals.
3 Witkin Cal. Proc. 5th Actions § 369, Hearing, Determination, and Security.

§ 391.4. Dismissal for failure to furnish security

When security that has been ordered furnished is not furnished as ordered, the litigation shall be dismissed as to the defendant for whose benefit it was ordered furnished. *(Added by Stats.1963, c. 1471, p. 3038, § 1.)*

Research References

Rutter, Cal. Practice Guide: Civil Appeals & Writs Ch. 2-C, C. Nonappealable Orders.
Rutter, Cal. Practice Guide: Civ. Pro. Before Trial Ch. 1-G, G. Prior Court Order Required for Certain Pleadings.
Rutter, Cal. Practice Guide: Civ. Pro. Before Trial Ch. 11-B, B. Involuntary Dismissals.
Rutter, Cal. Practice Guide: Civ. Pro. Before Trial Gen. Matls., Highlights.
3 Witkin Cal. Proc. 5th Actions § 369, Hearing, Determination, and Security.

§ 391.6. Stay of proceedings

Except as provided in subdivision (b) of Section 391.3, when a motion pursuant to Section 391.1 is filed prior to trial the litigation is stayed, and the moving defendant need not plead, until 10 days after the motion shall have been denied, or if granted, until 10 days after the required security has been furnished and the moving defendant given written notice thereof. When a motion pursuant to Section 391.1 is made at any time thereafter, the litigation shall be stayed for such period after the denial of the motion or the furnishing of the required security as the court shall determine. *(Added by Stats.1963, c. 1471, p. 3038, § 1. Amended by Stats.1975, c. 381, p. 855, § 2; Stats.2012, c. 417 (A.B.2274), § 4.)*

Research References

Rutter, Cal. Practice Guide: Civ. Pro. Before Trial Ch. 1-G, G. Prior Court Order Required for Certain Pleadings.
3 Witkin Cal. Proc. 5th Actions § 368, Motion and Grounds.

§ 391.7. Prefiling order prohibiting the filing of new litigation; contempt; conditions

(a) In addition to any other relief provided in this title, the court may, on its own motion or the motion of any party, enter a prefiling order which prohibits a vexatious litigant from filing any new litigation in the courts of this state in propria persona without first obtaining leave of the presiding justice or presiding judge of the court where the litigation is proposed to be filed.

Disobedience of the order by a vexatious litigant may be punished as a contempt of court.

(b) The presiding justice or presiding judge shall permit the filing of that litigation only if it appears that the litigation has merit and has not been filed for the purposes of harassment or delay. The presiding justice or presiding judge may condition the filing of the litigation upon the furnishing of security for the benefit of the defendants as provided in Section 391.3.

(c) The clerk may not file any litigation presented by a vexatious litigant subject to a prefiling order unless the vexatious litigant first obtains an order from the presiding justice or presiding judge permitting the filing. If the clerk mistakenly files the litigation without the order, any party may file with the clerk and serve, or the presiding justice or presiding judge may direct the clerk to file and serve, on the plaintiff and other parties a notice stating that the plaintiff is a vexatious litigant subject to a prefiling order as set forth in subdivision (a). The filing of the notice shall automatically stay the litigation. The litigation shall be automatically dismissed unless the plaintiff within 10 days of the filing of that notice obtains an order from the presiding justice or presiding judge permitting the filing of the litigation as set forth in subdivision (b). If the presiding justice or presiding judge issues an order permitting the filing, the stay of the litigation shall remain in effect, and the defendants need not plead, until 10 days after the defendants are served with a copy of the order.

(d) For purposes of this section, "litigation" includes any petition, application, or motion other than a discovery motion, in a proceeding under the Family Code or Probate Code, for any order.

(e) The presiding justice or presiding judge of a court may designate a justice or judge of the same court to act on his or her behalf in exercising the authority and responsibilities provided under subdivisions (a) to (c), inclusive.

(f) The clerk of the court shall provide the Judicial Council a copy of any prefiling orders issued pursuant to subdivision (a). The Judicial Council shall maintain a record of vexatious litigants subject to those prefiling orders and shall annually disseminate a list of those persons to the clerks of the courts of this state. *(Added by Stats.1990, c. 621 (S.B.2675), § 3. Amended by Stats.2002, c. 1118 (A.B.1938), § 1; Stats.2011, c. 49 (S.B.731), § 1.)*

Research References

Rutter, Cal. Practice Guide: Civil Appeals & Writs Ch. 2-D, D. Standing to Appeal.
Rutter, Cal. Practice Guide: Civil Appeals & Writs Ch. 5-B, B. Types of Motions, Applications and Requests.
Rutter, Cal. Practice Guide: Civil Appeals & Writs Ch. 8-C, C. Standards of Appellate Review.
Rutter, Cal. Practice Guide: Civil Appeals & Writs Ch. 11-E, E. Appellate Costs and Sanctions.
Rutter, Cal. Practice Guide: Civ. Pro. Before Trial Ch. 1-G, G. Prior Court Order Required for Certain Pleadings.
Rutter, Cal. Practice Guide: Civ. Pro. Before Trial Gen. Matls., Highlights.
Rutter, Cal. Practice Guide: Civil Trials & Evidence Ch. 1-K, K. Continuance Motions.
Rutter, Cal. Practice Guide: Family Law Gen. Matls, Highlights.
Rutter, Cal. Practice Guide: Prof. Responsibility Ch. 8-B, B. Accepting or Rejecting Employment.
3 Witkin Cal. Proc. 5th Actions § 365, (S 365) in General.
3 Witkin Cal. Proc. 5th Actions § 368, Motion and Grounds.
3 Witkin Cal. Proc. 5th Actions § 370, Order Prohibiting Filing of New Litigation.

§ 391.8. Filing application to vacate prefiling order and remove name from Judicial Council's list

(a) A vexatious litigant subject to a prefiling order under Section 391.7 may file an application to vacate the prefiling order and remove his or her name from the Judicial Council's list of vexatious litigants subject to prefiling orders. The application shall be filed in the court that entered the prefiling order, either in the action in which the prefiling order was entered or in conjunction with a request to the presiding justice or presiding judge to file new litigation under Section 391.7. The application shall be made before the justice or judge who entered the order, if that justice or judge is available. If that justice or judge who entered the order is not available, the application shall be made before the presiding justice or presiding judge, or his or her designee.

(b) A vexatious litigant whose application under subdivision (a) was denied shall not be permitted to file another application on or before 12 months has elapsed after the date of the denial of the previous application.

(c) A court may vacate a prefiling order and order removal of a vexatious litigant's name from the Judicial Council's list of vexatious litigants subject to prefiling orders upon a showing of a material change in the facts upon which the order was granted and that the ends of justice would be served by vacating the order. *(Added by Stats.2011, c. 49 (S.B.731), § 2.)*

Research References

Rutter, Cal. Practice Guide: Civ. Pro. Before Trial Ch. 1-G, G. Prior Court Order Required for Certain Pleadings.
Rutter, Cal. Practice Guide: Family Law Gen. Matls, Highlights.
3 Witkin Cal. Proc. 5th Actions § 370, Order Prohibiting Filing of New Litigation.

Title 4

OF THE PLACE OF TRIAL, RECLASSIFICATION, AND COORDINATION OF CIVIL ACTIONS

CHAPTER 1. PLACE OF TRIAL

§ 392. Real property actions; proper court

(a) Subject to the power of the court to transfer actions and proceedings as provided in this title, the superior court in the county where the real property that is the subject of the action, or some part thereof, is situated, is the proper court for the trial of the following actions:

(1) For the recovery of real property, or of an estate or interest therein, or for the determination in any form, of that right or interest, and for injuries to real property.

(2) For the foreclosure of all liens and mortgages on real property.

(b) In the court designated as the proper court in subdivision (a), the proper court location for trial of a proceeding for an unlawful detainer, as defined in Section 1161, is the location where the court tries that type of proceeding that is nearest or most accessible to where the real property that is the subject of the action, or some part thereof, is situated. Otherwise any location of the superior court designated as the proper court in subdivision (a) is a proper court location for the trial. The court may specify by local rule the nearest or most accessible court location where the court tries that type of case. *(Enacted in 1872. Amended by Code Am.1875–76, c. 117, p. 90, § 1; Stats.1889, c. 342, p. 352, § 1; Stats.1907, c. 369, p. 700, § 1; Stats.1933, c. 744, p. 1837, § 3; Stats.1951, c. 869, p. 2383, § 1; Stats.1976, c. 73, p. 110, § 3; Stats.1998, c. 931 (S.B.2139), § 60, eff. Sept. 28, 1998; Stats.2002, c. 806 (A.B.3027), § 7.)*

Law Revision Commission Comments

Recommendations relating to partition of real and personal property. 13 Cal.L.Rev.Comm. Reports 401 (1975), 1691 (1976).

Section 392 is amended to reflect the elimination of the justice court. Cal. Const. art. VI, §§ 1, 5(b). In a county in which there is no municipal court, the superior court has jurisdiction of matters that would be within the subject matter jurisdiction of the municipal court. Cal. Const. art. VI, 10 (superior court jurisdiction); Code Civ. Proc. §§ 85, 85.1 (limited civil cases). [28 Cal.L.Rev.Comm. Reports 51 (1998)].

Research References

Rutter, Cal. Practice Guide: Civ. Pro. Before Trial Ch. 3-D, D. Venue.
Rutter, Cal. Practice Guide: Fed.Civ.Pro. Before Trial Ch. 4-G, G. Special Venue Rules.
Rutter, Cal. Practice Guide: Fed.Civ.Pro. Before Trial Ch. 1-D, D. Choosing Between State and Federal Courts.
Miller and Starr California Real Estate § 29:1, General Observations; Theories of Liability.
Miller and Starr California Real Estate § 28:55, Venue.
Miller and Starr California Real Estate § 19:166, Jurisdiction, Venue, Summons and Complaint.
Miller and Starr California Real Estate § 19:219, Jurisdiction and Venue.
3 Witkin Cal. Proc. 5th Actions § 779, in General.
3 Witkin Cal. Proc. 5th Actions § 782, (S 782) Former Justice and Municipal Courts.
3 Witkin Cal. Proc. 5th Actions § 783, (S 783) Consolidation of Trial Courts.
3 Witkin Cal. Proc. 5th Actions § 793, Nature and Classes.
3 Witkin Cal. Proc. 5th Actions § 794, Land in More Than One County.
3 Witkin Cal. Proc. 5th Actions § 795, Ejectment and Unlawful Detainer.

Civ. Pro.

3 Witkin Cal. Proc. 5th Actions § 796, Quiet Title.
3 Witkin Cal. Proc. 5th Actions § 797, Actions Involving Deeds, Contracts, or Trusts.
3 Witkin Cal. Proc. 5th Actions § 799, (S 799) Enforcement of Lien.
3 Witkin Cal. Proc. 5th Actions § 801, Physical Injuries.
3 Witkin Cal. Proc. 5th Actions § 802, Indirect or Consequential Injuries.
3 Witkin Cal. Proc. 5th Actions § 806, (S 806) Proceeding Under Trust Law.
3 Witkin Cal. Proc. 5th Actions § 845, Actions on Installment Contracts.
3 Witkin Cal. Proc. 5th Actions § 849, (S 849) in General.
3 Witkin Cal. Proc. 5th Actions § 883, (S 883) Mixed Action.
3 Witkin Cal. Proc. 5th Actions § 884, (S 884) Joinder of Local and Transitory Causes.
8 Witkin Cal. Proc. 5th Enforcement of Judgment § 453, (S 453) Jurisdiction and Venue.
12 Witkin, California Summary 10th Real Property § 728, Jurisdiction, Venue, and Process.
13 Witkin, California Summary 10th Trusts § 225, (S 225) Venue.

§ 393. Actions to recover penalty or forfeiture; actions against public officers; proper court

Subject to the power of the court to transfer actions and proceedings as provided in this title, the county in which the cause, or some part of the cause, arose, is the proper county for the trial of the following actions:

(a) For the recovery of a penalty or forfeiture imposed by statute, except, that when it is imposed for an offense committed on a lake, river, or other stream of water, situated in two or more counties, the action may be tried in any county bordering on the lake, river, or stream, and opposite to the place where the offense was committed.

(b) Against a public officer or person especially appointed to execute the duties of a public officer, for an act done by the officer or person in virtue of the office, or against a person who, by the officer's command or in the officer's aid, does anything touching the duties of the officer. *(Enacted in 1872. Amended by Stats.1933, c. 744, p. 1838, § 4; Stats.1951, c. 869, p. 2384, § 2; Stats.1998, c. 931 (S.B.2139), § 61, eff. Sept. 28, 1998; Stats.2003, c. 449 (A.B.1712), § 7.)*

Law Revision Commission Comments

Section 393 is amended to reflect the elimination of the justice court. Cal. Const. art. VI, 5(b). In a county in which there is no municipal court, the superior court has jurisdiction of matters that would be within the subject matter jurisdiction of the municipal court. Cal. Const. art. VI, 10 (superior court jurisdiction); Code Civ. Proc. §§ 85, 85.1 (limited civil cases). [28 Cal.L.Rev.Comm. Reports 51 (1998)].

Research References

Rutter, Cal. Practice Guide: Civ. Pro. Before Trial Ch. 3-D, D. Venue.
Rutter, Cal. Practice Guide: Insurance Litigation Ch. 14-B, B. Courts and Regulation.
3 Witkin Cal. Proc. 5th Actions § 782, (S 782) Former Justice and Municipal Courts.
3 Witkin Cal. Proc. 5th Actions § 804, Recovery of Penalty or Forfeiture.
3 Witkin Cal. Proc. 5th Actions § 845, Actions on Installment Contracts.
3 Witkin Cal. Proc. 5th Actions § 862, Nature of Problem.
3 Witkin Cal. Proc. 5th Actions § 869, Statutory Rule.
3 Witkin Cal. Proc. 5th Actions § 870, Illustrations.
8 Witkin Cal. Proc. 5th Extraordinary Writs § 301, Venue.

§ 394. Actions by or against a city, county, city and county or local agency; transfer of cases; proper court

(a) An action or proceeding against a county, or city and county, a city, or local agency, may be tried in the county, or city and county, or the county in which the city or local agency is situated, unless the action or proceeding is brought by a county, or city and county, a city, or local agency, in which case it may be tried in any county, or city and county, not a party thereto and in which the city or local agency is not situated. Except for actions initiated by the local child support agency pursuant to Section 17400, 17402, 17404, or 17416 of the Family Code, any action or proceeding brought by a county, city and county, city, or local agency within a certain county, or city and county, against a resident of another county, city and county, or city, or a corporation doing business in the latter, shall be, on motion of either party, transferred for trial to a county, or city and county, other than the plaintiff, if the plaintiff is a county, or city and county, and other than that in which the plaintiff is situated, if the plaintiff is a city, or a local agency, and other than that in which the defendant resides, or is doing business, or is situated. Whenever an action or proceeding is brought against a county, city and county, city, or local agency, in any county, or city and county, other than the defendant, if the defendant is a county, or city and county, or, if the defendant is a city, or local agency, other than that in which the defendant is situated, the action or proceeding must be, on motion of that defendant, transferred for trial to a county, or city and county, other than that in which the plaintiff, or any of the plaintiffs, resides, or is doing business, or is situated, and other than the plaintiff county, or city and county, or county in which that plaintiff city or local agency is situated, and other than the defendant county, or city and county, or county in which the defendant city or local agency is situated; provided, however, that any action or proceeding against the city, county, city and county, or local agency for injury occurring within the city, county, or city and county, or within the county in which the local agency is situated, to person or property or person and property caused by the negligence or alleged negligence of the city, county, city and county, local agency, or its agents or employees, shall be tried in that county, or city and county, or if a city is a defendant, in the city or in the county in which the city is situated, or if a local agency is a defendant, in the county in which the local agency is situated. In that action or proceeding, the parties thereto may, by stipulation in writing, or made in open court, and entered in the minutes, agree upon any county, or city and county, for the place of trial thereof. When the action or proceeding is one in which a jury is not of right, or in case a jury is waived, then in lieu of transferring the cause, the court in the original county may request the chairperson of the Judicial Council to assign a disinterested judge from a neutral county to hear that cause and all proceedings in connection therewith. When the action or proceeding is transferred to another county for trial, a witness required to respond to a subpoena for a hearing within the original county shall be compelled to attend hearings in the county to which the cause is transferred. If the demand for transfer is made by one party and the opposing party does not consent thereto, the additional costs of the nonconsenting party occasioned by the transfer of the cause, including living and traveling expenses of the nonconsenting party and material witnesses, found by the court to be material, and called by the nonconsenting party, not to exceed five dollars ($5) per day each in excess of witness fees and mileage otherwise allowed by law, shall be assessed by the court hearing the cause against the party requesting the transfer. To the extent of that excess, those costs shall be awarded to the nonconsenting party regardless of the outcome of the trial. This section shall apply to actions or proceedings now pending or hereafter brought.

(b) For the purposes of this section, "local agency" shall mean any governmental district, board, or agency, or any other local governmental body or corporation, but shall not include the State of California or any of its agencies, departments, commissions, or boards. *(Enacted in 1872. Amended by Stats.1881, c. 30, p. 23, § 1; Stats.1891, c. 61, p. 56, § 1; Stats.1907, c. 369, p. 700, § 2; Stats.1915, c. 434, p. 721, § 1; Stats.1921, c. 382, p. 573, § 1; Stats.1929, c. 112, p. 198, § 1; Stats.1931, c. 942, p. 1948, § 1; Stats.1933, c. 744, p. 1838, § 5; Stats.1970, c. 604, p. 1184, § 1; Stats.1971, c. 957, p. 1865, § 1; Stats.1994, c. 1269*

(A.B.2208), § 2.2; Stats.2002, c. 784 (S.B.1316), § 52; Stats. 2002, c. 927 (A.B.3032), § 1.)

Law Revision Commission Comments

Subdivision (b) of Section 394 is deleted to reflect unification of the municipal and superior courts pursuant to Article VI, Section 5(e), of the California Constitution. [32 Cal.L.Rev.Comm. Reports 116].

Research References

Rutter, Cal. Practice Guide: Civ. Pro. Before Trial Ch. 3-D, D. Venue.
Miller and Starr California Real Estate § 30A:49, Jurisdiction and Venue.
Miller and Starr California Real Estate § 30A:54, Withdrawal of Deposit.
3 Witkin Cal. Proc. 5th Actions § 783, (S 783) Consolidation of Trial Courts.
3 Witkin Cal. Proc. 5th Actions § 785, (S 785) General Rule: Agreement Fixing Venue is Void.
3 Witkin Cal. Proc. 5th Actions § 815, (S 815) Other Proceedings.
3 Witkin Cal. Proc. 5th Actions § 871, (S 871) in General.
3 Witkin Cal. Proc. 5th Actions § 872, (S 872) Parties Covered.
3 Witkin Cal. Proc. 5th Actions § 873, (S 873) Parties Excluded.
3 Witkin Cal. Proc. 5th Actions § 874, Negligence Action Against City or County.
3 Witkin Cal. Proc. 5th Actions § 875, County Child Support or Paternity Proceeding.
3 Witkin Cal. Proc. 5th Actions § 876, Individual Defendant.
3 Witkin Cal. Proc. 5th Actions § 877, Corporation Defendant.
3 Witkin Cal. Proc. 5th Actions § 879, Condemnation.
3 Witkin Cal. Proc. 5th Actions § 880, (S 880) in General.
3 Witkin Cal. Proc. 5th Actions § 881, (S 881) Distinctions and Clarifications.
3 Witkin Cal. Proc. 5th Actions § 904, (S 904) Joinder of Private and Governmental Defendants.
3 Witkin Cal. Proc. 5th Actions § 915, Exceptions.
3 Witkin Cal. Proc. 5th Actions § 955, (S 955) Procedure.
3 Witkin Cal. Proc. 5th Actions § 958, Removal to Neutral County.
8 Witkin, California Summary 10th Constitutional Law § 1204, Jurisdiction and Venue.
13 Witkin, California Summary 10th Equity § 148, (S 148) Action and Temporary Relief.

§ 395. Actions generally; proper court; waiver

(a) Except as otherwise provided by law and subject to the power of the court to transfer actions or proceedings as provided in this title, the superior court in the county where the defendants or some of them reside at the commencement of the action is the proper court for the trial of the action. If the action is for injury to person or personal property or for death from wrongful act or negligence, the superior court in either the county where the injury occurs or the injury causing death occurs or the county where the defendants, or some of them reside at the commencement of the action, is a proper court for the trial of the action. In a proceeding for dissolution of marriage, the superior court in the county where either the petitioner or respondent has been a resident for three months next preceding the commencement of the proceeding is the proper court for the trial of the proceeding. In a proceeding for nullity of marriage or legal separation of the parties, the superior court in the county where either the petitioner or respondent resides at the commencement of the proceeding is the proper court for the trial of the proceeding. In a proceeding to enforce an obligation of support under Section 3900 of the Family Code, the superior court in the county where the child resides is the proper court for the trial of the action. In a proceeding to establish and enforce a foreign judgment or court order for the support of a minor child, the superior court in the county where the child resides is the proper court for the trial of the action. Subject to subdivision (b), if a defendant has contracted to perform an obligation in a particular county, the superior court in the county where the obligation is to be performed, where the contract in fact was entered into, or where the defendant or any defendant resides at the commencement of the action is a proper court for the trial of an action founded on that obligation, and the county where the obligation is incurred is the county where it is to be performed, unless there is a special contract in writing to the contrary. If none of the defendants reside in the state or if they reside in the state and the county where they reside is unknown to the plaintiff, the action may be tried in the superior court in any county that the plaintiff may designate in his or her complaint, and, if the defendant is about to depart from the state, the action may be tried in the superior court in any county where either of the parties reside or service is made. If any person is improperly joined as a defendant or has been made a defendant solely for the purpose of having the action tried in the superior court in the county where he or she resides, his or her residence shall not be considered in determining the proper place for the trial of the action.

(b) Subject to the power of the court to transfer actions or proceedings as provided in this title, in an action arising from an offer or provision of goods, services, loans or extensions of credit intended primarily for personal, family or household use, other than an obligation described in Section 1812.10 or Section 2984.4 of the Civil Code, or an action arising from a transaction consummated as a proximate result of either an unsolicited telephone call made by a seller engaged in the business of consummating transactions of that kind or a telephone call or electronic transmission made by the buyer or lessee in response to a solicitation by the seller, the superior court in the county where the buyer or lessee in fact signed the contract, where the buyer or lessee resided at the time the contract was entered into, or where the buyer or lessee resides at the commencement of the action is the proper court for the trial of the action. In the superior court designated in this subdivision as the proper court, the proper court location for trial of a case is the location where the court tries that type of case that is nearest or most accessible to where the buyer or lessee resides, where the buyer or lessee in fact signed the contract, where the buyer or lessee resided at the time the contract was entered into, or where the buyer or lessee resides at the commencement of the action. Otherwise, any location of the superior court designated as the proper court in this subdivision is a proper court location for the trial. The court may specify by local rule the nearest or most accessible court location where the court tries that type of case.

(c) Any provision of an obligation described in subdivision (b) waiving that subdivision is void and unenforceable. *(Enacted in 1872. Amended by Stats.1907, c. 369, p. 700, § 3; Stats.1911, c. 421, p. 847, § 1; Stats.1933, c. 744, p. 1840, § 6; Stats.1939, c. 981, p. 2733, § 1; Stats.1951, c. 869, p. 2384, § 3; Stats.1955, c. 832, p. 1447, § 1; Stats.1969, c. 1608, p. 3344, § 11, operative Jan. 1, 1970; Stats.1970, c. 75, p. 88, § 1; Stats.1971, c. 1640, p. 3540, § 1; Stats.1972, c. 1117, § 1; Stats.1972, c. 1118, § 3; Stats.1972, c. 1119, § 3; Stats.1976, c. 610, p. 1460, § 1; Stats.1991, c. 228 (A.B.1889), § 3; Stats.1992, c. 163 (A.B.2641), § 17, operative Jan. 1, 1994; Stats.1994, c. 1269 (A.B.2208), § 2.4; Stats.1998, c. 473 (A.B.2134), § 1; Stats.1998, c. 931 (S.B.2139), § 62, eff. Sept. 28, 1998; Stats.1998, c. 931 (S.B.2139), § 62.5, eff. Sept. 28, 1998, operative Jan. 1, 1999; Stats.2002, c. 806 (A.B.3027), § 8.)*

Law Revision Commission Comments

Subdivision (a) of Section 395 is amended to substitute a reference to the Family Code provision that replaced the former Civil Code provision. The part of the fourth sentence of subdivision (a) relating to an action to determine parental relations has been deleted because it was inconsistent with and in effect replaced by Family Code Section 7620(b). [22 Cal.L.Rev.Comm.Reports 1 (1992)].

Section 395 is amended to reflect the elimination of the justice court. Cal. Const. art. VI, §§ 1, 5(b). In a county in which there is no municipal court, the superior court has jurisdiction of matters that would be within the subject matter jurisdiction of the municipal court. Cal. Const. art. VI, 10 (superior court jurisdiction); Code Civ. Proc. §§ 85, 85.1 (limited civil cases). [28 Cal.L.Rev.Comm. Reports 51 (1998)].

Research References

Rutter, Cal. Practice Guide: Civ. Pro. Before Trial Ch. 3-D, D. Venue.

Rutter, Cal. Practice Guide: Civ. Pro. Before Trial Ch. 5-G, G. Relief from Default.

Rutter, Cal. Practice Guide: Civ. Pro. Before Trial Ch. 6-B, B. Complaints.

California Practice Guide: Employment Litigation Ch. 19-A, A. Plaintiff's Forum Selection.

Rutter, Cal. Practice Guide: Enforcing Judgments/Debts Ch. 3-C, C. Prelawsuit Considerations.

Rutter, Cal. Practice Guide: Fed.Civ.Pro. Before Trial Ch. 1-D, D. Choosing Between State and Federal Courts.

3 Witkin Cal. Proc. 5th Actions § 782, (S 782) Former Justice and Municipal Courts.

3 Witkin Cal. Proc. 5th Actions § 785, (S 785) General Rule: Agreement Fixing Venue is Void.

3 Witkin Cal. Proc. 5th Actions § 802, Indirect or Consequential Injuries.

3 Witkin Cal. Proc. 5th Actions § 806, (S 806) Proceeding Under Trust Law.

3 Witkin Cal. Proc. 5th Actions § 810, Former Law: Petitioner's Residence.

3 Witkin Cal. Proc. 5th Actions § 811, Current Law: Either Party's Residence.

3 Witkin Cal. Proc. 5th Actions § 812, Former Law: Respondent's Residence.

3 Witkin Cal. Proc. 5th Actions § 813, Current Law: Either Party's Residence.

3 Witkin Cal. Proc. 5th Actions § 815, (S 815) Other Proceedings.

3 Witkin Cal. Proc. 5th Actions § 817, (S 817) Nature of Right.

3 Witkin Cal. Proc. 5th Actions § 821, (S 821) Personal Torts Other Than Physical Injury or Death.

3 Witkin Cal. Proc. 5th Actions § 822, (S 822) Torts to Personal Property Other Than Physical Injury.

3 Witkin Cal. Proc. 5th Actions § 831, (S 831) Actions to Recover Money: in General.

3 Witkin Cal. Proc. 5th Actions § 832, (S 832) Actions for Personal Injury or Death.

3 Witkin Cal. Proc. 5th Actions § 833, (S 833) Actions for Injury to Personal Property.

3 Witkin Cal. Proc. 5th Actions § 834, (S 834) Nature of Statute.

3 Witkin Cal. Proc. 5th Actions § 837, (S 837) in General.

3 Witkin Cal. Proc. 5th Actions § 841, (S 841) Effect of Limiting Proviso: "Obligation Incurred.".

3 Witkin Cal. Proc. 5th Actions § 844, Promise to Pay Seller's Assignee.

3 Witkin Cal. Proc. 5th Actions § 845, Actions on Installment Contracts.

3 Witkin Cal. Proc. 5th Actions § 846, Actions on Consumer Obligations.

3 Witkin Cal. Proc. 5th Actions § 847, Defendant Nonresident or Residence Unknown.

3 Witkin Cal. Proc. 5th Actions § 848, Defendant About to Depart.

3 Witkin Cal. Proc. 5th Actions § 854, Where Contract is Made.

3 Witkin Cal. Proc. 5th Actions § 855, (S 855) in General.

3 Witkin Cal. Proc. 5th Actions § 859, (S 859) Tort Actions.

3 Witkin Cal. Proc. 5th Actions § 870, Illustrations.

3 Witkin Cal. Proc. 5th Actions § 871, (S 871) in General.

3 Witkin Cal. Proc. 5th Actions § 874, Negligence Action Against City or County.

3 Witkin Cal. Proc. 5th Actions § 886, (S 886) Action Under Fair Employment and Housing Act.

3 Witkin Cal. Proc. 5th Actions § 888, (S 888) Distinction: Action Under Consumers Legal Remedies Act.

3 Witkin Cal. Proc. 5th Actions § 889, Effect of Proper Joinder.

3 Witkin Cal. Proc. 5th Actions § 890, Effect of Improper Joinder.

3 Witkin Cal. Proc. 5th Actions § 891, Amendment or Dismissal After Motion.

3 Witkin Cal. Proc. 5th Actions § 894, (S 894) Two Tests.

3 Witkin Cal. Proc. 5th Actions § 897, (S 897) Insufficiency Appearing from Pleading.

3 Witkin Cal. Proc. 5th Actions § 903, County Where Neither Resides is Improper.

3 Witkin Cal. Proc. 5th Actions § 904, (S 904) Joinder of Private and Governmental Defendants.

3 Witkin Cal. Proc. 5th Actions § 933, (S 933) Points and Authorities.

3 Witkin Cal. Proc. 5th Actions § 958, Removal to Neutral County.

4 Witkin Cal. Proc. 5th Pleading § 472, Limited Civil Cases.

5 Witkin Cal. Proc. 5th Pleading § 762, Filing at Improper Venue.

11 Witkin, California Summary 10th Husband and Wife § 73, (S 73) Residence and Venue.

11 Witkin, California Summary 10th Husband and Wife § 146, Proceedings.

11 Witkin, California Summary 10th Husband and Wife § 170, (S 170) Venue, Limitations, Parties, and Pleadings.

5 Witkin, California Summary 10th Torts § 5, (S 5) Classification of Torts.

5 Witkin, California Summary 10th Torts § 525, Action Disregarding Venue Statutes.

8 Witkin, California Summary 10th Constitutional Law § 951, Judicial Enforcement.

13 Witkin, California Summary 10th Trusts § 225, (S 225) Venue.

§ 395.1. Executor, administrator, guardian, conservator, or trustee in official or representative capacity

Except as otherwise provided in Section 17005 of the Probate Code pertaining to trustees, when a defendant is sued in an official or representative capacity as executor, administrator, guardian, conservator, or trustee on a claim for the payment of money or for the recovery of personal property, the county which has jurisdiction of the estate which the defendant represents shall be the proper county for the trial of the action. *(Added by Stats.1943, c. 1043, p. 2979, § 1. Amended by Stats.1979, c. 730, p. 2476, § 20, operative Jan. 1, 1981; Stats.1986, c. 820, § 16, operative July 1, 1987.)*

Law Revision Commission Comments

Recommendations relating to Guardianship-Conservatorship Law 14 Cal.L.Rev.Comm. Reports 501 (1978).

Section 395.1 is amended to add the reference to a conservator. [1979]

Section 395.1 is amended to recognize the special venue provisions relating to internal affairs of trusts. See also Prob. Code §§ 17000(a) (exclusive jurisdiction over internal affairs of trusts), 17300–17304 (proceedings involving trust subject to continuing court jurisdiction). [18 Cal.L.Rev.Comm. Reports 501 (1986)].

Research References

Rutter, Cal. Practice Guide: Civ. Pro. Before Trial Ch. 3-D, D. Venue.

3 Witkin Cal. Proc. 5th Actions § 805, (S 805) Proceeding Against Executor or Other Representative.

3 Witkin Cal. Proc. 5th Actions § 822, (S 822) Torts to Personal Property Other Than Physical Injury.

3 Witkin Cal. Proc. 5th Actions § 824, Accounting.

3 Witkin Cal. Proc. 5th Actions § 831, (S 831) Actions to Recover Money: in General.

3 Witkin Cal. Proc. 5th Actions § 937, Award of Expenses and Fees to Prevailing Party.

14 Witkin, California Summary 10th Wills and Probate § 647, Procedure.

§ 395.2. Unincorporated associations

If an unincorporated association has filed a statement with the Secretary of State pursuant to statute, designating its principal office in this state, the proper county for the trial of an action against the unincorporated association is the same as it would be if the unincorporated association were a corporation and, for the purpose of determining the proper county, the principal place of business of the unincorporated association shall be deemed to be the principal office in this state listed in the statement. *(Added by Stats.1967, c. 1324, p. 3150, § 2. Amended by Stats.2004, c. 178 (S.B.1746), § 2.)*

Law Revision Commission Comments

Section 395.2 is amended to reflect that an unincorporated association may file a statement designating its principal office under sections other than former Corporations Code Section 24003 (continued without substantive change in Corporations Code Section 18200). See, e.g., Corp. Code §§ 15621(a)(4) (limited partnership), 16309 (general partnership), 16953(a)(3) (limited liability partnership), 17051(a)(4) (limited liability company), 17060(a)(2) (limited liability company). [33 Cal.L.Rev.Comm. Reports 770 (2004)].

Recommendation and study relating to suit by or against an unincorporated association, 8 Cal.L.Rev.Comm. Reports 901 (1966).

Research References

Rutter, Cal. Practice Guide: Civ. Pro. Before Trial Ch. 3-D, D. Venue.
3 Witkin Cal. Proc. 5th Actions § 850, (S 850) Unincorporated Associations.
3 Witkin Cal. Proc. 5th Actions § 851, (S 851) Corporate or Association Residence.
3 Witkin Cal. Proc. 5th Actions § 852, Domestic Corporation or Association.

§ 395.5. Actions against corporations or associations; place of trial

A corporation or association may be sued in the county where the contract is made or is to be performed, or where the obligation or liability arises, or the breach occurs; or in the county where the principal place of business of such corporation is situated, subject to the power of the court to change the place of trial as in other cases. *(Added by Stats.1972, c. 118, § 1, eff. June 5, 1972.)*

Research References

Rutter, Cal. Practice Guide: Civ. Pro. Before Trial Ch. 3-D, D. Venue.
California Practice Guide: Employment Litigation Ch. 19-A, A. Plaintiff's Forum Selection.
Rutter, Cal. Practice Guide: Insurance Litigation Ch. 15-D, D. Filing Considerations.
3 Witkin Cal. Proc. 5th Actions § 849, (S 849) in General.
3 Witkin Cal. Proc. 5th Actions § 850, (S 850) Unincorporated Associations.
3 Witkin Cal. Proc. 5th Actions § 852, Domestic Corporation or Association.
3 Witkin Cal. Proc. 5th Actions § 855, (S 855) in General.
3 Witkin Cal. Proc. 5th Actions § 861, (S 861) Action Based on Statutory Liability.
3 Witkin Cal. Proc. 5th Actions § 887, (S 887) Action to Dissolve Corporation.
3 Witkin Cal. Proc. 5th Actions § 903, County Where Neither Resides is Improper.

§ 396. Superior court lacking jurisdiction of appeal or petition; transfer to court having jurisdiction

(a) No appeal or petition filed in the superior court shall be dismissed solely because the appeal or petition was not filed in the proper state court.

(b) If the superior court lacks jurisdiction of an appeal or petition, and a court of appeal or the Supreme Court would have jurisdiction, the appeal or petition shall be transferred to the court having jurisdiction upon terms as to costs or otherwise as may be just, and proceeded with as if regularly filed in the court having jurisdiction. *(Added by Stats.2008, c. 56 (S.B.1182), § 2.)*

Law Revision Commission Comments

Section 396 requires a superior court to transfer an appeal or petition over which the superior court lacks jurisdiction to an appellate court that has jurisdiction. The provision continues a policy that requires transfer and prohibits dismissal of a cause simply because it was filed in the wrong court. See, e.g., former Section 396 (2002 Cal. Stat. ch. 806, § 9); Gov't Code § 68915; see Friends of Mammoth v. Bd. of Supervisors, 8 Cal.3d 247, 268–69, 502 P.2d 1049, 104 Cal.Rptr. 761 (1972); Morgan v. Somervell, 40 Cal.App.2d 398, 400, 104 P.2d 866 (1940). [37 Cal.L.Rev. Comm. Reports 195 (2007)].

Section 396 is repealed due to trial court unification. The provision directed a court not to dismiss but to transfer a case if the court lacked subject matter jurisdiction and another state court would have such jurisdiction. The provision was often invoked when a municipal court transferred a case outside its jurisdiction to the superior court, or vice versa. See, e.g., Walker v. Superior Court, 53 Cal.3d 257, 807 P.2d 418, 279 Cal.Rptr. 576 (1991); Cal. Employment Stabilization Comm'n v. Municipal Court, 62 Cal.App.2d 781, 145 P.2d 361 (1944). After unification of the municipal and superior courts, it no longer served that purpose.

There was a split of authority regarding whether the provision authorized a superior court lacking jurisdiction to transfer a case to a court of appeal or the state Supreme Court. Compare TrafficSchoolOnline, Inc. v. Superior Court, 89 Cal.App.4th 222, 225, 107 Cal.Rptr.2d 412 (2001) ("[T]he superior court is not vested with the authority by Code of Civil Procedure Section 396 to transfer a case to the Court of Appeal or the Supreme Court."), with Padilla v. Dep't of Alcoholic Beverage Control, 43 Cal.App.4th 1151, 1154, 51 Cal.Rptr.2d 133 (1996) (Transfer requirement of Section 396 applies "in the case of proceedings filed in the superior court which, by statute, may be filed only in the Supreme Court or the Court of Appeal."); see also Pajaro Valley Water Mgmt. Agency v. McGrath, 128 Cal.App.4th 1093, 1104 n.4, 27 Cal.Rptr.3d 741 (2005) ("It is possible, though a point of disagreement, that [Section 396] retains vitality as empowering the superior court to transfer cases within the exclusive original jurisdiction of the appellate courts." (emphasis in original)).

Consistent with the key policy of deciding a case on its merits even if it is filed in the wrong tribunal, new Section 396 makes clear that if a superior court lacks jurisdiction of a matter and a state appellate court would have jurisdiction, the superior court must transfer the matter instead of dismissing it. [37 Cal.L.Rev.Comm. Reports 195 (2007)].

Research References

Rutter, Cal. Practice Guide: Real Prop. Transactions Ch. 4-F, F. Use of an Escrow.
3 Witkin Cal. Proc. 5th Actions § 19, Repeal of Jurisdictional Statute.
3 Witkin Cal. Proc. 5th Actions § 780, Illustrations.
3 Witkin Cal. Proc. 5th Actions § 786, (S 786) Distinctions and Exceptions.
3 Witkin Cal. Proc. 5th Actions § 872, (S 872) Parties Covered.
3 Witkin Cal. Proc. 5th Actions § 933, (S 933) Points and Authorities.
2 Witkin Cal. Proc. 5th Courts § 281, (S 281) in General.
2 Witkin Cal. Proc. 5th Courts § 287, (S 287) Restrictions on Transfer.
8 Witkin Cal. Proc. 5th Enforcement of Judgment § 453, (S 453) Jurisdiction and Venue.
8 Witkin Cal. Proc. 5th Extraordinary Writs § 261, (S 261) in General.
2 Witkin Cal. Proc. 5th Jurisdiction § 23, (S 23) Actual Recovery is Not Controlling.
2 Witkin Cal. Proc. 5th Jurisdiction § 27, (S 27) Waiver of Excess Recovery.
2 Witkin Cal. Proc. 5th Jurisdiction § 29, (S 29) Effect of Puffing.
2 Witkin Cal. Proc. 5th Jurisdiction § 52, (S 52) in General.
2 Witkin Cal. Proc. 5th Jurisdiction § 399, Nature and Purpose of Statute.
2 Witkin Cal. Proc. 5th Jurisdiction § 401, Review of Improper Transfer.
2 Witkin Cal. Proc. 5th Jurisdiction § 402, Plaintiff's Case is Beyond Jurisdiction.
2 Witkin Cal. Proc. 5th Jurisdiction § 403, Cross-Complaint is Beyond Jurisdiction.
2 Witkin Cal. Proc. 5th Jurisdiction § 405, Subject Matter Jurisdiction is Vested Elsewhere by Statute.
2 Witkin Cal. Proc. 5th Jurisdiction § 406, in General.
2 Witkin Cal. Proc. 5th Jurisdiction § 407, Determination of Lack of Jurisdiction.
2 Witkin Cal. Proc. 5th Jurisdiction § 408, Proceeding is Deemed Commenced in New Court.
2 Witkin Cal. Proc. 5th Jurisdiction § 409, (S 409) Discretionary Where Defect Appears During Trial.
4 Witkin Cal. Proc. 5th Pleading § 451, (S 451) Allegations Control Title or Prayer.
6 Witkin Cal. Proc. 5th Proceedings Without Trial § 392, Tolling on Transfer for Lack of Jurisdiction.

§ 396a. Specified actions or proceedings; statement of jurisdictional facts; transfers; consent to retention of case

In a case that is subject to Sections 1812.10 and 2984.4 of the Civil Code, or subdivision (b) of Section 395 of the Code of Civil Procedure, or in an action or proceeding for an unlawful detainer as defined in Section 1161 of the Code of Civil Procedure:

(a) The plaintiff shall state facts in the complaint, verified by the plaintiff's oath, or the oath of the plaintiff's attorney, or in an affidavit of the plaintiff or of the plaintiff's attorney filed with the complaint, showing that the action has been commenced in the proper superior court and the proper court location for the trial of the action or proceeding, and showing that the action is subject to the provisions of Sections 1812.10 and 2984.4 of the

Civil Code or subdivision (b) of Section 395 of the Code of Civil Procedure, or is an action for an unlawful detainer. When the affidavit is filed with the complaint, a copy thereof shall be served with the summons. Except as provided in this section, if the complaint or affidavit is not filed pursuant to this subdivision, no further proceedings may occur in the action or proceeding, except to dismiss the action or proceeding without prejudice. However, the court may, on terms that are just, permit the affidavit to be filed after the filing of the complaint, and a copy of the affidavit shall be served on the defendant and the time to answer or otherwise plead shall date from that service.

(b) If it appears from the complaint or affidavit, or otherwise, that the superior court or court location where the action or proceeding is commenced is not the proper court or court location for the trial, the court where the action or proceeding is commenced, or a judge thereof, shall, whenever that fact appears, transfer it to the proper court or court location, on its own motion, or on motion of the defendant, unless the defendant consents in writing, or in open court (consent in open court being entered in the minutes of the court), to the keeping of the action or proceeding in the court or court location where commenced. If that consent is given, the action or proceeding may continue in the court or court location where commenced. Notwithstanding Section 1801.1 and subdivision (f) of Section 2983.7 of the Civil Code, that consent may be given by a defendant who is represented by counsel at the time the consent is given, and if an action or proceeding is subject to subdivision (b) of Section 395 or is for an unlawful detainer, that consent may only be given by a defendant who is represented by counsel at the time the consent is given.

(c) In any case where the transfer of the action or proceeding is ordered under subdivision (a) or (b), if summons is served prior to the filing of the action or proceeding in the superior court or court location to which it is transferred, as to any defendant, so served, who has not appeared in the action or proceeding, the time to answer or otherwise plead shall date from service upon that defendant of written notice of the filing.

(d) If it appears from the complaint or affidavit of the plaintiff that the superior court and court location where the action or proceeding is commenced are a proper court and court location for the trial thereof, all proper proceedings may be had, and the action or proceeding may be tried in that court at that location.

(e) A motion for a transfer of the action or proceeding to a different superior court may be made as in other cases, within the time, upon the grounds, and in the manner provided in this title, and if upon that motion it appears that the action or proceeding is not pending in the proper court, or should for other cause be transferred, the action or proceeding shall be ordered transferred as provided in this title.

If any action or proceeding is ordered transferred to another court as provided in this section, proceedings shall be had, and the costs and fees shall be paid, as provided in Sections 398 and 399.

(f) If a motion is made for transfer of an action or proceeding to a different court location within the same superior court as provided in this section, proceedings shall be had as provided by local rules of the superior court. (Added by Stats.1933, c. 744, p. 1841, § 8. Amended by Stats.1935, c. 722, p. 1948, § 2; Stats.1937, c. 97, p. 336, § 1; Stats.1949, c. 1286, p. 2270, § 3; Stats.1951, c. 869, p. 2386, § 5; Stats.1970, c. 725, p. 1353, § 3; Stats.1976, c. 1288, p. 5763, § 11; Stats.1982, c. 38, p. 75, § 1; Stats.1998, c. 931 (S.B.2139), § 65, eff. Sept. 28, 1998; Stats.2002, c. 806 (A.B.3027), § 10; Stats.2007, c. 263 (A.B.310), § 5.)

Law Revision Commission Comments

Section 396a is amended to accommodate unification of the municipal and superior courts in a county. Cal. Const. art. VI, § 5(e). It is also amended to reflect elimination of the justice court. Cal. Const. art. VI, §§ 1, 5(b). Formerly, each county had one or more municipal courts and a superior court, and Section 396a applied to matters commenced in the municipal courts. A limited civil case is equivalent to a matter within the original jurisdiction of the municipal court under former law, so Section 396a as amended continues the effect of former law. Cf. Sections 85, 85.1 (limited civil cases). [28 Cal.L.Rev.Comm. Reports 51 (1998)].

Subdivision (b) of Section 396a is amended to delete the reference to a "docket," because courts no longer maintain a record denominated a "docket" in civil cases. Actions taken in open court are now recorded in the minutes of a superior court. See Gov't Code § 69844 (minutes of superior court); see also Copley Press v. Superior Court, 6 Cal.App.4th 106, 110, 7 Cal.Rptr.2d 841 (1992). [35 Cal.L.Rev.Comm. Reports 219 (2007)].

Research References

Rutter, Cal. Practice Guide: Civ. Pro. Before Trial Ch. 3-D, D. Venue.
Rutter, Cal. Practice Guide: Civ. Pro. Before Trial Ch. 6-B, B. Complaints.
Miller and Starr California Real Estate § 19:221, Complaint and Summons.
3 Witkin Cal. Proc. 5th Actions § 780, Illustrations.
3 Witkin Cal. Proc. 5th Actions § 783, (S 783) Consolidation of Trial Courts.
3 Witkin Cal. Proc. 5th Actions § 795, Ejectment and Unlawful Detainer.
3 Witkin Cal. Proc. 5th Actions § 845, Actions on Installment Contracts.
3 Witkin Cal. Proc. 5th Actions § 846, Actions on Consumer Obligations.
3 Witkin Cal. Proc. 5th Actions § 907, Necessity of Motion.
3 Witkin Cal. Proc. 5th Actions § 1008, (S 1008) Delivery to Defendant.
4 Witkin Cal. Proc. 5th Pleading § 472, Limited Civil Cases.
5 Witkin Cal. Proc. 5th Pleading § 762, Filing at Improper Venue.
6 Witkin Cal. Proc. 5th Proceedings Without Trial § 147, Default After Granting Motion to Strike or Transfer.

§ 396b. Trial in court having jurisdiction of subject matter but not proper court; transfer; domestic relations cases; retention of cause for convenience of witnesses; time to file response upon denial of motion for transfer

(a) Except as otherwise provided in Section 396a, if an action or proceeding is commenced in a court having jurisdiction of the subject matter thereof, other than the court designated as the proper court for the trial thereof, under this title, the action may, notwithstanding, be tried in the court where commenced, unless the defendant, at the time he or she answers, demurs, or moves to strike, or, at his or her option, without answering, demurring, or moving to strike and within the time otherwise allowed to respond to the complaint, files with the clerk, a notice of motion for an order transferring the action or proceeding to the proper court, together with proof of service, upon the adverse party, of a copy of those papers. Upon the hearing of the motion the court shall, if it appears that the action or proceeding was not commenced in the proper court, order the action or proceeding transferred to the proper court.

(b) In its discretion, the court may order the payment to the prevailing party of reasonable expenses and attorney's fees incurred in making or resisting the motion to transfer whether or not that party is otherwise entitled to recover his or her costs of action. In determining whether that order for expenses and fees shall be made, the court shall take into consideration (1) whether an offer to stipulate to change of venue was reasonably made and rejected, and (2) whether the motion or selection of venue was made in good faith given the facts and law the party making the motion or selecting the venue knew or should have known. As between the party and his or her attorney, those expenses and fees shall be the personal liability of the attorney not chargeable to the party. Sanctions shall not be imposed pursuant to this subdivision except on notice contained in a party's papers, or on the court's own noticed motion, and after opportunity to be heard.

(c) The court in a proceeding for dissolution of marriage or legal separation or under the Uniform Parentage Act (Part 3 (commencing with Section 7600) of Division 12 of the Family Code) may, prior to the determination of the motion to transfer, consider and determine motions for allowance of temporary spousal support, support of children, and counsel fees and costs, and motions to determine custody of and visitation with children, and may make all necessary and proper orders in connection therewith.

(d) In any case, if an answer is filed, the court may consider opposition to the motion to transfer, if any, and may retain the action in the county where commenced if it appears that the convenience of the witnesses or the ends of justice will thereby be promoted.

(e) If the motion to transfer is denied, the court shall allow the defendant time to move to strike, demur, or otherwise plead if the defendant has not previously filed a response. *(Added by Stats.1933, c. 744, p. 1842, § 8a. Amended by Stats.1939, c. 149, p. 1263, § 1; Stats.1951, c. 869, p. 2387, § 6; Stats.1969, c. 345, p. 720, § 1; Stats.1969, c. 1608, p. 3345, § 12; Stats.1969, c. 1609, p. 3360, § 28, operative Jan. 1, 1970; Stats.1974, c. 1369, p. 2964, § 2; Stats.1981, c. 122, p. 856, § 1; Stats.1982, c. 704, p. 2856, § 1; Stats.1983, c. 1167, § 1; Stats.1989, c. 1416, § 11; Stats. 1989, c. 1417, § 3.5; Stats.1992, c. 163 (A.B.2641), § 18, operative Jan. 1, 1994; Stats.2005, c. 706 (A.B.1742), § 10.)*

Law Revision Commission Comments

Subdivision (c) of Section 396b is amended to conform to the language of the Family Code. [22 Cal.L.Rev.Comm.Reports 1 (1992)].

Retention of venue for convenience of witnesses; recommendation and study. Cal.Law Revision Comm. (1957) Vol. 1, p. L–5.

Research References

Rutter, Cal. Practice Guide: Civ. Pro. Before Trial Ch. 3-D, D. Venue.
Rutter, Cal. Practice Guide: Civ. Pro. Before Trial Ch. 6-B, B. Complaints.
Rutter, Cal. Practice Guide: Civ. Pro. Before Trial Ch. 11-A, A. Voluntary Dismissals.
Rutter, Cal. Practice Guide: Civ. Pro. Before Trial Ch. 9(III)-A, A. Sources of Sanctions Power.
Rutter, Cal. Practice Guide: Civ. Pro. Before Trial Ch. 9(III)-D, D. Other Sanctions Statutes and Rules.
California Practice Guide: Employment Litigation Ch. 19-B, B. Defendant's Challenges to Forum Plaintiff Selects.
Rutter, Cal. Practice Guide: Insurance Litigation Ch. 15-D, D. Filing Considerations.
Rutter, Cal. Practice Guide: Prof. Responsibility Ch. 8-E, E. Consequences of Improper Advocacy.
3 Witkin Cal. Proc. 5th Actions § 780, Illustrations.
3 Witkin Cal. Proc. 5th Actions § 812, Former Law: Respondent's Residence.
3 Witkin Cal. Proc. 5th Actions § 815, (S 815) Other Proceedings.
3 Witkin Cal. Proc. 5th Actions § 913, Stipulation to Grant Motion.
3 Witkin Cal. Proc. 5th Actions § 915, Exceptions.
3 Witkin Cal. Proc. 5th Actions § 922, Form of Notice.
3 Witkin Cal. Proc. 5th Actions § 924, Time of Notice.
3 Witkin Cal. Proc. 5th Actions § 925, Waiver by Failure to Comply.
3 Witkin Cal. Proc. 5th Actions § 926, Former Affidavit of Merits.
3 Witkin Cal. Proc. 5th Actions § 927, (S 927) Nature of Affidavit.
3 Witkin Cal. Proc. 5th Actions § 935, Selection of Proper Court.
3 Witkin Cal. Proc. 5th Actions § 937, Award of Expenses and Fees to Prevailing Party.
3 Witkin Cal. Proc. 5th Actions § 938, Payment of Costs of Transfer or Award.
3 Witkin Cal. Proc. 5th Actions § 939, (S 939) Pleading After Denial of Motion.
3 Witkin Cal. Proc. 5th Actions § 940, in General.
3 Witkin Cal. Proc. 5th Actions § 942, Time for Notice of Motion.
3 Witkin Cal. Proc. 5th Actions § 944, (S 944) in General.
3 Witkin Cal. Proc. 5th Actions § 945, (S 945) Counteraffidavits.
1 Witkin Cal. Proc. 5th Attorneys § 163, (S 163) Agreement With Client.
2 Witkin Cal. Proc. 5th Jurisdiction § 290, (S 290) Procedural Error or Omission.
6 Witkin Cal. Proc. 5th Proceedings Without Trial § 55, (S 55) Statutory Authorization.
6 Witkin Cal. Proc. 5th Proceedings Without Trial § 138, Responses Preventing Entry of Default.
6 Witkin Cal. Proc. 5th Proceedings Without Trial § 146, Filing of Motion Prevents Default.
6 Witkin Cal. Proc. 5th Proceedings Without Trial § 147, Default After Granting Motion to Strike or Transfer.
6 Witkin Cal. Proc. 5th Proceedings Without Trial § 148, Default After Denial of Motions.
6 Witkin Cal. Proc. 5th Proceedings Without Trial § 291, Motion to Change Venue Pending.
7 Witkin Cal. Proc. 5th Trial § 226, (S 226) in General.
12 Witkin, California Summary 10th Real Property § 728, Jurisdiction, Venue, and Process.
11 Witkin, California Summary 10th Husband and Wife § 73, (S 73) Residence and Venue.

§ 397. Change of place of trial; grounds

The court may, on motion, change the place of trial in the following cases:

(a) When the court designated in the complaint is not the proper court.

(b) When there is reason to believe that an impartial trial cannot be had therein.

(c) When the convenience of witnesses and the ends of justice would be promoted by the change.

(d) When from any cause there is no judge of the court qualified to act.

(e) When a proceeding for dissolution of marriage has been filed in the county in which the petitioner has been a resident for three months next preceding the commencement of the proceeding, and the respondent at the time of the commencement of the proceeding is a resident of another county in this state, to the county of the respondent's residence when the ends of justice would be promoted by the change. If a motion to change the place of trial is made pursuant to this paragraph, the court may, prior to the determination of such motion, consider and determine motions for allowance of temporary spousal support, support of children, temporary restraining orders, attorneys' fees, and costs, and make all necessary and proper orders in connection therewith. *(Enacted in 1872. Amended by Stats. 1907, c. 369, p. 701, § 5; Stats.1933, c. 744, p. 1843, § 9; Stats.1955, c. 832, p. 1448, § 2; Stats.1969, c. 1608, p. 3346, § 13, operative Jan. 1, 1970; Stats.1992, c. 163 (A.B.2641), § 19, operative Jan. 1, 1994.)*

Law Revision Commission Comments

The subdivisions of Section 397 are redesignated and subdivision (e) is amended to more closely conform to the language of Sections 259(f) and 396b(c). [22 Cal.L.Rev.Comm.Reports 1 (1992)].

Research References

Rutter, Cal. Practice Guide: Civ. Pro. Before Trial Ch. 3-D, D. Venue.
Rutter, Cal. Practice Guide: Civ. Pro. Before Trial Ch. 5-G, G. Relief from Default.
California Practice Guide: Employment Litigation Ch. 19-A, A. Plaintiff's Forum Selection.
California Practice Guide: Employment Litigation Ch. 19-B, B. Defendant's Challenges to Forum Plaintiff Selects.
Rutter, Cal. Practice Guide: Fed.Civ.Pro. Before Trial Ch. 1-D, D. Choosing Between State and Federal Courts.
Rutter, Cal. Practice Guide: Insurance Litigation Ch. 15-D, D. Filing Considerations.
Miller and Starr California Real Estate § 19:219, Jurisdiction and Venue.
3 Witkin Cal. Proc. 5th Actions § 810, Former Law: Petitioner's Residence.
3 Witkin Cal. Proc. 5th Actions § 811, Current Law: Either Party's Residence.
3 Witkin Cal. Proc. 5th Actions § 812, Former Law: Respondent's Residence.
3 Witkin Cal. Proc. 5th Actions § 867, Actions by Cities, Counties, and Local Agencies.

Civ. Pro.

3 Witkin Cal. Proc. 5th Actions § 886, (S 886) Action Under Fair Employment and Housing Act.
3 Witkin Cal. Proc. 5th Actions § 905, Statutory Grounds.
3 Witkin Cal. Proc. 5th Actions § 907, Necessity of Motion.
3 Witkin Cal. Proc. 5th Actions § 915, Exceptions.
3 Witkin Cal. Proc. 5th Actions § 940, in General.
3 Witkin Cal. Proc. 5th Actions § 941, Form of Notice of Motion.
3 Witkin Cal. Proc. 5th Actions § 955, (S 955) Procedure.
3 Witkin Cal. Proc. 5th Actions § 957, Disqualified Judge.
9 Witkin Cal. Proc. 5th Administrative Proceedings § 106, Time and Place.
11 Witkin, California Summary 10th Husband and Wife § 73, (S 73) Residence and Venue.

§ 397.5. Proceedings related to continuation of marriage; transfer from county

In any proceeding for dissolution or nullity of marriage or legal separation of the parties under the Family Code, where it appears that both petitioner and respondent have moved from the county rendering the order, the court may, when the ends of justice and the convenience of the parties would be promoted by the change, order that the proceedings be transferred to the county of residence of either party. *(Added by Stats.1971, c. 1210, p. 2328, § 7. Amended by Stats.1980, c. 234, p. 477, § 2; Stats.1994, c. 1269 (A.B.2208), § 2.6.)*

Law Revision Commission Comments

Section 397.5 is amended to correct a reference to the former Family Law Act (former Civ. Code § 4000 *et seq.*) and to conform to Family Code terminology. This is a technical, nonsubstantive change. [24 Cal.L.Rev. Comm. Reports 621 (1994)].

Research References

Rutter, Cal. Practice Guide: Civ. Pro. Before Trial Ch. 3-D, D. Venue.
Rutter, Cal. Practice Guide: Civil Trials & Evidence Ch. 4-G, G. Motion to Sever or Bifurcate.
3 Witkin Cal. Proc. 5th Actions § 811, Current Law: Either Party's Residence.
3 Witkin Cal. Proc. 5th Actions § 813, Current Law: Either Party's Residence.
3 Witkin Cal. Proc. 5th Actions § 847, Defendant Nonresident or Residence Unknown.
3 Witkin Cal. Proc. 5th Actions § 905, Statutory Grounds.
10 Witkin, California Summary 10th Parent and Child § 285, (S 285) in General.
11 Witkin, California Summary 10th Husband and Wife § 73, (S 73) Residence and Venue.
11 Witkin, California Summary 10th Husband and Wife § 146, Proceedings.
11 Witkin, California Summary 10th Husband and Wife § 170, (S 170) Venue, Limitations, Parties, and Pleadings.

§ 398. Transfer; proper court having jurisdiction

If, for any cause, specified in subdivisions 2, 3 and 4 of section 397, the court orders the transfer of an action or proceeding, it must be transferred to a court having jurisdiction of the subject matter of the action which the parties may agree upon, by stipulation in writing, or made in open court and entered in the minutes or docket; or, if they do not so agree, then to the nearest or most accessible court, where the like objection or cause for making the order does not exist.

If an action or proceeding is commenced in a court, other than one designated as a proper court for the trial thereof by the provisions of this title, and the same be ordered transferred for that reason, it must be transferred to any such proper court which the parties may agree upon by stipulation in writing, or made in open court and entered in the minutes or docket; if the parties do not so agree, then to any such proper court in the county in which the action or proceeding was commenced which the defendant may designate, or, if there be no such proper court in such county, to any such proper court, in a proper county, designated by the defendant; if the parties do not so agree, and the defendant does not so designate the court, as herein provided, or where the court orders the transfer of an action on its own motion as provided in this title, to such proper court as the court in which the action or proceeding is pending may determine.

The designation of the court by the defendant, herein provided for, may be made in the notice of motion for change of venue or in open court, entered in the minutes or docket, at the time the order for transfer is made. *(Enacted in 1872. Amended by Stats.1881, c. 30, p. 23, § 2; Stats.1897, c. 124, p. 184, § 1; Stats.1925, c. 438, p. 948, § 1; Stats.1927, c. 744, p. 1406, § 2; Stats.1933, c. 744, p. 1843, § 10.)*

Research References

3 Witkin Cal. Proc. 5th Actions § 910, Where Ground is Impartial Trial.
3 Witkin Cal. Proc. 5th Actions § 935, Selection of Proper Court.
3 Witkin Cal. Proc. 5th Actions § 940, in General.
3 Witkin Cal. Proc. 5th Actions § 955, (S 955) Procedure.
3 Witkin Cal. Proc. 5th Actions § 957, Disqualified Judge.

§ 399. Transfer; transmission of pleadings, papers, etc.; fees and costs; notice; jurisdiction of transferee court

(a) When an order is made transferring an action or proceeding under any of the provisions of this title, the clerk shall, after expiration of the time within which a petition for writ of mandate could have been filed pursuant to Section 400, or if a writ petition is filed after judgment denying the writ becomes final, and upon payment of the costs and fees, transmit the pleadings and papers therein (or if the pleadings be oral a transcript of the same) to the clerk of the court to which the same is transferred. When the transfer is sought on any ground specified in subdivision (b), (c), (d), or (e) of Section 397, the costs and fees thereof, and of filing the papers in the court to which the transfer is ordered, shall be paid at the time the notice of motion is filed, by the party making the motion for the transfer. When the transfer is sought solely, or is ordered, because the action or proceeding was commenced in a court other than that designated as proper by this title, those costs and fees (including any expenses and attorney's fees awarded to the defendant pursuant to Section 396b) shall be paid by the plaintiff before the transfer is made; and if the defendant has paid those costs and fees at the time of filing a notice of motion, the same shall be repaid to the defendant, upon the making of the transfer order. If those costs and fees have not been so paid by the plaintiff within five days after service of notice of the transfer order, then any other party interested therein, whether named in the complaint as a party or not, may pay those costs and fees, and the clerk shall thereupon transmit the papers and pleadings therein as if those costs and fees had been originally paid by the plaintiff, and the same shall be a proper item of costs of the party so paying the same, recoverable by that party in the event that party prevails in the action; otherwise, the same shall be offset against and deducted from the amount, if any, awarded the plaintiff in the event the plaintiff prevails against that party in the action. The cause of action shall not be further prosecuted in any court until those costs and fees are paid. If those costs and fees are not paid within 30 days after service of notice of the transfer order, or if a copy of a petition for writ of mandate pursuant to Section 400 is filed in the trial court, or if an appeal is taken pursuant to Section 904.2, then within 30 days after notice of finality of the order of transfer, the court on a duly noticed motion by any party may dismiss the action without prejudice to the cause on the condition that no other action on the cause may be commenced in another court prior to satisfaction of the court's order for costs and fees. When a petition for writ of mandate or appeal does not result in a stay of proceedings, the time for payment of those costs shall be 60 days after service of the notice of the order.

(b) At the time of transmittal of the papers and pleadings, the clerk shall mail notice to all parties who have appeared in the action or special proceeding, stating the date on which transmittal occurred. Promptly upon receipt of the papers and pleadings, the clerk of the court to which the action or proceeding is transferred shall mail notice to all parties who have appeared in the action or special proceeding, stating the date of the filing of the case and number assigned to the case in the court.

(c) The court to which an action or proceeding is transferred under this title shall have and exercise over the same the like jurisdiction as if it had been originally commenced therein, all prior proceedings being saved, and the court may require amendment of the pleadings, the filing and service of amended, additional, or supplemental pleadings, and the giving of notice, as may be necessary for the proper presentation and determination of the action or proceeding in the court. *(Enacted in 1872. Amended by Stats.1909, c. 723, p. 1097, § 1; Stats.1933, c. 744, p. 1844, § 11; Stats.1935, c. 722, p. 1949, § 3; Stats.1951, c. 869, p. 2388, § 7; Stats.1955, c. 832, p. 1449, § 3; Stats.1959, c. 1487, p. 3780, § 2; Stats.1961, c. 1059, p. 2747, § 1; Stats.1969, c. 345, p. 721, § 2; Stats.1974, c. 1369, p. 2965, § 3; Stats.1989, c. 1417, § 4; Stats.2007, c. 43 (S.B.649), § 4.)*

Law Revision Commission Comments

Section 399 is amended to delete an obsolete cross-reference to former Section 904.3, relating to appeals from justice courts. The justice courts no longer exist and former Section 904.3 was repealed. See 1994 Cal. Stat. res. ch. 113 (SCA 7) (Prop. 191, approved Nov. 8, 1994); 1976 Cal. Stat. ch. 1288, § 13.

Section 399 is also amended to correct the cross-references to subdivisions of Section 397. Former subdivisions (2)-(5) were relabeled as subdivisions (b)-(e). See 1992 Cal. Stat. ch. 163, § 19. Section 399 is revised to reflect that change.

Section 399 is further amended to insert subdivisions and make stylistic revisions. [36 Cal.L.Rev.Comm. Reports 305 (2007)].

Research References

Rutter, Cal. Practice Guide: Civ. Pro. Before Trial Ch. 3-D, D. Venue.
Rutter, Cal. Practice Guide: Civ. Pro. Before Trial Ch. 11-B, B. Involuntary Dismissals.
3 Witkin Cal. Proc. 5th Actions § 913, Stipulation to Grant Motion.
3 Witkin Cal. Proc. 5th Actions § 916, (S 916) Effect of Order Granting Change.
3 Witkin Cal. Proc. 5th Actions § 920, Procedure on Mandamus.
3 Witkin Cal. Proc. 5th Actions § 936, Transmission of Papers.
3 Witkin Cal. Proc. 5th Actions § 938, Payment of Costs of Transfer or Award.
3 Witkin Cal. Proc. 5th Actions § 940, in General.
2 Witkin Cal. Proc. 5th Courts § 366, (S 366) Miscellaneous Duties.
2 Witkin Cal. Proc. 5th Jurisdiction § 401, Review of Improper Transfer.
2 Witkin Cal. Proc. 5th Jurisdiction § 406, in General.
6 Witkin Cal. Proc. 5th Proceedings Without Trial § 392, Tolling on Transfer for Lack of Jurisdiction.

§ 400. Petition for writ of mandate by party aggrieved

When an order is made by the superior court granting or denying a motion to change the place of trial, the party aggrieved by the order may, within 20 days after service of a written notice of the order, petition the court of appeal for the district in which the court granting or denying the motion is situated for a writ of mandate requiring trial of the case in the proper court. The superior court may, for good cause, and prior to the expiration of the initial 20–day period, extend the time for one additional period not to exceed 10 days. The petitioner shall file a copy of the petition in the trial court immediately after the petition is filed in the court of appeal. The court of appeal may stay all proceedings in the case, pending judgment on the petition becoming final. The clerk of the court of appeal shall file with the clerk of the trial court, a copy of any final order or final judgment immediately after the order or judgment becomes final. *(Added by Stats.1961, c. 1059, p. 2748, § 3. Amended by*

Stats.1963, c. 461, p. 1309, § 1; Stats.1967, c. 17, p. 828, § 12; Stats.1984, c. 145, § 1; Stats.1989, c. 1416, § 12; Stats.1998, c. 931 (S.B.2139), § 67, eff. Sept. 28, 1998; Stats.1999, c. 344 (S.B.210), § 10, eff. Sept. 7, 1999.)

Law Revision Commission Comments

Section 400 is amended to accommodate unification of the municipal and superior courts in a county. Cal. Const. art. VI, § 5(e). See Section 85 (limited civil cases) & Comment. [28 Cal.L.Rev.Comm. Reports 51 (1998)].

Section 400 is amended for organizational clarity. The references to reclassification are continued without substantive change in Section 403.080 (petition for writ of mandate). [29 Cal.L.Rev.Comm. Reports App. 5 (1999)].

Research References

Rutter, Cal. Practice Guide: Civil Appeals & Writs Ch. 2-C, C. Nonappealable Orders.
Rutter, Cal. Practice Guide: Civil Appeals & Writs Ch. 15-C, C. Statutory Writs.
Rutter, Cal. Practice Guide: Civ. Pro. Before Trial Ch. 3-D, D. Venue.
Rutter, Cal. Practice Guide: Civ. Pro. Before Trial Ch. 5-B, B. Entry of Default.
California Practice Guide: Employment Litigation Ch. 19-T, T. Appeals.
3 Witkin Cal. Proc. 5th Actions § 919, Mandamus and Appeal.
3 Witkin Cal. Proc. 5th Actions § 920, Procedure on Mandamus.
3 Witkin Cal. Proc. 5th Actions § 958, Removal to Neutral County.
9 Witkin Cal. Proc. 5th Appeal § 170, Orders Dealing With Venue.
9 Witkin Cal. Proc. 5th Appeal § 288, Where Judgment is Not Stayed by Appeal or Undertaking.
8 Witkin Cal. Proc. 5th Extraordinary Writs § 105, (S 105) Venue and Inconvenient Forum.
2 Witkin Cal. Proc. 5th Jurisdiction § 401, Review of Improper Transfer.

§ 401. Actions involving state; county or city and county in which attorney general has office

(1) Whenever it is provided by any law of this State that an action or proceeding against the State or a department, institution, board, commission, bureau, officer or other agency thereof shall or may be commenced in, tried in, or removed to the County of Sacramento, the same may be commenced and tried in any city or city and county of this State in which the Attorney General has an office.

(2) Whenever it is provided by any law of this State that the State or a department, institution, board, commission, bureau, officer or other agency thereof shall or may commence an action or proceeding in the County of Sacramento, the same, on motion of the defendants or some of them, shall be removed for trial to the county or city and county in which the Attorney General has an office nearest to the county in which the defendants or some of them reside or have their principal office in this State. *(Added by Stats.1947, c. 306, p. 866, § 1.)*

Research References

Rutter, Cal. Practice Guide: Civ. Pro. Before Trial Ch. 3-D, D. Venue.
Rutter, Cal. Practice Guide: Insurance Litigation Ch. 14-B, B. Courts and Regulation.
3 Witkin Cal. Proc. 5th Actions § 816, Miscellaneous Local Proceedings.
3 Witkin Cal. Proc. 5th Actions § 863, Where Attorney General Has Office.
3 Witkin Cal. Proc. 5th Actions § 865, Local Actions.
3 Witkin Cal. Proc. 5th Actions § 866, Transitory Actions.
3 Witkin Cal. Proc. 5th Actions § 868, (S 868) Actions Against State Agency.

§ 402. Local rules; court location

(a) Except as otherwise provided by law:

(1) A superior court may specify by local rule the locations where certain types of actions or proceedings are to be filed.

(2) A superior court may specify by local rule the locations where certain types of actions or proceedings are to be heard or tried.

(3) A superior court may not dismiss a case, and the clerk may not reject a case for filing, because it is filed, or a person seeks to file it, in a court location other than the location specified by local rule. However, the court may transfer the case on its own motion to the proper court location.

(b) A superior court may transfer an action or proceeding filed in one location to another location of the superior court. This section does not affect the authority of the presiding judge to apportion the business of the court as provided by the California Rules of Court. *(Added by Stats.2002, c. 806 (A.B. 3027), § 12.)*

Research References

Rutter, Cal. Practice Guide: Civ. Pro. Before Trial Ch. 3-D, D. Venue.
3 Witkin Cal. Proc. 5th Actions § 783, (S 783) Consolidation of Trial Courts.

§ 403.   Transfer motion; coordination of actions; notice; consolidation; rules

A judge may, on motion, transfer an action or actions from another court to that judge's court for coordination with an action involving a common question of fact or law within the meaning of Section 404. The motion shall be supported by a declaration stating facts showing that the actions meet the standards specified in Section 404.1, are not complex as defined by the Judicial Council and that the moving party has made a good faith effort to obtain agreement to the transfer from all parties to each action. Notice of the motion shall be served on all parties to each action and on each court in which an action is pending. Any party to that action may file papers opposing the motion within the time permitted by rule of the Judicial Council. The court to which a case is transferred may order the cases consolidated for trial pursuant to Section 1048 without any further motion or hearing.

The Judicial Council may adopt rules to implement this section, including rules prescribing procedures for preventing duplicative or conflicting transfer orders issued by different courts. *(Added by Stats.1996, c. 713 (S.B.1726), § 1, eff. Sept. 23, 1996. Amended by Stats.2000, c. 688 (A.B.1669), § 2; Stats.2002, c. 784 (S.B.1316), § 55.)*

Law Revision Commission Comments

Section 403 is amended to reflect unification of the municipal and superior courts pursuant to Article VI, Section 5(e), of the California Constitution. *Cf.* Sections 404–404.8 (coordination of complex cases). [32 Cal.L.Rev.Comm. Reports 120 (2002)].

Research References

Rutter, Cal. Practice Guide: Civ. Pro. Before Trial Ch. 6-B, B. Complaints.
Rutter, Cal. Practice Guide: Civ. Pro. Before Trial Ch. 12(I)-E, E. Consolidation, Coordination and Bifurcation.
Rutter, Cal. Practice Guide: Civil Trials & Evidence Ch. 4-H, H. Motions to Consolidate or Coordinate Separate Cases.
Rutter, Cal. Practice Guide: Personal Injury Ch. 5-E, E. Selected Pleading Issues.
Rutter, Cal. Practice Guide: Personal Injury Ch. 9-A, A. Assignment to Trial.
4 Witkin Cal. Proc. 5th Pleading § 364, What Constitutes Complex Case.
4 Witkin Cal. Proc. 5th Pleading § 366, (S 366) Transfer of Noncomplex Actions.

4 Witkin Cal. Proc. 5th Pleading § 375, (S 375) Coordination of Related Cases.

CHAPTER 2.   RECLASSIFICATION OF CIVIL ACTIONS AND PROCEEDINGS

§ 403.010.   Expansion or limitations with respect to this chapter

Nothing in this chapter expands or limits the law on whether a plaintiff, cross-complainant, or petitioner may file an amended complaint or other amended initial pleading. Nothing in this chapter expands or limits the law on whether, and to what extent, an amendment relates back to the date of filing the original complaint or other initial pleading. *(Added by Stats.1999, c. 344 (S.B.210), § 11, eff. Sept. 7, 1999. Amended by Stats.2002, c. 784 (S.B.1316), § 56.)*

Law Revision Commission Comments

Subdivision (a) of Section 403.010 makes clear that this chapter is limited to counties in which the trial courts have unified. For transfer between superior and municipal courts in counties in which the courts have not unified, see Chapter 1 (commencing with Section 392).

The first sentence of subdivision (b) continues former Section 395.9(e) without substantive change. The second sentence clarifies that this chapter does not affect the running of the statute of limitations. [29 Cal.L.Rev. Comm. Reports App. 5 (1999)].

Section 403.010 is amended to reflect unification of the municipal and superior courts pursuant to Article VI, Section 5(e), of the California Constitution. [32 Cal.L.Rev.Comm. Reports 121 (2002)].

Research References

Rutter, Cal. Practice Guide: Civil Appeals & Writs Ch. 8-C, C. Standards of Appellate Review.
9 Witkin Cal. Proc. 5th Appeal § 167, Order Dealing With Jurisdictional Reclassification.
2 Witkin Cal. Proc. 5th Jurisdiction § 6, (S 6) Jurisdictional Classification.
2 Witkin Cal. Proc. 5th Jurisdiction § 407, Determination of Lack of Jurisdiction.
2 Witkin Cal. Proc. 5th Jurisdiction § 411, (S 411) in General.

§ 403.020.   Amended complaint or other initial pleading; changed jurisdictional classification; reclassification

(a) If a plaintiff, cross-complainant, or petitioner files an amended complaint or other amended initial pleading that changes the jurisdictional classification from limited to unlimited, the party at the time of filing the pleading shall pay the reclassification fee provided in Section 403.060, and the clerk shall promptly reclassify the case. If the amendment changes the jurisdictional classification from unlimited to limited, no reclassification fee is required, and the clerk shall promptly reclassify the case.

(b) For purposes of this chapter, an amendment to an initial pleading shall be treated in the same manner as an amended initial pleading. *(Added by Stats.1999, c. 344 (S.B.210), § 11, eff.*

Sept. 7, 1999. Amended by Stats.2001, c. 159 (S.B.662), § 38; Stats.2001, c. 824 (A.B.1700), § 2.)

Law Revision Commission Comments

Section 403.020 is added to provide guidance where a plaintiff recognizes and acknowledges the need for reclassification. It does not affect whether a plaintiff is entitled to amend the complaint or other initial pleading. See Section 403.010 (application and effect of chapter). For authority to amend pleadings, see Sections 426.50 (amending to add cause of action), 472 (amendment once of course), 473 (amendment requiring leave of court).

See also Sections 32.5 (jurisdictional classification), 403.030 (reclassification of limited civil case by cross-complaint), 403.040 (motion for reclassification), 422.030 (caption). [29 Cal.L.Rev.Comm. Reports App. 5 (1999)].

Research References

Rutter, Cal. Practice Guide: Civ. Pro. Before Trial Ch. 3-A, A. Subject Matter Jurisdiction (Competency).
2 Witkin Cal. Proc. 5th Jurisdiction § 411, (S 411) in General.
4 Witkin Cal. Proc. 5th Pleading § 17, Format of First Page.

§ 403.030. Limited civil cases; cross-complainant; caption change; reclassification

If a party in a limited civil case files a cross-complaint that causes the action or proceeding to exceed the maximum amount in controversy for a limited civil case or otherwise fail to satisfy the requirements for a limited civil case as prescribed by Section 85, the caption of the cross-complaint shall state that the action or proceeding is a limited civil case to be reclassified by cross-complaint, or words to that effect. The party at the time of filing the cross-complaint shall pay the reclassification fees provided in Section 403.060, and the clerk shall promptly reclassify the case. *(Added by Stats.1999, c. 344 (S.B.210), § 11, eff. Sept. 7, 1999. Amended by Stats.2001, c. 824 (A.B.1700), § 3.)*

Law Revision Commission Comments

Section 403.030 is added to provide guidance where a cross-complainant in a limited civil case recognizes and acknowledges the need for reclassification.

See also Sections 403.020 (reclassification by amending initial pleading), 403.040 (motion for reclassification), 422.30 (caption). [29 Cal.L.Rev. Comm. Reports App. 5 (1999)].

Research References

Rutter, Cal. Practice Guide: Civ. Pro. Before Trial Ch. 3-A, A. Subject Matter Jurisdiction (Competency).
Rutter, Cal. Practice Guide: Civ. Pro. Before Trial Ch. 6-D, D. Cross-Complaint.
Rutter, Cal. Practice Guide: Personal Injury Ch. 5-D, D. Classification as Limited or Unlimited Civil Case.
2 Witkin Cal. Proc. 5th Jurisdiction § 36, (S 36) Large Demand by Cross-Complaint.
2 Witkin Cal. Proc. 5th Jurisdiction § 411, (S 411) in General.
4 Witkin Cal. Proc. 5th Pleading § 17, Format of First Page.

§ 403.040. Motion for reclassification

(a) The plaintiff, cross-complainant, or petitioner may file a motion for reclassification within the time allowed for that party to amend the initial pleading. The defendant or cross-defendant may file a motion for reclassification within the time allowed for that party to respond to the initial pleading. The court, on its own motion, may reclassify a case at any time. A motion for reclassification does not extend the moving party's time to amend or answer or otherwise respond. The court shall grant the motion and enter an order for reclassification, regardless of any fault or lack of fault, if the case has been classified in an incorrect jurisdictional classification.

(b) If a party files a motion for reclassification after the time for that party to amend that party's initial pleading or to respond to a complaint, cross-complaint, or other initial pleading, the court shall grant the motion and enter an order for reclassification only if both of the following conditions are satisfied:

(1) The case is incorrectly classified.

(2) The moving party shows good cause for not seeking reclassification earlier.

(c) If the court grants a motion for reclassification, the payment of the reclassification fee shall be determined, unless the court orders otherwise, as follows:

(1) If a case is reclassified as an unlimited civil case, the party whose pleading causes the action or proceeding to exceed the maximum amount in controversy for a limited civil case or otherwise fails to satisfy the requirements of a limited civil case under Section 85 shall pay the reclassification fee provided in Section 403.060.

(2) If a case is reclassified as a limited civil case, no reclassification fee is required.

(d) If the court grants an order for reclassification of an action or proceeding pursuant to this section, the reclassification shall proceed as follows:

(1) If the required reclassification fee is paid pursuant to Section 403.060 or no reclassification fee is required, the clerk shall promptly reclassify the case.

(2) An action that has been reclassified pursuant to this section shall not be further prosecuted in any court until the required reclassification fee is paid. If the required reclassification fee has not been paid within five days after service of notice of the order for reclassification, any party interested in the case, regardless of whether that party is named in the complaint, may pay the fee, and the clerk shall promptly reclassify the case as if the fee had been paid as provided in Section 403.060. The fee shall then be a proper item of costs of the party paying it, recoverable if that party prevails in the action or proceeding. Otherwise, the fee shall be offset against and deducted from the amount, if any, awarded to the party responsible for the fee, if that party prevails in the action or proceeding.

(3) If the fee is not paid within 30 days after service of notice of an order of reclassification, the court on its own motion or the motion of any party may order the case to proceed as a limited civil case, dismiss the action or cross-action without prejudice on the condition that no other action or proceeding on the same matters may be commenced in any other court until the reclassification fee is paid, or take such other action as the court may deem appropriate.

(e) Nothing in this section shall be construed to require the superior court to reclassify an action or proceeding because the judgment to be rendered, as determined at the trial or hearing, is one that might have been rendered in a limited civil case.

(f) In any case where the misclassification is due solely to an excess in the amount of the demand, the excess may be remitted and the action may continue as a limited civil case. *(Added by Stats.1999, c. 344 (S.B.210), § 11, eff. Sept. 7, 1999. Amended by Stats.2001, c. 824 (A.B.1700), § 4.)*

Law Revision Commission Comments

Subdivision (a) of Section 403.040 continues the first and third sentences of former Section 399.5(a) without substantive change. A new clause is added to expressly negate any inference that a motion for reclassification may only be granted upon a finding of fault. This is declarative of existing law.

Subdivision (b) continues former Section 395.9(b), with revisions to improve clarity. The reference to a motion by the court is deleted as redundant. See subdivision (a).

Subdivisions (c)-(d) continue former Section 395.9(f)-(g) without substantive change.

For the procedure on granting a motion for reclassification, see Sections 403.060 (proceedings on order granting motion for reclassification), 403.070 (reclassified action or proceeding). For reclassification fees, see Section 403.050. See also Sections 403.020 (reclassification by amending initial pleading), 403.030 (reclassification of limited civil case by cross-complaint). [29 Cal.L.Rev.Comm. Reports App. 5 (1999)].

Research References

Rutter, Cal. Practice Guide: Civil Appeals & Writs Ch. 15-C, C. Statutory Writs.
Rutter, Cal. Practice Guide: Civ. Pro. Before Trial Ch. 1-B, B. Prelawsuit Investigations, Research and Analysis.
Rutter, Cal. Practice Guide: Civ. Pro. Before Trial Ch. 3-A, A. Subject Matter Jurisdiction (Competency).
Rutter, Cal. Practice Guide: Civ. Pro. Before Trial Ch. 5-B, B. Entry of Default.
Rutter, Cal. Practice Guide: Civ. Pro. Before Trial Ch. 6-B, B. Complaints.
Rutter, Cal. Practice Guide: Personal Injury Ch. 5-D, D. Classification as Limited or Unlimited Civil Case.
2 Witkin Cal. Proc. 5th Jurisdiction § 27, (S 27) Waiver of Excess Recovery.
2 Witkin Cal. Proc. 5th Jurisdiction § 29, (S 29) Effect of Puffing.
2 Witkin Cal. Proc. 5th Jurisdiction § 409, (S 409) Discretionary Where Defect Appears During Trial.
2 Witkin Cal. Proc. 5th Jurisdiction § 411, (S 411) in General.
2 Witkin Cal. Proc. 5th Jurisdiction § 412, (S 412) Reclassification Fees.

§ 403.050. Stipulation as to reclassification

(a) The parties to the action or proceeding may stipulate to reclassification of the case within the time allowed to respond to the initial pleading.

(b) If the stipulation for reclassification changes the jurisdictional classification of the case from limited to unlimited, the reclassification fee provided in Section 403.060 shall be paid at the time the stipulation is filed.

(c) Upon filing of the stipulation and, if required under subdivision (b), the payment of the reclassification fee provided in Section 403.060, the clerk shall promptly reclassify the case. *(Added by Stats.2001, c. 824 (A.B.1700), § 6.)*

Research References

Rutter, Cal. Practice Guide: Civ. Pro. Before Trial Ch. 3-A, A. Subject Matter Jurisdiction (Competency).
2 Witkin Cal. Proc. 5th Jurisdiction § 411, (S 411) in General.
4 Witkin Cal. Proc. 5th Pleading § 17, Format of First Page.

§ 403.060. Reclassification fees

(a) For reclassification of a case from a limited civil case to an unlimited civil case, a fee shall be charged as provided in Section 70619 of the Government Code. This reclassification fee shall be in addition to any other fee due for that appearance or filing in a limited civil case. No additional amounts shall be charged for appearance or filing fees paid prior to reclassification. After reclassification, the fees ordinarily charged in an unlimited case shall be charged.

(b) If a reclassification fee is required and is not paid at the time an amended complaint or other initial pleading, a cross-complaint, or a stipulation for reclassification is filed under Section 403.020, 403.030, or 403.050, the clerk shall not reclassify the case and the case shall remain and proceed as a limited civil case.

(c) No fee shall be charged for reclassification of a case from an unlimited civil case to a limited civil case. The fees ordinarily required for filing or appearing in a limited civil case shall be charged at the time of filing a pleading that reclassifies the case. Parties are not entitled to a refund of the difference between any fees previously paid for appearance or filing in an unlimited civil case and the fees due in a limited civil case. After reclassification, the fees ordinarily charged in a limited civil case shall be charged. *(Added by Stats.2001, c. 824 (A.B.1700), § 8. Amend-*

ed by Stats.2005, c. 75 (A.B.145), § 29, eff. July 19, 2005, operative Jan. 1, 2006.)

Research References

Rutter, Cal. Practice Guide: Civ. Pro. Before Trial Ch. 3-A, A. Subject Matter Jurisdiction (Competency).
Rutter, Cal. Practice Guide: Personal Injury Ch. 5-D, D. Classification as Limited or Unlimited Civil Case.
2 Witkin Cal. Proc. 5th Jurisdiction § 411, (S 411) in General.
2 Witkin Cal. Proc. 5th Jurisdiction § 412, (S 412) Reclassification Fees.
4 Witkin Cal. Proc. 5th Pleading § 26, Additional Fees.

§ 403.070. Commencement of action; court authority

(a) An action or proceeding that is reclassified shall be deemed to have been commenced at the time the complaint or petition was initially filed, not at the time of reclassification.

(b) The court shall have and exercise over the reclassified action or proceeding the same authority as if the action or proceeding had been originally commenced as reclassified, all prior proceedings being saved. The court may allow or require whatever amendment of the pleadings, filing and service of amended, additional, or supplemental pleadings, or giving of notice, or other appropriate action, as may be necessary for the proper presentation and determination of the action or proceeding as reclassified. *(Added by Stats.1999, c. 344 (S.B.210), § 11, eff. Sept. 7, 1999.)*

Law Revision Commission Comments

Subdivision (a) of Section 403.070 continues former Section 399.5(d) without substantive change. Subdivision (b) continues without substantive change former Section 399.5(e) and the second sentence of former Section 395.9(a).

See also Sections 403.020 (reclassification by amending initial pleading), 403.030 (reclassification of limited civil case by cross-complaint), 403.040 (motion for reclassification), 403.050 (reclassification fees), 422.30 (caption). [29 Cal.L.Rev.Comm. Reports App. 5 (1999)].

Research References

Rutter, Cal. Practice Guide: Civil Appeals & Writs Ch. 16-A, A. Introduction.
Rutter, Cal. Practice Guide: Civ. Pro. Before Trial Ch. 3-A, A. Subject Matter Jurisdiction (Competency).
2 Witkin Cal. Proc. 5th Jurisdiction § 413, (S 413) Effect of Reclassification or Failure to Reclassify.

§ 403.080. Petition for writ of mandate for proper classification; time limits; stay; final order

When an order is made by the superior court granting or denying a motion to reclassify an action or proceeding pursuant to Section 403.040, the party aggrieved by the order may, within 20 days after service of a written notice of the order, petition the court of appeal for the district in which the court granting or denying the motion is situated for a writ of mandate requiring proper classification of the action or proceeding pursuant to Section 403.040. The superior court may, for good cause, and prior to the expiration of the initial 20–day period, extend the time for one additional period not to exceed 10 days. The petitioner shall file a copy of the petition in the superior court immediately after the petition is filed in the court of appeal. The court of appeal may stay all proceedings in the case, pending judgment on the petition becoming final. The clerk of the court of appeal shall file with the clerk of the superior court, a copy of any final order or final judgment immediately after the order or judgment becomes final. *(Added by Stats.1999, c. 344 (S.B.210), § 11, eff. Sept. 7, 1999.)*

Law Revision Commission Comments

Section 403.080 continues without substantive change the references to reclassification deleted from Section 400. [29 Cal.L.Rev.Comm. Reports App. 5 (1999)].

Research References

Rutter, Cal. Practice Guide: Civil Appeals & Writs Ch. 2-B, B. Appealable Judgments and Orders.

Rutter, Cal. Practice Guide: Civil Appeals & Writs Ch. 15-C, C. Statutory Writs.

Rutter, Cal. Practice Guide: Civ. Pro. Before Trial Ch. 3-A, A. Subject Matter Jurisdiction (Competency).

9 Witkin Cal. Proc. 5th Appeal § 167, Order Dealing With Jurisdictional Reclassification.

2 Witkin Cal. Proc. 5th Jurisdiction § 414, (S 414) Review.

§ 403.090. Rules

The Judicial Council may prescribe rules, not inconsistent with statute, governing the procedure for reclassification of civil actions and proceedings. *(Added by Stats.1999, c. 344 (S.B.210), § 11, eff. Sept. 7, 1999.)*

Law Revision Commission Comments

Section 403.090 is added to facilitate refinement of the procedures governing reclassification of civil actions. See also Section 403.050 (Judicial Council authority to prescribe rules governing manner of paying reclassification fees and consequences of failure to make payment). [29 Cal.L.Rev.Comm. Reports App. 5 (1999)].

Research References

Rutter, Cal. Practice Guide: Civ. Pro. Before Trial Ch. 3-A, A. Subject Matter Jurisdiction (Competency).

Rutter, Cal. Practice Guide: Personal Injury Ch. 5-D, D. Classification as Limited or Unlimited Civil Case.

CHAPTER 3. COORDINATION

Section

404.   Civil actions sharing common question of fact or law; petition for coordination or motion for permission to submit petition; supporting declaration; assignment of judge.

404.1.   Promotion of ends of justice; standards.

404.2.   Selection of reviewing court.

404.3.   Order coordinating actions; assignment of judges.

404.4.   Coordinated actions; request to include pending action.

404.5.   Stay.

404.6.   Writ of mandate.

404.7.   Practice and procedure; duty of judicial council.

404.8.   Expenses.

404.9.   Delegation of duties of presiding judge.

§ 404. Civil actions sharing common question of fact or law; petition for coordination or motion for permission to submit petition; supporting declaration; assignment of judge

When civil actions sharing a common question of fact or law are pending in different courts, a petition for coordination may be submitted to the Chairperson of the Judicial Council, by the presiding judge of any such court, or by any party to one of the actions after obtaining permission from the presiding judge, or by all of the parties plaintiff or defendant in any such action. A petition for coordination, or a motion for permission to submit a petition, shall be supported by a declaration stating facts showing that the actions are complex, as defined by the Judicial Council and that the actions meet the standards specified in Section 404.1. On receipt of a petition for coordination, the Chairperson of the Judicial Council may assign a judge to determine whether the actions are complex, and if so, whether coordination of the actions is appropriate, or the Chairperson of the Judicial Council may authorize the presiding judge of a court to assign the matter to judicial officers of the court to make the determination in the same manner as assignments are made in

other civil cases. *(Added by Stats.1972, c. 1162, § 2, operative Jan. 1, 1974. Amended by Stats.1982, c. 250, p. 798, § 1; Stats.1996, c. 713 (S.B.1726), § 3, eff. Sept. 23, 1996; Stats.2000, c. 688 (A.B.1669), § 3; Stats.2002, c. 784 (S.B.1316), § 57.)*

Law Revision Commission Comments

Section 404 is amended to reflect unification of the municipal and superior courts pursuant to Article VI, Section 5(e), of the California Constitution. *Cf.* Section 403 (transfer and coordination of noncomplex cases). [32 Cal.L.Rev.Comm. Reports 121 (2002)].

Research References

Rutter, Cal. Practice Guide: Civ. Pro. Before Trial Ch. 2-C, C. Joinder of Parties.

Rutter, Cal. Practice Guide: Civ. Pro. Before Trial Ch. 6-B, B. Complaints.

Rutter, Cal. Practice Guide: Civ. Pro. Before Trial Ch. 9(I)-D, D. Hearing.

Rutter, Cal. Practice Guide: Civ. Pro. Before Trial Ch. 12(I)-E, E. Consolidation, Coordination and Bifurcation.

Rutter, Cal. Practice Guide: Civil Trials & Evidence Ch. 3-B, B. Peremptory Challenge of Judge (CCP § 170.6).

Rutter, Cal. Practice Guide: Civil Trials & Evidence Ch. 4-H, H. Motions to Consolidate or Coordinate Separate Cases.

Rutter, Cal. Practice Guide: Personal Injury Ch. 5-E, E. Selected Pleading Issues.

Rutter, Cal. Practice Guide: Personal Injury Ch. 9-A, A. Assignment to Trial.

9 Witkin Cal. Proc. 5th Appeal § 805, (S 805) Suggestions to Judge.

4 Witkin Cal. Proc. 5th Pleading § 352, (S 352) in General.

4 Witkin Cal. Proc. 5th Pleading § 353, (S 353) Test: Common Question in Different Courts.

4 Witkin Cal. Proc. 5th Pleading § 357, in General.

4 Witkin Cal. Proc. 5th Pleading § 359, (S 359) Motion in Court.

4 Witkin Cal. Proc. 5th Pleading § 361, Assignment of Coordination Motion Judge.

4 Witkin Cal. Proc. 5th Pleading § 364, What Constitutes Complex Case.

4 Witkin Cal. Proc. 5th Pleading § 366, (S 366) Transfer of Noncomplex Actions.

4 Witkin Cal. Proc. 5th Pleading § 375, (S 375) Coordination of Related Cases.

12 Witkin, California Summary 10th Real Property § 736, Trial.

9 Witkin, California Summary 10th Taxation § 297, (S 297) Constitutional Restriction.

§ 404.1. Promotion of ends of justice; standards

Coordination of civil actions sharing a common question of fact or law is appropriate if one judge hearing all of the actions for all purposes in a selected site or sites will promote the ends of justice taking into account whether the common question of fact or law is predominating and significant to the litigation; the convenience of parties, witnesses, and counsel; the relative development of the actions and the work product of counsel; the efficient utilization of judicial facilities and manpower; the calendar of the courts; the disadvantages of duplicative and inconsistent rulings, orders, or judgments; and, the likelihood of settlement of the actions without further litigation should coordination be denied. *(Added by Stats.1972, c. 1162, § 2, operative Jan. 1, 1974.)*

Research References

Rutter, Cal. Practice Guide: Civ. Pro. Before Trial Ch. 12(I)-E, E. Consolidation, Coordination and Bifurcation.

Rutter, Cal. Practice Guide: Civil Trials & Evidence Ch. 4-H, H. Motions to Consolidate or Coordinate Separate Cases.

Rutter, Cal. Practice Guide: Personal Injury Ch. 5-E, E. Selected Pleading Issues.

4 Witkin Cal. Proc. 5th Pleading § 353, (S 353) Test: Common Question in Different Courts.

4 Witkin Cal. Proc. 5th Pleading § 357, in General.

4 Witkin Cal. Proc. 5th Pleading § 359, (S 359) Motion in Court.

4 Witkin Cal. Proc. 5th Pleading § 366, (S 366) Transfer of Noncomplex Actions.

Civ. Pro.

4 Witkin Cal. Proc. 5th Pleading § 370, Remand of Action or Claim.
4 Witkin Cal. Proc. 5th Pleading § 374, (S 374) Review.

§ 404.2. Selection of reviewing court

A judge assigned pursuant to Section 404 who determines that coordination is appropriate shall select the reviewing court having appellate jurisdiction if the actions to be coordinated are within the jurisdiction of more than one reviewing court. The assigned judge shall select the reviewing court which will promote the ends of justice as determined under the standards specified in Section 404.1. *(Added by Stats.1972, c. 1162, § 2, operative Jan. 1, 1974. Amended by Stats.1996, c. 713 (S.B.1726), § 4, eff. Sept. 23, 1996.)*

Research References

California Practice Guide: Employment Litigation Ch. 19-T, T. Appeals.
4 Witkin Cal. Proc. 5th Pleading § 374, (S 374) Review.

§ 404.3. Order coordinating actions; assignment of judges

A judge assigned pursuant to Section 404 who determines that coordination is appropriate shall order the actions coordinated, report that fact to the Chairperson of the Judicial Council, and the Chairperson of the Judicial Council shall either assign a judge to hear and determine the actions in the site or sites the assigned judge finds appropriate or authorize the presiding judge of a court to assign the matter to judicial officers of the court in the same manner as assignments are made in other civil cases. *(Added by Stats.1972, c. 1162, § 2, operative Jan. 1, 1974. Amended by Stats.1980, c. 318, p. 654, § 1; Stats.1996, c. 713 (S.B.1726), § 5, eff. Sept. 23, 1996; Stats.2002, c. 784 (S.B.1316), § 58.)*

Law Revision Commission Comments

Section 404.3 is amended to reflect unification of the municipal and superior courts pursuant to Article VI, Section 5(e), of the California Constitution. *Cf.* Section 403 (transfer and coordination of noncomplex cases). [32 Cal.L.Rev.Comm. Reports 122 (2002)].

Research References

Rutter, Cal. Practice Guide: Personal Injury Ch. 9-A, A. Assignment to Trial.
4 Witkin Cal. Proc. 5th Pleading § 353, (S 353) Test: Common Question in Different Courts.
4 Witkin Cal. Proc. 5th Pleading § 365, Determination and Order.
4 Witkin Cal. Proc. 5th Pleading § 367, in General.

§ 404.4. Coordinated actions; request to include pending action

The presiding judge of any court in which there is pending an action sharing a common question of fact or law with actions coordinated pursuant to Section 404, on the court's own motion or the motion of any party supported by an affidavit stating facts showing that the action meets the standards specified in Section 404.1, or all the parties plaintiff or defendant in any such action, supported by an affidavit stating facts showing that the action meets the standards specified in Section 404.1, may request the judge assigned to hear the coordinated actions for an order coordinating the action. Coordination of the action shall be determined under the standards specified in Section 404.1. *(Added by Stats.1972, c. 1162, § 2, operative Jan. 1, 1974. Amended by Stats.1996, c. 713 (S.B.1726), § 6, eff. Sept. 23, 1996.)*

Research References

4 Witkin Cal. Proc. 5th Pleading § 372, Add-On Cases.

§ 404.5. Stay

Pending any determination of whether coordination is appropriate, the judge making that determination may stay any action being considered for, or affecting an action being considered for, coordination. *(Added by Stats.1972, c. 1162, § 2, operative Jan. 1, 1974.)*

Research References

4 Witkin Cal. Proc. 5th Pleading § 362, Stay Pending Determination.

§ 404.6. Writ of mandate

Within 20 days after service upon him or her of a written notice of entry of an order of the court under this chapter, any party may petition the appropriate reviewing court for a writ of mandate to require the court to make such order as the reviewing court finds appropriate. The superior court may, for good cause, and prior to the expiration of the initial 20-day period, extend the time for one additional period not to exceed 10 days. *(Added by Stats.1972, c. 1162, § 2, operative Jan. 1, 1974. Amended by Stats.1989, c. 1416, § 13.)*

Research References

Rutter, Cal. Practice Guide: Civil Appeals & Writs Ch. 15-C, C. Statutory Writs.
8 Witkin Cal. Proc. 5th Extraordinary Writs § 110, in General.
4 Witkin Cal. Proc. 5th Pleading § 374, (S 374) Review.

§ 404.7. Practice and procedure; duty of judicial council

Notwithstanding any other provision of law, the Judicial Council shall provide by rule the practice and procedure for coordination of civil actions in convenient courts, including provision for giving notice and presenting evidence. *(Added by Stats.1972, c. 1162, § 2, operative Jan. 1, 1974.)*

Research References

Rutter, Cal. Practice Guide: Civ. Pro. Before Trial Ch. 12(I)-E, E. Consolidation, Coordination and Bifurcation.
Rutter, Cal. Practice Guide: Civil Trials & Evidence Ch. 4-H, H. Motions to Consolidate or Coordinate Separate Cases.
4 Witkin Cal. Proc. 5th Pleading § 353, (S 353) Test: Common Question in Different Courts.
4 Witkin Cal. Proc. 5th Pleading § 354, (S 354) Applicable Procedure.
4 Witkin Cal. Proc. 5th Pleading § 355, (S 355) Peremptory Challenge of Assigned Judge.

§ 404.8. Expenses

Expenses of the assigned judge, other necessary judicial officers and employees, and facilities for cases coordinated under Section 404 shall be paid or reimbursed by the state from funds appropriated to the Judicial Council. *(Added by Stats.1972, c. 1162, § 2, operative Jan. 1, 1974. Amended by Stats.1996, c. 713 (S.B.1726), § 7, eff. Sept. 23, 1996.)*

Research References

Rutter, Cal. Practice Guide: Civ. Pro. Before Trial Ch. 12(I)-E, E. Consolidation, Coordination and Bifurcation.
4 Witkin Cal. Proc. 5th Pleading § 352, (S 352) in General.

§ 404.9. Delegation of duties of presiding judge

Any duties of the presiding judge specified in this chapter may be delegated by the presiding judge to another judge of the court. *(Added by Stats.1996, c. 713 (S.B.1726), § 8, eff. Sept. 23, 1996. Amended by Stats.2002, c. 784 (S.B.1316), § 59.)*

Law Revision Commission Comments

Section 404.9 is amended to reflect unification of the municipal and superior courts pursuant to Article VI, Section 5(e), of the California Constitution.

The first paragraph is amended to delete language referring to the sole judge. Every superior court has at least two judgeships as a result of trial court unification. See Gov't Code § 69580 *et seq.* (number of judges). Where a court has only one judge due to a vacancy or otherwise, the reference to the "presiding judge" means the sole judge of the court. See Gov't Code § 69508.5 (presiding judge).

The second paragraph is deleted as unnecessary. The provision relating to proceedings for transfer from a municipal court is obsolete. The provision for coordination rules is redundant. See Section 404.7 (rules for coordination of complex cases). *Cf.* Section 403 (transfer and coordination of noncomplex cases). [32 Cal.L.Rev.Comm. Reports 123 (2002)].

Research References

4 Witkin Cal. Proc. 5th Pleading § 352, (S 352) in General.

Title 4.5

RECORDING NOTICE OF CERTAIN ACTIONS

CHAPTER 1. DEFINITIONS AND GENERAL PROVISIONS

§ 405. Definitions; construction

The definitions in this chapter govern the construction of this title. *(Added by Stats.1992, c. 883 (A.B.3620), § 2.)*

Research References

Rutter, Cal. Practice Guide: Civil Appeals & Writs Ch. 15-C, C. Statutory Writs.
Rutter, Cal. Practice Guide: Real Prop. Transactions Ch. 8-B, B. Options to Purchase.
Rutter, Cal. Practice Guide: Real Prop. Transactions Ch. 11-D, D. Buyer's Remedies Upon Seller's Breach-Damages and Specific Performance.
Rutter, Cal. Practice Guide: Real Prop. Transactions Ch. 11-H, H. Other Remedies.
Rutter, Cal. Practice Guide: Real Prop. Transactions Ch. 11-I, I. Lis Pendens.
Miller and Starr California Real Estate § 11:148, Nature and Effect of a Lis Pendens.
Miller and Starr California Real Estate § 11:150, Actions in Which a Lis Pendens May or Must be Recorded.
3 Witkin Cal. Proc. 5th Actions § 373, (S 373) 1992 Revision.
14 Witkin, California Summary 10th Wills and Probate § 375, Lis Pendens.

§ 405.1. Claimant

"Claimant" means a party to an action who asserts a real property claim and records a notice of the pendency of the action. *(Added by Stats.1992, c. 883 (A.B.3620), § 2.)*

Research References

Rutter, Cal. Practice Guide: Civ. Pro. Before Trial Ch. 9(I)-J, J. Motion to Expunge Lis Pendens.

Rutter, Cal. Practice Guide: Real Prop. Transactions Ch. 11-I, I. Lis Pendens.
Miller and Starr California Real Estate § 5:66, Authority to Sell.
Miller and Starr California Real Estate § 11:148, Nature and Effect of a Lis Pendens.
Miller and Starr California Real Estate § 11:149, Procedural and Formal Requirements for a Lis Pendens.
3 Witkin Cal. Proc. 5th Actions § 374, (S 374) Definitions.

§ 405.2. Notice of pendency of action or notice

"Notice of pendency of action" or "notice" means a notice of the pendency of an action in which a real property claim is alleged. *(Added by Stats.1992, c. 883 (A.B.3620), § 2.)*

Research References

Miller and Starr California Real Estate § 11:6, Instruments Subject to Recording--List of Recordable Documents.
Miller and Starr California Real Estate § 11:148, Nature and Effect of a Lis Pendens.
Miller and Starr California Real Estate § 11:149, Procedural and Formal Requirements for a Lis Pendens.
3 Witkin Cal. Proc. 5th Actions § 374, (S 374) Definitions.

§ 405.3. Probable validity

"Probable validity," with respect to a real property claim, means that it is more likely than not that the claimant will obtain a judgment against the defendant on the claim. *(Added by Stats.1992, c. 883 (A.B.3620), § 2.)*

Research References

Rutter, Cal. Practice Guide: Civ. Pro. Before Trial Ch. 9(I)-J, J. Motion to Expunge Lis Pendens.
Rutter, Cal. Practice Guide: Real Prop. Transactions Ch. 11-I, I. Lis Pendens.
Miller and Starr California Real Estate § 11:149, Procedural and Formal Requirements for a Lis Pendens.
Miller and Starr California Real Estate § 11:153, Expungement of a Lis Pendens--Policy.
Miller and Starr California Real Estate § 11:154, Expungement of a Lis Pendens--Procedure and Grounds for Expungement.
17 NO. 6 Miller & Starr, California Real Estate Newsalert 10, Recording and Priorities.
3 Witkin Cal. Proc. 5th Actions § 374, (S 374) Definitions.
3 Witkin Cal. Proc. 5th Actions § 394, Burden and Degree of Proof.

§ 405.4. Real property claim

"Real property claim" means the cause or causes of action in a pleading which would, if meritorious, affect (a) title to, or the right to possession of, specific real property or (b) the use of an easement identified in the pleading, other than an easement obtained pursuant to statute by any regulated public utility. *(Added by Stats.1992, c. 883 (A.B.3620), § 2.)*

Research References

Rutter, Cal. Practice Guide: Civ. Pro. Before Trial Ch. 9(I)-J, J. Motion to Expunge Lis Pendens.
Rutter, Cal. Practice Guide: Enforcing Judgments/Debts Ch. 6G-4, Creditor's Suit.
Rutter, Cal. Practice Guide: Real Prop. Transactions Ch. 11-I, I. Lis Pendens.
Miller and Starr California Real Estate § 12:51, Management and Control--Sale or Encumbrance of Real Property.
Miller and Starr California Real Estate § 15:72, Remedies for Interference With the Use of an Easement.
Miller and Starr California Real Estate § 11:148, Nature and Effect of a Lis Pendens.
Miller and Starr California Real Estate § 11:149, Procedural and Formal Requirements for a Lis Pendens.
Miller and Starr California Real Estate § 11:150, Actions in Which a Lis Pendens May or Must be Recorded.
Miller and Starr California Real Estate § 11:153, Expungement of a Lis Pendens--Policy.

14 NO. 1 Miller & Starr, California Real Estate Newsalert 13, Recording and Priorities.
15 NO. 4 Miller & Starr, California Real Estate Newsalert 33, Recording and Priorities.
16 NO. 2 Miller & Starr, California Real Estate Newsalert 16, Recording and Priorities.
22 NO. 3 Miller & Starr, California Real Estate Newsalert 19, Recording and Priorities.
3 Witkin Cal. Proc. 5th Actions § 374, (S 374) Definitions.
3 Witkin Cal. Proc. 5th Actions § 376, (S 376) Real Property Claim.
3 Witkin Cal. Proc. 5th Actions § 383, (S 383) Signature of Attorney or Approval of Court.
3 Witkin Cal. Proc. 5th Actions § 396, (S 396) in General.
3 Witkin Cal. Proc. 5th Actions § 398, (S 398) Action to Impose Constructive Trust.
3 Witkin Cal. Proc. 5th Actions § 399, (S 399) Action to Impose Equitable Lien.
3 Witkin Cal. Proc. 5th Actions § 401, (S 401) Claim of Easement.

§ 405.5. Application of title

This title applies to an action pending in any United States District Court in the same manner that it applies to an action pending in the courts of this state. *(Added by Stats.1992, c. 883 (A.B.3620), § 2.)*

Research References

Rutter, Cal. Practice Guide: Real Prop. Transactions Ch. 11-I, I. Lis Pendens.
Miller and Starr California Real Estate § 11:148, Nature and Effect of a Lis Pendens.
Miller and Starr California Real Estate § 11:150, Actions in Which a Lis Pendens May or Must be Recorded.
3 Witkin Cal. Proc. 5th Actions § 377, (S 377) Federal District Court Action.

§ 405.6. Actions by public agency in eminent domain; law governing

In an action by a public agency in eminent domain pursuant to Title 7 (commencing with Section 1230.010) of Part 3, the issuance, service, and recordation of a notice of pendency of action shall be governed by Section 1250.150 and shall not be subject to Chapter 2 (commencing with Section 405.20). *(Added by Stats.1992, c. 883 (A.B.3620), § 2.)*

Research References

Miller and Starr California Real Estate § 11:149, Procedural and Formal Requirements for a Lis Pendens.
Miller and Starr California Real Estate § 11:150, Actions in Which a Lis Pendens May or Must be Recorded.
3 Witkin Cal. Proc. 5th Actions § 378, (S 378) Condemnation Action.
3 Witkin Cal. Proc. 5th Actions § 383, (S 383) Signature of Attorney or Approval of Court.
3 Witkin Cal. Proc. 5th Actions § 384, (S 384) Service and Filing.

§ 405.7. Actions declaring buildings uninhabitable; recording notice

Whenever an action is commenced to declare a building uninhabitable, the plaintiff public agency, at the time of filing the complaint, shall record in the office of the recorder of the county in which the building is situated, a notice of the pendency of the action, containing the names of the parties and a description of the real property upon which the building affected by the action is situated. *(Added by Stats.1992, c. 883 (A.B.3620), § 2.)*

Research References

Rutter, Cal. Practice Guide: Civ. Pro. Before Trial Ch. 9(I)-J, J. Motion to Expunge Lis Pendens.
Rutter, Cal. Practice Guide: Real Prop. Transactions Ch. 11-I, I. Lis Pendens.
Miller and Starr California Real Estate § 11:150, Actions in Which a Lis Pendens May or Must be Recorded.

3 Witkin Cal. Proc. 5th Actions § 381, (S 381) Specific Mandatory Statutes.
12 Witkin, California Summary 10th Real Property § 318, (S 318) Unusual Instruments.

§ 405.8. Availability of other relief

Nothing in this title precludes any party from seeking an attachment, injunction, or other relief in connection with a real property claim or the expungement of a notice of pending action. *(Added by Stats.1992, c. 883 (A.B.3620), § 2.)*

Research References

Rutter, Cal. Practice Guide: Civ. Pro. Before Trial Ch. 9(I)-J, J. Motion to Expunge Lis Pendens.
Rutter, Cal. Practice Guide: Real Prop. Transactions Ch. 11-I, I. Lis Pendens.
Miller and Starr California Real Estate § 11:148, Nature and Effect of a Lis Pendens.
3 Witkin Cal. Proc. 5th Actions § 373, (S 373) 1992 Revision.
3 Witkin Cal. Proc. 5th Actions § 398, (S 398) Action to Impose Constructive Trust.

CHAPTER 2. RECORDATION SERVICE AND FILING

§ 405.20. Place of recording; contents

A party to an action who asserts a real property claim may record a notice of pendency of action in which that real property claim is alleged. The notice may be recorded in the office of the recorder of each county in which all or part of the real property is situated. The notice shall contain the names of all parties to the action and a description of the property affected by the action. *(Added by Stats.1992, c. 883 (A.B.3620), § 2. Amended by Stats.2004, c. 227 (S.B.1102), § 10, eff. Aug. 16, 2004.)*

Research References

Rutter, Cal. Practice Guide: A.D.R. Ch. 5-D, D. Defenses to Enforcement.
Rutter, Cal. Practice Guide: Enforcing Judgments/Debts Ch. 6G-4, Creditor's Suit.
Rutter, Cal. Practice Guide: Real Prop. Transactions Ch. 11-D, D. Buyer's Remedies Upon Seller's Breach-Damages and Specific Performance.
Rutter, Cal. Practice Guide: Real Prop. Transactions Ch. 11-I, I. Lis Pendens.
Miller and Starr California Real Estate § 11:6, Instruments Subject to Recording--List of Recordable Documents.
Miller and Starr California Real Estate § 11:148, Nature and Effect of a Lis Pendens.
Miller and Starr California Real Estate § 11:149, Procedural and Formal Requirements for a Lis Pendens.
Miller and Starr California Real Estate § 11:150, Actions in Which a Lis Pendens May or Must be Recorded.
16 NO. 2 Miller & Starr, California Real Estate Newsalert 16, Recording and Priorities.
19 NO. 6 Miller & Starr, California Real Estate Newsalert 18, Recording and Priorities.
3 Witkin Cal. Proc. 5th Actions § 373, (S 373) 1992 Revision.
3 Witkin Cal. Proc. 5th Actions § 376, (S 376) Real Property Claim.
3 Witkin Cal. Proc. 5th Actions § 382, (S 382) Form of Notice.

3 Witkin Cal. Proc. 5th Actions § 385, (S 385) Recordation.

§ 405.21. Prerequisites to recording

An attorney of record in an action may sign a notice of pendency of action. Alternatively, a judge of the court in which an action that includes a real property claim is pending may, upon request of a party thereto, approve a notice of pendency of action. A notice of pendency of action shall not be recorded unless (a) it has been signed by the attorney of record, (b) it is signed by a party acting in propria persona and approved by a judge as provided in this section, or (c) the action is subject to Section 405.6. *(Added by Stats.1992, c. 883 (A.B.3620), § 2. Amended by Stats.1994, c. 146 (A.B.3601), § 20.)*

Research References

Rutter, Cal. Practice Guide: Real Prop. Transactions Ch. 11-I, I. Lis Pendens.
Miller and Starr California Real Estate § 11:23, Purpose and Effect; Required for Recordation.
Miller and Starr California Real Estate § 11:149, Procedural and Formal Requirements for a Lis Pendens.
3 Witkin Cal. Proc. 5th Actions § 383, (S 383) Signature of Attorney or Approval of Court.

§ 405.22. Service

Except in actions subject to Section 405.6, the claimant shall, prior to recordation of the notice, cause a copy of the notice to be mailed, by registered or certified mail, return receipt requested, to all known addresses of the parties to whom the real property claim is adverse and to all owners of record of the real property affected by the real property claim as shown by the latest county assessment roll. If there is no known address for service on an adverse party or owner, then as to that party or owner a declaration under penalty of perjury to that effect may be recorded instead of the proof of service required above, and the service on that party or owner shall not be required. Immediately following recordation, a copy of the notice shall also be filed with the court in which the action is pending. Service shall also be made immediately and in the same manner upon each adverse party later joined in the action. *(Added by Stats.1992, c. 883 (A.B.3620), § 2. Amended by Stats.1996, c. 1159 (A.B.3471), § 9; Stats.2004, c. 227 (S.B.1102), § 11, eff. Aug. 16, 2004.)*

Research References

Rutter, Cal. Practice Guide: Civ. Pro. Before Trial Ch. 9(I)-J, J. Motion to Expunge Lis Pendens.
Rutter, Cal. Practice Guide: Real Prop. Transactions Ch. 11-I, I. Lis Pendens.
Miller and Starr California Real Estate § 11:149, Procedural and Formal Requirements for a Lis Pendens.
Miller and Starr California Real Estate § 11:154, Expungement of a Lis Pendens--Procedure and Grounds for Expungement.
3 Witkin Cal. Proc. 5th Actions § 384, (S 384) Service and Filing.
3 Witkin Cal. Proc. 5th Actions § 385, (S 385) Recordation.

§ 405.23. Service upon adverse parties and owners; requirements; proof of service

Any notice of pendency of action shall be void and invalid as to any adverse party or owner of record unless the requirements of Section 405.22 are met for that party or owner and a proof of service in the form and content specified in Section 1013a has been recorded with the notice of pendency of action. *(Added by Stats.1992, c. 883 (A.B.3620), § 2.)*

Research References

Rutter, Cal. Practice Guide: Civ. Pro. Before Trial Ch. 9(I)-J, J. Motion to Expunge Lis Pendens.
Rutter, Cal. Practice Guide: Real Prop. Transactions Ch. 11-I, I. Lis Pendens.

Miller and Starr California Real Estate § 11:149, Procedural and Formal Requirements for a Lis Pendens.
Miller and Starr California Real Estate § 11:154, Expungement of a Lis Pendens--Procedure and Grounds for Expungement.
3 Witkin Cal. Proc. 5th Actions § 385, (S 385) Recordation.
3 Witkin Cal. Proc. 5th Actions § 390, 1992 Revision.
3 Witkin Cal. Proc. 5th Actions § 391, in General.
3 Witkin Cal. Proc. 5th Actions § 394, Burden and Degree of Proof.
3 Witkin Cal. Proc. 5th Actions § 395, Invalid and Void Lis Pendens.
3 Witkin Cal. Proc. 5th Actions § 410, (S 410) Attorneys' Fees and Costs.

§ 405.24. Constructive notice; time of recording; rights and interests relate back to date recording

From the time of recording the notice of pendency of action, a purchaser, encumbrancer, or other transferee of the real property described in the notice shall be deemed to have constructive notice of the pendency of the noticed action as it relates to the real property and only of its pendency against parties not fictitiously named. The rights and interest of the claimant in the property, as ultimately determined in the pending noticed action, shall relate back to the date of the recording of the notice. *(Added by Stats.1992, c. 883 (A.B.3620), § 2.)*

Research References

Rutter, Cal. Practice Guide: Real Prop. Transactions Ch. 11-D, D. Buyer's Remedies Upon Seller's Breach-Damages and Specific Performance.
Rutter, Cal. Practice Guide: Real Prop. Transactions Ch. 11-I, I. Lis Pendens.
Miller and Starr California Real Estate § 11:6, Instruments Subject to Recording--List of Recordable Documents.
Miller and Starr California Real Estate § 11:22, When Recording is Complete--For Constructive Notice.
Miller and Starr California Real Estate § 11:148, Nature and Effect of a Lis Pendens.
Miller and Starr California Real Estate § 11:149, Procedural and Formal Requirements for a Lis Pendens.
Miller and Starr California Real Estate § 11:150, Actions in Which a Lis Pendens May or Must be Recorded.
Miller and Starr California Real Estate § 11:151, Effect of Recorded Lis Pendens on Subsequent Interests.
Miller and Starr California Real Estate § 11:152, Effect of Lis Pendens on Prior Interests.
17 NO. 5 Miller & Starr, California Real Estate Newsalert 15, Recording and Priorities.
3 Witkin Cal. Proc. 5th Actions § 387, (S 387) Constructive Notice.
3 Witkin Cal. Proc. 5th Actions § 388, (S 388) Where Notice is Ineffective.

CHAPTER 3. EXPUNGEMENT AND OTHER RELIEF

Section

405.39.   Appeal of orders or other actions; review; writ of mandate; filing and service.

§ 405.30. Application to court for expungement; parties or nonparties with interest; evidence; burden of proof

At any time after notice of pendency of action has been recorded, any party, or any nonparty with an interest in the real property affected thereby, may apply to the court in which the action is pending to expunge the notice. However, a person who is not a party to the action shall obtain leave to intervene from the court at or before the time the party brings the motion to expunge the notice. Evidence or declarations may be filed with the motion to expunge the notice. The court may permit evidence to be received in the form of oral testimony, and may make any orders it deems just to provide for discovery by any party affected by a motion to expunge the notice. The claimant shall have the burden of proof under Sections 405.31 and 405.32. *(Added by Stats.1992, c. 883 (A.B.3620), § 2.)*

Research References

Rutter, Cal. Practice Guide: Civil Appeals & Writs Ch. 15-C, C. Statutory Writs.
Rutter, Cal. Practice Guide: Civ. Pro. Before Trial Ch. 9(I)-J, J. Motion to Expunge Lis Pendens.
Rutter, Cal. Practice Guide: Real Prop. Transactions Ch. 11-I, I. Lis Pendens.
Miller and Starr California Real Estate § 11:148, Nature and Effect of a Lis Pendens.
Miller and Starr California Real Estate § 11:149, Procedural and Formal Requirements for a Lis Pendens.
Miller and Starr California Real Estate § 11:154, Expungement of a Lis Pendens--Procedure and Grounds for Expungement.
19 NO. 4 Miller & Starr, California Real Estate Newsalert 48, Recording and Priorities.
3 Witkin Cal. Proc. 5th Actions § 373, (S 373) 1992 Revision.
3 Witkin Cal. Proc. 5th Actions § 390, 1992 Revision.
3 Witkin Cal. Proc. 5th Actions § 391, in General.
3 Witkin Cal. Proc. 5th Actions § 392, Time for Bringing Motion.
3 Witkin Cal. Proc. 5th Actions § 393, Evidence and Discovery.
3 Witkin Cal. Proc. 5th Actions § 394, Burden and Degree of Proof.
3 Witkin Cal. Proc. 5th Actions § 396, (S 396) in General.
3 Witkin Cal. Proc. 5th Actions § 403, (S 403) Current Law.
3 Witkin Cal. Proc. 5th Actions § 407, (S 407) Procedure.
3 Witkin Cal. Proc. 5th Actions § 410, (S 410) Attorneys' Fees and Costs.
3 Witkin Cal. Proc. 5th Actions § 411, (S 411) Review by Mandamus.

§ 405.31. Pleading; real property claim

In proceedings under this chapter, the court shall order the notice expunged if the court finds that the pleading on which the notice is based does not contain a real property claim. The court shall not order an undertaking to be given as a condition of expunging the notice where the court finds the pleading does not contain a real property claim. *(Added by Stats.1992, c. 883 (A.B.3620), § 2.)*

Research References

Rutter, Cal. Practice Guide: Civil Appeals & Writs Ch. 15-C, C. Statutory Writs.
Rutter, Cal. Practice Guide: Civ. Pro. Before Trial Ch. 9(I)-J, J. Motion to Expunge Lis Pendens.
Rutter, Cal. Practice Guide: Real Prop. Transactions Ch. 11-I, I. Lis Pendens.
Rutter, Cal. Practice Guide: Real Prop. Transactions Form 11:B, Motion to Expunge Lis Pendens.
Miller and Starr California Real Estate § 11:148, Nature and Effect of a Lis Pendens.
Miller and Starr California Real Estate § 11:149, Procedural and Formal Requirements for a Lis Pendens.
Miller and Starr California Real Estate § 11:150, Actions in Which a Lis Pendens May or Must be Recorded.

Miller and Starr California Real Estate § 11:153, Expungement of a Lis Pendens--Policy.
Miller and Starr California Real Estate § 11:154, Expungement of a Lis Pendens--Procedure and Grounds for Expungement.
15 NO. 1 Miller & Starr, California Real Estate Newsalert 14, Recording and Priorities.
3 Witkin Cal. Proc. 5th Actions § 390, 1992 Revision.
3 Witkin Cal. Proc. 5th Actions § 391, in General.
3 Witkin Cal. Proc. 5th Actions § 394, Burden and Degree of Proof.
3 Witkin Cal. Proc. 5th Actions § 396, (S 396) in General.
3 Witkin Cal. Proc. 5th Actions § 401, (S 401) Claim of Easement.
3 Witkin Cal. Proc. 5th Actions § 403, (S 403) Current Law.
3 Witkin Cal. Proc. 5th Actions § 408, Nature and Purpose of Remedy.
3 Witkin Cal. Proc. 5th Actions § 409, Procedure.
3 Witkin Cal. Proc. 5th Actions § 410, (S 410) Attorneys' Fees and Costs.

§ 405.32. Standard of proof

In proceedings under this chapter, the court shall order that the notice be expunged if the court finds that the claimant has not established by a preponderance of the evidence the probable validity of the real property claim. The court shall not order an undertaking to be given as a condition of expunging the notice if the court finds the claimant has not established the probable validity of the real property claim. *(Added by Stats.1992, c. 883 (A.B.3620), § 2.)*

Research References

Rutter, Cal. Practice Guide: Civil Appeals & Writs Ch. 15-C, C. Statutory Writs.
Rutter, Cal. Practice Guide: Civ. Pro. Before Trial Ch. 1-C, C. Prelawsuit Notices, Claims and Demands.
Rutter, Cal. Practice Guide: Civ. Pro. Before Trial Ch. 9(I)-J, J. Motion to Expunge Lis Pendens.
Rutter, Cal. Practice Guide: Real Prop. Transactions Ch. 11-I, I. Lis Pendens.
Rutter, Cal. Practice Guide: Real Prop. Transactions Form 11:B, Motion to Expunge Lis Pendens.
Miller and Starr California Real Estate § 11:46, Privileged Publication.
Miller and Starr California Real Estate § 11:150, Actions in Which a Lis Pendens May or Must be Recorded.
Miller and Starr California Real Estate § 11:153, Expungement of a Lis Pendens--Policy.
Miller and Starr California Real Estate § 11:154, Expungement of a Lis Pendens--Procedure and Grounds for Expungement.
15 NO. 4 Miller & Starr, California Real Estate Newsalert 33, Recording and Priorities.
16 NO. 3 Miller & Starr, California Real Estate Newsalert 13, Recording and Priorities.
17 NO. 6 Miller & Starr, California Real Estate Newsalert 10, Recording and Priorities.
3 Witkin Cal. Proc. 5th Actions § 390, 1992 Revision.
3 Witkin Cal. Proc. 5th Actions § 391, in General.
3 Witkin Cal. Proc. 5th Actions § 392, Time for Bringing Motion.
3 Witkin Cal. Proc. 5th Actions § 394, Burden and Degree of Proof.
3 Witkin Cal. Proc. 5th Actions § 396, (S 396) in General.
3 Witkin Cal. Proc. 5th Actions § 398, (S 398) Action to Impose Constructive Trust.
3 Witkin Cal. Proc. 5th Actions § 403, (S 403) Current Law.
3 Witkin Cal. Proc. 5th Actions § 404, (S 404) in General.
3 Witkin Cal. Proc. 5th Actions § 408, Nature and Purpose of Remedy.
3 Witkin Cal. Proc. 5th Actions § 409, Procedure.
3 Witkin Cal. Proc. 5th Actions § 410, (S 410) Attorneys' Fees and Costs.

§ 405.33. Giving of an undertaking; conditional expungement of notice; fulfillment of condition; recovery; presumption

In proceedings under this chapter, the court shall order that the notice be expunged if the court finds that the real property claim has probable validity, but adequate relief can be secured to the claimant by the giving of an undertaking. The expungement order shall be conditioned upon the giving of the undertaking of such nature and in such amount as will indemnify the claimant for all damages proximately resulting from the expungement which the claimant may incur if the claimant prevails upon the real property claim. In its order conditionally expunging the notice, the court shall set a return date for the moving party to show fulfillment of the condition, and if the moving party fails to show fulfillment of the condition on the return day, the court shall deny the motion to expunge without further notice or hearing. Recovery may be had on the undertaking pursuant to Section 996.440.

For purposes only of determining under this section whether the giving of an undertaking will secure adequate relief to the claimant, the presumption of Section 3387 of the Civil Code that real property is unique shall not apply, except in the case of real property improved with a single-family dwelling which the claimant intends to occupy. *(Added by Stats.1992, c. 883 (A.B.3620), § 2.)*

Research References

Rutter, Cal. Practice Guide: Civil Appeals & Writs Ch. 15-C, C. Statutory Writs.
Rutter, Cal. Practice Guide: Civ. Pro. Before Trial Ch. 9(I)-J, J. Motion to Expunge Lis Pendens.
Rutter, Cal. Practice Guide: Real Prop. Transactions Ch. 11-I, I. Lis Pendens.
Rutter, Cal. Practice Guide: Real Prop. Transactions Form 11:B, Motion to Expunge Lis Pendens.
Miller and Starr California Real Estate § 11:153, Expungement of a Lis Pendens--Policy.
Miller and Starr California Real Estate § 11:154, Expungement of a Lis Pendens--Procedure and Grounds for Expungement.
Miller and Starr California Real Estate § 11:155, Expungement of a Lis Pendens--Recovery on an Undertaking.
18 NO. 5 Miller & Starr, California Real Estate Newsalert 20, Remedies.
3 Witkin Cal. Proc. 5th Actions § 390, 1992 Revision.
3 Witkin Cal. Proc. 5th Actions § 391, in General.
3 Witkin Cal. Proc. 5th Actions § 394, Burden and Degree of Proof.
3 Witkin Cal. Proc. 5th Actions § 404, (S 404) in General.
3 Witkin Cal. Proc. 5th Actions § 405, (S 405) Amount and Nature of Undertaking.
3 Witkin Cal. Proc. 5th Actions § 407, (S 407) Procedure.
3 Witkin Cal. Proc. 5th Actions § 408, Nature and Purpose of Remedy.
3 Witkin Cal. Proc. 5th Actions § 409, Procedure.
3 Witkin Cal. Proc. 5th Actions § 410, (S 410) Attorneys' Fees and Costs.
6 Witkin Cal. Proc. 5th Provisional Remedies § 9, Scope of Bond and Undertaking Law.

§ 405.34. Giving of undertaking as condition of maintaining notice; nonparties; evidence; compliance; recovery

Subject to the provisions of Sections 405.31 and 405.32, at any time after a notice of pendency of action has been recorded, and regardless of whether a motion to expunge has been filed, the court may, upon motion by any person with an interest in the property, require the claimant to give the moving party an undertaking as a condition of maintaining the notice in the record title. However, a person who is not a party to the action shall obtain leave to intervene from the court at or before the time the person moves to require an undertaking. The court may permit evidence to be received in the form of oral testimony and may make any orders it deems just to provide for discovery by any affected party. An undertaking required pursuant to this section shall be of such nature and in such amount as the court may determine to be just. In its order requiring an undertaking, the court shall set a return date for the claimant to show compliance and if the claimant fails to show compliance on the return date, the court shall order the notice of pendency of action expunged without further notice or hearing.

Recovery on an undertaking required pursuant to this section may be had in an amount not to exceed the undertaking, pursuant to Section 996.440, upon a showing (a) that the claimant did not prevail on the real property claim and (b) that the person seeking recovery suffered damages as a result of the maintenance of the notice. In assessing these damages, the court shall not consider the claimant's intent or the presence or absence of probable cause. *(Added by Stats.1992, c. 883 (A.B.3620), § 2.)*

Research References

Rutter, Cal. Practice Guide: Civ. Pro. Before Trial Ch. 9(I)-J, J. Motion to Expunge Lis Pendens.
Rutter, Cal. Practice Guide: Real Prop. Transactions Ch. 11-I, I. Lis Pendens.
Miller and Starr California Real Estate § 11:154, Expungement of a Lis Pendens--Procedure and Grounds for Expungement.
Miller and Starr California Real Estate § 11:155, Expungement of a Lis Pendens--Recovery on an Undertaking.
3 Witkin Cal. Proc. 5th Actions § 390, 1992 Revision.
3 Witkin Cal. Proc. 5th Actions § 391, in General.
3 Witkin Cal. Proc. 5th Actions § 398, (S 398) Action to Impose Constructive Trust.
3 Witkin Cal. Proc. 5th Actions § 408, Nature and Purpose of Remedy.
3 Witkin Cal. Proc. 5th Actions § 409, Procedure.
3 Witkin Cal. Proc. 5th Actions § 410, (S 410) Attorneys' Fees and Costs.
6 Witkin Cal. Proc. 5th Provisional Remedies § 9, Scope of Bond and Undertaking Law.

§ 405.35. Effective date and recording of order expunging notice of pendency

No order expunging a notice of pendency of action shall be effective, nor shall it be recorded in the office of any county recorder, until the time within which a petition for writ of mandate may be filed pursuant to Section 405.39 has expired. No order expunging a notice of pendency of action shall be effective, nor shall it be recorded in the office of any county recorder, after a petition for writ of mandate has been timely filed pursuant to Section 405.39, until the proceeding commenced by the petition is finally adjudicated. This section imposes no duty on the county recorder to determine whether the requirements of this section or of any order expunging a notice of pendency of action have been met. *(Added by Stats.1992, c. 883 (A.B.3620), § 2.)*

Research References

Rutter, Cal. Practice Guide: Civil Appeals & Writs Ch. 15-C, C. Statutory Writs.
Rutter, Cal. Practice Guide: Civ. Pro. Before Trial Ch. 9(I)-J, J. Motion to Expunge Lis Pendens.
Rutter, Cal. Practice Guide: Real Prop. Transactions Ch. 11-I, I. Lis Pendens.
Miller and Starr California Real Estate § 11:151, Effect of Recorded Lis Pendens on Subsequent Interests.
Miller and Starr California Real Estate § 11:154, Expungement of a Lis Pendens--Procedure and Grounds for Expungement.
Miller and Starr California Real Estate § 11:156, Effect of an Expungement or Withdrawal; Appellate Review.
3 Witkin Cal. Proc. 5th Actions § 413, When Expungement Becomes Effective.

§ 405.36. Expungement of notice of pending action; subsequent notice as to affected property; recording

Once a notice of pending action has been expunged, the claimant may not record another notice of pending action as to the affected property without leave of the court in which the action is pending. *(Added by Stats.1992, c. 883 (A.B.3620), § 2.)*

Research References

Rutter, Cal. Practice Guide: Civ. Pro. Before Trial Ch. 9(I)-J, J. Motion to Expunge Lis Pendens.
Rutter, Cal. Practice Guide: Real Prop. Transactions Ch. 11-I, I. Lis Pendens.
Miller and Starr California Real Estate § 11:149, Procedural and Formal Requirements for a Lis Pendens.
Miller and Starr California Real Estate § 11:156, Effect of an Expungement or Withdrawal; Appellate Review.

3 Witkin Cal. Proc. 5th Actions § 415, Second Notice Requires Court Approval.

§ 405.37. Exoneration or modification of undertaking; conditional order

After notice and hearing, for good cause and upon such terms as are just, the court may exonerate or modify any undertaking required by an order issued pursuant to Section 405.33 or 405.34 or pursuant to a stipulation made in lieu of such an order. An order of the court under this section may be made conditional upon the giving of a new undertaking under Section 405.33 or 405.34. *(Added by Stats.1992, c. 883 (A.B.3620), § 2.)*

Research References

Miller and Starr California Real Estate § 11:154, Expungement of a Lis Pendens--Procedure and Grounds for Expungement.
3 Witkin Cal. Proc. 5th Actions § 407, (S 407) Procedure.
3 Witkin Cal. Proc. 5th Actions § 409, Procedure.

§ 405.38. Attorney's fees and costs

The court shall direct that the party prevailing on any motion under this chapter be awarded the reasonable attorney's fees and costs of making or opposing the motion unless the court finds that the other party acted with substantial justification or that other circumstances make the imposition of attorney's fees and costs unjust. *(Added by Stats.1992, c. 883 (A.B.3620), § 2.)*

Research References

Rutter, Cal. Practice Guide: Civil Appeals & Writs Ch. 15-C, C. Statutory Writs.
Rutter, Cal. Practice Guide: Civ. Pro. Before Trial Ch. 9(I)-J, J. Motion to Expunge Lis Pendens.
Rutter, Cal. Practice Guide: Real Prop. Transactions Ch. 11-C, C. Seller's Remedies Upon Buyer's Breach-Damages and Specific Performance.
Rutter, Cal. Practice Guide: Real Prop. Transactions Ch. 11-I, I. Lis Pendens.
Miller and Starr California Real Estate § 34:66, Examples of Actions in Which Fees Can be Recovered.
Miller and Starr California Real Estate § 11:154, Expungement of a Lis Pendens--Procedure and Grounds for Expungement.
14 NO. 5 Miller & Starr, California Real Estate Newsalert 20, Recording and Priorities.
17 NO. 5 Miller & Starr, California Real Estate Newsalert 15, Recording and Priorities.
3 Witkin Cal. Proc. 5th Actions § 391, in General.
3 Witkin Cal. Proc. 5th Actions § 394, Burden and Degree of Proof.
3 Witkin Cal. Proc. 5th Actions § 407, (S 407) Procedure.
3 Witkin Cal. Proc. 5th Actions § 409, Procedure.
3 Witkin Cal. Proc. 5th Actions § 410, (S 410) Attorneys' Fees and Costs.

§ 405.39. Appeal of orders or other actions; review; writ of mandate; filing and service

No order or other action of the court under this chapter shall be appealable. Any party aggrieved by an order made on a motion under this chapter may petition the proper reviewing court to review the order by writ of mandate. The petition for writ of mandate shall be filed and served within 20 days of service of written notice of the order by the court or any party. The court which issued the order may, within the initial 20-day period, extend the initial 20-day period for one additional period not to exceed 10 days. A copy of the petition for writ of mandate shall be delivered to the clerk of the court which issued the order with a request that it be placed in the court file. *(Added by Stats.1992, c. 883 (A.B.3620), § 2.)*

Research References

Rutter, Cal. Practice Guide: Civil Appeals & Writs Ch. 2-C, C. Nonappealable Orders.
Rutter, Cal. Practice Guide: Civil Appeals & Writs Ch. 15-C, C. Statutory Writs.

Rutter, Cal. Practice Guide: Civ. Pro. Before Trial Ch. 9(I)-J, J. Motion to Expunge Lis Pendens.
Rutter, Cal. Practice Guide: Real Prop. Transactions Ch. 11-I, I. Lis Pendens.
Miller and Starr California Real Estate § 11:151, Effect of Recorded Lis Pendens on Subsequent Interests.
Miller and Starr California Real Estate § 11:154, Expungement of a Lis Pendens--Procedure and Grounds for Expungement.
Miller and Starr California Real Estate § 11:156, Effect of an Expungement or Withdrawal; Appellate Review.
17 NO. 5 Miller & Starr, California Real Estate Newsalert 15, Recording and Priorities.
3 Witkin Cal. Proc. 5th Actions § 391, in General.
3 Witkin Cal. Proc. 5th Actions § 392, Time for Bringing Motion.
3 Witkin Cal. Proc. 5th Actions § 407, (S 407) Procedure.
3 Witkin Cal. Proc. 5th Actions § 409, Procedure.
3 Witkin Cal. Proc. 5th Actions § 411, (S 411) Review by Mandamus.
3 Witkin Cal. Proc. 5th Actions § 413, When Expungement Becomes Effective.

CHAPTER 4. WITHDRAWAL

Section
405.50.   Notice of withdrawal; recording; acknowledgement.

§ 405.50. Notice of withdrawal; recording; acknowledgement

At any time after notice of pendency of an action has been recorded pursuant to this title or other law, the notice may be withdrawn by recording in the office of the recorder in which the notice of pendency was recorded a notice of withdrawal executed by the party who recorded the notice of pendency of action or by the party's successor in interest. The notice of withdrawal shall be acknowledged. *(Added by Stats.1992, c. 883 (A.B.3620), § 2.)*

Research References

Rutter, Cal. Practice Guide: Civ. Pro. Before Trial Ch. 9(I)-J, J. Motion to Expunge Lis Pendens.
Rutter, Cal. Practice Guide: Real Prop. Transactions Ch. 11-I, I. Lis Pendens.
Miller and Starr California Real Estate § 11:151, Effect of Recorded Lis Pendens on Subsequent Interests.
Miller and Starr California Real Estate § 11:156, Effect of an Expungement or Withdrawal; Appellate Review.
3 Witkin Cal. Proc. 5th Actions § 373, (S 373) 1992 Revision.
3 Witkin Cal. Proc. 5th Actions § 412, (S 412) Withdrawal of Notice.

CHAPTER 5. EFFECT OF WITHDRAWAL OR EXPUNGEMENT OF NOTICE

Section
405.60.   Actual or constructive notice.
405.61.   Actual knowledge; nonfictitious parties; legislative intent.

§ 405.60. Actual or constructive notice

Upon the withdrawal of a notice of pendency of action pursuant to Section 405.50 or upon recordation of a certified copy of an order expunging a notice of pendency of action pursuant to this title, neither the notice nor any information derived from it, prior to the recording of a certified copy of the judgment or decree issued in the action, shall constitute actual or constructive notice of any of the matters contained, claimed, alleged, or contended therein, or of any of the matters related to the action, or create a duty of inquiry in any person thereafter dealing with the affected property. *(Added by Stats.1992, c. 883 (A.B.3620), § 2.)*

Research References

Rutter, Cal. Practice Guide: Civ. Pro. Before Trial Ch. 9(I)-J, J. Motion to Expunge Lis Pendens.

Rutter, Cal. Practice Guide: Real Prop. Transactions Ch. 11-I, I. Lis Pendens.

Miller and Starr California Real Estate § 11:6, Instruments Subject to Recording--List of Recordable Documents.

Miller and Starr California Real Estate § 11:65. Recorded Documents that Do Not Give Constructive Notice--Documents Not Specifically Stated to Impart Constructive Notice by Statute or Which Are Specifically Stated Not to Impart Constructive...

Miller and Starr California Real Estate § 11:147, Priority of Judgments and Pending Litigation; in General.

Miller and Starr California Real Estate § 11:148, Nature and Effect of a Lis Pendens.

Miller and Starr California Real Estate § 11:150, Actions in Which a Lis Pendens May or Must be Recorded.

Miller and Starr California Real Estate § 11:151, Effect of Recorded Lis Pendens on Subsequent Interests.

Miller and Starr California Real Estate § 11:156, Effect of an Expungement or Withdrawal; Appellate Review.

3 Witkin Cal. Proc. 5th Actions § 373, (S 373) 1992 Revision.

3 Witkin Cal. Proc. 5th Actions § 414, Recording Expungement Order or Notice of Withdrawal.

§ 405.61. Actual knowledge; nonfictitious parties; legislative intent

Upon the withdrawal of a notice of pendency of action pursuant to Section 405.50 or upon recordation of a certified copy of an order expunging a notice of pendency of action pursuant to this title, no person except a nonfictitious party to the action at the time of recording of the notice of withdrawal or order, who thereafter becomes, by conveyance recorded prior to the recording of a certified copy of the judgment or decree issued in the action, a purchaser, transferee, mortgagee, or other encumbrancer for a valuable consideration of any interest in the real property subject to the action, shall be deemed to have actual knowledge of the action or any of the matters contained, claimed, or alleged therein, or of any of the matters related to the action, irrespective of whether that person possessed actual knowledge of the action or matter and irrespective of when or how the knowledge was obtained.

It is the intent of the Legislature that this section shall provide for the absolute and complete free transferability of real property after the expungement or withdrawal of a notice of pendency of action. *(Added by Stats.1992, c. 883 (A.B.3620), § 2.)*

Research References

Rutter, Cal. Practice Guide: Civ. Pro. Before Trial Ch. 9(I)-J, J. Motion to Expunge Lis Pendens.

Rutter, Cal. Practice Guide: Real Prop. Transactions Ch. 11-I, I. Lis Pendens.

Miller and Starr California Real Estate § 11:6, Instruments Subject to Recording--List of Recordable Documents.

Miller and Starr California Real Estate § 11:65. Recorded Documents that Do Not Give Constructive Notice--Documents Not Specifically Stated to Impart Constructive Notice by Statute or Which Are Specifically Stated Not to Impart Constructive...

Miller and Starr California Real Estate § 11:147, Priority of Judgments and Pending Litigation; in General.

Miller and Starr California Real Estate § 11:148, Nature and Effect of a Lis Pendens.

Miller and Starr California Real Estate § 11:151, Effect of Recorded Lis Pendens on Subsequent Interests.

Miller and Starr California Real Estate § 11:156, Effect of an Expungement or Withdrawal; Appellate Review.

3 Witkin Cal. Proc. 5th Actions § 373, (S 373) 1992 Revision.

3 Witkin Cal. Proc. 5th Actions § 400, (S 400) Action to Set Aside Fraudulent Conveyance.

3 Witkin Cal. Proc. 5th Actions § 414, Recording Expungement Order or Notice of Withdrawal.

Title 5

JURISDICTION AND SERVICE OF PROCESS

CHAPTER 1. JURISDICTION AND FORUM

ARTICLE 1. JURISDICTION

Section
410.10. Basis.

§ 410.10. Basis

A court of this state may exercise jurisdiction on any basis not inconsistent with the Constitution of this state or of the United States. *(Added by Stats.1969, c. 1610, p. 3363, § 3, operative July 1, 1970.)*

Research References

Rutter, Cal. Practice Guide: A.D.R. Ch. 5-K, K. Arbitration of International Commercial Disputes.

Rutter, Cal. Practice Guide: Civ. Pro. Before Trial Ch. 3-B, B. Jurisdiction Over Parties-Personal Jurisdiction.

Rutter, Cal. Practice Guide: Civ. Pro. Before Trial Ch. 4-A, A. Requirements-In General.

California Practice Guide: Employment Litigation Ch. 19-A, A. Plaintiff's Forum Selection.

Rutter, Cal. Practice Guide: Fed.Civ.Pro. Before Trial Ch. 1-D, D. Choosing Between State and Federal Courts.

Rutter, Cal. Practice Guide: Fed.Civ.Pro. Before Trial Ch. 3-C, C. State "Long Arm" Statutes.

Rutter, Cal. Practice Guide: Fed.Civ.Pro. Before Trial Ch. 5-B, B. Service of Summons and Personal Jurisdiction.

Rutter, Cal. Practice Guide: Fed.Civ.Pro. Before Trial Ch. 5-F, F. Manner of Service (Where Service Not Waived).

Rutter, Cal. Practice Guide: Fed.Civ.Pro. Before Trial Ch. 5-B, Outline B.

Rutter, Cal. Practice Guide: Insurance Litigation Ch. 15-D, D. Filing Considerations.

3 Witkin Cal. Proc. 5th Actions § 967, (S 967) Statutory Revision of 1969.

3 Witkin Cal. Proc. 5th Actions § 1024, Nonresident Insurer.

2 Witkin Cal. Proc. 5th Jurisdiction § 8, (S 8) in General.

2 Witkin Cal. Proc. 5th Jurisdiction § 9, (S 9) All Judicially Recognized Bases Are Approved.

2 Witkin Cal. Proc. 5th Jurisdiction § 107, California Jurisdiction Statute.

2 Witkin Cal. Proc. 5th Jurisdiction § 108, General Principles.

2 Witkin Cal. Proc. 5th Jurisdiction § 126, Person Immune from Process.

2 Witkin Cal. Proc. 5th Jurisdiction § 128, Minimum Contacts Are Required.

2 Witkin Cal. Proc. 5th Jurisdiction § 151, (S 151) Child Custody and Support.

2 Witkin Cal. Proc. 5th Jurisdiction § 158, (S 158) Ownership, Possession, or Use of Property.

2 Witkin Cal. Proc. 5th Jurisdiction § 185, (S 185) Jurisdiction Over Foreign Representative.

2 Witkin Cal. Proc. 5th Jurisdiction § 186, (S 186) in General.

2 Witkin Cal. Proc. 5th Jurisdiction § 199, (S 199) Distinction: General Appearance After Judgment.

2 Witkin Cal. Proc. 5th Jurisdiction § 250, Former Rule: Attachment Allowed.

9 Witkin, California Summary 10th Taxation § 356, Tax on Buyer Collected by Retailer.

11 Witkin, California Summary 10th Community Property § 169, Hearing and Incidental Proceedings.

7 Witkin, California Summary 10th Constitutional Law § 644, (S 644) Actions in Personam.

13 Witkin, California Summary 10th Trusts § 218, (S 218) Bases of Jurisdiction.

14 Witkin, California Summary 10th Wills and Probate § 70, Jurisdiction Over Foreign Representative.

14 Witkin, California Summary 10th Wills and Probate § 668, Judicial Proceedings.

14 Witkin, California Summary 10th Wills and Probate § 844, (S 844) Conflict of Law Rules.

14 Witkin, California Summary 10th Wills and Probate § 874, (S 874) Petition.

14 Witkin, California Summary 10th Wills and Probate § 898, (S 898) Petition.

ARTICLE 2. FORUM

Section
410.30. Stay or dismissal of action; general appearance.
410.40. Foreign or nonresident parties; maintenance of actions; choice of state law; application.
410.42. Construction subcontracts; unenforceability of provisions requiring dispute resolution outside state.

§ 410.30. Stay or dismissal of action; general appearance

(a) When a court upon motion of a party or its own motion finds that in the interest of substantial justice an action should be heard in a forum outside this state, the court shall stay or dismiss the action in whole or in part on any conditions that may be just.

(b) The provisions of Section 418.10 do not apply to a motion to stay or dismiss the action by a defendant who has made a general appearance. *(Added by Stats.1969, c. 1610, p. 3363, § 3, operative July 1, 1970. Amended by Stats.1972, c. 601, § 1; Stats.1986, c. 968, § 4, eff. Sept. 22, 1986; Stats.1972, c. 601, § 1, operative Jan. 1, 1992.)*

Research References

Rutter, Cal. Practice Guide: Civil Appeals & Writs Ch. 8-D, D. Limits on Assertion of Issues on Appeal.

Rutter, Cal. Practice Guide: Civ. Pro. Before Trial Ch. 3-B, B. Jurisdiction Over Parties-Personal Jurisdiction.

Rutter, Cal. Practice Guide: Civ. Pro. Before Trial Ch. 3-C, C. Forum Non Conveniens.

Rutter, Cal. Practice Guide: Civ. Pro. Before Trial Ch. 7(I)-A, A. Demurrers.

Rutter, Cal. Practice Guide: Insurance Litigation Ch. 15-D, D. Filing Considerations.

Rutter, Cal. Practice Guide: Insurance Litigation Ch. 15-F, F. Pretrial Motions.

3 Witkin Cal. Proc. 5th Actions § 20, Repeal of Statute Creating Cause of Action.

2 Witkin Cal. Proc. 5th Jurisdiction § 355, Modern Rule.

2 Witkin Cal. Proc. 5th Jurisdiction § 377, in General.

2 Witkin Cal. Proc. 5th Jurisdiction § 380, California Statute.

2 Witkin Cal. Proc. 5th Jurisdiction § 384, (S 384) Statutory Amendment.

2 Witkin Cal. Proc. 5th Jurisdiction § 387, (S 387) Distinction: Plaintiff's Election of Two Forums.

2 Witkin Cal. Proc. 5th Jurisdiction § 398, Methods of Prevention.

6 Witkin Cal. Proc. 5th Proceedings Without Trial § 474, in General.

13 Witkin, California Summary 10th Trusts § 218, (S 218) Bases of Jurisdiction.

14 Witkin, California Summary 10th Wills and Probate § 875, (S 875) Hearing, Determination, and Appeal.

14 Witkin, California Summary 10th Wills and Probate § 899, (S 899) Hearing, Determination, and Appeal.

§ 410.40. Foreign or nonresident parties; maintenance of actions; choice of state law; application

Any person may maintain an action or proceeding in a court of this state against a foreign corporation or nonresident person where the action or proceeding arises out of or relates to any contract, agreement, or undertaking for which a choice of California law has been made in whole or in part by the parties thereto and which (a) is a contract, agreement, or undertaking, contingent or otherwise, relating to a transaction involving in the aggregate not less than one million dollars ($1,000,000), and (b)

contains a provision or provisions under which the foreign corporation or nonresident agrees to submit to the jurisdiction of the courts of this state.

This section applies to contracts, agreements, and undertakings entered into before, on, or after its effective date; it shall be fully retroactive. Contracts, agreements, and undertakings selecting California law entered into before the effective date of this section shall be valid, enforceable, and effective as if this section had been in effect on the date they were entered into; and actions and proceedings commencing in a court of this state before the effective date of this section may be maintained as if this section were in effect on the date they were commenced. *(Added by Stats.1992, c. 615 (S.B.1804), § 5.)*

Research References

Rutter, Cal. Practice Guide: Civ. Pro. Before Trial Ch. 3-C, C. Forum Non Conveniens.

2 Witkin Cal. Proc. 5th Jurisdiction § 392, Effect of Choice of Law Provision.

§ 410.42. Construction subcontracts; unenforceability of provisions requiring dispute resolution outside state

(a) The following provisions of a contract between the contractor and a subcontractor with principal offices in this state, for the construction of a public or private work of improvement in this state, shall be void and unenforceable:

(1) A provision which purports to require any dispute between the parties to be litigated, arbitrated, or otherwise determined outside this state.

(2) A provision which purports to preclude a party from commencing such a proceeding or obtaining a judgment or other resolution in this state or the courts of this state.

(b) For purposes of this section, "construction" means any work or services performed on, or materials provided for, a work of improvement, as defined in Section 8050 of the Civil Code, and for which a lien may be claimed pursuant to Section 8400 of the Civil Code (whether or not a lien is in fact claimed) or for which such a lien could be claimed but for Section 8160 of the Civil Code. *(Added by Stats.1991, c. 582 (A.B.1051), § 1. Amended by Stats.2010, c. 697 (S.B.189), § 22, operative July 1, 2012.)*

Law Revision Commission Comments

Section 410.42 is amended to correct cross-references and technical stylistic revisions. [37 Cal.L.Rev.Comm. Reports 527 (2007)].

Research References

Rutter, Cal. Practice Guide: A.D.R. Ch. 5-C, C. Enforceability of Arbitration Agreements-In General.

Rutter, Cal. Practice Guide: A.D.R. Ch. 3B-B, B. ADR Options in Construction Disputes.

Rutter, Cal. Practice Guide: Civ. Pro. Before Trial Ch. 3-B, B. Jurisdiction Over Parties-Personal Jurisdiction.

Miller and Starr California Real Estate § 35:3, Mediations--Various Applications.

Miller and Starr California Real Estate § 27:47, Provisions for Arbitration and Mediation of Disputes--Generally.

Miller and Starr California Real Estate § 29:76, Systems for Resolving Defective Construction Disputes.

17 NO. 3 Miller & Starr, California Real Estate Newsalert 3, Construction Contracts.

17 NO. 3 Miller & Starr, California Real Estate Newsalert 11, Mechanics' Liens.

2 Witkin Cal. Proc. 5th Jurisdiction § 359, Subcontractor's Contract.

6 Witkin Cal. Proc. 5th Proceedings Without Trial § 531, in General.

1 Witkin Cal. Summ. 10th Contracts § 452, General Principle.

ARTICLE 3. JURISDICTION IN ACTION

Section

410.50. Time of acquisition; general appearance as equivalent to personal service of summons.
410.60. Corporation dissolved or charter forfeited; jurisdiction over trustees, stockholders, etc.
410.70. Multiple defendants; joint and several liability on contracts.

§ 410.50. Time of acquisition; general appearance as equivalent to personal service of summons

(a) Except as otherwise provided by statute, the court in which an action is pending has jurisdiction over a party from the time summons is served on him as provided by Chapter 4 (commencing with Section 413.10). A general appearance by a party is equivalent to personal service of summons on such party.

(b) Jurisdiction of the court over the parties and the subject matter of an action continues throughout subsequent proceedings in the action. *(Added by Stats.1969, c. 1610, p. 3363, § 3, operative July 1, 1970.)*

Research References

Rutter, Cal. Practice Guide: Civ. Pro. Before Trial Ch. 3-B, B. Jurisdiction Over Parties-Personal Jurisdiction.
Rutter, Cal. Practice Guide: Civil Trials & Evidence Ch. 18-C, C. Other Post-Trial Motions.
Rutter, Cal. Practice Guide: Enforcing Judgments/Debts Ch. 6A-1, Jurisdiction to Enforce Judgments.
3 Witkin Cal. Proc. 5th Actions § 960, (S 960) Summons in Civil Action.
2 Witkin Cal. Proc. 5th Jurisdiction § 192, Definition and Scope of Doctrine.
2 Witkin Cal. Proc. 5th Jurisdiction § 198, (S 198) in General.
2 Witkin Cal. Proc. 5th Jurisdiction § 199, (S 199) Distinction: General Appearance After Judgment.
2 Witkin Cal. Proc. 5th Jurisdiction § 415, (S 415) in General.
2 Witkin Cal. Proc. 5th Jurisdiction § 418, General Rule.
9 Witkin, California Summary 10th Partnership § 176, (S 176) Action Against Dissolved Company.
13 Witkin, California Summary 10th Trusts § 218, (S 218) Bases of Jurisdiction.

§ 410.60. Corporation dissolved or charter forfeited; jurisdiction over trustees, stockholders, etc.

In an action against a corporation which has forfeited its charter or right to do business, or has dissolved, the court in which the action is pending has jurisdiction over all the trustees of such corporation and of its stockholders or members from the time summons is served on one of the trustees as provided by Chapter 4 (commencing with Section 413.10). *(Added by Stats.1969, c. 1610, p. 3363, § 3, operative July 1, 1970.)*

Research References

2 Witkin Cal. Proc. 5th Jurisdiction § 180, (S 180) Jurisdiction Over Defunct Corporation.
4 Witkin Cal. Proc. 5th Pleading § 91, Dissolved Corporation.
9 Witkin, California Summary 10th Partnership § 176, (S 176) Action Against Dissolved Company.

§ 410.70. Multiple defendants; joint and several liability on contracts

In an action against two or more persons who are jointly, jointly and severally, or severally liable on a contract, the court in which the action is pending has jurisdiction to proceed against such of the defendants as are served as if they were the only defendants. *(Added by Stats.1969, c. 1610, p. 3363, § 3, operative July 1, 1970.)*

Research References

Rutter, Cal. Practice Guide: Enforcing Judgments/Debts Ch. 6G-12, Enforcement Against Joint Debtors.
8 Witkin Cal. Proc. 5th Enforcement of Judgment § 398, (S 398) Nature of Remedy.
7 Witkin Cal. Proc. 5th Judgment § 39, (S 39) Defendants: Contract Actions.
2 Witkin Cal. Proc. 5th Jurisdiction § 184, (S 184) Jurisdiction Over Joint Debtors.
1 Witkin Cal. Summ. 10th Contracts § 112, Action and Judgment.

CHAPTER 2. COMMENCING CIVIL ACTIONS

Section

411.10. Complaint.
411.20. Tender of amount of filing fees paid by check; insufficient funds; acceptance or voidability of filed papers; notice; time to tender amount; presumptions; administrative fees.
411.21. Tender of amount less than required for filing fees; notice; time to tender amount; procedural effect; administrative charge.
411.35. Malpractice actions; architects, engineers, or surveyors; certificate of review and consultation; res ipsa loquitur exception; failure to file.

§ 411.10. Complaint

A civil action is commenced by filing a complaint with the court. *(Added by Stats.1969, c. 1610, p. 3363, § 3, operative July 1, 1970.)*

Research References

Rutter, Cal. Practice Guide: Civ. Pro. Before Trial Ch. 11-B, B. Involuntary Dismissals.
3 Witkin Cal. Proc. 5th Actions § 994, Issuance.
2 Witkin Cal. Proc. 5th Courts § 26, Distinction: Judge at Home.
2 Witkin Cal. Proc. 5th Courts § 259, (S 259) Local Standards and Procedure.
4 Witkin Cal. Proc. 5th Pleading § 19, in General.
4 Witkin Cal. Proc. 5th Pleading § 470, Nature of Pleading.
5 Witkin Cal. Proc. 5th Pleading § 1139, What Constitutes Pendency.

§ 411.20. Tender of amount of filing fees paid by check; insufficient funds; acceptance or voidability of filed papers; notice; time to tender amount; presumptions; administrative fees

(a) If the clerk accepts for filing a complaint or other first paper, or any subsequent filing, and payment is made by check which is later returned without payment, the clerk shall, by mail, notify the party who tendered the check that (1) the check has been returned without payment, (2) the administrative charge specified in subdivision (g) has been imposed to reimburse the court for the costs of processing the returned check and providing the notice specified in this subdivision, and (3) the party has 20 days from the date of mailing of the notice within which to pay the filing fee and the administrative charge, except as provided in subdivision (e). The notice also shall state that the administrative charge and the filing fee shall be paid in cash, by certified check, or by other means specified by the court, but not by traveler's check or personal check. If the person who tendered the check is not a party to the action or proposed action, but only is acting on behalf of a party, the clerk shall notify not only the person who tendered the check, but also the party or that party's attorney if the party is represented. The clerk's certificate as to the mailing of notice pursuant to this section establishes a rebuttable presumption that the fees were not paid. This presumption is a presumption affecting the burden of producing evidence.

Civ. Pro.

(b) The clerk shall void the filing if the party who tendered a returned check or on whose behalf a returned check was tendered has not paid the full amount of the fee and the administrative charge by a means specified in subdivision (a) within 20 days of the date on which the notice required by subdivision (a) was mailed. Any filing voided by this section can be disposed of immediately after the 20 days have elapsed without preserving a copy in the court records, notwithstanding Section 68152 of the Government Code.

(c) If an adverse party files a response to a complaint, paper or filing referred to in subdivision (a), together with a filing fee, and the original filing is voided pursuant to subdivision (b), the responsive filing is not required and shall be voided. The court shall, by mail, provide notice to the parties or their attorneys that the initial paper and the response have been voided. The responding party's filing fee shall be refunded upon request, provided that the request for a refund is made within 20 days from the date on which the notice was mailed. Upon receipt of the request, the court shall refund the responding party's filing fee without imposing any administrative charge. A refund under this subdivision is available if the adverse party has filed only a responsive pleading, but not if the party has also filed a cross-complaint or other first paper seeking affirmative relief for which there is a filing fee.

(d) If an adverse party, or a person acting on behalf of the adverse party, tenders a check for a required filing fee that is later returned without payment, the procedures in subdivisions (a) and (b) shall apply.

(e) If any trial or other hearing is scheduled to be heard prior to the expiration of the 20–day period provided for in subdivision (a), the fee shall be paid prior to the trial or hearing. Failure of the party to pay the fee prior to the trial or hearing date shall cause the court to void the filing and proceed as if it had not been filed.

(f) If the clerk performs a service or issues any document for which a fee is required and payment is made by check which is later returned without payment, the court may order further proceedings suspended as to the party for whom the check was tendered. If the court so orders, the clerk shall, by mail, notify the party who tendered the check that proceedings have been suspended until the receipt of payment of the required fee and the administrative charge specified in subdivision (g), by cash cashier's check, or other means specified by the court, but not by personal check or traveler's check. If the person who tendered the check is not a party to the action or proposed action, but only is acting on behalf of a party, the clerk shall notify not only the person who tendered the check, but also the party or that party's attorney if the party is represented. The clerk's certificate as to the mailing of notice pursuant to this section establishes a rebuttable presumption that the fees were not paid. This presumption is a presumption affecting the burden of producing evidence.

(g) The clerk shall impose an administrative charge for providing notice that a check submitted for a filing fee has been returned without payment and for all related administrative, clerical, and other costs incurred under this section. The administrative charge shall, in each instance, be either twenty-five dollars ($25) or a reasonable amount that does not exceed the actual cost incurred by the court, as determined by the court. The notices provided by the court under subdivisions (a) and (f) shall state the specific amount of the administrative charge that shall be paid to the court. Each administrative charge collected shall be distributed to the court that incurred the charge as described in Section 68085.1 of the Government Code. *(Added by Stats.1982, c. 1543, p. 6007, § 3. Amended by Stats.1994, c. 587 (A.B.3600), § 3.7; Stats.2004, c. 171 (A.B.3078), § 2; Stats.*

2005, c. 75 (A.B.145), § 30, eff. July 19, 2005, operative Jan. 1, 2006.)

Research References

Rutter, Cal. Practice Guide: Civ. Pro. Before Trial Ch. 1-H, H. Filing Fee Considerations.
Rutter, Cal. Practice Guide: Civ. Pro. Before Trial Ch. 9(I)-B, B. Preparing and Filing Motions.
3 Witkin Cal. Proc. 5th Actions § 994, Issuance.
8 Witkin Cal. Proc. 5th Attack Judgment Trial Court § 147, (S 147) in General.
2 Witkin Cal. Proc. 5th Courts § 367, (S 367) Fees.
2 Witkin Cal. Proc. 5th Jurisdiction § 91, (S 91) Violation of Jurisdictional Time Limit.
4 Witkin Cal. Proc. 5th Pleading § 19, in General.

§ 411.21.   Tender of amount less than required for filing fees; notice; time to tender amount; procedural effect; administrative charge

(a) If a complaint or other first paper is accompanied by payment by check in an amount less than the required fee, the clerk shall accept the paper for filing, but shall not issue a summons until the court receives full payment of the required fee. The clerk shall, by mail, notify the party tendering the check that (1) the check was made out for an amount less than the required filing fee, (2) the administrative charge specified in subdivision (g) has been imposed to reimburse the court for the costs of processing the partial payment and providing the notice specified in this subdivision, and (3) the party has 20 days from the date of mailing of the notice within which to pay the remainder of the required fee and the administrative charge, except as provided in subdivision (f). If the person who tendered the check is not a party to the action or proposed action, but only is acting on behalf of a party, the clerk shall notify not only the person who tendered the check, and also the party or that party's attorney, if the party is represented. The clerk's certificate as to the mailing of notice pursuant to this section establishes a rebuttable presumption that the fees were not paid. This presumption is a presumption affecting the burden of producing evidence. This subdivision does not apply to an unlawful detainer action.

(b) The clerk shall void the filing if the party who tendered a check in an amount less than the required filing fee or on whose behalf a check in an amount less than the required filing fee was tendered has not paid the full amount of the fee and the administrative charge by a means specified in subdivision (a) within 20 days of the date on which the notice required by subdivision (a) was mailed. Any filing voided by this section may be disposed of immediately after the 20 days have elapsed without preserving a copy in the court records notwithstanding Section 68152 of the Government Code.

(c) If a check for less than the required fee was tendered, the remainder of the required fee and the administrative charge were not paid within the period specified in subdivision (a), and a refund of the partial payment has not been requested in a writing mailed or presented by the party or person who tendered the check within 20 days from the date on which the remainder of the required fee was due, the partial payment shall be remitted to the State Treasurer to be deposited in the Trial Court Trust Fund, except for the amount of the administrative charge described in subdivision (g), that shall be deducted from the partial payment and shall be distributed as described in subdivision (g) to the court which incurred the charge. If the party or person who tendered the check for partial payment requests a refund of the partial payment, in writing, within the time specified in this subdivision, the clerk shall refund the amount of the partial payment less the amount of the administrative charge imposed by that court. All partial payments that the court received before January 1, 2006, and that remain on deposit for filings that the clerk voided pursuant to this section, once three years have passed from the date that the filing was voided, shall be remitted to the State Treasurer for deposit into the Trial Court Trust Fund.

(d) If an adverse party files a response to a complaint or other first paper referred to in subdivision (a), together with a filing fee, and the original filing is voided pursuant to subdivision (b), the responsive filing is not required and shall be voided. The court shall, by mail, provide notice to the parties that the initial paper and the response have been voided. The responding party's filing fee shall be refunded upon request, provided that the request for a refund is made in writing within 20 days from the date on which the notice was mailed. Upon receipt of the request, the court shall reimburse the responding party's filing fee without imposing any administrative charge. A refund under this subdivision is available if the adverse party has filed only a responsive pleading, but not if the party has also filed a cross-complaint or other first paper seeking affirmative relief for which there is a filing fee.

(e) If an adverse party, or a person acting on behalf of the adverse party, tenders a check for a required filing fee in an amount less than the required fee, the procedures in subdivisions (a), (b), and (c) shall apply.

(f) If any trial or other hearing is scheduled to be heard prior to the expiration of the 20-day period provided for in subdivision (a), the fee shall be paid prior to the trial or hearing. Failure of the party to pay the fee prior to the trial or hearing date shall cause the court to void the filing and proceed as if it had not been filed.

(g) The clerk shall impose an administrative charge for providing notice that a check submitted for a filing fee is in an amount less than the required fee and for all related administrative, clerical, and other costs incurred under this section. The administrative charge shall, in each instance, be either twenty-five dollars ($25) or a reasonable amount that does not exceed the actual cost incurred by the court, as determined by the court. The notices provided by the court under subdivision (a) shall state the specific amount of the administrative charge that shall be paid to the court. Each administrative charge collected shall be distributed to the court that incurred the charge as described in Section 68085.1 of the Government Code. When a partial payment is to be remitted to the State Treasurer under subdivision (c), the court shall notify the Administrative Office of the Courts of the amount of (1) the partial payment collected, and (2) the administrative charge to be deducted from the payment and to be distributed to the court. *(Added by Stats.2005, c. 75 (A.B.145), § 31, eff. July 19, 2005, operative Jan. 1, 2006. Amended by Stats.2007, c. 738 (A.B.1248), § 5.)*

Research References

Rutter, Cal. Practice Guide: Civ. Pro. Before Trial Ch. 1-H, H. Filing Fee Considerations.
4 Witkin Cal. Proc. 5th Pleading § 19, in General.

§ 411.35. Malpractice actions; architects, engineers, or surveyors; certificate of review and consultation; res ipsa loquitur exception; failure to file

(a) In every action, including a cross-complaint for damages or indemnity, arising out of the professional negligence of a person holding a valid architect's certificate issued pursuant to Chapter 3 (commencing with Section 5500) of Division 3 of the Business and Professions Code, or of a person holding a valid registration as a professional engineer issued pursuant to Chapter 7 (commencing with Section 6700) of Division 3 of the Business and Professions Code, or a person holding a valid land surveyor's license issued pursuant to Chapter 15 (commencing with Section 8700) of Division 3 of the Business and Professions

Code on or before the date of service of the complaint or cross-complaint on any defendant or cross-defendant, the attorney for the plaintiff or cross-complainant shall file and serve the certificate specified by subdivision (b).

(b) A certificate shall be executed by the attorney for the plaintiff or cross-complainant declaring one of the following:

(1) That the attorney has reviewed the facts of the case, that the attorney has consulted with and received an opinion from at least one architect, professional engineer, or land surveyor who is licensed to practice and practices in this state or any other state, or who teaches at an accredited college or university and is licensed to practice in this state or any other state, in the same discipline as the defendant or cross-defendant and who the attorney reasonably believes is knowledgeable in the relevant issues involved in the particular action, and that the attorney has concluded on the basis of this review and consultation that there is reasonable and meritorious cause for the filing of this action. The person consulted may not be a party to the litigation. The person consulted shall render his or her opinion that the named defendant or cross-defendant was negligent or was not negligent in the performance of the applicable professional services.

(2) That the attorney was unable to obtain the consultation required by paragraph (1) because a statute of limitations would impair the action and that the certificate required by paragraph (1) could not be obtained before the impairment of the action. If a certificate is executed pursuant to this paragraph, the certificate required by paragraph (1) shall be filed within 60 days after filing the complaint.

(3) That the attorney was unable to obtain the consultation required by paragraph (1) because the attorney had made three separate good faith attempts with three separate architects, professional engineers, or land surveyors to obtain this consultation and none of those contacted would agree to the consultation.

(c) Where a certificate is required pursuant to this section, only one certificate shall be filed, notwithstanding that multiple defendants have been named in the complaint or may be named at a later time.

(d) Where the attorney intends to rely solely on the doctrine of "res ipsa loquitur," as defined in Section 646 of the Evidence Code, or exclusively on a failure to inform of the consequences of a procedure, or both, this section shall be inapplicable. The attorney shall certify upon filing of the complaint that the attorney is solely relying on the doctrines of "res ipsa loquitur" or failure to inform of the consequences of a procedure or both, and for that reason is not filing a certificate required by this section.

(e) For purposes of this section, and subject to Section 912 of the Evidence Code, an attorney who submits a certificate as required by paragraph (1) or (2) of subdivision (b) has a privilege to refuse to disclose the identity of the architect, professional engineer, or land surveyor consulted and the contents of the consultation. The privilege shall also be held by the architect, professional engineer, or land surveyor so consulted. If, however, the attorney makes a claim under paragraph (3) of subdivision (b) that he or she was unable to obtain the required consultation with the architect, professional engineer, or land surveyor, the court may require the attorney to divulge the names of architects, professional engineers, or land surveyors refusing the consultation.

(f) A violation of this section may constitute unprofessional conduct and be grounds for discipline against the attorney, except that the failure to file the certificate required by paragraph (1) of subdivision (b), within 60 days after filing the complaint and certificate provided for by paragraph (2) of subdivision (b), shall not be grounds for discipline against the attorney.

(g) The failure to file a certificate in accordance with this section shall be grounds for a demurrer pursuant to Section 430.10 or a motion to strike pursuant to Section 435.

(h) Upon the favorable conclusion of the litigation with respect to any party for whom a certificate of merit was filed or for whom a certificate of merit should have been filed pursuant to this section, the trial court may, upon the motion of a party or upon the court's own motion, verify compliance with this section, by requiring the attorney for the plaintiff or cross-complainant who was required by subdivision (b) to execute the certificate to reveal the name, address, and telephone number of the person or persons consulted with pursuant to subdivision (b) that were relied upon by the attorney in preparation of the certificate of merit. The name, address, and telephone number shall be disclosed to the trial judge in an in-camera proceeding at which the moving party shall not be present. If the trial judge finds there has been a failure to comply with this section, the court may order a party, a party's attorney, or both, to pay any reasonable expenses, including attorney's fees, incurred by another party as a result of the failure to comply with this section.

(i) For purposes of this section, "action" includes a complaint or cross-complaint for equitable indemnity arising out of the rendition of professional services whether or not the complaint or cross-complaint specifically asserts or utilizes the terms "professional negligence" or "negligence." *(Added by Stats. 1979, c. 973, p. 3334, § 1. Amended by Stats.1983, c. 414, § 1; Stats.1986, c. 1231, § 1; Stats.1988, c. 1070, § 1; Stats.1990, c, 204 (S.B.2089), § 1; Stats.1991, c. 272 (S.B.527), § 1; Stats.1995, c. 241 (S.B.934), § 1; Stats.1999, c. 176 (A.B.540), § 1.)*

Research References

Rutter, Cal. Practice Guide: Civ. Pro. Before Trial Ch. 1-D, D. Prelawsuit Consultation Requirement in Certain Professional Negligence Actions.
Rutter, Cal. Practice Guide: Civ. Pro. Before Trial Ch. 8C-4, Attorney Work Product Protection.
Rutter, Cal. Practice Guide: Civ. Pro. Before Trial Ch. 7(I)-A, A. Demurrers.
Rutter, Cal. Practice Guide: Civ. Pro. Before Trial Ch. 7(I)-B, B. Motions to Strike.
Rutter, Cal. Practice Guide: Fed.Civ.Pro. Before Trial Ch. 1-B, B. Federal vs. State Law.
Miller and Starr California Real Estate § 29:61, Certificates of Merit.
20 NO. 4 Miller & Starr, California Real Estate Newsalert 27, Defective Construction.
3 Witkin Cal. Proc. 5th Actions § 209, (S 209) Certificate of Merit in Malpractice Action Against Architect, Engineer, or Land Surveyor.
7 Witkin Cal. Proc. 5th Judgment § 229, (S 229) Actions Involving Personal Injury or Intentional Torts.
5 Witkin Cal. Proc. 5th Pleading § 951, in General.
5 Witkin Cal. Proc. 5th Pleading § 978, No Certificate Filed.

CHAPTER 3. SUMMONS

§ 412.10.   Issuance of copy of summons by clerk; retention of original

After payment of all applicable fees, the plaintiff may have the clerk issue one or more summons for any defendant. The clerk shall keep each original summons in the court records and provide a copy of each summons issued to the plaintiff who requested issuance of the summons. *(Added by Stats.1969, c. 1610, p. 3363, § 3, operative July 1, 1970. Amended by Stats.2005, c. 300 (A.B.496), § 2.)*

Research References

Rutter, Cal. Practice Guide: Civ. Pro. Before Trial Ch. 4-B, B. Issuance of Summons.
3 Witkin Cal. Proc. 5th Actions § 960, (S 960) Summons in Civil Action.
3 Witkin Cal. Proc. 5th Actions § 967, (S 967) Statutory Revision of 1969.
3 Witkin Cal. Proc. 5th Actions § 993, (S 993) Probate Proceedings.
3 Witkin Cal. Proc. 5th Actions § 994, Issuance.
3 Witkin Cal. Proc. 5th Actions § 995, Amended or Supplemental Complaint.
3 Witkin Cal. Proc. 5th Actions § 996, Loss or Failure to Serve.
2 Witkin Cal. Proc. 5th Courts § 259, (S 259) Local Standards and Procedure.
4 Witkin Cal. Proc. 5th Pleading § 19, in General.
5 Witkin Cal. Proc. 5th Pleading § 1247, (S 1247) Procedure.
14 Witkin, California Summary 10th Wills and Probate § 577, (S 577) Objection, Summons, and Response.

§ 412.20.   Summons; formalities; contents

(a) Except as otherwise required by statute, a summons shall be directed to the defendant, signed by the clerk and issued under the seal of the court in which the action is pending, and it shall contain:

(1) The title of the court in which the action is pending.

(2) The names of the parties to the action.

(3) A direction that the defendant file with the court a written pleading in response to the complaint within 30 days after summons is served on him or her.

(4) A notice that, unless the defendant so responds, his or her default will be entered upon application by the plaintiff, and the plaintiff may apply to the court for the relief demanded in the complaint, which could result in garnishment of wages, taking of money or property, or other relief.

(5) The following statement in boldface type: "You may seek the advice of an attorney in any matter connected with the complaint or this summons. Such attorney should be consulted promptly so that your pleading may be filed or entered within the time required by this summons."

(6) The following introductory legend at the top of the summons above all other matter, in boldface type, in English and Spanish:

"Notice! You have been sued. The court may decide against you without your being heard unless you respond within 30 days. Read information below."

(b) Each county may, by ordinance, require that the legend contained in paragraph (6) of subdivision (a) be set forth in every summons issued out of the courts of that county in any additional foreign language, if the legend in the additional foreign language is set forth in the summons in the same manner as required in that paragraph.

(c) A summons in a form approved by the Judicial Council is deemed to comply with this section. *(Added by Stats.1969, c. 1610, p. 3363, § 3, operative July 1, 1970. Amended by Stats.1974, c. 363, p. 697, § 1; Stats.1989, c. 79, § 1, eff. June 30, 1989; Stats.1989, c. 1105, § 6.)*

Research References

Rutter, Cal. Practice Guide: Civ. Pro. Before Trial Ch. 4-B, B. Issuance of Summons.
Rutter, Cal. Practice Guide: Civ. Pro. Before Trial Ch. 4-C, C. Content of Summons.
Rutter, Cal. Practice Guide: Civ. Pro. Before Trial Ch. 5-B, B. Entry of Default.

Rutter, Cal. Practice Guide: Civ. Pro. Before Trial Ch. 6-B, B. Complaints.

Rutter, Cal. Practice Guide: Civ. Pro. Before Trial Ch. 6-C, C. Answer.

Rutter, Cal. Practice Guide: Civ. Pro. Before Trial Ch. 12(I)-B, B. Case Management ("Fast Track") System.

Rutter, Cal. Practice Guide: Fed.Civ.Pro. Before Trial Ch. 5-E, E. Waiver of Service.

Miller and Starr California Real Estate § 19:221, Complaint and Summons.

3 Witkin Cal. Proc. 5th Actions § 981, (S 981) in General.

3 Witkin Cal. Proc. 5th Actions § 982, in General.

3 Witkin Cal. Proc. 5th Actions § 983, Names of Parties.

3 Witkin Cal. Proc. 5th Actions § 984, (S 984) in General.

3 Witkin Cal. Proc. 5th Actions § 986, Other Requirements.

2 Witkin Cal. Proc. 5th Courts § 29, (S 29) Use of English.

2 Witkin Cal. Proc. 5th Courts § 262, Minimum Time Standards.

2 Witkin Cal. Proc. 5th Courts § 363, (S 363) Process and Notices.

4 Witkin Cal. Proc. 5th Pleading § 7, (S 7) Time Prescribed by Statute.

12 Witkin, California Summary 10th Real Property § 69, Summons.

10 Witkin, California Summary 10th Parent and Child § 51, Protective Orders.

§ 412.30. Action against corporation or unincorporated association; notice; contents; default judgment

In an action against a corporation or an unincorporated association (including a partnership), the copy of the summons that is served shall contain a notice stating in substance: "To the person served: You are hereby served in the within action (or special proceeding) on behalf of (here state the name of the corporation or the unincorporated association) as a person upon whom a copy of the summons and of the complaint may be delivered to effect service on said party under the provisions of (here state appropriate provisions of Chapter 4 (commencing with Section 413.10) of the Code of Civil Procedure)." If service is also made on such person as an individual, the notice shall also indicate that service is being made on such person as an individual as well as on behalf of the corporation or the unincorporated association.

If such notice does not appear on the copy of the summons served, no default may be taken against such corporation or unincorporated association or against such person individually, as the case may be. *(Added by Stats.1969, c. 1610, p. 3363, § 3, operative July 1, 1970.)*

Research References

Rutter, Cal. Practice Guide: Civ. Pro. Before Trial Ch. 4-C, C. Content of Summons.

Rutter, Cal. Practice Guide: Civ. Pro. Before Trial Ch. 4-D, D. Service of Summons.

3 Witkin Cal. Proc. 5th Actions § 989, (S 989) Actions Against Corporation or Association.

3 Witkin Cal. Proc. 5th Actions § 1068, Personal Delivery or Leaving Copy.

6 Witkin Cal. Proc. 5th Proceedings Without Trial § 353, (S 353) Extension of Time as Estoppel.

CHAPTER 4. SERVICE OF SUMMONS

ARTICLE 1. GENERAL

§ 413.10. Law governing service

Except as otherwise provided by statute, a summons shall be served on a person:

(a) Within this state, as provided in this chapter.

(b) Outside this state but within the United States, as provided in this chapter or as prescribed by the law of the place where the person is served.

(c) Outside the United States, as provided in this chapter or as directed by the court in which the action is pending, or, if the court before or after service finds that the service is reasonably calculated to give actual notice, as prescribed by the law of the place where the person is served or as directed by the foreign authority in response to a letter rogatory. These rules are subject to the provisions of the Convention on the "Service Abroad of Judicial and Extrajudicial Documents" in Civil or Commercial Matters (Hague Service Convention). *(Added by Stats.1969, c. 1610, p. 3363, § 3, operative July 1, 1970. Amended by Stats.1984, c. 191, § 1.)*

Research References

Rutter, Cal. Practice Guide: Civ. Pro. Before Trial Ch. 4-A, A. Requirements-In General.

Rutter, Cal. Practice Guide: Civ. Pro. Before Trial Ch. 4-D, D. Service of Summons.

Rutter, Cal. Practice Guide: Enforcing Judgments/Debts Ch. 4-B, B. Claim and Delivery.

Rutter, Cal. Practice Guide: Fed.Civ.Pro. Before Trial Ch. 5-F, F. Manner of Service (Where Service Not Waived).

Rutter, Cal. Practice Guide: Personal Injury Ch. 5-E, E. Selected Pleading Issues.

3 Witkin Cal. Proc. 5th Actions § 967, (S 967) Statutory Revision of 1969.

3 Witkin Cal. Proc. 5th Actions § 989, (S 989) Actions Against Corporation or Association.

3 Witkin Cal. Proc. 5th Actions § 993, (S 993) Probate Proceedings.

3 Witkin Cal. Proc. 5th Actions § 1001, (S 1001) Statutory Revision of 1969.

3 Witkin Cal. Proc. 5th Actions § 1002, (S 1002) Service Within California.

3 Witkin Cal. Proc. 5th Actions § 1003, (S 1003) Service Outside California But Within United States.

3 Witkin Cal. Proc. 5th Actions § 1004, Statutory Requirements.

3 Witkin Cal. Proc. 5th Actions § 1005, Hague Service Convention Requirements.

3 Witkin Cal. Proc. 5th Actions § 1007, (S 1007) Method Devised by Court.

3 Witkin Cal. Proc. 5th Actions § 1021, in General.

3 Witkin Cal. Proc. 5th Actions § 1027, (S 1027) Service and Effect.

3 Witkin Cal. Proc. 5th Actions § 1051, Domestic Corporation.

3 Witkin Cal. Proc. 5th Actions § 1055, Foreign Partnership.

3 Witkin Cal. Proc. 5th Actions § 1073, Under Foreign Law.

3 Witkin Cal. Proc. 5th Actions § 1074, Under Court Order.

1 Witkin Cal. Proc. 5th Attorneys § 231, Trial After Arbitration.

8 Witkin Cal. Proc. 5th Enforcement of Judgment § 27, Manner of Service.

8 Witkin Cal. Proc. 5th Enforcement of Judgment § 28, Proof of Service.

2 Witkin Cal. Proc. 5th Jurisdiction § 121, Jurisdiction and Process Statute.

2 Witkin Cal. Proc. 5th Jurisdiction § 126, Person Immune from Process.

4 Witkin Cal. Proc. 5th Pleading § 29, (S 29) Service.

6 Witkin Cal. Proc. 5th Proceedings Without Trial § 13, General Rule.

6 Witkin Cal. Proc. 5th Provisional Remedies § 88, (S 88) Service.

6 Witkin Cal. Proc. 5th Provisional Remedies § 257, Noticed Motion.

12 Witkin, California Summary 10th Real Property § 728, Jurisdiction, Venue, and Process.

9 Witkin, California Summary 10th Corporations § 231, (S 231) Service of Process.

9 Witkin, California Summary 10th Partnership § 67, (S 67) Agent and Service of Process.

9 Witkin, California Summary 10th Partnership § 141, (S 141) Agent and Service of Process.

9 Witkin, California Summary 10th Partnership § 176, (S 176) Action Against Dissolved Company.

13 Witkin, California Summary 10th Trusts § 231, (S 231) Notice.

13 Witkin, California Summary 10th Trusts § 264, (S 264) Immunity for Good Faith Acts or Omissions.

13 Witkin, California Summary 10th Trusts § 280, (S 280) Notice of Hearing.

13 Witkin, California Summary 10th Trusts § 284, (S 284) Notice of Hearing.

14 Witkin, California Summary 10th Wills and Probate § 357, Notice.

14 Witkin, California Summary 10th Wills and Probate § 398, (S 398) Citation.

14 Witkin, California Summary 10th Wills and Probate § 577, (S 577) Objection, Summons, and Response.

14 Witkin, California Summary 10th Wills and Probate § 616, Immunity for Good Faith Acts or Omissions.

14 Witkin, California Summary 10th Wills and Probate § 707, Expenses of Administration.

14 Witkin, California Summary 10th Wills and Probate § 875, (S 875) Hearing, Determination, and Appeal.

14 Witkin, California Summary 10th Wills and Probate § 899, (S 899) Hearing, Determination, and Appeal.

§ 413.20.   Service by mail; time not extended

If a summons is served by mail pursuant to this chapter, the provisions of Section 1013 that extend the time for exercising a right or doing an act shall not extend any time specified in this title. *(Added by Stats.1969, c. 1610, p. 3363, § 3, operative July 1, 1970.)*

Research References

Rutter, Cal. Practice Guide: Civ. Pro. Before Trial Ch. 4-D, D. Service of Summons.

3 Witkin Cal. Proc. 5th Actions § 1020, (S 1020) No Extension of Time.

6 Witkin Cal. Proc. 5th Proceedings Without Trial § 31, Express Limitations.

§ 413.30.   Procedure when no provision made for service; proof of service

Where no provision is made in this chapter or other law for the service of summons, the court in which the action is pending may direct that summons be served in a manner which is reasonably calculated to give actual notice to the party to be served and that proof of such service be made as prescribed by the court. *(Added by Stats.1969, c. 1610, p. 3363, § 3, operative July 1, 1970.)*

Research References

3 Witkin Cal. Proc. 5th Actions § 417, (S 417) Constitutional Right in Marital Case.

3 Witkin Cal. Proc. 5th Actions § 1007, (S 1007) Method Devised by Court.

14 Witkin, California Summary 10th Wills and Probate § 39, Major Changes.

14 Witkin, California Summary 10th Wills and Probate § 391, (S 391) in General.

14 Witkin, California Summary 10th Wills and Probate § 392, (S 392) Manner of Mailing.

14 Witkin, California Summary 10th Wills and Probate § 393, Personal Delivery.

§ 413.40.   Service in violation of law governing process servers

Any service of summons which complies with the provisions of this chapter shall not be rendered invalid or ineffective because it was made by a person in violation of Chapter 16 (commencing with Section 22350) of Division 8 of the Business and Professions Code. *(Added by Stats.1971, c. 1661, p. 3578, § 2, operative July 1, 1972.)*

Research References

Rutter, Cal. Practice Guide: Civ. Pro. Before Trial Ch. 4-D, D. Service of Summons.

3 Witkin Cal. Proc. 5th Actions § 998, (S 998) Registered Process Server.

ARTICLE 2.   PERSONS WHO MAY SERVE SUMMONS

Section
414.10.   Authorized persons.

§ 414.10.   Authorized persons

A summons may be served by any person who is at least 18 years of age and not a party to the action. *(Added by Stats.1969, c. 1610, p. 3363, § 3, operative July 1, 1970.)*

Research References

Rutter, Cal. Practice Guide: Civ. Pro. Before Trial Ch. 4-D, D. Service of Summons.

Rutter, Cal. Practice Guide: Civ. Pro. Before Trial Ch. 8E-6, Subpoena to Nonparty Deponent or Business Records Custodian.

3 Witkin Cal. Proc. 5th Actions § 997, (S 997) Officer or Private Person.

3 Witkin Cal. Proc. 5th Actions § 1067, (S 1067) Affidavit or Certificate.

ARTICLE 3.   MANNER OF SERVICE OF SUMMONS

Section
415.10.   Personal delivery of copy of summons and complaint; date.

415.20.   Leaving copy of summons and complaint at office, dwelling house, usual place of abode or business or usual mailing address; mailing copy.

415.21.   Access to gated communities; identification.

415.30.   Service by mail.

415.40.   Service on person outside state.

415.45.   Unlawful detainer; service by posting and mailing or other manner.

415.46.   Prejudgment claim of right to possession.

415.47.   Unlawful detainer; intent of lessee not to abandon premises; service.

415.50.   Service by publication.

415.95.   Service of summons on a business organization, form unknown.

§ 415.10.   Personal delivery of copy of summons and complaint; date

A summons may be served by personal delivery of a copy of the summons and of the complaint to the person to be served. Service of a summons in this manner is deemed complete at the time of such delivery.

The date upon which personal delivery is made shall be entered on or affixed to the face of the copy of the summons at the time of its delivery. However, service of a summons without such date shall be valid and effective. *(Added by Stats.1969, c. 1610, p. 3363, § 3, operative July 1, 1970.   Amended by Stats.1976, c. 789, p. 1827, § 1.)*

Research References

Rutter, Cal. Practice Guide: Civ. Pro. Before Trial Ch. 4-D, D. Service of Summons.

Rutter, Cal. Practice Guide: Civ. Pro. Before Trial Ch. 11-B, B. Involuntary Dismissals.

Rutter, Cal. Practice Guide: Enforcing Judgments/Debts Ch. 6F-3, Issuance and Service of Earnings Withholding Orders.

Rutter, Cal. Practice Guide: Enforcing Judgments/Debts Ch. 6A-10, Service of Writs, Notices and Other Papers in Enforcement Proceedings.

Rutter, Cal. Practice Guide: Family Law Ch. 7-F, F. Visitation Rights.

Rutter, Cal. Practice Guide: Fed.Civ.Pro. Before Trial Ch. 5-F, F. Manner of Service (Where Service Not Waived).

3 Witkin Cal. Proc. 5th Actions § 1002, (S 1002) Service Within California.

3 Witkin Cal. Proc. 5th Actions § 1008, (S 1008) Delivery to Defendant.

3 Witkin Cal. Proc. 5th Actions § 1019, Service on Corporation.

3 Witkin Cal. Proc. 5th Actions § 1068, Personal Delivery or Leaving Copy.

8 Witkin Cal. Proc. 5th Enforcement of Judgment § 27, Manner of Service.

8 Witkin Cal. Proc. 5th Enforcement of Judgment § 28, Proof of Service.

8 Witkin Cal. Proc. 5th Enforcement of Judgment § 254, in General.

8 Witkin Cal. Proc. 5th Enforcement of Judgment § 278, (S 278) Examination of Judgment Debtor.

8 Witkin Cal. Proc. 5th Enforcement of Judgment § 457, (S 457) Notice of Entry.

2 Witkin Cal. Proc. 5th Jurisdiction § 116, (S 116) Personal Service.

2 Witkin Cal. Proc. 5th Jurisdiction § 121, Jurisdiction and Process Statute.

4 Witkin Cal. Proc. 5th Pleading § 514, Statement Preserving Right to Seek Punitive Damages.

6 Witkin Cal. Proc. 5th Provisional Remedies § 269, (S 269) Service of Writ and Undertaking.

6 Witkin Cal. Proc. 5th Provisional Remedies § 401, (S 401) Service of Motion to Modify Permanent Injunction.

6 Witkin Cal. Proc. 5th Provisional Remedies § 407, Service of Motion to Dissolve Permanent Injunction.

12 Witkin, California Summary 40th Real Property § 112, (S 112) Liens.

12 Witkin, California Summary 10th Real Property § 112B, (New)-Higher Value or Longer Delinquency.

10 Witkin, California Summary 10th Parent and Child § 387, (S 387) Application and Order or Response.

14 Witkin, California Summary 10th Wills and Probate § 511, Procedure.

14 Witkin, California Summary 10th Wills and Probate § 562, Determination Whether Act Constitutes Contest.

14 Witkin, California Summary 10th Wills and Probate § 723, (S 723) in General.

14 Witkin, California Summary 10th Wills and Probate § 750, (S 750) Petition to Revoke or Limit Authority.

14 Witkin, California Summary 10th Wills and Probate § 762, (S 762) Restraining Order to Prevent Proposed Action.

14 Witkin, California Summary 10th Wills and Probate § 920, (S 920) in General.

14 Witkin, California Summary 10th Wills and Probate § 940, (S 940) Citation to Proposed Conservatee.

14 Witkin, California Summary 10th Wills and Probate § 1061, (S 1061) Termination of Limited Conservatorship.

§ 415.20. Leaving copy of summons and complaint at office, dwelling house, usual place of abode or business or usual mailing address; mailing copy

(a) In lieu of personal delivery of a copy of the summons and complaint to the person to be served as specified in Section 416.10, 416.20, 416.30, 416.40, or 416.50, a summons may be served by leaving a copy of the summons and complaint during usual office hours in his or her office or, if no physical address is known, at his or her usual mailing address, other than a United States Postal Service post office box, with the person who is apparently in charge thereof, and by thereafter mailing a copy of the summons and complaint by first- class mail, postage prepaid to the person to be served at the place where a copy of the summons and complaint were left. When service is effected by leaving a copy of the summons and complaint at a mailing address, it shall be left with a person at least 18 years of age, who shall be informed of the contents thereof. Service of a summons in this manner is deemed complete on the 10th day after the mailing.

(b) If a copy of the summons and complaint cannot with reasonable diligence be personally delivered to the person to be served, as specified in Section 416.60, 416.70, 416.80, or 416.90, a summons may be served by leaving a copy of the summons and complaint at the person's dwelling house, usual place of abode, usual place of business, or usual mailing address other than a United States Postal Service post office box, in the presence of a competent member of the household or a person apparently in charge of his or her office, place of business, or usual mailing address other than a United States Postal Service post office box, at least 18 years of age, who shall be informed of the contents thereof, and by thereafter mailing a copy of the summons and of the complaint by first-class mail, postage prepaid to the person to be served at the place where a copy of the summons and complaint were left. Service of a summons in this manner is deemed complete on the 10th day after the mailing. *(Added by Stats.1969, c. 1610, p. 3363, § 3, operative July 1, 1970. Amended by Stats.1989, c. 1416, § 15; Stats.2003, c. 128 (A.B.418), § 1.)*

Research References

Rutter, Cal. Practice Guide: Civ. Pro. Before Trial Ch. 4-D, D. Service of Summons.

Rutter, Cal. Practice Guide: Civ. Pro. Before Trial Ch. 11-B, B. Involuntary Dismissals.

Rutter, Cal. Practice Guide: Civ. Pro. Before Trial Ch. 9(II)-D, D. Attachment.

California Practice Guide: Employment Litigation Ch. 11-J, J. Enforcing California Laws Regulating Employee Compensation.

Rutter, Cal. Practice Guide: Enforcing Judgments/Debts Ch. 6F-3, Issuance and Service of Earnings Withholding Orders.

Rutter, Cal. Practice Guide: Enforcing Judgments/Debts Ch. 6A-10, Service of Writs, Notices and Other Papers in Enforcement Proceedings.

Rutter, Cal. Practice Guide: Fed.Civ.Pro. Before Trial Ch. 5-F, F. Manner of Service (Where Service Not Waived).

Rutter, Cal. Practice Guide: Fed.Civ.Pro. Before Trial Ch. 6-B, B. Expiration of Time to Respond.

Rutter, Cal. Practice Guide: Insurance Litigation Ch. 6I-B, B. Particular Surety Bond Coverages.

Miller and Starr California Real Estate § 28:28, Statutory Provisions Governing Notice.

Miller and Starr California Real Estate § 28:36, Time and Method for Service of the Preliminary Notice.

Miller and Starr California Real Estate § 28:73, Service of the Stop Payment Notice.

Miller and Starr California Real Estate § 28:83, Suit to Enforce the Stop Payment Notice.

Miller and Starr California Real Estate § 28:87, Requirement for and Contents of a Preliminary Notice.

Miller and Starr California Real Estate § 28:89, Duty of Public Agency After Receipt of Stop Payment Notice.

Miller and Starr California Real Estate § 28:90, Release of the Stop Payment Notice.

Miller and Starr California Real Estate § 28:98, Notice as Condition Precedent to Surety's Liability on Payment Bond.

Miller and Starr California Real Estate § 28:122, Action by Claimants and Others on Public Works Payment Bond--Procedure and Notice.

3 Witkin Cal. Proc. 5th Actions § 1002, (S 1002) Service Within California.

3 Witkin Cal. Proc. 5th Actions § 1010, (S 1010) Corporation, Association, or Public Entity Defendant.

3 Witkin Cal. Proc. 5th Actions § 1011, Attempted Physical Delivery is Required.

3 Witkin Cal. Proc. 5th Actions § 1012, Effectuating Substituted Service.

3 Witkin Cal. Proc. 5th Actions § 1013, (S 1013) Business Organization of Unknown Form.

3 Witkin Cal. Proc. 5th Actions § 1014, (S 1014) Service at Gated Communities.

3 Witkin Cal. Proc. 5th Actions § 1068, Personal Delivery or Leaving Copy.

3 Witkin Cal. Proc. 5th Actions § 221C, (S 221C) (New)-Private Property: Preliminary Notice.

2 Witkin Cal. Proc. 5th Courts § 294, (S 294) Notice to Appear.

8 Witkin Cal. Proc. 5th Enforcement of Judgment § 27, Manner of Service.

8 Witkin Cal. Proc. 5th Enforcement of Judgment § 28, Proof of Service.

8 Witkin Cal. Proc. 5th Enforcement of Judgment § 254, in General.

2 Witkin Cal. Proc. 5th Jurisdiction § 116, (S 116) Personal Service.

2 Witkin Cal. Proc. 5th Jurisdiction § 121, Jurisdiction and Process Statute.

Civ. Pro.

4 Witkin, California Summary 10th Security Transactions in Real Property § 31E, (New)-Preliminary Notice.

§ 415.21.   Access to gated communities; identification

(a) Notwithstanding any other law, any person shall be granted access to a gated community for a reasonable period of time for the sole purpose of performing lawful service of process or service of a subpoena, upon identifying to the guard the person or persons to be served, and upon displaying a current driver's license or other identification, and one of the following:

(1) A badge or other confirmation that the individual is acting in his or her capacity as a representative of a county sheriff or marshal.

(2) Evidence of current registration as a process server pursuant to Chapter 16 (commencing with Section 22350) of Division 8 of the Business and Professions Code or of licensure as a private investigator pursuant to Chapter 11.3 (commencing with Section 7512) of Division 3 of the Business and Professions Code.

(b) This section shall only apply to a gated community that is staffed at the time service of process is attempted by a guard or other security personnel assigned to control access to the community. *(Added by Stats.1994, c. 691 (A.B.3307), § 1. Amended by Stats.2005, c. 706 (A.B.1742), § 11; Stats.2012, c. 113 (A.B.1720), § 1.)*

Research References

Rutter, Cal. Practice Guide: Civ. Pro. Before Trial Ch. 4-D, D. Service of Summons.
Rutter, Cal. Practice Guide: Civ. Pro. Before Trial Ch. 8E-6, Subpoena to Nonparty Deponent or Business Records Custodian.
3 Witkin Cal. Proc. 5th Actions § 1014, (S 1014) Service at Gated Communities.

§ 415.30.   Service by mail

(a) A summons may be served by mail as provided in this section. A copy of the summons and of the complaint shall be mailed (by first-class mail or airmail, postage prepaid) to the person to be served, together with two copies of the notice and acknowledgment provided for in subdivision (b) and a return envelope, postage prepaid, addressed to the sender.

(b) The notice specified in subdivision (a) shall be in substantially the following form:

(Title of court and cause, with action number, to be inserted by the sender prior to mailing)

NOTICE

To: (Here state the name of the person to be served.)

This summons is served pursuant to Section 415.30 of the California Code of Civil Procedure. Failure to complete this form and return it to the sender within 20 days may subject you (or the party on whose behalf you are being served) to liability for the payment of any expenses incurred in serving a summons upon you in any other manner permitted by law. If you are served on behalf of a corporation, unincorporated association (including a partnership), or other entity, this form must be signed in the name of such entity by you or by a person authorized to receive service of process on behalf of such entity. In all other cases, this form must be signed by you personally or by a person authorized by you to acknowledge receipt of summons. Section 415.30 provides that this summons is deemed served on the date of execution of an acknowledgment of receipt of summons.

_____

Signature of sender

ACKNOWLEDGMENT OF RECEIPT OF SUMMONS

This acknowledges receipt on (insert date) of a copy of the summons and of the complaint at (insert address).

Date: _____

(Date this acknowledgment is executed)

_____

Signature of person acknowledging receipt, with title if acknowledgment is made on behalf of another person

(c) Service of a summons pursuant to this section is deemed complete on the date a written acknowledgment of receipt of summons is executed, if such acknowledgment thereafter is returned to the sender.

(d) If the person to whom a copy of the summons and of the complaint are mailed pursuant to this section fails to complete and return the acknowledgment form set forth in subdivision (b) within 20 days from the date of such mailing, the party to whom the summons was mailed shall be liable for reasonable expenses thereafter incurred in serving or attempting to serve the party by another method permitted by this chapter, and, except for good cause shown, the court in which the action is pending, upon motion, with or without notice, shall award the party such expenses whether or not he is otherwise entitled to recover his costs in the action.

(e) A notice or acknowledgment of receipt in form approved by the Judicial Council is deemed to comply with this section. *(Added by Stats.1969, c. 1610, p. 3363, § 3, operative July 1, 1970.)*

Research References

Rutter, Cal. Practice Guide: Civ. Pro. Before Trial Ch. 4-D, D. Service of Summons.
Rutter, Cal. Practice Guide: Enforcing Judgments/Debts Ch. 6A-10, Service of Writs, Notices and Other Papers in Enforcement Proceedings.
Rutter, Cal. Practice Guide: Fed.Civ.Pro. Before Trial Ch. 5-E, E. Waiver of Service.
Rutter, Cal. Practice Guide: Fed.Civ.Pro. Before Trial Ch. 5-F, F. Manner of Service (Where Service Not Waived).
3 Witkin Cal. Proc. 5th Actions § 1002, (S 1002) Service Within California.
3 Witkin Cal. Proc. 5th Actions § 1015, in General.
3 Witkin Cal. Proc. 5th Actions § 1016, Notice.
3 Witkin Cal. Proc. 5th Actions § 1017, Acknowledgment of Receipt.
3 Witkin Cal. Proc. 5th Actions § 1018, in General.
3 Witkin Cal. Proc. 5th Actions § 1069, Service by Mail.
7 Witkin Cal. Proc. 5th Judgment § 87, (S 87) Distinctions.
2 Witkin Cal. Proc. 5th Jurisdiction § 121, Jurisdiction and Process Statute.
8 Witkin, California Summary 10th Constitutional Law § 1202, (S 1202) Remedies If Proceeding is Not Promptly Commenced.
14 Witkin, California Summary 10th Wills and Probate § 511, Procedure.
14 Witkin, California Summary 10th Wills and Probate § 562, Determination Whether Act Constitutes Contest.
14 Witkin, California Summary 10th Wills and Probate § 723, (S 723) in General.
14 Witkin, California Summary 10th Wills and Probate § 750, (S 750) Petition to Revoke or Limit Authority.
14 Witkin, California Summary 10th Wills and Probate § 762, (S 762) Restraining Order to Prevent Proposed Action.
14 Witkin, California Summary 10th Wills and Probate § 910, General Notice Requirement.
14 Witkin, California Summary 10th Wills and Probate § 920, (S 920) in General.
14 Witkin, California Summary 10th Wills and Probate § 940, (S 940) Citation to Proposed Conservatee.

14 Witkin, California Summary 10th Wills and Probate § 1061, (S 1061) Termination of Limited Conservatorship.

§ 415.40. Service on person outside state

A summons may be served on a person outside this state in any manner provided by this article or by sending a copy of the summons and of the complaint to the person to be served by first-class mail, postage prepaid, requiring a return receipt. Service of a summons by this form of mail is deemed complete on the 10th day after such mailing. *(Added by Stats.1969, c. 1610, p. 3363, § 3, operative July 1, 1970. Amended by Stats.1982, c. 249, p. 797, § 1.)*

Research References

Rutter, Cal. Practice Guide: Civ. Pro. Before Trial Ch. 4-D, D. Service of Summons.
Rutter, Cal. Practice Guide: Civ. Pro. Before Trial Ch. 4-E, E. Proof of Service of Summons.
Rutter, Cal. Practice Guide: Civ. Pro. Before Trial Ch. 11-B, B. Involuntary Dismissals.
Rutter, Cal. Practice Guide: Enforcing Judgments/Debts Ch. 6A-10, Service of Writs, Notices and Other Papers in Enforcement Proceedings.
Rutter, Cal. Practice Guide: Fed.Civ.Pro. Before Trial Ch. 3-A, A. Nature of Requirement.
Rutter, Cal. Practice Guide: Fed.Civ.Pro. Before Trial Ch. 5-B, B. Service of Summons and Personal Jurisdiction.
Rutter, Cal. Practice Guide: Fed.Civ.Pro. Before Trial Ch. 5-F, F. Manner of Service (Where Service Not Waived).
Rutter, Cal. Practice Guide: Fed.Civ.Pro. Before Trial Ch. 2D-7, Time for Removal.
Rutter, Cal. Practice Guide: Insurance Litigation Ch. 15-D, D. Filing Considerations.
Miller and Starr California Real Estate § 5:5, California Broker Dealing With Out-Of-State Property.
3 Witkin Cal. Proc. 5th Actions § 1018, in General.
3 Witkin Cal. Proc. 5th Actions § 1019, Service on Corporation.
3 Witkin Cal. Proc. 5th Actions § 1026, (S 1026) in General.
3 Witkin Cal. Proc. 5th Actions § 1049, Officer or Designated Agent.
3 Witkin Cal. Proc. 5th Actions § 1071, (S 1071) Statutory Requirements.
2 Witkin Cal. Proc. 5th Jurisdiction § 121, Jurisdiction and Process Statute.
10 Witkin, California Summary 10th Parent and Child § 387, (S 387) Application and Order or Response.
14 Witkin, California Summary 10th Wills and Probate § 940, (S 940) Citation to Proposed Conservatee.

§ 415.45. Unlawful detainer; service by posting and mailing or other manner

(a) A summons in an action for unlawful detainer of real property may be served by posting if upon affidavit it appears to the satisfaction of the court in which the action is pending that the party to be served cannot with reasonable diligence be served in any manner specified in this article other than publication and that:

(1) A cause of action exists against the party upon whom service is to be made or he is a necessary or proper party to the action; or

(2) The party to be served has or claims an interest in real property in this state that is subject to the jurisdiction of the court or the relief demanded in the action consists wholly or in part in excluding such party from any interest in such property.

(b) The court shall order the summons to be posted on the premises in a manner most likely to give actual notice to the party to be served and direct that a copy of the summons and of the complaint be forthwith mailed by certified mail to such party at his last known address.

(c) Service of summons in this manner is deemed complete on the 10th day after posting and mailing.

(d) Notwithstanding an order for posting of the summons, a summons may be served in any other manner authorized by this article, except publication, in which event such service shall supersede any posted summons. *(Added by Stats.1972, c. 719, p. 1312, § 1. Amended by Stats.1978, c. 625, p. 2077, § 1.)*

Research References

Rutter, Cal. Practice Guide: Civ. Pro. Before Trial Ch. 4-D, D. Service of Summons.
Miller and Starr California Real Estate § 19:222, Complaint and Summons--Service of the Summons and Complaint; Claim to Right of Possession.
3 Witkin Cal. Proc. 5th Actions § 1045, Posting in Unlawful Detainer.
3 Witkin Cal. Proc. 5th Actions § 1070, Other Methods of Service.
3 Witkin Cal. Proc. 5th Actions § 1071, (S 1071) Statutory Requirements.
12 Witkin, California Summary 10th Real Property § 728, Jurisdiction, Venue, and Process.

§ 415.46. Prejudgment claim of right to possession

(a) In addition to the service of a summons and complaint in an action for unlawful detainer upon a tenant and subtenant, if any, as prescribed by this article, a prejudgment claim of right to possession may also be served on any person who appears to be or who may claim to have occupied the premises at the time of the filing of the action. Service upon occupants shall be made pursuant to subdivision (c) by serving a copy of a prejudgment claim of right to possession, as specified in subdivision (f), attached to a copy of the summons and complaint at the same time service is made upon the tenant and subtenant, if any.

(b) Service of the prejudgment claim of right to possession in this manner shall be effected by a marshal, sheriff, or registered process server.

(c)(1) When serving the summons and complaint upon a tenant and subtenant, if any, the marshal, sheriff, or registered process server shall make a reasonably diligent effort to ascertain whether there are other adult occupants of the premises who are not named in the summons and complaint by inquiring of the person or persons who are being personally served, or any person of suitable age and discretion who appears to reside upon the premises, whether there are other occupants of the premises.

(2) If the identity of such an occupant is disclosed to the officer or process server and the occupant is present at the premises, the officer or process server shall serve that occupant with a copy of the prejudgment claim of right to possession attached to a copy of the summons and complaint. If personal service cannot be made upon that occupant at that time, service may be effected by leaving a copy of a prejudgment claim of right to possession attached to a copy of the summons and complaint addressed to that occupant with a person of suitable age and discretion at the premises, affixing the same so that it is not readily removable in a conspicuous place on the premises in a manner most likely to give actual notice to that occupant, and sending the same addressed to that occupant by first-class mail.

(3) In addition to the service on an identified occupant, or if no occupant is disclosed to the officer or process server, or if substituted service is made upon the tenant and subtenant, if any, the officer or process server shall serve a prejudgment claim of right to possession for all other persons who may claim to occupy the premises at the time of the filing of the action by leaving a copy of a prejudgment claim of right to possession attached to a copy of the summons and complaint at the premises at the same time service is made upon the tenant and subtenant, if any, affixing the same so that it is not readily removable in a conspicuous place on the premises so that it is likely to give actual notice to an occupant, and sending the same addressed to "all occupants in care of the named tenant" to the premises by first-class mail.

(4) The person serving process shall state the date of service on the prejudgment claim of right to possession form. However, the absence of the date of service on the prejudgment claim of right to possession does not invalidate the claim.

(d) Proof of service under this section shall be filed with the court and shall include a statement that service was made pursuant to this section. Service on occupants in accordance with this section shall not alter or affect service upon the tenant or subtenant, if any.

(e)(1) If an owner or his or her agent has directed and obtained service of a prejudgment claim of right to possession in accordance with this section, no occupant of the premises, whether or not that occupant is named in the judgment for possession, may object to the enforcement of that judgment as prescribed in Section 1174.3.

(2) In any action for unlawful detainer resulting from a foreclosure sale of a rental housing unit pursuant to Section 1161a, paragraph (1) shall not limit the right of any tenant or subtenant of the property to file a prejudgment claim of right of possession pursuant to subdivision (a) of Section 1174.25 at any time before judgment, or to object to enforcement of a judgment for possession as prescribed in Section 1174.3, whether or not the tenant or subtenant was served with a prejudgment claim of right to possession.

(f) The prejudgment claim of right to possession shall be made on the following form:

NOTICE

EVERYONE WHO LIVES IN THIS RENTAL UNIT MAY BE EVICTED BY COURT ORDER. READ THIS FORM IF YOU LIVE HERE AND YOUR NAME IS NOT ON THE ATTACHED SUMMONS AND COMPLAINT.

If you live here and you do not complete and submit this form within 10 days of the date of service shown on this form, you will be evicted without further hearing by the court along with the persons named in the summons and complaint.

If you file this form, your claim will be determined in the eviction action against the persons named in the complaint.

If you do not file this form, you will be evicted without further hearing.

CLAIMANT OR CLAIMANT'S ATTORNEY (Name and Address):	**TELEPHONE NO.**	**FOR COURT USE ONLY**

ATTORNEY FOR (Name):

NAME OF COURT:
 STREET ADDRESS:
MAILING ADDRESS:
CITY AND ZIP CODE:
BRANCH NAME:

PLAINTIFF:
DEFENDANT:

PREJUDGMENT CLAIM OF RIGHT TO POSSESSION

CASE NUMBER:

DATE OF SERVICE:
(Date that form is served or delivered, posted and mailed by the officer or process server)

Complete this form only if ALL of these statements are true:
1. You are NOT named in the accompanying Summons and Complaint.
2. You occupied the subject premises on or before the date the unlawful detainer (eviction) complaint was filed. (The date is in the accompanying Summons and Complaint.)
3. You still occupy the subject premises.

I DECLARE THE FOLLOWING UNDER PENALTY OF PERJURY:
1. My name is (specify):
2. I reside at (street address, unit no., city and ZIP code):
3. The address of "the premises" subject to this claim is (address):
4. On (insert date): _____, the landlord or the landlord's authorized agent filed a complaint to recover possession of the premises. (This date is in the accompanying Summons and Complaint.)
5. I occupied the premises on the date the complaint was filed (the date in item 4). I have continued to occupy the premises ever since.
6. I was at least 18 years of age on the date the complaint was filed (the date in item 4).

7.   I claim a right to possession of the premises because I occupied the premises on the date the complaint was filed (the date in item 4).

8.   I was not named in the Summons and Complaint.

9.   I understand that if I make this claim of possession, I will be added as a defendant to the unlawful detainer (eviction) action.

10.   (Filing fee) I understand that I must go to the court and pay a filing fee of $_____ or file with the court "Application for Waiver of Court Fees and Costs." I understand that if I don't pay the filing fee or file the form for waiver of court fees within 10 days from the date of service on the form (excluding court holidays), I will not be entitled to make a claim of right to possession. I also understand that I will have 5 days (excluding court holidays) to file a response to the Summons and Complaint after I file this claim of possession.

NOTICE: If you fail to file this claim, you will be evicted without further hearing.

---

11.   Rental agreement. I have (check all that apply to you):

    a. ☐   an oral rental agreement with the landlord.

    b. ☐   a written rental agreement with the landlord.

    c. ☐   an oral rental agreement with a person other than the landlord.

    d. ☐   a written rental agreement with a person other than the landlord.

    e. ☐   other (explain):

I declare under penalty of perjury under the laws of the State of California that the foregoing is true and correct.

WARNING: Perjury is a felony punishable by imprisonment in the state prison.

Date:

....   ►_____

       (TYPE OR PRINT NAME)   (SIGNATURE OF CLAIMANT)

NOTICE: If you file this claim to possession, the unlawful detainer action against you will be determined at trial. At trial, you may be found liable for rent, costs, and, in some cases, treble damages.

NOTICE TO OCCUPANTS

YOU MUST ACT AT ONCE IF ALL THE FOLLOWING ARE TRUE:

(1)   You are not named in the accompanying Summons and Complaint.

(2)   You occupied the premises on or before the date the unlawful detainer (eviction) complaint was filed.

(3)   You still occupy the premises.

You can complete and **SUBMIT THIS CLAIM FORM** within 10 days from the date of service (on the form) at the court where the unlawful detainer (eviction) complaint was filed.

   If you do not complete and submit this form (and pay a filing fee or file the form for proceeding in forma pauperis if you cannot pay the fee), YOU WILL BE EVICTED.

   After this form is properly filed, you will be added as a defendant in the unlawful detainer (eviction) action and your right to occupy the premises will be decided by the court. If you do not file this claim, you will be evicted without a hearing.

PREJUDGMENT CLAIM OF RIGHT TO POSSESSION

(Added by Stats.1990, c. 1535 (S.B.2508), § 1. Amended by Stats.1991, c. 57 (S.B.323), § 1, eff. June 17, 1991; Stats.2012, c. 562 (A.B.2610), § 2.)

Research References

Rutter, Cal. Practice Guide: Enforcing Judgments/Debts Ch. 6I-1, Writ of Possession or Sale.

Rutter, Cal. Practice Guide: Enforcing Judgments/Debts Ch. 6I-3, Enforcement of Judgment for Possession of Real Property.

Rutter, Cal. Practice Guide: Enforcing Judgments/Debts Ch. 6I-1, Outline 1.

Miller and Starr California Real Estate § 19:222, Complaint and Summons--Service of the Summons and Complaint; Claim to Right of Possession.

3 Witkin Cal. Proc. 5th Actions § 987, (S 987) Actions Involving Real Property.

3 Witkin Cal. Proc. 5th Actions § 1045, Posting in Unlawful Detainer.

8 Witkin Cal. Proc. 5th Enforcement of Judgment § 332, (S 332) in General.

8 Witkin Cal. Proc. 5th Enforcement of Judgment § 334, in General.

8 Witkin Cal. Proc. 5th Enforcement of Judgment § 336, (S 336) Failure to Vacate Property.

12 Witkin, California Summary 10th Real Property § 728, Jurisdiction, Venue, and Process.

12 Witkin, California Summary 10th Real Property § 729, Parties.

§ 415.47. Unlawful detainer; intent of lessee not to abandon premises; service

(a) Where the lessee has given the lessor written notice of the lessee's intent not to abandon leased real property as provided in Section 1951.3 of the Civil Code, the summons in an action for unlawful detainer of the real property may be served on the lessee by certified mail, postage prepaid, addressed to the lessee at the address stated in the lessee's notice of intent not to abandon if such summons is deposited in the mail within 60 days from the date the lessee's notice of intent not to abandon is received by the lessor. Service in this manner is deemed completed on the 10th day after such mailing.

(b) Where the lessee has given the lessor written notice of the lessee's intent not to abandon leased real property as provided in Section 1951.3 of the Civil Code, but failed to include in such notice an address at which the lessee may be served by certified mail in any action for unlawful detainer of the real property, the summons in an action for unlawful detainer of the real property may be served on the lessee by certified mail, postage prepaid, addressed to the lessee at (1) the same address or addresses to which the lessor's notice of belief of abandonment was addressed if that notice was given by mail or (2) the address of the real property if the lessor's notice of belief of abandonment was personally served on the lessee. Service may not be made pursuant to this subdivision unless the summons is deposited in the mail within 60 days from the date the lessee's notice of intent not to abandon is received by the lessor. Service in the manner authorized by this subdivision is deemed completed on the 10th day after such mailing.

(c) This section provides an alternative method of service on the lessee and does not preclude service in any other manner authorized by this chapter. *(Added by Stats.1974, c. 332, p. 663, § 2.)*

Research References

Miller and Starr California Real Estate § 19:222, Complaint and Summons--Service of the Summons and Complaint; Claim to Right of Possession.

3 Witkin Cal. Proc. 5th Actions § 1022, Unlawful Detainer.

12 Witkin, California Summary 10th Real Property § 728, Jurisdiction, Venue, and Process.

§ 415.50. Service by publication

(a) A summons may be served by publication if upon affidavit it appears to the satisfaction of the court in which the action is pending that the party to be served cannot with reasonable diligence be served in another manner specified in this article and that either:

(1) A cause of action exists against the party upon whom service is to be made or he or she is a necessary or proper party to the action.

(2) The party to be served has or claims an interest in real or personal property in this state that is subject to the jurisdiction of the court or the relief demanded in the action consists wholly or in part in excluding the party from any interest in the property.

(b) The court shall order the summons to be published in a named newspaper, published in this state, that is most likely to give actual notice to the party to be served. If the party to be served resides or is located out of this state, the court may also order the summons to be published in a named newspaper outside this state that is most likely to give actual notice to that party. The order shall direct that a copy of the summons, the complaint, and the order for publication be forthwith mailed to the party if his or her address is ascertained before expiration of the time prescribed for publication of the summons. Except as otherwise provided by statute, the publication shall be made as provided by Section 6064 of the Government Code unless the court, in its discretion, orders publication for a longer period.

(c) Service of a summons in this manner is deemed complete as provided in Section 6064 of the Government Code.

(d) Notwithstanding an order for publication of the summons, a summons may be served in another manner authorized by this chapter, in which event the service shall supersede any published summons.

(e) As a condition of establishing that the party to be served cannot with reasonable diligence be served in another manner specified in this article, the court may not require that a search be conducted of public databases where access by a registered process server to residential addresses is prohibited by law or by published policy of the agency providing the database, including, but not limited to, voter registration rolls and records of the Department of Motor Vehicles. *(Added by Stats.1969, c. 1610, p. 3363, § 3, operative July 1, 1970. Amended by Stats.1972, c. 601, § 2; Stats.1984, c. 352, § 1; Stats.2002, c. 197 (A.B.2493), § 2; Stats.2003, c. 449 (A.B.1712), § 8.)*

Research References

Rutter, Cal. Practice Guide: Civ. Pro. Before Trial Ch. 2-C, C. Joinder of Parties.

Rutter, Cal. Practice Guide: Civ. Pro. Before Trial Ch. 4-D, D. Service of Summons.

Rutter, Cal. Practice Guide: Civ. Pro. Before Trial Ch. 11-B, B. Involuntary Dismissals.

Rutter, Cal. Practice Guide: Enforcing Judgments/Debts Ch. 6A-10, Service of Writs, Notices and Other Papers in Enforcement Proceedings.

Rutter, Cal. Practice Guide: Fed.Civ.Pro. Before Trial Ch. 5-F, F. Manner of Service (Where Service Not Waived).

Rutter, Cal. Practice Guide: Personal Injury Ch. 5-E, E. Selected Pleading Issues.

3 Witkin Cal. Proc. 5th Actions § 1002, (S 1002) Service Within California.

3 Witkin Cal. Proc. 5th Actions § 1033, Statutory Revision of 1969.

3 Witkin Cal. Proc. 5th Actions § 1035, Necessity.

3 Witkin Cal. Proc. 5th Actions § 1038, (S 1038) Inquiry of Persons.

3 Witkin Cal. Proc. 5th Actions § 1039, (S 1039) Search of Directories and Records.

3 Witkin Cal. Proc. 5th Actions § 1040, (S 1040) Statutory Conditions.

3 Witkin Cal. Proc. 5th Actions § 1041, (S 1041) Sufficiency of Averments.

3 Witkin Cal. Proc. 5th Actions § 1042, (S 1042) Order.

3 Witkin Cal. Proc. 5th Actions § 1043, Publication.

3 Witkin Cal. Proc. 5th Actions § 1044, Where Defendant's Address is Ascertained.

3 Witkin Cal. Proc. 5th Actions § 1070, Other Methods of Service.

2 Witkin Cal. Proc. 5th Jurisdiction § 121, Jurisdiction and Process Statute.

6 Witkin Cal. Proc. 5th Proceedings Without Trial § 343, Amenability to Service Only by Publication.

11 Witkin, California Summary 10th Husband and Wife § 68, in General.

§ 415.95. Service of summons on a business organization, form unknown

(a) A summons may be served on a business organization, form unknown, by leaving a copy of the summons and complaint during usual office hours with the person who is apparently in charge of the office of that business organization, and by thereafter mailing a copy of the summons and complaint by first-class mail, postage prepaid, to the person to be served at the place where a copy of the summons and complaint was left. Service of a summons in this manner is deemed complete on the 10th day after the mailing.

(b) Service of a summons pursuant to this section is not valid for a corporation with a registered agent for service of process listed with the Secretary of State. *(Added by Stats.2003, c. 128 (A.B.418), § 2.)*

Research References

Rutter, Cal. Practice Guide: Civ. Pro. Before Trial Ch. 4-C, C. Content of Summons.

Rutter, Cal. Practice Guide: Civ. Pro. Before Trial Ch. 4-D, D. Service of Summons.

Rutter, Cal. Practice Guide: Civ. Pro. Before Trial Ch. 4-E, E. Proof of Service of Summons.

Rutter, Cal. Practice Guide: Civ. Pro. Before Trial Ch. 6-B, B. Complaints.

3 Witkin Cal. Proc. 5th Actions § 1002, (S 1002) Service Within California.

3 Witkin Cal. Proc. 5th Actions § 1013, (S 1013) Business Organization of Unknown Form.

3 Witkin Cal. Proc. 5th Actions § 1019, Service on Corporation.

ARTICLE 4. PERSONS UPON WHOM SUMMONS MAY BE SERVED

Section
416.10.   Corporations generally.
416.20.   Corporation dissolved or charter forfeited.
416.30.   Joint stock company or association.
416.40.   Unincorporated association.
416.50.   Public entity.
416.60.   Minors.
416.70.   Wards and conservatees.
416.80.   Political candidates.
416.90.   Persons not otherwise specified.

§ 416.10. Corporations generally

A summons may be served on a corporation by delivering a copy of the summons and the complaint by any of the following methods:

(a) To the person designated as agent for service of process as provided by any provision in Section 202, 1502, 2105, or 2107 of the Corporations Code (or Sections 3301 to 3303, inclusive, or Sections 6500 to 6504, inclusive, of the Corporations Code, as in

effect on December 31, 1976, with respect to corporations to which they remain applicable).

(b) To the president, chief executive officer, or other head of the corporation, a vice president, a secretary or assistant secretary, a treasurer or assistant treasurer, a controller or chief financial officer, a general manager, or a person authorized by the corporation to receive service of process.

(c) If the corporation is a bank, to a cashier or assistant cashier or to a person specified in subdivision (a) or (b).

(d) If authorized by any provision in Section 1701, 1702, 2110, or 2111 of the Corporations Code (or Sections 3301 to 3303, inclusive, or Sections 6500 to 6504, inclusive, of the Corporations Code, as in effect on December 31, 1976, with respect to corporations to which they remain applicable), as provided by that provision. *(Added by Stats.1969, c. 1610, p. 3363, § 3, operative July 1, 1970. Amended by Stats.1975, c. 682, p. 1515, § 3, eff. Jan. 1, 1977; Stats.1976, c. 641, p. 1508, § 1.1, eff. Jan. 1, 1977; Stats.2006, c. 567 (A.B.2303), § 7.)*

Research References

Rutter, Cal. Practice Guide: Civ. Pro. Before Trial Ch. 2-B, B. Capacity to Sue or Defend.

Rutter, Cal. Practice Guide: Civ. Pro. Before Trial Ch. 4-A, A. Requirements-In General.

Rutter, Cal. Practice Guide: Civ. Pro. Before Trial Ch. 4-C, C. Content of Summons.

Rutter, Cal. Practice Guide: Civ. Pro. Before Trial Ch. 4-D, D. Service of Summons.

Rutter, Cal. Practice Guide: Enforcing Judgments/Debts Ch. 6B-6, Duration of Real Property Judgment Lien.

Rutter, Cal. Practice Guide: Enforcing Judgments/Debts Ch. 6F-3, Issuance and Service of Earnings Withholding Orders.

Rutter, Cal. Practice Guide: Fed.Civ.Pro. Before Trial Ch. 3-D, D. Traditional Bases for Personal Jurisdiction.

Rutter, Cal. Practice Guide: Fed.Civ.Pro. Before Trial Ch. 5-F, F. Manner of Service (Where Service Not Waived).

Rutter, Cal. Practice Guide: Insurance Litigation Ch. 15-D, D. Filing Considerations.

Miller and Starr California Real Estate § 30A:48, The Complaint.

3 Witkin Cal. Proc. 5th Actions § 972, Abrogation of Common Law Rule.

3 Witkin Cal. Proc. 5th Actions § 989, (S 989) Actions Against Corporation or Association.

3 Witkin Cal. Proc. 5th Actions § 1010, (S 1010) Corporation, Association, or Public Entity Defendant.

3 Witkin Cal. Proc. 5th Actions § 1019, Service on Corporation.

3 Witkin Cal. Proc. 5th Actions § 1046, Officer or Designated Agent.

3 Witkin Cal. Proc. 5th Actions § 1048, Secretary of State.

3 Witkin Cal. Proc. 5th Actions § 1049, Officer or Designated Agent.

3 Witkin Cal. Proc. 5th Actions § 1050, Secretary of State.

3 Witkin Cal. Proc. 5th Actions § 1051, Domestic Corporation.

3 Witkin Cal. Proc. 5th Actions § 1052, Foreign Corporation.

3 Witkin Cal. Proc. 5th Actions § 1053, (S 1053) Joint Stock Company.

3 Witkin Cal. Proc. 5th Actions § 1054, Domestic Association.

3 Witkin Cal. Proc. 5th Actions § 1063, (S 1063) Other Persons.

8 Witkin Cal. Proc. 5th Enforcement of Judgment § 254, in General.

2 Witkin Cal. Proc. 5th Jurisdiction § 179, (S 179) After Interstate Business.

§ 416.20. Corporation dissolved or charter forfeited

A summons may be served on a corporation that has forfeited its charter or right to do business, or has dissolved, by delivering a copy of the summons and of the complaint:

(a) To a person who is a trustee of the corporation and of its stockholders or members; or

(b) When authorized by any provision in Sections 2011 or 2114 of the Corporations Code (or Sections 3301 to 3303, inclusive, or Sections 6500 to 6504, inclusive, of the Corporations Code as in effect on December 31, 1976, with respect to corporations to which they remain applicable), as provided by such provision. *(Added by Stats.1969, c. 1610, p. 3363, § 3, operative July 1, 1970. Amended by Stats.1970, c. 585, p. 1166,*

§ 1; Stats.1975, c. 682, p. 1615, § 4, eff. Jan. 1, 1977; Stats.1977, c. 235, p. 1032, § 1.1.)

Research References

Rutter, Cal. Practice Guide: Civ. Pro. Before Trial Ch. 2-B, B. Capacity to Sue or Defend.
Rutter, Cal. Practice Guide: Civ. Pro. Before Trial Ch. 4-C, C. Content of Summons.
Rutter, Cal. Practice Guide: Civ. Pro. Before Trial Ch. 4-D, D. Service of Summons.
3 Witkin Cal. Proc. 5th Actions § 1010, (S 1010) Corporation, Association, or Public Entity Defendant.
3 Witkin Cal. Proc. 5th Actions § 1019, Service on Corporation.
3 Witkin Cal. Proc. 5th Actions § 1049, Officer or Designated Agent.
3 Witkin Cal. Proc. 5th Actions § 1051, Domestic Corporation.
3 Witkin Cal. Proc. 5th Actions § 1053, (S 1053) Joint Stock Company.

§ 416.30.   Joint stock company or association

A summons may be served on a joint stock company or association by delivering a copy of the summons and of the complaint as provided by Section 416.10 or 416.20. *(Added by Stats.1969, c. 1610, p. 3363, § 3, operative July 1, 1970.)*

Research References

Rutter, Cal. Practice Guide: Civ. Pro. Before Trial Ch. 4-D, D. Service of Summons.
3 Witkin Cal. Proc. 5th Actions § 1010, (S 1010) Corporation, Association, or Public Entity Defendant.
3 Witkin Cal. Proc. 5th Actions § 1053, (S 1053) Joint Stock Company.

§ 416.40.   Unincorporated association

A summons may be served on an unincorporated association (including a partnership) by delivering a copy of the summons and of the complaint:

(a) If the association is a general or limited partnership, to the person designated as agent for service of process in a statement filed with the Secretary of State or to a general partner or the general manager of the partnership;

(b) If the association is not a general or limited partnership, to the person designated as agent for service of process in a statement filed with the Secretary of State or to the president or other head of the association, a vice president, a secretary or assistant secretary, a treasurer or assistant treasurer, a general manager, or a person authorized by the association to receive service of process;

(c) When authorized by Section 18220 of the Corporations Code, as provided by that section. *(Added by Stats.1969, c. 1610, p. 3363, § 3, operative July 1, 1970. Amended by Stats.2004, c. 178 (S.B.1746), § 3.)*

Law Revision Commission Comments

Section 416.40 is amended to reflect that an unincorporated association may designate an agent for service of process under sections other than former Corporations Code Section 24003 (continued without substantive change in Corporations Code Section 18200). See, e.g., Corp. Code §§ 15621(a)(4) (limited partnership), 16309 (general partnership), 16953(a)(3) (limited liability partnership), 17051(a)(4) (limited liability company), 17060(a)(2) (limited liability company). [33 Cal.L.Rev.Comm. Reports 771 (2004)].

Section 416.40 continues the law, including various changes enacted by the 1968 Legislature, that governs service of process on an individual on behalf of an unincorporated association (including a partnership), with one exception. The list of persons who may be served has been expanded to follow more closely the rules governing service on a corporation. (Compare Section 416.10.)

A partnership or other unincorporated association may sue and be sued in its own name, and accordingly it may be so served. (Cal.Code Civ.Proc. § 388; cf. Fed.R.Civ.P., Rule 4(d)(3); see Cal.Corp.Code §§ 15006(1), 24000–24007; Comment, 42 Cal.L.Rev. 812.)

Service may be made upon an agent designated by the partnership or association to receive service of process or upon a general partner or an

officer named in subdivision (a) or (b), as the case may be, or, when authorized by Section 24007 of the Corporations Code, upon one or more of the association's members named in a court order and by mailing a copy of the process to the association at its last known address.

Subdivision (c) incorporates by reference the law dealing with service upon a foreign partnership doing business in this state in actions arising out of such business. Section 15700 of the Corporations Code requires such a partnership, if it does not have a regular place of business within this state, to designate an agent for service of process and authorizes service on the Secretary of State if no agent is designated. The Secretary of State must give telegraphic notice and forward the process by registered mail. (See 37 Cal.L.Rev. 93.)

Research References

Rutter, Cal. Practice Guide: Civ. Pro. Before Trial Ch. 4-C, C. Content of Summons.
Rutter, Cal. Practice Guide: Civ. Pro. Before Trial Ch. 4-D, D. Service of Summons.
Rutter, Cal. Practice Guide: Fed.Civ.Pro. Before Trial Ch. 3-D, D. Traditional Bases for Personal Jurisdiction.
Rutter, Cal. Practice Guide: Fed.Civ.Pro. Before Trial Ch. 5-F, F. Manner of Service (Where Service Not Waived).
3 Witkin Cal. Proc. 5th Actions § 1010, (S 1010) Corporation, Association, or Public Entity Defendant.
3 Witkin Cal. Proc. 5th Actions § 1054, Domestic Association.
9 Witkin, California Summary 10th Partnership § 126, (S 126) Agent for Service of Process.

§ 416.50.   Public entity

(a) A summons may be served on a public entity by delivering a copy of the summons and of the complaint to the clerk, secretary, president, presiding officer, or other head of its governing body.

(b) As used in this section, "public entity" includes the state and any office, department, division, bureau, board, commission, or agency of the state, the Regents of the University of California, a county, city, district, public authority, public agency, and any other political subdivision or public corporation in this state. *(Added by Stats.1969, c. 1610, p. 3363, § 3, operative July 1, 1970.)*

Research References

Rutter, Cal. Practice Guide: Civ. Pro. Before Trial Ch. 4-D, D. Service of Summons.
Rutter, Cal. Practice Guide: Fed.Civ.Pro. Before Trial Ch. 5-F, F. Manner of Service (Where Service Not Waived).
3 Witkin Cal. Proc. 5th Actions § 1010, (S 1010) Corporation, Association, or Public Entity Defendant.
3 Witkin Cal. Proc. 5th Actions § 1056, in General.
3 Witkin Cal. Proc. 5th Actions § 1057, Officers.
5 Witkin, California Summary 10th Torts § 217, (S 217) Statutory Framework.

§ 416.60.   Minors

A summons may be served on a minor by delivering a copy of the summons and of the complaint to his parent, guardian, conservator, or similar fiduciary, or, if no such person can be found with reasonable diligence, to any person having the care or control of such minor or with whom he resides or by whom he is employed, and to the minor if he is at least 12 years of age. *(Added by Stats.1969, c. 1610, p. 3, § 1, operative July 1, 1970. Amended by Stats.1972, c. 579, § 14.5.)*

Research References

Rutter, Cal. Practice Guide: Civ. Pro. Before Trial Ch. 4-C, C. Content of Summons.
Rutter, Cal. Practice Guide: Civ. Pro. Before Trial Ch. 4-D, D. Service of Summons.
Rutter, Cal. Practice Guide: Fed.Civ.Pro. Before Trial Ch. 5-F, F. Manner of Service (Where Service Not Waived).
3 Witkin Cal. Proc. 5th Actions § 1011, Attempted Physical Delivery is Required.

3 Witkin Cal. Proc. 5th Actions § 1060, (S 1060) Minor.

§ 416.70. Wards and conservatees

A summons may be served on a person (other than a minor) for whom a guardian, conservator, or similar fiduciary has been appointed by delivering a copy of the summons and of the complaint to his guardian, conservator, or similar fiduciary and to such person, but, for good cause shown, the court in which the action is pending may dispense with delivery to such person. *(Added by Stats.1969, c. 1610, p. 3363, § 3, operative July 1, 1970. Amended by Stats.1972, c. 579, § 15.)*

Research References

Rutter, Cal. Practice Guide: Civ. Pro. Before Trial Ch. 4-C, C. Content of Summons.
Rutter, Cal. Practice Guide: Civ. Pro. Before Trial Ch. 4-D, D. Service of Summons.
Rutter, Cal. Practice Guide: Fed.Civ.Pro. Before Trial Ch. 5-F, F. Manner of Service (Where Service Not Waived).
3 Witkin Cal. Proc. 5th Actions § 1011, Attempted Physical Delivery is Required.
3 Witkin Cal. Proc. 5th Actions § 1061, (S 1061) Ward or Conservatee.
10 Witkin, California Summary 10th Parent and Child § 610, (S 610) Notice of Hearing.

§ 416.80. Political candidates

When authorized by Section 12 of the Elections Code, a summons may be served as provided by that section. *(Added by Stats.1969, c. 1610, p. 3363, § 3, operative July 1, 1970. Amended by Stats.1976, c. 1438, p. 6476, § 24.1; Stats.1994, c. 923 (S.B.1546), § 2; Stats.2009, c. 140 (A.B.1164), § 38.)*

Research References

Rutter, Cal. Practice Guide: Civ. Pro. Before Trial Ch. 4-D, D. Service of Summons.
3 Witkin Cal. Proc. 5th Actions § 1011, Attempted Physical Delivery is Required.
3 Witkin Cal. Proc. 5th Actions § 1062, (S 1062) Candidate for Public Office.

§ 416.90. Persons not otherwise specified

A summons may be served on a person not otherwise specified in this article by delivering a copy of the summons and of the complaint to such person or to a person authorized by him to receive service of process. *(Added by Stats.1969, c. 1610, p. 3363, § 3, operative July 1, 1970.)*

Research References

Rutter, Cal. Practice Guide: Civ. Pro. Before Trial Ch. 2-C, C. Joinder of Parties.
Rutter, Cal. Practice Guide: Civ. Pro. Before Trial Ch. 4-C, C. Content of Summons.
Rutter, Cal. Practice Guide: Civ. Pro. Before Trial Ch. 4-D, D. Service of Summons.
3 Witkin Cal. Proc. 5th Actions § 1011, Attempted Physical Delivery is Required.
3 Witkin Cal. Proc. 5th Actions § 1063, (S 1063) Other Persons.

ARTICLE 5. PROOF OF SERVICE

Section

417.10. Service within state; manner.
417.20. Service outside state; manner.
417.30. Filing proof of service of summons; exception.
417.40. Proof of service signed by registered process server; additional contents.

§ 417.10. Service within state; manner

Proof that a summons was served on a person within this state shall be made:

(a) If served under Section 415.10, 415.20, or 415.30, by the affidavit of the person making the service showing the time, place, and manner of service and facts showing that the service was made in accordance with this chapter. The affidavit shall recite or in other manner show the name of the person to whom a copy of the summons and of the complaint were delivered, and, if appropriate, his or her title or the capacity in which he or she is served, and that the notice required by Section 412.30 appeared on the copy of the summons served, if in fact it did appear.

If service is made by mail pursuant to Section 415.30, proof of service shall include the acknowledgment of receipt of summons in the form provided by that section or other written acknowledgment of receipt of summons satisfactory to the court.

(b) If served by publication pursuant to Section 415.50, by the affidavit of the publisher or printer, or his or her foreperson or principal clerk, showing the time and place of publication, and an affidavit showing the time and place a copy of the summons and of the complaint were mailed to the party to be served, if in fact mailed.

(c) If served pursuant to another law of this state, in the manner prescribed by that law or, if no manner is prescribed, in the manner prescribed by this section for proof of a similar manner of service.

(d) By the written admission of the party.

(e) If served by posting pursuant to Section 415.45, by the affidavit of the person who posted the premises, showing the time and place of posting, and an affidavit showing the time and place copies of the summons and of the complaint were mailed to the party to be served, if in fact mailed.

(f) All proof of personal service shall be made on a form adopted by the Judicial Council. *(Added by Stats.1969, c. 1610, p. 3363, § 3, operative July 1, 1970. Amended by Stats.1972, c. 719, § 2; Stats.1980, c. 676, § 65; Stats.1986, c. 953, § 2, operative July 1, 1987; Stats.2006, c. 538 (S.B.1852), § 63.)*

Research References

Rutter, Cal. Practice Guide: Civ. Pro. Before Trial Ch. 4-E, E. Proof of Service of Summons.
3 Witkin Cal. Proc. 5th Actions § 1064, (S 1064) in General.
3 Witkin Cal. Proc. 5th Actions § 1067, (S 1067) Affidavit or Certificate.
3 Witkin Cal. Proc. 5th Actions § 1068, Personal Delivery or Leaving Copy.
3 Witkin Cal. Proc. 5th Actions § 1069, Service by Mail.
3 Witkin Cal. Proc. 5th Actions § 1070, Other Methods of Service.
3 Witkin Cal. Proc. 5th Actions § 1071, (S 1071) Statutory Requirements.
8 Witkin Cal. Proc. 5th Enforcement of Judgment § 28, Proof of Service.
8 Witkin Cal. Proc. 5th Enforcement of Judgment § 457, (S 457) Notice of Entry.

§ 417.20. Service outside state; manner

Proof that a summons was served on a person outside this state shall be made:

(a) If served in a manner specified in a statute of this state, as prescribed by Section 417.10, and if service is made by mail pursuant to Section 415.40, proof of service shall include evidence satisfactory to the court establishing actual delivery to the person to be served, by a signed return receipt or other evidence;

(b) In the manner prescribed by the court order pursuant to which the service is made;

(c) Subject to any additional requirements that may be imposed by the court in which the action is pending, in the manner prescribed by the law of the place where the person is served for proof of service in an action in its courts of general jurisdiction; or

(d) By the written admission of the party.

(e) If served by posting pursuant to Section 415.45, by the affidavit of the person who posted the premises, showing the time and place of posting, and an affidavit showing the time and place copies of the summons and of the complaint were mailed to the party to be served, if in fact mailed. *(Added by Stats.1969, c. 1610, p. 3363, § 3. Amended by Stats.1972, c. 719, § 3.)*

Research References

Rutter, Cal. Practice Guide: Civ. Pro. Before Trial Ch. 4-E, E. Proof of Service of Summons.
3 Witkin Cal. Proc. 5th Actions § 1019, Service on Corporation.
3 Witkin Cal. Proc. 5th Actions § 1064, (S 1064) in General.
3 Witkin Cal. Proc. 5th Actions § 1071, (S 1071) Statutory Requirements.
3 Witkin Cal. Proc. 5th Actions § 1072, (S 1072) Illustrations.
3 Witkin Cal. Proc. 5th Actions § 1073, Under Foreign Law.
3 Witkin Cal. Proc. 5th Actions § 1074, Under Court Order.
6 Witkin Cal. Proc. 5th Proceedings Without Trial § 323, Return Within 3 Years and 60 Days.

§ 417.30. Filing proof of service of summons; exception

After a summons has been served on a person, proof of service of the summons as provided in Section 417.10 or 417.20 shall be filed, unless the defendant has previously made a general appearance. *(Added by Stats.1969, c. 1610, p. 3363, § 3, operative July 1, 1970. Amended by Stats.1971, c. 1366, § 1; Stats.2005, c. 300 (A.B.496), § 3.)*

Research References

Rutter, Cal. Practice Guide: Civ. Pro. Before Trial Ch. 4-E, E. Proof of Service of Summons.
3 Witkin Cal. Proc. 5th Actions § 1064, (S 1064) in General.
6 Witkin Cal. Proc. 5th Proceedings Without Trial § 350, Other Illustrations of Strict Construction.

§ 417.40. Proof of service signed by registered process server; additional contents

Any proof of service which is signed by a person registered under Chapter 16 (commencing with Section 22350) of Division 8 of the Business and Professions Code or his employee or independent contractor shall indicate the county in which he is registered and the number assigned to him pursuant to Section 22355 of the Business and Professions Code. *(Added by Stats.1971, c. 1661, p. 3578, § 3, operative July 1, 1972.)*

Research References

Rutter, Cal. Practice Guide: Civ. Pro. Before Trial Ch. 4-E, E. Proof of Service of Summons.
3 Witkin Cal. Proc. 5th Actions § 1002, (S 1002) Service Within California.
3 Witkin Cal. Proc. 5th Actions § 1003, (S 1003) Service Outside California But Within United States.
3 Witkin Cal. Proc. 5th Actions § 1004, Statutory Requirements.
3 Witkin Cal. Proc. 5th Actions § 1067, (S 1067) Affidavit or Certificate.

CHAPTER 5. OBJECTION TO JURISDICTION

Section
418.10. Motion to quash service of summons or to stay or dismiss action; procedure; appearance; waiver.
418.11. Appearance for ex parte relief or provisional remedy; not general appearance nor waiver of motion rights.

§ 418.10. Motion to quash service of summons or to stay or dismiss action; procedure; appearance; waiver

(a) A defendant, on or before the last day of his or her time to plead or within any further time that the court may for good cause allow, may serve and file a notice of motion for one or more of the following purposes:

(1) To quash service of summons on the ground of lack of jurisdiction of the court over him or her.

(2) To stay or dismiss the action on the ground of inconvenient forum.

(3) To dismiss the action pursuant to the applicable provisions of Chapter 1.5 (commencing with Section 583.110) of Title 8.

(b) The notice shall designate, as the time for making the motion, a date not more than 30 days after filing of the notice. The notice shall be served in the same manner, and at the same times, prescribed by subdivision (b) of Section 1005. The service and filing of the notice shall extend the defendant's time to plead until 15 days after service upon him or her of a written notice of entry of an order denying his or her motion, except that for good cause shown the court may extend the defendant's time to plead for an additional period not exceeding 20 days.

(c) If the motion is denied by the trial court, the defendant, within 10 days after service upon him or her of a written notice of entry of an order of the court denying his or her motion, or within any further time not exceeding 20 days that the trial court may for good cause allow, and before pleading, may petition an appropriate reviewing court for a writ of mandate to require the trial court to enter its order quashing the service of summons or staying or dismissing the action. The defendant shall file or enter his or her responsive pleading in the trial court within the time prescribed by subdivision (b) unless, on or before the last day of the defendant's time to plead, he or she serves upon the adverse party and files with the trial court a notice that he or she has petitioned for a writ of mandate. The service and filing of the notice shall extend the defendant's time to plead until 10 days after service upon him or her of a written notice of the final judgment in the mandate proceeding. The time to plead may for good cause shown be extended by the trial court for an additional period not exceeding 20 days.

(d) No default may be entered against the defendant before expiration of his or her time to plead, and no motion under this section, or under Section 473 or 473.5 when joined with a motion under this section, or application to the court or stipulation of the parties for an extension of the time to plead, shall be deemed a general appearance by the defendant.

(e) A defendant or cross-defendant may make a motion under this section and simultaneously answer, demur, or move to strike the complaint or cross-complaint.

(1) Notwithstanding Section 1014, no act by a party who makes a motion under this section, including filing an answer, demurrer, or motion to strike constitutes an appearance, unless the court denies the motion made under this section. If the court denies the motion made under this section, the defendant or cross-defendant is not deemed to have generally appeared until entry of the order denying the motion.

(2) If the motion made under this section is denied and the defendant or cross-defendant petitions for a writ of mandate pursuant to subdivision (c), the defendant or cross-defendant is not deemed to have generally appeared until the proceedings on the writ petition have finally concluded.

(3) Failure to make a motion under this section at the time of filing a demurrer or motion to strike constitutes a waiver of the issues of lack of personal jurisdiction, inadequacy of process, inadequacy of service of process, inconvenient forum, and delay in prosecution. *(Added by Stats.1969, c. 1610, p. 3363, § 3, operative July 1, 1970. Amended by Stats.1989, c. 693, § 1; Stats.1993, c. 456 (A.B.58), § 1; Stats.2002, c. 69 (S.B.1325), § 1.)*

Research References

Rutter, Cal. Practice Guide: Civil Appeals & Writs Ch. 2-B, B. Appealable Judgments and Orders.

§ 418.11. Appearance for ex parte relief or provisional remedy; not general appearance nor waiver of motion rights

An appearance at a hearing at which ex parte relief is sought, or an appearance at a hearing for which an ex parte application for a provisional remedy is made, is not a general appearance and does not constitute a waiver of the right to make a motion under Section 418.10. *(Added by Stats.1987, c. 62, § 1.)*

Research References

Title 6

OF THE PLEADINGS IN CIVIL ACTIONS

CHAPTER 1. THE PLEADINGS IN GENERAL

§ 420. Pleadings defined

DEFINITION OF PLEADINGS. The pleadings are the formal allegations by the parties of their respective claims and defenses, for the judgment of the Court. *(Enacted in 1872.)*

Research References

Rutter, Cal. Practice Guide: Civ. Pro. Before Trial Ch. 9(III)-C, C. Sanctions Under CCP § 128.7.
4 Witkin Cal. Proc. 5th Pleading § 4, (S 4) in General.

§ 421. Forms and rules

THIS CODE PRESCRIBES THE FORM AND RULES OF PLEADINGS. The forms of pleading in civil actions, and the rules by which the sufficiency of the pleadings is to be determined, are those prescribed in this Code. *(Enacted in 1872.)*

Research References

4 Witkin Cal. Proc. 5th Pleading § 13, in General.

§ 422.10. Allowable pleadings

The pleadings allowed in civil actions are complaints, demurrers, answers, and cross-complaints. *(Added by Stats.1971, c. 244, p. 378, § 18, operative July 1, 1972.)*

Law Revision Commission Comments

Section 422.10 supersedes the first paragraph of former Code of Civil Procedure Section 422. However, unlike Section 422 which specified the pleadings to which a demurrer or answer could be filed, Section 422.10 merely lists the pleadings allowed; the circumstances where a particular pleading is required or permitted are specified in subsequent sections. See also Section 411.10 ("A civil action is commenced by filing a complaint with the court."). The pleadings that can request affirmative relief are complaints and cross-complaints; a counterclaim is no longer permitted. See Code of Civil Procedure § 428.80.

Research References

Rutter, Cal. Practice Guide: Civ. Pro. Before Trial Ch. 6-A, A. Introduction.
Rutter, Cal. Practice Guide: Civ. Pro. Before Trial Ch. 7(I)-A, A. Demurrers.
Rutter, Cal. Practice Guide: Civ. Pro. Before Trial Ch. 9(III)-C, C. Sanctions Under CCP § 128.7.
Rutter, Cal. Practice Guide: Civil Trials & Evidence Ch. 8D-D, D. Hearsay Exceptions.
Rutter, Cal. Practice Guide: Insurance Litigation Ch. 15-E, E. Pleadings.
4 Witkin Cal. Proc. 5th Pleading § 4, (S 4) in General.
4 Witkin Cal. Proc. 5th Pleading § 453, (S 453) Distinctions.
5 Witkin Cal. Proc. 5th Pleading § 946, Raising Issue of Law.

§ 422.30. Caption; contents

(a) Every pleading shall contain a caption setting forth:

(1) The name of the court and county in which the action is brought.

(2) The title of the action.

(b) In a limited civil case, the caption shall state that the case is a limited civil case, and the clerk shall classify the case accordingly. *(Added by Stats.1971, c. 244, p. 378, § 20, operative July 1, 1972. Amended by Stats.1998, c. 931 (S.B.2139), § 71, eff. Sept. 28, 1998; Stats.1999, c. 344 (S.B.210), § 13, eff. Sept. 7, 1999; Stats.2002, c. 784 (S.B.1316), § 60.)*

Law Revision Commission Comments

Section 422.30 retains the substance of the portion of subdivision 1 of former Code of Civil Procedure Section 426 which prescribed the caption to be used on a complaint. However, unlike the provision of former Section 426, Section 422.30 applies to all pleadings rather than merely to the complaint. This extension of the caption requirement is consistent with former practice. Cal.Rules of Ct., Rules 201(c) (superior court), 501(c) (municipal court).

Section 422.30 is amended to accommodate unification of the municipal and superior courts in a county. Cal. Const. art. VI, § 5(e). Subdivision (b) facilitates identification of limited civil cases in a county in which the municipal and superior courts have unified their operations in the superior court. See Section 85 (limited civil cases) & Comment. For guidance on procedures for challenging a caption stating, or failing to state, that an action or proceeding is a limited civil case, see Sections 395.9 (misclassification as limited civil case or otherwise), 399.5 (reclassification pursuant to Section 395.9), 400 (petition for writ of mandate).

Section 422.30 is also amended to reflect the elimination of the justice court. Cal. Const. art. VI, §§ 1, 5(b). [28 Cal.L.Rev.Comm. Reports 51 (1998)].

Subdivision (c) of Section 422.30 is amended to clarify that the clerk is to rely on the caption in determining how to classify a civil case that is brought in a unified superior court. For the rules governing reclassification, see Sections 403.010–403.090. See also Section 32.5 (jurisdictional classification). [29 Cal.L.Rev.Comm. Reports App. 5 (1999)].

Section 422.30 is amended to reflect unification of the municipal and superior courts pursuant to Article VI, Section 5(e), of the California Constitution. See Section 38 (judicial district). *Cf.* Gov't Code § 71042.5 (preservation of judicial districts for purpose of publication). [32 Cal.L.Rev.Comm. Reports 123 (2002)].

Research References

Rutter, Cal. Practice Guide: Civ. Pro. Before Trial Ch. 6-B, B. Complaints.
Rutter, Cal. Practice Guide: Personal Injury Ch. 5-E, E. Selected Pleading Issues.
4 Witkin Cal. Proc. 5th Pleading § 17, Format of First Page.
4 Witkin Cal. Proc. 5th Pleading § 471, Superior Court.
4 Witkin Cal. Proc. 5th Pleading § 472, Limited Civil Cases.
4 Witkin Cal. Proc. 5th Pleading § 496, Form.
4 Witkin Cal. Proc. 5th Pleading § 500, Other Procedures Distinguished.
4 Witkin Cal. Proc. 5th Pleading § 511, (S 511) in General.

§ 422.40. Names of parties in complaint; names in other pleadings

In the complaint, the title of the action shall include the names of all the parties; but, except as otherwise provided by statute or rule of the Judicial Council, in other pleadings it is sufficient to state the name of the first party on each side with an appropriate indication of other parties. *(Added by Stats.1971, c. 244, p. 378, § 21, operative July 1, 1972.)*

Law Revision Commission Comments

Section 422.40 continues the requirement found in subdivision 1 of former Code of Civil Procedure Section 426 that the complaint include the names of the parties and adds a new provision applying to other pleadings. The inclusion of the phrase "*et al.*" would be "an appropriate indication of other parties" for the purposes of Section 422.40. Section 422.40 is based on the second sentence of Rule 10(a) of the Federal Rules of Civil Procedure.

Research References

Rutter, Cal. Practice Guide: Civ. Pro. Before Trial Ch. 6-B, B. Complaints.
Rutter, Cal. Practice Guide: Civ. Pro. Before Trial Ch. 6-C, C. Answer.
Rutter, Cal. Practice Guide: Civ. Pro. Before Trial Ch. 6-D, D. Cross-Complaint.
3 Witkin Cal. Proc. 5th Actions § 239, (S 239) Claims in Class Actions.
4 Witkin Cal. Proc. 5th Pleading § 13, in General.
4 Witkin Cal. Proc. 5th Pleading § 471, Superior Court.

4 Witkin Cal. Proc. 5th Pleading § 473, Natural Persons.

CHAPTER 2. PLEADINGS DEMANDING RELIEF

ARTICLE 1.   GENERAL PROVISIONS

§ 425.10. Statement of facts; demand for judgment

(a) A complaint or cross-complaint shall contain both of the following:

(1) A statement of the facts constituting the cause of action, in ordinary and concise language.

(2) A demand for judgment for the relief to which the pleader claims to be entitled. If the recovery of money or damages is demanded, the amount demanded shall be stated.

(b) Notwithstanding subdivision (a), where an action is brought to recover actual or punitive damages for personal injury or wrongful death, the amount demanded shall not be stated, but the complaint shall comply with Section 422.30 and, in a limited civil case, with subdivision (b) of Section 70613 of the Government Code. (Added by Stats.1971, c. 244, p. 379, § 23, operative July 1, 1972. Amended by Stats.1974, c. 1481, p. 3239, § 1; Stats.1979, c. 778, p. 2662, § 2; Stats.1998, c. 931 (S.B.2139), § 72, eff. Sept. 28, 1998; Stats.2001, c. 812 (A.B.223), § 1; Stats.2005, c. 75 (A.B.145), § 32, eff. July 19, 2005, operative Jan. 1, 2006.)

Law Revision Commission Comments

Section 425.10 continues requirements found in subdivision 2 and subdivision 3 (first portion) of former Code of Civil Procedure Section 426. However, Section 425.10 applies to both complaints and cross-complaints while Section 426 by its terms applied to "complaint[s]."

Section 425.10 is amended to accommodate unification of the municipal and superior courts in a county. Cal. Const. art. VI, § 5(e). See Section 85

(limited civil cases) & Comment. [28 Cal.L.Rev.Comm. Reports 51 (1998)].

Section 425.10 is amended to conform the pleading requirements in limited and unlimited civil cases. In a complaint seeking actual or punitive damages for personal injury or wrongful death, the amount demanded should not be stated, regardless of the jurisdictional classification of the action. If the case is a limited civil case, however, the first page of the complaint must (1) identify the case as a limited civil case as required by Section 422.30, and (2) state whether the amount demanded exceeds $10,000, so as to permit determination of the filing fee. See Gov't Code 72055 (first filing fee in limited civil case). For format requirements, see Cal. R. Ct. Rule 201(f)(8).

Technical changes are also made for conformity with preferred drafting style. [31 Cal.L.Rev.Comm. Reports 85 (2001)].

Recommendation and study relating to counterclaims and cross-complaints, joinder of causes of action, and related provisions. 10 Cal.L.Revision Comm.Reports 501 (1971); Report of Senate Committee on Judiciary on Senate Bill 201, S.Journal, April 1, 1971; Communication From Assembly Committee on Judiciary on Senate Bill 201, A.Journal, June 16, 1971.

Research References

Rutter, Cal. Practice Guide: Civ. Pro. Before Trial Ch. 2-B, B. Capacity to Sue or Defend.

Rutter, Cal. Practice Guide: Civ. Pro. Before Trial Ch. 3-A, A. Subject Matter Jurisdiction (Competency).

Rutter, Cal. Practice Guide: Civ. Pro. Before Trial Ch. 5-B, B. Entry of Default.

Rutter, Cal. Practice Guide: Civ. Pro. Before Trial Ch. 5-E, E. Limitations on Default Judgments.

Rutter, Cal. Practice Guide: Civ. Pro. Before Trial Ch. 6-A, A. Introduction.

Rutter, Cal. Practice Guide: Civ. Pro. Before Trial Ch. 6-B, B. Complaints.

Rutter, Cal. Practice Guide: Civ. Pro. Before Trial Ch. 8D-4, "Pinning Down" Your Opponent.

Rutter, Cal. Practice Guide: Civ. Pro. Before Trial Ch. 8K-1, Request for Statement of Damages (Personal Injury or Death Cases).

California Practice Guide: Employment Litigation Ch. 19-C, C. Plaintiff's Complaint.

Rutter, Cal. Practice Guide: Fed.Civ.Pro. Before Trial Ch. 1-B, B. Federal vs. State Law.

Rutter, Cal. Practice Guide: Fed.Civ.Pro. Before Trial Ch. 2D-4, What Cases and Claims Are Removable.

Rutter, Cal. Practice Guide: Personal Injury Ch. 5-D, D. Classification as Limited or Unlimited Civil Case.

Rutter, Cal. Practice Guide: Personal Injury Ch. 5-E, E. Selected Pleading Issues.

Miller and Starr California Real Estate § 34:92, Punitive Damages-- Constitutional Validity and Limits.

9 Witkin Cal. Proc. 5th Appeal § 361, Appeal from Default Judgment.

4 Witkin Cal. Proc. 5th Pleading § 378, Requirement of Pleading Facts.

4 Witkin Cal. Proc. 5th Pleading § 379, Notice Pleading and Federal Rules.

4 Witkin Cal. Proc. 5th Pleading § 471, Superior Court.

4 Witkin Cal. Proc. 5th Pleading § 480, Amendment to Allege Initial Ignorance.

4 Witkin Cal. Proc. 5th Pleading § 495, Nature of Prayer.

4 Witkin Cal. Proc. 5th Pleading § 496, Form.

4 Witkin Cal. Proc. 5th Pleading § 500, Other Procedures Distinguished.

4 Witkin Cal. Proc. 5th Pleading § 511, (S 511) in General.

4 Witkin Cal. Proc. 5th Pleading § 513, (S 513) Effect of Statement on Amount of Actual Award.

4 Witkin Cal. Proc. 5th Pleading § 514, Statement Preserving Right to Seek Punitive Damages.

6 Witkin Cal. Proc. 5th Proceedings Without Trial § 150, Prayer for Damages According to Proof.

6 Witkin Cal. Proc. 5th Proceedings Without Trial § 153, Action for Accounting.

6 Witkin Cal. Proc. 5th Proceedings Without Trial § 154, (S 154) Notice of Damages.

6 Witkin Cal. Proc. 5th Proceedings Without Trial § 155, (S 155) Effect of Other Claims.

6 Witkin Cal. Proc. 5th Proceedings Without Trial § 158, (S 158) Requirement of Notice of Amount Sought.

7 Witkin Cal. Proc. 5th Trial § 276, Amount of Demand.

Civ. Pro.

6 Witkin, California Summary 10th Torts § 1749, Judgment by Default.

§ 425.11.　Personal injury or wrongful death actions; statement of nature and amount of damages; service of statement

(a)　As used in this section:

(1)　"Complaint" includes a cross-complaint.

(2)　"Plaintiff" includes a cross-complainant.

(3)　"Defendant" includes a cross-defendant.

(b)　When a complaint is filed in an action to recover damages for personal injury or wrongful death, the defendant may at any time request a statement setting forth the nature and amount of damages being sought.　The request shall be served upon the plaintiff, who shall serve a responsive statement as to the damages within 15 days.　In the event that a response is not served, the defendant, on notice to the plaintiff, may petition the court in which the action is pending to order the plaintiff to serve a responsive statement.

(c)　If no request is made for the statement referred to in subdivision (b), the plaintiff shall serve the statement on the defendant before a default may be taken.

(d)　The statement referred to in subdivision (b) shall be served in the following manner:

(1)　If a party has not appeared in the action, the statement shall be served in the same manner as a summons.

(2)　If a party has appeared in the action, the statement shall be served upon the party's attorney, or upon the party if the party has appeared without an attorney, in the manner provided for service of a summons or in the manner provided by Chapter 5 (commencing with Section 1010) of Title 14 of Part 2.

(e)　The statement referred to in subdivision (b) may be combined with the statement described in Section 425.115. *(Added by Stats.1974, c. 1481, p. 3239, § 2.　Amended by Stats.1993, c. 456 (A.B.58), § 2; Stats.1995, c. 796 (S.B.45), § 2; Stats.1998, c. 931 (S.B.2139), § 73, eff. Sept. 28, 1998; Stats.2001, c. 812 (A.B.223), § 2; Stats.2006, c. 538 (S.B.1852), § 63.5.)*

Law Revision Commission Comments

Section 425.11 is amended to accommodate unification of the municipal and superior courts in a county. Cal. Const. art. VI, § 5(e). See Section 85 (limited civil cases) & Comment. [28 Cal.L.Rev.Comm. Reports 51 (1998)].

Section 425.11 is amended to conform to the pleading requirements of limited and unlimited civil cases. See Section 425.10. Technical changes are also made for conformity with preferred drafting style. [30 Cal.L.Rev. Comm. Reports 443 (2000)].

Research References

Rutter, Cal. Practice Guide: Civ. Pro. Before Trial Ch. 3-A, A. Subject Matter Jurisdiction (Competency).

Rutter, Cal. Practice Guide: Civ. Pro. Before Trial Ch. 4-D, D. Service of Summons.

Rutter, Cal. Practice Guide: Civ. Pro. Before Trial Ch. 5-B, B. Entry of Default.

Rutter, Cal. Practice Guide: Civ. Pro. Before Trial Ch. 5-C, C. Default Judgment by Clerk.

Rutter, Cal. Practice Guide: Civ. Pro. Before Trial Ch. 5-E, E. Limitations on Default Judgments.

Rutter, Cal. Practice Guide: Civ. Pro. Before Trial Ch. 5-G, G. Relief from Default.

Rutter, Cal. Practice Guide: Civ. Pro. Before Trial Ch. 6-B, B. Complaints.

Rutter, Cal. Practice Guide: Civ. Pro. Before Trial Ch. 8A-6, Statutory Procedures Outside Discovery Act.

Rutter, Cal. Practice Guide: Civ. Pro. Before Trial Ch. 8D-4, "Pinning Down" Your Opponent.

Rutter, Cal. Practice Guide: Civ. Pro. Before Trial Ch. 8D-5, Selecting Proper Discovery Tools.

Rutter, Cal. Practice Guide: Civ. Pro. Before Trial Ch. 8D-6, Determining Sequence of Discovery Procedures.

Rutter, Cal. Practice Guide: Civ. Pro. Before Trial Ch. 8F-8, Sanctions in Enforcing Discovery.

Rutter, Cal. Practice Guide: Civ. Pro. Before Trial Ch. 8K-1, Request for Statement of Damages (Personal Injury or Death Cases).

Rutter, Cal. Practice Guide: Civ. Pro. Before Trial Ch. 4-D, Outline D.

Rutter, Cal. Practice Guide: Civ. Pro. Before Trial Ch. 5-B, Outline B.

Rutter, Cal. Practice Guide: Civ. Pro. Before Trial Ch. 5-E, Outline E.

Rutter, Cal. Practice Guide: Civ. Pro. Before Trial Ch. 8D-4, Outline 4.

Rutter, Cal. Practice Guide: Civ. Pro. Before Trial Ch. 8D-5, Outline 5.

Rutter, Cal. Practice Guide: Civ. Pro. Before Trial Ch. 8F-8, Outline 8.

Rutter, Cal. Practice Guide: Civil Trials & Evidence Ch. 1-A, A. Importance of Statewide and Local Rules of Court.

Rutter, Cal. Practice Guide: Insurance Litigation Form 12:B, Sample Excess Liability Letter.

Rutter, Cal. Practice Guide: Personal Injury Ch. 3-A, A. Introduction.

Rutter, Cal. Practice Guide: Personal Injury Ch. 5-D, D. Classification as Limited or Unlimited Civil Case.

Rutter, Cal. Practice Guide: Personal Injury Ch. 5-E, E. Selected Pleading Issues.

8 Witkin Cal. Proc. 5th Attack Judgment Trial Court § 12, Lack of Jurisdiction Shown by Record.

4 Witkin Cal. Proc. 5th Pleading § 382, (S 382) Judicial Council Forms.

4 Witkin Cal. Proc. 5th Pleading § 511, (S 511) in General.

4 Witkin Cal. Proc. 5th Pleading § 512, (S 512) Service and Filing of Statement.

4 Witkin Cal. Proc. 5th Pleading § 513, (S 513) Effect of Statement on Amount of Actual Award.

4 Witkin Cal. Proc. 5th Pleading § 514, Statement Preserving Right to Seek Punitive Damages.

5 Witkin Cal. Proc. 5th Pleading § 1245, Where Defendant Does Not Appear.

6 Witkin Cal. Proc. 5th Proceedings Without Trial § 150, Prayer for Damages According to Proof.

6 Witkin Cal. Proc. 5th Proceedings Without Trial § 151, Default Entered as Discovery Sanction.

6 Witkin Cal. Proc. 5th Proceedings Without Trial § 153, Action for Accounting.

6 Witkin Cal. Proc. 5th Proceedings Without Trial § 154, (S 154) Notice of Damages.

6 Witkin Cal. Proc. 5th Proceedings Without Trial § 155, (S 155) Effect of Other Claims.

6 Witkin Cal. Proc. 5th Proceedings Without Trial § 156, (S 156) Special and General Damages.

6 Witkin Cal. Proc. 5th Proceedings Without Trial § 157, (S 157) Time for Response.

6 Witkin Cal. Proc. 5th Proceedings Without Trial § 159, (S 159) Damages Statement Preserves Right to Recover.

6 Witkin, California Summary 10th Torts § 1749, Judgment by Default.

§ 425.115.　Punitive damages; service of statement; form

(a)　As used in this section:

(1)　"Complaint" includes a cross-complaint.

(2)　"Plaintiff" includes a cross-complainant.

(3)　"Defendant" includes a cross-defendant.

(b)　The plaintiff preserves the right to seek punitive damages pursuant to Section 3294 of the Civil Code on a default judgment by serving upon the defendant the following statement, or its substantial equivalent:

NOTICE TO _____:

　　　　　(Insert name of defendant or cross-defendant)

_____ reserves the right to seek

(Insert name of plaintiff or cross-
　　　complainant)

$ _____ in punitive damages

　　　　(Insert dollar amount)

when _____ seeks a judgment in the

　　　(Insert name of plaintiff or
　　　　cross-complainant)

suit filed against you.

_____　　_____

　　(Insert name of attorney or　　　　　(Date)
party appearing in propria persona)

(c) If the plaintiff seeks punitive damages pursuant to Section 3294 of the Civil Code, and if the defendant appears in the action, the plaintiff shall not be limited to the amount set forth in the statement served on the defendant pursuant to this section.

(d) A plaintiff who serves a statement on the defendant pursuant to this section shall be deemed to have complied with Sections 425.10 and 580 of this code and Section 3295 of the Civil Code.

(e) The plaintiff may serve a statement upon the defendant pursuant to this section, and may serve the statement as part of the statement required by Section 425.11.

(f) The plaintiff shall serve the statement upon the defendant pursuant to this section before a default may be taken, if the motion for default judgment includes a request for punitive damages.

(g) The statement referred to in subdivision (b) shall be served by one of the following methods:

(1) If the party has not appeared in the action, the statement shall be served in the same manner as a summons pursuant to Article 3 (commencing with Section 415.10) of Chapter 4 of Title 5 of Part 2 of the Code of Civil Procedure.

(2) If the party has appeared in the action, the statement shall be served upon his or her attorney, or upon the party if he or she has appeared without an attorney, either in the same manner as a summons pursuant to Article 3 (commencing with Section 415.10) of Chapter 4 or in the manner provided by Chapter 5 (commencing with Section 1010) of Title 14. *(Added by Stats.1995, c. 796 (S.B.45), § 3. Amended by Stats.2005, c. 706 (A.B.1742), § 12.)*

Research References

Rutter, Cal. Practice Guide: Civ. Pro. Before Trial Ch. 5-B, B. Entry of Default.
Rutter, Cal. Practice Guide: Civ. Pro. Before Trial Ch. 5-C, C. Default Judgment by Clerk.
Rutter, Cal. Practice Guide: Civ. Pro. Before Trial Ch. 5-E, E. Limitations on Default Judgments.
Rutter, Cal. Practice Guide: Civ. Pro. Before Trial Ch. 6-B, B. Complaints.
Rutter, Cal. Practice Guide: Civ. Pro. Before Trial Ch. 8K-1, Request for Statement of Damages (Personal Injury or Death Cases).
Rutter, Cal. Practice Guide: Personal Injury Ch. 3-E, E. Punitive Damages.
Rutter, Cal. Practice Guide: Personal Injury Ch. 5-E, E. Selected Pleading Issues.
Miller and Starr California Real Estate § 34:92, Punitive Damages--Constitutional Validity and Limits.
4 Witkin Cal. Proc. 5th Pleading § 382, (S 382) Judicial Council Forms.
4 Witkin Cal. Proc. 5th Pleading § 514, Statement Preserving Right to Seek Punitive Damages.
6 Witkin Cal. Proc. 5th Proceedings Without Trial § 154, (S 154) Notice of Damages.
6 Witkin Cal. Proc. 5th Proceedings Without Trial § 159, (S 159) Damages Statement Preserves Right to Recover.
6 Witkin, California Summary 10th Torts § 1559, Nature and Purpose of Award.
6 Witkin, California Summary 10th Torts § 1749, Judgment by Default.

§ 425.12. Official forms for use in trial court; development and approval; consultation with advisory committee

(a) The Judicial Council shall develop and approve official forms for use in trial courts of this state for any complaint, cross-complaint or answer in any action based upon personal injury, property damage, wrongful death, unlawful detainer, breach of contract or fraud.

(b) The Judicial Council shall develop and approve an official form for use as a statement of damages pursuant to Sections 425.11 and 425.115.

(c) In developing the forms required by this section, the Judicial Council shall consult with a representative advisory committee which shall include, but not be limited to, representatives of the plaintiff's bar, the defense bar, the public interest bar, court administrators and the public. The forms shall be drafted in nontechnical language and shall be made available through the office of the clerk of the appropriate trial court. *(Added by Stats.1979, c. 843, p. 2934, § 1. Amended by Stats.1982, c. 272, p. 861, § 1; Stats.1984, c. 354, § 1; Stats.1995, c. 796 (S.B.45), § 4.)*

Research References

Rutter, Cal. Practice Guide: Civ. Pro. Before Trial Ch. 6-A, A. Introduction.
Rutter, Cal. Practice Guide: Civ. Pro. Before Trial Ch. 6-B, B. Complaints.
Rutter, Cal. Practice Guide: Insurance Litigation Ch. 11-C, C. Fraud.
Rutter, Cal. Practice Guide: Personal Injury Ch. 5-E, E. Selected Pleading Issues.
4 Witkin Cal. Proc. 5th Pleading § 382, (S 382) Judicial Council Forms.

§ 425.13. Negligence actions against health care providers; claims for punitive damages; amended pleadings

(a) In any action for damages arising out of the professional negligence of a health care provider, no claim for punitive damages shall be included in a complaint or other pleading unless the court enters an order allowing an amended pleading that includes a claim for punitive damages to be filed. The court may allow the filing of an amended pleading claiming punitive damages on a motion by the party seeking the amended pleading and on the basis of the supporting and opposing affidavits presented that the plaintiff has established that there is a substantial probability that the plaintiff will prevail on the claim pursuant to Section 3294 of the Civil Code. The court shall not grant a motion allowing the filing of an amended pleading that includes a claim for punitive damages if the motion for such an order is not filed within two years after the complaint or initial pleading is filed or not less than nine months before the date the matter is first set for trial, whichever is earlier.

(b) For the purposes of this section, "health care provider" means any person licensed or certified pursuant to Division 2 (commencing with Section 500) of the Business and Professions Code, or licensed pursuant to the Osteopathic Initiative Act, or the Chiropractic Initiative Act, or licensed pursuant to Chapter 2.5 (commencing with Section 1440) of Division 2 of the Health and Safety Code; and any clinic, health dispensary, or health facility, licensed pursuant to Division 2 (commencing with Section 1200) of the Health and Safety Code. "Health care provider" includes the legal representatives of a health care provider. *(Added by Stats.1987, c. 1498, § 7. Amended by Stats.1988, c. 1204, § 1; Stats.1988, c. 1205, § 1.)*

Research References

Rutter, Cal. Practice Guide: Civil Appeals & Writs Ch. 8-C, C. Standards of Appellate Review.
Rutter, Cal. Practice Guide: Civil Appeals & Writs Ch. 13-A, A. General Considerations.
Rutter, Cal. Practice Guide: Civ. Pro. Before Trial Ch. 1-C, C. Prelawsuit Notices, Claims and Demands.
Rutter, Cal. Practice Guide: Civ. Pro. Before Trial Ch. 1-G, G. Prior Court Order Required for Certain Pleadings.
Rutter, Cal. Practice Guide: Civ. Pro. Before Trial Ch. 6-B, B. Complaints.
Rutter, Cal. Practice Guide: Civ. Pro. Before Trial Ch. 6-E, E. Amended and Supplemental Pleadings.
Rutter, Cal. Practice Guide: Civ. Pro. Before Trial Ch. 8C-5, Privacy Protection.
Rutter, Cal. Practice Guide: Civ. Pro. Before Trial Ch. 7(I)-B, B. Motions to Strike.
Rutter, Cal. Practice Guide: Civ. Pro. Before Trial Ch. 12(I)-B, B. Case Management ("Fast Track") System.

Rutter, Cal. Practice Guide: Personal Injury Ch. 3-E, E. Punitive Damages.

Rutter, Cal. Practice Guide: Personal Injury Ch. 3-F, F. MICRA Provisions Affecting Damages.

Rutter, Cal. Practice Guide: Personal Injury Ch. 5-E, E. Selected Pleading Issues.

Rutter, Cal. Practice Guide: Personal Injury Ch. 6-A, A. Scope of Discovery and Limitations.

Rutter, Cal. Practice Guide: Personal Injury Ch. 8-A, A. Case Management.

Rutter, Cal. Practice Guide: Personal Injury Ch. 3-E, Outline E.

3 Witkin Cal. Proc. 5th Actions § 748, Statute in Second Action Not Tolled.

2 Witkin Cal. Proc. 5th Jurisdiction § 290, (S 290) Procedural Error or Omission.

5 Witkin Cal. Proc. 5th Pleading § 935, (S 935) Pleading Punitive or Exemplary Damages.

5 Witkin Cal. Proc. 5th Pleading § 1034, (S 1034) in General.

7 Witkin Cal. Proc. 5th Trial § 66, (S 66) in General.

7 Witkin Cal. Proc. 5th Trial § 71, (S 71) Party's Survival in Doubt.

6 Witkin, California Summary 10th Torts § 936, (S 936) Health Care Provider.

6 Witkin, California Summary 10th Torts § 1600, (S 1600) in General.

6 Witkin, California Summary 10th Torts § 1601, (S 1601) Arising Out of Professional Negligence.

6 Witkin, California Summary 10th Torts § 1602, (S 1602) Substantial Probability that Plaintiff Will Prevail.

6 Witkin, California Summary 10th Torts § 1603, (S 1603) Time Limits.

6 Witkin, California Summary 10th Torts § 1604, (S 1604) Action Based on Intentional Tort or Crime.

6 Witkin, California Summary 10th Torts § 1605, Action Against Religious Corporation.

6 Witkin, California Summary 10th Torts § 1686, Statutory Remedies.

§ 425.14. Actions against religious corporations or religious corporation soles; claims for punitive or exemplary damages; amended pleadings; discovery

No claim for punitive or exemplary damages against a religious corporation or religious corporation sole shall be included in a complaint or other pleading unless the court enters an order allowing an amended pleading that includes a claim for punitive or exemplary damages to be filed. The court may allow the filing of an amended pleading claiming punitive or exemplary damages on a motion by the party seeking the amended pleading and upon a finding, on the basis of the supporting and opposing affidavits presented, that the plaintiff has established evidence which substantiates that plaintiff will meet the clear and convincing standard of proof under Section 3294 of the Civil Code.

Nothing in this section is intended to affect the plaintiff's right to discover evidence on the issue of punitive or exemplary damages. *(Added by Stats.1988, c. 1410, § 1.)*

Research References

Rutter, Cal. Practice Guide: Civ. Pro. Before Trial Ch. 1-G, G. Prior Court Order Required for Certain Pleadings.

Rutter, Cal. Practice Guide: Civ. Pro. Before Trial Ch. 6-B, B. Complaints.

Rutter, Cal. Practice Guide: Civ. Pro. Before Trial Ch. 7(I)-B, B. Motions to Strike.

Rutter, Cal. Practice Guide: Personal Injury Ch. 3-E, E. Punitive Damages.

Rutter, Cal. Practice Guide: Personal Injury Ch. 5-E, E. Selected Pleading Issues.

5 Witkin Cal. Proc. 5th Pleading § 935, (S 935) Pleading Punitive or Exemplary Damages.

5 Witkin Cal. Proc. 5th Pleading § 1034, (S 1034) in General.

7 Witkin Cal. Proc. 5th Trial § 80, California Constitution and Statutes.

6 Witkin, California Summary 10th Torts § 1605, Action Against Religious Corporation.

§ 425.15. Actions against directors or officers of nonprofit corporations; court order; pleadings; discovery; exceptions

(a) No cause of action against a person serving without compensation as a director or officer of a nonprofit corporation described in this section, on account of any negligent act or omission by that person within the scope of that person's duties as a director acting in the capacity of a board member, or as an officer acting in the capacity of, and within the scope of the duties of, an officer, shall be included in a complaint or other pleading unless the court enters an order allowing the pleading that includes that claim to be filed after the court determines that the party seeking to file the pleading has established evidence that substantiates the claim. The court may allow the filing of a pleading that includes that claim following the filing of a verified petition therefor accompanied by the proposed pleading and supporting affidavits stating the facts upon which the liability is based. The court shall order service of the petition upon the party against whom the action is proposed to be filed and permit that party to submit opposing affidavits prior to making its determination. The filing of the petition, proposed pleading, and accompanying affidavits shall toll the running of any applicable statute of limitations until the final determination of the matter, which ruling, if favorable to the petitioning party, shall permit the proposed pleading to be filed.

(b) Nothing in this section shall affect the right of the plaintiff to discover evidence on the issue of damages.

(c) Nothing in this section shall be construed to affect any action against a nonprofit corporation for any negligent action or omission of a volunteer director or officer occurring within the scope of the person's duties.

(d) For the purposes of this section, "compensation" means remuneration whether by way of salary, fee, or other consideration for services rendered. However, the payment of per diem, mileage, or other reimbursement expenses to a director or officer shall not constitute compensation.

(e)(1) This section applies only to officers and directors of nonprofit corporations that are subject to Part 2 (commencing with Section 5110), Part 3 (commencing with Section 7110), or Part 4 (commencing with Section 9110) of Division 2 of Title 1 of the Corporations Code that are organized to provide charitable, educational, scientific, social, or other forms of public service and that are exempt from federal income taxation under Section 501(c)(1), except any credit union, or Section 501(c)(4), 501(c)(5), 501(c)(7), or 501(c)(19) of the Internal Revenue Code[1].

(2) This section does not apply to any corporation that unlawfully restricts membership, services, or benefits conferred on the basis of political affiliation, age, or any characteristic listed or defined in subdivision (b) or (e) of Section 51 of the Civil Code. *(Added by Stats.1992, c. 726 (S.B.1264), § 1. Amended by Stats.2007, c. 568 (A.B.14), § 16.)*

[1] 26 U.S.C.A. § 501(c).

Research References

Rutter, Cal. Practice Guide: Civ. Pro. Before Trial Ch. 1-G, G. Prior Court Order Required for Certain Pleadings.

Rutter, Cal. Practice Guide: Civ. Pro. Before Trial Ch. 6-B, B. Complaints.

Rutter, Cal. Practice Guide: Personal Injury Ch. 5-E, E. Selected Pleading Issues.

9 Witkin, California Summary 10th Corporations § 299, (S 299) Scope of Liability.

5 Witkin, California Summary 10th Torts § 35, Volunteer Directors or Officers of Nonprofit Corporations.

§ 425.16. Anti–SLAPP motion

(a) The Legislature finds and declares that there has been a disturbing increase in lawsuits brought primarily to chill the valid exercise of the constitutional rights of freedom of speech and petition for the redress of grievances. The Legislature finds and declares that it is in the public interest to encourage continued participation in matters of public significance, and that this participation should not be chilled through abuse of the judicial process. To this end, this section shall be construed broadly.

(b)(1) A cause of action against a person arising from any act of that person in furtherance of the person's right of petition or free speech under the United States Constitution or the California Constitution in connection with a public issue shall be subject to a special motion to strike, unless the court determines that the plaintiff has established that there is a probability that the plaintiff will prevail on the claim.

(2) In making its determination, the court shall consider the pleadings, and supporting and opposing affidavits stating the facts upon which the liability or defense is based.

(3) If the court determines that the plaintiff has established a probability that he or she will prevail on the claim, neither that determination nor the fact of that determination shall be admissible in evidence at any later stage of the case, or in any subsequent action, and no burden of proof or degree of proof otherwise applicable shall be affected by that determination in any later stage of the case or in any subsequent proceeding.

(c)(1) Except as provided in paragraph (2), in any action subject to subdivision (b), a prevailing defendant on a special motion to strike shall be entitled to recover his or her attorney's fees and costs. If the court finds that a special motion to strike is frivolous or is solely intended to cause unnecessary delay, the court shall award costs and reasonable attorney's fees to a plaintiff prevailing on the motion, pursuant to Section 128.5.

(2) A defendant who prevails on a special motion to strike in an action subject to paragraph (1) shall not be entitled to attorney's fees and costs if that cause of action is brought pursuant to Section 6259, 11130, 11130.3, 54960, or 54960.1 of the Government Code. Nothing in this paragraph shall be construed to prevent a prevailing defendant from recovering attorney's fees and costs pursuant to subdivision (d) of Section 6259, 11130.5, or 54690.5[1].

(d) This section shall not apply to any enforcement action brought in the name of the people of the State of California by the Attorney General, district attorney, or city attorney, acting as a public prosecutor.

(e) As used in this section, "act in furtherance of a person's right of petition or free speech under the United States or California Constitution in connection with a public issue" includes: (1) any written or oral statement or writing made before a legislative, executive, or judicial proceeding, or any other official proceeding authorized by law, (2) any written or oral statement or writing made in connection with an issue under consideration or review by a legislative, executive, or judicial body, or any other official proceeding authorized by law, (3) any written or oral statement or writing made in a place open to the public or a public forum in connection with an issue of public interest, or (4) any other conduct in furtherance of the exercise of the constitutional right of petition or the constitutional right of free speech in connection with a public issue or an issue of public interest.

(f) The special motion may be filed within 60 days of the service of the complaint or, in the court's discretion, at any later time upon terms it deems proper. The motion shall be scheduled by the clerk of the court for a hearing not more than 30 days after the service of the motion unless the docket conditions of the court require a later hearing.

(g) All discovery proceedings in the action shall be stayed upon the filing of a notice of motion made pursuant to this section. The stay of discovery shall remain in effect until notice of entry of the order ruling on the motion. The court, on noticed motion and for good cause shown, may order that specified discovery be conducted notwithstanding this subdivision.

(h) For purposes of this section, "complaint" includes "cross-complaint" and "petition," "plaintiff" includes "cross-complainant" and "petitioner," and " defendant" includes "cross-defendant" and " respondent."

(i) An order granting or denying a special motion to strike shall be appealable under Section 904.1.

(j)(1) Any party who files a special motion to strike pursuant to this section, and any party who files an opposition to a special motion to strike, shall, promptly upon so filing, transmit to the Judicial Council, by e-mail or facsimile, a copy of the endorsed, filed caption page of the motion or opposition, a copy of any related notice of appeal or petition for a writ, and a conformed copy of any order issued pursuant to this section, including any order granting or denying a special motion to strike, discovery, or fees.

(2) The Judicial Council shall maintain a public record of information transmitted pursuant to this subdivision for at least three years, and may store the information on microfilm or other appropriate electronic media. *(Added by Stats.1992, c. 726 (S.B.1264), § 2. Amended by Stats.1993, c. 1239 (S.B.9), § 1; Stats.1997, c. 271 (S.B.1296), § 1; Stats.1999, c. 960 (A.B.1675), § 1, eff. Oct. 10, 1999; Stats.2005, c. 535 (A.B.1158), § 1, eff. Oct. 5, 2005; Stats.2009, c. 65 (S.B.786), § 1; Stats.2010, c. 328 (S.B.1330), § 34.)*

[1] So in enrolled bill. Probably should be "54960.5".

Research References

Rutter, Cal. Practice Guide: A.D.R. Ch. 5-E, E. Claims Subject to Arbitration (Arbitrability).

Rutter, Cal. Practice Guide: Civil Appeals & Writs Ch. 2-B, B. Appealable Judgments and Orders.

Rutter, Cal. Practice Guide: Civil Appeals & Writs Ch. 2-C, C. Nonappealable Orders.

Rutter, Cal. Practice Guide: Civil Appeals & Writs Ch. 2-D, D. Standing to Appeal.

Rutter, Cal. Practice Guide: Civil Appeals & Writs Ch. 3-B, B. Filing Deadlines.

Rutter, Cal. Practice Guide: Civil Appeals & Writs Ch. 7-A, A. Overview.

Rutter, Cal. Practice Guide: Civil Appeals & Writs Ch. 7-C, C. Stay by Posting Security (Bond or Undertaking).

Rutter, Cal. Practice Guide: Civil Appeals & Writs Ch. 8-B, B. Presumption of Correctness.

Rutter, Cal. Practice Guide: Civil Appeals & Writs Ch. 8-C, C. Standards of Appellate Review.

Rutter, Cal. Practice Guide: Civil Appeals & Writs Ch. 8-D, D. Limits on Assertion of Issues on Appeal.

Rutter, Cal. Practice Guide: Civil Appeals & Writs Ch. 14-B, B. Recovery of Appellate Costs and Attorney Fees.

Rutter, Cal. Practice Guide: Civil Appeals & Writs Ch. 14-D, D. Precedential Effect of Appellate Court Opinions.

Rutter, Cal. Practice Guide: Civil Appeals & Writs Ch. 15-C, C. Statutory Writs.

Rutter, Cal. Practice Guide: Civil Appeals & Writs Gen. Matls., Highlights.

Rutter, Cal. Practice Guide: Civ. Pro. Before Trial Ch. 1-A, A. Accepting a New Case.

Rutter, Cal. Practice Guide: Civ. Pro. Before Trial Ch. 1-B, B. Prelawsuit Investigations, Research and Analysis.

Rutter, Cal. Practice Guide: Civ. Pro. Before Trial Ch. 2-C, C. Joinder of Parties.

Rutter, Cal. Practice Guide: Civ. Pro. Before Trial Ch. 6-E, E. Amended and Supplemental Pleadings.

Rutter, Cal. Practice Guide: Civ. Pro. Before Trial Ch. 10-G, G. Ruling on Motion.

Rutter, Cal. Practice Guide: Civ. Pro. Before Trial Ch. 11-A, A. Voluntary Dismissals.

Rutter, Cal. Practice Guide: Civ. Pro. Before Trial Ch. 8B-3, Limitations on Right to Discovery.

Rutter, Cal. Practice Guide: Civ. Pro. Before Trial Ch. 7(I)-B, B. Motions to Strike.

Rutter, Cal. Practice Guide: Civ. Pro. Before Trial Ch. 7(II)-A, A. Introduction.

Rutter, Cal. Practice Guide: Civ. Pro. Before Trial Ch. 7(II)-B, B. Exemptions (Actions Not Subject to SLAPP Statutes).

Rutter, Cal. Practice Guide: Civ. Pro. Before Trial Ch. 7(II)-C, C. "Persons" Protected by Anti-SLAPP Statute.

Rutter, Cal. Practice Guide: Civ. Pro. Before Trial Ch. 7(II)-D, D. Activities Protected by Anti-SLAPP Statute.

Rutter, Cal. Practice Guide: Civ. Pro. Before Trial Ch. 7(II)-E, E. Causes of Action Subject to Being Stricken.

Rutter, Cal. Practice Guide: Civ. Pro. Before Trial Ch. 7(II)-F, F. Procedure.

Rutter, Cal. Practice Guide: Civ. Pro. Before Trial Ch. 7(II)-G, G. "SLAPPback" Motions.

Rutter, Cal. Practice Guide: Civ. Pro. Before Trial Gen. Matls., Highlights.

Rutter, Cal. Practice Guide: Civ. Pro. Before Trial Ch. 9(III)-B, B. Sanctions Under CCP § 128.5 (Pre-1995 and SLAPP Cases).

Rutter, Cal. Practice Guide: Civil Trials & Evidence Ch. 17-E, E. Attorney Fees as Costs.

California Practice Guide: Employment Litigation Ch. 1-B, B. Plaintiffs' Evaluation of Claims.

California Practice Guide: Employment Litigation Ch. 10-E, E. Harasser's Individual Liability.

California Practice Guide: Employment Litigation Ch. 19-D, D. Defendant's Challenges and Responses to Complaint.

Rutter, Cal. Practice Guide: Enforcing Judgments/Debts Ch. 2-C, C. Tort Liability.

Rutter, Cal. Practice Guide: Enforcing Judgments/Debts Ch. 6A-5, Amount Recoverable Under Judgment.

Rutter, Cal. Practice Guide: Enforcing Judgments/Debts Ch. 6D-6, Debtor's Recourse Against Execution Levy.

Rutter, Cal. Practice Guide: Enforcing Judgments/Debts Ch. 6A-5, Outline 5.

Rutter, Cal. Practice Guide: Fed.Civ.Pro. Before Trial Ch. 9-D, D. Motions to Dismiss (Rule 12(B)).

Rutter, Cal. Practice Guide: Fed.Civ.Pro. Before Trial Ch. 1-B, B. Federal vs. State Law.

Rutter, Cal. Practice Guide: Fed.Civ.Pro. Before Trial Ch. 16-G, G. Voluntary Dismissals.

Rutter, Cal. Practice Guide: Insurance Litigation Ch. 11-J, J. Other Torts Not Necessarily Related to Insurer "Bad Faith".

Rutter, Cal. Practice Guide: Insurance Litigation Ch. 15-F, F. Pretrial Motions.

Rutter, Cal. Practice Guide: Insurance Litigation Ch. 12D-N, N. Anti-SLAPP Motions.

Rutter, Cal. Practice Guide: Insurance Litigation Ch. 11-J, Outline J.

Rutter, Cal. Practice Guide: Landlord-Tenant Gen. Matls, Highlights.

Rutter, Cal. Practice Guide: Personal Injury Ch. 3-A, A. Introduction.

Rutter, Cal. Practice Guide: Personal Injury Ch. 5-E, E. Selected Pleading Issues.

Rutter, Cal. Practice Guide: Personal Injury Ch. 6-A, A. Scope of Discovery and Limitations.

Rutter, Cal. Practice Guide: Personal Injury Ch. 9-M, M. Verdicts and Judgment.

Rutter, Cal. Practice Guide: Personal Injury Ch. 9-M, Outline M.

Rutter, Cal. Practice Guide: Real Prop. Transactions Ch. 6-I, I. Real Property Foreclosures and Antideficiency Laws.

Rutter, Cal. Practice Guide: Prof. Responsibility Ch. 2-F, F. Print Media Advertising.

Rutter, Cal. Practice Guide: Prof. Responsibility Ch. 4-G, G. Procedural Considerations for Disqualification Based on Conflict of Interest.

Rutter, Cal. Practice Guide: Prof. Responsibility Ch. 6-D, D. Professional Liability.

Miller and Starr California Real Estate § 23:18, Remedies.

Miller and Starr California Real Estate § 27:20, Private Remedies.

Miller and Starr California Real Estate § 29:76, Systems for Resolving Defective Construction Disputes.

Miller and Starr California Real Estate § 34:64, Recovery of Attorney's Fees; Basis for Recovery.

Miller and Starr California Real Estate § 34:66, Examples of Actions in Which Fees Can be Recovered.

Miller and Starr California Real Estate § 35:50, Defenses to Petition to Compel Arbitration--In General.

Miller and Starr California Real Estate § 10:144, Remedies for Violation.

Miller and Starr California Real Estate § 10:185, Recording and Mailing.

Miller and Starr California Real Estate § 19:102, Enforcement and Remedies.

Miller and Starr California Real Estate § 19:217, Restrictions on Access and Reporting of Unlawful Detainer Actions.

Miller and Starr California Real Estate § 25A:15, Procedures for Preparing an Environmental Impact Report.

Miller and Starr California Real Estate § 34:146, "Anti-SLAPP" Litigation.

Miller and Starr California Real Estate § 25B:17.10, Members--Anti-SLAPP Motions.

14 NO. 1 Miller & Starr, California Real Estate Newsalert 9, Landlord and Tenant.

14 NO. 3 Miller & Starr, California Real Estate Newsalert 10, Landowners' Liability.

15 NO. 2 Miller & Starr, California Real Estate Newsalert 1, SLAPP Happy: An Analysis of California's Anti-SLAPP (Strategic Lawsuits Against Public Participation) Statute.

17 NO. 4 Miller & Starr, California Real Estate Newsalert 3, Commercial Arbitration.

18 NO. 2 Miller & Starr, California Real Estate Newsalert 7, Contracts.

18 NO. 6 Miller & Starr, California Real Estate Newsalert 8, Deeds of Trust.

18 NO. 2 Miller & Starr, California Real Estate Newsalert 12, Discrimination.

19 NO. 2 Miller & Starr, California Real Estate Newsalert 1, Anti-SLAPP Motions in Real Estate Litigation: an Update.

19 NO. 6 Miller & Starr, California Real Estate Newsalert 3, Alternative Dispute Resolution.

19 NO. 3 Miller & Starr, California Real Estate Newsalert 24, Remedies.

20 NO. 5 Miller & Starr, California Real Estate Newsalert 16, Judicial Remedies.

20 NO. 2 Miller & Starr, California Real Estate Newsalert 18, Landlord and Tenant.

20 NO. 4 Miller & Starr, California Real Estate Newsalert 34, Judicial Remedies.

20 NO. 4 Miller & Starr, California Real Estate Newsalert 40, Recording and Priorities.

21 NO. 5 Miller & Starr, California Real Estate Newsalert 18, Judicial Remedies.

22 NO. 2 Miller & Starr, California Real Estate Newsalert 6, Common Interest Developments.

22 NO. 2 Miller & Starr, California Real Estate Newsalert 15, Judicial Remedies.

22 NO. 1 Miller & Starr, California Real Estate Newsalert 19, Judicial Remedies.

23 NO. 1 Miller & Starr, California Real Estate Newsalert 14, Judicial Remedies.

Rutter Practice Guide: Fed.Civ.Pro. Bef.Trial(5th Cir) Ch. 1-B, B. Federal vs. State Law.

9 Witkin Cal. Proc. 5th Appeal § 172, Order on Special Motion to Strike SLAPP Suit.

9 Witkin Cal. Proc. 5th Appeal § 230, Money or Payment of Money.

7 Witkin Cal. Proc. 5th Judgment § 222, (S 222) Actions in Bad Faith.

7 Witkin Cal. Proc. 5th Judgment § 301, Fees Determined by Trial Court.

7 Witkin Cal. Proc. 5th Judgment § 312, Use of Lodestar Approach.

2 Witkin Cal. Proc. 5th Jurisdiction § 316, (S 316) Judgment Against.

5 Witkin Cal. Proc. 5th Pleading § 1009, Statutory Provisions.

5 Witkin Cal. Proc. 5th Pleading § 1017, (S 1017) Statutory Framework.

5 Witkin Cal. Proc. 5th Pleading § 1018, (S 1018) Statute is Constitutional.

5 Witkin Cal. Proc. 5th Pleading § 1019, (S 1019) in General.

5 Witkin Cal. Proc. 5th Pleading § 1020, (S 1020) Scope of "Arising From" Requirement.

5 Witkin Cal. Proc. 5th Pleading § 1021, (S 1021) Cases Involving Right of Petition.

5 Witkin Cal. Proc. 5th Pleading § 1022, in General.

5 Witkin Cal. Proc. 5th Pleading § 1023, Illustrations.

5 Witkin Cal. Proc. 5th Pleading § 1024, (S 1024) When Statement Need Not Concern Issue of Public Significance.

5 Witkin Cal. Proc. 5th Pleading § 1025, (S 1025) in General.

5 Witkin Cal. Proc. 5th Pleading § 1026, in General.

5 Witkin Cal. Proc. 5th Pleading § 1027, Illustrations.

5 Witkin Cal. Proc. 5th Pleading § 1028, (S 1028) Public Significance, Issue, or Interest Lacking.

5 Witkin Cal. Proc. 5th Pleading § 1029, (S 1029) Action Did Not Arise from Protected Activity.

5 Witkin Cal. Proc. 5th Pleading § 1030, (S 1030) Illegal Speech.

5 Witkin Cal. Proc. 5th Pleading § 1031, (S 1031) Miscellaneous Cases.

5 Witkin Cal. Proc. 5th Pleading § 1032, Parties.

§ 425.17. Legislative findings and declarations regarding California Anti-SLAPP Law; application of § 425.16

(a) The Legislature finds and declares that there has been a disturbing abuse of Section 425.16, the California Anti–SLAPP Law, which has undermined the exercise of the constitutional rights of freedom of speech and petition for the redress of grievances, contrary to the purpose and intent of Section 425.16. The Legislature finds and declares that it is in the public interest to encourage continued participation in matters of public significance, and that this participation should not be chilled through abuse of the judicial process or Section 425.16.

(b) Section 425.16 does not apply to any action brought solely in the public interest or on behalf of the general public if all of the following conditions exist:

(1) The plaintiff does not seek any relief greater than or different from the relief sought for the general public or a class of which the plaintiff is a member. A claim for attorney's fees, costs, or penalties does not constitute greater or different relief for purposes of this subdivision.

(2) The action, if successful, would enforce an important right affecting the public interest, and would confer a significant benefit, whether pecuniary or nonpecuniary, on the general public or a large class of persons.

(3) Private enforcement is necessary and places a disproportionate financial burden on the plaintiff in relation to the plaintiff's stake in the matter.

(c) Section 425.16 does not apply to any cause of action brought against a person primarily engaged in the business of selling or leasing goods or services, including, but not limited to, insurance, securities, or financial instruments, arising from any statement or conduct by that person if both of the following conditions exist:

(1) The statement or conduct consists of representations of fact about that person's or a business competitor's business operations, goods, or services, that is made for the purpose of obtaining approval for, promoting, or securing sales or leases of, or commercial transactions in, the person's goods or services, or the statement or conduct was made in the course of delivering the person's goods or services.

(2) The intended audience is an actual or potential buyer or customer, or a person likely to repeat the statement to, or otherwise influence, an actual or potential buyer or customer, or the statement or conduct arose out of or within the context of a regulatory approval process, proceeding, or investigation, except where the statement or conduct was made by a telephone corporation in the course of a proceeding before the California Public Utilities Commission and is the subject of a lawsuit brought by a competitor, notwithstanding that the conduct or statement concerns an important public issue.

(d) Subdivisions (b) and (c) do not apply to any of the following:

(1) Any person enumerated in subdivision (b) of Section 2 of Article I of the California Constitution or Section 1070 of the Evidence Code, or any person engaged in the dissemination of ideas or expression in any book or academic journal, while engaged in the gathering, receiving, or processing of information for communication to the public.

(2) Any action against any person or entity based upon the creation, dissemination, exhibition, advertisement, or other similar promotion of any dramatic, literary, musical, political, or artistic work, including, but not limited to, a motion picture or television program, or an article published in a newspaper or magazine of general circulation.

(3) Any nonprofit organization that receives more than 50 percent of its annual revenues from federal, state, or local government grants, awards, programs, or reimbursements for services rendered.

(e) If any trial court denies a special motion to strike on the grounds that the action or cause of action is exempt pursuant to this section, the appeal provisions in subdivision (i) of Section 425.16 and paragraph (13) of subdivision (a) of Section 904.1 do not apply to that action or cause of action. *(Added by Stats.2003, c. 338 (S.B.515), § 1. Amended by Stats.2011, c. 296 (A.B.1023), § 36.5.)*

Research References

Rutter, Cal. Practice Guide: Civil Appeals & Writs Ch. 2-B, B. Appealable Judgments and Orders.

Rutter, Cal. Practice Guide: Civil Appeals & Writs Ch. 2-C, C. Nonappealable Orders.

Rutter, Cal. Practice Guide: Civ. Pro. Before Trial Ch. 7(II)-A, A. Introduction.

Rutter, Cal. Practice Guide: Civ. Pro. Before Trial Ch. 7(II)-B, B. Exemptions (Actions Not Subject to SLAPP Statutes).

Rutter, Cal. Practice Guide: Civ. Pro. Before Trial Ch. 7(II)-C, C. "Persons" Protected by Anti-SLAPP Statute.

Rutter, Cal. Practice Guide: Civ. Pro. Before Trial Ch. 7(II)-D, D. Activities Protected by Anti-SLAPP Statute.

Rutter, Cal. Practice Guide: Civ. Pro. Before Trial Ch. 7(II)-F, F. Procedure.

Rutter, Cal. Practice Guide: Personal Injury Ch. 5-E, E. Selected Pleading Issues.

Rutter, Cal. Practice Guide: Prof. Responsibility Ch. 2-F, F. Print Media Advertising.

Rutter, Cal. Practice Guide: Prof. Responsibility Ch. 6-D, D. Professional Liability.

Miller and Starr California Real Estate § 27:20, Private Remedies.

Miller and Starr California Real Estate § 34:146, "Anti-SLAPP" Litigation.

Miller and Starr California Real Estate § 25B:17.10, Members--Anti-SLAPP Motions.

15 NO. 2 Miller & Starr, California Real Estate Newsalert 1, SLAPP Happy: An Analysis of California's Anti-SLAPP (Strategic Lawsuits Against Public Participation) Statute.

9 Witkin Cal. Proc. 5th Appeal § 172, Order on Special Motion to Strike SLAPP Suit.

5 Witkin Cal. Proc. 5th Pleading § 1017, (S 1017) Statutory Framework.

5 Witkin Cal. Proc. 5th Pleading § 1026, in General.

5 Witkin Cal. Proc. 5th Pleading § 1027, Illustrations.

5 Witkin Cal. Proc. 5th Pleading § 1028, (S 1028) Public Significance, Issue, or Interest Lacking.

5 Witkin Cal. Proc. 5th Pleading § 1031, (S 1031) Miscellaneous Cases.

5 Witkin Cal. Proc. 5th Pleading § 1039, Appeal.
5 Witkin Cal. Proc. 5th Pleading § 1041, (S 1041) Right of Prevailing Plaintiff.

§ 425.18. SLAPPback actions; motion to strike; limitations periods; discovery; remedies

(a) The Legislature finds and declares that a SLAPPback is distinguishable in character and origin from the ordinary malicious prosecution action. The Legislature further finds and declares that a SLAPPback cause of action should be treated differently, as provided in this section, from an ordinary malicious prosecution action because a SLAPPback is consistent with the Legislature's intent to protect the valid exercise of the constitutional rights of free speech and petition by its deterrent effect on SLAPP (strategic lawsuit against public participation) litigation and by its restoration of public confidence in participatory democracy.

(b) For purposes of this section, the following terms have the following meanings:

(1) "SLAPPback" means any cause of action for malicious prosecution or abuse of process arising from the filing or maintenance of a prior cause of action that has been dismissed pursuant to a special motion to strike under Section 425.16.

(2) "Special motion to strike" means a motion made pursuant to Section 425.16.

(c) The provisions of subdivisions (c), (f), (g), and (i) of Section 425.16, and paragraph (13) of subdivision (a) of Section 904.1, shall not apply to a special motion to strike a SLAPPback.

(d)(1) A special motion to strike a SLAPPback shall be filed within any one of the following periods of time, as follows:

(A) Within 120 days of the service of the complaint.

(B) At the court's discretion, within six months of the service of the complaint.

(C) At the court's discretion, at any later time in extraordinary cases due to no fault of the defendant and upon written findings of the court stating the extraordinary case and circumstance.

(2) The motion shall be scheduled by the clerk of the court for a hearing not more than 30 days after the service of the motion unless the docket conditions of the court require a later hearing.

(e) A party opposing a special motion to strike a SLAPPback may file an ex parte application for a continuance to obtain necessary discovery. If it appears that facts essential to justify opposition to that motion may exist, but cannot then be presented, the court shall grant a reasonable continuance to permit the party to obtain affidavits or conduct discovery or may make any other order as may be just.

(f) If the court finds that a special motion to strike a SLAPPback is frivolous or solely intended to cause unnecessary delay, the court shall award costs and reasonable attorney's fees to a plaintiff prevailing on the motion, pursuant to Section 128.5.

(g) Upon entry of an order denying a special motion to strike a SLAPPback claim, or granting the special motion to strike as to some but less than all causes of action alleged in a complaint containing a SLAPPback claim, an aggrieved party may, within 20 days after service of a written notice of the entry of the order, petition an appropriate reviewing court for a peremptory writ.

(h) A special motion to strike may not be filed against a SLAPPback by a party whose filing or maintenance of the prior cause of action from which the SLAPPback arises was illegal as a matter of law.

(i) This section does not apply to a SLAPPback filed by a public entity. (Added by Stats.2005, c. 535 (A.B.1158), § 2, eff. Oct. 5, 2005.)

Research References

Rutter, Cal. Practice Guide: Civil Appeals & Writs Ch. 2-B, B. Appealable Judgments and Orders.
Rutter, Cal. Practice Guide: Civil Appeals & Writs Ch. 15-C, C. Statutory Writs.
Rutter, Cal. Practice Guide: Civ. Pro. Before Trial Ch. 7(II)-D, D. Activities Protected by Anti-SLAPP Statute.
Rutter, Cal. Practice Guide: Civ. Pro. Before Trial Ch. 7(II)-G, G. "SLAPPback" Motions.
Rutter, Cal. Practice Guide: Enforcing Judgments/Debts Ch. 2-C, C. Tort Liability.
Rutter, Cal. Practice Guide: Enforcing Judgments/Debts Ch. 2-C, Outline C.
Rutter, Cal. Practice Guide: Personal Injury Ch. 3-A, A. Introduction.
Rutter, Cal. Practice Guide: Personal Injury Ch. 5-E, E. Selected Pleading Issues.
Rutter, Cal. Practice Guide: Prof. Responsibility Ch. 6-D, D. Professional Liability.
Rutter, Cal. Practice Guide: Prof. Responsibility Ch. 6-D, Outline D.
Miller and Starr California Real Estate § 34:146, "Anti-SLAPP" Litigation.
19 NO. 2 Miller & Starr, California Real Estate Newsalert 1, Anti-SLAPP Motions in Real Estate Litigation: an Update.
9 Witkin Cal. Proc. 5th Appeal § 172, Order on Special Motion to Strike SLAPP Suit.
5 Witkin Cal. Proc. 5th Pleading § 1043, in General.
5 Witkin Cal. Proc. 5th Pleading § 1044, Exceptions.
5 Witkin, California Summary 10th Torts § 469, Nature of Tort.
5 Witkin, California Summary 10th Torts § 517, (S 517) Nature of Tort.

§ 425.50. Allegation of construction-related accessibility claim; statement of facts in complaint; verification by plaintiff; amendment of complaint

(a) An allegation of a construction-related accessibility claim in a complaint, as defined in subdivision (a) of Section 55.52 of the Civil Code, shall state facts sufficient to allow a reasonable person to identify the basis of the violation or violations supporting the claim, including all of the following:

(1) A plain language explanation of the specific access barrier or barriers the individual encountered, or by which the individual alleges he or she was deterred, with sufficient information about the location of the alleged barrier to enable a reasonable person to identify the access barrier.

(2) The way in which the barrier denied the individual full and equal use or access, or in which it deterred the individual, on each particular occasion.

(3) The date or dates of each particular occasion on which the claimant encountered the specific access barrier, or on which he or she was deterred.

(b) A complaint alleging a construction-related accessibility claim, as those terms are defined in subdivision (a) of Section 55.3 of the Civil Code, shall be verified by the plaintiff. A complaint filed without verification shall be subject to a motion to strike.

(c) Nothing in this section shall limit the right of a plaintiff to amend a complaint under Section 472, or with leave of the court under Section 473. However, an amended pleading alleging a construction-related accessibility claim shall be pled as required by subdivision (a).

(d) This section shall become operative on January 1, 2013. (Added by Stats.2012, c. 383 (S.B.1186), § 13, eff. Sept. 19, 2012, operative Jan. 1, 2013. Amended by Stats.2013, c. 76 (A.B.383), § 22.)

ARTICLE 2.   COMPULSORY CROSS–COMPLAINTS

§ 426.10. Definitions

As used in this article:

(a) "Complaint" means a complaint or cross-complaint.

(b) "Plaintiff" means a person who files a complaint or cross-complaint.

(c) "Related cause of action" means a cause of action which arises out of the same transaction, occurrence, or series of transactions or occurrences as the cause of action which the plaintiff alleges in his complaint. *(Added by Stats.1971, c. 244, p. 379, § 23, operative July 1, 1972.)*

Law Revision Commission Comments

The definition in Section 426.10 of "related cause of action" provides a convenient means for referring to a cause of action which arises out of the same transaction or occurrence. Subdivision (c) follows prior law (former Code of Civil Procedure Section 439) which was judicially interpreted to include a series of related acts or conduct. Brunswig Drug Co. v. Springer, 55 Cal.App.2d 444, 130 P.2d 758 (1942) ("transaction" embraces the entire series of acts and mutual conduct of the parties); Sylvester v. Soulsburg, 252 Cal.App.2d 185, 60 Cal.Rptr. 218 (1967) (a continuous sequence of acts by vendors of real and personal property—including suit to terminate sale contracts, entry upon the real property, taking possession of the personal property, and remaining in possession for a time—constituted a single transaction giving rise to purchasers' claim for damages for trespass).

Recommendation and study relating to counterclaims and cross-complaints, joinder of causes of action, and related provisions. 10 Cal.L.Revision and Comm.Reports 501 (1971); Report of Senate Committee on Judiciary on Senate Bill 201, S.Journal, April 1, 1971; Communication From Assembly Committee on Judiciary on Senate Bill 201, A.Journal, June 16, 1971.

Research References

Rutter, Cal. Practice Guide: Civ. Pro. Before Trial Ch. 6-D, D. Cross-Complaint.
Rutter, Cal. Practice Guide: Insurance Litigation Ch. 15-B, B. Actions by Insurers.
Rutter, Cal. Practice Guide: Personal Injury Ch. 5-E, E. Selected Pleading Issues.
5 Witkin Cal. Proc. 5th Pleading § 1177, Failure to Plead as Bar.
5 Witkin Cal. Proc. 5th Pleading § 1179, (S 1179) Other Exceptions.

§ 426.30. Waiver of related cause of action; exceptions

(a) Except as otherwise provided by statute, if a party against whom a complaint has been filed and served fails to allege in a cross-complaint any related cause of action which (at the time of serving his answer to the complaint) he has against the plaintiff, such party may not thereafter in any other action assert against the plaintiff the related cause of action not pleaded.

(b) This section does not apply if either of the following is established:

(1) The court in which the action is pending does not have jurisdiction to render a personal judgment against the person who failed to plead the related cause of action.

(2) The person who failed to plead the related cause of action did not file an answer to the complaint against him. *(Added by Stats.1971, c. 244, p. 379, § 23, operative July 1, 1972.)*

Research References

Rutter, Cal. Practice Guide: Civ. Pro. Before Trial Ch. 6-D, D. Cross-Complaint.

Research References

Rutter, Cal. Practice Guide: Civ. Pro. Before Trial Ch. 11-A, A. Voluntary Dismissals.
California Practice Guide: Employment Litigation Ch. 19-D, D. Defendant's Challenges and Responses to Complaint.
Rutter, Cal. Practice Guide: Insurance Litigation Ch. 15-B, B. Actions by Insurers.
Rutter, Cal. Practice Guide: Insurance Litigation Ch. 7B-E, E. Scope of Duty to Defend.
Rutter, Cal. Practice Guide: Insurance Litigation Ch. 7B-L, L. Defense Counsel's Obligations-Professional Responsibility Considerations.
Rutter, Cal. Practice Guide: Insurance Litigation Ch. 12B-C, C. Bad Faith Liability Despite Settlement of Third Party Claims.
Rutter, Cal. Practice Guide: Personal Injury Ch. 5-E, E. Selected Pleading Issues.
Miller and Starr California Real Estate § 19:215, Nature of the Remedy--Effect of Tenant's Abandonment Before Trial.
14 NO. 3 Miller & Starr, California Real Estate Newsalert 13, Remedies.
3 Witkin Cal. Proc. 5th Actions § 449, (S 449) Cross-Demands Deemed Compensated.
7 Witkin Cal. Proc. 5th Judgment § 99, (S 99) General Rule in Superior Court.
7 Witkin Cal. Proc. 5th Judgment § 348, Waiver and Estoppel.
5 Witkin Cal. Proc. 5th Pleading § 1166, When Setoff is Improper.
5 Witkin Cal. Proc. 5th Pleading § 1177, Failure to Plead as Bar.
5 Witkin Cal. Proc. 5th Pleading § 1178, (S 1178) Court Without Jurisdiction.
5 Witkin Cal. Proc. 5th Pleading § 1179, (S 1179) Other Exceptions.
12 Witkin, California Summary 10th Real Property § 733, Governing Law.

§ 426.40. Application

This article does not apply if any of the following are established:

(a) The cause of action not pleaded requires for its adjudication the presence of additional parties over whom the court cannot acquire jurisdiction.

(b) Both the court in which the action is pending and any other court to which the action is transferrable pursuant to Section 396 are prohibited by the federal or state constitution or by a statute from entertaining the cause of action not pleaded.

(c) At the time the action was commenced, the cause of action not pleaded was the subject of another pending action. *(Added by Stats.1971, c. 244, p. 379, § 23, operative July 1, 1972.)*

Research References

Rutter, Cal. Practice Guide: Civ. Pro. Before Trial Ch. 6-D, D. Cross-Complaint.
Rutter, Cal. Practice Guide: Civ. Pro. Before Trial Ch. 11-A, A. Voluntary Dismissals.
Rutter, Cal. Practice Guide: Personal Injury Ch. 5-E, E. Selected Pleading Issues.
5 Witkin Cal. Proc. 5th Pleading § 1178, (S 1178) Court Without Jurisdiction.
5 Witkin Cal. Proc. 5th Pleading § 1179, (S 1179) Other Exceptions.

§ 426.50. Failure to plead cause of action; notice; amendment

A party who fails to plead a cause of action subject to the requirements of this article, whether through oversight, inadvertence, mistake, neglect, or other cause, may apply to the court for leave to amend his pleading, or to file a cross-complaint, to assert such cause at any time during the course of the action. The court, after notice to the adverse party, shall grant, upon such terms as may be just to the parties, leave to amend the pleading, or to file the cross-complaint, to assert such cause if the party who failed to plead the cause acted in good faith. This subdivision shall be liberally construed to avoid forfeiture of causes of action. *(Added by Stats.1971, c. 244, p. 379, § 23, operative July 1, 1972.)*

Research References

Rutter, Cal. Practice Guide: Civ. Pro. Before Trial Ch. 6-D, D. Cross-Complaint.
Rutter, Cal. Practice Guide: Civ. Pro. Before Trial Ch. 11-A, A. Voluntary Dismissals.
Rutter, Cal. Practice Guide: Personal Injury Ch. 5-E, E. Selected Pleading Issues.
3 Witkin Cal. Proc. 5th Actions § 453, (S 453) Amended Cross-Complaint.
5 Witkin Cal. Proc. 5th Pleading § 1177, Failure to Plead as Bar.
5 Witkin Cal. Proc. 5th Pleading § 1180, Relief from Failure to Plead.

§ 426.60. Application to civil actions; exceptions

(a) This article applies only to civil actions and does not apply to special proceedings.

(b) This article does not apply to actions in the small claims court.

(c) This article does not apply where the only relief sought is a declaration of the rights and duties of the respective parties in an action for declaratory relief under Chapter 8 (commencing with Section 1060) of Title 14 of this part. *(Added by Stats.1971, c. 244, p. 380, § 23, operative July 1, 1971.)*

Research References

Rutter, Cal. Practice Guide: Civ. Pro. Before Trial Ch. 6-D, D. Cross-Complaint.
Rutter, Cal. Practice Guide: Personal Injury Ch. 5-E, E. Selected Pleading Issues.
5 Witkin Cal. Proc. 5th Pleading § 1179, (S 1179) Other Exceptions.

§ 426.70. Eminent domain; application of article; related cause of action

(a) Notwithstanding subdivision (a) of Section 426.60, this article applies to eminent domain proceedings.

(b) The related cause of action may be asserted by cross-complaint in an eminent domain proceeding whether or not the party asserting such cause of action has presented a claim in compliance with Part 3 (commencing with Section 900) of Division 3.6 of Title 1 of the Government Code to the plaintiff in the original eminent domain proceeding. *(Added by Stats.1975, c. 1240, p. 3160, § 3, operative July 1, 1976.)*

Law Revision Commission Comments

Subdivision (a) of Section 426.70—by making this article applicable to eminent domain proceedings—codifies the principle that a related cause of action must be asserted against the plaintiff in an eminent domain action or it is barred. Klopping v. City of Whittier, 8 Cal.3d 39, 58, 500 P.2d 1345, 1360, 104 Cal.Rptr. 1, 16 (1972) (damages caused by pre-condemnation announcements). The related cause must be asserted as a cross-complaint. See Section 426.30.

Subdivision (b) of Section 426.70 dispenses with the requirement that a claim be presented to a public entity as a condition to bringing a compulsory cross-complaint against the public entity in an eminent domain proceeding. Compare Govt. Code §§ 905, 905.2; County of San Luis Obispo v. Ranchita Cattle Co., 16 Cal.App.3d 383, 94 Cal.Rptr. 73 (1971). Accordingly, the cause of action is not barred by mere failure to present the claim within the time specified in the public entity claims statute, and the cause may be asserted by cross-complaint in the eminent domain action whether or not a claim has been presented to the public entity. However, subdivision (b) eliminates the requirement only as against the plaintiff. Actions against third parties are not affected, nor are any relevant statutes of limitations.

Eminent domain law. 13 Cal.L.Rev.Comm. Reports 1001 (1975).

Research References

Miller and Starr California Real Estate § 30A:60, Cross-Complaint.

5 Witkin Cal. Proc. 5th Pleading § 1179, (S 1179) Other Exceptions.

ARTICLE 3. PERMISSIVE JOINDER OF CAUSES OF ACTION

§ 427.10. Joinder of other causes of action by plaintiff

(a) A plaintiff who in a complaint, alone or with coplaintiffs, alleges a cause of action against one or more defendants may unite with such cause any other causes which he has either alone or with any coplaintiffs against any of such defendants.

(b) Causes of action may be joined in a cross-complaint in accordance with Sections 428.10 and 428.30. *(Added by Stats. 1971, c. 244, p. 380, § 23, operative July 1, 1972.)*

Research References

Rutter, Cal. Practice Guide: Civ. Pro. Before Trial Ch. 2-C, C. Joinder of Parties.
Rutter, Cal. Practice Guide: Civ. Pro. Before Trial Ch. 6-B, B. Complaints.
Rutter, Cal. Practice Guide: Fed.Civ.Pro. Before Trial Ch. 1-D, D. Choosing Between State and Federal Courts.
Rutter, Cal. Practice Guide: Fed.Civ.Pro. Before Trial Ch. 2B-1, General Considerations.
Rutter, Cal. Practice Guide: Fed.Civ.Pro. Before Trial Ch. 2D-4, What Cases and Claims Are Removable.
Rutter, Cal. Practice Guide: Personal Injury Ch. 5-C, C. Selected Issues Affecting Parties.
Rutter, Cal. Practice Guide: Personal Injury Ch. 5-E, E. Selected Pleading Issues.
3 Witkin Cal. Proc. 5th Actions § 882, (S 882) One Cause of Action.
4 Witkin Cal. Proc. 5th Pleading § 54, (S 54) Injuries to Person and Property from One Act.
4 Witkin Cal. Proc. 5th Pleading § 337, (S 337) Unrestricted Joinder of Causes.
4 Witkin Cal. Proc. 5th Pleading § 339, (S 339) Cause Need Not Affect All Parties.

ARTICLE 4. CROSS–COMPLAINTS

§ 428.10. Filing of cross-complaint; causes of action

A party against whom a cause of action has been asserted in a complaint or cross-complaint may file a cross-complaint setting forth either or both of the following:

(a) Any cause of action he has against any of the parties who filed the complaint or cross-complaint against him. Nothing in this subdivision authorizes the filing of a cross-complaint against the plaintiff in an action commenced under Title 7 (commencing with Section 1230.010) of Part 3.

(b) Any cause of action he has against a person alleged to be liable thereon, whether or not such person is already a party to the action, if the cause of action asserted in his cross-complaint (1) arises out of the same transaction, occurrence, or series of transactions or occurrences as the cause brought against him or (2) asserts a claim, right, or interest in the property or controversy which is the subject of the cause brought against him. *(Added by Stats.1971, c. 244, p. 380, § 23, operative July 1, 1972. Amended by Stats.1975, c. 1240, p. 3160, § 4, operative July 1, 1976.)*

Law Revision Commission Comments

Section 428.10 is amended to conform to the numbering of the Eminent Domain Law.

Research References

Rutter, Cal. Practice Guide: Civ. Pro. Before Trial Ch. 6-D, D. Cross-Complaint.

Rutter, Cal. Practice Guide: Insurance Litigation Ch. 7B-E, E. Scope of Duty to Defend.

Rutter, Cal. Practice Guide: Personal Injury Ch. 5-E, E. Selected Pleading Issues.

Miller and Starr California Real Estate § 3:36, Tort Liability and Vicarious Liability; Generally.

Miller and Starr California Real Estate § 10:76, Payment by Setoff; General Rules.

Miller and Starr California Real Estate § 29:75, Indemnity and the 10-Year Period of Repose.

3 Witkin Cal. Proc. 5th Actions § 613, (S 613) Exception Held Applicable.

3 Witkin Cal. Proc. 5th Actions § 614, (S 614) Exception Held Inapplicable.

3 Witkin Cal. Proc. 5th Actions § 617, Defects in Construction of Residential Real Property: Ten Years.

4 Witkin Cal. Proc. 5th Pleading § 67, (S 67) Designation of Parties.

4 Witkin Cal. Proc. 5th Pleading § 337, (S 337) Unrestricted Joinder of Causes.

5 Witkin Cal. Proc. 5th Pleading § 1167, (S 1167) Nature and Scope.

5 Witkin Cal. Proc. 5th Pleading § 1169, in General.

5 Witkin Cal. Proc. 5th Pleading § 1170, Exceptions.

5 Witkin Cal. Proc. 5th Pleading § 1171, Related Causes of Action.

5 Witkin Cal. Proc. 5th Pleading § 1172, Joinder of Cross-Defendants.

5 Witkin Cal. Proc. 5th Pleading § 1173, (S 1173) New Party Cross-Complainant.

5 Witkin Cal. Proc. 5th Pleading § 1174, (S 1174) Joinder of Causes of Action.

5 Witkin Cal. Proc. 5th Pleading § 1175, (S 1175) Cross-Complaint to Cross-Complaint.

5 Witkin Cal. Proc. 5th Pleading § 1170A, (S 1170A) (New)-Unrestricted Cross-Complaint Against Codefendant.

6 Witkin, California Summary 10th Torts § 1357, Adoption of Doctrine.

4 Witkin, California Summary 10th Negotiable Instruments § 82, (S 82) in General.

8 Witkin, California Summary 10th Constitutional Law § 1276, (S 1276) Cross-Complaint in Condemnation Action.

§ 428.20. Joinder of person as cross-party

When a person files a cross-complaint as authorized by Section 428.10, he may join any person as a cross-complainant or cross-defendant, whether or not such person is already a party to the action, if, had the cross-complaint been filed as an independent action, the joinder of that party would have been permitted by the statutes governing joinder of parties. *(Added by Stats. 1971, c. 244, p. 380, § 23, operative July 1, 1972.)*

Law Revision Commission Comments

Section 428.20 makes clear that, when a cross-complaint is permitted under Section 428.10, persons may be joined as cross-complainants who were not previously parties to the action and the cross-complaint may be brought against persons who were not previously parties to the action. Thus, Section 428.20 is consistent with the general principle that a cross-complaint is to be treated as if it were a complaint in an independent action.

Section 428.20 retains prior law that a cross-complaint may be brought against a person or persons not previously parties to the action if it asserts a cause of action that arises out of the same transaction or occurrence; there is no requirement that it assert a cause of action against a person already a party to the action. See former Code of Civil Procedure Section 442. However, where the cause of action asserted in the cross-complaint does not arise out of the same transaction or occurrence. Section 428.20 provides a more liberal rule than prior law. Formerly, a counterclaim could be brought against a plaintiff only; a third person could not be

joined because this was precluded by the "several judgment" requirement of former Code of Civil Procedure Section 438. This limitation on joinder of parties is not continued in Section 428.20. For further discussion, see Friedenthal, Joinder of Claims, Counterclaims, and Cross-Complaints: Suggested Revision of the California Provisions, 23 Stan. L. Rev. 1, 21–23 (1970).

Research References

Rutter, Cal. Practice Guide: Civ. Pro. Before Trial Ch. 6-D, D. Cross-Complaint.

Rutter, Cal. Practice Guide: Personal Injury Ch. 5-E, E. Selected Pleading Issues.

4 Witkin Cal. Proc. 5th Pleading § 67, (S 67) Designation of Parties.

4 Witkin Cal. Proc. 5th Pleading § 216, Other Procedures Compared.

5 Witkin Cal. Proc. 5th Pleading § 1172, Joinder of Cross-Defendants.

5 Witkin Cal. Proc. 5th Pleading § 1173, (S 1173) New Party Cross-Complainant.

6 Witkin, California Summary 10th Torts § 1357, Adoption of Doctrine.

§ 428.30. Joinder of other causes of action by cross-complainant

Where a person files a cross-complaint as authorized by Section 428.10, he may unite with the cause of action asserted in the cross-complaint any other causes of action he has against any of the cross-defendants, other than the plaintiff in an eminent domain proceeding, whether or not such cross-defendant is already a party to the action. *(Added by Stats.1971, c. 244, p. 381, § 23, operative July 1, 1972.)*

Research References

Rutter, Cal. Practice Guide: Civ. Pro. Before Trial Ch. 6-D, D. Cross-Complaint.

Rutter, Cal. Practice Guide: Personal Injury Ch. 5-E, E. Selected Pleading Issues.

4 Witkin Cal. Proc. 5th Pleading § 67, (S 67) Designation of Parties.

4 Witkin Cal. Proc. 5th Pleading § 337, (S 337) Unrestricted Joinder of Causes.

5 Witkin Cal. Proc. 5th Pleading § 1174, (S 1174) Joinder of Causes of Action.

§ 428.40. Separate document

The cross-complaint shall be a separate document. *(Added by Stats.1971, c. 244, p. 381, § 23, operative July 1, 1972.)*

Law Revision Commission Comments

Section 428.40 requires the cross-complaint to be a separate document. Under prior practice, a counterclaim could be a part of the answer. However, the counterclaim is now abolished. See Section 428.80.

Research References

Rutter, Cal. Practice Guide: Civ. Pro. Before Trial Ch. 6-D, D. Cross-Complaint.

5 Witkin Cal. Proc. 5th Pleading § 1167, (S 1167) Nature and Scope.

§ 428.50. Filing of cross-complaint; leave of court

(a) A party shall file a cross-complaint against any of the parties who filed the complaint or cross-complaint against him or her before or at the same time as the answer to the complaint or cross-complaint.

(b) Any other cross-complaint may be filed at any time before the court has set a date for trial.

(c) A party shall obtain leave of court to file any cross-complaint except one filed within the time specified in subdivision (a) or (b). Leave may be granted in the interest of justice at any time during the course of the action. *(Added by Stats.1971, c. 244, p. 381, § 23, operative July 1, 1972. Amended by Stats.1983, c. 176, § 1.)*

Research References

Rutter, Cal. Practice Guide: Civ. Pro. Before Trial Ch. 6-D, D. Cross-Complaint.

Rutter, Cal. Practice Guide: Civ. Pro. Before Trial Ch. 11-A, A. Voluntary Dismissals.

Rutter, Cal. Practice Guide: Personal Injury Ch. 5-E, E. Selected Pleading Issues.

Miller and Starr California Real Estate § 19:215, Nature of the Remedy-- Effect of Tenant's Abandonment Before Trial.

5 Witkin Cal. Proc. 5th Pleading § 1168, (S 1168) Time to File.

§ 428.60. Service; appearance

A cross-complaint shall be served on each of the parties in an action in the following manner:

(1) If a party has not appeared in the action, a summons upon the cross-complaint shall be issued and served upon him in the same manner as upon commencement of an original action.

(2) If a party has appeared in the action, the cross-complaint shall be served upon his attorney, or upon the party if he has appeared without an attorney, in the manner provided for service of summons or in the manner provided by Chapter 5 (commencing with Section 1010) of Title 14 of Part 2 of this code. *(Added by Stats.1971, c. 244, p. 381, § 23, operative July 1, 1972. Amended by Stats.1974, c. 429, p. 1041, § 1.)*

Law Revision Commission Comments

Section 428.60 continues without substantive change requirements that were imposed under former Code of Civil Procedure Section 442.

Research References

Rutter, Cal. Practice Guide: Civ. Pro. Before Trial Ch. 6-D, D. Cross-Complaint.

3 Witkin Cal. Proc. 5th Actions § 1020, (S 1020) No Extension of Time.

5 Witkin Cal. Proc. 5th Pleading § 1167, (S 1167) Nature and Scope.

§ 428.70. Definitions

(a) As used in this section:

(1) "Third-party plaintiff" means a person against whom a cause of action has been asserted in a complaint or cross-complaint, who claims the right to recover all or part of any amounts for which he may be held liable on such cause of action from a third person, and who files a cross-complaint stating such claim as a cause of action against the third person.

(2) "Third-party defendant" means the person who is alleged in a cross-complaint filed by a third-party plaintiff to be liable to the third-party plaintiff if the third-party plaintiff is held liable on the claim against him.

(b) In addition to the other rights and duties a third-party defendant has under this article, he may, at the time he files his answer to the cross-complaint, file as a separate document a special answer alleging against the person who asserted the cause of action against the third-party plaintiff any defenses which the third-party plaintiff has to such cause of action. The special answer shall be served on the third-party plaintiff and on the person who asserted the cause of action against the third-party plaintiff. *(Added by Stats.1971, c. 244, p. 381, § 23, operative July 1, 1972.)*

Law Revision Commission Comments

Section 428.70 makes clear that, in addition to all rights and duties of a party against whom a cross-complaint has been filed, a third-party defendant has the right to assert any defenses which the third-party plaintiff could have asserted against the party who pleaded the cause of action against the third-party plaintiff.

The special answer provided by Section 428.70 is designed primarily to meet the problem that arises where a plaintiff sues a defendant and the defendant cross-complains against a third party for indemnity. To protect himself from the defendant's failure or neglect to assert a proper defense to the plaintiff's action, through collusion or otherwise, the third-party defendant is allowed to assert any defenses available to the original defendant directly against the plaintiff.

Research References

Rutter, Cal. Practice Guide: Civil Appeals & Writs Ch. 2-B, B. Appealable Judgments and Orders.

Rutter, Cal. Practice Guide: Civ. Pro. Before Trial Ch. 6-D, D. Cross-Complaint.

Rutter, Cal. Practice Guide: Personal Injury Ch. 5-E, E. Selected Pleading Issues.

9 Witkin Cal. Proc. 5th Appeal § 111, (S 111) Order Striking Special Answer by Third-Party Defendant.

4 Witkin Cal. Proc. 5th Pleading § 67, (S 67) Designation of Parties.

5 Witkin Cal. Proc. 5th Pleading § 1176, (S 1176) Special Answer by Third-Party Defendant.

§ 428.80. Abolition of counterclaim

The counterclaim is abolished. Any cause of action that formerly was asserted by a counterclaim shall be asserted by a cross-complaint. Where any statute refers to asserting a cause of action as a counterclaim, such cause shall be asserted as a cross-complaint. The erroneous designation of a pleading as a counterclaim shall not affect its validity, but such pleading shall be deemed to be a cross-complaint. *(Added by Stats.1971, c. 244, p. 381, § 23, operative July 1, 1972.)*

Law Revision Commission Comments

Section 428.80 abolishes the counterclaim. Section 428.10 provides for a cross-complaint that permits a party to assert any cause of action he formerly could have asserted as a counterclaim. There is no provision for counterclaims under the revised pleading rules. However, although conforming changes have been made in various codes, sections may be found that refer to counterclaims. *E.g.*, Com.Code § 1201(1), (2), (13). Section 428.80 makes clear that these statutes are to be interpreted in a manner consistent with the revised pleading provisions and that the causes of action referred to in these statutes are to be asserted as cross-complaints, not as counterclaims.

Research References

3 Witkin Cal. Proc. 5th Actions § 448, Statute Runs If Affirmative Relief is Sought.

5 Witkin Cal. Proc. 5th Pleading § 1167, (S 1167) Nature and Scope.

ARTICLE 5. CONTENTS OF DOCUMENTS IN PARTICULAR ACTIONS OR PROCEEDINGS

Section
429.30. Contents of complaint.

§ 429.30. Contents of complaint

(a) As used in this section:

(1) "Complaint" includes a cross-complaint.

(2) "Plaintiff" includes the person filing a cross-complaint.

(b) If the complaint contains a demand for relief on account of the alleged infringement of the plaintiff's rights in and to a literary, artistic, or intellectual production, there shall be attached to the complaint a copy of the production as to which the infringement is claimed and a copy of the alleged infringing production. If, by reason of bulk or the nature of the production, it is not practicable to attach a copy to the complaint, that fact and the reasons why it is impracticable to attach a copy of the production to the complaint shall be alleged; and the court, in connection with any demurrer, motion, or other proceedings in the cause in which a knowledge of the contents of such production may be necessary or desirable, shall make such order for a view of the production not attached as will suit the convenience of the court to the end that the contents of such production may be deemed to be a part of the complaint to the same extent and with the same force as though such production had been capable of being and had been attached to the complaint. The attachment of any such production in accordance with the provisions of this section shall not be deemed a making public of the production within the meaning of Section 983 of the Civil Code. *(Added by Stats.1971, c. 244, p. 382, § 23, operative July 1, 1972.)*

Law Revision Commission Comments

Section 429.30 continues the provisions of the last portion of subdivision 3 of former Section 426 of the Code of Civil Procedure, but subdivision (a) has been added to extend these provisions to cross-complaints.

Research References

4 Witkin Cal. Proc. 5th Pleading § 471, Superior Court.
5 Witkin Cal. Proc. 5th Pleading § 708, Copy or View of Production.

CHAPTER 3. OBJECTIONS TO PLEADINGS; DENIALS AND DEFENSES

ARTICLE 1. OBJECTIONS TO PLEADINGS

§ 430.10. Objection by defendant; grounds

The party against whom a complaint or cross-complaint has been filed may object, by demurrer or answer as provided in Section 430.30, to the pleading on any one or more of the following grounds:

(a) The court has no jurisdiction of the subject of the cause of action alleged in the pleading.

(b) The person who filed the pleading does not have the legal capacity to sue.

(c) There is another action pending between the same parties on the same cause of action.

(d) There is a defect or misjoinder of parties.

(e) The pleading does not state facts sufficient to constitute a cause of action.

(f) The pleading is uncertain. As used in this subdivision, "uncertain" includes ambiguous and unintelligible.

(g) In an action founded upon a contract, it cannot be ascertained from the pleading whether the contract is written, is oral, or is implied by conduct.

(h) No certificate was filed as required by Section 411.35.

(i) No certificate was filed as required by Section 411.36. *(Added by Stats.1971, c. 244, p. 383, § 29, operative July 1, 1972. Amended by Stats.1973, c. 828, p. 1476, § 2; Stats.1979, c. 973, p. 3336, § 2; Stats.1979, c. 988, p. 3367, § 2; Stats.1980, c. 163, p. 362, § 2; Stats.1980, c. 500, p. 1047, § 1; Stats.1990, c. 216 (S.B.2510), § 8; Stats.1993, c. 456 (A.B.58), § 3.)*

Research References

Rutter, Cal. Practice Guide: Civil Appeals & Writs Ch. 2-B, B. Appealable Judgments and Orders.
Rutter, Cal. Practice Guide: Civil Appeals & Writs Ch. 8-C, C. Standards of Appellate Review.
Rutter, Cal. Practice Guide: Civ. Pro. Before Trial Ch. 1-D, D. Prelawsuit Consultation Requirement in Certain Professional Negligence Actions.
Rutter, Cal. Practice Guide: Civ. Pro. Before Trial Ch. 2-C, C. Joinder of Parties.
Rutter, Cal. Practice Guide: Civ. Pro. Before Trial Ch. 3-A, A. Subject Matter Jurisdiction (Competency).
Rutter, Cal. Practice Guide: Civ. Pro. Before Trial Ch. 5-B, B. Entry of Default.
Rutter, Cal. Practice Guide: Civ. Pro. Before Trial Ch. 6-B, B. Complaints.
Rutter, Cal. Practice Guide: Civ. Pro. Before Trial Ch. 6-C, C. Answer.
Rutter, Cal. Practice Guide: Civ. Pro. Before Trial Ch. 11-B, B. Involuntary Dismissals.
Rutter, Cal. Practice Guide: Civ. Pro. Before Trial Ch. 7(I)-A, A. Demurrers.
Rutter, Cal. Practice Guide: Civ. Pro. Before Trial Ch. 9(I)-A, A. Introduction.
Rutter, Cal. Practice Guide: Civ. Pro. Before Trial Ch. 7(I)-A, Outline a.
California Practice Guide: Employment Litigation Ch. 19-D, D. Defendant's Challenges and Responses to Complaint.
California Practice Guide: Employment Litigation Ch. 19-T, T. Appeals.
Rutter, Cal. Practice Guide: Fed.Civ.Pro. Before Trial Ch. 9-A, Introduction.
Rutter, Cal. Practice Guide: Insurance Litigation Ch. 15-F, F. Pretrial Motions.
Rutter, Cal. Practice Guide: Personal Injury Ch. 5-A, A. Prelawsuit Filings.
Rutter, Cal. Practice Guide: Personal Injury Ch. 5-C, C. Selected Issues Affecting Parties.
Rutter, Cal. Practice Guide: Personal Injury Ch. 5-E, E. Selected Pleading Issues.
Miller and Starr California Real Estate § 29:61, Certificates of Merit.
3 Witkin Cal. Proc. 5th Actions § 593, (S 593) Statutory Rule.
2 Witkin Cal. Proc. 5th Jurisdiction § 428, (S 428) in General.
2 Witkin Cal. Proc. 5th Jurisdiction § 429, (S 429) Where Parties Were Not Adverse in Previous Action.
4 Witkin Cal. Proc. 5th Pleading § 522, Pleading Legal Effect.
5 Witkin Cal. Proc. 5th Pleading § 951, in General.
5 Witkin Cal. Proc. 5th Pleading § 961, (S 961) Form.
5 Witkin Cal. Proc. 5th Pleading § 962, Statute of Limitations.
5 Witkin Cal. Proc. 5th Pleading § 968, (S 968) Form.
5 Witkin Cal. Proc. 5th Pleading § 969, No Jurisdiction of Subject Matter.
5 Witkin Cal. Proc. 5th Pleading § 970, Lack of Capacity to Sue.
5 Witkin Cal. Proc. 5th Pleading § 971, Other Action Pending.
5 Witkin Cal. Proc. 5th Pleading § 972, Nonjoinder of Parties.
5 Witkin Cal. Proc. 5th Pleading § 973, Misjoinder of Parties.
5 Witkin Cal. Proc. 5th Pleading § 974, (S 974) in General.
5 Witkin Cal. Proc. 5th Pleading § 975, (S 975) When Demurrer Will be Sustained.
5 Witkin Cal. Proc. 5th Pleading § 977, Failure to Disclose Oral Contract.
5 Witkin Cal. Proc. 5th Pleading § 978, No Certificate Filed.
5 Witkin Cal. Proc. 5th Pleading § 1129, Nature of Plea.
5 Witkin Cal. Proc. 5th Pleading § 1138, General Rule and Theory.
5 Witkin Cal. Proc. 5th Pleading § 1141, Distinction: Action Pending in Another State.
5 Witkin Cal. Proc. 5th Pleading § 1144, Special Rules Under Probate Code.
5 Witkin Cal. Proc. 5th Pleading § 1151, Earlier Theory of Defense of Substance.

§ 430.20. Objections by plaintiff; grounds

A party against whom an answer has been filed may object, by demurrer as provided in Section 430.30, to the answer upon any one or more of the following grounds:

(a) The answer does not state facts sufficient to constitute a defense.

(b) The answer is uncertain. As used in this subdivision, "uncertain" includes ambiguous and unintelligible.

(c) Where the answer pleads a contract, it cannot be ascertained from the answer whether the contract is written or oral. *(Added by Stats.1971, c. 244, p. 384, § 29, operative July 1, 1972.)*

Law Revision Commission Comments

Section 430.20 continues without substantive change the portions of former Code of Civil Procedure Section 444 that specified the grounds for objection to the answer except that the grounds for objection to what formerly would have been a counterclaim are now the same as the grounds for objecting to a complaint. See Section 430.10.

Research References

Rutter, Cal. Practice Guide: Civ. Pro. Before Trial Ch. 6-C, C. Answer.
Rutter, Cal. Practice Guide: Civ. Pro. Before Trial Ch. 7(I)-A, A. Demurrers.
5 Witkin Cal. Proc. 5th Pleading § 1182, (S 1182) Grounds.

§ 430.30.   Objections by demurrer and answer

(a) When any ground for objection to a complaint, cross-complaint, or answer appears on the face thereof, or from any matter of which the court is required to or may take judicial notice, the objection on that ground may be taken by a demurrer to the pleading.

(b) When any ground for objection to a complaint or cross-complaint does not appear on the face of the pleading, the objection may be taken by answer.

(c) A party objecting to a complaint or cross-complaint may demur and answer at the same time. *(Added by Stats.1971, c. 244, p. 384, § 29, operative July 1, 1972.)*

Research References

Rutter, Cal. Practice Guide: Civ. Pro. Before Trial Ch. 6-C, C. Answer.
Rutter, Cal. Practice Guide: Civ. Pro. Before Trial Ch. 7(I)-A, A. Demurrers.
Rutter, Cal. Practice Guide: Civil Trials & Evidence Ch. 8C-J, J. Judicial Notice.
California Practice Guide: Employment Litigation Ch. 19-D, D. Defendant's Challenges and Responses to Complaint.
Rutter, Cal. Practice Guide: Personal Injury Ch. 5-E, E. Selected Pleading Issues.
2 Witkin Cal. Proc. 5th Jurisdiction § 398, Methods of Prevention.
4 Witkin Cal. Proc. 5th Pleading § 440, General Principle.
5 Witkin Cal. Proc. 5th Pleading § 946, Raising Issue of Law.
5 Witkin Cal. Proc. 5th Pleading § 947, (S 947) General Rule and Applications.
5 Witkin Cal. Proc. 5th Pleading § 948, (S 948) Exceptions and Distinctions.
5 Witkin Cal. Proc. 5th Pleading § 949, Filing With Answer or Motion to Strike.
5 Witkin Cal. Proc. 5th Pleading § 1129, Nature of Plea.
5 Witkin Cal. Proc. 5th Pleading § 1131, (S 1131) Waiver by Delay in Raising Objection.

§ 430.40.   Demurrer; time

(a) A person against whom a complaint or cross-complaint has been filed may, within 30 days after service of the complaint or cross-complaint, demur to the complaint or cross-complaint.

(b) A party who has filed a complaint or cross-complaint may, within 10 days after service of the answer to his pleading, demur to the answer. *(Added by Stats.1971, c. 244, p. 384, § 29, operative July 1, 1972.)*

Law Revision Commission Comments

Section 430.40 is consistent with the times specified in former Sections 430, 442, and 443 of the Code of Civil Procedure. See also Sections 412.20(a)(3) and 432.10.

Research References

Rutter, Cal. Practice Guide: Civ. Pro. Before Trial Ch. 6-E, E. Amended and Supplemental Pleadings.

Rutter, Cal. Practice Guide: Civ. Pro. Before Trial Ch. 7(I)-A, A. Demurrers.
4 Witkin Cal. Proc. 5th Pleading § 7, (S 7) Time Prescribed by Statute.
5 Witkin Cal. Proc. 5th Pleading § 979, (S 979) Service and Filing.
5 Witkin Cal. Proc. 5th Pleading § 1181, (S 1181) Nature of Pleading.
5 Witkin Cal. Proc. 5th Pleading § 1193, (S 1193) Amendment of Answer.
6 Witkin Cal. Proc. 5th Proceedings Without Trial § 193, (S 193) Time of Motion.

§ 430.50.   Demurrer to all or part of pleadings

(a) A demurrer to a complaint or cross-complaint may be taken to the whole complaint or cross-complaint or to any of the causes of action stated therein.

(b) A demurrer to an answer may be taken to the whole answer or to any one or more of the several defenses set up in the answer. *(Added by Stats.1971, c. 244, p. 384, § 29, operative July 1, 1972.)*

Law Revision Commission Comments

Section 430.50 is consistent with prior law but provides specifically that cross-complaints (which include what formerly were counterclaims) are treated the same as complaints. See former Code of Civil Procedure Sections 431 (complaints) and 441 and 443 (answers).

Research References

Rutter, Cal. Practice Guide: Civ. Pro. Before Trial Ch. 7(I)-A, A. Demurrers.
5 Witkin Cal. Proc. 5th Pleading § 949, Filing With Answer or Motion to Strike.
5 Witkin Cal. Proc. 5th Pleading § 954, Demurrer to Entire Complaint.
5 Witkin Cal. Proc. 5th Pleading § 1183, (S 1183) Procedure.

§ 430.60.   Specification of grounds

A demurrer shall distinctly specify the grounds upon which any of the objections to the complaint, cross-complaint, or answer are taken. Unless it does so, it may be disregarded. *(Added by Stats.1971, c. 244, p. 384, § 29, operative July 1, 1972.)*

Law Revision Commission Comments

Section 430.60 continues the rule formerly found in Section 431 of the Code of Civil Procedure except that the rule has been extended—in accordance with the former practice—to cover specifically cross-complaints and answers.

Research References

Rutter, Cal. Practice Guide: Civ. Pro. Before Trial Ch. 7(I)-A, A. Demurrers.
5 Witkin Cal. Proc. 5th Pleading § 961, (S 961) Form.
5 Witkin Cal. Proc. 5th Pleading § 968, (S 968) Form.

§ 430.70.   Demurrer based on matter of which court may take judicial notice; specification

When the ground of demurrer is based on a matter of which the court may take judicial notice pursuant to Section 452 or 453 of the Evidence Code, such matter shall be specified in the demurrer, or in the supporting points and authorities for the purpose of invoking such notice, except as the court may otherwise permit. *(Added by Stats.1971, c. 244, p. 384, § 29, operative July 1, 1972.)*

Law Revision Commission Comments

Section 430.70 continues without change the provisions of former Code of Civil Procedure Section 431.5.

Research References

Rutter, Cal. Practice Guide: Civ. Pro. Before Trial Ch. 7(I)-A, A. Demurrers.
5 Witkin Cal. Proc. 5th Pleading § 961, (S 961) Form.

5 Witkin Cal. Proc. 5th Pleading § 971, Other Action Pending.

§ 430.80. Failure to object by demurrer or answer; waiver; exceptions

(a) If the party against whom a complaint or cross-complaint has been filed fails to object to the pleading, either by demurrer or answer, that party is deemed to have waived the objection unless it is an objection that the court has no jurisdiction of the subject of the cause of action alleged in the pleading or an objection that the pleading does not state facts sufficient to constitute a cause of action.

(b) If the party against whom an answer has been filed fails to demur thereto, that party is deemed to have waived the objection unless it is an objection that the answer does not state facts sufficient to constitute a defense. *(Added by Stats.1971, c. 244, p. 385, § 29, operative July 1, 1972. Amended by Stats.1983, c. 1167, § 2.)*

Law Revision Commission Comments

Section 430.80 is the same in substance as former Code of Civil Procedure Section 434 except that Section 430.80 makes clear that the rule applies to objections to cross-complaints.

Research References

Rutter, Cal. Practice Guide: Civil Appeals & Writs Ch. 8-D, D. Limits on Assertion of Issues on Appeal.
Rutter, Cal. Practice Guide: Civ. Pro. Before Trial Ch. 2-A, A. Standing to Sue-"Real Party in Interest" Requirement.
Rutter, Cal. Practice Guide: Civ. Pro. Before Trial Ch. 2-C, C. Joinder of Parties.
Rutter, Cal. Practice Guide: Civ. Pro. Before Trial Ch. 3-A, A. Subject Matter Jurisdiction (Competency).
Rutter, Cal. Practice Guide: Civ. Pro. Before Trial Ch. 6-C, C. Answer.
Rutter, Cal. Practice Guide: Civ. Pro. Before Trial Ch. 7(I)-A, A. Demurrers.
Rutter, Cal. Practice Guide: Civ. Pro. Before Trial Ch. 7(I)-C, C. Motion for Judgment on the Pleadings.
California Practice Guide: Employment Litigation Ch. 16-E, E. Statute of Limitations.
Rutter, Cal. Practice Guide: Insurance Litigation Ch. 15-F, F. Pretrial Motions.
Rutter, Cal. Practice Guide: Personal Injury Ch. 5-C, C. Selected Issues Affecting Parties.
Rutter, Cal. Practice Guide: Personal Injury Ch. 5-E, E. Selected Pleading Issues.
Rutter, Cal. Practice Guide: Personal Injury Ch. 9-L, L. Motions to Terminate Trial Before Verdict.
5 Witkin Cal. Proc. 5th Pleading § 958, Defects of Substance Are Not Waived.
5 Witkin Cal. Proc. 5th Pleading § 959, Defects of Form Raised by General Demurrer.
5 Witkin Cal. Proc. 5th Pleading § 960, Defects of Form Raised by Special Demurrer.
5 Witkin Cal. Proc. 5th Pleading § 961, (S 961) Form.
5 Witkin Cal. Proc. 5th Pleading § 981, (S 981) Hearing.
5 Witkin Cal. Proc. 5th Pleading § 1131, (S 1131) Waiver by Delay in Raising Objection.
6 Witkin Cal. Proc. 5th Proceedings Without Trial § 194, (S 194) Effect of Failure to File General Demurrer.
10 Witkin, California Summary 10th Parent and Child § 706, Waiver of Appellate Review.

§ 430.90. Removal of civil action to federal court; filing response; time

(a) Where the defendant has removed a civil action to federal court without filing a response in the original court and the case is later remanded for improper removal, the time to respond shall be as follows:

(1) If the defendant has not generally appeared in either the original or federal court, then 30 days from the day the original court receives the case on remand to move to dismiss the action pursuant to Section 583.250 or to move to quash service of

summons or to stay or dismiss the action pursuant to Section 418.10, if the court has not ruled on a similar motion filed by the defendant prior to the removal of the action to federal court.

(2) If the defendant has not filed an answer in the original court, then 30 days from the day the original court receives the case on remand to do any of the following:

(A) Answer the complaint.

(B) Demur or move to strike all or a portion of the complaint if: (i) an answer was not filed in the federal court, and (ii) a demurrer or motion to strike raising the same or similar issues was not filed and ruled upon by the original court prior to the removal of the action to federal court or was not filed and ruled upon in federal court prior to the remand. If the demurrer or motion to strike is denied by the court, the defendant shall have 30 days to answer the complaint unless an answer was filed with the demurrer or motion to strike.

(b) For the purposes of this section, time shall be calculated from the date of the original court's receipt of the order of remand. *(Added by Stats.1995, c. 796 (S.B.45), § 5.)*

Research References

Rutter, Cal. Practice Guide: Civ. Pro. Before Trial Ch. 5-B, B. Entry of Default.
Rutter, Cal. Practice Guide: Fed.Civ.Pro. Before Trial Ch. 6-B, B. Expiration of Time to Respond.
4 Witkin Cal. Proc. 5th Pleading § 7, (S 7) Time Prescribed by Statute.

ARTICLE 2. DENIALS AND DEFENSES

Section
431.10. Material and immaterial allegations, defined.
431.20. Uncontroverted allegations deemed true; new matter in answer deemed controverted.
431.30. Answer; contents; information and belief; denials; defenses.
431.40. Actions involving $1000 or less; general written denial; cross-complaints.
431.50. Actions on insurance contracts; claim of exemption from liability.
431.70. Cross demands for money; defense in answer; failure to assert defense; effect of assignment or death; money judgments.

§ 431.10. Material and immaterial allegations, defined

(a) A material allegation in a pleading is one essential to the claim or defense and which could not be stricken from the pleading without leaving it insufficient as to that claim or defense.

(b) An immaterial allegation in a pleading is any of the following:

(1) An allegation that is not essential to the statement of a claim or defense.

(2) An allegation that is neither pertinent to nor supported by an otherwise sufficient claim or defense.

(3) A demand for judgment requesting relief not supported by the allegations of the complaint or cross-complaint.

(c) An "immaterial allegation" means "irrelevant matter" as that term is used in Section 436. *(Added by Stats.1971, c. 244, p. 384, § 29, operative July 1, 1972. Amended by Stats.1982, c. 704, p. 2857, § 2; Stats.1983, c. 1167, § 3; Stats.1986, c. 540, § 2.)*

Law Revision Commission Comments

Section 431.10 continues without substantive change the provisions of former Code of Civil Procedure Section 463.

Research References

Rutter, Cal. Practice Guide: Civ. Pro. Before Trial Ch. 6-C, C. Answer.
Rutter, Cal. Practice Guide: Civ. Pro. Before Trial Ch. 7(I)-B, B. Motions to Strike.
5 Witkin Cal. Proc. 5th Pleading § 1047, in General.

§ 431.20. Uncontroverted allegations deemed true; new matter in answer deemed controverted

(a) Every material allegation of the complaint or cross-complaint, not controverted by the answer, shall, for the purposes of the action, be taken as true.

(b) The statement of any new matter in the answer, in avoidance or constituting a defense, shall, on the trial, be deemed controverted by the opposite party. *(Added by Stats. 1971, c. 244, p. 385, § 29, operative July 1, 1972.)*

Law Revision Commission Comments

Section 431.20 continues without substantive change the provisions of former Section 462 of the Code of Civil Procedure except that the section is made specifically applicable to a cross-complaint. Under prior law, an answer to a cross-complaint was required, but no answer to a counterclaim was required. Since cross-complaints now include what formerly were counterclaims, an answer is now required in some cases where one was not previously required. For further discussion, see Friedenthal, Joinder of Claims, Counterclaims, and Cross-Complaints: Suggested Revision of the California Provisions, 23 Stan. L. Rev. 1, 23–24 (1970).

Research References

Rutter, Cal. Practice Guide: Civ. Pro. Before Trial Ch. 6-C, C. Answer.
Rutter, Cal. Practice Guide: Civil Trials & Evidence Ch. 8D-D, D. Hearsay Exceptions.
Rutter, Cal. Practice Guide: Insurance Litigation Ch. 15-E, E. Pleadings.
Rutter, Cal. Practice Guide: Personal Injury Ch. 5-E, E. Selected Pleading Issues.
4 Witkin Cal. Proc. 5th Pleading § 4, (S 4) in General.
4 Witkin Cal. Proc. 5th Pleading § 452, (S 452) Nature of Judicial Admission.
5 Witkin Cal. Proc. 5th Pleading § 1050, General Rule.
5 Witkin Cal. Proc. 5th Pleading § 1051, (S 1051) Immaterial or Improper Allegations.
5 Witkin Cal. Proc. 5th Pleading § 1052, (S 1052) Other Exceptions and Distinctions.
5 Witkin Cal. Proc. 5th Pleading § 1083, New Matter is Deemed Controverted.
5 Witkin Cal. Proc. 5th Pleading § 1184, Answer to Cross-Complaint.

§ 431.30. Answer; contents; information and belief; denials; defenses

(a) As used in this section:

(1) "Complaint" includes a cross-complaint.

(2) "Defendant" includes a person filing an answer to a cross-complaint.

(b) The answer to a complaint shall contain:

(1) The general or specific denial of the material allegations of the complaint controverted by the defendant.

(2) A statement of any new matter constituting a defense.

(c) Affirmative relief may not be claimed in the answer.

(d) If the complaint is subject to Article 2 (commencing with Section 90) of Chapter 5.1 of Title 1 of Part 1 or is not verified, a general denial is sufficient but only puts in issue the material allegations of the complaint. If the complaint is verified, unless the complaint is subject to Article 2 (commencing with Section 90) of Chapter 5.1 of Title 1 of Part 1, the denial of the allegations shall be made positively or according to the information and belief of the defendant. However, if the cause of action is a claim assigned to a third party for collection and the complaint is verified, the denial of the allegations shall be made positively or according to the information and belief of the

defendant, even if the complaint is subject to Article 2 (commencing with Section 90) of Chapter 5.1 of Title 1 of Part 1.

(e) If the defendant has no information or belief upon the subject sufficient to enable him or her to answer an allegation of the complaint, he or she may so state in his or her answer and place his or her denial on that ground.

(f) The denials of the allegations controverted may be stated by reference to specific paragraphs or parts of the complaint; or by express admission of certain allegations of the complaint with a general denial of all of the allegations not so admitted; or by denial of certain allegations upon information and belief, or for lack of sufficient information or belief, with a general denial of all allegations not so denied or expressly admitted.

(g) The defenses shall be separately stated, and the several defenses shall refer to the causes of action which they are intended to answer, in a manner by which they may be intelligibly distinguished. *(Added by Stats.1971, c. 244, p. 385, § 29, operative July 1, 1972. Amended by Stats.1979, c. 212, p. 456, § 2; Stats.1985, c. 621, § 1; Stats.1986, c. 281, § 1; Stats.2003, c. 149 (S.B.79), § 8.)*

Law Revision Commission Comments

Subdivisions (a), (b), (d), (e), and (f) of Section 431.30 are the same in substance as former Code of Civil Procedure Section 437 except that they have been broadened to specifically include cross-complaints. See the Comment to Section 431.20. Subdivision (c) makes clear that affirmative relief may not be claimed in the answer. The former counterclaim is abolished. See Section 428.80; *cf.* Section 431.70 (set-off). Subdivision (g) is the same in substance as the second sentence of former Code of Civil Procedure Section 441.

Subdivision (d) of Section 431.30 is amended to correct the reference to former Chapter 5. [33 Cal.L.Rev.Comm. Reports 191 (2003)].

Research References

Rutter, Cal. Practice Guide: Civ. Pro. Before Trial Ch. 6-B, B. Complaints.
Rutter, Cal. Practice Guide: Civ. Pro. Before Trial Ch. 6-C, C. Answer.
Rutter, Cal. Practice Guide: Civ. Pro. Before Trial Ch. 11-A, A. Voluntary Dismissals.
Rutter, Cal. Practice Guide: Civ. Pro. Before Trial Ch. 9(III)-C, C. Sanctions Under CCP § 128.7.
California Practice Guide: Employment Litigation Ch. 19-D, D. Defendant's Challenges and Responses to Complaint.
California Practice Guide: Employment Litigation Form 19:B, Answer to Complaint for Damages for Sexual Harassment, Retaliation, Breach of Contract, Wrongful Discharge in Violation of Public Policy.
Rutter, Cal. Practice Guide: Fed.Civ.Pro. Before Trial Ch. 1-D, D. Choosing Between State and Federal Courts.
Rutter, Cal. Practice Guide: Fed.Civ.Pro. Before Trial Ch. 8-E, E. Answer.
Rutter, Cal. Practice Guide: Fed.Civ.Pro. Before Trial Ch. 2D-9, Effect of Removal.
Rutter, Cal. Practice Guide: Insurance Litigation Ch. 15-E, E. Pleadings.
Rutter, Cal. Practice Guide: Insurance Litigation Ch. 7B-E, E. Scope of Duty to Defend.
Rutter, Cal. Practice Guide: Personal Injury Ch. 5-E, E. Selected Pleading Issues.
Miller and Starr California Real Estate § 28:113, Statute of Limitations--Action by Owner or Obligee.
Miller and Starr California Real Estate § 28:119, Statute of Limitations--Action by Claimant.
Rutter Practice Guide: Fed.Civ.Pro. Bef.Trial(5th Cir) Ch. 1-D, D. Choosing Between State and Federal Courts.
4 Witkin Cal. Proc. 5th Pleading § 398, (S 398) Right to Plead.
4 Witkin Cal. Proc. 5th Pleading § 459, (S 459) Nature of Verification.
5 Witkin Cal. Proc. 5th Pleading § 1047, in General.
5 Witkin Cal. Proc. 5th Pleading § 1059, Where Complaint is Not Verified.
5 Witkin Cal. Proc. 5th Pleading § 1061, Where Complaint is Verified.
5 Witkin Cal. Proc. 5th Pleading § 1063, (S 1063) Specific Denial by Parts and Qualified General Denial.
5 Witkin Cal. Proc. 5th Pleading § 1064, (S 1064) Information and Belief.

5 Witkin Cal. Proc. 5th Pleading § 1065, (S 1065) Lack of Information or Belief.
5 Witkin Cal. Proc. 5th Pleading § 1075, Defenses to Common Counts.
5 Witkin Cal. Proc. 5th Pleading § 1081, Distinguished from Denial.
5 Witkin Cal. Proc. 5th Pleading § 1084, in General.
5 Witkin Cal. Proc. 5th Pleading § 1085, (S 1085) Right to Plead.
5 Witkin Cal. Proc. 5th Pleading § 1087, (S 1087) Limitations on Right.

§ 431.40. Actions involving $1000 or less; general written denial; cross-complaints

(a) Any provision of law to the contrary notwithstanding, in any action in which the demand, exclusive of interest, or the value of the property in controversy does not exceed one thousand dollars ($1000), the defendant at his option, in lieu of demurrer or other answer, may file a general written denial and a brief statement of any new matter constituting a defense.

(b) Nothing in this section excuses the defendant from complying with the provisions of law applicable to a cross-complaint, and any cross-complaint of the defendant shall be subject to the requirements applicable in any other action.

(c) The general written denial described in subdivision (a) shall be on a blank available at the place of filing and shall be in a form prescribed by the Judicial Council. This form need not be verified. (Added by Stats.1971, c. 244, p. 386, § 29, operative July 1, 1972. Amended by Stats.1972, c. 562, § 1; Stats.1976, c. 1389, p. 6297, § 1; Stats.1977, c. 93, p. 514, § 1.)

Law Revision Commission Comments

Section 431.40 continues the provisions of former Code of Civil Procedure Section 437b except that the relaxed requirements under the former section for counterclaims (now asserted a cross-complaints) are not continued.

Research References

Rutter, Cal. Practice Guide: Civ. Pro. Before Trial Ch. 6-C, C. Answer.
5 Witkin Cal. Proc. 5th Pleading § 1060, Where Demand or Value is Small.
12 Witkin, California Summary 10th Real Property § 730, Pleadings.

§ 431.50. Actions on insurance contracts; claim of exemption from liability

In an action to recover upon a contract of insurance wherein the defendant claims exemption from liability upon the ground that, although the proximate cause of the loss was a peril insured against, the loss was remotely caused by or would not have occurred but for a peril excepted in the contract of insurance, the defendant shall in his answer set forth and specify the peril which was the proximate cause of the loss, in what manner the peril excepted contributed to the loss or itself caused the peril insured against, and if he claims that the peril excepted caused the peril insured against, he shall in his answer set forth and specify upon what premises or at what place the peril excepted caused the peril insured against. (Added by Stats.1971, c. 244, p. 386, § 29, operative July 1, 1972.)

Law Revision Commission Comments

Section 431.50 is the same as former Code of Civil Procedure Section 437a.

Research References

Rutter, Cal. Practice Guide: Civ. Pro. Before Trial Ch. 6-C, C. Answer.
Rutter, Cal. Practice Guide: Insurance Litigation Ch. 15-E, E. Pleadings.
5 Witkin Cal. Proc. 5th Pleading § 1047, in General.

§ 431.70. Cross demands for money; defense in answer; failure to assert defense; effect of assignment or death; money judgments

Where cross-demands for money have existed between persons at any point in time when neither demand was barred by the statute of limitations, and an action is thereafter commenced by one such person, the other person may assert in the answer the defense of payment in that the two demands are compensated so far as they equal each other, notwithstanding that an independent action asserting the person's claim would at the time of filing the answer be barred by the statute of limitations. If the cross-demand would otherwise be barred by the statute of limitations, the relief accorded under this section shall not exceed the value of the relief granted to the other party. The defense provided by this section is not available if the cross-demand is barred for failure to assert it in a prior action under Section 426.30. Neither person can be deprived of the benefits of this section by the assignment or death of the other. For the purposes of this section, a money judgment is a "demand for money" and, as applied to a money judgment, the demand is barred by the statute of limitations when enforcement of the judgment is barred under Chapter 3 (commencing with Section 683.010) of Division 1 of Title 9. (Added by Stats.1971, c. 244, p. 386, § 29, operative July 1, 1972. Amended by Stats.1982, c. 497, p. 2154, § 32, operative July 1, 1983.)

Law Revision Commission Comments

Section 431.70 is amended to codify the case law rule that applies the offset principle where one of the claims to be offset is a judgment. See, e.g., Erlich v. Superior Court, 63 Cal.2d 551, 555, 407 P.2d 649, 651, 47 Cal.Rptr. 473, 475 (1965); Harrison v. Adams, 20 Cal.2d 646, 648–49, 128 P.2d 9, 11–12 (1942); Machado v. Borges, 170 Cal. 501, 150 P. 351 (1915); Coonan v. Loewenthal, 147 Cal. 218, 223, 81 P. 527, 528 (1905); Nash v. Krelig, 136 Cal. 627, 69 P. 418 (1902). A judgment on which the time limit on enforceability has run (see Section 683.020) is analogous to a claim barred by the statute of limitations. The policy which allows the offsetting of cross-demands that have coexisted at some point in time, notwithstanding that one of the claims is now barred by the statute of limitations (see Jones v. Mortimer, 28 Cal.2d 627, 632–33, 170 P.2d 893, 896–97 (1946); Sunrise Produce Co. v. Malovich, 101 Cal.App.2d 520, 522–23, 225 P.2d 973, 974–75 (1950)), applies equally to cross-demands where one of the demands which coexisted is a judgment on which the time for enforcement has expired. Section 431.70 as amended allows the offset of a judgment if the claim of the judgment debtor existed during the period during which the judgment was enforceable. However, where the judgment debtor's claim arises after the period for enforcement of the judgment has run, the judgment cannot be offset against the judgment debtor's claim; in this case, the demands have not "existed between persons at any point in time when neither demand was barred by the statute of limitations" (15 Cal.L.Rev.Comm. Reports 2001).

Research References

Rutter, Cal. Practice Guide: Civ. Pro. Before Trial Ch. 6-C, C. Answer.
Rutter, Cal. Practice Guide: Civ. Pro. Before Trial Ch. 6-D, D. Cross-Complaint.
Rutter, Cal. Practice Guide: Civ. Pro. Before Trial Ch. 9(II)-D, D. Attachment.
Rutter, Cal. Practice Guide: Enforcing Judgments/Debts Ch. 4-A, A. Attachment.
Rutter, Cal. Practice Guide: Fed.Civ.Pro. Before Trial Ch. 8-F, F. Counterclaims, Crossclaims and Third Party Claims.
Rutter, Cal. Practice Guide: Insurance Litigation Ch. 15-E, E. Pleadings.
Rutter, Cal. Practice Guide: Insurance Litigation Ch. 7B-E, E. Scope of Duty to Defend.
Rutter, Cal. Practice Guide: Personal Injury Ch. 5-E, E. Selected Pleading Issues.
Rutter, Cal. Practice Guide: Prof. Responsibility Ch. 6-D, D. Professional Liability.
Miller and Starr California Real Estate § 10:76, Payment by Setoff; General Rules.
Miller and Starr California Real Estate § 10:77, Offset Against Secured Debt Prior to Foreclosure Sale.
Miller and Starr California Real Estate § 25B:87, Members' Assessments.
3 Witkin Cal. Proc. 5th Actions § 449, (S 449) Cross-Demands Deemed Compensated.
8 Witkin Cal. Proc. 5th Enforcement of Judgment § 512, (S 512) Nature of Right.
5 Witkin Cal. Proc. 5th Pleading § 1165, Revised Law of Setoff.
5 Witkin Cal. Proc. 5th Pleading § 1166, When Setoff is Improper.

6 Witkin Cal. Proc. 5th Provisional Remedies § 98, (S 98) in General.
6 Witkin, California Summary 10th Torts § 1372, (S 1372) Setoff.
7 Witkin, California Summary 10th Constitutional Law § 619, in General.

ARTICLE 3. TIME TO RESPOND TO CROSS–COMPLAINT

Section
432.10. Motion, demurrer or other plea; time.

§ 432.10. Motion, demurrer or other plea; time

A party served with a cross-complaint may within 30 days after service move, demur, or otherwise plead to the cross-complaint in the same manner as to an original complaint. *(Added by Stats.1971, c. 244, p. 387, § 29, operative July 1, 1972.)*

Law Revision Commission Comments

Section 432.10 is the same as the last sentence of former Code of Civil Procedure Section 442.

Research References

Rutter, Cal. Practice Guide: Civ. Pro. Before Trial Ch. 6-D, D. Cross-Complaint.
4 Witkin Cal. Proc. 5th Pleading § 4, (S 4) in General.
4 Witkin Cal. Proc. 5th Pleading § 7, (S 7) Time Prescribed by Statute.
5 Witkin Cal. Proc. 5th Pleading § 1184, Answer to Cross-Complaint.
5 Witkin Cal. Proc. 5th Pleading § 1185, Demurrer to Cross-Complaint.

CHAPTER 4. MOTION TO STRIKE

Section
435. Notice of motion to strike whole or part of complaint.
436. Discretion of court to strike pleadings or portions of pleadings.
437. Grounds for motion to strike; judicial notice; specification.

§ 435. Notice of motion to strike whole or part of complaint

(a) As used in this section:

(1) The term "complaint" includes a cross-complaint.

(2) The term "pleading" means a demurrer, answer, complaint, or cross-complaint.

(b)(1) Any party, within the time allowed to respond to a pleading may serve and file a notice of motion to strike the whole or any part thereof, but this time limitation shall not apply to motions specified in subdivision (e).

(2) A notice of motion to strike the answer or the complaint, or a portion thereof, shall specify a hearing date set in accordance with Section 1005.

(3) A notice of motion to strike a demurrer, or a portion thereof, shall set the hearing thereon concurrently with the hearing on the demurrer.

(c) If a party serves and files a notice of motion to strike without demurring to the complaint, the time to answer is extended and no default may be entered against that defendant, except as provided in Sections 585 and 586.

(d) The filing of a notice of motion to strike an answer or complaint, or portion thereof, shall not extend the time within which to demur.

(e) A motion to strike, as specified in this section, may be made as part of a motion pursuant to subparagraph (A) of paragraph (1) of subdivision (i) of Section 438. *(Added by Stats.1955, c. 1452, p. 2640, § 3a. Amended by Stats.1971, c. 244, p. 387, § 33, operative July 1, 1972; Stats.1982, c. 704, p. 2857, § 3; Stats.1993, c. 456 (A.B.58), § 3.5.)*

Law Revision Commission Comments

Section 435 is amended to make its provisions specifically applicable to cross-complaints. With respect to a cross-complaint that would have been a cross-complaint under prior law, Section 435 continues prior law under former Code of Civil Procedure Section 442. Section 435 also makes clear that a motion to strike may be directed to a cross-complaint that formerly would have been asserted as a counterclaim in the answer. The prior law was not clear on this point. But see Code Civ.Proc. § 453 (striking sham or irrelevant answer).

Research References

Rutter, Cal. Practice Guide: Civil Appeals & Writs Ch. 8-C, C. Standards of Appellate Review.
Rutter, Cal. Practice Guide: Civ. Pro. Before Trial Ch. 3-A, A. Subject Matter Jurisdiction (Competency).
Rutter, Cal. Practice Guide: Civ. Pro. Before Trial Ch. 6-C, C. Answer.
Rutter, Cal. Practice Guide: Civ. Pro. Before Trial Ch. 6-E, E. Amended and Supplemental Pleadings.
Rutter, Cal. Practice Guide: Civ. Pro. Before Trial Ch. 7(I)-B, B. Motions to Strike.
California Practice Guide: Employment Litigation Ch. 19-H, H. Other Pretrial Procedures.
Rutter, Cal. Practice Guide: Insurance Litigation Ch. 15-F, F. Pretrial Motions.
Rutter, Cal. Practice Guide: Personal Injury Ch. 5-A, A. Prelawsuit Filings.
3 Witkin Cal. Proc. 5th Actions § 593, (S 593) Statutory Rule.
4 Witkin Cal. Proc. 5th Pleading § 10, Extension to Ordinary Party.
5 Witkin Cal. Proc. 5th Pleading § 949, Filing With Answer or Motion to Strike.
5 Witkin Cal. Proc. 5th Pleading § 1008, Nature of Motion.
5 Witkin Cal. Proc. 5th Pleading § 1009, Statutory Provisions.
5 Witkin Cal. Proc. 5th Pleading § 1013, (S 1013) Sham Pleading.
5 Witkin Cal. Proc. 5th Pleading § 1014, (S 1014) in General.
5 Witkin Cal. Proc. 5th Pleading § 1015, (S 1015) Motion With or Without Demurrer.
5 Witkin Cal. Proc. 5th Pleading § 1057, Nature of Power.
6 Witkin Cal. Proc. 5th Proceedings Without Trial § 5, (S 5) Time of Motion.
6 Witkin Cal. Proc. 5th Proceedings Without Trial § 7, General Requirement of Notice.

§ 436. Discretion of court to strike pleadings or portions of pleadings

The court may, upon a motion made pursuant to Section 435, or at any time in its discretion, and upon terms it deems proper:

(a) Strike out any irrelevant, false, or improper matter inserted in any pleading.

(b) Strike out all or any part of any pleading not drawn or filed in conformity with the laws of this state, a court rule, or an order of the court. *(Added by Stats.1982, c. 704, p. 2857, § 3.5. Amended by Stats.1983, c. 1167, p. 2857, § 4.)*

Research References

Rutter, Cal. Practice Guide: Civil Appeals & Writs Ch. 8-C, C. Standards of Appellate Review.
Rutter, Cal. Practice Guide: Civ. Pro. Before Trial Ch. 6-B, B. Complaints.
Rutter, Cal. Practice Guide: Civ. Pro. Before Trial Ch. 7(I)-A, A. Demurrers.
Rutter, Cal. Practice Guide: Civ. Pro. Before Trial Ch. 7(I)-B, B. Motions to Strike.
Rutter, Cal. Practice Guide: Civ. Pro. Before Trial Ch. 7(I)-C, C. Motion for Judgment on the Pleadings.
California Practice Guide: Employment Litigation Ch. 19-D, D. Defendant's Challenges and Responses to Complaint.
Rutter, Cal. Practice Guide: Insurance Litigation Ch. 15-F, F. Pretrial Motions.
5 Witkin Cal. Proc. 5th Pleading § 986, (S 986) Striking and Right to Answer.
5 Witkin Cal. Proc. 5th Pleading § 1009, Statutory Provisions.
5 Witkin Cal. Proc. 5th Pleading § 1010, (S 1010) Irrelevant and Redundant Matter.

5 Witkin Cal. Proc. 5th Pleading § 1011, (S 1011) Procedural Defects Not Subject to Demurrer.
5 Witkin Cal. Proc. 5th Pleading § 1013, (S 1013) Sham Pleading.
5 Witkin Cal. Proc. 5th Pleading § 1014, (S 1014) in General.
5 Witkin Cal. Proc. 5th Pleading § 1057, Nature of Power.
6 Witkin Cal. Proc. 5th Proceedings Without Trial § 198, (S 198) Further Proceedings Where Leave to Amend is Granted.
6 Witkin Cal. Proc. 5th Proceedings Without Trial § 207, Motion to Dismiss or Strike.
7 Witkin Cal. Proc. 5th Trial § 238, Signing and Certification.

§ 437. Grounds for motion to strike; judicial notice; specification

(a) The grounds for a motion to strike shall appear on the face of the challenged pleading or from any matter of which the court is required to take judicial notice.

(b) Where the motion to strike is based on matter of which the court may take judicial notice pursuant to Section 452 or 453 of the Evidence Code, such matter shall be specified in the notice of motion, or in the supporting points and authorities, except as the court may otherwise permit. *(Added by Stats.1982, c. 704, p. 2858, § 4.)*

Research References

Rutter, Cal. Practice Guide: Civ. Pro. Before Trial Ch. 3-A, A. Subject Matter Jurisdiction (Competency).
Rutter, Cal. Practice Guide: Civ. Pro. Before Trial Ch. 10-F, F. Burden of Proof on Motion.
Rutter, Cal. Practice Guide: Civ. Pro. Before Trial Ch. 7(I)-B, B. Motions to Strike.
California Practice Guide: Employment Litigation Ch. 19-H, H. Other Pretrial Procedures.
Rutter, Cal. Practice Guide: Insurance Litigation Ch. 15-F, F. Pretrial Motions.
5 Witkin Cal. Proc. 5th Pleading § 1009, Statutory Provisions.
6 Witkin Cal. Proc. 5th Proceedings Without Trial § 207, Motion to Dismiss or Strike.

CHAPTER 5. SUMMARY JUDGMENTS AND MOTIONS FOR JUDGMENT ON THE PLEADINGS

§ 437c. Grounds for and effect of summary judgment; procedure on motion

Section operative until January 1, 2015. See, also, section operative January 1, 2015.

(a) Any party may move for summary judgment in any action or proceeding if it is contended that the action has no merit or that there is no defense to the action or proceeding. The motion may be made at any time after 60 days have elapsed since the general appearance in the action or proceeding of each party against whom the motion is directed or at any earlier time after the general appearance that the court, with or without notice and upon good cause shown, may direct. Notice of the motion and supporting papers shall be served on all other parties to the action at least 75 days before the time appointed for hearing. However, if the notice is served by mail, the required 75–day period of notice shall be increased by five days if the place of address is within the State of California, 10 days if the place of address is outside the State of California but within the United States, and 20 days if the place of address is outside the United

States, and if the notice is served by facsimile transmission, Express Mail, or another method of delivery providing for overnight delivery, the required 75–day period of notice shall be increased by two court days. The motion shall be heard no later than 30 days before the date of trial, unless the court for good cause orders otherwise. The filing of the motion shall not extend the time within which a party must otherwise file a responsive pleading.

(b)(1) The motion shall be supported by affidavits, declarations, admissions, answers to interrogatories, depositions, and matters of which judicial notice shall or may be taken. The supporting papers shall include a separate statement setting forth plainly and concisely all material facts which the moving party contends are undisputed. Each of the material facts stated shall be followed by a reference to the supporting evidence. The failure to comply with this requirement of a separate statement may in the court's discretion constitute a sufficient ground for denial of the motion.

(2) Any opposition to the motion shall be served and filed not less than 14 days preceding the noticed or continued date of hearing, unless the court for good cause orders otherwise. The opposition, where appropriate, shall consist of affidavits, declarations, admissions, answers to interrogatories, depositions, and matters of which judicial notice shall or may be taken.

(3) The opposition papers shall include a separate statement that responds to each of the material facts contended by the moving party to be undisputed, indicating whether the opposing party agrees or disagrees that those facts are undisputed. The statement also shall set forth plainly and concisely any other material facts that the opposing party contends are disputed. Each material fact contended by the opposing party to be disputed shall be followed by a reference to the supporting evidence. Failure to comply with this requirement of a separate statement may constitute a sufficient ground, in the court's discretion, for granting the motion.

(4) Any reply to the opposition shall be served and filed by the moving party not less than five days preceding the noticed or continued date of hearing, unless the court for good cause orders otherwise.

(5) Evidentiary objections not made at the hearing shall be deemed waived.

(6) Except for subdivision (c) of Section 1005 relating to the method of service of opposition and reply papers, Sections 1005 and 1013, extending the time within which a right may be exercised or an act may be done, do not apply to this section.

(7) Any incorporation by reference of matter in the court's file shall set forth with specificity the exact matter to which reference is being made and shall not incorporate the entire file.

(c) The motion for summary judgment shall be granted if all the papers submitted show that there is no triable issue as to any material fact and that the moving party is entitled to a judgment as a matter of law. In determining whether the papers show that there is no triable issue as to any material fact the court shall consider all of the evidence set forth in the papers, except that to which objections have been made and sustained by the court, and all inferences reasonably deducible from the evidence, except summary judgment may not be granted by the court based on inferences reasonably deducible from the evidence, if contradicted by other inferences or evidence, which raise a triable issue as to any material fact.

(d) Supporting and opposing affidavits or declarations shall be made by any person on personal knowledge, shall set forth admissible evidence, and shall show affirmatively that the affiant is competent to testify to the matters stated in the affidavits or declarations. Any objections based on the failure to comply with the requirements of this subdivision shall be made at the hearing or shall be deemed waived.

(e) If a party is otherwise entitled to a summary judgment pursuant to this section, summary judgment may not be denied on grounds of credibility or for want of cross-examination of witnesses furnishing affidavits or declarations in support of the summary judgment, except that summary judgment may be denied in the discretion of the court, where the only proof of a material fact offered in support of the summary judgment is an affidavit or declaration made by an individual who was the sole witness to that fact; or where a material fact is an individual's state of mind, or lack thereof, and that fact is sought to be established solely by the individual's affirmation thereof.

(f)(1) A party may move for summary adjudication as to one or more causes of action within an action, one or more affirmative defenses, one or more claims for damages, or one or more issues of duty, if that party contends that the cause of action has no merit or that there is no affirmative defense thereto, or that there is no merit to an affirmative defense as to any cause of action, or both, or that there is no merit to a claim for damages, as specified in Section 3294 of the Civil Code, or that one or more defendants either owed or did not owe a duty to the plaintiff or plaintiffs. A motion for summary adjudication shall be granted only if it completely disposes of a cause of action, an affirmative defense, a claim for damages, or an issue of duty.

(2) A motion for summary adjudication may be made by itself or as an alternative to a motion for summary judgment and shall proceed in all procedural respects as a motion for summary judgment. However, a party may not move for summary judgment based on issues asserted in a prior motion for summary adjudication and denied by the court, unless that party establishes to the satisfaction of the court, newly discovered facts or circumstances or a change of law supporting the issues reasserted in the summary judgment motion.

(g) Upon the denial of a motion for summary judgment, on the ground that there is a triable issue as to one or more material facts, the court shall, by written or oral order, specify one or more material facts raised by the motion as to which the court has determined there exists a triable controversy. This determination shall specifically refer to the evidence proffered in support of and in opposition to the motion which indicates that a triable controversy exists. Upon the grant of a motion for summary judgment, on the ground that there is no triable issue of material fact, the court shall, by written or oral order, specify the reasons for its determination. The order shall specifically refer to the evidence proffered in support of, and if applicable in opposition to, the motion which indicates that no triable issue exists. The court shall also state its reasons for any other determination. The court shall record its determination by court reporter or written order.

(h) If it appears from the affidavits submitted in opposition to a motion for summary judgment or summary adjudication or both that facts essential to justify opposition may exist but cannot, for reasons stated, then be presented, the court shall deny the motion, or order a continuance to permit affidavits to be obtained or discovery to be had or may make any other order as may be just. The application to continue the motion to obtain necessary discovery may also be made by ex parte motion at any time on or before the date the opposition response to the motion is due.

(i) If, after granting a continuance to allow specified additional discovery, the court determines that the party seeking summary judgment has unreasonably failed to allow the discovery to be conducted, the court shall grant a continuance to permit the discovery to go forward or deny the motion for summary judgment or summary adjudication. This section does not affect or limit the ability of any party to compel discovery under the Civil Discovery Act (Title 4 (commencing with Section 2016.010) of Part 4).

(j) If the court determines at any time that any of the affidavits are presented in bad faith or solely for purposes of delay, the court shall order the party presenting the affidavits to pay the other party the amount of the reasonable expenses which the filing of the affidavits caused the other party to incur. Sanctions may not be imposed pursuant to this subdivision, except on notice contained in a party's papers, or on the court's own noticed motion, and after an opportunity to be heard.

(k) Except when a separate judgment may properly be awarded in the action, no final judgment may be entered on a motion for summary judgment prior to the termination of the action, but the final judgment shall, in addition to any matters determined in the action, award judgment as established by the summary proceeding herein provided for.

(l) In actions which arise out of an injury to the person or to property, if a motion for summary judgment was granted on the basis that the defendant was without fault, no other defendant during trial, over plaintiff's objection, may attempt to attribute fault to or comment on the absence or involvement of the defendant who was granted the motion.

(m)(1) A summary judgment entered under this section is an appealable judgment as in other cases. Upon entry of any order pursuant to this section, except the entry of summary judgment, a party may, within 20 days after service upon him or her of a written notice of entry of the order, petition an appropriate reviewing court for a peremptory writ. If the notice is served by mail, the initial period within which to file the petition shall be increased by five days if the place of address is within the State of California, 10 days if the place of address is outside the State of California but within the United States, and 20 days if the place of address is outside the United States. If the notice is served by facsimile transmission, Express Mail, or another method of delivery providing for overnight delivery, the initial period within which to file the petition shall be increased by two court days. The superior court may, for good cause, and prior to the expiration of the initial period, extend the time for one additional period not to exceed 10 days.

(2) Before a reviewing court affirms an order granting summary judgment or summary adjudication on a ground not relied upon by the trial court, the reviewing court shall afford the parties an opportunity to present their views on the issue by submitting supplemental briefs. The supplemental briefing may include an argument that additional evidence relating to that ground exists, but that the party has not had an adequate opportunity to present the evidence or to conduct discovery on the issue. The court may reverse or remand based upon the supplemental briefing to allow the parties to present additional evidence or to conduct discovery on the issue. If the court fails to allow supplemental briefing, a rehearing shall be ordered upon timely petition of any party.

(n)(1) If a motion for summary adjudication is granted, at the trial of the action, the cause or causes of action within the action, affirmative defense or defenses, claim for damages, or issue or issues of duty as to the motion which has been granted shall be deemed to be established and the action shall proceed as to the cause or causes of action, affirmative defense or defenses, claim for damages, or issue or issues of duty remaining.

(2) In the trial of the action, the fact that a motion for summary adjudication is granted as to one or more causes of action, affirmative defenses, claims for damages, or issues of duty within the action shall not operate to bar any cause of action, affirmative defense, claim for damages, or issue of duty as to which summary adjudication was either not sought or denied.

(3) In the trial of an action, neither a party, nor a witness, nor the court shall comment upon the grant or denial of a motion for summary adjudication to a jury.

(*o*) A cause of action has no merit if either of the following exists:

(1) One or more of the elements of the cause of action cannot be separately established, even if that element is separately pleaded.

(2) A defendant establishes an affirmative defense to that cause of action.

(p) For purposes of motions for summary judgment and summary adjudication:

(1) A plaintiff or cross-complainant has met his or her burden of showing that there is no defense to a cause of action if that party has proved each element of the cause of action entitling the party to judgment on that cause of action. Once the plaintiff or cross-complainant has met that burden, the burden shifts to the defendant or cross-defendant to show that a triable issue of one or more material facts exists as to that cause of action or a defense thereto. The defendant or cross-defendant may not rely upon the mere allegations or denials of its pleadings to show that a triable issue of material fact exists but, instead, shall set forth the specific facts showing that a triable issue of material fact exists as to that cause of action or a defense thereto.

(2) A defendant or cross-defendant has met his or her burden of showing that a cause of action has no merit if that party has shown that one or more elements of the cause of action, even if not separately pleaded, cannot be established, or that there is a complete defense to that cause of action. Once the defendant or cross-defendant has met that burden, the burden shifts to the plaintiff or cross-complainant to show that a triable issue of one or more material facts exists as to that cause of action or a defense thereto. The plaintiff or cross-complainant may not rely upon the mere allegations or denials of its pleadings to show that a triable issue of material fact exists but, instead, shall set forth the specific facts showing that a triable issue of material fact exists as to that cause of action or a defense thereto.

(q) This section does not extend the period for trial provided by Section 1170.5.

(r) Subdivisions (a) and (b) do not apply to actions brought pursuant to Chapter 4 (commencing with Section 1159) of Title 3 of Part 3.

(s)(1) Notwithstanding subdivision (f), a party may move for summary adjudication of a legal issue or a claim for damages other than punitive damages that does not completely dispose of a cause of action, an affirmative defense, or an issue of duty.

(2) This motion may be brought only upon the stipulation of the parties whose claims or defenses are put at issue by the motion and a prior determination and order by the court that the motion will further the interests of judicial economy, by reducing the time to be consumed in trial, or significantly increase the ability of the parties to resolve the case by settlement.

(3) Before a motion may be filed pursuant to this subdivision, the parties shall submit to the court a joint stipulation clearly setting forth the issue or issues to be adjudicated, with a declaration from each stipulating party demonstrating that a ruling on the motion will further the interests of judicial economy by reducing the time to be consumed in trial or significantly increasing the probability of settlement. Within 15 days of the court's receipt of the stipulation and declarations, unless the court has good cause for extending the time in which to make the determination, the court shall notify the submitting parties as to whether the motion may be filed. If the court elects not to allow the filing of the motion, the stipulating parties may request, and upon that request the court shall conduct, an informal conference with the stipulating parties to permit further evaluation of the proposed stipulation; but no further papers may be filed by the parties in support of the proposed motion.

(4) Any motion for summary adjudication brought under this subdivision shall contain the following language, or its substantial equivalent, in the notice of motion:

"This motion is made pursuant to subdivision (s) of Section 437c of the Code of Civil Procedure. The parties to this motion stipulate that the court shall hear the motion and that the resolution of this motion will either further the interests of judicial economy by reducing the time to be consumed in trial or significantly increase the ability of the parties to resolve the case by settlement."

(5) The notice of motion shall be signed by counsel for all parties, and by those parties in propia persona, to the motion.

(6) The joint stipulation shall be served on all parties, if any, who are not parties to the motion specified in paragraph (1). If, within 10 days of the submission of the stipulation, any nonstipulating party files an objection to the determination of the issue, the court may consider the objection in determining whether or not to allow the motion to be filed.

(7) A motion for summary adjudication brought pursuant to this subdivision may be made by itself or as an alternative to a motion for summary judgment and shall proceed in all procedural respects as a motion for summary judgment.

(t) For the purposes of this section, a change in law does not include a later enacted statute without retroactive application.

(u) This section shall remain in effect only until January 1, 2015, and as of that date is repealed, unless a later enacted statute, that is enacted before January 1, 2015, deletes or extends that date. (*Added by Stats.1973, c. 366, p. 807, § 2. Amended by Stats.1976, c. 675, p. 1664, § 1; Stats.1978, c. 949, p. 2930, § 2; Stats.1980, c. 57, p. 151, § 1; Stats.1982, c. 1510, p. 5855, § 1; Stats.1983, c. 490, § 1; Stats.1984, c. 171, § 1; Stats.1986, c. 540, § 3; Stats.1989, c. 1416, § 16; Stats.1990, c. 1561 (S.B.2594), § 2; Stats.1992, c. 339 (S.B.1409), § 1; Stats.1992, c. 1348 (A.B.2616), § 1; Stats.1993, c. 276 (A.B.498), § 1; Stats.1994, c. 493 (A.B.651), § 1, eff. Sept. 12, 1994; Stats.2002, c. 448 (S.B.688), § 5; Stats.2003, c. 62 (S.B.600), § 24; Stats.2004, c. 182 (A.B.3081), § 9, operative July 1, 2005; Stats.2011, c. 419 (S.B.384), § 3.*)

Validity

This statute was held unconstitutional to the extent that it limits the court's ability to reconsider its prior interim orders to correct its own errors, in Le Francois v. Goel (2005) 29 Cal.Rptr.3d 249, 35 Cal.4th 1094, 112 P.3d 636, as modified.

Repeal

For repeal of this section, see its terms.

Law Revision Commission Comments

Subdivision (i) of Section 437c is amended to reflect nonsubstantive reorganization of the rules governing civil discovery. [33 Cal.L.Rev. Comm. Reports 983 (2004)].

Research References

Rutter, Cal. Practice Guide: A.D.R. Ch. 1-E, E. Enforcing ADR Settlements.

Rutter, Cal. Practice Guide: A.D.R. Ch. 5-H, H. Conduct of Arbitration Proceedings.

Rutter, Cal. Practice Guide: A.D.R. Ch. 3B-C, C. Statutorily-Mandated ADR.

§ 437c. Grounds for and effect of summary judgment; procedure on motion

Section operative January 1, 2015. See, also, section operative until January 1, 2015.

(a) Any party may move for summary judgment in any action or proceeding if it is contended that the action has no merit or that there is no defense to the action or proceeding. The motion may be made at any time after 60 days have elapsed since the general appearance in the action or proceeding of each party against whom the motion is directed or at any earlier time after the general appearance that the court, with or without notice and upon good cause shown, may direct. Notice of the motion and supporting papers shall be served on all other parties to the action at least 75 days before the time appointed for hearing. However, if the notice is served by mail, the required 75–day period of notice shall be increased by five days if the place of address is within the State of California, 10 days if the place of address is outside the State of California but within the United States, and 20 days if the place of address is outside the United States, and if the notice is served by facsimile transmission,

Express Mail, or another method of delivery providing for overnight delivery, the required 75–day period of notice shall be increased by two court days. The motion shall be heard no later than 30 days before the date of trial, unless the court for good cause orders otherwise. The filing of the motion shall not extend the time within which a party must otherwise file a responsive pleading.

(b)(1) The motion shall be supported by affidavits, declarations, admissions, answers to interrogatories, depositions, and matters of which judicial notice shall or may be taken. The supporting papers shall include a separate statement setting forth plainly and concisely all material facts which the moving party contends are undisputed. Each of the material facts stated shall be followed by a reference to the supporting evidence. The failure to comply with this requirement of a separate statement may in the court's discretion constitute a sufficient ground for denial of the motion.

(2) Any opposition to the motion shall be served and filed not less than 14 days preceding the noticed or continued date of hearing, unless the court for good cause orders otherwise. The opposition, where appropriate, shall consist of affidavits, declarations, admissions, answers to interrogatories, depositions, and matters of which judicial notice shall or may be taken.

(3) The opposition papers shall include a separate statement that responds to each of the material facts contended by the moving party to be undisputed, indicating whether the opposing party agrees or disagrees that those facts are undisputed. The statement also shall set forth plainly and concisely any other material facts that the opposing party contends are disputed. Each material fact contended by the opposing party to be disputed shall be followed by a reference to the supporting evidence. Failure to comply with this requirement of a separate statement may constitute a sufficient ground, in the court's discretion, for granting the motion.

(4) Any reply to the opposition shall be served and filed by the moving party not less than five days preceding the noticed or continued date of hearing, unless the court for good cause orders otherwise.

(5) Evidentiary objections not made at the hearing shall be deemed waived.

(6) Except for subdivision (c) of Section 1005 relating to the method of service of opposition and reply papers, Sections 1005 and 1013, extending the time within which a right may be exercised or an act may be done, do not apply to this section.

(7) Any incorporation by reference of matter in the court's file shall set forth with specificity the exact matter to which reference is being made and shall not incorporate the entire file.

(c) The motion for summary judgment shall be granted if all the papers submitted show that there is no triable issue as to any material fact and that the moving party is entitled to a judgment as a matter of law. In determining whether the papers show that there is no triable issue as to any material fact the court shall consider all of the evidence set forth in the papers, except that to which objections have been made and sustained by the court, and all inferences reasonably deducible from the evidence, except summary judgment may not be granted by the court based on inferences reasonably deducible from the evidence, if contradicted by other inferences or evidence, which raise a triable issue as to any material fact.

(d) Supporting and opposing affidavits or declarations shall be made by any person on personal knowledge, shall set forth admissible evidence, and shall show affirmatively that the affiant is competent to testify to the matters stated in the affidavits or declarations. Any objections based on the failure to comply with the requirements of this subdivision shall be made at the hearing or shall be deemed waived.

(e) If a party is otherwise entitled to a summary judgment pursuant to this section, summary judgment may not be denied on grounds of credibility or for want of cross-examination of witnesses furnishing affidavits or declarations in support of the summary judgment, except that summary judgment may be denied in the discretion of the court, where the only proof of a material fact offered in support of the summary judgment is an affidavit or declaration made by an individual who was the sole witness to that fact; or where a material fact is an individual's state of mind, or lack thereof, and that fact is sought to be established solely by the individual's affirmation thereof.

(f)(1) A party may move for summary adjudication as to one or more causes of action within an action, one or more affirmative defenses, one or more claims for damages, or one or more issues of duty, if that party contends that the cause of action has no merit or that there is no affirmative defense thereto, or that there is no merit to an affirmative defense as to any cause of action, or both, or that there is no merit to a claim for damages, as specified in Section 3294 of the Civil Code, or that one or more defendants either owed or did not owe a duty to the plaintiff or plaintiffs. A motion for summary adjudication shall be granted only if it completely disposes of a cause of action, an affirmative defense, a claim for damages, or an issue of duty.

(2) A motion for summary adjudication may be made by itself or as an alternative to a motion for summary judgment and shall proceed in all procedural respects as a motion for summary judgment. However, a party may not move for summary judgment based on issues asserted in a prior motion for summary adjudication and denied by the court, unless that party establishes to the satisfaction of the court, newly discovered facts or circumstances or a change of law supporting the issues reasserted in the summary judgment motion.

(g) Upon the denial of a motion for summary judgment, on the ground that there is a triable issue as to one or more material facts, the court shall, by written or oral order, specify one or more material facts raised by the motion as to which the court has determined there exists a triable controversy. This determination shall specifically refer to the evidence proffered in support of and in opposition to the motion which indicates that a triable controversy exists. Upon the grant of a motion for summary judgment, on the ground that there is no triable issue of material fact, the court shall, by written or oral order, specify the reasons for its determination. The order shall specifically refer to the evidence proffered in support of, and if applicable in opposition to, the motion which indicates that no triable issue exists. The court shall also state its reasons for any other determination. The court shall record its determination by court reporter or written order.

(h) If it appears from the affidavits submitted in opposition to a motion for summary judgment or summary adjudication or both that facts essential to justify opposition may exist but cannot, for reasons stated, then be presented, the court shall deny the motion, or order a continuance to permit affidavits to be obtained or discovery to be had or may make any other order as may be just. The application to continue the motion to obtain necessary discovery may also be made by ex parte motion at any time on or before the date the opposition response to the motion is due.

(i) If, after granting a continuance to allow specified additional discovery, the court determines that the party seeking summary judgment has unreasonably failed to allow the discovery to be conducted, the court shall grant a continuance to permit the discovery to go forward or deny the motion for summary judgment or summary adjudication. This section does not affect or limit the ability of any party to compel discovery under the Civil Discovery Act (Title 4 (commencing with Section 2016.010) of Part 4).

(j) If the court determines at any time that any of the affidavits are presented in bad faith or solely for purposes of delay, the court shall order the party presenting the affidavits to pay the other party the amount of the reasonable expenses which the filing of the affidavits caused the other party to incur. Sanctions may not be imposed pursuant to this subdivision, except on notice contained in a party's papers, or on the court's own noticed motion, and after an opportunity to be heard.

(k) Except when a separate judgment may properly be awarded in the action, no final judgment may be entered on a motion for summary judgment prior to the termination of the action, but the final judgment shall, in addition to any matters determined in the action, award judgment as established by the summary proceeding herein provided for.

(*l*) In actions which arise out of an injury to the person or to property, if a motion for summary judgment was granted on the basis that the defendant was without fault, no other defendant during trial, over plaintiff's objection, may attempt to attribute fault to or comment on the absence or involvement of the defendant who was granted the motion.

(m)(1) A summary judgment entered under this section is an appealable judgment as in other cases. Upon entry of any order pursuant to this section, except the entry of summary judgment, a party may, within 20 days after service upon him or her of a written notice of entry of the order, petition an appropriate reviewing court for a peremptory writ. If the notice is served by mail, the initial period within which to file the petition shall be increased by five days if the place of address is within the State of California, 10 days if the place of address is outside the State of California but within the United States, and 20 days if the place of address is outside the United States. If the notice is served by facsimile transmission, Express Mail, or another method of delivery providing for overnight delivery, the initial period within which to file the petition shall be increased by two court days. The superior court may, for good cause, and prior to the expiration of the initial period, extend the time for one additional period not to exceed 10 days.

(2) Before a reviewing court affirms an order granting summary judgment or summary adjudication on a ground not relied upon by the trial court, the reviewing court shall afford the parties an opportunity to present their views on the issue by submitting supplemental briefs. The supplemental briefing may include an argument that additional evidence relating to that ground exists, but that the party has not had an adequate opportunity to present the evidence or to conduct discovery on the issue. The court may reverse or remand based upon the supplemental briefing to allow the parties to present additional evidence or to conduct discovery on the issue. If the court fails to allow supplemental briefing, a rehearing shall be ordered upon timely petition of any party.

(n)(1) If a motion for summary adjudication is granted, at the trial of the action, the cause or causes of action within the action, affirmative defense or defenses, claim for damages, or issue or issues of duty as to the motion which has been granted shall be deemed to be established and the action shall proceed as to the cause or causes of action, affirmative defense or defenses, claim for damages, or issue or issues of duty remaining.

(2) In the trial of the action, the fact that a motion for summary adjudication is granted as to one or more causes of action, affirmative defenses, claims for damages, or issues of duty within the action shall not operate to bar any cause of action, affirmative defense, claim for damages, or issue of duty as to which summary adjudication was either not sought or denied.

(3) In the trial of an action, neither a party, nor a witness, nor the court shall comment upon the grant or denial of a motion for summary adjudication to a jury.

(*o*) A cause of action has no merit if either of the following exists:

(1) One or more of the elements of the cause of action cannot be separately established, even if that element is separately pleaded.

(2) A defendant establishes an affirmative defense to that cause of action.

(p) For purposes of motions for summary judgment and summary adjudication:

(1) A plaintiff or cross-complainant has met his or her burden of showing that there is no defense to a cause of action if that party has proved each element of the cause of action entitling the party to judgment on that cause of action. Once the plaintiff or cross-complainant has met that burden, the burden shifts to the defendant or cross-defendant to show that a triable issue of one or more material facts exists as to that cause of action or a defense thereto. The defendant or cross-defendant may not rely upon the mere allegations or denials of its pleadings to show that a triable issue of material fact exists but, instead, shall set forth the specific facts showing that a triable issue of material fact exists as to that cause of action or a defense thereto.

(2) A defendant or cross-defendant has met his or her burden of showing that a cause of action has no merit if that party has shown that one or more elements of the cause of action, even if not separately pleaded, cannot be established, or that there is a complete defense to that cause of action. Once the defendant or cross-defendant has met that burden, the burden shifts to the plaintiff or cross-complainant to show that a triable issue of one or more material facts exists as to that cause of action or a defense thereto. The plaintiff or cross-complainant may not rely upon the mere allegations or denials of its pleadings to show that a triable issue of material fact exists but, instead, shall set forth the specific facts showing that a triable issue of material fact exists as to that cause of action or a defense thereto.

(q) This section does not extend the period for trial provided by Section 1170.5.

(r) Subdivisions (a) and (b) do not apply to actions brought pursuant to Chapter 4 (commencing with Section 1159) of Title 3 of Part 3.

(s) For the purposes of this section, a change in law does not include a later enacted statute without retroactive application.

(t) This section shall become operative on January 1, 2015. (*Added by Stats.2011, c. 419 (S.B.384), § 4, operative Jan. 1, 2015.*)

Research References

Rutter, Cal. Practice Guide: A.D.R. Ch. 1-E, E. Enforcing ADR Settlements.
Rutter, Cal. Practice Guide: A.D.R. Ch. 5-H, H. Conduct of Arbitration Proceedings.
Rutter, Cal. Practice Guide: A.D.R. Ch. 3B-C, C. Statutorily-Mandated ADR.
Rutter, Cal. Practice Guide: Civil Appeals & Writs Ch. 2-C, C. Nonappealable Orders.
Rutter, Cal. Practice Guide: Civil Appeals & Writs Ch. 8-C, C. Standards of Appellate Review.
Rutter, Cal. Practice Guide: Civil Appeals & Writs Ch. 8-D, D. Limits on Assertion of Issues on Appeal.
Rutter, Cal. Practice Guide: Civil Appeals & Writs Ch. 9-B, B. Approaches to Briefwriting.
Rutter, Cal. Practice Guide: Civil Appeals & Writs Ch. 9-D, D. Procedural Rules.
Rutter, Cal. Practice Guide: Civil Appeals & Writs Ch. 11-C, C. Rendition of Opinion and Judgment.

§ 438. Judgment on the pleadings; grounds; motions; conditions for motions; amended complaint or answer

(a) As used in this section:

(1) "Complaint" includes a cross-complaint.

(2) "Plaintiff" includes a cross-complainant.

(3) "Defendant" includes a cross-defendant.

(b)(1) A party may move for judgment on the pleadings.

(2) The court may upon its own motion grant a motion for judgment on the pleadings.

(c)(1) The motion provided for in this section may only be made on one of the following grounds:

(A) If the moving party is a plaintiff, that the complaint states facts sufficient to constitute a cause or causes of action against the defendant and the answer does not state facts sufficient to constitute a defense to the complaint.

(B) If the moving party is a defendant, that either of the following conditions exist:

(i) The court has no jurisdiction of the subject of the cause of action alleged in the complaint.

(ii) The complaint does not state facts sufficient to constitute a cause of action against that defendant.

(2) The motion provided for in this section may be made as to either of the following:

(A) The entire complaint or cross-complaint or as to any of the causes of action stated therein.

(B) The entire answer or one or more of the affirmative defenses set forth in the answer.

(3) If the court on its own motion grants the motion for judgment on the pleadings, it shall be on one of the following bases:

(A) If the motion is granted in favor of the plaintiff, it shall be based on the grounds that the complaint states facts sufficient to constitute a cause or causes of action against the defendant and the answer does not state facts sufficient to constitute a defense to the complaint.

(B) If the motion is granted in favor of the defendant, that either of the following conditions exist:

(i) The court has no jurisdiction of the subject of the cause of action alleged in the complaint.

(ii) The complaint does not state facts sufficient to constitute a cause of action against that defendant.

(d) The grounds for motion provided for in this section shall appear on the face of the challenged pleading or from any matter of which the court is required to take judicial notice. Where the motion is based on a matter of which the court may take judicial notice pursuant to Section 452 or 453 of the Evidence Code, the matter shall be specified in the notice of motion, or in the supporting points and authorities, except as the court may otherwise permit.

(e) No motion may be made pursuant to this section if a pretrial conference order has been entered pursuant to Section 575, or within 30 days of the date the action is initially set for trial, whichever is later, unless the court otherwise permits.

(f) The motion provided for in this section may be made only after one of the following conditions has occurred:

(1) If the moving party is a plaintiff, and the defendant has already filed his or her answer to the complaint and the time for the plaintiff to demur to the answer has expired.

(2) If the moving party is a defendant, and the defendant has already filed his or her answer to the complaint and the time for the defendant to demur to the complaint has expired.

(g) The motion provided for in this section may be made even though either of the following conditions exist:

(1) The moving party has already demurred to the complaint or answer, as the case may be, on the same grounds as is the basis for the motion provided for in this section and the demurrer has been overruled, provided that there has been a material change in applicable case law or statute since the ruling on the demurrer.

(2) The moving party did not demur to the complaint or answer, as the case may be, on the same grounds as is the basis for the motion provided for in this section.

(h)(1) The motion provided for in this section may be granted with or without leave to file an amended complaint or answer, as the case may be.

(2) Where a motion is granted pursuant to this section with leave to file an amended complaint or answer, as the case may be, then the court shall grant 30 days to the party against whom the motion was granted to file an amended complaint or answer, as the case may be.

(3) If the motion is granted with respect to the entire complaint or answer without leave to file an amended complaint or answer, as the case may be, then judgment shall be entered forthwith in accordance with the motion granting judgment to the moving party.

(4) If the motion is granted with leave to file an amended complaint or answer, as the case may be, then the following procedures shall be followed:

(A) If an amended complaint is filed after the time to file an amended complaint has expired, then the court may strike the complaint pursuant to Section 436 and enter judgment in favor of that defendant against that plaintiff or a plaintiff.

(B) If an amended answer is filed after the time to file an amended answer has expired, then the court may strike the answer pursuant to Section 436 and proceed to enter judgment in favor of that plaintiff and against that defendant or a defendant.

(C) Except where subparagraphs (A) and (B) apply, if the motion is granted with respect to the entire complaint or answer with leave to file an amended complaint or answer, as the case may be, but an amended complaint or answer is not filed, then after the time to file an amended complaint or answer, as the case may be, has expired, judgment shall be entered forthwith in favor of the moving party.

(i)(1) Where a motion for judgment on the pleadings is granted with leave to amend, the court shall not enter a judgment in favor of a party until the following proceedings are had:

(A) If an amended pleading is filed and the moving party contends that pleading is filed after the time to file an amended pleading has expired or that the pleading is in violation of the court's prior ruling on the motion, then that party shall move to strike the pleading and enter judgment in its favor.

(B) If no amended pleading is filed, then the party shall move for entry of judgment in its favor.

(2) All motions made pursuant to this subdivision shall be made pursuant to Section 1010.

(3) At the hearing on the motion provided for in this subdivision, the court shall determine whether to enter judgment in favor of a particular party. *(Added by Stats.1993, c. 456 (A.B.58), § 5. Amended by Stats.1994, c. 493 (A.B.651), § 2, eff. Sept. 12, 1994.)*

Research References

Rutter, Cal. Practice Guide: Civil Appeals & Writs Ch. 8-C, C. Standards of Appellate Review.

Rutter, Cal. Practice Guide: Civ. Pro. Before Trial Ch. 10-B, B. Role of Pleadings in Summary Judgment Procedure.

Rutter, Cal. Practice Guide: Civ. Pro. Before Trial Ch. 7(I)-C, C. Motion for Judgment on the Pleadings.

Rutter, Cal. Practice Guide: Civil Trials & Evidence Ch. 4-I, I. Other Motions at Final Status Conference.

Rutter, Cal. Practice Guide: Insurance Litigation Ch. 15-F, F. Pretrial Motions.

Rutter, Cal. Practice Guide: Personal Injury Ch. 9-L, L. Motions to Terminate Trial Before Verdict.

Miller and Starr California Real Estate § 10:76, Payment by Setoff; General Rules.

16 NO. 6 Miller & Starr, California Real Estate Newsalert 4, Broker's Compensation.

5 Witkin Cal. Proc. 5th Pleading § 1002, Motion for Judgment on Pleadings.

5 Witkin Cal. Proc. 5th Pleading § 1156, Nature of Former Restricted Cross-Complaint.

6 Witkin Cal. Proc. 5th Proceedings Without Trial § 186, (S 186) Statutory Motion.

6 Witkin Cal. Proc. 5th Proceedings Without Trial § 187, (S 187) General Demurrer Compared.

6 Witkin Cal. Proc. 5th Proceedings Without Trial § 189, (S 189) Statutory Requirements.

6 Witkin Cal. Proc. 5th Proceedings Without Trial § 190, (S 190) Motion by Defendant.

6 Witkin Cal. Proc. 5th Proceedings Without Trial § 192, (S 192) Notice.

6 Witkin Cal. Proc. 5th Proceedings Without Trial § 193, (S 193) Time of Motion.

6 Witkin Cal. Proc. 5th Proceedings Without Trial § 194, (S 194) Effect of Failure to File General Demurrer.

6 Witkin Cal. Proc. 5th Proceedings Without Trial § 195, (S 195) Effect of Prior Overruling of General Demurrer.

CHAPTER 6. VERIFICATION OF PLEADINGS

Section

446. Subscription of pleadings; necessity of verification; affidavit of party; who may verify; verification by attorney or by officer of corporation or agency; affidavit; assertion of truth under penalty of perjury.

§ 446. Subscription of pleadings; necessity of verification; affidavit of party; who may verify; verification by attorney or by officer of corporation or agency; affidavit; assertion of truth under penalty of perjury

(a) Every pleading shall be subscribed by the party or his or her attorney. When the state, any county thereof, city, school district, district, public agency, or public corporation, or any officer of the state, or of any county thereof, city, school district, district, public agency, or public corporation, in his or her official capacity, is plaintiff, the answer shall be verified, unless an admission of the truth of the complaint might subject the party to a criminal prosecution, or, unless a county thereof, city, school district, district, public agency, or public corporation, or an officer of the state, or of any county, city, school district, district, public agency, or public corporation, in his or her official capacity, is defendant. When the complaint is verified, the answer shall be verified. In all cases of a verification of a pleading, the affidavit of the party shall state that the same is true of his own knowledge, except as to the matters which are therein stated on his or her information or belief, and as to those matters that he or she believes it to be true; and where a pleading is verified, it shall be by the affidavit of a party, unless the parties are absent from the county where the attorney has his or her office, or from some cause unable to verify it, or the facts are within the knowledge of his or her attorney or other person verifying the same. When the pleading is verified by the attorney, or any other person except one of the parties, he or she shall set forth in the affidavit the reasons why it is not made by one of the parties.

When a corporation is a party, the verification may be made by any officer thereof. When the state, any county thereof, city, school district, district, public agency, or public corporation, or an officer of the state, or of any county thereof, city, school district, district, public agency, or public corporation, in his or her official capacity is plaintiff, the complaint need not be verified; and if the state, any county thereof, city, school district, district, public agency, or public corporation, or an officer of such state, county, city, school district, district, public agency, or public corporation, in his or her official capacity is defendant, its or his or her answer need not be verified.

When the verification is made by the attorney for the reason that the parties are absent from the county where he or she has his or her office, or from some other cause are unable to verify it, or when the verification is made on behalf of a corporation or public agency by any officer thereof, the attorney's or officer's affidavit shall state that he or she has read the pleading and that he or she is informed and believes the matters therein to be true and on that ground alleges that the matters stated therein are true. However, in those cases the pleadings shall not otherwise be considered as an affidavit or declaration establishing the facts therein alleged.

A person verifying a pleading need not swear to the truth or his or her belief in the truth of the matters stated therein but may, instead, assert the truth or his or her belief in the truth of those matters "under penalty of perjury."

(b) This section shall become operative on January 1, 1999, unless a statute that becomes effective on or before this date extends or deletes the repeal date of Section 446, as amended by Assembly Bill 3594 of the 1993–94 Regular Session. *(Added by Stats.1994, c. 1062 (A.B.3594), § 5, operative Jan. 1, 1999.)*

Research References

Rutter, Cal. Practice Guide: Civil Appeals & Writs Ch. 15-E, E. Procedures on Writ Review.
Rutter, Cal. Practice Guide: Civ. Pro. Before Trial Ch. 6-B, B. Complaints.
Rutter, Cal. Practice Guide: Civ. Pro. Before Trial Ch. 6-C, C. Answer.
Rutter, Cal. Practice Guide: Civ. Pro. Before Trial Ch. 9(I)-B, B. Preparing and Filing Motions.
Rutter, Cal. Practice Guide: Civ. Pro. Before Trial Ch. 9(II)-A, A. Injunctions.
Rutter, Cal. Practice Guide: Civ. Pro. Before Trial Ch. 9(II)-D, D. Attachment.
Rutter, Cal. Practice Guide: Civil Trials & Evidence Ch. 3-A, A. Challenges for Cause.
California Practice Guide: Employment Litigation Ch. 13-H, H. Contesting Citations and Related Orders and Notices.
Rutter, Cal. Practice Guide: Enforcing Judgments/Debts Ch. 4-A, A. Attachment.
Rutter, Cal. Practice Guide: Enforcing Judgments/Debts Ch. 4-B, B. Claim and Delivery.
Rutter, Cal. Practice Guide: Enforcing Judgments/Debts Ch. 4-C, C. Receiverships.
8 Witkin Cal. Proc. 5th Extraordinary Writs § 172, Verification.
4 Witkin Cal. Proc. 5th Pleading § 398, (S 398) Right to Plead.
4 Witkin Cal. Proc. 5th Pleading § 459, (S 459) Nature of Verification.
4 Witkin Cal. Proc. 5th Pleading § 461, (S 461) Who May Verify.
4 Witkin Cal. Proc. 5th Pleading § 462, Affidavit or Declaration.
4 Witkin Cal. Proc. 5th Pleading § 464, (S 464) Statement of Reasons.
4 Witkin Cal. Proc. 5th Pleading § 465, (S 465) Verification by Attorney or Officer.
4 Witkin Cal. Proc. 5th Pleading § 466, Complaint or Petition.
4 Witkin Cal. Proc. 5th Pleading § 467, Answer.
4 Witkin Cal. Proc. 5th Pleading § 471, Superior Court.
6 Witkin Cal. Proc. 5th Provisional Remedies § 103, Notice of Opposition.
6 Witkin Cal. Proc. 5th Provisional Remedies § 377, Showing by Verified Complaint.
12 Witkin, California Summary 10th Real Property § 730, Pleadings.

CHAPTER 7. GENERAL RULES OF PLEADING

Section

461.   Libel and slander; answer; evidence of mitigating circumstances.

464.   Supplemental pleadings.

465.   Subsequent pleadings and proof of service; filing; service.

§ 452.   Liberal construction

PLEADINGS TO BE LIBERALLY CONSTRUED. In the construction of a pleading, for the purpose of determining its effect, its allegations must be liberally construed, with a view to substantial justice between the parties. *(Enacted in 1872.)*

Research References

Rutter, Cal. Practice Guide: Civ. Pro. Before Trial Ch. 7(I)-A, A. Demurrers.

Rutter, Cal. Practice Guide: Civ. Pro. Before Trial Ch. 7(I)-B, B. Motions to Strike.

4 Witkin Cal. Proc. 5th Pleading § 442, General Rule.

§ 454.   Pleading accounts; delivery of copy after demand; exclusion from evidence; further account; verification

It is not necessary for a party to set forth in a pleading the items of an account therein alleged, but he must deliver to the adverse party, within ten days after a demand thereof in writing, a copy of the account, or be precluded from giving evidence thereof. The court or judge thereof may order a further account when the one delivered is too general, or is defective in any particular.

If the pleading is verified the account must be verified by the affidavit of the party to the effect that he believes it to be true; or if the facts are within the personal knowledge of the agent or attorney for the party, or the party is not within the county where the attorney has his office or from some cause unable to make the affidavit, by the affidavit of the agent or attorney. *(Enacted in 1872. Amended by Code Am.1880, c. 14, p. 2, § 2; Stats.1939, c. 63, p. 1005, § 1.)*

Research References

Rutter, Cal. Practice Guide: Civ. Pro. Before Trial Ch. 6-B, B. Complaints.

Rutter, Cal. Practice Guide: Civ. Pro. Before Trial Ch. 8A-6, Statutory Procedures Outside Discovery Act.

Rutter, Cal. Practice Guide: Civ. Pro. Before Trial Ch. 8D-5, Selecting Proper Discovery Tools.

Rutter, Cal. Practice Guide: Civ. Pro. Before Trial Ch. 8D-6, Determining Sequence of Discovery Procedures.

Rutter, Cal. Practice Guide: Civ. Pro. Before Trial Ch. 8K-2, Demand for Bill of Particulars.

Rutter, Cal. Practice Guide: Civ. Pro. Before Trial Ch. 8D-5, Outline 5.

Rutter, Cal. Practice Guide: Fed.Civ.Pro. Before Trial Ch. 9-A, Introduction.

4 Witkin Cal. Proc. 5th Pleading § 471, Superior Court.

4 Witkin Cal. Proc. 5th Pleading § 499, Limited to Action on Account.

4 Witkin Cal. Proc. 5th Pleading § 501, (S 501) Ordinary Contract and Quasi-Contract Actions.

4 Witkin Cal. Proc. 5th Pleading § 502, (S 502) Account Stated or Other Superseding Contract.

4 Witkin Cal. Proc. 5th Pleading § 503, (S 503) Defendant's Demand.

4 Witkin Cal. Proc. 5th Pleading § 504, (S 504) Delivery of Account.

4 Witkin Cal. Proc. 5th Pleading § 505, (S 505) Amendment or Further Account.

4 Witkin Cal. Proc. 5th Pleading § 507, (S 507) in General.

4 Witkin Cal. Proc. 5th Pleading § 510, (S 510) Relief from Default.

§ 455.   Real estate; description with certainty

DESCRIPTION OF REAL PROPERTY IN A PLEADING. In an action for the recovery of real property, it must be described in the complaint with such certainty as to enable an officer, upon execution, to identify it. *(Enacted in 1872.)*

Research References

4 Witkin Cal. Proc. 5th Pleading § 471, Superior Court.

5 Witkin Cal. Proc. 5th Pleading § 635, Elements of Cause of Action.

§ 456.   Pleading judgments or determinations; establishment of jurisdictional facts

In pleading a judgment or other determination of a court, officer, or board, it is not necessary to state the facts conferring jurisdiction, but such judgment or determination may be stated to have been duly given or made and to have become final. If such allegation be controverted, the party pleading must establish on the trial the facts conferring jurisdiction and creating finality. *(Enacted in 1872. Amended by Stats.1957, c. 1365, p. 2700, § 1.)*

Research References

4 Witkin Cal. Proc. 5th Pleading § 390, (S 390) Judgment or Administrative Determination.

5 Witkin Cal. Proc. 5th Pleading § 902, (S 902) Personal Representative.

§ 457.   Performance of conditions precedent; pleading and proof

CONDITIONS PRECEDENT, HOW TO BE PLEADED. In pleading the performance of conditions precedent in a contract, it is not necessary to state the facts showing such performance, but it may be stated generally that the party duly performed all the conditions on his part, and if such allegation be controverted, the party pleading must establish, on the trial, the facts showing such performance. *(Enacted in 1872.)*

Research References

Rutter, Cal. Practice Guide: Civ. Pro. Before Trial Ch. 6-B, B. Complaints.

4 Witkin Cal. Proc. 5th Pleading § 388, (S 388) Conditions Precedent.

4 Witkin Cal. Proc. 5th Pleading § 530, (S 530) Conditions Precedent.

5 Witkin Cal. Proc. 5th Pleading § 801, (S 801) Forms of Allegation.

§ 458.   Statute of limitations; pleading and proof

STATUTE OF LIMITATIONS, HOW PLEADED. In pleading the Statute of Limitations it is not necessary to state the facts showing the defense, but it may be stated generally that the cause of action is barred by the provisions of Section ____ (giving the number of the section and subdivision thereof, if it is so divided, relied upon) of the Code of Civil Procedure; and if such allegation be controverted, the party pleading must establish, on the trial, the facts showing that the cause of action is so barred. *(Enacted in 1872.)*

Research References

Rutter, Cal. Practice Guide: Civ. Pro. Before Trial Ch. 6-C, C. Answer.

Rutter, Cal. Practice Guide: Civ. Pro. Before Trial Ch. 7(I)-A, A. Demurrers.

California Practice Guide: Employment Litigation Ch. 16-E, E. Statute of Limitations.

Rutter, Cal. Practice Guide: Insurance Litigation Ch. 15-E, E. Pleadings.

Rutter, Cal. Practice Guide: Personal Injury Ch. 5-E, E. Selected Pleading Issues.

4 Witkin Cal. Proc. 5th Pleading § 391, (S 391) Other Matters.

5 Witkin Cal. Proc. 5th Pleading § 1120, Pleading Section Where No Subdivision.

5 Witkin Cal. Proc. 5th Pleading § 1121, Pleading Subdivision.

§ 459.   Private statutes, ordinances or rights thereunder; performance of conditions precedent; pleading and proof

In pleading a private statute, or an ordinance of a county or municipal corporation, or a right derived therefrom, it is sufficient to refer to such statute or ordinance by its title and the day of its passage. In pleading the performance of conditions precedent under a statute or an ordinance of a county or municipal corporation, or of a right derived therefrom, it is not necessary to state the facts showing such performance, but it may be stated generally that the party duly performed all the conditions on his part required thereby; if such allegations be controverted the party pleading must establish on the trial the facts showing such performance. *(Enacted in 1872. Amended by Stats.1907, c. 372, p. 707, § 10.)*

Research References

4 Witkin Cal. Proc. 5th Pleading § 388, (S 388) Conditions Precedent.
4 Witkin Cal. Proc. 5th Pleading § 389, (S 389) Ordinance or Private Statute.
4 Witkin Cal. Proc. 5th Pleading § 487, (S 487) Forms of Allegation.
4 Witkin Cal. Proc. 5th Pleading § 621, Elements of Cause of Action.

§ 460. Libel and slander; pleading and proof

LIBEL AND SLANDER, HOW STATED IN COMPLAINT. NOT NECESSARY TO ALLEGE OR PROVE SPECIAL DAMAGES. In an action for libel or slander it is not necessary to state in the complaint any extrinsic facts for the purpose of showing the application to the plaintiff of the defamatory matter out of which the cause of action arose; but it is sufficient to state, generally, that the same was published or spoken concerning the plaintiff; and if such allegation be controverted, the plaintiff must establish on the trial that it was so published or spoken. *(Enacted in 1872.)*

Research References

4 Witkin Cal. Proc. 5th Pleading § 391, (S 391) Other Matters.
4 Witkin Cal. Proc. 5th Pleading § 471, Superior Court.
5 Witkin Cal. Proc. 5th Pleading § 744, Colloquium: Publication Concerning Plaintiff.

§ 460.5. Libel and slander; application to shorten time of response to complaint; order; precedence in setting for hearing or trial

(a) In any action for libel or slander, for good cause shown upon ex parte written application, the court may order that the time to respond to the complaint is 20 days after the service of summons on the defendant. The application shall be supported by an affidavit stating facts showing, among other things, that the alleged defamatory matter has been continuously published and that there is a reasonable likelihood that the publication will continue. The order shall direct the clerk to endorse the summons to show that the time to respond has been shortened pursuant to this section. A copy of the application, affidavit, and order shall be served with the summons.

(b) In any such action, unless otherwise ordered by the court for good cause shown, the time allowed the defendant to respond to the complaint or amend the answer under Section 586 shall not exceed 10 days.

(c) The court shall give any such action precedence over all other civil actions, except actions to which special precedence is given by law, in the matter of the setting the case for hearing or trial, and in hearing the case, to the end that all such actions shall be quickly heard and determined. Except for good cause shown, the court shall not grant a continuance in excess of 10 days without the consent of the adverse party.

(d) For purposes of this section, "continuously published" means three or more publications within 15 days. *(Added by Stats.1972, c. 594, § 1.)*

Research References

Rutter, Cal. Practice Guide: Civ. Pro. Before Trial Ch. 12(I)-C, C. Claims for Trial Setting Preference.
3 Witkin Cal. Proc. 5th Actions § 985, (S 985) Special Statutes.

7 Witkin Cal. Proc. 5th Trial § 72, (S 72) Miscellaneous Statutes.

§ 460.7. Libel and slander; election campaign; time to respond to pleadings; precedence; expedition

(a) In any action by a candidate or former candidate for elective public office against a holder of elective public office or an opposing candidate for libel or slander that is alleged to have occurred during the course of an election campaign, the court shall order that the time to respond to the complaint is 20 days after the service of summons on the defendant. The order shall direct the clerk to endorse the summons to show that the time to respond has been shortened pursuant to this section. A copy of the affidavit and order shall be served with the summons.

(b) In any action described in subdivision (a), unless otherwise ordered by the court for good cause shown, the time allowed the defendant to respond to the complaint or amend the answer under Section 586 shall not exceed 10 days.

(c) The court shall give any action described in subdivision (a) precedence over all other civil actions, except actions to which special precedence is given by law, in the matter of the setting of the case of hearing or trial, and in hearing the case, to the end that all actions described in subdivision (a) shall be quickly heard and determined. Except for good cause shown, the court shall not grant a continuance in excess of 10 days without the consent of the adverse party. *(Added by Stats.1982, c. 1642, p. 6676, § 2. Amended by Stats.2006, c. 538 (S.B.1852), § 64.)*

Research References

7 Witkin Cal. Proc. 5th Trial § 72, (S 72) Miscellaneous Statutes.

§ 461. Libel and slander; answer; evidence of mitigating circumstances

In any action within Section 460 or 460.5, the defendant may, in his answer, allege both the truth of the matter charged as defamatory, and any mitigating circumstances, to reduce the amount of damages. Whether he proves the justification or not, he may give in evidence the mitigating circumstances. *(Enacted in 1872. Amended by Stats.1972, c. 594, § 2.)*

Research References

5 Witkin Cal. Proc. 5th Pleading § 738, (S 738) Pleading of Falsity is Not Required.
5 Witkin Cal. Proc. 5th Pleading § 1101, Justification or Privilege.
5 Witkin Cal. Proc. 5th Pleading § 1106, Mitigation of Damages.
6 Witkin, California Summary 10th Torts § 1630, (S 1630) Other Mitigating Factors.

§ 464. Supplemental pleadings

(a) The plaintiff and defendant, respectively, may be allowed, on motion, to make a supplemental complaint or answer, alleging facts material to the case occurring after the former complaint or answer.

(b) The plaintiff and defendant, or petitioner and respondent, may, in any action in which the support of children is an issue, file a supplemental complaint seeking a judgment or order of paternity or support for a child of the mother and father of the child whose paternity and support are already in issue before the court. A supplemental complaint for paternity or child support may be filed without leave of court either before or after final judgment in the underlying action.

(c) Upon the filing of a supplemental complaint, the court clerk shall issue an amended or supplemental summons pursuant to Section 412.10. Service of the supplemental summons and complaint shall be made in the manner provided for the initial service of a summons by this code. *(Enacted in 1872. Amended by Stats.1994, c. 1269 (A.B.2208), § 2.8.)*

Research References

Rutter, Cal. Practice Guide: Civ. Pro. Before Trial Ch. 6-E, E. Amended and Supplemental Pleadings.
Rutter, Cal. Practice Guide: Family Law Ch. 6-A, A. Child Support.
5 Witkin Cal. Proc. 5th Pleading § 1246, (S 1246) Nature of Supplemental Pleadings.
5 Witkin Cal. Proc. 5th Pleading § 1247, (S 1247) Procedure.
5 Witkin Cal. Proc. 5th Pleading § 1252, Distinctions and Qualifications.
11 Witkin, California Summary 10th Husband and Wife § 83, Petition.
11 Witkin, California Summary 10th Husband and Wife § 324, (S 324) Pleadings.

§ 465. Subsequent pleadings and proof of service; filing; service

Except with leave of the court, all pleadings subsequent to the complaint, together with proof of service unless a summons need be issued, shall be filed with the clerk or judge, and copies thereof served upon the adverse party or his or her attorney. *(Enacted in 1872. Amended by Code Am.1873–74, c. 383, p. 301, § 57; Stats.1933, c. 744, p. 1850, § 30; Stats.1951, c. 1737, p. 4103, § 55; Stats.1979, c. 212, p. 457, § 3; Stats.1986, c. 953, § 3.)*

Research References

Rutter, Cal. Practice Guide: Civ. Pro. Before Trial Ch. 6-C, C. Answer.
4 Witkin Cal. Proc. 5th Pleading § 19, in General.
4 Witkin Cal. Proc. 5th Pleading § 29, (S 29) Service.
5 Witkin Cal. Proc. 5th Pleading § 979, (S 979) Service and Filing.
5 Witkin Cal. Proc. 5th Pleading § 1242, in General.

CHAPTER 8. VARIANCE—MISTAKES IN PLEADINGS AND AMENDMENTS

Section

§ 469. Variance; when material; order for amendment

No variance between the allegation in a pleading and the proof is to be deemed material, unless it has actually misled the adverse party to his prejudice in maintaining his action or defense upon the merits. Whenever it appears that a party has been so misled, the Court may order the pleading to be amended, upon such terms as may be just. *(Enacted in 1872. Amended by Code Am. 1873–74, c. 383, p. 302, § 58.)*

Research References

Rutter, Cal. Practice Guide: Civ. Pro. Before Trial Ch. 6-A, A. Introduction.
Rutter, Cal. Practice Guide: Civ. Pro. Before Trial Ch. 10-F, F. Burden of Proof on Motion.
5 Witkin Cal. Proc. 5th Pleading § 1210, Immaterial Variance.
5 Witkin Cal. Proc. 5th Pleading § 1211, (S 1211) Liberal Allowance of Amendment.
5 Witkin Cal. Proc. 5th Pleading § 1214, Substantial Variance Cured by Trial.
10 Witkin, California Summary 10th Parent and Child § 564, in General.
10 Witkin, California Summary 10th Parent and Child § 654, (S 654) Power to Modify or Correct.
10 Witkin, California Summary 10th Parent and Child § 774, Variance and Amendment.
11 Witkin, California Summary 10th Husband and Wife § 117, (S 117) Power to Enter Judgment.

§ 470. Immaterial variance; findings; amendment

Where the variance is not material, as provided in Section 469 the court may direct the fact to be found according to the evidence, or may order an immediate amendment, without costs. *(Enacted in 1872. Amended by Stats.1986, c. 540, § 4.)*

Research References

Rutter, Cal. Practice Guide: Civ. Pro. Before Trial Ch. 10-F, F. Burden of Proof on Motion.
5 Witkin Cal. Proc. 5th Pleading § 1210, Immaterial Variance.
10 Witkin, California Summary 10th Parent and Child § 654, (S 654) Power to Modify or Correct.

§ 471. Variance distinguished from failure of proof

Where, however, the allegation of the claim or defense to which the proof is directed, is unproved, not in some particular or particulars only, but in its general scope and meaning, it is not to be deemed a case of variance, within the meaning of Sections 469 and 470, but a failure of proof. *(Enacted in 1872. Amended by Stats.1986, c. 540, § 5.)*

Research References

Rutter, Cal. Practice Guide: Civ. Pro. Before Trial Ch. 6-A, A. Introduction.
5 Witkin Cal. Proc. 5th Pleading § 1215, Noncurable Failure of Proof.

§ 471.5. Amended complaint; filing; answer; time

(a) If the complaint is amended, a copy of the amendments shall be filed, or the court may, in its discretion, require the complaint as amended to be filed, and a copy of the amendments or amended complaint must be served upon the defendants affected thereby. The defendant shall answer the amendments, or the complaint as amended, within 30 days after service thereof, or such other time as the court may direct, and judgment by default may be entered upon failure to answer, as in other cases. For the purposes of this subdivision, "complaint" includes a cross-complaint, and "defendant" includes a person against whom a cross-complaint is filed.

(b) If the answer is amended, the adverse party has 10 days after service thereof, or such other time as the court may direct, in which to demur to the amended answer. *(Added by Stats. 1972, c. 73, p. 94, § 2, eff. May 15, 1972, operative July 1, 1972.)*

Research References

Rutter, Cal. Practice Guide: Civ. Pro. Before Trial Ch. 5-B, B. Entry of Default.
Rutter, Cal. Practice Guide: Civ. Pro. Before Trial Ch. 6-E, E. Amended and Supplemental Pleadings.
Rutter, Cal. Practice Guide: Civ. Pro. Before Trial Ch. 7(I)-A, A. Demurrers.

4 Witkin Cal. Proc. 5th Pleading § 8, (S 8) Time Prescribed by Court.
5 Witkin Cal. Proc. 5th Pleading § 1241, (S 1241) Amendment or Amended Pleading.
5 Witkin Cal. Proc. 5th Pleading § 1242, in General.

§ 472. Amendment once of course

Any pleading may be amended once by the party of course, and without costs, at any time before the answer or demurrer is filed, or after demurrer and before the trial of the issue of law thereon, by filing the same as amended and serving a copy on the adverse party, and the time in which the adverse party must respond thereto shall be computed from the date of notice of the amendment. *(Enacted in 1872. Amended by Code Am.1873–74, c. 383, p. 302, § 59; Stats.1933, c. 744, p. 1850, § 31; Stats.1951, c. 1737, p. 4103, § 56, operative Jan. 1, 1952; Stats.1972, c. 73, p. 95, § 3; Stats.1977, c. 1257, § 13, eff. Jan. 3, 1977; Stats.1983, c. 142, § 4.)*

Research References

Rutter, Cal. Practice Guide: Civ. Pro. Before Trial Ch. 3-A, A. Subject Matter Jurisdiction (Competency).
Rutter, Cal. Practice Guide: Civ. Pro. Before Trial Ch. 6-E, E. Amended and Supplemental Pleadings.
Rutter, Cal. Practice Guide: Civ. Pro. Before Trial Ch. 7(I)-A, A. Demurrers.
5 Witkin Cal. Proc. 5th Pleading § 1040, (S 1040) Right of Prevailing Defendant.
5 Witkin Cal. Proc. 5th Pleading § 1186, (S 1186) Right to Amend Pleadings.
5 Witkin Cal. Proc. 5th Pleading § 1192, (S 1192) in General.
5 Witkin Cal. Proc. 5th Pleading § 1193, (S 1193) Amendment of Answer.
5 Witkin Cal. Proc. 5th Pleading § 1240, (S 1240) Application and Notice.

§ 472a. Demurrers; motion to strike; motion to dismiss relating to service of summons

(a) A demurrer is not waived by an answer filed at the same time.

(b) Except as otherwise provided by rule adopted by the Judicial Council, when a demurrer to a complaint or to a cross-complaint is overruled and there is no answer filed, the court shall allow an answer to be filed upon such terms as may be just. If a demurrer to the answer is overruled, the action shall proceed as if no demurrer had been interposed, and the facts alleged in the answer shall be considered as denied to the extent mentioned in Section 431.20.

(c) When a demurrer is sustained, the court may grant leave to amend the pleading upon any terms as may be just and shall fix the time within which the amendment or amended pleading shall be filed. When a demurrer is stricken pursuant to Section 436 and there is no answer filed, the court shall allow an answer to be filed on terms that are just.

(d) When a motion to strike is granted pursuant to Section 436, the court may order that an amendment or amended pleading be filed upon terms it deems proper. When a motion to strike a complaint or cross-complaint, or portion thereof, is denied, the court shall allow the party filing the motion to strike to file an answer.

(e) When a motion to dismiss an action pursuant to Article 2 (commencing with Section 583.210) of Chapter 1.5 of Title 8 is denied, the court shall allow a pleading to be filed. *(Added by Stats.1933, c. 744, p. 1851, § 32. Amended by Stats.1951, c. 1737, p. 4103, § 57, operative Jan. 1, 1952; Stats.1971, c. 1475, p. 2913, § 1; Stats.1982, c. 704, p. 2858, § 6; Stats.1983, c. 142, § 5; Stats.1983, c. 1167, § 5; Stats.1984, c. 572, § 2; Stats.1989, c. 1416, § 17; Stats.1993, c. 456 (A.B.58), § 6.)*

Research References

Rutter, Cal. Practice Guide: Civ. Pro. Before Trial Ch. 5-B, B. Entry of Default.

Rutter, Cal. Practice Guide: Civ. Pro. Before Trial Ch. 6-E, E. Amended and Supplemental Pleadings.
Rutter, Cal. Practice Guide: Civ. Pro. Before Trial Ch. 11-B, B. Involuntary Dismissals.
Rutter, Cal. Practice Guide: Civ. Pro. Before Trial Ch. 7(I)-A, A. Demurrers.
Rutter, Cal. Practice Guide: Civ. Pro. Before Trial Ch. 7(I)-B, B. Motions to Strike.
8 Witkin Cal. Proc. 5th Extraordinary Writs § 201, (S 201) Where Demurrer Alone is Filed.
4 Witkin Cal. Proc. 5th Pleading § 8, (S 8) Time Prescribed by Court.
5 Witkin Cal. Proc. 5th Pleading § 949, Filing With Answer or Motion to Strike.
5 Witkin Cal. Proc. 5th Pleading § 982, Overruling or Sustaining.
5 Witkin Cal. Proc. 5th Pleading § 985, (S 985) Overruling and Right to Answer.
5 Witkin Cal. Proc. 5th Pleading § 986, (S 986) Striking and Right to Answer.
5 Witkin Cal. Proc. 5th Pleading § 987, Specification of Grounds.
5 Witkin Cal. Proc. 5th Pleading § 1014, (S 1014) in General.
5 Witkin Cal. Proc. 5th Pleading § 1241, (S 1241) Amendment or Amended Pleading.
6 Witkin Cal. Proc. 5th Proceedings Without Trial § 146, Filing of Motion Prevents Default.
6 Witkin Cal. Proc. 5th Proceedings Without Trial § 356, Ruling on Motion.

§ 472b. Running of time for pleading following ruling on demurrer, reversal or remand

When a demurrer to any pleading is sustained or overruled, and time to amend or answer is given, the time so given runs from the service of notice of the decision or order, unless the notice is waived in open court, and the waiver entered in the minutes. When an order sustaining a demurrer without leave to amend is reversed or otherwise remanded by any order issued by a reviewing court, any amended complaint shall be filed within 30 days after the clerk of the reviewing court mails notice of the issuance of the remittitur. *(Formerly § 476, added by Code Am.1873–74, c. 383, p. 304, § 61. Renumbered § 472b and amended by Stats.1933, c. 744, p. 1851, § 33. Amended by Stats.1994, c. 146 (A.B.3601), § 24; Stats.1994, c. 41 (A.B.911), § 1; Stats.2001, c. 44 (S.B.562), § 3.)*

Law Revision Commission Comments

Section 472b is amended to delete the reference to a "docket," because courts no longer maintain a record denominated a "docket" in civil cases. Formerly, justice courts maintained a docket in civil cases, which was a record of actions taken in open court, as well as documents filed and other proceedings in the case. See former Government Code 71614 (1953 Cal. Stat. ch. 206, 1, repealed by 1977 Cal. Stat. ch. 1257, 71) (judge of justice court shall keep a book denominated a "docket"), 71614.5 (1959 Cal. Stat. ch. 671, 2, repealed by 1977 Cal. Stat. ch. 1257, 72) (clerk or judge of justice court shall keep the "docket" and other records of the court). Now actions taken in open court are recorded in the minutes of a superior court. Government Code 69844; see also Copley Press v. Superior Court, 6 Cal.App.4th 106, 110, 7 Cal.Rptr.2d 841 (1992). Documents filed or lodged and other proceedings in a civil case are recorded in the register of actions. See Government Code 69845 (clerk of superior court may keep a register of actions), 69845.5 (alternative to maintaining register of actions in superior court). Because the minutes are the proper record for reflecting a waiver in open court, and Section 472b already refers to the minutes, the reference to the "docket" may be deleted without substituting a reference to the register of actions. [30 Cal.L.Rev.Comm. Reports 479 (2000)].

Research References

Rutter, Cal. Practice Guide: Civil Appeals & Writs Ch. 14-C, C. Trial Court Proceedings After Reversal.
Rutter, Cal. Practice Guide: Civ. Pro. Before Trial Ch. 5-B, B. Entry of Default.
Rutter, Cal. Practice Guide: Civ. Pro. Before Trial Ch. 7(I)-A, A. Demurrers.
Rutter, Cal. Practice Guide: Civ. Pro. Before Trial Ch. 9(I)-B, B. Preparing and Filing Motions.

Rutter, Cal. Practice Guide: Civ. Pro. Before Trial Ch. 9(I)-E, E. Posthearing Procedures.
5 Witkin Cal. Proc. 5th Pleading § 982, Overruling or Sustaining.
5 Witkin Cal. Proc. 5th Pleading § 983, Notification and Service of Notice.
6 Witkin Cal. Proc. 5th Proceedings Without Trial § 45, (S 45) Notification and Notice.
6 Witkin Cal. Proc. 5th Proceedings Without Trial § 144, Failure to Answer After Demurrer is Overruled.

§ 472c. Sustained demurrers

(a) When any court makes an order sustaining a demurrer without leave to amend the question as to whether or not such court abused its discretion in making such an order is open on appeal even though no request to amend such pleading was made.

(b) The following orders shall be deemed open on appeal where an amended pleading is filed after the court's order:

(1) An order sustaining a demurrer to a cause of action within a complaint or cross-complaint where the order did not sustain the demurrer as to the entire complaint or cross-complaint.

(2) An order sustaining a demurrer to an affirmative defense within an answer where the order sustaining the demurrer did not sustain the demurrer as to the entire answer.

(3) An order granting a motion to strike a portion of a pleading where the order granting the motion to strike did not strike the entire pleading.

(c) As used in this section, "open on appeal" means that a party aggrieved by an order listed in subdivision (b) may claim the order as error in an appeal from the final judgment in the action. (Added by Stats.1939, c. 714, p. 2235, § 1. Amended by Stats.1993, c. 456 (A.B.58), § 7.)

Research References

Rutter, Cal. Practice Guide: Civil Appeals & Writs Ch. 2-C, C. Nonappealable Orders.
Rutter, Cal. Practice Guide: Civil Appeals & Writs Ch. 8-C, C. Standards of Appellate Review.
Rutter, Cal. Practice Guide: Civ. Pro. Before Trial Ch. 7(I)-A, A. Demurrers.
Rutter, Cal. Practice Guide: Civ. Pro. Before Trial Ch. 7(I)-B, B. Motions to Strike.
5 Witkin Cal. Proc. 5th Pleading § 1000, Review of Order.

§ 472d. Statement of grounds for decision or order sustaining demurrer

Whenever a demurrer in any action or proceeding is sustained, the court shall include in its decision or order a statement of the specific ground or grounds upon which the decision or order is based which may be by reference to appropriate pages and paragraphs of the demurrer.

The party against whom a demurrer has been sustained may waive these requirements. (Added by Stats.1961, c. 727, p. 1969, § 1.)

Research References

Rutter, Cal. Practice Guide: Civil Appeals & Writs Ch. 8-D, D. Limits on Assertion of Issues on Appeal.
Rutter, Cal. Practice Guide: Civ. Pro. Before Trial Ch. 7(I)-A, A. Demurrers.
Rutter, Cal. Practice Guide: Civ. Pro. Before Trial Ch. 9(I)-E, E. Posthearing Procedures.
5 Witkin Cal. Proc. 5th Pleading § 987, Specification of Grounds.

§ 473. Amendments permitted by court; enlargement of time to answer or demur; continuance, costs; relief from judgment, etc., taken by mistake, inadvertence, surprise, or excusable neglect; vacating default judgment; compensatory costs and legal fees; penalties; clerical mistakes in judgment or order; relief

(a)(1) The court may, in furtherance of justice, and on any terms as may be proper, allow a party to amend any pleading or proceeding by adding or striking out the name of any party, or by correcting a mistake in the name of a party, or a mistake in any other respect; and may, upon like terms, enlarge the time for answer or demurrer. The court may likewise, in its discretion, after notice to the adverse party, allow, upon any terms as may be just, an amendment to any pleading or proceeding in other particulars; and may upon like terms allow an answer to be made after the time limited by this code.

(2) When it appears to the satisfaction of the court that the amendment renders it necessary, the court may postpone the trial, and may, when the postponement will by the amendment be rendered necessary, require, as a condition to the amendment, the payment to the adverse party of any costs as may be just.

(b) The court may, upon any terms as may be just, relieve a party or his or her legal representative from a judgment, dismissal, order, or other proceeding taken against him or her through his or her mistake, inadvertence, surprise, or excusable neglect. Application for this relief shall be accompanied by a copy of the answer or other pleading proposed to be filed therein, otherwise the application shall not be granted, and shall be made within a reasonable time, in no case exceeding six months, after the judgment, dismissal, order, or proceeding was taken. However, in the case of a judgment, dismissal, order, or other proceeding determining the ownership or right to possession of real or personal property, without extending the six-month period, when a notice in writing is personally served within the State of California both upon the party against whom the judgment, dismissal, order, or other proceeding has been taken, and upon his or her attorney of record, if any, notifying that party and his or her attorney of record, if any, that the order, judgment, dismissal, or other proceeding was taken against him or her and that any rights the party has to apply for relief under the provisions of Section 473 of the Code of Civil Procedure shall expire 90 days after service of the notice, then the application shall be made within 90 days after service of the notice upon the defaulting party or his or her attorney of record, if any, whichever service shall be later. No affidavit or declaration of merits shall be required of the moving party. Notwithstanding any other requirements of this section, the court shall, whenever an application for relief is made no more than six months after entry of judgment, is in proper form, and is accompanied by an attorney's sworn affidavit attesting to his or her mistake, inadvertence, surprise, or neglect, vacate any (1) resulting default entered by the clerk against his or her client, and which will result in entry of a default judgment, or (2) resulting default judgment or dismissal entered against his or her client, unless the court finds that the default or dismissal was not in fact caused by the attorney's mistake, inadvertence, surprise, or neglect. The court shall, whenever relief is granted based on an attorney's affidavit of fault, direct the attorney to pay reasonable compensatory legal fees and costs to opposing counsel or parties. However, this section shall not lengthen the time within which an action shall be brought to trial pursuant to Section 583.310.

(c)(1) Whenever the court grants relief from a default, default judgment, or dismissal based on any of the provisions of this section, the court may do any of the following:

(A) Impose a penalty of no greater than one thousand dollars ($1,000) upon an offending attorney or party.

(B) Direct that an offending attorney pay an amount no greater than one thousand dollars ($1,000) to the State Bar Client Security Fund.

(C) Grant other relief as is appropriate.

(2) However, where the court grants relief from a default or default judgment pursuant to this section based upon the

affidavit of the defaulting party's attorney attesting to the attorney's mistake, inadvertence, surprise, or neglect, the relief shall not be made conditional upon the attorney's payment of compensatory legal fees or costs or monetary penalties imposed by the court or upon compliance with other sanctions ordered by the court.

(d) The court may, upon motion of the injured party, or its own motion, correct clerical mistakes in its judgment or orders as entered, so as to conform to the judgment or order directed, and may, on motion of either party after notice to the other party, set aside any void judgment or order. *(Enacted in 1872. Amended by Code Am.1873–74, c. 383, p. 302, § 60; Code Am.1880, c. 14, p. 2, § 3; Stats.1917, c. 159, p. 242, § 1; Stats.1933, c. 744, p. 1851, § 34; Stats.1961, c. 722, p. 1965, § 1; Stats.1981, c. 122, p. 857, § 2; Stats.1988, c. 1131, § 1; Stats.1991, c. 1003 (S.B.882), § 1; Stats.1992, c. 427 (A.B.3355), § 16; Stats.1992, c. 876 (A.B.3296), § 4; Stats.1996, c. 60 (S.B.52), § 1.)*

Research References

Rutter, Cal. Practice Guide: A.D.R. Ch. 4-B, B. Judicial Arbitration.

Rutter, Cal. Practice Guide: A.D.R. Ch. 5-D, D. Defenses to Enforcement.

Rutter, Cal. Practice Guide: A.D.R. Ch. 5-G, G. Procedures to Enforce Arbitration.

Rutter, Cal. Practice Guide: A.D.R. Ch. 5-J, J. Challenging and Enforcing Arbitrator's Award in Court.

Rutter, Cal. Practice Guide: A.D.R. Ch. 6-B, B. Temporary Judges.

Rutter, Cal. Practice Guide: A.D.R. Ch. 5-D, Outline D.

Rutter, Cal. Practice Guide: A.D.R. Ch. 5-J, Outline J.

Rutter, Cal. Practice Guide: Civil Appeals & Writs Ch. 2-B, B. Appealable Judgments and Orders.

Rutter, Cal. Practice Guide: Civil Appeals & Writs Ch. 2-D, D. Standing to Appeal.

Rutter, Cal. Practice Guide: Civil Appeals & Writs Ch. 3-A, A. Necessity of Timely Filing for Appeal.

Rutter, Cal. Practice Guide: Civil Appeals & Writs Ch. 3-C, C. Extensions of Filing Deadline.

Rutter, Cal. Practice Guide: Civil Appeals & Writs Ch. 4-A, A. General Considerations.

Rutter, Cal. Practice Guide: Civil Appeals & Writs Ch. 5-B, B. Types of Motions, Applications and Requests.

Rutter, Cal. Practice Guide: Civil Appeals & Writs Ch. 7-A, A. Overview.

Rutter, Cal. Practice Guide: Civil Appeals & Writs Ch. 8-C, C. Standards of Appellate Review.

Rutter, Cal. Practice Guide: Civil Appeals & Writs Ch. 8-D, D. Limits on Assertion of Issues on Appeal.

Rutter, Cal. Practice Guide: Civil Appeals & Writs Ch. 14-B, B. Recovery of Appellate Costs and Attorney Fees.

Rutter, Cal. Practice Guide: Civil Appeals & Writs Ch. 14-C, C. Trial Court Proceedings After Reversal.

Rutter, Cal. Practice Guide: Civil Appeals & Writs Ch. 15-A, A. Overview.

Rutter, Cal. Practice Guide: Civil Appeals & Writs Ch. 3-A, Outline a.

Rutter, Cal. Practice Guide: Civil Appeals & Writs Ch. 8-C, Outline C.

Rutter, Cal. Practice Guide: Civ. Pro. Before Trial Ch. 1-A, A. Accepting a New Case.

Rutter, Cal. Practice Guide: Civ. Pro. Before Trial Ch. 1-C, C. Prelawsuit Notices, Claims and Demands.

Rutter, Cal. Practice Guide: Civ. Pro. Before Trial Ch. 1-H, H. Filing Fee Considerations.

Rutter, Cal. Practice Guide: Civ. Pro. Before Trial Ch. 2-G, G. Substitution of Parties.

Rutter, Cal. Practice Guide: Civ. Pro. Before Trial Ch. 3-A, A. Subject Matter Jurisdiction (Competency).

Rutter, Cal. Practice Guide: Civ. Pro. Before Trial Ch. 3-B, B. Jurisdiction Over Parties-Personal Jurisdiction.

Rutter, Cal. Practice Guide: Civ. Pro. Before Trial Ch. 5-A, A. General.

Rutter, Cal. Practice Guide: Civ. Pro. Before Trial Ch. 5-B, B. Entry of Default.

Rutter, Cal. Practice Guide: Civ. Pro. Before Trial Ch. 5-D, D. Default Judgment by Court.

Rutter, Cal. Practice Guide: Civ. Pro. Before Trial Ch. 5-E, E. Limitations on Default Judgments.

Rutter, Cal. Practice Guide: Civ. Pro. Before Trial Ch. 5-G, G. Relief from Default.

Rutter, Cal. Practice Guide: Civ. Pro. Before Trial Ch. 6-B, B. Complaints.

Rutter, Cal. Practice Guide: Civ. Pro. Before Trial Ch. 6-E, E. Amended and Supplemental Pleadings.

Rutter, Cal. Practice Guide: Civ. Pro. Before Trial Ch. 8G-7, Motion to Compel Further Answers.

Rutter, Cal. Practice Guide: Civ. Pro. Before Trial Ch. 8H-8, Enforcing Demand.

Rutter, Cal. Practice Guide: Civ. Pro. Before Trial Ch. 10-C, C. Procedural Requirements-Moving Party.

Rutter, Cal. Practice Guide: Civ. Pro. Before Trial Ch. 10-F, F. Burden of Proof on Motion.

Rutter, Cal. Practice Guide: Civ. Pro. Before Trial Ch. 10-H, H. Entry of Judgment or Order.

Rutter, Cal. Practice Guide: Civ. Pro. Before Trial Ch. 10-I, I. Challenging Judgment or Order in Trial Court.

Rutter, Cal. Practice Guide: Civ. Pro. Before Trial Ch. 11-A, A. Voluntary Dismissals.

Rutter, Cal. Practice Guide: Civ. Pro. Before Trial Ch. 11-B, B. Involuntary Dismissals.

Rutter, Cal. Practice Guide: Civ. Pro. Before Trial Ch. 13-F, F. Arbitration Award.

Rutter, Cal. Practice Guide: Civ. Pro. Before Trial Ch. 13-G, G. Trial De Novo.

Rutter, Cal. Practice Guide: Civ. Pro. Before Trial Ch. 8A-3, Civil Discovery Act.

Rutter, Cal. Practice Guide: Civ. Pro. Before Trial Ch. 8F-5, Responding to Interrogatories.

Rutter, Cal. Practice Guide: Civ. Pro. Before Trial Ch. 8F-7, Motion to Compel Answers.

Rutter, Cal. Practice Guide: Civ. Pro. Before Trial Ch. 8F-8, Sanctions in Enforcing Discovery.

Rutter, Cal. Practice Guide: Civ. Pro. Before Trial Ch. 8G-6, Effect of Delay or Failure to Respond to Rfas.

Rutter, Cal. Practice Guide: Civ. Pro. Before Trial Ch. 8G-8, Amending or Withdrawing Admissions.

Rutter, Cal. Practice Guide: Civ. Pro. Before Trial Ch. 8H-6, Responding to Demand.

Rutter, Cal. Practice Guide: Civ. Pro. Before Trial Ch. 8I-2, Physical Examination by Demand in Personal Injury Cases.

Rutter, Cal. Practice Guide: Civ. Pro. Before Trial Ch. 8J-3, Deadline for Demand.

Rutter, Cal. Practice Guide: Civ. Pro. Before Trial Ch. 8K-2, Demand for Bill of Particulars.

Rutter, Cal. Practice Guide: Civ. Pro. Before Trial Ch. 8L-2, Special Discovery Procedures Permitted.

Rutter, Cal. Practice Guide: Civ. Pro. Before Trial Ch. 8E-14, Deposition Transcript.

Rutter, Cal. Practice Guide: Civ. Pro. Before Trial Ch. 8E-16, Sanctions Re Depositions.

Rutter, Cal. Practice Guide: Civ. Pro. Before Trial Ch. 8J-10, Relief from Exclusion Sanction.

Rutter, Cal. Practice Guide: Civ. Pro. Before Trial Ch. 1-C, Outline C.

Rutter, Cal. Practice Guide: Civ. Pro. Before Trial Ch. 1-H, Outline H.

Rutter, Cal. Practice Guide: Civ. Pro. Before Trial Ch. 5-E, Outline E.

Rutter, Cal. Practice Guide: Civ. Pro. Before Trial Ch. 5-G, Outline G.

Rutter, Cal. Practice Guide: Civ. Pro. Before Trial Ch. 7(I)-A, A. Demurrers.

Rutter, Cal. Practice Guide: Civ. Pro. Before Trial Ch. 7(I)-C, C. Motion for Judgment on the Pleadings.

Rutter, Cal. Practice Guide: Civ. Pro. Before Trial Ch. 9(I)-A, A. Introduction.

Rutter, Cal. Practice Guide: Civ. Pro. Before Trial Ch. 9(I)-B, B. Preparing and Filing Motions.

Rutter, Cal. Practice Guide: Civ. Pro. Before Trial Ch. 9(I)-C, C. Opposing the Motion-And Rebutting the Opposition.

Rutter, Cal. Practice Guide: Civ. Pro. Before Trial Ch. 9(I)-E, E. Posthearing Procedures.

Rutter, Cal. Practice Guide: Civ. Pro. Before Trial Ch. 9(I)-F, F. Ex Parte Motions.

Rutter, Cal. Practice Guide: Civ. Pro. Before Trial Ch. 10-H, Outline H.

Rutter, Cal. Practice Guide: Civ. Pro. Before Trial Ch. 11-B, Outline B.

Rutter, Cal. Practice Guide: Civ. Pro. Before Trial Ch. 13-F, Outline F.

Rutter, Cal. Practice Guide: Civ. Pro. Before Trial Ch. 8A-3, Outline 3.

Rutter, Cal. Practice Guide: Civ. Pro. Before Trial Ch. 8F-5, Outline 5.

Rutter, Cal. Practice Guide: Civ. Pro. Before Trial Ch. 8G-6, Outline 6.

Rutter, Cal. Practice Guide: Civ. Pro. Before Trial Ch. 8G-8, Outline 8.

Rutter, Cal. Practice Guide: Civ. Pro. Before Trial Ch. 8H-6, Outline 6.

Rutter, Cal. Practice Guide: Civ. Pro. Before Trial Ch. 8I-2, Outline 2.

Rutter, Cal. Practice Guide: Civ. Pro. Before Trial Gen. Matls., Highlights.

Rutter, Cal. Practice Guide: Civ. Pro. Before Trial Ch. 12(II)-C, C. Statutory Offer to Compromise (CCP § 998).

Rutter, Cal. Practice Guide: Civ. Pro. Before Trial Ch. 12(II)-F, F. Motion to Enforce Settlement (CCP §§ 664.6, 664.7).

Rutter, Cal. Practice Guide: Civ. Pro. Before Trial Ch. 12(II)-G, G. Motion for Relief from Settlement.

Rutter, Cal. Practice Guide: Civ. Pro. Before Trial Ch. 9(I)-E, Outline E.

Rutter, Cal. Practice Guide: Civ. Pro. Before Trial Ch. 12(II)-C, Outline C.

Rutter, Cal. Practice Guide: Civil Trials & Evidence Ch. 1-J, J. Notice of Trial.

Rutter, Cal. Practice Guide: Civil Trials & Evidence Ch. 2-B, B. What Constitutes Jury Trial.

Rutter, Cal. Practice Guide: Civil Trials & Evidence Ch. 2-F, F. Relief from Waiver.

Rutter, Cal. Practice Guide: Civil Trials & Evidence Ch. 4-I, I. Other Motions at Final Status Conference.

Rutter, Cal. Practice Guide: Civil Trials & Evidence Ch. 11-A, A. Direct Examination of Expert Witnesses.

Rutter, Cal. Practice Guide: Civil Trials & Evidence Ch. 12-B, B. Motion for Nonsuit.

Rutter, Cal. Practice Guide: Civil Trials & Evidence Ch. 12-D, D. Other Motions During Trial.

Rutter, Cal. Practice Guide: Civil Trials & Evidence Ch. 17-D, D. Costs.

Rutter, Cal. Practice Guide: Civil Trials & Evidence Ch. 17-E, E. Attorney Fees as Costs.

Rutter, Cal. Practice Guide: Civil Trials & Evidence Ch. 18-A, A. Motion for Judgment Notwithstanding the Verdict ("JNOV").

Rutter, Cal. Practice Guide: Civil Trials & Evidence Ch. 18-B, B. Motion for New Trial.

Rutter, Cal. Practice Guide: Civil Trials & Evidence Ch. 18-C, C. Other Post-Trial Motions.

Rutter, Cal. Practice Guide: Civil Trials & Evidence Ch. 8C-K, K. Stipulations.

Rutter, Cal. Practice Guide: Civil Trials & Evidence Ch. 8D-D, D. Hearsay Exceptions.

Rutter, Cal. Practice Guide: Civil Trials & Evidence Ch. 1-J, Outline J.

Rutter, Cal. Practice Guide: Civil Trials & Evidence Gen. Matls., Highlights.

Rutter, Cal. Practice Guide: Civil Trials & Evidence Ch. 18-B, Outline B.

Rutter, Cal. Practice Guide: Civil Trials & Evidence Ch. 18-C, Outline C.

California Practice Guide: Employment Litigation Ch. 11-J, J. Enforcing California Laws Regulating Employee Compensation.

California Practice Guide: Employment Litigation Ch. 13-H, H. Contesting Citations and Related Orders and Notices.

California Practice Guide: Employment Litigation Ch. 19-G, G. Summary Judgment/Summary Adjudication.

California Practice Guide: Employment Litigation Ch. 13-H, Outline H.

Rutter, Cal. Practice Guide: Enforcing Judgments/Debts Ch. 3-C, C. Prelawsuit Considerations.

Rutter, Cal. Practice Guide: Enforcing Judgments/Debts Ch. 6E-3, Procedures for Claiming Exemptions.

Rutter, Cal. Practice Guide: Enforcing Judgments/Debts Ch. 6J-2, Enforcing Sister State Judgments in California.

Rutter, Cal. Practice Guide: Family Law Ch. 5-F, F. Special Provisions for Pendente Lite "Expedited Child Support Order".

Rutter, Cal. Practice Guide: Family Law Ch. 6-A, A. Child Support.

Rutter, Cal. Practice Guide: Family Law Ch. 6-B, B. Spousal Support.

Rutter, Cal. Practice Guide: Family Law Ch. 17-B, B. Spousal Support.

Rutter, Cal. Practice Guide: Family Law Ch. 6-B, Outline B.

Rutter, Cal. Practice Guide: Family Law Gen. Matls, Highlights.

Rutter, Cal. Practice Guide: Insurance Litigation Ch. 10-A, A. Conservatorship and Liquidation Proceedings.

Rutter, Cal. Practice Guide: Insurance Litigation Ch. 15-A, A. Actions Against Insurers.

Rutter, Cal. Practice Guide: Insurance Litigation Ch. 15-K, K. Judgment Creditor's Action to Enforce Judgment Debtor's Liability Insurance (INS.C. § 11580(B)(2)).

Rutter, Cal. Practice Guide: Insurance Litigation Ch. 15-A, Outline a.

Rutter, Cal. Practice Guide: Personal Injury Ch. 4-D, D. Techniques Where Settlement Not Forthcoming.

Rutter, Cal. Practice Guide: Personal Injury Ch. 4-G, G. Concluding and Enforcing Settlement.

Rutter, Cal. Practice Guide: Personal Injury Ch. 5-A, A. Prelawsuit Filings.

Rutter, Cal. Practice Guide: Personal Injury Ch. 5-B, B. When to Sue-Statute of Limitations.

Rutter, Cal. Practice Guide: Personal Injury Ch. 6-B, B. Overview of Selected Discovery Procedures.

Rutter, Cal. Practice Guide: Personal Injury Ch. 6-D, D. Expert Witness Information Exchanges (CCP § 2034.210 et seq.).

Rutter, Cal. Practice Guide: Personal Injury Ch. 6-E, E. Special Discovery Rules and Procedures in Limited Civil Cases.

Rutter, Cal. Practice Guide: Personal Injury Ch. 7-H, H. Arbitration Award and Judgment.

Rutter, Cal. Practice Guide: Personal Injury Ch. 7-I, I. Trial De Novo After Arbitration Award.

Rutter, Cal. Practice Guide: Personal Injury Ch. 8-B, B. After Trial Date Set (Three to Four Months Before Trial).

Rutter, Cal. Practice Guide: Personal Injury Ch. 9-N, N. Special Trial Rules in Limited Civil Cases (CCP § 90 et seq.).

Rutter, Cal. Practice Guide: Personal Injury Ch. 10-C, C. Motion to Vacate and Enter Different Judgment.

Rutter, Cal. Practice Guide: Personal Injury Ch. 4-D, Outline D.

Rutter, Cal. Practice Guide: Personal Injury Ch. 4-G, Outline G.

Rutter, Cal. Practice Guide: Personal Injury Ch. 5-A, Outline a.

Rutter, Cal. Practice Guide: Personal Injury Ch. 5-B, Outline B.

Rutter, Cal. Practice Guide: Personal Injury Ch. 6-B, Outline B.

Rutter, Cal. Practice Guide: Personal Injury Ch. 7-I, Outline I.

Rutter, Cal. Practice Guide: Real Prop. Transactions Ch. 1-C, C. Attorney Fees and Costs Agreements.

Rutter, Cal. Practice Guide: Real Prop. Transactions Ch. 6-I, I. Real Property Foreclosures and Antideficiency Laws.

Rutter, Cal. Practice Guide: Prof. Responsibility Ch. 3-D, D. Authority of Client vs. Authority of Attorney.

Rutter, Cal. Practice Guide: Prof. Responsibility Ch. 5-K, K. Fee Recovery/Enforcing Fee Agreements.

Rutter, Cal. Practice Guide: Prof. Responsibility Ch. 6-A, A. Sources of Duty of Competence.

Rutter, Cal. Practice Guide: Prof. Responsibility Ch. 6-B, B. Elements of Attorney Competence.

Rutter, Cal. Practice Guide: Prof. Responsibility Ch. 10-D, D. Termination by Completion of Engagement.

Rutter, Cal. Practice Guide: Prof. Responsibility Ch. 11-H, H. Proceedings Before Trial.

Rutter, Cal. Practice Guide: Prof. Responsibility Ch. 5-K, Outline K.

Rutter, Cal. Practice Guide: Prof. Responsibility Ch. 6-A, Outline a.

Miller and Starr California Real Estate § 5:68, Confirmation of Sale; Additional Offers.

Miller and Starr California Real Estate § 5:71, Broker's Contract Rights to a Commission; Probate Listings.

Miller and Starr California Real Estate § 27:19, Civil Wage and Penalty Assessments.

Miller and Starr California Real Estate § 35:46, Venue and Service of the Petition and Response.

Miller and Starr California Real Estate § 35:92, Petition to Correct an Arbitrator's Award.

Miller and Starr California Real Estate § 35:94, Grounds for Vacating an Award.

Miller and Starr California Real Estate § 25A:23, Type of Action; Time to File; Preparation of Administrative Record.

13 NO. 5 Miller & Starr, California Real Estate Newsalert 15, Subdivisions.

14 NO. 5 Miller & Starr, California Real Estate Newsalert 9, Discrimination.

15 NO. 3 Miller & Starr, California Real Estate Newsalert 18, Subdivisions.

21 NO. 5 Miller & Starr, California Real Estate Newsalert 6, Construction Law and Contracting.

22 NO. 5 Miller & Starr, California Real Estate Newsalert 4, Common Interest Developments.

22 NO. 4 Miller & Starr, California Real Estate Newsalert 36, Judicial Remedies.

3 Witkin Cal. Proc. 5th Actions § 290, Theory of Relief.

3 Witkin Cal. Proc. 5th Actions § 292, (S 292) Calendaring Mistake.

3 Witkin Cal. Proc. 5th Actions § 295, (S 295) Failure to File Second Claim.

§ 473.1. Court assuming jurisdiction over attorney's practice; relief from judgment, order or proceeding

The court may, upon such terms as may be just, relieve a party from a judgment, order, or other proceeding taken against him or her, including dismissal of an action pursuant to Section 581 or Chapter 1.5 (commencing with Section 583.110) of Title 8, where a court of this state has assumed jurisdiction, pursuant to Section 6180 or 6190 of the Business and Professions Code, over the law practice of the attorney for the party and the judgment, order or other proceeding was taken against the party after the application for the court to assume jurisdiction over the practice was filed. Application for this relief shall be made within a reasonable period of time, in no case exceeding six months, after the court takes jurisdiction over the practice. However, in the case of a judgment, order, or other proceeding determining the ownership or right to possession of real or personal property, without extending the six-month period, when a notice in writing is personally served within the state both upon the party against whom the judgment, order, or other proceeding has been taken, and upon the attorney appointed pursuant to Section 6180.5 of the Business and Professions Code to act under the court's direction, notifying the party and the appointed attorney that the order, judgment, or other proceeding was taken against him or her and that any rights the party has to apply for relief under the provisions of the section shall expire 90 days after service of notice, then application for relief must be made within 90 days after service of the notice upon the defaulting party or the attorney appointed to act under the court's direction pursuant to Section 6180.5 of the Business and Professions Code, whichever service is later. No affidavit or declaration of merits shall be required of the moving party. *(Added by Stats.1983, c. 254, § 4. Amended by Stats.1993, c. 589 (A.B.2211), § 25.)*

Law Revision Commission Comments

Section 473.1 is amended to substitute a reference to the provisions that replaced former Sections 581a and 583. This is a technical, nonsubstantive change. [23 Cal.L.Rev.Comm. Reports 901 (1993) (Annual Report, App. 6)].

Research References

8 Witkin Cal. Proc. 5th Attack Judgment Trial Court § 144, (S 144) Nature of Relief.

1 Witkin Cal. Proc. 5th Attorneys § 89, Relief Available to Clients.

§ 473.5. Motion to set aside default and for leave to defend action

(a) When service of a summons has not resulted in actual notice to a party in time to defend the action and a default or default judgment has been entered against him or her in the action, he or she may serve and file a notice of motion to set aside the default or default judgment and for leave to defend the action. The notice of motion shall be served and filed within a reasonable time, but in no event exceeding the earlier of: (i) two years after entry of a default judgment against him or her; or (ii) 180 days after service on him or her of a written notice that the default or default judgment has been entered.

(b) A notice of motion to set aside a default or default judgment and for leave to defend the action shall designate as the time for making the motion a date prescribed by subdivision (b) of Section 1005, and it shall be accompanied by an affidavit showing under oath that the party's lack of actual notice in time to defend the action was not caused by his or her avoidance of service or inexcusable neglect. The party shall serve and file with the notice a copy of the answer, motion, or other pleading proposed to be filed in the action.

(c) Upon a finding by the court that the motion was made within the period permitted by subdivision (a) and that his or her lack of actual notice in time to defend the action was not caused by his or her avoidance of service or inexcusable neglect, it may set aside the default or default judgment on whatever terms as may be just and allow the party to defend the action. *(Added by Stats.1969, c. 1610, p. 3373, § 23, operative July 1, 1970. Amended by Stats.1990, c. 1491 (A.B.3765), § 5.)*

Research References

Rutter, Cal. Practice Guide: Civil Appeals & Writs Ch. 2-B, B. Appealable Judgments and Orders.

Rutter, Cal. Practice Guide: Civ. Pro. Before Trial Ch. 3-B, B. Jurisdiction Over Parties-Personal Jurisdiction.

Rutter, Cal. Practice Guide: Civ. Pro. Before Trial Ch. 4-F, F. Procedures for Challenging Service of Summons.

Rutter, Cal. Practice Guide: Civ. Pro. Before Trial Ch. 5-B, B. Entry of Default.

Rutter, Cal. Practice Guide: Civ. Pro. Before Trial Ch. 5-G, G. Relief from Default.

Rutter, Cal. Practice Guide: Civ. Pro. Before Trial Ch. 5-G, Outline G.

Rutter, Cal. Practice Guide: Enforcing Judgments/Debts Ch. 6A-7, Period During Which Judgment Enforceable; Renewal Procedures.

9 Witkin Cal. Proc. 5th Administrative Proceedings § 98, Service.

9 Witkin Cal. Proc. 5th Appeal § 198, (S 198) No Effective Appeal from Judgment.

9 Witkin Cal. Proc. 5th Appeal § 200, (S 200) Statutory Motions.

8 Witkin Cal. Proc. 5th Attack Judgment Trial Court § 209, (S 209) Timeliness of Motion.

8 Witkin Cal. Proc. 5th Attack Judgment Trial Court § 210, Nature of Relief.

8 Witkin Cal. Proc. 5th Attack Judgment Trial Court § 211, (S 211) Statutory Rule.

8 Witkin Cal. Proc. 5th Attack Judgment Trial Court § 212, (S 212) Strict Construction.

8 Witkin Cal. Proc. 5th Attack Judgment Trial Court § 213, (S 213) Notice of Motion.

8 Witkin Cal. Proc. 5th Attack Judgment Trial Court § 214, (S 214) Order.

8 Witkin Cal. Proc. 5th Attack Judgment Trial Court § 224, (S 224) Void Judgment.

8 Witkin Cal. Proc. 5th Enforcement of Judgment § 38, (S 38) Vacation or Modification.

2 Witkin Cal. Proc. 5th Jurisdiction § 192, Definition and Scope of Doctrine.

2 Witkin Cal. Proc. 5th Jurisdiction § 222, (S 222) Motion Coupled With Motion to Vacate.

§ 474. Defendant designated by fictitious name; amendment; requirements for default judgment; notice to person served

When the plaintiff is ignorant of the name of a defendant, he must state that fact in the complaint, or the affidavit if the action is commenced by affidavit, and such defendant may be designated in any pleading or proceeding by any name, and when his true name is discovered, the pleading or proceeding must be amended accordingly; provided, that no default or default judgment shall be entered against a defendant so designated, unless it appears that the copy of the summons or other process, or, if there be no summons or process, the copy of the first pleading or notice served upon such defendant bore on the face thereof a notice stating in substance: "To the person served: You are hereby served in the within action (or proceedings) as (or on behalf of) the person sued under the fictitious name of (designating it)." The certificate or affidavit of service must state the fictitious name under which such defendant was served and the fact that notice of identity was given by endorsement upon the document served as required by this section. The foregoing requirements for entry of a default or default judgment shall be applicable only as to fictitious names designated pursuant to this section and not in the event the plaintiff has sued the defendant by an erroneous name and shall not be applicable to entry of a default or default judgment based upon service, in the manner otherwise provided by law, of an amended pleading, process or notice designating defendant by his true name. *(Enacted in 1872. Amended by Stats.1953, c. 1244, p. 2807, § 1; Stats.1955, c. 886, p. 1516, § 1.)*

Research References

Rutter, Cal. Practice Guide: Civ. Pro. Before Trial Ch. 1-B, B. Prelawsuit Investigations, Research and Analysis.

Rutter, Cal. Practice Guide: Civ. Pro. Before Trial Ch. 1-C, C. Prelawsuit Notices, Claims and Demands.

Rutter, Cal. Practice Guide: Civ. Pro. Before Trial Ch. 4-C, C. Content of Summons.

Rutter, Cal. Practice Guide: Civ. Pro. Before Trial Ch. 4-D, D. Service of Summons.

Rutter, Cal. Practice Guide: Civ. Pro. Before Trial Ch. 4-E, E. Proof of Service of Summons.

Rutter, Cal. Practice Guide: Civ. Pro. Before Trial Ch. 5-E, E. Limitations on Default Judgments.

Rutter, Cal. Practice Guide: Civ. Pro. Before Trial Ch. 6-B, B. Complaints.

Rutter, Cal. Practice Guide: Civ. Pro. Before Trial Ch. 6-E, E. Amended and Supplemental Pleadings.

Rutter, Cal. Practice Guide: Fed.Civ.Pro. Before Trial Ch. 1-B, B. Federal vs. State Law.

Rutter, Cal. Practice Guide: Fed.Civ.Pro. Before Trial Ch. 1-D, D. Choosing Between State and Federal Courts.

Rutter, Cal. Practice Guide: Fed.Civ.Pro. Before Trial Ch. 8-D, D. Complaints.

Rutter, Cal. Practice Guide: Fed.Civ.Pro. Before Trial Ch. 2D-4, What Cases and Claims Are Removable.

Rutter, Cal. Practice Guide: Personal Injury Ch. 5-A, A. Prelawsuit Filings.

Rutter, Cal. Practice Guide: Personal Injury Ch. 5-E, E. Selected Pleading Issues.

Miller and Starr California Real Estate § 28:58, Parties.

3 Witkin Cal. Proc. 5th Actions § 436, (S 436) Illustration: Product Liability Action.

3 Witkin Cal. Proc. 5th Actions § 496, in General.

3 Witkin Cal. Proc. 5th Actions § 722, (S 722) in General.

3 Witkin Cal. Proc. 5th Actions § 983, Names of Parties.

3 Witkin Cal. Proc. 5th Actions § 991, (S 991) Persons Sued by Fictitious Name.

2 Witkin Cal. Proc. 5th Jurisdiction § 316, (S 316) Judgment Against.

4 Witkin Cal. Proc. 5th Pleading § 478, in General.

4 Witkin Cal. Proc. 5th Pleading § 479, True Name Known.

4 Witkin Cal. Proc. 5th Pleading § 480, Amendment to Allege Initial Ignorance.

4 Witkin Cal. Proc. 5th Pleading § 481, (S 481) Actual Ignorance.

4 Witkin Cal. Proc. 5th Pleading § 484, (S 484) Problem and Rule.

4 Witkin Cal. Proc. 5th Pleading § 485, (S 485) Illustrations.

4 Witkin Cal. Proc. 5th Pleading § 486, (S 486) Exception: Public Entity Defendant.

4 Witkin Cal. Proc. 5th Pleading § 487, (S 487) Forms of Allegation.

4 Witkin Cal. Proc. 5th Pleading § 489, Application and Order.

4 Witkin Cal. Proc. 5th Pleading § 494, Effect of Failure to Amend.

5 Witkin Cal. Proc. 5th Pleading § 1226, in General.

5 Witkin Cal. Proc. 5th Pleading § 1235, (S 1235) Modern View.

6 Witkin Cal. Proc. 5th Proceedings Without Trial § 177, Wrongly or Fictitiously Named Defendant.

6 Witkin Cal. Proc. 5th Proceedings Without Trial § 444, (S 444) Doe Defendant.

§ 475. Errors, etc. not affecting substantial rights disregarded; reversal only for prejudicial error; presumptions

The court must, in every stage of an action, disregard any error, improper ruling, instruction, or defect, in the pleadings or proceedings which, in the opinion of said court, does not affect the substantial rights of the parties. No judgment, decision, or decree shall be reversed or affected by reason of any error, ruling, instruction, or defect, unless it shall appear from the record that such error, ruling, instruction, or defect was prejudicial, and also that by reason of such error, ruling, instruction, or defect, the said party complaining or appealing sustained and suffered substantial injury, and that a different result would have been probable if such error, ruling, instruction, or defect had not occurred or existed. There shall be no presumption that error is prejudicial, or that injury was done if error is shown. *(Enacted in 1872. Amended by Stats.1897, c. 47, p. 44, § 1.)*

Research References

Rutter, Cal. Practice Guide: Civil Appeals & Writs Ch. 8-E, E. Limits on Reversal or Modification-"Prejudicial Error" Rule.

Rutter, Cal. Practice Guide: Civil Trials & Evidence Ch. 14-G, G. Appellate Review of Instructions Given and Refused.

Rutter, Cal. Practice Guide: Enforcing Judgments/Debts Ch. 6B-3, Creation of Judgment Lien.

Miller and Starr California Real Estate § 25A:21, Judicial Review for Environmental Impact Report.

9 Witkin Cal. Proc. 5th Appeal § 416, (S 416) Development of California Doctrine.

9 Witkin Cal. Proc. 5th Appeal § 418, Review of Entire Record.

4 Witkin Cal. Proc. 5th Pleading § 442, General Rule.

5 Witkin Cal. Proc. 5th Pleading § 1210, Immaterial Variance.

Title 6.5

ATTACHMENT

CHAPTER 1. WORDS AND PHRASES DEFINED

§ 481.010. Definitions to govern construction of title

Unless the provision or context otherwise requires, the definitions in this chapter govern the construction of this title. *(Added by Stats.1974, c. 1516, p. 3337, § 9, operative Jan. 1, 1977.)*

Law Revision Commission Comments

Section 481.010 is a standard provision found in the definitional portion of recently enacted California codes. See, *e.g.*, Evid.Code § 100; Veh.Code § 100.

Additional definitions are found in the preliminary provisions of the Code of Civil Procedure. *E.g.*, Section 17 provides "the singular number includes the plural and the plural the singular."

Research References

Rutter, Cal. Practice Guide: A.D.R. Ch. 5-G, G. Procedures to Enforce Arbitration.

Rutter, Cal. Practice Guide: Civil Appeals & Writs Ch. 15-A, A. Overview.

Rutter, Cal. Practice Guide: Civ. Pro. Before Trial Ch. 9(II)-D, D. Attachment.

Rutter, Cal. Practice Guide: Enforcing Judgments/Debts Ch. 4-A, A. Attachment.

Rutter, Cal. Practice Guide: Fed.Civ.Pro. Before Trial Ch. 13-A, A. Introduction.

Rutter, Cal. Practice Guide: Real Prop. Transactions Ch. 6-I, I. Real Property Foreclosures and Antideficiency Laws.

Miller and Starr California Real Estate § 32:17, Unsecured Obligation.

3 Witkin Cal. Proc. 5th Actions § 187, (S 187) Attachment.

2 Witkin Cal. Proc. 5th Courts § 289, (S 289) in General.

8 Witkin Cal. Proc. 5th Enforcement of Judgment § 68, (S 68) Relation Back and Priorities.

8 Witkin Cal. Proc. 5th Enforcement of Judgment § 176, (S 176) Time for Determining Exemptions.

8 Witkin Cal. Proc. 5th Enforcement of Judgment § 498, (S 498) Remedies of Creditors.

6 Witkin Cal. Proc. 5th Proceedings Without Trial § 529, (S 529) in General.

6 Witkin Cal. Proc. 5th Provisional Remedies § 1, (S 1) in General.

6 Witkin Cal. Proc. 5th Provisional Remedies § 52, Enactment.

6 Witkin Cal. Proc. 5th Provisional Remedies § 53, Nature and Scope.

6 Witkin Cal. Proc. 5th Provisional Remedies § 55, General Definitions.

4 Witkin, California Summary 10th Secured Transactions in Personal Property § 64, (S 64) in Proceeds.

§ 481.020. Account debtor defined

"Account debtor" means "account debtor" as defined in paragraph (3) of subdivision (a) of Section 9102 of the Commercial Code. *(Added by Stats.1974, c. 1516, p. 3337, § 9, operative Jan. 1, 1977. Amended by Stats.1982, c. 1198, p. 4274, § 1, operative July 1, 1983; Stats.1999, c. 991 (S.B.45), § 11.5, operative July 1, 2001.)*

Law Revision Commission Comments

Section 481.020 is based on the definition of "account debtor" provided by paragraph (a) of subdivision (1) of Section 9105 of the Commercial Code. This paragraph provides: " 'Account debtor' means the person who is obligated on an account, chattel paper, contract right or general intangible . . . . ."

Section 481.020 merely substitutes the term "account receivable" for "account" and "chose in action" for "general intangible." See Sections 481.030 ("account receivable" defined), 481.050 ("chose in action" defined). Attachment of a "contract right" (as that term is defined by Section 9106 of the Commercial Code) is not permitted. "Chattel paper" is defined by Section 481.040 in substantially the same manner as under the Commercial Code.

Section 481.020 is amended to conform to Section 680.120 (Enforcement of Judgments Law) (16 Cal.L.Rev.Comm. Reports 701).

Research References

6 Witkin Cal. Proc. 5th Provisional Remedies § 56, Commercial Code Definitions.

6 Witkin Cal. Proc. 5th Provisional Remedies § 174, Accounts Receivable and General Intangibles.

§ 481.030. Account receivable defined

"Account receivable" means "account" as defined in paragraph (2) of subdivision (a) of Section 9102 of the Commercial Code. *(Added by Stats.1974, c. 1516, p. 3337, § 9, operative Jan. 1, 1977. Amended by Stats.1982, c. 1198, p. 4274, § 2, operative July 1, 1983; Stats.1999, c. 991 (S.B.45), § 12, operative July 1, 2001.)*

Law Revision Commission Comments

Section 481.030 is based on the definition of "account" provided by Section 9106 of the Commercial Code. However, the term "account receivable" is used in this title because it is more descriptive than "account" and because it avoids confusion with the term "deposit account." Compare Section 481.080 ("deposit account" defined). Section 481.030 also substitutes the terms "negotiable instrument" and "security" for the term "instrument" used in Section 9106. However, the substance of the Commercial Code is retained. *Compare* Sections 481.160 ("negotiable instrument" defined) and 481.210 ("security" defined) *with* Commercial Code Section 9105(1)(g) ("instrument" defined).

Section 481.030 also makes clear that the right to payment must have been earned at the time of levy. This continues former attachment law. See, *e.g.*, Brunskill v. Stutman, 186 Cal.App.2d 97, 8 Cal.Rptr. 910 (1960); Philbrook v. Mercantile Trust Co., 84 Cal.App. 187, 257 P. 882 (1927). See also Dawson v. Bank of America, 100 Cal.App.2d 305, 223 P.2d 280 (1950).

The method of levy on an account receivable is provided by Section 488.370.

Section 481.030 is amended to conform to Section 680.130 (Enforcement of Judgments Law) (16 Cal.L.Rev.Comm. Reports 701).

Research References

Rutter, Cal. Practice Guide: Enforcing Judgments/Debts Ch. 4-A, A. Attachment.

6 Witkin Cal. Proc. 5th Provisional Remedies § 56, Commercial Code Definitions.

6 Witkin Cal. Proc. 5th Provisional Remedies § 174, Accounts Receivable and General Intangibles.

§ 481.040. Chattel paper defined

"Chattel paper" means "chattel paper" as defined in paragraph (11) of subdivision (a) of Section 9102 of the Commercial Code. *(Added by Stats.1974, c. 1516, p. 3337, § 9, operative Jan. 1, 1977. Amended by Stats.1982, c. 1198, p. 4274, § 3, operative July 1, 1983; Stats.1999, c. 991 (S.B.45), § 12.1, operative July 1, 2001.)*

Law Revision Commission Comments

Section 481.040 is substantively the same as paragraph (b) of subdivision (1) of Section 9105 of the Commercial Code. The term "instrument" used in paragraph (b) of subdivision (1) of Section 9105 is defined in paragraph (g) of subdivision (1) of Section 9105. Section 481.040 incorporates the same definition in its third sentence. Thus, "chattel paper" under this title has basically the same meaning as "chattel paper" under Section 9105 of the Commercial Code, and the following excerpt from the Comment to Section 9105 should help to explain the term:

A dealer sells a tractor to a farmer on conditional sales contract. The conditional sales contract is a "security agreement", the farmer is the "debtor", the dealer is the "secured party" and the tractor is the type of "collateral" defined in Section 9–109 as "equipment". But now the dealer transfers the contract to his bank, either by outright sale or to secure a loan. Since the conditional sales contract is a security agreement relating to specific equipment the conditional sales contract is now the type of collateral called "chattel paper". In this transaction between the dealer and his bank, the bank is the "secured party", the dealer is the "debtor", and the farmer is the "account debtor".

Under the definition of "security interest" in Section 1–201(37) a lease does not create a security interest unless intended as security. Whether or not the lease itself is a security agreement, it is chattel paper when transferred if it relates to specific goods. Thus, if the dealer enters into a straight lease of the tractor to the farmer (not intended as security), and then arranges to borrow money on the security of the lease, the lease is chattel paper.

The method of levy on chattel paper is provided by Section 488.380.

Section 481.040 is amended to conform to Section 680.140 (Enforcement of Judgments Law) (16 Cal.L.Rev.Comm. Reports 701).

Research References

6 Witkin Cal. Proc. 5th Provisional Remedies § 56, Commercial Code Definitions.

6 Witkin Cal. Proc. 5th Provisional Remedies § 158, Property Governed by Enforcement of Judgments Law.

§ 481.055. Costs defined

"Costs" means costs and disbursements, including, but not limited to, statutory fees, charges, commissions, and expenses. *(Added by Stats.1982, c. 1198, p. 4274, § 5, operative July 1, 1983.)*

Research References

6 Witkin Cal. Proc. 5th Provisional Remedies § 55, General Definitions.

6 Witkin Cal. Proc. 5th Provisional Remedies § 99, (S 99) Costs and Attorneys' Fees.

§ 481.060. Complaint defined

"Complaint" includes a cross-complaint. *(Added by Stats. 1974, c. 1516, p. 3338, § 9, operative Jan. 1, 1977.)*

Law Revision Commission Comments

Section 481.060 continues former law. See, *e.g.*, Allers v. Beverly Hills Laundry, Inc., 98 Cal.App. 580, 277 P. 337 (1929).

Research References

Miller and Starr California Real Estate § 32:6, Who Can Attach.

6 Witkin Cal. Proc. 5th Provisional Remedies § 55, General Definitions.

§ 481.070. Defendant defined

"Defendant" includes a cross-defendant. *(Added by Stats. 1974, c. 1516, p. 3338, § 9, operative Jan. 1, 1977.)*

Law Revision Commission Comments

See Comment to Section 481.060.

Research References

6 Witkin Cal. Proc. 5th Provisional Remedies § 55, General Definitions.

§ 481.080. Deposit account defined

"Deposit account" means "deposit account" as defined in paragraph (29) of subdivision (a) of Section 9102 of the Commercial Code. *(Added by Stats.1974, c. 1516, p. 3338, § 9, operative Jan. 1, 1977. Amended by Stats.1982, c. 1198, p. 4274, § 6, operative July 1, 1983; Stats.1999, c. 991 (S.B.45), § 12.2, operative July 1, 2001.)*

Law Revision Commission Comments

Section 481.080 defines "deposit account" as the term is used in this title. The method of levy on deposit accounts is provided by Section 488.390. See also Section 488.400.

Section 481.080 is amended to conform to Section 680.170 (Enforcement of Judgments Law) (16 Cal.L.Rev.Comm. Reports 701).

Research References

6 Witkin Cal. Proc. 5th Provisional Remedies § 56, Commercial Code Definitions.

6 Witkin Cal. Proc. 5th Provisional Remedies § 175, (S 175) in General.

§ 481.090. Document of title defined

"Document of title" means "document" as defined in paragraph (30) of subdivision (a) of Section 9102 of the Commercial Code. A document of title is negotiable if it is negotiable within the meaning of Section 7104 of the Commercial Code. *(Added by Stats.1974, c. 1516, p. 3338, § 9, operative Jan. 1, 1977.*

Amended by Stats.1982, c. 1198, p. 4274, § 7, operative July 1, 1983; Stats.1999, c. 991 (S.B.45), § 12.3, operative July 1, 2001.)

Law Revision Commission Comments

Section 481.090 defines "document" by incorporating by reference the term "document of title" defined by subdivision (15) of Section 1201 of the Commercial Code. A negotiable document is levied upon in the same manner as a negotiable instrument (Section 488.400), and goods subject to a negotiable document may not be attached. See Section 488.330(d). On the other hand, goods subject to a nonnegotiable document may be levied upon pursuant to Section 488.330.

Section 481.090 is amended to conform to Section 680.180 (Enforcement of Judgments Law) (16 Cal.L.Rev.Comm. Reports 701).

Research References

6 Witkin Cal. Proc. 5th Provisional Remedies § 56, Commercial Code Definitions.
6 Witkin Cal. Proc. 5th Provisional Remedies § 158, Property Governed by Enforcement of Judgments Law.

§ 481.100. Equipment defined

"Equipment" means tangible personal property in the possession of the defendant and used or bought for use primarily in the defendant's trade, business, or profession if it is not included in the definitions of inventory or farm products. *(Added by Stats.1974, c. 1516, p. 3338, § 9, operative Jan. 1, 1977.)*

Law Revision Commission Comments

Section 481.100 is based on the definition of "equipment" provided by Section 9109 of the Commercial Code. (11 Cal.L.Rev.Comm. Reports 701, amended by 16 Cal.L.Rev.Comm. Reports 1611).

Research References

6 Witkin Cal. Proc. 5th Provisional Remedies § 55, General Definitions.
6 Witkin Cal. Proc. 5th Provisional Remedies § 161, (S 161) in General.

§ 481.110. Farm products defined

"Farm products" means crops or livestock or supplies used or produced in farming operations or products of crops or livestock in their unmanufactured states (such as ginned cotton, wool clip, maple syrup, milk, and eggs), while in the possession of a defendant engaged in raising, fattening, grazing, or other farming operations. If tangible personal property is a farm product, it is neither equipment nor inventory. *(Added by Stats.1974, c. 1516, p. 3338, § 9, operative Jan. 1, 1977. Amended by Stats.1982, c. 1198, p. 4274, § 8, operative July 1, 1983.)*

Law Revision Commission Comments

Section 481.110 is based on the definition of "farm products" provided by Section 9109 of the Commercial Code. Equipment and inventory are defined by Sections 481.100 and 481.120, respectively. (11 Cal.L.Rev. Comm. Reports 701, amended by 16 Cal.L.Rev.Comm. Reports 1611).

Section 481.110 is amended to delete honey from the list of farm products, consistent with the amendment of Section 9109 of the Commercial Code. See 1974 Cal.Stats. ch. 997, § 12 (16 Cal.L.Rev.Comm. Reports 1611).

The method of levy on farm products is provided in Section 488.360. (11 Cal.L.Rev.Comm. Reports 701, amended by 16 Cal.L.Rev.Comm. Reports 701).

Research References

Rutter, Cal. Practice Guide: Enforcing Judgments/Debts Ch. 4-A, A. Attachment.
6 Witkin Cal. Proc. 5th Provisional Remedies § 55, General Definitions.
6 Witkin Cal. Proc. 5th Provisional Remedies § 146, Effect.
6 Witkin Cal. Proc. 5th Provisional Remedies § 168, (S 168) in General.

§ 481.113. Financial institution defined

"Financial institution" means a state or national bank, state or federal savings and loan association or credit union, or like organization, and includes a corporation engaged in a safe deposit business. *(Added by Stats.1982, c. 1198, p. 4274, § 9, operative July 1, 1983.)*

Law Revision Commission Comments

Section 481.113 is new and is the same as Section 680.200 (Enforcement of Judgments Law) (16 Cal.L.Rev.Comm. Reports 1612).

Research References

6 Witkin Cal. Proc. 5th Provisional Remedies § 55, General Definitions.
6 Witkin Cal. Proc. 5th Provisional Remedies § 146, Effect.
6 Witkin Cal. Proc. 5th Provisional Remedies § 175, (S 175) in General.
6 Witkin Cal. Proc. 5th Provisional Remedies § 177, Safe Deposit Boxes.

§ 481.115. General intangibles defined

"General intangibles" means "general intangibles," as defined in paragraph (42) of subdivision (a) of Section 9102 of the Commercial Code, consisting of rights to payment. *(Added by Stats.1982, c. 1198, p. 4275, § 10, operative July 1, 1983. Amended by Stats.1999, c. 991 (S.B.45), § 13, operative July 1, 2001.)*

Law Revision Commission Comments

Section 481.115 is the same as Section 680.210 (Enforcement of Judgments Law) and supersedes former Section 481.050 ("chose in action" defined). The limitation to debts arising out of the conduct of a trade, business, or profession found in former Section 481.050 is continued in Section 487.010(c) (2) (property subject to attachment) (16 Cal.L.Rev.Comm. Reports 1612).

Research References

Rutter, Cal. Practice Guide: Enforcing Judgments/Debts Ch. 4-A, A. Attachment.
6 Witkin Cal. Proc. 5th Provisional Remedies § 56, Commercial Code Definitions.
6 Witkin Cal. Proc. 5th Provisional Remedies § 174, Accounts Receivable and General Intangibles.

§ 481.117. Instrument defined

"Instrument" means "instrument" as defined in paragraph (47) of subdivision (a) of Section 9102 of the Commercial Code. *(Added by Stats.1982, c. 1198, p. 4275, § 11, operative July 1, 1983. Amended by Stats.1999, c. 991 (S.B.45), § 13.1, operative July 1, 2001.)*

Law Revision Commission Comments

Section 481.117 is the same as Section 680.220 (Enforcement of Judgments Law) and supersedes a portion of former Section 481.050 ("chose in action" includes nonnegotiable instrument) and former Section 481.160 ("negotiable instrument" defined) (16 Cal.L.Rev.Comm. Reports 1612).

Research References

6 Witkin Cal. Proc. 5th Provisional Remedies § 56, Commercial Code Definitions.
6 Witkin Cal. Proc. 5th Provisional Remedies § 158, Property Governed by Enforcement of Judgments Law.

§ 481.120. Inventory defined

"Inventory" means tangible personal property in the possession of a defendant that (a) is held by the defendant for sale or lease or to be furnished under contracts of service or (b) is raw materials, work in process, or materials used or consumed in his trade, business, or profession. Inventory of a person is not to be classified as his equipment. *(Added by Stats.1974, c. 1516, p. 3338, § 9, operative Jan. 1, 1977.)*

Law Revision Commission Comments

Section 481.120 is based on the definition of "inventory" provided by Section 9109 of the Commercial Code. The phrase "or if he has leased or so furnished them" contained in Section 9109 has been omitted here to make clear that inventory under this title is limited to property in the possession of the defendant. (11 Cal.L.Rev.Comm. Reports 701, amended by 11 Cal.L.Rev.Comm. Reports 1612).

Research References

Rutter, Cal. Practice Guide: Enforcing Judgments/Debts Ch. 4-A, A. Attachment.
6 Witkin Cal. Proc. 5th Provisional Remedies § 55, General Definitions.
6 Witkin Cal. Proc. 5th Provisional Remedies § 146, Effect.
6 Witkin Cal. Proc. 5th Provisional Remedies § 168, (S 168) in General.

§ 481.140.   Levying officer defined

"Levying officer" means the sheriff or marshal who is directed to execute a writ or order issued under this title. *(Added by Stats.1974, c. 1516, p. 3338, § 9, operative Jan. 1, 1977. Amended by Stats.1996, c. 872 (A.B.3472), § 12.)*

Research References

6 Witkin Cal. Proc. 5th Provisional Remedies § 55, General Definitions.

§ 481.170.   Person defined

"Person" includes a natural person, a corporation, a partnership or other unincorporated association, a limited liability company, and a public entity. *(Added by Stats.1974, c. 1516, p. 3338, § 9, operative Jan. 1, 1977. Amended by Stats.1982, c. 1198, p. 4275, § 14, operative July 1, 1983; Stats.1994, c. 1010 (S.B.2053), § 58.)*

Law Revision Commission Comments

Section 481.170 is amended to conform to Section 680.280 (Enforcement of Judgments Law) (16 Cal.L.Rev.Comm. Reports 1613).

Research References

Rutter, Cal. Practice Guide: Enforcing Judgments/Debts Ch. 4-A, A. Attachment.
6 Witkin Cal. Proc. 5th Provisional Remedies § 55, General Definitions.

§ 481.175.   Personal property defined

"Personal property" includes both tangible and intangible personal property. *(Added by Stats.1982, c. 1198, p. 4275, § 15, operative July 1, 1983.)*

Law Revision Commission Comments

Section 481.175 is new and is the same as Section 680.290 (Enforcement of Judgments Law) (16 Cal.L.Rev.Comm. Reports 1613).

Research References

6 Witkin Cal. Proc. 5th Provisional Remedies § 55, General Definitions.
6 Witkin Cal. Proc. 5th Provisional Remedies § 160, (S 160) Current Attachment Law.

§ 481.180.   Plaintiff defined

"Plaintiff" means a person who files a complaint or cross-complaint. *(Added by Stats.1974, c. 1516, p. 3338, § 9, operative Jan. 1, 1977.)*

Law Revision Commission Comments

See Comment to Section 481.060.

Research References

6 Witkin Cal. Proc. 5th Provisional Remedies § 47, Main Action.
6 Witkin Cal. Proc. 5th Provisional Remedies § 55, General Definitions.

§ 481.190.   Probable validity defined

A claim has "probable validity" where it is more likely than not that the plaintiff will obtain a judgment against the defendant on that claim. *(Added by Stats.1974, c. 1516, p. 3338, § 9, operative Jan. 1, 1977.)*

Law Revision Commission Comments

The definition of "probable validity" in Section 481.190 requires that, at the hearing on the application for a writ, the plaintiff must at least establish a prima facie case. If the defendant makes an appearance, the court must then consider the relative merits of the positions of the respective parties and make a determination of the probable outcome of the litigation.

Research References

Rutter, Cal. Practice Guide: Civ. Pro. Before Trial Ch. 9(II)-D, D. Attachment.
Rutter, Cal. Practice Guide: Enforcing Judgments/Debts Ch. 4-A, A. Attachment.
17 NO. 5 Miller & Starr, California Real Estate Newsalert 4, Construction Contracts.
6 Witkin Cal. Proc. 5th Provisional Remedies § 55, General Definitions.
6 Witkin Cal. Proc. 5th Provisional Remedies § 108, Burden of Proof.
6 Witkin Cal. Proc. 5th Provisional Remedies § 111, (S 111) Right to Attach Order.
6 Witkin Cal. Proc. 5th Provisional Remedies § 131, (S 131) Order and Writ.
6 Witkin Cal. Proc. 5th Provisional Remedies § 143, (S 143) Ex Parte Hearing and Determination.

§ 481.195.   Property defined

"Property" includes real and personal property and any interest therein. *(Added by Stats.1982, c. 1198, p. 4275, § 16, operative July 1, 1983.)*

Law Revision Commission Comments

Section 481.195 is new and is the same as Section 680.310 (Enforcement of Judgments Law) (16 Cal.L.Rev.Comm. Reports 1614).

Research References

Miller and Starr California Real Estate § 17:37, Generally; Definitions.
6 Witkin Cal. Proc. 5th Provisional Remedies § 55, General Definitions.

§ 481.200.   Public entity defined

"Public entity" includes the state, the Regents of the University of California, a county, a city, district, public authority, public agency, and any other political subdivision or public corporation in the state. *(Added by Stats.1974, c. 1516, p. 3338, § 9, operative Jan. 1, 1977.)*

Law Revision Commission Comments

Section 481.200 adopts the language of the definition found in Section 811.2 of the Government Code.

Research References

7 Witkin Cal. Proc. 5th Judgment § 136, (S 136) Jury Fees and Expenses.
6 Witkin Cal. Proc. 5th Provisional Remedies § 55, General Definitions.

§ 481.203.   Real property defined

"Real property" includes any right in real property, including, but not limited to, a leasehold interest in real property. *(Added by Stats.1982, c. 1198, p. 4275, § 17, operative July 1, 1983.)*

Law Revision Commission Comments

Section 481.203 is new and is the same as Section 680.320 (Enforcement of Judgments Law) (16 Cal.L.Rev.Comm. Reports 1614).

Research References

Miller and Starr California Real Estate § 19:2, Lease as Personal Property or Real Property.
Miller and Starr California Real Estate § 17:37, Generally; Definitions.
6 Witkin Cal. Proc. 5th Provisional Remedies § 55, General Definitions.

6 Witkin Cal. Proc. 5th Provisional Remedies § 158, Property Governed by Enforcement of Judgments Law.

§ 481.205. Registered process server defined

"Registered process server" means a person registered as a process server pursuant to Chapter 16 (commencing with Section 22350) of Division 8 of the Business and Professions Code. *(Added by Stats.1982, c. 1198, p. 4275, § 18, operative July 1, 1983.)*

Law Revision Commission Comments

Section 481.205 is new and is the same as Section 680.330 (Enforcement of Judgments Law) (16 Cal.L.Rev.Comm. Report 1614).

Research References

6 Witkin Cal. Proc. 5th Provisional Remedies § 55, General Definitions.
6 Witkin Cal. Proc. 5th Provisional Remedies § 152, Levy by Registered Process Server.

§ 481.207. Secured party defined

Section operative until July 1, 2014. See, also, section operative July 1, 2014.

"Secured party" means "secured party" as defined in paragraph (72) of subdivision (a) of Section 9102 of the Commercial Code. *(Added by Stats.1982, c. 1198, p. 4275, § 19, operative July 1, 1983. Amended by Stats.1999, c. 991 (S.B.45), § 13.2, operative July 1, 2001.)*

§ 481.207. Secured party defined

Section operative July 1, 2014. See, also, section operative until July 1, 2014.

"Secured party" means "secured party" as defined in paragraph (73) of subdivision (a) of Section 9102 of the Commercial Code. *(Added by Stats.1982, c. 1198, p. 4275, § 19, operative July 1, 1983. Amended by Stats.1999, c. 991 (S.B.45), § 13.2, operative July 1, 2001; Stats.2013, c. 531 (A.B.502), § 2, operative July 1, 2014.)*

Law Revision Commission Comments

Section 481.207 is new and is the same as Section 680.340 (Enforcement of Judgments Law) (16 Cal.L.Rev.Comm. Reports 1614).

Research References

6 Witkin Cal. Proc. 5th Provisional Remedies § 56, Commercial Code Definitions.

§ 481.210. Security defined

"Security" means a "security" as defined by Section 8102 of the Commercial Code. *(Added by Stats.1974, c. 1516, p. 3339, § 9, operative Jan. 1, 1977.)*

Law Revision Commission Comments

Section 481.210 defines "security" by incorporating by reference the same term as defined by Section 8102 of the Commercial Code. The method of levy on a security is provided by Section 488.410.

Research References

6 Witkin Cal. Proc. 5th Provisional Remedies § 56, Commercial Code Definitions.
6 Witkin Cal. Proc. 5th Provisional Remedies § 179, Securities.

§ 481.220. Security agreement defined

Section operative until July 1, 2014. See, also, section operative July 1, 2014.

"Security agreement" means a "security agreement" as defined by paragraph (73) of subdivision (a) of Section 9102 of the Commercial Code. *(Added by Stats.1974, c. 1516, p. 3339, § 9,*

operative Jan. 1, 1977. Amended by Stats.1999, c. 991 (S.B.45), § 13.3, operative July 1, 2001.)

§ 481.220. Security agreement defined

Section operative July 1, 2014. See, also, section operative until July 1, 2014.

"Security agreement" means a "security agreement" as defined by paragraph (74) of subdivision (a) of Section 9102 of the Commercial Code. *(Added by Stats.1974, c. 1516, p. 3339, § 9, operative Jan. 1, 1977. Amended by Stats.1999, c. 991 (S.B.45), § 13.3, operative July 1, 2001; Stats.2013, c. 531 (A.B.502), § 3, operative July 1, 2014.)*

Law Revision Commission Comments

Section 481.220 defines "security agreement" by incorporating by reference the same term as defined by paragraph (h) of subdivision (1) of Section 9105 of the Commercial Code.

Research References

6 Witkin Cal. Proc. 5th Provisional Remedies § 56, Commercial Code Definitions.

§ 481.223. Security interest defined

"Security interest" means "security interest" as defined in Section 1201 of the Commercial Code. *(Added by Stats.1982, c. 1198, p. 4275, § 20, operative July 1, 1983.)*

Law Revision Commission Comments

Section 481.223 is new and is the same as Section 680.360 (Enforcement of Judgments Law) (16 Cal.L.Rev.Comm. Reports 1615).

Research References

6 Witkin Cal. Proc. 5th Provisional Remedies § 56, Commercial Code Definitions.

§ 481.225. Tangible personal property defined

"Tangible personal property" includes chattel paper, documents of title, instruments, securities, and money. *(Added by Stats.1982, c. 1198, p. 4275, § 21, operative July 1, 1983.)*

Law Revision Commission Comments

Section 481.225 is new and is the same as Section 680.370 (Enforcement of Judgments Law) (16 Cal.L.Rev.Comm. Reports 1615).

Research References

Rutter, Cal. Practice Guide: Enforcing Judgments/Debts Ch. 4-A, A. Attachment.
6 Witkin Cal. Proc. 5th Provisional Remedies § 55, General Definitions.

CHAPTER 2. GENERAL PROVISIONS

Section

482.110. Estimate of costs and attorney fees; application for right to attach order and writ.

482.120. Interest of defendant in property in excess of amount necessary for security; authority of court.

§ 482.010. Short title

This title shall be known and may be cited as "The Attachment Law." *(Added by Stats.1974, c. 1516, p. 3339, § 9, operative Jan. 1, 1977.)*

Research References

6 Witkin Cal. Proc. 5th Provisional Remedies § 53, Nature and Scope.

§ 482.020. Injunctive relief available

Nothing in this title precludes the granting of relief pursuant to Chapter 3 (commencing with Section 525) of Title 7. *(Added by Stats.1974, c. 1516, p. 3339, § 9, operative Jan. 1, 1977.)*

Law Revision Commission Comments

Section 482.020 deals with certain problems of integration of this title with Chapter 3 of Title 7 of this part. The remedies provided by this title are not intended to be exclusive. In some circumstances, the relief provided, while theoretically available, may be impractical or ineffectual. In other cases, relief hereunder may be denied due to a close factual question of liability. In these situations, an injunction may provide a more satisfactory remedy and the ruling on an application for injunctive relief pursuant to the other provisions of this code should not be prejudiced by reason of the theoretical availability of a remedy at law.

Research References

Rutter, Cal. Practice Guide: Enforcing Judgments/Debts Ch. 4-A, A. Attachment.
6 Witkin Cal. Proc. 5th Provisional Remedies § 49, Nonexclusive Remedy.

§ 482.030. Judicial Council rules

(a) The Judicial Council may provide by rule for the practice and procedure in proceedings under this title.

(b) The Judicial Council shall prescribe the form of the applications, notices, orders, and other documents required by this title. *(Added by Stats.1974, c. 1516, p. 3339, § 9, operative Jan. 1, 1977.)*

Law Revision Commission Comments

Section 482.030 imposes certain duties on the Judicial Council. Subdivision (b) requires the Judicial Council to prescribe the forms necessary for the purposes of this title. The Judicial Council has authority to adopt and revise forms as necessary but must act in a manner consistent with the provisions of this title.

Research References

Rutter, Cal. Practice Guide: Civ. Pro. Before Trial Ch. 9(II)-D, D. Attachment.
Rutter, Cal. Practice Guide: Enforcing Judgments/Debts Ch. 4-A, A. Attachment.
6 Witkin Cal. Proc. 5th Provisional Remedies § 92, (S 92) Judicial Council Forms.

§ 482.040. Affidavits; statement of facts; affiant; verified complaint

The facts stated in each affidavit filed pursuant to this title shall be set forth with particularity. Except where matters are specifically permitted by this title to be shown by information and belief, each affidavit shall show affirmatively that the affiant, if sworn as a witness, can testify competently to the facts stated therein. As to matters shown by information and belief, the affidavit shall state the facts on which the affiant's belief is based, showing the nature of his information and the reliability of his informant. The affiant may be any person, whether or not a party to the action, who has knowledge of the facts. A verified complaint that satisfies the requirements of this section may be used in lieu of or in addition to an affidavit. *(Added by Stats.1974, c. 1516, p. 3339, § 9, operative Jan. 1, 1977.)*

Research References

Rutter, Cal. Practice Guide: Civ. Pro. Before Trial Ch. 9(II)-D, D. Attachment.
Rutter, Cal. Practice Guide: Enforcing Judgments/Debts Ch. 4-A, A. Attachment.
6 Witkin Cal. Proc. 5th Provisional Remedies § 89, (S 89) Affidavits.
6 Witkin Cal. Proc. 5th Provisional Remedies § 96, Affidavit.
6 Witkin Cal. Proc. 5th Provisional Remedies § 103, Notice of Opposition.
6 Witkin Cal. Proc. 5th Provisional Remedies § 125, (S 125) Application and Supporting Affidavit.
6 Witkin Cal. Proc. 5th Provisional Remedies § 130, (S 130) Application and Affidavit.
6 Witkin Cal. Proc. 5th Provisional Remedies § 138, Application and Affidavit.
6 Witkin Cal. Proc. 5th Provisional Remedies § 142, (S 142) Application and Affidavit.
6 Witkin Cal. Proc. 5th Provisional Remedies § 253, (S 253) Affidavits.

§ 482.050. Delayed public disclosure

(a) If the plaintiff so requests in writing at the time he files his complaint, the clerk of the court with whom the complaint is filed shall not make available to the public the records and documents in such action before either (1) 30 days after the filing of the complaint or (2) the filing pursuant to this title of the return of service of the notice of hearing and any temporary protective order, or of the writ of attachment if issued without notice, whichever event occurs first.

(b) Notwithstanding subdivision (a), the clerk of the court shall make the entire file in the action available for inspection at any time to any party named in the complaint or to his attorney.

(c) The request by plaintiff that the fact of filing of a complaint or application for relief not be made public may take the form of a notation to that effect, made by rubber stamp or other suitable means, at the top of the first page of the complaint filed with the clerk. *(Added by Stats.1974, c. 1516, p. 3339, § 9, operative Jan. 1, 1977.)*

Law Revision Commission Comments

Section 482.050 is substantively the same as former Section 537.5.

Research References

Rutter, Cal. Practice Guide: Civ. Pro. Before Trial Ch. 9(II)-D, D. Attachment.
Rutter, Cal. Practice Guide: Enforcing Judgments/Debts Ch. 4-A, A. Attachment.
Miller and Starr California Real Estate § 32:34, Procedure for Issuance of the Writ.
6 Witkin Cal. Proc. 5th Provisional Remedies § 94, (S 94) Request for Secrecy.

§ 482.060. Judicial duties; subordinate duties performable by appointed officers

(a) Except as otherwise provided in subdivision (b), the judicial duties to be performed under this title are subordinate judicial duties within the meaning of Section 22 of Article VI of the California Constitution and may be performed by appointed officers such as court commissioners.

(b) The judicial duties to be performed in the determination of the following matters are not subordinate judicial duties:

(1) A contested claim of exemption.

(2) A contested motion for determination of the liability and damages for wrongful attachment.

(3) A contested third-party claim.

(4) A contested proceeding to enforce a third person's liability.

(c) Nothing in subdivision (b) limits the power of a court to appoint a temporary judge pursuant to Section 21 of Article VI of the California Constitution. *(Added by Stats.1978, c. 151, § 1. Amended by Stats.1982, c. 1198, p. 4276, § 23, operative July 1, 1983.)*

Law Revision Commission Comments

Section 482.060 authorizes the use of court commissioners to perform judicial duties arising under this title, subject to the exceptions noted in subdivision (b).

Contested exemption claims, described in paragraph (1) of subdivision (b), may arise under Sections 482.100 (postlevy exemption claims based on changed circumstances), 484.070 (claim of exemption and notice of opposition in procedure for issuance of writ of attachment after a noticed hearing), 484.350–484.360 (claim of exemption and notice of opposition in procedure for issuance of additional writ after a noticed hearing), 484.530 (claim of exemption after levy of ex parte additional writ), 485.610 (claim of exemption after levy of ex parte writ or additional writ), or 492.040–492.050 (release of exempt property where nonresident defendant files general appearance). [A contested exemption claim may also arise under Section 487.030 (claim of exemption for real property)].

Motions for determination of liability and damages for wrongful attachment arise under [former] Sections 490.030 and 490.050 [superseded by Sections 996.440 and 996.460]. Third-party claims are made and determined in the manner provided by [former] Section 689 which [was] incorporated by [former] Section 488.090 [superseded by Section 488.110]. [See also Section 491.170.] Actions to enforce a garnishee's liability may be brought pursuant to [former] Section 488.550 [superseded by Sections 488.600, 488.610 491.310–491.370, and 701.010–701.020].

Subdivision (c) recognizes that a qualified commissioner or other person may be appointed as a temporary judge, upon stipulation of the parties, to determine a matter pursuant to the authority of Section 21 of Article VI of the California Constitution (11 Cal.L.Rev.Comm. Reports 701, amended by 16 Cal.L.Rev.Comm. Reports 1618).

Subdivision (b)(4) of Section 482.060 is revised to make clear its application to proceedings under Sections 488.600, 488.610, 491.170, and 491.310 (16 Cal.L.Rev.Comm. Reports 1618).

Research References

Rutter, Cal. Practice Guide: Civ. Pro. Before Trial Ch. 9(I)-D, D. Hearing.

Rutter, Cal. Practice Guide: Civ. Pro. Before Trial Ch. 9(II)-D, D. Attachment.

Rutter, Cal. Practice Guide: Enforcing Judgments/Debts Ch. 4-A, A. Attachment.

2 Witkin Cal. Proc. 5th Courts § 344, (S 344) Statutory Duties.

6 Witkin Cal. Proc. 5th Provisional Remedies § 93, (S 93) Courts and Court Commissioners.

6 Witkin Cal. Proc. 5th Provisional Remedies § 106, in General.

6 Witkin Cal. Proc. 5th Provisional Remedies § 156, Third-Party Claims.

6 Witkin Cal. Proc. 5th Provisional Remedies § 201, (S 201) Nature of Action.

6 Witkin Cal. Proc. 5th Provisional Remedies § 232, (S 232) Statutory Remedy.

§ 482.070. Method and proof of service of legal process

(a)(1) Except as otherwise provided in this title, legal process required or permitted to be served under this title may be served personally or by mail.

(2) For purposes of this title, the term "legal process" shall refer to each and all of the writs, notices, orders, or other papers required or permitted to be served pursuant to this title.

(b) Except as otherwise provided in this section, service of legal process under this title is governed by Article 1 (commencing with Section 684.010) and Article 2 (commencing with Section 684.110) of Chapter 4 of Division 1 of Title 9, including the provisions of Section 684.120 extending time when service is made by mail.

(c) For the purpose of subdivision (b), in Article 1 (commencing with Section 684.010) and Article 2 (commencing with Section 684.110) of Chapter 4 of Division 1 of Title 9:

(1) References to the "judgment debtor" shall be deemed references to the defendant.

(2) References to the "judgment creditor" shall be deemed references to the plaintiff.

(3) References to a "writ" shall be deemed references to a writ of attachment.

(4) References to a "notice of levy" shall be deemed references to a notice of attachment.

(d) If the defendant has not appeared in the action and legal process is required to be personally served on the defendant under this title, service shall be made in the same manner as a summons is served under Chapter 4 (commencing with Section 413.10) of Title 5.

(e) Except for service of a subpoena or other process to require the attendance of the defendant or service of a paper to bring the defendant into contempt, if the defendant has an attorney of record in the action, service shall be made on the attorney rather than on the defendant.

(f) Proof of service under this title is governed by Article 3 (commencing with Section 684.210) of Chapter 4 of Division 1 of Title 9. *(Added by Stats.1974, c. 1516, p. 3340, § 9, operative Jan. 1, 1977. Amended by Stats.1982, c. 1198, p. 4276, § 24, operative July 1, 1983; Stats.2012, c. 484 (A.B.2364), § 1.)*

Law Revision Commission Comments

Section 482.070 is amended to incorporate generally the detailed provisions in the Enforcement of Judgments Law governing the manner of service, the persons to be served, and proof of service. See Sections 684.010–684.220 (16 Cal.L.Rev.Comm. Reports 1620).

Research References

Rutter, Cal. Practice Guide: Enforcing Judgments/Debts Ch. 4-A, A. Attachment.

6 Witkin Cal. Proc. 5th Provisional Remedies § 88, (S 88) Service.

6 Witkin Cal. Proc. 5th Provisional Remedies § 153, Notice and Service.

§ 482.080. Order for transfer of property or documentary evidence of title to levying officer; service; notice regarding failure to comply

(a) If a writ of attachment is issued, the court may also issue an order directing the defendant to transfer to the levying officer either or both of the following:

(1) Possession of the property to be attached if the property is sought to be attached by taking it into custody.

(2) Possession of documentary evidence of title to property of or a debt owed to the defendant that is sought to be attached. An order pursuant to this paragraph may be served when the property or debt is levied upon or thereafter.

(b) The order shall be personally served on the defendant and shall contain a notice to the defendant that failure to comply with the order may subject the defendant to arrest and punishment for contempt of court. *(Added by Stats.1974, c. 1516, p. 3340, § 9, operative Jan. 1, 1977. Amended by Stats.1976, c. 437, p. 1117, § 2; Stats.1982, c. 1198, p. 4277, § 25, operative July 1, 1983.)*

Law Revision Commission Comments

Section 482.080 is new. It makes clear that the court has power to issue a "turnover" order directing the defendant to cooperate in transferring possession. Such order is not issued in lieu of a writ but rather in addition to or in aid of a writ. Compare Section 512.070 ("turnover" order under claim and delivery procedure).

Section 482.080 is amended to make clear that an order may be issued under subdivision (a) (1) only where the property is sought to be attached by taking it into custody.

Subdivision (a) (2) is added to Section 482.080 to provide for issuance of a "turnover" order directing the defendant to transfer to the levying officer the muniments of title to property, or documentary evidence of a debt, which is attached. Issuance of an order under subdivision (a) (2) is appropriate, for example, where a motor vehicle has been or is to be attached and the certificate of ownership is sought. Possession of such muniments of title is useful to facilitate sale (such as in the case of the certificate of ownership of a motor vehicle) and to prevent a transfer.

An order may be issued pursuant to this section when the writ of attachment is issued or thereafter.

Subdivision (b) of Section 482.080 is amended to delete the words "or arrest" from the last sentence. This amendment makes clear that the defendant is not subject to arrest independent of contempt proceedings. See Code Civ.Proc. § 501 (civil arrest abolished). A person may still be arrested in the course of contempt proceedings. See Code Civ.Proc. §§ 1212, 1214 (13 Cal.L.Rev.Comm. Reports 801, amended by 16 Cal.L.Rev.Comm. Reports 1621).

Section 482.080 is amended to make clear that personal service of the order is required. See also Sections 482.070 (manner of service) and 684.030 (service on defendant rather than defendant's attorney required) (16 Cal.L.Rev.Comm. Reports 701).

Research References

Rutter, Cal. Practice Guide: Civ. Pro. Before Trial Ch. 9(II)-D, D. Attachment.

Rutter, Cal. Practice Guide: Enforcing Judgments/Debts Ch. 4-A, A. Attachment.

Miller and Starr California Real Estate § 32:34, Procedure for Issuance of the Writ.

6 Witkin Cal. Proc. 5th Provisional Remedies § 114, (S 114) Turnover Order.

6 Witkin Cal. Proc. 5th Provisional Remedies § 167, (S 167) Rights of Bona Fide Purchaser.

§ 482.090. Multiple writs; alias writ of attachment; date of issuance

(a) Several writs in the same form may be issued simultaneously or from time to time upon the same undertaking, whether or not any writ previously issued has been returned.

(b) After the return of the writ of attachment, or upon the filing by the plaintiff of an affidavit setting forth the loss of the writ of attachment, the clerk, upon demand of the plaintiff at any time before judgment, may issue an alias writ which shall be in the same form as the original without requirement of a new undertaking.

(c) The date of issuance of a writ of attachment shall be deemed to be the date the writ is first issued. *(Added by Stats.1974, c. 1516, p. 3340, § 9, operative Jan. 1, 1977.)*

Law Revision Commission Comments

Subdivision (a) of Section 482.090 makes clear that the court has the power to issue multiple writs where necessary—*e.g.*, to levy upon property located in different counties. No time limit is prescribed as to when additional writs may be issued under this subdivision. Compare last paragraph of former Section 540. However, subdivision (c) makes clear that the date of issuance of a writ is the date the writ is *first* issued, and the expiration of the lien created by a levy of attachment is determined accordingly. Hence, subdivision (c), in combination with Section 488.510, provides a time limit of a little less than three years. Subdivision (a) deals only with writs *in the same form*. The procedure for obtaining additional writs in a new form is provided by Articles 2 and 3 of Chapter 4, Article 3 of Chapter 5, and Sections 492.060–492.090 of Chapter 12.

Subdivision (b) is substantively the same as former Section 559½.

Research References

Rutter, Cal. Practice Guide: Civ. Pro. Before Trial Ch. 9(II)-D, D. Attachment.

Rutter, Cal. Practice Guide: Enforcing Judgments/Debts Ch. 4-A, A. Attachment.

6 Witkin Cal. Proc. 5th Provisional Remedies § 117, (S 117) Multiple Writs.

6 Witkin Cal. Proc. 5th Provisional Remedies § 118, Nature and Purpose.

§ 482.100. Claim of exemption; change of circumstances; procedure; support of individual and household

(a) The defendant may claim an exemption provided in Section 487.020 for property levied upon pursuant to a writ issued under this title if the right to the exemption is the result of a change in circumstances occurring after (1) the denial of a claim of exemption for the property earlier in the action or (2) the expiration of the time for claiming the exemption earlier in the action.

(b) A claim of exemption under this section shall follow the procedure provided in Article 2 (commencing with Section 703.510) of Chapter 4 of Division 2 of Title 9 except that, subject to subdivision (a), the defendant may claim the exemption at any time. For this purpose, references in Article 2 (commencing with Section 703.510) of Chapter 4 of Division 2 of Title 9 to the "judgment debtor" shall be deemed references to the defendant, and references to the "judgment creditor" shall be deemed references to the plaintiff.

(c) The exemption provided by subdivision (b) of Section 487.020 may be claimed at the defendant's option either pursuant to subdivision (b) of this section or by following the procedure provided in this subdivision. The claim shall be made by filing with the court and serving on the plaintiff a notice of motion. Service on the plaintiff shall be made not less than three days prior to the date set for the hearing. The hearing shall be held not more than five days after the filing of the notice of motion unless, for good cause shown, the court orders otherwise. The notice of motion shall state the relief requested and shall be accompanied by an affidavit supporting any factual issues raised and points and authorities supporting any legal issues raised. At the hearing on the motion, the defendant has the burden of showing that the property is exempt pursuant to subdivision (b) of Section 487.020. Upon this showing and the showing required by subdivision (a), the court shall order the release of the property. *(Added by Stats.1976, c. 437, p. 1117, § 3. Amended by Stats.1982, c. 1198, p. 4277, § 26, operative July 1, 1983.)*

Law Revision Commission Comments

Section 482.100 provides the procedure for making postlevy claims of exemption under this title where the right to the exemption is based upon a change in circumstances occurring after the exemption has previously been denied or the defendant has previously failed to make a timely claim. See generally Sections 484.070 and 484.350 (claiming exemptions at a noticed hearing on issuance of a writ) and Sections 484.530 and 485.610 (claiming exemptions within 30 days after notice of levy of an ex parte writ).

The requirement that the defendant show a change in circumstances giving rise to the exemption in any case where the exemption has previously been claimed but denied or where the exemption was required to be claimed within a specified time but the defendant failed to do so is applicable, for example, where the defendant failed to claim an exemption for property described in the plaintiff's application for a writ issuable after a noticed hearing (Section 484.070(a)), where the defendant made a claim of exemption as to property not described in the plaintiff's application for a writ issuable after a noticed hearing but failed to prove the exemption (Section 484.070(b)), or where the defendant failed to claim the exemption within the time for making a claim of exemption after levy of an ex parte writ of attachment or additional writ (Section 484.530 or 485.610). If the defendant fails to make a timely claim of exemption, the exemption is waived for purposes of both attachment and execution unless the defendant or judgment debtor shows a change of circumstances affecting his right to the exemption. See, e.g., Section 484.070.

Subdivision (b) incorporates the procedure provided by [the Enforcement of Judgments Law] for claiming exemptions after levy of any writ issued under Chapter 4 or 5.

The provisions for claiming exemptions after levy apply as well in the case of a nonresident defendant whose property has been levied upon pursuant to a writ issued under Chapter 12 except that the nonresident defendant must first have filed a general appearance. See Sections 492.040 and 492.050. Under Chapter 12, the initial determination of exemptions is made when the defendant makes a general appearance. See Sections 492.040 and 492.050. The procedures of Section 482.100 are applicable where the right to the exemption is the result of a change in circumstances occurring after that time.

A claim of exemption made pursuant to subdivision (b) may be made at any time after levy so long as the defendant can show, pursuant to subdivision (a), that the right to claim the exemption is the result of a change in circumstances occurring after the claim was previously denied or the time for previously making the claim had expired.

A more expeditious procedure is provided by subdivision (c) for claiming a hardship exemption. See Section 487.020(b) (exemption of property necessary for the support of an individual defendant or the defendant's family supported in whole or in part by the defendant). . . . Subdivision (b) of former Section 537.3 permitted the defendant to claim a hardship exemption at any time after levy upon five days' notice to the plaintiff. See Sections 484.530(b) and 485.610(b) (incorporating procedure of Section 482.100(c) but without the necessity of showing a change in circumstances). It should be noted that an exemption for necessities may also be claimed, at the defendant's option, pursuant to the procedures provided by subdivision (b) of this section. The defendant may elect to use the subdivision (b) procedure, for example, where there is no need for the more expeditious procedure provided by subdivision (c).

After levy, the defendant may claim an exemption only for property which has been levied upon. Contrast Section 484.070 which permits the defendant to claim an exemption for property which is not described in the plaintiff's application (13 Cal.L.Rev.Comm. Reports 801, amended by 16 Cal.L.Rev.Comm. Reports 1623).

Section 482.100 is amended to substitute a reference to the provisions that replaced former Section 690.50 and to make other conforming revisions. See also Section 482.070 (manner of service) (16 Cal.L.Rev. Comm. Reports 1624).

Research References

Rutter, Cal. Practice Guide: Civ. Pro. Before Trial Ch. 9(II)-D, D. Attachment.
Rutter, Cal. Practice Guide: Enforcing Judgments/Debts Ch. 4-A, A. Attachment.
Rutter, Cal. Practice Guide: Enforcing Judgments/Debts Ch. 6G-23, Enforcement After Judgment Debtor's Death.
Miller and Starr California Real Estate § 32:27, Procedure to Claim an Exemption.
Miller and Starr California Real Estate § 32:35, Noticed Hearing Procedure.
6 Witkin Cal. Proc. 5th Provisional Remedies § 87, (S 87) Claim of Real Property Exemption.
6 Witkin Cal. Proc. 5th Provisional Remedies § 104, Defendant's Claim of Exemption.
6 Witkin Cal. Proc. 5th Provisional Remedies § 121, (S 121) Defendant's Claim of Exemption.
6 Witkin Cal. Proc. 5th Provisional Remedies § 127, (S 127) Defendant's Claim of Exemption.
6 Witkin Cal. Proc. 5th Provisional Remedies § 140, (S 140) Defendant's Claim of Exemption.
6 Witkin Cal. Proc. 5th Provisional Remedies § 169, (S 169) Custody of Keeper or Levying Officer.
6 Witkin Cal. Proc. 5th Provisional Remedies § 222, (S 222) Claim of Exemption.
13 Witkin, California Summary 10th Trusts § 267, (S 267) Claims Established by Judgment.
14 Witkin, California Summary 10th Wills and Probate § 628, (S 628) Conversion of Attachment Lien to Judgment Lien.

§ 482.110. Estimate of costs and attorney fees; application for right to attach order and writ

(a) The plaintiff's application for a right to attach order and a writ of attachment pursuant to this title may include an estimate of the costs and allowable attorney's fees.

(b) In the discretion of the court, the amount to be secured by the attachment may include an estimated amount for costs and allowable attorney's fees. *(Added by Stats.1976, c. 437, p. 1118, § 4.)*

Law Revision Commission Comments

Section 482.110 makes clear that, upon the plaintiff's application therefor, the "amount to be secured by the attachment" may include costs and attorney's fees, in the court's discretion. [See Sections 483.015, 483.020.] See also Sections 484.020, [484.050,] 484.090, 484.320, 484.370, 484.520, 485.220, 485.520, 485.540, [486.020, 486.060, 488.465, 488.720,] 489.310, 489.320, [491.420,] 492.030, 492.070, 492.090 [, 493.040]. This section does not provide any authority for the award of costs or attorney's fees not otherwise made recoverable by contract or statute (13 Cal.L.Rev. Comm. Reports 801, amended by 16 Cal.L.Rev.Comm. Reports 1625).

Research References

Rutter, Cal. Practice Guide: Civ. Pro. Before Trial Ch. 9(II)-D, D. Attachment.
Rutter, Cal. Practice Guide: Enforcing Judgments/Debts Ch. 4-A, A. Attachment.
Miller and Starr California Real Estate § 32:16, Amount of Obligation Subject to Attachment.
Miller and Starr California Real Estate § 32:35, Noticed Hearing Procedure.
6 Witkin Cal. Proc. 5th Provisional Remedies § 98, (S 98) in General.
6 Witkin Cal. Proc. 5th Provisional Remedies § 99, (S 99) Costs and Attorneys' Fees.
6 Witkin Cal. Proc. 5th Provisional Remedies § 100, (S 100) Unlawful Detainer.
6 Witkin Cal. Proc. 5th Provisional Remedies § 102, Contents of Notice.

§ 482.120. Interest of defendant in property in excess of amount necessary for security; authority of court

If the court determines at the hearing on issuance of a writ of attachment under this title that the value of the defendant's interest in the property described in the plaintiff's application clearly exceeds the amount necessary to satisfy the amount to be secured by the attachment, the court may direct the order of levy on the property described in the writ or restrict the amount of the property to be levied upon. *(Added by Stats.1976, c. 437, p. 1118, § 5.)*

Law Revision Commission Comments

Section 482.120 provides a procedure whereby the court may protect against an excessive attachment before levy. After levy, the defendant may seek an order releasing an excessive attachment pursuant to [former] Section 488.555 [superseded by Section 488.720]. The provision in Section 482.120 for an order directing the order of levy continues the substance of a provision of former law. See the last sentence of former Section 538.4. The provision for an order restricting the amount of property to be levied upon recognizes the court's discretion to examine the plaintiff's application and to seek to avoid the attachment of an excessive amount of the defendant's property by ordering issuance of a writ describing a lesser amount of the defendant's property than is described in the plaintiff's application for the writ. This provision makes explicit the authority formerly implied by the last sentence of subdivision (b) of Section 484.090. Similar provisions formerly appeared in Sections 484.370, 484.520, 485.220(b), 485.540, 492.030(b), and 492.090. The enactment of this provision is not intended to require a more detailed description of property in the plaintiff's application than that which satisfies subdivision (e) of Section 484.020 (13 Cal.L.Rev.Comm. Reports 801, amended by 16 Cal.L.Rev.Comm. Reports 1625).

Research References

Rutter, Cal. Practice Guide: Enforcing Judgments/Debts Ch. 4-A, A. Attachment.
Miller and Starr California Real Estate § 32:35, Noticed Hearing Procedure.
6 Witkin Cal. Proc. 5th Provisional Remedies § 102, Contents of Notice.
6 Witkin Cal. Proc. 5th Provisional Remedies § 113, Writ Restricting Amount of Levy.

Civ. Pro.

6 Witkin Cal. Proc. 5th Provisional Remedies § 220, (S 220) Nature of Remedy.

CHAPTER 3.　ACTIONS IN WHICH ATTACHMENT AUTHORIZED

Section

483.010. Claims subject to attachment; minimum amount; secured claims; claims against natural persons; other relief.

483.012. Actions to foreclose mortgages or deeds of trust; pursuit of remedies; effect.

483.013. Federal disability benefits awarded to veterans for service-connected disabilities; exemptions.

483.015. Amount to be secured by attachment.

483.020. Unlawful detainer proceedings; amount to be secured.

§ 483.010. Claims subject to attachment; minimum amount; secured claims; claims against natural persons; other relief

(a) Except as otherwise provided by statute, an attachment may be issued only in an action on a claim or claims for money, each of which is based upon a contract, express or implied, where the total amount of the claim or claims is a fixed or readily ascertainable amount not less than five hundred dollars ($500) exclusive of costs, interest, and attorney's fees.

(b) An attachment may not be issued on a claim which is secured by any interest in real property arising from agreement, statute, or other rule of law (including any mortgage or deed of trust of realty and any statutory, common law, or equitable lien on real property, but excluding any security interest in fixtures subject to Division 9 (commencing with Section 9101) of the Commercial Code). However, an attachment may be issued where the claim was originally so secured but, without any act of the plaintiff or the person to whom the security was given, the security has become valueless or has decreased in value to less than the amount then owing on the claim, in which event the amount to be secured by the attachment shall not exceed the lesser of the amount of the decrease or the difference between the value of the security and the amount then owing on the claim.

(c) If the action is against a defendant who is a natural person, an attachment may be issued only on a claim which arises out of the conduct by the defendant of a trade, business, or profession. An attachment may not be issued on a claim against a defendant who is a natural person if the claim is based on the sale or lease of property, a license to use property, the furnishing of services, or the loan of money where the property sold or leased, or licensed for use, the services furnished, or the money loaned was used by the defendant primarily for personal, family, or household purposes.

(d) An attachment may be issued pursuant to this section whether or not other forms of relief are demanded. *(Added by Stats.1974, c. 1516, p. 3340, § 9, operative Jan. 1, 1977. Amended by Stats.1976, c. 437, p. 1118, § 6; Stats.1982, c. 1198, p. 4278, § 27, operative July 1, 1983; Stats.1990, c. 943 (S.B.2170), § 1; Stats.1993, c. 589 (A.B.2211), § 26; Stats.1995, c. 591 (A.B.1689), § 1; Stats.1997, c. 222 (A.B.1258), § 1.)*

Law Revision Commission Comments

Section 483.010 is based on subdivision (a) of former Section 537.1. Subdivision (a) of former Section 537.1 was designed to limit attachment to cases arising out of commercial transactions. (The title to the 1972 enactment provides that it is one "relating to attachment in commercial actions.") Section 483.010 continues this purpose. Subdivision (a) limits the claims on which an attachment may be issued to those based on a contract, express or implied, where the total amount claimed is $500 or more, exclusive of costs, interest, and attorney's fees. Subdivision (c) further carries out this purpose by providing that, if the defendant is an individual, an attachment may be issued only if the contract claim "arises out of the conduct by the individual of a trade, business, or profession" and only if the goods, services, or money furnished were not used primarily for the defendant's personal, family, or household purposes. *Cf.* Advance Transformer Co. v. Superior Court, 44 Cal.App.3d 127, 142, 118 Cal.Rptr. 350, 360 (1974) (construing former Sections 537.1 and 537.2 as "limiting the attachment to situations in which the claim arises out of defendant's conduct of his business"). Compare Civil Code Section 1802.1 (retail sales). However, Section 483.010 is intended to encompass each of the situations described in paragraphs (1) through (4) of subdivision (a) of former Section 537.1. In this respect, it should be noted that the term "contract" used in subdivision (a) includes a lease of either real or personal property. See Stanford Hotel Co. v. M. Schwind Co., 180 Cal. 348, 181 P. 780 (1919) (realty); Walker v. Phillips, 205 Cal.App.2d 26, 22 Cal.Rptr. 727 (1962) (personalty). In addition, unlike former Section 537.2, Section 483.010 permits attachment on such claims against corporations and partnerships and other unincorporated associations which are not organized for profit or engaged in an activity for profit. Under Section 483.010, the court is not faced with the potentially difficult and complex problem of determining whether a corporation, partnership, or association is engaged in a trade, business, or profession.

Claims may be aggregated, but the total amount claimed in the action must be not less than $500. Generally an expeditious remedy will be available for lesser amounts under the small claims procedure. See Section 116.110 *et seq.* The claim must be for a "fixed or readily ascertainable" amount. This provision continues former law. E.g., Lewis v. Steifel, 98 Cal.App.2d 648, 220 P.2d 769 (1950).

The introductory clause of Section 483.010 recognizes the authority to attach granted by other miscellaneous statutory provisions. See, e.g., Civ. Code §§ 3065a, 3152; Fin. Code § 3144; Food & Agric. Code § 281; Harb. & Nav. Code § 495.1; Health and Safety Code § 11501; Lab. Code § 5600; Rev. & Tax. Code §§ 6713, 7864, 8972, 11472, 12680, 18833, 26251, 30302, 32352. See also Section 492.010 (nonresident attachment).

The attachment remedy is not available where the plaintiff's claim is secured by real property unless, without act of the plaintiff, the security has become valueless or has decreased in value to less than the amount then owing on the claim. See subdivision (b). Moreover, the security cannot simply be waived. As to a claim secured by personal property, see Section 483.015(b)(4). Special rules also apply in unlawful detainer cases. See Section 483.020. [26 Cal.L.Rev.Comm. Reports 307 (1996)].

The last clause of subdivision (b) of Section 483.010 is omitted as obsolete. This exception was applicable to personal property formerly covered by the general rule against attachment on a claim secured by personal property.

Subdivision (e) is deleted to remove the sunset provision that was enacted in 1990 and extended in 1995. See 1990 Cal. Stat. ch. 943, § 1; 1995 Cal. Stat. ch. 591, § 1. [26 Cal.L.Rev.Comm. Reports 307 (1996)].

Research References

California Real Estate Forms (Miller & Starr) § 3:8, Deed of Trust, Security Agreement, and Fixture Filing With Assignment of Rents and Agreements.

California Real Estate Forms (Miller & Starr) § 3:14, Construction Deed of Trust, Security Agreement, and Fixture Filing With Assignment of Rents and Agreements.

Rutter, Cal. Practice Guide: Civ. Pro. Before Trial Ch. 9(II)-D, D. Attachment.

California Practice Guide: Employment Litigation Ch. 6-D, D. Worker Adjustment and Retraining Notification Act (Warn Act).

Rutter, Cal. Practice Guide: Enforcing Judgments/Debts Ch. 4-A, A. Attachment.

Rutter, Cal. Practice Guide: Fed.Civ.Pro. Before Trial Ch. 13-C, C. Requirements for Injunctive Relief.

Rutter, Cal. Practice Guide: Real Prop. Transactions Form 6:I, Deed of Trust (Complex).

Miller and Starr California Real Estate § 28:2, Alternative (Cumulative) Remedies of the Claimant.

Miller and Starr California Real Estate § 32:6, Who Can Attach.

Miller and Starr California Real Estate § 32:9, Former Attachment Law.

Miller and Starr California Real Estate § 10:10, Requirement of Some Debt or Obligation.

Miller and Starr California Real Estate § 32:10, Current Attachment Law.

Miller and Starr California Real Estate § 32:11, Availability of Attachment--In General.

Miller and Starr California Real Estate § 32:12, Against Individual Defendants.

Miller and Starr California Real Estate § 32:13, Against Nonindividual Defendants.

Miller and Starr California Real Estate § 32:16, Amount of Obligation Subject to Attachment.

Miller and Starr California Real Estate § 32:17, Unsecured Obligation.

Miller and Starr California Real Estate § 32:18, Inadequate Security.

Miller and Starr California Real Estate § 32:39, Statutory Recovery on the Undertaking.

Miller and Starr California Real Estate § 10:155, Who May Enforce the One-Action Rule.

Miller and Starr California Real Estate § 10:263, Definitions; Guarantor, Surety.

Miller and Starr California Real Estate § 10:264, Definitions; Comaker, Accommodation.

Miller and Starr California Real Estate § 10:266, Application of "Exhaustion of the Security" Requirement.

Miller and Starr California Real Estate § 19:227, Prejudgment Remedies; Attachment and Receivership.

20 NO. 3 Miller & Starr, California Real Estate Newsalert 17, Involuntary Liens.

21 NO. 1 Miller & Starr, California Real Estate Newsalert 9, Deeds of Trust.

6 Witkin Cal. Proc. 5th Provisional Remedies § 53, Nature and Scope.

6 Witkin Cal. Proc. 5th Provisional Remedies § 57, (S 57) in General.

6 Witkin Cal. Proc. 5th Provisional Remedies § 58, in General.

6 Witkin Cal. Proc. 5th Provisional Remedies § 59, Express and Implied in Fact Contracts.

6 Witkin Cal. Proc. 5th Provisional Remedies § 64, Where Other Relief is Also Sought.

6 Witkin Cal. Proc. 5th Provisional Remedies § 65, (S 65) Minimum Amount Claimed.

6 Witkin Cal. Proc. 5th Provisional Remedies § 67, (S 67) Current Attachment Law.

6 Witkin Cal. Proc. 5th Provisional Remedies § 68, (S 68) Security Without Value or Decreased in Value.

6 Witkin Cal. Proc. 5th Provisional Remedies § 70, Statutory Development.

6 Witkin Cal. Proc. 5th Provisional Remedies § 71, Persons and Entities Subject to Attachment.

6 Witkin Cal. Proc. 5th Provisional Remedies § 73, Trade or Business Requirement.

6 Witkin Cal. Proc. 5th Provisional Remedies § 100, (S 100) Unlawful Detainer.

6 Witkin Cal. Proc. 5th Provisional Remedies § 102, Contents of Notice.

6 Witkin Cal. Proc. 5th Provisional Remedies § 233, (S 233) Acts Constituting Wrongful Attachment.

6 Witkin Cal. Proc. 5th Provisional Remedies § 237, Action for Money.

7 Witkin Cal. Proc. 5th Trial § 35, Improper Expenses.

12 Witkin, California Summary 10th Real Property § 734, Illustrations.

§ 483.012. Actions to foreclose mortgages or deeds of trust; pursuit of remedies; effect

Subject to the restrictions of Sections 580b and 580d, in an action to foreclose a mortgage or deed of trust on real property or an estate for years therein, pursuit of any remedy provided by this title shall not constitute an action for the recovery of a debt for purposes of subdivision (a) of Section 726 or a failure to comply with any other statutory or judicial requirement to proceed first against security. (Added by Stats.1997, c. 222 (A.B.1258), § 3.)

Research References

Rutter, Cal. Practice Guide: Civ. Pro. Before Trial Ch. 9(II)-D, D. Attachment.

Rutter, Cal. Practice Guide: Enforcing Judgments/Debts Ch. 4-A, A. Attachment.

Rutter, Cal. Practice Guide: Real Prop. Transactions Ch. 6-I, I. Real Property Foreclosures and Antideficiency Laws.

Rutter, Cal. Practice Guide: Real Prop. Transactions Ch. 6-I Outline, Outline I.

Miller and Starr California Real Estate § 32:17, Unsecured Obligation.

6 Witkin Cal. Proc. 5th Provisional Remedies § 68, (S 68) Security Without Value or Decreased in Value.

§ 483.013. Federal disability benefits awarded to veterans for service-connected disabilities; exemptions

Notwithstanding Section 483.010, federal disability benefits awarded to veterans for service-connected disabilities pursuant to Chapter 11 of Title 38 of the United States Code shall be exempt from the claim of creditors, and shall not be liable to attachment, levy, or seizure by or under any legal or equitable process whatsoever, as provided by federal law. This section does not apply to that portion of service-connected disability benefits that are subject to child and spousal support enforcement under Section 659(h)(1)(A)(ii)(V) of Title 42 of the United States Code. (Added by Stats.2009, c. 162 (S.B.285), § 2.)

Research References

Rutter, Cal. Practice Guide: Enforcing Judgments/Debts Ch. 6E-5, Specific Exempt Property.

§ 483.015. Amount to be secured by attachment

(a) Subject to subdivision (b) and to Section 483.020, the amount to be secured by an attachment is the sum of the following:

(1) The amount of the defendant's indebtedness claimed by the plaintiff.

(2) Any additional amount included by the court under Section 482.110.

(b) The amount described in subdivision (a) shall be reduced by the sum of the following:

(1) The amount of any money judgment in favor of the defendant and against the plaintiff that remains unsatisfied and is enforceable.

(2) The amount of any indebtedness of the plaintiff that the defendant has claimed in a cross-complaint filed in the action if the defendant's claim is one upon which an attachment could be issued.

(3) The amount of any claim of the defendant asserted as a defense in the answer pursuant to Section 431.70 if the defendant's claim is one upon which an attachment could be issued had an action been brought on the claim when it was not barred by the statute of limitations.

(4) The value of any security interest in the property of the defendant held by the plaintiff to secure the defendant's indebtedness claimed by the plaintiff, together with the amount by which the value of the security interest has decreased due to the act of the plaintiff or a prior holder of the security interest. (Added by Stats.1982, p. 4278, § 28, operative July 1, 1983. Amended by Stats.1983, c. 155, § 1, eff. June 30, 1983, operative July 1, 1983; Stats.1990, c. 943 (S.B.2170), § 2; Stats.1993, c. 589 (A.B.2211), § 27; Stats.1995, c. 591 (A.B.1689), § 3; Stats.1997, c. 222 (A.B.1258), § 4.)

Law Revision Commission Comments

Section 483.015 governs the amount for which an attachment may issue. Subdivision (b) clarifies the nature of claims that will reduce the amount to be secured by attachment. This subdivision makes clear, for example, that the amount to be secured by the attachment is not reduced by a tort claim that has not been reduced to judgment. The defendant may seek to have the amount secured by the attachment reduced as provided in Sections 484.060 and 485.240. Under subdivision (b), if a claim may be offset only if it is "one upon which an attachment could be issued," the claim must meet the requirements of Section 483.010 as to amount and nature of the claim. [26 Cal.L.Rev.Comm. Reports 307 (1996)].

Subdivision (c) of Section 483.015 is deleted to remove the sunset provision that was enacted in 1990 and amended in 1995. See 1990 Cal. Stat. ch. 943, § 2; 1995 Cal. Stat. ch. 591, § 3. For a special limitation on the reduction factor in subdivision (b)(4), see Section 483.020(e) (unlawful detainer). Subdivision (b)(4) is amended for clarity. This is a technical, nonsubstantive change. [26 Cal.L.Rev.Comm. Reports 307 (1996)].

Research References

Rutter, Cal. Practice Guide: Civ. Pro. Before Trial Ch. 9(II)-D, D. Attachment.

Rutter, Cal. Practice Guide: Enforcing Judgments/Debts Ch. 4-A, A. Attachment.

Miller and Starr California Real Estate § 32:16, Amount of Obligation Subject to Attachment.

Miller and Starr California Real Estate § 19:227, Prejudgment Remedies; Attachment and Receivership.

6 Witkin Cal. Proc. 5th Provisional Remedies § 98, (S 98) in General.

6 Witkin Cal. Proc. 5th Provisional Remedies § 100, (S 100) Unlawful Detainer.

6 Witkin Cal. Proc. 5th Provisional Remedies § 102, Contents of Notice.

6 Witkin Cal. Proc. 5th Provisional Remedies § 111, (S 111) Right to Attach Order.

6 Witkin Cal. Proc. 5th Provisional Remedies § 135, (S 135) Noticed Motion.

§ 483.020. Unlawful detainer proceedings; amount to be secured

(a) Subject to subdivisions (d) and (e), the amount to be secured by the attachment in an unlawful detainer proceeding is the sum of the following:

(1) The amount of the rent due and unpaid as of the date of filing the complaint in the unlawful detainer proceeding.

(2) Any additional amount included by the court under subdivision (c).

(3) Any additional amount included by the court under Section 482.110.

(b) In an unlawful detainer proceeding, the plaintiff's application for a right to attach order and a writ of attachment pursuant to this title may include (in addition to the rent due and unpaid as of the date of the filing of the complaint and any additional estimated amount authorized by Section 482.110) an amount equal to the rent for the period from the date the complaint is filed until the estimated date of judgment or such earlier estimated date as possession has been or is likely to be delivered to the plaintiff, such amount to be computed at the rate provided in the lease.

(c) The amount to be secured by the attachment in the unlawful detainer proceeding may, in the discretion of the court, include an additional amount equal to the amount of rent for the period from the date the complaint is filed until the estimated date of judgment or such earlier estimated date as possession has been or is likely to be delivered to the plaintiff, such amount to be computed at the rate provided in the lease.

(d) Except as provided in subdivision (e), the amount to be secured by the attachment as otherwise determined under this section shall be reduced by the amounts described in subdivision (b) of Section 483.015.

(e) Where the plaintiff has received a payment or holds a deposit to secure (1) the payment of rent and the performance of other obligations under the lease or (2) only the performance of other obligations under the lease, the amount of the payment or deposit shall not be subtracted in determining the amount to be secured by the attachment. *(Added by Stats.1978, c. 273, § 2. Amended by Stats.1982, c. 1198, p. 4279, § 29, operative July 1, 1983; Stats.1997, c. 222 (A.B.1258), § 6.)*

Law Revision Commission Comments

Section 483.020 makes clear that, on the plaintiff's application, the "amount to be secured by the attachment" in an unlawful detainer proceeding may include, in the court's discretion, an amount for the use and occupation of the premises by the defendant during the period from the time the complaint is filed until either the time of judgment or such

earlier time as possession has been or is likely to be delivered to the plaintiff. One factor the court should consider in deciding whether to allow the additional amount is the likelihood that the unlawful detainer proceeding will be contested. There may be a considerable delay in bringing the unlawful detainer proceeding to trial if it is contested. In this case, there may be a greater need for attachment to include an additional amount to cover rent accruing after the complaint is filed. It should be noted that, in the case of a defendant who is a natural person, attachment is permitted only where the premises were leased for trade, business, or professional purposes. See Section 483.010.

The amount authorized under subdivision (c) is in addition to (1) the amount in which the attachment would otherwise issue (unpaid rent due and owing at the time of the filing of the complaint) and (2) the additional amount for costs and attorney's fees that the court may authorize under Section 482.110.

Subdivision (d) makes clear that the amount of a deposit (such as a deposit described in Civil Code Section 1950.7) held by the plaintiff solely to secure the payment of rent is to be subtracted in determining the amount to be secured by the attachment. However, the amount of the deposit is not subtracted in determining the amount to be secured by the attachment where, for example, the deposit is to secure both the payment of rent and the repair and cleaning of the premises on termination of the tenancy. Under former law, it was held that a deposit in connection with a lease of real property was not "security" such as to preclude an attachment under former Section 537(4), superseded by Section 483.010(b). See Garfinkle v. Montgomery, 113 Cal.App.2d 149, 155–57, 248 P.2d 52, 56–57 (1952). [26 Cal.L.Rev.Comm. Reports 307 (1996)].

Section 483.020 is amended to conform this section to Sections 483.010 and 483.015, as amended in 1990. The "notwithstanding" clause formerly in subdivision (d) is unnecessary, since Section 483.010 has been amended to eliminate the categorical restriction on attachment where a claim is secured by personal property. See 1990 Cal. Stat. ch. 943, § 1. Former subdivision (e) is deleted as surplus, since the appropriate reduction in the amount of the attachment is covered by subdivision (d), which incorporates the reduction factors in Section 483.015. See 1990 Cal. Stat. ch. 943, § 2, which added paragraph (4) to Section 483.015(b).

As revised, this section is consistent with the rule that an attachment is available where a claim is partially secured by personal property (Section 483.010(b)), with the amount of the attachment reduced by the value of any security interest (Section 483.015(b)(4)) that is applicable exclusively to the rental obligation. If the security may be applied to any obligation other than rent, subdivision (e) makes clear that the amount of the attachment is not reduced by the amount of the security. [26 Cal.L.Rev. Comm. Reports 307 (1996)].

Research References

Rutter, Cal. Practice Guide: Civ. Pro. Before Trial Ch. 9(II)-D, D. Attachment.

Rutter, Cal. Practice Guide: Enforcing Judgments/Debts Ch. 4-A, A. Attachment.

Miller and Starr California Real Estate § 32:13, Against Nonindividual Defendants.

Miller and Starr California Real Estate § 32:16, Amount of Obligation Subject to Attachment.

Miller and Starr California Real Estate § 19:227, Prejudgment Remedies; Attachment and Receivership.

6 Witkin Cal. Proc. 5th Provisional Remedies § 59, Express and Implied in Fact Contracts.

6 Witkin Cal. Proc. 5th Provisional Remedies § 100, (S 100) Unlawful Detainer.

6 Witkin Cal. Proc. 5th Provisional Remedies § 102, Contents of Notice.

6 Witkin Cal. Proc. 5th Provisional Remedies § 111, (S 111) Right to Attach Order.

CHAPTER 4. NOTICED HEARING PROCEDURE FOR OBTAINING WRIT OF ATTACHMENT

Civ. Pro.

Law Revision Commission Comments

Chapters 4, 5, and 6 provide the general procedures for obtaining a temporary protective order, a right to attach order, and a writ of attachment. See also Chapter 12 (commencing with Section 492.010) (nonresident attachment). At the time the plaintiff files his complaint, or at any time thereafter, he may apply for a temporary protective order, a right to attach order, and a writ of attachment in the court where his action is brought. Sections 484.010, 485.210, and 486.010.

Noticed hearing procedure. In the absence of exceptional circumstances, the plaintiff must apply under a notice hearing procedure. See Section 485.010. Notice of the hearing on the application, a copy of the summons and complaint, and a copy of the plaintiff's application and affidavit must be served on the defendant at least 20 days before the hearing. Section 484.040. The defendant, if he wishes to oppose the issuance of the right to attach order, must file and serve on the plaintiff at least five days before the date of the hearing a notice of opposition. Section 484.060(a). If he also desires to make a claim of exemption from attachment, the defendant [may] include such claim with his notice of opposition. Section 484.060(b). If he does not wish to oppose the issuance of the right to attach order, the defendant may still claim an exemption from attachment by filing and serving on the plaintiff any such claim together with supporting affidavits at least five days before the hearing. Section 484.070 . . . . The defendant may claim exemptions as to [real property and as to personal] property not described in the plaintiff's application but, if he fails to prove that such property is exempt, he may not again claim an exemption as to such property unless he shows that there has been a change in circumstances. Section 484.070 (b). As to [personal] property described in the plaintiff's application, the defendant must make his claim within the time provided, or the claim is barred, absent changed circumstances occurring after the hearing on the plaintiff's application. Section 484.070(a).

If the plaintiff wants to contest a claim of exemption, he must serve on the defendant a notice of opposition to such claim at least two days before the hearing. Section 484.070(f). If the plaintiff does not oppose a defendant's claim in this manner, then the property claimed to be exempt may not be attached and, if all the property sought to be attached is thus exempted, the hearing will not be held. Id.

If the defendant neither makes a claim of exemption nor serves a notice of opposition, he may not oppose the application for a right to attach order and a writ of attachment (Section 484.060(a)), but the court is still required to review the application to see if the plaintiff has made an adequate showing to entitle him to the order and writ. Section 484.090.

Temporary protective order procedure. When the plaintiff applies for a right to attach order, he may also apply for a temporary protective order. Section 486.010. An ex parte hearing is then held upon such application and, if the plaintiff shows that he would suffer great or irreparable injury (under the same requirements provided for an ex parte right to attach order), the court issues the order on such terms as are considered just. Sections 486.020, 486.040. The statute does, however, provided certain limitations applicable to any temporary protective order. Sections 486.050, 486.060. If the temporary protective order is granted, notice of that fact is served on the defendant along with the notice of the hearing on plaintiff's application for the order and writ. Section 486.080. The temporary protective order expires generally 40 days after its issuance, or when a levy of attachment on the affected property is made by the plaintiff, or when the defendant gives an undertaking to secure the payment of the plaintiff's judgment, whichever occurs first. Section 486.090. The defendant may apply for the vacation or modification of the temporary protective order, and the court may order its vacation or modification either ex parte or, in its discretion, after a noticed hearing. Section 486.100.

Ex parte procedure. When extraordinary circumstances are thought to exist, the plaintiff may seek an ex parte right to attach order and writ of attachment. However, the plaintiff must be able to show that he would suffer great or irreparable injury if the issuance of the order were delayed until notice and an opportunity for a hearing could be given the defendant. Section 485.010.

On application for an ex parte right to attach order and writ of attachment, the court may issue a temporary protective order in lieu of a writ and require the plaintiff to proceed for his order and writ pursuant to the noticed hearing procedure. Section 486.030. If he does this, the procedures described above requiring notice to the defendant and a hearing on the application apply. Id. The plaintiff is still required to show that extraordinary circumstances exist, but the protective order is issued in lieu of the writ where the latter form of relief seems unnecessary or unreasonable. Id.

Where the right to attach order and writ are issued ex parte, the defendant may apply for an order to set aside the right to attach order and to quash the writ and, if any property has been levied upon, to release such property. Section 485.240. This application is served on the plaintiff and, at the noticed hearing, the court determines if the plaintiff is entitled to the right to attach order. Id. The defendant may also claim pursuant to [the procedure provided by the Enforcement of Judgments Law] an exemption as to any property attached under the ex parte procedure. Section [485.610]. Such claim may be joined with the application in opposition to the order.

For a diagram outlining these procedures, see Recommendation Relating to Prejudgment Attachment, 11 Cal.L. Revision Comm'n Reports 701, 905 (1973) (11 Cal.L.Rev.Comm. Reports 701, amended by 16 Cal.L.Rev.Comm. Reports 1632).

ARTICLE 1. RIGHT TO ATTACH ORDER; ISSUANCE OF WRIT OF ATTACHMENT

Section
484.010.   Filing application.
484.020.   Execution and contents of application.
484.030.   Affidavit.
484.040.   Hearing; service on defendant.
484.050.   Information provided defendant by notice of application and hearing.
484.060.   Notice of opposition; claim of exemption.
484.070.   Claim of exemption; failure to make or prove claim; time; exceptions; notice of opposition; temporary order; burden of proof.
484.080.   Plaintiff not ready; denial of application; continuance; extension of protective order.
484.090.   Hearing; findings; orders; additional evidence.
484.100.   Effect of determinations.
484.110.   Effect of failure to oppose right to attach or reduction of amount secured or to rebut evidence.

§ 484.010. Filing application

Upon the filing of the complaint or at any time thereafter, the plaintiff may apply pursuant to this article for a right to attach order and a writ of attachment by filing an application for the order and writ with the court in which the action is brought. *(Added by Stats.1974, c. 1516, p. 3341, § 9, operative Jan. 1, 1977.)*

Law Revision Commission Comments

Section 484.010 is similar in content and purpose to former Section 537. This chapter provides a noticed hearing procedure for the issuance of a writ of attachment which should be utilized in most situations. A procedure for the ex parte issuance of a writ of attachment prior to a noticed hearing on the probable validity of the plaintiff's claim is provided in Chapter 5 (commencing with Section 485.010) for use in exceptional circumstances. See also Chapter 12 (commencing with Section 492.010) (nonresident attachment); Chapter 6 (commencing with Section 486.010) (temporary protective order).

Attachment is, of course, a prejudgment remedy; after final judgment, the plaintiff may, if necessary, proceed by way of execution.

Research References

Rutter, Cal. Practice Guide: Civ. Pro. Before Trial Ch. 9(II)-D, D. Attachment.
Rutter, Cal. Practice Guide: Enforcing Judgments/Debts Ch. 4-A, A. Attachment.
Miller and Starr California Real Estate § 32:10, Current Attachment Law.
Miller and Starr California Real Estate § 32:27, Procedure to Claim an Exemption.
Miller and Starr California Real Estate § 32:34, Procedure for Issuance of the Writ.
6 Witkin Cal. Proc. 5th Provisional Remedies § 47, Main Action.
6 Witkin Cal. Proc. 5th Provisional Remedies § 53, Nature and Scope.
6 Witkin Cal. Proc. 5th Provisional Remedies § 95, in General.
6 Witkin Cal. Proc. 5th Provisional Remedies § 119, (S 119) Application.
6 Witkin Cal. Proc. 5th Provisional Remedies § 123, (S 123) Hearing and Issuance of Writ.

6 Witkin Cal. Proc. 5th Provisional Remedies § 125, (S 125) Application and Supporting Affidavit.

6 Witkin Cal. Proc. 5th Provisional Remedies § 126, (S 126) Ex Parte Hearing and Issuance of Writ.

6 Witkin Cal. Proc. 5th Provisional Remedies § 242, Hearing, Order, and Writ.

§ 484.020. Execution and contents of application

The application shall be executed under oath and shall include all of the following:

(a) A statement showing that the attachment is sought to secure the recovery on a claim upon which an attachment may be issued.

(b) A statement of the amount to be secured by the attachment.

(c) A statement that the attachment is not sought for a purpose other than the recovery on the claim upon which the attachment is based.

(d) A statement that the applicant has no information or belief that the claim is discharged in a proceeding under Title 11 of the United States Code (Bankruptcy) or that the prosecution of the action is stayed in a proceeding under Title 11 of the United States Code (Bankruptcy).

(e) A description of the property to be attached under the writ of attachment and a statement that the plaintiff is informed and believes that such property is subject to attachment. Where the defendant is a corporation, a reference to "all corporate property which is subject to attachment pursuant to subdivision (a) of Code of Civil Procedure Section 487.010" satisfies the requirements of this subdivision. Where the defendant is a partnership or other unincorporated association, a reference to "all property of the partnership or other unincorporated association which is subject to attachment pursuant to subdivision (b) of Code of Civil Procedure Section 487.010" satisfies the requirements of this subdivision. Where the defendant is a natural person, the description of the property shall be reasonably adequate to permit the defendant to identify the specific property sought to be attached. *(Added by Stats.1974, c. 1516, p. 3341, § 9, operative Jan. 1, 1977. Amended by Stats.1982, c. 1198, p. 4279, § 30, operative July 1, 1983.)*

Law Revision Commission Comments

Section 484.020, together with Section 484.030, is substantively similar to former Section 538. However, where the defendant is an individual, subdivision (e) of Section 484.020 requires the plaintiff to include in his application a description of the property sought to be attached which is reasonably adequate to permit the defendant to identify such property. The writ issued pursuant to Section 484.090 is limited to the property described in the plaintiff's application. Thus, the defendant can determine whether he desires to make a claim of exemption as to that property. It is believed that, in many cases, the defendant will be willing to waive his claim and that this will result in a substantial saving in the time of court and counsel. It should be noted, however, that, if a right to attach order is issued under this article, the plaintiff may subsequently apply ex parte for additional writs pursuant to Article 3 (commencing with Section 484.510). To protect himself from such future levies, the defendant may claim as exempt any property not described in the plaintiff's application. See Section 484.070. A specific description is required only where the defendant is an individual. Corporations and partnerships generally have no exempt property. See Sections 487.010 and 487.020 and the Comments thereto. Hence, it is unnecessary to include a specific description for the purpose of either limiting the property sought to be attached or facilitating a claim of exemption.

Subdivision (b) of Section 484.020 is amended to reflect the addition of Section 483.015 which provides for the calculation of the amount to be secured by the attachment. Subdivision (d) is amended to provide references to the new Bankruptcy Code. The amendment of subdivision (e) conforms the subdivision to subdivision (e) of Section 487.010 (16 Cal.L.Rev.Comm. Reports 1636).

Research References

Rutter, Cal. Practice Guide: Civ. Pro. Before Trial Ch. 9(II)-D, D. Attachment.

Rutter, Cal. Practice Guide: Enforcing Judgments/Debts Ch. 4-A, A. Attachment.

Miller and Starr California Real Estate § 32:20, Individual Defendants.

Miller and Starr California Real Estate § 32:21, Nonindividual Defendants.

Miller and Starr California Real Estate § 32:27, Procedure to Claim an Exemption.

Miller and Starr California Real Estate § 32:35, Noticed Hearing Procedure.

6 Witkin Cal. Proc. 5th Provisional Remedies § 95, in General.

6 Witkin Cal. Proc. 5th Provisional Remedies § 97, Specific Description of Property.

6 Witkin Cal. Proc. 5th Provisional Remedies § 111, (S 111) Right to Attach Order.

6 Witkin Cal. Proc. 5th Provisional Remedies § 119, (S 119) Application.

6 Witkin Cal. Proc. 5th Provisional Remedies § 130, (S 130) Application and Affidavit.

6 Witkin Cal. Proc. 5th Provisional Remedies § 138, Application and Affidavit.

6 Witkin Cal. Proc. 5th Provisional Remedies § 241, Application and Affidavit.

6 Witkin Cal. Proc. 5th Provisional Remedies § 243, Additional Writs.

§ 484.030. Affidavit

The application shall be supported by an affidavit showing that the plaintiff on the facts presented would be entitled to a judgment on the claim upon which the attachment is based. *(Added by Stats.1974, c. 1516, p. 3341, § 9, operative Jan. 1, 1977.)*

Law Revision Commission Comments

Section 484.030 continues the requirement of former Section 538 that the plaintiff's application for the issuance of a writ of attachment be supported by appropriate affidavits. General requirements for these affidavits are provided in Section 482.040. Of course, several affidavits may be used which together provide evidence sufficient to entitle the plaintiff to a judgment in the action. See Code Civ.Proc. § 17 (singular number includes the plural). Moreover, the application itself may contain the necessary supporting evidence and, since it is executed under oath, it may constitute a sufficient affidavit for the purposes of this section.

Research References

Rutter, Cal. Practice Guide: Enforcing Judgments/Debts Ch. 4-A, A. Attachment.

Miller and Starr California Real Estate § 32:35, Noticed Hearing Procedure.

6 Witkin Cal. Proc. 5th Provisional Remedies § 2, (S 2) Use of Affidavit.

6 Witkin Cal. Proc. 5th Provisional Remedies § 96, Affidavit.

§ 484.040. Hearing; service on defendant

No order or writ shall be issued under this article except after a hearing. At the times prescribed by subdivision (b) of Section 1005, the defendant shall be served with all of the following:

(a) A copy of the summons and complaint.

(b) A notice of application and hearing.

(c) A copy of the application and of any affidavit in support of the application. *(Added by Stats.1974, c. 1516, p. 3341, § 9, operative Jan. 1, 1977. Amended by Stats.1989, c. 693, § 2.)*

Law Revision Commission Comments

Section 484.040 is similar to former Section 538.2. As to the manner of service, see Section 482.070.

Research References

Rutter, Cal. Practice Guide: Civ. Pro. Before Trial Ch. 9(II)-D, D. Attachment.

Rutter, Cal. Practice Guide: Enforcing Judgments/Debts Ch. 4-A, A. Attachment.

Miller and Starr California Real Estate § 32:35, Noticed Hearing Procedure.

Civ. Pro.

6 Witkin Cal. Proc. 5th Provisional Remedies § 101, Statutory Requirement.

6 Witkin Cal. Proc. 5th Provisional Remedies § 106, in General.

6 Witkin Cal. Proc. 5th Provisional Remedies § 120, (S 120) Notice to Defendant.

6 Witkin Cal. Proc. 5th Provisional Remedies § 141, (S 141) Nature and Purpose.

6 Witkin Cal. Proc. 5th Provisional Remedies § 144, in General.

§ 484.050. Information provided defendant by notice of application and hearing

The notice of application and hearing shall inform the defendant of all of the following:

(a) A hearing will be held at a place and at a time, to be specified in the notice, on plaintiff's application for a right to attach order and a writ of attachment.

(b) The order will be issued if the court finds that the plaintiff's claim is probably valid and the other requirements for issuing the order are established. The hearing is not for the purpose of determining whether the claim is actually valid. The determination of the actual validity of the claim will be made in subsequent proceedings in the action and will not be affected by the decisions at the hearing on the application for the order.

(c) The amount to be secured by the attachment is determined pursuant to Sections 482.110, 483.010, 483.015, and 483.020, which statutes shall be summarized in the notice.

(d) If the right to attach order is issued, a writ of attachment will be issued to attach the property described in the plaintiff's application unless the court determines that such property is exempt from attachment or that its value clearly exceeds the amount necessary to satisfy the amount to be secured by the attachment. However, additional writs of attachment may be issued to attach other nonexempt property of the defendant on the basis of the right to attach order.

(e) If the defendant desires to oppose the issuance of the order, the defendant shall file with the court and serve on the plaintiff a notice of opposition and supporting affidavit as required by Section 484.060 not later than five court days prior to the date set for hearing.

(f) If the defendant claims that the personal property described in the application, or a portion thereof, is exempt from attachment, the defendant shall include that claim in the notice of opposition filed and served pursuant to Section 484.060 or file and serve a separate claim of exemption with respect to the property as provided in Section 484.070. If the defendant does not do so, the claim of exemption will be barred in the absence of a showing of a change in circumstances occurring after the expiration of the time for claiming exemptions.

(g) The defendant may obtain a determination at the hearing whether real or personal property not described in the application or real property described in the application is exempt from attachment by including the claim in the notice of opposition filed and served pursuant to Section 484.060 or by filing and serving a separate claim of exemption with respect to the property as provided in Section 484.070, but the failure to so claim that the property is exempt from attachment will not preclude the defendant from making a claim of exemption with respect to the property at a later time.

(h) Either the defendant or the defendant's attorney or both of them may be present at the hearing.

(i) The notice shall contain the following statement: "You may seek the advice of an attorney as to any matter connected with the plaintiff's application. The attorney should be consulted promptly so that the attorney may assist you before the time set for hearing." (Added by Stats.1974, c. 1516, p. 3342, § 9, operative Jan. 1, 1977. Amended by Stats.1976, c. 437, p. 1119,

§ 7; Stats.1982, c. 1198, p. 4280, § 31, operative July 1, 1983; Stats.1983, c. 155, § 2, eff. June 30, 1983, operative July 1, 1983; Stats.1994, c. 587 (A.B.3600), § 4; Stats.1997, c. 222 (A.B.1258), § 7.)

Law Revision Commission Comments

Section 484.050 outlines the basic requirements for the "notice of application and hearing." See Section 482.030 (Judicial Council to prescribe forms). No comparable provision existed under former law.

Subdivision (c) of Section 484.050 [since redesignated as subdivision (d)] is amended to recognize the authority of the court under Section 482.120 to prevent an excessive attachment. Subdivisions (d) and (e) [since redesignated as subdivisions (e) and (f)] of Section 484.050 are amended to conform to Sections 484.060 and 484.070. See Section 482.100 (procedure for claiming exemptions based upon a showing of changed circumstances). Exemptions not claimed as provided by Section 484.070 [for personal property described in the application] are waived for purposes of both attachment and execution except as provided by Section 482.100 [13 Cal.L.Rev.Comm. Reports 801, amended by 16 Cal.L.Rev. Comm. Reports 1638].

Section 484.050 is amended to add a new subdivision (c) to conform to subdivision (b) of Section 483.015. Subdivisions (f) and (g) are revised to conform to amended Section 484.070. The other changes are non-substantive [16 Cal.L.Rev.Comm. Reports 1639].

Subdivision (c) of Section 484.050 is amended to conform to Section 483.015 as amended. [16 Cal.L.Rev.Comm. Reports 2175 (1982)].

Subdivision (c) of Section 484.050 is amended for conformity with the substantive rules governing the amount of an attachment. The notice is required to set out the substance of the rules in Sections 482.110, 483.010, 483.015, and 483.020. See Section 482.030(b) (Judicial Council to prescribe form of notices). [26 Cal.L.Rev.Comm. Reports 307 (1996)].

Research References

Rutter, Cal. Practice Guide: Civ. Pro. Before Trial Ch. 9(II)-D, D. Attachment.

Rutter, Cal. Practice Guide: Enforcing Judgments/Debts Ch. 4-A, A. Attachment.

Miller and Starr California Real Estate § 32:16, Amount of Obligation Subject to Attachment.

Miller and Starr California Real Estate § 32:21, Nonindividual Defendants.

Miller and Starr California Real Estate § 32:27, Procedure to Claim an Exemption.

Miller and Starr California Real Estate § 32:35, Noticed Hearing Procedure.

6 Witkin Cal. Proc. 5th Provisional Remedies § 102, Contents of Notice.

6 Witkin Cal. Proc. 5th Provisional Remedies § 120, (S 120) Notice to Defendant.

§ 484.060. Notice of opposition; claim of exemption

(a) If the defendant desires to oppose the issuance of the right to attach order sought by plaintiff or objects to the amount sought to be secured by the attachment, the defendant shall file and serve upon the plaintiff no later than five court days prior to the date set for the hearing a notice of opposition. The notice shall state the grounds on which the defendant opposes the issuance of the order or objects to the amount sought to be secured by the attachment and shall be accompanied by an affidavit supporting any factual issues raised and points and authorities supporting any legal issues raised. If the defendant fails to file a notice of opposition within the time prescribed, the defendant shall not be permitted to oppose the issuance of the order.

(b) If a defendant filing a notice of opposition desires to make any claim of exemption as provided in Section 484.070, the defendant may include that claim in the notice of opposition filed pursuant to this section.

(c) The plaintiff may file and serve upon the opposing party a reply two court days prior to the date set for the hearing. (Added by Stats.1974, c. 1516, p. 3342, § 9, operative Jan. 1, 1977. Amended by Stats.1983, c. 155, § 3, eff. June 30, 1983, operative July 1, 1983; Stats.1990, c. 1491 (A.B.3765), § 6.)

Law Revision Commission Comments

Section 484.060 is new. No precisely comparable provision existed under former law. Former Section 538.4 did require each party to "serve upon the other at least 24 hours before the hearing any affidavits intended to be introduced at the hearing, unless the court at the hearing for good cause shown permits the introduction of affidavits not previously served." See also former Sections 556 and 557. However, Section 484.060 requires the defendant to file a notice of opposition, supporting affidavits, and points and authorities in every case where he seeks to oppose issuance of a writ. In turn, the plaintiff is required to file any counteraffidavits in opposition to a claim of exemption not later than two days before the hearing date. See Section 484.070.

Subdivision (a) of Section 484.060 is amended to make clear that the defendant may seek the reduction of the amount of the attachment by the amounts specified in subdivision (b) of Section 483.015. [16 Cal.L.Rev. Comm. Reports 2175 (1982)].

Research References

Rutter, Cal. Practice Guide: Civ. Pro. Before Trial Ch. 9(II)-D, D. Attachment.
Rutter, Cal. Practice Guide: Enforcing Judgments/Debts Ch. 4-A, A. Attachment.
Miller and Starr California Real Estate § 32:16, Amount of Obligation Subject to Attachment.
Miller and Starr California Real Estate § 32:35, Noticed Hearing Procedure.
6 Witkin Cal. Proc. 5th Provisional Remedies § 98, (S 98) in General.
6 Witkin Cal. Proc. 5th Provisional Remedies § 102, Contents of Notice.
6 Witkin Cal. Proc. 5th Provisional Remedies § 103, Notice of Opposition.
6 Witkin Cal. Proc. 5th Provisional Remedies § 108, Burden of Proof.

§ 484.070. Claim of exemption; failure to make or prove claim; time; exceptions; notice of opposition; temporary order; burden of proof

(a) If the defendant claims that the personal property described in the plaintiff's application, or a portion of such property, is exempt from attachment, the defendant shall claim the exemption as provided in this section. If the defendant fails to make the claim or makes the claim but fails to prove that the personal property is exempt, the defendant may not later claim the exemption except as provided in Section 482.100.

(b) If the defendant desires to claim at the hearing that real or personal property not described in the plaintiff's application or real property described in the plaintiff's application is exempt from attachment, in whole or in part, the defendant shall claim the exemption as provided in this section. Failure to make claim does not preclude the defendant from later claiming the exemption. If the claim is made as provided in this section but the defendant fails to prove that the property is exempt from attachment, the defendant may not later claim that the property, or a portion thereof, is exempt except as provided in Section 482.100.

(c) The claim of exemption shall:

(1) Describe the property claimed to be exempt.

(2) Specify the statute section supporting the claim.

(d) The claim of exemption shall be accompanied by an affidavit supporting any factual issues raised by the claim and points and authorities supporting any legal issues raised.

(e) The claim of exemption, together with any supporting affidavit and points and authorities, shall be filed and served on the plaintiff not less than five court days before the date set for the hearing.

(f) If the plaintiff desires to oppose the claim of exemption, the plaintiff shall file and serve on the defendant, not less than two days before the date set for the hearing, a notice of opposition to the claim of exemption, accompanied by an affidavit supporting any factual issues raised and points and authorities supporting any legal issues raised. If the plaintiff

does not file and serve a notice of opposition as provided in this subdivision, no writ of attachment shall be issued as to the property claimed to be exempt. If all of the property described in the plaintiff's application is claimed to be exempt and the plaintiff does not file and serve a notice of opposition as provided in this subdivision, no hearing shall be held and no right to attach order or writ of attachment shall be issued and any temporary protective order issued pursuant to Chapter 6 (commencing with Section 486.010) immediately expires.

(g) If the plaintiff files and serves a notice of opposition to the claim as provided in this section, the defendant has the burden of proving that the property is exempt from attachment. *(Added by Stats.1974, c. 1516, p. 3343, § 9, operative Jan. 1, 1977. Amended by Stats.1976, c. 437, p. 1120, § 8; Stats.1982, c. 1198, p. 4281, § 32, operative July 1, 1983; Stats.1998, c. 932 (A.B.1094), § 14.)*

Law Revision Commission Comments

Section 484.070 provides a prelevy procedure for claiming an exemption from attachment. Compare [Sections 482.100, 484.530, 485.610, 487.030] (postlevy claim). [See also Section 488.720 (release of excess property).] See also former Section 537.3 (authorizing defendant's prelevy claim of exemption for property "necessary for support") (11 Cal.L.Rev.Comm. Reports 701, amended by 16 Cal.L.Rev.Comm. Reports 1641).

Subdivisions (a) and (b) of Section 484.070 are amended to reflect the enactment of Section 482.100 (procedure for claiming exemptions based upon a showing of changed circumstances). Exemptions [for personal property described in the plaintiff's application] not claimed as provided by this section are waived for purposes of both attachment and execution except as provided by Section 482.100. Subdivision (f) is amended to provide for automatic expiration of a temporary protective order upon the plaintiff's failure to oppose a claim of exemption as to all the defendant's property described in the plaintiff's application. This amendment eliminates any necessity in such cases for proceeding under Section 486.100 for early vacation of the order. See Section 486.090 and Comment thereto (13 Cal.L.Rev.Comm. Reports 801, amended by 16 Cal.L.Rev.Comm. Reports 1641).

Subdivision (a) of Section 484.070 is amended to make clear that the defendant is not required to claim an exemption for real property at the hearing on issuance of the right to attach order and writ of attachment. See Section 487.020 (exemptions from attachment). Consequently, if the defendant's real property dwelling is sought to be attached, a failure to claim an exemption for it does not constitute a waiver of the exemption. However, subdivision (b) permits the defendant to claim an exemption in real property at the hearing on issuance of the right to attach order if the defendant so desires. If the plaintiff who has attached a dwelling recovers judgment in the action and levies on the dwelling under a writ of execution, the exemption may then be determined as provided in Section 704.710 et seq. in the Enforcement of Judgments Law. The other changes in Section 484.070 are technical. See Section 482.070 (manner of service) (16 Cal.L.Rev.Comm. Reports 1641).

Research References

Rutter, Cal. Practice Guide: Civ. Pro. Before Trial Ch. 9(II)-D, D. Attachment.
Rutter, Cal. Practice Guide: Enforcing Judgments/Debts Ch. 4-A, A. Attachment.
Miller and Starr California Real Estate § 32:27, Procedure to Claim an Exemption.
Miller and Starr California Real Estate § 32:35, Noticed Hearing Procedure.
6 Witkin Cal. Proc. 5th Provisional Remedies § 87, (S 87) Claim of Real Property Exemption.
6 Witkin Cal. Proc. 5th Provisional Remedies § 102, Contents of Notice.
6 Witkin Cal. Proc. 5th Provisional Remedies § 104, Defendant's Claim of Exemption.
6 Witkin Cal. Proc. 5th Provisional Remedies § 105, Plaintiff's Opposition to Claim.
6 Witkin Cal. Proc. 5th Provisional Remedies § 108, Burden of Proof.
6 Witkin Cal. Proc. 5th Provisional Remedies § 121, (S 121) Defendant's Claim of Exemption.
6 Witkin Cal. Proc. 5th Provisional Remedies § 122, (S 122) Plaintiff's Opposition to Claim.
6 Witkin Cal. Proc. 5th Provisional Remedies § 145, Expiration, Modification, and Vacation.

6 Witkin Cal. Proc. 5th Provisional Remedies § 179, Securities.
6 Witkin Cal. Proc. 5th Provisional Remedies § 181, Interest in Estate Personal Property.
6 Witkin Cal. Proc. 5th Provisional Remedies § 207, (S 207) After Creation of Lien.

§ 484.080. Plaintiff not ready; denial of application; continuance; extension of protective order

(a) At the time set for the hearing, the plaintiff shall be ready to proceed. If the plaintiff is not ready, or if he has failed to comply with Section 484.040, the court may either deny the application for the order or, for good cause shown, grant the plaintiff a continuance for a reasonable period. If such a continuance is granted, the effective period of any protective order issued pursuant to Chapter 6 (commencing with Section 486.010) may be extended by the court for a period ending not more than 10 days after the new hearing date if the plaintiff shows a continuing need for such protective order.

(b) The court may, in its discretion and for good cause shown, grant the defendant a continuance for a reasonable period to enable him to oppose the issuance of the right to attach order. If such a continuance is granted, the court shall extend the effective period of any protective order issued pursuant to Chapter 6 (commencing with Section 486.010) for a period ending not more than 10 days after the new hearing date unless the defendant shows pursuant to Section 486.100 that the protective order should be modified or vacated. *(Added by Stats.1974, c. 1516, p. 3344, § 9, operative Jan: 1, 1977.)*

Law Revision Commission Comments

Section 484.080 is new. No comparable provision existed under former law.

Research References

Rutter, Cal. Practice Guide: Enforcing Judgments/Debts Ch. 4-A, A. Attachment.
Miller and Starr California Real Estate § 32:35, Noticed Hearing Procedure.
6 Witkin Cal. Proc. 5th Provisional Remedies § 106, in General.
6 Witkin Cal. Proc. 5th Provisional Remedies § 145, Expiration, Modification, and Vacation.

§ 484.090. Hearing; findings; orders; additional evidence

(a) At the hearing, the court shall consider the showing made by the parties appearing and shall issue a right to attach order, which shall state the amount to be secured by the attachment determined by the court in accordance with Section 483.015 or 483.020, if it finds all of the following:

(1) The claim upon which the attachment is based is one upon which an attachment may be issued.

(2) The plaintiff has established the probable validity of the claim upon which the attachment is based.

(3) The attachment is not sought for a purpose other than the recovery on the claim upon which the attachment is based.

(4) The amount to be secured by the attachment is greater than zero.

(b) If, in addition to the findings required by subdivision (a), the court finds that the defendant has failed to prove that all the property sought to be attached is exempt from attachment, it shall order a writ of attachment to be issued upon the filing of an undertaking as provided by Sections 489.210 and 489.220.

(c) If the court determines that property of the defendant is exempt from attachment, in whole or in part, the right to attach order shall describe the exempt property and prohibit attachment of the property.

(d) The court's determinations shall be made upon the basis of the pleadings and other papers in the record; but, upon good cause shown, the court may receive and consider at the hearing additional evidence, oral or documentary, and additional points and authorities, or it may continue the hearing for the production of the additional evidence or points and authorities. *(Added by Stats.1974, c. 1516, p. 3344, § 9, operative Jan. 1, 1977. Amended by Stats.1976, c. 437, p. 1121, § 9; Stats.1982, c. 1198, p. 4282, § 33, operative July 1, 1983; Stats.1997, c. 222 (A.B. 1258), § 8.)*

Law Revision Commission Comments

Section 484.090 is similar in content and purpose to former Section 538.4. However, former Section 538.4 provided a preference for hearing which is not continued. Also, the explicit direction that a writ be issued automatically if the defendant fails to appear is eliminated. Instead, Section 484.060 requires the defendant to file a notice of opposition if he plans to oppose the issuance of a writ; if he does not so file, he may not oppose the application. The court must still review the application to determine whether or not the plaintiff has made a prima facie showing for the issuance of the writ. Whether or not the defendant appears in opposition, the plaintiff has the burden of proving (1) that his claim is one upon which an attachment may be issued and (2) the probable validity of such claim. See Section 481.190.

Former Section 538.4 authorized either party to submit oral evidence at the hearing. Section 484.090 contemplates that, in the usual case, the court's determinations will be made on the basis of the pleadings, affidavits, and points and authorities filed prior to the hearing and that an additional evidentiary showing at the hearing will be allowed only upon good cause. This procedure should result in a conservation of judicial time without prejudicing the rights of the parties and should avoid converting the hearing on a preliminary matter into a full-dress trial of the merits of the action.

The time limits for filing the required affidavits are provided in Sections 484.060 and 484.070.

Section 484.090 does not continue the requirement of former Section 538.4 that the defendant make himself or an agent or officer available for examination regarding the plaintiff's claim.

Although no special finding is required, no right to attach order will be issued if the defendant shows that such order would violate the National Bankruptcy Act. See Section 484.020(d).

Subdivision (b) of Section 484.090 [formerly required] the writ to state the amount to be secured by the attachment and describe the property to be levied upon. [See 1976 Amendment Comment.] The writ does not require that levy be made in any particular order. Contrast the last sentence of former Section 538.4 . . . . . .

As to multiple writs, alias writs, and additional writs, see Sections 482.090 and 484.310 and the Comments thereto (12 Cal.L.Rev.Comm. Reports 558, amended by 16 Cal.Law.Rev.Comm. Reports 1643).

The introductory sentence of subdivision (a) is amended to provide that the right to attach order state the amount to be secured by the attachment. The first sentence of subdivision (b) is amended to make clear that the court orders the clerk to issue the writ. The second sentence of subdivision (b) has been deleted, but its substance is continued in subdivision (a) of Section 488.010.

The introductory clause of subdivision (a) of Section 484.090 is revised to reflect the addition of subdivision (b) to Section 483.015 (16 Cal.L.Rev. Comm. Reports 1644).

Paragraph (4) is added to subdivision (a) of Section 484.090 to make clear that the court is not to issue a right to attach order and writ of attachment if there is no amount to be secured by the attachment. This amendment establishes the principle that a right to attach order cannot be issued if there is no amount for which a writ of attachment can be issued and avoids the theoretical possibility of the court's making a right to attach order with no amount to be secured by the attachment. Prior to the 1990 amendments to Section 483.015, this was not likely to occur even in theory, but with the change in the rules concerning issuance of attachment where the plaintiff's claim is secured by personal property, the statutes read literally would permit issuance of a right to attach order under Section 484.090 even though the value of the security exceeded the amount of the claim. See Section 483.015(b)(4); see also Section 485.240 (application to set aside right to attach order). [26 Cal.L.Rev.Comm. Reports 307 (1996)].

Research References

Rutter, Cal. Practice Guide: Civ. Pro. Before Trial Ch. 9(II)-D, D. Attachment.

Rutter, Cal. Practice Guide: Enforcing Judgments/Debts Ch. 4-A, A. Attachment.

Rutter, Cal. Practice Guide: Insurance Litigation Ch. 15-L, L. Effect of Insured's Bankruptcy.

Miller and Starr California Real Estate § 32:10, Current Attachment Law.

Miller and Starr California Real Estate § 32:11, Availability of Attachment--In General.

Miller and Starr California Real Estate § 32:18, Inadequate Security.

Miller and Starr California Real Estate § 32:35, Noticed Hearing Procedure.

Miller and Starr California Real Estate § 11:154, Expungement of a Lis Pendens--Procedure and Grounds for Expungement.

20 NO. 3 Miller & Starr, California Real Estate Newsalert 17, Involuntary Liens.

3 Witkin Cal. Proc. 5th Actions § 403, (S 403) Current Law.

3 Witkin Cal. Proc. 5th Actions § 963, (S 963) Writ.

6 Witkin Cal. Proc. 5th Provisional Remedies § 107, Evidence.

6 Witkin Cal. Proc. 5th Provisional Remedies § 108, Burden of Proof.

6 Witkin Cal. Proc. 5th Provisional Remedies § 111, (S 111) Right to Attach Order.

6 Witkin Cal. Proc. 5th Provisional Remedies § 112, in General.

6 Witkin Cal. Proc. 5th Provisional Remedies § 123, (S 123) Hearing and Issuance of Writ.

6 Witkin Cal. Proc. 5th Provisional Remedies § 137, (S 137) Hearing and Determination.

§ 484.100. Effect of determinations

The court's determinations under this chapter shall have no effect on the determination of any issues in the action other than issues relevant to proceedings under this chapter nor shall they affect the rights of the plaintiff or defendant in any other action arising out of the same claim of the plaintiff or defendant. The court's determinations under this chapter shall not be given in evidence nor referred to at the trial of any such action. *(Added by Stats.1974, c. 1516, p. 3344, § 9, operative Jan. 1, 1977. Amended by Stats.1982, c. 1198, p. 4283, § 34, operative July 1, 1983.)*

Law Revision Commission Comments

Section 484.100 makes clear that the determinations of the court under this chapter have no effect on the determination of the validity of the plaintiff's claim in the action he has brought against the defendant nor do they affect the defendant's right to oppose an attachment or to claim that property is exempt in another action brought on the same claim. However, if the court determines that the plaintiff is not entitled to an attachment because he has failed to establish the probable validity of his claim or that certain property of the defendant is exempt, such determinations are binding on the plaintiff in a subsequent action on the same claim unless the defendant is no longer entitled to the exemption because of changed circumstances. Section 484.100 does not, however, make inadmissible any affidavit filed under this chapter. The admissibility of such an affidavit is determined by rules of evidence otherwise applicable.

Section 484.100 is amended to reflect that the defendant may seek to reduce the amount to be secured by the attachment on the ground that defendant has a claim against the plaintiff. See Section 483.015(b) (16 Cal.L.Rev.Comm. Reports 1645).

Research References

Rutter, Cal. Practice Guide: Civ. Pro. Before Trial Ch. 9(II)-D, D. Attachment.

Rutter, Cal. Practice Guide: Enforcing Judgments/Debts Ch. 4-A, A. Attachment.

Miller and Starr California Real Estate § 32:35, Noticed Hearing Procedure.

6 Witkin Cal. Proc. 5th Provisional Remedies § 102, Contents of Notice.

6 Witkin Cal. Proc. 5th Provisional Remedies § 109, Effect of Determinations.

6 Witkin Cal. Proc. 5th Provisional Remedies § 110, (S 110) Renewed Application.

§ 484.110. Effect of failure to oppose right to attach or reduction of amount secured or to rebut evidence

(a) Neither the failure of the defendant to oppose the issuance of a right to attach order under this chapter nor the defendant's failure to rebut any evidence produced by the plaintiff in connection with proceedings under this chapter shall constitute a waiver of any defense to the plaintiff's claim in the action or any other action or have any effect on the right of the defendant to produce or exclude evidence at the trial of any such action.

(b) Neither the failure of the plaintiff to oppose the issuance of an order reducing the amount to be secured by the attachment under this chapter nor the plaintiff's failure to rebut any evidence produced by the defendant in connection with proceedings under this chapter shall constitute a waiver of any defense to the defendant's claim in the action or any other action or have any effect on the right of the plaintiff to produce or exclude evidence at the trial of any such action. *(Added by Stats.1974, c. 1516, p. 3345, § 9, operative Jan. 1, 1977. Amended by Stats.1982, c. 1198, p. 4283, § 35, operative July 1, 1983.)*

Law Revision Commission Comments

Section 484.110 is amended to recognize that the defendant may seek to reduce the amount to be secured by the attachment on the ground that plaintiff has a claim against the plaintiff. See Section 483.015(b) (16 Cal.L.Rev.Comm. Reports 1646).

Research References

Rutter, Cal. Practice Guide: Civ. Pro. Before Trial Ch. 9(II)-D, D. Attachment.

Rutter, Cal. Practice Guide: Enforcing Judgments/Debts Ch. 4-A, A. Attachment.

Miller and Starr California Real Estate § 32:10, Current Attachment Law.

Miller and Starr California Real Estate § 32:27, Procedure to Claim an Exemption.

Miller and Starr California Real Estate § 32:34, Procedure for Issuance of the Writ.

6 Witkin Cal. Proc. 5th Provisional Remedies § 109, Effect of Determinations.

ARTICLE 2. NOTICED HEARING PROCEDURE FOR OBTAINING ADDITIONAL WRITS

§ 484.310. Filing application

At any time after a right to attach order has been issued under Article 1 (commencing with Section 484.010) or after the court has found pursuant to Section 485.240 that the plaintiff is entitled to a right to attach order, the plaintiff may apply for a writ of attachment under this article by filing an application with the court in which the action is brought. *(Added by Stats.1974, c. 1516, p. 3345, § 9, operative Jan. 1, 1977.)*

Law Revision Commission Comments

Article 2 (commencing with Section 484.310) provides a noticed hearing procedure for the issuance of a writ of attachment after the plaintiff has established at a noticed hearing that he is entitled to a right to attach order. The purpose of the noticed hearing here is to determine whether the defendant can establish that the [personal] property sought to be levied upon is exempt. If no claim of exemption is made, the writ is issued and any claim of exemption is barred [with respect to the personal property] subject to a change in circumstances occurring after the hearing. See Section 484.350. An alternative ex parte procedure for the issuance of a writ is provided by Article 3 (commencing with Section 484.510). Under the latter procedure, the defendant can establish that property is exempt after it is levied upon if he has not previously claimed . . . that the property was exempt. [See Section 484.530.]

Both Article 2 and Article 3 serve the purpose of providing a procedure for the issuance of additional writs in a new form where a right to attach order has already been issued. It should be noted that these procedures are necessary only where the defendant is an individual. In an action against a corporation or partnership, the writ issued pursuant to Section 484.090 will generally refer to all corporate or all partnership property subject to attachment pursuant to Section 487.010. Hence, the only "additional" writs necessary will be in the same form. See Section 482.090 (11 Cal.L.Rev.Comm. Reports 701, amended by 16 Cal.L.Rev. Comm. Reports 1646).

Research References

Rutter, Cal. Practice Guide: Enforcing Judgments/Debts Ch. 4-A, A. Attachment.
Miller and Starr California Real Estate § 32:34, Procedure for Issuance of the Writ.
Miller and Starr California Real Estate § 32:35, Noticed Hearing Procedure.
6 Witkin Cal. Proc. 5th Provisional Remedies § 102, Contents of Notice.
6 Witkin Cal. Proc. 5th Provisional Remedies § 118, Nature and Purpose.
6 Witkin Cal. Proc. 5th Provisional Remedies § 119, (S 119) Application.
6 Witkin Cal. Proc. 5th Provisional Remedies § 137, (S 137) Hearing and Determination.
6 Witkin Cal. Proc. 5th Provisional Remedies § 243, Additional Writs.

§ 484.320. Execution and contents of application

The application shall be executed under oath and shall include all of the following:

(a) A statement that the plaintiff has been issued a right to attach order under Article 1 (commencing with Section 484.010) or that the court has found pursuant to Section 485.240 that the plaintiff is entitled to a right to attach order.

(b) A statement of the amount to be secured by the attachment.

(c) A description of the property to be attached under the writ of attachment and a statement that the plaintiff is informed and believes that the property is subject to attachment. The description shall satisfy the requirements of Section 484.020.

(d) A statement that the applicant has no information or belief that the claim is discharged in a proceeding under Title 11 of the United States Code (Bankruptcy) or that the prosecution of the action is stayed in a proceeding under Title 11 of the United States Code (Bankruptcy). *(Added by Stats.1974, c. 1516, p. 3345, § 9, operative Jan. 1, 1977. Amended by Stats.1982, c. 1198, p. 4283, § 36, operative July 1, 1983.)*

Law Revision Commission Comments

Section 484.320 is comparable to Section 484.020 except that a statement that the plaintiff has established that he is entitled to a right to attach order is substituted for certain prerequisites to that order.

Subdivision (b) of Section 484.320 is amended to reflect the addition of Section 483.015 which provides for the calculation of the amount to be secured by the attachment. Subdivision (d) is amended to provide references to the new Bankruptcy Code (16 Cal.L.Rev.Comm. Reports 1647).

Research References

Rutter, Cal. Practice Guide: Enforcing Judgments/Debts Ch. 4-A, A. Attachment.

Miller and Starr California Real Estate § 32:35, Noticed Hearing Procedure.
6 Witkin Cal. Proc. 5th Provisional Remedies § 119, (S 119) Application.
6 Witkin Cal. Proc. 5th Provisional Remedies § 125, (S 125) Application and Supporting Affidavit.

§ 484.330. Hearing; service on defendant

No writ of attachment shall be issued under this article except after a hearing. At least 15 days prior to the hearing, the defendant shall be served with both of the following:

(a) A notice of application and hearing.

(b) A copy of the application. *(Added by Stats.1974, c. 1516, p. 3345, § 9, operative Jan. 1, 1977. Amended by Stats.1991, c. 1090 (A.B.1484), § 2.)*

Law Revision Commission Comments

Section 484.330 is comparable to Section 484.040. Service of a copy of the summons and complaint is not required here because it will have already been accomplished.

Research References

Rutter, Cal. Practice Guide: Enforcing Judgments/Debts Ch. 4-A, A. Attachment.
Miller and Starr California Real Estate § 32:27, Procedure to Claim an Exemption.
6 Witkin Cal. Proc. 5th Provisional Remedies § 120, (S 120) Notice to Defendant.
6 Witkin Cal. Proc. 5th Provisional Remedies § 123, (S 123) Hearing and Issuance of Writ.

§ 484.340. Information provided defendant by notice of application and hearing

The notice of application and hearing shall inform the defendant of all of the following:

(a) The plaintiff has applied for a writ of attachment to attach the property described in the application.

(b) A hearing will be held at a place and at a time, to be specified in the notice, to determine whether the plaintiff is entitled to the writ.

(c) A writ of attachment will be issued to attach the property described in the plaintiff's application unless the court determines that the property is exempt from attachment or that its value clearly exceeds the amount necessary to satisfy the amount to be secured by the attachment.

(d) If the defendant claims that the property described in the application, or a portion thereof, is exempt from attachment, the defendant may file with the court and serve on the plaintiff a claim of exemption with respect to the property as provided in Section 484.350 not later than five days prior to the date set for hearing. If the defendant fails to make such a claim with respect to personal property, the defendant may not later claim the exemption in the absence of a showing of a change in circumstances occurring after the expiration of the time for claiming exemptions.

(e) Either the defendant or the defendant's attorney or both of them may be present at the hearing.

(f) The notice shall contain the following statement: "You may seek the advice of an attorney as to any matter connected with the plaintiff's application. The attorney should be consulted promptly so that the attorney may assist you before the time set for hearing." *(Added by Stats.1974, c. 1516, p. 3345, § 9, operative Jan. 1, 1977. Amended by Stats.1976, c. 437, p. 1122, § 10; Stats.1982, c. 1198, p. 4283, § 37, operative July 1, 1983.)*

Law Revision Commission Comments

Section 484.340 is comparable to Section 484.050. Of course, the hearing here is concerned only with the defendant's right, if any, to an exemption and the notice is accordingly so limited.

Subdivision (c) of Section 484.340 is amended to recognize the authority of the court under Section 482.120 to prevent an excessive attachment. Subdivision (d) is amended to conform to the provisions of Section 484.350. See Section 482.100 (procedure for claiming exemptions based upon a showing of changed circumstances). Exemptions [for personal property] not claimed as provided by Section 484.350 are waived for purposes of both attachment and execution except as provided by Section 482.100 (13 Cal.L.Rev.Comm. Reports 801, amended by 16 Cal.L.Rev. Comm. Reports 1649).

Subdivision (d) of Section 484.340 is amended to conform to amended Section 484.350. See the Comment to Section 484.350 (16 Cal.L.Rev. Comm. Reports 1649).

Research References

Rutter, Cal. Practice Guide: Enforcing Judgments/Debts Ch. 4-A, A. Attachment.
Miller and Starr California Real Estate § 32:35, Noticed Hearing Procedure.
6 Witkin Cal. Proc. 5th Provisional Remedies § 120, (S 120) Notice to Defendant.

§ 484.350.   Claim of exemption

(a) If the defendant claims that the property described in the plaintiff's application, or a portion of such property, is exempt from attachment, the defendant may claim the exemption as provided in this section. If the defendant fails to make a claim with respect to personal property, or makes a claim with respect to real or personal property but fails to prove that the property is exempt, the defendant may not later claim the exemption except as provided in Section 482.100.

(b) The claim of exemption shall:

(1) Describe the property claimed to be exempt.

(2) Specify the statute section supporting the claim.

(c) The claim of exemption shall be accompanied by an affidavit supporting any factual issues raised by the claim and points and authorities supporting any legal issues raised.

(d) The claim of exemption, together with any supporting affidavit and points and authorities, shall be filed and served on the plaintiff not less than five court days before the date set for the hearing. *(Added by Stats.1974, c. 1516, p. 3346, § 9, operative Jan. 1, 1977. Amended by Stats.1976, c. 437, p. 1122, § 11; Stats.1982, c. 1198, p. 4284, § 38, operative July 1, 1983; Stats.1998, c. 932 (A.B.1094), § 15.)*

Law Revision Commission Comments

Section 484.350 is comparable to subdivisions (a), (c), (d), and (e) of Section 484.070.

Subdivision (a) of Section 484.350 is amended to reflect the enactment of Section 482.100 (procedure for claiming exemptions based upon a showing of changed circumstances). Exemptions [for personal property] not claimed as provided by this section are waived for purposes of both attachment and execution except as provided by Section 482.100 (13 Cal.L.Rev.Comm. Reports 801, amended by 16 Cal.L.Rev.Comm. Reports 1650).

Subdivision (a) of Section 484.350 is amended to make clear that the defendant does not waive an exemption for real property by failure to claim it at the hearing on issuance of the writ. See the Comment to Section 484.070. See also Section 482.070 (manner of service) (16 Cal.L.Rev.Comm. Reports 1650).

Research References

Rutter, Cal. Practice Guide: Enforcing Judgments/Debts Ch. 4-A, A. Attachment.
Miller and Starr California Real Estate § 32:35, Noticed Hearing Procedure.

6 Witkin Cal. Proc. 5th Provisional Remedies § 87, (S 87) Claim of Real Property Exemption.
6 Witkin Cal. Proc. 5th Provisional Remedies § 120, (S 120) Notice to Defendant.
6 Witkin Cal. Proc. 5th Provisional Remedies § 121, (S 121) Defendant's Claim of Exemption.
6 Witkin Cal. Proc. 5th Provisional Remedies § 179, Securities.
6 Witkin Cal. Proc. 5th Provisional Remedies § 181, Interest in Estate Personal Property.

§ 484.360.   Notice of opposition to claim of exemption; burden of proof

(a) If the defendant files and serves a claim of exemption and the plaintiff desires to oppose the claim, he shall file and serve on the defendant, not less than two days before the date set for the hearing, a notice of opposition to the claim of exemption, accompanied by an affidavit supporting any factual issues raised and points and authorities supporting any legal issues raised.

(b) If the defendant files and serves a claim of exemption and supporting affidavit as provided in Section 484.350 and the plaintiff does not file and serve a notice of opposition as provided in this section, no writ of attachment shall be issued as to the property claimed to be exempt. If all of the property described in the plaintiff's application is claimed to be exempt and the plaintiff does not file and serve a notice of opposition as provided in this section, no hearing shall be held and no writ of attachment shall be issued.

(c) If the plaintiff files and serves a notice of opposition to the claim as provided in this section, the defendant has the burden of proving that the property is exempt from attachment. *(Added by Stats.1974, c. 1516, p. 3346, § 9, operative Jan. 1, 1977.)*

Law Revision Commission Comments

Section 484.360 is comparable to subdivisions (f) and (g) of Section 484.070.

Research References

Rutter, Cal. Practice Guide: Enforcing Judgments/Debts Ch. 4-A, A. Attachment.
6 Witkin Cal. Proc. 5th Provisional Remedies § 122, (S 122) Plaintiff's Opposition to Claim.

§ 484.370.   Hearing; issuance of writ; findings

The hearing shall be conducted in the manner prescribed in Section 484.090 and the court shall order a writ of attachment to be issued upon the filing of an undertaking as provided by Sections 489.210 and 489.220, if it finds both of the following:

(a) A right to attach order has been issued in the action pursuant to Article 1 (commencing with Section 484.010) or the court has found pursuant to Section 485.240 that the plaintiff is entitled to a right to attach order.

(b) The defendant has failed to prove that the property sought to be attached, or the portion thereof to be described in the writ, is exempt from attachment. *(Added by Stats.1974, c. 1516, p. 3347, § 9, operative Jan. 1, 1977. Amended by Stats.1976, c. 437, p. 1122, § 12.)*

Law Revision Commission Comments

Section 484.370 is comparable to Section 484.090.

The introductory sentence of Section 484.370 is amended to make clear that the court orders the clerk to issue the writ and to delete language concerning the content of the writ of attachment. The deleted language is continued in Section 488.010.

Research References

Rutter, Cal. Practice Guide: Enforcing Judgments/Debts Ch. 4-A, A. Attachment.
Miller and Starr California Real Estate § 32:34, Procedure for Issuance of the Writ.

Miller and Starr California Real Estate § 32:35, Noticed Hearing Procedure.
6 Witkin Cal. Proc. 5th Provisional Remedies § 91, (S 91) Undertakings.
6 Witkin Cal. Proc. 5th Provisional Remedies § 123, (S 123) Hearing and Issuance of Writ.

ARTICLE 3. EX PARTE PROCEDURE FOR OBTAINING ADDITIONAL WRITS

Section
484.510.   Application; filing; affidavits.
484.520.   Issuance of writ; findings.
484.530.   Claim of exemption.

§ 484.510. Application; filing; affidavits

(a) At any time after a right to attach order has been issued under Article 1 (commencing with Section 484.010) or after the court has found pursuant to Section 485.240 that the plaintiff is entitled to a right to attach order, the plaintiff may apply for a writ of attachment under this article by filing an application which meets the requirements of Section 484.320 with the court in which the action is brought.

(b) The application shall be accompanied by an affidavit showing that the property sought to be attached is not exempt from attachment. Such affidavit may be based on the affiant's information and belief. *(Added by Stats.1974, c. 1516, p. 3347, § 9, operative Jan. 1, 1977.)*

Law Revision Commission Comments

Article 3 (commencing with Section 484.510) provides an ex parte procedure for the issuance of a writ after a right to attach order has been issued following a noticed hearing. See Comment to Section 484.310. In contrast, Chapter 5 (commencing with Section 485.010) provides a procedure for the ex parte issuance of both the right to attach order and a writ. Such relief is, however, available only in exceptional circumstances. See Section 485.010 and Comment thereto.

Research References

Rutter, Cal. Practice Guide: Enforcing Judgments/Debts Ch. 4-A, A. Attachment.
Miller and Starr California Real Estate § 32:34, Procedure for Issuance of the Writ.
Miller and Starr California Real Estate § 32:35, Noticed Hearing Procedure.
6 Witkin Cal. Proc. 5th Provisional Remedies § 124, (S 124) in General.
6 Witkin Cal. Proc. 5th Provisional Remedies § 125, (S 125) Application and Supporting Affidavit.
6 Witkin Cal. Proc. 5th Provisional Remedies § 137, (S 137) Hearing and Determination.
6 Witkin Cal. Proc. 5th Provisional Remedies § 138, Application and Affidavit.
6 Witkin Cal. Proc. 5th Provisional Remedies § 233, (S 233) Acts Constituting Wrongful Attachment.
6 Witkin Cal. Proc. 5th Provisional Remedies § 243, Additional Writs.

§ 484.520. Issuance of writ; findings

The court shall examine the application and supporting affidavit and shall order a writ of attachment to be issued upon the filing of an undertaking as provided by Sections 489.210 and 489.220, if it finds both of the following:

(a) A right to attach order has been issued in the action pursuant to Article 1 (commencing with Section 484.010) or the court has found pursuant to Section 485.240 that the plaintiff is entitled to a right to attach order.

(b) The affidavit accompanying the application shows that the property sought to be attached, or the portion thereof to be described in the writ, is not exempt from attachment. *(Added by Stats.1974, c. 1516, p. 3347, § 9, operative Jan. 1, 1977. Amended by Stats.1976, c. 437, p. 1123, § 13.)*

Law Revision Commission Comments

Section 484.520 is comparable to Section 484.370 except here the determinations are made ex parte and the plaintiff must show that the property sought to be attached is not exempt from attachment. This determination may be subsequently challenged by the defendant. See Section 484.530. [But see Section 484.530(c)] [11 Cal.L.Rev.Comm. Reports 701, amended by 16 Cal.L.Rev.Comm. Reports 1652].

Section 484.520 is amended in the same manner as Section 484.370. See Comment to Section 484.370.

Research References

Rutter, Cal. Practice Guide: Enforcing Judgments/Debts Ch. 4-A, A. Attachment.
Miller and Starr California Real Estate § 32:35, Noticed Hearing Procedure.
6 Witkin Cal. Proc. 5th Provisional Remedies § 91, (S 91) Undertakings.
6 Witkin Cal. Proc. 5th Provisional Remedies § 126, (S 126) Ex Parte Hearing and Issuance of Writ.

§ 484.530. Claim of exemption

(a) The defendant may claim an exemption as to real or personal property levied upon pursuant to a writ issued under this article by following the procedure set forth in Article 2 (commencing with Section 703.510) of Chapter 4 of Division 2 of Title 9, except that the defendant shall claim the exemption as to personal property not later than 30 days after the levying officer serves the defendant with the notice of attachment describing such property. For this purpose, references in Article 2 (commencing with Section 703.510) of Chapter 4 of Division 2 of Title 9 to the "judgment debtor" shall be deemed references to the defendant, and references to the "judgment creditor" shall be deemed references to the plaintiff.

(b) The defendant may claim the exemption provided by subdivision (b) of Section 487.020 within the time provided by subdivision (a) of this section either (1) by following the procedure set forth in Article 2 (commencing with Section 703.510) of Chapter 4 of Division 2 of Title 9 or (2) by following the procedure set forth in subdivision (c) of Section 482.100 except that the requirement of showing changed circumstances under subdivision (a) of Section 482.100 does not apply.

(c) Notwithstanding subdivisions (a) and (b), a claim of exemption shall be denied if the claim has been denied earlier in the action and there is no change in circumstances affecting the claim. *(Added by Stats.1974, c. 1516, p. 3347, § 9, operative Jan. 1, 1977. Amended by Stats.1976, c. 437, p. 1123, § 14; Stats. 1982, c. 1198, p. 4284, § 39, operative July 1, 1983.)*

Law Revision Commission Comments

A notice of attachment (see Section [488.060]) will be served on the defendant at or about the time his property is levied upon. [See Section 488.305.] The notice will advise him of his right to make a claim of exemption where the writ has been issued ex parte (11 Cal.L.Rev.Comm. Reports 701, amended by 16 Cal.L.Rev.Comm. Reports 1653).

Subdivision (a) of Section 484.530 is amended to provide that the defendant may claim an exemption for property that has been levied upon not later than 30 days after the levying officer serves the defendant with a notice of attachment describing the property. See [Sections 488.060] ([contents of] notice of attachment) [, 488.305 (service of notice of attachment)].

Subdivision (b) permits the defendant to claim an exemption of necessities by the expeditious procedure provided by subdivision (c) of Section 482.100 as an alternative to the procedure provided by [the Enforcement of Judgments Law] and incorporated by subdivision (a) of this section. However, as subdivision (b) provides, the defendant is not required to show that his right to claim the exemption is the result of a change of circumstances as is required when a claim is made under Section 482.100 after the time for claiming exemptions has passed.

Subdivision (c) applies where the defendant has made a claim of exemption pursuant to Section 484.070 for [personal] property not described in the plaintiff's application [or for real property] but failed to prove his right to the exemption. See also Section 482.100 (postlevy claims of exemption on grounds of changed circumstances).

Exemptions [for personal property] not claimed as provided by this section are waived for purposes both of attachment and of execution except as provided by Section 482.100 (13 Cal.L.Rev.Comm. Reports 801, amended by 16 Cal.L.Rev.Comm. Reports 1653).

Research References

Rutter, Cal. Practice Guide: Enforcing Judgments/Debts Ch. 4-A, A. Attachment.

Miller and Starr California Real Estate § 32:34, Procedure for Issuance of the Writ.

Miller and Starr California Real Estate § 32:35, Noticed Hearing Procedure.

6 Witkin Cal. Proc. 5th Provisional Remedies § 87, (S 87) Claim of Real Property Exemption.

6 Witkin Cal. Proc. 5th Provisional Remedies § 127, (S 127) Defendant's Claim of Exemption.

6 Witkin Cal. Proc. 5th Provisional Remedies § 179, Securities.

6 Witkin Cal. Proc. 5th Provisional Remedies § 181, Interest in Estate Personal Property.

CHAPTER 5. EX PARTE HEARING PROCEDURE FOR OBTAINING WRIT OF ATTACHMENT

ARTICLE 1. GREAT OR IRREPARABLE INJURY REQUIREMENT

§ 485.010. Affidavit; showing; review of issuance of writ; time

(a) Except as otherwise provided by statute, no right to attach order or writ of attachment may be issued pursuant to this chapter unless it appears from facts shown by affidavit that great or irreparable injury would result to the plaintiff if issuance of the order were delayed until the matter could be heard on notice.

(b) The requirement of subdivision (a) is satisfied if any of the following are shown:

(1) Under the circumstances of the case, it may be inferred that there is a danger that the property sought to be attached would be concealed, substantially impaired in value, or otherwise made unavailable to levy if issuance of the order were delayed until the matter could be heard on notice.

(2) Under the circumstances of the case, it may be inferred that the defendant has failed to pay the debt underlying the requested attachment and the defendant is insolvent in the sense that the defendant is generally not paying his or her debts as those debts become due, unless the debts are subject to a bona fide dispute. Plaintiff's affidavit filed in support of the ex parte attachment shall state, in addition to the requirements of Section 485.530, the known undisputed debts of the defendant, that the debts are not subject to bona fide dispute, and the basis for plaintiff's determination that the defendant's debts are undisputed.

(3) A bulk sales notice has been recorded and published pursuant to Division 6 (commencing with Section 6101) of the Commercial Code with respect to a bulk transfer by the defendant.

(4) An escrow has been opened pursuant to the provisions of Section 24074 of the Business and Professions Code with respect to the sale by the defendant of a liquor license.

(5) Any other circumstance showing that great or irreparable injury would result to the plaintiff if issuance of the order were delayed until the matter could be heard on notice.

(c) Upon a writ being issued solely on a showing under paragraph (2) of subdivision (b), if the defendant requests the court to review the issuance of the writ, the court shall conduct a hearing within five court days after the plaintiff is served with notice of the defendant's request. A writ issued solely on a showing under paragraph (3) of subdivision (b) shall be limited to the property covered by the bulk sales notice or the proceeds of the sale of such property. In addition to any other service required by this title, such writ shall be served by the levying officer on the transferee or auctioneer identified by the bulk sales notice not more than five days after the levy of such writ. A writ issued solely on a showing under paragraph (4) of subdivision (b) shall be limited to the plaintiff's pro rata share of the proceeds of the sale in escrow. *(Added by Stats.1974, c. 1516, p. 3348, § 9, operative Jan. 1, 1977. Amended by Stats.1976, c. 437, p. 1123, § 14.5; Stats.1988, c. 727, § 1.)*

Law Revision Commission Comments

Section 485.010 is based on former Section 538.5. Subdivision (a) of former Section 538.5 has been replaced by the substantively similar provisions of paragraphs (2) and (3) of subdivision (b) and subdivision (c) of Section 485.010. Paragraph (3) of subdivision (b) does not, however, modify the exclusive scheme of priorities provided by Section 24074 of the Business and Professions Code (see Grover Escrow Corp. v. Cole, 71 Cal.2d 61, 453 P.2d 461, 77 Cal.Rptr. 21 (1969)) but merely provides for levy in the circumstances contemplated in the last paragraph of Section 24074. Subdivisions (b) and (c) of former Section 538.5 have been replaced by paragraphs (1) and (4) of subdivision (b) of Section 485.010. These two paragraphs authorize ex parte relief on a showing of circumstances from which it may be inferred that there is a danger that property will be concealed, substantially impaired in value, or otherwise made unavailable to levy or a showing of any other circumstance that indicates that the plaintiff would suffer great or irreparable injury if issuance of the writ were delayed until the matter could be heard on notice.

The introductory clause to Section 485.010 recognizes the specific authorization to issue an ex parte attachment provided by other statutes. See e.g., Harb. & Nav.Code § 495.1; Health & Saf.Code § 11501; Rev. & Tax.Code §§ 6713, 7864, 8972, 11472, 12680, 18833, 26251, 30302, and 32352. See also Chapter 12 (commencing with Section 492.010) (nonresident attachment).

Research References

Rutter, Cal. Practice Guide: A.D.R. Ch. 5-G, G. Procedures to Enforce Arbitration.

Rutter, Cal. Practice Guide: Civ. Pro. Before Trial Ch. 9(II)-D, D. Attachment.

Rutter, Cal. Practice Guide: Enforcing Judgments/Debts Ch. 4-A, A. Attachment.

Miller and Starr California Real Estate § 32:10, Current Attachment Law.

Miller and Starr California Real Estate § 32:34, Procedure for Issuance of the Writ.

Miller and Starr California Real Estate § 32:36, Ex Parte Procedure.

6 Witkin Cal. Proc. 5th Provisional Remedies § 53, Nature and Scope.

6 Witkin Cal. Proc. 5th Provisional Remedies § 128, Requirement.

6 Witkin Cal. Proc. 5th Provisional Remedies § 129, Sufficient Showing.

6 Witkin Cal. Proc. 5th Provisional Remedies § 130, (S 130) Application and Affidavit.

6 Witkin Cal. Proc. 5th Provisional Remedies § 131, (S 131) Order and Writ.

6 Witkin Cal. Proc. 5th Provisional Remedies § 136, (S 136) No Review of Finding of Great or Irreparable Injury.

6 Witkin Cal. Proc. 5th Provisional Remedies § 138, Application and Affidavit.

6 Witkin Cal. Proc. 5th Provisional Remedies § 139, Issuance of Writ.

6 Witkin Cal. Proc. 5th Provisional Remedies § 141, (S 141) Nature and Purpose.

6 Witkin Cal. Proc. 5th Provisional Remedies § 142, (S 142) Application and Affidavit.
6 Witkin Cal. Proc. 5th Provisional Remedies § 143, (S 143) Ex Parte Hearing and Determination.
6 Witkin Cal. Proc. 5th Provisional Remedies § 233, (S 233) Acts Constituting Wrongful Attachment.

ARTICLE 2.　ORDER DETERMINING RIGHT TO ATTACH; ISSUANCE OF WRIT OF ATTACHMENT

§ 485.210.　Application; filing; showing; supporting affidavit

(a) Upon the filing of the complaint or at any time thereafter, the plaintiff may apply pursuant to this article for a right to attach order and a writ of attachment by filing an application for the order and writ with the court in which the action is brought.

(b) The application shall satisfy the requirements of Section 484.020 and, in addition, shall include a statement showing that the requirement of Section 485.010 is satisfied.

(c) The application shall be supported by an affidavit showing all of the following:

(1) The plaintiff on the facts presented would be entitled to a judgment on the claim upon which the attachment is based.

(2) The plaintiff would suffer great or irreparable injury (within the meaning of Section 485.010) if issuance of the order were delayed until the matter could be heard on notice.

(3) The property sought to be attached is not exempt from attachment.

(d) An affidavit in support of the showing required by paragraph (3) of subdivision (c) may be based on the affiant's information and belief. *(Added by Stats.1974, c. 1516, p. 3348, § 9, operative Jan. 1, 1977.)*

Law Revision Commission Comments

Section 485.210 provides the procedure for applying ex parte for the issuance of a writ of attachment prior to a noticed hearing on the probable validity of the plaintiff's claim. Compare Sections 484.010–484.030 and 484.510. Compare also the first paragraph of former Section 538.5.

Research References

Rutter, Cal. Practice Guide: Enforcing Judgments/Debts Ch. 4-A, A. Attachment.
Miller and Starr California Real Estate § 32:36, Ex Parte Procedure.
6 Witkin Cal. Proc. 5th Provisional Remedies § 130, (S 130) Application and Affidavit.

§ 485.220.　Issuance of order and writ; findings; denial of order

(a) The court shall examine the application and supporting affidavit and, except as provided in Section 486.030, shall issue a right to attach order, which shall state the amount to be secured by the attachment, and order a writ of attachment to be issued upon the filing of an undertaking as provided by Sections 489.210 and 489.220, if it finds all of the following:

(1) The claim upon which the attachment is based is one upon which an attachment may be issued.

(2) The plaintiff has established the probable validity of the claim upon which the attachment is based.

(3) The attachment is not sought for a purpose other than the recovery upon the claim upon which the attachment is based.

(4) The affidavit accompanying the application shows that the property sought to be attached, or the portion thereof to be specified in the writ, is not exempt from attachment.

(5) The plaintiff will suffer great or irreparable injury (within the meaning of Section 485.010) if issuance of the order is delayed until the matter can be heard on notice.

(6) The amount to be secured by the attachment is greater than zero.

(b) If the court finds that the application and the supporting affidavit do not satisfy the requirements of Section 485.010, it shall so state and deny the order. If denial is solely on the ground that Section 485.010 is not satisfied, the court shall so state and such denial does not preclude the plaintiff from applying for a right to attach order and writ of attachment under Chapter 4 (commencing with Section 484.010) with the same affidavits and supporting papers. *(Added by Stats.1974, c. 1516, p. 3349, § 9, operative Jan. 1, 1977. Amended by Stats.1976, c. 437, p. 1124, § 15; Stats.1997, c. 222 (A.B.1258), § 9.)*

Law Revision Commission Comments

Section 485.220 provides the procedure for the ex parte issuance of a writ of attachment prior to a noticed hearing on the probable validity of the plaintiff's claim. Compare Section 484.090.

The exception provided in subdivision (a) recognizes that the court may, in its discretion, issue a temporary protective order in lieu of a writ of attachment even where the requirements of this section are satisfied. See Section 486.030 and Comment thereto.

Section 485.220 is amended in the same manner as Section 484.090. See Comment to Section 484.090.

Paragraph (6) is added to subdivision (a) of Section 485.220 to make clear that the court is not to issue a right to attach order and writ of attachment if there is no amount to be secured by the attachment. This amendment is consistent with Section 484.090. See Section 484.090 Comment. [26 Cal.L.Rev.Comm. Reports 307 (1996)].

Research References

Rutter, Cal. Practice Guide: Civ. Pro. Before Trial Ch. 9(II)-D, D. Attachment.
Rutter, Cal. Practice Guide: Enforcing Judgments/Debts Ch. 4-A, A. Attachment.
Miller and Starr California Real Estate § 32:35, Noticed Hearing Procedure.
Miller and Starr California Real Estate § 32:36, Ex Parte Procedure.
6 Witkin Cal. Proc. 5th Provisional Remedies § 131, (S 131) Order and Writ.

§ 485.230.　Discovery; property in which defendant has an interest

Where a right to attach order has been issued by the court, a plaintiff may discover, through any means provided for by, and subject to the protections included in, Title 4 (commencing with Section 2016.010) of Part 4, the identity, location, and value of property in which the defendant has an interest. *(Added by Stats.1992, c. 1348 (A.B.2616), § 2. Amended by Stats.2004, c. 182 (A.B.3081), § 10, operative July 1, 2005.)*

Law Revision Commission Comments

Section 485.230 is amended to reflect nonsubstantive reorganization of the rules governing civil discovery. [33 Cal.L.Rev.Comm. Reports 991 (2003)].

Research References

Rutter, Cal. Practice Guide: Civ. Pro. Before Trial Ch. 8E-3, Whose Deposition May be Taken.

Rutter, Cal. Practice Guide: Enforcing Judgments/Debts Ch. 4-A, A. Attachment.

6 Witkin Cal. Proc. 5th Provisional Remedies § 90, (S 90) Discovery.

§ 485.240. Application to set aside order or reduce amount secured; notice of motion; hearing and determination

(a) Any defendant whose property has been attached pursuant to a writ issued under this chapter may apply for an order (1) that the right to attach order be set aside, the writ of attachment quashed, and any property levied upon pursuant to the writ be released, or (2) that the amount to be secured by the attachment be reduced as provided in Section 483.015. Such application shall be made by filing with the court and serving on the plaintiff a notice of motion.

(b) The notice of motion shall state the grounds on which the motion is based and shall be accompanied by an affidavit supporting any factual issues raised and points and authorities supporting any legal issues raised. It shall not be grounds to set aside an order that the plaintiff would not have suffered great or irreparable injury (within the meaning of Section 485.010) if issuance of the order had been delayed until the matter could have been heard on notice.

(c) At the hearing on the motion, the court shall determine whether the plaintiff is entitled to the right to attach order or whether the amount to be secured by the attachment should be reduced. If the court finds that the plaintiff is not entitled to the right to attach order, it shall order the right to attach order set aside, the writ of attachment quashed, and any property levied on pursuant to the writ released. If the court finds that the plaintiff is entitled to the right to attach order, thereafter the plaintiff may apply for additional writs pursuant to Article 2 (commencing with Section 484.310) or Article 3 (commencing with Section 484.510) of Chapter 4.

(d) The court's determinations shall be made upon the basis of the pleadings and other papers in the record; but, upon good cause shown, the court may receive and consider at the hearing additional evidence, oral or documentary, and additional points and authorities, or it may continue the hearing for the production of such additional evidence or points and authorities.

(e) The hearing provided for in this section shall take precedence over all other civil matters on the calendar of that day except older matters of the same character. *(Added by Stats.1974, c. 1516, p. 3349, § 9, operative Jan. 1, 1977. Amended by Stats.1983, c. 155, § 4, eff. June 30, 1983, operative July 1, 1983.)*

Law Revision Commission Comments

Subdivisions (a) and (c) of Section 485.240 are amended to make clear that the defendant may seek the reduction of the amount of the attachment by the amounts specified in subdivision (b) of Section 483.015. [16 Cal.L.Rev.Comm. Reports 2175 (1982)].

Research References

Rutter, Cal. Practice Guide: Civ. Pro. Before Trial Ch. 9(II)-D, D. Attachment.

Rutter, Cal. Practice Guide: Enforcing Judgments/Debts Ch. 4-A, A. Attachment.

Miller and Starr California Real Estate § 32:16, Amount of Obligation Subject to Attachment.

Miller and Starr California Real Estate § 32:36, Ex Parte Procedure.

6 Witkin Cal. Proc. 5th Proceedings Without Trial § 7, General Requirement of Notice.

6 Witkin Cal. Proc. 5th Provisional Remedies § 98, (S 98) in General.

6 Witkin Cal. Proc. 5th Provisional Remedies § 119, (S 119) Application.

6 Witkin Cal. Proc. 5th Provisional Remedies § 123, (S 123) Hearing and Issuance of Writ.

6 Witkin Cal. Proc. 5th Provisional Remedies § 125, (S 125) Application and Supporting Affidavit.

6 Witkin Cal. Proc. 5th Provisional Remedies § 126, (S 126) Ex Parte Hearing and Issuance of Writ.

6 Witkin Cal. Proc. 5th Provisional Remedies § 135, (S 135) Noticed Motion.

6 Witkin Cal. Proc. 5th Provisional Remedies § 136, (S 136) No Review of Finding of Great or Irreparable Injury.

6 Witkin Cal. Proc. 5th Provisional Remedies § 137, (S 137) Hearing and Determination.

ARTICLE 3. PROCEDURE FOR OBTAINING ADDITIONAL WRITS

Section

§ 485.510. Application; filing

At any time after a right to attach order and writ of attachment have been issued under Article 2 (commencing with Section 485.210), the plaintiff may apply for an additional writ of attachment under this article by filing an application with the court in which the action is brought. *(Added by Stats.1974, c. 1516, p. 3350, § 9, operative Jan. 1, 1977.)*

Law Revision Commission Comments

Sections 485.510 through 485.530 are comparable to Section 484.510 only here the plaintiff must show that exceptional circumstances continue his need for the ex parte issuance of a writ. Nothing, of course precludes the plaintiff from applying for a new order and writ pursuant to Article 1 of Chapter 4. Moreover, where there has been a hearing pursuant to Section 485.240 and the plaintiff's right to attach has been upheld, the plaintiff may apply for an additional writ pursuant to the procedures provided in Article 2 (commencing with Section 484.310) and Article 3 (commencing with Section 484.510) of Chapter 4. See Section 485.240(c).

Research References

Rutter, Cal. Practice Guide: Enforcing Judgments/Debts Ch. 4-A, A. Attachment.

Miller and Starr California Real Estate § 32:36, Ex Parte Procedure.

6 Witkin Cal. Proc. 5th Provisional Remedies § 124, (S 124) in General.

6 Witkin Cal. Proc. 5th Provisional Remedies § 138, Application and Affidavit.

§ 485.520. Application; execution; contents

The application shall be executed under oath and shall include all of the following:

(a) A statement that the plaintiff has been issued a right to attach order and writ of attachment pursuant to Article 2 (commencing with Section 485.210) in the action.

(b) A statement of the amount to be secured by the attachment under the right to attach order.

(c) A description of the property to be attached under the writ of attachment and a statement that the plaintiff is informed and believes that the property is not exempt from attachment. The description shall satisfy the requirements of Section 484.020.

(d) A statement showing that the requirement of Section 485.010 has been satisfied. *(Added by Stats.1974, c. 1516, p. 3350, § 9, operative Jan. 1, 1977. Amended by Stats.1982, c. 1198, p. 4285, § 41, operative July 1, 1983.)*

Law Revision Commission Comments

See Comment to Section 485.510.

Section 485.520 is amended to reflect the addition of Section 483.015 which provides for the calculation of the amount to be secured by the attachment (16 Cal.L.Rev.Comm. Reports 701).

§ 485.530. Supporting affidavit

(a) The application shall be supported by an affidavit showing both of the following:

(1) The plaintiff would suffer great or irreparable injury (within the meaning of Section 485.010) if the issuance of the writ of attachment were delayed until the matter could be heard on notice.

(2) The property sought to be attached is not exempt from attachment.

(b) The affidavit in support of the showing required by paragraph (2) of subdivision (a) may be based on the affiant's information and belief. *(Added by Stats.1974, c. 1516, p. 3351, § 9, operative Jan. 1, 1977. Amended by Stats.1976, c. 437, p. 437, § 17.)*

Law Revision Commission Comments

See Comment to Section 485.510.

The amendment of Section 485.530 is a clarifying, nonsubstantive change. Under this article, the plaintiff applies for a writ of attachment, not a right to attach order.

§ 485.540. Issuance of writ; findings

The court shall examine the application and supporting affidavit and shall order a writ of attachment to be issued upon the filing of an undertaking as provided by Sections 489.210 and 489.220, if it finds all of the following:

(a) A right to attach order has been issued in the action pursuant to Article 2 (commencing with Section 485.210).

(b) The affidavit accompanying the application shows that the property sought to be attached, or the portion thereof to be specified in the writ, is not exempt from attachment.

(c) The plaintiff will suffer great or irreparable injury (within the meaning of Section 485.010) if issuance of the writ of attachment is delayed until the matter can be heard on notice. *(Added by Stats.1974, c. 1516, p. 3351, § 9, operative Jan. 1, 1977. Amended by Stats.1976, c. 437, p. 1125, § 18.)*

Law Revision Commission Comments

Section 485.540 is comparable to Section 484.520 except here the court must make a finding that great or irreparable injury would result to the plaintiff if issuance of the order were delayed until the matter could be heard on notice. See Comment to Section 485.510.

The introductory clause of Section 485.540 is amended in the same manner as Section 484.370. See Comment to Section 484.370. The amendment of subdivision (c) reflects the fact that the plaintiff is applying for a writ of attachment; a right to attach order must already have been issued as subdivision (a) provides.

ARTICLE 4. CLAIM OF EXEMPTION

Section

485.610. Procedure; time; support of individual and household.

§ 485.610. Procedure; time; support of individual and household

(a) The defendant may claim an exemption as to real or personal property levied upon pursuant to a writ of attachment issued under this chapter by following the procedure set forth in Article 2 (commencing with Section 703.510) of Chapter 4 of Division 2 of Title 9, except that the defendant shall claim the exemption as to personal property not later than 30 days after the levying officer serves the defendant with the notice of attachment describing such property and may claim an exemption for real property within the time provided in Section 487.030. For this purpose, references in Article 2 (commencing with Section 703.510) of Chapter 4 of Division 2 of Title 9 to the "judgment debtor" shall be deemed references to the defendant, and references to the "judgment creditor" shall be deemed references to the plaintiff.

(b) The defendant may claim the exemption provided by subdivision (b) of Section 487.020 within the time provided by subdivision (a) of this section either (1) by following the procedure set forth in Article 2 (commencing with Section 703.510) of Chapter 4 of Division 2 of Title 9 or (2) by following the procedure set forth in subdivision (c) of Section 482.100 except that the requirement of showing changed circumstances under subdivision (a) of Section 482.100 does not apply. *(Added by Stats.1976, c. 437, p. 1125, § 19. Amended by Stats.1982, c. 1198, p. 4285, § 42, operative July 1, 1983; Stats.1984, c. 538, § 2.)*

Law Revision Commission Comments

Section 485.610 provides a procedure for claiming exemptions for property levied upon under a writ of attachment issued pursuant to Article 2 (commencing with Section 485.210) or Article 3 (commencing with Section 485.510). Section 485.610 supersedes former Section 485.230. The defendant may claim an exemption only for property which has been levied upon. Exemptions [for personal property] not claimed as provided by this section are waived for purposes of both attachment and execution except as provided by Section 482.100 (postlevy claims of exemption on grounds of changed circumstances).

Subdivision (a) incorporates the procedure provided by [the Enforcement of Judgments Law] for claiming exemptions but provides special time limits.

Subdivision (b) permits the defendant to claim an exemption of necessities by the expeditious procedure provided by subdivision (c) of Section 482.100 as an alternative to the procedure provided by [the Enforcement of Judgments Law] and incorporated by subdivision (a) of this section. However, as subdivision (b) provides, the defendant is not required to show that his right to claim the exemption is the result of a change of circumstances as is required when a claim is made under Section 482.100 after the time for claiming exemptions has passed (13 Cal.L.Rev.Comm. Reports 801, amended by 16 Cal.L.Rev.Comm. Reports 701).

Subdivision (a) of Section 485.610 is amended to make clear that the defendant does not waive an exemption for real property by failure to claim it within the time prescribed. The other changes in Section 485.610 are technical (16 Cal.L.Rev.Comm. Reports 701).

Subdivision (a) of Section 485.610 is amended to provide a cross-reference to Section 487.030 which permits claims of exemption for real property to be made at any time before judgment in the action regardless of the time that has expired since the property was attached or notice was given the defendant. This amendment makes no substantive change. [17 Cal.L.Rev.Comm. Reports 975 (1984)].

Research References

Rutter, Cal. Practice Guide: Enforcing Judgments/Debts Ch. 4-A, A. Attachment.
Miller and Starr California Real Estate § 32:35, Noticed Hearing Procedure.
Miller and Starr California Real Estate § 32:36, Ex Parte Procedure.
6 Witkin Cal. Proc. 5th Provisional Remedies § 85, Property Not Made Subject to Attachment.
6 Witkin Cal. Proc. 5th Provisional Remedies § 87, (S 87) Claim of Real Property Exemption.
6 Witkin Cal. Proc. 5th Provisional Remedies § 140, (S 140) Defendant's Claim of Exemption.
6 Witkin Cal. Proc. 5th Provisional Remedies § 179, Securities.
6 Witkin Cal. Proc. 5th Provisional Remedies § 181, Interest in Estate Personal Property.
13 Witkin, California Summary 10th Trusts § 267, (S 267) Claims Established by Judgment.

CHAPTER 6.   TEMPORARY PROTECTIVE ORDER

§ 486.010.   Application; filing; contents

(a) At the time of applying for a right to attach order under Chapter 4 (commencing with Section 484.010), the plaintiff may apply pursuant to this chapter for a temporary protective order by filing an application for the order with the court in which the action is brought.

(b) The application shall state what relief is requested and shall be supported by an affidavit, which may be based on information and belief, showing that the plaintiff would suffer great or irreparable injury (within the meaning of Section 485.010) if the temporary protective order were not issued. *(Added by Stats.1974, c. 1516, p. 3351, § 9, operative Jan. 1, 1977.)*

Law Revision Commission Comments

Section 486.010 replaces former Section 538.1. In contrast to former Section 538.1 which provided for the issuance of a temporary restraining order as a matter of right in every case, Section 486.010 requires the plaintiff to apply for relief and show that such relief is required to avoid great or irreparable injury to him.

The application required by this section will accompany that required by Section 484.020, thus permitting the court to make the determinations required by Section 486.020.

Sections 486.010 and 486.020 provide for the situation where the plaintiff specifically applies for a temporary protective order. A temporary protective order may also be issued on the court's own motion in lieu of the ex parte issuance of a writ of attachment pursuant to Section 486.030.

Research References

Rutter, Cal. Practice Guide: Civ. Pro. Before Trial Ch. 9(II)-D, D. Attachment.
Rutter, Cal. Practice Guide: Enforcing Judgments/Debts Ch. 4-A, A. Attachment.
Miller and Starr California Real Estate § 32:10, Current Attachment Law.
Miller and Starr California Real Estate § 32:34, Procedure for Issuance of the Writ.

Miller and Starr California Real Estate § 32:37, Temporary Protective Orders.
6 Witkin Cal. Proc. 5th Provisional Remedies § 53, Nature and Scope.
6 Witkin Cal. Proc. 5th Provisional Remedies § 142, (S 142) Application and Affidavit.

§ 486.020.   Examination of applicant; issuance of order; undertaking; findings

The court shall examine the application, supporting affidavit, and other papers on record and shall issue a temporary protective order, which shall state the amount sought to be secured by the attachment under the application for the right to attach order, upon the filing of an undertaking as provided by Sections 489.210 and 489.220, if it finds all of the following:

(a) The claim upon which the application for attachment is based is one upon which an attachment may be issued.

(b) The plaintiff has established the probable validity of the claim upon which the application for the attachment is based.

(c) The order is not sought for a purpose other than the recovery upon the claim upon which the application for the attachment is based.

(d) The plaintiff will suffer great or irreparable injury (within the meaning of Section 485.010) if the temporary protective order is not issued. *(Added by Stats.1974, c. 1516, p. 3351, § 9, operative Jan. 1, 1977. Amended by Stats.1976, c. 437, p. 1126, § 19.5; Stats.1982, c. 1198, p. 4286, § 42.5, operative July 1, 1983.)*

Law Revision Commission Comments

Section 486.020 provides for an ex parte determination of the right to a temporary protective order. See generally Comment to Section 486.010.

Section 486.020 is amended to add the requirement that the temporary protective order state the amount sought to be secured by the attachment under the application for the right to attach order. This addition implements subdivision (c) (1) of Section 486.060 and subdivision (b) of Section 489.320 (16 Cal.L.Rev.Comm. Reports 1663).

Research References

Rutter, Cal. Practice Guide: Enforcing Judgments/Debts Ch. 4-A, A. Attachment.
Miller and Starr California Real Estate § 32:37, Temporary Protective Orders.
6 Witkin Cal. Proc. 5th Provisional Remedies § 91, (S 91) Undertakings.
6 Witkin Cal. Proc. 5th Provisional Remedies § 143, (S 143) Ex Parte Hearing and Determination.

§ 486.030.   Temporary protective order in lieu of writ of attachment

(a) In any case where the plaintiff has applied for a right to attach order and writ of attachment under Chapter 5 (commencing with Section 485.010), the court may in its discretion deny the application for the order and writ and issue instead a temporary protective order under this chapter if it determines that the requirements of Section 485.220 are satisfied but that the issuance of the temporary protective order instead of the right to attach order and writ would be in the interest of justice and equity to the parties, taking into account the effect on the defendant of issuing a writ of attachment ex parte, the effect on the plaintiff of issuing the temporary protective order instead of the writ, and other factors that bear on equity and justice under the circumstances of the particular case.

(b) If the court issues a temporary protective order under this section, the plaintiff's application for a right to attach order and writ shall be treated as an application for a right to attach order and writ under Article 1 (commencing with Section 484.010) of Chapter 4 and the plaintiff shall comply with the requirements of service provided in Section 484.040. *(Added by Stats.1974, c. 1516, p. 3352, § 9, operative Jan. 1, 1977.)*

Law Revision Commission Comments

Section 486.030 is new. No similar provision existed under former law. See Comment to Section 486.010. Where a temporary protective order is issued in lieu of a right to attach order and writ, the plaintiff's application for the order and writ is treated as an application under Article 1 of Chapter 4. The plaintiff must serve the application, notice of application, and other papers required by Section 484.040 and the procedures provided thereafter are then followed.

Research References

Rutter, Cal. Practice Guide: Enforcing Judgments/Debts Ch. 4-A, A. Attachment.

Miller and Starr California Real Estate § 32:37, Temporary Protective Orders.

6 Witkin Cal. Proc. 5th Provisional Remedies § 131, (S 131) Order and Writ.

6 Witkin Cal. Proc. 5th Provisional Remedies § 141, (S 141) Nature and Purpose.

§ 486.040. Contents of order

The temporary protective order issued under this chapter shall contain such provisions as the court determines would be in the interest of justice and equity to the parties, taking into account the effects on both the defendant and the plaintiff under the circumstances of the particular case. (*Added by Stats.1974, c. 1516, p. 3352, § 9, operative Jan. 1, 1977.*)

Law Revision Commission Comments

Section 486.040 is new; no similar provision existed under former law. This section directs the court to consider what provisions in the temporary protective order would be fair and equitable for both parties. Included in such provisions may be a specific expiration date. See Section 486.090(a).

Research References

Rutter, Cal. Practice Guide: Enforcing Judgments/Debts Ch. 4-A, A. Attachment.

Miller and Starr California Real Estate § 32:37, Temporary Protective Orders.

6 Witkin Cal. Proc. 5th Provisional Remedies § 144, in General.

6 Witkin Cal. Proc. 5th Provisional Remedies § 146, Effect.

§ 486.050. Scope of order

(a) Except as otherwise provided in Section 486.040, the temporary protective order may prohibit a transfer by the defendant of any of the defendant's property in this state subject to the levy of the writ of attachment. The temporary protective order shall describe the property in a manner adequate to permit the defendant to identify the property subject to the temporary protective order.

(b) Notwithstanding subdivision (a), if the property is farm products held for sale or is inventory, the temporary protective order shall not prohibit the defendant from transferring the property in the ordinary course of business, but the temporary protective order may impose appropriate restrictions on the disposition of the proceeds from that type of transfer. (*Added by Stats.1974, c. 1516, p. 3352, § 9, operative Jan. 1, 1977. Amended by Stats.1976, c. 437, p. 1126, § 20; Stats.2008, c. 179 (S.B.1498), § 35.*)

Law Revision Commission Comments

Section 486.050 is based on a comparable provision in former Section 538.3. Exceptions similar to those provided by Section 486.060 were also provided by Section 538.3. Section 538.3 also provided:

> Without limiting the generality of the phrase "not in the ordinary course of business", the payment by the defendant of an antecedent debt shall not be considered in the ordinary course of business within the meaning of this section.

This clause has been eliminated. The court should be able to frame an effective order under the guidelines provided in Sections 486.050 and 486.060. Such order may, in appropriate circumstances, prohibit the payment of antecedent debts.

Section 486.050 merely authorizes the issuance of an order prohibiting transfers where appropriate (see Section 486.040); former Section 538.3 seemed to always require the issuance of an order prohibiting transfers.

Subdivision (a) of Section 486.050 is amended to prescribe the manner of describing property that is subject to the temporary protective order. The description in a temporary protective order restraining the transfer of property of an individual defendant or a portion of the property of a corporation or a partnership should be sufficiently specific to permit accurate identification.

The temporary protective order should restrain the transfer only of an amount of the defendant's property that is reasonably necessary to protect the plaintiff's interest until a writ of attachment can be issued. Where an excessive amount of property is subject to the temporary protective order, the plaintiff may be liable for abuse of process. Cf. White Lighting Co. v. Wolfson, 68 Cal.2d 336, 438 P.2d 345, 66 Cal.Rptr. 697 (1968).

The amendments to the introductory portion of subdivision (a) and to subdivision (b) are technical and make no substantive change.

Research References

Rutter, Cal. Practice Guide: Enforcing Judgments/Debts Ch. 4-A, A. Attachment.

Miller and Starr California Real Estate § 32:37, Temporary Protective Orders.

6 Witkin Cal. Proc. 5th Provisional Remedies § 144, in General.

6 Witkin Cal. Proc. 5th Provisional Remedies § 146, Effect.

§ 486.060. Authority of defendant to issue checks; restrictions

(a) Notwithstanding any terms of the temporary protective order, the defendant may issue any number of checks against any of the defendant's accounts in a financial institution in this state to the extent permitted by this section.

(b) The defendant may issue any number of checks in any amount for the following purposes:

(1) Payment of any payroll expense (including fringe benefits and taxes and premiums for workers' compensation and unemployment insurance) falling due in the ordinary course of business prior to the levy of a writ of attachment.

(2) Payment for goods thereafter delivered to the defendant C.O.D. for use in the defendant's trade, business, or profession.

(3) Payment of taxes if payment is necessary to avoid penalties which will accrue if there is any further delay in payment.

(4) Payment of reasonable legal fees and reasonable costs and expenses required for the representation of the defendant in the action.

(c) In addition to the checks permitted to be issued by subdivision (b), the defendant may issue any number of checks for any purpose so long as the total amount of the checks does not exceed the greater of the following:

(1) The amount by which the total amount on deposit exceeds the sum of the amount sought to be secured by the attachment and the amounts permitted to be paid pursuant to subdivision (b).

(2) One thousand dollars ($1,000). (*Added by Stats.1974, c. 1516, p. 3353, § 9, operative Jan. 1, 1977. Amended by Stats.1976, c. 437, p. 1126, § 21; Stats.1982, c. 1198, p. 4286, § 43, operative July 1, 1983.*)

Law Revision Commission Comments

Section 486.060 is based on comparable provisions in former Section 538.3. See the Comment to Section 486.050.

Section 486.060, as enacted, and its predecessor, former Section 538.3, failed to state clearly the rules permitting a defendant who is subject to a temporary protective order to write checks. Section 486.060, as amended, makes clear that, if funds are available, the defendant may write checks, regardless of the plaintiff's claim, for a total of $1,000 for any purpose and for any amount for the purposes listed in subdivision (b). Section 486.060 does not require the defendant to write checks for the purposes described in subdivision (b) nor does it establish a preference of one of these purposes over any other. Subdivision (c)(1) provides that the defendant may write checks for purposes, other than those described in subdivision (b), in excess of $1,000 only if the defendant reserves sufficient funds to cover checks permitted to be written by subdivision (b) and to pay the plaintiff's claim. Subdivision (c)(1) is intended to prevent a temporary protective order issued on a small claim from tying up large accounts. The defendant may always write checks in the total amount of $1,000 as provided in subdivision (c)(2) even though the amount remaining on deposit is insufficient to secure the plaintiff's claim.

In the following examples illustrating the application of Section 486.060, assume that the defendant has deposit accounts totaling $10,000 in this state and the plaintiff has a $5,000 claim:

(1) If expenses under subdivision (b) total $2,000, the defendant may write checks to pay them and then write additional checks totaling $3,000 under subdivision (c), reserving $5,000 to cover the plaintiff's claim.

(2) If, in the first example, the defendant had decided for some reason to defer payment of the $2,000 payable under subdivision (b), he could still write an additional check for not more than $3,000 since subdivision (c) allows checks to be written in amounts in addition to the total amounts permitted to be paid under subdivision (b) and the amount of the plaintiff's claim.

(3) If expenses under subdivision (b) total $8,000, the defendant may write checks for any purpose in an aggregate amount of not more than $1,000 under subdivision (c). If the defendant has deferred paying the $8,000 under subdivision (b), he may write checks under subdivision (c) totaling not more than $1,000 since the total amount on deposit ($10,000) is less than the sum of the plaintiff's claim ($5,000) and expenses under subdivision (b) ($8,000). Checks may be written under subdivision (c) for the same amount where the defendant has already paid the $8,000 under subdivision (b); he may then write checks totaling not more than $1,000 since the total amount remaining on deposit ($2,000) is less than the amount of the plaintiff's claim ($5,000).

(4) If the defendant has no expenses under subdivision (b), he may write checks totaling $5,000 for any purpose under subdivision (c).

(5) In the fourth example, if the defendant writes checks for $5,000 under subdivision (c) and later discovers that he has expenses of a type described in subdivision (b) and so writes checks for such purposes, the defendant has violated the temporary protective order.

The introductory clause of Section 486.060 is amended to make clear that the defendant may issue checks for the purposes and in the amount provided regardless of the temporary protective order. The form of the temporary protective order is prescribed by the Judicial Council. See Section 482.030(b).

Subdivision (a) of Section 486.060 is amended to recognize that checks may be issued against accounts in financial institutions (defined in Section 481.113) other than banks. The amendment to subdivision (c)(1) is clarifying. See Section 483.015 (16 Cal.L.Rev.Comm. Reports 1668).

Research References

Rutter, Cal. Practice Guide: Enforcing Judgments/Debts Ch. 4-A, A. Attachment.
Miller and Starr California Real Estate § 32:37, Temporary Protective Orders.
6 Witkin Cal. Proc. 5th Provisional Remedies § 146, Effect.

§ 486.070. Application of order

Except as otherwise provided by Section 486.110, a temporary protective order issued under this chapter binds only the defendant, whether or not any other person knows of or is served with a copy of the temporary protective order. *(Added by Stats.1974, c. 1516, p. 3353, § 9, operative Jan. 1, 1977. Amended by Stats.1976, c. 437, p. 1127, § 22.)*

Law Revision Commission Comments

Section 486.070 expands the policy of a provision in former Section 538.1 which absolved any bank from observing the terms of a restraining order. Section 486.070 does not, however, affect any other provisions of law such as the law relating to fraudulent conveyances. See Civil Code §§ 3439–3440.1.

The amendment of Section 486.070 makes clear that a person other than the defendant is not bound by the temporary protective order even where such person knows of the order or is served with a copy of the order. This provision is based on a similar provision in the last sentence of former Section 538.1. Section 486.070 does not affect any other

provisions of law such as the law relating to fraudulent conveyances. See Civil Code §§ 3439–3440.1.

Research References

Rutter, Cal. Practice Guide: Enforcing Judgments/Debts Ch. 4-A, A. Attachment.
6 Witkin Cal. Proc. 5th Provisional Remedies § 144, in General.

§ 486.080. Service of order and documents

The temporary protective order shall be personally served on the defendant together with the documents referred to in Section 484.040. *(Added by Stats.1974, c. 1516, p. 3353, § 9, operative Jan. 1, 1977. Amended by Stats.1982, c. 1198, p. 4287, § 44, operative July 1, 1983.)*

Law Revision Commission Comments

Section 486.080 is amended to make clear that personal service on the defendant is required. Since the temporary protective order binds only the defendant (Section 486.070), it is enforced by contempt proceedings and hence must be served on the defendant rather than the defendant's attorney. See Sections 482.070 and 684.030 (16 Cal.L.Rev.Comm. Reports 1669).

Research References

Rutter, Cal. Practice Guide: Enforcing Judgments/Debts Ch. 4-A, A. Attachment.
6 Witkin Cal. Proc. 5th Provisional Remedies § 144, in General.

§ 486.090. Expiration of order

Except as otherwise provided in this title, the temporary protective order shall expire at the earliest of the following times:

(a) Forty days after the issuance of the order or, if an earlier date is prescribed by the court in the order, on such earlier date.

(b) As to specific property described in the order, when a levy of attachment upon that property is made by the plaintiff. *(Added by Stats.1974, c. 1516, p. 3353, § 9, operative Jan. 1, 1977. Amended by Stats.1976, c. 437, p. 1127, § 23.)*

Law Revision Commission Comments

Section 486.090 is based on a comparable provision in former Section 538.3. See also Section 489.320 (court order terminating temporary protective order).

The amendment to the introductory clause of Section 486.090 is technical and makes no substantive change. The effective date of the temporary protective order may be extended pursuant to Section 484.080 in the case of a continuance. The court may modify or vacate a temporary protective order pursuant to Section 486.100 (on application of defendant) or terminate the order pursuant to Section 489.320 (undertaking to secure termination). It should also be noted that, where the defendant claims an exemption for all the property described in the plaintiff's application for a writ and the plaintiff does not oppose the claim of exemption, the temporary protective order expires without a hearing or further court action. Section 484.070(f). In cases where the court determines at a hearing that property is exempt, or that a writ of attachment may not issue for any other reason, the defendant may move the court to vacate or modify the protective order pursuant to Section 486.100.

Research References

Rutter, Cal. Practice Guide: Enforcing Judgments/Debts Ch. 4-A, A. Attachment.
Miller and Starr California Real Estate § 32:37, Temporary Protective Orders.
6 Witkin Cal. Proc. 5th Provisional Remedies § 145, Expiration, Modification, and Vacation.

§ 486.100. Modification or vacation of order

Upon ex parte application of the defendant or, if the court so orders, after a noticed hearing, the court may modify or vacate the temporary protective order if it determines that such action would be in the interest of justice and equity to the parties, taking into account the effect on the defendant of the continuance of the original order, the effect on the plaintiff of modifying or vacating the order, and any other factors. *(Added by Stats.1974, c. 1516, p. 3353, § 9, operative Jan. 1, 1977.)*

Law Revision Commission Comments

Section 486.100 expands a comparable provision in former Section 538.3.

Research References

Rutter, Cal. Practice Guide: Civ. Pro. Before Trial Ch. 9(II)-D, D. Attachment.
Rutter, Cal. Practice Guide: Enforcing Judgments/Debts Ch. 4-A, A. Attachment.
Miller and Starr California Real Estate § 32:37, Temporary Protective Orders.
6 Witkin Cal. Proc. 5th Provisional Remedies § 106, in General.
6 Witkin Cal. Proc. 5th Provisional Remedies § 145, Expiration, Modification, and Vacation.

§ 486.110. Lien

(a) The service upon the defendant of a temporary protective order pursuant to Section 486.080 creates a lien upon any property, or the proceeds thereof, which is described in the order, is owned by the defendant at the time of such service, and is subject to attachment pursuant to this title. The lien continues on property subject to the lien, notwithstanding the transfer or encumbrance of the property subject to the lien, unless the person receiving the property, whether real or personal, is a person listed in Section 697.740.

(b) The lien terminates upon the date of expiration of the temporary protective order except with respect to property levied upon while the temporary protective order is in effect under a writ of attachment issued upon application of the plaintiff. *(Added by Stats.1974, c. 1516, p. 3353, § 9, operative Jan. 1, 1977. Amended by Stats.1982, c. 1198, p. 4287, § 45, operative July 1, 1983; Stats.1984, c. 538, § 2.5.)*

Law Revision Commission Comments

Section 486.110 is based on former Section 542b. The levy of a writ of attachment perfects only the lien that could be initially created by the temporary protective order; hence, levy of a writ does not affect the prior rights of bona fide purchasers or buyers in the ordinary course of business who are not bound by the temporary protective order. [See Section 697.740.] Of course, transfers subsequent to the levy are subject to the lien of attachment. See Section 488.500 (11 Cal.L.Rev.Comm. Reports 701, amended by 16 Cal.L.Rev.Comm. Reports 1671).

Subdivision (a) of Section 486.110 is amended for consistency with the Enforcement of Judgments Law. See also Section 488.500 (attachment lien). The provision formerly contained in subdivision (b) governing the interplay between the lien of the temporary protective order and the attachment lien is superseded by Section 488.500(1) (16 Cal.L.Rev.Comm. Reports 1671).

The amendment to subdivision (a) of Section 486.110 is a nonsubstantive revision to make clear that Section 697.740 applies to transferees or encumbrancers of property subject to the lien of a temporary protective order whether the property is real or personal. [17 Cal.L.Rev.Comm. Reports 975 (1984); 18 Cal.L.Rev.Comm. Reports 94 (1984)].

Research References

Rutter, Cal. Practice Guide: Civ. Pro. Before Trial Ch. 9(II)-D, D. Attachment.
Rutter, Cal. Practice Guide: Enforcing Judgments/Debts Ch. 4-A, A. Attachment.
Miller and Starr California Real Estate § 32:4, Effect.
Miller and Starr California Real Estate § 32:10, Current Attachment Law.
Miller and Starr California Real Estate § 32:34, Procedure for Issuance of the Writ.
Miller and Starr California Real Estate § 32:37, Temporary Protective Orders.
6 Witkin Cal. Proc. 5th Provisional Remedies § 144, in General.

6 Witkin Cal. Proc. 5th Provisional Remedies § 147, (S 147) Lien.
6 Witkin Cal. Proc. 5th Provisional Remedies § 179, Securities.
6 Witkin Cal. Proc. 5th Provisional Remedies § 184, Nature and Effect of Lien.

CHAPTER 7. PROPERTY SUBJECT TO ATTACHMENT

Section
487.010.   Subject property.
487.020.   Exempt property.
487.025.   Homestead; effect of recording declaration; extent of attachment lien.
487.030.   Timeliness of exemption claim.

§ 487.010. Subject property

The following property of the defendant is subject to attachment:

(a) Where the defendant is a corporation, all corporate property for which a method of levy is provided by Article 2 (commencing with Section 488.300) of Chapter 8.

(b) Where the defendant is a partnership or other unincorporated association, all partnership or association property for which a method of levy is provided by Article 2 (commencing with Section 488.300) of Chapter 8.

(c) Where the defendant is a natural person, all of the following property:

(1) Interests in real property except leasehold estates with unexpired terms of less than one year.

(2) Accounts receivable, chattel paper, and general intangibles arising out of the conduct by the defendant of a trade, business, or profession, except any such individual claim with a principal balance of less than one hundred fifty dollars ($150).

(3) Equipment.

(4) Farm products.

(5) Inventory.

(6) Final money judgments arising out of the conduct by the defendant of a trade, business, or profession.

(7) Money on the premises where a trade, business, or profession is conducted by the defendant and, except for the first one thousand dollars ($1,000), money located elsewhere than on such premises and deposit accounts, but, if the defendant has more than one deposit account or has at least one deposit account and money located elsewhere than on the premises where a trade, business, or profession is conducted by the defendant, the court, upon application of the plaintiff, may order that the writ of attachment be levied so that an aggregate amount of one thousand dollars ($1,000) in the form of such money and in such accounts remains free of levy.

(8) Negotiable documents of title.

(9) Instruments.

(10) Securities.

(11) Minerals or the like (including oil and gas) to be extracted.

(d) In the case of a defendant described in subdivision (c), community property of a type described in subdivision (c) is subject to attachment if the community property would be subject to enforcement of the judgment obtained in the action in which the attachment is sought. Unless the provision or context otherwise requires, if community property that is subject to attachment is sought to be attached:

(1) Any provision of this title that applies to the property of the defendant or to obligations owed to the defendant also

applies to the community property interest of the spouse of the defendant and to obligations owed to either spouse that are community property.

(2) Any provision of this title that applies to property in the possession or under the control of the defendant also applies to community property in the possession or under the control of the spouse of the defendant. *(Added by Stats.1974, c. 1516, p. 3353, § 9, operative Jan. 1, 1977. Amended by Stats.1976, c. 437, p. 1127, § 24; Stats.1982, c. 1198, p. 4287, § 46, operative July 1, 1983.)*

Law Revision Commission Comments

The amendment of the introductory clause of Section 487.010 makes clear that only the defendant's property is subject to attachment. All other property is exempt from attachment in the action as provided by subdivision (d) of Section 487.020. The fact that the defendant's property is subject to attachment does not in any way mean that the plaintiff may cause it to be attached in a particular action without incurring liability for abuse of process should the levy be excessive.

Subdivision (b) is amended to make clear that, where the defendant is an unincorporated association, all the property of the association for which a method of levy is provided is subject to attachment.

Subdivision (c) is amended to make clear that leasehold estates with an unexpired term of less than one year are not subject to attachment where the defendant is an individual. This amendment continues former law. See former Section 537.3(b) (6).

The provision concerning deposit accounts—formerly appearing in paragraph (2) of subdivision (c)—has been combined with the provision concerning money in paragraph (7). The effect of this amendment is that all of an individual defendant's money on the premises where he conducts a trade, business, or profession is subject to attachment. In addition, all but $1,000 of the individual's deposit accounts and money not located on the premises where he conducts a trade, business, or profession is subject to attachment. However, where the individual defendant either has more than one deposit account or has one or more deposit accounts and money not on the premises, the plaintiff must apply to the court in order to levy on such money or on the deposit accounts so that the total remaining free from attachment is $1,000. The plaintiff may apply for such order at the time of the hearing on issuance of the writ or thereafter.

Where an individual is sued for his individual liability as a partner or a member of an association, subdivision (c) provides the property of the individual which may be reached by the attachment. Consequently,...all individuals against whom attachment may properly be issued pursuant to Section 483.010 are treated the same regardless of whether their personal liability arises out of their conduct of a trade, business, or profession as a sole proprietor, a partner, or a member of an association (13 Cal.L.Rev. Comm. Reports 801, amended by 16 Cal.L.Rev.Comm. Reports 1673).

Subdivisions (a) and (b) of Section 487.010 are amended to correct cross-references. Subdivision (c) is amended to conform to Sections 481.090 ("document of title" defined), 481.115 ("general intangibles" defined), 481.117 ("instrument" defined), 481.170 ("person" defined), 488.325 (levy on minerals and the like to be extracted), and 488.480 (levy on final money judgment). Subdivision (d) is new and is analogous to Section 695.020 in the Enforcement of Judgments Law (16 Cal.L.Rev. Comm. Reports 652, 1613).

Research References

Rutter, Cal. Practice Guide: Civ. Pro. Before Trial Ch. 9(II)-D, D. Attachment.

Rutter, Cal. Practice Guide: Enforcing Judgments/Debts Ch. 4-A, A. Attachment.

Miller and Starr California Real Estate § 19:2, Lease as Personal Property or Real Property.

Miller and Starr California Real Estate § 12:63, Liability for Debts and Judgments.

Miller and Starr California Real Estate § 17:21, Minerals--In General.

Miller and Starr California Real Estate § 17:23, Minerals--Oil and Gas.

Miller and Starr California Real Estate § 31:63, Enforcement of a Money Judgment Against a Mobilehome.

Miller and Starr California Real Estate § 32:10, Current Attachment Law.

Miller and Starr California Real Estate § 32:13, Against Nonindividual Defendants.

Miller and Starr California Real Estate § 32:19, Property Subject to Attachment--In General.

Miller and Starr California Real Estate § 32:20, Individual Defendants.

Miller and Starr California Real Estate § 32:21, Nonindividual Defendants.

Miller and Starr California Real Estate § 32:25, Other Exemptions.

Miller and Starr California Real Estate § 32:26, Claim of Exemption.

Miller and Starr California Real Estate § 32:28, Attachment of Real Property.

Miller and Starr California Real Estate § 32:50, Community Property.

Miller and Starr California Real Estate § 32:62, Property of a Partner or Partnership.

Miller and Starr California Real Estate § 11:122, Recordation of the Attachment Lien.

6 Witkin Cal. Proc. 5th Provisional Remedies § 53, Nature and Scope.

6 Witkin Cal. Proc. 5th Provisional Remedies § 75, in General.

6 Witkin Cal. Proc. 5th Provisional Remedies § 76, Property of Corporation.

6 Witkin Cal. Proc. 5th Provisional Remedies § 77, Property of Partnership or Other Unincorporated Association.

6 Witkin Cal. Proc. 5th Provisional Remedies § 78, (S 78) in General.

6 Witkin Cal. Proc. 5th Provisional Remedies § 79, (S 79) Community Property.

6 Witkin Cal. Proc. 5th Provisional Remedies § 80, (S 80) Individual Liability as Partner or Member of Association.

6 Witkin Cal. Proc. 5th Provisional Remedies § 85, Property Not Made Subject to Attachment.

6 Witkin Cal. Proc. 5th Provisional Remedies § 97, Specific Description of Property.

6 Witkin Cal. Proc. 5th Provisional Remedies § 175, (S 175) in General.

6 Witkin Cal. Proc. 5th Provisional Remedies § 238, Property Subject to Attachment.

§ 487.020. Exempt property

Except as provided in paragraph (2) of subdivision (a) of Section 3439.07 of the Civil Code, the following property is exempt from attachment:

(a) All property exempt from enforcement of a money judgment.

(b) Property which is necessary for the support of a defendant who is a natural person or the family of such defendant supported in whole or in part by the defendant.

(c) "Earnings" as defined by Section 706.011.

(d) All property not subject to attachment pursuant to Section 487.010. *(Added by Stats.1974, c. 1516, p. 3354, § 9, operative Jan. 1, 1977. Amended by Stats.1976, c. 437, p. 1128, § 25; Stats.1982, c. 1198, p. 4288, § 47, operative July 1, 1983; Stats.1986, c. 383, § 7.)*

Law Revision Commission Comments

The introductory phrase of Section 487.020, reading "Notwithstanding Section 487.010," is deleted since it was confusing when read with subdivision (d); this amendment makes no substantive change. The language of subdivision (b) is amended to make clear that an individual defendant is entitled to the exemption as well as a defendant with a family and that the exemption applies where members of the defendant's family supported by the defendant are not living in the defendant's household.

Research References

Rutter, Cal. Practice Guide: Civ. Pro. Before Trial Ch. 9(II)-D, D. Attachment.

California Practice Guide: Employment Litigation Ch. 11-D, D. Payment of Wages.

Rutter, Cal. Practice Guide: Enforcing Judgments/Debts Ch. 4-A, A. Attachment.

Rutter, Cal. Practice Guide: Enforcing Judgments/Debts Ch. 6E-1, Introduction.

Rutter, Cal. Practice Guide: Enforcing Judgments/Debts Ch. 6G-23, Enforcement After Judgment Debtor's Death.

Miller and Starr California Real Estate § 6:16, Funds Held in Trust; Restrictions on Disbursement.

Miller and Starr California Real Estate § 13:48, Determination of the Liens Against the Homestead; Priorities.

Miller and Starr California Real Estate § 32:10, Current Attachment Law.

Miller and Starr California Real Estate § 32:23, Earnings.

Miller and Starr California Real Estate § 32:24, Homestead.
Miller and Starr California Real Estate § 32:25, Other Exemptions.
Miller and Starr California Real Estate § 32:27, Procedure to Claim an Exemption.
5 Witkin Cal. Proc. 5th Pleading § 1166, When Setoff is Improper.
6 Witkin Cal. Proc. 5th Provisional Remedies § 51, (S 51) Requisites of Valid Statute.
6 Witkin Cal. Proc. 5th Provisional Remedies § 80, (S 80) Individual Liability as Partner or Member of Association.
6 Witkin Cal. Proc. 5th Provisional Remedies § 81, Fraudulently Transferred Property.
6 Witkin Cal. Proc. 5th Provisional Remedies § 82, Property Exempt from Enforcement of Money Judgment.
6 Witkin Cal. Proc. 5th Provisional Remedies § 83, Property Necessary for Support.
6 Witkin Cal. Proc. 5th Provisional Remedies § 84, Earnings.
6 Witkin Cal. Proc. 5th Provisional Remedies § 85, Property Not Made Subject to Attachment.
6 Witkin Cal. Proc. 5th Provisional Remedies § 86, (S 86) Homestead.
6 Witkin Cal. Proc. 5th Provisional Remedies § 87, (S 87) Claim of Real Property Exemption.
6 Witkin Cal. Proc. 5th Provisional Remedies § 127, (S 127) Defendant's Claim of Exemption.
6 Witkin Cal. Proc. 5th Provisional Remedies § 140, (S 140) Defendant's Claim of Exemption.
6 Witkin Cal. Proc. 5th Provisional Remedies § 169, (S 169) Custody of Keeper or Levying Officer.
6 Witkin Cal. Proc. 5th Provisional Remedies § 222, (S 222) Claim of Exemption.
6 Witkin Cal. Proc. 5th Provisional Remedies § 238, Property Subject to Attachment.
3 Witkin, California Summary 10th Agency and Employment § 259, (S 259) Illustrations: Recovery Upheld.
3 Witkin, California Summary 10th Agency and Employment § 399, (S 399) Wilful Failure.
3 Witkin, California Summary 10th Agency and Employment § 400, (S 400) in General.
13 Witkin, California Summary 10th Trusts § 267, (S 267) Claims Established by Judgment.
14 Witkin, California Summary 10th Wills and Probate § 628, (S 628) Conversion of Attachment Lien to Judgment Lien.

§ 487.025. Homestead; effect of recording declaration; extent of attachment lien

(a) The recording of a homestead declaration (as defined in Section 704.910) does not limit or affect the right of a plaintiff to attach the declared homestead described in the homestead declaration, whether the homestead declaration is recorded before or after the declared homestead is attached.

(b) An attachment lien attaches to a homestead (as defined in Section 704.710) in the amount of any surplus over the total of the following:

(1) All liens and encumbrances on the homestead at the time the attachment lien is created.

(2) The homestead exemption set forth in Section 704.730.

(c) Nothing in subdivision (a) or (b) limits the right of the defendant to an exemption under subdivision (b) of Section 487.020.

(d) Notwithstanding subdivision (b), a homestead (as defined in Section 704.710) is exempt from sale to the extent provided in Section 704.800 when it is sought to be sold to enforce the judgment obtained in the action in which the attachment was obtained. *(Added by Stats.1982, c. 1198, p. 4288, § 47.5, operative July 1, 1983.)*

Research References

Rutter, Cal. Practice Guide: Enforcing Judgments/Debts Ch. 4-A, A. Attachment.
Miller and Starr California Real Estate § 13:48, Determination of the Liens Against the Homestead; Priorities.
Miller and Starr California Real Estate § 32:24, Homestead.

6 Witkin Cal. Proc. 5th Provisional Remedies § 86, (S 86) Homestead.

§ 487.030. Timeliness of exemption claim

(a) At any time prior to the entry of judgment in the action, the defendant may claim any exemption provided by subdivision (a) of Section 487.020 with respect to real property by following the procedure set forth in Article 2 (commencing with Section 703.510) of Chapter 4 of Division 2 of Title 9. A claim of exemption under this subdivision shall be denied if the claim has been denied earlier in the action.

(b) At any time prior to the entry of judgment in the action, the defendant may claim the exemption provided by subdivision (b) of Section 487.020 with respect to real property either (1) by following the procedure set forth in Article 2 (commencing with Section 703.510) of Chapter 4 of Division 2 of Title 9 or (2) by following the procedure set forth in subdivision (c) of Section 482.100 except that the requirement of showing changed circumstances under subdivision (a) of Section 482.100 does not apply. A claim of exemption under this subdivision shall be denied if the claim has been denied earlier in the action and there is no change in circumstances affecting the claim.

(c) For the purposes of this section, references in Article 2 (commencing with Section 703.510) of Chapter 4 of Division 2 of Title 9 to the "judgment debtor" shall be deemed references to the defendant, and references to the "judgment creditor" shall be deemed references to the plaintiff.

(d) Nothing in this section limits the right to claim after the entry of judgment a homestead exemption for real property under Article 4 (commencing with Section 704.710) of Chapter 4 of Division 2 of Title 9 unless prior to entry of judgment the defendant has claimed the exemption provided by subdivision (a) of Section 487.020 with respect to such property and the claim has been denied. *(Added by Stats.1982, c. 1198, p. 4289, § 48, operative July 1, 1983.)*

Law Revision Commission Comments

Section 487.030 provides a procedure for claiming an exemption for real property under this title. This procedure supplements the other provisions of this title that permit, but do not require, the defendant to claim an exemption for real property. See Sections 484.070, 484.350, 484.530, 485.610. (16 Cal.L.Rev.Comm. Reports 1678).

Research References

Rutter, Cal. Practice Guide: Enforcing Judgments/Debts Ch. 4-A, A. Attachment.
Miller and Starr California Real Estate § 32:24, Homestead.
Miller and Starr California Real Estate § 32:27, Procedure to Claim an Exemption.
Miller and Starr California Real Estate § 32:35, Noticed Hearing Procedure.
6 Witkin Cal. Proc. 5th Provisional Remedies § 87, (S 87) Claim of Real Property Exemption.
6 Witkin Cal. Proc. 5th Provisional Remedies § 140, (S 140) Defendant's Claim of Exemption.

CHAPTER 8. LEVY PROCEDURES; LIEN OF ATTACHMENT; MANAGEMENT AND DISPOSITION OF ATTACHED PROPERTY

ARTICLE 1. GENERAL PROVISIONS

Section

§ 488.010. Writ of attachment; contents

The writ of attachment shall include the following information:

(a) The date of issuance of the writ.

(b) The title of the court that issued the writ and the cause and number of the action.

(c) The name and address of the plaintiff and the name and last known address of the defendant.

(d) The amount to be secured by the attachment.

(e) A description of the property to be levied upon to satisfy the attachment. *(Added by Stats.1982, c. 1198, p. 4290, § 50, operative July 1, 1983.)*

Research References

Miller and Starr California Real Estate § 17:31, Timber.
Miller and Starr California Real Estate § 32:31, Creation and Extension of the Attachment Lien.
Miller and Starr California Real Estate § 32:35, Noticed Hearing Procedure.
Miller and Starr California Real Estate § 11:123, Relation to Subsequent Interests.
6 Witkin Cal. Proc. 5th Provisional Remedies § 53, Nature and Scope.
6 Witkin Cal. Proc. 5th Provisional Remedies § 112, in General.
6 Witkin Cal. Proc. 5th Provisional Remedies § 158, Property Governed by Enforcement of Judgments Law.

§ 488.020. Levying officer; direction of writ; instructions; duties; liability

(a) A writ of attachment shall be directed to a levying officer in the county in which property of the defendant described in the writ may be located and to any registered process server.

(b) Upon the receipt of written instructions from the plaintiff's attorney of record or, if the plaintiff has no attorney of record, from the plaintiff, the levying officer to whom the writ is directed and delivered shall levy the writ without delay in the manner provided in this chapter on the property described in the writ or so much thereof as is clearly sufficient to satisfy the amount to be secured by the attachment. The levying officer is not liable for a determination made in good faith under this subdivision.

(c) If a copy of the summons and complaint has not previously been served on the defendant, the instructions to the levying officer shall instruct the levying officer to make the service at the same time the levying officer serves the defendant with a copy of the writ of attachment. *(Added by Stats.1982, c. 1198, p. 4290, § 50, operative July 1, 1983.)*

Research References

Rutter, Cal. Practice Guide: Enforcing Judgments/Debts Ch. 4-A, A. Attachment.
6 Witkin Cal. Proc. 5th Provisional Remedies § 149, Instructions to Levying Officer.
6 Witkin Cal. Proc. 5th Provisional Remedies § 151, Levy by Levying Officer.
6 Witkin Cal. Proc. 5th Provisional Remedies § 157, Limited Liability of Officer.

§ 488.030. Plaintiff's instructions to levying officer; action and reliance by officer

(a) The plaintiff shall give the levying officer instructions in writing. The instructions shall be signed by the plaintiff's attorney of record or, if the plaintiff does not have an attorney of record, by the plaintiff. The instructions shall contain the information needed or requested by the levying officer to comply with the provisions of this title, including but not limited to:

(1) An adequate description of any property to be levied upon.

(2) A statement whether the property is a dwelling.

(3) If the property is a dwelling, whether it is real or personal property.

(b) Subject to subdivision (c), the levying officer shall act in accordance with the written instructions to the extent the actions are taken in conformance with the provisions of this title.

(c) Except to the extent the levying officer has actual knowledge that the information is incorrect, the levying officer may rely on any information contained in the written instructions. *(Added by Stats.1982, c. 1198, p. 4290, § 50, operative July 1, 1983.)*

Law Revision Commission Comments

Section 488.030 supersedes a portion of the instruction provision formerly included in Section 488.010(a) and is drawn from Section 687.010 (Enforcement of Judgments Law). See also Section 488.040 (instructions to include name and address of persons to be served) and Section 488.020 (instructions concerning service of copy of summons and complaint) (16 Cal.L.Rev.Comm. Reports 1682).

Research References

Rutter, Cal. Practice Guide: Enforcing Judgments/Debts Ch. 4-A, A. Attachment.
Miller and Starr California Real Estate § 32:33, Release of Attachment Lien.
6 Witkin Cal. Proc. 5th Provisional Remedies § 149, Instructions to Levying Officer.
6 Witkin Cal. Proc. 5th Provisional Remedies § 151, Levy by Levying Officer.
6 Witkin Cal. Proc. 5th Provisional Remedies § 152, Levy by Registered Process Server.

§ 488.040. Persons to be served; names and addresses; reliance

(a) If the levying officer is required by any provision of this title to serve any writ, order, notice, or other paper on any person, the plaintiff shall include in the instructions to the levying officer the correct name and address of the person. The plaintiff shall use reasonable diligence to ascertain the correct name and address of the person.

(b) Unless the levying officer has actual knowledge that the name or address included in the instructions is incorrect, the levying officer shall rely on the instructions in serving the writ, order, notice, or other paper on the person. *(Added by Stats.1982, c. 1198, p. 4290, § 50, operative July 1, 1983.)*

Law Revision Commission Comments

Section 488.040 supersedes a portion of the instruction provision formerly included in Section 488.010(a) and is drawn from Section 684.130 (Enforcement of Judgments Law) (16 Cal.L.Rev.Comm. Reports 1683).

Research References

Rutter, Cal. Practice Guide: Enforcing Judgments/Debts Ch. 4-A, A. Attachment.
6 Witkin Cal. Proc. 5th Provisional Remedies § 149, Instructions to Levying Officer.
6 Witkin Cal. Proc. 5th Provisional Remedies § 151, Levy by Levying Officer.

§ 488.050.   Deposits for costs

(a) Except as otherwise provided by law:

(1) As a prerequisite to the performance by the levying officer of a duty under this title, the plaintiff shall deposit a sum of money with the levying officer sufficient to pay the costs of performing the duty.

(2) As a prerequisite to the taking of property into custody by the levying officer under this chapter, whether by keeper or otherwise, the plaintiff shall deposit with the levying officer a sum of money sufficient to pay the costs of taking the property and keeping it safely for a period not to exceed 15 days. If continuation of the custody of the property is required, the levying officer shall, from time to time, demand orally or in writing that the plaintiff deposit additional amounts to cover estimated costs for periods not to exceed 30 days each. A written demand may be mailed or delivered to the plaintiff. The plaintiff has not less than three business days after receipt of the demand within which to comply with the demand. If the amount demanded is not paid within the time specified in the oral or written demand, the levying officer shall release the property.

(b) The levying officer is not liable for failure to take or hold property unless the plaintiff has complied with the provisions of this section. *(Added by Stats.1982, c. 1198, p. 4291, § 50, operative July 1, 1983.)*

Law Revision Commission Comments

Subdivision (a) of Section 488.050 supersedes former Section 488.050 and conforms to Section 685.100 (Enforcement of Judgments Law). See the Comment to Section 685.100. The provision of former Section 488.050 requiring release of property to the defendant is not continued. Property is released to the proper person as prescribed by Section 488.730. See also Section 481.055 ("costs" defined). Subdivision (b) continues the substance of former subdivision (a) of Section 488.060 (16 Cal.L.Rev. Comm. Reports 1684).

Research References

Rutter, Cal. Practice Guide: Enforcing Judgments/Debts Ch. 4-A, A. Attachment.
6 Witkin Cal. Proc. 5th Provisional Remedies § 150, Deposit to Cover Expenses.
6 Witkin Cal. Proc. 5th Provisional Remedies § 157, Limited Liability of Officer.

§ 488.060.   Notice of attachment

The notice of attachment shall inform the person notified of all of the following:

(a) The capacity in which the person is notified.

(b) The specific property which is sought to be attached.

(c) The person's rights under the attachment, including the right to make a third-party claim pursuant to Division 4 (commencing with Section 720.010) of Title 9.

(d) The person's duties under the attachment. *(Added by Stats.1982, c. 1198, p. 4291, § 50, operative July 1, 1983.)*

Law Revision Commission Comments

Section 488.060 continues the substance of former Section 488.020. The former section has been revised to correct a cross-reference and to make other nonsubstantive changes. The notice of attachment also must identify any person (other than the defendant) in whose name real property or growing crops, timber to be cut, or minerals and the like stands upon the records of the county. See Section 700.015 (adopted by reference by Section 488.315) and Section 700.020 (adopted by reference by Section 488.325). [See also Section 489.230 (notice to defendant that undertaking has been filed and right to object to undertaking) (16 Cal.L.Rev.Comm. Reports 1684)].

Research References

6 Witkin Cal. Proc. 5th Provisional Remedies § 153, Notice and Service.

§ 488.065.   Notice of attachment; copy of notice served upon third party

A copy of the original notice of attachment which has been served upon a third party holding the property sought to be attached, if served upon the defendant or any other party, shall suffice as the notice of attachment to that person. *(Added by Stats.1984, c. 759, § 1.)*

Research References

Miller and Starr California Real Estate § 32:31, Creation and Extension of the Attachment Lien.
6 Witkin Cal. Proc. 5th Provisional Remedies § 153, Notice and Service.

§ 488.070.   Property located in a private place of defendant

If a writ of attachment has been issued and personal property sought to be attached under the writ is located in a private place of the defendant:

(a) The levying officer shall comply with the provisions of Section 699.030.

(b) The plaintiff may obtain the relief provided under Section 699.030 in the manner and subject to the requirements of that section. *(Added by Stats.1982, c. 1198, p. 4291, § 50, operative July 1, 1983.)*

Law Revision Commission Comments

Section 488.070 is new and adopts by reference the procedure provided in the Enforcement of Judgments Law (16 Cal.L.Rev.Comm. Reports 1685).

Research References

Rutter, Cal. Practice Guide: Enforcing Judgments/Debts Ch. 4-A, A. Attachment.
6 Witkin Cal. Proc. 5th Provisional Remedies § 154, Custody.

§ 488.080.   Levy of writ by registered process server; types of property

(a) A registered process server may levy under a writ of attachment on the following types of property:

(1) Real property, pursuant to Section 488.315.

(2) Growing crops, timber to be cut, or minerals or the like (including oil and gas) to be extracted or accounts receivable resulting from the sale thereof at the wellhead or minehead, pursuant to Section 488.325.

(3) Personal property in the custody of a levying officer, pursuant to Section 488.355.

(4) Equipment of a going business, pursuant to Section 488.375.

(5) Motor vehicles, vessels, mobilehomes, or commercial coaches used as equipment of a going business, pursuant to Section 488.385.

(6) Farm products or inventory of a going business, pursuant to Section 488.405.

(7) Personal property used as a dwelling, pursuant to subdivision (a) of Section 700.080.

(8) Deposit accounts, pursuant to Section 488.455.

(9) Property in a safe-deposit box, pursuant to Section 488.460.

(10) Accounts receivable or general intangibles, pursuant to Section 488.470.

(11) Final money judgments, pursuant to Section 488.480.

(12) Interest of a defendant in personal property in the estate of a decedent, pursuant to Section 488.485.

(b) Before levying under the writ of attachment, the registered process server shall deposit a copy of the writ with the levying officer and pay the fee provided by Section 26721 of the Government Code.

(c) If a registered process server levies on property pursuant to subdivision (a), the registered process server shall do both of the following:

(1) Comply with the applicable levy, posting, and service provisions of Article 2 (commencing with Section 488.300).

(2) Request any third person served to give a garnishee's memorandum to the levying officer in compliance with Section 488.610 on a form provided by the registered process server.

(d) Within five court days after levy under this section, all of the following shall be filed with the levying officer:

(1) The writ of attachment.

(2) A proof of service by the registered process server stating the manner of levy performed.

(3) Proof of service of the copy of the writ and notice of attachment on other persons, as required by Article 2 (commencing with Section 488.300).

(4) Instructions in writing, as required by the provisions of Section 488.030.

(e) If the fee provided by Section 26721 of the Government Code has been paid, the levying officer shall perform all other duties under the writ as if the levying officer had levied under the writ and shall return the writ to the court. If the registered process server does not comply with subdivisions (b) and (d), the levy is ineffective and the levying officer is not required to perform any duties under the writ and may issue a release for any property sought to be attached. The levying officer is not liable for actions taken in conformance with the provisions of this title in reliance on information provided to the levying officer under subdivision (d), except to the extent that the levying officer has actual knowledge that the information is incorrect. Nothing in this subdivision limits any liability the plaintiff or registered process server may have if the levying officer acts on the basis of incorrect information provided under subdivision (d).

(f) The fee for services of a registered process server under this section shall be allowed as a recoverable cost pursuant to Section 1033.5. *(Added by Stats.1982, c. 1198, p. 4309, § 50.5, operative July 1, 1983. Amended by Stats.1983, c. 155, § 5, eff. June 30, 1983, operative July 1, 1983; Stats.1984, c. 538, § 3; Stats.1984, c. 759, § 2.5; Stats.1987, c. 1080, § 2; Stats.2007, c. 15 (A.B.859), § 1.)*

Law Revision Commission Comments

Section 488.080 is new and is drawn from Section 699.080 (Enforcement of Judgments Law). See the Comment to Section 699.080. See also Section 481.205 ("registered process server" defined) (16 Cal.L.Rev. Comm. Reports 701).

A new subdivision (b) is added to Section 488.080 to require a registered process server to file a copy of the writ with the appropriate levying officer before attempting to levy. This requirement gives the levying officer an early opportunity to establish a file which facilitates handling exemption claims and third-party claims, garnishees' memorandums, and payments by garnishees or by the defendant. Subdivision (e) is amended for consistency with new subdivision (b). [16 Cal.L.Rev.Comm. Reports 2175 (1982)].

Research References

Rutter, Cal. Practice Guide: Enforcing Judgments/Debts Ch. 4-A, A. Attachment.
Miller and Starr California Real Estate § 32:31, Creation and Extension of the Attachment Lien.
6 Witkin Cal. Proc. 5th Provisional Remedies § 99, (S 99) Costs and Attorneys' Fees.
6 Witkin Cal. Proc. 5th Provisional Remedies § 152, Levy by Registered Process Server.
6 Witkin Cal. Proc. 5th Provisional Remedies § 157, Limited Liability of Officer.

§ 488.090.   Method of taking property into custody

Except as otherwise provided by statute, where the method of levy upon property requires that property be taken into custody or where the levying officer is otherwise directed to take property into custody, the levying officer may do so by any of the following methods:

(a) Removing the property to a place of safekeeping.

(b) Installing a keeper.

(c) Otherwise obtaining possession or control of the property. *(Added by Stats.1982, c. 1198, p. 4292, § 50, operative July 1, 1983.)*

Law Revision Commission Comments

Section 488.090 supersedes former Section 488.045 and conforms to Section 687.030 (Enforcement of Judgments Law) (16 Cal.L.Rev.Comm. Reports 701).

Research References

Rutter, Cal. Practice Guide: Enforcing Judgments/Debts Ch. 4-A, A. Attachment.
6 Witkin Cal. Proc. 5th Provisional Remedies § 154, Custody.
6 Witkin Cal. Proc. 5th Provisional Remedies § 160, (S 160) Current Attachment Law.

§ 488.100.   Lien for levying officer's costs

The levying officer has a special lien, dependent upon possession, on personal property levied upon in the amount of the levying officer's costs for which an advance has not been made. *(Added by Stats.1982, c. 1198, p. 4293, § 50, operative July 1, 1983.)*

Law Revision Commission Comments

Section 488.100, which continues the substance of a portion of former Civil Code Section 3057, is the same as Section 687.050 (Enforcement of Judgments Law) (16 Cal.L.Rev.Comm. Reports 701).

Research References

Rutter, Cal. Practice Guide: Enforcing Judgments/Debts Ch. 4-A, A. Attachment.
6 Witkin Cal. Proc. 5th Provisional Remedies § 150, Deposit to Cover Expenses.

§ 488.110.   Third person claiming interest in attached property

A third person shall claim an interest in property attached in the manner provided for third-party claims under Division 4 (commencing with Section 720.010) of Title 9. *(Added by Stats.1982, c. 1198, p. 4293, § 50, operative July 1, 1983.)*

Law Revision Commission Comments

Section 488.110 continues the substance of former Section 488.090 (16 Cal.L.Rev.Comm. Reports 701).

Research References

Rutter, Cal. Practice Guide: Enforcing Judgments/Debts Ch. 4-A, A. Attachment.
6 Witkin Cal. Proc. 5th Provisional Remedies § 156, Third-Party Claims.
6 Witkin Cal. Proc. 5th Provisional Remedies § 178, Deposit Accounts and Boxes in Third Person's Name.

§ 488.120. Attachment lien; effect of failure to post, serve, or mail writ and notice of attachment

In any case where property has been levied upon and, pursuant to a levy, a copy of the writ of attachment and a notice of attachment are required by statute to be posted or to be served on or mailed to the defendant or other person, failure to post, serve, or mail the copy of the writ and the notice does not affect the attachment lien created by the levy. *(Added by Stats.1982, c. 1198, p. 4293, § 50, operative July 1, 1983.)*

Law Revision Commission Comments

Section 488.120 is drawn from Section 699.550 (Enforcement of Judgments Law). See the Comment to Section 699.550. Section 488.120 continues the substance of portions of former Sections 488.310–488.430 (16 Cal.L.Rev.Comm. Reports 701).

Research References

Rutter, Cal. Practice Guide: Enforcing Judgments/Debts Ch. 4-A, A. Attachment.
Miller and Starr California Real Estate § 32:31, Creation and Extension of the Attachment Lien.
6 Witkin Cal. Proc. 5th Provisional Remedies § 153, Notice and Service.

§ 488.130. Return of writ of attachment; report; inventory

(a) The levying officer to whom the writ of attachment is delivered shall return the writ to the court from which the writ issued, together with a report of the levying officer's actions. The return shall be made promptly in accordance with the plaintiff's instructions given to the levying officer but in no event later than 60 days after the levying officer receives the writ.

(b) The levying officer shall make a full inventory of property attached and return the inventory with the writ. *(Added by Stats.1982, c. 1198, p. 4293, § 50, operative July 1, 1983.)*

Law Revision Commission Comments

Subdivision (a) of Section 488.130 continues the substance of former Section 488.070 and is consistent with a portion of Section 699.560 (Enforcement of Judgments Law). Subdivision (b) continues the substance of a provision that appeared in former Section 488.080 (16 Cal.L.Rev.Comm. Reports 701).

Research References

Rutter, Cal. Practice Guide: Enforcing Judgments/Debts Ch. 4-A, A. Attachment.
6 Witkin Cal. Proc. 5th Provisional Remedies § 155, Return and Inventory.

§ 488.140. Liability of levying officer or process server

(a) The levying officer or registered process server is not liable for actions taken in conformance with the provisions of this title, including actions taken in conformance with the provisions of this title in reliance on information contained in the written instructions of the plaintiff except to the extent the levying officer or registered process server has actual knowledge that the information is incorrect. Nothing in this subdivision limits any liability the plaintiff may have if the levying officer or registered process server acts on the basis of incorrect information given in the written instructions.

(b) Unless the levying officer is negligent in the care or handling of the property, the levying officer is not liable to either the plaintiff or the defendant for loss by fire, theft, injury, or damage of any kind to personal property while (1) in the possession of the levying officer either in a warehouse or other storage place or in the custody of a keeper or (2) in transit to or from a warehouse or other storage place. *(Added by Stats.1982, c. 1198, p. 4293, § 50, operative July 1, 1983. Amended by Stats.1983, c. 155, § 5.5, eff. June 30, 1983, operative July 1, 1983.)*

Law Revision Commission Comments

Section 488.140 is consistent with Section 687.040 (Enforcement of Judgments Law). Subdivision (b) continues the substance of former Section 488.060(b) (16 Cal.L.Rev.Comm. Reports 701).

Research References

Rutter, Cal. Practice Guide: Enforcing Judgments/Debts Ch. 4-A, A. Attachment.
Miller and Starr California Real Estate § 17:59, Subsequent Parties; Notice of Prior Interests--Encumbrancers.
6 Witkin Cal. Proc. 5th Provisional Remedies § 152, Levy by Registered Process Server.
6 Witkin Cal. Proc. 5th Provisional Remedies § 157, Limited Liability of Officer.

ARTICLE 2. METHODS OF LEVY

Section

488.485.   Decedents' estates; defendants' interests in personal property.

§ 488.300. Definitions

If the method of levy under a writ of execution is incorporated by this article, for the purposes of this article references in Article 4 (commencing with Section 700.010) of Chapter 3 of Division 2 of Title 9 to:

(a) "Judgment creditor" shall be deemed references to the plaintiff.

(b) "Judgment debtor" shall be deemed references to the defendant.

(c) "Notice of levy" shall be deemed references to a notice of attachment.

(d) "Writ" shall be deemed references to a writ of attachment. *(Added by Stats.1982, c. 1198, p. 4293, § 50, operative July 1, 1983.)*

Law Revision Commission Comments

Section 488.300 facilitates the incorporation by reference in this article of the applicable method of levy under a writ of execution provided in the Enforcement of Judgments Law (16 Cal.L.Rev.Comm. Reports 701).

Research References

Rutter, Cal. Practice Guide: Civ. Pro. Before Trial Ch. 9(II)-D, D. Attachment.

Rutter, Cal. Practice Guide: Enforcing Judgments/Debts Ch. 4-A, A. Attachment.

Rutter, Cal. Practice Guide: Enforcing Judgments/Debts Ch. 6D-4, Levy on Specific Property.

Miller and Starr California Real Estate § 32:21, Nonindividual Defendants.

6 Witkin Cal. Proc. 5th Provisional Remedies § 76, Property of Corporation.

6 Witkin Cal. Proc. 5th Provisional Remedies § 77, Property of Partnership or Other Unincorporated Association.

6 Witkin Cal. Proc. 5th Provisional Remedies § 152, Levy by Registered Process Server.

6 Witkin Cal. Proc. 5th Provisional Remedies § 158, Property Governed by Enforcement of Judgments Law.

6 Witkin Cal. Proc. 5th Provisional Remedies § 174, Accounts Receivable and General Intangibles.

6 Witkin Cal. Proc. 5th Provisional Remedies § 238, Property Subject to Attachment.

§ 488.305. Levy; service of writ and notice of attachment

At the time of levy pursuant to this article or promptly thereafter, the levying officer shall serve a copy of the writ of attachment and a notice of attachment on the defendant. *(Added by Stats.1982, c. 1198, p. 4293, § 50, operative July 1, 1983.)*

Law Revision Commission Comments

Section 488.305 is drawn from Section 700.010 (Enforcement of Judgments Law). Section 488.305 continues the requirement of former Sections 488.310–488.430 that the defendant be given notice of attachment. The requirement of former law that notice be given within 15 days (see former Section 488.310) or 45 days (see former Section 488.330) is superseded by the requirement of Section 488.305 that notice be given promptly after levy. For the manner of service, see Section 482.070. Under Section 482.070, service may be made personally or by mail (16 Cal.L.Rev.Comm. Reports 701).

Research References

Rutter, Cal. Practice Guide: Enforcing Judgments/Debts Ch. 4-A, A. Attachment.

Miller and Starr California Real Estate § 32:31, Creation and Extension of the Attachment Lien.

Miller and Starr California Real Estate § 11:122, Recordation of the Attachment Lien.

6 Witkin Cal. Proc. 5th Provisional Remedies § 153, Notice and Service.

§ 488.315. Real property

To attach real property, the levying officer shall comply with Section 700.015 and the recorder shall index the copy of the writ of attachment and a notice of attachment as provided in that section. *(Added by Stats.1982, c. 1198, p. 4294, § 50, operative July 1, 1983.)*

Law Revision Commission Comments

Section 488.315 is new and supersedes former Section 488.310. See also Sections 481.203 ("real property" defined), 488.300 (incorporated terms). For the effect of the attachment lien created under this section, see Section 488.500(b) (16 Cal.L.Rev.Comm. Reports 701).

Research References

Rutter, Cal. Practice Guide: Enforcing Judgments/Debts Ch. 4-A, A. Attachment.

Miller and Starr California Real Estate § 11:6, Instruments Subject to Recording--List of Recordable Documents.

Miller and Starr California Real Estate § 32:28, Attachment of Real Property.

Miller and Starr California Real Estate § 32:31, Creation and Extension of the Attachment Lien.

Miller and Starr California Real Estate § 11:122, Recordation of the Attachment Lien.

6 Witkin Cal. Proc. 5th Provisional Remedies § 152, Levy by Registered Process Server.

6 Witkin Cal. Proc. 5th Provisional Remedies § 158, Property Governed by Enforcement of Judgments Law.

6 Witkin Cal. Proc. 5th Provisional Remedies § 161, (S 161) in General.

§ 488.325. Growing crops; timber to be cut; minerals, etc., to be extracted or accounts receivable from sale thereof at wellhead or minehead

To attach (1) growing crops, (2) timber to be cut, or (3) minerals or the like (including oil and gas) to be extracted or accounts receivable resulting from the sale thereof at the wellhead or minehead, the levying officer shall comply with Section 700.020 and the recorder shall index the copy of the writ of attachment and a notice of attachment as provided in that section. *(Added by Stats.1982, c. 1198, p. 4294, § 50, operative July 1, 1983.)*

Law Revision Commission Comments

Section 488.325 is new and supersedes a portion of former Section 488.360(c). See also Section 488.300 (incorporated terms). The provisions in Section 488.325 relating to attachment of minerals or the like (including oil and gas) to be extracted and accounts receivable resulting from the sale thereof at the wellhead or minehead were not found in prior attachment law. See the Comment to Section 700.020. Once the crops are harvested, the timber is cut, or the minerals are extracted, the property may be attached pursuant to Sections 488.335–488.365 (tangible personal property), 488.395 (keeper for farm products), or 488.405 (lien on farm products), whichever is appropriate. The levying officer or a receiver may cultivate, care for, harvest, pack, and sell the attached property, if necessary, pursuant to court order under Section 488.700. See also Sections 488.120 (effect of failure to give notice of attachment), 488.305 (service of notice of attachment on defendant), 482.070 (manner of service) (16 Cal.L.Rev.Comm. Reports 701).

Research References

Rutter, Cal. Practice Guide: Enforcing Judgments/Debts Ch. 4-A, A. Attachment.

Miller and Starr California Real Estate § 17:21, Minerals--In General.

Miller and Starr California Real Estate § 17:23, Minerals--Oil and Gas.

Miller and Starr California Real Estate § 17:31, Timber.

Miller and Starr California Real Estate § 17:33, Crops--Encumbrance of Crops.

Miller and Starr California Real Estate § 32:31, Creation and Extension of the Attachment Lien.

6 Witkin Cal. Proc. 5th Provisional Remedies § 152, Levy by Registered Process Server.

6 Witkin Cal. Proc. 5th Provisional Remedies § 173, Crops, Timber, and Minerals.

§ 488.335. Personal property in defendant's possession or control

Unless another method of attachment is provided by this article, to attach tangible personal property in the possession or under the control of the defendant, the levying officer shall take the property into custody. *(Added by Stats.1982, c. 1198, p. 4294, § 50, operative July 1, 1983.)*

Law Revision Commission Comments

Section 488.335 is drawn from Section 700.030 (Enforcement of Judgments Law) and continues the substance of former Section 488.320(a). See also Sections 482.070 (manner of service), 488.090 (manner of taking property into custody), 488.120 (effect of failure to give notice of attachment), 488.305 (service of notice of attachment on defendant) (16 Cal.L.Rev.Comm. Reports 701).

Research References

Rutter, Cal. Practice Guide: Enforcing Judgments/Debts Ch. 4-A, A. Attachment.
6 Witkin Cal. Proc. 5th Provisional Remedies § 114, (S 114) Turnover Order.
6 Witkin Cal. Proc. 5th Provisional Remedies § 160, (S 160) Current Attachment Law.
6 Witkin Cal. Proc. 5th Provisional Remedies § 161, (S 161) in General.
6 Witkin Cal. Proc. 5th Provisional Remedies § 173, Crops, Timber, and Minerals.

§ 488.345. Personal property in third person's possession or control

Unless another method of attachment is provided by this article, to attach tangible personal property in the possession or under the control of a third person, the levying officer shall comply with Section 700.040. *(Added by Stats.1982, c. 1198, p. 4294, § 50, operative July 1, 1983.)*

Law Revision Commission Comments

Section 488.345 supersedes subdivisions (a) and (d) of former Section 488.330. The method of levy provided by Section 700.040(a) continues the substance of former Section 488.330(a). Subdivision (b) of Section 700.040 supersedes former Section 488.330(d). See also Sections 482.070 (manner of service), 488.120 (effect of failure to give notice of attachment), 488.300 (incorporated terms), 488.305 (service of notice of attachment on defendant) (16 Cal.L.Rev.Comm. Reports 701).

Research References

Rutter, Cal. Practice Guide: Enforcing Judgments/Debts Ch. 4-A, A. Attachment.
6 Witkin Cal. Proc. 5th Provisional Remedies § 158, Property Governed by Enforcement of Judgments Law.

§ 488.355. Personal property in levying officer's custody

(a) To attach personal property in the custody of a levying officer, the plaintiff or levying officer shall comply with subdivision (a) of Section 700.050.

(b) The levying officer having custody of the property shall comply with the writs in the order they are received and is not subject to the provisions of Article 4 (commencing with Section 488.600). *(Added by Stats.1982, c. 1198, p. 4294, § 50, operative July 1, 1983.)*

Law Revision Commission Comments

Section 488.355 is new. Subdivision (b) is drawn from Section 700.050(b). See also Sections 482.070 (manner of service), 488.120 (effect of failure to give notice of attachment), 488.300 (incorporated terms), 488.305 (service of notice of attachment on defendant) (16 Cal.L.Rev. Comm. Reports 701).

Research References

Rutter, Cal. Practice Guide: Enforcing Judgments/Debts Ch. 4-A, A. Attachment.
6 Witkin Cal. Proc. 5th Provisional Remedies § 152, Levy by Registered Process Server.
6 Witkin Cal. Proc. 5th Provisional Remedies § 158, Property Governed by Enforcement of Judgments Law.

§ 488.365. Goods in possession of bailee not issuing a negotiable document of title

To attach goods in the possession of a bailee (as defined in Section 7102 of the Commercial Code) other than one who has issued a negotiable document of title therefor, the levying officer shall comply with Section 700.060. *(Added by Stats.1982, c. 1198, p. 4294, § 50, operative July 1, 1983.)*

Law Revision Commission Comments

Section 488.365 is new. Attachment of property in the possession of a third person was formerly governed by Section 488.330. See also Sections 482.070 (manner of service), 488.120 (effect of failure to give notice of attachment), 488.300 (incorporated terms), 488.305 (service of notice of attachment on defendant) (16 Cal.L.Rev.Comm. Reports 701).

Research References

Rutter, Cal. Practice Guide: Enforcing Judgments/Debts Ch. 4-A, A. Attachment.
6 Witkin Cal. Proc. 5th Provisional Remedies § 158, Property Governed by Enforcement of Judgments Law.

§ 488.375. Equipment of going business; possession or control by defendant

(a) Except as provided by Section 488.385, to attach equipment of a going business in the possession or under the control of the defendant, the levying officer shall file with the office of the Secretary of State a notice of attachment, in the form prescribed by the Secretary of State, which shall contain all of the following:

(1) The name and mailing address of the plaintiff.

(2) The name and last known mailing address of the defendant.

(3) The title of the court where the action is pending and the cause and number of the action.

(4) A description of the specific property attached.

(5) A statement that the plaintiff has acquired an attachment lien on the specified property of the defendant.

(b) Upon presentation of a notice of attachment under this section for filing, and tender of the filing fee to the office of the Secretary of State, the notice of attachment shall be filed, marked, and indexed in the same manner as a financing statement. The fee for filing in the office of the Secretary of State is the same as the fee for filing a financing statement in the standard form.

(c) Upon the request of any person, the Secretary of State shall issue a certificate showing whether there is on file in that office on the date and hour stated therein any notice of attachment filed against the equipment of a particular person named in the request. If a notice of attachment is on file, the certificate shall state the date and hour of filing of each such notice and any notice affecting any such notice of attachment and the name and address of the plaintiff. Upon request, the Secretary of State shall furnish a copy of any notice of attachment or notice affecting a notice of attachment. The certificate shall be issued as part of a combined certificate pursuant to Section 9528 of the Commercial Code, and the fee for the certificate and copies shall be in accordance with that section.

(d) The fee for filing, indexing, and furnishing filing data for a notice of extension of attachment is the same as the fee for a continuation statement under Section 9525 of the Commercial Code. The fee for filing, indexing, and furnishing filing data for a notice of release of attachment is the same as the fee for a statement of release under Section 9525 of the Commercial Code.

(e) If property subject to an attachment lien under this section becomes a fixture (as defined in Section 9313 of the Commercial Code), the attachment lien under this section is extinguished. *(Added by Stats.1982, c. 1198, p. 4294, § 50, operative July 1, 1983. Amended by Stats.1983, c. 155, § 6, eff. June 30, 1983, operative July 1, 1983; Stats.1988, c. 393, § 7; Stats.1999, c. 991 (S.B.45), § 13.4, operative July 1, 2001.)*

Law Revision Commission Comments

Subdivision (a) of Section 488.375 continues the substance of former Section 488.340(a). See Section 481.100 ("equipment" defined). As under former law, if there is doubt whether the property is equipment or a fixture, the plaintiff may desire to attach pursuant to both this section and Section 488.315 (real property). Since this section is limited to the attachment of equipment of a going business, Section 488.335 (tangible personal property in defendant's possession) provides the appropriate method of levy where the business has failed or ceased to operate. For the effect of a lien created under this section, see Section 488.500(c). See also Sections 488.120 (effect of failure to give notice of attachment), 488.305 (service of notice of attachment on defendant).

Subdivision (b) is drawn from Section 697.570 (filing notice of judgment lien on personal property) and supersedes a portion of former Section 488.340(c). Subdivision (c) continues the substance of the first, second, and fourth sentences of former Section 488.340(d) and is drawn from Section 697.580. See also Com. Code § 9409 (combined certificate). Subdivision (d) supersedes a portion of former Section 488.340(c) and is drawn in part from a portion of Section 697.650(c). Subdivisions (b), (c), and (d) incorporate the fee provisions in the Commercial Code rather than provide specific fees as did former Section 488.340 for the sake of consistency (16 Cal.L.Rev.Comm. Reports 701).

Subdivision (e) is added to Section 488.375 to make clear that the lien on equipment is extinguished if the equipment becomes a fixture. This subdivision is the same as Sections 488.385 (attachment lien on vehicle, vessel, mobilehome, or commercial coach that is equipment), 488.405(e) (attachment lien on inventory), and 697.530(e) (judgment lien on certain business property). [16 Cal.L.Rev.Comm. Reports 2175 (1982)].

Research References

Rutter, Cal. Practice Guide: Enforcing Judgments/Debts Ch. 4-A, A. Attachment.

Miller and Starr California Real Estate § 11:122, Recordation of the Attachment Lien.

6 Witkin Cal. Proc. 5th Provisional Remedies § 152, Levy by Registered Process Server.

6 Witkin Cal. Proc. 5th Provisional Remedies § 161, (S 161) in General.

6 Witkin Cal. Proc. 5th Provisional Remedies § 162, (S 162) Lien.

6 Witkin Cal. Proc. 5th Provisional Remedies § 163, (S 163) Fees.

4 Witkin, California Summary 10th Secured Transactions in Personal Property § 93, (S 93) Acknowledgments and Responses to Requests.

§ 488.385. Vehicle or vessel; equipment of going business; possession or control by defendant

(a) To attach a vehicle or vessel for which a certificate of ownership has been issued by the Department of Motor Vehicles, or a mobilehome or commercial coach for which a certificate of title has been issued by the Department of Housing and Community Development, which is equipment of a going business in the possession or under the control of the defendant, the levying officer shall file with the appropriate department a notice of attachment, in the form prescribed by the appropriate department, which shall contain all of the following:

(1) The name and mailing address of the plaintiff.

(2) The name and last known mailing address of the defendant.

(3) The title of the court where the action is pending and the cause and number of the action.

(4) A description of the specific property attached.

(5) A statement that the plaintiff has acquired an attachment lien on the specific property of the defendant.

(b) Upon presentation of a notice of attachment, notice of extension, or notice of release under this section for filing and tender of the filing fee to the appropriate department, the notice shall be filed and indexed. The fee for filing and indexing the notice is fifteen dollars ($15).

(c) Upon the request of any person, the department shall issue its certificate showing whether there is on file in that department on the date and hour stated therein any notice of attachment filed against the property of a particular person named in the request. If a notice of attachment is on file, the certificate shall state the date and hour of filing of each such notice of attachment and any notice affecting any such notice of attachment and the name and address of the plaintiff. The fee for the certificate issued pursuant to this subdivision is fifteen dollars ($15). Upon request, the department shall furnish a copy of any notice of attachment or notice affecting a notice of attachment for a fee of one dollar ($1) per page.

(d) If property subject to an attachment lien under this section becomes a fixture (as defined in paragraph (41) of subdivision (a) of Section 9102 of the Commercial Code), the attachment lien under this section is extinguished. *(Added by Stats.1982, c. 1198, p. 4295, § 50, operative July 1, 1983. Amended by Stats.1983, c. 155, § 7, eff. June 30, 1983, operative July 1, 1983; Stats.1999, c. 991 (S.B.45), § 13.5, operative July 1, 2001; Stats.2003, c. 719 (S.B.1055), § 1.)*

Law Revision Commission Comments

Subdivision (a) of Section 488.385 continues the substance of former Section 488.350(a) and recognizes the transfer of jurisdiction over mobilehomes and commercial coaches to the Department of Housing and Community Development. See, e.g., Health and Safety Code §§ 18075, 18075.29, 18076.21, 18077.1–18077.3. See also Veh. Code §§ 6300, 6301 (motor vehicles), 9919, 9920 (vessels). For the effect of a lien created under this section, see Section 488.500(d). Section 488.385 governs attachment of vehicles, vessels, mobilehomes, and commercial coaches that are equipment; this section does not deal with inventory (see Sections 488.395 and 488.405) or such items that are neither equipment nor inventory. See Sections 481.100 ("equipment" defined), 488.335 (levy on tangible personal property in defendant's possession), 488.345 (levy on tangible personal property in third person's possession), 488.355 (levy on property in custody of levying officer). See also Sections 487.010 (property subject to attachment), 488.120 (effect of failure to give notice of attachment), 488.305 (service of notice of attachment on defendant), 488.425 (notice to legal owner), 488.500 (attachment lien).

Subdivision (b) is drawn from Section 697.570 (filing notice of judgment lien on personal property) and continues the first sentence of former Section 488.350(f). Subdivision (c) continues the substance of the second, third, and fourth sentences of former Section 488.350(f), but the fee for a certificate under subdivision (c) is raised from $2 to $3 (16 Cal.L.Rev. Comm. Reports 701).

Subdivision (d) is added to Section 488.385 to make clear that the lien on equipment under this section is extinguished if the equipment, such as a mobilehome, becomes a fixture. This subdivision is the same as Sections 488.375(e) (attachment lien on equipment generally), 488.405(e) (attachment lien on inventory), and 697.530(e) (judgment lien on certain business property). [16 Cal.L.Rev.Comm. Reports 2175 (1982)].

Research References

Rutter, Cal. Practice Guide: Enforcing Judgments/Debts Ch. 4-A, A. Attachment.

Miller and Starr California Real Estate § 17:59, Subsequent Parties; Notice of Prior Interests--Encumbrancers.

Miller and Starr California Real Estate § 31:63, Enforcement of a Money Judgment Against a Mobilehome.

Miller and Starr California Real Estate § 32:20, Individual Defendants.

Miller and Starr California Real Estate § 32:31, Creation and Extension of the Attachment Lien.
6 Witkin Cal. Proc. 5th Provisional Remedies § 152, Levy by Registered Process Server.
6 Witkin Cal. Proc. 5th Provisional Remedies § 161, (S 161) in General.
6 Witkin Cal. Proc. 5th Provisional Remedies § 164, (S 164) in General.
6 Witkin Cal. Proc. 5th Provisional Remedies § 165, (S 165) Lien.
6 Witkin Cal. Proc. 5th Provisional Remedies § 166, (S 166) Fees.
6 Witkin Cal. Proc. 5th Provisional Remedies § 167, (S 167) Rights of Bona Fide Purchaser.
6 Witkin Cal. Proc. 5th Provisional Remedies § 171, Lien.

§ 488.395. Farm products or inventory of going business; possession or control by defendant

Except as specified in subdivision (e) and as provided by Sections 488.325 and 488.405:

(a) To attach farm products or inventory of a going business in the possession or under the control of the defendant, the levying officer shall place a keeper in charge of the property for the period prescribed by subdivisions (b) and (c). During the keeper period, the business may continue to operate in the ordinary course of business provided that all sales are final and are for cash or its equivalent. For the purpose of this subdivision, a check is the equivalent of cash. The levying officer is not liable for accepting payment in the form of a cash equivalent. The keeper shall take custody of the proceeds from all sales unless otherwise directed by the plaintiff.

(b) Subject to subdivision (c), the period during which the business may continue to operate under the keeper is:

(1) Ten days, if the defendant is a natural person and the writ of attachment has been issued ex parte pursuant to Article 3 (commencing with Section 484.510) of Chapter 4 or pursuant to Chapter 5 (commencing with Section 485.010).

(2) Two days, in cases not described in paragraph (1).

(c) Unless some other disposition is agreed upon by the plaintiff and the defendant, the levying officer shall take the farm products or inventory into exclusive custody at the earlier of the following times:

(1) At any time the defendant objects to placement of a keeper in charge of the business.

(2) At the conclusion of the applicable period prescribed by subdivision (b).

(d) A defendant described in paragraph (1) of subdivision (b) may claim an exemption pursuant to subdivision (b) of Section 487.020 by following the procedure set forth in subdivision (c) of Section 482.100 except that the requirement of showing changed circumstances under subdivision (a) of Section 482.100 does not apply. Upon a showing that the property is exempt pursuant to subdivision (b) of Section 487.020, the court shall order the release of the exempt property and may make such further order as the court deems appropriate to protect against frustration of the collection of the plaintiff's claim. The order may permit the plaintiff to attach farm products or inventory of the going business and proceeds or after-acquired property, or both, by filing pursuant to Section 488.405 and may provide reasonable restrictions on the disposition of the property previously attached.

(e) This section does not apply to the placement of a keeper in a business for the purpose of attaching tangible personal property consisting solely of money or equivalent proceeds of sales, which shall be conducted in the same manner as provided in Section 700.070. *(Added by Stats.1982, c. 1198, p. 4296, § 50, operative July 1, 1983. Amended by Stats.1996, c. 1159 (A.B. 3471), § 10.)*

Law Revision Commission Comments

Section 488.395 supersedes subdivisions (a) and (b) of former Section 488.360. See Sections 481.110 ("farm products" defined), 481.120 ("inventory" defined). The introductory clause of Section 488.395 recognizes exceptions to the method of levy provided by this section. Section 488.325 provides the exclusive method of attaching growing crops and timber to be cut. Section 488.405 provides an alternative method of attaching farm products and inventory and their cash proceeds by filing with the Secretary of State.

Subdivisions (a)–(c) of Section 488.395 continue the substance of former Section 488.360(a), except that subdivision (b) provides new rules governing the length of the keeper period. Former Section 488.360(a) provided a 10-day keeper in all cases, whereas subdivision (b) of this section limits the 10-day keeper to defendants who may have the need to claim an exemption, i.e., natural persons who have not had the opportunity at a noticed hearing to claim the necessities exemption provided by Section 487.020(b). Subdivision (d) continues the substance of former Section 488.360(b) but incorporates the procedure of Section 482.100(c) (16 Cal.L.Rev.Comm. Reports 701).

Research References

Rutter, Cal. Practice Guide: Enforcing Judgments/Debts Ch. 4-A, A. Attachment.
Miller and Starr California Real Estate § 32:31, Creation and Extension of the Attachment Lien.
6 Witkin Cal. Proc. 5th Provisional Remedies § 157, Limited Liability of Officer.
6 Witkin Cal. Proc. 5th Provisional Remedies § 164, (S 164) in General.
6 Witkin Cal. Proc. 5th Provisional Remedies § 168, (S 168) in General.
6 Witkin Cal. Proc. 5th Provisional Remedies § 169, (S 169) Custody of Keeper or Levying Officer.
6 Witkin Cal. Proc. 5th Provisional Remedies § 173, Crops, Timber, and Minerals.

§ 488.405. Farm products or inventory of going business; possession or control by defendant; alternative attachment method

(a) This section provides an alternative method of attaching farm products or inventory of a going business in the possession or under the control of the defendant, but this section does not apply to property described in Section 488.325. This section applies if the plaintiff instructs the levying officer to attach the farm products or inventory under this section.

(b) To attach under this section farm products or inventory of a going business in the possession or under the control of the defendant, the levying officer shall file a notice of attachment with the Secretary of State.

(c) Except as provided in subdivisions (d) and (e), the filing of the notice of attachment gives the plaintiff an attachment lien on all of the following:

(1) The farm products or inventory described in the notice.

(2) Identifiable cash proceeds (as that term is used in Section 9315 of the Commercial Code).

(3) If permitted by the writ of attachment or court order, after-acquired property.

(d) The attachment lien created by the filing of the notice of attachment under this section does not extend to either of the following:

(1) A vehicle or vessel required to be registered with the Department of Motor Vehicles or a mobilehome or commercial coach required to be registered pursuant to the Health and Safety Code.

(2) The inventory of a retail merchant held for sale except to the extent that the inventory of the retail merchant consists of durable goods having a unit retail value of at least five hundred dollars ($500). For the purposes of this paragraph, "retail merchant" does not include (A) a person whose sales for resale exceeded 75 percent in dollar volume of the person's total sales of all goods during the 12 months preceding the filing of the

notice of attachment or (B) a cooperative association organized pursuant to Chapter 1 (commencing with Section 54001) of Division 20 of the Food and Agricultural Code (agricultural cooperative associations) or Part 3 (commencing with Section 13200) of Division 3 of Title 1 of the Corporations Code (Fish Marketing Act).

(e) If property subject to an attachment lien under this section becomes a fixture (as defined in paragraph (41) of subdivision (a) of Section 9102 of the Commercial Code), the attachment lien under this section is extinguished.

(f) The notice of attachment shall be in the form prescribed by the Secretary of State and shall contain all of the following:

(1) The name and mailing address of the plaintiff.

(2) The name and last known mailing address of the defendant.

(3) The title of the court where the action is pending and the cause and number of the action.

(4) A description of the farm products and inventory attached.

(5) A statement that the plaintiff has acquired an attachment lien on the described property and on identifiable cash proceeds (as that term is used in Section 9315 of the Commercial Code) and, if permitted by the writ of attachment or court order, on after-acquired property.

(g) Upon presentation of a notice of attachment under this section for filing and tender of the filing fee to the office of the Secretary of State, the notice of attachment shall be filed, marked, and indexed in the same manner as a financing statement. The fee for filing in the office of the Secretary of State is the same as the fee for filing a financing statement in the standard form.

(h) Upon the request of any person, the Secretary of State shall issue a certificate showing whether there is on file in that office on the date and hour stated therein any notice of attachment filed against the farm products or inventory of a particular person named in the request. If a notice of attachment is on file, the certificate shall state the date and hour of filing of each such notice of attachment and any notice affecting any such notice of attachment and the name and address of the plaintiff. Upon request, the Secretary of State shall furnish a copy of any notice of attachment or notice affecting a notice of attachment. The certificate shall be issued as part of a combined certificate pursuant to Section 9528 of the Commercial Code, and the fee for the certificate and copies shall be in accordance with that section.

(i) The fee for filing, indexing, and furnishing filing data for a notice of extension of attachment is the same as the fee for a continuation statement under Section 9525 of the Commercial Code. The fee for filing, indexing, and furnishing filing data for a notice of release of attachment is the same as the fee for a statement of release under Section 9519 of the Commercial Code. *(Added by Stats.1982, c. 1198, p. 4297, § 50, operative July 1, 1983. Amended by Stats.1988, c. 393, § 8; Stats.1999, c. 991 (S.B.45), § 14, operative July 1, 2001.)*

Law Revision Commission Comments

Section 488.405 supersedes former Section 488.360(c). See Sections 481.110 ("farm products" defined), 481.120 ("inventory" defined). This section provides an alternate to the method of attaching farm products and inventory under Section 488.395 (keeper levy). As under former Section 488.360(c), Section 488.405 provides the plaintiff with a floating lien on the defendant's farm products or inventory, cash proceeds, and after-acquired property. Subdivision (c) provides for the automatic coverage of identifiable cash proceeds, consistent with Commercial Code Sections 9203(3) and 9306(3)(b). Former Section 488.360(c) required specific authorization in a writ or order before identifiable cash proceeds

were covered by the lien. Subdivisions (d) and (e) are provisions new to the Attachment Law that prescribe limitations on the property covered by the lien. These limitations are the same as those applicable to a judgment lien on personal property. See Section 697.530(d), (e). For a limitation on the coverage of the lien in insolvency proceedings, see Section 697.620 (incorporated by Section 488.500(c)). See also Sections 488.120 (effect of failure to give notice of attachment), 488.305 (service of notice of attachment on defendant).

Subdivision (f) continues the substance of former Section 488.360(c) pertaining to the form of the notice of attachment and is analogous to Section 697.550 (contents of notice of judgment lien on personal property).

Subdivision (g) continues the substance of a portion of the sixth sentence of former Section 488.360(c) and is analogous to Section 697.570 (filing notice of judgment lien on personal property). Subdivision (h) continues the substance of the seventh, eighth, and tenth sentences of former Section 488.360(c) and is analogous to Section 697.580. See also Com. Code § 9409 (Combined certificate). Subdivision (i) supersedes a portion of the sixth sentence of former Section 488.360(c) and is drawn in part from a portion of Section 697.650(c). Subdivisions (g), (h), and (i) incorporate the fee provisions in the Commercial Code rather than provide specific fees as did former Section 488.360(c) (16 Cal.L.Rev. Comm. Reports 701).

Research References

Rutter, Cal. Practice Guide: Enforcing Judgments/Debts Ch. 4-A, A. Attachment.
Miller and Starr California Real Estate § 32:31, Creation and Extension of the Attachment Lien.
Miller and Starr California Real Estate § 11:122, Recordation of the Attachment Lien.
6 Witkin Cal. Proc. 5th Provisional Remedies § 152, Levy by Registered Process Server.
6 Witkin Cal. Proc. 5th Provisional Remedies § 164, (S 164) in General.
6 Witkin Cal. Proc. 5th Provisional Remedies § 168, (S 168) in General.
6 Witkin Cal. Proc. 5th Provisional Remedies § 169, (S 169) Custody of Keeper or Levying Officer.
6 Witkin Cal. Proc. 5th Provisional Remedies § 170, in General.
6 Witkin Cal. Proc. 5th Provisional Remedies § 171, Lien.
6 Witkin Cal. Proc. 5th Provisional Remedies § 172, Fees.
6 Witkin Cal. Proc. 5th Provisional Remedies § 173, Crops, Timber, and Minerals.
4 Witkin, California Summary 10th Secured Transactions in Personal Property § 93, (S 93) Acknowledgments and Responses to Requests.

§ 488.415. Personal property used as dwelling

To attach personal property used as a dwelling, the levying officer shall comply with Section 700.080. *(Added by Stats.1982, c. 1198, p. 4298, § 50, operative July 1, 1983.)*

Law Revision Commission Comments

Section 488.415 is new. See also Sections 482.070 (manner of service), 488.120 (effect of failure to give notice of attachment), 488.300 (incorporated terms), 488.305 (service of notice of attachment on defendant) (16 Cal.L.Rev.Comm. Reports 701).

Research References

Rutter, Cal. Practice Guide: Enforcing Judgments/Debts Ch. 4-A, A. Attachment.
Miller and Starr California Real Estate § 31:63, Enforcement of a Money Judgment Against a Mobilehome.
Miller and Starr California Real Estate § 32:31, Creation and Extension of the Attachment Lien.
6 Witkin Cal. Proc. 5th Provisional Remedies § 158, Property Governed by Enforcement of Judgments Law.

§ 488.425. Vehicles or vessels; certificates of ownership or title in effect

If a vehicle or vessel is attached and a certificate of ownership has been issued by the Department of Motor Vehicles for the vehicle or vessel and the certificate of ownership is still in effect, or if a mobilehome or commercial coach is attached and a certificate of title has been issued by the Department of Housing and Community Development for the mobilehome or commercial coach and the certificate of title is still in effect, the levying officer shall comply with Section 700.090. *(Added by Stats.1982, c. 1198, p. 4298, § 50, operative July 1, 1983.)*

Law Revision Commission Comments

Section 488.425 supersedes former Section 488.350(c). See also Sections 482.070 (manner of service), 488.120 (effect of failure to give notice of attachment), 488.300 (incorporated terms), 488.305 (service of notice of attachment on defendant) (16 Cal.L.Rev.Comm. Reports 701).

Research References

Miller and Starr California Real Estate § 31:63, Enforcement of a Money Judgment Against a Mobilehome.

Miller and Starr California Real Estate § 32:31, Creation and Extension of the Attachment Lien.

6 Witkin Cal. Proc. 5th Provisional Remedies § 158, Property Governed by Enforcement of Judgments Law.

6 Witkin Cal. Proc. 5th Provisional Remedies § 164, (S 164) in General.

§ 488.435. Chattel papers

(a) To attach chattel paper, the levying officer shall comply with Section 700.100.

(b) In addition to any other rights created by a levy on chattel paper, the levy creates a lien on the defendant's rights in specific goods subject to the chattel paper. *(Added by Stats.1982, c. 1198, p. 4298, § 50, operative July 1, 1983.)*

Law Revision Commission Comments

Section 488.435 supersedes former Section 488.380. See Section 481.040 ("chattel paper" defined). Subdivision (a) of Section 700.100 continues the method of levy provided by former Section 488.380(a). Subdivision (b) of Section 700.100 supersedes former Section 488.380(c) and provides new preconditions for giving notice of attachment to the account debtor. Subdivision (b) of Section 488.435 is the same as Section 700.100(c). See also Sections 482.070 (manner of service), 488.120 (effect of failure to give notice of attachment), 488.300 (incorporated terms), 488.305 (service of notice of attachment on defendant) (16 Cal.L.Rev. Comm. Reports 701).

Research References

Rutter, Cal. Practice Guide: Enforcing Judgments/Debts Ch. 4-A, A. Attachment.

6 Witkin Cal. Proc. 5th Provisional Remedies § 114, (S 114) Turnover Order.

6 Witkin Cal. Proc. 5th Provisional Remedies § 158, Property Governed by Enforcement of Judgments Law.

§ 488.440. Instruments

To attach an instrument, the levying officer shall comply with Section 700.110. *(Added by Stats.1982, c. 1198, p. 4298, § 50, operative July 1, 1983.)*

Law Revision Commission Comments

Section 488.440 supersedes the portions of former Section 488.400 relating to attachment of negotiable instruments. See Section 481.117 ("instrument" defined). Subdivision (a) of Section 700.110 continues the method of levy provided by former Section 488.400(a). Subdivision (b) of Section 700.110 supersedes former Section 488.400(c) and provides new preconditions for giving notice of attachment to the obligor. See also Sections 482.070 (manner of service), 488.120 (effect of failure to give notice of attachment), 488.300 (incorporated terms), 488.305 (service of notice of attachment on defendant). (16 Cal.L.Rev.Comm. Reports 701).

Research References

Rutter, Cal. Practice Guide: Enforcing Judgments/Debts Ch. 4-A, A. Attachment.

Miller and Starr California Real Estate § 32:61, Property Interests Subject to Execution.

6 Witkin Cal. Proc. 5th Provisional Remedies § 114, (S 114) Turnover Order.

6 Witkin Cal. Proc. 5th Provisional Remedies § 158, Property Governed by Enforcement of Judgments Law.

6 Witkin Cal. Proc. 5th Provisional Remedies § 175, (S 175) in General.

§ 488.445. Negotiable documents of title

To attach a negotiable document of title, the levying officer shall comply with Section 700.120. *(Added by Stats.1982, c. 1198, p. 4298, § 50, operative July 1, 1983.)*

Law Revision Commission Comments

Section 488.445 continues the substance of a portion of former Section 488.400(a) relating to the method of attachment of negotiable documents. See also Sections 481.090 ("document of title" defined), 482.070 (manner of service), 488.120 (effect of failure to give notice of attachment), 488.300 (incorporated terms), 488.305 (service of notice of attachment on defendant) (16 Cal.L.Rev.Comm. Reports 701).

Research References

Rutter, Cal. Practice Guide: Enforcing Judgments/Debts Ch. 4-A, A. Attachment.

6 Witkin Cal. Proc. 5th Provisional Remedies § 114, (S 114) Turnover Order.

6 Witkin Cal. Proc. 5th Provisional Remedies § 158, Property Governed by Enforcement of Judgments Law.

§ 488.450. Securities

To attach a security, the levying officer shall comply with Section 8112 of the Commercial Code. The legal process referred to in Section 8112 of the Commercial Code means the legal process required by the state in which the chief executive office of the issuer of the security is located and, where that state is California, means personal service by the levying officer of a copy of the writ of attachment and notice of attachment on the person who is to be served. *(Added by Stats.1982, c. 1198, p. 4298, § 50, operative July 1, 1983. Amended by Stats.1984, c. 927, § 1; Stats.1985, c. 41, § 1; Stats.1996, c. 497 (S.B.1591), § 1.5, operative Jan. 1, 1997.)*

Law Revision Commission Comments

Section 488.450 supersedes former Section 488.410 and is drawn from Section 700.130 (Enforcement of Judgments Law). See Section 481.210 ("security" defined). The substance of former Section 488.410 relating to attachment of securities is prescribed in Commercial Code Section 8317. See also Sections 482.070 (manner of service), 488.120 (effect of failure to give notice of attachment), 488.305 (service of notice of attachment on defendant) (16 Cal.L.Rev.Comm. Reports 701).

Section 488.450 is amended to correct a technical defect. Chapter 927 of the Statutes of 1984 amended Section 488.450 in connection with a revision of the Commercial Code provisions relating to uncertificated securities. The second sentence, as added to Section 488.450, erroneously referred to a writ of execution and notice of levy whereas the correct reference under the Attachment Law is to a writ of attachment and notice of attachment. [18 Cal.R.Rev.Comm. Reports 361 (1985)].

Research References

Rutter, Cal. Practice Guide: Enforcing Judgments/Debts Ch. 4-A, A. Attachment.

6 Witkin Cal. Proc. 5th Provisional Remedies § 114, (S 114) Turnover Order.

6 Witkin Cal. Proc. 5th Provisional Remedies § 179, Securities.

§ 488.455. Deposit accounts

(a) Subject to Sections 488.465 and 684.115, to attach a deposit account, the levying officer shall personally serve a copy of the writ of attachment and a notice of attachment on the financial institution with which the deposit account is maintained.

(b) The attachment lien that arises upon service of a writ of attachment and notice of attachment reaches only amounts in a deposit account at the time of service on the financial institution, including the amount of any deposit not yet finally collected, unless the deposit is returned unpaid to the financial institution.

(c) The levying officer shall serve a copy of the writ of attachment and a notice of attachment on any third person in whose name any deposit account described therein stands. That service shall be made personally or by mail as follows:

(1) At the time of levy or promptly thereafter, if the party seeking the levy informs the levying officer of that person and his, her, or its residence or business address.

(2) Promptly following the levying officer's receipt of a garnishee's memorandum if service was not accomplished pursuant to paragraph (1), if the garnishee's memorandum identifies that person and his, her, or its residence or business address.

(d) The financial institution shall not honor a withdrawal request or a check or other order for the payment of money from the deposit account if presentation of that withdrawal request or item to the financial institution occurs during the time the attachment lien is in effect unless, following that withdrawal or payment, sufficient funds are available to cover the levy. For these purposes, a withdrawal from the deposit account to cover the financial institution's standard fee or charge for processing the levy shall not be considered a payment of money from the account in violation of this subdivision.

(e) During the time the attachment lien is in effect, the financial institution is not liable to any person for any of the following:

(1) Performance of the duties of a garnishee under the levy.

(2) Nonpayment of a check or other order for the payment or transfer of money drawn or presented against the deposit account if the nonpayment is pursuant to the requirements of subdivision (d).

(3) Refusal to pay a withdrawal from the deposit account if the refusal is pursuant to the requirements of subdivision (d).

(f) For the purposes of this section, none of the following is a third person in whose name the deposit account stands:

(1) A person who is only a person named as the beneficiary of a Totten trust account.

(2) A person who is only a payee designated in a pay-on-death provision in an account pursuant to Section 18318.5 of the Financial Code or Section 5140 of the Probate Code, or other similar provision.

(3) A person who is only acting in a representative or custodial capacity with respect to benefits paid or payable by the United States government. Rather, accounts maintained by the representative or custodian shall be deemed to stand in that beneficiary's name, and the amounts therein shall be covered by a levy against that beneficiary.

(g) For purposes of this section, final payment of a deposit shall be deemed to have occurred in accordance with Section 4215 or 11210 of the Commercial Code or with automated clearinghouse or Federal Reserve System rule, regulation, operating circular, or similar governing document, as applicable to the deposit. If, for any reason, a deposit is returned by the financial institution upon which it is drawn, that deposit shall not be deemed finally collected for purposes of this subdivision regardless of any later payment by the financial institution upon which the deposit is drawn.

(h) When a deposit account has been attached, as an alternative to paying the amount of the deposit account that is attached to the levying officer as required by Section 488.600, the financial institution may continue to hold the deposit account until the deposit account is levied upon after judgment in the action or is earlier released, the deposit account to be held in one of the following manners:

(1) If the entire deposit account is attached, the financial institution may hold the deposit account on the terms applicable before the attachment, subject to the requirements of subdivision (d).

(2) If less than the entire deposit account is attached:

(A) With the consent of the defendant, and any third person in whose name the deposit account stands, the financial institution may hold in the deposit account on the same terms an amount larger than the attached amount as necessary to avoid a penalty or a reduction of the rate of interest.

(B) If the defendant, and any third person in whose name the deposit account stands, do not consent as provided in subparagraph (A), the financial institution may hold the attached amount on the same terms affecting the deposit account before the attachment, subject to the requirements of subdivision (d).

(3) The financial institution may hold the attached deposit account in any other manner agreed upon by the plaintiff, the defendant, and any third person in whose name the deposit account stands.

(i) Subdivision (h) does not prevent a financial institution that is holding an attached deposit account as provided in subdivision (h) from paying the attached amount to the levying officer before the time the financial institution otherwise is required to pay the amount under subdivision (h). *(Added by Stats.1982, c. 1198, p. 4299, § 50, operative July 1, 1983. Amended by Stats.1983, c. 155, § 8, eff. June 30, 1983, operative July 1, 1983; Stats.1984, c. 538, § 4; Stats.2002, c. 664 (A.B.3034), § 47; Stats.2003, c. 110 (A.B.690), § 1; Stats.2012, c. 484 (A.B.2364), § 2.)*

Law Revision Commission Comments

Section 488.455 supersedes former Section 488.390 and is drawn from Section 700.140 (Enforcement of Judgments Law). Subdivision (a) continues the substance of former Section 488.390(a) relating to the method of attachment of deposit accounts. A deposit account evidenced by a negotiable certificate of deposit is a negotiable instrument and may be attached pursuant to Section 488.440, not pursuant to this section. See Sections 481.080 (incorporating definition of "deposit account" in Commercial Code Section 9105) and 481.117 (incorporating definition of "instrument" in Commercial Code Section 9105 which includes a "negotiable instrument" as defined by Commercial Code Section 3104).

Subdivision (b) continues the substance of a portion of former Section 488.390(b). See also Sections 482.070 (manner of service), 488.120 (effect of failure to give notice of attachment), 488.305 (service of notice of attachment on defendant).

Subdivision (c) is a new provision that was not found in former attachment law. It is comparable to Section 700.140(c). The introductory clause of subdivision (c) recognizes that special rules apply where the deposit account stands in the name of a third person.

Subdivision (d) continues the substance of former Section 488.390(c) (16 Cal.L.Rev.Comm. Reports 701).

Research References

Rutter, Cal. Practice Guide: Civ. Pro. Before Trial Ch. 9(II)-D, D. Attachment.

Rutter, Cal. Practice Guide: Enforcing Judgments/Debts Ch. 4-A, A. Attachment.

20 NO. 2 Miller & Starr, California Real Estate Newsalert 1, Policy Considerations Trump Statutory Construction, Giving Stop Notice Claimants a Big Advantage Over Construction Lenders.

6 Witkin Cal. Proc. 5th Provisional Remedies § 152, Levy by Registered Process Server.

6 Witkin Cal. Proc. 5th Provisional Remedies § 175, (S 175) In General.

6 Witkin Cal. Proc. 5th Provisional Remedies § 176, (S 176) Retention of Account by Financial Institution.

6 Witkin Cal. Proc. 5th Provisional Remedies § 178, Deposit Accounts and Boxes in Third Person's Name.

§ 488.460. Property in safe-deposit box; written notice to judgment creditors

(a) Subject to Sections 488.465 and 684.115, to attach property in a safe-deposit box, the levying officer shall personally serve a copy of the writ of attachment and a notice of attachment on the financial institution with which the safe-deposit box is maintained.

(b) At the time of levy or promptly thereafter, the levying officer shall serve a copy of the writ of attachment and a notice of attachment on any third person in whose name the safe-deposit box stands.

(c) During the time the attachment lien is in effect, the financial institution may not permit the removal of any of the contents of the safe-deposit box except as directed by the levying officer.

(d) Upon receipt of a garnishee's memorandum from the financial institution, as required by Section 488.610, indicating a safe-deposit box is under levy, the levying officer shall promptly mail a written notice to the judgment creditor demanding an additional fee as required by Section 26723 of the Government Code, plus the costs to open the safe-deposit box and seize and store the contents. The levying officer shall release the levy on the safe-deposit box if the plaintiff does not pay the required fee, plus costs, within three business days plus the extended time period specified in subdivision (a) of Section 1013 for service by mail by the levying officer.

(e) The levying officer may first give the person in whose name the safe-deposit box stands an opportunity to open the safe-deposit box to permit the removal pursuant to the attachment of the attached property. The financial institution may refuse to permit the forcible opening of the safe-deposit box to permit the removal of the attached property unless the plaintiff or levying officer pays in advance the cost of forcibly opening the safe-deposit box and of repairing any damage caused thereby.

(f) During the time the attachment lien is in effect, the financial institution is not liable to any person for any of the following:

(1) Performance of the duties of a garnishee under the attachment.

(2) Refusal to permit access to the safe-deposit box by the person in whose name it stands.

(3) Removal of any of the contents of the safe-deposit box pursuant to the attachment.

(g) If the levying officer removes any property from the safe-deposit box to satisfy the levy, but allows other property to remain in the safe-deposit box, the attachment lien is released automatically with respect to any property that remains in the safe-deposit box. *(Added by Stats.1982, c. 1198, p. 4299, § 50, operative July 1, 1983. Amended by Stats.1984, c. 538, § 5; Stats.2003, c. 888 (A.B.394), § 1; Stats.2012, c. 484 (A.B.2364), § 3.)*

Law Revision Commission Comments

Section 488.460 is new and is drawn from Section 700.150 (Enforcement of Judgments Law). Former law providing methods of attachment did not provide special rules governing attachment of property in a safe deposit box, unless the box was rented to a person other than the defendant. See former Section 489.240. See also Sections 482.070 (manner of service), 488.120 (effect of failure to give notice of attachment), 488.305 (service of notice of attachment on defendant) (16 Cal.L.Rev.Comm. Reports 701).

Research References

Rutter, Cal. Practice Guide: Enforcing Judgments/Debts Ch. 4-A, A. Attachment.
6 Witkin Cal. Proc. 5th Provisional Remedies § 152, Levy by Registered Process Server.
6 Witkin Cal. Proc. 5th Provisional Remedies § 177, Safe Deposit Boxes.

6 Witkin Cal. Proc. 5th Provisional Remedies § 178, Deposit Accounts and Boxes in Third Person's Name.

§ 488.465. Deposit accounts or safe-deposit boxes standing in name of person other than defendant; levy authorized by court order; levies in which court order not required; obligation of financial institution

(a) Except as provided in subdivision (b), a deposit account or safe-deposit box standing in the name of a person other than the defendant, either alone or together with other third persons, is not subject to levy under Section 488.455 or 488.460 unless the levy is authorized by court order. The levying officer shall serve a copy of the court order on the third person at the time the copy of the writ of attachment and the notice of attachment are served on the third person.

(b) A court order is not required as a prerequisite to levy on a deposit account or safe-deposit box standing in the name of any of the following:

(1) The defendant, whether alone or together with third persons.

(2) The defendant's spouse, whether alone or together with other third persons. An affidavit showing that the person in whose name the account stands is the defendant's spouse shall be delivered to the financial institution at the time of levy.

(3) A fictitious business name if an unexpired fictitious business name statement filed pursuant to Chapter 5 (commencing with Section 17900) of Part 3 of Division 7 of the Business and Professions Code lists as the persons doing business under the fictitious business name either (A) the defendant or (B) the defendant's spouse or (C) the defendant and the defendant's spouse, but does not list any other person. A copy of a fictitious business name statement, certified as provided in Section 17926 of the Business and Professions Code, that satisfies these requirements shall be delivered to the financial institution at the time of levy and, if a person other than the defendant is listed in the statement, an affidavit showing that the other person is the defendant's spouse shall also be delivered to the financial institution at the time of levy.

(c) In any case where a deposit account in the name of a person other than the defendant, whether alone or together with the defendant, is levied upon, the financial institution shall not pay to the levying officer the amount levied upon until being notified to do so by the levying officer. The levying officer may not require the financial institution to pay the amount levied upon until the expiration of 15 days after service of notice of attachment on the third person. *(Added by Stats.1984, c. 538, § 6.3.)*

Research References

Rutter, Cal. Practice Guide: Enforcing Judgments/Debts Ch. 4-A, A. Attachment.
6 Witkin Cal. Proc. 5th Provisional Remedies § 175, (S 175) in General.
6 Witkin Cal. Proc. 5th Provisional Remedies § 177, Safe Deposit Boxes.
6 Witkin Cal. Proc. 5th Provisional Remedies § 178, Deposit Accounts and Boxes in Third Person's Name.

§ 488.470. Account receivable or general intangible

(a) Unless another method of attachment is provided by this article, to attach an account receivable or general intangible, the levying officer shall personally serve a copy of the writ of attachment and a notice of attachment on the account debtor.

(b) If an attachment is made under subdivision (a) and payments on the account receivable or general intangible are made to a person other than the defendant (whether pursuant to a security agreement, assignment for collection, or otherwise), the levying officer shall, if so instructed by the plaintiff, personally serve a copy of the writ of attachment and a notice of attachment on such third person. Service of the copy of the writ and notice of attachment on the third person is an attachment of any amounts owed to the defendant by the third person. *(Added by Stats.1982, c. 1198, p. 4301, § 50, operative July 1, 1983.)*

Law Revision Commission Comments

Section 488.470 supersedes former Section 488.370 and is drawn from Section 700.170 (Enforcement of Judgments Law). Section 488.470 uses the term "general intangible" in place of "chose in action" which was used in former Section 488.370. See Section 481.115 ("general intangibles" defined). Subdivision (a) continues the method of levy provided by former Section 488.370(a). Subdivision (b) supersedes a portion of former Section 488.370(b) providing for service on a co-obligee. See also Sections 482.070 (manner of service), 488.120 (effect of failure to give notice of attachment), 488.305 (service of notice of attachment on defendant) (16 Cal.L.Rev.Comm. Reports 701).

Research References

Rutter, Cal. Practice Guide: Civ. Pro. Before Trial Ch. 9(II)-D, D. Attachment.

Rutter, Cal. Practice Guide: Enforcing Judgments/Debts Ch. 4-A, A. Attachment.

20 NO. 2 Miller & Starr, California Real Estate Newsalert 1, Policy Considerations Trump Statutory Construction, Giving Stop Notice Claimants a Big Advantage Over Construction Lenders.

6 Witkin Cal. Proc. 5th Provisional Remedies § 152, Levy by Registered Process Server.

6 Witkin Cal. Proc. 5th Provisional Remedies § 174, Accounts Receivable and General Intangibles.

§ 488.475. Property that is the subject of a pending action or special proceeding

(a) The following property may be attached pursuant to this article notwithstanding that the property levied upon is the subject of a pending action or special proceeding:

(1) Real property.

(2) Growing crops, timber to be cut, or minerals or the like (including oil and gas) to be extracted or accounts receivable resulting from the sale thereof at the wellhead or minehead.

(3) Tangible personal property in the possession or under the control of the defendant or in the custody of a levying officer.

(4) The interest of a defendant in personal property in the estate of a decedent, whether the interest arises by testate or intestate succession.

(b) Except as provided in subdivision (a), attachment of property that is the subject of an action or special proceeding pending at the time of the attachment is not effective.

(c) If attachment is attempted but is ineffective under subdivision (b) and the levying officer has requested a garnishee's memorandum under Section 488.610 in connection with the ineffective attachment, the garnishee's memorandum shall include the following information in addition to that required by Section 488.610:

(1) A statement that the attachment of the property is not effective because the property is the subject of a pending action or special proceeding.

(2) The title of the court and the cause and number of the pending action or proceeding.

(d) For the purpose of this section, an action or proceeding is pending from the time the action or proceeding is commenced until judgment has been entered and the time for appeal has expired or, if an appeal is filed, until the appeal has been finally determined.

(e) Nothing in this section affects or limits the right of the plaintiff to obtain a lien pursuant to Article 3 (commencing with Section 491.410) of Chapter 11. *(Added by Stats.1982, c. 1198, p. 4301, § 50, operative July 1, 1983.)*

Law Revision Commission Comments

Section 488.475 is new and is drawn from Section 700.180 (Enforcement of Judgments Law). See also Sections 491.410–491.460 (lien in pending action or proceeding) (16 Cal.L.Rev.Comm. Reports 701).

Research References

Rutter, Cal. Practice Guide: Enforcing Judgments/Debts Ch. 4-A, A. Attachment.

Miller and Starr California Real Estate § 32:28, Attachment of Real Property.

6 Witkin Cal. Proc. 5th Provisional Remedies § 179, Securities.

6 Witkin Cal. Proc. 5th Provisional Remedies § 182, Property Subject of Pending Action.

6 Witkin Cal. Proc. 5th Provisional Remedies § 194, (S 194) Content and Form.

§ 488.480. Final money judgment

(a) As used in this section, "final money judgment" means a money judgment after the time for appeal from the judgment has expired or, if an appeal is filed, after the appeal has been finally determined.

(b) To attach a final money judgment, the levying officer shall file a copy of the writ of attachment and a notice of attachment with the clerk of the court that entered the final money judgment. The court clerk shall endorse upon the judgment a statement of the existence of the attachment lien and the time it was created. If an abstract of the judgment is issued, it shall include a statement of the attachment lien in favor of the plaintiff.

(c) At the time of levy or promptly thereafter, the levying officer shall serve a copy of the writ of attachment and a notice of attachment on the judgment debtor obligated to pay the final money judgment attached. *(Added by Stats.1982, c. 1198, p. 4302, § 50, operative July 1, 1983. Amended by Stats.1984, c. 538, § 6.5.)*

Law Revision Commission Comments

Section 488.480 supersedes former Section 488.420 and is drawn from Section 700.190 (Enforcement of Judgments Law). Subdivision (a) continues the substance of former Section 488.420(c). Subdivision (b) supersedes former Section 488.420(a) which required both filing and service on the defendant's judgment debtor to attach a judgment. Subdivision (c) provides for notice to the defendant's judgment debtor, but such notice is not a prerequisite of a valid attachment. See also Sections 482.070 (manner of service), 488.120 (effect of failure to give notice of attachment), 488.305 (service of notice of attachment on defendant) (16 Cal.L.Rev.Comm. Reports 701).

Research References

Rutter, Cal. Practice Guide: Enforcing Judgments/Debts Ch. 4-A, A. Attachment.

6 Witkin Cal. Proc. 5th Provisional Remedies § 152, Levy by Registered Process Server.

6 Witkin Cal. Proc. 5th Provisional Remedies § 179, Securities.

6 Witkin Cal. Proc. 5th Provisional Remedies § 180, (L)--Final Money Judgments.

§ 488.485. Decedents' estates; defendants' interests in personal property

(a) To attach the interest of the defendant in personal property in the estate of a decedent, whether the interest arises by testate or intestate succession, the levying officer shall personally serve a copy of the writ of attachment and a notice of attachment on the personal representative of the decedent. The attachment does not impair the powers of the representative over the property for the purposes of administration.

(b) The personal representative shall report the attachment to the court in which the estate is being administered when any petition for distribution is filed. If a decree orders distribution to the defendant, the court making the decree shall order the attached property to be deliverd[1] to the levying officer. The property may not be delivered to the levying officer until the decree distributing the propety[2] has become final. To the extent the property delivered to the levying officer is not necessary to satisfy the attachment, it shall be released to the defendant.

(c) Promptly after the property is delivered to the levying officer pursuant to subdivision (b), the levying officer shall serve a notice describing the property on the defendant. Notwithstanding Sections 484.070, 484.350, 484.530, and 485.610, a claim of exemption for the property described in the notice may be made within 10 days after the notice was served on the defendant. *(Added by Stats.1982, c. 1198, p. 4302, § 50, operative July 1, 1983.)*

[1] So in chaptered bill.
[2] So in chaptered bill.

Law Revision Commission Comments

Section 488.485 supersedes former Section 488.430 and is drawn from Section 700.200(a)–(c) (Enforcement of Judgments Law). Subdivision (a) does not continue the requirement of former Section 488.430 that the writ and notice be filed in the office of the court clerk as a condition of a valid attachment. See also Sections 482.070 (manner of service), 488.120 (effect of failure to give notice of attachment), 488.305 (service of notice of attachment on defendant) (16 Cal.L.Rev.Comm. Reports 701).

Research References

Rutter, Cal. Practice Guide: Civ. Pro. Before Trial Ch. 9(II)-D, D. Attachment.
Rutter, Cal. Practice Guide: Enforcing Judgments/Debts Ch. 4-A, A. Attachment.
Rutter, Cal. Practice Guide: Enforcing Judgments/Debts Ch. 6D-4, Levy on Specific Property.
Miller and Starr California Real Estate § 32:28, Attachment of Real Property.
6 Witkin Cal. Proc. 5th Provisional Remedies § 152, Levy by Registered Process Server.
6 Witkin Cal. Proc. 5th Provisional Remedies § 179, Securities.
6 Witkin Cal. Proc. 5th Provisional Remedies § 181, Interest in Estate Personal Property.
14 Witkin, California Summary 10th Wills and Probate § 645, Right to Bring Action.

ARTICLE 3. LIEN OF ATTACHMENT

Section
488.500.   Creation and extent of lien.
488.510.   Term of lien.

§ 488.500. Creation and extent of lien

(a) A levy on property under a writ of attachment creates an attachment lien on the property from the time of levy until the expiration of the time provided by Section 488.510.

(b) Except as provided in subdivisions (c) and (d), if property subject to an attachment lien is transferred or encumbered, the property transferred or encumbered remains subject to the lien after the transfer or encumbrance to the same extent that the property would remain subject to an execution lien pursuant to Sections 697.720 to 697.750, inclusive.

(c) Except as otherwise provided in this title, if equipment is attached pursuant to Section 488.375 or farm products or inventory is attached pursuant to Section 488.405, the attachment lien on the property covered by the attachment lien has the same force and effect as a judgment lien on personal property created at the same time would have pursuant to Sections 697.590 to 697.620, inclusive.

(d) If equipment consisting of a vehicle, vessel, mobilehome, or commercial coach is attached pursuant to Section 488.385, the attachment lien on the specified property does not affect the

rights of a person who is a bona fide purchaser or encumbrancer and obtains possession of both the property and its certificate of ownership issued by the Department of Motor Vehicles or its certificate of title or registration card issued by the Department of Housing and Community Development. If the levying officer obtains possession of the certificate of ownership or certificate of title or registration card, the attachment lien has the priority of the lien of a lien creditor under Sections 9317 and 9323 of the Commercial Code as of the time possession is obtained by the levying officer. If the levying officer does not obtain possession of the certificate of ownership or certificate of title or registration card, the attachment lien has the same force and effect as an unperfected security interest that attached at the same time as the notice of attachment was filed.

(e) If an attachment lien is created on property that is subject to the lien of a temporary protective order or a lien under Article 1 (commencing with Section 491.110) of Chapter 11, the priority of the attachment lien relates back to the date the earlier lien was created. Nothing in this subdivision affects priorities or rights of third persons established while the lien of the temporary protective order or the lien under Article 1 (commencing with Section 491.110) of Chapter 11 was in effect as determined under the law governing the effect of such lien. *(Added by Stats.1982, c. 1198, p. 4303, § 50, operative July 1, 1983. Amended by Stats.1999, c. 991 (S.B.45), § 15, operative July 1, 2001.)*

Law Revision Commission Comments

Section 488.500 supersedes former Section 488.500. Subdivision (a) states the effective date of attachment liens provided in subdivisions (b)–(h) of the former section. This is consistent with Section 697.710 (Enforcement of Judgments Law). The provision of subdivision (a) of former Section 488.500 concerning the effect of an attachment lien is superseded by subdivisions (b), (c), and (d).

Subdivision (b) provides the general rule which incorporates the provisions governing the effect of execution liens. See the Comments to Sections 697.720–697.750.

Subdivision (c) supersedes the eleventh sentence of subdivision (c) of former Section 488.360 (farm products and inventory). Note that the lien on inventory under Section 488.405 does not attach to (1) vehicles, vessels, mobilehomes, or commercial coaches required to be registered or (2) inventory of a retail merchant unless the inventory consists of durable goods having a unit retail value of at least $500. See subdivision (d) of Section 488.405. Likewise, the lien does not continue if the property becomes a fixture. See Section 488.405(e). The provision pertaining to the attachment lien on equipment is new; former Section 488.340 provided no special rules governing the effect of an attachment lien on equipment.

Subdivision (d) continues the substance of subdivision (d) of former Section 488.350 and provides new rules governing the effect and priority of an attachment lien depending upon whether the levying officer has obtained possession of the certificate of ownership of a vehicle or vessel or the certificate of title or registration card of a mobilehome or commercial coach. Possession of the certificate may be obtained in an appropriate case by a turnover order issued pursuant to Section 482.080. See also Health and Safety Code §§ 18077.1, 18077.2; Veh. Code §§ 6300, 6301, 9919, 9920.

Subdivision (e) continues the substance of subdivision (i) of former Section 488.500 and a provision formerly contained in subdivision (b) of Section 486.110. As to the effect of a lien of a temporary protective order, see Section 486.110. As to the lien of an examination proceeding under Article 1 (commencing with Section 491.110) of Chapter 11, see Sections 491.110 and 491.190 (creation and duration of liens), 491.200 (effect of lien) (16 Cal.L.Rev.Comm. Reports 701).

Research References

Rutter, Cal. Practice Guide: Enforcing Judgments/Debts Ch. 4-A, A. Attachment.
Miller and Starr California Real Estate § 32:3, Purpose.
Miller and Starr California Real Estate § 32:4, Effect.
Miller and Starr California Real Estate § 31:63, Enforcement of a Money Judgment Against a Mobilehome.

Miller and Starr California Real Estate § 32:31, Creation and Extension of the Attachment Lien.

Miller and Starr California Real Estate § 11:122, Recordation of the Attachment Lien.

Miller and Starr California Real Estate § 11:123, Relation to Subsequent Interests.

6 Witkin Cal. Proc. 5th Provisional Remedies § 162, (S 162) Lien.

6 Witkin Cal. Proc. 5th Provisional Remedies § 165, (S 165) Lien.

6 Witkin Cal. Proc. 5th Provisional Remedies § 167, (S 167) Rights of Bona Fide Purchaser.

6 Witkin Cal. Proc. 5th Provisional Remedies § 171, Lien.

6 Witkin Cal. Proc. 5th Provisional Remedies § 175, (S 175) in General.

6 Witkin Cal. Proc. 5th Provisional Remedies § 179, Securities.

6 Witkin Cal. Proc. 5th Provisional Remedies § 184, Nature and Effect of Lien.

§ 488.510.　Term of lien

(a) Unless sooner released or discharged, any attachment shall cease to be of any force or effect, and the property levied upon shall be released from the operation of the attachment, at the expiration of three years from the date of issuance of the writ of attachment under which the levy was made.

(b) Notwithstanding subdivision (a), upon motion of the plaintiff, made not less than 10 or more than 60 days before the expiration of the three-year period and upon notice of not less than five days to the defendant whose property is attached, the court in which the action is pending may, by order filed prior to the expiration of the period and for good cause, extend the time of the attachment for a period not exceeding one year from the date on which the attachment would otherwise expire.

(c) The levying officer shall serve notice of the order upon any person holding property pursuant to an attachment and shall record or file the notice in any office where the writ and notice of attachment are recorded or filed prior to the expiration of the period described in subdivision (a) or any extension thereof. Where the attached property is real property, the plaintiff or the plaintiff's attorney, instead of the levying officer, may record the required notice.

(d) Any attachment may be extended from time to time in the manner prescribed in this section, but the maximum period of the attachment, including the extensions, shall not exceed eight years from the date of issuance of the writ of attachment under which the levy of attachment was made.

(e) The death of the defendant whose property is attached does not terminate the attachment. *(Added by Stats.1982, c. 1198, p. 4304, § 50, operative July 1, 1983.)*

Law Revision Commission Comments

Section 488.510 continues former Section 488.510 without change (16 Cal.L.Rev.Comm. Reports 701).

Research References

Rutter, Cal. Practice Guide: Civ. Pro. Before Trial Ch. 9(II)-D, D. Attachment.

Rutter, Cal. Practice Guide: Enforcing Judgments/Debts Ch. 4-A, A. Attachment.

Miller and Starr California Real Estate § 32:31, Creation and Extension of the Attachment Lien.

Miller and Starr California Real Estate § 32:32, Termination of the Attachment Lien.

Miller and Starr California Real Estate § 32:33, Release of Attachment Lien.

Miller and Starr California Real Estate § 11:122, Recordation of the Attachment Lien.

Miller and Starr California Real Estate § 11:123, Relation to Subsequent Interests.

6 Witkin Cal. Proc. 5th Provisional Remedies § 179, Securities.

6 Witkin Cal. Proc. 5th Provisional Remedies § 184, Nature and Effect of Lien.

6 Witkin Cal. Proc. 5th Provisional Remedies § 187, Duration and Extension.

ARTICLE 4.　DUTIES AND LIABILITIES OF THIRD PERSONS AFTER LEVY

§ 488.600.　Duties and liabilities; definitions

(a) Sections 701.010, 701.020, 701.040, 701.050, 701.060, and 701.070 prescribe duties and liabilities of a third person under a levy made under this title.

(b) For the purposes of this section, references in Sections 701.010, 701.020, 701.040, 701.050, and 701.060 to:

(1) "Amount required to satisfy the judgment" shall be deemed references to the amount required to satisfy the amount to be secured by the attachment.

(2) "Execution lien" or "lien" shall be deemed references to the attachment lien.

(3) "Judgment creditor" shall be deemed references to the plaintiff.

(4) "Judgment debtor" shall be deemed references to the defendant.

(5) "Levy" shall be deemed references to levy of attachment.

(6) "Notice of levy" shall be deemed references to notice of attachment.

(7) "Release" of property shall be deemed references to release of property pursuant to this title.

(8) "Satisfaction or discharge of the judgment" shall be deemed references to the satisfaction or termination of the attachment.

(9) "Writ" or "writ of execution" shall be deemed references to a writ of attachment.

(c) For the purposes of this section, references in Section 701.070 to:

(1) "Levy" shall be deemed references to levy of attachment.

(2) "Notice of the levy" shall be deemed references to notice of attachment. *(Added by Stats.1982, c. 1198, p. 4304, § 50, operative July 1, 1983. Amended by Stats.1984, c. 538, § 6.7; Stats.2012, c. 484 (A.B.2364), § 4.)*

Law Revision Commission Comments

Section 488.600 makes applicable to attachment the provisions of the Enforcement of Judgments Law governing the duties and liabilities of third persons after levy. See also Section 488.610 (garnishee's memorandum). Section 488.600 supersedes subdivision (b) of former Section 488.330 and portions of former Sections 488.540 and 488.550 (16 Cal.L.Rev.Comm. Reports 701).

Research References

Rutter, Cal. Practice Guide: Enforcing Judgments/Debts Ch. 4-A, A. Attachment.

Miller and Starr California Real Estate § 11:123, Relation to Subsequent Interests.

6 Witkin Cal. Proc. 5th Provisional Remedies § 158, Property Governed by Enforcement of Judgments Law.

6 Witkin Cal. Proc. 5th Provisional Remedies § 176, (S 176) Retention of Account by Financial Institution.

6 Witkin Cal. Proc. 5th Provisional Remedies § 192, Enforcement of Judgments Law is Applicable.

§ 488.610. Garnishee's memorandum

(a) At the time of service of a copy of the writ of attachment and a notice of attachment on a third person, the levying officer shall request the third person to give the levying officer a garnishee's memorandum containing the information required by this section. Within 10 days after the request is made, the third person shall mail or deliver the garnishee's memorandum to the levying officer whether or not the levy is effective.

(b) The garnishee's memorandum shall be executed under oath and shall contain the following information:

(1) A description of any property of the defendant sought to be attached that is not delivered to the levying officer and the reason for not delivering the property.

(2) A statement of the amount and terms of any obligation to the defendant sought to be attached that is due and payable and is not paid to the levying officer and the reason for not paying the obligation.

(3) A statement of the amount and terms of any obligation to the defendant sought to be attached that is not due and payable at the time of levy.

(4) A description of claims and rights of other persons to the attached property or obligation that are known to the third person and the names and addresses of those other persons.

(5) A statement that the garnishee holds neither any property nor any obligations in favor of the judgment debtor.

(c) If a garnishee's memorandum is received from the third person, the levying officer shall promptly mail or deliver a copy of the memorandum to the plaintiff and attach the original to the writ when it is returned to the court. If a garnishee's memorandum is not received from the third person, the levying officer shall so state in the return.

(d) Except as provided in subdivisions (e) and (f), if a third person does not give the levying officer a garnishee's memorandum within the time provided in subdivision (a) or does not provide complete information, the third person may, in the court's discretion, be required to pay the costs and reasonable attorney's fees incurred in any proceedings to obtain the information required in the garnishee's memorandum.

(e) Notwithstanding subdivision (a), where a deposit account or property in a safe-deposit box is attached, the financial institution need not give a garnishee's memorandum to the levying officer if the financial institution fully complies with the levy and, if a garnishee's memorandum is required, the garnishee's memorandum need provide information with respect only to property which is carried on the records available at the office or branch where the levy is made, unless the levy has been served at a central location designated by a financial institution in accordance with Section 684.115, in which case the garnishee's memorandum shall apply to all offices and branches of the financial institution except to the extent acceptance of the levy at that central location is limited pursuant to paragraph (3) of subdivision (a) of Section 684.115.

(f) Notwithstanding subdivision (a), the third person need not give a garnishee's memorandum to the levying officer if both of the following conditions are satisfied:

(1) The third person has delivered to the levying officer all of the property sought to be attached.

(2) The third person has paid to the levying officer the amount due at the time of levy on any obligation to the defendant that was attached and there is no additional amount that thereafter will become payable on the obligation levied

upon. *(Added by Stats.1982, c. 1198, p. 4305, § 50, operative July 1, 1983. Amended by Stats.2012, c. 484 (A.B.2364), § 5.)*

Law Revision Commission Comments

Section 488.610 supersedes former Section 488.080(b) and is drawn from Section 701.030 (Enforcement of Judgments Law). See the Comment to Section 701.030. Subdivision (a) continues the substance of a portion of the first sentence and the second sentence of former Section 488.080(b). Subdivision (b) supersedes the portion of former Section 488.080(b) that prescribed the information to be given by the garnishee. Subdivision (b) does not require the garnishee to state the amount owed, if the entire debt is paid over to the levying officer. Subdivision (c) continues the substance of the fourth sentence of former Section 488.080(b). Subdivision (d) continues the substance of the last sentence of former Section 488.080(b); the liability for attorney's fees is new to the Attachment Law. Subdivisions (e) and (f) are consistent with the comparable provisions of Section 701.030 (16 Cal.L.Rev.Comm. Reports 701).

Research References

Rutter, Cal. Practice Guide: Enforcing Judgments/Debts Ch. 4-A, A. Attachment.

20 NO. 2 Miller & Starr, California Real Estate Newsalert 1, Policy Considerations Trump Statutory Construction, Giving Stop Notice Claimants a Big Advantage Over Construction Lenders.

6 Witkin Cal. Proc. 5th Provisional Remedies § 152, Levy by Registered Process Server.

6 Witkin Cal. Proc. 5th Provisional Remedies § 177, Safe Deposit Boxes.

6 Witkin Cal. Proc. 5th Provisional Remedies § 193, (S 193) in General.

6 Witkin Cal. Proc. 5th Provisional Remedies § 194, (S 194) Content and Form.

§ 488.620. Disclosure in garnishee's memorandum; liability

A third person who gives a garnishee's memorandum pursuant to this title is not liable to any person for the disclosure in the garnishee's memorandum of any information contained in the garnishee's memorandum. *(Added by Stats.1983, c. 155, § 8.3, eff. June 30, 1983, operative July 1, 1983.)*

Research References

6 Witkin Cal. Proc. 5th Provisional Remedies § 193, (S 193) in General.

ARTICLE 5. MANAGEMENT AND DISPOSITION OF ATTACHED PROPERTY

Section

488.700.   Preservation of attached property; sales; receivers.

488.710.   Instruments for withdrawal of money.

488.720.   Orders releasing attachment to extent attachment is excessive.

488.730.   Release of attached property; basis; mode; procedure.

488.740.   Defendant prevailing over plaintiff; disposition of proceeds and property.

§ 488.700. Preservation of attached property; sales; receivers

(a) If property has been or is sought to be attached, the court may appoint a receiver or order the levying officer to take any action the court orders that is necessary to preserve the value of the property, including but not limited to selling the property, if the court determines that the property is perishable or will greatly deteriorate or greatly depreciate in value or that for some other reason the interests of the parties will be best served by the order. An order may be made under this subdivision upon application of the plaintiff, the defendant, or a person who has filed a third-party claim pursuant to Division 4 (commencing with Section 720.010) of Title 9. The application shall be made on noticed motion if the court so directs or a court rule so requires. Otherwise, the application may be made ex parte.

Civ. Pro.

(b) If the levying officer determines that property is extremely perishable or will greatly deteriorate or greatly depreciate in value before a court order pursuant to subdivision (a) could be obtained, the levying officer may take any action necessary to preserve the value of the property or may sell the property. The levying officer is not liable for a determination made in good faith under this subdivision.

(c) Except as otherwise provided by order of the court, a sale of the property pursuant to this section shall be made in the manner provided by Article 6 (commencing with Section 701.510) of Chapter 3 of Division 2 of Title 9 and the proceeds shall be deposited in the court to abide the judgment in the action. Notwithstanding subdivisions (b) and (d) of Section 701.530, notice of sale shall be posted and served at a reasonable time before sale, considering the character and condition of the property.

(d) If a receiver is appointed, the court shall fix the daily fee of the receiver and may order the plaintiff to pay the fees and expenses of the receiver in advance or may direct that the whole or any part of the fees and expenses be paid from the proceeds of any sale of the property. Except as otherwise provided in this section, the provisions of Chapter 5 (commencing with Section 564) and Chapter 5a (commencing with Section 571) of Title 7 govern the appointment, qualifications, powers, rights, and duties of a receiver appointed under this section. (Added by Stats.1982, c. 1198, p. 4306, § 50, operative July 1, 1983.)

Law Revision Commission Comments

Section 488.700 supersedes former Section 488.530 and is drawn from Section 699.070 (Enforcement of Judgments Law) (16 Cal.L.Rev.Comm. Reports 701).

Research References

Rutter, Cal. Practice Guide: Civ. Pro. Before Trial Ch. 9(II)-B, B. Receiverships.
Rutter, Cal. Practice Guide: Enforcing Judgments/Debts Ch. 4-A, A. Attachment.
Miller and Starr California Real Estate § 33:1, Nature of Receiverships; in General.
8 Witkin Cal. Proc. 5th Enforcement of Judgment § 102, (S 102) Preservation of Property.
6 Witkin Cal. Proc. 5th Provisional Remedies § 157, Limited Liability of Officer.
6 Witkin Cal. Proc. 5th Provisional Remedies § 173, Crops, Timber, and Minerals.
6 Witkin Cal. Proc. 5th Provisional Remedies § 179, Securities.
6 Witkin Cal. Proc. 5th Provisional Remedies § 191, Depreciating Property.

§ 488.710.　Instruments for withdrawal of money

(a) As used in this section, "instrument" means a check, draft, money order, or other order for the withdrawal of money from a financial institution, the United States, any state, or any public entity within any state.

(b) If an instrument is payable to the defendant on demand and comes into the possession of a levying officer pursuant to this title, the levying officer shall promptly endorse and present the instrument for payment.

(c) The levying officer shall endorse the instrument by writing on the instrument (1) the name of the defendant, (2) the name and official title of the levying officer, and (3) the title of the court and the cause in which the writ was issued. The endorsement is as valid as if the instrument were endorsed by the defendant. No financial institution or public entity on which the instrument is drawn is liable to any person for payment of the instrument to the levying officer rather than to the defendant by reason of the endorsement. No levying officer is liable by reason of endorsing, presenting, and obtaining payment of the instrument. The funds or credit resulting from the payment of

the instrument shall be held by the levying officer subject to the lien of attachment.

(d) If it appears from the face of the instrument that it has been tendered to the defendant in satisfaction of a claim or demand and that endorsement of the instrument is considered a release and satisfaction by the defendant of the claim or demand, the levying officer shall not endorse the instrument unless the defendant has first endorsed it to the levying officer. If the defendant does not endorse the instrument to the levying officer, the levying officer shall hold the instrument for 30 days and is not liable to the defendant or to any other person for delay in presenting it for payment. At the end of the 30-day holding period, the levying officer shall return the instrument to the maker. (Added by Stats.1982, c. 1198, p. 4307, § 50, operative July 1, 1983.)

Law Revision Commission Comments

Section 488.710 supersedes former Section 488.520 and is drawn from Section 687.020 (Enforcement of Judgments Law). The provision in subdivision (d) for the return of an instrument to the maker after 30 days in certain circumstances is new to attachment law (16 Cal.L.Rev.Comm. Reports 701).

Research References

Rutter, Cal. Practice Guide: Enforcing Judgments/Debts Ch. 4-A, A. Attachment.
6 Witkin Cal. Proc. 5th Provisional Remedies § 157, Limited Liability of Officer.
6 Witkin Cal. Proc. 5th Provisional Remedies § 179, Securities.
6 Witkin Cal. Proc. 5th Provisional Remedies § 190, Commercial Paper.
4 Witkin, California Summary 10th Negotiable Instruments § 17, (S 17) Payee.

§ 488.720.　Orders releasing attachment to extent attachment is excessive

(a) The defendant may apply by noticed motion to the court in which the action is pending or in which the judgment in the action was entered for an order releasing the attachment of property to the extent that the value of the defendant's interest in the property clearly exceeds the amount necessary to satisfy the amount to be secured by the attachment.

(b) The notice of motion shall state the grounds on which the motion is based and shall be accompanied by an affidavit supporting any factual issues raised and points and authorities supporting any legal issues raised.

(c) At the hearing on the motion, the court shall determine the value of the defendant's interest in the property and order the release of the attachment of the property to the extent that the value of the defendant's interest in the property attached clearly exceeds the amount necessary to satisfy the amount to be secured by the attachment. After entry of judgment in the action in which the property was attached, the court shall also take into consideration in determining whether the attachment is clearly excessive the value of any property not attached in the action that (1) has been levied upon pursuant to a writ of execution issued to satisfy the judgment in the action or (2) otherwise has been sought to be applied to the satisfaction of the judgment in the action.

(d) The court's determinations shall be made upon the basis of the pleadings and other papers in the record; but, upon good cause shown, the court may receive and consider at the hearing additional evidence, oral or documentary, and additional points and authorities, or it may continue the hearing for the production of the additional evidence or points and authorities. (Added by Stats.1982, c. 1198, p. 4307, § 50, operative July 1, 1983.)

Civ. Pro.

Research References

Rutter, Cal. Practice Guide: Enforcing Judgments/Debts Ch. 4-A, A. Attachment.
Miller and Starr California Real Estate § 32:21, Nonindividual Defendants.
Miller and Starr California Real Estate § 32:33, Release of Attachment Lien.
Miller and Starr California Real Estate § 32:39, Statutory Recovery on the Undertaking.
6 Witkin Cal. Proc. 5th Provisional Remedies § 116, Amount.
6 Witkin Cal. Proc. 5th Provisional Remedies § 220, (S 220) Nature of Remedy.
6 Witkin Cal. Proc. 5th Provisional Remedies § 221, (S 221) Procedure.

§ 488.730. Release of attached property; basis; mode; procedure

(a) The levying officer shall release attached property when the levying officer receives a written direction to release the property from the plaintiff's attorney of record or, if the plaintiff does not have an attorney of record, from the plaintiff or when the levying officer receives a certified copy of a court order for release or when otherwise required to release the property. The release extinguishes any attachment lien in favor of the plaintiff on the property released.

(b) If the property to be released has been taken into custody under the levy, it shall be released to the person from whom it was taken unless otherwise ordered by the court. If the person does not claim the property to be released, the levying officer shall retain custody of the property and shall serve on the person a notice of where possession of the property may be obtained. If the person does not claim the property within 30 days after the notice is served, the levying officer shall sell the property (other than cash which does not have a value exceeding its face value) in the manner provided by Article 6 (commencing with Section 701.510) of Chapter 3 of Division 2 of Title 9. The levying officer shall deposit the proceeds of sale and cash, after first deducting the levying officer's costs, with the county treasurer of the county where the property is located payable to the order of the person. If the amount deposited is not claimed by the person or the legal representative of the person within five years after the deposit is made, by making application to the treasurer or other official designated by the county, it shall be paid into the general fund of the county.

(c) If the property to be released has not been taken into custody under the levy, the levying officer shall release the attachment by issuing a written notice of release and serving it on the person who was served with a copy of the writ and a notice of attachment to create the lien.

(d) If the property to be released was levied upon by recording or filing a copy of the writ and a notice of attachment, the levying officer shall record or file a written notice of release in the same office. If the notice of attachment had been filed with the Secretary of State, any release shall have the effect prescribed in Section 697.650.

(e) The levying officer is not liable for releasing an attachment in accordance with this section and no other person is liable for acting in conformity with the release. *(Added by Stats.1982, c. 1198, p. 4308, § 50, operative July 1, 1983. Amended by Stats.1983, c. 155, § 9, eff. June 30, 1983, operative July 1, 1983; Stats.1989, c. 445, § 1.)*

Law Revision Commission Comments

Section 488.730 supersedes former Section 488.560 and is drawn from Section 699.060 (Enforcement of Judgments Law). See also Sections 481.055 ("costs" defined), 482.070 (manner of service) (16 Cal.L.Rev. Comm. Reports 701).

Subdivision (b) of Section 488.730 is amended to delete erroneous language. See Section 699.060(b) (release from execution). [16 Cal. L.Rev.Comm. Reports 2175 (1982)].

Research References

Rutter, Cal. Practice Guide: Enforcing Judgments/Debts Ch. 4-A, A. Attachment.
Miller and Starr California Real Estate § 32:33, Release of Attachment Lien.
Miller and Starr California Real Estate § 11:122, Recordation of the Attachment Lien.
6 Witkin Cal. Proc. 5th Provisional Remedies § 157, Limited Liability of Officer.
6 Witkin Cal. Proc. 5th Provisional Remedies § 179, Securities.
6 Witkin Cal. Proc. 5th Provisional Remedies § 189, (S 189) Release of Attached Property.
6 Witkin Cal. Proc. 5th Provisional Remedies § 210, (S 210) Right to Release.
6 Witkin Cal. Proc. 5th Provisional Remedies § 211, (S 211) Redelivery or Sale of Property in Custody.
6 Witkin Cal. Proc. 5th Provisional Remedies § 212, (S 212) Written Release of Property Not in Custody.

§ 488.740. Defendant prevailing over plaintiff; disposition of proceeds and property

If the defendant recovers judgment against the plaintiff and no timely motion for vacation of judgment or for judgment notwithstanding the verdict or for a new trial is filed and served and is pending and no appeal is perfected and undertaking executed and filed as provided in Section 921, any undertaking received from the defendant in the action, all the proceeds of sales and money collected by the levying officer, and all the property attached remaining in the levying officer's hands shall be delivered to the person from whom it was collected or taken, unless otherwise ordered by the court; and the court shall order the discharge of any attachment made in the action and the release of any property held thereunder. *(Added by Stats.1982, c. 1198, p. 4309, § 50, operative July 1, 1983.)*

Law Revision Commission Comments

Section 488.740 continues former Section 488.570 (16 Cal.L.Rev. Comm. Reports 701).

Research References

Rutter, Cal. Practice Guide: Enforcing Judgments/Debts Ch. 4-A, A. Attachment.
Miller and Starr California Real Estate § 32:32, Termination of the Attachment Lien.
Miller and Starr California Real Estate § 32:33, Release of Attachment Lien.
Miller and Starr California Real Estate § 11:123, Relation to Subsequent Interests.
6 Witkin Cal. Proc. 5th Provisional Remedies § 215, (S 215) Final Judgment for Defendant.

CHAPTER 9. UNDERTAKINGS

ARTICLE 1. GENERAL PROVISIONS

§ 489.010. Application of Bond and Undertaking Law

The Bond and Undertaking Law (Chapter 2 (commencing with Section 995.010) of Title 14) applies to a bond given pursuant to this title, except to the extent this title prescribes a different rule or is inconsistent. *(Added by Stats.1985, c. 41 § 2.)*

Law Revision Commission Comments

Section 489.010 makes clear that the Bond and Undertaking Law applies in attachment. This makes no change in the law. See the Comment to the repeal of former Sections 489.010–489.050. [18 Cal. L.Rev.Comm. Reports 361 (1985)].

Research References

Rutter, Cal. Practice Guide: Civ. Pro. Before Trial Ch. 11-A, A. Voluntary Dismissals.
Rutter, Cal. Practice Guide: Enforcing Judgments/Debts Ch. 4-A, A. Attachment.
6 Witkin Cal. Proc. 5th Provisional Remedies § 53, Nature and Scope.
6 Witkin Cal. Proc. 5th Provisional Remedies § 91, (S 91) Undertakings.

§ 489.060. Approval; filing

(a) Except as provided in subdivision (b), all undertakings given pursuant to this title shall be presented to a proper court for approval and upon approval shall be filed with the court in which the action is pending.

(b) If the surety on the undertaking is an admitted surety insurer, the undertaking is not required to be approved by the court. *(Added by Stats.1974, c. 1516, p. 3368, § 9, operative Jan. 1, 1977. Amended by Stats.1976, c. 437, p. 1136, § 36.5; Stats.1982, c. 517, p. 2336, § 107.)*

Law Revision Commission Comments

[Subdivision (a) of] Section 489.060 requires approval of any undertaking under this title by a court before it may be filed [, except as provided in subdivision (b)]. This makes the requirement of former Section 540 (undertaking for release of attached property) applicable to all undertakings authorized or required by this title. The court approves the undertaking if it determines that the undertaking on its face and the affidavits of the sureties are sufficient. Such approval has no effect on the right of the beneficiary to object to the sufficiency of the undertaking. It should be noted that in some instances an undertaking may be approved by a court in a county other than the county in which the action is pending. See Section 489.310. However, following approval, all undertakings must be filed with the court in which the action is pending. Under prior law, the undertaking was filed with the court in some instances (former Section 540) and with the levying officer in others (former Section 539a) .... (11 Cal.L.Rev.Comm. Reports 801, amended by 16 Cal. L.Rev.Comm. Reports 701).

Subdivision (a) of Section 489.060 is amended to delete language made unnecessary by Section 995.420 (time undertaking becomes effective). Subdivision (b) is amended for consistency with the Bond and Undertaking Law. See Section 995.120 ("admitted surety insurer" defined). Subdivision (c) is superseded by Section 995.410 (approval of undertaking) [16 Cal.L.Rev.Comm. Reports 501 (1982)].

Research References

Rutter, Cal. Practice Guide: Enforcing Judgments/Debts Ch. 4-A, A. Attachment.
Miller and Starr California Real Estate § 32:35, Noticed Hearing Procedure.
6 Witkin Cal. Proc. 5th Provisional Remedies § 91, (S 91) Undertakings.

§ 489.130. Failure to increase undertaking; order of court; effect

Where the court orders the amount of the undertaking increased pursuant to Section 489.220 or 489.410, the plaintiff's failure to increase the amount of the undertaking is not a wrongful attachment within the meaning of Section 490.010. *(Added by Stats.1976, c. 437, p. 1136, § 37.)*

Law Revision Commission Comments

Section 489.130 makes clear that the mere failure of the plaintiff to increase the amount of an undertaking when ordered to do so pursuant to Section 489.220 (undertaking to obtain a writ of attachment or protective order) or Section 489.410 (undertaking on appeal) is not a wrongful attachment under Section 490.010. The insufficient undertaking remains in effect pursuant to [Section 995.960(b) (2)], and the plaintiff's liability for wrongful attachment pursuant to Section 490.010 is limited to the amount of the insufficient undertaking by subdivision (b) of Section 490.020. However, where an order to increase the amount of the undertaking is not complied with, the rights which the plaintiff obtained by filing the original undertaking cease as provided in [Section 995.960(b) (1)] and subdivision (a) of Section 489.410. Hence, if a temporary protective order has been issued, it is vacated; if a writ of attachment has been issued and levied, the writ is quashed and the property released (13 Cal.L.Rev.Comm. Reports 801, amended by 16 Cal.L.Rev.Comm. Reports 701).

Research References

Rutter, Cal. Practice Guide: Enforcing Judgments/Debts Ch. 4-A, A. Attachment.
6 Witkin Cal. Proc. 5th Provisional Remedies § 233, (S 233) Acts Constituting Wrongful Attachment.

ARTICLE 2. UNDERTAKINGS TO OBTAIN WRIT OF ATTACHMENT OR PROTECTIVE ORDER

Section

§ 489.210. Undertaking prerequisite to attachment or order

Before issuance of a writ of attachment, a temporary protective order, or an order under subdivision (b) of Section 491.415, the plaintiff shall file an undertaking to pay the defendant any amount the defendant may recover for any wrongful attachment by the plaintiff in the action. *(Added by Stats.1974, c. 1516, p. 3369, § 9, operative Jan. 1, 1977. Amended by Stats.1976, c. 437, p. 1136, § 37.5; Stats.1984, c. 538, § 7.)*

Law Revision Commission Comments

Section 489.210 supersedes the first sentence of former Section 539. For damages on wrongful attachment, see Chapter 10 (commencing with Section 490.010). The recovery for a wrongful attachment includes not only damages but also attorney's fees. See Section 490.020. See also Section 490.010 (acts constituting wrongful attachment).

Section 489.210 is amended to require the giving of an undertaking as a prerequisite to obtaining an order permitting creation of a lien in a pending action. [17 Cal.L.Rev.Comm. Reports 975 (1984)].

Research References

Rutter, Cal. Practice Guide: Enforcing Judgments/Debts Ch. 4-A, A. Attachment.
Miller and Starr California Real Estate § 32:35, Noticed Hearing Procedure.
Miller and Starr California Real Estate § 32:39, Statutory Recovery on the Undertaking.
6 Witkin Cal. Proc. 5th Provisional Remedies § 91, (S 91) Undertakings.
6 Witkin Cal. Proc. 5th Provisional Remedies § 115, Necessity.
6 Witkin Cal. Proc. 5th Provisional Remedies § 204, Plaintiff's Application.
6 Witkin Cal. Proc. 5th Provisional Remedies § 225, Amount of Recovery.

§ 489.220. Amount of undertaking

(a) Except as provided in subdivision (b), the amount of an undertaking filed pursuant to this article shall be ten thousand dollars ($10,000).

(b) If, upon objection to the undertaking, the court determines that the probable recovery for wrongful attachment exceeds the amount of the undertaking, it shall order the amount of the undertaking increased to the amount it determines to be the probable recovery for wrongful attachment if it is ultimately determined that the attachment was wrongful. *(Added by Stats.1974, c. 1516, p. 3369, § 9, operative Jan. 1, 1977. Amended by Stats.1976, c. 437, p. 1136, § 38; Stats.1977, c. 1257, § 14, eff. Jan. 3, 1977; Stats.1998, c. 931 (S.B.2139), § 74, eff. Sept. 28, 1998; Stats.2001, c. 812 (A.B.223), § 3.)*

Law Revision Commission Comments

Section 489.220 supersedes portions of former Section 539. Unlike Section 539, this section provides no authorization for decreasing the amount of an undertaking. Instead, subdivision (a) provides certain minimum amounts which the defendant can then move to have increased where the circumstances indicate that the damages due to the attachment may exceed such amount. Compare the second sentence of former Section 539. Under former law, the undertaking could be increased but no guide existed as to the proper amount. See the last sentence of former Section 539(a).

Section 489.220 is amended to provide for the amount of the undertaking in justice court.

Section 489.220 is amended to accommodate unification of the municipal and superior courts in a county. Cal. Const. art. VI, § 5(e). It is also amended to reflect elimination of the justice court. Cal. Const. art. VI, §§ 1, 5(b). Formerly, each county had one or more municipal courts and a superior court, and Section 489.220 required an undertaking of $2,500 for an action in municipal court and $7,500 for an action in superior court. A limited civil case is equivalent to a matter within the original jurisdiction of the municipal court, so Section 489.220 as amended continues the effect of former law. See Section 85 (limited civil cases) & Comment. [28 Cal.L.Rev.Comm. Reports 51 (1998)].

Section 489.220 is amended to provide for the same attachment undertaking, regardless of the jurisdictional classification of the case. Formerly, the amount of the initial undertaking depended on whether the case was a limited civil case or an unlimited civil case. 1998 Cal.Stat. c.931, 74. [30 Cal.L.Rev.Comm. Reports 443 (2000)].

Research References

Rutter, Cal. Practice Guide: Civ. Pro. Before Trial Ch. 9(II)-D, D. Attachment.

Rutter, Cal. Practice Guide: Enforcing Judgments/Debts Ch. 4-A, A. Attachment.

Rutter, Cal. Practice Guide: Insurance Litigation Ch. 6I-B, B. Particular Surety Bond Coverages.

Miller and Starr California Real Estate § 32:35, Noticed Hearing Procedure.

6 Witkin Cal. Proc. 5th Provisional Remedies § 91, (S 91) Undertakings.

6 Witkin Cal. Proc. 5th Provisional Remedies § 116, Amount.

6 Witkin Cal. Proc. 5th Provisional Remedies § 204, Plaintiff's Application.

6 Witkin Cal. Proc. 5th Provisional Remedies § 221, (S 221) Procedure.

§ 489.230. Necessary statements in notice of attachment and protective order

(a) The notice of attachment shall include a statement, in a form adopted by the Judicial Council, advising the defendant that the undertaking has been filed and informing the defendant of the right to object to the undertaking.

(b) The form for the temporary protective order shall include a statement comparable to the one required by subdivision (a). *(Added by Stats.1974, c. 1516, p. 3369, § 9, operative Jan. 1, 1977. Amended by Stats.1976, c. 437, p. 1137, § 39; Stats.1982, c. 517, p. 2336, § 114.)*

Law Revision Commission Comments

Section 489.230 is new. No comparable provision existed under former law. See Section [488.060] (notice of attachment) (11 Cal.L.Rev.Comm. Reports 701, amended by 16 Cal.L.Rev.Comm. Reports 701).

Section 489.230 is amended to make clear that the statement required by subdivision (a) is to be included in the notice of attachment provided by Section [488.060]. The amendment of subdivision (b) is technical (13

Cal.L.Rev.Comm. Reports 801, amended by 16 Cal.L.Rev.Comm. Reports 701).

Subdivision (a) of Section 489.230 is amended to delete an incorrect section reference [16 Cal.L.Rev.Comm. Reports 501 (1982)].

Research References

Miller and Starr California Real Estate § 32:35, Noticed Hearing Procedure.

6 Witkin Cal. Proc. 5th Provisional Remedies § 144, in General.

6 Witkin Cal. Proc. 5th Provisional Remedies § 153, Notice and Service.

ARTICLE 3. UNDERTAKING TO OBTAIN RELEASE OF ATTACHMENT OR PROTECTIVE ORDER

Section

489.310. Application for order for substitution of undertaking for property; undertaking.

489.320. Application to terminate protective order; undertaking.

§ 489.310. Application for order for substitution of undertaking for property; undertaking

(a) Whenever a writ is issued, a defendant who has appeared in the action may apply by noticed motion to the court in which the action is pending for an order permitting the defendant to substitute an undertaking for any of his property in the state which has been or is subject to being attached.

(b) In a case (1) where the defendant applies for an order to release a portion of property which has been attached or (2) where the defendant applies for an order preventing the attachment of property and the amount of the undertaking to be given is less than the amount to be secured by the attachment, the application shall include a statement, executed under oath, describing the property to be so released or so protected from attachment.

(c) The defendant shall file an undertaking to pay the plaintiff the value of the property released not exceeding the amount of any judgment which may be recovered by the plaintiff in the action against the defendant. The amount of the undertaking filed pursuant to this section shall be equal to the lesser of (1) the value of the property attached or prevented from being attached or (2) the amount specified by the writ to be secured by the attachment. The court shall issue such order upon the condition that a sufficient undertaking be filed.

(d) Where an action is against more than one defendant, any defendant may make such application. The filing of an undertaking by such defendant shall not subject him to any demand against any other defendant; however, the levying officer shall not be prevented thereby from attaching, or be obliged to release from attachment, any property of any other defendant. Where all the defendants do not join in the application, the application shall include a statement, executed under oath, describing the character of the defendant's title to the property and the manner in which the defendant acquired such title and stating whether any other defendant who has not joined in the application has an interest in the property. Where two or more defendants have an interest in the same property, a joint application and undertaking shall be filed to secure the release of such property. *(Added by Stats.1974, c. 1516, p. 3370, § 9, operative Jan. 1, 1977. Amended by Stats.1976, c. 437, p. 1137, § 40.)*

Law Revision Commission Comments

Section 489.310 is based on former Sections 540, 554, and 555. It should be noted that subdivision (a) [prior to the 1976 amendments required] only "reasonable" notice to the plaintiff. Depending on the circumstances, this period may be very short. For example, where a keeper has been placed in the defendant's business under a writ of attachment issued ex parte, the impact on the defendant may be devastating and permission to file an undertaking in lieu of the attachment should be expedited (11 Cal.L.Rev.Comm. Reports 701, amended by 16 Cal.L.Rev.Comm. Reports 701).

Research References

Rutter, Cal. Practice Guide: Civ. Pro. Before Trial Ch. 9(II)-D, D. Attachment.
Rutter, Cal. Practice Guide: Enforcing Judgments/Debts Ch. 4-A, A. Attachment.
Rutter, Cal. Practice Guide: Insurance Litigation Ch. 6I-B, B. Particular Surety Bond Coverages.
Miller and Starr California Real Estate § 32:27, Procedure to Claim an Exemption.
Miller and Starr California Real Estate § 32:33, Release of Attachment Lien.
Miller and Starr California Real Estate § 11:122, Recordation of the Attachment Lien.
6 Witkin Cal. Proc. 5th Provisional Remedies § 91, (S 91) Undertakings.
6 Witkin Cal. Proc. 5th Provisional Remedies § 213, (S 213) Application and Undertaking.
6 Witkin Cal. Proc. 5th Provisional Remedies § 225, Amount of Recovery.

§ 489.320. Application to terminate protective order; undertaking

(a) A defendant who has been served with a temporary protective order and who has appeared in the action may apply by noticed motion to the court in which the action is pending for an order terminating the temporary protective order with respect to that defendant.

(b) The defendant shall file an undertaking to pay the plaintiff the amount of any judgment recovered by the plaintiff in the action against the defendant. The amount of the undertaking filed pursuant to this section shall be equal to the amount sought to be secured by the attachment. The court shall issue the order terminating the temporary protective order with respect to the defendant upon the condition that a sufficient undertaking is filed. *(Added by Stats.1974, c. 1516, p. 3371, § 9, operative Jan. 1, 1977. Amended by Stats.1976, c. 437, p. 1138, § 41; Stats.1982, c. 1198, p. 4310, § 52, operative July 1, 1983.)*

Law Revision Commission Comments

Section 489.320 is based on former Sections 540, 554, and 555. See also Section 486.090 (expiration of temporary protective order) and the Comment to Section 489.310.

Subdivision (a) of Section 489.320 is amended to provide that an application for an order under this section is made by noticed motion.

The amendment to Section 489.320 is clarifying. See Section 483.015 (16 Cal.L.Rev.Comm. Reports 701).

Research References

Rutter, Cal. Practice Guide: Enforcing Judgments/Debts Ch. 4-A, A. Attachment.
Miller and Starr California Real Estate § 32:37, Temporary Protective Orders.
6 Witkin Cal. Proc. 5th Provisional Remedies § 91, (S 91) Undertakings.
6 Witkin Cal. Proc. 5th Provisional Remedies § 145, Expiration, Modification, and Vacation.
6 Witkin Cal. Proc. 5th Provisional Remedies § 148, (S 148) Undertaking to Terminate Order.

ARTICLE 4. UNDERTAKING ON APPEAL

§ 489.410. Increase to continue attachment after judgment; appeal; effect of postjudgment motions

(a) At any time after entry of judgment in favor of the defendant and before perfection of an appeal under Section 921, upon motion of the defendant, the trial court may order an increase in the amount of the original undertaking on attachment in such amount, if any, as is justified by the detriment reasonably to be anticipated by continuing the attachment. Unless such undertaking is filed within 10 days after such order, the attachment shall be set aside and the property released therefrom.

(b) If an order increasing the undertaking is made, the amount of the undertaking on appeal required by Section 921 shall be the same as the amount fixed by the trial court in such order.

(c) Neither the pendency nor granting of a motion timely filed and served by the plaintiff for vacation of judgment or for judgment notwithstanding the verdict or for new trial shall continue an attachment in force unless an undertaking is given by the plaintiff to pay all costs and damages sustained by continuing the attachment. The undertaking may be included in the undertaking specified in Section 921. If not so included, the same procedure shall apply as in case of an undertaking pursuant to Section 921. *(Added by Stats.1974, c. 1516, p. 3371, § 9, operative Jan. 1, 1977.)*

Law Revision Commission Comments

Section 489.410 is based on former Section 553.

Research References

Rutter, Cal. Practice Guide: Civil Appeals & Writs Ch. 7-C, C. Stay by Posting Security (Bond or Undertaking).
Rutter, Cal. Practice Guide: Enforcing Judgments/Debts Ch. 4-A, A. Attachment.
Miller and Starr California Real Estate § 32:32, Termination of the Attachment Lien.
Miller and Starr California Real Estate § 32:35, Noticed Hearing Procedure.
6 Witkin Cal. Proc. 5th Provisional Remedies § 91, (S 91) Undertakings.
6 Witkin Cal. Proc. 5th Provisional Remedies § 216, (S 216) Plaintiff's Appeal Without Undertaking.
6 Witkin Cal. Proc. 5th Provisional Remedies § 217, (S 217) Plaintiff's Motion Without Undertaking.
6 Witkin Cal. Proc. 5th Provisional Remedies § 225, Amount of Recovery.

§ 489.420. Defendant's undertaking on appeal; release of attachment

If a defendant appeals and the enforcement of the judgment against the defendant is stayed by the filing of a sufficient undertaking on appeal as provided by this code, all property of the defendant which has been attached in the action shall be released from the attachment upon the failure of the respondent to object to the undertaking within the time prescribed by statute or, if an objection is made, upon a determination that the undertaking is sufficient. *(Added by Stats.1974, c. 1516, p. 3371, § 9, operative Jan. 1, 1977. Amended by Stats.1982, c. 517, p. 2336, § 115.)*

Law Revision Commission Comments

Section 489.420 is based on former Section 553.5. Section 489.420 provides for release where the defendant appeals and the trial court in its discretion requires an undertaking and the undertaking is given. See Section 917.9. Perfection of an appeal by the defendant stays the enforcement of the judgment but does not otherwise affect the lien of attachment. See Section 916. The defendant may, of course, have already obtained a release pursuant to Section 489.310. The provision for the levying officer's fees has been eliminated. These can be recovered eventually as costs, pending the final determination in the action.

Section 489.420 is amended for consistency with the Bond and Undertaking Law. See Section 995.910 (objections to undertakings) [16 Cal.L.Rev.Comm. Reports 501 (1982)].

Research References

Rutter, Cal. Practice Guide: Enforcing Judgments/Debts Ch. 4-A, A. Attachment.
Miller and Starr California Real Estate § 32:32, Termination of the Attachment Lien.
Miller and Starr California Real Estate § 32:35, Noticed Hearing Procedure.
6 Witkin Cal. Proc. 5th Provisional Remedies § 91, (S 91) Undertakings.
6 Witkin Cal. Proc. 5th Provisional Remedies § 219, (S 219) Defendant's Appeal With Undertaking.

CHAPTER 10. LIABILITY FOR WRONGFUL ATTACHMENT

Section
490.010.   Wrongful attachment defined.
490.020.   Scope of liability; limitation.
490.040.   Offset against amount of recovery.
490.060.   Common law recovery.

§ 490.010. Wrongful attachment defined

A wrongful attachment consists of any of the following:

(a) The levy under a writ of attachment or the service of a temporary protective order in an action in which attachment is not authorized, except that it is not a wrongful attachment if both of the following are established:

(1) The levy was not authorized solely because of the prohibition of subdivision (c) of Section 483.010.

(2) The person who sold or leased, or licensed for use, the property, furnished the services, or loaned the money reasonably believed that it would not be used primarily for personal, family, or household purposes.

(b) The levy under a writ of attachment or the service of a temporary protective order in an action in which the plaintiff does not recover judgment.

(c) The levy under writ of attachment obtained pursuant to Article 3 (commencing with Section 484.510) of Chapter 4 or Chapter 5 (commencing with Section 485.010) on property exempt from attachment except where the plaintiff shows that the plaintiff reasonably believed that the property attached was not exempt from attachment. *(Added by Stats.1974, c. 1516, p. 3372, § 9, operative Jan. 1, 1977. Amended by Stats.1976, c. 437, p. 1138, § 42; Stats.1982, c. 1198, p. 4310, § 53, operative July 1, 1983.)*

Law Revision Commission Comments

Section 490.010 is amended to delete subdivision (d) which related to wrongful attachment of property of third persons. A third person whose property is levied upon may resort to the remedies provided by Division 4 (commencing with Section 720.010) of Title 9 (third-party claim) or to common law remedies (16 Cal.L.Rev.Comm. Reports 701).

Research References

Rutter, Cal. Practice Guide: Civ. Pro. Before Trial Ch. 9(II)-D, D. Attachment.
Rutter, Cal. Practice Guide: Enforcing Judgments/Debts Ch. 4-A, A. Attachment.
Rutter, Cal. Practice Guide: Insurance Litigation Ch. 6I-B, B. Particular Surety Bond Coverages.
Miller and Starr California Real Estate § 32:38, Wrongful Attachment--In General.
Miller and Starr California Real Estate § 32:39, Statutory Recovery on the Undertaking.
6 Witkin Cal. Proc. 5th Provisional Remedies § 53, Nature and Scope.

6 Witkin Cal. Proc. 5th Provisional Remedies § 232, (S 232) Statutory Remedy.
6 Witkin Cal. Proc. 5th Provisional Remedies § 233, (S 233) Acts Constituting Wrongful Attachment.
6 Witkin Cal. Proc. 5th Provisional Remedies § 234, (S 234) Measure of Plaintiff's Liability.
5 Witkin, California Summary 10th Torts § 523, (S 523) Improper or Excessive Attachment.

§ 490.020. Scope of liability; limitation

(a) The liability of a plaintiff for causing a wrongful attachment under Section 490.010 includes both of the following:

(1) All damages proximately caused to the defendant by the wrongful attachment.

(2) All costs and expenses, including attorney's fees, reasonably expended in defeating the attachment.

(b) The liability of a plaintiff for wrongful attachment pursuant to Section 490.010 is limited by the amount of the undertaking. *(Added by Stats.1974, c. 1516, p. 3372, § 9, operative Jan. 1, 1977. Amended by Stats.1982, c. 1198, p. 4311, § 54, operative July 1, 1983.)*

Law Revision Commission Comments

Section 490.020 is amended to make clear that only the defendant may recover for a wrongful attachment pursuant to Section 490.010. A third person is entitled to protection pursuant to Division 4 (commencing with Section 720.010) of Title 9 (third-party claims). See also Section 488.465 (objection by third person to undertaking where joint account or safe deposit box in name of third person) (16 Cal.L.Rev.Comm. Reports 701).

Research References

Rutter, Cal. Practice Guide: Civ. Pro. Before Trial Ch. 9(II)-D, D. Attachment.
Rutter, Cal. Practice Guide: Enforcing Judgments/Debts Ch. 2-C, C. Tort Liability.
Rutter, Cal. Practice Guide: Enforcing Judgments/Debts Ch. 4-A, A. Attachment.
Rutter, Cal. Practice Guide: Insurance Litigation Ch. 6I-B, B. Particular Surety Bond Coverages.
Miller and Starr California Real Estate § 32:38, Wrongful Attachment--In General.
Miller and Starr California Real Estate § 32:39, Statutory Recovery on the Undertaking.
6 Witkin Cal. Proc. 5th Provisional Remedies § 225, Amount of Recovery.
6 Witkin Cal. Proc. 5th Provisional Remedies § 234, (S 234) Measure of Plaintiff's Liability.

§ 490.040. Offset against amount of recovery

The amount of any recovery for wrongful attachment shall be offset insofar as possible against any unsatisfied amounts owed to the plaintiff by the defendant on the judgment in the action for which wrongful attachment damages are awarded. *(Added by Stats.1974, c. 1516, p. 3373, § 9, operative Jan. 1, 1977.)*

Research References

Rutter, Cal. Practice Guide: Enforcing Judgments/Debts Ch. 4-A, A. Attachment.
Miller and Starr California Real Estate § 32:39, Statutory Recovery on the Undertaking.
6 Witkin Cal. Proc. 5th Provisional Remedies § 234, (S 234) Measure of Plaintiff's Liability.

§ 490.060. Common law recovery

Nothing in this chapter limits the right to recover for damages caused by an attachment or protective order on any common law theory of recovery. *(Added by Stats.1974, c. 1516, p. 3373, § 9, operative Jan. 1, 1977.)*

Law Revision Commission Comments

Section 490.060 makes clear that this chapter does not limit the common law remedies for wrongful attachment such as malicious prosecution and abuse of process. See, e.g., White Lighting Co. v. Wolfson, 68 Cal.2d 336, 438 P.2d 345, 66 Cal.Rptr. 697 (1968).

Research References

Rutter, Cal. Practice Guide: Civ. Pro. Before Trial Ch. 9(II)-D, D. Attachment.

Rutter, Cal. Practice Guide: Enforcing Judgments/Debts Ch. 2-C, C. Tort Liability.

Rutter, Cal. Practice Guide: Enforcing Judgments/Debts Ch. 4-A, A. Attachment.

Miller and Starr California Real Estate § 32:38, Wrongful Attachment--In General.

6 Witkin Cal. Proc. 5th Provisional Remedies § 232, (S 232) Statutory Remedy.

CHAPTER 11. ATTACHING PLAINTIFF'S MISCELLANEOUS REMEDIES

ARTICLE 1. EXAMINATION OF THIRD PERSON

§ 491.110. Application and affidavit; order for appearance; service of order; lien

(a) Upon ex parte application by the plaintiff and proof by the plaintiff by affidavit or otherwise to the satisfaction of the proper court that the plaintiff has a right to attach order and that a third person has possession or control of property in which the defendant has an interest or is indebted to the defendant in an amount exceeding two hundred fifty dollars ($250), the court shall make an order directing the third person to appear before the court, or before a referee appointed by the court, at a time and place specified in the order, to answer concerning the property or debt. The affidavit in support of the plaintiff's application may be based on the affiant's information and belief.

(b) Not less than 10 days prior to the date set for the examination, a copy of the order shall be:

(1) Served personally on the third person.

(2) Served personally or by mail on the defendant.

(c) If the property or the debt is described in the affidavit or application for an order under subdivision (a) in a manner reasonably adequate to permit it to be identified, service of the order on the third person creates a lien on the defendant's interest in the property in the third person's possession or control or on the debt owed by the third person to the defendant. The lien continues for a period of one year from the date of the order unless extended or sooner terminated by the court.

(d) The order shall contain the following statement in 14-point boldface type if printed or in capital letters if typed: "NOTICE TO PERSON SERVED. If you fail to appear at the time and place specified in this order, you may be subject to arrest and punishment for contempt of court and the court may make an order requiring you to pay the reasonable attorney's fees incurred by the plaintiff in this proceeding."

(e) The order is not effective unless, at the time it is served on the third person, the person serving the order tenders to the third person fees for the mileage necessary to be traveled from the third person's residence to the place of examination. The fees shall be in the same amount generally provided for witnesses when legally required to attend civil proceedings in the court where the examination proceeding is to be conducted. *(Added by Stats.1982, c. 1198, p. 4311, § 57, operative July 1, 1983.)*

Law Revision Commission Comments

Section 491.110 supersedes the first and third sentences of subdivision (a) and all of subdivision (b) of former Section 491.010. Section 491.110 is drawn from subdivisions (a), (b), (c), (e) (1), and (f) of Section 708.120 (Enforcement of Judgments Law). See also Section 482.070 (manner of service). The provision in subdivision (a) limiting examinations to third persons owing more than $250 and the provisions of subdivisions (c), (d), and (e) are new in the Attachment Law. Consistent with former law, Section 491.110 does not permit the general examination of the defendant (16 Cal.L.Rev.Comm. Reports 701).

Research References

Rutter, Cal. Practice Guide: Civ. Pro. Before Trial Ch. 9(II)-D, D. Attachment.

Rutter, Cal. Practice Guide: Enforcing Judgments/Debts Ch. 4-A, A. Attachment.

Miller and Starr California Real Estate § 32:30, When Property Held by Third Party.

Miller and Starr California Real Estate § 11:124, Relation to Prior Interests.

6 Witkin Cal. Proc. 5th Provisional Remedies § 53, Nature and Scope.

6 Witkin Cal. Proc. 5th Provisional Remedies § 178, Deposit Accounts and Boxes in Third Person's Name.

6 Witkin Cal. Proc. 5th Provisional Remedies § 179, Securities.

6 Witkin Cal. Proc. 5th Provisional Remedies § 184, Nature and Effect of Lien.

6 Witkin Cal. Proc. 5th Provisional Remedies § 195, (S 195) in General.

6 Witkin Cal. Proc. 5th Provisional Remedies § 196, (S 196) Application.

6 Witkin Cal. Proc. 5th Provisional Remedies § 197, (S 197) Order to Appear.

6 Witkin Cal. Proc. 5th Provisional Remedies § 198, (S 198) Examination.

§ 491.120. Witnesses

In any proceeding for the examination of a third person under this article, witnesses, including the defendant, may be required to appear and testify before the court or referee in the same manner as upon the trial of an issue. *(Added by Stats.1982, c. 1198, p. 4312, § 57, operative July 1, 1983.)*

Law Revision Commission Comments

Section 491.120 continues the substance of former Section 491.040 (16 Cal.L.Rev.Comm. Reports 701).

Research References

Rutter, Cal. Practice Guide: Civ. Pro. Before Trial Ch. 9(II)-D, D. Attachment.

Rutter, Cal. Practice Guide: Enforcing Judgments/Debts Ch. 4-A, A. Attachment.

6 Witkin Cal. Proc. 5th Provisional Remedies § 198, (S 198) Examination.

§ 491.130. Referee; powers

(a) The examination proceedings authorized by this article may be conducted by a referee appointed by the court. The referee may issue, modify, or vacate an order authorized by Section 491.190, may make a protective order authorized by

Section 491.180, and may issue a warrant authorized by Section 491.160, and has the same power as the court to grant adjournments, to preserve order, and to subpoena witnesses to attend the examination, but only the court that ordered the reference has power to do any of the following:

(1) Punish for contempt for disobeying an order of the referee.

(2) Make an award of attorney's fees pursuant to Section 491.160.

(3) Determine a third-party claim under Section 491.170.

(b) Only a member of the State Bar of California is eligible for appointment as a referee pursuant to this article.

(c) Nothing in subdivision (a) limits the power of a court to appoint a temporary judge pursuant to Section 21 of Article VI of the California Constitution. *(Added by Stats.1982, c. 1198, p. 4312, § 57, operative July 1, 1983.)*

Law Revision Commission Comments

Section 491.130 is new and is drawn from Section 708.140 (Enforcement of Judgments Law) (16 Cal.Rev.Comm. Reports 701).

Research References

Rutter, Cal. Practice Guide: Enforcing Judgments/Debts Ch. 4-A, A. Attachment.
6 Witkin Cal. Proc. 5th Provisional Remedies § 198, (S 198) Examination.

§ 491.140. Organizations; specified individuals; designation of persons to appear

(a) If a corporation, partnership, association, trust, or other organization is served with an order to appear for an examination, it shall designate to appear and be examined one or more officers, directors, managing agents, or other persons who are familiar with its property and debts.

(b) If the order to appear for an examination requires the appearance of a specified individual, the specified individual shall appear for the examination and may be accompanied by one or more officers, directors, managing agents, or other persons familiar with the property and debts of the corporation, partnership, association, trust, or other organization.

(c) If the order to appear for the examination does not require the appearance of a specified individual, the order shall advise the corporation, partnership, association, trust, or other organization of its duty to make a designation under subdivision (a).

(d) A corporation, partnership, association, trust, or other organization, whether or not a party, may appear at an examination through any authorized officer, director, or employee, whether or not the person is an attorney. *(Added by Stats.1982, c. 1198, p. 4312, § 57, operative July 1, 1983. Amended by Stats.1984, c. 538, § 7.5.)*

Law Revision Commission Comments

Section 491.140 supersedes the second sentence of subdivision (a) of former Section 490.010 and is drawn from Section 708.150 (Enforcement of Judgments Law). See the Comment to Section 708.150 (16 Cal.L.Rev. Comm. Reports 701).

Research References

Rutter, Cal. Practice Guide: Enforcing Judgments/Debts Ch. 4-A, A. Attachment.
6 Witkin Cal. Proc. 5th Provisional Remedies § 198, (S 198) Examination.

§ 491.150. Proper court for examination; procedure of court other than court that issued writ; fees

(a) Except as otherwise provided in this section, the proper court for examination of a person under this article is the court that issued the writ of attachment.

(b) A person sought to be examined may not be required to attend an examination before a court located outside the county in which the person resides or has a place of business unless the distance from the person's place of residence or place of business to the place of examination is less than 150 miles.

(c) If a person sought to be examined does not reside or have a place of business in the county where the court that issued the writ is located, the superior court in the county where the person resides or has a place of business is a proper court for examination of the person.

(d) If the plaintiff seeks an examination of a person before a court other than the court that issued the writ, the plaintiff shall file an application that shall include all of the following:

(1) A certified copy of the complaint in the pending action.

(2) An affidavit in support of the application stating the place of residence or place of business of the person sought to be examined.

(3) Any necessary affidavit or showing for the examination as required by Section 491.110.

(4) The filing fee for a motion as provided in subdivision (a) of Section 70617 of the Government Code. *(Added by Stats. 1982, c. 1198, p. 4313, § 57, operative July 1, 1983. Amended by Stats.2005, c. 75 (A.B.145), § 33, eff. July 19, 2005, operative Jan. 1, 2006.)*

Law Revision Commission Comments

Section 491.150 is drawn from Section 708.160 (Enforcement of Judgments Law). Subdivision (b) continues the substance of former Section 491.020. Subdivisions (c) and (d) continue the substance of former Section 491.030 (16 Cal.L.Rev.Comm. Reports 701).

Research References

Rutter, Cal. Practice Guide: Enforcing Judgments/Debts Ch. 4-A, A. Attachment.
6 Witkin Cal. Proc. 5th Provisional Remedies § 195, (S 195) in General.
6 Witkin Cal. Proc. 5th Provisional Remedies § 196, (S 196) Application.

§ 491.160. Failure to appear; wilfully making improper service

(a) If an order requiring a person to appear for an examination was served by a sheriff, marshal, a person specially appointed by the court in the order, or a registered process server, and the person fails to appear:

(1) The court may do either of the following:

(A) Pursuant to a warrant, have the person brought before the court to answer for the failure to appear and may punish the person for contempt.

(B) Issue a warrant for the arrest of the person who failed to appear as required by the court order, pursuant to Section 1993.

(2) If the person's failure to appear is without good cause, the plaintiff shall be awarded reasonable attorney's fees incurred in the examination proceeding.

(b) A person who willfully makes an improper service of an order for an examination which subsequently results in the arrest pursuant to subdivision (a) of the person who fails to appear is guilty of a misdemeanor. *(Added by Stats.1982, c. 1198, p. 4313, § 57, operative July 1, 1983. Amended by Stats.1996, c. 872 (A.B.3472), § 13; Stats.2006, c. 277 (A.B.2369), § 1.)*

Law Revision Commission Comments

Subdivision (a)(1) of Section 491.160 continues the substance of former Section 491.010(c); the remainder of Section 491.160 is new and is consistent with Section 708.170 (Enforcement of Judgments Law). See also Section 481.205 ("registered process server" defined). The substance of the provision of Section 708.170 relating to attorney's fees awarded against the debtor is not included in Section 491.160 since the defendant is not permitted to be directly examined under this chapter (16 Cal.L.Rev. Comm. Reports 701).

§ 491.170. Determination of adverse interest or debt; orders of court; undertaking; modifying or vacating order

(a) Subject to subdivision (b), if a third person examined pursuant to this article claims an interest in the property adverse to the defendant or denies the debt, the court may, if the plaintiff so requests, determine the interests in the property or the existence of the debt. Such a determination is conclusive as to the plaintiff, the defendant, and the third person, but an appeal may be taken from the determination in the manner provided for appeals from the court in which the proceeding takes place. The court may grant a continuance for a reasonable time for discovery proceedings, the production of evidence, or other preparation for the hearing.

(b) The court may not make the determination provided in subdivision (a) if the third person's claim is made in good faith and any of the following conditions is satisfied:

(1) The court would not be a proper court for the trial of an independent civil action (including a creditor's suit) for the determination of the interests in the property or the existence of the debt, and the third person objects to the determination of the matter under subdivision (a).

(2) At the time an order for examination pursuant to this article is served on the third person a civil action (including a creditor's suit) is pending with respect to the interests in the property or the existence of the debt.

(3) The court determines that the interests in the property or the existence of the debt should be determined in a creditor's suit.

(c) Upon application of the plaintiff made ex parte, the court may make an order forbidding transfer of the property to the defendant or payment of the debt to the defendant until the interests in the property or the existence of the debt is determined pursuant to subdivision (a) or until a creditor's suit may be commenced and an order obtained pursuant to Section 491.340. An undertaking may be required in the discretion of the court. The court may modify or vacate the order at any time with or without a hearing on such terms as are just.

(d) Upon application of the plaintiff upon noticed motion, the court, if it determines that the defendant probably owns an interest in the property or that the debt probably is owed to the defendant, may make an order forbidding the transfer or other disposition of the property to any person or forbidding payment of the debt until the interests in the property or the existence of the debt is determined pursuant to subdivision (a) or until a creditor's suit may be commenced and an order obtained pursuant to Section 491.340. The court shall require the plaintiff to furnish an undertaking as provided in Section 529. The court may modify or vacate the order at any time after notice and hearing on such terms as are just. *(Added by Stats.1982, c. 1198, p. 4314, § 57, operative July 1, 1983.)*

Law Revision Commission Comments

Section 491.170 is new and is drawn from Section 708.180 (Enforcement of Judgments Law). See the Comment to Section 708.180. Under former Section 491.010, the court was not permitted in an examination proceeding to determine an adverse claim of a third person to the property sought to be attached. See also Sections 491.190 (order attaching property or for payment of debt or delivery of property to

levying officer), 491.310 (creditor's suit) (16 Cal.L.Rev.Comm. Reports 701).

§ 491.180. Protective orders

In any proceeding under this article, the court may, on motion of the person to be examined or on its own motion, make such protective orders as justice may require. *(Added by Stats.1982, c. 1198, p. 4314, § 57, operative July 1, 1983.)*

Law Revision Commission Comments

Section 491.180 is new and is drawn from Section 708.200 (Enforcement of Judgments Law) (16 Cal.L.Rev.Comm. Reports 701).

§ 491.190. Conclusion of proceedings; orders of court; claim of adverse interest or debt

(a) Except as provided in subdivision (b), at the conclusion of a proceeding pursuant to this article:

(1) The court may order the defendant's interest in the property in the possession or under the control of the third person or a debt owed by the third person to the defendant to be attached in the manner and under the conditions provided by this title or to be delivered or paid to the levying officer if the levying officer has a writ of attachment permitting the attachment of the property or debt. After the property or debt has been attached, the order may be enforced as provided in Section 491.360. The order creates a lien on the property or debt. The lien continues for a period of one year from the date of the order unless the court extends or reduces the period of the existence of the lien.

(2) If the property or debt has previously been attached, the court may make an order determining the third person's liability, and the order may be enforced as provided in Section 491.360.

(b) If a third person examined pursuant to this article claims an interest in the property adverse to the defendant or denies the debt and the court does not determine the matter as provided in subdivision (a) of Section 491.170, the court may not make an order under subdivision (a) of this section, but may make an order pursuant to subdivision (c) or (d) of Section 491.170 forbidding transfer or payment to the extent authorized by that section. *(Added by Stats.1982, c. 1198, p. 4315, § 57, operative July 1, 1983.)*

Law Revision Commission Comments

Section 491.190 supersedes former Section 491.010(d) and is drawn in part from Section 708.205 (Enforcement of Judgments Law). See the Comment to Section 708.205. See also Section 488.500(e) (relation back of attachment lien) (16 Cal.L.Rev.Comm. Reports 701).

Research References

Rutter, Cal. Practice Guide: Civ. Pro. Before Trial Ch. 9(II)-D, D. Attachment.

Rutter, Cal. Practice Guide: Enforcing Judgments/Debts Ch. 4-A, A. Attachment.

6 Witkin Cal. Proc. 5th Provisional Remedies § 198, (S 198) Examination.

6 Witkin Cal. Proc. 5th Provisional Remedies § 199, (S 199) Determination and Order.

§ 491.200. Lien attaching to property

A lien created under this article continues on property subject to the lien notwithstanding the transfer or encumbrance of the property subject to the lien unless the transfer or encumbrance is made to a person listed in Section 697.740. *(Added by Stats. 1982, c. 1198, p. 4315, § 57, operative July 1, 1983.)*

Law Revision Commission Comments

Section 491.200 is drawn from Section 697.920 (Enforcement of Judgments Law) (16 Cal.L.Rev.Comm. Reports 701).

Research References

Rutter, Cal. Practice Guide: Enforcing Judgments/Debts Ch. 4-A, A. Attachment.

Miller and Starr California Real Estate § 32:4, Effect.

Miller and Starr California Real Estate § 32:30, When Property Held by Third Party.

Miller and Starr California Real Estate § 11:123, Relation to Subsequent Interests.

Miller and Starr California Real Estate § 11:124, Relation to Prior Interests.

6 Witkin Cal. Proc. 5th Provisional Remedies § 197, (S 197) Order to Appear.

ARTICLE 2. CREDITOR'S SUIT

§ 491.310. Right of action against third person

If a third person has possession or control of property in which the defendant has an interest or is indebted to the defendant and the property or debt has been subjected to an attachment lien, the plaintiff may bring an action against the third person to enforce the third person's liability under this title. *(Added by Stats.1982, c. 1198, p. 4315, § 57, operative July 1, 1983.)*

Law Revision Commission Comments

Section 491.310 supersedes a portion of subdivision (c) of former Section 488.550 and is drawn from Section 708.210 (Enforcement of Judgments Law). Section 491.310 retains the requirement of former Section 488.550 that the property or debt have been attached. The procedure provided by this article is available only to enforce attachment liens. If a plaintiff has obtained only a lien in an examination proceeding (Section 491.110, 491.190), the plaintiff may not bring a creditor's suit until the property or debt is levied upon under a writ of attachment (16 Cal.L.Rev.Comm. Reports 701).

Research References

Rutter, Cal. Practice Guide: Civ. Pro. Before Trial Ch. 9(II)-D, D. Attachment.

Rutter, Cal. Practice Guide: Enforcing Judgments/Debts Ch. 4-A, A. Attachment.

Miller and Starr California Real Estate § 32:30, When Property Held by Third Party.

6 Witkin Cal. Proc. 5th Provisional Remedies § 178, Deposit Accounts and Boxes in Third Person's Name.

6 Witkin Cal. Proc. 5th Provisional Remedies § 201, (S 201) Nature of Action.

§ 491.320. Joinder of defendant; venue

The defendant shall be joined in an action brought pursuant to this article but is not an indispensable party. The residence of the defendant may not be considered in the determination of proper venue unless otherwise provided by contract between the defendant and the third person. *(Added by Stats.1982, c. 1198, p. 4315, § 57, operative July 1, 1983.)*

Law Revision Commission Comments

Section 491.320 supersedes the third sentence of subdivision (c) of former Section 488.550 and is drawn from Section 708.220 (Enforcement of Judgments Law). See the Comment to Section 708.220 (16 Cal.L.Rev. Comm. Reports 701).

Research References

Rutter, Cal. Practice Guide: Enforcing Judgments/Debts Ch. 4-A, A. Attachment.

6 Witkin Cal. Proc. 5th Provisional Remedies § 201, (S 201) Nature of Action.

§ 491.330. Limitation of actions; lien

(a) Except as provided in subdivision (b), an action shall be commenced pursuant to this article before the expiration of the later of the following times:

(1) The time when the defendant may bring an action against the third person concerning the property or debt.

(2) One year after creation of an attachment lien on the property or debt pursuant to this title if the lien is created at the time when the defendant may bring an action against the third person concerning the property or debt.

(b) An action may not be commenced pursuant to this article if the attachment lien is not in effect.

(c) If an action is commenced pursuant to this article within the time permitted in this section, the action may be prosecuted to judgment so long as the attachment lien or a lien of the plaintiff on the same property pursuant to Title 9 (commencing with Section 680.010) is in effect. *(Added by Stats.1982, c. 1198, p. 4315, § 57, operative July 1, 1983.)*

Law Revision Commission Comments

Section 491.330 supersedes a portion of subdivision (c) of former Section 488.550 and is drawn from Section 708.230 (Enforcement of Judgments Law) (16 Cal.L.Rev.Comm. Reports 701).

Research References

Rutter, Cal. Practice Guide: Enforcing Judgments/Debts Ch. 4-A, A. Attachment.

6 Witkin Cal. Proc. 5th Provisional Remedies § 201, (S 201) Nature of Action.

§ 491.340. Restraining orders; injunction

The plaintiff may apply to the court in which an action under this article is pending for either or both of the following:

(a) An order restraining the third person from transferring the attached property to the defendant or from paying the attached debt to the defendant. The order shall be made on noticed motion if the court so directs or a court rule so requires. Otherwise, the order may be made on ex parte application. The order shall remain in effect until judgment is entered in the action or until such earlier time as the court may provide in the order. An undertaking may be required in the discretion of the court. The court may modify or vacate the order at any time with or without a hearing on such terms as are just.

(b) A temporary restraining order or a preliminary injunction or both, restraining the third person from transferring to any person or otherwise disposing of the attached property, pursuant to Chapter 3 (commencing with Section 525) of Title 7, and the court may make, dissolve, and modify such orders as provided therein. *(Added by Stats.1982, c. 1198, p. 4316, § 57, operative July 1, 1983.)*

Law Revision Commission Comments

Section 491.340 is new and is drawn from Section 708.240 (Enforcement of Judgments Law) (16 Cal.L.Rev.Comm. Reports 701).

Research References

Rutter, Cal. Practice Guide: Enforcing Judgments/Debts Ch. 4-A, A. Attachment.
6 Witkin Cal. Proc. 5th Provisional Remedies § 91, (S 91) Undertakings.
6 Witkin Cal. Proc. 5th Provisional Remedies § 199, (S 199) Determination and Order.
6 Witkin Cal. Proc. 5th Provisional Remedies § 202, (S 202) Order and Judgment.

§ 491.350.　Jury trial

There is no right to a jury trial in an action under this article. *(Added by Stats.1982, c. 1198, p. 4316, § 57, operative July 1, 1983.)*

Law Revision Commission Comments

Section 491.350 is new and is the same as Section 708.270 (Enforcement of Judgments Law). See the Comment to Section 708.270 (16 Cal.L.Rev. Comm. Reports 701).

Research References

6 Witkin Cal. Proc. 5th Provisional Remedies § 201, (S 201) Nature of Action.

§ 491.360.　Judgment; enforcement

If the plaintiff establishes the liability of the third person, the court shall render judgment accordingly. The judgment may be enforced in the same manner as it could be enforced if it had been obtained by the defendant against the third party; but, prior to entry of judgment in favor of the plaintiff against the defendant, any money or property obtained in enforcing the judgment against the third party shall be paid or delivered into court to abide the judgment in the action of the plaintiff against the defendant or shall be held by a levying officer, or otherwise held, as ordered by the court. *(Added by Stats.1982, c. 1198, p. 4316, § 57, operative July 1, 1983.)*

Law Revision Commission Comments

Section 491.360 is new. The amount of the liability of the third person is determined under Section 488.600 which incorporates by reference the provisions of the Enforcement of Judgments Law, including subdivision (a) of Section 701.020 (16 Cal.L.Rev.Comm. Reports 701).

Research References

Rutter, Cal. Practice Guide: Enforcing Judgments/Debts Ch. 4-A, A. Attachment.
6 Witkin Cal. Proc. 5th Provisional Remedies § 199, (S 199) Determination and Order.
6 Witkin Cal. Proc. 5th Provisional Remedies § 202, (S 202) Order and Judgment.

§ 491.370.　Costs

Costs incurred by or taxed against the plaintiff in an action under this article may not be recovered from the defendant. *(Added by Stats.1982, c. 1198, p. 4316, § 57, operative July 1, 1983.)*

Law Revision Commission Comments

Section 491.370 is new and is analogous to subdivision (b) of Section 708.290 (Enforcement of Judgments Law) (16 Cal.L.Rev.Comm. Reports 701).

Research References

Rutter, Cal. Practice Guide: Enforcing Judgments/Debts Ch. 4-A, A. Attachment.
Miller and Starr California Real Estate § 32:30, When Property Held by Third Party.
6 Witkin Cal. Proc. 5th Provisional Remedies § 202, (S 202) Order and Judgment.

ARTICLE 3.　LIEN IN PENDING ACTION OR PROCEEDING

Section
491.410.　Right to attach order; extent of lien; notice of lien; service on parties; pendency of appeal.
491.415.　Defendant's cause of action and rights to money or property as property subject to attachment; application for order permitting creation of lien; undertaking; exemption.
491.420.　Notice of lien; contents.
491.430.　Intervention; plaintiff deemed to be a party.
491.440.　Consent of plaintiff to enforcement of judgment in favor of defendant, compromise, etc.; order of court.
491.450.　Statement of lien.
491.460.　Order for attachment; transfer of property; judgment against third party; enforcement; judicial custody of money or property.
491.470.　Money or property recovered by defendant in action or proceeding; exemption; termination of lien.

§ 491.410.　Right to attach order; notice of lien; service on parties; pendency of appeal

(a) If the defendant is a party to a pending action or special proceeding, the plaintiff may obtain a lien under this article, to the extent required to secure the amount to be secured by the attachment, on both of the following:

(1) Any cause of action of the defendant for money or property that is the subject of the other action or proceeding, if the money or property would be subject to attachment if the defendant prevails in the action or proceedings.

(2) The rights of the defendant to money or property under any judgment subsequently procured in the other action or proceeding, if the money or property would be subject to attachment.

(b) To obtain a lien under this article, the plaintiff shall file all of the following in the other pending action or special proceeding:

(1) A notice of lien.

(2) A copy of the right to attach order.

(3) A copy of an order permitting creation of a lien under this article made by the court that issued the right to attach order.

(c) At the time of the filing under subdivision (b) or promptly thereafter, the plaintiff shall serve on all parties who, prior thereto, have made an appearance in the other action or special proceeding a copy of the notice of lien and a statement of the date when the notice of lien was filed in the other action or special proceeding. Failure to serve all parties as required by this subdivision does not affect the lien created by the filing under subdivision (b), but the rights of a party are not affected by the lien until the party has notice of the lien.

(d) For the purpose of this article, an action or special proceeding is pending until the time for appeal from the judgment has expired or, if an appeal is filed, until the appeal has been finally determined. *(Added by Stats.1982, c. 1198, p. 4316, § 57, operative July 1, 1983. Amended by Stats.1984, c. 538, § 8.)*

Law Revision Commission Comments

Section 491.410 is new and is drawn from Section 708.410 (Enforcement of Judgments Law). See also Sections 482.070 (manner of service), 483.015 (amount to be secured by attachment) (16 Cal.L.Rev.Comm. Reports 701).

Subdivision (a) of Section 491.410 is amended to provide that a lien may not be created under this article if the money or property the defendant seeks would not be subject to attachment should the defendant prevail in the action or special proceeding. See, e.g., Section 487.010 (property subject to attachment). Subdivision (b) is amended to require the plaintiff to file a court order permitting creation of a lien under this article. [17 Cal.L.Rev.Comm.Reports 975 (1984)].

Research References

Rutter, Cal. Practice Guide: Enforcing Judgments/Debts Ch. 4-A, A. Attachment.
Rutter, Cal. Practice Guide: Prof. Responsibility Ch. 5-F, F. Formalizing Fee Agreements.
Miller and Starr California Real Estate § 32:20, Individual Defendants.
Miller and Starr California Real Estate § 32:21, Nonindividual Defendants.
1 Witkin Cal. Proc. 5th Attorneys § 172, (S 172) Priority.
6 Witkin Cal. Proc. 5th Provisional Remedies § 179, Securities.
6 Witkin Cal. Proc. 5th Provisional Remedies § 182, Property Subject of Pending Action.
6 Witkin Cal. Proc. 5th Provisional Remedies § 203, Nature of Lien.
6 Witkin Cal. Proc. 5th Provisional Remedies § 204, Plaintiff's Application.
6 Witkin Cal. Proc. 5th Provisional Remedies § 205, Notice.
6 Witkin Cal. Proc. 5th Provisional Remedies § 208, Effect on Judgment in Action.

§ 491.415. Defendant's cause of action and rights to money or property as property subject to attachment; application for order permitting creation of lien; undertaking; exemption

(a) For the purpose of applying for a right to attach order, the defendant's cause of action that is the subject of the pending action or proceeding and the defendant's rights to money or property under a judgment procured in the action or proceeding shall be treated as property subject to attachment.

(b) At the time the plaintiff applies for a right to attach order, the plaintiff may apply for an order permitting creation of a lien under this article. If the plaintiff has already obtained a right to attach order, an application for an order permitting creation of a lien under this article may be applied for in the same manner as a writ of attachment. As a prerequisite to obtaining an order under this subdivision, the plaintiff shall file an undertaking as provided by Sections 489.210 and 489.220.

(c) The defendant may, but is not required to, claim an exemption in a proceeding initiated by the plaintiff for an order permitting creation of a lien under this article. An exemption may be claimed if the money or property sought by the defendant would be exempt from attachment should the defendant prevail in the other action or proceeding. The exemption shall be claimed and determined pursuant to this subdivision in the same manner as an exemption is claimed and determined upon application for a writ of attachment. *(Added by Stats.1984, c. 538, § 9.)*

Law Revision Commission Comments

Subdivision (a) of Section 491.415 facilitates applying for a right to attach order in a situation where the plaintiff seeks to create a lien under this article. See Section 484.020 (application for right to attach order). Subdivision (b) imposes a new requirement that the plaintiff obtain a court order permitting creation of the lien; this requirement is analogous

to obtain a writ of attachment which describes the property to be attached. See Section 488.010 (contents of writ of attachment). Subdivision (b) also makes clear that an undertaking is required. If an undertaking has already been given to obtain a writ of attachment, this provision does not require another undertaking.

Subdivision (c) permits the defendant to make an exemption claim in the proceedings initiated by the plaintiff to obtain a right to attach order and an order permitting creation of a lien in a pending action. This subdivision incorporates the procedures applicable to claiming attachment exemptions generally. The defendant may also claim exemptions pursuant to the procedure provided in Section 491.470, if the exemption has not been determined under subdivision (c) of Section 491.415. Proceedings under Section 491.415 are in the court where the plaintiff's action against the defendant is pending, whereas proceedings under Section 491.470 are in the court where the action involving the defendant's right to money or property is pending. [17 Cal.L.Rev.Comm.Reports 975 (1984)].

Research References

Rutter, Cal. Practice Guide: Enforcing Judgments/Debts Ch. 4-A, A. Attachment.
6 Witkin Cal. Proc. 5th Provisional Remedies § 204, Plaintiff's Application.
6 Witkin Cal. Proc. 5th Provisional Remedies § 206, (S 206) Before Creation of Lien.
6 Witkin Cal. Proc. 5th Provisional Remedies § 207, (S 207) After Creation of Lien.

§ 491.420. Notice of lien; contents

The notice of lien under Section 491.410 shall contain all of the following:

(a) A statement that a lien has been created under this article and the title of the court and the cause and number of the pending action or proceeding in which the notice of lien is filed.

(b) The name and last known address of the defendant.

(c) The name and address of the plaintiff.

(d) The title of the court where the plaintiff's action against the defendant is pending and the cause and number of the action.

(e) The amount required to secure the amount to be secured by the attachment at the time the notice of lien is filed in the action or proceeding.

(f) A statement that the lien attaches to any cause of action of the defendant that is the subject of such action or proceeding and to the defendant's rights to money or property under any judgment subsequently procured in the action or proceeding.

(g) A statement that no compromise, dismissal, settlement, or satisfaction of the pending action or proceeding or any of the defendant's rights to money or property under any judgment procured therein may be entered into by or on behalf of the defendant, and that the defendant may not enforce the defendant's rights to money or property under any judgment procured in the pending action or proceeding by a writ or otherwise, unless one of the following requirements is satisfied:

(1) The prior approval by order of the court in which the action or proceeding is pending has been obtained.

(2) The written consent of the plaintiff has been obtained or the plaintiff has released the lien. *(Added by Stats.1982, c. 1198, p. 4317, § 57, operative July 1, 1983.)*

Law Revision Commission Comments

Section 491.420 is drawn from Section 708.420(a)–(g) (Enforcement of Judgments Law) (16 Cal.L.Rev.Comm. Reports 701).

Research References

Rutter, Cal. Practice Guide: Enforcing Judgments/Debts Ch. 4-A, A. Attachment.

6 Witkin Cal. Proc. 5th Provisional Remedies § 205, Notice.

§ 491.430.   Intervention; plaintiff deemed to be a party

(a) The court in which the action or special proceeding subject to the lien under this article is pending may permit the plaintiff who has obtained the lien to intervene in the action or proceeding pursuant to Section 387.

(b) For the purposes of subdivision (a) of Section 491.460 and Section 491.470, a plaintiff shall be deemed to be a party to the action or special proceeding even though the plaintiff has not become a party to the action or proceeding under subdivision (a). *(Added by Stats.1982, c. 1198, p. 4317, § 57, operative July 1, 1983. Amended by Stats.1984, c. 538, § 10.)*

Law Revision Commission Comments

Section 491.430 is drawn from Section 708.430 (Enforcement of Judgments Law) (16 Cal.L.Rev.Comm. Reports 701).

Subdivision (b) of Section 491.430 is amended to take account of the enactment of Section 491.470 (exemption claim in court where action pending). [17 Cal.L.Rev.Comm.Reports 975 (1984)].

Research References

Rutter, Cal. Practice Guide: Enforcing Judgments/Debts Ch. 4-A, A. Attachment.
6 Witkin Cal. Proc. 5th Provisional Remedies § 207, (S 207) After Creation of Lien.
6 Witkin Cal. Proc. 5th Provisional Remedies § 209, Enforcement of Lien.

§ 491.440.   Consent of plaintiff to enforcement of judgment in favor of defendant, compromise, etc.; order of court

(a) Except as provided in subdivision (c) of Section 491.410, unless the lien is released, the judgment recovered in the action or special proceeding in favor of the defendant may not be enforced by a writ or otherwise, and no compromise, dismissal, settlement, or satisfaction of the pending action or special proceeding or the judgment procured therein may be entered into by or on behalf of the defendant, without the written consent of the plaintiff or authorization by order of the court obtained under subdivision (b).

(b) Upon application by the defendant, the court in which the action or special proceeding subject to the lien under this article is pending or the judgment procured therein is entered may, in its discretion, after a hearing, make an order described in subdivision (a) that may include such terms and conditions as the court deems necessary. The application for an order under this subdivision shall be made on noticed motion. The notice of motion shall be served on the plaintiff. *(Added by Stats.1982, c. 1198, p. 4318, § 57, operative July 1, 1983.)*

Research References

Rutter, Cal. Practice Guide: Enforcing Judgments/Debts Ch. 4-A, A. Attachment.
Miller and Starr California Real Estate § 32:21, Nonindividual Defendants.
6 Witkin Cal. Proc. 5th Provisional Remedies § 208, Effect on Judgment in Action.

§ 491.450.   Statement of lien

(a) If a lien is created pursuant to this article, the court clerk shall endorse upon the judgment recovered in the action or special proceeding a statement of the existence of the lien and the time it was created.

(b) Any abstract issued upon the judgment shall include a statement of the lien in favor of the plaintiff. *(Added by Stats.1982, c. 1198, p. 4318, § 57, operative July 1, 1983.)*

Law Revision Commission Comments

Section 491.450 is drawn from Section 708.460 (Enforcement of Judgments Law) (16 Cal.L.Rev.Comm. Reports 701).

Research References

6 Witkin Cal. Proc. 5th Provisional Remedies § 208, Effect on Judgment in Action.

§ 491.460.   Order for attachment; transfer of property; judgment against third party; enforcement; judicial custody of money or property

(a) If the defendant is entitled to money or property under the judgment in the action or special proceeding and a lien created under this article exists, upon application of any party to the action or special proceeding, the court may order that the defendant's rights to money or property under the judgment be attached or otherwise applied to the satisfaction of the lien created under this article as ordered by the court. Application for an order under this section shall be on noticed motion. The notice of motion shall be served on all other parties.

(b) If the judgment determines that the defendant has an interest in property, the court may order the party having custody or control of the property not to transfer the property until it can be attached or otherwise applied to the satisfaction of the lien created under this article.

(c) If the court determines that a party (other than the defendant) having notice of the lien created under this article has transferred property that was subject to the lien, or has paid an amount to the defendant that was subject to the lien, the court shall render judgment against the party in an amount equal to the lesser of the following:

(1) The value of the defendant's interest in the property or the amount paid to the defendant.

(2) The amount of the plaintiff's lien created under this article.

(d) A judgment or order under this section may be enforced in the same manner as it could be enforced if it had been obtained by the defendant against the third party; but, prior to entry of judgment in favor of the plaintiff against the defendant, any money or property obtained in enforcing the judgment or order against the third party shall be paid or delivered into court to abide the judgment in the action of the plaintiff against the defendant or shall be held by a levying officer, or otherwise held, as ordered by the court. *(Added by Stats.1982, c. 1198, p. 4318, § 57, operative July 1, 1983.)*

Law Revision Commission Comments

Section 491.460 is drawn from Section 708.470 (Enforcement of Judgments Law). See also Sections 482.070 (manner of service), 483.015 (amount to be secured by attachment) (16 Cal.L.Rev.Comm. Reports 701).

Research References

Rutter, Cal. Practice Guide: Enforcing Judgments/Debts Ch. 4-A, A. Attachment.
6 Witkin Cal. Proc. 5th Provisional Remedies § 207, (S 207) After Creation of Lien.
6 Witkin Cal. Proc. 5th Provisional Remedies § 209, Enforcement of Lien.

§ 491.470.   Money or property recovered by defendant in action or proceeding; exemption; termination of lien

(a) If a lien is created under this article, the defendant may claim that all or any portion of the money or property that the defendant may recover in the action or special proceeding is exempt from attachment. The claim shall be made by application on noticed motion to the court in which the action or special proceeding is pending, filed, and served on the plaintiff not later than 30 days after the defendant has notice of the creation of lien. The defendant shall execute an affidavit in support of the application that includes the matters set forth in subdivision (c) of Section 484.070. No notice of opposition to the claim of exemption is required. The failure of the defendant to make a claim of exemption under this section constitutes a waiver of the exemption.

(b) The court may determine the exemption claim at any time prior to the entry of judgment in the action or special proceeding or may consolidate the exemption hearing with the hearing on a motion pursuant to Section 491.460.

(c) If the defendant establishes to the satisfaction of the court that the money or property that the defendant may recover in the action or special proceeding is all or partially exempt from attachment, the court shall order the termination of the lien created under this article on the exempt portion of the money or property. *(Added by Stats.1984, c. 538, § 11.)*

Law Revision Commission Comments

Section 491.470 provides the procedure for the making and determination of an exemption claimed for the defendant's prospective recovery that is subject to a lien created under this article. This procedure is drawn from Section 708.450. The plaintiff is deemed to be a party for the purposes of this section. See Section 491.430(b). See also Section 482.070 (manner of service).

An exemption claim may also be made and determined as provided in Section 491.415(c). See the Comment to Section 491.415(c). [17 Cal.L.Rev.Comm.Reports 975 (1984)].

Research References

Rutter, Cal. Practice Guide: Enforcing Judgments/Debts Ch. 4-A, A. Attachment.
6 Witkin Cal. Proc. 5th Provisional Remedies § 207, (S 207) After Creation of Lien.

CHAPTER 12. NONRESIDENT ATTACHMENT

Section

§ 492.010. Persons and entities subject to attachment

Notwithstanding subdivision (a) of Section 483.010, an attachment may be issued in any action for the recovery of money brought against any of the following:

(a) A natural person who does not reside in this state.

(b) A foreign corporation not qualified to do business in this state under the provisions of Chapter 21 (commencing with Section 2100) of Division 1 of Title 1 of the Corporations Code.

(c) A foreign partnership which has not filed a designation pursuant to Section 15700 of the Corporations Code. *(Added by Stats.1974, c. 1516, p. 3374, § 9, operative Jan. 1, 1977. Amended by Stats.1975, c. 682, p. 1512, § 5, operative Jan. 1, 1977; Stats.1982, c. 1198, p. 4319, § 58, operative July 1, 1983.)*

Law Revision Commission Comments

Section 492.010 is based upon subdivision (b) of former Section 537.1 and subdivision (d) of former Section 537.2. As under prior law, Section 492.010 authorizes issuance of an attachment in any action for the recovery of money against a nonresident individual, a foreign corporation not qualified to do business in this state, or a foreign partnership which has not designated an agent for service of process. This authority supplements that provided by Section 483.010 and other miscellaneous statutory authorizations. See Section 483.010 and Comment thereto. Special procedures for the issuance of an attachment under this chapter are provided in Sections 492.020 and 492.030. See also Sections 492.060–492.090. A procedure for setting aside an attachment issued under this chapter and a significant limitation on this authority to attach are provided in Section 492.050.

Section 492.010 is amended for consistency with Section 481.170 ("person" defined) (16 Cal.L.Rev.Comm. Reports 701).

Research References

Rutter, Cal. Practice Guide: Civ. Pro. Before Trial Ch. 3-B, B. Jurisdiction Over Parties-Personal Jurisdiction.
Rutter, Cal. Practice Guide: Civ. Pro. Before Trial Ch. 9(II)-D, D. Attachment.
Rutter, Cal. Practice Guide: Enforcing Judgments/Debts Ch. 4-A, A. Attachment.
Miller and Starr California Real Estate § 32:2, Nature of an Attachment Lien.
Miller and Starr California Real Estate § 32:9, Former Attachment Law.
Miller and Starr California Real Estate § 32:10, Current Attachment Law.
Miller and Starr California Real Estate § 32:11, Availability of Attachment--In General.
Miller and Starr California Real Estate § 32:12, Against Individual Defendants.
Miller and Starr California Real Estate § 32:14, Against Nonresident Individual Defendants.
Miller and Starr California Real Estate § 32:17, Unsecured Obligation.
Miller and Starr California Real Estate § 32:21, Nonindividual Defendants.
6 Witkin Cal. Proc. 5th Provisional Remedies § 53, Nature and Scope.
6 Witkin Cal. Proc. 5th Provisional Remedies § 57, (S 57) in General.
6 Witkin Cal. Proc. 5th Provisional Remedies § 237, Action for Money.
6 Witkin Cal. Proc. 5th Provisional Remedies § 239, Natural Person Not Residing in State.
6 Witkin Cal. Proc. 5th Provisional Remedies § 240, Foreign Corporation or Partnership.
6 Witkin Cal. Proc. 5th Provisional Remedies § 241, Application and Affidavit.
6 Witkin Cal. Proc. 5th Provisional Remedies § 242, Hearing, Order, and Writ.
6 Witkin Cal. Proc. 5th Provisional Remedies § 244, Motion to Set Aside and Quash.

§ 492.020. Application

(a) Upon the filing of the complaint or at any time thereafter, the plaintiff may apply pursuant to this chapter for a right to attach order and a writ of attachment by filing an application for the order and writ with the court in which the action is brought.

(b) The application shall satisfy the requirements of Section 484.020 and shall be supported by an affidavit showing all of the following:

(1) The action is one described in Section 492.010 and is brought against a defendant described in Section 492.010.

(2) The plaintiff on the facts presented would be entitled to a judgment on the claim upon which the attachment is based.

(3) The property sought to be attached is subject to attachment pursuant to Section 492.040.

(c) The affidavit in support of the showing required by paragraph (3) of subdivision (b) may be based on the affiant's information and belief. *(Added by Stats.1974, c. 1516, p. 3374, § 9, operative Jan. 1, 1977.)*

Law Revision Commission Comments

Sections 492.020 and 492.030 provide an ex parte procedure for the issuance of an attachment pursuant to the authority granted by Section 492.010. Compare Sections 485.210–485.220. See also subdivision (d) of former Section 538.5.

Research References

Rutter, Cal. Practice Guide: Enforcing Judgments/Debts Ch. 4-A, A. Attachment.

Miller and Starr California Real Estate § 32:21, Nonindividual Defendants.

6 Witkin Cal. Proc. 5th Provisional Remedies § 241, Application and Affidavit.

§ 492.030. Findings

(a) The court shall examine the application and supporting affidavit and shall issue a right to attach order, which shall state the amount to be secured by the attachment, and order a writ of attachment to be issued upon the filing of an undertaking as provided by Sections 489.210 and 489.220, if it finds all of the following:

(1) The claim upon which the attachment is based is one upon which an attachment may be issued.

(2) The plaintiff has established the probable validity of the claim upon which the attachment is based.

(3) The defendant is one described in Section 492.010.

(4) The attachment is not sought for a purpose other than the recovery on the claim upon which the attachment is based.

(5) The affidavit accompanying the application shows that the property sought to be attached, or the portion thereof to be specified in the writ, is subject to attachment pursuant to Section 492.040.

(6) The amount to be secured by the attachment is greater than zero.

(b) If the court finds that the application and supporting affidavit do not satisfy the requirements of this chapter, it shall so state and deny the order. If denial is solely on the ground that the defendant is not one described in Section 492.010, the judicial officer shall so state and such denial does not preclude the plaintiff from applying for a right to attach order and writ of attachment under Chapter 4 (commencing with Section 484.010) with the same affidavits and supporting papers. *(Added by Stats.1974, c. 1516, p. 3374, § 9, operative Jan. 1, 1977. Amended by Stats.1976, c. 437, p. 1139, § 44; Stats.1997, c. 222 (A.B.1258), § 10.)*

Law Revision Commission Comments

Section 492.030 is amended in the same manner as Section 484.090. See Comment to Section 484.090.

Paragraph (6) is added to subdivision (a) of Section 492.030 to make clear that the court is not to issue a right to attach order and writ of attachment if there is no amount to be secured by the attachment. This amendment is consistent with Section 484.090. See Section 484.090 Comment. [26 Cal.L.Rev.Comm. Reports 307 (1996)].

Research References

Rutter, Cal. Practice Guide: Civ. Pro. Before Trial Ch. 9(II)-D, D. Attachment.

Rutter, Cal. Practice Guide: Enforcing Judgments/Debts Ch. 4-A, A. Attachment.

Miller and Starr California Real Estate § 32:21, Nonindividual Defendants.

Miller and Starr California Real Estate § 32:35, Noticed Hearing Procedure.

6 Witkin Cal. Proc. 5th Provisional Remedies § 242, Hearing, Order, and Writ.

6 Witkin Cal. Proc. 5th Provisional Remedies § 243, Additional Writs.

§ 492.040. Property subject to attachment

Notwithstanding Sections 487.010 and 487.020, a writ of attachment issued under this chapter may be levied upon any property of a defendant for which a method of levy is provided by Article 2 (commencing with Section 488.300) of Chapter 8. However, after the defendant has filed a general appearance in the action, only nonexempt property of the defendant may be levied upon and property previously levied upon which is exempt under Section 487.020 shall be released upon order of the court.

(Added by Stats.1974, c. 1516, p. 3375, § 9, operative Jan. 1, 1977. Amended by Stats.1982, c. 1198, p. 4319, § 59, operative July 1, 1983.)

Law Revision Commission Comments

Section 492.040 describes the property which is subject to attachment under a writ issued pursuant to this chapter. Any property of any defendant for which a method of levy is provided by this title is subject initially to attachment. The limitations of Sections 487.010 and 487.020 do not apply until after the defendant has filed a general appearance in the action. However, after the defendant files a general appearance, he may secure either (1) a release of all property attached if there is no authorization for the attachment apart from the provisions of this chapter or (2) a release of any property exempt from attachment under Section 487.020 if an attachment is authorized under Section 483.010. See Section 483.010 and the Comment thereto. See also Section 492.050 and the Comment thereto.

Section 492.040 is amended to correct the reference to Article 2 of Chapter 8 (16 Cal.L.Rev.Comm. Reports 701).

Research References

Rutter, Cal. Practice Guide: Enforcing Judgments/Debts Ch. 4-A, A. Attachment.

Miller and Starr California Real Estate § 32:10, Current Attachment Law.

Miller and Starr California Real Estate § 32:14, Against Nonresident Individual Defendants.

Miller and Starr California Real Estate § 32:21, Nonindividual Defendants.

6 Witkin Cal. Proc. 5th Provisional Remedies § 75, in General.

6 Witkin Cal. Proc. 5th Provisional Remedies § 238, Property Subject to Attachment.

6 Witkin Cal. Proc. 5th Provisional Remedies § 241, Application and Affidavit.

6 Witkin Cal. Proc. 5th Provisional Remedies § 242, Hearing, Order, and Writ.

6 Witkin Cal. Proc. 5th Provisional Remedies § 243, Additional Writs.

6 Witkin Cal. Proc. 5th Provisional Remedies § 244, Motion to Set Aside and Quash.

§ 492.050. Application to quash attachment and release property; hearing; determination

(a) Any defendant whose property has been attached pursuant to a writ issued under this chapter may apply for an order that the right to attach order be set aside, the writ of attachment quashed, and any property levied upon pursuant to the writ released. Such application shall be made by filing with the court and serving on the plaintiff a notice of motion.

(b) The notice of motion shall state the grounds on which the motion is based and shall be accompanied by an affidavit supporting any factual issues raised and points and authorities supporting any legal issues raised.

(c) If the defendant has filed a general appearance in the action, the right to attach order shall be set aside unless the plaintiff shows that his right to attach is authorized by a provision other than Section 492.010.

(d) At the hearing on the motion, the court shall determine whether the plaintiff is entitled to a right to attach order. If the court finds that the plaintiff is not entitled to a right to attach order, it shall order the right to attach order set aside, the writ of attachment quashed, and any property levied upon pursuant to the writ released. If the court finds that the plaintiff is entitled to a right to attach order, the attachment shall continue in effect except as provided in Section 492.040 and, thereafter, the plaintiff may apply for additional writs pursuant to Article 2 (commencing with Section 484.310) or Article 3 (commencing with Section 484.510) of Chapter 4.

(e) The court's determination shall be made upon the basis of the pleadings and other papers in the record; but, upon good cause shown, the court may receive and consider at the hearing additional evidence, oral or documentary, and additional points and authorities, or it may continue the hearing for the production of such additional evidence or points and authorities.

(f) The hearing provided for in this section shall take precedence over all other civil matters on the calendar of that day except older matters of the same character. *(Added by Stats. 1974, c. 1516, p. 3375, § 9, operative Jan. 1, 1977.)*

Law Revision Commission Comments

Section 492.050 provides a procedure for testing and setting aside a right to attach order and writ of attachment issued pursuant to this chapter. The noticed motion procedure is comparable to that provided by Section 485.240. Substantively, however, subdivision (c) requires the plaintiff to show that his attachment is authorized by a provision other than Section 492.010 if the defendant files a general appearance in the action. This continues an innovation introduced in 1972 (see former Section 538.5(d), Cal.Stats.1972, Ch. 550, § 13) and demonstrates the jurisdictional nature of an attachment secured pursuant to this chapter. Even if the plaintiff can continue the attachment pursuant to some other statutory authority, *e.g.*, Section 483.010, the defendant is entitled to have such attachment limited to property subject to attachment under Sections 487.010 and 487.020. See Section 492.040 and Comment thereto. This section does not, of course, affect any right a defendant may have to a stay or dismissal of the action pursuant to Sections 410.30 and 418.10.

Research References

Rutter, Cal. Practice Guide: Civ. Pro. Before Trial Ch. 9(II)-D, D. Attachment.
Rutter, Cal. Practice Guide: Enforcing Judgments/Debts Ch. 4-A, A. Attachment.
6 Witkin Cal. Proc. 5th Provisional Remedies § 243, Additional Writs.
6 Witkin Cal. Proc. 5th Provisional Remedies § 244, Motion to Set Aside and Quash.

§ 492.060. Application for additional writ; time; filing

At any time after a right to attach order and writ of attachment have been issued under this chapter and before the hearing provided by Section 492.050, the plaintiff may apply for an additional writ of attachment under this chapter as provided in Sections 492.060 to 492.090, inclusive. The application shall be filed with the court in which the action is brought. *(Added by Stats.1974, c. 1516, p. 3376, § 9, operative Jan. 1, 1977.)*

Law Revision Commission Comments

Sections 492.060–492.090 provide a procedure which permits a plaintiff to secure additional writs under this chapter prior to the hearing contemplated by Section 492.050. Where there has been a hearing pursuant to Section 492.050 and the plaintiff's right to attach has been upheld, the plaintiff may apply for an additional writ pursuant to the procedures provided in Articles 2 and 3 of Chapter 4. See Section 492.050(d).

Research References

Rutter, Cal. Practice Guide: Enforcing Judgments/Debts Ch. 4-A, A. Attachment.
Miller and Starr California Real Estate § 32:21, Nonindividual Defendants.
6 Witkin Cal. Proc. 5th Provisional Remedies § 243, Additional Writs.

§ 492.070. Application for additional writ; execution; contents

The application shall be executed under oath and shall include all of the following:

(a) A statement that the plaintiff has been issued a right to attach order and writ of attachment pursuant to Section 492.030.

(b) A statement of the amount to be secured by the attachment.

(c) A description of the property to be attached under the writ of attachment and a statement that the plaintiff is informed and believes that such property is subject to attachment pursuant to Section 492.040. The description shall satisfy the requirements

of Section 484.020. *(Added by Stats.1974, c. 1516, p. 3376, § 9, operative Jan. 1, 1977. Amended by Stats.1982, c. 1198, p. 4319, § 60, operative July 1, 1983.)*

Law Revision Commission Comments

See Comment to Section 492.060.

The amendment to Section 492.070 is clarifying and conforms to the amendments made to Sections 484.020, 484.320, and 485.520 (16 Cal. L.Rev.Comm. Reports 701).

Research References

6 Witkin Cal. Proc. 5th Provisional Remedies § 243, Additional Writs.

§ 492.090. Application for writ; examination; issuance of writ; findings

The court shall examine the application and supporting affidavit and shall order a writ of attachment to be issued upon the filing of an undertaking as provided by Sections 489.210 and 489.220, if it finds both of the following:

(a) A right to attach order has been issued in the action pursuant to Section 492.030.

(b) The affidavit accompanying the application shows that the property sought to be attached, or the portion thereof to be specified in the writ, is subject to attachment pursuant to Section 492.040. *(Added by Stats.1974, c. 1516, p. 3376, § 9, operative Jan. 1, 1977. Amended by Stats.1976, c. 437, p. 1140, § 45.)*

Law Revision Commission Comments

See Comment to Section 492.060.

Section 492.090 is amended in the same manner as Section 484.370. See Comment to Section 484.370.

Research References

Rutter, Cal. Practice Guide: Enforcing Judgments/Debts Ch. 4-A, A. Attachment.
Miller and Starr California Real Estate § 32:2, Nature of an Attachment Lien.
Miller and Starr California Real Estate § 32:10, Current Attachment Law.
Miller and Starr California Real Estate § 32:11, Availability of Attachment--In General.
Miller and Starr California Real Estate § 32:14, Against Nonresident Individual Defendants.
Miller and Starr California Real Estate § 32:21, Nonindividual Defendants.
6 Witkin Cal. Proc. 5th Provisional Remedies § 243, Additional Writs.

CHAPTER 13. EFFECT OF BANKRUPTCY PROCEEDINGS AND GENERAL ASSIGNMENTS FOR THE BENEFIT OF CREDITORS

§ 493.010. General assignment for the benefit of creditors; requirements

As used in this chapter, "general assignment for the benefit of creditors" means an assignment which satisfies all of the following requirements:

(a) The assignment is an assignment of all the defendant's assets that are transferable and not exempt from enforcement of a money judgment.

(b) The assignment is for the benefit of all the defendant's creditors.

(c) The assignment does not itself create a preference of one creditor or class of creditors over any other creditor or class of creditors, but the assignment may recognize the existence of preferences to which creditors are otherwise entitled. *(Added by Stats.1977, c. 499, § 1. Amended by Stats.1982, c. 1198, p. 4319, § 61, operative July 1, 1983.)*

Law Revision Commission Comments

Section 493.010 is amended to conform to the terminology of Title 9 (commencing with Section 680.010) (Enforcement of Judgments Law). See, e.g., Section 703.010, (16 Cal.L.Rev.Comm. Reports 701).

Research References

Rutter, Cal. Practice Guide: Civ. Pro. Before Trial Ch. 9(II)-D, D. Attachment.
Rutter, Cal. Practice Guide: Enforcing Judgments/Debts Ch. 4-A, A. Attachment.
Rutter, Cal. Practice Guide: Enforcing Judgments/Debts Ch. 5-D, D. Involuntary Bankruptcy.
Miller and Starr California Real Estate § 32:37, Temporary Protective Orders.
8 Witkin Cal. Proc. 5th Enforcement of Judgment § 170, (S 170) Persons Entitled to Exemptions.
8 Witkin Cal. Proc. 5th Enforcement of Judgment § 489, in General.
8 Witkin Cal. Proc. 5th Enforcement of Judgment § 505, (S 505) Avoidance of Preferential Transfers by Assignee for Benefit of Creditors.
6 Witkin Cal. Proc. 5th Provisional Remedies § 53, Nature and Scope.
6 Witkin Cal. Proc. 5th Provisional Remedies § 179, Securities.
6 Witkin Cal. Proc. 5th Provisional Remedies § 188, (S 188) in General.
1 Witkin Cal. Summ. 10th Contracts § 710, (S 710) in General.

§ 493.020. Authority of defendant to make a general assignment for benefit of creditors

Notwithstanding any other provision of this title, the defendant may make a general assignment for the benefit of creditors. *(Added by Stats.1977, c. 499, § 1.)*

Law Revision Commission Comments

Section 493.020 makes clear that, regardless of the terms of any writ of attachment, temporary protective order (Sections 486.010–486.110), or turnover order (Section 482.080), the defendant may make a general assignment for the benefit of creditors. Section 493.020 and the remainder of Chapter 13 reflect the policy favoring general assignments for the benefit of creditors (which contemplate the ratable distribution to creditors of the assignor's assets) over attachment (which permits an unsecured creditor to establish a priority over other unsecured creditors).

Research References

6 Witkin Cal. Proc. 5th Provisional Remedies § 179, Securities.
6 Witkin Cal. Proc. 5th Provisional Remedies § 188, (S 188) in General.

§ 493.030. Termination of lien of temporary protective order or of attachment upon assignment; effect of filing bankruptcy petition

(a) The making of a general assignment for the benefit of creditors terminates a lien of a temporary protective order or of attachment if the lien was created within 90 days prior to the making of the general assignment.

(b) The filing of a petition commencing a voluntary or involuntary case under Title 11 of the United States Code (Bankruptcy) [1] terminates a lien of a temporary protective order or of attachment if the lien was created within 90 days prior to the filing of the petition.

(c) Subdivisions (a) and (b) do not apply unless all liens of attachment on the defendant's property in other states that were created within 90 days prior to the making of a general assignment for the benefit of creditors or the filing of a petition commencing a case under Title 11 of the United States Code (Bankruptcy) have terminated. *(Added by Stats.1977, c. 499, § 1. Amended by Stats.1979, c. 177, p. 395, § 1, eff. June 29, 1979, operative Oct. 1, 1979.)*

[1] 11 U.S.C.A. § 101 et seq.

Law Revision Commission Comments

Section 493.030 provides for the termination of the lien of a temporary protective order or of an attachment upon the making of a general assignment for the benefit of creditors (defined in Section 493.010) or the commencement of bankruptcy proceedings within [90 days] after the creation of the lien. See also Sections 486.090 (expiration of temporary protective order), 486.110 (lien of temporary protective order from time of service), 488.500 (lien of attachment), 488.510 (duration of lien of attachment).

Section 493.030 is derived from a portion of former Section 542b which provided for the termination of the lien created by service of the notice of attachment hearing and the temporary restraining order when the defendant filed a proceeding under the Bankruptcy Act or made a general assignment for the benefit of creditors. It broadens the former section to provide for the automatic termination of the lien of attachment, thereby making it unnecessary to initiate court proceedings under the Bankruptcy Act to have the lien of attachment declared void. This principle is also applied where the defendant makes a general assignment for the benefit of creditors (defined in Section 493.010) within the specified time. . . .

Subdivision (c) prevents the termination of attachment liens under this section in a case where attachment liens on the defendant's property in other states are not terminated. This provision recognizes that, in another state, the lien may not be voided under Section 67a(1) of the Bankruptcy Act, 11 U.S.C. § 107(a) (1) (1970), or under the applicable laws in that state relating to general assignments for the benefit of creditors. For example, if the law relating to general assignments in another state does not provide for the termination of an attachment lien in that state, the making of a general assignment would not terminate the attachment lien in California if there is an attachment lien on the defendant's property located elsewhere that would not be terminated. Similarly, if the trustee in bankruptcy does not obtain a court order voiding an attachment lien in another state, an attachment lien in California will not be automatically terminated under subdivision (b) of this section.

This chapter does not affect other provisions voiding liens arising under this title. See, e.g., Ins. Code § 1034 (voidable preferences in insolvency proceedings applicable to insurers) (14 Cal.L.Rev.Comm. Reports 61, amended by 16 Cal.L.Rev.Comm. Reports 701).

Section 493.030 is amended to conform to the 90-day preference period prescribed by the Bankruptcy Reform Act of 1978 (Pub.L. No. 95–598), 11 U.S.C. § 547. Other changes in this section conform to the terminology of the new act. The provision relating to general assignments is made uniform with the bankruptcy provision. The reference to preservation of liens for the benefit of the estate is superseded by Section 493.060. See Comment to Section 493.060.

Research References

Rutter, Cal. Practice Guide: Civ. Pro. Before Trial Ch. 9(II)-D, D. Attachment.
Rutter, Cal. Practice Guide: Enforcing Judgments/Debts Ch. 4-A, A. Attachment.
Rutter, Cal. Practice Guide: Enforcing Judgments/Debts Ch. 5-D, D. Involuntary Bankruptcy.
Miller and Starr California Real Estate § 32:32, Termination of the Attachment Lien.
Miller and Starr California Real Estate § 32:37, Temporary Protective Orders.
6 Witkin Cal. Proc. 5th Provisional Remedies § 147, (S 147) Lien.

6 Witkin Cal. Proc. 5th Provisional Remedies § 179, Securities.
6 Witkin Cal. Proc. 5th Provisional Remedies § 188, (S 188) in General.

§ 493.040. Release of attachment after lien terminates; procedure

(a) Where a lien of attachment terminates pursuant to Section 493.030, the assignee under a general assignment for the benefit of creditors or, in the case of a bankruptcy, the trustee, interim trustee, or the debtor in possession if there is no trustee or interim trustee, may secure the release of the attached property by filing with the levying officer a request for release of attachment stating the grounds for release and describing the property to be released, executed under oath, together with a copy thereof.

(b) In the case of an assignee, the request shall include two copies of the general assignment for the benefit of creditors.

(c) In the case of a trustee, interim trustee, or debtor in possession, the request shall include a certified copy of the petition in bankruptcy, together with a copy thereof.

(d) If immediate release of the attachment is sought, the request shall be accompanied by an undertaking to pay the plaintiff any damages resulting from an improper release of the attachment, in the amount to be secured by the attachment, executed by an admitted surety insurer.

(e) Within five days after the filing of the request for release of attachment, the levying officer shall mail to the plaintiff:

(1) A copy of the request for release of the attachment, including the copy of the document filed pursuant to subdivision (b) or (c).

(2) If an undertaking has not been given, a notice that the attachment will be released pursuant to the request for release of attachment unless otherwise ordered by a court within 10 days after the date of mailing the notice.

(3) If an undertaking has been given, a notice that the attachment has been released.

(f) Unless otherwise ordered by a court, if an undertaking has not been given, the levying officer shall release the attachment pursuant to the request for release of attachment after the expiration of 10 days from the date of mailing the papers referred to in subdivision (e) to the plaintiff. If an undertaking has been given, the levying officer shall immediately release the attachment pursuant to the request for release of attachment.

(g) Where the attached property has been taken into custody, it shall be released to the person making the request for release of attachment or some other person designated in the request. Where the attached property has not been taken into custody, it shall be released as provided in subdivision (c) or (d) of Section 488.730.

(h) The levying officer is not liable for releasing an attachment in accordance with this section nor is any other person liable for acting in conformity with the release. (Added by Stats.1977, c. 499, § 1. Amended by Stats.1979, c. 177, p. 395, § 2, eff. June 29, 1979, operative Oct. 1, 1979; Stats.1982, c. 517, p. 2337, § 117; Stats.1982, c. 1198, p. 4321, § 62.5, operative July 1, 1983.)

Law Revision Commission Comments

Section 493.040 provides a procedure for releasing property from an attachment the lien of which has terminated pursuant to Section 493.030. Under Section 493.040, the levying officer is provided with sufficient information to dispose of the attached property in an expeditious and orderly manner. By giving the plaintiff notice before the release takes place, the plaintiff in an appropriate case is able to protect his or her interests in preserving the attachment priority. In the alternative, where the person seeking release has given a proper undertaking, the property is released from attachment immediately and the plaintiff is protected by the

undertaking in the amount of the plaintiff's claim to be secured by the attachment. Under the release provisions of Section . . . . . . [488.730], which are incorporated by Section 493.040(g), garnishees are informed that they are relieved of the duties and liabilities of a garnishee arising from service of the notice and writ of attachment. Subdivision (h) protects persons acting in conformity with the release provisions of this section and is the same . . . . . . [in substance as Section 488.730(e)] (14 Cal.L.Rev.Comm. Reports 61, amended by 16 Cal.L.Rev.Comm. Reports 701).

Section 493.040 is amended to conform to the elimination of receivers and the creation of interim trustees by the Bankruptcy Reform Act of 1978 (Pub.L. No. 95–598), 11 U.S.C. §§ 105, 303, 701.

Section 493.040 is amended [by Stats.1982, c. 1198] to insert a reference to Section 488.730 which replaced former Section 488.560 (16 Cal.L.Rev. Comm. Reports 701).

Research References

Rutter, Cal. Practice Guide: Enforcing Judgments/Debts Ch. 4-A, A. Attachment.
Miller and Starr California Real Estate § 32:32, Termination of the Attachment Lien.
6 Witkin Cal. Proc. 5th Provisional Remedies § 91, (S 91) Undertakings.
6 Witkin Cal. Proc. 5th Provisional Remedies § 157, Limited Liability of Officer.
6 Witkin Cal. Proc. 5th Provisional Remedies § 179, Securities.
6 Witkin Cal. Proc. 5th Provisional Remedies § 189, (S 189) Release of Attached Property.

§ 493.050. Reinstatement of lien of temporary protective order or attachment; particular cases

(a) The lien of a temporary protective order or of attachment, which has terminated pursuant to Section 493.030, is reinstated with the same effect as if it had not been terminated in the following cases:

(1) Where the termination is the result of the making of a general assignment for the benefit of creditors and the general assignment for the benefit of creditors is set aside otherwise than by the filing of a petition commencing a case under Title 11 of the United States Code (Bankruptcy).[1]

(2) Where the termination is the result of the filing of a petition commencing a case under Title 11 of the United States Code (Bankruptcy) and the petition is dismissed.

(3) Where the termination is the result of the filing of a petition commencing a case under Title 11 of the United States Code (Bankruptcy) and the trustee abandons property which had been subject to the lien of the temporary protective order or of attachment.

(b) The period from the making of a general assignment for the benefit of creditors until reinstatement of the lien of the temporary protective order or of attachment is not counted in determining the duration of the temporary protective order or the lien of attachment. (Added by Stats.1977, c. 499, § 1. Amended by Stats.1979, c. 177, p. 396, § 3, eff. June 29, 1979, operative Oct. 1, 1979.)

[1] 11 U.S.C.A. § 101 et seq.

Law Revision Commission Comments

Section 493.050 provides for reinstatement of the terminated lien where the general assignment for the benefit of creditors is set aside, the [petition commencing a case under Title 11 of the United States Code is dismissed], or the trustee in bankruptcy abandons property that had been subject to a terminated lien. Paragraph (2) of subdivision (a) is derived from a proviso contained in Section 67a(1) of the Bankruptcy Act, 11 U.S.C. § 107(a) (1) (1970). Paragraph (1) applies this principle to the analogous situation where the general assignment for the benefit of creditors fails. Paragraph (3) codifies for the purposes of this chapter the principle that, after abandonment, the property is restored to its former status as if it had never been held by the trustee. See Pounds v. Chicago Ins. Co., 298 So.2d 134 (La.Ct.App.1974).

Subdivision (b) provides for the tolling of the running of the effective periods of the temporary protective under Section 486.090 and the lien of attachment under Section 488.510 when the defendant makes a general assignment for the benefit of creditors. Federal law provides for the tolling of state statutes of limitation upon the filing of a petition in bankruptcy. Bankruptcy Act § 11f, 11 U.S.C. § 29(f) (1970); Booloodian v. Ohanesian, 13 Cal.App.3d 635, 91 Cal.Rptr. 923 (1970) (tolling of period of attachment lien under former Section 542b). Note that the effective date of the lien of the reinstated attachment may relate back to the date of service of a temporary protective order as provided in Section 488.500 (14 Cal.L.Rev.Comm. Reports 61, amended by 16 Cal.L.Rev. Comm. Reports 701).

Section 493.050 is amended to conform to the terminology of the Bankruptcy Reform Act of 1978 (Pub.L. No. 95–598), 11 U.S.C. § 303.

Research References

Rutter, Cal. Practice Guide: Enforcing Judgments/Debts Ch. 4-A, A. Attachment.
6 Witkin Cal. Proc. 5th Provisional Remedies § 179, Securities.
6 Witkin Cal. Proc. 5th Provisional Remedies § 188, (S 188) in General.

§ 493.060. Subrogation; preservation of lien

(a) Upon the making of a general assignment for the benefit of creditors that terminates a lien under this chapter, the assignee is subrogated to the rights of the plaintiff under the temporary protective order or attachment.

(b) Upon the filing of a petition commencing a case under Title 11 of the United States Code (Bankruptcy), a lien terminated pursuant to this chapter is preserved for the benefit of the estate. *(Added by Stats.1977, c. 499, § 1. Amended by Stats.1979, c. 177, p. 397, § 4, eff. June 29, 1979, operative Oct. 1, 1979.)*

Law Revision Commission Comments

Section 493.060 subrogates the assignee under the general assignment for the benefit of creditors to the rights of the attaching plaintiff in order to prevent the termination of the lien of the temporary protective order or of attachment from benefiting a lienholder whose lien was subordinate to the plaintiff's lien but whose lien is not terminated by the making of the general assignment. Hence, where the plaintiff has attached property of the defendant and the property later becomes subject to a security interest, a general assignment by the defendant gives the assignee the priority of the attaching plaintiff whose lien is terminated by Section 493.030(a). Without this provision, the secured party whose interest would otherwise be prior to the assignee's would move up in the line of priorities and the termination of the attachment lien would benefit the secured party rather than the entire estate under control of the assignee. This provision is analogous in effect to the provision in the Bankruptcy Act which permits the trustee to be subrogated to the rights of a lienholder whose lien is void. See Bankruptcy Act § 67a(3), 11 U.S.C. § 107(a)(3) (1970).

Subdivision (b) is added to Section 493.060 for consistency with the Bankruptcy Reform Act of 1978 (Pub.L. No. 95–598), 11 U.S.C. § 551. This subdivision supersedes the provision formerly found in Section 493.030(b) relating to a court order preserving the lien for the benefit of the bankrupt estate.

Research References

Rutter, Cal. Practice Guide: Civ. Pro. Before Trial Ch. 9(II)-D, D. Attachment.
Rutter, Cal. Practice Guide: Enforcing Judgments/Debts Ch. 4-A, A. Attachment.
Rutter, Cal. Practice Guide: Enforcing Judgments/Debts Ch. 5-D, D. Involuntary Bankruptcy.
Rutter, Cal. Practice Guide: Fed.Civ.Pro. Before Trial Ch. 13-A, A. Introduction.
Miller and Starr California Real Estate § 32:32, Termination of the Attachment Lien.
6 Witkin Cal. Proc. 5th Provisional Remedies § 179, Securities.

6 Witkin Cal. Proc. 5th Provisional Remedies § 188, (S 188) in General.

Title 7

OTHER PROVISIONAL REMEDIES IN CIVIL ACTIONS

Law Revision Commission Comments

A new heading for Title 7 (now commencing with Section 500) has been enacted by Section 10 of the session law chapter which contained this section.

CHAPTER 1.   GENERAL PROVISIONS

Section
501. Imprisonment for debt or tort prohibited.

Law Revision Commission Comments

Chapter 1 (commencing with Section 477), repealed by this section [Stats.1974, c. 1516, § 8], has been reenacted without change as Chapter 1 (commencing with Section 500) of Title 7 of Part 2 of the Code of Civil Procedure.

§ 501.   Imprisonment for debt or tort prohibited

A person may not be imprisoned in a civil action for debt or tort, whether before or after judgment. Nothing in this section affects any power a court may have to imprison a person who violates a court order. *(Added by Stats.1974, c. 1516, p. 3377, § 11, operative Jan. 1, 1977.)*

Law Revision Commission Comments

Section 501 continues former Section 478 without change.

Research References

Rutter, Cal. Practice Guide: Enforcing Judgments/Debts Ch. 6A-13, Creating an Enforcement of Judgment Plan.
8 Witkin Cal. Proc. 5th Enforcement of Judgment § 3, (S 3) Civil Arrest Abolished.
6 Witkin Cal. Proc. 5th Provisional Remedies § 5, (S 5) Abolition of Civil Arrest.

CHAPTER 2.   CLAIM AND DELIVERY OF PERSONAL PROPERTY

ARTICLE 1.   WORDS AND PHRASES DEFINED

Section
511.010. Construction.
511.020. Complaint.
511.030. Defendant.

§ 511.010. Construction

Unless the provision or context otherwise requires, the definitions in this article govern the construction of this chapter. *(Added by Stats.1973, c. 526, p. 1013, § 2, operative July 1, 1974.)*

Law Revision Commission Comments

Section 511.010 is a standard provision found in the definitional portion of recently enacted California codes. See, *e.g.*, Evid.Code § 100; Veh.Code § 100.

Additional definitions are found in the preliminary provisions of the Code of Civil Procedure. *E.g.*, Section 17 provides "the singular number includes the plural and the plural the singular."

Research References

California Practice Guide: Employment Litigation Ch. 2-I, I. Investigations.
Miller and Starr California Real Estate § 31:69, Judicial Remedies.
14 NO. 1 Miller & Starr, California Real Estate Newsalert 2, Commercial Arbitration.
6 Witkin Cal. Proc. 5th Provisional Remedies § 1, (S 1) in General.
6 Witkin Cal. Proc. 5th Provisional Remedies § 250, (S 250) in General.
6 Witkin Cal. Proc. 5th Provisional Remedies § 251, (S 251) Definitions.
5 Witkin, California Summary 10th Torts § 700, Remedies.

§ 511.020. Complaint

"Complaint" includes a cross-complaint. *(Added by Stats. 1973, c. 526, p. 1013, § 2, operative July 1, 1974.)*

Research References

6 Witkin Cal. Proc. 5th Provisional Remedies § 251, (S 251) Definitions.

§ 511.030. Defendant

"Defendant" includes a cross-defendant. *(Added by Stats. 1973, c. 526, p. 1013, § 2, operative July 1, 1974.)*

Research References

6 Witkin Cal. Proc. 5th Provisional Remedies § 251, (S 251) Definitions.

§ 511.040. Farm products

"Farm products" means crops or livestock or supplies used or produced in farming operations or products of crops or livestock in their unmanufactured states (such as ginned cotton, wool clip, maple syrup, honey, milk, and eggs) while in the possession of a defendant engaged in raising, fattening, grazing, or other farming operations. If tangible personal property is a farm product, it is not inventory. *(Added by Stats.1973, c. 526, p. 1013, § 2, operative July 1, 1974.)*

Law Revision Commission Comments

Section 511.040 is based on the definition of "farm products" provided by Section 9109 of the Commercial Code. Section 9109 provides in part:
9109. Goods are . . . "farm products" if they are crops or livestock or supplies used or produced in farming operations or if they are products of crops or livestock in their unmanufactured states (such as ginned cotton, wool clip, maple syrup, honey, milk and eggs), and if they are in the possession of a debtor engaged in raising, fattening, grazing or other farming operations. If goods are farm products they are neither equipment nor inventory . . . .

Inventory is defined by Section 511.050. A definition of "equipment" is unnecessary. Farm products and inventory are defined only because the terms are used in connection with provisions which permit sale of such property in the ordinary course of business despite the issuance of a temporary restraining order. See Section 513.020. Equipment would not by its nature usually be sold in the ordinary course of business and is not, therefore, included in the exception permitting transfer.

Research References

6 Witkin Cal. Proc. 5th Provisional Remedies § 266, (S 266) Provisions of Order.

§ 511.050. Inventory

"Inventory" means tangible personal property in the possession of a defendant who holds it for sale or lease or to be furnished under contracts of service. *(Added by Stats.1973, c. 526, p. 1013, § 2, operative July 1, 1974.)*

Law Revision Commission Comments

Section 511.050 is based on the definition of "inventory" provided by Section 9109 of the Commercial Code. Section 9109 provides in part:
9109. Goods are . . . "inventory" if they are held by a person who holds them for sale or lease or to be furnished under contracts of service or if he has leased or so furnished them or if they are raw materials, work in process or materials used or consumed in a business. Inventory of a person is not to be classified as his equipment.

The phrase "or if he has leased or so furnished them" has been deleted to make clear that inventory under this title is limited to property in the possession of the defendant. See also Comment to Section 511.040. The phrase "raw materials, work in process, or materials used or consumed in" the defendant's business has also been deleted. This property would not be sold in the ordinary course of business anyway; hence, it does not need to be included in the exception permitting transfer. See Sections 511.040 and 513.020 and Comments thereto.

Research References

6 Witkin Cal. Proc. 5th Provisional Remedies § 266, (S 266) Provisions of Order.

§ 511.060. Levying officer

"Levying officer" means the sheriff or marshal who is directed to execute a writ of possession issued under this chapter. *(Added by Stats.1973, c. 526, p. 1013, § 2, operative July 1, 1974. Amended by Stats.1996, c. 872 (A.B.3472), § 14.)*

Research References

6 Witkin Cal. Proc. 5th Provisional Remedies § 251, (S 251) Definitions.

§ 511.070. Person

"Person" includes an individual, a corporation, a partnership or other unincorporated association, a limited liability company, and a public entity. *(Added by Stats.1973, c. 526, p. 1013, § 2, operative July 1, 1974. Amended by Stats.1994, c. 1010 (S.B. 2053), § 59.)*

Research References

6 Witkin Cal. Proc. 5th Provisional Remedies § 251, (S 251) Definitions.

§ 511.080. Plaintiff

"Plaintiff" means a person who files a complaint or cross-complaint. *(Added by Stats.1973, c. 526, p. 1013, § 2, operative July 1, 1974.)*

Research References

6 Witkin Cal. Proc. 5th Provisional Remedies § 251, (S 251) Definitions.

§ 511.090. Probable validity

A claim has "probable validity" where it is more likely than not that the plaintiff will obtain a judgment against the defendant on that claim. *(Added by Stats.1973, c. 526, p. 1013, § 2, operative July 1, 1974.)*

Research References

Rutter, Cal. Practice Guide: Civ. Pro. Before Trial Ch. 9(II)-C, C. Writ of Possession ("Claim and Delivery").

Rutter, Cal. Practice Guide: Enforcing Judgments/Debts Ch. 4-B, B. Claim and Delivery.

6 Witkin Cal. Proc. 5th Provisional Remedies § 261, Issuance of Writ.

§ 511.100. Public entity

"Public entity" includes the state, the Regents of the University of California, a county, city, district, public authority, public agency, and any other political subdivision or public corporation in the state. *(Added by Stats.1973, c. 526, p. 1013, § 2, operative July 1, 1974.)*

Research References

6 Witkin Cal. Proc. 5th Provisional Remedies § 251, (S 251) Definitions.

ARTICLE 2.   WRIT OF POSSESSION

Section
512.010.   Application for writ; time; contents.
512.020.   Issuance after hearing; exceptions; ex parte upon probable cause; documents served on defendant; application to quash; order.
512.030.   Service of documents on defendant prior to hearing.
512.040.   Notice of application and hearing for writ; contents.
512.050.   Filing of affidavits and briefs with court; duty of court.
512.060.   Issuance of writ; requirements; probable cause for entry of private place.
512.070.   Order for transfer of possession to plaintiff; failure to comply; contempt or arrest.
512.080.   Writ of possession; requirements.
512.090.   Seizure of property at place not specified in writ; ex parte endorsement; probable cause.
512.100.   Failure of defendant to oppose issuance of writ or to rebut evidence; no waiver of defenses in main action.
512.110.   Effect of court determinations under this chapter; admissibility.
512.120.   Failure of plaintiff to recover judgment; redelivery of property to defendant; liability for damages.

§ 512.010. Application for writ; time; contents

(a) Upon the filing of the complaint or at any time thereafter, the plaintiff may apply pursuant to this chapter for a writ of possession by filing a written application for the writ with the court in which the action is brought.

(b) The application shall be executed under oath and shall include all of the following:

(1) A showing of the basis of the plaintiff's claim and that the plaintiff is entitled to possession of the property claimed. If the basis of the plaintiff's claim is a written instrument, a copy of the instrument shall be attached.

(2) A showing that the property is wrongfully detained by the defendant, of the manner in which the defendant came into possession of the property, and, according to the best knowledge, information, and belief of the plaintiff, of the reason for the detention.

(3) A particular description of the property and a statement of its value.

(4) A statement, according to the best knowledge, information, and belief of the plaintiff, of the location of the property and, if the property, or some part of it, is within a private place which may have to be entered to take possession, a showing that there is probable cause to believe that such property is located there.

(5) A statement that the property has not been taken for a tax, assessment, or fine, pursuant to a statute; or seized under an execution against the property of the plaintiff; or, if so seized, that it is by statute exempt from such seizure.

(c) The requirements of subdivision (b) may be satisfied by one or more affidavits filed with the application. *(Added by Stats.1973, c. 526, p. 1013, § 2, operative July 1, 1974.)*

Research References

Rutter, Cal. Practice Guide: A.D.R. Ch. 5-G, G. Procedures to Enforce Arbitration.

Rutter, Cal. Practice Guide: Civ. Pro. Before Trial Ch. 9(II)-C, C. Writ of Possession ("Claim and Delivery").

Rutter, Cal. Practice Guide: Enforcing Judgments/Debts Ch. 4-B, B. Claim and Delivery.

Rutter, Cal. Practice Guide: Fed.Civ.Pro. Before Trial Ch. 13-A, A. Introduction.

Miller and Starr California Real Estate § 31:69, Judicial Remedies.

5 Witkin Cal. Proc. 5th Pleading § 692, (S 692) in General.

6 Witkin Cal. Proc. 5th Proceedings Without Trial § 529, (S 529) in General.

6 Witkin Cal. Proc. 5th Provisional Remedies § 250, (S 250) in General.

6 Witkin Cal. Proc. 5th Provisional Remedies § 253, (S 253) Affidavits.

6 Witkin Cal. Proc. 5th Provisional Remedies § 255, in General.

6 Witkin Cal. Proc. 5th Provisional Remedies § 256, Content.

§ 512.020. Issuance after hearing; exceptions; ex parte upon probable cause; documents served on defendant; application to quash; order

(a) Except as otherwise provided in this section, no writ shall be issued under this chapter except after a hearing on a noticed motion.

(b) A writ of possession may be issued ex parte pursuant to this subdivision if probable cause appears that any of the following conditions exists:

(1) The defendant gained possession of the property by feloniously taking the property from the plaintiff. This subdivision shall not apply where the defendant has fraudulently appropriated property entrusted to him or obtained possession by false or fraudulent representation or pretense or by embezzlement.

(2) The property is a credit card.

(3) The defendant acquired possession of the property in the ordinary course of his trade or business for commercial purposes and:

(i) The property is not necessary for the support of the defendant or his family; and

(ii) There is an immediate danger that the property will become unavailable to levy by reason of being transferred, concealed, or removed from the state or will become substantially impaired in value by acts of destruction or by failure to take care of the property in a reasonable manner; and

(iii) The ex parte issuance of a writ of possession is necessary to protect the property.

The plaintiff's application for the writ shall satisfy the requirements of Section 512.010 and, in addition, shall include a showing that the conditions required by this subdivision exist. A writ of possession may issue if the court finds that the conditions required by this subdivision exist and the requirements of Section 512.060 are met. Where a writ of possession has been issued pursuant to this subdivision, a copy of the summons and complaint, a copy of the application and any affidavit in support thereof, and a notice which satisfies the requirements of subdivisions (c) and (d) of Section 512.040 and informs the defendant of his rights under this subdivision shall be served upon the defendant and any other person required by Section 514.020 to be served with a writ of possession. Any defendant whose property has been taken pursuant to a writ of possession issued under this subdivision may apply for an order that the writ be quashed and any property levied on pursuant to the writ be released. Such application shall be made by noticed motion, and the provisions of Section 512.050 shall apply. Pending the hearing on the defendant's application, the court may order that delivery pursuant to Section 514.030 of any property previously levied upon be stayed. If the court determines that the plaintiff is not entitled to a writ of possession, the court shall quash the writ of possession and order the release and redelivery of any property previously levied upon, and shall award the defendant any damages sustained by him which were proximately caused by the levy of the writ of possession and the loss of possession of the property pursuant to such levy. *(Added by Stats.1973, c. 526, p. 1013, § 2, operative July 1, 1974.)*

Law Revision Commission Comments

Subdivision (a) of Section 512.020 and Sections 512.030 and 512.040 replace subdivision (b) of former Section 510. Section 510 required an initial judicial review of the plaintiff's application for a writ of possession followed by the issuance of an order directed to the defendant to show cause why a writ should not issue. This procedure was both inefficient and unnecessary and has been replaced here by a noticed motion procedure in most situations.

Subdivision (b) of Section 512.020 provides an ex parte issuance procedure available only in certain circumstances. Compare former Section 510(c). Subdivision (b) authorizes the court to issue a writ ex parte where the property claimed (1) has been stolen from the plaintiff and is still in the possession of the thief, (2) is a credit card, or (3) is commercial property which is not necessary for the support of the defendant or his family and which is likely to be unavailable for levy if the matter is heard upon noticed motion. Paragraph (1) does not apply where the property is in the possession of a person who did not take the property from the plaintiff, nor does it apply where possession was obtained by fraud, trick or device, or similar means. These limitations do not completely deprive the plaintiff of a remedy; rather, they compel the use of either the noticed motion procedure provided by this chapter or criminal process. See Penal Code §§ 1407–1413, 1523–1542. See also Recommendation Relating to the Claim and Delivery Statute, 11 Cal.L.Revision Comm'n Reports 301, 317 n. 45 (1973).

Subdivision (b) outlines the procedures for the ex parte issuance of a writ and the review of such issuance. The plaintiff's application is basically the same as that required under the noticed motion procedure but must also include a showing of the special circumstances that permit ex parte issuance. The plaintiff must, of course, show the probable validity of his claim and probable cause for the entry and taking of property from a private place. See Section 512.010 and the Comment thereto. The court may, in its discretion, issue a writ ex parte if it finds that the special circumstances required by subdivision (b) exist, that the plaintiff has established probable validity, and that the plaintiff has filed the proper undertaking. See Section 512.060 and the Comment thereto. The writ, a copy of the summons and complaint, a copy of the application for the writ and affidavits in support thereof, and a notice informing the defendant of his rights must be served on the defendant and any other person required to be served by Section 514.020. Following issuance, the defendant may apply by noticed motion for an order quashing the writ. The rules governing the time for service and the manner of service are the same as for motions generally. See Comment to Section 512.030. A special provision for an order shortening time is unnecessary since the provisions of Section 1005 authorizing such an order apply. Contrast former Section 510(c). Of course, nothing in subdivision (b) precludes the defendant from obtaining the release of the property by posting the undertaking required by Section 515.020. If the writ is quashed, Section 512.020 requires that the defendant be awarded any damages sustained by him which were proximately caused by the levy. This right does not depend upon whether the defendant ultimately prevails in the action.

Research References

Rutter, Cal. Practice Guide: Civ. Pro. Before Trial Ch. 9(II)-C, C. Writ of Possession ("Claim and Delivery").
Rutter, Cal. Practice Guide: Enforcing Judgments/Debts Ch. 4-B, B. Claim and Delivery.
Miller and Starr California Real Estate § 31:69, Judicial Remedies.
6 Witkin Cal. Proc. 5th Provisional Remedies § 257, Noticed Motion.

6 Witkin Cal. Proc. 5th Provisional Remedies § 259, Conditions.
6 Witkin Cal. Proc. 5th Provisional Remedies § 260, Procedure.
6 Witkin Cal. Proc. 5th Provisional Remedies § 265, (S 265) Nature of Remedy.

§ 512.030.   Service of documents on defendant prior to hearing

(a) Prior to the hearing required by subdivision (a) of Section 512.020, the defendant shall be served with all of the following:

(1) A copy of the summons and complaint.

(2) A Notice of Application and Hearing.

(3) A copy of the application and any affidavit in support thereof.

(b) If the defendant has not appeared in the action, and a writ, notice, order, or other paper is required to be personally served on the defendant under this title, service shall be made in the same manner as a summons is served under Chapter 4 (commencing with Section 413.10) of Title 5. *(Added by Stats.1973, c. 526, p. 1013, § 2, operative July 1, 1974. Amended by Stats.2007, c. 15 (A.B.859), § 2.)*

Law Revision Commission Comments

Section 512.030 replaces a portion of former Section 510. The rules governing the time for service and the manner of service are the same as for motions generally. See Chapters 4 (commencing with Section 1003) and 5 (commencing with Section 1010) of Title 14 of this part. The contents of the Notice of Application and Hearing are prescribed by Section 512.040.

Research References

Rutter, Cal. Practice Guide: Enforcing Judgments/Debts Ch. 4-B, B. Claim and Delivery.
Miller and Starr California Real Estate § 31:69, Judicial Remedies.
6 Witkin Cal. Proc. 5th Provisional Remedies § 257, Noticed Motion.
6 Witkin Cal. Proc. 5th Provisional Remedies § 269, (S 269) Service of Writ and Undertaking.

§ 512.040.   Notice of application and hearing for writ; contents

The "Notice of Application and Hearing" shall inform the defendant of all of the following:

(a) A hearing will be held at a place and at a time, to be specified in the notice, on plaintiff's application for a writ of possession.

(b) The writ will be issued if the court finds that the plaintiff's claim is probably valid and the other requirements for issuing the writ are established. The hearing is not for the purpose of determining whether the claim is actually valid. The determination of the actual validity of the claim will be made in subsequent proceedings in the action and will not be affected by the decision at the hearing on the application for the writ.

(c) If the defendant desires to oppose the issuance of the writ, he shall file with the court either an affidavit providing evidence sufficient to defeat the plaintiff's right to issuance of the writ or an undertaking to stay the delivery of the property in accordance with Section 515.020.

(d) The notice shall contain the following statement: "If you believe the plaintiff may not be entitled to possession of the property claimed, you may wish to seek the advice of an attorney. Such attorney should be consulted promptly so that he may assist you before the time set for the hearing." *(Added by Stats.1973, c. 526, p. 1013, § 2, operative July 1, 1974.)*

Law Revision Commission Comments

Section 512.040 is based on a portion of subdivision (b) of former Section 510. Under the former procedure, the order to show cause informed the defendant of the time and place of the hearing and the defendant's right to appear and oppose the issuance of the writ or to file an undertaking. Section 512.040 requires the notice to do these things as well as inform the defendant of the purpose of the hearing and the need for prompt action in response to the notice.

Research References

Rutter, Cal. Practice Guide: Civ. Pro. Before Trial Ch. 9(II)-C, C. Writ of Possession ("Claim and Delivery").
Rutter, Cal. Practice Guide: Enforcing Judgments/Debts Ch. 4-B, B. Claim and Delivery.
Miller and Starr California Real Estate § 31:69, Judicial Remedies.
6 Witkin Cal. Proc. 5th Provisional Remedies § 257, Noticed Motion.
6 Witkin Cal. Proc. 5th Provisional Remedies § 260, Procedure.

§ 512.050. Filing of affidavits and briefs with court; duty of court

Each party shall file with the court and serve upon the other party within the time prescribed by rule any affidavits and points and authorities intended to be relied upon at the hearing. At the hearing, the court shall make its determinations upon the basis of the pleadings and other papers in the record; but, upon good cause shown, the court may receive and consider additional evidence and authority produced at the hearing or may continue the hearing for the production of such additional evidence, oral or documentary, or the filing of other affidavits or points and authorities. *(Added by Stats.1973, c. 526, p. 1013, § 2, operative July 1, 1974.)*

Law Revision Commission Comments

Section 512.050 is new. Subdivision (b) of former Section 510 apparently permitted the defendant to delay indicating his opposition to issuance of a writ until his appearance at the hearing. Section 512.050 is intended to encourage an earlier framing of the parties' contentions and an exchange of support therefor. The time limit for filing is left to rules adopted by the Judicial Council, but the trial court may grant relief from such limits upon a showing of good cause.

Research References

Rutter, Cal. Practice Guide: Enforcing Judgments/Debts Ch. 4-B, B. Claim and Delivery.
Rutter, Cal. Practice Guide: Enforcing Judgments/Debts Form 4:Y, Notice of Defendant's Rights.
Miller and Starr California Real Estate § 31:69, Judicial Remedies.
6 Witkin Cal. Proc. 5th Provisional Remedies § 2, (S 2) Use of Affidavit.
6 Witkin Cal. Proc. 5th Provisional Remedies § 258, Determination.
6 Witkin Cal. Proc. 5th Provisional Remedies § 260, Procedure.

§ 512.060. Issuance of writ; requirements; probable cause for entry of private place

(a) At the hearing, a writ of possession shall issue if both of the following are found:

(1) The plaintiff has established the probable validity of the plaintiff's claim to possession of the property.

(2) The undertaking requirements of Section 515.010 are satisfied.

(b) No writ directing the levying officer to enter a private place to take possession of any property shall be issued unless the plaintiff has established that there is probable cause to believe that the property is located there. *(Added by Stats.1973, c. 526, § 1013, § 2, operative July 1, 1974. Amended by Stats.2002, c. 68 (S.B.1322), § 1.)*

Law Revision Commission Comments

Subdivision (a)(2) of Section 512.060 is amended to recognize that an undertaking is not required in certain cases. See Section 515.010. [31 Cal.L.Rev.Comm. Reports 135 (2002)].

Research References

Rutter, Cal. Practice Guide: Civ. Pro. Before Trial Ch. 9(II)-C, C. Writ of Possession ("Claim and Delivery").
Rutter, Cal. Practice Guide: Enforcing Judgments/Debts Ch. 4-B, B. Claim and Delivery.

Miller and Starr California Real Estate § 31:69, Judicial Remedies.
Miller and Starr California Real Estate § 11:154, Expungement of a Lis Pendens--Procedure and Grounds for Expungement.
6 Witkin Cal. Proc. 5th Provisional Remedies § 256, Content.
6 Witkin Cal. Proc. 5th Provisional Remedies § 260, Procedure.
6 Witkin Cal. Proc. 5th Provisional Remedies § 261, Issuance of Writ.
6 Witkin Cal. Proc. 5th Provisional Remedies § 268, (S 268) Search and Seizure.

§ 512.070. Order for transfer of possession to plaintiff; failure to comply; contempt or arrest

If a writ of possession is issued, the court may also issue an order directing the defendant to transfer possession of the property to the plaintiff. Such order shall contain a notice to the defendant that failure to turn over possession of such property to plaintiff may subject the defendant to being held in contempt of court. *(Added by Stats.1973, c. 526, p. 1013, § 2, operative July 1, 1974. Amended by Stats.1976, c. 145, p. 230, § 1.)*

Law Revision Commission Comments

Section 512.070 is new. It makes clear that the court has power to issue a "turnover" order directing the defendant to cooperate in transferring possession. Such order is not issued in lieu of a writ but rather in addition to or in aid of a writ, permitting the plaintiff to select a more informal and less expensive means of securing possession.

Section 512.070 is amended to delete the reference to the party or person in possession in the provision requiring the order to state that failure to comply may subject such person to contempt of court. Since the order is directed only to the defendant, it would be inappropriate to hold some other person in contempt for failure to obey it.

Section 512.070 is also amended to delete the words "or arrest" from the last sentence. This amendment makes clear that the defendant is not subject to arrest independent of contempt proceedings. See Code Civ.Proc. § 501 (civil arrest abolished). A person may still be arrested in the course of contempt proceedings. See Code Civ.Proc. §§ 1212, 1214, 1220.

Research References

Rutter, Cal. Practice Guide: Civ. Pro. Before Trial Ch. 9(II)-C, C. Writ of Possession ("Claim and Delivery").
Rutter, Cal. Practice Guide: Enforcing Judgments/Debts Ch. 4-B, B. Claim and Delivery.
Miller and Starr California Real Estate § 31:69, Judicial Remedies.
6 Witkin Cal. Proc. 5th Provisional Remedies § 263, Turnover Order.
6 Witkin Cal. Proc. 5th Provisional Remedies § 271, (S 271) Defendant's Undertaking to Protect Possession.
6 Witkin Cal. Proc. 5th Provisional Remedies § 273, Effect of Judgment in Main Action.
6 Witkin Cal. Proc. 5th Provisional Remedies § 368, (S 368) in General.

§ 512.080. Writ of possession; requirements

The writ of possession shall meet all of the following requirements:

(a) Be directed to the levying officer within whose jurisdiction the property is located.

(b) Describe the specific property to be seized.

(c) Specify any private place that may be entered to take possession of the property or some part of it.

(d) Direct the levying officer to levy on the property pursuant to Section 514.010 if found and to retain it in custody until released or sold pursuant to Section 514.030.

(e) Inform the defendant of the right to object to the plaintiff's undertaking, a copy of which shall be attached to the writ, or to obtain redelivery of the property by filing an undertaking as prescribed by Section 515.020. *(Added by Stats.1973, c. 526, p. 1013, § 2, operative July 1, 1974. Amended by Stats.1982, c. 517, p. 2338, § 118.)*

Law Revision Commission Comments

Section 512.080 is substantively the same as subdivision (a) of former Section 512.

Section 512.080 is amended for consistency with the Bond and Undertaking Law. See Section 995.910 (objections to undertakings). The other changes in Section 512.080 are technical. [16 Cal.L.Rev. Comm. Reports 501 (1982)].

Research References

Rutter, Cal. Practice Guide: Civ. Pro. Before Trial Ch. 9(II)-C, C. Writ of Possession ("Claim and Delivery").
Rutter, Cal. Practice Guide: Enforcing Judgments/Debts Ch. 4-B, B. Claim and Delivery.
Miller and Starr California Real Estate § 31:69, Judicial Remedies.
6 Witkin Cal. Proc. 5th Provisional Remedies § 262, Form and Content of Writ.

§ 512.090. Seizure of property at place not specified in writ; ex parte endorsement; probable cause

(a) The plaintiff may apply ex parte in writing to the court in which the action was brought for an endorsement on the writ directing the levying officer to seize the property at a private place not specified in the writ.

(b) The court shall make the endorsement if the plaintiff establishes by affidavit that there is probable cause to believe that the property or some part of it may be found at that place. *(Added by Stats.1973, c. 526, p. 1013, § 2, operative July 1, 1974.)*

Law Revision Commission Comments

Section 512.090 is based on subdivision (b) of former Section 512.

Research References

Rutter, Cal. Practice Guide: Civ. Pro. Before Trial Ch. 9(II)-C, C. Writ of Possession ("Claim and Delivery").
Rutter, Cal. Practice Guide: Enforcing Judgments/Debts Ch. 4-B, B. Claim and Delivery.
6 Witkin Cal. Proc. 5th Provisional Remedies § 262, Form and Content of Writ.

§ 512.100. Failure of defendant to oppose issuance of writ or to rebut evidence; no waiver of defenses in main action

Neither the failure of the defendant to oppose the issuance of a writ of possession under this chapter nor his failure to rebut any evidence produced by the plaintiff in connection with proceedings under this chapter shall constitute a waiver of any defense to plaintiff's claim in the action or any other action or have any effect on the right of the defendant to produce or exclude evidence at the trial of any such action. *(Added by Stats.1973, c. 526, p. 1013, § 2, operative July 1, 1974.)*

Research References

Rutter, Cal. Practice Guide: Enforcing Judgments/Debts Ch. 4-B, B. Claim and Delivery.
Miller and Starr California Real Estate § 31:69, Judicial Remedies.
6 Witkin Cal. Proc. 5th Provisional Remedies § 250, (S 250) in General.

§ 512.110. Effect of court determinations under this chapter; admissibility

The determinations of the court under this chapter shall have no effect on the determination of any issues in the action other than the issues relevant to proceedings under this chapter, nor shall they affect the rights of any party in any other action arising out of the same claim. The determinations of the court under this chapter shall not be given in evidence nor referred to in the trial of any such action. *(Added by Stats.1973, c. 526, p. 1013, § 2, operative July 1, 1974.)*

Law Revision Commission Comments

Section 512.110 makes clear that the determinations of the court under this article have no effect on the determination of the validity of the plaintiff's claim in the action he has brought against the defendant nor do they affect the rights of any party in any other action. Section 512.110 does not, however, make inadmissible any affidavit filed under this chapter. The admissibility of such an affidavit is determined by the rules of evidence otherwise applicable.

Research References

Rutter, Cal. Practice Guide: Enforcing Judgments/Debts Ch. 4-B, B. Claim and Delivery.
Miller and Starr California Real Estate § 31:69, Judicial Remedies.
6 Witkin Cal. Proc. 5th Provisional Remedies § 250, (S 250) in General.

§ 512.120. Failure of plaintiff to recover judgment; redelivery of property to defendant; liability for damages

If the plaintiff fails to recover judgment in the action, he shall redeliver the property to the defendant and be liable for all damages sustained by the defendant which are proximately caused by operation of the temporary restraining order and preliminary injunction, if any, the levy of the writ of possession, and the loss of possession of the property pursuant to levy of the writ of possession or in compliance with an order issued under Section 512.070. *(Added by Stats.1973, c. 526, p. 1013, § 2, operative July 1, 1974.)*

Research References

Rutter, Cal. Practice Guide: Enforcing Judgments/Debts Ch. 4-B, B. Claim and Delivery.
6 Witkin Cal. Proc. 5th Provisional Remedies § 273, Effect of Judgment in Main Action.

ARTICLE 3. TEMPORARY RESTRAINING ORDER

Section
513.010. Law governing; application for order; grounds; requirements for ex parte issuance.
513.020. Prohibition of certain acts by defendant.

§ 513.010. Law governing; application for order; grounds; requirements for ex parte issuance

(a) Except as otherwise provided by this chapter, the provisions of Chapter 3 (commencing with Section 525) of this title relating to the issuance of a temporary restraining order apply. At or after the time he files his application for writ of possession, the plaintiff may apply for a temporary restraining order by setting forth in the application a statement of grounds justifying the issuance of such order.

(b) A temporary restraining order may issue ex parte if all of the following are found:

(1) The plaintiff has established the probable validity of his claim to possession of the property.

(2) The plaintiff has provided an undertaking as required by Section 515.010.

(3) The plaintiff has established the probability that there is an immediate danger that the property claimed may become unavailable to levy by reason of being transferred, concealed, or removed or may become substantially impaired in value.

(c) If at the hearing on issuance of the writ of possession the court determines that the plaintiff is not entitled to a writ of possession, the court shall dissolve any temporary restraining order; otherwise, the court may issue a preliminary injunction to remain in effect until the property claimed is seized pursuant to the writ of possession. *(Added by Stats.1973, c. 526, p. 1013, § 2, operative July 1, 1974.)*

Research References

Rutter, Cal. Practice Guide: Civ. Pro. Before Trial Ch. 9(II)-C, C. Writ of Possession ("Claim and Delivery").

Rutter, Cal. Practice Guide: Enforcing Judgments/Debts Ch. 4-B, B. Claim and Delivery.

Rutter, Cal. Practice Guide: Insurance Litigation Ch. 6I-B, B. Particular Surety Bond Coverages.

6 Witkin Cal. Proc. 5th Provisional Remedies § 250, (S 250) in General.

6 Witkin Cal. Proc. 5th Provisional Remedies § 256, Content.

6 Witkin Cal. Proc. 5th Provisional Remedies § 265, (S 265) Nature of Remedy.

6 Witkin Cal. Proc. 5th Provisional Remedies § 267, (S 267) Procedure After Hearing on Writ.

§ 513.020. Prohibition of certain acts by defendant

In the discretion of the court, the temporary restraining order may prohibit the defendant from doing any or all of the following:

(a) Transferring any interest in the property by sale, pledge, or grant of security interest, or otherwise disposing of, or encumbering, the property. If the property is farm products held for sale or lease or is inventory, the order may not prohibit the defendant from transferring the property in the ordinary course of business, but the order may impose appropriate restrictions on the disposition of the proceeds from such transfer.

(b) Concealing or otherwise removing the property in such a manner as to make it less available to seizure by the levying officer.

(c) Impairing the value of the property either by acts of destruction or by failure to care for the property in a reasonable manner. *(Added by Stats.1973, c. 526, p. 1013, § 2, operative July 1, 1974.)*

Law Revision Commission Comments

Section 513.020 provides specificity with respect to the nature of the temporary restraining order authorized by Section 513.010. Compare subdivision (d) of former Section 510. The court in its discretion, may generally prohibit transfers of the property in question. This should not, however, cause interference with a manufacturer's processing of raw materials or work in process. Moreover, where the property is farm goods or inventory (defined in Sections 511.040 and 511.050, respectively), subdivision (a) requires that such property be permitted to be sold in the ordinary course of business, subject to limitations on the disposition of the proceeds from sale.

The rare case in which the property will perish or deteriorate, for example, if not refrigerated or, in the case of animals, if not cared for properly is taken care of in subdivision (c) under which the defendant can be ordered to take whatever precautions are necessary to preserve the property until the time of the hearing.

Research References

Rutter, Cal. Practice Guide: Civ. Pro. Before Trial Ch. 9(II)-C, C. Writ of Possession ("Claim and Delivery").

Rutter, Cal. Practice Guide: Enforcing Judgments/Debts Ch. 4-B, B. Claim and Delivery.

6 Witkin Cal. Proc. 5th Provisional Remedies § 266, (S 266) Provisions of Order.

ARTICLE 4. LEVY AND CUSTODY

§ 514.010. Seizure of property; retention by officer; property used as dwelling; property located in private place

(a) Except as otherwise provided in this section, upon receipt of the writ of possession the levying officer shall search for and take custody of the specified property, if it be in the possession of the defendant or his agent, either by removing the property to a place of safekeeping or by installing a keeper.

(b) If the specified property is used as a dwelling, such as a mobilehome or boat, levy shall be made by placing a keeper in charge of the property for two days, at the plaintiff's expense, after which period the levying officer shall remove the occupants and any contents not specified in the writ and shall take exclusive possession of the property.

(c) If the specified property or any part of it is in a private place, the levying officer shall at the time he demands possession of the property announce his identity, purpose, and authority. If the property is not voluntarily delivered, the levying officer may cause any building or enclosure where the property may be located to be broken open in such a manner as he reasonably believes will cause the least damage and may call upon the power of the county to aid and protect him, but, if he reasonably believes that entry and seizure of the property will involve a substantial risk of death or serious bodily harm to any person, he shall refrain from seizing the property and shall promptly make a return to the court from which the writ issued setting forth the reasons for his belief that the risk exists. In such case, the court shall make such orders as may be appropriate.

(d) Nothing in this section authorizes the levying officer to enter or search any private place not specified in the writ of possession or other order of the court. *(Added by Stats.1973, c. 526, p. 1013, § 2, operative July 1, 1974.)*

Law Revision Commission Comments

Section 514.010 is substantively the same as the first two paragraphs of former Section 513.

Research References

Rutter, Cal. Practice Guide: Civ. Pro. Before Trial Ch. 9(II)-C, C. Writ of Possession ("Claim and Delivery").

Rutter, Cal. Practice Guide: Enforcing Judgments/Debts Ch. 4-B, B. Claim and Delivery.

Miller and Starr California Real Estate § 31:69, Judicial Remedies.

6 Witkin Cal. Proc. 5th Provisional Remedies § 250, (S 250) in General.

6 Witkin Cal. Proc. 5th Provisional Remedies § 262, Form and Content of Writ.

6 Witkin Cal. Proc. 5th Provisional Remedies § 268, (S 268) Search and Seizure.

§ 514.020. Delivery of copy of writ and plaintiff's undertaking by officer to defendant

(a) At the time of levy, the levying officer shall deliver to the person in possession of the property a copy of the writ of possession, a copy of the plaintiff's undertaking, if any, and a copy of the order for issuance of the writ.

(b) If no one is in possession of the property at the time of levy, the levying officer shall subsequently serve the writ and attached undertaking on the defendant. If the defendant has appeared in the action, service shall be accomplished in the manner provided by Chapter 5 (commencing with Section 1010) of Title 14. If the defendant has not appeared in the action, service shall be accomplished in the manner provided for the service of summons and complaint by Article 3 (commencing with Section 415.10) of Chapter 4 of Title 5. *(Added by Stats.1973, c. 526, p. 1013, § 2, operative July 1, 1974. Amended by Stats.2002, c. 68 (S.B.1322), § 2.)*

Law Revision Commission Comments

Section 514.020 is similar in effect to the last paragraph of former Section 513. Section 514.020 does not require a second service of the summons and complaint and application for writ of possession. That has presumably been accomplished pursuant to Section 512.030. See also Section 512.020 (service of summons and complaint required where writ issued ex parte). Moreover, Section 514.020 requires service of the writ of possession on the defendant only if he is the person in possession or no one is in possession of the property at the time of levy. Service is in no event a condition to levy. Levy is accomplished by taking the property into custody.

Subdivision (a) of Section 514.020 is amended to recognize that an undertaking is not required in certain cases. See Section 515.010. A copy of the order for issuance of the writ is included so that the person served will receive the necessary information in cases where there is no undertaking.

The amendments in subdivision (b) are technical, nonsubstantive revisions to eliminate surplus language. [31 Cal.L.Rev.Comm. Reports 135 (2002)].

Research References

Rutter, Cal. Practice Guide: Civ. Pro. Before Trial Ch. 9(II)-C, C. Writ of Possession ("Claim and Delivery").
Rutter, Cal. Practice Guide: Enforcing Judgments/Debts Ch. 4-B, B. Claim and Delivery.
6 Witkin Cal. Proc. 5th Provisional Remedies § 260, Procedure.
6 Witkin Cal. Proc. 5th Provisional Remedies § 269, (S 269) Service of Writ and Undertaking.

§ 514.030. Custody of seized property; delivery to plaintiff; redelivery to defendant; sale of perishable property

(a) After the levying officer takes possession pursuant to a writ of possession, the levying officer shall keep the property in a secure place. Except as otherwise provided by Sections 512.020 and 514.050:

(1) If notice of the filing of an undertaking for redelivery or notice of objection to the plaintiff's undertaking is not received by the levying officer within 10 days after levy of the writ of possession, the levying officer shall deliver the property to plaintiff, upon receiving the fees for taking and necessary expenses for keeping the property.

(2) If notice of the filing of an undertaking for redelivery is received by the levying officer within 10 days after levy of the writ of possession and defendant's undertaking is not objected to, the levying officer shall redeliver the property to defendant upon expiration of the time to so object, upon receiving the fees for taking and necessary expenses for keeping the property not already paid or advanced by the plaintiff.

(3) If notice of objection to the plaintiff's undertaking or notice of the filing of an undertaking for redelivery is received within 10 days after levy of the writ of possession and defendant's undertaking is objected to, the levying officer shall not deliver or redeliver the property until the time provided in Section 515.030.

(b) Notwithstanding subdivision (a), where not otherwise provided by contract and where an undertaking for redelivery has not been filed, upon a showing that the property is perishable or will greatly deteriorate or depreciate in value or for some other reason that the interests of the parties will be best served thereby, the court may order that the property be sold and the proceeds deposited in the court to abide the judgment in the action. *(Added by Stats.1973, c. 526, p. 1013, § 2, operative July 1, 1974. Amended by Stats.1982, c. 517, p. 2338, § 119.)*

Law Revision Commission Comments

Section 514.030 is amended for consistency with the Bond and Undertaking Law. See Section 995.910 (objections to undertakings). The other changes in Section 514.030 are technical. [16 Cal.L.Rev. Comm. Reports 501 (1982)].

Research References

Rutter, Cal. Practice Guide: Civ. Pro. Before Trial Ch. 9(II)-C, C. Writ of Possession ("Claim and Delivery").
Rutter, Cal. Practice Guide: Enforcing Judgments/Debts Ch. 4-B, B. Claim and Delivery.
Rutter, Cal. Practice Guide: Enforcing Judgments/Debts Form 4:Y, Notice of Defendant's Rights.
Miller and Starr California Real Estate § 31:69, Judicial Remedies.
6 Witkin Cal. Proc. 5th Provisional Remedies § 262, Form and Content of Writ.
6 Witkin Cal. Proc. 5th Provisional Remedies § 270, (S 270) Custody, Delivery, Redelivery, or Sale of Property.

§ 514.040. Return by officer

The levying officer shall return the writ of possession, with his proceedings thereon, to the court in which the action is pending within 30 days after levy but in no event more than 60 days after the writ is issued. *(Added by Stats.1973, c. 526, p. 1013, § 2, operative July 1, 1974.)*

Law Revision Commission Comments

Section 514.040 is substantively similar to former Section 518. Section 514.040 has, however, been revised to provide a date certain for the return of all writs—even those under which the sheriff has not been able to levy.

Research References

Rutter, Cal. Practice Guide: Enforcing Judgments/Debts Ch. 4-B, B. Claim and Delivery.
6 Witkin Cal. Proc. 5th Provisional Remedies § 272, (S 272) Return of Writ.

§ 514.050. Third party claims

Where the property taken is claimed by a third person, the rules and proceedings applicable in cases of third-party claims under Division 4 (commencing with Section 720.010) of Title 9 apply. *(Added by Stats.1973, c. 526, p. 1013, § 2, operative July 1, 1974. Amended by Stats.1982, c. 497, p. 2155, § 33, operative July 1, 1983.)*

Law Revision Commission Comments

Section 514.050 is substantively identical to former Section 517.

Section 514.050 is amended to insert a reference to the appropriate provisions of the Enforcement of Judgments Law (15 Cal.L.Rev.Comm. Reports 2001).

Research References

Rutter, Cal. Practice Guide: Civ. Pro. Before Trial Ch. 9(II)-C, C. Writ of Possession ("Claim and Delivery").
Rutter, Cal. Practice Guide: Enforcing Judgments/Debts Ch. 4-B, B. Claim and Delivery.
6 Witkin Cal. Proc. 5th Provisional Remedies § 245, (S 245) Nature of Remedy.

ARTICLE 5. UNDERTAKINGS

Section

§ 515.010. Necessity of plaintiff filing an undertaking prior to issuance of temporary restraining order or writ of possession; requirements; defendant's undertaking

(a) Except as provided in subdivision (b), the court shall not issue a temporary restraining order or a writ of possession until the plaintiff has filed an undertaking with the court. The undertaking shall provide that the sureties are bound to the defendant for the return of the property to the defendant, if return of the property is ordered, and for the payment to the defendant of any sum recovered against the plaintiff. The undertaking shall be in an amount not less than twice the value of the defendant's interest in the property or in a greater amount. The value of the defendant's interest in the property is determined by the market value of the property less the amount due and owing on any conditional sales contract or security agreement and all liens and encumbrances on the property, and any other factors necessary to determine the defendant's interest in the property.

(b) If the court finds that the defendant has no interest in the property, the court shall waive the requirement of the plaintiff's undertaking and shall include in the order for issuance of the writ the amount of the defendant's undertaking sufficient to satisfy the requirements of subdivision (b) of Section 515.020. *(Added by Stats.1973, c. 526, p. 1013, § 2, operative July 1, 1974. Amended by Stats.1978, c. 373, § 1; Stats.1981, c. 975, p. 3722, § 2; Stats.1982, c. 517, p. 2339, § 120; Stats.1984, c. 538, § 12; Stats.2002, c. 68 (S.B.1322), § 3.)*

Law Revision Commission Comments

Section 515.010 is amended to provide for an undertaking in the amount of the defendant's interest in the property in all cases. It is also amended to delete provisions duplicated in the Bond and Undertaking Law. See Sections 995.320 (contents of undertaking), 995.310 (sureties on undertaking), 995.910 (objections to undertakings). The other changes in Section 515.010 are technical. [16 Cal.L.Rev.Comm. Reports 501].

The reference in the second sentence of Section 515.010 to the limitation of liability to the amount of the undertaking is deleted as unnecessary. See Section 996.470 (limitation on liability of surety). The third sentence is amended to make clear that the plaintiff may give an undertaking in an amount that exceeds twice the value of the defendant's interest. This is not a substantive change. Under Section 515.020 the defendant can obtain the release of the property or prevent its seizure by giving an undertaking in the same amount as the plaintiff's undertaking. Under Section 515.010 the plaintiff may set the amount of the undertaking at a level sufficient to protect the plaintiff's interest in the property should the defendant give a release undertaking pursuant to Section 515.020. [17 Cal.L.Rev.Comm.Reports 975 (1984)].

Subdivision (b) is added to Section 515.010 to dispense with the plaintiff's undertaking where the defendant has no interest in the property. This provision avoids the idle act of requiring an undertaking in the amount of zero dollars. Where there is no plaintiff's undertaking, the last clause of subdivision (b) makes clear that the court must set an amount of the defendant's undertaking to retain or regain possession under Section 515.020 sufficient to pay costs and damages the plaintiff may sustain by reason of the loss of possession of the property. See Section 515.020(b). [31 Cal.L.Rev.Comm. Reports 136 (2002)].

Research References

Rutter, Cal. Practice Guide: Civ. Pro. Before Trial Ch. 9(II)-C, C. Writ of Possession ("Claim and Delivery").
Rutter, Cal. Practice Guide: Enforcing Judgments/Debts Ch. 4-B, B. Claim and Delivery.
Rutter, Cal. Practice Guide: Insurance Litigation Ch. 6I-B, B. Particular Surety Bond Coverages.
Miller and Starr California Real Estate § 31:69, Judicial Remedies.
6 Witkin Cal. Proc. 5th Provisional Remedies § 250, (S 250) in General.
6 Witkin Cal. Proc. 5th Provisional Remedies § 254, (S 254) Undertakings.
6 Witkin Cal. Proc. 5th Provisional Remedies § 261, Issuance of Writ.
6 Witkin Cal. Proc. 5th Provisional Remedies § 264, (S 264) Undertaking.
6 Witkin Cal. Proc. 5th Provisional Remedies § 265, (S 265) Nature of Remedy.
6 Witkin Cal. Proc. 5th Provisional Remedies § 271, (S 271) Defendant's Undertaking to Protect Possession.

§ 515.020. Defendant's undertaking; requirements; redelivery

(a) The defendant may prevent the plaintiff from taking possession of property pursuant to a writ of possession or regain possession of property so taken by filing with the court in which the action was brought an undertaking in an amount equal to the amount of the plaintiff's undertaking pursuant to subdivision (a) of Section 515.010 or in the amount determined by the court pursuant to subdivision (b) of Section 515.010.

(b) The undertaking shall state that, if the plaintiff recovers judgment on the action, the defendant shall pay all costs awarded to the plaintiff and all damages that the plaintiff may sustain by reason of the loss of possession of the property. The damages recoverable by the plaintiff pursuant to this section shall include all damages proximately caused by the plaintiff's failure to gain or retain possession.

(c) The defendant's undertaking may be filed at any time before or after levy of the writ of possession. A copy of the undertaking shall be mailed to the levying officer.

(d) If an undertaking for redelivery is filed and the defendant's undertaking is not objected to, the levying officer shall deliver the property to the defendant, or, if the plaintiff has previously been given possession of the property, the plaintiff shall deliver the property to the defendant. If an undertaking for redelivery is filed and the defendant's undertaking is objected to, the provisions of Section 515.030 apply. *(Added by Stats. 1973, c. 526, p. 1013, § 2, operative July 1, 1974. Amended by Stats.1978, c. 373, § 2; Stats.1982, c. 517, p. 2339, § 121; Stats.1984, c. 538, § 13; Stats.2002, c. 68 (S.B.1322), § 4.)*

Law Revision Commission Comments

Section 515.020 is amended to conform to Section 515.010. It is also amended to delete provisions duplicated in the Bond and Undertaking Law. See Sections 995.320 (contents of undertaking), 995.310 (sureties on undertaking), 995.910 (objections to undertakings), 995.370 (service of copy of undertaking), 995.240 (waiver in cases of indigency). [16 Cal.L.Rev.Comm. Reports 501].

The provision in subdivision (a) of Section 515.020 limiting liability to the amount of the undertaking is deleted as unnecessary. See Section 996.470 (limitation on liability of surety). This amendment makes no substantive change. [17 Cal.L.Rev.Comm.Reports 975 (1984)].

Subdivision (a) of Section 515.020 is amended to recognize that the amount of the defendant's undertaking may be set by the court pursuant to Section 515.010(b). The section is retabulated to permit easy reference to the contents of the undertaking. See Section 515.010(b). [31 Cal. L.Rev.Comm. Reports 137 (2002)].

Research References

Rutter, Cal. Practice Guide: Civ. Pro. Before Trial Ch. 9(II)-C, C. Writ of Possession ("Claim and Delivery").
Rutter, Cal. Practice Guide: Enforcing Judgments/Debts Ch. 4-B, B. Claim and Delivery.
Rutter, Cal. Practice Guide: Insurance Litigation Ch. 6I-B, B. Particular Surety Bond Coverages.
Miller and Starr California Real Estate § 31:69, Judicial Remedies.
8 Witkin Cal. Proc. 5th Attack Judgment Trial Court § 146, (S 146) When Relief is Not Available.
6 Witkin Cal. Proc. 5th Provisional Remedies § 254, (S 254) Undertakings.
6 Witkin Cal. Proc. 5th Provisional Remedies § 257, Noticed Motion.
6 Witkin Cal. Proc. 5th Provisional Remedies § 260, Procedure.
6 Witkin Cal. Proc. 5th Provisional Remedies § 262, Form and Content of Writ.
6 Witkin Cal. Proc. 5th Provisional Remedies § 264, (S 264) Undertaking.
6 Witkin Cal. Proc. 5th Provisional Remedies § 271, (S 271) Defendant's Undertaking to Protect Possession.

§ 515.030. Objection to plaintiff's or defendant's undertaking; determination; order

(a) The defendant may object to the plaintiff's undertaking not later than 10 days after levy of the writ of possession. The defendant shall mail notice of objection to the levying officer.

(b) The plaintiff may object to the defendant's undertaking not later than 10 days after the defendant's undertaking is filed. The plaintiff shall mail notice of objection to the levying officer.

(c) If the court determines that the plaintiff's undertaking is insufficient and a sufficient undertaking is not filed within the time required by statute, the court shall vacate the temporary restraining order or preliminary injunction, if any, and the writ of possession and, if levy has occurred, order the levying officer or the plaintiff to return the property to the defendant. If the court determines that the plaintiff's undertaking is sufficient, the court shall order the levying officer to deliver the property to the plaintiff.

(d) If the court determines that the defendant's undertaking is insufficient and a sufficient undertaking is not filed within the time required by statute, the court shall order the levying officer to deliver the property to the plaintiff, or, if the plaintiff has previously been given possession of the property, the plaintiff shall retain possession. If the court determines that the defendant's undertaking is sufficient, the court shall order the levying officer or the plaintiff to deliver the property to the defendant. *(Added by Stats.1973, c. 526, p. 1013, § 2, operative July 1, 1974. Amended by Stats.1982, c. 517, p. 2339, § 122; Stats.1984, c. 538, § 14.)*

Law Revision Commission Comments

Section 515.030 is amended for consistency with the Bond and Undertaking Law. See Sections 995.910–995.960 (objections to undertakings). [16 Cal.L.Rev.Comm. Reports 501].

Subdivision (b) of Section 515.030 is amended for consistency with the Bond and Undertaking Law. See Section 995.920 (objection to undertaking). This amendment makes no substantive change. [17 Cal.L.Rev.Comm.Reports 975 (1984)].

Research References

Rutter, Cal. Practice Guide: Civ. Pro. Before Trial Ch. 9(II)-C, C. Writ of Possession ("Claim and Delivery").
Rutter, Cal. Practice Guide: Enforcing Judgments/Debts Ch. 4-B, B. Claim and Delivery.
Miller and Starr California Real Estate § 31:69, Judicial Remedies.
6 Witkin Cal. Proc. 5th Provisional Remedies § 254, (S 254) Undertakings.
6 Witkin Cal. Proc. 5th Provisional Remedies § 264, (S 264) Undertaking.
6 Witkin Cal. Proc. 5th Provisional Remedies § 270, (S 270) Custody, Delivery, Redelivery, or Sale of Property.
6 Witkin Cal. Proc. 5th Provisional Remedies § 271, (S 271) Defendant's Undertaking to Protect Possession.

ARTICLE 6. MISCELLANEOUS PROVISIONS

Section

§ 516.010. Judicial Council; rules of practice and procedure

The Judicial Council may provide by rule for the practice and procedure in proceedings under this chapter. *(Added by Stats. 1973, c. 526, p. 1013, § 2, operative July 1, 1974.)*

Research References

6 Witkin Cal. Proc. 5th Provisional Remedies § 250, (S 250) in General.

§ 516.020. Judicial Council; forms

The Judicial Council shall prescribe the form of the applications, notices, orders, and other documents required by this chapter. *(Added by Stats.1973, c. 526, p. 1013, § 2, operative July 1, 1974.)*

Law Revision Commission Comments

Section 516.020 requires the Judicial Council to prescribe the forms necessary for the purposes of this chapter. The Judicial Council has authority to adopt and revise forms as necessary but must act in a manner consistent with the provisions of this chapter.

Research References

Rutter, Cal. Practice Guide: Civ. Pro. Before Trial Ch. 9(II)-C, C. Writ of Possession ("Claim and Delivery").
Rutter, Cal. Practice Guide: Enforcing Judgments/Debts Ch. 4-B, B. Claim and Delivery.
6 Witkin Cal. Proc. 5th Provisional Remedies § 252, (S 252) Judicial Council Forms.

§ 516.030. Affidavits

The facts stated in each affidavit filed pursuant to this chapter shall be set forth with particularity. Except where matters are specifically permitted by this chapter to be shown by information and belief, each affidavit shall show affirmatively that the affiant, if sworn as a witness, can testify competently to the facts stated therein. The affiant may be any person, whether or not a party to the action, who has knowledge of the facts. A verified complaint that satisfies the requirements of this section may be used in lieu of or in addition to an ordinary affidavit. *(Added by Stats.1973, c. 526, p. 1013, § 2, operative July 1, 1974.)*

Law Revision Commission Comments

Section 516.030 provides standards for affidavits filed pursuant to this chapter. These standards are comparable to but not as restrictive as those provided for affidavits filed in support of or in opposition to a motion for summary judgment. Compare Section 437c. A verified complaint that satisfies the requirements of this section may be used in lieu of or in addition to an ordinary affidavit. It should be noted that under Section 512.010 certain matters may be shown to the best of the plaintiff's knowledge, information, and belief. In such situations, the facts stated in the affidavit will be the facts on which his belief is based and may include the nature of his information and the reliability of his informant.

Research References

Rutter, Cal. Practice Guide: Civ. Pro. Before Trial Ch. 9(II)-C, C. Writ of Possession ("Claim and Delivery").
Rutter, Cal. Practice Guide: Enforcing Judgments/Debts Ch. 4-B, B. Claim and Delivery.
6 Witkin Cal. Proc. 5th Provisional Remedies § 89, (S 89) Affidavits.
6 Witkin Cal. Proc. 5th Provisional Remedies § 253, (S 253) Affidavits.
6 Witkin Cal. Proc. 5th Provisional Remedies § 255, in General.

§ 516.040. Subordinate judicial duties

The judicial duties to be performed under this chapter are "subordinate judicial duties" within the meaning of Section 22 of Article VI of the California Constitution and may be performed by appointed officers such as court commissioners. *(Added by Stats.1973, c. 526, p. 1013, § 2, operative July 1, 1974.)*

Research References

Rutter, Cal. Practice Guide: Civ. Pro. Before Trial Ch. 9(I)-D, D. Hearing.
6 Witkin Cal. Proc. 5th Provisional Remedies § 250, (S 250) in General.

§ 516.050. Injunction

Nothing in this chapter shall preclude the granting of relief pursuant to Chapter 3 (commencing with Section 525) of this title. *(Added by Stats.1973, c. 526, p. 1013, § 2, operative July 1, 1974.)*

Research References

Rutter, Cal. Practice Guide: Enforcing Judgments/Debts Ch. 4-B, B. Claim and Delivery.
Rutter, Cal. Practice Guide: Fed.Civ.Pro. Before Trial Ch. 13-A, A. Introduction.
Miller and Starr California Real Estate § 31:69, Judicial Remedies.

CHAPTER 3.   INJUNCTION

§ 525.   Definition; grant; enforcement

An injunction is a writ or order requiring a person to refrain from a particular act. It may be granted by the court in which the action is brought, or by a judge thereof; and when granted by a judge, it may be enforced as an order of the court. *(Enacted in 1872. Amended by Code Am.1880, c. 15, p. 3, § 3; Stats.1907, c. 272, p. 340, § 1.)*

Research References

Rutter, Cal. Practice Guide: Civ. Pro. Before Trial Ch. 9(II)-A, A. Injunctions.
Rutter, Cal. Practice Guide: Enforcing Judgments/Debts Ch. 4-B, B. Claim and Delivery.
Rutter, Cal. Practice Guide: Enforcing Judgments/Debts Ch. 6G-4, Creditor's Suit.
Rutter, Cal. Practice Guide: Real Prop. Transactions Ch. 7-B, B. Sale of Ground Lease Tenant's Interest-Preliminary Concerns Re Assignment and Subletting.
3 Witkin Cal. Proc. 5th Actions § 370, Order Prohibiting Filing of New Litigation.
3 Witkin Cal. Proc. 5th Actions § 963, (S 963) Writ.
9 Witkin Cal. Proc. 5th Administrative Proceedings § 138, (S 138) in General.
8 Witkin Cal. Proc. 5th Enforcement of Judgment § 293, (S 293) Order Forbidding Transfer or Payment.
5 Witkin Cal. Proc. 5th Pleading § 822, (S 822) Nature of Action.
6 Witkin Cal. Proc. 5th Provisional Remedies § 1, (S 1) in General.
6 Witkin Cal. Proc. 5th Provisional Remedies § 202, (S 202) Order and Judgment.
6 Witkin Cal. Proc. 5th Provisional Remedies § 250, (S 250) in General.
6 Witkin Cal. Proc. 5th Provisional Remedies § 265, (S 265) Nature of Remedy.
6 Witkin Cal. Proc. 5th Provisional Remedies § 267, (S 267) Procedure After Hearing on Writ.
6 Witkin Cal. Proc. 5th Provisional Remedies § 274, in General.
6 Witkin Cal. Proc. 5th Provisional Remedies § 278, (S 278) in General.
6 Witkin Cal. Proc. 5th Provisional Remedies § 280, (S 280) in General.
6 Witkin Cal. Proc. 5th Provisional Remedies § 289, (S 289) Conditions.

§ 526.   Cases in which authorized;   restrictions on grant

(a) An injunction may be granted in the following cases:

(1) When it appears by the complaint that the plaintiff is entitled to the relief demanded, and the relief, or any part thereof, consists in restraining the commission or continuance of the act complained of, either for a limited period or perpetually.

(2) When it appears by the complaint or affidavits that the commission or continuance of some act during the litigation would produce waste, or great or irreparable injury, to a party to the action.

(3) When it appears, during the litigation, that a party to the action is doing, or threatens, or is about to do, or is procuring or suffering to be done, some act in violation of the rights of another party to the action respecting the subject of the action, and tending to render the judgment ineffectual.

(4) When pecuniary compensation would not afford adequate relief.

(5) Where it would be extremely difficult to ascertain the amount of compensation which would afford adequate relief.

(6) Where the restraint is necessary to prevent a multiplicity of judicial proceedings.

(7) Where the obligation arises from a trust.

(b) An injunction cannot be granted in the following cases:

(1) To stay a judicial proceeding pending at the commencement of the action in which the injunction is demanded, unless the restraint is necessary to prevent a multiplicity of proceedings.

(2) To stay proceedings in a court of the United States.

(3) To stay proceedings in another state upon a judgment of a court of that state.

(4) To prevent the execution of a public statute by officers of the law for the public benefit.

(5) To prevent the breach of a contract the performance of which would not be specifically enforced, other than a contract in writing for the rendition of personal services from one to another where the promised service is of a special, unique, unusual, extraordinary, or intellectual character, which gives it peculiar

value, the loss of which cannot be reasonably or adequately compensated in damages in an action at law, and where the compensation for the personal services is as follows:

(A) As to contracts entered into on or before December 31, 1993, the minimum compensation provided in the contract for the personal services shall be at the rate of six thousand dollars ($6,000) per annum.

(B) As to contracts entered into on or after January 1, 1994, the criteria of clause (i) or (ii), as follows, are satisfied:

(i) The compensation is as follows:

(I) The minimum compensation provided in the contract shall be at the rate of nine thousand dollars ($9,000) per annum for the first year of the contract, twelve thousand dollars ($12,000) per annum for the second year of the contract, and fifteen thousand dollars ($15,000) per annum for the third to seventh years, inclusive, of the contract.

(II) In addition, after the third year of the contract, there shall actually have been paid for the services through and including the contract year during which the injunctive relief is sought, over and above the minimum contractual compensation specified in subclause (I), the amount of fifteen thousand dollars ($15,000) per annum during the fourth and fifth years of the contract, and thirty thousand dollars ($30,000) per annum during the sixth and seventh years of the contract. As a condition to petitioning for an injunction, amounts payable under this clause may be paid at any time prior to seeking injunctive relief.

(ii) The aggregate compensation actually received for the services provided under a contract that does not meet the criteria of subparagraph (A), is at least 10 times the applicable aggregate minimum amount specified in subclauses (I) and (II) of clause (i) through and including the contract year during which the injunctive relief is sought. As a condition to petitioning for an injunction, amounts payable under this subparagraph may be paid at any time prior to seeking injunctive relief.

(C) Compensation paid in any contract year in excess of the minimums specified in clauses (i) and (ii) of subparagraph (B) shall apply to reduce the compensation otherwise required to be paid under those provisions in any subsequent contract years. However, an injunction may be granted to prevent the breach of a contract entered into between any nonprofit cooperative corporation or association and a member or stockholder thereof, in respect to any provision regarding the sale or delivery to the corporation or association of the products produced or acquired by the member or stockholder.

(6) To prevent the exercise of a public or private office, in a lawful manner, by the person in possession.

(7) To prevent a legislative act by a municipal corporation. (Enacted in 1872. Amended by Stats.1907, c. 272, p. 341, § 2; Stats.1919, c. 224, p. 325, § 1; Stats.1925, c. 408, p. 828, § 1; Stats.1992, c. 177 (S.B.1459), § 2; Stats.1993, c. 836 (S.B.487), § 2.)

Research References

Rutter, Cal. Practice Guide: A.D.R. Ch. 5-G, G. Procedures to Enforce Arbitration.

Rutter, Cal. Practice Guide: Civ. Pro. Before Trial Ch. 9(II)-A, A. Injunctions.

California Practice Guide: Employment Litigation Ch. 17-A, A. Equitable Relief.

Rutter, Cal. Practice Guide: Enforcing Judgments/Debts Ch. 6G-1, Examination of Judgment Debtor and Third Parties.

Rutter, Cal. Practice Guide: Real Prop. Transactions Ch. 7-B, B. Sale of Ground Lease Tenant's Interest-Preliminary Concerns Re Assignment and Subletting.

Miller and Starr California Real Estate § 16:6, Nature of Possession Required--Possession by a Tenant.

Miller and Starr California Real Estate § 10:56, Beneficiary's Remedies for Injuries to the Collateral Caused by Third Persons.

Miller and Starr California Real Estate § 34:10, Ancillary Remedies-- Injunction or Lien to Secure Recovery.

Miller and Starr California Real Estate § 34:23, Availability of Injunction.

Miller and Starr California Real Estate § 35:58, Provisional Remedies While Arbitration Pending.

Miller and Starr California Real Estate § 19:223, Cross-Complaint; Affirmative Defenses.

Miller and Starr California Real Estate § 30B:29, Procedural Considerations.

9 Witkin Cal. Proc. 5th Administrative Proceedings § 146, (S 146) Injunction.

2 Witkin Cal. Proc. 5th Jurisdiction § 325, Interference With Law Enforcement.

4 Witkin Cal. Proc. 5th Pleading § 348, Nature of Remedy.

5 Witkin Cal. Proc. 5th Pleading § 822, (S 822) Nature of Action.

5 Witkin Cal. Proc. 5th Pleading § 827, (S 827) Threatened Multiplicity of Actions.

6 Witkin Cal. Proc. 5th Proceedings Without Trial § 529, (S 529) in General.

6 Witkin Cal. Proc. 5th Provisional Remedies § 289, (S 289) Conditions.

6 Witkin Cal. Proc. 5th Provisional Remedies § 294, Inadequacy of Other Remedies.

6 Witkin Cal. Proc. 5th Provisional Remedies § 295, Irreparable Injury.

6 Witkin Cal. Proc. 5th Provisional Remedies § 296, Multiplicity of Actions.

6 Witkin Cal. Proc. 5th Provisional Remedies § 297, (S 297) in General.

6 Witkin Cal. Proc. 5th Provisional Remedies § 299, (S 299) Waste.

6 Witkin Cal. Proc. 5th Provisional Remedies § 305, (S 305) in General.

6 Witkin Cal. Proc. 5th Provisional Remedies § 306, (S 306) Unique Personal Services.

6 Witkin Cal. Proc. 5th Provisional Remedies § 308, (S 308) Other Contracts.

6 Witkin Cal. Proc. 5th Provisional Remedies § 309, Business and Personal Property Interests.

6 Witkin Cal. Proc. 5th Provisional Remedies § 331, (S 331) Injunction Against Enforcement.

6 Witkin Cal. Proc. 5th Provisional Remedies § 332, (S 332) Injunction Against Enactment.

6 Witkin Cal. Proc. 5th Provisional Remedies § 333, Judicial Proceeding.

6 Witkin Cal. Proc. 5th Provisional Remedies § 334, Arbitration Proceeding.

6 Witkin Cal. Proc. 5th Provisional Remedies § 338, (S 338) Judicial Remedy.

7 Witkin, California Summary 10th Constitutional Law § 98, (S 98) in General.

13 Witkin, California Summary 10th Equity § 37, (S 37) Other Contracts.

13 Witkin, California Summary 10th Equity § 51, (S 51) Nature and Purpose of Statute.

13 Witkin, California Summary 10th Equity § 52, (S 52) Option to Pay is Insufficient.

13 Witkin, California Summary 10th Trusts § 123, Enjoining Threatened Breach.

13 Witkin, California Summary 10th Trusts § 232, (S 232) Orders and Appeal.

§ 526a. Actions against officers; scope of section; municipal bonds

An action to obtain a judgment, restraining and preventing any illegal expenditure of, waste of, or injury to, the estate, funds, or other property of a county, town, city or city and county of the state, may be maintained against any officer thereof, or any agent, or other person, acting in its behalf, either by a citizen resident therein, or by a corporation, who is assessed for and is liable to pay, or, within one year before the commencement of the action, has paid, a tax therein. This section does not affect any right of action in favor of a county, city, town, or city and county, or any public officer; provided, that no injunction shall be granted restraining the offering for sale, sale, or issuance of any municipal bonds for public improvements or public utilities.

An action brought pursuant to this section to enjoin a public improvement project shall take special precedence over all civil matters on the calendar of the court except those matters to which equal precedence on the calendar is granted by law. *(Added by Stats.1909, c. 348, p. 578, § 1. Amended by Stats.1911, c. 71, p. 87, § 1; Stats.1967, c. 706, p. 2080, § 1.)*

Research References

Rutter, Cal. Practice Guide: Civ. Pro. Before Trial Ch. 2-A, A. Standing to Sue-"Real Party in Interest" Requirement.

Rutter, Cal. Practice Guide: Civ. Pro. Before Trial Ch. 14-D, D. Representative Suits.

Rutter, Cal. Practice Guide: Civ. Pro. Before Trial Ch. 12(I)-C, C. Claims for Trial Setting Preference.

Rutter, Cal. Practice Guide: Civ. Pro. Before Trial Ch. 9(II)-A, A. Injunctions.

Miller and Starr California Real Estate § 27:35, Public Works Competitive Bidding--Bid Protests and Judicial Review of Award of a Public Contract.

4 Witkin Cal. Proc. 5th Pleading § 121, (S 121) Statement of Doctrine.

4 Witkin Cal. Proc. 5th Pleading § 156, Supervision of Charitable Trust.

4 Witkin Cal. Proc. 5th Pleading § 158, (S 158) Validating Action.

4 Witkin Cal. Proc. 5th Pleading § 162, in General.

4 Witkin Cal. Proc. 5th Pleading § 164, Action Against State Agency or Officer.

4 Witkin Cal. Proc. 5th Pleading § 166, Where Issue Becomes Moot.

4 Witkin Cal. Proc. 5th Pleading § 168, Action Involving Agency's Discretion.

4 Witkin Cal. Proc. 5th Pleading § 169, Action Involving Judicial Function.

4 Witkin Cal. Proc. 5th Pleading § 306, (S 306) Other Situations.

6 Witkin Cal. Proc. 5th Provisional Remedies § 246, Blair Case.

6 Witkin Cal. Proc. 5th Provisional Remedies § 312, Taxpayer's Action.

6 Witkin Cal. Proc. 5th Provisional Remedies § 331, (S 331) Injunction Against Enforcement.

6 Witkin Cal. Proc. 5th Provisional Remedies § 344, Public Interest.

7 Witkin Cal. Proc. 5th Trial § 72, (S 72) Miscellaneous Statutes.

9 Witkin, California Summary 10th Taxation § 296, (S 296) Statutory Restriction.

5 Witkin, California Summary 10th Torts § 766, (S 766) Other Privileges.

7 Witkin, California Summary 10th Constitutional Law § 80, State or Local Taxpayer.

8 Witkin, California Summary 10th Constitutional Law § 734, in General.

§ 526b. Municipal utility bonds; restraining issuance, sale, etc.; liability for costs

Every person or corporation bringing, instigating, exciting or abetting, any suit to obtain an injunction, restraining or enjoining the issuance, sale, offering for sale, or delivery, of bonds, or other securities, or the expenditure of the proceeds of the sale of such bonds or other securities, of any city, city and county, town, county, or other district organized under the laws of this state, or any other political subdivision of this state, proposed to be issued, sold, offered for sale or delivered by such city, city and county, town, county, district or other political subdivision, for the purpose of acquiring, constructing, completing, improving or extending water works, electric works, gas works or other public utility works or property, shall, if the injunction sought is finally denied, and if such person or corporation owns, controls, or is operating or interested in, a public utility business of the same nature as that for which such bonds or other securities are proposed to be issued, sold, offered for sale, or delivered, be liable to the defendant for all costs, damages and necessary expenses resulting to such defendant by reason of the filing of such suit. *(Added by Stats.1921, c. 384, p. 575, § 1.)*

Research References

7 Witkin Cal. Proc. 5th Judgment § 234, in General.

§ 527. Grants before judgment upon verified complaint or affidavits; service; notice; procedures; application; fees

(a) A preliminary injunction may be granted at any time before judgment upon a verified complaint, or upon affidavits if the complaint in the one case, or the affidavits in the other, show satisfactorily that sufficient grounds exist therefor. No preliminary injunction shall be granted without notice to the opposing party.

(b) A temporary restraining order or a preliminary injunction, or both, may be granted in a class action, in which one or more of the parties sues or defends for the benefit of numerous parties upon the same grounds as in other actions, whether or not the class has been certified.

(c) No temporary restraining order shall be granted without notice to the opposing party, unless both of the following requirements are satisfied:

(1) It appears from facts shown by affidavit or by the verified complaint that great or irreparable injury will result to the applicant before the matter can be heard on notice.

(2) The applicant or the applicant's attorney certifies one of the following to the court under oath:

(A) That within a reasonable time prior to the application the applicant informed the opposing party or the opposing party's attorney at what time and where the application would be made.

(B) That the applicant in good faith attempted but was unable to inform the opposing party and the opposing party's attorney, specifying the efforts made to contact them.

(C) That for reasons specified the applicant should not be required to so inform the opposing party or the opposing party's attorney.

(d) In case a temporary restraining order is granted without notice in the contingency specified in subdivision (c):

(1) The matter shall be made returnable on an order requiring cause to be shown why a preliminary injunction should not be granted, on the earliest day that the business of the court will admit of, but not later than 15 days or, if good cause appears to the court, 22 days from the date the temporary restraining order is issued.

(2) The party who obtained the temporary restraining order shall, within five days from the date the temporary restraining order is issued or two days prior to the hearing, whichever is earlier, serve on the opposing party a copy of the complaint if not previously served, the order to show cause stating the date, time, and place of the hearing, any affidavits to be used in the application, and a copy of the points and authorities in support of the application. The court may for good cause, on motion of the applicant or on its own motion, shorten the time required by this paragraph for service on the opposing party.

(3) When the matter first comes up for hearing, if the party who obtained the temporary restraining order is not ready to proceed, or if the party has failed to effect service as required by paragraph (2), the court shall dissolve the temporary restraining order.

(4) The opposing party is entitled to one continuance for a reasonable period of not less than 15 days or any shorter period requested by the opposing party, to enable the opposing party to meet the application for a preliminary injunction. If the opposing party obtains a continuance under this paragraph, the temporary restraining order shall remain in effect until the date of the continued hearing.

(5) Upon the filing of an affidavit by the applicant that the opposing party could not be served within the time required by paragraph (2), the court may reissue any temporary restraining order previously issued. The reissued order shall be made returnable as provided by paragraph (1), with the time for hearing measured from the date of reissuance. No fee shall be charged for reissuing the order.

(e) The opposing party may, in response to an order to show cause, present affidavits relating to the granting of the preliminary injunction, and if the affidavits are served on the applicant at least two days prior to the hearing, the applicant shall not be entitled to any continuance on account thereof. On the day the order is made returnable, the hearing shall take precedence over all other matters on the calendar of the day, except older matters of the same character, and matters to which special precedence may be given by law. When the cause is at issue it shall be set for trial at the earliest possible date and shall take precedence over all other cases, except older matters of the same character, and matters to which special precedence may be given by law.

(f) Notwithstanding failure to satisfy the time requirements of this section, the court may nonetheless hear the order to show cause why a preliminary injunction should not be granted if the moving and supporting papers are served within the time required by Section 1005 and one of the following conditions is satisfied:

(1) The order to show cause is issued without a temporary restraining order.

(2) The order to show cause is issued with a temporary restraining order, but is either not set for hearing within the time required by paragraph (1) of subdivision (d), or the party who obtained the temporary restraining order fails to effect service within the time required by paragraph (2) of subdivision (d).

(g) This section does not apply to an order issued under the Family Code.

(h) As used in this section:

(1) "Complaint" means a complaint or a cross-complaint.

(2) "Court" means the court in which the action is pending. *(Enacted in 1872. Amended by Stats.1895, c. 49, p. 51, § 1; Stats.1907, c. 272, p. 341, § 3; Stats.1911, c. 42, p. 59, § 1; Stats.1963, c. 878, p. 2125, § 2; Stats.1970, c. 488, p. 969, § 1; Stats.1977, c. 720, § 1; Stats.1978, c. 346, § 1; Stats.1979, c. 129, p. 316, § 1; Stats.1979, c. 795, p. 2707, § 7, operative July 1, 1980; Stats.1981, c. 182, p. 1100, § 1; Stats.1982, c. 812, p. 3100, § 1; Stats.1992, c. 163 (A.B.2641), § 23, operative Jan. 1, 1994; Stats.1993, c. 583 (A.B.284), § 1; Stats.1994, c. 587 (A.B.3600), § 5; Stats.1995, c. 796 (S.B.45), § 6; Stats.2000, c. 688 (A.B. 1669), § 4.)*

Law Revision Commission Comments

Section 527 is amended to delete provisions that applied only to orders described in Family Code Section 240, which are now governed by Part 4 (commencing with Section 240) of Division 2 of the Family Code, not by this section.

The provision formerly in subdivision (b) is continued in Family Code Section 245. The new language in subdivision (b) makes clear that the section does not apply to an order described in Family Code Section 240. The provisions of Section 527 that applied to the orders described in Family Code Section 240 have been duplicated in Part 4 (commencing with Section 240) of Division 2 of the Family Code. [22 Cal.L.Rev.Comm.Reports 1 (1992)].

Paragraph (1) of subdivision (d) of Section 527 is amended to increase from five to seven days the additional time the court may for good cause allow to hear an order to show cause with a temporary restraining order. This permits a court that hears such matters one day a week to extend the hearing until the next regular day for hearing.

A provision is added in paragraph (2) of subdivision (d) to require the moving papers to be served within five days after issuance of the temporary restraining order or two days before the hearing, whichever is earlier. Although paragraph (2) permits the order to show cause to be served less than 15 days before the hearing (the general requirement for a notice of motion under Section 1005), the short time permitted for service is ameliorated by paragraph (4) of subdivision (d) which gives the opposing party the right to a continuance to prepare for the hearing.

A provision is added in paragraph (2) of subdivision (d) to include a copy of the order to show cause with the documents that must be served. A copy of the complaint must be served only if not previously served. (The former second sentence of subdivision (a), which required a copy of the complaint or of the affidavits on which the "injunction" was granted to be served if not previously served, is deleted. Neither a preliminary nor a permanent injunction may be granted without notice.) Paragraph (2) of subdivision (d) requires the order to show cause to state the date, time, and place of the hearing. This is consistent with Section 1010 (notice of motion must state when it will be made).

A provision is added in paragraph (2) of subdivision (d) to give the court authority to shorten the time for service. This is consistent with Family Code Section 243. The requirement of good cause for shortening time is taken from Rule 305 of the California Rules of Court.

A provision is added in paragraph (4) of subdivision (d) to provide that if the opposing party obtains a continuance, the temporary restraining order is continued in effect until the hearing. This codifies the rule of International Molders & Allied Workers Union, Local 164 v. Superior Court, 70 Cal.App.3d 395, 407, 138 Cal.Rptr. 794 (1977).

Paragraph (5) is added to subdivision (d) to give the court authority to reissue a temporary restraining order not served within the required time. This is consistent with McDonald v. Superior Court, 18 Cal.App.2d 652, 655–56, 64 P.2d 738 (1937), and with Family Code Section 245.

Subdivision (f) is added to make clear that if the time requirements of this section are not satisfied or if the order to show cause is issued without a temporary restraining order, the court may still hear the matter if the papers are served within the time provided by Section 1005 for a notice of motion (15 days, with additional time if mailed). This changes the result in McDonald v. Superior Court, *supra*, and treats an order to show cause without a temporary restraining order the same as a notice of motion for a preliminary injunction without a temporary restraining order. See Gilbert & Kaplan, *Injunctions*, in 2 California Civil Procedure Before Trial § 39.43 (Cal. Cont. Ed. Bar 3d ed. 1992).

The other revisions to Section 527 are technical. [24 Cal.L.Rev.Comm. Reports 603 (1994)].

Research References

Rutter, Cal. Practice Guide: A.D.R. Ch. 5-G, G. Procedures to Enforce Arbitration.

Rutter, Cal. Practice Guide: Civ. Pro. Before Trial Ch. 6-B, B. Complaints.

Rutter, Cal. Practice Guide: Civ. Pro. Before Trial Ch. 14-C, C. Procedural Issues.

Rutter, Cal. Practice Guide: Civ. Pro. Before Trial Ch. 9(I)-B, B. Preparing and Filing Motions.

Rutter, Cal. Practice Guide: Civ. Pro. Before Trial Ch. 12(I)-C, C. Claims for Trial Setting Preference.

Rutter, Cal. Practice Guide: Civ. Pro. Before Trial Ch. 9(II)-A, A. Injunctions.

Rutter, Cal. Practice Guide: Civ. Pro. Before Trial Ch. 9(II)-C, C. Writ of Possession ("Claim and Delivery").

Rutter, Cal. Practice Guide: Civil Trials & Evidence Ch. 1-A, A. Importance of Statewide and Local Rules of Court.

Rutter, Cal. Practice Guide: Civil Trials & Evidence Ch. 8D-B, B. Hearsay vs. Nonhearsay.

Rutter, Cal. Practice Guide: Enforcing Judgments/Debts Ch. 4-B, B. Claim and Delivery.

2 Witkin Cal. Proc. 5th Jurisdiction § 320, (S 320) Granting of Relief as Excess of Jurisdiction.

4 Witkin Cal. Proc. 5th Pleading § 466, Complaint or Petition.

5 Witkin Cal. Proc. 5th Pleading § 822, (S 822) Nature of Action.

5 Witkin Cal. Proc. 5th Pleading § 824, (S 824) Where Complaint is Used as Affidavit.

5 Witkin Cal. Proc. 5th Pleading § 990, (S 990) Dismissal on Failure to Amend.

6 Witkin Cal. Proc. 5th Proceedings Without Trial § 529, (S 529) in General.

6 Witkin Cal. Proc. 5th Provisional Remedies § 2, (S 2) Use of Affidavit.

6 Witkin Cal. Proc. 5th Provisional Remedies § 284, Temporary Restraining Order.

6 Witkin Cal. Proc. 5th Provisional Remedies § 291, (S 291) Special Statutes.

6 Witkin Cal. Proc. 5th Provisional Remedies § 315, Domestic Violence.

6 Witkin Cal. Proc. 5th Provisional Remedies § 321, (S 321) Petition, Service, and Response.

6 Witkin Cal. Proc. 5th Provisional Remedies § 329, (S 329) Petition, Service, and Response.

6 Witkin Cal. Proc. 5th Provisional Remedies § 334, Arbitration Proceeding.

6 Witkin Cal. Proc. 5th Provisional Remedies § 363, Ex Parte Issuance.

6 Witkin Cal. Proc. 5th Provisional Remedies § 364, Order to Show Cause and Restraining Order.

6 Witkin Cal. Proc. 5th Provisional Remedies § 365, Return Date.

6 Witkin Cal. Proc. 5th Provisional Remedies § 368, (S 368) in General.

6 Witkin Cal. Proc. 5th Provisional Remedies § 370, (S 370) in General.

6 Witkin Cal. Proc. 5th Provisional Remedies § 372, (S 372) Time.

6 Witkin Cal. Proc. 5th Provisional Remedies § 373, to Defendant.

6 Witkin Cal. Proc. 5th Provisional Remedies § 374, to Plaintiff.

6 Witkin Cal. Proc. 5th Provisional Remedies § 376, Necessity for Showing.

6 Witkin Cal. Proc. 5th Provisional Remedies § 380, Showing by Affidavit.

6 Witkin Cal. Proc. 5th Provisional Remedies § 448, Confirmation of Appointment.

6 Witkin Cal. Proc. 5th Provisional Remedies § 330D, (S 330D) (New)-Petition, Service, and Response.

7 Witkin Cal. Proc. 5th Trial § 31, (S 31) Particular Actions and Proceedings.

7 Witkin Cal. Proc. 5th Trial § 72, (S 72) Miscellaneous Statutes.

10 Witkin, California Summary 10th Parent and Child § 453, Jurisdiction Over Adults.

11 Witkin, California Summary 10th Husband and Wife § 371, (S 371) Civil Remedies.

7 Witkin, California Summary 10th Constitutional Law § 371, Restrictions on Motion Pictures and Plays.

7 Witkin, California Summary 10th Constitutional Law § 397, (S 397) by Labor Organizations.

7 Witkin, California Summary 10th Constitutional Law § 656, (S 656) Restraining Criminal Nuisance.

§ 527.3. Labor disputes; jurisdiction of court

(a) In order to promote the rights of workers to engage in concerted activities for the purpose of collective bargaining, picketing or other mutual aid or protection, and to prevent the evils which frequently occur when courts interfere with the normal processes of dispute resolution between employers and recognized employee organizations, the equity jurisdiction of the courts in cases involving or growing out of a labor dispute shall be no broader than as set forth in subdivision (b) of this section, and the provisions of subdivision (b) of this section shall be strictly construed in accordance with existing law governing labor disputes with the purpose of avoiding any unnecessary judicial interference in labor disputes.

(b) The acts enumerated in this subdivision, whether performed singly or in concert, shall be legal, and no court nor any judge nor judges thereof, shall have jurisdiction to issue any restraining order or preliminary or permanent injunction which, in specific or general terms, prohibits any person or persons, whether singly or in concert, from doing any of the following:

(1) Giving publicity to, and obtaining or communicating information regarding the existence of, or the facts involved in, any labor dispute, whether by advertising, speaking, patrolling any public street or any place where any person or persons may lawfully be, or by any other method not involving fraud, violence or breach of the peace.

(2) Peaceful picketing or patrolling involving any labor dispute, whether engaged in singly or in numbers.

(3) Assembling peaceably to do any of the acts specified in paragraphs (1) and (2) or to promote lawful interests.

(4) Except as provided in subparagraph (iv), for purposes of this section, "labor dispute" is defined as follows:

(i) A case shall be held to involve or to grow out of a labor dispute when the case involves persons who are engaged in the same industry, trade, craft, or occupation; or have direct or indirect interests therein; or who are employees of the same employer; or who are members of the same or an affiliated organization of employers or employees; whether such dispute is (a) between one or more employers or associations of employers and one or more employees or associations of employees; (b) between one or more employers or associations of employers and one or more employers or associations of employers; or (c) between one or more employees or associations of employees

and one or more employees or associations of employees; or when the case involves any conflicting or competing interests in a "labor dispute" of "persons participating or interested" therein (as defined in subparagraph (ii)).

(ii) A person or association shall be held to be a person participating or interested in a labor dispute if relief is sought against him or it, and if he or it is engaged in the same industry, trade, craft, or occupation in which such dispute occurs, or has a direct or indirect interest therein, or is a member, officer, or agent of any association composed in whole or in part of employers or employees engaged in such industry, trade, craft, or occupation.

(iii) The term "labor dispute" includes any controversy concerning terms or conditions of employment, or concerning the association or representation of persons in negotiating, fixing, maintaining, changing, or seeking to arrange terms or conditions of employment regardless of whether or not the disputants stand in the proximate relation of employer and employee.

(iv) The term "labor dispute" does not include a jurisdictional strike as defined in Section 1118 of the Labor Code.

(c) Nothing contained in this section shall be construed to alter or supersede the provisions of Chapter 1 of the 1975–76 Third Extraordinary Session [1], and to the extent of any conflict between the provisions of this act and that chapter, the provisions of the latter shall prevail.

(d) Nothing contained in this section shall be construed to alter the legal rights of public employees or their employers, nor shall this section alter the rights of parties to collective-bargaining agreements under the provisions of Section 1126 of the Labor Code.

(e) It is not the intent of this section to permit conduct that is unlawful including breach of the peace, disorderly conduct, the unlawful blocking of access or egress to premises where a labor dispute exists, or other similar unlawful activity. *(Added by Stats.1975, c. 1156, p. 2845, § 2.)*

[1] Labor Code § 1140 et seq.

Research References

Rutter, Cal. Practice Guide: Civ. Pro. Before Trial Ch. 9(II)-A, A. Injunctions.

California Practice Guide: Employment Litigation Ch. 15-C, C. Labor Management Relations Act Preemption (Including Nlra).

Miller and Starr California Real Estate § 22:80, Use of Common Area for Exercise of First Amendment Rights.

6 Witkin Cal. Proc. 5th Provisional Remedies § 313, Labor Dispute.

6 Witkin Cal. Proc. 5th Provisional Remedies § 326, (S 326) Nature and Scope of Statute.

6 Witkin Cal. Proc. 5th Provisional Remedies § 363, Ex Parte Issuance.

6 Witkin Cal. Proc. 5th Provisional Remedies § 330A, (S 330A) (New)-Nature and Scope of Statute.

5 Witkin, California Summary 10th Torts § 596, (S 596) Request for Information.

3 Witkin, California Summary 10th Agency and Employment § 632, (S 632) Nature and Scope of Act.

3 Witkin, California Summary 10th Agency and Employment § 650, (S 650) Private Property.

3 Witkin, California Summary 10th Agency and Employment § 652, (S 652) in General.

3 Witkin, California Summary 10th Agency and Employment § 653, (S 653) Scope of Permissible Injunction.

3 Witkin, California Summary 10th Agency and Employment § 654, (S 654) Procedure for Injunctive Relief.

3 Witkin, California Summary 10th Agency and Employment § 669, Jurisdiction of Court.

§ 527.6. Harassment; temporary restraining order and injunction; procedure; domestic violence; support person; costs and attorney fees; punishment

Section operative until July 1, 2014. See, also, section operative July 1, 2014.

(a)(1) A person who has suffered harassment as defined in subdivision (b) may seek a temporary restraining order and an injunction prohibiting harassment as provided in this section.

(2) A minor, under 12 years of age, accompanied by a duly appointed and acting guardian ad litem, shall be permitted to appear in court without counsel for the limited purpose of requesting or opposing a request for a temporary restraining order or injunction, or both, under this section as provided in Section 374.

(b) For the purposes of this section:

(1) "Course of conduct" is a pattern of conduct composed of a series of acts over a period of time, however short, evidencing a continuity of purpose, including following or stalking an individual, making harassing telephone calls to an individual, or sending harassing correspondence to an individual by any means, including, but not limited to, the use of public or private mails, interoffice mail, facsimile, or computer email. Constitutionally protected activity is not included within the meaning of "course of conduct."

(2) "Credible threat of violence" is a knowing and willful statement or course of conduct that would place a reasonable person in fear for his or her safety, or the safety of his or her immediate family, and that serves no legitimate purpose.

(3) "Harassment" is unlawful violence, a credible threat of violence, or a knowing and willful course of conduct directed at a specific person that seriously alarms, annoys, or harasses the person, and that serves no legitimate purpose. The course of conduct must be such as would cause a reasonable person to suffer substantial emotional distress, and must actually cause substantial emotional distress to the petitioner.

(4) "Petitioner" means the person to be protected by the temporary restraining order and injunction and, if the court grants the petition, the protected person.

(5) "Respondent" means the person against whom the temporary restraining order and injunction are sought and, if the petition is granted, the restrained person.

(6) "Temporary restraining order" and "injunction" mean orders that include any of the following restraining orders, whether issued ex parte or after notice and hearing:

(A) An order enjoining a party from harassing, intimidating, molesting, attacking, striking, stalking, threatening, sexually assaulting, battering, abusing, telephoning, including, but not limited to, making annoying telephone calls, as described in Section 653m of the Penal Code, destroying personal property, contacting, either directly or indirectly, by mail or otherwise, or coming within a specified distance of, or disturbing the peace of, the petitioner.

(B) An order enjoining a party from specified behavior that the court determines is necessary to effectuate orders described in subparagraph (A).

(7) "Unlawful violence" is any assault or battery, or stalking as prohibited in Section 646.9 of the Penal Code, but shall not include lawful acts of self-defense or defense of others.

(c) In the discretion of the court, on a showing of good cause, a temporary restraining order or injunction issued under this section may include other named family or household members.

(d) Upon filing a petition for an injunction under this section, the petitioner may obtain a temporary restraining order in accordance with Section 527, except to the extent this section provides a rule that is inconsistent. The temporary restraining order may include any of the restraining orders described in paragraph (6) of subdivision (b). A temporary restraining order may be issued with or without notice, based on a declaration that, to the satisfaction of the court, shows reasonable proof of harassment of the petitioner by the respondent, and that great or irreparable harm would result to the petitioner.

(e) A request for the issuance of a temporary restraining order without notice under this section shall be granted or denied on the same day that the petition is submitted to the court, unless the petition is filed too late in the day to permit effective review, in which case the order shall be granted or denied on the next day of judicial business in sufficient time for the order to be filed that day with the clerk of the court.

(f) A temporary restraining order issued under this section shall remain in effect, at the court's discretion, for a period not to exceed 21 days, or, if the court extends the time for hearing under subdivision (g), not to exceed 25 days, unless otherwise modified or terminated by the court.

(g) Within 21 days, or, if good cause appears to the court, 25 days from the date that a petition for a temporary order is granted or denied, a hearing shall be held on the petition for the injunction. If no request for temporary orders is made, the hearing shall be held within 21 days, or, if good cause appears to the court, 25 days, from the date that the petition is filed.

(h) The respondent may file a response that explains, excuses, justifies, or denies the alleged harassment or may file a cross-petition under this section.

(i) At the hearing, the judge shall receive any testimony that is relevant, and may make an independent inquiry. If the judge finds by clear and convincing evidence that unlawful harassment exists, an injunction shall issue prohibiting the harassment.

(j)(1) In the discretion of the court, an order issued after notice and hearing under this section may have a duration of not more than three years, subject to termination or modification by further order of the court either on written stipulation filed with the court or on the motion of a party. These orders may be renewed, upon the request of a party, for a duration of not more than three additional years, without a showing of any further harassment since the issuance of the original order, subject to termination or modification by further order of the court either on written stipulation filed with the court or on the motion of a party. The request for renewal may be brought at any time within the three months before the expiration of the order.

(2) The failure to state the expiration date on the face of the form creates an order with a duration of three years from the date of issuance.

(3) If an action is filed for the purpose of terminating or modifying a protective order prior to the expiration date specified in the order by a party other than the protected party, the party who is protected by the order shall be given notice, pursuant to subdivision (b) of Section 1005, of the proceeding by personal service or, if the protected party has satisfied the requirements of Chapter 3.1 (commencing with Section 6205) of Division 7 of Title 1 of the Government Code, by service on the Secretary of State. If the party who is protected by the order cannot be notified prior to the hearing for modification or termination of the protective order, the court shall deny the motion to modify or terminate the order without prejudice or continue the hearing until the party who is protected can be properly noticed and may, upon a showing of good cause, specify another method for service of process that is reasonably designed to afford actual notice to the protected party. The protected party may waive his or her right to notice if he or she is physically present in court and does not challenge the sufficiency of the notice.

(k) This section does not preclude either party from representation by private counsel or from appearing on the party's own behalf.

(*l*) In a proceeding under this section if there are allegations of unlawful violence or credible threats of violence, a support person may accompany a party in court and, if the party is not represented by an attorney, may sit with the party at the table that is generally reserved for the party and the party's attorney. The support person is present to provide moral and emotional support for a person who alleges he or she is a victim of violence. The support person is not present as a legal adviser and may not provide legal advice. The support person may assist the person who alleges he or she is a victim of violence in feeling more confident that he or she will not be injured or threatened by the other party during the proceedings if the person who alleges he or she is a victim of violence and the other party are required to be present in close proximity. This subdivision does not preclude the court from exercising its discretion to remove the support person from the courtroom if the court believes the support person is prompting, swaying, or influencing the party assisted by the support person.

(m) Upon the filing of a petition for an injunction under this section, the respondent shall be personally served with a copy of the petition, temporary restraining order, if any, and notice of hearing of the petition. Service shall be made at least five days before the hearing. The court may for good cause, on motion of the petitioner or on its own motion, shorten the time for service on the respondent.

(n) A notice of hearing under this section shall notify the respondent that if he or she does not attend the hearing, the court may make orders against him or her that could last up to three years.

(*o*)(1) The court may, upon the filing of a declaration by the petitioner that the respondent could not be served within the time required by statute, reissue an order previously issued and dissolved by the court for failure to serve the respondent. The reissued order shall remain in effect until the date set for the hearing.

(2) The reissued order shall state on its face the date of expiration of the order.

(p)(1) If a respondent, named in a restraining order issued after a hearing, has not been served personally with the order but has received actual notice of the existence and substance of the order through personal appearance in court to hear the terms of the order from the court, no additional proof of service is required for enforcement of the order.

(2) If the respondent named in a temporary restraining order is personally served with the order and notice of hearing with respect to a restraining order or protective order based on the temporary restraining order, but the respondent does not appear at the hearing, either personally or by an attorney, and the terms and conditions of the restraining order or protective order issued at the hearing are identical to the temporary restraining order, except for the duration of the order, then the restraining order or protective order issued at the hearing may be served on the respondent by first-class mail sent to the respondent at the most current address for the respondent available to the court.

(3) The Judicial Council form for temporary orders issued pursuant to this subdivision shall contain a statement in substantially the following form:

"If you have been personally served with this temporary restraining order and notice of hearing, but you do not appear at the hearing either in person or by a lawyer, and a restraining order that is the same as this temporary restraining order except for the expiration date is issued at the hearing, a copy of the restraining order will be served on you by mail at the following address: ____.

If that address is not correct or you wish to verify that the temporary restraining order was converted to a restraining order

at the hearing without substantive change and to find out the duration of that order, contact the clerk of the court."

(q)(1) Information on any temporary restraining order or injunction relating to civil harassment issued by a court pursuant to this section shall be transmitted to the Department of Justice in accordance with either paragraph (2) or (3).

(2) The court shall order the petitioner or the attorney for the petitioner to deliver a copy of an order issued under this section, or reissuance, extension, modification, or termination of the order, and any subsequent proof of service, by the close of the business day on which the order, reissuance, extension, modification, or termination was made, to a law enforcement agency having jurisdiction over the residence of the petitioner and to any additional law enforcement agencies within the court's discretion as are requested by the petitioner.

(3) Alternatively, the court or its designee shall transmit, within one business day, to law enforcement personnel all information required under subdivision (b) of Section 6380 of the Family Code regarding any order issued under this section, or a reissuance, extension, modification, or termination of the order, and any subsequent proof of service, by either one of the following methods:

(A) Transmitting a physical copy of the order or proof of service to a local law enforcement agency authorized by the Department of Justice to enter orders into the California Law Enforcement Telecommunications System (CLETS).

(B) With the approval of the Department of Justice, entering the order or proof of service into CLETS directly.

(4) Each appropriate law enforcement agency shall make available information as to the existence and current status of these orders to law enforcement officers responding to the scene of reported harassment.

(5) An order issued under this section shall, on request of the petitioner, be served on the respondent, whether or not the respondent has been taken into custody, by any law enforcement officer who is present at the scene of reported harassment involving the parties to the proceeding. The petitioner shall provide the officer with an endorsed copy of the order and a proof of service that the officer shall complete and send to the issuing court.

(6) Upon receiving information at the scene of an incident of harassment that a protective order has been issued under this section, or that a person who has been taken into custody is the subject of an order, if the protected person cannot produce a certified copy of the order, a law enforcement officer shall immediately attempt to verify the existence of the order.

(7) If the law enforcement officer determines that a protective order has been issued, but not served, the officer shall immediately notify the respondent of the terms of the order and shall at that time also enforce the order. Verbal notice of the terms of the order shall constitute service of the order and is sufficient notice for the purposes of this section and for the purposes of Section 29825 of the Penal Code.

(r) The prevailing party in any action brought under this section may be awarded court costs and attorney's fees, if any.

(s) Any willful disobedience of any temporary restraining order or injunction granted under this section is punishable pursuant to Section 273.6 of the Penal Code.

(t)(1) A person subject to a protective order issued under this section shall not own, possess, purchase, receive, or attempt to purchase or receive a firearm or ammunition while the protective order is in effect.

(2) The court shall order a person subject to a protective order issued under this section to relinquish any firearms he or she owns or possesses pursuant to Section 527.9.

(3) Every person who owns, possesses, purchases, or receives, or attempts to purchase or receive, a firearm or ammunition while the protective order is in effect is punishable pursuant to Section 29825 of the Penal Code.

(u) This section does not apply to any action or proceeding covered by Title 1.6C (commencing with Section 1788) of Part 4 of Division 3 of the Civil Code or by Division 10 (commencing with Section 6200) of the Family Code. This section does not preclude a petitioner from using other existing civil remedies.

(v)(1) The Judicial Council shall develop forms, instructions, and rules relating to matters governed by this section. The petition and response forms shall be simple and concise, and their use by parties in actions brought pursuant to this section shall be mandatory.

(2) A temporary restraining order or injunction relating to civil harassment issued by a court pursuant to this section shall be issued on forms adopted by the Judicial Council of California and that have been approved by the Department of Justice pursuant to subdivision (i) of Section 6380 of the Family Code. However, the fact that an order issued by a court pursuant to this section was not issued on forms adopted by the Judicial Council and approved by the Department of Justice shall not, in and of itself, make the order unenforceable.

(w) There is no filing fee for a petition that alleges that a person has inflicted or threatened violence against the petitioner, or stalked the petitioner, or acted or spoken in any other manner that has placed the petitioner in reasonable fear of violence, and that seeks a protective or restraining order or injunction restraining stalking or future violence or threats of violence, in any action brought pursuant to this section. No fee shall be paid for a subpoena filed in connection with a petition alleging these acts. No fee shall be paid for filing a response to a petition alleging these acts.

(x)(1) Subject to paragraph (4) of subdivision (b) of Section 6103.2 of the Government Code, there shall be no fee for the service of process by a sheriff or marshal of a protective order, restraining order, or injunction to be issued, if either of the following conditions applies:

(A) The protective order, restraining order, or injunction issued pursuant to this section is based upon stalking, as prohibited by Section 646.9 of the Penal Code.

(B) The protective order, restraining order, or injunction issued pursuant to this section is based upon unlawful violence or a credible threat of violence.

(2) The Judicial Council shall prepare and develop forms for persons who wish to avail themselves of the services described in this subdivision.

<u>(y) This section shall remain in effect only until July 1, 2014, and as of that date is repealed, unless a later enacted statute, that is enacted before July 1, 2014, deletes or extends that date.</u>
(Added by Stats.2002, c. 1009 (A.B.2030), § 2, operative Jan. 1, 2007. Amended by Stats.2003, c. 498 (S.B.226), § 2, operative Jan. 1, 2007; Stats.2006, c. 476 (A.B.2695), § 1; Stats.2010, c. 178 (S.B.1115), § 20, operative Jan. 1, 2012; Stats.2010, c. 572 (A.B.1596), § 1, operative Jan. 1, 2012; Stats.2011, c. 285 (A.B.1402), § 1; Stats.2011, c. 101 (A.B.454), § 1; Stats.2012, c. 162 (S.B.1171), § 12; Stats.2013, c. 158 (A.B.499), § 1.)

Repeal

For repeal of this section, see its terms.

Research References

Rutter, Cal. Practice Guide: Civil Appeals & Writs Ch. 8-C, C. Standards of Appellate Review.

Rutter, Cal. Practice Guide: Civil Appeals & Writs Gen. Matls., Highlights.

Rutter, Cal. Practice Guide: Civ. Pro. Before Trial Ch. 2-B, B. Capacity to Sue or Defend.

Rutter, Cal. Practice Guide: Civ. Pro. Before Trial Ch. 11-A, A. Voluntary Dismissals.

Rutter, Cal. Practice Guide: Civ. Pro. Before Trial Ch. 9(I)-A, A. Introduction.

Rutter, Cal. Practice Guide: Civ. Pro. Before Trial Ch. 12(I)-C, C. Claims for Trial Setting Preference.

Rutter, Cal. Practice Guide: Civ. Pro. Before Trial Ch. 7(II)-D, D. Activities Protected by Anti-SLAPP Statute.

Rutter, Cal. Practice Guide: Civ. Pro. Before Trial Ch. 7(II)-E, E. Causes of Action Subject to Being Stricken.

Rutter, Cal. Practice Guide: Civ. Pro. Before Trial Ch. 9(II)-A, A. Injunctions.

Rutter, Cal. Practice Guide: Civ. Pro. Before Trial Gen. Matls., Highlights.

Rutter, Cal. Practice Guide: Civil Trials & Evidence Ch. 17-E, E. Attorney Fees as Costs.

Rutter, Cal. Practice Guide: Civil Trials & Evidence Ch. 8D-B, B. Hearsay vs. Nonhearsay.

Rutter, Cal. Practice Guide: Civil Trials & Evidence Ch. 8D-C, C. General Parameters Re Admissibility of Hearsay Evidence.

Rutter, Cal. Practice Guide: Personal Injury Ch. 1-B, B. Initial Evaluation of Case: Decision to Accept or Reject Employment or Undertake Further Evaluation of Claim.

Miller and Starr California Real Estate § 15:72, Remedies for Interference With the Use of an Easement.

Miller and Starr California Real Estate § 19:32, Tenancy at Sufferance.

Miller and Starr California Real Estate § 34:66, Examples of Actions in Which Fees Can be Recovered.

Miller and Starr California Real Estate § 34:74, Effect of Dismissal of Action Before Judgment.

2 Witkin Cal. Proc. 5th Courts § 29, (S 29) Use of English.

2 Witkin Cal. Proc. 5th Courts § 199, (S 199) in General.

8 Witkin Cal. Proc. 5th Enforcement of Judgment § 515, (S 515) Automatic Stay.

7 Witkin Cal. Proc. 5th Judgment § 223, (S 223) Civil Rights Actions.

4 Witkin Cal. Proc. 5th Pleading § 73, (S 73) Exception: Injunction or Protective Order.

5 Witkin Cal. Proc. 5th Pleading § 1019, (S 1019) in General.

6 Witkin Cal. Proc. 5th Provisional Remedies § 316, (S 316) Nature and Scope of Statute.

6 Witkin Cal. Proc. 5th Provisional Remedies § 317, (S 317) Definitions.

6 Witkin Cal. Proc. 5th Provisional Remedies § 318, (S 318) Constitutionally Protected Activity.

6 Witkin Cal. Proc. 5th Provisional Remedies § 319, (S 319) Restriction on Possession of Firearms.

6 Witkin Cal. Proc. 5th Provisional Remedies § 320, (S 320) Judicial Council Forms.

6 Witkin Cal. Proc. 5th Provisional Remedies § 321, (S 321) Petition, Service, and Response.

6 Witkin Cal. Proc. 5th Provisional Remedies § 322, (S 322) Hearing, Determination, and Enforcement Response.

6 Witkin Cal. Proc. 5th Provisional Remedies § 375, on Court's Own Motion.

12 Witkin, California Summary 10th Real Property § 703, (S 703) Nature of Remedy.

11 Witkin, California Summary 10th Husband and Wife § 371, (S 371) Civil Remedies.

11 Witkin, California Summary 10th Husband and Wife § 374, (S 374) Definitions.

11 Witkin, California Summary 10th Husband and Wife § 384, (S 384) Orders After Notice and Hearing.

11 Witkin, California Summary 10th Husband and Wife § 387, (S 387) Electronic Transmission and Recording of Data.

5 Witkin, California Summary 10th Torts § 660, (S 660) in General.

5 Witkin, California Summary 10th Torts § 662, (S 662) Stalking.

5 Witkin, California Summary 10th Torts § 496A, (S 496A) (New)- Petition to Enjoin Harassment.

Civ. Pro.

5 Witkin, California Summary 10th Torts § 496B, (S 496B) (New)-Petition to Enjoin Workplace Violence or Threats.

§ 527.6. Harassment; temporary restraining order and injunction; procedure; allegations or threats of violence; support person; costs and attorney fees; punishment

Section operative July 1, 2014. See, also,
section operative until July 1, 2014.

(a)(1) A person who has suffered harassment as defined in subdivision (b) may seek a temporary restraining order and an injunction prohibiting harassment as provided in this section.

(2) A minor, under 12 years of age, accompanied by a duly appointed and acting guardian ad litem, shall be permitted to appear in court without counsel for the limited purpose of requesting or opposing a request for a temporary restraining order or injunction, or both, under this section as provided in Section 374.

(b) For the purposes of this section:

(1) "Course of conduct" is a pattern of conduct composed of a series of acts over a period of time, however short, evidencing a continuity of purpose, including following or stalking an individual, making harassing telephone calls to an individual, or sending harassing correspondence to an individual by any means, including, but not limited to, the use of public or private mails, interoffice mail, facsimile, or computer email. Constitutionally protected activity is not included within the meaning of "course of conduct."

(2) "Credible threat of violence" is a knowing and willful statement or course of conduct that would place a reasonable person in fear for his or her safety, or the safety of his or her immediate family, and that serves no legitimate purpose.

(3) "Harassment" is unlawful violence, a credible threat of violence, or a knowing and willful course of conduct directed at a specific person that seriously alarms, annoys, or harasses the person, and that serves no legitimate purpose. The course of conduct must be such as would cause a reasonable person to suffer substantial emotional distress, and must actually cause substantial emotional distress to the petitioner.

(4) "Petitioner" means the person to be protected by the temporary restraining order and injunction and, if the court grants the petition, the protected person.

(5) "Respondent" means the person against whom the temporary restraining order and injunction are sought and, if the petition is granted, the restrained person.

(6) "Temporary restraining order" and "injunction" mean orders that include any of the following restraining orders, whether issued ex parte or after notice and hearing:

(A) An order enjoining a party from harassing, intimidating, molesting, attacking, striking, stalking, threatening, sexually assaulting, battering, abusing, telephoning, including, but not limited to, making annoying telephone calls, as described in Section 653m of the Penal Code, destroying personal property, contacting, either directly or indirectly, by mail or otherwise, or coming within a specified distance of, or disturbing the peace of, the petitioner.

(B) An order enjoining a party from specified behavior that the court determines is necessary to effectuate orders described in subparagraph (A).

(7) "Unlawful violence" is any assault or battery, or stalking as prohibited in Section 646.9 of the Penal Code, but shall not include lawful acts of self-defense or defense of others.

(c) In the discretion of the court, on a showing of good cause, a temporary restraining order or injunction issued under this section may include other named family or household members.

(d) Upon filing a petition for an injunction under this section, the petitioner may obtain a temporary restraining order in accordance with Section 527, except to the extent this section provides a rule that is inconsistent. The temporary restraining order may include any of the restraining orders described in paragraph (6) of subdivision (b). A temporary restraining order may be issued with or without notice, based on a declaration that, to the satisfaction of the court, shows reasonable proof of harassment of the petitioner by the respondent, and that great or irreparable harm would result to the petitioner.

(e) A request for the issuance of a temporary restraining order without notice under this section shall be granted or denied on the same day that the petition is submitted to the court, unless the petition is filed too late in the day to permit effective review, in which case the order shall be granted or denied on the next day of judicial business in sufficient time for the order to be filed that day with the clerk of the court.

(f) A temporary restraining order issued under this section shall remain in effect, at the court's discretion, for a period not to exceed 21 days, or, if the court extends the time for hearing under subdivision (g), not to exceed 25 days, unless otherwise modified or terminated by the court.

(g) Within 21 days, or, if good cause appears to the court, 25 days from the date that a petition for a temporary order is granted or denied, a hearing shall be held on the petition for the injunction. If no request for temporary orders is made, the hearing shall be held within 21 days, or, if good cause appears to the court, 25 days, from the date that the petition is filed.

(h) The respondent may file a response that explains, excuses, justifies, or denies the alleged harassment or may file a cross-petition under this section.

(i) At the hearing, the judge shall receive any testimony that is relevant, and may make an independent inquiry. If the judge finds by clear and convincing evidence that unlawful harassment exists, an injunction shall issue prohibiting the harassment.

(j)(1) In the discretion of the court, an order issued after notice and hearing under this section may have a duration of not more than five years, subject to termination or modification by further order of the court either on written stipulation filed with the court or on the motion of a party. The order may be renewed, upon the request of a party, for a duration of not more than five additional years, without a showing of any further harassment since the issuance of the original order, subject to termination or modification by further order of the court either on written stipulation filed with the court or on the motion of a party. A request for renewal may be brought at any time within the three months before the expiration of the order.

(2) The failure to state the expiration date on the face of the form creates an order with a duration of three years from the date of issuance.

(3) If an action is filed for the purpose of terminating or modifying a protective order prior to the expiration date specified in the order by a party other than the protected party, the party who is protected by the order shall be given notice, pursuant to subdivision (b) of Section 1005, of the proceeding by personal service or, if the protected party has satisfied the requirements of Chapter 3.1 (commencing with Section 6205) of Division 7 of Title 1 of the Government Code, by service on the Secretary of State. If the party who is protected by the order cannot be notified prior to the hearing for modification or termination of the protective order, the court shall deny the motion to modify or terminate the order without prejudice or continue the hearing until the party who is protected can be properly noticed and may, upon a showing of good cause, specify another method for service of process that is reasonably designed to afford actual notice to the protected party. The

protected party may waive his or her right to notice if he or she is physically present in court and does not challenge the sufficiency of the notice.

(k) This section does not preclude either party from representation by private counsel or from appearing on the party's own behalf.

(*l*) In a proceeding under this section if there are allegations of unlawful violence or credible threats of violence, a support person may accompany a party in court and, if the party is not represented by an attorney, may sit with the party at the table that is generally reserved for the party and the party's attorney. The support person is present to provide moral and emotional support for a person who alleges he or she is a victim of violence. The support person is not present as a legal adviser and may not provide legal advice. The support person may assist the person who alleges he or she is a victim of violence in feeling more confident that he or she will not be injured or threatened by the other party during the proceedings if the person who alleges he or she is a victim of violence and the other party are required to be present in close proximity. This subdivision does not preclude the court from exercising its discretion to remove the support person from the courtroom if the court believes the support person is prompting, swaying, or influencing the party assisted by the support person.

(m) Upon the filing of a petition for an injunction under this section, the respondent shall be personally served with a copy of the petition, temporary restraining order, if any, and notice of hearing of the petition. Service shall be made at least five days before the hearing. The court may for good cause, on motion of the petitioner or on its own motion, shorten the time for service on the respondent.

(n) A notice of hearing under this section shall notify the respondent that if he or she does not attend the hearing, the court may make orders against him or her that could last up to three years.

(*o*)(1) The court may, upon the filing of a declaration by the petitioner that the respondent could not be served within the time required by statute, reissue an order previously issued and dissolved by the court for failure to serve the respondent. The reissued order shall remain in effect until the date set for the hearing.

(2) The reissued order shall state on its face the date of expiration of the order.

(p)(1) If a respondent, named in a restraining order issued after a hearing, has not been served personally with the order but has received actual notice of the existence and substance of the order through personal appearance in court to hear the terms of the order from the court, no additional proof of service is required for enforcement of the order.

(2) If the respondent named in a temporary restraining order is personally served with the order and notice of hearing with respect to a restraining order or protective order based on the temporary restraining order, but the respondent does not appear at the hearing, either personally or by an attorney, and the terms and conditions of the restraining order or protective order issued at the hearing are identical to the temporary restraining order, except for the duration of the order, then the restraining order or protective order issued at the hearing may be served on the respondent by first-class mail sent to the respondent at the most current address for the respondent available to the court.

(3) The Judicial Council form for temporary orders issued pursuant to this subdivision shall contain a statement in substantially the following form:

"If you have been personally served with this temporary restraining order and notice of hearing, but you do not appear at the hearing either in person or by a lawyer, and a restraining order that is the same as this temporary restraining order except for the expiration date is issued at the hearing, a copy of the restraining order will be served on you by mail at the following address: ____.

If that address is not correct or you wish to verify that the temporary restraining order was converted to a restraining order at the hearing without substantive change and to find out the duration of that order, contact the clerk of the court."

(q)(1) Information on any temporary restraining order or injunction relating to civil harassment issued by a court pursuant to this section shall be transmitted to the Department of Justice in accordance with either paragraph (2) or (3).

(2) The court shall order the petitioner or the attorney for the petitioner to deliver a copy of an order issued under this section, or reissuance, extension, modification, or termination of the order, and any subsequent proof of service, by the close of the business day on which the order, reissuance, extension, modification, or termination was made, to a law enforcement agency having jurisdiction over the residence of the petitioner and to any additional law enforcement agencies within the court's discretion as are requested by the petitioner.

(3) Alternatively, the court or its designee shall transmit, within one business day, to law enforcement personnel all information required under subdivision (b) of Section 6380 of the Family Code regarding any order issued under this section, or a reissuance, extension, modification, or termination of the order, and any subsequent proof of service, by either one of the following methods:

(A) Transmitting a physical copy of the order or proof of service to a local law enforcement agency authorized by the Department of Justice to enter orders into the California Law Enforcement Telecommunications System (CLETS).

(B) With the approval of the Department of Justice, entering the order or proof of service into CLETS directly.

(4) Each appropriate law enforcement agency shall make available information as to the existence and current status of these orders to law enforcement officers responding to the scene of reported harassment.

(5) An order issued under this section shall, on request of the petitioner, be served on the respondent, whether or not the respondent has been taken into custody, by any law enforcement officer who is present at the scene of reported harassment involving the parties to the proceeding. The petitioner shall provide the officer with an endorsed copy of the order and a proof of service that the officer shall complete and send to the issuing court.

(6) Upon receiving information at the scene of an incident of harassment that a protective order has been issued under this section, or that a person who has been taken into custody is the subject of an order, if the protected person cannot produce a certified copy of the order, a law enforcement officer shall immediately attempt to verify the existence of the order.

(7) If the law enforcement officer determines that a protective order has been issued, but not served, the officer shall immediately notify the respondent of the terms of the order and shall at that time also enforce the order. Verbal notice of the terms of the order shall constitute service of the order and is sufficient notice for the purposes of this section and for the purposes of Section 29825 of the Penal Code.

(r) The prevailing party in any action brought under this section may be awarded court costs and attorney's fees, if any.

(s) Any willful disobedience of any temporary restraining order or injunction granted under this section is punishable pursuant to Section 273.6 of the Penal Code.

(t)(1) A person subject to a protective order issued under this section shall not own, possess, purchase, receive, or attempt to purchase or receive a firearm or ammunition while the protective order is in effect.

(2) The court shall order a person subject to a protective order issued under this section to relinquish any firearms he or she owns or possesses pursuant to Section 527.9.

(3) Every person who owns, possesses, purchases, or receives, or attempts to purchase or receive, a firearm or ammunition while the protective order is in effect is punishable pursuant to Section 29825 of the Penal Code.

(u) This section does not apply to any action or proceeding covered by Title 1.6C (commencing with Section 1788) of Part 4 of Division 3 of the Civil Code or by Division 10 (commencing with Section 6200) of the Family Code. This section does not preclude a petitioner from using other existing civil remedies.

(v)(1) The Judicial Council shall develop forms, instructions, and rules relating to matters governed by this section. The petition and response forms shall be simple and concise, and their use by parties in actions brought pursuant to this section shall be mandatory.

(2) A temporary restraining order or injunction relating to civil harassment issued by a court pursuant to this section shall be issued on forms adopted by the Judicial Council of California and that have been approved by the Department of Justice pursuant to subdivision (i) of Section 6380 of the Family Code. However, the fact that an order issued by a court pursuant to this section was not issued on forms adopted by the Judicial Council and approved by the Department of Justice shall not, in and of itself, make the order unenforceable.

(w) There is no filing fee for a petition that alleges that a person has inflicted or threatened violence against the petitioner, or stalked the petitioner, or acted or spoken in any other manner that has placed the petitioner in reasonable fear of violence, and that seeks a protective or restraining order or injunction restraining stalking or future violence or threats of violence, in any action brought pursuant to this section. No fee shall be paid for a subpoena filed in connection with a petition alleging these acts. No fee shall be paid for filing a response to a petition alleging these acts.

(x)(1) Subject to paragraph (4) of subdivision (b) of Section 6103.2 of the Government Code, there shall be no fee for the service of process by a sheriff or marshal of a protective order, restraining order, or injunction to be issued, if either of the following conditions applies:

(A) The protective order, restraining order, or injunction issued pursuant to this section is based upon stalking, as prohibited by Section 646.9 of the Penal Code.

(B) The protective order, restraining order, or injunction issued pursuant to this section is based upon unlawful violence or a credible threat of violence.

(2) The Judicial Council shall prepare and develop forms for persons who wish to avail themselves of the services described in this subdivision.

(y) This section shall become operative on July 1, 2014. *(Added by Stats.2013, c. 158 (A.B.499), § 2, operative July 1, 2014.)*

§ 527.7. Groups meeting, advocating and acting in furtherance of unlawful force or violence against persons; injunctions; bad faith actions

(a) It shall be unlawful for any group, association, organization, society, or other assemblage of two or more persons to meet and to advocate, and to take substantial action in furtherance of, the commission of an unlawful act of violence or force

directed to and likely to produce the imminent and unlawful infliction of serious bodily injury or death of another person within this state.

(b) Whenever it reasonably appears that any group, association, society, or other assemblage of two or more persons has met and taken substantial action in furtherance of the commission of an act of violence made unlawful by subdivision (a) and will engage in those acts in the future, any aggrieved individual may bring a civil action in the superior court to enjoin the advocacy of the commission of any act of violence made unlawful by subdivision (a) at any future meeting or meetings. Upon a proper showing by clear and convincing evidence, a permanent or preliminary injunction, restraining order, or writ of mandate shall be granted.

(c) Whenever it appears that an action brought under this section was groundless and brought in bad faith for the purpose of harassment, the trial court or any appellate court may award to the defendant attorney's fees and court costs incurred for the purpose of defending the action. *(Added by Stats.1982, c. 1624, p. 6489, § 1.)*

Research References

Rutter, Cal. Practice Guide: Civ. Pro. Before Trial Ch. 9(II)-A, A. Injunctions.
2 Witkin Cal. Proc. 5th Courts § 199, (S 199) in General.
6 Witkin Cal. Proc. 5th Provisional Remedies § 335, Crime that is Enjoinable Tort.
7 Witkin, California Summary 10th Constitutional Law § 457, in General.
13 Witkin, California Summary 10th Equity § 74, Exception: Statutory Authorization.

§ 527.8. Employees subject to unlawful violence or threat of violence at the workplace; temporary restraining order; injunction; constitutional protections for speech and activities

(a) Any employer, whose employee has suffered unlawful violence or a credible threat of violence from any individual, that can reasonably be construed to be carried out or to have been carried out at the workplace, may seek a temporary restraining order and an injunction on behalf of the employee and, at the discretion of the court, any number of other employees at the workplace, and, if appropriate, other employees at other workplaces of the employer.

(b) For the purposes of this section:

(1) "Course of conduct" is a pattern of conduct composed of a series of acts over a period of time, however short, evidencing a continuity of purpose, including following or stalking an employee to or from the place of work; entering the workplace; following an employee during hours of employment; making telephone calls to an employee; or sending correspondence to an employee by any means, including, but not limited to, the use of the public or private mails, interoffice mail, facsimile, or computer email.

(2) "Credible threat of violence" is a knowing and willful statement or course of conduct that would place a reasonable person in fear for his or her safety, or the safety of his or her immediate family, and that serves no legitimate purpose.

(3) "Employer" and "employee" mean persons defined in Section 350 of the Labor Code. "Employer" also includes a federal agency, the state, a state agency, a city, county, or district, and a private, public, or quasi-public corporation, or any public agency thereof or therein. "Employee" also includes the members of boards of directors of private, public, and quasi-public corporations and elected and appointed public officers. For purposes of this section only, "employee" also includes a volunteer or independent contractor who performs services for the employer at the employer's worksite.

(4) "Petitioner" means the employer that petitions under subdivision (a) for a temporary restraining order and injunction.

(5) "Respondent" means the person against whom the temporary restraining order and injunction are sought and, if the petition is granted, the restrained person.

(6) "Temporary restraining order" and "injunction" mean orders that include any of the following restraining orders, whether issued ex parte or after notice and hearing:

(A) An order enjoining a party from harassing, intimidating, molesting, attacking, striking, stalking, threatening, sexually assaulting, battering, abusing, telephoning, including, but not limited to, making annoying telephone calls as described in Section 653m of the Penal Code, destroying personal property, contacting, either directly or indirectly, by mail or otherwise, or coming within a specified distance of, or disturbing the peace of, the employee.

(B) An order enjoining a party from specified behavior that the court determines is necessary to effectuate orders described in subparagraph (A).

(7) "Unlawful violence" is any assault or battery, or stalking as prohibited in Section 646.9 of the Penal Code, but shall not include lawful acts of self-defense or defense of others.

(c) This section does not permit a court to issue a temporary restraining order or injunction prohibiting speech or other activities that are constitutionally protected, or otherwise protected by Section 527.3 or any other provision of law.

(d) In the discretion of the court, on a showing of good cause, a temporary restraining order or injunction issued under this section may include other named family or household members, or other persons employed at the employee's workplace or workplaces.

(e) Upon filing a petition for an injunction under this section, the petitioner may obtain a temporary restraining order in accordance with subdivision (a) of Section 527, if the petitioner also files a declaration that, to the satisfaction of the court, shows reasonable proof that an employee has suffered unlawful violence or a credible threat of violence by the respondent, and that great or irreparable harm would result to an employee. The temporary restraining order may include any of the protective orders described in paragraph (6) of subdivision (b).

(f) A request for the issuance of a temporary restraining order without notice under this section shall be granted or denied on the same day that the petition is submitted to the court, unless the petition is filed too late in the day to permit effective review, in which case the order shall be granted or denied on the next day of judicial business in sufficient time for the order to be filed that day with the clerk of the court.

(g) A temporary restraining order granted under this section shall remain in effect, at the court's discretion, for a period not to exceed 21 days, or if the court extends the time for hearing under subdivision (h), not to exceed 25 days, unless otherwise modified or terminated by the court.

(h) Within 21 days, or if good cause appears to the court, 25 days from the date that a petition for a temporary order is granted or denied, a hearing shall be held on the petition for the injunction. If no request for temporary orders is made, the hearing shall be held within 21 days, or, if good cause appears to the court, 25 days, from the date that the petition is filed.

(i) The respondent may file a response that explains, excuses, justifies, or denies the alleged unlawful violence or credible threats of violence.

(j) At the hearing, the judge shall receive any testimony that is relevant and may make an independent inquiry. Moreover, if the respondent is a current employee of the entity requesting the injunction, the judge shall receive evidence concerning the employer's decision to retain, terminate, or otherwise discipline the respondent. If the judge finds by clear and convincing evidence that the respondent engaged in unlawful violence or made a credible threat of violence, an injunction shall issue prohibiting further unlawful violence or threats of violence.

(k)(1) In the discretion of the court, an order issued after notice and hearing under this section may have a duration of not more than three years, subject to termination or modification by further order of the court either on written stipulation filed with the court or on the motion of a party. These orders may be renewed, upon the request of a party, for a duration of not more than three years, without a showing of any further violence or threats of violence since the issuance of the original order, subject to termination or modification by further order of the court either on written stipulation filed with the court or on the motion of a party. The request for renewal may be brought at any time within the three months before the expiration of the order.

(2) The failure to state the expiration date on the face of the form creates an order with a duration of three years from the date of issuance.

(3) If an action is filed for the purpose of terminating or modifying a protective order prior to the expiration date specified in the order by a party other than the protected party, the party who is protected by the order shall be given notice, pursuant to subdivision (b) of Section 1005, of the proceeding by personal service or, if the protected party has satisfied the requirements of Chapter 3.1 (commencing with Section 6205) of Division 7 of Title 1 of the Government Code, by service on the Secretary of State. If the party who is protected by the order cannot be notified prior to the hearing for modification or termination of the protective order, the court shall deny the motion to modify or terminate the order without prejudice or continue the hearing until the party who is protected can be properly noticed and may, upon a showing of good cause, specify another method for service of process that is reasonably designed to afford actual notice to the protected party. The protected party may waive his or her right to notice if he or she is physically present in court and does not challenge the sufficiency of the notice.

(l) This section does not preclude either party from representation by private counsel or from appearing on his or her own behalf.

(m) Upon filing of a petition for an injunction under this section, the respondent shall be personally served with a copy of the petition, temporary restraining order, if any, and notice of hearing of the petition. Service shall be made at least five days before the hearing. The court may, for good cause, on motion of the petitioner or on its own motion, shorten the time for service on the respondent.

(n) A notice of hearing under this section shall notify the respondent that, if he or she does not attend the hearing, the court may make orders against him or her that could last up to three years.

(o)(1) The court may, upon the filing of a declaration by the petitioner that the respondent could not be served within the time required by statute, reissue an order previously issued and dissolved by the court for failure to serve the respondent. The reissued order shall remain in effect until the date set for the hearing.

(2) The reissued order shall state on its face the date of expiration of the order.

(p)(1) If a respondent, named in a restraining order issued under this section after a hearing, has not been served personally with the order but has received actual notice of the existence and substance of the order through personal appearance in court to hear the terms of the order from the court, no additional proof of service is required for enforcement of the order.

(2) If the respondent named in a temporary restraining order is personally served with the order and notice of hearing with respect to a restraining order or protective order based on the temporary restraining order, but the person does not appear at the hearing, either personally or by an attorney, and the terms and conditions of the restraining order or protective order issued at the hearing are identical to the temporary restraining order, except for the duration of the order, then the restraining order or protective order issued at the hearing may be served on the person by first-class mail sent to that person at the most current address for the person available to the court.

(3) The Judicial Council form for temporary orders issued pursuant to this subdivision shall contain a statement in substantially the following form:

"If you have been personally served with this temporary restraining order and notice of hearing, but you do not appear at the hearing either in person or by a lawyer, and a restraining order that is the same as this restraining order except for the expiration date is issued at the hearing, a copy of the order will be served on you by mail at the following address: _____

If that address is not correct or you wish to verify that the temporary restraining order was converted to a restraining order at the hearing without substantive change and to find out the duration of that order, contact the clerk of the court."

(q)(1) Information on any temporary restraining order or injunction relating to workplace violence issued by a court pursuant to this section shall be transmitted to the Department of Justice in accordance with either paragraph (2) or (3).

(2) The court shall order the petitioner or the attorney for the petitioner to deliver a copy of any order issued under this section, or a reissuance, extension, modification, or termination of the order, and any subsequent proof of service, by the close of the business day on which the order, reissuance, extension, modification, or termination was made, to each law enforcement agency having jurisdiction over the residence of the petitioner and to any additional law enforcement agencies within the court's discretion as are requested by the petitioner.

(3) Alternatively, the court or its designee shall transmit, within one business day, to law enforcement personnel all information required under subdivision (b) of Section 6380 of the Family Code regarding any order issued under this section, or a reissuance, extension, modification, or termination of the order, and any subsequent proof of service, by either one of the following methods:

(A) Transmitting a physical copy of the order or proof of service to a local law enforcement agency authorized by the Department of Justice to enter orders into the California Law Enforcement Telecommunications System (CLETS).

(B) With the approval of the Department of Justice, entering the order or proof of service into CLETS directly.

(4) Each appropriate law enforcement agency shall make available information as to the existence and current status of these orders to law enforcement officers responding to the scene of reported unlawful violence or a credible threat of violence.

(5) At the request of the petitioner, an order issued under this section shall be served on the respondent, regardless of whether the respondent has been taken into custody, by any law enforcement officer who is present at the scene of reported unlawful violence or a credible threat of violence involving the

parties to the proceedings. The petitioner shall provide the officer with an endorsed copy of the order and proof of service that the officer shall complete and send to the issuing court.

(6) Upon receiving information at the scene of an incident of unlawful violence or a credible threat of violence that a protective order has been issued under this section, or that a person who has been taken into custody is the subject of an order, if the petitioner or the protected person cannot produce an endorsed copy of the order, a law enforcement officer shall immediately attempt to verify the existence of the order.

(7) If the law enforcement officer determines that a protective order has been issued, but not served, the officer shall immediately notify the respondent of the terms of the order and obtain the respondent's address. The law enforcement officer shall at that time also enforce the order, but may not arrest or take the respondent into custody for acts in violation of the order that were committed prior to the verbal notice of the terms and conditions of the order. The law enforcement officer's verbal notice of the terms of the order shall constitute service of the order and constitutes sufficient notice for the purposes of this section and for the purposes of Section 29825 of the Penal Code. The petitioner shall mail an endorsed copy of the order to the respondent's mailing address provided to the law enforcement officer within one business day of the reported incident of unlawful violence or a credible threat of violence at which a verbal notice of the terms of the order was provided by a law enforcement officer.

(r)(1) A person subject to a protective order issued under this section shall not own, possess, purchase, receive, or attempt to purchase or receive a firearm or ammunition while the protective order is in effect.

(2) The court shall order a person subject to a protective order issued under this section to relinquish any firearms he or she owns or possesses pursuant to Section 527.9.

(3) Every person who owns, possesses, purchases or receives, or attempts to purchase or receive a firearm or ammunition while the protective order is in effect is punishable pursuant to Section 29825 of the Penal Code.

(s) Any intentional disobedience of any temporary restraining order or injunction granted under this section is punishable pursuant to Section 273.6 of the Penal Code.

(t) Nothing in this section may be construed as expanding, diminishing, altering, or modifying the duty, if any, of an employer to provide a safe workplace for employees and other persons.

(u)(1) The Judicial Council shall develop forms, instructions, and rules for relating to matters governed by this section. The forms for the petition and response shall be simple and concise, and their use by parties in actions brought pursuant to this section shall be mandatory.

(2) A temporary restraining order or injunction relating to unlawful violence or a credible threat of violence issued by a court pursuant to this section shall be issued on forms adopted by the Judicial Council of California and that have been approved by the Department of Justice pursuant to subdivision (i) of Section 6380 of the Family Code. However, the fact that an order issued by a court pursuant to this section was not issued on forms adopted by the Judicial Council and approved by the Department of Justice shall not, in and of itself, make the order unenforceable.

(v) There is no filing fee for a petition that alleges that a person has inflicted or threatened violence against an employee of the petitioner, or stalked the employee, or acted or spoken in any other manner that has placed the employee in reasonable fear of violence, and that seeks a protective or restraining order or injunction restraining stalking or future violence or threats of violence, in any action brought pursuant to this section. No fee shall be paid for a subpoena filed in connection with a petition alleging these acts. No fee shall be paid for filing a response to a petition alleging these acts.

(w)(1) Subject to paragraph (4) of subdivision (b) of Section 6103.2 of the Government Code, there shall be no fee for the service of process by a sheriff or marshal of a temporary restraining order or injunction to be issued pursuant to this section if either of the following conditions applies:

(A) The temporary restraining order or injunction issued pursuant to this section is based upon stalking, as prohibited by Section 646.9 of the Penal Code.

(B) The temporary restraining order or injunction issued pursuant to this section is based on unlawful violence or a credible threat of violence.

(2) The Judicial Council shall prepare and develop forms for persons who wish to avail themselves of the services described in this subdivision. *(Added by Stats.1993–94, 1st Ex.Sess., c. 29 (A.B.68), § 2, eff. Nov. 30, 1994. Amended by Stats.1998, c. 581 (A.B.2801), § 3; Stats.1999, c. 661 (A.B.825), § 2; Stats.2000, c. 688 (A.B.1669), § 6; Stats.2002, c. 1008 (A.B.3028), § 3; Stats. 2003, c. 498 (S.B.226), § 3; Stats.2005, c. 467 (A.B.429), § 1; Stats.2006, c. 476 (A.B.2695), § 2; Stats.2010, c. 178 (S.B.1115), § 21, operative Jan. 1, 2012; Stats.2010, c. 572 (A.B.1596), § 2, operative Jan. 1, 2012; Stats.2011, c. 285 (A.B.1402), § 2; Stats. 2011, c. 101 (A.B.454), § 2; Stats.2012, c. 162 (S.B.1171), § 13.)*

Research References

Rutter, Cal. Practice Guide: Civ. Pro. Before Trial Ch. 2-A, A. Standing to Sue-"Real Party in Interest" Requirement.
Rutter, Cal. Practice Guide: Civ. Pro. Before Trial Ch. 2-B, B. Capacity to Sue or Defend.
Rutter, Cal. Practice Guide: Civ. Pro. Before Trial Ch. 9(I)-A, A. Introduction.
Rutter, Cal. Practice Guide: Civ. Pro. Before Trial Ch. 7(II)-B, B. Exemptions (Actions Not Subject to SLAPP Statutes).
Rutter, Cal. Practice Guide: Civ. Pro. Before Trial Ch. 7(II)-D, D. Activities Protected by Anti-SLAPP Statute.
Rutter, Cal. Practice Guide: Civ. Pro. Before Trial Ch. 7(II)-E, E. Causes of Action Subject to Being Stricken.
Rutter, Cal. Practice Guide: Civ. Pro. Before Trial Ch. 9(II)-A, A. Injunctions.
Rutter, Cal. Practice Guide: Civ. Pro. Before Trial Gen. Matls., Highlights.
California Practice Guide: Employment Litigation Ch. 5-A, A. Wrongful Discharge in Violation of Public Policy (Tameny Claims).
California Practice Guide: Employment Litigation Ch. 13-I, I. Collateral (Non-Osh) Actions Relating to Occupational Safety and Health.
Miller and Starr California Real Estate § 35:97, Arbitrators Exceeded Their Powers.
2 Witkin Cal. Proc. 5th Courts § 29, (S 29) Use of English.
2 Witkin Cal. Proc. 5th Courts § 199, (S 199) in General.
4 Witkin Cal. Proc. 5th Pleading § 73, (S 73) Exception: Injunction or Protective Order.
5 Witkin Cal. Proc. 5th Pleading § 1019, (S 1019) in General.
5 Witkin Cal. Proc. 5th Pleading § 1037, (S 1037) Plaintiff's Inability to Meet Burden as Matter of Law.
6 Witkin Cal. Proc. 5th Provisional Remedies § 319, (S 319) Restriction on Possession of Firearms.
6 Witkin Cal. Proc. 5th Provisional Remedies § 326, (S 326) Nature and Scope of Statute.
6 Witkin Cal. Proc. 5th Provisional Remedies § 327, (S 327) Definitions.
6 Witkin Cal. Proc. 5th Provisional Remedies § 328, (S 328) Judicial Council Forms.
6 Witkin Cal. Proc. 5th Provisional Remedies § 329, (S 329) Petition, Service, and Response.
6 Witkin Cal. Proc. 5th Provisional Remedies § 330, (S 330) Hearing, Determination, and Enforcement.
11 Witkin Cal. Summary 10th Husband and Wife § 371, (S 371) Civil Remedies.
11 Witkin, California Summary 10th Husband and Wife § 387, (S 387) Electronic Transmission and Recording of Data.
5 Witkin, California Summary 10th Torts § 496B, (S 496B) (New)- Petition to Enjoin Workplace Violence or Threats.
3 Witkin, California Summary 10th Agency and Employment § 246, Policy Delineated in Constitution, Statute, Regulation, or Rule.
3 Witkin, California Summary 10th Agency and Employment § 375, Work Violence Safety Act.

§ 527.85. Officers authorized to maintain order on school campus or facility; threat of violence made off school campus; temporary restraining order and injunction; violation of restraining order

(a) Any chief administrative officer of a postsecondary educational institution, or an officer or employee designated by the chief administrative officer to maintain order on the school campus or facility, a student of which has suffered a credible threat of violence made off the school campus or facility from any individual, which can reasonably be construed to be carried out or to have been carried out at the school campus or facility, may, with the written consent of the student, seek a temporary restraining order and an injunction, on behalf of the student and, at the discretion of the court, any number of other students at the campus or facility who are similarly situated.

(b) For the purposes of this section, the following definitions shall apply:

(1) "Chief administrative officer" means the principal, president, or highest ranking official of the postsecondary educational institution.

(2) "Course of conduct" means a pattern of conduct composed of a series of acts over a period of time, however short, evidencing a continuity of purpose, including any of the following:

(A) Following or stalking a student to or from school.

(B) Entering the school campus or facility.

(C) Following a student during school hours.

(D) Making telephone calls to a student.

(E) Sending correspondence to a student by any means, including, but not limited to, the use of the public or private mails, interoffice mail, facsimile, or computer email.

(3) "Credible threat of violence" means a knowing and willful statement or course of conduct that would place a reasonable person in fear for his or her safety, or the safety of his or her immediate family, and that serves no legitimate purpose.

(4) "Petitioner" means the chief administrative officer, or his or her designee, who petitions under subdivision (a) for a temporary restraining order and injunction.

(5) "Postsecondary educational institution" means a private institution of vocational, professional, or postsecondary education.

(6) "Respondent" means the person against whom the temporary restraining order and injunction are sought and, if the petition is granted, the restrained person.

(7) "Student" means an adult currently enrolled in or applying for admission to a postsecondary educational institution.

(8) "Temporary restraining order" and "injunction" mean orders that include any of the following restraining orders, whether issued ex parte, or after notice and hearing:

(A) An order enjoining a party from harassing, intimidating, molesting, attacking, striking, stalking, threatening, sexually assaulting, battering, abusing, telephoning, including, but not limited to, making annoying telephone calls as described in Section 653m of the Penal Code, destroying personal property, contacting, either directly or indirectly, by mail or otherwise, or coming within a specified distance of, or disturbing the peace of, the student.

(B) An order enjoining a party from specified behavior that the court determines is necessary to effectuate orders described in subparagraph (A).

(9) "Unlawful violence" means any assault or battery, or stalking as prohibited in Section 646.9 of the Penal Code, but shall not include lawful acts of self-defense or defense of others.

(c) This section does not permit a court to issue a temporary restraining order or injunction prohibiting speech or other activities that are constitutionally protected, or otherwise protected by Section 527.3 or any other provision of law.

(d) In the discretion of the court, on a showing of good cause, a temporary restraining order or injunction issued under this section may include other named family or household members of the student, or other students at the campus or facility.

(e) Upon filing a petition for an injunction under this section, the petitioner may obtain a temporary restraining order in accordance with subdivision (a) of Section 527, if the petitioner also files a declaration that, to the satisfaction of the court, shows reasonable proof that a student has suffered a credible threat of violence made off the school campus or facility by the respondent, and that great or irreparable harm would result to the student. The temporary restraining order may include any of the protective orders described in paragraph (8) of subdivision (b).

(f) A request for the issuance of a temporary restraining order without notice under this section shall be granted or denied on the same day that the petition is submitted to the court, unless the petition is filed too late in the day to permit effective review, in which case the order shall be granted or denied on the next day of judicial business in sufficient time for the order to be filed that day with the clerk of the court.

(g) A temporary restraining order granted under this section shall remain in effect, at the court's discretion, for a period not to exceed 21 days, or if the court extends the time for hearing under subdivision (h), not to exceed 25 days, unless otherwise modified or terminated by the court.

(h) Within 21 days, or if good cause appears to the court, within 25 days, from the date that a petition for a temporary order is granted or denied, a hearing shall be held on the petition for the injunction. If no request for temporary orders is made, the hearing shall be held within 21 days, or if good cause appears to the court, 25 days, from the date the petition is filed.

(i) The respondent may file a response that explains, excuses, justifies, or denies the alleged credible threats of violence.

(j) At the hearing, the judge shall receive any testimony that is relevant and may make an independent inquiry. Moreover, if the respondent is a current student of the entity requesting the injunction, the judge shall receive evidence concerning the decision of the postsecondary educational institution decision to retain, terminate, or otherwise discipline the respondent. If the judge finds by clear and convincing evidence that the respondent made a credible threat of violence off the school campus or facility, an injunction shall be issued prohibiting further threats of violence.

(k)(1) In the discretion of the court, an order issued after notice and hearing under this section may have a duration of not more than three years, subject to termination or modification by further order of the court either on written stipulation filed with the court or on the motion of a party. These orders may be renewed, upon the request of a party, for a duration of not more than three years, without a showing of any further violence or threats of violence since the issuance of the original order, subject to termination or modification by further order of the

court either on written stipulation filed with the court or on the motion of a party. The request for renewal may be brought at any time within the three months before the expiration of the order.

(2) The failure to state the expiration date on the face of the form creates an order with a duration of three years from the date of issuance.

(3) If an action is filed for the purpose of terminating or modifying a protective order prior to the expiration date specified in the order by a party other than the protected party, the party who is protected by the order shall be given notice, pursuant to subdivision (b) of Section 1005, of the proceeding by personal service or, if the protected party has satisfied the requirements of Chapter 3.1 (commencing with Section 6205) of Division 7 of Title 1 of the Government Code, by service on the Secretary of State. If the party who is protected by the order cannot be notified prior to the hearing for modification or termination of the protective order, the court shall deny the motion to modify or terminate the order without prejudice or continue the hearing until the party who is protected can be properly noticed and may, upon a showing of good cause, specify another method for service of process that is reasonably designed to afford actual notice to the protected party. The protected party may waive his or her right to notice if he or she is physically present in court and does not challenge the sufficiency of the notice.

(*l*) This section does not preclude either party from representation by private counsel or from appearing on his or her own behalf.

(m) Upon filing of a petition for an injunction under this section, the respondent shall be personally served with a copy of the petition, temporary restraining order, if any, and notice of hearing of the petition. Service shall be made at least five days before the hearing. The court may, for good cause, on motion of the petitioner or on its own motion, shorten the time for service on the respondent.

(n) A notice of hearing under this section shall notify the respondent that if he or she does not attend the hearing, the court may make orders against him or her that could last up to three years.

(*o*)(1) The court may, upon the filing of a declaration by the petitioner that the respondent could not be served within the time required by statute, reissue an order previously issued and dissolved by the court for failure to serve the respondent. The reissued order shall remain in effect until the date set for the hearing.

(2) The reissued order shall state on its face the date of expiration of the order.

(p)(1) If a respondent, named in an order issued under this section after a hearing, has not been served personally with the order but has received actual notice of the existence and substance of the order through personal appearance in court to hear the terms of the order from the court, no additional proof of service is required for enforcement of the order.

(2) If the respondent named in a temporary restraining order is personally served with the order and notice of hearing with respect to a restraining order or protective order based on the temporary restraining order, but the respondent does not appear at the hearing, either personally or by an attorney, and the terms and conditions of the restraining order or protective order issued at the hearing are identical to the temporary restraining order, except for the duration of the order, then the restraining order or protective order issued at the hearing may be served on the respondent by first-class mail sent to that person at the most current address for the respondent available to the court.

(3) The Judicial Council form for temporary orders issued pursuant to this subdivision shall contain a statement in substantially the following form:

"If you have been personally served with a temporary restraining order and notice of hearing, but you do not appear at the hearing either in person or by a lawyer, and a restraining order that is the same as this temporary restraining order except for the expiration date is issued at the hearing, a copy of the order will be served on you by mail at the following address:____.

If that address is not correct or you wish to verify that the temporary restraining order was converted to a restraining order at the hearing without substantive change and to find out the duration of that order, contact the clerk of the court."

(q)(1) Information on any temporary restraining order or injunction relating to schoolsite violence issued by a court pursuant to this section shall be transmitted to the Department of Justice in accordance with either paragraph (2) or (3).

(2) The court shall order the petitioner or the attorney for the petitioner to deliver a copy of any order issued under this section, or a reissuance, extension, modification, or termination of the order, and any subsequent proof of service, by the close of the business day on which the order, reissuance, or termination of the order, and any proof of service, was made, to each law enforcement agency having jurisdiction over the residence of the petition and to any additional law enforcement agencies within the court's discretion as are requested by the petitioner.

(3) Alternatively, the court or its designee shall transmit, within one business day, to law enforcement personnel all information required under subdivision (b) of Section 6380 of the Family Code regarding any order issued under this section, or a reissuance, extension, modification, or termination of the order, and any subsequent proof of service, by either one of the following methods:

(A) Transmitting a physical copy of the order or proof of service to a local law enforcement agency authorized by the Department of Justice to enter orders into the California Law Enforcement Telecommunications System (CLETS).

(B) With the approval of the Department of Justice, entering the order of proof of service into CLETS directly.

(4) Each appropriate law enforcement agency shall make available information as to the existence and current status of these orders to law enforcement officers responding to the scene of reported unlawful violence or a credible threat of violence.

(5) At the request of the petitioner, an order issued under this section shall be served on the respondent, regardless of whether the respondent has been taken into custody, by any law enforcement officer who is present at the scene of reported unlawful violence or a credible threat of violence involving the parties to the proceedings. The petitioner shall provide the officer with an endorsed copy of the order and proof of service that the officer shall complete and send to the issuing court.

(6) Upon receiving information at the scene of an incident of unlawful violence or a credible threat of violence that a protective order has been issued under this section, or that a person who has been taken into custody is the subject of an order, if the petitioner or the protected person cannot produce an endorsed copy of the order, a law enforcement officer shall immediately attempt to verify the existence of the order.

(7) If the law enforcement officer determines that a protective order has been issued, but not served, the officer shall immediately notify the respondent of the terms of the order and obtain the respondent's address. The law enforcement officer shall at that time also enforce the order, but may not arrest or take the respondent into custody for acts in violation of the order that were committed prior to the verbal notice of the terms and conditions of the order. The law enforcement officer's verbal notice of the terms of the order shall constitute service of the order and constitutes sufficient notice for the purposes of this section, and Section 29825 of the Penal Code. The petitioner shall mail an endorsed copy of the order to the respondent's mailing address provided to the law enforcement officer within one business day of the reported incident of unlawful violence or a credible threat of violence at which a verbal notice of the terms of the order was provided by a law enforcement officer.

(r)(1) A person subject to a protective order issued under this section shall not own, possess, purchase, receive, or attempt to purchase or receive a firearm or ammunition while the protective order is in effect.

(2) The court shall order a person subject to a protective order issued under this section to relinquish any firearms he or she owns or possesses pursuant to Section 527.9.

(3) Every person who owns, possesses, purchases, or receives, or attempts to purchase or receive a firearm or ammunition while the protective order is in effect is punishable pursuant to Section 29825 of the Penal Code.

(s) Any intentional disobedience of any temporary restraining order or injunction granted under this section is punishable pursuant to Section 273.6 of the Penal Code.

(t) Nothing in this section may be construed as expanding, diminishing, altering, or modifying the duty, if any, of a postsecondary educational institution to provide a safe environment for students and other persons.

(u)(1) The Judicial Council shall develop forms, instructions, and rules relating to matters governed by this section. The forms for the petition and response shall be simple and concise, and their use by parties in actions brought pursuant to this section shall be mandatory.

(2) A temporary restraining order or injunction relating to unlawful violence or a credible threat of violence issued by a court pursuant to this section shall be issued on forms adopted by the Judicial Council and that have been approved by the Department of Justice pursuant to subdivision (i) of Section 6380 of the Family Code. However, the fact that an order issued by a court pursuant to this section was not issued on forms adopted by the Judicial Council and approved by the Department of Justice shall not, in and of itself, make the order unenforceable.

(v) There is no filing fee for a petition that alleges that a person has threatened violence against a student of the petitioner, or stalked the student, or acted or spoken in any other manner that has placed the student in reasonable fear of violence, and that seeks a protective or restraining order or injunction restraining stalking or future threats of violence, in any action brought pursuant to this section. No fee shall be paid for a subpoena filed in connection with a petition alleging these acts. No fee shall be paid for filing a response to a petition alleging these acts.

(w)(1) Subject to paragraph (4) of subdivision (b) of Section 6103.2 of the Government Code, there shall be no fee for the service of process by a sheriff or marshal of a temporary restraining order or injunction to be issued pursuant to this section if either of the following conditions applies:

(A) The temporary restraining order or injunction issued pursuant to this section is based upon stalking, as prohibited by Section 646.9 of the Penal Code.

(B) The temporary restraining order or injunction issued pursuant to this section is based upon a credible threat of violence.

(2) The Judicial Council shall prepare and develop forms for persons who wish to avail themselves of the services described in this subdivision. *(Added by Stats.2009, c. 566 (S.B.188), § 1. Amended by Stats.2010, c. 178 (S.B.1115), § 22, operative Jan. 1, 2012; Stats.2010, c. 572 (A.B.1596), § 4, operative Jan. 1, 2012; Stats.2011, c. 285 (A.B.1402), § 3; Stats.2011, c. 101 (A.B.454), § 3; Stats.2012, c. 162 (S.B.1171), § 14.)*

Research References

Rutter, Cal. Practice Guide: Civ. Pro. Before Trial Ch. 9(II)-A, A. Injunctions.

6 Witkin Cal. Proc. 5th Provisional Remedies § 330A, (S 330A) (New)- Nature and Scope of Statute.

6 Witkin Cal. Proc. 5th Provisional Remedies § 330B, (S 330B) (New)- Definitions.

6 Witkin Cal. Proc. 5th Provisional Remedies § 330C, (S 330C) (New)- Judicial Council Forms.

6 Witkin Cal. Proc. 5th Provisional Remedies § 330D, (S 330D) (New)- Petition, Service, and Response.

6 Witkin Cal. Proc. 5th Provisional Remedies § 330E, (S 330E) (New)- Hearing, Determination, and Enforcement.

11 Witkin, California Summary 10th Husband and Wife § 387, (S 387) Electronic Transmission and Recording of Data.

§ 527.9. Relinquishment of firearms; persons subject to protective orders

(a) A person subject to a temporary restraining order or injunction issued pursuant to Section 527.6, 527.8, or 527.85 or subject to a restraining order issued pursuant to Section 136.2 of the Penal Code, or Section 15657.03 of the Welfare and Institutions Code, shall relinquish the firearm pursuant to this section.

(b) Upon the issuance of a protective order against a person pursuant to subdivision (a), the court shall order that person to relinquish any firearm in that person's immediate possession or control, or subject to that person's immediate possession or control, within 24 hours of being served with the order, either by surrendering the firearm to the control of local law enforcement officials, or by selling the firearm to a licensed gun dealer, as specified in Article 1 (commencing with Section 26700) and Article 2 (commencing with Section 26800) of Chapter 2 of Division 6 of Title 4 of Part 6 of the Penal Code. A person ordered to relinquish any firearm pursuant to this subdivision shall file with the court a receipt showing the firearm was surrendered to the local law enforcement agency or sold to a licensed gun dealer within 48 hours after receiving the order. In the event that it is necessary to continue the date of any hearing due to a request for a relinquishment order pursuant to this section, the court shall ensure that all applicable protective orders described in Section 6218 of the Family Code remain in effect or bifurcate the issues and grant the permanent restraining order pending the date of the hearing.

(c) A local law enforcement agency may charge the person subject to the order or injunction a fee for the storage of any firearm relinquished pursuant to this section. The fee shall not exceed the actual cost incurred by the local law enforcement agency for the storage of the firearm. For purposes of this subdivision, "actual cost" means expenses directly related to taking possession of a firearm, storing the firearm, and surrendering possession of the firearm to a licensed dealer as defined in Section 26700 of the Penal Code or to the person relinquishing the firearm.

(d) The restraining order requiring a person to relinquish a firearm pursuant to subdivision (b) shall state on its face that the respondent is prohibited from owning, possessing, purchasing, or receiving a firearm while the protective order is in effect and that the firearm shall be relinquished to the local law enforcement agency for that jurisdiction or sold to a licensed gun dealer, and that proof of surrender or sale shall be filed with the court within a specified period of receipt of the order. The order shall also state on its face the expiration date for relinquishment. Nothing in this section shall limit a respondent's right under existing law to petition the court at a later date for modification of the order.

(e) The restraining order requiring a person to relinquish a firearm pursuant to subdivision (b) shall prohibit the person from possessing or controlling any firearm for the duration of the order. At the expiration of the order, the local law enforcement agency shall return possession of any surrendered firearm to the respondent, within five days after the expiration of the relinquishment order, unless the local law enforcement agency determines that (1) the firearm has been stolen, (2) the respondent is prohibited from possessing a firearm because the respondent is in any prohibited class for the possession of firearms, as defined in Chapter 2 (commencing with Section 29800) and Chapter 3 (commencing with Section 29900) of Division 9 of Title 4 of Part 6 of the Penal Code and Sections 8100 and 8103 of the Welfare and Institutions Code, or (3) another successive restraining order is issued against the respondent under this section. If the local law enforcement agency determines that the respondent is the legal owner of any firearm deposited with the local law enforcement agency and is prohibited from possessing any firearm, the respondent shall be entitled to sell or transfer the firearm to a licensed dealer as defined in Section 26700 of the Penal Code. If the firearm has been stolen, the firearm shall be restored to the lawful owner upon his or her identification of the firearm and proof of ownership.

(f) The court may, as part of the relinquishment order, grant an exemption from the relinquishment requirements of this section for a particular firearm if the respondent can show that a particular firearm is necessary as a condition of continued employment and that the current employer is unable to reassign the respondent to another position where a firearm is unnecessary. If an exemption is granted pursuant to this subdivision, the order shall provide that the firearm shall be in the physical possession of the respondent only during scheduled work hours and during travel to and from his or her place of employment. In any case involving a peace officer who as a condition of employment and whose personal safety depends on the ability to carry a firearm, a court may allow the peace officer to continue to carry a firearm, either on duty or off duty, if the court finds by a preponderance of the evidence that the officer does not pose a threat of harm. Prior to making this finding, the court shall require a mandatory psychological evaluation of the peace officer and may require the peace officer to enter into counseling or other remedial treatment program to deal with any propensity for domestic violence.

(g) During the period of the relinquishment order, a respondent is entitled to make one sale of all firearms that are in the possession of a local law enforcement agency pursuant to this section. A licensed gun dealer, who presents a local law enforcement agency with a bill of sale indicating that all firearms owned by the respondent that are in the possession of the local law enforcement agency have been sold by the respondent to the licensed gun dealer, shall be given possession of those firearms, at the location where a respondent's firearms are stored, within five days of presenting the local law enforcement agency with a bill of sale. *(Added by Stats.2003, c. 498 (S.B.226), § 4. Amended by Stats.2006, c. 474 (A.B.2129), § 1; Stats.2010, c. 178 (S.B.1115), § 23, operative Jan. 1, 2012; Stats.2010, c. 572 (A.B.1596), § 5, operative Jan. 1, 2012; Stats.2011, c. 285 (A.B.1402), § 4.)*

Law Revision Commission Comments

Subdivisions (b), (c), and (e) of Section 527.9 (as it reads in 2010 Cal. Stat. ch. 572, § 5) are amended to reflect nonsubstantive reorganization of the statutes governing control of deadly weapons. [41 Cal.L.Rev.Comm. Reports 135 (2011)].

Research References

6 Witkin Cal. Proc. 5th Provisional Remedies § 319, (S 319) Restriction on Possession of Firearms.

6 Witkin Cal. Proc. 5th Provisional Remedies § 326, (S 326) Nature and Scope of Statute.

6 Witkin Cal. Proc. 5th Provisional Remedies § 330A, (S 330A) (New)- Nature and Scope of Statute.

§ 527.10. Addresses or locations of persons protected under court order; prohibition upon certain enjoined parties from acting to obtain such information

(a) The court shall order that any party enjoined pursuant to Section 527.6, 527.8, or 527.85 be prohibited from taking any action to obtain the address or location of any protected person, unless there is good cause not to make that order.

(b) The Judicial Council shall develop forms necessary to effectuate this section. *(Added by Stats.2005, c. 472 (A.B.978), § 1. Amended by Stats.2010, c. 572 (A.B.1596), § 3, operative Jan. 1, 2012.)*

Research References

6 Witkin Cal. Proc. 5th Provisional Remedies § 316, (S 316) Nature and Scope of Statute.

6 Witkin Cal. Proc. 5th Provisional Remedies § 326, (S 326) Nature and Scope of Statute.

6 Witkin Cal. Proc. 5th Provisional Remedies § 330A, (S 330A) (New)- Nature and Scope of Statute.

11 Witkin, California Summary 10th Husband and Wife § 370, (S 370) in General.

§ 528. Grant after answer; notice; order to show cause; temporary restraint

An injunction cannot be allowed after the defendant has answered, unless upon notice, or upon an order to show cause; but in such case the defendant may be restrained until the decision of the Court or Judge granting or refusing the injunction. *(Enacted in 1872.)*

Research References

6 Witkin Cal. Proc. 5th Provisional Remedies § 368, (S 368) in General.

§ 529. Undertaking; objection; insufficiency; dissolution of injunction; exceptions

(a) On granting an injunction, the court or judge must require an undertaking on the part of the applicant to the effect that the applicant will pay to the party enjoined any damages, not exceeding an amount to be specified, the party may sustain by reason of the injunction, if the court finally decides that the applicant was not entitled to the injunction. Within five days after the service of the injunction, the person enjoined may object to the undertaking. If the court determines that the applicant's undertaking is insufficient and a sufficient undertaking is not filed within the time required by statute, the order granting the injunction must be dissolved.

(b) This section does not apply to any of the following persons:

(1) Either spouse against the other in a proceeding for legal separation or dissolution of marriage.

(2) The applicant for an order described in Division 10 (commencing with Section 6200) of the Family Code.

(3) A public entity or officer described in Section 995.220. *(Enacted in 1872. Amended by Code Am.1873–74, c. 624, p. 405, § 1; Code Am.1880, c. 64, p. 62, § 1; Stats.1907, c. 272, p. 342, § 4; Stats.1931, c. 140, p. 201, § 1; Stats.1933, c. 744, p. 1858, § 66; Stats.1979, c. 795, p. 2710, § 9, operative July 1, 1980; Stats.1982, c. 517, p. 2340, § 123; Stats.1992, c. 163 (A.B.2641), § 25, operative Jan. 1, 1994; Stats.1993, c. 219 (A.B.1500), § 63.7.)*

Law Revision Commission Comments

Section 529 is amended for consistency with the Bond and Undertaking Law. See Sections 995.220 (undertaking not required of public entity or officer), 995.310 (sureties on undertaking), 995.920 (grounds for objection), 995.930 (manner of making objection), 995.950 (hearing on objection), 995.960 (determination of sufficiency of undertaking). Unlike Section 995.930, Section 529 requires objection to an undertaking to be made within 5 days after service of the injunction, rather than within 10 days after service of the undertaking. The other changes in Section 529 are technical. [16 Cal.L.Rev.Comm. Reports 501 (1982)].

Subdivision (b) of Section 529 is amended to refer to the Family Code provisions that replaced the Code of Civil Procedure and Civil Code provisions. The reference to "applicant" has been substituted for the former reference to "plaintiff." This is not a substantive change. [23 Cal.L.Rev.Comm. Reports 1 (1993)].

Research References

Rutter, Cal. Practice Guide: Civil Appeals & Writs Ch. 2-C, C. Nonappealable Orders.

Rutter, Cal. Practice Guide: Civ. Pro. Before Trial Ch. 1-A, A. Accepting a New Case.

Rutter, Cal. Practice Guide: Civ. Pro. Before Trial Ch. 8K-4, Injunctions in Aid of Discovery.

Rutter, Cal. Practice Guide: Civ. Pro. Before Trial Ch. 9(II)-A, A. Injunctions.

California Practice Guide: Employment Litigation Ch. 14-C, C. Misappropriation of Employer's Trade Secrets.

California Practice Guide: Employment Litigation Ch. 19-F, F. Discovery.

Rutter, Cal. Practice Guide: Enforcing Judgments/Debts Ch. 6G-1, Examination of Judgment Debtor and Third Parties.

Rutter, Cal. Practice Guide: Family Law Gen. Matls. Highlights.

Rutter, Cal. Practice Guide: Insurance Litigation Ch. 6I-B, B. Particular Surety Bond Coverages.

Rutter, Cal. Practice Guide: Real Prop. Transactions Ch. 7-B, B. Sale of Ground Lease Tenant's Interest-Preliminary Concerns Re Assignment and Subletting.

Miller and Starr California Real Estate § 33:6, Procedures for Appointment.

Miller and Starr California Real Estate § 25:54, Judicial Review.

Miller and Starr California Real Estate § 25A:24, Remedies; Attorney's Fees.

3 Witkin Cal. Proc. 5th Actions § 421, Injunction Bond.

6 Witkin Cal. Proc. 5th Provisional Remedies § 6, Former Law.

6 Witkin Cal. Proc. 5th Provisional Remedies § 366, Undertaking.

6 Witkin Cal. Proc. 5th Provisional Remedies § 382, (S 382) in General.

6 Witkin Cal. Proc. 5th Provisional Remedies § 383, (S 383) Exemptions.

6 Witkin Cal. Proc. 5th Provisional Remedies § 384, (S 384) Amount and Form.

6 Witkin Cal. Proc. 5th Provisional Remedies § 414, Nature of Liability.

6 Witkin Cal. Proc. 5th Provisional Remedies § 415, Final Termination of Main Action.

6 Witkin Cal. Proc. 5th Provisional Remedies § 383A, (S 383A) (New)- Waiver or Forfeiture.

§ 529.1. Construction project; undertaking

(a) In all actions in which the court has granted an injunction sought by any plaintiff to enjoin a construction project which has received all legally required licenses and permits, the defendant may apply to the court by noticed motion for an order requiring the plaintiff to furnish an undertaking as security for costs and any damages that may be incurred by the defendant by the conclusion of the action or proceeding as the result of a delay in the construction of the project. The motion shall be made on the grounds that there is no reasonable possibility that the plaintiff will obtain a judgment against the moving defendant and that the plaintiff will not suffer undue economic hardship by filing the undertaking.

(b) If the court, after hearing, determines that the grounds for the motion have been established, the court shall order that the plaintiff file the undertaking in an amount specified in the court's order as security for costs and damages of the defendant. The liability of the plaintiff pursuant to this section for the costs and damages of the defendant shall not exceed five hundred thousand dollars ($500,000).

(c) As used in this section, a construction project includes, but is not restricted to, the construction, surveying, design, specifications, alteration, repair, improvement, maintenance, removal, or demolition of any building, highway, road, parking facility, bridge, railroad, airport, pier or dock, excavation or other structure, development or other improvement to real or personal property. *(Added by Stats.1979, c. 750, p. 2601, § 1. Amended by Stats.1982, c. 517, p. 2340, § 124; Stats.2004, c. 193 (S.B.111), § 11.)*

Law Revision Commission Comments

Section 529.1 is amended for consistency with the Bond and Undertaking Law. See Sections 995.220 (undertaking note required of public entity), 995.320 (contents of undertaking), 996.410–996.495 (liability of sureties). Unlike Section 996.470 (limitation on liability of surety), Section 529.1 imposes a $500,000 limitation on liability. [16 Cal.L.Rev. Comm. Reports 501 (1982)].

Section 529.1 is amended to delete reference to an obsolete reporting requirement. The required report was to be completed by January 1, 1985. [33 Cal.L.Rev.Comm. Reports 291 (2003)].

Research References

Rutter, Cal. Practice Guide: Insurance Litigation Ch. 6I-B, B. Particular Surety Bond Coverages.
Miller and Starr California Real Estate § 25:54, Judicial Review.
Miller and Starr California Real Estate § 25:67, Criminal and Civil Remedies.
Miller and Starr California Real Estate § 25A:24, Remedies; Attorney's Fees.
3 Witkin Cal. Proc. 5th Actions § 360, Action Challenging Construction Project.
6 Witkin Cal. Proc. 5th Provisional Remedies § 382, (S 382) in General.

§ 529.2. Action to challenge housing project; undertaking by plaintiff

(a) In all civil actions, including, but not limited to, actions brought pursuant to Section 21167 of the Public Resources Code, brought by any plaintiff to challenge a housing project which is a development project, as defined by Section 65928 of the Government Code, and which meets or exceeds the requirements for low- or moderate-income housing as set forth in Section 65915 of the Government Code, a defendant may, if the bringing of the action or the seeking by the plaintiff of particular relief including, but not limited to, injunctions, has the effect of preventing or delaying the project from being carried out, apply to the court by noticed motion for an order requiring the plaintiff to furnish an undertaking as security for costs and any damages that may be incurred by the defendant by the conclusion of the action or proceeding as the result of a delay in carrying out the development project. The motion shall be made on the grounds that: (1) the action was brought in bad faith, vexatiously, for the purpose of delay, or to thwart the low- or moderate-income nature of the housing development project, and (2) the plaintiff will not suffer undue economic hardship by filing the undertaking.

(b) If the court, after hearing, determines that the grounds for the motion have been established, the court shall order that the plaintiff file the undertaking in an amount specified in the court's order as security for costs and damages of the defendant. The liability of the plaintiff pursuant to this section for the costs and damages of the defendant shall not exceed five hundred thousand dollars ($500,000).

(c) If at any time after the plaintiff has filed an undertaking the housing development plan is changed by the developer in bad faith so that it fails to meet or exceed the requirements for low- or moderate-income housing as set forth in Section 65915 of the Government Code, the developer shall be liable to the

plaintiff for the cost of obtaining the undertaking. *(Added by Stats.1981, c. 970, p. 3700, § 1. Amended by Stats.1982, c. 517, p. 2300, § 124.5.)*

Research References

Miller and Starr California Real Estate § 25:54, Judicial Review.
3 Witkin Cal. Proc. 5th Actions § 360, Action Challenging Construction Project.
6 Witkin Cal. Proc. 5th Provisional Remedies § 382, (S 382) in General.

§ 530. Diversion, diminution or increase in flow of water; notice; denial upon giving bond

In all actions which may be hereafter brought when an injunction or restraining order may be applied for to prevent the diversion, diminution or increase of the flow of water in its natural channels, to the ordinary flow of which the plaintiff claims to be entitled, the court shall first require due notice of the application to be served upon the defendant, unless it shall appear from the verified complaint or affidavits upon which the application therefor is made, that, within ten days prior to the time of such application, the plaintiff has been in the peaceable possession of the flow of such water, and that, within such time, said plaintiff has been deprived of the flow thereof by the wrongful diversion of such flow by the defendant, or that the plaintiff, at the time of such application, is, and for ten days prior thereto, has been, in possession of the flow of said water, and that the defendant threatens to divert the flow of such water; and if such notice of such application be given and upon the hearing thereof, it be made to appear to the court that plaintiff is entitled to the injunction, but that the issuance thereof pending the litigation will entail great damage upon defendant, and that plaintiff will not be greatly damaged by the acts complained of pending the litigation, and can be fully compensated for such damage as he may suffer, the court may refuse the injunction upon the defendant giving a bond such as is provided for in section five hundred and thirty-two; and upon the trial the same proceedings shall be had, and with the same effect as in said section provided. *(Enacted in 1872. Amended by Stats.1887, c. 188, p. 240; Stats.1907, c. 272, p. 342, § 5; Stats.1911, c. 733, p. 1421, § 1.)*

Research References

Miller and Starr California Real Estate § 22:3, Nuisance Per Se.
Miller and Starr California Real Estate § 23:68, Nuisance.
8 Witkin Cal. Proc. 5th Enforcement of Judgment § 490, Insolvency.
6 Witkin Cal. Proc. 5th Provisional Remedies § 301, (S 301) Interference With Water Rights.

§ 531. Suspension of business of corporation

An injunction to suspend the general and ordinary business of a corporation cannot be granted without due notice of the application therefor to the proper officers or managing agent of the corporation, except when the people of this state are a party to the proceeding. *(Enacted in 1872. Amended by Stats.1907, c. 272, p. 342, § 6.)*

Research References

Miller and Starr California Real Estate § 35:23, Public Policy in Favor of Arbitration.
6 Witkin Cal. Proc. 5th Provisional Remedies § 368, (S 368) in General.

§ 532. Application to dissolve or modify; opposition; bond for dissolution or modification; damages; attorney's fees

(a) If an injunction is granted without notice to the person enjoined, the person may apply, upon reasonable notice to the judge who granted the injunction, or to the court in which the action was brought, to dissolve or modify the injunction. The application may be made upon the complaint or the affidavit on which the injunction was granted, or upon affidavit on the part of the person enjoined, with or without the answer. If the application is made upon affidavits on the part of the person enjoined, but not otherwise, the person against whom the application is made may oppose the application by affidavits or other evidence in addition to that on which the injunction was granted.

(b) In all actions in which an injunction or restraining order has been or may be granted or applied for, to prevent the diversion, pending the litigation, of water used, or to be used, for irrigation or domestic purposes only, if it is made to appear to the court that great damage will be suffered by the person enjoined, in case the injunction is continued, and that the person in whose behalf it issued can be fully compensated for any damages suffered by reason of the continuance of the acts enjoined during the pendency of the litigation, the court in its discretion, may dissolve or modify the injunction. The dissolution or modification shall be subject to the person enjoined giving a bond in such amount as may be fixed by the court or judge, conditioned that the enjoined person will pay all damages which the person in whose behalf the injunction issued may suffer by reason of the continuance, during the litigation, of the acts complained of. Upon the trial the amount of the damages must be ascertained, and in case judgment is rendered for the person in whose behalf the injunction was granted, the amount fixed as damages must be included in the judgment, together with reasonable attorney's fees. In any proceedings to enforce the liability on the bond, the amount of the damages as fixed in the judgment is conclusive. *(Enacted in 1872. Amended by Stats.1887, c. 188, p. 241; Stats.1907, c. 272, p. 342, § 7; Stats.1982, c. 517, p. 2341, § 125.)*

Law Revision Commission Comments

Section 532 is amended for consistency with the Bond and Undertaking Law. See Sections 995.910 (objections to bonds) and 996.410 (enforcement of liability on bond). The other changes in Section 532 are technical. [16 Cal.L.Rev.Comm. Reports 501 (1982)].

Research References

Rutter, Cal. Practice Guide: Civ. Pro. Before Trial Ch. 9(II)-A, A. Injunctions.
7 Witkin Cal. Proc. 5th Judgment § 230, (S 230) Actions Involving Real Property or Environmental Issues.
6 Witkin Cal. Proc. 5th Provisional Remedies § 267, (S 267) Procedure After Hearing on Writ.
6 Witkin Cal. Proc. 5th Provisional Remedies § 399, (S 399) Statutory Authority and Inherent Power.
6 Witkin Cal. Proc. 5th Provisional Remedies § 406, in General.

§ 533. Modification or dissolution of injunction or temporary restraining order

In any action, the court may on notice modify or dissolve an injunction or temporary restraining order upon a showing that there has been a material change in the facts upon which the injunction or temporary restraining order was granted, that the law upon which the injunction or temporary restraining order was granted has changed, or that the ends of justice would be served by the modification or dissolution of the injunction or temporary restraining order. *(Added by Stats.1995, c. 796 (S.B.45), § 8.)*

Research References

Rutter, Cal. Practice Guide: Civ. Pro. Before Trial Ch. 9(II)-A, A. Injunctions.
3 Witkin Cal. Proc. 5th Actions § 370, Order Prohibiting Filing of New Litigation.
6 Witkin Cal. Proc. 5th Provisional Remedies § 399, (S 399) Statutory Authority and Inherent Power.
6 Witkin Cal. Proc. 5th Provisional Remedies § 406, in General.

11 Witkin, California Summary 10th Husband and Wife § 384, (S 384) Orders After Notice and Hearing.

§ 534. Actions concerning diversion or use of water; defense of irrigation or other public use; reply; jurisdiction; evidence; fixing time, manner and extent of water appropriation; damages; appeals; jury trial

In any action brought by a riparian owner to enjoin the diversion of water appropriated or proposed to be appropriated, or the use thereof, against any person or persons appropriating or proposing to appropriate such waters, the defendant may set up in his answer that the water diverted or proposed to be diverted is for the irrigation of land or other public use, and, in such case, he shall also in such answer set forth the quantity of water desired to be taken and necessary to such irrigation of land or the public use, the nature of such use, the place where the same is used or proposed to be used, the duration and extent of the diversion or the proposed diversion, including the stages of the flow of the stream at and during the time in which the water is to be diverted, and that the same may be diverted without interfering with the actual and necessary beneficial uses of the plaintiff, and that such defendant so answering desires that the court shall ascertain and fix the damages, if any, that will result to the plaintiff or to his riparian lands from the appropriation of the water so appropriated or intended to be appropriated by defendant.

The plaintiff may serve and file a reply to the defendant's answer stating plaintiff's rights to the water and the damage plaintiff will suffer by the defendant's taking of the water, and plaintiff may implead as parties to the action all persons necessary to a full determination of the rights of plaintiff to the water and the damages plaintiff will suffer by the proposed taking by defendant, and the court shall have jurisdiction to hear and determine all the rights to water of the plaintiff and other parties to the action, and said parties shall have a right to state and prove their rights, and shall be bound by the judgment rendered the same as though made parties plaintiff at the commencement of the action.

Upon the trial of the case the court shall receive and hear evidence on behalf of the respective parties, and if the court finds that the allegations of such answer are true as to the aforesaid matters, and that the appropriation and diversion of such waters is for irrigation of land or other public use and that, after allowing sufficient water for the actual and necessary beneficial uses of the plaintiff and other parties, there is water available to be beneficially appropriated by such defendant so answering, the court shall fix the time and manner and extent of such appropriation and the actual damages, if any, resulting to the plaintiff or other parties on account of the same, and in fixing such damages the court shall be guided by Article 5 (commencing with Section 1263.410) of Chapter 9 of Title 7 of Part 3, and if, upon the ascertainment and fixing of such damages the defendant, within the time allowed in Section 1268.010 for the payment of damages in proceedings in eminent domain, shall pay into court the amount of damages fixed and the costs adjudged to be paid by such defendant, or give a good and sufficient bond to pay the same upon the final settlement of the case, the injunction prayed for by the plaintiff shall be denied to the extent of the amount the defendant is permitted to appropriate, as aforesaid, and the temporary injunction, if any has been granted, shall be vacated to the extent aforesaid; provided, that any of the parties may appeal from such judgment as in other cases; and provided, further, that if such judgment is in favor of the defendant and if he upon and pending such appeal shall keep on deposit with the clerk of said court the amount of such damages and costs, or the bond, if it be given, so awarded to be paid to the plaintiff or other parties in the event such judgment shall be affirmed, no injunction against the appropriation of the amount the defendant is permitted to appropriate as aforesaid shall be granted or enforced pending such appeal, and, upon the acceptance by the plaintiff or other parties of such amount so awarded or upon the affirmation of such decision on appeal so that such judgment shall become final, the defendant shall have the right to divert and appropriate from such stream, against such plaintiff or other parties and his successors in interest, the quantity of water therein adjudged and allowed. Upon the filing of such answer as is herein provided for, the parties plaintiff or other parties and defendant shall be entitled to a jury trial upon the issues as to damages so raised, as provided in Title 7 (commencing with Section 1230.010) of Part 3, applying to proceedings in eminent domain. *(Added by Stats.1917, c. 553, p. 745, § 1. Amended by Stats.1975, c. 1240, p. 3160, § 5, operative July 1, 1976.)*

Law Revision Commission Comments

Section 534 is amended to replace the references to former Sections 1248 and 1251 with references to the statutory provisions that supersede those sections.

Research References

Miller and Starr California Real Estate § 17:25, Water Rights.
6 Witkin Cal. Proc. 5th Provisional Remedies § 301, (S 301) Interference With Water Rights.
3 Witkin, California Summary 10th Agency and Employment § 435, Contracts and Fees.

CHAPTER 5. RECEIVERS

§ 564. Appointment; cases in which authorized; definitions

(a) A receiver may be appointed, in the manner provided in this chapter, by the court in which an action or proceeding is pending in any case in which the court is empowered by law to appoint a receiver.

(b) A receiver may be appointed by the court in which an action or proceeding is pending, or by a judge thereof, in the following cases:

(1) In an action by a vendor to vacate a fraudulent purchase of property, or by a creditor to subject any property or fund to the creditor's claim, or between partners or others jointly owning or interested in any property or fund, on the application of the plaintiff, or of any party whose right to or interest in the property or fund, or the proceeds thereof, is probable, and where it is shown that the property or fund is in danger of being lost, removed, or materially injured.

(2) In an action by a secured lender for the foreclosure of a deed of trust or mortgage and sale of property upon which there is a lien under a deed of trust or mortgage, where it appears that the property is in danger of being lost, removed, or materially injured, or that the condition of the deed of trust or mortgage has not been performed, and that the property is probably insufficient to discharge the deed of trust or mortgage debt.

(3) After judgment, to carry the judgment into effect.

(4) After judgment, to dispose of the property according to the judgment, or to preserve it during the pendency of an appeal, or pursuant to the Enforcement of Judgments Law (Title 9 (commencing with Section 680.010)), or after sale of real property pursuant to a decree of foreclosure, during the redemption period, to collect, expend, and disburse rents as directed by the court or otherwise provided by law.

(5) Where a corporation has been dissolved, as provided in Section 565.

(6) Where a corporation is insolvent, or in imminent danger of insolvency, or has forfeited its corporate rights.

(7) In an action of unlawful detainer.

(8) At the request of the Public Utilities Commission pursuant to Section 855 or 5259.5 of the Public Utilities Code.

(9) In all other cases where necessary to preserve the property or rights of any party.

(10) At the request of the Office of Statewide Health Planning and Development, or the Attorney General, pursuant to Section 129173 of the Health and Safety Code.

(11) In an action by a secured lender for specific performance of an assignment of rents provision in a deed of trust, mortgage, or separate assignment document. The appointment may be continued after entry of a judgment for specific performance if appropriate to protect, operate, or maintain real property encumbered by a deed of trust or mortgage or to collect rents therefrom while a pending nonjudicial foreclosure under power of sale in a deed of trust or mortgage is being completed.

(12) In a case brought by an assignee under an assignment of leases, rents, issues, or profits pursuant to subdivision (g) of Section 2938 of the Civil Code.

(c) A receiver may be appointed, in the manner provided in this chapter, including, but not limited to, Section 566, by the superior court in an action brought by a secured lender to enforce the rights provided in Section 2929.5 of the Civil Code, to enable the secured lender to enter and inspect the real property security for the purpose of determining the existence, location, nature, and magnitude of any past or present release or threatened release of any hazardous substance into, onto, beneath, or from the real property security. The secured lender shall not abuse the right of entry and inspection or use it to harass the borrower or tenant of the property. Except in case of an emergency, when the borrower or tenant of the property has abandoned the premises, or if it is impracticable to do so, the secured lender shall give the borrower or tenant of the property reasonable notice of the secured lender's intent to enter and shall enter only during the borrower's or tenant's normal business hours. Twenty-four hours' notice shall be presumed to be reasonable notice in the absence of evidence to the contrary.

(d) Any action by a secured lender to appoint a receiver pursuant to this section shall not constitute an action within the meaning of subdivision (a) of Section 726.

(e) For purposes of this section:

(1) "Borrower" means the trustor under a deed of trust, or a mortgagor under a mortgage, where the deed of trust or mortgage encumbers real property security and secures the performance of the trustor or mortgagor under a loan, extension of credit, guaranty, or other obligation. The term includes any successor in interest of the trustor or mortgagor to the real property security before the deed of trust or mortgage has been discharged, reconveyed, or foreclosed upon.

Civ. Pro.

(2) "Hazardous substance" means any of the following:

(A) Any "hazardous substance" as defined in subdivision (h) of Section 25281 of the Health and Safety Code.

(B) Any "waste" as defined in subdivision (d) of Section 13050 of the Water Code.

(C) Petroleum including crude oil or any fraction thereof, natural gas, natural gas liquids, liquefied natural gas, or synthetic gas usable for fuel, or any mixture thereof.

(3) "Real property security" means any real property and improvements, other than a separate interest and any related interest in the common area of a residential common interest development, as the terms "separate interest," "common area," and "common interest development" are defined in Section 4095, 4100, and 4185 of the Civil Code, or real property consisting of one acre or less that contains 1 to 15 dwelling units.

(4) "Release" means any spilling, leaking, pumping, pouring, emitting, emptying, discharging, injecting, escaping, leaching, dumping, or disposing into the environment, including continuing migration, of hazardous substances into, onto, or through soil, surface water, or groundwater.

(5) "Secured lender" means the beneficiary under a deed of trust against the real property security, or the mortgagee under a mortgage against the real property security, and any successor in interest of the beneficiary or mortgagee to the deed of trust or mortgage. *(Enacted in 1872. Amended by Stats.1919, c. 166, p. 251, § 1; Stats.1933, c. 744, p. 1867, § 85a; Stats.1941, c. 444, p. 1736, § 1; Stats.1980, c. 1078, p. 3438, § 1; Stats.1982, c. 497, p. 2155, § 34, operative July 1, 1983; Stats.1991, c. 1167 (A.B.1735), § 2; Stats.1992, c. 167 (A.B.2750), § 2; Stats.1994, c. 414 (S.B.1705), § 2, eff. Sept. 1, 1994; Stats.1995, c. 384 (A.B.1110), § 1; Stats.1996, c. 1023 (S.B.1497), § 29, eff. Sept. 29, 1996; Stats.1996, c. 49 (S.B.947), § 4; Stats.1996, c. 1154 (A.B.3020), § 2, eff. Sept. 30, 1996; Stats.1996, c. 1154 (A.B.3020), § 2.1, eff. Sept. 30, 1996, operative Jan. 1, 1997; Stats.1998, c. 931 (S.B. 2139), § 75, eff. Sept. 28, 1998; Stats.2001, c. 44 (S.B.562), § 4; Stats.2002, c. 999 (A.B.2481), § 3; Stats.2012, c. 181 (A.B.806), § 44, operative Jan. 1, 2014.)*

Law Revision Commission Comments

Subdivision 4 of Section 564 is amended to conform to the Enforcement of Judgments Law. Proceedings in aid of execution are entitled examination proceedings under the new law. See Sections 708.110–708.205. The prerequisite that an execution be returned unsatisfied or that the debtor refuse to apply property to the satisfaction of the judgment is not continued. See Section 708.620 and the Comment thereto. The provision for appointment of a receiver during the redemption period applies in a more limited class of cases. See Sections 726(e), 729.010. Redemption is no longer available after execution sales. See Section 701.680. See also Section 712.060 (receiver to enforce judgment for possession or sale of property) (15 Cal.L.Rev.Comm. Reports 2001; 82 A.J. 9356).

Section 564 is amended to accommodate unification of the municipal and superior courts in a county. Cal. Const. art. VI, § 5(e). See Section 85 (limited civil cases) & Comment. [28 Cal.L.Rev.Comm. Reports 51 (1998)].

For purposes of simplification, Section 564 is broadened to govern appointment of a receiver in all cases, regardless of the jurisdictional classification of the case. Formerly, a separate provision governed appointment of a receiver in a limited civil case. 1998 Cal. Stat. ch. 931, 29 (former Section 86(a)(8)).

Although Section 564 covers both limited and unlimited civil cases, some of the types of actions listed in the statute may only be brought as an unlimited civil case. For example, Section 564(b)(7) refers to appointment of a receiver where the Public Utilities Commission requests a receiver pursuant to Public Utilities Code Section 855 or 5259.5. Such a proceeding may only be brought as an unlimited civil case. See Section 85 & Comment.

To aid practitioners, subdivision (b)(5) of Section 564 is amended to refer to Section 565 (appointment of receiver on dissolution of corporation).

Subdivision (b)(9) (former subdivision (b)(8)) is amended to delete language authorizing appointment of a receiver "where receivers have heretofore been appointed by the usages of courts of equity," and insert more readily understandable language formerly found in Section 86. This is not a substantive change. The deleted language conferred broad authority to appoint a receiver, but only where other remedies were found to be inadequate. See, e.g., Golden State Glass Corp. v. Superior Court, 13 Cal.2d 384, 393, 90 P.2d 75 (1939) (superior court should appoint receiver only where necessary to "adequately protect the rights of the parties"); Alhambra–Shumway Mines, Inc. v. Alhambra Gold Mine Corp., 116 Cal.App.2d 869, 873, 254 P.2d 599 (1953) (where less severe remedy will adequately protect parties, court ordinarily should not appoint receiver); see also Murray v. Murray, 115 Cal. 266, 275, 47 P. 37 (1896) (in equity, receiver may be appointed where plaintiff has equitable claim to property and "receiver is necessary to preserve the same from loss"). Similarly, subdivision (b)(9) authorizes appointment of a receiver only "where *necessary* to preserve the property or rights of any party." (Emphasis added.)

As before, the general language of subdivision (b)(9) does not override specific requirements enumerated elsewhere in the statute. See, e.g., Marsch v. Williams, 23 Cal.App.4th 238, 246 n.8, 28 Cal.Rptr.2d 402 (1994); Dabney Oil Co. v. Providence Oil Co., 22 Cal.App. 233, 237, 133 P. 1155 (1913).

Subdivision (b)(10) (former subdivision (b)(9)) is amended to correct the cross-reference. Health and Safety Code Section 436.222 was repealed in 1995 and its substance recodified in Section 129173. See 1995 Cal. Stat. ch. 415, 9, 79.5.

For other provisions concerning receivers, see Sections 565–570, 708.610–708.630, 712.060, 1422. See also Civ. Code 3439.07; Corp. Code 1801, 1803, 16504; Fam. Code 290; Ins. Code 1064.1–1064.12. [30 Cal.L.Rev.Comm. Reports 291 (2000)].

Section 564 is amended to correct cross-references to former Civil Code Section 1351(b), (c), (l). [40 Cal.L.Rev.Comm. Reports 235 (2010)].

Research References

Rutter, Cal. Practice Guide: A.D.R. Ch. 5-G, G. Procedures to Enforce Arbitration.

Rutter, Cal. Practice Guide: Civ. Pro. Before Trial Ch. 9(II)-B, B. Receiverships.

Rutter, Cal. Practice Guide: Enforcing Judgments/Debts Ch. 4-C, C. Receiverships.

Rutter, Cal. Practice Guide: Enforcing Judgments/Debts Ch. 6G-6, Receiver to Enforce Judgment-EJL Provisions.

Rutter, Cal. Practice Guide: Enforcing Judgments/Debts Ch. 6G-7, Charging Orders Against Debtor Partnership/LLC Interests.

Rutter, Cal. Practice Guide: Real Prop. Transactions Ch. 6-H, H. Security for Promissory Note.

Rutter, Cal. Practice Guide: Real Prop. Transactions Ch. 6-I, I. Real Property Foreclosures and Antideficiency Laws.

Rutter, Cal. Practice Guide: Real Prop. Transactions Ch. 6-K, K. Environmental Indemnities.

Rutter, Cal. Practice Guide: Real Prop. Transactions Form 6:I, Deed of Trust (Complex).

Miller and Starr California Real Estate § 33:1, Nature of Receiverships; in General.

Miller and Starr California Real Estate § 33:4, Standards for Appointment.

Miller and Starr California Real Estate § 33:8, Appeals, Generally.

Miller and Starr California Real Estate § 10:50, Enforcement of the Assignment Required.

Miller and Starr California Real Estate § 10:52, Receiver to Collect Rents.

Miller and Starr California Real Estate § 10:54, Remedies and Measure of Damages for Waste.

Miller and Starr California Real Estate § 12:15, Right of Partition--Procedure in Partition Action.

Miller and Starr California Real Estate § 22:28, Actions by Public Entities.

Miller and Starr California Real Estate § 22:30, Appointment of a Receiver When Residential Property a Nuisance; Tenant Rights When Receiver Appointed.

Miller and Starr California Real Estate § 33:11, Preservation and Management--Power of Possession and Control; Rights of Others.

Miller and Starr California Real Estate § 33:15, Preservation and Management--Power to Demolish Substandard Structures.

Miller and Starr California Real Estate § 33:23, Actions in Which a Receiver May be Appointed--In General.

Miller and Starr California Real Estate § 33:24, Actions in Which a Receiver May be Appointed--By Vendor to Vacate Fraudulent Purchase.

Miller and Starr California Real Estate § 33:25, Actions in Which a Receiver May be Appointed--By Creditor to Subject Property or Fund to Creditor Claim.

Miller and Starr California Real Estate § 33:26, Actions in Which a Receiver May be Appointed--Between Partners or Joint Venturers.

Miller and Starr California Real Estate § 33:27, Actions in Which a Receiver May be Appointed--Between Parties With Joint or Probable Interests in Property.

Miller and Starr California Real Estate § 33:28, Actions in Which a Receiver May be Appointed--Partition.

Miller and Starr California Real Estate § 33:29, Actions in Which a Receiver May be Appointed--Unlawful Detainer.

Miller and Starr California Real Estate § 33:32, Enforcement Actions After Entry of Judgment.

Miller and Starr California Real Estate § 33:33, Secured Creditor Actions--In General.

Miller and Starr California Real Estate § 33:34, Secured Creditor Actions--To Preserve Property in Danger of Being Lost, Removed, or Materially Injured, or Insufficient to Discharge the Debt.

Miller and Starr California Real Estate § 33:35, Secured Creditor Actions--To Specifically Enforce Possessory Rights or Assignments of Rents and Profits.

Miller and Starr California Real Estate § 33:38, Secured Creditor Actions--To Preserve Guarantor's Claimed Rights in Collateral.

Miller and Starr California Real Estate § 33:39, Secured Creditor Actions--Inspection for Hazardous Substances.

Miller and Starr California Real Estate § 33:40, Secured Creditor Actions--Unlawful Detainer After Foreclosure.

Miller and Starr California Real Estate § 35:83, Authority of the Arbitrators; Issues and Remedies.

Miller and Starr California Real Estate § 10:157, Exception; Environmentally Impaired Property.

Miller and Starr California Real Estate § 10:163, Action for Possession.

Miller and Starr California Real Estate § 10:230, Possession and Rents During the Redemption Period.

Miller and Starr California Real Estate § 11:101, Effect of Foreclosure on Rights of Tenants in Possession.

Miller and Starr California Real Estate § 19:227, Prejudgment Remedies; Attachment and Receivership.

14 NO. 4 Miller & Starr, California Real Estate Newsalert 28, Receivers.

15 NO. 4 Miller & Starr, California Real Estate Newsalert 1, California's "One Form of Action" and "Security First" Rules: Have They Cleared the Minefields Yet?

18 NO. 4 Miller & Starr, California Real Estate Newsalert 39, Receivers.

8 Witkin Cal. Proc. 5th Enforcement of Judgment § 102, (S 102) Preservation of Property.

8 Witkin Cal. Proc. 5th Enforcement of Judgment § 310, (S 310) in General.

6 Witkin Cal. Proc. 5th Proceedings Without Trial § 529, (S 529) in General.

6 Witkin Cal. Proc. 5th Provisional Remedies § 1, (S 1) in General.

6 Witkin Cal. Proc. 5th Provisional Remedies § 179, Securities.

6 Witkin Cal. Proc. 5th Provisional Remedies § 191, Depreciating Property.

6 Witkin Cal. Proc. 5th Provisional Remedies § 419, (S 419) Nature of Receivership.

6 Witkin Cal. Proc. 5th Provisional Remedies § 423, Specific Statutory Enumeration.

6 Witkin Cal. Proc. 5th Provisional Remedies § 424, Other Bases.

6 Witkin Cal. Proc. 5th Provisional Remedies § 425, (S 425) Action by Vendor or Creditor.

6 Witkin Cal. Proc. 5th Provisional Remedies § 426, (S 426) Action by Secured Lender.

6 Witkin Cal. Proc. 5th Provisional Remedies § 427, (S 427) Action by Office of Statewide Health Planning and Development.

6 Witkin Cal. Proc. 5th Provisional Remedies § 428, (S 428) Action Between Partners or Joint Owners.

6 Witkin Cal. Proc. 5th Provisional Remedies § 429, Statutory Authorization.

6 Witkin Cal. Proc. 5th Provisional Remedies § 430, Clause Authorizing Appointment.

6 Witkin Cal. Proc. 5th Provisional Remedies § 431, (S 431) Specific Performance of Assignment of Rents.

6 Witkin Cal. Proc. 5th Provisional Remedies § 432, (S 432) Action by Assignee Under Assignment of Rents, Issues, or Profits.

6 Witkin Cal. Proc. 5th Provisional Remedies § 433, (S 433) Unlawful Detainer.

6 Witkin Cal. Proc. 5th Provisional Remedies § 434, (S 434) Operation of Water or Sewer System.

6 Witkin Cal. Proc. 5th Provisional Remedies § 435, (S 435) Abandonment of Stored Household Property.

6 Witkin Cal. Proc. 5th Provisional Remedies § 436, Insolvency.

6 Witkin Cal. Proc. 5th Provisional Remedies § 437, Fraud or Mismanagement.

6 Witkin Cal. Proc. 5th Provisional Remedies § 438, Dissolution or Forfeiture.

6 Witkin Cal. Proc. 5th Provisional Remedies § 439, (S 439) Family Law Action.

6 Witkin Cal. Proc. 5th Provisional Remedies § 441, Motion.

11 Witkin, California Summary 10th Husband and Wife § 206, Other Remedies.

11 Witkin, California Summary 10th Husband and Wife § 266, (S 266) Appointment of Receiver.

4 Witkin, California Summary 10th Security Transactions in Real Property § 101, Receiver.

4 Witkin, California Summary 10th Security Transactions in Real Property § 128, Remedy is Not Action.

4 Witkin, California Summary 10th Security Transactions in Real Property § 170, (S 170) Possession, Rents, and Profits.

4 Witkin, California Summary 10th Security Transactions in Real Property § 171, in General.

4 Witkin, California Summary 10th Security Transactions in Real Property § 208, (S 208) Nature and Scope of Legislation.

4 Witkin, California Summary 10th Security Transactions in Real Property § 209, (S 209) Inspection of Property.

13 Witkin, California Summary 10th Trusts § 125, Receiver or Temporary Trustee.

§ 565. Appointment upon dissolution of corporation

Upon the dissolution of any corporation, the Superior Court of the county in which the corporation carries on its business or has its principal place of business, on application of any creditor of the corporation, or of any stockholder or member thereof, may appoint one or more persons to be receivers or trustees of the corporation, to take charge of the estate and effects thereof, and to collect the debts and property due and belonging to the corporation, and to pay the outstanding debts thereof, and to divide the moneys and other property that shall remain over among the stockholders or members. *(Enacted in 1872. Amended by Code Am.1880, c. 15, p. 4, § 7.)*

Research References

Rutter, Cal. Practice Guide: Enforcing Judgments/Debts Ch. 4-C, C. Receiverships.

Miller and Starr California Real Estate § 33:1, Nature of Receiverships; in General.

Miller and Starr California Real Estate § 33:4, Standards for Appointment.

Miller and Starr California Real Estate § 33:23, Actions in Which a Receiver May be Appointed--In General.

6 Witkin Cal. Proc. 5th Provisional Remedies § 423, Specific Statutory Enumeration.

6 Witkin Cal. Proc. 5th Provisional Remedies § 438, Dissolution or Forfeiture.

§ 566. Persons ineligible to appointment; consent; undertaking on ex parte application

(a) No party, or attorney of a party, or person interested in an action, or related to any judge of the court by consanguinity or affinity within the third degree, can be appointed receiver therein without the written consent of the parties, filed with the clerk.

Civ. Pro.

(b) If a receiver is appointed upon an ex parte application, the court, before making the order, must require from the applicant an undertaking in an amount to be fixed by the court, to the effect that the applicant will pay to the defendant all damages the defendant may sustain by reason of the appointment of the receiver and the entry by the receiver upon the duties, in case the applicant shall have procured the appointment wrongfully, maliciously, or without sufficient cause. *(Enacted in 1872. Amended by Code Am.1873–74, c. 383, p. 309, § 73; Stats.1897, c. 69, p. 60, § 1; Stats.1907, c. 374, p. 710, § 1; Stats.1982, c. 517, p. 2342, § 127.)*

Law Revision Commission Comments

Section 566 is amended to delete provisions duplicated in the Bond and Undertaking Law. See Sections 995.310 (sureties on undertaking) and 996.010 (insufficient undertakings). The other changes in Section 566 are technical. [16 Cal.L.Rev.Comm. Reports 501 (1982)].

Research References

Rutter, Cal. Practice Guide: Civ. Pro. Before Trial Ch. 9(II)-B, B. Receiverships.
Rutter, Cal. Practice Guide: Enforcing Judgments/Debts Ch. 4-C, C. Receiverships.
Rutter, Cal. Practice Guide: Insurance Litigation Ch. 6I-B, B. Particular Surety Bond Coverages.
Miller and Starr California Real Estate § 33:3, Who May Act as Receiver; Restrictions on Special Arrangements.
Miller and Starr California Real Estate § 33:6, Procedures for Appointment.
Miller and Starr California Real Estate § 33:7, Undertakings, Bonds, Receiver's Oath, and Related Claims.
6 Witkin Cal. Proc. 5th Provisional Remedies § 443, Appointment.
6 Witkin Cal. Proc. 5th Provisional Remedies § 447, Undertaking.

§ 567. Oath and undertaking of receiver

Before entering upon the duties of a receiver:

(a) The receiver must be sworn to perform the duties faithfully.

(b) The receiver shall give an undertaking to the State of California, in such sum as the court or judge may direct, to the effect that the receiver will faithfully discharge the duties of receiver in the action and obey the orders of the court therein. The receiver shall be allowed the cost of the undertaking. *(Enacted in 1872. Amended by Stats.1907, c. 374, p. 710, § 2; Stats.1982, c. 517, p. 2342, § 128.)*

Law Revision Commission Comments

Section 567 is amended for consistency with the Bond and Undertaking Law. See Sections 995.310 (sureties on undertaking), and 995.840 (court approval of undertaking). The last sentence of subdivision (b) continues the substance of a portion of former Section 1042. The other changes in Section 567 are technical. [16 Cal.L.Rev.Comm. Reports 501 (1982)].

Research References

Rutter, Cal. Practice Guide: Civ. Pro. Before Trial Ch. 9(II)-B, B. Receiverships.
Rutter, Cal. Practice Guide: Enforcing Judgments/Debts Ch. 4-C, C. Receiverships.
Rutter, Cal. Practice Guide: Insurance Litigation Ch. 6I-B, B. Particular Surety Bond Coverages.
Miller and Starr California Real Estate § 33:6, Procedures for Appointment.
Miller and Starr California Real Estate § 33:7, Undertakings, Bonds, Receiver's Oath, and Related Claims.
Miller and Starr California Real Estate § 33:9, Sources of Receiver's Limited Authority; Court Approval and Instructions.
Miller and Starr California Real Estate § 33:18, Liabilities of a Receiver.

6 Witkin Cal. Proc. 5th Provisional Remedies § 444, Qualification and Undertaking.

§ 568. Powers

The receiver has, under the control of the Court, power to bring and defend actions in his own name, as receiver; to take and keep possession of the property, to receive rents, collect debts, to compound for and compromise the same, to make transfers, and generally to do such acts respecting the property as the Court may authorize. *(Enacted in 1872.)*

Research References

Rutter, Cal. Practice Guide: Civ. Pro. Before Trial Ch. 9(II)-B, B. Receiverships.
Rutter, Cal. Practice Guide: Enforcing Judgments/Debts Ch. 4-C, C. Receiverships.
Miller and Starr California Real Estate § 33:2, Receiver as a Neutral Agent of the Court.
Miller and Starr California Real Estate § 33:9, Sources of Receiver's Limited Authority; Court Approval and Instructions.
Miller and Starr California Real Estate § 33:10, Preservation and Management--Generally.
Miller and Starr California Real Estate § 33:11, Preservation and Management--Power of Possession and Control; Rights of Others.
Miller and Starr California Real Estate § 33:16, Preservation and Management--Power to Bring and Defend Actions.
4 Witkin Cal. Proc. 5th Pleading § 148, (S 148) Receiver.
6 Witkin Cal. Proc. 5th Provisional Remedies § 451, in General.
6 Witkin Cal. Proc. 5th Provisional Remedies § 452, Right to Sue and be Sued.
6 Witkin Cal. Proc. 5th Provisional Remedies § 454, Possession and Control of Property.
3 Witkin, California Summary 10th Agency and Employment § 330, (S 330) Employee Housing Act.
2 Witkin Cal. Summ. 10th Workers' Compensation § 159, (S 159) in General.

§ 568.1. Deposit of securities in securities depository

Any securities in the hands of a receiver may, under the control of the court, be deposited by the receiver in a securities depository, as defined in Section 30004 of the Financial Code, which is licensed under Section 30200 of the Financial Code or exempted from licensing thereunder by Section 30005 or 30006 of the Financial Code, and such securities may be held by such securities depository in the manner authorized by Section 775 of the Financial Code. *(Added by Stats.1972, c. 1057, p. 1955, § 9.)*

Research References

Miller and Starr California Real Estate § 33:20, Duties of a Receiver--Investment of Funds.
6 Witkin Cal. Proc. 5th Provisional Remedies § 454, Possession and Control of Property.

§ 568.2. Notification to court of order or notice to correct substandard or unsafe condition of rental housing

(a) A receiver of real property containing rental housing shall notify the court of the existence of any order or notice to correct any substandard or unsafe condition, as defined in Section 17920.3 or 17920.10 of the Health and Safety Code, with which the receiver cannot comply within the time provided by the order or notice.

(b) The notice shall be filed within 30 days after the receiver's appointment or, if the substandard condition occurs subsequently, within 15 days of its occurrence.

(c) The notice shall inform the court of all of the following:

(1) The substandard conditions that exist.

(2) The threat or danger that the substandard conditions pose to any occupant of the property or the public.

(3) The approximate cost and time involved in abating the conditions. If more time is needed to approximate the cost,

then the notice shall provide the date on which the approximate cost will be filed with the court and that date shall be within 10 days of the filing.

(4) Whether the receivership estate is likely to contain sufficient funds to abate the conditions.

(d) If the receivership estate does not contain sufficient funds to abate the conditions, the receiver shall request further instructions or orders from the court.

(e) The court, upon receipt of a notice pursuant to subdivision (d), shall consider appropriate orders or instructions to enable the receiver to correct the substandard conditions or to terminate or limit the period of receivership. *(Added by Stats.2001, c. 414 (A.B.472), § 1. Amended by Stats.2005, c. 595 (S.B.253), § 3.)*

Research References

Rutter, Cal. Practice Guide: Enforcing Judgments/Debts Ch. 4-C, C. Receiverships.
Miller and Starr California Real Estate § 33:4, Standards for Appointment.
Miller and Starr California Real Estate § 33:14, Preservation and Management--Power to Improve or Upgrade.
Miller and Starr California Real Estate § 33:31, Actions in Which a Receiver May be Appointed--To Abate Substandard Conditions in Residential Buildings.
Miller and Starr California Real Estate § 19:121, Tenant's Remedies for Landlord's Breach of the Implied Warranty.
Miller and Starr California Real Estate § 19:227, Prejudgment Remedies; Attachment and Receivership.
16 NO. 4 Miller & Starr, California Real Estate Newsalert 16, Receivers.
16 NO. 5 Miller & Starr, California Real Estate Newsalert 26. State Board of Equalization Issues Comprehensive Summary and Qs and As for Transfers of Base Year Values of Principal Residences State Board of Equalization Issues Comprehensive Summary and Qs and As for Transfers of...
6 Witkin Cal. Proc. 5th Provisional Remedies § 454, Possession and Control of Property.

§ 568.3. Motion in receivership actions; who may file motion; conditions

Any tenant of real property that is subject to receivership, a tenant association or organization, or any federal, state, or local enforcement agency, may file a motion in a receivership action for the purpose of seeking further instructions or orders from the court, if either of the following is true:

(a) Substandard conditions exist, as defined by Section 17920.3 or 17920.10 of the Health and Safety Code.

(b) A dispute or controversy exists concerning the powers or duties of the receiver affecting a tenant or the public. *(Added by Stats.2001, c. 414 (A.B.472), § 2. Amended by Stats.2005, c. 595 (S.B.253), § 4.)*

Research References

Rutter, Cal. Practice Guide: Enforcing Judgments/Debts Ch. 4-C, C. Receiverships.
Miller and Starr California Real Estate § 33:31, Actions in Which a Receiver May be Appointed--To Abate Substandard Conditions in Residential Buildings.
Miller and Starr California Real Estate § 19:121, Tenant's Remedies for Landlord's Breach of the Implied Warranty.
Miller and Starr California Real Estate § 19:227, Prejudgment Remedies; Attachment and Receivership.
16 NO. 4 Miller & Starr, California Real Estate Newsalert 16, Receivers.
16 NO. 5 Miller & Starr, California Real Estate Newsalert 26. State Board of Equalization Issues Comprehensive Summary and Qs and As for Transfers of Base Year Values of Principal Residences State Board of Equalization Issues Comprehensive Summary and Qs and As for Transfers of...

6 Witkin Cal. Proc. 5th Provisional Remedies § 454, Possession and Control of Property.

§ 568.5. Sales; authority; manner; confirmation

A receiver may, pursuant to an order of the court, sell real or personal property in the receiver's possession upon the notice and in the manner prescribed by Article 6 (commencing with Section 701.510) of Chapter 3 of Division 2 of Title 9. The sale is not final until confirmed by the court. *(Added by Stats.1939, c. 374, p. 1709, § 1. Amended by Stats.1982, c. 497, p. 2156, § 35, operative July 1, 1983.)*

Research References

Rutter, Cal. Practice Guide: Civ. Pro. Before Trial Ch. 9(II)-B, B. Receiverships.
Rutter, Cal. Practice Guide: Enforcing Judgments/Debts Ch. 4-C, C. Receiverships.
Rutter, Cal. Practice Guide: Enforcing Judgments/Debts Ch. 6D-8, Special Requirements for Sale of Real Property Dwellings.
Rutter, Cal. Practice Guide: Enforcing Judgments/Debts Ch. 6G-6, Receiver to Enforce Judgment-EJL Provisions.
Miller and Starr California Real Estate § 33:13, Preservation and Management--Power to Sell Assets.
6 Witkin Cal. Proc. 5th Provisional Remedies § 437, Fraud or Mismanagement.
6 Witkin Cal. Proc. 5th Provisional Remedies § 455, Sale of Property.

§ 569. Interest bearing accounts; deposit of funds; conditions

Funds in the hands of a receiver may be deposited in one or more interest bearing accounts in the name and for the benefit of the receivership estate with one or more financial institutions, provided that all of the following conditions are satisfied:

(a) The deposits are fully guaranteed or insured under federal law.

(b) The financial institution in which the funds are deposited is not a party to the action in which the receiver was appointed.

(c) The receiver does not own 1 percent or more in value of the outstanding stock of the financial institution, is not an officer, director, or employee of the financial institution, and is not a sibling, whether by the whole or half-blood, spouse, aunt, uncle, nephew, niece, ancestor, or lineal descendant of an owner, officer, employee, or director. *(Enacted in 1872. Amended by Stats.1998, c. 932 (A.B.1094), § 16.)*

Research References

Rutter, Cal. Practice Guide: Civ. Pro. Before Trial Ch. 9(II)-B, B. Receiverships.
Rutter, Cal. Practice Guide: Enforcing Judgments/Debts Ch. 4-C, C. Receiverships.
Miller and Starr California Real Estate § 33:20, Duties of a Receiver--Investment of Funds.
6 Witkin Cal. Proc. 5th Provisional Remedies § 454, Possession and Control of Property.

§ 570. Unclaimed funds; publication of notice; payment to State Treasury; rights of owner; expense of notice

A receiver having any funds in his hands belonging to a person whose whereabouts are unknown to him, shall, before receiving his discharge as such receiver, publish a notice, in one or more newspapers published in the county, at least once a week for four consecutive weeks, setting forth the name of the owner of any unclaimed funds, the last known place of residence or post office address of such owner and the amount of such unclaimed funds. Any funds remaining in his hands unclaimed for 30 days after the date of the last publication of such notice, shall be reported to the court, and upon order of the court, all such funds must be paid into the State Treasury accompanied with a copy of the order, which must set forth the facts required in the notice herein provided. Such funds shall be deemed to have been received by the State under Chapter 7 (commencing with Section

1500) of Title 10 of Part 3 of this code and may be recovered in the manner prescribed therein.

All costs and expenses connected with such advertising shall be paid out of the funds the whereabouts of whose owners are unknown. *(Added by Stats.1913, c. 87, p. 92, § 1. Amended by Stats.1915, c. 83, p. 107, § 1; Stats.1917, c. 138, p. 203, § 1; Stats.1963, c. 1762, p. 3516, § 1.)*

Research References

Miller and Starr California Real Estate § 33:9, Sources of Receiver's Limited Authority; Court Approval and Instructions.
Miller and Starr California Real Estate § 33:21, Duties of a Receiver--To Account and Secure Discharge.
6 Witkin Cal. Proc. 5th Provisional Remedies § 454, Possession and Control of Property.
13 Witkin, California Summary 10th Personal Property § 39, (S 39) Other Statutes Dealing With Unclaimed Property.

CHAPTER 5A. UNDERTAKING OF PERSONS HANDLING PRIVATE PROPERTY OR FUNDS

Section
571.   Provision of order of appointment.

§ 571. Provision of order of appointment

If a referee or commissioner is appointed by a court and the duties of the referee or commissioner will, or are reasonably anticipated to, involve the custody of personal property or the receipt or disbursement of moneys, the order of appointment shall provide that before entering upon the duties, the referee or commissioner shall execute an undertaking to the State of California, to the effect that the referee or commissioner will faithfully discharge the duties of referee or commissioner, as the case may be, and obey the orders of the court therein. The order of appointment shall specify the amount of the undertaking, but a failure to so specify shall not invalidate the order. *(Added by Stats.1963, c. 575, p. 1453, § 1. Amended by Stats.1977, c. 1257, § 16, eff. Jan. 3, 1977; Stats.1982, c. 517, p. 2343, § 129.)*

Law Revision Commission Comments

Section 571 is amended for consistency with the Bond and Undertaking Law. See Sections 995.310 (sureties on undertaking) and 995.840 (court approval of undertaking). The other changes in Section 571 are technical. [16 Cal.L.Rev.Comm. Reports 501 (1982)].

Research References

Rutter, Cal. Practice Guide: A.D.R. Ch. 6-C, C. Referees.
Rutter, Cal. Practice Guide: Civil Trials & Evidence Ch. 16-G, G. Trial by Reference.
2 Witkin Cal. Proc. 5th Courts § 343, (S 343) in General.
2 Witkin Cal. Proc. 5th Courts § 346, (S 346) in General.
8 Witkin Cal. Proc. 5th Enforcement of Judgment § 102, (S 102) Preservation of Property.
8 Witkin Cal. Proc. 5th Enforcement of Judgment § 310, (S 310) in General.
6 Witkin Cal. Proc. 5th Provisional Remedies § 179, Securities.
6 Witkin Cal. Proc. 5th Provisional Remedies § 191, Depreciating Property.

CHAPTER 6. DEPOSIT IN COURT

Section
572.   Order for deposit; when authorized.
573.   Deposit with court's treasury.
574.   Order for deposit; enforcement.

§ 572. Order for deposit; when authorized

When it is admitted by the pleadings, or shown upon the examination of a party to the action, that he or she has in his or her possession, or under his or her control, any money or other thing capable of delivery, which, being the subject of litigation, is held by him or her as trustee for another party, or which belongs or which is due to another party or which should, under the circumstances of the case be held by the court pending final disposition of the action, the court may order the same, upon motion, to be deposited in court or delivered to such party, upon those conditions that may be just, subject to the further direction of the court. *(Enacted in 1872. Amended by Stats.1907, c. 375, p. 710, § 1; Stats.1986, c. 540, § 6.)*

Research References

2 Witkin Cal. Proc. 5th Courts § 216, Concurrent Jurisdiction of Appellate Court.
6 Witkin Cal. Proc. 5th Provisional Remedies § 1, (S 1) in General.
6 Witkin Cal. Proc. 5th Provisional Remedies § 461, Nature of Remedy.
6 Witkin Cal. Proc. 5th Provisional Remedies § 462, Limitations.
6 Witkin Cal. Proc. 5th Provisional Remedies § 463, Procedure.
6 Witkin, California Summary 10th Torts § 1653, (S 1653) Insurer's Settlement Offer as Abrogating Obligation to Pay Prejudgment Interest.

§ 573. Deposit with court's treasury

Whenever money is paid into or deposited in the court under this chapter, it shall be deposited with the court's treasury as provided in Section 68084 of the Government Code. *(Added by Stats.2005, c. 75 (A.B.145), § 35, eff. July 19, 2005, operative Jan. 1, 2006.)*

Research References

2 Witkin Cal. Proc. 5th Courts § 366, (S 366) Miscellaneous Duties.
6 Witkin Cal. Proc. 5th Provisional Remedies § 463, Procedure.

§ 574. Order for deposit; enforcement

Whenever, in the exercise of its authority, a court has ordered the deposit or delivery of money, or other thing, and the order is disobeyed, the court, beside punishing the disobedience, may make an order requiring the sheriff or marshal to take the money, or thing, and deposit or deliver it in conformity with the direction of the court. *(Enacted in 1872. Amended by Stats. 1933, c. 744, p. 1868, § 87; Stats.1996, c. 872 (A.B.3472), § 15.)*

Research References

6 Witkin Cal. Proc. 5th Provisional Remedies § 463, Procedure.

Title 7a

PRETRIAL CONFERENCES

Section
575.   Promulgation of rules by Judicial Council.
575.1.   Local rules; scope; purpose; promulgation.
575.2.   Noncompliance with local rules; effects.
576.   Amendment of pleadings or pretrial conference order.

§ 575. Promulgation of rules by Judicial Council

The Judicial Council may promulgate rules governing pretrial conferences, and the time, manner and nature thereof, in civil cases at issue, or in one or more classes thereof, in the superior courts. *(Added by Stats.1955, c. 632, p. 1130, § 1. Amended by Stats.1977, c. 1257, § 17, eff. Jan. 3, 1977; Stats.1998, c. 931 (S.B.2139), § 76, eff. Sept. 28, 1998; Stats.2002, c. 784 (S.B.1316), § 61.)*

Law Revision Commission Comments

Section 575 is amended to reflect the elimination of the justice court. Cal. Const. art. VI, §§ 1, 5(b). [28 Cal.L.Rev.Comm. Reports 51 (1998)].

Section 575 is amended to reflect unification of the municipal and superior courts pursuant to Article VI, Section 5(e), of the California Constitution. [32 Cal.L.Rev.Comm. Reports 124 (2002)]. [32 Cal.L.Rev. Comm. Reports 124 (2002)].

Research References

Rutter, Cal. Practice Guide: Civil Trials & Evidence Ch. 4-I, I. Other Motions at Final Status Conference.

Rutter, Cal. Practice Guide: Personal Injury Ch. 9-L, L. Motions to Terminate Trial Before Verdict.

2 Witkin Cal. Proc. 5th Courts § 182, Broad Rule-Making Power.

6 Witkin Cal. Proc. 5th Proceedings Without Trial § 193, (S 193) Time of Motion.

7 Witkin Cal. Proc. 5th Trial § 45, Current Procedure.

§ 575.1. Local rules; scope; purpose; promulgation

(a) The presiding judge of each superior court may prepare, with the assistance of appropriate committees of the court, proposed local rules designed to expedite and facilitate the business of the court. The rules need not be limited to those actions on the civil active list, but may provide for the supervision and judicial management of actions from the date they are filed. Rules prepared pursuant to this section shall be submitted for consideration to the judges of the court and, upon approval by a majority of the judges, the judges shall have the proposed rules published and submitted to the local bar and others, as specified by the Judicial Council, for consideration and recommendations.

(b) After a majority of the judges have officially adopted the rules, they shall be filed with the Judicial Council as required by Section 68071 of the Government Code and as specified in rules adopted by the Judicial Council. The Judicial Council shall prescribe rules to ensure that a complete current set of local rules and amendments, for each county in the state, is made available for public examination in each county. The local rules shall also be published for general distribution in accordance with rules adopted by the Judicial Council. Each court shall make its local rules available for inspection and copying in every location of the court that generally accepts filing of papers. The court may impose a reasonable charge for copying the rules and may impose a reasonable page limit on copying. The rules shall be accompanied by a notice indicating where a full set of the rules may be purchased.

(c) If a judge of a court adopts a rule that applies solely to cases in that judge's courtroom, or a particular branch or district of a court adopts a rule that applies solely to cases in that particular branch or district of a court, the court shall publish these rules as part of the general publication of rules required by the California Rules of Court. The court shall organize the rules so that rules on a common subject, whether individual, branch, district, or courtwide appear sequentially. Individual judges' rules and branch and district rules are local rules of court for purposes of this section and for purposes of the adoption, publication, comment, and filing requirements set forth in the Judicial Council rules applicable to local court rules. *(Added by Stats.1982, c. 1402, p. 5354, § 1. Amended by Stats.1989, c. 1416, § 19; Stats.1993, c. 925 (S.B.425), § 1; Stats.1993, c. 926 (A.B.2205), § 3.5; Stats.1998, c. 931 (S.B.2139), § 77, eff. Sept. 28, 1998; Stats.2003, c. 149 (S.B.79), § 9.)*

Law Revision Commission Comments

Section 575.1 is amended to reflect the elimination of the justice court. Cal. Const. art. VI, §§ 1, 5(b). [28 Cal.L.Rev.Comm. Reports 51 (1998)].

Subdivision (a) of Section 575.1 is amended to reflect unification of the municipal and superior courts pursuant to former Section 5(e) of Article VI of the California Constitution.

Subdivision (b) is amended to be consistent with the approach used in California Rule of Court 981, as amended effective January 1, 2003, regarding preparation of and public access to local rules. Rules of Court adopted by the Judicial Council pursuant to this section cannot be inconsistent with statute. See Cal. Const. art. VI, § 6. [33 Cal.L.Rev. Comm. Reports 192 (2003)].

Research References

Rutter, Cal. Practice Guide: Civ. Pro. Before Trial Ch. 9(I)-A, A. Introduction.

Rutter, Cal. Practice Guide: Civ. Pro. Before Trial Ch. 12(I)-B, B. Case Management ("Fast Track") System.

Rutter, Cal. Practice Guide: Civil Trials & Evidence Ch. 1-A, A. Importance of Statewide and Local Rules of Court.

Rutter, Cal. Practice Guide: Civil Trials & Evidence Ch. 4-A, A. General Considerations.

Rutter, Cal. Practice Guide: Personal Injury Ch. 8-A, A. Case Management.

2 Witkin Cal. Proc. 5th Courts § 200, (S 200) Adoption and Publication.

2 Witkin Cal. Proc. 5th Courts § 264, in General.

6 Witkin Cal. Proc. 5th Proceedings Without Trial § 281, Local Rules.

7 Witkin Cal. Proc. 5th Trial § 39, (S 39) Management and Distribution of Court Business.

7 Witkin Cal. Proc. 5th Trial § 58, (S 58) in General.

7 Witkin Cal. Proc. 5th Trial § 60, in General.

§ 575.2. Noncompliance with local rules; effects

(a) Local rules promulgated pursuant to Section 575.1 may provide that if any counsel, a party represented by counsel, or a party if in pro se, fails to comply with any of the requirements thereof, the court on motion of a party or on its own motion may strike out all or any part of any pleading of that party, or, dismiss the action or proceeding or any part thereof, or enter a judgment by default against that party, or impose other penalties of a lesser nature as otherwise provided by law, and may order that party or his or her counsel to pay to the moving party the reasonable expenses in making the motion, including reasonable attorney fees. No penalty may be imposed under this section without prior notice to, and an opportunity to be heard by, the party against whom the penalty is sought to be imposed.

(b) It is the intent of the Legislature that if a failure to comply with these rules is the responsibility of counsel and not of the party, any penalty shall be imposed on counsel and shall not adversely affect the party's cause of action or defense thereto. *(Added by Stats.1982, c. 1402, p. 5354, § 2. Amended by Stats.2002, c. 806 (A.B.3027), § 14.)*

Research References

Rutter, Cal. Practice Guide: A.D.R. Ch. 4-B, B. Judicial Arbitration.

Rutter, Cal. Practice Guide: A.D.R. Ch. 4-C, C. Statutorily-Mandated Court Mediation Programs.

Rutter, Cal. Practice Guide: Civil Appeals & Writs Ch. 8-C, C. Standards of Appellate Review.

Rutter, Cal. Practice Guide: Civ. Pro. Before Trial Ch. 5-B, B. Entry of Default.

Rutter, Cal. Practice Guide: Civ. Pro. Before Trial Ch. 11-A, A. Voluntary Dismissals.

Rutter, Cal. Practice Guide: Civ. Pro. Before Trial Ch. 11-B, B. Involuntary Dismissals.

Rutter, Cal. Practice Guide: Civ. Pro. Before Trial Ch. 13-E, E. the Arbitration Hearing.

Rutter, Cal. Practice Guide: Civ. Pro. Before Trial Ch. 9(I)-A, A. Introduction.

Rutter, Cal. Practice Guide: Civ. Pro. Before Trial Ch. 9(I)-D, D. Hearing.

Rutter, Cal. Practice Guide: Civ. Pro. Before Trial Ch. 12(I)-B, B. Case Management ("Fast Track") System.

Rutter, Cal. Practice Guide: Civ. Pro. Before Trial Ch. 9(III)-A, A. Sources of Sanctions Power.

Rutter, Cal. Practice Guide: Civ. Pro. Before Trial Ch. 9(III)-D, D. Other Sanctions Statutes and Rules.

Rutter, Cal. Practice Guide: Civ. Pro. Before Trial Ch. 9(III)-D, Outline D.

Rutter, Cal. Practice Guide: Personal Injury Ch. 7-F, F. Preparing for Arbitration.

Rutter, Cal. Practice Guide: Personal Injury Ch. 8-A, A. Case Management.

Rutter, Cal. Practice Guide: Personal Injury Ch. 9-B, B. In-Chambers Conference Before Commencement of Trial.

Rutter, Cal. Practice Guide: Prof. Responsibility Ch. 1-A, A. Sources of Regulation of Practice of Law in California-Overview.

Rutter, Cal. Practice Guide: Prof. Responsibility Ch. 3-D, D. Authority of Client vs. Authority of Attorney.

Rutter, Cal. Practice Guide: Prof. Responsibility Ch. 8-E, E. Consequences of Improper Advocacy.

2 Witkin Cal. Proc. 5th Courts § 177, (S 177) Imposition of Money Sanctions.

2 Witkin Cal. Proc. 5th Courts § 199, (S 199) in General.

2 Witkin Cal. Proc. 5th Courts § 202, (S 202) Duty of Clerk to Accept Filing Inconsistent With Local Rule.

2 Witkin Cal. Proc. 5th Courts § 264, in General.

2 Witkin Cal. Proc. 5th Courts § 265, Sanctions Proper.

2 Witkin Cal. Proc. 5th Courts § 266, Sanctions Improper.

6 Witkin Cal. Proc. 5th Proceedings Without Trial § 55, (S 55) Statutory Authorization.

6 Witkin Cal. Proc. 5th Proceedings Without Trial § 284, (S 284) Effect of Fast Track Rules.

7 Witkin Cal. Proc. 5th Trial § 58, (S 58) in General.

7 Witkin Cal. Proc. 5th Trial § 60, in General.

7 Witkin Cal. Proc. 5th Trial § 61, Sanctions for Attorney's Negligence.

7 Witkin Cal. Proc. 5th Trial § 64, (S 64) Right to Hearing.

7 Witkin Cal. Proc. 5th Trial § 226, (S 226) in General.

§ 576. Amendment of pleadings or pretrial conference order

Any judge, at any time before or after commencement of trial, in the furtherance of justice, and upon such terms as may be proper, may allow the amendment of any pleading or pretrial conference order. *(Added by Stats.1963, c. 882, p. 2129, § 1.)*

Research References

Rutter, Cal. Practice Guide: Civ. Pro. Before Trial Ch. 6-E, E. Amended and Supplemental Pleadings.

Rutter, Cal. Practice Guide: Civ. Pro. Before Trial Ch. 7(I)-B, B. Motions to Strike.

Rutter, Cal. Practice Guide: Civil Trials & Evidence Ch. 4-I, I. Other Motions at Final Status Conference.

Rutter, Cal. Practice Guide: Civil Trials & Evidence Ch. 12-D, D. Other Motions During Trial.

Rutter, Cal. Practice Guide: Family Law Ch. 6-B, B. Spousal Support.

5 Witkin Cal. Proc. 5th Pleading § 1186, (S 1186) Right to Amend Pleadings.

5 Witkin Cal. Proc. 5th Pleading § 1204, (S 1204) Amendment Permitted.

7 Witkin Cal. Proc. 5th Trial § 47, Preparation of Conference Order.

Title 8

OF THE TRIAL AND JUDGMENT IN CIVIL ACTIONS

CHAPTER 1. JUDGMENT IN GENERAL

§ 577. Judgment defined

A judgment is the final determination of the rights of the parties in an action or proceeding. *(Enacted in 1872.)*

Research References

Rutter, Cal. Practice Guide: Enforcing Judgments/Debts Ch. 6A-3, "Judgment," "Judgment Debtor" and "Judgment Creditor" Defined.

7 Witkin Cal. Proc. 5th Judgment § 1, Nature and Classification of Judgment.

4 Witkin Cal. Proc. 5th Pleading § 256, (S 256) Nature of Trial.

§ 577.5. Amount; computation and statement in dollars and cents; fractions rejected

In any judgment, or execution upon such judgment, the amount shall be computed and stated in dollars and cents, rejecting fractions. *(Added by Stats.1951, c. 655, p. 1850, § 21.)*

Research References

Rutter, Cal. Practice Guide: Enforcing Judgments/Debts Ch. 6D-2, Writ of Execution.

7 Witkin Cal. Proc. 5th Judgment § 30, in General.

§ 578. Judgment for or against one or more of several parties; determination of rights between parties

Judgment may be given for or against one or more of several plaintiffs, and for or against one or more of several defendants; and it may, when the justice of the case requires it, determine the ultimate rights of the parties on each side, as between themselves. *(Enacted in 1872.)*

Research References

Rutter, Cal. Practice Guide: Civ. Pro. Before Trial Ch. 9(II)-B, B. Receiverships.

Rutter, Cal. Practice Guide: Civil Trials & Evidence Ch. 17-C, C. Entry of Judgment.

7 Witkin Cal. Proc. 5th Judgment § 38, (S 38) in General.

5 Witkin Cal. Proc. 5th Pleading § 1137, Misjoinder.

1 Witkin Cal. Summ. 10th Contracts § 112, Action and Judgment.

§ 579. Judgment against one or more defendants; action proceeding against others

In an action against several defendants, the Court may, in its discretion, render judgment against one or more of them, leaving the action to proceed against the others, whenever a several judgment is proper. *(Enacted in 1872.)*

Research References

Rutter, Cal. Practice Guide: Civ. Pro. Before Trial Ch. 5-C, C. Default Judgment by Clerk.

Rutter, Cal. Practice Guide: Civ. Pro. Before Trial Ch. 5-D, D. Default Judgment by Court.

Rutter, Cal. Practice Guide: Civ. Pro. Before Trial Ch. 5-E, E. Limitations on Default Judgments.

Rutter, Cal. Practice Guide: Civ. Pro. Before Trial Ch. 12(I)-E, E. Consolidation, Coordination and Bifurcation.

Rutter, Cal. Practice Guide: Civil Trials & Evidence Ch. 17-C, C. Entry of Judgment.

7 Witkin Cal. Proc. 5th Judgment § 38, (S 38) in General.

6 Witkin Cal. Proc. 5th Proceedings Without Trial § 135, (S 135) Default of Fewer Than All Defendants.

1 Witkin Cal. Summ. 10th Contracts § 112, Action and Judgment.

§ 580. Relief granted; no answer; limited civil case

(a) The relief granted to the plaintiff, if there is no answer, cannot exceed that demanded in the complaint, in the statement required by Section 425.11, or in the statement provided for by Section 425.115; but in any other case, the court may grant the plaintiff any relief consistent with the case made by the complaint and embraced within the issue. The court may impose liability, regardless of whether the theory upon which liability is sought to be imposed involves legal or equitable principles.

(b) Notwithstanding subdivision (a), the following types of relief may not be granted in a limited civil case:

(1) Relief exceeding the maximum amount in controversy for a limited civil case as provided in Section 85, exclusive of attorney's fees, interest, and costs.

(2) A permanent injunction, except as otherwise authorized by statute.

(3) A determination of title to real property.

(4) Declaratory relief, except as authorized by Section 86. *(Enacted in 1872. Amended by Stats.1993, c. 456 (A.B.58), § 8; Stats.1995, c. 796 (S.B.45), § 9; Stats.1998, c. 931 (S.B.2139), § 78, eff. Sept. 28, 1998; Stats.2006, c. 86 (A.B.2126), § 1; Stats.2007, c. 43 (S.B.649), § 5.)*

Law Revision Commission Comments

Section 580 is amended to accommodate unification of the municipal and superior courts in a county. Cal. Const. art. VI, § 5(e).

The last sentence of subdivision (a) continues former Section 86(c) without substantive change.

Subdivision (b)(1) makes explicit that although the jurisdiction of a unified superior court includes matters in which the amount in controversy exceeds the maximum for a limited civil case as provided in Section 85, the court cannot grant substantive relief exceeding that maximum in a limited civil case. Formerly, each county had one or more municipal courts and a superior court, and the jurisdictional limit of the municipal courts constrained the relief awardable in matters tried in those courts. *See* Stokus v. Marsh, 217 Cal.App.3d 647, 653, 266 Cal.Rptr. 90 (1990) ("we view the jurisdictional limit of Code of Civil Procedure section 86 as applying to the substantive judgment and not the award of costs, including reasonable attorneys' fees"); Bakkebo v. Municipal Court, 124 Cal.App.3d 229, 235, 177 Cal.Rptr. 239 (1981) ("Since the substantive demand is the touchstone of jurisdiction it follows that if the recovery on that demand is within the jurisdiction of the municipal court, that court retains jurisdiction to award costs and attorney fees even though those items, when added to the substantive portion of the judgment, aggregate an amount in excess of the jurisdictional limit."); *see also* Section 396 ("In any case where the lack of jurisdiction is due solely to an excess in the amount of the demand, the excess may be remitted and the action may continue in the court where it is pending."). A limited civil case is equivalent to a matter within the original jurisdiction of the municipal court under former law, so Section 580(b)(1) as amended continues and codifies the effect of former law.

Similarly, subdivisions (b)(2)-(b)(5) reflect and preserve limitations on the types of equitable relief awardable in a municipal court. See R. Weil & I. Brown, Jr., California Practice Guide: Civil Procedure Before Trial, *Jurisdiction and Venue* 3:12–3:18.1, at 3–6 to 3–7 (1997). *See also* St. James Church of Christ Holiness v. Superior Court, 135 Cal.App.2d 352, 362, 287 P.2d 387 (1955) (municipal court lacks jurisdiction to grant permanent injunction); Pasadena Inv. Co. v. Peerless Casualty Co., 134 Cal.App.2d Supp. 902, 286 P.2d 1014 (1955) (municipal court lacks jurisdiction to grant declaratory relief). On enforcement of orders under the Family Code, see Fam. Code 200, 290; *In re* Marriage of Lackey, 143 Cal.App.3d 698, 191 Cal.Rptr. 309 (1983).

Cf. Sections 85, 85.1 (limited civil cases). [28 Cal.L.Rev.Comm. Reports App. 7 (1998)].

Section 580 is amended to authorize the enforcement of a Family Code judgment in a limited civil case. The change would affect two judgment enforcement procedures: (1) a creditor's suit (Sections 708.210-708.270), and (2) a lien filed against a judgment debtor's interest in a pending case (Sections 708.410-708.480).

Other judgment enforcement procedures, which do not give rise to enforcement in a limited civil case, are not affected by the amendment. Those procedures fall into one of the following categories:

(1) A procedure conducted without a court hearing. See Sections 697.310-697.410 (judgment lien on real property), 697.510-697.670 (judgment lien on personal property), 699.010-701.830 (execution), 708.010-708.030 (written interrogatory or inspection demand), 712.010-716.030 (enforcement of writ of possession or sale).

(2) A procedure conducted in the same court that entered the judgment to be enforced (or in a court of the same or higher jurisdiction). See Sections 708.110-708.205 (debtor examination), 708.310-708.320 (charging order), 708.510-708.560 (assignment order), 708.610-708.630 (appointment of receiver), 708.710-708.795 (enforcement against obligation of public entity), 708.910-708.930 (enforcement against franchise), 709.020 (action against nonvested property interest).

(3) A special proceeding under the Probate Code. See Sections 709.010 (enforcement against debtor's interest as beneficiary of trust), 709.030 (enforcement against debtor's interest in guardianship or conservatorship estate).

The changes to subdivision (a) are nonsubstantive. [35 Cal.L.Rev. Comm. Reports 175 (2005)].

Subdivision (b) of Section 580 is amended to clarify its interrelationship with provisions such as Business and Professions Code Section 12606, under which a court in a limited civil case is authorized to grant relief that might be considered a permanent injunction (e.g., an order to destroy property packed in misleading containers). See also Bus. & Prof. Code § 12606.2; Food & Agric. Code §§ 25564, 29733, 43039, 59289. [36 Cal.L.Rev.Comm. Reports 305 (2006)].

Research References

California Real Estate Forms (Miller & Starr) § 3:8, Deed of Trust, Security Agreement, and Fixture Filing With Assignment of Rents and Agreements.

California Real Estate Forms (Miller & Starr) § 3:14, Construction Deed of Trust, Security Agreement, and Fixture Filing With Assignment of Rents and Agreements.

California Real Estate Forms (Miller & Starr) § 3:21, Deed of Trust, Assignment of Rents, Security Agreement and Fixture Filing– Conduit Loan.

California Real Estate Forms (Miller & Starr) § 3:34, Short Form Deed of Trust and Assignment of Rents.

California Real Estate Forms (Miller & Starr) § 3:35, Long Form Deed of Trust and Assignment of Rents.

Rutter, Cal. Practice Guide: A.D.R. Ch. 5-J, J. Challenging and Enforcing Arbitrator's Award in Court.

Rutter, Cal. Practice Guide: Civil Appeals & Writs Ch. 8-C, C. Standards of Appellate Review.

Rutter, Cal. Practice Guide: Civ. Pro. Before Trial Ch. 3-A, A. Subject Matter Jurisdiction (Competency).

Rutter, Cal. Practice Guide: Civ. Pro. Before Trial Ch. 5-E, E. Limitations on Default Judgments.

Rutter, Cal. Practice Guide: Civ. Pro. Before Trial Ch. 6-B, B. Complaints.

Rutter, Cal. Practice Guide: Family Law Ch. 6-B, B. Spousal Support.

Rutter, Cal. Practice Guide: Personal Injury Ch. 5-D, D. Classification as Limited or Unlimited Civil Case.

Rutter, Cal. Practice Guide: Personal Injury Ch. 5-E, E. Selected Pleading Issues.

Rutter, Cal. Practice Guide: Personal Injury Ch. 8-B, B. After Trial Date Set (Three to Four Months Before Trial).

Miller and Starr California Real Estate § 34:92, Punitive Damages-- Constitutional Validity and Limits.

Miller and Starr California Real Estate § 10:175, Single Security for Separate Debts.

2 Witkin Cal. Proc. 5th Courts § 242, (S 242) Conditions for Limited Civil Cases.

2 Witkin Cal. Proc. 5th Courts § 245, (S 245) in General.

2 Witkin Cal. Proc. 5th Jurisdiction § 2, (S 2) Power to Apply Substantive Law Remedies.

2 Witkin Cal. Proc. 5th Jurisdiction § 313, Default Judgment Outside the Issues.

4 Witkin Cal. Proc. 5th Pleading § 32, Contract, Tort, and Other Forms.

4 Witkin Cal. Proc. 5th Pleading § 497, (S 497) Contested Case.

4 Witkin Cal. Proc. 5th Pleading § 498, (S 498) Default Case.

4 Witkin Cal. Proc. 5th Pleading § 513, (S 513) Effect of Statement on Amount of Actual Award.

4 Witkin Cal. Proc. 5th Pleading § 514, Statement Preserving Right to Seek Punitive Damages.

5 Witkin Cal. Proc. 5th Pleading § 850, (S 850) Nature of Action.

6 Witkin Cal. Proc. 5th Proceedings Without Trial § 149, General Rule: Recovery is Limited to Amount Alleged.

6 Witkin Cal. Proc. 5th Proceedings Without Trial § 150, Prayer for Damages According to Proof.

6 Witkin Cal. Proc. 5th Proceedings Without Trial § 151, Default Entered as Discovery Sanction.

6 Witkin Cal. Proc. 5th Proceedings Without Trial § 152, Prayer on Dissolution Petition Form.

6 Witkin Cal. Proc. 5th Proceedings Without Trial § 154, (S 154) Notice of Damages.

6 Witkin Cal. Proc. 5th Proceedings Without Trial § 563, Remedies.

6 Witkin Cal. Proc. 5th Provisional Remedies § 276, Jurisdiction.

11 Witkin, California Summary 10th Husband and Wife § 243, Request in Petition.

11 Witkin, California Summary 10th Husband and Wife § 274, (S 274) Default Award.

6 Witkin, California Summary 10th Torts § 1749, Judgment by Default.

§ 580a. Action for deficiency judgment after foreclosure or trustee's sale; complaint; appraisal; deficiency computed on basis of fair market value; limitation of actions; necessity of sale

Whenever a money judgment is sought for the balance due upon an obligation for the payment of which a deed of trust or mortgage with power of sale upon real property or any interest therein was given as security, following the exercise of the power of sale in such deed of trust or mortgage, the plaintiff shall set forth in his or her complaint the entire amount of the indebtedness which was secured by the deed of trust or mortgage at the time of sale, the amount for which the real property or interest therein was sold and the fair market value thereof at the date of sale and the date of that sale. Upon the application of either party made at least 10 days before the time of trial the court shall, and upon its own motion the court at any time may, appoint one of the probate referees provided for by law to appraise the property or the interest therein sold as of the time of sale. The referee shall file his or her appraisal with the clerk and that appraisal shall be admissible in evidence. The referee shall take and subscribe an oath to be attached to the appraisal that he or she has truly, honestly and impartially appraised the property to the best of his or her knowledge and ability. Any referee so appointed may be called and examined as a witness by any party or by the court itself. The court must fix the compensation of the referee in an amount as determined by the court to be reasonable, but those fees shall not exceed similar fees for similar services in the community where the services are rendered, which may be taxed and allowed in like manner as other costs. Before rendering any judgment the court shall find the fair market value of the real property, or interest therein sold, at the time of sale. The court may render judgment for not more than the amount by which the entire amount of the indebtedness due at the time of sale exceeded the fair market value of the real property or interest therein sold at the time of sale with interest thereon from the date of the sale; provided, however, that in no event shall the amount of the judgment, exclusive of interest after the date of sale, exceed the difference between the amount for which the property was sold and the entire amount of the indebtedness secured by the deed of trust or mortgage. Any such action must be brought within three months of the time of sale under the deed of trust or mortgage. No judgment shall be rendered in any such action until the real property or interest therein has first been sold pursuant to the terms of the deed of trust or mortgage, unless the real property or interest therein has become valueless. *(Added by Stats.1933, c. 642, p. 1672, § 4. Reenacted by Stats.1935, c. 650, p. 1805, § 4. Amended by Stats.1968, c. 450, p. 1070, § 2; Stats.1970, c. 1282, p. 2320, § 1, eff. July 1, 1971; Stats.1982, c. 1535, p. 5965, § 1; Stats.1988, c. 1199, § 6, operative July 1, 1989.)*

Law Revision Commission Comments

Section 580a is amended to correct terminology. See Prob.Code §§ 400–453 (probate referees). [19 Cal.L.Rev.Comm. Reports 103.5 (1988)].

Research References

California Real Estate Forms (Miller & Starr) § 3:7, Promissory Note.

California Real Estate Forms (Miller & Starr) § 3:8, Deed of Trust, Security Agreement, and Fixture Filing With Assignment of Rents and Agreements.

California Real Estate Forms (Miller & Starr) § 3:9, Assignment of Lessor's Interest in Leases and Seller's Interest in Contracts for Sale.

California Real Estate Forms (Miller & Starr) § 3:13, Promissory Note Secured by Construction Deed of Trust.

California Real Estate Forms (Miller & Starr) § 3:14, Construction Deed of Trust, Security Agreement, and Fixture Filing With Assignment of Rents and Agreements.

California Real Estate Forms (Miller & Starr) § 3:20, Promissory Note– Conduit Loan.

California Real Estate Forms (Miller & Starr) § 3:22, Assignment of Leases and Rents–Conduit Loans.

California Real Estate Forms (Miller & Starr) § 3:29, Exceptions to Non-Recourse Guaranty–Conduit Loan.

California Real Estate Forms (Miller & Starr) § 3:30, Environmental Indemnity–Conduit Loan.

California Real Estate Forms (Miller & Starr) § 3:37, Continuing Guaranty.

§ 580b. Contract of sale; deed of trust or mortgage; credit transaction; chattel mortgage; no deficiency to be owed or collected and deficiency judgments prohibited; exception for liability of guarantor, pledgor, or other surety

(a) Except as provided in subdivision (c), no deficiency shall be owed or collected, and no deficiency judgment shall lie * * * ₂ for any of the following:

(1) After a sale of real property or an estate for years therein for failure of the purchaser to complete his or her contract of sale.

(2) Under a deed of trust or mortgage given to the vendor to secure payment of the balance of the purchase price of that real property or estate for years therein.

(3) Under a deed of trust or mortgage on a dwelling for not more than four families given to a lender to secure repayment of a loan * * * that was used to pay all or part of the purchase price of that dwelling, occupied entirely or in part by the purchaser. * * * For purposes of subdivision (b), a loan described in this paragraph * * * is a "purchase money loan."

(b) No deficiency shall be owed or collected, and no deficiency judgment shall lie * * *, on a loan, refinance, or other credit transaction (collectively, a "credit transaction") that is used to refinance a purchase money loan, or subsequent refinances of a purchase money loan, except to the extent that in a credit transaction * * * the lender or creditor advances new principal (hereafter "new advance") that is not applied to an obligation owed or to be owed under the purchase money loan, or to fees, costs, or related expenses of the credit transaction. A new credit transaction shall be deemed to be a purchase money loan except as to the principal amount of a new advance. For purposes of this section, any payment of principal shall be deemed to be applied first to the principal balance of the purchase money loan, and then to the principal balance of a new advance, and interest payments shall be applied to any interest due and owing. * * * This subdivision applies only * * * to credit transactions that are executed on or after January 1, 2013.

(c) The fact that no deficiency shall be owed or collected under the circumstances set forth in subdivisions (a) and (b) does not affect the liability that a guarantor, pledgor or other surety might otherwise have with respect to the deficiency, or that might otherwise be satisfied in whole or in part from other collateral pledged to secure the obligation that is the subject of the deficiency.

(d) When both a chattel mortgage and a deed of trust or mortgage have been given to secure payment of the balance of the combined purchase price of both real and personal property, no deficiency judgment shall lie * * * under any one thereof if no deficiency judgment would lie under the deed of trust or mortgage on the real property or estate for years therein. *(Added by Stats.1933, c. 642, p. 1673, § 5. Re-enacted and amended by Stats.1935, c. 650, p. 1806, § 5. Amended by Stats.1935, c. 680, p. 1869, § 1; Stats.1949, c. 1599, p. 2846, § 1; Stats.1963, c. 2158, p. 4500, § 1; Stats.1989, c. 698, § 12; Stats.2012, c. 64 (S.B.1069), § 1; Stats.2013, c. 65 (S.B.426), § 2.)*

Research References

California Real Estate Forms (Miller & Starr) § 3:7, Promissory Note.

Civ. Pro.

§ 580c. Mortgage foreclosure or trustee's sale; liability for actual costs and reasonable fees

In all cases where existing deeds of trust or mortgages are judicially foreclosed, unless a different amount is set up in the mortgage or deed of trust, and in all cases of mortgages and deeds of trust executed after this act takes effect, the mortgagor or trustor may be required to pay only such amount as trustee's or attorney's fees for processing the judicial foreclosure as the court may find reasonable and also the actual cost of publishing, recording, mailing and posting notices, litigation guarantee, and litigation cost of suit. *(Added by Stats.1933, c. 642, p. 1673, § 6. Re-enacted by Stats.1935, c. 650, p. 1806, § 6. Amended by Stats.1984, c. 1730, § 6.)*

Research References

Rutter, Cal. Practice Guide: Real Prop. Transactions Ch. 6-F, F. Promissory Note.

Miller and Starr California Real Estate § 10:236, Policy Objectives; the "Standard" Transaction.

7 Witkin Cal. Proc. 5th Judgment § 167, Other Contracts.

4 Witkin, California Summary 10th Security Transactions in Real Property § 125, Security is Not Mortgage.

§ 580d. Real property or estate for years sold under power of sale; no deficiency to be owed or collected and deficiency judgments prohibited; exception for liability of guarantor, pledgor, or other surety

* * * (a) Except as provided in subdivision (b), no deficiency shall be owed or collected, and no deficiency judgment shall be rendered for a deficiency on a note secured by a deed of trust or mortgage on real property or an estate for years therein * * * executed in any case in which the real property or estate for years therein has been sold by the mortgagee or trustee under power of sale contained in the mortgage or deed of trust.

(b) The fact that no deficiency shall be owed or collected under the circumstances set forth in subdivision (a) does not affect the liability that a guarantor, pledgor or other surety might otherwise have with respect to the deficiency, or that might otherwise be satisfied in whole or in part from other collateral pledged to secure the obligation that is the subject of the deficiency.

(c) This section does not apply to a deed of trust, mortgage, or other lien given to secure the payment of bonds or other evidences of indebtedness authorized or permitted to be issued by the Commissioner of Corporations, or which is made by a public utility subject to the Public Utilities Act (Part 1 (commencing with Section 201) of Division 1 of the Public Utilities Code). *(Added by Stats.1940, Ex.Sess., c. 29, p. 84, § 2. Amended by Stats.1989, c. 698, § 13; Stats.2013, c. 65 (S.B.426), § 3.)*

Research References

California Real Estate Forms (Miller & Starr) § 3:7, Promissory Note.

California Real Estate Forms (Miller & Starr) § 3:8, Deed of Trust, Security Agreement, and Fixture Filing With Assignment of Rents and Agreements.

California Real Estate Forms (Miller & Starr) § 3:9, Assignment of Lessor's Interest in Leases and Seller's Interest in Contracts for Sale.

California Real Estate Forms (Miller & Starr) § 3:13, Promissory Note Secured by Construction Deed of Trust.

California Real Estate Forms (Miller & Starr) § 3:14, Construction Deed of Trust, Security Agreement, and Fixture Filing With Assignment of Rents and Agreements.

California Real Estate Forms (Miller & Starr) § 3:20, Promissory Note-- Conduit Loan.

California Real Estate Forms (Miller & Starr) § 3:21, Deed of Trust, Assignment of Rents, Security Agreement and Fixture Filing-- Conduit Loan.

California Real Estate Forms (Miller & Starr) § 3:22, Assignment of Leases and Rents--Conduit Loans.

California Real Estate Forms (Miller & Starr) § 3:29, Exceptions to Non-Recourse Guaranty--Conduit Loan.

California Real Estate Forms (Miller & Starr) § 3:30, Environmental Indemnity--Conduit Loan.

California Real Estate Forms (Miller & Starr) § 3:36, Contingent Interest Agreement.

California Real Estate Forms (Miller & Starr) § 3:37, Continuing Guaranty.

California Real Estate Forms (Miller & Starr) § 3:38, Completion Guaranty.

California Real Estate Forms (Miller & Starr) § 3:40, Assignment of Membership Interest.

California Real Estate Forms (Miller & Starr) § 3:55, Subordination, Nondisturbance, and Attornment Agreement.

California Real Estate Forms (Miller & Starr) § 3:66, Deed in Lieu of Foreclosure--Transfer Agreement.

California Real Estate Forms (Miller & Starr) § 3:75, Third-Party Waivers--Deed of Trust.

Rutter, Cal. Practice Guide: Enforcing Judgments/Debts Ch. 3-A, A. Evaluating the Claim.

Rutter, Cal. Practice Guide: Enforcing Judgments/Debts Ch. 4-A, A. Attachment.

Rutter, Cal. Practice Guide: Enforcing Judgments/Debts Ch. 6A-13, Creating an Enforcement of Judgment Plan.

Rutter, Cal. Practice Guide: Real Prop. Transactions Ch. 6-I, I. Real Property Foreclosures and Antideficiency Laws.

Rutter, Cal. Practice Guide: Real Prop. Transactions Ch. 6-J, J. Guaranty of the Obligation.

Rutter, Cal. Practice Guide: Real Prop. Transactions Form 6:L, Guaranty.

Rutter, Cal. Practice Guide: Real Prop. Transactions Form 9:A, Sample Opinion Letter (By Borrower's Counsel).

Rutter, Cal. Practice Guide: Real Prop. Transactions Ch. 6-I Outline, Outline I.

Miller and Starr California Real Estate § 17:7, UCC Provisions, Generally.

Miller and Starr California Real Estate § 10:59, Payment of Taxes and Assessments.

Miller and Starr California Real Estate § 10:79, Offset of Deficiency by Beneficiary After Nonjudicial Foreclosure Sale.

Miller and Starr California Real Estate § 10:118, Recovery of Amount Omitted from Demand; Effect of Antideficiency Limitations.

Miller and Starr California Real Estate § 10:119, Partial Releases; Definition; Procedure.

Miller and Starr California Real Estate § 10:124, Choice of Remedies.

Miller and Starr California Real Estate § 10:125, Effect of Antideficiency Legislation.

Miller and Starr California Real Estate § 10:127, Conflict of Laws.

Miller and Starr California Real Estate § 10:146, Effect of Beneficiary's or Trustor's Intervening Death or Incapacity.

Miller and Starr California Real Estate § 10:159, Exception; Sold-Out Junior Lien.

Miller and Starr California Real Estate § 10:164, Action Against the Trustor for Fraud or Other Claims.

Miller and Starr California Real Estate § 10:170, Enforcement of a Personal Property Lien.

Miller and Starr California Real Estate § 10:171, Requirements for a Unified Sale.

Miller and Starr California Real Estate § 10:172, Beneficiary's Alternative Remedies.

Miller and Starr California Real Estate § 10:176, Separate Security for Separate Debts.

Miller and Starr California Real Estate § 10:191, Attorney's or Trustee's Fees.

Miller and Starr California Real Estate § 10:204, Who Can Bid at the Sale.

Miller and Starr California Real Estate § 10:214, Deficiency Judgment.

Miller and Starr California Real Estate § 10:215, Exception; Recovery from Additional Security.

Miller and Starr California Real Estate § 10:216, Tort or Other Liability After the Foreclosure Sale.

Miller and Starr California Real Estate § 10:217, Liability for "Bad-Faith" Waste.

Miller and Starr California Real Estate § 10:226, The Judicial Sale.

Miller and Starr California Real Estate § 10:234, Determination of "Fair Value".

Miller and Starr California Real Estate § 10:235, Potentially Liable Persons.

Miller and Starr California Real Estate § 10:241, Conflict of Laws; Loans Held by Federal Agency.

Miller and Starr California Real Estate § 10:261, Exception; Action for Fraud.

Miller and Starr California Real Estate § 10:263, Definitions; Guarantor, Surety.

Miller and Starr California Real Estate § 10:265, Waiver of Guarantor's Defenses.

Miller and Starr California Real Estate § 10:268, Liability for Deficiency After Nonjudicial Foreclosure.

Miller and Starr California Real Estate § 10:66.10, Short Sales; Short-Pay Demand Statement.

15 NO. 4 Miller & Starr, California Real Estate Newsalert 1, California's "One Form of Action" and "Security First" Rules: Have They Cleared the Minefields Yet?

15 NO. 5 Miller & Starr, California Real Estate Newsalert 5, Deeds of Trust.

16 NO. 2 Miller & Starr, California Real Estate Newsalert 1, Trustee Sales: the "Terminator" of Debtors' Equities.

16 NO. 4 Miller & Starr, California Real Estate Newsalert 26, Deeds of Trust.

22 NO. 3 Miller & Starr, California Real Estate Newsalert 8, Deeds of Trust.

22 NO. 2 Miller & Starr, California Real Estate Newsalert 9, Deeds of Trust.

22 NO. 6 Miller & Starr, California Real Estate Newsalert 11, Deeds of Trust.

23 NO. 1 Miller & Starr, California Real Estate Newsalert 9, Deeds of Trust.

9 Witkin Cal. Proc. 5th Appeal § 354, (S 354) Proper Consideration.

5 Witkin Cal. Proc. 5th Pleading § 1211, (S 1211) Liberal Allowance of Amendment.

6 Witkin Cal. Proc. 5th Provisional Remedies § 68, (S 68) Security Without Value or Decreased in Value.

4 Witkin, California Summary 10th Security Transactions in Real Property § 132, in General.

4 Witkin, California Summary 10th Security Transactions in Real Property § 136, Mixed Collateral: Real and Personal Property.

4 Witkin, California Summary 10th Security Transactions in Real Property § 179, (S 179) Nature and Scope of Statutes.

4 Witkin, California Summary 10th Security Transactions in Real Property § 181, (S 181) Sold-Out Junior Lienor.

4 Witkin, California Summary 10th Security Transactions in Real Property § 184, (S 184) Distinctions.

4 Witkin, California Summary 10th Security Transactions in Real Property § 195, (S 195) Purported Guaranty.

Civ. Pro.

4 Witkin, California Summary 10th Security Transactions in Real Property § 197, (S 197) in General.

4 Witkin, California Summary 10th Security Transactions in Real Property § 198, (S 198) Bad Faith Waste.

4 Witkin, California Summary 10th Security Transactions in Real Property § 199, (S 199) in General.

4 Witkin, California Summary 10th Security Transactions in Real Property § 200, (S 200) Where Additional Security is Given.

4 Witkin, California Summary 10th Security Transactions in Real Property § 201, (S 201) Where Part of Note Unsecured.

4 Witkin, California Summary 10th Security Transactions in Real Property § 202, (S 202) in General.

4 Witkin, California Summary 10th Security Transactions in Real Property § 203, (S 203) Where Purported Guarantor is Principal.

4 Witkin, California Summary 10th Security Transactions in Real Property § 204, (S 204) Waiver of Defenses.

4 Witkin, California Summary 10th Security Transactions in Real Property § 205, Action by Sold-Out Junior Lienor.

4 Witkin, California Summary 10th Security Transactions in Real Property § 206, Defense of Action to Enjoin Sale.

4 Witkin, California Summary 10th Security Transactions in Real Property § 207, (S 207) Constitutionality of Restrictions.

4 Witkin, California Summary 10th Security Transactions in Real Property § 210, (S 210) Waiver of Lien.

4 Witkin, California Summary 10th Security Transactions in Real Property § 211, (S 211) Breach of Environmental Provision.

4 Witkin, California Summary 10th Security Transactions in Real Property § 207A, (S 207A) (New)-Nonjudicial Sale: C.C.P. 580e (Short Sale).

7 Witkin, California Summary 10th Constitutional Law § 624, Clarification of Existing Law.

§ 580e. Deficiency collection and judgment following short sale with consent of trustee or mortgagee prohibited; circumstances; exception for fraud; non-application of section; waivers void and against public policy

(a)(1) No deficiency shall be owed or collected, and no deficiency judgment shall be requested or rendered for any deficiency upon a note secured solely by a deed of trust or mortgage for a dwelling of not more than four units, in any case in which the trustor or mortgagor sells the dwelling for a sale price less than the remaining amount of the indebtedness outstanding at the time of sale, in accordance with the written consent of the holder of the deed of trust or mortgage, provided that both of the following have occurred:

(A) Title has been voluntarily transferred to a buyer by grant deed or by other document of conveyance that has been recorded in the county where all or part of the real property is located.

(B) The proceeds of the sale have been tendered to the mortgagee, beneficiary, or the agent of the mortgagee or beneficiary, in accordance with the parties' agreement.

(2) In circumstances not described in paragraph (1), when a note is not secured solely by a deed of trust or mortgage for a dwelling of not more than four units, no judgment shall be rendered for any deficiency upon a note secured by a deed of trust or mortgage for a dwelling of not more than four units, if the trustor or mortgagor sells the dwelling for a sale price less than the remaining amount of the indebtedness outstanding at the time of sale, in accordance with the written consent of the holder of the deed of trust or mortgage. Following the sale, in accordance with the holder's written consent, the voluntary transfer of title to a buyer by grant deed or by other document of conveyance recorded in the county where all or part of the real property is located, and the tender to the mortgagee, beneficiary, or the agent of the mortgagee or beneficiary of the sale proceeds, as agreed, the rights, remedies, and obligations of any holder, beneficiary, mortgagee, trustor, mortgagor, obligor, obligee, or guarantor of the note, deed of trust, or mortgage, and with respect to any other property that secures the note, shall be treated and determined as if the dwelling had been sold through foreclosure under a power of sale contained in the deed of trust

or mortgage for a price equal to the sale proceeds received by the holder, in the manner contemplated by Section 580d.

(b) A holder of a note shall not require the trustor, mortgagor, or maker of the note to pay any additional compensation, aside from the proceeds of the sale, in exchange for the written consent to the sale.

(c) If the trustor or mortgagor commits either fraud with respect to the sale of, or waste with respect to, the real property that secures the deed of trust or mortgage, this section shall not limit the ability of the holder of the deed of trust or mortgage to seek damages and use existing rights and remedies against the trustor or mortgagor or any third party for fraud or waste.

(d)(1) This section shall not apply if the trustor or mortgagor is a corporation, limited liability company, limited partnership, or political subdivision of the state.

(2) This section shall not apply to any deed of trust, mortgage, or other lien given to secure the payment of bonds or other evidence of indebtedness authorized, or permitted to be issued, by the Commissioner of Corporations, or that is made by a public utility subject to the Public Utilities Act (Part 1 (commencing with Section 201) of Division 1 of the Public Utilities Code).

(e) Any purported waiver of subdivision (a) or (b) shall be void and against public policy. *(Added by Stats.2010, c. 701 (S.B.931), § 1. Amended by Stats.2011, c. 82 (S.B.458), § 1, eff. July 15, 2011.)*

Research References

Rutter, Cal. Practice Guide: Real Prop. Transactions Ch. 6-I, I. Real Property Foreclosures and Antideficiency Laws.

Rutter, Cal. Practice Guide: Real Prop. Transactions Ch. 6-I Outline, Outline I.

Miller and Starr California Real Estate § 10:118, Recovery of Amount Omitted from Demand; Effect of Antideficiency Limitations.

Miller and Starr California Real Estate § 10:119, Partial Releases; Definition; Procedure.

Miller and Starr California Real Estate § 10:156, Waiver; Trustor's Election.

Miller and Starr California Real Estate § 10:158, Exception; Valueless Security.

Miller and Starr California Real Estate § 10:214, Deficiency Judgment.

Miller and Starr California Real Estate § 10:235, Potentially Liable Persons.

Miller and Starr California Real Estate § 10:66.10, Short Sales; Short-Pay Demand Statement.

21 NO. 4 Miller & Starr, California Real Estate Newsalert 11, Deeds of Trust.

22 NO. 1 Miller & Starr, California Real Estate Newsalert 2, Deeds of Trust.

22 NO. 3 Miller & Starr, California Real Estate Newsalert 8, Deeds of Trust.

22 NO. 4 Miller & Starr, California Real Estate Newsalert 10, Deeds of Trust.

4 Witkin, California Summary 10th Security Transactions in Real Property § 207A, (S 207A) (New)-Nonjudicial Sale: C.C.P. 580e (Short Sale).

§ 580.5. Secured obligations supported by letter of credit; presentment, receipt of payment or enforcement by beneficiary of letter of credit; honor or payment; demand or receipt of reimbursement by issuer

(a) For purposes of this section:

(1) "Beneficiary" means a "beneficiary" as defined in paragraph (3) of subdivision (a) of Section 5102 of the Commercial Code.

(2) "Issuer" means an "issuer" as defined in paragraph (9) of subdivision (a) of Section 5102 of the Commercial Code.

(3) "Letter of credit" means a "letter of credit" as defined in paragraph (10) of subdivision (a) of Section 5102 of the Commercial Code whether or not the engagement is governed by

Division 5 (commencing with Section 5101) of the Commercial Code.

(b) With respect to an obligation which is secured by a mortgage or a deed of trust upon real property or an estate for years therein and which is also supported by a letter of credit, neither the presentment, receipt of payment, or enforcement of a draft or demand for payment under the letter of credit by the beneficiary of the letter of credit nor the honor or payment of, or the demand for reimbursement, receipt of reimbursement or enforcement of any contractual, statutory or other reimbursement obligation relating to, the letter of credit by the issuer of the letter of credit shall, whether done before or after the judicial or nonjudicial foreclosure of the mortgage or deed of trust or conveyance in lieu thereof, constitute any of the following:

(1) An action within the meaning of subdivision (a) of Section 726, or a failure to comply with any other statutory or judicial requirement to proceed first against security.

(2) A money judgment for a deficiency or a deficiency judgment within the meaning of Section 580a, 580b, or 580d, or subdivision (b) of Section 726, or the functional equivalent of any such judgment.

(3) A violation of Section 580a, 580b, 580d, or 726. *(Added by Stats.1994, c. 611 (S.B.1612), § 2, eff. Sept. 16, 1994. Amended by Stats.1996, c. 176 (S.B.1599), § 2.)*

Research References

Rutter, Cal. Practice Guide: Real Prop. Transactions Ch. 6-I, I. Real Property Foreclosures and Antideficiency Laws.
Miller and Starr California Real Estate § 10:173, Debt Secured by Deed of Trust and Letter of Credit.
Miller and Starr California Real Estate § 10:215, Exception; Recovery from Additional Security.
4 Witkin, California Summary 10th Security Transactions in Real Property § 125, Security is Not Mortgage.
4 Witkin, California Summary 10th Security Transactions in Real Property § 200, (S 200) Where Additional Security is Given.
7 Witkin, California Summary 10th Constitutional Law § 624, Clarification of Existing Law.

§ 580.7. Loan transactions; circumstances rendering letter of credit unenforceable

(a) For purposes of this section:

(1) "Beneficiary" means a "beneficiary" as defined in paragraph (3) of subdivision (a) of Section 5102 of the Commercial Code.

(2) "Customer" means an "applicant" as defined in paragraph (2) of subdivision (a) of Section 5102 of the Commercial Code.

(3) "Letter of credit" means a "letter of credit" as defined in paragraph (10) of subdivision (a) of Section 5102 of the Commercial Code whether or not the engagement is governed by Division 5 (commencing with Section 5101) of the Commercial Code.

(b) No letter of credit shall be enforceable by any party thereto in a loan transaction in which all of the following circumstances exist:

(1) The customer is a natural person.

(2) The letter of credit is issued to the beneficiary to avoid a default of the existing loan.

(3) The existing loan is secured by a purchase money deed of trust or purchase money mortgage on real property containing one to four residential units, at least one of which is owned and occupied, or was intended at the time the existing loan was made, to be occupied by the customer.

(4) The letter of credit is issued after the effective date of this section. *(Added by Stats.1994, c. 611 (S.B.1612), § 3, eff. Sept. 16, 1994. Amended by Stats.1996, c. 176 (S.B.1599), § 3.)*

Research References

Rutter, Cal. Practice Guide: Real Prop. Transactions Ch. 6-I, I. Real Property Foreclosures and Antideficiency Laws.
Miller and Starr California Real Estate § 10:173, Debt Secured by Deed of Trust and Letter of Credit.
Miller and Starr California Real Estate § 10:215, Exception; Recovery from Additional Security.
4 Witkin, California Summary 10th Security Transactions in Real Property § 125, Security is Not Mortgage.
4 Witkin, California Summary 10th Security Transactions in Real Property § 200, (S 200) Where Additional Security is Given.
7 Witkin, California Summary 10th Constitutional Law § 624, Clarification of Existing Law.

§ 581. Dismissal; definitions

(a) As used in this section:

(1) "Action" means any civil action or special proceeding.

(2) "Complaint" means a complaint and a cross-complaint.

(3) "Court" means the court in which the action is pending.

(4) "Defendant" includes a cross-defendant.

(5) "Plaintiff" includes a cross-complainant.

(6) "Trial." A trial shall be deemed to actually commence at the beginning of the opening statement or argument of any party or his or her counsel, or if there is no opening statement, then at the time of the administering of the oath or affirmation to the first witness, or the introduction of any evidence.

(b) An action may be dismissed in any of the following instances:

(1) With or without prejudice, upon written request of the plaintiff to the clerk, filed with papers in the case, or by oral or written request to the court at any time before the actual commencement of trial, upon payment of the costs, if any.

(2) With or without prejudice, by any party upon the written consent of all other parties.

(3) By the court, without prejudice, when no party appears for trial following 30 days' notice of time and place of trial.

(4) By the court, without prejudice, when dismissal is made pursuant to the applicable provisions of Chapter 1.5 (commencing with Section 583.110).

(5) By the court, without prejudice, when either party fails to appear on the trial and the other party appears and asks for dismissal.

(c) A plaintiff may dismiss his or her complaint, or any cause of action asserted in it, in its entirety, or as to any defendant or defendants, with or without prejudice prior to the actual commencement of trial.

(d) Except as otherwise provided in subdivision (e), the court shall dismiss the complaint, or any cause of action asserted in it, in its entirety or as to any defendant, with prejudice, when upon the trial and before the final submission of the case, the plaintiff abandons it.

(e) After the actual commencement of trial, the court shall dismiss the complaint, or any causes of action asserted in it, in its entirety or as to any defendants, with prejudice, if the plaintiff requests a dismissal, unless all affected parties to the trial consent to dismissal without prejudice or by order of the court dismissing the same without prejudice on a showing of good cause.

(f) The court may dismiss the complaint as to that defendant when:

(1) Except where Section 597 applies, after a demurrer to the complaint is sustained without leave to amend and either party moves for dismissal.

(2) Except where Section 597 applies, after a demurrer to the complaint is sustained with leave to amend, the plaintiff fails to amend it within the time allowed by the court and either party moves for dismissal.

(3) After a motion to strike the whole of a complaint is granted without leave to amend and either party moves for dismissal.

(4) After a motion to strike the whole of a complaint or portion thereof is granted with leave to amend the plaintiff fails to amend it within the time allowed by the court and either party moves for dismissal.

(g) The court may dismiss without prejudice the complaint in whole, or as to that defendant, when dismissal is made under the applicable provisions of Chapter 1.5 (commencing with Section 583.110).

(h) The court may dismiss without prejudice the complaint in whole, or as to that defendant, when dismissal is made pursuant to Section 418.10.

(i) No dismissal of an action may be made or entered, or both, under paragraph (1) of subdivision (b) where affirmative relief has been sought by the cross-complaint of a defendant or if there is a motion pending for an order transferring the action to another court under the provisions of Section 396b.

(j) No dismissal may be made or entered, or both, under paragraph (1) or (2) of subdivision (b) except upon the written consent of the attorney for the party or parties applying therefor, or if consent of the attorney is not obtained, upon order of dismissal by the court after notice to the attorney.

(k) No action may be dismissed which has been determined to be a class action under the provisions of this code unless and until notice that the court deems adequate has been given and the court orders the dismissal.

(*l*) The court may dismiss, without prejudice, the complaint in whole, or as to that defendant when either party fails to appear at the trial and the other party appears and asks for the dismissal.

(m) The provisions of this section shall not be deemed to be an exclusive enumeration of the court's power to dismiss an action or dismiss a complaint as to a defendant. *(Added by Stats.1986, c. 540, § 8. Amended by Stats.1987, c. 1080, § 3; Stats.1993, c. 456 (A.B.58), § 9.)*

Research References

Rutter, Cal. Practice Guide: A.D.R. Ch. 5-G, G. Procedures to Enforce Arbitration.

Rutter, Cal. Practice Guide: Civil Appeals & Writs Ch. 8-C, C. Standards of Appellate Review.

Rutter, Cal. Practice Guide: Civ. Pro. Before Trial Ch. 3-B, B. Jurisdiction Over Parties-Personal Jurisdiction.

Rutter, Cal. Practice Guide: Civ. Pro. Before Trial Ch. 3-C, C. Forum Non Conveniens.

Rutter, Cal. Practice Guide: Civ. Pro. Before Trial Ch. 11-A, A. Voluntary Dismissals.

Rutter, Cal. Practice Guide: Civ. Pro. Before Trial Ch. 11-B, B. Involuntary Dismissals.

Rutter, Cal. Practice Guide: Civ. Pro. Before Trial Ch. 13-G, G. Trial De Novo.

Rutter, Cal. Practice Guide: Civ. Pro. Before Trial Ch. 8G-9, Evidentiary Effect of Admissions.

Rutter, Cal. Practice Guide: Civ. Pro. Before Trial Ch. 7(I)-A, A. Demurrers.

Rutter, Cal. Practice Guide: Civ. Pro. Before Trial Ch. 7(I)-B, B. Motions to Strike.

Rutter, Cal. Practice Guide: Civ. Pro. Before Trial Ch. 7(I)-D, D. Motion to Dismiss.

Rutter, Cal. Practice Guide: Civ. Pro. Before Trial Ch. 9(I)-F, F. Ex Parte Motions.

Rutter, Cal. Practice Guide: Civ. Pro. Before Trial Ch. 9(III)-A, A. Sources of Sanctions Power.

Rutter, Cal. Practice Guide: Civil Trials & Evidence Ch. 1-K, K. Continuance Motions.

Rutter, Cal. Practice Guide: Civil Trials & Evidence Ch. 4-I, I. Other Motions at Final Status Conference.

Rutter, Cal. Practice Guide: Civil Trials & Evidence Ch. 12-D, D. Other Motions During Trial.

Rutter, Cal. Practice Guide: Civil Trials & Evidence Ch. 16-E, E. Statement of Decision.

Miller and Starr California Real Estate § 12:15, Right of Partition--Procedure in Partition Action.

Miller and Starr California Real Estate § 19:89, Municipal Regulation of Rent ("Rent Control"); Authority to Enact an Ordinance.

Miller and Starr California Real Estate § 34:74, Effect of Dismissal of Action Before Judgment.

Miller and Starr California Real Estate § 35:22, Nature of Arbitration.

16 NO. 3 Miller & Starr, California Real Estate Newsalert 11, Landlord and Tenant.

21 NO. 6 Miller & Starr, California Real Estate Newsalert 3, Alternative Dispute Resolution.

3 Witkin Cal. Proc. 5th Actions § 184, Manifestation by Suit.

3 Witkin Cal. Proc. 5th Actions § 915, Exceptions.

8 Witkin Cal. Proc. 5th Attack Judgment Trial Court § 196, (S 196) in General.

2 Witkin Cal. Proc. 5th Courts § 203, Invalid Rules.

2 Witkin Cal. Proc. 5th Courts § 266, Sanctions Improper.

2 Witkin Cal. Proc. 5th Courts § 319, No Power to Consolidate or Dismiss Action.

8 Witkin Cal. Proc. 5th Enforcement of Judgment § 348, (S 348) Hearing.

7 Witkin Cal. Proc. 5th Judgment § 48, Formal Order of Dismissal or Nonsuit.

7 Witkin Cal. Proc. 5th Judgment § 380, (S 380) Refusal to Comply With Discovery Order.

7 Witkin Cal. Proc. 5th Judgment § 383, Effect of Recitals in Judgment.

2 Witkin Cal. Proc. 5th Jurisdiction § 97, (S 97) Other Illustrations: Civil Cases.

2 Witkin Cal. Proc. 5th Jurisdiction § 326, (L)--Disregard of Voluntary Dismissal.

4 Witkin Cal. Proc. 5th Pleading § 328, (S 328) Plaintiff's Duty to Continue Action.

5 Witkin Cal. Proc. 5th Pleading § 990, (S 990) Dismissal on Failure to Amend.

5 Witkin Cal. Proc. 5th Pleading § 997, Necessity of Judgment.

5 Witkin Cal. Proc. 5th Pleading § 999, Dismissal on Court's Own Motion.

5 Witkin Cal. Proc. 5th Pleading § 1014, (S 1014) in General.

6 Witkin Cal. Proc. 5th Proceedings Without Trial § 58, (S 58) in General.

6 Witkin Cal. Proc. 5th Proceedings Without Trial § 280, in General.

6 Witkin Cal. Proc. 5th Proceedings Without Trial § 282, Inherent Power of Court.

6 Witkin Cal. Proc. 5th Proceedings Without Trial § 283, (S 283) in General.

6 Witkin Cal. Proc. 5th Proceedings Without Trial § 284, (S 284) Effect of Fast Track Rules.

6 Witkin Cal. Proc. 5th Proceedings Without Trial § 286, (S 286) Fewer Than All Defendants.

6 Witkin Cal. Proc. 5th Proceedings Without Trial § 287, (S 287) Fewer Than All Causes.

6 Witkin Cal. Proc. 5th Proceedings Without Trial § 288, (S 288) in General.

6 Witkin Cal. Proc. 5th Proceedings Without Trial § 289, (S 289) Form of Affirmative Relief Sought.

6 Witkin Cal. Proc. 5th Proceedings Without Trial § 290, Complaint in Intervention Filed.

6 Witkin Cal. Proc. 5th Proceedings Without Trial § 291, Motion to Change Venue Pending.

6 Witkin Cal. Proc. 5th Proceedings Without Trial § 292, Plaintiff Not Sole Party in Interest.

6 Witkin Cal. Proc. 5th Proceedings Without Trial § 293, (S 293) in General.

6 Witkin Cal. Proc. 5th Proceedings Without Trial § 294, (S 294) Right to Dismiss After Motion for Summary Judgment.

6 Witkin Cal. Proc. 5th Proceedings Without Trial § 295, (S 295) Statutory Definition.

6 Witkin Cal. Proc. 5th Proceedings Without Trial § 296, (S 296) Demurrer Sustained Without Leave to Amend.

6 Witkin Cal. Proc. 5th Proceedings Without Trial § 297, (S 297) Demurrer Sustained With Leave to Amend.

6 Witkin Cal. Proc. 5th Proceedings Without Trial § 298, (S 298) Default on Request for Admissions.

6 Witkin Cal. Proc. 5th Proceedings Without Trial § 305, Request and Clerk's Entry.

6 Witkin Cal. Proc. 5th Proceedings Without Trial § 308, Res Judicata and Collateral Estoppel.

6 Witkin Cal. Proc. 5th Proceedings Without Trial § 311, (S 311) Dismissal on Request of Plaintiff.

6 Witkin Cal. Proc. 5th Proceedings Without Trial § 312, (S 312) Dismissal on Abandonment.

6 Witkin Cal. Proc. 5th Proceedings Without Trial § 313, (S 313) Effect of Dismissal.

6 Witkin Cal. Proc. 5th Proceedings Without Trial § 314, by Consent of Adverse Party.

6 Witkin Cal. Proc. 5th Proceedings Without Trial § 357, Effect of Dismissal.

6 Witkin Cal. Proc. 5th Proceedings Without Trial § 368, Effect of Dismissal.

6 Witkin Cal. Proc. 5th Proceedings Without Trial § 473, Effect of Dismissal.

6 Witkin Cal. Proc. 5th Proceedings Without Trial § 474, in General.

6 Witkin Cal. Proc. 5th Proceedings Without Trial § 475, (S 475) When Dismissal is Proper.

6 Witkin Cal. Proc. 5th Proceedings Without Trial § 476, (S 476) Trial of Uncontested Matter as Alternative to Dismissal.

6 Witkin Cal. Proc. 5th Proceedings Without Trial § 477, Demurrer Sustained.

6 Witkin Cal. Proc. 5th Proceedings Without Trial § 478, Motion to Strike Granted.

6 Witkin Cal. Proc. 5th Proceedings Without Trial § 604, Sanctions for Failure to Participate.

6 Witkin Cal. Proc. 5th Proceedings Without Trial § 620, (S 620) Subsequent Voluntary Dismissal.

7 Witkin Cal. Proc. 5th Trial § 1, (S 1) in General.

7 Witkin Cal. Proc. 5th Trial § 3, Trial on the Law.

11 Witkin, California Summary 10th Husband and Wife § 202, Hearing and Determination.

14 Witkin, California Summary 10th Wills and Probate § 579, (S 579) Orders and Judgment.

14 Witkin, California Summary 10th Wills and Probate § 583, Who May Petition.

14 Witkin, California Summary 10th Wills and Probate § 918, (S 918) Who May File.

2 Witkin Cal. Summ. 10th Workers' Compensation § 84, (S 84) Reimbursement.

§ 581c. Nonsuit; partial grant of motion; effect

(a) Only after, and not before, the plaintiff has completed his or her opening statement, or after the presentation of his or her evidence in a trial by jury, the defendant, without waiving his or her right to offer evidence in the event the motion is not granted, may move for a judgment of nonsuit.

(b) If it appears that the evidence presented, or to be presented, supports the granting of the motion as to some but not all of the issues involved in the action, the court shall grant the motion as to those issues and the action shall proceed as to the issues remaining. Despite the granting of the motion, no final judgment shall be entered prior to the termination of the action, but the final judgment in the action shall, in addition to any matters determined in the trial, award judgment as determined by the motion herein provided for.

(c) If the motion is granted, unless the court in its order for judgment otherwise specifies, the judgment of nonsuit operates as an adjudication upon the merits.

(d) In actions which arise out of an injury to the person or to property, when a motion for judgment of nonsuit was granted on the basis that the defendant was without fault, no other defendant during trial, over plaintiff's objection, may attempt to attribute fault to or comment on the absence or involvement of the defendant who was granted the motion. *(Added by Stats. 1947, c. 990, p. 2257, § 2. Amended by Stats.1961, c. 692, p. 1927,*

§ 1; Stats.1980, c. 187, p. 409, § 1; Stats.1982, c. 1510, p. 5857, § 2; Stats.1998, c. 200 (S.B.1556), § 1.)

Research References

Rutter, Cal. Practice Guide: Civil Trials & Evidence Ch. 6-F, F. Challenging Legally-Deficient Opening Statement (Motion for Nonsuit or Directed Verdict).

Rutter, Cal. Practice Guide: Civil Trials & Evidence Ch. 12-B, B. Motion for Nonsuit.

Rutter, Cal. Practice Guide: Civil Trials & Evidence Ch. 12-C, C. Motion for Directed Verdict.

Rutter, Cal. Practice Guide: Civil Trials & Evidence Ch. 16-C, C. Motion for Judgment (CCP § 631.8).

California Practice Guide: Employment Litigation Ch. 19-P, P. Motions During Trial.

Rutter, Cal. Practice Guide: Personal Injury Ch. 9-D, D. Opening Statements.

Rutter, Cal. Practice Guide: Personal Injury Ch. 9-L, L. Motions to Terminate Trial Before Verdict.

7 Witkin Cal. Proc. 5th Judgment § 48, Formal Order of Dismissal or Nonsuit.

7 Witkin Cal. Proc. 5th Judgment § 345, Discretion Rejected.

7 Witkin Cal. Proc. 5th Judgment § 380, (S 380) Refusal to Comply With Discovery Order.

7 Witkin Cal. Proc. 5th Judgment § 381, Nonsuit in Jury Trial.

7 Witkin Cal. Proc. 5th Judgment § 382, Judgment on Motion in Court Trial.

7 Witkin Cal. Proc. 5th Trial § 406, (S 406) Nature of Motion.

7 Witkin Cal. Proc. 5th Trial § 407, (S 407) Partial Nonsuit.

7 Witkin Cal. Proc. 5th Trial § 412, (S 412) Necessity of Motion.

7 Witkin Cal. Proc. 5th Trial § 413, After Evidence is Presented.

7 Witkin Cal. Proc. 5th Trial § 414, After Plaintiff's Opening Statement.

7 Witkin Cal. Proc. 5th Trial § 419, (S 419) Order.

§ 581d. Dismissal; entry; form

A written dismissal of an action shall be entered in the clerk's register and is effective for all purposes when so entered.

All dismissals ordered by the court shall be in the form of a written order signed by the court and filed in the action and those orders when so filed shall constitute judgments and be effective for all purposes, and the clerk shall note those judgments in the register of actions in the case. *(Added by Stats.1947, c. 990, p. 2257, § 3. Amended by Stats.1951, c. 1737, p. 4112, § 84, operative Jan. 1, 1952; Stats.1959, c. 346, p. 2269, § 1; Stats.1963, c. 875, p. 2123, § 1; Stats.1977, c. 1257, p. 4761, § 18, eff. Jan. 3, 1977; Stats.1998, c. 931 (S.B.2139), § 79, eff. Sept. 28, 1998.)*

Law Revision Commission Comments

Section 581d is amended to reflect the elimination of the justice court. Cal. Const. art. VI, §§ 1, 5(b). [28 Cal.L.Rev.Comm. Reports 51 (1998)].

Research References

Rutter, Cal. Practice Guide: Civil Appeals & Writs Ch. 2-B, B. Appealable Judgments and Orders.

Rutter, Cal. Practice Guide: Civil Appeals & Writs Ch. 2-C, C. Nonappealable Orders.

Rutter, Cal. Practice Guide: Civ. Pro. Before Trial Ch. 9(I)-E, E. Posthearing Procedures.

Rutter, Cal. Practice Guide: Civil Trials & Evidence Ch. 12-B, B. Motion for Nonsuit.

Rutter, Cal. Practice Guide: Enforcing Judgments/Debts Ch. 6A-3, "Judgment," "Judgment Debtor" and "Judgment Creditor" Defined.

9 Witkin Cal. Proc. 5th Appeal § 144, Dismissal and Nonsuit.

9 Witkin Cal. Proc. 5th Appeal § 612, Where Formal Order is Required.

7 Witkin Cal. Proc. 5th Judgment § 48, Formal Order of Dismissal or Nonsuit.

7 Witkin Cal. Proc. 5th Judgment § 52, Dismissals and Nonsuits.

7 Witkin Cal. Proc. 5th Judgment § 57, Purpose and Entry.

6 Witkin Cal. Proc. 5th Proceedings Without Trial § 280, in General.

6 Witkin Cal. Proc. 5th Proceedings Without Trial § 305, Request and Clerk's Entry.

6 Witkin Cal. Proc. 5th Proceedings Without Trial § 366, (S 366) Order Granting Dismissal.

6 Witkin Cal. Proc. 5th Proceedings Without Trial § 477, Demurrer Sustained.

7 Witkin Cal. Proc. 5th Trial § 419, (S 419) Order.

§ 581.5. Consumer debt buyer collection actions; debt buyer failure to appear; dismissal; award of costs for trial preparation

In a case involving consumer debt, as defined in Section 1788.2 of the Civil Code, and as regulated under Title 1.6C.5 (commencing with Section 1788.50) of Part 4 of Division 3 of the Civil Code, if the defendant debtor appears for trial on the scheduled trial date, and the plaintiff debt buyer either fails to appear or is not prepared to proceed to trial, and the court does not find a good cause for continuance, the court may, in its discretion, dismiss the action with or without prejudice. Notwithstanding any other law, in this instance, the court may award the defendant debtor's costs of preparing for trial, including, but not limited to, lost wages and transportation expenses. *(Added by Stats.2013, c. 64 (S.B.233), § 3.)*

§ 582. Judgment on merits

In all other cases judgment shall be rendered on the merits. *(Enacted in 1872. Amended by Stats.1907, c. 376, p. 712, § 3; Stats.1947, c. 990, p. 2257, § 4.)*

Research References

7 Witkin Cal. Proc. 5th Judgment § 380, (S 380) Refusal to Comply With Discovery Order.

§ 582.5. Payment of judgment by defendant in limited civil case; terms and conditions

In a limited civil case in which the defendant has appeared, if the judgment or order is for the payment of money by the defendant, the defendant shall pay the judgment immediately or at any time and upon terms and conditions, including installment payments, that the court may prescribe. The court may amend the terms and conditions for payment of the judgment or order at any time to provide for installment payments for good cause upon motion by a party and notice to all affected parties, regardless of the nature of the underlying debt and regardless of whether the moving party appeared before entry of the judgment or order. In any determination regarding the imposition of terms and conditions upon the payment of the judgment, the court shall consider any factors that would be relevant to the determination of a claim for exemption pursuant to Chapter 4 (commencing with Section 703.010) of Division 2 of Title 9 of Part 2 or the examination of a debtor pursuant to Article 2 (commencing with Section 708.110) of Chapter 6 of Division 2 of Title 9. *(Added by Stats.1998, c. 931 (S.B.2139), § 80, eff. Sept. 28, 1998.)*

Law Revision Commission Comments

Section 582.5 continues former Section 85 without substantive change, except that former Section 85 referred to the municipal courts, whereas Section 582.5 pertains to a limited civil case. A limited civil case is equivalent to a matter within the original jurisdiction of the municipal court under former law, so Section 582.5 as amended continues the effect of former law. See Section 85 (limited civil cases) & Comment. [28 Cal.L.Rev.Comm. Reports 51 (1998)].

Research References

Rutter, Cal. Practice Guide: Enforcing Judgments/Debts Ch. 6B-5, Amount of Judgment Lien.

Rutter, Cal. Practice Guide: Enforcing Judgments/Debts Ch. 6C-4, Amount of Lien.

8 Witkin Cal. Proc. 5th Enforcement of Judgment § 69, in General.

8 Witkin Cal. Proc. 5th Enforcement of Judgment § 75, (S 75) Amount of Lien.

8 Witkin Cal. Proc. 5th Enforcement of Judgment § 85, (S 85) Amount of Lien.

8 Witkin Cal. Proc. 5th Enforcement of Judgment § 507, Payment or Compromise by Judgment Debtor.

7 Witkin Cal. Proc. 5th Judgment § 31, Installment Payments.

CHAPTER 1.5. DISMISSAL FOR DELAY IN PROSECUTION

ARTICLE 1. DEFINITIONS AND GENERAL PROVISIONS

§ 583.110. Definitions

As used in this chapter, unless the provision or context otherwise requires:

(a) "Action" includes an action commenced by cross-complaint or other pleading that asserts a cause of action or claim for relief.

(b) "Complaint" includes a cross-complaint or other initial pleading.

(c) "Court" means the court in which the action is pending.

(d) "Defendant" includes a cross-defendant or other person against whom an action is commenced.

(e) "Plaintiff" includes a cross-complainant or other person by whom an action is commenced.

(f) "Service" includes return of summons. *(Added by Stats. 1984, c. 1705, § 5.)*

Research References

Rutter, Cal. Practice Guide: A.D.R. Ch. 4-C, C. Statutorily-Mandated Court Mediation Programs.

Rutter, Cal. Practice Guide: Civil Appeals & Writs Ch. 15-B, B. Common Law Writs.

Rutter, Cal. Practice Guide: Civil Appeals & Writs Ch. 15-C, C. Statutory Writs.

Rutter, Cal. Practice Guide: Civ. Pro. Before Trial Ch. 11-B, B. Involuntary Dismissals.

Rutter, Cal. Practice Guide: Civ. Pro. Before Trial Ch. 13-A, A. Introduction.

Rutter, Cal. Practice Guide: Civ. Pro. Before Trial Ch. 7(I)-D, D. Motion to Dismiss.

Rutter, Cal. Practice Guide: Civ. Pro. Before Trial Ch. 11-B, Outline B.

Rutter, Cal. Practice Guide: Family Law Ch. 6-A, A. Child Support.

§ 583.120. Civil actions; special proceedings

(a) This chapter applies to a civil action and does not apply to a special proceeding except to the extent incorporated by reference in the special proceeding.

(b) Notwithstanding subdivision (a), the court may, by rule or otherwise under inherent authority of the court, apply this chapter to a special proceeding or part of a special proceeding except to the extent such application would be inconsistent with the character of the special proceeding or the statute governing the special proceeding. *(Added by Stats.1984, c. 1705, § 5.)*

Law Revision Commission Comments

Section 583.120 is new. Subdivision (a) preserves the effect of existing law. See, e.g., Big Bear Mun. Water Dist. v. Superior Court, 269 Cal.App.2d 919, 75 Cal.Rptr. 580 (1969) (dismissal provisions applicable in eminent domain proceedings by virtue of incorporation by reference of civil procedures); Rules of Court 1233 (dismissal for lack of prosecution provisions incorporated specifically in family law proceedings).

Subdivision (b) gives the court latitude to apply the provisions of this chapter in special proceedings where appropriate. The application would be inconsistent with the character of a special proceeding such as a decedent's estate. See, e.g., Horney v. Superior Court, 83 Cal.App.2d 262, 188 P.2d 552 (1948). In addition, a special proceeding may prescribe different rules. *Cf.* Civil Code § 3147 (discretionary dismissal of action to foreclose mechanics lien). [17 Cal.L.Rev.Comm. Reports 905 (1984)].

Research References

§ 583.130. Plaintiff to proceed with reasonable diligence; stipulations and disposition of action on merits favored

It is the policy of the state that a plaintiff shall proceed with reasonable diligence in the prosecution of an action but that all parties shall cooperate in bringing the action to trial or other disposition. Except as otherwise provided by statute or by rule of court adopted pursuant to statute, the policy favoring the right of parties to make stipulations in their own interests and the policy favoring trial or other disposition of an action on the merits are generally to be preferred over the policy that requires dismissal for failure to proceed with reasonable diligence in the prosecution of an action in construing the provisions of this chapter. *(Added by Stats.1984, c. 1705, § 5.)*

Law Revision Commission Comments

Section 583.130 is new. It is consistent with statements in the cases of the preference for trial on the merits. See, e.g., Hocharian v. Superior Court, 28 Cal.3d 714, 621 P.2d 829, 170 Cal.Rptr. 790 (1981); General Ins. Co. v. Superior Court, 15 Cal.3d 449, 541 P.2d 289, 124 Cal.Rptr. 745 (1975); Denham v. Superior Court, 2 Cal.3d 557, 468 P.2d 193, 86 Cal.Rptr. 65 (1970); Weeks v. Roberts, 68 Cal.2d 802, 442 P.2d 361, 69 Cal.Rptr. 305 (1968). [17 Cal.L.Rev.Comm. Reports 905 (1984)].

Research References

§ 583.140. Waiver and estoppel

Nothing in this chapter abrogates or otherwise affects the principles of waiver and estoppel. *(Added by Stats.1984, c. 1705, § 5.)*

Law Revision Commission Comments

Section 583.140 continues and expands a provision of former Section 581a(f)(1). This chapter does not alter and is supplemented by general rules of waiver and estoppel. See, e.g., Southern Pac. v. Seaboard Mills, 207 Cal.App.2d 97, 24 Cal.Rptr. 236 (1962) (waiver of failure to timely bring to trial); Tresway Aero, Inc. v. Superior Court, 5 Cal.3d 431, 487 P.2d 1211, 96 Cal.Rptr. 571 (1971) (estoppel to assert failure to timely serve and return summons); Borglund v. Bombardier, Ltd., 121 Cal. App.3d 276, 175 Cal.Rptr. 150 (1981) (estoppel to assert failure to timely bring to trial); Holder v. Sheet Metal Worker's Int'l Ass'n, 121 Cal.App.3d 321, 175 Cal.Rptr. 313 (1981) (waiver or estoppel to assert failure to timely bring to new trial following reversal on appeal). [17 Cal.L.Rev.Comm. Reports 905 (1984)].

Research References

6 Witkin Cal. Proc. 5th Proceedings Without Trial § 351, (S 351) Development of Estoppel Exception.

6 Witkin Cal. Proc. 5th Proceedings Without Trial § 354, (S 354) Waiver of Right to Dismiss.

6 Witkin Cal. Proc. 5th Proceedings Without Trial § 418, (S 418) Estoppel Against Defendant.

6 Witkin Cal. Proc. 5th Proceedings Without Trial § 420, (S 420) Waiver by Going to Trial.

6 Witkin Cal. Proc. 5th Proceedings Without Trial § 434, in General.

6 Witkin Cal. Proc. 5th Proceedings Without Trial § 437, Estoppel.

§ 583.150. Dismissal or sanction imposed under rule

This chapter does not limit or affect the authority of a court to dismiss an action or impose other sanctions under a rule adopted by the court pursuant to Section 575.1 or by the Judicial Council pursuant to statute, or otherwise under inherent authority of the court. *(Added by Stats.1984, c. 1705, § 5.)*

Law Revision Commission Comments

Section 583.150 makes clear that although this chapter is by its terms limited in scope, it does not affect other law or authority relating to delay in prosecution. See, e.g., Section 575.1 (court rules); Section 583.410 (Judicial Council rules); Blue Chip Enterprises, Inc. v. Brentwood Sav. & Loan Ass'n, 71 Cal.App.3d 706, 139 Cal.Rptr. 651 (1977) (inherent authority). Inherent authority of the court may not be exercised contrary to statute and may not be used to justify a lesser sanction where dismissal is mandated. Sections 583.250 and 583.360 (mandatory dismissal). See, e.g., Weeks v. Roberts, 68 Cal.2d 802, 442 P.2d 361, 69 Cal.Rptr. 305 (1968). This chapter is supplemented by general provisions of law such as the right of the defendant to appear and compel discovery and the right of the defendant to set or advance trial date. [17 Cal.L.Rev.Comm. Reports 905 (1984)].

Research References

Rutter, Cal. Practice Guide: Civ. Pro. Before Trial Ch. 11-B, B. Involuntary Dismissals.

Rutter, Cal. Practice Guide: Civ. Pro. Before Trial Ch. 9(III)-A, A. Sources of Sanctions Power.

6 Witkin Cal. Proc. 5th Proceedings Without Trial § 281, Local Rules.

6 Witkin Cal. Proc. 5th Proceedings Without Trial § 282, Inherent Power of Court.

6 Witkin Cal. Proc. 5th Proceedings Without Trial § 315, (S 315) Governing Law.

§ 583.160. Application of chapter

This chapter applies to a motion for dismissal made in an action commenced before, on, or after the effective date of this chapter, except that in the case of an action commenced before the effective date of this chapter:

(a) A motion for dismissal made pursuant to notice given before, on, or within one year after the effective date of this chapter is governed by the applicable law in effect immediately before the effective date and for this purpose the law in effect immediately before the effective date continues in effect.

(b) This chapter does not affect an order dismissing an action made before the effective date of this chapter. *(Added by Stats.1984, c. 1705, § 5.)*

§ 583.161. Petition for separation or dissolution of marriage, nullity, or termination of domestic partnership, or petition filed under the Uniform Parentage Act; existence of child support, child custody, visitation, or spousal support orders, personal conduct restraining order, or bifurcated case; dismissal prohibited

A petition filed pursuant to Section 299, 2250, 2330, or 7600 of the Family Code shall not be dismissed pursuant to this chapter if any of the following conditions exist:

(a) An order for child support or an order regarding child custody or visitation has been issued in connection with the proceeding and the order has not been (1) terminated by the court or (2) terminated by operation of law pursuant to Sections 3022, 3900, 3901, 4007, and 4013 of the Family Code.

(b) An order for spousal support has been issued in connection with the proceeding and the order has not been terminated by the court.

(c) A personal conduct restraining order has been issued pursuant to the Domestic Violence Prevention Act (Division 10 (commencing with Section 6200) of the Family Code) and the order has not been terminated by operation of law or by the court.

(d) An issue in the case has been bifurcated and one of the following has occurred:

* * * (1) A separate trial * * * has been conducted pursuant to Section 2337 of the Family Code.

(2) A separate trial has been conducted pursuant to the California Rules of Court. *(Added by Stats.1986, c. 366, § 2. Amended by Stats.1992, c. 163 (A.B.2641), § 26, operative Jan. 1, 1994; Stats.1993, c. 219 (A.B.1500), § 65; Stats.1994, c. 1269 (A.B.2208), § 3; Stats.2013, c. 40 (A.B.522), § 1.)*

Law Revision Commission Comments

Section 583.161 is amended to substitute references to the Family Code provisions that replaced the former Civil Code provisions and to conform it to Family Code Section 3601. [23 Cal.L.Rev.Comm. Reports 1 (1993)].

Research References

Rutter, Cal. Practice Guide: Civ. Pro. Before Trial Ch. 11-B, B. Involuntary Dismissals.

Rutter, Cal. Practice Guide: Family Law Ch. 6-A, A. Child Support.

6 Witkin Cal. Proc. 5th Proceedings Without Trial § 317, (S 317) Proceedings for Dissolution or Legal Separation.

6 Witkin Cal. Proc. 5th Proceedings Without Trial § 318, (S 318) Nondissolution Proceedings Involving Child Support Order.

6 Witkin Cal. Proc. 5th Proceedings Without Trial § 363, (S 363) Dissolution or Separation.

6 Witkin Cal. Proc. 5th Proceedings Without Trial § 429, (S 429) After Mistrial or Jury Disagreement.

ARTICLE 2. MANDATORY TIME FOR SERVICE OF SUMMONS

Section

583.210. Time of service of summons and complaint; time for filing proof of service.

583.220. Exceptions; written stipulation; general appearance.

583.230. Extension of time for service.

583.240. Computation of time.

583.250. Failure to make timely service; mandatory nature of article.

§ 583.210. Time of service of summons and complaint; time for filing proof of service

(a) The summons and complaint shall be served upon a defendant within three years after the action is commenced against the defendant. For the purpose of this subdivision, an action is commenced at the time the complaint is filed.

(b) Proof of service of the summons shall be filed within 60 days after the time the summons and complaint must be served upon a defendant. *(Added by Stats.1984, c. 1705, § 5. Amended by Stats.2005, c. 300 (A.B.496), § 4.)*

Research References

Rutter, Cal. Practice Guide: A.D.R. Ch. 5-H, H. Conduct of Arbitration Proceedings.

Rutter, Cal. Practice Guide: Civil Appeals & Writs Ch. 15-B, B. Common Law Writs.

Rutter, Cal. Practice Guide: Civ. Pro. Before Trial Ch. 4-A, A. Requirements-In General.

Rutter, Cal. Practice Guide: Civ. Pro. Before Trial Ch. 4-D, D. Service of Summons.

Rutter, Cal. Practice Guide: Civ. Pro. Before Trial Ch. 4-E, E. Proof of Service of Summons.

Rutter, Cal. Practice Guide: Civ. Pro. Before Trial Ch. 4-F, F. Procedures for Challenging Service of Summons.

Rutter, Cal. Practice Guide: Civ. Pro. Before Trial Ch. 5-G, G. Relief from Default.

Rutter, Cal. Practice Guide: Civ. Pro. Before Trial Ch. 6-B, B. Complaints.

Rutter, Cal. Practice Guide: Civ. Pro. Before Trial Ch. 11-B, B. Involuntary Dismissals.

Rutter, Cal. Practice Guide: Enforcing Judgments/Debts Ch. 6G-12, Enforcement Against Joint Debtors.

Rutter, Cal. Practice Guide: Fed.Civ.Pro. Before Trial Ch. 1-B, B. Federal vs. State Law.

Rutter, Cal. Practice Guide: Fed.Civ.Pro. Before Trial Ch. 5-A, A. General Considerations.

Rutter, Cal. Practice Guide: Fed.Civ.Pro. Before Trial Ch. 5-G, G. Time Limit for Service-"120-Day Dismissal Statute".

Rutter, Cal. Practice Guide: Fed.Civ.Pro. Before Trial Ch. 2D-9, Effect of Removal.

Rutter, Cal. Practice Guide: Personal Injury Ch. 1-B, B. Initial Evaluation of Case: Decision to Accept or Reject Employment or Undertake Further Evaluation of Claim.

Rutter, Cal. Practice Guide: Personal Injury Ch. 5-B, B. When to Sue-Statute of Limitations.

Rutter, Cal. Practice Guide: Personal Injury Ch. 5-C, C. Selected Issues Affecting Parties.

Rutter, Cal. Practice Guide: Personal Injury Ch. 5-E, E. Selected Pleading Issues.

Rutter, Cal. Practice Guide: Personal Injury Ch. 8-A, A. Case Management.

Rutter, Cal. Practice Guide: Personal Injury Ch. 8-B, B. After Trial Date Set (Three to Four Months Before Trial).

Miller and Starr California Real Estate § 27:129, Private Enforcement of False Claims.

3 Witkin Cal. Proc. 5th Actions § 990, (S 990) Proceedings Against Unserved Joint Debtors.

3 Witkin Cal. Proc. 5th Actions § 1065, (S 1065) Nature of Return.

8 Witkin Cal. Proc. 5th Attack Judgment Trial Court § 196, (S 196) in General.

2 Witkin Cal. Proc. 5th Jurisdiction § 192, Definition and Scope of Doctrine.

4 Witkin Cal. Proc. 5th Pleading § 490, Delay in Seeking Amendment.

6 Witkin Cal. Proc. 5th Proceedings Without Trial § 138, Responses Preventing Entry of Default.

6 Witkin Cal. Proc. 5th Proceedings Without Trial § 315, (S 315) Governing Law.

6 Witkin Cal. Proc. 5th Proceedings Without Trial § 319, Authority.

6 Witkin Cal. Proc. 5th Proceedings Without Trial § 322, Service Within 3 Years.

6 Witkin Cal. Proc. 5th Proceedings Without Trial § 323, Return Within 3 Years and 60 Days.

6 Witkin Cal. Proc. 5th Proceedings Without Trial § 324, Agreement for Shorter Time.

6 Witkin Cal. Proc. 5th Proceedings Without Trial § 325, (S 325) General Rule.

6 Witkin Cal. Proc. 5th Proceedings Without Trial § 326, (S 326) Claim Based on Different Operative Facts.

6 Witkin Cal. Proc. 5th Proceedings Without Trial § 330, (S 330) Nature and Scope of Exception.

6 Witkin Cal. Proc. 5th Proceedings Without Trial § 334, Appearance After Period Has Run.

6 Witkin Cal. Proc. 5th Proceedings Without Trial § 343, Amenability to Service Only by Publication.

6 Witkin Cal. Proc. 5th Proceedings Without Trial § 349, Improper Dismissal of Action.

6 Witkin Cal. Proc. 5th Proceedings Without Trial § 356, Ruling on Motion.

6 Witkin Cal. Proc. 5th Proceedings Without Trial § 441, Extensions, Exceptions, and Excuses.

6 Witkin Cal. Proc. 5th Proceedings Without Trial § 444, (S 444) Doe Defendant.

2 Witkin Cal. Summ. 10th Workers' Compensation § 86, (S 86) Action by Employee: Joinder or Intervention by Employer.

§ 583.220. Exceptions; written stipulation; general appearance

The time within which service must be made pursuant to this article does not apply if the defendant enters into a stipulation in writing or does another act that constitutes a general appearance in the action. For the purpose of this section none of the following constitutes a general appearance in the action:

(a) A stipulation pursuant to Section 583.230 extending the time within which service must be made.

(b) A motion to dismiss made pursuant to this chapter, whether joined with a motion to quash service or a motion to set aside a default judgment, or otherwise.

(c) An extension of time to plead after a motion to dismiss made pursuant to this chapter. *(Added by Stats.1984, c. 1705, § 5.)*

Law Revision Commission Comments

Section 583.220 continues the substance of the last portion of subdivisions (a) and (b) and subdivision (e) of former Section 581a. It adopts case law that a defendant may make a general appearance for the purpose of this section by an act outside the record that shows an intent to submit to the general jurisdiction of the court. See, e.g., General Ins. Co. v. Superior Court, 15 Cal.3d 449, 541 P.2d 289, 124 Cal.Rptr. 745 (1975) (stipulation). However, the combination of a motion to dismiss with other relevant motions does not constitute a general appearance. See, e.g., Dresser v. Superior Court, 231 Cal.App.2d 68, 41 Cal.Rptr. 473 (1964) (motion to quash and dismiss); Pease v. City of San Diego, 93 Cal.App.2d 706, 209 P.2d 843 (1949) (motion to set aside default judgment and dismiss). For other acts constituting a general appearance, see Sections 396b and 1014. Section 583.220 applies to a cross-defendant only to the extent the cross-defendant has made a general appearance for the purposes of the cross-complaint. See Section 583.110 ("action" and "defendant" defined). [17 Cal.L.Rev.Comm. Reports 905 (1984)].

Research References

Rutter, Cal. Practice Guide: Civ. Pro. Before Trial Ch. 4-F, F. Procedures for Challenging Service of Summons.

Rutter, Cal. Practice Guide: Civ. Pro. Before Trial Ch. 11-B, B. Involuntary Dismissals.

2 Witkin Cal. Proc. 5th Jurisdiction § 229, Motion to Dismiss for Failure to Return Summons.

6 Witkin Cal. Proc. 5th Proceedings Without Trial § 319, Authority.

6 Witkin Cal. Proc. 5th Proceedings Without Trial § 329, Statutory Basis.

6 Witkin Cal. Proc. 5th Proceedings Without Trial § 330, (S 330) Nature and Scope of Exception.

6 Witkin Cal. Proc. 5th Proceedings Without Trial § 331, Motion to Dismiss for Delay in Prosecution.

6 Witkin Cal. Proc. 5th Proceedings Without Trial § 332, Extension of Time to Plead.

6 Witkin Cal. Proc. 5th Proceedings Without Trial § 337, Other Acts.

6 Witkin Cal. Proc. 5th Proceedings Without Trial § 338, Stipulation Extending Time for Service.

§ 583.230. Extension of time for service

The parties may extend the time within which service must be made pursuant to this article by the following means:

(a) By written stipulation. The stipulation need not be filed but, if it is not filed, the stipulation shall be brought to the attention of the court if relevant to a motion for dismissal.

(b) By oral agreement made in open court, if entered in the minutes of the court or a transcript is made. *(Added by Stats.1984, c. 1705, § 5.)*

Law Revision Commission Comments

Subdivision (a) of Section 583.230 is drawn from the last portion of subdivisions (a) and (b) of former Section 581a. The requirement that the stipulation be filed is not continued; it was unduly restrictive.

Subdivision (b) is consistent with Section 583.330(b) (extension of time). [17 Cal.L.Rev.Comm. Reports 905 (1984)].

Research References

Rutter, Cal. Practice Guide: Civ. Pro. Before Trial Ch. 11-B, B. Involuntary Dismissals.
6 Witkin Cal. Proc. 5th Proceedings Without Trial § 319, Authority.
6 Witkin Cal. Proc. 5th Proceedings Without Trial § 329, Statutory Basis.
6 Witkin Cal. Proc. 5th Proceedings Without Trial § 337, Other Acts.
6 Witkin Cal. Proc. 5th Proceedings Without Trial § 338, Stipulation Extending Time for Service.
6 Witkin Cal. Proc. 5th Proceedings Without Trial § 441, Extensions, Exceptions, and Excuses.

§ 583.240. Computation of time

In computing the time within which service must be made pursuant to this article, there shall be excluded the time during which any of the following conditions existed:

(a) The defendant was not amenable to the process of the court.

(b) The prosecution of the action or proceedings in the action was stayed and the stay affected service.

(c) The validity of service was the subject of litigation by the parties.

(d) Service, for any other reason, was impossible, impracticable, or futile due to causes beyond the plaintiff's control. Failure to discover relevant facts or evidence is not a cause beyond the plaintiff's control for the purpose of this subdivision. *(Added by Stats.1984, c. 1705, § 5.)*

Law Revision Commission Comments

Subdivision (a) of Section 583.240 continues the substance of subdivision (d) of former Section 581a. Subdivision (b) is based on an exception to the three-year service period stated in appellate decisions. Subdivision (c) is new; it applies where the person to be served is aware of the action but challenges jurisdiction of the court or sufficiency of service.

Subdivision (d) continues the substance of subdivision (f)(2) of former Section 581a. It is based on appellate decisions, but it also makes clear that there is only an excuse for causes beyond the plaintiff's control and that failure to discover relevant facts or evidence does not excuse compliance. This overrules Hocharian v. Superior Court, 28 Cal.3d 714, 621 P.2d 829, 170 Cal.Rptr. 790 (1981). The excuse of impossibility, impracticability, or futility should be strictly construed in light of the need to give a defendant adequate notice of the action so that the defendant can take necessary steps to preserve evidence. Contrast Section 583.340 and Comment thereto (liberal construction of excuse for failure to bring to trial within a prescribed time). This difference in treatment is consistent with one aspect of the policy announced in Section 583.130—plaintiff must exercise diligence—and recognizes that service, unlike bringing to trial, is ordinarily within the control of the plaintiff. [17 Cal.L.Rev.Comm. Reports 905 (1984)].

Research References

Rutter, Cal. Practice Guide: Civ. Pro. Before Trial Ch. 4-D, D. Service of Summons.
Rutter, Cal. Practice Guide: Civ. Pro. Before Trial Ch. 11-B, B. Involuntary Dismissals.
21 NO. 1 Miller & Starr, California Real Estate Newsalert 23, Subdivisions, Land Use Planning, and Approvals.
6 Witkin Cal. Proc. 5th Proceedings Without Trial § 339, Statutory Development.
6 Witkin Cal. Proc. 5th Proceedings Without Trial § 342, Marriage or Death of Defendant.
6 Witkin Cal. Proc. 5th Proceedings Without Trial § 343, Amenability to Service Only by Publication.
6 Witkin Cal. Proc. 5th Proceedings Without Trial § 344, (S 344) Stay Affecting Service.
6 Witkin Cal. Proc. 5th Proceedings Without Trial § 345, (S 345) Validity of Service Disputed.
6 Witkin Cal. Proc. 5th Proceedings Without Trial § 346, Judicial Rule and Codification.
6 Witkin Cal. Proc. 5th Proceedings Without Trial § 347, Strict Construction.
6 Witkin Cal. Proc. 5th Proceedings Without Trial § 349, Improper Dismissal of Action.
6 Witkin Cal. Proc. 5th Proceedings Without Trial § 350, Other Illustrations of Strict Construction.
6 Witkin Cal. Proc. 5th Proceedings Without Trial § 396, Codification of Exceptions.
6 Witkin Cal. Proc. 5th Proceedings Without Trial § 407, Defendant Not Amendable to Process.
6 Witkin Cal. Proc. 5th Proceedings Without Trial § 441, Extensions, Exceptions, and Excuses.

§ 583.250. Failure to make timely service; mandatory nature of article

(a) If service is not made in an action within the time prescribed in this article:

(1) The action shall not be further prosecuted and no further proceedings shall be held in the action.

(2) The action shall be dismissed by the court on its own motion or on motion of any person interested in the action, whether named as a party or not, after notice to the parties.

(b) The requirements of this article are mandatory and are not subject to extension, excuse, or exception except as expressly provided by statute. *(Added by Stats.1984, c. 1705, § 5.)*

Research References

Rutter, Cal. Practice Guide: Civ. Pro. Before Trial Ch. 4-A, A. Requirements-In General.
Rutter, Cal. Practice Guide: Civ. Pro. Before Trial Ch. 4-D, D. Service of Summons.
Rutter, Cal. Practice Guide: Civ. Pro. Before Trial Ch. 5-B, B. Entry of Default.
Rutter, Cal. Practice Guide: Civ. Pro. Before Trial Ch. 5-G, G. Relief from Default.
Rutter, Cal. Practice Guide: Civ. Pro. Before Trial Ch. 11-B, B. Involuntary Dismissals.
Rutter, Cal. Practice Guide: Fed.Civ.Pro. Before Trial Ch. 1-D, D. Choosing Between State and Federal Courts.
Rutter, Cal. Practice Guide: Fed.Civ.Pro. Before Trial Ch. 5-A, A. General Considerations.
Rutter, Cal. Practice Guide: Fed.Civ.Pro. Before Trial Ch. 5-G, G. Time Limit for Service-"120-Day Dismissal Statute".
Rutter, Cal. Practice Guide: Personal Injury Ch. 5-B, B. When to Sue-Statute of Limitations.
2 Witkin Cal. Proc. 5th Jurisdiction § 91, (S 91) Violation of Jurisdictional Time Limit.
2 Witkin Cal. Proc. 5th Jurisdiction § 229, Motion to Dismiss for Failure to Return Summons.
2 Witkin Cal. Proc. 5th Jurisdiction § 233, Objection to Interrogatories.
4 Witkin Cal. Proc. 5th Pleading § 7, (S 7) Time Prescribed by Statute.
6 Witkin Cal. Proc. 5th Proceedings Without Trial § 148, Default After Denial of Motions.
6 Witkin Cal. Proc. 5th Proceedings Without Trial § 319, Authority.
6 Witkin Cal. Proc. 5th Proceedings Without Trial § 321, Scope of Statute.
6 Witkin Cal. Proc. 5th Proceedings Without Trial § 329, Statutory Basis.
6 Witkin Cal. Proc. 5th Proceedings Without Trial § 355, Motion to Dismiss.
6 Witkin Cal. Proc. 5th Proceedings Without Trial § 356, Ruling on Motion.
6 Witkin Cal. Proc. 5th Proceedings Without Trial § 357, Effect of Dismissal.
8 Witkin, California Summary 10th Constitutional Law § 1207, Process.
2 Witkin Cal. Summ. 10th Workers' Compensation § 86, (S 86) Action by Employee: Joinder or Intervention by Employer.

ARTICLE 3. MANDATORY TIME FOR BRINGING ACTION TO TRIAL OR NEW TRIAL

Section

583.330. Extension of time.
583.340. Computation of time.
583.350. Tolling or extension of time resulting in less than six months to bring action.
583.360. Dismissal on motion of court or defendant; mandatory nature of article.

§ 583.310. Time to bring action to trial

An action shall be brought to trial within five years after the action is commenced against the defendant. *(Added by Stats. 1984, c. 1705, § 5.)*

Law Revision Commission Comments

Section 583.310 is drawn from a portion of subdivision (b) of former Section 583. For exceptions and exclusions, see Sections 583.330 (extension of time) and 583.340 (computation of time). [17 Cal.L.Rev. Comm. Reports 905 (1984)].

Research References

Rutter, Cal. Practice Guide: A.D.R. Ch. 4-B, B. Judicial Arbitration.
Rutter, Cal. Practice Guide: A.D.R. Ch. 5-D, D. Defenses to Enforcement.
Rutter, Cal. Practice Guide: A.D.R. Ch. 5-G, G. Procedures to Enforce Arbitration.
Rutter, Cal. Practice Guide: A.D.R. Ch. 5-H, H. Conduct of Arbitration Proceedings.
Rutter, Cal. Practice Guide: Civil Appeals & Writs Ch. 2-C, C. Nonappealable Orders.
Rutter, Cal. Practice Guide: Civil Appeals & Writs Ch. 7-A, A. Overview.
Rutter, Cal. Practice Guide: Civil Appeals & Writs Ch. 8-C, C. Standards of Appellate Review.
Rutter, Cal. Practice Guide: Civil Appeals & Writs Ch. 14-C, C. Trial Court Proceedings After Reversal.
Rutter, Cal. Practice Guide: Civil Appeals & Writs Ch. 15-B, B. Common Law Writs.
Rutter, Cal. Practice Guide: Civ. Pro. Before Trial Ch. 5-A, A. General.
Rutter, Cal. Practice Guide: Civ. Pro. Before Trial Ch. 6-D, D. Cross-Complaint.
Rutter, Cal. Practice Guide: Civ. Pro. Before Trial Ch. 11-B, B. Involuntary Dismissals.
Rutter, Cal. Practice Guide: Civ. Pro. Before Trial Ch. 13-G, G. Trial De Novo.
Rutter, Cal. Practice Guide: Civ. Pro. Before Trial Ch. 11-B, Outline B.
Rutter, Cal. Practice Guide: Civ. Pro. Before Trial Ch. 12(II)-D, D. Plaintiff's Duties Upon Settlement.
Rutter, Cal. Practice Guide: Civil Trials & Evidence Ch. 1-A, A. Importance of Statewide and Local Rules of Court.
Rutter, Cal. Practice Guide: Civil Trials & Evidence Ch. 1-J, J. Notice of Trial.
Rutter, Cal. Practice Guide: Civil Trials & Evidence Ch. 3-B, B. Peremptory Challenge of Judge (CCP § 170.6).
Rutter, Cal. Practice Guide: Family Law Ch. 6-A, A. Child Support.
Rutter, Cal. Practice Guide: Fed.Civ.Pro. Before Trial Ch. 1-D, D. Choosing Between State and Federal Courts.
Rutter, Cal. Practice Guide: Personal Injury Ch. 3-G, G. Independent Damages Claims.
Rutter, Cal. Practice Guide: Personal Injury Ch. 4-F, F. Court-Conducted Settlement Proceedings.
Rutter, Cal. Practice Guide: Personal Injury Ch. 4-G, G. Concluding and Enforcing Settlement.
Rutter, Cal. Practice Guide: Personal Injury Ch. 5-B, B. When to Sue-Statute of Limitations.
Rutter, Cal. Practice Guide: Personal Injury Ch. 5-E, E. Selected Pleading Issues.
Rutter, Cal. Practice Guide: Personal Injury Ch. 7-B, B. Tactical Considerations-Pros and Cons of Judicial Arbitration.
Rutter, Cal. Practice Guide: Personal Injury Ch. 7-I, I. Trial De Novo After Arbitration Award.
Rutter, Cal. Practice Guide: Personal Injury Ch. 8-A, A. Case Management.
Rutter, Cal. Practice Guide: Personal Injury Ch. 4-G, Outline G.
Rutter, Cal. Practice Guide: Prof. Responsibility Ch. 5-K, K. Fee Recovery/Enforcing Fee Agreements.

Rutter, Cal. Practice Guide: Prof. Responsibility Ch. 6-D, D. Professional Liability.
Miller and Starr California Real Estate § 35:13, Procedural Aspects of Civil Action Mediation.
21 NO. 4 Miller & Starr, California Real Estate Newsalert 32, Inverse Condemnation.
3 Witkin Cal. Proc. 5th Actions § 639, (S 639) Conflicting Decisions in Courts of Appeal.
3 Witkin Cal. Proc. 5th Actions § 641, (S 641) Illustrations.
3 Witkin Cal. Proc. 5th Actions § 709, Disability of Attorney.
8 Witkin Cal. Proc. 5th Attack Judgment Trial Court § 147, (S 147) in General.
8 Witkin Cal. Proc. 5th Attack Judgment Trial Court § 192, (S 192) Governing Provisions.
8 Witkin Cal. Proc. 5th Attack Judgment Trial Court § 196, (S 196) in General.
2 Witkin Cal. Proc. 5th Courts § 348, (S 348) Nature of Position.
4 Witkin Cal. Proc. 5th Pleading § 362, Stay Pending Determination.
5 Witkin Cal. Proc. 5th Pleading § 1180, Relief from Failure to Plead.
5 Witkin Cal. Proc. 5th Pleading § 1188, (S 1188) Statute of Limitations and Dismissal.
6 Witkin Cal. Proc. 5th Proceedings Without Trial § 315, (S 315) Governing Law.
6 Witkin Cal. Proc. 5th Proceedings Without Trial § 317, (S 317) Proceedings for Dissolution or Legal Separation.
6 Witkin Cal. Proc. 5th Proceedings Without Trial § 358, Statutory Framework.
6 Witkin Cal. Proc. 5th Proceedings Without Trial § 362, (S 362) Coordinated Actions.
6 Witkin Cal. Proc. 5th Proceedings Without Trial § 369, 5-Year Period.
6 Witkin Cal. Proc. 5th Proceedings Without Trial § 370, (S 370) in General.
6 Witkin Cal. Proc. 5th Proceedings Without Trial § 371, (S 371) Addition of New Parties.
6 Witkin Cal. Proc. 5th Proceedings Without Trial § 374, (S 374) in General.
6 Witkin Cal. Proc. 5th Proceedings Without Trial § 413, in General.
6 Witkin Cal. Proc. 5th Proceedings Without Trial § 416, Plaintiff's Duty to Monitor Resetting.
6 Witkin Cal. Proc. 5th Proceedings Without Trial § 423, Extension Where Less Than 6 Months Remain.
6 Witkin Cal. Proc. 5th Proceedings Without Trial § 428, (S 428) in General.
6 Witkin Cal. Proc. 5th Proceedings Without Trial § 432, Judgment Reversed With Remand for New Trial.
6 Witkin Cal. Proc. 5th Proceedings Without Trial § 434, in General.
6 Witkin Cal. Proc. 5th Proceedings Without Trial § 441, Extensions, Exceptions, and Excuses.
6 Witkin Cal. Proc. 5th Proceedings Without Trial § 490, Time for Mediation.
6 Witkin Cal. Proc. 5th Proceedings Without Trial § 587, Effect of Submission.
10 Witkin, California Summary 10th Parent and Child § 385, Support During Action.
7 Witkin, California Summary 10th Constitutional Law § 631, Efficient Remedy Must be Left.

§ 583.320. New trial; time to bring action to trial

(a) If a new trial is granted in the action the action shall again be brought to trial within the following times:

(1) If a trial is commenced but no judgment is entered because of a mistrial or because a jury is unable to reach a decision, within three years after the order of the court declaring the mistrial or the disagreement of the jury is entered.

(2) If after judgment a new trial is granted and no appeal is taken, within three years after the order granting the new trial is entered.

(3) If on appeal an order granting a new trial is affirmed or a judgment is reversed and the action remanded for a new trial, within three years after the remittitur is filed by the clerk of the trial court.

Civ. Pro.

(b) Nothing in this section requires that an action again be brought to trial before expiration of the time prescribed in Section 583.310. *(Added by Stats.1984, c. 1705, § 5.)*

Law Revision Commission Comments

Section 583.320 is drawn from portions of subdivisions (c) and (d) of former Section 583. For exceptions and exclusions, see Sections 583.330 (extension of time) and 583.340 (computation of time). [17 Cal.L.Rev. Comm. Reports 905 (1984)].

Research References

Rutter, Cal. Practice Guide: Civil Appeals & Writs Ch. 14-A, A. Remittitur.
Rutter, Cal. Practice Guide: Civil Appeals & Writs Ch. 14-C, C. Trial Court Proceedings After Reversal.
Rutter, Cal. Practice Guide: Civ. Pro. Before Trial Ch. 11-B, B. Involuntary Dismissals.
Rutter, Cal. Practice Guide: Personal Injury Ch. 5-B, B. When to Sue-Statute of Limitations.
6 Witkin Cal. Proc. 5th Proceedings Without Trial § 428, (S 428) in General.
6 Witkin Cal. Proc. 5th Proceedings Without Trial § 429, (S 429) After Mistrial or Jury Disagreement.
6 Witkin Cal. Proc. 5th Proceedings Without Trial § 430, (S 430) After New Trial is Granted.
6 Witkin Cal. Proc. 5th Proceedings Without Trial § 431, Order Granting New Trial.
6 Witkin Cal. Proc. 5th Proceedings Without Trial § 432, Judgment Reversed With Remand for New Trial.
6 Witkin Cal. Proc. 5th Proceedings Without Trial § 433, Distinction: Judgment Reversed Without Remand for New Trial.
6 Witkin Cal. Proc. 5th Proceedings Without Trial § 434, in General.
6 Witkin Cal. Proc. 5th Proceedings Without Trial § 436, (S 436) Requirement of Reasonable Diligence.
6 Witkin Cal. Proc. 5th Proceedings Without Trial § 437, Estoppel.

§ 583.330. Extension of time

The parties may extend the time within which an action must be brought to trial pursuant to this article by the following means:

(a) By written stipulation. The stipulation need not be filed but, if it is not filed, the stipulation shall be brought to the attention of the court if relevant to a motion for dismissal.

(b) By oral agreement made in open court, if entered in the minutes of the court or a transcript is made. *(Added by Stats.1984, c. 1705, § 5.)*

Law Revision Commission Comments

Subdivision (a) of Section 583.330 continues the substance of portions of subdivisions (c) and (d) of former Section 583, and extends to actions in which there has been an appeal. This overrules prior case law. See, e.g., cases cited in Good v. State, 273 Cal.App.2d 587, 590, 78 Cal.Rptr. 316 (1969). The requirement that the stipulation be filed is not continued; it was unduly restrictive. Subdivision (b) codifies existing case law. See, e.g., Govea v. Superior Court, 26 Cal.App.2d 27, 78 P.2d 433 (1938); Preiss v. Good Samaritan Hospital, 171 Cal.App.2d 559, 340 P.2d 661 (1959). [17 Cal.L.Rev.Comm. Reports 905 (1984)].

Research References

Rutter, Cal. Practice Guide: Civil Appeals & Writs Ch. 14-C, C. Trial Court Proceedings After Reversal.
Rutter, Cal. Practice Guide: Civ. Pro. Before Trial Ch. 11-B, B. Involuntary Dismissals.
6 Witkin Cal. Proc. 5th Proceedings Without Trial § 382, (S 382) in General.
6 Witkin Cal. Proc. 5th Proceedings Without Trial § 428, (S 428) in General.
6 Witkin Cal. Proc. 5th Proceedings Without Trial § 433, Distinction: Judgment Reversed Without Remand for New Trial.
6 Witkin Cal. Proc. 5th Proceedings Without Trial § 434, in General.
6 Witkin Cal. Proc. 5th Proceedings Without Trial § 437, Estoppel.

6 Witkin Cal. Proc. 5th Proceedings Without Trial § 441, Extensions, Exceptions, and Excuses.

§ 583.340. Computation of time

In computing the time within which an action must be brought to trial pursuant to this article, there shall be excluded the time during which any of the following conditions existed:

(a) The jurisdiction of the court to try the action was suspended.

(b) Prosecution or trial of the action was stayed or enjoined.

(c) Bringing the action to trial, for any other reason, was impossible, impracticable, or futile. *(Added by Stats.1984, c. 1705, § 5.)*

Law Revision Commission Comments

Subdivision (a) of Section 583.340 continues the substance of the last portion of subdivision (f) of former Section 583. Subdivision (b) codifies existing case law. See, e.g., Marcus v. Superior Court, 75 Cal.App.3d 204, 141 Cal.Rptr. 890 (1977).

Subdivision (c) codifies the case law "impossible, impractical, or futile" standard. The provisions of subdivision (c) must be interpreted liberally, consistent with the policy favoring trial on the merits. See Section 583.130 (policy statement). Contrast Section 583.240 and Comment thereto (strict construction of excuse for failure to serve within prescribed time). This difference in treatment recognizes that bringing an action to trial, unlike service, may be impossible, impracticable, or futile due to factors not reasonably within the control of the plaintiff.

Under Section 583.340 the time within which an action must be brought to trial is tolled for the period of the excuse, regardless whether a reasonable time remained at the end of the period of the excuse to bring the action to trial. This overrules cases such as State of California v. Superior Court, 98 Cal.App.3d 643, 159 Cal.Rptr. 650 (1979), and Brown v. Superior Court, 62 Cal.App.3d 197, 132 Cal.Rptr. 916 (1976). [17 Cal.L.Rev.Comm. Reports 905 (1984)].

Research References

Rutter, Cal. Practice Guide: A.D.R. Ch. 5-G, G. Procedures to Enforce Arbitration.
Rutter, Cal. Practice Guide: Civil Appeals & Writs Ch. 7-A, A. Overview.
Rutter, Cal. Practice Guide: Civil Appeals & Writs Ch. 8-C, C. Standards of Appellate Review.
Rutter, Cal. Practice Guide: Civil Appeals & Writs Ch. 14-C, C. Trial Court Proceedings After Reversal.
Rutter, Cal. Practice Guide: Civ. Pro. Before Trial Ch. 5-G, G. Relief from Default.
Rutter, Cal. Practice Guide: Civ. Pro. Before Trial Ch. 11-B, B. Involuntary Dismissals.
Rutter, Cal. Practice Guide: Civil Trials & Evidence Ch. 2-D, D. Securing Trial by Jury.
Rutter, Cal. Practice Guide: Civil Trials & Evidence Ch. 3-B, B. Peremptory Challenge of Judge (CCP § 170.6).
Rutter, Cal. Practice Guide: Personal Injury Ch. 4-F, F. Court-Conducted Settlement Proceedings.
Rutter, Cal. Practice Guide: Personal Injury Ch. 5-B, B. When to Sue-Statute of Limitations.
Miller and Starr California Real Estate § 35:62, Effect of Five-Year Period to Bring Litigation to Trial.
3 Witkin Cal. Proc. 5th Actions § 641, (S 641) Illustrations.
6 Witkin Cal. Proc. 5th Proceedings Without Trial § 347, Strict Construction.
6 Witkin Cal. Proc. 5th Proceedings Without Trial § 389, in General.
6 Witkin Cal. Proc. 5th Proceedings Without Trial § 392, Tolling on Transfer for Lack of Jurisdiction.
6 Witkin Cal. Proc. 5th Proceedings Without Trial § 393, in General.
6 Witkin Cal. Proc. 5th Proceedings Without Trial § 396, Codification of Exceptions.
6 Witkin Cal. Proc. 5th Proceedings Without Trial § 400, Duration of Tolling.
6 Witkin Cal. Proc. 5th Proceedings Without Trial § 403, Death or Illness.
6 Witkin Cal. Proc. 5th Proceedings Without Trial § 405, Interlocutory Review.
6 Witkin Cal. Proc. 5th Proceedings Without Trial § 407, Defendant Not Amendable to Process.

6 Witkin Cal. Proc. 5th Proceedings Without Trial § 412, (S 412) Submission to Contractual Arbitration.

6 Witkin Cal. Proc. 5th Proceedings Without Trial § 417, Impracticability and Diligence.

6 Witkin Cal. Proc. 5th Proceedings Without Trial § 422, (S 422) Compromise Agreement.

6 Witkin Cal. Proc. 5th Proceedings Without Trial § 434, in General.

6 Witkin Cal. Proc. 5th Proceedings Without Trial § 435, (S 435) in General.

6 Witkin Cal. Proc. 5th Proceedings Without Trial § 441, Extensions, Exceptions, and Excuses.

§ 583.350. Tolling or extension of time resulting in less than six months to bring action

If the time within which an action must be brought to trial pursuant to this article is tolled or otherwise extended pursuant to statute with the result that at the end of the period of tolling or extension less than six months remains within which the action must be brought to trial, the action shall not be dismissed pursuant to this article if the action is brought to trial within six months after the end of the period of tolling or extension. *(Added by Stats.1984, c. 1705, § 5.)*

Research References

Rutter, Cal. Practice Guide: Civil Appeals & Writs Ch. 14-C, C. Trial Court Proceedings After Reversal.

Rutter, Cal. Practice Guide: Civ. Pro. Before Trial Ch. 11-B, B. Involuntary Dismissals.

6 Witkin Cal. Proc. 5th Proceedings Without Trial § 317, (S 317) Proceedings for Dissolution or Legal Separation.

6 Witkin Cal. Proc. 5th Proceedings Without Trial § 399, Diligence.

6 Witkin Cal. Proc. 5th Proceedings Without Trial § 405, Interlocutory Review.

6 Witkin Cal. Proc. 5th Proceedings Without Trial § 423, Extension Where Less Than 6 Months Remain.

6 Witkin Cal. Proc. 5th Proceedings Without Trial § 431, Order Granting New Trial.

6 Witkin Cal. Proc. 5th Proceedings Without Trial § 432, Judgment Reversed With Remand for New Trial.

6 Witkin Cal. Proc. 5th Proceedings Without Trial § 434, in General.

§ 583.360. Dismissal on motion of court or defendant; mandatory nature of article

(a) An action shall be dismissed by the court on its own motion or on motion of the defendant, after notice to the parties, if the action is not brought to trial within the time prescribed in this article.

(b) The requirements of this article are mandatory and are not subject to extension, excuse, or exception except as expressly provided by statute. *(Added by Stats.1984, c. 1705, § 5.)*

Law Revision Commission Comments

Subdivision (a) of Section 583.360 continues the substance of portions of subdivisions (b), (c), and (d) of former Section 583, with the exception of the references to due notice to the plaintiff, which duplicated general provisions. See Sections 1005 and 1005.5 (notice of motion). Subdivision (b) is consistent with subdivision (b) of Section 583.250 (mandatory dismissal for failure to serve summons). [17 Cal.L.Rev.Comm. Reports 905 (1984)].

Research References

Rutter, Cal. Practice Guide: A.D.R. Ch. 4-B, B. Judicial Arbitration.

Rutter, Cal. Practice Guide: A.D.R. Ch. 5-D, D. Defenses to Enforcement.

Rutter, Cal. Practice Guide: A.D.R. Ch. 5-G, G. Procedures to Enforce Arbitration.

Rutter, Cal. Practice Guide: A.D.R. Ch. 5-H, H. Conduct of Arbitration Proceedings.

Rutter, Cal. Practice Guide: Civil Appeals & Writs Ch. 8-C, C. Standards of Appellate Review.

Rutter, Cal. Practice Guide: Civil Appeals & Writs Ch. 14-C, C. Trial Court Proceedings After Reversal.

Rutter, Cal. Practice Guide: Civil Appeals & Writs Ch. 15-B, B. Common Law Writs.

Rutter, Cal. Practice Guide: Civ. Pro. Before Trial Ch. 11-B, B. Involuntary Dismissals.

Rutter, Cal. Practice Guide: Civ. Pro. Before Trial Ch. 13-G, G. Trial De Novo.

Rutter, Cal. Practice Guide: Personal Injury Ch. 5-B, B. When to Sue-Statute of Limitations.

Rutter, Cal. Practice Guide: Personal Injury Ch. 7-I, I. Trial De Novo After Arbitration Award.

Rutter, Cal. Practice Guide: Prof. Responsibility Ch. 5-K, K. Fee Recovery/Enforcing Fee Agreements.

Miller and Starr California Real Estate § 35:62, Effect of Five-Year Period to Bring Litigation to Trial.

21 NO. 4 Miller & Starr, California Real Estate Newsalert 32, Inverse Condemnation.

2 Witkin Cal. Proc. 5th Jurisdiction § 91, (S 91) Violation of Jurisdictional Time Limit.

2 Witkin Cal. Proc. 5th Jurisdiction § 228, Motion to Dismiss for Lack of Prosecution.

6 Witkin Cal. Proc. 5th Proceedings Without Trial § 358, Statutory Framework.

6 Witkin Cal. Proc. 5th Proceedings Without Trial § 364, Motion to Dismiss.

6 Witkin Cal. Proc. 5th Proceedings Without Trial § 365, Ruling on Motion.

6 Witkin Cal. Proc. 5th Proceedings Without Trial § 369, 5-Year Period.

6 Witkin Cal. Proc. 5th Proceedings Without Trial § 374, (S 374) in General.

6 Witkin Cal. Proc. 5th Proceedings Without Trial § 376, Impanelment.

6 Witkin Cal. Proc. 5th Proceedings Without Trial § 392, Tolling on Transfer for Lack of Jurisdiction.

6 Witkin Cal. Proc. 5th Proceedings Without Trial § 428, (S 428) in General.

10 Witkin, California Summary 10th Parent and Child § 385, Support During Action.

ARTICLE 4. DISCRETIONARY DISMISSAL FOR DELAY

Section

583.410.   Discretion to dismiss under appropriate circumstances; procedure.

583.420.   Grounds for dismissal; computation of time.

583.430.   Conditions for dismissal; orders.

§ 583.410. Discretion to dismiss under appropriate circumstances; procedure

(a) The court may in its discretion dismiss an action for delay in prosecution pursuant to this article on its own motion or on motion of the defendant if to do so appears to the court appropriate under the circumstances of the case.

(b) Dismissal shall be pursuant to the procedure and in accordance with the criteria prescribed by rules adopted by the Judicial Council. *(Added by Stats.1984, c. 1705, § 5.)*

Law Revision Commission Comments

Section 583.410 continues the substance of subdivision (a) of former Section 583. It makes clear the authority of the Judicial Council to prescribe criteria. See subdivision (e) of Rule 203.5 of the California Rules of Court (matters considered by court in ruling on motion). [17 Cal.L.Rev.Comm. Reports 905 (1984)].

Research References

Rutter, Cal. Practice Guide: A.D.R. Ch. 4-B, B. Judicial Arbitration.

Rutter, Cal. Practice Guide: Civil Appeals & Writs Ch. 8-C, C. Standards of Appellate Review.

Rutter, Cal. Practice Guide: Civil Appeals & Writs Ch. 14-C, C. Trial Court Proceedings After Reversal.

Rutter, Cal. Practice Guide: Civ. Pro. Before Trial Ch. 4-D, D. Service of Summons.

Rutter, Cal. Practice Guide: Civ. Pro. Before Trial Ch. 5-G, G. Relief from Default.

Rutter, Cal. Practice Guide: Civ. Pro. Before Trial Ch. 11-B, B. Involuntary Dismissals.

Rutter, Cal. Practice Guide: Civ. Pro. Before Trial Ch. 13-C, C. Civil Proceedings Subject to Judicial Arbitration.

Rutter, Cal. Practice Guide: Civ. Pro. Before Trial Ch. 13-G, G. Trial De Novo.

Rutter, Cal. Practice Guide: Civ. Pro. Before Trial Ch. 8D-1, Discovery Plan-Reasons for Plan.

Rutter, Cal. Practice Guide: Civ. Pro. Before Trial Ch. 9(I)-F, F. Ex Parte Motions.

Rutter, Cal. Practice Guide: Civ. Pro. Before Trial Ch. 11-B, Outline B.

Rutter, Cal. Practice Guide: Personal Injury Ch. 5-C, C. Selected Issues Affecting Parties.

Rutter, Cal. Practice Guide: Personal Injury Ch. 7-I, I. Trial De Novo After Arbitration Award.

Rutter, Cal. Practice Guide: Personal Injury Ch. 8-A, A. Case Management.

Miller and Starr California Real Estate § 35:48, Hearing and Order on the Petition.

9 Witkin Cal. Proc. 5th Appeal § 163, (S 163) Notice of Ruling.

8 Witkin Cal. Proc. 5th Attack Judgment Trial Court § 196, (S 196) in General.

6 Witkin Cal. Proc. 5th Proceedings Without Trial § 315, (S 315) Governing Law.

6 Witkin Cal. Proc. 5th Proceedings Without Trial § 416, Plaintiff's Duty to Monitor Resetting.

6 Witkin Cal. Proc. 5th Proceedings Without Trial § 438, Power to Dismiss.

6 Witkin Cal. Proc. 5th Proceedings Without Trial § 439, Criteria Governing Exercise of Discretion.

6 Witkin Cal. Proc. 5th Proceedings Without Trial § 440, Premature Dismissal is Improper.

6 Witkin Cal. Proc. 5th Proceedings Without Trial § 458, Effect of Trial Preference.

6 Witkin Cal. Proc. 5th Proceedings Without Trial § 468, (S 468) Absent or Incorrect Statement of Grounds.

6 Witkin Cal. Proc. 5th Proceedings Without Trial § 469, (S 469) in General.

6 Witkin Cal. Proc. 5th Proceedings Without Trial § 472, (S 472) Relief Under.

7 Witkin Cal. Proc. 5th Trial § 70, (S 70) Party Under Age 14.

2 Witkin Cal. Summ. 10th Workers' Compensation § 85, (S 85) Action by Employer: Intervention by Employee.

§ 583.420. Grounds for dismissal; computation of time

(a) The court may not dismiss an action pursuant to this article for delay in prosecution except after one of the following conditions has occurred:

(1) Service is not made within two years after the action is commenced against the defendant.

(2) The action is not brought to trial within the following times:

(A) Three years after the action is commenced against the defendant unless otherwise prescribed by rule under subparagraph (B).

(B) Two years after the action is commenced against the defendant if the Judicial Council by rule adopted pursuant to Section 583.410 so prescribes for the court because of the condition of the court calendar or for other reasons affecting the conduct of litigation or the administration of justice.

(3) A new trial is granted and the action is not again brought to trial within the following times:

(A) If a trial is commenced but no judgment is entered because of a mistrial or because a jury is unable to reach a decision, within two years after the order of the court declaring the mistrial or the disagreement of the jury is entered.

(B) If after judgment a new trial is granted and no appeal is taken, within two years after the order granting the new trial is entered.

(C) If on appeal an order granting a new trial is affirmed or a judgment is reversed and the action remanded for a new trial,

within two years after the remittitur is filed by the clerk of the trial court.

(b) The times provided in subdivision (a) shall be computed in the manner provided for computation of the comparable times under Articles 2 (commencing with Section 583.210) and 3 (commencing with Section 583.310). *(Added by Stats.1984, c. 1705, § 5.)*

Research References

Rutter, Cal. Practice Guide: A.D.R. Ch. 4-B, B. Judicial Arbitration.

Rutter, Cal. Practice Guide: Civil Appeals & Writs Ch. 14-A, A. Remittitur.

Rutter, Cal. Practice Guide: Civil Appeals & Writs Ch. 14-C, C. Trial Court Proceedings After Reversal.

Rutter, Cal. Practice Guide: Civ. Pro. Before Trial Ch. 4-A, A. Requirements-In General.

Rutter, Cal. Practice Guide: Civ. Pro. Before Trial Ch. 4-D, D. Service of Summons.

Rutter, Cal. Practice Guide: Civ. Pro. Before Trial Ch. 11-B, B. Involuntary Dismissals.

Rutter, Cal. Practice Guide: Civ. Pro. Before Trial Ch. 13-C, C. Civil Proceedings Subject to Judicial Arbitration.

Rutter, Cal. Practice Guide: Fed.Civ.Pro. Before Trial Ch. 1-D, D. Choosing Between State and Federal Courts.

Rutter, Cal. Practice Guide: Fed.Civ.Pro. Before Trial Ch. 5-A, A. General Considerations.

Rutter, Cal. Practice Guide: Fed.Civ.Pro. Before Trial Ch. 5-G, G. Time Limit for Service-"120-Day Dismissal Statute".

Rutter, Cal. Practice Guide: Fed.Civ.Pro. Before Trial Ch. 2D-9, Effect of Removal.

Rutter, Cal. Practice Guide: Personal Injury Ch. 8-A, A. Case Management.

Miller and Starr California Real Estate § 35:48, Hearing and Order on the Petition.

9 Witkin Cal. Proc. 5th Appeal § 163, (S 163) Notice of Ruling.

6 Witkin Cal. Proc. 5th Proceedings Without Trial § 417, Impracticability and Diligence.

6 Witkin Cal. Proc. 5th Proceedings Without Trial § 440, Premature Dismissal is Improper.

6 Witkin Cal. Proc. 5th Proceedings Without Trial § 441, Extensions, Exceptions, and Excuses.

6 Witkin Cal. Proc. 5th Proceedings Without Trial § 442, in General.

6 Witkin Cal. Proc. 5th Proceedings Without Trial § 443, (S 443) Amended Complaint.

6 Witkin Cal. Proc. 5th Proceedings Without Trial § 444, (S 444) Doe Defendant.

6 Witkin Cal. Proc. 5th Proceedings Without Trial § 445, (S 445) Complaint in Intervention.

6 Witkin Cal. Proc. 5th Proceedings Without Trial § 447, (S 447) Sufficiency of Showing.

6 Witkin Cal. Proc. 5th Proceedings Without Trial § 449, (S 449) Dismissal Upheld.

6 Witkin Cal. Proc. 5th Proceedings Without Trial § 451, in General.

6 Witkin Cal. Proc. 5th Proceedings Without Trial § 458, Effect of Trial Preference.

6 Witkin Cal. Proc. 5th Proceedings Without Trial § 464, (S 464) Delay in New Trial.

6 Witkin Cal. Proc. 5th Proceedings Without Trial § 472, (S 472) Relief Under.

7 Witkin Cal. Proc. 5th Trial § 70, (S 70) Party Under Age 14.

§ 583.430. Conditions for dismissal; orders

(a) In a proceeding for dismissal of an action pursuant to this article for delay in prosecution the court in its discretion may require as a condition of granting or denial of dismissal that the parties comply with such terms as appear to the court proper to effectuate substantial justice.

(b) The court may make any order necessary to effectuate the authority provided in this section, including, but not limited to, provisional and conditional orders. *(Added by Stats.1984, c. 1705, § 5.)*

Law Revision Commission Comments

Section 583.430 is new. It codifies a portion of Rule 203.5 of the California Rules of Court. In exercising its authority under Section 583.430, the court must consider the criteria prescribed in Rule 203.5 as well as the policy of the state favoring trial on the merits. See Sections 583.410(b) (discretionary dismissal) and 583.130 (policy statement). The authority of the court to condition an order granting dismissal includes but is not limited to such matters as waiver by the defendant of a statute of limitation or dismissal by the defendant of a cross-complaint. The authority of the court to condition an order denying dismissal includes but is not limited to such matters as completion of discovery, certificate of readiness for trial, or motion to advance trial date. [17 Cal.L.R.Comm. Reports 905 (1984)].

Research References

Rutter, Cal. Practice Guide: Civil Appeals & Writs Ch. 8-C, C. Standards of Appellate Review.

Rutter, Cal. Practice Guide: Civ. Pro. Before Trial Ch. 11-B, B. Involuntary Dismissals.

Rutter, Cal. Practice Guide: Personal Injury Ch. 7-I, I. Trial De Novo After Arbitration Award.

6 Witkin Cal. Proc. 5th Proceedings Without Trial § 467, (S 467) Ruling May be Conditioned.

CHAPTER 2. JUDGMENT UPON FAILURE TO ANSWER

Section
585.   Judgment on default.
585.5.   Affidavit accompanying application to enter default; motion to set aside default and for leave to defend; procedure.
586.   Proceedings and judgment as if defendant had failed to answer; cases where applicable.
587.   Affidavit of mailing application for entry of default judgment.
587.5.   Application of terms.

§ 585. Judgment on default

Judgment may be had, if the defendant fails to answer the complaint, as follows:

(a) In an action arising upon contract or judgment for the recovery of money or damages only, if the defendant has, or if more than one defendant, if any of the defendants have, been served, other than by publication, and no answer, demurrer, notice of motion to strike of the character specified in subdivision (f), notice of motion to transfer pursuant to Section 396b, notice of motion to dismiss pursuant to Article 2 (commencing with Section 583.210) of Chapter 1.5 of Title 8, notice of motion to quash service of summons or to stay or dismiss the action pursuant to Section 418.10, or notice of the filing of a petition for writ of mandate as provided in Section 418.10 has been filed with the clerk of the court within the time specified in the summons, or within further time as may be allowed, the clerk, upon written application of the plaintiff, and proof of the service of summons, shall enter the default of the defendant or defendants, so served, and immediately thereafter enter judgment for the principal amount demanded in the complaint, in the statement required by Section 425.11, or in the statement provided for in Section 425.115, or a lesser amount if credit has been acknowledged, together with interest allowed by law or in accordance with the terms of the contract, and the costs against the defendant, or defendants, or against one or more of the defendants. If, by rule of court, a schedule of attorneys' fees to be allowed has been adopted, the clerk may include in the judgment attorneys' fees in accordance with the schedule (1) if the contract provides that attorneys' fees shall be allowed in the event of an action thereon, or (2) if the action is one in which the plaintiff is entitled by statute to recover attorneys' fees in addition to money or damages. The plaintiff shall file a written request at the time of application for entry of the default of the defendant or defendants, to have attorneys' fees fixed by the court, whereupon, after the entry of the default, the court shall hear the application for determination of the attorneys' fees and shall render judgment for the attorneys' fees and for the other relief demanded in the complaint, in the statement required by Section 425.11, or in the statement provided for in Section 425.115, or a lesser amount if credit has been acknowledged, and the costs against the defendant, or defendants, or against one or more of the defendants.

(b) In other actions, if the defendant has been served, other than by publication, and no answer, demurrer, notice of motion to strike of the character specified in subdivision (f), notice of motion to transfer pursuant to Section 396b, notice of motion to dismiss pursuant to Article 2 (commencing with Section 583.210) of Chapter 1.5 of Title 8, notice of motion to quash service of summons or to stay or dismiss the action pursuant to Section 418.10 or notice of the filing of a petition for writ of mandate as provided in Section 418.10 has been filed with the clerk of the court within the time specified in the summons, or within further time as may be allowed, the clerk, upon written application of the plaintiff, shall enter the default of the defendant. The plaintiff thereafter may apply to the court for the relief demanded in the complaint. The court shall hear the evidence offered by the plaintiff, and shall render judgment in the plaintiff's favor for that relief, not exceeding the amount stated in the complaint, in the statement required by Section 425.11, or in the statement provided for by Section 425.115, as appears by the evidence to be just. If the taking of an account, or the proof of any fact, is necessary to enable the court to give judgment or to carry the judgment into effect, the court may take the account or hear the proof, or may, in its discretion, order a reference for that purpose. If the action is for the recovery of damages, in whole or in part, the court may order the damages to be assessed by a jury; or if, to determine the amount of damages, the examination of a long account is involved, by a reference as above provided.

(c) In all actions where the service of the summons was by publication, upon the expiration of the time for answering, and upon proof of the publication and that no answer, demurrer, notice of motion to strike of the character specified in subdivision (f), notice of motion to transfer pursuant to Section 396b, notice of motion to dismiss pursuant to Article 2 (commencing with Section 583.210) of Chapter 1.5 of Title 8, notice of motion to quash service of summons or to stay or dismiss the action pursuant to Section 418.10, or notice of the filing of a petition for writ of mandate as provided in Section 418.10 has been filed, the clerk, upon written application of the plaintiff, shall enter the default of the defendant. The plaintiff thereafter may apply to the court for the relief demanded in the complaint; and the court shall hear the evidence offered by the plaintiff, and shall render judgment in the plaintiff's favor for that relief, not exceeding the amount stated in the complaint, in the statement required by Section 425.11, or in the statement provided for in Section 425.115, as appears by the evidence to be just. If the defendant is not a resident of the state, the court shall require the plaintiff, or the plaintiff's agent, to be examined, on oath, respecting any payments that have been made to the plaintiff, or to anyone for the plaintiff's use, on account of any demand mentioned in the complaint, in the statement required by Section 425.11, or in the statement provided for in Section 425.115, and may render judgment for the amount that the plaintiff is entitled to recover. In all cases affecting the title to or possession of real property, where the service of the summons was by publication and the defendant has failed to answer, no judgment shall be rendered upon proof of mere occupancy, unless the occupancy has continued for the time and has been of the character necessary to confer title by prescription. In all cases where the plaintiff bases a claim upon a paper title, the court shall require evidence establishing the plaintiff's equitable right to judgment before rendering judgment. In actions involving only the possession of real property where the complaint is verified and shows by proper allegations that no party to the action claims title to the real property involved, either by prescription, accession, transfer, will, or succession, but only the possession thereof, the court may render judgment upon proof of occupancy by plaintiff and ouster by defendant.

(d) In the cases referred to in subdivisions (b) and (c), or upon an application to have attorneys' fees fixed by the court pursuant to subdivision (a), the court in its discretion may permit the use of affidavits, in lieu of personal testimony, as to all or any part of the evidence or proof required or permitted to be offered, received, or heard in those cases. The facts stated in the affidavit or affidavits shall be within the personal knowledge of the affiant and shall be set forth with particularity, and each affidavit shall show affirmatively that the affiant, if sworn as a witness, can testify competently thereto.

(e) If a defendant files a cross-complaint against another defendant or the plaintiff, a default may be entered against that party on that cross-complaint if the plaintiff or that cross-defendant has been served with that cross-complaint and has failed to file an answer, demurrer, notice of motion to strike of the character specified in subdivision (f), notice of motion to transfer pursuant to Section 396b, notice of motion to dismiss pursuant to Article 2 (commencing with Section 583.210) of Chapter 1.5 of Title 8, notice of motion to quash service of summons or to stay or dismiss the action pursuant to Section 418.10, or notice of the filing of a petition for a writ of mandate as provided in Section 418.10 within the time specified in the summons, or within another time period as may be allowed. However, no judgment may separately be entered on that cross-complaint unless a separate judgment may, in fact, be properly awarded on that cross-complaint and the court finds that a separate judgment on that cross-complaint would not substantially delay the final disposition of the action between the parties.

(f) A notice of motion to strike within the meaning of this section is a notice of motion to strike the whole or any part of a pleading filed within the time which the moving party is required otherwise to plead to that pleading. The notice of motion to strike shall specify a hearing date set in accordance with Section 1005. The filing of a notice of motion does not extend the time within which to demur. *(Enacted in 1872. Amended by Stats.1905, c. 47, p. 42, § 1; Stats.1907, c. 376, p. 712, § 4; Stats.1915, c. 553, p. 932, § 1; Stats.1931, c. 285, p. 692, § 1; Stats.1933, c. 744, p. 1870, § 92; Stats.1951, c. 1737, p. 4112, § 85, operative Jan. 1, 1952; Stats.1955, c. 512, p. 989, § 1; Stats.1955, c. 1452, p. 2641, § 6; Stats.1961, c. 393, p. 1445, § 1; Stats.1967, c. 135, p. 1168, § 1; Stats.1969, c. 345, p. 722, § 3; Stats.1969, c. 567, p. 1195, 1.5; Stats.1969, c. 1611, p. 3386, § 6.7, operative July 1, 1970; Stats.1973, c. 312, p. 729, § 1; Stats.1980, c. 367, p. 736, § 2; Stats.1982, c. 704, p. 2858, § 6.5; Stats.1986, c. 540, § 9; Stats.1993, c. 456 (A.B.58), § 10; Stats.1995, c. 796 (S.B.45), § 10; Stats.2007, c. 263 (A.B.310), § 6.)*

Law Revision Commission Comments

Section 585 is amended to delete unnecessary language authorizing the judge to substitute for the clerk if there is no clerk. See Code Civ. Proc. § 167 (judge may perform any act court clerk may perform); Gov't Code §§ 69840–69848 (duties of clerk of superior court), 71620(b) (executive or administrative officer has authority of clerk of court).

Section 585 is also amended to make stylistic revisions. [35 Cal.L.Rev. Comm. Reports 219 (2006)].

Research References

Rutter, Cal. Practice Guide: Civ. Pro. Before Trial Ch. 3-D, D. Venue.

Rutter, Cal. Practice Guide: Civ. Pro. Before Trial Ch. 5-A, A. General.

Rutter, Cal. Practice Guide: Civ. Pro. Before Trial Ch. 5-B, B. Entry of Default.

Rutter, Cal. Practice Guide: Civ. Pro. Before Trial Ch. 5-C, C. Default Judgment by Clerk.

Rutter, Cal. Practice Guide: Civ. Pro. Before Trial Ch. 5-D, D. Default Judgment by Court.

Rutter, Cal. Practice Guide: Civ. Pro. Before Trial Ch. 5-E, E. Limitations on Default Judgments.

Rutter, Cal. Practice Guide: Civ. Pro. Before Trial Ch. 11-B, B. Involuntary Dismissals.

Rutter, Cal. Practice Guide: Civ. Pro. Before Trial Ch. 7(I)-A, A. Demurrers.

Rutter, Cal. Practice Guide: Civ. Pro. Before Trial Ch. 7(I)-B, B. Motions to Strike.

Rutter, Cal. Practice Guide: Enforcing Judgments/Debts Ch. 3-C, C. Prelawsuit Considerations.

8 Witkin Cal. Proc. 5th Attack Judgment Trial Court § 193, in General.

2 Witkin Cal. Proc. 5th Courts § 254, Disclosure of Witnesses and Evidence.

2 Witkin Cal. Proc. 5th Courts § 364, in General.

8 Witkin Cal. Proc. 5th Enforcement of Judgment § 46, in General.

7 Witkin Cal. Proc. 5th Judgment § 95, (S 95) Prevailing Party in Specified Actions.

5 Witkin Cal. Proc. 5th Pleading § 946, Raising Issue of Law.

5 Witkin Cal. Proc. 5th Pleading § 999, Dismissal on Court's Own Motion.

5 Witkin Cal. Proc. 5th Pleading § 1015, (S 1015) Motion With or Without Demurrer.

6 Witkin Cal. Proc. 5th Proceedings Without Trial § 63, (S 63) Nature and Purpose.

6 Witkin Cal. Proc. 5th Proceedings Without Trial § 133, (S 133) Nature and Effect.

6 Witkin Cal. Proc. 5th Proceedings Without Trial § 135, (S 135) Default of Fewer Than All Defendants.

6 Witkin Cal. Proc. 5th Proceedings Without Trial § 136, (S 136) Default Against Corporation Under Fictitious Business Name.

6 Witkin Cal. Proc. 5th Proceedings Without Trial § 137, (S 137) Restrictions on Default Judgments.

6 Witkin Cal. Proc. 5th Proceedings Without Trial § 138, Responses Preventing Entry of Default.

6 Witkin Cal. Proc. 5th Proceedings Without Trial § 140, Types of Actions.

6 Witkin Cal. Proc. 5th Proceedings Without Trial § 141, Failure to Answer or Demur to Complaint.

6 Witkin Cal. Proc. 5th Proceedings Without Trial § 142, Failure to Answer or Demur to Cross-Complaint.

6 Witkin Cal. Proc. 5th Proceedings Without Trial § 143, Failure to Answer or Demur to Amended Complaint.

6 Witkin Cal. Proc. 5th Proceedings Without Trial § 146, Filing of Motion Prevents Default.

6 Witkin Cal. Proc. 5th Proceedings Without Trial § 147, Default After Granting Motion to Strike or Transfer.

6 Witkin Cal. Proc. 5th Proceedings Without Trial § 149, General Rule: Recovery is Limited to Amount Alleged.

6 Witkin Cal. Proc. 5th Proceedings Without Trial § 150, Prayer for Damages According to Proof.

6 Witkin Cal. Proc. 5th Proceedings Without Trial § 154, (S 154) Notice of Damages.

6 Witkin Cal. Proc. 5th Proceedings Without Trial § 160, (S 160) Nature of Clerk's Power.

6 Witkin Cal. Proc. 5th Proceedings Without Trial § 161, (S 161) Application and Affidavit.

6 Witkin Cal. Proc. 5th Proceedings Without Trial § 163, (S 163) Entry and Memorandum.

6 Witkin Cal. Proc. 5th Proceedings Without Trial § 165, When Clerk May Act.

6 Witkin Cal. Proc. 5th Proceedings Without Trial § 166, Contents of Judgment.

6 Witkin Cal. Proc. 5th Proceedings Without Trial § 168, Contract Actions: No Definite Sum Demanded.

6 Witkin Cal. Proc. 5th Proceedings Without Trial § 169, (S 169) Procedure.

6 Witkin Cal. Proc. 5th Proceedings Without Trial § 170, (S 170) Nature of Hearing.

6 Witkin Cal. Proc. 5th Proceedings Without Trial § 171, Defendant Served by Publication.

6 Witkin Cal. Proc. 5th Proceedings Without Trial § 172, Judgment on Cross-Complaint.

6 Witkin Cal. Proc. 5th Proceedings Without Trial § 178, Case Not Within Clerk's Power.

6 Witkin Cal. Proc. 5th Proceedings Without Trial § 181, Entry Without Proof of Service.

11 Witkin, California Summary 10th Husband and Wife § 198, Order to Show Cause or Motion.

6 Witkin, California Summary 10th Torts § 1749, Judgment by Default.

§ 585.5. Affidavit accompanying application to enter default; motion to set aside default and for leave to defend; procedure

(a) Every application to enter default under subdivision (a) of Section 585 shall include, or be accompanied by, an affidavit stating facts showing that the action is or is not subject to Section 1812.10 or 2984.4 of the Civil Code or subdivision (b) of Section 395.

(b) When a default or default judgment has been entered without full compliance with Section 1812.10 or 2984.4 of the Civil Code, or subdivision (b) of Section 395, the defendant may serve and file a notice of motion to set aside the default or default judgment and for leave to defend the action in the proper court. The notice of motion shall be served and filed within 60 days after the defendant first receives notice of levy under a writ of execution, or notice of any other procedure for enforcing, the default judgment.

(c) A notice of motion to set aside a default or default judgment and for leave to defend the action in the proper court shall designate as the time for making the motion a date prescribed by subdivision (b) of Section 1005, and it shall be accompanied by an affidavit showing under oath that the action was not commenced in the proper court according to Section 1812.10 or 2984.4 of the Civil Code or subdivision (b) of Section 395. The party shall serve and file with the notice a copy of the answer, motion, or other pleading proposed to be filed in the action.

(d) Upon a finding by the court that the motion was made within the period permitted by subdivision (b) and that the action was not commenced in the proper court, it shall set aside the default or default judgment on such terms as may be just and shall allow such a party to defend the action in the proper court.

(e) Unless the plaintiff can show that the plaintiff used reasonable diligence to avoid filing the action in the improper court, upon a finding that the action was commenced in the improper court the court shall award the defendant actual damages and costs, including reasonable attorney's fees. *(Added by Stats.1970, c. 725, p. 1354, § 4. Amended by Stats.1971, c. 1640, p. 3541, § 2; Stats.1982, c. 497, p. 2156, § 36, operative July 1, 1983; Stats.1983, c. 142, § 6; Stats.1991, c. 1090 (A.B.1484), § 3.)*

Law Revision Commission Comments

Subdivision (b) of Section 585.5 is amended to clarify the time within which a motion to set aside a default must be made. The 60-day period runs from the date notice of enforcement proceedings (whether levy, examination, or some other procedure) is received by the defendant rather than the date of levy itself. See Sections 699.010–701.830 (execution), 708.010–709.030 (miscellaneous creditors' remedies) (15 Cal.L.Rev.Comm. Reports 2001).

Research References

Rutter, Cal. Practice Guide: Civ. Pro. Before Trial Ch. 5-B, B. Entry of Default.

Rutter, Cal. Practice Guide: Civ. Pro. Before Trial Ch. 5-G, G. Relief from Default.

8 Witkin Cal. Proc. 5th Attack Judgment Trial Court § 144, (S 144) Nature of Relief.

6 Witkin Cal. Proc. 5th Proceedings Without Trial § 161, (S 161) Application and Affidavit.

§ 586. Proceedings and judgment as if defendant had failed to answer; cases where applicable

(a) In the following cases the same proceedings shall be had, and judgment shall be rendered in the same manner, as if the defendant had failed to answer:

(1) If the complaint has been amended, and the defendant fails to answer it, as amended, or demur thereto, or file a notice of motion to strike, of the character specified in Section 585, within 30 days after service thereof or within the time allowed by the court.

(2) If the demurrer to the complaint is overruled and a motion to strike, of the character specified in Section 585, is denied, or where only one thereof is filed, if the demurrer is overruled or the motion to strike is denied, and the defendant fails to answer the complaint within the time allowed by the court.

(3) If a motion to strike, of the character specified in Section 585, is granted in whole or in part, and the defendant fails to answer the unstricken portion of the complaint within the time allowed by the court, no demurrer having been sustained or being then pending.

(4) If a motion to quash service of summons or to stay or dismiss the action has been filed, or writ of mandate sought and notice thereof given, as provided in Section 418.10, and upon denial of the motion or writ, the defendant fails to respond to the complaint within the time provided in that section or as otherwise provided by law.

(5) If the demurrer to the answer is sustained and the defendant fails to amend the answer within the time allowed by the court.

(6)(A) If a motion to transfer pursuant to Section 396b is denied and the defendant fails to respond to the complaint within the time allowed by the court pursuant to subdivision (e) of Section 396b or within the time provided in subparagraph (C).

(B) If a motion to transfer pursuant to Section 396b is granted and the defendant fails to respond to the complaint within 30 days of the mailing of notice of the filing and case number by the clerk of the court to which the action or proceeding is transferred or within the time provided in subparagraph (C).

(C) If the order granting or denying a motion to transfer pursuant to Section 396a or 396b is the subject of an appeal pursuant to Section 904.2 in which a stay is granted or of a mandate proceeding pursuant to Section 400, the court having jurisdiction over the trial, upon application or on its own motion after the appeal or mandate proceeding becomes final or upon earlier termination of a stay, shall allow the defendant a reasonable time to respond to the complaint. Notice of the order allowing the defendant further time to respond to the complaint shall be promptly served by the party who obtained the order or by the clerk if the order is made on the court's own motion.

(7) If a motion to strike the answer in whole, of the character specified in Section 585, is granted without leave to amend, or if a motion to strike the answer in whole or in part, of the character specified in Section 585, is granted with leave to amend and the defendant fails to amend the answer within the time allowed by the court.

(8) If a motion to dismiss pursuant to Section 583.250 is denied and the defendant fails to respond within the time allowed by the court.

(b) For the purposes of this section, "respond" means to answer, to demur, or to move to strike. *(Formerly § 872, enacted* in 1872. *Amended by Stats.1921, c. 127, p. 122, § 1. Renumbered § 586 and amended by Stats.1933, c. 744, p. 1871, § 93. Amended by Stats.1955, c. 1452, p. 2643, § 7; Stats.1969, c. 345, p. 724, § 4; Stats.1969, c. 1611, p. 3389, § 7.5, operative July 1, 1970; Stats.1970, c. 587, p. 1167, § 1; Stats.1973, c. 167, p. 469, § 12; Stats.1982, c. 704, p. 2860, § 7; Stats.1983, c. 1167, § 7; Stats.1991, c. 1090 (A.B.1484), § 4; Stats.1993, c. 456 (A.B.58), § 11; Stats.1995, c. 796 (S.B.45), § 11; Stats.2007, c. 43 (S.B. 649), § 6.)*

Law Revision Commission Comments

Subdivision (a)(6)(C) of Section 586 is amended to delete an obsolete cross-reference to former Section 904.3, relating to appeals from justice courts. The justice courts no longer exist and former Section 904.3 was repealed. See 1994 Cal. Stat. res. ch. 113 (SCA 7) (Prop. 191, approved Nov. 8, 1994); 1976 Cal. Stat. ch. 1288, § 13.

Section 586 is further amended to make stylistic revisions. [36 Cal. L.Rev.Comm. Reports 305 (2006)].

Research References

Rutter, Cal. Practice Guide: Civ. Pro. Before Trial Ch. 3-D, D. Venue.
Rutter, Cal. Practice Guide: Civ. Pro. Before Trial Ch. 5-B, B. Entry of Default.
Rutter, Cal. Practice Guide: Civ. Pro. Before Trial Ch. 7(I)-B, B. Motions to Strike.
Miller and Starr California Real Estate § 19:222, Complaint and Summons--Service of the Summons and Complaint; Claim to Right of Possession.
3 Witkin Cal. Proc. 5th Actions § 920, Procedure on Mandamus.
3 Witkin Cal. Proc. 5th Actions § 936, Transmission of Papers.
4 Witkin Cal. Proc. 5th Pleading § 8, (S 8) Time Prescribed by Court.
5 Witkin Cal. Proc. 5th Pleading § 999, Dismissal on Court's Own Motion.
5 Witkin Cal. Proc. 5th Pleading § 1014, (S 1014) in General.
5 Witkin Cal. Proc. 5th Pleading § 1015, (S 1015) Motion With or Without Demurrer.
6 Witkin Cal. Proc. 5th Proceedings Without Trial § 143, Failure to Answer or Demur to Amended Complaint.
6 Witkin Cal. Proc. 5th Proceedings Without Trial § 144, Failure to Answer After Demurrer is Overruled.
6 Witkin Cal. Proc. 5th Proceedings Without Trial § 145, Failure to Amend After Demurrer is Sustained.
6 Witkin Cal. Proc. 5th Proceedings Without Trial § 147, Default After Granting Motion to Strike or Transfer.
6 Witkin Cal. Proc. 5th Proceedings Without Trial § 148, Default After Denial of Motions.
6 Witkin Cal. Proc. 5th Proceedings Without Trial § 157, (S 157) Time for Response.
11 Witkin, California Summary 10th Husband and Wife § 198, Order to Show Cause or Motion.

§ 587. Affidavit of mailing application for entry of default judgment

An application by a plaintiff for entry of default under subdivision (a), (b), or (c) of Section 585 or Section 586 shall include an affidavit stating that a copy of the application has been mailed to the defendant's attorney of record or, if none, to the defendant at his or her last known address and the date on which the copy was mailed. If no such address of the defendant is known to the plaintiff or plaintiff's attorney, the affidavit shall state that fact.

No default under subdivision (a), (b), or (c) of Section 585 or Section 586 shall be entered, unless the affidavit is filed. The nonreceipt of the notice shall not invalidate or constitute ground for setting aside any judgment. *(Added by Stats.1969, c. 567, p. 1197, § 2. Amended by Stats.1970, c. 105, p. 326, § 1; Stats. 1983, c. 142, § 7; Stats.1995, c. 796 (S.B.45), § 12.)*

Research References

Rutter, Cal. Practice Guide: Civ. Pro. Before Trial Ch. 5-B, B. Entry of Default.

Rutter, Cal. Practice Guide: Civ. Pro. Before Trial Ch. 5-D, D. Default Judgment by Court.
Rutter, Cal. Practice Guide: Civ. Pro. Before Trial Ch. 9(I)-B, B. Preparing and Filing Motions.
Rutter, Cal. Practice Guide: Personal Injury Ch. 5-E, E. Selected Pleading Issues.
2 Witkin Cal. Proc. 5th Jurisdiction § 290, (S 290) Procedural Error or Omission.
6 Witkin Cal. Proc. 5th Proceedings Without Trial § 161, (S 161) Application and Affidavit.
6 Witkin Cal. Proc. 5th Proceedings Without Trial § 162, (S 162) Notice to Defendant.
6 Witkin Cal. Proc. 5th Proceedings Without Trial § 171, Defendant Served by Publication.
6 Witkin Cal. Proc. 5th Proceedings Without Trial § 180, Entry Without Affidavit of Notice.

§ 587.5. Application of terms

As used in this chapter, unless the context otherwise specifically requires, the following terms apply:

(a) "Complaint" includes a cross-complaint.

(b) "Defendant" includes a cross-defendant.

(c) "Plaintiff" includes a cross-complainant. *(Added by Stats. 1986, c. 540, § 10.)*

Research References

6 Witkin Cal. Proc. 5th Proceedings Without Trial § 142, Failure to Answer or Demur to Cross-Complaint.

CHAPTER 3. ISSUES—THE MODE OF TRIAL AND POSTPONEMENTS

Section
588. Issues defined; kinds of issues.
589. Issue of law.
590. Issue of fact.
591. Issue of law; trial.
592. Issue of fact; jury trial; waiver; reference; issues of law disposed of first.
594. Bringing issues to trial or hearing; absence of adversary; proof of notice.
594a. Postponement; court's own motion.
595. Postponement; action on administrative hearing; party, attorney or principal witness a Member of the Legislature.
595.1. "Proceeding in a court" defined.
595.2. Postponement; duration; stipulation.
595.3. Postponement; mining claims.
595.4. Postponement; absence of evidence.
596. Postponement; deposition of witness.
597. Special defenses not involving merits; trial; judgment for defendant pleading issue; interlocutory judgment on defense of another action pending or demurrer; decision for plaintiff; trial of other issues; applicability to cross-complaints and demurrers.
597.5. Professional negligence; statute of limitations as special defense; separate trial.
598. Precedence of issues; motion.

§ 588. Issues defined; kinds of issues

Issues arise upon the pleadings when a fact or a conclusion of law is maintained by the one party and is controverted by the other. They are of two kinds:

1. Of law; and,

2. Of fact. *(Enacted in 1872.)*

§ 589. Issue of law

An issue of law arises:

(a) Upon a demurrer to the complaint, cross-complaint, or answer, or to some part thereof.

(b) Upon a motion to strike made pursuant to Section 435, 436, or 473. *(Enacted in 1872. Amended by Stats.1982, c. 704, p. 2861, § 8; Stats.1983, c. 1167, § 8.)*

Research References

Rutter, Cal. Practice Guide: Civ. Pro. Before Trial Ch. 7(I)-A, A. Demurrers.
Rutter, Cal. Practice Guide: Civil Trials & Evidence Ch. 2-B, B. What Constitutes Jury Trial.
5 Witkin Cal. Proc. 5th Pleading § 946, Raising Issue of Law.
7 Witkin Cal. Proc. 5th Trial § 81, Jury Tries Issues of Fact Only.

§ 590. Issue of fact

An issue of fact arises:

1. Upon a material allegation in the complaint controverted by the answer; and,

2. Upon new matters in the answer, except an issue of law is joined thereon. *(Enacted in 1872.)*

Research References

Rutter, Cal. Practice Guide: Civil Trials & Evidence Ch. 2-B, B. What Constitutes Jury Trial.
5 Witkin Cal. Proc. 5th Pleading § 1045, (S 1045) Nature and Purpose of Answer.
7 Witkin Cal. Proc. 5th Trial § 81, Jury Tries Issues of Fact Only.

§ 591. Issue of law; trial

An issue of law must be tried by the court, unless it is referred upon consent; provided, however, that failure on the part of any person filing any demurrer to prosecute the same may be construed as a waiver of such demurrer, except as otherwise provided in Section 430.80 of this code. *(Enacted in 1872. Amended by Stats.1929, c. 484, p. 847, § 1; Stats.1982, c. 704, p. 2861, § 9.)*

Research References

Rutter, Cal. Practice Guide: Civil Trials & Evidence Ch. 1-A, A. Importance of Statewide and Local Rules of Court.
Rutter, Cal. Practice Guide: Civil Trials & Evidence Ch. 2-B, B. What Constitutes Jury Trial.
Rutter, Cal. Practice Guide: Civil Trials & Evidence Ch. 4-G, G. Motion to Sever or Bifurcate.
Rutter, Cal. Practice Guide: Personal Injury Ch. 9-E, E. Order of Trial and Proof and Related Matters.
5 Witkin Cal. Proc. 5th Pleading § 958, Defects of Substance Are Not Waived.
5 Witkin Cal. Proc. 5th Pleading § 981, (S 981) Hearing.
7 Witkin Cal. Proc. 5th Trial § 81, Jury Tries Issues of Fact Only.

§ 592. Issue of fact; jury trial; waiver; reference; issues of law disposed of first

In actions for the recovery of specific, real, or personal property, with or without damages, or for money claimed as due upon contract, or as damages for breach of contract, or for injuries, an issue of fact must be tried by a jury, unless a jury trial is waived, or a reference is ordered, as provided in this Code. Where in these cases there are issues both of law and fact, the issue of law must be first disposed of. In other cases, issues of fact must be tried by the Court, subject to its power to order any such issue to be tried by a jury, or to be referred to a referee, as provided in this Code. *(Enacted in 1872. Amended by Code Am.1873–74, c. 383, p. 310, § 74.)*

Research References

Rutter, Cal. Practice Guide: Civ. Pro. Before Trial Ch. 12(I)-D, D. Demand for Jury Trial and Waiver.
Rutter, Cal. Practice Guide: Civ. Pro. Before Trial Ch. 12(I)-E, E. Consolidation, Coordination and Bifurcation.
Rutter, Cal. Practice Guide: Civ. Pro. Before Trial Ch. 12(I)-E, Outline E.
Rutter, Cal. Practice Guide: Civil Trials & Evidence Ch. 2-A, A. Sources of Right to Jury Trial.
Rutter, Cal. Practice Guide: Civil Trials & Evidence Ch. 2-B, B. What Constitutes Jury Trial.
Rutter, Cal. Practice Guide: Civil Trials & Evidence Ch. 2-C, C. Cases in Which Jury Trial May be Demanded.
Rutter, Cal. Practice Guide: Civil Trials & Evidence Ch. 2-E, E. Waiver of Jury Trial.
Rutter, Cal. Practice Guide: Civil Trials & Evidence Ch. 4-G, G. Motion to Sever or Bifurcate.
Rutter, Cal. Practice Guide: Civil Trials & Evidence Ch. 16-G, G. Trial by Reference.
California Practice Guide: Employment Litigation Ch. 19-I, I. Right to Jury Trial.
Rutter, Cal. Practice Guide: Personal Injury Ch. 9-E, E. Order of Trial and Proof and Related Matters.
Miller and Starr California Real Estate § 19:230, Trial; Judgment; Stay of Execution.
4 Witkin Cal. Proc. 5th Pleading § 256, (S 256) Nature of Trial.
7 Witkin Cal. Proc. 5th Trial § 80, California Constitution and Statutes.
7 Witkin Cal. Proc. 5th Trial § 81, Jury Tries Issues of Fact Only.
7 Witkin Cal. Proc. 5th Trial § 109, (S 109) Where Jury is Not Matter of Right.
7 Witkin Cal. Proc. 5th Trial § 149, (S 149) Order of Proof: in General.
11 Witkin, California Summary 10th Husband and Wife § 343, (S 343) CalWORKs Aid.

§ 594. Bringing issues to trial or hearing; absence of adversary; proof of notice

(a) In superior courts either party may bring an issue to trial or to a hearing, and, in the absence of the adverse party, unless the court, for good cause, otherwise directs, may proceed with the case and take a dismissal of the action, or a verdict, or judgment, as the case may require; provided, however, if the issue to be tried is an issue of fact, proof shall first be made to the satisfaction of the court that the adverse party has had 15 days' notice of such trial or five days' notice of the trial in an unlawful detainer action as specified in subdivision (b). If the adverse party has served notice of trial upon the party seeking the dismissal, verdict, or judgment at least five days prior to the trial, the adverse party shall be deemed to have had notice.

(b) The notice to the adverse party required by subdivision (a) shall be served by mail on all the parties by the clerk of the court not less than 20 days prior to the date set for trial. In an unlawful detainer action where notice is served by mail that service shall be mailed not less than 10 days prior to the date set for trial. If notice is not served by the clerk as required by this subdivision, it may be served by mail by any party on the adverse party not less than 15 days prior to the date set for trial, and in an unlawful detainer action where notice is served by mail that service shall be mailed not less than 10 days prior to the date set for trial. The time provisions of Section 1013 shall not serve to extend the notice of trial requirements under this subdivision for unlawful detainer actions. If notice is served by the clerk, proof thereof may be made by introduction into evidence of the clerk's certificate pursuant to subdivision (3) of Section 1013a or other competent evidence. If notice is served by a party, proof may be made by introduction into evidence of an affidavit or certificate pursuant to subdivision (1) or (2) of Section 1013a or other competent evidence. The provisions of this subdivision are exclusive. *(Enacted in 1872. Amended by Stats.1899, c. 6, p. 5, § 1; Stats.1933, c. 744, p. 1871, § 94; Stats.1935, c. 722, p. 1954, § 8; Stats.1951, c. 1737, p. 4113, § 86, operative Jan. 1, 1952; Stats.1969, c. 85, p. 205, § 1; Stats.1975, c. 1001, p. 2345, § 1; Stats.1976, c. 406, p. 1056, § 1; Stats.1977, c. 685, p. 2211, § 1;*

Stats.1977, c. 1257, p. 4761, § 19, eff. Oct. 3, 1977; Stats.1977, c. 1257, p. 4762, § 19.5, eff. Oct. 3, 1977, operative Jan. 1, 1978; Stats.1998, c. 931 (S.B.2139), § 81, eff. Sept. 28, 1998; Stats.2002, c. 784 (S.B.1316), § 62.)

Law Revision Commission Comments

Section 594 is amended to reflect the elimination of the justice court. Cal. Const. art. VI, §§ 1, 5(b). [28 Cal.L.Rev.Comm. Reports 51 (1998)].

Subdivision (a) of Section 594 is amended to reflect unification of the municipal and superior courts pursuant to Article VI, Section 5(e), of the California Constitution. [32 Cal.L.Rev.Comm. Reports 124 (2002)].

Research References

Rutter, Cal. Practice Guide: Civil Appeals & Writs Ch. 8-E, E. Limits on Reversal or Modification-"Prejudicial Error" Rule.

Rutter, Cal. Practice Guide: Civ. Pro. Before Trial Ch. 6-B, B. Complaints.

Rutter, Cal. Practice Guide: Civ. Pro. Before Trial Ch. 12(I)-C, C. Claims for Trial Setting Preference.

Rutter, Cal. Practice Guide: Civil Trials & Evidence Ch. 1-A, A. Importance of Statewide and Local Rules of Court.

Rutter, Cal. Practice Guide: Civil Trials & Evidence Ch. 1-J, J. Notice of Trial.

Rutter, Cal. Practice Guide: Civil Trials & Evidence Gen. Matls., Highlights.

2 Witkin Cal. Proc. 5th Jurisdiction § 287, (S 287) General Principle.

2 Witkin Cal. Proc. 5th Jurisdiction § 327, Miscellaneous Unauthorized Orders.

5 Witkin Cal. Proc. 5th Pleading § 981, (S 981) Hearing.

6 Witkin Cal. Proc. 5th Proceedings Without Trial § 31, Express Limitations.

6 Witkin Cal. Proc. 5th Proceedings Without Trial § 374, (S 374) in General.

6 Witkin Cal. Proc. 5th Proceedings Without Trial § 475, (S 475) When Dismissal is Proper.

6 Witkin Cal. Proc. 5th Proceedings Without Trial § 476, (S 476) Trial of Uncontested Matter as Alternative to Dismissal.

7 Witkin Cal. Proc. 5th Trial § 16, When Continuance Will be Granted.

7 Witkin Cal. Proc. 5th Trial § 75, (S 75) Statutory Provisions.

7 Witkin Cal. Proc. 5th Trial § 76, (S 76) Mandatory Requirement.

7 Witkin Cal. Proc. 5th Trial § 77, (S 77) Exceptions and Waiver.

7 Witkin Cal. Proc. 5th Trial § 78, (S 78) Resumption of Trial After Continuance.

10 Witkin, California Summary 10th Parent and Child § 805, Presence at Trial.

3 Witkin, California Summary 10th Agency and Employment § 74, Effect of Judgment.

§ 594a. Postponement; court's own motion

The court may, of its own motion, postpone the trial, if at the time fixed for the trial the court is engaged in the trial of another action; or if, as provided in section 473 of this code, an amendment of the pleadings, or the allowance of time to make such amendment, or to plead, renders a postponement necessary. *(Added by Stats.1933, c. 744, p. 1873, § 95.)*

Research References

7 Witkin Cal. Proc. 5th Trial § 8, (S 8) Limitations.

7 Witkin Cal. Proc. 5th Trial § 21, (S 21) Absence of Judge.

7 Witkin Cal. Proc. 5th Trial § 25, (S 25) Changes in Parties or Pleadings.

§ 595. Postponement; action on administrative hearing; party, attorney or principal witness a Member of the Legislature

The trial of any civil action, or proceeding in a court, or of any administrative proceeding before a state board or commission or officer, irrespective of the date of the filing thereof or when it became at issue, or the hearing of any motion, demurrer, or other proceeding, shall be postponed to a date certain when it appears to the court, board, commission, or officer before which such action or proceeding is pending that either a party thereto, or any attorney of record therein (whether he became an attorney of record before or after the commencement of a legislative session or before or after his appointment to a legislative committee), or a principal witness, is a Member of the Legislature of this state and that the Legislature is in session or in recess (not exceeding a recess of forty (40) days) or that a legislative interim committee of which he is a duly appointed member is meeting, or is to meet within a period which the court finds does not exceed the time reasonably necessary to enable the member to reach the committee meeting by the ordinary mode of travel. When the Legislature is in session or in recess such action or proceeding shall not, without the consent of the attorney of record therein, be brought on for trial or hearing before the expiration of thirty (30) days next following final adjournment of the Legislature or the commencement of a recess of more than forty (40) days. If a date is available during recess, continuance shall be given if possible to such earlier date. When a legislative committee is meeting or is to meet within a period which the court finds does not exceed the time reasonably necessary to enable the member to reach the committee meeting by the ordinary mode of travel, such action or proceeding shall not, without the consent of the attorney of record therein, be brought on for trial or hearing before the expiration of such period necessary following the adjournment or recess of the committee meeting as the court finds is reasonably necessary to enable the member to reach the place of trial or hearing by the ordinary mode of travel from the place of the committee meeting, unless at the expiration of that period the Legislature is to be in session; and in that case the action or proceeding shall not, without such consent, be brought on for trial or hearing before the expiration of thirty (30) days next following final adjournment or the commencement of a recess of more than forty (40) days. If a date is available during the recess, continuance shall be given to such earlier date. However, any postponement granted under the provisions of this paragraph shall suspend for the same period of time as the postponement, the running of any period of time for any ruling or proceeding by a court, board, commission, or officer, or for the performance by any party of any act affected by said postponement.

Granting of a continuance pursuant to this section is mandatory unless the court determines that such continuance would defeat or abridge a right to relief pendente lite in a paternity action or a right to invoke a provisional remedy such as pendente lite support in a domestic relations controversy, attachment and sale of perishable goods, receivership of a failing business, and temporary restraining order or preliminary injunction, and that the continuance should not be granted. *(Enacted in 1872. Amended by Code Am.1880, c. 13, p. 1, § 1; Stats.1911, c. 744, p. 1448, § 1; Stats.1931, c. 1078, p. 2282, § 1; Stats.1933, c. 282, p. 851, § 1; Stats.1933, c. 744, p. 1873, § 96; Stats.1945, c. 1512, p. 2822, § 1, eff. July 18, 1945; Stats.1955, c. 926, p. 1553, § 1; Stats.1963, c. 1468, p. 3034, § 1; Stats.1965, c. 1989, p. 4516, § 1; Stats.1968, c. 698, p. 1396, § 1.)*

Research References

Rutter, Cal. Practice Guide: Civil Trials & Evidence Ch. 1-K, K. Continuance Motions.

4 Witkin Cal. Proc. 5th Pleading § 11, Extension to Legislator.

6 Witkin Cal. Proc. 5th Proceedings Without Trial § 18, Extension by Stipulation or Court Order.

7 Witkin Cal. Proc. 5th Trial § 8, (S 8) Limitations.

7 Witkin Cal. Proc. 5th Trial § 26, Persons Entitled.

7 Witkin Cal. Proc. 5th Trial § 27, Proceedings Covered.

7 Witkin Cal. Proc. 5th Trial § 28, Extent of Continuance.

7 Witkin Cal. Proc. 5th Trial § 29, Exceptions to Mandatory Right.

§ 595.1. "Proceeding in a court" defined

The term "proceeding in a court" as it is used in Section 595 shall include any discovery proceeding, pretrial conference, deposition, interrogatory, or any other proceeding arising out of a pending civil action.

The enactment of this section at the 1965 Regular Session of the Legislature does not constitute a change in, but is declaratory of, the preexisting law. *(Added by Stats.1965, c. 1890, p. 4359, § 1.)*

Research References

7 Witkin Cal. Proc. 5th Trial § 27, Proceedings Covered.

§ 595.2. Postponement; duration; stipulation

In all cases, the court shall postpone a trial, or the hearing of any motion or demurrer, for a period not to exceed thirty (30) days, when all attorneys of record of parties who have appeared in the action agree in writing to such postponement. *(Added by Stats.1965, c. 1989, p. 4517, § 3.)*

Research References

Rutter, Cal. Practice Guide: Civ. Pro. Before Trial Ch. 9(I)-D, D. Hearing.
Rutter, Cal. Practice Guide: Civ. Pro. Before Trial Ch. 12(I)-F, F. Motions to Continue Trial.
Rutter, Cal. Practice Guide: Civil Trials & Evidence Ch. 1-K, K. Continuance Motions.
Rutter, Cal. Practice Guide: Civil Trials & Evidence Ch. 1-K, Outline K.
Rutter, Cal. Practice Guide: Personal Injury Ch. 9-A, A. Assignment to Trial.
7 Witkin Cal. Proc. 5th Trial § 36, (S 36) Stipulation.

§ 595.3. Postponement; mining claims

In actions involving the title to mining claims, or involving trespass for damage upon mining claims, if it be made to appear to the satisfaction of the court that, in order that justice may be done and the action fairly tried on its merits, it is necessary that further developments should be made, underground or upon the surface of the mining claims involved in such action, the court shall grant the postponement of the trial of the action, giving the party a reasonable time in which to prepare for trial and to do said development work. *(Added by Stats.1965, c. 1989, p. 4517, § 4.)*

Research References

Rutter, Cal. Practice Guide: Civil Trials & Evidence Ch. 1-K, K. Continuance Motions.
7 Witkin Cal. Proc. 5th Trial § 31, (S 31) Particular Actions and Proceedings.

§ 595.4. Postponement; absence of evidence

A motion to postpone a trial on the ground of the absence of evidence can only be made upon affidavit showing the materiality of the evidence expected to be obtained, and that due diligence has been used to procure it. The court may require the moving party, where application is made on account of the absence of a material witness, to state upon affidavit the evidence which he expects to obtain; and if the adverse party thereupon admits that such evidence would be given, and that it be considered as actually given on the trial, or offered and overruled as improper, the trial must not be postponed. *(Added by Stats.1965, c. 1989, p. 4517, § 2.)*

Research References

Rutter, Cal. Practice Guide: Civil Trials & Evidence Ch. 1-K, K. Continuance Motions.
Rutter, Cal. Practice Guide: Personal Injury Ch. 9-A, A. Assignment to Trial.
7 Witkin Cal. Proc. 5th Trial § 18, (S 18) Absence of Evidence.
7 Witkin Cal. Proc. 5th Trial § 20, Showing of Necessity.
7 Witkin Cal. Proc. 5th Trial § 33, (S 33) Affidavits and Deposition.

§ 596. Postponement; deposition of witness

The party obtaining a postponement of a trial, if required by the adverse party, must consent that the testimony of any witness of such adverse party, who is in attendance, be then taken by deposition before a judge or clerk of the court in which the case is pending, or before such notary public as the court may indicate, which must accordingly be done; and the testimony so taken may be read on the trial, with the same effect, and subject to the same objections, as if the witnesses were produced. *(Enacted in 1872. Amended by Stats.1933, c. 744, p. 1874, § 97; Stats.1951, c. 1737, p. 4114, § 87, operative Jan. 1, 1952.)*

Research References

Rutter, Cal. Practice Guide: Civil Trials & Evidence Ch. 1-K, K. Continuance Motions.
7 Witkin Cal. Proc. 5th Trial § 33, (S 33) Affidavits and Deposition.

§ 597. Special defenses not involving merits; trial; judgment for defendant pleading issue; interlocutory judgment on defense of another action pending or demurrer; decision for plaintiff; trial of other issues; applicability to cross-complaints and demurrers

When the answer pleads that the action is barred by the statute of limitations, or by a prior judgment, or that another action is pending upon the same cause of action, or sets up any other defense not involving the merits of the plaintiff's cause of action but constituting a bar or ground of abatement to the prosecution thereof, the court may, either upon its own motion or upon the motion of any party, proceed to the trial of the special defense or defenses before the trial of any other issue in the case, and if the decision of the court, or the verdict of the jury, upon any special defense so tried (other than the defense of another action pending) is in favor of the defendant pleading the same, judgment for the defendant shall thereupon be entered and no trial of other issues in the action shall be had unless that judgment shall be reversed on appeal or otherwise set aside or vacated; and where the defense of another action pending or a demurrer based upon subdivision (c) of Section 430.10 is sustained (and no other special defense is sustained) an interlocutory judgment shall be entered in favor of the defendant pleading the same to the effect that no trial of other issues shall be had until the final determination of that other action, and the plaintiff may appeal from the interlocutory judgment in the same manner and within the same time as is now or may be hereafter provided by law for appeals from judgments. If the decision of the court, or the verdict of the jury, upon the special defense or defenses so tried is in favor of the plaintiff, trial of the other issues shall thereafter be had either upon the court's own motion or upon the motion of any party, and judgment shall be entered thereon in the same manner and with the same effect as if all the issues in the case had been tried at one time. In such an event any and all decisions or verdicts upon the special defense or defenses, and all rulings on the trial thereof shall be deemed excepted to and may be reviewed on motion for a new trial or upon appeal from the judgment.

This section also applies to the trial of special defenses pleaded in an answer to a cross-complaint or a demurrer based upon subdivision (c) of Section 430.10, and if the decision of the court or the verdict of the jury upon the special defense or defenses is in favor of the cross-defendant, no further trial shall be had upon the issues raised by the cross-complaint, but trial of the other issues in the action shall thereafter be had either upon the court's own motion or upon the motion of any party, and after the trial thereof the judgment shall be entered in the action as is justified by the decision or verdict on such other issues, considered in connection with the decision or verdict upon the trial of such an affirmative defense raised in the answer to the cross-complaint. *(Added by Stats.1939, c. 715, p. 2235, § 1. Amended by Stats.1969, c. 201, p. 485, § 1; Stats.1979, c. 216, p. 461, § 1; Stats.1986, c. 540, § 11.)*

Research References

Rutter, Cal. Practice Guide: Civil Appeals & Writs Ch. 2-B, B. Appealable Judgments and Orders.

Rutter, Cal. Practice Guide: Civ. Pro. Before Trial Ch. 3-A, A. Subject Matter Jurisdiction (Competency).

Rutter, Cal. Practice Guide: Civ. Pro. Before Trial Ch. 11-B, B. Involuntary Dismissals.

Rutter, Cal. Practice Guide: Civ. Pro. Before Trial Ch. 12(I)-E, E. Consolidation, Coordination and Bifurcation.

Rutter, Cal. Practice Guide: Civ. Pro. Before Trial Ch. 12(I)-E, Outline E.

Rutter, Cal. Practice Guide: Civil Trials & Evidence Ch. 2-C, C. Cases in Which Jury Trial May be Demanded.

Rutter, Cal. Practice Guide: Civil Trials & Evidence Ch. 4-G, G. Motion to Sever or Bifurcate.

Rutter, Cal. Practice Guide: Civil Trials & Evidence Ch. 4-G, Outline G.

California Practice Guide: Employment Litigation Ch. 19-T, T. Appeals.

Rutter, Cal. Practice Guide: Insurance Litigation Ch. 15-I, I. Trial.

Rutter, Cal. Practice Guide: Personal Injury Ch. 9-E, E. Order of Trial and Proof and Related Matters.

3 Witkin Cal. Proc. 5th Actions § 431, (S 431) Statutory Classification.

9 Witkin Cal. Proc. 5th Appeal § 118, (S 118) Multiple Causes of Action.

9 Witkin Cal. Proc. 5th Appeal § 138, (S 138) Appealable Interlocutory Judgments.

9 Witkin Cal. Proc. 5th Appeal § 159, Orders at Trial.

7 Witkin Cal. Proc. 5th Judgment § 21, Statutory Types.

4 Witkin Cal. Proc. 5th Pleading § 377, (S 377) California Statute.

5 Witkin Cal. Proc. 5th Pleading § 946, Raising Issue of Law.

5 Witkin Cal. Proc. 5th Pleading § 971, Other Action Pending.

5 Witkin Cal. Proc. 5th Pleading § 1005, (S 1005) Principal Grounds for Motion.

5 Witkin Cal. Proc. 5th Pleading § 1129, Nature of Plea.

5 Witkin Cal. Proc. 5th Pleading § 1149, (S 1149) Plea Sustained.

6 Witkin Cal. Proc. 5th Proceedings Without Trial § 114, (S 114) Former Motion Procedure.

6 Witkin Cal. Proc. 5th Proceedings Without Trial § 210, Trial of Special Defenses.

6 Witkin Cal. Proc. 5th Proceedings Without Trial § 477, Demurrer Sustained.

7 Witkin Cal. Proc. 5th Trial § 84, Actions Classified as Legal.

7 Witkin Cal. Proc. 5th Trial § 150, Nature and Scope of Statute.

7 Witkin Cal. Proc. 5th Trial § 151, Special Defenses Covered.

7 Witkin Cal. Proc. 5th Trial § 152, Decision for Defendant.

7 Witkin Cal. Proc. 5th Trial § 153, Decision for Plaintiff.

7 Witkin Cal. Proc. 5th Trial § 154, in General.

§ 597.5. Professional negligence; statute of limitations as special defense; separate trial

In an action against a physician or surgeon, dentist, registered nurse, dispensing optician, optometrist, registered physical therapist, podiatrist, licensed psychologist, osteopathic physician and surgeon, chiropractor, clinical laboratory bioanalyst, clinical laboratory technologist, veterinarian, or a licensed hospital as the employer of any such person, based upon the person's alleged professional negligence, or for rendering professional services without consent, or for error or omission in the person's practice, if the answer pleads that the action is barred by the statute of limitations, and if any party so moves or the court upon its own motion requires, the issues raised thereby must be tried separately and before any other issues in the case are tried. If the issue raised by the statute of limitations is finally determined in favor of the plaintiff, the remaining issues shall then be tried. *(Added by Stats.1968, c. 1104, p. 2116, § 1. Amended by Stats.1979, c. 216, p. 462, § 2; Stats.1993, c. 226 (A.B.1987), § 5.)*

Research References

Rutter, Cal. Practice Guide: Civ. Pro. Before Trial Ch. 12(I)-E, E. Consolidation, Coordination and Bifurcation.

Rutter, Cal. Practice Guide: Civil Trials & Evidence Ch. 4-G, G. Motion to Sever or Bifurcate.

Rutter, Cal. Practice Guide: Civil Trials & Evidence Ch. 4-G, Outline G.

Rutter, Cal. Practice Guide: Personal Injury Ch. 9-E, E. Order of Trial and Proof and Related Matters.

4 Witkin Cal. Proc. 5th Pleading § 377, (S 377) California Statute.

7 Witkin Cal. Proc. 5th Trial § 151, Special Defenses Covered.

7 Witkin Cal. Proc. 5th Trial § 154, in General.

§ 598. Precedence of issues; motion

The court may, when the convenience of witnesses, the ends of justice, or the economy and efficiency of handling the litigation would be promoted thereby, on motion of a party, after notice and hearing, make an order, no later than the close of pretrial conference in cases in which such pretrial conference is to be held, or, in other cases, no later than 30 days before the trial date, that the trial of any issue or any part thereof shall precede the trial of any other issue or any part thereof in the case, except for special defenses which may be tried first pursuant to Sections 597 and 597.5. The court, on its own motion, may make such an order at any time. Where either the issue of liability as to all causes of action precedes the trial of other issues or parts thereof, and the decision of the court, or the verdict of the jury upon such issue so tried is in favor of any party on whom liability is sought to be imposed, judgment in favor of such party shall thereupon be entered and no trial of other issues in the action as against such party shall be had unless such judgment shall be reversed upon appeal or otherwise set aside or vacated.

If the decision of the court, or the verdict of the jury upon the issue of liability so tried shall be against any party on whom liability is sought to be imposed, or if the decision of the court or the verdict of the jury upon any other issue or part thereof so tried does not result in a judgment being entered pursuant to this chapter, then the trial of the other issues or parts thereof shall thereafter be had at such time, and if a jury trial, before the same or another jury, as ordered by the court either upon its own motion or upon the motion of any party, and judgment shall be entered in the same manner and with the same effect as if all the issues in the case had been tried at one time. *(Added by Stats.1963, c. 1205, p. 2705, § 1. Amended by Stats.1977, c. 57, p. 447, § 1; Stats.1979, c. 216, p. 462, § 3; Stats.1979, c. 349, p. 1213, § 1.)*

Research References

Rutter, Cal. Practice Guide: Civil Appeals & Writs Ch. 2-B, B. Appealable Judgments and Orders.

Rutter, Cal. Practice Guide: Civ. Pro. Before Trial Ch. 12(I)-B, B. Case Management ("Fast Track") System.

Rutter, Cal. Practice Guide: Civ. Pro. Before Trial Ch. 12(I)-E, E. Consolidation, Coordination and Bifurcation.

Rutter, Cal. Practice Guide: Civ. Pro. Before Trial Ch. 12(I)-E, Outline E.

Rutter, Cal. Practice Guide: Civil Trials & Evidence Ch. 4-B, B. Preliminary Matters Discussed in Final Status Conference or In-Chambers Conference.

Rutter, Cal. Practice Guide: Civil Trials & Evidence Ch. 4-G, G. Motion to Sever or Bifurcate.

Rutter, Cal. Practice Guide: Civil Trials & Evidence Ch. 18-A, A. Motion for Judgment Notwithstanding the Verdict ("JNOV").

Rutter, Cal. Practice Guide: Civil Trials & Evidence Ch. 8G-B, B. Procedures on Objection.

Rutter, Cal. Practice Guide: Civil Trials & Evidence Ch. 4-G, Outline G.

California Practice Guide: Employment Litigation Ch. 19-H, H. Other Pretrial Procedures.

Rutter, Cal. Practice Guide: Insurance Litigation Ch. 15-F, F. Pretrial Motions.

Rutter, Cal. Practice Guide: Personal Injury Ch. 9-E, E. Order of Trial and Proof and Related Matters.

9 Witkin Cal. Proc. 5th Appeal § 119, (S 119) Order in Bifurcated Trial.

9 Witkin Cal. Proc. 5th Appeal § 159, Orders at Trial.

9 Witkin Cal. Proc. 5th Appeal § 193, (S 193) Order Denying Judgment Notwithstanding Verdict.

4 Witkin Cal. Proc. 5th Pleading § 377, (S 377) California Statute.

6 Witkin Cal. Proc. 5th Proceedings Without Trial § 405, Interlocutory Review.

7 Witkin Cal. Proc. 5th Trial § 154, in General.

7 Witkin Cal. Proc. 5th Trial § 155, Motion and Order.

7 Witkin Cal. Proc. 5th Trial § 156, Proceedings After Decision.

CHAPTER 4. TRIAL BY JURY

ARTICLE 2. CONDUCT OF THE TRIAL

§ 607. Order of proceedings

When the jury has been sworn, the trial must proceed in the following order, unless the court, for special reasons otherwise directs:

1. The plaintiff may state the issue and his case;

2. The defendant may then state his defense, if he so wishes, or wait until after plaintiff has produced his evidence;

3. The plaintiff must then produce the evidence on his part;

4. The defendant may then open his defense, if he has not done so previously;

5. The defendant may then produce the evidence on his part;

6. The parties may then respectively offer rebutting evidence only, unless the court, for good reason, in furtherance of justice, permit them to offer evidence upon their original case;

7. When the evidence is concluded, unless the case is submitted to the jury on either side or on both sides without argument, the plaintiff must commence and may conclude the argument;

8. If several defendants having separate defenses, appear by different counsel, the court must determine their relative order in the evidence and argument;

9. The court may then charge the jury. *(Enacted in 1872. Amended by Stats.1933, c. 744, p. 1874, § 100; Stats.1965, c. 841, p. 2437, § 1.)*

Research References

Rutter, Cal. Practice Guide: Civil Trials & Evidence Ch. 1-M, M. Order of Proceedings.
Rutter, Cal. Practice Guide: Civil Trials & Evidence Ch. 4-G, G. Motion to Sever or Bifurcate.
Rutter, Cal. Practice Guide: Civil Trials & Evidence Ch. 4-I, I. Other Motions at Final Status Conference.
Rutter, Cal. Practice Guide: Civil Trials & Evidence Ch. 6-A, A. General Considerations.

Rutter, Cal. Practice Guide: Civil Trials & Evidence Ch. 6-B, B. Order of Presentation of Opening Statements.
Rutter, Cal. Practice Guide: Civil Trials & Evidence Ch. 7-B, B. Explanations, Admonitions and Preinstructions.
Rutter, Cal. Practice Guide: Civil Trials & Evidence Ch. 9-H, H. Rebuttal and Surrebuttal.
Rutter, Cal. Practice Guide: Civil Trials & Evidence Ch. 12-D, D. Other Motions During Trial.
Rutter, Cal. Practice Guide: Civil Trials & Evidence Ch. 13-A, A. Procedural Considerations Re Closing Argument.
Rutter, Cal. Practice Guide: Civil Trials & Evidence Ch. 14-F, F. Instructing the Jury.
Rutter, Cal. Practice Guide: Civil Trials & Evidence Ch. 16-A, A. General Considerations Re Nonjury Trials.
Rutter, Cal. Practice Guide: Personal Injury Ch. 9-D, D. Opening Statements.
Rutter, Cal. Practice Guide: Personal Injury Ch. 9-E, E. Order of Trial and Proof and Related Matters.
Rutter, Cal. Practice Guide: Personal Injury Ch. 9-J, J. Final Arguments Upon Close of Evidence.
Rutter, Cal. Practice Guide: Personal Injury Ch. 9-K, K. Submission of Case to Jury.
7 Witkin Cal. Proc. 5th Trial § 147, Trial by Jury.
7 Witkin Cal. Proc. 5th Trial § 160, Opening Statements.
7 Witkin Cal. Proc. 5th Trial § 162, (S 162) Trial by Jury.
7 Witkin Cal. Proc. 5th Trial § 165, (S 165) Waiver.
7 Witkin Cal. Proc. 5th Trial § 256, (S 256) Nature of Instruction.
7 Witkin Cal. Proc. 5th Trial § 289, (S 289) Power to Instruct.

§ 607a. Proposed jury instructions

In every case which is being tried before the court with a jury, it shall be the duty of counsel for the respective parties, before the first witness is sworn, to deliver to the judge presiding at the trial and serve upon opposing counsel, all proposed instructions to the jury covering the law as disclosed by the pleadings. Thereafter, and before the commencement of the argument, counsel may deliver to such judge, and serve upon opposing counsel, additional proposed instructions to the jury upon questions of law developed by the evidence and not disclosed by the pleadings. All proposed instructions shall be typewritten, each on a separate sheet of paper. Before the commencement of the argument, the court, on request of counsel, must: (1) decide whether to give, refuse, or modify the proposed instructions; (2) decide which instructions shall be given in addition to those proposed, if any; and (3) advise counsel of all instructions to be given. However, if, during the argument, issues are raised which have not been covered by instructions given or refused, the court may, on request of counsel, give additional instructions on the subject matter thereof. *(Added by Stats.1929, c. 481, p. 845, § 1. Amended by Stats.1933, c. 744, p. 1874, § 101; Stats.1951, c. 1737, p. 4115, § 89, operative Jan. 1, 1952; Stats.1957, c. 1698, p. 3073, § 1.)*

Research References

Rutter, Cal. Practice Guide: Civil Trials & Evidence Ch. 4-C, C. Jury Matters.
Rutter, Cal. Practice Guide: Civil Trials & Evidence Ch. 13-A, A. Procedural Considerations Re Closing Argument.
Rutter, Cal. Practice Guide: Civil Trials & Evidence Ch. 14-A, A. General Considerations.
Rutter, Cal. Practice Guide: Civil Trials & Evidence Ch. 14-C, C. Procedural Requirements.
Rutter, Cal. Practice Guide: Civil Trials & Evidence Ch. 14-D, D. Preparing Jury Instructions.
Rutter, Cal. Practice Guide: Civil Trials & Evidence Ch. 14-E, E. Argument and Settlement Re Proposed Instructions.
California Practice Guide: Employment Litigation Ch. 19-R, R. Jury Instructions.
Rutter, Cal. Practice Guide: Insurance Litigation Ch. 13-C, C. Punitive Damages.
Rutter, Cal. Practice Guide: Personal Injury Ch. 8-D, D. Final Preparation (One Month Before Trial).
Rutter, Cal. Practice Guide: Personal Injury Ch. 9-B, B. In-Chambers Conference Before Commencement of Trial.

Rutter, Cal. Practice Guide: Personal Injury Ch. 9-K, K. Submission of
　　Case to Jury.
7 Witkin Cal. Proc. 5th Trial § 262, Timely Presentation.
7 Witkin Cal. Proc. 5th Trial § 263, Formal Requisites.
7 Witkin Cal. Proc. 5th Trial § 264, (S 264) in General.
7 Witkin Cal. Proc. 5th Trial § 265, (S 265) Modification by Judge.

§ 608.　Charge to jury; written statement of points of law

In charging the jury the Court may state to them all matters of
law which it thinks necessary for their information in giving their
verdict; and, if it state the testimony of the case, it must inform
the jury that they are the exclusive judges of all questions of fact.
The Court must furnish to either party, at the time, upon
request, a statement in writing of the points of law contained in
the charge, or sign, at the time, a statement of such points
prepared and submitted by the counsel of either party. *(Enacted
in 1872.)*

Research References

Rutter, Cal. Practice Guide: Civil Trials & Evidence Ch. 12-A, A. Motion
　　for Mistrial.
Rutter, Cal. Practice Guide: Civil Trials & Evidence Ch. 14-A, A. General
　　Considerations.
Rutter, Cal. Practice Guide: Civil Trials & Evidence Ch. 14-E, E.
　　Argument and Settlement Re Proposed Instructions.
California Practice Guide: Employment Litigation Ch. 19-R, R. Jury
　　Instructions.
Rutter, Cal. Practice Guide: Personal Injury Ch. 9-K, K. Submission of
　　Case to Jury.
7 Witkin Cal. Proc. 5th Trial § 256, (S 256) Nature of Instruction.
7 Witkin Cal. Proc. 5th Trial § 261, (S 261) Instructions on Court's Own
　　Motion.
7 Witkin Cal. Proc. 5th Trial § 264, (S 264) in General.
7 Witkin Cal. Proc. 5th Trial § 289, (S 289) Power to Instruct.

§ 609.　Special instructions

Where either party asks special instructions to be given to the
jury, the Court must either give such instruction, as requested, or
refuse to do so, or give the instruction with a modification, in
such manner that it may distinctly appear what instructions were
given in whole or in part. *(Enacted in 1872.)*

Research References

Rutter, Cal. Practice Guide: Civil Trials & Evidence Ch. 14-A, A. General
　　Considerations.
Rutter, Cal. Practice Guide: Civil Trials & Evidence Ch. 14-E, E.
　　Argument and Settlement Re Proposed Instructions.
7 Witkin Cal. Proc. 5th Trial § 264, (S 264) in General.
7 Witkin Cal. Proc. 5th Trial § 265, (S 265) Modification by Judge.

§ 611.　Separation of jury; prohibition on research, dissemination of information, and conversation; admonishment

If the jury are permitted to separate, either during the trial or
after the case is submitted to them, they shall be admonished by
the court that it is their duty not to conduct research, disseminate information, or converse with, or permit themselves to be
addressed by, any other person on any subject of the trial, and
that it is their duty not to form or express an opinion thereon
until the case is finally submitted to them. The court shall
clearly explain, as part of the admonishment, that the prohibition
on research, dissemination of information, and conversation
applies to all forms of electronic and wireless communication.
(Enacted in 1872. Amended by Stats.2011, c. 181 (A.B.141), § 1.)

Research References

Rutter, Cal. Practice Guide: Civil Trials & Evidence Ch. 4-C, C. Jury
　　Matters.
Rutter, Cal. Practice Guide: Civil Trials & Evidence Ch. 7-B, B.
　　Explanations, Admonitions and Preinstructions.
Rutter, Cal. Practice Guide: Civil Trials & Evidence Ch. 7-C, C. Access to
　　Evidence During Trial.

Rutter, Cal. Practice Guide: Civil Trials & Evidence Ch. 7-F, F. Juror
　　Misconduct During Trial.
Rutter, Cal. Practice Guide: Civil Trials & Evidence Ch. 12-A, A. Motion
　　for Mistrial.
Rutter, Cal. Practice Guide: Civil Trials & Evidence Ch. 15-A, A. General
　　Considerations.
Rutter, Cal. Practice Guide: Civil Trials & Evidence Ch. 15-F, F. Juror
　　Misconduct During Deliberations.
Rutter, Cal. Practice Guide: Civil Trials & Evidence Ch. 7-B, Outline B.
Rutter, Cal. Practice Guide: Civil Trials & Evidence Gen. Matls.,
　　Highlights.
Rutter, Cal. Practice Guide: Personal Injury Ch. 9-B, B. In-Chambers
　　Conference Before Commencement of Trial.
Rutter, Cal. Practice Guide: Personal Injury Ch. 9-K, K. Submission of
　　Case to Jury.
7 Witkin Cal. Proc. 5th Trial § 318, (S 318) in General.
7 Witkin Cal. Proc. 5th Trial § 333, Unauthorized Discussion or
　　Separation.

§ 612.　Items which may be taken into jury room

Upon retiring for deliberation the jury may take with them all
papers which have been received as evidence in the cause, except
depositions, or copies of such papers as ought not, in the opinion
of the court, to be taken from the person having them in
possession; and they may also take with them any exhibits which
the court may deem proper, notes of the testimony or other
proceedings on the trial, taken by themselves or any of them, but
none taken by any other person. *(Enacted in 1872. Amended by
Stats.1939, c. 753, p. 2283, § 1.)*

Research References

Rutter, Cal. Practice Guide: Civil Trials & Evidence Ch. 1-C, C.
　　Marshalling the Evidence.
Rutter, Cal. Practice Guide: Civil Trials & Evidence Ch. 15-C, C. Matters
　　Allowed in Jury Room During Deliberations.
Rutter, Cal. Practice Guide: Civil Trials & Evidence Ch. 15-D, D. Juror
　　Requests for Additional Information During Deliberations.
Rutter, Cal. Practice Guide: Personal Injury Ch. 9-K, K. Submission of
　　Case to Jury.
7 Witkin Cal. Proc. 5th Trial § 323, (S 323) Papers and Exhibits in Jury
　　Room.
7 Witkin Cal. Proc. 5th Trial § 327, Unauthorized Papers in Jury Room.

§ 612.5.　Written instructions; copy with jury upon retiring for deliberation

Upon the jury retiring for deliberation, the court shall advise
the jury of the availability of a written copy of the jury
instructions. The court may, at its discretion, provide the jury
with a copy of the written instructions given. However, if the
jury requests the court to supply a copy of the written instructions, the court shall supply the jury with a copy. *(Added by
Stats.1975, c. 461, § 1. Amended by Stats.1986, c. 1045, § 1.)*

Research References

Rutter, Cal. Practice Guide: Civil Trials & Evidence Ch. 14-F, F.
　　Instructing the Jury.
Rutter, Cal. Practice Guide: Civil Trials & Evidence Ch. 15-C, C. Matters
　　Allowed in Jury Room During Deliberations.
Rutter, Cal. Practice Guide: Personal Injury Ch. 9-K, K. Submission of
　　Case to Jury.
7 Witkin Cal. Proc. 5th Trial § 323, (S 323) Papers and Exhibits in Jury
　　Room.
7 Witkin Cal. Proc. 5th Trial § 325, (S 325) Return for Instructions.

§ 613.　Decision in court; deliberation; communications

When the case is finally submitted to the jury, they may decide
in court or retire for deliberation. If they retire, they must be
kept together in some convenient place, under charge of an
officer, until at least three-fourths of them agree upon a verdict
or are discharged by the court. Unless by order of the court, the
officer having them under his or her charge shall not permit any
communication to be made to them, including any form of

electronic or wireless communication, or make any himself or herself, except to ask them if they or three-fourths of them are agreed upon a verdict. The officer shall not, before their verdict is rendered, communicate to any person the state of their deliberations, or the verdict agreed upon. *(Enacted in 1872. Amended by Code Am.1880, c. 21, p. 10, § 1; Stats.2011, c. 181 (A.B.141), § 2.)*

Research References

Rutter, Cal. Practice Guide: Civil Trials & Evidence Ch. 15-A, A. General Considerations.
Rutter, Cal. Practice Guide: Civil Trials & Evidence Ch. 15-B, B. Custody and Care of Jurors During Deliberations.
Rutter, Cal. Practice Guide: Civil Trials & Evidence Ch. 15-F, F. Juror Misconduct During Deliberations.
Rutter, Cal. Practice Guide: Personal Injury Ch. 9-K, K. Submission of Case to Jury.
7 Witkin Cal. Proc. 5th Trial § 318, (S 318) in General.
7 Witkin Cal. Proc. 5th Trial § 319, (S 319) Length of Deliberations.
7 Witkin Cal. Proc. 5th Trial § 330, (S 330) in General.
7 Witkin Cal. Proc. 5th Trial § 332, (S 332) With Judge or Court Officer.
7 Witkin Cal. Proc. 5th Trial § 333, Unauthorized Discussion or Separation.

§ 614. Return to court for information; notice to parties or counsel

After the jury have retired for deliberation, if there be a disagreement between them as to any part of the testimony, or if they desire to be informed of any point of law arising in the cause, they may require the officer to conduct them into Court. Upon their being brought into Court, the information required must be given in the presence of, or after notice to, the parties or counsel. *(Enacted in 1872.)*

Research References

Rutter, Cal. Practice Guide: Civil Trials & Evidence Ch. 14-F, F. Instructing the Jury.
Rutter, Cal. Practice Guide: Civil Trials & Evidence Ch. 15-D, D. Juror Requests for Additional Information During Deliberations.
Rutter, Cal. Practice Guide: Personal Injury Ch. 9-K, K. Submission of Case to Jury.
7 Witkin Cal. Proc. 5th Trial § 324, (S 324) Return for Reading of Testimony.
7 Witkin Cal. Proc. 5th Trial § 325, (S 325) Return for Instructions.
7 Witkin Cal. Proc. 5th Trial § 332, (S 332) With Judge or Court Officer.

§ 614.5. Reading prior testimony to jury; presence of judge

Except for good cause shown, the judge in his or her discretion need not be present in the court while testimony previously received in evidence is read to the jury. *(Added by Stats.1987, c. 88, § 1, eff. July 2, 1987.)*

Research References

Rutter, Cal. Practice Guide: Civil Trials & Evidence Ch. 15-D, D. Juror Requests for Additional Information During Deliberations.
Rutter, Cal. Practice Guide: Personal Injury Ch. 9-B, B. In-Chambers Conference Before Commencement of Trial.
Rutter, Cal. Practice Guide: Personal Injury Ch. 9-K, K. Submission of Case to Jury.
7 Witkin Cal. Proc. 5th Trial § 324, (S 324) Return for Reading of Testimony.

§ 616. Discharge without verdict or prevention from giving verdict; retrial

In all cases where the jury are discharged without having rendered a verdict, or are prevented from giving a verdict, by reason of accident or other cause, during the progress of the trial, or after the cause is submitted to them, except as provided in Section 630, the action may be again tried immediately, or at a future time, as the court may direct. *(Enacted in 1872. Amended by Stats.1947, c. 984, p. 2252, § 1.)*

Research References

Rutter, Cal. Practice Guide: Civil Trials & Evidence Ch. 12-A, A. Motion for Mistrial.
Rutter, Cal. Practice Guide: Civil Trials & Evidence Ch. 12-C, C. Motion for Directed Verdict.
Rutter, Cal. Practice Guide: Civil Trials & Evidence Ch. 18-B, B. Motion for New Trial.
Rutter, Cal. Practice Guide: Personal Injury Ch. 9-L, L. Motions to Terminate Trial Before Verdict.
8 Witkin Cal. Proc. 5th Attack Judgment Trial Court § 18, (S 18) Nature and Object of Motion.
7 Witkin Cal. Proc. 5th Trial § 167, Mistrial.

§ 617. Adjournment during absence of jury; sealed verdict

While the jury are absent the Court may adjourn from time to time, in respect to other business; but it is nevertheless open for every purpose connected with the cause submitted to the jury, until a verdict is rendered or the jury discharged. The Court may direct the jury to bring in a sealed verdict, at the opening of the Court, in case of an agreement during a recess or adjournment for the day. *(Enacted in 1872. Amended by Code Am.1880, c. 21, p. 10, § 2.)*

Research References

Rutter, Cal. Practice Guide: Civil Trials & Evidence Ch. 15-D, D. Juror Requests for Additional Information During Deliberations.
7 Witkin Cal. Proc. 5th Trial § 339, Receipt of Verdict.

§ 618. Verdict; polling jury

When the jury, or three-fourths of them, have agreed upon a verdict, they must be conducted into court and the verdict rendered by their foreperson. The verdict must be in writing, signed by the foreperson, and must be read to the jury by the clerk, and the inquiry made whether it is their verdict. Either party may require the jury to be polled, which is done by the court or clerk, asking each juror if it is the juror's verdict. If upon inquiry or polling, more than one-fourth of the jurors disagree thereto, the jury must be sent out again, but if no disagreement is expressed, the verdict is complete and the jury discharged from the case. *(Enacted in 1872. Amended by Code Am.1880, c. 21, p. 10, § 3; Stats.1933, c. 744, p. 1875, § 102; Stats.1935, c. 722, p. 1956, § 9; Stats.1978, c. 258, p. 542, § 1; Stats.2007, c. 263 (A.B.310), § 7.)*

Law Revision Commission Comments

Section 618 is amended to delete unnecessary language authorizing the judge to substitute for the clerk if there is no clerk. See Code Civ. Proc. § 167 (judge may perform any act court clerk may perform); Gov't Code §§ 69840–69848 (duties of clerk of superior court), 71620(b) (executive or administrative officer has authority of clerk of court).

Section 618 is also amended to make stylistic revisions and make the statute gender neutral. [35 Cal.L.Rev.Comm. Reports 219 (2006)].

Research References

Rutter, Cal. Practice Guide: Civil Trials & Evidence Ch. 17-A, A. Verdicts.
California Practice Guide: Employment Litigation Ch. 19-K, K. Jury Selection.
Rutter, Cal. Practice Guide: Personal Injury Ch. 9-M, M. Verdicts and Judgment.
2 Witkin Cal. Proc. 5th Courts § 366, (S 366) Miscellaneous Duties.
7 Witkin Cal. Proc. 5th Trial § 339, Receipt of Verdict.
7 Witkin Cal. Proc. 5th Trial § 350, Polling Jury.

§ 619. Informal or insufficient verdict; correction

When the verdict is announced, if it is informal or insufficient, in not covering the issue submitted, it may be corrected by the jury under the advice of the Court, or the jury may be again sent out. *(Enacted in 1872.)*

Research References

Rutter, Cal. Practice Guide: Civil Trials & Evidence Ch. 17-A, A. Verdicts.

Rutter, Cal. Practice Guide: Civil Trials & Evidence Ch. 18-A, A. Motion for Judgment Notwithstanding the Verdict ("JNOV").

Rutter, Cal. Practice Guide: Personal Injury Ch. 9-M, M. Verdicts and Judgment.

7 Witkin Cal. Proc. 5th Trial § 358, (S 358) Joint Liability.

7 Witkin Cal. Proc. 5th Trial § 371, (S 371) Judge's Power to Order Correction.

7 Witkin Cal. Proc. 5th Trial § 372, (S 372) Judge's Duty to Order Correction.

7 Witkin Cal. Proc. 5th Trial § 374, (S 374) Distinction: Verdict Erroneous But Not Defective.

ARTICLE 3. THE VERDICT

Section

624. General and special verdicts defined.
625. Special verdict or findings; punitive damages; filing and entry upon minutes; general verdict controlled by special findings.
626. Actions or cross-complaints for recovery of money.
627. Action for recovery of specific personal property.
628. Entry.
629. Judgment notwithstanding verdict.
630. Motion for directed verdict; granting of motion for all or part of issues involved; effect; ordering judgment after discharge of jury and failure to grant directed verdict.

§ 624. General and special verdicts defined

The verdict of a jury is either general or special. A general verdict is that by which they pronounce generally upon all or any of the issues, either in favor of the plaintiff or defendant; a special verdict is that by which the jury find the facts only, leaving the judgment to the Court. The special verdict must present the conclusions of fact as established by the evidence, and not the evidence to prove them; and those conclusions of fact must be so presented as that nothing shall remain to the Court but to draw from them conclusions of law. *(Enacted in 1872.)*

Research References

Rutter, Cal. Practice Guide: Civil Trials & Evidence Ch. 17-A, A. Verdicts.

Rutter, Cal. Practice Guide: Fed.Civ.Pro. Before Trial Ch. 1-D, D. Choosing Between State and Federal Courts.

Rutter, Cal. Practice Guide: Personal Injury Ch. 9-M, M. Verdicts and Judgment.

7 Witkin Cal. Proc. 5th Trial § 341, (S 341) General Verdict.

7 Witkin Cal. Proc. 5th Trial § 342, Nature of Special Verdict.

§ 625. Special verdict or findings; punitive damages; filing and entry upon minutes; general verdict controlled by special findings

In all cases the court may direct the jury to find a special verdict in writing, upon all, or any of the issues, and in all cases may instruct them, if they render a general verdict, to find upon particular questions of fact, to be stated in writing, and may direct a written finding thereon. In all cases in which the issue of punitive damages is presented to the jury the court shall direct the jury to find a special verdict in writing separating punitive damages from compensatory damages. The special verdict or finding must be filed with the clerk and entered upon the minutes. Where a special finding of facts is inconsistent with the general verdict, the former controls the latter, and the court must give judgment accordingly. *(Enacted in 1872. Amended by Stats.1905, c. 62, p. 56, § 1; Stats.1909, c. 121, p. 193, § 1; Stats.1957, c. 1443, p. 2771, § 1; Stats.1983, c. 176, § 2.)*

Research References

Rutter, Cal. Practice Guide: Civil Trials & Evidence Ch. 13-E, E. Presentation of Closing Argument.

Rutter, Cal. Practice Guide: Civil Trials & Evidence Ch. 17-A, A. Verdicts.

Rutter, Cal. Practice Guide: Insurance Litigation Ch. 13-C, C. Punitive Damages.

Rutter, Cal. Practice Guide: Personal Injury Ch. 3-E, E. Punitive Damages.

Rutter, Cal. Practice Guide: Personal Injury Ch. 3-F, F. MICRA Provisions Affecting Damages.

Rutter, Cal. Practice Guide: Personal Injury Ch. 9-M, M. Verdicts and Judgment.

7 Witkin Cal. Proc. 5th Trial § 340, Entry of Verdict.

7 Witkin Cal. Proc. 5th Trial § 342, Nature of Special Verdict.

7 Witkin Cal. Proc. 5th Trial § 343, Partial Acceptance of Special Verdict.

7 Witkin Cal. Proc. 5th Trial § 345, Punitive Damages.

7 Witkin Cal. Proc. 5th Trial § 347, Nature of Special Findings.

7 Witkin Cal. Proc. 5th Trial § 353, Special Findings to Test General Verdict.

7 Witkin Cal. Proc. 5th Trial § 364, Special Findings Inconsistent With General Verdict.

§ 626. Actions or cross-complaints for recovery of money

When a verdict is found for the plaintiff in an action for the recovery of money, or for the cross-complainant when a cross-complaint for the recovery of money is established, the jury must also find the amount of the recovery. *(Enacted in 1872. Amended by Stats.1971, c. 244, p. 391, § 52, operative July 1, 1972.)*

Law Revision Commission Comments

The amendment to Section 626 substitutes a reference to "cross-complaint" for the former reference to "counterclaim" and makes other conforming changes to reflect the fact that counterclaims have been abolished and claims formerly asserted as counterclaims are now to be asserted as cross-complaints. See Code of Civil Procedure Section 428.80.

§ 627. Action for recovery of specific personal property

In an action for the recovery of specific personal property, if the property has not been delivered to the plaintiff, or the defendant, by his answer, claim a return thereof, the jury, if their verdict be in favor of the plaintiff, or, if being in favor of defendant, they also find that he is entitled to a return thereof, must find the value of the property, and, if so instructed, the value of specific portions thereof, and may at the same time assess the damages, if any are claimed in the complaint or answer, which the prevailing party has sustained by reason of the taking or detention of such property. *(Enacted in 1872. Amended by Code Am.1873–74, c. 383, p. 311, § 77.)*

Research References

5 Witkin Cal. Proc. 5th Pleading § 692, (S 692) in General.

6 Witkin Cal. Proc. 5th Provisional Remedies § 273, Effect of Judgment in Main Action.

§ 628. Entry

In superior courts upon receipt of a verdict, an entry must be made in the minutes of the court, specifying the time of trial, the names of the jurors and witnesses, and setting out the verdict at length; and where a special verdict is found, either the judgment rendered thereon, or if the case is reserved for argument or further consideration, the order thus reserving it. *(Enacted in 1872. Amended by Stats.1933, c. 744, p. 1875, § 103; Stats.1951, c. 1737, p. 4115, § 90, operative Jan. 1, 1952; Stats.1965, c. 205, p. 1171, § 2; Stats.1977, c. 1257, p. 4763, § 21, eff. Jan. 3, 1977; Stats.1998, c. 931 (S.B.2139), § 82, eff. Sept. 28, 1998; Stats.2002, c. 784 (S.B.1316), § 63.)*

Civ. Pro.

Law Revision Commission Comments

Section 628 is amended to reflect the elimination of the justice court. Cal. Const. art. VI, §§ 1, 5(b). [28 Cal.L.Rev.Comm. Reports 51 (1998)].

Section 628 is amended to reflect unification of the municipal and superior courts pursuant to Article VI, Section 5(e), of the California Constitution. [32 Cal.L.Rev.Comm. Reports 125 (2002)].

Research References

Rutter, Cal. Practice Guide: Civil Trials & Evidence Ch. 17-A, A. Verdicts.
Rutter, Cal. Practice Guide: Civil Trials & Evidence Ch. 17-C, C. Entry of Judgment.
Rutter, Cal. Practice Guide: Personal Injury Ch. 9-M, M. Verdicts and Judgment.
7 Witkin Cal. Proc. 5th Trial § 340, Entry of Verdict.
7 Witkin Cal. Proc. 5th Trial § 343, Partial Acceptance of Special Verdict.

§ 629. Judgment notwithstanding verdict

The court, before the expiration of its power to rule on a motion for a new trial, either of its own motion, after five days' notice, or on motion of a party against whom a verdict has been rendered, shall render judgment in favor of the aggrieved party notwithstanding the verdict whenever a motion for a directed verdict for the aggrieved party should have been granted had a previous motion been made.

A motion for judgment notwithstanding the verdict shall be made within the period specified by Section 659 of this code in respect of the filing and serving of notice of intention to move for a new trial. The making of a motion for judgment notwithstanding the verdict shall not extend the time within which a party may file and serve notice of intention to move for a new trial. The court shall not rule upon the motion for judgment notwithstanding the verdict until the expiration of the time within which a motion for a new trial must be served and filed, and if a motion for a new trial has been filed with the court by the aggrieved party, the court shall rule upon both motions at the same time. The power of the court to rule on a motion for judgment notwithstanding the verdict shall not extend beyond the last date upon which it has the power to rule on a motion for a new trial. If a motion for judgment notwithstanding the verdict is not determined before such date, the effect shall be a denial of such motion without further order of the court.

If the motion for judgment notwithstanding the verdict be denied and if a new trial be denied, the appellate court shall, when it appears that the motion for judgment notwithstanding the verdict should have been granted, order judgment to be so entered on appeal from the judgment or from the order denying the motion for judgment notwithstanding the verdict.

Where a new trial is granted to the party moving for judgment notwithstanding the verdict, and the motion for judgment notwithstanding the verdict is denied, the order denying the motion for judgment notwithstanding the verdict shall nevertheless be reviewable on appeal from said order by the aggrieved party. If the court grants the motion for judgment notwithstanding the verdict or of its own motion directs the entry of judgment notwithstanding the verdict and likewise grants the motion for a new trial, the order granting the new trial shall be effective only if, on appeal, the judgment notwithstanding the verdict is reversed, and the order granting a new trial is not appealed from or, if appealed from, is affirmed. *(Added by States.1923, c. 366, p. 750, § 1. Amended by Stats.1935, c. 722, p. 1956, § 10; Stats.1937, c. 551, p. 1579, § 1; Stats.1951, c. 801, p. 2288, eff. Jan. 1, 1952; Stats.1961, c. 604, p. 1752, § 1; Stats.1963, c. 205, p. 1943, § 1.)*

Research References

Rutter, Cal. Practice Guide: Civil Appeals & Writs Ch. 2-B, B. Appealable Judgments and Orders.

Rutter, Cal. Practice Guide: Civil Appeals & Writs Ch. 3-C, C. Extensions of Filing Deadline.
Rutter, Cal. Practice Guide: Civil Appeals & Writs Ch. 3-F, F. Cross-Appeals.
Rutter, Cal. Practice Guide: Civil Appeals & Writs Ch. 11-D, D. Disposition.
Rutter, Cal. Practice Guide: Civil Appeals & Writs Ch. 14-C, C. Trial Court Proceedings After Reversal.
Rutter, Cal. Practice Guide: Civil Appeals & Writs Ch. 15-A, A. Overview.
Rutter, Cal. Practice Guide: Civil Trials & Evidence Ch. 12-C, C. Motion for Directed Verdict.
Rutter, Cal. Practice Guide: Civil Trials & Evidence Ch. 18-A, A. Motion for Judgment Notwithstanding the Verdict ("JNOV").
Rutter, Cal. Practice Guide: Civil Trials & Evidence Ch. 18-B, B. Motion for New Trial.
California Practice Guide: Employment Litigation Ch. 19-S, S. Post-Trial Proceedings.
Rutter, Cal. Practice Guide: Insurance Litigation Ch. 13-C, C. Punitive Damages.
Rutter, Cal. Practice Guide: Personal Injury Ch. 10-A, A. Motion for New Trial.
Rutter, Cal. Practice Guide: Personal Injury Ch. 10-B, B. Motion for Judgment Notwithstanding the Verdict.
Miller and Starr California Real Estate § 34:99, Punitive Damages--Judicial Review.
9 Witkin Cal. Proc. 5th Appeal § 192, (S 192) Order Granting New Trial.
9 Witkin Cal. Proc. 5th Appeal § 193, (S 193) Order Denying Judgment Notwithstanding Verdict.
9 Witkin Cal. Proc. 5th Appeal § 871, Distinction: Reversal for Insufficiency of Evidence.
9 Witkin Cal. Proc. 5th Appeal § 873, (S 873) Reversal of Judgment Notwithstanding Verdict.
8 Witkin Cal. Proc. 5th Attack Judgment Trial Court § 47, Motion Improperly Labeled.
7 Witkin Cal. Proc. 5th Trial § 156, Proceedings After Decision.
7 Witkin Cal. Proc. 5th Trial § 436, (S 436) Nature of Power.
7 Witkin Cal. Proc. 5th Trial § 438, (S 438) Motion for Directed Verdict is Unnecessary.
7 Witkin Cal. Proc. 5th Trial § 439, (S 439) Motion.
7 Witkin Cal. Proc. 5th Trial § 440, (S 440) With Motion for New Trial.
7 Witkin Cal. Proc. 5th Trial § 441, (S 441) Ruling on Motion.
7 Witkin Cal. Proc. 5th Trial § 442, (S 442) Granting on Court's Own Motion.
7 Witkin Cal. Proc. 5th Trial § 443, (S 443) Partial Judgment.
7 Witkin Cal. Proc. 5th Trial § 444, (S 444) Orders Denying Both Motions.
7 Witkin Cal. Proc. 5th Trial § 445, (S 445) Order Granting New Trial Motion.
7 Witkin Cal. Proc. 5th Trial § 446, (S 446) Orders Granting Both Motions.

§ 630. Motion for directed verdict; granting of motion for all or part of issues involved; effect; ordering judgment after discharge of jury and failure to grant directed verdict

(a) Unless the court specified an earlier time for making a motion for directed verdict, after all parties have completed the presentation of all of their evidence in a trial by jury, any party may, without waiving his or her right to trial by jury in the event the motion is not granted, move for an order directing entry of a verdict in its favor.

(b) If it appears that the evidence presented supports the granting of the motion as to some, but not all, of the issues involved in the action, the court shall grant the motion as to those issues and the action shall proceed on any remaining issues. Despite the granting of such a motion, no final judgment shall be entered prior to the termination of the action, but the final judgment, in addition to any matter determined in the trial, shall reflect the verdict ordered by the court as determined by the motion for directed verdict.

(c) If the motion is granted, unless the court in its order directing entry of the verdict specifies otherwise, it shall operate as an adjudication upon the merits.

(d) In actions which arise out of an injury to a person or property, when a motion for directed verdict was granted on the basis that a defendant was without fault, no other defendant during trial, over plaintiff's objection, shall attempt to attribute fault to or comment on the absence or involvement of the defendant who was granted the motion.

(e) The order of the court granting the motion for directed verdict is effective without any assent of the jury.

(f) When the jury for any reason has been discharged without having rendered a verdict, the court on its own motion or upon motion of a party, notice of which was given within 10 days after discharge of the jury, may order judgment to be entered in favor of a party whenever a motion for directed verdict for that party should have been granted had a previous motion been made. Except as otherwise provided in Section 12a, the power of the court to act under the provisions of this section shall expire 30 days after the day upon which the jury was discharged, and if judgment has not been ordered within that time the effect shall be the denial of any motion for judgment without further order of the court. *(Added by Stats.1947, c. 984, p. 2252, § 2. Amended by Stats.1967, c. 625, p. 1972, § 1; Stats.1986, c. 540, § 12.)*

Research References

Rutter, Cal. Practice Guide: Civil Trials & Evidence Ch. 12-A, A. Motion for Mistrial.
Rutter, Cal. Practice Guide: Civil Trials & Evidence Ch. 12-B, B. Motion for Nonsuit.
Rutter, Cal. Practice Guide: Civil Trials & Evidence Ch. 12-C, C. Motion for Directed Verdict.
Rutter, Cal. Practice Guide: Civil Trials & Evidence Ch. 18-A, A. Motion for Judgment Notwithstanding the Verdict ("JNOV").
California Practice Guide: Employment Litigation Ch. 19-P, P. Motions During Trial.
Rutter, Cal. Practice Guide: Personal Injury Ch. 9-L, L. Motions to Terminate Trial Before Verdict.
9 Witkin Cal. Proc. 5th Appeal § 159, Orders at Trial.
7 Witkin Cal. Proc. 5th Trial § 167, Mistrial.
7 Witkin Cal. Proc. 5th Trial § 420, in General.
7 Witkin Cal. Proc. 5th Trial § 424, Time for Motion.
7 Witkin Cal. Proc. 5th Trial § 427, Duty of Jurors to Comply.
7 Witkin Cal. Proc. 5th Trial § 428, Order by Judge After Jury is Discharged.
7 Witkin Cal. Proc. 5th Trial § 443, (S 443) Partial Judgment.

CHAPTER 4.5.   EXPEDITED JURY TRIALS

Repeal

For repeal of Chapter 4.5, see Code of Civil Procedure § 630.12.

§ 630.01.   Definitions

For purposes of this chapter:

(a) "Expedited jury trial" means a consensual, binding jury trial before a reduced jury panel and a judicial officer.

(b) "High/low agreement" means a written agreement entered into by the parties that specifies a minimum amount of damages that a plaintiff is guaranteed to receive from the defendant, and a maximum amount of damages that the defendant will be liable for, regardless of the ultimate verdict returned by the jury. Neither the existence of, nor the amounts contained in, any high/low agreements may be disclosed to the jury.

(c) "Post-trial motions" does not include motions relating to costs and attorney's fees, motions to correct a judgment for a clerical error, and motions to enforce a judgment. *(Added by Stats.2010, c. 674 (A.B.2284), § 2. Amended by Stats.2011, c. 296 (A.B.1023), § 37.)*

Repeal

For repeal of Chapter 4.5, see Code of Civil Procedure § 630.12.

Research References

Rutter, Cal. Practice Guide: A.D.R. Ch. 6-B, B. Temporary Judges.
Rutter, Cal. Practice Guide: Civil Appeals & Writs Ch. 2-A, A. Overview.
Rutter, Cal. Practice Guide: Civil Appeals & Writs Ch. 2-D, D. Standing to Appeal.
Rutter, Cal. Practice Guide: Civ. Pro. Before Trial Ch. 12(I)-H, H. Expedited Jury Trials.
Rutter, Cal. Practice Guide: Civil Trials & Evidence Ch. 2-A, A. Sources of Right to Jury Trial.
Rutter, Cal. Practice Guide: Civil Trials & Evidence Ch. 4-A, A. General Considerations.
Rutter, Cal. Practice Guide: Civil Trials & Evidence Ch. 4-B, B. Preliminary Matters Discussed in Final Status Conference or In-Chambers Conference.
Rutter, Cal. Practice Guide: Civil Trials & Evidence Ch. 8A-A, A. Types of Evidence.
Rutter, Cal. Practice Guide: Personal Injury Ch. 8-A, A. Case Management.
9 Witkin Cal. Proc. 5th Appeal § 84A, (S 84A) (New)-Expedited Jury Trial.
8 Witkin Cal. Proc. 5th Attack Judgment Trial Court § 22, in General.
8 Witkin Cal. Proc. 5th Attack Judgment Trial Court § 139, Nature and Grounds.
8 Witkin Cal. Proc. 5th Attack Judgment Trial Court § 144, (S 144) Nature of Relief.
8 Witkin Cal. Proc. 5th Attack Judgment Trial Court § 206, in General.
8 Witkin Cal. Proc. 5th Attack Judgment Trial Court § 215, (S 215) in General.
7 Witkin Cal. Proc. 5th Trial § 6A, (S 6A) (New)-In General.
7 Witkin Cal. Proc. 5th Trial § 6C, (S 6C) (New)-Conduct of Trial.

§ 630.02.   Rules and procedures applicable to expedited jury trials

The rules and procedures applicable to expedited jury trials are as follows:

(a) The procedures in this chapter and in the implementing rules of court shall apply to expedited jury trials, unless the parties agree otherwise, as permitted under subparagraph (E) of paragraph (1) of subdivision (e) of Section 630.03, and the court so orders.

(b) Any matters not expressly addressed in this chapter, in the implementing rules of court, or in a consent order authorized by this chapter and the implementing rules, are governed by applicable statutes and rules governing civil actions. *(Added by Stats.2010, c. 674 (A.B.2284), § 2.)*

Repeal

For repeal of Chapter 4.5, see Code of Civil Procedure § 630.12.

Research References

7 Witkin Cal. Proc. 5th Trial § 6A, (S 6A) (New)-In General.

§ 630.03. Proposed consent order; exceptions to binding nature of agreement; timing of agreement; approval of agreement; contents of proposed consent order

(a) All parties agreeing to participate in an expedited jury trial and, if represented, their counsel, shall sign a proposed consent order granting an expedited jury trial.

(b) Except as provided in subdivision (d), the agreement to participate in the expedited jury trial process is binding upon the parties, unless either of the following occurs:

(1) All parties stipulate to end the agreement to participate.

(2) The court, on its own motion or at the request of a party by noticed motion, finds that good cause exists for the action not to proceed under the rules of this chapter.

(c) Any agreement to participate in an expedited jury trial under this chapter may be entered into only after a dispute has arisen and an action has been filed.

(d) The court shall approve the use of an expedited jury trial and any high/low agreements or other stipulations for an expedited jury trial involving either of the following:

(1) A self-represented litigant.

(2) A minor, an incompetent person, or a person for whom a conservator has been appointed.

(e) The proposed consent order submitted to the court shall include all of the following:

(1) A preliminary statement that each named party and any insurance carrier responsible for providing coverage or defense on behalf of that party, individually identified in the proposed consent order, have been informed of the rules and procedures for an expedited jury trial and provided with a Judicial Council information sheet regarding expedited jury trials, have agreed to take part in or, in the case of a responsible insurance carrier, not object to, the expedited jury trial process, and have agreed to all the specific provisions set forth in the consent order.

(2) The parties' agreement to all of the following:

(A) That all parties waive all rights to appeal and to move for directed verdict or make any post-trial motions, except as provided in Sections 630.08 and 630.09.

(B) That each side shall have up to three hours in which to present its case.

(C) That the jury shall be composed of eight or fewer jurors with no alternates.

(D) That each side shall be limited to three peremptory challenges, unless the court permits an additional challenge in cases with more than two sides as provided in Section 630.04.

(E) That the trial and pretrial matters will proceed under subparagraphs (A) to (D), inclusive, and, unless the parties expressly agree otherwise in the proposed consent order, under all other provisions in this chapter and in the implementing rules of court.

(f) The court shall issue the consent order as proposed by the parties, unless the court finds good cause why the action should not proceed through the expedited jury trial process, in which case the court shall deny the proposed consent order in its entirety. *(Added by Stats.2010, c. 674 (A.B.2284), § 2.)*

Repeal

For repeal of Chapter 4.5, see Code of Civil Procedure § 630.12.

Research References

Rutter, Cal. Practice Guide: Civ. Pro. Before Trial Ch. 12(I)-H, H. Expedited Jury Trials.

Rutter, Cal. Practice Guide: Civil Trials & Evidence Ch. 2-A, A. Sources of Right to Jury Trial.

Rutter, Cal. Practice Guide: Civil Trials & Evidence Ch. 2-B, B. What Constitutes Jury Trial.

Rutter, Cal. Practice Guide: Personal Injury Ch. 8-A, A. Case Management.

9 Witkin Cal. Proc. 5th Appeal § 84A, (S 84A) (New)-Expedited Jury Trial.

7 Witkin Cal. Proc. 5th Trial § 6A, (S 6A) (New)-In General.

§ 630.04. Juries in expedited jury trial cases; number of jurors; peremptory challenges

(a) Juries in expedited jury trial cases shall be composed of eight jurors, unless the parties have agreed to fewer. No alternates shall be selected.

(b) The court shall allow each side three peremptory challenges. If there are more than two parties in a case and more than two sides, as determined by the court under subdivision (c) of Section 231, the parties may request one additional peremptory challenge each, which is to be granted by the court as the interests of justice may require. *(Added by Stats.2010, c. 674 (A.B.2284), § 2.)*

Repeal

For repeal of Chapter 4.5, see Code of Civil Procedure § 630.12.

Research References

Rutter, Cal. Practice Guide: Civ. Pro. Before Trial Ch. 12(I)-H, H. Expedited Jury Trials.

Rutter, Cal. Practice Guide: Civil Trials & Evidence Ch. 2-B, B. What Constitutes Jury Trial.

Rutter, Cal. Practice Guide: Civil Trials & Evidence Ch. 4-C, C. Jury Matters.

Rutter, Cal. Practice Guide: Civil Trials & Evidence Ch. 5-I, I. Challenging Prospective Jurors.

Rutter, Cal. Practice Guide: Civil Trials & Evidence Ch. 5-J, J. Alternate Jurors.

Rutter, Cal. Practice Guide: Personal Injury Ch. 8-A, A. Case Management.

7 Witkin Cal. Proc. 5th Trial § 6A, (S 6A) (New)-In General.

7 Witkin Cal. Proc. 5th Trial § 6C, (S 6C) (New)-Conduct of Trial.

§ 630.05. Jury deliberation in expedited cases

Nothing in this chapter is intended to preclude a jury from deliberating as long as needed. *(Added by Stats.2010, c. 674 (A.B.2284), § 2.)*

Repeal

For repeal of Chapter 4.5, see Code of Civil Procedure § 630.12.

Research References

Rutter, Cal. Practice Guide: Civ. Pro. Before Trial Ch. 12(I)-H, H. Expedited Jury Trials.

7 Witkin Cal. Proc. 5th Trial § 6C, (S 6C) (New)-Conduct of Trial.

7 Witkin Cal. Proc. 5th Trial § 319, (S 319) Length of Deliberations.

§ 630.06. Applicability of rules of evidence; waiver or stipulation not to affect privilege; right to issue subpoenas and notices to appear

(a) The rules of evidence apply in expedited jury trials, unless the parties stipulate otherwise.

(b) Any stipulation by the parties to use relaxed rules of evidence may not be construed to eliminate, or in any way affect, the right of a witness or party to invoke any applicable privilege or other law protecting confidentiality.

(c) The right to issue subpoenas and notices to appear to secure the attendance of witnesses or the production of documents at trial shall be in accordance with this code. *(Added by Stats.2010, c. 674 (A.B.2284), § 2.)*

Repeal

For repeal of Chapter 4.5, see Code of Civil Procedure § 630.12.

Research References

Rutter, Cal. Practice Guide: Civ. Pro. Before Trial Ch. 12(I)-H, H. Expedited Jury Trials.
Rutter, Cal. Practice Guide: Civil Trials & Evidence Ch. 4-B, B. Preliminary Matters Discussed in Final Status Conference or In-Chambers Conference.
Rutter, Cal. Practice Guide: Civil Trials & Evidence Ch. 8A-A, A. Types of Evidence.
7 Witkin Cal. Proc. 5th Trial § 6C, (S 6C) (New)-Conduct of Trial.

§ 630.07. Binding nature of agreement; vote of jurors

(a) The verdict in an expedited jury trial case is binding, subject to any written high/low agreement or other stipulations concerning the amount of the award agreed upon by the parties.

(b) A vote of six of the eight jurors is required for a verdict, unless the parties stipulate otherwise. *(Added by Stats.2010, c. 674 (A.B.2284), § 2.)*

Repeal

For repeal of Chapter 4.5, see Code of Civil Procedure § 630.12.

Research References

Rutter, Cal. Practice Guide: Civ. Pro. Before Trial Ch. 12(I)-H, H. Expedited Jury Trials.
Rutter, Cal. Practice Guide: Personal Injury Ch. 8-A, A. Case Management.
Rutter, Cal. Practice Guide: Personal Injury Ch. 9-M, M. Verdicts and Judgment.
7 Witkin Cal. Proc. 5th Trial § 6C, (S 6C) (New)-Conduct of Trial.

§ 630.08. Waiver of motions for directed verdict, to set aside verdict or judgment rendered by jury, or for new trial based on amount of damages; limitation of court's authority to direct verdict, enter judgment as a matter of law, or order new trial

(a) By agreeing to participate in the expedited jury trial process, the parties agree to waive any motions for directed verdict, motions to set aside the verdict or any judgment rendered by the jury, or motions for a new trial on the basis of inadequate or excessive damages.

(b) The court shall not set aside any verdict or any judgment, shall not direct that judgment be entered in favor of a party entitled to judgment as a matter of law, and shall not order a new trial, except on the grounds stated in Section 630.09. *(Added by Stats.2010, c. 674 (A.B.2284), § 2. Amended by Stats.2011, c. 296 (A.B.1023), § 38.)*

Repeal

For repeal of Chapter 4.5, see Code of Civil Procedure § 630.12.

Research References

Rutter, Cal. Practice Guide: Civil Trials & Evidence Ch. 2-A, A. Sources of Right to Jury Trial.
Rutter, Cal. Practice Guide: Civil Trials & Evidence Ch. 2-C, C. Cases in Which Jury Trial May be Demanded.
Rutter, Cal. Practice Guide: Civil Trials & Evidence Ch. 12-C, C. Motion for Directed Verdict.
Rutter, Cal. Practice Guide: Civil Trials & Evidence Ch. 18-A, A. Motion for Judgment Notwithstanding the Verdict ("JNOV").
Rutter, Cal. Practice Guide: Civil Trials & Evidence Ch. 18-B, B. Motion for New Trial.
Rutter, Cal. Practice Guide: Civil Trials & Evidence Ch. 18-C, C. Other Post-Trial Motions.
8 Witkin Cal. Proc. 5th Attack Judgment Trial Court § 22, in General.
8 Witkin Cal. Proc. 5th Attack Judgment Trial Court § 139, Nature and Grounds.
8 Witkin Cal. Proc. 5th Attack Judgment Trial Court § 144, (S 144) Nature of Relief.
8 Witkin Cal. Proc. 5th Attack Judgment Trial Court § 206, in General.
8 Witkin Cal. Proc. 5th Attack Judgment Trial Court § 215, (S 215) in General.
7 Witkin Cal. Proc. 5th Trial § 6A, (S 6A) (New)-In General.
7 Witkin Cal. Proc. 5th Trial § 6D, (S 6D) (New)-Post-Trial Proceedings.
7 Witkin Cal. Proc. 5th Trial § 420, in General.
7 Witkin Cal. Proc. 5th Trial § 436, (S 436) Nature of Power.

§ 630.09. Waiver of right to bring post-trial motions or appeal; exceptions; procedures

(a) By agreeing to participate in the expedited jury trial process, the parties agree to waive the right to bring post-trial motions or to appeal from the determination of the matter, except as provided in this section. The only grounds on which a party may move for a new trial or appeal are any of the following:

(1) Judicial misconduct that materially affected the substantial rights of a party.

(2) Misconduct of the jury.

(3) Corruption, fraud, or other undue means employed in the proceedings of the court, jury, or adverse party that prevented a party from having a fair trial.

(b) Within 10 court days of the entry of a jury verdict, a party may file with the clerk and serve on each adverse party a notice of the intention to move for a new trial on any of the grounds specified in subdivision (a). The notice shall be deemed to be a motion for a new trial.

(c) Except as provided in subdivision (b), parties to an expedited jury trial shall not make any post-trial motions except for motions relating to costs and attorney's fees, motions to correct a judgment for clerical error, and motions to enforce a judgment.

(d) Before filing an appeal, a party shall make a motion for a new trial under subdivision (b). If the motion for a new trial is denied, the party may appeal the judgment to the appropriate court with appellate jurisdiction and seek a new trial on any of the grounds specified in subdivision (a). Parties to an expedited jury trial may not appeal on any other ground. *(Added by Stats.2010, c. 674 (A.B.2284), § 2.)*

Repeal

For repeal of Chapter 4.5, see Code of Civil Procedure § 630.12.

Research References

Rutter, Cal. Practice Guide: Civil Appeals & Writs Ch. 2-A, A. Overview.
Rutter, Cal. Practice Guide: Civil Appeals & Writs Ch. 2-D, D. Standing to Appeal.

Rutter, Cal. Practice Guide: Civil Appeals & Writs Ch. 8-D, D. Limits on Assertion of Issues on Appeal.

Rutter, Cal. Practice Guide: Civ. Pro. Before Trial Ch. 12(I)-H, H. Expedited Jury Trials.

Rutter, Cal. Practice Guide: Civil Trials & Evidence Ch. 12-C, C. Motion for Directed Verdict.

Rutter, Cal. Practice Guide: Civil Trials & Evidence Ch. 18-A, A. Motion for Judgment Notwithstanding the Verdict ("JNOV").

Rutter, Cal. Practice Guide: Civil Trials & Evidence Ch. 18-B, B. Motion for New Trial.

Rutter, Cal. Practice Guide: Civil Trials & Evidence Ch. 18-C, C. Other Post-Trial Motions.

Rutter, Cal. Practice Guide: Civil Trials & Evidence Ch. 8B-C, C. Procedural Considerations.

Rutter, Cal. Practice Guide: Personal Injury Ch. 8-A, A. Case Management.

9 Witkin Cal. Proc. 5th Appeal § 84A, (S 84A) (New)-Expedited Jury Trial.

8 Witkin Cal. Proc. 5th Attack Judgment Trial Court § 22, in General.

8 Witkin Cal. Proc. 5th Attack Judgment Trial Court § 139, Nature and Grounds.

8 Witkin Cal. Proc. 5th Attack Judgment Trial Court § 144, (S 144) Nature of Relief.

8 Witkin Cal. Proc. 5th Attack Judgment Trial Court § 206, in General.

8 Witkin Cal. Proc. 5th Attack Judgment Trial Court § 215, (S 215) in General.

7 Witkin Cal. Proc. 5th Trial § 6A, (S 6A) (New)-In General.

7 Witkin Cal. Proc. 5th Trial § 6D, (S 6D) (New)-Post-Trial Proceedings.

§ 630.10. Applicability of statutes and rules governing costs and attorney's fees

All statutes and rules governing costs and attorney's fees shall apply in expedited jury trials, unless the parties agree otherwise in the consent order. *(Added by Stats.2010, c. 674 (A.B.2284), § 2.)*

Repeal

For repeal of Chapter 4.5, see Code of Civil Procedure § 630.12.

Research References

7 Witkin Cal. Proc. 5th Trial § 6D, (S 6D) (New)-Post-Trial Proceedings.

§ 630.11. Rules and forms to establish uniform procedures implementing chapter

The Judicial Council shall, on or before January 1, 2011, adopt rules and forms to establish uniform procedures implementing the provisions of this chapter, including, but not limited to, rules for all of the following:

(a) Additional content of proposed consent orders.

(b) Pretrial exchanges and submissions.

(c) Pretrial conferences.

(d) Time limits for jury selection.

(e) Time limits for trial, including presentation of evidence and argument.

(f) Presentation of evidence and testimony.

(g) Any other procedures necessary to implement the provisions of this chapter. *(Added by Stats.2010, c. 674 (A.B.2284), § 2.)*

Repeal

For repeal of Chapter 4.5, see Code of Civil Procedure § 630.12.

Research References

7 Witkin Cal. Proc. 5th Trial § 6A, (S 6A) (New)-In General.

§ 630.12. Duration of chapter

This chapter shall remain in effect only until January 1, 2016, and as of that date is repealed, unless a later enacted statute, that is enacted before January 1, 2016, deletes or extends that date. *(Added by Stats.2010, c. 674 (A.B.2284), § 2.)*

Research References

8 Witkin Cal. Proc. 5th Attack Judgment Trial Court § 22, in General.

8 Witkin Cal. Proc. 5th Attack Judgment Trial Court § 139, Nature and Grounds.

8 Witkin Cal. Proc. 5th Attack Judgment Trial Court § 144, (S 144) Nature of Relief.

8 Witkin Cal. Proc. 5th Attack Judgment Trial Court § 206, in General.

8 Witkin Cal. Proc. 5th Attack Judgment Trial Court § 215, (S 215) in General.

7 Witkin Cal. Proc. 5th Trial § 6A, (S 6A) (New)-In General.

CHAPTER 5. TRIAL BY COURT

Section

§ 631. Right to jury trial; demand for jury trial; payment of nonrefundable fee by at least one party on each side of case; failure to timely pay fee; daily deposit of sum equal to that day's fees and mileage of the jury; waiver of jury trial

(a) The right to a trial by jury as declared by Section 16 of Article I of the California Constitution shall be preserved to the parties inviolate. In civil cases, a jury may only be waived pursuant to subdivision (f).

(b) At least one party demanding a jury on each side of a civil case shall pay a nonrefundable fee of one hundred fifty dollars ($150), unless the fee has been paid by another party on the same side of the case. The fee shall offset the costs to the state of providing juries in civil cases. If there are more than two parties to the case, for purposes of this section only, all plaintiffs shall be considered one side of the case, and all other parties shall be considered the other side of the case. Payment of the fee by a party on one side of the case shall not relieve parties on the other side of the case from waiver pursuant to subdivision (f).

(c) The fee described in subdivision (b) shall be due on or before the date scheduled for the initial case management conference in the action, except as follows:

(1) In unlawful detainer actions, the fees shall be due at least five days before the date set for trial.

(2) If no case management conference is scheduled in a civil action, or the initial case management conference occurred before June 28, 2012, and the initial complaint was filed on or after July 1, 2011, the fee shall be due no later than 365 calendar days after the filing of the initial complaint.

(3) If the initial case management conference occurred before June 28, 2012, and the initial complaint in the case was filed before July 1, 2011, the fee shall be due at least 25 calendar days before the date initially set for trial.

(4) If the party requesting a jury has not appeared before the initial case management conference, or first appeared more than 365 calendar days after the filing of the initial complaint, the fee shall be due at least 25 calendar days before the date initially set for trial.

(d) If a party failed to timely pay the fee described in subdivision (b) that was due between June 27, 2012, and November 30, 2012, the party will be relieved of a jury waiver on that basis only if the party pays the fee on or before December 31, 2012, or 25 calendar days before the date initially set for trial, whichever is earlier.

(e) The parties demanding a jury trial shall deposit with the clerk or judge, at the beginning of the second and each succeeding day's session, a sum equal to that day's fees and mileage of the jury, including the fees and mileage for the trial jury panel if the trial jury has not yet been selected and sworn. If more than one party has demanded a jury, the respective amount to be paid daily by each party demanding a jury shall be determined by stipulation of the parties or by order of the court.

(f) A party waives trial by jury in any of the following ways:

(1) By failing to appear at the trial.

(2) By written consent filed with the clerk or judge.

(3) By oral consent, in open court, entered in the minutes.

(4) By failing to announce that a jury is required, at the time the cause is first set for trial, if it is set upon notice or stipulation, or within five days after notice of setting if it is set without notice or stipulation.

(5) By failing to timely pay the fee described in subdivision (b), unless another party on the same side of the case has paid that fee.

(6) By failing to deposit with the clerk or judge, at the beginning of the second and each succeeding day's session, the sum provided in subdivision (e).

(g) The court may, in its discretion upon just terms, allow a trial by jury although there may have been a waiver of a trial by jury.

(h) The court shall transmit the fee described in subdivision (b) to the State Treasury for deposit in the Trial Court Trust Fund within 45 calendar days after the end of the month in which the fee is paid to the court. *(Added by Stats.1988, c. 10, § 3, eff. Feb. 17, 1988. Amended by Stats.1988, c. 278, § 1; Stats.1989, c. 15, § 2, eff. May 10, 1989; Stats.1998, c. 931 (S.B.2139), § 83, eff. Sept. 28, 1998; Stats.1999, c. 83 (S.B.966), § 24; Stats.2000, c. 127 (A.B.2866), § 2, eff. July 10, 2000; Stats.2002, c. 806 (A.B.3027), § 15; Stats.2012, c. 41 (S.B.1021), § 3, eff. June 27, 2012; Stats.2012, c. 342 (A.B.1481), § 1, eff. Sept. 17, 2012.)*

Law Revision Commission Comments

Section 631 is amended to accommodate unification of the municipal and superior courts in a county. Cal. Const. art. VI, § 5(e). See Section 85 (limited civil cases) & Comment. [28 Cal.L.Rev.Comm. Reports 51 (1998)].

Research References

Rutter, Cal. Practice Guide: A.D.R. Ch. 3-A, A. General Considerations.
Rutter, Cal. Practice Guide: Civ. Pro. Before Trial Ch. 12(I)-D, D. Demand for Jury Trial and Waiver.
Rutter, Cal. Practice Guide: Civil Trials & Evidence Ch. 1-A, A. Importance of Statewide and Local Rules of Court.
Rutter, Cal. Practice Guide: Civil Trials & Evidence Ch. 2-A, A. Sources of Right to Jury Trial.
Rutter, Cal. Practice Guide: Civil Trials & Evidence Ch. 2-C, C. Cases in Which Jury Trial May be Demanded.
Rutter, Cal. Practice Guide: Civil Trials & Evidence Ch. 2-D, D. Securing Trial by Jury.

Rutter, Cal. Practice Guide: Civil Trials & Evidence Ch. 2-E, E. Waiver of Jury Trial.
Rutter, Cal. Practice Guide: Civil Trials & Evidence Ch. 2-F, F. Relief from Waiver.
Rutter, Cal. Practice Guide: Civil Trials & Evidence Ch. 16-A, A. General Considerations Re Nonjury Trials.
California Practice Guide: Employment Litigation Ch. 18-C, C. Contractual Arbitration.
California Practice Guide: Employment Litigation Ch. 19-E, E. Jury Demand.
Rutter, Cal. Practice Guide: Fed.Civ.Pro. Before Trial Ch. 1-D, D. Choosing Between State and Federal Courts.
Rutter, Cal. Practice Guide: Fed.Civ.Pro. Before Trial Ch. 2D-9, Effect of Removal.
Rutter, Cal. Practice Guide: Landlord-Tenant Form 2:C, Office Lease.
Rutter, Cal. Practice Guide: Personal Injury Ch. 8-A, A. Case Management.
Rutter, Cal. Practice Guide: Personal Injury Ch. 9-B, B. In-Chambers Conference Before Commencement of Trial.
Rutter, Cal. Practice Guide: Personal Injury Ch. 9-C, C. Impanelment of Jury.
Rutter, Cal. Practice Guide: Personal Injury Gen. Matls., Highlights.
Miller and Starr California Real Estate § 1:6, Void and Voidable Contracts.
16 NO. 2 Miller & Starr, California Real Estate Newsalert 5, Contracts.
17 NO. 2 Miller & Starr, California Real Estate Newsalert 5, Contracts.
19 NO. 2 Miller & Starr, California Real Estate Newsalert 6, Common Interest Developments.
23 NO. 1 Miller & Starr, California Real Estate Newsalert 3, Alternative Dispute Resolution.
3 Witkin Cal. Proc. 5th Actions § 105, Waiver of Jury Trial.
7 Witkin Cal. Proc. 5th Judgment § 136, (S 136) Jury Fees and Expenses.
6 Witkin Cal. Proc. 5th Proceedings Without Trial § 210, Trial of Special Defenses.
7 Witkin Cal. Proc. 5th Trial § 98, (S 98) Demand.
7 Witkin Cal. Proc. 5th Trial § 99, Advance and Subsequent Deposits.
7 Witkin Cal. Proc. 5th Trial § 101, (S 101) in General.
7 Witkin Cal. Proc. 5th Trial § 102, in General.
7 Witkin Cal. Proc. 5th Trial § 103, Predispute Agreement.
7 Witkin Cal. Proc. 5th Trial § 104, (S 104) Noncompliance With Requirements.
7 Witkin Cal. Proc. 5th Trial § 106, Discretion and Policy.
7 Witkin Cal. Proc. 5th Trial § 107, Denial of Relief.
7 Witkin Cal. Proc. 5th Trial § 108, Review of Order Denying Relief.

§ 631.2.   Superior court payment of jury fees;   reimbursement

(a) Notwithstanding any other provision of law, the superior court may pay jury fees in civil cases from general funds of the court available therefor. Nothing in this section shall be construed to change the requirements for the deposit of jury fees in any civil case by the appropriate party to the litigation at the time and in the manner otherwise provided by law. Nothing in this section shall preclude the right of the superior court to be reimbursed by the party to the litigation liable therefor for any payment of jury fees pursuant to this section. Nothing in this section shall preclude the right of the county to be reimbursed by the party to the litigation liable therefor for any payment of jury fees pursuant to this section as it read in Section 4 of Chapter 10 of the Statutes of 1988, or pursuant to former Section 631.1 as it read in Section 1 of Chapter 144 of the Statutes of 1971.

(b) The party who has demanded trial by jury shall reimburse the superior court for the fees and mileage of all jurors appearing for voir dire examination, except those jurors who are excused and subsequently on the same day are called for voir dire examination in another case. *(Added by Stats.1988, c. 10, § 4, eff. Feb. 17, 1988. Amended by Stats.2012, c. 470 (A.B.1529), § 6.)*

Law Revision Commission Comments

Section 631.2 is amended to reflect enactment of the Lockyer–Isenberg Trial Court Funding Act. See Sections 77003 ("court operations" defined), 77200 (state funding of "court operations"); see also Cal. R. Ct.

10.810(d), Function 2 (jury services). [39 Cal.L.Rev.Comm. Reports 157 (2009)].

Research References

Rutter, Cal. Practice Guide: Civil Trials & Evidence Ch. 2-D, D. Securing Trial by Jury.
Rutter, Cal. Practice Guide: Civil Trials & Evidence Ch. 5-A, A. Obtaining Prospective Jurors.
Rutter, Cal. Practice Guide: Personal Injury Ch. 9-C, C. Impanelment of Jury.
7 Witkin Cal. Proc. 5th Judgment § 136, (S 136) Jury Fees and Expenses.
7 Witkin Cal. Proc. 5th Trial § 99, Advance and Subsequent Deposits.

§ 631.3. Forfeiture of jury fees deposited; disposition of fees

(a) Notwithstanding any other law, when a party to the litigation has deposited jury fees with the judge or clerk and that party waives a jury or obtains a continuance of the trial, or the case is settled, none of the deposit shall be refunded if the court finds there has been insufficient time to notify the jurors that the trial would not proceed at the time set. If the jury fees so deposited are not refunded for any of these reasons, or if a refund of jury fees deposited with the judge or clerk has not been requested, in writing, by the depositing party within 20 business days from the date on which the jury is waived or the action is settled, dismissed, or a continuance thereof granted, the fees shall be transmitted to the Controller for deposit into the Trial Court Trust Fund.

(b) All jury fees and mileage fees that may accrue by reason of a juror serving on more than one case in the same day shall be transmitted to the Controller for deposit into the Trial Court Trust Fund. All jury fees that were deposited with the court in advance of trial pursuant to Section 631 prior to January 1, 1999, and that remain on deposit in cases that were settled, dismissed, or otherwise disposed of, and three years have passed since the date the case was settled, dismissed, or otherwise disposed of, shall be transmitted to the Controller for deposit into the Trial Court Trust Fund.

(c) The fee described in subdivision (b) of Section 631 shall be nonrefundable and is not subject to this section. *(Added by Stats.1949, c. 444, p. 790, § 1. Amended by Stats.1955, c. 511, p. 988, § 1; Stats.1963, c. 678, p. 1683, § 1; Stats.1998, c. 1003 (S.B.1520), § 1; Stats.1998, c. 1004 (A.B.1935), § 1; Stats.2000, c. 447 (S.B.1533), § 2; Stats.2001, c. 824 (A.B.1700), § 9; Stats.2012, c. 41 (S.B.1021), § 4, eff. June 27, 2012; Stats.2012, c. 342 (A.B.1481), § 2, eff. Sept. 17, 2012.)*

Research References

Rutter, Cal. Practice Guide: Civ. Pro. Before Trial Ch. 12(I)-D, D. Demand for Jury Trial and Waiver.
Rutter, Cal. Practice Guide: Civil Trials & Evidence Ch. 2-D, D. Securing Trial by Jury.
Rutter, Cal. Practice Guide: Personal Injury Ch. 8-A, A. Case Management.
7 Witkin Cal. Proc. 5th Trial § 100, Refund or Forfeiture.

§ 631.5. Deposit of jury fees; eminent domain cases

In all cases of eminent domain the deposits of jury fees and mileage provided for in section 631 of this code shall be made by the party seeking condemnation regardless of which party shall have demanded a jury trial, and the trial shall not proceed until such deposits are made. *(Added by Stats.1939, c. 806, p. 2345, § 1.)*

Research References

Rutter, Cal. Practice Guide: Civil Trials & Evidence Ch. 2-D, D. Securing Trial by Jury.
Miller and Starr California Real Estate § 30A:70, Right to Jury Trial.

7 Witkin Cal. Proc. 5th Trial § 99, Advance and Subsequent Deposits.

§ 631.7. Order of proceedings

Ordinarily, unless the court otherwise directs, the trial of a civil action tried by the court without a jury shall proceed in the order specified in Section 607. *(Added by Stats.1965, c. 299, p. 1358, § 20, operative Jan. 1, 1967.)*

Law Revision Commission Comments

The second sentence of Code of Civil Procedure Section 2042 reads: "Ordinarily, the party beginning the case must exhaust his evidence before the other party begins." Section 631.7 supersedes this sentence insofar as it relates to nonjury civil cases; it states the existing law more accurately than does the sentence which it replaces, insofar as the superseded sentence relates to other actions, it is unnecessary because of Code of Civil Procedure Section 607 (civil jury cases) and Penal Code Sections 1093 and 1094 (criminal actions).

Research References

Rutter, Cal. Practice Guide: Civil Trials & Evidence Ch. 6-A, A. General Considerations.
Rutter, Cal. Practice Guide: Civil Trials & Evidence Ch. 6-B, B. Order of Presentation of Opening Statements.
Rutter, Cal. Practice Guide: Civil Trials & Evidence Ch. 16-A, A. General Considerations Re Nonjury Trials.
Rutter, Cal. Practice Guide: Personal Injury Ch. 9-D, D. Opening Statements.
Rutter, Cal. Practice Guide: Personal Injury Ch. 9-E, E. Order of Trial and Proof and Related Matters.
Rutter, Cal. Practice Guide: Personal Injury Ch. 9-J, J. Final Arguments Upon Close of Evidence.
7 Witkin Cal. Proc. 5th Judgment § 136, (S 136) Jury Fees and Expenses.
7 Witkin Cal. Proc. 5th Trial § 148, Trial by Court.

§ 631.8. Motion for judgment; partial grant of motion; effect

(a) After a party has completed his presentation of evidence in a trial by the court, the other party, without waiving his right to offer evidence in support of his defense or in rebuttal in the event the motion is not granted, may move for a judgment. The court as trier of the facts shall weigh the evidence and may render a judgment in favor of the moving party, in which case the court shall make a statement of decision as provided in Sections 632 and 634, or may decline to render any judgment until the close of all the evidence. The court may consider all evidence received, provided, however, that the party against whom the motion for judgment has been made shall have had an opportunity to present additional evidence to rebut evidence received during the presentation of evidence deemed by the presenting party to have been adverse to him, and to rehabilitate the testimony of a witness whose credibility has been attacked by the moving party. Such motion may also be made and granted as to any cross-complaint.

(b) If it appears that the evidence presented supports the granting of the motion as to some but not all the issues involved in the action, the court shall grant the motion as to those issues and the action shall proceed as to the issues remaining. Despite the granting of such a motion, no final judgment shall be entered prior to the termination of the action, but the final judgment in such action shall, in addition to any matters determined in the trial, award judgment as determined by the motion herein provided for.

(c) If the motion is granted, unless the court in its order for judgment otherwise specifies, such judgment operates as an adjudication upon the merits. *(Added by Stats.1961, c. 692, p. 1927, § 2. Amended by Stats.1971, c. 244, p. 391, § 53, operative July 1, 1972; Stats.1978, c. 372, p. 1114, § 1; Stats.1980, c. 187, p. 409, § 2; Stats.1986, c. 540, § 13.)*

Law Revision Commission Comments

The amendment to Section 631.8 merely deletes the reference to a "counterclaim." Counterclaims have been abolished; claims that formerly were asserted as counterclaims are now asserted as cross-complaints. See Code of Civil Procedure Section 428.80.

Research References

Rutter, Cal. Practice Guide: Civil Appeals & Writs Ch. 8-C, C. Standards of Appellate Review.

Rutter, Cal. Practice Guide: Civil Appeals & Writs Ch. 8-C, Outline C.

Rutter, Cal. Practice Guide: Civ. Pro. Before Trial Ch. 9(III)-D, D. Other Sanctions Statutes and Rules.

Rutter, Cal. Practice Guide: Civil Trials & Evidence Ch. 12-A, A. Motion for Mistrial.

Rutter, Cal. Practice Guide: Civil Trials & Evidence Ch. 12-B, B. Motion for Nonsuit.

Rutter, Cal. Practice Guide: Civil Trials & Evidence Ch. 16-B, B. Judge's Role as Trier of Fact.

Rutter, Cal. Practice Guide: Civil Trials & Evidence Ch. 16-C, C. Motion for Judgment (CCP § 631.8).

Rutter, Cal. Practice Guide: Personal Injury Ch. 1-B, B. Initial Evaluation of Case: Decision to Accept or Reject Employment or Undertake Further Evaluation of Claim.

Rutter, Cal. Practice Guide: Personal Injury Ch. 3-A, A. Introduction.

Rutter, Cal. Practice Guide: Personal Injury Ch. 5-A, A. Prelawsuit Filings.

Rutter, Cal. Practice Guide: Personal Injury Ch. 9-A, A. Assignment to Trial.

Rutter, Cal. Practice Guide: Personal Injury Ch. 9-L, L. Motions to Terminate Trial Before Verdict.

Rutter, Cal. Practice Guide: Personal Injury Ch. 9-M, M. Verdicts and Judgment.

Rutter, Cal. Practice Guide: Personal Injury Ch. 9-L, Outline L.

16 NO. 6 Miller & Starr, California Real Estate Newsalert 13, Inverse Condemnation.

18 NO. 1 Miller & Starr, California Real Estate Newsalert 12, Easements.

21 NO. 3 Miller & Starr, California Real Estate Newsalert 1, to Do or Not to Do-Whose Instructions to Follow in Closing an Escrow.

8 Witkin Cal. Proc. 5th Attack Judgment Trial Court § 38, Power and Duty to Weigh Evidence.

1 Witkin Cal. Proc. 5th Attorneys § 288, (S 288) Standard of Care.

7 Witkin Cal. Proc. 5th Judgment § 235, (S 235) Statutory Authorization.

7 Witkin Cal. Proc. 5th Judgment § 382, Judgment on Motion in Court Trial.

7 Witkin Cal. Proc. 5th Trial § 408, (S 408) Other Proceedings Distinguished.

7 Witkin Cal. Proc. 5th Trial § 412, (S 412) Necessity of Motion.

7 Witkin Cal. Proc. 5th Trial § 430, Motion.

7 Witkin Cal. Proc. 5th Trial § 431, (S 431) Statutory Rule.

7 Witkin Cal. Proc. 5th Trial § 433, (S 433) All Evidence and Opportunity to Rebut.

7 Witkin Cal. Proc. 5th Trial § 434, (S 434) in General.

7 Witkin Cal. Proc. 5th Trial § 435, (S 435) New Trial and Appeal.

12 Witkin, California Summary 10th Real Property § 47, Contribution.

5 Witkin, California Summary 10th Torts § 457, Acts of Landlords.

6 Witkin, California Summary 10th Torts § 1137, (S 1137) Warning of Danger.

§ 632. Statement of decision

In superior courts, upon the trial of a question of fact by the court, written findings of fact and conclusions of law shall not be required. The court shall issue a statement of decision explaining the factual and legal basis for its decision as to each of the principal controverted issues at trial upon the request of any party appearing at the trial. The request must be made within 10 days after the court announces a tentative decision unless the trial is concluded within one calendar day or in less than eight hours over more than one day in which event the request must be made prior to the submission of the matter for decision. The request for a statement of decision shall specify those controverted issues as to which the party is requesting a statement of decision. After a party has requested the statement, any party may make proposals as to the content of the statement of decision.

The statement of decision shall be in writing, unless the parties appearing at trial agree otherwise; however, when the trial is concluded within one calendar day or in less than 8 hours over more than one day, the statement of decision may be made orally on the record in the presence of the parties. *(Enacted in 1872. Amended by Code Am.1873–74, c. 383, p. 312, § 79; Stats.1933, c. 744, p. 1876, § 105; Stats.1951, c. 1737, p. 4116, § 92, operative Jan. 1, 1952; Stats.1959, c. 637, p. 2613, § 1; Stats.1968, c. 716, p. 1417, § 1, operative Jan. 1, 1969; Stats.1969, c. 339, p. 713, § 1; Stats.1975, c. 301, § 2; Stats.1977, c. 1257, p. 4763, § 22, eff. Jan. 3, 1977; Stats.1981, c. 900, p. 3425, § 1; Stats.1987, c. 207, § 1; Stats.1998, c. 931 (S.B.2139), § 84, eff. Sept. 28, 1998; Stats.2002, c. 784 (S.B.1316), § 64.)*

Law Revision Commission Comments

Section 632 is amended to require the court to state in its announcement of intended decision or in its findings, if findings are requested, which findings are based primarily on evidence obtained at a view pursuant to Section 651. In addition, the court must state its observations at the view which support the indicated findings. This provision changes the rule as stated in Gates v. McKinnon, 18 Cal.2d 179, 114 P.2d 576 (1941), that an appellate court will assume that the evidence acquired at a view by the trial judge is sufficient to sustain the findings. See also South Santa Clara Valley Water Cons. Dist. v. Johnson, 231 Cal.App.2d 388, 41 Cal.Rptr. 846 (1964); Stegner v. Bahr & Ledoyen, Inc., 126 Cal.App.2d 220, 272 P.2d 106 (1954); Orchard v. Cecil F. White Ranches, Inc., 97 Cal.App.2d 35, 217 P.2d 143 (1950); Estate of Sullivan, 86 Cal.App.2d 890, 195 P.2d 894 (1948); Chatterton v. Boone, 81 Cal.App.2d 943, 185 P.2d 610 (1947). If the court does not state that a finding is primarily supported by evidence obtained at a view and also state the observations supporting the finding, the finding will not be sustained by the appellate court in the absence of substantial evidence in the record to support it.

Section 632 is amended to reflect the elimination of the justice court. Cal. Const. art. VI, §§ 1, 5(b). [28 Cal.L.Rev.Comm. Reports 51 (1998)].

Section 632 is amended to reflect unification of the municipal and superior courts pursuant to Article VI, Section 5(e), of the California Constitution. [32 Cal.L.Rev.Comm. Reports 125 (2002)].

Research References

Rutter, Cal. Practice Guide: A.D.R. Ch. 5-G, G. Procedures to Enforce Arbitration.

Rutter, Cal. Practice Guide: A.D.R. Ch. 5-J, J. Challenging and Enforcing Arbitrator's Award in Court.

Rutter, Cal. Practice Guide: A.D.R. Ch. 6-B, B. Temporary Judges.

Rutter, Cal. Practice Guide: A.D.R. Ch. 6-C, C. Referees.

Rutter, Cal. Practice Guide: Civil Appeals & Writs Ch. 8-B, B. Presumption of Correctness.

Rutter, Cal. Practice Guide: Civil Appeals & Writs Ch. 8-D, D. Limits on Assertion of Issues on Appeal.

Rutter, Cal. Practice Guide: Civil Appeals & Writs Ch. 8-E, E. Limits on Reversal or Modification-"Prejudicial Error" Rule.

Rutter, Cal. Practice Guide: Civil Appeals & Writs Gen. Matls., Highlights.

Rutter, Cal. Practice Guide: Civ. Pro. Before Trial Ch. 9(I)-E, E. Posthearing Procedures.

Rutter, Cal. Practice Guide: Civ. Pro. Before Trial Ch. 9(II)-A, A. Injunctions.

Rutter, Cal. Practice Guide: Civil Trials & Evidence Ch. 16-C, C. Motion for Judgment (CCP § 631.8).

Rutter, Cal. Practice Guide: Civil Trials & Evidence Ch. 16-E, E. Statement of Decision.

Rutter, Cal. Practice Guide: Civil Trials & Evidence Ch. 17-B, B. Decision in Nonjury Trials.

Rutter, Cal. Practice Guide: Civil Trials & Evidence Ch. 18-B, B. Motion for New Trial.

Rutter, Cal. Practice Guide: Civil Trials & Evidence Ch. 18-C, C. Other Post-Trial Motions.

Rutter, Cal. Practice Guide: Family Law Ch. 6-A, A. Child Support.

Rutter, Cal. Practice Guide: Family Law Ch. 6-B, B. Spousal Support.

Rutter, Cal. Practice Guide: Family Law Ch. 7-C, C. Custody Awards, Generally.

Rutter, Cal. Practice Guide: Family Law Ch. 7-D, D. Joint Custody.

Rutter, Cal. Practice Guide: Personal Injury Ch. 7-H, H. Arbitration Award and Judgment.

Rutter, Cal. Practice Guide: Personal Injury Ch. 9-M, M. Verdicts and Judgment.

Miller and Starr California Real Estate § 35:54, Review of Order Granting or Denying Petition to Compel Arbitration.

Miller and Starr California Real Estate § 35:57, Stay of Arbitration Pending Litigation.

Miller and Starr California Real Estate § 35:90, Petition to Confirm an Award.

Miller and Starr California Real Estate § 35:92, Petition to Correct an Arbitrator's Award.

Miller and Starr California Real Estate § 35:103, Order of Confirmation; Judgment; Court's Award of Costs.

Miller and Starr California Real Estate § 35:105, Appeal of Judgment Based on Confirmation, or Order Denying Confirmation or Vacating an Arbitration Award.

9 Witkin Cal. Proc. 5th Appeal § 349, (S 349) Exceptions.

9 Witkin Cal. Proc. 5th Appeal § 350, in General.

9 Witkin Cal. Proc. 5th Appeal § 457, (S 457) Failure to Issue Sufficient Statement of Decision.

8 Witkin Cal. Proc. 5th Enforcement of Judgment § 458, (S 458) in General.

8 Witkin Cal. Proc. 5th Extraordinary Writs § 335, (S 335) Judgment Denying Relief.

7 Witkin Cal. Proc. 5th Judgment § 9, (S 9) Announcement of Decision and Proposed Judgment.

7 Witkin Cal. Proc. 5th Judgment § 47, Judgment After Trial or Hearing.

6 Witkin Cal. Proc. 5th Provisional Remedies § 387, (S 387) in General.

7 Witkin Cal. Proc. 5th Trial § 389, (S 389) Former Law on Findings and Conclusions.

7 Witkin Cal. Proc. 5th Trial § 390, (S 390) Nature and Scope of Requirement.

7 Witkin Cal. Proc. 5th Trial § 391, (S 391) When Statement is Required.

7 Witkin Cal. Proc. 5th Trial § 392, (S 392) When Statement is Not Required.

7 Witkin Cal. Proc. 5th Trial § 394, (S 394) Announcement of Tentative Decision.

7 Witkin Cal. Proc. 5th Trial § 395, (S 395) Request by Party.

7 Witkin Cal. Proc. 5th Trial § 396, (S 396) Preparation of Statement.

7 Witkin Cal. Proc. 5th Trial § 400, (S 400) Procedure in Bifurcated Trial.

7 Witkin Cal. Proc. 5th Trial § 401, (S 401) in General.

7 Witkin Cal. Proc. 5th Trial § 402, (S 402) Insufficient Statement.

7 Witkin Cal. Proc. 5th Trial § 404, (S 404) Waiver by Failure to Object.

10 Witkin, California Summary 10th Parent and Child § 218, (S 218) Statutory Rule.

10 Witkin, California Summary 10th Parent and Child § 285, (S 285) in General.

11 Witkin, California Summary 10th Community Property § 241, Statutory Requirement of Division.

11 Witkin, California Summary 10th Husband and Wife § 107, (S 107) Statement of Decision.

14 Witkin, California Summary 10th Wills and Probate § 472, Summary Determination of Disputes.

14 Witkin, California Summary 10th Wills and Probate § 998, (S 998) Summary Determination of Disputes.

§ 634. Omission or ambiguity brought to attention of trial court; inference

When a statement of decision does not resolve a controverted issue, or if the statement is ambiguous and the record shows that the omission or ambiguity was brought to the attention of the trial court either prior to entry of judgment or in conjunction with a motion under Section 657 or 663, it shall not be inferred on appeal or upon a motion under Section 657 or 663 that the trial court decided in favor of the prevailing party as to those facts or on that issue. *(Enacted in 1872. Amended by Stats.1913, c. 58, p. 58, § 1; Stats.1933, c. 744, p. 1877, § 106; Stats.1959, c. 637, p. 2614, § 2; Stats.1963, c. 378, p. 1167, § 1; Stats.1968, c. 716, p. 1418, § 2, operative Jan. 1, 1969; Stats.1981, c. 900, p. 3425, § 2.)*

Research References

Rutter, Cal. Practice Guide: A.D.R. Ch. 6-C, C. Referees.

Rutter, Cal. Practice Guide: Civil Appeals & Writs Ch. 8-B, B. Presumption of Correctness.

Rutter, Cal. Practice Guide: Civil Trials & Evidence Ch. 16-E, E. Statement of Decision.

Rutter, Cal. Practice Guide: Personal Injury Ch. 9-M, M. Verdicts and Judgment.

9 Witkin Cal. Proc. 5th Appeal § 350, in General.

8 Witkin Cal. Proc. 5th Enforcement of Judgment § 458, (S 458) in General.

7 Witkin Cal. Proc. 5th Trial § 398, (S 398) Objections.

7 Witkin Cal. Proc. 5th Trial § 404, (S 404) Waiver by Failure to Object.

§ 635. Formal judgment or order; signature by presiding judge in absence of trial judge

In all cases where the decision of the court has been entered in its minutes, and when the judge who heard or tried the case is unavailable, the formal judgment or order conforming to the minutes may be signed by the presiding judge of the court or by a judge designated by the presiding judge. *(Added by Stats.1965, c. 1942, p. 4470, § 1. Amended by Stats.1981, c. 900, p. 3426, § 3; Stats.1992, c. 876 (A.B.3296), § 5.)*

Research References

Rutter, Cal. Practice Guide: Civil Trials & Evidence Ch. 16-E, E. Statement of Decision.

Rutter, Cal. Practice Guide: Civil Trials & Evidence Ch. 17-C, C. Entry of Judgment.

Rutter, Cal. Practice Guide: Personal Injury Ch. 9-M, M. Verdicts and Judgment.

8 Witkin Cal. Proc. 5th Enforcement of Judgment § 458, (S 458) in General.

7 Witkin Cal. Proc. 5th Judgment § 45, Decision by Judge Who Tried Case.

7 Witkin Cal. Proc. 5th Trial § 394, (S 394) Announcement of Tentative Decision.

§ 636. Proceedings after judgment upon issue of law

Proceedings after determination of issue of law. On a judgment for the plaintiff upon an issue of law, he may proceed in the manner prescribed by the first two subdivisions of Section 585, upon the failure of the defendant to answer. If judgment be for the defendant upon an issue of law, and the taking of an account, or the proof of any fact, be necessary to enable the Court to complete the judgment, a reference may be ordered, as in that section provided. *(Enacted in 1872.)*

CHAPTER 6. OF REFERENCES AND TRIALS BY REFEREES

§ 638. Appointment of referee; agreement of parties

A referee may be appointed upon the agreement of the parties filed with the clerk, or judge, or entered in the minutes, or upon the motion of a party to a written contract or lease that provides that any controversy arising therefrom shall be heard by a referee if the court finds a reference agreement exists between the parties:

(a) To hear and determine any or all of the issues in an action or proceeding, whether of fact or of law, and to report a statement of decision.

(b) To ascertain a fact necessary to enable the court to determine an action or proceeding.

(c) In any matter in which a referee is appointed pursuant to this section, a copy of the order shall be forwarded to the office of the presiding judge. The Judicial Council shall, by rule, collect information on the use of these referees. The Judicial Council shall also collect information on fees paid by the parties for the use of referees to the extent that information regarding those fees is reported to the court. The Judicial Council shall report thereon to the Legislature by July 1, 2003. This subdivision shall become inoperative on January 1, 2004. *(Enacted in 1872. Amended by Stats.1933, c. 744, p. 1877, § 107; Stats.1951, c. 1737, p. 4117, § 93, operative Jan. 1, 1952; Stats.1982, c. 440, p. 1810, § 1; Stats.1984, c. 350, § 1; Stats. 2000, c. 644 (A.B.2912), § 1; Stats.2001, c. 44 (S.B.562), § 5; Stats.2002, c. 1008 (A.B.3028), § 4.)*

Law Revision Commission Comments

Section 638 is amended to delete the reference to a "docket," because courts no longer maintain a record denominated a "docket" in civil cases. Formerly, justice courts maintained a docket in civil cases, which was a record of actions taken in open court, as well as documents filed and other proceedings in the case. See former Gov't Code 71614 (1953 Cal. Stat. ch. 206, 1, repealed by 1977 Cal. Stat. ch. 1257, 71) (judge of justice court shall keep a book denominated a "docket"), 71614.5 (1959 Cal. Stat. ch. 671, 2, repealed by 1977 Cal. Stat. ch. 1257, 72) (clerk or judge of justice court shall keep the "docket" and other records of the court). Now actions taken in open court are recorded in the minutes of a superior court. Gov't Code 69844; see also Copley Press v. Superior Court, 6 Cal.App.4th 106, 110, 7 Cal.Rptr.2d 841 (1992). Documents filed or lodged and other proceedings in a civil case are recorded in the register of actions. See Gov't Code 69845 (clerk of superior court may keep a register of actions), 69845.5 (alternative to maintaining register of actions in superior court). Because the minutes are the proper record for reflecting an appointment in open court, and Section 638 already refers to the minutes, the reference to the "docket" may be deleted without substituting a reference to the register of actions.

A technical change is also made for conformity with preferred drafting style. [30 Cal.L.Rev.Comm. Reports 479 (2000)].

Research References

California Real Estate Forms (Miller & Starr) § 3:55, Subordination, Nondisturbance, and Attornment Agreement.

Rutter, Cal. Practice Guide: A.D.R. Ch. 1-D, D. Planning for Private ADR.

Rutter, Cal. Practice Guide: A.D.R. Ch. 5-J, J. Challenging and Enforcing Arbitrator's Award in Court.

Rutter, Cal. Practice Guide: A.D.R. Ch. 6-A, A. General Considerations.

Rutter, Cal. Practice Guide: A.D.R. Ch. 6-C, C. Referees.

Rutter, Cal. Practice Guide: A.D.R. Ch. 7-A, A. Mediators.

Rutter, Cal. Practice Guide: A.D.R. Ch. 7-D, D. Referees.

Rutter, Cal. Practice Guide: A.D.R. Ch. 8-D, D. Drafting Considerations-In General.

Rutter, Cal. Practice Guide: A.D.R. Ch. 3B-B, B. ADR Options in Construction Disputes.

Rutter, Cal. Practice Guide: A.D.R. App. D Form 14, Two-Step ADR Clause (Mediation/Adjudication) (Short Form).

Rutter, Cal. Practice Guide: A.D.R. App. D Form 83, ADR Clause for Disputes Between Financial Institutions.

Rutter, Cal. Practice Guide: A.D.R. App. D Form 126, ADR Clause (Submission of Disputes to Referee).

Rutter, Cal. Practice Guide: A.D.R. App. D Form 127, ADR Clause (Conduct of Reference Proceeding).

Rutter, Cal. Practice Guide: A.D.R. App. D Form 128, ADR Clause (Trial by Reference of Discovery Issues).

Rutter, Cal. Practice Guide: A.D.R. App. D Form 129, ADR Clause (Referee for Purposes of Case Management in Event of Litigation).

Rutter, Cal. Practice Guide: A.D.R. App. D Form 130, Motion for Order of Reference (CCP §§ 638.

Rutter, Cal. Practice Guide: A.D.R. App. D Form 131, Order Granting Motion for Reference.

Rutter, Cal. Practice Guide: A.D.R. App. D Form 132, Stipulation for General Reference Order.

Rutter, Cal. Practice Guide: A.D.R. App. D Form 133, Stipulation and Order for Appointment of Referee (Long Form).

Rutter, Cal. Practice Guide: A.D.R. App. D Form 138, Stipulation and Order for General Reference.

Rutter, Cal. Practice Guide: A.D.R. App. D Form 139, Stipulation and Order for General Reference.

Rutter, Cal. Practice Guide: A.D.R. App. D Form 141, Stipulation and Order of Reference for Case Management Purposes.

Rutter, Cal. Practice Guide: A.D.R. Ch. 6-C, Outline C.

Rutter, Cal. Practice Guide: A.D.R. App. D Form Intro. 5, Orders of Reference.

Rutter, Cal. Practice Guide: Civil Appeals & Writs Ch. 2-E, E. Appealability of Private Judge Decisions.

Rutter, Cal. Practice Guide: Civ. Pro. Before Trial Ch. 1-B, B. Prelawsuit Investigations, Research and Analysis.

Rutter, Cal. Practice Guide: Civ. Pro. Before Trial Ch. 6-B, B. Complaints.

Rutter, Cal. Practice Guide: Civ. Pro. Before Trial Ch. 8K-5, Appointment of Referee in Aid of Discovery.

Rutter, Cal. Practice Guide: Civ. Pro. Before Trial Ch. 9(I)-D, D. Hearing.

Rutter, Cal. Practice Guide: Civ. Pro. Before Trial Ch. 12(I)-D, D. Demand for Jury Trial and Waiver.

Rutter, Cal. Practice Guide: Civ. Pro. Before Trial Ch. 12(II)-F, F. Motion to Enforce Settlement (CCP §§ 664.6, 664.7).

Rutter, Cal. Practice Guide: Civil Trials & Evidence Ch. 2-E, E. Waiver of Jury Trial.

Rutter, Cal. Practice Guide: Civil Trials & Evidence Ch. 16-G, G. Trial by Reference.

Rutter, Cal. Practice Guide: Civil Trials & Evidence Ch. 2-E, Outline E.

Rutter, Cal. Practice Guide: Civil Trials & Evidence Ch. 16-G, Outline G.

California Practice Guide: Employment Litigation Ch. 18-D, D. Private Trials.

California Practice Guide: Employment Litigation Ch. 18-F, F. Selecting the Neutral.

California Practice Guide: Employment Litigation Ch. 18-D, Outline D.

Rutter, Cal. Practice Guide: Family Law Ch. 7-B, B. Contested Custody Proceedings, Generally.

Rutter, Cal. Practice Guide: Personal Injury Ch. 4-G, G. Concluding and Enforcing Settlement.

Rutter, Cal. Practice Guide: Real Prop. Transactions Ch. 4-E, E. Drafting the Purchase and Sale Agreement-Terms and Conditions.

Rutter, Cal. Practice Guide: Real Prop. Transactions Form 4:H, (Attorney-Drafted) Purchase and Sale Agreement and Joint Escrow Instructions.

Rutter, Cal. Practice Guide: Prof. Responsibility Ch. 8-D, D. Restrictions on Speech and Behavior Outside Courtroom.

Miller and Starr California Real Estate § 1:6, Void and Voidable Contracts.

Miller and Starr California Real Estate § 24:26, Rights of Enforcement--Remedies for Breach.

Miller and Starr California Real Estate § 29:76, Systems for Resolving Defective Construction Disputes.

Miller and Starr California Real Estate § 35:18, Reference Compared to Other ADR Procedures.

Miller and Starr California Real Estate § 35:19, Contract Provisions and Enforceability.

Miller and Starr California Real Estate § 35:20, The Reference Procedure.

Miller and Starr California Real Estate § 25B:113, Arbitration or Other Resolution of Disputes With the Subdivider.

13 NO. 6 Miller & Starr, California Real Estate Newsalert 1, Using Basura to Make Construction Defect Claims Arbitrable, or Woodside to Send Them to a Referee.

13 NO. 6 Miller & Starr, California Real Estate Newsalert 3, Commercial Arbitration.

14 NO. 6 Miller & Starr, California Real Estate Newsalert 3, Commercial Arbitration.

15 NO. 2 Miller & Starr, California Real Estate Newsalert 8, Eminent Domain.

16 NO. 2 Miller & Starr, California Real Estate Newsalert 4, Commercial Arbitration.

17 NO. 2 Miller & Starr, California Real Estate Newsalert 5, Contracts.

19 NO. 2 Miller & Starr, California Real Estate Newsalert 6, Common Interest Developments.

21 NO. 2 Miller & Starr, California Real Estate Newsalert 2, Alternative Dispute Resolution.

21 NO. 5 Miller & Starr, California Real Estate Newsalert 3, Alternative Dispute Resolution.

21 NO. 4 Miller & Starr, California Real Estate Newsalert 19, Alternative Dispute Resolution.

22 NO. 5 Miller & Starr, California Real Estate Newsalert 1, Real Estate Transactions With Native American Tribes.

9 Witkin Cal. Proc. 5th Appeal § 767, (S 767) Reference.

1 Witkin Cal. Proc. 5th Attorneys § 275, Other Matters Relating to Trial.

2 Witkin Cal. Proc. 5th Courts § 191, (S 191) Civil Rules.

2 Witkin Cal. Proc. 5th Courts § 262, Minimum Time Standards.

2 Witkin Cal. Proc. 5th Courts § 345, (S 345) Scope of Authority.

2 Witkin Cal. Proc. 5th Courts § 346, (S 346) in General.

4 Witkin Cal. Proc. 5th Pleading § 17, Format of First Page.

6 Witkin Cal. Proc. 5th Proceedings Without Trial § 63, (S 63) Nature and Purpose.

6 Witkin Cal. Proc. 5th Proceedings Without Trial § 64, (S 64) Voluntary Reference.

6 Witkin Cal. Proc. 5th Proceedings Without Trial § 67, Improper Reference.

6 Witkin Cal. Proc. 5th Proceedings Without Trial § 68, (S 68) Motion.

6 Witkin Cal. Proc. 5th Proceedings Without Trial § 69, (S 69) Appointment of Referee.

6 Witkin Cal. Proc. 5th Proceedings Without Trial § 74, (S 74) Report.

6 Witkin Cal. Proc. 5th Proceedings Without Trial § 123, Agreement Made in Mediation.

6 Witkin Cal. Proc. 5th Proceedings Without Trial § 496, (S 496) Voluntary Reference.

6 Witkin Cal. Proc. 5th Proceedings Without Trial § 497, (S 497) Temporary Judge.

7 Witkin Cal. Proc. 5th Trial § 103, Predispute Agreement.

7 Witkin Cal. Proc. 5th Trial § 390, (S 390) Nature and Scope of Requirement.

11 Witkin, California Summary 10th Husband and Wife § 107, (S 107) Statement of Decision.

14 Witkin, California Summary 10th Wills and Probate § 597, Powers of Probate Referee.

14 Witkin, California Summary 10th Wills and Probate § 998, (S 998) Summary Determination of Disputes.

§ 639. Appointment of referee

(a) When the parties do not consent, the court may, upon the written motion of any party, or of its own motion, appoint a referee in the following cases pursuant to the provisions of subdivision (b) of Section 640:

(1) When the trial of an issue of fact requires the examination of a long account on either side; in which case the referees may be directed to hear and decide the whole issue, or report upon any specific question of fact involved therein.

(2) When the taking of an account is necessary for the information of the court before judgment, or for carrying a judgment or order into effect.

(3) When a question of fact, other than upon the pleadings, arises upon motion or otherwise, in any stage of the action.

(4) When it is necessary for the information of the court in a special proceeding.

(5) When the court in any pending action determines that it is necessary for the court to appoint a referee to hear and determine any and all discovery motions and disputes relevant to discovery in the action and to report findings and make a recommendation thereon.

(b) In a discovery matter, a motion to disqualify an appointed referee pursuant to Section 170.6 shall be made to the court by a party either:

(A) Within 10 days after notice of the appointment, or if the party has not yet appeared in the action, a motion shall be made within 10 days after the appearance, if a discovery referee has been appointed for all discovery purposes.

(B) At least five days before the date set for hearing, if the referee assigned is known at least 10 days before the date set for hearing and the discovery referee has been assigned only for limited discovery purposes.

(c) When a referee is appointed pursuant to paragraph (5) of subdivision (a), the order shall indicate whether the referee is being appointed for all discovery purposes in the action.

(d) All appointments of referees pursuant to this section shall be by written order and shall include the following:

(1) When the referee is appointed pursuant to paragraph (1), (2), (3), or (4) of subdivision (a), a statement of the reason the referee is being appointed.

(2) When the referee is appointed pursuant to paragraph (5) of subdivision (a), the exceptional circumstances requiring the reference, which must be specific to the circumstances of the particular case.

(3) The subject matter or matters included in the reference.

(4) The name, business address, and telephone number of the referee.

(5) The maximum hourly rate the referee may charge and, at the request of any party, the maximum number of hours for which the referee may charge. Upon the written application of any party or the referee, the court may, for good cause shown, modify the maximum number of hours subject to any findings as set forth in paragraph (6).

(6)(A) Either a finding that no party has established an economic inability to pay a pro rata share of the referee's fee or a finding that one or more parties has established an economic inability to pay a pro rata share of the referee's fees and that another party has agreed voluntarily to pay that additional share of the referee's fee. A court shall not appoint a referee at a cost to the parties if neither of these findings is made.

(B) In determining whether a party has established an inability to pay the referee's fees under subparagraph (A), the court shall consider only the ability of the party, not the party's counsel, to pay these fees. If a party is proceeding in forma pauperis, the party shall be deemed by the court to have an economic inability to pay the referee's fees. However, a determination of economic inability to pay the fees shall not be limited to parties that proceed in forma pauperis. For those parties who are not proceeding in forma pauperis, the court, in determining whether a party has established an inability to pay the fees, shall consider, among other things, the estimated cost of the referral and the impact of the proposed fees on the party's ability to proceed with the litigation.

(e) In any matter in which a referee is appointed pursuant to paragraph (5) of subdivision (a), a copy of the order appointing the referee shall be forwarded to the office of the presiding judge of the court. The Judicial Council shall, by rule, collect information on the use of these references and the reference fees charged to litigants, and shall report thereon to the Legislature by July 1, 2003. This subdivision shall become inoperative on January 1, 2004. *(Enacted in 1872. Amended by Stats.1933, c. 744, p. 1877, § 108; Stats.1951, c. 1737, p. 4117, § 94, operative Jan. 1, 1952; Stats.1977, c. 1257, p. 4764, § 23, eff. Jan. 3, 1977; Stats.1981, c. 299, p. 1429, § 1; Stats.2000, c. 644 (A.B.2912), § 2; Stats.2000, c. 1011 (S.B.2153), § 1.5; Stats.2001, c. 362 (S.B.475), § 1.)*

Research References

Rutter, Cal. Practice Guide: A.D.R. Ch. 3-C, C. Confidentiality.

Rutter, Cal. Practice Guide: A.D.R. Ch. 6-C, C. Referees.

Rutter, Cal. Practice Guide: A.D.R. Ch. 7-A, A. Mediators.

Rutter, Cal. Practice Guide: A.D.R. Ch. 7-D, D. Referees.

Rutter, Cal. Practice Guide: A.D.R. Ch. 3B-B, B. ADR Options in Construction Disputes.

Civ. Pro.

Rutter, Cal. Practice Guide: A.D.R. App. D Form 129, ADR Clause (Referee for Purposes of Case Management in Event of Litigation).

Rutter, Cal. Practice Guide: A.D.R. App. D Form 138, Stipulation and Order for General Reference.

Rutter, Cal. Practice Guide: A.D.R. App. D Form 142, Notice of Motion for Appointment of Referee for Discovery Purposes.

Rutter, Cal. Practice Guide: A.D.R. App. D Form 143, Order Appointing Referee for the Purpose of Discovery.

Rutter, Cal. Practice Guide: A.D.R. App. D Form 144, Motion for Reference for Case Management Purposes.

Rutter, Cal. Practice Guide: A.D.R. App. D Form 145, Order of Reference for Case Management.

Rutter, Cal. Practice Guide: A.D.R. Ch. 6-C, Outline C.

Rutter, Cal. Practice Guide: A.D.R. App. D Form Intro. 5, Orders of Reference.

Rutter, Cal. Practice Guide: Civ. Pro. Before Trial Ch. 1-B, B. Prelawsuit Investigations, Research and Analysis.

Rutter, Cal. Practice Guide: Civ. Pro. Before Trial Ch. 5-D, D. Default Judgment by Court.

Rutter, Cal. Practice Guide: Civ. Pro. Before Trial Ch. 6-B, B. Complaints.

Rutter, Cal. Practice Guide: Civ. Pro. Before Trial Ch. 13-A, A. Introduction.

Rutter, Cal. Practice Guide: Civ. Pro. Before Trial Ch. 8F-7, Motion to Compel Answers.

Rutter, Cal. Practice Guide: Civ. Pro. Before Trial Ch. 8K-5, Appointment of Referee in Aid of Discovery.

Rutter, Cal. Practice Guide: Civ. Pro. Before Trial Ch. 8E-11, Protective Orders.

Rutter, Cal. Practice Guide: Civ. Pro. Before Trial Ch. 8E-12, Conduct of Deposition.

Rutter, Cal. Practice Guide: Civ. Pro. Before Trial Ch. 9(I)-D, D. Hearing.

Rutter, Cal. Practice Guide: Civ. Pro. Before Trial Ch. 12(II)-A, A. Mandatory Settlement Conference ("Msc").

Rutter, Cal. Practice Guide: Civil Trials & Evidence Ch. 16-G, G. Trial by Reference.

Rutter, Cal. Practice Guide: Civil Trials & Evidence Ch. 16-G, Outline G.

California Practice Guide: Employment Litigation Ch. 18-F, F. Selecting the Neutral.

Rutter, Cal. Practice Guide: Enforcing Judgments/Debts Ch. 6G-7, Charging Orders Against Debtor Partnership/LLC Interests.

Rutter, Cal. Practice Guide: Personal Injury Ch. 4-G, G. Concluding and Enforcing Settlement.

Rutter, Cal. Practice Guide: Personal Injury Ch. 8-B, B. After Trial Date Set (Three to Four Months Before Trial).

Rutter, Cal. Practice Guide: Personal Injury Ch. 9-A, A. Assignment to Trial.

Rutter, Cal. Practice Guide: Prof. Responsibility Ch. 8-D, D. Restrictions on Speech and Behavior Outside Courtroom.

Miller and Starr California Real Estate § 29:76, Systems for Resolving Defective Construction Disputes.

9 Witkin Cal. Proc. 5th Appeal § 767, (S 767) Reference.

2 Witkin Cal. Proc. 5th Courts § 191, (S 191) Civil Rules.

2 Witkin Cal. Proc. 5th Courts § 262, Minimum Time Standards.

2 Witkin Cal. Proc. 5th Courts § 346, (S 346) in General.

4 Witkin Cal. Proc. 5th Pleading § 17, Format of First Page.

6 Witkin Cal. Proc. 5th Proceedings Without Trial § 63, (S 63) Nature and Purpose.

6 Witkin Cal. Proc. 5th Proceedings Without Trial § 65, in General.

6 Witkin Cal. Proc. 5th Proceedings Without Trial § 66, Proper Reference.

6 Witkin Cal. Proc. 5th Proceedings Without Trial § 67, Improper Reference.

6 Witkin Cal. Proc. 5th Proceedings Without Trial § 68, (S 68) Motion.

6 Witkin Cal. Proc. 5th Proceedings Without Trial § 69, (S 69) Appointment of Referee.

6 Witkin Cal. Proc. 5th Proceedings Without Trial § 70, (S 70) Objection to Referee.

6 Witkin Cal. Proc. 5th Proceedings Without Trial § 74, (S 74) Report.

10 Witkin, California Summary 10th Parent and Child § 281, (S 281) Recommendations.

11 Witkin, California Summary 10th Husband and Wife § 201, Case Management Plan.

14 Witkin, California Summary 10th Wills and Probate § 371, General Rules of Practice.

§ 640. Selection of referees

(a) The court shall appoint as referee or referees the person or persons, not exceeding three, agreed upon by the parties.

(b) If the parties do not agree on the selection of the referee or referees, each party shall submit to the court up to three nominees for appointment as referee and the court shall appoint one or more referees, not exceeding three, from among the nominees against whom there is no legal objection. If no nominations are received from any of the parties, the court shall appoint one or more referees, not exceeding three, against whom there is no legal objection, or the court may appoint a court commissioner of the county where the cause is pending as a referee.

(c) Participation in the referee selection procedure pursuant to this section does not constitute a waiver of grounds for objection to the appointment of a referee under Section 641 or 641.2. *(Enacted in 1872. Amended by Stats.1913, c. 166, p. 246, § 1; Stats.1933, c. 744, p. 1877, § 109; Stats.1951, c. 1737, p. 4117, § 95, operative Jan. 1, 1952; Stats.1975, c. 1240, § 6, operative July 1, 1976; Stats.2000, c. 644 (A.B.2912), § 3.)*

Law Revision Commission Comments

The portion of Section 640 relating to the residence of referees in eminent domain proceedings is deleted because it serves no useful purpose and tends unnecessarily to complicate eminent domain law. The last sentence is deleted as unnecessary. See Cal.Const., Art. XII, § 23a and Pub.Util.Code §§ 1401–1421.

Research References

Rutter, Cal. Practice Guide: A.D.R. Ch. 1-D, D. Planning for Private ADR.

Rutter, Cal. Practice Guide: A.D.R. Ch. 6-C, C. Referees.

Rutter, Cal. Practice Guide: A.D.R. App. D Form 83, ADR Clause for Disputes Between Financial Institutions.

Rutter, Cal. Practice Guide: A.D.R. App. D Form 126, ADR Clause (Submission of Disputes to Referee).

Rutter, Cal. Practice Guide: A.D.R. App. D Form 128, ADR Clause (Trial by Reference of Discovery Issues).

Rutter, Cal. Practice Guide: A.D.R. App. D Form 129, ADR Clause (Referee for Purposes of Case Management in Event of Litigation).

Rutter, Cal. Practice Guide: A.D.R. App. D Form 130, Motion for Order of Reference (CCP §§ 638.

Rutter, Cal. Practice Guide: Civ. Pro. Before Trial Ch. 8K-5, Appointment of Referee in Aid of Discovery.

Rutter, Cal. Practice Guide: Civ. Pro. Before Trial Ch. 9(I)-D, D. Hearing.

Rutter, Cal. Practice Guide: Civil Trials & Evidence Ch. 16-G, G. Trial by Reference.

Rutter, Cal. Practice Guide: Civil Trials & Evidence Ch. 8G-D, D. Burdens and Standards of Proof.

Rutter, Cal. Practice Guide: Real Prop. Transactions Form 4:H, (Attorney-Drafted) Purchase and Sale Agreement and Joint Escrow Instructions.

Miller and Starr California Real Estate § 35:20, The Reference Procedure.

2 Witkin Cal. Proc. 5th Courts § 346, (S 346) in General.

2 Witkin Cal. Proc. 5th Courts § 347, (S 347) Court Commissioner as Referee.

6 Witkin Cal. Proc. 5th Proceedings Without Trial § 65, in General.

6 Witkin Cal. Proc. 5th Proceedings Without Trial § 69, (S 69) Appointment of Referee.

§ 640.5. Judicial Council report on the practice and cost of referring discovery disputes to outside referees

It is the intent of the Legislature that the practice and cost of referring discovery disputes to outside referees be thoroughly reviewed. Therefore, in addition to the requirements of subdivision (e) of Section 639, the Judicial Council shall collect information from the trial courts on the use of referees in discovery matters pursuant to either Sections 638 and 639. The collected data shall include information on the number of referees, the cost to the parties, and the time spent by the discovery referee. The Judicial Council shall report thereon to the Legislature by July 1, 2003. *(Added by Stats.2001, c. 362 (S.B.475), § 2.)*

§ 641. Objections to referee; grounds

A party may object to the appointment of any person as referee, on one or more of the following grounds:

(a) A want of any of the qualifications prescribed by statute to render a person competent as a juror, except a requirement of residence within a particular county in the state.

(b) Consanguinity or affinity, within the third degree, to either party, or to an officer of a corporation which is a party, or to any judge of the court in which the appointment shall be made.

(c) Standing in the relation of guardian and ward, conservator and conservatee, master and servant, employer and clerk, or principal and agent, to either party; or being a member of the family of either party; or a partner in business with either party; or security on any bond or obligation for either party.

(d) Having served as a juror or been a witness on any trial between the same parties.

(e) Interest on the part of the person in the event of the action, or in the main question involved in the action.

(f) Having formed or expressed an unqualified opinion or belief as to the merits of the action.

(g) The existence of a state of mind in the potential referee evincing enmity against or bias toward either party. *(Enacted in 1872. Amended by Stats.1897, c. 69, p. 60, § 2; Stats.1907, c. 378, p. 714, § 1; Stats.1933, c. 744, p. 1878, § 110; Stats.1951, c. 1737, p. 4118, § 96, operative Jan. 1, 1952; Stats.1979, c. 730, p. 2477, § 22, operative Jan. 1, 1981; Stats.1997, c. 724 (A.B.1172), § 1; Stats.2000, c. 644 (A.B.2912), § 4.)*

Law Revision Commission Comments

Section 641 is amended to add the reference to conservator and conservatee in subdivision 3.

Research References

Rutter, Cal. Practice Guide: A.D.R. Ch. 6-C, C. Referees.
Rutter, Cal. Practice Guide: A.D.R. Ch. 7-D, D. Referees.
Rutter, Cal. Practice Guide: A.D.R. App. D Form 127, ADR Clause (Conduct of Reference Proceeding).
Rutter, Cal. Practice Guide: Civ. Pro. Before Trial Ch. 8K-5, Appointment of Referee in Aid of Discovery.
Rutter, Cal. Practice Guide: Civ. Pro. Before Trial Ch. 9(I)-D, D. Hearing.
Rutter, Cal. Practice Guide: Civil Trials & Evidence Ch. 16-G, G. Trial by Reference.
California Practice Guide: Employment Litigation Ch. 13-H, H. Contesting Citations and Related Orders and Notices.
Miller and Starr California Real Estate § 35:20, The Reference Procedure.
2 Witkin Cal. Proc. 5th Courts § 346, (S 346) in General.
6 Witkin Cal. Proc. 5th Proceedings Without Trial § 69, (S 69) Appointment of Referee.
6 Witkin Cal. Proc. 5th Proceedings Without Trial § 70, (S 70) Objection to Referee.

§ 641.2. Environmental actions; objection to referee on grounds of technical qualifications

In any action brought under Article 8 (commencing with Section 12600) of Chapter 6, Part 2, Division 3, Title 3[1] of the Government Code, a party may object to the appointment of any person as referee on the ground that the person is not technically qualified with respect to the particular subject matter of the

proceeding. *(Added by Stats.1971, c. 1518, p. 2994, § 2. Amended by Stats.2000, c. 644 (A.B.2912), § 5.)*

1 So in enrolled bill. Probably should read "Title 2".

Research References

Rutter, Cal. Practice Guide: A.D.R. Ch. 6-C, C. Referees.
Rutter, Cal. Practice Guide: A.D.R. Ch. 7-D, D. Referees.
Rutter, Cal. Practice Guide: Civ. Pro. Before Trial Ch. 8K-5, Appointment of Referee in Aid of Discovery.
Rutter, Cal. Practice Guide: Civil Trials & Evidence Ch. 16-G, G. Trial by Reference.
Miller and Starr California Real Estate § 35:20, The Reference Procedure.
4 Witkin Cal. Proc. 5th Pleading § 161, Action by Attorney General.
6 Witkin Cal. Proc. 5th Proceedings Without Trial § 69, (S 69) Appointment of Referee.
6 Witkin Cal. Proc. 5th Proceedings Without Trial § 70, (S 70) Objection to Referee.

§ 642. Objections to reference or to referee

Objections, if any, to a reference or to the referee or referees appointed by the court shall be made in writing, and must be heard and disposed of by the court, not by the referee. *(Added by Stats.2000, c. 644 (A.B.2912), § 7.)*

Research References

Rutter, Cal. Practice Guide: A.D.R. Ch. 7-D, D. Referees.
Rutter, Cal. Practice Guide: Civ. Pro. Before Trial Ch. 8K-5, Appointment of Referee in Aid of Discovery.
Rutter, Cal. Practice Guide: Civ. Pro. Before Trial Ch. 9(I)-D, D. Hearing.
Rutter, Cal. Practice Guide: Civil Trials & Evidence Ch. 16-G, G. Trial by Reference.
Miller and Starr California Real Estate § 35:20, The Reference Procedure.
2 Witkin Cal. Proc. 5th Courts § 346, (S 346) in General.
6 Witkin Cal. Proc. 5th Proceedings Without Trial § 70, (S 70) Objection to Referee.
12 Witkin, California Summary 10th Real Property § 556, (S 556) Illustration of Permissible Restraint on Right.

§ 643. Written report; time; objections

(a) Unless otherwise directed by the court, the referees or commissioner must report their statement of decision in writing to the court within 20 days after the hearing, if any, has been concluded and the matter has been submitted.

(b) A referee appointed pursuant to Section 638 shall report as agreed by the parties and approved by the court.

(c) A referee appointed pursuant to Section 639 shall file with the court a report that includes a recommendation on the merits of any disputed issue, a statement of the total hours spent and the total fees charged by the referee, and the referee's recommended allocation of payment. The referee shall serve the report on all parties. Any party may file an objection to the referee's report or recommendations within 10 days after the referee serves and files the report, or within another time as the court may direct. The objection shall be served on the referee and all other parties. Responses to the objections shall be filed with the court and served on the referee and all other parties within 10 days after the objection is served. The court shall review any objections to the report and any responses submitted to those objections and shall thereafter enter appropriate orders. Nothing in this section is intended to deprive the court of its power to change the terms of the referee's appointment or to modify or disregard the referee's recommendations, and this overriding power may be exercised at any time, either on the motion of any party for good cause shown or on the court's own motion. *(Enacted in 1872. Amended by Stats.1984, c. 350, § 2; Stats.2000, c. 644 (A.B.2912), § 8.)*

Research References

Rutter, Cal. Practice Guide: A.D.R. Ch. 6-C, C. Referees.

Rutter, Cal. Practice Guide: A.D.R. App. D Form 127, ADR Clause (Conduct of Reference Proceeding).

Rutter, Cal. Practice Guide: Civ. Pro. Before Trial Ch. 8K-5, Appointment of Referee in Aid of Discovery.

Rutter, Cal. Practice Guide: Civ. Pro. Before Trial Ch. 9(I)-D, D. Hearing.

Rutter, Cal. Practice Guide: Civil Trials & Evidence Ch. 16-G, G. Trial by Reference.

Rutter, Cal. Practice Guide: Personal Injury Ch. 8-B, B. After Trial Date Set (Three to Four Months Before Trial).

Miller and Starr California Real Estate § 35:20, The Reference Procedure.

6 Witkin Cal. Proc. 5th Proceedings Without Trial § 74, (S 74) Report.

7 Witkin Cal. Proc. 5th Trial § 390, (S 390) Nature and Scope of Requirement.

§ 644. Effect of referee or commissioner's decision

(a) In the case of a consensual general reference pursuant to Section 638, the decision of the referee or commissioner upon the whole issue must stand as the decision of the court, and upon filing of the statement of decision with the clerk of the court, judgment may be entered thereon in the same manner as if the action had been tried by the court.

(b) In the case of all other references, the decision of the referee or commissioner is only advisory. The court may adopt the referee's recommendations, in whole or in part, after independently considering the referee's findings and any objections and responses thereto filed with the court. *(Enacted in 1872. Amended by Stats.1933, c. 744, p. 1878, § 111; Stats.1951, c. 1737, p. 4118, § 97, operative Jan. 1, 1952; Stats.1984, c. 350, § 3; Stats.2000, c. 644 (A.B.2912), § 9; Stats.2007, c. 263 (A.B.310), § 8.)*

Law Revision Commission Comments

Section 644 is amended to delete unnecessary language authorizing the judge to substitute for the clerk if there is no clerk. See Code Civ. Proc. § 167 (judge may perform any act court clerk may perform); Gov't Code §§ 69840–69848 (duties of clerk of superior court), 71620(b) (executive or administrative officer has authority of clerk of court). [35 Cal.L.Rev. Comm. Reports 219 (2006)].

Research References

California Real Estate Forms (Miller & Starr) § 3:55, Subordination, Nondisturbance, and Attornment Agreement.

Rutter, Cal. Practice Guide: A.D.R. Ch. 6-C, C. Referees.

Rutter, Cal. Practice Guide: A.D.R. App. D Form 127, ADR Clause (Conduct of Reference Proceeding).

Rutter, Cal. Practice Guide: A.D.R. App. D Form 133, Stipulation and Order for Appointment of Referee (Long Form).

Rutter, Cal. Practice Guide: Civil Appeals & Writs Ch. 2-E, E. Appealability of Private Judge Decisions.

Rutter, Cal. Practice Guide: Civ. Pro. Before Trial Ch. 9(I)-D, D. Hearing.

Rutter, Cal. Practice Guide: Civil Trials & Evidence Ch. 16-G, G. Trial by Reference.

Rutter, Cal. Practice Guide: Personal Injury Ch. 4-G, G. Concluding and Enforcing Settlement.

Rutter, Cal. Practice Guide: Personal Injury Ch. 8-B, B. After Trial Date Set (Three to Four Months Before Trial).

Miller and Starr California Real Estate § 35:20, The Reference Procedure.

15 NO. 2 Miller & Starr, California Real Estate Newsalert 8, Eminent Domain.

6 Witkin Cal. Proc. 5th Proceedings Without Trial § 67, Improper Reference.

6 Witkin Cal. Proc. 5th Proceedings Without Trial § 74, (S 74) Report.

6 Witkin Cal. Proc. 5th Proceedings Without Trial § 75, (S 75) Review of General Reference.

6 Witkin Cal. Proc. 5th Proceedings Without Trial § 123, Agreement Made in Mediation.

6 Witkin Cal. Proc. 5th Proceedings Without Trial § 496, (S 496) Voluntary Reference.

§ 645. Exception and review; decision as special verdict

The decision of the referee appointed pursuant to Section 638 or commissioner may be excepted to and reviewed in like manner as if made by the court. When the reference is to report the facts, the decision reported has the effect of a special verdict. *(Enacted in 1872. Amended by Stats.1984, c. 350, § 4; Stats. 2000, c. 644 (A.B.2912), § 10.)*

Research References

California Real Estate Forms (Miller & Starr) § 3:55, Subordination, Nondisturbance, and Attornment Agreement.

Rutter, Cal. Practice Guide: A.D.R. Ch. 6-C, C. Referees.

Rutter, Cal. Practice Guide: A.D.R. App. D Form 141, Stipulation and Order of Reference for Case Management Purposes.

Rutter, Cal. Practice Guide: Civil Appeals & Writs Ch. 2-E, E. Appealability of Private Judge Decisions.

Rutter, Cal. Practice Guide: Civil Trials & Evidence Ch. 16-G, G. Trial by Reference.

Miller and Starr California Real Estate § 35:20, The Reference Procedure.

6 Witkin Cal. Proc. 5th Proceedings Without Trial § 67, Improper Reference.

6 Witkin Cal. Proc. 5th Proceedings Without Trial § 74, (S 74) Report.

6 Witkin Cal. Proc. 5th Proceedings Without Trial § 75, (S 75) Review of General Reference.

6 Witkin Cal. Proc. 5th Proceedings Without Trial § 76, (S 76) Review of Special Reference.

§ 645.1. Payment of referee's fees; court order

(a) When a referee is appointed pursuant to Section 638, the referee's fees shall be paid as agreed by the parties. If the parties do not agree on the payment of fees and request the matter to be resolved by the court, the court may order the parties to pay the referee's fees as set forth in subdivision (b).

(b) When a referee is appointed pursuant to Section 639, at any time after a determination of ability to pay is made as specified in paragraph (6) of subdivision (d) of Section 639, the court may order the parties to pay the fees of referees who are not employees or officers of the court at the time of appointment, as fixed pursuant to Section 1023, in any manner determined by the court to be fair and reasonable, including an apportionment of the fees among the parties. For purposes of this section, the term "parties" does not include parties' counsel. *(Added by Stats.1981, c. 299, p. 1430, § 2. Amended by Stats.2000, c. 644 (A.B.2912), § 11; Stats.2001, c. 159 (S.B.662), § 38.5.)*

Research References

Rutter, Cal. Practice Guide: A.D.R. Ch. 6-C, C. Referees.

Rutter, Cal. Practice Guide: A.D.R. App. D Form 132, Stipulation for General Reference Order.

Rutter, Cal. Practice Guide: A.D.R. App. D Form 141, Stipulation and Order of Reference for Case Management Purposes.

Rutter, Cal. Practice Guide: Civ. Pro. Before Trial Ch. 8K-5, Appointment of Referee in Aid of Discovery.

Rutter, Cal. Practice Guide: Civ. Pro. Before Trial Ch. 8E-12, Conduct of Deposition.

Rutter, Cal. Practice Guide: Civ. Pro. Before Trial Ch. 9(I)-D, D. Hearing.

Rutter, Cal. Practice Guide: Civil Trials & Evidence Ch. 16-G, G. Trial by Reference.

Rutter, Cal. Practice Guide: Personal Injury Ch. 8-B, B. After Trial Date Set (Three to Four Months Before Trial).

Miller and Starr California Real Estate § 35:19, Contract Provisions and Enforceability.

Miller and Starr California Real Estate § 35:20, The Reference Procedure.

Miller and Starr California Real Estate § 25B:113, Arbitration or Other Resolution of Disputes With the Subdivider.

14 NO. 6 Miller & Starr, California Real Estate Newsalert 3, Commercial Arbitration.

16 NO. 2 Miller & Starr, California Real Estate Newsalert 4, Commercial Arbitration.

6 Witkin Cal. Proc. 5th Proceedings Without Trial § 77, in General.

6 Witkin Cal. Proc. 5th Proceedings Without Trial § 78, Consideration of Economic Hardship.

1 Witkin Cal. Summ. 10th Contracts § 337, Other Contract or Provision.

§ 645.2. Adoption of rules

The Judicial Council shall adopt all rules of court necessary to implement this chapter. *(Added by Stats.2000, c. 644 (A.B.2912), § 12.)*

CHAPTER 7. PROVISIONS RELATING TO TRIALS IN GENERAL

ARTICLE 1. EXCEPTIONS

§ 646. Definition; time for taking

An exception is an objection upon a matter of law to a decision made, either before or after judgment, by a Court, tribunal, Judge, or other judicial officer, in an action or proceeding. The exception must be taken at the time the decision is made, except as provided in section six hundred and forty-seven. *(Enacted in 1872. Amended by Code Am.1873–74, c. 383, p. 312, § 81; Code Am.1875–76, c. 517, p. 91, § 1.)*

Research References

9 Witkin Cal. Proc. 5th Appeal § 403, (S 403) Formal Exceptions Abolished.

§ 647. Matters considered excepted to

All of the following are deemed excepted to: the verdict of the jury; the final decision in an action or proceeding; an interlocutory order or decision, finally determining the rights of the parties, or some of them; an order or decision from which an appeal may be taken; an order sustaining or overruling a demurrer, allowing or refusing to allow an amendment to a pleading, striking out or refusing to strike out a pleading or a portion thereof, or refusing a continuance; an order made upon ex parte application, giving an instruction, refusing to give an instruction, or modifying an instruction requested; an order or decision made in the absence of the party or an order granting or denying a nonsuit or a motion to strike out evidence or testimony; a ruling sustaining or overruling an objection to evidence; and any statement or other action of the court in commenting upon or in summarizing the evidence. If the party, at the time when the order, ruling, action or decision is sought or made, or within a reasonable time thereafter, makes known his position thereon, by objection or otherwise, all other orders, rulings, actions or decisions are deemed to have been excepted to. *(Enacted in 1872. Amended by Code Am.1875–76, c. 517, p. 92, § 2; Stats.1907, c. 379, p. 715, § 1; Stats.1909, c. 355, p. 586, § 1; Stats.1939, c. 335, p. 1674, § 1; Stats.1941, c. 1256, p. 3201, § 1; Stats.1953, c. 715, p. 1984, § 1; Stats.1963, c. 99, p. 735, § 1.)*

Research References

Rutter, Cal. Practice Guide: Civil Appeals & Writs Ch. 8-D, D. Limits on Assertion of Issues on Appeal.

Rutter, Cal. Practice Guide: Civil Appeals & Writs Form 7:D, Petition for Writ of Supersedeas or Other Stay Order.

Rutter, Cal. Practice Guide: Civil Trials & Evidence Ch. 2-E, E. Waiver of Jury Trial.

Rutter, Cal. Practice Guide: Civil Trials & Evidence Ch. 12-A, A. Motion for Mistrial.

Rutter, Cal. Practice Guide: Civil Trials & Evidence Ch. 14-E, E. Argument and Settlement Re Proposed Instructions.

Rutter, Cal. Practice Guide: Civil Trials & Evidence Ch. 18-B, B. Motion for New Trial.

California Practice Guide: Employment Litigation Ch. 19-R, R. Jury Instructions.

Rutter, Cal. Practice Guide: Personal Injury Ch. 10-A, A. Motion for New Trial.

9 Witkin Cal. Proc. 5th Appeal § 403, (S 403) Formal Exceptions Abolished.

8 Witkin Cal. Proc. 5th Attack Judgment Trial Court § 44, (S 44) Error in Law.

7 Witkin Cal. Proc. 5th Trial § 304, (S 304) Automatic Exception.

ARTICLE 1.5. VIEW BY TRIER OF FACT

§ 651. View; subject matter; personnel; procedure

(a) On its own motion or on the motion of a party, where the court finds that such a view would be proper and would aid the trier of fact in its determination of the case, the court may order a view of any of the following:

(1) The property which is the subject of litigation.

(2) The place where any relevant event occurred.

(3) Any object, demonstration, or experiment, a view of which is relevant and admissible in evidence in the case and which cannot with reasonable convenience be viewed in the courtroom.

(b) On such occasion, the entire court, including the judge, jury, if any, court reporter, if any, and any necessary officers, shall proceed to the place, property, object, demonstration, or experiment to be viewed. The court shall be in session throughout the view. At the view, the court may permit testimony of witnesses. The proceedings at the view shall be recorded to the same extent as the proceedings in the courtroom. *(Added by Stats.1975, c. 301, § 3.)*

Research References

Rutter, Cal. Practice Guide: Civil Trials & Evidence Ch. 4-B, B. Preliminary Matters Discussed in Final Status Conference or In-Chambers Conference.

Rutter, Cal. Practice Guide: Civil Trials & Evidence Ch. 4-C, C. Jury Matters.

Rutter, Cal. Practice Guide: Civil Trials & Evidence Ch. 6-G, G. Preparing Opening Statement.

Rutter, Cal. Practice Guide: Civil Trials & Evidence Ch. 7-C, C. Access to Evidence During Trial.

Rutter, Cal. Practice Guide: Civil Trials & Evidence Ch. 15-F, F. Juror Misconduct During Deliberations.

Rutter, Cal. Practice Guide: Civil Trials & Evidence Ch. 8C-F, F. Jury Views.

Rutter, Cal. Practice Guide: Personal Injury Ch. 9-I, I. Use of Writings, Exhibits and Demonstrative Evidence.

7 Witkin Cal. Proc. 5th Trial § 328, Unauthorized Reception of Evidence.

ARTICLE 2. NEW TRIALS

Section

657.   Relief available on motion for new trial; causes; specification of grounds and reasons; new trial for insufficient evidence; manner of making and entering order; appeal.

657.1. Death or disability of court reporter or loss or destruction of notes.

658.   Application; affidavits; minutes of court.

659.   Notice of motion; filing and service, time; contents; extension of time.

659a.   Supporting and counter-affidavits; time for service and filing; maximum extension of time.

660.   Hearing; reference to pleadings, orders, depositions, documentary evidence, transcript, recollection of judge; attendance of reporter; precedence; time for ruling; automatic denial; determination; minute order.

661.   Judge; designation and notice of time for argument; time for hearing by judge other than trial judge.

662.   Cause tried by court; powers of judge on motion for new trial.

662.5. Inadequate or excessive damages as grounds; conditional orders.

663.   Setting aside judgment or decree; entry of new judgment; grounds.

663a.   Notice of intention to move to set aside and vacate judgment; contents; power of court to rule; extension of time; appeal of court order.

663.1. Loss or destruction of papers by conflagration or calamity.

663.2. Loss or destruction of papers by conflagration or calamity; time for motion.

§ 656. New trial defined

A new trial is a re-examination of an issue of fact in the same court after a trial and decision by a jury, court, or referee. *(Enacted in 1872. Amended by Stats.1907, c. 380, p. 717, § 1.)*

Research References

Rutter, Cal. Practice Guide: Civil Appeals & Writs Ch. 14-C, C. Trial Court Proceedings After Reversal.

Rutter, Cal. Practice Guide: Civil Trials & Evidence Ch. 3-B, B. Peremptory Challenge of Judge (CCP § 170.6).

Rutter, Cal. Practice Guide: Civil Trials & Evidence Ch. 18-B, B. Motion for New Trial.

California Practice Guide: Employment Litigation Ch. 19-S, S. Post-Trial Proceedings.

Rutter, Cal. Practice Guide: Personal Injury Ch. 9-A, A. Assignment to Trial.

Rutter, Cal. Practice Guide: Personal Injury Ch. 10-A, A. Motion for New Trial.

8 Witkin Cal. Proc. 5th Attack Judgment Trial Court § 18, (S 18) Nature and Object of Motion.

8 Witkin Cal. Proc. 5th Attack Judgment Trial Court § 22, in General.

8 Witkin Cal. Proc. 5th Attack Judgment Trial Court § 55, After Decision.

2 Witkin Cal. Proc. 5th Courts § 151, (S 151) New Trial After Reversal.

6 Witkin Cal. Proc. 5th Proceedings Without Trial § 75, (S 75) Review of General Reference.

6 Witkin Cal. Proc. 5th Proceedings Without Trial § 432, Judgment Reversed With Remand for New Trial.

§ 657. Relief available on motion for new trial; causes; specification of grounds and reasons; new trial for insufficient evidence; manner of making and entering order; appeal

The verdict may be vacated and any other decision may be modified or vacated, in whole or in part, and a new or further trial granted on all or part of the issues, on the application of the party aggrieved, for any of the following causes, materially affecting the substantial rights of such party:

1. Irregularity in the proceedings of the court, jury or adverse party, or any order of the court or abuse of discretion by which either party was prevented from having a fair trial.

2. Misconduct of the jury; and whenever any one or more of the jurors have been induced to assent to any general or special verdict, or to a finding on any question submitted to them by the court, by a resort to the determination of chance, such misconduct may be proved by the affidavit of any one of the jurors.

3. Accident or surprise, which ordinary prudence could not have guarded against.

4. Newly discovered evidence, material for the party making the application, which he could not, with reasonable diligence, have discovered and produced at the trial.

5. Excessive or inadequate damages.

6. Insufficiency of the evidence to justify the verdict or other decision, or the verdict or other decision is against law.

7. Error in law, occurring at the trial and excepted to by the party making the application.

When a new trial is granted, on all or part of the issues, the court shall specify the ground or grounds upon which it is granted and the court's reason or reasons for granting the new trial upon each ground stated.

A new trial shall not be granted upon the ground of insufficiency of the evidence to justify the verdict or other decision, nor upon the ground of excessive or inadequate damages, unless after weighing the evidence the court is convinced from the entire record, including reasonable inferences therefrom, that the court or jury clearly should have reached a different verdict or decision.

The order passing upon and determining the motion must be made and entered as provided in Section 660 and if the motion is granted must state the ground or grounds relied upon by the court, and may contain the specification of reasons. If an order granting such motion does not contain such specification of reasons, the court must, within 10 days after filing such order, prepare, sign and file such specification of reasons in writing with the clerk. The court shall not direct the attorney for a party to prepare either or both said order and said specification of reasons.

On appeal from an order granting a new trial the order shall be affirmed if it should have been granted upon any ground stated in the motion, whether or not specified in the order or specification of reasons, except that (a) the order shall not be affirmed upon the ground of the insufficiency of the evidence to justify the verdict or other decision, or upon the ground of excessive or inadequate damages, unless such ground is stated in the order granting the motion and (b) on appeal from an order granting a new trial upon the ground of the insufficiency of the evidence to justify the verdict or other decision, or upon the ground of excessive or inadequate damages, it shall be conclusively presumed that said order as to such ground was made only for the reasons specified in said order or said specification of reasons, and such order shall be reversed as to such ground only if there is no substantial basis in the record for any of such reasons. *(Enacted in 1872. Amended by Stats.1919, c. 100, p. 141, § 1; Stats.1929, c. 479, p. 841, § 2; Stats.1939, c. 713, p. 2234, § 1; Stats.1965, c. 1749, p. 3922, § 1; Stats.1967, c. 72, p. 970, § 1.)*

Research References

Rutter, Cal. Practice Guide: A.D.R. Ch. 3-C, C. Confidentiality.

Rutter, Cal. Practice Guide: A.D.R. Ch. 6-C, C. Referees.

Rutter, Cal. Practice Guide: A.D.R. App. D Form 138, Stipulation and Order for General Reference.

Rutter, Cal. Practice Guide: Civil Appeals & Writs Ch. 8-B, B. Presumption of Correctness.

Civ. Pro.

6 Witkin, California Summary 10th Torts § 1740, Discretion of Jury and Trial Court.

§ 657.1. Death or disability of court reporter or loss or destruction of notes

A new trial may also be granted as provided in Section 914 of this code. *(Added by Stats.1968, c. 387, p. 821, § 1.)*

Research References

Rutter, Cal. Practice Guide: Civil Trials & Evidence Ch. 18-B, B. Motion for New Trial.
Rutter, Cal. Practice Guide: Personal Injury Ch. 10-A, A. Motion for New Trial.
Rutter, Cal. Practice Guide: Personal Injury Ch. 10-A, Outline a.
8 Witkin Cal. Proc. 5th Attack Judgment Trial Court § 45, (S 45) Other Grounds.

§ 658. Application; affidavits; minutes of court

When the application is made for a cause mentioned in the first, second, third and fourth subdivisions of Section 657, it must be made upon affidavits; otherwise it must be made on the minutes of the court. *(Enacted in 1872. Amended by Code Am.1873–74, c. 383, p. 314, § 84; Stats.1915, c. 107, p. 201, § 1; Stats.1983, c. 1167, § 9.)*

Research References

Rutter, Cal. Practice Guide: Civil Trials & Evidence Ch. 15-F, F. Juror Misconduct During Deliberations.
Rutter, Cal. Practice Guide: Civil Trials & Evidence Ch. 18-B, B. Motion for New Trial.
Rutter, Cal. Practice Guide: Personal Injury Ch. 10-A, A. Motion for New Trial.
8 Witkin Cal. Proc. 5th Attack Judgment Trial Court § 20, (S 20) Statutory Procedure is Mandatory.
8 Witkin Cal. Proc. 5th Attack Judgment Trial Court § 48, (S 48) Statutory Requirements.
8 Witkin Cal. Proc. 5th Attack Judgment Trial Court § 49, (S 49) Failure to Designate Whether Motion is Made on Minutes or Affidavits.
8 Witkin Cal. Proc. 5th Attack Judgment Trial Court § 65, (S 65) Affidavits and Counteraffidavits.
8 Witkin Cal. Proc. 5th Attack Judgment Trial Court § 69, No Oral Testimony.
7 Witkin Cal. Proc. 5th Trial § 386, (S 386) No-Knowledge Affidavit of Attorney and Party.

§ 659. Notice of motion; filing and service, time; contents; extension of time

(a) The party intending to move for a new trial shall file with the clerk and serve upon each adverse party a notice of his or her intention to move for a new trial, designating the grounds upon which the motion will be made and whether the same will be made upon affidavits or the minutes of the court, or both, either:

(1) After the decision is rendered and before the entry of judgment.

(2) Within 15 days of the date of mailing notice of entry of judgment by the clerk of the court pursuant to Section 664.5, or service upon him or her by any party of written notice of entry of judgment, or within 180 days after the entry of judgment, whichever is earliest; provided, that upon the filing of the first notice of intention to move for a new trial by a party, each other party shall have 15 days after the service of that notice upon him or her to file and serve a notice of intention to move for a new trial.

(b) That notice of intention to move for a new trial shall be deemed to be a motion for a new trial on all the grounds stated in the notice. The times specified in paragraphs (1) and (2) of subdivision (a) shall not be extended by order or stipulation or by those provisions of Section 1013 that extend the time for exercising a right or doing an act where service is by mail. *(Enacted in 1872. Amended by Code Am.1873–74, c. 383, p. 315,*

§ 85; Stats.1907, c. 380, p. 717, § 2; Stats.1915, c. 107, p. 201, § 2; Stats.1923, c. 367, p. 751, § 1; Stats.1929, c. 479, p. 841, § 3; Stats.1951, c. 801, p. 2289, § 2, eff. Jan. 1, 1952; Stats.1959, c. 469, p. 2404, § 1; Stats.1961, c. 604, p. 1753, § 2; Stats.1965, c. 1890, p. 4359, § 1.5; Stats.1967, c. 169, p. 1266, § 1; Stats.1970, c. 621, p. 1232, § 1; Stats.2012, c. 83 (A.B.2106), § 1.)*

Research References

Rutter, Cal. Practice Guide: A.D.R. Ch. 6-B, B. Temporary Judges.
Rutter, Cal. Practice Guide: Civil Appeals & Writs Ch. 3-C, C. Extensions of Filing Deadline.
Rutter, Cal. Practice Guide: Civil Appeals & Writs Ch. 15-B, B. Common Law Writs.
Rutter, Cal. Practice Guide: Civ. Pro. Before Trial Ch. 3-A, A. Subject Matter Jurisdiction (Competency).
Rutter, Cal. Practice Guide: Civ. Pro. Before Trial Ch. 5-G, G. Relief from Default.
Rutter, Cal. Practice Guide: Civ. Pro. Before Trial Ch. 10-I, I. Challenging Judgment or Order in Trial Court.
Rutter, Cal. Practice Guide: Civ. Pro. Before Trial Ch. 9(I)-B, B. Preparing and Filing Motions.
Rutter, Cal. Practice Guide: Civil Trials & Evidence Ch. 17-F, F. Prejudgment Interest.
Rutter, Cal. Practice Guide: Civil Trials & Evidence Ch. 18-A, A. Motion for Judgment Notwithstanding the Verdict ("JNOV").
Rutter, Cal. Practice Guide: Civil Trials & Evidence Ch. 18-B, B. Motion for New Trial.
California Practice Guide: Employment Litigation Ch. 19-S, S. Post-Trial Proceedings.
Rutter, Cal. Practice Guide: Enforcing Judgments/Debts Ch. 3-C, C. Prelawsuit Considerations.
Rutter, Cal. Practice Guide: Family Law Ch. 6-A, A. Child Support.
Rutter, Cal. Practice Guide: Personal Injury Ch. 10-A, A. Motion for New Trial.
Rutter, Cal. Practice Guide: Personal Injury Ch. 10-B, B. Motion for Judgment Notwithstanding the Verdict.
Rutter, Cal. Practice Guide: Personal Injury Ch. 10-D, D. Government Entity Defendant Post-Trial Elections, Requests, Motions and Hearings.
9 Witkin Cal. Proc. 5th Appeal § 587, (S 587) Purpose of Rule.
9 Witkin Cal. Proc. 5th Appeal § 590, (S 590) Forms of Extension.
8 Witkin Cal. Proc. 5th Attack Judgment Trial Court § 46, in General.
8 Witkin Cal. Proc. 5th Attack Judgment Trial Court § 48, (S 48) Statutory Requirements.
8 Witkin Cal. Proc. 5th Attack Judgment Trial Court § 50, (S 50) Other Defects.
8 Witkin Cal. Proc. 5th Attack Judgment Trial Court § 51, Service on Adverse Party.
8 Witkin Cal. Proc. 5th Attack Judgment Trial Court § 52, Filing Fee.
8 Witkin Cal. Proc. 5th Attack Judgment Trial Court § 53, (S 53) in General.
8 Witkin Cal. Proc. 5th Attack Judgment Trial Court § 54, (S 54) Late Filing is Void.
8 Witkin Cal. Proc. 5th Attack Judgment Trial Court § 55, After Decision.
8 Witkin Cal. Proc. 5th Attack Judgment Trial Court § 56, What Constitutes Decision.
8 Witkin Cal. Proc. 5th Attack Judgment Trial Court § 58, Notice of Entry by Clerk.
8 Witkin Cal. Proc. 5th Attack Judgment Trial Court § 59, Notice of Entry by Party.
8 Witkin Cal. Proc. 5th Attack Judgment Trial Court § 60, Form of Notice.
8 Witkin Cal. Proc. 5th Attack Judgment Trial Court § 62, Commencement and Running of Period.
8 Witkin Cal. Proc. 5th Attack Judgment Trial Court § 63, (S 63) Fifteen Days After Other Party's Notice of Motion.
8 Witkin Cal. Proc. 5th Attack Judgment Trial Court § 64, (S 64) One Hundred Eighty Days After Entry of Judgment.
8 Witkin Cal. Proc. 5th Attack Judgment Trial Court § 67, in General.
8 Witkin Cal. Proc. 5th Attack Judgment Trial Court § 97, (S 97) Nature of Power.
8 Witkin Cal. Proc. 5th Attack Judgment Trial Court § 141, Notice of Motion.
2 Witkin Cal. Proc. 5th Courts § 321, No Appeal or Motion Attacking Judgment.

8 Witkin Cal. Proc. 5th Enforcement of Judgment § 433, (S 433) Postjudgment Settlement Conference.

8 Witkin Cal. Proc. 5th Enforcement of Judgment § 435, (S 435) Reduction of Judgment for Collateral Source Payments.

7 Witkin Cal. Proc. 5th Judgment § 57, Purpose and Entry.

7 Witkin Cal. Proc. 5th Judgment § 58, Notice by Party.

6 Witkin Cal. Proc. 5th Proceedings Without Trial § 5, (S 5) Time of Motion.

6 Witkin Cal. Proc. 5th Proceedings Without Trial § 259, (S 259) Challenging Judgment in Trial Court.

7 Witkin Cal. Proc. 5th Trial § 439, (S 439) Motion.

7 Witkin Cal. Proc. 5th Trial § 442, (S 442) Granting on Court's Own Motion.

5 Witkin, California Summary 10th Torts § 234, Conference on Satisfaction of Judgment.

6 Witkin, California Summary 10th Torts § 1638, Motion, Discovery, and Settlement Conference.

§ 659a. Supporting and counter-affidavits; time for service and filing; maximum extension of time

Within 10 days of filing the notice, the moving party shall serve upon all other parties and file any affidavits intended to be used upon such motion. Such other parties shall have ten days after such service within which to serve upon the moving party and file counter-affidavits. The time herein specified may, for good cause shown by affidavit or by written stipulation of the parties, be extended by any judge for an additional period of not exceeding 20 days. *(Added by Stats.1929, c. 479, p. 841, § 4. Amended by Stats.1933, c. 744, p. 1881, § 118; Stats.1935, c. 722, p. 1958, § 13; Stats.1989, c. 1416, § 20.)*

Research References

Rutter, Cal. Practice Guide: Civil Trials & Evidence Ch. 18-A, A. Motion for Judgment Notwithstanding the Verdict ("JNOV").

Rutter, Cal. Practice Guide: Civil Trials & Evidence Ch. 18-B, B. Motion for New Trial.

Rutter, Cal. Practice Guide: Personal Injury Ch. 10-A, A. Motion for New Trial.

8 Witkin Cal. Proc. 5th Attack Judgment Trial Court § 65, (S 65) Affidavits and Counteraffidavits.

7 Witkin Cal. Proc. 5th Trial § 386, (S 386) No-Knowledge Affidavit of Attorney and Party.

7 Witkin Cal. Proc. 5th Trial § 387, (S 387) Jurors' Affidavits of Misconduct.

§ 660. Hearing; reference to pleadings, orders, depositions, documentary evidence, transcript, recollection of judge; attendance of reporter; precedence; time for ruling; automatic denial; determination; minute order

On the hearing of such motion, reference may be had in all cases to the pleadings and orders of the court on file, and when the motion is made on the minutes, reference may also be had to any depositions and documentary evidence offered at the trial and to the report of the proceedings on the trial taken by the phonographic reporter, or to any certified transcript of such report or if there be no such report or certified transcript, to such proceedings occurring at the trial as are within the recollection of the judge; when the proceedings at the trial have been phonographically reported, but the reporter's notes have not been transcribed, the reporter must upon request of the court or either party, attend the hearing of the motion and shall read his notes, or such parts thereof as the court, or either party, may require.

The hearing and disposition of the motion for a new trial shall have precedence over all other matters except criminal cases, probate matters and cases actually on trial, and it shall be the duty of the court to determine the same at the earliest possible moment.

Except as otherwise provided in Section 12a of this code, the power of the court to rule on a motion for a new trial shall expire 60 days from and after the mailing of notice of entry of judgment by the clerk of the court pursuant to Section 664.5 or 60 days from and after service on the moving party by any party of written notice of the entry of the judgment, whichever is earlier, or if such notice has not theretofore been given, then 60 days after filing of the first notice of intention to move for a new trial. If such motion is not determined within said period of 60 days, or within said period as thus extended, the effect shall be a denial of the motion without further order of the court. A motion for a new trial is not determined within the meaning of this section until an order ruling on the motion (1) is entered in the permanent minutes of the court or (2) is signed by the judge and filed with the clerk. The entry of a new trial order in the permanent minutes of the court shall constitute a determination of the motion even though such minute order as entered expressly directs that a written order be prepared, signed and filed. The minute entry shall in all cases show the date on which the order actually is entered in the permanent minutes, but failure to comply with this direction shall not impair the validity or effectiveness of the order. *(Enacted in 1872. Amended by Code Am.1873–74, c. 383, p. 317, § 86; Stats.1907, c. 380, p. 718, § 3; Stats.1915, c. 107, p. 202, § 3; Stats.1917, c. 156, p. 240, § 1; Stats.1923, c. 105, p. 233, § 1; Stats.1929, c. 479, p. 842, § 5; Stats.1933, c. 29, p. 305, § 5; Stats.1959, c. 468, p. 2403, § 1; Stats.1969, c. 87, p. 209, § 1; Stats.1970, c. 621, p. 1232, § 2.)*

Research References

California Real Estate Forms (Miller & Starr) § 3:8, Deed of Trust, Security Agreement, and Fixture Filing With Assignment of Rents and Agreements.

California Real Estate Forms (Miller & Starr) § 3:14, Construction Deed of Trust, Security Agreement, and Fixture Filing With Assignment of Rents and Agreements.

Rutter, Cal. Practice Guide: Civil Appeals & Writs Ch. 3-B, B. Filing Deadlines.

Rutter, Cal. Practice Guide: Civil Appeals & Writs Ch. 3-C, C. Extensions of Filing Deadline.

Rutter, Cal. Practice Guide: Civil Appeals & Writs Ch. 11-D, D. Disposition.

Rutter, Cal. Practice Guide: Civil Appeals & Writs Ch. 15-B, B. Common Law Writs.

Rutter, Cal. Practice Guide: Civ. Pro. Before Trial Ch. 10-I, I. Challenging Judgment or Order in Trial Court.

Rutter, Cal. Practice Guide: Civil Trials & Evidence Ch. 18-A, A. Motion for Judgment Notwithstanding the Verdict ("JNOV").

Rutter, Cal. Practice Guide: Civil Trials & Evidence Ch. 18-B, B. Motion for New Trial.

Rutter, Cal. Practice Guide: Civil Trials & Evidence Gen. Matls., Highlights.

Rutter, Cal. Practice Guide: Personal Injury Ch. 10-A, A. Motion for New Trial.

Rutter, Cal. Practice Guide: Personal Injury Gen. Matls., Highlights.

9 Witkin Cal. Proc. 5th Appeal § 577, (S 577) in General.

9 Witkin Cal. Proc. 5th Appeal § 600, in General.

9 Witkin Cal. Proc. 5th Appeal § 609, Order Entered in Minutes.

9 Witkin Cal. Proc. 5th Appeal § 616, (S 616) Cases Departing from Jurisdictional Rule.

8 Witkin Cal. Proc. 5th Attack Judgment Trial Court § 56, What Constitutes Decision.

8 Witkin Cal. Proc. 5th Attack Judgment Trial Court § 59, Notice of Entry by Party.

8 Witkin Cal. Proc. 5th Attack Judgment Trial Court § 63, (S 63) Fifteen Days After Other Party's Notice of Motion.

8 Witkin Cal. Proc. 5th Attack Judgment Trial Court § 67, in General.

8 Witkin Cal. Proc. 5th Attack Judgment Trial Court § 68, Evidence and Argument.

8 Witkin Cal. Proc. 5th Attack Judgment Trial Court § 71, (S 71) New Judge.

8 Witkin Cal. Proc. 5th Attack Judgment Trial Court § 72, (S 72) in General.

8 Witkin Cal. Proc. 5th Attack Judgment Trial Court § 73, (S 73) Commencement of Period.

8 Witkin Cal. Proc. 5th Attack Judgment Trial Court § 74, (S 74) Extensions.

8 Witkin Cal. Proc. 5th Attack Judgment Trial Court § 75, (S 75) Time is Jurisdictional.

8 Witkin Cal. Proc. 5th Attack Judgment Trial Court § 76, (S 76) Failure to Meet Deadline.

8 Witkin Cal. Proc. 5th Attack Judgment Trial Court § 77, (S 77) in General.

8 Witkin Cal. Proc. 5th Attack Judgment Trial Court § 80, No Nunc Pro Tunc Correction.

8 Witkin Cal. Proc. 5th Attack Judgment Trial Court § 115, Compliance After Jurisdictional Time Limit Expires.

8 Witkin Cal. Proc. 5th Attack Judgment Trial Court § 124, Minute Entry or Signed Order.

8 Witkin Cal. Proc. 5th Attack Judgment Trial Court § 125, Permanent Minutes.

2 Witkin Cal. Proc. 5th Courts § 27, (S 27) Powers of Judge Out of County.

2 Witkin Cal. Proc. 5th Courts § 365, Permanent Minutes.

7 Witkin Cal. Proc. 5th Judgment § 57, Purpose and Entry.

2 Witkin Cal. Proc. 5th Jurisdiction § 329, Act in Excess of Jurisdiction.

7 Witkin Cal. Proc. 5th Trial § 441, (S 441) Ruling on Motion.

§ 661. Judge; designation and notice of time for argument; time for hearing by judge other than trial judge

The motion for a new trial shall be heard and determined by the judge who presided at the trial; provided, however, that in case of the inability of such judge or if at the time noticed for hearing thereon he is absent from the county where the trial was had, the same shall be heard and determined by any other judge of the same court. Upon the expiration of the time to file counter affidavits the clerk forthwith shall call the motion to the attention of the judge who presided at the trial, or the judge acting in his place, as the case may be, and such judge thereupon shall designate the time for oral argument, if any, to be had on said motion. Five (5) days' notice by mail shall be given of such oral argument, if any, by the clerk to the respective parties. Such motion, if heard by a judge other than the trial judge shall be argued orally or shall be submitted without oral argument, as the judge may direct, not later than ten (10) days before the expiration of the time within which the court has power to pass on the same. *(Added by Stats.1929, c. 479, p. 842, § 6. Amended by Stats.1931, c. 768, p. 1608, § 1; Stats.1933, c. 744, p. 1881, § 119.)*

Research References

Rutter, Cal. Practice Guide: Civil Trials & Evidence Ch. 18-A, A. Motion for Judgment Notwithstanding the Verdict ("JNOV").

Rutter, Cal. Practice Guide: Civil Trials & Evidence Ch. 18-B, B. Motion for New Trial.

Rutter, Cal. Practice Guide: Civil Trials & Evidence Ch. 18-C, C. Other Post-Trial Motions.

Rutter, Cal. Practice Guide: Personal Injury Ch. 10-A, A. Motion for New Trial.

8 Witkin Cal. Proc. 5th Attack Judgment Trial Court § 67, in General.

8 Witkin Cal. Proc. 5th Attack Judgment Trial Court § 68, Evidence and Argument.

8 Witkin Cal. Proc. 5th Attack Judgment Trial Court § 70, (S 70) Trial Judge.

8 Witkin Cal. Proc. 5th Attack Judgment Trial Court § 71, (S 71) New Judge.

8 Witkin Cal. Proc. 5th Attack Judgment Trial Court § 142, Hearing and Determination.

2 Witkin Cal. Proc. 5th Courts § 19, What Successor Can Do.

6 Witkin Cal. Proc. 5th Proceedings Without Trial § 75, (S 75) Review of General Reference.

§ 662. Cause tried by court; powers of judge on motion for new trial

In ruling on such motion, in a cause tried without a jury, the court may, on such terms as may be just, change or add to the statement of decision, modify the judgment, in whole or in part, vacate the judgment, in whole or in part, and grant a new trial on all or part of the issues, or, in lieu of granting a new trial, may vacate and set aside the statement of decision and judgment and

reopen the case for further proceedings and the introduction of additional evidence with the same effect as if the case had been reopened after the submission thereof and before a decision had been filed or judgment rendered. Any judgment thereafter entered shall be subject to the provisions of sections 657 and 659. *(Added by Stats.1929, c. 479, p. 843, § 7. Amended by Stats.1981, c. 900, p. 3426, § 4.)*

Research References

Rutter, Cal. Practice Guide: A.D.R. Ch. 6-C, C. Referees.

Rutter, Cal. Practice Guide: Civil Appeals & Writs Ch. 2-A, A. Overview.

Rutter, Cal. Practice Guide: Civil Appeals & Writs Ch. 2-B, B. Appealable Judgments and Orders.

Rutter, Cal. Practice Guide: Civil Appeals & Writs Ch. 2-C, C. Nonappealable Orders.

Rutter, Cal. Practice Guide: Civil Appeals & Writs Ch. 15-A, A. Overview.

Rutter, Cal. Practice Guide: Civil Appeals & Writs Ch. 2-B, Outline B.

Rutter, Cal. Practice Guide: Civil Appeals & Writs Ch. 2-C, Outline C.

Rutter, Cal. Practice Guide: Civil Trials & Evidence Ch. 16-E, E. Statement of Decision.

Rutter, Cal. Practice Guide: Civil Trials & Evidence Ch. 18-B, B. Motion for New Trial.

Rutter, Cal. Practice Guide: Personal Injury Ch. 10-A, A. Motion for New Trial.

9 Witkin Cal. Proc. 5th Appeal § 98, (S 98) Distinctions.

9 Witkin Cal. Proc. 5th Appeal § 164, Order Denying New Trial.

9 Witkin Cal. Proc. 5th Appeal § 312, (S 312) No Fact-Finding.

9 Witkin Cal. Proc. 5th Appeal § 583, (S 583) Where Judgment is Modified.

9 Witkin Cal. Proc. 5th Appeal § 874, (S 874) Nature of Power.

8 Witkin Cal. Proc. 5th Attack Judgment Trial Court § 62, Commencement and Running of Period.

8 Witkin Cal. Proc. 5th Attack Judgment Trial Court § 97, (S 97) Nature of Power.

8 Witkin Cal. Proc. 5th Attack Judgment Trial Court § 99, (S 99) Procedure.

8 Witkin Cal. Proc. 5th Attack Judgment Trial Court § 100, Grant of New Trial Treated as Denial.

8 Witkin Cal. Proc. 5th Attack Judgment Trial Court § 101, Order Directing Reopening of Case.

8 Witkin Cal. Proc. 5th Attack Judgment Trial Court § 102, Motions Made Both for New Trial and to Vacate Judgment.

8 Witkin Cal. Proc. 5th Attack Judgment Trial Court § 103, (S 103) Where Motion is Heard by New Judge.

8 Witkin Cal. Proc. 5th Attack Judgment Trial Court § 104, (S 104) Nature of Power.

8 Witkin Cal. Proc. 5th Attack Judgment Trial Court § 142, Hearing and Determination.

7 Witkin Cal. Proc. 5th Trial § 399, (S 399) Signing, Filing, and Amending.

11 Witkin, California Summary 10th Husband and Wife § 108, (S 108) Former Two-Judgment Procedure.

§ 662.5. Inadequate or excessive damages as grounds; conditional orders

(a) In any civil action where after trial by jury an order granting a new trial limited to the issue of damages would be proper, the trial court may in its discretion:

(1) If the ground for granting a new trial is inadequate damages, issue a conditional order granting the new trial unless the party against whom the verdict has been rendered consents to the addition of damages in an amount the court in its independent judgment determines from the evidence to be fair and reasonable.

(2) If the ground for granting a new trial is excessive damages, issue a conditional order granting the new trial unless the party in whose favor the verdict has been rendered consents to the reduction of so much thereof as the court in its independent judgment determines from the evidence to be fair and reasonable.

(b) If a deadline for acceptance or rejection of the addition or reduction of damages is not set forth in the conditional order, the deadline is 30 days from the date the conditional order is served by the clerk of the court. Failure to respond to the order in accordance with this section shall be deemed a rejection of the addition or reduction of damages and a new trial limited to the issue of damages shall be granted automatically.

(c) A party filing and serving an acceptance of a conditionally ordered addition or reduction of damages shall concurrently serve and submit to the court a proposed amended judgment reflecting the modified judgment amount, as well as any other uncontested judgment awards. *(Added by Stats.1967, c. 72, p. 972, § 2. Amended by Stats.1969, c. 115, p. 252, § 1; Stats.2011, c. 409 (A.B.1403), § 2.)*

Law Revision Commission Comments

Section 662.5 makes it clear that additur may be used in certain cases as an alternative to granting a motion for a new trial on the ground of inadequacy of damages. The section is permissive in nature; it does not require that additur be used merely because the conditions stated in the section are satisfied. The section does not preclude the use of additur in any other case where it is appropriate, nor does the section affect existing remittitur practice.

Subdivision (a). Subdivision (a) authorizes additur only where after weighing the evidence the court is convinced from the entire record, including reasonable inferences therefrom, that the verdict, *although supported by substantial evidence*, is clearly inadequate. See Code Civ.Proc. § 657. In addition, the defendant must consent to the additional damages; otherwise, the condition upon which the court's order denying the new trial is predicated will not have been satisfied and, insofar as the order grants a new trial, it will become effective as the order of the court. These conditions are designed to meet the constitutional objections to additur in unliquidated damages cases that were raised in Dorsey v. Barba, 38 Cal.2d 350, 240 P.2d 604 (1952). See the discussion in 8 Cal.Law Revision Comm'n, Rep., Rec. & Studies 608–609 (1967).

The exercise of additur authority under subdivision (a) is limited to cases where "an order granting a new trial limited to the issue of damages would . . . be proper." This limitation prevents the use of additur where the inadequate damages are the result of a compromise on liability. A new trial limited to the issue of damages is not appropriate in such a case. E.g., Hamasaki v. Flotho, 39 Cal.2d 602, 248 P.2d 910 (1952); Leipert v. Honold, 39 Cal.2d 462, 247 P.2d 324 (1952).

Subdivision (a) applies only to civil actions where there has been a trial by jury. Sufficient statutory authority for the exercise of discretionary additur authority in cases tried by the court without a jury is provided by Code of Civil Procedure Section 662.

Subdivision (a) grants additur authority to trial courts only; existing appellate additur practice is unaffected. See Code Civ.Proc. § 53; Cal.Rules of Court, Rule 24(b).

Subdivision (b). This subdivision makes it clear that Section 662.5 does not preclude the exercise of additur authority in any other case in which it may appropriately be exercised. It appears from the holdings and discussion in various cases that additur is permissible not only under the circumstances specified in subdivision (a) but also in the following cases:

(1) In any case where damages are certain and ascertainable by a fixed standard. In such a case—e.g., where plaintiff sues on a $25,000 note and the jury has returned a verdict for $20,000—the court by an additur order merely fixes damages in the only amount justified by the evidence and the only amount that a jury properly could find; any variance in that amount would either be excessive or inadequate as a matter of law. See Pierce v. Schaden, 62 Cal. 283 (1882); Adamson v. County of Los Angeles, 52 Cal.App. 125, 198 P. 52 (1921).

(2) In any case where the court's additur order requires the consent of both plaintiff and defendant. Failure of either party to consent will result in granting a new trial; hence, the plaintiff retains control over whether or not he will receive a second jury trial. Since consent of both parties operates to waive each party's right to a jury trial, there can be no complaint as to this form of additur. Hall v. Murphy, 187 Cal.App.2d 296, 9 Cal.Rptr. 547 (1960).

(3) In any case where the court, with the consent of the defendant, fixes damages in the highest amount which the evidence will support. Since any larger amount would be excessive as a matter of law, the plaintiff is not prejudiced by denial of a second jury trial. See Dorsey v. Barba, 38 Cal.2d 350, 358, 240 P.2d 604, 608 (1952) ("[T]he plaintiff has actually been injured [only] if, under the evidence, he could have obtained a still larger award from a second jury."); Dorsey v. Barba, 226 P.2d 677, 690 (Cal.Dist.Ct.App.1951); Comment, 40 Cal.L.Rev. 276, 285–286 (1952).

Subdivision (b) also leaves the California Supreme Court free to modify, limit, or even overrule its decision in the Dorsey case and allow additur practice in cases where the jury verdict on damages is *not* supported by substantial evidence.

Subdivision (c). Subdivision (c) makes it clear that this section has no effect on existing remittitur practice.

As amended, this section merely recognizes that additur and remittitur practice exists in California. The section incorporates the general standard for granting additur and remittitur as set out in Jehl v. Southern Pacific Co.:

There is no essential difference between the procedures appropriate for remittitur and additur, and we may therefore look to remittitur cases a determine the proper procedure for additur.

Upon a motion for new trial grounded on insufficiency of the evidence because the damages are inadequate, the court should first determine whether the damages are clearly inadequate and, if so, whether the case would be a proper one for granting a motion for new trial limited to damages. . . . If both conditions exist, the court in its discretion may issue an order granting the motion for new trial unless the defendant consents to an additur as determined by the court. The court's power extends to all such cases. It is not limited to those cases in which an appellate court would sustain either the granting or denial of a motion for new trial on the ground of insufficiency of the evidence. The court shall prescribe the time within which the defendant must accept the additur, and in no case may this time be longer than the jurisdictional period for granting a new trial. . . . If the defendant fails to consent within the prescribed time, the order granting the new trial becomes final.

If the court decides to order an additur, it should set the amount that it determines from the evidence to be fair and reasonable. In this respect it should exercise its completely independent judgment. It need not fix either the minimum or maximum amount that it would have sustained on a motion for new trial or the minimum or maximum amount that would be supported by substantial evidence and therefore sustainable on appeal. If the defendant deems the additur excessive, he may reject it and seek to sustain the jury's award on an appeal from the order granting a new trial. If the plaintiff deems the additur insufficient, he may raise the issue on an appeal from the judgment as modified by the additur. [66 Cal.2d 821, 832–833, 427 P.2d 988, 995, 59 Cal.Rptr. 276, 283 (1967). *Citations omitted.*]

It should be noted that the additur and remittitur procedure under Section 662.5 is not specified in the section. The section does not affect any procedural limitations on additur and remittitur, whether established by statutory or decisional law (such as the time within which the additur or remittitur must be accepted) or by rules of practice and procedure adopted by the Judicial Council pursuant to Section 6 of Article VI of the California Constitution. Compare Jehl v. Southern Pacific Co., 66 Cal.2d 821, 427 P.2d 988, 59 Cal.Rptr. 276 (1967), with Alberton v. Superior Court, 265 Adv.Cal.App. 921, 71 Cal.Rptr. 553 (1968), concerning the time within which the additur or remittitur must be accepted.

Research References

Rutter, Cal. Practice Guide: Civil Appeals & Writs Ch. 2-D, D. Standing to Appeal.

Rutter, Cal. Practice Guide: Civil Trials & Evidence Ch. 18-A, A. Motion for Judgment Notwithstanding the Verdict ("JNOV").

Rutter, Cal. Practice Guide: Civil Trials & Evidence Ch. 18-B, B. Motion for New Trial.

Rutter, Cal. Practice Guide: Civil Trials & Evidence Gen. Matls., Highlights.

California Practice Guide: Employment Litigation Ch. 19-S, S. Post-Trial Proceedings.

Rutter, Cal. Practice Guide: Insurance Litigation Ch. 13-C, C. Punitive Damages.

Rutter, Cal. Practice Guide: Personal Injury Ch. 10-A, A. Motion for New Trial.

Rutter, Cal. Practice Guide: Personal Injury Ch. 10-B, B. Motion for Judgment Notwithstanding the Verdict.

8 Witkin Cal. Proc. 5th Attack Judgment Trial Court § 113, Specification Requirement.

8 Witkin Cal. Proc. 5th Attack Judgment Trial Court § 116, Nature of Remittitur.

8 Witkin Cal. Proc. 5th Attack Judgment Trial Court § 117, Reapportionment of Liability is Not Proper.

8 Witkin Cal. Proc. 5th Attack Judgment Trial Court § 118, Form of Order.

8 Witkin Cal. Proc. 5th Attack Judgment Trial Court § 119, Effect of Failure to Remit.

8 Witkin Cal. Proc. 5th Attack Judgment Trial Court § 120, Judicial Recognition of Power.

8 Witkin Cal. Proc. 5th Attack Judgment Trial Court § 121, Statutory Authorization.

8 Witkin Cal. Proc. 5th Attack Judgment Trial Court § 122, Scope of Additur.

8 Witkin Cal. Proc. 5th Attack Judgment Trial Court § 123, Procedure.

§ 663. Setting aside judgment or decree; entry of new judgment; grounds

A judgment or decree, when based upon a decision by the court, or the special verdict of a jury, may, upon motion of the party aggrieved, be set aside and vacated by the same court, and another and different judgment entered, for either of the following causes, materially affecting the substantial rights of the party and entitling the party to a different judgment:

1. Incorrect or erroneous legal basis for the decision, not consistent with or not supported by the facts; and in such case when the judgment is set aside, the statement of decision shall be amended and corrected.

2. A judgment or decree not consistent with or not supported by the special verdict. *(Added by Stats.1897, c. 67, p. 58, § 1. Amended by Stats.1933, c. 744, p. 1881, § 120; Stats.1981, c. 900, p. 3426, § 5.)*

Research References

Rutter, Cal. Practice Guide: A.D.R. Ch. 6-C, C. Referees.

Rutter, Cal. Practice Guide: Civil Appeals & Writs Ch. 2-B, B. Appealable Judgments and Orders.

Rutter, Cal. Practice Guide: Civil Appeals & Writs Ch. 2-D, D. Standing to Appeal.

Rutter, Cal. Practice Guide: Civil Appeals & Writs Ch. 3-C, C. Extensions of Filing Deadline.

Rutter, Cal. Practice Guide: Civil Appeals & Writs Ch. 7-A, A. Overview.

Rutter, Cal. Practice Guide: Civil Appeals & Writs Ch. 8-B, B. Presumption of Correctness.

Rutter, Cal. Practice Guide: Civil Appeals & Writs Ch. 15-A, A. Overview.

Rutter, Cal. Practice Guide: Civ. Pro. Before Trial Ch. 3-A, A. Subject Matter Jurisdiction (Competency).

Rutter, Cal. Practice Guide: Civ. Pro. Before Trial Ch. 10-I, I. Challenging Judgment or Order in Trial Court.

Rutter, Cal. Practice Guide: Civil Trials & Evidence Ch. 16-E, E. Statement of Decision.

Rutter, Cal. Practice Guide: Civil Trials & Evidence Ch. 18-B, B. Motion for New Trial.

Rutter, Cal. Practice Guide: Civil Trials & Evidence Ch. 18-C, C. Other Post-Trial Motions.

Rutter, Cal. Practice Guide: Civil Trials & Evidence Ch. 18-B, Outline B.

Rutter, Cal. Practice Guide: Insurance Litigation Ch. 15-A, A. Actions Against Insurers.

Rutter, Cal. Practice Guide: Insurance Litigation Ch. 15-A, Outline a.

Rutter, Cal. Practice Guide: Personal Injury Ch. 4-D, D. Techniques Where Settlement Not Forthcoming.

Rutter, Cal. Practice Guide: Personal Injury Ch. 9-M, M. Verdicts and Judgment.

Rutter, Cal. Practice Guide: Personal Injury Ch. 10-A, A. Motion for New Trial.

Rutter, Cal. Practice Guide: Personal Injury Ch. 10-C, C. Motion to Vacate and Enter Different Judgment.

Miller and Starr California Real Estate § 35:20, The Reference Procedure.

9 Witkin Cal. Proc. 5th Appeal § 26, (S 26) Motion to Vacate.

9 Witkin Cal. Proc. 5th Appeal § 194, General Rule: Appealable.

9 Witkin Cal. Proc. 5th Appeal § 197, General Rule: Nonappealable.

9 Witkin Cal. Proc. 5th Appeal § 200, (S 200) Statutory Motions.

9 Witkin Cal. Proc. 5th Appeal § 595, (S 595) Nature of Motion.

9 Witkin Cal. Proc. 5th Appeal § 596, (S 596) Motion on Any Ground.

8 Witkin Cal. Proc. 5th Attack Judgment Trial Court § 24, Exception: Complete Statutory Plan Excluding Motion.

8 Witkin Cal. Proc. 5th Attack Judgment Trial Court § 47, Motion Improperly Labeled.

8 Witkin Cal. Proc. 5th Attack Judgment Trial Court § 102, Motions Made Both for New Trial and to Vacate Judgment.

8 Witkin Cal. Proc. 5th Attack Judgment Trial Court § 139, Nature and Grounds.

8 Witkin Cal. Proc. 5th Attack Judgment Trial Court § 140, Motion for New Trial Distinguished.

8 Witkin Cal. Proc. 5th Attack Judgment Trial Court § 141, Notice of Motion.

8 Witkin Cal. Proc. 5th Attack Judgment Trial Court § 142, Hearing and Determination.

8 Witkin Cal. Proc. 5th Attack Judgment Trial Court § 143, Review on Appeal.

8 Witkin Cal. Proc. 5th Attack Judgment Trial Court § 147, (S 147) in General.

2 Witkin Cal. Proc. 5th Courts § 19, What Successor Can Do.

2 Witkin Cal. Proc. 5th Courts § 23, in General.

2 Witkin Cal. Proc. 5th Courts § 321, No Appeal or Motion Attacking Judgment.

7 Witkin Cal. Proc. 5th Judgment § 421, (S 421) in General.

6 Witkin Cal. Proc. 5th Proceedings Without Trial § 432, Judgment Reversed With Remand for New Trial.

7 Witkin Cal. Proc. 5th Trial § 398, (S 398) Objections.

10 Witkin, California Summary 10th Parent and Child § 700, (S 700) Right to Appeal.

5 Witkin, California Summary 10th Torts § 76, Time of Settlement.

8 Witkin, California Summary 10th Constitutional Law § 1171, Definitions.

§ 663a. Notice of intention to move to set aside and vacate judgment; contents; power of court to rule; extension of time; appeal of court order

(a) A party intending to make a motion to set aside and vacate a judgment, as described in Section 663, shall file with the clerk and serve upon the adverse party a notice of his or her intention, designating the grounds upon which the motion will be made, and specifying the particulars in which the legal basis for the decision is not consistent with or supported by the facts, or in which the judgment or decree is not consistent with the special verdict, either:

(1) After the decision is rendered and before the entry of judgment.

(2) Within 15 days of the date of mailing of notice of entry of judgment by the clerk of the court pursuant to Section 664.5, or service upon him or her by any party of written notice of entry of judgment, or within 180 days after the entry of judgment, whichever is earliest.

(b) Except as otherwise provided in Section 12a, the power of the court to rule on a motion to set aside and vacate a judgment shall expire 60 days from the mailing of notice of entry of judgment by the clerk of the court pursuant to Section 664.5, or 60 days after service upon the moving party by any party of written notice of entry of the judgment, whichever is earlier, or if that notice has not been given, then 60 days after filing of the first notice of intention to move to set aside and vacate the judgment. If that motion is not determined within the 60–day period, or within that period, as extended, the effect shall be a denial of the motion without further order of the court. A motion to set aside and vacate a judgment is not determined within the meaning of this section until an order ruling on the motion is (1) entered in the permanent minutes of the court, or (2) signed by the judge and filed with the clerk. The entry of an order to set aside and vacate the judgment in the permanent minutes of the court shall constitute a determination of the motion, even though that minute order, as entered, expressly directs that a written order be prepared, signed, and filed. The minute entry shall, in all cases, show the date on which the order actually is entered in the permanent minutes, but failure to comply with this direction shall not impair the validity or effectiveness of the order.

(c) The provisions of Section 1013 extending the time for exercising a right or doing an act where service is by mail shall not apply to extend the times specified in paragraphs (1) and (2) of subdivision (a).

(d) An order of the court granting a motion may be reviewed on appeal in the same manner as a special order made after final judgment. *(Formerly § 663½, added by Stats.1897, c. 67, p. 59, § 1. Renumbered § 663a, and amended by Stats.1907, c. 380, p. 719, § 4. Amended by Stats.1915, c. 108, p. 203, § 1; Stats.1959, c. 469, p. 2404, § 2; Stats.1965, c. 1890, p. 4360, § 2; Stats.1967, c. 119, p. 1041, § 1; Stats.1967, c. 169, p. 1266, § 2; Stats.1983, c. 302, § 1; Stats.2012, c. 83 (A.B.2106), § 2.)*

Research References

Rutter, Cal. Practice Guide: A.D.R. Ch. 6-B, B. Temporary Judges.
Rutter, Cal. Practice Guide: Civil Appeals & Writs Ch. 2-B, B. Appealable Judgments and Orders.
Rutter, Cal. Practice Guide: Civil Appeals & Writs Ch. 7-A, A. Overview.
Rutter, Cal. Practice Guide: Civil Appeals & Writs Ch. 15-A, A. Overview.
Rutter, Cal. Practice Guide: Civ. Pro. Before Trial Ch. 9(I)-B, B. Preparing and Filing Motions.
Rutter, Cal. Practice Guide: Civil Trials & Evidence Ch. 18-C, C. Other Post-Trial Motions.
Rutter, Cal. Practice Guide: Personal Injury Ch. 10-C, C. Motion to Vacate and Enter Different Judgment.
9 Witkin Cal. Proc. 5th Appeal § 194, General Rule: Appealable.
9 Witkin Cal. Proc. 5th Appeal § 595, (S 595) Nature of Motion.
8 Witkin Cal. Proc. 5th Attack Judgment Trial Court § 141, Notice of Motion.
8 Witkin Cal. Proc. 5th Attack Judgment Trial Court § 143, Review on Appeal.
7 Witkin Cal. Proc. 5th Judgment § 57, Purpose and Entry.
7 Witkin Cal. Proc. 5th Judgment § 58, Notice by Party.
4 Witkin Cal. Proc. 5th Pleading § 24, (S 24) Electronic Service.
6 Witkin Cal. Proc. 5th Proceedings Without Trial § 31, Express Limitations.

§ 663.1. Loss or destruction of papers by conflagration or calamity

The court may grant a new trial of any action or proceeding when all of the following conditions exist:

(a) Any proposed bill of exceptions or statement of the case on motion for a new trial is lost or destroyed by reason of conflagration or other public calamity.

(b) No other record of the proceedings upon the trial thereof can be obtained.

(c) Such action or proceeding is subject to review by motion for new trial pending at the time of such loss or destruction.

(d) The court in which such action or proceeding is pending deems it impossible or impracticable to restore such proceedings and to settle a bill of exceptions or statement of the case containing such proceedings, so as to enable the court to review the judgment or order therein by motion for new trial.

(e) At the time of such loss or destruction a motion for new trial was pending.

In order to grant such new trial, it shall be unnecessary to have any bill of exceptions or statement of the case settled, but upon the facts recited in this section being shown to the satisfaction of the court by affidavit or otherwise, the court may grant such new trial. *(Added by Stats.1953, c. 52, p. 697, § 2.)*

Research References

Rutter, Cal. Practice Guide: Civil Trials & Evidence Ch. 18-B, B. Motion for New Trial.

8 Witkin Cal. Proc. 5th Attack Judgment Trial Court § 45, (S 45) Other Grounds.

§ 663.2. Loss or destruction of papers by conflagration or calamity; time for motion

Pending the hearing of a motion pursuant to Section 663.1 to grant a new trial, the time within which a bill of exceptions may be prepared, served, or presented for settlement shall be extended and shall not commence to run until the decision upon the motion. The motion must be made within 30 days after the loss or destruction of the records. *(Added by Stats.1953, c. 52, p. 697, § 3.)*

Research References

Rutter, Cal. Practice Guide: Civil Appeals & Writs Ch. 8-C, C. Standards of Appellate Review.
Rutter, Cal. Practice Guide: Civil Trials & Evidence Ch. 18-B, B. Motion for New Trial.
Rutter, Cal. Practice Guide: Personal Injury Ch. 10-A, A. Motion for New Trial.
8 Witkin Cal. Proc. 5th Attack Judgment Trial Court § 45, (S 45) Other Grounds.

CHAPTER 8. THE MANNER OF GIVING AND ENTERING JUDGMENT

Section

§ 664. Entry of judgment; time; conformity to verdict or decision; automatic stay on motion for judgment NOV; necessity of entry

When trial by jury has been had, judgment must be entered by the clerk, in conformity to the verdict within 24 hours after the rendition of the verdict, whether or not a motion for judgment notwithstanding the verdict be pending, unless the court order the case to be reserved for argument or further consideration, or grant a stay of proceedings. If the trial has been had by the court, judgment must be entered by the clerk, in conformity to the decision of the court, immediately upon the filing of such decision. In no case is a judgment effectual for any purpose until entered. *(Enacted in 1872. Amended by Stats.1907, c. 381, p. 719, § 1; Stats.1933, c. 744, p. 1882, § 121; Stats.1951, c. 1737, p. 4118, § 98, operative Jan. 1, 1952; Stats.1961, c. 604, p. 1753, § 3; Stats.1977, c. 1257, p. 4765, § 25, eff. Oct. 3, 1977.)*

Research References

Rutter, Cal. Practice Guide: A.D.R. Ch. 6-C, C. Referees.

Rutter, Cal. Practice Guide: Civil Appeals & Writs Ch. 3-B, B. Filing Deadlines.

Rutter, Cal. Practice Guide: Civil Trials & Evidence Ch. 16-F, F. Preparation and Entry of Judgment.

Rutter, Cal. Practice Guide: Civil Trials & Evidence Ch. 17-C, C. Entry of Judgment.

Rutter, Cal. Practice Guide: Civil Trials & Evidence Ch. 18-A, A. Motion for Judgment Notwithstanding the Verdict ("JNOV").

Rutter, Cal. Practice Guide: Enforcing Judgments/Debts Ch. 6A-4, "Entry" of Judgment.

Rutter, Cal. Practice Guide: Enforcing Judgments/Debts Ch. 6A-7, Period During Which Judgment Enforceable; Renewal Procedures.

Rutter, Cal. Practice Guide: Personal Injury Ch. 3-B, B. Potential Claimants in a Personal Injury Case.

Rutter, Cal. Practice Guide: Personal Injury Ch. 3-F, F. MICRA Provisions Affecting Damages.

Rutter, Cal. Practice Guide: Personal Injury Ch. 9-M, M. Verdicts and Judgment.

9 Witkin Cal. Proc. 5th Appeal § 578, Used in Place of Notice of Entry.

9 Witkin Cal. Proc. 5th Appeal § 597, Cross-Appeal Where Motion is Granted.

9 Witkin Cal. Proc. 5th Appeal § 867, Other Defective Judgments.

9 Witkin Cal. Proc. 5th Appeal § 873, (S 873) Reversal of Judgment Notwithstanding Verdict.

2 Witkin Cal. Proc. 5th Courts § 364, in General.

7 Witkin Cal. Proc. 5th Judgment § 9, (S 9) Announcement of Decision and Proposed Judgment.

7 Witkin Cal. Proc. 5th Judgment § 47, Judgment After Trial or Hearing.

7 Witkin Cal. Proc. 5th Judgment § 49, (S 49) in General.

7 Witkin Cal. Proc. 5th Judgment § 50, (S 50) Judgment is Ineffectual Until Entry.

7 Witkin Cal. Proc. 5th Judgment § 53, Probate Orders.

7 Witkin Cal. Proc. 5th Judgment § 55, Judgments.

7 Witkin Cal. Proc. 5th Judgment § 57, Purpose and Entry.

7 Witkin Cal. Proc. 5th Trial § 389, (S 389) Former Law on Findings and Conclusions.

7 Witkin Cal. Proc. 5th Trial § 397, (S 397) Proposed Judgment Where Statement is Not Required.

7 Witkin Cal. Proc. 5th Trial § 399, (S 399) Signing, Filing, and Amending.

7 Witkin Cal. Proc. 5th Trial § 439, (S 439) Motion.

6 Witkin, California Summary 10th Torts § 970, Attorneys' Fees When Periodic Payments Are Awarded.

§ 664.5. Notice of entry of judgment; mailing

(a) In any contested action or special proceeding other than a small claims action or an action or proceeding in which a prevailing party is not represented by counsel, the party submitting an order or judgment for entry shall prepare and mail a copy of the notice of entry of judgment to all parties who have appeared in the action or proceeding and shall file with the court the original notice of entry of judgment together with the proof of service by mail. This subdivision does not apply in a proceeding for dissolution of marriage, for nullity of marriage, or for legal separation.

(b) Promptly upon entry of judgment in a contested action or special proceeding in which a prevailing party is not represented by counsel, the clerk of the court shall mail notice of entry of judgment to all parties who have appeared in the action or special proceeding and shall execute a certificate of such mailing and place it in the court's file in the cause.

(c) For purposes of this section, "judgment" includes any judgment, decree, or signed order from which an appeal lies.

(d) Upon order of the court in any action or special proceeding, the clerk shall mail notice of entry of any judgment or ruling, whether or not appealable.

(e) The Judicial Council shall, by January 1, 1999, adopt a rule of court for the purposes of providing that, upon entry of judgment in a contested action or special proceeding in which a state statute or regulation has been declared unconstitutional by the court, the Attorney General is promptly notified of the judgment and that a certificate of that mailing is placed in the court's file in the cause. *(Added by Stats.1965, c. 1890, p. 4360, § 3. Amended by Stats.1967, c. 169, p. 1267, § 3; Stats.1967, c. 1428, p. 3355, § 1; Stats.1969, c. 87, p. 209, § 2; Stats.1977, c. 1257, p. 4765, § 26, eff. Oct. 3, 1977; Stats.1981, c. 904, p. 3437, § 1; Stats.1982, c. 559, p. 2505, § 1, eff. Aug. 24, 1982; Stats.1993, c. 158 (A.B.392), § 3.05, eff. July 21, 1993; Stats.1996, c. 1061 (S.B.1033), § 1; Stats.1997, c. 259 (A.B.380), § 1.)*

Law Revision Commission Comments

Section 664.5 is amended to delete references to former Civil Code provisions. The reference to a proceeding for "summary dissolution" is omitted from Section 664.5 as unnecessary, since summary dissolution is included under the language "dissolution of marriage" used in the amended section. See Chapter 5(commencing with Section 2400) of Part 3 of Division 6 of the Family Code. [26 Cal.L.Rev.Comm. Reports 107 (1996) (App. 5)].

Research References

Rutter, Cal. Practice Guide: A.D.R. Ch. 6-B, B. Temporary Judges.

Rutter, Cal. Practice Guide: Civil Appeals & Writs Ch. 2-D, D. Standing to Appeal.

Rutter, Cal. Practice Guide: Civil Appeals & Writs Ch. 3-B, B. Filing Deadlines.

Rutter, Cal. Practice Guide: Civil Appeals & Writs Ch. 3-C, C. Extensions of Filing Deadline.

Rutter, Cal. Practice Guide: Civ. Pro. Before Trial Ch. 11-A, A. Voluntary Dismissals.

Rutter, Cal. Practice Guide: Civ. Pro. Before Trial Ch. 7(I)-A, A. Demurrers.

Rutter, Cal. Practice Guide: Civil Trials & Evidence Ch. 17-C, C. Entry of Judgment.

Rutter, Cal. Practice Guide: Civil Trials & Evidence Ch. 17-D, D. Costs.

Rutter, Cal. Practice Guide: Civil Trials & Evidence Ch. 18-A, A. Motion for Judgment Notwithstanding the Verdict ("JNOV").

Rutter, Cal. Practice Guide: Civil Trials & Evidence Ch. 18-B, B. Motion for New Trial.

California Practice Guide: Employment Litigation Ch. 19-T, T. Appeals.

Rutter, Cal. Practice Guide: Personal Injury Ch. 9-M, M. Verdicts and Judgment.

Rutter, Cal. Practice Guide: Personal Injury Ch. 10-A, A. Motion for New Trial.

Rutter, Cal. Practice Guide: Personal Injury Ch. 10-B, B. Motion for Judgment Notwithstanding the Verdict.

Rutter, Cal. Practice Guide: Personal Injury Ch. 10-C, C. Motion to Vacate and Enter Different Judgment.

9 Witkin Cal. Proc. 5th Appeal § 30, Intervention by Attorney General.

9 Witkin Cal. Proc. 5th Appeal § 576, Who May Give Notice of Entry.

9 Witkin Cal. Proc. 5th Appeal § 577, (S 577) in General.

9 Witkin Cal. Proc. 5th Appeal § 579, as Equivalent to Notice of Entry.

9 Witkin Cal. Proc. 5th Appeal § 580, (S 580) Erroneous or Inadequate Notice.

8 Witkin Cal. Proc. 5th Attack Judgment Trial Court § 58, Notice of Entry by Clerk.

8 Witkin Cal. Proc. 5th Attack Judgment Trial Court § 59, Notice of Entry by Party.

8 Witkin Cal. Proc. 5th Attack Judgment Trial Court § 73, (S 73) Commencement of Period.

8 Witkin Cal. Proc. 5th Enforcement of Judgment § 457, (S 457) Notice of Entry.

7 Witkin Cal. Proc. 5th Judgment § 57, Purpose and Entry.

7 Witkin Cal. Proc. 5th Judgment § 58, Notice by Party.

7 Witkin Cal. Proc. 5th Judgment § 59, Notice by Clerk.

7 Witkin Cal. Proc. 5th Judgment § 140, Time Limits.

5 Witkin Cal. Proc. 5th Pleading § 897, (S 897) Judgment and Request for Judgment.

5 Witkin Cal. Proc. 5th Pleading § 983, Notification and Service of Notice.

6 Witkin Cal. Proc. 5th Proceedings Without Trial § 45, (S 45) Notification and Notice.

7 Witkin Cal. Proc. 5th Trial § 440, (S 440) With Motion for New Trial.

§ 664.6. Entry of judgment pursuant to terms of stipulation for settlement

If parties to pending litigation stipulate, in a writing signed by the parties outside the presence of the court or orally before the court, for settlement of the case, or part thereof, the court, upon motion, may enter judgment pursuant to the terms of the settlement. If requested by the parties, the court may retain jurisdiction over the parties to enforce the settlement until performance in full of the terms of the settlement. *(Added by Stats.1981, c. 904, p. 3437, § 2. Amended by Stats.1993, c. 768 (S.B.252), § 1; Stats.1994, c. 587 (A.B.3600), § 7.)*

Research References

Rutter, Cal. Practice Guide: A.D.R. Ch. 1-D, D. Planning for Private ADR.

Rutter, Cal. Practice Guide: A.D.R. Ch. 1-E, E. Enforcing ADR Settlements.

Rutter, Cal. Practice Guide: A.D.R. Ch. 2-F, F. Wrapping Up Settlement.

Rutter, Cal. Practice Guide: A.D.R. Ch. 3-A, A. General Considerations.

Rutter, Cal. Practice Guide: A.D.R. Ch. 3-C, C. Confidentiality.

Rutter, Cal. Practice Guide: A.D.R. Ch. 3-E, E. Voluntary Settlement Conference (Vsc) (Evaluative Mediation).

Rutter, Cal. Practice Guide: A.D.R. Ch. 4-D, D. Mandatory Settlement Conferences.

Rutter, Cal. Practice Guide: A.D.R. Ch. 5-A, A. General Considerations.

Rutter, Cal. Practice Guide: A.D.R. Gen. Matls., Highlights.

Rutter, Cal. Practice Guide: A.D.R. Ch. 1-E, Outline E.

Rutter, Cal. Practice Guide: Civil Appeals & Writs Ch. 2-A, A. Overview.

Rutter, Cal. Practice Guide: Civil Appeals & Writs Ch. 2-B, B. Appealable Judgments and Orders.

Rutter, Cal. Practice Guide: Civil Appeals & Writs Ch. 2-C, C. Nonappealable Orders.

Rutter, Cal. Practice Guide: Civil Appeals & Writs Ch. 2-D, D. Standing to Appeal.

Rutter, Cal. Practice Guide: Civil Appeals & Writs Ch. 8-C, C. Standards of Appellate Review.

Rutter, Cal. Practice Guide: Civil Appeals & Writs Ch. 11-E, E. Appellate Costs and Sanctions.

Rutter, Cal. Practice Guide: Civil Appeals & Writs Ch. 14-D, D. Precedential Effect of Appellate Court Opinions.

Rutter, Cal. Practice Guide: Civil Appeals & Writs Ch. 2-B, Outline B.

Rutter, Cal. Practice Guide: Civil Appeals & Writs Ch. 2-C, Outline C.

Rutter, Cal. Practice Guide: Civil Appeals & Writs Ch. 8-C, Outline C.

Rutter, Cal. Practice Guide: Civ. Pro. Before Trial Ch. 11-A, A. Voluntary Dismissals.

Rutter, Cal. Practice Guide: Civ. Pro. Before Trial Ch. 11-B, B. Involuntary Dismissals.

Rutter, Cal. Practice Guide: Civ. Pro. Before Trial Gen. Matls., Highlights.

Rutter, Cal. Practice Guide: Civ. Pro. Before Trial Ch. 12(II)-A, A. Mandatory Settlement Conference ("Msc").

Rutter, Cal. Practice Guide: Civ. Pro. Before Trial Ch. 12(II)-B, B. Settlements on Behalf of Minors or Incompetents.

Rutter, Cal. Practice Guide: Civ. Pro. Before Trial Ch. 12(II)-F, F. Motion to Enforce Settlement (CCP §§ 664.6, 664.7).

Rutter, Cal. Practice Guide: Civ. Pro. Before Trial Ch. 12(II)-A, Outline a.

Rutter, Cal. Practice Guide: Civ. Pro. Before Trial Ch. 12(II)-B, Outline B.

Rutter, Cal. Practice Guide: Civ. Pro. Before Trial Ch. 12(II)-F, Outline F.

Rutter, Cal. Practice Guide: Civil Trials & Evidence Ch. 8C-K, K. Stipulations.

California Practice Guide: Employment Litigation Ch. 18-A, A. Settlement Considerations.

Rutter, Cal. Practice Guide: Enforcing Judgments/Debts Ch. 6A-13, Creating an Enforcement of Judgment Plan.

Rutter, Cal. Practice Guide: Enforcing Judgments/Debts Ch. 6A-13, Tline 13.

Rutter, Cal. Practice Guide: Family Law Ch. 6-A, A. Child Support.

Rutter, Cal. Practice Guide: Family Law Ch. 17-A, A. Child Support.

Rutter, Cal. Practice Guide: Fed.Civ.Pro. Before Trial Ch. 1-D, D. Choosing Between State and Federal Courts.

Rutter, Cal. Practice Guide: Insurance Litigation Ch. 15-H, H. Settlement of Third Party Claims Against Insured.

Rutter, Cal. Practice Guide: Insurance Litigation Ch. 7K-D, D. Policy Provisions.

Rutter, Cal. Practice Guide: Personal Injury Ch. 4-C, C. Effective Settlement Negotiations.

Rutter, Cal. Practice Guide: Personal Injury Ch. 4-D, D. Techniques Where Settlement Not Forthcoming.

Rutter, Cal. Practice Guide: Personal Injury Ch. 4-G, G. Concluding and Enforcing Settlement.

Rutter, Cal. Practice Guide: Personal Injury Ch. 4-G, Outline G.

Rutter, Cal. Practice Guide: Real Prop. Transactions Ch. 4-D, D. Selecting the Form of Written Agreement.

Rutter, Cal. Practice Guide: Prof. Responsibility Ch. 3-D, D. Authority of Client vs. Authority of Attorney.

Rutter, Cal. Practice Guide: Prof. Responsibility Ch. 11-H, H. Proceedings Before Trial.

Rutter, Cal. Practice Guide: Prof. Responsibility Ch. 3-D, Outline D.

Miller and Starr California Real Estate § 1:69, Contract for the Sale, Gift, or Financing of Real Property.

Miller and Starr California Real Estate § 1:81, Written Authority Required; the Equal Dignities Rule.

Miller and Starr California Real Estate § 35:6, --Confidentiality in Mediation.

Miller and Starr California Real Estate § 29:76, Systems for Resolving Defective Construction Disputes.

Miller and Starr California Real Estate § 34:38, Liquidated Damages--In Real Property Marketing Contracts.

Miller and Starr California Real Estate § 35:17, Efficacy of the Mediation Process; Enforceability.

Miller and Starr California Real Estate § 35:18, Reference Compared to Other ADR Procedures.

Miller and Starr California Real Estate § 35:67, Qualifications and Compensation of an Arbitrator.

13 NO. 6 Miller & Starr, California Real Estate Newsalert 13, Remedies - Breach of Contract.

17 NO. 5 Miller & Starr, California Real Estate Newsalert 5, Contracts.

23 NO. 1 Miller & Starr, California Real Estate Newsalert 3, Alternative Dispute Resolution.

9 Witkin Cal. Proc. 5th Appeal § 69, (S 69) Acceptance of Benefits of Settlement.

9 Witkin Cal. Proc. 5th Appeal § 549, (S 549) Settlement Must be Signed by Parties.

1 Witkin Cal. Proc. 5th Attorneys § 246, Compromise and Consent Judgments.

7 Witkin Cal. Proc. 5th Judgment § 46, Minute Order on Motion.

7 Witkin Cal. Proc. 5th Judgment § 51, Judgments.

2 Witkin Cal. Proc. 5th Jurisdiction § 13, General Principle.

2 Witkin Cal. Proc. 5th Jurisdiction § 421, in General.

4 Witkin Cal. Proc. 5th Pleading § 80, Nature and Scope of Power.

6 Witkin Cal. Proc. 5th Proceedings Without Trial § 64, (S 64) Voluntary Reference.

6 Witkin Cal. Proc. 5th Proceedings Without Trial § 113, Nature and Effect.

6 Witkin Cal. Proc. 5th Proceedings Without Trial § 115, in General.

6 Witkin Cal. Proc. 5th Proceedings Without Trial § 116, Litigation Must be Pending.

6 Witkin Cal. Proc. 5th Proceedings Without Trial § 117, Insurance-Funded Settlements.

6 Witkin Cal. Proc. 5th Proceedings Without Trial § 118, (S 118) in General.

6 Witkin Cal. Proc. 5th Proceedings Without Trial § 119, (S 119) Signatures.

6 Witkin Cal. Proc. 5th Proceedings Without Trial § 120, (S 120) Authority of Attorney.

6 Witkin Cal. Proc. 5th Proceedings Without Trial § 121, (S 121) Oral Stipulations.

6 Witkin Cal. Proc. 5th Proceedings Without Trial § 122, Agreement Made in Arbitration.

6 Witkin Cal. Proc. 5th Proceedings Without Trial § 123, Agreement Made in Mediation.

6 Witkin Cal. Proc. 5th Proceedings Without Trial § 124, Preservation of Right to Indemnity.

6 Witkin Cal. Proc. 5th Proceedings Without Trial § 125, Retention of Jurisdiction.

6 Witkin Cal. Proc. 5th Proceedings Without Trial § 126, (S 126) Other Means of Enforcement.

6 Witkin Cal. Proc. 5th Proceedings Without Trial § 211, Motion to Enforce Settlement.

11 Witkin, California Summary 10th Husband and Wife § 273, (S 273) Continuing Jurisdiction.

11 Witkin, California Summary 10th Husband and Wife § 350, Purposes of Incorporation.

§ 664.7. Construction defect action; entry of judgment pursuant to terms of stipulation for settlement

(a) Notwithstanding Section 664.6, if parties to a pending construction defect action stipulate personally or, where a party's contribution is paid on its behalf pursuant to a policy of insurance, the parties stipulate through their respective counsel, in a writing signed by the parties outside the presence of the court or orally before the court, for settlement of the case, or part thereof, the court, upon motion, may enter judgment pursuant to the terms of the settlement. If requested by the parties, the court may retain jurisdiction over the parties to enforce the settlement until performance in full of the terms of the settlement.

(b) It is the intent of the Legislature that this section modify the holding of Levy v. Superior Court (1995), 10 Cal. 4th 578, regarding the authority of counsel in a construction defect action to bind a party to a settlement.

(c) For purposes of this section, "construction defect action" shall mean any civil action that seeks monetary recovery against a developer, builder, design professional, general contractor, material supplier, or subcontractor of any residential dwelling based upon a claim for alleged defects in the design or construction of the residential dwelling unit. (Added by Stats. 1998, c. 856 (A.B.1950), § 1.)

Research References

Rutter, Cal. Practice Guide: A.D.R. Ch. 1-E, E. Enforcing ADR Settlements.

Rutter, Cal. Practice Guide: Civ. Pro. Before Trial Ch. 12(II)-F, F. Motion to Enforce Settlement (CCP §§ 664.6, 664.7).

Rutter, Cal. Practice Guide: Enforcing Judgments/Debts Ch. 3-C, C. Prelawsuit Considerations.

Rutter, Cal. Practice Guide: Enforcing Judgments/Debts Ch. 6A-13, Creating an Enforcement of Judgment Plan.

Rutter, Cal. Practice Guide: Personal Injury Ch. 4-G, G. Concluding and Enforcing Settlement.

Rutter, Cal. Practice Guide: Prof. Responsibility Ch. 3-D, D. Authority of Client vs. Authority of Attorney.

Miller and Starr California Real Estate § 1:81, Written Authority Required; the Equal Dignities Rule.

Miller and Starr California Real Estate § 29:76, Systems for Resolving Defective Construction Disputes.

9 Witkin Cal. Proc. 5th Appeal § 549, (S 549) Settlement Must be Signed by Parties.

2 Witkin Cal. Proc. 5th Jurisdiction § 420, (S 420) Express Reservation.

6 Witkin Cal. Proc. 5th Proceedings Without Trial § 120, (S 120) Authority of Attorney.

§ 665. Case reserved for argument; bringing before court

CASE MAY BE BROUGHT BEFORE THE COURT FOR ARGUMENT. When the case is reserved for argument or further consideration, as mentioned in the last section, it may be brought by either party before the Court for argument. (Enacted in 1872.)

§ 666. Judgment on cross-complaint exceeding cross-defendant's demand; affirmative relief; remission of amount in excess of jurisdiction

If a claim asserted in a cross-complaint is established at the trial and the amount so established exceeds the demand established by the party against whom the cross-complaint is asserted,

judgment for the party asserting the cross-complaint must be given for the excess; or if it appears that the party asserting the cross-complaint is entitled to any other affirmative relief, judgment must be given accordingly.

When the amount found due to either party exceeds the sum for which the court is authorized to enter judgment, such party may remit the excess, and judgment may be rendered for the residue. (Enacted in 1872. Amended by Stats.1933, c. 744, p. 1882, § 122; Stats.1971, c. 244, p. 391, § 54, operative July 1, 1972.)

Law Revision Commission Comments

The amendment of Section 666 deletes the reference to a "counterclaim" and makes other conforming changes. Counterclaims have been abolished; claims that formerly were asserted as counterclaims are now asserted as cross-complaints. See Code of Civil Procedure Section 428.80. [10 Cal.L.Rev.Comm.Reports 573 (1970].

Research References

7 Witkin Cal. Proc. 5th Judgment § 91, Party Who Obtains Net Monetary Recovery.

6 Witkin, California Summary 10th Torts § 1372, (S 1372) Setoff.

§ 667. Personal property; judgment for possession or value

In an action to recover the possession of personal property, judgment for the plaintiff may be for the possession or the value thereof, in case a delivery cannot be had, and damages for the detention. If the property has been delivered to the plaintiff, and the defendant claim a return thereof judgment for the defendant may be for a return of the property or the value thereof, in case a return cannot be had, and damages for taking and withholding the same. (Enacted in 1872. Amended by Stats.1933, c. 744, p. 1882, § 123; Stats.1973, c. 20, p. 34, § 7; Stats.1982, c. 497, p. 2156, § 37, operative July 1, 1983.)

Law Revision Commission Comments

Section 667 is amended to reflect the fact that execution may no longer issue against the person of the judgment debtor in a civil action. See Code Civ.Proc. § 478 and Comment thereto. [11 Cal.L.Rev.Comm.Reports 14 (1972)].

Section 667 is amended to delete the portion relating to payment in a specified kind of money or currency. This provision is superseded by Section 577.5, which requires a judgment shall be computed and stated in dollars and cents. See also 65 Harv.L.Rev. 887 (1952) (if an obligation is payable in foreign currency, the judgment converts it into dollars). The deleted language dates back to 1851 (Cal.Stats.1851 ch. 5, § 200 p. 82) and was applied, for example, to a judgment on a notice containing a promise to pay in gold coin. [16 Cal.L.Rev.Comm. Reports 1789 (1982)].

Research References

7 Witkin Cal. Proc. 5th Judgment § 32, (S 32) Specific Recovery of Personal Property.

5 Witkin Cal. Proc. 5th Pleading § 692, (S 692) in General.

5 Witkin Cal. Proc. 5th Pleading § 693, (S 693) Common Law Forms.

5 Witkin Cal. Proc. 5th Pleading § 701, Value of Property.

6 Witkin Cal. Proc. 5th Provisional Remedies § 273, Effect of Judgment in Main Action.

6 Witkin, California Summary 10th Torts § 1724, in General.

§ 667.7. Action against health care provider; periodic payments of future damages; contempt; legislative intent

(a) In any action for injury or damages against a provider of health care services, a superior court shall, at the request of either party, enter a judgment ordering that money damages or its equivalent for future damages of the judgment creditor be paid in whole or in part by periodic payments rather than by a lump-sum payment if the award equals or exceeds fifty thousand dollars ($50,000) in future damages. In entering a judgment ordering the payment of future damages by periodic payments, the court shall make a specific finding as to the dollar amount of periodic payments which will compensate the judgment creditor for such future damages. As a condition to authorizing periodic payments of future damages, the court shall require the judgment debtor who is not adequately insured to post security adequate to assure full payment of such damages awarded by the judgment. Upon termination of periodic payments of future damages, the court shall order the return of this security, or so much as remains, to the judgment debtor.

(b)(1) The judgment ordering the payment of future damages by periodic payments shall specify the recipient or recipients of the payments, the dollar amount of the payments, the interval between payments, and the number of payments or the period of time over which payments shall be made. Such payments shall only be subject to modification in the event of the death of the judgment creditor.

(2) In the event that the court finds that the judgment debtor has exhibited a continuing pattern of failing to make the payments, as specified in paragraph (1), the court shall find the judgment debtor in contempt of court and, in addition to the required periodic payments, shall order the judgment debtor to pay the judgment creditor all damages caused by the failure to make such periodic payments, including court costs and attorney's fees.

(c) However, money damages awarded for loss of future earnings shall not be reduced or payments terminated by reason of the death of the judgment creditor, but shall be paid to persons to whom the judgment creditor owed a duty of support, as provided by law, immediately prior to his death. In such cases the court which rendered the original judgment, may, upon petition of any party in interest, modify the judgment to award and apportion the unpaid future damages in accordance with this subdivision.

(d) Following the occurrence or expiration of all obligations specified in the periodic payment judgment, any obligation of the judgment debtor to make further payments shall cease and any security given, pursuant to subdivision (a) shall revert to the judgment debtor.

(e) As used in this section:

(1) "Future damages" includes damages for future medical treatment, care or custody, loss of future earnings, loss of bodily function, or future pain and suffering of the judgment creditor.

(2) "Periodic payments" means the payment of money or delivery of other property to the judgment creditor at regular intervals.

(3) "Health care provider" means any person licensed or certified pursuant to Division 2 (commencing with Section 500) of the Business and Professions Code, or licensed pursuant to the Osteopathic Initiative Act, or the Chiropractic Initiative Act, or licensed pursuant to Chapter 2.5 (commencing with Section 1440) of Division 2 of the Health and Safety Code; and any clinic, health dispensary, or health facility, licensed pursuant to Division 2 (commencing with Section 1200) of the Health and Safety Code. "Health care provider" includes the legal representatives of a health care provider.

(4) "Professional negligence" means a negligent act or omission to act by a health care provider in the rendering of professional services, which act or omission is the proximate cause of a personal injury or wrongful death, provided that such services are within the scope of services for which the provider is licensed and which are not within any restriction imposed by the licensing agency or licensed hospital.

(f) It is the intent of the Legislature in enacting this section to authorize the entry of judgments in malpractice actions against health care providers which provide for the payment of future damages through periodic payments rather than lump-sum payments. By authorizing periodic payment judgments, it is the further intent of the Legislature that the courts will utilize such judgments to provide compensation sufficient to meet the needs of an injured plaintiff and those persons who are dependent on the plaintiff for whatever period is necessary while eliminating the potential windfall from a lump-sum recovery which was intended to provide for the care of an injured plaintiff over an extended period who then dies shortly after the judgment is paid, leaving the balance of the judgment award to persons and purposes for which it was not intended. It is also the intent of the Legislature that all elements of the periodic payment program be specified with certainty in the judgment ordering such payments and that the judgment not be subject to modification at some future time which might alter the specifications of the original judgment. *(Added by Stats.1975, 2nd Ex.Sess., c. 1, p. 3971, § 26. Amended by Stats.1975, 2nd Ex.Sess., c. 2, p. 3993, § 1.194, eff. Sept. 24, 1975, operative Dec. 12, 1975.)*

Research References

Rutter, Cal. Practice Guide: Civil Appeals & Writs Ch. 7-C, C. Stay by Posting Security (Bond or Undertaking).

Rutter, Cal. Practice Guide: Civ. Pro. Before Trial Ch. 12(II)-C, C. Statutory Offer to Compromise (CCP § 998).

Rutter, Cal. Practice Guide: Civ. Pro. Before Trial Ch. 12(II)-E, E. Motion to Determine "Good Faith" of "Piecemeal" Settlement (CCP § 877.6).

Rutter, Cal. Practice Guide: Civil Trials & Evidence Ch. 17-C, C. Entry of Judgment.

Rutter, Cal. Practice Guide: Civil Trials & Evidence Ch. 17-D, D. Costs.

Rutter, Cal. Practice Guide: Enforcing Judgments/Debts Ch. 6A-6, Payment of Final Judgments Against Public Entities.

Rutter, Cal. Practice Guide: Enforcing Judgments/Debts Ch. 6B-3, Creation of Judgment Lien.

Rutter, Cal. Practice Guide: Enforcing Judgments/Debts Ch. 6B-5, Amount of Judgment Lien.

Rutter, Cal. Practice Guide: Enforcing Judgments/Debts Ch. 6B-6, Duration of Real Property Judgment Lien.

Rutter, Cal. Practice Guide: Personal Injury Ch. 3-A, A. Introduction.

Rutter, Cal. Practice Guide: Personal Injury Ch. 3-C, C. Specific Items of Compensatory Damages.

Rutter, Cal. Practice Guide: Personal Injury Ch. 3-F, F. MICRA Provisions Affecting Damages.

Rutter, Cal. Practice Guide: Personal Injury Ch. 4-D, D. Techniques Where Settlement Not Forthcoming.

Rutter, Cal. Practice Guide: Personal Injury Ch. 9-M, M. Verdicts and Judgment.

Rutter, Cal. Practice Guide: Personal Injury Ch. 10-D, D. Government Entity Defendant Post-Trial Elections, Requests, Motions and Hearings.

Rutter, Cal. Practice Guide: Personal Injury Ch. 3-F, Outline F.

Rutter, Cal. Practice Guide: Prof. Responsibility Ch. 5-C, C. Other Statutory Limits on Fees and Fee Agreements.

1 Witkin Cal. Proc. 5th Attorneys § 182, Statutory Provisions.

1 Witkin Cal. Proc. 5th Attorneys § 187, Method of Payment.

8 Witkin Cal. Proc. 5th Enforcement of Judgment § 71, Installment Judgment for Support or Health Care.

8 Witkin Cal. Proc. 5th Enforcement of Judgment § 434, (S 434) Periodic Payments.

7 Witkin Cal. Proc. 5th Judgment § 31, Installment Payments.

2 Witkin Cal. Proc. 5th Jurisdiction § 329, Act in Excess of Jurisdiction.

6 Witkin Cal. Proc. 5th Proceedings Without Trial § 106, Value of Periodic Payments.

7 Witkin Cal. Proc. 5th Trial § 344, Future Damages.

5 Witkin, California Summary 10th Torts § 235, Periodic Payment of Judgment.

6 Witkin, California Summary 10th Torts § 941, (S 941) Constitutionality of Act.

6 Witkin, California Summary 10th Torts § 942, Statutory Provisions.

6 Witkin, California Summary 10th Torts § 964, Periodic Payments.

6 Witkin, California Summary 10th Torts § 966, Authorization.

6 Witkin, California Summary 10th Torts § 967, Purpose.

6 Witkin, California Summary 10th Torts § 968, Procedure.

6 Witkin, California Summary 10th Torts § 969, No Interest on Periodic Payments.

Civ. Pro.

6 Witkin, California Summary 10th Torts § 970, Attorneys' Fees When Periodic Payments Are Awarded.

§ 668. Judgment book

Except as provided in Section 668.5, the clerk of the superior court, must keep, with the records of the court, a book called the "judgment book," in which judgments must be entered. *(Enacted in 1872. Amended by Stats.1933, c. 744, p. 1883, § 124; Stats.1951, c. 1737, p. 4119, § 100, operative Jan. 1, 1952; Stats.1973, c. 185, p. 487, § 1; Stats.1974, c. 219, p. 418, § 1; Stats.1974, c. 1169, p. 2503, § 1; Stats.1977, c. 1257, p. 4765, § 28, eff. Oct. 3, 1977; Stats.1998, c. 931 (S.B.2139), § 86, eff. Sept. 28, 1998; Stats.2002, c. 784 (S.B.1316), § 66.)*

Law Revision Commission Comments

Section 668 is amended to reflect the elimination of the justice court. Cal. Const. art. VI, §§ 1, 5(b). [28 Cal.L.Rev.Comm. Reports 51 (1998)].

Section 668 is amended to reflect unification of the municipal and superior courts pursuant to Article VI, Section 5(e), of the California Constitution. [32 Cal.L.Rev.Comm. Reports 126 (2002)].

Research References

Rutter, Cal. Practice Guide: A.D.R. Ch. 6-B, B. Temporary Judges.
Rutter, Cal. Practice Guide: Civil Trials & Evidence Ch. 17-C, C. Entry of Judgment.
Rutter, Cal. Practice Guide: Civil Trials & Evidence Ch. 18-B, B. Motion for New Trial.
Rutter, Cal. Practice Guide: Enforcing Judgments/Debts Ch. 6A-4, "Entry" of Judgment.
9 Witkin Cal. Proc. 5th Appeal § 608, (S 608) Judgment and Decree of Distribution.
2 Witkin Cal. Proc. 5th Courts § 364, in General.
7 Witkin Cal. Proc. 5th Judgment § 51, Judgments.
7 Witkin Cal. Proc. 5th Judgment § 53, Probate Orders.

§ 668.5. Microfilm copies, or entry into register of actions or electronic data-processing system in lieu of entry in judgment book

In those counties where the clerk of the court places individual judgments in the file of actions and either a microfilm copy of the individual judgment is made, or the judgment is entered in the register of actions, or into the court's electronic data-processing system, prior to placement of the judgment in the file of actions, the clerk shall not be required to enter judgments in a judgment book, and the date of filing the judgment with the clerk shall constitute the date of its entry. *(Added by Stats.1974, c. 1169, p. 2503, § 2. Amended by Stats.1983, c. 464, § 1.)*

Research References

Rutter, Cal. Practice Guide: Civil Appeals & Writs Ch. 3-B, B. Filing Deadlines.
Rutter, Cal. Practice Guide: Civil Appeals & Writs Ch. 16-C, C. Notice of Appeal.
Rutter, Cal. Practice Guide: Civil Trials & Evidence Ch. 17-C, C. Entry of Judgment.
Rutter, Cal. Practice Guide: Civil Trials & Evidence Ch. 18-B, B. Motion for New Trial.
Rutter, Cal. Practice Guide: Enforcing Judgments/Debts Ch. 6A-4, "Entry" of Judgment.
9 Witkin Cal. Proc. 5th Appeal § 608, (S 608) Judgment and Decree of Distribution.
2 Witkin Cal. Proc. 5th Courts § 364, in General.
7 Witkin Cal. Proc. 5th Judgment § 49, (S 49) in General.
7 Witkin Cal. Proc. 5th Judgment § 51, Judgments.
7 Witkin Cal. Proc. 5th Judgment § 55, Judgments.

§ 669. Death of party after trial and submission to judge sitting without jury or after verdict and before judgment; rendition of judgment

If a party dies after trial and submission of the case to a judge sitting without a jury for decision or after a verdict upon any issue of fact, and before judgment, the court may nevertheless render judgment thereon. *(Enacted in 1872. Amended by Stats.1965, c. 1636, p. 3730, § 1; Stats.1980, c. 124, p. 294, § 2.)*

Law Revision Commission Comments

Section 669 is amended to delete the second sentence. Enforcement of a judgment against a deceased party is governed by the Probate Code. See Section 686.020. See also Prob. Code §§ 730, 732 (enforcement of judgments after death). [15 Cal.L.Rev.Comm. Reports 1336 (1979)].

Research References

Rutter, Cal. Practice Guide: Civil Trials & Evidence Ch. 17-C, C. Entry of Judgment.
California Practice Guide: Employment Litigation Ch. 19-H, H. Other Pretrial Procedures.
Rutter, Cal. Practice Guide: Personal Injury Ch. 3-B, B. Potential Claimants in a Personal Injury Case.
3 Witkin Cal. Proc. 5th Actions § 17, (S 17) Illustrations.
8 Witkin Cal. Proc. 5th Enforcement of Judgment § 65, (S 65) Former Law.
7 Witkin Cal. Proc. 5th Judgment § 5, (S 5) After Verdict or Submission.
7 Witkin Cal. Proc. 5th Judgment § 62, Death of Party.
4 Witkin Cal. Proc. 5th Pleading § 261, Where Substitution is Unnecessary.
11 Witkin, California Summary 10th Husband and Wife § 119, (S 119) Entry After Death of Party.
14 Witkin, California Summary 10th Wills and Probate § 520, (S 520) Cause of Action Against Decedent.

§ 670. Judgment roll; contents

In superior courts the following papers, without being attached together, shall constitute the judgment roll:

(a) In case the complaint is not answered by any defendant, the summons, with the affidavit or proof of service; the complaint; the request for entry of default with a memorandum indorsed thereon that the default of the defendant in not answering was entered, and a copy of the judgment; if defendant has appeared by demurrer, and the demurrer has been overruled, then notice of the overruling thereof served on defendant's attorney, together with proof of the service; and in case the service so made is by publication, the affidavit for publication of summons, and the order directing the publication of summons.

(b) In all other cases, the pleadings, all orders striking out any pleading in whole or in part, a copy of the verdict of the jury, the statement of decision of the court, or finding of the referee, and a copy of any order made on demurrer, or relating to a change of parties, and a copy of the judgment; if there are two or more defendants in the action, and any one of them has allowed judgment to pass against him or her by default, the summons, with proof of its service, on the defendant, and if the service on the defaulting defendant be by publication, then the affidavit for publication, and the order directing the publication of summons. *(Enacted in 1872. Amended by Code Am.1873–74, c. 383, p. 319, § 89; Code Am.1875–76, c. 168, p. 93, § 1; Stats.1895, c. 40, p. 45, § 1; Stats.1907, c. 381, p. 720, § 2; Stats.1933, c. 744, p. 1883, § 125; Stats.1939, c. 733, p. 2259, § 1; Stats.1970, c. 218, p. 470, § 1; Stats.1977, c. 1257, p. 4765, § 29, eff. Oct. 3, 1977; Stats.1981, c. 900, p. 3426, § 6; Stats.1998, c. 931 (S.B.2139), § 87, eff. Sept. 28, 1998; Stats.2002, c. 784 (S.B.1316), § 67.)*

Law Revision Commission Comments

Section 670 is amended to reflect the elimination of the justice court. Cal. Const. art. VI, §§ 1, 5(b). [28 Cal.L.Rev.Comm. Reports 51 (1998)].

Section 670 is amended to reflect unification of the municipal and superior courts pursuant to Article VI, Section 5(e), of the California Constitution. [32 Cal.L.Rev.Comm. Reports 126 (2002)].

Research References

9 Witkin Cal. Proc. 5th Appeal § 667, (S 667) Nature of Record.

6 Witkin Cal. Proc. 5th Proceedings Without Trial § 163, (S 163) Entry and Memorandum.

§ 673. Assignee of right may become assignee of record; procedure; acknowledgment of assignment of judgment

(a) An assignee of a right represented by a judgment may become an assignee of record by filing with the clerk of the court which entered the judgment an acknowledgment of assignment of judgment.

(b) An acknowledgment of assignment of judgment shall contain all of the following:

(1) The title of the court where the judgment is entered and the cause and number of the action.

(2) The date of entry of the judgment and of any renewals of the judgment and where entered in the records of the court.

(3) The name and address of the judgment creditor and name and last known address of the judgment debtor.

(4) A statement describing the right represented by the judgment that is assigned to the assignee.

(5) The name and address of the assignee.

(c) The acknowledgment of assignment of judgment shall be:

(1) Made in the manner of an acknowledgment of a conveyance of real property.

(2) Executed and acknowledged by the judgment creditor or by the prior assignee of record if there is one.

(d) This section is in addition to, and does not limit or restrict, any other means by which an assignee may become an assignee of record. *(Added by Stats.1982, c. 497, p. 2157, § 38, operative July 1, 1983.)*

Law Revision Commission Comments

Section 673 is a new provision that prescribes the content and manner of execution of an acknowledgment of assignment of judgment. Although prior law referred to an "assignee of record" (see reference in former Section 675 relating to satisfaction of judgment), it was unclear how a person became an "assignee of record." Section 673 fills this gap, but the section does not limit or restrict the use of any other means by which an assignee may become an assignee of record. See subdivision (d).

The required contents and manner of execution of the acknowledgment of assignment of judgment are comparable to those specified in Section 724.060 (contents and manner of execution of acknowledgment of satisfaction of judgment).

The filing of the acknowledgment of assignment with the court under this section does not, of itself, give notice to the judgment debtor so as to invalidate any payments made by the judgment debtor to the judgment creditor or a prior assignee of record. See Civil Code § 954.5(c). The filing with the court, however, affects the priorities between conflicting assignments. See Civil Code § 954.5(b).

Nothing in Section 673 requires the filing of the acknowledgment of assignment of judgment with the court in order to accomplish the transfer of the interest in the judgment. See Civil Code § 954.5(a). But, unless the assignee becomes an assignee of record by some other means, the failure to file an acknowledgment of assignment of judgment precludes the use by the assignee of a writ of execution and other enforcement remedies. See Section 681.020. [16 Cal.L.Rev.Comm. Reports 1790 (1982)].

Research References

Rutter, Cal. Practice Guide: Enforcing Judgments/Debts Ch. 6G-11, Enforcement of Judgment by Assignees.

Miller and Starr California Real Estate § 32:61, Property Interests Subject to Execution.

Miller and Starr California Real Estate § 32:68, Conditions to Conducting the Sale.

19 NO. 3 Miller & Starr, California Real Estate Newsalert 16, Homesteads.

8 Witkin Cal. Proc. 5th Enforcement of Judgment § 24, Enforcement by Assignee.

§ 674. Abstract of judgment or decree; contents; amendment

(a) Except as otherwise provided in Section 4506 of the Family Code, an abstract of a judgment or decree requiring the payment of money shall be certified by the clerk of the court where the judgment or decree was entered and shall contain all of the following:

(1) The title of the court where the judgment or decree is entered and cause and number of the action.

(2) The date of entry of the judgment or decree and of any renewals of the judgment or decree and where entered in the records of the court.

(3) The name and last known address of the judgment debtor and the address at which the summons was either personally served or mailed to the judgment debtor or the judgment debtor's attorney of record.

(4) The name and address of the judgment creditor.

(5) The amount of the judgment or decree as entered or as last renewed.

(6) The last four digits of the social security number and driver's license number of the judgment debtor if they are known to the judgment creditor. If either or both of those sets of numbers are not known to the judgment creditor, that fact shall be indicated on the abstract of judgment.

(7) Whether a stay of enforcement has been ordered by the court and, if so, the date the stay ends.

(8) The date of issuance of the abstract.

(b) An abstract of judgment, recorded after January 1, 1979, that does not list the social security number and driver's license number of the judgment debtor, or either of them, as required by subdivision (a) or by Section 4506 of the Family Code, may be amended by the recording of a document entitled "Amendment to Abstract of Judgment." The Amendment to Abstract of Judgment shall contain all of the information required by this section or by Section 4506 of the Family Code, and shall set forth the date of recording and the book and page location in the records of the county recorder of the original abstract of judgment.

A recorded Amendment to Abstract of Judgment shall have priority as of the date of recordation of the original abstract of judgment, except as to any purchaser, encumbrancer, or lessee who obtained their interest after the recordation of the original abstract of judgment but prior to the recordation of the Amendment to Abstract of Judgment without actual notice of the original abstract of judgment. The purchaser, encumbrancer, or lessee without actual notice may assert as a defense against enforcement of the abstract of judgment the failure to comply with this section or Section 4506 of the Family Code regarding the contents of the original abstract of judgment notwithstanding the subsequent recordation of an Amendment to Abstract of Judgment. With respect to an abstract of judgment recorded between January 1, 1979, and July 10, 1985, the defense against enforcement for failure to comply with this section or Section 4506 of the Family Code may not be asserted by the holder of another abstract of judgment or involuntary lien, recorded without actual notice of the prior abstract, unless refusal to allow the defense would result in prejudice and substantial injury as used in Section 475. The recordation of an Amendment to Abstract of Judgment does not extend or otherwise alter the computation of time as provided in Section 697.310.

(c)(1) The abstract of judgment shall be certified in the name of the judgment debtor as listed on the judgment and may also include the additional name or names by which the judgment debtor is known as set forth in the affidavit of identity, as defined in Section 680.135, filed by the judgment creditor with the application for issuance of the abstract of judgment. Prior to the clerk of the court certifying an abstract of judgment containing any additional name or names by which the judgment debtor is known that are not listed on the judgment, the court shall approve the affidavit of identity. If the court determines, without a hearing or a notice, that the affidavit of identity states sufficient facts upon which the judgment creditor has identified the additional names of the judgment debtor, the court shall authorize the certification of the abstract of judgment with the additional name or names.

(2) The remedies provided in Section 697.410 apply to a recorded abstract of a money judgment based upon an affidavit of identity that appears to create a judgment lien on real property of a person who is not the judgment debtor. *(Enacted in 1872. Amended by Stats.1907, c. 381, p. 720, § 4; Stats.1923, c. 368, p. 752, § 3; Stats.1927, c. 493, p. 830, § 1; Stats.1933, c. 744, p. 1884, § 129; Stats.1935, c. 298, p. 1017, § 1; Stats.1947, c. 116, p. 638, § 1; Stats.1951, c. 1737, p. 4119, § 101, operative Jan. 1, 1952; Stats.1955, c. 781, p. 1380, § 1; Stats.1957, c. 43, p. 603, § 6; Stats.1973, c. 797, p. 1413, § 1; Stats.1974, c. 211, p. 405, § 1; Stats.1974, c. 1169, p. 2503, § 3; Stats.1976, c. 1000, p. 2368, § 1, operative July 1, 1977; Stats.1977, c. 1257, p. 4766, § 30, eff. Oct. 3, 1977; Stats.1978, c. 203, § 1; Stats.1980, c. 1281, p. 4326, § 2; Stats.1982, c. 517, p. 2344, § 131; Stats.1982, c. 497, p. 2157, § 39, operative July 1, 1983; Stats.1988, c. 153, § 6; Stats.1988, c. 1411, § 1; Stats.1992, c. 163 (A.B.2641), § 28, operative Jan. 1, 1994; Stats.2000, c. 639 (A.B.2405), § 1; Stats.2001, c. 159 (S.B.662), § 39; Stats.2007, c. 189 (S.B.644), § 1.)*

Law Revision Commission Comments

Section 674 is amended to make clear that the section applies to judgments entered pursuant to Title 11 (commencing with Section 1710.10) of Part 3 of this code. [11 Cal.L.Rev.Comm.Reports 674 (1973)].

Section 674 is amended to delete subdivisions (b) and (c), which are continued without substantive change in Family Code Section 4506 and to make conforming revisions. [22 Cal.L.Rev.Comm.Reports 1 (1992)].

Research References

Rutter, Cal. Practice Guide: Enforcing Judgments/Debts Ch. 2-C, C. Tort Liability.

Rutter, Cal. Practice Guide: Enforcing Judgments/Debts Ch. 6B-3, Creation of Judgment Lien.

Rutter, Cal. Practice Guide: Enforcing Judgments/Debts Ch. 6B-11, Release of Real Property Judgment Lien.

Rutter, Cal. Practice Guide: Real Prop. Transactions Ch. 11-H, H. Other Remedies.

Miller and Starr California Real Estate § 11:10, Required Form and Contents--In General.

Miller and Starr California Real Estate § 32:47, Contents of the Abstract of Judgment.

Miller and Starr California Real Estate § 32:48, Nature and Creation.

Miller and Starr California Real Estate § 32:49, Real Property Subject to the Judgment Lien.

Miller and Starr California Real Estate § 32:67, Stay of Execution Sale.

Miller and Starr California Real Estate § 11:164, Personal Property Tax Liens.

16 NO. 2 Miller & Starr, California Real Estate Newsalert 13, Involuntary Liens.

2 Witkin Cal. Proc. 5th Courts § 303, (S 303) Enforcement and Stay.

8 Witkin Cal. Proc. 5th Enforcement of Judgment § 65, (S 65) Former Law.

8 Witkin Cal. Proc. 5th Enforcement of Judgment § 70, Abstract of Judgment.

8 Witkin Cal. Proc. 5th Enforcement of Judgment § 81, Release of Erroneous Lien.

8 Witkin Cal. Proc. 5th Enforcement of Judgment § 220, (S 220) Application.

7 Witkin Cal. Proc. 5th Judgment § 64, Abstract of Judgment.

10 Witkin, California Summary 10th Parent and Child § 432, Assets Subject to Order.

Title 8.5

UNIFORM FOREIGN–MONEY CLAIMS ACT

Section

§ 676. Short title

This title shall be known and may be cited as the Uniform Foreign-Money Claims Act. *(Added by Stats.1991, c. 932 (A.B.1646), § 1.)*

Research References

Rutter, Cal. Practice Guide: Enforcing Judgments/Debts Ch. 6J-5, Uniform Foreign-Money Claims Act.

8 Witkin Cal. Proc. 5th Enforcement of Judgment § 468, in General.

§ 676.1. Definitions

As used in this title:

(1) "Action" means a judicial proceeding or arbitration in which a payment in money may be awarded or enforced with respect to a foreign-money claim.

(2) "Bank-offered spot rate" means the spot rate of exchange at which a bank will sell foreign money at a spot rate.

(3) "Conversion date" means the banking day next preceding the date on which money, in accordance with this title, is (i) paid to a claimant in an action or distribution proceeding, (ii) paid to the official designated by law to enforce a judgment or award on behalf of a claimant, or (iii) used to recoup, setoff, or counterclaim in different moneys in an action or distribution proceeding.

(4) "Distribution proceeding" means a judicial or nonjudicial proceeding for the distribution of a fund in which one or more foreign-money claims is asserted and includes an accounting, an assignment for the benefit of creditors, a foreclosure, the liquidation or rehabilitation of a corporation or other entity, and the distribution of an estate, trust, or other fund.

(5) "Foreign money" means money other than money of the United States of America.

(6) "Foreign-money claim" means a claim upon an obligation to pay, or a claim for recovery of a loss, expressed in or measured by a foreign money.

(7) "Money" means a medium of exchange for the payment of obligations or a store of value authorized or adopted by a government or by intergovernmental agreement.

(8) "Money of the claim" means the money determined as proper pursuant to Section 676.4.

(9) "Person" means an individual, a corporation, government or governmental subdivision or agency, business trust, estate, trust, joint venture, partnership, association, two or more persons having a joint or common interest, or any other legal or commercial entity.

(10) "Rate of exchange" means the rate at which money of one country may be converted into money of another country in a free financial market convenient to or reasonably usable by a person obligated to pay or to state a rate of conversion. If separate rates of exchange apply to different kinds of transactions, the term means the rate applicable to the particular transaction giving rise to the foreign-money claim.

(11) "Spot rate" means the rate of exchange at which foreign money is sold by a bank or other dealer in foreign exchange for immediate or next day availability or for settlement by immediate payment in cash or equivalent, by charge to an account, or by an agreed delayed settlement not exceeding two days.

(12) "State" means a State of the United States, the District of Columbia, the Commonwealth of Puerto Rico, or a territory or insular possession subject to the jurisdiction of the United States. *(Added by Stats.1991, c. 932 (A.B.1646), § 1.)*

Research References

8 Witkin Cal. Proc. 5th Enforcement of Judgment § 468, in General.
8 Witkin Cal. Proc. 5th Enforcement of Judgment § 471, Determining Amount of Money Owed on Claim.
8 Witkin Cal. Proc. 5th Enforcement of Judgment § 473, Judgment or Award.
8 Witkin Cal. Proc. 5th Enforcement of Judgment § 476, Enforcement of Judgment Rendered in Another Jurisdiction.

§ 676.2. Application of title

(a) This title applies only to a foreign-money claim in an action or distribution proceeding.

(b) This title applies to foreign-money issues even if other law under the conflict-of-laws rules of this state applies to other issues in the action or distribution proceeding. *(Added by Stats.1991, c. 932 (A.B.1646), § 1.)*

Research References

8 Witkin Cal. Proc. 5th Enforcement of Judgment § 468, in General.

§ 676.3. Agreement of parties

(a) The effect of this title may be varied by agreement of the parties made before or after commencement of an action or distribution proceeding or the entry of judgment.

(b) Parties to a transaction may agree upon the money to be used in a transaction giving rise to a foreign-money claim and may agree to use different moneys for different aspects of the transaction. Stating the price in a foreign money for one aspect of a transaction does not alone require the use of that money for other aspects of the transaction. *(Added by Stats.1991, c. 932 (A.B.1646), § 1.)*

Research References

8 Witkin Cal. Proc. 5th Enforcement of Judgment § 468, in General.

§ 676.4. Proper money of claim for payment

(a) The money in which the parties to a transaction have agreed that payment is to be made is the proper money of the claim for payment.

(b) If the parties to a transaction have not otherwise agreed, the proper money of the claim, as in each case may be appropriate, is one of the following:

(1) The money regularly used between the parties as a matter of usage or course of dealing.

(2) The money used at the time of a transaction in international trade, by trade usage or common practice, for valuing or settling transactions in the particular commodity or service involved.

(3) The money in which the loss was ultimately felt or will be incurred by the party claimant. *(Added by Stats.1991, c. 932 (A.B.1646), § 1.)*

Research References

8 Witkin Cal. Proc. 5th Enforcement of Judgment § 470, Determining Proper Money of Claim.

§ 676.5. Amount contracted to be paid in foreign money measured by specified amount of different money; determination; conversion date; payment

(a) If an amount contracted to be paid in a foreign money is measured by a specified amount of a different money, the amount to be paid is determined on the conversion date.

(b) If an amount contracted to be paid in a foreign money is to be measured by a different money at the rate of exchange prevailing on a date before default, that rate of exchange applies only to payments made within a reasonable time after default, not exceeding 30 days. Thereafter, conversion is made at the bank-offered spot rate on the conversion date.

(c) A monetary claim is neither usurious nor unconscionable because the agreement on which it is based provides that the amount of the debtor's obligation to be paid in the debtor's money, when received by the creditor, shall equal a specified amount of the foreign money of the country of the creditor. If, because of unexcused delay in payment of a judgment or award, the amount received by the creditor does not equal the amount of the foreign money specified in the agreement, the court or arbitrator shall amend the judgment or award accordingly. *(Added by Stats.1991, c. 932 (A.B.1646), § 1.)*

Research References

8 Witkin Cal. Proc. 5th Enforcement of Judgment § 471, Determining Amount of Money Owed on Claim.
8 Witkin Cal. Proc. 5th Enforcement of Judgment § 473, Judgment or Award.

§ 676.6. Claim in a specified foreign money or not; defenses; proper money question

(a) A person may assert a claim in a specified foreign money. If a foreign-money claim is not asserted, the claimant makes the claim in United States dollars.

(b) An opposing party may allege and prove that a claim, in whole or in part, is in a different money than that asserted by the claimant.

(c) A person may assert a defense, setoff, recoupment, or counterclaim in any money without regard to the money of other claims.

(d) The determination of the proper money of the claim is a question of law. *(Added by Stats.1991, c. 932 (A.B.1646), § 1.)*

Research References

8 Witkin Cal. Proc. 5th Enforcement of Judgment § 470, Determining Proper Money of Claim.

8 Witkin Cal. Proc. 5th Enforcement of Judgment § 472, Allegation and Proof of Money of Claim.

§ 676.7. Judgment or award on a foreign-money claim; amount stated in money of claim; form; entry; costs; payment; conversion

(a) Except as provided in subdivision (c), a judgment or award on a foreign-money claim shall be stated in an amount of the money of the claim.

(b) A judgment or award on a foreign-money claim is payable in that foreign money or, at the option of the debtor, in the amount of United States dollars which will purchase that foreign money on the conversion date at a bank-offered spot rate.

(c) Assessed costs shall be entered in United States dollars.

(d) Each payment in United States dollars shall be accepted and credited on a judgment or award on a foreign-money claim in the amount of the foreign money that could be purchased by the dollars at a bank-offered spot rate of exchange at or near the close of business on the conversion date for that payment.

(e) A judgment or award made in an action or distribution proceeding on both (1) a defense, setoff, recoupment, or counterclaim and (2) the adverse party's claim, shall be netted by converting the money of the smaller into the money of the larger, and by subtracting the smaller from the larger, and specify the rates of exchange used.

(f) A judgment substantially in the following form complies with subdivision (a):

"IT IS ADJUDGED AND ORDERED, that Defendant _____ pay to
                        (insert name)
plaintiff _____ the sum of _____
                (insert name)
_____
                (insert amount in the foreign money)
plus interest on that sum at the rate of _____
                        — (insert rate – see Section 676.9)
percent   a   year   or,
at the option of the judgement debtor, the number of United States dollars which will purchase the _____
_____ with interest due, at
        (insert name of foreign money)
a bank-offered spot rate at or near the close of business on the banking day next before the day of payment, together with assessed costs of _____
                        (insert amount)
United States dollars."

(g) If a contract claim is of the type covered by subdivision (a) or (b) of Section 676.5, the judgment or award shall be entered for the amount of money stated to measure the obligation to be paid in the money specified for payment or, at the option of the debtor, the number of United States dollars which will purchase the computed amount of the money of payment on the conversion date at a bank-offered spot rate.

(h) A judgment shall be entered in foreign money in the same manner, and has the same effect as a lien, as other judgments. It may be discharged by payment. *(Added by Stats.1991, c. 932 (A.B.1646), § 1.)*

Research References

8 Witkin Cal. Proc. 5th Enforcement of Judgment § 473, Judgment or Award.

8 Witkin Cal. Proc. 5th Enforcement of Judgment § 476, Enforcement of Judgment Rendered in Another Jurisdiction.

7 Witkin Cal. Proc. 5th Judgment § 30, in General.

§ 676.8. Distribution proceeding; foreign-money claimant; rate of exchange

The rate of exchange prevailing at or near the close of business on the day the distribution proceeding is initiated governs all exchanges of foreign money in a distribution proceeding. A foreign-money claimant in a distribution proceeding shall assert its claim in the named foreign money and show the amount of United States dollars resulting from a conversion as of the date the proceeding was initiated. *(Added by Stats.1991, c. 932 (A.B.1646), § 1.)*

Research References

8 Witkin Cal. Proc. 5th Enforcement of Judgment § 474, Conversion of Money in Distribution Proceeding.

7 Witkin Cal. Proc. 5th Judgment § 30, in General.

§ 676.9. Recovery of interest; rate

(a) With respect to a foreign-money claim, recovery of prejudgment or pre-award interest and the rate of interest to be applied in the action or distribution proceeding, except as provided in subdivision (b), are matters of the substantive law governing the right to recovery under the conflict-of-laws rules of this state.

(b) The court or arbitrator shall increase or decrease the amount of prejudgment or pre-award interest otherwise payable in a judgment or award in foreign money to the extent required by the law of this state governing a failure to make or accept an offer of settlement or offer of judgment, or conduct by a party or its attorney causing undue delay or expense.

(c) A judgment or award on a foreign-money claim bears interest at the rate applicable to judgments of this state. *(Added by Stats.1991, c. 932 (A.B.1646), § 1.)*

Research References

8 Witkin Cal. Proc. 5th Enforcement of Judgment § 475, Interest.

§ 676.10. Enforcement of foreign judgment expressed in foreign money

(a) If an action is brought to enforce a judgment of another jurisdiction expressed in a foreign money and the judgment is recognized in this state as enforceable, the enforcing judgment shall be entered as provided in Section 676.7, whether or not the foreign judgment confers an option to pay in an equivalent amount of United States dollars.

(b) A foreign judgment may be enforced in accordance with Title 11 (commencing with Section 1710.10) of Part 3.

(c) A satisfaction or partial payment made upon the foreign judgment, on proof thereof, shall be credited against the amount of foreign money specified in the judgment, notwithstanding the entry of judgment in this state.

(d) A judgment entered on a foreign-money claim only in United States dollars in another state shall be enforced in this state in United States dollars only. *(Added by Stats.1991, c. 932 (A.B.1646), § 1.)*

Research References

8 Witkin Cal. Proc. 5th Enforcement of Judgment § 476, Enforcement of Judgment Rendered in Another Jurisdiction.

§ 676.11. Provisional remedies; enforcement; computations of United States dollar equivalents to foreign money amounts claimed, etc.

(a) Computations under this section are for the limited purposes of the section and do not affect computation of the

United States dollar equivalent of the money of the judgment for the purpose of payment.

(b) For the limited purpose of facilitating the enforcement of provisional remedies in an action, the value in United States dollars of assets to be seized or restrained pursuant to a writ of attachment, garnishment, execution, or other legal process, the amount of United States dollars at issue for assessing costs, or the amount of United States dollars involved for a surety bond or other court-required undertaking, shall be ascertained as provided in subdivisions (c) and (d).

(c) A party seeking process, costs, bond, or other undertaking under subdivision (b) shall compute in United States dollars the amount of the foreign money claimed from a bank-offered spot rate prevailing at or near the close of business on the banking day next preceding the filing of a request or application for the issuance of process or for the determination of costs, or an application for a bond or other court-required undertaking.

(d) A party seeking the process, costs, bond, or other undertaking under subdivision (b) shall file with each request or application an affidavit or certificate executed in good faith by its counsel or a bank officer, stating the market quotation used and how it was obtained, and setting forth the calculation. Affected court officials incur no liability, after a filing of the affidavit or certificate, for acting as if the judgment were in the amount of United States dollars stated in the affidavit or certificate. *(Added by Stats.1991, c. 932 (A.B.1646), § 1.)*

Research References

8 Witkin Cal. Proc. 5th Enforcement of Judgment § 477, Determining Dollar Value of Claim for Limited Purposes.

§ 676.12. Substitution of new money by issuing or adopting country; rate of conversion

(a) If, after an obligation is expressed or a loss is incurred in a foreign money, the country issuing or adopting that money substitutes a new money in place of that money, the obligation or the loss is treated as if expressed or incurred in the new money at the rate of conversion the issuing country establishes for the payment of like obligations or losses denominated in the former money.

(b) If substitution under subdivision (a) occurs after a judgment or award is entered on a foreign-money claim, the court or arbitrator shall amend the judgment or award by a like conversion of the former money. *(Added by Stats.1991, c. 932 (A.B.1646), § 1.)*

Research References

8 Witkin Cal. Proc. 5th Enforcement of Judgment § 478, Effect of Issuing Country's Substitution of New Money for Old.

§ 676.13. Supplementary governing laws

Unless displaced by particular provisions of this title, the principles of law and equity, including the law merchant, and the law relative to capacity to contract, principal and agent, estoppel, fraud, misrepresentation, duress, coercion, mistake, bankruptcy, or other validating or invalidating causes supplement its provisions. *(Added by Stats.1991, c. 932 (A.B.1646), § 1.)*

Research References

8 Witkin Cal. Proc. 5th Enforcement of Judgment § 468, in General.

§ 676.14. Uniform application and construction

This title shall be applied and construed to effectuate its general purpose to make uniform the law with respect to the subject of this title among states enacting it. *(Added by Stats.1991, c. 932 (A.B.1646), § 1.)*

Research References

8 Witkin Cal. Proc. 5th Enforcement of Judgment § 468, in General.

§ 676.15. Severability

If any provision of this title or its application to any person or circumstance is held invalid, that invalidity does not affect other provisions or applications of this title which can be given effect without the invalid provision or application, and to this end the provisions of this title are severable. *(Added by Stats.1991, c. 932 (A.B.1646), § 1.)*

§ 676.16. Actions and distribution proceedings affected

This title applies to actions and distribution proceedings commenced on or after January 1, 1992. *(Added by Stats.1991, c. 932 (A.B.1646), § 1.)*

Title 9

ENFORCEMENT OF JUDGMENTS

Division 1

DEFINITIONS AND GENERAL PROVISIONS

CHAPTER 1. SHORT TITLE AND DEFINITIONS

Section

680.250.   Judgment debtor.
680.260.   Levying officer.
680.270.   Money judgment.
680.280.   Person.
680.290.   Personal property.
680.300.   Principal amount of the judgment.
680.310.   Property.
680.320.   Real property.
680.330.   Registered process server.
680.340.   Secured party.
680.340.   Secured party.
680.345.   Security.
680.350.   Security agreement.
680.350.   Security agreement.
680.360.   Security interest.
680.365.   Spousal support.
680.370.   Tangible personal property.
680.380.   Writ.

§ 680.010.   Short title

This title shall be known and may be cited as the Enforcement of Judgments Law. *(Added by Stats.1982, c. 1364, p. 5070, § 2, operative July 1, 1983.)*

Law Revision Commission Comments

Section 680.010 is new and provides a convenient means of referring to this title. See also Section 706.010 (Wage Garnishment Law). [15 Cal.L.Rev.Comm. Reports 1196 (1982)].

Research References

Rutter, Cal. Practice Guide: A.D.R. Ch. 4-B, B. Judicial Arbitration.
Rutter, Cal. Practice Guide: Civ. Pro. Before Trial Ch. 13-F, F. Arbitration Award.
Rutter, Cal. Practice Guide: Enforcing Judgments/Debts Ch. 6A-2, Enforcement of Judgments Law ("Ejl")-Background.
Rutter, Cal. Practice Guide: Enforcing Judgments/Debts Ch. 6C-2, Types of Property Subject to Jlpp.
Miller and Starr California Real Estate § 13:1, Overview; Scope and Terminology of Chapter.
Miller and Starr California Real Estate § 34:106, Statute of Limitations.
2 Witkin Cal. Proc. 5th Courts § 247, (S 247) Ancillary Remedies.
2 Witkin Cal. Proc. 5th Courts § 290, (S 290) Uniform Fees.
2 Witkin Cal. Proc. 5th Courts § 302, (S 302) in General.
2 Witkin Cal. Proc. 5th Courts § 303, (S 303) Enforcement and Stay.
8 Witkin Cal. Proc. 5th Enforcement of Judgment § 1, Organization of Chapter.
8 Witkin Cal. Proc. 5th Enforcement of Judgment § 18, (S 18) in General.
8 Witkin Cal. Proc. 5th Enforcement of Judgment § 429, (S 429) Against State.
8 Witkin Cal. Proc. 5th Enforcement of Judgment § 430, in General.
8 Witkin Cal. Proc. 5th Enforcement of Judgment § 432, Enforcement Mechanisms.
8 Witkin Cal. Proc. 5th Enforcement of Judgment § 436, Action on Judgment.
8 Witkin Cal. Proc. 5th Extraordinary Writs § 114, Enforcing or Vacating Judgment.
4 Witkin Cal. Proc. 5th Pleading § 215, Special Statutes.
4 Witkin Cal. Proc. 5th Pleading § 216, Other Procedures Compared.
6 Witkin Cal. Proc. 5th Provisional Remedies § 424, Other Bases.
4 Witkin, California Summary 10th Secured Transactions in Personal Property § 64, (S 64) in Proceeds.
13 Witkin, California Summary 10th Trusts § 267, (S 267) Claims Established by Judgment.
14 Witkin, California Summary 10th Wills and Probate § 379, Orders.
14 Witkin, California Summary 10th Wills and Probate § 627, (S 627) Money and Nonmoney Judgments.

§ 680.110.   Definitions

Unless the provision or context otherwise requires, the definitions in this chapter govern the construction of this title. *(Added by Stats.1982, c. 1364, p. 5070, § 2, operative July 1, 1983.)*

Law Revision Commission Comments

Section 680.110 is a standard provision found in the definitional portion of several California codes and laws. E.g., Code Civ.Proc. §§ 481.010, 1235.110; Evid. Code § 100; Veh. Code § 100. [15 Cal.L.Rev.Comm. Reports 1196 (1982)].

Research References

Rutter, Cal. Practice Guide: Enforcing Judgments/Debts Ch. 6A-3, "Judgment," "Judgment Debtor" and "Judgment Creditor" Defined.
8 Witkin Cal. Proc. 5th Enforcement of Judgment § 21, Definitions.

§ 680.120.   Account debtor

"Account debtor" means "account debtor" as defined in paragraph (3) of subdivision (a) of Section 9102 of the Commercial Code. *(Added by Stats.1982, c. 1364, p. 5070, § 2, operative July 1, 1983. Amended by Stats.1999, c. 991 (S.B.45), § 15.5, operative July 1, 2001.)*

Law Revision Commission Comments

Section 680.120 is new. The term "account debtor" is used in Sections 700.100, 700.170, and 701.050. [15 Cal.L.Rev.Comm. Reports 1197 (1982)].

Research References

8 Witkin Cal. Proc. 5th Enforcement of Judgment § 21, Definitions.
8 Witkin Cal. Proc. 5th Enforcement of Judgment § 135, (S 135) Accounts Receivable and General Intangibles.

§ 680.130.   Account receivable

"Account receivable" means "account" as defined in paragraph (2) of subdivision (a) of Section 9102 of the Commercial Code. *(Added by Stats.1982, c. 1364, p. 5070, § 2, operative July 1, 1983. Amended by Stats.1999, c. 991 (S.B.45), § 16, operative July 1, 2001.)*

Law Revision Commission Comments

Section 680.130 incorporates the Commercial Code definition of "account." The term "account receivable" is used in this title because it is more descriptive than "account" and because it avoids confusion with the term "deposit account." See Section 680.170 ("deposit account" defined). The term "account receivable" is used in Sections 697.530, 699.080, 700.170, 701.050, and 701.520. [16 Cal.L.Rev.Comm. Reports 1197 (1982)].

Research References

Rutter, Cal. Practice Guide: Enforcing Judgments/Debts Ch. 6D-4, Levy on Specific Property.
8 Witkin Cal. Proc. 5th Enforcement of Judgment § 21, Definitions.
8 Witkin Cal. Proc. 5th Enforcement of Judgment § 135, (S 135) Accounts Receivable and General Intangibles.

§ 680.135.   Affidavit of identity

"Affidavit of Identity" means an affidavit or declaration executed by a judgment creditor, under penalty of perjury, that is filed with the clerk of the court in which the judgment is entered at the time the judgment creditor files for a writ of execution or an abstract of judgment. The affidavit of identity shall set forth the case name and number, the name of the judgment debtor stated in the judgment, the additional name or names by which the judgment debtor is known, and the facts upon which the judgment creditor has relied in obtaining the judgment debtor's additional name or names. The affidavit of identity shall not include the name or names of persons, including any corporations, partnerships, or any legal entities not separately named in the judgment in which the judgment debtor is a partner, shareholder, or member, other than the judgment debtor. *(Added by Stats.2000, c. 639 (A.B.2405), § 2.)*

Research References

Rutter, Cal. Practice Guide: Enforcing Judgments/Debts Ch. 6B-3, Creation of Judgment Lien.

Rutter, Cal. Practice Guide: Enforcing Judgments/Debts Ch. 6D-2, Writ of Execution.

Miller and Starr California Real Estate § 32:47, Contents of the Abstract of Judgment.

Miller and Starr California Real Estate § 32:64, Creation, Duration, and Effect of Writ of Execution.

8 Witkin Cal. Proc. 5th Enforcement of Judgment § 21, Definitions.

8 Witkin Cal. Proc. 5th Enforcement of Judgment § 70, Abstract of Judgment.

8 Witkin Cal. Proc. 5th Enforcement of Judgment § 110, Writ Based on Affidavit of Identity.

§ 680.140. Chattel paper

"Chattel paper" means "chattel paper" as defined in paragraph (11) of subdivision (a) of Section 9102 of the Commercial Code. *(Added by Stats.1982, c. 1364, p. 5070, § 2, operative July 1, 1983. Amended by Stats.1999, c. 991 (S.B.45), § 16.1, operative July 1, 2001.)*

Law Revision Commission Comments

Section 680.140 is new. The term "chattel paper" is used in Sections 680.370, 697.530, 697.610, 697.740, 700.100, 701.050, and 701.520. [16 Cal.L.Rev.Comm. Reports 1197 (1982)].

Research References

8 Witkin Cal. Proc. 5th Enforcement of Judgment § 21, Definitions.

§ 680.145. Child support

"Child support" includes family support. *(Added by Stats. 1992, c. 163 (A.B.2641), § 29, operative Jan. 1, 1994.)*

Law Revision Commission Comments

Section 680.145 is a new provision that is consistent with Family Code Section 4501 (family support order enforceable in same manner and to same extent as child support order). [22 Cal.L.Rev.Comm.Reports 1 (1992)].

Research References

8 Witkin Cal. Proc. 5th Enforcement of Judgment § 21, Definitions.

§ 680.150. Costs

"Costs" means costs and disbursements, including but not limited to statutory fees, charges, commissions, and expenses. *(Added by Stats.1982, c. 1364, p. 5070, § 2, operative July 1, 1983.)*

Law Revision Commission Comments

Section 680.150 defines costs broadly to include all types of expenditures in the collection process. This permits use of the term "costs" throughout the title in place of such terms as fees, charges, commissions, expenses, and the like. Section 680.150 does not determine the extent to which an expenditure of a particular type is recoverable. See Sections 685.040–090. As used in this title, the term may in some cases be limited, such as in Section 685.100 (costs of levying officer). Attorney's fees incurred in enforcing a judgment are not included in costs collectible under this title unless otherwise provided by law. See Section 685.040. [16 Cal.L.Rev.Comm. Reports 1197 (1982)].

Research References

8 Witkin Cal. Proc. 5th Enforcement of Judgment § 21, Definitions.

§ 680.160. Court

"Court" means the court where the judgment sought to be enforced was entered. *(Added by Stats.1982, c. 1364, p. 5070, § 2, operative July 1, 1983.)*

Law Revision Commission Comments

The definition of "court" in Section 680.160 may in some cases be inapplicable. See, e.g., Section 708.160 (court of similar jurisdiction in another county). See also Section 680.110 (application of definitions). [16 Cal.L.Rev.Comm. Reports 1198 (1982)].

Research References

Rutter, Cal. Practice Guide: Enforcing Judgments/Debts Ch. 6H-4, Hearing on Third Party Claim.

2 Witkin Cal. Proc. 5th Courts § 303, (S 303) Enforcement and Stay.

8 Witkin Cal. Proc. 5th Enforcement of Judgment § 21, Definitions.

§ 680.170. Deposit account

"Deposit account" means "deposit account" as defined in paragraph (29) of subdivision (a) of Section 9102 of the Commercial Code. *(Added by Stats.1982, c. 1364, p. 5070, § 2, operative July 1, 1983. Amended by Stats.1999, c. 991 (S.B.45), § 16.2, operative July 1, 2001.)*

Law Revision Commission Comments

Section 680.170 is new. The term "deposit account" is used in Sections 684.110, 697.620, 699.080, 700.140, 700.160, 703.080, 704.070, and 704.080. [16 Cal.L.Rev.Comm. Reports 1198 (1982)].

Research References

8 Witkin Cal. Proc. 5th Enforcement of Judgment § 21, Definitions.

8 Witkin Cal. Proc. 5th Enforcement of Judgment § 132, (S 132) Deposit Accounts.

8 Witkin Cal. Proc. 5th Enforcement of Judgment § 174, (S 174) Tracing Exempt Funds.

§ 680.180. Document of title

"Document of title" means "document" as defined in paragraph (30) of subdivision (a) of Section 9102 of the Commercial Code. A document of title is negotiable if it is negotiable within the meaning of Section 7104 of the Commercial Code. *(Added by Stats.1982, c. 1364, p. 5070, § 2, operative July 1, 1983. Amended by Stats.1999, c. 991 (S.B.45), § 16.3, operative July 1, 2001.)*

Law Revision Commission Comments

Section 680.180 is new. The term "document of title" is used in Sections 680.370, 697.530, 697.610, 697.740, 700.040, 700.060, and 700.120. [16 Cal.L.Rev.Comm. Reports 1198 (1982)].

Research References

8 Witkin Cal. Proc. 5th Enforcement of Judgment § 21, Definitions.

8 Witkin Cal. Proc. 5th Enforcement of Judgment § 131, (S 131) Documents of Title and Securities.

§ 680.190. Equity

"Equity" means the fair market value of the interest of the judgment debtor in property, or in the case of community property the fair market value of the interest of the judgment debtor and the spouse of the judgment debtor in the property, over and above all liens and encumbrances on the interest superior to the judgment creditor's lien. *(Added by Stats.1982, c. 1364, p. 5071, § 2, operative July 1, 1983.)*

Law Revision Commission Comments

Section 680.190 is intended to simplify drafting. It makes clear that the judgment creditor's lien and junior liens are excluded in a determination of "equity" for purposes of applying certain exemptions. See, e.g., Sections 703.560, 704.030, and 704.060. See also Section 704.010 (use of used price guides in determining value of motor vehicle). [16 Cal.L.Rev. Comm. Reports 1198 (1982)].

Research References

Rutter, Cal. Practice Guide: Enforcing Judgments/Debts Ch. 6E-2, Rules Applicable to Exemptions from Enforcement of Money Judgments Generally.

Miller and Starr California Real Estate § 13:48, Determination of the Liens Against the Homestead; Priorities.

8 Witkin Cal. Proc. 5th Enforcement of Judgment § 21, Definitions.

8 Witkin Cal. Proc. 5th Enforcement of Judgment § 188, (S 188) Motor Vehicles.

8 Witkin Cal. Proc. 5th Enforcement of Judgment § 190, (S 190) Materials for Repair or Improvement of Dwelling.

8 Witkin Cal. Proc. 5th Enforcement of Judgment § 191, (S 191) Jewelry, Heirlooms, and Works of Art.

§ 680.200. Financial institution

"Financial institution" means a state or national bank, state or federal savings and loan association or credit union, or like organization, and includes a corporation engaged in a safe deposit business. *(Added by Stats.1982, c. 1364, p. 5071, § 2, operative July 1, 1983.)*

Law Revision Commission Comments

Section 680.200 is new. The term "financial institution" is used in Sections 694.110, 687.020, 700.140, 700.150, 700.160, 704.070, and 704.080. [16 Cal.L.Rev.Comm. Reports 1199 (1982)].

Research References

8 Witkin Cal. Proc. 5th Enforcement of Judgment § 21, Definitions.

8 Witkin Cal. Proc. 5th Enforcement of Judgment § 31, Indorsement and Collection of Instruments.

8 Witkin Cal. Proc. 5th Enforcement of Judgment § 132, (S 132) Deposit Accounts.

8 Witkin Cal. Proc. 5th Enforcement of Judgment § 133, (S 133) Safe Deposit Boxes.

14 Witkin, California Summary 10th Wills and Probate § 49, (S 49) Persons and Entities.

§ 680.210. General intangibles

"General intangibles" means "general intangibles," as defined in paragraph (42) of subdivision (a) of Section 9102 of the Commercial Code, consisting of rights to payment. *(Added by Stats.1982, c. 1364, p. 5071, § 2, operative July 1, 1983. Amended by Stats.1999, c. 991 (S.B.45), § 17, operative July 1, 2001.)*

Research References

Rutter, Cal. Practice Guide: Enforcing Judgments/Debts Ch. 6D-4, Levy on Specific Property.

8 Witkin Cal. Proc. 5th Enforcement of Judgment § 21, Definitions.

8 Witkin Cal. Proc. 5th Enforcement of Judgment § 135, (S 135) Accounts Receivable and General Intangibles.

§ 680.220. Instrument

"Instrument" means "instrument", as defined in paragraph (47) of subdivision (a) of Section 9102 of the Commercial Code. *(Added by Stats.1982, c. 1364, p. 5071, § 2, operative July 1, 1983. Amended by Stats.1999, c. 991 (S.B.45), § 17.1, operative July 1, 2001.)*

Research References

Rutter, Cal. Practice Guide: Enforcing Judgments/Debts Ch. 6D-4, Levy on Specific Property.

8 Witkin Cal. Proc. 5th Enforcement of Judgment § 21, Definitions.

8 Witkin Cal. Proc. 5th Enforcement of Judgment § 130, (S 130) Instruments.

§ 680.230. Judgment

"Judgment" means a judgment, order, or decree entered in a court of this state. *(Added by Stats.1982, c. 1364, p. 5071, § 2, operative July 1, 1983.)*

Law Revision Commission Comments

Section 680.230 is new and it continues the effect of former Section 1007 (order enforceable as judgment). For a discussion of the requirement that the judgment be entered "in a court of this state," see the Comment to Section 681.010. A judgment is not effectual for any purpose until entered. See Sections 664, 683.010. [16 Cal.L.Rev.Comm. Reports 1200 (1982)].

Research References

Rutter, Cal. Practice Guide: Civ. Pro. Before Trial Ch. 9(I)-E, E. Posthearing Procedures.

Rutter, Cal. Practice Guide: Civ. Pro. Before Trial Ch. 9(III)-E, E. Enforcement of Sanctions Orders.

Rutter, Cal. Practice Guide: Enforcing Judgments/Debts Ch. 6A-3, "Judgment," "Judgment Debtor" and "Judgment Creditor" Defined.

Rutter, Cal. Practice Guide: Enforcing Judgments/Debts Ch. 6D-2, Writ of Execution.

8 Witkin Cal. Proc. 5th Enforcement of Judgment § 21, Definitions.

8 Witkin Cal. Proc. 5th Enforcement of Judgment § 73, Sister State Judgment.

§ 680.240. Judgment creditor

"Judgment creditor" means the person in whose favor a judgment is rendered or, if there is an assignee of record, means the assignee of record. Unless the context otherwise requires, the term also includes the guardian or conservator of the estate, personal representative, or other successor in interest of the judgment creditor or assignee of record. *(Added by Stats.1982, c. 1364, p. 5071, § 2, operative July 1, 1983.)*

Law Revision Commission Comments

"Judgment creditor," as defined by Section 680.240, includes the person in whose favor the following types of judgments are rendered: money judgments, judgments for the possession of personal property, judgments for the possession of real property, and judgments for the sale of real or personal property. For special provisions on enforcement by an assignee or successor in interest, see Sections 681.020 (assignee), 686.010 (death of judgment creditor). [16 Cal.L.Rev.Comm. Reports 1200 (1982)].

Research References

Rutter, Cal. Practice Guide: Enforcing Judgments/Debts Ch. 6A-3, "Judgment," "Judgment Debtor" and "Judgment Creditor" Defined.

Miller and Starr California Real Estate § 32:68, Conditions to Conducting the Sale.

8 Witkin Cal. Proc. 5th Enforcement of Judgment § 21, Definitions.

8 Witkin Cal. Proc. 5th Enforcement of Judgment § 364, (S 364) Nature and Scope of Remedy.

§ 680.250. Judgment debtor

"Judgment debtor" means the person against whom a judgment is rendered. *(Added by Stats.1982, c. 1364, p. 5071, § 2, operative July 1, 1983.)*

Law Revision Commission Comments

"Judgment debtor," as defined by Section 680.250, includes persons against whom the following types of judgments are rendered: money judgments, judgments for the possession of personal property, judgments for the possession of real property, and judgments for the sale of real or personal property. [16 Cal.L.Rev.Comm. Reports 1200 (1982)].

Research References

Rutter, Cal. Practice Guide: Enforcing Judgments/Debts Ch. 6A-3, "Judgment," "Judgment Debtor" and "Judgment Creditor" Defined.

22 NO. 4 Miller & Starr, California Real Estate Newsalert 28, Deeds.

8 Witkin Cal. Proc. 5th Enforcement of Judgment § 21, Definitions.

8 Witkin Cal. Proc. 5th Enforcement of Judgment § 364, (S 364) Nature and Scope of Remedy.

§ 680.260. Levying officer

"Levying officer" means the sheriff or marshal. *(Added by Stats.1982, c. 1364, p. 5071, § 2, operative July 1, 1983. Amended by Stats.1996, c. 872 (A.B.3472), § 16.)*

Research References

Rutter, Cal. Practice Guide: Enforcing Judgments/Debts Ch. 6D-3, Levy of Writ of Execution-In General.

8 Witkin Cal. Proc. 5th Enforcement of Judgment § 21, Definitions.

§ 680.270. Money judgment

"Money judgment" means that part of a judgment that requires the payment of money. *(Added by Stats.1982, c. 1364, p. 5071, § 2, operative July 1, 1983.)*

Research References

Rutter, Cal. Practice Guide: Civ. Pro. Before Trial Ch. 9(I)-E, E. Posthearing Procedures.
Rutter, Cal. Practice Guide: Civ. Pro. Before Trial Ch. 9(III)-E, E. Enforcement of Sanctions Orders.
Rutter, Cal. Practice Guide: Enforcing Judgments/Debts Ch. 6D-2, Writ of Execution.
8 Witkin Cal. Proc. 5th Enforcement of Judgment § 21, Definitions.

§ 680.280. Person

"Person" includes a natural person, a corporation, a partnership or other unincorporated association, a general partner of a partnership, a limited liability company, and a public entity. *(Added by Stats.1982, c. 1364, p. 5071, § 2, operative July 1, 1983. Amended by Stats.1993, c. 1187 (S.B.70), § 1; Stats.1994, c. 1010 (S.B.2053), § 60.)*

Law Revision Commission Comments

Section 680.280 is new. See also Section 708.710 ("public entity" defined for purposes of collection of money judgment where judgment debtor is creditor of public entity). [16 Cal.L.Rev.Comm. Reports 1201 (1982)].

Research References

Rutter, Cal. Practice Guide: Enforcing Judgments/Debts Ch. 6A-3, "Judgment," "Judgment Debtor" and "Judgment Creditor" Defined.
Rutter, Cal. Practice Guide: Enforcing Judgments/Debts Gen. Matls., Highlights.
22 NO. 4 Miller & Starr, California Real Estate Newsalert 28, Deeds.
8 Witkin Cal. Proc. 5th Enforcement of Judgment § 21, Definitions.

§ 680.290. Personal property

"Personal property" includes both tangible and intangible personal property. *(Added by Stats.1982, c. 1364, p. 5071, § 2, operative July 1, 1983.)*

Law Revision Commission Comments

Section 680.290 is new. [16 Cal.L.Rev.Comm. Reports 1201 (1982)].

Research References

8 Witkin Cal. Proc. 5th Enforcement of Judgment § 21, Definitions.

§ 680.300. Principal amount of the judgment

"Principal amount of the judgment" means the total amount of the judgment as entered or as last renewed, together with the costs thereafter added to the judgment pursuant to Section 685.090, reduced by any partial satisfactions of such amount and costs and by any amounts no longer enforceable. *(Added by Stats.1982, c. 1364, p. 5071, § 2, operative July 1, 1983.)*

Law Revision Commission Comments

Section 680.300 is a new provision that recognizes that costs are a part of the principal amount of the judgment (Section 685.090) when the defined phrase is used in this title. [16 Cal.L.Rev.Comm. Reports 1201 (1982)].

Research References

Rutter, Cal. Practice Guide: Enforcing Judgments/Debts Ch. 6A-5, Amount Recoverable Under Judgment.
8 Witkin Cal. Proc. 5th Enforcement of Judgment § 21, Definitions.

8 Witkin Cal. Proc. 5th Enforcement of Judgment § 37, (S 37) Entry, Amount, and Notice.

§ 680.310. Property

"Property" includes real and personal property and any interest therein. *(Added by Stats.1982, c. 1364, p. 5071, § 2, operative July 1, 1983.)*

Law Revision Commission Comments

Section 680.310 is new. [16 Cal.L.Rev.Comm. Reports 1202 (1982)].

Research References

Miller and Starr California Real Estate § 17:37, Generally; Definitions.
8 Witkin Cal. Proc. 5th Enforcement of Judgment § 21, Definitions.

§ 680.320. Real property

"Real property" includes any right in real property, including but not limited to a leasehold interest in real property. *(Added by Stats.1982, c. 1364, p. 5071, § 2, operative July 1, 1983.)*

Research References

Rutter, Cal. Practice Guide: Enforcing Judgments/Debts Ch. 6D-4, Levy on Specific Property.
Miller and Starr California Real Estate § 19:2, Lease as Personal Property or Real Property.
Miller and Starr California Real Estate § 17:37, Generally; Definitions.
8 Witkin Cal. Proc. 5th Enforcement of Judgment § 21, Definitions.
8 Witkin Cal. Proc. 5th Enforcement of Judgment § 118, Property Subject to Levy.

§ 680.330. Registered process server

"Registered process server" means a person registered as a process server pursuant to Chapter 16 (commencing with Section 22350) of Division 8 of the Business and Professions Code. *(Added by Stats.1982, c. 1364, p. 5071, § 2, operative July 1, 1983.)*

Law Revision Commission Comments

Section 680.330 is drawn from subdivision (b) of former Section 687 and from subdivision (e) of former Section 723.101. The term "registered process server" is used in Sections 684.140, 699.080, 699.510, 706.101, and 708.170. [16 Cal.L.Rev.Comm. Reports 1202 (1982)].

Research References

8 Witkin Cal. Proc. 5th Enforcement of Judgment § 21, Definitions.
8 Witkin Cal. Proc. 5th Enforcement of Judgment § 103, (S 103) Levy by Registered Process Server.

§ 680.340. Secured party

Section operative until July 1, 2014. See, also, section operative July 1, 2014.

"Secured party" means "secured party" as defined in paragraph (72) of subdivision (a) of Section 9102 of the Commercial Code. *(Added by Stats.1982, c. 1364, p. 5071, § 2, operative July 1, 1983. Amended by Stats.1999, c. 991 (S.B.45), § 17.2, operative July 1, 2001.)*

§ 680.340. Secured party

Section operative July 1, 2014. See, also, section operative until July 1, 2014.

"Secured party" means "secured party" as defined in paragraph (73) of subdivision (a) of Section 9102 of the Commercial Code. *(Added by Stats.1982, c. 1364, p. 5071, § 2, operative July 1, 1983. Amended by Stats.1999, c. 991 (S.B.45), § 17.2, operative July 1, 2001; Stats.2013, c. 531 (A.B.502), § 4, operative July 1, 2014.)*

Law Revision Commission Comments

Section 680.340 is new. [16 Cal.L.Rev.Comm. Reports 1202 (1982)].

Civ. Pro.

Research References

8 Witkin Cal. Proc. 5th Enforcement of Judgment § 21, Definitions.

§ 680.345.   Security

"Security" means a "security" as defined in Section 8102 of the Commercial Code. *(Added by Stats.1982, c. 1364, p. 5072, § 2, operative July 1, 1983.)*

Research References

8 Witkin Cal. Proc. 5th Enforcement of Judgment § 21, Definitions.
8 Witkin Cal. Proc. 5th Enforcement of Judgment § 131, (S 131) Documents of Title and Securities.

§ 680.350.   Security agreement

Section operative until July 1, 2014. See, also, section operative July 1, 2014.

"Security agreement" means "security agreement" as defined in paragraph (73) of subdivision (a) of Section 9102 of the Commercial Code. *(Added by Stats.1982, c. 1364, p. 5072, § 2, operative July 1, 1983. Amended by Stats.1999, c. 991 (S.B.45), § 17.3, operative July 1, 2001.)*

§ 680.350.   Security agreement

Section operative July 1, 2014. See, also, section operative until July 1, 2014.

"Security agreement" means "security agreement" as defined in paragraph (74) of subdivision (a) of Section 9102 of the Commercial Code. *(Added by Stats.1982, c. 1364, p. 5072, § 2, operative July 1, 1983. Amended by Stats.1999, c. 991 (S.B.45), § 17.3, operative July 1, 2001; Stats.2013, c. 531 (A.B.502), § 5, operative July 1, 2014.)*

Law Revision Commission Comments

Section 680.350 is new. The term "security agreement" is used in Sections 700.100, 700.170, and 720.230. [16 Cal.L.Rev.Comm. Reports 1203 (1982)].

Research References

8 Witkin Cal. Proc. 5th Enforcement of Judgment § 21, Definitions.

§ 680.360.   Security interest

"Security interest" means "security interest" as defined in Section 1201 of the Commercial Code. *(Added by Stats.1982, c. 1364, p. 5072, § 2, operative July 1, 1983.)*

Law Revision Commission Comments

Section 680.360 is new. The term "security interest" is used in Sections 697.530, 697.590, 697.610, 697.620, 697.740, 700.060, 720.210, 720.230, 720.250, 720.280, 720.360, 720.530, 720.550, and 720.610. [16 Cal.L.Rev. Comm. Reports 1203 (1982)].

Research References

8 Witkin Cal. Proc. 5th Enforcement of Judgment § 21, Definitions.

§ 680.365.   Spousal support

"Spousal support" includes support for a former spouse. *(Added by Stats.1982, c. 1364, p. 5072, § 2, operative July 1, 1983.)*

Research References

8 Witkin Cal. Proc. 5th Enforcement of Judgment § 21, Definitions.

§ 680.370.   Tangible personal property

"Tangible personal property" includes chattel paper, documents of title, instruments, securities, and money. *(Added by Stats.1982, c. 1364, p. 5072, § 2, operative July 1, 1983.)*

Research References

8 Witkin Cal. Proc. 5th Enforcement of Judgment § 21, Definitions.

8 Witkin Cal. Proc. 5th Enforcement of Judgment § 126, Property of Going Business.

§ 680.380.   Writ

"Writ" includes a writ of execution, a writ of possession of personal property, a writ of possession of real property, and a writ of sale. *(Added by Stats.1982, c. 1364, p. 5072, § 2, operative July 1, 1983.)*

Law Revision Commission Comments

Section 680.380 defines "writ" for the purpose of general provisions pertaining to all writs issuable under this title. See also Section 680.110 (application of definitions). [16 Cal.L.Rev.Comm. Reports 1203 (1982)].

Research References

8 Witkin Cal. Proc. 5th Enforcement of Judgment § 21, Definitions.

CHAPTER 2.   GENERAL PROVISIONS

§ 681.010.   Judgments; provisions for enforcement

Except as otherwise provided by statute:

(a) A money judgment is enforceable as provided in Division 2 (commencing with Section 695.010).

(b) A judgment for possession of personal property is enforceable as provided in Chapter 2 (commencing with Section 714.010) of Division 3.

(c) A judgment for possession of real property is enforceable as provided in Chapter 3 (commencing with Section 715.010) of Division 3.

(d) A judgment for sale of real or personal property is enforceable as provided in Chapter 4 (commencing with Section 716.010) of Division 3.

(e) A judgment requiring performance of an act not described in subdivisions (a) to (d), inclusive, or requiring forbearance from performing an act, is enforceable as provided in Chapter 5 (commencing with Section 717.010) of Division 3. *(Added by Stats.1982, c. 1364, p. 5072, § 2, operative July 1, 1983.)*

Law Revision Commission Comments

Section 681.010 supersedes former Section 684. It refers to the provisions of this title that provide the means available for the enforcement of a judgment entered in this state. The introductory clause recognizes that this title does not provide the exclusive means for enforcing all judgments entered in this state. See, e.g., Civil Code §§ 4380 (enforcement of judgment, order, or decree under Family Law Act), 4701 (payment of child support enforceable by order for wage assignment), 4801.6 (payment of spousal support enforceable by order for wage assignment). See also Section 117.7 (enforcement of small claims court judgment); Section 695.050 and Gov't Code §§ 942, 965.6, 965.7, 965.8, 965.9, 970.1, 970.2 (enforcement of money judgments against public entities).

A money judgment entered in another state is not enforceable pursuant to this title until a California judgment has been entered based on the sister state money judgment. See Sections 1701.10(c) ("sister state judgment" defined), 1710.25 (entry of California judgment), 1710.35 (enforcement), 1710.60 (action on judgment). A support order issued in another state is enforceable in the same manner as a support order rendered in this state after it has been registered in California. See Sections 1698 (registration of foreign support order), 1699 (enforcement). A federal district court judgment entered or registered in this state is enforceable in the manner provided by federal law which to some extent incorporates state enforcement procedures. See Fed.R.Civ.P. 69(a) (enforcement of district court money judgment); 28 U.S.C. § 1963 (1976) (registration of judgment of one district court in another district). A money judgment of a court of a foreign nation is enforceable pursuant to Section 1713.3. [16 Cal.L.Rev.Comm. Reports 1204 (1982)].

Research References

Rutter, Cal. Practice Guide: Enforcing Judgments/Debts Ch. 6A-2, Enforcement of Judgments Law ("Ejl")-Background.
Rutter, Cal. Practice Guide: Enforcing Judgments/Debts Ch. 6I-6, Enforcing Other Judgments-Contempt.
8 Witkin Cal. Proc. 5th Enforcement of Judgment § 23, Enforcement of Particular Judgments.

§ 681.020. Enforcement by assignee

An assignee of a judgment is not entitled to enforce the judgment under this title unless an acknowledgment of assignment of judgment to that assignee has been filed under Section 673 or the assignee has otherwise become an assignee of record. *(Added by Stats.1982, c. 1364, p. 5072, § 2, operative July 1, 1983.)*

Law Revision Commission Comments

Section 681.020 is a new provision that codifies a requirement of former practice. The Commission has been advised that as a matter of practice under the former law an assignee of a judgment was not permitted to obtain a writ of execution unless the assignment was made a matter of record. [16 Cal.L.Rev.Comm. Reports 1205 (1982)].

Research References

Rutter, Cal. Practice Guide: Enforcing Judgments/Debts Ch. 6A-3, "Judgment," "Judgment Debtor" and "Judgment Creditor" Defined.
Rutter, Cal. Practice Guide: Enforcing Judgments/Debts Ch. 6G-11, Enforcement of Judgment by Assignees.
8 Witkin Cal. Proc. 5th Enforcement of Judgment § 24, Enforcement by Assignee.

§ 681.030. Rules; forms

(a) The Judicial Council may provide by rule for the practice and procedure in proceedings under this title.

(b) The Judicial Council may prescribe the form of the applications, notices, orders, writs, and other papers to be used under this title. The Judicial Council may prescribe forms in languages other than English. The timely completion and return of a Judicial Council form prescribed in a language other than English has the same force and effect as the timely completion and return of an English language form.

(c) The Judicial Council shall prepare a form containing all of the following:

(1) A list of each of the federal and this state's exemptions from enforcement of a money judgment against a natural person.

(2) A citation to the relevant statute of the United States or this state which creates each of the exemptions.

(3) Information on how to obtain the list of exemption amounts published pursuant to subdivision (d) of Section 703.150. *(Added by Stats.1982, c. 5072, § 2, operative July 1, 1983. Amended by Stats.1984, c. 538, § 15; Stats.1985, c. 41, § 3; Stats.2003, c. 379 (A.B.182), § 1.)*

Law Revision Commission Comments

Section 681.030 authorizes the Judicial Council to provide for practice and procedure under this title and to adopt and revise forms authorized or required by this title. The forms adopted are deemed to comply with this title and may contain additional information not specified in this title and may omit information otherwise required by a relevant provision of this title. The Judicial Council may adopt forms that supersede those provided in Chapter 19 (commencing with Section 693.010). The first sentence of subdivision (b) is comparable to Section 706.120 (wage garnishment). The last two sentences of subdivision (b) are drawn from comparable provisions contained in former Section 723.120 (wage garnish-

ment). See also Section 697.670 (certain forms prepared by Secretary of State), 706.081 (forms relating to withholding for taxes under Wage Garnishment Law), 706.100 (rules for practice and procedure under Wage Garnishment Law). [16 Cal.L.Rev.Comm. Reports 1206 (1982)].

Section 681.030 is amended to reflect the repeal of the statutory forms formerly provided in this title. [17 Cal.L.Rev.Comm.Reports 1001 (1983)].

Subdivision (b) of Section 681.030 is amended to provide a rule on the effect of the use of an official form in a language other than English. This amendment continues the substance of former Section 693.060(b) which related to the use of a Spanish language form in connection with the dwelling exemption. [18 Cal.L.Rev. Comm. Reports 361 (1985)].

Paragraph (3) is added to Section 681.030(c) to reflect the automatic triennial cost-of-living adjustment of personal property exemptions from enforcement of money judgments pursuant to Section 703.150. [33 Cal.L.Rev.Comm. Reports 127 (2003)].

Research References

Miller and Starr California Real Estate § 32:26, Claim of Exemption.
8 Witkin Cal. Proc. 5th Enforcement of Judgment § 25, Rules and Forms.
8 Witkin Cal. Proc. 5th Enforcement of Judgment § 117, (S 117) in General.

§ 681.035. Review and recommendations concerning enforcement of judgments

The California Law Revision Commission is authorized to maintain a continuing review of and submit recommendations to the Governor and the Legislature concerning enforcement of judgments. *(Added by Stats.2013, c. 15 (A.B.567), § 1.)*

Law Revision Commission Comments

Section 681.035 continues the last clause of former Section 703.120(b), without substantive change. [42 Cal.L.Rev.Comm. Reports 297 (2012)].

§ 681.040. Filing with levying officer

If a paper is required or permitted to be filed with a levying officer under this title, the paper is considered filed when it is actually received by the levying officer. *(Added by Stats.1982, c. 1364, p. 5073, § 2, operative July 1, 1983.)*

Research References

Rutter, Cal. Practice Guide: Enforcing Judgments/Debts Ch. 6E-3, Procedures for Claiming Exemptions.
8 Witkin Cal. Proc. 5th Enforcement of Judgment § 26, in General.

§ 681.050. Severability

If any provision or clause of this title or application thereof to any person or circumstances is held invalid, the invalidity does not affect other provisions or applications of this title which can be given effect without the invalid provision or application, and to this end the provisions of this title are severable. *(Added by Stats.1982, c. 1364, p. 5073, § 2, operative July 1, 1983.)*

Research References

Rutter, Cal. Practice Guide: Enforcing Judgments/Debts Ch. 6A-2, Enforcement of Judgments Law ("Ejl")-Background.

CHAPTER 3. PERIOD FOR ENFORCEMENT AND RENEWAL OF JUDGMENTS

ARTICLE 1. PERIOD FOR ENFORCEMENT OF JUDGMENTS

Section

§ 683.010.   Entry of judgment

Except as otherwise provided by statute or in the judgment, a judgment is enforceable under this title upon entry. *(Added by Stats.1982, c. 1364, p. 5073, § 2, operative July 1, 1983.)*

Law Revision Commission Comments

Section 683.010 continues the substance of a portion of former Section 681. Nothing in Section 683.010 limits the authority of the court to stay enforcement of a judgment under any other applicable statutory provisions, such as Sections 916–923. See also Sections 117.7 (automatic stay of small claims court judgment), 1174(c) (delay of enforcement of certain unlawful detainer judgments). Section 683.010 does not apply to judgments under the Family Law Act (Section 683.310) or to a money judgment against a public entity (Section 683.320). [16 Cal.L.Rev.Comm. Reports 1207 (1982)].

Research References

Rutter, Cal. Practice Guide: Enforcing Judgments/Debts Ch. 6A-4, "Entry" of Judgment.
Rutter, Cal. Practice Guide: Enforcing Judgments/Debts Ch. 6A-7, Period During Which Judgment Enforceable; Renewal Procedures.
Rutter, Cal. Practice Guide: Real Prop. Transactions Ch. 6-I, I. Real Property Foreclosures and Antideficiency Laws.
3 Witkin Cal. Proc. 5th Actions § 449, (S 449) Cross-Demands Deemed Compensated.
8 Witkin Cal. Proc. 5th Enforcement of Judgment § 18, (S 18) in General.
8 Witkin Cal. Proc. 5th Enforcement of Judgment § 34, in General.
8 Witkin Cal. Proc. 5th Enforcement of Judgment § 41, Exceptions to Application of Provisions.
8 Witkin Cal. Proc. 5th Enforcement of Judgment § 67, (S 67) Duration and Extinguishment.
5 Witkin Cal. Proc. 5th Pleading § 1165, Revised Law of Setoff.
10 Witkin, California Summary 10th Parent and Child § 902, (S 902) Restitution to Victim.
11 Witkin, California Summary 10th Husband and Wife § 5, Generally Applicable Procedures.

§ 683.020.   Period of enforceability

Except as otherwise provided by statute, upon the expiration of 10 years after the date of entry of a money judgment or a judgment for possession or sale of property:

(a) The judgment may not be enforced.

(b) All enforcement procedures pursuant to the judgment or to a writ or order issued pursuant to the judgment shall cease.

(c) Any lien created by an enforcement procedure pursuant to the judgment is extinguished. *(Added by Stats.1982, c. 1364, p. 5073, § 2, operative July 1, 1983.)*

Law Revision Commission Comments

Section 683.020 supersedes the first sentence of former Section 681 (which provided a 10-year enforcement period). Unless the judgment is renewed by action (see Section 683.050) or pursuant to Article 2 (commencing with Section 683.110), a judgment is enforceable only for 10 years; at the end of this period, enforcement of the judgment is barred and any liens created by the enforcement process are extinguished. No further action, including levy, sale, collection, or delivery pursuant to the judgment, or pursuant to a writ or order issued to enforce the judgment, may take place. The rule announced in Alonso Inv. Corp. v. Doff, 17

Cal.3d 539, 541–43, 551 P.2d 1243, 131 Cal.Rptr. 411 (1976), permitting the enforcement of a writ of execution after the expiration of the 10-year period if the writ had been timely issued, is not continued, subject to an exception where the judgment is renewed. See Section 683.200 (continuation of enforcement procedures upon renewal).

Section 683.020 applies only to money judgments and judgments for the possession or sale of property. Accordingly, other judgments—such as those governed by Section 717.010—are not subject to the 10-year rule of Section 683.020. Section 683.030 provides a special rule applicable to money judgments payable in installments. See also Sections 683.310 (judgments under Family Law Act excluded from this chapter), 683.320 (money judgment against public entity excluded from this chapter). As to judgments entered prior to the operative date of this section, see Section 694.030.

Unlike former Section 681, the 10-year period provided by Section 683.020 is not extended because enforcement of the judgment has been stayed or enjoined by court order or by operation of law. Nor is the 10-year period tolled for any reason. The statement in Nutt v. Nutt, 247 Cal.App.2d 166, 168, 55 Cal.Rptr. 380 (1966)—that the absence from the state of the judgment debtor and the debtor's property tolls the running of the time to seek a writ of execution under former Section 681—does not apply to this chapter. However, a judgment may be used as an offset after the expiration of the 10-year period if the claim of the judgment debtor (against which the judgment is offset) existed during the 10-year period during which the judgment was enforceable. See Section 431.70 and the Comment thereto. The judgment creditor may also be able to bring an action on the judgment after the 10-year enforcement period of this section has expired if the statute of limitations provided by Section 337.5 has not yet run. See Section 683.050 and the Comment thereto. [16 Cal.L.Rev.Comm. Reports 1207 (1982)].

Research References

Rutter, Cal. Practice Guide: Enforcing Judgments/Debts Ch. 6A-7, Period During Which Judgment Enforceable; Renewal Procedures.
Rutter, Cal. Practice Guide: Enforcing Judgments/Debts Ch. 6D-3, Levy of Writ of Execution-In General.
Rutter, Cal. Practice Guide: Enforcing Judgments/Debts Ch. 6G-1, Examination of Judgment Debtor and Third Parties.
Rutter, Cal. Practice Guide: Real Prop. Transactions Ch. 6-I, I. Real Property Foreclosures and Antideficiency Laws.
Miller and Starr California Real Estate § 32:55, Duration of the Judgment Lien.
15 NO. 4 Miller & Starr, California Real Estate Newsalert 28, Involuntary Liens.
8 Witkin Cal. Proc. 5th Enforcement of Judgment § 34, in General.
8 Witkin Cal. Proc. 5th Enforcement of Judgment § 35, (S 35) Right to Renew.
8 Witkin Cal. Proc. 5th Enforcement of Judgment § 39, (S 39) Extending Duration of Liens.
8 Witkin Cal. Proc. 5th Enforcement of Judgment § 69, in General.
8 Witkin Cal. Proc. 5th Enforcement of Judgment § 71, Installment Judgment for Support or Health Care.
8 Witkin Cal. Proc. 5th Enforcement of Judgment § 297, (S 297) Nature and Scope of Remedy.
8 Witkin Cal. Proc. 5th Enforcement of Judgment § 436, Action on Judgment.
10 Witkin, California Summary 10th Parent and Child § 902, (S 902) Restitution to Victim.

§ 683.030.   Period of enforceability; money judgments payable in installments

If a money judgment is payable in installments, the 10-year period of enforceability prescribed by Section 683.020 runs as to each installment from the date the installment becomes due and runs as to costs from the date the costs are added to the judgment pursuant to Section 685.090. *(Added by Stats.1982, c. 1364, p. 5073, § 2, operative July 1, 1983.)*

Law Revision Commission Comments

Section 683.030 codifies case law concerning the time within which installment judgments may be enforced. Cf. Wolfe v. Wolfe, 30 Cal.2d 1, 4, 180 P.2d 345 (1947) (installment judgment for support). For provisions authorizing installment judgments, see Civil Code § 3347 (installment payment of damages caused by slayer in a duel); Code Civ.Proc. §§ 85 (installment payment of municipal or justice court money judgment), 117 (time of payment of small claims court money judgment), 667.7 (periodic payment of certain future damages); Labor Code §§ 5801, 5806 (installment payment of workers' compensation award); Penal Code § 1205 (installment payment of fine); Veh. Code § 16380 (installment payment of vehicle accident damage judgment). Some installment judgments are not governed by this chapter. See Sections 683.310 (spousal or child support), 683.320 (money judgment against public entity). As to judgments entered prior to the operative date of this section, see Section 694.030. [16 Cal.L.Rev.Comm. Reports 1208 (1982)].

Research References

Miller and Starr California Real Estate § 32:55, Duration of the Judgment Lien.
8 Witkin Cal. Proc. 5th Enforcement of Judgment § 34, in General.

§ 683.040. Application more than 10 years after entry or renewal; affidavit

If the judgment creditor applies for a writ for the enforcement of a judgment and the application is made more than 10 years after the date the judgment was entered or renewed, the application shall be accompanied by an affidavit of a person having knowledge of the facts stating facts showing that the issuance of the writ sought in the application is not barred under this chapter. A copy of the affidavit shall be attached to the writ when issued. *(Added by Stats.1982, c. 1364, p. 5073, § 2, operative July 1, 1983.)*

Law Revision Commission Comments

Section 683.040 establishes a new requirement designed to provide information to the court clerk and levying officer when a writ of execution, possession, or sale is sought more than 10 years after the judgment was entered or renewed. Where the judgment is a money judgment payable in installments, the affidavit will be sufficient if it states that the 10-year limitation period (Section 683.030) has not run as to the installment or installments covered by the application for the writ. Section 683.040 does not apply to a judgment for child or spousal support; Civil Code Section 4380 requires the creditor to obtain a court order to enforce support obligations that are more than 10 years overdue. See Section 683.310. See also Civil Code Section 4383. As to the period of enforcement of a money judgment against a public entity, see Section 683.320 and Gov't Code §§ 965.5, 970.1. [16 Cal.L.Rev.Comm. Reports 1209 (1982)].

Research References

Rutter, Cal. Practice Guide: Enforcing Judgments/Debts Ch. 6D-2, Writ of Execution.
8 Witkin Cal. Proc. 5th Enforcement of Judgment § 34, in General.

§ 683.050. Judgment creditor's right to bring action; limitations

Nothing in this chapter limits any right the judgment creditor may have to bring an action on a judgment, but any such action shall be commenced within the period prescribed by Section 337.5. *(Added by Stats.1982, c. 1364, p. 5073, § 2, operative July 1, 1983.)*

Law Revision Commission Comments

Section 683.050 makes clear that the 10-year period of enforcement prescribed by Section 683.020 and the renewal procedure provided by Article 2 (commencing with Section 683.110) do not affect the right to bring an action on a judgment. The limitation period for commencing the action is prescribed by Section 337.5. The 10-year period provided by Section 683.020 and the 10-year statute of limitations provided by Section 337.5 are not coterminous. The period prescribed in Section 683.020 commences on the date of entry and is not tolled for any reason. The statute of limitations commences to run when the judgment is final (see Turner v. Donovan, 52 Cal.App.2d 236, 126 P.2d 187 (1942)) and may be tolled such as by the debtor's absence from the state (see Section 351). See also Section 683.220 (action on renewed judgment). [16 Cal.L.Rev. Comm. Reports 1210 (1982)].

Research References

Rutter, Cal. Practice Guide: Enforcing Judgments/Debts Ch. 6A-7, Period During Which Judgment Enforceable; Renewal Procedures.
14 NO. 5 Miller & Starr, California Real Estate Newsalert 15, Involuntary Liens.
8 Witkin Cal. Proc. 5th Enforcement of Judgment § 34, in General.
8 Witkin Cal. Proc. 5th Enforcement of Judgment § 35, (S 35) Right to Renew.
8 Witkin Cal. Proc. 5th Enforcement of Judgment § 436, Action on Judgment.

ARTICLE 2. RENEWAL OF JUDGMENTS

§ 683.110. Period of enforceability; extension; renewal of judgment

(a) The period of enforceability of a money judgment or a judgment for possession or sale of property may be extended by renewal of the judgment as provided in this article.

(b) A judgment shall not be renewed under this article if the application for renewal is filed within five years from the time the judgment was previously renewed under this article. *(Added by Stats.1982, c. 1364, p. 5073, § 2, operative July 1, 1983.)*

Law Revision Commission Comments

Sections 683.110–683.220 provide a new procedure for renewing judgments. This procedure is drawn from the procedure for enforcing sister state money judgments (Sections 1710.10–1710.65). Renewal under this article permits enforcement of a judgment beyond the 10-year period prescribed by Section 683.020. This procedure supersedes the procedure under former Section 685 pursuant to which a judgment could be enforced upon noticed motion after the expiration of 10 years in the discretion of the court upon a showing of the reasons for failure to enforce the judgment during the first 10 years. This article does not require the judgment creditor to demonstrate diligence in enforcing the judgment, but if renewal is not accomplished within 10 years after entry of the judgment, the judgment becomes unenforceable. See Sections 683.020, 683.130(a). See also Section 683.050 (right of action on judgment preserved). This article does not apply to a judgment under the Family Law Act (Section 683.310) or to a money judgment against a public entity (Section 683.320).

By preventing the renewal of a judgment more often than once every five years, subdivision (b) of Section 683.110 prevents the judgment creditor from renewing a judgment more frequently merely to compound the interest on the judgment. Renewal has the effect of compounding the interest on the judgment, since interest accrues on the total amount of the judgment as renewed (Sections 680.300, 685.010(a), 695.210) and the judgment as renewed includes accrued interest on the date of filing the application for renewal (Sections 683.150(b), 685.010(a), 695.210). [16 Cal.L.Rev.Comm. Reports 1210 (1982)].

Research References

Rutter, Cal. Practice Guide: Civil Trials & Evidence Ch. 18-C, C. Other Post-Trial Motions.
Rutter, Cal. Practice Guide: Enforcing Judgments/Debts Ch. 6A-5, Amount Recoverable Under Judgment.

Civ. Pro.

Rutter, Cal. Practice Guide: Enforcing Judgments/Debts Ch. 6A-7, Period During Which Judgment Enforceable; Renewal Procedures.

Rutter, Cal. Practice Guide: Real Prop. Transactions Ch. 6-I, I. Real Property Foreclosures and Antideficiency Laws.

Miller and Starr California Real Estate § 32:56, Renewal of the Judgment Lien.

Miller and Starr California Real Estate § 10:233, Deficiency Judgment.

8 Witkin Cal. Proc. 5th Enforcement of Judgment § 34, in General.

8 Witkin Cal. Proc. 5th Enforcement of Judgment § 35, (S 35) Right to Renew.

8 Witkin Cal. Proc. 5th Enforcement of Judgment § 37, (S 37) Entry, Amount, and Notice.

8 Witkin Cal. Proc. 5th Enforcement of Judgment § 403, Available Remedies.

8 Witkin Cal. Proc. 5th Enforcement of Judgment § 432, Enforcement Mechanisms.

8 Witkin Cal. Proc. 5th Enforcement of Judgment § 436, Action on Judgment.

11 Witkin, California Summary 10th Husband and Wife § 248, in General.

§ 683.120. Application for renewal; effect

(a) The judgment creditor may renew a judgment by filing an application for renewal of the judgment with the court in which the judgment was entered.

(b) Except as otherwise provided in this article, the filing of the application renews the judgment in the amount determined under Section 683.150 and extends the period of enforceability of the judgment as renewed for a period of 10 years from the date the application is filed.

(c) In the case of a money judgment payable in installments, for the purposes of enforcement and of any later renewal, the amount of the judgment as renewed shall be treated as a lump-sum money judgment entered on the date the application is filed. *(Added by Stats.1982, c. 1364, p. 5074, § 2, operative July 1, 1983.)*

Law Revision Commission Comments

Under Section 683.120 the enforceability of the judgment is extended until 10 years from the date the application for renewal is filed. Renewal under this article does not result in entry of a new judgment as would be the case where an action is brought on a California or sister state judgment or where a California judgment is entered on the basis of a sister state judgment. See Sections 683.050 (right of action on judgment preserved), 1710.25, 1710.35 (entry of California judgment on basis of sister state judgment).

Subdivision (c) makes clear that the application for renewal of an installment judgment reduces past due amounts of principal (including allowed costs) and interest (see Section 683.150) to a lump sum enforceable for an additional 10 years. Only those past due amounts that are not barred by the 10-year period of enforceability may be renewed. See Sections 683.030, 683.130(b), 683.150(c), (d). Future installments continue to accrue under the judgment as originally entered or as modified according to its terms.

This renewal procedure does not apply to the enforcement of judgments for support. See Section 683.310. See also Civil Code §§ 4380, 4384. [16 Cal.L.Rev.Comm. Reports 1211 (1982)].

Research References

Rutter, Cal. Practice Guide: Civ. Pro. Before Trial Ch. 5-G, G. Relief from Default.

Rutter, Cal. Practice Guide: Civil Trials & Evidence Ch. 18-C, C. Other Post-Trial Motions.

Rutter, Cal. Practice Guide: Enforcing Judgments/Debts Ch. 6A-7, Period During Which Judgment Enforceable; Renewal Procedures.

Miller and Starr California Real Estate § 32:55, Duration of the Judgment Lien.

Miller and Starr California Real Estate § 32:56, Renewal of the Judgment Lien.

8 Witkin Cal. Proc. 5th Enforcement of Judgment § 36, (S 36) Application.

§ 683.130. Application for renewal

(a) In the case of a lump-sum money judgment or a judgment for possession or sale of property, the application for renewal of the judgment may be filed at any time before the expiration of the 10–year period of enforceability provided by Section 683.020 or, if the judgment is a renewed judgment, at any time before the expiration of the 10–year period of enforceability of the renewed judgment provided by Section 683.120.

(b) In the case of a money judgment payable in installments, the application for renewal of the judgment may be filed:

(1) If the judgment has not previously been renewed, at any time as to past due amounts that at the time of filing are not barred by the expiration of the 10–year period of enforceability provided by Sections 683.020 and 683.030.

(2) If the judgment has previously been renewed, within the time specified by subdivision (a) as to the amount of the judgment as previously renewed and, as to any past due amounts that became due and payable after the previous renewal, at any time before the expiration of the 10–year period of enforceability provided by Sections 683.020 and 683.030. *(Added by Stats.1982, c. 1364, p. 5074, § 2, operative July 1, 1983. Amended by Stats.1991, c. 110 (S.B.101), § 14; Stats.1992, c. 163 (A.B.2641), § 30, operative Jan. 1, 1994; Stats.1992, c. 718 (A.B.568), § 4; Stats.1993, c. 219 (A.B.1500), § 66; Stats.1993, c. 876 (S.B.1068), § 8, eff. Oct. 6, 1993; Stats.2000, c. 808 (A.B.1358), § 4, eff. Sept. 28, 2000.)*

Law Revision Commission Comments

Subdivision (a) of Section 683.130 prescribes the general rule that renewal may be accomplished at any time when the judgment is still enforceable. See also Section 683.210 (renewal permitted during stay of enforcement). Renewal may take place during the initial 10-year period of enforcement (see Section 683.020) or during any subsequent renewal period (see subdivision (b) of Section 683.120). There is no limit on the number of renewals.

Subdivision (b) states a special application of the general rule to installment judgments. Renewal as to any installment must take place within 10 years after the installment becomes due. See Section 683.030 (time for enforcement of installment judgment). Subdivision (b) governs the type of installment judgments listed in the Comment to Section 683.030. When an installment judgment is renewed as to past due amounts, the renewed judgment is a lump-sum judgment (see subdivision (c) of Section 683.120) which thereafter is governed by subdivision (a) of Section 683.130 as to the amount of the renewed judgment. See also Section 683.150. Costs are included in the principal amount of the renewed judgment only if added to the judgment within the 10-year period. See Section 683.030.

This section does not apply to the enforcement of judgments for support. See Section 683.310. See also Civil Code §§ 4380, 4384. As to the renewal of judgments entered prior to the operative date of this section, see Section 694.030. [16 Cal.L.Rev.Comm. Reports 1213 (1982)].

Subdivision (c) of Section 683.130 is deleted as unnecessary because it duplicates rules in the Family Code. See Fam. Code §4502. This is not a substantive change. The exemption from renewal requirements for support orders in subdivision (c)(1) is unnecessary because Section 683.310 makes clear that this chapter does not apply to judgments or orders made or entered under the Family Code. Reimbursement for child support under Family Code Section 17402 is treated in the same fashion, as provided in Family Code Section 4502(a). The second sentence of subdivision (c)(1) is misplaced in this section pertaining to the time for filing an application for renewal. The period of enforceability of support orders is governed by Family Code Section 4502(a). The optional renewal procedure in Family Code Section 4502(b) continues the substance of subdivision (c)(2) of this section. See also Fam. Code §290 (methods of enforcement). [30 Cal.L.Rev.Comm. Reports 717 (2000)].

Research References

Rutter, Cal. Practice Guide: Civ. Pro. Before Trial Ch. 3-B, B. Jurisdiction Over Parties-Personal Jurisdiction.

Rutter, Cal. Practice Guide: Civ. Pro. Before Trial Ch. 4-F, F. Procedures for Challenging Service of Summons.

Rutter, Cal. Practice Guide: Enforcing Judgments/Debts Ch. 6A-7, Period During Which Judgment Enforceable; Renewal Procedures.

Miller and Starr California Real Estate § 32:55, Duration of the Judgment Lien.

Miller and Starr California Real Estate § 32:56, Renewal of the Judgment Lien.

13 NO. 4 Miller & Starr, California Real Estate Newsalert 21, Deeds of Trust.

15 NO. 4 Miller & Starr, California Real Estate Newsalert 28, Involuntary Liens.

8 Witkin Cal. Proc. 5th Enforcement of Judgment § 36, (S 36) Application.

8 Witkin Cal. Proc. 5th Enforcement of Judgment § 403, Available Remedies.

§ 683.140. Application for renewal; execution; contents

The application for renewal of the judgment shall be executed under oath and shall include all of the following:

(a) The title of the court where the judgment is entered and the cause and number of the action.

(b) The date of entry of the judgment and of any renewals of the judgment and where entered in the records of the court.

(c) The name and address of the judgment creditor and the name and last known address of the judgment debtor. However, the judgment creditor shall omit the name of a judgment debtor from the application for a writ of execution if the liability of that judgment debtor has ceased with regard to the judgment, including either of the following occurrences:

(1) The judgment debtor has obtained a discharge of the judgment pursuant to Title 11 of the United States Code and notice thereof has been filed with the court.

(2) The judgment creditor files an acknowledgment of satisfaction of judgment with regard to the judgment debtor pursuant to Chapter 1 (commencing with Section 724.010) of Division 5.

(d) In the case of a money judgment, the information necessary to compute the amount of the judgment as renewed. In the case of a judgment for possession or sale of property, a description of the performance remaining due. *(Added by Stats.1982, c. 1364, p. 5074, § 2, operative July 1, 1983. Amended by Stats.2013, c. 176 (S.B.551), § 1.)*

Law Revision Commission Comments

Section 683.140 sets forth the contents of the application for renewal of a judgment. It is drawn in part from Section 1710.15 (application for entry of judgment based on sister state judgment). As to the amount of the judgment as renewed, see Section 683.150. [16 Cal.L.Rev.Comm. Reports 1214 (1982)].

Research References

Rutter, Cal. Practice Guide: Enforcing Judgments/Debts Ch. 6A-7, Period During Which Judgment Enforceable; Renewal Procedures.

Miller and Starr California Real Estate § 32:56, Renewal of the Judgment Lien.

8 Witkin Cal. Proc. 5th Enforcement of Judgment § 36, (S 36) Application.

§ 683.150. Entry of renewal; amount of judgment as renewed

(a) Upon the filing of the application, the court clerk shall enter the renewal of the judgment in the court records.

(b) The fee for filing an application for renewal of judgment is as provided in subdivision (b) of Section 70626 of the Government Code.

(c) In the case of a money judgment, the entry of renewal shall show the amount of the judgment as renewed. Except as provided in subdivisions (d) and (e), this amount is the amount required to satisfy the judgment on the date of the filing of the application for renewal and includes the fee for the filing of the application for renewal.

(d) In the case of a money judgment payable in installments not previously renewed, the amount of the judgment as renewed is the total of the past due installments, the costs added to the judgment pursuant to Section 685.090, and the accrued interest, which remains unsatisfied and is enforceable on the date of the filing of the application for renewal and includes the fee for the filing of the application for renewal.

(e) In the case of a money judgment payable in installments previously renewed, the amount of the judgment as renewed under the latest renewal is the total of the following which remains unsatisfied and is enforceable on the date of the filing of the application for the latest renewal:

(1) The amount of the judgment as renewed under the previous renewal.

(2) The past due installments that became due and payable after the previous renewal.

(3) The costs that have been added to the judgment pursuant to Section 685.090 after the previous renewal.

(4) The interest that has accrued on the amounts described in paragraphs (1), (2), and (3) since the last renewal.

(5) The fee for filing the application for renewal.

(f) In the case of a judgment for possession or sale of property, the entry of renewal shall describe the performance remaining due. *(Added by Stats.1982, c. 1364, p. 5074, § 2, operative July 1, 1983. Amended by Stats.2005, c. 75 (A.B.145), § 36, eff. July 19, 2005, operative Jan. 1, 2006.)*

Law Revision Commission Comments

Section 683.150 requires that the court clerk enter the renewal of the judgment based on the application. The entry of the renewal by the court clerk is a ministerial act. In the case of a money judgment payable in installments, past due installments and costs that are not enforceable on the date of filing the application for renewal may not be renewed. See Section 683.030 (period of enforceability). [16 Cal.L.Rev.Comm. Reports 1215 (1982)].

Research References

Rutter, Cal. Practice Guide: Civil Trials & Evidence Ch. 18-C, C. Other Post-Trial Motions.

Rutter, Cal. Practice Guide: Enforcing Judgments/Debts Ch. 6A-7, Period During Which Judgment Enforceable; Renewal Procedures.

Miller and Starr California Real Estate § 32:56, Renewal of the Judgment Lien.

8 Witkin Cal. Proc. 5th Enforcement of Judgment § 35, (S 35) Right to Renew.

8 Witkin Cal. Proc. 5th Enforcement of Judgment § 36, (S 36) Application.

8 Witkin Cal. Proc. 5th Enforcement of Judgment § 37, (S 37) Entry, Amount, and Notice.

§ 683.160. Notice; service; filing proof of service

(a) The judgment creditor shall serve a notice of renewal of the judgment on the judgment debtor. Service shall be made personally or by first-class mail and proof of service shall be filed with the court clerk. The notice shall be in a form prescribed by the Judicial Council and shall inform the judgment debtor that the judgment debtor has 30 days within which to make a motion to vacate or modify the renewal.

(b) Until proof of service is filed pursuant to subdivision (a), no writ may be issued, nor may any enforcement proceedings be commenced to enforce the judgment, except to the extent that the judgment would be enforceable had it not been renewed. *(Added by Stats.1982, c. 1364, p. 5074, § 2, operative July 1, 1983. Amended by Stats.1985, c. 41, § 4; Stats.1988, c. 900, § 5.)*

Law Revision Commission Comments

Subdivision (a) of Section 683.160 is derived from subdivision (a) of Section 1710.30 and a portion of subdivision (b) of Section 1710.40 pertaining to sister state judgments. Under Section 683.150, the entry and filing of the renewal is a ministerial act. The judgment debtor is protected, however, by the provisions for notice under Section 683.160 and the opportunity to seek an order vacating or modifying the renewal pursuant to Section 683.170.

Subdivision (b) is designed to prevent enforcement after the 10-year period in a case where the judgment creditor has failed to serve notice of renewal on the judgment debtor. See also Section 683.040 (application for writ after 10 years). The notice of renewal may be served after the 10-year period has expired if the application for renewal is timely filed, and the judgment is enforceable after proof of service of the notice of renewal is filed unless the renewal is vacated. [16 Cal.L.Rev.Comm. Reports 1215 (1982)].

Subdivision (a) of Section 683.160 is amended to delete the reference to a repealed statutory form and substitute a reference to the form prepared by the Judicial Council. [18 Cal.L.Rev.Comm. Reports 361 (1985)].

Research References

Rutter, Cal. Practice Guide: Enforcing Judgments/Debts Ch. 6A-7, Period During Which Judgment Enforceable; Renewal Procedures.
Miller and Starr California Real Estate § 32:56, Renewal of the Judgment Lien.
8 Witkin Cal. Proc. 5th Enforcement of Judgment § 37, (S 37) Entry, Amount, and Notice.

§ 683.170. Vacation of renewal

(a) The renewal of a judgment pursuant to this article may be vacated on any ground that would be a defense to an action on the judgment, including the ground that the amount of the renewed judgment as entered pursuant to this article is incorrect, and shall be vacated if the application for renewal was filed within five years from the time the judgment was previously renewed under this article.

(b) Not later than 30 days after service of the notice of renewal pursuant to Section 683.160, the judgment debtor may apply by noticed motion under this section for an order of the court vacating the renewal of the judgment. The notice of motion shall be served on the judgment creditor. Service shall be made personally or by mail.

(c) Upon the hearing of the motion, the renewal may be ordered vacated upon any ground provided in subdivision (a), and another and different renewal may be entered, including, but not limited to, the renewal of the judgment in a different amount if the decision of the court is that the judgment creditor is entitled to renewal in a different amount. *(Added by Stats.1982, c. 1364, p. 5075, § 2, operative July 1, 1983.)*

Law Revision Commission Comments

Section 683.170 is derived from Section 1710.40 pertaining to sister state judgments. If it is determined at the hearing that the amount of the judgment as renewed (Section 683.150) is not correct, the court may order renewal in the correct amount pursuant to subdivision (c). On the other hand, if the court determines that the judgment has been fully satisfied or offset, the renewal should be vacated. If a motion to vacate is not made within the time stated in subdivision (b), the judgment remains enforceable in the amount stated in the entry of renewal. See Section 683.150. But nothing in this section affects or limits any remedies otherwise available to the judgment debtor after the time for making a motion to vacate has expired. [16 Cal.L.Rev.Comm. Reports 1216 (1982)].

Research References

Rutter, Cal. Practice Guide: Civil Appeals & Writs Ch. 2-B, B. Appealable Judgments and Orders.

Rutter, Cal. Practice Guide: Civ. Pro. Before Trial Ch. 4-F, F. Procedures for Challenging Service of Summons.
Rutter, Cal. Practice Guide: Civ. Pro. Before Trial Ch. 5-G, G. Relief from Default.
Rutter, Cal. Practice Guide: Enforcing Judgments/Debts Ch. 6A-7, Period During Which Judgment Enforceable; Renewal Procedures.
Miller and Starr California Real Estate § 32:56, Renewal of the Judgment Lien.
8 Witkin Cal. Proc. 5th Attack Judgment Trial Court § 237, Void Judgment.
8 Witkin Cal. Proc. 5th Enforcement of Judgment § 38, (S 38) Vacation or Modification.

§ 683.180. Judgment liens; effect of renewal

(a) If a judgment lien on an interest in real property has been created pursuant to a money judgment and the judgment is renewed pursuant to this article, the duration of the judgment lien is extended until 10 years from the date of the filing of the application for renewal if, before the expiration of the judgment lien, a certified copy of the application for renewal is recorded with the county recorder of the county where the real property subject to the judgment lien is located.

(b) A judgment lien on an interest in real property that has been transferred subject to the lien is not extended pursuant to subdivision (a) if the transfer was recorded before the application for renewal was filed unless both of the following requirements are satisfied:

(1) A copy of the application for renewal is personally served on the transferee.

(2) Proof of such service is filed with the court clerk within 90 days after the filing of the application for renewal. *(Added by Stats.1982, c. 1364, p. 5076, § 2, operative July 1, 1983. Amended by Stats.1983, c. 155, § 9.5, eff. June 30, 1983, operative July 1, 1983.)*

Law Revision Commission Comments

Section 683.180 provides a special procedure for extending the duration of a judgment lien on an interest in real property. See generally Article 2 (commencing with Section 697.310) of Chapter 2 of Division 2 (judgment liens on interests in real property). As to renewal of a judgment lien on real property under a judgment for support or against a health care provider, see Section 697.320. Section 683.180 does not apply to judgment liens under judgments for support. See Section 683.310. See also Civil Code §§ 4380, 4384.

Extension of the judgment lien for an additional 10 years under this section is analogous to the result obtained where a judgment in an action on a money judgment is recorded while a judgment lien under the original judgment is still in effect. See Provisor v. Nelson, 234 Cal.App.2d Supp. 876, 44 Cal.Rptr. 894 (1965). The priority of the judgment lien on an interest in real property remains the same, but the extension adds 10 years to the life of the lien dating from the time the application for renewal is filed. See also Section 697.030 (duration of liens). The judgment lien is extended only if the certified copy of the application for renewal is recorded while the judgment lien is still in effect. If the judgment lien is not so extended, the judgment creditor may record an abstract of the renewed judgment to obtain a new judgment lien dating from the recording of such abstract. As provided in subdivision (b), if the interest in real property has been transferred subject to the lien and the transfer has been recorded, an extension pursuant to this section extends the lien on the property in the hands of the transferee only if the transferee is served notice of the renewal and proof of service is filed within the prescribed time. [16 Cal.L.Rev.Comm. Reports 1217 (1982)].

Research References

Rutter, Cal. Practice Guide: Enforcing Judgments/Debts Ch. 6A-7, Period During Which Judgment Enforceable; Renewal Procedures.
Rutter, Cal. Practice Guide: Enforcing Judgments/Debts Ch. 6B-6, Duration of Real Property Judgment Lien.
Miller and Starr California Real Estate § 32:56, Renewal of the Judgment Lien.
Miller and Starr California Real Estate § 11:168, State Tax Liens--Personal Income and Corporate Franchise Tax Liens.

20 NO. 1 Miller & Starr, California Real Estate Newsalert 7, Deeds.
8 Witkin Cal. Proc. 5th Enforcement of Judgment § 34, in General.
8 Witkin Cal. Proc. 5th Enforcement of Judgment § 39, (S 39) Extending
    Duration of Liens.
8 Witkin Cal. Proc. 5th Enforcement of Judgment § 67, (S 67) Duration
    and Extinguishment.
8 Witkin Cal. Proc. 5th Enforcement of Judgment § 69, in General.

§ 683.190.   Liens other than judgment liens; effect of renewal

If a lien (other than a judgment lien on an interest in real property or an execution lien) has been created by an enforcement procedure pursuant to a judgment and the judgment is renewed pursuant to this article, the duration of the lien is extended, subject to any other limitations on its duration under this title, until 10 years from the date of the filing of the application for renewal of the judgment if, before the expiration of the lien, a certified copy of the application for renewal is served on or filed with the same person and in the same manner as the notice or order that created the lien. *(Added by Stats.1982, c. 1364, p. 5076, § 2, operative July 1, 1983.)*

Law Revision Commission Comments

Section 683.190 permits the continuation of liens, except for judgment liens on interests in real property and execution liens, both of which are governed by other provisions. Under Section 683.199, however, a lien of limited duration, such as a judgment lien on personal property (five years), is not increased in duration but is permitted to continue past the 10-year period specified in Section 683.020. See Section 697.510 (duration of judgment lien on personal property). A judgment lien on real property is continued by recording a certified copy of the application for renewal as provided in Section 683.180. An execution lien is continued by filing with the levying officer under Section 683.200. However, other liens governed by the general rule that the lien exists as long as the judgment is enforceable (see Section 697.030) are increased in duration pursuant to Section 683.190. [16 Cal.L.Rev.Comm. Reports 1218 (1982)].

Research References

Rutter, Cal. Practice Guide: Enforcing Judgments/Debts Ch. 6A-7, Period
    During Which Judgment Enforceable; Renewal Procedures.
Rutter, Cal. Practice Guide: Enforcing Judgments/Debts Ch. 6D-3, Levy
    of Writ of Execution-In General.
Rutter, Cal. Practice Guide: Enforcing Judgments/Debts Ch. 6G-8, Lien
    in Pending Action.
Miller and Starr California Real Estate § 32:56, Renewal of the Judgment
    Lien.
8 Witkin Cal. Proc. 5th Enforcement of Judgment § 39, (S 39) Extending
    Duration of Liens.

§ 683.200.   Enforcement proceedings; continuance

If a judgment is renewed pursuant to this article, any enforcement proceeding previously commenced pursuant to the judgment or to a writ or order issued pursuant to the judgment that would have ceased pursuant to Section 683.020 had the judgment not been renewed may be continued, subject to any other limitations provided in this title, if, before the expiration of the prior 10-year period of enforceability, a certified copy of the application for renewal of the judgment is filed with the levying officer, receiver, or other officer acting pursuant to such writ or order or, in other cases, is filed in the enforcement proceeding. *(Added by Stats.1982, c. 1364, p. 5076, § 2, operative July 1, 1983.)*

Law Revision Commission Comments

Section 683.200 permits the continuation of enforcement proceedings under this title that would otherwise have ceased because of the expiration of the period of enforceability. See Section 683.020. For example, a sale of real property pursuant to a writ of execution may proceed after the expiration of 10 years from the date of entry of the judgment if the judgment is renewed within the time allowed and a certified copy of the application for renewal is filed with the levying officer in charge of the sale before the expiration of the 10-year period. Likewise, an examination proceeding may continue if the certified copy of the application for

renewal is filed with the court that is to conduct the examination. [16 Cal.L.Rev.Comm. Reports 1219 (1982)].

Research References

Rutter, Cal. Practice Guide: Enforcing Judgments/Debts Ch. 6A-7, Period
    During Which Judgment Enforceable; Renewal Procedures.
Rutter, Cal. Practice Guide: Enforcing Judgments/Debts Ch. 6D-3, Levy
    of Writ of Execution-In General.
Miller and Starr California Real Estate § 32:56, Renewal of the Judgment
    Lien.
8 Witkin Cal. Proc. 5th Enforcement of Judgment § 34, in General.
8 Witkin Cal. Proc. 5th Enforcement of Judgment § 39, (S 39) Extending
    Duration of Liens.
8 Witkin Cal. Proc. 5th Enforcement of Judgment § 40, (S 40) Effect of
    Renewal on Enforcement.

§ 683.210.   Stay of enforcement

A judgment may be renewed notwithstanding any stay of enforcement of the judgment, but the renewal of the judgment does not affect the stay of enforcement. *(Added by Stats.1982, c. 1364, p. 5076, § 2, operative July 1, 1983.)*

Validity

For validity of this section, see In re Lobherr, Bkrtcy.C.D.Cal.2002, 282 B.R. 912.

Law Revision Commission Comments

Section 683.210 permits the judgment creditor to obtain an extension of the enforceability of a judgment even though a stay of enforcement is in effect. Renewal may be necessary if a judgment is temporarily stayed during the time that the 10-year enforcement period prescribed by Section 683.020 is running out. Renewal during a stay of enforcement does not affect the stay, but merely prevents the termination of the period of enforceability. [16 Cal.L.Rev.Comm. Reports 1219 (1982)].

Research References

Rutter, Cal. Practice Guide: Civil Appeals & Writs Ch. 7-A, A. Overview.
Rutter, Cal. Practice Guide: Enforcing Judgments/Debts Ch. 6A-7, Period
    During Which Judgment Enforceable; Renewal Procedures.
Miller and Starr California Real Estate § 32:56, Renewal of the Judgment
    Lien.
8 Witkin Cal. Proc. 5th Enforcement of Judgment § 40, (S 40) Effect of
    Renewal on Enforcement.

§ 683.220.   Application filing date; commencement of period for bringing action

If a judgment is renewed pursuant to this article, the date of the filing of the application for renewal shall be deemed to be the date that the period for commencing an action on the renewed judgment commences to run under Section 337.5. *(Added by Stats.1982, c. 1364, p. 5076, § 2, operative July 1, 1983.)*

Law Revision Commission Comments

Section 683.220 gives the judgment creditor a right to bring an action on a renewed judgment comparable to that which would have existed had the judgment creditor earlier resorted to an action on the judgment instead of the renewal procedure provided by this article. See Section 683.050 (right of action on judgment preserved). [16 Cal.L.Rev.Comm. Reports 1219 (1982)].

Research References

Rutter, Cal. Practice Guide: Real Prop. Transactions Ch. 6-I, I. Real
    Property Foreclosures and Antideficiency Laws.
Miller and Starr California Real Estate § 32:56, Renewal of the Judgment
    Lien.
8 Witkin Cal. Proc. 5th Enforcement of Judgment § 40, (S 40) Effect of
    Renewal on Enforcement.

ARTICLE 3.   APPLICATION OF CHAPTER

Civ. Pro.

§ 683.310. Judgments under Family Code; application of chapter

Except as otherwise provided in the Family Code, this chapter does not apply to a judgment or order made or entered pursuant to the Family Code. *(Added by Stats.1982, c. 1364, p. 5077, § 2, operative July 1, 1983. Amended by Stats.1991, c. 110 (S.B.101), § 15; Stats.1992, c. 163 (A.B.2641), § 31, operative Jan. 1, 1994; Stats.2000, c. 808 (A.B.1358), § 5, eff. Sept. 28, 2000.)*

Law Revision Commission Comments

Section 683.310 is amended to substitute a reference to the Family Code section that replaced the former Civil Code section and to substitute "a judgment or order made or entered pursuant to the Family Code" for the former reference to the former Family Law Act. Family Code Section 4502 provides that a judgment for child, family, or spousal support may be renewed in the manner specified in Article 2 (commencing with Section 683.110) of Chapter 3 of Title 9 of Part 2 of the Code of Civil Procedure. The methods of enforcement of a judgment or order made or entered pursuant to the Family Code are prescribed by Family Code Sections 290 and 291. [22 Cal.L.Rev.Comm.Reports 1 (1992)].

Section 683.310 is amended to accommodate other exceptions in the Family Code concerning enforcement of judgments and the likelihood of future revisions in the Family Code. This is a technical, nonsubstantive change. Family Code Section 4502 provides an important exception, making the ministerial renewal scheme under the Enforcement of Judgments Law available as an option for support judgments. Moreover, Family Code Section 291 makes this chapter applicable to enforceability and renewal of judgments for possession or sale entered under the Family Code. [30 Cal.L.Rev.Comm.Reports 717 (2000)].

Research References

Rutter, Cal. Practice Guide: Enforcing Judgments/Debts Ch. 6A-7, Period During Which Judgment Enforceable; Renewal Procedures.

Miller and Starr California Real Estate § 32:55, Duration of the Judgment Lien.

15 NO. 4 Miller & Starr, California Real Estate Newsalert 28, Involuntary Liens.

8 Witkin Cal. Proc. 5th Enforcement of Judgment § 41, Exceptions to Application of Provisions.

§ 683.320. Money judgments against public entities

This chapter does not apply to a money judgment against a public entity that is subject to Section 965.5 or 970.1 of the Government Code. *(Added by Stats.1982, c. 1364, p. 5077, § 2, operative July 1, 1983.)*

Law Revision Commission Comments

Section 683.320 recognizes that the period of enforceability of a money judgment against the state or a local public entity is governed by provisions of the Government Code. But see Gov't Code § 965.9 (judgment against the Regents of the University of California). The period of enforceability of a money judgment against a public entity may not be extended using the renewal procedure under Sections 683.110–683.220. This does not, however, affect the right to bring an action on the judgment. See Sections 337.5 and 683.050. See also Sections 695.050 (enforcement of money judgment against public entity), 712.070 (enforcement of nonmoney judgment against public entity). [16 Cal.L.Rev. Comm. Reports 1220 (1982)].

Research References

Rutter, Cal. Practice Guide: Enforcing Judgments/Debts Ch. 6A-7, Period During Which Judgment Enforceable; Renewal Procedures.

8 Witkin Cal. Proc. 5th Enforcement of Judgment § 41, Exceptions to Application of Provisions.

8 Witkin Cal. Proc. 5th Enforcement of Judgment § 432, Enforcement Mechanisms.

CHAPTER 4. MANNER OF SERVICE OF WRITS, NOTICES, AND OTHER PAPERS

ARTICLE 1. SERVICE ON ATTORNEY OF CREDITOR OR DEBTOR

§ 684.010. Judgment creditor; attorney of record

Subject to Chapter 1 (commencing with Section 283) of Title 5 of Part 1 of this code and Section 215 of the Family Code, when a notice, order, or other paper is required to be served under this title on the judgment creditor, it shall be served on the judgment creditor's attorney of record rather than on the judgment creditor if the judgment creditor has an attorney of record. *(Added by Stats.1982, c. 1364, p. 5077, § 2, operative July 1, 1983. Amended by Stats.1992, c. 163 (A.B.2641), § 32, operative Jan. 1, 1994.)*

Law Revision Commission Comments

Section 684.010 is drawn from the second and third sentences of Section 1015. The introductory clause recognizes (1) that, if the applicable procedure is followed, an attorney of record may withdraw from the case, be discharged, or be replaced by another attorney, and (2) that service must be made on the party rather than the attorney in certain Family Law Act matters after entry of final judgment. [16 Cal.L.Rev.Comm. Reports 1221 (1982)].

Section 684.010 is amended to substitute a reference to the Family Code section that replaced the former Civil Code section. [22 Cal.L.Rev.Comm.Reports 1 (1992)].

Research References

Rutter, Cal. Practice Guide: Enforcing Judgments/Debts Ch. 6A-5, Amount Recoverable Under Judgment.

Rutter, Cal. Practice Guide: Enforcing Judgments/Debts Ch. 6A-7, Period During Which Judgment Enforceable; Renewal Procedures.

Rutter, Cal. Practice Guide: Enforcing Judgments/Debts Ch. 6A-10, Service of Writs, Notices and Other Papers in Enforcement Proceedings.

Rutter, Cal. Practice Guide: Enforcing Judgments/Debts Ch. 6G-11, Enforcement of Judgment by Assignees.

8 Witkin Cal. Proc. 5th Enforcement of Judgment § 26, in General.

8 Witkin Cal. Proc. 5th Enforcement of Judgment § 27, Manner of Service.

6 Witkin Cal. Proc. 5th Provisional Remedies § 88, (S 88) Service.

§ 684.020. Judgment debtor; request for service on attorney; consent by attorney; revocation

(a) Except as provided in subdivision (b), when a writ, notice, order, or other paper is required to be served under this title on the judgment debtor, it shall be served on the judgment debtor instead of the attorney for the judgment debtor.

(b) The writ, notice, order, or other paper shall be served on the attorney specified by the judgment debtor rather than on the judgment debtor if all of the following requirements are satisfied:

(1) The judgment debtor has filed with the court and served on the judgment creditor a request that service on the judgment debtor under this title be made by serving the attorney specified in the request. Service on the judgment creditor of the request shall be made personally or by mail. The request shall include a

consent, signed by the attorney, to receive service under this title on behalf of the judgment debtor.

(2) The request has not been revoked by the judgment debtor.

(3) The consent to receive service has not been revoked by the attorney.

(c) A request or consent under subdivision (b) may be revoked by filing with the court a notice revoking the request or consent. A copy of the notice revoking the request or consent shall be served on the judgment creditor. Service shall be made personally or by mail. The judgment creditor is not bound by the revocation until the judgment creditor has received a copy of the notice revoking the request or consent. *(Added by Stats. 1982, c. 1364, p. 5077, § 2, operative July 1, 1983.)*

Research References

Rutter, Cal. Practice Guide: Enforcing Judgments/Debts Ch. 6A-10, Service of Writs, Notices and Other Papers in Enforcement Proceedings.
8 Witkin Cal. Proc. 5th Enforcement of Judgment § 26, in General.
8 Witkin Cal. Proc. 5th Enforcement of Judgment § 27, Manner of Service.

§ 684.030. Subpoenas; contempt papers

Sections 684.010 and 684.020 do not apply to either of the following:

(a) A subpoena or other process to require the attendance of a party.

(b) A paper to bring a party into contempt. *(Added by Stats.1982, c. 1364, p. 5077, § 2, operative July 1, 1983.)*

Law Revision Commission Comments

Section 684.030 is drawn from a provision of Section 1015. [16 Cal.L.Rev.Comm. Reports 1222 (1982)].

Research References

Rutter, Cal. Practice Guide: Enforcing Judgments/Debts Ch. 6A-10, Service of Writs, Notices and Other Papers in Enforcement Proceedings.
8 Witkin Cal. Proc. 5th Enforcement of Judgment § 26, in General.

§ 684.040. Service on attorney; procedure

If service on an attorney is required under this article, service on the attorney shall be made in any of the following ways:

(a) By personal delivery to the attorney.

(b) By service in the manner provided in subdivision (1) of Section 1011.

(c) By mail in the manner provided in Section 684.120. *(Added by Stats.1982, c. 1364, p. 5078, § 2, operative July 1, 1983.)*

Law Revision Commission Comments

Subdivisions (a) and (b) of Section 684.040 are comparable to the relevant portions of Section 1011. Subdivision (c) refers to a provision that is comparable to a portion of the first sentence of Section 1013(a). [16 Cal.L.Rev.Comm. Reports 1222 (1982)].

Research References

Rutter, Cal. Practice Guide: Enforcing Judgments/Debts Ch. 6A-10, Service of Writs, Notices and Other Papers in Enforcement Proceedings.
8 Witkin Cal. Proc. 5th Enforcement of Judgment § 26, in General.
8 Witkin Cal. Proc. 5th Enforcement of Judgment § 27, Manner of Service.

§ 684.050. Service on attorney as service on creditor or debtor

Service on the attorney for the judgment creditor or the judgment debtor pursuant to the provisions of this article constitutes service on the judgment creditor or judgment debtor

for the purposes of this title. *(Added by Stats.1982, c. 1364, p. 5078, § 2, operative July 1, 1983.)*

Law Revision Commission Comments

Section 684.050 makes clear that, subject to Section 684.040, service on the attorney pursuant to this article satisfies any requirement of this title that the judgment creditor or judgment debtor be served. [16 Cal.L.Rev. Comm. Reports 1223 (1982)].

Research References

Rutter, Cal. Practice Guide: Enforcing Judgments/Debts Ch. 6A-10, Service of Writs, Notices and Other Papers in Enforcement Proceedings.
8 Witkin Cal. Proc. 5th Enforcement of Judgment § 26, in General.

ARTICLE 2. MANNER OF SERVICE GENERALLY

Section
684.110. Personal service of legal process; definition; service on attorney; service on financial institution or other office in possession of property.
684.115. Financial institution with more than nine branches in state; designation of central location for service of process; notice of designation; failure to make designation; effect of service; modification or revocation of designation; online records of designation; effect of service at nondesignated location; service of other papers; application of section; requests for information; notification to debtor.
684.120. Service by mail.
684.130. Service by levying officer; instructions.
684.140. Service by levying officer; permission for personal service.

§ 684.110. Personal service of legal process; definition; service on attorney; service on financial institution or other office in possession of property

(a)(1) Subject to subdivisions (b), (c), and (d), if legal process is required to be personally served under this title, service shall be made in the same manner as a summons is served under Chapter 4 (commencing with Section 413.10) of Title 5.

(2) For purposes of this title, the term "legal process" shall refer to each and all of the writs, notices, orders, or other papers required or permitted to be served pursuant to this title.

(b) If the legal process is required to be personally served under this title and service on an attorney is required under Article 1 (commencing with Section 684.010), service shall be made on the attorney in the manner provided in Section 684.040.

(c) If the legal process is required to be personally served on (1) a financial institution in connection with a deposit account or with property held for safekeeping, as collateral for an obligation owed to the financial institution or in a safe-deposit box, (2) a title insurer (as defined in Section 12340.4 of the Insurance Code) or underwritten title company (as defined in Section 12340.5 of the Insurance Code), or (3) an industrial loan company (as defined in Section 18003 of the Financial Code), service shall be made at the office or branch that has actual possession of the property levied upon or at which a deposit account levied upon is carried and shall be made upon the officer, manager, or other person in charge of the office or branch at the time of service. For purposes of this section, the office or branch at which a deposit account levied upon is carried shall mean the branch, office, or other location where the financial institution maintains the account.

(d) Notwithstanding subdivision (c), with respect to legal process served on a financial institution, if the financial institution has designated a central location for service of legal process pursuant to Section 684.115, unless the financial institution elects to treat legal process served at a branch or office as effective, that legal process so served on the branch or office will not reach those accounts or property and need not be reported on the financial institution's garnishee memorandum.

(e) Notwithstanding subdivision (c), a financial institution, title insurer, or industrial loan company, in its discretion and without violating any obligation to its customer, may act upon service of legal process at any of its offices or branches, whether or not the office or branch is the location wherein accounts or property that may be reached by the process is or are maintained or located. *(Added by Stats.1982, c. 1364, p. 5078, § 2, operative July 1, 1983. Amended by Stats.2012, c. 484 (A.B.2364), § 6.)*

Research References

Rutter, Cal. Practice Guide: Enforcing Judgments/Debts Ch. 6B-6, Duration of Real Property Judgment Lien.

Rutter, Cal. Practice Guide: Enforcing Judgments/Debts Ch. 6D-4, Levy on Specific Property.

Rutter, Cal. Practice Guide: Enforcing Judgments/Debts Ch. 6A-10, Service of Writs, Notices and Other Papers in Enforcement Proceedings.

8 Witkin Cal. Proc. 5th Enforcement of Judgment § 27, Manner of Service.

6 Witkin Cal. Proc. 5th Provisional Remedies § 88, (S 88) Service.

§ 684.115. Financial institution with more than nine branches in state; designation of central location for service of process; notice of designation; failure to make designation; effect of service; modification or revocation of designation; online records of designation; effect of service at nondesignated location; service of other papers; application of section; requests for information; notification to debtor

(a) A financial institution may, and if it has more than nine branches or offices at which it conducts its business within this state * * * shall, designate one or more central locations for service of legal process within this state. Each designated location shall be referred to as a "central location." If a financial institution elects or is required to designate a central location for service of legal process, the financial institution shall file a notice of its designation with the Department of Financial Institutions, which filing shall be effective upon filing and shall contain all of the following:

(1) The physical address of the central location.

(2) The days and hours during which service will be accepted at the central location.

(3) If the central location will not accept service of legal process directed at deposit accounts maintained or property held at all of the financial institution's branches or offices within this state, or if the service accepted at the central location will not apply to safe-deposit boxes or other property of the judgment debtor held by or for the judgment debtor, the filing shall also contain sufficient information to permit a determination of the limitation or limitations, including, in the case of a limitation applicable to certain branches or offices, an identification of the branches or offices as to which service at the central location will not apply and the nature of the limitation applicable to those branches or offices. If the limitation will apply to all branches or offices of the financial institution within this state, the filing may indicate the nature of the limitation and that it applies to all branches or offices, in lieu of an identification of branches or offices as to which the limitation applies. To the extent that a financial institution's designation of a central location for service of legal process covers the process directed at deposit accounts, safe-deposit boxes, or other property of the judgment debtor held by or for the judgment debtor at a particular branch or

office located within this state, the branch or office shall be a branch or office covered by central process.

(b) Should a financial institution required to designate a central location fail to do so, each branch of that institution located in this state shall be deemed to be a central location at which service of legal process may be made, and all of the institution's branches or offices located within this state shall be deemed to be a branch or office covered by central process.

(c) Subject to any limitation noted pursuant to paragraph (3) of subdivision (a), service of legal process at a central location of a financial institution shall be effective against all deposit accounts and all property held for safekeeping, as collateral for an obligation owed to the financial institution or in a safe-deposit box if the same is described in the legal process and held by the financial institution at any branch or office covered by central process and located within this state. However, while service of legal process at the central location will establish a lien on all property, if any property other than deposit accounts is physically held by the financial institution in a county other than that in which the designated central location is located, the financial institution shall include in its garnishee's memorandum the location or locations of the property, and the judgment creditor shall obtain a writ of execution covering the property and directed to the levying officer in that county to accomplish the turnover of the property and shall forward the writ and related required documentation to the levying officer in the county in which the property is held.

(d) A financial institution may modify or revoke any designation made pursuant to subdivision (a) by filing the modification or revocation with the Department of Financial Institutions. The modification or revocation shall be effective when the Department of Financial Institutions' records have been updated to reflect the modification or revocation, provided that the judgment creditor may rely upon the superseded designation during the 30–day period following the effective date of the revocation or modification.

(e)(1) The Department of Financial Institutions shall update its online records to reflect a filing by a financial institution pursuant to subdivision (a) or a modification or revocation filed by a financial institution pursuant to subdivision (d) within 10 business days following the filing by the financial institution. The Department of Financial Institutions' Internet Web site shall reflect the date its online records for each financial institution have most recently been updated.

(2) The Department of Financial Institutions shall provide any person requesting it with a copy of each current filing made by a financial institution pursuant to subdivision (a). The Department of Financial Institutions may satisfy its obligation under this subdivision by posting all current designations of a financial institution, or the pertinent information therein, on an Internet Web site available to the public without charge, and if that information is made available, the Department of Financial Institutions may impose a reasonable fee for furnishing that information in any other manner.

(f) As to deposit accounts maintained or property held for safekeeping, as collateral for an obligation owed to the financial institution or in a safe-deposit box at a branch or office covered by central process, service of legal process at a location other than a central location designated by the financial institution shall not be effective unless the financial institution, in its absolute discretion, elects to act upon the process at that location as if it were effective. In the absence of an election, the financial institution may respond to the legal process by mailing or delivery of the garnishee's memorandum to the levying officer within the time otherwise provided therefor, with a statement on the garnishee's memorandum that the legal process was not properly served at the financial institution's designated location for receiving legal process, and, <u>therefore</u>, was not processed, and the address at which the financial institution is to receive legal process.

(g) If any legal process is served at a central location of a financial institution pursuant to this section, all related papers to be served on the financial institution shall be served at that location, unless agreed to the contrary between the serving party and the financial institution.

(h) This subdivision shall apply whenever a financial institution operates within this state at least one branch or office in addition to its head office or main office, as applicable, or a financial institution headquartered in another state operates more than one branch or office within this state, and no central location has been designated or deemed to have been designated by the institution for service of legal process relating to deposit accounts maintained at the financial institution's head office or main office, as applicable, and branches located within this state. If a judgment creditor reasonably believes that, pursuant to Section 700.140 and, if applicable, Section 700.160, any act of enforcement would be effective against a specific deposit account maintained at a financial institution described in this subdivision, the judgment creditor may file with the financial institution a written request that the financial institution identify the branch or office within this state at which a specified account might be maintained by the financial institution. The written request shall contain the following statements or information:

(1) The name of the person reasonably believed by the judgment creditor to be a person in whose name the specified deposit account stands.

(2) If the name of the person reasonably believed by the judgment creditor to be a person in whose name the specified deposit account stands is not a judgment debtor identified in the writ of execution, a statement that a person reasonably believed by the judgment creditor to be a person in whose name the specified deposit account stands will be appropriately identified in the legal process to be served pursuant to Section 700.160, including any supplementary papers, such as a court order or affidavit if the same will be required by Section 700.160.

(3) The specific identifying number of the account reasonably believed to be maintained with the financial institution and standing in the name of the judgment debtor or other person.

(4) The address of the requesting party.

(5) An affidavit by the judgment creditor or the judgment creditor's counsel stating substantially the following:

I hereby declare that this deposit account location request complies with Section 684.115 of the Code of Civil Procedure, that the account or accounts of the judgment debtor or other person or persons appropriately identified in the legal process and specified herein are subject to a valid writ of execution, or court order, that I have a reasonable belief, formed after an inquiry reasonable under the circumstances, that the financial institution receiving this deposit account location request has an account standing in the name of the judgment debtor or other person or persons appropriately identified in the legal process, and that information pertaining to the location of the account will assist the judgment creditor in enforcing the judgment.

(i) The affidavit contemplated by subdivision (h) shall be signed by the judgment creditor or the judgment creditor's counsel and filed at the financial institution's head office located within this state or, if the financial institution's head office is in another state, at one of its branches or offices within this state. Failure to comply with the requirements of subdivision (h) and this subdivision shall be sufficient basis for the financial institu-

tion to refuse to produce the information that would otherwise be required by subdivision (j).

(j) Within 10 banking days following receipt by a financial institution at the applicable location specified in subdivision (i) of a request contemplated by subdivision (h), as to each specific deposit account identified in the request contemplated by subdivision (h), the financial institution shall respond by mailing, by first-class mail with postage prepaid, to the requester's address as specified in the request a response indicating the branch or office location of the financial institution at which the specified deposit account might be maintained, or, if the specified deposit account, if it exists, would not be maintained at a specific location, at least one place within this state at which legal process relating to the deposit account should or may be served. The response to be furnished pursuant to this subdivision shall not require the financial institution to determine whether an account exists or, if an account does exist, whether it would be reached by the legal process, rather, the branch or office location shall be determined and reported by the financial institution based solely upon its determination that an account with the identifying number provided by the requester would be maintained at that branch if an account did exist, and the response shall not contain any information about the name in which the account stands or any other information concerning the account, if it exists. If more than one account number is specified in the request, the financial institution's responses as to some or all of those account numbers may be combined in a single writing.

(k) A response furnished in good faith by the financial institution pursuant to subdivision (j) shall not be deemed to violate the privacy of any person in whose name the specified deposit account stands nor the privacy of any other person, and shall not require the consent of the person in whose name the account stands nor that of any other person.

(*l*) A financial institution shall not notify the person in whose name the specified deposit account stands or any other person related to the specified account of the receipt of any request made pursuant to subdivision (h) and affecting that person's or persons' accounts at the financial institution, provided that the financial institution shall have no liability for its failure to comply with the provisions of this subdivision. *(Added by Stats.2012, c. 484 (A.B.2364), § 7. Amended by Stats.2013, c. 76 (A.B.383), § 23.)*

§ 684.120.   Service by mail

(a) Except as otherwise provided in this title, if a writ, notice, order, or other paper is to be served by mail under this title, it shall be sent by first-class mail (unless some other type of mail is specifically required) and shall be deposited in a post office, mailbox, sub-post office, substation, mail chute, or other like facility regularly maintained by the United States Postal Service, in a sealed envelope, with postage paid, addressed as follows:

(1) If an attorney is being served in place of the judgment creditor or judgment debtor as provided in Section 684.010 or 684.020, to the attorney at the last address given by the attorney on any paper filed in the proceeding and served on the party making the service.

(2) If any other person is being served, to such person at the person's current mailing address if known or, if unknown, at the address last given by the person on any paper filed in the proceeding and served on the party making the service.

(3) If the mailing cannot be made as provided in paragraph (1) or (2), to the person at the person's last known address.

(b) Service by mail is complete at the time of deposit; but, unless the court prescribes a shorter period of time, any prescribed period of notice and any right or duty to do any act or make any response within any prescribed period or on a date certain after a paper is served by mail is extended:

(1) Five days if the place of address is within the State of California.

(2) Ten days if the place of address is outside the State of California but within the United States.

(3) Twenty days if the place of address is outside the United States.

(c) The writ, notice, order, or other paper served by mail under this section shall bear a notation of the date and place of mailing or be accompanied by an unsigned copy of the affidavit or certificate of mailing. This subdivision is directory only. *(Added by Stats.1982, c. 1364, p. 5078, § 2, operative July 1, 1983.)*

Research References

Rutter, Cal. Practice Guide: Enforcing Judgments/Debts Ch. 6D-2, Writ of Execution.
Rutter, Cal. Practice Guide: Enforcing Judgments/Debts Ch. 6D-7, Sale and Collection of Property Levied Upon.
Rutter, Cal. Practice Guide: Enforcing Judgments/Debts Ch. 6D-8, Special Requirements for Sale of Real Property Dwellings.
Rutter, Cal. Practice Guide: Enforcing Judgments/Debts Ch. 6E-3, Procedures for Claiming Exemptions.
Rutter, Cal. Practice Guide: Enforcing Judgments/Debts Ch. 6E-4, Opposing Claim of Exemption.
Rutter, Cal. Practice Guide: Enforcing Judgments/Debts Ch. 6G-1, Examination of Judgment Debtor and Third Parties.
Rutter, Cal. Practice Guide: Enforcing Judgments/Debts Ch. 6A-10, Service of Writs, Notices and Other Papers in Enforcement Proceedings.
8 Witkin Cal. Proc. 5th Enforcement of Judgment § 26, in General.
8 Witkin Cal. Proc. 5th Enforcement of Judgment § 27, Manner of Service.
8 Witkin Cal. Proc. 5th Enforcement of Judgment § 28, Proof of Service.
8 Witkin Cal. Proc. 5th Enforcement of Judgment § 181, (S 181) Claim of Exemption.
8 Witkin Cal. Proc. 5th Enforcement of Judgment § 336, (S 336) Failure to Vacate Property.
6 Witkin Cal. Proc. 5th Provisional Remedies § 101, Statutory Requirement.

§ 684.130. Service by levying officer; instructions

(a) If the levying officer is required by any provision of this title to serve any writ, order, notice, or other paper on any person, the judgment creditor shall include in the instructions to the levying officer the correct name and address of the person. The judgment creditor shall use reasonable diligence to ascertain the correct name and address of the person.

(b) Unless the levying officer has actual knowledge that the name or address included in the instructions is incorrect, the levying officer shall rely on the instructions in serving the writ, order, notice, or other paper on the person. *(Added by Stats.1982, c. 1364, p. 5079, § 2, operative July 1, 1983.)*

Research References

Rutter, Cal. Practice Guide: Enforcing Judgments/Debts Ch. 6D-4, Levy on Specific Property.
Rutter, Cal. Practice Guide: Enforcing Judgments/Debts Ch. 6D-3, Levy of Writ of Execution-In General.
Rutter, Cal. Practice Guide: Enforcing Judgments/Debts Ch. 6A-10, Service of Writs, Notices and Other Papers in Enforcement Proceedings.
Miller and Starr California Real Estate § 32:27, Procedure to Claim an Exemption.
8 Witkin Cal. Proc. 5th Enforcement of Judgment § 26, in General.
8 Witkin Cal. Proc. 5th Enforcement of Judgment § 27, Manner of Service.

8 Witkin Cal. Proc. 5th Enforcement of Judgment § 29, Instructions from Judgment Creditor.

§ 684.140. Service by levying officer; permission for personal service

If a provision of this title provides for service by the levying officer of an order, notice, or other paper that runs in favor of a particular person, personal service of the paper may be made by the person or the person's agent if the levying officer gives permission. The levying officer's permission may be evidenced by a certificate signed by the levying officer. This section does not authorize the levying officer to give permission to serve a writ or notice of levy. If service is made by a person or the person's agent pursuant to this section, the cost of the service is not a recoverable cost. Nothing in this section limits the authority of a registered process server provided in this title. *(Added by Stats.1982, c. 1364, p. 5079, § 2, operative July 1, 1983.)*

Research References

Rutter, Cal. Practice Guide: Enforcing Judgments/Debts Ch. 6A-10, Service of Writs, Notices and Other Papers in Enforcement Proceedings.
8 Witkin Cal. Proc. 5th Enforcement of Judgment § 26, in General.
8 Witkin Cal. Proc. 5th Enforcement of Judgment § 27, Manner of Service.

ARTICLE 3. PROOF OF SERVICE

Section
684.210. Court hearings.
684.220. Manner of proof.

§ 684.210. Court hearings

If service of notice of a court hearing is required under this title, proof of service of the notice shall be made at or before the hearing to the satisfaction of the court. *(Added by Stats.1982, c. 1364, p. 5079, § 2, operative July 1, 1983.)*

Research References

Rutter, Cal. Practice Guide: Enforcing Judgments/Debts Ch. 6A-10, Service of Writs, Notices and Other Papers in Enforcement Proceedings.
8 Witkin Cal. Proc. 5th Enforcement of Judgment § 26, in General.
8 Witkin Cal. Proc. 5th Enforcement of Judgment § 28, Proof of Service.
6 Witkin Cal. Proc. 5th Provisional Remedies § 88, (S 88) Service.

§ 684.220. Manner of proof

Proof of service or of posting or publication under this title may be made by, but is not limited to, the following means:

(a) If service is made in the same manner as a summons is served under Chapter 4 (commencing with Section 413.10) of Title 5, proof of service may be made in the manner provided in Article 5 (commencing with Section 417.10) of that chapter.

(b) If service is made in the same manner as a summons is served under Section 415.10 or 415.20, proof of service may be made by affidavit of the person making the service showing the time, place, and manner of service and the facts showing that the service was made in accordance with the applicable statutory provisions. The affidavit shall recite or in other manner show the name of the person to whom the papers served were delivered and, if appropriate, the title of the person or the capacity in which the person was served.

(c) Proof of service by mail as provided in Section 684.120 may be made in the manner prescribed in Section 1013a.

(d) Proof of posting may be made by the affidavit of the person who posted the notice, showing the time and place of posting.

(e) Proof of publication may be made by the affidavit of the publisher or printer, or the foreman or principal clerk of the publisher or printer, showing the time and place of publication.

(f) Proof of service may be made by the written admission of the person served.

(g) Proof of service however made, or of posting or publication, may be made by testimonial evidence. *(Added by Stats. 1982, c. 1364, p. 5079, § 2, operative July 1, 1983.)*

Law Revision Commission Comments

Section 684.220 provides methods for proof of service or of posting or publication. Subdivision (a) incorporates the proof of service provisions applicable to service of summons and applies when this title requires service in the manner provided for service of a summons. See, e.g., Section 684.110(a). Subdivision (b) is drawn from Section 417.10 and applies when this title requires service in the manner provided for service of a summons under Sections 415.10 and 415.20. See, e.g., Section 684.110(d). Subdivision (c) applies where service by mail is made pursuant to Section 684.120. The remainder of Section 684.220 is consistent with civil practice generally. Subdivision (g) is an alternative to the other methods of proof provided in this section and permits proof to be made by testimonial evidence without regard to how the service was made. [16 Cal.L.Rev.Comm. Reports 1228 (1982)].

Research References

Rutter, Cal. Practice Guide: Enforcing Judgments/Debts Ch. 6A-10, Service of Writs, Notices and Other Papers in Enforcement Proceedings.

8 Witkin Cal. Proc. 5th Enforcement of Judgment § 26, in General.

8 Witkin Cal. Proc. 5th Enforcement of Judgment § 28, Proof of Service.

ARTICLE 4.　APPLICATION OF CHAPTER

Section

684.310.　Wage garnishment; applicability of service provisions.

§ 684.310.　Wage garnishment; applicability of service provisions

Except for Sections 684.130 and 684.140, the provisions of Article 1 (commencing with Section 684.010) and Article 2 (commencing with Section 684.110) do not apply to service under Chapter 5 (commencing with Section 706.010) of Division 2 (wage garnishment). *(Added by Stats.1982, c. 1364, p. 5080, § 2, operative July 1, 1983.)*

Law Revision Commission Comments

Section 684.310 makes certain service provisions of this chapter not applicable to wage garnishments. The Wage Garnishment Law contains special provisions governing service under that law. See, e.g., Sections 706.021, 706.101, and 706.104. [16 Cal.L.Rev.Comm. Reports 1228 (1982)].

Research References

Rutter, Cal. Practice Guide: Enforcing Judgments/Debts Ch. 6F-5, Earnings Exempt from Garnishment.

8 Witkin Cal. Proc. 5th Enforcement of Judgment § 26, in General.

CHAPTER 5.　INTEREST AND COSTS

Section
685.010.　Rate of interest.
685.020.　Interest; commencement of accrual.
685.030.　Money judgments; satisfaction in full; accrual of interest; writ of execution.
685.040.　Costs; attorney's fees.
685.050.　Levy under writ; costs and interests to be satisfied.
685.070.　Judgment creditor's costs; memorandum; motion to tax costs.

Section
685.080.　Motion to claim costs; notice; service; order.
685.090.　Costs added to judgment; inclusion in unsatisfied principal; outstanding writs; inclusion in amount of sale or collection distributed.
685.095.　Costs of service of writ by levying officer or registered process server added to judgment.
685.100.　Prerequisite to performance by levying officer of duty; prerequisite to taking property into custody; liability of levying officer.
685.110.　Prejudgment interest.

§ 685.010.　Rate of interest

(a) Interest accrues at the rate of 10 percent per annum on the principal amount of a money judgment remaining unsatisfied.

(b) The Legislature reserves the right to change the rate of interest provided in subdivision (a) at any time to a rate of less than 10 percent per annum, regardless of the date of entry of the judgment or the date any obligation upon which the judgment is based was incurred. A change in the rate of interest may be made applicable only to the interest that accrues after the operative date of the statute that changes the rate. *(Added by Stats.1982, c. 1364, p. 5080, § 2, operative July 1, 1983.)*

Research References

Rutter, Cal. Practice Guide: Civil Appeals & Writs Ch. 1-E, E. Preappeal Evaluation and "Housekeeping" Steps.

Rutter, Cal. Practice Guide: Civil Trials & Evidence Ch. 17-D, D. Costs.

Rutter, Cal. Practice Guide: Civil Trials & Evidence Ch. 17-F, F. Prejudgment Interest.

California Practice Guide: Employment Litigation Ch. 17-I, I. Interest.

Rutter, Cal. Practice Guide: Enforcing Judgments/Debts Ch. 6A-5, Amount Recoverable Under Judgment.

Rutter, Cal. Practice Guide: Enforcing Judgments/Debts Ch. 6D-2, Writ of Execution.

Rutter, Cal. Practice Guide: Family Law Ch. 6-A, A. Child Support.

Rutter, Cal. Practice Guide: Family Law Ch. 6-B, B. Spousal Support.

Rutter, Cal. Practice Guide: Fed.Civ.Pro. Before Trial Ch. 1-D, D. Choosing Between State and Federal Courts.

Rutter, Cal. Practice Guide: Insurance Litigation Ch. 13-A, A. Contract Damages.

Rutter, Cal. Practice Guide: Insurance Litigation Ch. 13-B, B. Extracontractual Compensatory Damages.

Rutter, Cal. Practice Guide: Personal Injury Ch. 4-D, D. Techniques Where Settlement Not Forthcoming.

Rutter, Cal. Practice Guide: Real Prop. Transactions Ch. 11-G, G. Rescission.

Miller and Starr California Real Estate § 21:1, Policy and Validity of the Usury Law.

Miller and Starr California Real Estate § 27:91, Prompt Payment of Progress Payments and Contract Retention.

Miller and Starr California Real Estate § 28:91, Suit to Enforce the Stop Payment Notice.

Miller and Starr California Real Estate § 34:35, Rate of Interest; Compound Interest.

Miller and Starr California Real Estate § 7:207, Tort Damages for Breach of the Duty to Defend.

Miller and Starr California Real Estate § 10:228, Procedure for Redemption.

20 NO. 3 Miller & Starr, California Real Estate Newsalert 18, Judicial Remedies.

8 Witkin Cal. Proc. 5th Enforcement of Judgment § 37, (S 37) Entry, Amount, and Notice.

8 Witkin Cal. Proc. 5th Enforcement of Judgment § 42, in General.

8 Witkin Cal. Proc. 5th Enforcement of Judgment § 53, Amount Satisfying Judgment.

8 Witkin Cal. Proc. 5th Enforcement of Judgment § 75, (S 75) Amount of Lien.

8 Witkin Cal. Proc. 5th Enforcement of Judgment § 394, (S 394) Demand for Acknowledgment.

7 Witkin Cal. Proc. 5th Judgment § 327, Rate of Interest.

7 Witkin Cal. Proc. 5th Judgment § 328, Rate Applicable to Local Public Entities.

6 Witkin, California Summary 10th Torts § 1650, (S 1650) Prejudgment Interest is Not Element of Damages.

3 Witkin, California Summary 10th Agency and Employment § 666, (S 666) Interest on Back Pay Award.

4 Witkin, California Summary 10th Negotiable Instruments § 47, (S 47) Additional Liability to Payee or Payee's Assignee.

14 Witkin, California Summary 10th Wills and Probate § 525, Statutory Framework.

14 Witkin, California Summary 10th Wills and Probate § 651, Interest.

14 Witkin, California Summary 10th Wills and Probate § 999, (S 999) Liability for Breach of Fiduciary Duty.

§ 685.020. Interest; commencement of accrual

(a) Except as provided in subdivision (b), interest commences to accrue on a money judgment on the date of entry of the judgment.

(b) Unless the judgment otherwise provides, if a money judgment is payable in installments, interest commences to accrue as to each installment on the date the installment becomes due. *(Added by Stats.1982, c. 1364, p. 5080, § 2, operative July 1, 1983. Amended by Stats.1983, c. 155, § 10, eff. June 30, 1983, operative July 1, 1983.)*

Law Revision Commission Comments

Subdivision (a) of Section 685.020 continues the general rule as to the time postjudgment interest commences to run. See former Section 682.2, Section 1033; Dixon Mobile Homes, Inc. v. Walters, 48 Cal.App.3d 964, 122 Cal.Rptr. 202 (1975). See also Sections 695.210 and 724.010 (amount to satisfy a judgment).

Subdivision (b) codifies the rule concerning accrual of interest on support judgments payable in installments and extends the rule to other judgments payable in installments. See, e.g., Huellmantel v. Huellmantel, 124 Cal. 583, 589–90, 57 P. 582 (1899); In re Marriage of Hoffee, 60 Cal.App.3d 337, 131 Cal.Rptr. 637 (1976). The introductory clause of subdivision (b) also recognizes that in certain circumstances the court may have the authority to order that interest accrues from the date of entry of a judgment rendered in an amount certain but payable in installments. See Section 85 (municipal or justice court may fix terms and conditions of payment of money judgment), 117 (small claims court may fix terms and conditions of payment).

Section 685.020 does not affect the rules that determine the extent to which prejudgment interest is to be included in a judgment. See Section 685.110. [16 Cal.L.Rev.Comm. Reports 2193 (1982)].

Research References

Rutter, Cal. Practice Guide: Civil Trials & Evidence Ch. 17-F, F. Prejudgment Interest.

Rutter, Cal. Practice Guide: Enforcing Judgments/Debts Ch. 6A-5, Amount Recoverable Under Judgment.

Rutter, Cal. Practice Guide: Family Law Ch. 6-A, A. Child Support.

Rutter, Cal. Practice Guide: Family Law Ch. 6-B, B. Spousal Support.

Rutter, Cal. Practice Guide: Personal Injury Ch. 9-M, M. Verdicts and Judgment.

Rutter, Cal. Practice Guide: Real Prop. Transactions Ch. 11-G, G. Rescission.

8 Witkin Cal. Proc. 5th Enforcement of Judgment § 43, When Accrual Commences.

8 Witkin Cal. Proc. 5th Enforcement of Judgment § 45, Support Orders.

11 Witkin, California Summary 10th Husband and Wife § 4, Definitions.

§ 685.030. Money judgments; satisfaction in full; accrual of interest; writ of execution

(a) If a money judgment is satisfied in full pursuant to a writ under this title, interest ceases to accrue on the judgment:

(1) If the proceeds of collection are paid in a lump sum, on the date of levy.

(2) If the money judgment is satisfied pursuant to an earnings withholding order, on the date and in the manner provided in Section 706.024 or Section 706.028.

(3) In any other case, on the date the proceeds of sale or collection are actually received by the levying officer.

(b) If a money judgment is satisfied in full other than pursuant to a writ under this title, interest ceases to accrue on the date the judgment is satisfied in full.

(c) If a money judgment is partially satisfied pursuant to a writ under this title or is otherwise partially satisfied, interest ceases to accrue as to the part satisfied on the date the part is satisfied.

(d) For the purposes of subdivisions (b) and (c), the date a money judgment is satisfied in full or in part is the earliest of the following times:

(1) The date satisfaction is actually received by the judgment creditor.

(2) The date satisfaction is tendered to the judgment creditor or deposited in court for the judgment creditor.

(3) The date of any other performance that has the effect of satisfaction.

(e) The clerk of a court may enter in the Register of Actions a writ of execution on a money judgment as returned wholly satisfied when the judgment amount, as specified on the writ, is fully collected and only an interest deficit of no more than ten dollars ($10) exists, due to automation of the continual daily interest accrual calculation. *(Added by Stats.1982, c. 1364, p. 5080, § 2, operative July 1, 1983. Amended by Stats.1991, c. 1090 (A.B.1484), § 4.5; Stats.1992, c. 283 (S.B.1372), § 1, eff. July 21, 1992; Stats.1998, c. 931 (S.B.2139), § 88, eff. Sept. 28, 1998; Stats.2001, c. 812 (A.B.223), § 4.)*

Law Revision Commission Comments

Subdivision (a) of Section 685.030 is amended to recognize the special rules applicable to cessation of interest with regard to collections by wage garnishment. See Sections 706.024 (amount required to satisfy earnings withholding order), 706.028 (final earnings withholding order for costs and interest). [21 Cal.L.Rev.Comm.Reports 135 (1991)].

Subdivision (e) of Section 685.030 is amended to accommodate unification of the municipal and superior courts in a county. Cal. Const. art. VI, § 5(e). It is also amended to reflect elimination of the justice court. Cal. Const. art. VI, §§ 1, 5(b). A limited civil case is equivalent to a matter within the original jurisdiction of the municipal court under former law, so Section 685.030 as amended continues the effect of former law. See Section 85 (limited civil cases) & Comment. [28 Cal.L.Rev.Comm. Reports 51 (1998)].

Subdivision (e) of Section 685.030 is amended to eliminate the difference in treatment between limited and unlimited civil cases.

For the register of actions in superior court, see Gov't Code 69845, 69845.5. For the register of actions in municipal court, see Code Civ. Proc. 1052, 1052.1.

A technical change is also made for conformity with preferred drafting style. [30 Cal.L.Rev.Comm. Reports 443 (2000)].

Research References

Rutter, Cal. Practice Guide: Enforcing Judgments/Debts Ch. 6A-5, Amount Recoverable Under Judgment.

8 Witkin Cal. Proc. 5th Enforcement of Judgment § 44, When Accrual Ceases.

§ 685.040. Costs; attorney's fees

The judgment creditor is entitled to the reasonable and necessary costs of enforcing a judgment. Attorney's fees incurred in enforcing a judgment are not included in costs collectible under this title unless otherwise provided by law. Attorney's fees incurred in enforcing a judgment are included as costs collectible under this title if the underlying judgment includes an award of attorney's fees to the judgment creditor pursuant to subparagraph (A) of paragraph (10) of subdivision (a) of Section 1033.5. *(Added by Stats.1982, c. 1364, p. 5081, § 2, operative July 1, 1983. Amended by Stats.1992, c. 1348 (A.B. 2616), § 3.)*

Research References

Rutter, Cal. Practice Guide: Civil Appeals & Writs Ch. 14-B, B. Recovery of Appellate Costs and Attorney Fees.

Rutter, Cal. Practice Guide: Civ. Pro. Before Trial Ch. 7(II)-F, F. Procedure.

Rutter, Cal. Practice Guide: Civil Trials & Evidence Ch. 17-E, E. Attorney Fees as Costs.

Rutter, Cal. Practice Guide: Enforcing Judgments/Debts Ch. 6A-5, Amount Recoverable Under Judgment.

Rutter, Cal. Practice Guide: Enforcing Judgments/Debts Ch. 6D-7, Sale and Collection of Property Levied Upon.

Rutter, Cal. Practice Guide: Enforcing Judgments/Debts Ch. 6G-4, Creditor's Suit.

Rutter, Cal. Practice Guide: Real Prop. Transactions Ch. 11-C, C. Seller's Remedies Upon Buyer's Breach-Damages and Specific Performance.

Miller and Starr California Real Estate § 34:66, Examples of Actions in Which Fees Can be Recovered.

Miller and Starr California Real Estate § 11:126, Relation to Subsequent Interests.

8 Witkin Cal. Proc. 5th Enforcement of Judgment § 46, in General.

8 Witkin Cal. Proc. 5th Enforcement of Judgment § 47, Memorandum of Costs.

8 Witkin Cal. Proc. 5th Enforcement of Judgment § 48, Motion for Costs.

8 Witkin Cal. Proc. 5th Enforcement of Judgment § 133, (S 133) Safe Deposit Boxes.

7 Witkin Cal. Proc. 5th Judgment § 137, (S 137) in General.

7 Witkin Cal. Proc. 5th Judgment § 138, (S 138) Attorneys' Fees.

§ 685.050. Levy under writ; costs and interests to be satisfied

(a) If a writ is issued pursuant to this title to enforce a judgment, the costs and interest to be satisfied in a levy under the writ are the following:

(1) The statutory fee for issuance of the writ.

(2) The amount of interest that has accrued from the date of entry or renewal of the judgment to the date of issuance of the writ, as adjusted for partial satisfactions, if the judgment creditor has filed an affidavit with the court clerk stating such amount.

(3) The amount of interest that accrues on the principal amount of the judgment remaining unsatisfied from the date of issuance of the writ until the date interest ceases to accrue.

(4) The levying officer's statutory costs for performing the duties under the writ.

(b) In a levy under the writ, the levying officer shall do all of the following:

(1) Collect the amount of costs and interest entered on the writ pursuant to paragraphs (1) and (2) of subdivision (a).

(2) Compute and collect the amount of additional interest required to be collected by paragraph (3) of subdivision (a) by reference to the daily interest entered on the writ. If amounts collected periodically do not fully satisfy the money judgment, the levying officer shall adjust the amount of daily interest to reflect the partial satisfactions, and make later collections by reference to the adjusted amount of daily interest.

(3) Determine and collect the amount of additional costs pursuant to paragraph (4) of subdivision (a). *(Added by Stats.1982, c. 1364, p. 5081, § 2, operative July 1, 1983. Amended by Stats.1992, c. 283 (S.B.1372), § 2, eff. July 21, 1992; Stats.2010, c. 4 (A.B.680), § 1.)*

Law Revision Commission Comments

Section 685.050 supersedes former Section 682.2 and a portion of former Section 1033.7. In addition to the costs collected pursuant to this section, the levying officer will also collect previously allowed costs that have been added to the judgment and are included in the principal amount of the judgment remaining unsatisfied. See Section 685.090. This section applies not only to writs of execution but also to writs of possession and of sale. See Section 712.040 (collection of money amounts included in judgment for possession or sale). For provisions applicable to

earnings withholding orders, see Section 706.010 et seq. [16 Cal.L.Rev. Comm. Reports 1232 (1982)].

Subdivision (b) of Section 685.050 is amended to permit recomputation of the amount of daily interest accruing on a money judgment in the case of partial satisfactions, in the discretion of the levying officer. See also Sections 685.010 (rate of interest on judgments), 685.030 (cessation of interest). The levying officer may condition recomputation on receiving adequate instructions from the judgment creditor. See Section 687.010. The benefit of recomputing the amount of daily interest is evident in the case of a continuing levy under an earnings withholding order. See Section 706.024 (amount required to satisfy earnings withholding order). The purpose of recomputation is to permit the full satisfaction of a money judgment during the course of a continuing levy, without the need to seek issuance of a new writ of execution or final earnings withholding order for costs and interest. See Section 685.030(a)(2), (c) (interest ceases to accrue on amount of partial satisfaction when amount received by levying officer); see also Sections 706.024(c) (cessation of interest on earnings withholding order), 706.028(d) (cessation of interest on final earnings withholding order for costs and interest). Recomputation also avoids the potential of collecting an excessive amount, which would occur if the full amount of daily interest noted on the writ of execution were collected without adjustment for partial satisfactions. [21 Cal.L.Rev.Comm.Reports 135 (1991)].

Research References

Rutter, Cal. Practice Guide: Enforcing Judgments/Debts Ch. 6A-5, Amount Recoverable Under Judgment.

Rutter, Cal. Practice Guide: Enforcing Judgments/Debts Ch. 6D-2, Writ of Execution.

8 Witkin Cal. Proc. 5th Enforcement of Judgment § 46, in General.

8 Witkin Cal. Proc. 5th Enforcement of Judgment § 47, Memorandum of Costs.

8 Witkin Cal. Proc. 5th Enforcement of Judgment § 54, Application of Money Received.

8 Witkin Cal. Proc. 5th Enforcement of Judgment § 158, (S 158) Order of Distribution.

8 Witkin Cal. Proc. 5th Enforcement of Judgment § 246, (S 246) Obtaining Full Satisfaction of Judgment.

§ 685.070. Judgment creditor's costs; memorandum; motion to tax costs

(a) The judgment creditor may claim under this section the following costs of enforcing a judgment:

(1) Statutory fees for preparing and issuing, and recording and indexing, an abstract of judgment or a certified copy of a judgment.

(2) Statutory fees for filing a notice of judgment lien on personal property.

(3) Statutory fees for issuing a writ for the enforcement of the judgment to the extent that the fees are not satisfied pursuant to Section 685.050.

(4) Statutory costs of the levying officer for performing the duties under a writ to the extent that the costs are not satisfied pursuant to Section 685.050 and the statutory fee of the levying officer for performing the duties under the Wage Garnishment Law to the extent that the fee has not been satisfied pursuant to the wage garnishment.

(5) Costs incurred in connection with any proceeding under Chapter 6 (commencing with Section 708.010) of Division 2 that have been approved as to amount, reasonableness, and necessity by the judge or referee conducting the proceeding.

(6) Attorney's fees, if allowed by Section 685.040.

(b) Before the judgment is fully satisfied but not later than two years after the costs have been incurred, the judgment creditor claiming costs under this section shall file a memorandum of costs with the court clerk and serve a copy on the judgment debtor. Service shall be made personally or by mail. The memorandum of costs shall be executed under oath by a person who has knowledge of the facts and shall state that to the person's best knowledge and belief the costs are correct, are reasonable and necessary, and have not been satisfied.

(c) Within 10 days after the memorandum of costs is served on the judgment debtor, the judgment debtor may apply to the court on noticed motion to have the costs taxed by the court. The notice of motion shall be served on the judgment creditor. Service shall be made personally or by mail. The court shall make an order allowing or disallowing the costs to the extent justified under the circumstances of the case.

(d) If no motion to tax costs is made within the time provided in subdivision (c), the costs claimed in the memorandum are allowed.

(e) If a memorandum of costs for the costs specified in subdivision (a) is filed at the same time as an application for a writ of execution, these statutory costs not already allowed by the court in an amount not to exceed one hundred dollars ($100) in the aggregate may be included in the amount specified in the writ of execution, subject to subsequent disallowance as ordered by the court pursuant to a motion to tax if filed by the debtor. The memorandum of costs shall contain the following statement: "The fees sought under this memorandum may be disallowed by a court upon a motion to tax filed by the debtor notwithstanding the fees having been included in the writ of execution." The inclusion of the above costs in the writ of execution or the pendency of the motion to tax on these costs shall not be cause for the clerk of the court to delay issuing the writ of execution or for the levying officer to delay enforcing the writ of execution.

(f) Section 1013, extending the time within which a right may be exercised or an act may be done, applies to this section. *(Added by Stats.1982, c. 1364, p. 5081, § 2, operative July 1, 1983. Amended by Stats.1990, c. 790 (S.B.2099), § 1; Stats.1992, c. 1348 (A.B.2616), § 4; Stats.1996, c. 60 (S.B.52), § 2.)*

Research References

Rutter, Cal. Practice Guide: Enforcing Judgments/Debts Ch. 6A-5, Amount Recoverable Under Judgment.
Rutter, Cal. Practice Guide: Enforcing Judgments/Debts Ch. 6G-4, Creditor's Suit.
Rutter, Cal. Practice Guide: Enforcing Judgments/Debts Ch. 6G-6, Receiver to Enforce Judgment-EJL Provisions.
Rutter, Cal. Practice Guide: Real Prop. Transactions Ch. 11-C, C. Seller's Remedies Upon Buyer's Breach-Damages and Specific Performance.
8 Witkin Cal. Proc. 5th Enforcement of Judgment § 46, in General.
8 Witkin Cal. Proc. 5th Enforcement of Judgment § 47, Memorandum of Costs.
8 Witkin Cal. Proc. 5th Enforcement of Judgment § 48, Motion for Costs.
8 Witkin Cal. Proc. 5th Enforcement of Judgment § 49, Addition of Costs to Judgment.
7 Witkin Cal. Proc. 5th Judgment § 137, (S 137) in General.
7 Witkin Cal. Proc. 5th Judgment § 139, (S 139) in General.
7 Witkin Cal. Proc. 5th Judgment § 143, (S 143) Memorandum or Motion After Judgment.
7 Witkin Cal. Proc. 5th Judgment § 144, (S 144) Motion to Strike or Tax Costs.

§ 685.080. Motion to claim costs; notice; service; order

(a) The judgment creditor may claim costs authorized by Section 685.040 by noticed motion. The motion shall be made before the judgment is satisfied in full, but not later than two years after the costs have been incurred. The costs claimed under this section may include, but are not limited to, costs that may be claimed under Section 685.070 and costs incurred but not approved by the court or referee in a proceeding under Chapter 6 (commencing with Section 708.010) of Division 2.

(b) The notice of motion shall describe the costs claimed, shall state their amount, and shall be supported by an affidavit of a person who has knowledge of the facts stating that to the person's best knowledge and belief the costs are correct, are reasonable and necessary, and have not been satisfied. The

notice of motion shall be served on the judgment debtor. Service shall be made personally or by mail.

(c) The court shall make an order allowing or disallowing the costs to the extent justified under the circumstances of the case. *(Added by Stats.1982, c. 1364, p. 5082, § 2, operative July 1, 1983.)*

Research References

Rutter, Cal. Practice Guide: Enforcing Judgments/Debts Ch. 6A-5, Amount Recoverable Under Judgment.
8 Witkin Cal. Proc. 5th Enforcement of Judgment § 48, Motion for Costs.
8 Witkin Cal. Proc. 5th Enforcement of Judgment § 333, (S 333) Execution of Writ of Possession.
7 Witkin Cal. Proc. 5th Judgment § 138, (S 138) Attorneys' Fees.
7 Witkin Cal. Proc. 5th Judgment § 143, (S 143) Memorandum or Motion After Judgment.

§ 685.090. Costs added to judgment; inclusion in unsatisfied principal; outstanding writs; inclusion in amount of sale or collection distributed

(a) Costs are added to and become a part of the judgment:

(1) Upon the filing of an order allowing the costs pursuant to this chapter.

(2) If a memorandum of costs is filed pursuant to Section 685.070 and no motion to tax is made, upon the expiration of the time for making the motion.

(3) As specified in Section 685.095.

(b) The costs added to the judgment pursuant to this section are included in the principal amount of the judgment remaining unsatisfied.

(c) If a writ or earnings withholding order is outstanding at the time the costs are added to the judgment pursuant to this section, the levying officer shall add the amount of those costs to the amount to be collected pursuant to the writ or earnings withholding order if the levying officer receives either of the following before the writ or earnings withholding order is returned:

(1) A certified copy of the court order allowing the costs.

(2) A certificate from the clerk of the court that the costs have been added to the judgment where the costs have been added to the judgment after a memorandum of costs has been filed pursuant to Section 685.070 and no motion to tax has been made within the time allowed for making the motion.

(d) The levying officer shall include the costs described in subdivision (c) in the amount of the sale or collection distributed to the judgment creditor only if the levying officer receives the certified copy of the court order or the clerk's certificate before the distribution is made. *(Added by Stats.1982, c. 1364, p. 5082, § 2, operative July 1, 1983. Amended by Stats.1992, c. 283 (S.B.1372), § 3, eff. July 21, 1992; Stats.1995, c. 576 (A.B.1225), § 3.)*

Law Revision Commission Comments

Subdivision (c) of Section 685.090 is amended to authorize the addition of costs to a judgment in a case where collection is being made under an earnings withholding order. See Sections 706.010–706.154 (Wage Garnishment Law). The procedure under subdivision (c) may by [sic] applied where the writ of execution has been returned pursuant to Section 699.560 and collection continues under the earnings withholding order. See Section 706.022. In this situation, costs may be added to the amount to be collected under the earnings withholding order without the need to obtain another writ of execution. [21 Cal.L.Rev.Comm.Reports 135 (1991)].

Research References

Rutter, Cal. Practice Guide: Civil Trials & Evidence Ch. 17-D, D. Costs.
Rutter, Cal. Practice Guide: Enforcing Judgments/Debts Ch. 6A-5, Amount Recoverable Under Judgment.

Rutter, Cal. Practice Guide: Enforcing Judgments/Debts Ch. 6F-8, Payment of Judgment Creditor; Satisfaction of Order; Duty to File Supplemental Return on Writ.

8 Witkin Cal. Proc. 5th Enforcement of Judgment § 21, Definitions.

8 Witkin Cal. Proc. 5th Enforcement of Judgment § 37, (S 37) Entry, Amount, and Notice.

8 Witkin Cal. Proc. 5th Enforcement of Judgment § 42, in General.

8 Witkin Cal. Proc. 5th Enforcement of Judgment § 46, in General.

8 Witkin Cal. Proc. 5th Enforcement of Judgment § 49, Addition of Costs to Judgment.

8 Witkin Cal. Proc. 5th Enforcement of Judgment § 53, Amount Satisfying Judgment.

8 Witkin Cal. Proc. 5th Enforcement of Judgment § 111, (S 111) Contents of Writ.

8 Witkin Cal. Proc. 5th Enforcement of Judgment § 246, (S 246) Obtaining Full Satisfaction of Judgment.

§ 685.095. Costs of service of writ by levying officer or registered process server added to judgment

When a writ is served by a levying officer or registered process server, the costs for that service, as determined pursuant to Section 1033.5, shall be added to and become part of the judgment. *(Added by Stats.1984, c. 759, § 3. Amended by Stats.1987, c. 1080, § 4.)*

Research References

8 Witkin Cal. Proc. 5th Enforcement of Judgment § 49, Addition of Costs to Judgment.

§ 685.100. Prerequisite to performance by levying officer of duty; prerequisite to taking property into custody; liability of levying officer

(a) Except as otherwise provided by law:

(1) As a prerequisite to the performance by the levying officer of a duty under this title, the judgment creditor shall deposit a sum of money with the levying officer sufficient to pay the costs of performing the duty.

(2) As a prerequisite to the taking of property into custody by the levying officer, whether by keeper or otherwise, the judgment creditor shall deposit with the levying officer a sum of money sufficient to pay the costs of taking the property and keeping it safely for a period not to exceed 15 days. If continuation of the custody of the property is required, the levying officer shall, from time to time, demand orally or in writing that the judgment creditor deposit additional amounts to cover estimated costs for periods not to exceed 30 days each. A written demand may be mailed or delivered to the judgment creditor. The judgment creditor has not less than three business days after receipt of the demand within which to comply with the demand. If the amount demanded is not paid within the time specified in the oral or written demand, the levying officer shall release the property.

(b) The levying officer is not liable for failure to take or hold property unless the judgment creditor has complied with the provisions of this section. *(Added by Stats.1982, c. 1364, p. 5083, § 2, operative July 1, 1983.)*

Law Revision Commission Comments

Subdivision (a)(1) of Section 685.100 makes more specific the requirement that costs of the levying officer be paid in advance. See Gov't Code §§ 6100, 24350.5. Subdivision (a)(2) is comparable to Section 488.050 (expenses in attachment) and recognizes the practice under former law of making an oral demand for costs.

The introductory clause of subdivision (a) recognizes that there are exceptions to the general rule stated in Section 685.100, such as where certain governmental agencies are judgment creditors. See, e.g., Labor Code § 101 (Labor Commissioner).

Similarly, certain creditors may not be required to prepay costs. See Section 1677 (collection of support payments under Uniform Reciprocal Enforcement of Support Act); Martin v. Superior Court, 176 Cal. 289, 296–97, 168 P. 135 (1917) (actions in forma pauperis).

Subdivision (b) is comparable to Section 488.060(a) (attachment). [16 Cal.L.Rev.Comm. Reports 1236 (1982)].

Research References

Rutter, Cal. Practice Guide: Enforcing Judgments/Debts Ch. 6D-3, Levy of Writ of Execution-In General.

Rutter, Cal. Practice Guide: Enforcing Judgments/Debts Ch. 6D-4, Levy on Specific Property.

Rutter, Cal. Practice Guide: Enforcing Judgments/Debts Ch. 6E-4, Opposing Claim of Exemption.

8 Witkin Cal. Proc. 5th Enforcement of Judgment § 30, Deposit to Cover Expenses.

8 Witkin Cal. Proc. 5th Enforcement of Judgment § 33, Liability of Officer.

8 Witkin Cal. Proc. 5th Enforcement of Judgment § 158, (S 158) Order of Distribution.

8 Witkin Cal. Proc. 5th Enforcement of Judgment § 186, (S 186) Disposition of Property During Proceedings.

§ 685.110. Prejudgment interest

Nothing in this chapter affects the law relating to prejudgment interest. *(Added by Stats.1982, c. 1364, p. 5083, § 2, operative July 1, 1983.)*

Research References

8 Witkin Cal. Proc. 5th Enforcement of Judgment § 42, in General.

CHAPTER 6. ENFORCEMENT AFTER DEATH OF JUDGMENT CREDITOR OR JUDGMENT DEBTOR

Section
686.010. Death of judgment creditor.
686.020. Death of judgment debtor.

§ 686.010. Death of judgment creditor

After the death of the judgment creditor, the judgment may be enforced as provided in this title by the judgment creditor's executor or administrator or successor in interest. *(Added by Stats.1982, c. 1364, p. 5084, § 2, operative July 1, 1983.)*

Law Revision Commission Comments

Section 686.010 continues former Section 686.010. The judgment is enforceable by the executor or administrator or successor in interest in the same manner as by a judgment creditor. [16 Cal.L.Rev.Comm. Reports 1237 (1982)].

Research References

Rutter, Cal. Practice Guide: Enforcing Judgments/Debts Ch. 6A-3, "Judgment," "Judgment Debtor" and "Judgment Creditor" Defined.

Rutter, Cal. Practice Guide: Enforcing Judgments/Debts Ch. 6G-22, Enforcement After Judgment Creditor's Death.

Miller and Starr California Real Estate § 32:55, Duration of the Judgment Lien.

8 Witkin Cal. Proc. 5th Enforcement of Judgment § 50, Enforcement After Death.

7 Witkin Cal. Proc. 5th Judgment § 6, (S 6) Effect on Enforcement of Judgment.

§ 686.020. Death of judgment debtor

After the death of the judgment debtor, enforcement of a judgment against property in the judgment debtor's estate is governed by the Probate Code, and not by this title. *(Added by Stats.1982, c. 1364, p. 5084, § 2, operative July 1, 1983. Amended by Stats.1989, c. 1416, § 21.)*

Law Revision Commission Comments

Section 686.020 continues former Section 686.020 and makes clear that, although various provisions of the Probate Code permit use of enforcement procedures provided in this title, the enforcement of a judgment against the judgment debtor after the death of the judgment debtor is governed by the Probate Code. See, e.g., Prob. Code §§ 716, 730, 732, 950. [16 Cal.L.Rev.Comm. Reports 1237 (1982)].

Section 686.020 is amended for conformity with the scope of the Probate Code provisions relating to enforcement of judgments. See Prob.Code §§ 9300–9304, 9391. As a consequence, property transferred subject to an enforcement lien before the death of the judgment debtor may be applied to the satisfaction of a money judgment using the same procedures that would have been available if the judgment debtor were still alive. See Section 695.070 (enforcement of lien after transfer). Under Section 686.020 and Probate Code Section 9300, after the death of a judgment debtor, enforcement of a judgment is governed by the Probate Code, not the Code of Civil Procedure. The language "and not by this title" is added to make this clear. For example, the filing of an abstract of judgment after death of the judgment debtor does not create a lien on estate property. See also Prob.Code § 9304 (conversion of attachment lien to judgment lien). [20 Cal.L.Rev.Comm.Reports 233 (1990)].

Research References

Rutter, Cal. Practice Guide: Enforcing Judgments/Debts Ch. 6G-23, Enforcement After Judgment Debtor's Death.
Miller and Starr California Real Estate § 32:32, Termination of the Attachment Lien.
Miller and Starr California Real Estate § 32:55, Duration of the Judgment Lien.
8 Witkin Cal. Proc. 5th Enforcement of Judgment § 50, Enforcement After Death.
7 Witkin Cal. Proc. 5th Judgment § 6, (S 6) Effect on Enforcement of Judgment.

CHAPTER 7. LEVYING OFFICERS

Section
687.010. Judgment creditor; instructions in writing; reliance on information; electronic transmission; instructions accompanied by writ of execution as electronic record.
687.020. Instruments; defined; endorsement.
687.030. Taking property into custody.
687.040. Liability; reliance on information; loss by fire, theft, injury or damage.
687.050. Levying officer's lien.

§ 687.010. Judgment creditor; instructions in writing; reliance on information; electronic transmission; instructions accompanied by writ of execution as electronic record

(a) The judgment creditor shall give the levying officer instructions in writing. The instructions shall * * * be signed by the judgment creditor's attorney of record or, if the judgment creditor does not have an attorney of record, by the judgment creditor. The instructions shall contain the information needed or requested by the levying officer to comply with this title, including, but not limited to, all of the following:

(1) An adequate description of any property to be levied upon.

(2) A statement whether the property is a dwelling.

(3) If the property is a dwelling, whether it is real or personal property.

(4) The name of the judgment debtor. If the judgment debtor is other than a natural person, the type of legal entity shall be stated.

(b) Subject to subdivision (c), the levying officer shall act in accordance with the written instructions to the extent the actions are taken in conformance with the provisions of this title.

(c) Except to the extent the levying officer has actual knowledge that the information is incorrect, the levying officer may rely on any information contained in the written instructions.

(d) The levying officer instructions may be transmitted electronically to the levying officer pursuant to Chapter 2 (commencing with Section 263) of Title 4 of Part 1.

(e) If the instructions directing the levying officer to perform a levy are accompanied by a writ of execution for money, possession, or sale of personal or real property issued by the court as an electronic record, as defined in subdivision (b) of Section 263.1, or a document printed from an electronic record issued by the court, the instructions shall also include all of the following information, as stated in the writ:

(1) The date of issuance of the writ.

(2) The name of each judgment creditor and judgment debtor.

(3) The amount of the total judgment for money, a description of the property subject to a judgment for possession or sale, or both the amount and the description.

(4) A statement indicating that the accompanying writ is either of the following:

(A) An original writ, or a copy of the original writ issued by the court as an electronic record, not already in the possession of the levying officer.

(B) A copy of the original writ already in possession of the levying officer.

(f) Except to the extent the levying officer has actual knowledge that the information in the electronic writ has been altered, the levying officer may proceed in the same manner as if in possession of a paper version of the original writ. *(Added by Stats.1982, c. 1364, p. 5084, § 2, operative July 1, 1983. Amended by Stats.2010, c. 680 (A.B.2394), § 5; Stats.2013, c. 156 (A.B. 1167), § 1.)*

Law Revision Commission Comments

Subdivision (a) of Section 687.010 is based on Section 488.010(a) (attachment) and on parts of subdivisions 2 and 3 of former Section 692 (sale of property). See also Sections 684.130 (address for notices), 699.530 (instructions for execution), 712.030 (instructions for writ of possession or sale).

Subdivisions (b) and (c) are consistent with Sections 262 (signed written instructions as excuse) and 687.040 (liability of levying officer). See also Section 684.130 (reliance on name and address given in instructions). [16 Cal.L.Rev.Comm. Reports 1238 (1982)].

Research References

Rutter, Cal. Practice Guide: Enforcing Judgments/Debts Ch. 6D-3, Levy of Writ of Execution-In General.
Rutter, Cal. Practice Guide: Enforcing Judgments/Debts Ch. 6D-4, Levy on Specific Property.
8 Witkin Cal. Proc. 5th Enforcement of Judgment § 29, Instructions from Judgment Creditor.
8 Witkin Cal. Proc. 5th Enforcement of Judgment § 103, (S 103) Levy by Registered Process Server.
8 Witkin Cal. Proc. 5th Enforcement of Judgment § 256, Service by Registered Process Server.
8 Witkin Cal. Proc. 5th Enforcement of Judgment § 333, (S 333) Execution of Writ of Possession.
5 Witkin, California Summary 10th Torts § 247, Illustrations Finding No Liability.

§ 687.020. Instruments; defined; endorsement

(a) As used in this section, "instrument" means a check, draft, money order, or other order for the withdrawal of money from a financial institution, the United States, any state, or any public entity within any state.

(b) If an instrument is payable to the judgment debtor on demand and comes into the possession of a levying officer pursuant to this title, the levying officer shall promptly endorse and present the instrument for payment.

(c) The levying officer shall endorse the instrument by writing on the instrument (1) the name of the judgment debtor, (2) the name and official title of the levying officer, (3) the title of the court where the judgment is entered, and (4) the date of entry of the judgment and where entered in the records of the court. The endorsement is as valid as if the instrument were endorsed by the judgment debtor. No financial institution or public entity on which the instrument is drawn is liable to any person for payment of the instrument to the levying officer rather than to the judgment debtor by reason of the endorsement. No levying officer is liable by reason of endorsing, presenting, and obtaining payment of the instrument.

(d) If it appears from the face of the instrument that it has been tendered to the judgment debtor in satisfaction of a claim or demand and that endorsement of the instrument is considered a release and satisfaction by the judgment debtor of the claim or demand, the levying officer shall not endorse the instrument unless the judgment debtor has first endorsed it to the levying officer. If the judgment debtor does not endorse the instrument to the levying officer, the levying officer shall hold the instrument for 30 days and is not liable to the judgment debtor or to any other person for delay in presenting it for payment. At the end of the 30-day holding period, the levying officer shall return the instrument to the maker. *(Added by Stats.1982, c. 1364, p. 5084, § 2, operative July 1, 1983.)*

Law Revision Commission Comments

Section 687.020 continues the substance of former Section 688(g) (which incorporated Section 488.520 in the Attachment Law by reference) except that (1) the former provision was limited to situations where an instrument comes into the possession of a levying officer or a receiver pursuant to a writ of execution whereas Section 687.020 is not so limited and (2) Section 687.020 adds a new provision in subdivision (d) for the return of the instrument to the maker after 30 days in certain cases. [16 Cal.L.Rev.Comm. Reports 1239 (1982)].

Research References

Rutter, Cal. Practice Guide: Enforcing Judgments/Debts Ch. 6D-4, Levy on Specific Property.
Rutter, Cal. Practice Guide: Enforcing Judgments/Debts Ch. 6D-7, Sale and Collection of Property Levied Upon.
8 Witkin Cal. Proc. 5th Enforcement of Judgment § 31, Indorsement and Collection of Instruments.
8 Witkin Cal. Proc. 5th Enforcement of Judgment § 33, Liability of Officer.
8 Witkin Cal. Proc. 5th Enforcement of Judgment § 130, (S 130) Instruments.
8 Witkin Cal. Proc. 5th Enforcement of Judgment § 143, (S 143) Duties of Obligor Under Instrument.
8 Witkin Cal. Proc. 5th Enforcement of Judgment § 144, (S 144) in General.

§ 687.030. Taking property into custody

Except as otherwise provided by statute, where the method of levy upon property requires that the property be taken into custody or where the levying officer is otherwise directed to take property into custody, the levying officer may do so by any of the following methods:

(a) Removing the property to a place of safekeeping.

(b) Installing a keeper.

(c) Otherwise obtaining possession or control of the property. *(Added by Stats.1982, c. 1364, p. 5085, § 2, operative July 1, 1983.)*

Law Revision Commission Comments

Section 687.030 continues the substance of the second sentence of former Section 688(c) except that Section 687.030 is not limited to custody under a writ of execution. The introductory clause recognizes exceptions to this general rule. See Sections 700.070 (keeper for tangible personal property of a going business), 700.080 (keeper for personal property used as dwelling).

Subdivision (c) is new and is intended to provide levying officers with a degree of flexibility in determining efficient and economical means of securing custody of personal property levied upon. Under this subdivision use of a keeper is not required in cases where the property is not moved to a place of safekeeping, but the custody obtained must be sufficient to prevent removal of the property. Such custody will be useful where property such as large construction equipment is levied upon. [16 Cal.L.Rev.Comm. Reports 1240 (1982)].

Research References

Rutter, Cal. Practice Guide: Enforcing Judgments/Debts Ch. 6D-4, Levy on Specific Property.
8 Witkin Cal. Proc. 5th Enforcement of Judgment § 32, Manner of Taking Custody of Property.
8 Witkin Cal. Proc. 5th Enforcement of Judgment § 124, Property in Possession of Debtor or Third Person.

§ 687.040. Liability; reliance on information; loss by fire, theft, injury or damage

(a) The levying officer or registered process server is not liable for actions taken in conformance with the provisions of this title, including actions taken in conformance with the provisions of this title in reliance on information contained in the written instructions of the judgment creditor, or in reliance on information provided to the levying officer by a registered process server pursuant to subdivision (d) of Section 699.080 or subdivision (e) of Section 706.101 or subdivision (b) of Section 715.040 or other provision, except to the extent the levying officer or registered process server has actual knowledge that the information is incorrect. Nothing in this subdivision limits any liability the judgment creditor may have if the levying officer or registered process server acts on the basis of incorrect information given in the written instructions.

(b) Unless the levying officer is negligent in the care or handling of the property, the levying officer is not liable to either the judgment debtor or the judgment creditor for loss by fire, theft, injury, or damage of any kind to personal property while (1) in the possession of the levying officer either in a warehouse or other storage place or in the custody of a keeper or (2) in transit to or from a warehouse or other storage place. *(Added by Stats.1982, c. 1364, p. 5085, § 2, operative July 1, 1983. Amended by Stats.1983, c. 155, § 11, eff. June 30, 1983, operative July 1, 1983.)*

Law Revision Commission Comments

Section 687.040 is amended to correct a cross-reference. [16 Cal. L.Rev.Comm. Reports 2194 (1982)].

Research References

Rutter, Cal. Practice Guide: Enforcing Judgments/Debts Ch. 6D-3, Levy of Writ of Execution-In General.
Rutter, Cal. Practice Guide: Enforcing Judgments/Debts Ch. 6D-4, Levy on Specific Property.
8 Witkin Cal. Proc. 5th Enforcement of Judgment § 33, Liability of Officer.
8 Witkin Cal. Proc. 5th Enforcement of Judgment § 103, (S 103) Levy by Registered Process Server.

§ 687.050. Levying officer's lien

The levying officer has a special lien, dependent upon possession, on personal property levied upon in the amount of the levying officer's costs for which an advance has not been made. *(Added by Stats.1982, c. 1364, p. 5085, § 2, operative July 1, 1983.)*

Research References

Rutter, Cal. Practice Guide: Enforcing Judgments/Debts Ch. 6D-3, Levy of Writ of Execution-In General.

8 Witkin Cal. Proc. 5th Enforcement of Judgment § 30, Deposit to Cover Expenses.

CHAPTER 8. ENFORCEMENT
OF STATE TAX LIABILITY

ARTICLE 1. ENFORCEMENT PURSUANT
TO WARRANT OR NOTICE OF LEVY

§ 688.010. Jurisdiction

A proceeding for the purpose of the remedies provided under this article is a limited civil case if (a) the amount of liability sought to be collected does not exceed the maximum amount in controversy for a limited civil case provided in Section 85, and (b) the legality of the liability being enforced is not contested by the person against whom enforcement is sought. *(Added by Stats.1982, c. 1364, p. 5085, § 2, operative July 1, 1983. Amended by Stats.1998, c. 931 (S.B.2139), § 89, eff. Sept. 28, 1998; Stats.2007, c. 43 (S.B.649), § 7.)*

Law Revision Commission Comments

Section 688.010 supersedes a portion of former Section 689d, a portion of the second sentence of former Section 690.51, and a portion of the second sentence of former Section 722.5. Under former law, jurisdiction was in the superior court exclusively. [16 Cal.L.Rev.Comm. Reports 1242 (1982)].

Section 688.010 is amended to reflect elimination of the justice court. Cal. Const. art. VI, §§ 1, 5(b). [28 Cal.L.Rev.Comm. Reports 51 (1998)].

Section 688.010 is amended to reflect unification of the municipal and superior courts pursuant to former Section 5(e) of Article VI of the California Constitution.

In a unified court system, the superior court has original jurisdiction of all causes except certain writ proceedings. Cal. Const. art. VI, § 10. Consequently, it is no longer necessary to specify which court has jurisdiction of a proceeding under this article. Language to that effect is deleted as obsolete.

Before unification, both the superior court and the municipal court had jurisdiction of a proceeding under this article if the amount sought was within the jurisdictional limit of the municipal court and the legality of the liability was uncontested. In a unified court system, that would be equivalent to permitting such a proceeding to be treated as either a limited civil case or an unlimited civil case. See Sections 85 & Comment (limited civil cases), 88 (unlimited civil cases). This concurrent jurisdiction feature is not continued. Under Section 688.010 as amended, it is mandatory, not optional, to treat a proceeding under this article as a limited civil case if the amount in controversy is within the maximum for a limited civil case and the legality of the liability is uncontested. [36 Cal.L.Rev.Comm. Reports 305 (2007)].

Research References

Rutter, Cal. Practice Guide: Civ. Pro. Before Trial Ch. 3-A, A. Subject Matter Jurisdiction (Competency).

Rutter, Cal. Practice Guide: Enforcing Judgments/Debts Ch. 6H-4, Hearing on Third Party Claim.

§ 688.020. Warrants issued by state; remedies; venue

(a) Except as otherwise provided by statute, if a warrant may properly be issued by the state, or by a department or agency of the state, pursuant to any provision of the Public Resources Code, Revenue and Taxation Code, or Unemployment Insurance Code, and the warrant may be levied with the same effect as a levy pursuant to a writ of execution, the state or the department or agency of the state authorized to issue the warrant may use any of the remedies available to a judgment creditor, including, but not limited to, those provided in Chapter 6 (commencing with Section 708.010) of Division 2.

(b) The proper court for the enforcement of those remedies is a court of any of the following counties:

(1) The county where the debtor resides.

(2) The county where the property against which enforcement is sought is located.

(3) If the debtor does not reside in this state, any county of this state.

(4) This section shall become operative on January 1, 2014. *(Added by Stats.2008, c. 552 (A.B.2578), § 2, operative Jan. 1, 2014.)*

Research References

8 Witkin Cal. Proc. 5th Enforcement of Judgment § 51, (S 51) in General.
8 Witkin Cal. Proc. 5th Enforcement of Judgment § 52, (S 52) Exemptions and Third-Party Claims.
8 Witkin Cal. Proc. 5th Enforcement of Judgment § 298, in General.
9 Witkin, California Summary 10th Taxation § 369, Enforcement and Collection.

§ 688.030. Levy upon property; exemptions; third party claims; notices; court hearing

(a) If pursuant to any provision of the Public Resources Code, Revenue and Taxation Code (excluding Sections 3201 to 3204, inclusive), or Unemployment Insurance Code, property is levied upon pursuant to a warrant or notice of levy issued by the state or by a department or agency of the state for the collection of a liability:

(1) If the debtor is a natural person, the debtor is entitled to the same exemptions to which a judgment debtor is entitled. Except as provided in subdivisions (b) and (c), the claim of exemption shall be made, heard, and determined as provided in Chapter 4 (commencing with Section 703.010) of Division 2 in the same manner as if the property were levied upon under a writ of execution.

(2) A third person may claim ownership or the right to possession of the property or a security interest in or lien on the property. Except as provided in subdivisions (b) and (c) or as otherwise provided by statute, the third-party claim shall be made, heard, and determined as provided in Division 4 (commencing with Section 720.010) in the same manner as if the property were levied upon under a writ of execution.

(b) In the case of a levy pursuant to a notice of levy:

(1) The claim of exemption or the third-party claim shall be filed with the state department or agency that issued the notice of levy.

(2) The state department or agency that issued the notice of levy shall perform the duties of the levying officer, except that the state department or agency need not give itself the notices that the levying officer is required to serve on a judgment creditor or creditor or the notices that a judgment creditor or creditor is required to give to the levying officer. The state department or agency in performing the duties of the levying

officer under this paragraph has no obligation to search public records or otherwise seek to determine whether any lien or encumbrance exists on property sold or collected.

(c) A claim of exemption or a third-party claim pursuant to this section shall be heard and determined in the superior court in the county where the property levied upon is located.

(d) This section shall become operative on January 1, 2014. *(Added by Stats.2008, c. 552 (A.B.2578), § 4, operative Jan. 1, 2014.)*

Research References

Rutter, Cal. Practice Guide: Enforcing Judgments/Debts Ch. 6D-7, Sale and Collection of Property Levied Upon.
Rutter, Cal. Practice Guide: Enforcing Judgments/Debts Ch. 6E-1, Introduction.
Rutter, Cal. Practice Guide: Enforcing Judgments/Debts Ch. 6E-3, Procedures for Claiming Exemptions.
Rutter, Cal. Practice Guide: Enforcing Judgments/Debts Ch. 6E-4, Opposing Claim of Exemption.
Rutter, Cal. Practice Guide: Enforcing Judgments/Debts Ch. 6H-2, Title or Possessory Claims to Real or Personal Property.
Rutter, Cal. Practice Guide: Enforcing Judgments/Debts Ch. 6H-4, Hearing on Third Party Claim.
8 Witkin Cal. Proc. 5th Enforcement of Judgment § 51, (S 51) in General.
8 Witkin Cal. Proc. 5th Enforcement of Judgment § 52, (S 52) Exemptions and Third-Party Claims.
8 Witkin Cal. Proc. 5th Enforcement of Judgment § 170, (S 170) Persons Entitled to Exemptions.

§ 688.040. Judgment creditor and judgment debtor defined

For the purpose of this article, as used in this title:

(a) "Judgment creditor" or "creditor" means the state or the department or agency of the state seeking to collect the liability.

(b) "Judgment debtor" or "debtor" means the debtor from whom the liability is sought to be collected. *(Added by Stats.1982, c. 1364, p. 5087, § 2, operative July 1, 1983.)*

Law Revision Commission Comments

Section 688.040 is new and is to make clear the meaning of the defined terms when applied in the context of this article. [16 Cal.L.Rev.Comm. Reports 1245 (1982)].

Research References

8 Witkin Cal. Proc. 5th Enforcement of Judgment § 51, (S 51) in General.

§ 688.050. Tax lien; date of creation

For the purpose of applying Section 694.080, 703.050, or 703.100, the date of creation of a tax lien is the earliest of the following times:

(a) The time when a notice of state tax lien is recorded or filed pursuant to Chapter 14 (commencing with Section 7150) of Division 7 of Title 1 of the Government Code.

(b) The time when the property is levied upon pursuant to a warrant or notice of levy or notice to withhold issued by the state or by a department or agency of the state.

(c) The time when any other act is performed that creates or perfects a lien on specific property as distinguished from a lien on the debtor's property generally. *(Added by Stats.1982, c. 1364, p. 5087, § 2, operative July 1, 1983.)*

Research References

8 Witkin Cal. Proc. 5th Enforcement of Judgment § 52, (S 52) Exemptions and Third-Party Claims.

ARTICLE 2. ENFORCEMENT OF JUDGMENT FOR TAXES

Section
688.110. Claim for taxes by public entity; enforcement of judgment.

§ 688.110. Claim for taxes by public entity; enforcement of judgment

Except as otherwise provided by statute, if a judgment is entered on a claim for taxes by a public entity, the judgment is enforceable pursuant to this title in the same manner as any other money judgment. *(Added by Stats.1982, c. 1364, p. 5087, § 2, operative July 1, 1983.)*

Law Revision Commission Comments

Section 688.110 is new and is consistent with Sections 3106, 6739, 14323, 14672, 16081, 16421, 18865, 32362, and 38524 of the Revenue and Taxation Code. For special provisions relating to wage garnishment for the collection of state taxes, see Sections 706.070–706.084. [16 Cal.L.Rev. Comm. Reports 1246 (1982)].

Research References

Rutter, Cal. Practice Guide: Enforcing Judgments/Debts Ch. 6A-2, Enforcement of Judgments Law ("Ejl")-Background.
8 Witkin Cal. Proc. 5th Enforcement of Judgment § 51, (S 51) in General.

CHAPTER 9. ENFORCEMENT OF SUPPORT JUDGMENTS

Section
689.010. Jurisdiction.
689.020. Issue and levy of warrants by local child support agency; remedies.
689.030. Levy on property; exemptions.
689.040. Authority of local child support agencies; delivery of writ of execution.
689.050. Definitions.

§ 689.010. Jurisdiction

For the purpose of the remedies provided under this chapter, jurisdiction is conferred upon the superior court. *(Added by Stats.1996, c. 957 (A.B.1058), § 4.)*

Research References

Rutter, Cal. Practice Guide: Enforcing Judgments/Debts Ch. 6H-4, Hearing on Third Party Claim.
8 Witkin Cal. Proc. 5th Enforcement of Judgment § 403, Available Remedies.
8 Witkin Cal. Proc. 5th Enforcement of Judgment § 405, Governmental Enforcement of Support Order.

§ 689.020. Issue and levy of warrants by local child support agency; remedies

(a) Except as otherwise provided by statute, whenever a warrant may properly be issued by a local child support agency pursuant to Section 17522 of the Family Code, and the warrant may be levied with the same effect as a levy pursuant to a writ of execution, the local child support agency may use any of the remedies available to a judgment creditor, including, but not limited to, those provided in Chapter 6 (commencing with Section 708.010) of Division 2.

(b) The proper court for the enforcement of the remedies provided under this chapter is the superior court in the county where the local child support agency enforcing the support obligation is located. *(Added by Stats.1996, c. 957 (A.B.1058), § 4. Amended by Stats.2000, c. 808 (A.B.1358), § 6, eff. Sept. 28, 2000.)*

Research References

Rutter, Cal. Practice Guide: Enforcing Judgments/Debts Ch. 6A-2, Enforcement of Judgments Law ("Ejl")-Background.
Rutter, Cal. Practice Guide: Enforcing Judgments/Debts Ch. 6E-4, Opposing Claim of Exemption.
Rutter, Cal. Practice Guide: Enforcing Judgments/Debts Ch. 6H-4, Hearing on Third Party Claim.

8 Witkin Cal. Proc. 5th Enforcement of Judgment § 405, Governmental Enforcement of Support Order.

11 Witkin, California Summary 10th Husband and Wife § 335, (S 335) Levy by Agency.

§ 689.030. Levy on property; exemptions

(a) Whenever the local child support agency, pursuant to Section 17522 of the Family Code, levies upon property pursuant to a warrant or notice of levy for the collection of a support obligation:

(1) If the debtor is a natural person, the debtor is entitled to the same exemptions to which a judgment debtor is entitled. Except as provided in subdivisions (b) and (c), the claim of exemption shall be made, heard, and determined as provided in Chapter 4 (commencing with Section 703.010) of Division 2 in the same manner as if the property were levied upon under a writ of execution.

(2) A third person may claim ownership or the right to possession of the property or a security interest in or lien on the property. Except as provided in subdivisions (b) and (c) or as otherwise provided by statute, the third-party claim shall be made, heard, and determined as provided in Division 4 (commencing with Section 720.010) in the same manner as if the property were levied upon under a writ of execution.

(b) In the case of a warrant or notice of levy issued pursuant to Section 17522 of the Family Code, the claim of exemption or the third-party claim shall be filed with the local child support agency that issued the warrant or notice of levy.

(c) A claim of exemption or a third-party claim pursuant to this section shall be heard and determined in the court specified in Section 689.010 in the county where the local child support agency enforcing the support obligation is located. *(Added by Stats.1996, c. 957 (A.B.1058), § 4. Amended by Stats.1997, c. 599 (A.B.573), § 1; Stats.2000, c. 808 (A.B.1358), § 7, eff. Sept. 28, 2000.)*

Research References

Rutter, Cal. Practice Guide: Enforcing Judgments/Debts Ch. 6E-1, Introduction.

Rutter, Cal. Practice Guide: Enforcing Judgments/Debts Ch. 6E-3, Procedures for Claiming Exemptions.

Rutter, Cal. Practice Guide: Enforcing Judgments/Debts Ch. 6E-4, Opposing Claim of Exemption.

Rutter, Cal. Practice Guide: Enforcing Judgments/Debts Ch. 6H-2, Title or Possessory Claims to Real or Personal Property.

Rutter, Cal. Practice Guide: Enforcing Judgments/Debts Ch. 6H-4, Hearing on Third Party Claim.

8 Witkin Cal. Proc. 5th Enforcement of Judgment § 180, (S 180) in General.

8 Witkin Cal. Proc. 5th Enforcement of Judgment § 364, (S 364) Nature and Scope of Remedy.

8 Witkin Cal. Proc. 5th Enforcement of Judgment § 405, Governmental Enforcement of Support Order.

11 Witkin, California Summary 10th Husband and Wife § 335, (S 335) Levy by Agency.

§ 689.040. Authority of local child support agencies; delivery of writ of execution

(a) Notwithstanding any other provision of law, in the case of a writ of execution issued by a court of competent jurisdiction pursuant to Chapter 3 (commencing with Section 699.010) and Chapter 5 (commencing with Section 706.010) of Division 2, the local child support agency, when enforcing a support obligation pursuant to Division 17 (commencing with Section 17000) of the Family Code, may perform the duties of the levying officer, except that the local child support agency need not give itself the notices that the levying officer is required to serve on a judgment creditor or creditor or the notices that a judgment creditor or creditor is required to give to the levying officer.

(b) Notwithstanding subdivision (a) of Section 700.140, if the writ of execution is for a deposit or credits or personal property in the possession or under the control of a bank or savings and loan association, the local child support agency may deliver or mail the writ of execution to a centralized location designated by the bank or savings and loan association. If the writ of execution is received at the designated central location, it will apply to all deposits and credits and personal property held by the bank or savings and loan association regardless of the location of that property. *(Added by Stats.1996, c. 957 (A.B.1058), § 4. Amended by Stats.2000, c. 808 (A.B.1358), § 8, eff. Sept. 28, 2000.)*

Research References

Rutter, Cal. Practice Guide: Enforcing Judgments/Debts Ch. 6D-3, Levy of Writ of Execution-In General.

Rutter, Cal. Practice Guide: Enforcing Judgments/Debts Ch. 6D-4, Levy on Specific Property.

Rutter, Cal. Practice Guide: Enforcing Judgments/Debts Ch. 6F-3, Issuance and Service of Earnings Withholding Orders.

Rutter, Cal. Practice Guide: Enforcing Judgments/Debts Ch. 6A-10, Service of Writs, Notices and Other Papers in Enforcement Proceedings.

8 Witkin Cal. Proc. 5th Enforcement of Judgment § 112, (S 112) Delivery and Execution of Writ.

8 Witkin Cal. Proc. 5th Enforcement of Judgment § 132, (S 132) Deposit Accounts.

8 Witkin Cal. Proc. 5th Enforcement of Judgment § 254, in General.

8 Witkin Cal. Proc. 5th Enforcement of Judgment § 405, Governmental Enforcement of Support Order.

11 Witkin, California Summary 10th Husband and Wife § 335, (S 335) Levy by Agency.

§ 689.050. Definitions

For the purpose of this chapter:

(a) "Judgment creditor" or "creditor" means the local child support agency seeking to collect a child or spousal support obligation pursuant to a support order.

(b) "Judgment debtor" or "debtor" means the debtor from whom the support obligation is sought to be collected. *(Added by Stats.1996, c. 957 (A.B.1058), § 4. Amended by Stats.2000, c. 808 (A.B.1358), § 9, eff. Sept. 28, 2000.)*

CHAPTER 20. TRANSITIONAL PROVISIONS

§ 694.010. Operative date and prior law defined

As used in this chapter:

(a) "Operative date" means July 1, 1983.

(b) "Prior law" means the applicable law in effect on June 30, 1983. *(Added by Stats.1982, c. 1364, p. 5102, § 2, operative July 1, 1983.)*

Research References

Rutter, Cal. Practice Guide: Enforcing Judgments/Debts Ch. 6A-2, Enforcement of Judgments Law ("Ejl")-Background.

8 Witkin Cal. Proc. 5th Enforcement of Judgment § 18, (S 18) in General.

§ 694.020.   Application of Title 9

Except as otherwise provided in this chapter, this title on and after its operative date applies to all proceedings commenced prior thereto unless in the opinion of the court application of a particular provision of this title would substantially interfere with the effective conduct of the proceedings or the rights of the parties or other interested persons, in which case the particular provision of this title does not apply and prior law applies. *(Added by Stats.1982, c. 1364, p. 5102, § 2, operative July 1, 1983.)*

Research References

Miller and Starr California Real Estate § 13:2, Basis for and Public Policy of the Homestead Exemptions.
Miller and Starr California Real Estate § 32:52, Previously Conveyed Property.

§ 694.030.   Period of enforcement; renewal

(a) Except for a judgment described in Section 683.310 or 683.320, the period for enforcement of a money judgment or a judgment for possession or sale of property entered prior to the operative date is governed on and after the operative date by Chapter 3 (commencing with Section 683.010).

(b) Notwithstanding subdivision (a), even though a judgment to which subdivision (a) applies is not renewable pursuant to Chapter 3 (commencing with Section 683.010) because the time for filing an application for renewal has expired, the judgment may be renewed under Chapter 3 (commencing with Section 683.010) if the court which entered the judgment determines, on noticed motion filed within two years after the operative date, that authority to enforce the judgment after the 10-year period provided in former Section 681 would have been granted if a motion had been made under former Section 685 and the court, in its discretion, makes an order authorizing the renewal of the judgment. The notice of motion shall be served personally or by mail on the judgment debtor. *(Added by Stats.1982, c. 1364, p. 5102, § 2, operative July 1, 1983.)*

Research References

Miller and Starr California Real Estate § 32:49, Real Property Subject to the Judgment Lien.
8 Witkin Cal. Proc. 5th Enforcement of Judgment § 18, (S 18) in General.

§ 694.040.   Enforcement procedures prior to operative date; prior law; manner of payment at sale

(a) Except as provided in subdivision (c), property levied upon or otherwise subjected to process for enforcement of a money judgment or a judgment for possession or sale of property prior to the operative date is subject to prior law relating to sale or delivery of possession.

(b) The duties to be performed in the execution of a writ or order for the enforcement of a money judgment or a judgment for possession or sale of property that is served prior to the operative date are governed by prior law.

(c) The manner of payment at a sale of property pursuant to a writ or order after the operative date is governed by Section 701.590. *(Added by Stats.1982, c. 1364, p. 5102, § 2, operative July 1, 1983.)*

Law Revision Commission Comments

Subdivisions (a) and (b) of Section 694.040 make clear that writs and orders served prior to the operative date are governed by prior law rather than this title, except that any sale is subject to the credit transaction provision of Section 701.590. [16 Cal.L.Rev.Comm. Reports 1262 (1982)].

§ 694.050.   Sale subject to right of redemption

(a) Except as provided in subdivision (b), property levied upon, or property to be sold upon which foreclosure or other proceedings for sale have been commenced, prior to the operative date that would have been sold subject to the right of redemption under prior law shall be sold subject to the right of redemption and may be redeemed as provided by prior law.

(b) If the judgment creditor and judgment debtor agree in writing, property described in subdivision (a) may be sold as provided in this title rather than subject to the right of redemption.

(c) Property sold prior to the operative date subject to the right of redemption under prior law may be redeemed as provided by prior law. *(Added by Stats.1982, c. 1364, p. 5102, § 2, operative July 1, 1983.)*

§ 694.060.   Creditor's suit against third party; commencement of action

Notwithstanding Section 708.230, an action may be commenced pursuant to Section 708.210 within one year after the operative date if the action could have been commenced under prior law on the day before the operative date. *(Added by Stats.1982, c. 1364, p. 5103, § 2, operative July 1, 1983.)*

Law Revision Commission Comments

Section 694.060 provides a one-year grace period for bringing a creditor's suit that would otherwise be barred by Section 708.230. [16 Cal.L.Rev.Comm. Reports 1263 (1982)].

§ 694.070.   Third party claims

(a) A third-party claim filed prior to the operative date is governed by prior law.

(b) A demand for a third-party claim served on a secured party prior to the operative date is governed by prior law. *(Added by Stats.1982, c. 1364, p. 5103, § 2, operative July 1, 1983.)*

Law Revision Commission Comments

Section 694.070 provides exceptions to the general rule governing application of this title provided by Section 694.020. [16 Cal.L.Rev. Comm. Reports 1264 (1982)].

§ 694.080.   Enforcement of money judgment; exemptions

The exemptions from enforcement of a money judgment provided by this title do not apply to property levied upon or otherwise subjected to a lien prior to the operative date. Whether such property is exempt is determined by the exemptions provided by law at the time the lien was created. *(Added by Stats.1982, c. 1364, p. 5103, § 2, operative July 1, 1983.)*

Law Revision Commission Comments

Section 694.080 facilitates the early application of Section 703.050 (exemptions in effect at time of lien govern). See Sections 703.050 and 703.060 and the Comments thereto. [16 Cal.L.Rev.Comm. Reports 1264 (1982)].

Research References

Rutter, Cal. Practice Guide: Enforcing Judgments/Debts Ch. 6E-1, Introduction.
Miller and Starr California Real Estate § 32:26, Claim of Exemption.
8 Witkin Cal. Proc. 5th Enforcement of Judgment § 18, (S 18) in General.
8 Witkin Cal. Proc. 5th Enforcement of Judgment § 52, (S 52) Exemptions and Third-Party Claims.

§ 694.090.   Declaration of homestead

On and after the operative date, a declaration of homestead made under prior law pursuant to Title 5 (commencing with Section 1237) of Part 4 of Division 2 of the Civil Code is effective only to the extent provided in Article 5 (commencing with

Section 704.910) of Chapter 4 of Division 2. *(Added by Stats.1982, c. 1364, p. 5103, § 2, operative July 1, 1983.)*

Research References

Rutter, Cal. Practice Guide: Enforcing Judgments/Debts Ch. 6E-6, "Homestead" Exemption.
8 Witkin Cal. Proc. 5th Enforcement of Judgment § 18, (S 18) in General.
8 Witkin Cal. Proc. 5th Enforcement of Judgment § 229, Development of Law.

Division 2

ENFORCEMENT OF MONEY JUDGMENTS

CHAPTER 1.   GENERAL PROVISIONS

ARTICLE 1.   PROPERTY SUBJECT TO ENFORCEMENT OF MONEY JUDGMENT

§ 695.010.   Property subject to enforcement generally

(a) Except as otherwise provided by law, all property of the judgment debtor is subject to enforcement of a money judgment.

(b) If property of the judgment debtor was attached in the action but was transferred before entry of the money judgment in favor of the judgment creditor, the property is subject to enforcement of the money judgment so long as the attachment lien remains effective. *(Added by Stats.1982, c. 1364, p. 5103, § 2, operative July 1, 1983. Amended by Stats.1984, c. 538, § 17.)*

Law Revision Commission Comments

Section 695.010 supersedes the first portion of subdivision (a) of former Section 688. The reference in former law to "any interest" in property and the enumeration of types of property subject to enforcement is not continued; all property of the judgment debtor, regardless of type or interest, is subject to enforcement of a money judgment unless an exception is provided by law. See also Civil Code §§ 1390.3, 1390.4 (enforcement against property subject to general power of appointment).

Some property that is not the judgment debtor's may also be subject to enforcement of a money judgment against the judgment debtor. See Section 695.020 (community property). For provisions governing liens on property that is transferred, see Sections 697.390 (judgment lien on real

property), 697.610 (judgment lien on personal property), 697.720–697.750 (execution lien). The introductory clause of Section 695.010 recognizes that some property of the judgment debtor is by law not subject to enforcement of a money judgment despite the general rule stated in Section 695.010. Property that is exempt by statute without the need to make an exemption claim is not subject to enforcement of a money judgment unless a particular exemption provision otherwise provides. See Section 703.030(b) (general rule). See also Sections 704.110(c) (public retirement plan benefits), 704.113 (public vacation credit), 704.115(c) (private retirement plan benefits), 706.052 (wage garnishment). Property of a public entity is not subject to enforcement of a money judgment under this division. See Section 695.050; Gov't Code §§ 965.5, 970.1. Property that is not transferable is generally not subject to enforcement. See Section 695.030. Certain property held in a fiduciary capacity may not be subject to enforcement. See, e.g., Civil Code § 986(a) (6) (amounts held for payment of artists); Educ.Code § 21116 (educational endowment property); Health & Saf.Code § 32508 (hospital endowment property); Labor Code § 270.5 (property held by logging employer as fund for wages). Specific property may be made not subject to enforcement by other statutes. See, e.g., Civil Code § 765 (estate at will); Health & Saf.Code § 7925 (cemetery funds); Labor Code § 4901 (workers' compensation). Federal law protects certain property from enforcement. See, e.g., 42 U.S.C. § 407 (social security).

Property of the judgment debtor that is by law not subject to enforcement of a money judgment may not be reached by any enforcement process, whether execution or otherwise. Certain property of the judgment debtor may be subject to enforcement by some, but not all, enforcement procedures. See, e.g., Section 699.720 (property not subject to execution but subject to other enforcement procedures. [16 Cal.L.Rev. Comm. Reports 1265 (1982)].

Subdivision (b) is added to Section 695.010 to make clear that property attached in the action is subject to enforcement even though it has been transferred. See Section 488.500 (attachment lien). Such property may be levied upon under a writ of execution after judgment without the need to bring a separate action to foreclose the lien. See Section 699.710 (property subject to execution). See also Section 697.340 (judgment lien does not reach real property transferred before judgment.) [17 Cal.L.Rev.Comm.Reports 1002 (1983)].

Research References

Rutter, Cal. Practice Guide: Enforcing Judgments/Debts Ch. 4-A, A. Attachment.
Rutter, Cal. Practice Guide: Enforcing Judgments/Debts Ch. 6B-2, Interests Subject to Judgment Lien.
Rutter, Cal. Practice Guide: Enforcing Judgments/Debts Ch. 6D-2, Writ of Execution.
Rutter, Cal. Practice Guide: Enforcing Judgments/Debts Ch. 6G-5, Assignment Order.
Rutter, Cal. Practice Guide: Enforcing Judgments/Debts Ch. 6G-7, Charging Orders Against Debtor Partnership/LLC Interests.
Rutter, Cal. Practice Guide: Enforcing Judgments/Debts Ch. 6I-3, Enforcement of Judgment for Possession of Real Property.
Rutter, Cal. Practice Guide: Enforcing Judgments/Debts Ch. 6A-11, Property Subject to Enforcement Procedures.
Miller and Starr California Real Estate § 19:2, Lease as Personal Property or Real Property.
Miller and Starr California Real Estate § 32:4, Effect.
Miller and Starr California Real Estate § 13:18, Termination by Voluntary Sale or Abandonment.
Miller and Starr California Real Estate § 13:48, Determination of the Liens Against the Homestead; Priorities.
Miller and Starr California Real Estate § 32:49, Real Property Subject to the Judgment Lien.
Miller and Starr California Real Estate § 32:52, Previously Conveyed Property.
Miller and Starr California Real Estate § 32:61, Property Interests Subject to Execution.
Miller and Starr California Real Estate § 11:125, Recordation of the Abstract of Judgment.
Miller and Starr California Real Estate § 11:127, Relation to Prior Interests.
Miller and Starr California Real Estate § 11:168, State Tax Liens--Personal Income and Corporate Franchise Tax Liens.
8 Witkin Cal. Proc. 5th Enforcement of Judgment § 23, Enforcement of Particular Judgments.
8 Witkin Cal. Proc. 5th Enforcement of Judgment § 55, (S 55) in General.

8 Witkin Cal. Proc. 5th Enforcement of Judgment § 58, (S 58) Community Property.

8 Witkin Cal. Proc. 5th Enforcement of Judgment § 59, (S 59) Attached Property Transferred Before Judgment.

8 Witkin Cal. Proc. 5th Enforcement of Judgment § 74, (S 74) Interests Subject to Lien.

8 Witkin Cal. Proc. 5th Enforcement of Judgment § 84, (S 84) Interests Subject to Lien.

8 Witkin Cal. Proc. 5th Enforcement of Judgment § 115, Property Subject to Execution.

8 Witkin Cal. Proc. 5th Enforcement of Judgment § 118, Property Subject to Levy.

§ 695.020. Community property

(a) Community property is subject to enforcement of a money judgment as provided in the Family Code.

(b) Unless the provision or context otherwise requires, if community property that is subject to enforcement of a money judgment is sought to be applied to the satisfaction of a money judgment:

(1) Any provision of this division that applies to the property of the judgment debtor or to obligations owed to the judgment debtor also applies to the community property interest of the spouse of the judgment debtor and to obligations owed to the other spouse that are community property.

(2) Any provision of this division that applies to property in the possession or under the control of the judgment debtor also applies to community property in the possession or under the control of the spouse of the judgment debtor. *(Added by Stats.1982, c. 1364, p. 5103, § 2, operative July 1, 1983. Amended by Stats.1983, c. 155, § 12, eff. June 30, 1983, operative July 1, 1983; Stats.1992, c. 163 (A.B.2641), § 33, operative Jan. 1, 1994.)*

Law Revision Commission Comments

Section 695.020 recognizes the rule that community property, including the interest of a nondebtor spouse, is generally subject to enforcement of a money judgment. For exceptions to this rule, see Civil Code Section 5100 et seq. [16 Cal.L.Rev.Comm. Reports 1266 (1982)].

Subdivision (b)(1) is amended to correct a typographical error. [16 Cal.L.Rev.Comm.Reports 2194 (1982)].

Subdivision (a) of Section 695.020 is amended to substitute a reference to the Family Code for the reference to the former Civil Code provisions. [22 Cal.L.Rev.Comm.Reports 1 (1992)].

Research References

Rutter, Cal. Practice Guide: Enforcing Judgments/Debts Ch. 6B-2, Interests Subject to Judgment Lien.

Rutter, Cal. Practice Guide: Enforcing Judgments/Debts Ch. 6D-7, Sale and Collection of Property Levied Upon.

Rutter, Cal. Practice Guide: Enforcing Judgments/Debts Form 6:P, Sample Levy Instructions.

Rutter, Cal. Practice Guide: Enforcing Judgments/Debts Ch. 6A-11, Property Subject to Enforcement Procedures.

Miller and Starr California Real Estate § 8:14, Deeds by Public or Court Officers.

Miller and Starr California Real Estate § 12:63, Liability for Debts and Judgments.

Miller and Starr California Real Estate § 32:50, Community Property.

Miller and Starr California Real Estate § 32:61, Property Interests Subject to Execution.

8 Witkin Cal. Proc. 5th Enforcement of Judgment § 55, (S 55) in General.

8 Witkin Cal. Proc. 5th Enforcement of Judgment § 58, (S 58) Community Property.

8 Witkin Cal. Proc. 5th Enforcement of Judgment § 173, (S 173) Application of Exemptions to Marital Property.

6 Witkin Cal. Proc. 5th Provisional Remedies § 79, (S 79) Community Property.

§ 695.030. Non-assignable and non-transferable property; interest in trust; cause of action for money or property

(a) Except as otherwise provided by statute, property of the judgment debtor that is not assignable or transferable is not subject to enforcement of a money judgment.

(b) The following property is subject to enforcement of a money judgment:

(1) An interest in a trust, to the extent provided by law.

(2) A cause of action for money or property that is the subject of a pending action or special proceeding. *(Added by Stats.1982, c. 1364, p. 5103, § 2, operative July 1, 1983. Amended by Stats.1986, c. 820, § 17, operative July 1, 1987.)*

Law Revision Commission Comments

Section 695.030 is amended to delete "spendthrift" from subdivision (b)(1) in recognition that trusts other than "spendthrift" trusts may be not assignable or transferable. See e.g., Prob.Code § 15302 (trust for support). [18 Cal.L.Rev.Comm. Reports 765 (1985)].

Research References

Rutter, Cal. Practice Guide: Enforcing Judgments/Debts Ch. 5-D, D. Involuntary Bankruptcy.

Rutter, Cal. Practice Guide: Enforcing Judgments/Debts Ch. 6G-7, Charging Orders Against Debtor Partnership/LLC Interests.

Rutter, Cal. Practice Guide: Enforcing Judgments/Debts Ch. 6A-11, Property Subject to Enforcement Procedures.

Rutter, Cal. Practice Guide: Insurance Litigation Ch. 12B-B, B. Bad Faith Refusal to Settle.

Miller and Starr California Real Estate § 28:77, Priority of Stop Payment Notices; Liability of Fund Holder.

Miller and Starr California Real Estate § 32:49, Real Property Subject to the Judgment Lien.

Miller and Starr California Real Estate § 32:61, Property Interests Subject to Execution.

8 Witkin Cal. Proc. 5th Enforcement of Judgment § 55, (S 55) in General.

8 Witkin Cal. Proc. 5th Enforcement of Judgment § 57, (S 57) Beneficial Interest in Trust.

8 Witkin Cal. Proc. 5th Enforcement of Judgment § 60, (S 60) in General.

8 Witkin Cal. Proc. 5th Enforcement of Judgment § 297, (S 297) Nature and Scope of Remedy.

13 Witkin, California Summary 10th Trusts § 23, Other Provisions Governing Trusts.

§ 695.035. Lessee's interest in real property; provisions in lease for termination or modification upon involuntary transfer or assignment

(a) A lessee's interest in real property may be applied to the satisfaction of a money judgment in any of the following circumstances:

(1) If the lessee has the right voluntarily to sublet the property or assign the interest in the lease.

(2) If the lessee has the right voluntarily to sublet the property or assign the interest in the lease subject to standards or conditions and the purchaser at the execution sale or other assignee agrees to comply with the standards or conditions that would have had to be complied with had the lessee voluntarily sublet the property or assigned the interest in the lease.

(3) If the lessee has the right voluntarily to sublet the property or assign the interest in the lease with the consent of the lessor, in which case the obligation of the lessor to consent to the assignment is subject to the same standard that would apply had the lessee voluntarily sublet the property or assigned the interest in the lease.

(4) In any other case, if the lessor consents in writing.

(b) A provision in a lease for the termination or modification of the lease upon an involuntary transfer or assignment of the lessee's interest is ineffective to the extent that such provision would prevent the application of the lessee's interest to the satisfaction of the money judgment under subdivision (a). *(Added by Stats.1982, c. 1364, p. 5104, § 2, operative July 1, 1983.)*

Research References

Rutter, Cal. Practice Guide: Enforcing Judgments/Debts Ch. 5-D, D. Involuntary Bankruptcy.

Civ. Pro.

Rutter, Cal. Practice Guide: Enforcing Judgments/Debts Ch. 6A-11, Property Subject to Enforcement Procedures.

Miller and Starr California Real Estate § 19:2, Lease as Personal Property or Real Property.

Miller and Starr California Real Estate § 19:69, Application of a Covenant or Condition Against Transfer.

Miller and Starr California Real Estate § 32:61, Property Interests Subject to Execution.

8 Witkin Cal. Proc. 5th Enforcement of Judgment § 55, (S 55) in General.

8 Witkin Cal. Proc. 5th Enforcement of Judgment § 56, (S 56) Leasehold Interest in Real Property.

§ 695.040.   Exempt property; release

Property that is not subject to enforcement of a money judgment may not be levied upon or in any other manner applied to the satisfaction of a money judgment. If property that is not subject to enforcement of a money judgment has been levied upon, the property may be released pursuant to the claim of exemption procedure provided in Article 2 (commencing with Section 703.510) of Chapter 4. *(Added by Stats.1982, c. 1364, p. 5104, § 2, operative July 1, 1983.)*

Law Revision Commission Comments

Section 695.040 is comparable to Section 703.510(b) (release of property exempt without making a claim). [16 Cal.L.Rev.Comm. Reports 1269 (1982)].

Research References

Rutter, Cal. Practice Guide: Enforcing Judgments/Debts Ch. 6A-11, Property Subject to Enforcement Procedures.

Miller and Starr California Real Estate § 32:61, Property Interests Subject to Execution.

8 Witkin Cal. Proc. 5th Enforcement of Judgment § 60, (S 60) in General.

8 Witkin Cal. Proc. 5th Enforcement of Judgment § 180, (S 180) in General.

§ 695.050.   Money judgment against public entity

A money judgment against a public entity is not enforceable under this division if the money judgment is subject to Chapter 1 (commencing with Section 965) of, or Article 1 (commencing with Section 970) of Chapter 2 of, Part 5 of Division 3.6 of Title 1 of the Government Code. *(Added by Stats.1982, c. 1364, p. 5104, § 2, operative July 1, 1983.)*

Law Revision Commission Comments

Section 695.050 continues existing law. See Government Code Sections 965.5(b) (state) and 970.1(b) (local public entities). See also Sections 683.320 and Comment to that section (period for enforcement of judgment), 712.070 (nonmoney judgments). [16 Cal.L.Rev.Comm. Reports 1269 (1982)].

Research References

Rutter, Cal. Practice Guide: Enforcing Judgments/Debts Ch. 6A-2, Enforcement of Judgments Law ("Ejl")-Background.

Rutter, Cal. Practice Guide: Enforcing Judgments/Debts Ch. 6D-2, Writ of Execution.

Rutter, Cal. Practice Guide: Enforcing Judgments/Debts Ch. 6I-1, Writ of Possession or Sale.

Miller and Starr California Real Estate § 32:61, Property Interests Subject to Execution.

8 Witkin Cal. Proc. 5th Enforcement of Judgment § 41, Exceptions to Application of Provisions.

8 Witkin Cal. Proc. 5th Enforcement of Judgment § 60, (S 60) in General.

8 Witkin Cal. Proc. 5th Enforcement of Judgment § 61, (S 61) Governmental Property.

8 Witkin Cal. Proc. 5th Enforcement of Judgment § 429, (S 429) Against State.

8 Witkin Cal. Proc. 5th Enforcement of Judgment § 432, Enforcement Mechanisms.

8 Witkin Cal. Proc. 5th Extraordinary Writs § 114, Enforcing or Vacating Judgment.

§ 695.060.   License to engage in business, profession or activity

Except as provided in Section 708.630, a license issued by a public entity to engage in any business, profession, or activity is not subject to enforcement of a money judgment. *(Added by Stats.1982, c. 1364, p. 5104, § 2, operative July 1, 1983.)*

Research References

Rutter, Cal. Practice Guide: Enforcing Judgments/Debts Ch. 5-D, D. Involuntary Bankruptcy.

Rutter, Cal. Practice Guide: Enforcing Judgments/Debts Ch. 6A-11, Property Subject to Enforcement Procedures.

Miller and Starr California Real Estate § 32:61, Property Interests Subject to Execution.

8 Witkin Cal. Proc. 5th Enforcement of Judgment § 60, (S 60) in General.

§ 695.070.   Transfer or encumbrance of property subject to lien

(a) Notwithstanding the transfer or encumbrance of property subject to a lien created under this division, if the property remains subject to the lien after the transfer or encumbrance, the money judgment may be enforced against the property in the same manner and to the same extent as if it had not been transferred or encumbered.

(b) If the judgment debtor dies after the transfer of property that remains subject to a lien created under this division, the money judgment may be enforced against the property as provided in subdivision (a). *(Added by Stats.1982, c. 1364, p. 5104, § 2, operative July 1, 1983. Amended by Stats.1989, c. 1416, § 22.)*

Law Revision Commission Comments

Section 695.070 is amended to clarify the manner of enforcement of a money judgment against property of a decedent in a situation where the property was transferred during the judgment debtor's lifetime subject to an enforcement lien. For provisions relating to continuation of liens after transfer, see Sections 697.390 (judgment line on real property), 697.610 (judgment lien on personal property), 697.720–697.750 (execution lien), 697.920 (other liens).

Under subdivision (b), the judgment creditor may enforce the money judgment against the transferred property after the judgment debtor's death using any appropriate procedure available before death. Thus, the death of the judgment debtor has no effect on the judgment creditor's remedies against property that was transferred subject to an enforcement lien. The judgment creditor may use a writ of execution, any other applicable enforcement procedure provided in this division, or an action against the owner of the property to foreclose the lien. Enforcement under this section may proceed only against the property subject to the lien and only in the amount of the lien on the transferred property, as is the case when enforcing a lien on transferred property while the judgment debtor is alive. See Sections 695.210 (amount required to satisfy judgment), 697.010 (amount of lien). As to enforcement of a judgment against property in the decedent's estate, see Code Civ.Proc. § 686.020 (enforcement against property in deceased judgment debtor's estate is governed by Probate Code); Prob.Code §§ 9300–9304 (enforcement of claims established by judgment). [20 Cal.L.Rev.Comm.Reports 233 (1990)].

Research References

Rutter, Cal. Practice Guide: Enforcing Judgments/Debts Ch. 6A-11, Property Subject to Enforcement Procedures.

Rutter, Cal. Practice Guide: Enforcing Judgments/Debts Ch. 6G-23, Enforcement After Judgment Debtor's Death.

Miller and Starr California Real Estate § 32:48, Nature and Creation.

Miller and Starr California Real Estate § 32:61, Property Interests Subject to Execution.

Miller and Starr California Real Estate § 11:123, Relation to Subsequent Interests.

Miller and Starr California Real Estate § 11:125, Recordation of the Abstract of Judgment.

Miller and Starr California Real Estate § 11:126, Relation to Subsequent Interests.

Miller and Starr California Real Estate § 11:127, Relation to Prior Interests.
Miller and Starr California Real Estate § 11:168, State Tax Liens--Personal Income and Corporate Franchise Tax Liens.
13 NO. 4 Miller & Starr, California Real Estate Newsalert 26, Involuntary Liens.
8 Witkin Cal. Proc. 5th Enforcement of Judgment § 55, (S 55) in General.
8 Witkin Cal. Proc. 5th Enforcement of Judgment § 92, (S 92) Creation and Duration.

ARTICLE 2. AMOUNT TO SATISFY MONEY JUDGMENT

Section
695.210. Amount required.
695.211. Interest accrual on arrearages; notice; statement of account; required contents.
695.220. Crediting of money received.
695.221. Crediting of money judgment for support.

§ 695.210. Amount required

The amount required to satisfy a money judgment is the total amount of the judgment as entered or renewed with the following additions and subtractions:

(a) The addition of costs added to the judgment pursuant to Section 685.090.

(b) The addition of interest added to the judgment as it accrues pursuant to Sections 685.010 to 685.030, inclusive.

(c) The subtraction of the amount of any partial satisfactions of the judgment.

(d) The subtraction of the amount of any portion of the judgment that is no longer enforceable. *(Added by Stats.1982, c. 1364, p. 5105, § 2, operative July 1, 1983. Amended by Stats.1992, c. 848 (S.B.1614), § 8, eff. Sept. 22, 1992; Stats.1993, c. 876 (S.B.1068), § 9, eff. Oct. 6, 1993.)*

Law Revision Commission Comments

Section 695.210 is new. For a related provision, see Section 680.300 ("principal amount of the judgment" defined). See also Section 577.5 (amount to be computed and stated in dollars and cents, rejecting fractions). [16 Cal.L.Rev.Comm. Reports 1270 (1982)].

Research References

Rutter, Cal. Practice Guide: Enforcing Judgments/Debts Ch. 6A-5, Amount Recoverable Under Judgment.
Rutter, Cal. Practice Guide: Enforcing Judgments/Debts Ch. 6B-5, Amount of Judgment Lien.
8 Witkin Cal. Proc. 5th Enforcement of Judgment § 53, Amount Satisfying Judgment.
8 Witkin Cal. Proc. 5th Enforcement of Judgment § 66, (S 66) Amount of Lien.
8 Witkin Cal. Proc. 5th Enforcement of Judgment § 75, (S 75) Amount of Lien.
8 Witkin Cal. Proc. 5th Enforcement of Judgment § 85, (S 85) Amount of Lien.
11 Witkin, California Summary 10th Husband and Wife § 250, (S 250) Definitions.

§ 695.211. Interest accrual on arrearages; notice; statement of account; required contents

(a) Every money judgment or order for child support shall provide notice that interest on arrearages accrues at the legal rate.

(b) The notice provisions required by this section shall be incorporated in the appropriate Judicial Council forms.

(c) Upon implementation of the California Child Support Automation System prescribed in Chapter 4 (commencing with Section 10080) of Part 1 of Division 9 of the Welfare and Institutions Code and certification of the California Child Support Automation System by the United States Department of Health and Human Services, whenever a statement of account is issued by the local child support agency in any child support action, the statement shall include a statement of an amount of current support, arrears, and interest due. *(Added by Stats.1994, c. 959 (A.B.3072), § 1, eff. Sept. 28, 1994. Amended by Stats. 2000, c. 808 (A.B.1358), § 10, eff. Sept. 28, 2000.)*

Research References

Rutter, Cal. Practice Guide: Family Law Ch. 6-A, A. Child Support.
8 Witkin Cal. Proc. 5th Enforcement of Judgment § 45, Support Orders.

§ 695.220. Crediting of money received

Money received in satisfaction of a money judgment, except a money judgment for support, is to be credited as follows:

(a) The money is first to be credited against the amounts described in subdivision (b) of Section 685.050 that are collected by the levying officer.

(b) Any remaining money is next to be credited against any fee due the court pursuant to Section 6103.5 or 68511.3 of the Government Code, which are to be remitted to the court by the levying officer.

(c) Any remaining money is next to be credited against the accrued interest that remains unsatisfied.

(d) Any remaining money is to be credited against the principal amount of the judgment remaining unsatisfied. If the judgment is payable in installments, the remaining money is to be credited against the matured installments in the order in which they matured. *(Added by Stats.1982, c. 1364, p. 5105, § 2, operative July 1, 1983. Amended by Stats.1992, c. 848 (S.B.1614), § 9, eff. Sept. 22, 1992; Stats.1993, c. 158 (A.B.392), § 3.2, eff. July 21, 1993; Stats.1993, c. 876 (S.B.1068), § 10, eff. Oct. 6, 1993; Stats.1993, c. 909 (S.B.15), § 1; Stats.1994, c. 146 (A.B. 3601), § 25; Stats.1994, c. 75 (A.B.1702), § 1, eff. May 20, 1994.)*

Law Revision Commission Comments

Section 695.220 is drawn from a portion of former Section 682.1 (writ of execution issued on money judgment), but Section 695.220 applies to any money received in satisfaction of the judgment not just that received pursuant to a levy of execution. See also the Comment to Section 724.010. [16 Cal.L.Rev.Comm. Reports 1270 (1982)].

Research References

Rutter, Cal. Practice Guide: Enforcing Judgments/Debts Ch. 6A-5, Amount Recoverable Under Judgment.
8 Witkin Cal. Proc. 5th Enforcement of Judgment § 54, Application of Money Received.
8 Witkin Cal. Proc. 5th Enforcement of Judgment § 58, (S 58) Community Property.
8 Witkin Cal. Proc. 5th Enforcement of Judgment § 158, (S 158) Order of Distribution.

§ 695.221. Crediting of money judgment for support

Satisfaction of a money judgment for support shall be credited as follows:

(a) The money shall first be credited against the current month's support.

(b) Any remaining money shall next be credited against the principal amount of the judgment remaining unsatisfied. If the judgment is payable in installments, the remaining money shall be credited against the matured installments in the order in which they matured.

(c) Any remaining money shall be credited against the accrued interest that remains unsatisfied.

(d) In cases enforced pursuant to Part D (commencing with Section 651) of Subchapter 4 of Chapter 7 of Title 42 of the United States Code, if a lump-sum payment is collected from a support obligor who has money judgments for support owing to more than one family, after the implementation of the California Child Support Automation System (CCSAS), all support collected shall be distributed pursuant to guidelines developed by the State Department of Child Support Services.

(e) Notwithstanding subdivisions (a), (b), and (c), a collection received as a result of a federal tax refund offset shall first be credited against the principal amount of past due support that has been assigned to the state pursuant to Section 11477 of the Welfare and Institutions Code and federal law and then any interest due on that past due support, prior to the principal amount of any other past due support remaining unsatisfied and then any interest due on that past due support.

(f) If federal law does not permit states to adopt the same order of distribution for the pre- and post-assistance child support arrears effective October 1, 1998, the following shall be the order of distribution of child support collections through September 30, 2000, except for federal tax refund offset collections, for child support received for families and children who are former recipients of Aid to Families with Dependent Children (AFDC) program benefits or former recipients of Temporary Assistance for Needy Families (TANF) program benefits:

(1) The money shall first be credited against the current month's support.

(2) Any remaining money shall next be credited against interest that accrued on arrearages owed to the family or children since leaving the AFDC program or the TANF program and then the arrearages.

(3) Any remaining money shall next be credited against interest that accrued on arrearages owed during the time the family or children received benefits under the AFDC program or the TANF program and then the arrearages.

(4) Any remaining money shall next be credited against interest that accrued on arrearages owed to the family or children prior to receiving benefits from the AFDC program or the TANF program and then the arrearages.

(g) If federal law does permit states to adopt the same order of distribution for the pre- and post-assistance child support arrears effective October 1, 1998, or effective October 1, 2000, whichever comes first, the following shall be the order of distribution of child support collections, except for federal tax refund offset collections, for child support received for families and children who are former recipients of AFDC program benefits or former recipients of TANF program benefits:

(1) The money shall first be credited against the current month's support.

(2) Any remaining money shall next be credited against the principal amount of the arrearages owed to the family or children since leaving the AFDC program or the TANF program and then the interest that accrued on those arrearages.

(3) Any remaining money shall next be credited against the principal amount of the arrearages owed to the family or children prior to receiving benefits from the AFDC program or the TANF program and then the interest that accrued on those arrearages.

(4) Any remaining money shall next be credited against the principal amount of the arrearages owed during the time the family or children received benefits under the AFDC program or the TANF program and then the interest that accrued on those arrearages.

(h) This section shall become operative on January 1, 2009. *(Added by Stats.2004, c. 305 (A.B.2669), § 2, operative Jan. 1, 2009.)*

Research References

Rutter, Cal. Practice Guide: Enforcing Judgments/Debts Ch. 6A-5, Amount Recoverable Under Judgment.
Rutter, Cal. Practice Guide: Family Law Ch. 6-A, A. Child Support.
8 Witkin Cal. Proc. 5th Enforcement of Judgment § 54, Application of Money Received.
8 Witkin Cal. Proc. 5th Enforcement of Judgment § 266, in General.
8 Witkin Cal. Proc. 5th Enforcement of Judgment § 403, Available Remedies.
10 Witkin, California Summary 10th Parent and Child § 393, Crediting Federal Retirement or Disability Payments.

CHAPTER 2.   LIENS

ARTICLE 1.   GENERAL PROVISIONS

§ 697.010.   Amount

Except as otherwise provided by statute, a lien created under this division or under Title 6.5 (commencing with Section 481.010) (attachment) is a lien for the amount required to satisfy the money judgment. *(Added by Stats.1982, c. 1364, p. 5105, § 2, operative July 1, 1983.)*

Law Revision Commission Comments

Section 697.010 makes clear that a lien is for the amount required to satisfy the judgment. See Section 695.210. For special rules as to the amount of the lien in the case of particular liens, see e.g., Sections 697.350 (judgment lien on real property), 697.540 (judgment lien on personal property), 706.029 (lien created by wage garnishment). These special rules prevail over Section 697.010 where applicable. [16 Cal.L.Rev. Comm. Reports 1271 (1982)].

Research References

Rutter, Cal. Practice Guide: Enforcing Judgments/Debts Ch. 4-A, A. Attachment.
Miller and Starr California Real Estate § 11:123, Relation to Subsequent Interests.
8 Witkin Cal. Proc. 5th Enforcement of Judgment § 64, (S 64) Statutory Basis for Lien.
8 Witkin Cal. Proc. 5th Enforcement of Judgment § 66, (S 66) Amount of Lien.

§ 697.020.   Priorities; third party rights

(a) If a lien is created on property pursuant to Title 6.5 (commencing with Section 481.010) (attachment) and after judgment in the action a lien is created pursuant to this division on the same property under the same claim while the earlier lien is in effect, the priority of the later lien relates back to the date the earlier lien was created.

(b) If a lien is created on property pursuant to this division and a later lien of the same or a different type is created pursuant to this division on the same property under the same judgment while the earlier lien is in effect, the priority of the later lien relates back to the date the earlier lien was created.

(c) Nothing in this section affects priorities or rights of third persons established while the earlier lien was in effect under the law governing the earlier lien. *(Added by Stats.1982, c. 1364, p. 5105, § 2, operative July 1, 1983.)*

Research References

Rutter, Cal. Practice Guide: Enforcing Judgments/Debts Ch. 4-A, A. Attachment.

Rutter, Cal. Practice Guide: Enforcing Judgments/Debts Ch. 6B-9, "Relation Back" to Attachment Lien.

Rutter, Cal. Practice Guide: Enforcing Judgments/Debts Ch. 6D-3, Levy of Writ of Execution-In General.

Rutter, Cal. Practice Guide: Enforcing Judgments/Debts Ch. 6D-7, Sale and Collection of Property Levied Upon.

Rutter, Cal. Practice Guide: Enforcing Judgments/Debts Ch. 6G-1, Examination of Judgment Debtor and Third Parties.

Rutter, Cal. Practice Guide: Enforcing Judgments/Debts Ch. 6G-4, Creditor's Suit.

Rutter, Cal. Practice Guide: Enforcing Judgments/Debts Ch. 6G-7, Charging Orders Against Debtor Partnership/LLC Interests.

Rutter, Cal. Practice Guide: Enforcing Judgments/Debts Ch. 6G-8, Lien in Pending Action.

Rutter, Cal. Practice Guide: Enforcing Judgments/Debts Ch. 6B-10, Enforcement of Real Property Judgment Lien; Execution Lien, Later-Created Real Property Judgment Lien "Relate Back" to Judgment Lien.

Miller and Starr California Real Estate § 32:4, Effect.

Miller and Starr California Real Estate § 8:14, Deeds by Public or Court Officers.

Miller and Starr California Real Estate § 32:48, Nature and Creation.

Miller and Starr California Real Estate § 32:56, Renewal of the Judgment Lien.

Miller and Starr California Real Estate § 32:64, Creation, Duration, and Effect of Writ of Execution.

Miller and Starr California Real Estate § 11:123, Relation to Subsequent Interests.

Miller and Starr California Real Estate § 11:126, Relation to Subsequent Interests.

Miller and Starr California Real Estate § 11:129, Priority of the Title of an Execution Sale Purchaser.

8 Witkin Cal. Proc. 5th Enforcement of Judgment § 68, (S 68) Relation Back and Priorities.

8 Witkin Cal. Proc. 5th Enforcement of Judgment § 77, (S 77) Priority of Liens.

8 Witkin Cal. Proc. 5th Enforcement of Judgment § 87, (S 87) Priority of Liens.

8 Witkin Cal. Proc. 5th Enforcement of Judgment § 92, (S 92) Creation and Duration.

8 Witkin Cal. Proc. 5th Enforcement of Judgment § 93, (S 93) Priorities.

§ 697.030. Duration

Subject to Sections 683.180 to 683.200, inclusive, and to Section 697.040, except where a shorter period is provided by statute, a lien created pursuant to this title is effective during the period of enforceability of the judgment. *(Added by Stats.1982, c. 1364, p. 5106, § 2, operative July 1, 1983.)*

Research References

Rutter, Cal. Practice Guide: Enforcing Judgments/Debts Ch. 6D-3, Levy of Writ of Execution-In General.

Rutter, Cal. Practice Guide: Enforcing Judgments/Debts Ch. 6F-2, Wage Garnishment-In General.

Rutter, Cal. Practice Guide: Enforcing Judgments/Debts Ch. 6G-4, Creditor's Suit.

Rutter, Cal. Practice Guide: Enforcing Judgments/Debts Ch. 6G-7, Charging Orders Against Debtor Partnership/LLC Interests.

Miller and Starr California Real Estate § 32:55, Duration of the Judgment Lien.

8 Witkin Cal. Proc. 5th Enforcement of Judgment § 67, (S 67) Duration and Extinguishment.

8 Witkin Cal. Proc. 5th Enforcement of Judgment § 69, in General.

8 Witkin Cal. Proc. 5th Enforcement of Judgment § 71, Installment Judgment for Support or Health Care.

§ 697.040. Stay of enforcement of judgment; effect on liens

(a) If enforcement of the judgment is stayed on appeal by the giving of a sufficient undertaking under Chapter 2 (commencing with Section 916) of Title 13:

(1) Existing liens created under this division are extinguished.

(2) New liens may not be created under this division during the period of the stay.

(b) Unless the court otherwise expressly orders, a stay of enforcement of the judgment under Section 918 does not extinguish or prevent the creation of a lien under Article 2 (commencing with Section 697.310) or Article 3 (commencing with Section 697.510); but, unless the court otherwise expressly orders, no other liens may be created or continued under this division during the period of the stay of enforcement.

(c) Unless the court expressly orders otherwise, if enforcement of the judgment is stayed pursuant to Section 1699 or 1710.50:

(1) Existing liens created under this division are extinguished.

(2) New liens may not be created under this division during the period of the stay. *(Added by Stats.1982, c. 1364, p. 5106, § 2, operative July 1, 1983.)*

Research References

Rutter, Cal. Practice Guide: Civil Appeals & Writs Ch. 7-C, C. Stay by Posting Security (Bond or Undertaking).

Rutter, Cal. Practice Guide: Enforcing Judgments/Debts Ch. 2-C, C. Tort Liability.

Rutter, Cal. Practice Guide: Enforcing Judgments/Debts Ch. 6D-6, Debtor's Recourse Against Execution Levy.

Rutter, Cal. Practice Guide: Enforcing Judgments/Debts Ch. 6F-2, Wage Garnishment-In General.

Rutter, Cal. Practice Guide: Enforcing Judgments/Debts Ch. 6G-7, Charging Orders Against Debtor Partnership/LLC Interests.

Rutter, Cal. Practice Guide: Enforcing Judgments/Debts Ch. 6J-2, Enforcing Sister State Judgments in California.

Miller and Starr California Real Estate § 32:58, Satisfaction or Release of the Judgment Lien.

8 Witkin Cal. Proc. 5th Enforcement of Judgment § 67, (S 67) Duration and Extinguishment.

§ 697.050. Lien extinguished; release

If a lien created pursuant to this division is extinguished, property held subject to the lien shall be released unless the property is to be held under another lien or the property is ordered by the court to be held pending resolution of a dispute concerning its proper disposition. *(Added by Stats.1982, c. 1364, p. 5106, § 2, operative July 1, 1983.)*

Law Revision Commission Comments

Section 697.050 is new and supersedes former subdivision (b) of Section 916. Section 697.050 requires the release of property when the lien is extinguished, except if it is subject to another lien (such as an execution lien in favor of another creditor) or if the court has ordered property to be retained (such as in proceedings on a third-party claim). See also Article 5 (commencing with Section 701.010) of Chapter 3 (duties and liabilities of third persons). If the property was levied upon by a levying officer, release is governed by Section 699.060. [16 Cal.L.Rev.Comm. Reports 1275 (1982)].

Research References

Rutter, Cal. Practice Guide: Civil Appeals & Writs Ch. 7-C, C. Stay by Posting Security (Bond or Undertaking).

Rutter, Cal. Practice Guide: Enforcing Judgments/Debts Ch. 6D-6, Debtor's Recourse Against Execution Levy.

Miller and Starr California Real Estate § 32:58, Satisfaction or Release of the Judgment Lien.

8 Witkin Cal. Proc. 5th Enforcement of Judgment § 67, (S 67) Duration and Extinguishment.

§ 697.060. Creation of judgment liens

(a) An abstract or certified copy of a money judgment of a court of the United States that is enforceable in this state may be recorded to create a judgment lien on real property pursuant to Article 2 (commencing with Section 697.310).

(b) A notice of judgment lien based on a money judgment of a court of the United States that is enforceable in this state may be filed to create a judgment lien on personal property pursuant to Article 3 (commencing with Section 697.510). *(Added by Stats.1982, c. 1364, p. 5106, § 2, operative July 1, 1983.)*

Research References

Rutter, Cal. Practice Guide: Enforcing Judgments/Debts Ch. 6B-3, Creation of Judgment Lien.
Rutter, Cal. Practice Guide: Enforcing Judgments/Debts Ch. 6C-3, Creation of Jlpp-Notice of Judgment Lien.
Miller and Starr California Real Estate § 32:48, Nature and Creation.
Miller and Starr California Real Estate § 11:125, Recordation of the Abstract of Judgment.
8 Witkin Cal. Proc. 5th Enforcement of Judgment § 69, in General.
8 Witkin Cal. Proc. 5th Enforcement of Judgment § 83, (S 83) Creation and Duration.

ARTICLE 2. JUDGMENT LIEN ON REAL PROPERTY

§ 697.310. Creation and duration of lien generally

(a) Except as otherwise provided by statute, a judgment lien on real property is created under this section by recording an abstract of a money judgment with the county recorder.

(b) Unless the money judgment is satisfied or the judgment lien is released, subject to Section 683.180 (renewal of judgment), a judgment lien created under this section continues until 10 years from the date of entry of the judgment.

(c) The creation and duration of a judgment lien under a money judgment entered pursuant to Section 117 or 582.5 of this code or Section 16380 of the Vehicle Code or under a similar judgment is governed by this section, notwithstanding that the judgment may be payable in installments. *(Added by Stats.1982, c. 1364, p. 5106, § 2, operative July 1, 1983. Amended by Stats.1998, c. 931 (S.B.2139), § 90, eff. Sept. 28, 1998.)*

Law Revision Commission Comments

Section 697.310 is amended to reflect relocation of the substance of former Section 85 to Section 582.5. [28 Cal.L.Rev.Comm. Reports 51 (1998)].

Research References

Rutter, Cal. Practice Guide: Enforcing Judgments/Debts Ch. 6B-2, Interests Subject to Judgment Lien.
Rutter, Cal. Practice Guide: Enforcing Judgments/Debts Ch. 6B-3, Creation of Judgment Lien.
Rutter, Cal. Practice Guide: Enforcing Judgments/Debts Ch. 6B-6, Duration of Real Property Judgment Lien.
Miller and Starr California Real Estate § 11:6, Instruments Subject to Recording--List of Recordable Documents.
Miller and Starr California Real Estate § 13:48, Determination of the Liens Against the Homestead; Priorities.
Miller and Starr California Real Estate § 31:63, Enforcement of a Money Judgment Against a Mobilehome.
Miller and Starr California Real Estate § 32:48, Nature and Creation.
Miller and Starr California Real Estate § 32:55, Duration of the Judgment Lien.
Miller and Starr California Real Estate § 11:152, Effect of Lis Pendens on Prior Interests.
Miller and Starr California Real Estate § 11:164, Personal Property Tax Liens.
Miller and Starr California Real Estate § 11:168, State Tax Liens--Personal Income and Corporate Franchise Tax Liens.
17 NO. 5 Miller & Starr, California Real Estate Newsalert 17, Remedies.
22 NO. 1 Miller & Starr, California Real Estate Newsalert 6, Common Interest Developments.
8 Witkin Cal. Proc. 5th Enforcement of Judgment § 69, in General.
8 Witkin Cal. Proc. 5th Enforcement of Judgment § 70, Abstract of Judgment.
8 Witkin Cal. Proc. 5th Enforcement of Judgment § 72, Workers' Compensation Award.
8 Witkin Cal. Proc. 5th Enforcement of Judgment § 73, Sister State Judgment.
8 Witkin Cal. Proc. 5th Enforcement of Judgment § 77, (S 77) Priority of Liens.
8 Witkin Cal. Proc. 5th Enforcement of Judgment § 78, (S 78) Transfer or Encumbrance of Interest.
8 Witkin Cal. Proc. 5th Enforcement of Judgment § 235, (S 235) Attachment of Judgment Lien.
8 Witkin Cal. Proc. 5th Enforcement of Judgment § 388, Creditor's Duty.
7 Witkin Cal. Proc. 5th Judgment § 64, Abstract of Judgment.

§ 697.320. Judgment for support payable in installments; judgment against health care provider requiring periodic payments; creation and duration

(a) A judgment lien on real property is created under this section by recording an abstract, a notice of support judgment, an interstate lien form promulgated by the federal Secretary of Health and Human Services pursuant to Section 652(a)(11) of Title 42 of the United States Code, or a certified copy of either of the following money judgments with the county recorder:

(1) A judgment for child, family, or spousal support payable in installments.

(2) A judgment entered pursuant to Section 667.7 (judgment against health care provider requiring periodic payments).

(b) Unless the money judgment is satisfied or the judgment lien is released, a judgment lien created under paragraph (1) of subdivision (a) or by recording an interstate lien form, as described in subdivision (a), continues during the period the judgment remains enforceable. Unless the money judgment is satisfied or the judgment lien is released, a judgment lien created under paragraph (2) of subdivision (a) continues for a period of 10 years from the date of its creation. The duration of a judgment lien created under paragraph (2) of subdivision (a) may be extended any number of times by recording, during the time the judgment lien is in existence, a certified copy of the judgment in the manner provided in this section for the initial recording; this rerecording has the effect of extending the duration of the judgment lien created under paragraph (2) of subdivision (a) until 10 years from the date of the rerecording. *(Added by Stats.1982, c. 1364, p. 5107, § 2, operative July 1, 1983. Amended by Stats.1986, c. 946, § 2; Stats.1992, c. 163 (A.B.2641), § 34, operative Jan. 1, 1994; Stats.1993, c. 876 (S.B.1068), § 12, eff. Oct. 6, 1993; Stats.1997, c. 599 (A.B.573), § 3; Stats.2002, c. 927 (A.B.3032), § 1.5.)*

Law Revision Commission Comments

Subdivision (a)(1) of Section 697.320 is amended to make clear that Section 697.320 applies to a judgment for family support. See Fam. Code § 4501 (family support order is enforceable in same manner and to same extent as child support order). See also Section 680.145 ("child support" includes family support). [22 Cal.L.Rev.Comm.Reports 1 (1992)].

Research References

Rutter, Cal. Practice Guide: Enforcing Judgments/Debts Ch. 6A-7, Period During Which Judgment Enforceable; Renewal Procedures.

Rutter, Cal. Practice Guide: Enforcing Judgments/Debts Ch. 6B-3, Creation of Judgment Lien.

Rutter, Cal. Practice Guide: Enforcing Judgments/Debts Ch. 6B-5, Amount of Judgment Lien.

Rutter, Cal. Practice Guide: Enforcing Judgments/Debts Ch. 6B-6, Duration of Real Property Judgment Lien.

Rutter, Cal. Practice Guide: Enforcing Judgments/Debts Ch. 6D-8, Special Requirements for Sale of Real Property Dwellings.

Rutter, Cal. Practice Guide: Enforcing Judgments/Debts Ch. 6E-6, "Homestead" Exemption.

Miller and Starr California Real Estate § 11:6, Instruments Subject to Recording--List of Recordable Documents.

Miller and Starr California Real Estate § 13:3, Effect of the Homestead Exemptions; in General.

Miller and Starr California Real Estate § 13:9, Effect of Death of an Owner, or Dissolution of the Marriage or Registered Domestic Partnership.

Miller and Starr California Real Estate § 32:48, Nature and Creation.

Miller and Starr California Real Estate § 32:56, Renewal of the Judgment Lien.

Miller and Starr California Real Estate § 11:126, Relation to Subsequent Interests.

8 Witkin Cal. Proc. 5th Enforcement of Judgment § 39, (S 39) Extending Duration of Liens.

8 Witkin Cal. Proc. 5th Enforcement of Judgment § 71, Installment Judgment for Support or Health Care.

8 Witkin Cal. Proc. 5th Enforcement of Judgment § 72, Workers' Compensation Award.

8 Witkin Cal. Proc. 5th Enforcement of Judgment § 75, (S 75) Amount of Lien.

8 Witkin Cal. Proc. 5th Enforcement of Judgment § 77, (S 77) Priority of Liens.

8 Witkin Cal. Proc. 5th Enforcement of Judgment § 78, (S 78) Transfer or Encumbrance of Interest.

8 Witkin Cal. Proc. 5th Enforcement of Judgment § 220, (S 220) Application.

8 Witkin Cal. Proc. 5th Enforcement of Judgment § 235, (S 235) Attachment of Judgment Lien.

8 Witkin Cal. Proc. 5th Enforcement of Judgment § 394, (S 394) Demand for Acknowledgment.

11 Witkin, California Summary 10th Husband and Wife § 267, (S 267) Judgment Lien.

§ 697.330. Workers' compensation orders; judgments for lump sum or payment in installments; creation and duration of lien

(a) In the case of a money judgment entered on an order, decision, or award made under Division 4 (commencing with Section 3200) of the Labor Code (workers' compensation):

(1) If the judgment is for a lump sum, a judgment lien on real property is created by recording an abstract of the judgment as provided in Section 697.310 and, except as otherwise provided in Division 4 (commencing with Section 3200) of the Labor Code, the judgment lien is governed by the provisions applicable to a judgment lien created under Section 697.310.

(2) If the judgment is for the payment of money in installments, a judgment lien on real property is created by recording a certified copy of the judgment as provided in Section 697.320 and, except as otherwise provided in Division 4 (commencing with Section 3200) of the Labor Code, the lien is governed by the provisions applicable to a judgment lien created under Section 697.320.

(b) Nothing in this section limits or affects any provision of Division 4 (commencing with Section 3200) of the Labor Code. *(Added by Stats.1982, c. 1364, p. 5107, § 2, operative July 1, 1983.)*

Law Revision Commission Comments

Section 697.330 is a new provision intended to make clear the effect of a judgment lien where the judgment is entered on a workers' compensation award. No cases have been found where a judgment lien (as distinguished from an execution lien) was sought to be created pursuant to a workers' compensation award. However, subdivision (a)(1) of Section 697.330 states the result that would appear to have been reached under former law, since an abstract of a lump-sum money judgment could be recorded to create a judgment lien under a provision formerly found in Section 674 and there was no exclusion of lump-sum judgments entered on workers' compensation awards. Subdivision (a)(2) treats an installment judgment entered on a workers' compensation award the same as an installment judgment for support.

Subdivision (a) is subject to the provisions of Division 4 of the Labor Code which provide the manner of enforcement of an order, decision, or award made under that division. See, e.g., Labor Code §§ 5300 (exclusive jurisdiction of appeals board for enforcement of award), 5808 (stay of execution of judgment entered upon an order, decision, or award), 5809 (order for entry of satisfaction of the judgment). See also Labor Code §§ 5600–5603 (issuance of writs of attachment upon order of appeals board), 5800 (interest on awards), 5806 (entry of judgment on award), 5955–6002 (stay of enforcement by court). It should be noted that the appeals board has authority to commute a workers' compensation award payable in installments to a lump sum. Labor Code §§ 5100–5106. If this authority is exercised, a judgment lien can then be created as provided in subdivision (a)(1) of Section 697.330. [16 Cal.L.Rev.Comm. Reports 1278 (1982)].

Research References

Rutter, Cal. Practice Guide: Enforcing Judgments/Debts Ch. 6A-7, Period During Which Judgment Enforceable; Renewal Procedures.

Rutter, Cal. Practice Guide: Enforcing Judgments/Debts Ch. 6B-3, Creation of Judgment Lien.

Rutter, Cal. Practice Guide: Enforcing Judgments/Debts Ch. 6B-6, Duration of Real Property Judgment Lien.

8 Witkin Cal. Proc. 5th Enforcement of Judgment § 39, (S 39) Extending Duration of Liens.

8 Witkin Cal. Proc. 5th Enforcement of Judgment § 72, Workers' Compensation Award.

§ 697.340. Interests in real property subject to attachment

Except as provided in Section 704.950:

(a) A judgment lien on real property attaches to all interests in real property in the county where the lien is created (whether present or future, vested or contingent, legal or equitable) that are subject to enforcement of the money judgment against the judgment debtor pursuant to Article 1 (commencing with Section 695.010) of Chapter 1 at the time the lien was created, but does not reach rental payments, a leasehold estate with an unexpired term of less than two years, the interest of a beneficiary under a trust, or real property that is subject to an attachment lien in favor of the creditor and was transferred before judgment.

(b) If any interest in real property in the county on which a judgment lien could be created under subdivision (a) is acquired after the judgment lien was created, the judgment lien attaches to such interest at the time it is acquired. *(Added by Stats.1982, c. 1364, p. 5107, § 2, operative July 1, 1983. Amended by Stats.1984, c. 538, § 18.)*

Research References

Rutter, Cal. Practice Guide: Enforcing Judgments/Debts Ch. 6B-2, Interests Subject to Judgment Lien.

Miller and Starr California Real Estate § 19:2, Lease as Personal Property or Real Property.

Miller and Starr California Real Estate § 13:48, Determination of the Liens Against the Homestead; Priorities.

§ 697.350.   Amount of lien

(a) Except as otherwise provided by statute, a judgment lien on real property is a lien for the amount required to satisfy the money judgment.

(b) A judgment lien on real property created under a money judgment payable in installments pursuant to Section 116.620 or 582.5 of this code or Section 16380 of the Vehicle Code or under a similar judgment is in the full amount required to satisfy the judgment, but the judgment lien may not be enforced for the amount of unmatured installments unless the court so orders.

(c) A judgment lien created pursuant to Section 697.320 is a lien for the amount of the installments as they mature under the terms of the judgment, plus accrued interest and the costs as they are added to the judgment pursuant to Chapter 5 (commencing with Section 685.010) of Division 1, and less the amount of any partial satisfactions, but does not become a lien for any installment until it becomes due and payable under the terms of the judgment. *(Added by Stats.1982, c. 1364, p. 5107, § 2, operative July 1, 1983. Amended by Stats.1998, c. 931 (S.B.2139), § 91, eff. Sept. 28, 1998; Stats.2009, c. 140 (A.B.1164), § 39.)*

Law Revision Commission Comments

Subdivision (a) of Section 697.350 provides the general rule governing the amount of judgment liens on real property. The lien is for the amount required to satisfy the judgment (Section 695.210).

Subdivision (b) makes clear that liens under three types of installment judgments are for the full amount required to satisfy the judgment (Section 695.210). This provision protects the judgment lienholder's priority over subsequent transferees and encumbrancers. See Section 697.390. However, as provided in subdivision (b), only the matured installments are enforceable in the absence of a court order. This will preclude enforcement of the judgment lien for amounts not yet due where such enforcement would defeat the purpose of permitting installment payments.

Subdivision (c) continues the substance of portions of former Sections 674.5 (support judgments) and 674.7 (installment judgment against health care provider) and provides the same rule for workers' compensation judgments payable in installments (Section 697.330). As to the duration of the lien, see Section 697.320(b) and the Comment to that section. [16 Cal.L.Rev.Comm. Reports 1280 (1982)].

Section 697.350 is amended to reflect relocation of the substance of former Section 85 to Section 582.5. [28 Cal.L.Rev.Comm. Reports 51 (1998)].

Research References

§ 697.360.   Modified judgments; creation and duration of lien; support judgments

(a) If a judgment lien on real property has been created under a money judgment that is thereafter modified as to its amount, an abstract of the modified judgment or a certified copy of the order modifying the judgment may be recorded in the same manner as an abstract of judgment or a certified copy of the judgment is recorded to create a judgment lien.

(b) If a judgment lien on real property has been created under a money judgment that is thereafter modified to reduce its amount, the judgment lien continues under the terms of the judgment as modified, whether or not the modification is recorded as provided in subdivision (a).

(c) If a judgment lien on real property has been created under a money judgment that is thereafter modified to increase its amount, the judgment lien continues under the terms of the original judgment until such time as the modification is recorded as provided in subdivision (a). Upon such recording, the judgment lien extends to the judgment as modified, but the priority for the additional amount under the judgment as modified dates from the time the modification is recorded.

(d) Notwithstanding subdivision (c), if a judgment lien on real property has been created under a money judgment, by recording of an abstract of support judgment under paragraph (1) of subdivision (a) of Section 697.320, and the support order is thereafter modified to increase its amount, the judgment lien extends to the judgment as modified without the need for recording of another abstract of support judgment, but the priority for the additional amount under the judgment dates from the time the modification is effective.

(e) A support obligee shall respond in a timely manner to (1) a title or escrow company request for a demand statement needed to close an escrow relating to a support judgment lien, or (2) a support obligor who claims an error exists in the amount of alleged arrears.

(f) A support obligor who complies with the procedure specified in Division 5 (commencing with Section 724.010) shall be entitled to the remedies specified therein. *(Added by Stats.1982, c. 1364, p. 5108, § 2, operative July 1, 1983. Amended by Stats.1995, c. 583 (A.B.554), § 1.)*

Law Revision Commission Comments

Section 697.360 governs the amount of the judgment lien in a case where the judgment is modified in amount. The most common application of the section will be a case where a support order requiring periodic payments is modified to change the amount of the periodic payment. Under subdivision (a) the abstract of the modified judgment or the certified copy of the order modifying the judgment may be recorded and has the effect of conforming the terms of the judgment lien with the modified judgment.

Under subdivision (b), a new recording is not required if the amount of the judgment has been reduced; the judgment lien may be enforced only for the judgment as so modified. However, subdivision (c) makes clear that, prior to recording, a modification that increases the amount of the judgment does not affect a judgment lien and that the priority as to the additional amounts dates from the time of recording; the priority as to the original amounts is not affected, whether or not the modification is recorded. [16 Cal.L.Rev.Comm. Reports 1281 (1982)].

Research References

Rutter, Cal. Practice Guide: Enforcing Judgments/Debts Ch. 6B-5, Amount of Judgment Lien.
Rutter, Cal. Practice Guide: Enforcing Judgments/Debts Ch. 6K-1, Acknowledgment of Full Satisfaction of Judgment.
Rutter, Cal. Practice Guide: Family Law Ch. 17-A, A. Child Support.
Rutter, Cal. Practice Guide: Family Law Ch. 17-B, B. Spousal Support.
Miller and Starr California Real Estate § 32:48, Nature and Creation.
Miller and Starr California Real Estate § 11:126, Relation to Subsequent Interests.
8 Witkin Cal. Proc. 5th Enforcement of Judgment § 75, (S 75) Amount of Lien.
11 Witkin, California Summary 10th Husband and Wife § 267, (S 267) Judgment Lien.

§ 697.370. Release or subordination

(a) The judgment creditor may do either of the following:

(1) Release from the judgment lien all or a part of the real property subject to the lien.

(2) Subordinate to another lien or encumbrance the judgment lien on all or a part of the real property subject to the judgment lien.

(b) A release or subordination is sufficient if it is executed by the judgment creditor in the same manner as an acknowledgment of satisfaction of judgment and contains all of the following:

(1) A description of the real property being released or on which the lien is being subordinated. If the judgment debtor does not have an interest of record in the real property, the release or subordination shall show the name of the record owner. If all of the real property of the judgment debtor in a county in which the lien is recorded is being released from the judgment lien, or if the judgment debtor has no known interest in any real property in that county, the release shall, in lieu of containing a description of the property being released, contain a statement substantially as follows: "This is a release from the judgment lien described herein of all of the interests in real property in _____ County presently owned or hereafter acquired of the herein named judgment debtor subject to the lien."

(2) The date the judgment lien was created and where in the records of the county the abstract of judgment or certified copy of the judgment was recorded to create the lien.

(3) The title of the court where the judgment is entered and the cause and number of the action.

(4) The date of entry of the judgment and of any subsequent renewals and where entered in the records of the court.

(5) The name and address of the judgment creditor, the judgment creditor's assignee, if any, and the judgment debtor whose interest in real property is released from the judgment lien or with respect to whom the judgment lien is subordinated.

(c) A release or subordination substantially complying with the requirements of this section is effective even though it contains minor errors that are not seriously misleading.

(d) The execution of a release or subordination of a judgment lien pursuant to this section does not release or subordinate the judgment lien as to judgment debtors not named in the release pursuant to paragraph (5) of subdivision (b). *(Added by Stats.1982, c. 1364, p. 5108, § 2, operative July 1, 1983. Amended by Stats.1986, c. 271, § 1; Stats.1987, c. 254, § 1.)*

Research References

Rutter, Cal. Practice Guide: Enforcing Judgments/Debts Ch. 6B-11, Release of Real Property Judgment Lien.
Miller and Starr California Real Estate § 11:6, Instruments Subject to Recording--List of Recordable Documents.
Miller and Starr California Real Estate § 32:58, Satisfaction or Release of the Judgment Lien.
Miller and Starr California Real Estate § 11:126, Relation to Subsequent Interests.
Miller and Starr California Real Estate § 11:200, "Subordination" Defined.
8 Witkin Cal. Proc. 5th Enforcement of Judgment § 79, (S 79) Recording Satisfaction of Judgment.
8 Witkin Cal. Proc. 5th Enforcement of Judgment § 80, in General.
10 Witkin, California Summary 10th Parent and Child § 431, Order for Deposit.
11 Witkin, California Summary 10th Husband and Wife § 267, (S 267) Judgment Lien.

§ 697.380. Priorities

(a) As used in this section:

(1) "Installment judgment lien" means a judgment lien created under Section 697.320.

(2) "Lump-sum judgment lien" means a judgment lien created under Section 697.310.

(b) Except as otherwise provided by law, the rules stated in this section govern the priorities of judgment liens on real property.

(c) A lump-sum judgment lien has priority over any other lump-sum judgment lien thereafter created.

(d) A lump-sum judgment lien has priority over an installment judgment lien as to all of the following:

(1) Installments that mature on the installment judgment after the lump-sum judgment lien is created.

(2) Interest that accrues on the installment judgment after the lump-sum judgment lien is created.

(3) Costs that are added to the installment judgment after the lump-sum judgment lien is created.

(e) An installment judgment lien has priority over a lump-sum judgment lien as to all of the following:

(1) Installments that have matured on the installment judgment before the lump-sum judgment lien is created.

(2) Interest that has accrued on the installment judgment before the lump-sum judgment lien is created.

(3) Costs that have been added to the installment judgment before the lump-sum judgment lien is created.

(f) If an installment judgment lien has been created and another installment judgment lien is thereafter created, the first installment judgment lien has priority over the second installment judgment lien as to the installments that have matured on the judgment at the time the second installment judgment lien is created, the interest that has accrued prior to that time on the judgment, and the costs that have been added prior to that time to the judgment pursuant to Chapter 5 (commencing with Section 685.010) of Division 1. Thereafter, priorities are determined by the time at which each installment matures on a judgment, the time the interest accrues on a judgment, and the time costs are added to a judgment pursuant to Chapter 5 (commencing with Section 685.010) of Division 1.

(g) For the purposes of this section, if two judgment liens attach to the same property at the same time under subdivision (b) of Section 697.340 (after-acquired property), the judgment lien that was first created has priority as to all amounts that are due and payable on that judgment at the time the property is acquired. *(Added by Stats.1982, c. 1364, p. 5109, § 2, operative July 1, 1983.)*

Law Revision Commission Comments

Section 697.380 provides general rules that determine priorities of judgment liens created under this article.

Subdivision (b) makes clear that the rules set out in this section are subject to specific rules provided by other sections. See, e.g., Section 697.020 (judgment lien dates back to effective date of prior lien).

Subdivision (c) gives a lien created by recording an abstract of a lump-sum money judgment priority over later lump-sum judgment liens unless the later lien relates back to an earlier time (as where the judgment lien is on property attached in the action in which the second judgment is obtained). See subdivision (b) (rules in this section subject to rules otherwise provided by law).

Subdivisions (d) and (e) set out the rules governing priorities where there is a competing lump-sum judgment lien and an installment judgment lien. Since the installment judgment lien is only a lien for installments as they mature (see subdivision (c) of Section 697.350), a lump-sum judgment lien is given priority over unmatured installments but not over matured installments. Subdivision (f) sets out the rules governing priorities where there are two competing installment judgment liens. In this case, the matured installments under each installment judgment have priority over later maturing installments under the other judgment. Prior law provided no rules for determining priority in these situations.

Subdivision (g) changes the former rule under which judgment liens on after-acquired property of the debtor in a county where two or more abstracts of judgments had been recorded were granted the same priority, but the creditor who acted first by levying upon the property under execution was given priority over the other judgment liens. See Hertweck v. Fearon, 180 Cal. 71, 75, 179 P. 190 (1919). [16 Cal.L.Rev.Comm. Reports 1284 (1982)].

Research References

Rutter, Cal. Practice Guide: Enforcing Judgments/Debts Ch. 6B-8, Priorities Among Real Property Judgment Liens.

Rutter, Cal. Practice Guide: Enforcing Judgments/Debts Ch. 6A-13, Creating an Enforcement of Judgment Plan.

Miller and Starr California Real Estate § 11:125, Recordation of the Abstract of Judgment.

Miller and Starr California Real Estate § 11:126, Relation to Subsequent Interests.

8 Witkin Cal. Proc. 5th Enforcement of Judgment § 68, (S 68) Relation Back and Priorities.

8 Witkin Cal. Proc. 5th Enforcement of Judgment § 77, (S 77) Priority of Liens.

§ 697.390. Interest subject to lien transferred or encumbered

If an interest in real property that is subject to a judgment lien is transferred or encumbered without satisfying or extinguishing the judgment lien:

(a) The interest transferred or encumbered remains subject to a judgment lien created pursuant to Section 697.310 in the same amount as if the interest had not been transferred or encumbered.

(b) The interest transferred or encumbered remains subject to a judgment lien created pursuant to Section 697.320 in the amount of the lien at the time of transfer or encumbrance plus interest thereafter accruing on such amount. *(Added by Stats. 1982, c. 1364, p. 5110, § 2, operative July 1, 1983. Amended by Stats.1984, c. 538, § 19.)*

Law Revision Commission Comments

Section 697.390 states rules governing judgment liens on interests in real property that have been transferred (sold, exchanged, or otherwise transferred) or encumbered. As to the continuation of the lien on transferred property after renewal of the judgment, see Section 683.180(b).

Under subdivision (a), the lien on the property interest transferred remains a lien in the same amount as is provided by subdivision (a) or (b) of Section 697.350 and includes interest that accrues and costs that are added to the judgment after the transfer. Under subdivision (a), the judgment lien has priority over any subsequent encumbrance in the same amount as is provided by subdivision (a) or (b) of Section 697.350 and this priority extends to interest that accrues and costs that are added to the judgment after the encumbrance of the interest. Subdivision (a) is consistent with prior case law. See, e.g., Kinney v. Vallentyne, 15 Cal.3d 475, 479, 541 P.2d 537, 124 Cal.Rptr. 897 (1975).

Subdivision (b) provides a special rule derived from portions of former Sections 674.5 and 674.7 applicable to the transfer of property subject to certain installment judgment liens. Subdivision (b) makes clear that interest accrues on the judgment lien for matured but unsatisfied installments after property is transferred or encumbered subject to the judgment lien. However, unmatured installments that fall due after the transfer or encumbrance, interest that accrues on such unmatured installments, and additional costs added to the judgment after the transfer or encumbrance are not added to the amount of the judgment lien on the property transferred or to the amount of the judgment lien given priority over the encumbrance.

Section 697.390 deals only with the situation where the transfer or encumbrance is made after the judgment lien is created. However, if the transfer is in fraud of the creditor, the creditor may follow the property into the hands of the transferee even if the transfer took place before the judgment lien attached. See, e.g., McGee v. Allen, 7 Cal.2d 468, 473, 60 P.2d 1026 (1936); Liuzza v. Bell, 40 Cal.App.2d 417, 429, 104 P.2d 1095 (1940). The same reasoning would require that preference be given to the judgment lien where an earlier encumbrance was in fraud of the creditor. [16 Cal.L.Rev.Comm. Reports 1285 (1982)].

Section 697.390 is amended to make clear that this section does not continue judgment liens that are otherwise extinguished. See, e.g., Section 701.630 (extinction of junior liens upon execution sale); Carpentier v. Brenham, 40 Cal. 221, 235 (1870) (effect on junior liens of foreclosure of senior lien); Hohn v. Riverside County Flood Control Dist., 228 Cal.App.2d 605, 613, 39 Cal.Rptr. 647 (1964) (purchaser at trustee's sale takes free of junior liens). [17 Cal.L.Rev.Comm.Reports 1003 (1983)].

Research References

Rutter, Cal. Practice Guide: Enforcing Judgments/Debts Ch. 6B-5, Amount of Judgment Lien.

Rutter, Cal. Practice Guide: Enforcing Judgments/Debts Ch. 6B-7, Property Transferred Subject to Real Property Judgment Lien.

Rutter, Cal. Practice Guide: Enforcing Judgments/Debts Ch. 6A-11, Property Subject to Enforcement Procedures.

Miller and Starr California Real Estate § 32:49, Real Property Subject to the Judgment Lien.

Miller and Starr California Real Estate § 32:51, Joint Tenancy Property.

Miller and Starr California Real Estate § 32:55, Duration of the Judgment Lien.

Miller and Starr California Real Estate § 32:61, Property Interests Subject to Execution.

Miller and Starr California Real Estate § 11:125, Recordation of the Abstract of Judgment.

Miller and Starr California Real Estate § 11:126, Relation to Subsequent Interests.

Miller and Starr California Real Estate § 11:127, Relation to Prior Interests.

13 NO. 4 Miller & Starr, California Real Estate Newsalert 26, Involuntary Liens.

8 Witkin Cal. Proc. 5th Enforcement of Judgment § 75, (S 75) Amount of Lien.

8 Witkin Cal. Proc. 5th Enforcement of Judgment § 78, (S 78) Transfer or Encumbrance of Interest.

8 Witkin Cal. Proc. 5th Enforcement of Judgment § 235, (S 235) Attachment of Judgment Lien.

§ 697.400. Satisfaction of judgment; release or subordination; recording

(a) The judgment creditor, judgment debtor, or owner of real property subject to a judgment lien on real property created under Section 697.310, may record in the office of the county recorder an acknowledgment of satisfaction of judgment executed as provided in Section 724.060 or a court clerk's certificate of satisfaction of judgment issued pursuant to Section 724.100. Upon such recording, the judgment lien created under the judgment that has been satisfied is extinguished as a matter of record.

(b) The judgment creditor, judgment debtor, or owner of real property subject to a judgment lien on real property created under Section 697.320, may record in the office of the county recorder an acknowledgment of satisfaction of matured installments under an installment judgment if the acknowledgment is executed as provided in Section 724.250. Upon such recording, the judgment lien is extinguished as a matter of record to the extent of the satisfied installments described in the acknowledgment of satisfaction.

(c) The judgment creditor, the judgment debtor, or the owner of real property subject to a judgment lien, including a property owner described in Section 697.410, may record in the office of the county recorder a release or subordination of a judgment lien on real property if the release or subordination is executed as provided in Section 697.370. *(Added by Stats.1982, c. 1364, p. 5110, § 2, operative July 1, 1983.)*

Law Revision Commission Comments

Section 697.400 is a new provision for recording the satisfaction of a judgment to extinguish as a matter of record the judgment lien on real property and for recording other documents affecting a judgment lien on real property. [16 Cal.L.Rev.Comm. Reports 1287 (1982)].

Research References

Rutter, Cal. Practice Guide: Enforcing Judgments/Debts Ch. 6K-1, Acknowledgment of Full Satisfaction of Judgment.
Rutter, Cal. Practice Guide: Enforcing Judgments/Debts Ch. 6K-3, Acknowledgment of Satisfaction of Matured Installments Under Installment Judgment.
Rutter, Cal. Practice Guide: Enforcing Judgments/Debts Ch. 6B-11, Release of Real Property Judgment Lien.
Miller and Starr California Real Estate § 11:6, Instruments Subject to Recording--List of Recordable Documents.
Miller and Starr California Real Estate § 32:58, Satisfaction or Release of the Judgment Lien.
Miller and Starr California Real Estate § 11:200, "Subordination" Defined.
8 Witkin Cal. Proc. 5th Enforcement of Judgment § 79, (S 79) Recording Satisfaction of Judgment.

§ 697.410. Erroneously identified property owner; lien; release; damages; attorney's fees

(a) If a recorded abstract of a money judgment or certified copy of a money judgment appears to create a judgment lien on real property of a person who is not the judgment debtor because the name of the property owner is the same as or similar to that of the judgment debtor, the erroneously identified property owner may deliver to the judgment creditor a written demand for a recordable document releasing the lien. The demand shall be accompanied by proof to the satisfaction of the judgment creditor that the property owner is not the judgment debtor and that the property is not subject to enforcement of the judgment against the judgment debtor.

(b) Within 15 days after receipt of the property owner's demand and proof satisfactory to the judgment creditor that the property owner is not the judgment debtor and that the property is not subject to enforcement of the judgment, the judgment creditor shall deliver to the property owner a recordable document releasing the lien on the property of such owner. If the judgment creditor improperly fails to deliver a recordable document releasing the lien within the time allowed, the judgment creditor is liable to the property owner for all damages sustained by reason of such failure and shall also forfeit one hundred dollars ($100) to the property owner.

(c) If the judgment creditor does not deliver a recordable document pursuant to subdivision (b), the property owner may apply to the court on noticed motion for an order releasing the judgment lien on the property of such owner. Notice of motion shall be served on the judgment creditor. Service shall be made

personally or by mail. Upon presentation of evidence to the satisfaction of the court that the property owner is not the judgment debtor and that the property is not subject to enforcement of the judgment, the court shall order the judgment creditor to prepare and deliver a recordable document releasing the lien or shall itself order the release of the judgment lien on the property of such owner. The court order may be recorded in the office of the county recorder with the same effect as the recordable document demanded by the property owner.

(d) The court shall award reasonable attorney's fees to the prevailing party in any proceeding maintained pursuant to this section.

(e) The damages provided by this section are not in derogation of any other damages or penalties to which an aggrieved person may be entitled by law. *(Added by Stats.1982, c. 1364, p. 5110, § 2, operative July 1, 1983.)*

Law Revision Commission Comments

Section 697.410 is drawn from subdivisions (e), (f), and (g) of former Section 675. The phrase "and that the property is not subject to the enforcement of the judgment" has been added in subdivision (a) to make clear that Section 697.410 does not permit a spouse who is not a judgment debtor to use this procedure to release a lien on community property that is subject to enforcement of a judgment obtained against the other spouse. [16 Cal.L.Rev.Comm. Reports 1288 (1982)].

Research References

Rutter, Cal. Practice Guide: Enforcing Judgments/Debts Ch. 6B-11, Release of Real Property Judgment Lien.
Miller and Starr California Real Estate § 11:6, Instruments Subject to Recording--List of Recordable Documents.
Miller and Starr California Real Estate § 32:58, Satisfaction or Release of the Judgment Lien.
8 Witkin Cal. Proc. 5th Enforcement of Judgment § 81, Release of Erroneous Lien.
8 Witkin Cal. Proc. 5th Enforcement of Judgment § 91, Release of Erroneous Lien.

ARTICLE 3. JUDGMENT LIEN ON PERSONAL PROPERTY

Section

697.660. Erroneously identified property owner; lien; release; damages; attorney's fees.

697.670. Forms prescribed by secretary of state.

Law Revision Commission Comments

Article 3 (Sections 697.510–697.670) provides a new procedure for obtaining a judgment lien on certain personal property (see Section 697.530) in a manner analogous to the procedure in the Commercial Code for perfecting a security interest by filing with the Secretary of State. As Section 697.520 makes clear, this procedure may be used in conjunction with other enforcement procedures (such as levy of execution or examination proceedings) or may be used alone as a means of establishing a priority over other creditors.

In certain cases, a judgment creditor will attempt to enforce a judgment through a procedure such as an examination proceeding (Sections 708.110–708.205) or a creditor's suit (Sections 708.210–708.290). In such a case, the judgment creditor will obtain a lien that can be defeated by the transfer of the property to a bona fide purchaser. See Section 697.920. However, use of the procedure provided in this article will in certain cases enable the judgment creditor to preclude transfer to a bona fide purchaser; the notice of judgment lien filed under this article is constructive notice to certain transferees. Section 697.610. See also Sections 697.590, 697.600 (priorities). Although the judgment lien will not protect against a transfer to a person described in Section 697.610, it may give the judgment creditor a priority over other creditors with respect to the identifiable cash proceeds (Section 697.620) or specified kinds of after-acquired property to which the judgment lien will automatically attach (Sections 697.530(b), 697.590(b), and 697.600(b)).

The judgment creditor may use the procedure provided in this article in order to establish a priority dating from the creation of the lien by filing with the Secretary of State. Although levy of execution creates an execution lien, a levy may be significantly delayed because of the time required to obtain a writ of execution and the time required by the levying officer to levy on property under the writ. Moreover, if the property is subject to a perfected security interest of a third person, the judgment creditor may not desire to levy upon the property because if the property is levied upon the judgment creditor may have to deal with a claim under the third-party claims procedure. See Section 720.010 et seq. The use of the procedure under this article gives the judgment creditor a priority over other unsecured creditors but avoids the need to levy on the property and thus avoids the possibility of the third-party claim by the secured party having priority.

If the lien on personal property is not voluntarily satisfied, it is anticipated that the normal remedy for enforcing the lien will be by levy of execution. See Chapter 3 (commencing with Section 699.010). In certain circumstances, the judgment creditor may need to use the remedies provided by Chapter 6 (commencing with Section 708.010). An action to foreclose the judgment lien on personal property may be necessary in certain circumstances, such as where the judgment debtor dies before the judgment is satisfied. See Section 686.020. In this sense the judgment lien on personal property is analogous to the judgment lien on real property which is normally enforced by execution and infrequently by foreclosure. However, absent the consent of the judgment debtor, the judgment creditor is not entitled to the other remedies provided in Chapter 5 (commencing with Section 9501) of Division 9 of the Commercial Code, such as self-help repossession or private sale.

General provisions concerning liens are set forth in Article 1 (commencing with Section 697.010). [16 Cal.L.Rev.Comm. Reports 1288 (1982)].

§ 697.510. Creation and duration; lapse; continuation statement; extinguishment

(a) A judgment lien on personal property described in Section 697.530 is created by filing a notice of judgment lien in the office of the Secretary of State pursuant to this article. A judgment lien may be created under this article only if the judgment is a money judgment that was first entered in this state after June 30, 1983. Except as provided in subdivision (b) of Section 697.540, a judgment lien may not be created under this article if the money judgment is payable in installments unless all of the installments under the judgment have become due and payable at the time the notice of judgment lien is filed.

(b) Except as otherwise provided in subdivision (c), (e), or (g), the judgment lien continues for five years from the date of filing.

(c) The effectiveness of a filed judgment lien lapses on the expiration of the period described in subdivision (b) unless, before the lapse, a continuation statement is filed pursuant to subdivision (d). Upon lapse, the judgment lien created by the filing of a notice pursuant to subdivision (a) ceases to be effective.

(d) A continuation statement may be filed only within the six-month period prior to the expiration of the five-year period specified in subdivision (b).

(e) A continuation statement that is not filed within the six-month period prescribed by subdivision (d) is ineffective. Upon timely filing of a continuation statement, the effectiveness of the initial notice of judgment lien continues for a period of five years commencing on the day on which the notice of judgment lien would have become ineffective in the absence of the filing. Upon the expiration of the five-year period, the notice of judgment lien lapses in the same manner as provided in subdivision (c), unless, before the lapse, another continuation statement is filed pursuant to subdivision (d). Succeeding continuation statements may be filed in the same manner to continue the effectiveness of the initial notice of judgment lien.

(f) For purposes of this section, "continuation statement" means an amendment of a notice of judgment lien that does both of the following:

(1) Identifies, by its file number, the initial notice of judgment lien to which it relates.

(2) Indicates that it is a continuation statement for, or that it is filed to continue the effectiveness of, the identified notice of judgment lien.

(g)(1) Notwithstanding any other provision of this section, the lien created by this section is extinguished at the earliest to occur of the following:

(A) The money judgment is satisfied.

(B) The period of enforceability of the judgment, including any extension thereof pursuant to Article 2 (commencing with Section 683.110) of Chapter 3 of Division 1, terminates.

(C) The judgment lien is terminated or released.

(2) If the lien created by this section is extinguished, the judgment creditor shall file a statement of release within 20 days after the judgment creditor receives an authenticated demand from the judgment debtor. For the purposes of this subdivision, "authenticated demand" means either a signed written demand or an executed or otherwise encrypted demand delivered electronically that identifies the judgment debtor and the demand for a statement of release.

(h) If a judgment creditor does not file a statement of release pursuant to subdivision (g), the person who made the demand may apply to the court on noticed motion for an order releasing the judgment lien. Notice of the motion shall be filed in the county where the judgment was rendered and notice of the motion shall be served on the judgment creditor. Service shall be made personally or by mail. Upon presentation of evidence to the satisfaction of the court that the judgment lien has been extinguished pursuant to subdivision (g), the court shall order the judgment creditor to prepare and file the statement of release or shall itself order the release of the judgment lien. The court order may be filed in the office of the Secretary of State and shall have the same effect as the statement of release demanded under subdivision (g).

(i) The court shall award reasonable attorney's fees to the prevailing party in any action or proceeding maintained pursuant to this section.

(j) Nothing in this section is in derogation of any other relief to which an aggrieved person may be entitled by law.

(k) The fees for filing and indexing a record under this section, or for responding to a request for information from the filing office, are as set forth in Section 9525 of the Commercial Code.

(*l*) The provisions of Sections 9522 and 9523 of the Commercial Code shall apply to a notice of judgment lien to the same extent as to a filed financing statement.

(m) Terms for which definitions are not set forth in Division 1 (commencing with Section 680.010) have the definitions set forth in the Commercial Code. *(Added by Stats.1982, c. 1364, p. 5111, § 2, operative July 1, 1983. Amended by Stats.2009, c. 410 (A.B.121), § 1.)*

Research References

Rutter, Cal. Practice Guide: Enforcing Judgments/Debts Ch. 6C-2, Types of Property Subject to Jlpp.
Rutter, Cal. Practice Guide: Enforcing Judgments/Debts Ch. 6C-3, Creation of Jlpp-Notice of Judgment Lien.
Rutter, Cal. Practice Guide: Enforcing Judgments/Debts Ch. 6C-4, Amount of Lien.
Rutter, Cal. Practice Guide: Enforcing Judgments/Debts Ch. 6C-5, Duration of Jlpp.
Miller and Starr California Real Estate § 11:164, Personal Property Tax Liens.
16 NO. 4 Miller & Starr, California Real Estate Newsalert 32, Involuntary Liens.
8 Witkin Cal. Proc. 5th Enforcement of Judgment § 67, (S 67) Duration and Extinguishment.
8 Witkin Cal. Proc. 5th Enforcement of Judgment § 68, (S 68) Relation Back and Priorities.
8 Witkin Cal. Proc. 5th Enforcement of Judgment § 82, (S 82) in General.
8 Witkin Cal. Proc. 5th Enforcement of Judgment § 83, (S 83) Creation and Duration.
8 Witkin Cal. Proc. 5th Enforcement of Judgment § 86, (S 86) Notice of Lien.
8 Witkin Cal. Proc. 5th Enforcement of Judgment § 87, (S 87) Priority of Liens.
8 Witkin Cal. Proc. 5th Enforcement of Judgment § 90, in General.
8 Witkin Cal. Proc. 5th Enforcement of Judgment § 126, Property of Going Business.
8 Witkin Cal. Proc. 5th Enforcement of Judgment § 129, (S 129) Chattel Paper.
8 Witkin Cal. Proc. 5th Enforcement of Judgment § 131, (S 131) Documents of Title and Securities.
8 Witkin Cal. Proc. 5th Enforcement of Judgment § 135, (S 135) Accounts Receivable and General Intangibles.
11 Witkin, California Summary 10th Husband and Wife § 336, (S 336) Lien on Personal Property.

§ 697.520. Alternative or additional lien

A judgment lien on personal property may be created pursuant to this article as an alternative or in addition to a lien created by levy under a writ of execution pursuant to Chapter 3 (commencing with Section 699.010) or by use of an enforcement procedure provided by Chapter 6 (commencing with Section 708.010). *(Added by Stats.1982, c. 1364, p. 5111, § 2, operative July 1, 1983.)*

Law Revision Commission Comments

Section 697.520 makes clear that the lien procedure under this article may be used in connection with other enforcement procedures (such as levy of execution or examination proceedings) or may be used alone as a means of establishing a priority over other creditors as to certain property. See the Comment to this article. [16 Cal.L.Rev.Comm. Reports 1291 (1982)].

Research References

Rutter, Cal. Practice Guide: Enforcing Judgments/Debts Ch. 6C-1, Practical Considerations.

8 Witkin Cal. Proc. 5th Enforcement of Judgment § 82, (S 82) in General.

§ 697.530. Interests in personal property subject to attachment; proceeds; exemptions; fixtures; obligations on accounts receivable or chattel paper; location in state

Section operative until July 1, 2014. See, also, section operative July 1, 2014.

(a) A judgment lien on personal property is a lien on all interests in the following personal property that are subject to enforcement of the money judgment against the judgment debtor pursuant to Article 1 (commencing with Section 695.010) of Chapter 1 at the time when the lien is created if the personal property is, at that time, any of the following:

(1) Accounts receivable, and the judgment debtor is located in this state.

(2) Tangible chattel paper, as defined in paragraph (78) of subdivision (a) of Section 9102 of the Commercial Code, and the judgment debtor is located in this state.

(3) Equipment, located within this state.

(4) Farm products, located within this state.

(5) Inventory, located within this state.

(6) Negotiable documents of title, located within this state.

(b) If any interest in personal property on which a judgment lien could be created under subdivision (a) is acquired after the judgment lien was created, the judgment lien attaches to the interest at the time it is acquired.

(c) To the extent provided by Section 697.620, a judgment lien on personal property continues on the proceeds received upon the sale, collection, or other disposition of the property subject to the judgment lien.

(d) Notwithstanding any other provision of this section, the judgment lien does not attach to:

(1) A vehicle or vessel required to be registered with the Department of Motor Vehicles or a mobilehome or commercial coach required to be registered pursuant to the Health and Safety Code.

(2) As-extracted collateral, as defined in paragraph (6) of subdivision (a) of Section 9102 of the Commercial Code, and timber to be cut.

(3) The inventory of a retail merchant held for sale except to the extent that the inventory of the retail merchant consists of durable goods having a unit retail value of at least five hundred dollars ($500). For the purposes of this paragraph, "retail merchant" does not include either of the following:

(A) A person whose sales for resale exceeded 75 percent in dollar volume of the person's total sales of all goods during the 12 months preceding the filing of the notice of judgment lien on personal property.

(B) A cooperative association organized pursuant to Chapter 1 (commencing with Section 54001) of Division 20 of the Food and Agricultural Code (agricultural cooperative associations) or Part 3 (commencing with Section 13200) of Division 3 of Title 1 of the Corporations Code (Fish Marketing Act).

(e) If property subject to a lien under this article becomes a fixture, as defined in paragraph (41) of subdivision (a) of Section 9102 of the Commercial Code, the judgment lien on that property is extinguished.

(f) Notwithstanding the filing of a notice of judgment lien, subject to the provisions of Chapter 6 (commencing with Section 708.010), a person obligated on an account receivable or chattel paper is authorized to pay or compromise the amount without notice to or consent of the judgment creditor unless and until there is a levy pursuant to Chapter 3 (commencing with Section 699.010).

(g) For purposes of this section, whether a person is located in this state is determined in accordance with Section 9307 of the Commercial Code, except that the location of a registered organization, as defined in paragraph (70) of subdivision (a) of Section 9102 of the Commercial Code, that is organized under the law of another state is determined without regard to subdivision (e) of Section 9307 of the Commercial Code. *(Added by Stats.1982, c. 1364, p. 5112, § 2, operative July 1, 1983. Amended by Stats.1999, c. 991 (S.B.45), § 17.4, operative July 1, 2001; Stats.2009, c. 153 (A.B.1549), § 1.)*

§ 697.530. Interests in personal property subject to attachment; proceeds; exemptions; fixtures; obligations on accounts receivable or chattel paper; location in state

Section operative July 1, 2014. See, also, section operative until July 1, 2014.

(a) A judgment lien on personal property is a lien on all interests in the following personal property that are subject to enforcement of the money judgment against the judgment debtor pursuant to Article 1 (commencing with Section 695.010) of Chapter 1 at the time when the lien is created if the personal property is, at that time, any of the following:

(1) Accounts receivable, and the judgment debtor is located in this state.

(2) Tangible chattel paper, as defined in paragraph (79) of subdivision (a) of Section 9102 of the Commercial Code, and the judgment debtor is located in this state.

(3) Equipment, located within this state.

(4) Farm products, located within this state.

(5) Inventory, located within this state.

(6) Negotiable documents of title, located within this state.

(b) If any interest in personal property on which a judgment lien could be created under subdivision (a) is acquired after the judgment lien was created, the judgment lien attaches to the interest at the time it is acquired.

(c) To the extent provided by Section 697.620, a judgment lien on personal property continues on the proceeds received upon the sale, collection, or other disposition of the property subject to the judgment lien.

(d) Notwithstanding any other provision of this section, the judgment lien does not attach to:

(1) A vehicle or vessel required to be registered with the Department of Motor Vehicles or a mobilehome or commercial coach required to be registered pursuant to the Health and Safety Code.

(2) As-extracted collateral, as defined in paragraph (6) of subdivision (a) of Section 9102 of the Commercial Code, and timber to be cut.

(3) The inventory of a retail merchant held for sale except to the extent that the inventory of the retail merchant consists of durable goods having a unit retail value of at least five hundred dollars ($500). For the purposes of this paragraph, "retail merchant" does not include either of the following:

(A) A person whose sales for resale exceeded 75 percent in dollar volume of the person's total sales of all goods during the 12 months preceding the filing of the notice of judgment lien on personal property.

(B) A cooperative association organized pursuant to Chapter 1 (commencing with Section 54001) of Division 20 of the Food and Agricultural Code (agricultural cooperative associations) or

Part 3 (commencing with Section 13200) of Division 3 of Title 1 of the Corporations Code (Fish Marketing Act).

(e) If property subject to a lien under this article becomes a fixture, as defined in paragraph (41) of subdivision (a) of Section 9102 of the Commercial Code, the judgment lien on that property is extinguished.

(f) Notwithstanding the filing of a notice of judgment lien, subject to the provisions of Chapter 6 (commencing with Section 708.010), a person obligated on an account receivable or chattel paper is authorized to pay or compromise the amount without notice to or consent of the judgment creditor unless and until there is a levy pursuant to Chapter 3 (commencing with Section 699.010).

(g) For purposes of this section, whether a person is located in this state is determined in accordance with Section 9307 of the Commercial Code, except that the location of a registered organization, as defined in paragraph (71) of subdivision (a) of Section 9102 of the Commercial Code, that is organized under the law of another state is determined without regard to subdivision (e) of Section 9307 of the Commercial Code. *(Added by Stats.1982, c. 1364, p. 5112, § 2, operative July 1, 1983. Amended by Stats.1999, c. 991 (S.B.45), § 17.4, operative July 1, 2001; Stats.2009, c. 153 (A.B.1549), § 1; Stats.2013, c. 531 (A.B.502), § 6, operative July 1, 2014.)*

Research References

Rutter, Cal. Practice Guide: Enforcing Judgments/Debts Ch. 6C-2, Types of Property Subject to Jlpp.

Rutter, Cal. Practice Guide: Enforcing Judgments/Debts, Ch. 6G-1, Examination of Judgment Debtor and Third Parties.

Miller and Starr California Real Estate § 17:56, Security Interests Given by Landlords and Lessees.

Miller and Starr California Real Estate § 31:63, Enforcement of a Money Judgment Against a Mobilehome.

Miller and Starr California Real Estate § 11:194, Priority Between a Deed of Trust and a Security Interest in Fixtures.

8 Witkin Cal. Proc. 5th Enforcement of Judgment § 84, (S 84) Interests Subject to Lien.

8 Witkin Cal. Proc. 5th Enforcement of Judgment § 86, (S 86) Notice of Lien.

8 Witkin Cal. Proc. 5th Enforcement of Judgment § 87, (S 87) Priority of Liens.

8 Witkin Cal. Proc. 5th Enforcement of Judgment § 88, (S 88) Transfer of Property.

§ 697.540. Amount of lien

(a) Except as otherwise provided by statute, a judgment lien on personal property is a lien for the amount required to satisfy the money judgment.

(b) A judgment lien on personal property created under a money judgment payable in installments pursuant to Section 117 or 582.5 of this code or pursuant to Section 16380 of the Vehicle Code is in the full amount required to satisfy the judgment, but the judgment lien may not be enforced for the amount of unmatured installments unless the court so orders. *(Added by Stats.1982, c. 1364, p. 5113, § 2, operative July 1, 1983. Amended by Stats.1998, c. 931 (S.B.2139), § 92, eff. Sept. 28, 1998.)*

Law Revision Commission Comments

Section 697.540 states the amount of the judgment lien. See Section 695.210 (amount required to satisfy the judgment). Section 697.540 is consistent with the treatment given lump-sum judgments under Section 697.350 (judgment lien on real property). Except as provided in subdivision (b) of this section, a judgment lien may not be created on personal property pursuant to an installment judgment if there are unmatured installments at the time of filing. See Section 697.510(a). [16 Cal.L.Rev.Comm. Reports 1294 (1982)].

Section 697.540 is amended to reflect relocation of the substance of former Section 85 to Section 582.5. [28 Cal.L.Rev.Comm. Reports 51 (1998)].

Research References

Rutter, Cal. Practice Guide: Enforcing Judgments/Debts Ch. 6C-4, Amount of Lien.

8 Witkin Cal. Proc. 5th Enforcement of Judgment 66, (S 66) Amount of Lien.

8 Witkin Cal. Proc. 5th Enforcement of Judgmen § 83, (S 83) Creation and Duration.

8 Witkin Cal. Proc. 5th Enforcement of Judgment § 85, (S 85) Amount of Lien.

§ 697.550. Notice of lien; execution; contents

The notice of judgment lien on personal property shall be executed under oath by the judgment creditor's attorney if the judgment creditor has an attorney of record or, if the judgment creditor does not have an attorney of record, by the judgment creditor and shall contain the following information:

(a) The name and mailing address of the judgment creditor.

(b) The name and last known mailing address of the judgment debtor.

(c) A statement that: "All property subject to enforcement of a money judgment against the judgment debtor to which a judgment lien on personal property may attach under Section 697.530 of the Code of Civil Procedure is subject to this judgment lien."

(d) The title of the court where the judgment is entered and the cause and number of the action.

(e) The date of entry of the judgment and of any subsequent renewals and where entered in the records of the court.

(f) The amount required to satisfy the judgment at the date of the notice.

(g) The date of the notice. *(Added by Stats.1982, c. 1364, p. 5113, § 2, operative July 1, 1983.)*

Law Revision Commission Comments

Section 697.550, which lists the contents of the notice of judgment lien, is subject to Section 697.670 which gives the Secretary of State authority to prepare a form of notice. [16 Cal.L.Rev.Comm. Reports 1295 (1982)].

Research References

Rutter, Cal. Practice Guide: Enforcing Judgments/Debts Ch. 6C-3, Creation of Jlpp-Notice of Judgment Lien.

16 NO. 4 Miller & Starr, California Real Estate Newsalert 32, Involuntary Liens.

8 Witkin Cal. Proc. 5th Enforcement of Judgment § 86, (S 86) Notice of Lien.

§ 697.560. Notice of lien; service

At the time of filing the notice of judgment lien on personal property or promptly thereafter, the judgment creditor shall serve a copy of the notice of judgment lien on the judgment debtor. Service shall be made personally or by mail. The failure to comply with this requirement does not affect the validity of the judgment lien. *(Added by Stats.1982, c. 1364, p. 5113, § 2, operative July 1, 1983.)*

Law Revision Commission Comments

Section 697.560 is analogous to provisions of this title concerning service of notice of levy on the judgment debtor. See Sections 699.550, 700.010. The last sentence applies only to the validity of the lien; it does not affect any liability the judgment creditor may have to the judgment debtor for failure to give the notice. This is consistent with the notice of levy provisions which provide that the levy is valid notwithstanding the failure to serve the required notice of levy on the judgment debtor. [16 Cal.L.Rev.Comm. Reports 1295 (1982)].

Research References

Rutter, Cal. Practice Guide: Enforcing Judgments/Debts Ch. 6C-3, Creation of Jlpp-Notice of Judgment Lien.

8 Witkin Cal. Proc. 5th Enforcement of Judgment § 86, (S 86) Notice of Lien.

§ 697.570. Notice of lien; filing; fee

Upon presentation of a notice of judgment lien on personal property for filing and tender of the filing fee to the office of the Secretary of State, the notice of judgment lien shall be filed, marked, and indexed in the same manner as a financing statement. The fee for filing in the office of the Secretary of State is the same as the fee for filing a financing statement in the standard form. A notice shall not be filed if it is presented for filing more than 10 days after the date of the notice. *(Added by Stats.1982, c. 1364, p. 5113, § 2, operative July 1, 1983.)*

Law Revision Commission Comments

Section 697.570 is adapted from Section 9403 of the Commercial Code. [16 Cal.L.Rev.Comm. Reports 1296 (1982)].

Research References

Rutter, Cal. Practice Guide: Enforcing Judgments/Debts Ch. 6C-3, Creation of Jlpp-Notice of Judgment Lien.

16 NO. 4 Miller & Starr, California Real Estate Newsalert 32, Involuntary Liens.

8 Witkin Cal. Proc. 5th Enforcement of Judgment § 86, (S 86) Notice of Lien.

§ 697.580. Certificate showing notice is on file; fee

(a) Upon the request of any person, the Secretary of State shall issue a certificate showing whether there is on file in that office on the date and hour stated therein any notice of judgment lien on personal property filed against the property of a particular person named in the request. If a notice of judgment lien is on file, the certificate shall state the date and hour of filing of each such notice and any notice affecting any such notice of judgment lien and the name and address of the judgment creditor.

(b) Upon request, the Secretary of State shall furnish a copy of any notice of judgment lien or notice affecting a notice of judgment lien. The certificate shall be issued as part of a combined certificate pursuant to Section 9528 of the Commercial Code, and the fee for the certificate and copies shall be in accordance with that section. *(Added by Stats.1982, c. 1364, p. 5113, § 2, operative July 1, 1983. Amended by Stats.1988, c. 393, § 9; Stats.1999, c. 991 (S.B.45), § 17.5, operative July 1, 2001.)*

Law Revision Commission Comments

Section 697.580 is based on portions of Sections 488.340 and 488.360 and of Commercial Code Section 9407. See also Com. Code § 9409 (combined certificate issued by Secretary of State). [16 Cal.L.Rev.Comm. Reports 1297 (1982)].

Research References

Rutter, Cal. Practice Guide: Enforcing Judgments/Debts Ch. 6C-3, Creation of Jlpp-Notice of Judgment Lien.

8 Witkin Cal. Proc. 5th Enforcement of Judgment § 86, (S 86) Notice of Lien.

4 Witkin, California Summary 10th Secured Transactions in Personal Property § 93, (S 93) Acknowledgments and Responses to Requests.

§ 697.590. Definitions; priorities; security interests or agricultural liens

(a) As used in this section:

(1) "Filing" means:

(A) With respect to a judgment lien on personal property, the filing of a notice of judgment lien in the office of the Secretary of State to create a judgment lien on personal property under this article.

(B) With respect to a security interest or agricultural lien, as defined in paragraph (5) of subdivision (a) of Section 9102 of the

Commercial Code, the filing of a financing statement pursuant to Division 9 (commencing with Section 9101) of the Commercial Code.

(2) "Perfection" means perfection of a security interest or agricultural lien pursuant to Division 9 (commencing with Section 9101) of the Commercial Code.

(3) "Personal property" means:

(A) With respect to a judgment lien on personal property, the property to which a judgment lien has attached pursuant to this article.

(B) With respect to a security interest, the collateral subject to a security interest pursuant to Division 9 (commencing with Section 9101) of the Commercial Code.

(C) With respect to an agricultural lien, the farm products subject to an agricultural lien pursuant to Division 9 (commencing with Section 9101) of the Commercial Code.

(4) "Purchase money security interest" has the same meaning as used in Section 9103 of the Commercial Code.

(b) Except as provided in subdivisions (d), (e), (g), and (h), priority between a judgment lien on personal property and a conflicting security interest or agricultural lien in the same personal property shall be determined according to this subdivision. Conflicting interests rank according to priority in time of filing or perfection. In the case of a judgment lien, priority dates from the time filing is first made covering the personal property. In the case of a security interest or agricultural lien, priority dates from the earlier of the time a filing is first made covering the personal property or the time the security interest or agricultural lien is first perfected, if there is no period thereafter when there is neither filing nor perfection.

(c) For the purposes of subdivision (b), a date of filing or perfection as to personal property is also a date of filing or perfection as to proceeds.

(d) A purchase money security interest has priority over a conflicting judgment lien on the same personal property or its proceeds if the purchase money security interest is perfected at the time the judgment debtor, as a debtor under the security agreement, receives possession of the personal property or within 20 days thereafter.

(e) If a purchase money security interest in inventory has priority over a judgment lien pursuant to subdivision (d) and a conflicting security interest has priority over the purchase money security interest in the same inventory pursuant to Section 9324 of the Commercial Code, the conflicting security interest also has priority over the judgment lien on the inventory subject to the purchase money security interest, notwithstanding that the conflicting security interest would not otherwise have priority over the judgment lien.

(f) A judgment lien that has attached to personal property, and that is also subordinate under subdivision (b) to a security interest in the same personal property, is subordinate to the security interest only to the extent that the security interest secures advances made before the judgment lien attached or within 45 days thereafter or made without knowledge of the judgment lien or pursuant to a commitment entered into without knowledge of the judgment lien. For the purpose of this subdivision, a secured party shall be deemed not to have knowledge of a judgment lien on personal property until (1) the judgment creditor serves a copy of the notice of judgment lien on the secured party personally or by mail and (2) the secured party has knowledge of the judgment lien on personal property, as "knowledge" is defined in Section 1201 of the Commercial Code. If service on the secured party is by mail, it shall be sent to the secured party at the address shown in the financing statement or security agreement.

(g) A perfected agricultural lien on personal property has priority over a judgment lien on the same personal property if the statute creating the agricultural lien so provides.

(h) A security interest in personal property perfected by the filing of a financing statement under the law of a jurisdiction other than this state, or perfected by another method pursuant to the law of a jurisdiction other than this state, has priority over a judgment lien in the same personal property. *(Added by Stats.1984, c. 538, § 19.6. Amended by Stats.1985, c. 41, § 5; Stats.1986, c. 248, § 20; Stats.1989, c. 445, § 2; Stats.1999, c. 991 (S.B.45), § 18, operative July 1, 2001; Stats.2009, c. 153 (A.B. 1549), § 2.)*

Law Revision Commission Comments

Subdivision (f) of Section 697.590 is amended to state directly the two requirements that must be satisfied before a secured party may be deemed to have knowledge of the judgment lien on personal property. This amendment makes no substantive change in prior law. [18 Cal.L.Rev. Comm. Reports 361 (1985)].

Research References

Rutter, Cal. Practice Guide: Enforcing Judgments/Debts Ch. 6C-3, Creation of Jlpp-Notice of Judgment Lien.
Rutter, Cal. Practice Guide: Enforcing Judgments/Debts Ch. 6C-6, Priority Rules.
Rutter, Cal. Practice Guide: Enforcing Judgments/Debts Ch. 6A-13, Creating an Enforcement of Judgment Plan.
8 Witkin Cal. Proc. 5th Enforcement of Judgment § 68, (S 68) Relation Back and Priorities.
8 Witkin Cal. Proc. 5th Enforcement of Judgment § 87, (S 87) Priority of Liens.
6 Witkin Cal. Proc. 5th Provisional Remedies § 162, (S 162) Lien.
6 Witkin Cal. Proc. 5th Provisional Remedies § 171, Lien.

§ 697.600. Priorities; liens

(a) A judgment lien on personal property has priority over any other judgment lien thereafter created on the property.

(b) For the purpose of this section, if two or more judgment liens attach to after-acquired property at the same time under subdivision (b) of Section 697.530, the judgment lien first filed has priority. *(Added by Stats.1982, c. 1364, p. 5114, § 2, operative July 1, 1983.)*

Law Revision Commission Comments

Section 697.600 establishes the rules of priority between competing judgment liens. Subdivision (b) governs the priority of liens on after-acquired property and is consistent with subdivision (g) of Section 697.380 (judgment lien on real property). See the Comment to Section 697.380. [16 Cal.L.Rev.Comm. Reports 1298 (1982)].

Research References

Rutter, Cal. Practice Guide: Enforcing Judgments/Debts Ch. 6C-6, Priority Rules.
Miller and Starr California Real Estate § 11:126, Relation to Subsequent Interests.
8 Witkin Cal. Proc. 5th Enforcement of Judgment § 68, (S 68) Relation Back and Priorities.
8 Witkin Cal. Proc. 5th Enforcement of Judgment § 84, (S 84) Interests Subject to Lien.
8 Witkin Cal. Proc. 5th Enforcement of Judgment § 87, (S 87) Priority of Liens.

§ 697.610. Disposition of property subject to lien; continuation of lien; exceptions

Except as provided in Sections 9617 and 9622 of the Commercial Code, a judgment lien on personal property continues notwithstanding the sale, exchange, or other disposition of the property, unless the person receiving the property is one of the following:

(a) A buyer in ordinary course of business (as defined in Section 1201 of the Commercial Code) who, under Section 9320 of the Commercial Code, would take free of a security interest created by the seller.

(b) A lessee in ordinary course of business (as defined in paragraph (15) of subdivision (a) of Section 10103 of the Commercial Code) who, under Section 9321 of the Commercial Code, would take free of a security interest created by the lessor.

(c) A holder to whom a negotiable document of title has been duly negotiated within the meaning of Section 7501 of the Commercial Code.

(d) A purchaser of chattel paper who, under Section 9330 of the Commercial Code, would have priority over another security interest in the chattel paper. *(Added by Stats.1982, c. 1364, p. 5114, § 2, operative July 1, 1983. Amended by Stats.1988, c. 1368, § 5, operative Jan. 1, 1990; Stats.1994, c. 668 (S.B.1405), § 5; Stats.1999, c. 991 (S.B.45), § 19, operative July 1, 2001.)*

Research References

Rutter, Cal. Practice Guide: Enforcing Judgments/Debts Ch. 6C-7, Effect of Transfer of Property Subject to Lien.
Rutter, Cal. Practice Guide: Enforcing Judgments/Debts Ch. 6A-11, Property Subject to Enforcement Procedures.
8 Witkin Cal. Proc. 5th Enforcement of Judgment § 88, (S 88) Transfer of Property.

§ 697.620. Proceeds; continuation of lien with same priority; insolvency

(a) As used in this section:

(1) "Cash proceeds" means money, checks, deposit accounts, and the like.

(2) "Proceeds" means identifiable cash proceeds received upon the sale, exchange, collection, or other disposition of property subject to a judgment lien on personal property.

(b) Except as provided in subdivision (c), the judgment lien on personal property continues in the proceeds with the same priority.

(c) In the event of insolvency proceedings (as defined in Section 1201 of the Commercial Code) instituted by or against the judgment debtor, the judgment lien continues under subdivision (b) only in the following proceeds:

(1) Proceeds in a separate deposit account containing only proceeds.

(2) Proceeds in the form of money which are neither commingled with other money nor deposited in a deposit account prior to the insolvency proceedings.

(3) Proceeds in the form of checks and the like which are not deposited in a deposit account prior to the insolvency proceedings. *(Added by Stats.1982, c. 1364, p. 5115, § 2, operative July 1, 1983.)*

Law Revision Commission Comments

Section 697.620 provides for the continuation of the judgment lien on identifiable cash proceeds of an interest in property subject to a judgment lien. For example, a judgment lien on inventory sold for identifiable cash proceeds continues on the proceeds. This is consistent with Commercial Code Section 9306(3)(b). The lien extends to the proceeds only if the lien of a perfected security interest would extend to the proceeds. As to proceeds not in the form of identifiable cash proceeds, the judgment lien will attach to the proceeds only if the proceeds are a type of property (such as inventory) that is subject to a judgment lien under this article. See Section 697.530(a). In this case, the lien will attach to the property as after-acquired property under subdivision (b) of Section 697.530. The lien will not attach if the proceeds are neither property of a type to which a judgment lien under this article would attach nor identifiable cash proceeds, since the lien will not attach under the after-acquired property provision of subdivision (b) of Section 697.530 nor under the identifiable

cash proceeds provision of this section. [16 Cal.L.Rev.Comm. Reports 1299 (1982)].

Research References

Rutter, Cal. Practice Guide: Enforcing Judgments/Debts Ch. 6C-2, Types of Property Subject to Jlpp.
Rutter, Cal. Practice Guide: Enforcing Judgments/Debts Ch. 6C-7, Effect of Transfer of Property Subject to Lien.
8 Witkin Cal. Proc. 5th Enforcement of Judgment § 84, (S 84) Interests Subject to Lien.
8 Witkin Cal. Proc. 5th Enforcement of Judgment § 88, (S 88) Transfer of Property.
6 Witkin Cal. Proc. 5th Provisional Remedies § 171, Lien.

§ 697.640. Satisfaction of judgment

(a) The judgment creditor, judgment debtor, owner of property subject to a judgment lien on personal property created under the judgment, or a person having a security interest in or a lien on the property subject to the judgment lien, may file in the office of the Secretary of State an acknowledgment of satisfaction of judgment executed as provided in Section 724.060 or a court clerk's certificate of satisfaction of judgment issued pursuant to Section 724.100, together with a statement containing the name of the judgment creditor, the name and address of the judgment debtor, and the file number of the notice of judgment lien. Upon such filing, the judgment lien created under the judgment that has been satisfied is extinguished as a matter of record. The fee for filing the acknowledgment or certificate is the same as the fee for filing a termination statement under Section 9404 of the Commercial Code.

(b) The filing officer shall treat an acknowledgment of satisfaction of judgment, or court clerk's certificate of satisfaction of judgment, and statement filed pursuant to this section in the same manner as a termination statement filed pursuant to Section 9525 of the Commercial Code. *(Added by Stats.1982, c. 1364, p. 5115, § 2, operative July 1, 1983. Amended by Stats.1983, c. 155, § 12.1, eff. June 30, 1983, operative July 1, 1983; Stats.1999, c. 991 (S.B.45), § 20, operative July 1, 2001.)*

Research References

Rutter, Cal. Practice Guide: Enforcing Judgments/Debts Ch. 6C-8, Extinguishing JLPP "As a Matter of Record".
Rutter, Cal. Practice Guide: Enforcing Judgments/Debts Ch. 6C-9, Release and Subordination.
Rutter, Cal. Practice Guide: Enforcing Judgments/Debts Ch. 6K-1, Acknowledgment of Full Satisfaction of Judgment.
8 Witkin Cal. Proc. 5th Enforcement of Judgment § 25, Rules and Forms.
8 Witkin Cal. Proc. 5th Enforcement of Judgment § 89, (S 89) Recording Satisfaction of Judgment.

§ 697.650. Release or subordination

(a) The judgment creditor may by a writing do any of the following:

(1) Release the judgment lien on all the personal property subject to the lien of a sole judgment debtor or of all the judgment debtors.

(2) If the notice of judgment lien names more than one judgment debtor, release the judgment lien on all the personal property subject to the lien of one or more but of less than all the judgment debtors.

(3) Release the judgment lien on all or a part of the personal property subject to the lien.

(4) Subordinate to a security interest or other lien or encumbrance the judgment lien on all or a part of the personal property subject to the judgment lien.

(b) A statement of release or subordination is sufficient if it is signed by the judgment creditor and contains the name and address of the judgment debtor, the file number of the notice of judgment lien, and wording appropriate to bring the statement within one of the paragraphs of subdivision (a). In the case of a release under paragraph (3) of subdivision (a), the statement of release shall also describe the property being released. In the case of a subordination under paragraph (4) of subdivision (a), the statement of subordination shall also describe the property on which the judgment lien is being subordinated and describe the security interest or other lien or encumbrance to which the judgment lien is being subordinated.

(c) The filing officer shall treat the filing of a statement of release pursuant to paragraph (1) of subdivision (a) of this section in the same manner as a termination statement filed pursuant to Sections 9513 and 9519 of the Commercial Code. The filing officer shall treat the filing of a statement of release pursuant to paragraph (2) of subdivision (a) of this section in the same manner as a comparable amendment filed pursuant to Sections 9512 and 9519 of the Commercial Code. The filing officer shall treat the filing of a statement of release pursuant to paragraph (3) of subdivision (a) of this section and the filing of a statement of subordination filed pursuant to paragraph (4) of subdivision (a) of this section in the same manner as a statement of release filed pursuant to Sections 9512 and 9519 of the Commercial Code.

(d) The fee for filing the statement is the same as that provided in Section 9525 of the Commercial Code. *(Added by Stats.1982, c. 1364, p. 5115, § 2, operative July 1, 1983. Amended by Stats.1983, c. 155, § 12.2, eff. June 30, 1983, operative July 1, 1983; Stats.1989, c. 445, § 3; Stats.1999, c. 991 (S.B.45), § 21, operative July 1, 2001.)*

Law Revision Commission Comments

Section 697.650 is drawn from Commercial Code Section 9405 for the sake of uniformity and provides a procedure for the release or subordination of the judgment lien on all or a part of the property subject to the judgment lien. The Secretary of State may provide a form for the statement of release or subordination. See Section 697.670. See also Section 697.660 (release of erroneous judgment lien). [16 Cal.L.Rev. Comm. Reports 1301 (1982)].

Research References

Rutter, Cal. Practice Guide: Enforcing Judgments/Debts Ch. 6C-9, Release and Subordination.
8 Witkin Cal. Proc. 5th Enforcement of Judgment § 90, in General.
6 Witkin Cal. Proc. 5th Provisional Remedies § 212, (S 212) Written Release of Property Not in Custody.

§ 697.660. Erroneously identified property owner; lien; release; damages; attorney's fees

(a) If a notice of judgment lien on personal property filed in the office of the Secretary of State appears to create a judgment lien on personal property of a person who is not the judgment debtor because the name of the property owner is the same as or similar to that of the judgment debtor, the erroneously identified property owner or a person having a security interest in or a lien on the property may deliver to the judgment creditor a written demand that the judgment creditor file in the office of the Secretary of State a statement releasing the lien as to the property of such owner. The demand shall be accompanied by proof to the satisfaction of the judgment creditor that the property owner is not the judgment debtor and that the property is not subject to enforcement of the judgment against the judgment debtor.

(b) Within 15 days after receipt of the demand and proof satisfactory to the judgment creditor that the property owner is not the judgment debtor and that the property is not subject to enforcement of the judgment, the judgment creditor shall file in the office of the Secretary of State a statement releasing the lien on the property of such owner. If the judgment creditor improperly fails to file the statement of release within the time

allowed, the judgment creditor is liable to the person who made the demand for all damages sustained by reason of such failure and shall also forfeit one hundred dollars ($100) to such person.

(c) If the judgment creditor does not file a statement of release pursuant to subdivision (b), the person who made the demand may apply to the court on noticed motion for an order releasing the judgment lien on the property of such owner. Notice of motion shall be served on the judgment creditor. Service shall be made personally or by mail. Upon presentation of evidence to the satisfaction of the court that the property owner is not the judgment debtor and that the property is not subject to enforcement of the judgment, the court shall order the judgment creditor to prepare and file the statement of release or shall itself order the release of the judgment lien on the property of such owner. The court order may be filed in the office of the Secretary of State with the same effect as the statement of release demanded under subdivision (a).

(d) The court shall award reasonable attorney's fees to the prevailing party in any action or proceeding maintained pursuant to this section.

(e) The damages provided by this section are not in derogation of any other damages or penalties to which an aggrieved person may be entitled by law.

(f) The fee for filing a statement of release or court order under this section is the same as that provided in Section 9525 of the Commercial Code. *(Added by Stats.1982, c. 1364, p. 5116, § 2, operative July 1, 1983. Amended by Stats.1999, c. 991 (S.B.45), § 21.5, operative July 1, 2001.)*

Research References

Rutter, Cal. Practice Guide: Enforcing Judgments/Debts Ch. 6C-10, Order for Release of Erroneously Identified Debtor.
8 Witkin Cal. Proc. 5th Enforcement of Judgment § 81, Release of Erroneous Lien.
8 Witkin Cal. Proc. 5th Enforcement of Judgment § 91, Release of Erroneous Lien.

§ 697.670. Forms prescribed by secretary of state

(a) The Secretary of State may prescribe, provided that a cost-savings would be achieved thereby:

(1) The forms for the notice of judgment lien on personal property and the statement of continuation, release, or subordination provided for in this article.

(2) The form for the statement provided for in Section 697.640 and the situations when that form is required or is not required.

(b) A form prescribed by the Secretary of State for a notice or statement pursuant to subdivision (a) is deemed to comply with this article and supersedes any requirements specified in this article for the notice or statement. *(Added by Stats.1982, c. 1364, p. 5117, § 2, operative July 1, 1983. Amended by Stats.1983, c. 155, § 12.3, eff. June 30, 1983, operative July 1, 1983; Stats.2009, c. 410 (A.B.121), § 2.)*

Law Revision Commission Comments

Section 697.670 is an exception to the general provision (Section 681.030) giving the Judicial Council authority to prescribe forms. The Secretary of State is authorized to prepare similar forms under the Attachment Law. See, e.g., Sections 488.340(a) (notice of attachment of equipment) and 488.360(c) (notice of attachment of farm products or inventory). [16 Cal.L.Rev.Comm. Reports 1303 (1982)].

Research References

Rutter, Cal. Practice Guide: Enforcing Judgments/Debts Ch. 6C-3, Creation of Jlpp-Notice of Judgment Lien.
Miller and Starr California Real Estate § 11:164, Personal Property Tax Liens.
8 Witkin Cal. Proc. 5th Enforcement of Judgment § 25, Rules and Forms.

8 Witkin Cal. Proc. 5th Enforcement of Judgment § 83, (S 83) Creation and Duration.

8 Witkin Cal. Proc. 5th Enforcement of Judgment § 86, (S 86) Notice of Lien.

8 Witkin Cal. Proc. 5th Enforcement of Judgment § 89, (S 89) Recording Satisfaction of Judgment.

8 Witkin Cal. Proc. 5th Enforcement of Judgment § 90, in General.

ARTICLE 4. EXECUTION LIEN

§ 697.710. Creation and duration of lien

A levy on property under a writ of execution creates an execution lien on the property from the time of levy until the expiration of two years after the date of issuance of the writ unless the judgment is sooner satisfied. *(Added by Stats.1982, c. 1364, p. 5117, § 2, operative July 1, 1983.)*

Research References

Rutter, Cal. Practice Guide: Enforcing Judgments/Debts Ch. 6B-2, Interests Subject to Judgment Lien.

Rutter, Cal. Practice Guide: Enforcing Judgments/Debts Ch. 6D-3, Levy of Writ of Execution-In General.

Rutter, Cal. Practice Guide: Enforcing Judgments/Debts Ch. 6D-4, Levy on Specific Property.

Rutter, Cal. Practice Guide: Enforcing Judgments/Debts Ch. 6E-6, "Homestead" Exemption.

Rutter, Cal. Practice Guide: Enforcing Judgments/Debts Ch. 6F-2, Wage Garnishment-In General.

Miller and Starr California Real Estate § 11:6, Instruments Subject to Recording--List of Recordable Documents.

Miller and Starr California Real Estate § 32:64, Creation, Duration, and Effect of Writ of Execution.

Miller and Starr California Real Estate § 11:128, Execution Lien; Recordation of the Writ of Execution.

8 Witkin Cal. Proc. 5th Enforcement of Judgment § 67, (S 67) Duration and Extinguishment.

8 Witkin Cal. Proc. 5th Enforcement of Judgment § 92, (S 92) Creation and Duration.

8 Witkin Cal. Proc. 5th Enforcement of Judgment § 99, (S 99) Nature of Execution.

8 Witkin Cal. Proc. 5th Enforcement of Judgment § 138, (S 138) Interest in Personal Property in Decedent's Estate.

8 Witkin Cal. Proc. 5th Enforcement of Judgment § 254, in General.

6 Witkin Cal. Proc. 5th Provisional Remedies § 179, Securities.

6 Witkin Cal. Proc. 5th Provisional Remedies § 184, Nature and Effect of Lien.

11 Witkin, California Summary 10th Husband and Wife § 264, (S 264) Enforcement Against Employee Benefit Plan.

§ 697.720. Interest in real property transferred or encumbered

Subject to Section 701.630, if an interest in real property subject to an execution lien is transferred or encumbered, the interest transferred or encumbered remains subject to the lien after the transfer or encumbrance. *(Added by Stats.1982, c. 1364, p. 5117, § 2, operative July 1, 1983.)*

Law Revision Commission Comments

Section 697.720 is a new provision that is consistent with case law. See, e.g., Kinney v. Vallentyne, 15 Cal.3d 475, 479, 541 P.2d 537, 124 Cal.Rptr.

897 (1975). See also Section 697.390 (effect of judgment lien on real property where property transferred or encumbered). [16 Cal.L.Rev. Comm. Reports 1304 (1982)].

Research References

Rutter, Cal. Practice Guide: Enforcing Judgments/Debts Ch. 6D-3, Levy of Writ of Execution-In General.

Rutter, Cal. Practice Guide: Enforcing Judgments/Debts Ch. 6A-11, Property Subject to Enforcement Procedures.

Miller and Starr California Real Estate § 32:4, Effect.

Miller and Starr California Real Estate § 31:63, Enforcement of a Money Judgment Against a Mobilehome.

Miller and Starr California Real Estate § 32:64, Creation, Duration, and Effect of Writ of Execution.

Miller and Starr California Real Estate § 11:123, Relation to Subsequent Interests.

Miller and Starr California Real Estate § 11:128, Execution Lien; Recordation of the Writ of Execution.

8 Witkin Cal. Proc. 5th Enforcement of Judgment § 94, (S 94) Transfer or Encumbrance of Real Property.

§ 697.730. Tangible personal property in custody of levying officer or of keeper in charge of business; continuation of lien after transfer, encumbrance, purchase or lease

(a) Subject to Section 701.630 and except as provided in subdivision (b), if tangible personal property subject to an execution lien is in the custody of a levying officer and is transferred or encumbered, the property remains subject to the lien after the transfer or encumbrance.

(b) If a levy upon tangible personal property of a going business is made by the levying officer placing a keeper in charge of the business, a purchaser or lessee of property subject to the execution lien takes the property free of the execution lien if the purchaser or lessee is one of the following:

(1) A buyer in ordinary course of business (as defined in Section 1201 of the Commercial Code) who, under Section 9320 of the Commercial Code, would take free of a security interest created by his or her seller.

(2) A lessee in ordinary course of business (as defined in paragraph (15) of subdivision (a) of Section 10103 of the Commercial Code) who, under Section 9321 of the Commercial Code, would take free of a security interest created by the lessor. *(Added by Stats.1982, c. 1364, p. 5117, § 2, operative July 1, 1983. Amended by Stats.1983, c. 155, § 12.4, eff. June 30, 1983, operative July 1, 1983; Stats.1988, c. 1368, § 6, operative Jan. 1, 1990; Stats.1994, c. 668 (S.B.1405), § 6; Stats.1999, c. 991 (S.B.45), § 22, operative July 1, 2001.)*

Law Revision Commission Comments

Section 697.730 is based on the principle that a potential transferee or encumbrancer of tangible personal property has a duty to determine whether the person attempting to transfer the property has possession of it and can deliver possession. Cf. Civil Code § 3440 (transfer without delivery conclusively presumed fraudulent). This principle applies where the property is in the levying officer's custody pursuant to execution. Compare Section 697.740 (effect of transfer or encumbrance where property not in custody of levying officer). See also Section 701.630 (extinction of lien upon execution sale). [16 Cal.L.Rev.Comm. Reports 1304 (1982)].

Research References

Rutter, Cal. Practice Guide: Enforcing Judgments/Debts Ch. 6D-3, Levy of Writ of Execution-In General.

Miller and Starr California Real Estate § 11:128, Execution Lien; Recordation of the Writ of Execution.

8 Witkin Cal. Proc. 5th Enforcement of Judgment § 95, Property in Levying Officer's Custody.

§ 697.740. Personal property not in custody of levying officer; continuation of lien after transfer or encumbrance; exceptions

Except as provided in Sections 9617 and 9622 of the Commercial Code and in Section 701.630, if personal property subject to an execution lien is not in the custody of a levying officer and the property is transferred or encumbered, the property remains subject to the lien after the transfer or encumbrance except where the transfer or encumbrance is made to one of the following persons:

(a) A person who acquires an interest in the property under the law of this state for reasonably equivalent value without knowledge of the lien. For purposes of this subdivision, value is given for a transfer or encumbrance if, in exchange for the transfer or encumbrance, property is transferred or an antecedent debt is secured or satisfied.

(b) A buyer in ordinary course of business (as defined in Section 1201 of the Commercial Code) who, under Section 9320 of the Commercial Code, would take free of a security interest created by the seller or encumbrancer.

(c) A lessee in ordinary course of business (as defined in paragraph (15) of subdivision (a) of Section 10103 of the Commercial Code) or a licensee in the ordinary course of business (as defined in subdivision (a) of Section 9321 of the Commercial Code) who, under Section 9321 of the Commercial Code, would take free of a security interest created by the lessor or the licensor.

(d) A holder in due course (as defined in Section 3302 of the Commercial Code) of a negotiable instrument within the meaning of Section 3104 of the Commercial Code.

(e) A holder to whom a negotiable document of title has been duly negotiated within the meaning of Section 7501 of the Commercial Code.

(f) A protected purchaser (as defined in Section 8303 of the Commercial Code) of a security or a person entitled to the benefits of Section 8502 or 8510 of the Commercial Code.

(g) A purchaser of chattel paper who gives new value and takes possession of the chattel paper in good faith and in the ordinary course of the purchaser's business or a purchaser of an instrument who gives value and takes possession of the instrument in good faith.

(h) A holder of a purchase money security interest (as defined in Section 9103 of the Commercial Code).

(i) A collecting bank holding a security interest in items being collected, accompanying documents and proceeds, pursuant to Section 4210 of the Commercial Code.

(j) A person who acquires any right or interest in letters of credit, advices of credit, or money.

(k) A person who acquires any right or interest in property subject to a certificate of title statute of another jurisdiction under the law of which indication of a security interest on the certificate of title is required as a condition of perfection of the security interest. *(Added by Stats.1982, c. 1364, p. 5117, § 2, operative July 1, 1983. Amended by Stats.1987, c. 40, § 4, eff. June 8, 1987; Stats.1988, c. 1368, § 7, operative Jan. 1, 1990; Stats. 1994, c. 668 (S.B.1405), § 7; Stats.1996, c. 497 (S.B.1591), § 2, operative Jan. 1, 1997; Stats.1999, c. 991 (S.B.45), § 23, operative July 1, 2001.)*

Law Revision Commission Comments

Section 697.740 is drawn from Government Code Section 7170(c) (state tax liens). Section 697.740 covers tangible personal property not covered by Section 697.730 and intangible personal property such as accounts receivable and general intangibles. See also Civil Code §§ 955, 955.1 (transfer of accounts and general intangibles). Although the section is based on the provision relating to state tax liens, it is also consistent with case law governing the effect of equitable liens. See Jud Whitehead Heater Co. v. Obler, 111 Cal.App.2d 861, 872–74, 245 P.2d 608, 616 (1952); Wagner v. Sariotti, 56 Cal.App.2d 693, 698, 133 P.2d 430, 433 (1943); cf. Taylor v. S & M Lamp Co., 190 Cal.App.2d 700, 711–13, 12 Cal.Rptr. 323 (1961). It should be noted that even if the transferee gives fair consideration and has no notice of the existence of a lien on the property, the transfer may in certain circumstances be attacked as a fraudulent conveyance. See Civil Code §§ 3439–3440. [16 Cal.L.Rev. Comm. Reports 1305 (1982)].

Research References

Rutter, Cal. Practice Guide: Enforcing Judgments/Debts Ch. 4-A, A. Attachment.
Rutter, Cal. Practice Guide: Enforcing Judgments/Debts Ch. 6C-1, Practical Considerations.
Rutter, Cal. Practice Guide: Enforcing Judgments/Debts Ch. 6D-3, Levy of Writ of Execution-In General.
Miller and Starr California Real Estate § 32:3, Purpose.
Miller and Starr California Real Estate § 32:4, Effect.
Miller and Starr California Real Estate § 31:63, Enforcement of a Money Judgment Against a Mobilehome.
Miller and Starr California Real Estate § 11:123, Relation to Subsequent Interests.
Miller and Starr California Real Estate § 11:128, Execution Lien; Recordation of the Writ of Execution.
8 Witkin Cal. Proc. 5th Enforcement of Judgment § 92, (S 92) Creation and Duration.
8 Witkin Cal. Proc. 5th Enforcement of Judgment § 96, Property Not in Levying Officer's Custody.
8 Witkin Cal. Proc. 5th Enforcement of Judgment § 97, Crops, Timber, and Minerals.
8 Witkin Cal. Proc. 5th Enforcement of Judgment § 98, Other Liens.
6 Witkin Cal. Proc. 5th Provisional Remedies § 147, (S 147) Lien.
6 Witkin Cal. Proc. 5th Provisional Remedies § 197, (S 197) Order to Appear.

§ 697.750. Growing crops; timber to be cut; minerals transferred or encumbered

Notwithstanding Section 697.740, except as provided in Section 9617 of the Commercial Code and in Section 701.630, if (1) growing crops, (2) timber to be cut, or (3) minerals or the like (including oil or gas) to be extracted or accounts receivable resulting from the sale thereof at wellhead or minehead are subject to an execution lien and are transferred or encumbered, the property remains subject to the execution lien after the transfer or encumbrance. *(Added by Stats.1982, c. 1364, p. 5118, § 2, operative July 1, 1983. Amended by Stats.1999, c. 991 (S.B.45), § 23.1, operative July 1, 2001.)*

Law Revision Commission Comments

Section 697.750 provides an exception to Section 697.740. Since a levy on growing crops, timber to be cut, or minerals to be extracted is accomplished by recording a copy of the writ and a notice of levy with the county recorder (Section 700.020), constructive notice is thereby given to any potential transferee or person taking an encumbrance on the property. Cf. Section 697.390 (effect of judgment lien on real property where property transferred or encumbered). [16 Cal.L.Rev.Comm. Reports 1306 (1982)].

Research References

Rutter, Cal. Practice Guide: Enforcing Judgments/Debts Ch. 6A-11, Property Subject to Enforcement Procedures.
Miller and Starr California Real Estate § 32:4, Effect.
Miller and Starr California Real Estate § 17:23, Minerals--Oil and Gas.
Miller and Starr California Real Estate § 17:31, Timber.
Miller and Starr California Real Estate § 17:33, Crops--Encumbrance of Crops.
Miller and Starr California Real Estate § 31:63, Enforcement of a Money Judgment Against a Mobilehome.

Miller and Starr California Real Estate § 32:64, Creation, Duration, and Effect of Writ of Execution.

Miller and Starr California Real Estate § 11:123, Relation to Subsequent Interests.

Miller and Starr California Real Estate § 11:128, Execution Lien; Recordation of the Writ of Execution.

8 Witkin Cal. Proc. 5th Enforcement of Judgment § 97, Crops, Timber, and Minerals.

ARTICLE 5. OTHER LIENS CREATED BY ENFORCEMENT PROCESS

Section

697.910. Application of article.

697.920. Continuation of lien; transfer or encumbrance of property subject to lien.

§ 697.910. Application of article

This article applies to liens created by any of the following:

(a) An examination proceeding as provided in Section 708.110, 708.120, or 708.205.

(b) A creditor's suit as provided in Section 708.250.

(c) A charging order as provided in Section 708.320. *(Added by Stats.1982, c. 1364, p. 5118, § 2, operative July 1, 1983.)*

Law Revision Commission Comments

Section 697.910 limits the scope of this chapter to the liens listed in the section. The effect of liens not covered by this article or other statutory provisions is determined, as under former law, by judicial decisions applicable to the particular provision. See also Sections 708.440 (effect of lien in pending action or proceeding), 708.530 (effect of assignment ordered by court). [16 Cal.L.Rev.Comm. Reports 1307 (1982)].

Research References

Rutter, Cal. Practice Guide: Enforcing Judgments/Debts Ch. 6C-1, Practical Considerations.

8 Witkin Cal. Proc. 5th Enforcement of Judgment § 98, Other Liens.

§ 697.920. Continuation of lien; transfer or encumbrance of property subject to lien

Except as provided in Section 9617 of the Commercial Code and in Section 701.630, a lien described in Section 697.910 continues on property subject to the lien, notwithstanding the transfer or encumbrance of the property subject to the lien, unless the transfer or encumbrance is made to a person listed in Section 697.740. *(Added by Stats.1982, c. 1364, p. 5118, § 2, operative July 1, 1983. Amended by Stats.1999, c. 991 (S.B.45), § 23.2, operative July 1, 2001.)*

Research References

Rutter, Cal. Practice Guide: Enforcing Judgments/Debts Ch. 6C-1, Practical Considerations.

Rutter, Cal. Practice Guide: Enforcing Judgments/Debts Ch. 6A-11, Property Subject to Enforcement Procedures.

Miller and Starr California Real Estate § 11:123, Relation to Subsequent Interests.

8 Witkin Cal. Proc. 5th Enforcement of Judgment § 98, Other Liens.

CHAPTER 3. EXECUTION

ARTICLE 1. GENERAL PROVISIONS

§ 699.010. Enforcement of money judgment by writ of execution

Except as otherwise provided by statute, this chapter governs enforcement of a money judgment by a writ of execution. *(Added by Stats.1982, c. 1364, p. 5118, § 2, operative July 1, 1983.)*

Law Revision Commission Comments

Section 699.010 makes clear that this chapter governs the procedure under a writ of execution. For provisions applicable to a wage garnishment, see Sections 706.010–706.154. For provisions applicable to property levied upon or otherwise subjected to process for enforcement prior to the operative date of this chapter, see Sections 694.040, 694.050. [16 Cal.L.Rev.Comm. Reports 1307 (1982)].

Research References

Rutter, Cal. Practice Guide: Enforcing Judgments/Debts Ch. 6D-2, Writ of Execution.

8 Witkin Cal. Proc. 5th Enforcement of Judgment § 82, (S 82) in General.

8 Witkin Cal. Proc. 5th Enforcement of Judgment § 84, (S 84) Interests Subject to Lien.

8 Witkin Cal. Proc. 5th Enforcement of Judgment § 99, (S 99) Nature of Execution.

8 Witkin Cal. Proc. 5th Enforcement of Judgment § 242, (S 242) Exclusive Procedure.

8 Witkin Cal. Proc. 5th Enforcement of Judgment § 405, Governmental Enforcement of Support Order.

§ 699.020. Satisfaction of judgment; receipt; discharge

At any time after delivery of a writ of execution to a levying officer and before its return, a person indebted to the judgment debtor may pay to the levying officer the amount of the debt or so much thereof as is necessary to satisfy the money judgment. The levying officer shall give a receipt for the amount paid and such receipt is a discharge for the amount paid. *(Added by Stats.1982, c. 1364, p. 5118, § 2, operative July 1, 1983.)*

Law Revision Commission Comments

Section 699.020 continues the substance of former Section 716. [16 Cal.L.Rev.Comm. Reports 1308 (1982)].

Research References

Rutter, Cal. Practice Guide: Enforcing Judgments/Debts Ch. 6D-3, Levy of Writ of Execution-In General.

Miller and Starr California Real Estate § 11:128, Execution Lien; Recordation of the Writ of Execution.

8 Witkin Cal. Proc. 5th Enforcement of Judgment § 105, (S 105) Payment by Debtor of Judgment Debtor.

§ 699.030. Personal property subject to levy; location in private place

If personal property sought to be levied upon is located in a private place of the judgment debtor:

(a) The levying officer making the levy shall demand delivery of the property by the judgment debtor and shall advise the judgment debtor that the judgment debtor may be liable for costs and attorney's fees incurred in any further proceedings to obtain delivery of the property. If the judgment debtor does not deliver the property, the levying officer shall make no further effort to obtain custody of the property and shall promptly notify the judgment creditor of the failure to obtain custody of the property.

(b) The judgment creditor may apply to the court ex parte, or on noticed motion if the court so directs or a court rule so requires, for an order directing the levying officer to seize the property in the private place. The application may be made whether or not a writ has been issued and whether or not demand has been made pursuant to subdivision (a). The application for the order shall describe with particularity both the property sought to be levied upon, and the place where it is to be found, according to the best knowledge, information, and belief of the judgment creditor. The court may not issue the order unless the judgment creditor establishes that there is probable cause to believe that property sought to be levied upon is located in the place described. The levying officer making the levy, at the time delivery of the property pursuant to the order is demanded, shall announce his or her identity, purpose, and authority. If the property is not voluntarily delivered, the levying officer may cause the building or enclosure where the property is believed to be located to be broken open in such manner as the levying officer reasonably believes will cause the least damage, but if the levying officer reasonably believes that entry and seizure of the property will involve a substantial risk of death or serious bodily harm to any person, the levying officer shall refrain from entering and shall promptly make a return to the court setting forth the reasons for believing that the risk exists. In such a case, the court shall make such orders as may be appropriate. *(Added by Stats.1982, c. 1364, p. 5118, § 2, operative July 1, 1983.)*

Law Revision Commission Comments

Subdivision (a) of Section 699.030 states the limit of a levying officer's authority to obtain property in a private place without further court authorization. Whether the judgment debtor who fails to deliver property is liable for costs of obtaining further court authorization depends on the circumstances of the case. See Sections 685.040 (reasonable and necessary costs) and 685.080 (motion for costs).

Subdivision (b) is based on comparable provisions relating to claim and delivery. See Sections 512.010, 512.060, 512.080, 514.010, and Comments thereto. If the levying officer gains entrance into a private place pursuant to an order issued under this section, the levying officer's authority to levy upon property is restricted by the terms of the order. [16 Cal.L.Rev. Comm. Reports 1309 (1982)].

Research References

Rutter, Cal. Practice Guide: Enforcing Judgments/Debts Ch. 4-A, A. Attachment.

Rutter, Cal. Practice Guide: Enforcing Judgments/Debts Ch. 6D-2, Writ of Execution.

Rutter, Cal. Practice Guide: Enforcing Judgments/Debts Ch. 6D-3, Levy of Writ of Execution-In General.

Rutter, Cal. Practice Guide: Enforcing Judgments/Debts Ch. 6D-4, Levy on Specific Property.

Rutter, Cal. Practice Guide: Enforcing Judgments/Debts Ch. 6I-2, Enforcement of Judgment for Possession of Personal Property.

Rutter, Cal. Practice Guide: Enforcing Judgments/Debts Ch. 6I-3, Enforcement of Judgment for Possession of Real Property.

8 Witkin Cal. Proc. 5th Enforcement of Judgment § 100, (S 100) Levy on Property in Private Place.

8 Witkin Cal. Proc. 5th Enforcement of Judgment § 329, (S 329) Writ of Possession.

6 Witkin Cal. Proc. 5th Provisional Remedies § 154, Custody.

§ 699.040. Order directing transfer of possession of property or possession of documentary evidence of title to property or debt owed; service; notice

(a) If a writ of execution is issued, the judgment creditor may apply to the court ex parte, or on noticed motion if the court so directs or a court rule so requires, for an order directing the judgment debtor to transfer to the levying officer either or both of the following:

(1) Possession of the property sought to be levied upon if the property is sought to be levied upon by taking it into custody.

(2) Possession of documentary evidence of title to property of or a debt owed to the judgment debtor that is sought to be levied upon. An order pursuant to this paragraph may be served when the property or debt is levied upon or thereafter.

(b) The court may issue an order pursuant to this section upon a showing of need for the order.

(c) The order shall be personally served on the judgment debtor and shall contain a notice to the judgment debtor that failure to comply with the order may subject the judgment debtor to arrest and punishment for contempt of court. *(Added by Stats.1982, c. 1364, p. 5119, § 2, operative July 1, 1983.)*

Law Revision Commission Comments

Section 699.040 is analogous to Section 482.080 (providing for turnover order when a writ of attachment is issued). See also Section 512.070 (providing for turnover order when writ of possession issued under claim and delivery statute). As to duty of a third person to execute and deliver any documents necessary to effect the transfer of property levied upon, see Section 701.010. [16 Cal.L.Rev.Comm. Reports 1310 (1982)].

Research References

Rutter, Cal. Practice Guide: Enforcing Judgments/Debts Ch. 6D-2, Writ of Execution.

Rutter, Cal. Practice Guide: Enforcing Judgments/Debts Ch. 6D-4, Levy on Specific Property.

8 Witkin Cal. Proc. 5th Enforcement of Judgment § 101, (S 101) Turnover Order.

8 Witkin Cal. Proc. 5th Enforcement of Judgment § 157, (S 157) Delivery of Possession, Certificate, or Deed.

8 Witkin Cal. Proc. 5th Enforcement of Judgment § 290, (S 290) Order Applying Property to Satisfaction of Judgment.

8 Witkin Cal. Proc. 5th Enforcement of Judgment § 331, (S 331) Turnover Order.

8 Witkin Cal. Proc. 5th Enforcement of Judgment § 339, (S 339) Turnover Order.

§ 699.060. Release; liability of levying officer; electronic transmission of directions

(a) The levying officer shall release property levied upon when the levying officer receives a written direction to release the property from the judgment creditor's attorney of record or, if the judgment creditor does not have an attorney of record, from the judgment creditor, or when the levying officer receives a certified copy of a court order for release, or when otherwise required to release the property. The release shall include the signature and name of the attorney or judgment creditor issuing the release. The release extinguishes any execution lien or attachment lien in favor of the judgment creditor on the property released.

(b) If the property to be released has been taken into custody under the levy, it shall be released to the person from whom it was taken unless otherwise ordered by the court. If the person does not claim the property to be released, the levying officer shall retain custody of the property and shall serve on the person a notice of where possession of the property may be obtained. Service shall be made personally or by mail. If the person does not claim the property within 30 days after the notice is served, the levying officer shall sell the property in the manner provided by Article 6 (commencing with Section 701.510), other than cash, which does not have a value exceeding its face value. The levying officer shall deposit the proceeds of sale and cash, after first deducting the levying officer's costs, with the county treasurer of the county where the property is located, payable to the order of the person. If the amount deposited is not claimed by the person, or the legal representative of the person, within five years after the deposit is made by making application to the treasurer or other official designated by the county, it shall be paid into the general fund of the county.

(c) If the property to be released has not been taken into custody under the levy, the levying officer shall release the property by issuing a written notice of release and serving it on the person who was served with a copy of the writ and a notice of levy to create the lien. Service shall be made personally or by mail.

(d) If the property to be released was levied upon by recording or filing a copy of the writ and a notice of levy, the levying officer shall record or file a written notice of release in the same office.

(e) The levying officer is not liable for releasing property in accordance with this section nor is any other person liable for acting in conformity with the release.

(f) The written direction to release property specified in subdivision (a) may be transmitted electronically to the levying officer pursuant to Chapter 2 (commencing with Section 263) of Title 4 of Part 1. *(Added by Stats.1982, c. 1364, p. 5119, § 2, operative July 1, 1983. Amended by Stats.2010, c. 680 (A.B.2394), § 6.)*

Research References

Rutter, Cal. Practice Guide: Civil Appeals & Writs Ch. 7-C, C. Stay by Posting Security (Bond or Undertaking).

Rutter, Cal. Practice Guide: Enforcing Judgments/Debts Ch. 6D-3, Levy of Writ of Execution-In General.

Rutter, Cal. Practice Guide: Enforcing Judgments/Debts Ch. 6D-6, Debtor's Recourse Against Execution Levy.

Rutter, Cal. Practice Guide: Enforcing Judgments/Debts Ch. 6E-4, Opposing Claim of Exemption.

Rutter, Cal. Practice Guide: Enforcing Judgments/Debts Ch. 6H-2, Title or Possessory Claims to Real or Personal Property.

Miller and Starr California Real Estate § 32:64, Creation, Duration, and Effect of Writ of Execution.

8 Witkin Cal. Proc. 5th Enforcement of Judgment § 33, Liability of Officer.

8 Witkin Cal. Proc. 5th Enforcement of Judgment § 67, (S 67) Duration and Extinguishment.

8 Witkin Cal. Proc. 5th Enforcement of Judgment § 106, (S 106) Release of Property.

8 Witkin Cal. Proc. 5th Enforcement of Judgment § 139, Delivery or Payment to Levying Officer.

8 Witkin Cal. Proc. 5th Enforcement of Judgment § 186, (S 186) Disposition of Property During Proceedings.

8 Witkin Cal. Proc. 5th Enforcement of Judgment § 371, (S 371) Release of Property.

8 Witkin Cal. Proc. 5th Enforcement of Judgment § 376, (S 376) Release of Property.

§ 699.070. Appointment of receiver; preservation of value of property; sale; application of proceeds to satisfaction of judgment

(a) The court may appoint a receiver or order the levying officer to take any action the court orders that is necessary to preserve the value of property levied upon, including but not limited to selling the property, if the court determines that the property is perishable or will greatly deteriorate or greatly depreciate in value or that for some other reason the interests of the parties will be best served by the order. An order may be made under this subdivision upon application of the judgment creditor, the judgment debtor, or a person who has filed a third-party claim pursuant to Division 4 (commencing with Section 720.010). The application shall be made on noticed motion if the court so directs or a court rule so requires. Otherwise, the application may be made ex parte.

(b) If the levying officer determines that property levied upon is extremely perishable or will greatly deteriorate or greatly depreciate in value before a court order pursuant to subdivision (a) could be obtained, the levying officer may take any action necessary to preserve the value of the property or may sell the property. The levying officer is not liable for a determination made in good faith under this subdivision.

(c) Except as otherwise provided by order of the court, a sale of property pursuant to this section shall be made in the manner provided by Article 6 (commencing with Section 701.510) and the proceeds shall be applied to the satisfaction of the money judgment in the manner provided by Article 7 (commencing with Section 701.810). Notwithstanding subdivisions (b) and (d) of Section 701.530, notice of sale shall be posted and served at a reasonable time before the sale, considering the character and condition of the property.

(d) If a receiver is appointed, the court shall fix the daily fee of the receiver and may order the judgment creditor to pay the fees and expenses of the receiver in advance or may direct that the whole or any part of the fees and expenses be paid from the proceeds of any sale of the property. Except as otherwise provided in this section, the provisions of Chapter 5 (commencing with Section 564) and Chapter 5a (commencing with Section 571) of Title 7 govern the appointment, qualifications, powers, rights, and duties of a receiver appointed under this section. *(Added by Stats.1982, c. 1364, p. 5120, § 2, operative July 1, 1983.)*

Law Revision Commission Comments

Section 699.070 is analogous to Section 488.530 (attachment) and supersedes provisions relating to disposition of perishable property in former Sections 689 (third-party claims proceedings) and 690.50(g) (exemption proceedings). See also Section 703.610 (disposition of property pending exemption proceedings). The second sentence of subdivision (c) continues the substance of subdivision 1 of former Section 692. As to the appointment of a receiver to enforce the judgment, see Sections 708.610–708.630. [16 Cal.L.Rev.Comm. Reports 1312 (1982)].

Research References

Rutter, Cal. Practice Guide: Enforcing Judgments/Debts Ch. 6D-2, Writ of Execution.

Rutter, Cal. Practice Guide: Enforcing Judgments/Debts Ch. 6D-7, Sale and Collection of Property Levied Upon.

Rutter, Cal. Practice Guide: Enforcing Judgments/Debts Ch. 6E-4, Opposing Claim of Exemption.

Miller and Starr California Real Estate § 32:64, Creation, Duration, and Effect of Writ of Execution.

Miller and Starr California Real Estate § 33:32, Enforcement Actions After Entry of Judgment.

8 Witkin Cal. Proc. 5th Enforcement of Judgment § 33, Liability of Officer.

8 Witkin Cal. Proc. 5th Enforcement of Judgment § 102, (S 102) Preservation of Property.

8 Witkin Cal. Proc. 5th Enforcement of Judgment § 121, in General.

8 Witkin Cal. Proc. 5th Enforcement of Judgment § 146, Sale of Personal Property.

8 Witkin Cal. Proc. 5th Enforcement of Judgment § 186, (S 186) Disposition of Property During Proceedings.

8 Witkin Cal. Proc. 5th Enforcement of Judgment § 310, (S 310) in General.

8 Witkin Cal. Proc. 5th Enforcement of Judgment § 369, (S 369) Effect of Filing or Not Filing Claim.

8 Witkin Cal. Proc. 5th Enforcement of Judgment § 374, (S 374) Effect of Filing or Not Filing Claim.

8 Witkin Cal. Proc. 5th Enforcement of Judgment § 381, (S 381) Proceedings and Determination.

8 Witkin Cal. Proc. 5th Enforcement of Judgment § 383, (S 383) Filing and Service of Demand.

§ 699.080. Types of property upon which levy may be made; duties of process server; documents filed; duties of levying officer; fees

(a) A registered process server may levy under a writ of execution on the following types of property:

(1) Real property, pursuant to Section 700.015.

(2) Growing crops, timber to be cut, or minerals or the like (including oil and gas) to be extracted or accounts receivable resulting from the sale thereof at the wellhead or minehead, pursuant to Section 700.020.

(3) Personal property in the custody of a levying officer, pursuant to Section 700.050.

(4) Personal property used as a dwelling, pursuant to subdivision (a) of Section 700.080.

(5) Deposit accounts, pursuant to Section 700.140.

(6) Property in a safe-deposit box, pursuant to Section 700.150.

(7) Accounts receivable or general intangibles, pursuant to Section 700.170.

(8) Final money judgments, pursuant to Section 700.190.

(9) Interest of a judgment debtor in personal property in the estate of a decedent, pursuant to Section 700.200.

(b) Before levying under the writ of execution, the registered process server shall deposit a copy of the writ with the levying officer and pay the fee provided by Section 26721 of the Government Code.

(c) If a registered process server levies on property pursuant to subdivision (a), the registered process server shall do both of the following:

(1) Comply with the applicable levy, posting, and service provisions of Article 4 (commencing with Section 700.010).

(2) Request any third person served to give a garnishee's memorandum to the levying officer in compliance with Section 701.030 on a form provided by the registered process server.

(d) Within five court days after levy under this section, all of the following shall be filed with the levying officer:

(1) The writ of execution.

(2) A proof of service by the registered process server stating the manner of levy performed.

(3) Proof of service of the copy of the writ and notice of levy on other persons, as required by Article 4 (commencing with Section 700.010).

(4) Instructions in writing, as required by the provisions of Section 687.010.

(e) If the fee provided by Section 26721 of the Government Code has been paid, the levying officer shall perform all other duties under the writ as if the levying officer had levied under the writ and shall return the writ to the court. If the registered process server does not comply with subdivisions (b) and (d), the levy is ineffective and the levying officer is not required to perform any duties under the writ and may issue a release for any property sought to be levied upon.

(f) The fee for services of a registered process server under this section shall be allowed as a recoverable cost pursuant to Section 1033.5.

(g) A registered process server may levy more than once under the same writ of execution, provided that the writ is still valid. *(Added by Stats.1982, c. 1364, p. 5121, § 2.1, operative July 1, 1983. Amended by Stats.1983, c. 155, § 13, eff. June 30, 1983, operative July 1, 1983; Stats.1984, c. 538, § 20; Stats.1984, c. 759, § 4.5; Stats.1987, c. 1080, § 5; Stats.2002, c. 197 (A.B.2493), § 3; Stats.2007, c. 15 (A.B.859), § 3.)*

Law Revision Commission Comments

Section 699.080 supersedes subdivisions (b) and (c) of former Section 687. This section expands and clarifies the role of the registered process server in levying on property pursuant to a writ of execution. See also Section 715.040 (service and posting of writ of possession of real property).

Subdivision (a) of Section 699.080 specifies the methods of levy that may be performed by a registered process server. This authority is limited to cases where the levy does not involve the possibility of taking immediate possession of the property.

Subdivision (c) makes clear that the registered process server is required to perform certain duties ancillary to the levy that would normally be performed by the levying officer at the time of levy or promptly thereafter. Subdivision (d) requires that the levying officer be provided with the information necessary to perform the remaining duties under the writ and to make a return on the writ. Subdivision (e) continues the substance of former Section 687(c). Subdivision (f) makes it discretionary with the court whether a fee for a registered process server will be allowed as costs. Whether the registered process server was used as a convenience to the judgment creditor or because service would not have been made if a public employee were used is an element to be considered by the court in exercising its discretion. If the court decides to allow a fee, subdivision (f) incorporates the general standard for recovery of the costs of employing a registered process server. For a limitation on this provision, see Section 706.101(e) (earnings withholding order).

Subdivision (b) is a new provision requiring a registered process server to file a copy of the writ with the appropriate levying officer and pay the standard fee before attempting to levy. This requirement gives the levying officer an early opportunity to establish a file which facilitates handling exemption claims and third-party claims, garnishees' memorandums, and payments by garnishees or by the judgment debtor. [16 Cal.L.Rev.Comm. Reports 2195 (1982)].

Research References

Rutter, Cal. Practice Guide: Enforcing Judgments/Debts Ch. 6A-5, Amount Recoverable Under Judgment.

Rutter, Cal. Practice Guide: Enforcing Judgments/Debts Ch. 6D-3, Levy of Writ of Execution-In General.

8 Witkin Cal. Proc. 5th Enforcement of Judgment § 48, Motion for Costs.

8 Witkin Cal. Proc. 5th Enforcement of Judgment § 103, (S 103) Levy by Registered Process Server.

8 Witkin Cal. Proc. 5th Enforcement of Judgment § 107, Application to Clerk.

§ 699.090. Property registered or recorded in name of owner; judgment debtor as owner; liability for levy

If property that is required by law to be registered or recorded in the name of the owner is levied upon under a writ of execution and it appears at the time of the levy that the judgment debtor was the registered or record owner of the property and the judgment creditor caused the levy to be made and the lien maintained in good faith and in reliance upon such registered or recorded ownership, neither the judgment creditor, the levying officer, nor the sureties on an undertaking given by the judgment creditor pursuant to Chapter 2 (commencing with Section 720.110) or Chapter 3 (commencing with Section 720.210) of Division 4 is liable to a third person for the levy itself. *(Added by Stats.1982, c. 1364, p. 5122, § 2, operative July 1, 1983.)*

Research References

Rutter, Cal. Practice Guide: Enforcing Judgments/Debts Ch. 6D-3, Levy of Writ of Execution-In General.

8 Witkin Cal. Proc. 5th Enforcement of Judgment § 33, Liability of Officer.

8 Witkin Cal. Proc. 5th Enforcement of Judgment § 104, (S 104) Levy Based on Record Ownership.

ARTICLE 2. WRIT OF EXECUTION AND NOTICE OF LEVY

Section

699.510.   Issuance of writ; judgments under Family Code.

699.520.   Directions to officer; contents of writ.

699.530.   Execution of writs; time for levy.

699.540.   Notice of levy.

699.545.   Notice of levy; copy of notice served on third party.

699.550.   Copy of writ and notice; failure to post, serve or mail.

699.560.   Time for return, report and accounting; electronic filing.

§ 699.510. Issuance of writ; judgments under Family Code

(a) Subject to subdivision (b), after entry of a money judgment, a writ of execution shall be issued by the clerk of the court, upon application of the judgment creditor, and shall be directed to the levying officer in the county where the levy is to be made and to any registered process server. The clerk of the court shall give priority to the application for, and issuance of, writs of execution on orders or judgments for child support and spousal support. A separate writ shall be issued for each county where a levy is to be made. Writs may be issued successively until the money judgment is satisfied, except that a new writ may not be issued for a county until the expiration of 180 days after the issuance of a prior writ for that county unless the prior writ is first returned.

(b) If the judgment creditor seeks a writ of execution to enforce a judgment made, entered, or enforceable pursuant to the Family Code, in addition to the requirements of this article, the judgment creditor shall satisfy the requirements of any applicable provisions of the Family Code.

(c)(1) The writ of execution shall be issued in the name of the judgment debtor as listed on the judgment, except that the judgment creditor shall omit the name of a judgment debtor from the application for a writ of execution if the liability of that judgment debtor has ceased with regard to the judgment, including either of the following occurrences:

(A) The judgment debtor has obtained a discharge of the judgment pursuant to Title 11 of the United States Code and notice thereof has been filed with the court.

(B) The judgment creditor files an acknowledgment of satisfaction of judgment with regard to the judgment debtor pursuant to Chapter 1 (commencing with Section 724.010) of Division 5.

* * * (2) The writ of execution * * * shall include the additional name or names, and the type of legal entity, by which the judgment debtor is known, as set forth in the affidavit of identity, as defined in Section 680.135, filed by the judgment creditor with the application for issuance of the writ of execution. Prior to the clerk of the court issuing a writ of execution containing any additional name or names by which the judgment debtor is known that are not listed on the judgment, the court shall approve the affidavit of identity. If the court determines, without a hearing or a notice, that the affidavit of identity states sufficient facts upon which the judgment creditor has identified the additional names of the judgment debtor, the court shall authorize the issuance of the writ of execution with the additional name or names.

(d) In any case where the writ of execution lists any name other than that listed on the judgment, the person in possession or control of the levied property, if other than the judgment debtor, shall not pay to the levying officer the amount or deliver the property being levied upon until being notified to do so by the levying officer. The levying officer may not require the person, if other than the judgment debtor, in possession or control of the levied property to pay the amount or deliver the property levied upon until the expiration of 15 days after service of notice of levy.

(e) If a person who is not the judgment debtor has property erroneously subject to an enforcement of judgment proceeding based upon an affidavit of identity, the person shall be entitled to the recovery of reasonable attorney's fees and costs from the judgment creditor incurred in releasing the person's property from a writ of execution, in addition to any other damages or penalties to which an aggrieved person may be entitled to by law, including Division 4 (commencing with Section 720.010). *(Added by Stats.1982, c. 1364, p. 5122, § 2, operative July 1, 1983. Amended by Stats.1992, c. 163 (A.B.2641), § 35, operative Jan. 1, 1994; Stats.2000, c. 639 (A.B.2405), § 3; Stats.2000, c. 808 (A.B.1358), § 12.1, eff. Sept. 28, 2000; Stats.2001, c. 159 (S.B. 662), § 40; Stats.2003, c. 17 (A.B.308), § 1; Stats.2010, c. 680 (A.B.2394), § 7; Stats.2013, c. 176 (S.B.551), § 2.)*

Law Revision Commission Comments

Subdivision (b) of Section 699.510 is revised to substitute a reference to the Family Code for the former reference to the former Family Law Act and to substitute references to the Family Code provisions that replaced the former Civil Code provisions. [22 Cal.L.Rev.Comm.Reports 1 (1992)].

The references to specific Family Code sections in subdivision (b) of Section 699.510 are deleted as unnecessary. If the court has made an order under Family Code Section 290 that affects the right to enforce support obligations by writ of execution, the order would have to be complied with. The reference to former Section 291 is obsolete; the new Section 291 does not apply to money judgments, and so is outside the scope of this section. References to Family Code Sections 2026 (reconciliation as amelioration of contempt) and 3556 (duty of support unaffected by failure or refusal of custody or visitation) are not relevant to issuance of a writ of execution under this section. The reference to Family Code Section 5100 *et seq.* is no longer relevant because the time limits on enforceability by writ have been removed from those sections. See former Fam. Code §§5100–5101, as amended by 1993 Cal. Stat. ch. 876, §§21–22. The general reference to compliance with any additional rules in the Family Code is retained to draw attention to the possibility that special rules may exist or may be enacted in the future.

The references to Family Code Sections 2026 (reconciliation of parties to be considered as ameliorating factor in considering contempt of existing order) and 3556 (duty of support not affected by failure or refusal of custodial parent to implement custody or visitation rights of noncustodial parent) are unrelated to the purpose of this section. Issuance of a writ of execution to enforce a money judgment does not have anything to do with enforcement by contempt. Use of the contempt power to enforce payment of support is distinct from enforcement by a writ of execution. Reference to Section 3556 seems irrelevant since that section provides that there is no excuse. The original intent of subdivision (b) was to recognize the court's authority to control enforcement by writ for amounts that were more than 10 years overdue, including the diligence rule in what became Family Code Section 291.

While the general authority of the court under Family Code Section 290 still exists, there are no limitations on writ issuance stated in the listed sections. Family Code Section 5100 provides that a writ may be used without prior court approval. [30 Cal.L.Rev.Comm.Reports 717 (2000)].

Research References

Rutter, Cal. Practice Guide: Civ. Pro. Before Trial Ch. 9(I)-E, E. Posthearing Procedures.

Rutter, Cal. Practice Guide: Civ. Pro. Before Trial Ch. 9(III)-E, E. Enforcement of Sanctions Orders.

Rutter, Cal. Practice Guide: Enforcing Judgments/Debts Ch. 6D-2, Writ of Execution.

Miller and Starr California Real Estate § 32:27, Procedure to Claim an Exemption.

Miller and Starr California Real Estate § 32:64, Creation, Duration, and Effect of Writ of Execution.

2 Witkin Cal. Proc. 5th Courts § 363, (S 363) Process and Notices.

8 Witkin Cal. Proc. 5th Enforcement of Judgment § 99, (S 99) Nature of Execution.

8 Witkin Cal. Proc. 5th Enforcement of Judgment § 107, Application to Clerk.

8 Witkin Cal. Proc. 5th Enforcement of Judgment § 108, Successive Writs.

8 Witkin Cal. Proc. 5th Enforcement of Judgment § 109, Writ to Enforce Support Order.

8 Witkin Cal. Proc. 5th Enforcement of Judgment § 110, Writ Based on Affidavit of Identity.

8 Witkin Cal. Proc. 5th Enforcement of Judgment § 111, (S 111) Contents of Writ.

8 Witkin Cal. Proc. 5th Enforcement of Judgment § 139, Delivery or Payment to Levying Officer.

8 Witkin Cal. Proc. 5th Enforcement of Judgment § 326, (S 326) Issuance of Writ of Possession or Sale.

§ 699.520. Directions to officer; contents of writ

The writ of execution shall require the levying officer to whom it is directed to enforce the money judgment and shall include the following information:

(a) The date of issuance of the writ.

(b) The title of the court where the judgment is entered and the cause and number of the action.

(c) The name and address of the judgment creditor and the name and last known address of the judgment debtor. If the judgment debtor is other than a natural person, the type of legal entity shall be stated.

(d) The date of the entry of the judgment and of any subsequent renewals and where entered in the records of the court.

(e) The total amount of the money judgment as entered or renewed, together with costs thereafter added to the judgment pursuant to Section 685. 090 and the accrued interest on the judgment from the date of entry or renewal of the judgment to the date of issuance of the writ, reduced by any partial satisfactions and by any amounts no longer enforceable.

(f) The amount required to satisfy the money judgment on the date the writ is issued.

(g) The amount of interest accruing daily on the principal amount of the judgment from the date the writ is issued.

(h) Whether any person has requested notice of sale under the judgment and, if so, the name and mailing address of that person.

(i) The sum of the fees and costs added to the judgment pursuant to Section 6103.5 or 68511.3 of the Government Code, and which is in addition to the amount owing to the judgment creditor on the judgment.

(j) Whether the writ of execution includes any additional names of the judgment debtor pursuant to an affidavit of identity, as defined in Section 680.135.

(k) A statement indicating whether the case is limited or unlimited. *(Added by Stats.1982, c. 1364, p. 5122, § 2, operative July 1, 1983. Amended by Stats.1993, c. 909 (S.B.15), § 2; Stats.2000, c. 639 (A.B.2405), § 4; Stats.2010, c. 680 (A.B.2394), § 8.)*

Law Revision Commission Comments

Section 699.520 prescribes the essential elements of a writ of execution. It supersedes a portion of the introductory paragraph and subdivision 1 of former Section 682, former Section 682.1, and portions of former Sections 682.2 and 692a. See also Section 699.530 (execution of writ). For the

statutory form of the writ, see Section 693.010. The writ of execution is directed to the levying officer and provides the basis for the levying officer's authority under this chapter. Some duties under the writ may be performed by a registered process server. See Section 699.080. See also Section 706.101(e) (wage garnishment).

Subdivision (g) provides for the computation of daily interest on the principal amount of the judgment (defined in Section 680.300). Under former Section 682.2, it appears that daily interest was computed on the total amount of the judgment remaining unpaid, including accrued interest. The change made by subdivision (g) avoids compounding of interest. [16 Cal.L.Rev.Comm. Reports 1318 (1982)].

Research References

Rutter, Cal. Practice Guide: Enforcing Judgments/Debts Ch. 6D-2, Writ of Execution.

Rutter, Cal. Practice Guide: Enforcing Judgments/Debts Ch. 6D-7, Sale and Collection of Property Levied Upon.

Rutter, Cal. Practice Guide: Enforcing Judgments/Debts Ch. 6A-13, Creating an Enforcement of Judgment Plan.

Miller and Starr California Real Estate § 32:64, Creation, Duration, and Effect of Writ of Execution.

8 Witkin Cal. Proc. 5th Enforcement of Judgment § 99, (S 99) Nature of Execution.

8 Witkin Cal. Proc. 5th Enforcement of Judgment § 107, Application to Clerk.

8 Witkin Cal. Proc. 5th Enforcement of Judgment § 111, (S 111) Contents of Writ.

§ 699.530. Execution of writs; time for levy

(a) Upon delivery of the writ of execution to the levying officer to whom the writ is directed, together with the written instructions of the judgment creditor, the levying officer shall execute the writ in the manner prescribed by law.

(b) The levying officer may not levy upon any property under the writ after the expiration of 180 days from the date the writ was issued. *(Added by Stats.1982, c. 1364, p. 5123, § 2, operative July 1, 1983.)*

Research References

Rutter, Cal. Practice Guide: Enforcing Judgments/Debts Ch. 6D-2, Writ of Execution.

Rutter, Cal. Practice Guide: Enforcing Judgments/Debts Ch. 6D-3, Levy of Writ of Execution-In General.

Rutter, Cal. Practice Guide: Enforcing Judgments/Debts Ch. 6F-3, Issuance and Service of Earnings Withholding Orders.

Miller and Starr California Real Estate § 32:27, Procedure to Claim an Exemption.

Miller and Starr California Real Estate § 32:64, Creation, Duration, and Effect of Writ of Execution.

8 Witkin Cal. Proc. 5th Enforcement of Judgment § 29, Instructions from Judgment Creditor.

8 Witkin Cal. Proc. 5th Enforcement of Judgment § 112, (S 112) Delivery and Execution of Writ.

8 Witkin Cal. Proc. 5th Enforcement of Judgment § 252, (S 252) Application for Order.

8 Witkin Cal. Proc. 5th Enforcement of Judgment § 253, (S 253) Issuance of Order.

8 Witkin Cal. Proc. 5th Enforcement of Judgment § 254, in General.

8 Witkin Cal. Proc. 5th Enforcement of Judgment § 256, Service by Registered Process Server.

8 Witkin Cal. Proc. 5th Enforcement of Judgment § 327, (S 327) Delivery, Execution, and Return of Writ.

§ 699.540. Notice of levy

The notice of levy required by Article 4 (commencing with Section 700.010) shall inform the person notified of all of the following:

(a) The capacity in which the person is notified.

(b) The property that is levied upon.

(c) The person's rights under the levy, including the right to claim an exemption pursuant to Chapter 4 (commencing with

Section 703.010) and the right to make a third-party claim pursuant to Division 4 (commencing with Section 720.010).

(d) The person's duties under the levy.

(e) All names listed in the writ of execution pursuant to an affidavit of identity, as defined in Section 680.135, if any. *(Added by Stats.1982, c. 1364, p. 5123, § 2, operative July 1, 1983. Amended by Stats.2000, c. 639 (A.B.2405), § 5.)*

Research References

Rutter, Cal. Practice Guide: Enforcing Judgments/Debts Ch. 6D-3, Levy of Writ of Execution-In General.

Miller and Starr California Real Estate § 32:64, Creation, Duration, and Effect of Writ of Execution.

8 Witkin Cal. Proc. 5th Enforcement of Judgment § 113, (S 113) Notice of Levy.

8 Witkin Cal. Proc. 5th Enforcement of Judgment § 313, (S 313) Filing, Notice, and Lien.

§ 699.545. Notice of levy; copy of notice served on third party

A copy of the original notice of levy which has been served upon a third party holding the property sought to be levied upon and the affidavit of identity, as defined in Section 680.135, if any, if served upon the judgment debtor or any other party, shall suffice as the notice of levy to that person. *(Added by Stats.1984, c. 759, § 5. Amended by Stats.2000, c. 639 (A.B.2405), § 6.)*

Research References

8 Witkin Cal. Proc. 5th Enforcement of Judgment § 113, (S 113) Notice of Levy.

§ 699.550. Copy of writ and notice; failure to post, serve or mail

In any case where property has been levied upon and, pursuant to a levy, a copy of the writ of execution and a notice of levy are required by statute to be posted or to be served on or mailed to the judgment debtor or other person, failure to post, serve, or mail the copy of the writ and the notice does not affect the execution lien created by the levy. Failure to serve on or mail to the judgment debtor a list of exemptions does not affect the execution lien created by the levy. *(Added by Stats.1982, c. 1364, p. 5123, § 2, operative July 1, 1983.)*

Law Revision Commission Comments

Section 699.550 is analogous to portions of Sections 488.310–488.430 (method of levy in attachment) which were incorporated by former Section 688. This section is intended to preserve the validity of a levy in a case where additional postings, service, or mailings have been omitted. For example, an instrument in the hands of a third person is levied upon at the time the third person is served. See Section 700.110(a) (2). The levy is effective to create a lien even though no notice is given the judgment debtor (as required by Section 700.010) or the obligor under the instrument (as provided by Section 700.110(b)), but the rights of the obligor are not affected until the obligor knows or has reason to know of the levy (see Sections 701.010, 701.060). As to failure to give notice of a sale, see Section 701.560. [16 Cal.L.Rev.Comm. Reports 1320 (1982)].

Research References

Rutter, Cal. Practice Guide: Enforcing Judgments/Debts Ch. 6D-3, Levy of Writ of Execution-In General.

Rutter, Cal. Practice Guide: Enforcing Judgments/Debts Ch. 6D-4, Levy on Specific Property.

Miller and Starr California Real Estate § 32:27, Procedure to Claim an Exemption.

Miller and Starr California Real Estate § 32:64, Creation, Duration, and Effect of Writ of Execution.

8 Witkin Cal. Proc. 5th Enforcement of Judgment § 92, (S 92) Creation and Duration.

8 Witkin Cal. Proc. 5th Enforcement of Judgment § 117, (S 117) in General.

§ 699.560. Time for return, report and accounting; electronic filing

(a) Except as provided in subdivisions (b) and (c), the writ expires and the levying officer to whom the writ of execution is delivered shall return the writ to the court, or store the writ as provided in Section 263.6, and file a return with the court reporting the levying officer's actions and an accounting of amounts collected, and costs incurred, at the earliest of the following times:

(1) Two years from the date of issuance of the writ, unless paragraph (1) of subdivision (a) of Section 706.022 is applicable.

(2) Promptly after all of the duties under the writ are performed.

(3) When return is requested in writing by the judgment creditor.

(4) If no levy takes place under the writ within 180 days after its issuance, promptly after the expiration of the 180–day period.

(5) Upon expiration of the time for enforcement of the money judgment.

(b) If a levy has been made under Section 700.200 upon an interest in personal property in the estate of a decedent, the writ shall be returned within the time prescribed in Section 700.200.

(c) If a levy has been made under Section 5103 of the Family Code on the judgment debtor's right to the payment of benefits from an employee pension benefit plan, the writ shall be returned within the time prescribed in that section.

(d) If a levy has been made under the Wage Garnishment Law (Chapter 5 (commencing with Section 706.010)), and the earnings withholding order remains in effect, the writ of execution shall be returned as provided in subdivision (a) and a supplemental return shall be made as provided in Section 706.033.

(e) Subject to the limitations in subdivision (c) of Section 263, a levying officer may electronically file with the court the return, containing the information required by subdivision (a), pursuant to Chapter 2 (commencing with Section 263) of Title 4 of Part 1. *(Added by Stats.1982, c. 1364, p. 5123, § 2, operative July 1, 1983. Amended by Stats.1985, c. 362, § 5; Stats.1992, c. 163 (A.B.2641), § 361; Stats.1992, c. 283 (S.B.1372), § 4, eff. July 26, 1992; Stats.1993, c. 219 (A.B.1500), § 67; Stats.2010, c. 680 (A.B.2394), § 9.)*

Law Revision Commission Comments

Subdivision (d) is added to Section 699.560 to recognize the special rule concerning returns where an earnings withholding order continues in force after the writ of execution is required to be returned. [21 Cal.L.Rev.Comm.Reports 135 (1991)].

Subdivision (c) of Section 699.560 is amended to substitute a reference to the Family Code section that replaced the former Civil Code section. [23 Cal.L.Rev.Comm. Reports 1 (1993)].

Research References

Rutter, Cal. Practice Guide: Enforcing Judgments/Debts Ch. 6D-3, Levy of Writ of Execution-In General.

Rutter, Cal. Practice Guide: Enforcing Judgments/Debts Ch. 6D-7, Sale and Collection of Property Levied Upon.

8 Witkin Cal. Proc. 5th Enforcement of Judgment § 114, (S 114) Return of Writ.

8 Witkin Cal. Proc. 5th Enforcement of Judgment § 138, (S 138) Interest in Personal Property in Decedent's Estate.

8 Witkin Cal. Proc. 5th Enforcement of Judgment § 259, (S 259) Payment of Amounts Withheld.

8 Witkin Cal. Proc. 5th Enforcement of Judgment § 260, (S 260) Continuation of Order After Return of Writ.

Civ. Pro.

8 Witkin Cal. Proc. 5th Enforcement of Judgment § 327, (S 327) Delivery, Execution, and Return of Writ.

ARTICLE 3. PROPERTY SUBJECT TO EXECUTION

§ 699.710. Property subject to enforcement of money judgment subject to levy

Except as otherwise provided by law, all property that is subject to enforcement of a money judgment pursuant to Article 1 (commencing with Section 695.010) of Chapter 1 is subject to levy under a writ of execution to satisfy a money judgment. *(Added by Stats.1982, c. 1364, p. 5124, § 2, operative July 1, 1983.)*

Research References

Rutter, Cal. Practice Guide: Enforcing Judgments/Debts Ch. 6D-2, Writ of Execution.
Miller and Starr California Real Estate § 19:2, Lease as Personal Property or Real Property.
Miller and Starr California Real Estate § 32:61, Property Interests Subject to Execution.
8 Witkin Cal. Proc. 5th Enforcement of Judgment § 115, Property Subject to Execution.
8 Witkin Cal. Proc. 5th Enforcement of Judgment § 118, Property Subject to Levy.

§ 699.720. Property not subject to execution

(a) The following types of property are not subject to execution:

(1) An alcoholic beverage license that is transferable under Article 5 (commencing with Section 24070) of Chapter 6 of Division 9 of the Business and Professions Code.

(2) The interest of a partner in a partnership or member in a limited liability company if the partnership or the limited liability company is not a judgment debtor.

(3) A cause of action that is the subject of a pending action or special proceeding.

(4) A judgment in favor of the judgment debtor prior to the expiration of the time for appeal from the judgment or, if an appeal is filed, prior to the final determination of the appeal.

(5) A debt (other than earnings) owing and unpaid by a public entity.

(6) The loan value of an unmatured life insurance, endowment, or annuity policy.

(7) A franchise granted by a public entity and all the rights and privileges of the franchise.

(8) The interest of a trust beneficiary.

(9) A contingent remainder, executory interest, or other interest in property that is not vested.

(10) Property in a guardianship or conservatorship estate.

(b) Nothing in subdivision (a) affects or limits the right of the judgment creditor to apply property to the satisfaction of a money judgment pursuant to any applicable procedure other than execution. *(Added by Stats.1982, c. 1364, p. 5124, § 2, operative July 1, 1983. Amended by Stats.1996, c. 57 (S.B.141), § 1, eff. June 6, 1996.)*

Research References

Rutter, Cal. Practice Guide: Enforcing Judgments/Debts Ch. 4-A, A. Attachment.
Rutter, Cal. Practice Guide: Enforcing Judgments/Debts Ch. 6D-2, Writ of Execution.

Rutter, Cal. Practice Guide: Enforcing Judgments/Debts Ch. 6G-5, Assignment Order.
Rutter, Cal. Practice Guide: Enforcing Judgments/Debts Ch. 6G-7, Charging Orders Against Debtor Partnership/LLC Interests.
Rutter, Cal. Practice Guide: Enforcing Judgments/Debts Ch. 6G-8, Lien in Pending Action.
Rutter, Cal. Practice Guide: Enforcing Judgments/Debts Ch. 6G-9, Collection of Debts Owed Judgment Debtors by State or Local Public Entities.
Rutter, Cal. Practice Guide: Enforcing Judgments/Debts Ch. 6G-10, Enforcement Against Franchises.
Rutter, Cal. Practice Guide: Enforcing Judgments/Debts Ch. 6G-17, Enforcement Against Beneficiary's Trust Interests.
Rutter, Cal. Practice Guide: Enforcing Judgments/Debts Ch. 6G-18, Enforcement Against Nonvested Contingent Interests.
Miller and Starr California Real Estate § 32:61, Property Interests Subject to Execution.
Miller and Starr California Real Estate § 32:62, Property of a Partner or Partnership.
8 Witkin Cal. Proc. 5th Enforcement of Judgment § 116, Property Not Subject to Execution.
8 Witkin Cal. Proc. 5th Enforcement of Judgment § 199, (S 199) Life Insurance Policies.
8 Witkin Cal. Proc. 5th Enforcement of Judgment § 296, Charging Order.
8 Witkin Cal. Proc. 5th Enforcement of Judgment § 297, (S 297) Nature and Scope of Remedy.
8 Witkin Cal. Proc. 5th Enforcement of Judgment § 305, (S 305) Nature and Procedure.
8 Witkin Cal. Proc. 5th Enforcement of Judgment § 311, (S 311) Transfer of Alcoholic Beverage License.
8 Witkin Cal. Proc. 5th Enforcement of Judgment § 320, (S 320) Franchise.
8 Witkin Cal. Proc. 5th Enforcement of Judgment § 321, Enforcement of Judgments Law.
8 Witkin Cal. Proc. 5th Enforcement of Judgment § 323, (S 323) Contingent Interest.
8 Witkin Cal. Proc. 5th Enforcement of Judgment § 324, (S 324) Guardianship or Conservatorship Estate.

ARTICLE 4. METHODS OF LEVY

Section

700.160.   Safe-deposit box in name of person other than debtor alone or with third person; court order; exceptions; payment by financial institution.

700.170.   Account receivable or general intangible.

700.180.   Property subject of pending action or special proceeding; ineffective levy; garnishee's memorandum.

700.190.   Final money judgment.

700.200.   Interest in personal property in estate of decedent.

§ 700.010.   Service on judgment debtor

(a) At the time of levy pursuant to this article or promptly thereafter, the levying officer shall serve a copy of the following on the judgment debtor:

(1) The writ of execution.

(2) A notice of levy.

(3) If the judgment debtor is a natural person, a copy of the form listing exemptions prepared by the Judicial Council pursuant to subdivision (c) of Section 681.030, the list of exemption amounts published pursuant to subdivision (e) of Section 703.150, a copy of the form that the judgment debtor may use to make a claim of exemption pursuant to Section 703.520, and a copy of the form the judgment debtor may use to provide a financial statement pursuant to Section 703.530.

(4) Any affidavit of identity, as defined in Section 680.135, for names of the debtor listed on the writ of execution.

(b) Service under this section shall be made personally or by mail. *(Added by Stats.1982, c. 1364, p. 5124, § 2, operative July 1, 1983. Amended by Stats.2000, c. 639 (A.B.2405), § 7; Stats.2003, c. 379 (A.B.182), § 2; Stats.2013, c. 64 (S.B.233), § 4.)*

Law Revision Commission Comments

Section 700.010 continues the requirement of former Section 682.1 and of the second sentence of subdivision (b) of former Section 688 that a copy of the writ be served on the judgment debtor and adds the requirement that a notice of levy also be served on the judgment debtor. The judgment creditor has the responsibility of furnishing the levying officer with the information necessary to comply with this provision. See Section 687.010 (instructions to levying officer). See also Section 699.080 (levy by registered process server). Failure to comply with Section 700.010 does not affect the validity of the execution lien created by the levy. See Section 699.550. [16 Cal.L.Rev.Comm. Reports 1324 (1982)].

Section 700.010 is amended to reflect the automatic triennial cost-of-living adjustment of personal property exemptions from enforcement of money judgments pursuant to Section 703.150. [33 Cal.L.Rev.Commn. Reports 128 (2003)].

Research References

Rutter, Cal. Practice Guide: Enforcing Judgments/Debts Ch. 6D-3, Levy of Writ of Execution-In General.

Rutter, Cal. Practice Guide: Enforcing Judgments/Debts Ch. 6D-4, Levy on Specific Property.

Miller and Starr California Real Estate § 31:63, Enforcement of a Money Judgment Against a Mobilehome.

Miller and Starr California Real Estate § 32:26, Claim of Exemption.

Miller and Starr California Real Estate § 32:27, Procedure to Claim an Exemption.

Miller and Starr California Real Estate § 32:64, Creation, Duration, and Effect of Writ of Execution.

Miller and Starr California Real Estate § 10:226, The Judicial Sale.

8 Witkin Cal. Proc. 5th Enforcement of Judgment § 99, (S 99) Nature of Execution.

8 Witkin Cal. Proc. 5th Enforcement of Judgment § 103, (S 103) Levy by Registered Process Server.

8 Witkin Cal. Proc. 5th Enforcement of Judgment § 113, (S 113) Notice of Levy.

8 Witkin Cal. Proc. 5th Enforcement of Judgment § 117, (S 117) in General.

8 Witkin Cal. Proc. 5th Enforcement of Judgment § 124, Property in Possession of Debtor or Third Person.

8 Witkin Cal. Proc. 5th Enforcement of Judgment § 135, (S 135) Accounts Receivable and General Intangibles.

8 Witkin Cal. Proc. 5th Enforcement of Judgment § 147, Sale of Real Property.

8 Witkin Cal. Proc. 5th Enforcement of Judgment § 338, (S 338) Writ of Sale.

6 Witkin Cal. Proc. 5th Provisional Remedies § 158, Property Governed by Enforcement of Judgments Law.

§ 700.015.   Real property; copies of writ and notice of levy; recording; service and posting

(a) To levy upon real property, the levying officer shall record with the recorder of the county where the real property is located a copy of the writ of execution and a notice of levy that describes the property levied upon and states that the judgment debtor's interest in the described property has been levied upon. If the judgment debtor's interest in the real property stands upon the records of the county in the name of a person other than the judgment debtor, the notice of levy shall identify the third person and the recorder shall index the copy of the writ and notice of levy in the names of both the judgment debtor and the third person.

(b) At the time of levy or promptly thereafter, the levying officer shall serve a copy of the writ and a notice of levy on any third person in whose name the judgment debtor's interest in the real property stands upon the records of the county. Service shall be made personally or by mail. If service on the third person is by mail, it shall be sent to the person at the address for such person, if any, shown by the records of the office of the tax assessor of the county where the real property is located or, if no address is so shown, to the person at the address used by the county recorder for the return of the instrument creating the interest of the third person in the property.

(c) At the time of levy or promptly thereafter, the levying officer shall serve a copy of the writ and a notice of levy on one occupant of the real property. Service on the occupant shall be made by leaving the copy of the writ and a notice of levy with the occupant personally or, in the occupant's absence, with a person of suitable age and discretion found upon the real property when service is attempted who is either an employee or agent of the occupant or a member of the occupant's household. If unable to serve such an occupant at the time service is attempted, the levying officer shall post the copy of the writ and the notice of levy in a conspicuous place on the real property. If the real property described in the notice of levy consists of more than one distinct lot, parcel, or governmental subdivision and any of the lots, parcels, or governmental subdivisions lies with relation to any of the others so as to form one or more continuous, unbroken tracts, only one service or posting need be made under this subdivision as to each continuous, unbroken tract. *(Added by Stats.1982, c. 1364, p. 5125, § 2, operative July 1, 1983.)*

Research References

Rutter, Cal. Practice Guide: Enforcing Judgments/Debts Ch. 4-A, A. Attachment.

Rutter, Cal. Practice Guide: Enforcing Judgments/Debts Ch. 6D-4, Levy on Specific Property.

Miller and Starr California Real Estate § 11:6, Instruments Subject to Recording--List of Recordable Documents.

Miller and Starr California Real Estate § 31:63, Enforcement of a Money Judgment Against a Mobilehome.

Miller and Starr California Real Estate § 32:27, Procedure to Claim an Exemption.

Miller and Starr California Real Estate § 32:31, Creation and Extension of the Attachment Lien.

Miller and Starr California Real Estate § 32:64, Creation, Duration, and Effect of Writ of Execution.

Miller and Starr California Real Estate § 11:122, Recordation of the Attachment Lien.

Miller and Starr California Real Estate § 11:128, Execution Lien; Recordation of the Writ of Execution.

8 Witkin Cal. Proc. 5th Enforcement of Judgment § 118, Property Subject to Levy.

8 Witkin Cal. Proc. 5th Enforcement of Judgment § 119, Recording With County Recorder.

8 Witkin Cal. Proc. 5th Enforcement of Judgment § 120, Service of Writ and Notice.

8 Witkin Cal. Proc. 5th Enforcement of Judgment § 136, (S 136) Property Subject of Pending Action.

6 Witkin Cal. Proc. 5th Provisional Remedies § 158, Property Governed by Enforcement of Judgments Law.

14 Witkin, California Summary 10th Wills and Probate § 645, Right to Bring Action.

§ 700.020.   Growing crops, timber to be cut or minerals

(a) To levy upon (1) growing crops, (2) timber to be cut, or (3) minerals or the like (including oil and gas) to be extracted or accounts receivable resulting from the sale thereof at the wellhead or minehead, the levying officer shall record with the recorder of the county where those crops, timber, or minerals or the like are located a copy of the writ of execution and a notice of levy that describes the property levied upon and states that the judgment debtor's interest in the described property has been levied upon and describes the real property where the crops, timber, or minerals or the like are located. If the judgment debtor's interest in the crops, timber, minerals or the like, or if the real property where the crops, timber, or minerals or the like are located, stands upon the records of the county in the name of a person other than the judgment debtor, the notice of levy shall identify the third person and the recorder shall index the copy of the writ and notice of levy in the names of both the judgment debtor and the third person.

(b) At the time of levy or promptly thereafter, the levying officer shall serve a copy of the writ and a notice of levy personally or by mail on the following persons:

(1) Any third person in whose name the judgment debtor's interest in the crops, timber, minerals or the like stands upon the records of the county and any third person in whose name the real property stands upon the records of the county. If service on the third person is by mail, it shall be sent to the person at the address for the person, if any, shown by the records of the office of the assessor of the county where the real property is located or, if no address is so shown, to the person at the address used by the county recorder for the return of the instrument creating the interest of the third person in the property.

(2) Any secured party who has filed a financing statement with respect to the crops, timber, or minerals or the like or the accounts receivable, prior to the date of levy on the property.

(c) At the time of levy or promptly thereafter, the levying officer shall serve a copy of the writ and a notice of levy on one occupant of the real property where the crops, timber, or minerals or the like are located. Service on the occupant shall be made by leaving the copy of the writ and a notice of levy with the occupant personally or, in the occupant's absence, with a person of suitable age and discretion found upon the real property when service is attempted who is either an employee or agent of the occupant or a member of the occupant's household. If he or she is unable to serve an occupant or suitable person at the time service is attempted, the levying officer shall post the copy of the writ and the notice of levy in a conspicuous place on the real property. However, the posting requirement of the preceding sentence shall not apply where the levy is made upon minerals or the like (but not including oil or gas) and no dwelling is located on the real property. If the real property described in the notice of levy consists of more than one distinct lot, parcel, or governmental subdivision and any of the lots, parcels, or

governmental subdivisions lies with relation to any of the others so as to form one or more continuous, unbroken tracts, only one service or posting need be made under this subdivision as to each continuous, unbroken tract. *(Added by Stats.1982, c. 1364, p. 5125, § 2, operative July 1, 1983. Amended by Stats.1993, c. 1187 (S.B.70), § 1.5.)*

Research References

Rutter, Cal. Practice Guide: Enforcing Judgments/Debts Ch. 4-A, A. Attachment.

Rutter, Cal. Practice Guide: Enforcing Judgments/Debts Ch. 6D-4, Levy on Specific Property.

Miller and Starr California Real Estate § 17:21, Minerals--In General.

Miller and Starr California Real Estate § 17:23, Minerals--Oil and Gas.

Miller and Starr California Real Estate § 17:31, Timber.

Miller and Starr California Real Estate § 17:33, Crops--Encumbrance of Crops.

Miller and Starr California Real Estate § 32:31, Creation and Extension of the Attachment Lien.

Miller and Starr California Real Estate § 11:128, Execution Lien; Recordation of the Writ of Execution.

8 Witkin Cal. Proc. 5th Enforcement of Judgment § 97, Crops, Timber, and Minerals.

8 Witkin Cal. Proc. 5th Enforcement of Judgment § 121, in General.

8 Witkin Cal. Proc. 5th Enforcement of Judgment § 122, Recording With County Recorder.

8 Witkin Cal. Proc. 5th Enforcement of Judgment § 123, Service of Writ and Notice.

8 Witkin Cal. Proc. 5th Enforcement of Judgment § 135, (S 135) Accounts Receivable and General Intangibles.

8 Witkin Cal. Proc. 5th Enforcement of Judgment § 136, (S 136) Property Subject of Pending Action.

6 Witkin Cal. Proc. 5th Provisional Remedies § 173, Crops, Timber, and Minerals.

§ 700.030.   Tangible personal property in possession or control of debtor

Unless another method of levy is provided by this article, to levy upon tangible personal property in the possession or under the control of the judgment debtor, the levying officer shall take the property into custody. *(Added by Stats.1982, c. 1364, p. 5126, § 2, operative July 1, 1983.)*

Research References

Rutter, Cal. Practice Guide: Enforcing Judgments/Debts Ch. 6D-4, Levy on Specific Property.

Rutter, Cal. Practice Guide: Enforcing Judgments/Debts Form 6:P, Sample Levy Instructions.

8 Witkin Cal. Proc. 5th Enforcement of Judgment § 121, in General.

8 Witkin Cal. Proc. 5th Enforcement of Judgment § 124, Property in Possession of Debtor or Third Person.

8 Witkin Cal. Proc. 5th Enforcement of Judgment § 126, Property of Going Business.

8 Witkin Cal. Proc. 5th Enforcement of Judgment § 136, (S 136) Property Subject of Pending Action.

§ 700.040.   Tangible personal property in possession or control of third person; bailees

(a) Unless another method of levy is provided by this article, to levy upon tangible personal property in the possession or under the control of a third person, the levying officer shall personally serve a copy of the writ of execution and a notice of levy on the third person.

(b) If goods are in the possession of a bailee who has issued a negotiable document of title therefor, the goods may not be levied upon but the negotiable document of title may be levied upon in the manner provided by Section 700.120. If goods are in the possession of a bailee other than one who has issued a negotiable document of title therefor, the goods may be levied upon in the manner provided by Section 700.060. As used in this subdivision, "bailee" means "bailee" as defined in Section

7102 of the Commercial Code. *(Added by Stats.1982, c. 1364, p. 5126, § 2, operative July 1, 1983.)*

Research References

Rutter, Cal. Practice Guide: Enforcing Judgments/Debts Ch. 6D-4, Levy on Specific Property.
8 Witkin Cal. Proc. 5th Enforcement of Judgment § 124, Property in Possession of Debtor or Third Person.
8 Witkin Cal. Proc. 5th Enforcement of Judgment § 131, (S 131) Documents of Title and Securities.
6 Witkin Cal. Proc. 5th Provisional Remedies § 158, Property Governed by Enforcement of Judgments Law.

§ 700.050. Personal property in custody of levying officer

(a) To levy upon personal property in the custody of a levying officer:

(1) If the writ of execution is directed to the levying officer having custody of the property, the judgment creditor shall deliver the writ to the levying officer.

(2) If the writ of execution is directed to a levying officer other than the levying officer having custody of the property, the levying officer to whom the writ is directed shall serve a copy of the writ and a notice of levy on the levying officer having custody. Service shall be made personally or by mail.

(b) The levying officer having custody of the property shall comply with the writs in the order they are received and is not subject to the provisions of Article 5 (commencing with Section 701.010) (duties and liabilities of third persons after levy). *(Added by Stats.1982, c. 1364, p. 5127, § 2, operative July 1, 1983.)*

Research References

Rutter, Cal. Practice Guide: Enforcing Judgments/Debts Ch. 6D-4, Levy on Specific Property.
8 Witkin Cal. Proc. 5th Enforcement of Judgment § 124, Property in Possession of Debtor or Third Person.
8 Witkin Cal. Proc. 5th Enforcement of Judgment § 125, Property in Custody of Levying Officer.
8 Witkin Cal. Proc. 5th Enforcement of Judgment § 136, (S 136) Property Subject of Pending Action.
8 Witkin Cal. Proc. 5th Enforcement of Judgment § 139, Delivery or Payment to Levying Officer.
6 Witkin Cal. Proc. 5th Provisional Remedies § 158, Property Governed by Enforcement of Judgments Law.

§ 700.060. Service on bailee and secured party

(a) To levy upon goods in the possession of a bailee (as defined in Section 7102 of the Commercial Code) other than one who has issued a negotiable document of title therefor, the levying officer shall personally serve a copy of the writ of execution and a notice of levy on the bailee.

(b) If the goods described in subdivision (a) are subject to a security interest, the levying officer shall, if so instructed by the judgment creditor, serve a copy of the writ of execution and a notice of levy on the secured party. Service shall be made personally or by mail. *(Added by Stats.1982, c. 1364, p. 5127, § 2, operative July 1, 1983.)*

Research References

Rutter, Cal. Practice Guide: Enforcing Judgments/Debts Ch. 6D-3, Levy of Writ of Execution-In General.
Rutter, Cal. Practice Guide: Enforcing Judgments/Debts Ch. 6D-4, Levy on Specific Property.
Rutter, Cal. Practice Guide: Enforcing Judgments/Debts Ch. 6D-7, Sale and Collection of Property Levied Upon.
8 Witkin Cal. Proc. 5th Enforcement of Judgment § 124, Property in Possession of Debtor or Third Person.

6 Witkin Cal. Proc. 5th Provisional Remedies § 158, Property Governed by Enforcement of Judgments Law.

§ 700.070. Tangible personal property of going business in possession or control of debtor

To levy upon tangible personal property of a going business in the possession or under the control of the judgment debtor, the levying officer shall comply with Section 700.030, except to the extent that the judgment creditor instructs that levy be made in the following manner:

(a) The levying officer shall place a keeper in charge of the business for the period requested by the judgment creditor. During the period, the business may continue to operate in the ordinary course of business provided that all sales are final and are for cash or its equivalent. For the purpose of this subdivision, a check is the equivalent of cash. The levying officer is not liable for accepting payment in the form of a cash equivalent. The keeper shall take custody of the proceeds from all sales unless otherwise directed by the judgment creditor.

(b) The levying officer shall take the tangible personal property into exclusive custody at the earliest of the following times:

(1) At any time the judgment debtor objects to placement of a keeper in charge of the business.

(2) At any time when requested by the judgment creditor.

(3) At the end of 10 days from the time the keeper is placed in charge of the business.

(c) Where a keeper is placed in a business for the purpose of taking into custody tangible personal property consisting solely of money or equivalent proceeds of sales, the provisions of subdivision (b) shall not apply, and the levying officer shall take such property into exclusive custody at the end of each daily keeper period. *(Added by Stats.1982, c. 1364, p. 5127, § 2, operative July 1, 1983. Amended by Stats.1996, c. 1159 (A.B. 3471), § 11.)*

Research References

Rutter, Cal. Practice Guide: Enforcing Judgments/Debts Ch. 4-A, A. Attachment.
Rutter, Cal. Practice Guide: Enforcing Judgments/Debts Ch. 6D-4, Levy on Specific Property.
Rutter, Cal. Practice Guide: Enforcing Judgments/Debts Form 6:P, Sample Levy Instructions.
8 Witkin Cal. Proc. 5th Enforcement of Judgment § 33, Liability of Officer.
8 Witkin Cal. Proc. 5th Enforcement of Judgment § 124, Property in Possession of Debtor or Third Person.
8 Witkin Cal. Proc. 5th Enforcement of Judgment § 126, Property of Going Business.
6 Witkin Cal. Proc. 5th Provisional Remedies § 169, (S 169) Custody of Keeper or Levying Officer.

§ 700.080. Personal property used as dwelling

(a) To levy upon personal property used as a dwelling, the levying officer shall serve a copy of the writ of execution and a notice of levy on one occupant of the property. Service on the occupant shall be made by leaving the copy of the writ and the notice of levy with the occupant personally or, in the occupant's absence, with a person of suitable age and discretion found at the property when service is attempted who is a member of the occupant's family or household. If unable to serve the occupant at the time service is attempted, the levying officer shall make the levy by posting the copy of the writ and the notice of levy in a conspicuous place on the property.

(b) If the judgment creditor so instructs, the levying officer shall place a keeper in charge of the property for a period requested by the judgment creditor.

(c) The judgment creditor may apply to the court on noticed motion for an order directing the levying officer to remove the occupants. The notice of motion shall be served on any legal owner and any junior lienholder who was served pursuant to Section 700.090, on the occupant, and, if the judgment debtor is not the occupant, on the judgment debtor. Service shall be made personally or by mail. At the hearing on the motion the court shall determine the occupant's right to possession and shall make an order including terms and conditions that are appropriate under the circumstances of the case.

(d) Personal property used as a dwelling shall include a mobilehome, whether the mobilehome is occupied or unoccupied at the time of the levy. *(Added by Stats.1982, c. 1364, p. 5128, § 2, operative July 1, 1983. Amended by Stats.1983, c. 1124, § 9, operative Jan. 1, 1984; Stats.1995, c. 446 (S.B.69), § 2.)*

Research References

Rutter, Cal. Practice Guide: Enforcing Judgments/Debts Ch. 6D-4, Levy on Specific Property.
Rutter, Cal. Practice Guide: Enforcing Judgments/Debts Ch. 6I-2, Enforcement of Judgment for Possession of Personal Property.
Miller and Starr California Real Estate § 31:63, Enforcement of a Money Judgment Against a Mobilehome.
Miller and Starr California Real Estate § 32:27, Procedure to Claim an Exemption.
Miller and Starr California Real Estate § 32:31, Creation and Extension of the Attachment Lien.
Miller and Starr California Real Estate § 32:61, Property Interests Subject to Execution.
Miller and Starr California Real Estate § 32:64, Creation, Duration, and Effect of Writ of Execution.
Miller and Starr California Real Estate § 19:232, Recovery of Possession; Writ of Possession.
8 Witkin Cal. Proc. 5th Enforcement of Judgment § 124, Property in Possession of Debtor or Third Person.
8 Witkin Cal. Proc. 5th Enforcement of Judgment § 127, Property Used as Dwelling.
8 Witkin Cal. Proc. 5th Enforcement of Judgment § 329, (S 329) Writ of Possession.
6 Witkin Cal. Proc. 5th Provisional Remedies § 152, Levy by Registered Process Server.
6 Witkin Cal. Proc. 5th Provisional Remedies § 158, Property Governed by Enforcement of Judgments Law.

§ 700.090. Vehicle, vessel, manufactured home, mobilehome or commercial coach; determination of legal owner

If a vehicle or vessel is levied upon and a certificate of ownership has been issued by the Department of Motor Vehicles for such vehicle or vessel and the certificate of ownership is still in effect, or if a manufactured home, mobilehome, or commercial coach is levied upon and a permanent title record has been established by the Department of Housing and Community Development for such manufactured home, mobilehome, or commercial coach the levying officer shall determine from the appropriate department the name and address of the legal owner and each junior lienholder of the property levied upon. If the legal owner or junior lienholder is not the judgment debtor and is not in possession of the vehicle, vessel, manufactured home, mobilehome, or commercial coach, the levying officer shall at the time of levy or promptly thereafter serve a copy of the writ of execution and a notice of levy on the legal owner or junior lienholder. Service shall be made personally or by mail. *(Added by Stats.1982, c. 1364, p. 5128, § 2, operative July 1, 1983. Amended by Stats.1983, c. 1124, § 10, operative Jan. 1, 1984.)*

Law Revision Commission Comments

Section 700.090 supersedes subdivision (1) of former Section 689b. The provision for determining the legal owner of a mobilehome or commercial coach is new. See generally Health & Saf. Code §§ 18075–18077.4 (registration and titling of mobilehomes). Former law required notice to be given the legal owner if different from the registered owner.

This section is worded so as to avoid duplicate notice in any case where the legal owner has already received notice in the course of the levy. [16 Cal.L.Rev.Comm. Reports 1334 (1982)].

Research References

Rutter, Cal. Practice Guide: Enforcing Judgments/Debts Ch. 6D-4, Levy on Specific Property.
Rutter, Cal. Practice Guide: Enforcing Judgments/Debts Form 6:P, Sample Levy Instructions.
Miller and Starr California Real Estate § 31:63, Enforcement of a Money Judgment Against a Mobilehome.
Miller and Starr California Real Estate § 32:31, Creation and Extension of the Attachment Lien.
Miller and Starr California Real Estate § 32:64, Creation, Duration, and Effect of Writ of Execution.
8 Witkin Cal. Proc. 5th Enforcement of Judgment § 127, Property Used as Dwelling.
8 Witkin Cal. Proc. 5th Enforcement of Judgment § 128, Motor Vehicles, Vessels, Manufactured Homes, Mobilehomes, and Coaches.
6 Witkin Cal. Proc. 5th Provisional Remedies § 158, Property Governed by Enforcement of Judgments Law.
6 Witkin Cal. Proc. 5th Provisional Remedies § 164, (S 164) in General.

§ 700.100. Chattel paper; lien on rights in goods subject to the paper

(a) To levy upon chattel paper, the levying officer shall:

(1) If the chattel paper is in the possession of the judgment debtor, take the chattel paper into custody.

(2) If the chattel paper is in the possession of a third person, personally serve a copy of the writ of execution and a notice of levy on the third person.

(b) If the levying officer obtains custody of the chattel paper or if pursuant to a security agreement the judgment debtor has liberty to collect or compromise the chattel paper or to accept the return of goods or make repossessions, the levying officer shall, if so instructed by the judgment creditor, serve a copy of the writ of execution and a notice of levy on the account debtor. Service shall be made personally or by mail.

(c) In addition to any other rights created by a levy on chattel paper, the levy creates a lien on the judgment debtor's rights in specific goods subject to the chattel paper. *(Added by Stats.1982, c. 1364, p. 5128, § 2, operative July 1, 1983.)*

Research References

Rutter, Cal. Practice Guide: Enforcing Judgments/Debts Ch. 6D-4, Levy on Specific Property.
8 Witkin Cal. Proc. 5th Enforcement of Judgment § 129, (S 129) Chattel Paper.
8 Witkin Cal. Proc. 5th Enforcement of Judgment § 142, (S 142) Duties of Account Debtor.
6 Witkin Cal. Proc. 5th Provisional Remedies § 114, (S 114) Turnover Order.
6 Witkin Cal. Proc. 5th Provisional Remedies § 158, Property Governed by Enforcement of Judgments Law.

§ 700.110. Instruments

(a) To levy upon an instrument, the levying officer shall:

(1) If the instrument is in the possession of the judgment debtor, take the instrument into custody.

(2) If the instrument is in the possession of a third person, personally serve a copy of the writ of execution and a notice of levy on the third person.

(b) If the levying officer obtains custody of the instrument, the levying officer shall, if the judgment creditor so instructs, serve a copy of the writ of execution and a notice of levy on the obligor. Service shall be made personally or by mail. *(Added by Stats.1982, c. 1364, p. 5129, § 2, operative July 1, 1983.)*

Civ. Pro.

Research References

Rutter, Cal. Practice Guide: Enforcing Judgments/Debts Ch. 6D-4, Levy on Specific Property.

Rutter, Cal. Practice Guide: Enforcing Judgments/Debts Ch. 6D-5, Duties, Rights and Liabilities of Third Persons After Levy.

Rutter, Cal. Practice Guide: Enforcing Judgments/Debts Form 6:P, Sample Levy Instructions.

Miller and Starr California Real Estate § 32:61, Property Interests Subject to Execution.

8 Witkin Cal. Proc. 5th Enforcement of Judgment § 130, (S 130) Instruments.

8 Witkin Cal. Proc. 5th Enforcement of Judgment § 143, (S 143) Duties of Obligor Under Instrument.

6 Witkin Cal. Proc. 5th Provisional Remedies § 114, (S 114) Turnover Order.

6 Witkin Cal. Proc. 5th Provisional Remedies § 158, Property Governed by Enforcement of Judgments Law.

§ 700.120.　Negotiable documents of title

To levy upon a negotiable document of title, the levying officer shall:

(a) If the negotiable document of title is in the possession of the judgment debtor, take the negotiable document of title into custody.

(b) If the negotiable document of title is in the possession of a third person, personally serve a copy of the writ of execution and a notice of levy on the third person. *(Added by Stats.1982, c. 1364, p. 5129, § 2, operative July 1, 1983.)*

Research References

Rutter, Cal. Practice Guide: Enforcing Judgments/Debts Ch. 6D-4, Levy on Specific Property.

8 Witkin Cal. Proc. 5th Enforcement of Judgment § 124, Property in Possession of Debtor or Third Person.

8 Witkin Cal. Proc. 5th Enforcement of Judgment § 131, (S 131) Documents of Title and Securities.

6 Witkin Cal. Proc. 5th Provisional Remedies § 114, (S 114) Turnover Order.

6 Witkin Cal. Proc. 5th Provisional Remedies § 158, Property Governed by Enforcement of Judgments Law.

§ 700.130.　Securities

To levy upon a security, the levying officer shall comply with Section 8112 of the Commercial Code. The legal process referred to in Section 8112 of the Commercial Code means the legal process required by the state in which the chief executive office of the issuer of the security is located and, where that state is California, means personal service by the levying officer of a copy of the writ of execution and notice of levy on the person who is to be served. *(Added by Stats.1982, c. 1364, p. 5129, § 2, operative July 1, 1983. Amended by Stats.1984, c. 927, § 2; Stats.1996, c. 497 (S.B.1591), § 3, operative Jan. 1, 1997.)*

Research References

Rutter, Cal. Practice Guide: Enforcing Judgments/Debts Ch. 6D-4, Levy on Specific Property.

Rutter, Cal. Practice Guide: Enforcing Judgments/Debts Ch. 6J-3, Enforcing California Judgments Against Debtor's Out-Of-State Property.

8 Witkin Cal. Proc. 5th Enforcement of Judgment § 131, (S 131) Documents of Title and Securities.

§ 700.140.　Deposit accounts; execution lien; liability of financial institution; termination of lien; final payment of deposit defined

(a) Subject to Sections 684.115 and 700.160, to levy upon a deposit account, the levying officer shall personally serve a copy of the writ of execution and a notice of levy on the financial institution with which the deposit account is maintained.

(b) The execution lien that arises upon service of a writ of execution and notice of levy reaches only amounts in a deposit account at the time of service on the financial institution, including the amount of any deposit not yet finally collected unless the deposit is returned unpaid to the financial institution.

(c) The levying officer shall serve a copy of the writ of execution and a notice of levy on any third person in whose name any deposit account described therein stands. Service shall be made personally or by mail as follows:

(1) At the time of levy or promptly thereafter, if the party seeking the levy informs the levying officer of the person and his, her, or its residence or business address.

(2) Promptly following the levying officer's receipt of a garnishee's memorandum if service was not accomplished pursuant to paragraph (1) if the garnishee's memorandum identifies the person and his, her, or its residence or business address.

(d) The financial institution shall not honor a withdrawal request or a check or other order for the payment of money from the deposit account if presentment of the withdrawal request or item to the financial institution occurs during the time the execution lien is in effect unless, following the withdrawal or payment, sufficient funds are available to cover the levy. For these purposes, a withdrawal from the deposit account to cover the financial institution's standard fee or charge for processing the levy shall not be considered a payment of money from the account in violation of this subdivision.

(e) During the time the execution lien is in effect, the financial institution is not liable to any person for any of the following:

(1) Performance of the duties of a garnishee under the levy.

(2) Nonpayment of a check or other order for the payment or transfer of money drawn or presented against the deposit account if the nonpayment is pursuant to the requirements of subdivision (d).

(3) Refusal to pay a withdrawal from the deposit account if the refusal is pursuant to the requirements of subdivision (d).

(f) When the amount levied upon pursuant to this section is paid to the levying officer, the execution lien on the deposit account levied upon terminates.

(g) For the purposes of this section, none of the following is a third person in whose name the deposit account stands:

(1) A person who is only a person named as the beneficiary of a Totten trust account.

(2) A person who is only a payee designated in a pay-on-death provision in an account pursuant to Section 18318.5 of the Financial Code or Section 5140 of the Probate Code, or other similar provision.

(3) A person who is only acting in a representative or custodial capacity with respect to benefits paid or payable by the United States government. Rather, accounts maintained by the representative or custodian shall be deemed to stand in the beneficiary's name, and the amounts therein shall be covered by a levy against the beneficiary.

(h) For purposes of this section, final payment of a deposit shall be deemed to have occurred in accordance with Section 4215 or 11210 of the Commercial Code or with automated clearinghouse or Federal Reserve System rule, regulation, operating circular, or similar governing document, as applicable to the deposit. If, for any reason, a deposit is returned by the financial institution upon which it is drawn, the deposit shall not be deemed finally collected for purposes of this subdivision regardless of any later payment by the financial institution upon which the deposit is drawn. *(Added by Stats.1982, c. 1364, p. 5129, § 2, operative July 1, 1983. Amended by Stats.1983, c. 155, § 14, eff. June 30, 1983, operative July 1, 1983; Stats.1984, c. 538, § 21; Stats.2002, c. 664 (A.B.3034), § 48; Stats.2003, c. 110*

(A.B.690), § 2; Stats.2009, c. 153 (A.B.1549), § 3; Stats.2012, c. 484 (A.B.2364), § 8.)

Law Revision Commission Comments

Section 700.140 is analogous to Section 488.390 (attachment of deposit accounts), which was incorporated by former Section 688(b). Withdrawals made after the time of levy reduce any applicable exemption. See Section 704.070(f). For provisions governing levy on a deposit account standing in the name of a person other than the judgment debtor, see Section 700.160. [16 Cal.L.Rev.Comm. Reports 1338 (1982)].

Research References

Rutter, Cal. Practice Guide: Enforcing Judgments/Debts Ch. 4-A, A. Attachment.
Rutter, Cal. Practice Guide: Enforcing Judgments/Debts Ch. 6D-4, Levy on Specific Property.
Miller and Starr California Real Estate § 32:64, Creation, Duration, and Effect of Writ of Execution.
8 Witkin Cal. Proc. 5th Enforcement of Judgment § 132, (S 132) Deposit Accounts.
8 Witkin Cal. Proc. 5th Enforcement of Judgment § 134, (S 134) Deposit Accounts and Boxes in Third Person's Name.
8 Witkin Cal. Proc. 5th Enforcement of Judgment § 135, (S 135) Accounts Receivable and General Intangibles.
8 Witkin Cal. Proc. 5th Enforcement of Judgment § 405, Governmental Enforcement of Support Order.

§ 700.150. Property in safe-deposit box; service of write of execution and notice of levy; execution lien; notice to judgment creditor regarding fees and costs; advance notice; liability of financial institution; property not removed

(a) Subject to Section 700.160, to levy upon property in a safe-deposit box, the levying officer shall personally serve a copy of the writ of execution and a notice of levy on the financial institution with which the safe-deposit box is maintained.

(b) At the time of the levy or promptly thereafter, the levying officer shall serve a copy of the writ of execution and a notice of levy on any third person in whose name the safe-deposit box stands. Service shall be made personally or by mail.

(c) During the time the execution lien is in effect, the financial institution may not permit the removal of any of the contents of the safe-deposit box except as directed by the levying officer.

(d) Upon receipt of a garnishee's memorandum from the financial institution indicating a safe-deposit box is under levy, the levying officer shall promptly mail a written notice to the judgment creditor demanding an additional fee as required by Section 26723 of the Government Code, plus the costs to open the safe-deposit box and seize and store the contents. The levying officer shall release the levy on the safe-deposit box if the judgment creditor does not pay the required fee, plus costs, within three business days plus the extended time period specified in subdivision (a) of Section 1013 for service by mail by the levying officer.

(e) The levying officer may first give the person in whose name the safe-deposit box stands an opportunity to open the safe-deposit box to permit the removal pursuant to the levy of the property levied upon. The financial institution may refuse to permit the forcible opening of the safe-deposit box to permit the removal of the property levied upon unless the levying officer or the judgment creditor pays in advance the cost of forcibly opening the safe-deposit box and of repairing any damage caused thereby.

(f) The levying officer shall give the judgment creditor at least three court days' advance notice of the date and time the levying officer will open the safe-deposit box and seize the contents thereof, and the judgment creditor shall be entitled to be present at that time.

(g) During the time the execution lien is in effect, the financial institution is not liable to any person for any of the following:

(1) Performance of the duties of a garnishee under the levy.

(2) Refusal to permit access to the safe-deposit box by the person in whose name it stands.

(3) Removal of any of the contents of the safe-deposit box pursuant to the levy.

(h) If the levying officer removes any property from the safe-deposit box to satisfy the levy, but allows other property to remain in the safe-deposit box, the execution lien is released automatically with respect to any property that remains in the safe-deposit box. *(Added by Stats.1982, c. 1364, p. 5130, § 2, operative July 1, 1983. Amended by Stats.1984, c. 538, § 22; Stats.2003, c. 888 (A.B.394), § 2; Stats.2012, c. 484 (A.B.2364), § 9.)*

Research References

Rutter, Cal. Practice Guide: Enforcing Judgments/Debts Ch. 4-A, A. Attachment.
Rutter, Cal. Practice Guide: Enforcing Judgments/Debts Ch. 6D-4, Levy on Specific Property.
Miller and Starr California Real Estate § 32:64, Creation, Duration, and Effect of Writ of Execution.
8 Witkin Cal. Proc. 5th Enforcement of Judgment § 124, Property in Possession of Debtor or Third Person.
8 Witkin Cal. Proc. 5th Enforcement of Judgment § 133, (S 133) Safe Deposit Boxes.
8 Witkin Cal. Proc. 5th Enforcement of Judgment § 134, (S 134) Deposit Accounts and Boxes in Third Person's Name.

§ 700.160. Safe-deposit box in name of person other than debtor alone or with third person; court order; exceptions; payment by financial institution

(a) Except as provided in subdivision (b), a deposit account or safe-deposit box standing in the name of a person other than the judgment debtor, either alone or together with third persons, is not subject to levy under Section 700.140 or 700.150 unless the legal process served on the third party includes a court order authorizing the levy.

(b) A court order is not required to levy on a deposit account or safe-deposit box standing in the name of any of the following:

(1) The judgment debtor, whether alone or together with third persons.

(2) The judgment debtor's spouse or registered domestic partner, whether alone or together with other persons, provided an affidavit is delivered to the financial institution at the time of levy showing that person is the judgment debtor's spouse or registered domestic partner.

(3) A fictitious business name, provided a copy of an unexpired statement certified in accordance with Section 17926 of the Business and Professions Code is delivered to the financial institution at the time of levy, the fictitious business name statement does not list any person other than the judgment debtor, the judgment debtor's spouse or the judgment debtor's registered domestic partner as the person or persons doing business under the fictitious business name, and, if a person other than the judgment debtor is listed in the statement, an affidavit stating that the other person is the judgment debtor's spouse or registered domestic partner is delivered to the financial institution at the time of the levy.

(4) The additional name of a judgment debtor listed on the legal process pursuant to an affidavit of identity as provided by Section 680.135, whether alone or together with third persons.

(c) In any case where a deposit account in the name of a person other than the judgment debtor, whether alone or together with the judgment debtor, is levied upon, the financial institution shall not pay to the levying officer the amount levied upon until being notified to do so by the levying officer. The levying officer may not require the financial institution to pay the amount levied upon until the expiration of 15 days after service of notice of levy on the third person. *(Added by Stats.1984, c. 538, § 23.5. Amended by Stats.2000, c. 639 (A.B.2405), § 8; Stats.2011, c. 308 (S.B.647), § 3; Stats.2012, c. 484 (A.B.2364), § 10.)*

Research References

Rutter, Cal. Practice Guide: Enforcing Judgments/Debts Ch. 4-A, A. Attachment.
Rutter, Cal. Practice Guide: Enforcing Judgments/Debts Ch. 6D-4, Levy on Specific Property.
Rutter, Cal. Practice Guide: Enforcing Judgments/Debts Form 6:R, Affidavit Under CCP § 700.160(B)(3).
Rutter, Cal. Practice Guide: Enforcing Judgments/Debts Ch. 6G-17, Enforcement Against Beneficiary's Trust Interests.
8 Witkin Cal. Proc. 5th Enforcement of Judgment § 124, Property in Possession of Debtor or Third Person.
8 Witkin Cal. Proc. 5th Enforcement of Judgment § 132, (S 132) Deposit Accounts.
8 Witkin Cal. Proc. 5th Enforcement of Judgment § 133, (S 133) Safe Deposit Boxes.
8 Witkin Cal. Proc. 5th Enforcement of Judgment § 134, (S 134) Deposit Accounts and Boxes in Third Person's Name.

§ 700.170. Account receivable or general intangible

(a) Unless another method of levy is provided by this article, to levy upon an account receivable or general intangible, the levying officer shall personally serve a copy of the writ of execution and a notice of levy on the account debtor.

(b) If a levy is made under subdivision (a) and payments on the account receivable or general intangible are made to a person other than the judgment debtor (whether pursuant to a security agreement, assignment for collection, or otherwise), the levying officer shall, if so instructed by the judgment creditor, personally serve a copy of the writ of execution and a notice of levy on such third person. Service of the copy of the writ and notice of levy on such third person is a levy on any amounts owed to the judgment debtor by such third person. *(Added by Stats.1982, c. 1364, p. 5132, § 2, operative July 1, 1983.)*

Research References

Rutter, Cal. Practice Guide: Enforcing Judgments/Debts Ch. 6B-2, Interests Subject to Judgment Lien.
Rutter, Cal. Practice Guide: Enforcing Judgments/Debts Ch. 6D-4, Levy on Specific Property.
Rutter, Cal. Practice Guide: Enforcing Judgments/Debts Form 6:P, Sample Levy Instructions.
8 Witkin Cal. Proc. 5th Enforcement of Judgment § 74, (S 74) Interests Subject to Lien.
8 Witkin Cal. Proc. 5th Enforcement of Judgment § 135, (S 135) Accounts Receivable and General Intangibles.
8 Witkin Cal. Proc. 5th Enforcement of Judgment § 142, (S 142) Duties of Account Debtor.
11 Witkin, California Summary 10th Husband and Wife § 254, (S 254) Priorities.

§ 700.180. Property subject of pending action or special proceeding; ineffective levy; garnishee's memorandum

(a) The following property may be levied upon pursuant to this article notwithstanding that the property levied upon is the subject of a pending action or special proceeding:

(1) Real property.

(2) Growing crops, timber to be cut, or minerals or the like (including oil and gas) to be extracted or accounts receivable resulting from the sale thereof at the wellhead or minehead.

(3) Tangible personal property in the possession or under the control of the judgment debtor or in the custody of a levying officer.

(4) The interest of a judgment debtor in personal property in the estate of a decedent, whether the interest arises by testate or intestate succession.

(b) Except as provided in subdivision (a), a levy upon property that is the subject of an action or special proceeding pending at the time of the levy is not effective.

(c) If a levy is attempted but is ineffective under subdivision (b) and the levying officer has requested a garnishee's memorandum under Section 701.030 in connection with the ineffective levy, the garnishee's memorandum shall include the following information in addition to that required by Section 701.030:

(1) A statement that the levy on the property is not effective because the property is the subject of a pending action or special proceeding.

(2) The title of the court, cause, and number of the pending action or proceeding.

(d) For the purpose of this section, an action or proceeding is pending from the time the action or proceeding is commenced until judgment has been entered and the time for appeal has expired or, if an appeal is filed, until the appeal has been finally determined.

(e) Nothing in this section affects or limits the right of the judgment creditor to obtain a lien pursuant to Article 5 (commencing with Section 708.410) of Chapter 6. *(Added by Stats.1982, c. 1364, p. 5132, § 2, operative July 1, 1983.)*

Research References

Rutter, Cal. Practice Guide: Enforcing Judgments/Debts Ch. 4-A, A. Attachment.
Rutter, Cal. Practice Guide: Enforcing Judgments/Debts Ch. 6D-4, Levy on Specific Property.
Rutter, Cal. Practice Guide: Enforcing Judgments/Debts Ch. 6D-5, Duties, Rights and Liabilities of Third Persons After Levy.
Rutter, Cal. Practice Guide: Enforcing Judgments/Debts Ch. 6G-8, Lien in Pending Action.
Miller and Starr California Real Estate § 32:28, Attachment of Real Property.
Miller and Starr California Real Estate § 32:64, Creation, Duration, and Effect of Writ of Execution.
8 Witkin Cal. Proc. 5th Enforcement of Judgment § 136, (S 136) Property Subject of Pending Action.
8 Witkin Cal. Proc. 5th Enforcement of Judgment § 140, Garnishee's Memorandum.
8 Witkin Cal. Proc. 5th Enforcement of Judgment § 297, (S 297) Nature and Scope of Remedy.
8 Witkin Cal. Proc. 5th Enforcement of Judgment § 304, After Final Judgment.

§ 700.190. Final money judgment

(a) As used in this section, "final money judgment" means a money judgment after the time for appeal from the judgment has expired or, if an appeal is filed, after the appeal has been finally determined.

(b) To levy upon a final money judgment, the levying officer shall file a copy of the writ of execution and a notice of levy with the clerk of the court that entered the final money judgment. The court clerk shall endorse upon the judgment a statement of the existence of the execution lien and the time it was created. If an abstract of the judgment is issued, it shall include a statement of the execution lien in favor of the judgment creditor.

(c) At the time of levy or promptly thereafter, the levying officer shall serve a copy of the writ of execution and a notice of levy on the judgment debtor obligated to pay the final money judgment levied upon. Service shall be made personally or by mail. *(Added by Stats.1982, c. 1364, p. 5133, § 2, operative July 1, 1983. Amended by Stats.1984, c. 538, § 25.3.)*

Law Revision Commission Comments

Section 700.190, which establishes the manner and effect of a levy upon a final money judgment, is drawn in part from Section 488.420 (attachment). Where a final judgment is not a money judgment, Section 700.190 has no effect on the manner of levy. A levy is made on tangible property just as if there were no final judgment relating to that property. The effect of the final judgment in such a case is its relevance as a determination of the judgment debtor's ownership of or other interest in the property. As to levy on property that is the subject of a pending action or proceeding, see Section 700.180 and Comment thereto. See also Article 5 (commencing with Section 708.410) of Chapter 6 (lien in a pending action or proceeding).

Subdivision (b) of former Section 688 provided that the manner of levy of execution was the same as in attachment, and the Attachment Law (Section 488.420) provides for the attachment of a final judgment. Section 700.190, like Section 488.420, requires the filing of a copy of the writ and notice of levy in the court in which the judgment levied upon was entered. However, unlike Section 488.420, Section 700.190 does not require service of a copy of the writ and notice on the judgment debtor obligated to pay the judgment levied upon as an essential element of the levy. Although Section 700.190 requires the levying officer to serve a copy of the writ and notice on that judgment debtor, service is not a requisite for a valid levy under Section 700.190. See Section 699.550. However, subdivision (c) protects the judgment debtor obligated to pay the judgment levied upon who pays the judgment creditor under that judgment without notice of the levy. In this respect, Section 700.190 is consistent with Civil Code Section 954.5 (payment where acknowledgment of assignment of judgment is filed). [16 Cal.L.Rev.Comm. Reports 1345 (1982)].

Research References

Rutter, Cal. Practice Guide: Enforcing Judgments/Debts Ch. 4-A, A. Attachment.
Rutter, Cal. Practice Guide: Enforcing Judgments/Debts Ch. 6D-4, Levy on Specific Property.
8 Witkin Cal. Proc. 5th Enforcement of Judgment § 137, (S 137) Final Money Judgment.
8 Witkin Cal. Proc. 5th Enforcement of Judgment § 304, After Final Judgment.

§ 700.200. Interest in personal property in estate of decedent

(a) To levy upon the interest of the judgment debtor in personal property in the estate of a decedent, whether the interest arises by testate or intestate succession, the levying officer shall personally serve a copy of the writ and a notice of levy on the personal representative of the decedent. The levy does not impair the powers of the representative over the property for the purposes of administration.

(b) The personal representative shall report the levy to the court in which the estate is being administered when any petition for distribution is filed. If a decree orders distribution to the judgment debtor, the court making the decree shall order the property levied upon to be delivered to the levying officer. The property may not be delivered to the levying officer until the decree distributing the property has become final. To the extent the property delivered to the levying officer is not necessary to satisfy the money judgment, it shall be released to the judgment debtor.

(c) Promptly after the property is delivered to the levying officer pursuant to subdivision (b), the levying officer shall serve a notice describing the property on the judgment debtor. Service shall be made personally or by mail. Notwithstanding Section 703.520, a claim of exemption for the property described in the notice may be made within 10 days after the notice was served on the judgment debtor.

(d) Notwithstanding Section 697.710, an execution lien created by a levy pursuant to this section continues for a period of one year after the decree distributing the interest has become final unless the judgment is sooner satisfied.

(e) A writ under which a levy is made pursuant to this section shall be returned not later than one year after the date the decree distributing the interest has become final. *(Added by Stats.1982, c. 1364, p. 5133, § 2, operative July 1, 1983.)*

Law Revision Commission Comments

Subdivisions (a) and (b) of Section 700.200 provide a method of levy analogous to Section 488.430 (attachment of an interest in personal property of a decedent's estate) which was incorporated by former Section 688(b). Subdivision (c) affords the judgment debtor an opportunity to claim any available exemption for the property once it is delivered to the levying officer. The time for claiming the exemption is extended if service is by mail. See Section 684.120. Subdivision (d) supersedes a portion of the first sentence of former Section 688(e) and extends the period the execution lien is effective beyond the period set by Section 697.710 for execution liens generally. Subdivision (e) provides an exception to the general rules governing return of a writ of execution. [16 Cal.L.Rev. Comm. Reports 1347 (1982)].

Research References

Rutter, Cal. Practice Guide: Enforcing Judgments/Debts Ch. 4-A, A. Attachment.
Rutter, Cal. Practice Guide: Enforcing Judgments/Debts Ch. 6D-3, Levy of Writ of Execution-In General.
Rutter, Cal. Practice Guide: Enforcing Judgments/Debts Ch. 6D-4, Levy on Specific Property.
8 Witkin Cal. Proc. 5th Enforcement of Judgment § 92, (S 92) Creation and Duration.
8 Witkin Cal. Proc. 5th Enforcement of Judgment § 114, (S 114) Return of Writ.
8 Witkin Cal. Proc. 5th Enforcement of Judgment § 136, (S 136) Property Subject of Pending Action.
8 Witkin Cal. Proc. 5th Enforcement of Judgment § 138, (S 138) Interest in Personal Property in Decedent's Estate.
8 Witkin Cal. Proc. 5th Enforcement of Judgment § 139, Delivery or Payment to Levying Officer.

ARTICLE 5. DUTIES AND LIABILITIES OF THIRD PERSONS AFTER LEVY

§ 701.010. Duties of third persons; good cause defined

(a) Except as otherwise provided by statute, when a levy is made by service of a copy of the writ of execution and a notice of levy on a third person, the third person at the time of levy or promptly thereafter shall comply with this section.

(b) Unless the third person has good cause for failure or refusal to do so:

(1) The third person shall deliver to the levying officer any of the property levied upon that is in the possession or under the control of the third person at the time of levy unless the third person claims the right to possession of the property.

(2) To the extent that the third person does not deny an obligation levied upon, or claim a priority over the judgment creditor's lien, the third person shall pay to the levying officer both of the following:

(A) The amount of the obligation levied upon that is due and payable to the judgment debtor at the time of levy.

(B) Amounts that become due and payable to the judgment debtor on the obligation levied upon during the period of the execution lien.

(3) If the third person makes a delivery or payment to the levying officer pursuant to this section, the third person shall execute and deliver any documents necessary to effect the transfer of the property.

(c) For the purposes of this section, "good cause" includes, but is not limited to, a showing that the third person did not know or have reason to know of the levy from all the facts and circumstances known to the third person. *(Added by Stats.1982, c. 1364, p. 5134, § 2, operative July 1, 1983.)*

Law Revision Commission Comments

Section 701.010 is new. Service of the copy of the writ of execution and a notice of levy on the third person creates a lien on any personal property or obligation that is subject to levy of execution even if the garnishee refuses to turn the property over or to pay the obligation to the levying officer. See Section 697.710 (execution lien); Nordstrom v. Corona City Water Co., 155 Cal. 206, 212, 100 P. 242 (1909). See also Section 701.020 (liability of third person).

The introductory portion of subdivision (a) recognizes exceptions to the duty of the garnishee. See, e.g., Sections 700.160 (delay by a financial institution), 700.050 (paper levy on a levying officer), 700.200 (power of personal representative over property in estate of a decedent), and 701.050 (duty of account debtor). [16 Cal.L.Rev.Comm. Reports 1348 (1982)].

Research References

Rutter, Cal. Practice Guide: Enforcing Judgments/Debts Ch. 4-A, A. Attachment.
Rutter, Cal. Practice Guide: Enforcing Judgments/Debts Ch. 6D-4, Levy on Specific Property.
Rutter, Cal. Practice Guide: Enforcing Judgments/Debts Ch. 6D-5, Duties, Rights and Liabilities of Third Persons After Levy.
Rutter, Cal. Practice Guide: Enforcing Judgments/Debts Ch. 6D-7, Sale and Collection of Property Levied Upon.
Rutter, Cal. Practice Guide: Enforcing Judgments/Debts Ch. 6G-4, Creditor's Suit.
Rutter, Cal. Practice Guide: Enforcing Judgments/Debts Gen. Matls., Highlights.
8 Witkin Cal. Proc. 5th Enforcement of Judgment § 125, Property in Custody of Levying Officer.
8 Witkin Cal. Proc. 5th Enforcement of Judgment § 129, (S 129) Chattel Paper.
8 Witkin Cal. Proc. 5th Enforcement of Judgment § 139, Delivery or Payment to Levying Officer.
8 Witkin Cal. Proc. 5th Enforcement of Judgment § 157, (S 157) Delivery of Possession, Certificate, or Deed.
8 Witkin Cal. Proc. 5th Enforcement of Judgment § 196, Limitation on Withdrawal of Balance.
8 Witkin Cal. Proc. 5th Enforcement of Judgment § 291, (S 291) Nature of Action.
6 Witkin Cal. Proc. 5th Provisional Remedies § 192, Enforcement of Judgments Law is Applicable.

§ 701.020. Liability of third persons

(a) If a third person is required by this article to deliver property to the levying officer or to make payments to the levying officer and the third person fails or refuses without good cause to do so, the third person is liable to the judgment creditor for whichever of the following is the lesser amount:

(1) The value of the judgment debtor's interest in the property or the amount of the payments required to be made.

(2) The amount required to satisfy the judgment pursuant to which the levy is made.

(b) The third person's liability continues until the earliest of the following times:

(1) The time when the property levied upon is delivered to the levying officer or the payments are made to the levying officer.

(2) The time when the property levied upon is released pursuant to Section 699.060.

(3) The time when the judgment is satisfied or discharged.

(c) If the third person's liability is established, the court that determines the liability may, in its discretion, require the third person to pay the costs and reasonable attorney's fees incurred by the judgment creditor in establishing the liability. *(Added by Stats.1982, c. 1364, p. 5134, § 2, operative July 1, 1983.)*

Law Revision Commission Comments

Section 701.020 is new and is comparable to Section 488.550 (attachment). The judgment creditor may seek to enforce compliance with the levy under Section 701.020 or to impose liability on the third person pursuant to Article 2 (commencing with Section 708.110) (examination proceedings) or Article 3 (commencing with Section 708.210) (creditor's suit) of Chapter 6. See also Section 697.710 (execution lien). [16 Cal.L.Rev.Comm. Reports 1349 (1982)].

Research References

Rutter, Cal. Practice Guide: Enforcing Judgments/Debts Ch. 6A-5, Amount Recoverable Under Judgment.
Rutter, Cal. Practice Guide: Enforcing Judgments/Debts Ch. 6D-4, Levy on Specific Property.
Rutter, Cal. Practice Guide: Enforcing Judgments/Debts Ch. 6D-5, Duties, Rights and Liabilities of Third Persons After Levy.
Rutter, Cal. Practice Guide: Enforcing Judgments/Debts Gen. Matls., Highlights.
8 Witkin Cal. Proc. 5th Enforcement of Judgment § 139, Delivery or Payment to Levying Officer.
8 Witkin Cal. Proc. 5th Enforcement of Judgment § 295, (S 295) Judgment.
8 Witkin Cal. Proc. 5th Enforcement of Judgment § 306, (S 306) Effect of Assignment.
6 Witkin Cal. Proc. 5th Provisional Remedies § 192, Enforcement of Judgments Law is Applicable.

§ 701.030. Garnishee's memorandum; contents; copy to judgment creditor; effect of failure to provide; exceptions

(a) At the time of service of a copy of the legal process on a third person, the levying officer shall request the third person to give the levying officer a garnishee's memorandum containing the information required by this section. Within 10 days after the legal process is served, the third person shall mail or deliver the garnishee's memorandum to the levying officer whether or not the levy is effective.

(b) The garnishee's memorandum shall be executed under oath and shall contain the following information, as applicable:

(1) A description of any property of the judgment debtor sought to be levied upon that is not delivered to the levying officer and the reason for not delivering the property.

(2) A description of any property of the judgment debtor not sought to be levied upon that is in the possession or under the control of the third person at the time of levy.

(3) A statement of the amount and terms of any obligation to the judgment debtor sought to be levied upon that is due and payable and is not paid to the levying officer, and the reason for not paying the obligation.

(4) A statement of the amount and terms of any obligation to the judgment debtor sought to be levied upon that is not due and payable at the time of levy.

Civ. Pro.

(5) A statement of the amount and terms of any obligation to the judgment debtor at the time of levy not sought to be levied upon.

(6) A description of claims and rights of other persons to the property or obligation levied upon that are known to the third person and the names and addresses of those other persons.

(7) A statement that the garnishee holds neither any property nor any obligations in favor of the judgment debtor.

(c) If a garnishee's memorandum is received from the third person, the levying officer shall retain a copy and promptly mail or deliver a copy of the memorandum to the judgment creditor.

(d) Except as provided in subdivisions (e) and (f), if a third person does not give the levying officer a garnishee's memorandum within the time provided in subdivision (a), or does not provide complete information, the third person may, in the court's discretion, be required to pay the costs and reasonable attorney's fees incurred in any proceedings to obtain the information required in the garnishee's memorandum.

(e) Notwithstanding subdivision (a), when the levy is made upon a deposit account or upon property in a safe-deposit box, the financial institution need not give a garnishee's memorandum to the levying officer if the financial institution fully complies with the levy and, if a garnishee's memorandum is required, the garnishee's memorandum needs to provide information with respect only to property that is carried on the records available at the office or branch where the levy is made provided that if a levy has been served at a central location designated by a financial institution in accordance with Section 684.115, the garnishee's memorandum shall apply to all offices and branches of the financial institution except to the extent acceptance of the levy at those central locations is limited pursuant to paragraph (3) of subdivision (a) of Section 684.115.

(f) Notwithstanding subdivision (a), the third person need not give a garnishee's memorandum to the levying officer if both of the following conditions are satisfied:

(1) The third person has delivered to the levying officer all of the property sought to be levied upon.

(2) The third person has paid to the levying officer the amount due at the time of levy on any obligation to the judgment debtor that was levied upon, and there is no additional amount that thereafter will become payable on the obligation levied upon.

(g) The garnishee may electronically transmit the garnishee's memorandum to the levying officer pursuant to Chapter 2 (commencing with Section 263) of Title 4 of Part 1. *(Added by Stats.1982, c. 1364, p. 5134, § 2, operative July 1, 1983. Amended by Stats.2010, c. 680 (A.B.2394), § 10; Stats.2012, c. 484 (A.B. 2364), § 11.)*

Law Revision Commission Comments

Section 701.030 is derived from Section 488.080(b) but requires the garnishee to provide a broader range of information. The garnishee's memorandum may serve as an inexpensive alternative to an examination proceeding under Section 708.120. Subdivision (a) makes clear that the third person has a duty to give a memorandum even though the levy is ineffective. See, e.g., Section 700.180 (levy on certain personal property ineffective where the property is the subject of a pending action or proceeding). Additional information may be required by another provision (see Section 700.180) where a levy is ineffective. [16 Cal.L.Rev. Comm. Reports 1351 (1982)].

Research References

Rutter, Cal. Practice Guide: Enforcing Judgments/Debts Ch. 6D-3, Levy of Writ of Execution-In General.
Rutter, Cal. Practice Guide: Enforcing Judgments/Debts Ch. 6D-5, Duties, Rights and Liabilities of Third Persons After Levy.

Rutter, Cal. Practice Guide: Enforcing Judgments/Debts Gen. Matls., Highlights.
8 Witkin Cal. Proc. 5th Enforcement of Judgment § 103, (S 103) Levy by Registered Process Server.
8 Witkin Cal. Proc. 5th Enforcement of Judgment § 133, (S 133) Safe Deposit Boxes.
8 Witkin Cal. Proc. 5th Enforcement of Judgment § 140, Garnishee's Memorandum.

§ 701.035. Liability of third person for disclosure in garnishee's memorandum

A third person who gives a garnishee's memorandum pursuant to this title is not liable to any person for the disclosure in the garnishee's memorandum of any information contained in the garnishee's memorandum. *(Added by Stats.1983, c. 155, § 14.6, eff. June 30, 1983, operative July 1, 1983.)*

Research References

Rutter, Cal. Practice Guide: Enforcing Judgments/Debts Ch. 6D-5, Duties, Rights and Liabilities of Third Persons After Levy.
8 Witkin Cal. Proc. 5th Enforcement of Judgment § 140, Garnishee's Memorandum.

§ 701.040. Property subject to security interest attached prior to levy; lien with priority; duties of secured party

(a) Except as otherwise ordered by the court upon a determination that the judgment creditor's lien has priority over the security interest, if property levied upon is subject to a security interest that attached prior to levy, the property or obligation is subject to enforcement of the security interest without regard to the levy unless the property is in the custody of the levying officer; but, if the execution lien has priority over the security interest, the secured party is liable to the judgment creditor for any proceeds received by the secured party from the property to the extent of the execution lien.

(b) After the security interest is satisfied, the secured party shall deliver any excess property, and pay any excess payments or proceeds of property, remaining in the possession of the secured party to the levying officer for the purposes of the levy, as provided in Section 9615 of the Commercial Code, unless otherwise ordered by the court or directed by the levying officer. *(Added by Stats.1990, c. 1125 (A.B.3881), § 1.5, operative Jan. 1, 2002. Amended by Stats.1999, c. 991 (S.B.45), § 24.5, operative Jan. 1, 2002.)*

Research References

Rutter, Cal. Practice Guide: Enforcing Judgments/Debts Ch. 6D-3, Levy of Writ of Execution-In General.
Rutter, Cal. Practice Guide: Enforcing Judgments/Debts Ch. 6D-4, Levy on Specific Property.
Rutter, Cal. Practice Guide: Enforcing Judgments/Debts Ch. 6D-5, Duties, Rights and Liabilities of Third Persons After Levy.
Rutter, Cal. Practice Guide: Enforcing Judgments/Debts Ch. 6D-7, Sale and Collection of Property Levied Upon.
8 Witkin Cal. Proc. 5th Enforcement of Judgment § 124, Property in Possession of Debtor or Third Person.
8 Witkin Cal. Proc. 5th Enforcement of Judgment § 141, (S 141) Rights and Duties of Secured Party.
8 Witkin Cal. Proc. 5th Enforcement of Judgment § 142, (S 142) Duties of Account Debtor.
6 Witkin Cal. Proc. 5th Provisional Remedies § 192, Enforcement of Judgments Law is Applicable.
4 Witkin, California Summary 10th Secured Transactions in Personal Property § 177, Application of Proceeds.
4 Witkin, California Summary 10th Secured Transactions in Personal Property § 185, (S 185) in General.
4 Witkin, California Summary 10th Secured Transactions in Personal Property § 186, (S 186) Right to Surplus and Liability for Deficiency.

4 Witkin, California Summary 10th Secured Transactions in Personal Property § 200, Consumer Transactions.

§ 701.050. Account receivable, chattel paper, or general intangible; duties of account debtor

After service of a copy of the writ of execution and a notice of levy on an account debtor obligated on an account receivable, chattel paper, or general intangible:

(a) If the account debtor has been making payments or is required to make payments to the judgment debtor, the account debtor shall make payments to the levying officer as they become due unless otherwise directed by court order or by the levying officer. Payments made to the judgment debtor after the account debtor has received notice of the levy do not discharge the obligation of the account debtor to make payments as required by this subdivision.

(b) If the account debtor has been making payments to a third person or is required to make payments to a third person (whether pursuant to a security agreement, assignment for collection, or otherwise), the account debtor shall continue to make such payments to the third person notwithstanding the levy until the account debtor receives notice that the obligation to the third person is satisfied or is otherwise directed by court order or by the third person. After the account debtor receives notice that the obligation to the third person is satisfied, the account debtor shall make payments to the levying officer as they become due unless otherwise directed by court order or by the levying officer.

(c) If pursuant to a security agreement the judgment debtor has liberty to accept the return of goods or make repossessions under the account receivable or chattel paper, the account debtor shall deliver to the levying officer property returnable to the judgment debtor unless otherwise directed by court order or by the levying officer. *(Added by Stats.1982, c. 1364, p. 5136, § 2, operative July 1, 1983.)*

Law Revision Commission Comments

Section 701.050 sets forth the duties of an account debtor obligated on an account receivable, chattel paper, or general intangible. Like Section 701.040, this section is intended to preserve the status quo between the account debtor and a third person to whom the account debtor has been making or is required to make payments. See also the Comment to Section 701.040. Subdivisions (a) and (c) provide significant exceptions to this principle, however, in cases where the judgment debtor has the liberty to accept payments or the return of property. See Com. Code § 9205 (liberty in debtor to collect accounts and chattel paper). [16 Cal.L.Rev.Comm. Reports 1353 (1982)].

Research References

Rutter, Cal. Practice Guide: Enforcing Judgments/Debts Ch. 6D-4, Levy on Specific Property.
Rutter, Cal. Practice Guide: Enforcing Judgments/Debts Ch. 6D-5, Duties, Rights and Liabilities of Third Persons After Levy.
8 Witkin Cal. Proc. 5th Enforcement of Judgment § 142, (S 142) Duties of Account Debtor.
8 Witkin Cal. Proc. 5th Enforcement of Judgment § 306, (S 306) Effect of Assignment.
6 Witkin Cal. Proc. 5th Provisional Remedies § 192, Enforcement of Judgments Law is Applicable.

§ 701.060. Payments under instrument to levying officer

If the levying officer obtains custody of an instrument levied upon and serves the obligor under the instrument pursuant to the levy, the obligor shall make payments to the levying officer as they become due. Payments made to a person other than the levying officer do not discharge the obligation of the obligor to make payments as required by this section if the payments are made after the obligor has received notice of the levy. *(Added by Stats.1982, c. 1364, p. 5137, § 2, operative July 1, 1983.)*

Research References

Rutter, Cal. Practice Guide: Enforcing Judgments/Debts Ch. 6D-4, Levy on Specific Property.
Rutter, Cal. Practice Guide: Enforcing Judgments/Debts Ch. 6D-5, Duties, Rights and Liabilities of Third Persons After Levy.
8 Witkin Cal. Proc. 5th Enforcement of Judgment § 130, (S 130) Instruments.
8 Witkin Cal. Proc. 5th Enforcement of Judgment § 143, (S 143) Duties of Obligor Under Instrument.
6 Witkin Cal. Proc. 5th Provisional Remedies § 192, Enforcement of Judgments Law is Applicable.

§ 701.070. Payment to levying officer

If a final money judgment has been levied upon and the levying officer has served the judgment debtor under the final money judgment levied upon, the judgment debtor shall make any payments due under the judgment to the levying officer. Payments made to a person other than the levying officer do not discharge the obligation of the judgment debtor under the final money judgment levied upon if the payments are made after the judgment debtor has received notice of the levy. *(Added by Stats.1984, c. 538, § 25.5.)*

Research References

Rutter, Cal. Practice Guide: Enforcing Judgments/Debts Ch. 4-A, A. Attachment.
Rutter, Cal. Practice Guide: Enforcing Judgments/Debts Ch. 6D-4, Levy on Specific Property.
8 Witkin Cal. Proc. 5th Enforcement of Judgment § 137, (S 137) Final Money Judgment.
6 Witkin Cal. Proc. 5th Provisional Remedies § 192, Enforcement of Judgments Law is Applicable.

ARTICLE 6. SALE AND COLLECTION

Section

§ 701.510. Property subject to sale

Subject to Sections 687.020 and 701.520, the levying officer shall sell all property that has been levied upon except:

(a) Tangible personal property may not be sold until the levying officer obtains custody of the property.

(b) Cash may not be sold unless it has a value exceeding its face value. *(Added by Stats.1982, c. 1364, p. 5137, § 2, operative July 1, 1983.)*

Law Revision Commission Comments

Section 701.510 continues the general authority of the levying officer to sell property after levy. See former Section 691. If sale is not made during the period of the lien of execution, the property must be released unless the property is to be held under another lien or is to be held pending resolution of a dispute as to its disposition. Section 697.050. After sale, the proceeds are applied in the manner provided by Section 701.810. Subdivisions (a) and (b) provide exceptions to the general rule. See also Section 701.520 (sale of collectible property). As to sale of property levied upon prior to operative date of this article, see Sections 694.040, 694.050. [16 Cal.L.Rev.Comm. Reports 1354 (1982)].

Research References

Rutter, Cal. Practice Guide: Civ. Pro. Before Trial Ch. 9(II)-B, B. Receiverships.

Rutter, Cal. Practice Guide: Enforcing Judgments/Debts Ch. 4-C, C. Receiverships.

Rutter, Cal. Practice Guide: Enforcing Judgments/Debts Ch. 6D-7, Sale and Collection of Property Levied Upon.

Miller and Starr California Real Estate § 32:66, Notice of Sale.

Miller and Starr California Real Estate § 33:13, Preservation and Management--Power to Sell Assets.

Miller and Starr California Real Estate § 11:128, Execution Lien; Recordation of the Writ of Execution.

Miller and Starr California Real Estate § 11:172, Assessment and Bond Liens--Special Tax Liens Under the Mello-Roos Community Facilities Act.

8 Witkin Cal. Proc. 5th Enforcement of Judgment § 99, (S 99) Nature of Execution.

8 Witkin Cal. Proc. 5th Enforcement of Judgment § 102, (S 102) Preservation of Property.

8 Witkin Cal. Proc. 5th Enforcement of Judgment § 106, (S 106) Release of Property.

8 Witkin Cal. Proc. 5th Enforcement of Judgment § 144, (S 144) in General.

8 Witkin Cal. Proc. 5th Enforcement of Judgment § 148, Notice to Bidders and Persons Requesting Notice.

8 Witkin Cal. Proc. 5th Enforcement of Judgment § 155, Default of Bidder.

8 Witkin Cal. Proc. 5th Enforcement of Judgment § 222, (S 222) Determination and Order.

8 Witkin Cal. Proc. 5th Enforcement of Judgment § 290, (S 290) Order Applying Property to Satisfaction of Judgment.

8 Witkin Cal. Proc. 5th Enforcement of Judgment § 304, After Final Judgment.

8 Witkin Cal. Proc. 5th Enforcement of Judgment § 338, (S 338) Writ of Sale.

6 Witkin Cal. Proc. 5th Provisional Remedies § 179, Securities.

6 Witkin Cal. Proc. 5th Provisional Remedies § 191, Depreciating Property.

6 Witkin Cal. Proc. 5th Provisional Remedies § 211, (S 211) Redelivery or Sale of Property in Custody.

6 Witkin Cal. Proc. 5th Provisional Remedies § 455, Sale of Property.

10 Witkin, California Summary 10th Parent and Child § 435, Use or Sale of Assets.

§ 701.520. Property to be collected; intention to sell; orders

(a) Except as provided in this section, any of the following property that has been levied upon shall be collected rather than sold:

(1) Accounts receivable.

(2) Chattel paper.

(3) General intangibles.

(4) Final money judgments.

(5) Instruments that are not customarily transferred in an established market.

(6) Instruments that represent an obligation arising out of the sale or lease of property, a license to use property, the furnishing of services, or the loan of money where the property sold or leased or licensed for use, the services furnished, or the money loaned was used by an individual primarily for personal, family, or household purposes.

(b) At the time of levy on property described in subdivision (a) or thereafter, the judgment creditor may serve a notice of intended sale of the property on the judgment debtor. Service shall be made personally or by mail. A copy of the notice of intended sale and proof of service on the judgment debtor shall be filed with the court and with the levying officer. The notice of intended sale shall describe the property and state that it will be sold at an execution sale unless, within the time allowed after service of the notice of intended sale, the judgment debtor applies to the court on noticed motion for an order that the property be collected rather than sold.

(c) Within 10 days after service of the notice of intended sale, the judgment debtor may apply to the court on noticed motion for an order that the property be collected rather than sold. A judgment debtor who so applies shall, within the time allowed for the application, serve a copy of the notice of motion on the judgment creditor and file a copy of the notice of motion with the levying officer. Service of the copy of the notice of motion on the judgment creditor shall be made personally or by mail. If the copy of the notice of motion is not filed with the levying officer within the time allowed, the levying officer shall proceed to sell the property. If a copy of the notice of motion is filed with the levying officer within the time allowed, the levying officer shall continue to collect the property until otherwise ordered by the court.

(d) At the hearing on the motion, the court may in its discretion order that the property be sold or be collected depending on the equities and circumstances of the particular case. If the court orders that the property be sold, the order may specify terms and conditions of sale. If the court orders that the property be collected, the court may condition its order on an assignment of the property by the judgment debtor to the judgment creditor pursuant to Article 6 (commencing with Section 708.510) of Chapter 6. *(Added by Stats.1982, c. 1364, p. 5137, § 2, operative July 1, 1983.)*

Law Revision Commission Comments

Subdivision (a) of Section 701.520 provides a degree of protection for types of property that are particularly susceptible to sacrifice and speculative sales. Former law did not contain such exceptions to the general rule that property levied upon is to be sold on execution (see Section 701.510), although former Section 691 directed the levying officer to collect or sell things in action. Section 701.520 clarifies the manner of applying a judgment in favor of the judgment debtor to the satisfaction of the judgment creditor's money judgment. See subdivision (a) (4). Prior law provided for the attachment of final judgments (see subdivision 5 of former Section 542, superseded by Section 488.420), but appeared to forbid levy and sale under execution (see former Section 688(f)). See also Sections 700.180 (levy on property that is subject of pending action), 700.190 (levy on final money judgment), 708.470--708.480 (enforcement of lien obtained in pending action). The effect of paragraphs (5) and (6) of subdivision (a) is to permit sale without court order of instruments that are regularly transferred on established markets so long as the instruments are not consumer paper. See Section 701.510.

Subdivisions (b)--(d) provide a procedure through which the judgment creditor may have the property sold if the judgment debtor does not object within 10 days. The time for objecting is extended if the judgment debtor is served by mail. See Section 684.120. The objection is made in the form of a motion that the property be collected rather than sold. Subdivision (d) provides the court with broad authority to determine whether a sale should take place depending, for example, on such factors as whether the obligation is currently being paid, the probable proceeds of a sale of the obligation, the costs of collection if it is not sold, and the availability of other useful remedies. If a sale is permitted, the court may set a minimum price or require court confirmation of sale. The sale may be conducted in the same manner as other execution sales or may be conducted in some other manner, e.g., as a negotiated private sale through some commercial channel. [16 Cal.L.Rev.Comm. Reports 1356 (1982)].

Research References

Rutter, Cal. Practice Guide: Enforcing Judgments/Debts Ch. 6D-7, Sale and Collection of Property Levied Upon.

Miller and Starr California Real Estate § 32:64, Creation, Duration, and Effect of Writ of Execution.

8 Witkin Cal. Proc. 5th Enforcement of Judgment § 144, (S 144) in General.

8 Witkin Cal. Proc. 5th Enforcement of Judgment § 145, (S 145) Property to be Collected Rather Than Sold.

8 Witkin Cal. Proc. 5th Enforcement of Judgment § 304, After Final Judgment.

§ 701.530. Notice of sale of personal property; posting and service; time for sale

(a) Notice of sale of personal property shall be in writing, shall state the date, time, and place of sale, and shall describe the property to be sold.

(b) Not less than 10 days before a sale of personal property, notice of sale shall be posted and served on the judgment debtor by the levying officer. Service shall be made personally or by mail.

(c) Posting under this section shall be in three public places in:

(1) The city in which the property is to be sold if it is to be sold in a city.

(2) The county in which the property is to be sold if it is not to be sold in a city.

(d) A sale of personal property of an individual may not take place until the expiration of the time during which the judgment debtor may make a claim of exemption under subdivision (a) of Section 703.520. *(Added by Stats.1982, c. 1364, p. 5138, § 2, operative July 1, 1983. Amended by Stats.2002, c. 784 (S.B.1316), § 68.)*

Law Revision Commission Comments

Subdivision (c)(2) of Section 701.530 is amended to reflect unification of the municipal and superior courts pursuant to Article VI, Section 5(e), of the California Constitution. See Section 38 (judicial district). [32 Cal.L.Rev.Comm. Reports 127 (2002)].

Research References

Rutter, Cal. Practice Guide: Enforcing Judgments/Debts Ch. 6D-7, Sale and Collection of Property Levied Upon.

8 Witkin Cal. Proc. 5th Enforcement of Judgment § 146, Sale of Personal Property.

8 Witkin Cal. Proc. 5th Enforcement of Judgment § 148, Notice to Bidders and Persons Requesting Notice.

§ 701.540. Notice of sale of interest in real property; service, mailing and posting; publication; notice to lienholders

(a) Notice of sale of an interest in real property shall be in writing, shall state the date, time, and place of sale, shall describe the interest to be sold, and shall give a legal description of the real property and its street address or other common designation, if any. If the real property has no street address or other common designation, the notice of sale shall include a statement that directions to its location may be obtained from the levying officer upon oral or written request or, in the discretion of the levying officer, the notice of sale may contain directions to its location. Directions are sufficient if information as to the location of the real property is given by reference to the direction and approximate distance from the nearest crossroads, frontage road, or access road. If an accurate legal description of the real property is given, the validity of the notice and sale is not affected by the fact that the street address or other common designation, or directions to its location, are erroneous or omitted.

(b) Not less than 20 days before the date of sale, notice of sale of an interest in real property shall be served, mailed, and posted by the levying officer as provided in subdivisions (c), (d), (e), and (f).

(c) Notice of sale shall be served on the judgment debtor. Service shall be made personally or by mail.

(d) Notice of sale shall be posted in the following places:

(1) One public place in the city in which the interest in the real property is to be sold if it is to be sold in a city or, if not to be sold in a city, one public place in the county in which the interest in the real property is to be sold.

(2) A conspicuous place on the real property.

(e) At the time notice is posted pursuant to paragraph (2) of subdivision (d), notice of sale shall be served or service shall be attempted on one occupant of the real property. Service on the occupant shall be made by leaving the notice with the occupant personally or, in the occupant's absence, with any person of suitable age and discretion found upon the real property at the time service is attempted who is either an employee or agent of the occupant or a member of the occupant's household. If the levying officer is unable to serve such an occupant at the time service is attempted, the levying officer is not required to make any further attempts to serve an occupant.

(f) If the property described in the notice of sale consists of more than one distinct lot, parcel, or governmental subdivision and any of the lots, parcels, or governmental subdivisions lies with relation to any of the others so as to form one or more continuous, unbroken tracts, only one service pursuant to subdivision (e) and posting pursuant to paragraph (2) of subdivision (d) need be made as to each continuous, unbroken tract.

(g) Notice of sale shall be published pursuant to Section 6063 of the Government Code, with the first publication at least 20 days prior to the time of sale, in a newspaper of general circulation published in the city in which the real property or a part thereof is situated if any part thereof is situated in a city or, if not, in a newspaper of general circulation published in the judicial district in which the real property or a part thereof is situated. If no newspaper of general circulation is published in the city or judicial district, notice of sale shall be published in a newspaper of general circulation in the county in which the real property or a part thereof is situated.

(h) Not earlier than 30 days after the date of levy, the judgment creditor shall determine the names of all persons having liens on the real property on the date of levy that are of record in the office of the county recorder and shall instruct the levying officer to mail notice of sale to each such person at the address used by the county recorder for the return of the instrument creating the person's lien after recording. The levying officer shall mail notice to each such person, at the address given in the instructions, not less than 20 days before the date of sale. *(Added by Stats.1982, c. 1364, p. 5138, § 2, operative July 1, 1983. Amended by Stats.2002, c. 784 (S.B.1316), § 69.)*

Law Revision Commission Comments

Section 701.540 supersedes subdivision 3 of former Section 692. Notice of sale may not be given until the expiration of the period provided in Section 701.545. The responsibility of the levying officer under subdivision (a) to give directions to the location of property that has no street address or other common designation is derived from the provision of former Section 692 for giving directions by the beneficiary of a deed of trust. See also Section 687.010 (instructions to levying officer). Subdivision (b) continues a portion of subdivision 3 of former Section 692. Subdivision (c) requires personal service on the judgment debtor whereas subdivision 3 of former Section 692 permitted service by certified mail. Subdivisions (e) and (f) are the same as portions of Section 700.015(c) (notice of levy). Subdivisions (d) and (g) continue the substance of portions of subdivision 3 of former Section 692. Subdivision (h) requires notice not required by former law. For special provisions applicable to sale of a dwelling to enforce a money judgment, see Sections 704.770, 704.790. [16 Cal.L.Rev.Comm. Reports 1359 (1982)].

Subdivision (d)(1) of Section 701.540 is amended to reflect unification of the municipal and superior courts pursuant to Article VI, Section 5(e), of the California Constitution. See Section 38 (judicial district). *Cf.* Gov't Code § 71042.5 (preservation of judicial districts for purpose of publication). [32 Cal.L.Rev.Comm. Reports 128 (2002)].

Research References

Rutter, Cal. Practice Guide: Enforcing Judgments/Debts Ch. 6D-4, Levy on Specific Property.
Rutter, Cal. Practice Guide: Enforcing Judgments/Debts Ch. 6D-7, Sale and Collection of Property Levied Upon.
Miller and Starr California Real Estate § 32:66, Notice of Sale.
Miller and Starr California Real Estate § 10:226, The Judicial Sale.
8 Witkin Cal. Proc. 5th Enforcement of Judgment § 29, Instructions from Judgment Creditor.
8 Witkin Cal. Proc. 5th Enforcement of Judgment § 147, Sale of Real Property.
8 Witkin Cal. Proc. 5th Enforcement of Judgment § 148, Notice to Bidders and Persons Requesting Notice.
12 Witkin, California Summary 10th Real Property § 79, Procedure.

§ 701.545. Notice of sale of interest in real property other than leasehold estate with unexpired term under two years at levy

Notice of sale of an interest in real property, other than a leasehold estate with an unexpired term of less than two years at the time of levy, may not be given pursuant to Section 701.540 until the expiration of 120 days after the date notice of levy on the interest in real property was served on the judgment debtor. *(Added by Stats.1982, c. 1364, p. 5139, § 2, operative July 1, 1983.)*

Research References

Rutter, Cal. Practice Guide: Enforcing Judgments/Debts Ch. 6D-4, Levy on Specific Property.
Rutter, Cal. Practice Guide: Enforcing Judgments/Debts Ch. 6D-7, Sale and Collection of Property Levied Upon.
Miller and Starr California Real Estate § 32:66, Notice of Sale.
Miller and Starr California Real Estate § 11:128, Execution Lien; Recordation of the Writ of Execution.
Miller and Starr California Real Estate § 11:171, Assessment and Bond Liens--Enforcement of 1911 Improvement Act Bonds.
Miller and Starr California Real Estate § 11:172, Assessment and Bond Liens--Special Tax Liens Under the Mello-Roos Community Facilities Act.
8 Witkin Cal. Proc. 5th Enforcement of Judgment § 147, Sale of Real Property.
10 Witkin, California Summary 10th Parent and Child § 432, Assets Subject to Order.

§ 701.547. Contents of notice; provisions governing

A notice of sale shall contain the substance of the following statement: "Prospective bidders should refer to Sections 701.510 to 701.680, inclusive, of the Code of Civil Procedure for provisions governing the terms, conditions, and effect of the sale and the liability of defaulting bidders." *(Added by Stats.1982, c. 1364, p. 5140, § 2, operative July 1, 1983.)*

Research References

Rutter, Cal. Practice Guide: Enforcing Judgments/Debts Ch. 6D-7, Sale and Collection of Property Levied Upon.
Miller and Starr California Real Estate § 32:66, Notice of Sale.

8 Witkin Cal. Proc. 5th Enforcement of Judgment § 148, Notice to Bidders and Persons Requesting Notice.

§ 701.550. Request for notice

(a) In addition to the notice of sale required by this article, the levying officer shall, at the time notice of sale is posted pursuant to Section 701.530 or 701.540, mail notice of sale to any person who has requested notice of the sale pursuant to this section.

(b) A request for notice of sale under this section made prior to the issuance of the writ shall be in writing and shall be filed with the clerk of the court where the judgment is entered. The request shall specify the title of the court, the cause and number of the action in which the judgment was entered, and the date of entry thereof, and shall state the address to which the notice of sale is to be mailed. The name and address of the person requesting notice of sale under this subdivision shall be noted on the writ.

(c) A person who desires notice of sale of particular property that has been levied upon may file a request for notice of sale with the levying officer who will conduct the sale. The request shall contain the information specified by the levying officer as needed in order to comply with the request. *(Added by Stats.1982, c. 1364, p. 5140, § 2, operative July 1, 1983.)*

Research References

Rutter, Cal. Practice Guide: Enforcing Judgments/Debts Ch. 6D-7, Sale and Collection of Property Levied Upon.
Miller and Starr California Real Estate § 32:66, Notice of Sale.
Miller and Starr California Real Estate § 10:226, The Judicial Sale.
8 Witkin Cal. Proc. 5th Enforcement of Judgment § 148, Notice to Bidders and Persons Requesting Notice.

§ 701.555. Advertisement of sale

In addition to the notice of sale required by this article, the judgment creditor may advertise the sale in the classified or other advertising section of a newspaper of general circulation or other publication and may recover reasonable costs of such advertising. The judgment debtor may also advertise the sale at the judgment debtor's own expense. *(Added by Stats.1982, c. 1364, p. 5140, § 2, operative July 1, 1983.)*

Research References

Rutter, Cal. Practice Guide: Enforcing Judgments/Debts Ch. 6D-7, Sale and Collection of Property Levied Upon.
Miller and Starr California Real Estate § 32:66, Notice of Sale.
Miller and Starr California Real Estate § 10:226, The Judicial Sale.
8 Witkin Cal. Proc. 5th Enforcement of Judgment § 149, Advertising by Creditor or Debtor.

§ 701.560. Failure to give notice; liability of officer

(a) Failure to give notice of sale as required by this article does not invalidate the sale.

(b) A levying officer who sells property without giving the required notice is liable to the judgment creditor and the judgment debtor for actual damages caused by failure to give notice. *(Added by Stats.1982, c. 1364, p. 5140, § 2, operative July 1, 1983.)*

Law Revision Commission Comments

Subdivision (a) of Section 701.560 codifies existing law. See Smith v. Randall, 6 Cal. 47, 50 (1856); Hamilton v. Carpenter, 52 Cal.App.2d 447, 448, 126 P.2d 395 (1942). Subdivision (b) continues the levying officer's liability for actual damages for failure to give proper notice of sale provided by former Section 693. Former Section 693 provided for liability to the "aggrieved party." See Sheehy v. Graves, 58 Cal. 449 (1881) (judgment creditor as aggrieved party); Bellmer v. Blessington, 136 Cal. 3, 68 P. 111 (1902) (judgment debtor as aggrieved party); Kelley v. Desmond, 63 Cal. 517, 518 (1883) (purchaser at execution sale not aggrieved party). The forfeiture of $100 by the levying officer to the aggrieved party under former Section 693 is not continued. [16 Cal. L.Rev.Comm. Reports 1362 (1982)].

Research References

Rutter, Cal. Practice Guide: Enforcing Judgments/Debts Ch. 6D-3, Levy of Writ of Execution-In General.
Rutter, Cal. Practice Guide: Enforcing Judgments/Debts Ch. 6D-4, Levy on Specific Property.
Rutter, Cal. Practice Guide: Enforcing Judgments/Debts Ch. 6D-7, Sale and Collection of Property Levied Upon.
Miller and Starr California Real Estate § 32:66, Notice of Sale.
Miller and Starr California Real Estate § 10:226, The Judicial Sale.
8 Witkin Cal. Proc. 5th Enforcement of Judgment § 33, Liability of Officer.
8 Witkin Cal. Proc. 5th Enforcement of Judgment § 150, Effect of Sale Without Notice.

§ 701.570. Sale; date, time and place; auction; view of property; sale by group or lot

(a) A sale of property shall be held at the date, time, and place specified in the notice of sale, which shall be in the county where the property or a part thereof is situated and between the hours of nine in the morning and five in the afternoon. Subject to subdivision (d), real property consisting of one parcel, or of two or more contiguous parcels, situated in two or more counties may be sold in one county as instructed by the judgment creditor.

(b) The sale shall be made at auction to the highest bidder.

(c) If personal property capable of manual delivery is to be sold, it shall be within the view of those who attend the sale unless, upon application of the judgment creditor or the judgment debtor, the court orders otherwise.

(d) Property shall be sold separately or in such groups or lots as are likely to bring the highest price. The judgment debtor may request that the property be sold separately or together and may request that the property be sold in a particular order. If the judgment debtor is not present at the sale, the request may be made in writing and delivered to the levying officer prior to the sale. The levying officer shall honor the request if, in the opinion of the levying officer, the requested manner of sale is likely to yield an amount at least equal to any other manner of sale or the amount required to satisfy the money judgment. The levying officer is not liable for a decision made in good faith under this subdivision.

(e) After sufficient property has been sold to yield the amount required to satisfy the money judgment, no more shall be sold. *(Added by Stats.1982, c. 1364, p. 5140, § 2, operative July 1, 1983.)*

Law Revision Commission Comments

Subdivisions (a) and (b) of Section 701.570 continue the substance of the first sentence of former Section 694. Subdivision (c) supersedes a portion of the fourth sentence of former Section 694 which required personal property to be in the view of the persons attending the sale.

Subdivision (d) supersedes a portion of the fourth sentence and the fifth sentence of former Section 694. See also the last sentence of former Section 691. Although former Section 694 appeared to require that real property must be sold in separate parcels, the cases interpreting that section suggest that sale en masse constitutes at most an irregularity and that the true test is whether separate sale would produce a higher price. See 5 B. Witkin, California Procedure Enforcement of Judgment § 80, at 3451 (2d ed. 1971). There may be cases where sale as a unit will produce a substantially higher price than separate sale.

Subdivision (d) permits the judgment debtor to make reasonable requests concerning the manner of sale, but the levying officer is empowered to accept or reject the request. Under former Section 694, the judgment debtor appeared to have absolute control over the order and lots in which the property was sold. The authority for the judgment debtor to make a request in writing when not present at the sale is not found in prior law.

Subdivision (e) continues the second sentence of former Section 694. [16 Cal.L.Rev.Comm. Reports 1363 (1982)].

Research References

Rutter, Cal. Practice Guide: Enforcing Judgments/Debts Ch. 6D-7, Sale and Collection of Property Levied Upon.
Miller and Starr California Real Estate § 32:69, Conduct of Sale.
Miller and Starr California Real Estate § 10:226, The Judicial Sale.
8 Witkin Cal. Proc. 5th Enforcement of Judgment § 33, Liability of Officer.
8 Witkin Cal. Proc. 5th Enforcement of Judgment § 146, Sale of Personal Property.
8 Witkin Cal. Proc. 5th Enforcement of Judgment § 151, in General.
12 Witkin, California Summary 10th Real Property § 79, Procedure.

§ 701.580. Postponement of sale

The judgment debtor and judgment creditor together may request in writing that a sale be postponed to an agreed day and hour. The request shall be delivered to the levying officer conducting the sale, and the levying officer shall, by public declaration at the time and place originally fixed for the sale, postpone the sale to the day and hour fixed in the request. Notice of any additional postponements shall be given by public declaration by the levying officer at the time and place last appointed for the sale. No other notice of postponed sale need be given. A postponed sale shall be held at the place originally fixed for the sale. *(Added by Stats.1982, c. 1364, p. 5141, § 2, operative July 1, 1983.)*

Law Revision Commission Comments

Section 701.580 continues the substance of the second paragraph of former Section 694. [16 Cal.L.Rev.Comm. Reports 1364 (1982)].

Research References

Rutter, Cal. Practice Guide: Enforcing Judgments/Debts Ch. 6D-7, Sale and Collection of Property Levied Upon.
Miller and Starr California Real Estate § 10:226, The Judicial Sale.
8 Witkin Cal. Proc. 5th Enforcement of Judgment § 152, Postponement of Sale.

§ 701.590. Form of payment; creditor's bid

(a) Except as otherwise provided in this section, the purchaser at a sale shall pay in cash or by certified check or cashier's check.

(b) The judgment creditor may bid by giving the levying officer a written receipt crediting all or part of the amount required to satisfy the judgment, except that the levying officer's costs remaining unsatisfied and the amount of preferred labor claims, exempt proceeds, and any other claim that is required by statute to be satisfied, shall be paid in cash or by certified check or cashier's check.

(c) If the highest bid for an interest in real property sold exceeds five thousand dollars ($5,000), the highest bidder may elect to treat the sale as a credit transaction. A person who makes the election shall deposit at least five thousand dollars ($5,000) or 10 percent of the amount bid, whichever is greater, and within 10 days after the date of the sale shall pay the balance due plus costs accruing with regard to the property sold and interest accruing at the rate on money judgments on the balance of the amount bid from the date of sale until the date of payment.

(d) If the highest bid for an item, group, or lot of personal property sold exceeds two thousand five hundred dollars ($2,500), the highest bidder may elect to treat the sale as a credit transaction. A person who makes the election shall deposit at least two thousand five hundred dollars ($2,500) or 10 percent of the amount bid, whichever is greater, and within 10 days after the date of the sale shall pay the balance due plus costs accruing with regard to the property sold and interest accruing at the rate on money judgments on the balance of the amount bid from the date of sale until the date of payment.

(e) A person who makes the election under subdivision (c) or (d) is not entitled to possession of the property sold until the amount bid, plus accruing costs and interest, have been paid. *(Added by Stats.1982, c. 1364, p. 5141, § 2, operative July 1, 1983.)*

Research References

Rutter, Cal. Practice Guide: Enforcing Judgments/Debts Ch. 6D-7, Sale and Collection of Property Levied Upon.
Miller and Starr California Real Estate § 32:69, Conduct of Sale.
Miller and Starr California Real Estate § 10:226, The Judicial Sale.
8 Witkin Cal. Proc. 5th Enforcement of Judgment § 154, Manner of Payment.
8 Witkin Cal. Proc. 5th Enforcement of Judgment § 155, Default of Bidder.

§ 701.600. Failure to pay; application of deposit; liability; subsequent bids

If the highest bidder does not pay the amount bid as prescribed by Section 701.590:

(a) The levying officer shall sell the property:

(1) If the default occurs at the sale, either to the next highest bidder at the amount of the next highest bid if such bidder agrees or to the highest bidder at a new sale held immediately.

(2) If the default occurs after the sale to a credit bidder pursuant to subdivision (c) of Section 701.590, to the highest bidder at a new sale.

(b) The levying officer shall apply the amount of any deposit made pursuant to subdivision (c) of Section 701.590 in the following order:

(1) To the satisfaction of costs accruing with regard to the property sold from the date of the sale until the date the property is resold, including costs of resale.

(2) To the satisfaction of interest at the rate on money judgments on the amount bid from the date of the sale until the date the property is resold.

(3) To the amount required to satisfy the money judgment in the order of distribution prescribed by Section 701.810 or Section 704.850, whichever is applicable.

(c) If there is a sale to the next highest bidder or to the highest bidder at a new sale, the defaulting bidder is liable for the following amounts in an action by the judgment creditor or judgment debtor:

(1) The amount bid, less the amount obtained from the resale of the property and the amount of any deposit applied pursuant to subdivision (b). The amount recovered pursuant to this paragraph shall be distributed in the manner prescribed by Section 701.810 or Section 704.850, whichever is applicable.

(2) Any costs accruing with regard to the property sold from the date of sale until the date the property is resold, including costs of resale.

(3) Interest at the rate on money judgments on the amount bid from the date of the sale until the date the property is resold.

(4) Costs and attorney's fees incurred in the action under this subdivision.

(d) The levying officer may, in the levying officer's discretion, reject any subsequent bid of the defaulting bidder. *(Added by Stats.1982, c. 1364, p. 5142, § 2, operative July 1, 1983.)*

Research References

Rutter, Cal. Practice Guide: Enforcing Judgments/Debts Ch. 6D-7, Sale and Collection of Property Levied Upon.
Miller and Starr California Real Estate § 32:69, Conduct of Sale.
Miller and Starr California Real Estate § 10:226, The Judicial Sale.

8 Witkin Cal. Proc. 5th Enforcement of Judgment § 155, Default of Bidder.

§ 701.610. Levying officer; conflict of interest

The levying officer may not be a purchaser or have an interest in any purchase at a sale. *(Added by Stats.1982, c. 1364, p. 5142, § 2, operative July 1, 1983.)*

Law Revision Commission Comments

Section 701.610 continues the substance of the third sentence of former Section 694. [16 Cal.L.Rev.Comm. Reports 1367 (1982)].

Research References

Rutter, Cal. Practice Guide: Enforcing Judgments/Debts Ch. 6D-7, Sale and Collection of Property Levied Upon.
8 Witkin Cal. Proc. 5th Enforcement of Judgment § 153, in General.

§ 701.620. Minimum bid required; failure to receive minimum

(a) Property may not be sold unless the amount bid exceeds the total of the following amounts:

(1) The amount of all preferred labor claims that are required by Section 1206 to be satisfied from the proceeds.

(2) The amount of any state tax lien (as defined in Section 7162 of the Government Code) that is superior to the judgment creditor's lien.

(3) If the purchaser is not the judgment creditor, the amount of any deposit made pursuant to Section 720.260 with interest thereon at the rate on money judgments from the date of the deposit to the date of the sale.

(b) Property for which a proceeds exemption is provided by Section 704.010 (motor vehicle), 704.020 (household furnishings and other personal effects), or 704.060 (tools of trade), may not be sold unless the amount bid exceeds the sum of any amount under subdivision (a) and the amount of the proceeds exemption.

(c) If a minimum bid required for the sale of property pursuant to this section is not received, the levying officer shall promptly release the property. *(Added by Stats.1982, c. 1364, p. 5142, § 2, operative July 1, 1983.)*

Research References

Rutter, Cal. Practice Guide: Enforcing Judgments/Debts Ch. 6D-7, Sale and Collection of Property Levied Upon.
Miller and Starr California Real Estate § 10:226, The Judicial Sale.
8 Witkin Cal. Proc. 5th Enforcement of Judgment § 153, in General.
8 Witkin Cal. Proc. 5th Enforcement of Judgment § 154, Manner of Payment.

§ 701.630. Liens extinguished

If property is sold pursuant to this article, the lien under which it is sold, any liens subordinate thereto, and any state tax lien (as defined in Section 7162 of the Government Code) on the property sold are extinguished. *(Added by Stats.1982, c. 1364, p. 5143, § 2, operative July 1, 1983.)*

Research References

Rutter, Cal. Practice Guide: Enforcing Judgments/Debts Ch. 6D-3, Levy of Writ of Execution-In General.
Rutter, Cal. Practice Guide: Enforcing Judgments/Debts Ch. 6D-7, Sale and Collection of Property Levied Upon.
Miller and Starr California Real Estate § 8:14, Deeds by Public or Court Officers.
Miller and Starr California Real Estate § 32:69, Conduct of Sale.
Miller and Starr California Real Estate § 10:223, Joinder of Parties.
Miller and Starr California Real Estate § 10:227, Statutory Redemption; Who Can Redeem.
Miller and Starr California Real Estate § 10:231, Sheriff's Deed; Purchaser's Title.

Miller and Starr California Real Estate § 11:100, Priority of the Purchaser's Title from a Foreclosure Sale.

Miller and Starr California Real Estate § 11:126, Relation to Subsequent Interests.

Miller and Starr California Real Estate § 11:129, Priority of the Title of an Execution Sale Purchaser.

Miller and Starr California Real Estate § 11:172, Assessment and Bond Liens--Special Tax Liens Under the Mello-Roos Community Facilities Act.

8 Witkin Cal. Proc. 5th Enforcement of Judgment § 94, (S 94) Transfer or Encumbrance of Real Property.

8 Witkin Cal. Proc. 5th Enforcement of Judgment § 95, Property in Levying Officer's Custody.

8 Witkin Cal. Proc. 5th Enforcement of Judgment § 96, Property Not in Levying Officer's Custody.

8 Witkin Cal. Proc. 5th Enforcement of Judgment § 97, Crops, Timber, and Minerals.

8 Witkin Cal. Proc. 5th Enforcement of Judgment § 98, Other Liens.

8 Witkin Cal. Proc. 5th Enforcement of Judgment § 156, (S 156) Effect of Sale.

§ 701.640. Interests acquired

The purchaser of property at an execution sale acquires any interest of the judgment debtor in the property sold (1) that is held on the effective date of the lien under which the property was sold or (2) that is acquired between such effective date and the date of sale. *(Added by Stats.1982, c. 1364, p. 5143, § 2, operative July 1, 1983.)*

Law Revision Commission Comments

Section 701.640 supersedes former Section 700 and portions of former Sections 698 and 699 and provides a single rule covering both real and personal property. It makes clear that the sale on execution conveys the interest that was liable for the satisfaction of the judgment on the date of levy or the date that the judgment became a lien on the property and any such interest in the property subject to the lien that is acquired before the date of sale, assuming that the lien has been maintained throughout such period. See Section 697.020 (relation back of liens); Kenyon v. Quinn, 41 Cal. 325, 329–30 (1871); Frink v. Roe, 70 Cal. 296, 305, 11 P. 820 (1886). If the property sold is community property, the interest of the judgment debtor's spouse also is sold. See Section 695.020. The interest of the execution sale purchaser is no longer subject to the statutory right of redemption formerly provided by Sections 700a–707. See Section 701.680 and the Comment thereto. [16 Cal.L.Rev.Comm. Reports 1369 (1982)].

Research References

Rutter, Cal. Practice Guide: Enforcing Judgments/Debts Ch. 6D-4, Levy on Specific Property.

Rutter, Cal. Practice Guide: Enforcing Judgments/Debts Ch. 6D-7, Sale and Collection of Property Levied Upon.

Rutter, Cal. Practice Guide: Enforcing Judgments/Debts Ch. 6A-11, Property Subject to Enforcement Procedures.

Miller and Starr California Real Estate § 8:14, Deeds by Public or Court Officers.

Miller and Starr California Real Estate § 32:53, Subsequently Acquired Property.

Miller and Starr California Real Estate § 32:69, Conduct of Sale.

Miller and Starr California Real Estate § 10:231, Sheriff's Deed; Purchaser's Title.

Miller and Starr California Real Estate § 11:126, Relation to Subsequent Interests.

Miller and Starr California Real Estate § 11:129, Priority of the Title of an Execution Sale Purchaser.

Miller and Starr California Real Estate § 11:177, Priorities Among State and Local Tax and Assessment Liens--Priority Between Assessment Liens.

8 Witkin Cal. Proc. 5th Enforcement of Judgment § 156, (S 156) Effect of Sale.

4 Witkin, California Summary 10th Security Transactions in Real Property § 169, (S 169) Passage of Title.

§ 701.650. Delivery of property; certificate of sale; title

(a) When the purchaser of personal property pays the amount due:

(1) If the property is capable of manual delivery, the levying officer shall deliver the property to the purchaser and, if the purchaser so requests, shall execute and deliver a certificate of sale to the purchaser.

(2) If the property is not tangible personal property or if it is otherwise not capable of manual delivery, the levying officer shall execute and deliver a certificate of sale to the purchaser.

(b) If property or a certificate is delivered pursuant to subdivision (a), the levying officer shall sign or endorse any document or instrument in the levying officer's possession relating to the title to or the right to possession of the property and deliver it to the purchaser. *(Added by Stats.1982, c. 1364, p. 5143, § 2, operative July 1, 1983.)*

Law Revision Commission Comments

Subdivision (a) of Section 701.650 supersedes portions of former Sections 698 and 699. Subdivision (b) is new. See also Sections 699.040 (turnover order for documentary evidence of title), 701.010 (delivery by third person of documents necessary to transfer title). [16 Cal.L.Rev. Comm. Reports 1370 (1982)].

Research References

Rutter, Cal. Practice Guide: Enforcing Judgments/Debts Ch. 6D-7, Sale and Collection of Property Levied Upon.

8 Witkin Cal. Proc. 5th Enforcement of Judgment § 157, (S 157) Delivery of Possession, Certificate, or Deed.

§ 701.660. Deed of sale; recordation

When the purchaser of an interest in real property pays the amount due to the levying officer, including any amount required to be paid as a documentary transfer tax pursuant to Section 11911 of the Revenue and Taxation Code, the levying officer conducting the sale shall execute and deliver a deed of sale to the purchaser, record a duplicate of the deed of sale in the office of the county recorder, and forward to the county or city and county any documentary transfer tax paid by the purchaser. *(Added by Stats.1982, c. 1364, p. 5143, § 2, operative July 1, 1983. Amended by Stats.2010, c. 680 (A.B.2394), § 11.)*

Law Revision Commission Comments

Section 701.660 continues a portion of the third sentence of subdivision (a) of former Section 700a. [16 Cal.L.Rev.Comm. Reports 1370 (1982)].

Research References

Rutter, Cal. Practice Guide: Enforcing Judgments/Debts Ch. 6D-7, Sale and Collection of Property Levied Upon.

Miller and Starr California Real Estate § 11:6, Instruments Subject to Recording--List of Recordable Documents.

Miller and Starr California Real Estate § 10:231, Sheriff's Deed; Purchaser's Title.

Miller and Starr California Real Estate § 11:126, Relation to Subsequent Interests.

8 Witkin Cal. Proc. 5th Enforcement of Judgment § 157, (S 157) Delivery of Possession, Certificate, or Deed.

§ 701.670. Contents of certificate or deed of sale

The certificate of sale or deed of sale shall contain all of the following:

(a) The title of the court where the judgment was entered under which the sale was made and the cause and number of the action.

(b) The date of entry of the judgment and of any subsequent renewals and where entered in the records of the court.

(c) The name and address of the judgment creditor and the name and last known address of the judgment debtor.

(d) A description of the property sold.

(e) The date of sale. *(Added by Stats.1982, c. 1364, p. 5143, § 2, operative July 1, 1983.)*

Research References

Rutter, Cal. Practice Guide: Enforcing Judgments/Debts Ch. 6D-7, Sale and Collection of Property Levied Upon.

Miller and Starr California Real Estate § 10:228, Procedure for Redemption.

Miller and Starr California Real Estate § 10:231, Sheriff's Deed; Purchaser's Title.

8 Witkin Cal. Proc. 5th Enforcement of Judgment § 157, (S 157) Delivery of Possession, Certificate, or Deed.

§ 701.680. Sale absolute; reversed, vacated or set aside judgment; irregularities in proceedings; remedies

(a) Except as provided in paragraph (1) of subdivision (c), a sale of property pursuant to this article is absolute and may not be set aside for any reason.

(b) If the judgment is reversed, vacated, or otherwise set aside, the judgment debtor may recover from the judgment creditor the proceeds of a sale pursuant to the judgment with interest at the rate on money judgments to the extent the proceeds were applied to the satisfaction of the judgment.

(c) If the sale was improper because of irregularities in the proceedings, because the property sold was not subject to execution, or for any other reason:

(1) The judgment debtor, or the judgment debtor's successor in interest, may commence an action within 90 days after the date of sale to set aside the sale if the purchaser at the sale is the judgment creditor. Subject to paragraph (2), if the sale is set aside, the judgment of the judgment creditor is revived to reflect the amount that was satisfied from the proceeds of the sale and the judgment creditor is entitled to interest on the amount of the judgment as so revived as if the sale had not been made. Any liens extinguished by the sale of the property are revived and reattach to the property with the same priority and effect as if the sale had not been made.

(2) The judgment debtor, or the judgment debtor's successor in interest, may recover damages caused by the impropriety. If damages are recovered against the judgment creditor, they shall be offset against the judgment to the extent the judgment is not satisfied. If damages are recovered against the levying officer, they shall be applied to the judgment to the extent the judgment is not satisfied.

(d) For the purposes of subdivision (c), the purchaser of the property at the sale is not a successor in interest. *(Added by Stats.1982, c. 1364, p. 5143, § 2, operative July 1, 1983. Amended by Stats.1985, c. 41, § 6; Stats.1985, c. 157, § 3; Stats.1989, c. 1416, § 23.)*

Law Revision Commission Comments

Subdivision (c)(1) of Section 701.680 is amended to make clear that where a sale is improper the judgment debtor (or successor in interest) is permitted to bring an action to set aside the sale within six months if the property was purchased by the judgment creditor, but not if it was purchased by a third person. The limitation of this right to the judgment debtor (and the judgment debtor's successor in interest) was not clearly stated in the former statute. The amendment of subdivision (c)(1) makes this limitation clear.

Subdivision (c) is also amended to make clear that a successor in interest of the judgment debtor may seek to overturn a sale, or seek to recover damages caused by the impropriety, pursuant to this section. This provision is consistent with Section 729.020 which determines who may redeem from a foreclosure sale. [18 Cal.L.Rev.Comm. Reports 361 (1985)].

Subdivision (c)(1) of Section 701.680 is revised to provide for the reattachment of liens on property sold at an execution sale that is later held to be improper. In this case, the liens that were extinguished by operation of Section 701.630, including the lien of the judgment creditor sought to be satisfied by the sale, are revived and reattached to the property as if the execution sale had not taken place. Other things being equal, revived liens attach in the amounts and with the priority that they

would have had if not extinguished by the sale under the superior lien of the judgment creditor.

Subdivision (c)(1) is also amended to shorten the time for bringing an action to set aside the sale from six months to 90 days. [19 Cal.L.Rev.Comm.Reports 1260 (1988)].

Research References

Rutter, Cal. Practice Guide: Enforcing Judgments/Debts Ch. 6D-7, Sale and Collection of Property Levied Upon.

Rutter, Cal. Practice Guide: Real Prop. Transactions Ch. 6-I, I. Real Property Foreclosures and Antideficiency Laws.

Miller and Starr California Real Estate § 13:50, Attack on the Validity of the Sale.

Miller and Starr California Real Estate § 31:69, Judicial Remedies.

Miller and Starr California Real Estate § 32:66, Notice of Sale.

Miller and Starr California Real Estate § 32:73, Attack on Validity of Sale.

Miller and Starr California Real Estate § 32:74, Debtor's Right of Redemption.

Miller and Starr California Real Estate § 10:232, Attack on Validity of the Sale.

Miller and Starr California Real Estate § 11:126, Relation to Subsequent Interests.

Miller and Starr California Real Estate § 11:128, Execution Lien; Recordation of the Writ of Execution.

Miller and Starr California Real Estate § 11:171, Assessment and Bond Liens--Enforcement of 1911 Improvement Act Bonds.

Miller and Starr California Real Estate § 11:172, Assessment and Bond Liens--Special Tax Liens Under the Mello-Roos Community Facilities Act.

13 NO. 3 Miller & Starr, California Real Estate Newsalert 7, Deeds of Trust.

14 NO. 2 Miller & Starr, California Real Estate Newsalert 12, Homesteads.

17 NO. 6 Miller & Starr, California Real Estate Newsalert 10, Recording and Priorities.

22 NO. 4 Miller & Starr, California Real Estate Newsalert 35, Involuntary Liens.

3 Witkin Cal. Proc. 5th Actions § 678, Illustrations.

8 Witkin Cal. Proc. 5th Enforcement of Judgment § 20, Redemption.

8 Witkin Cal. Proc. 5th Enforcement of Judgment § 33, Liability of Officer.

8 Witkin Cal. Proc. 5th Enforcement of Judgment § 148, Notice to Bidders and Persons Requesting Notice.

8 Witkin Cal. Proc. 5th Enforcement of Judgment § 156, (S 156) Effect of Sale.

8 Witkin Cal. Proc. 5th Enforcement of Judgment § 164, in General.

8 Witkin Cal. Proc. 5th Enforcement of Judgment § 166, (S 166) Restitution After Reversal.

8 Witkin Cal. Proc. 5th Enforcement of Judgment § 167, (S 167) Damages for Improper Sale.

8 Witkin Cal. Proc. 5th Enforcement of Judgment § 219, (S 219) in General.

4 Witkin, California Summary 10th Secured Transactions in Personal Property § 8, (S 8) Remedies of Pledgee.

ARTICLE 7. DISTRIBUTION OF PROCEEDS OF SALE OR COLLECTION

§ 701.810. Order of distribution

Except as otherwise provided by statute, the levying officer shall distribute the proceeds of sale or collection in the following order:

(a) To persons having preferred labor claims that are required by Section 1206 to be satisfied from the proceeds, in the amounts required by Section 1206 to be satisfied.

(b) To the state department or agency having a state tax lien (as defined in Section 7162 of the Government Code) that is superior to the judgment creditor's lien, in the amount of the lien.

(c) If a deposit has been made pursuant to Section 720.260 and the purchaser at the sale is not the judgment creditor, to the judgment creditor in the amount required to repay the deposit with interest thereon at the rate on money judgments from the date of the deposit.

(d) To the judgment debtor in the amount of any applicable exemption of proceeds pursuant to Section 704.010 (motor vehicle), 704.020 (household furnishings and other personal effects), or 704.060 (tools of trade), except that such proceeds shall be used to satisfy all of the following in the order of their respective priorities:

(1) Any consensual liens and encumbrances, and any liens for labor or materials, that are subordinate to the judgment creditor's lien.

(2) Subject to Section 688.030, any state tax lien (as defined in Section 7162 of the Government Code) on the property sold if the notice of state tax lien on the property has been recorded or filed pursuant to Section 7171 of the Government Code prior to the time the levying officer received the proceeds of the sale or collection.

(e) To the levying officer for the reimbursement of the levying officer's costs for which an advance has not been made.

(f) To the judgment creditor to satisfy the following, in the following order:

(1) First, any costs and interest accruing on the judgment after issuance of the writ pursuant to which the sale or collection is conducted.

(2) Second, the principal amount due on the judgment with costs and interest, as entered on the writ.

(g) To any other judgment creditors who have delivered writs to the levying officer, accompanied by instructions to levy upon the judgment debtor's property or the proceeds of its sale or collection, or any other persons actually known by the levying officer to have a claim, lien, or other interest subordinate to the judgment creditor's lien that is extinguished by the sale and that is not otherwise satisfied pursuant to this section, in the amounts to which they are entitled in order of their respective priorities.

(h) To the judgment debtor in the amount remaining. *(Added by Stats.1982, c. 1364, p. 5144, § 2, operative July 1, 1983. Amended by Stats.2010, c. 4 (A.B.680), § 2.)*

Research References

Rutter, Cal. Practice Guide: Enforcing Judgments/Debts Ch. 6D-7, Sale and Collection of Property Levied Upon.

Miller and Starr California Real Estate § 32:71, Distribution of Sale Proceeds.

Miller and Starr California Real Estate § 10:226, The Judicial Sale.

Miller and Starr California Real Estate § 11:126, Relation to Subsequent Interests.

Miller and Starr California Real Estate § 11:129, Priority of the Title of an Execution Sale Purchaser.

8 Witkin Cal. Proc. 5th Enforcement of Judgment § 102, (S 102) Preservation of Property.

8 Witkin Cal. Proc. 5th Enforcement of Judgment § 155, Default of Bidder.

8 Witkin Cal. Proc. 5th Enforcement of Judgment § 156, (S 156) Effect of Sale.

8 Witkin Cal. Proc. 5th Enforcement of Judgment § 158, (S 158) Order of Distribution.

8 Witkin Cal. Proc. 5th Enforcement of Judgment § 160, (S 160) Conflicting Claims to Proceeds.

8 Witkin Cal. Proc. 5th Enforcement of Judgment § 227, (S 227) Distribution of Proceeds.

8 Witkin Cal. Proc. 5th Enforcement of Judgment § 377, (S 377) Payment to Secured Party or Lienholder.

8 Witkin Cal. Proc. 5th Enforcement of Judgment § 383, (S 383) Filing and Service of Demand.

10 Witkin, California Summary 10th Parent and Child § 435, Use or Sale of Assets.

§ 701.820. Distribution or deposit; time for payment; receipt of noncash payment; officer's liability; application for ex parte order

(a) Promptly after a sale or collection under this title, the levying officer shall distribute the proceeds to the persons entitled thereto or, in cases covered by Section 701.830, deposit the proceeds with the court.

(b) Except as otherwise provided by statute, the proceeds shall be paid to the persons entitled thereto within 30 days after the proceeds are received by the levying officer.

(c) If the proceeds are not received by the levying officer in one payment, the levying officer may accumulate proceeds received during a 30–day period and the accumulated proceeds shall be paid to the persons entitled thereto not later than 10 days after the expiration of the 30–day period.

(d) When proceeds are received by the levying officer in the form of a check or other form of noncash payment that is to be honored upon presentation by the levying officer for payment, the proceeds are not received for the purposes of this section until the check or other form of noncash payment has actually been honored upon presentation for payment.

(e) The provisions of Section 26680 of the Government Code apply to the levying officer only if all of the following conditions are satisfied:

(1) The levying officer has failed to pay the proceeds or deposit them with the court as provided in this article within the time provided in this section.

(2) Upon such failure, a person entitled to any of the proceeds has filed, in person or by certified mail, with the levying officer a written demand for the payment of the proceeds to the persons entitled thereto.

(3) The levying officer has failed within 10 days after the demand is filed to pay to the person filing the demand the proceeds to which that person is entitled.

(f) If all proceeds have not been received within 10 days after the filing of the demand specified by paragraph (3) of subdivision (e), a judgment creditor may file an ex parte application for an order directing the levying officer to show cause why relief should not be granted pursuant to Section 26680 of the Government Code. The order shall name a date and time for the levying officer to appear not less than 20 and not more than 30 days after filing of the application. If the levying officer pays all proceeds as provided in subdivision (e) of Section 701.810 to the judgment creditor no later than 10 days prior to the hearing, the judgment creditor shall notify the court of full payment no later than three days prior to the hearing and the court shall withdraw the order and vacate the hearing.

(g) An ex parte application filed pursuant to subdivision (f) shall state the date and manner of all of the following:

(1) Delivery of the writ of execution to the levying officer.

(2) Remittance of the proceeds to the levying officer.

(3) Filing of the 10–day demand pursuant to subdivision (e).

(h) If the court finds that the facts alleged in the ex parte application filed pursuant to subdivision (f) to be knowingly false, or made in bad faith, the court may award costs and reasonable attorney fees to the levying officer. *(Added by Stats.1982, c. 1364, p. 5144, § 2, operative July 1, 1983. Amended by Stats.2010, c. 4 (A.B.680), § 3.)*

Research References

Rutter, Cal. Practice Guide: Enforcing Judgments/Debts Ch. 6D-7, Sale and Collection of Property Levied Upon.

Miller and Starr California Real Estate § 13:49, Conduct of the Sale; Distribution of Proceeds.

Miller and Starr California Real Estate § 32:71, Distribution of Sale Proceeds.

3 Witkin Cal. Proc. 5th Actions § 240, (S 240) in General.

8 Witkin Cal. Proc. 5th Enforcement of Judgment § 33, Liability of Officer.

8 Witkin Cal. Proc. 5th Enforcement of Judgment § 159, (S 159) Time for Distribution.

8 Witkin Cal. Proc. 5th Enforcement of Judgment § 227, (S 227) Distribution of Proceeds.

§ 701.830. Conflicting claims

(a) If there are conflicting claims to all or a portion of the proceeds of sale or collection known to the levying officer before the proceeds are distributed, the levying officer may deposit with the court the proceeds that are the subject of the conflicting claims instead of distributing such proceeds under Section 701.810. Any interested person may apply on noticed motion for an order for the distribution of the proceeds deposited with the court. A copy of the notice of motion shall be served on such persons as the court shall by order determine in such manner as the court prescribes. Any interested person may request time for filing a response to the motion for an order for the distribution of the proceeds, for discovery proceedings in connection with the motion, or for other preparation for the hearing on the motion, and the court shall grant a continuance for a reasonable time for any of these purposes.

(b) Except as provided in subdivision (c), at the hearing on the motion the court shall determine the issues presented by the motion and make an order for the distribution of the proceeds deposited with the court.

(c) The court shall not determine the issues presented by the motion and instead shall abate the hearing until the issues presented by the motion can be determined in a civil action in the following cases if:

(1) The court is not the proper court under any other provision of law for the trial of a civil action with respect to the subject matter of the motion and any interested person at or prior to the hearing objects to the determination of the issues presented by the motion by the court.

(2) A civil action is pending with respect to the subject matter of the motion and jurisdiction has been obtained in the court in which the civil action is pending.

(3) The court determines that the matter should be determined in a civil action. *(Added by Stats.1982, c. 1364, p. 5146, § 2, operative July 1, 1983.)*

Research References

Rutter, Cal. Practice Guide: Enforcing Judgments/Debts Ch. 6D-7, Sale and Collection of Property Levied Upon.

Miller and Starr California Real Estate § 13:49, Conduct of the Sale; Distribution of Proceeds.

Miller and Starr California Real Estate § 32:71, Distribution of Sale Proceeds.

8 Witkin Cal. Proc. 5th Enforcement of Judgment § 159, (S 159) Time for Distribution.

8 Witkin Cal. Proc. 5th Enforcement of Judgment § 160, (S 160) Conflicting Claims to Proceeds.

8 Witkin Cal. Proc. 5th Enforcement of Judgment § 227, (S 227) Distribution of Proceeds.

CHAPTER 4. EXEMPTIONS

OFFICIAL FORMS
CURRENT DOLLAR AMOUNTS OF EXEMPTIONS FROM ENFORCEMENT OF JUDGMENTS

Code of Civil Procedure sections 703.140(b) and 704.010 et seq.

EXEMPTIONS UNDER SECTION 703.140(b)

The following lists the current dollar amounts of exemptions from enforcement of judgment under Code of Civil Procedure section 703.140(b).

These amounts are effective April 1, 2013. Unless otherwise provided by statute after that date, they will be adjusted at each three-year interval, ending on March 31. The amount of the adjustment to the prior amounts is based on the change in the annual California Consumer Price Index for All Urban Consumers for the most recent three-year period ending on the preceding December 31, with each adjusted amount rounded to the nearest $25. (See Code Civ. Proc., § 703.150(d).)

Code Civ. Proc., § 703.140(b)	Type of Property	Amount of Exemption
(1)	The debtor's aggregate interest in real property or personal property that the debtor or a dependent of the debtor uses as a residence, in a cooperative that owns property that the debtor or a dependent of the debtor uses as a residence, or in a burial plot for the debtor or a dependent of the debtor	$25,075
(2)	The debtor's interest in one motor vehicle	$ 5,100
(3)	The debtor's interest in household furnishings, household goods, wearing apparel, appliances, books, animals, crops, or musical instruments, that are held primarily for the personal, family, or household use of the debtor or a dependent of the debtor (value is of any particular item)	$ 650
(4)	The debtor's aggregate interest in jewelry held primarily for the personal, family, or household use of the debtor or a dependent of the debtor	$ 1,525

Civ. Pro.

Code Civ. Proc., § 703.140(b)	Type of Property	Amount of Exemption
(5)	The debtor's aggregate interest, plus any unused amount of the exemption provided under paragraph (1), in any property	$ 1,350
(6)	The debtor's aggregate interest in any implements, professional books, or tools of the trade of the debtor or the trade of a dependent of the debtor	$ 7,575
(8)	The debtor's aggregate interest in any accrued dividend or interest under, or loan value of, any unmatured life insurance contract owned by the debtor under which the insured is the debtor or an individual of whom the debtor is a dependent	$13,675
(11)(D)	The debtor's right to receive, or property traceable to, a payment on account of personal bodily injury, not including pain and suffering or compensation for actual pecuniary loss, of the debtor or an individual of whom the debtor is a dependent	$25,575

EXEMPTIONS UNDER SECTION 704.010 et seq.

The following lists the current dollar amounts of exemptions from enforcement of judgment under title 9, division 2, chapter 4, article 3 (commencing with section 704.010) of the Code of Civil Procedure.

These amounts are effective April 1, 2013. Unless otherwise provided by statute after that date, they will be adjusted at each three-year interval, ending on March 31. The amount of the adjustment to the prior amounts is based on the change in the annual California Consumer Price Index for All Urban Consumers for the most recent three-year period ending on the preceding December 31, with each adjusted amount rounded to the nearest $25. (See Code Civ. Proc., § 703.150(d).)

Code Civ. Proc. Section	Type of Property	Amount of Exemption
704.010	Motor vehicle (any combination of aggregate equity, proceeds of execution sale, and proceeds of insurance or other indemnification for loss, damage, or destruction)	$ 2,900
704.030	Material to be applied to repair or maintenance of residence	$ 3,050

Code Civ. Proc. Section	Type of Property	Amount of Exemption
704.040	Jewelry, heirlooms, art	$ 7,625
704.060	Personal property used in debtor's or debtor's spouse's trade, business, or profession (amount of exemption for commercial motor vehicle not to exceed $4,850)	$ 7,625
704.060	Personal property used in debtor's and spouse's common trade, business, or profession (amount of exemption for commercial motor vehicle not to exceed $9,700)	$15,250
704.080	Deposit account with direct payment of social security or public benefits (exemption without claim, section 704.080(b)) [1]	
	• Public benefits, one depositor is designated payee	$ 1,525
	• Social security benefits, one depositor is designated payee	$ 3,050
	• Public benefits, two or more depositors are designated payees [2]	$ 2,275
	• Social security benefits, two or more depositors are designated payees [2]	$ 4,575
704.090	Inmate trust account	$ 1,525
	Inmate trust account (restitution fine or order)	$ 300 [3]
704.100	Aggregate loan value of unmatured life insurance policies	$12,225

[1] The amount of a deposit account that exceeds exemption amounts is also exempt to the extent it consists of payments of public benefits or social security benefits. (Code Civ. Proc., § 704.080(c).)

[2] If only one joint payee is a beneficiary of the payment, the exemption is in the amount available to a single designated payee. (Code Civ. Proc., § 704.080(b)(3) and (4).)

[3] This amount is not subject to adjustments under Code Civ. Proc., § 703.150.

ARTICLE 1. GENERAL PROVISIONS

Section
703.010. Application of exemptions.
703.020. Persons who may claim exemptions.
703.030. Claiming exemptions; time and manner; waiver; relief for failure to claim.
703.040. Prior waivers void.
703.050. Determination; judgments affected; levy of execution.
703.060. Power of state to repeal, alter, or add to exemptions.
703.070. Judgment for child, family, or spousal support.
703.080. Tracing exempt funds.
703.090. Levy on exempt property; recovery of collection costs.
703.100. Time for determination; circumstances considered.
703.110. Married judgment debtor; determination and application of exemption.
703.115. Exemption based upon need; consideration of property.

Section

703.130.   Federal bankruptcy exemptions; not authorized.
703.140.   Federal bankruptcy; applicable exemptions.
703.150.   Adjustment of exemption amounts; three-year intervals; increases; determination by Judicial Council; publication of list; application of adjustments.

§ 703.010.   Application of exemptions

Except as otherwise provided by statute:

(a) The exemptions provided by this chapter or by any other statute apply to all procedures for enforcement of a money judgment.

(b) The exemptions provided by this chapter or by any other statute do not apply if the judgment to be enforced is for the foreclosure of a mortgage, deed of trust, or other lien or encumbrance on the property other than a lien created pursuant to this division or pursuant to Title 6.5 (commencing with Section 481.010) (attachment). *(Added by Stats.1982, c. 1364, p. 5146, § 2, operative July 1, 1983.)*

Law Revision Commission Comments

Subdivision (a) of Section 703.010 makes clear that exemptions apply regardless of the procedure selected for the enforcement of a money judgment. Subdivision (a) is comparable to but broader than former Section 690 in that subdivision (a) applies to exemptions prescribed by statute apart from this chapter and applies to all procedures for enforcement of a money judgment and not just execution. For exemptions not included in this chapter, see e.g., Civil Code § 986(a) (6) (artist's residual payment); Code Civ.Proc. §§ 706.050–706.052 (earnings); Health & Safety Code § 32508 (hospital endowments); 10 U.S.C. § 1035 (servicemen savings); 38 U.S.C. § 3101 (veterans benefits); 42 U.S.C. § 407 (federal OASDI benefits); 45 U.S.C. § 231m (railroad retirement pensions). The exemptions apply to the enforcement of costs and damages under nonmoney judgments. See Section 712.040.

For the application of exemptions to enforcement of support judgments, see Section 703.070. For the application of exemptions to tax obligations, see Section 688.030. As to the exemptions applicable where the property was levied upon or otherwise subject to a lien prior to the operative date of this chapter, see Section 694.080.

Subdivision (b) continues the substance of a portion of former Section 690.52. See also former Civil Code § 1241; former Code Civ.Proc. §§ 690.28, 690.31(b) (3). The portion of former Section 690.52 that made exemptions inapplicable in the case of a judgment for the purchase price of the property is not continued because it was unenforceable in practice and because a security interest may be obtained in such a case. [16 Cal.L.Rev.Comm. Reports 1377 (1982)].

Research References

Rutter, Cal. Practice Guide: Enforcing Judgments/Debts Ch. 6D-7, Sale and Collection of Property Levied Upon.
Rutter, Cal. Practice Guide: Enforcing Judgments/Debts Ch. 6E-1, Introduction.
Rutter, Cal. Practice Guide: Enforcing Judgments/Debts Ch. 6E-6, "Homestead" Exemption.
Rutter, Cal. Practice Guide: Enforcing Judgments/Debts Ch. 6I-5, Enforcement of Money Judgment Included in Judgment for Possession or Sale.
Miller and Starr California Real Estate § 10:2, Lien Versus Title Theories.
Miller and Starr California Real Estate § 13:5, Voluntary or Involuntary Sale of Homestead; Reinvestment of Proceeds.
Miller and Starr California Real Estate § 13:12, Waiver of the Homestead Exemption.
Miller and Starr California Real Estate § 13:18, Termination by Voluntary Sale or Abandonment.
Miller and Starr California Real Estate § 13:48, Determination of the Liens Against the Homestead; Priorities.
Miller and Starr California Real Estate § 13:54, Election of Federal or State Exemptions.
Miller and Starr California Real Estate § 32:25, Other Exemptions.
Miller and Starr California Real Estate § 32:61, Property Interests Subject to Execution.

2 Witkin Cal. Proc. 5th Courts § 304, Terms and Conditions.
8 Witkin Cal. Proc. 5th Enforcement of Judgment § 113, (S 113) Notice of Levy.
8 Witkin Cal. Proc. 5th Enforcement of Judgment § 169, (S 169) Scope and Application of Exemption Statutes.
8 Witkin Cal. Proc. 5th Enforcement of Judgment § 170, (S 170) Persons Entitled to Exemptions.
8 Witkin Cal. Proc. 5th Enforcement of Judgment § 178, (S 178) Exemptions in Bankruptcy.
8 Witkin Cal. Proc. 5th Enforcement of Judgment § 179, (S 179) Periodic Adjustments.
8 Witkin Cal. Proc. 5th Enforcement of Judgment § 218, Nature and Scope of Exemption.
8 Witkin Cal. Proc. 5th Enforcement of Judgment § 280, Judgment Debtor's Claim of Exemption.
8 Witkin Cal. Proc. 5th Enforcement of Judgment § 294, (S 294) Debtor's Claim of Exemption.
8 Witkin Cal. Proc. 5th Enforcement of Judgment § 302, (S 302) Debtor's Claim of Exemption.
8 Witkin Cal. Proc. 5th Enforcement of Judgment § 307, (S 307) Debtor's Claim of Exemption.
8 Witkin Cal. Proc. 5th Enforcement of Judgment § 316, (S 316) Procedure After Deposit in Court.
8 Witkin Cal. Proc. 5th Enforcement of Judgment § 328, (S 328) Collection of Included Money Judgment.
8 Witkin Cal. Proc. 5th Enforcement of Judgment § 405, Governmental Enforcement of Support Order.
9 Witkin, California Summary 10th Taxation § 124, (S 124) Provisions.
11 Witkin, California Summary 10th Husband and Wife § 250, (S 250) Definitions.
4 Witkin, California Summary 10th Negotiable Instruments § 84, (S 84) Statutory Limitations on Exercise of Setoff.
13 Witkin, California Summary 10th Trusts § 259, (S 259) Rights During Settlor's Lifetime.
2 Witkin Cal. Summ. 10th Workers' Compensation § 155, Recovery from Employer.

§ 703.020.   Persons who may claim exemptions

(a) The exemptions provided by this chapter apply only to property of a natural person.

(b) The exemptions provided in this chapter may be claimed by any of the following persons:

(1) In all cases, by the judgment debtor or a person acting on behalf of the judgment debtor.

(2) In the case of community property, by the spouse of the judgment debtor, whether or not the spouse is also a judgment debtor under the judgment. *(Added by Stats.1982, c. 1364, p. 5146, § 2, operative July 1, 1983.)*

Law Revision Commission Comments

Subdivision (a) of Section 703.020 codifies the rule of Canal-Randolph Anaheim, Inc. v. Wilkoski, 103 Cal.App.3d 282, 163 Cal.Rptr. 30 (1980).

The persons entitled to claim an exemption on behalf of a judgment debtor under subdivision (b) include the judgment debtor's agent and other persons acting on behalf of a judgment debtor, such as a public or private retirement plan (see Sections 704.110, 704.115). If community property is sought to be applied to the satisfaction of a judgment, either the judgment debtor or the spouse of the judgment debtor may claim exemptions for the property. Cf. White v. Gobey, 130 Cal.App.Supp. 789, 791, 19 P.2d 876 (1933) (nondebtor spouse permitted to claim wage garnishment exemption). See also Section 703.110 (application of exemptions to marital property) and the Comment thereto.

Section 703.020 is limited to exemptions provided by this chapter; the scope of exemptions provided by other statutes is determined by the other statutes, not by Section 703.020. [16 Cal.L.Rev.Comm. Reports 1378 (1982)].

Research References

Rutter, Cal. Practice Guide: Enforcing Judgments/Debts Ch. 4-A, A. Attachment.
Rutter, Cal. Practice Guide: Enforcing Judgments/Debts Ch. 6E-1, Introduction.

Rutter, Cal. Practice Guide: Enforcing Judgments/Debts Ch. 6E-3, Procedures for Claiming Exemptions.
Miller and Starr California Real Estate § 32:24, Homestead.
Miller and Starr California Real Estate § 32:26, Claim of Exemption.
Miller and Starr California Real Estate § 32:54, Effect of Homestead Exemption.
20 NO. 6 Miller & Starr, California Real Estate Newsalert 13, Homesteads.
8 Witkin Cal. Proc. 5th Enforcement of Judgment § 170, (S 170) Persons Entitled to Exemptions.
8 Witkin Cal. Proc. 5th Enforcement of Judgment § 230, Definitions.

§ 703.030. Claiming exemptions; time and manner; waiver; relief for failure to claim

(a) An exemption for property that is described in this chapter or in any other statute as exempt may be claimed within the time and in the manner prescribed in the applicable enforcement procedure. If the exemption is not so claimed, the exemption is waived and the property is subject to enforcement of a money judgment.

(b) Except as otherwise specifically provided by statute, property that is described in this chapter or in any other statute as exempt without making a claim is not subject to any procedure for enforcement of a money judgment.

(c) Nothing in this section limits the authority of the court pursuant to Section 473 to relieve a person upon such terms as may be just from failure to claim an exemption within the time and in the manner prescribed in the applicable enforcement procedure. *(Added by Stats.1982, c. 1364, p. 5147, § 2, operative July 1, 1983.)*

Research References

Rutter, Cal. Practice Guide: Enforcing Judgments/Debts Ch. 6D-4, Levy on Specific Property.
Rutter, Cal. Practice Guide: Enforcing Judgments/Debts Ch. 6E-3, Procedures for Claiming Exemptions.
Rutter, Cal. Practice Guide: Enforcing Judgments/Debts Ch. 6E-5, Specific Exempt Property.
Rutter, Cal. Practice Guide: Enforcing Judgments/Debts Ch. 6A-11, Property Subject to Enforcement Procedures.
Miller and Starr California Real Estate § 13:12, Waiver of the Homestead Exemption.
Miller and Starr California Real Estate § 13:46, Hearing on the Application; Marshalling of Assets.
Miller and Starr California Real Estate § 32:25, Other Exemptions.
Miller and Starr California Real Estate § 32:26, Claim of Exemption.
Miller and Starr California Real Estate § 32:27, Procedure to Claim an Exemption.
8 Witkin Cal. Proc. 5th Enforcement of Judgment § 171, (S 171) Claim Requirement and Waiver of Exemption.
8 Witkin Cal. Proc. 5th Enforcement of Judgment § 180, (S 180) in General.
8 Witkin Cal. Proc. 5th Enforcement of Judgment § 280, Judgment Debtor's Claim of Exemption.

§ 703.040. Prior waivers void

A purported contractual or other prior waiver of the exemptions provided by this chapter or by any other statute, other than a waiver by failure to claim an exemption required to be claimed or otherwise made at the time enforcement is sought, is against public policy and void. *(Added by Stats.1982, c. 1364, p. 5147, § 2, operative July 1, 1983.)*

Law Revision Commission Comments

Section 703.040 codifies existing case law. See, e.g., Industrial Loan & Inv. Co. v. Superior Court, 189 Cal. 546, 209 P. 360 (1922). Of course, exemptions do not apply if the judgment to be enforced is for the foreclosure of a mortgage or other lien not created under this division. See Section 703.010(b). [16 Cal.L.Rev.Comm. Reports 1380 (1982)].

Research References

Rutter, Cal. Practice Guide: Enforcing Judgments/Debts Ch. 6E-2, Rules Applicable to Exemptions from Enforcement of Money Judgments Generally.
Miller and Starr California Real Estate § 13:12, Waiver of the Homestead Exemption.
Miller and Starr California Real Estate § 32:26, Claim of Exemption.
8 Witkin Cal. Proc. 5th Enforcement of Judgment § 171, (S 171) Claim Requirement and Waiver of Exemption.

§ 703.050. Determination; judgments affected; levy of execution

(a) The determination whether property is exempt or the amount of an exemption shall be made by application of the exemption statutes in effect (1) at the time the judgment creditor's lien on the property was created or (2) if the judgment creditor's lien on the property is the latest in a series of overlapping liens created when an earlier lien on the property in favor of the judgment creditor was in effect, at the time the earliest lien in the series of overlapping liens was created.

(b) This section applies to all judgments, whether based upon tort, contract, or other legal theory or cause of action that arose before or after the operative date of this section, and whether the judgment was entered before or after the operative date of this section.

(c) Notwithstanding subdivision (a), in the case of a levy of execution, the procedures to be followed in levying upon, selling, or releasing property, claiming, processing, opposing, and determining exemptions, and paying exemption proceeds, shall be governed by the law in effect at the time the levy of execution is made on the property. *(Added by Stats.1982, c. 1364, p. 5147, § 2, operative July 1, 1983.)*

Law Revision Commission Comments

Section 703.050 applies exemptions in effect at the time a lien is created on the property. This is consistent with the holding in San Diego White Truck Co. v. Swift, 96 Cal.App.3d 88, 157 Cal.Rptr. 745 (1979), and National Collection Agency, Inc. v. Fabila, 93 Cal.App.3d Supp. 1, 155 Cal.Rptr. 356 (1979), and rejects the case law rule that the judgment debtor could take advantage only of the exemptions in effect at the time an obligation was incurred. See, e.g., In re Rauer's Collection Co., 87 Cal.App.2d 248, 253–54, 196 P.2d 803 (1948); Daylin Medical & Surgical Supply, Inc. v. Thomas, 69 Cal.App.3d Supp. 37, 40–42, 138 Cal.Rptr. 878 (1977); Smith v. Hume, 29 Cal.App.2d Supp. 747, 749–51, 74 P.2d 566 (1937); Medical Fin. Ass'n v. Wood, 20 Cal.App.2d Supp. 749, 63 P.2d 1219 (1936). See also Comment, The Contract Clause and the Constitutionality of Retroactive Application of Exemption Statutes: A reconsideration, 9 Pac.L.J. 889 (1978). [16 Cal.L.Rev.Comm. Reports 1381 (1982)].

Research References

Rutter, Cal. Practice Guide: Enforcing Judgments/Debts Ch. 6B-1, Practical Considerations.
Rutter, Cal. Practice Guide: Enforcing Judgments/Debts Ch. 6D-8, Special Requirements for Sale of Real Property Dwellings.
Rutter, Cal. Practice Guide: Enforcing Judgments/Debts Ch. 6E-1, Introduction.
Rutter, Cal. Practice Guide: Enforcing Judgments/Debts Ch. 6E-2, Rules Applicable to Exemptions from Enforcement of Money Judgments Generally.
Rutter, Cal. Practice Guide: Enforcing Judgments/Debts Ch. 6E-6, "Homestead" Exemption.
Miller and Starr California Real Estate § 13:2, Basis for and Public Policy of the Homestead Exemptions.
Miller and Starr California Real Estate § 32:4, Effect.
Miller and Starr California Real Estate § 13:39, Amount of Exemption-- Determination of Amount.
Miller and Starr California Real Estate § 13:41, Amount of Exemption-- Effect of Statutory Increase on Existing Creditors.
Miller and Starr California Real Estate § 13:42, Statutory Proceedings Mandatory.
Miller and Starr California Real Estate § 13:48, Determination of the Liens Against the Homestead; Priorities.

Civ. Pro.

Miller and Starr California Real Estate § 32:22, Property Exempt from Attachment--In General.

Miller and Starr California Real Estate § 32:26, Claim of Exemption.

Miller and Starr California Real Estate § 32:48, Nature and Creation.

8 Witkin Cal. Proc. 5th Enforcement of Judgment § 18, (S 18) in General.

8 Witkin Cal. Proc. 5th Enforcement of Judgment § 52, (S 52) Exemptions and Third-Party Claims.

8 Witkin Cal. Proc. 5th Enforcement of Judgment § 169, (S 169) Scope and Application of Exemption Statutes.

8 Witkin Cal. Proc. 5th Enforcement of Judgment § 179, (S 179) Periodic Adjustments.

8 Witkin Cal. Proc. 5th Enforcement of Judgment § 235, (S 235) Attachment of Judgment Lien.

§ 703.060. Power of state to repeal, alter, or add to exemptions

(a) The Legislature finds and declares that generally persons who enter into contracts do not do so in reliance on an assumption that the exemptions in effect at the time of the contract will govern enforcement of any judgment based on the contract, that liens imposed on property are imposed not as a matter of right but as a matter of privilege granted by statute for purposes of priority, that no vested rights with respect to exemptions are created by the making of a contract or imposition of a lien, that application of exemptions and exemption procedures in effect at the time of enforcement of a judgment is essential to the proper balance between the rights of judgment debtors and judgment creditors and has a minimal effect on the economic stability essential for the maintenance of private and public faith in commercial matters, and that it is the policy of the state to treat all judgment debtors equally with respect to exemptions and exemption procedures in effect at the time of enforcement of a money judgment. To this end, the Legislature reserves the right to repeal, alter, or add to the exemptions and the procedures therefor at any time and intends, unless otherwise provided by statute, that any repeals, alterations, or additions apply upon their operative date to enforcement of all money judgments, whether based upon tort, contract, or other legal theory or cause of action that arose before or after the operative date of the repeals, alterations, or additions, whether the judgment was entered before or after the operative date of the repeals, alterations, or additions.

(b) All contracts shall be deemed to have been made and all liens on property shall be deemed to have been created in recognition of the power of the state to repeal, alter, and add to statutes providing for liens and exemptions from the enforcement of money judgments. *(Added by Stats.1982, c. 1364, p. 5147, § 2, operative July 1, 1983.)*

Law Revision Commission Comments

Section 703.060 reserves the power of the state to change and add to existing exemptions in line with recent decisions in other jurisdictions. See, e.g., Wilkinson v. Carpenter, 277 Or. 557, 561 P.2d 607, 610–11 (1977); Hooter v. Wilson, 273 So.2d 516, 521–22 (La.1973). Section 703.060 makes clear that the Legislature may make changes in exemptions applicable to all enforcement proceedings after the operative date of the change, without regard to when the judgment was entered or when the underlying obligation or liability was created or arose. [16 Cal.L.Rev. Comm. Reports 1382 (1982)].

Research References

Rutter, Cal. Practice Guide: Enforcing Judgments/Debts Ch. 6E-2, Rules Applicable to Exemptions from Enforcement of Money Judgments Generally.

Miller and Starr California Real Estate § 13:2, Basis for and Public Policy of the Homestead Exemptions.

Miller and Starr California Real Estate § 13:41, Amount of Exemption--Effect of Statutory Increase on Existing Creditors.

Miller and Starr California Real Estate § 32:22, Property Exempt from Attachment--In General.

8 Witkin Cal. Proc. 5th Enforcement of Judgment § 169, (S 169) Scope and Application of Exemption Statutes.

§ 703.070. Judgment for child, family, or spousal support

Except as otherwise provided by statute:

(a) The exemptions provided by this chapter or by any other statute apply to a judgment for child, family, or spousal support.

(b) If property is exempt without making a claim, the property is not subject to being applied to the satisfaction of a judgment for child, family, or spousal support.

(c) Except as provided in subdivision (b), if property sought to be applied to the satisfaction of a judgment for child, family, or spousal support is shown to be exempt under subdivision (a) in appropriate proceedings, the court shall, upon noticed motion of the judgment creditor, determine the extent to which the exempt property nevertheless shall be applied to the satisfaction of the judgment. In making this determination, the court shall take into account the needs of the judgment creditor, the needs of the judgment debtor and all the persons the judgment debtor is required to support, and all other relevant circumstances. The court shall effectuate its determination by an order specifying the extent to which the otherwise exempt property is to be applied to the satisfaction of the judgment. *(Added by Stats.1982, c. 1364, p. 5148, § 2, operative July 1, 1983. Amended by Stats.1992, c. 163 (A.B.2641), § 37, operative Jan. 1, 1994.)*

Law Revision Commission Comments

Subdivisions (a) and (b) of Section 703.070 codify the case law rule that exemptions apply to the enforcement of support unless there is a specific exception. See, e.g., Miller v. Superior Court, 69 Cal.2d 14, 442 P.2d 663, 69 Cal.Rptr. 583 (1968); Ogle v. Heim, 69 Cal.2d 7, 442 P.2d 659, 69 Cal.Rptr. 579 (1968); Yager v. Yager, 7 Cal.2d 213, 60 P.2d 422 (1936). Except to the extent that a particular exemption otherwise provides, property that is exempt without making a claim may not be applied to enforcement of a judgment for support. Section 703.070(b). As to property that is exempt if the exemption is claimed, subdivision (c) of Section 703.070 permits the court, when the exemption is claimed, to nevertheless make an equitable division of the otherwise exempt property based on the needs of the parties. Subdivision (c) is drawn from older case law concerning the equitable division of earnings levied upon to enforce a support judgment. See Rankins v. Rankins, 52 Cal.App.2d 231, 126 P.2d 125 (1942). See also Section 706.052 (equitable division of earnings). The introductory clause of Section 703.070 recognizes that other provisions may make some types of property that are exempt without making a claim subject to the enforcement of a support judgment and that other provisions may prescribe the extent to which particular types of property are subject to enforcement of a support judgment. See Sections 704.110(c) (public retirement plan benefits), 704.113 (public vacation credits), 704.115(c) (private retirement plan benefits), 706.052 (wage garnishment). [16 Cal.L.Rev.Comm. Reports 1383 (1982)].

Section 703.070 is amended to add references to "family" support. See Fam. Code § 4501 (family support order enforceable in same manner and to same extent as child support order). See also Section 680.145 ("child support" includes family support). [22 Cal.L.Rev.Comm.Reports 1 (1992)].

Research References

Rutter, Cal. Practice Guide: Enforcing Judgments/Debts Ch. 6E-1, Introduction.

Miller and Starr California Real Estate § 32:26, Claim of Exemption.

Miller and Starr California Real Estate § 32:27, Procedure to Claim an Exemption.

8 Witkin Cal. Proc. 5th Enforcement of Judgment § 172, (S 172) Application of Exemptions to Judgment for Support.

8 Witkin Cal. Proc. 5th Enforcement of Judgment § 201, (S 201) in General.

8 Witkin Cal. Proc. 5th Enforcement of Judgment § 202, (S 202) Effect of Support Judgment.

8 Witkin Cal. Proc. 5th Enforcement of Judgment § 204, Private Retirement Benefits.

8 Witkin Cal. Proc. 5th Enforcement of Judgment § 205, (S 205) Unemployment and Strike Benefits.

8 Witkin Cal. Proc. 5th Enforcement of Judgment § 209, (S 209) Workers' Compensation.
10 Witkin, California Summary 10th Parent and Child § 432, Assets Subject to Order.
11 Witkin, California Summary 10th Husband and Wife § 262, (S 262) in General.

§ 703.080. Tracing exempt funds

(a) Subject to any limitation provided in the particular exemption, a fund that is exempt remains exempt to the extent that it can be traced into deposit accounts or in the form of cash or its equivalent.

(b) The exemption claimant has the burden of tracing an exempt fund.

(c) The tracing of exempt funds in a deposit account shall be by application of the lowest intermediate balance principle unless the exemption claimant or the judgment creditor shows that some other method of tracing would better serve the interests of justice and equity under the circumstances of the case. *(Added by Stats.1982, c. 1364, p. 5148, § 2, operative July 1, 1983.)*

Research References

Rutter, Cal. Practice Guide: Enforcing Judgments/Debts Ch. 6E-2, Rules Applicable to Exemptions from Enforcement of Money Judgments Generally.
Rutter, Cal. Practice Guide: Enforcing Judgments/Debts Ch. 6E-5, Specific Exempt Property.
Miller and Starr California Real Estate § 13:5, Voluntary or Involuntary Sale of Homestead; Reinvestment of Proceeds.
Miller and Starr California Real Estate § 32:26, Claim of Exemption.
8 Witkin Cal. Proc. 5th Enforcement of Judgment § 174, (S 174) Tracing Exempt Funds.
8 Witkin Cal. Proc. 5th Enforcement of Judgment § 194, (S 194) Paid Earnings.
8 Witkin Cal. Proc. 5th Enforcement of Judgment § 204, Private Retirement Benefits.

§ 703.090. Levy on exempt property; recovery of collection costs

If a judgment creditor has failed to oppose a claim of exemption within the time allowed by Section 703.550 or if property has been determined by a court to be exempt, and the judgment creditor thereafter levies upon or otherwise seeks to apply the property toward the satisfaction of the same money judgment, the judgment creditor is not entitled to recover the subsequent costs of collection unless the property is applied to satisfaction of the judgment. *(Added by Stats.1982, c. 1364, p. 5149, § 2, operative July 1, 1983.)*

Law Revision Commission Comments

Section 703.090 is intended to limit repeated levies on the same property by the judgment creditor. Nothing in this section affects any right the judgment debtor may have to recover damages for abuse of process. In the case of a dwelling, if a minimum bid is not received at the sale, the dwelling is released and is not thereafter subject to execution sale at the behest of the same judgment creditor for one year. See Section 704.800. [16 Cal.L.Rev.Comm. Reports 1385 (1982)].

Research References

Miller and Starr California Real Estate § 32:35, Noticed Hearing Procedure.
8 Witkin Cal. Proc. 5th Enforcement of Judgment § 175, (S 175) Effect of Levy on Exempt Property.

§ 703.100. Time for determination; circumstances considered

(a) Subject to subdivision (b), the determination whether property is exempt shall be made under the circumstances existing at the earliest of the following times:

(1) The time of levy on the property.

(2) The time of the commencement of court proceedings for the application of the property to the satisfaction of the money judgment.

(3) The time a lien is created under Title 6.5 (commencing with Section 481.010) (attachment) or under this title.

(b) The court, in its discretion, may take into consideration any of the following changes that have occurred between the time of levy or commencement of enforcement proceedings or creation of the lien and the time of the hearing:

(1) A change in the use of the property if the exemption is based upon the use of property and if the property was used for the exempt purpose at the time of the levy or the commencement of enforcement proceedings or the creation of the lien but is used for a nonexempt purpose at the time of the hearing.

(2) A change in the value of the property if the exemption is based upon the value of the property.

(3) A change in the financial circumstances of the judgment debtor and spouse and dependents of the judgment debtor if the exemption is based upon their needs. *(Added by Stats.1982, c. 1364, p. 5149, § 2, operative July 1, 1983.)*

Research References

Rutter, Cal. Practice Guide: Enforcing Judgments/Debts Ch. 6B-1, Practical Considerations.
Rutter, Cal. Practice Guide: Enforcing Judgments/Debts Ch. 6D-8, Special Requirements for Sale of Real Property Dwellings.
Rutter, Cal. Practice Guide: Enforcing Judgments/Debts Ch. 6E-1, Introduction.
Rutter, Cal. Practice Guide: Enforcing Judgments/Debts Ch. 6E-2, Rules Applicable to Exemptions from Enforcement of Money Judgments Generally.
Rutter, Cal. Practice Guide: Enforcing Judgments/Debts Ch. 6E-4, Opposing Claim of Exemption.
Miller and Starr California Real Estate § 13:2, Basis for and Public Policy of the Homestead Exemptions.
Miller and Starr California Real Estate § 13:16, Residency, Ownership and Use.
Miller and Starr California Real Estate § 13:48, Determination of the Liens Against the Homestead; Priorities.
Miller and Starr California Real Estate § 32:22, Property Exempt from Attachment--In General.
Miller and Starr California Real Estate § 32:26, Claim of Exemption.
Miller and Starr California Real Estate § 32:27, Procedure to Claim an Exemption.
8 Witkin Cal. Proc. 5th Enforcement of Judgment § 52, (S 52) Exemptions and Third-Party Claims.
8 Witkin Cal. Proc. 5th Enforcement of Judgment § 176, (S 176) Time for Determining Exemptions.
8 Witkin Cal. Proc. 5th Enforcement of Judgment § 217, (S 217) Homestead.
8 Witkin Cal. Proc. 5th Enforcement of Judgment § 290, (S 290) Order Applying Property to Satisfaction of Judgment.

§ 703.110. Married judgment debtor; determination and application of exemption

If the judgment debtor is married:

(a) The exemptions provided by this chapter or by any other statute apply to all property that is subject to enforcement of a money judgment, including the interest of the spouse of the judgment debtor in community property. The fact that one or both spouses are judgment debtors under the judgment or that property sought to be applied to the satisfaction of the judgment is separate or community does not increase or reduce the number or amount of the exemptions. Where the property exempt under a particular exemption is limited to a specified maximum dollar amount, unless the exemption provision specifically provides otherwise, the two spouses together are entitled to one exemption limited to the specified maximum dollar amount, whether one or both of the spouses are judgment debtors under the judgment and whether the property sought to be applied to the satisfaction of the judgment is separate or community.

(b) If an exemption is required by statute to be applied first to property not before the court and then to property before the court, the application of the exemption to property not before the court shall be made to the community property and separate property of both spouses, whether or not such property is subject to enforcement of the money judgment.

(c) If the same exemption is claimed by the judgment debtor and the spouse of the judgment debtor for different property, and the property claimed by one spouse, but not both, is exempt, the exemption shall be applied as the spouses agree. If the spouses are unable to agree, the exemption shall be applied as directed by the court in its discretion. *(Added by Stats.1982, c. 1364, p. 5149, § 2, operative July 1, 1983. Amended by Stats.1983, c. 155, § 14.7, eff. June 30, 1983, operative July 1, 1983.)*

Research References

Rutter, Cal. Practice Guide: Enforcing Judgments/Debts Ch. 6E-2, Rules Applicable to Exemptions from Enforcement of Money Judgments Generally.
Rutter, Cal. Practice Guide: Enforcing Judgments/Debts Ch. 6E-6, "Homestead" Exemption.
Miller and Starr California Real Estate § 32:23, Earnings.
Miller and Starr California Real Estate § 32:26, Claim of Exemption.
Miller and Starr California Real Estate § 32:50, Community Property.
8 Witkin Cal. Proc. 5th Enforcement of Judgment § 173, (S 173) Application of Exemptions to Marital Property.
8 Witkin Cal. Proc. 5th Enforcement of Judgment § 218, Nature and Scope of Exemption.

§ 703.115. Exemption based upon need; consideration of property

In determining an exemption based upon the needs of the judgment debtor and the spouse and dependents of the judgment debtor or an exemption based upon the needs of the judgment debtor and the family of the judgment debtor, the court shall take into account all property of the judgment debtor and, to the extent the judgment debtor has a spouse and dependents or family, all property of such spouse and dependents or family, including community property and separate property of the spouse, whether or not such property is subject to enforcement of the money judgment. *(Added by Stats.1983, c. 155, § 15, eff. June 30, 1983, operative July 1, 1983.)*

Research References

Rutter, Cal. Practice Guide: Enforcing Judgments/Debts Ch. 4-A, A. Attachment.
Rutter, Cal. Practice Guide: Enforcing Judgments/Debts Ch. 6E-2, Rules Applicable to Exemptions from Enforcement of Money Judgments Generally.
Rutter, Cal. Practice Guide: Enforcing Judgments/Debts Ch. 6F-5, Earnings Exempt from Garnishment.
8 Witkin Cal. Proc. 5th Enforcement of Judgment § 177, (S 177) Determination of Exemptions Based on Need.

§ 703.130. Federal bankruptcy exemptions; not authorized

Pursuant to the authority of paragraph (2) of subsection (b) of Section 522 of Title 11 of the United States Code, the exemptions set forth in subsection (d) of Section 522 of Title 11 of the United States Code (Bankruptcy) are not authorized in this state. *(Added by Stats.1984, c. 218, § 1.5. Amended by Stats.2009, c. 500 (A.B.1059), § 14.)*

Research References

Rutter, Cal. Practice Guide: Enforcing Judgments/Debts Ch. 6E-1, Introduction.
Miller and Starr California Real Estate § 13:54, Election of Federal or State Exemptions.
Miller and Starr California Real Estate § 32:26, Claim of Exemption.

8 Witkin Cal. Proc. 5th Enforcement of Judgment § 178, (S 178) Exemptions in Bankruptcy.
8 Witkin Cal. Proc. 5th Enforcement of Judgment § 514, (S 514) in General.

§ 703.140. Federal bankruptcy; applicable exemptions

(a) In a case under Title 11 of the United States Code, all of the exemptions provided by this chapter, including the homestead exemption, other than the provisions of subdivision (b) are applicable regardless of whether there is a money judgment against the debtor or whether a money judgment is being enforced by execution sale or any other procedure, but the exemptions provided by subdivision (b) may be elected in lieu of all other exemptions provided by this chapter, as follows:

(1) If a husband and wife are joined in the petition, they jointly may elect to utilize the applicable exemption provisions of this chapter other than the provisions of subdivision (b), or to utilize the applicable exemptions set forth in subdivision (b), but not both.

(2) If the petition is filed individually, and not jointly, for a husband or a wife, the exemptions provided by this chapter other than the provisions of subdivision (b) are applicable, except that, if both the husband and the wife effectively waive in writing the right to claim, during the period the case commenced by filing the petition is pending, the exemptions provided by the applicable exemption provisions of this chapter, other than subdivision (b), in any case commenced by filing a petition for either of them under Title 11 of the United States Code, then they may elect to instead utilize the applicable exemptions set forth in subdivision (b).

(3) If the petition is filed for an unmarried person, that person may elect to utilize the applicable exemption provisions of this chapter other than subdivision (b), or to utilize the applicable exemptions set forth in subdivision (b), but not both.

(b) The following exemptions may be elected as provided in subdivision (a):

(1) The debtor's aggregate interest, not to exceed twenty-four thousand sixty dollars ($24,060) in value, in real property or personal property that the debtor or a dependent of the debtor uses as a residence, in a cooperative that owns property that the debtor or a dependent of the debtor uses as a residence.

(2) The debtor's interest, not to exceed four thousand eight hundred dollars ($4,800) in value, in one or more motor vehicles.

(3) The debtor's interest, not to exceed six hundred dollars ($600) in value in any particular item, in household furnishings, household goods, wearing apparel, appliances, books, animals, crops, or musical instruments, that are held primarily for the personal, family, or household use of the debtor or a dependent of the debtor.

(4) The debtor's aggregate interest, not to exceed one thousand four hundred twenty-five dollars ($1,425) in value, in jewelry held primarily for the personal, family, or household use of the debtor or a dependent of the debtor.

(5) The debtor's aggregate interest, not to exceed in value one thousand two hundred eighty dollars ($1,280) plus any unused amount of the exemption provided under paragraph (1), in any property.

(6) The debtor's aggregate interest, not to exceed seven thousand one hundred seventy-five dollars ($7,175) in value, in any implements, professional books, or tools of the trade of the debtor or the trade of a dependent of the debtor.

(7) Any unmatured life insurance contract owned by the debtor, other than a credit life insurance contract.

(8) The debtor's aggregate interest, not to exceed in value twelve thousand eight hundred sixty dollars ($12,860), in any

accrued dividend or interest under, or loan value of, any unmatured life insurance contract owned by the debtor under which the insured is the debtor or an individual of whom the debtor is a dependent.

(9) Professionally prescribed health aids for the debtor or a dependent of the debtor.

(10) The debtor's right to receive any of the following:

(A) A social security benefit, unemployment compensation, or a local public assistance benefit.

(B) A veterans' benefit.

(C) A disability, illness, or unemployment benefit.

(D) Alimony, support, or separate maintenance, to the extent reasonably necessary for the support of the debtor and any dependent of the debtor.

(E) A payment under a stock bonus, pension, profit-sharing, annuity, or similar plan or contract on account of illness, disability, death, age, or length of service, to the extent reasonably necessary for the support of the debtor and any dependent of the debtor, unless all of the following apply:

(i) That plan or contract was established by or under the auspices of an insider that employed the debtor at the time the debtor's rights under the plan or contract arose.

(ii) The payment is on account of age or length of service.

(iii) That plan or contract does not qualify under Section 401(a), 403(a), 403(b), 408, or 408A of the Internal Revenue Code of 1986.

(11) The debtor's right to receive, or property that is traceable to, any of the following:

(A) An award under a crime victim's reparation law.

(B) A payment on account of the wrongful death of an individual of whom the debtor was a dependent, to the extent reasonably necessary for the support of the debtor and any dependent of the debtor.

(C) A payment under a life insurance contract that insured the life of an individual of whom the debtor was a dependent on the date of that individual's death, to the extent reasonably necessary for the support of the debtor and any dependent of the debtor.

(D) A payment, not to exceed twenty-four thousand sixty dollars ($24,060), on account of personal bodily injury of the debtor or an individual of whom the debtor is a dependent.

(E) A payment in compensation of loss of future earnings of the debtor or an individual of whom the debtor is or was a dependent, to the extent reasonably necessary for the support of the debtor and any dependent of the debtor. *(Added by Stats.1984, c. 218, § 2. Amended by Stats.1993, c. 1111 (S.B.651), § 1, eff. Oct. 11, 1993; Stats.1995, c. 196 (S.B.832), § 1, eff. July 31, 1995; Stats.1999, c. 98 (S.B.469), § 1; Stats.2000, c. 135 (A.B.2539), § 15; Stats.2001, c. 42 (A.B.1704), § 1; Stats.2003, c. 379 (A.B.182), § 3; Stats.2012, c. 678 (A.B.929), § 1.)*

Explanatory Note

For a list of the amounts of exemptions as adjusted by the Judicial Council and required by Code of Civil Procedure § 703.150, which authorizes the Judicial Council to publish cost-of-living adjustments every three years, see the Judicial Council Form reproduced under Chapter 4, preceding Code of Civil Procedure § 703.010 (for electronic publications, see Refs & Annos).

Law Revision Commission Comments

Section 703.140 is amended to conform to the amounts in the federal Bankruptcy Code and to correct references to sections in the Internal Revenue Code. See 11 U.S.C. § 522. [25 Cal.L.Rev.Comm. Reports 1 (1995)].

Section 703.140 is amended to delete subdivision (c), which is superseded by the automatic cost-of-living adjustment provided in Section 703.150. [33 Cal.L.Rev.Commn. Reports 132 (2003)].

Research References

Rutter, Cal. Practice Guide: Enforcing Judgments/Debts Ch. 6D-3, Levy of Writ of Execution-In General.

Rutter, Cal. Practice Guide: Enforcing Judgments/Debts Ch. 6E-1, Introduction.

Rutter, Cal. Practice Guide: Enforcing Judgments/Debts Ch. 6E-1, Outline 1.

Rutter, Cal. Practice Guide: Insurance Litigation Ch. 15-L, L. Effect of Insured's Bankruptcy.

Miller and Starr California Real Estate § 13:54, Election of Federal or State Exemptions.

Miller and Starr California Real Estate § 32:26, Claim of Exemption.

Miller and Starr California Real Estate § 32:46, Effect of Debtor's Bankruptcy.

14 NO. 6 Miller & Starr, California Real Estate Newsalert 10, Homesteads.

20 NO. 4 Miller & Starr, California Real Estate Newsalert 32, Homesteads.

20 NO. 4 Miller & Starr, California Real Estate Newsalert 33, Involuntary Liens.

8 Witkin Cal. Proc. 5th Enforcement of Judgment § 178, (S 178) Exemptions in Bankruptcy.

8 Witkin Cal. Proc. 5th Enforcement of Judgment § 179, (S 179) Periodic Adjustments.

8 Witkin Cal. Proc. 5th Enforcement of Judgment § 514, (S 514) in General.

§ 703.150. Adjustment of exemption amounts; three-year intervals; increases; determination by Judicial Council; publication of list; application of adjustments

(a) On April 1, 2004, and at each three-year interval ending on April 1 thereafter, the dollar amounts of exemptions provided in subdivision (b) of Section 703.140 in effect immediately before that date shall be adjusted as provided in subdivision (d).

(b) On April 1, 2007, and at each three-year interval ending on April 1 thereafter, the dollar amounts of exemptions provided in Article 3 (commencing with Section 704.010) in effect immediately before that date shall be adjusted as provided in subdivision (d).

(c) On April 1, 2013, and at each three-year interval ending on April 1 thereafter, the Judicial Council shall submit to the Legislature the amount by which the dollar amounts of exemptions provided in subdivision (a) of Section 704.730 in effect immediately before that date may be increased as provided in subdivision (d). Those increases shall not take effect unless they are approved by the Legislature.

(d) The Judicial Council shall determine the amount of the adjustment based on the change in the annual California Consumer Price Index for All Urban Consumers, published by the Department of Industrial Relations, Division of Labor Statistics, for the most recent three-year period ending on December 31 preceding the adjustment, with each adjusted amount rounded to the nearest twenty-five dollars ($25).

(e) Beginning April 1, 2004, the Judicial Council shall publish a list of the current dollar amounts of exemptions provided in subdivision (b) of Section 703.140 and in Article 3 (commencing with Section 704.010), together with the date of the next scheduled adjustment. In any year that the Legislature votes to increase the exemptions provided in subdivision (a) of Section 704.730, the Judicial Council shall publish a list of current dollar amounts of exemptions.

(f) Adjustments made under subdivision (a) do not apply with respect to cases commenced before the date of the adjustment, subject to any contrary rule applicable under the federal

Bankruptcy Code. The applicability of adjustments made under subdivisions (b) and (c) is governed by Section 703.050. *(Added by Stats.2003, c. 379 (A.B.182), § 4. Amended by Stats.2009, c. 499 (A.B.1046), § 1; Stats.2010, c. 212 (A.B.2767), § 1; Stats. 2012, c. 678 (A.B.929), § 2.)*

Explanatory Note

For a list of the amounts of exemptions as adjusted by the Judicial Council and required by Code of Civil Procedure § 703.150, which authorizes the Judicial Council to publish cost-of-living adjustments every three years, see the Judicial Council Form reproduced under Chapter 4, preceding Code of Civil Procedure § 703.010 (for electronic publications, see Refs & Annos).

Law Revision Commission Comments

Section 703.150 provides a new automatic triennial cost-of-living adjustment (COLA) for personal property exemptions applicable to enforcement of judgments and in bankruptcy. Subdivision (a) supersedes former subdivision (c) of Section 703.140, which coordinated the bankruptcy-only exemptions in Section 703.140(b) with triennial adjustments under the federal Bankruptcy Code. The automatic COLA applicable to the bankruptcy-only exemptions in Section 703.140(b) begins in 2004.

Under subdivision (b), the automatic COLA applicable to the Article 3 enforcement of judgments exemptions (Sections 704.010–704.210) is deferred until 2007, because these amounts are adjusted by statute operative January 1, 2004. For an exception to the adjustment provided in subdivision (b), see Section 704.090(b) (inmate trust fund exemption as to crime victim's claim).

The triennial adjustment period under this section is the same as that provided under the Bankruptcy Code. See 11 U.S.C. § 104(b)(1)(A). The $25 rounding factor in subdivision (c) is also drawn from federal law. See 11 U.S.C. § 104(b)(1)(B).

Subdivision (e) clarifies the application of adjusted exemption amounts. As to bankruptcy, the rule is the same as provided by 11 U.S.C. § 104(c). The rule as to adjusted exemption amounts in state enforcement of judgment proceedings is consistent with the general rule under this title.

See also Sections 681.030(c)(3) (list of exemption amounts published pursuant to subdivision (d) referenced in Judicial Council form), 700.010 (list of exemption amounts published pursuant to subdivision (d) served with notice of levy). [33 Cal.L.Rev.Comm. Reports 133 (2003)].

Research References

Rutter, Cal. Practice Guide: Enforcing Judgments/Debts Ch. 6E-1, Introduction.
Rutter, Cal. Practice Guide: Enforcing Judgments/Debts Ch. 6E-5, Specific Exempt Property.
Rutter, Cal. Practice Guide: Enforcing Judgments/Debts Ch. 6E-6, "Homestead" Exemption.
Miller and Starr California Real Estate § 13:39, Amount of Exemption--Determination of Amount.
Miller and Starr California Real Estate § 13:41, Amount of Exemption--Effect of Statutory Increase on Existing Creditors.
Miller and Starr California Real Estate § 13:53, Equity Included or Excluded from the Bankruptcy Estate; Appreciation of Judgment Liens.
Miller and Starr California Real Estate § 32:24, Homestead.
Miller and Starr California Real Estate § 32:25, Other Exemptions.
Miller and Starr California Real Estate § 32:26, Claim of Exemption.
Miller and Starr California Real Estate § 32:54, Effect of Homestead Exemption.
14 NO. 4 Miller & Starr, California Real Estate Newsalert 9, Involuntary Liens.
20 NO. 4 Miller & Starr, California Real Estate Newsalert 11, Homesteads.
8 Witkin Cal. Proc. 5th Enforcement of Judgment § 25, Rules and Forms.
8 Witkin Cal. Proc. 5th Enforcement of Judgment § 117, (S 117) in General.

8 Witkin Cal. Proc. 5th Enforcement of Judgment § 179, (S 179) Periodic Adjustments.

ARTICLE 2. PROCEDURE FOR CLAIMING EXEMPTIONS AFTER LEVY

Section
703.510. Claiming exemptions after levy; property exempt without claim; release.
703.520. Claim of exemption; filing; contents.
703.530. Financial statement.
703.540. Copy of claim and notice; service.
703.550. Notice of opposition and motion for determination.
703.560. Contents of notice of opposition.
703.570. Hearing; time; service of notice.
703.580. Pleadings; burden of proof; evidence; order; release or satisfaction.
703.590. Extension of time.
703.600. Appeal.
703.610. Disposition of property pending final determination and appeal.

§ 703.510. Claiming exemptions after levy; property exempt without claim; release

(a) Except as otherwise provided by statute, property that has been levied upon may be claimed to be exempt as provided in this article.

(b) If property that is exempt without making a claim is levied upon, it may be released pursuant to the exemption procedure provided in this article. *(Added by Stats.1982, c. 1364, p. 5151, § 2, operative July 1, 1983.)*

Research References

Rutter, Cal. Practice Guide: Enforcing Judgments/Debts Ch. 4-A, A. Attachment.
Rutter, Cal. Practice Guide: Enforcing Judgments/Debts Ch. 6E-3, Procedures for Claiming Exemptions.
Rutter, Cal. Practice Guide: Enforcing Judgments/Debts Ch. 6E-4, Opposing Claim of Exemption.
Miller and Starr California Real Estate § 13:42, Statutory Proceedings Mandatory.
Miller and Starr California Real Estate § 32:25, Other Exemptions.
Miller and Starr California Real Estate § 32:61, Property Interests Subject to Execution.
8 Witkin Cal. Proc. 5th Enforcement of Judgment § 60, (S 60) in General.
8 Witkin Cal. Proc. 5th Enforcement of Judgment § 163, (S 163) Motion to Recall or Quash.
8 Witkin Cal. Proc. 5th Enforcement of Judgment § 180, (S 180) in General.
8 Witkin Cal. Proc. 5th Enforcement of Judgment § 197, Determination of Exempt Balance.
8 Witkin Cal. Proc. 5th Enforcement of Judgment § 219, (S 219) in General.
8 Witkin Cal. Proc. 5th Enforcement of Judgment § 261, (S 261) in General.
8 Witkin Cal. Proc. 5th Enforcement of Judgment § 405, Governmental Enforcement of Support Order.
6 Witkin Cal. Proc. 5th Provisional Remedies § 87, (S 87) Claim of Real Property Exemption.
6 Witkin Cal. Proc. 5th Provisional Remedies § 127, (S 127) Defendant's Claim of Exemption.
6 Witkin Cal. Proc. 5th Provisional Remedies § 140, (S 140) Defendant's Claim of Exemption.
6 Witkin Cal. Proc. 5th Provisional Remedies § 222, (S 222) Claim of Exemption.

§ 703.520. Claim of exemption; filing; contents

(a) The claimant may make a claim of exemption by filing with the levying officer a claim of exemption together with a copy thereof. The claim shall be made within 10 days after the date the notice of levy on the property claimed to be exempt was served on the judgment debtor.

(b) The claim of exemption shall be executed under oath and shall include all of the following:

(1) The name of the claimant and the mailing address where service of a notice of opposition to the claim may be made upon the claimant.

(2) The name and last known address of the judgment debtor if the claimant is not the judgment debtor.

(3) A description of the property claimed to be exempt. If an exemption is claimed pursuant to Section 704.010 or 704.060, the claimant shall describe all other property of the same type (including exempt proceeds of property of the same type) owned by the judgment debtor alone or in combination with others on the date of levy and identify the property, whether or not levied upon, to which the exemption is to be applied. If an exemption is claimed pursuant to subdivision (b) of Section 704.100, the claimant shall state the nature and amount of all other property of the same type owned by the judgment debtor or the spouse of the judgment debtor alone or in combination with others on the date of levy.

(4) A financial statement if required by Section 703.530.

(5) A citation of the provision of this chapter or other statute upon which the claim is based.

(6) A statement of the facts necessary to support the claim. *(Added by Stats.1982, c. 1364, p. 5151, § 2, operative July 1, 1983.)*

Research References

Rutter, Cal. Practice Guide: Enforcing Judgments/Debts Ch. 6E-3, Procedures for Claiming Exemptions.
Rutter, Cal. Practice Guide: Enforcing Judgments/Debts Ch. 6G-1, Examination of Judgment Debtor and Third Parties.
Miller and Starr California Real Estate § 32:27, Procedure to Claim an Exemption.
Miller and Starr California Real Estate § 32:35, Noticed Hearing Procedure.
8 Witkin Cal. Proc. 5th Enforcement of Judgment § 138, (S 138) Interest in Personal Property in Decedent's Estate.
8 Witkin Cal. Proc. 5th Enforcement of Judgment § 146, Sale of Personal Property.
8 Witkin Cal. Proc. 5th Enforcement of Judgment § 181, (S 181) Claim of Exemption.
8 Witkin Cal. Proc. 5th Enforcement of Judgment § 280, Judgment Debtor's Claim of Exemption.
8 Witkin Cal. Proc. 5th Enforcement of Judgment § 294, (S 294) Debtor's Claim of Exemption.
8 Witkin Cal. Proc. 5th Enforcement of Judgment § 302, (S 302) Debtor's Claim of Exemption.
8 Witkin Cal. Proc. 5th Enforcement of Judgment § 307, (S 307) Debtor's Claim of Exemption.
8 Witkin Cal. Proc. 5th Enforcement of Judgment § 316, (S 316) Procedure After Deposit in Court.

§ 703.530. Financial statement

(a) If property is claimed as exempt pursuant to a provision exempting property to the extent necessary for the support of the judgment debtor and the spouse and dependents of the judgment debtor, the claim of exemption shall include a financial statement.

(b) The financial statement shall include all of the following information:

(1) The name of the spouse of the judgment debtor.

(2) The name, age, and relationship of all persons dependent upon the judgment debtor or the spouse of the judgment debtor for support.

(3) All sources and the amounts of earnings and other income of the judgment debtor and the spouse and dependents of the judgment debtor.

(4) A list of the assets of the judgment debtor and the spouse and dependents of the judgment debtor and the value of such assets.

(5) All outstanding obligations of the judgment debtor and the spouse and dependents of the judgment debtor.

(c) The financial statement shall be executed under oath by the judgment debtor and, unless the spouses are living separate and apart, by the spouse of the judgment debtor. *(Added by Stats.1982, c. 1364, p. 5151, § 2, operative July 1, 1983.)*

Law Revision Commission Comments

Section 703.530 is drawn in part from former Section 723.124 (wage garnishment), but Section 703.530 requires a more comprehensive financial statement and requires that it be executed by the spouse of the judgment debtor (as well as by the judgment debtor) unless they are living separate and apart. An exemption based upon the need of the judgment debtor and the spouse and dependents of the judgment debtor must take into account the property of the spouse and dependents. See Section 703.110(b). Additional information is required in the financial statement in case of a wage garnishment. See Section 706.124. [16 Cal.L.Rev. Comm. Reports 1393 (1982)].

Research References

Rutter, Cal. Practice Guide: Civ. Pro. Before Trial Ch. 9(II)-D, D. Attachment.
Rutter, Cal. Practice Guide: Enforcing Judgments/Debts Ch. 6E-3, Procedures for Claiming Exemptions.
8 Witkin Cal. Proc. 5th Enforcement of Judgment § 181, (S 181) Claim of Exemption.
8 Witkin Cal. Proc. 5th Enforcement of Judgment § 261, (S 261) in General.

§ 703.540. Copy of claim and notice; service

Promptly after the filing of the claim of exemption, the levying officer shall serve both of the following on the judgment creditor personally or by mail:

(a) A copy of the claim of exemption.

(b) A notice of claim of exemption stating that the claim of exemption has been made and that the levying officer will release the property unless, within the time allowed as specified in the notice, both of the following are filed with the levying officer:

(1) A copy of the notice of opposition to the claim of exemption.

(2) A copy of the notice of motion for an order determining the claim of exemption. *(Added by Stats.1982, c. 1364, p. 5152, § 2, operative July 1, 1983.)*

Law Revision Commission Comments

Section 703.540 supersedes subdivision (b) of former Section 690.50. [16 Cal.L.Rev.Comm. Reports 1394 (1982)].

Research References

Rutter, Cal. Practice Guide: Enforcing Judgments/Debts Ch. 6E-3, Procedures for Claiming Exemptions.
Miller and Starr California Real Estate § 32:27, Procedure to Claim an Exemption.
Miller and Starr California Real Estate § 32:35, Noticed Hearing Procedure.
8 Witkin Cal. Proc. 5th Enforcement of Judgment § 182, (S 182) Notice of Claim.

§ 703.550. Notice of opposition and motion for determination

Within 10 days after service of the notice of claim of exemption, a judgment creditor who opposes the claim of exemption shall file with the court a notice of opposition to the claim of exemption and a notice of motion for an order

Civ. Pro.

determining the claim of exemption and shall file with the levying officer a copy of the notice of opposition and a copy of the notice of motion. Upon the filing of the copies of the notice of opposition and notice of motion, the levying officer shall promptly file the claim of exemption with the court. If copies of the notice of opposition and notice of motion are not filed with the levying officer within the time allowed, the levying officer shall immediately release the property to the extent it is claimed to be exempt. *(Added by Stats.1982, c. 1364, p. 5152, § 2, operative July 1, 1983.)*

Research References

Rutter, Cal. Practice Guide: Enforcing Judgments/Debts Ch. 6E-4, Opposing Claim of Exemption.
Miller and Starr California Real Estate § 32:27, Procedure to Claim an Exemption.
Miller and Starr California Real Estate § 32:35, Noticed Hearing Procedure.
8 Witkin Cal. Proc. 5th Enforcement of Judgment § 175, (S 175) Effect of Levy on Exempt Property.
8 Witkin Cal. Proc. 5th Enforcement of Judgment § 183, (S 183) Opposition to Claim.

§ 703.560. Contents of notice of opposition

The notice of opposition to the claim of exemption shall be executed under oath and shall include both of the following:

(a) An allegation either (1) that the property is not exempt under the provision of this chapter or other statute relied upon or (2) that the equity in the property claimed to be exempt is in excess of the amount provided in the applicable exemption.

(b) A statement of the facts necessary to support the allegation. *(Added by Stats.1982, c. 1364, p. 5152, § 2, operative July 1, 1983.)*

Law Revision Commission Comments

Section 703.560 supersedes a portion of subdivision (c) of former Section 690.50. [16 Cal.L.Rev.Comm. Reports 1395 (1982)].

Research References

Rutter, Cal. Practice Guide: Enforcing Judgments/Debts Ch. 6E-4, Opposing Claim of Exemption.
Miller and Starr California Real Estate § 32:27, Procedure to Claim an Exemption.
8 Witkin Cal. Proc. 5th Enforcement of Judgment § 183, (S 183) Opposition to Claim.
8 Witkin Cal. Proc. 5th Enforcement of Judgment § 316, (S 316) Procedure After Deposit in Court.

§ 703.570. Hearing; time; service of notice

(a) The hearing on the motion shall be held not later than 30 days from the date the notice of motion was filed with the court unless continued by the court for good cause.

(b) Not less than 10 days prior to the hearing, the judgment creditor shall serve a notice of the hearing and a copy of the notice of opposition to the claim of exemption on the claimant and on the judgment debtor, if other than the claimant. Service shall be made personally or by mail. *(Added by Stats.1982, c. 1364, p. 5152, § 2, operative July 1, 1983. Amended by Stats.2012, c. 484 (A.B.2364), § 12.)*

Research References

Rutter, Cal. Practice Guide: Enforcing Judgments/Debts Ch. 6E-4, Opposing Claim of Exemption.
Miller and Starr California Real Estate § 32:27, Procedure to Claim an Exemption.
Miller and Starr California Real Estate § 32:35, Noticed Hearing Procedure.

8 Witkin Cal. Proc. 5th Enforcement of Judgment § 184, (S 184) Hearing.

§ 703.580. Pleadings; burden of proof; evidence; order; release or satisfaction

(a) The claim of exemption and notice of opposition to the claim of exemption constitute the pleadings, subject to the power of the court to permit amendments in the interest of justice.

(b) At a hearing under this section, the exemption claimant has the burden of proof.

(c) The claim of exemption is deemed controverted by the notice of opposition to the claim of exemption and both shall be received in evidence. If no other evidence is offered, the court, if satisfied that sufficient facts are shown by the claim of exemption (including the financial statement if one is required) and the notice of opposition, may make its determination thereon. If not satisfied, the court shall order the hearing continued for the production of other evidence, oral or documentary.

(d) At the conclusion of the hearing, the court shall determine by order whether or not the property is exempt in whole or in part. Subject to Section 703.600, the order is determinative of the right of the judgment creditor to apply the property to the satisfaction of the judgment. No findings are required in a proceeding under this section.

(e) The court clerk shall promptly transmit a certified copy of the order to the levying officer. Subject to Section 703.610, the levying officer shall, in compliance with the order, release the property or apply the property to the satisfaction of the money judgment.

(f) Unless otherwise ordered by the court, if an exemption is not determined within the time provided by Section 703.570, the property claimed to be exempt shall be released. *(Added by Stats.1982, c. 1364, p. 5153, § 2, operative July 1, 1983. Amended by Stats.2002, c. 68 (S.B.1322), § 5.)*

Law Revision Commission Comments

Subdivisions (a)-(d) of Section 703.580 continue the substance of a portion of subdivision (i) of former Section 690.50. Subdivision (e) continues the substance of the first sentence of subdivision (j) of former Section 690.50. [16 Cal.L.Rev.Comm. Reports 1396 (1982)].

Subdivision (f) is added to Section 703.580 to govern the disposition of property where the matter is not determined within the 20-day statutory time limit, such as where the hearing on the exemption claim has been taken off calendar or for any other reason. [31 Cal.L.Rev.Comm. Reports 138 (2002)].

Research References

Rutter, Cal. Practice Guide: Enforcing Judgments/Debts Ch. 5-D, D. Involuntary Bankruptcy.
Rutter, Cal. Practice Guide: Enforcing Judgments/Debts Ch. 6E-2, Rules Applicable to Exemptions from Enforcement of Money Judgments Generally.
Rutter, Cal. Practice Guide: Enforcing Judgments/Debts Ch. 6E-4, Opposing Claim of Exemption.
8 Witkin Cal. Proc. 5th Enforcement of Judgment § 184, (S 184) Hearing.
8 Witkin Cal. Proc. 5th Enforcement of Judgment § 185, (S 185) Order.
8 Witkin Cal. Proc. 5th Enforcement of Judgment § 316, (S 316) Procedure After Deposit in Court.

§ 703.590. Extension of time

If the court extends the time allowed for an act to be done under this article, written notice of the extension shall be filed with the levying officer and, unless notice is waived, shall be served promptly on the opposing party. Service shall be made personally or by mail. *(Added by Stats.1982, c. 1364, p. 5153, § 2, operative July 1, 1983.)*

Civ. Pro.

§ 703.600. Appeal

An appeal lies from any order made under this article. *(Added by Stats.1982, c. 1364, p. 5153, § 2, operative July 1, 1983. Amended by Stats.1998, c. 931 (S.B.2139), § 93, eff. Sept. 28, 1998.)*

§ 703.610. Disposition of property pending final determination and appeal

(a) Except as otherwise provided by statute or ordered by the court, the levying officer shall not release, sell, or otherwise dispose of the property for which an exemption is claimed until an appeal is waived, the time to file an appeal has expired, or the exemption is finally determined.

(b) At any time while the exemption proceedings are pending, upon motion of the judgment creditor or a claimant, or upon its own motion, the court may make any orders for disposition of the property that may be proper under the circumstances of the case. The order may be modified or vacated by the court at any time during the pendency of the exemption proceedings upon any terms that are just.

(c) If an appeal of the determination of a claim of exemption is taken, notice of the appeal shall be given to the levying officer and the levying officer shall hold, release, or dispose of the property in accordance with the provisions governing enforcement and stay of enforcement of money judgments pending appeal. *(Added by Stats.1982, c. 1364, p. 5153, § 2, operative July 1, 1983. Amended by Stats.2002, c. 68 (S.B.1322), § 6.)*

ARTICLE 3. EXEMPT PROPERTY

§ 704.010. Motor vehicles; equity and proceeds of sale or insurance

(a) Any combination of the following is exempt in the amount of two thousand three hundred dollars ($2,300):

(1) The aggregate equity in motor vehicles.

(2) The proceeds of an execution sale of a motor vehicle.

(3) The proceeds of insurance or other indemnification for the loss, damage, or destruction of a motor vehicle.

(b) Proceeds exempt under subdivision (a) are exempt for a period of 90 days after the time the proceeds are actually received by the judgment debtor.

(c) For the purpose of determining the equity, the fair market value of a motor vehicle shall be determined by reference to used car price guides customarily used by California automobile dealers unless the motor vehicle is not listed in such price guides.

(d) If the judgment debtor has only one motor vehicle and it is sold at an execution sale, the proceeds of the execution sale are exempt in the amount of two thousand three hundred dollars ($2,300) without making a claim. The levying officer shall consult and may rely upon the records of the Department of Motor Vehicles in determining whether the judgment debtor has only one motor vehicle. In the case covered by this subdivision, the exemption provided by subdivision (a) is not available. *(Added by Stats.1982, c. 1364, p. 5154, § 2, operative July 1, 1983. Amended by Stats.1995, c. 196 (S.B.832), § 2, eff. July 31, 1995; Stats.2003, c. 379 (A.B.182), § 5.)*

Explanatory Note

For the current amount of exemption under this section, as adjusted by the Judicial Council and required by Code of Civil Procedure § 703.150, which authorizes the Judicial Council to publish cost-of-living adjustments every three years, see the Judicial Council Form reproduced under Chapter 4, preceding Code of Civil Procedure § 703.010 (for electronic publications, see Refs & Annos).

Law Revision Commission Comments

Section 704.010 is amended to increase the exemption amounts from $1,200 to $1,900. [25 Cal.L.Rev.Comm. Reports 707 (1995)].

Section 704.010 is amended to adjust the exemption amount for cost-of-living increases since the section was last amended in 1995. See 1995 Cal. Stat. ch. 196, § 2. Adjusted amounts were determined by applying the California Consumer Price Index (August 2002) for all urban consumers and rounding to the nearest $25. For future automatic triennial adjustments, see Section 703.150. [33 Cal.L.Rev.Commn. Reports 134 (2003)].

Research References

Rutter, Cal. Practice Guide: Civ. Pro. Before Trial Ch. 9(II)-D, D. Attachment.
Rutter, Cal. Practice Guide: Enforcing Judgments/Debts Ch. 6D-7, Sale and Collection of Property Levied Upon.
Rutter, Cal. Practice Guide: Enforcing Judgments/Debts Ch. 6E-2, Rules Applicable to Exemptions from Enforcement of Money Judgments Generally.
Rutter, Cal. Practice Guide: Enforcing Judgments/Debts Ch. 6E-5, Specific Exempt Property.
Miller and Starr California Real Estate § 32:22, Property Exempt from Attachment--In General.
Miller and Starr California Real Estate § 32:25, Other Exemptions.
Miller and Starr California Real Estate § 32:26, Claim of Exemption.
8 Witkin Cal. Proc. 5th Enforcement of Judgment § 153, in General.
8 Witkin Cal. Proc. 5th Enforcement of Judgment § 158, (S 158) Order of Distribution.
8 Witkin Cal. Proc. 5th Enforcement of Judgment § 174, (S 174) Tracing Exempt Funds.
8 Witkin Cal. Proc. 5th Enforcement of Judgment § 179, (S 179) Periodic Adjustments.
8 Witkin Cal. Proc. 5th Enforcement of Judgment § 187, (S 187) in General.
8 Witkin Cal. Proc. 5th Enforcement of Judgment § 188, (S 188) Motor Vehicles.
8 Witkin Cal. Proc. 5th Enforcement of Judgment § 193, (S 193) Personal Property Used in Trade, Business, or Profession.

§ 704.020. Household furnishings, appliances, provisions, wearing apparel and other personal effects; items of extraordinary value

(a) Household furnishings, appliances, provisions, wearing apparel, and other personal effects are exempt in the following cases:

(1) If ordinarily and reasonably necessary to, and personally used or procured for use by, the judgment debtor and members of the judgment debtor's family at the judgment debtor's principal place of residence.

(2) Where the judgment debtor and the judgment debtor's spouse live separate and apart, if ordinarily and reasonably necessary to, and personally used or procured for use by, the spouse and members of the spouse's family at the spouse's principal place of residence.

(b) In determining whether an item of property is "ordinarily and reasonably necessary" under subdivision (a), the court shall take into account both of the following:

(1) The extent to which the particular type of item is ordinarily found in a household.

(2) Whether the particular item has extraordinary value as compared to the value of items of the same type found in other households.

(c) If an item of property for which an exemption is claimed pursuant to this section is an item of the type ordinarily found in a household but is determined not to be exempt because the item has extraordinary value as compared to the value of items of the same type found in other households, the proceeds obtained at an execution sale of the item are exempt in the amount determined by the court to be a reasonable amount sufficient to purchase a replacement of ordinary value if the court determines that a replacement is reasonably necessary. Proceeds exempt under this subdivision are exempt for a period of 90 days after the proceeds are actually received by the judgment debtor. *(Added by Stats.1982, c. 1364, p. 5154, § 2, operative July 1, 1983.)*

Research References

Rutter, Cal. Practice Guide: Enforcing Judgments/Debts Ch. 6D-7, Sale and Collection of Property Levied Upon.
Rutter, Cal. Practice Guide: Enforcing Judgments/Debts Ch. 6E-2, Rules Applicable to Exemptions from Enforcement of Money Judgments Generally.
Rutter, Cal. Practice Guide: Enforcing Judgments/Debts Ch. 6E-5, Specific Exempt Property.
Miller and Starr California Real Estate § 32:25, Other Exemptions.
8 Witkin Cal. Proc. 5th Enforcement of Judgment § 153, in General.
8 Witkin Cal. Proc. 5th Enforcement of Judgment § 158, (S 158) Order of Distribution.
8 Witkin Cal. Proc. 5th Enforcement of Judgment § 174, (S 174) Tracing Exempt Funds.
8 Witkin Cal. Proc. 5th Enforcement of Judgment § 177, (S 177) Determination of Exemptions Based on Need.
8 Witkin Cal. Proc. 5th Enforcement of Judgment § 189, (S 189) Household Furnishings and Personal Effects.

§ 704.030. Material for repair or improvement of residence

Material that in good faith is about to be applied to the repair or improvement of a residence is exempt if the equity in the material does not exceed two thousand four hundred twenty-five dollars ($2,425) in the following cases:

(a) If purchased in good faith for use in the repair or improvement of the judgment debtor's principal place of residence.

(b) Where the judgment debtor and the judgment debtor's spouse live separate and apart, if purchased in good faith for use in the repair or improvement of the spouse's principal place of residence. *(Added by Stats.1982, c. 1364, p. 5155, § 2, operative July 1, 1983. Amended by Stats.1995, c. 196 (S.B.832), § 3, eff. July 31, 1995; Stats.2003, c. 379 (A.B.182), § 6.)*

Explanatory Note

For the current amount of exemption under this section, as adjusted by the Judicial Council and required by Code of Civil Procedure § 703.150, which authorizes the

Judicial Council to publish cost-of-living adjustments every three years, see the Judicial Council Form reproduced under Chapter 4, preceding Code of Civil Procedure § 703.010 (for electronic publications, see Refs & Annos).

Law Revision Commission Comments

Section 704.030 continues a portion of former Section 690.17 and makes clear that a second exemption is available where the sponser live separate and apart. [16 Cal.L.Rev.Comm.Reports 1400 (1982)].

Section 704.030 is amended to double the exemption amount. [25 Cal.L.Rev.Comm. Reports 1 (1995)].

Section 704.030 is amended to adjust the exemption amount for cost-of-living increases since the section was last amended in 1995. See 1995 Cal. Stat. ch. 196, § 3. Adjusted amounts were determined by applying the California Consumer Price Index (August 2002) for all urban consumers and rounding to the nearest $25. For future automatic triennial adjustments, see Section 703.150. [33 Cal.L.Rev.Commn. Reports 135 (2003)].

Research References

Rutter, Cal. Practice Guide: Enforcing Judgments/Debts Ch. 6E-2, Rules Applicable to Exemptions from Enforcement of Money Judgments Generally.
Rutter, Cal. Practice Guide: Enforcing Judgments/Debts Ch. 6E-5, Specific Exempt Property.
Miller and Starr California Real Estate § 32:25, Other Exemptions.
8 Witkin Cal. Proc. 5th Enforcement of Judgment § 173, (S 173) Application of Exemptions to Marital Property.
8 Witkin Cal. Proc. 5th Enforcement of Judgment § 190, (S 190) Materials for Repair or Improvement of Dwelling.

§ 704.040. Jewelry, heirlooms, and works of art

Jewelry, heirlooms, and works of art are exempt to the extent that the aggregate equity therein does not exceed six thousand seventy-five dollars ($6,075). *(Added by Stats.1982, c. 1364, p. 5155, § 2, operative July 1, 1983. Amended by Stats.1995, c. 196 (S.B.832), § 4, eff. July 31, 1995; Stats.2003, c. 379 (A.B.182), § 7.)*

Explanatory Note

For the current amount of exemptions under this section, as adjusted by the Judicial Council and required by Code of Civil Procedure § 703.150, which authorizes the Judicial Council to publish cost-of-living adjustments every three years, see the Judicial Council Form reproduced under Chapter 4, preceding Code of Civil Procedure § 703.010 (for electronic publications, see Refs & Annos).

Law Revision Commission Comments

Section 704.040 is amended to double the exemption amount. [25 Cal.L.Rev.Comm. Reports 1 (1995)].

Section 704.040 is amended to adjust the exemption amount for cost-of-living increases since the section was last amended in 1995. See 1995 Cal. Stat. ch. 196, § 4. Adjusted amounts were determined by applying the California Consumer Price Index (August 2002) for all urban consumers and rounding to the nearest $25. For future automatic triennial adjustments, see Section 703.150. [33 Cal.L.Rev.Commn. Reports 135 (2003)].

Research References

Rutter, Cal. Practice Guide: Enforcing Judgments/Debts Ch. 6E-2, Rules Applicable to Exemptions from Enforcement of Money Judgments Generally.
Rutter, Cal. Practice Guide: Enforcing Judgments/Debts Ch. 6E-5, Specific Exempt Property.
Miller and Starr California Real Estate § 32:25, Other Exemptions.
8 Witkin Cal. Proc. 5th Enforcement of Judgment § 191, (S 191) Jewelry, Heirlooms, and Works of Art.

§ 704.050. Health aids; prosthetic and orthopedic appliances

Health aids reasonably necessary to enable the judgment debtor or the spouse or a dependent of the judgment debtor to work or sustain health, and prosthetic and orthopedic appliances, are exempt. *(Added by Stats.1982, c. 1364, p. 5155, § 2, operative July 1, 1983.)*

Law Revision Commission Comments

Section 704.050 supersedes former Section 690.5 which exempted prosthetic and orthopedic appliances used by the debtor. Section 704.050 is based on Section 5(2) of the Uniform Exemptions Act (1976). The requirement that health aids be reasonably necessary to enable the individual to work or sustain health permits the exemption of such items as a wheel chair for a person unable to walk to work or an air conditioner for a person afflicted with asthma, but does not permit the exemption of a swimming pool, sauna, bicycle, or golf clubs merely because their use is necessary to sustain good health. [16 Cal.L.Rev.Comm. Reports 1401 (1982)].

Research References

Rutter, Cal. Practice Guide: Enforcing Judgments/Debts Ch. 6E-5, Specific Exempt Property.
8 Witkin Cal. Proc. 5th Enforcement of Judgment § 177, (S 177) Determination of Exemptions Based on Need.
8 Witkin Cal. Proc. 5th Enforcement of Judgment § 192, (S 192) Health Aids.

§ 704.060. Personal property necessary to and used in exercise of trade, business or profession

(a) Tools, implements, instruments, materials, uniforms, furnishings, books, equipment, one commercial motor vehicle, one vessel, and other personal property are exempt to the extent that the aggregate equity therein does not exceed:

(1) Six thousand seventy-five dollars $6,075)[1], if reasonably necessary to and actually used by the judgment debtor in the exercise of the trade, business, or profession by which the judgment debtor earns a livelihood.

(2) Six thousand seventy-five dollars ($6,075), if reasonably necessary to and actually used by the spouse of the judgment debtor in the exercise of the trade, business, or profession by which the spouse earns a livelihood.

(3) Twice the amount of the exemption provided in paragraph (1), if reasonably necessary to and actually used by the judgment debtor and by the spouse of the judgment debtor in the exercise of the same trade, business, or profession by which both earn a livelihood. In the case covered by this paragraph, the exemptions provided in paragraphs (1) and (2) are not available.

(b) If property described in subdivision (a) is sold at an execution sale, or if it has been lost, damaged, or destroyed, the proceeds of the execution sale or of insurance or other indemnification are exempt for a period of 90 days after the proceeds are actually received by the judgment debtor or the judgment debtor's spouse. The amount exempt under this subdivision is the amount specified in subdivision (a) that applies to the particular case less the aggregate equity of any other property to which the exemption provided by subdivision (a) for the particular case has been applied.

(c) Notwithstanding subdivision (a), a motor vehicle is not exempt under subdivision (a) if there is a motor vehicle exempt under Section 704.010 which is reasonably adequate for use in the trade, business, or profession for which the exemption is claimed under this section.

(d) Notwithstanding subdivisions (a) and (b):

(1) The amount of the exemption for a commercial motor vehicle under paragraph (1) or (2) of subdivision (a) is limited to four thousand eight hundred fifty dollars ($4,850).

(2) The amount of the exemption for a commercial motor vehicle under paragraph (3) of subdivision (a) is limited to twice the amount of the exemption provided in paragraph (1) of this subdivision. *(Added by Stats.1982, c. 1364, p. 5155, § 2, operative*

July 1, 1983.   Amended by Stats.1995, c. 196 (S.B.832), § 5, eff. July 31, 1995; Stats.2003, c. 379 (A.B.182), § 8.)

1 So in chaptered copy.

Explanatory Note

For the current amount of exemption under this section, as adjusted by the Judicial Council and required by Code of Civil Procedure § 703.150, which authorizes the Judicial Council to publish cost-of-living adjustments every three years, see the Judicial Council Form reproduced under Chapter 4, preceding Code of Civil Procedure § 703.010 (for electronic publications, see Refs & Annos).

Law Revision Commission Comments

Section 704.060 is amended to double the exemption amounts for the general tools of the trade exemption. However, the exemption for a commercial motor vehicle under this section is limited as provided in subdivision (d). This limitation is generally consistent with the motor vehicle exemption under Section 704.010. [25 Cal.L.Rev.Comm. Reports 707 (1995)].

Section 704.060 is amended to adjust the exemption amount for cost-of-living increases since the section was last amended in 1995. See 1995 Cal. Stat. ch. 196, § 5. Adjusted amounts were determined by applying the California Consumer Price Index (August 2002) for all urban consumers and rounding to the nearest $25, except that the amounts in subdivisions (a)(3) and (d)(2) are determined by doubling the amounts in subdivisions (a)(1) and (d)(1), respectively. [33 Cal.L.Rev.Commn. Reports 137 (2003)].

Research References

Rutter, Cal. Practice Guide: Enforcing Judgments/Debts Ch. 6D-7, Sale and Collection of Property Levied Upon.
Rutter, Cal. Practice Guide: Enforcing Judgments/Debts Ch. 6E-2, Rules Applicable to Exemptions from Enforcement of Money Judgments Generally.
Rutter, Cal. Practice Guide: Enforcing Judgments/Debts Ch. 6E-5, Specific Exempt Property.
Miller and Starr California Real Estate § 32:25, Other Exemptions.
8 Witkin Cal. Proc. 5th Enforcement of Judgment § 153, in General.
8 Witkin Cal. Proc. 5th Enforcement of Judgment § 158, (S 158) Order of Distribution.
8 Witkin Cal. Proc. 5th Enforcement of Judgment § 173, (S 173) Application of Exemptions to Marital Property.
8 Witkin Cal. Proc. 5th Enforcement of Judgment § 174, (S 174) Tracing Exempt Funds.
8 Witkin Cal. Proc. 5th Enforcement of Judgment § 193, (S 193) Personal Property Used in Trade, Business, or Profession.

§ 704.070. Paid earnings; earnings withholding order; wage assignment for support

(a) As used in this section:

(1) "Earnings withholding order" means an earnings withholding order under Chapter 5 (commencing with Section 706.010) (Wage Garnishment Law).

(2) "Paid earnings" means earnings as defined in Section 706.011 that were paid to the employee during the 30-day period ending on the date of the levy. For the purposes of this paragraph, where earnings that have been paid to the employee are sought to be subjected to the enforcement of a money judgment other than by a levy, the date of levy is deemed to be the date the earnings were otherwise subjected to the enforcement of the judgment.

(3) "Earnings assignment order for support" means an earnings assignment order for support as defined in Section 706.011.

(b) Paid earnings that can be traced into deposit accounts or in the form of cash or its equivalent as provided in Section 703.080 are exempt in the following amounts:

(1) All of the paid earnings are exempt if prior to payment to the employee they were subject to an earnings withholding order or an earnings assignment order for support.

(2) Seventy-five percent of the paid earnings that are levied upon or otherwise sought to be subjected to the enforcement of a money judgment are exempt if prior to payment to the employee they were not subject to an earnings withholding order or an earnings assignment order for support. *(Added by Stats.1982, c. 1364, p. 5156, § 2, operative July 1, 1983. Amended by Stats.1992, c. 163 (A.B.2641), § 38, operative Jan. 1, 1994.)*

Law Revision Commission Comments

Section 704.070 is amended to conform to the terminology of the Family Code. See Chapter 8 (commencing with Section 5200) of Part 5 of Division 9 of the Family Code (earnings assignment order for support). [22 Cal.L.Rev.Comm.Reports 1 (1992)].

Research References

Rutter, Cal. Practice Guide: Enforcing Judgments/Debts Ch. 6D-4, Levy on Specific Property.
Rutter, Cal. Practice Guide: Enforcing Judgments/Debts Ch. 6E-2, Rules Applicable to Exemptions from Enforcement of Money Judgments Generally.
Rutter, Cal. Practice Guide: Enforcing Judgments/Debts Ch. 6E-5, Specific Exempt Property.
Rutter, Cal. Practice Guide: Enforcing Judgments/Debts Ch. 6G-5, Assignment Order.
Miller and Starr California Real Estate § 32:23, Earnings.
8 Witkin Cal. Proc. 5th Enforcement of Judgment § 194, (S 194) Paid Earnings.
8 Witkin Cal. Proc. 5th Enforcement of Judgment § 243, (S 243) Definitions.
11 Witkin, California Summary 10th Husband and Wife § 209, Money Judgment Distinguished.

§ 704.080. Deposit account; social security benefits; public benefits

(a) For the purposes of this section:

(1) "Deposit account" means a deposit account in which payments of public benefits or social security benefits are directly deposited by the government or its agent.

(2) "Social security benefits" means payments authorized by the Social Security Administration for regular retirement and survivors' benefits, supplemental security income benefits, coal miners' health benefits, and disability insurance benefits. "Public benefits" means aid payments authorized pursuant to subdivision (a) of Section 11450 of the Welfare and Institutions Code, payments for supportive services as described in Section 11323.2 of the Welfare and Institutions Code, and general assistance payments made pursuant to Section 17000.5 of the Welfare and Institutions Code.

(b) A deposit account is exempt without making a claim in the following amount:

(1) One thousand two hundred twenty-five dollars ($1,225) where one depositor is the designated payee of the directly deposited public benefits payments.

(2) Two thousand four hundred twenty-five dollars ($2,425) where one depositor is the designated payee of directly deposited social security payments.

(3) One thousand eight hundred twenty-five dollars ($1,825) where two or more depositors are the designated payees of the directly deposited public benefits payments, unless those depositors are joint payees of directly deposited payments that represent a benefit to only one of the depositors, in which case the exemption under paragraph (1) applies.

(4) Three thousand six hundred fifty dollars ($3,650) where two or more depositors are the designated payees of directly deposited social security payments, unless those depositors are

joint payees of directly deposited payments that represent a benefit to only one of the depositors, in which case the exemption under paragraph (2) applies.

(c) The amount of a deposit account that exceeds the exemption provided in subdivision (b) is exempt to the extent that it consists of payments of public benefits or social security benefits.

(d) Notwithstanding Article 5 (commencing with Section 701.010) of Chapter 3, when a deposit account is levied upon or otherwise sought to be subjected to the enforcement of a money judgment, the financial institution that holds the deposit account shall either place the amount that exceeds the exemption provided in subdivision (b) in a suspense account or otherwise prohibit withdrawal of that amount pending notification of the failure of the judgment creditor to file the affidavit required by this section or the judicial determination of the exempt status of the amount. Within 10 business days after the levy, the financial institution shall provide the levying officer with a written notice stating (1) that the deposit account is one in which payments of public benefits or social security benefits are directly deposited by the government or its agent and (2) the balance of the deposit account that exceeds the exemption provided by subdivision (b). Promptly upon receipt of the notice, the levying officer shall serve the notice on the judgment creditor. Service shall be made personally or by mail.

(e) Notwithstanding the procedure prescribed in Article 2 (commencing with Section 703.510), whether there is an amount exempt under subdivision (c) shall be determined as follows:

(1) Within five days after the levying officer serves the notice on the judgment creditor under subdivision (d), a judgment creditor who desires to claim that the amount is not exempt shall file with the court an affidavit alleging that the amount is not exempt and file a copy with the levying officer. The affidavit shall be in the form of the notice of opposition provided by Section 703.560, and a hearing shall be set and held, and notice given, as provided by Sections 703.570 and 703.580. For the purpose of this subdivision, the "notice of opposition to the claim of exemption" in Sections 703.570 and 703.580 means the affidavit under this subdivision.

(2) If the judgment creditor does not file the affidavit with the levying officer and give notice of hearing pursuant to Section 703.570 within the time provided in paragraph (1), the levying officer shall release the deposit account and shall notify the financial institution.

(3) The affidavit constitutes the pleading of the judgment creditor, subject to the power of the court to permit amendments in the interest of justice. The affidavit is deemed controverted and no counteraffidavit is required.

(4) At a hearing under this subdivision, the judgment debtor has the burden of proving that the excess amount is exempt.

(5) At the conclusion of the hearing, the court by order shall determine whether or not the amount of the deposit account is exempt pursuant to subdivision (c) in whole or in part and shall make an appropriate order for its prompt disposition. No findings are required in a proceeding under this subdivision.

(6) Upon determining the exemption claim for the deposit account under subdivision (c), the court shall immediately transmit a certified copy of the order of the court to the financial institution and to the levying officer. If the order determines that all or part of the excess is exempt under subdivision (c), with respect to the amount of the excess which is exempt, the financial institution shall transfer the exempt excess from the suspense account or otherwise release any restrictions on its withdrawal by the judgment debtor. The transfer or release shall be effected within three business days of the receipt of the certified copy of the court order by the financial institution.

(f) If the judgment debtor claims that a portion of the amount is exempt other than pursuant to subdivision (c), the claim of exemption shall be made pursuant to Article 2 (commencing with Section 703.510). If the judgment debtor also opposes the judgment creditor's affidavit regarding an amount exempt pursuant to subdivision (c), both exemptions shall be determined at the same hearing, provided the judgment debtor has complied with Article 2 (commencing with Section 703.510). *(Added by Stats.1982, c. 1364, p. 5156, § 2, operative July 1, 1983. Amended by Stats.1995, c. 196 (S.B.832), § 6, eff. July 31, 1995; Stats.1998, c. 290 (A.B.2724), § 1, operative Jan. 1, 2000; Stats.2003, c. 379 (A.B.182), § 9.)*

Explanatory Note

For the current amount of exemptions under this section, as adjusted by the Judicial Council and required by Code of Civil Procedure § 703.150, which authorizes the Judicial Council to publish cost-of-living adjustments every three years, see the Judicial Council Form reproduced under Chapter 4, preceding Code of Civil Procedure § 703.010 (for electronic publications, see Refs & Annos).

Validity

For validity of this section, see Lopez v. Washington Mut. Bank, FA, C.A.9 (Cal.)2002, 302 F.3d 900, opinion amended on denial of rehearing 311 F.3d 928.

Law Revision Commission Comments

Section 704.080 is amended to quadruple the exemption amounts. [25 Cal.L.Rev.Comm. Reports 1 (1995)].

Section 704.080 is amended to adjust the social security payments exemption amounts for cost-of-living increases since the section was last amended in 1995. See 1995 Cal. Stat. ch. 196, § 6. The public benefits exemption amounts are also adjusted for consistency with the scheme enacted in 1998 of setting this exemption at 50% of the social security payments exemption (subject to rounding to nearest $25). See 1998 Cal. Stat. ch. 290, § 1. Adjusted amounts were determined by applying the California Consumer Price Index (August 2002) for all urban consumers and rounding to the nearest $25. For future automatic triennial adjustments, see Section 703.150. [33 Cal.L.Rev.Commn. Reports 140, 141 (2003)].

Research References

Rutter, Cal. Practice Guide: Enforcing Judgments/Debts Ch. 6D-4, Levy on Specific Property.
Rutter, Cal. Practice Guide: Enforcing Judgments/Debts Ch. 6E-2, Rules Applicable to Exemptions from Enforcement of Money Judgments Generally.
Rutter, Cal. Practice Guide: Enforcing Judgments/Debts Ch. 6E-5, Specific Exempt Property.
Miller and Starr California Real Estate § 32:25, Other Exemptions.
8 Witkin Cal. Proc. 5th Enforcement of Judgment § 173, (S 173) Application of Exemptions to Marital Property.
8 Witkin Cal. Proc. 5th Enforcement of Judgment § 180, (S 180) in General.
8 Witkin Cal. Proc. 5th Enforcement of Judgment § 195, Nature and Amount of Exemption.
8 Witkin Cal. Proc. 5th Enforcement of Judgment § 196, Limitation on Withdrawal of Balance.
8 Witkin Cal. Proc. 5th Enforcement of Judgment § 197, Determination of Exempt Balance.

§ 704.090. Correctional facility inmates; funds in trust

(a) The funds of a judgment debtor confined in a prison or facility under the jurisdiction of the Department of Corrections or the Department of the Youth Authority or confined in any county or city jail, road camp, industrial farm, or other local correctional facility, held in trust for or to the credit of the judgment debtor, in an inmate's trust account or similar account by the state, county, or city, or any agency thereof, are exempt without making a claim in the amount of one thousand two hundred twenty-five dollars ($1,225). If the judgment debtor is married, each spouse is entitled to a separate exemption under this section or the spouses may combine their exemptions.

(b) Notwithstanding subdivision (a), if the judgment is for a restitution fine or order imposed pursuant to subdivision (a) of Section 13967 of the Government Code, as operative on or before September 28, 1994, or Section 1203.04 of the Penal Code, as operative on or before August 2, 1995, or Section 1202.4 of the Penal Code, the funds held in trust for, or to the credit of, a judgment debtor described in subdivision (a) are exempt in the amount of three hundred dollars ($300) without making a claim. The exemption provided in this subdivision is not subject to adjustment under Section 703.150. *(Added by Stats.1982, c. 1364, p. 5158, § 2, operative July 1, 1983. Amended by Stats.1996, c. 1077 (A.B.2898), § 1; Stats.2003, c. 379 (A.B. 182), § 10.)*

Explanatory Note

For the current amount of exemption under this section, as adjusted by the Judicial Council and required by Code of Civil Procedure § 703.150, which authorizes the Judicial Council to publish cost-of-living adjustments every three years, see the Judicial Council Form reproduced under Chapter 4, preceding Code of Civil Procedure § 703.010 (for electronic publications, see Refs & Annos).

Law Revision Commission Comments

Section 704.090 supersedes former Section 690.21, which provided an exemption of $40. [16 Cal.L.Rev.Comm. Reports 1407 (1982)].

Subdivision (a) of Section 704.090 is amended to adjust the exemption amount for cost-of-living increases since the section was last amended in 1995. See 1995 Cal. Stat. ch. 196, § 2. Adjusted amounts were determined by applying the California Consumer Price Index (August 2002) for all urban consumers and rounding to the nearest $25. For future automatic triennial adjustments, see Section 703.150.

Subdivision (b) is amended to provide an exception to the automatic triennial adjustment for this special type of exemption. [33 Cal.L.Rev. Commn. Reports 141, 142 (2003)].

Research References

Rutter, Cal. Practice Guide: Enforcing Judgments/Debts Ch. 6E-2, Rules Applicable to Exemptions from Enforcement of Money Judgments Generally.
Rutter, Cal. Practice Guide: Enforcing Judgments/Debts Ch. 6E-5, Specific Exempt Property.
8 Witkin Cal. Proc. 5th Enforcement of Judgment § 62, (S 62) Property in Custody of Law.
8 Witkin Cal. Proc. 5th Enforcement of Judgment § 63, (S 63) Property Found on Arrested Person.
8 Witkin Cal. Proc. 5th Enforcement of Judgment § 173, (S 173) Application of Exemptions to Marital Property.
8 Witkin Cal. Proc. 5th Enforcement of Judgment § 198, (S 198) Inmate's Trust Account.

§ 704.100.   Life insurance policies

(a) Unmatured life insurance policies (including endowment and annuity policies), but not the loan value of such policies, are exempt without making a claim.

(b) The aggregate loan value of unmatured life insurance policies (including endowment and annuity policies) is subject to the enforcement of a money judgment but is exempt in the amount of nine thousand seven hundred dollars ($9,700). If the judgment debtor is married, each spouse is entitled to a separate exemption under this subdivision, and the exemptions of the spouses may be combined, regardless of whether the policies belong to either or both spouses and regardless of whether the spouse of the judgment debtor is also a judgment debtor under the judgment. The exemption provided by this subdivision shall be first applied to policies other than the policy before the court

and then, if the exemption is not exhausted, to the policy before the court.

(c) Benefits from matured life insurance policies (including endowment and annuity policies) are exempt to the extent reasonably necessary for the support of the judgment debtor and the spouse and dependents of the judgment debtor. *(Added by Stats.1982, c. 1364, p. 5158, § 2, operative July 1, 1983. Amended by Stats.1995, c. 196 (S.B.832), § 7, eff. July 31, 1995; Stats.2003, c. 379 (A.B.182), § 11.)*

Explanatory Note

For the current amount of exemption under this section, as adjusted by the Judicial Council and required by Code of Civil Procedure § 703.150, which authorizes the Judicial Council to publish cost-of-living adjustments every three years, see the Judicial Council Form reproduced under Chapter 4, preceding Code of Civil Procedure § 703.010 (for electronic publications, see Refs & Annos).

Law Revision Commission Comments

Section 704.100 is amended to adjust the exemption amount for cost-of-living increases since the section was last amended in 1995. See 1995 Cal. Stat. ch. 196, § 7. Adjusted amounts were determined by applying the California Consumer Price Index (August 2002) for all urban consumers and rounding to the nearest $25. For future automatic triennial adjustments, see Section 703.150. [33 Cal.L.Rev.Comm. Reports 142 (2003)].

Research References

Rutter, Cal. Practice Guide: Enforcing Judgments/Debts Ch. 6E-2, Rules Applicable to Exemptions from Enforcement of Money Judgments Generally.
Rutter, Cal. Practice Guide: Enforcing Judgments/Debts Ch. 6E-3, Procedures for Claiming Exemptions.
Rutter, Cal. Practice Guide: Enforcing Judgments/Debts Ch. 6E-5, Specific Exempt Property.
Rutter, Cal. Practice Guide: Insurance Litigation Ch. 15-L, L. Effect of Insured's Bankruptcy.
Miller and Starr California Real Estate § 32:25, Other Exemptions.
8 Witkin Cal. Proc. 5th Enforcement of Judgment § 116, Property Not Subject to Execution.
8 Witkin Cal. Proc. 5th Enforcement of Judgment § 173, (S 173) Application of Exemptions to Marital Property.
8 Witkin Cal. Proc. 5th Enforcement of Judgment § 177, (S 177) Determination of Exemptions Based on Need.
8 Witkin Cal. Proc. 5th Enforcement of Judgment § 199, (S 199) Life Insurance Policies.
8 Witkin Cal. Proc. 5th Enforcement of Judgment § 305, (S 305) Nature and Procedure.

§ 704.110.   Public retirement benefits; rights and benefits under public retirement system; return of contributions from public entity

(a) As used in this section:

(1) "Public entity" means the state, or a city, city and county, county, or other political subdivision of the state, or a public trust, public corporation, or public board, or the governing body of any of them, but does not include the United States except where expressly so provided.

(2) "Public retirement benefit" means a pension or an annuity, or a retirement, disability, death, or other benefit, paid or payable by a public retirement system.

(3) "Public retirement system" means a system established pursuant to statute by a public entity for retirement, annuity, or pension purposes or payment of disability or death benefits.

(b) All amounts held, controlled, or in process of distribution by a public entity derived from contributions by the public entity or by an officer or employee of the public entity for public retirement benefit purposes, and all rights and benefits accrued or accruing to any person under a public retirement system, are exempt without making a claim.

(c) Notwithstanding subdivision (b), where an amount described in subdivision (b) becomes payable to a person and is sought to be applied to the satisfaction of a judgment for child, family, or spousal support against that person:

(1) Except as provided in paragraphs (2) and (3), the amount is exempt only to the extent that the court determines under subdivision (c) of Section 703.070.

(2) If the amount sought to be applied to the satisfaction of the judgment is payable periodically, the amount payable is subject to an earnings assignment order for support as defined in Section 706.011, or any other applicable enforcement procedure, but the amount to be withheld pursuant to the assignment order or other procedure shall not exceed the amount permitted to be withheld on an earnings withholding order for support under Section 706.052. The paying entity may deduct from the payment being made to the judgment debtor, for each payment made pursuant to an earnings assignment order under this paragraph, an amount reflecting the actual cost of administration caused by the assignment order of up to two dollars ($2) for each payment.

(3) If the intercept procedure provided for in Section 11357 of the Welfare and Institutions Code is used for benefits that are payable periodically, the amount to be withheld shall not exceed the amount permitted to be withheld on an earnings withholding order for support under Section 706.052.

(4) If the amount sought to be applied to the satisfaction of the judgment is payable as a lump-sum distribution, the amount payable is subject to the intercept procedure provided in Section 11357 of the Welfare and Institutions Code or any other applicable enforcement procedure.

(d) All amounts received by any person, a resident of the state, as a public retirement benefit or as a return of contributions and interest thereon from the United States or a public entity or from a public retirement system are exempt. *(Added by Stats.1982, c. 1364, p. 5158, § 2, operative July 1, 1983. Amended by Stats.1992, c. 163 (A.B.2341), § 39, operative Jan. 1, 1994; Stats.1996, c. 912 (A.B.1751), § 1; Stats.1996, c. 927 (S.B.468), § 1.5.)*

Law Revision Commission Comments

Section 704.110 continues the substance of subdivisions (a) and (b) of former Section 690.18, with drafting changes for purposes of clarity and uniformity. Subdivision (c) governs the application of the exemption for payable but unpaid benefits against the enforcement of child or spousal support judgments. Subdivision (c) (1) applies the general rule governing exemptions in support cases. Subdivision (c) (2) incorporates the standard applicable to wage garnishments to enforce support judgments. See Section 706.052 and the Comment thereto. See also Civil Code §§ 4701 (wage assignment for child support), 4801.6 (wage assignment for spousal support). The one dollar fee for administrative costs provided by former Section 690.18(b) is increased to two dollars in subdivision (c) (2) of this section. The two dollar fee is the same as that formerly provided in Government Code Section 21201 (public employees' retirement).

The exemption provided in subdivision (d) applies whether the benefits are in the actual possession of the retirement benefit recipient or have been deposited. See Section 703.080 (tracing exempt funds). The general rule governing exemptions in support cases provided by Section 703.070 applies to benefits after they have been paid. For the exemption of vacation credits, see Section 704.113. For the exemption of benefits under the Unemployment Insurance Code, see Section 704.120. [16 Cal.L.Rev.Comm. Reports 1410 (1982)].

Section 704.110 is amended to conform to the terminology of the Family Code. See Chapter 8 (commencing with Section 5200) of Part 5 of Division 9 of the Family Code (earnings assignment order for support). A reference to "family" support has been added to subdivision (c). See Fam. Code § 4501 (family support order enforceable in same manner and to same extent as child support order). See also Section 680.145 ("child

support" includes family support). [22 Cal.L.Rev.Comm.Reports 1 (1992)].

Research References

Rutter, Cal. Practice Guide: Enforcing Judgments/Debts Ch. 6E-5, Specific Exempt Property.
Miller and Starr California Real Estate § 32:25, Other Exemptions.
8 Witkin Cal. Proc. 5th Enforcement of Judgment § 172, (S 172) Application of Exemptions to Judgment for Support.
8 Witkin Cal. Proc. 5th Enforcement of Judgment § 201, (S 201) in General.
8 Witkin Cal. Proc. 5th Enforcement of Judgment § 202, (S 202) Effect of Support Judgment.
11 Witkin, California Summary 10th Husband and Wife § 250, (S 250) Definitions.

§ 704.113. Vacation credits

(a) As used in this section, "vacation credits" means vacation credits accumulated by a state employee pursuant to Section 18050 of the Government Code or by any other public employee pursuant to any law for the accumulation of vacation credits applicable to the employee.

(b) All vacation credits are exempt without making a claim.

(c) Amounts paid periodically or as a lump sum representing vacation credits are subject to any earnings withholding order served under Chapter 5 (commencing with Section 706.010) or any earnings assignment order for support as defined in Section 706.011 and are exempt to the same extent as earnings of a judgment debtor. *(Added by Stats.1982, c. 1364, p. 5159, § 2, operative July 1, 1983. Amended by Stats.1992, c. 163 (A.B.2641), § 40, operative Jan. 1, 1994.)*

Law Revision Commission Comments

Subdivision (c) of Section 704.113 is amended to conform to Section 706.011(b). [22 Cal.L.Rev.Comm.Reports 1 (1992)].

Research References

Rutter, Cal. Practice Guide: Enforcing Judgments/Debts Ch. 6E-5, Specific Exempt Property.
Miller and Starr California Real Estate § 32:23, Earnings.
8 Witkin Cal. Proc. 5th Enforcement of Judgment § 203, Public Employee Vacation Credits.
11 Witkin, California Summary 10th Husband and Wife § 250, (S 250) Definitions.

§ 704.114. Service of earnings assignment orders for support on public entity; return to employee contributions; written notice of receipt of funds; use of monies

(a) Notwithstanding any other provision of law, service of an earnings assignment order for support, or an order or notice to withhold income for child support on any public entity described in Section 704.110, other than the United States government, creates a lien on all employee contributions in the amount necessary to satisfy a support judgment as determined under Section 695.210 to the extent that the judgment remains enforceable.

(b) The public entity shall comply with any request for a return of employee contributions by an employee named in the order or notice to withhold by delivering the contributions to the clerk of the court in which the support order was awarded or last registered, unless the entity has received a certified copy of an order or administrative notice terminating the earnings assignment order for support.

(c) Upon receipt of moneys pursuant to this section, the clerk of the court, within 10 days, shall send written notice of the receipt of the deposit to the parties and to the local child support agency enforcing any order pursuant to Section 17400 of the Family Code.

(d) Moneys received pursuant to this section are subject to any procedure available to enforce an order for support, but if no enforcement procedure is commenced after 30 days have elapsed from the date the notice of receipt is sent, the clerk shall, upon request, return the moneys to the public entity that delivered the moneys to the court unless the public entity has informed the court in writing that the moneys shall be released to the employee.

(e) A court shall not directly or indirectly condition the issuance, modification, or termination of, or condition the terms or conditions of, any order for support upon the making of a request for the return of employee contributions by an employee. *(Added by Stats.1989, c. 1359, § 8. Amended by Stats.1992, c. 163 (A.B.2641), § 41; Stats.1992, c. 851 (S.B.1530), § 2, eff. Sept. 22, 1992; Stats.1993, c. 219 (A.B.1500), § 68; Stats.2000, c. 808 (A.B.1358), § 13, eff. Sept. 28, 2000.)*

Law Revision Commission Comments

Section 704.114 is amended to conform to the terminology of the Family Code. See Chapter 8 (commencing with Section 5200) of Part 5 of Division 9 of the Family Code (earnings assignment order for support). The section has also been divided into subdivisions and revised for clarity. See Section 706.011 ("earnings assignment order for support" defined). [23 Cal.L.Rev.Comm. Reports 1 (1993)].

Research References

Rutter, Cal. Practice Guide: Enforcing Judgments/Debts Ch. 6F-2, Wage Garnishment-In General.
8 Witkin Cal. Proc. 5th Enforcement of Judgment § 202, (S 202) Effect of Support Judgment.

§ 704.115. Private retirement plans; exemption; periodic payments

(a) As used in this section, "private retirement plan" means:

(1) Private retirement plans, including, but not limited to, union retirement plans.

(2) Profit–sharing plans designed and used for retirement purposes.

(3) Self–employed retirement plans and individual retirement annuities or accounts provided for in the Internal Revenue Code of 1986, [1] as amended, including individual retirement accounts qualified under Section 408 or 408A of that code, to the extent the amounts held in the plans, annuities, or accounts do not exceed the maximum amounts exempt from federal income taxation under that code.

(b) All amounts held, controlled, or in process of distribution by a private retirement plan, for the payment of benefits as an annuity, pension, retirement allowance, disability payment, or death benefit from a private retirement plan are exempt.

(c) Notwithstanding subdivision (b), where an amount described in subdivision (b) becomes payable to a person and is sought to be applied to the satisfaction of a judgment for child, family, or spousal support against that person:

(1) Except as provided in paragraph (2), the amount is exempt only to the extent that the court determines under subdivision (c) of Section 703.070.

(2) If the amount sought to be applied to the satisfaction of the judgment is payable periodically, the amount payable is subject to an earnings assignment order for support as defined in Section 706.011 or any other applicable enforcement procedure, but the amount to be withheld pursuant to the assignment order or other procedure shall not exceed the amount permitted to be withheld on an earnings withholding order for support under Section 706.052.

(d) After payment, the amounts described in subdivision (b) and all contributions and interest thereon returned to any member of a private retirement plan are exempt.

(e) Notwithstanding subdivisions (b) and (d), except as provided in subdivision (f), the amounts described in paragraph (3) of subdivision (a) are exempt only to the extent necessary to provide for the support of the judgment debtor when the judgment debtor retires and for the support of the spouse and dependents of the judgment debtor, taking into account all resources that are likely to be available for the support of the judgment debtor when the judgment debtor retires. In determining the amount to be exempt under this subdivision, the court shall allow the judgment debtor such additional amount as is necessary to pay any federal and state income taxes payable as a result of the applying of an amount described in paragraph (3) of subdivision (a) to the satisfaction of the money judgment.

(f) Where the amounts described in paragraph (3) of subdivision (a) are payable periodically, the amount of the periodic payment that may be applied to the satisfaction of a money judgment is the amount that may be withheld from a like amount of earnings under Chapter 5 (commencing with Section 706.010) (Wage Garnishment Law). To the extent a lump-sum distribution from an individual retirement account is treated differently from a periodic distribution under this subdivision, any lump-sum distribution from an account qualified under Section 408A of the Internal Revenue Code shall be treated the same as a lump-sum distribution from an account qualified under Section 408 of the Internal Revenue Code for purposes of determining whether any of that payment may be applied to the satisfaction of a money judgment. *(Added by Stats.1982, c. 1364, p. 5159, § 2, operative July 1, 1983. Amended by Stats.1992, c. 163 (A.B.2641), § 42, operative Jan. 1, 1994; Stats.1999, c. 98 (S.B.469), § 2; Stats.2000, c. 135 (A.B.2539), § 16.)*

1 Internal Revenue Code sections are in Title 26 of U.S.C.A.

Law Revision Commission Comments

Subdivision (c) of Section 704.115 is amended to conform to the terminology of the Family Code. See Chapter 8 (commencing with Section 5200) of Part 5 of Division 9 of the Family Code (earnings assignment order for support). A reference to "family" support has been added to subdivision (c). See Fam. Code § 4501 (family support order enforceable in same manner and to same extent as child support order). See also Section 680.145 ("child support" includes family support). [22 Cal.L.Rev.Comm.Reports 1 (1992)].

Research References

Rutter, Cal. Practice Guide: Enforcing Judgments/Debts Ch. 6E-5, Specific Exempt Property.
Rutter, Cal. Practice Guide: Family Law Ch. 6-B, B. Spousal Support.
Miller and Starr California Real Estate § 32:25, Other Exemptions.
8 Witkin Cal. Proc. 5th Enforcement of Judgment § 172, (S 172) Application of Exemptions to Judgment for Support.
8 Witkin Cal. Proc. 5th Enforcement of Judgment § 204, Private Retirement Benefits.
11 Witkin, California Summary 10th Husband and Wife § 250, (S 250) Definitions.

§ 704.120. Unemployment insurance and compensation funds; exemption; child support judgments

(a) Contributions by workers payable to the Unemployment Compensation Disability Fund and by employers payable to the Unemployment Fund are exempt without making a claim.

(b) Before payment, amounts held for payment of the following benefits are exempt without making a claim:

(1) Benefits payable under Division 1 (commencing with Section 100) of the Unemployment Insurance Code.

(2) Incentives payable under Division 2 (commencing with Section 5000) of the Unemployment Insurance Code.

(3) Benefits payable under an employer's plan or system to supplement unemployment compensation benefits of the employees generally or for a class or group of employees.

(4) Unemployment benefits payable by a fraternal organization to its bona fide members.

(5) Benefits payable by a union due to a labor dispute.

(c) After payment, the benefits described in subdivision (b) are exempt.

(d) During the payment of benefits described in paragraph (1) of subdivision (b) to a judgment debtor under a support judgment, the judgment creditor may, through the appropriate local child support agency, seek to apply the benefit payment to satisfy the judgment as provided by Section 17518 of the Family Code.

(e) During the payment of benefits described in paragraphs (2) to (5), inclusive, of subdivision (b) to a judgment debtor under a support judgment, the judgment creditor may, directly or through the appropriate local child support agency, seek to apply the benefit payments to satisfy the judgment by an earnings assignment order for support as defined in Section 706.011 or any other applicable enforcement procedure. If the benefit is payable periodically, the amount to be withheld pursuant to the assignment order or other procedure shall be 25 percent of the amount of each periodic payment or any lower amount specified in writing by the judgment creditor or court order, rounded down to the nearest whole dollar. Otherwise the amount to be withheld shall be the amount the court determines under subdivision (c) of Section 703.070. The paying entity may deduct from each payment made pursuant to an assignment order under this subdivision an amount reflecting the actual cost of administration caused by the assignment order up to two dollars ($2) for each payment. *(Added by Stats.1982, c. 1364, p. 5161, § 2, operative July 1, 1983. Amended by Stats.1983, c. 155, § 16, eff. June 30, 1983, operative July 1, 1983; Stats.1988, c. 261, § 1, eff. July 5, 1988; Stats.1992, c. 163 (A.B.2641), § 43, operative Jan. 1, 1994; Stats.2000, c. 808 (A.B.1358), § 14, eff. Sept. 28, 2000.)*

Law Revision Commission Comments

Subdivision (e) of Section 704.120 is amended to conform to the terminology of the Family Code. See Chapter 8 (commencing with Section 5200) of Part 5 of Division 9 of the Family Code (earnings assignment order for support). [22 Cal.L.Rev.Comm.Reports 1 (1992)].

Research References

Rutter, Cal. Practice Guide: Enforcing Judgments/Debts Ch. 6D-4, Levy on Specific Property.
Rutter, Cal. Practice Guide: Enforcing Judgments/Debts Ch. 6E-5, Specific Exempt Property.
Miller and Starr California Real Estate § 32:25, Other Exemptions.
8 Witkin Cal. Proc. 5th Enforcement of Judgment § 205, (S 205) Unemployment and Strike Benefits.
4 Witkin, California Summary 10th Negotiable Instruments § 83, (S 83) Validity of Setoff.

§ 704.130. Disability or health insurance benefits; exemption

(a) Before payment, benefits from a disability or health insurance policy or program are exempt without making a claim. After payment, the benefits are exempt.

(b) Subdivision (a) does not apply to benefits that are paid or payable to cover the cost of health care if the judgment creditor is a provider of health care whose claim is the basis on which the benefits are paid or payable.

(c) During the payment of disability benefits described in subdivision (a) to a judgment debtor under a support judgment, the judgment creditor or local child support agency may seek to apply the benefit payments to satisfy the judgment by an earnings

assignment order for support, as defined in Section 706.011, or any other applicable enforcement procedure, but the amount to be withheld pursuant to the earnings assignment order or other procedure shall not exceed the amount permitted to be withheld on an earnings assignment order for support under Section 706.052. *(Added by Stats.1982, c. 1364, p. 5161, § 2, operative July 1, 1983. Amended by Stats.1997, c. 599 (A.B.573), § 4; Stats.2000, c. 808 (A.B.1358), § 15, eff. Sept. 28, 2000.)*

Research References

Rutter, Cal. Practice Guide: Enforcing Judgments/Debts Ch. 6E-5, Specific Exempt Property.
Miller and Starr California Real Estate § 32:25, Other Exemptions.
8 Witkin Cal. Proc. 5th Enforcement of Judgment § 172, (S 172) Application of Exemptions to Judgment for Support.
8 Witkin Cal. Proc. 5th Enforcement of Judgment § 206, (S 206) Disability and Health Benefits.
11 Witkin, California Summary 10th Husband and Wife § 262, (S 262) in General.

§ 704.140. Personal injury causes of action, damages or settlement; exemption; exception; periodic payment

(a) Except as provided in Article 5 (commencing with Section 708.410) of Chapter 6, a cause of action for personal injury is exempt without making a claim.

(b) Except as provided in subdivisions (c) and (d), an award of damages or a settlement arising out of personal injury is exempt to the extent necessary for the support of the judgment debtor and the spouse and dependents of the judgment debtor.

(c) Subdivision (b) does not apply if the judgment creditor is a provider of health care whose claim is based on the providing of health care for the personal injury for which the award or settlement was made.

(d) Where an award of damages or a settlement arising out of personal injury is payable periodically, the amount of such periodic payment that may be applied to the satisfaction of a money judgment is the amount that may be withheld from a like amount of earnings under Chapter 5 (commencing with Section 706.010) (Wage Garnishment Law). *(Added by Stats.1982, c. 1364, p. 5162, § 2, operative July 1, 1983.)*

Law Revision Commission Comments

Section 704.140 is new. An award or settlement that will result from a cause of action that is the subject of a pending action may be reached by the lien procedure provided by Article 5 (commencing with Section 708.410) of Chapter 6, but the exemption provided by subdivision (b) of Section 704.140 may be claimed in the pending action. See Section 704.450. See also Section 695.030 (property not subject to enforcement of money judgment). [16 Cal.L.Rev.Comm. Reports 1416 (1982)].

Research References

Rutter, Cal. Practice Guide: Enforcing Judgments/Debts Ch. 6E-5, Specific Exempt Property.
Miller and Starr California Real Estate § 32:25, Other Exemptions.
8 Witkin Cal. Proc. 5th Enforcement of Judgment § 177, (S 177) Determination of Exemptions Based on Need.
8 Witkin Cal. Proc. 5th Enforcement of Judgment § 207, (S 207) Damages for Personal Injury.
8 Witkin Cal. Proc. 5th Enforcement of Judgment § 219, (S 219) in General.

§ 704.150. Wrongful death causes of action, damages or settlement; exemption; periodic payments

(a) Except as provided in Article 5 (commencing with Section 708.410) of Chapter 6, a cause of action for wrongful death is exempt without making a claim.

(b) Except as provided in subdivision (c), an award of damages or a settlement arising out of the wrongful death of the judgment debtor's spouse or a person on whom the judgment debtor or the judgment debtor's spouse was dependent is exempt to the extent reasonably necessary for support of the judgment debtor and the spouse and dependents of the judgment debtor.

(c) Where an award of damages or a settlement arising out of the wrongful death of the judgment debtor's spouse or a person on whom the judgment debtor or the judgment debtor's spouse was dependent is payable periodically, the amount of such a periodic payment that may be applied to the satisfaction of a money judgment is the amount that may be withheld from a like amount of earnings under Chapter 5 (commencing with Section 706.010) (Wage Garnishment Law). *(Added by Stats.1982, c. 1364, p. 5162, § 2, operative July 1, 1983.)*

Law Revision Commission Comments

Section 704.150 is new. An award or settlement that will result from a cause of action that is the subject of a pending action may be reached by the lien procedure provided by Article 5 (commencing with Section 708.410) of Chapter 6. See the Comment to Section 704.140. See also Section 695.030 (property not subject to enforcement of money judgment). [16 Cal.L.Rev.Comm. Reports 1416 (1982)].

Research References

Rutter, Cal. Practice Guide: Enforcing Judgments/Debts Ch. 6E-5, Specific Exempt Property.
Miller and Starr California Real Estate § 32:25, Other Exemptions.
8 Witkin Cal. Proc. 5th Enforcement of Judgment § 177, (S 177) Determination of Exemptions Based on Need.
8 Witkin Cal. Proc. 5th Enforcement of Judgment § 208, (S 208) Damages for Wrongful Death.

§ 704.160. Workers' compensation claim or award; temporary benefits; exemption

(a) Except as provided by Chapter 1 (commencing with Section 4900) of Part 3 of Division 4 of the Labor Code, before payment, a claim for workers' compensation or workers' compensation awarded or adjudged is exempt without making a claim. Except as specified in subdivision (b), after payment, the award is exempt.

(b) Notwithstanding any other provision of law, during the payment of workers' compensation temporary disability benefits described in subdivision (a) to a support judgment debtor, the support judgment creditor may, through the appropriate local child support agency, seek to apply the workers' compensation temporary disability benefit payment to satisfy the support judgment as provided by Section 17404 of the Family Code.

(c) Notwithstanding any other provision of law, during the payment of workers' compensation temporary disability benefits described in subdivision (a) to a support judgment debtor under a support judgment, including a judgment for reimbursement of public assistance, the judgment creditor may, directly or through the appropriate local child support agency, seek to apply the temporary disability benefit payments to satisfy the support judgment by an earnings assignment order for support, as defined in Section 5208 of the Family Code, or any other applicable enforcement procedure. The amount to be withheld pursuant to the earnings assignment order for support or other enforcement procedure shall be 25 percent of the amount of each periodic payment or any lower amount specified in writing by the judgment creditor or court order, rounded down to the nearest dollar. Otherwise, the amount to be withheld shall be the amount the court determines under subdivision (c) of Section 703.070. The paying entity may deduct from each payment made pursuant to an order assigning earnings under this subdivision an amount reflecting the actual cost of administration of this assignment, up to two dollars ($2) for each payment.

(d) Unless the provision or context otherwise requires, the following definitions govern the construction of this section.

(1) "Judgment debtor" or "support judgment debtor" means a person who is owing a duty of support.

(2) "Judgment creditor" or "support judgment creditor" means the person to whom support has been ordered to be paid.

(3) "Support" refers to an obligation owing on behalf of a child, spouse, or family; or an amount owing pursuant to Section 17402 of the Family Code. It also includes past due support or arrearage when it exists. *(Added by Stats.1982, c. 1364, p. 5162, § 2, operative July 1, 1983. Amended by Stats.1992, c. 848 (S.B.1614), § 10, eff. Sept. 22, 1992; Stats.1993, c. 219 (A.B. 1500), § 69; Stats.2000, c. 808 (A.B.1358), § 16, eff. Sept. 28, 2000.)*

Law Revision Commission Comments

Section 704.160 continues the substance of former Section 690.15. [16 Cal.L.Rev.Comm. Reports 1417 (1982)].

Section 704.160 is amended to substitute references to "earnings assignment order for support" and the Family Code section defining the term. These are not substantive changes. [23 Cal.L.Rev.Comm. Reports 1 (1993)].

Research References

Rutter, Cal. Practice Guide: Enforcing Judgments/Debts Ch. 6E-5, Specific Exempt Property.
Miller and Starr California Real Estate § 32:25, Other Exemptions.
8 Witkin Cal. Proc. 5th Enforcement of Judgment § 209, (S 209) Workers' Compensation.

§ 704.170. Social services aid; exemption

Before payment, aid provided pursuant to Division 9 (commencing with Section 10000) of the Welfare and Institutions Code or similar aid provided by a charitable organization or a fraternal benefit society as defined in Section 10990 of the Insurance Code, is exempt without making a claim. After payment, the aid is exempt. *(Added by Stats.1982, c. 1364, p. 5162, § 2, operative July 1, 1983.)*

Law Revision Commission Comments

Section 704.170 is based on former Sections 690.14 and 690.19. Section 704.170 exempts local aid as well as federal aid administered by the state pursuant to the Welfare and Institutions Code. See also Welf. & Inst. Code § 10052 ("aid" defined). Section 704.170 also expands the category of nongovernmental aid that is exempt. Former Section 690.14 applied only to fraternal benefit societies. [16 Cal.L.Rev.Comm. Reports 1417 (1982)].

Research References

Rutter, Cal. Practice Guide: Enforcing Judgments/Debts Ch. 6E-5, Specific Exempt Property.
8 Witkin Cal. Proc. 5th Enforcement of Judgment § 210, (S 210) Aid to Needy Persons.

§ 704.180. Relocation benefits; exemption

Before payment, relocation benefits for displacement from a dwelling which are to be paid pursuant to Chapter 16 (commencing with Section 7260) of Division 7 of Title 1 of the Government Code or the federal "Uniform Relocation Assistance and Real Property Acquisition Policies Act of 1970" (42 U.S.C. Sec. 4601 et seq.), as amended, are exempt without making a claim. After payment, the benefits are exempt. *(Added by Stats.1982, c. 1364, p. 5163, § 2, operative July 1, 1983.)*

Law Revision Commission Comments

Section 704.180 supersedes Section 690.8a. Section 704.180 expands the former exemption to include relocation benefits paid or payable by a public utility (Pub.Util. Code § 600) or a quasi-public entity (Gov't. Code § 7260). The last sentence of this section requires the debtor to claim an exemption for such benefits after payment, whereas under former law these benefits were designated as exempt without filing a claim. [16 Cal.L.Rev.Comm. Reports 1417 (1982)].

Research References

Rutter, Cal. Practice Guide: Enforcing Judgments/Debts Ch. 6E-5, Specific Exempt Property.
8 Witkin Cal. Proc. 5th Enforcement of Judgment § 211, (S 211) Relocation Benefits.

§ 704.190. Institution of higher education, defined; financial aid exemption

(a) As used in this section, "institution of higher education" means "institution of higher education" as defined in Section 1141(a) of Title 20 of the United States Code, as amended.

(b) Before payment, financial aid for expenses while attending school provided to a student by an institution of higher education is exempt without making a claim. After payment, the aid is exempt. *(Added by Stats.1982, c. 1364, p. 5163, § 2, operative July 1, 1983.)*

Research References

Rutter, Cal. Practice Guide: Enforcing Judgments/Debts Ch. 6E-5, Specific Exempt Property.
8 Witkin Cal. Proc. 5th Enforcement of Judgment § 212, (S 212) Financial Aid to Students.

§ 704.200. Definitions; family and cemetery plots; exemption

(a) As used in this section:

(1) "Cemetery" has the meaning provided by Section 7003 of the Health and Safety Code.

(2) "Family plot" is a plot that satisfies the requirements of Section 8650 of the Health and Safety Code.

(3) "Plot" has the meaning provided by Section 7022 of the Health and Safety Code.

(b) A family plot is exempt without making a claim.

(c) Except as provided in subdivision (d), a cemetery plot for the judgment debtor and the spouse of the judgment debtor is exempt.

(d) Land held for the purpose of sale or disposition as cemetery plots or otherwise is not exempt. *(Added by Stats.1982, c. 1364, p. 5163, § 2, operative July 1, 1983.)*

Law Revision Commission Comments

Section 704.200 supersedes portions of former Section 690.24 which provided an exemption for a cemetery lot not exceeding one-quarter of an acre in size or, in the case of a religious or benevolent association or corporation, five acres in size. Subdivision (b) recognizes that family plots are inalienable. See Health & Saf. Code § 8650. Subdivision (c) exempts cemetery plots for the judgment debtor and spouse. See also Health & Saf. Code § 8601 (spouse's vested right of interment). Subdivision (d) continues the substance of the third paragraph of former Section 690.24. The fourth paragraph of former Section 690.24, relating to the application of the exemption against a judgment for the purchase price, is not continued because it is not longer necessary. See Comment to Section 703.010(b). The portion of land containing graves of human beings is not subject to enforcement of a money judgment. See Peebler v. Danziger, 104 Cal.App.2d 491, 493, 231 P.2d 895 (1951). [16 Cal.L.Rev. Comm. Reports 1419 (1982)].

Research References

Rutter, Cal. Practice Guide: Enforcing Judgments/Debts Ch. 6E-5, Specific Exempt Property.
Miller and Starr California Real Estate § 32:25, Other Exemptions.
8 Witkin Cal. Proc. 5th Enforcement of Judgment § 213, (S 213) Cemetery Plots.

§ 704.210. Property not subject to enforcement of money judgment; exemption

Property that is not subject to enforcement of a money judgment is exempt without making a claim. *(Added by Stats. 1982, c. 1364, p. 5163, § 2, operative July 1, 1983.)*

Law Revision Commission Comments

Section 704.210 is consistent with Section 695.040 (release of the property not subject to enforcement). [16 Cal.L.Rev.Comm. Reports 1419 (1982)].

Research References

8 Witkin Cal. Proc. 5th Enforcement of Judgment § 60, (S 60) in General.
8 Witkin Cal. Proc. 5th Enforcement of Judgment § 180, (S 180) in General.

ARTICLE 4. HOMESTEAD EXEMPTION

§ 704.710. Definitions

As used in this article:

(a) "Dwelling" means a place where a person resides and may include but is not limited to the following:

(1) A house together with the outbuildings and the land upon which they are situated.

(2) A mobilehome together with the outbuildings and the land upon which they are situated.

(3) A boat or other waterborne vessel.

(4) A condominium, as defined in Section 783 of the Civil Code.

(5) A planned development, as defined in Section 11003 of the Business and Professions Code.

(6) A stock cooperative, as defined in Section 11003.2 of the Business and Professions Code.

(7) A community apartment project, as defined in Section 11004 of the Business and Professions Code.

(b) "Family unit" means any of the following:

(1) The judgment debtor and the judgment debtor's spouse if the spouses reside together in the homestead.

(2) The judgment debtor and at least one of the following persons who the judgment debtor cares for or maintains in the homestead:

(A) The minor child or minor grandchild of the judgment debtor or the judgment debtor's spouse or the minor child or grandchild of a deceased spouse or former spouse.

(B) The minor brother or sister of the judgment debtor or judgment debtor's spouse or the minor child of a deceased brother or sister of either spouse.

(C) The father, mother, grandfather, or grandmother of the judgment debtor or the judgment debtor's spouse or the father, mother, grandfather, or grandmother of a deceased spouse.

(D) An unmarried relative described in this paragraph who has attained the age of majority and is unable to take care of or support himself or herself.

(3) The judgment debtor's spouse and at least one of the persons listed in paragraph (2) who the judgment debtor's spouse cares for or maintains in the homestead.

(c) "Homestead" means the principal dwelling (1) in which the judgment debtor or the judgment debtor's spouse resided on the date the judgment creditor's lien attached to the dwelling, and (2) in which the judgment debtor or the judgment debtor's spouse resided continuously thereafter until the date of the court determination that the dwelling is a homestead. Where exempt proceeds from the sale or damage or destruction of a homestead are used toward the acquisition of a dwelling within the six-month period provided by Section 704.720, "homestead" also means the dwelling so acquired if it is the principal dwelling in which the judgment debtor or the judgment debtor's spouse resided continuously from the date of acquisition until the date of the court determination that the dwelling is a homestead, whether or not an abstract or certified copy of a judgment was recorded to create a judgment lien before the dwelling was acquired.

(d) "Spouse" does not include a married person following entry of a judgment decreeing legal separation of the parties, unless such married persons reside together in the same dwelling. *(Added by Stats.1982, c. 1364, p. 5163, § 2, operative July 1, 1983. Amended by Stats.1983, c. 155, § 17, eff. June 30, 1983, operative July 1, 1983; Stats.1983, c. 1159, § 11, operative July 1, 1984.)*

Research References

Rutter, Cal. Practice Guide: Enforcing Judgments/Debts Ch. 6E-6, "Homestead" Exemption.

Miller and Starr California Real Estate § 11:6, Instruments Subject to Recording--List of Recordable Documents.

Miller and Starr California Real Estate § 13:1, Overview; Scope and Terminology of Chapter.

Miller and Starr California Real Estate § 13:2, Basis for and Public Policy of the Homestead Exemptions.

Miller and Starr California Real Estate § 13:3, Effect of the Homestead Exemptions; in General.

Miller and Starr California Real Estate § 13:4, Comparison of Declared Homestead and Automatic Exemption.

Miller and Starr California Real Estate § 13:5, Voluntary or Involuntary Sale of Homestead; Reinvestment of Proceeds.

Miller and Starr California Real Estate § 13:7, Destruction of the Homestead; Exemption of Insurance Proceeds.

Miller and Starr California Real Estate § 13:9, Effect of Death of an Owner, or Dissolution of the Marriage or Registered Domestic Partnership.

Miller and Starr California Real Estate § 13:15, Automatic Exemption--In General.

Miller and Starr California Real Estate § 13:16, Residency, Ownership and Use.

Miller and Starr California Real Estate § 13:17, Types of Property that Qualify.

Miller and Starr California Real Estate § 13:18, Termination by Voluntary Sale or Abandonment.

Miller and Starr California Real Estate § 13:21, Marital Homestead; Either Spouse.

Miller and Starr California Real Estate § 13:22, Residency, Ownership and Use.

Miller and Starr California Real Estate § 13:23, Improvements; Amount of Property Included.

Miller and Starr California Real Estate § 13:25, Qualified Property Interests.

Miller and Starr California Real Estate § 13:26, Equitable Interests.

Miller and Starr California Real Estate § 13:27, Declaration on Community and Separate Property.

Miller and Starr California Real Estate § 13:28, Statutory Contents Mandatory.

Miller and Starr California Real Estate § 13:34, Abandonment of the Declared Homestead.

Miller and Starr California Real Estate § 13:38, Amount of Exemption--Classification Based on Age, Disability, and Membership in a Family Unit.

Miller and Starr California Real Estate § 13:40, Amount of Exemption--After Judgment of Dissolution or Legal Separation; Effect of Reconciliation.

Miller and Starr California Real Estate § 13:42, Statutory Proceedings Mandatory.

Miller and Starr California Real Estate § 13:43, Commencement of Proceedings.

Miller and Starr California Real Estate § 13:46, Hearing on the Application; Marshalling of Assets.

Miller and Starr California Real Estate § 13:48, Determination of the Liens Against the Homestead; Priorities.

Miller and Starr California Real Estate § 13:50, Attack on the Validity of the Sale.

Miller and Starr California Real Estate § 13:51, Effect of Debtor's Bankruptcy; Residency Requirement.

Miller and Starr California Real Estate § 13:59, Relationship of Probate Homestead to Declared and Automatic Exemptions.

Miller and Starr California Real Estate § 13:61, Creation of the Probate Homestead.

Miller and Starr California Real Estate § 13:63, Liability of the Probate Homestead.

Miller and Starr California Real Estate § 25B:5, Condominiums--Definition and Description.

Miller and Starr California Real Estate § 25B:7, Community Apartment Projects.

Miller and Starr California Real Estate § 25B:8, Stock Cooperatives.

Miller and Starr California Real Estate § 25B:9, Planned Developments.

Miller and Starr California Real Estate § 32:24, Homestead.

Miller and Starr California Real Estate § 32:26, Claim of Exemption.

Miller and Starr California Real Estate § 32:54, Effect of Homestead Exemption.

14 NO. 3 Miller & Starr, California Real Estate Newsalert 8, Homesteads.

17 NO. 4 Miller & Starr, California Real Estate Newsalert 12, Homesteads.

19 NO. 1 Miller & Starr, California Real Estate Newsalert 16, Homesteads.

20 NO. 6 Miller & Starr, California Real Estate Newsalert 13, Homesteads.

9 Witkin Cal. Proc. 5th Appeal § 185, Orders Dealing With Enforcement.

1 Witkin Cal. Proc. 5th Attorneys § 518, (S 518) False and Misleading Communications.

8 Witkin Cal. Proc. 5th Enforcement of Judgment § 176, (S 176) Time for Determining Exemptions.

8 Witkin Cal. Proc. 5th Enforcement of Judgment § 180, (S 180) in General.

8 Witkin Cal. Proc. 5th Enforcement of Judgment § 215, (S 215) in General.

8 Witkin Cal. Proc. 5th Enforcement of Judgment § 216, (S 216) in General.

8 Witkin Cal. Proc. 5th Enforcement of Judgment § 217, (S 217) Homestead.

8 Witkin Cal. Proc. 5th Enforcement of Judgment § 218, Nature and Scope of Exemption.

8 Witkin Cal. Proc. 5th Enforcement of Judgment § 219, (S 219) in General.

8 Witkin Cal. Proc. 5th Enforcement of Judgment § 222, (S 222) Determination and Order.

8 Witkin Cal. Proc. 5th Enforcement of Judgment § 225, (S 225) Acceleration Clauses and Prepayment Penalties.

8 Witkin Cal. Proc. 5th Enforcement of Judgment § 226, (S 226) Where Debtor is Partial Owner.

8 Witkin Cal. Proc. 5th Enforcement of Judgment § 230, Definitions.

8 Witkin Cal. Proc. 5th Enforcement of Judgment § 232, (S 232) Residence Requirement.

8 Witkin Cal. Proc. 5th Enforcement of Judgment § 236, (S 236) Levy of Execution.

8 Witkin Cal. Proc. 5th Enforcement of Judgment § 240, Regulation of Homestead Filing Services.

6 Witkin Cal. Proc. 5th Provisional Remedies § 87, (S 87) Claim of Real Property Exemption.

12 Witkin, California Summary 10th Real Property § 86, (S 86) Other Statutes.

14 Witkin, California Summary 10th Wills and Probate § 772, (S 772) Liability of Property.

§ 704.720. Extent of homestead exemption; exemption for proceeds of sale, insurance, indemnification or compensation; separate homesteads of debtor and spouse

(a) A homestead is exempt from sale under this division to the extent provided in Section 704.800.

(b) If a homestead is sold under this division or is damaged or destroyed or is acquired for public use, the proceeds of sale or of insurance or other indemnification for damage or destruction of the homestead or the proceeds received as compensation for a homestead acquired for public use are exempt in the amount of the homestead exemption provided in Section 704.730. The proceeds are exempt for a period of six months after the time the proceeds are actually received by the judgment debtor, except that, if a homestead exemption is applied to other property of the judgment debtor or the judgment debtor's spouse during that period, the proceeds thereafter are not exempt.

(c) If the judgment debtor and spouse of the judgment debtor reside in separate homesteads, only the homestead of one of the spouses is exempt and only the proceeds of the exempt homestead are exempt.

(d) If a judgment debtor is not currently residing in the homestead, but his or her separated or former spouse continues to reside in or exercise control over possession of the homestead, that judgment debtor continues to be entitled to an exemption under this article until entry of judgment or other legally enforceable agreement dividing the community property between the judgment debtor and the separated or former spouse, or until a later time period as specified by court order. Nothing in this subdivision shall entitle the judgment debtor to more than one exempt homestead. Notwithstanding subdivision (d) of Section 704.710, for purposes of this article, "spouse" may include a separated or former spouse consistent with this subdivision. *(Added by Stats.1982, c. 1364, p. 5164, § 2, operative July 1, 1983. Amended by Stats.2007, c. 153 (S.B.433), § 1.)*

Research References

Rutter, Cal. Practice Guide: Enforcing Judgments/Debts Ch. 6E-2, Rules Applicable to Exemptions from Enforcement of Money Judgments Generally.

Rutter, Cal. Practice Guide: Enforcing Judgments/Debts Ch. 6E-6, "Homestead" Exemption.

Miller and Starr California Real Estate § 13:1, Overview; Scope and Terminology of Chapter.

Miller and Starr California Real Estate § 13:3, Effect of the Homestead Exemptions; in General.

Miller and Starr California Real Estate § 13:4, Comparison of Declared Homestead and Automatic Exemption.

Miller and Starr California Real Estate § 13:5, Voluntary or Involuntary Sale of Homestead; Reinvestment of Proceeds.

Miller and Starr California Real Estate § 13:7, Destruction of the Homestead; Exemption of Insurance Proceeds.

Miller and Starr California Real Estate § 13:8, Condemnation of the Homestead; Exemption of the Award.

Miller and Starr California Real Estate § 13:9, Effect of Death of an Owner, or Dissolution of the Marriage or Registered Domestic Partnership.

Miller and Starr California Real Estate § 12:60, Disposition on Dissolution.

Miller and Starr California Real Estate § 13:15, Automatic Exemption-- In General.

Miller and Starr California Real Estate § 13:16, Residency, Ownership and Use.

Miller and Starr California Real Estate § 13:18, Termination by Voluntary Sale or Abandonment.

Miller and Starr California Real Estate § 13:19, Amount of the Automatic Exemption.

Miller and Starr California Real Estate § 13:24, Occupation of Residence Used for Production of Income.

Miller and Starr California Real Estate § 13:38, Amount of Exemption-- Classification Based on Age, Disability, and Membership in a Family Unit.

Miller and Starr California Real Estate § 13:48, Determination of the Liens Against the Homestead; Priorities.

Miller and Starr California Real Estate § 13:59, Relationship of Probate Homestead to Declared and Automatic Exemptions.

16 NO. 2 Miller & Starr, California Real Estate Newsalert 12, Homesteads.

18 NO. 4 Miller & Starr, California Real Estate Newsalert 14, Homesteads.

18 NO. 4 Miller & Starr, California Real Estate Newsalert 45, Table of Statutes (Newsalert Vol 18).

8 Witkin Cal. Proc. 5th Enforcement of Judgment § 173, (S 173) Application of Exemptions to Marital Property.

8 Witkin Cal. Proc. 5th Enforcement of Judgment § 174, (S 174) Tracing Exempt Funds.

8 Witkin Cal. Proc. 5th Enforcement of Judgment § 216, (S 216) in General.

8 Witkin Cal. Proc. 5th Enforcement of Judgment § 217, (S 217) Homestead.

8 Witkin Cal. Proc. 5th Enforcement of Judgment § 218, Nature and Scope of Exemption.

8 Witkin, California Summary 10th Constitutional Law § 1272, (S 1272) Authorized Payments and Assistance.

§ 704.730. Amount of homestead exemption

(a) The amount of the homestead exemption is one of the following:

(1) Seventy-five thousand dollars ($75,000) unless the judgment debtor or spouse of the judgment debtor who resides in the homestead is a person described in paragraph (2) or (3).

(2) One hundred thousand dollars ($100,000) if the judgment debtor or spouse of the judgment debtor who resides in the homestead is at the time of the attempted sale of the homestead a member of a family unit, and there is at least one member of the family unit who owns no interest in the homestead or whose only interest in the homestead is a community property interest with the judgment debtor.

(3) One hundred seventy-five thousand dollars ($175,000) if the judgment debtor or spouse of the judgment debtor who resides in the homestead is at the time of the attempted sale of the homestead any one of the following:

(A) A person 65 years of age or older.

(B) A person physically or mentally disabled who as a result of that disability is unable to engage in substantial gainful employment. There is a rebuttable presumption affecting the burden of proof that a person receiving disability insurance benefit payments under Title II or supplemental security income payments under Title XVI of the federal Social Security Act satisfies the requirements of this paragraph as to his or her inability to engage in substantial gainful employment.

(C) A person 55 years of age or older with a gross annual income of not more than twenty-five thousand dollars ($25,000) or, if the judgment debtor is married, a gross annual income, including the gross annual income of the judgment debtor's spouse, of not more than thirty-five thousand dollars ($35,000) and the sale is an involuntary sale.

(b) Notwithstanding any other provision of this section, the combined homestead exemptions of spouses on the same judgment shall not exceed the amount specified in paragraph (2) or (3), whichever is applicable, of subdivision (a), regardless of whether the spouses are jointly obligated on the judgment and regardless of whether the homestead consists of community or separate property or both. Notwithstanding any other provision of this article, if both spouses are entitled to a homestead exemption, the exemption of proceeds of the homestead shall be apportioned between the spouses on the basis of their proportionate interests in the homestead. *(Added by Stats.1982, c. 1364, p. 5165, § 2, operative July 1, 1983. Amended by Stats.1984, c. 454, § 1; Stats.1986, c. 1000, § 1; Stats.1986, c. 1001, § 1; Stats.1988, c. 1168, § 1; Stats.1990, c. 155 (A.B.2562), § 1; Stats.1997, c. 82 (A.B.451), § 1; Stats.2003, c. 64 (S.B.804), § 1; Stats.2009, c. 499 (A.B.1046), § 2; Stats.2012, c. 678 (A.B.929), § 3.)*

Research References

Rutter, Cal. Practice Guide: Enforcing Judgments/Debts Ch. 6B-1, Practical Considerations.

Rutter, Cal. Practice Guide: Enforcing Judgments/Debts Ch. 6E-2, Rules Applicable to Exemptions from Enforcement of Money Judgments Generally.

Rutter, Cal. Practice Guide: Enforcing Judgments/Debts Ch. 6E-6, "Homestead" Exemption.

Miller and Starr California Real Estate § 13:1, Overview; Scope and Terminology of Chapter.

Miller and Starr California Real Estate § 13:3, Effect of the Homestead Exemptions; in General.

Miller and Starr California Real Estate § 13:4, Comparison of Declared Homestead and Automatic Exemption.

Miller and Starr California Real Estate § 13:9, Effect of Death of an Owner, or Dissolution of the Marriage or Registered Domestic Partnership.

Miller and Starr California Real Estate § 13:16, Residency, Ownership and Use.

Miller and Starr California Real Estate § 13:21, Marital Homestead; Either Spouse.

Miller and Starr California Real Estate § 13:37, Amount of Exemption-- In General.

Miller and Starr California Real Estate § 13:38, Amount of Exemption-- Classification Based on Age, Disability, and Membership in a Family Unit.

Miller and Starr California Real Estate § 13:39, Amount of Exemption-- Determination of Amount.

Miller and Starr California Real Estate § 13:41, Amount of Exemption-- Effect of Statutory Increase on Existing Creditors.

Miller and Starr California Real Estate § 13:54, Election of Federal or State Exemptions.

Miller and Starr California Real Estate § 13:59, Relationship of Probate Homestead to Declared and Automatic Exemptions.

Miller and Starr California Real Estate § 32:24, Homestead.

Miller and Starr California Real Estate § 32:26, Claim of Exemption.

Miller and Starr California Real Estate § 32:54, Effect of Homestead Exemption.

14 NO. 4 Miller & Starr, California Real Estate Newsalert 8, Homesteads.

20 NO. 4 Miller & Starr, California Real Estate Newsalert 11, Homesteads.

20 NO. 6 Miller & Starr, California Real Estate Newsalert 13, Homesteads.

22 NO. 6 Miller & Starr, California Real Estate Newsalert 16, Homesteads.

8 Witkin Cal. Proc. 5th Enforcement of Judgment § 173, (S 173) Application of Exemptions to Marital Property.

8 Witkin Cal. Proc. 5th Enforcement of Judgment § 179, (S 179) Periodic Adjustments.

8 Witkin Cal. Proc. 5th Enforcement of Judgment § 218, Nature and Scope of Exemption.

8 Witkin Cal. Proc. 5th Enforcement of Judgment § 232, (S 232) Residence Requirement.

8 Witkin Cal. Proc. 5th Enforcement of Judgment § 234, (S 234) Sale or Other Disposition of Property.

8 Witkin Cal. Proc. 5th Enforcement of Judgment § 235, (S 235) Attachment of Judgment Lien.

8 Witkin Cal. Proc. 5th Enforcement of Judgment § 238, Effect of Death of Owner.

6 Witkin Cal. Proc. 5th Provisional Remedies § 86, (S 86) Homestead.

§ 704.740. Sale of dwelling to enforce money judgment

(a) Except as provided in subdivision (b), the interest of a natural person in a dwelling may not be sold under this division to enforce a money judgment except pursuant to a court order for sale obtained under this article and the dwelling exemption shall be determined under this article.

(b) If the dwelling is personal property or is real property in which the judgment debtor has a leasehold estate with an unexpired term of less than two years at the time of levy:

(1) A court order for sale is not required and the procedures provided in this article relating to the court order for sale do not apply.

(2) An exemption claim shall be made and determined as provided in Article 2 (commencing with Section 703.510). *(Added by Stats.1982, c. 1364, p. 5165, § 2, operative July 1, 1983. Amended by Stats.1984, c. 538, § 26.)*

Law Revision Commission Comments

Subdivision (a) of Section 704.740 supersedes portions of former Civil Code Sections 1245, 1249, and 1250 and former Code of Civil Procedure Section 690.31(c) and (f).

Subdivision (b) incorporates the general procedures for claiming an exemption where the dwelling levied upon is not subject to the delay of sale provision of Section 701.545 (120-day delay of notice of sale of an interest in real property other than a leasehold estate with an unexpired term of less than two years). Under former law, a housetrailer, mobilehome, houseboat, boat, or other waterborne vessel in which the judgment debtor or the judgment debtor's family actually resided could be claimed as exempt in a similar manner. See former Sections 690(a), 690.3, 690.50. This section also applies to claims of exemption for certain mobilehomes that under former law would have been determined as provided in former Section 690.31 (judgment creditor's application for writ of execution on dwelling, including a mobilehome as defined by Health & Safety Code § 18008). See also Health & Saf. Code § 18551(c) (mobilehome installed on foundation system deemed a fixture and a real property improvement). The judgment creditor's instructions to the levying officer must indicate whether property to be levied on is a dwelling. See Section 687.010. [16 Cal.L.Rev.Comm. Reports 1424 (1982)].

Research References

Rutter, Cal. Practice Guide: Enforcing Judgments/Debts Ch. 6D-4, Levy on Specific Property.

Rutter, Cal. Practice Guide: Enforcing Judgments/Debts Ch. 6D-8, Special Requirements for Sale of Real Property Dwellings.

Miller and Starr California Real Estate § 13:1, Overview; Scope and Terminology of Chapter.

Miller and Starr California Real Estate § 13:3, Effect of the Homestead Exemptions; in General.

Miller and Starr California Real Estate § 13:4, Comparison of Declared Homestead and Automatic Exemption.

Miller and Starr California Real Estate § 19:2, Lease as Personal Property or Real Property.

Miller and Starr California Real Estate § 13:12, Waiver of the Homestead Exemption.

Miller and Starr California Real Estate § 13:15, Automatic Exemption-- In General.

Miller and Starr California Real Estate § 13:16, Residency, Ownership and Use.

Miller and Starr California Real Estate § 13:42, Statutory Proceedings Mandatory.

Miller and Starr California Real Estate § 13:43, Commencement of Proceedings.

Miller and Starr California Real Estate § 32:24, Homestead.

Miller and Starr California Real Estate § 32:54, Effect of Homestead Exemption.

Miller and Starr California Real Estate § 32:68, Conditions to Conducting the Sale.

Miller and Starr California Real Estate § 33:13, Preservation and Management--Power to Sell Assets.
Miller and Starr California Real Estate § 33:32, Enforcement Actions After Entry of Judgment.
14 NO. 2 Miller & Starr, California Real Estate Newsalert 12, Homesteads.
19 NO. 3 Miller & Starr, California Real Estate Newsalert 16, Homesteads.
20 NO. 2 Miller & Starr, California Real Estate Newsalert 16, Homesteads.
8 Witkin Cal. Proc. 5th Enforcement of Judgment § 219, (S 219) in General.
8 Witkin Cal. Proc. 5th Enforcement of Judgment § 240, Regulation of Homestead Filing Services.

§ 704.750. Notice of levy; application for order of sale; filing abstract or copy of judgment; fees

(a) Promptly after a dwelling is levied upon (other than a dwelling described in subdivision (b) of Section 704.740), the levying officer shall serve notice on the judgment creditor that the levy has been made and that the property will be released unless the judgment creditor complies with the requirements of this section. Service shall be made personally or by mail. Within 20 days after service of the notice, the judgment creditor shall apply to the court for an order for sale of the dwelling and shall file a copy of the application with the levying officer. If the judgment creditor does not file the copy of the application for an order for sale of the dwelling within the allowed time, the levying officer shall release the dwelling.

(b) If the dwelling is located in a county other than the county where the judgment was entered:

(1) The judgment creditor shall apply to the superior court of the county where the dwelling is located.

(2) The judgment creditor shall file with the application an abstract of judgment in the form prescribed by Section 674 or, in the case of a judgment described in Section 697.320, a certified copy of the judgment.

(3) The judgment creditor shall pay the filing fee for a motion as provided in subdivision (a) of Section 70617 of the Government Code. *(Added by Stats.1982, c. 1364, p. 5165, § 2, operative July 1, 1983. Amended by Stats.2005, c. 75 (A.B.145), § 37, eff. July 19, 2005, operative Jan. 1, 2006.)*

Law Revision Commission Comments

Section 704.750 supersedes the introductory portion and the last two paragraphs of former Civil Code Section 1245 and former Code of Civil Procedure Section 690.31(c). Unlike the former provisions which required the judgment creditor to apply for issuance of a writ of execution, Section 704.750 requires the judgment creditor to apply for an order for sale after the execution levy. This ensures that all writs will be issued out of the court in which the judgment is entered. The 20-day period allowed to apply for the order and to file the copy of the application is extended if the notice of levy is served by mail. See Section 684.120. Notice of the application for an order for sale of the property must be given the levying officer or the dwelling will be released. This requirement applies only to real property dwellings and not to personal property dwellings or to dwellings with less than a two-year leasehold. See Section 704.740(b). [16 Cal.L.Rev.Comm. Reports 1426 (1982)].

Research References

Rutter, Cal. Practice Guide: Enforcing Judgments/Debts Ch. 6D-8, Special Requirements for Sale of Real Property Dwellings.
Miller and Starr California Real Estate § 13:1, Overview; Scope and Terminology of Chapter.
Miller and Starr California Real Estate § 13:39, Amount of Exemption--Determination of Amount.
Miller and Starr California Real Estate § 13:42, Statutory Proceedings Mandatory.
Miller and Starr California Real Estate § 13:43, Commencement of Proceedings.

Miller and Starr California Real Estate § 32:68, Conditions to Conducting the Sale.
8 Witkin Cal. Proc. 5th Enforcement of Judgment § 220, (S 220) Application.

§ 704.760. Application for order for sale; contents

The judgment creditor's application shall be made under oath, shall describe the dwelling, and shall contain all of the following:

(a) A statement whether or not the records of the county tax assessor indicate that there is a current homeowner's exemption or disabled veteran's exemption for the dwelling and the person or persons who claimed any such exemption.

(b) A statement, which may be based on information and belief, whether the dwelling is a homestead and the amount of the homestead exemption, if any, and a statement whether or not the records of the county recorder indicate that a homestead declaration under Article 5 (commencing with Section 704.910) that describes the dwelling has been recorded by the judgment debtor or the spouse of the judgment debtor.

(c) A statement of the amount of any liens or encumbrances on the dwelling, the name of each person having a lien or encumbrance on the dwelling, and the address of such person used by the county recorder for the return of the instrument creating such person's lien or encumbrance after recording. *(Added by Stats.1982, c. 1364, p. 5166, § 2, operative July 1, 1983.)*

Law Revision Commission Comments

Section 704.760 supersedes subdivisions (a)–(c) of former Civil Code Section 1245 and paragraphs (1)–(2) of former Code of Civil Procedure Section 690.31(c). [16 Cal.L.Rev.Comm. Reports 1427 (1982)].

Research References

Rutter, Cal. Practice Guide: Enforcing Judgments/Debts Ch. 6D-8, Special Requirements for Sale of Real Property Dwellings.
Miller and Starr California Real Estate § 13:12, Waiver of the Homestead Exemption.
Miller and Starr California Real Estate § 13:42, Statutory Proceedings Mandatory.
Miller and Starr California Real Estate § 13:44, Contents of the Application for an Order Authorizing Sale.
Miller and Starr California Real Estate § 13:50, Attack on the Validity of the Sale.
Miller and Starr California Real Estate § 32:68, Conditions to Conducting the Sale.
8 Witkin Cal. Proc. 5th Enforcement of Judgment § 220, (S 220) Application.

§ 704.770. Time set for hearing; order to show cause; service of copy of order and documents

(a) Upon the filing of the application by the judgment creditor, the court shall set a time and place for hearing and order the judgment debtor to show cause why an order for sale should not be made in accordance with the application. The time set for hearing shall be not later than 45 days after the application is filed or such later time as the court orders upon a showing of good cause.

(b) Not later than 30 days before the time set for hearing, the judgment creditor shall do both of the following:

(1) Serve on the judgment debtor a copy of the order to show cause, a copy of the application of the judgment creditor, and a copy of the notice of the hearing in the form prescribed by the Judicial Council. Service shall be made personally or by mail.

(2) Personally serve a copy of each document listed in paragraph (1) on an occupant of the dwelling or, if there is no occupant present at the time service is attempted, post a copy of each document in a conspicuous place at the dwelling. *(Added by Stats.1982, c. 1364, p. 5166, § 2, operative July 1, 1983. Amended by Stats.1985, c. 41, § 7.)*

Law Revision Commission Comments

Subdivision (a) of Section 704.770 supersedes the introductory portions of former Civil Code Section 1246 and former Code of Civil Procedure Section 690.31(d). Subdivision (b) supersedes former Civil Code Section 1257 and former Code of Civil Procedure Section 690.31(1). A longer period of notice is required under subdivision (b) if the judgment debtor is served by mail. See Section 684.120. [16 Cal.L.Rev.Comm. Reports 1247 (1982)].

Subdivision(b)(1) of Section 704.770 is amended to delete the reference to a repealed statutory form and substitute a reference to the form prepared by the Judicial Council. [18 Cal.L.Rev.Comm. Reports 361 (1985)].

Research References

Rutter, Cal. Practice Guide: Enforcing Judgments/Debts Ch. 6D-7, Sale and Collection of Property Levied Upon.
Rutter, Cal. Practice Guide: Enforcing Judgments/Debts Ch. 6D-8, Special Requirements for Sale of Real Property Dwellings.
Miller and Starr California Real Estate § 13:45, Service of Application; Notice of Hearing.
Miller and Starr California Real Estate § 13:46, Hearing on the Application; Marshalling of Assets.
Miller and Starr California Real Estate § 13:48, Determination of the Liens Against the Homestead; Priorities.
Miller and Starr California Real Estate § 32:68, Conditions to Conducting the Sale.
8 Witkin Cal. Proc. 5th Enforcement of Judgment § 221, (S 221) Time and Notice of Hearing.

§ 704.780. Burden of proof; determination of exemption and fair market value; order for sale; transmittal of copies of order; appointment of appraiser

(a) The burden of proof at the hearing is determined in the following manner:

(1) If the records of the county tax assessor indicate that there is a current homeowner's exemption or disabled veteran's exemption for the dwelling claimed by the judgment debtor or the judgment debtor's spouse, the judgment creditor has the burden of proof that the dwelling is not a homestead. If the records of the county tax assessor indicate that there is not a current homeowner's exemption or disabled veteran's exemption for the dwelling claimed by the judgment debtor or the judgment debtor's spouse, the burden of proof that the dwelling is a homestead is on the person who claims that the dwelling is a homestead.

(2) If the application states the amount of the homestead exemption, the person claiming the homestead exemption has the burden of proof that the amount of the exemption is other than the amount stated in the application.

(b) The court shall determine whether the dwelling is exempt. If the court determines that the dwelling is exempt, the court shall determine the amount of the homestead exemption and the fair market value of the dwelling. The court shall make an order for sale of the dwelling subject to the homestead exemption, unless the court determines that the sale of the dwelling would not be likely to produce a bid sufficient to satisfy any part of the amount due on the judgment pursuant to Section 704.800. The order for sale of the dwelling subject to the homestead exemption shall specify the amount of the proceeds of the sale that is to be distributed to each person having a lien or encumbrance on the dwelling and shall include the name and address of each such person. Subject to the provisions of this article, the sale is governed by Article 6 (commencing with Section 701.510) of Chapter 3. If the court determines that the dwelling is not exempt, the court shall make an order for sale of the property in the manner provided in Article 6 (commencing with Section 701.510) of Chapter 3.

(c) The court clerk shall transmit a certified copy of the court order (1) to the levying officer and (2) if the court making the order is not the court in which the judgment was entered, to the clerk of the court in which the judgment was entered.

(d) The court may appoint a qualified appraiser to assist the court in determining the fair market value of the dwelling. If the court appoints an appraiser, the court shall fix the compensation of the appraiser in an amount determined by the court to be reasonable, not to exceed similar fees for similar services in the community where the dwelling is located. *(Added by Stats.1982, c. 1364, p. 5166, § 2, operative July 1, 1983. Amended by Stats.1984, c. 538, § 26.5; Stats.1995, c. 196 (S.B.832), § 8, eff. July 31, 1995.)*

Law Revision Commission Comments

Subdivision (b) of Section 704.780 is amended to make clear that the court is not required to order a sale if the proceeds are not likely to be sufficient to satisfy any part of the creditor's judgment. This amendment avoids futile sale orders and is made in response to the court's decision in Abbett Electric Corp. v. Storek, 22 Cal.App.4th 1460, 27 Cal.Rptr.2d 845 (1994). See also Sections 704.800 (minimum bid), 704.850 (distribution of proceeds of sale of homestead). [25 Cal.L.Rev.Comm. Reports 1 (1995)].

Research References

Rutter, Cal. Practice Guide: Enforcing Judgments/Debts Ch. 6D-8, Special Requirements for Sale of Real Property Dwellings.
Miller and Starr California Real Estate § 13:41, Amount of Exemption-- Effect of Statutory Increase on Existing Creditors.
Miller and Starr California Real Estate § 13:42, Statutory Proceedings Mandatory.
Miller and Starr California Real Estate § 13:46, Hearing on the Application; Marshalling of Assets.
Miller and Starr California Real Estate § 13:48, Determination of the Liens Against the Homestead; Priorities.
Miller and Starr California Real Estate § 13:50, Attack on the Validity of the Sale.
Miller and Starr California Real Estate § 32:54, Effect of Homestead Exemption.
Miller and Starr California Real Estate § 32:68, Conditions to Conducting the Sale.
8 Witkin Cal. Proc. 5th Enforcement of Judgment § 222, (S 222) Determination and Order.
8 Witkin Cal. Proc. 5th Enforcement of Judgment § 224, (S 224) Minimum Bid.
8 Witkin Cal. Proc. 5th Enforcement of Judgment § 240, Regulation of Homestead Filing Services.

§ 704.790. Service of copy and notice of order upon failure to appear; proof of service; declaration concerning failure to appear; hearing

(a) This section applies in any case where the court makes an order for sale of the dwelling upon a hearing at which none of the following appeared:

(1) The judgment debtor.

(2) The judgment debtor's spouse.

(3) The attorney for the judgment debtor.

(4) The attorney for the judgment debtor's spouse.

(b) Not later than 10 days after the date of the order for sale, the judgment creditor shall serve a copy of the order and a notice of the order in the form prescribed by the Judicial Council:

(1) Personally or by mail on the judgment debtor and the judgment debtor's spouse.

(2) Personally on an occupant of the dwelling or, if there is no occupant present at the time service is attempted, post a copy of the order and notice in a conspicuous place at the dwelling.

(c) Proof of service and of any posting shall be filed with the court and with the levying officer. If the judgment creditor fails to comply with this subdivision and with subdivision (b) in any case where this section applies, the dwelling may not be sold under the order for sale.

(d) If, within 10 days after service of notice of the order, the judgment debtor or the judgment debtor's spouse files with the levying officer a declaration that the absence of the judgment debtor and the judgment debtor's spouse or the attorney for the judgment debtor or the judgment debtor's spouse from the hearing was due to mistake, inadvertence, surprise, or excusable neglect and that the judgment debtor or spouse of the judgment debtor wishes to assert the homestead exemption, the levying officer shall transmit the declaration forthwith to the court. Upon receipt of the declaration, the court shall set a time and place for hearing to determine whether the determinations of the court should be modified. The time set for hearing shall be not later than 20 days after receipt of the declaration. The court clerk shall cause notice of the hearing promptly to be given to the parties. *(Added by Stats.1982, c. 1364, p. 5167, § 2, operative July 1, 1983. Amended by Stats.1985, c. 41, § 8.)*

Law Revision Commission Comments

Subdivision (b) of Section 704.790 is amended to delete the reference to a repealed statutory form and substitute a reference to the form prepared by the Judicial Council. [18 Cal.L.Rev.Comm. Reports 361 (1985)].

Subdivision (a) of Section 704.790 supersedes former Civil Code Sections 1251 and 1257 and former Code of Civil Procedure Section 690.31(g) and (*l*). Subdivision (d) supersedes former Civil Code Section 1252 and former Code of Civil Procedure Section 690.31(h). (16 Cal.L.Rev.Comm. Reports 1430 (1986)].

Research References

Rutter, Cal. Practice Guide: Enforcing Judgments/Debts Ch. 6D-8, Special Requirements for Sale of Real Property Dwellings.
Miller and Starr California Real Estate § 13:1, Overview; Scope and Terminology of Chapter.
Miller and Starr California Real Estate § 13:46, Hearing on the Application; Marshalling of Assets.
Miller and Starr California Real Estate § 13:48, Determination of the Liens Against the Homestead; Priorities.
Miller and Starr California Real Estate § 32:68, Conditions to Conducting the Sale.
8 Witkin Cal. Proc. 5th Enforcement of Judgment § 147, Sale of Real Property.
8 Witkin Cal. Proc. 5th Enforcement of Judgment § 223, (S 223) Where Debtor Defaults.

§ 704.800. Insufficient sale bids

(a) If no bid is received at a sale of a homestead pursuant to a court order for sale that exceeds the amount of the homestead exemption plus any additional amount necessary to satisfy all liens and encumbrances on the property, including but not limited to any attachment or judgment lien, the homestead shall not be sold and shall be released and is not thereafter subject to a court order for sale upon subsequent application by the same judgment creditor for a period of one year.

(b) If no bid is received at the sale of a homestead pursuant to a court order for sale that is 90 percent or more of the fair market value determined pursuant to Section 704.780, the homestead shall not be sold unless the court, upon motion of the judgment creditor, does one of the following:

(1) Grants permission to accept the highest bid that exceeds the amount of the minimum bid required by subdivision (a).

(2) Makes a new order for sale of the homestead. *(Added by Stats.1982, c. 1364, p. 5168, § 2, operative July 1, 1983.)*

Research References

Rutter, Cal. Practice Guide: Enforcing Judgments/Debts Ch. 4-A, A. Attachment.
Rutter, Cal. Practice Guide: Enforcing Judgments/Debts Ch. 5-D, D. Involuntary Bankruptcy.
Rutter, Cal. Practice Guide: Enforcing Judgments/Debts Ch. 6D-7, Sale and Collection of Property Levied Upon.

Rutter, Cal. Practice Guide: Enforcing Judgments/Debts Ch. 6D-8, Special Requirements for Sale of Real Property Dwellings.
Rutter, Cal. Practice Guide: Enforcing Judgments/Debts Ch. 6E-6, "Homestead" Exemption.
Miller and Starr California Real Estate § 13:12, Waiver of the Homestead Exemption.
Miller and Starr California Real Estate § 13:15, Automatic Exemption--In General.
Miller and Starr California Real Estate § 13:19, Amount of the Automatic Exemption.
Miller and Starr California Real Estate § 13:48, Determination of the Liens Against the Homestead; Priorities.
Miller and Starr California Real Estate § 13:49, Conduct of the Sale; Distribution of Proceeds.
Miller and Starr California Real Estate § 32:24, Homestead.
Miller and Starr California Real Estate § 32:54, Effect of Homestead Exemption.
Miller and Starr California Real Estate § 32:68, Conditions to Conducting the Sale.
Miller and Starr California Real Estate § 10:226, The Judicial Sale.
8 Witkin Cal. Proc. 5th Enforcement of Judgment § 153, in General.
8 Witkin Cal. Proc. 5th Enforcement of Judgment § 218, Nature and Scope of Exemption.
8 Witkin Cal. Proc. 5th Enforcement of Judgment § 222, (S 222) Determination and Order.
8 Witkin Cal. Proc. 5th Enforcement of Judgment § 224, (S 224) Minimum Bid.
8 Witkin Cal. Proc. 5th Enforcement of Judgment § 228, (S 228) Costs, Extensions, and Appeal.
8 Witkin Cal. Proc. 5th Enforcement of Judgment § 235, (S 235) Attachment of Judgment Lien.
8 Witkin Cal. Proc. 5th Enforcement of Judgment § 497, Requirement of Injury to Creditor.
6 Witkin Cal. Proc. 5th Provisional Remedies § 86, (S 86) Homestead.

§ 704.810. Homestead subject to lien or encumbrance

Levy on a homestead that is subject to a lien or encumbrance is not by itself grounds for acceleration of the obligation secured by the lien or encumbrance, notwithstanding any provision of the obligation, lien, or encumbrance and if the homestead is sold pursuant to court order under this article the amount payable to satisfy a lien or encumbrance shall not include any penalty for prepayment. *(Added by Stats.1982, c. 1364, p. 5168, § 2, operative July 1, 1983.)*

Research References

Rutter, Cal. Practice Guide: Enforcing Judgments/Debts Ch. 6D-8, Special Requirements for Sale of Real Property Dwellings.
Rutter, Cal. Practice Guide: Enforcing Judgments/Debts Ch. 6E-6, "Homestead" Exemption.
Miller and Starr California Real Estate § 13:5, Voluntary or Involuntary Sale of Homestead; Reinvestment of Proceeds.
Miller and Starr California Real Estate § 10:97, Prepayment Fee--Obligation for Payment.
Miller and Starr California Real Estate § 32:68, Conditions to Conducting the Sale.
Miller and Starr California Real Estate § 10:109, Acceleration on Further Encumbrance; "Due on Encumbrance" Clause.
8 Witkin Cal. Proc. 5th Enforcement of Judgment § 155, Default of Bidder.
8 Witkin Cal. Proc. 5th Enforcement of Judgment § 225, (S 225) Acceleration Clauses and Prepayment Penalties.

§ 704.820. Joint tenancy, tenancy in common or interest less than fee

If the dwelling is owned by the judgment debtor as a joint tenant or tenant in common or if the interest of the judgment debtor in the dwelling is a leasehold or other interest less than a fee interest:

(a) At an execution sale of a dwelling, the interest of the judgment debtor in the dwelling and not the dwelling shall be sold. If there is more than one judgment debtor of the judgment creditor, the interests of the judgment debtors in the dwelling shall be sold together and each of the judgment debtors entitled to a homestead exemption is entitled to apply his or her exemption to his or her own interest.

(b) For the purposes of this section, all references in this article to the "dwelling" or "homestead" are deemed to be references to the interest of the judgment debtor in the dwelling or homestead. *(Added by Stats.1982, c. 1364, p. 5168, § 2, operative July 1, 1983.)*

Law Revision Commission Comments

Section 704.820 implements the intent of this article not to restrict the interest of the judgment debtor for which a homestead exemption is available. A homestead exemption is available to a judgment debtor regardless of whether the judgment debtor's interest is a fee, leasehold, or lesser interest. See Section 704.710(a) and Comment thereto. If the judgment debtor's interest is an interest in community property, the whole community interest is subject to enforcement of the judgment. See Section 695.020 (liability of community property). [16 Cal.L.Rev.Comm. Reports 1431 (1982)].

Research References

Rutter, Cal. Practice Guide: Enforcing Judgments/Debts Ch. 5-D, D. Involuntary Bankruptcy.
Rutter, Cal. Practice Guide: Enforcing Judgments/Debts Ch. 6D-8, Special Requirements for Sale of Real Property Dwellings.
Rutter, Cal. Practice Guide: Enforcing Judgments/Debts Ch. 6E-6, "Homestead" Exemption.
Miller and Starr California Real Estate § 13:16, Residency, Ownership and Use.
Miller and Starr California Real Estate § 13:25, Qualified Property Interests.
Miller and Starr California Real Estate § 13:47, Sale of an Undivided Interest.
Miller and Starr California Real Estate § 13:57, Sale of Homestead in Bankruptcy.
8 Witkin Cal. Proc. 5th Enforcement of Judgment § 226, (S 226) Where Debtor is Partial Owner.

§ 704.830. Written notice of extension; appeal

The provisions of Sections 703.590 and 703.600 apply to proceedings under this article. *(Added by Stats.1982, c. 1364, p. 5169, § 2, operative July 1, 1983.)*

Law Revision Commission Comments

Section 704.830 continues the substance of former Civil Code Sections 1258 (portion incorporating Code of Civil Procedure Section 690.50(*l*)) and 1259.1, and former Code of Civil Procedure Section 690.31(m) (portion incorporating Code of Civil Procedure Section 690.50(*l*)) and (n). It incorporates the provisions in the general exemption procedure pertaining to extensions of time and appeals. [16 Cal.L.Rev.Comm. Reports 1432 (1982)].

Research References

Miller and Starr California Real Estate § 13:46, Hearing on the Application; Marshalling of Assets.
8 Witkin Cal. Proc. 5th Enforcement of Judgment § 228, (S 228) Costs, Extensions, and Appeal.

§ 704.840. Costs

(a) Except as provided in subdivision (b), the judgment creditor is entitled to recover reasonable costs incurred in a proceeding under this article.

(b) If no bid is received at a sale of a homestead pursuant to a court order for sale that exceeds the amount of the homestead exemption plus any additional amount necessary to satisfy all liens and encumbrances on the property, the judgment creditor is not entitled to recover costs incurred in a proceeding under this article or costs of sale. *(Added by Stats.1982, c. 1364, p. 5169, § 2, operative July 1, 1983.)*

Law Revision Commission Comments

Section 704.840 supersedes former Civil Code Section 1259. [16 Cal.L.Rev.Comm. Reports 1432 (1982)].

Research References

Rutter, Cal. Practice Guide: Enforcing Judgments/Debts Ch. 6D-8, Special Requirements for Sale of Real Property Dwellings.
Miller and Starr California Real Estate § 13:3, Effect of the Homestead Exemptions; in General.
Miller and Starr California Real Estate § 13:43, Commencement of Proceedings.
Miller and Starr California Real Estate § 13:49, Conduct of the Sale; Distribution of Proceeds.
Miller and Starr California Real Estate § 32:24, Homestead.
8 Witkin Cal. Proc. 5th Enforcement of Judgment § 228, (S 228) Costs, Extensions, and Appeal.

§ 704.850. Distribution of proceeds of sale

(a) The levying officer shall distribute the proceeds of sale of a homestead in the following order:

(1) To the discharge of all liens and encumbrances, if any, on the property.

(2) To the judgment debtor in the amount of any applicable exemption of proceeds pursuant to Section 704.720.

(3) To the levying officer for the reimbursement of the levying officer's costs for which an advance has not been made.

(4) To the judgment creditor to satisfy the following:

(A) First, costs and interest accruing after issuance of the writ pursuant to which the sale is conducted.

(B) Second, the amount due on the judgment with costs and interest, as entered on the writ.

(5) To the judgment debtor in the amount remaining.

(b) Sections 701.820 and 701.830 apply to distribution of proceeds under this section. *(Added by Stats.1982, c. 1364, p. 5169, § 2, operative July 1, 1983.)*

Research References

Rutter, Cal. Practice Guide: Enforcing Judgments/Debts Ch. 6D-4, Levy on Specific Property.
Rutter, Cal. Practice Guide: Enforcing Judgments/Debts Ch. 6D-7, Sale and Collection of Property Levied Upon.
Rutter, Cal. Practice Guide: Enforcing Judgments/Debts Ch. 6D-8, Special Requirements for Sale of Real Property Dwellings.
Rutter, Cal. Practice Guide: Enforcing Judgments/Debts Ch. 6E-6, "Homestead" Exemption.
Miller and Starr California Real Estate § 11:6, Instruments Subject to Recording--List of Recordable Documents.
Miller and Starr California Real Estate § 13:1, Overview; Scope and Terminology of Chapter.
Miller and Starr California Real Estate § 13:2, Basis for and Public Policy of the Homestead Exemptions.
Miller and Starr California Real Estate § 13:3, Effect of the Homestead Exemptions; in General.
Miller and Starr California Real Estate § 13:4, Comparison of Declared Homestead and Automatic Exemption.
Miller and Starr California Real Estate § 13:5, Voluntary or Involuntary Sale of Homestead; Reinvestment of Proceeds.
Miller and Starr California Real Estate § 13:12, Waiver of the Homestead Exemption.
Miller and Starr California Real Estate § 13:16, Residency, Ownership and Use.
Miller and Starr California Real Estate § 13:19, Amount of the Automatic Exemption.
Miller and Starr California Real Estate § 13:42, Statutory Proceedings Mandatory.
Miller and Starr California Real Estate § 13:47, Sale of an Undivided Interest.
Miller and Starr California Real Estate § 13:48, Determination of the Liens Against the Homestead; Priorities.

Miller and Starr California Real Estate § 13:49, Conduct of the Sale; Distribution of Proceeds.

8 Witkin Cal. Proc. 5th Enforcement of Judgment § 155, Default of Bidder.

8 Witkin Cal. Proc. 5th Enforcement of Judgment § 158, (S 158) Order of Distribution.

8 Witkin Cal. Proc. 5th Enforcement of Judgment § 227, (S 227) Distribution of Proceeds.

ARTICLE 5. DECLARED HOMESTEADS

§ 704.910. Definitions

As used in this article:

(a) "Declared homestead" means the dwelling described in a homestead declaration.

(b) "Declared homestead owner" includes both of the following:

(1) The owner of an interest in the declared homestead who is named as a declared homestead owner in a homestead declaration recorded pursuant to this article.

(2) The declarant named in a declaration of homestead recorded prior to July 1, 1983, pursuant to former Title 5 (commencing with Section 1237) of Part 4 of Division 2 of the Civil Code and the spouse of such declarant.

(c) "Dwelling" means any interest in real property (whether present or future, vested or contingent, legal or equitable) that is a "dwelling" as defined in Section 704.710, but does not include a leasehold estate with an unexpired term of less than two years or the interest of the beneficiary of a trust.

(d) "Homestead declaration" includes both of the following:

(1) A homestead declaration recorded pursuant to this article.

(2) A declaration of homestead recorded prior to July 1, 1983, pursuant to former Title 5 (commencing with former Section 1237) of Part 4 of Division 2 of the Civil Code.

(e) "Spouse" means a "spouse" as defined in Section 704.710. *(Added by Stats.1982, c. 1364, p. 5169, § 2, operative July 1, 1983.)*

Research References

Rutter, Cal. Practice Guide: Enforcing Judgments/Debts Ch. 6E-6, "Homestead" Exemption.

Miller and Starr California Real Estate § 13:1, Overview; Scope and Terminology of Chapter.

Miller and Starr California Real Estate § 13:4, Comparison of Declared Homestead and Automatic Exemption.

Miller and Starr California Real Estate § 19:2, Lease as Personal Property or Real Property.

Miller and Starr California Real Estate § 13:14, Regulation of Homestead Declaration Filing Services.

Miller and Starr California Real Estate § 13:20, Who Can Declare a Homestead.

Miller and Starr California Real Estate § 13:21, Marital Homestead; Either Spouse.

Miller and Starr California Real Estate § 13:22, Residency, Ownership and Use.

Miller and Starr California Real Estate § 13:25, Qualified Property Interests.

Miller and Starr California Real Estate § 13:26, Equitable Interests.

Miller and Starr California Real Estate § 13:27, Declaration on Community and Separate Property.

Miller and Starr California Real Estate § 13:28, Statutory Contents Mandatory.

Miller and Starr California Real Estate § 13:36, Effect of a Conveyance or Encumbrance of the Declared Homestead.

Miller and Starr California Real Estate § 13:39, Amount of Exemption-- Determination of Amount.

Miller and Starr California Real Estate § 13:40, Amount of Exemption-- After Judgment of Dissolution or Legal Separation; Effect of Reconciliation.

Miller and Starr California Real Estate § 13:59, Relationship of Probate Homestead to Declared and Automatic Exemptions.

8 Witkin Cal. Proc. 5th Enforcement of Judgment § 18, (S 18) in General.

8 Witkin Cal. Proc. 5th Enforcement of Judgment § 215, (S 215) in General.

8 Witkin Cal. Proc. 5th Enforcement of Judgment § 220, (S 220) Application.

8 Witkin Cal. Proc. 5th Enforcement of Judgment § 229, Development of Law.

8 Witkin Cal. Proc. 5th Enforcement of Judgment § 230, Definitions.

8 Witkin Cal. Proc. 5th Enforcement of Judgment § 231, (S 231) Recording Declaration.

6 Witkin Cal. Proc. 5th Provisional Remedies § 86, (S 86) Homestead.

12 Witkin, California Summary 10th Real Property § 53, (S 53) Homestead.

12 Witkin, California Summary 10th Real Property § 86, (S 86) Other Statutes.

14 Witkin, California Summary 10th Wills and Probate § 768, (S 768) Relationship Between Probate Homestead and Declared Homestead.

§ 704.920. Selection of declared homestead

A dwelling in which an owner or spouse of an owner resides may be selected as a declared homestead pursuant to this article by recording a homestead declaration in the office of the county recorder of the county where the dwelling is located. From and after the time of recording, the dwelling is a declared homestead for the purposes of this article. *(Added by Stats.1982, c. 1364, p. 5170, § 2, operative July 1, 1983.)*

Research References

Rutter, Cal. Practice Guide: Enforcing Judgments/Debts Ch. 6E-6, "Homestead" Exemption.

Miller and Starr California Real Estate § 11:6, Instruments Subject to Recording--List of Recordable Documents.

Miller and Starr California Real Estate § 13:1, Overview; Scope and Terminology of Chapter.

Miller and Starr California Real Estate § 13:4, Comparison of Declared Homestead and Automatic Exemption.

Miller and Starr California Real Estate § 13:20, Who Can Declare a Homestead.

Miller and Starr California Real Estate § 13:21, Marital Homestead; Either Spouse.

Miller and Starr California Real Estate § 13:22, Residency, Ownership and Use.

Miller and Starr California Real Estate § 13:25, Qualified Property Interests.

Miller and Starr California Real Estate § 13:26, Equitable Interests.

Miller and Starr California Real Estate § 13:28, Statutory Contents Mandatory.

Miller and Starr California Real Estate § 13:30, Required Contents of the Declaration--Statement of Residence.

Miller and Starr California Real Estate § 13:33, Recordation.

Miller and Starr California Real Estate § 13:34, Abandonment of the Declared Homestead.

Miller and Starr California Real Estate § 13:38, Amount of Exemption-- Classification Based on Age, Disability, and Membership in a Family Unit.

Miller and Starr California Real Estate § 13:40, Amount of Exemption-- After Judgment of Dissolution or Legal Separation; Effect of Reconciliation.

Miller and Starr California Real Estate § 13:59, Relationship of Probate Homestead to Declared and Automatic Exemptions.

8 Witkin Cal. Proc. 5th Enforcement of Judgment § 231, (S 231) Recording Declaration.

8 Witkin Cal. Proc. 5th Enforcement of Judgment § 232, (S 232) Residence Requirement.

12 Witkin, California Summary 10th Real Property § 53, (S 53) Homestead.

§ 704.930. Homestead declaration; contents; execution and acknowledgment; statement of facts and authority

(a) A homestead declaration recorded pursuant to this article shall contain all of the following:

(1) The name of the declared homestead owner. A husband and wife both may be named as declared homestead owners in the same homestead declaration if each owns an interest in the dwelling selected as the declared homestead.

(2) A description of the declared homestead.

(3) A statement that the declared homestead is the principal dwelling of the declared homestead owner or such person's spouse, and that the declared homestead owner or such person's spouse resides in the declared homestead on the date the homestead declaration is recorded.

(b) The homestead declaration shall be executed and acknowledged in the manner of an acknowledgment of a conveyance of real property by at least one of the following persons:

(1) The declared homestead owner.

(2) The spouse of the declared homestead owner.

(3) The guardian or conservator of the person or estate of either of the persons listed in paragraph (1) or (2). The guardian or conservator may execute, acknowledge, and record a homestead declaration without the need to obtain court authorization.

(4) A person acting under a power of attorney or otherwise authorized to act on behalf of a person listed in paragraph (1) or (2).

(c) The homestead declaration shall include a statement that the facts stated in the homestead declaration are known to be true as of the personal knowledge of the person executing and acknowledging the homestead declaration. If the homestead declaration is executed and acknowledged by a person listed in paragraph (3) or (4) of subdivision (b), it shall also contain a statement that the person has authority to so act on behalf of the declared homestead owner or the spouse of the declared homestead owner and the source of the person's authority. *(Added by Stats.1982, c. 1364, p. 5170, § 2, operative July 1, 1983. Amended by Stats.1983, c. 155, § 18, eff. June 30, 1983, operative July 1, 1983.)*

Research References

Rutter, Cal. Practice Guide: Enforcing Judgments/Debts Ch. 6E-6, "Homestead" Exemption.

Miller and Starr California Real Estate § 13:4, Comparison of Declared Homestead and Automatic Exemption.

Miller and Starr California Real Estate § 11:23, Purpose and Effect; Required for Recordation.

Miller and Starr California Real Estate § 13:20, Who Can Declare a Homestead.

Miller and Starr California Real Estate § 13:21, Marital Homestead; Either Spouse.

Miller and Starr California Real Estate § 13:22, Residency, Ownership and Use.

Miller and Starr California Real Estate § 13:25, Qualified Property Interests.

Miller and Starr California Real Estate § 13:28, Statutory Contents Mandatory.

Miller and Starr California Real Estate § 13:29, Required Contents of the Declaration--In General.

Miller and Starr California Real Estate § 13:30, Required Contents of the Declaration--Statement of Residence.

Miller and Starr California Real Estate § 13:31, Required Contents of the Declaration--Property Description.

Miller and Starr California Real Estate § 13:32, Execution and Acknowledgment.

8 Witkin Cal. Proc. 5th Enforcement of Judgment § 230, Definitions.

8 Witkin Cal. Proc. 5th Enforcement of Judgment § 231, (S 231) Recording Declaration.

8 Witkin Cal. Proc. 5th Enforcement of Judgment § 232, (S 232) Residence Requirement.

§ 704.940. Declaration as restriction or limitation on right to convey or encumber; evidentiary value of declaration

A homestead declaration does not restrict or limit any right to convey or encumber the declared homestead. A homestead declaration, when properly recorded, is prima facie evidence of the facts therein stated, and conclusive evidence thereof in favor of a purchaser or encumbrancer in good faith and for a valuable consideration. *(Added by Stats.1982, c. 1364, p. 5170, § 2, operative July 1, 1983.)*

Research References

Rutter, Cal. Practice Guide: Enforcing Judgments/Debts Ch. 6E-6, "Homestead" Exemption.

Miller and Starr California Real Estate § 13:3, Effect of the Homestead Exemptions; in General.

Miller and Starr California Real Estate § 13:5, Voluntary or Involuntary Sale of Homestead; Reinvestment of Proceeds.

Miller and Starr California Real Estate § 13:6, Proceeds from a Refinance of the Homestead.

Miller and Starr California Real Estate § 13:12, Waiver of the Homestead Exemption.

Miller and Starr California Real Estate § 13:22, Residency, Ownership and Use.

Miller and Starr California Real Estate § 13:25, Qualified Property Interests.

Miller and Starr California Real Estate § 13:28, Statutory Contents Mandatory.

Miller and Starr California Real Estate § 13:46, Hearing on the Application; Marshalling of Assets.

Miller and Starr California Real Estate § 13:48, Determination of the Liens Against the Homestead; Priorities.

8 Witkin Cal. Proc. 5th Enforcement of Judgment § 231, (S 231) Recording Declaration.

8 Witkin Cal. Proc. 5th Enforcement of Judgment § 232, (S 232) Residence Requirement.

8 Witkin Cal. Proc. 5th Enforcement of Judgment § 234, (S 234) Sale or Other Disposition of Property.

8 Witkin Cal. Proc. 5th Enforcement of Judgment § 235, (S 235) Attachment of Judgment Lien.

§ 704.950. Judgment lien on real property; attachment to declared homestead

(a) Except as provided in subdivisions (b) and (c), a judgment lien on real property created pursuant to Article 2 (commencing with Section 697.310) of Chapter 2 does not attach to a declared homestead if both of the following requirements are satisfied:

(1) A homestead declaration describing the declared homestead was recorded prior to the time the abstract or certified copy of the judgment was recorded to create the judgment lien.

(2) The homestead declaration names the judgment debtor or the spouse of the judgment debtor as a declared homestead owner.

(b) This section does not apply to a judgment lien created under Section 697.320 by recording a certified copy of a judgment for child, family, or spousal support.

(c) A judgment lien attaches to a declared homestead in the amount of any surplus over the total of the following:

(1) All liens and encumbrances on the declared homestead at the time the abstract of judgment or certified copy of the judgment is recorded to create the judgment lien.

(2) The homestead exemption set forth in Section 704.730. *(Added by Stats.1982, c. 1364, p. 5171, § 2, operative July 1, 1983. Amended by Stats.1992, c. 163 (A.B.2641), § 44, operative Jan. 1, 1994.)*

Law Revision Commission Comments

Subdivision (b) of Section 704.950 is amended to make clear that the section applies to a judgment for family support. See Fam. Code § 4501 (family support order enforceable in same manner and to same extent as child support order). See also Section 680.145 ("child support" includes family support). [22 Cal.L.Rev.Comm.Reports 1 (1992)].

Research References

Rutter, Cal. Practice Guide: Enforcing Judgments/Debts Ch. 6B-2, Interests Subject to Judgment Lien.
Rutter, Cal. Practice Guide: Enforcing Judgments/Debts Ch. 6E-6, "Homestead" Exemption.
Miller and Starr California Real Estate § 13:3, Effect of the Homestead Exemptions; in General.
Miller and Starr California Real Estate § 13:4, Comparison of Declared Homestead and Automatic Exemption.
Miller and Starr California Real Estate § 13:9, Effect of Death of an Owner, or Dissolution of the Marriage or Registered Domestic Partnership.
Miller and Starr California Real Estate § 13:37, Amount of Exemption-- In General.
Miller and Starr California Real Estate § 13:38, Amount of Exemption-- Classification Based on Age, Disability, and Membership in a Family Unit.
Miller and Starr California Real Estate § 13:39, Amount of Exemption-- Determination of Amount.
Miller and Starr California Real Estate § 13:48, Determination of the Liens Against the Homestead; Priorities.
Miller and Starr California Real Estate § 32:54, Effect of Homestead Exemption.
16 NO. 2 Miller & Starr, California Real Estate Newsalert 12, Homesteads.
8 Witkin Cal. Proc. 5th Enforcement of Judgment § 74, (S 74) Interests Subject to Lien.
8 Witkin Cal. Proc. 5th Enforcement of Judgment § 235, (S 235) Attachment of Judgment Lien.

§ 704.960. Exemption of proceeds from voluntary sale; investment in new dwelling and homestead declaration thereon

(a) If a declared homestead is voluntarily sold, the proceeds of sale are exempt in the amount provided by Section 704.730 for a period of six months after the date of sale.

(b) If the proceeds of a declared homestead are invested in a new dwelling within six months after the date of a voluntary sale or within six months after proceeds of an execution sale or of insurance or other indemnification for damage or destruction are received, the new dwelling may be selected as a declared homestead by recording a homestead declaration within the applicable six-month period. In such case, the homestead declaration has the same effect as if it had been recorded at the time the prior homestead declaration was recorded. *(Added by Stats.1982, c. 1364, p. 5171, § 2, operative July 1, 1983.)*

Research References

Rutter, Cal. Practice Guide: Enforcing Judgments/Debts Ch. 6E-2, Rules Applicable to Exemptions from Enforcement of Money Judgments Generally.
Rutter, Cal. Practice Guide: Enforcing Judgments/Debts Ch. 6E-6, "Homestead" Exemption.
Miller and Starr California Real Estate § 13:1, Overview; Scope and Terminology of Chapter.
Miller and Starr California Real Estate § 13:3, Effect of the Homestead Exemptions; in General.
Miller and Starr California Real Estate § 13:4, Comparison of Declared Homestead and Automatic Exemption.
Miller and Starr California Real Estate § 13:5, Voluntary or Involuntary Sale of Homestead; Reinvestment of Proceeds.
Miller and Starr California Real Estate § 13:7, Destruction of the Homestead; Exemption of Insurance Proceeds.
Miller and Starr California Real Estate § 13:8, Condemnation of the Homestead; Exemption of the Award.
Miller and Starr California Real Estate § 13:24, Occupation of Residence Used for Production of Income.
Miller and Starr California Real Estate § 13:36, Effect of a Conveyance or Encumbrance of the Declared Homestead.
Miller and Starr California Real Estate § 13:37, Amount of Exemption-- In General.
Miller and Starr California Real Estate § 13:38, Amount of Exemption-- Classification Based on Age, Disability, and Membership in a Family Unit.
Miller and Starr California Real Estate § 13:39, Amount of Exemption-- Determination of Amount.
8 Witkin Cal. Proc. 5th Enforcement of Judgment § 174, (S 174) Tracing Exempt Funds.
8 Witkin Cal. Proc. 5th Enforcement of Judgment § 218, Nature and Scope of Exemption.
8 Witkin Cal. Proc. 5th Enforcement of Judgment § 234, (S 234) Sale or Other Disposition of Property.
8 Witkin Cal. Proc. 5th Enforcement of Judgment § 235, (S 235) Attachment of Judgment Lien.

§ 704.965. Increase in amount of homestead exemption pursuant to § 704.730; effect on prior recorded homestead declaration

If a homestead declaration is recorded prior to the operative date of an amendment to Section 704.730 which increases the amount of the homestead exemption, the amount of the exemption for the purposes of subdivision (c) of Section 704.950 and Section 704.960 is the increased amount, except that, if the judgment creditor obtained a lien on the declared homestead prior to the operative date of the amendment to Section 704.730, the exemption for the purposes of subdivision (c) of Section 704.950 and Section 704.960 shall be determined as if that amendment to Section 704.730 had not been enacted. *(Added by Stats.1984, c. 454, § 2.)*

Research References

Rutter, Cal. Practice Guide: Enforcing Judgments/Debts Ch. 6B-1, Practical Considerations.
Rutter, Cal. Practice Guide: Enforcing Judgments/Debts Ch. 6E-1, Introduction.
Rutter, Cal. Practice Guide: Enforcing Judgments/Debts Ch. 6E-6, "Homestead" Exemption.
Miller and Starr California Real Estate § 13:37, Amount of Exemption-- In General.
Miller and Starr California Real Estate § 13:41, Amount of Exemption-- Effect of Statutory Increase on Existing Creditors.
8 Witkin Cal. Proc. 5th Enforcement of Judgment § 234, (S 234) Sale or Other Disposition of Property.
8 Witkin Cal. Proc. 5th Enforcement of Judgment § 235, (S 235) Attachment of Judgment Lien.

§ 704.970. Levy pursuant to writ of execution

Whether or not a homestead declaration has been recorded:

(a) Nothing in this article affects the right of levy pursuant to a writ of execution.

(b) Any levy pursuant to a writ of execution on a dwelling (as defined in Section 704.710) and the sale pursuant thereto shall be made in compliance with Article 4 (commencing with Section 704.710) and the judgment debtor and the judgment creditor shall have all the rights and benefits provided by that article. *(Added by Stats.1982, c. 1364, p. 5171, § 2, operative July 1, 1983.)*

Research References

Rutter, Cal. Practice Guide: Enforcing Judgments/Debts Ch. 6E-6, "Homestead" Exemption.
Miller and Starr California Real Estate § 13:4, Comparison of Declared Homestead and Automatic Exemption.
Miller and Starr California Real Estate § 13:20, Who Can Declare a Homestead.
Miller and Starr California Real Estate § 13:25, Qualified Property Interests.
Miller and Starr California Real Estate § 13:42, Statutory Proceedings Mandatory.
Miller and Starr California Real Estate § 13:43, Commencement of Proceedings.
Miller and Starr California Real Estate § 13:50, Attack on the Validity of the Sale.
8 Witkin Cal. Proc. 5th Enforcement of Judgment § 236, (S 236) Levy of Execution.
8 Witkin Cal. Proc. 5th Enforcement of Judgment § 240, Regulation of Homestead Filing Services.

§ 704.980. Declaration of abandonment

(a) A declared homestead may be abandoned by a declaration of abandonment under this section, whether the homestead declaration was recorded pursuant to this article or pursuant to former Title 5 (commencing with former Section 1237) of Part 4 of Division 2 of the Civil Code.

(b) A declaration of abandonment shall be executed and acknowledged in the manner of an acknowledgment of a conveyance of real property. It shall be executed and acknowledged by a declared homestead owner or by a person authorized to act on behalf of a declared homestead owner. If it is executed and acknowledged by a person authorized to act on behalf of a declared homestead owner, the declaration shall contain a statement that the person has authority to act on behalf of the declared homestead owner and the source of the person's authority.

(c) The declaration of abandonment does not affect the declared homestead of any person other than the declared homestead owner named in the declaration of abandonment. *(Added by Stats.1982, c. 1364, p. 5171, § 2, operative July 1, 1983.)*

Research References

Rutter, Cal. Practice Guide: Enforcing Judgments/Debts Ch. 6E-6, "Homestead" Exemption.
Miller and Starr California Real Estate § 11:6, Instruments Subject to Recording--List of Recordable Documents.
Miller and Starr California Real Estate § 13:4, Comparison of Declared Homestead and Automatic Exemption.
Miller and Starr California Real Estate § 11:23, Purpose and Effect; Required for Recordation.
Miller and Starr California Real Estate § 13:22, Residency, Ownership and Use.
Miller and Starr California Real Estate § 13:34, Abandonment of the Declared Homestead.
Miller and Starr California Real Estate § 13:36, Effect of a Conveyance or Encumbrance of the Declared Homestead.
8 Witkin Cal. Proc. 5th Enforcement of Judgment § 239, Abandonment.

§ 704.990. Abandonment by operation of law; prior valid declaration

(a) A declared homestead is abandoned by operation of law as to a declared homestead owner if the declared homestead owner or a person authorized to act on behalf of the declared homestead owner executes, acknowledges, and records a new homestead declaration for the declared homestead owner on different property. An abandonment under this subdivision does not affect the declared homestead of any person other than the declared homestead owner named in the new homestead declaration.

(b) Notwithstanding subdivision (a), if a homestead declaration is recorded which includes property described in a previously recorded homestead declaration, to the extent that the prior homestead declaration is still valid, the new homestead declaration shall not be considered an abandonment of the prior declared homestead. *(Added by Stats.1982, c. 1364, p. 5172, § 2, operative July 1, 1983.)*

Research References

Rutter, Cal. Practice Guide: Enforcing Judgments/Debts Ch. 6E-6, "Homestead" Exemption.
Miller and Starr California Real Estate § 13:21, Marital Homestead; Either Spouse.
Miller and Starr California Real Estate § 13:22, Residency, Ownership and Use.
Miller and Starr California Real Estate § 13:34, Abandonment of the Declared Homestead.
8 Witkin Cal. Proc. 5th Enforcement of Judgment § 239, Abandonment.

§ 704.995. Protection of homestead; continuation after death

(a) The protection of the declared homestead from any creditor having an attachment lien, execution lien, or judgment lien on the dwelling continues after the death of the declared homestead owner if, at the time of the death, the dwelling was the principal dwelling of one or more of the following persons to whom all or part of the interest of the deceased declared homestead owner passes:

(1) The surviving spouse of the decedent.

(2) A member of the family of the decedent.

(b) The protection of the declared homestead provided by subdivision (a) continues regardless of whether the decedent was the sole owner of the declared homestead or owned the declared homestead with the surviving spouse or a member of the decedent's family and regardless of whether the surviving spouse or the member of the decedent's family was a declared homestead owner at the time of the decedent's death.

(c) The amount of the homestead exemption is determined pursuant to Section 704.730 depending on the circumstances of the case at the time the amount is required to be determined. *(Added by Stats.1984, c. 538, § 27.)*

Law Revision Commission Comments

Section 704.995 is added to make clear that the surviving spouse or resident family does not lose the declared homestead right by the death of a declared homestead owner. Hence, the protection afforded the declared homestead from creditors continues even though the person who recorded the homestead declaration or who was the sole or joint owner is dead. This section rejects a contrary dictum in Estate of Grigsby, 134 Cal.App.3d 611, 615, 184 Cal.Rptr. 886, 888 (1982) ("... the declared homestead does not survive the death of one of the spouses."). See also Prob.Code § 6528 (effect of probate homestead on declared homestead). Subdivision (c) makes clear that where the right to a declared homestead continues, the amount of the homestead exemption is determined under the normal rules. For example, if the surviving spouse is not 65 years of age or older and does not have another family member living in the dwelling, the dollar amount of the declared homestead that is protected from creditors will be reduced. See Sections 704.730 (amount of homestead exemption), 704.950 (attachment of judgment lien to surplus value). [17 Cal.L.Rev.Comm. Reports 1013 (1983)].

Research References

Rutter, Cal. Practice Guide: Enforcing Judgments/Debts Ch. 6E-6, "Homestead" Exemption.
Miller and Starr California Real Estate § 13:1, Overview; Scope and Terminology of Chapter.

Miller and Starr California Real Estate § 13:2, Basis for and Public Policy of the Homestead Exemptions.

Miller and Starr California Real Estate § 13:4, Comparison of Declared Homestead and Automatic Exemption.

Miller and Starr California Real Estate § 13:9, Effect of Death of an Owner, or Dissolution of the Marriage or Registered Domestic Partnership.

Miller and Starr California Real Estate § 13:12, Waiver of the Homestead Exemption.

Miller and Starr California Real Estate § 13:37, Amount of Exemption-- In General.

Miller and Starr California Real Estate § 13:48, Determination of the Liens Against the Homestead; Priorities.

Miller and Starr California Real Estate § 13:59, Relationship of Probate Homestead to Declared and Automatic Exemptions.

Miller and Starr California Real Estate § 32:24, Homestead.

Miller and Starr California Real Estate § 32:54, Effect of Homestead Exemption.

Miller and Starr California Real Estate § 32:61, Property Interests Subject to Execution.

8 Witkin Cal. Proc. 5th Enforcement of Judgment § 238, Effect of Death of Owner.

CHAPTER 5. WAGE GARNISHMENT

ARTICLE 1. SHORT TITLE; DEFINITIONS

§ 706.010. Short title

This chapter shall be known and may be cited as the "Wage Garnishment Law." *(Added by Stats.1982, c. 1364, p. 5172, § 2, operative July 1, 1983.)*

Law Revision Commission Comments

Section 706.010 substitutes the more descriptive term "Wage Garnishment Law" for the term "Employees' Earnings Protection Law" used in former Section 723.010. [16 Cal.L.Rev.Comm. Reports 1442 (1982)].

Research References

Rutter, Cal. Practice Guide: Enforcing Judgments/Debts Ch. 6D-4, Levy on Specific Property.

Rutter, Cal. Practice Guide: Enforcing Judgments/Debts Ch. 6E-5, Specific Exempt Property.

8 Witkin Cal. Proc. 5th Enforcement of Judgment § 2, (S 2) in General.

8 Witkin Cal. Proc. 5th Enforcement of Judgment § 18, (S 18) in General.

8 Witkin Cal. Proc. 5th Enforcement of Judgment § 21, Definitions.

8 Witkin Cal. Proc. 5th Enforcement of Judgment § 114, (S 114) Return of Writ.

8 Witkin Cal. Proc. 5th Enforcement of Judgment § 180, (S 180) in General.

8 Witkin Cal. Proc. 5th Enforcement of Judgment § 203, Public Employee Vacation Credits.

8 Witkin Cal. Proc. 5th Enforcement of Judgment § 204, Private Retirement Benefits.

8 Witkin Cal. Proc. 5th Enforcement of Judgment § 207, (S 207) Damages for Personal Injury.

8 Witkin Cal. Proc. 5th Enforcement of Judgment § 208, (S 208) Damages for Wrongful Death.

8 Witkin Cal. Proc. 5th Enforcement of Judgment § 241, (S 241) Statutory Development.

8 Witkin Cal. Proc. 5th Enforcement of Judgment § 309, (S 309) Limitations on Recovery.

8 Witkin Cal. Proc. 5th Enforcement of Judgment § 312, (S 312) Nature and Scope of Remedy.

8 Witkin Cal. Proc. 5th Enforcement of Judgment § 328, (S 328) Collection of Included Money Judgment.

8 Witkin Cal. Proc. 5th Enforcement of Judgment § 405, Governmental Enforcement of Support Order.

§ 706.011. Definitions

As used in this chapter:

(a) "Disposable earnings" means the portion of an individual's earnings that remains after deducting all amounts required to be withheld by law.

(b) "Earnings" means compensation payable by an employer to an employee for personal services performed by such employee, whether denominated as wages, salary, commission, bonus, or otherwise.

(c) "Earnings withholding order for elder or dependent adult financial abuse" means an earnings withholding order, made pursuant to Article 5 (commencing with Section 706.100) and based on a money judgment in an action for elder or adult dependent financial abuse under Section 15657.5 of the Welfare and Institutions Code.

(d) "Earnings assignment order for support" means an order, made pursuant to Chapter 8 (commencing with Section 5200) of Part 5 of Division 9 of the Family Code or Section 3088 of the Probate Code, which requires an employer to withhold earnings for support.

(e) "Employee" means a public officer and any individual who performs services subject to the right of the employer to control both what shall be done and how it shall be done.

(f) "Employer" means a person for whom an individual performs services as an employee.

(g) "Judgment creditor," as applied to the state, means the specific state agency seeking to collect a judgment or tax liability.

(h) "Judgment debtor" includes a person from whom the state is seeking to collect a tax liability under Article 4 (commencing with Section 706.070), whether or not a judgment has been obtained on such tax liability.

(i) "Person" includes an individual, a corporation, a partnership or other unincorporated association, a limited liability company, and a public entity. *(Added by Stats.1982, c. 1364, p. 5172, § 2, operative July 1, 1983. Amended by Stats.1990, c. 1493 (A.B.3974), § 30.5; Stats.1992, c. 163 (A.B.2641), § 45, operative Jan. 1, 1994; Stats.1994, c. 1010 (S.B.2053), § 61; Stats.2010, c. 64 (A.B.2619), § 1, operative Jan. 1, 2012; Stats.2012, c. 474 (A.B.1775), § 1, operative July 1, 2013.)*

Law Revision Commission Comments

Section 706.011 is amended to conform to the terminology of the Family Code and to substitute references to the Family Code provisions that replaced the former Civil Code provisions. See Chapter 8 (commencing with Section 5200) of Part 5 of Division 9 of the Family Code (earnings assignment order for support). The term "wage assignment for support" in former subdivision (g) has been replaced by "earnings assignment for support" in new subdivision (b), and other subdivisions have been redesignated to keep the definitions in alphabetical order. [22 Cal.L.Rev.Comm.Reports 1 (1992)].

Research References

Rutter, Cal. Practice Guide: Enforcing Judgments/Debts Ch. 6E-5, Specific Exempt Property.

Rutter, Cal. Practice Guide: Enforcing Judgments/Debts Ch. 6F-2, Wage Garnishment-In General.

Rutter, Cal. Practice Guide: Enforcing Judgments/Debts Ch. 6G-5, Assignment Order.

8 Witkin Cal. Proc. 5th Enforcement of Judgment § 194, (S 194) Paid Earnings.

8 Witkin Cal. Proc. 5th Enforcement of Judgment § 202, (S 202) Effect of Support Judgment.

8 Witkin Cal. Proc. 5th Enforcement of Judgment § 204, Private Retirement Benefits.

8 Witkin Cal. Proc. 5th Enforcement of Judgment § 205, (S 205) Unemployment and Strike Benefits.

8 Witkin Cal. Proc. 5th Enforcement of Judgment § 206, (S 206) Disability and Health Benefits.

8 Witkin Cal. Proc. 5th Enforcement of Judgment § 243, (S 243) Definitions.

8 Witkin Cal. Proc. 5th Enforcement of Judgment § 245, (S 245) Priority of Withholding Orders.

8 Witkin Cal. Proc. 5th Enforcement of Judgment § 268, (S 268) Earnings Assignment Order for Support.

8 Witkin Cal. Proc. 5th Enforcement of Judgment § 269, (S 269) in General.

8 Witkin Cal. Proc. 5th Enforcement of Judgment § 274A, (New)- Earnings Withholding Order for Elder or Dependent Adult Financial Abuse.

6 Witkin Cal. Proc. 5th Provisional Remedies § 84, Earnings.

11 Witkin, California Summary 10th Husband and Wife § 250, (S 250) Definitions.

ARTICLE 2.   GENERAL PROVISIONS

§ 706.020.   Application of chapter

Except for an earning assignment order for support, the earnings of an employee shall not be required to be withheld by an employer for payment of a debt by means of any judicial procedure other than pursuant to this chapter. *(Added by Stats.1982, c. 1364, p. 5173, § 2, operative July 1, 1983. Amended by Stats.1992, c. 163 (A.B.2641), § 46, operative Jan. 1, 1994.)*

Law Revision Commission Comments

Section 706.020 makes clear that, with the exception of wage assignments for support (defined in subdivision (g) of Section 706.011), the Wage Garnishment Law is the exclusive judicial method of compelling an employer to withhold earnings. The section continues former Section 723.020. Attachment of earnings before judgment is abolished by Section 487.020(c). For provisions relating to voluntary wage assignments, see Labor Code Section 300. This chapter has no effect on judgment collection procedures that do not involve the withholding of an employee's earnings. However, where an employee's earnings are sought to be garnished, the creditor must comply with the provisions of this chapter. This rule applies to public entities as well as private persons. This chapter, for example, imposes limitations on the state's ability to garnish wages for tax delinquencies pursuant to its warrant and notice procedures. See Article 4 (commencing with Section 706.070).

The Wage Garnishment Law has no effect on matters that are preempted by federal law, such as federal bankruptcy proceedings and federal tax collection procedures. E.g., I.R.C. § 6334(c). Nor does this chapter apply to deductions which an employer is authorized by statute to make for such items as insurance premiums and payments to health, welfare, or pension plans. See, e.g., Gov't Code §§ 1156–1158, Labor Code §§ 224, 300. Finally, this chapter does not affect the procedures for the examination of a debtor of the judgment debtor provided in Article 2 (commencing with Section 708.110) of Chapter 6. See also Comment to Section 706.154. [16 Cal.L.Rev.Comm. Reports 1443 (1982)].

Section 706.020 is amended to conform to the terminology of the Family Code. See Chapter 8 (commencing with Section 5200) of Part 5 of Division 9 of the Family Code (earnings assignment order for support). "Earnings assignment order for support" is defined in Section 706.011. [22 Cal.L.Rev.Comm.Reports 1 (1992)].

Research References

Rutter, Cal. Practice Guide: Enforcing Judgments/Debts Ch. 6F-2, Wage Garnishment-In General.

Rutter, Cal. Practice Guide: Enforcing Judgments/Debts Ch. 6G-5, Assignment Order.

8 Witkin Cal. Proc. 5th Enforcement of Judgment § 242, (S 242) Exclusive Procedure.

§ 706.021.   Procedure for levy of execution upon employee earnings

Notwithstanding any other provision of this title, a levy of execution upon the earnings of an employee shall be made by service of an earnings withholding order upon the employer in accordance with this chapter. *(Added by Stats.1982, c. 1364, p. 5173, § 2, operative July 1, 1983.)*

Law Revision Commission Comments

Section 706.021 continues former Section 723.021 except that a reference to "this title" is substituted for the reference to former Section 688 in the introductory clause. Section 706.021 makes clear that a levy of execution on earnings is made as provided in this chapter rather than under Chapter 3 (commencing with Section 699.010). [16 Cal.L.Rev. Comm. Reports 1444 (1982)].

Research References

8 Witkin Cal. Proc. 5th Enforcement of Judgment § 242, (S 242) Exclusive Procedure.

§ 706.022.   Withholding period, defined; amount withheld; employer liability for amounts withheld and paid prior to service of order

(a) As used in this section, "withholding period" means the period which commences on the 10th day after service of an earnings withholding order upon the employer and which continues until the earliest of the following dates:

(1) The date the employer has withheld the full amount required to satisfy the order.

(2) The date of termination specified in a court order served on the employer.

(3) The date of termination specified in a notice of termination served on the employer by the levying officer.

(4) The date of termination of a dormant or suspended earnings withholding order as determined pursuant to Section 706.032.

(b) Except as otherwise provided by statute, an employer shall withhold the amounts required by an earnings withholding order from all earnings of the employee payable for any pay period of the employee which ends during the withholding period.

(c) An employer is not liable for any amounts withheld and paid over to the levying officer pursuant to an earnings withholding order prior to service upon the employer pursuant to paragraph (2) or (3) of subdivision (a). *(Added by Stats.1982, c. 1364, p. 5173, § 2, operative July 1, 1983. Amended by Stats.1989, c. 263, § 1; Stats.1992, c. 283 (S.B.1372), § 5, eff. July 21, 1992.)*

Law Revision Commission Comments

Subdivision (a)(1) of Section 706.022 is amended for conformity with Section 706.024 (amount required to satisfy earnings withholding order). Subdivision (a)(4) is added to reflect the automatic termination of earnings withholding orders under Section 706.032.

The remainder of this Comment is drawn from the Comment to Section 706.022 as enacted in 1982, with revisions to reflect the amendment of this section in 1989. See 1982 Cal.Stat. ch. 1364, § 2; 1989 Cal.Stat. ch. 263, § 1.

Section 706.022 states the basic rules governing the employer's duty to withhold pursuant to an earnings withholding order.

Subdivision (b) requires the employer to withhold from all earnings of an employee payable for any pay period of such employee which *ends* during the "withholding period." The "withholding period" is described in subdivision (a). It should be noted that *only* earnings for a pay period ending during the withholding period are subject to levy. Earnings for prior periods, even though still in the possession of the employer, are not subject to the order. An employer may not, however, defer or accelerate any payment of earnings to an employee with the intent to defeat or diminish the satisfaction of a judgment pursuant to this chapter. See Section 706.153.

Under subdivision (a), the withholding period generally commences 10 calendar days (not working or business days) after service of an earnings withholding order is completed. See Section 706.101 (when service completed). For example, if an order is served on Friday, the withholding period would commence on the second following Monday. See Section 12 (computation of time). The 10-day delay affords the employer time to process the order within its organization, i.e., deliver the order to the employer's bookkeeper, make bookkeeping adjustments, and so on.

The introductory clause to subdivision (b) recognizes certain exceptions to the general rule stated in subdivision (b). An employer is not generally required to withhold pursuant to two orders at the same time, except in special cases involving withholding orders for support or taxes. Thus, an ordinary earnings withholding order served when an earlier order is in place will not be given effect. See Section 706.023 (priority of orders) & Comment. See also Section 706.104(a) (no withholding if debtor not employed and no earnings due).

The withholding period does not end until the first of the events described in paragraphs (1) through (4) of subdivision (a) occurs. The employer has a *continuing* duty to withhold during the withholding period. See also Section 706.032 (termination of dormant or suspended order).

Paragraph (1) requires the employer to stop withholding when the full amount required to satisfy the earnings withholding order has been withheld. See Section 706.024 (amount required to satisfy order).

Paragraph (2) reflects the fact that the court may order the termination of the earnings withholding order. See Section 706.105(g). Of course, in some situations, the court will only modify the prior order, and the employer then must comply with the order as modified for the remainder of the withholding period.

Paragraph (3) requires the employer to stop withholding when served with a notice of termination. See Section 706.101 (manner of service). A notice of termination is served (1) where the levying officers is notified of the satisfaction of the judgment or (2) where the judgment debtor has claimed an exemption for the entire amount of earnings but the judgment creditor has failed within the time allowed to file with the levying officer a notice of opposition to claim of exemption and a notice of the hearing on the exemption. See Sections 706.027 (satisfaction of judgment), 706.105(f) (grounds for termination of withholding order in exemption proceeding). The levying officer may also serve a notice of termination where the order has been dormant or suspended for 180 days. See Section 706.032 (termination for dormancy or suspension).

Paragraph (4) recognizes the special rule for termination of earnings withholding orders that have been dormant or suspended for a period of 180 days. See Section 706.032 & Comment.

The judgment creditor has an affirmative duty to inform the levying officer of the satisfaction of the judgment. See Section 706.027.

Service of an order for the collection of state taxes suspends the duty of an employer to withhold pursuant to a prior order (other than an order for support). See Section 706.077 (tax orders). However, this is only a suspension. After the tax order is satisfied, if the withholding period for the prior order has not ended, the employer must again withhold pursuant to the prior order. See Section 706.032 (termination in case of suspension for 180 days by supervening order).

Similarly, the duty to withhold is not terminated by the layoff, discharge, or suspension of an employee and, if the employee is rehired or returns to work during the withholding period, the employer must resume withholding pursuant to the order. See Section 706.032 (termination in case of dormancy for 180 days).

The termination of certain types of orders—orders for the collection of state taxes and support orders—is governed by separate rules. See Sections 706.030 (support orders), 706.078 (tax orders).

Sometimes an order will be terminated without the employer's prior knowledge. Subdivision (c) makes clear that an employer will not be subject to liability for having withheld and paid over amounts pursuant to an order prior to service of a written notice of termination of the order. In such a case, the employee must look to the judgment creditor for the recovery of amounts previously paid to the judgment creditor. See Section 706.154 (employer entitled to rely on documents actually served). See also Section 706.105(i) (recovery from levying officer or judgment creditor of amounts received after order terminated).

An earnings withholding order may also be affected by federal bankruptcy proceedings. See Comment to Section 706.020. [21 Cal.L.Rev.Comm.Reports 135 (1991)].

Research References

Rutter, Cal. Practice Guide: Enforcing Judgments/Debts Ch. 6D-3, Levy of Writ of Execution-In General.

Rutter, Cal. Practice Guide: Enforcing Judgments/Debts Ch. 6D-7, Sale and Collection of Property Levied Upon.

Rutter, Cal. Practice Guide: Enforcing Judgments/Debts Ch. 6F-2, Wage Garnishment-In General.

Rutter, Cal. Practice Guide: Enforcing Judgments/Debts Ch. 6F-5, Earnings Exempt from Garnishment.

Rutter, Cal. Practice Guide: Enforcing Judgments/Debts Ch. 6F-7, Employer Duties and Liabilities Under Wgl.

8 Witkin Cal. Proc. 5th Enforcement of Judgment § 114, (S 114) Return of Writ.

8 Witkin Cal. Proc. 5th Enforcement of Judgment § 244, (S 244) Withholding Period.

8 Witkin Cal. Proc. 5th Enforcement of Judgment § 247, (S 247) Satisfaction of Judgment Before Termination of Withholding Order.

8 Witkin Cal. Proc. 5th Enforcement of Judgment § 258, (S 258) Withholding by Employer.

8 Witkin Cal. Proc. 5th Enforcement of Judgment § 264, (S 264) Debtor's Recovery of Amounts Withheld.

8 Witkin Cal. Proc. 5th Enforcement of Judgment § 274, (S 274) Commencement and Termination of Withholding.

§ 706.023. Multiple earnings withholding orders; earnings withholding orders for elder or dependent adult financial abuse

Except as otherwise provided in this chapter:

(a) An employer shall comply with the first earnings withholding order served upon the employer.

(b) If the employer is served with two or more earnings withholding orders on the same day, the employer shall comply with the order issued pursuant to the judgment first entered. If two or more orders served on the same day are based on judgments entered upon the same day, the employer shall comply with whichever one of the orders the employer selects.

(c) If an earnings withholding order is served while an employer is required to comply with another earnings withholding order with respect to the earnings of the same employee, the subsequent order is ineffective and the employer shall not

Civ. Pro.

withhold earnings pursuant to the subsequent order, except as provided in subdivision (d).

(d) Notwithstanding any other provisions of this section, a withholding order for elder or dependent adult financial abuse has priority over any other earning withholding order except for a withholding order for support under Section 706.030 and a withholding order for taxes under Section 706.072.

(1) An employer upon whom a withholding order for elder or dependent adult financial abuse is served shall withhold and pay over earnings of the employee pursuant to that order notwithstanding the requirements of another earnings withholding order except as provided in paragraph (2).

(2) An employer shall not withhold earnings of an employee pursuant to an earnings withholding order for elder or dependent adult financial abuse if a withholding order for support or for taxes is in effect or if a prior withholding order for elder or dependent adult financial abuse is in effect. In that case, the subsequent withholding order for elder or dependent financial abuse is ineffective.

(3) When an employer is required to cease withholding earnings pursuant to a prior earnings withholding order, the employer shall notify the levying officer who served the prior earnings withholding order that a supervening earnings withholding order for elder or dependent financial abuse is in effect. *(Added by Stats.1982, c. 1364, p. 5173, § 2, operative July 1, 1983. Amended by Stats.2010, c. 64 (A.B.2619), § 2, operative Jan. 1, 2012.)*

Research References

Rutter, Cal. Practice Guide: Enforcing Judgments/Debts Ch. 6F-3, Issuance and Service of Earnings Withholding Orders.
Rutter, Cal. Practice Guide: Enforcing Judgments/Debts Ch. 6F-6, Priority Among Earnings Withholding Orders.
8 Witkin Cal. Proc. 5th Enforcement of Judgment § 245, (S 245) Priority of Withholding Orders.
8 Witkin Cal. Proc. 5th Enforcement of Judgment § 274A, (New)-Earnings Withholding Order for Elder or Dependent Adult Financial Abuse.

§ 706.024.   Amount required to satisfy earnings withholding order; discretionary notice; accrual of interest

(a) The amount required to satisfy an earnings withholding order is the total amount required to satisfy the writ of execution on the date the order is issued, with the following additions and subtractions:

(1) The addition of the statutory fee for service of the order and any other statutory fees for performing duties under the order.

(2) The addition of costs added to the order pursuant to Section 685.090.

(3) The subtraction of the amount of any partial satisfactions.

(4) The addition of daily interest accruing after issuance of the order, as adjusted for partial satisfactions.

(b) From time to time the levying officer, in the levying officer's discretion, may give written notice to the employer of the amount required to satisfy the earnings withholding order and the employer shall determine the total amount to withhold based upon the levying officer's notice, notwithstanding a different amount stated in the order originally served on the employer.

(c) If the full amount required to satisfy the earnings withholding order as stated in the order or in the levying officer's notice under subdivision (b) is withheld from the judgment debtor's earnings, interest ceases to accrue on that amount. *(Added by Stats.1992, c. 283 (S.B.1372), § 6, eff. July 21, 1992.)*

Law Revision Commission Comments

Section 706.024 is new. This section provides for adjustment of the total amount required to satisfy an earnings withholding order. Since an active order continues in force until it is satisfied, full satisfaction of the judgment may not occur unless the total amount due as stated in the order as issued is adjusted as provided in subdivision (a).

See also Sections 685.030 (accrual of interest and satisfaction), 685.050 (costs and interest under writ), 685.090(c) (costs added to writ or order after issuance), 695.210 (amount required to satisfy money judgment), 699.520(e) (amount enforceable under writ of execution), 706.101(c) (notice by first class mail). [21 Cal.L.Rev.Comm.Reports 135 (1991)].

Research References

Rutter, Cal. Practice Guide: Enforcing Judgments/Debts Ch. 6F-8, Payment of Judgment Creditor; Satisfaction of Order; Duty to File Supplemental Return on Writ.
8 Witkin Cal. Proc. 5th Enforcement of Judgment § 44, When Accrual Ceases.
8 Witkin Cal. Proc. 5th Enforcement of Judgment § 246, (S 246) Obtaining Full Satisfaction of Judgment.
8 Witkin Cal. Proc. 5th Enforcement of Judgment § 259, (S 259) Payment of Amounts Withheld.
8 Witkin Cal. Proc. 5th Enforcement of Judgment § 260, (S 260) Continuation of Order After Return of Writ.

§ 706.025.   Payments to levying officer

(a) Except as provided in subdivision (b), the amount required to be withheld pursuant to an earnings withholding order shall be paid monthly to the levying officer not later than the 15th day of each month. The initial monthly payment shall include all amounts required to be withheld from the earnings of the employee during the preceding calendar month up to the close of the employee's pay period ending closest to the last day of that month, and thereafter each monthly payment shall include amounts withheld from the employee's earnings for services rendered in the interim up to the close of the employee's pay period ending closest to the last day of the preceding calendar month.

(b) The employer may elect to pay the amounts withheld to the levying officer more frequently than monthly. If the employer so elects, payment of the amount withheld from the employee's earnings for each pay period shall be made not later than 10 days after the close of the pay period. *(Added by Stats.1982, c. 1364, p. 5173, § 2, operative July 1, 1983.)*

Law Revision Commission Comments

Section 706.025 specifies when the amounts withheld pursuant to an earnings withholding order must be paid over to the levying officer. As to payment to the employee if an exemption claim is allowed, see Section 706.105(i). Regardless whether payment is required, the employer is required to send an employer's return to the levying officer. See Sections 706.104 and 706.126. Section 706.025 continues former Section 723.025. [16 Cal.L.Rev.Comm. Reports 1448 (1982)].

Research References

Rutter, Cal. Practice Guide: Enforcing Judgments/Debts Ch. 6F-2, Wage Garnishment-In General.
Rutter, Cal. Practice Guide: Enforcing Judgments/Debts Ch. 6F-7, Employer Duties and Liabilities Under Wgl.
8 Witkin Cal. Proc. 5th Enforcement of Judgment § 258, (S 258) Withholding by Employer.
8 Witkin Cal. Proc. 5th Enforcement of Judgment § 259, (S 259) Payment of Amounts Withheld.

§ 706.026.   Levying officer; receipt, accounting, and payment of amounts received; electronic filing

(a) The levying officer shall receive and account for all amounts paid by the employer pursuant to Section 706.025 and shall pay the amounts so received over to the person entitled thereto at least once every 30 days.

(b) At least once every two years, the levying officer shall file an accounting with the court, as provided by Section 699.560, for all amounts collected under the earnings withholding order, including costs and interest added to the amount due. Subject to the limitations in subdivision (c) of Section 263, the levying officer may electronically file the accounting with the court, pursuant to Chapter 2 (commencing with Section 263) of Title 4 of Part 1. *(Added by Stats.1982, c. 1364, p. 5174, § 2, operative July 1, 1983. Amended by Stats.1992, c. 283 (S.B.1372), § 7, eff. July 21, 1992; Stats.2010, c. 680 (A.B.2394), § 12.)*

Law Revision Commission Comments

Section 706.026 continues subdivision (a) of former Section 723.026. The remainder of former Section 723.026 (which in effect extended the time for return of the writ of execution) has not been continued because this portion is no longer necessary in view of Section 699.560 which extends generally the time for return of writs of execution. [16 Cal.L.Rev.Comm. Reports 1449 (1982)].

Subdivision (b) is added to Section 706.026 to provide for an accounting to the court of activities under an earnings withholding order. See Section 680.160 ("court" defined). This account is in the nature of a return on a writ and is required whether or not the writ has been returned. See Section 699.560 (return of writ of execution). When the earnings withholding order terminates, the levying officer is to make a supplemental return on the writ. See Section 706.033 (supplemental return).

The change in subdivision (a) is a technical, nonsubstantive change intended to conform the language of this section to Section 706.025. [21 Cal.L.Rev.Comm.Reports 135 (1991)].

Research References

Rutter, Cal. Practice Guide: Enforcing Judgments/Debts Ch. 6F-8, Payment of Judgment Creditor; Satisfaction of Order; Duty to File Supplemental Return on Writ.
8 Witkin Cal. Proc. 5th Enforcement of Judgment § 259, (S 259) Payment of Amounts Withheld.
8 Witkin Cal. Proc. 5th Enforcement of Judgment § 260, (S 260) Continuation of Order After Return of Writ.

§ 706.027. Notice of satisfaction of judgment

If the judgment pursuant to which the earnings withholding order is issued is satisfied before the order otherwise terminates pursuant to Section 706.022, the judgment creditor shall promptly notify the levying officer who shall promptly terminate the order by serving a notice of termination on the employer. *(Added by Stats.1982, c. 1364, p. 5174, § 2, operative July 1, 1983.)*

Law Revision Commission Comments

Section 706.027 continues former Section 723.027 and requires the judgment creditor to give notice of satisfaction of the judgment to the levying officer if the earnings withholding order has not yet terminated. See Section 706.022 (withholding period). In some cases, the employer will be aware of the satisfaction by virtue of the employer's having withheld the amount necessary to satisfy the judgment. See Section 706.022(a) (2). In this case, Section 706.027 does not apply. However, the judgment may be satisfied by additional payments from the debtor or through other debt collection procedures instituted by the judgment creditor. If this is the case, Section 706.027 applies, and the judgment creditor has the duty to notify the levying officer promptly of the satisfaction so that the levying officer may serve a notice of termination on the employer. Service of the notice of termination is to be made on the person, and at the address, indicated in the employer's return. See Sections 706.101(c) and 706.126(b) (6). As to the general duty of a creditor to furnish a debtor a satisfaction of judgment, see Chapter 1 (commencing with Section 724.010) of Division 5. Failure to perform the duty imposed by this section may make the judgment creditor liable in an action for abuse of process. See White Lighting Co. v. Wolfson, 68 Cal.2d 336, 347–51, 438 P.2d 345, 351–54, 66 Cal.Rptr. 697, 703–06 (1968). [16 Cal.L.Rev.Comm. Reports 1449 (1982)].

Research References

Rutter, Cal. Practice Guide: Enforcing Judgments/Debts Ch. 6F-8, Payment of Judgment Creditor; Satisfaction of Order; Duty to File Supplemental Return on Writ.

8 Witkin Cal. Proc. 5th Enforcement of Judgment § 247, (S 247) Satisfaction of Judgment Before Termination of Withholding Order.
8 Witkin Cal. Proc. 5th Enforcement of Judgment § 274, (S 274) Commencement and Termination of Withholding.

§ 706.028. Final earnings withholding order for costs and interest

(a) "Final earnings withholding order for costs and interest" means an earnings withholding order for the collection only of unsatisfied costs and interest, which is issued after an earlier earnings withholding order has been returned satisfied.

(b) After the amount stated as owing in a prior earnings withholding order is paid, the judgment creditor may obtain a final earnings withholding order for costs and interest to collect amounts of costs and interest that were not collected under the prior earnings withholding order.

(c) A final earnings withholding order for costs and interest shall be enforced in the same manner as other earnings withholding orders.

(d) Satisfaction of the amount stated as owing in a final earnings withholding order for costs and interest is equivalent to satisfaction of the money judgment. For this purpose, interest ceases to accrue on the date of issuance of the final earnings withholding order and no additional costs may be added after that date, except for the statutory fee for service of the order and any other statutory fees for performing duties under the order. *(Added by Stats.1992, c. 283 (S.B.1372), § 9, eff. July 21, 1992.)*

Law Revision Commission Comments

Section 706.028 is new. This section provides for a final earnings withholding order for costs and interest and supersedes former Section 706.028 (subsequent order for costs and interest). The new "final order" differs from the "subsequent order" under former law since it permits a full satisfaction of the money judgment through wage garnishment by stopping the running of interest on the remaining balance due on the judgment (which balance comprises earlier costs and interest). The amount stated as due on a final earnings withholding order may be increased only by statutory costs. See Gov't Code §§ 26746 (disbursement fee), 26750 (fee for service and other duties under earnings withholding order). In other respects, as provided in subdivision (c), a final earnings withholding order is treated the same as any other earnings withholding order.

If the principal amount of the judgment is not fully satisfied before an earnings withholding order is terminated, another order may be issued to collect the balance due on the judgment pursuant to this chapter. See Section 706.102 (issuance of earnings withholding order). This later earnings withholding order is distinct from a final earnings withholding order for costs and interest provided by this section.

A final earnings withholding order is not available where the full amount due on the judgment has been collected under the initial earnings withholding order pursuant to the optional procedure set forth in Section 706.024. [21 Cal.L.Rev.Comm.Reports 135 (1991)].

Research References

Rutter, Cal. Practice Guide: Enforcing Judgments/Debts Ch. 6A-5, Amount Recoverable Under Judgment.
Rutter, Cal. Practice Guide: Enforcing Judgments/Debts Ch. 6F-3, Issuance and Service of Earnings Withholding Orders.
8 Witkin Cal. Proc. 5th Enforcement of Judgment § 44, When Accrual Ceases.
8 Witkin Cal. Proc. 5th Enforcement of Judgment § 246, (S 246) Obtaining Full Satisfaction of Judgment.

§ 706.029. Service of order creating lien; duration

Service of an earnings withholding order creates a lien upon the earnings of the judgment debtor that are required to be withheld pursuant to the order and upon all property of the employer subject to the enforcement of a money judgment in the amount required to be withheld pursuant to such order. The lien continues for a period of one year from the date the earnings of the judgment debtor become payable unless the amount required to be withheld pursuant to the order is paid as required by law. *(Added by Stats.1982, c. 1364, p. 5174, § 2, operative July 1, 1983.)*

Research References

Rutter, Cal. Practice Guide: Enforcing Judgments/Debts Ch. 6F-2, Wage Garnishment-In General.
8 Witkin Cal. Proc. 5th Enforcement of Judgment § 66, (S 66) Amount of Lien.
8 Witkin Cal. Proc. 5th Enforcement of Judgment § 254, in General.
11 Witkin, California Summary 10th Husband and Wife § 249, (S 249) in General.

§ 706.030. Withholding order for support; operation with earnings withholding order

(a) A "withholding order for support" is an earnings withholding order issued on a writ of execution to collect delinquent amounts payable under a judgment for the support of a child, or spouse or former spouse, of the judgment debtor. A withholding order for support shall be denoted as such on its face.

(b) The local child support agency may issue a withholding order for support on a notice of levy pursuant to Section 17522 of the Family Code to collect a support obligation.

(1) When the local child support agency issues a withholding order for support, a reference in this chapter to a levying officer is deemed to mean the local child support agency who issues the withholding order for support.

(2) Service of a withholding order for support issued by the local child support agency may be made by first-class mail or in any other manner described in Section 706.101. Service of a withholding order for support issued by the local child support agency is complete when it is received by the employer or a person described in paragraph (1) or (2) of subdivision (a) of Section 706.101, or if service is by first-class mail, service is complete as specified in Section 1013.

(3) The local child support agency shall serve upon the employer the withholding order for support, a copy of the order, and a notice informing the support obligor of the effect of the order and of his or her right to hearings and remedies provided in this chapter and in the Family Code. The notice shall be accompanied by the forms necessary to obtain an administrative review and a judicial hearing and instructions on how to file the forms. Within 10 days from the date of service, the employer shall deliver to the support obligor a copy of the withholding order for support, the forms to obtain an administrative review and judicial hearing, and the notice. If the support obligor is no longer employed by the employer and the employer does not owe the support obligor any earnings, the employer shall inform the local child support agency that the support obligor is no longer employed by the employer.

(4) An employer who fails to comply with paragraph (3) shall be subject to a civil penalty of five hundred dollars ($500) for each occurrence.

(5) The local child support agency shall provide for an administrative review to reconsider or modify the amount to be withheld for arrearages pursuant to the withholding order for support, if the support obligor requests a review at any time after service of the withholding order. The local child support agency shall provide the review in the same manner and timeframes provided for resolution of a complaint pursuant to Section 17800 of the Family Code. The local child support agency shall notify the employer if the review results in any modifications to the withholding order for support. If the local child support agency cannot complete the administrative review within 30 calendar days of receipt of the complaint, the local child support agency shall notify the employer to suspend withholding any disputed amount pending the completion of the review and the determination by the local child support agency.

(6) Nothing in this section prohibits the support obligor from seeking a judicial determination of arrearages pursuant to subdivision (c) of Section 17256 of the Family Code or from filing a motion for equitable division of earnings pursuant to Section 706.052 either prior to or after the administrative review provided by this section. Within five business days after receiving notice of the obligor having filed for judicial relief pursuant to this section, the local child support agency shall notify the employer to suspend withholding any disputed amount pending a determination by the court. The employer shall then adjust the withholding within not more than nine days of receiving the notice from the local child support agency.

(c) Notwithstanding any other provision of this chapter:

(1) An employer shall continue to withhold pursuant to a withholding order for support until the earliest of the dates specified in paragraph (1), (2), or (3) of subdivision (a) of Section 706.022, except that a withholding order for support shall automatically terminate one year after the employment of the employee by the employer terminates.

(2) A withholding order for support has priority over any other earnings withholding order. An employer upon whom a withholding order for support is served shall withhold and pay over earnings of the employee pursuant to that order notwithstanding the requirements of another earnings withholding order.

(3) Subject to paragraph (2) and to Article 3 (commencing with Section 706.050), an employer shall withhold earnings pursuant to both a withholding order for support and another earnings withholding order simultaneously.

(4) An employer who willfully fails to withhold and forward support pursuant to a valid earnings withholding order for support issued and served upon the employer pursuant to this chapter is liable to the support obligee, as defined in Section 5214 of the Family Code, for the amount of support not withheld, forwarded, or otherwise paid to the support obligee.

(5) Notwithstanding any other provision of law, an employer shall send all earnings withheld pursuant to a withholding order for support to the levying officer or the State Disbursement Unit as described in Section 17309 of the Family Code within the time period specified by federal law.

(6) Once the State Disbursement Unit as described in Section 17309 of the Family Code is operational, all support payments made pursuant to an earnings withholding order shall be made to that unit.

(7) Earnings withheld pursuant to an earnings withholding order for support shall be credited toward satisfaction of a support judgment as specified in Section 695.221. *(Added by Stats.1982, c. 1364, p. 5174, § 2, operative July 1, 1983. Amended by Stats.1992, c. 283 (S.B.1372), § 10, eff. July 21, 1992; Stats. 1997, c. 599 (A.B.573), § 5; Stats.2000, c. 808 (A.B.1358), § 17, eff. Sept. 28, 2000; Stats.2001, c. 755 (S.B.943), § 1, eff. Oct. 12, 2001; Stats.2003, c. 387 (A.B.739), § 1.)*

Law Revision Commission Comments

Section 706.030 continues former Section 723.030 and provides special rules for an earnings withholding order to enforce a judgment for delinquent support payments for a child or spouse or former spouse of the judgment debtor. An earnings withholding order for support is given a different effect than other withholding orders: It is effective until the employer has withheld the full amount specified in the order or he is served with a notice of termination, in which case the date of termination will be specified in the notice. See subdivision (b)(1). Thus, the withholding order for support does not terminate 100 days after service (it may, of course, be modified). The withholding order for support is subject to special exemption rules (see Section 706.052). Even when in effect, it does not necessarily preclude withholding on either a prior or subsequent earnings withholding order. If not earlier terminated, the withholding order for support automatically terminates one year after the employment of the employee terminates. Thus, for example, if the employee returns to work for the same employer within one year from the date his employment terminated, the employer must withhold pursuant to the withholding order for support. On the other hand, if the employee does not return to work until more than one year from the date his employment terminated, the order expires at the end of the year, and nothing is withheld pursuant to the order when the employee returns to work.

The earnings withholding order for support is given priority over any other earnings withholding order. But see Section 706.031 (wage assignment for support given priority). However, a prior earnings withholding order remains in effect, and a judgment creditor may still obtain an earnings withholding order even where there is already in effect a prior earnings withholding order for support. Thus, where there are two earnings withholding orders in effect—one for support and one for another obligation—the amount withheld for support is deducted from the employee's earnings first. The amount, if any, that may be withheld pursuant to the other earnings withholding order is determined by subtracting the amount withheld pursuant to the withholding order for support from the amount that otherwise could be withheld pursuant to the other earnings withholding order. See Sections 706.077, 706.050, and 706.051 and the Comments thereto. [16 Cal.L.Rev.Comm. Reports 1452 (1982)].

Research References

Rutter, Cal. Practice Guide: Enforcing Judgments/Debts Ch. 6A-5, Amount Recoverable Under Judgment.

Rutter, Cal. Practice Guide: Enforcing Judgments/Debts Ch. 6F-2, Wage Garnishment-In General.

Rutter, Cal. Practice Guide: Enforcing Judgments/Debts Ch. 6F-3, Issuance and Service of Earnings Withholding Orders.

Rutter, Cal. Practice Guide: Enforcing Judgments/Debts Ch. 6F-4, Automatic Termination; Dormant or Suspended Earnings Withholding Orders; Automatic Stay.

Rutter, Cal. Practice Guide: Enforcing Judgments/Debts Ch. 6F-6, Priority Among Earnings Withholding Orders.

Rutter, Cal. Practice Guide: Enforcing Judgments/Debts Ch. 6F-7, Employer Duties and Liabilities Under Wgl.

Rutter, Cal. Practice Guide: Enforcing Judgments/Debts Ch. 6F-8, Payment of Judgment Creditor; Satisfaction of Order; Duty to File Supplemental Return on Writ.

8 Witkin Cal. Proc. 5th Enforcement of Judgment § 245, (S 245) Priority of Withholding Orders.

8 Witkin Cal. Proc. 5th Enforcement of Judgment § 251, Restrictions on Earnings Withholding.

8 Witkin Cal. Proc. 5th Enforcement of Judgment § 261, (S 261) in General.

8 Witkin Cal. Proc. 5th Enforcement of Judgment § 266, in General.

8 Witkin Cal. Proc. 5th Enforcement of Judgment § 267, Issuance by Local Child Support Agency.

8 Witkin Cal. Proc. 5th Enforcement of Judgment § 268, (S 268) Earnings Assignment Order for Support.

8 Witkin Cal. Proc. 5th Enforcement of Judgment § 273, (S 273) Priority.

8 Witkin Cal. Proc. 5th Enforcement of Judgment § 274, (S 274) Commencement and Termination of Withholding.

8 Witkin Cal. Proc. 5th Enforcement of Judgment § 403, Available Remedies.

8 Witkin Cal. Proc. 5th Enforcement of Judgment § 405, Governmental Enforcement of Support Order.

11 Witkin, California Summary 10th Husband and Wife § 262, (S 262) in General.

11 Witkin, California Summary 10th Husband and Wife § 335, (S 335) Levy by Agency.

13 Witkin, California Summary 10th Trusts § 164, in General.

§ 706.031. Earnings assignment order for support; operation with earnings withholding order

(a) Nothing in this chapter affects an earnings assignment order for support.

(b) An earnings assignment order for support shall be given priority over any earnings withholding order. An employer upon whom an earnings assignment order for support is served shall withhold and pay over the earnings of the employee pursuant to the assignment order notwithstanding the requirements of any earnings withholding order. When an employer is required to cease withholding earnings pursuant to an earnings withholding order, the employer shall notify the levying officer who served the earnings withholding order that a supervening earnings assignment order for support is in effect.

(c) Subject to subdivisions (b), (d), and (e), an employer shall withhold earnings of an employee pursuant to both an earnings assignment order for support and an earnings withholding order.

(d) The employer shall withhold pursuant to an earnings withholding order only to the extent that the sum of the amount withheld pursuant to any earnings assignment order for support and the amount withheld pursuant to the earnings withholding order does not exceed the amount that may be withheld under Article 3 (commencing with Section 706.050).

(e) The employer shall withhold pursuant to an earnings withholding order for taxes only to the extent that the sum of the amount withheld pursuant to any earnings assignment order for support and the amount withheld pursuant to the earnings withholding order for taxes does not exceed the amount that may be withheld under Article 4 (commencing with Section 706.070). *(Added by Stats.1982, c. 1364, p. 5175, § 2, operative July 1, 1983. Amended by Stats.1992, c. 163 (A.B.2641), § 47, operative Jan. 1, 1994.)*

Law Revision Commission Comments

Section 706.031 continues former Section 723.031 and states the effect of a wage assignment for support (defined in subdivision (g) of Section 706.011) on an earnings withholding order.

Subdivision (a) makes clear that nothing in this chapter affects the wage assignment for support, and subdivision (b) makes clear that the wage assignment has priority over any earnings withholding order, including a withholding order for support under Section 706.030. Under subdivision (b), the employer is required to notify the levying officer who earlier served an earnings withholding order if that order is completely superseded by the wage assignment. It should be noted that "levying officer" includes the state agency where a withholding order for taxes is superseded. See Section 706.073.

Subdivisions (b) and (d) of Section 706.031 make clear that, where any wage assignment for support is in effect, the amount withheld from the debtor's earnings pursuant to any such wage assignment is deducted from the amount that otherwise would be withheld under Section 706.050 on an earnings withholding order to enforce an ordinary money judgment or that otherwise would be withheld where a portion of the debtor's earnings have been determined to be exempt under Section 706.051. Suppose, for example, that a wage assignment for support is in effect which requires that $40 per week be withheld. Assume that Section 706.050 limits the amount that may be withheld to $56. To determine the maximum amount that may be withheld pursuant to the earnings withholding order (absent any exemption allowed under Section 706.051), the $40 withheld pursuant to the wage assignment for support is subtracted from the $56, leaving $16 as the maximum amount that may be withheld pursuant to the earnings withholding order. For a special rule applicable when the earnings withholding order is on a judgment for delinquent amounts payable for child or spousal support, see Sections 706.030 and 706.052. The rule stated in subdivision (d) of Section 706.031 is required to avoid conflict with the federal Consumer Credit Protection Act. That act requires that the amount withheld pursuant to any wage assignment for support be included in determining whether any amount may be withheld pursuant to an earnings withholding order on an ordinary judgment. See subdivision (c) of Section 302 of the act, 15 U.S.C. § 1672(c) (1970) ("garnishment" means "any legal or equitable procedure through which the earnings of any individual are required to be withheld for payment of any debt") and [1969–1973 Transfer Binder] Lab.L.Rep. (CCH) para. 30.813.

Under subdivision (e), the amount that could be withheld pursuant to a withholding order for taxes would be computed in the same manner as for an ordinary earnings withholding order pursuant to Section 706.050 unless the withholding order for taxes is obtained under Section 706.076. [16 Cal.L.Rev.Comm. Reports 1454 (1982)].

Civ. Pro.

Section 706.031 is amended to conform to the terminology of the Family Code. See Chapter 8 (commencing with Section 5200) of Part 5 of Division 9 of the Family Code (earnings assignment order for support). "Earnings assignment order for support" is defined in Section 706.011. [22 Cal.L.Rev.Comm.Reports 1 (1992)].

Research References

Rutter, Cal. Practice Guide: Enforcing Judgments/Debts Ch. 6D-2, Writ of Execution.
Rutter, Cal. Practice Guide: Enforcing Judgments/Debts Ch. 6F-2, Wage Garnishment-In General.
Rutter, Cal. Practice Guide: Enforcing Judgments/Debts Ch. 6F-6, Priority Among Earnings Withholding Orders.
8 Witkin Cal. Proc. 5th Enforcement of Judgment § 245, (S 245) Priority of Withholding Orders.
8 Witkin Cal. Proc. 5th Enforcement of Judgment § 251, Restrictions on Earnings Withholding.
8 Witkin Cal. Proc. 5th Enforcement of Judgment § 266, in General.
8 Witkin Cal. Proc. 5th Enforcement of Judgment § 268, (S 268) Earnings Assignment Order for Support.
8 Witkin Cal. Proc. 5th Enforcement of Judgment § 273, (S 273) Priority.
8 Witkin Cal. Proc. 5th Enforcement of Judgment § 405, Governmental Enforcement of Support Order.
11 Witkin, California Summary 10th Husband and Wife § 249, (S 249) in General.
11 Witkin, California Summary 10th Husband and Wife § 254, (S 254) Priorities.

§ 706.032. Termination of earnings withholding orders

(a) Except as otherwise provided by statute:

(1) If withholding under an earnings withholding order ceases because the judgment debtor's employment has terminated, the earnings withholding order terminates at the conclusion of a continuous 180-day period during which no amounts are withheld under the order.

(2) If withholding under an earnings withholding order ceases because the judgment debtor's earnings are subject to an order or assignment with higher priority, the earnings withholding order terminates at the conclusion of a continuous two-year period during which no amounts are withheld under the order.

(b) If an earnings withholding order has terminated pursuant to subdivision (a), the employer shall return the order to the levying officer along with a statement of the reasons for returning the order. *(Added by Stats.1992, c. 283 (S.B.1372), § 11, eff. July 21, 1992.)*

Law Revision Commission Comments

Section 706.032 is new. This section provides for the automatic termination of dormant or suspended earnings withholding orders in favor of general creditors. If the debtor leaves employment after an earnings withholding order has become effective, the duty to withhold continues for 180 days under subdivision (a)(1). If the debtor returns to work during this period, the employer is required to resume withholding pursuant to the order. If withholding under a general creditor's earnings withholding order is suspended because of withholding under an earnings withholding order or assignment for support or an earnings withholding order for taxes, the suspended order remains in effect until two years have elapsed with no withholding. See Sections 706.030 (support orders), 706.031 (wage assignment for support), 706.078 (tax orders).

The employer has a duty under subdivision (b) to determine whether an earnings withholding order has terminated under subdivision (a) and to return the order to the levying officer.

For a special rule concerning termination of earnings withholding orders for support, see Section 706.030(b)(1). For a special rule concerning termination of earnings withholding orders for taxes, see Section 706.078(c).

If the debtor is not employed and no earnings are due when the withholding period would begin under Section 706.022, the service of the order is ineffective and is not subject to the 180-day rule or two-year rule in this section. See Section 706.104(a). [22 Cal.L.Rev.Comm.Reports 987 (1992)].

Research References

Rutter, Cal. Practice Guide: Enforcing Judgments/Debts Ch. 6F-2, Wage Garnishment-In General.
Rutter, Cal. Practice Guide: Enforcing Judgments/Debts Ch. 6F-4, Automatic Termination; Dormant or Suspended Earnings Withholding Orders; Automatic Stay.
8 Witkin Cal. Proc. 5th Enforcement of Judgment § 244, (S 244) Withholding Period.
8 Witkin Cal. Proc. 5th Enforcement of Judgment § 245, (S 245) Priority of Withholding Orders.
8 Witkin Cal. Proc. 5th Enforcement of Judgment § 248, (S 248) Termination of Dormant or Suspended Withholding Order.
8 Witkin Cal. Proc. 5th Enforcement of Judgment § 258, (S 258) Withholding by Employer.

§ 706.033. Return of writ before earnings withholding order terminates; supplemental return on writ

If the writ is returned before the earnings withholding order terminates, on termination of the earnings withholding order the levying officer shall make a supplemental return on the writ. The supplemental return shall contain the same information as an original return pursuant to Section 699.560. *(Added by Stats.1992, c. 283 (S.B.1372), § 12, eff. July 21, 1992.)*

Law Revision Commission Comments

Section 706.033 is new. This section provides explicit authority for making a supplemental return on a writ where withholding under an earnings withholding order continues after the writ is returned. See also Section 706.026 (account of levying officer for amounts collected). [21 Cal.L.Rev.Comm.Reports 135 (1991)].

Research References

Rutter, Cal. Practice Guide: Enforcing Judgments/Debts Ch. 6D-3, Levy of Writ of Execution-In General.
Rutter, Cal. Practice Guide: Enforcing Judgments/Debts Ch. 6F-8, Payment of Judgment Creditor; Satisfaction of Order; Duty to File Supplemental Return on Writ.
8 Witkin Cal. Proc. 5th Enforcement of Judgment § 114, (S 114) Return of Writ.
8 Witkin Cal. Proc. 5th Enforcement of Judgment § 260, (S 260) Continuation of Order After Return of Writ.

§ 706.034. Deduction from employee earnings for payments made in accordance with earnings withholding order

The employer may deduct from the earnings of the employee the sum of one dollar and fifty cents ($1.50) for each payment made in accordance with an earnings withholding order issued pursuant to this chapter. *(Added by Stats.1997, c. 137 (A.B.519), § 1. Amended by Stats.2004, c. 520 (A.B.2530), § 1.)*

Research References

Rutter, Cal. Practice Guide: Enforcing Judgments/Debts Ch. 6F-7, Employer Duties and Liabilities Under Wgl.
8 Witkin Cal. Proc. 5th Enforcement of Judgment § 259, (S 259) Payment of Amounts Withheld.

ARTICLE 3. RESTRICTIONS ON EARNINGS WITHHOLDING

§ 706.050. Amount of disposable earnings of an individual judgment debtor subject to levy

(a) Except as otherwise provided in this chapter, the maximum amount of disposable earnings of an individual judgment debtor for any workweek that is subject to levy under an earnings withholding order shall not exceed the lesser of the following:

(1) Twenty-five percent of the individual's disposable earnings for that week.

(2) The amount by which the individual's disposable earnings for that week exceed 40 times the state minimum hourly wage in effect at the time the earnings are payable.

(b) For any pay period other than weekly, the following multipliers shall be used to determine the maximum amount of disposable earnings subject to levy under an earnings withholding order that is proportional in effect to the calculation described in paragraph (2) of subdivision (a), except as specified in paragraph (1):

(1) For a daily pay period, the amounts shall be identical to the amounts described in subdivision (a).

(2) For a biweekly pay period, multiply the state hourly minimum wage by 80 work hours.

(3) For a semimonthly pay period, multiply the state hourly minimum wage by 86 ⅔ work hours.

(4) For a monthly pay period, multiply the state hourly minimum wage by 173 ⅓ work hours. *(Added by Stats.1982, c. 1364, p. 5175, § 2, operative July 1, 1983. Amended by Stats.2012, c. 474 (A.B.1775), § 2, operative July 1, 2013.)*

Research References

California Practice Guide: Employment Litigation Ch. 11-D, D. Payment of Wages.
Rutter, Cal. Practice Guide: Enforcing Judgments/Debts Ch. 6F-5, Earnings Exempt from Garnishment.
8 Witkin Cal. Proc. 5th Enforcement of Judgment § 251, Restrictions on Earnings Withholding.
8 Witkin Cal. Proc. 5th Enforcement of Judgment § 266, in General.
8 Witkin Cal. Proc. 5th Enforcement of Judgment § 268, (S 268) Earnings Assignment Order for Support.
8 Witkin Cal. Proc. 5th Enforcement of Judgment § 271, (S 271) Issuance of Order.
13 Witkin, California Summary 10th Trusts § 164, in General.

§ 706.051. Amount necessary for support of judgment debtor or family; exemption

(a) For the purposes of this section, "family of the judgment debtor" includes the spouse or former spouse of the judgment debtor.

(b) Except as provided in subdivision (c), the portion of the judgment debtor's earnings that the judgment debtor proves is necessary for the support of the judgment debtor or the judgment debtor's family supported in whole or in part by the judgment debtor is exempt from levy under this chapter.

(c) The exemption provided in subdivision (b) is not available if any of the following exceptions applies:

(1) The debt was incurred pursuant to an order or award for the payment of attorney's fees under Section 2030, 3121, or 3557 of the Family Code.

(2) The debt was incurred for personal services rendered by an employee or former employee of the judgment debtor.

(3) The order is a withholding order for support under Section 706.030.

(4) The order is one governed by Article 4 (commencing with Section 706.070) (state tax order). *(Added by Stats.1982, c. 1364, p. 5175, § 2, operative July 1, 1983. Amended by Stats.2011, c. 694 (A.B.1388), § 1.)*

Research References

Rutter, Cal. Practice Guide: Enforcing Judgments/Debts Ch. 6E-2, Rules Applicable to Exemptions from Enforcement of Money Judgments Generally.
Rutter, Cal. Practice Guide: Enforcing Judgments/Debts Ch. 6F-5, Earnings Exempt from Garnishment.
Rutter, Cal. Practice Guide: Enforcing Judgments/Debts Gen. Matls., Highlights.
Rutter, Cal. Practice Guide: Family Law Gen. Matls, Highlights.
3 Witkin Cal. Proc. 5th Actions § 429D, (S 429D) (New)-Eligibility Criteria.
8 Witkin Cal. Proc. 5th Enforcement of Judgment § 251, Restrictions on Earnings Withholding.
8 Witkin Cal. Proc. 5th Enforcement of Judgment § 261, (S 261) in General.
8 Witkin Cal. Proc. 5th Enforcement of Judgment § 271, (S 271) Issuance of Order.
13 Witkin, California Summary 10th Trusts § 164, in General.

§ 706.052. Disposable earnings and earnings withheld pursuant to earning assignment order for support; exemption; equitable division of earnings by court

(a) Except as provided in subdivision (b), one-half of the disposable earnings (as defined by Section 1672 of Title 15 of the United States Code) of the judgment debtor, plus any amount withheld from the judgment debtor's earnings pursuant to any earnings assignment order for support, is exempt from levy under this chapter where the earnings withholding order is a withholding order for support under Section 706.030.

(b) Except as provided in subdivision (c), upon motion of any interested party, the court shall make an equitable division of the judgment debtor's earnings that takes into account the needs of all the persons the judgment debtor is required to support and shall effectuate such division by an order determining the amount to be withheld from the judgment debtor's earnings pursuant to the withholding order for support.

(c) An order made under subdivision (b) may not authorize the withholding of an amount in excess of the amount that may be withheld for support under federal law under Section 1673 of Title 15 of the United States Code. *(Added by Stats.1982, c. 1364, p. 5176, § 2, operative July 1, 1983. Amended by Stats.1992, c. 163 (A.B.2641), § 48, operative Jan. 1, 1994.)*

Law Revision Commission Comments

Section 706.052 continues former Section 723.052 except that subdivision (c) is added to reflect that the court's authority under subdivision (b) is limited by the maximum amounts that may be withheld under federal law. See 15 U.S.C. § 1673(b) (2) (Supp.1979).

Subdivision (a) of Section 706.052 prescribes the exemption applicable to a wage garnishment for the collection of delinquent child or spousal support payments except in cases where the court has made an equitable division pursuant to subdivision (b). The judgment debtor's earnings that are subject to the 50 percent exemption under subdivision (a) are "disposable earnings" as defined by the federal Consumer Credit Protection Act, 15 U.S.C. § 1672 (1976). Unlike federal law, however, subdivision (a) protects the same amount of earnings regardless of whether the judgment debtor is supporting a present and a former spouse or is more than 12 weeks delinquent. Federal law permits garnishment of 50 percent of the employee's earnings if the employee is supporting a spouse or dependent other than the person who caused the garnishment and 60 percent if the employee is not supporting such additional persons; these percentages are increased to 55 percent and 65 percent, respectively, if the support payments are more than 12 weeks delinquent. See 15 U.S.C. § 1673(b) (2) (Supp.1979).

Subdivision (a) also makes clear that, in applying the 50 percent exemption, the amount withheld from the earnings of the judgment debtor pursuant to any wage assignment for support (defined in subdivision (g) of Section 706.011) is included in computing the 50 percent of the judgment debtor's earnings that may be withheld. For example, if 30 percent of the judgment debtor's earnings are withheld pursuant to a wage assignment for support, an additional 20 percent may be withheld pursuant to the earnings withholding order for the collection of delinquent amounts payable for child or spousal support.

Subdivision (b) makes the 50 percent standard provided by subdivision (a) subject to the power of the court to make an order that more or less of the judgment debtor's earnings be withheld where the earnings withholding order is issued to collect delinquent child or spousal support payments. Subdivision (c) makes clear that the court may not order the withholding of an amount in excess of that permitted by federal law. This maximum amount varies depending upon whether the judgment debtor is supporting more than one person or is more than 12 weeks delinquent. The authority of the court to make an equitable division of the judgment debtor's earnings between, for example, the debtor and a former spouse, or between a former spouse and a present family, is based on decisions under a former statute. See, e.g., Rankins v. Rankins, 52 Cal.App.2d 231, 126 P.2d 125 (1942).

Under this section, an employer who receives an earnings withholding order for support will know that 50 percent of disposable earnings is to be withheld unless the employer is served with a court order requiring a greater or lesser amount to be withheld.

For rules relating to the priority to be given a withholding order for support, see Section 706.030. [16 Cal.L.Rev.Comm. Reports 1457 (1982)].

Subdivision (a) of Section 706.052 is amended to conform to the terminology of the Family Code. See Chapter 8 (commencing with Section 5200) of Part 5 of Division 9 of the Family Code (earnings assignment order for support). "Earnings assignment order for support" is defined in Section 706.011. [22 Cal.L.Rev.Comm.Reports 1 (1992)].

Research References

Rutter, Cal. Practice Guide: Enforcing Judgments/Debts Ch. 6E-5, Specific Exempt Property.

Rutter, Cal. Practice Guide: Enforcing Judgments/Debts Ch. 6F-5, Earnings Exempt from Garnishment.

8 Witkin Cal. Proc. 5th Enforcement of Judgment § 202, (S 202) Effect of Support Judgment.

8 Witkin Cal. Proc. 5th Enforcement of Judgment § 204, Private Retirement Benefits.

8 Witkin Cal. Proc. 5th Enforcement of Judgment § 206, (S 206) Disability and Health Benefits.

8 Witkin Cal. Proc. 5th Enforcement of Judgment § 251, Restrictions on Earnings Withholding.

8 Witkin Cal. Proc. 5th Enforcement of Judgment § 267, Issuance by Local Child Support Agency.

10 Witkin, California Summary 10th Parent and Child § 416, (S 416) Application and Order.

11 Witkin, California Summary 10th Husband and Wife § 334, (S 334) in General.

ARTICLE 4. EARNINGS WITHHOLDING ORDER FOR TAXES

Section
706.070. Definitions.

706.071. Limitations on state's right to collect state tax liability.

706.072. Withholding order for taxes, defined; issuance requirements; notice of proposed issuance.

706.073. Application of chapter and article to withholding order for taxes; levying officer, defined.

706.074. Issuance of withholding order by state; contents; amount.

706.075. Service and delivery of copy of order and notice; hearing; employer liability.

706.076. Withholding amounts in excess of order issued under section 706.074; application to court for order; setting for hearing and notice; issuance of order; temporary earnings holding order.

706.077. Employer withholding; prior earnings withholding orders.

706.078. Pay periods to which withholding order applicable; jeopardy withholding order for taxes; termination of order.

Section
706.080. Manner of service of order, notice or other document.

706.081. Form of order, notice or other document.

706.082. Court proceedings for review of taxpayer's liability.

706.084. Warrant, notice of levy or notice or order to withhold.

§ 706.070. Definitions

As used in this article:

(a) "State" means the State of California and includes any officer, department, board, or agency thereof.

(b) "State tax liability" means an amount for which the state has a state tax lien as defined in Section 7162 of the Government Code excluding a state tax lien created pursuant to the Fish and Game Code.

(c) For purposes of an earnings withholding order for taxes issued by the Franchise Tax Board, "state tax liability" also includes any liability under Part 10 (commencing with Section 17001), Part 10.2 (commencing with Section 18401), or Part 11 (commencing with Section 23001) of Division 2 of the Revenue and Taxation Code that is due and payable within the meaning of subdivision (b) of Section 19221 of the Revenue and Taxation Code, and unpaid. The amendments to this section by the act [1] adding this subdivision shall apply to any amount that is unpaid on or after the effective date of that act, or any amount that first becomes due and payable, and unpaid, after the effective date of that act. *(Added by Stats.1982, c. 1364, p. 5176, § 2, operative July 1, 1983. Amended by Stats.2012, c. 37 (S.B.1015), § 1, eff. June 27, 2012.)*

[1] Stats.2012, c. 37 (S.B.1015), eff. June 27, 2012.

Law Revision Commission Comments

Section 706.070 provides definitions for terms used in this article.

Subdivision (a) continues subdivision (a) of former Section 723.070. "State" means the state or any agency thereof. Where the term "state" is used in this article, it refers to the particular state agency that administers the particular tax law under which recovery of the delinquent tax is sought. See Section 706.011(d).

Subdivision (b) supersedes subdivision (b) of former Section 723.070 and substitutes a general reference to the amount for which the state has a state tax lien for the listing of the sections of various tax laws in former Section 723.070(b). Subdivision (b) continues former law by permitting an earnings withholding order for taxes in the case of sales and use taxes (Rev. & Tax. Code § 6757), vehicle fuel license taxes (Rev. & Tax. Code § 7872), use fuel taxes (Rev. & Tax. Code § 8996), gift taxes (Rev. & Tax. Code § 16063), personal income taxes (Rev. & Tax. Code § 18881), bank and corporation taxes (Rev. & Tax. Code § 26161), cigarette taxes (Rev. & Tax. Code § 30322), alcoholic beverage taxes (Rev. & Tax. Code § 32363), and unemployment compensation contributions (Unemp.Ins. Code § 1703). Subdivision (b) adds new authority for an earnings withholding order for taxes in the case of the timber yield tax (Rev. & Tax. Code § 38532), oil and gas conservation charges (Pub.Res. Code § 3423) and geothermal resources charges (Pub.Res. Code § 3772). The former provision permitting an earnings withholding order for taxes in the case of private car taxes under Section 11451 of the Revenue and Taxation Code is not continued. [16 Cal.L.Rev.Comm. Reports 1459 (1982)].

Research References

Rutter, Cal. Practice Guide: Enforcing Judgments/Debts Ch. 6F-2, Wage Garnishment-In General.

8 Witkin Cal. Proc. 5th Enforcement of Judgment § 243, (S 243) Definitions.

8 Witkin Cal. Proc. 5th Enforcement of Judgment § 250, (S 250) Rules and Forms.

8 Witkin Cal. Proc. 5th Enforcement of Judgment § 251, Restrictions on Earnings Withholding.

8 Witkin Cal. Proc. 5th Enforcement of Judgment § 261, (S 261) in General.

8 Witkin Cal. Proc. 5th Enforcement of Judgment § 268, (S 268) Earnings Assignment Order for Support.

8 Witkin Cal. Proc. 5th Enforcement of Judgment § 269, (S 269) in General.

§ 706.071. Limitations on state's right to collect state tax liability

This chapter does not limit the state's right to collect a state tax liability except that (a) no levy upon earnings of an employee held by an employer is effective unless such levy is made in accordance with the provisions of this chapter and (b) other methods of collection may not be used to require an employer to withhold earnings of an employee in payment of a state tax liability. (*Added by Stats.1982, c. 1364, p. 5176, § 2, operative July 1, 1983.*)

Law Revision Commission Comments

Section 706.071 continues the substance of former Section 723.071. The substitution of "other methods of collection" for "the methods of collection referred to in subdivision (b) of Section 723.070" is not a substantive change; this change merely conforms to the change made by Section 706.070 in the language found in former Section 723.070.

Section 706.071 makes clear that the levy procedure for withholding earnings of an employee for the collection of state tax liability provided in the Wage Garnishment Law is exclusive. The authorization, for example, to direct orders to third persons who owe the taxpayer money found in Section 18817 (personal income tax) and Section 26132 (bank and corporation taxes) of the Revenue and Taxation Code is limited by Section 706.071. This article deals, however, only with levy on earnings to collect certain state taxes. The collection of federal taxes is accomplished pursuant to federal law and cannot be limited by state law. See I.R.C. § 6334. As to other taxes not within the scope of this article, the tax obligation must be reduced to judgment, and the taxing authority may then obtain an earnings withholding order like any other creditor; such order is treated the same as any other earnings withholding order, and this article does not apply. [16 Cal.L.Rev.Comm. Reports 1460 (1982)].

Research References

8 Witkin Cal. Proc. 5th Enforcement of Judgment § 269, (S 269) in General.

§ 706.072. Withholding order for taxes, defined; issuance requirements; notice of proposed issuance

(a) A "withholding order for taxes" is an earnings withholding order issued pursuant to this article to collect a state tax liability and shall be denoted as a withholding order for taxes on its face.

(b) A withholding order for taxes may only be issued under one of the following circumstances:

(1) The existence of the state tax liability appears on the face of the taxpayer's return, including a case where such tax liability is disclosed from the taxpayer's return after errors in mathematical computations in the return have been corrected.

(2) The state tax liability has been assessed or determined as provided by statute and the taxpayer had notice of the proposed assessment or determination and had available an opportunity to have the proposed assessment or determination reviewed by appropriate administrative procedures. If the taxpayer makes a timely request for review of the assessment or determination, the state shall not issue a withholding order for taxes until the administrative review procedure is completed. If the taxpayer is given notice of the proposed assessment or determination but does not make a timely request for review, the state may issue a withholding order for taxes.

(c) In any case where a state tax liability has been assessed or determined prior to July 1, 1983, and the state determines that the requirement of subdivision (b) may not have been satisfied, the state may send a "Notice of Proposed Issuance of Withholding Order for Taxes" to the taxpayer at the taxpayer's last known address by first-class mail, postage prepaid. The notice shall advise the taxpayer that the taxpayer may have the assessment or determination reviewed by appropriate administrative proce-

dures and state how such a review may be obtained. If the taxpayer is sent such a notice and requests such a review within 30 days from the date the notice was mailed to the taxpayer, the state shall provide appropriate administrative procedures for review of the assessment or determination and shall not issue the withholding order for taxes until the administrative review procedure is completed. If the taxpayer is sent such a notice and does not request such a review within 30 days from the date the notice was mailed to the taxpayer, the state may issue the withholding order for taxes.

(d) A withholding order for taxes may be issued whether or not the state tax liability has been reduced to judgment. (*Added by Stats.1982, c. 1364, p. 5176, § 2, operative July 1, 1983.*)

Research References

Rutter, Cal. Practice Guide: Enforcing Judgments/Debts Ch. 6F-2, Wage Garnishment-In General.

8 Witkin Cal. Proc. 5th Enforcement of Judgment § 269, (S 269) in General.

8 Witkin Cal. Proc. 5th Enforcement of Judgment § 270, (S 270) Conditions for Order.

§ 706.073. Application of chapter and article to withholding order for taxes; levying officer, defined

Except as otherwise provided in this article, the provisions of this chapter govern the procedures and proceedings concerning a withholding order for taxes. For the purposes of this article, a reference in this chapter to a "levying officer" shall be deemed to mean the specific state agency seeking to collect a state tax liability under this article. (*Added by Stats.1982, c. 1364, p. 5177, § 2, operative July 1, 1983.*)

Law Revision Commission Comments

Section 706.073 continues former Section 723.073 and makes clear that the provisions of this chapter governing earnings withholding orders are applicable to withholding orders for taxes except to the extent that this article contains special provisions applicable to such orders. [16 Cal. L.Rev.Comm. Reports 1462 (1982)].

Research References

8 Witkin Cal. Proc. 5th Enforcement of Judgment § 269, (S 269) in General.

§ 706.074. Issuance of withholding order by state; contents; amount

(a) The state may itself issue a withholding order for taxes under this section to collect a state tax liability. The order shall specify the total amount required to be withheld pursuant to the order (unpaid tax liability including any penalties, accrued interest, and costs).

(b) Unless a lesser amount is specified in the order, the amount to be withheld by the employer each pay period pursuant to an order issued under this section is the amount required to be withheld under Section 1673(a) of Title 15 of the United States Code, and is not subject to the exception provided in Section 1673(b) of Title 15 of the United States Code. (*Added by Stats.1982, c. 1364, p. 5177, § 2, operative July 1, 1983.*)

Law Revision Commission Comments

Section 706.074 continues the substance of former Section 723.074. The reference to the relevant provision of federal law has been substituted for the reference to former Section 723.050. This makes clear that an order issued under this section is limited to the amount that can be withheld on a garnishment by an ordinary creditor. A court-issued order can require the withholding of a greater amount. See Section 706.076.

Section 706.074 specifies the procedure to be followed when the state taxing agency itself issues the withholding order for taxes. In such case, no application to a court for the order is required. Under an order issued pursuant to Section 706.074, the employer may be required to withhold the same amount as if the earnings withholding order were issued at the behest of a judgment creditor. This amount must be withheld by the employer unless the order itself specifies a lesser amount or the amount to be withheld is reduced pursuant to subdivision (c) of Section 706.075. As to the priority of a withholding order for support, see Sections 706.030 and 706.077 and Comments thereto. As to the effect of a wage assignment for support (defined in subdivision (g) of Section 706.011), see subdivision (e) of Section 706.031 and the Comment thereto. [16 Cal.L.Rev.Comm. Reports 1463 (1982)].

Research References

Rutter, Cal. Practice Guide: Enforcing Judgments/Debts Ch. 6F-5, Earnings Exempt from Garnishment.
8 Witkin Cal. Proc. 5th Enforcement of Judgment § 271, (S 271) Issuance of Order.

§ 706.075. Service and delivery of copy of order and notice; hearing; employer liability

(a) This section applies to any withholding order for taxes issued under this article.

(b) Together with the withholding order for taxes, the state shall serve upon the employer an additional copy of the order and a notice informing the taxpayer of the effect of the order and of his right to hearings and remedies provided in this chapter. Within 10 days from the date of service, the employer shall deliver to the taxpayer a copy of the order and the notice, except that immediate delivery shall be made where a jeopardy withholding order for taxes has been served. If the taxpayer is no longer employed by the employer and the employer does not owe the taxpayer any earnings, the employer is not required to make such delivery.

(c) The state shall provide for an administrative hearing to reconsider or modify the amount to be withheld pursuant to the withholding order for taxes, and the taxpayer may request such a hearing at any time after service of the order. If the taxpayer requests a hearing, the hearing shall be provided, and the matter shall be determined, within 15 days after the request is received by the state. The determination of the amount to be withheld is subject to the standard provided in subdivision (b) of Section 706.051. Judicial review of the determination made pursuant to this subdivision by the state may be had only if a petition for a writ of mandate pursuant to Section 1094.5 is filed within 90 days from the date that written notice of the state's determination was delivered or mailed to the taxpayer.

(d) The employer is not subject to any civil liability for failure to comply with subdivision (b). Nothing in this subdivision limits the power of a court to hold the employer in contempt of court for failure to comply with subdivision (b). *(Added by Stats.1982, c. 1364, p. 5178, § 2, operative July 1, 1983.)*

Research References

8 Witkin Cal. Proc. 5th Enforcement of Judgment § 257, (S 257) Employer's Duties on Service of Withholding Order.
8 Witkin Cal. Proc. 5th Enforcement of Judgment § 269, (S 269) in General.
8 Witkin Cal. Proc. 5th Enforcement of Judgment § 271, (S 271) Issuance of Order.
8 Witkin Cal. Proc. 5th Enforcement of Judgment § 272, (S 272) Service and Form of Documents.

§ 706.076. Withholding amounts in excess of order issued under section 706.074; application to court for order; setting for hearing and notice; issuance of order; temporary earnings holding order

(a) A withholding order for taxes may be issued pursuant to this section requiring the employer of the taxpayer to withhold an amount in excess of the amount that may be required to be withheld pursuant to an order issued under Section 706.074.

(b) The state may, at any time, apply to a court of record in the county where the taxpayer was last known to reside for the issuance of a withholding order for taxes under this section to collect a state tax liability.

(c) The application for the order shall include a statement under oath that the state has served upon the taxpayer both of the following:

(1) A copy of the application.

(2) A notice informing the taxpayer of the purpose of the application and the right of the taxpayer to appear at the court hearing on the application.

(d) Upon the filing of the application, the court shall immediately set the matter for hearing and the court clerk shall send a notice of the time and place of the hearing by first-class mail, postage prepaid, to the state and the taxpayer. The notice shall be deposited in the mail at least 10 days before the day set for the hearing.

(e) After hearing, the court shall issue a withholding order for taxes which shall require the taxpayer's employer to withhold and pay over all earnings of the taxpayer other than that amount which the taxpayer proves is exempt under subdivision (b) of Section 706.051, but in no event shall the amount to be withheld be less than that permitted to be withheld under Section 706.050.

(f) The state may issue a temporary earnings holding order, which shall be denoted as such on its face, in any case where the state intends to apply for a withholding order for taxes under this section and has determined that the collection of the state tax liability will be jeopardized in whole or in part if the temporary earnings holding order is not issued. The temporary earnings holding order shall be directed to the taxpayer's employer and shall require the employer to retain in the employer's possession or under the employer's control all or such portion of the earnings of the taxpayer then or thereafter due as is specified in the order. Together with the temporary earnings holding order, the state shall serve upon the employer an additional copy of the order and a notice informing the taxpayer of the effect of the order and of the right to the remedies provided in this chapter. Upon receipt of the order, the employer shall deliver to the taxpayer a copy of the order and notice. If the taxpayer is no longer employed by the employer and the employer does not owe the taxpayer any earnings, the employer is not required to make such delivery. The temporary earnings holding order expires 15 days from the date it is served on the employer unless it is extended by the court on ex parte application for good cause shown. If a temporary earnings holding order is served on an employer, the state may not thereafter, for a period of six months, serve on the same employer another temporary earnings holding order for the same employee unless the court for good cause shown otherwise orders. Sections 706.153 and 706.154 apply to temporary earnings holding orders issued under this section. *(Added by Stats.1982, c. 1364, p. 5178, § 2, operative July 1, 1983.)*

Law Revision Commission Comments

Section 706.076 continues former Section 723.076. Section 706.076 provides a procedure whereby the taxing agency can obtain an order, after court hearing, that requires the employer to withhold all of the employee's earnings in excess of the amount necessary for the support of the taxpayer or his family. An order may be obtained under Section 706.076 that requires the withholding of more than the amount that the state taxing agency could require the employer to withhold pursuant to an order issued by the agency itself under Section 706.074. This grant of authority is not intended as a directive that such authority be used generally. This extreme remedy could be harsh in its application and should be used sparingly.

Provision is made in subdivision (f) of Section 706.076 for a temporary order directing the employer to hold any earnings of the employee then or thereafter due. Such orders should be used only in rare and unusual cases. The temporary order prevents the employer from paying to the employee all or a specified portion of the employee's earnings for a limited period in order to permit the court to act on the state's application for an earnings withholding order for taxes. [16 Cal.L.Rev.Comm. Reports 1466 (1982)].

Research References

Rutter, Cal. Practice Guide: Enforcing Judgments/Debts Ch. 6F-5, Earnings Exempt from Garnishment.
8 Witkin Cal. Proc. 5th Enforcement of Judgment § 257, (S 257) Employer's Duties on Service of Withholding Order.
8 Witkin Cal. Proc. 5th Enforcement of Judgment § 271, (S 271) Issuance of Order.
8 Witkin Cal. Proc. 5th Enforcement of Judgment § 272, (S 272) Service and Form of Documents.

§ 706.077. Employer withholding; prior earnings withholding orders

(a) Subject to subdivision (b), an employer upon whom a withholding order for taxes is served shall withhold and pay over earnings of the employee pursuant to such order and shall cease to withhold earnings pursuant to any prior earnings withholding order except that a withholding order for support shall be given priority as provided in Section 706.030. When an employer is required to cease withholding earnings pursuant to an earlier earnings withholding order, the employer shall notify the levying officer who served the earlier earnings withholding order that a supervening withholding order for taxes is in effect.

(b) An employer shall not withhold earnings of an employee pursuant to a withholding order for taxes if a prior withholding order for taxes is in effect, and, in such case, the subsequent withholding order for taxes is ineffective. *(Added by Stats.1982, c. 1364, p. 5179, § 2, operative July 1, 1983.)*

Law Revision Commission Comments

Section 706.077 continues former Section 723.077 and deals with the priority a tax withholding order is to be given with respect to other earnings withholding orders. A withholding order for taxes takes priority over any prior earnings withholding order except one for support or another withholding order for taxes. As indicated in the Comment to Section 706.030, a withholding order for support always takes priority over any other earnings withholding order. Thus, where a withholding order for support is in effect and a subsequent tax order is received, the employer will continue to withhold pursuant to the withholding order for support, and the amount withheld pursuant to the tax order will be reduced by the amount withheld pursuant to the withholding order for support. Similarly, where a tax order is in effect and a withholding order for support is served, the withholding order for support again takes priority. See the Comments to Sections 706.030 and 706.050. However, where the prior earnings withholding order is for the collection of a debt other than for taxes or delinquent support, the tax order displaces the prior earnings withholding order, and the employer must withhold only pursuant to the tax order until the tax debt is completely paid. If the earnings withholding order for taxes is satisfied during the withholding period of the prior earnings withholding order (Section 706.022), the employer must then again withhold pursuant to the prior earnings withholding order. Where there is a prior tax order in effect, the second tax order is ineffective; the employer may not withhold pursuant to the second order and must promptly notify the agency which issued or obtained the second order of the reason for his action. See Section 706.104(b).

As to the effect of a wage assignment for support (defined in subdivision (g) of Section 706.011), see Section 706.031(e). As indicated in the Comment to Section 706.031, a wage assignment for support takes priority over any earnings withholding order. Thus, where a wage assignment for support is in effect and a subsequent tax order is received, the employer will continue to withhold pursuant to the wage assignment, and the amount withheld pursuant to the tax order will be reduced by the amount withheld pursuant to the wage assignment for support. Similarly, where a tax order is in effect and a wage assignment for support is served, the wage assignment takes priority. See the Comments to Sections 706.031 and 706.050. [16 Cal.L.Rev.Comm. Reports 1467 (1982)].

Research References

Rutter, Cal. Practice Guide: Enforcing Judgments/Debts Ch. 6F-6, Priority Among Earnings Withholding Orders.
8 Witkin Cal. Proc. 5th Enforcement of Judgment § 245, (S 245) Priority of Withholding Orders.
8 Witkin Cal. Proc. 5th Enforcement of Judgment § 258, (S 258) Withholding by Employer.
8 Witkin Cal. Proc. 5th Enforcement of Judgment § 273, (S 273) Priority.

§ 706.078. Pay periods to which withholding order applicable; jeopardy withholding order for taxes; termination of order

(a) Except as provided in subdivision (b), the employer shall not withhold pursuant to a withholding order for taxes from earnings of the employee payable for any pay period of such employee that ends prior to the 10th day after service of the order.

(b) A "jeopardy withholding order for taxes," which shall be denoted as such on its face, is a withholding order for taxes that requires that the employer withhold pursuant to the order from earnings due to the employee at the time of service of the order on the employer and from earnings thereafter due. A jeopardy withholding order for taxes may be issued only where the state has determined that the collection of a state tax liability will be jeopardized in whole or in part by delaying the time when withholding from earnings commences.

(c) An employer shall continue to withhold pursuant to a withholding order for taxes until the amount specified in the order has been paid in full or the order is withdrawn, except that the order automatically terminates one year after the employment of the employee by the employer terminates. The state shall promptly serve on the employer a notice terminating the withholding order for taxes if the state tax liability for which the withholding order for taxes was issued is satisfied before the employer has withheld the full amount specified in the order, and the employer shall discontinue withholding in compliance with such notice. *(Added by Stats.1982, c. 1364, p. 5180, § 2, operative July 1, 1983.)*

Law Revision Commission Comments

Section 706.078 continues former Section 723.078. Subdivision (a) requires the employer to withhold commencing at the same time as with any other order. See Section 706.022. Subdivision (b) provides for a jeopardy withholding order that requires immediate withholding. Such an order should be used only in rare and unusual cases. Subdivision (c) requires the employer to withhold earnings pursuant to a withholding order for taxes until the amount specified in the order has been paid in full and provides for a notice if the tax liability is satisfied before the full amount specified in the order has been withheld. The notice required by Section 706.078 is in lieu of the notice provided by Section 706.027. If not earlier terminated by the court, the order automatically terminates one year after the employment of the employee by the employer terminates. See the discussion of a comparable provision in the Comment to Section 706.030. [16 Cal.L.Rev.Comm. Reports 1486 (1982)].

Research References

8 Witkin Cal. Proc. 5th Enforcement of Judgment § 274, (S 274) Commencement and Termination of Withholding.

§ 706.080. Manner of service of order, notice or other document

Service of a withholding order for taxes or of any other notice or document required under this chapter in connection with a withholding order for taxes may be made by the state by first-class mail, postage prepaid, or by any authorized state employee. Service of a withholding order for taxes is complete when it is received by the employer or a person described in paragraph (1) or (2) of subdivision (a) of Section 706.101. Service of, or the providing of, any other notice or document required to be served or provided under this chapter in connection with a withholding order for taxes is complete when the notice or document is deposited in the mail addressed to the last known address of the person on whom it is served or to whom it is to be provided. *(Added by Stats.1982, c. 1364, p. 5180, § 2, operative July 1, 1983.)*

Law Revision Commission Comments

Section 706.080 continues the substance of former Section 723.080 and provides special provisions for service of notices, documents, and orders under this article. This special service provision is in lieu of the one prescribed by Section 706.101. [16 Cal.L.Rev.Comm. Reports 1470 (1982)].

Research References

8 Witkin Cal. Proc. 5th Enforcement of Judgment § 254, in General.
8 Witkin Cal. Proc. 5th Enforcement of Judgment § 272, (S 272) Service and Form of Documents.

§ 706.081.   Form of order, notice or other document

Except for the forms referred to in Section 706.076, the state shall prescribe the form of any order, notice, or other document required by this chapter in connection with a withholding order for taxes notwithstanding Sections 706.100 and 706.120, and any form so prescribed is deemed to comply with this chapter. *(Added by Stats.1982, c. 1364, p. 5180, § 2, operative July 1, 1983.)*

Law Revision Commission Comments

Section 706.081 continues former Section 723.081. The section requires that forms used in connection with this article be prescribed by the state taxing agency administering the particular tax law except that the Judicial Council prescribes the forms used in connection with court issued orders under Section 706.076. See Section 706.120. [16 Cal.L.Rev. Comm. Reports 1470 (1982)].

Research References

Rutter, Cal. Practice Guide: Enforcing Judgments/Debts Ch. 6F-3, Issuance and Service of Earnings Withholding Orders.
8 Witkin Cal. Proc. 5th Enforcement of Judgment § 25, Rules and Forms.
8 Witkin Cal. Proc. 5th Enforcement of Judgment § 250, (S 250) Rules and Forms.
8 Witkin Cal. Proc. 5th Enforcement of Judgment § 272, (S 272) Service and Form of Documents.

§ 706.082.   Court proceedings for review of taxpayer's liability

No review of the taxpayer's tax liability shall be permitted in any court proceedings under this chapter. *(Added by Stats.1982, c. 1364, p. 5180, § 2, operative July 1, 1983.)*

Law Revision Commission Comments

Section 706.082 continues former Section 723.082 and makes clear that the court, in a proceeding under this chapter, may not review the taxpayer's tax liability. [16 Cal.L.Rev.Comm. Reports 1470 (1982)].

Research References

8 Witkin Cal. Proc. 5th Enforcement of Judgment § 269, (S 269) in General.

§ 706.084.   Warrant, notice of levy or notice or order to withhold

Where a warrant, notice of levy, or notice or order to withhold is served on the employer to enforce a state tax liability of a person who is an employee of that employer, it shall be deemed to be a withholding order for taxes as to any earnings that are subject to the provisions of this chapter if both of the following requirements are satisfied:

(a) The form provides notice on its face that it is to be treated as a withholding order for taxes as to any earnings that are subject to the provisions of this chapter.

(b) The form provides all the information provided in a withholding order for taxes. *(Added by Stats.1982, c. 1364, p. 5180, § 2, operative July 1, 1983.)*

Law Revision Commission Comments

Section 706.084 continues the substance of former Section 723.084. The section has been revised to reflect the revised definition of "state tax liability" in Section 706.070.

Section 706.084 deals with the situation where it is not clear whether an employer-employee relationship exists. The warrant, notice of levy, or notice or order to withhold may be issued on the assumption the taxpayer is an independent contractor. However, so that the taxpayer cannot avoid the withholding by claiming that he is an employee and that his earnings may be withheld only pursuant to an earnings withholding order, Section 706.084 provides that the warrant, notice, or order may require that it be treated as an earnings withholding order if the taxpayer is an employee. The contents of the forms (except for a court issued withholding order for taxes) are prescribed by the state. See Section 706.081. The form for the court issued withholding order for taxes is prescribed by the Judicial Council. See Section 706.120. [16 Cal.L.Rev.Comm. Reports 1471 (1982)].

Research References

Rutter, Cal. Practice Guide: Enforcing Judgments/Debts Ch. 6F-2, Wage Garnishment-In General.
8 Witkin Cal. Proc. 5th Enforcement of Judgment § 269, (S 269) in General.
8 Witkin Cal. Proc. 5th Enforcement of Judgment § 272, (S 272) Service and Form of Documents.

ARTICLE 5.   PROCEDURE FOR EARNINGS WITHHOLDING ORDERS AND EXEMPTION CLAIMS

Section

§ 706.100.   Practice and procedure in proceedings under this chapter; rules

Notwithstanding any other provision of law, the Judicial Council may provide by rule for the practice and procedure in proceedings under this chapter except for the state's administrative hearings provided by Article 4 (commencing with Section 706.070). *(Added by Stats.1982, c. 1364, p. 5181, § 2, operative July 1, 1983.)*

Law Revision Commission Comments

Section 706.100 continues former Section 723.100. Article 5 outlines generally the procedure for issuance and review of an earnings withholding order; however, Section 706.100 authorizes the Judicial Council to provide by rule for the practice and procedure in proceedings under this chapter. As to the broad authority of the Judicial Council under a comparable provision, see In re Marriage of Lusk, 86 Cal.App.3d 228, 150 Cal.Rptr. 63 (1978) (Family Law Act rules). The state tax agency prescribes the rules of procedure for administrative hearings under Article 4 (withholding orders for taxes). The Judicial Council also prescribes the forms to be used under this chapter. See Section 706.120. But see Section 706.081 (forms used in connection with withholding orders for taxes—other than the form of a court issued order—are prescribed by state). [16 Cal.L.Rev.Comm. Reports 1471 (1982)].

Research References

8 Witkin Cal. Proc. 5th Enforcement of Judgment § 25, Rules and Forms.
8 Witkin Cal. Proc. 5th Enforcement of Judgment § 243, (S 243) Definitions.
8 Witkin Cal. Proc. 5th Enforcement of Judgment § 250, (S 250) Rules and Forms.

§ 706.101.　Service of order by delivery; earnings withholding order

(a) An earnings withholding order shall be served by the levying officer upon the employer by delivery of the order to any of the following:

(1) The managing agent or person in charge, at the time of service, of the branch or office where the employee works or the office from which the employee is paid. In the case of a state employee, the office from which the employee is paid does not include the Controller's office unless the employee works directly for the Controller's office.

(2) Any person to whom a copy of the summons and of the complaint may be delivered to make service on the employer under Article 4 (commencing with Section 416.10) of Chapter 4 of Title 5.

(b) Service of an earnings withholding order shall be made by personal delivery as provided in Section 415.10 or 415.20 or by delivery by first-class mail, postage prepaid. When service is made by first-class mail, service is complete at the time of receipt of the earnings withholding order, as indicated in the employer's return, or the date of mailing if the date of receipt is not indicated on the employer's return. If the levying officer attempts service by first-class mail under this subdivision and does not receive the employer's return within 15 days from the date of mailing, the levying officer shall make service as provided in Article 3 (commencing with Section 415.10) of Chapter 4 of Title 5. For purposes of this section, "employer's return" refers to the Judicial Council-issued form specified by Section 706.126.

(c) The state may issue an earnings withholding order directly, without the use of a levying officer, for purposes of collecting overpayments of unemployment compensation or disability benefits pursuant to Article 4 (commencing with Section 1375) of Chapter 5 of Part 1 of, and Article 5 (commencing with Section 2735) of Chapter 2 of Part 2 of, Division 1 of the Unemployment Insurance Code. The earnings withholding order shall be served by registered or certified mail, postage prepaid, with return receipt requested. Service is deemed complete at the time the return receipt is executed by, or on behalf of, the recipient. If the state does not receive a return receipt within 15 days from the date of deposit in the mail of the withholding order, the state shall refer the earnings withholding order to a levying officer for service in accordance with subdivision (b).

(d) Except as provided in subdivision (b) or (c), service of any notice or document under this chapter may be made by first-class mail, postage prepaid. If service is made on the employer after the employer's return has been received by the levying officer, the service shall be made by first-class mail, postage prepaid, on the person designated in the employer's return to receive notices and at the address indicated in the employer's return, whether or not that address is within the county. This subdivision does not preclude service by personal delivery (1) on the employer before the employer's return has been received by the levying officer or (2) on the person designated in the employer's return after its receipt.

(e) Notwithstanding subdivision (b), if the judgment creditor so requests, the levying officer shall make service of the earnings withholding order by personal delivery as provided in Section

415.10 or 415.20.   *(Added by Stats.1982, c. 1364, p. 5181, § 2.2, operative July 1, 1983.   Amended by Stats.1984, c. 538, § 28; Stats.1989, c. 1416, § 24; Stats.2002, c. 890 (A.B.2929), § 1; Stats.2010, c. 680 (A.B.2394), § 13.)*

Law Revision Commission Comments

Former subdivision (e) of Section 706.101 is superseded by Section 706.108 (issuance and service of earnings withholding order by registered process server). [17 Cal.L.Rev.Comm. Reports 1015 (1983)].

Research References

Rutter, Cal. Practice Guide: Enforcing Judgments/Debts Ch. 6F-3, Issuance and Service of Earnings Withholding Orders.
8 Witkin Cal. Proc. 5th Enforcement of Judgment § 244, (S 244) Withholding Period.
8 Witkin Cal. Proc. 5th Enforcement of Judgment § 253, (S 253) Issuance of Order.
8 Witkin Cal. Proc. 5th Enforcement of Judgment § 254, in General.
8 Witkin Cal. Proc. 5th Enforcement of Judgment § 267, Issuance by Local Child Support Agency.
8 Witkin Cal. Proc. 5th Enforcement of Judgment § 272, (S 272) Service and Form of Documents.

§ 706.102.　Issuance of earnings withholding order where writ of execution issued and time for levy on property under writ not yet expired

(a) If a writ of execution has been issued to the county where the judgment debtor's employer is to be served and the time specified in subdivision (b) of Section 699.530 for levy on property under the writ has not expired, a judgment creditor may apply for the issuance of an earnings withholding order by filing an application with a levying officer in such county who shall promptly issue an earnings withholding order.

(b) This section does not apply where the earnings withholding order is a withholding order for taxes.   *(Added by Stats.1982, c. 1364, p. 5182, § 2, operative July 1, 1983.)*

Research References

Rutter, Cal. Practice Guide: Enforcing Judgments/Debts Ch. 6F-3, Issuance and Service of Earnings Withholding Orders.
8 Witkin Cal. Proc. 5th Enforcement of Judgment § 252, (S 252) Application for Order.
8 Witkin Cal. Proc. 5th Enforcement of Judgment § 253, (S 253) Issuance of Order.

§ 706.103.　Service of documents by levying officer on employer

(a) The levying officer shall serve upon the designated employer all of the following:

(1) The original and one copy of the earnings withholding order.

(2) The form for the employer's return.

(3) The notice to employee of earnings withholding order.

(4) A copy of the form that the judgment debtor may use to make a claim of exemption.

(5) A copy of the form the judgment debtor may use to provide a financial statement.

(b) At the time the levying officer makes service pursuant to subdivision (a), the levying officer shall provide the employer with a copy of the employer's instructions referred to in Section 706.127. The Judicial Council may adopt rules prescribing the circumstances when compliance with this subdivision is not required.

(c) No earnings withholding order shall be served upon the employer after the time specified in subdivision (b) of Section 699.530.   *(Added by Stats.1982, c. 1364, p. 5182, § 2, operative July 1, 1983.   Amended by Stats.2013, c. 64 (S.B.233), § 5.)*

Research References

Rutter, Cal. Practice Guide: Enforcing Judgments/Debts Ch. 6F-3, Issuance and Service of Earnings Withholding Orders.

8 Witkin Cal. Proc. 5th Enforcement of Judgment § 254, in General.

8 Witkin Cal. Proc. 5th Enforcement of Judgment § 255, What Must be Served.

§ 706.104. Delivery of copy of order, notice of earnings withholding, copy of form for claim of exemption, and copy of form to provide financial statement; completion of employer return

Any employer who is served with an earnings withholding order shall:

(a) Deliver to the judgment debtor a copy of the earnings withholding order, the notice to employee of earnings withholding, a copy of the form that the judgment debtor may use to make a claim of exemption, and a copy of the form the judgment debtor may use to provide a financial statement within 10 days from the date of service. If the judgment debtor is no longer employed by the employer and the employer does not owe the employee any earnings, the employer is not required to make such delivery. The employer is not subject to any civil liability for failure to comply with this subdivision. Nothing in this subdivision limits the power of a court to hold the employer in contempt of court for failure to comply with this subdivision.

(b) Complete the employer's return on the form provided by the levying officer and mail it by first-class mail, postage prepaid, to the levying officer within 15 days from the date of service. If the earnings withholding order is ineffective, the employer shall state in the employer's return that the order will not be complied with for this reason and shall return the order to the levying officer with the employer's return. *(Added by Stats.1982, c. 1364, p. 5182, § 2, operative July 1, 1983. Amended by Stats.2013, c. 64 (S.B.233), § 6.)*

Law Revision Commission Comments

Section 706.104 continues former Section 723.104 and imposes certain duties on an employer who is served with an earnings withholding order. The section applies to all earnings withholding orders, including those for support and taxes. See Sections 706.030(a) (support), 706.072(a) (taxes).

Subdivision (a) requires the employer to deliver to the employee a copy of the order and a notice advising the employee of his rights. See also Section 706.075 (withholding order for taxes). There is a special provision, however, concerning the time for such delivery when the order is a jeopardy withholding order for taxes. See Sections 706.073, 706.075(b). See also Section 706.076(f) (notice of temporary earnings holding order).

The last two sentences of subdivision (a) make clear that an employer is not liable for civil damages for failure to give the employee the notice concerning the employee's rights. Section 706.104 does not preclude the Labor Commissioner from taking action under the Labor Code if the employer consistently fails to give employees the notice required under subdivision (a). Moreover, although the employer is not civilly liable, the employer may be subject to punishment for contempt. This would be appropriate where the employer fails to give the employee notice out of malice or willful neglect but would not be appropriate where the employer merely inadvertently fails to give the notice.

Subdivision (b) requires the employer to fill out and mail an employer's return to the levying officer who served the earnings withholding order. In the case of a withholding order for taxes, the return is made to the state agency seeking to collect the tax. See Section 706.073. Under subdivision (b), if the earnings withholding order is ineffective (see Comment to Section 706.023), the employer must state in the return that the order will not be complied with for this reason and also return the order. The form of the return is prescribed by the Judicial Council. See Section 706.120. See also Sections 706.126 (contents of return), 706.081 (form of return for withholding order for taxes is prescribed by state). [16 Cal.L.Rev.Comm. Reports 1476 (1982)].

Research References

Rutter, Cal. Practice Guide: Enforcing Judgments/Debts Ch. 6F-6, Priority Among Earnings Withholding Orders.

Rutter, Cal. Practice Guide: Enforcing Judgments/Debts Ch. 6F-7, Employer Duties and Liabilities Under Wgl.

8 Witkin Cal. Proc. 5th Enforcement of Judgment § 257, (S 257) Employer's Duties on Service of Withholding Order.

8 Witkin Cal. Proc. 5th Enforcement of Judgment § 273, (S 273) Priority.

§ 706.105. Claim of exemption under § 706.051

(a) A judgment debtor may claim an exemption under Section 706.051 under either of the following circumstances:

(1) No prior hearing has been held with respect to the earnings withholding order.

(2) There has been a material change in circumstances since the time of the last prior hearing on the earnings withholding order.

(b) A claim of exemption shall be made by filing with the levying officer an original and one copy of (1) the judgment debtor's claim of exemption and (2) the judgment debtor's financial statement.

(c) Upon filing of the claim of exemption, the levying officer shall promptly send to the judgment creditor, at the address stated in the application for the earnings withholding order, by first-class mail, postage prepaid, all of the following:

(1) A copy of the claim of exemption.

(2) A copy of the financial statement.

(3) A notice of claim of exemption. The notice shall state that the claim of exemption has been filed and that the earnings withholding order will be terminated, or modified to reflect the amount of earnings claimed to be exempt in the claim of exemption, unless a notice of opposition to the claim of exemption is filed with the levying officer by the judgment creditor within 10 days after the date of the mailing of the notice of claim of exemption.

(d) A judgment creditor who desires to contest a claim of exemption shall, within 10 days after the date of the mailing of the notice of claim of exemption, file with the levying officer a notice of opposition to the claim of exemption.

(e) If a notice of opposition to the claim of exemption is filed with the levying officer within the 10–day period, the judgment creditor is entitled to a hearing on the claim of exemption. If the judgment creditor desires a hearing on the claim of exemption, the judgment creditor shall file a notice of motion for an order determining the claim of exemption with the court within 10 days after the date the levying officer mailed the notice of claim of exemption. If the notice of motion is so filed, the hearing on the motion shall be held not later than 30 days from the date the notice of motion was filed unless continued by the court for good cause. At the time prescribed by subdivision (b) of Section 1005, the judgment creditor shall give written notice of the hearing to the levying officer and shall serve a notice of the hearing and a copy of the notice of opposition to the claim of exemption on the judgment debtor and, if the claim of exemption so requested, on the attorney for the judgment debtor. Service is deemed made when the notice of the hearing and a copy of the notice of opposition to the claim of exemption are deposited in the mail, postage prepaid, addressed to the judgment debtor at the address stated in the claim of exemption and, if service on the attorney for the judgment debtor was requested in the claim of exemption, to the attorney at the address stated in the claim of exemption. The judgment creditor shall file proof of the service with the court. After receiving the notice of the hearing and before the date set for the hearing, the levying officer shall file the claim of exemption and the notice of opposition to the claim of exemption with the court.

(f) If the levying officer does not receive a notice of opposition to the claim of exemption within the 10–day period after the date of mailing of the notice of claim of exemption and a notice of the hearing not later than 10 days after the filing of the notice of opposition to the claim of exemption, the levying officer shall serve on the employer one of the following:

(1) A notice that the earnings withholding order has been terminated if all of the judgment debtor's earnings were claimed to be exempt.

(2) A modified earnings withholding order that reflects the amount of earnings claimed to be exempt in the claim of exemption if only a portion of the judgment debtor's earnings was claimed to be exempt.

(g) If, after hearing, the court orders that the earnings withholding order be modified or terminated, the clerk shall promptly transmit a certified copy of the order to the levying officer who shall promptly serve on the employer of the judgment debtor (1) a copy of the modified earnings withholding order or (2) a notice that the earnings withholding order has been terminated. The court may order that the earnings withholding order be terminated as of a date that precedes the date of hearing. If the court determines that any amount withheld pursuant to the earnings withholding order shall be paid to the judgment debtor, the court shall make an order directing the person who holds that amount to pay it promptly to the judgment debtor.

(h) If the earnings withholding order is terminated by the court, unless the court otherwise orders or unless there is a material change of circumstances since the time of the last prior hearing on the earnings withholding order, the judgment creditor may not apply for another earnings withholding order directed to the same employer with respect to the same judgment debtor for a period of 100 days following the date of service of the earnings withholding order or 60 days after the date of the termination of the order, whichever is later.

(i) If an employer has withheld and paid over amounts pursuant to an earnings withholding order after the date of termination of the order but prior to the receipt of notice of its termination, the judgment debtor may recover those amounts only from the levying officer if the levying officer still holds those amounts or, if those amounts have been paid over to the judgment creditor, from the judgment creditor. If the employer has withheld amounts pursuant to an earnings withholding order after termination of the order but has not paid over those amounts to the levying officer, the employer shall promptly pay those amounts to the judgment debtor.

(j) An appeal lies from any court order under this section denying a claim of exemption or modifying or terminating an earnings withholding order. An appeal by the judgment creditor from an order modifying or terminating the earnings withholding order does not stay the order from which the appeal is taken. Notwithstanding the appeal, until the order modifying or terminating the earnings withholding order is set aside or modified, the order allowing the claim of exemption in whole or in part shall be given the same effect as if the appeal had not been taken.

(k) This section does not apply to a withholding order for support or a withholding order for taxes. *(Added by Stats.1982, c. 1364, p. 5183, § 2, operative July 1, 1983. Amended by Stats.1989, c. 693, § 3; Stats.1998, c. 931 (S.B.2139), § 94, eff. Sept. 28, 1998.)*

Law Revision Commission Comments

Section 706.105 is amended to accommodate unification of the municipal and superior courts in a county. Cal. Const. art. VI, § 5(e). See Sections 85 (limited civil cases), 86(a)(8) (enforcement of judgment in limited civil case), 904.1 (taking appeal), 904.2 (taking appeal in limited civil case). See also Section 85 Comment. [28 Cal.L.Rev.Comm. Reports 51 (1998)].

Research References

Rutter, Cal. Practice Guide: Enforcing Judgments/Debts Ch. 6F-5, Earnings Exempt from Garnishment.
Rutter, Cal. Practice Guide: Enforcing Judgments/Debts Ch. 6F-7, Employer Duties and Liabilities Under Wgl.
8 Witkin Cal. Proc. 5th Enforcement of Judgment § 261, (S 261) in General.
8 Witkin Cal. Proc. 5th Enforcement of Judgment § 262, (S 262) Notice, Opposition, and Hearing.
8 Witkin Cal. Proc. 5th Enforcement of Judgment § 263, (S 263) Modification or Termination of Withholding Order.
8 Witkin Cal. Proc. 5th Enforcement of Judgment § 264, (S 264) Debtor's Recovery of Amounts Withheld.
8 Witkin Cal. Proc. 5th Enforcement of Judgment § 265, (S 265) Restriction on New Withholding Orders.

§ 706.106. Findings in court proceedings

No findings are required in court proceedings under this chapter. *(Added by Stats.1982, c. 1364, p. 5185, § 2, operative July 1, 1983.)*

Law Revision Commission Comments

Section 706.106 continues former Section 723.106 and is comparable to a provision found in subdivision (d) of Section 703.580 (claims of exemption). [16 Cal.L.Rev.Comm. Reports 1482 (1982)].

Research References

Rutter, Cal. Practice Guide: Enforcing Judgments/Debts Ch. 6F-5, Earnings Exempt from Garnishment.
8 Witkin Cal. Proc. 5th Enforcement of Judgment § 263, (S 263) Modification or Termination of Withholding Order.

§ 706.108. Earnings withholding order; service and filing requirements; duties of levying officer

(a) If a writ of execution has been issued to the county where the judgment debtor's employer is to be served and the time specified in subdivision (b) of Section 699.530 for levy on property under the writ has not expired, a judgment creditor may deliver an application for issuance of an earnings withholding order to a registered process server who may then issue an earnings withholding order.

(b) If the registered process server has issued the earnings withholding order, the registered process server, before serving the earnings withholding order, shall deposit with the levying officer a copy of the writ of execution, the application for issuance of an earnings withholding order, and a copy of the earnings withholding order, and shall pay the fee provided by Section 26750 of the Government Code.

(c) A registered process server may serve an earnings withholding order on an employer whether the earnings withholding order was issued by a levying officer or by a registered process server, but no earnings withholding order may be served after the time specified in subdivision (b) of Section 699.530. In performing this function, the registered process server shall serve upon the designated employer all of the following:

(1) The original and one copy of the earnings withholding order.

(2) The form for the employer's return.

(3) The notice to the employee of the earnings withholding order.

(4) A copy of the form that the judgment debtor may use to make a claim of exemption.

(5) A copy of the form the judgment debtor may use to provide a financial statement.

(6) A copy of the employer's instructions referred to in Section 706.127, except as otherwise prescribed in rules adopted by the Judicial Council.

(d) Within five court days after service under this section, all of the following shall be filed with the levying officer:

(1) The writ of execution, if it is not already in the hands of the levying officer.

(2) Proof of service on the employer of the papers listed in subdivision (c).

(3) Instructions in writing, as required by the provisions of Section 687.010.

(e) If the fee provided by Section 26750 of the Government Code has been paid, the levying officer shall perform all other duties required by this chapter as if the levying officer had served the earnings withholding order. If the registered process server does not comply with subdivisions (b), where applicable, and (d), the service of the earnings withholding order is ineffective and the levying officer is not required to perform any duties under the order and may terminate the order and may release any withheld earnings to the judgment debtor.

(f) The fee for services of a registered process server under this section shall be allowed as a recoverable cost pursuant to Section 1033.5. *(Added by Stats.1984, c. 538, § 29. Amended by Stats.1987, c. 1080, § 6; Stats.2002, c. 197 (A.B.2493), § 4; Stats.2009, c. 54 (S.B.544), § 6; Stats.2013, c. 64 (S.B.233), § 7.)*

Law Revision Commission Comments

Section 706.108 supersedes former subdivision (e) of Section 706.101 which provided for service of an earnings withholding order by a registered process server. The authority of the registered process server to issue an earnings withholding order provided in subdivision (a) is new. This is comparable to the authority of a levying officer under Section 706.102. See also Section 706.121 (contents of application for earnings withholding order).

Subdivision (b) is comparable to subdivision (b) of Section 699.080 (levying by registered process server under writ of execution). The papers are required to be filed with the levying officer under this subdivision to give the levying officer an early opportunity to establish a file, thereby facilitating the handling of any exemption claim, the employer's return, and payments by the employer or judgment debtor. Of course, if the levying officer has issued the earnings withholding order, this step is not required since the necessary papers will already be on file before service on the employer.

Subdivision (c) is the same in substance as Section 706.103 which applies to service by a levying officer. The first sentence continues the authority provided by former subdivision (e) of Section 706.101.

Subdivision (d) is drawn from subdivision (d) of Section 699.080 (levy by registered process server under writ of execution). If the levying officer has issued the earnings withholding order, the writ of execution will already be in the hands of the levying officer, as is recognized in subdivision (d)(1). If the registered process server has issued the earnings withholding order, however, only a copy of the writ of execution is delivered to the levying officer under subdivision (b) and the writ itself is retained and filed with the levying officer only after service on the employer is complete.

Subdivision (e) continues the substance of the second sentence of former subdivision (e) of Section 706.101 and is comparable to subdivision (e) of Section 699.080 (duties of levying officer after levy by registered process server under writ of execution).

Subdivision (f) continues the limitation on the extra fee that may be allowed provided by former subdivision (e) of Section 706.101. Subdivision (f) is comparable in other respects to subdivision (f) of Section 699.080 (fee for levy under writ of execution). [17 Cal.L.Rev.Comm. Reports 1017 (1983)].

Research References

Rutter, Cal. Practice Guide: Enforcing Judgments/Debts Ch. 6F-3, Issuance and Service of Earnings Withholding Orders.
8 Witkin Cal. Proc. 5th Enforcement of Judgment § 48, Motion for Costs.

8 Witkin Cal. Proc. 5th Enforcement of Judgment § 253, (S 253) Issuance of Order.
8 Witkin Cal. Proc. 5th Enforcement of Judgment § 254, in General.
8 Witkin Cal. Proc. 5th Enforcement of Judgment § 256, Service by Registered Process Server.

§ 706.109. Earnings withholding order; issuance against spouse of judgment debtor

An earnings withholding order may not be issued against the earnings of the spouse of the judgment debtor except by court order upon noticed motion. *(Added by Stats.1984, c. 1671, § 20.)*

Research References

Rutter, Cal. Practice Guide: Enforcing Judgments/Debts Ch. 6F-3, Issuance and Service of Earnings Withholding Orders.
8 Witkin Cal. Proc. 5th Enforcement of Judgment § 251, Restrictions on Earnings Withholding.
11 Witkin, California Summary 10th Community Property § 177, (S 177) General Rule.

ARTICLE 6. FORMS; EMPLOYER'S INSTRUCTIONS

§ 706.120. Form of documents

Except as provided in Section 706.081, the Judicial Council shall prescribe the form of the applications, notices, claims of exemption, orders, and other documents required by this chapter as provided in Section 681.030, and only such forms may be used to implement this chapter. *(Added by Stats.1982, c. 1364, p. 5185, § 2, operative July 1, 1983.)*

Law Revision Commission Comments

Section 706.120 continues the substance of former Section 723.120. The last two sentences of former Section 723.120 have been omitted as unnecessary in view of the inclusion of the substance of these sentences in the general provisions of Section 681.030.

Section 706.120 requires the Judicial Council to prescribe the forms necessary for the purposes of this chapter. Various sections prescribe information to the contained in the forms; but the Judicial Council has complete authority to adopt and revise the forms as necessary and may require additional information in the forms or may omit information from the forms that it determines is unnecessary. See also Section 706.081 (forms in connection with withholding order for taxes). [16 Cal.L.Rev. Comm. Reports 1484 (1982)].

Research References

Rutter, Cal. Practice Guide: Enforcing Judgments/Debts Ch. 6F-3, Issuance and Service of Earnings Withholding Orders.
8 Witkin Cal. Proc. 5th Enforcement of Judgment § 25, Rules and Forms.

8 Witkin Cal. Proc. 5th Enforcement of Judgment § 250, (S 250) Rules and Forms.

§ 706.121. Application for issuance of earnings withholding order; form and contents

The "application for issuance of earnings withholding order" shall be executed under oath and shall include all of the following:

(a) The name, the last known address, and, if known, the social security number of the judgment debtor.

(b) The name and address of the judgment creditor.

(c) The court where the judgment was entered and the date the judgment was entered.

(d) Whether the judgment is based in whole or in part on a claim for elder or dependent adult financial abuse and, if in part, how much of the judgment arises from that claim.

(e) The date of issuance of a writ of execution to the county where the earnings withholding order is sought.

(f) The total amount required to satisfy the order on the date of issuance (which may not exceed the amount required to satisfy the writ of execution on the date of issuance of the order plus the levying officer's statutory fee for service of the order).

(g) The name and address of the employer to whom the order will be directed.

(h) The name and address of the person to whom the withheld money is to be paid by the levying officer. *(Added by Stats.1982, c. 1364, p. 5185, § 2, operative July 1, 1983. Amended by Stats.1992, c. 283 (S.B.1372), § 14, eff. July 21, 1992; Stats. 2010, c. 64 (A.B.2619), § 3, operative Jan. 1, 2012.)*

Law Revision Commission Comments

Section 706.121 continues former Section 723.121 but a reference has been added to the amount of the fee of the levying officer for the service of the earnings withholding order. See the Comment to Section 706.125.

The form for the application for an earnings withholding order is prescribed by the Judicial Council. See Section 706.120. [16 Cal.L.Rev. Comm. Reports 1484 (1982)].

Subdivision (e) of Section 706.121 is amended for consistency with Section 706.024 which governs the amount required to satisfy an earnings withholding order and Section 706.125(e) (contents of earnings withholding order). See Section 706.024 & Comment. [21 Cal.L.Rev.Comm.Reports 135 (1991)].

Research References

Rutter, Cal. Practice Guide: Enforcing Judgments/Debts Ch. 6F-3, Issuance and Service of Earnings Withholding Orders.
8 Witkin Cal. Proc. 5th Enforcement of Judgment § 252, (S 252) Application for Order.

§ 706.122. Notice to employee of earnings withholding order; form and contents

The "notice to employee of earnings withholding order" shall contain a statement that informs the employee in simple terms of the nature of a wage garnishment, the right to an exemption, the procedure for claiming an exemption, and any other information the Judicial Council determines would be useful to the employee and appropriate for inclusion in the notice, including all of the following:

(a) The named employer has been ordered to withhold from the earnings of the judgment debtor the amounts required to be withheld under Section 706.050, or such other amounts as are specified in the earnings withholding order, and to pay these amounts over to the levying officer for transmittal to the person specified in the order in payment of the judgment described in the order.

(b) The manner of computing the amounts required to be withheld pursuant to Section 706.050.

(c) The judgment debtor may be able to keep more or all of the judgment debtor's earnings if the judgment debtor proves that the additional earnings are necessary for the support of the judgment debtor or the judgment debtor's family supported in whole or in part by the judgment debtor.

(d) If the judgment debtor wishes a court hearing to prove that amounts should not be withheld from the judgment debtor's earnings because they are necessary for the support of the judgment debtor or the judgment debtor's family supported in whole or in part by the judgment debtor, the judgment debtor shall file with the levying officer an original and one copy of the "judgment debtor's claim of exemption" and an original and one copy of the "judgment debtor's financial statement." * * * *(Added by Stats.1982, c. 1364, p. 5186, § 2, operative July 1, 1983. Amended by Stats.2013, c. 64 (S.B.233), § 8.)*

Research References

8 Witkin Cal. Proc. 5th Enforcement of Judgment § 255, What Must be Served.

§ 706.123. Judgment debtor's claim of exemption; form and contents

The "judgment debtor's claim of exemption" shall be executed under oath. The claim of exemption shall indicate how much the judgment debtor believes should be withheld from the judgment debtor's earnings each pay period by the employer pursuant to the earnings withholding order and shall state the judgment debtor's present mailing address. *(Added by Stats. 1982, c. 1364, p. 5186, § 2, operative July 1, 1983.)*

Law Revision Commission Comments

Section 706.123 continues former Section 723.123. The form for the claim of exemption is prescribed by the Judicial Council. See Section 706.120. Levying officers must provide copies of the forms without charge. See Section 706.129. The "present mailing address" may or may not be the judgment debtor's residence address. [16 Cal.L.Rev.Comm. Reports 1486 (1982)].

Research References

Rutter, Cal. Practice Guide: Enforcing Judgments/Debts Ch. 6F-5, Earnings Exempt from Garnishment.
8 Witkin Cal. Proc. 5th Enforcement of Judgment § 261, (S 261) in General.

§ 706.124. Judgment debtor's financial statement; form and contents

The "judgment debtor's financial statement" shall be executed as provided in Section 703.530 and contain all of the information required by that section and the following additional information:

(a) Whether any earnings withholding orders are in effect with respect to the earnings of the judgment debtor or the spouse or dependents of the judgment debtor.

(b) Whether any earnings assignment orders for support are in effect with respect to the earnings of the judgment debtor or the spouse or dependents of the judgment debtor. *(Added by Stats.1982, c. 1364, p. 5186, § 2, operative July 1, 1983. Amended by Stats.1992, c. 163 (A.B.2641), § 49, operative Jan. 1, 1994.)*

Law Revision Commission Comments

Subdivision (b) of Section 706.124 is amended to conform to the terminology of the Family Code. See Chapter 8 (commencing with Section 5200) of Part 5 of Division 9 of the Family Code (earnings assignment order for support). "Earnings assignment order for support" is defined in Section 706.011. [22 Cal.L.Rev.Comm.Reports 1 (1992)].

Research References

Rutter, Cal. Practice Guide: Enforcing Judgments/Debts Ch. 6E-3, Procedures for Claiming Exemptions.
8 Witkin Cal. Proc. 5th Enforcement of Judgment § 181, (S 181) Claim of Exemption.
8 Witkin Cal. Proc. 5th Enforcement of Judgment § 261, (S 261) in General.

§ 706.125. Earnings withholding order; contents

The "earnings withholding order" shall include all of the following:

(a) The name, address, and, if known, the social security number of the judgment debtor.

(b) The name and address of the employer to whom the order is directed.

(c) The court where the judgment was entered, the date the judgment was entered, and the name of the judgment creditor.

(d) Whether the judgment is based in whole or in part on a claim for elder or dependent adult financial abuse and, if in part, how much of the judgment arises from the claim.

(e) The date of issuance of the writ of execution to the county where the earnings withholding order is sought.

(f) The total amount required to satisfy the order on the date of issuance (which may not exceed the amount required to satisfy the writ of execution on the date of issuance of the order plus the levying officer's statutory fee for service of the order).

(g) A description of the withholding period and an order to the employer to withhold from the earnings of the judgment debtor for each pay period the amount required to be withheld under Section 706.050 or the amount specified in the order subject to Section 706.024, as the case may be, for the pay periods ending during the withholding period.

(h) An order to the employer to pay over to the levying officer at a specified address the amount required to be withheld and paid over pursuant to the order in the manner and within the times provided by law.

(i) An order that the employer fill out the "employer's return" and return it by first-class mail, postage prepaid, to the levying officer at a specified address within 15 days after service of the earnings withholding order.

(j) An order that the employer deliver to the judgment debtor a copy of the earnings withholding order and the "notice to employee of earnings withholding order" within 10 days after service of the earnings withholding order; but, if the judgment debtor is no longer employed by the employer and the employer does not owe the employee any earnings, the employer is not required to make the delivery.

(k) The name and address of the levying officer. *(Added by Stats.1982, c. 1364, p. 5187, § 2, operative July 1, 1983. Amended by Stats.1992, c. 283 (S.B.1372), § 15, eff. July 21, 1992; Stats. 2010, c. 64 (A.B.2619), § 4, operative Jan. 1, 2012.)*

Law Revision Commission Comments

Section 706.125 specifies the information to be included in the earnings withholding order. The form of the order is prescribed by the Judicial Council. See Section 706.120. Special forms are prescribed for earnings withholding orders for taxes. See Section 706.081.

Section 706.125 continues former Section 723.125 but adds a reference to the levying officer's fee for service of the earnings withholding order (see Gov't Code § 26750). This reference is added to make clear that the amount to be withheld by the employer includes the amount of the fee for service of the earnings withholding order. [16 Cal.L.Rev.Comm. Reports 1488 (1982)].

Subdivisions (e) and (f) of Section 706.125 are amended for consistency with Section 706.024 which governs the amount required to satisfy an earnings withholding order. See Section 706.024 & Comment. [21 Cal.L.Rev.Comm.Reports 135 (1991)].

Research References

Rutter, Cal. Practice Guide: Enforcing Judgments/Debts Ch. 6F-3, Issuance and Service of Earnings Withholding Orders.
8 Witkin Cal. Proc. 5th Enforcement of Judgment § 47, Memorandum of Costs.
8 Witkin Cal. Proc. 5th Enforcement of Judgment § 253, (S 253) Issuance of Order.

§ 706.126. Employer's return; form and contents

(a) The "employer's return" shall be executed under oath. The form for the return provided to the employer shall state all of the following information:

(1) The name and address of the levying officer to whom the form is to be returned.

(2) A direction that the form be mailed to the levying officer by first-class mail, postage prepaid, no later than 15 days after the date of service of the earnings withholding order.

(3) The name, the address, and, if known, the social security number of the judgment debtor.

(b) In addition, the employer's return form shall require the employer to supply all of the following information:

(1) The date the earnings withholding order was served on the employer.

(2) Whether the judgment debtor is employed by the employer or whether the employer otherwise owes earnings to the employee.

(3) If the judgment debtor is employed by the employer or the employer otherwise owes earnings to the employee, the amount of the employee's earnings for the last pay period and the length of this pay period.

(4) Whether the employer was required on the date of service to comply with an earlier earnings withholding order and, if so, the name of the judgment creditor who secured the earlier order, the levying officer who served such order, the date it was issued, the date it was served, the expiration date of such order, and which of the earnings withholding orders the employer is required to comply with under the applicable statutory rules concerning the priority of such orders.

(5) Whether the employer was required on the date of service to comply with an earnings assignment order for support and, if so, the court which issued such assignment order and the date it was issued and any other information the Judicial Council determines is needed to identify the order.

(6) The name and address of the person to whom notices to the employer are to be sent. *(Added by Stats.1982, c. 1364, p. 5187, § 2, operative July 1, 1983. Amended by Stats.1992, c. 163 (A.B.2641), § 50, operative Jan. 1, 1994.)*

Law Revision Commission Comments

Section 706.126 continues former Section 723.126 and specifies the information to be included in the employer's return. The form for the return is prescribed by the Judicial Council (see Section 706.120) or, in the case of a return in connection with a withholding order for taxes, by the state (see Section 706.081). [16 Cal.L.Rev.Comm. Reports 1489 (1982)].

Subdivision (b)(5) of Section 706.126 is amended to conform to the terminology of the Family Code. See Chapter 8 (commencing with Section 5200) of Part 5 of Division 9 of the Family Code (earnings assignment order for support). "Earnings assignment order for support" is defined in Section 706.011. [22 Cal.L.Rev.Comm.Reports 1 (1992)].

Research References

Rutter, Cal. Practice Guide: Enforcing Judgments/Debts Ch. 6F-7, Employer Duties and Liabilities Under Wgl.

8 Witkin Cal. Proc. 5th Enforcement of Judgment § 255, What Must be Served.

§ 706.127. Employer's instructions; preparation, revision and supplementation; supplying to levying officers

(a) The Judicial Council shall prepare "employer's instructions" for employers and revise or supplement these instructions to reflect changes in the law or rules regulating the withholding of earnings.

(b) Except to the extent that they are included in the forms required to be provided by the employer to the levying officer, the Judicial Council shall publish and provide to the levying officers copies of the employer's instructions. *(Added by Stats. 1982, c. 1364, p. 5188, § 2, operative July 1, 1983.)*

Law Revision Commission Comments

Section 706.127 continues former Section 723.127 and requires the preparation of employer's instructions that provide the employer with the information he needs to comply with the law. The levying officer provides the employer with a copy of the employer's instructions with the earnings withholding order. See Section 706.103. [16 Cal.L.Rev.Comm. Reports 1490 (1982)].

Research References

8 Witkin Cal. Proc. 5th Enforcement of Judgment § 250, (S 250) Rules and Forms.
8 Witkin Cal. Proc. 5th Enforcement of Judgment § 255, What Must be Served.

§ 706.128. Judgment creditor's notice of opposition to claim of exemption; form and contents

The "judgment creditor's notice of opposition to the claim of exemption" shall be executed under oath and shall include all of the following:

(a) The name, last known address, and, if known, the social security number of the judgment debtor.

(b) The name and address of the judgment creditor.

(c) The date of mailing of the notice of claim of exemption.

(d) The amount of the judgment debtor's claim of exemption which the judgment creditor claims is not exempt.

(e) The factual and legal grounds for the judgment creditor's opposition to the claim of exemption. *(Added by Stats.1982, c. 1364, p. 5188, § 2, operative July 1, 1983.)*

Law Revision Commission Comments

Section 706.128 continues former Section 723.128 and specifies the information to be included in the judgment creditor's notice of opposition to the claim of exemption. The form is prescribed by the Judicial Council. See Section 706.120. [16 Cal.L.Rev.Comm. Reports 1490 (1982)].

Research References

Rutter, Cal. Practice Guide: Enforcing Judgments/Debts Ch. 6F-5, Earnings Exempt from Garnishment.
8 Witkin Cal. Proc. 5th Enforcement of Judgment § 262, (S 262) Notice, Opposition, and Hearing.

§ 706.129. Copies of forms available from levying officers

The levying officer shall have copies of the forms for the "judgment debtor's claim of exemption" and "judgment debtor's financial statement" available at the levying officer's office for distribution without charge to a person who desires to make a claim of exemption under Section 706.051. *(Added by Stats. 1982, c. 1364, p. 5188, § 2, operative July 1, 1983.)*

Law Revision Commission Comments

Section 706.129 continues former Section 723.129 and implements the last sentence of subdivision (d) of Section 706.122. The forms are

prescribed by the Judicial Council. See Section 706.120. [16 Cal.L.Rev. Comm. Reports 1490 (1982)].

Research References

8 Witkin Cal. Proc. 5th Enforcement of Judgment § 250, (S 250) Rules and Forms.
8 Witkin Cal. Proc. 5th Enforcement of Judgment § 261, (S 261) in General.

ARTICLE 7. ADMINISTRATION AND ENFORCEMENT

Section
706.151. Acts required as conditions to exemption from provisions of federal consumer credit protection act.
706.152. Withholding with intent to defraud.
706.153. Deferral or acceleration of payments to employee; civil actions.
706.154. Failure of employer to withhold or pay over; liability for compliance with orders or notices purporting to be in accordance with chapter provisions.

§ 706.151. Acts required as conditions to exemption from provisions of federal consumer credit protection act

The Judicial Council may perform all acts required by the Administrator of the Wage and Hour Division of the United States Department of Labor as conditions to exemption of this state from the earnings garnishment provisions of the Consumer Credit Protection Act of 1968 (15 U.S.C. Secs. 1671–1677), including, but not limited to:

(a) Representing and acting on behalf of the state in relation to the Administrator of the Wage and Hour Division and the administrator's representatives with regard to any matter relating to, or arising out of, the application, interpretation, and enforcement of the laws of this state regulating withholding of earnings.

(b) Submitting to the Administrator of the Wage and Hour Division in duplicate and on a current basis, a certified copy of every statute of this state affecting earnings withholding, and a certified copy of any decision in any case involving any of those statutes, made by the Supreme Court of this state.

(c) Submitting to the Administrator of the Wage and Hour Division any information relating to the enforcement of earnings withholding laws of this state which the administrator may request. *(Added by Stats.1982, c. 1364, p. 5189, § 2, operative July 1, 1983.)*

Law Revision Commission Comments

Section 706.151 continues former Section 723.151 and authorizes the Judicial Council to do whatever is required by the federal administrator to obtain and maintain a state exemption from the earnings garnishment provisions of the Consumer Credit Protection Act. Subdivisions (a), (b), and (c) are based on the language of 29 Code of Federal Regulations Section 870.55(a), requiring the state representative to act as liaison with the federal administrator. [16 Cal.L.Rev.Comm. Reports 1491 (1982)].

§ 706.152. Withholding with intent to defraud

If an employer withholds earnings pursuant to this chapter and, with the intent to defraud either the judgment creditor or the judgment debtor, fails to pay such withheld earnings over to the levying officer, the employer is guilty of a misdemeanor. *(Added by Stats.1982, c. 1364, p. 5189, § 2, operative July 1, 1983.)*

Law Revision Commission Comments

Section 706.152 continues former Section 723.152. [16 Cal.L.Rev. Comm. Reports 1492 (1982)].

Research References

Rutter, Cal. Practice Guide: Enforcing Judgments/Debts Ch. 6F-7, Employer Duties and Liabilities Under Wgl.
8 Witkin Cal. Proc. 5th Enforcement of Judgment § 249, (S 249) Liability of Employer.

§ 706.153. Deferral or acceleration of payments to employee; civil actions

(a) No employer shall defer or accelerate any payment of earnings to an employee with the intent to defeat or diminish the judgment creditor's rights under an earnings withholding order issued pursuant to the procedures provided by this chapter.

(b) If an employer violates this section, the judgment creditor may bring a civil action against the employer to recover the amount that would have been withheld and paid over pursuant to this chapter had the employer not violated this section. The remedy provided by this subdivision is not exclusive. *(Added by Stats.1982, c. 1364, p. 5189, § 2, operative July 1, 1983.)*

Law Revision Commission Comments

Section 706.153 continues former Section 723.153 and makes clear that an employer may neither defer nor accelerate payment of earnings to an employee in an attempt to avoid compliance with an earnings withholding order and specifies the measure of damages in case of violation. [16 Cal.L.Rev.Comm. Reports 1492 (1982)].

Research References

Rutter, Cal. Practice Guide: Enforcing Judgments/Debts Ch. 6F-2, Wage Garnishment-In General.
Rutter, Cal. Practice Guide: Enforcing Judgments/Debts Ch. 6F-7, Employer Duties and Liabilities Under Wgl.
8 Witkin Cal. Proc. 5th Enforcement of Judgment § 249, (S 249) Liability of Employer.
8 Witkin Cal. Proc. 5th Enforcement of Judgment § 271, (S 271) Issuance of Order.

§ 706.154. Failure of employer to withhold or pay over; liability for compliance with orders or notices purporting to be in accordance with chapter provisions

(a) If an employer fails to withhold or to pay over the amount the employer is required to withhold and pay over pursuant to this chapter, the judgment creditor may bring a civil action against the employer to recover such amount. The remedy provided by this subdivision is not exclusive.

(b) Notwithstanding subdivision (a), an employer who complies with any written order or written notice which purports to be given or served in accordance with the provisions of this chapter is not subject to any civil or criminal liability for such compliance unless the employer has actively participated in a fraud. *(Added by Stats.1982, c. 1364, p. 5189, § 2, operative July 1, 1983.)*

Law Revision Commission Comments

Section 706.154 continues former Section 723.154. The section authorizes suit by a creditor against an employer both where the employer fails to withhold properly and where he fails to pay over amounts withheld. This remedy is independent of the procedure for examination of a debtor of the judgment debtor under Section 708.120.

Subdivision (b) makes clear that an employer is protected from liability where he complies with an order or written notice which appears proper on its face. Occasionally, through mistake, inadvertence, or even deliberate misconduct, an employer may be sent an order or notice which appears valid but which has been improperly obtained or served. For example, a creditor may fail to observe the 10-day moratorium on service of a second earnings withholding order. See Section 706.107 and Comment thereto. The employer is not required in such circumstances to go beyond the document itself and is not subject to liability where he complies with its directions and is not actively participating in a fraud. The remedy of the injured party in such a case is to proceed against the person who falsified the document or who improperly obtained the document or caused it prematurely to be served.

This section also makes clear that, where an employer is complying with a prior order, he is not liable for failing to comply with a subsequent valid order—even though the prior order is in fact invalid—unless he is actively participating in a fraud. [16 Cal.L.Rev.Comm. Reports 1493 (1982)].

Research References

Rutter, Cal. Practice Guide: Enforcing Judgments/Debts Ch. 6D-4, Levy on Specific Property.
Rutter, Cal. Practice Guide: Enforcing Judgments/Debts Ch. 6F-7, Employer Duties and Liabilities Under Wgl.
8 Witkin Cal. Proc. 5th Enforcement of Judgment § 249, (S 249) Liability of Employer.
8 Witkin Cal. Proc. 5th Enforcement of Judgment § 271, (S 271) Issuance of Order.

CHAPTER 6. MISCELLANEOUS CREDITORS' REMEDIES

ARTICLE 1. WRITTEN INTERROGATORIES TO JUDGMENT DEBTOR

§ 708.010. Procedure used when money judgment enforceable; stay of proceedings

(a) Except as provided in this section and in subdivision (b) of Section 708.020, the procedure in this article may be used at any time a money judgment is enforceable.

(b) If enforcement of the judgment is stayed on appeal by the giving of a sufficient undertaking under Chapter 2 (commencing with Section 916) of Title 13, all proceedings under this article are stayed. In any other case where the enforcement of the judgment is stayed, all proceedings under this article are stayed unless the court otherwise expressly orders. *(Added by Stats. 1982, c. 1364, p. 5190, § 2, operative July 1, 1983.)*

Research References

Rutter, Cal. Practice Guide: Enforcing Judgments/Debts Ch. 6G-2, Written Interrogatories to Judgment Debtor.
Rutter, Cal. Practice Guide: Enforcing Judgments/Debts Ch. 6G-3, Inspection Demand to Judgment Debtor.
8 Witkin Cal. Proc. 5th Enforcement of Judgment § 47, Memorandum of Costs.
8 Witkin Cal. Proc. 5th Enforcement of Judgment § 48, Motion for Costs.
8 Witkin Cal. Proc. 5th Enforcement of Judgment § 51, (S 51) in General.
8 Witkin Cal. Proc. 5th Enforcement of Judgment § 82, (S 82) in General.
8 Witkin Cal. Proc. 5th Enforcement of Judgment § 84, (S 84) Interests Subject to Lien.
8 Witkin Cal. Proc. 5th Enforcement of Judgment § 275, Written Interrogatories to Judgment Debtor.
8 Witkin Cal. Proc. 5th Enforcement of Judgment § 328, (S 328) Collection of Included Money Judgment.

8 Witkin Cal. Proc. 5th Enforcement of Judgment § 381, (S 381) Proceedings and Determination.

8 Witkin Cal. Proc. 5th Enforcement of Judgment § 405, Governmental Enforcement of Support Order.

§ 708.020.   Written interrogatories

(a) The judgment creditor may propound written interrogatories to the judgment debtor, in the manner provided in Chapter 13 (commencing with Section 2030.010) of Title 4 of Part 4, requesting information to aid in enforcement of the money judgment. The judgment debtor shall answer the interrogatories in the manner and within the time provided by Chapter 13 (commencing with Section 2030.010) of Title 4 of Part 4.

(b) The judgment creditor may not serve interrogatories pursuant to this section within 120 days after the judgment debtor has responded to interrogatories previously served pursuant to this section or within 120 days after the judgment debtor has been examined pursuant to Article 2 (commencing with Section 708.110), and the judgment debtor is not required to respond to any interrogatories so served.

(c) Interrogatories served pursuant to this section may be enforced, to the extent practicable, in the same manner as interrogatories in a civil action.

(d) The limitation provided by Chapter 13 (commencing with Section 2030.010) of Title 4 of Part 4 on the number of interrogatories that may be propounded applies to each set of interrogatories propounded from time to time pursuant to this section, but does not apply cumulatively to interrogatories propounded by the judgment creditor to the judgment debtor. *(Added by Stats.1982, c. 1364, p. 5190, § 2, operative July 1, 1983. Amended by Stats.1992, c. 283 (S.B.1372), § 16, eff. July 21, 1992; Stats.2004, c. 182 (A.B.3081), § 11, operative July 1, 2005.)*

Law Revision Commission Comments

Subdivision (a) of Section 708.020 is the same in substance as the first sentence of former Section 714.5, except that the limitation of former Section 714.5 that interrogatories could be propounded only to a judgment debtor represented by counsel is not continued. This change is consistent with Section 2030 (interrogatories in civil actions generally). The provision that the interrogatories request information to aid in enforcement of the judgment is new, and is consistent with Section 2016 (examination regarding matter relevant to subject matter of the action). The provision of former Section 714.5 that written interrogatories to the judgment debtor are cumulative and in addition to the examination procedure is omitted as unnecessary. Sections 708.010 and 708.020 make clear that written interrogatories may be used at any time the money judgment is enforceable if there has been no stay and the judgment debtor has not responded to interrogatories or been examined within the preceding 120 days.

Subdivision (b) is the same in substance as the last sentence of former Section 714.5.

Subdivision (c) continues the substance of the third sentence of former Section 714.5. Under subdivision (c), if the judgment debtor fails to answer interrogatories without substantial justification, sanctions may include an award of attorney's fees. Section 2034(a). If the court orders the judgment debtor to answer and the judgment debtor refuses to do so, the refusal is punishable as a contempt. Section 2034(b); MacDonald v. Superior Court, 75 Cal.App.3d 692, 696, 141 Cal.Rptr. 667 (1977). The court is also authorized to make such protective orders for the benefit of the judgment debtor as justice may require. See Section 2030(c). [16 Cal.L.Rev.Comm. Reports 1494 (1982)].

Subdivision (d) is added to Section 708.020 to make clear that the 35 interrogatory limit in Section 2030(c) is not a cumulative limitation on interrogatories to judgment debtors. Thus, for example, a judgment creditor may propound 25 interrogatories to the judgment debtor and then 120 days later propound 30 more interrogatories without running afoul of the limitations in Section 2030. See also Section 2016(c) (discovery article applies in enforcement of judgment as provided in this article). [21 Cal.L.Rev.Comm.Reports 135 (1991)].

Subdivisions (a) and (d) of Section 708.020 are amended to reflect nonsubstantive reorganization of the rules governing civil discovery. [33 Cal.L.Rev.Comm. Reports 992 (2004)].

Research References

Rutter, Cal. Practice Guide: Civ. Pro. Before Trial Ch. 8B-3, Limitations on Right to Discovery.

Rutter, Cal. Practice Guide: Enforcing Judgments/Debts Ch. 6A-5, Amount Recoverable Under Judgment.

Rutter, Cal. Practice Guide: Enforcing Judgments/Debts Ch. 6G-2, Written Interrogatories to Judgment Debtor.

8 Witkin Cal. Proc. 5th Enforcement of Judgment § 275, Written Interrogatories to Judgment Debtor.

8 Witkin Cal. Proc. 5th Enforcement of Judgment § 276, Demand for Inspection of Documents.

8 Witkin Cal. Proc. 5th Enforcement of Judgment § 278, (S 278) Examination of Judgment Debtor.

8 Witkin Cal. Proc. 5th Enforcement of Judgment § 289, (S 289) Protective Orders.

§ 708.030.   Inspection of documents;   service of subsequent interrogatories or demands

(a) The judgment creditor may demand that any judgment debtor produce and permit the party making the demand, or someone acting on that party's behalf, to inspect and to copy a document that is in the possession, custody, or control of the party on whom the demand is made in the manner provided in Chapter 14 (commencing with Section 2031.010) of Title 4 of Part 4, if the demand requests information to aid in enforcement of the money judgment. The judgment debtor shall respond and comply with the demand in the manner and within the time provided by Chapter 14 (commencing with Section 2031.010) of Title 4 of Part 4.

(b) The judgment creditor may not serve interrogatories or inspection demands pursuant to this section or Section 708.020 within 120 days after the judgment debtor has responded to the interrogatories or demands previously served pursuant to this section or Section 708.020, or within 120 days after the judgment debtor has been examined pursuant to Article 2 (commencing with Section 708.110), and the judgment debtor is not required to respond to any discovery so served.

(c) Inspection demands served pursuant to this section may be enforced to the extent practicable, in the same manner as inspection demands in a civil action. *(Added by Stats.1992, c. 1348 (A.B.2616), § 5. Amended by Stats.2004, c. 182 (A.B.3081), § 12, operative July 1, 2005.)*

Law Revision Commission Comments

Subdivision (a) of Section 708.030 is amended to reflect nonsubstantive reorganization of the rules governing civil discovery. [33 Cal.L.Rev. Comm. Reports 993 (2004)].

Research References

Rutter, Cal. Practice Guide: Enforcing Judgments/Debts Ch. 6G-2, Written Interrogatories to Judgment Debtor.

Rutter, Cal. Practice Guide: Enforcing Judgments/Debts Ch. 6G-3, Inspection Demand to Judgment Debtor.

8 Witkin Cal. Proc. 5th Enforcement of Judgment § 275, Written Interrogatories to Judgment Debtor.

8 Witkin Cal. Proc. 5th Enforcement of Judgment § 276, Demand for Inspection of Documents.

ARTICLE 2.   EXAMINATION PROCEEDINGS

Civ. Pro.

§ 708.110.   Order for examination; service; contents

(a) The judgment creditor may apply to the proper court for an order requiring the judgment debtor to appear before the court, or before a referee appointed by the court, at a time and place specified in the order, to furnish information to aid in enforcement of the money judgment.

(b) If the judgment creditor has not caused the judgment debtor to be examined under this section during the preceding 120 days, the court shall make the order upon ex parte application of the judgment creditor.

(c) If the judgment creditor has caused the judgment debtor to be examined under this section during the preceding 120 days, the court shall make the order if the judgment creditor by affidavit or otherwise shows good cause for the order. The application shall be made on noticed motion if the court so directs or a court rule so requires. Otherwise, it may be made ex parte.

(d) The judgment creditor shall personally serve a copy of the order on the judgment debtor not less than 10 days before the date set for the examination. Service shall be made in the manner specified in Section 415.10. Service of the order creates a lien on the personal property of the judgment debtor for a period of one year from the date of the order unless extended or sooner terminated by the court.

(e) The order shall contain the following statement in 14-point boldface type if printed or in capital letters if typed: "NOTICE TO JUDGMENT DEBTOR. If you fail to appear at the time and place specified in this order, you may be subject to arrest and punishment for contempt of court and the court may make an order requiring you to pay the reasonable attorney's fees incurred by the judgment creditor in this proceeding." *(Added by Stats.1982, c. 1364, p. 5190, § 2, operative July 1, 1983. Amended by Stats.1984, c. 538, § 30; Stats.1993, c. 793 (A.B.504), § 1.)*

Law Revision Commission Comments

Subdivision (a) of Section 708.110 supersedes the first sentences of former Sections 714 and 715. The former language requiring the judgment debtor to answer concerning his property has been revised to require the judgment debtor to furnish information to aid in enforcement of the judgment. This might include, for example, information concerning future employment prospects. The proper court for an examination under this section is prescribed in Section 708.160. The judgment debtor may not be ordered to appear when the judgment is no longer enforceable. See Section 683.020.

Under subdivision (b), the judgment creditor may obtain an order of examination if the judgment creditor has not caused the judgment debtor to be examined within the preceding 120 days. Subdivision (b) permits the judgment creditor to obtain an order of examination even though the judgment debtor may have been required to respond to written interrogatories under Section 708.020 within the 120-day period. The provision in subdivision (b) that the order of examination is made upon ex parte application codifies case law. See Lewis v. Neblett, 188 Cal.App.2d 290, 297, 10 Cal.Rptr. 441 (1961).

The good cause requirement of subdivision (c) for examination more frequently than every 120 days supersedes the requirement of former Section 715 that the judgment debtor have property that the judgment debtor "unjustly refuses" to apply toward the satisfaction of the judgment.

The first sentence of subdivision (d) is new. The second sentence of subdivision (d) codifies the rule in Nordstrom v. Corona City Water Co., 155 Cal. 206, 212–13, 100 P. 242, 245 (1909). No duration is specified for the lien. However, it may not be enforced beyond the time for enforcement of the judgment. See Sections 683.010–683.220. See also Sections 697.020 (relation back of liens), 697.920 (effect of liens).

Subdivision (e) continues the substance of the third paragraph of former Section 714 and adds the requirement that the notice advise the judgment debtor that failure to appear may result in attorney's fees being imposed. See Section 708.170. [16 Cal.L.Rev.Comm. Reports 1496 (1982)].

Subdivision (d) of Section 708.110 is amended to prescribe a one-year duration for the lien created under this section. This is consistent with the duration of a lien created under Section 703.120 (examination of third person). [17 Cal.L.Rev.Comm. Reports 1018 (1983)].

Research References

Rutter, Cal. Practice Guide: Enforcing Judgments/Debts Ch. 5-B, B. Overview of Substantive Bankruptcy Law.

Rutter, Cal. Practice Guide: Enforcing Judgments/Debts Ch. 6A-5, Amount Recoverable Under Judgment.

Rutter, Cal. Practice Guide: Enforcing Judgments/Debts Ch. 6D-4, Levy on Specific Property.

Rutter, Cal. Practice Guide: Enforcing Judgments/Debts Ch. 6G-1, Examination of Judgment Debtor and Third Parties.

Rutter, Cal. Practice Guide: Personal Injury Ch. 4-G, G. Concluding and Enforcing Settlement.

8 Witkin Cal. Proc. 5th Enforcement of Judgment § 139, Delivery or Payment to Levying Officer.

8 Witkin Cal. Proc. 5th Enforcement of Judgment § 141, (S 141) Rights and Duties of Secured Party.

8 Witkin Cal. Proc. 5th Enforcement of Judgment § 242, (S 242) Exclusive Procedure.

8 Witkin Cal. Proc. 5th Enforcement of Judgment § 275, Written Interrogatories to Judgment Debtor.

8 Witkin Cal. Proc. 5th Enforcement of Judgment § 276, Demand for Inspection of Documents.

8 Witkin Cal. Proc. 5th Enforcement of Judgment § 277, (S 277) Development of Law.

8 Witkin Cal. Proc. 5th Enforcement of Judgment § 278, (S 278) Examination of Judgment Debtor.

8 Witkin Cal. Proc. 5th Enforcement of Judgment § 286, Testimony Concerning Settlement Negotiations.

8 Witkin Cal. Proc. 5th Enforcement of Judgment § 287, (S 287) Proper Court for Examination.

8 Witkin Cal. Proc. 5th Enforcement of Judgment § 310, (S 310) in General.

§ 708.120.   Orders where property in possession or control of third party

(a) Upon ex parte application by a judgment creditor who has a money judgment and proof by the judgment creditor by affidavit or otherwise to the satisfaction of the proper court that a third person has possession or control of property in which the judgment debtor has an interest or is indebted to the judgment debtor in an amount exceeding two hundred fifty dollars ($250), the court shall make an order directing the third person to appear before the court, or before a referee appointed by the court, at a time and place specified in the order, to answer concerning such property or debt. The affidavit in support of the judgment creditor's application may be based on the affiant's information and belief.

(b) Not less than 10 days prior to the date set for the examination, a copy of the order shall be:

(1) Served personally on the third person.

(2) Served personally or by mail on the judgment debtor.

(c) If the property in the third person's possession or control in which the judgment debtor has an interest or the debt owed by the third person to the judgment debtor is described in the affidavit or application for an order under subdivision (a) in a manner reasonably adequate to permit it to be identified, service of the order on the third person creates a lien on the judgment debtor's interest in the property or on the debt for a period of one year from the date of the order unless extended or sooner terminated by the court.

(d) The judgment debtor may claim that all or any portion of the property or debt is exempt from enforcement of a money judgment by application to the court on noticed motion, filed with the court and personally served on the judgment creditor not later than three days before the date set for the examination. The judgment debtor shall execute an affidavit in support of the application that includes all of the matters set forth in subdivision (b) of Section 703.520. If a claim of exemption is made pursuant to this section, a notice of opposition to the claim of exemption is not required. The court shall determine any claim of exemption made pursuant to this section. Failure of the judgment debtor to make a claim of exemption does not preclude the judgment debtor from later claiming the exemption unless the property or debt is described in the order in a manner reasonably adequate to permit it to be identified and the judgment debtor receives notice of the examination proceeding at least 10 days before the date set for the examination.

(e) An order made pursuant to subdivision (a) shall contain the following statements in 14–point boldface type if printed or in capital letters if typed:

(1) "NOTICE TO PERSON SERVED. If you fail to appear at the time and place specified in this order, you may be subject to arrest and punishment for contempt of court and the court may make an order requiring you to pay the reasonable attorney's fees incurred by the judgment creditor in this proceeding."

(2) "NOTICE TO JUDGMENT DEBTOR. The person in whose favor the judgment was entered in this action claims that the person to be examined pursuant to this order has possession or control of property which is yours or owes you a debt. This property or debt is as follows: (Description of property or debt). If you claim that all or any portion of this property or debt is exempt from enforcement of the money judgment, you must file your exemption claim in writing with the court and personally serve a copy on the judgment creditor not later than three days before the date set for the examination. You must appear at the time and place set for this examination to establish your claim of exemption or your exemption may be waived."

(f) An order made pursuant to subdivision (a) is not effective unless, at the time it is served on the third person, the person serving the order tenders to the third person fees for the mileage necessary to be traveled from the third person's residence to the place of examination. The mileage fees shall be in the same amount generally provided for witnesses when legally required to attend civil proceedings in the court where the examination proceeding is to be conducted. *(Added by Stats.1982, c. 1364, p. 5191, § 2, operative July 1, 1983. Amended by Stats.1995, c. 576 (A.B.1225), § 3.6.)*

Research References

Rutter, Cal. Practice Guide: Enforcing Judgments/Debts Ch. 6D-5, Duties, Rights and Liabilities of Third Persons After Levy.
Rutter, Cal. Practice Guide: Enforcing Judgments/Debts Ch. 6G-1, Examination of Judgment Debtor and Third Parties.
8 Witkin Cal. Proc. 5th Enforcement of Judgment § 134, (S 134) Deposit Accounts and Boxes in Third Person's Name.
8 Witkin Cal. Proc. 5th Enforcement of Judgment § 140, Garnishee's Memorandum.
8 Witkin Cal. Proc. 5th Enforcement of Judgment § 279, Issuance and Service of Order.

8 Witkin Cal. Proc. 5th Enforcement of Judgment § 280, Judgment Debtor's Claim of Exemption.
8 Witkin Cal. Proc. 5th Enforcement of Judgment § 287, (S 287) Proper Court for Examination.
8 Witkin Cal. Proc. 5th Enforcement of Judgment § 290, (S 290) Order Applying Property to Satisfaction of Judgment.
8 Witkin Cal. Proc. 5th Enforcement of Judgment § 294, (S 294) Debtor's Claim of Exemption.
6 Witkin Cal. Proc. 5th Provisional Remedies § 195, (S 195) in General.

§ 708.130. Witnesses; privilege

(a) Witnesses may be required to appear and testify before the court or referee in an examination proceeding under this article in the same manner as upon the trial of an issue.

(b) The privilege prescribed by Article 4 (commencing with Section 970) of Chapter 4 of Division 8 of the Evidence Code does not apply in an examination proceeding under this article. *(Added by Stats.1982, c. 1364, p. 5192, § 2, operative July 1, 1983.)*

Law Revision Commission Comments

Subdivision (a) of Section 708.130 continues former Section 718. Subdivision (b) is new and changes the rule set forth in the second sentence of former Section 717 (marital privilege applicable in proceedings to examine debtor of judgment debtor in the absence of a waiver). [16 Cal.L.Rev.Comm. Reports 1501 (1982)].

Research References

Rutter, Cal. Practice Guide: Enforcing Judgments/Debts Ch. 6G-1, Examination of Judgment Debtor and Third Parties.
8 Witkin Cal. Proc. 5th Enforcement of Judgment § 284, in General.
8 Witkin Cal. Proc. 5th Enforcement of Judgment § 285, Privileges.

§ 708.140. Proceedings conducted by referee or temporary judge

(a) The examination proceedings authorized by this article may be conducted by a referee appointed by the court. The referee may issue, modify, or vacate an order authorized by Section 708.205, may make a protective order authorized by Section 708.200, and may issue a warrant authorized by Section 708.170, and has the same power as the court to grant adjournments, to preserve order, and to subpoena witnesses to attend the examination, but only the court that ordered the reference has power to do the following:

(1) Punish for contempt for disobeying an order of the referee.

(2) Make an award of attorney's fees pursuant to Section 708.170.

(3) Determine a contested claim of exemption or determine a third-party claim under Section 708.180.

(b) Only a member of the State Bar of California is eligible for appointment as a referee pursuant to this article. A person who was duly appointed as a referee prior to July 1, 1983, pursuant to the law in operation at the time of appointment, and who is available to perform the duties of a referee on July 1, 1983, shall be exempt from the requirements of this subdivision.

(c) Nothing in subdivision (a) limits the power of a court to appoint a temporary judge pursuant to Section 21 of Article VI of the California Constitution. *(Added by Stats.1982, c. 1364, p. 5192, § 2, operative July 1, 1983. Amended by Stats.1983, c. 155, § 19, eff. June 30, 1983, operative July 1, 1983.)*

Law Revision Commission Comments

Subdivision (a) of Section 708.140 continues the authority of a referee appointed by the court provided in former Sections 714–715, 717–721, and 723. The authority to modify and vacate orders is generalized from former Section 720. The authority to compel the appearance of a person at the examination and to control the proceeding generalizes the authority of a referee appointed by a superior court formerly provided by Section 723. The limitation on the power to punish for contempt provided in paragraph (1) of subdivision (a) continues the substance of former Section 721. Paragraph (2) of subdivision (a) is new. Paragraph (3) is drawn from Section 482.060 (subordinate judicial duties in attachment).

Subdivision (b) supersedes the portion of former Section 723 that required a referee to have been a member of the State Bar for at least five years. Former Section 723 was applicable to a referee appointed by a superior court in a county or city and county having a population of one million or more.

Subdivision (c) is drawn from Section 482.060 (attachment). [16 Cal.L.Rev.Comm. Reports 1502 (1982)].

Research References

Rutter, Cal. Practice Guide: Enforcing Judgments/Debts Ch. 6G-1, Examination of Judgment Debtor and Third Parties.

8 Witkin Cal. Proc. 5th Enforcement of Judgment § 280, Judgment Debtor's Claim of Exemption.

8 Witkin Cal. Proc. 5th Enforcement of Judgment § 281, (S 281) Right to Determination.

8 Witkin Cal. Proc. 5th Enforcement of Judgment § 284, in General.

8 Witkin Cal. Proc. 5th Enforcement of Judgment § 288, (S 288) Failure to Appear for Examination.

8 Witkin Cal. Proc. 5th Enforcement of Judgment § 342, Enforceable Judgments and Orders.

7 Witkin Cal. Proc. 5th Trial § 169, Any Judicial Tribunal.

§ 708.150. Order for examination in case of corporation, partnership, etc.

(a) If a corporation, partnership, association, trust, or other organization is served with an order to appear for an examination, it shall designate to appear and be examined one or more officers, directors, managing agents, or other persons who are familiar with its property and debts.

(b) If the order to appear for an examination requires the appearance of a specified individual, the specified individual shall appear for the examination and may be accompanied by one or more officers, directors, managing agents, or other persons familiar with the property and debts of the corporation, partnership, association, trust, or other organization.

(c) If the order to appear for the examination does not require the appearance of a specified individual, the order shall advise the corporation, partnership, association, trust, or other organization of its duty to make a designation under subdivision (a).

(d) A corporation, partnership, association, trust, or other organization, whether or not a party, may appear at an examination through any authorized officer, director, or employee, whether or not the person is an attorney. *(Added by Stats.1982, c. 1364, p. 5192, § 2, operative July 1, 1983. Amended by Stats.1984, c. 538, § 30.5.)*

Law Revision Commission Comments

Subdivision (a) of Section 708.150 is derived from Section 2019(a) (6). Former Section 717 provided for the appearance of a "corporation or any officer or member thereof." Subdivision (b) permits the order to specify that a designated person appear for the examination. Subdivision (c) is comparable to the third sentence of Section 2019(a) (6).

If an organization described in subdivision (a) is served with an order to appear for an examination and no specified individual is required to appear by the order, the organization itself may nonetheless be held in contempt of court for its failure to appear. See Section 1209 (disobedience of lawful order is a contempt); 14 Cal.Jur.3d Contempt § 30 (1974) (corporations and other organizations may be held in contempt). If a specified individual is designated to appear in the order under subdivision (b), the designated individual is subject to the contempt sanction. See also Section 708.170 (reasonable attorneys' fees may be awarded for failure to appear). [16 Cal.L.Rev.Comm. Reports 1503 (1982)].

Research References

Rutter, Cal. Practice Guide: Enforcing Judgments/Debts Ch. 6G-1, Examination of Judgment Debtor and Third Parties.

8 Witkin Cal. Proc. 5th Enforcement of Judgment § 284, in General.

§ 708.160. Venue for examination

(a) Except as otherwise provided in this section, the proper court for examination of a person under this article is the court in which the money judgment is entered.

(b) A person sought to be examined may not be required to attend an examination before a court located outside the county in which the person resides or has a place of business unless the distance from the person's place of residence or place of business to the place of examination is less than 150 miles.

(c) If a person sought to be examined does not reside or have a place of business in the county where the judgment is entered, the superior court in the county where the person resides or has a place of business is a proper court for examination of the person.

(d) If the judgment creditor seeks an examination of a person before a court other than the court in which the judgment is entered, the judgment creditor shall file an application that shall include all of the following:

(1) An abstract of judgment in the form prescribed by Section 674.

(2) An affidavit in support of the application stating the place of residence or place of business of the person sought to be examined.

(3) Any necessary affidavit or showing for the examination as required by Section 708.110 or 708.120.

(4) The filing fee for a motion as provided in subdivision (a) of Section 70617 of the Government Code. *(Added by Stats. 1982, c. 1364, p. 5193, § 2, operative July 1, 1983. Amended by Stats.2005, c. 75 (A.B.145), § 38, eff. July 19, 2005, operative Jan. 1, 2006.)*

Law Revision Commission Comments

Subdivision (a) of Section 708.160 is new and makes clear what was implicit under former law. Subdivision (b) continues the substance of the first sentence of former Section 717.1. Subdivisions (c) and (d) continue the substance of former Section 722. Paragraph (2) of subdivision (d) sets forth the required contents of the affidavit in greater detail than did former Section 722. Paragraph (4) of subdivision (d) continues the filing fee under former Section 722. [16 Cal.L.Rev.Comm. Reports 1504 (1982)].

Research References

Rutter, Cal. Practice Guide: Enforcing Judgments/Debts Ch. 6G-1, Examination of Judgment Debtor and Third Parties.

8 Witkin Cal. Proc. 5th Enforcement of Judgment § 287, (S 287) Proper Court for Examination.

§ 708.170. Failure to appear after service of order; improper service

(a) If an order requiring a person to appear for an examination was served by a sheriff, marshal, a person specially appointed by the court in the order, or a registered process server, and the person fails to appear:

(1) The court may do either of the following:

(A) Pursuant to a warrant, have the person brought before the court to answer for the failure to appear and may punish the person for contempt.

(B) Issue a warrant for the arrest of the person who failed to appear as required by the court order, pursuant to Section 1993.

(2) If the person's failure to appear is without good cause, the judgment creditor shall be awarded reasonable attorney's fees incurred in the examination proceeding. Attorney's fees awarded against the judgment debtor shall be added to and become part of the principal amount of the judgment.

(b) A person who willfully makes an improper service of an order for an examination which subsequently results in the arrest pursuant to subdivision (a) of the person who fails to appear is guilty of a misdemeanor. *(Added by Stats.1982, c. 1364, p. 5193, § 2, operative July 1, 1983. Amended by Stats.1996, c. 872 (A.B.3472), § 17; Stats.2006, c. 277 (A.B.2369), § 2.)*

Law Revision Commission Comments

Subdivision (a) (1) of Section 708.170 continues the substance of the second paragraph of former Section 714 and the second paragraph of former Section 717. Subdivision (a) (2) is new and does not limit any right to attorney's fees the parties may have under a contract or statute.

Subdivision (b) continues the substance of the last paragraphs of former Sections 714 and 717, respectively. The authority provided by former Section 715 for arresting the judgment debtor where there is a danger of the debtor absconding and for imprisoning the judgment debtor for failure to give an undertaking when ordered to do so is not continued, consistent with the repeal of the civil arrest provisions. See 1973 Cal.Stats. ch. 20. Section 708.170 does not limit the contempt power of the court under Sections 1209–1222. [16 Cal.L.Rev.Comm. Reports 1505 (1982)].

Research References

Rutter, Cal. Practice Guide: Enforcing Judgments/Debts Ch. 6A-5, Amount Recoverable Under Judgment.

Rutter, Cal. Practice Guide: Enforcing Judgments/Debts Ch. 6G-1, Examination of Judgment Debtor and Third Parties.

2 Witkin Cal. Proc. 5th Courts § 302, (S 302) in General.

8 Witkin Cal. Proc. 5th Enforcement of Judgment § 284, in General.

8 Witkin Cal. Proc. 5th Enforcement of Judgment § 288, (S 288) Failure to Appear for Examination.

8 Witkin Cal. Proc. 5th Enforcement of Judgment § 342, Enforceable Judgments and Orders.

3 Witkin, California Summary 10th Agency and Employment § 321, (S 321) Judgment.

§ 708.180. Adverse claim of, or denial of debt by third party

(a) Subject to subdivision (b), if a third person examined pursuant to Section 708.120 claims an interest in the property adverse to the judgment debtor or denies the debt, the court may, if the judgment creditor so requests, determine the interests in the property or the existence of the debt. The determination is conclusive as to the parties to the proceeding and the third person, but an appeal may be taken from the determination. The court may grant a continuance for a reasonable time for discovery proceedings, the production of evidence, or other preparation for the hearing.

(b) The court may not make the determination provided in subdivision (a) if the third person's claim is made in good faith and any of the following conditions is satisfied:

(1) The court would not be a proper court for the trial of an independent civil action (including a creditor's suit) for the determination of the interests in the property or the existence of the debt, and the third person objects to the determination of the matter under subdivision (a).

(2) At the time an order for examination pursuant to Section 708.120 is served on the third person a civil action (including a creditor's suit) is pending with respect to the interests in the property or the existence of the debt.

(3) The court determines that the interests in the property or the existence of the debt should be determined in a creditor's suit.

(c) Upon application of the judgment creditor made ex parte, the court may make an order forbidding transfer of the property to the judgment debtor or payment of the debt to the judgment debtor until the interests in the property or the existence of the debt is determined pursuant to subdivision (a) or until a creditor's suit may be commenced and an order obtained pursuant to Section 708.240. An undertaking may be required in the discretion of the court. The court may modify or vacate

the order at any time with or without a hearing on such terms as are just.

(d) Upon application of the judgment creditor upon noticed motion, the court may, if it determines that the judgment debtor probably owns an interest in the property or that the debt probably is owed to the judgment debtor, make an order forbidding the transfer or other disposition of the property to any person or forbidding payment of the debt until the interests in the property or the existence of the debt is determined pursuant to subdivision (a) or until a creditor's suit may be commenced and an order obtained pursuant to Section 708.240. The court shall require the judgment creditor to furnish an undertaking as provided in Section 529. The court may modify or vacate the order at any time after notice and hearing on such terms as are just. *(Added by Stats.1982, c. 1364, p. 5194, § 2, operative July 1, 1983. Amended by Stats.1998, c. 931 (S.B.2139), § 95, eff. Sept. 28, 1998.)*

Law Revision Commission Comments

Section 708.180 is amended to accommodate unification of the municipal and superior courts in a county. Cal. Const. art. VI, § 5(e). See Sections 85 (limited civil cases), 86(a)(8) (enforcement of judgment in limited civil case), 904.1 (taking appeal), 904.2 (taking appeal in limited civil case). See also Section 85 Comment. [28 Cal.L.Rev.Comm. Reports 51 (1998)].

Research References

Rutter, Cal. Practice Guide: Enforcing Judgments/Debts Ch. 6F-7, Employer Duties and Liabilities Under Wgl.

Rutter, Cal. Practice Guide: Enforcing Judgments/Debts Ch. 6G-1, Examination of Judgment Debtor and Third Parties.

8 Witkin Cal. Proc. 5th Enforcement of Judgment § 134, (S 134) Deposit Accounts and Boxes in Third Person's Name.

8 Witkin Cal. Proc. 5th Enforcement of Judgment § 281, (S 281) Right to Determination.

8 Witkin Cal. Proc. 5th Enforcement of Judgment § 282, (S 282) Restrictions on Transfer or Payment.

8 Witkin Cal. Proc. 5th Enforcement of Judgment § 283, (S 283) Intervention.

8 Witkin Cal. Proc. 5th Enforcement of Judgment § 284, in General.

8 Witkin Cal. Proc. 5th Enforcement of Judgment § 290, (S 290) Order Applying Property to Satisfaction of Judgment.

8 Witkin Cal. Proc. 5th Enforcement of Judgment § 291, (S 291) Nature of Action.

8 Witkin Cal. Proc. 5th Enforcement of Judgment § 293, (S 293) Order Forbidding Transfer or Payment.

§ 708.190. Intervention of third party

The court may permit a person claiming an interest in the property or debt sought to be applied in an examination proceeding to intervene in the proceeding and may determine the person's rights in the property or debt pursuant to Section 708.180. *(Added by Stats.1982, c. 1364, p. 5195, § 2, operative July 1, 1983.)*

Law Revision Commission Comments

Section 708.190 is new. In a proper case, this section permits the early resolution of a third-party claim to property that is the subject of an examination proceeding. For the procedure applicable to third-party claims after levy, see Division 4 (commencing with Section 720.010). [16 Cal.L.Rev.Comm. Reports 1507 (1982)].

Research References

Rutter, Cal. Practice Guide: Enforcing Judgments/Debts Ch. 6G-1, Examination of Judgment Debtor and Third Parties.

Rutter, Cal. Practice Guide: Enforcing Judgments/Debts Ch. 6H-1, Introduction.

8 Witkin Cal. Proc. 5th Enforcement of Judgment § 283, (S 283) Intervention.

8 Witkin Cal. Proc. 5th Enforcement of Judgment § 283, (S 283) Intervention.

Civ. Pro.

8 Witkin Cal. Proc. 5th Enforcement of Judgment § 365, (S 365) Alternative Remedies.

4 Witkin Cal. Proc. 5th Pleading § 215, Special Statutes.

§ 708.200. Protective orders

In any proceeding under this article, the court may, on motion of the person to be examined or on its own motion, make such protective orders as justice may require. *(Added by Stats.1982, c. 1364, p. 5195, § 2, operative July 1, 1983.)*

Law Revision Commission Comments

Section 708.200 is new and is comparable to the court's authority under Section 708.020 (which incorporates Section 2030) to make a protective order with respect to written interrogatories to the judgment debtor. Under Section 708.200, the court is authorized to make the order on its own motion as well as on motion of the person to be examined. [16 Cal.L.Rev.Comm. Reports 1507 (1982)].

Research References

Rutter, Cal. Practice Guide: Enforcing Judgments/Debts Ch. 6G-1, Examination of Judgment Debtor and Third Parties.

8 Witkin Cal. Proc. 5th Enforcement of Judgment § 284, in General.

8 Witkin Cal. Proc. 5th Enforcement of Judgment § 289, (S 289) Protective Orders.

§ 708.205. Order for satisfaction of money judgment or forbidding transfer or payment

(a) Except as provided in subdivision (b), at the conclusion of a proceeding pursuant to this article, the court may order the judgment debtor's interest in the property in the possession or under the control of the judgment debtor or the third person or a debt owed by the third person to the judgment debtor to be applied toward the satisfaction of the money judgment if the property is not exempt from enforcement of a money judgment. Such an order creates a lien on the property or debt.

(b) If a third person examined pursuant to Section 708.120 claims an interest in the property adverse to the judgment debtor or denies the debt and the court does not determine the matter as provided in subdivision (a) of Section 708.180, the court may not order the property or debt to be applied toward the satisfaction of the money judgment but may make an order pursuant to subdivision (c) or (d) of Section 708.180 forbidding transfer or payment to the extent authorized by that section. *(Added by Stats.1982, c. 1364, p. 5195, § 2, operative July 1, 1983.)*

Law Revision Commission Comments

Subdivision (a) of Section 708.205 continues the broad authority provided by former Section 719 for the court to order any nonexempt property or debt to be applied toward the satisfaction of the judgment. See also the last portion of the first sentence of former Section 715. Under subdivision (a), the person examined—whether the judgment debtor or a third person—may be ordered to deliver property or funds to the levying officer. See Lewis v. Neblett, 188 Cal.App.2d 290, 295, 10 Cal.Rptr. 441, 444 (1961) (funds in hands of administrator of estate). The person examined may also be ordered to pay the judgment creditor directly. See Hustead v. Superior Court, 2 Cal.App.3d 780, 783–87, 83 Cal.Rptr. 26, 27–30 (1969) (sublessee of judgment debtor ordered to pay rent to judgment creditor, order held invalid on other grounds). A receiver may be appointed with the powers ordered by the court, and the judgment debtor may be ordered to make any necessary assignments or deliveries to the receiver for the purpose of sale or collection. See Habenicht v. Lissak, 78 Cal. 351, 357–58, 20 P. 874, 877 (1899) (seat on stock exchange); Pacific Bank v. Robinson, 57 Cal. 520, 524 (1881) (patent rights); Hathaway v. Brady, 26 Cal. 581, 593–94 (1864) (note); Tucker v. Fontes, 70 Cal.App.2d 768, 771–72, 161 P.2d 697, 701 (1945) (business assets). The court may order execution to be issued to collect the amount due. See William Deering & Co. v. Richardson-Kimball Co., 109 Cal. 73, 41 P. 801 (1895) (funds in bank). If property is to be sold pursuant to the court's order under subdivision (a), it will be sold either by a levying officer (in which case there must be a valid writ of execution outstanding) or by a receiver appointed by the court. Orders made in examination proceedings are enforceable by contempt. See Section 1209.

Subdivision (b) supersedes the portion of former Section 719 that precluded a court order applying property in every case where the third person claimed an adverse interest in the property or denied the debt. Under subdivision (b), this rule applies only if the interest of the third person has not been determined pursuant to Section 708.180. The judgment creditor may then proceed by way of a creditor's suit pursuant to Article 3 (commencing with Section 708.210) or an independent civil action. [16 Cal.L.Rev.Comm. Reports 1508 (1982)].

Research References

Rutter, Cal. Practice Guide: Enforcing Judgments/Debts Ch. 6G-1, Examination of Judgment Debtor and Third Parties.

Rutter, Cal. Practice Guide: Enforcing Judgments/Debts Ch. 6J-3, Enforcing California Judgments Against Debtor's Out-Of-State Property.

8 Witkin Cal. Proc. 5th Enforcement of Judgment § 199, (S 199) Life Insurance Policies.

8 Witkin Cal. Proc. 5th Enforcement of Judgment § 284, in General.

8 Witkin Cal. Proc. 5th Enforcement of Judgment § 290, (S 290) Order Applying Property to Satisfaction of Judgment.

8 Witkin Cal. Proc. 5th Enforcement of Judgment § 295, (S 295) Judgment.

ARTICLE 3. CREDITOR'S SUIT

Law Revision Commission Comments

Article 3 (commencing with Section 708.210) authorizes the judgment creditor to bring suit against third persons indebted to or in possession of property of the judgment debtor. It is anticipated, however, that less expensive and less cumbersome enforcement procedures will be used in the normal case and that the creditor's suit will be used where the third person has failed to perform the duties of a garnishee (see Section 701.010 et seq.), where the court does not determine disputed ownership of the property or the existence of the debt under Section 708.180, or where for some other reason the judgment creditor believes that the third person will not cooperate. Disputes concerning the interests of a third person and a judgment debtor in personal property may also be resolved through the third-party claims procedure. See Division 4 (commencing with Section 720.010). [16 Cal.L.Rev.Comm. Reports 1509 (1982)].

§ 708.210. Actions against third party in possession or control of property or indebted to judgment debtor

If a third person has possession or control of property in which the judgment debtor has an interest or is indebted to the judgment debtor, the judgment creditor may bring an action against the third person to have the interest or debt applied to the satisfaction of the money judgment. *(Added by Stats.1982, c. 1364, p. 5195, § 2, operative July 1, 1983.)*

Law Revision Commission Comments

Section 708.210 supersedes the first portion of the first sentence of former Section 720. An action may be brought under this article without the necessity of first levying under a writ of execution, examining the third person, or resorting to any other procedure for the satisfaction of the judgment. The rule under former law—requiring the exhaustion of remedies at law before the equitable remedy of the creditor's suit could be employed—is not continued. For the former rule, see Farmers & Merchants Bank v. Bank of Italy, 216 Cal. 452, 455–58, 14 P.2d 527, 528–

29 (1932) (resort to supplementary proceedings required); Bond v. Bulgheroni, 215 Cal. 7, 10–11, 8 P.2d 130, 132 (1932) (resort to supplementary proceedings not required if inadequate or futile). [16 Cal.L.Rev.Comm. Reports 1509 (1982)].

Research References

Rutter, Cal. Practice Guide: Civ. Pro. Before Trial Ch. 3-A, A. Subject Matter Jurisdiction (Competency).
Rutter, Cal. Practice Guide: Enforcing Judgments/Debts Ch. 4-A, A. Attachment.
Rutter, Cal. Practice Guide: Enforcing Judgments/Debts Ch. 6D-5, Duties, Rights and Liabilities of Third Persons After Levy.
Rutter, Cal. Practice Guide: Enforcing Judgments/Debts Ch. 6G-4, Creditor's Suit.
Rutter, Cal. Practice Guide: Enforcing Judgments/Debts Ch. 6J-3, Enforcing California Judgments Against Debtor's Out-Of-State Property.
Miller and Starr California Real Estate § 32:30, When Property Held by Third Party.
Miller and Starr California Real Estate § 32:49, Real Property Subject to the Judgment Lien.
3 Witkin Cal. Proc. 5th Actions § 129, Miscellaneous Actions.
2 Witkin Cal. Proc. 5th Courts § 247, (S 247) Ancillary Remedies.
8 Witkin Cal. Proc. 5th Enforcement of Judgment § 2, (S 2) in General.
8 Witkin Cal. Proc. 5th Enforcement of Judgment § 134, (S 134) Deposit Accounts and Boxes in Third Person's Name.
8 Witkin Cal. Proc. 5th Enforcement of Judgment § 139, Delivery or Payment to Levying Officer.
8 Witkin Cal. Proc. 5th Enforcement of Judgment § 141, (S 141) Rights and Duties of Secured Party.
8 Witkin Cal. Proc. 5th Enforcement of Judgment § 291, (S 291) Nature of Action.
2 Witkin, California Summary 10th Insurance § 307, No Liability for Failure to Settle.

§ 708.220. Parties; venue

The judgment debtor shall be joined in an action brought pursuant to this article but is not an indispensable party. The residence of the judgment debtor may not be considered in the determination of proper venue unless otherwise provided by contract between the judgment debtor and the third person. *(Added by Stats.1982, c. 1364, p. 5195, § 2, operative July 1, 1983.)*

Law Revision Commission Comments

Section 708.220 is new. If the judgment debtor cannot be joined, the creditor's suit should proceed, the judgment debtor not being an indispensable party. See Section 389(b). The second sentence makes clear the rules of venue in a creditor's suit. Under this sentence, the venue in a creditor's suit is the same as it would be had the judgment debtor brought the action against the third person. See also Holstein v. Superior Court, 275 Cal.App.2d 708, 710, 80 Cal.Rptr. 301, 302 (1969). [16 Cal.L.Rev.Comm. Reports 1510 (1982)].

Research References

Rutter, Cal. Practice Guide: Enforcing Judgments/Debts Ch. 6G-4, Creditor's Suit.
8 Witkin Cal. Proc. 5th Enforcement of Judgment § 291, (S 291) Nature of Action.

§ 708.230. Limitation of actions

(a) Except as provided in subdivision (b), an action shall be commenced pursuant to this article before the expiration of the later of the following times:

(1) The time when the judgment debtor may bring an action against the third person concerning the property or debt.

(2) One year after creation of a lien on the property or debt pursuant to this title if the lien is created at the time when the judgment debtor may bring an action against the third person concerning the property or debt.

(b) An action may not be commenced pursuant to this article after the period for enforcement of the money judgment has expired.

(c) Notwithstanding Section 683.020, if an action is commenced pursuant to this article within the time permitted in this section, the action may be prosecuted to judgment. *(Added by Stats.1982, c. 1364, p. 5195, § 2, operative July 1, 1983.)*

Law Revision Commission Comments

Section 708.230 is new and provides a statute of limitations for bringing a creditor's suit. Under prior law, the general four-year statute of limitations was applicable and began to run from the return of the writ of execution unsatisfied. See Sherman v. S.K.D. Oil Co., 185 Cal. 534, 538, 545, 197 P. 799, 801 (1921). Under Section 708.230, the statute of limitations is no longer tied to the return of the writ unsatisfied or the failure of examination proceedings because the judgment creditor is not required to exhaust these remedies before resorting to a creditor's suit. See Section 708.210 and the Comment thereto. For a transitional provision, see Section 694.060.

The extension of time provided by paragraph (2) of subdivision (a) may be effectuated by the creation of an enforcement lien on the property, as for example, an execution lien (see Section 697.710), a judgment lien on personal property (see Sections 697.510–697.670), or a lien created by service of an order of examination on the third person (see Section 708.120).

A creditor's suit commenced within the period prescribed by this section may be pursued to judgment after the money judgment is no longer enforceable against the original judgment debtor notwithstanding Section 683.020. The judgment in the creditor's suit may then be enforced as provided in Section 708.280, and the 10-year period of enforceability (subject to renewal) provided by Section 683.020 applies to the judgment in the creditor's suit. [16 Cal.L.Rev.Comm. Reports 1511 (1982)].

Research References

Rutter, Cal. Practice Guide: Enforcing Judgments/Debts Ch. 6G-4, Creditor's Suit.
Miller and Starr California Real Estate § 32:49, Real Property Subject to the Judgment Lien.
8 Witkin Cal. Proc. 5th Enforcement of Judgment § 292, (S 292) Time for Bringing Action.

§ 708.240. Application for restraining order, temporary restraining order or injunction

The judgment creditor may apply to the court in which an action under this article is pending for either or both of the following:

(a) An order restraining the third person from transferring to the judgment debtor the property in which the judgment debtor is claimed to have an interest or from paying to the judgment debtor the alleged debt. The order shall be made on noticed motion if the court so directs or a court rule so requires. Otherwise, the order shall be made on ex parte application. The order shall remain in effect until judgment is entered in the action or until such earlier time as the court may provide in the order. An undertaking may be required in the discretion of the court. The court may modify or vacate the order at any time with or without a hearing on such terms as are just.

(b) A temporary restraining order or a preliminary injunction or both, restraining the third person from transferring to any person or otherwise disposing of the property in which the judgment debtor is claimed to have an interest, pursuant to Chapter 3 (commencing with Section 525) of Title 7, and the court may make, dissolve, and modify such orders as provided therein. *(Added by Stats.1982, c. 1364, p. 5196, § 2, operative July 1, 1983.)*

Law Revision Commission Comments

Section 708.240 supersedes a portion of former Section 720. See also Section 708.180(c)–(d) (order in examination proceedings forbidding transfer or payment). Although an order may be made under subdivision (a) without notice and of long duration, its effect is narrowly limited to orders forbidding transfer or payment to the judgment debtor. By incorporating Chapter 3 (commencing with Section 525) of Title 7 (injunctions), subdivision (b) provides the third person with procedural safeguards which were not present in former Section 720. [16 Cal.L.Rev. Comm. Reports 1512 (1982)].

Research References

Rutter, Cal. Practice Guide: Enforcing Judgments/Debts Ch. 6G-4, Creditor's Suit.
Miller and Starr California Real Estate § 32:49, Real Property Subject to the Judgment Lien.
8 Witkin Cal. Proc. 5th Enforcement of Judgment § 282, (S 282) Restrictions on Transfer or Payment.
8 Witkin Cal. Proc. 5th Enforcement of Judgment § 293, (S 293) Order Forbidding Transfer or Payment.

§ 708.250. Service of summons creating lien

Service of summons on the third person creates a lien on the interest of the judgment debtor in the property or on the debt owed to the judgment debtor that is the subject of an action under this article. *(Added by Stats.1982, c. 1364, p. 5196, § 2, operative July 1, 1983.)*

Law Revision Commission Comments

Section 708.250 codifies case law. See Canfield v. Security-First Nat'l Bank, 13 Cal.2d 1, 28–30, 87 P.2d 830, 844 (1939); Nordstrom v. Corona City Water Co., 155 Cal. 206, 212–13, 100 P. 242, 245 (1909); cf. Seymour v. McAvoy, 121 Cal. 438, 441, 53 P. 946, 947 (1898) (filing bill in equity creates equitable lien). [16 Cal.L.Rev.Comm. Reports 1512 (1982)].

Research References

Rutter, Cal. Practice Guide: Enforcing Judgments/Debts Ch. 6G-4, Creditor's Suit.
Miller and Starr California Real Estate § 32:49, Real Property Subject to the Judgment Lien.
8 Witkin Cal. Proc. 5th Enforcement of Judgment § 291, (S 291) Nature of Action.

§ 708.260. Claim of exemption

(a) In an action brought pursuant to this article, the judgment debtor may claim that all or any portion of the property or debt is exempt from enforcement of a money judgment. The claim shall be made by application to the court on noticed motion, filed with the court and served on the judgment creditor not later than 30 days before the date set for trial. Service shall be made personally or by mail. The judgment debtor shall execute an affidavit in support of the application that includes all of the matters set forth in subdivision (b) of Section 703.520. No notice of opposition to the claim of exemption is required. If the judgment debtor has not been named as a party to the action, the judgment debtor may obtain an order under Section 389 that the judgment debtor be made a party. Except as provided in subdivision (b), failure of the judgment debtor to make a claim of exemption is a waiver of the exemption.

(b) Failure of the judgment debtor to make a claim of exemption in an action brought pursuant to this article is not a waiver of the exemption if both of the following conditions are satisfied:

(1) The judgment debtor has not been served with process in the action that contains a description of the property or debt reasonably adequate to permit it to be identified.

(2) The judgment debtor does not have actual notice of the pendency of the action and the identity of the property or the nature of the debt in issue. *(Added by Stats.1982, c. 1364, p. 5196, § 2, operative July 1, 1983.)*

Research References

Rutter, Cal. Practice Guide: Enforcing Judgments/Debts Ch. 6G-4, Creditor's Suit.
Miller and Starr California Real Estate § 32:49, Real Property Subject to the Judgment Lien.

8 Witkin Cal. Proc. 5th Enforcement of Judgment § 280, Judgment Debtor's Claim of Exemption.
8 Witkin Cal. Proc. 5th Enforcement of Judgment § 291, (S 291) Nature of Action.
8 Witkin Cal. Proc. 5th Enforcement of Judgment § 294, (S 294) Debtor's Claim of Exemption.

§ 708.270. Right to jury trial

There is no right to a jury trial in an action under this article. *(Added by Stats.1982, c. 1364, p. 5197, § 2, operative July 1, 1983.)*

Law Revision Commission Comments

Section 708.270 is new and codifies what appears to be California law. Cf. Misrach v. Liederman, 14 Cal.App.2d Supp. 757, 58 P.2d 746 (1936). See generally 21 Am.Jur.2d Creditors' Bills § 9, at 10 (1965); 21 C.J.S. Creditors' Suits § 73, at 1125 (1940). [16 Cal.L.Rev.Comm. Reports 1513 (1982)].

Research References

Rutter, Cal. Practice Guide: Enforcing Judgments/Debts Ch. 6G-4, Creditor's Suit.
8 Witkin Cal. Proc. 5th Enforcement of Judgment § 291, (S 291) Nature of Action.

§ 708.280. Court determination of exemption claim; rendering of judgment; order concerning transfer of property

(a) The court shall determine any exemption claim made in the action. If the judgment debtor establishes to the satisfaction of the court that the property or debt is exempt from enforcement of a money judgment, the court shall so adjudge and may not make the orders referred to in subdivisions (b), (c), and (d).

(b) If the judgment creditor establishes that the third person has property in which the judgment debtor has an interest or is indebted to the judgment debtor, the court shall render judgment accordingly. The property or debt may be applied to the satisfaction of the judgment creditor's judgment against the judgment debtor as ordered by the court.

(c) If the court determines that the third person has property in which the judgment debtor has an interest, the court may order the third person not to transfer the property until it can be levied upon or otherwise applied to the satisfaction of the judgment.

(d) If the court determines that the third person has transferred property that was subject to a lien in favor of the judgment creditor or, contrary to court order of which the third person has notice, has paid the debt to the judgment debtor or has transferred the property, the court shall render judgment against the third person in an amount equal to the lesser of the following:

(1) The value of the judgment debtor's interest in the property or the amount of the debt.

(2) The amount of the judgment creditor's judgment against the judgment debtor remaining unsatisfied. *(Added by Stats. 1982, c. 1364, p. 5197, § 2, operative July 1, 1983.)*

Law Revision Commission Comments

Section 708.280 is new. Subdivision (a) recognizes that only nonexempt property may be applied to the satisfaction of the judgment. See Section 703.010 (exemptions apply to all procedures for enforcement of money judgments). At the conclusion of a creditor's suit, the property may be applied toward the satisfaction of the judgment in a manner appropriate to the particular type of property. See the Comment to Section 708.205. Ordinarily, the property or debt that has been determined in the creditor's suit to belong to or to be owing to the judgment debtor will be levied upon under a writ of execution. If the judgment creditor does not have a valid writ of execution, the judgment creditor may apply for an order under subdivision (c) preventing the third person from transferring the property until it can be applied to the satisfaction of the judgment. If the property cannot be levied upon, some other manner of enforcement will be necessary. [16 Cal.L.Rev.Comm. Reports 1514 (1982)].

Research References

Rutter, Cal. Practice Guide: Enforcing Judgments/Debts Ch. 6G-4, Creditor's Suit.
Miller and Starr California Real Estate § 32:49, Real Property Subject to the Judgment Lien.
8 Witkin Cal. Proc. 5th Enforcement of Judgment § 292, (S 292) Time for Bringing Action.
8 Witkin Cal. Proc. 5th Enforcement of Judgment § 295, (S 295) Judgment.

§ 708.290. Costs

Costs incurred by or taxed against the judgment creditor in an action under this article may not be recovered from the judgment debtor as a cost of enforcing the judgment. *(Added by Stats. 1982, c. 1364, p. 5197, § 2, operative July 1, 1983.)*

Research References

Rutter, Cal. Practice Guide: Enforcing Judgments/Debts Ch. 6G-4, Creditor's Suit.
Miller and Starr California Real Estate § 32:30, When Property Held by Third Party.
8 Witkin Cal. Proc. 5th Enforcement of Judgment § 295, (S 295) Judgment.

ARTICLE 4. CHARGING ORDERS

Section
708.310. Money judgment against partner or member.
708.320. Creation of lien on a judgment creditor's interest in partnership or limited liability company; conditions; effect of issuing charging order.

§ 708.310. Money judgment against partner or member

If a money judgment is rendered against a partner or member but not against the partnership or limited liability company, the judgment debtor's interest in the partnership or limited liability company may be applied toward the satisfaction of the judgment by an order charging the judgment debtor's interest pursuant to Section 15907.3, 16504, or 17705.03 of the Corporations Code. *(Added by Stats.1982, c. 1364, p. 5197, § 2, operative July 1, 1983. Amended by Stats.1985, c. 41, § 9; Stats.2002, c. 451 (A.B.2355), § 1; Stats.2012, c. 419 (S.B.323), § 4, operative Jan. 1, 2014.)*

Law Revision Commission Comments

Section 708.310 is amended to delete the reference to former Corporations Code Section 15573 and substitute a reference to Corporations Code Section 15673 which superseded the former statute. See 1983 Cal.Stats. ch. 1223, §§ 9–10.

Research References

Rutter, Cal. Practice Guide: Enforcing Judgments/Debts Ch. 4-A, A. Attachment.
Rutter, Cal. Practice Guide: Enforcing Judgments/Debts Ch. 6G-7, Charging Orders Against Debtor Partnership/LLC Interests.
Rutter, Cal. Practice Guide: Enforcing Judgments/Debts Ch. 6J-3, Enforcing California Judgments Against Debtor's Out-Of-State Property.
Rutter, Cal. Practice Guide: Enforcing Judgments/Debts Form 6:YY.3, Notice of Motion to Charge LLC Member's Interst.
Miller and Starr California Real Estate § 33:1, Nature of Receiverships; in General.
Miller and Starr California Real Estate § 32:21, Nonindividual Defendants.
Miller and Starr California Real Estate § 32:30, When Property Held by Third Party.
Miller and Starr California Real Estate § 32:49, Real Property Subject to the Judgment Lien.
8 Witkin Cal. Proc. 5th Enforcement of Judgment § 116, Property Not Subject to Execution.
8 Witkin Cal. Proc. 5th Enforcement of Judgment § 296, Charging Order.

11 Witkin, California Summary 10th Husband and Wife § 268, (S 268) Charging Order Against Interest in Partnership or Limited Liability Company.

§ 708.320. Creation of lien on a judgment creditor's interest in partnership or limited liability company; conditions; effect of issuing charging order

(a) A lien on a judgment debtor's interest in a partnership or limited liability company is created by service of a notice of motion for a charging order on the judgment debtor and on either of the following:

(1) All partners or the partnership.

(2) All members or the limited liability company.

(b) If a charging order is issued, the lien created pursuant to subdivision (a) continues under the terms of the order. If issuance of the charging order is denied, the lien is extinguished. *(Added by Stats.1982, c. 1364, p. 5197, § 2, operative July 1, 1983. Amended by Stats.2002, c. 451 (A.B.2355), § 2.)*

Law Revision Commission Comments

Section 708.320 is new. Former statutory law did not explicitly provide for a lien of a charging order. The lien of a charging order was recognized in case law, but the time of its creation and its effect were unclear. See Taylor v. S & M Lamp Co., 190 Cal.App.2d 700, 707–12, 12 Cal.Rptr. 323, 329–31 (1961). Section 708.320 establishes the time of creation of the lien by reference to service of notice of motion for the charging order. Cf. Ribero v. Callaway, 87 Cal.App.2d 135, 138, 196 P.2d 109 (1948) (charging orders issued on noticed motion). This provision is analogous to the creation of a lien in an examination proceeding under Article 2 (commencing with Section 708.110) by service of the order of examination. See also Section 416.40 (service on partnership). [16 Cal.L.Rev.Comm. Reports 1516 (1982)].

Research References

Rutter, Cal. Practice Guide: Enforcing Judgments/Debts Ch. 6G-7, Charging Orders Against Debtor Partnership/LLC Interests.
Miller and Starr California Real Estate § 33:1, Nature of Receiverships; in General.
Miller and Starr California Real Estate § 32:49, Real Property Subject to the Judgment Lien.
8 Witkin Cal. Proc. 5th Enforcement of Judgment § 296, Charging Order.
11 Witkin, California Summary 10th Husband and Wife § 268, (S 268) Charging Order Against Interest in Partnership or Limited Liability Company.

ARTICLE 5. LIEN IN PENDING ACTION OR PROCEEDING

Section
708.410. Interests subject to lien; filing notice of lien and abstract or copy of judgment; service; pending, defined.
708.420. Contents of notice of lien.
708.430. Intervention; party to action.
708.440. Enforcement of judgment recovered in favor of judgment debtor; compromise, dismissal, etc.; court-ordered terms and conditions.
708.450. Claim of exemption; determination; termination of lien.
708.460. Statement concerning lien endorsed on judgment; inclusion in abstract.
708.470. Order for satisfaction of lien; order not to transfer property; judgment rendered against parties transferring property or making payment to judgment debtor.
708.480. Enforcement of lien.

§ 708.410. Interests subject to lien; filing notice of lien and abstract or copy of judgment; service; pending, defined

(a) A judgment creditor who has a money judgment against a judgment debtor who is a party to a pending action or special proceeding may obtain a lien under this article, to the extent required to satisfy the judgment creditor's money judgment, on both of the following:

(1) Any cause of action of such judgment debtor for money or property that is the subject of the action or proceeding.

(2) The rights of such judgment debtor to money or property under any judgment subsequently procured in the action or proceeding.

(b) To obtain a lien under this article, the judgment creditor shall file a notice of lien and an abstract or certified copy of the judgment creditor's money judgment in the pending action or special proceeding.

(c) At the time of the filing under subdivision (b) or promptly thereafter, the judgment creditor shall serve on all parties who, prior thereto, have made an appearance in the action or special proceeding a copy of the notice of lien and a statement of the date when the notice of lien was filed in the action or special proceeding. Service shall be made personally or by mail. Failure to serve all parties as required by this subdivision does not affect the lien created by the filing under subdivision (b), but the rights of a party are not affected by the lien until the party has notice of the lien.

(d) For the purpose of this article, an action or special proceeding is pending until the time for appeal from the judgment has expired or, if an appeal is filed, until the appeal has been finally determined. *(Added by Stats.1982, c. 1364, p. 5197, § 2, operative July 1, 1983.)*

Research References

Rutter, Cal. Practice Guide: Civ. Pro. Before Trial Ch. 2-E, E. Intervention.
Rutter, Cal. Practice Guide: Enforcing Judgments/Debts Ch. 6D-4, Levy on Specific Property.
Rutter, Cal. Practice Guide: Enforcing Judgments/Debts Ch. 6G-8, Lien in Pending Action.
Rutter, Cal. Practice Guide: Personal Injury Ch. 1-C, C. Formation of Attorney-Client Relationship: the Employment Agreement.
Miller and Starr California Real Estate § 32:28, Attachment of Real Property.
9 Witkin Cal. Proc. 5th Appeal § 143, (S 143) Motion as Special Proceeding.
1 Witkin Cal. Proc. 5th Attorneys § 172, (S 172) Priority.
8 Witkin Cal. Proc. 5th Enforcement of Judgment § 55, (S 55) in General.
8 Witkin Cal. Proc. 5th Enforcement of Judgment § 116, Property Not Subject to Execution.
8 Witkin Cal. Proc. 5th Enforcement of Judgment § 136, (S 136) Property Subject of Pending Action.
8 Witkin Cal. Proc. 5th Enforcement of Judgment § 207, (S 207) Damages for Personal Injury.
8 Witkin Cal. Proc. 5th Enforcement of Judgment § 208, (S 208) Damages for Wrongful Death.
8 Witkin Cal. Proc. 5th Enforcement of Judgment § 297, (S 297) Nature and Scope of Remedy.
8 Witkin Cal. Proc. 5th Enforcement of Judgment § 298, in General.
8 Witkin Cal. Proc. 5th Enforcement of Judgment § 300, (S 300) Notice.
8 Witkin Cal. Proc. 5th Enforcement of Judgment § 301, (S 301) Restrictions on Compromise, Dismissal, Settlement, Satisfaction, or Enforcement.
8 Witkin Cal. Proc. 5th Enforcement of Judgment § 302, (S 302) Debtor's Claim of Exemption.
8 Witkin Cal. Proc. 5th Enforcement of Judgment § 312, (S 312) Nature and Scope of Remedy.

8 Witkin Cal. Proc. 5th Enforcement of Judgment § 317, in General.

§ 708.420. Contents of notice of lien

The notice of lien under Section 708.410 shall contain all of the following:

(a) A statement that a lien has been created under this article and the title of the court and the cause and number of the pending action or proceeding in which the notice of lien is filed.

(b) The name and last known address of the judgment debtor.

(c) The name and address of the judgment creditor.

(d) The title of the court where the judgment creditor's money judgment is entered and the cause and number of the action, the date of entry of the judgment, and the date of any subsequent renewals, and where entered in the records of the court.

(e) The amount required to satisfy the judgment creditor's money judgment at the time the notice of lien is filed in the action or proceeding.

(f) A statement that the lien attaches to any cause of action of the judgment debtor that is the subject of the action or proceeding and to the judgment debtor's rights to money or property under any judgment subsequently procured in the action or proceeding.

(g) A statement that no compromise, dismissal, settlement, or satisfaction of the pending action or proceeding or any of the judgment debtor's rights to money or property under any judgment procured therein may be entered into by or on behalf of the judgment debtor, and that the judgment debtor may not enforce the judgment debtor's rights to money or property under any judgment procured in the action or proceeding by a writ or otherwise, unless one of the following requirements is satisfied:

(1) The prior approval by order of the court in which the action or proceeding is pending has been obtained.

(2) The written consent of the judgment creditor has been obtained or the judgment creditor has released the lien.

(3) The money judgment of the judgment creditor has been satisfied.

(h) A statement that the judgment debtor may claim an exemption for all or any portion of the money or property within 30 days after the judgment debtor has notice of the creation of the lien and a statement that, if the exemption is not claimed within the time allowed, the exemption is waived. *(Added by Stats.1982, c. 1364, p. 5198, § 2, operative July 1, 1983.)*

Law Revision Commission Comments

Section 708.420 is new and is designed to advise the parties to the pending action or proceeding of the relevant facts and of the consequences of the filing of a notice of lien under this article. [16 Cal.L.Rev.Comm. Reports 1519 (1982)].

Research References

Rutter, Cal. Practice Guide: Enforcing Judgments/Debts Ch. 6G-8, Lien in Pending Action.
Miller and Starr California Real Estate § 32:49, Real Property Subject to the Judgment Lien.
8 Witkin Cal. Proc. 5th Enforcement of Judgment § 300, (S 300) Notice.

§ 708.430. Intervention; party to action

(a) The court in which the action or special proceeding is pending may permit a judgment creditor who has obtained a lien under this article to intervene in the action or proceeding pursuant to Section 387.

(b) For the purposes of Sections 708.450 and 708.470, a judgment creditor shall be deemed to be a party to the action or special proceeding even though the judgment creditor has not become a party to the action or proceeding under subdivision (a). *(Added by Stats.1982, c. 1364, p. 5199, § 2, operative July 1, 1983.)*

Law Revision Commission Comments

Subdivision (a) of Section 708.430 continues the substance of a portion of the first sentence of former Section 688.1(a). Subdivision (b) permits a judgment creditor who has not intervened to oppose a claim of exemption pursuant to Section 708.450 or to seek an order applying the property to the satisfaction of the judgment creditor's judgment pursuant to Section 708.470. [16 Cal.L.Rev.Comm. Reports 1520 (1982)].

Research References

Rutter, Cal. Practice Guide: Civ. Pro. Before Trial Ch. 2-E, E. Intervention.

Rutter, Cal. Practice Guide: Enforcing Judgments/Debts Ch. 6G-8, Lien in Pending Action.

8 Witkin Cal. Proc. 5th Enforcement of Judgment § 297, (S 297) Nature and Scope of Remedy.

8 Witkin Cal. Proc. 5th Enforcement of Judgment § 302, (S 302) Debtor's Claim of Exemption.

8 Witkin Cal. Proc. 5th Enforcement of Judgment § 303, in General.

§ 708.440. Enforcement of judgment recovered in favor of judgment debtor; compromise, dismissal, etc.; court-ordered terms and conditions

(a) Except as provided in subdivision (c) of Section 708.410, unless the judgment creditor's money judgment is first satisfied or the lien is released, the judgment recovered in the action or special proceeding in favor of the judgment debtor may not be enforced by a writ or otherwise, and no compromise, dismissal, settlement, or satisfaction of the pending action or special proceeding or the judgment procured therein may be entered into by or on behalf of the judgment debtor, without the written consent of the judgment creditor or authorization by order of the court obtained under subdivision (b).

(b) Upon application by the judgment debtor, the court in which the action or special proceeding is pending or the judgment procured therein is entered may, in its discretion, after a hearing, make an order described in subdivision (a) that may include such terms and conditions as the court deems necessary. The application for an order under this subdivision shall be made on noticed motion. The notice of motion shall be served on the judgment creditor. Service shall be made personally or by mail. *(Added by Stats.1982, c. 1364, p. 5199, § 2, operative July 1, 1983.)*

Law Revision Commission Comments

Section 708.440 supersedes a portion of the second sentence of former Section 688.1. The provision permitting compromise, dismissal, settlement, or satisfaction pursuant to court order despite the opposition of the judgment creditor is new and has been added to prevent, for example, the judgment creditor from forcing the judgment debtor to proceed with the action when the court concludes that it is in the best interests of the parties to settle. See also Abatti v. Eldridge, 112 Cal.App.3d 411, 169 Cal.Rptr. 330 (1980) (power of court to approve settlement that does not fully satisfy lien). The introductory clause of subdivision (a) recognizes that, notwithstanding this section, the rights of a party who settles without notice of the lien are unaffected by the lien. See Section 708.410(c). [16 Cal.L.Rev.Comm. Reports 1521 (1982)].

Research References

Rutter, Cal. Practice Guide: Enforcing Judgments/Debts Ch. 6G-8, Lien in Pending Action.

8 Witkin Cal. Proc. 5th Enforcement of Judgment § 301, (S 301) Restrictions on Compromise, Dismissal, Settlement, Satisfaction, or Enforcement.

8 Witkin Cal. Proc. 5th Enforcement of Judgment § 303, in General.

§ 708.450. Claim of exemption; determination; termination of lien

(a) If a lien is created under this article, the judgment debtor may claim that all or any portion of the money or property that the judgment debtor may recover in the action or special proceeding is exempt from enforcement of a money judgment. The claim shall be made by application on noticed motion to the court in which the action or special proceeding is pending, filed and served on the judgment creditor not later than 30 days after the judgment debtor has notice of the creation of the lien. Service shall be made personally or by mail. The judgment debtor shall execute an affidavit in support of the application that includes all the matters set forth in subdivision (b) of Section 703.520. No notice of opposition to the claim of exemption is required. The failure of the judgment debtor to make a claim of exemption under this section constitutes a waiver of the exemption.

(b) The court may determine the exemption claim at any time prior to the entry of judgment in the action or special proceeding or may consolidate the exemption hearing with the hearing on a motion pursuant to Section 708.470.

(c) If the judgment debtor establishes to the satisfaction of the court that the right of the judgment debtor to money or property under the judgment in the action or special proceeding is all or partially exempt from enforcement of a money judgment, the court shall order the termination of the lien created under this article on the exempt portion of the money or property. *(Added by Stats.1982, c. 1364, p. 5199, § 2, operative July 1, 1983. Amended by Stats.1984, c. 538, § 31.)*

Law Revision Commission Comments

Section 708.450 provides the procedure for the making and determination of any exemption claimed for the judgment debtor's prospective recovery that is subject to a lien created under this article. This procedure is drawn from Sections 708.260 and 708.280 (creditor's suit). The judgment creditor is deemed to be a party for the purposes of this section. See Section 708.430(b). [16 Cal.L.Rev.Comm. Reports 1522 (1982)].

Subdivision (b) of Section 708.450 is amended to clarify the procedure for determining exemptions. [17 Cal.L.Rev.Comm. Reports 1019 (1983)].

Research References

Rutter, Cal. Practice Guide: Enforcing Judgments/Debts Ch. 6G-8, Lien in Pending Action.

8 Witkin Cal. Proc. 5th Enforcement of Judgment § 297, (S 297) Nature and Scope of Remedy.

8 Witkin Cal. Proc. 5th Enforcement of Judgment § 302, (S 302) Debtor's Claim of Exemption.

§ 708.460. Statement concerning lien endorsed on judgment; inclusion in abstract

(a) If a lien is created pursuant to this article, the court clerk shall endorse upon the judgment recovered in the action or special proceeding a statement of the existence of the lien and the time it was created.

(b) Any abstract issued upon the judgment shall include a statement of the lien in favor of the judgment creditor. *(Added by Stats.1982, c. 1364, p. 5200, § 2, operative July 1, 1983.)*

Law Revision Commission Comments

Section 708.460 supersedes the third sentence of former Section 688.1. Section 708.460 is consistent with the last two sentences of subdivision (b) of Section 700.190 (execution lien on final money judgment). [16 Cal.L.Rev.Comm. Reports 1522 (1982)].

Research References

Rutter, Cal. Practice Guide: Enforcing Judgments/Debts Ch. 6G-8, Lien in Pending Action.

8 Witkin Cal. Proc. 5th Enforcement of Judgment § 297, (S 297) Nature and Scope of Remedy.

§ 708.470. Order for satisfaction of lien; order not to transfer property; judgment rendered against parties transferring property or making payment to judgment debtor

(a) If the judgment debtor is entitled to money or property under the judgment in the action or special proceeding and a lien created under this article exists, upon application of any party to the action or special proceeding, the court may order that the judgment debtor's rights to money or property under the judgment be applied to the satisfaction of the lien created under this article as ordered by the court. Application for an order under this section shall be on noticed motion. The notice of motion shall be served on all other parties. Service shall be made personally or by mail.

(b) If the judgment determines that the judgment debtor has an interest in property, the court may order the party having custody or control of the property not to transfer the property until it can be levied upon or otherwise applied to the satisfaction of the lien created under this article.

(c) If the court determines that a party (other than the judgment debtor) having notice of the lien created under this article has transferred property that was subject to the lien or has paid an amount to the judgment debtor that was subject to the lien, the court shall render judgment against the party in an amount equal to the lesser of the following:

(1) The value of the judgment debtor's interest in the property or the amount paid the judgment debtor.

(2) The amount of the judgment creditor's lien created under this article. *(Added by Stats.1982, c. 1364, p. 5200, § 2, operative July 1, 1983.)*

Law Revision Commission Comments

Section 708.470 is drawn from subdivisions (b)–(d) of Section 708.280 (creditor's suit). The judgment creditor is deemed to be a party for the purposes of this section. See Section 708.430(b). [16 Cal.L.Rev.Comm. Reports 1523 (1982)].

Research References

Rutter, Cal. Practice Guide: Enforcing Judgments/Debts Ch. 6G-8, Lien in Pending Action.

Rutter, Cal. Practice Guide: Enforcing Judgments/Debts Ch. 6G-8, Outline 8.

Rutter, Cal. Practice Guide: Prof. Responsibility Ch. 5-F, F. Formalizing Fee Agreements.

8 Witkin Cal. Proc. 5th Enforcement of Judgment § 297, (S 297) Nature and Scope of Remedy.

8 Witkin Cal. Proc. 5th Enforcement of Judgment § 302, (S 302) Debtor's Claim of Exemption.

8 Witkin Cal. Proc. 5th Enforcement of Judgment § 303, in General.

§ 708.480. Enforcement of lien

A lien created under this article may be enforced by any applicable procedure:

(a) After the judgment subject to the lien is entered and the time for appeal from the judgment has expired.

(b) If an appeal is filed from the judgment subject to the lien, after the appeal is finally determined. *(Added by Stats.1982, c. 1364, p. 5200, § 2, operative July 1, 1983.)*

Research References

Rutter, Cal. Practice Guide: Enforcing Judgments/Debts Ch. 6G-8, Lien in Pending Action.

8 Witkin Cal. Proc. 5th Enforcement of Judgment § 304, After Final Judgment.

ARTICLE 6. ASSIGNMENT ORDER

§ 708.510. Assignment of right to payments; service of notice; factors considered in ordering assignment; amount assigned

(a) Except as otherwise provided by law, upon application of the judgment creditor on noticed motion, the court may order the judgment debtor to assign to the judgment creditor or to a receiver appointed pursuant to Article 7 (commencing with Section 708.610) all or part of a right to payment due or to become due, whether or not the right is conditioned on future developments, including but not limited to the following types of payments:

(1) Wages due from the federal government that are not subject to withholding under an earnings withholding order.

(2) Rents.

(3) Commissions.

(4) Royalties.

(5) Payments due from a patent or copyright.

(6) Insurance policy loan value.

(b) The notice of the motion shall be served on the judgment debtor. Service shall be made personally or by mail.

(c) Subject to subdivisions (d), (e), and (f), in determining whether to order an assignment or the amount of an assignment pursuant to subdivision (a), the court may take into consideration all relevant factors, including the following:

(1) The reasonable requirements of a judgment debtor who is a natural person and of persons supported in whole or in part by the judgment debtor.

(2) Payments the judgment debtor is required to make or that are deducted in satisfaction of other judgments and wage assignments, including earnings assignment orders for support.

(3) The amount remaining due on the money judgment.

(4) The amount being or to be received in satisfaction of the right to payment that may be assigned.

(d) A right to payment may be assigned pursuant to this article only to the extent necessary to satisfy the money judgment.

(e) When earnings or periodic payments pursuant to a pension or retirement plan are assigned pursuant to subdivision (a), the amount of the earnings or the periodic payments assigned shall not exceed the amount that may be withheld from a like amount of earnings under Chapter 5 (commencing with Section 706.010) (Wage Garnishment Law).

(f) Where a specific amount of the payment or payments to be assigned is exempt by another statutory provision, the amount of the payment or payments to be assigned pursuant to subdivision (a) shall not exceed the amount by which the payment or payments exceed the exempt amount. *(Added by Stats.1982, c.*

1364, p. 5201, § 2, operative July 1, 1983. Amended by Stats.1992, c. 163 (A.B.2641), § 51, operative Jan. 1, 1994.)

Law Revision Commission Comments

Subdivision (c)(2) of Section 708.510 is amended to make clear that the court is to take into consideration any earnings assignment order for support. "Earnings assignment order for support" is defined in Section 706.011. [22 Cal.L.Rev.Comm.Reports 1 (1992)].

Research References

Rutter, Cal. Practice Guide: Enforcing Judgments/Debts Ch. 6D-4, Levy on Specific Property.

Rutter, Cal. Practice Guide: Enforcing Judgments/Debts Ch. 6G-5, Assignment Order.

Rutter, Cal. Practice Guide: Enforcing Judgments/Debts Ch. 6J-3, Enforcing California Judgments Against Debtor's Out-Of-State Property.

Rutter, Cal. Practice Guide: Enforcing Judgments/Debts Ch. 6G-18, Enforcement Against Nonvested Contingent Interests.

Miller and Starr California Real Estate § 11:129, Priority of the Title of an Execution Sale Purchaser.

8 Witkin Cal. Proc. 5th Enforcement of Judgment § 74, (S 74) Interests Subject to Lien.

8 Witkin Cal. Proc. 5th Enforcement of Judgment § 145, (S 145) Property to be Collected Rather Than Sold.

8 Witkin Cal. Proc. 5th Enforcement of Judgment § 199, (S 199) Life Insurance Policies.

8 Witkin Cal. Proc. 5th Enforcement of Judgment § 304, After Final Judgment.

8 Witkin Cal. Proc. 5th Enforcement of Judgment § 305, (S 305) Nature and Procedure.

8 Witkin Cal. Proc. 5th Enforcement of Judgment § 309, (S 309) Limitations on Recovery.

1 Witkin Cal. Summ. 10th Contracts § 95, (S 95) Assignment as Between Assignee and Assignor.

§ 708.520. Order restraining assignment by judgment debtor

(a) When an application is made pursuant to Section 708.510 or thereafter, the judgment creditor may apply to the court for an order restraining the judgment debtor from assigning or otherwise disposing of the right to payment that is sought to be assigned. The application shall be made on noticed motion if the court so directs or a court rule so requires. Otherwise, it may be made ex parte.

(b) The court may issue an order pursuant to this section upon a showing of need for the order. The court, in its discretion, may require the judgment creditor to provide an undertaking.

(c) The court may modify or vacate the order at any time with or without a hearing on such terms as are just.

(d) The order shall be personally served upon the judgment debtor and shall contain a notice to the judgment debtor that failure to comply with the order may subject the judgment debtor to being held in contempt of court. *(Added by Stats.1982, c. 1364, p. 5201, § 2, operative July 1, 1983.)*

Law Revision Commission Comments

Section 708.520 affords injunctive relief in an appropriate case, pending determination of the judgment creditor's application for an assignment order. [16 Cal.L.Rev.Comm. Reports 1527 (1982)].

Research References

Rutter, Cal. Practice Guide: Enforcing Judgments/Debts Ch. 6G-5, Assignment Order.

8 Witkin Cal. Proc. 5th Enforcement of Judgment § 305, (S 305) Nature and Procedure.

§ 708.530. Effect and priority of assignment

(a) Except as provided in subdivision (b), the effect and priority of an assignment ordered pursuant to this article is governed by Section 955.1 of the Civil Code. For the purpose of priority, an assignee of a right to payment pursuant to this article

shall be deemed to be a bona fide assignee for value under the terms of Section 955.1 of the Civil Code.

(b) An assignment of the right to future rent ordered under this article is recordable as an instrument affecting real property and the priority of such an assignment is governed by Section 1214 of the Civil Code. *(Added by Stats.1982, c. 1364, p. 5202, § 2, operative July 1, 1983. Amended by Stats.1984, c. 538, § 32.)*

Law Revision Commission Comments

Section 708.530 incorporates the rule generally applicable to assignments of general intangibles and other rights to payment. Under Civil Code Section 955.1 and this section, the judgment creditor who has obtained an assignment under this article will have priority over another assignee of the same right for value and without notice only if the judgment creditor first gives notice to the obligor. See also Section 708.540. [16 Cal.L.Rev.Comm. Reports 1527 (1982)].

Section 708.530 is amended to provide a special rule governing assignments of rights to future rent. Subdivision (b) recognizes such assignments as instruments affecting real property subject to the recording act. [17 Cal.L.Rev.Comm. Reports 1020 (1983)].

Research References

Rutter, Cal. Practice Guide: Enforcing Judgments/Debts Ch. 6G-5, Assignment Order.

Miller and Starr California Real Estate § 11:129, Priority of the Title of an Execution Sale Purchaser.

8 Witkin Cal. Proc. 5th Enforcement of Judgment § 306, (S 306) Effect of Assignment.

§ 708.540. Rights of obligor; obligor, defined

The rights of an obligor are not affected by an order assigning the right to payment until notice of the order is received by the obligor. For the purpose of this section, "obligor" means the person who is obligated to make payments to the judgment debtor or who may become obligated to make payments to the judgment debtor depending upon future developments. *(Added by Stats.1982, c. 1364, p. 5202, § 2, operative July 1, 1983.)*

Law Revision Commission Comments

Section 708.540 makes clear that the person obligated to make payments to the judgment debtor or who will become obligated is not affected by the assignment order until notice of the order is received. This section is analogous to provisions governing the effect of an execution levy. See, e.g., Sections 701.020 (liability of third person under levy), 701.050 (duty of account debtor). See also Civil Code § 955.1 (rights of certain obligors upon assignment); Com.Code § 9318 (rights of account debtor). [16 Cal.L.Rev.Comm. Reports 1528 (1982)].

Research References

Rutter, Cal. Practice Guide: Enforcing Judgments/Debts Ch. 6G-5, Assignment Order.

8 Witkin Cal. Proc. 5th Enforcement of Judgment § 306, (S 306) Effect of Assignment.

§ 708.550. Claim of exemption

(a) The judgment debtor may claim that all or a portion of the right to payment is exempt from enforcement of a money judgment by application to the court on noticed motion filed not later than three days before the date set for the hearing on the judgment creditor's application for an assignment order. The judgment debtor shall execute an affidavit in support of the application that includes all of the matters set forth in subdivision (b) of Section 703.520. Failure of the judgment debtor to make a claim of exemption is a waiver of the exemption.

(b) The notice of the motion shall be personally served on the judgment creditor not later than three days before the date set for the hearing.

(c) The court shall determine any claim of exemption made pursuant to this section at the hearing on issuance of the assignment order. *(Added by Stats.1982, c. 1364, p. 5202, § 2, operative July 1, 1983.)*

Law Revision Commission Comments

Section 708.550 provides a motion procedure for claiming exemptions in a proceeding under this article. Exemptions not claimed as provided in this section are waived. See Section 703.030. [16 Cal.L.Rev.Comm. Reports 1528 (1982)].

Research References

Rutter, Cal. Practice Guide: Enforcing Judgments/Debts Ch. 6G-5, Assignment Order.
8 Witkin Cal. Proc. 5th Enforcement of Judgment § 307, (S 307) Debtor's Claim of Exemption.

§ 708.560. Order to modify or set aside assignment order

(a) Either the judgment creditor or the judgment debtor may apply to the court on noticed motion for an order to modify or set aside the assignment order. The notice of motion shall be served on the other party. Service shall be made personally or by mail.

(b) The court shall make an order modifying or setting aside the assignment order upon a showing that there has been a material change in circumstances since the time of the previous hearing on the assignment order. The court may order a reassignment of the right to payments as necessary. The order shall state whether and to what extent it applies to payments already made. *(Added by Stats.1982, c. 1364, p. 5202, § 2, operative July 1, 1983.)*

Law Revision Commission Comments

Section 708.560 gives the court broad discretion to modify or set aside an assignment order depending upon the circumstances of the case. [16 Cal.L.Rev.Comm. Reports 1529 (1982)].

Research References

Rutter, Cal. Practice Guide: Enforcing Judgments/Debts Ch. 6G-5, Assignment Order.
Miller and Starr California Real Estate § 32:28, Attachment of Real Property.
8 Witkin Cal. Proc. 5th Enforcement of Judgment § 308, (S 308) Modifying or Setting Aside Order.

ARTICLE 7. RECEIVER TO ENFORCE JUDGMENT

Section
708.610. Appointment, qualification, etc. of receiver.
708.620. Circumstances under which appointment of receiver appropriate.
708.630. Interest of judgment debtor in alcoholic beverage license.

§ 708.610. Appointment, qualification, etc. of receiver

The provisions of Chapter 5 (commencing with Section 564) and Chapter 5a (commencing with Section 571) of Title 7 govern the appointment, qualifications, powers, rights, and duties of a receiver appointed under this article. *(Added by Stats.1982, c. 1364, p. 5203, § 2, operative July 1, 1983.)*

Law Revision Commission Comments

Section 708.610 makes clear that the general receiver provisions continue to apply to receivers for enforcement of judgments. The appointment of a receiver is subject to the general rules concerning the time within which judgments may be enforced. See Chapter 3 (commencing with Section 683.010) of Division 1. [16 Cal.L.Rev.Comm. Reports 1529 (1982)].

Research References

Rutter, Cal. Practice Guide: Enforcing Judgments/Debts Ch. 4-C, C. Receiverships.

Rutter, Cal. Practice Guide: Enforcing Judgments/Debts Ch. 6G-6, Receiver to Enforce Judgment-EJL Provisions.
Miller and Starr California Real Estate § 33:1, Nature of Receiverships; in General.
8 Witkin Cal. Proc. 5th Enforcement of Judgment § 2, (S 2) In General.
8 Witkin Cal. Proc. 5th Enforcement of Judgment § 305, (S 305) Nature and Procedure.
8 Witkin Cal. Proc. 5th Enforcement of Judgment § 310, (S 310) in General.
8 Witkin Cal. Proc. 5th Enforcement of Judgment § 325, (S 325) Nature and Scope of Law.

§ 708.620. Circumstances under which appointment of receiver appropriate

The court may appoint a receiver to enforce the judgment where the judgment creditor shows that, considering the interests of both the judgment creditor and the judgment debtor, the appointment of a receiver is a reasonable method to obtain the fair and orderly satisfaction of the judgment. *(Added by Stats.1982, c. 1364, p. 5203, § 2, operative July 1, 1983.)*

Research References

Rutter, Cal. Practice Guide: Enforcing Judgments/Debts Ch. 6G-1, Examination of Judgment Debtor and Third Parties.
Rutter, Cal. Practice Guide: Enforcing Judgments/Debts Ch. 6G-6, Receiver to Enforce Judgment-EJL Provisions.
Miller and Starr California Real Estate § 33:32, Enforcement Actions After Entry of Judgment.
20 NO. 2 Miller & Starr, California Real Estate Newsalert 16, Homesteads.
8 Witkin Cal. Proc. 5th Enforcement of Judgment § 304, After Final Judgment.
8 Witkin Cal. Proc. 5th Enforcement of Judgment § 310, (S 310) in General.

§ 708.630. Interest of judgment debtor in alcoholic beverage license

(a) The judgment debtor's interest in an alcoholic beverage license may be applied to the satisfaction of a money judgment only as provided in this section.

(b) The court may appoint a receiver for the purpose of transferring the judgment debtor's interest in an alcoholic beverage license that is transferable under Article 5 (commencing with Section 24070) of Chapter 6 of Division 9 of the Business and Professions Code, unless the judgment debtor shows in the proceeding to appoint a receiver that the amount of delinquent taxes described in Section 24049 of the Business and Professions Code and claims of creditors with priority over the judgment creditor pursuant to Section 24074 of the Business and Professions Code exceed the probable sale price of the license.

(c) The receiver may exercise the powers of the licensee as necessary and in exercising such powers shall comply with the applicable provisions of Division 9 (commencing with Section 23000) of the Business and Professions Code and applicable regulations of the Department of Alcoholic Beverage Control. An application shall be filed to transfer the license to the receiver and a temporary retail permit shall be obtained during the pendency of the transfer. *(Added by Stats.1982, c. 1364, p. 5203, § 2, operative July 1, 1983.)*

Research References

Rutter, Cal. Practice Guide: Enforcing Judgments/Debts Ch. 4-C, C. Receiverships.
Rutter, Cal. Practice Guide: Enforcing Judgments/Debts Ch. 5-D, D. Involuntary Bankruptcy.
Rutter, Cal. Practice Guide: Enforcing Judgments/Debts Ch. 6D-2, Writ of Execution.
Rutter, Cal. Practice Guide: Enforcing Judgments/Debts Ch. 6G-6, Receiver to Enforce Judgment-EJL Provisions.
Rutter, Cal. Practice Guide: Enforcing Judgments/Debts Ch. 6A-11, Property Subject to Enforcement Procedures.

Miller and Starr California Real Estate § 33:1, Nature of Receiverships; in General.

Miller and Starr California Real Estate § 33:32, Enforcement Actions After Entry of Judgment.

8 Witkin Cal. Proc. 5th Enforcement of Judgment § 55, (S 55) in General.

8 Witkin Cal. Proc. 5th Enforcement of Judgment § 60, (S 60) in General.

8 Witkin Cal. Proc. 5th Enforcement of Judgment § 116, Property Not Subject to Execution.

8 Witkin Cal. Proc. 5th Enforcement of Judgment § 311, (S 311) Transfer of Alcoholic Beverage License.

ARTICLE 8. COLLECTION OF JUDGMENT WHERE JUDGMENT DEBTOR IS CREDITOR OF PUBLIC ENTITY

§ 708.710. Definitions

As used in this article:

(a) "Local public entity" means any public entity other than the state.

(b) "Public entity" means the state, a county, city, district, public authority, public agency, and any other political subdivision in the state.

(c) "State" means the State of California.

(d) "State agency" means a state office, officer, department, division, bureau, board, commission or agency claims against which are paid by warrants drawn by the Controller. *(Added by Stats.1982, c. 1364, p. 5203, § 2, operative July 1, 1983.)*

Law Revision Commission Comments

Section 708.710 defines several terms used in this article but makes no substantive change in former law. See former Section 710. Subdivision (d) is drawn from Section 900.6 of the Government Code and reflects the fact that Section 708.740 applies only to state agencies which present claims to the State Controller. As to claims which are not presented to the State Controller, Section 708.750 applies. [16 Cal.L.Rev.Comm. Reports 1532 (1982)].

Research References

Rutter, Cal. Practice Guide: Enforcing Judgments/Debts Ch. 6D-2, Writ of Execution.

Rutter, Cal. Practice Guide: Enforcing Judgments/Debts Ch. 6D-3, Levy of Writ of Execution-In General.

Rutter, Cal. Practice Guide: Enforcing Judgments/Debts Ch. 6G-1, Examination of Judgment Debtor and Third Parties.

Rutter, Cal. Practice Guide: Enforcing Judgments/Debts Ch. 6G-9, Collection of Debts Owed Judgment Debtors by State or Local Public Entities.

8 Witkin Cal. Proc. 5th Enforcement of Judgment § 2, (S 2) in General.

8 Witkin Cal. Proc. 5th Enforcement of Judgment § 116, Property Not Subject to Execution.

8 Witkin Cal. Proc. 5th Enforcement of Judgment § 304, After Final Judgment.

8 Witkin Cal. Proc. 5th Enforcement of Judgment § 312, (S 312) Nature and Scope of Remedy.

8 Witkin Cal. Proc. 5th Enforcement of Judgment § 313, (S 313) Filing, Notice, and Lien.

8 Witkin Cal. Proc. 5th Enforcement of Judgment § 317, in General.

§ 708.720. Procedures governing; earnings of public officer or employee; obligation subject of pending action or special proceeding

(a) If a public entity owes money to the judgment debtor, the obligation of the public entity may be applied to the satisfaction of the money judgment against the judgment debtor only in the manner provided by (1) this article, (2) Chapter 5 (commencing with Section 706.010) (wage garnishment), or (3) Article 5 (commencing with Section 708.410) (lien in pending action or proceeding).

(b) The earnings of a public officer or employee shall not be withheld pursuant to this article. Except as expressly provided by law, the earnings of a public officer or employee may be withheld for the payment of a money judgment only pursuant to Chapter 5 (commencing with Section 706.010).

(c) If the obligation of a public entity to pay money to the judgment debtor is the subject of a pending action or special proceeding, the procedure in this article does not apply. The payment of the obligation that is the subject of the pending action or special proceeding may be applied to the satisfaction of the money judgment against the judgment debtor only in the manner provided in Article 5 (commencing with Section 708.410). *(Added by Stats.1982, c. 1364, p. 5203, § 2, operative July 1, 1983.)*

Law Revision Commission Comments

Section 708.720 makes clear the procedures available to apply the obligation of a public entity to pay money to the judgment debtor to the satisfaction of a money judgment against the judgment debtor. The section continues the substance of former Section 710(h) (wage garnishment) and makes clear that a lien may be obtained in a pending action or proceeding to which the public entity is a party. [16 Cal.L.Rev.Comm. Reports 1533 (1982)].

Research References

Rutter, Cal. Practice Guide: Enforcing Judgments/Debts Ch. 6F-2, Wage Garnishment-In General.

Rutter, Cal. Practice Guide: Enforcing Judgments/Debts Ch. 6F-3, Issuance and Service of Earnings Withholding Orders.

Rutter, Cal. Practice Guide: Enforcing Judgments/Debts Ch. 6G-9, Collection of Debts Owed Judgment Debtors by State or Local Public Entities.

8 Witkin Cal. Proc. 5th Enforcement of Judgment § 312, (S 312) Nature and Scope of Remedy.

§ 708.730. Money owed by public entity; filing abstract or copy of judgment and affidavit; service of notice; submission of claim; judgment for support

(a) If money is owing and unpaid to the judgment debtor by a public entity, the judgment creditor may file, in the manner provided in this article, an abstract of the money judgment or a certified copy of the money judgment, together with an affidavit that states that the judgment creditor desires the relief provided by this article and states the exact amount then required to satisfy the judgment. The judgment creditor may state in the affidavit any fact tending to establish the identity of the judgment debtor.

(b) Promptly after filing the abstract or certified copy of the judgment and the affidavit with the public entity, the judgment creditor shall serve notice of the filing on the judgment debtor. Service shall be made personally or by mail.

(c) If the judgment is for support and related costs and money is owing and unpaid to the judgment debtor by a state agency, including, but not limited to, money owing and unpaid to the judgment debtor by a state agency on a claim for refund from the Franchise Tax Board under the Personal Income Tax Law, Part 10 (commencing with Section 17001) of Division 2 of the Revenue and Taxation Code, or the Bank and Corporation Tax Law, Part 11 (commencing with Section 23001) of Division 2 of the Revenue and Taxation Code or as a result of the judgment debtor's winnings in the California State Lottery, and the local child support agency is enforcing the support obligation pursuant to Section 17400 of the Family Code, the claim may be submitted as follows: The local child support agency may file the affidavit referred to in subdivision (a) without filing an abstract or certified copy of the judgment. In lieu thereof, the affidavit shall also state that an abstract of the judgment could be obtained. Where there is more than one judgment debtor, the local child support agency may include all the judgment debtors in a single affidavit. Separate affidavits need not be submitted for each judgment debtor. The affidavit need not on its face separately identify each judgment debtor or the exact amount required to satisfy the judgment, so long as it incorporates by reference forms or other automated data transmittals, as required by the Department of Child Support Services, which contain this information. Affidavits submitted pursuant to this subdivision by the local child support agency shall meet the standards and procedures prescribed by the state agency to which the affidavit is submitted, except that those affidavits submitted with respect to moneys owed and unpaid to the judgment debtor as a result of a claim for refund from the Franchise Tax Board under the Personal Income Tax Law, Part 10 (commencing with Section 17001) of Division 2 of the Revenue and Taxation Code, or the Bank and Corporation Tax Law, Part 11 (commencing with Section 23001) of Division 2 of the Revenue and Taxation Code, shall meet the standards and procedures prescribed by the Franchise Tax Board.

In serving the notice required by subdivision (b), the Director of the Department of Child Support Services or his or her designee may act in lieu of the judgment creditor as to judgments enforced under this division.

(d) If the judgment is for child, spousal, or family support and related costs and money is owing and unpaid to the judgment debtor by a state agency on a claim for refund from the Franchise Tax Board under the Personal Income Tax Law, Part 10 (commencing with Section 17001) of Division 2 of the Revenue and Taxation Code, or the Bank and Corporation Tax Law, Part 11 (commencing with Section 23001) of Division 2 of the Revenue and Taxation Code, or as a result of the judgment debtor's winnings in the California State Lottery, the judgment creditor may file with the court an abstract or a certified copy of the judgment ordering the payment of child, spousal, or family support, together with a request that the court issue a Notice of Support Arrearage, as provided in Section 708.780, to which any personal income tax refunds and lottery winnings owed the judgment debtor by the State of California will be subject. The request shall be accompanied by an affidavit, signed under penalty of perjury, which shall state that the judgment creditor desires the relief provided by this subdivision and shall state the exact amount then required to satisfy the judgment. In addition, the affidavit shall specify the beginning and ending dates of all periods during which the arrearage for support occurred, specify the arrearage for each month, and state that the support is at least 90 days overdue or is overdue in an amount equal to 90 days of support. It shall also certify that the child or children are not recipients, and during the period for which payment is requested, were not recipients, of Aid to Families with Dependent Children and there was no assignment to a state or county agency of support and shall certify on information and belief that there is not current or past action by a district attorney pending for support or support enforcement on the judgment creditor's behalf.

The request shall have attached a proof of service showing that copies of the request, the affidavit, and the abstract or certified copy of the judgment ordering the payment of support have been served on the judgment debtor and the district attorney of the county in which the support judgment is entered. Service shall be by certified mail, postage prepaid, return receipt requested, to the last known address of the party to be served, or by personal service.

This subdivision does not apply in any instance in which a district attorney initiated or participated as counsel in the action for support or if support is required to be paid through a district attorney's office.

The Department of Child Support Services shall, upon request, inform the Legislature of the use and effect of this subdivision on or before December 31, 2000.

This subdivision shall become operative on January 1, 1996, and shall become inoperative on December 31, 2000.

(e) For purposes of this section, "support" means an obligation owing on behalf of a child, spouse, or family, or combination thereof. *(Added by Stats.1982, c. 1364, p. 5204, § 2, operative July 1, 1983. Amended by Stats.1983, c. 1010, § 1; Stats.1984, c. 1007, § 1; Stats.1986, c. 436, § 1, eff. July 22, 1986; Stats.1988, c. 1017, § 1, operative July 1, 1989; Stats.1989, c. 1359, § 9; Stats.1992, c. 163 (A.B.2641), § 52, operative Jan. 1, 1994; Stats.1995, c. 459 (A.B.1515), § 1; Stats.2000, c. 808 (A.B.1358), § 18, eff. Sept. 28, 2000.)*

Law Revision Commission Comments

Subdivision (a) of Section 708.730 continues the substance of the introductory paragraph of subdivision (a) and the first sentence of subdivision (e) of former Section 710.

Money is "owing and unpaid" under these provisions when there is an existing and unsatisfied legal liability on the part of the public entity. McDaniel v. City & County of San Francisco, 259 Cal.App.2d 356, 361, 66 Cal.Rptr. 384, 387 (1968); Department of Water & Power v. Inyo Chem. Co., 16 Cal.2d 744, 751–53, 108 P.2d 410 (1940).

Subdivision (b) is new. Former Section 710 did not provide for a notice of filing. See McDaniel v. City & County of San Francisco, 259 Cal.App.2d 356, 363, 66 Cal.Rptr. 384 (1968). This notice serves the same purpose as a notice of levy under a writ of execution. See Section 699.540.

The procedure provided by this article also applies in cases where money is owed to the judgment debtor by reason of an award in an eminent domain proceeding. Former Section 710(d) provided a distinct but similar procedure for reaching such awards. Under this title, the judgment creditor may seek to apply such property toward the satisfaction of a money judgment through the procedures normally applicable, depending upon the status of the money at the time when it is sought to be reached. Hence, if an eminent domain proceeding has been commenced, the judgment creditor may obtain a lien in the pending eminent domain proceeding pursuant to Article 5 (commencing with Section 708.410). If the judgment in the eminent domain proceeding is final and the public entity has not paid the award to the judgment debtor, the judgment creditor may file an abstract or certified copy of the judgment and an affidavit with the public entity pursuant to this article. If the public entity has deposited the amount of the award with the court where the eminent domain proceeding was held and the judgment creditor has not obtained a lien under Article 5, the judgment creditor may use some other appropriate procedure, such as garnishment or motion. See, e.g., Kimball v. Richardson-Kimball Co., 111 Cal. 386, 394, 43 P. 1111 (1896) (levy of attachment); Phoenix v. Kovacevich, 246 Cal.App.2d 774, 778–79, 55 Cal.Rptr. 135 (1966) (permission to levy by court order); Credit Bureau of San Diego, Inc. v. Getty, 61 Cal.App.2d Supp. 823, 826–29, 142 P.2d 105 (1943) (affidavit procedure of former Section 710 not effective where court deposited money with county); Colver v. W.B. Scarborough Co., 73 Cal.App. 455, 457–59, 238 P. 1110 (1925) (levy of execution). [16 Cal.L.Rev.Comm. Reports 1533 (1982)].

Section 708.730 is amended to delete the phrase "or decree," which was used in several places in the section. See Section 680.230 (defining "judgment" to include decree). [22 Cal.L.Rev.Comm.Reports 1 (1992)].

Research References

Rutter, Cal. Practice Guide: Enforcing Judgments/Debts Ch. 6G-9, Collection of Debts Owed Judgment Debtors by State or Local Public Entities.

8 Witkin Cal. Proc. 5th Enforcement of Judgment § 297, (S 297) Nature and Scope of Remedy.

8 Witkin Cal. Proc. 5th Enforcement of Judgment § 312, (S 312) Nature and Scope of Remedy.

8 Witkin Cal. Proc. 5th Enforcement of Judgment § 313, (S 313) Filing, Notice, and Lien.

8 Witkin Cal. Proc. 5th Enforcement of Judgment § 317, in General.

8 Witkin Cal. Proc. 5th Enforcement of Judgment § 318, Support Judgment.

§ 708.740. Filing of abstract or copy of money judgment and affidavit where money owed by state agency; duties of agency; duties of controller; judgment for support; selection among multiple claims; status as refunds of tax overpayments to judgment debtor

(a) Except as provided in subdivision (e), if money is owing and unpaid to the judgment debtor by a state agency, the judgment creditor shall file the abstract or certified copy of the judgment and the affidavit with the state agency owing the money to the judgment debtor prior to the time the state agency presents the claim of the judgment debtor to the Controller. Where the affidavit is prepared under subdivision (c) of Section 708.730, the affidavit shall be filed with the Department of Child Support Services, and no abstract need be filed. Filing of the affidavit with the department shall be sufficient to require the Controller to transfer the funds claimed by the judgment debtor, notwithstanding that the claim of the judgment debtor has been filed with another state agency.

(b) When presenting the claim of the judgment debtor to the Controller, the state agency shall do all of the following:

(1) Note the fact of the filing of the abstract or certified copy of the judgment and the affidavit.

(2) State the amount required to satisfy the judgment as shown by the affidavit.

(3) State any amounts advanced to the judgment debtor by the state, or owed by the judgment debtor to the state, for expenses or for any other purpose.

(c) Except as provided in subdivisions (d) and (e), to discharge the claim of the judgment debtor, the Controller shall (1) deposit with the court, by a warrant or check payable to the court, the amount due the judgment debtor (after deducting an amount sufficient to reimburse the state for any amounts advanced to the judgment debtor or owed by the judgment debtor to the state) required to satisfy the money judgment as shown by the affidavit in full or to the greatest extent and (2) pay the balance thereof, if any, to the judgment debtor.

(d) Where an affidavit stating the existence of a judgment for support has been submitted to the Department of Child Support Services, pursuant to subdivision (c) of Section 708.730, to discharge the claim of a judgment debtor, the Controller shall direct payment to the county agency designated by the local child support agency in his or her affidavit.

(e) Where the judgment is for support and the money owed is for lottery winnings or a refund of overpayment of tax, penalty, interest, or interest allowable with respect to an overpayment under Part 10 (commencing with Section 17001) of Division 2 of the Revenue and Taxation Code, and the support obligation is not being enforced pursuant to Section 17400 of the Family Code, the judgment creditor may file the abstract or certified copy of the judgment with the local child support agency of the county in which the support judgment is entered or registered. The local child support agency shall then file the claim of the judgment creditor pursuant to subdivision (c) of Section 708.730. When funds are received by the local child support agency, it shall discharge any claim of the judgment debtor by forwarding those sums to the clerk of the court pursuant to subdivision (c) of this section. Any and all notices otherwise required of a judgment creditor or the clerk of the court, and any litigation to enforce rights under this subdivision shall be the responsibility of the judgment creditor, the same as if service had been directly on the Controller without the intervention of the local child support agency.

(f) Where the claim of the judgment debtor is less than ten dollars ($10) and the claim of the judgment creditor arises under an affidavit filed pursuant to subdivision (c) of Section 708.730, the Controller may disregard the claim of the judgment creditor and forward any and all sums due to the judgment debtor. In the event that there is more than one claimant for a refund, the Franchise Tax Board shall have discretion in allocating the overpayment among claimants.

(g) Should two or more local child support agencies submit claims on behalf of a judgment creditor, the Controller in his or her discretion may select which claim or claims he or she shall honor.

(h) Any claims which are honored in behalf of a judgment creditor shall be considered as refunds of tax overpayments to the judgment debtor.

(i) For purposes of this section, "support" means an obligation owing on behalf of a child, spouse, or family, or combination thereof. *(Added by Stats.1982, c. 1364, p. 5204, § 2, operative July 1, 1983. Amended by Stats.1983, c. 1010, § 2; Stats.1984, c. 1007, § 2; Stats.1988, c. 1017, § 1.5; Stats.1989, c. 1359, § 9.3; Stats.2000, c. 808 (A.B.1358), § 19, eff. Sept. 28, 2000.)*

Law Revision Commission Comments

Section 708.740 continues the substance of paragraph 1 of subdivision (a) of former Section 710. [16 Cal.L.Rev.Comm. Reports 1535 (1982)].

Research References

Rutter, Cal. Practice Guide: Enforcing Judgments/Debts Ch. 6G-9, Collection of Debts Owed Judgment Debtors by State or Local Public Entities.

8 Witkin Cal. Proc. 5th Enforcement of Judgment § 314, (S 314) Collection of Debt Owed by State Agency.

8 Witkin Cal. Proc. 5th Enforcement of Judgment § 318, Support Judgment.

8 Witkin Cal. Proc. 5th Enforcement of Judgment § 319, Debt Owed Under Public Works Contract.

6 Witkin Cal. Proc. 5th Provisional Remedies § 461, Nature of Remedy.

§ 708.750. Filing abstract or copy of judgment and affidavit where money owed by public entity other than state agency; procedure to discharge claim of judgment debtor

If money is owing and unpaid to the judgment debtor by a public entity other than a state agency, the judgment creditor shall file the abstract or certified copy of the judgment and the affidavit with the auditor of the public entity or, if there is no auditor, with the official whose duty corresponds to that of auditor. To discharge the claim of the judgment debtor, the auditor or other official shall (1) deposit with the court by a warrant or check payable to the court, the amount due the judgment debtor (after deducting an amount sufficient to reimburse the public entity for any amounts advanced to the judgment debtor or owed by the judgment debtor to the public entity) required to satisfy the money judgment as shown by the affidavit in full or to the greatest extent and (2) pay the balance thereof, if any, to the judgment debtor. *(Added by Stats.1982, c. 1364, p. 5205, § 2, operative July 1, 1983.)*

Law Revision Commission Comments

Section 708.750 continues the substance of paragraph 2 of subdivision (a) of former Section 710. The reference to deductions for advances to, or amounts owed by, the judgment debtor did not appear in the former law applicable to local public entities, but has been included in Section 708.750 to make it parallel to Section 708.740, applicable to the state agencies. [16 Cal.L.Rev.Comm. Reports 1536 (1982)].

Research References

Rutter, Cal. Practice Guide: Enforcing Judgments/Debts Ch. 6G-9, Collection of Debts Owed Judgment Debtors by State or Local Public Entities.

8 Witkin Cal. Proc. 5th Enforcement of Judgment § 315, (S 315) Collection of Debt Owed by Public Entity Other Than State Agency.

8 Witkin Cal. Proc. 5th Enforcement of Judgment § 319, Debt Owed Under Public Works Contract.

6 Witkin Cal. Proc. 5th Provisional Remedies § 461, Nature of Remedy.

§ 708.755. Lottery prize paid in annual installments; lien of judgment creditor; procedures for continued effect; expiration

(a) Upon compliance with this section, the lien of a judgment creditor pursuant to this article is created against a lottery prize to be paid in annual installments and shall continue in force and effect until the judgment is paid or expires, whichever occurs first. For the lien to continue in effect, the judgment creditor shall do all of the following:

(1) Commencing with the second installment against which the judgment lien creditor asserts its lien, annually file with the lottery an affidavit stating that the judgment has not been satisfied and the amount of the remaining unsatisfied judgment, including interest and costs, if any. This affidavit shall be filed with the lottery not less than 45 days, nor more than 90 days, before the annual payment due date on the prize that is the subject of the judgment lien.

(2) If the judgment lien is renewed, file with the lottery a certified copy of the renewal application, as authorized in this code not less than 45 days, nor more than 90 days, before the annual payment due date on the prize that is the subject of the judgment lien, in order for the judgment lien to be effective in continuing the existing judgment lien against the annual lottery prize payments.

(b) If the judgment lien creditor fails to file the annual statement, renewal of judgment, or renewal of abstract, the lien shall expire. Expiration of a lien for failure to comply with this section shall not preclude the judgment creditor from commenc-

ing a new procedure under this article to enforce the judgment, to the extent that the judgment otherwise continues to be enforceable under applicable law. *(Formerly § 708.750, added by Stats.1995, c. 363 (A.B.218), § 1, eff. Aug. 4, 1995. Renumbered § 708.755 and amended by Stats.1996, c. 124 (A.B.3470), § 14.)*

Research References

Rutter, Cal. Practice Guide: Enforcing Judgments/Debts Ch. 6A-7, Period During Which Judgment Enforceable; Renewal Procedures.

Rutter, Cal. Practice Guide: Enforcing Judgments/Debts Ch. 6G-9, Collection of Debts Owed Judgment Debtors by State or Local Public Entities.

8 Witkin Cal. Proc. 5th Enforcement of Judgment § 317, in General.

§ 708.760. Procedure where judgment debtor is a contractor upon a public work

(a) If the judgment debtor named in the abstract or certified copy of the judgment filed pursuant to this article is a contractor upon a public work, the cost of which is to be paid out of public moneys voted, appropriated, or otherwise set apart for such purpose, only so much of the contract price shall be deemed owing and unpaid within the meaning of Section 708.740 or 708.750 as may remain payable under the terms of the contractor's contract, upon the completion thereof, after deducting sums due and to become due to persons described in Section 9100 of the Civil Code. In ascertaining the sums due or to become due to such persons, only claims which are filed against the moneys due or to become due to the judgment debtor in accordance with Chapter 4 (commencing with Section 9350) of Title 3 of Part 6 of Division 4 of the Civil Code shall be considered.

(b) The Controller, auditor, or other public disbursing officer whose duty it is to make payments under the provisions of the contract may not deposit an amount with the court pursuant to this article until the contract is completed, but may deposit an amount with the court to satisfy the claim of the judgment debtor before the payments specified in subdivision (a) are made so long as a sufficient amount is retained for the satisfaction of the claims of persons described in Section 9100 of the Civil Code. *(Added by Stats.1982, c. 1364, p. 5205, § 2, operative July 1, 1983. Amended by Stats.2010, c. 697 (S.B.189), § 23, operative July 1, 2012.)*

Law Revision Commission Comments

Subdivision (a) of Section 708.760 continues the substance of the first and second sentences of former Section 710a. Subdivision (b) supersedes the last sentence of former Section 710a. Subdivision (b) is intended to permit payment to the judgment creditor without the necessity of awaiting the resolution of disputes concerning payment to other contractors. [16 Cal.L.Rev.Comm. Reports 1536 (1982)].

Section 708.760 is amended to correct cross-references. [37 Cal.L.Rev. Comm. Reports 527 (2007)].

Research References

Rutter, Cal. Practice Guide: Enforcing Judgments/Debts Ch. 6G-9, Collection of Debts Owed Judgment Debtors by State or Local Public Entities.

8 Witkin Cal. Proc. 5th Enforcement of Judgment § 319, Debt Owed Under Public Works Contract.

6 Witkin Cal. Proc. 5th Provisional Remedies § 461, Nature of Remedy.

§ 708.770. Service of notice of deposit; claim of exemption

(a) Except as provided in subdivision (g), promptly after deposit with the court by the public entity, the court clerk shall cause a notice of deposit to be served on the judgment debtor. Service shall be made personally or by mail.

(b) Within 10 days after service of the notice of deposit pursuant to subdivision (a), the judgment debtor who claims an exemption shall do both of the following:

(1) File with the court a claim of exemption and a notice of motion for an order determining the claim of exemption. The claim of exemption shall include all of the matters set forth in subdivision (b) of Section 703.520.

(2) Serve on the judgment creditor a copy of the notice of motion, a copy of the claim of exemption, and a notice of hearing on the motion. Service shall be made personally or by mail.

(c) The hearing on the motion shall be held not later than 30 days from the date the notice of motion was filed with the court unless continued by the court for good cause.

(d) Within 10 days after the judgment creditor is served under subdivision (b), the judgment creditor who opposes the motion shall do both of the following:

(1) File with the court a notice of opposition to the claim of exemption. The notice of opposition to the claim of exemption shall be executed under oath and shall include all of the matters set forth in Section 703.560.

(2) Serve on the judgment debtor a copy of the notice of opposition to the claim of exemption. Service shall be made personally or by mail.

(e) Subdivisions (a) to (d), inclusive, of Section 703.580 and Sections 703.590 and 703.600 apply to a claim of exemption made pursuant to this section.

(f) The failure of the judgment debtor to make a claim of exemption under this section constitutes a waiver of the exemption.

(g) In lieu of service of the notice of deposit described herein, where a state agency has been served with an affidavit pursuant to subdivision (c) of Section 708.730 and has presented the claim of the judgment creditor to the Controller pursuant to subdivision (a) of Section 708.740, the state agency shall cause a notice of deposit to be sent to the judgment debtor instructing the judgment debtor to file any and all requests for relief with the district attorney who filed the affidavit, or the court clerk if the seizure arises under subdivision (e) of Section 708.740. Except in those cases arising under subdivision (e) of Section 708.740, the judgment debtor shall file the request for relief with the district attorney within 15 days after service of notice from the public agency, or the judgment debtor shall be deemed to have waived any claim he or she might otherwise have. If the matter cannot be resolved with the district attorney, the district attorney shall so advise the judgment debtor and the judgment debtor shall then be authorized to commence proceedings under this section or any other appropriate provision of law. The notice from the district attorney shall for any limitation have the same effect as a notice of deposit under subdivision (a). Service of any notice or request under this subdivision shall be made personally or by mail.

Claims arising from the filing of an abstract or certified copy of a judgment, under subdivision (e) of Section 708.740 shall be governed by the procedure and limitations set forth in subdivisions (a) through (f). *(Added by Stats.1982, c. 1364, p. 5205, § 2, operative July 1, 1983. Amended by Stats.1983, c. 1010, § 3.)*

Research References

Rutter, Cal. Practice Guide: Enforcing Judgments/Debts Ch. 6G-9, Collection of Debts Owed Judgment Debtors by State or Local Public Entities.
8 Witkin Cal. Proc. 5th Enforcement of Judgment § 316, (S 316) Procedure After Deposit in Court.
8 Witkin Cal. Proc. 5th Enforcement of Judgment § 318, Support Judgment.

§ 708.775. Disposition by court

After the expiration of the period allowed for claiming an exemption under Section 708.770 if no exemption has been claimed, or after the determination of the claim of exemption if an exemption is claimed within the period allowed for claiming the exemption under Section 708.770, the court shall pay the nonexempt portion of the money deposited to which the judgment creditor is entitled to the judgment creditor and the balance thereof, if any, to the judgment debtor, unless some other disposition is required by law. *(Added by Stats.1982, c. 1364, p. 5206, § 2, operative July 1, 1983.)*

Law Revision Commission Comments

Section 708.775 supersedes subdivision (c) of former Section 710. Section 708.775 recognizes that the judgment debtor may not be entitled to the excess, such as, for example, where a second judgment creditor has a lien subordinate to that of the first judgment creditor. See Section 701.810 (distribution of proceeds). [16 Cal.L.Rev.Comm. Reports 1538 (1982)].

Research References

Rutter, Cal. Practice Guide: Enforcing Judgments/Debts Ch. 6G-9, Collection of Debts Owed Judgment Debtors by State or Local Public Entities.
8 Witkin Cal. Proc. 5th Enforcement of Judgment § 316, (S 316) Procedure After Deposit in Court.

§ 708.780. Amount of lien created; affidavits filed pursuant to subds. (c) and (d) of § 708.730

(a) Filing of the abstract or certified copy of the judgment and the affidavit pursuant to this article creates a lien on the money owing and unpaid to the judgment debtor by the public entity in an amount equal to that which may properly be applied to the satisfaction of the money judgment under this article.

(b) When an affidavit is filed pursuant to subdivision (c) of Section 708.730, it shall apply to all claims for refund from the Franchise Tax Board under the Personal Income Tax Law, Part 10 (commencing with Section 17001) of Division 2 of the Revenue and Taxation Code, or the Bank and Corporation Tax Law, Part 11 (commencing with Section 23001) of Division 2 of the Revenue and Taxation Code, which the judgment debtor subsequently claims during a period one year after filing of the affidavit, or October 1 of the year following the filing of the affidavit, whichever occurs later, the same as if claims for these overpayments were filed by the judgment debtor with the appropriate state agency on the date the affidavit was filed.

(c) When a request is filed pursuant to subdivision (d) of Section 708.730 with the court, the clerk of the court shall issue a Notice of Support Arrearage. The clerk of the court shall issue the notice 30 days after the request was filed pursuant to subdivision (d) of Section 708.730 without a hearing if no objection has been raised by the judgment debtor pursuant to this subdivision. If an objection has been raised, the notice shall not be ordered until after a hearing. The notice shall contain the name of the person ordered to pay support and his or her social security number; the amount of the arrearage determined by the court; whether the arrearage is for child, spousal, or family support and the specific combination thereof; a statement of how the recipient may challenge the statement of arrearage; and the name, address, and social security number of the person to whom the arrearage is owed. Upon the clerk of the court issuing the Notice of Support Arrearage, a copy of the request, the affidavit, and the notice shall be served by the party who requested the court to issue the Notice of Support Arrearage upon the person ordered to pay support and the Controller. Service may be personal, in accordance with Section 1011, or by mail, in accordance with Section 1013. Service upon the Controller shall be at the Controller's office in Sacramento.

The judgment debtor may object to the request or affidavit upon any of the following grounds: (1) there is an error in the amount of the arrearage stated in the affidavit; (2) the alleged judgment debtor is not the judgment debtor from whom the support is due; (3) the amount to be intercepted exceeds that allowable under federal law; (4) a default in payment of the support for 30 days has not occurred; or (5) other necessary factual allegations contained in the affidavit are erroneous.

Upon receipt of the Notice of Support Arrearage, the Controller shall take reasonable measures to deduct from any personal income tax refunds and lottery winnings owed and processed for payment to the judgment debtor and deposit with the court a warrant, subject to Sections 708.770 and 708.775, with service of a copy of the warrant upon the local child support agency of the county in which the support judgment is entered, payable to the court, the amount due the judgment creditor (after deducting an amount sufficient to reimburse the state for any amounts advanced to the judgment debtor or owed by the judgment debtor to the state) required to satisfy the money judgment as shown by the affidavit in full or to the greatest extent, and pay the balance thereof, if any, to the judgment debtor. At any hearing pursuant to Section 708.770, the judgment debtor may challenge the distribution of these funds on exemption or other grounds, including, but not limited to, an allegation that the judgment has been satisfied or that service was improper. The notice shall not apply to any money which is exempt by law from execution. The Controller shall determine the cost of enforcing the notice and may establish a notice filing fee not to exceed five dollars ($5).

Service of the Notice of Support Arrearage and of the request and affidavit pursuant to this subdivision creates a lien on the money owing and unpaid to the judgment debtor which shall become effective 30 days following service upon the Controller. This notice shall remain in effect for four years from the date of its issuance or until the arrearage for which the notice was issued is satisfied, whichever occurs first.

Any person who files a request with the court to issue a Notice of Support Arrearage pursuant to subdivision (d) of Section 708.730 shall notify the court and the Controller of any satisfaction of the arrearage after the Notice of Support Arrearage has been issued by the clerk of the court. The notice to the court and the Controller shall be filed with the court and the Controller and served upon the local child support agency of the county in which the support judgment is entered within 30 days of the satisfaction or discharge and shall show a partial or full satisfaction of the arrearage or any other resolution of the arrearage.

Upon filing and service, the Notice of Support Arrearage shall be of no force and effect.

The State Department of Social Services shall, upon request, inform the Legislature of the use and effect of this subdivision on or before December 31, 2001.

This subdivision shall become operative on January 1, 1996, and shall become inoperative on December 31, 2001.

(d) For purposes of this section, "support" means an obligation owing on behalf of a child, spouse, or family, or combination thereof. *(Added by Stats.1982, c. 1364, p. 5206, § 2, operative July 1, 1983. Amended by Stats.1983, c. 1010, § 3.5; Stats.1988, c. 1017, § 2, operative July 1, 1989; Stats.1989, c. 1359, § 9.5; Stats.1990, c. 1493 (A.B.3974), § 31; Stats.1995, c. 459 (A.B.1515), § 2; Stats.1999, c. 652 (S.B.240), § 2.)*

Inoperative Date

Subd. (c) became inoperative on Dec. 31, 2001, by its own terms.

Law Revision Commission Comments

Section 708.780 provides for the creation of a lien as of the time of filing with the public entity by the judgment creditor under Section 708.740 or 708.750. This principle is consistent with decisions under former law which equated filing with levy and determined priority as of the time of filing. See Department of Water & Power v. Inyo Chem. Co., 16 Cal.2d 744, 751–53, 108 P.2d 410 (1940); Ott Hardware Co. v. Davis, 165 Cal. 795, 800, 134 P. 973 (1913). [16 Cal.L.Rev.Comm. Reports 1538 (1982)].

Research References

Rutter, Cal. Practice Guide: Enforcing Judgments/Debts Ch. 6G-9, Collection of Debts Owed Judgment Debtors by State or Local Public Entities.

8 Witkin Cal. Proc. 5th Enforcement of Judgment § 313, (S 313) Filing, Notice, and Lien.

8 Witkin Cal. Proc. 5th Enforcement of Judgment § 318, Support Judgment.

§ 708.785. Filing fees

(a) The judgment creditor upon filing the abstract or certified copy of the judgment and the affidavit shall pay a fee of six dollars ($6) to the public entity with which it is filed.

(b) Fees received by the state under this section shall be deposited to the credit of the fund from which payments were, or would be, made on account of collection under this article. *(Added by Stats.1982, c. 1364, p. 5206, § 2, operative July 1, 1983.)*

Law Revision Commission Comments

Subdivision (a) of Section 708.785 continues the substance of subdivision (b) of former Section 710. Subdivision (b) continues the substance of subdivision (g) of former Section 710. [16 Cal.L.Rev.Comm. Reports 1539 (1982)].

Research References

Rutter, Cal. Practice Guide: Enforcing Judgments/Debts Ch. 6G-9, Collection of Debts Owed Judgment Debtors by State or Local Public Entities.

8 Witkin Cal. Proc. 5th Enforcement of Judgment § 313, (S 313) Filing, Notice, and Lien.

§ 708.790. Liability of public officer or employee; office, defined

No public officer or employee is liable for failure to perform a duty imposed by this article unless sufficient information is furnished by the abstract or certified copy of the judgment together with the affidavit to enable the officer or employee in the exercise of reasonable diligence to ascertain the identity of the judgment debtor therefrom and from the papers and records on file in the office in which the officer or employee works. The word "office" as used in this section does not include any branch or subordinate office located in a different city. *(Added by Stats.1982, c. 1364, p. 5206, § 2, operative July 1, 1983.)*

Law Revision Commission Comments

Section 708.790 continues the substance of the last two sentences of subdivision (e) of former Section 710. See also Section 708.730 (judgment creditor may state additional information in affidavit to establish identity of judgment debtor). [16 Cal.L.Rev.Comm. Reports 1539 (1982)].

Research References

Rutter, Cal. Practice Guide: Enforcing Judgments/Debts Ch. 6G-9, Collection of Debts Owed Judgment Debtors by State or Local Public Entities.

8 Witkin Cal. Proc. 5th Enforcement of Judgment § 312, (S 312) Nature and Scope of Remedy.

§ 708.795. Filing against overpayment of tax, penalty or interest

Except as to sums due and unpaid under a judgment for support, nothing in this article authorizes the filing against an overpayment of tax, penalty, or interest, or interest allowable with respect to an overpayment, under Part 10 (commencing with Section 17001), or Part 11 (commencing with Section 23001) of Division 2 of the Revenue and Taxation Code or under

Division 6 (commencing with Section 13000) of the Unemployment Insurance Code. *(Added by Stats.1982, c. 1364, p. 5206, § 2, operative July 1, 1983. Amended by Stats.1983, c. 1010, § 4; Stats.1984, c. 1007, § 3.)*

Research References

Rutter, Cal. Practice Guide: Enforcing Judgments/Debts Ch. 6G-1, Examination of Judgment Debtor and Third Parties.
Rutter, Cal. Practice Guide: Enforcing Judgments/Debts Ch. 6G-9, Collection of Debts Owed Judgment Debtors by State or Local Public Entities.
8 Witkin Cal. Proc. 5th Enforcement of Judgment § 317, in General.

ARTICLE 9. ENFORCEMENT AGAINST FRANCHISE

Section
708.910. Franchise, defined.
708.920. Procedure for order for application of franchise to satisfaction of money judgment.
708.930. Laws governing order for application of franchise.

§ 708.910. Franchise, defined

As used in this article, "franchise" means a franchise granted by a public entity and all the rights and privileges thereof, other than the franchise of being a corporation. *(Added by Stats.1982, c. 1364, p. 5207, § 2, operative July 1, 1983.)*

Law Revision Commission Comments

Section 708.910 makes clear that this article applies only to franchises from public entities. Private franchises are governed by the general rules relating to application of property to satisfaction of a money judgment. [16 Cal.L.Rev.Comm. Reports 1540 (1982)].

Research References

Rutter, Cal. Practice Guide: Enforcing Judgments/Debts Ch. 6G-10, Enforcement Against Franchises.
8 Witkin Cal. Proc. 5th Enforcement of Judgment § 320, (S 320) Franchise.

§ 708.920. Procedure for order for application of franchise to satisfaction of money judgment

(a) The court may, in its discretion, order a franchise applied to the satisfaction of a money judgment upon application by the judgment creditor made on noticed motion. The notice of motion shall be served on the judgment debtor and the public entity that granted the franchise. Service shall be made personally or by mail. In exercising its discretion, the court shall determine whether application of the franchise to the satisfaction of the judgment is proper taking into account all the circumstances of the case, including but not limited to the nature of the franchise, whether the franchise is by its terms transferable, and the likelihood that application of the franchise to the satisfaction of the judgment will yield a substantial amount.

(b) If the court orders application of the franchise to the satisfaction of the judgment, application shall be by such means as appears proper to the court, including but not limited to sale of the franchise, assignment of the franchise or proceeds of the franchise, or appointment of a receiver. The court may include in its order, or make additional orders containing, provisions to effectuate the application of the franchise to the satisfaction of the judgment, including but not limited to provisions relating to the place of sale of the franchise, possession of the property of the judgment debtor necessary for the exercise of the franchise, receipt of proceeds of the franchise, recovery of penalties imposed by law and recoverable for injury to the franchise or for damages or other cause, and the judgment debtor's powers, duties, and liability for penalties and forfeitures. *(Added by Stats.1982, c. 1364, p. 5207, § 2, operative July 1, 1983.)*

Law Revision Commission Comments

Subdivision (a) of Section 708.920 supersedes former Section 724a. A franchise is no longer subject to levy and sale under execution but may only be applied to the satisfaction of a judgment pursuant to court order made in the court's discretion. See Section 699.720 and Comment thereto (property not subject to execution) and Section 965.010 (property subject to enforcement of money judgment). Subdivision (b) supersedes former Sections 724b-724e. See also Cal. Const. Art. XX, § 4 (liability of franchise or property held thereunder). [16 Cal.L.Rev.Comm. Reports 1541 (1982)].

Research References

Rutter, Cal. Practice Guide: Enforcing Judgments/Debts Ch. 6D-2, Writ of Execution.
Rutter, Cal. Practice Guide: Enforcing Judgments/Debts Ch. 6G-6, Receiver to Enforce Judgment-EJL Provisions.
Rutter, Cal. Practice Guide: Enforcing Judgments/Debts Ch. 6G-10, Enforcement Against Franchises.
Miller and Starr California Real Estate § 33:32, Enforcement Actions After Entry of Judgment.
8 Witkin Cal. Proc. 5th Enforcement of Judgment § 116, Property Not Subject to Execution.
8 Witkin Cal. Proc. 5th Enforcement of Judgment § 310, (S 310) in General.
8 Witkin Cal. Proc. 5th Enforcement of Judgment § 320, (S 320) Franchise.

§ 708.930. Laws governing order for application of franchise

Notwithstanding any other provision of this article, an order for application of a franchise to the satisfaction of a money judgment is subject to all applicable laws governing sale, transfer, or other actions concerning the franchise, including but not limited to any necessary approvals by the Public Utilities Commission or local public entities and compliance with statutory or administrative regulations. *(Added by Stats.1982, c. 1364, p. 5207, § 2, operative July 1, 1983.)*

Law Revision Commission Comments

Section 708.930 incorporates limitations on sale and other actions affecting franchises. See, e.g., City of South Pasadena v. Pasadena Land and Water Co., 152 Cal. 579, 93 P. 490 (1908) (franchise not transferable unless transferee continues exercise of franchise). [16 Cal.L.Rev.Comm. Reports 1541 (1982)].

Research References

Rutter, Cal. Practice Guide: Enforcing Judgments/Debts Ch. 6G-10, Enforcement Against Franchises.
8 Witkin Cal. Proc. 5th Enforcement of Judgment § 320, (S 320) Franchise.

ARTICLE 10. OTHER ENFORCEMENT PROCEDURES

Section
709.010. Trust defined; enforcement of money judgment against interest in trust.
709.020. Order applying nonvested property interest to satisfaction of money judgment.
709.030. Property in guardianship or conservatorship estate.

§ 709.010. Trust defined; enforcement of money judgment against interest in trust

(a) As used in this section, "trust" has the meaning provided in Section 82 of the Probate Code.

(b) The judgment debtor's interest as a beneficiary of a trust is subject to enforcement of a money judgment only upon petition under this section by a judgment creditor to a court having jurisdiction over administration of the trust as prescribed in Part 5 (commencing with Section 17000) of Division 9 of the Probate Code. The judgment debtor's interest in the trust may be applied to the satisfaction of the money judgment by such means as the court, in its discretion, determines are proper, including but not limited to imposition of a lien on or sale of the judgment debtor's interest, collection of trust income, and liquidation and transfer of trust property by the trustee.

(c) Nothing in this section affects the limitations on the enforcement of a money judgment against the judgment debtor's interest in a trust under Chapter 2 (commencing with Section 15300) of Part 2 of Division 9 of the Probate Code, and the provisions of this section are subject to the limitations of that chapter. *(Added by Stats.1982, c. 1364, p. 5207, § 2, operative July 1, 1983. Amended by Stats.1984, c. 493, § 1; Stats.1984, c. 892, § 2.5; Stats.1986, c. 820, § 18, operative July 1, 1987.)*

Law Revision Commission Comments

Subdivision (a) of Section 709.010 incorporates provisions that make clear that this section applies only to written, voluntary, express trusts (testamentary or inter vivos) and not to such trusts as Totten trusts, investment trusts, and deeds of trust.

Subdivision (b) provides for the application of the judgment debtor's beneficial interest in a trust to the satisfaction of a money judgment. Section 699.720(a) (8) (property not subject to execution) reverses the case law rule that the judgment debtor's beneficial interest in a trust is subject to execution. See, e.g., Houghton v. Pacific Southwest Trust & Sav. Bank, 111 Cal.App. 509, 295 P. 1079 (1931). Enforcement processes may not reach specific trust assets or the judgment debtor's interest in the trust (see, e.g., Poindexter v. Los Angeles Stone Co., 60 Cal.App. 686, 214 P. 241 (1923) (judgment lien)) except pursuant to court order applying the interest or assets to satisfaction of the judgment.

Subdivision (c) makes clear that this section does not affect the validity of a spendthrift provision in a trust instrument but permits the surplus income from a spendthrift trust to be reached under Section 709.010 to the extent that such income is liable for payment of a judgment under the law otherwise applicable. The remedy provided by Section 709.010 replaces the remedy of a creditor's suit which was used under former law. See Canfield v. Security-First Nat'l Bank, 13 Cal.2d 1, 34, 87 P.2d 830 (1939). See also Civil Code § 859; *In re* Lawrence's Estate, 267 Cal.App.2d 77, 82–83, 72 Cal.Rptr. 851 (1968). [16 Cal.L.Rev.Comm. Reports 1542 (1982)].

Research References

Rutter, Cal. Practice Guide: Enforcing Judgments/Debts Ch. 6D-2, Writ of Execution.
Rutter, Cal. Practice Guide: Enforcing Judgments/Debts Ch. 6G-17, Enforcement Against Beneficiary's Trust Interests.
Miller and Starr California Real Estate § 32:49, Real Property Subject to the Judgment Lien.
8 Witkin Cal. Proc. 5th Enforcement of Judgment § 57, (S 57) Beneficial Interest in Trust.
8 Witkin Cal. Proc. 5th Enforcement of Judgment § 74, (S 74) Interests Subject to Lien.
8 Witkin Cal. Proc. 5th Enforcement of Judgment § 116, Property Not Subject to Execution.
8 Witkin Cal. Proc. 5th Enforcement of Judgment § 321, Enforcement of Judgments Law.
8 Witkin Cal. Proc. 5th Enforcement of Judgment § 322, Limitations Under Trust Law.
13 Witkin, California Summary 10th Trusts § 23, Other Provisions Governing Trusts.
13 Witkin, California Summary 10th Trusts § 143, (S 143) Beneficiary's Equitable Estate.
13 Witkin, California Summary 10th Trusts § 151, Nature and Validity of Spendthrift Trusts.
13 Witkin, California Summary 10th Trusts § 156, (S 156) Law Revision Commission Report.
13 Witkin, California Summary 10th Trusts § 157, (S 157) Restraints on Transfer.
13 Witkin, California Summary 10th Trusts § 159, (S 159) Discretionary Trust.
13 Witkin, California Summary 10th Trusts § 161, Claims for Child or Spousal Support.
13 Witkin, California Summary 10th Trusts § 162, Liability for Public Support.
13 Witkin, California Summary 10th Trusts § 164, in General.

13 Witkin, California Summary 10th Trusts § 165, Reaching Surplus Income.

§ 709.020. Order applying nonvested property interest to satisfaction of money judgment

The judgment creditor may apply to the court on noticed motion for an order applying to the satisfaction of a money judgment a contingent remainder, executory interest, or other interest of the judgment debtor in property that is not vested in the judgment debtor. The interest of the judgment debtor may be applied to the satisfaction of the money judgment by such means as the court, in its discretion, determines are proper to protect the interests of both the judgment debtor and judgment creditor, including but not limited to the imposition of a lien on or the sale of the judgment debtor's interest. *(Added by Stats.1982, c. 1364, p. 5208, § 2, operative July 1, 1983.)*

Law Revision Commission Comments

Section 709.020 reverses the rule of such cases as Anglo California Nat'l Bank v. Kidd, 58 Cal.App.2d 651, 137 P.2d 460 (1943), which held that contingent interests are not subject to satisfaction of a money judgment. Section 699.720(a) (9) continues the rule that such interests are not subject to execution. Section 709.020 is intended to permit the court, in an examination proceeding or creditor's suit or otherwise, to fashion a suitable remedy through its equitable powers in order to prevent a sacrifice sale of the judgment debtor's interest while preserving the rights of the judgment creditor. [16 Cal.L.Rev.Comm. Reports 1543 (1982)].

Research References

Rutter, Cal. Practice Guide: Enforcing Judgments/Debts Ch. 6D-2, Writ of Execution.
Rutter, Cal. Practice Guide: Enforcing Judgments/Debts Ch. 6G-18, Enforcement Against Nonvested Contingent Interests.
Miller and Starr California Real Estate § 32:49, Real Property Subject to the Judgment Lien.
8 Witkin Cal. Proc. 5th Enforcement of Judgment § 116, Property Not Subject to Execution.
8 Witkin Cal. Proc. 5th Enforcement of Judgment § 323, (S 323) Contingent Interest.

§ 709.030. Property in guardianship or conservatorship estate

Property in a guardianship or conservatorship estate is not subject to enforcement of a money judgment by a procedure provided in this division, but the judgment creditor may apply to the court in which the guardianship or conservatorship proceeding is pending under Division 4 (commencing with Section 1400) of the Probate Code for an order requiring payment of the judgment. *(Added by Stats.1982, c. 1364, p. 5208, § 2, operative July 1, 1983.)*

Law Revision Commission Comments

Section 709.030 codifies the rule of McCracken v. Lott, 3 Cal.2d 164, 44 P.2d 355 (1935). If the guardian or conservator fails, neglects, or refuses to pay the judgment, the judgment creditor may apply to the court having jurisdiction of the guardianship or conservatorship proceeding pursuant to Probate Code Section 2404. [16 Cal.L.Rev.Comm. Reports 1544 (1982)].

Research References

Rutter, Cal. Practice Guide: Enforcing Judgments/Debts Ch. 6D-2, Writ of Execution.
Rutter, Cal. Practice Guide: Enforcing Judgments/Debts Ch. 6G-21, Enforcement Against Property in Guardianship or Conservatorship Estate.
Miller and Starr California Real Estate § 13:18, Termination by Voluntary Sale or Abandonment.
8 Witkin Cal. Proc. 5th Enforcement of Judgment § 116, Property Not Subject to Execution.

8 Witkin Cal. Proc. 5th Enforcement of Judgment § 324, (S 324) Guardianship or Conservatorship Estate.

Division 3

ENFORCEMENT OF NONMONEY JUDGMENTS

CHAPTER 1. GENERAL PROVISIONS

§ 712.010. Issuance of writ of possession or sale

After entry of a judgment for possession or sale of property, a writ of possession or sale shall be issued by the clerk of the court upon application of the judgment creditor and shall be directed to the levying officer in the county where the judgment is to be enforced. The application shall include a declaration under penalty of perjury stating the daily rental value of the property as of the date the complaint for unlawful detainer was filed. A separate writ shall be issued for each county where the judgment is to be enforced. Writs may be issued successively until the judgment is satisfied, except that a new writ may not be issued for a county until the expiration of 180 days after the issuance of a prior writ for that county unless the prior writ is first returned. *(Added by Stats.1982, c. 1364, p. 5208, § 2, operative July 1, 1983. Amended by Stats.1988, c. 1405, § 1.)*

Law Revision Commission Comments

Section 712.010 is a general provision applicable to the issuance of writs of possession or sale that may be used to enforce judgments for possession or sale under this division. The section is analogous to subdivision (a) of Section 699.510 relating to writs of execution. See also the Comment to Section 699.510. It is based in part on former Sections 681, 684, and 687. Section 712.010 authorizes issuance of writs to more than one county; it will be a rare case, however, in which a writ of sale or possession of real property is needed in a county other than that where the judgment is entered. See, e.g., Sections 392 (venue for actions concerning real property), 701.570(a) (execution sale of parcel of real property located in more than one county), 726(d) (place of sale of mortgaged premises). The last sentence providing for successive writs, is made necessary by the provisions of Section 712.050 concerning the return of the writ. In certain unlawful detainer cases, a writ of possession of real property may not be issued until the expiration of five days after entry of the judgment. See Section 1174(c). [16 Cal.L.Rev.Comm. Reports 1544 (1982)].

Research References

Rutter, Cal. Practice Guide: Civil Appeals & Writs Ch. 15-A, A. Overview.

Rutter, Cal. Practice Guide: Enforcing Judgments/Debts Ch. 2-C, C. Tort Liability.

Rutter, Cal. Practice Guide: Enforcing Judgments/Debts Ch. 6D-2, Writ of Execution.

Rutter, Cal. Practice Guide: Enforcing Judgments/Debts Ch. 6I-1, Writ of Possession or Sale.

Miller and Starr California Real Estate § 10:226, The Judicial Sale.

Miller and Starr California Real Estate § 19:232, Recovery of Possession; Writ of Possession.

8 Witkin Cal. Proc. 5th Enforcement of Judgment § 61, (S 61) Governmental Property.

8 Witkin Cal. Proc. 5th Enforcement of Judgment § 325, (S 325) Nature and Scope of Law.

8 Witkin Cal. Proc. 5th Enforcement of Judgment § 326, (S 326) Issuance of Writ of Possession or Sale.

8 Witkin Cal. Proc. 5th Enforcement of Judgment § 329, (S 329) Writ of Possession.

8 Witkin Cal. Proc. 5th Enforcement of Judgment § 332, (S 332) in General.

8 Witkin Cal. Proc. 5th Enforcement of Judgment § 338, (S 338) Writ of Sale.

12 Witkin, California Summary 10th Real Property § 732, (S 732) Immediate Possession.

12 Witkin, California Summary 10th Real Property § 741, (S 741) in General.

§ 712.020. Contents of writ

A writ of possession or sale issued pursuant to this division shall require the levying officer to whom it is directed to enforce the judgment and shall include the following information:

(a) The date of issuance of the writ.

(b) The title of the court where the judgment for possession or sale is entered and the cause and number of the action.

(c) The name and address of the creditor and the name and last known address of the judgment debtor. If the judgment debtor is other than a natural person, the type of legal entity shall be stated.

(d) The date the judgment was entered, and the date of any subsequent renewals, and where entered in the records of the court.

(e) If the judgment for possession or sale includes a money judgment, the amount required to satisfy the money judgment on the date the writ is issued, and the amount of interest accruing daily on the principal amount of the judgment from the date the writ is issued may be included on the writ at the option of the creditor.

(f) Whether any person has requested notice of sale under the judgment and, if so, the name and address of that person.

(g) Any other information required to be included in the particular writ.

(h) A statement indicating whether the case is limited or unlimited. *(Added by Stats.1982, c. 1364, p. 5208, § 2, operative July 1, 1983. Amended by Stats.1988, c. 1405, § 2; Stats.1989, c. 12, § 1, eff. April 28, 1989, operative May 1, 1989; Stats.1993, c. 926 (A.B.2205), § 4; Stats.2010, c. 680 (A.B.2394), § 14.)*

Law Revision Commission Comments

Section 712.020 prescribes the essential elements of a writ of possession or sale issued to enforce a judgment under this division. This section is analogous to Section 699.520 (contents of writ of execution). Additional information is required depending upon the type of writ. See Sections 714.010, 715.010, 716.010. A statutory form of the writ of is provided in Section 693.010. The Judicial Council has authority to supersede the statutory form. See Section 681.030(b). [16 Cal.L.Rev.Comm. Reports 1545 (1982)].

Research References

Rutter, Cal. Practice Guide: Enforcing Judgments/Debts Ch. 6D-2, Writ of Execution.

Rutter, Cal. Practice Guide: Enforcing Judgments/Debts Ch. 6I-1, Writ of Possession or Sale.

Miller and Starr California Real Estate § 10:226, The Judicial Sale.

Civ. Pro.

Miller and Starr California Real Estate § 19:232, Recovery of Possession; Writ of Possession.
8 Witkin Cal. Proc. 5th Enforcement of Judgment § 326, (S 326) Issuance of Writ of Possession or Sale.
8 Witkin Cal. Proc. 5th Enforcement of Judgment § 329, (S 329) Writ of Possession.
8 Witkin Cal. Proc. 5th Enforcement of Judgment § 332, (S 332) in General.
8 Witkin Cal. Proc. 5th Enforcement of Judgment § 338, (S 338) Writ of Sale.

§ 712.030.   Execution of writ; time for levy or seizure

(a) Upon delivery of the writ of possession or sale to the levying officer to whom the writ is directed, together with the written instructions of the judgment creditor, the levying officer shall execute the writ in the manner prescribed by law.

(b) The levying officer may not levy upon or otherwise seize property under the writ after the expiration of 180 days from the date the writ was issued. *(Added by Stats.1982, c. 1364, p. 5209, § 2, operative July 1, 1983.)*

Law Revision Commission Comments

Section 712.030 is analogous to Section 699.530 (delivery and execution of writ of execution). See also the Comment to Section 699.530. [16 Cal.L.Rev.Comm. Reports 1546 (1982)].

Research References

Rutter, Cal. Practice Guide: Enforcing Judgments/Debts Ch. 6I-1, Writ of Possession or Sale.
Miller and Starr California Real Estate § 10:226, The Judicial Sale.
8 Witkin Cal. Proc. 5th Enforcement of Judgment § 327, (S 327) Delivery, Execution, and Return of Writ.

§ 712.040.   Enforcement of writ of possession or sale as writ of execution to satisfy money judgment; other available remedies

(a) A writ of possession or sale may be enforced as a writ of execution to satisfy any money judgment included in the judgment for possession or sale. If amounts due under the judgment are not satisfied pursuant to the writ of possession or sale, the judgment creditor may use a writ of execution to satisfy any money judgment included in the judgment after the writ of possession or sale has been returned or 180 days after its issuance, whichever is earlier. If the judgment creditor does not desire issuance of a writ of possession or sale (because possession has been voluntarily surrendered, the secured obligation has been voluntarily satisfied, or other reason), a writ of execution may be issued to satisfy any money judgment included in the judgment.

(b) Whether or not a writ of possession or sale has been issued, enforced, or returned, the judgment creditor may use any available remedies provided by Chapter 5 (commencing with Section 706.010) or Chapter 6 (commencing with Section 708.010) of Division 2 to satisfy any money judgment included in the judgment.

(c) Notwithstanding subdivisions (a) and (b), if so ordered in a judgment for sale, a money judgment included in the judgment may only be enforced as ordered by the court. *(Added by Stats.1982, c. 1364, p. 5209, § 2, operative July 1, 1983.)*

Research References

Rutter, Cal. Practice Guide: Enforcing Judgments/Debts Ch. 6I-5, Enforcement of Money Judgment Included in Judgment for Possession or Sale.
Miller and Starr California Real Estate § 10:226, The Judicial Sale.
8 Witkin Cal. Proc. 5th Enforcement of Judgment § 325, (S 325) Nature and Scope of Law.

8 Witkin Cal. Proc. 5th Enforcement of Judgment § 328, (S 328) Collection of Included Money Judgment.

§ 712.050.   Return of writ

The return of a writ of possession or sale is governed by Section 699.560 (return of writ of execution). *(Added by Stats.1982, c. 1364, p. 5209, § 2, operative July 1, 1983.)*

Law Revision Commission Comments

Section 712.050 is new; prior statutory law did not provide for the return of a writ of possession or sale. See former Section 683. This section differs from the rule applied in Magnaud v. Traeger, 66 Cal.App. 526, 530–31, 226 P. 990 (1924), where it was held that a writ of possession of real property remained in force insofar as it directed the levying officer to levy on property to satisfy the part of the judgment awarding damages. [16 Cal.L.Rev.Comm. Reports 1547 (1982)].

Research References

Rutter, Cal. Practice Guide: Enforcing Judgments/Debts Ch. 6I-1, Writ of Possession or Sale.
8 Witkin Cal. Proc. 5th Enforcement of Judgment § 327, (S 327) Delivery, Execution, and Return of Writ.

§ 712.060.   Appointment of receiver

The court may appoint a receiver pursuant to Article 7 (commencing with Section 708.610) of Chapter 6 of Division 2 to enforce a judgment for possession or sale of property. *(Added by Stats.1982, c. 1364, p. 5209, § 2, operative July 1, 1983.)*

Law Revision Commission Comments

Section 712.060 makes clear that a receiver may be appointed to enforce a judgment for possession or sale of property under this division. Under former law, receivers were not expressly authorized to enforce such judgments. See the former provision of Section 726 for appointment of elisor or commissioner to sell property at conclusion of foreclosure action. See also Ramsey v. Furlott, 14 Cal.App.2d 145, 148, 57 P.2d 1007 (1936) (appointment of "receiver and commissioner" to gather property and sell it is in effect appointment of commissioner). Receivers have been appointed at the commencement of a foreclosure action and continued in possession until sale. Boyd v. Benneyan, 204 Cal. 23, 25, 266 P. 278 (1928). The appointment of a receiver is subject to the general rules concerning the time within which a judgment may be enforced. See Sections 683.010–683.220. [16 Cal.L.Rev.Comm. Reports 1547 (1982)].

Research References

Rutter, Cal. Practice Guide: Enforcing Judgments/Debts Ch. 6G-6, Receiver to Enforce Judgment-EJL Provisions.
Rutter, Cal. Practice Guide: Enforcing Judgments/Debts Ch. 6I-1, Writ of Possession or Sale.
Rutter, Cal. Practice Guide: Enforcing Judgments/Debts Ch. 6I-2, Enforcement of Judgment for Possession of Personal Property.
Rutter, Cal. Practice Guide: Enforcing Judgments/Debts Ch. 6I-4, Enforcement of Judgment for Sale of Property.
Rutter, Cal. Practice Guide: Enforcing Judgments/Debts Ch. 6A-13, Creating an Enforcement of Judgment Plan.
Miller and Starr California Real Estate § 33:32, Enforcement Actions After Entry of Judgment.
Miller and Starr California Real Estate § 10:226, The Judicial Sale.
Miller and Starr California Real Estate § 10:230, Possession and Rents During the Redemption Period.
8 Witkin Cal. Proc. 5th Enforcement of Judgment § 310, (S 310) in General.
8 Witkin Cal. Proc. 5th Enforcement of Judgment § 325, (S 325) Nature and Scope of Law.
4 Witkin, California Summary 10th Security Transactions in Real Property § 142, Pleading and Decree.
4 Witkin, California Summary 10th Security Transactions in Real Property § 143, Manner of Sale.

§ 712.070.   Enforcement of judgment against public entity

Except as provided in Section 695.050, a judgment against a public entity is enforceable under this division. *(Added by Stats.1982, c. 1364, p. 5210, § 2, operative July 1, 1983.)*

Law Revision Commission Comments

Section 712.070 makes clear that nonmoney judgments against public entities are governed by this title even though money judgments are not. See Section 695.050 and Comment thereto. [16 Cal.L.Rev.Comm. Reports 1548 (1982)].

Research References

8 Witkin Cal. Proc. 5th Enforcement of Judgment § 41, Exceptions to Application of Provisions.
8 Witkin Cal. Proc. 5th Enforcement of Judgment § 61, (S 61) Governmental Property.

CHAPTER 2. JUDGMENT FOR POSSESSION OF PERSONAL PROPERTY

Section
714.010.   Writ of possession of personal property; contents.
714.020.   Execution of writ.
714.030.   Order for transfer of possession and/or evidence of title.

§ 714.010. Writ of possession of personal property; contents

(a) A judgment for possession of personal property may be enforced by a writ of possession of personal property issued pursuant to Section 712.010.

(b) In addition to the information required by Section 712.020, the writ of possession of personal property shall contain the following:

(1) A description of the property to be delivered to the judgment creditor in satisfaction of the judgment.

(2) The value of the property if specified in the judgment or a supplemental order. *(Added by Stats.1982, c. 1364, p. 5210, § 2, operative July 1, 1983.)*

Law Revision Commission Comments

Section 714.010 supersedes portions of subdivision 4 of former Section 682 and of former Section 684. Under this chapter, a judgment for possession of personal property is enforced by a writ of possession rather than a writ of execution. A statutory form for the writ of possession is provided in Section 693.010. The Judicial Council has authority to supersede the statutory form. See Section 681.030(b). [16 Cal.L.Rev. Comm. Reports 1548 (1982)].

Research References

Rutter, Cal. Practice Guide: Enforcing Judgments/Debts Ch. 6I-1, Writ of Possession or Sale.
8 Witkin Cal. Proc. 5th Enforcement of Judgment § 23, Enforcement of Particular Judgments.
8 Witkin Cal. Proc. 5th Enforcement of Judgment § 325, (S 325) Nature and Scope of Law.
8 Witkin Cal. Proc. 5th Enforcement of Judgment § 326, (S 326) Issuance of Writ of Possession or Sale.
8 Witkin Cal. Proc. 5th Enforcement of Judgment § 329, (S 329) Writ of Possession.

§ 714.020. Execution of writ

(a) To execute the writ of possession of personal property, the levying officer shall search for the property specified in the writ and, if the property is in the possession of the judgment debtor or an agent of the judgment debtor, take custody of the property in the same manner as a levy under a writ of execution on such property in the possession of the judgment debtor. Custody of personal property used as a dwelling shall be taken as provided by Section 700.080. Custody of property in a private place shall be taken as provided by Section 699.030. If the levying officer obtains possession of the property specified in the writ of possession, the levying officer shall deliver the property to the judgment creditor in satisfaction of the judgment.

(b) If the property specified in the writ of possession cannot be taken into custody, the levying officer shall make a demand upon the judgment debtor for the property if the judgment debtor can be located. If custody of the property is not then obtained, the levying officer shall so state in the return. Thereafter the judgment for the possession of the property may be enforced in the same manner as a money judgment for the value of the property as specified in the judgment or a supplemental order.

(c) The writ of possession of personal property may, under the circumstances described in subdivision (b), be treated as a writ of execution. *(Added by Stats.1982, c. 1364, p. 5210, § 2, operative July 1, 1983.)*

Law Revision Commission Comments

Section 714.020 supersedes a portion of subdivision 4 of former Section 682 and former Section 684.1 (incorporating the manner of enforcing prejudgment writs of possession pursuant to Section 514.010). By incorporating the manner of levy under a writ of execution, subdivision (a) continues the general substance of prior law. See, e.g., Sections 699.030 (property in private place), 700.030 (property in judgment debtor's possession), 700.070 (property of going business), 700.080 (personal property dwelling).

Under subdivision (b), the value of the property is substituted only where the property cannot be delivered. See Section 667; Drinkhouse v. Van Ness, 202 Cal. 359, 374, 260 P. 869 (1927). The value of the property is generally alleged and determined in the action. See Sections 627, 667; 3 B. Witkin, California Procedure Pleading § 555, at 2197, § 563, at 2202–03 (2d ed. 1971). The judgment creditor is not obligated to accept merely the value of the property if the property itself is available. Griffith v. Reddick, 41 Cal.App. 458, 461–62, 182 P. 984 (1919). [16 Cal.L.Rev. Comm. Reports 1549 (1982)].

Research References

Rutter, Cal. Practice Guide: Enforcing Judgments/Debts Ch. 6I-2, Enforcement of Judgment for Possession of Personal Property.
8 Witkin Cal. Proc. 5th Enforcement of Judgment § 329, (S 329) Writ of Possession.
8 Witkin Cal. Proc. 5th Enforcement of Judgment § 330, (S 330) Where Property Cannot be Taken Into Custody.

§ 714.030. Order for transfer of possession and/or evidence of title

(a) After entry of a judgment for possession of personal property, and whether or not a writ of possession of personal property has been issued, the judgment creditor may apply to the court for an order directing the judgment debtor to transfer possession of the property or documentary evidence of title to the property or both to the judgment creditor. The application shall be made on noticed motion if the court so directs or a court rule so requires. Otherwise, the application may be made ex parte.

(b) The court may issue an order pursuant to this section upon a showing of need for the order.

(c) The order shall be personally served on the judgment debtor and shall contain a notice to the judgment debtor that failure to comply with the order may subject the judgment debtor to being held in contempt of court. *(Added by Stats.1982, c. 1364, p. 5210, § 2, operative July 1, 1983.)*

Law Revision Commission Comments

Section 714.030 is based on comparable provisions applicable before judgment (Section 512.070) and to money judgments (Section 699.040). Section 714.030 makes clear that the court has power to issue a turnover order directing the judgment debtor to transfer possession of the specified property directly to the judgment creditor. The order may be used in lieu of or in addition to a writ of possession. [16 Cal.L.Rev.Comm. Reports 1550 (1982)].

Research References

Rutter, Cal. Practice Guide: Enforcing Judgments/Debts Ch. 6I-2, Enforcement of Judgment for Possession of Personal Property.

Rutter, Cal. Practice Guide: Enforcing Judgments/Debts Ch. 6J-3, Enforcing California Judgments Against Debtor's Out-Of-State Property.

8 Witkin Cal. Proc. 5th Enforcement of Judgment § 331, (S 331) Turnover Order.

CHAPTER 3. JUDGMENT FOR POSSESSION OF REAL PROPERTY

Section

§ 715.010. Writ of possession of real property; application; contents; service

(a) A judgment for possession of real property may be enforced by a writ of possession of real property issued pursuant to Section 712.010. The application for the writ shall provide a place to indicate that the writ applies to all tenants, subtenants, if any, name of claimants, if any, and any other occupants of the premises.

(b) In addition to the information required by Section 712.020, the writ of possession of real property shall contain the following:

(1) A description of the real property, possession of which is to be delivered to the judgment creditor in satisfaction of the judgment.

(2) A statement that if the real property is not vacated within five days from the date of service of a copy of the writ on the occupant or, if the copy of the writ is posted, within five days from the date a copy of the writ is served on the judgment debtor, the levying officer will remove the occupants from the real property and place the judgment creditor in possession.

(3) A statement that any personal property, except a mobilehome, remaining on the real property after the judgment creditor has been placed in possession will be sold or otherwise disposed of in accordance with Section 1174 unless the judgment debtor or other owner pays the judgment creditor the reasonable cost of storage and takes possession of the personal property not later than 15 days after the time the judgment creditor takes possession of the real property.

(4) The date the complaint was filed in the action that resulted in the judgment of possession.

(5) The date or dates on which the court will hear objections to enforcement of a judgment of possession that are filed pursuant to Section 1174.3, unless a summons, complaint, and prejudgment claim of right to possession were served upon the occupants in accordance with Section 415.46.

(6) The daily rental value of the property as of the date the complaint for unlawful detainer was filed unless a summons, complaint, and prejudgment claim of right of possession were served upon the occupants in accordance with Section 415.46.

(7) If a summons, complaint, and prejudgment claim of right to possession were served upon the occupants in accordance with Section 415.46, a statement that the writ applies to all tenants, subtenants, if any, named claimants, if any, and any other occupants of the premises.

(c) At the time the writ of possession is served or posted, the levying officer shall also serve or post a copy of the form for a claim of right to possession, unless a summons, complaint, and prejudgment claim of right to possession were served upon the occupants in accordance with Section 415.46. *(Added by Stats. 1982, c. 1364, p. 5211, § 2, operative July 1, 1983. Amended by Stats.1986, c. 1220, § 1; Stats.1989, c. 12, § 2, eff. April 28, 1989, operative May 1, 1989; Stats.1990, c. 1535 (S.B.2508), § 1.5; Stats.1991, c. 57 (S.B.323), § 3, eff. June 17, 1991; Stats.1995, c. 446 (S.B.69), § 3; Stats.2004, c. 183 (A.B.3082), § 43.)*

Law Revision Commission Comments

Section 715.010 supersedes a portion of subdivision 4 of former Section 682, a portion of former Section 684, and portions of Section 1174 (unlawful detainer). Under this chapter, a judgment for possession of real property is enforced by a writ of possession rather than a writ of execution or a writ of restitution. A statutory form for the writ of possession is provided in Section 693.010. The Judicial Council has authority to supersede the statutory form. See Section 681.030(b). Subdivision (b)(3) continues a provision formerly found in Section 1174(d). [16 Cal.L.Rev.Comm. Reports 1551 (1982)].

Research References

Rutter, Cal. Practice Guide: Enforcing Judgments/Debts Ch. 6I-1, Writ of Possession or Sale.

Miller and Starr California Real Estate § 19:232, Recovery of Possession; Writ of Possession.

8 Witkin Cal. Proc. 5th Enforcement of Judgment § 23, Enforcement of Particular Judgments.

8 Witkin Cal. Proc. 5th Enforcement of Judgment § 325, (S 325) Nature and Scope of Law.

8 Witkin Cal. Proc. 5th Enforcement of Judgment § 326, (S 326) Issuance of Writ of Possession or Sale.

8 Witkin Cal. Proc. 5th Enforcement of Judgment § 332, (S 332) in General.

8 Witkin Cal. Proc. 5th Enforcement of Judgment § 334, in General.

§ 715.020. Execution of writ

To execute the writ of possession of real property:

(a) The levying officer shall serve a copy of the writ of possession on one occupant of the property. Service on the occupant shall be made by leaving the copy of the writ with the occupant personally or, in the occupant's absence, with a person of suitable age and discretion found upon the property when service is attempted who is either an employee or agent of the occupant or a member of the occupant's household.

(b) If unable to serve an occupant described in subdivision (a) at the time service is attempted, the levying officer shall execute the writ of possession by posting a copy of the writ in a conspicuous place on the property and serving a copy of the writ of possession on the judgment debtor. Service shall be made personally or by mail. If the judgment debtor's address is not known, the copy of the writ may be served by mailing it to the address of the property.

(c) If the judgment debtor, members of the judgment debtor's household, and any other occupants holding under the judgment debtor do not vacate the property within five days from the date of service on an occupant pursuant to subdivision (a) or on the judgment debtor pursuant to subdivision (b), the levying officer shall remove the occupants from the property and place the judgment creditor in possession. The provisions of Section 684.120 extending time do not apply to the five-day period specified in this subdivision.

(d) Notwithstanding subdivision (c), unless the person is named in the writ, the levying officer may not remove any person from the property who claims a right to possession of the

Civ. Pro.

property accruing prior to the commencement of the unlawful detainer action or who claims to have been in possession of the property on the date of the filing of the unlawful detainer action. However, if the summons, complaint, and prejudgment claim of right to possession were served upon the occupants in accordance with Section 415.46, no occupant of the premises, whether or not the occupant is named in the judgment for possession, may object to the enforcement of the judgment as prescribed in Section 1174.3. *(Added by Stats.1982, c. 1364, p. 5211, § 2, operative July 1, 1983. Amended by Stats.1991, c. 57, (S.B.323), § 4, eff. June 17, 1991.)*

Law Revision Commission Comments

Section 715.020 continues and generalizes provisions formerly contained in Section 1174(d) (unlawful detainer). [16 Cal.L.Rev.Comm. Reports 1552 (1982)].

Research References

Rutter, Cal. Practice Guide: Enforcing Judgments/Debts Ch. 6I-3, Enforcement of Judgment for Possession of Real Property.
Miller and Starr California Real Estate § 19:220, Parties.
Miller and Starr California Real Estate § 19:232, Recovery of Possession; Writ of Possession.
8 Witkin Cal. Proc. 5th Enforcement of Judgment § 332, (S 332) in General.
8 Witkin Cal. Proc. 5th Enforcement of Judgment § 333, (S 333) Execution of Writ of Possession.
8 Witkin Cal. Proc. 5th Enforcement of Judgment § 334, in General.
8 Witkin Cal. Proc. 5th Enforcement of Judgment § 336, (S 336) Failure to Vacate Property.

§ 715.030. Disposition of personal property remaining on real property

The disposition of personal property remaining on the real property after the judgment creditor is placed in possession thereof pursuant to the writ of possession is governed by subdivisions (e) to (m), inclusive, of Section 1174. For this purpose, references in Section 1174 and in provisions incorporated by reference in Section 1174 to the "landlord" shall be deemed to be references to the judgment creditor and references to the "tenant" shall be deemed to be references to the judgment debtor or other occupant. *(Added by Stats.1982, c. 1364, p. 5212, § 2, operative July 1, 1983.)*

Law Revision Commission Comments

Section 715.030 makes the procedure for disposition of personal property remaining on the premises where a tenant has vacated in an unlawful detainer action applicable to all cases where personal property remains on the premises after possession is delivered to a judgment creditor pursuant to a writ of possession of real property. [16 Cal.L.Rev. Comm. Reports 1553 (1982)].

Research References

Rutter, Cal. Practice Guide: Enforcing Judgments/Debts Ch. 6I-3, Enforcement of Judgment for Possession of Real Property.
8 Witkin Cal. Proc. 5th Enforcement of Judgment § 332, (S 332) in General.
8 Witkin Cal. Proc. 5th Enforcement of Judgment § 337, (S 337) Disposition of Personal Property.

§ 715.040. Execution of writ by registered process server; filing with levying officer; duties of levying officer; fees

(a) A registered process server may execute the writ of possession of real property as provided in subdivisions (a) and (b) of Section 715.020 if a proper writ of possession is delivered to the sheriff or marshal and that officer does not execute the writ as provided in subdivisions (a) and (b) of Section 715.020 within three days (Saturday, Sunday, and legal holidays excluded) from the day the writ is delivered to that officer. If the writ is not executed within that time, the levying officer shall upon request give the writ to the judgment creditor or to a registered process server designated by the judgment creditor.

(b) Within five days after executing the writ under this section, all of the following shall be filed with the levying officer:

(1) The writ of possession of real property.

(2) An affidavit of the registered process server stating the manner in which the writ was executed.

(3) Proof of service of the writ.

(4) Instructions in writing, as required by the provisions of Section 687.010.

(c) If the writ is executed by a registered process server, the levying officer shall perform all other duties under the writ and shall return the writ to the court.

(d) The fee for services of a registered process server under this section may, in the court's discretion, be allowed as a recoverable cost upon a motion pursuant to Section 685.080. If allowed, the amount of the fee to be allowed is governed by Section 1033.5. *(Added by Stats.1982, c. 1364, p. 5212, § 2.3, operative July 1, 1983. Amended by Stats.1983, c. 155, § 20, eff. June 30, 1983, operative July 1, 1983; Stats.1987, c. 1080, § 7; Stats.1996, c. 872 (A.B.3472), § 18.)*

Law Revision Commission Comments

Subdivision (a) of Section 715.040 is amended to make clear that if the levying officer does not serve or post pursuant to the writ within the three days allowed, the writ is to be returned to the judgment creditor or registered process server so that the writ can be executed pursuant to this section. Subdivision (c) is amended to avoid any implication that a second fee must be paid to the levying officer for the performance of remaining duties under the writ. The fee provided by Government Code Section 26733 is paid when the writ is delivered to the levying officer as required in subdivision (a). [16 Cal. L. Rev. Comm. Reports 2175 (1982)].

Research References

Rutter, Cal. Practice Guide: Enforcing Judgments/Debts Ch. 6I-3, Enforcement of Judgment for Possession of Real Property.
Miller and Starr California Real Estate § 19:232, Recovery of Possession; Writ of Possession.
8 Witkin Cal. Proc. 5th Enforcement of Judgment § 48, Motion for Costs.
8 Witkin Cal. Proc. 5th Enforcement of Judgment § 333, (S 333) Execution of Writ of Possession.

§ 715.050. Writ of possession; enforcement without delay; exception for mobilehomes or manufactured homes

Except with respect to enforcement of a judgment for money, a writ of possession issued pursuant to a judgment for possession in an unlawful detainer action shall be enforced pursuant to this chapter without delay, notwithstanding receipt of notice of the filing by the defendant of a bankruptcy proceeding.

This section does not apply to a writ of possession issued for possession of a mobilehome or manufactured home, as those terms are defined in subdivision (a) of Section 1161a, and does not apply to a writ of possession issued for possession of real property in a mobilehome park subject to the Mobilehome Residency Law (Chapter 2.5 (commencing with Section 798) of Title 2 of Part 2 of Division 2 of the Civil Code), or to a manufactured housing community, as defined in Section 18801 of the Health and Safety Code. *(Added by Stats.1994, c. 898 (S.B.690), § 2.)*

Validity

For validity of this section, see In re Butler, Bkrtcy.C.D.Cal.2002, 271 B.R. 867.

Research References

Rutter, Cal. Practice Guide: Enforcing Judgments/Debts Ch. 6I-3, Enforcement of Judgment for Possession of Real Property.

Miller and Starr California Real Estate § 19:179, Insolvency or Bankruptcy of the Tenant.

Miller and Starr California Real Estate § 19:228, Prejudgment Remedies; Attachment and Receivership--Writ of Possession Before Trial.

Miller and Starr California Real Estate § 19:232, Recovery of Possession; Writ of Possession.

8 Witkin Cal. Proc. 5th Enforcement of Judgment § 332, (S 332) in General.

12 Witkin, California Summary 10th Real Property § 741, (S 741) in General.

CHAPTER 4.　JUDGMENT FOR SALE OF PROPERTY

Section

716.010.　Writ of sale; contents; copy of judgment for sale.

716.020.　Execution of writ.

716.030.　Order for transfer to levying officer.

§ 716.010.　Writ of sale; contents; copy of judgment for sale

(a) A judgment for sale of real or personal property may be enforced by a writ of sale issued pursuant to Section 712.010.

(b) In addition to the information required by Section 712.020, the writ of sale shall contain a description of the property to be sold in satisfaction of the judgment for sale.

(c) The writ of sale delivered to the levying officer shall be accompanied by a certified copy of the judgment for sale. *(Added by Stats.1982, c. 1364, p. 5213, § 2, operative July 1, 1983.)*

Law Revision Commission Comments

Section 716.010 supersedes a portion of former Section 684. Under this chapter, judgments for the sale of real or personal property are no longer enforced without resort to a writ of sale. The judgment is not enforced through an order of sale or a writ of enforcement as was formerly the practice. See, e.g., Laubisch v. Roberdo, 43 Cal.2d 702, 713, 277 P.2d 9 (1954); Knapp v. Rose, 32 Cal.2d 530, 534, 197 P.2d 7 (1948). A statutory form for the writ of sale is provided in Section 693.010. The Judicial Council has authority to supersede the statutory form. See Section 681.030(b). A levy is required in every case whereas under former law no levy was required since the property was directed to be sold by the judgment—a practice arising from distinctions between the manner of enforcing common law judgments and equitable decrees. See Southern Cal. Lumber Co. v. Ocean Beach Hotel Co., 94 Cal. 217, 222–24, 29 P. 627 (1892). Subdivision (c) requires delivery of a certified copy of the judgment to enable the levying officer to follow the terms of the judgment. See, e.g., Section 716.020(c) (application of proceeds in conformity with judgment). The judgment may also direct that a single parcel or contiguous parcels of real property situated in two or more counties be sold in one of the counties as if it were all situated therein. See Sections 701.570(a), 726(d). [16 Cal.L.Rev.Comm. Reports 1554 (1982)].

Research References

Rutter, Cal. Practice Guide: Enforcing Judgments/Debts Ch. 6I-4, Enforcement of Judgment for Sale of Property.

Miller and Starr California Real Estate § 10:226, The Judicial Sale.

8 Witkin Cal. Proc. 5th Enforcement of Judgment § 23, Enforcement of Particular Judgments.

8 Witkin Cal. Proc. 5th Enforcement of Judgment § 325, (S 325) Nature and Scope of Law.

8 Witkin Cal. Proc. 5th Enforcement of Judgment § 326, (S 326) Issuance of Writ of Possession or Sale.

8 Witkin Cal. Proc. 5th Enforcement of Judgment § 338, (S 338) Writ of Sale.

§ 716.020.　Execution of writ

To execute the writ of sale, the levying officer shall:

(a) Levy upon the property described in the writ of sale in the manner prescribed by Article 4 (commencing with Section 700.010) of Chapter 3 of Division 2 for levy under a writ of execution.

(b) Except as otherwise ordered by the court, give notice of sale and sell the property described in the writ of sale in the manner prescribed by Article 6 (commencing with Section 701.510) of Chapter 3 of Division 2 for giving notice and selling under a writ of execution.

(c) Apply the proceeds of the sale of the property in conformity with the judgment for sale. *(Added by Stats.1982, c. 1364, p. 5213, § 2, operative July 1, 1983.)*

Research References

Rutter, Cal. Practice Guide: Enforcing Judgments/Debts Ch. 6I-4, Enforcement of Judgment for Sale of Property.

Miller and Starr California Real Estate § 32:73, Attack on Validity of Sale.

Miller and Starr California Real Estate § 10:226, The Judicial Sale.

Miller and Starr California Real Estate § 10:227, Statutory Redemption; Who Can Redeem.

8 Witkin Cal. Proc. 5th Enforcement of Judgment § 338, (S 338) Writ of Sale.

4 Witkin, California Summary 10th Security Transactions in Real Property § 143, Manner of Sale.

§ 716.030.　Order for transfer to levying officer

(a) If a writ of sale is issued, the judgment creditor may apply to the court ex parte, or on noticed motion if the court so directs or a court rule so requires, for an order directing the judgment debtor to transfer to the levying officer:

(1) Possession of the property to be sold if the prescribed method of levy is by taking the property into custody.

(2) Possession of any documentary evidence of title to property to be sold. An order pursuant to this paragraph may be served when the property is levied upon or thereafter.

(b) The court may issue an order pursuant to this section upon a showing of need for the order.

(c) The order shall be personally served on the judgment debtor and shall contain a notice to the judgment debtor that failure to comply with the order may subject the judgment debtor to being held in contempt of court. *(Added by Stats.1982, c. 1364, p. 5213, § 2, operative July 1, 1983.)*

Law Revision Commission Comments

Section 716.030 is comparable to Section 699.040 (turnover order in aid of execution) and Section 714.030 (turnover order in aid of writ of possession of personal property). [16 Cal.L.Rev.Comm. Reports 1556 (1982)].

Research References

Rutter, Cal. Practice Guide: Enforcing Judgments/Debts Ch. 6I-4, Enforcement of Judgment for Sale of Property.

Rutter, Cal. Practice Guide: Enforcing Judgments/Debts Ch. 6J-3, Enforcing California Judgments Against Debtor's Out-Of-State Property.

8 Witkin Cal. Proc. 5th Enforcement of Judgment § 339, (S 339) Turnover Order.

CHAPTER 5.　OTHER JUDGMENTS

Section

717.010.　Judgments not otherwise enforceable pursuant to title.

§ 717.010.　Judgments not otherwise enforceable pursuant to title

A judgment not otherwise enforceable pursuant to this title may be enforced by personally serving a certified copy of the judgment on the person required to obey it and invoking the power of the court to punish for contempt. *(Added by Stats. 1982, c. 1364, p. 5213, § 2, operative July 1, 1983.)*

Law Revision Commission Comments

Section 717.010 continues the substance of a portion of former Section 684. [16 Cal.L.Rev.Comm. Reports 1556 (1982)].

Research References

Rutter, Cal. Practice Guide: Enforcing Judgments/Debts Ch. 6I-6, Enforcing Other Judgments-Contempt.

Miller and Starr California Real Estate § 11:147, Priority of Judgments and Pending Litigation; in General.

8 Witkin Cal. Proc. 5th Enforcement of Judgment § 23, Enforcement of Particular Judgments.

8 Witkin Cal. Proc. 5th Enforcement of Judgment § 325, (S 325) Nature and Scope of Law.

8 Witkin Cal. Proc. 5th Enforcement of Judgment § 340, Nature and Scope of Power.

14 Witkin, California Summary 10th Wills and Probate § 487, Decedent's Partnership Business.

Division 4

THIRD–PARTY CLAIMS AND RELATED PROCEDURES

CHAPTER 1. DEFINITIONS

§ 720.010. Construction

Unless the provision or context otherwise requires, the definitions in this chapter govern the construction of this division. *(Added by Stats.1982, c. 1364, p. 5213, § 2, operative July 1, 1983.)*

Law Revision Commission Comments

This chapter provides special definitions of "creditor" and "debtor" which are necessary because this division also governs third-party claims to property levied upon under writs of attachment and prejudgment writs of possession. See, e.g., Section 720.110 (chapter extends to attachment and prejudgment writ of possession). [16 Cal.L.Rev.Comm. Reports 1557 (1982)].

Research References

Rutter, Cal. Practice Guide: Civ. Pro. Before Trial Ch. 9(II)-D, D. Attachment.

Rutter, Cal. Practice Guide: Enforcing Judgments/Debts Ch. 4-B, B. Claim and Delivery.

Rutter, Cal. Practice Guide: Enforcing Judgments/Debts Ch. 6D-2, Writ of Execution.

Miller and Starr California Real Estate § 33:1, Nature of Receiverships; in General.

8 Witkin Cal. Proc. 5th Enforcement of Judgment § 21, Definitions.

8 Witkin Cal. Proc. 5th Enforcement of Judgment § 102, (S 102) Preservation of Property.

8 Witkin Cal. Proc. 5th Enforcement of Judgment § 113, (S 113) Notice of Levy.

8 Witkin Cal. Proc. 5th Enforcement of Judgment § 129, (S 129) Chattel Paper.

8 Witkin Cal. Proc. 5th Enforcement of Judgment § 134, (S 134) Deposit Accounts and Boxes in Third Person's Name.

8 Witkin Cal. Proc. 5th Enforcement of Judgment § 139, Delivery or Payment to Levying Officer.

8 Witkin Cal. Proc. 5th Enforcement of Judgment § 163, (S 163) Motion to Recall or Quash.

8 Witkin Cal. Proc. 5th Enforcement of Judgment § 291, (S 291) Nature of Action.

8 Witkin Cal. Proc. 5th Enforcement of Judgment § 364, (S 364) Nature and Scope of Remedy.

8 Witkin Cal. Proc. 5th Enforcement of Judgment § 405, Governmental Enforcement of Support Order.

6 Witkin Cal. Proc. 5th Provisional Remedies § 156, Third-Party Claims.

6 Witkin Cal. Proc. 5th Provisional Remedies § 179, Securities.

6 Witkin Cal. Proc. 5th Provisional Remedies § 191, Depreciating Property.

6 Witkin Cal. Proc. 5th Provisional Remedies § 232, (S 232) Statutory Remedy.

6 Witkin Cal. Proc. 5th Provisional Remedies § 245, (S 245) Nature of Remedy.

13 Witkin, California Summary 10th Personal Property § 227, Levy on Property.

§ 720.020. Creditor, defined

"Creditor" means the judgment creditor or, in the case of a levy under a writ of attachment or prejudgment writ of possession of personal property, the plaintiff. *(Added by Stats.1982, c. 1364, p. 5214, § 2, operative July 1, 1983.)*

Law Revision Commission Comments

See the Comment to Section 720.010. See also Section 680.240 ("judgment creditor" defined). [16 Cal.L.Rev.Comm. Reports 1557 (1982)].

Research References

8 Witkin Cal. Proc. 5th Enforcement of Judgment § 364, (S 364) Nature and Scope of Remedy.

§ 720.030. Debtor, defined

"Debtor" means the judgment debtor or, in the case of a levy under a writ of attachment or prejudgment writ of possession of personal property, the defendant. *(Added by Stats.1982, c. 1364, p. 5214, § 2, operative July 1, 1983.)*

Law Revision Commission Comments

See the Comment to Section 720.010. See also Section 680.250 ("judgment debtor" defined). [16 Cal.L.Rev.Comm. Reports 1557 (1982)].

Research References

8 Witkin Cal. Proc. 5th Enforcement of Judgment § 364, (S 364) Nature and Scope of Remedy.

CHAPTER 2. THIRD–PARTY CLAIMS OF OWNERSHIP AND POSSESSION

Section

720.160. Undertaking by creditor; notice of opposition in case of public entity.

720.170. Release of property.

§ 720.110. Third-party claims allowed

A third person claiming ownership or the right to possession of property may make a third-party claim under this chapter in any of the following cases if the interest claimed is superior to the creditor's lien on the property:

(a) Where real property has been levied upon under a writ of attachment or a writ of execution.

(b) Where personal property has been levied upon under a writ of attachment, a writ of execution, a prejudgment or postjudgment writ of possession, or a writ of sale. *(Added by Stats.1982, c. 1364, p. 5214, § 2, operative July 1, 1983.)*

Law Revision Commission Comments

Section 720.110 supersedes a portion of the first paragraph of former Section 689 which permitted claims of title and the right to possession of personal property only.

Subdivision (a) of Section 720.110 makes the summary third-party claims procedure available to a person claiming a superior ownership or possessory right in real property that is subjected to attachment or execution to satisfy a money obligation. Under former law, a quiet title action was the usual remedy where real property was wrongfully sold on execution. See First Nat'l Bank v. Kinslow, 8 Cal.2d 339, 345, 65 P.2d 796, 799 (1937). Nothing in this division precludes the use of a quiet title action; Section 720.110 merely makes available the additional remedy of the summary third-party claims procedure. See also Section 720.150 (third-party's interest not affected by failure to make third-party claim).

Subdivision (b) sets forth the cases in which the procedure of this chapter is available to assert superior claims of ownership or right to possession where personal property has been levied upon. Former Section 689 applied to cases where the property was levied upon under execution and also was incorporated for prejudgment remedies. See Section 488.090 (attachment) and Section 514.050 (claim and delivery). The former procedure was also available to determine third-party claims to property seized to satisfy a judgment foreclosing a chattel mortgage. See Lawler v. Solus, 101 Cal.App.2d 816, 226 P.2d 348 (1951). Subdivision (b) makes clear that this procedure applies in prejudgment remedy cases and also where property is levied upon under a postjudgment writ of possession. As to a third-party claim of a security interest or lien on the property levied upon, see Chapter 3 (commencing with Section 720.210). See also Section 688.030 (third-party claims where tax liability enforced). For a transitional provision applicable to claims filed prior to the operative date of this chapter, see Section 694.070. [16 Cal.L.Rev.Comm. Reports 1558 (1982)].

Research References

Rutter, Cal. Practice Guide: Enforcing Judgments/Debts Ch. 6H-1, Introduction.

Miller and Starr California Real Estate § 19:67, Liability of the Parties--Between Tenant-Sublessor and Subtenant.

Miller and Starr California Real Estate § 32:30, When Property Held by Third Party.

Miller and Starr California Real Estate § 32:61, Property Interests Subject to Execution.

3 Witkin Cal. Proc. 5th Actions § 916, (S 916) Effect of Order Granting Change.

8 Witkin Cal. Proc. 5th Enforcement of Judgment § 104, (S 104) Levy Based on Record Ownership.

8 Witkin Cal. Proc. 5th Enforcement of Judgment § 364, (S 364) Nature and Scope of Remedy.

8 Witkin Cal. Proc. 5th Enforcement of Judgment § 365, (S 365) Alternative Remedies.

8 Witkin Cal. Proc. 5th Enforcement of Judgment § 367, (S 367) Right to File Claim.

8 Witkin Cal. Proc. 5th Enforcement of Judgment § 386, (S 386) Filing and Service of Undertaking and Release of Property.

4 Witkin Cal. Proc. 5th Pleading § 216, Other Procedures Compared.

§ 720.120. Time for filing claim

A person making a third-party claim under this chapter shall file the claim with the levying officer, together with two copies of the claim, after levy on the property but before the levying officer does any of the following:

(a) Sells the property.

(b) Delivers possession of the property to the creditor.

(c) Pays proceeds of collection to the creditor. *(Added by Stats.1982, c. 1364, p. 5214, § 2, operative July 1, 1983.)*

Law Revision Commission Comments

Section 720.120 supersedes a portion of the first paragraph of former Section 689. See the Comment to Section 720.110. Two copies of the claim are required to be filed so that one may be served on the debtor and one on the creditor. See Section 720.140. The former statute, unlike Section 720.120, did not specify the time within which a third-party claim could be filed, but in National Bank of New Zealand v. Finn, 81 Cal.App. 317, 337, 253 P. 757, 766 (1927), involving attachment of a check, it was stated that the claim must be made before the property was sold or otherwise applied to the satisfaction of the plaintiff's demand. [16 Cal.L.Rev.Comm. Reports 1559 (1982)].

Research References

Rutter, Cal. Practice Guide: Enforcing Judgments/Debts Ch. 6H-2, Title or Possessory Claims to Real or Personal Property.

Miller and Starr California Real Estate § 32:30, When Property Held by Third Party.

Miller and Starr California Real Estate § 32:64, Creation, Duration, and Effect of Writ of Execution.

8 Witkin Cal. Proc. 5th Enforcement of Judgment § 368, (S 368) Time and Manner of Making Claim.

8 Witkin Cal. Proc. 5th Enforcement of Judgment § 378, (S 378) Application and Notice.

8 Witkin Cal. Proc. 5th Enforcement of Judgment § 379, (S 379) Papers Filed by Levying Officer.

§ 720.130. Form and contents of claim; copy of writing upon which claim based

(a) The third-party claim shall be executed under oath and shall contain all of the following:

(1) The name of the third person and an address in this state where service by mail may be made on the third person.

(2) A description of the property in which an interest is claimed.

(3) A description of the interest claimed, including a statement of the facts upon which the claim is based.

(4) An estimate of the market value of the interest claimed.

(b) A copy of any writing upon which the claim is based shall be attached to the third-party claim. At a hearing on the third-party claim, the court in its discretion may exclude from evidence any writing a copy of which was not attached to the third-party claim. *(Added by Stats.1982, c. 1364, p. 5214, § 2, operative July 1, 1983.)*

Law Revision Commission Comments

Section 720.130 supersedes a portion of the first paragraph of former Section 689. [16 Cal.L.Rev.Comm. Reports 1559 (1982)].

Research References

Rutter, Cal. Practice Guide: Enforcing Judgments/Debts Ch. 6H-2, Title or Possessory Claims to Real or Personal Property.

8 Witkin Cal. Proc. 5th Enforcement of Judgment § 368, (S 368) Time and Manner of Making Claim.

8 Witkin Cal. Proc. 5th Enforcement of Judgment § 381, (S 381) Proceedings and Determination.

§ 720.140. Service by levying officer upon creditor and debtor; time for objections

(a) Not later than five days after the third-party claim is filed with the levying officer, the levying officer shall serve the following personally or by mail on the creditor:

(1) A copy of the third-party claim.

(2) A statement whether the third person has filed an undertaking to release the property pursuant to Chapter 6 (commencing with Section 720.610).

(3) If the third person has filed an undertaking to release the property, a notice that the property will be released unless, within the time allowed as specified in the notice, the creditor objects to the undertaking.

(4) If the third person has not filed an undertaking to release the property, a notice that the property will be released unless, within the time allowed as specified in the notice, the creditor files with the levying officer an undertaking that satisfies the requirements of Section 720.160.

(b) The time allowed the creditor for objecting to the third person's undertaking to release the property or for filing an undertaking is 10 days after service under subdivision (a).

(c) Within the time allowed for service on the creditor under subdivision (a), the levying officer shall serve a copy of the papers specified in subdivision (a) on the debtor. Service shall be made personally or by mail.

(d) The levying officer may serve the copy of the third-party claim and the statement and notice pursuant to this section notwithstanding any defect, informality, or insufficiency of the claim. *(Added by Stats.1982, c. 1364, p. 5214, § 2, operative July 1, 1983.)*

Law Revision Commission Comments

Subdivision (a) of Section 720.140 supersedes a portion of the first paragraph of former Section 689. Paragraphs (3) and (4) recognize that it is unnecessary for the creditor to file an undertaking to preserve the lien on the property if the third person has filed an undertaking to release it. Subdivision (b) allows the creditor at least 10 days within which to respond to the claim, whereas the first paragraph of former Section 689 allowed five days. Subdivision (c) is new. Subdivision (d) continues the substance of the first sentence of the sixth paragraph of former Section 689. [16 Cal.L.Rev.Comm. Reports 1560 (1982)].

Research References

Rutter, Cal. Practice Guide: Enforcing Judgments/Debts Ch. 6H-2, Title or Possessory Claims to Real or Personal Property.
Rutter, Cal. Practice Guide: Enforcing Judgments/Debts Ch. 6H-7, Statutory Requirements for Undertakings.
Miller and Starr California Real Estate § 32:64, Creation, Duration, and Effect of Writ of Execution.
8 Witkin Cal. Proc. 5th Enforcement of Judgment § 368, (S 368) Time and Manner of Making Claim.
8 Witkin Cal. Proc. 5th Enforcement of Judgment § 370, (S 370) Creditor's Undertaking.
8 Witkin Cal. Proc. 5th Enforcement of Judgment § 386, (S 386) Filing and Service of Undertaking and Release of Property.

§ 720.150. Limitations on powers of levying officer; failure to file claim

(a) Except as otherwise provided by statute, if a third-party claim is timely filed, the levying officer may not do any of the following with respect to the property in which an interest is claimed:

(1) Sell the property.

(2) Deliver possession of the property to the creditor.

(3) Pay proceeds of collection to the creditor.

(b) The interest of the third person in the property levied upon is not affected by the third person's failure to file a third-party claim under this chapter. *(Added by Stats.1982, c. 1364, p. 5215, § 2, operative July 1, 1983.)*

Research References

Rutter, Cal. Practice Guide: Enforcing Judgments/Debts Ch. 6D-3, Levy of Writ of Execution-In General.
Rutter, Cal. Practice Guide: Enforcing Judgments/Debts Ch. 6D-7, Sale and Collection of Property Levied Upon.
Rutter, Cal. Practice Guide: Enforcing Judgments/Debts Ch. 6H-1, Introduction.
Rutter, Cal. Practice Guide: Enforcing Judgments/Debts Ch. 6H-2, Title or Possessory Claims to Real or Personal Property.
Miller and Starr California Real Estate § 32:64, Creation, Duration, and Effect of Writ of Execution.
8 Witkin Cal. Proc. 5th Enforcement of Judgment § 369, (S 369) Effect of Filing or Not Filing Claim.

§ 720.160. Undertaking by creditor; notice of opposition in case of public entity

(a) If the creditor files with the levying officer an undertaking that satisfies the requirements of this section within the time allowed under subdivision (b) of Section 720.140:

(1) The levying officer shall execute the writ in the manner provided by law unless the third person files an undertaking to release the property pursuant to Chapter 6 (commencing with Section 720.610).

(2) After sale, payment, or delivery of the property pursuant to the writ, the property is free of all claims of the third person for which the creditor has given the undertaking.

(b) Subject to Sections 720.770 and 996.010, unless the creditor elects to file an undertaking in a larger amount, the amount of the undertaking filed by the creditor under this section shall be in the amount of ten thousand dollars ($10,000), or twice the amount of the execution lien as of the date of levy or other enforcement lien as of the date it was created, whichever is the lesser amount.

(c) An undertaking given by the creditor under this chapter shall:

(1) Be made in favor of the third person.

(2) Indemnify the third person against any loss, liability, damages, costs, and attorney's fees, incurred by reason of the enforcement proceedings.

(3) Be conditioned on a final judgment that the third person owns or has the right of possession of the property.

(d) If the creditor is a public entity exempt from giving an undertaking, the public entity shall, in lieu of filing the undertaking, file with the levying officer a notice stating that the public entity opposes the claim of the third person. When so filed, the notice is deemed to satisfy the requirement of this section that an undertaking be filed. *(Added by Stats.1982, c. 1364, p. 5215, § 2, operative July 1, 1983. Amended by Stats.1985, c. 41, § 10; Stats.1998, c. 931 (S.B.2139), § 96, eff. Sept. 28, 1998; Stats.2001, c. 812 (A.B.223), § 5.)*

Law Revision Commission Comments

Subdivision (a) of Section 720.160 supersedes the seventh paragraph of former Section 689. Subdivisions (b) and (c) supersede portions of the first and second paragraphs of former Section 689. The option of giving an undertaking in a flat amount pursuant to subdivision (b) is new. The amounts are the same as the amounts set for an initial undertaking in attachment. See Section 489.220(a). The third person (1) may apply to the court for an order requiring an undertaking in a greater amount pursuant to Sections 720.760–720.770 or (2) may obtain the release of the property by giving an undertaking pursuant to Chapter 6 (commencing with Section 720.610) in the same amount as the creditor's undertaking.

Whether or not the creditor has filed an undertaking, the debtor may in some circumstances forestall a sale or other proceeding under the writ by obtaining a stay pursuant to Section 720.380.

Subdivision (d) is new and is drawn from existing practice developed as a result of Section 1058 which provides that public entities are generally exempt from giving statutory undertakings. See California State Sheriffs' Ass'n. Civil Procedural Manual 13.02 (rev.1980). [16 Cal.L.Rev.Comm. Reports 1562 (1982)].

Subdivision (b) of Section 720.160 is amended to refer to Section 996.010 in the Bond and Undertaking Law which supersedes material formerly included in Section 720.770. [18 Cal.L.Rev.Comm. Reports 363 (1985)].

Section 720.160 is amended to accommodate unification of the municipal and superior courts in a county. Cal. Const. art. VI, § 5(e). It is also amended to reflect elimination of the justice court. Cal. Const. art. VI, §§ 1, 5(b). Formerly, each county had one or more municipal courts and a superior court, and Section 720.160 required an undertaking of $2,500 for an action in municipal court and $7,500 for an action in superior court. A limited civil case is equivalent to a matter within the original jurisdiction of the municipal court under former law, so Section 720.160 as amended continues the effect of former law. See Section 85 (limited civil cases) & Comment. [28 Cal.L.Rev.Comm. Reports 51 (1998)].

Section 720.160 is amended to provide for an undertaking of $10,000 (or twice the amount of the execution lien, whichever is less), regardless of the jurisdictional classification of the case. The $10,000 undertaking amount is the same as the amount of an attachment undertaking. See Section 489.220 (attachment undertaking). [30 Cal.L.Rev.Comm. Reports 443 (2000)].

Research References

Rutter, Cal. Practice Guide: Enforcing Judgments/Debts Ch. 6H-2, Title or Possessory Claims to Real or Personal Property.
Miller and Starr California Real Estate § 32:64, Creation, Duration, and Effect of Writ of Execution.
8 Witkin Cal. Proc. 5th Enforcement of Judgment § 366, (S 366) General Rules Governing Undertakings.
8 Witkin Cal. Proc. 5th Enforcement of Judgment § 368, (S 368) Time and Manner of Making Claim.
8 Witkin Cal. Proc. 5th Enforcement of Judgment § 369, (S 369) Effect of Filing or Not Filing Claim.
8 Witkin Cal. Proc. 5th Enforcement of Judgment § 370, (S 370) Creditor's Undertaking.
8 Witkin Cal. Proc. 5th Enforcement of Judgment § 371, (S 371) Release of Property.
8 Witkin Cal. Proc. 5th Enforcement of Judgment § 379, (S 379) Papers Filed by Levying Officer.
8 Witkin Cal. Proc. 5th Enforcement of Judgment § 381, (S 381) Proceedings and Determination.
8 Witkin Cal. Proc. 5th Enforcement of Judgment § 385, (S 385) Nature of Undertaking.

§ 720.170. Release of property

(a) In a case where the third person has not filed with the levying officer an undertaking to release the property pursuant to Chapter 6 (commencing with Section 720.610), if the creditor does not within the time allowed under subdivision (b) of Section 720.140 file with the levying officer an undertaking (or file a notice if the creditor is a public entity) that satisfies the requirements of Section 720.160, the levying officer shall release the property unless it is to be held under another lien or unless otherwise ordered by the court.

(b) Except as otherwise provided in this section, release is governed by Section 699.060.

(c) If personal property that has been taken into custody is to be released to the debtor pursuant to Section 699.060 and the debtor has not claimed the property within 10 days after notice was served pursuant to Section 699.060, the levying officer shall release the property to the third person making the claim.

(d) A hearing may be had on the third-party claim pursuant to Chapter 4 (commencing with Section 720.310) notwithstanding the release of the property pursuant to this section. (*Added by Stats.1982, c. 1364, p. 5216, § 2, operative July 1, 1983.*)

Law Revision Commission Comments

Subdivision (a) of Section 720.170 Supersedes a portion of the first paragraph of former Section 689. The introductory clause recognizes that this section applies only where the third person has not filed an undertaking to release the property. The time allowed the creditor for filing an undertaking depends on the manner of service of the third-party claim pursuant to Section 720.140. See Section 684.120 (service by mail).

Subdivision (b) makes clear that the general rules governing release of property apply except as provided in this section. Accordingly, if a third person to whom property is to be released pursuant to subdivision (b) or subdivision (c) does not claim property in the levying officer's custody, the property generally will be sold and the proceeds deposited with the county in the name of the third person. See Section 699.060(b).

Subdivision (c) supersedes former Section 689.5. If the property to be released was levied upon in the possession of the debtor, the property will be released to the debtor as provided by the general rules governing release. See Section 699.060 (tangible personal property released to person from whom it was taken). However, if the debtor does not claim the property, the third person who claimed it under this chapter is entitled to its possession as provided in subdivision (c). This is an exception to the general release provision that, if the debtor does not claim the property, it is to be sold and the proceeds deposited in the name of the debtor. See Section 699.060(b).

Subdivision (d) makes clear that the third-party claim may be determined under the appropriate procedure even though the property has been released because the creditor has not filed an undertaking. See Sections 720.310–720.430. If the creditor prevails at the hearing, the released property may again be levied upon as provided in Section 720.430. [16 Cal.L.Rev.Comm. Reports 1563 (1982)].

Research References

Rutter, Cal. Practice Guide: Enforcing Judgments/Debts Ch. 6H-2, Title or Possessory Claims to Real or Personal Property.
Rutter, Cal. Practice Guide: Enforcing Judgments/Debts Ch. 6H-4, Hearing on Third Party Claim.
Miller and Starr California Real Estate § 32:64, Creation, Duration, and Effect of Writ of Execution.
8 Witkin Cal. Proc. 5th Enforcement of Judgment § 371, (S 371) Release of Property.
8 Witkin Cal. Proc. 5th Enforcement of Judgment § 382, (S 382) Satisfaction from Released Property.
8 Witkin Cal. Proc. 5th Enforcement of Judgment § 383, (S 383) Filing and Service of Demand.
8 Witkin Cal. Proc. 5th Enforcement of Judgment § 386, (S 386) Filing and Service of Undertaking and Release of Property.

CHAPTER 3. THIRD–PARTY CLAIM OF SECURITY INTEREST OR LIEN

Section

§ 720.210. Claim allowable; security interest in fixtures

(a) Where personal property has been levied upon under a writ of attachment, a writ of execution, a prejudgment or postjudgment writ of possession, or a writ of sale, a third person claiming a security interest in or lien on the personal property may make a third-party claim under this chapter if the security interest or lien claimed is superior to the creditor's lien on the property.

(b) A secured party claiming a security interest in fixtures may make a third-party claim pursuant to this chapter if the security interest claimed is superior to the creditor's lien on the property. For this purpose, references in this division to "personal property" shall be deemed references to fixtures. *(Added by Stats.1982, c. 1364, p. 5216, § 2, operative July 1, 1983.)*

Research References

Rutter, Cal. Practice Guide: Enforcing Judgments/Debts Ch. 6H-1, Introduction.

8 Witkin Cal. Proc. 5th Enforcement of Judgment § 104, (S 104) Levy Based on Record Ownership.

8 Witkin Cal. Proc. 5th Enforcement of Judgment § 364, (S 364) Nature and Scope of Remedy.

8 Witkin Cal. Proc. 5th Enforcement of Judgment § 372, (S 372) Right to File Claim.

8 Witkin Cal. Proc. 5th Enforcement of Judgment § 386, (S 386) Filing and Service of Undertaking and Release of Property.

§ 720.220. Time for filing claim and copies

A person making a third-party claim under this chapter shall file the claim with the levying officer, together with two copies of the claim, after levy on the personal property but before the levying officer does any of the following:

(a) Sells the property.

(b) Delivers possession of the property to the creditor.

(c) Pays proceeds of collection to the creditor. *(Added by Stats.1982, c. 1364, p. 5216, § 2, operative July 1, 1983.)*

Law Revision Commission Comments

Section 720.220 supersedes the first sentence of former Section 689b(2). See the Comment to Section 720.210. Two copies of the claim are required to be filed so that one may be served on the debtor and one on the creditor. See Section 720.240. As to the specification in Section 720.220 of the time within which the third-party claim must be filed, see the Comment to Section 720.120. [16 Cal.L.Rev.Comm. Reports 1565 (1982)].

Research References

Rutter, Cal. Practice Guide: Enforcing Judgments/Debts Ch. 6H-2, Title or Possessory Claims to Real or Personal Property.

Rutter, Cal. Practice Guide: Enforcing Judgments/Debts Ch. 6H-3, Claim of Security Interest in or Lien on Personal Property or Fixtures.

8 Witkin Cal. Proc. 5th Enforcement of Judgment § 373, (S 373) Time and Manner of Making Claim.

8 Witkin Cal. Proc. 5th Enforcement of Judgment § 378, (S 378) Application and Notice.

8 Witkin Cal. Proc. 5th Enforcement of Judgment § 379, (S 379) Papers Filed by Levying Officer.

§ 720.230. Form and contents of claim; copy of security agreement, financing statement or writing upon which claim based

(a) The third-party claim shall be executed under oath and shall contain all of the following:

(1) The name of the secured party or lienholder and an address in this state where service by mail may be made on the secured party or lienholder.

(2) A description of the personal property in which a security interest or lien is claimed.

(3) A detailed description of the security interest or lien claimed, including a statement of the facts upon which it is based.

(4) A statement of the total amount of sums due or to accrue under the security interest or lien and the applicable rate of interest on amounts due.

(b) In the case of a security interest, a copy of the security agreement and any financing statement shall be attached to the third-party claim. In the case of a lien, a copy of any writing upon which the claim is based shall be attached to the third-party claim. At a hearing on the third-party claim, the court in its discretion may exclude from evidence any writing a copy of which was not attached to the third-party claim. *(Added by Stats.1982, c. 1364, p. 5217, § 2, operative July 1, 1983.)*

Law Revision Commission Comments

Section 720.230 supersedes a portion of former Section 689b(2). [16 Cal.L.Rev.Comm. Reports 1566 (1982)].

Research References

Rutter, Cal. Practice Guide: Enforcing Judgments/Debts Ch. 6H-3, Claim of Security Interest in or Lien on Personal Property or Fixtures.

8 Witkin Cal. Proc. 5th Enforcement of Judgment § 373, (S 373) Time and Manner of Making Claim.

8 Witkin Cal. Proc. 5th Enforcement of Judgment § 375, (S 375) Creditor's Undertaking.

8 Witkin Cal. Proc. 5th Enforcement of Judgment § 381, (S 381) Proceedings and Determination.

§ 720.240. Service by levying officer on creditor and debtor; time for objections

(a) Not later than five days after the third-party claim is filed with the levying officer, the levying officer shall serve the following personally or by mail on the creditor:

(1) A copy of the third-party claim.

(2) A statement whether the third person has filed an undertaking to release the property pursuant to Chapter 6 (commencing with Section 720.610).

(3) If the third person has filed an undertaking to release the property, a notice that the property will be released unless, within the time allowed as specified in the notice, the creditor objects to the undertaking.

(4) If the third person has not filed an undertaking to release the property, a notice that the property will be released unless, within the time allowed as specified in the notice, the creditor does one of the following:

(A) Files with the levying officer an undertaking that satisfies the requirements of Section 720.260 and a statement under Section 720.280.

(B) Deposits with the levying officer the amount claimed plus interest at the applicable rate to the estimated date of tender to the secured party or lienholder.

(b) The time allowed the creditor for objecting to the third person's undertaking to release the property or for filing an undertaking and statement or making a deposit pursuant to subdivision (a) is 10 days after service under subdivision (a).

(c) Within the time allowed for service on the creditor under subdivision (a), the levying officer shall serve a copy of the papers specified in subdivision (a) on the debtor. Service shall be made personally or by mail.

(d) The levying officer may serve the copy of the third-party claim and the statement and notice pursuant to this section notwithstanding any defect, informality, or insufficiency of the claim. *(Added by Stats.1982, c. 1364, p. 5217, § 2, operative July 1, 1983.)*

Law Revision Commission Comments

Subdivision (a) of Section 720.240 supersedes subdivision (3) and a portion of the first paragraph of subdivision (9) of former Section 689b. Paragraphs (3) and (4) recognize that it is unnecessary for the creditor to file an undertaking to preserve the lien on the property or to pay off the secured party or lienholder if the property is to be released on a third person's undertaking. The creditor may make a deposit pursuant to

Section 1054a in lieu of an undertaking, but such a deposit has the effect of an undertaking given under this chapter rather than a deposit made to satisfy the claim of the secured party or lienholder.

Subdivision (b) allows the creditor at least 10 days within which to respond to the claim, whereas former Section 689b(4) allowed five days after receipt. Subdivision (c) is new. Subdivision (d) continues the substance of the second sentence of former Section 689b(2). [16 Cal.L.Rev.Comm. Reports 1567 (1982)].

Research References

Rutter, Cal. Practice Guide: Enforcing Judgments/Debts Ch. 6H-3, Claim of Security Interest in or Lien on Personal Property or Fixtures.
Rutter, Cal. Practice Guide: Enforcing Judgments/Debts Ch. 6H-7, Statutory Requirements for Undertakings.
8 Witkin Cal. Proc. 5th Enforcement of Judgment § 373, (S 373) Time and Manner of Making Claim.
8 Witkin Cal. Proc. 5th Enforcement of Judgment § 375, (S 375) Creditor's Undertaking.
8 Witkin Cal. Proc. 5th Enforcement of Judgment § 386, (S 386) Filing and Service of Undertaking and Release of Property.

§ 720.250. Limitations on power of levying officer; failure to file claim

(a) Except as otherwise provided by statute, if a third-party claim is timely filed, the levying officer may not do any of the following with respect to the personal property in which the security interest or lien is claimed:

(1) Sell the property.

(2) Deliver possession of the property to the creditor.

(3) Pay proceeds of collection to the creditor.

(b) The interest of a secured party or lienholder in the property levied upon is not affected by the failure of the secured party or lienholder to file a third-party claim under this chapter. *(Added by Stats.1982, c. 1364, p. 5218, § 2, operative July 1, 1983.)*

Law Revision Commission Comments

Section 720.250 is new. See the Comment to Section 720.150. See also Section 720.260 (effect of undertaking or deposit). Subdivision (b) makes clear that a secured party or lienholder does not waive a superior interest in the property levied upon by failure to make a third-party claim pursuant to this chapter. See the Comment to Section 720.150. [16 Cal.L.Rev. Comm. Reports 1568 (1982)].

Research References

Rutter, Cal. Practice Guide: Enforcing Judgments/Debts Ch. 6H-1, Introduction.
Rutter, Cal. Practice Guide: Enforcing Judgments/Debts Ch. 6H-3, Claim of Security Interest in or Lien on Personal Property or Fixtures.
Miller and Starr California Real Estate § 32:64, Creation, Duration, and Effect of Writ of Execution.
8 Witkin Cal. Proc. 5th Enforcement of Judgment § 374, (S 374) Effect of Filing or Not Filing Claim.

§ 720.260. Undertaking by creditor; notice of opposition in case of public entity

(a) If the creditor within the time allowed under subdivision (b) of Section 720.240 either files with the levying officer an undertaking that satisfies the requirements of this section and a statement that satisfies the requirements of Section 720.280 or makes a deposit with the levying officer of the amount claimed under Section 720.230:

(1) The levying officer shall execute the writ in the manner provided by law unless, in a case where the creditor has filed an undertaking, the secured party or lienholder files an undertaking to release the property pursuant to Chapter 6 (commencing with Section 720.610).

(2) After sale, payment, or delivery of the property pursuant to the writ, the property is free of all claims or liens of the secured party or lienholder for which the creditor has given the undertaking or made the deposit.

(b) Subject to Sections 720.770 and 996.010, unless the creditor elects to file an undertaking in a larger amount, the amount of the undertaking filed by the creditor under this section shall be in the amount of ten thousand dollars ($10,000) or twice the amount of the execution lien as of the date of levy or other enforcement lien as of the date it was created, whichever is the lesser amount.

(c) An undertaking given by the creditor under this chapter shall:

(1) Be made in favor of the secured party or lienholder.

(2) Indemnify the secured party or lienholder against any loss, liability, damages, costs, and attorney's fees, incurred by reason of the enforcement proceedings.

(3) Be conditioned on a final judgment that the security interest or lien of the third person is entitled to priority over the creditor's lien.

(d) If the creditor is a public entity exempt from giving an undertaking, the public entity shall, in lieu of filing the undertaking, file with the levying officer a notice stating that the public entity opposes the claim of the third person. When so filed, the notice is deemed to satisfy the requirement of this section that an undertaking be filed. *(Added by Stats.1982, c. 1364, p. 5218, § 2, operative July 1, 1983. Amended by Stats.1985, c. 41, § 11; Stats.1998, c. 931 (S.B.2139), § 97, eff. Sept. 28, 1998; Stats.2001, c. 812 (A.B.223), § 6.)*

Law Revision Commission Comments

Subdivision (a) of Section 720.260 supersedes parts of subdivisions (8) and (9) of former Section 689b. Under paragraph (2) of subdivision (a), the property may be sold free of all interests for which an undertaking is given or deposit is made. However, whether or not the creditor has filed an undertaking or made a deposit, the secured party or lienholder may prevent a sale in an appropriate case by obtaining a stay pursuant to Section 720.380.

Subdivisions (b) and (c) supersede portions of the first and second paragraphs of subdivision (9) of former Section 689b. The option of giving an undertaking in a flat amount pursuant to subdivision (b) is new. The amounts are the same as the amounts set for an initial undertaking in attachment. See Section 489.220(a). The secured party or lienholder (1) may apply to the court for an order requiring an undertaking in a greater amount pursuant to Sections 720.760–720.770 or (2) may obtain the release of the property by giving an undertaking pursuant to Chapter 6 (commencing with Section 720.610) in the same amount as the creditor's undertaking.

Subdivision (d) is new and is drawn from existing practice developed as a result of Section 1058 which provides that public entities are generally exempt from giving statutory undertakings. See California State Sheriffs' Ass'n Civil Procedural Manual 13.02 (rev.ed.1980). [16 Cal.L.Rev. Comm. Reports 1569 (1982)].

Subdivision (b) of Section 720.260 is amended to refer to Section 996.010 in the Bond and Undertaking Law which supersedes material formerly included in Section 720.770. [18 Cal.L.Rev.Comm. Reports 363 (1985)].

Section 720.260 is amended to accommodate unification of the municipal and superior courts in a county. Cal. Const. art. VI, § 5(e). It is also amended to reflect elimination of the justice court. Cal. Const. art. VI, §§ 1, 5(b). Formerly, each county had one or more municipal courts and a superior court, and Section 720.260 required an undertaking of $2,500 for an action in municipal court and $7,500 for an action in superior court. A limited civil case is equivalent to a matter within the original jurisdiction of the municipal court under former law, so Section 720.260 as amended continues the effect of former law. See Section 85 (limited civil cases) & Comment. [28 Cal.L.Rev.Comm. Reports App. 7 (1998)].

Section 720.260 is amended to provide for an undertaking of $10,000 (or twice the amount of the execution lien, whichever is less), regardless of the jurisdictional classification of the case. The $10,000 undertaking amount is the same as the amount of an attachment undertaking. See

Section 489.220 (attachment undertaking). [30 Cal.L.Rev.Comm. Reports 443 (2000)].

Research References

Rutter, Cal. Practice Guide: Enforcing Judgments/Debts Ch. 6D-7, Sale and Collection of Property Levied Upon.

Rutter, Cal. Practice Guide: Enforcing Judgments/Debts Ch. 6E-5, Specific Exempt Property.

Rutter, Cal. Practice Guide: Enforcing Judgments/Debts Ch. 6H-3, Claim of Security Interest in or Lien on Personal Property or Fixtures.

Rutter, Cal. Practice Guide: Enforcing Judgments/Debts Ch. 6H-4, Hearing on Third Party Claim.

8 Witkin Cal. Proc. 5th Enforcement of Judgment § 153, in General.

8 Witkin Cal. Proc. 5th Enforcement of Judgment § 158, (S 158) Order of Distribution.

8 Witkin Cal. Proc. 5th Enforcement of Judgment § 366, (S 366) General Rules Governing Undertakings.

8 Witkin Cal. Proc. 5th Enforcement of Judgment § 373, (S 373) Time and Manner of Making Claim.

8 Witkin Cal. Proc. 5th Enforcement of Judgment § 374, (S 374) Effect of Filing or Not Filing Claim.

8 Witkin Cal. Proc. 5th Enforcement of Judgment § 375, (S 375) Creditor's Undertaking.

8 Witkin Cal. Proc. 5th Enforcement of Judgment § 376, (S 376) Release of Property.

8 Witkin Cal. Proc. 5th Enforcement of Judgment § 379, (S 379) Papers Filed by Levying Officer.

8 Witkin Cal. Proc. 5th Enforcement of Judgment § 381, (S 381) Proceedings and Determination.

8 Witkin Cal. Proc. 5th Enforcement of Judgment § 385, (S 385) Nature of Undertaking.

8 Witkin Cal. Proc. 5th Enforcement of Judgment § 375A, (S 375A) (New)-Action on Undertaking.

§ 720.270. Release of property

(a) In a case where the third person has not filed with the levying officer an undertaking to release the property pursuant to Chapter 6 (commencing with Section 720.610), if the creditor does not within the time allowed under subdivision (b) of Section 720.240 file with the levying officer an undertaking (or file a notice if the creditor is a public entity) that satisfies the requirements of Section 720.260 and a statement under Section 720.280, or deposit with the levying officer the amount claimed under Section 720.230, the levying officer shall release the personal property unless it is to be held under another lien or unless otherwise ordered by the court.

(b) Except as otherwise provided in this section, release is governed by Section 699.060.

(c) If property that has been taken into custody is to be released to the debtor pursuant to Section 699.060 and the debtor has not claimed the property within 10 days after notice was served pursuant to Section 699.060, the levying officer shall release the property to the secured party or lienholder making the claim.

(d) A hearing may be had on the third-party claim pursuant to Chapter 4 (commencing with Section 720.310) notwithstanding the release of the property pursuant to this section. *(Added by Stats.1982, c. 1364, p. 5219, § 2, operative July 1, 1983.)*

Law Revision Commission Comments

Subdivision (a) of Section 720.270 supersedes subdivision (4) and a portion of the first paragraph of subdivision (9) of former Section 689b. The introductory clause recognizes that this section applies only where the third person has not filed an undertaking to release the property. The time allowed the creditor for filing an undertaking and statement or making a deposit depends on the manner of service of the third-party claim pursuant to Section 720.240. See Section 684.120 (service by mail). Subdivision (b) makes clear that the general rules governing release of property apply except as provided in this section. See the Comment to Section 720.170(b). Subdivision (c) supersedes former Section 689.5. See the Comment to Section 720.170(c). Subdivision (d) makes clear that the claim of the secured party or lienholder may be determined under the appropriate procedure even though the property has been released because the creditor has not filed an undertaking and statement or made a deposit. See Sections 720.310–720.430. If the creditor prevails at the hearing, the released property may again be levied upon as provided in Section 720.430. [16 Cal.L.Rev.Comm. Reports 1570 (1982)].

Research References

Rutter, Cal. Practice Guide: Enforcing Judgments/Debts Ch. 6H-3, Claim of Security Interest in or Lien on Personal Property or Fixtures.

Rutter, Cal. Practice Guide: Enforcing Judgments/Debts Ch. 6H-4, Hearing on Third Party Claim.

8 Witkin Cal. Proc. 5th Enforcement of Judgment § 376, (S 376) Release of Property.

8 Witkin Cal. Proc. 5th Enforcement of Judgment § 382, (S 382) Satisfaction from Released Property.

8 Witkin Cal. Proc. 5th Enforcement of Judgment § 383, (S 383) Filing and Service of Demand.

§ 720.280. Creditor duties upon filing undertaking

At the time the creditor files an undertaking with the levying officer in response to a third-party claim by a secured party, the creditor shall do all of the following:

(a) File with the levying officer a statement executed under oath that the security interest is invalid, that the security interest is not entitled to priority over the creditor's lien, or that the amount demanded in the claim exceeds the amount to which the secured party is entitled, for the reasons specified therein.

(b) Serve a copy of the statement on the secured party. Service shall be made personally or by mail.

(c) Serve a copy of the statement on the debtor. Service shall be made personally or by mail. *(Added by Stats.1982, c. 1364, p. 5219, § 2, operative July 1, 1983.)*

Law Revision Commission Comments

Section 720.280 supersedes a portion of the first paragraph of subdivision (9) of former Section 689b. This section permits the creditor to resist the claim of the secured party on the grounds that the security interest is not entitled to priority or is excessive, whereas former law required a statement that the chattel mortgage or conditional sale was void or invalid. See Section 720.210 (application of article); Com. Code § 9301 (priority of lien creditor over unperfected security interest). [16 Cal.L.Rev.Comm. Reports 1571 (1982)].

Research References

Rutter, Cal. Practice Guide: Enforcing Judgments/Debts Ch. 6H-3, Claim of Security Interest in or Lien on Personal Property or Fixtures.

Rutter, Cal. Practice Guide: Enforcing Judgments/Debts Ch. 6H-4, Hearing on Third Party Claim.

8 Witkin Cal. Proc. 5th Enforcement of Judgment § 373, (S 373) Time and Manner of Making Claim.

8 Witkin Cal. Proc. 5th Enforcement of Judgment § 375, (S 375) Creditor's Undertaking.

8 Witkin Cal. Proc. 5th Enforcement of Judgment § 376, (S 376) Release of Property.

8 Witkin Cal. Proc. 5th Enforcement of Judgment § 379, (S 379) Papers Filed by Levying Officer.

8 Witkin Cal. Proc. 5th Enforcement of Judgment § 380, (S 380) Creditor's Statement Opposing Claim of Secured Party.

§ 720.290. Tender or payment of deposit

(a) If the levying officer receives a sufficient deposit from the creditor, the levying officer shall promptly tender or pay the deposit to the secured party or lienholder who made the third-party claim except that, if the deposit is made by personal check, the levying officer is allowed a reasonable time for the check to clear.

(b) If the tender is accepted, the interest of the secured party or lienholder in the property for which deposit is made passes to the creditor making the deposit and, on distribution of any proceeds under Section 701.810, the creditor who makes the deposit shall be entitled to the proceeds to the extent of the deposit in the priority of the interest for which the deposit is made.

(c) If the tender is refused, the amount of the deposit shall be deposited with the county treasurer payable to the order of the secured party or lienholder. *(Added by Stats.1982, c. 1364, p. 5219, § 2, operative July 1, 1983.)*

Law Revision Commission Comments

Section 720.290 continues the substance of subdivisions (5)–(7) of former Section 689b, except that the officer is required to tender or pay promptly rather than within five days. [16 Cal.L.Rev.Comm. Reports 1572 (1982)].

Research References

Rutter, Cal. Practice Guide: Enforcing Judgments/Debts Ch. 6H-3, Claim of Security Interest in or Lien on Personal Property or Fixtures.
8 Witkin Cal. Proc. 5th Enforcement of Judgment § 377, (S 377) Payment to Secured Party or Lienholder.

CHAPTER 4. HEARING ON THIRD–PARTY CLAIM

Section
720.310. Petition for hearing; time for hearing.
720.320. Service of notice of hearing; filing of copy; contents of notice.
720.330. Filing of papers with court.
720.340. Procedure where creditor has not filed statement in opposition.
720.350. Pleadings and amendments; third-party claim deemed controverted.
720.360. Burden of proof.
720.370. Dismissal of petition or proceedings.
720.380. Order staying sale or enjoining transfer or disposition.
720.390. Judgment and order for disposition.
720.400. Findings.
720.410. Right to jury trial.
720.420. Appeals.
720.430. Levy upon or application of property to satisfaction of judgment after release.

§ 720.310. Petition for hearing; time for hearing

(a) Not later than 15 days after the third-party claim is filed with the levying officer pursuant to Section 720.120 or 720.220, or 15 days after filing an undertaking pursuant to Section 720.610, either the creditor or the third person may petition the court for a hearing to determine the validity of the third-party claim and the proper disposition of the property that is the subject of the claim.

(b) The hearing may be held whether or not an undertaking has been filed but not if a deposit has been made pursuant to Section 720.260.

(c) The hearing shall be held within 20 days after the filing of the petition unless continued by the court for good cause shown. *(Added by Stats.1982, c. 1364, p. 5220, § 2, operative July 1, 1983. Amended by Stats.1986, c. 672, § 1.)*

Law Revision Commission Comments

Subdivisions (a) and (b) of Section 720.310 continue the substance of the first two sentences of the eighth paragraph of former Section 689 and the first sentence of subdivision (10) of former Section 689b. Subdivision (c) continues the substance of the third and fifth sentences of the eighth paragraph of former Section 689 and the second and fourth sentences of subdivision (10) of former Section 689b. [16 Cal.L.Rev. Comm. Reports 1572 (1982)].

Research References

Rutter, Cal. Practice Guide: Enforcing Judgments/Debts Ch. 6H-3, Claim of Security Interest in or Lien on Personal Property or Fixtures.
Rutter, Cal. Practice Guide: Enforcing Judgments/Debts Ch. 6H-4, Hearing on Third Party Claim.
Miller and Starr California Real Estate § 32:64, Creation, Duration, and Effect of Writ of Execution.
8 Witkin Cal. Proc. 5th Enforcement of Judgment § 371, (S 371) Release of Property.
8 Witkin Cal. Proc. 5th Enforcement of Judgment § 376, (S 376) Release of Property.
8 Witkin Cal. Proc. 5th Enforcement of Judgment § 378, (S 378) Application and Notice.
8 Witkin Cal. Proc. 5th Enforcement of Judgment § 380, (S 380) Creditor's Statement Opposing Claim of Secured Party.
8 Witkin Cal. Proc. 5th Enforcement of Judgment § 381, (S 381) Proceedings and Determination.

§ 720.320. Service of notice of hearing; filing of copy; contents of notice

(a) At the time prescribed in subdivision (b) of Section 1005, the petitioner shall do both of the following:

(1) Serve notice of the time and place of the hearing on the creditor or the third person (whichever person is not the petitioner) and on the debtor. Service shall be made personally or by mail.

(2) File a copy of the notice of hearing with the levying officer.

(b) The notice of the hearing shall include a statement that the purpose of the hearing is to determine the validity of the third-party claim and the proper disposition of the property that is the subject of the third-party claim. *(Added by Stats.1982, c. 1364, p. 5220, § 2, operative July 1, 1983. Amended by Stats.1989, c. 693, § 4.)*

Law Revision Commission Comments

Section 720.320 supersedes the fourth sentence of the eighth paragraph of Section 689 and the second sentence of subdivision (10) of former Section 689b. This section also requires notice to be given to the debtor to avoid the misapplication of funds that could occur under former law. See Rubin v. Barasch, 275 Cal.App.2d 835, 80 Cal.Rptr. 337 (1969). [16 Cal.L.Rev.Comm. Reports 1573 (1982)].

Research References

Rutter, Cal. Practice Guide: Enforcing Judgments/Debts Ch. 6H-4, Hearing on Third Party Claim.
Miller and Starr California Real Estate § 32:64, Creation, Duration, and Effect of Writ of Execution.
8 Witkin Cal. Proc. 5th Enforcement of Judgment § 378, (S 378) Application and Notice.
8 Witkin Cal. Proc. 5th Enforcement of Judgment § 380, (S 380) Creditor's Statement Opposing Claim of Secured Party.

§ 720.330. Filing of papers with court

Promptly after receipt of the notice of the hearing on the third-party claim, the levying officer shall file the following papers with the court:

(a) The third-party claim that was filed with the levying officer pursuant to Section 720.120 or 720.220.

(b) Any statement filed by the creditor with the levying officer pursuant to Section 720.280 in opposition to the third-party claim of a secured party.

(c) Any undertaking of the creditor filed with the levying officer pursuant to Section 720.160 or Section 720.260.

(d) Any undertaking to release filed by a third person pursuant to Chapter 6 (commencing with Section 720.610).

(e) Any notice filed by a public entity pursuant to Section 720.160 or 720.260. *(Added by Stats.1982, c. 1364, p. 5220, § 2, operative July 1, 1983.)*

Civ. Pro.

Law Revision Commission Comments

Section 720.330 supersedes a portion of the eleventh sentence of the eighth paragraph of former Section 689. Former law did not require the levying officer to file the creditor's statement or undertaking with the court. See former Sections 689, 689b. An undertaking in the possession of the levying officer that is not filed with the court pursuant to this section should be filed pursuant to Section 720.800. [16 Cal.L.Rev. Comm. Reports 1573 (1982)].

Research References

Rutter, Cal. Practice Guide: Enforcing Judgments/Debts Ch. 6H-4, Hearing on Third Party Claim.
Miller and Starr California Real Estate § 32:64, Creation, Duration, and Effect of Writ of Execution.
8 Witkin Cal. Proc. 5th Enforcement of Judgment § 379, (S 379) Papers Filed by Levying Officer.

§ 720.340. Procedure where creditor has not filed statement in opposition

If the creditor has not filed a statement with the levying officer pursuant to Section 720.280 in opposition to a third-party claim by a secured party:

(a) In a case where the creditor petitions for a hearing on the third-party claim, the creditor shall file the statement with the court at the time the petition is filed and shall serve a copy thereof on the secured party with notice of the hearing served pursuant to Section 720.320.

(b) In a case where the secured party has petitioned for a hearing on the third-party claim, the creditor shall file the statement with the court and serve a copy of the statement on the secured party not later than five days before the date set for the hearing. Service shall be made personally or by mail. *(Added by Stats.1982, c. 1364, p. 5220, § 2, operative July 1, 1983.)*

Law Revision Commission Comments

Section 720.340 is new. [16 Cal.L.Rev.Comm. Reports 1574 (1982)].

Research References

Rutter, Cal. Practice Guide: Enforcing Judgments/Debts Ch. 6H-4, Hearing on Third Party Claim.
8 Witkin Cal. Proc. 5th Enforcement of Judgment § 380, (S 380) Creditor's Statement Opposing Claim of Secured Party.

§ 720.350. Pleadings and amendments; third-party claim deemed controverted

(a) Subject to the power of the court to permit an amendment in the interest of justice:

(1) The third-party claim constitutes the pleading of the third person.

(2) In the case of a third-party claim by a secured party, the creditor's statement constitutes the pleading of the creditor.

(b) A third-party claim of ownership, right to possession, or a lien, shall be deemed controverted by the creditor. *(Added by Stats.1982, c. 1364, p. 5221, § 2, operative July 1, 1983.)*

Law Revision Commission Comments

Subdivision (a)(1) of Section 720.350 continues the substance of a portion of the eleventh sentence of the eighth paragraph of former Section 689. Unlike subdivision (a)(2), former Section 689b did not prescribe the effect of the creditor's statement in opposition to the claim of a secured party. Subdivision (b) continues the substance of a portion of the eleventh sentence of the eighth paragraph of former Section 689; but subdivision (b) is limited to third-party claims of ownership, right to possession, or a lien, whereas the former provision applied to all claims under former Section 689 or 689b. [16 Cal.L.Rev.Comm. Reports 1574 (1982)].

Research References

Rutter, Cal. Practice Guide: Enforcing Judgments/Debts Ch. 6H-4, Hearing on Third Party Claim.
8 Witkin Cal. Proc. 5th Enforcement of Judgment § 381, (S 381) Proceedings and Determination.

§ 720.360. Burden of proof

At a hearing on a third-party claim, the third person has the burden of proof. *(Added by Stats.1982, c. 1364, p. 5221, § 2, operative July 1, 1983.)*

Research References

Rutter, Cal. Practice Guide: Enforcing Judgments/Debts Ch. 6H-4, Hearing on Third Party Claim.
Miller and Starr California Real Estate § 32:64, Creation, Duration, and Effect of Writ of Execution.
8 Witkin Cal. Proc. 5th Enforcement of Judgment § 381, (S 381) Proceedings and Determination.

§ 720.370. Dismissal of petition or proceedings

If the petition for a hearing was made by the third person, neither the petition nor the proceedings pursuant thereto may be dismissed without the consent of the creditor. If the petition for a hearing was made by the creditor, neither the petition nor the proceedings pursuant thereto may be dismissed without the consent of the third person. *(Added by Stats.1982, c. 1364, p. 5221, § 2, operative July 1, 1983.)*

Research References

Rutter, Cal. Practice Guide: Enforcing Judgments/Debts Ch. 6H-4, Hearing on Third Party Claim.
8 Witkin Cal. Proc. 5th Enforcement of Judgment § 381, (S 381) Proceedings and Determination.

§ 720.380. Order staying sale or enjoining transfer or disposition

(a) Notwithstanding any other provision of this title, the court may make an order staying the sale of the property under a writ or enjoining any transfer or other disposition of the property levied upon under a writ until proceedings for the determination of the rights of a third person can be commenced and prosecuted to termination and may require such undertaking as it considers necessary as a condition for making the order.

(b) After the filing of a third-party claim, notwithstanding Sections 720.160 and 720.260, the creditor, the debtor, or the third person may apply to the court for an order staying the sale of the property under a writ or enjoining any transfer or other disposition of the property until proceedings under this article can be commenced and prosecuted to termination. The application shall be made on noticed motion if the court so directs or a court rule otherwise so requires. Otherwise, the application may be made ex parte.

(c) An order made pursuant to this section may be modified or vacated by the court at any time prior to the termination of the proceedings upon such terms as are just. *(Added by Stats.1982, c. 1364, p. 5221, § 2, operative July 1, 1983.)*

Law Revision Commission Comments

Subdivisions (a) and (b) of Section 720.380 supersede the eighth sentence of the eighth paragraph of former Section 689. Subdivision (c) continues the substance of the ninth sentence of the eighth paragraph of former Section 689. See Section 699.070 (disposition of perishable property). [16 Cal.L.Rev.Comm. Reports 1576 (1982)].

Research References

Rutter, Cal. Practice Guide: Enforcing Judgments/Debts Ch. 6H-4, Hearing on Third Party Claim.
Miller and Starr California Real Estate § 32:64, Creation, Duration, and Effect of Writ of Execution.

8 Witkin Cal. Proc. 5th Enforcement of Judgment § 381, (S 381) Proceedings and Determination.

§ 720.390.   Judgment and order for disposition

At the conclusion of the hearing, the court shall give judgment determining the validity of the third-party claim and may order the disposition of the property or its proceeds in accordance with the respective interests of the parties.   Subject to Section 720.420, the judgment is conclusive between the parties to the proceeding. *(Added by Stats.1982, c. 1364, p. 5221, § 2, operative July 1, 1983.)*

Law Revision Commission Comments

Section 720.390 continues the substance of a portion of the fourteenth and fifteenth sentences of the eighth paragraph of former Section 689 and the third sentence of subdivision (10) of former Section 689b. See also Section 699.070 (disposition of perishable property). [16 Cal.L.Rev. Comm. Reports 1576 (1982)].

Research References

Rutter, Cal. Practice Guide: Enforcing Judgments/Debts Ch. 6H-4, Hearing on Third Party Claim.
Miller and Starr California Real Estate § 19:67, Liability of the Parties-- Between Tenant-Sublessor and Subtenant.
Miller and Starr California Real Estate § 32:61, Property Interests Subject to Execution.
Miller and Starr California Real Estate § 32:64, Creation, Duration, and Effect of Writ of Execution.
9 Witkin Cal. Proc. 5th Appeal § 185, Orders Dealing With Enforcement.
8 Witkin Cal. Proc. 5th Enforcement of Judgment § 381, (S 381) Proceedings and Determination.

§ 720.400.   Findings

No findings are required in proceedings under this chapter. *(Added by Stats.1982, c. 1364, p. 5221, § 2, operative July 1, 1983.)*

Law Revision Commission Comments

Section 720.400 continues the substance of the thirteenth sentence of the eighth paragraph of former Section 689. [16 Cal.L.Rev.Comm. Reports 1576 (1982)].

Research References

Rutter, Cal. Practice Guide: Enforcing Judgments/Debts Ch. 6H-4, Hearing on Third Party Claim.
8 Witkin Cal. Proc. 5th Enforcement of Judgment § 381, (S 381) Proceedings and Determination.

§ 720.410.   Right to jury trial

There is no right to a jury trial in a proceeding pursuant to this chapter. *(Added by Stats.1982, c. 1364, p. 5222, § 2, operative July 1, 1983.)*

Law Revision Commission Comments

Section 720.410 codifies the holding in Misrach v. Liederman, 14 Cal.App.2d Supp. 757, 58 P.2d 746 (1936). [16 Cal.L.Rev.Comm. Reports 1576 (1982)].

Research References

Rutter, Cal. Practice Guide: Enforcing Judgments/Debts Ch. 6H-4, Hearing on Third Party Claim.
8 Witkin Cal. Proc. 5th Enforcement of Judgment § 381, (S 381) Proceedings and Determination.

§ 720.420.   Appeals

An appeal may be taken from a judgment given pursuant to Section 720.390. *(Added by Stats.1982, c. 1364, p. 5222, § 2, operative July 1, 1983. Amended by Stats.1998, c. 931 (S.B.2139), § 98, eff. Sept. 28, 1998.)*

Law Revision Commission Comments

Section 720.420 continues the substance of the seventeenth sentence of the eighth paragraph of former Section 689. [16 Cal.L.Rev.Comm. Reports 1577 (1982)].

Section 720.420 is amended to accommodate unification of the municipal and superior courts in a county. Cal. Const. art. VI, § 5(e). See Sections 85 (limited civil cases), 86(a)(8) (enforcement of judgment in limited civil case), 904.1 (taking appeal), 904.2 (taking appeal in limited civil case). See also Section 85 Comment. [28 Cal.L.Rev.Comm. Reports 51 (1998)].

Research References

Rutter, Cal. Practice Guide: Enforcing Judgments/Debts Ch. 6H-4, Hearing on Third Party Claim.
8 Witkin Cal. Proc. 5th Enforcement of Judgment § 381, (S 381) Proceedings and Determination.

§ 720.430.   Levy upon or application of property to satisfaction of judgment after release

If property has been released pursuant to Section 720.170, 720.270, or 720.660, it may be levied upon or otherwise sought to be applied to the satisfaction of the judgment only if it is determined in the hearing on the third-party claim that the debtor has an interest in the property that may be levied upon or otherwise applied to the satisfaction of the judgment. *(Added by Stats.1982, c. 1364, p. 5222, § 2, operative July 1, 1983.)*

Law Revision Commission Comments

Section 720.430 supersedes the sixteenth sentence of the eighth paragraph of former Section 689 and the second paragraph of subdivision (10) of former Section 689b. Former law referred only to relevy upon property that had been released, but Section 720.430 recognizes that other enforcement procedures may also be employed. See, e.g., Chapter 6 (commencing with Section 708.010) (miscellaneous creditor's remedies) of Division 2. [16 Cal.L.Rev.Comm. Reports 1577 (1982)].

Research References

Rutter, Cal. Practice Guide: Enforcing Judgments/Debts Ch. 6H-2, Title or Possessory Claims to Real or Personal Property.
Rutter, Cal. Practice Guide: Enforcing Judgments/Debts Ch. 6H-4, Hearing on Third Party Claim.
Miller and Starr California Real Estate § 32:64, Creation, Duration, and Effect of Writ of Execution.
8 Witkin Cal. Proc. 5th Enforcement of Judgment § 369, (S 369) Effect of Filing or Not Filing Claim.
8 Witkin Cal. Proc. 5th Enforcement of Judgment § 374, (S 374) Effect of Filing or Not Filing Claim.
8 Witkin Cal. Proc. 5th Enforcement of Judgment § 382, (S 382) Satisfaction from Released Property.

CHAPTER 5.   CREDITOR'S DEMAND FOR THIRD–PARTY CLAIM BY SECURED PARTY OR LIENHOLDER

§ 720.510.   Demand by creditor

A creditor may make a demand as provided in this chapter that a secured party or lienholder file a third-party claim to personal property that has been levied upon under a writ of attachment or a writ of execution. *(Added by Stats.1982, c. 1364, p. 5222, § 2, operative July 1, 1983.)*

Civ. Pro.

Research References

Rutter, Cal. Practice Guide: Enforcing Judgments/Debts Ch. 6H-5, Creditor's Demand for Third Party Claim by Secured Party.
8 Witkin Cal. Proc. 5th Enforcement of Judgment § 383, (S 383) Filing and Service of Demand.

§ 720.520. Filing of demand and copy; service

(a) The creditor's demand for a third-party claim by the secured party or lienholder, together with a copy of the demand, shall be filed with the levying officer after levy on the personal property but before the levying officer sells the property or pays proceeds of collection to the creditor.

(b) Promptly after the demand and a copy thereof are filed, the levying officer shall personally serve the demand on the secured party or lienholder. Service of the demand on the secured party or lienholder shall be attested by the certificate of the levying officer and the certificate shall be filed in the action promptly after service.

(c) The demand shall be served by the levying officer who levied on the property or by any other levying officer whose office is closer to the place of service. If service is made by another levying officer, such levying officer's costs shall be paid out of the costs prepaid to the levying officer who levied on the property. *(Added by Stats.1982, c. 1364, p. 5222, § 2, operative July 1, 1983.)*

Research References

Rutter, Cal. Practice Guide: Enforcing Judgments/Debts Ch. 6H-5, Creditor's Demand for Third Party Claim by Secured Party.
8 Witkin Cal. Proc. 5th Enforcement of Judgment § 383, (S 383) Filing and Service of Demand.

§ 720.530. Contents of demand

The demand for a third-party claim served on a secured party or lienholder shall contain all of the following:

(a) The name and address of the secured party or lienholder.

(b) The name and address of the creditor.

(c) A detailed description of the personal property levied upon and the date of levy.

(d) A statement that if the secured party or lienholder does not file a third-party claim pursuant to Chapter 3 (commencing with Section 720.210) within 30 days after service of the demand, the secured party or lienholder shall be deemed to have waived any priority the security interest or lien may have over the creditor's lien on the property levied upon unless the property levied upon is released from the creditor's lien.

(e) A statement that if any priority of the security interest or lien is waived, the secured party or lienholder may have a right to share in any excess proceeds of an execution sale of the property as provided in Section 701.810. *(Added by Stats.1982, c. 1364, p. 5222, § 2, operative July 1, 1983.)*

Research References

Rutter, Cal. Practice Guide: Enforcing Judgments/Debts Ch. 6H-5, Creditor's Demand for Third Party Claim by Secured Party.
8 Witkin Cal. Proc. 5th Enforcement of Judgment § 383, (S 383) Filing and Service of Demand.

§ 720.540. Release, sale or disposition of property described in demand

Except as otherwise provided by statute, the levying officer may not release, sell, or otherwise dispose of the personal property described in the demand before the expiration of 30 days after service of the demand on the secured party or lienholder. *(Added by Stats.1982, c. 1364, p. 5223, § 2, operative July 1, 1983.)*

Research References

Rutter, Cal. Practice Guide: Enforcing Judgments/Debts Ch. 6H-5, Creditor's Demand for Third Party Claim by Secured Party.
8 Witkin Cal. Proc. 5th Enforcement of Judgment § 383, (S 383) Filing and Service of Demand.

§ 720.550. Failure to file claim after demand; priority

(a) If the secured party or lienholder does not file a third-party claim with the levying officer pursuant to Chapter 3 (commencing with Section 720.210) within 30 days after service of the demand, the secured party or lienholder shall be deemed to have waived any priority the security interest or lien may have over the creditor's lien on the personal property levied upon and the property may be applied toward the satisfaction of the judgment free of the security interest or lien.

(b) If the secured party or lienholder is deemed to have waived any priority over the creditor's lien pursuant to subdivision (a) and the creditor's lien on the personal property is released, the security interest or lien is restored to its former position of priority. *(Added by Stats.1982, c. 1364, p. 5223, § 2, operative July 1, 1983.)*

Research References

Rutter, Cal. Practice Guide: Enforcing Judgments/Debts Ch. 6H-5, Creditor's Demand for Third Party Claim by Secured Party.

8 Witkin Cal. Proc. 5th Enforcement of Judgment § 384, (S 384) Effect of
    Failure to Make Claim.

CHAPTER 6.   THIRD–PARTY UNDERTAKING
TO RELEASE PROPERTY

Section
720.610.   Cases in which undertaking applicable.
720.620.   Time for filing undertaking and copies.
720.630.   Contents and amount of undertaking.
720.640.   Service of copy of undertaking on creditor and
             debtor.
720.650.   Undertaking effective upon release of property.
720.660.   Release of property.

§ 720.610.   Cases in which undertaking applicable

A third person may give an undertaking to release property
pursuant to this chapter in the following cases:

(a) Where the third person claims ownership or the right to
possession of real property that has been levied upon under a
writ of attachment or a writ of execution.

(b) Where the third person claims ownership or the right to
possession of personal property that has been levied under
a writ of attachment, a writ of execution, or a writ of sale.

(c) Where the third person claims a security interest in or a
lien on personal property that has been levied upon under a writ
of attachment, a writ of execution, or a writ of sale. (*Added by
Stats.1982, c. 1364, p. 5223, § 2, operative July 1, 1983.*)

Law Revision Commission Comments

Section 720.610 supersedes former Section 710b which applied only to
personal property levied upon to satisfy a money judgment in a case where
the third person "claimed" the property. Compare former Section 689
(paragraph seven of which referred to release under former Section 710b)
with former Section 689b (which contained no reference to former Section
710b). [16 Cal.L.Rev.Comm. Reports 1580 (1982)].

Research References

Rutter, Cal. Practice Guide: Enforcing Judgments/Debts Ch. 6H-6, Third
    Party Undertaking to Release Property.
Miller and Starr California Real Estate § 32:30, When Property Held by
    Third Party.
Miller and Starr California Real Estate § 32:64, Creation, Duration, and
    Effect of Writ of Execution.
8 Witkin Cal. Proc. 5th Enforcement of Judgment § 368, (S 368) Time
    and Manner of Making Claim.
8 Witkin Cal. Proc. 5th Enforcement of Judgment § 370, (S 370)
    Creditor's Undertaking.
8 Witkin Cal. Proc. 5th Enforcement of Judgment § 371, (S 371) Release
    of Property.
8 Witkin Cal. Proc. 5th Enforcement of Judgment § 373, (S 373) Time
    and Manner of Making Claim.
8 Witkin Cal. Proc. 5th Enforcement of Judgment § 375, (S 375)
    Creditor's Undertaking.
8 Witkin Cal. Proc. 5th Enforcement of Judgment § 376, (S 376) Release
    of Property.
8 Witkin Cal. Proc. 5th Enforcement of Judgment § 378, (S 378)
    Application and Notice.
8 Witkin Cal. Proc. 5th Enforcement of Judgment § 379, (S 379) Papers
    Filed by Levying Officer.
8 Witkin Cal. Proc. 5th Enforcement of Judgment § 385, (S 385) Nature
    of Undertaking.

§ 720.620.   Time for filing undertaking and copies

The third person shall file the undertaking to release property
with the levying officer, together with two copies of the
undertaking:

(a) At the time the third person files a third-party claim
pursuant to Chapter 2 (commencing with Section 720.110) or
Chapter 3 (commencing with Section 720.210).

(b) If the third person has previously filed a third-party claim
to the property, at any time before the levying officer does any of
the following:

(1) Sells the property.

(2) Delivers possession of the property to the creditor.

(3) Pays proceeds of collection to the creditor. (*Added by
Stats.1982, c. 1364, p. 5223, § 2, operative July 1, 1983.*)

Research References

Rutter, Cal. Practice Guide: Enforcing Judgments/Debts Ch. 6H-6, Third
    Party Undertaking to Release Property.
Miller and Starr California Real Estate § 32:64, Creation, Duration, and
    Effect of Writ of Execution.
8 Witkin Cal. Proc. 5th Enforcement of Judgment § 386, (S 386) Filing
    and Service of Undertaking and Release of Property.

§ 720.630.   Contents and amount of undertaking

(a) The undertaking to release property shall contain a
description of the property to be released and shall describe the
interest of the third person.

(b) The undertaking shall be made in favor of the creditor and
shall provide that, if the debtor is finally adjudged to have an
interest in the property levied upon, the third person shall pay to
the creditor the lesser of the following:

(1) The amount required to satisfy the judgment against the
debtor of the creditor who had the lien on the property.

(2) A sum equal to the market value of the debtor's interest in
the property levied upon.

(c) Except as provided in subdivision (d) and unless the third
person elects to file an undertaking in a larger amount, the
amount of the undertaking shall be the lesser of the following
amounts:

(1) Twice the market value of the property sought to be
released.

(2) Twice the amount of the creditor's lien on the property
sought to be released.

(d) If the creditor has given an undertaking in response to the
third person's claim regarding the property pursuant to Section
720.160 or 720.260, the third person's undertaking shall be in the
amount of the creditor's undertaking. (*Added by Stats.1982, c.
1364, p. 5223, § 2, operative July 1, 1983.*)

Law Revision Commission Comments

Section 720.630 supersedes portions of former Section 710c. Subdivision (b) recognizes that the creditor is not entitled to a greater satisfaction
from the third person's undertaking than from the debtor. Subdivision
(c) continues the substance of a portion of former Section 710c, subject to
the exception provided in subdivision (d). Subdivision (d) enables the
third person to obtain the release of the property only by giving an
undertaking in the amount of the creditor's undertaking filed in response
to the third-party's claim. [16 Cal.L.Rev.Comm. Reports 1582 (1982)].

Research References

Rutter, Cal. Practice Guide: Enforcing Judgments/Debts Ch. 6H-2, Title
    or Possessory Claims to Real or Personal Property.
Rutter, Cal. Practice Guide: Enforcing Judgments/Debts Ch. 6H-6, Third
    Party Undertaking to Release Property.
Miller and Starr California Real Estate § 32:64, Creation, Duration, and
    Effect of Writ of Execution.
8 Witkin Cal. Proc. 5th Enforcement of Judgment § 385, (S 385) Nature
    of Undertaking.

§ 720.640.   Service of copy of undertaking on creditor and
debtor

(a) If the undertaking to release property is filed with the
levying officer at the time the third-party claim is filed, the
levying officer shall serve a copy of the undertaking on the

1691   ENFORCEMENT OF JUDGMENTS   § 720.770

creditor and on the debtor with the notice of the filing of the third-party claim served pursuant to Section 720.140 or 720.240.

(b) If the undertaking to release property is filed with the levying officer after the third-party claim is filed, not later than five days after the undertaking is filed, the levying officer shall serve a copy of the undertaking on the creditor and on the debtor with a notice that the property will be released unless, within the time allowed as specified in the notice, the creditor objects to the undertaking. Service shall be made personally or by mail. *(Added by Stats.1982, c. 1364, p. 5224, § 2, operative July 1, 1983.)*

Law Revision Commission Comments

Section 720.640 is new. Under former Section 711, the third person was required to serve a copy of the undertaking on the creditor. [16 Cal.L.Rev.Comm. Reports 1582 (1982)].

Research References

Rutter, Cal. Practice Guide: Enforcing Judgments/Debts Ch. 6H-6, Third Party Undertaking to Release Property.
Miller and Starr California Real Estate § 32:64, Creation, Duration, and Effect of Writ of Execution.
8 Witkin Cal. Proc. 5th Enforcement of Judgment § 386, (S 386) Filing and Service of Undertaking and Release of Property.

§ 720.650. Undertaking effective upon release of property

The third person's undertaking becomes effective when the property described therein is released pursuant to this chapter. *(Added by Stats.1982, c. 1364, p. 5224, § 2, operative July 1, 1983.)*

Law Revision Commission Comments

Section 720.650 supersedes former Section 713½ which provided that the undertaking was effective 10 days after service on the creditor or, if an objection to the undertaking was made, when a new undertaking was given. Under Section 720.650, the undertaking is effective when it achieves its purpose—the release of the property it describes—by which time the period for making an objection will have expired. See Section 720.760. [16 Cal.L.Rev.Comm. Reports 1583 (1982)].

Research References

8 Witkin Cal. Proc. 5th Enforcement of Judgment § 386, (S 386) Filing and Service of Undertaking and Release of Property.

§ 720.660. Release of property

The levying officer shall release the property described in the third person's undertaking in the manner provided by Section 720.170 promptly after the expiration of the time allowed for objecting to the undertaking, unless the creditor has objected to the undertaking, and filed with the levying officer a copy of the notice of motion as required by Section 720.760, prior to the expiration of that time. *(Added by Stats.1982, c. 1364, p. 5224, § 2, operative July 1, 1983. Amended by Stats.1985, c. 41, § 12.)*

Law Revision Commission Comments

Section 720.660 supersedes a portion of the seventh paragraph of former Section 689 and a portion of former Section 713½. [16 Cal.L.Rev. Comm. Reports 1583 (1982)].

Section 720.660 is amended to delete a reference to former subdivision (b) of Section 720.760 which is superseded by a provision of the Bond and Undertaking Law. See Section 995.930(b) (time for objecting to undertaking). [18 Cal.L.Rev.Comm. Reports 363 (1985)].

Research References

Rutter, Cal. Practice Guide: Enforcing Judgments/Debts Ch. 6E-4, Opposing Claim of Exemption.
Rutter, Cal. Practice Guide: Enforcing Judgments/Debts Ch. 6H-2, Title or Possessory Claims to Real or Personal Property.
Rutter, Cal. Practice Guide: Enforcing Judgments/Debts Ch. 6H-6, Third Party Undertaking to Release Property.
Miller and Starr California Real Estate § 32:64, Creation, Duration, and Effect of Writ of Execution.

8 Witkin Cal. Proc. 5th Enforcement of Judgment § 186, (S 186) Disposition of Property During Proceedings.
8 Witkin Cal. Proc. 5th Enforcement of Judgment § 382, (S 382) Satisfaction from Released Property.
8 Witkin Cal. Proc. 5th Enforcement of Judgment § 386, (S 386) Filing and Service of Undertaking and Release of Property.

CHAPTER 7. UNDERTAKINGS

Section

720.710.   Application of Bond and Undertaking Law.
720.760.   Objection; filing notice of motion.
720.770.   Hearing on objection; decrease in amount of undertaking.
720.800.   Undertaking filed with levying officer.

§ 720.710. Application of Bond and Undertaking Law

The Bond and Undertaking Law (Chapter 2 (commencing with Section 995.010) of Title 14) applies to a bond given pursuant to this title, except to the extent this title prescribes a different rule or is inconsistent. *(Added by Stats.1985, c. 41, § 13.)*

Law Revision Commission Comments

Section 720.710 makes clear that the Bond and Undertaking Law applies under the Enforcement of Judgments Law. This makes no change in the law. See the Comment to the repeal of former Sections 720.710–720.750. [18 Cal.L.Rev.Comm. Reports 363 (1985)].

Research References

Rutter, Cal. Practice Guide: Enforcing Judgments/Debts Ch. 6H-7, Statutory Requirements for Undertakings.
8 Witkin Cal. Proc. 5th Enforcement of Judgment § 366, (S 366) General Rules Governing Undertakings.

§ 720.760. Objection; filing notice of motion

A copy of a notice of motion objecting to an undertaking shall be filed with the levying officer. *(Added by Stats.1982, c. 1364, p. 5225, § 2, operative July 1, 1983. Amended by Stats.1983, c. 18, § 14, eff. April 21, 1983, operative July 1, 1983.)*

Law Revision Commission Comments

Section 720.760 continues the substance of Sections 489.070 and 489.080 (attachment) which were incorporated by former Sections 689 and 689b, and supersedes a portion of former Section 711½. The time for objecting to an undertaking has been changed from five days after notice of receipt of the undertaking (see the third paragraph of former Section 689) to 10 days after service. [16 Cal.L.Rev.Comm. Reports 1585 (1982)].

Section 720.760 is amended to delete provisions duplicated in the Bond and Undertaking Law. See Sections 995.920 (grounds for objection), 995.930 (manner of making objection), 995.030 (manner of service), and 995.940 (objection to sufficiency of undertaking based on market value). [16 Cal. L. Rev. Comm. Reports 2246 (1982)].

Research References

Rutter, Cal. Practice Guide: Enforcing Judgments/Debts Ch. 6H-7, Statutory Requirements for Undertakings.
8 Witkin Cal. Proc. 5th Enforcement of Judgment § 366, (S 366) General Rules Governing Undertakings.
8 Witkin Cal. Proc. 5th Enforcement of Judgment § 386, (S 386) Filing and Service of Undertaking and Release of Property.

§ 720.770. Hearing on objection; decrease in amount of undertaking

Unless the parties otherwise agree, the hearing on an objection to an undertaking shall be held not less than 10 nor more than 15 days after service of the notice of motion. The court may order the amount of the undertaking decreased below the amount prescribed by Section 720.160 or 720.260 if the court determines the amount prescribed exceeds the probable recovery of the beneficiary if the beneficiary ultimately prevails in

Civ. Pro.

proceedings to enforce the liability on the undertaking. *(Added by Stats.1982, c. 1364, p. 5225, § 2, operative July 1, 1983. Amended by Stats.1983, c. 18, § 15, eff. April 21, 1983, operative July 1, 1983.)*

Law Revision Commission Comments

Section 720.770 is drawn from Section 489.090 (attachment) which was incorporated by former Sections 689 and 689b, and supersedes portions of former Sections 712 and 712½ (undertaking to release property). Subdivision (f) is derived from Section 489.220(b) (undertakings in attachment). The amount of the undertaking may not be decreased on the principal's initiative but only in a situation where the beneficiary has objected to the amount of the undertaking and the court finds that it is more than adequate. [16 Cal.L.Rev.Comm. Reports 1586 (1982)].

Section 720.770 is amended to delete provisions duplicated in the Bond and Undertaking Law. See Sections 995.950 (hearing on objection), 995.960 (determination of sufficiency of undertaking), and 996.010–996.030 (insufficient and excessive undertakings). [16 Cal. L. Rev. Comm. Reports 2246 (1982)].

Research References

Rutter, Cal. Practice Guide: Enforcing Judgments/Debts Ch. 6H-7, Statutory Requirements for Undertakings.
Miller and Starr California Real Estate § 32:64, Creation, Duration, and Effect of Writ of Execution.
8 Witkin Cal. Proc. 5th Enforcement of Judgment § 366, (S 366) General Rules Governing Undertakings.
8 Witkin Cal. Proc. 5th Enforcement of Judgment § 370, (S 370) Creditor's Undertaking.
8 Witkin Cal. Proc. 5th Enforcement of Judgment § 375, (S 375) Creditor's Undertaking.

§ 720.800.   Undertaking filed with levying officer

If an undertaking has been filed with a levying officer pursuant to this division, and the undertaking remains in the levying officer's possession when the writ is to be returned, the levying officer shall file the undertaking with the court at the time the writ is returned. *(Added by Stats.1982, c. 1364, p. 5226, § 2, operative July 1, 1983.)*

Research References

Rutter, Cal. Practice Guide: Enforcing Judgments/Debts Ch. 6H-7, Statutory Requirements for Undertakings.
Miller and Starr California Real Estate § 32:30, When Property Held by Third Party.
8 Witkin Cal. Proc. 5th Enforcement of Judgment § 366, (S 366) General Rules Governing Undertakings.
8 Witkin Cal. Proc. 5th Enforcement of Judgment § 379, (S 379) Papers Filed by Levying Officer.

Division 5

SATISFACTION OF JUDGMENT

CHAPTER 1.   SATISFACTION OF JUDGMENT

§ 724.010.   Satisfaction by payment in full or acceptance of lesser sum; obligation to give or file acknowledgment

(a) A money judgment may be satisfied by payment of the full amount required to satisfy the judgment or by acceptance by the judgment creditor of a lesser sum in full satisfaction of the judgment.

(b) Where a money judgment is satisfied by levy, the obligation of the judgment creditor to give or file an acknowledgment of satisfaction arises only when the judgment creditor has received the full amount required to satisfy the judgment from the levying officer.

(c) Where a money judgment is satisfied by payment to the judgment creditor by check or other form of noncash payment that is to be honored upon presentation by the judgment creditor for payment, the obligation of the judgment creditor to give or file an acknowledgment of satisfaction of judgment arises only when the check or other form of noncash payment has actually been honored upon presentation for payment. *(Added by Stats.1982, c. 1364, p. 5226, § 2, operative July 1, 1983.)*

Research References

Rutter, Cal. Practice Guide: Civil Appeals & Writs Ch. 2-D, D. Standing to Appeal.
Rutter, Cal. Practice Guide: Enforcing Judgments/Debts Ch. 6K-1, Acknowledgment of Full Satisfaction of Judgment.
Miller and Starr California Real Estate § 32:58, Satisfaction or Release of the Judgment Lien.
9 Witkin Cal. Proc. 5th Appeal § 78, Executing Satisfaction of Judgment.
1 Witkin Cal. Proc. 5th Attorneys § 255, (S 255) in General.
8 Witkin Cal. Proc. 5th Enforcement of Judgment § 75, (S 75) Amount of Lien.
8 Witkin Cal. Proc. 5th Enforcement of Judgment § 387, (S 387) in General.
8 Witkin Cal. Proc. 5th Enforcement of Judgment § 388, Creditor's Duty.
8 Witkin Cal. Proc. 5th Enforcement of Judgment § 507, Payment or Compromise by Judgment Debtor.
1 Witkin Cal. Summ. 10th Contracts § 959, Rule and Theory.

§ 724.020.   Time for entry of satisfaction of judgment

The court clerk shall enter satisfaction of a money judgment in the register of actions when the following occur:

(a) A writ is returned satisfied for the full amount of a lump-sum judgment.

(b) An acknowledgment of satisfaction of judgment is filed with the court.

(c) The court orders entry of satisfaction of judgment. *(Added by Stats.1982, c. 1364, p. 5226, § 2, operative July 1, 1983.)*

Law Revision Commission Comments

Section 724.020 continues the substance of portions of subdivision (a) of former Section 675. [16 Cal.L.Rev.Comm. Reports 1589 (1982)].

Research References

Rutter, Cal. Practice Guide: Enforcing Judgments/Debts Ch. 6K-1, Acknowledgment of Full Satisfaction of Judgment.
8 Witkin Cal. Proc. 5th Enforcement of Judgment § 387, (S 387) in General.

8 Witkin Cal. Proc. 5th Enforcement of Judgment § 388, Creditor's Duty.
1 Witkin Cal. Summ. 10th Contracts § 959, Rule and Theory.

§ 724.030.   Acknowledgment by judgment creditor

When a money judgment is satisfied, the judgment creditor immediately shall file with the court an acknowledgment of satisfaction of judgment. This section does not apply where the judgment is satisfied in full pursuant to a writ. (Added by Stats.1982, c. 1364, p. 5227, § 2, operative July 1, 1983.)

Research References

Rutter, Cal. Practice Guide: Enforcing Judgments/Debts Ch. 6K-1, Acknowledgment of Full Satisfaction of Judgment.
Miller and Starr California Real Estate § 32:58, Satisfaction or Release of the Judgment Lien.
8 Witkin Cal. Proc. 5th Enforcement of Judgment § 388, Creditor's Duty.

§ 724.040.   Procedure after satisfaction where abstract of judgment recorded

If an abstract of a money judgment has been recorded with the recorder of any county and the judgment is satisfied, the judgment creditor shall immediately do both of the following:

(a) File an acknowledgment of satisfaction of judgment with the court.

(b) Serve an acknowledgment of satisfaction of judgment on the judgment debtor. Service shall be made personally or by mail. (Added by Stats.1982, c. 1364, p. 5227, § 2, operative July 1, 1983.)

Research References

Rutter, Cal. Practice Guide: Enforcing Judgments/Debts Ch. 6K-1, Acknowledgment of Full Satisfaction of Judgment.
Rutter, Cal. Practice Guide: Enforcing Judgments/Debts Ch. 6B-11, Release of Real Property Judgment Lien.
Miller and Starr California Real Estate § 32:58, Satisfaction or Release of the Judgment Lien.
8 Witkin Cal. Proc. 5th Enforcement of Judgment § 388, Creditor's Duty.

§ 724.050.   Demand upon judgment creditor

(a) If a money judgment has been satisfied, the judgment debtor, the owner of real or personal property subject to a judgment lien created under the judgment, or a person having a security interest in or a lien on personal property subject to a judgment lien created under the judgment may serve personally or by mail on the judgment creditor a demand in writing that the judgment creditor do one or both of the following:

(1) File an acknowledgment of satisfaction of judgment with the court.

(2) Execute, acknowledge, and deliver an acknowledgment of satisfaction of judgment to the person who made the demand.

(b) The demand shall include the following statement: "Important warning. If this judgment has been satisfied, the law requires that you comply with this demand not later than 15 days after you receive it. If a court proceeding is necessary to compel you to comply with this demand, you will be required to pay my reasonable attorney's fees in the proceeding if the court determines that the judgment has been satisfied and that you failed to comply with the demand. In addition, if the court determines that you failed without just cause to comply with this demand within the 15 days allowed, you will be liable for all damages I sustain by reason of such failure and will also forfeit one hundred dollars to me."

(c) If the judgment has been satisfied, the judgment creditor shall comply with the demand not later than 15 days after actual receipt of the demand.

(d) If the judgment creditor does not comply with the demand within the time allowed, the person making the demand may apply to the court on noticed motion for an order requiring the judgment creditor to comply with the demand. The notice of motion shall be served on the judgment creditor. Service shall be made personally or by mail. If the court determines that the judgment has been satisfied and that the judgment creditor has not complied with the demand, the court shall either (1) order the judgment creditor to comply with the demand or (2) order the court clerk to enter satisfaction of the judgment.

(e) If the judgment has been satisfied and the judgment creditor fails without just cause to comply with the demand within the time allowed, the judgment creditor is liable to the person who made the demand for all damages sustained by reason of such failure and shall also forfeit one hundred dollars ($100) to such person. Liability under this subdivision may be determined in the proceedings on the motion pursuant to subdivision (d) or in an action. (Added by Stats.1982, c. 1364, p. 5227, § 2, operative July 1, 1983.)

Research References

Rutter, Cal. Practice Guide: A.D.R. Ch. 5-J, J. Challenging and Enforcing Arbitrator's Award in Court.
Rutter, Cal. Practice Guide: Enforcing Judgments/Debts Ch. 6K-1, Acknowledgment of Full Satisfaction of Judgment.
Rutter, Cal. Practice Guide: Personal Injury Ch. 4-D, D. Techniques Where Settlement Not Forthcoming.
Miller and Starr California Real Estate § 32:58, Satisfaction or Release of the Judgment Lien.
Miller and Starr California Real Estate § 10:213, Disposition of Sales Proceeds.
8 Witkin Cal. Proc. 5th Enforcement of Judgment § 389, Demand for Acknowledgment.
8 Witkin Cal. Proc. 5th Enforcement of Judgment § 393, Acknowledgment of Partial Satisfaction.
7 Witkin Cal. Proc. 5th Judgment § 424, Property Actions.
4 Witkin, California Summary 10th Security Transactions in Real Property § 206, Defense of Action to Enjoin Sale.

§ 724.060.   Form and contents of acknowledgment of satisfaction

(a) An acknowledgment of satisfaction of judgment shall contain the following information:

(1) The title of the court.

(2) The cause and number of the action.

(3) The names and addresses of the judgment creditor, the judgment debtor, and the assignee of record if any. If an abstract of the judgment has been recorded in any county, the judgment debtor's name shall appear on the acknowledgment of satisfaction of judgment as it appears on the abstract of judgment.

(4) The date of entry of judgment and of any renewals of the judgment and where entered in the records of the court.

(5) A statement either that the judgment is satisfied in full or that the judgment creditor has accepted payment or performance other than that specified in the judgment in full satisfaction of the judgment.

(6) A statement whether an abstract of the judgment has been recorded in any county and, if so, a statement of each county where the abstract has been recorded and the book and page of the county records where the abstract has been recorded, and a notice that the acknowledgment of satisfaction of judgment (or a court clerk's certificate of satisfaction of judgment) will have to be recorded with the county recorder of each county where the abstract of judgment has been recorded in order to release the judgment lien on real property in that county.

(7) A statement whether a notice of judgment lien has been filed in the office of the Secretary of State and, if such a notice has been filed, a statement of the file number of such notice, and a notice that the acknowledgment of satisfaction of judgment (or

a court clerk's certificate of satisfaction of judgment) will have to be filed in that office in order to terminate the judgment lien on personal property.

(b) The acknowledgment of satisfaction of judgment shall be made in the manner of an acknowledgment of a conveyance of real property.

(c) The acknowledgment of satisfaction of judgment shall be executed and acknowledged by one of the following:

(1) The judgment creditor.

(2) The assignee of record.

(3) The attorney for the judgment creditor or assignee of record unless a revocation of the attorney's authority is filed.

(4) The local child support agency director or his or her designee, if the local child support agency has been providing child support services pursuant to Section 17400 of the Family Code. The acknowledgment of satisfaction of judgment may be recorded by the local child support agency pursuant to Section 27282 of the Government Code. *(Added by Stats.1982, c. 1364, p. 5228, § 2, operative July 1, 1983. Amended by Stats.1983, c. 155, § 21, eff. June 30, 1983, operative July 1, 1983; Stats.2004, c. 339 (A.B.1704), § 1.)*

Law Revision Commission Comments

Section 724.060 supersedes portions of subdivisions (a) and (b) of former Section 675. The required contents of the acknowledgment of satisfaction of judgment are drawn from the official form approved by the Judicial Council. See Form for Acknowledgment of Full Satisfaction of Judgment (Form Approved by the Judicial Council of California, effective July 1, 1975). The reference to a notice of judgment lien on personal property filed in the office of the Secretary of State is new and will alert the judgment debtor as to the need to take action to terminate the judgment lien on personal property. See Section 697.640. As to the effect of an acknowledgment of satisfaction executed by the attorney, see Wherry v. Rambo, 97 Cal.App.2d 569, 218 P.2d 142 (1950). [16 Cal.L.Rev.Comm. Reports 1594 (1982)].

Research References

Rutter, Cal. Practice Guide: Enforcing Judgments/Debts Ch. 6C-8, Extinguishing JLPP "As a Matter of Record".

Rutter, Cal. Practice Guide: Enforcing Judgments/Debts Ch. 6K-1, Acknowledgment of Full Satisfaction of Judgment.

Rutter, Cal. Practice Guide: Enforcing Judgments/Debts Ch. 6B-11, Release of Real Property Judgment Lien.

Miller and Starr California Real Estate § 32:58, Satisfaction or Release of the Judgment Lien.

Miller and Starr California Real Estate § 11:126, Relation to Subsequent Interests.

15 NO. 4 Miller & Starr, California Real Estate Newsalert 15, Recording and Priorities.

8 Witkin Cal. Proc. 5th Enforcement of Judgment § 24, Enforcement by Assignee.

8 Witkin Cal. Proc. 5th Enforcement of Judgment § 79, (S 79) Recording Satisfaction of Judgment.

8 Witkin Cal. Proc. 5th Enforcement of Judgment § 89, (S 89) Recording Satisfaction of Judgment.

8 Witkin Cal. Proc. 5th Enforcement of Judgment § 390, Execution and Content of Acknowledgment.

8 Witkin Cal. Proc. 5th Enforcement of Judgment § 393, Acknowledgment of Partial Satisfaction.

8 Witkin Cal. Proc. 5th Enforcement of Judgment § 395, (S 395) Execution and Content of Acknowledgment.

8 Witkin Cal. Proc. 5th Enforcement of Judgment § 405, Governmental Enforcement of Support Order.

§ 724.070. Conditional delivery of acknowledgment

(a) If a judgment creditor intentionally conditions delivery of an acknowledgment of satisfaction of judgment upon the performance of any act or the payment of an amount in excess of that to which the judgment creditor is entitled under the judgment, the judgment creditor is liable to the judgment debtor

for all damages sustained by reason of such action or two hundred fifty dollars ($250), whichever is the greater amount.

(b) Subdivision (a) does not apply if the judgment creditor has agreed to deliver an acknowledgment of satisfaction of judgment to the judgment debtor prior to full satisfaction of the judgment in consideration for the judgment debtor's agreement either to furnish security or to execute a promissory note, or both, the principal amount of which does not exceed the amount to which the judgment creditor is entitled under the judgment. *(Added by Stats.1982, c. 1364, p. 5229, § 2, operative July 1, 1983.)*

Law Revision Commission Comments

Section 724.070 continues the substance of subdivision (d) of former Section 675. [16 Cal.L.Rev.Comm. Reports 1595 (1982)].

Research References

Rutter, Cal. Practice Guide: Enforcing Judgments/Debts Ch. 6K-1, Acknowledgment of Full Satisfaction of Judgment.

Miller and Starr California Real Estate § 32:55, Duration of the Judgment Lien.

Miller and Starr California Real Estate § 32:58, Satisfaction or Release of the Judgment Lien.

8 Witkin Cal. Proc. 5th Enforcement of Judgment § 388, Creditor's Duty.

§ 724.080. Attorney's fees

In an action or proceeding maintained pursuant to this chapter, the court shall award reasonable attorney's fees to the prevailing party. *(Added by Stats.1982, c. 1364, p. 5229, § 2, operative July 1, 1983.)*

Law Revision Commission Comments

Section 724.080 continues the substance of a portion of subdivision (f) of former Section 675. [16 Cal.L.Rev.Comm. Reports 1595 (1982)].

Research References

Miller and Starr California Real Estate § 32:58, Satisfaction or Release of the Judgment Lien.

8 Witkin Cal. Proc. 5th Enforcement of Judgment § 387, (S 387) in General.

8 Witkin Cal. Proc. 5th Enforcement of Judgment § 393, Acknowledgment of Partial Satisfaction.

7 Witkin Cal. Proc. 5th Judgment § 222, (S 222) Actions in Bad Faith.

§ 724.090. Damages

The damages recoverable pursuant to this chapter are not in derogation of any other damages or penalties to which an aggrieved person may be entitled by law. *(Added by Stats.1982, c. 1364, p. 5229, § 2, operative July 1, 1983.)*

Law Revision Commission Comments

Section 724.090 continues the substance of former Section 675(g). [16 Cal.L.Rev.Comm. Reports 1595 (1982)].

Research References

Rutter, Cal. Practice Guide: Enforcing Judgments/Debts Ch. 6K-1, Acknowledgment of Full Satisfaction of Judgment.

Miller and Starr California Real Estate § 32:58, Satisfaction or Release of the Judgment Lien.

8 Witkin Cal. Proc. 5th Enforcement of Judgment § 387, (S 387) in General.

§ 724.100. Certificate of satisfaction of judgment; fee; contents

(a) If satisfaction of a judgment has been entered in the register of actions, the court clerk shall issue a certificate of satisfaction of judgment upon application therefor and payment of the fee as provided in subdivision (a) of Section 70626 of the Government Code.

(b) The certificate of satisfaction of judgment shall contain the following information:

(1) The title of the court.

(2) The cause and number of the action.

(3) The names of the judgment creditor and the judgment debtor.

(4) The date of entry of judgment and of any renewals of the judgment and where entered in the records of the court.

(5) The date of entry of satisfaction of judgment and where it was entered in the register of actions. *(Added by Stats.1982, c. 1364, p. 5229, § 2, operative July 1, 1983. Amended by Stats.2005, c. 75 (A.B.145), § 39, eff. July 19, 2005, operative Jan. 1, 2006.)*

Law Revision Commission Comments

Section 724.100 is new. The certificate of satisfaction of judgment serves the same function as an acknowledgment of satisfaction of judgment and can be used, for example, where an acknowledgment of satisfaction of judgment cannot be easily obtained. [16 Cal.L.Rev.Comm. Reports 1596 (1982)].

Research References

Rutter, Cal. Practice Guide: Enforcing Judgments/Debts Ch. 6C-8, Extinguishing JLPP "As a Matter of Record".
Rutter, Cal. Practice Guide: Enforcing Judgments/Debts Ch. 6K-1, Acknowledgment of Full Satisfaction of Judgment.
8 Witkin Cal. Proc. 5th Enforcement of Judgment § 79, (S 79) Recording Satisfaction of Judgment.
8 Witkin Cal. Proc. 5th Enforcement of Judgment § 89, (S 89) Recording Satisfaction of Judgment.
8 Witkin Cal. Proc. 5th Enforcement of Judgment § 388, Creditor's Duty.
8 Witkin Cal. Proc. 5th Enforcement of Judgment § 391, (S 391) Certificate of Satisfaction.

CHAPTER 2. ACKNOWLEDGMENT OF PARTIAL SATISFACTION OF JUDGMENT

Section
724.110. Demand upon judgment creditor for acknowledgment of partial satisfaction of judgment.
724.120. Form and contents of acknowledgment.

§ 724.110. Demand upon judgment creditor for acknowledgment of partial satisfaction of judgment

(a) The judgment debtor or the owner of real or personal property subject to a judgment lien created under a money judgment may serve on the judgment creditor a demand in writing that the judgment creditor execute, acknowledge, and deliver an acknowledgment of partial satisfaction of judgment to the person who made the demand. Service shall be made personally or by mail. If the judgment has been partially satisfied, the judgment creditor shall comply with the demand not later than 15 days after actual receipt of the demand.

(b) If the judgment creditor does not comply with the demand within the time allowed, the judgment debtor or the owner of the real or personal property subject to a judgment lien created under the judgment may apply to the court on noticed motion for an order requiring the judgment creditor to comply with the demand. The notice of motion shall be served on the judgment creditor. Service shall be made personally or by mail. If the court determines that the judgment has been partially satisfied and that the judgment creditor has not complied with the demand, the court shall make an order determining the amount of the partial satisfaction and may make an order requiring the judgment creditor to comply with the demand. *(Added by Stats.1982, c. 1364, p. 5229, § 2, operative July 1, 1983.)*

Law Revision Commission Comments

Section 724.110 is a new provision that provides a procedure whereby the judgment debtor or owner of property subject to a judgment lien may obtain an acknowledgment of partial satisfaction of judgment or a court

determination of the amount of partial satisfaction if the judgment creditor does not comply with a demand for an acknowledgment of partial satisfaction. Former statutory law did not provide for a similar procedure, but such a procedure was apparently allowed. See Campbell v. Southern Pacific Co., 22 Cal.3d 51, 583 P.2d 121, 148 Cal.Rptr. 596 (1978); Kaplan v. Hacker, 113 Cal.App.2d 571, 248 P.2d 464 (1952). See also Dallman v. Dallman, 179 Cal.App.2d 27, 3 Cal.Rptr. 383 (1960) (motion to compel plaintiff to acknowledge partial satisfaction of terms of interlocutory divorce decree). Unlike the procedure for compelling the judgment creditor to deliver an acknowledgment of full satisfaction of judgment, Section 724.110 does not provide a sanction for failure to comply with the demand (compare subdivision (e) of Section 724.050) or for attorney's fees to the prevailing party (compare Section 724.080). [16 Cal.L.Rev.Comm. Reports 1597 (1982)].

Research References

Rutter, Cal. Practice Guide: Enforcing Judgments/Debts Ch. 6K-2, Acknowledgment of Partial Satisfaction of Judgment.
Rutter, Cal. Practice Guide: Personal Injury Ch. 4-D, D. Techniques Where Settlement Not Forthcoming.
Rutter, Cal. Practice Guide: Personal Injury Ch. 4-D, Outline D.
Miller and Starr California Real Estate § 32:58, Satisfaction or Release of the Judgment Lien.
8 Witkin Cal. Proc. 5th Enforcement of Judgment § 393, Acknowledgment of Partial Satisfaction.
5 Witkin, California Summary 10th Torts § 98, Settlement Offsetting Entire Judgment.

§ 724.120. Form and contents of acknowledgment

An acknowledgment of partial satisfaction of judgment shall be made in the same manner and by the same person as an acknowledgment of satisfaction of judgment and shall contain the following information:

(a) The title of the court.

(b) The cause and number of the action.

(c) The names and addresses of the judgment creditor, the judgment debtor, and the assignee of record if any. If an abstract of the judgment has been recorded in any county, the judgment debtor's name shall appear on the acknowledgment of partial satisfaction of judgment as it appears on the abstract of judgment.

(d) The date of entry of judgment and of any renewals of the judgment and where entered in the records of the court.

(e) A statement of the amount received by the judgment creditor in partial satisfaction of the judgment.

(f) A statement whether an abstract of judgment has been recorded in any county and, if so, a statement of each county where the abstract has been recorded and the book and page of the county records where the abstract has been recorded.

(g) A statement whether a notice of judgment lien has been filed in the office of the Secretary of State and, if so, the file number of the notice. *(Added by Stats.1982, c. 1364, p. 5230, § 2, operative July 1, 1983.)*

Law Revision Commission Comments

Section 724.120 is adapted from Section 724.060 which prescribes the contents and manner of execution of an acknowledgment of full satisfaction of judgment. [16 Cal.L.Rev.Comm. Reports 1598 (1982)].

Research References

Miller and Starr California Real Estate § 32:58, Satisfaction or Release of the Judgment Lien.
8 Witkin Cal. Proc. 5th Enforcement of Judgment § 393, Acknowledgment of Partial Satisfaction.

5 Witkin, California Summary 10th Torts § 98, Settlement Offsetting
   Entire Judgment.

CHAPTER 3. ACKNOWLEDGMENT OF SATIS-
FACTION OF MATURED INSTALLMENTS
UNDER INSTALLMENT JUDGMENT

§ 724.210.   Definitions

As used in this chapter:

(a) "Installment judgment" means a money judgment under
which a lien may be created on an interest in real property under
Section 697.320.

(b) "Matured installments" means the sum of all of the
following:

(1) All amounts and installments that have matured under an
installment judgment on or before the date specified in the
demand for an acknowledgment of satisfaction of matured
installments under an installment judgment.

(2) The interest that has accrued on the installment judgment
on the date specified in the demand.

(3) The costs that have been added to the installment
judgment on or before the date specified in the demand pursuant
to Chapter 5 (commencing with Section 685.010) of Division 1.
(Added by Stats.1982, c. 1364, p. 5230, § 2, operative July 1, 1983.)

Law Revision Commission Comments

Section 724.210 is included to provide a convenient reference to the
installment judgments that constitute a judgment lien on real property
under Section 697.320 (judgment for periodic spousal or child support,
judgment against health care provider requiring periodic payments, and
workers' compensation award judgment payable in installments). [16
Cal.L.Rev.Comm. Reports 1598 (1982)].

Research References

Rutter, Cal. Practice Guide: Enforcing Judgments/Debts Ch. 6K-3,
   Acknowledgment of Satisfaction of Matured Installments Under
   Installment Judgment.
Miller and Starr California Real Estate § 32:58, Satisfaction or Release of
   the Judgment Lien.
8 Witkin Cal. Proc. 5th Enforcement of Judgment § 394, (S 394) Demand
   for Acknowledgment.
8 Witkin Cal. Proc. 5th Enforcement of Judgment § 396, (S 396) Liability
   for Failure to Comply.
11 Witkin, California Summary 10th Husband and Wife § 267, (S 267)
   Judgment Lien.

§ 724.220.   Demand for acknowledgment of satisfaction of
matured installments

(a) If real property is subject to a judgment lien created under
an installment judgment, the judgment debtor or the owner of
real property subject to the judgment lien may serve on the
judgment creditor a demand in writing that the judgment
creditor execute, acknowledge, and deliver to the person who
made the demand an acknowledgment of satisfaction of matured
installments under an installment judgment. Service shall be
made personally or by mail.

(b) The demand shall include the following statement: "Important warning. If the matured installments on this judgment
have been satisfied as of date specified in this demand, the law
requires that you comply with this demand not later than 15 days
after you receive it. (The 'matured installments' are all amounts
and installments that are due and payable on or before the date
specified in this demand together with the accrued interest to
that date and costs added to the judgment on or before that
date.) If a court proceeding is necessary to compel you to
comply with this demand, you will be required to pay my
reasonable attorney's fees in the proceeding if the court determines that the matured installments have been satisfied and that
you failed to comply with the demand. In addition, if the court
determines that you failed without just cause to comply with this
demand within the 15 days allowed, you will be liable for all
damages I sustain by reason of such failure and will also forfeit
one hundred dollars to me."

(c) If the matured installments have been satisfied as of the
date specified in the demand, the judgment creditor shall comply
with the demand not later than 15 days after actual receipt of the
demand. *(Added by Stats.1982, c. 1364, p. 5231, § 2, operative
July 1, 1983.)*

Law Revision Commission Comments

Section 724.220 is adapted from subdivisions (a)–(c) of Section 724.050.
If real property is subject to a judgment lien, the acknowledgment of
satisfaction of matured installments permits the judgment debtor or other
owner to transfer the property free of the lien. See Section 697.400(b).
[16 Cal.L.Rev.Comm. Reports 1599 (1982)].

Research References

Rutter, Cal. Practice Guide: Enforcing Judgments/Debts Ch. 6K-3,
   Acknowledgment of Satisfaction of Matured Installments Under
   Installment Judgment.
8 Witkin Cal. Proc. 5th Enforcement of Judgment § 394, (S 394) Demand
   for Acknowledgment.

§ 724.230.   Order requiring compliance with demand

If the judgment creditor does not comply with the demand
within the time allowed, the judgment debtor or the owner of the
real property subject to a judgment lien created under the
installment judgment may apply to the court on noticed motion
for an order requiring the judgment creditor to comply with the
demand. The notice of motion shall be served on the judgment
creditor. Service shall be made personally or by mail. If the
court determines that the matured installments have been
satisfied as of the date specified in the demand and that the
judgment creditor has not complied with the demand, the court
shall either (1) order the judgment creditor to comply with the
demand or (2) make an order determining that the matured
installments as of the date specified in the demand have been
satisfied. *(Added by Stats.1982, c. 1364, p. 5231, § 2, operative
July 1, 1983.)*

Law Revision Commission Comments

Section 724.230 is drawn from subdivision (d) of Section 724.050. [16
Cal.L.Rev.Comm. Reports 1600 (1982)].

Research References

Rutter, Cal. Practice Guide: Enforcing Judgments/Debts Ch. 6K-3,
   Acknowledgment of Satisfaction of Matured Installments Under
   Installment Judgment.
8 Witkin Cal. Proc. 5th Enforcement of Judgment § 394, (S 394) Demand
   for Acknowledgment.
8 Witkin Cal. Proc. 5th Enforcement of Judgment § 396, (S 396) Liability
   for Failure to Comply.

§ 724.240.   Liability of judgment creditor for damages

(a) If the matured installments under the installment judgment have been satisfied as of the date specified in the demand

and the judgment creditor fails without just cause to comply with the demand within the time allowed, the judgment creditor is liable to the person who made the demand for all damages sustained by reason of such failure and shall also forfeit one hundred dollars ($100) to such person. Liability under this subdivision may be determined in the proceedings on a motion pursuant to Section 724.230 or in an action.

(b) The damages recoverable pursuant to subdivision (a) are not in derogation of any other damages or penalties to which an aggrieved person may be entitled by law. *(Added by Stats.1982, c. 1364, p. 5231, § 2, operative July 1, 1983.)*

Law Revision Commission Comments

Section 724.240 is drawn from subdivision (e) of Section 724.050 and from Section 724.090. [16 Cal.L.Rev.Comm. Reports 1600 (1982)].

Research References

Rutter, Cal. Practice Guide: Enforcing Judgments/Debts Ch. 6K-3, Acknowledgment of Satisfaction of Matured Installments Under Installment Judgment.
8 Witkin Cal. Proc. 5th Enforcement of Judgment § 396, (S 396) Liability for Failure to Comply.

§ 724.250. Form and contents of acknowledgment; child or spousal support orders

(a) An acknowledgment of satisfaction of matured installments under an installment judgment shall be made in the same manner and by the same person as an acknowledgment of satisfaction of judgment and shall contain the following information:

(1) The title of the court.

(2) The cause and number of the action.

(3) The names and addresses of the judgment creditor, the judgment debtor, and the assignee of record if any. The judgment debtor's name shall appear on the acknowledgment of satisfaction of matured installments as it appears on the certified copy of the judgment that was recorded to create the judgment lien.

(4) The date of entry of the judgment and of any renewals of the judgment and where entered in the records of the court.

(5) A statement that the matured installments under the installment judgment had been satisfied as of a specified date.

(6) A statement whether a certified copy or abstract of the judgment has been recorded in any county and, if so, a statement of each county where the certified or abstract copy has been recorded and the book and page of the county records where the certified copy or abstract of the judgment has been recorded.

(b) If any amount of child or spousal support provided in a support order has been directed to be made to an officer designated by statute or by the court pursuant to Article 4 (commencing with Section 4200) of Chapter 2 of Part 2 of Division 9 of the Family Code or Chapter 4 (commencing with Section 4350) of Part 3 of Division 9 of the Family Code or any other provision of law and the directive is set forth in the certified copy or abstract of the judgment that was recorded to create the judgment lien on real property, or in a similarly recorded certified copy or abstract of an amended or supplemental order, the acknowledgment of satisfaction of matured installments under the installment judgment is not effective and does not affect the judgment lien unless the acknowledgment is executed by or approved in writing by the designated officer. *(Added by Stats.1982, c. 1364, p. 5232, § 2, operative July 1, 1983. Amended by Stats.1986, c. 946, § 3; Stats.1992, c. 163 (A.B.2641), § 53, operative Jan. 1, 1994.)*

Law Revision Commission Comments

Subdivision (b) of Section 724.250 is amended to substitute a reference to the Family Code provisions that replaced former Civil Code Section 4702. A reference to former Civil Code Section 4801.7, now Chapter 4 (commencing with Section 4350) of Part 3 of Division 9 of the Family Code, has been added to subdivision (b), conforming this section to Code of Civil Procedure Section 704.114. [22 Cal.L.Rev.Comm.Reports 1 (1992)].

Research References

Rutter, Cal. Practice Guide: Enforcing Judgments/Debts Ch. 6K-3, Acknowledgment of Satisfaction of Matured Installments Under Installment Judgment.
Miller and Starr California Real Estate § 32:58, Satisfaction or Release of the Judgment Lien.
8 Witkin Cal. Proc. 5th Enforcement of Judgment § 79, (S 79) Recording Satisfaction of Judgment.
8 Witkin Cal. Proc. 5th Enforcement of Judgment § 395, (S 395) Execution and Content of Acknowledgment.

§ 724.260. Attorney's fees

In an action or proceeding maintained pursuant to this chapter, the court shall award reasonable attorney's fees to the prevailing party. *(Added by Stats.1982, c. 1364, p. 5235, § 2, operative July 1, 1983.)*

Law Revision Commission Comments

Section 724.260 is drawn from Section 724.080. [16 Cal.L.Rev.Comm. Reports 1602 (1982)].

Research References

Rutter, Cal. Practice Guide: Enforcing Judgments/Debts Ch. 6A-2, Enforcement of Judgments Law ("Ejl")-Background.
Rutter, Cal. Practice Guide: Enforcing Judgments/Debts Ch. 6K-3, Acknowledgment of Satisfaction of Matured Installments Under Installment Judgment.
8 Witkin Cal. Proc. 5th Enforcement of Judgment § 396, (S 396) Liability for Failure to Comply.

Title 10

ACTIONS IN PARTICULAR CASES

CHAPTER 1. ACTIONS FOR THE FORECLOSURE OF MORTGAGES

§ 725a. Mortgage or trust deed with power of sale; parties entitled to sue

The beneficiary or trustee named in a deed of trust or mortgagee named in a mortgage with power of sale upon real property or any interest therein to secure a debt or other obligation, or if there be a successor or successors in interest of such beneficiary, trustee or mortgagee, then such successor or successors in interest, shall have the right to bring suit to foreclose the same in the manner and subject to the provisions, rights and remedies relating to the foreclosure of a mortgage upon such property. *(Added by Stats.1933, c. 642, p. 1673, § 7. Re-enacted by Stats.1935, c. 650, p. 1807, § 7. Amended by Stats.1939, c. 584, p. 1990, § 1; Stats.1941, c. 446, p. 1738, § 1; Stats.1982, c. 497, p. 2158, § 45, operative July 1, 1983.)*

Research References

Rutter, Cal. Practice Guide: Civ. Pro. Before Trial Ch. 2-A, A. Standing to Sue-"Real Party in Interest" Requirement.

Rutter, Cal. Practice Guide: Enforcing Judgments/Debts Ch. 1-A, A. Lawyer's Role in Debt Collection Process.

Rutter, Cal. Practice Guide: Enforcing Judgments/Debts Ch. 3-A, A. Evaluating the Claim.

Rutter, Cal. Practice Guide: Enforcing Judgments/Debts Ch. 4-C, C. Receiverships.

Miller and Starr California Real Estate § 10:123, Nature of Foreclosure; Termination of Redemption.

Miller and Starr California Real Estate § 10:124, Choice of Remedies.

Miller and Starr California Real Estate § 10:221, Comparison With Nonjudicial Foreclosure.

Miller and Starr California Real Estate § 10:223, Joinder of Parties.

18 NO. 2 Miller & Starr, California Real Estate Newsalert 1, The Marketable Record Title Act- Is Private Foreclosure Barred Ten Years After Maturity, or Not?

22 NO. 3 Miller & Starr, California Real Estate Newsalert 1, Show Me Your Papers: Sales and Assignments of Secured Real Estate Loans and the California Foreclosure Process.

22 NO. 4 Miller & Starr, California Real Estate Newsalert 1, Show Me Your Papers: Sales and Assignments of Secured Real Estate Loans and the California Foreclosure Process (Part II).

23 NO. 2 Miller & Starr, California Real Estate Newsalert 8, Deeds of Trust.

12 Witkin, California Summary 10th Real Property § 338, Ancient Mortgages and Deeds of Trust.

4 Witkin, California Summary 10th Security Transactions in Real Property § 3, Mortgage.

4 Witkin, California Summary 10th Security Transactions in Real Property § 7, (S 7) Strict Trust Compared and Distinguished.

4 Witkin, California Summary 10th Security Transactions in Real Property § 122, Deed of Trust.

4 Witkin, California Summary 10th Security Transactions in Real Property § 124, (S 124) in General: C.C.P. 726.

4 Witkin, California Summary 10th Security Transactions in Real Property § 137, in General.

4 Witkin, California Summary 10th Security Transactions in Real Property § 179, (S 179) Nature and Scope of Statutes.

4 Witkin, California Summary 10th Security Transactions in Real Property § 207, (S 207) Constitutionality of Restrictions.

8 Witkin, California Summary 10th Constitutional Law § 1287, (S 1287) Valid Changes in Remedy or Procedure.

§ 726. Form of action; procedure; action for borrower fraud

(a) There can be but one form of action for the recovery of any debt or the enforcement of any right secured by mortgage upon real property or an estate for years therein, which action shall be in accordance with the provisions of this chapter. In the action the court may, by its judgment, direct the sale of the encumbered real property or estate for years therein (or so much of the real property or estate for years as may be necessary), and the application of the proceeds of the sale to the payment of the costs of court, the expenses of levy and sale, and the amount due plaintiff, including, where the mortgage provides for the payment of attorney's fees, the sum for attorney's fees as the court shall find reasonable, not exceeding the amount named in the mortgage.

(b) The decree for the foreclosure of a mortgage or deed of trust secured by real property or estate for years therein shall declare the amount of the indebtedness or right so secured and, unless judgment for any deficiency there may be between the sale price and the amount due with costs is waived by the judgment creditor or a deficiency judgment is prohibited by Section 580b, shall determine the personal liability of any defendant for the payment of the debt secured by the mortgage or deed of trust and shall name the defendants against whom a deficiency judgment may be ordered following the proceedings prescribed in this section. In the event of waiver, or if the prohibition of Section 580b is applicable, the decree shall so declare and there shall be no judgment for a deficiency. In the event that a deficiency is not waived or prohibited and it is decreed that any defendant is personally liable for the debt, then upon application of the plaintiff filed at any time within three months of the date of the foreclosure sale and after a hearing thereon at which the court shall take evidence and at which hearing either party may present evidence as to the fair value of the real property or estate for years therein sold as of the date of sale, the court shall render a money judgment against the defendant or defendants for the amount by which the amount of the indebtedness with interest and costs of levy and sale and of action exceeds the fair value of the real property or estate for years therein sold as of the date of sale. In no event shall the amount of the judgment, exclusive of interest from the date of sale and of costs exceed the difference between the amount for which the real property or estate for years therein was sold and the entire amount of the indebtedness secured by the mortgage or deed of trust. Notice of the hearing shall be served upon all defendants who have appeared in the action and against whom a deficiency judgment is sought, or upon their attorneys of record, at least 15 days before the date set for the hearing. Upon application of any party made at least 10 days before the date set for the hearing the court shall, and upon its own motion the court at any time may, appoint one of the probate referees provided for by law to appraise the real property or estate for years therein sold as of the time of sale. The probate referee shall file the appraisal with the clerk and the appraisal is admissible in evidence. The probate referee shall take and subscribe an oath to be attached to the appraisal that the referee has truly, honestly and impartially appraised the real property or estate for years therein to the best of the referee's knowledge and ability. Any probate referee so appointed may be called and examined as a witness by any party or by the court itself. The court shall fix the compensation, in an amount as determined by the court to be reasonable, but the fees shall not exceed similar fees for similar services in the community where the services are rendered, which may be taxed and allowed in like manner as other costs.

(c) No person holding a conveyance from or under the mortgagor of real property or estate for years therein, or having a lien thereon, which conveyance or lien does not appear of record in the proper office at the time of the commencement of the action need be made a party to the action, and the judgment therein rendered, and the proceedings therein had, are as conclusive against the person holding the unrecorded conveyance or lien as if the person had been a party to the action. Notwithstanding Section 701.630, the sale of the encumbered real property or estate for years therein does not affect the interest of a person who holds a conveyance from or under the mortgagor of the real property or estate for years therein mortgaged, or has a lien thereon, if the conveyance or lien appears of record in the proper office at the time of the commencement of the action and the person holding the recorded conveyance or lien is not made a party to the action.

(d) If the real property or estate for years therein mortgaged consists of a single parcel, or two or more parcels, situated in two or more counties, the court may, in its judgment, direct the whole thereof to be sold in one of the counties, and upon these proceedings, and with like effect, as if the whole of the property were situated in that county.

(e) If a deficiency judgment is waived or prohibited, the real property or estate for years therein shall be sold as provided in Section 716.020. If a deficiency judgment is not waived or prohibited, the real property or estate for years therein shall be sold subject to the right of redemption as provided in Sections 729.010 to 729.090, inclusive.

(f) Notwithstanding this section or any other provision of law to the contrary, any person authorized by this state to make or arrange loans secured by real property or any successor in interest thereto, that originates, acquires, or purchases, in whole or in part, any loan secured directly or collaterally, in whole or in part, by a mortgage or deed of trust on real property or an estate for years therein, may bring an action for recovery of damages, including exemplary damages not to exceed 50 percent of the actual damages, against a borrower where the action is based on fraud under Section 1572 of the Civil Code and the fraudulent conduct by the borrower induced the original lender to make that loan.

(g) Subdivision (f) does not apply to loans secured by single-family, owner-occupied residential real property, when the property is actually occupied by the borrower as represented to the lender in order to obtain the loan and the loan is for an amount of one hundred fifty thousand dollars ($150,000) or less, as adjusted annually, commencing on January 1, 1987, to the

Consumer Price Index as published by the United States Department of Labor.

(h) Any action maintained pursuant to subdivision (f) for damages shall not constitute a money judgment for deficiency, or a deficiency judgment within the meaning of Section 580a, 580b, or 580d of the Code of Civil Procedure. *(Enacted in 1872. Amended by Stats.1893, c. 101, p. 118, § 1; Stats.1895, c. 108, p. 99, § 1; Stats.1901, c. 43, p. 48, § 1; Stats.1933, c. 793, p. 2118, § 1; Stats.1937, c. 353, p. 770, § 1; Stats.1963, c. 819, p. 2007, § 26, eff. Jan. 1, 1965; Stats.1967, c. 1003, p. 2594, § 1; Stats.1968, c. 450, p. 1009, § 3; Stats.1970, c. 1282, p. 2321, § 2, eff. July 1, 1971; Stats.1982, c. 497, p. 2158, § 46; Stats.1982, c. 517, p. 2352, § 152; Stats.1982, c. 1535, p. 5966, § 2; Stats.1983, c. 18, § 18, eff. April 21, 1983; Stats.1983, c. 155, § 22, eff. June 30, 1983, operative July 1, 1983; Stats.1987, c. 180, § 1; Stats. 1989, c. 698, § 14; Stats.1992, c. 1095 (A.B.2734), § 4.)*

Law Revision Commission Comments

Section 726 is amended to delete provisions duplicated in the Bond and Undertaking Law. See Sections 995.820 (undertaking by officer of court) and 995.840 (court approval of undertaking). [16 Cal.L.Rev.Comm. Reports 2239 (1982)].

The provisions of Section 726 relating to commissioners appointed to sell real property under a judgment of foreclosure are repealed. Pursuant to Section 712.060 a receiver may be appointed to sell the property under the direction of the court. See also Sections 567 (oath and undertaking of receiver), 568 (powers of receiver), 568.5 (sales by receiver), 708.620 (appointment of receiver). The provisions concerning the qualification and duties of receivers and commissioners were essentially the same under former law. Consequently, special commissioners have been eliminated in favor of the uniform provisions concerning receivers. The provisions of Section 726 concerning elisors are unnecessary. See, e.g., Section 262.8.

A provision for the application of proceeds to satisfy the costs of levy is added to Section 726(a) because Section 716.010 requires levy under a writ of sale if the judgment is enforced by a levying officer.

Subdivision (c) codifies the rule in Carpentier v. Brenham, 40 Cal. 221, 235 (1870), to the effect that the interest of a junior lienholder of record is not affected by the foreclosure of a senior lien if the junior lienholder is not joined.

Subdivision (e) specifies the manner of sale depending upon whether the property is to be sold subject to the right of redemption.

See Chapter 1 (commencing with Section 712.010) and Chapter 4 (commencing with Section 716.010) of Division 3 of Title 9 for provisions governing the enforcement of judgments for sale of real property. [16 Cal.L.Rev.Comm. Reports 2175 (1982)].

Research References

California Real Estate Forms (Miller & Starr) § 3:7, Promissory Note..
California Real Estate Forms (Miller & Starr) § 3:8, Deed of Trust, Security Agreement, and Fixture Filing With Assignment of Rents and Agreements.
California Real Estate Forms (Miller & Starr) § 3:9, Assignment of Lessor's Interest in Leases and Seller's Interest in Contracts for Sale.
California Real Estate Forms (Miller & Starr) § 2:23, Retail Lease--Small Strip-Shopping Center.
California Real Estate Forms (Miller & Starr) § 2:24, Retail Lease--Restaurant.
California Real Estate Forms (Miller & Starr) § 2:36, Consent to Sublease.
California Real Estate Forms (Miller & Starr) § 3:13, Promissory Note Secured by Construction Deed of Trust.
California Real Estate Forms (Miller & Starr) § 3:14, Construction Deed of Trust, Security Agreement, and Fixture Filing With Assignment of Rents and Agreements.
California Real Estate Forms (Miller & Starr) § 3:15, Construction Loan Agreement.
California Real Estate Forms (Miller & Starr) § 3:20, Promissory Note--Conduit Loan.

Civ. Pro.

Civ. Pro.

§ 726.5. Environmental impairment to real property security interest where borrower is in default; remedies of lender

(a) Notwithstanding subdivision (a) of Section 726 or any other provision of law, except subdivision (d) of this section, a secured lender may elect between the following where the real property security is environmentally impaired and the borrower's obligations to the secured lender are in default:

(1)(A) Waiver of its lien against (i) any parcel of real property security that is environmentally impaired or is an affected parcel, and (ii) all or any portion of the fixtures and personal property attached to the parcels; and

(B) Exercise of (i) the rights and remedies of an unsecured creditor, including reduction of its claim against the borrower to judgment, and (ii) any other rights and remedies permitted by law.

(2) Exercise of (i) the rights and remedies of a creditor secured by a deed of trust or mortgage and, if applicable, a lien against fixtures or personal property attached to the real property security, and (ii) any other rights and remedies permitted by law.

(b) Before the secured lender may waive its lien against any parcel of real property security pursuant to paragraph (1) of subdivision (a) on the basis of the environmental impairment contemplated by paragraph (3) of subdivision (e), (i) the secured lender shall provide written notice of the default to the borrower, and (ii) the value of the subject real property security shall be established and its environmentally impaired status shall be confirmed by an order of a court of competent jurisdiction in an action brought by the secured lender against the borrower. The complaint for a valuation and confirmation action may include causes of action for a money judgment for all or part of the secured obligation, in which case the waiver of the secured lender's liens under paragraph (1) of subdivision (a) shall result only if and when a final money judgment is obtained against the borrower.

(c) If a secured lender elects the rights and remedies permitted by paragraph (1) of subdivision (a) and the borrower's obligations are also secured by other real property security, fixtures, or personal property, the secured lender shall first foreclose against the additional collateral to the extent required by applicable law in which case the amount of the judgment of the secured lender pursuant to paragraph (1) of subdivision (a) shall be limited to the extent Section 580a or 580d, or subdivision (b) of Section 726 apply to the foreclosures of additional real property security. The borrower may waive or modify the foreclosure requirements of this subdivision provided that the waiver or modification is in writing and signed by the borrower after default.

(d) Subdivision (a) shall be inapplicable if all of the following are true:

(1) The release or threatened release was not knowingly or negligently caused or contributed to, or knowingly or willfully permitted or acquiesced to, by any of the following:

(A) The borrower or any related party.

(B) Any affiliate or agent of the borrower or any related party.

(2) In conjunction with the making, renewal, or modification of the loan, extension of credit, guaranty, or other obligation secured by the real property security, neither the borrower, any related party, nor any affiliate or agent of either the borrower or any related party had actual knowledge or notice of the release or threatened release, or if a person had knowledge or notice of the release or threatened release, the borrower made written disclosure thereof to the secured lender after the secured lender's written request for information concerning the environmental condition of the real property security, or the secured lender otherwise obtained actual knowledge thereof, prior to the making, renewal, or modification of the obligation.

(e) For purposes of this section:

(1) "Affected parcel" means any portion of a parcel of real property security that is (A) contiguous to the environmentally impaired parcel, even if separated by roads, streets, utility easements, or railroad rights-of-way, (B) part of an approved or proposed subdivision within the meaning of Section 66424 of the Government Code, of which the environmentally impaired parcel is also a part, or (C) within 2,000 feet of the environmentally impaired parcel.

(2) "Borrower" means the trustor under a deed of trust, or a mortgagor under a mortgage, where the deed of trust or mortgage encumbers real property security and secures the performance of the trustor or mortgagor under a loan, extension of credit, guaranty, or other obligation. The term includes any successor-in-interest of the trustor or mortgagor to the real property security before the deed of trust or mortgage has been discharged, reconveyed, or foreclosed upon.

(3) "Environmentally impaired" means that the estimated costs to clean up and remediate a past or present release or threatened release of any hazardous substance into, onto, beneath, or from the real property security, not disclosed in writing to, or otherwise actually known by, the secured lender prior to the making of the loan or extension of credit secured by the real property security, exceeds 25 percent of the higher of the aggregate fair market value of all security for the loan or extension of credit (A) at the time of the making of the loan or extension of credit, or (B) at the time of the discovery of the release or threatened release by the secured lender. For the purposes of this definition, the estimated cost to clean up and remediate the contamination caused by the release or threatened release shall include only those costs that would be incurred reasonably and in good faith, and fair market value shall be determined without giving consideration to the release or threatened release, and shall be exclusive of the amount of all liens and encumbrances against the security that are senior in priority to the lien of the secured lender. Notwithstanding the foregoing, the real property security for any loan or extension of credit secured by a single parcel of real property which is included in the National Priorities List pursuant to Section 9605 of Title 42 of the United States Code, or in any list published by the Department of Toxic Substances Control pursuant to subdivision (b) of Section 25356 of the Health and Safety Code, shall be deemed to be environmentally impaired.

(4) "Hazardous substance" means any of the following:

(A) Any "hazardous substance" as defined in subdivision (h) of Section 25281 of the Health and Safety Code.

(B) Any "waste" as defined in subdivision (d) of Section 13050 of the Water Code.

(C) Petroleum, including crude oil or any fraction thereof, natural gas, natural gas liquids, liquefied natural gas, or synthetic gas usable for fuel, or any mixture thereof.

(5) "Real property security" means any real property and improvements, other than a separate interest and any related interest in the common area of a residential common interest development, as the terms "separate interest," "common area," and "common interest development" are defined in Sections 4095, 4100, and 4185 of the Civil Code, or real property which contains only 1 to 15 dwelling units, which in either case (A) is solely used (i) for residential purposes, or (ii) if reasonably contemplated by the parties to the deed of trust or mortgage, for residential purposes as well as limited agricultural or commercial purposes incidental thereto, and (B) is the subject of an issued certificate of occupancy unless the dwelling is to be owned and occupied by the borrower.

(6) "Related party" means any person who shares an ownership interest with the borrower in the real property security, or is a partner or joint venturer with the borrower in a partnership or joint venture, the business of which includes the acquisition, development, use, lease, or sale of the real property security.

(7) "Release" means any spilling, leaking, pumping, pouring, emitting, emptying, discharging, injecting, escaping, leaching, dumping, or disposing into the environment, including continu-

ing migration, of hazardous substances into, onto, or through soil, surface water, or groundwater. The term does not include actions directly relating to the incorporation in a lawful manner of building materials into a permanent improvement to the real property security.

(8) "Secured lender" means the beneficiary under a deed of trust against the real property security, or the mortgagee under a mortgage against the real property security, and any successor-in-interest of the beneficiary or mortgagee to the deed of trust or mortgage.

(f) This section shall not be construed to invalidate or otherwise affect in any manner any rights or obligations arising under contract in connection with a loan or extension of credit, including, without limitation, provisions limiting recourse.

(g) This section shall only apply to loans, extensions of credit, guaranties, or other obligations secured by real property security made, renewed, or modified on or after January 1, 1992. *(Added by Stats.1991, c. 1167 (A.B.1735), § 3. Amended by Stats.1992, c. 167 (A.B.2750), § 3; Stats.1999, c. 60 (S.B.328), § 1; Stats.2002, c. 999 (A.B.2481), § 4; Stats.2012, c. 181 (A.B.806), § 45, operative Jan. 1, 2014.)*

Law Revision Commission Comments

Section 726.5 is amended to correct cross-references to former Civil Code Section 1351(b), (c), (*l*). [40 Cal.L.Rev.Comm. Reports 235 (2010)].

Research References

California Real Estate Forms (Miller & Starr) § 3:7, Promissory Note.
California Real Estate Forms (Miller & Starr) § 3:8, Deed of Trust, Security Agreement, and Fixture Filing With Assignment of Rents and Agreements.
California Real Estate Forms (Miller & Starr) § 3:10, Environmental Certification, Agreement, and Indemnity of Borrower.
California Real Estate Forms (Miller & Starr) § 3:13, Promissory Note Secured by Construction Deed of Trust.
California Real Estate Forms (Miller & Starr) § 3:14, Construction Deed of Trust, Security Agreement, and Fixture Filing With Assignment of Rents and Agreements.
California Real Estate Forms (Miller & Starr) § 3:21, Deed of Trust, Assignment of Rents, Security Agreement and Fixture Filing-- Conduit Loan.
California Real Estate Forms (Miller & Starr) § 3:30, Environmental Indemnity--Conduit Loan.
Rutter, Cal. Practice Guide: Real Prop. Transactions Ch. 6-K, K. Environmental Indemnities.
Rutter, Cal. Practice Guide: Real Prop. Transactions Form 6:I, Deed of Trust (Complex).
Rutter, Cal. Practice Guide: Real Prop. Transactions Form 9:A, Sample Opinion Letter (By Borrower's Counsel).
Miller and Starr California Real Estate § 10:156, Waiver; Trustor's Election.
Miller and Starr California Real Estate § 10:157, Exception; Environmentally Impaired Property.
4 Witkin, California Summary 10th Security Transactions in Real Property § 208, (S 208) Nature and Scope of Legislation.
4 Witkin, California Summary 10th Security Transactions in Real Property § 210, (S 210) Waiver of Lien.

§ 727. Surplus; deposit in court; payment

SURPLUS MONEY TO BE DEPOSITED IN COURT. If there be surplus money remaining, after payment of the amount due on the mortgage, lien, or incumbrance, with costs, the Court may cause the same to be paid to the person entitled to it, and in the meantime may direct it to be deposited in Court. *(Enacted in 1872.)*

Research References

Miller and Starr California Real Estate § 10:225, Foreclosure Decree.
8 Witkin Cal. Proc. 5th Enforcement of Judgment § 62, (S 62) Property in Custody of Law.

§ 728. Proceedings when debt secured is not all due

PROCEEDINGS WHEN DEBT SECURED FALLS DUE AT DIFFERENT TIMES. If the debt for which the mortgage, lien, or incumbrance is held is not all due, as soon as sufficient of the property has been sold to pay the amount due, with costs, the sale must cease; and afterwards, as often as more becomes due, for principal or interest, the Court may, on motion, order more to be sold. But if the property cannot be sold in portions, without injury to the parties, the whole may be ordered to be sold in the first instance, and the entire debt and costs paid, there being a rebate of interest where such rebate is proper. *(Enacted in 1872.)*

Research References

Miller and Starr California Real Estate § 10:103, Acceleration on Default; Validity.

§ 729.010. Sale subject to right of redemption; procedure; notice of sale

(a) If the decree of foreclosure of a mortgage or deed of trust on real property pursuant to Section 726 determines that a deficiency judgment may be ordered against the defendant, the real property (other than a leasehold estate with an unexpired term of less than two years at the time of levy) shall be sold subject to the right of redemption.

(b) If the property is to be sold subject to the right of redemption, the sale is governed by Section 716.020, except that:

(1) The notice of sale of the property shall state that the property will be sold subject to the right of redemption and shall state the amount of the secured indebtedness with interest and costs.

(2) Notice of sale may be given upon entry of the judgment for sale of the property and the provision of Section 701.545 delaying notice of sale does not apply.

(3) Notice of sale may be given to persons having liens on the property upon entry of the judgment for sale of the property and the provision of subdivision (h) of Section 701.540 delaying such notice does not apply. *(Added by Stats.1982, c. 497, p. 2160, § 48, operative July 1, 1983.)*

Research References

Rutter, Cal. Practice Guide: Enforcing Judgments/Debts Ch. 6D-7, Sale and Collection of Property Levied Upon.
Rutter, Cal. Practice Guide: Real Prop. Transactions Ch. 6-I, I. Real Property Foreclosures and Antideficiency Laws.
Miller and Starr California Real Estate § 18:7, The Unclaimed Property Law--Property Unclaimed or Abandoned.
Miller and Starr California Real Estate § 32:73, Attack on Validity of Sale.
Miller and Starr California Real Estate § 10:226, The Judicial Sale.
Miller and Starr California Real Estate § 10:227, Statutory Redemption; Who Can Redeem.
Miller and Starr California Real Estate § 25B:93, Foreclosure of Lien by Sale; Redemption Rights.
16 NO. 2 Miller & Starr, California Real Estate Newsalert 1, Trustee Sales: the "Terminator" of Debtors' Equities.
16 NO. 3 Miller & Starr, California Real Estate Newsalert 1, Assessment Liens and Foreclosure in Common Interest Developments.
8 Witkin Cal. Proc. 5th Enforcement of Judgment § 20, Redemption.
4 Witkin, California Summary 10th Security Transactions in Real Property § 143, Manner of Sale.

4 Witkin, California Summary 10th Security Transactions in Real Property § 233, (S 233) Scope and Manner of Exercise.

§ 729.020. Parties who may redeem

Property sold subject to the right of redemption may be redeemed only by the judgment debtor or the judgment debtor's successor in interest. For the purpose of this article, the purchaser of the property at the foreclosure sale is not a successor in interest. *(Added by Stats.1982, c. 497, p. 2160, § 49, operative July 1, 1983.)*

Research References

Rutter, Cal. Practice Guide: Enforcing Judgments/Debts Ch. 6B-2, Interests Subject to Judgment Lien.
Miller and Starr California Real Estate § 10:227, Statutory Redemption; Who Can Redeem.
4 Witkin, California Summary 10th Security Transactions in Real Property § 233, (S 233) Scope and Manner of Exercise.

§ 729.030. Redemption period

The redemption period during which property may be redeemed from a foreclosure sale under this chapter ends:

(a) Three months after the date of sale if the proceeds of the sale are sufficient to satisfy the secured indebtedness with interest and costs of action and of sale.

(b) One year after the date of sale if the proceeds of the sale are not sufficient to satisfy the secured indebtedness with interest and costs of action and of sale. *(Added by Stats.1982, c. 497, p. 2160, § 50, operative July 1, 1983.)*

Research References

Rutter, Cal. Practice Guide: Enforcing Judgments/Debts Ch. 6B-2, Interests Subject to Judgment Lien.
Miller and Starr California Real Estate § 10:228, Procedure for Redemption.
16 NO. 2 Miller & Starr, California Real Estate Newsalert 1, Trustee Sales: the "Terminator" of Debtors' Equities.
4 Witkin, California Summary 10th Security Transactions in Real Property § 233, (S 233) Scope and Manner of Exercise.

§ 729.035. Sales of a separate interest in a common interest development; right of redemption

Notwithstanding any provision of law to the contrary, the sale of a separate interest in a common interest development is subject to the right of redemption within 90 days after the sale if the sale arises from a foreclosure by the association of a common interest development pursuant to Sections 5700, 5710, and 5735 of the Civil Code, subject to the conditions of Sections 5705, 5715, and 5720 of the Civil Code. *(Added by Stats.2005, c. 452 (S.B.137), § 8. Amended by Stats.2012, c. 181 (A.B.806), § 46, operative Jan. 1, 2014.)*

Law Revision Commission Comments

Section 729.035 is amended to correct cross-references to former Civil Code Sections 1367.1 and 1367.4. [40 Cal.L.Rev.Comm. Reports 235 (2010)].

Research References

Rutter, Cal. Practice Guide: Real Prop. Transactions Ch. 6-I, I. Real Property Foreclosures and Antideficiency Laws.
Miller and Starr California Real Estate § 10:179, Nature and Basis of Power of Sale.
Miller and Starr California Real Estate § 10:197, Mode of Redemption.
Miller and Starr California Real Estate § 10:219, Redemption After Trustee's Sale.
Miller and Starr California Real Estate § 10:228, Procedure for Redemption.
Miller and Starr California Real Estate § 10:230, Possession and Rents During the Redemption Period.
16 NO. 3 Miller & Starr, California Real Estate Newsalert 1, Assessment Liens and Foreclosure in Common Interest Developments.

16 NO. 4 Miller & Starr, California Real Estate Newsalert 19, Subdivisions.
16 NO. 5 Miller & Starr, California Real Estate Newsalert 26. State Board of Equalization Issues Comprehensive Summary and Qs and As for Transfers of Base Year Values of Principal Residences State Board of Equalization Issues Comprehensive Summary and Qs and As for Transfers of...
21 NO. 6 Miller & Starr, California Real Estate Newsalert 5, Common Interest Developments.
12 Witkin, California Summary 10th Real Property § 112, (S 112) Liens.

§ 729.040. Sale of real property sold subject to a right of redemption; certificate of sale; contents

(a) Notwithstanding Section 701.660, when the purchaser of an interest in real property sold subject to the right of redemption pays the amount due, the levying officer conducting the sale shall execute and deliver a certificate of sale to the purchaser and record a duplicate of the certificate of sale in the office of the county recorder.

(b) The certificate of sale shall contain either:

(1) In the case of a judicial foreclosure, the information required by Section 701.670.

(2) In the case of a nonjudicial foreclosure, all of the information required by subdivisions (c), (d), and (e) of Section 701.670.

(c) In addition to the information required by subdivision (b), the certificate of sale shall also contain the following:

(1) The price paid for each distinct lot or parcel of real property sold subject to the right of redemption.

(2) The total price paid.

(3) A statement that the property is subject to the right of redemption, indicating the applicable redemption period. *(Added by Stats.1982, c. 497, p. 2160, § 51, operative July 1, 1983. Amended by Stats.2006, c. 575 (A.B.2624), § 6.)*

Research References

Rutter, Cal. Practice Guide: Real Prop. Transactions Ch. 13(I)-E, E. Property Tax Valuation of Purchased Property.
Miller and Starr California Real Estate § 10:226, The Judicial Sale.
Miller and Starr California Real Estate § 10:228, Procedure for Redemption.
17 NO. 4 Miller & Starr, California Real Estate Newsalert 2, Statutory Update:.
17 NO. 6 Miller & Starr, California Real Estate Newsalert 20, Table of Statutes (Newsalert Vol 17).
9 Witkin, California Summary 10th Taxation § 151, in General.
4 Witkin, California Summary 10th Security Transactions in Real Property § 233, (S 233) Scope and Manner of Exercise.

§ 729.050. Property sold subject to right of redemption; notice to judgment debtor

If property is sold subject to the right of redemption, promptly after the sale the levying officer or trustee who conducted the sale shall serve notice of the right of redemption on the judgment debtor. Service shall be made personally or by mail. The notice of the right of redemption shall indicate the applicable redemption period. *(Added by Stats.1982, c. 497, p. 2161, § 52, operative July 1, 1983. Amended by Stats.2006, c. 575 (A.B.2624), § 7.)*

Research References

Miller and Starr California Real Estate § 10:226, The Judicial Sale.
Miller and Starr California Real Estate § 10:228, Procedure for Redemption.
16 NO. 3 Miller & Starr, California Real Estate Newsalert 1, Assessment Liens and Foreclosure in Common Interest Developments.
17 NO. 4 Miller & Starr, California Real Estate Newsalert 2, Statutory Update:.

17 NO. 6 Miller & Starr, California Real Estate Newsalert 20, Table of Statutes (Newsalert Vol 17).

4 Witkin, California Summary 10th Security Transactions in Real Property § 233, (S 233) Scope and Manner of Exercise.

§ 729.060. Redemption; procedure; redemption price; offset for rents and profits

(a) A person who seeks to redeem the property shall deposit the redemption price with the levying officer who conducted the sale before the expiration of the redemption period. If a successor in interest to the judgment debtor seeks to redeem the property, the successor in interest shall, at the time the redemption price is deposited, file with the levying officer either (1) a certified copy of a recorded conveyance or (2) a copy of an assignment or any other evidence of the interest verified by an affidavit of the successor in interest or of a subscribing witness thereto.

(b) The redemption price is the total of the following amounts, less any offset allowed under subdivision (c).

(1) The purchase price at the sale.

(2) The amount of any assessments or taxes and reasonable amounts for fire insurance, maintenance, upkeep, and repair of improvements on the property.

(3) Any amount paid by the purchaser on a prior obligation secured by the property to the extent that the payment was necessary for the protection of the purchaser's interest.

(4) Interest on the amounts described in paragraphs (1), (2), and (3) at the rate of interest on money judgments from the time such amount was paid until the date the deposit is made.

(5) If the purchaser at the sale has any liens subordinate to the lien under which the property was sold, the amount of the purchaser's lien, plus interest at the rate of interest on money judgments from the date of the sale until the date the deposit is made.

(c) Rents and profits from the property paid to the purchaser or the value of the use and occupation of the property to the purchaser may be offset against the amounts described in subdivision (b). *(Added by Stats.1982, c. 497, p. 2161, § 53, operative July 1, 1983. Amended by Stats.1984, c. 538, § 32.5.)*

Research References

Miller and Starr California Real Estate § 18:7, The Unclaimed Property Law--Property Unclaimed or Abandoned.

Miller and Starr California Real Estate § 10:179, Nature and Basis of Power of Sale.

Miller and Starr California Real Estate § 10:197, Mode of Redemption.

Miller and Starr California Real Estate § 10:219, Redemption After Trustee's Sale.

Miller and Starr California Real Estate § 10:228, Procedure for Redemption.

Miller and Starr California Real Estate § 10:230, Possession and Rents During the Redemption Period.

16 NO. 2 Miller & Starr, California Real Estate Newsalert 1, Trustee Sales: the "Terminator" of Debtors' Equities.

16 NO. 3 Miller & Starr, California Real Estate Newsalert 1, Assessment Liens and Foreclosure in Common Interest Developments.

21 NO. 6 Miller & Starr, California Real Estate Newsalert 5, Common Interest Developments.

4 Witkin, California Summary 10th Security Transactions in Real Property § 170, (S 170) Possession, Rents, and Profits.

4 Witkin, California Summary 10th Security Transactions in Real Property § 233, (S 233) Scope and Manner of Exercise.

§ 729.070. Redemption price; disagreement between purchaser and redeemer; court order; petition; hearing

(a) If the purchaser and the person seeking to redeem the property disagree on the redemption price or as to whether the person is entitled to redeem the property, or if the purchaser refuses the tender of the redemption price pursuant to Section 729.080, the person seeking to redeem may file a petition with the court for an order determining the redemption price or whether the person is entitled to redeem the property. The petition shall be filed before the expiration of the redemption period. At the time the petition is filed, the petitioner shall deposit the undisputed amount of the redemption price with the levying officer, if deposit has not previously been made, and give written notice to the levying officer or trustee of the filing of the petition.

(b) The petition shall be in writing and shall include the following statements:

(1) The amounts demanded to which the person seeking to redeem objects and the reasons for the objection.

(2) Any amounts offset to which the purchaser objects and the justification for the offset.

(3) The status of the petitioner that qualifies the petitioner to redeem the property. A copy of the papers required by subdivision (a) of Section 729.060 shall be filed with the petition.

(c) The hearing on the petition shall be held not later than 20 days after the date the petition was filed unless continued by the court for good cause.

(d) Not less than 10 days before the hearing, the person seeking to redeem the property shall personally serve on the purchaser a copy of the petition together with a notice of the time and place of the hearing.

(e) At the hearing on the petition, the person seeking to redeem the property has the burden of proof.

(f) At the conclusion of the hearing, the court shall determine by order the amount required to redeem the property. The determination shall be made upon affidavit or evidence satisfactory to the court.

(g) If an amount in addition to that deposited with the levying officer is required to redeem the property, the person seeking to redeem shall, within 10 days after the issuance of the order, pay the additional amount to the levying officer. *(Added by Stats. 1982, c. 497, p. 2161, § 54, operative July 1, 1983. Amended by Stats.2006, c. 575 (A.B.2624), § 8.)*

Research References

Miller and Starr California Real Estate § 10:179, Nature and Basis of Power of Sale.

Miller and Starr California Real Estate § 10:197, Mode of Redemption.

Miller and Starr California Real Estate § 10:219, Redemption After Trustee's Sale.

Miller and Starr California Real Estate § 10:228, Procedure for Redemption.

Miller and Starr California Real Estate § 10:230, Possession and Rents During the Redemption Period.

Miller and Starr California Real Estate § 25B:93, Foreclosure of Lien by Sale; Redemption Rights.

16 NO. 3 Miller & Starr, California Real Estate Newsalert 1, Assessment Liens and Foreclosure in Common Interest Developments.

17 NO. 4 Miller & Starr, California Real Estate Newsalert 2, Statutory Update:.

17 NO. 6 Miller & Starr, California Real Estate Newsalert 20, Table of Statutes (Newsalert Vol 17).

12 Witkin, California Summary 10th Real Property § 112, (S 112) Liens.

4 Witkin, California Summary 10th Security Transactions in Real Property § 233, (S 233) Scope and Manner of Exercise.

§ 729.080. Procedure upon deposit or non-deposit of redemption price; refusal of tender; effect of redemption

(a) If the redemption price is not deposited pursuant to Section 729.060 before the expiration of the redemption period, or if no additional deposit is made pursuant to subdivision (g) of Section 729.070 before the expiration of the time provided, the levying officer who conducted the sale shall promptly execute and deliver to the purchaser a deed of sale that complies with the requirements of Section 701.670, or the nonjudicial foreclosure trustee pursuant to Section 729.035 shall deliver an executed trustee's deed and comply with the requirements of Section 2924j of the Civil Code.

(b) If the person seeking to redeem the property deposits the redemption price pursuant to Section 729.060 or 729.070 during the redemption period, the levying officer shall tender the deposit to the purchaser. If the purchaser accepts the tender or if the redemption price determined by court order is tendered, the levying officer or trustee shall promptly execute and deliver a certificate of redemption to the person seeking to redeem and shall immediately record a duplicate of the certificate in the office of the recorder of the county where the property is located.

(c) Tender of the redemption price determined by court order or agreed upon by the purchaser and the person seeking to redeem the property is equivalent to payment. If the tender is refused, the levying officer shall deposit the amount tendered with the county treasurer of the county where the property is located, payable to the order of the purchaser. If the amount deposited is not claimed by the purchaser, or the legal representative of the purchaser, within five years after the deposit is made, by making application to the treasurer or other official designated by the county, it shall be paid into the general fund of the county.

(d) Except as provided in subdivision (e), upon redemption the effect of the sale is terminated and the person who redeemed the property is restored to the estate therein sold at the sale.

(e) Liens extinguished by the sale, as provided in Section 701.630, do not reattach to the property after redemption, and the property that was subject to the extinguished lien may not be applied to the satisfaction of the claim or judgment under which the lien was created. *(Added by Stats.1982, c. 497, p. 2162, § 55, operative July 1, 1983. Amended by Stats.2006, c. 575 (A.B.2624), § 9.)*

Research References

Miller and Starr California Real Estate § 11:6, Instruments Subject to Recording--List of Recordable Documents.
Miller and Starr California Real Estate § 18:7, The Unclaimed Property Law--Property Unclaimed or Abandoned.
Miller and Starr California Real Estate § 10:228, Procedure for Redemption.
Miller and Starr California Real Estate § 10:229, Effect of Redemption.
Miller and Starr California Real Estate § 10:231, Sheriff's Deed; Purchaser's Title.
Miller and Starr California Real Estate § 11:100, Priority of the Purchaser's Title from a Foreclosure Sale.
16 NO. 3 Miller & Starr, California Real Estate Newsalert 1, Assessment Liens and Foreclosure in Common Interest Developments.
17 NO. 4 Miller & Starr, California Real Estate Newsalert 2, Statutory Update:.
17 NO. 6 Miller & Starr, California Real Estate Newsalert 20, Table of Statutes (Newsalert Vol 17).
4 Witkin, California Summary 10th Security Transactions in Real Property § 233, (S 233) Scope and Manner of Exercise.

§ 729.090.   Rents and profits; purchaser's right of entry

(a) From the time of the sale until a redemption, the purchaser is entitled to receive from the person in possession the rents and profits from the property or the value of the use and occupation of the property.

(b) Notwithstanding subdivision (a), the purchaser is liable to the person who redeems for any rents or profits that have been received by the purchaser pursuant to subdivision (a).

(c) The purchaser, from the time of sale until redemption, is entitled to enter the property during reasonable hours to repair and maintain the premises and is entitled to an order restraining waste on the property from the court. Such order may be granted with or without notice in the discretion of the court. *(Added by Stats.1982, c. 497, p. 2163, § 56, operative July 1, 1983.)*

Research References

Rutter, Cal. Practice Guide: Enforcing Judgments/Debts Ch. 6D-7, Sale and Collection of Property Levied Upon.
Rutter, Cal. Practice Guide: Real Prop. Transactions Ch. 6-I, I. Real Property Foreclosures and Antideficiency Laws.
Miller and Starr California Real Estate § 32:73, Attack on Validity of Sale.
Miller and Starr California Real Estate § 10:226, The Judicial Sale.
Miller and Starr California Real Estate § 10:227, Statutory Redemption; Who Can Redeem.
Miller and Starr California Real Estate § 10:230, Possession and Rents During the Redemption Period.
Miller and Starr California Real Estate § 25B:93, Foreclosure of Lien by Sale; Redemption Rights.
21 NO. 6 Miller & Starr, California Real Estate Newsalert 5, Common Interest Developments.
4 Witkin, California Summary 10th Security Transactions in Real Property § 170, (S 170) Possession, Rents, and Profits.

§ 730.   Attorney's fees fixed by court

In all cases of foreclosure of mortgage the attorney's fee shall be fixed by the court in which the proceedings are had, any stipulation in the mortgage to the contrary notwithstanding. *(Added by Stats.1953, c. 52, p. 697, § 4.)*

Research References

Rutter, Cal. Practice Guide: Real Prop. Transactions Ch. 6-F, F. Promissory Note.
Rutter, Cal. Practice Guide: Real Prop. Transactions Ch. 6-H, H. Security for Promissory Note.
Rutter, Cal. Practice Guide: Real Prop. Transactions Ch. 6-H Outline, Outline H.
Miller and Starr California Real Estate § 10:225, Foreclosure Decree.
7 Witkin Cal. Proc. 5th Judgment § 230, (S 230) Actions Involving Real Property or Environmental Issues.
4 Witkin, California Summary 10th Security Transactions in Real Property § 142, Pleading and Decree.

§ 730.5.   Security interests in personal property or fixtures; applicability of certain sections

Except as otherwise provided by Section 9604 of the Commercial Code, none of the provisions of this chapter or of Section 580a, 580b, 580c, or 580d applies to any security interest in personal property or fixtures governed by the Commercial Code. *(Added by Stats.1980, c. 1156, p. 3857, § 1. Amended by Stats.1992, c. 1095 (A.B.2734), § 5; Stats.1999, c. 991 (S.B.45), § 25, operative July 1, 2001.)*

Research References

Miller and Starr California Real Estate § 17:7, UCC Provisions, Generally.
Miller and Starr California Real Estate § 10:170, Enforcement of a Personal Property Lien.
Miller and Starr California Real Estate § 10:172, Beneficiary's Alternative Remedies.

CHAPTER 2. ACTIONS FOR NUISANCE, WASTE, AND WILLFUL TRESPASS, IN CERTAIN CASES, ON REAL PROPERTY

Section

Section

731c.   Nuisance; injury to oil or gas wells or formations as result of secondary recovery operations.

731.5.   Public trails; closure; injunction; attorney's fees; costs.

732.   Waste; parties to action; right of action; treble damages.

733.   Trespass; cutting, carrying off, or injuring trees; treble damages.

734.   Trespass; cutting, carrying off, or injuring trees; actual damages for timber from uncultivated woodland for certain purposes.

735.   Forcible or unlawful entry; treble damages.

736.   Breach of environmental provision; remedies; damages; applicability of section; definitions.

§ 731. Nuisance; action to abate, damages; parties authorized to sue; public nuisance

An action may be brought by any person whose property is injuriously affected, or whose personal enjoyment is lessened by a nuisance, as defined in Section 3479 of the Civil Code, and by the judgment in that action the nuisance may be enjoined or abated as well as damages recovered therefor. A civil action may be brought in the name of the people of the State of California to abate a public nuisance, as defined in Section 3480 of the Civil Code, by the district attorney or county counsel of any county in which the nuisance exists, or by the city attorney of any town or city in which the nuisance exists. Each of those officers shall have concurrent right to bring an action for a public nuisance existing within a town or city. The district attorney, county counsel, or city attorney of any county or city in which the nuisance exists shall bring an action whenever directed by the board of supervisors of the county, or whenever directed by the legislative authority of the town or city. *(Enacted in 1872. Amended by Stats.1905, c. 128, p. 130, § 1; Stats.2010, c. 570 (A.B.1502), § 2.)*

Research References

Miller and Starr California Real Estate § 14:5, Remedies--Injunction.

Miller and Starr California Real Estate § 15:72, Remedies for Interference With the Use of an Easement.

Miller and Starr California Real Estate § 22:11, Indecent or Offensive Acts--Adult Entertainment; First Amendment Protection.

Miller and Starr California Real Estate § 22:19, Alternative Remedies.

Miller and Starr California Real Estate § 22:28, Actions by Public Entities.

21 NO. 4 Miller & Starr, California Real Estate Newsalert 15, Landowners' Liability.

4 Witkin Cal. Proc. 5th Pleading § 170, (S 170) Other Examples.

13 Witkin, California Summary 10th Equity § 133, (S 133) Statutory Framework.

13 Witkin, California Summary 10th Equity § 153, (S 153) Against Private Nuisance.

13 Witkin, California Summary 10th Equity § 154, Abatement and Injunction.

13 Witkin, California Summary 10th Equity § 155, Action by State for Damages.

§ 731a. Nuisance; uses in industrial, commercial or airport zones; restriction on right of abatement

Whenever any city, city and county, or county shall have established zones or districts under authority of law wherein certain manufacturing or commercial or airport uses are expressly permitted, except in an action to abate a public nuisance brought in the name of the people of the State of California, no person or persons, firm or corporation shall be enjoined or restrained by the injunctive process from the reasonable and necessary operation in any such industrial or commercial zone or airport of any use expressly permitted therein, nor shall such use be deemed a nuisance without evidence of the employment of

unnecessary and injurious methods of operation. Nothing in this act shall be deemed to apply to the regulation and working hours of canneries, fertilizing plants, refineries and other similar establishments whose operation produce offensive odors. *(Added by Stats.1935, c. 511, p. 1584, § 1. Amended by Stats.1947, c. 913, p. 2112, § 1; Stats.1959, c. 795, p. 2808, § 2.)*

Research References

Miller and Starr California Real Estate § 22:7, Nuisance Because of Location.

Miller and Starr California Real Estate § 3:44, Negligence Liability--Duty to Inspect Property Being Sold.

Miller and Starr California Real Estate § 1:144, Duty of Seller of Real Property to Disclose--Statutory Duty of Disclosure.

Miller and Starr California Real Estate § 22:33, in General; Coming to the Nuisance.

Miller and Starr California Real Estate § 22:34, Compliance With Zoning Law.

Miller and Starr California Real Estate § 24:26, Rights of Enforcement--Remedies for Breach.

12 Witkin, California Summary 10th Real Property § 440, California Law.

12 Witkin, California Summary 10th Real Property § 493, (S 493) Military, Industrial, and Airport Influences.

13 Witkin, California Summary 10th Equity § 136, (S 136) Trespass Distinguished.

13 Witkin, California Summary 10th Equity § 165, (S 165) Zoning Regulations.

§ 731b. Nuisance; airport or airpark; presumption; prima facie evidence

In any action or proceeding to abate the use of an airport or an airpark, proof that the airport or airpark has been in existence for three years constitutes a rebuttable presumption which shall be prima facie evidence that the operation of the airport or airpark does not constitute a nuisance. *(Added by Stats.1953, c. 52, p. 697, § 5.)*

§ 731c. Nuisance; injury to oil or gas wells or formations as result of secondary recovery operations

Injury to formations bearing oil or gas or to oil or gas wells caused by the subsurface migration of any substance as a result of secondary recovery operations for oil or gas conducted in accordance with good oilfield practices shall not be grounds for enjoining the secondary recovery operations if an undertaking is given for the payment of any compensable damages to which the owners of interests in the formations or wells may be entitled resulting from the injury. Any benefit to the injured property from the secondary recovery operation shall be considered in mitigation of damages for the injury. *(Added by Stats.1961, c. 2200, p. 4545, § 1. Amended by Stats.1982, c. 517, p. 2354, § 154.)*

Law Revision Commission Comments

Section 731c is amended for consistency with the Bond and Undertaking Law. See Code Civ.Proc. § 995.020 (application of provisions) 16 Cal.L.Rev.Comm. Reports 501).

Research References

6 Witkin Cal. Proc. 5th Provisional Remedies § 344, Public Interest.

§ 731.5. Public trails; closure; injunction; attorney's fees; costs

Whenever any person unlawfully closes any public trail, any person who uses such trail or would use such trail, and any association, corporation or other entity whose membership as a whole is adversely affected by such closure may bring an action to enjoin such closure.

The prevailing party in such action shall be entitled to recover reasonable attorney's fees, in addition to court costs.

As used in this section, a public trail is any trail to which the public in general has a right of access, which right is established pursuant to a recorded document conveying to a political corporation or governmental agency, specifying the nature of such public trail, specifically describing the location thereof, and naming the record owners of the real property over which such trail exists if created by a license, permit or easement. It includes, but is not limited to, pedestrian, equestrian, and boating trails, but does not include any public street, road, or highway. *(Added by Stats.1979, c. 682, § 1.)*

Research References

Miller and Starr California Real Estate § 15:72, Remedies for Interference With the Use of an Easement.
13 Witkin, California Summary 10th Equity § 158, No Private Remedy.

§ 732. Waste; parties to action; right of action; treble damages

If a guardian, conservator, tenant for life or years, joint tenant, or tenant in common of real property, commit waste thereon, any person aggrieved by the waste may bring an action against him therefor, in which action there may be judgment for treble damages. *(Enacted in 1872. Amended by Stats.1979, c. 730, § 23, operative Jan. 1, 1981.)*

Law Revision Commission Comments

Section 732 is amended to add the reference to a conservator.

Research References

Rutter, Cal. Practice Guide: Personal Injury Ch. 3-E, E. Punitive Damages.
Miller and Starr California Real Estate § 12:7, Waste by a Cotenant.
Miller and Starr California Real Estate § 2:16, Sale or Assignment.
Miller and Starr California Real Estate § 2:19, Right to Possession; Waste.
Miller and Starr California Real Estate § 9:22, Duties and Liabilities; Waste.
Miller and Starr California Real Estate § 17:31, Timber.
Miller and Starr California Real Estate § 34:99, Punitive Damages-- Judicial Review.
Miller and Starr California Real Estate § 19:126, Waste.
Miller and Starr California Real Estate § 19:130, Landlord's Remedies.
12 Witkin, California Summary 10th Real Property § 21, (S 21) Rights of Owner.
12 Witkin, California Summary 10th Real Property § 31, (S 31) Waste and Permissible Use.
12 Witkin, California Summary 10th Real Property § 41, (S 41) in General.
12 Witkin, California Summary 10th Real Property § 370, (S 370) Prohibition and Remedies.
6 Witkin, California Summary 10th Torts § 1570, Treble Damages.

§ 733. Trespass; cutting, carrying off, or injuring trees; treble damages

TRESPASS FOR CUTTING OR CARRYING AWAY TREES, ETC., ACTIONS FOR. Any person who cuts down or carries off any wood or underwood, tree, or timber, or girdles or otherwise injures any tree or timber on the land of another person, or on the street or highway in front of any person's house, village, or city lot, or cultivated grounds; or on the commons or public grounds of any city or town, or on the street or highway in front thereof, without lawful authority, is liable to the owner of such land, or to such city or town, for treble the amount of damages which may be assessed therefor, in a civil action, in any Court having jurisdiction. *(Enacted in 1872.)*

Research References

Rutter, Cal. Practice Guide: Personal Injury Ch. 3-E, E. Punitive Damages.
Miller and Starr California Real Estate § 14:9, Self-Help for Encroaching Trees.

Miller and Starr California Real Estate § 14:11, Damages.
Miller and Starr California Real Estate § 17:31, Timber.
Miller and Starr California Real Estate § 34:99, Punitive Damages-- Judicial Review.
6 Witkin, California Summary 10th Torts § 1570, Treble Damages.
6 Witkin, California Summary 10th Torts § 1734, Wilful and Malicious Trespass: Treble Damages.

§ 734. Trespass; cutting, carrying off, or injuring trees; actual damages for timber from uncultivated woodland for certain purposes

MEASURE OF DAMAGES IN CERTAIN CASES UNDER THE LAST SECTION. Nothing in the last section authorizes the recovery of more than the just value of the timber taken from uncultivated woodland for the repair of a public highway or bridge upon the land, or adjoining it. *(Enacted in 1872.)*

Research References

Miller and Starr California Real Estate § 17:31, Timber.

§ 735. Forcible or unlawful entry; treble damages

DAMAGES IN ACTIONS FOR FORCIBLE ENTRY, ETC., MAY BE TREBLED. If a person recover damages for a forcible or unlawful entry in or upon, or detention of any building or any cultivated real property, judgment may be entered for three times the amount at which the actual damages are assessed. *(Enacted in 1872.)*

Research References

California Real Estate Forms (Miller & Starr) § 3:14, Construction Deed of Trust, Security Agreement, and Fixture Filing With Assignment of Rents and Agreements.
California Real Estate Forms (Miller & Starr) § 3:21, Deed of Trust, Assignment of Rents, Security Agreement and Fixture Filing-- Conduit Loan.
Rutter, Cal. Practice Guide: Personal Injury Ch. 3-E, E. Punitive Damages.
Miller and Starr California Real Estate § 19:167, Defenses.
Miller and Starr California Real Estate § 19:168, Judgment; Damages.
6 Witkin, California Summary 10th Torts § 1570, Treble Damages.

§ 736. Breach of environmental provision; remedies; damages; applicability of section; definitions

(a) Notwithstanding any other provision of law, a secured lender may bring an action for breach of contract against a borrower for breach of any environmental provision made by the borrower relating to the real property security, for the recovery of damages, and for the enforcement of the environmental provision, and that action or failure to foreclose first against collateral shall not constitute an action within the meaning of subdivision (a) of Section 726, or constitute a money judgment for a deficiency or a deficiency judgment within the meaning of Section 580a, 580b, or 580d, or subdivision (b) of Section 726. No injunction for the enforcement of an environmental provision may be issued after (1) the obligation secured by the real property security has been fully satisfied, or (2) all of the borrower's rights, title, and interest in and to the real property security has been transferred in a bona fide transaction to an unaffiliated third party for fair value.

(b) The damages a secured lender may recover pursuant to subdivision (a) shall be limited to reimbursement or indemnification of the following:

(1) If not pursuant to an order of any federal, state, or local governmental agency relating to the cleanup, remediation, or other response action required by applicable law, those costs relating to a reasonable and good faith cleanup, remediation, or other response action concerning a release or threatened release of hazardous substances which is anticipated by the environmental provision.

(2) If pursuant to an order of any federal, state, or local governmental agency relating to the cleanup, remediation, or other response action required by applicable law which is anticipated by the environmental provision, all amounts reasonably advanced in good faith by the secured lender in connection therewith, provided that the secured lender negotiated, or attempted to negotiate, in good faith to minimize the amounts it was required to advance under the order.

(3) Indemnification against all liabilities of the secured lender to any third party relating to the breach and not arising from acts, omissions, or other conduct which occur after the borrower is no longer an owner or operator of the real property security, and provided the secured lender is not responsible for the environmentally impaired condition of the real property security in accordance with the standards set forth in subdivision (d) of Section 726.5. For purposes of this paragraph, the term "owner or operator" means those persons described in Section 101(20)(A) of the Comprehensive Environmental Response, Compensation, and Liability Act of 1980, as amended (42 U.S.C. Sec. 9601, et seq.).

(4) Attorneys' fees and costs incurred by the secured lender relating to the breach.

The damages a secured lender may recover pursuant to subdivision (a) shall not include (i) any part of the principal amount or accrued interest of the secured obligation, except for any amounts advanced by the secured lender to cure or mitigate the breach of the environmental provision that are added to the principal amount, and contractual interest thereon, or (ii) amounts which relate to a release which was knowingly permitted, caused, or contributed to by the secured lender or any affiliate or agent of the secured lender.

(c) A secured lender may not recover damages against a borrower pursuant to subdivision (a) for amounts advanced or obligations incurred for the cleanup or other remediation of real property security, and related attorneys' fees and costs, if all of the following are true:

(1) The original principal amount of, or commitment for, the loan or other obligation secured by the real property security did not exceed two hundred thousand dollars ($200,000).

(2) In conjunction with the secured lender's acceptance of the environmental provision, the secured lender agreed in writing to accept the real property security on the basis of a completed environmental site assessment and other relevant information from the borrower.

(3) The borrower did not permit, cause, or contribute to the release or threatened release.

(4) The deed of trust or mortgage covering the real property security has not been discharged, reconveyed, or foreclosed upon.

(d) This section is not intended to establish, abrogate, modify, limit, or otherwise affect any cause of action other than that provided by subdivision (a) that a secured lender may have against a borrower under an environmental provision.

(e) This section shall apply only to environmental provisions contracted in conjunction with loans, extensions of credit, guaranties, or other obligations made, renewed, or modified on or after January 1, 1992. Notwithstanding the foregoing, this section shall not be construed to validate, invalidate, or otherwise affect in any manner the rights and obligations of the parties to, or the enforcement of, environmental provisions contracted before January 1, 1992.

(f) For purposes of this section:

(1) "Borrower" means the trustor under a deed of trust, or a mortgagor under a mortgage, where the deed of trust or mortgage encumbers real property security and secures the performance of the trustor or mortgagor under a loan, extension of credit, guaranty, or other obligation. The term includes any successor-in-interest of the trustor or mortgagor to the real property security before the deed of trust or mortgage has been discharged, reconveyed, or foreclosed upon.

(2) "Environmental provision" means any written representation, warranty, indemnity, promise, or covenant relating to the existence, location, nature, use, generation, manufacture, storage, disposal, handling, or past, present, or future release or threatened release, of any hazardous substance into, onto, beneath, or from the real property security, or to past, present, or future compliance with any law relating thereto, made by a borrower in conjunction with the making, renewal, or modification of a loan, extension of credit, guaranty, or other obligation involving the borrower, whether or not the representation, warranty, indemnity, promise, or covenant is or was contained in or secured by the deed of trust or mortgage, and whether or not the deed of trust or mortgage has been discharged, reconveyed, or foreclosed upon.

(3) "Hazardous substance" means any of the following:

(A) Any "hazardous substance" as defined in subdivision (h) of Section 25281 of the Health and Safety Code.

(B) Any "waste" as defined in subdivision (d) of Section 13050 of the Water Code.

(C) Petroleum, including crude oil or any fraction thereof, natural gas, natural gas liquids, liquefied natural gas, or synthetic gas usable for fuel, or any mixture thereof.

(4) "Real property security" means any real property and improvements, other than a separate interest and any related interest in the common area of a residential common interest development, as the terms "separate interest," "common area," and "common interest development" are defined in Sections 4095, 4100, and 4185 of the Civil Code, or real property which contains only 1 to 15 dwelling units, which in either case (A) is solely used (i) for residential purposes, or (ii) if reasonably contemplated by the parties to the deed of trust or mortgage, for residential purposes as well as limited agricultural or commercial purposes incidental thereto, and (B) is the subject of an issued certificate of occupancy unless the dwelling is to be owned and occupied by the borrower.

(5) "Release" means any spilling, leaking, pumping, pouring, emitting, emptying, discharging, injecting, escaping, leaching, dumping, or disposing into the environment, including continuing migration, of hazardous substances into, onto, or through soil, surface water, or groundwater. The term does not include actions directly relating to the incorporation in a lawful manner of building materials into a permanent improvement to the real property security.

(6) "Secured lender" means the beneficiary under a deed of trust against the real property security, or the mortgagee under a mortgage against the real property security, and any successor-in-interest of the beneficiary or mortgagee to the deed of trust or mortgage. *(Added by Stats.1991, c. 1167 (A.B.1735), § 4. Amended by Stats.1992, c. 167 (A.B.2750), § 4; Stats.1999, c. 60 (S.B.328), § 2; Stats.2002, c. 999 (A.B.2481), § 5; Stats.2012, c. 181 (A.B.806), § 47, operative Jan. 1, 2014.)*

Law Revision Commission Comments

Section 736 is amended to correct cross-references to former Civil Code Section 1351(b), (c), (*l*). [40 Cal.L.Rev.Comm. Reports 235 (2010)].

Research References

California Real Estate Forms (Miller & Starr) § 3:7, Promissory Note.

California Real Estate Forms (Miller & Starr) § 3:8, Deed of Trust, Security Agreement, and Fixture Filing With Assignment of Rents and Agreements.

California Real Estate Forms (Miller & Starr) § 3:10, Environmental Certification, Agreement, and Indemnity of Borrower.

California Real Estate Forms (Miller & Starr) § 3:13, Promissory Note Secured by Construction Deed of Trust.

California Real Estate Forms (Miller & Starr) § 3:14, Construction Deed of Trust, Security Agreement, and Fixture Filing With Assignment of Rents and Agreements.

California Real Estate Forms (Miller & Starr) § 3:21, Deed of Trust, Assignment of Rents, Security Agreement and Fixture Filing--Conduit Loan.

California Real Estate Forms (Miller & Starr) § 3:30, Environmental Indemnity--Conduit Loan.

Rutter, Cal. Practice Guide: Real Prop. Transactions Ch. 6-K, K. Environmental Indemnities.

Rutter, Cal. Practice Guide: Real Prop. Transactions Form 6:I, Deed of Trust (Complex).

Miller and Starr California Real Estate § 10:157, Exception; Environmentally Impaired Property.

4 Witkin, California Summary 10th Security Transactions in Real Property § 126, Action is Not to Recover Debt.

4 Witkin, California Summary 10th Security Transactions in Real Property § 179, (S 179) Nature and Scope of Statutes.

4 Witkin, California Summary 10th Security Transactions in Real Property § 208, (S 208) Nature and Scope of Legislation.

4 Witkin, California Summary 10th Security Transactions in Real Property § 211, (S 211) Breach of Environmental Provision.

CHAPTER 3. ACTIONS FOR THE RECOVERY OF REAL PROPERTY, AND OTHER PROVISIONS RELATING TO ACTIONS CONCERNING REAL PROPERTY

Law Revision Commission Comments

The heading of Chapter 3 is amended to reflect the relocation to Chapter 4 (commencing with Section 760.010) (quiet title) of provisions relating to actions to determine conflicting claims to real property.

§ 740. Recovery of property; termination of right during pendency of action; damages for withholding property

In an action for the recovery of property, where the plaintiff shows a right to recover at the time the action was commenced, but it appears that his right has terminated during the pendency of the action, the verdict and judgment must be according to the fact, and the plaintiff may recover damages for withholding the property. *(Enacted in 1872. Amended by Stats.1907, c. 363, p. 686, § 1.)*

Research References

Miller and Starr California Real Estate § 34:104, Who Can Bring the Action.

§ 741. Damages for withholding property; value of improvements as set-off

(a) As used in this section, "good faith improver" has the meaning given that term by Section 871.1.

(b) When damages are claimed for withholding the property recovered, and improvements have been made on the property by a defendant or his predecessor in interest as a good faith improver, the amount by which such improvements enhance the value of the land must be allowed as a setoff against such damages. *(Enacted in 1872. Amended by Stats.1968, c. 150, p. 373, § 2.)*

Law Revision Commission Comments

Section 741 has been amended to eliminate the condition that the defendant claim the property under "color of title." The amended section requires a setoff if the defendant is a good faith improver as defined in Section 871.1. This amendment makes Section 741 consistent with later enacted Civil Code Section 1013.5. See the Comment to Section 871.1. Thus, the limited protection afforded by Section 741 is extended to include the situation, for example, where the defendant owns one lot but builds on the plaintiff's lot by mistake.

The amendment also substitutes "the amount by which such improvements enhance the value of the land" for "the value of such improvements." The new language clarifies the former wording and assures that the value of the improvement, for purposes of setoff, will be measured by the extent to which the improvement has increased the market value of the land.

Research References

Miller and Starr California Real Estate § 17:43, Where Improver Does Not Believe He or She Owns the Improved Property.

Miller and Starr California Real Estate § 34:104, Who Can Bring the Action.

12 Witkin, California Summary 10th Real Property § 462, (S 462) Other Relief.

§ 742. Order for survey and measurement of land or mining tunnels, etc.

The Court in which an action is pending for the recovery of real property, or for damages for an injury thereto, or a Judge thereof may, on motion, upon notice by either party for good cause shown, grant an order allowing to such party the right to enter upon the property and make survey and measurement thereof, and of any tunnels, shafts, or drifts therein, for the purpose of the action, even though entry for such purpose has to be made through other lands belonging to parties to the action. *(Enacted in 1872. Amended by Code Am.1880, c. 22, p. 11, § 1.)*

Research References

Miller and Starr California Real Estate § 34:104, Who Can Bring the Action.

§ 743. Order for survey and measurement; contents; service; authority to enter; injuries to property

ORDER, WHAT TO CONTAIN AND HOW SERVED. IF UNNECESSARY INJURY DONE, THE PARTY SURVEYING TO BE LIABLE THEREFOR. The order must describe the property, and a copy thereof must be served on the owner or occupant; and thereupon such party may enter upon the property, with necessary surveyors and assistants, and make such survey and measurement; but if any unnecessary injury be done to the property he is liable therefor. *(Enacted in 1872.)*

Research References

Miller and Starr California Real Estate § 34:104, Who Can Bring the Action.

§ 744. Mortgage not a conveyance

A MORTGAGE MUST NOT BE DEEMED A CONVEYANCE, WHATEVER ITS TERMS. A mortgage of real property shall not be deemed a conveyance, whatever its terms, so as to enable the owner of the mortgage to recover possession of the real property without a foreclosure and sale. *(Enacted in 1872.)*

Research References

Miller and Starr California Real Estate § 10:2, Lien Versus Title Theories.
Miller and Starr California Real Estate § 10:163, Action for Possession.

§ 745. Injunction against injury to real property

The court may, by injunction, on good cause shown, restrain the party in possession from doing any act to the injury of real property:

(a) During the foreclosure of a mortgage on the property.

(b) After levy on the property and before the possession of the property is transferred pursuant to sale under the levy. *(Enacted in 1872. Amended by Stats.1982, c. 497, p. 2163, § 57, operative July 1, 1983.)*

Research References

Miller and Starr California Real Estate § 10:54, Remedies and Measure of Damages for Waste.
Miller and Starr California Real Estate § 32:64, Creation, Duration, and Effect of Writ of Execution.
Miller and Starr California Real Estate § 10:230, Possession and Rents During the Redemption Period.

§ 746. Damages for injury to real property; recovery by purchaser after levy

When real property has been sold pursuant to a levy, the purchaser of the property, or any person who has succeeded to the interest of the purchaser, may recover damages from the person causing the injury for injury to the property after levy and before possession is delivered to the purchaser or the person who has succeeded to the interest of the purchaser. *(Enacted in 1872. Amended by Stats.1982, c. 497, p. 2163, § 58, operative July 1, 1983.)*

Research References

Miller and Starr California Real Estate § 10:54, Remedies and Measure of Damages for Waste.
Miller and Starr California Real Estate § 32:64, Creation, Duration, and Effect of Writ of Execution.
Miller and Starr California Real Estate § 10:230, Possession and Rents During the Redemption Period.

§ 747. Action for recovery of real estate; alienation by defendant; effect

ACTION NOT TO BE PREJUDICED BY ALIENATION PENDING SUIT. An action for the recovery of real property against a person in possession cannot be prejudiced by any alienation made by such person, either before or after the commencement of the action. *(Enacted in 1872.)*

Research References

Miller and Starr California Real Estate § 19:220, Parties.

Miller and Starr California Real Estate § 34:104, Who Can Bring the Action.

§ 748. Mining claims; local customs, usages or regulations

MINING CLAIMS, ACTIONS CONCERNING TO BE GOVERNED BY LOCAL RULES. In actions, respecting mining claims, proof must be admitted of the customs, usages, or regulations established and in force at the bar or diggings embracing such claim; and such customs, usages, or regulations, when not in conflict with the laws of this State, must govern the decision of the action. *(Enacted in 1872.)*

§ 749. Action for damages against beneficiary of trust deed; forged instruments; treble damages; application and effect of section

(a) In an action for damages by a homeowner or trustor against a beneficiary of a trust deed on real property consisting of a single-family residence containing not more than four dwelling units, or against an assignee or successor in interest thereof, wherein it is established the trust deed was forged in whole or in part by the beneficiary, judgment may be entered for three times the amount at which the actual damages are assessed.

(b) An assignee or successor in interest of a beneficiary or a transferee of a prior assignee or of a prior successor in interest shall not be subject to treble damages unless it is established that the person purchased or obtained the deed of trust with actual knowledge of the forgery of the deed of trust.

(c) This section shall not apply to any person who does not purchase and sell four or more deeds of trust in any calendar year.

(d) This section shall not limit or affect the availability of punitive damages, if any, to the injured party.

(e) This section shall apply to any action filed on or after July 1, 1983, provided that any action filed prior to the effective date of this section is pending at that time in the court of original jurisdiction. *(Added by Stats.1984, c. 1397, § 1.)*

Research References

Miller and Starr California Real Estate § 10:7, Execution and Delivery.
Miller and Starr California Real Estate § 4:72, Sale or Assignment of Secured Obligations.
Miller and Starr California Real Estate § 8:52, Forgery.
Miller and Starr California Real Estate § 11:13, Required Form and Contents--Effect of a Forgery.
Miller and Starr California Real Estate § 10:236, Policy Objectives; the "Standard" Transaction.
3 Witkin Cal. Proc. 5th Actions § 381, (S 381) Specific Mandatory Statutes.
4 Witkin, California Summary 10th Security Transactions in Real Property § 41, (S 41) Deed of Trust.

§ 749.5. Forged trust deeds; single-family residences; treble damages; application of section

(a) In an action for damages by an assignee or a successor in interest against a beneficiary of a trust deed on real property consisting of a single-family residence containing not more than four dwelling units, wherein it is established the trust deed was forged in whole or in part by the beneficiary, judgment may be entered for three times the amount at which the actual damages are assessed.

(b) This section shall not apply to any person who does not purchase and sell four or more deeds of trust in any calendar year.

(c) This section shall not limit or affect the availability of punitive damages, if any, to the injured party.

Civ. Pro.

(d) This section shall apply to any action filed on or after January 1, 1984. *(Added by Stats.1984, c. 1397, § 2.)*

Research References

Miller and Starr California Real Estate § 10:7, Execution and Delivery.

Miller and Starr California Real Estate § 4:72, Sale or Assignment of Secured Obligations.

Miller and Starr California Real Estate § 8:52, Forgery.

Miller and Starr California Real Estate § 11:13, Required Form and Contents--Effect of a Forgery.

Miller and Starr California Real Estate § 10:236, Policy Objectives; the "Standard" Transaction.

4 Witkin, California Summary 10th Security Transactions in Real Property § 41, (S 41) Deed of Trust.

CHAPTER 3.5. ACTIONS TO RE–ESTABLISH DESTROYED LAND RECORDS

§ 751.01. Short title

This chapter may be cited as the Destroyed Land Records Relief Law. *(Added by Stats.1953, c. 52, p. 697, § 6.)*

Research References

Miller and Starr California Real Estate § 11:9, Destruction of Public Records; Proof of Recorded Document.

Miller and Starr California Real Estate § 34:108, Types of Actions for Quiet Title.

3 Witkin Cal. Proc. 5th Actions § 985, (S 985) Special Statutes.

2 Witkin Cal. Proc. 5th Jurisdiction § 245, Illustrations.

5 Witkin Cal. Proc. 5th Pleading § 655, (S 655) Other Actions Distinguished.

§ 751.02. Right of action; grounds; venue

Whenever the public records in the office of the county recorder of any county are lost or destroyed in whole or in any material part by flood, fire, earthquake, enemy attack, or from any other cause, any person who claims an estate of inheritance or for life in, and who is by himself, or his tenant or other person holding under him in the actual and peaceable possession of, any real property in the county may bring and maintain an action in rem against all the world, in the superior court for the county in which such real property is situate, to establish his title to such property and to determine all adverse claims thereto.

Such action may also be brought in the county in which the real property is situate if any real property is in another county, but was formerly in the county of which all or a material part of the records were so lost or destroyed, and if the lost or destroyed records included all or a material part of the public records in the office of the county recorder covering all or a material part of the time when the real property was in the county whose records were so lost or destroyed. *(Added by Stats.1953, c. 52, p. 697, § 6.)*

Research References

Miller and Starr California Real Estate § 11:9, Destruction of Public Records; Proof of Recorded Document.

§ 751.03. Separate parcels in same action

Any number of separate parcels of land claimed by the plaintiff may be included in the same action. *(Added by Stats.1953, c. 52, p. 698, § 6.)*

§ 751.04. Commencement of action; parties; contents of complaint

The action shall be commenced by the filing of a verified complaint. The party commencing the action shall be named as plaintiff, and the defendants shall be described as "all persons claiming any interest in, or lien upon, the real property herein described, or any part thereof." The complaint shall contain a statement of the facts enumerated in Section 751.02, a particular description of the real property, and a specification of the estate, title, or interest of the plaintiff in the property. *(Added by Stats.1953, c. 52, p. 698, § 6.)*

Research References

Miller and Starr California Real Estate § 11:9, Destruction of Public Records; Proof of Recorded Document.

§ 751.05. Summons; issuance; form

Upon the filing of the complaint, a summons shall be issued under the seal of the court. The summons shall contain the name of the court and county in which the action is brought, and the name of the plaintiff and a particular description of the real property involved, and shall be directed to "all persons claiming any interest in, or lien upon, the real property herein described, or any part thereof," as defendants, and shall be substantially in the following form:

"IN THE SUPERIOR COURT OF THE STATE OF CALIFORNIA IN AND FOR THE COUNTY (OR CITY AND COUNTY) OF . . . .

. . . .)
                        Plaintiff,)
                 vs.   )
All Persons Claiming Any Interest in,) Action No. . . . . .
   or Lien Upon, the Real Property   )
   Herein Described or Any Part   )
   thereof,   )
                    Defendants.)

The people of the State of California, to all persons claiming any interest in, or lien upon, the real property herein described, or any part thereof, defendants, greeting:

You are hereby required to appear and answer the complaint of . . . ., plaintiff, filed with the clerk of the above-entitled court and county, within three months after the first publication of this summons, and to set forth what interest or lien, if any, you have in or upon that certain real property or any part thereof, situated in the County (or City and County) of . . . ., State of California, particularly described as follows: (here insert description.)

And you are hereby notified that, unless you so appear and answer, the plaintiff will apply to the court for the relief demanded in the complaint, to wit: (here insert a statement of the relief so demanded.)

Witness my hand and the seal of said court, this . . . . day of . . . .,A.D. . . . . (SEAL)

. . . ., Clerk."

(Added by Stats.1953, c. 52, p. 698, § 6.)

Research References

Rutter, Cal. Practice Guide: Civ. Pro. Before Trial Ch. 4-C, C. Content of Summons.
Miller and Starr California Real Estate § 11:9, Destruction of Public Records; Proof of Recorded Document.
3 Witkin Cal. Proc. 5th Actions § 987, (S 987) Actions Involving Real Property.

§ 751.06. Summons; publication

The summons shall be published in a newspaper of general circulation published in the county in which the action is brought. The newspaper in which publication is to be made shall be designated by an order of the court or a judge thereof to be signed and filed with the clerk. No other order for the publication of the summons shall be necessary, nor shall any affidavit therefor be required, nor need any copy of the complaint be served, except as required by this chapter. The summons shall be published pursuant to Section 6065 of the Government Code, and to each publication thereof shall be appended a memorandum in substance as follows:

"The first publication of this summons was made in . . . . (here insert name) newspaper on the . . . . . . day of . . . . . . A.D. . . . .," (inserting the date). *(Added by Stats.1953, c. 52, p. 699, § 6.)*

Research References

Miller and Starr California Real Estate § 11:9, Destruction of Public Records; Proof of Recorded Document.
3 Witkin Cal. Proc. 5th Actions § 1034, Special Statutes.

§ 751.07. Plaintiff's affidavit; statement of persons claiming adverse interest

If the affidavit provided for in Section 751.09 discloses the name of any person claiming an interest in the property or a lien thereon adverse to the plaintiff, that fact and the name and address, if given, of the person shall be stated in a memorandum to be appended to the summons in substance as follows:

"The following persons are said to claim an interest in, or lien upon, said property adverse to plaintiff," (giving their names and addresses as above provided). *(Added by Stats.1953, c. 52, p. 699, § 6.)*

Research References

Miller and Starr California Real Estate § 11:9, Destruction of Public Records; Proof of Recorded Document.
3 Witkin Cal. Proc. 5th Actions § 987, (S 987) Actions Involving Real Property.

§ 751.08. Summons; posting

A copy of the summons and a copy of the memorandum shall be posted in a conspicuous place on each separate parcel of the property described in the complaint within 15 days after the first publication of the summons. *(Added by Stats.1953, c. 52, p. 699, § 6.)*

Research References

Miller and Starr California Real Estate § 11:9, Destruction of Public Records; Proof of Recorded Document.

§ 751.09. Plaintiff's affidavit; contents; inclusion in judgment roll

At the time of filing the complaint the plaintiff shall file with it his affidavit fully and explicitly setting forth and showing:

(a) The character of the plaintiff's estate, right, title, interest, or claim in, and possession of, the property, the period it has existed, and from whom obtained.

(b) Whether or not the plaintiff has ever made any conveyance of all or any part of the property, or any interest therein, and if so when and to whom, and a statement of any and all subsisting mortgages, deeds of trust, and other liens thereon.

(c) That the plaintiff does not know and has never been informed of any other person who claims or who may claim any interest in or lien upon all or any part of the property adversely to the plaintiff, or if the plaintiff does know or has been informed of any such person, the name and address of such person.

If the plaintiff is unable to state any of the required matters, the plaintiff shall set forth and show fully and explicitly the reasons for such inability. Such affidavit shall constitute a part of the judgment-roll. If the plaintiff is a corporation, the affidavit shall be made by an officer thereof. If the plaintiff is a person under guardianship or conservatorship, the affidavit shall be made by the guardian or conservator. *(Added by Stats.1953, c. 52, p. 699, § 6. Amended by Stats.1979, c. 730, § 24, operative Jan. 1, 1981.)*

Law Revision Commission Comments

Section 751.09 is amended to add the references to conservator and conservatorship.

Research References

Miller and Starr California Real Estate § 11:9, Destruction of Public Records; Proof of Recorded Document.

§ 751.10. Summons; service on disclosed defendants

If the affidavit discloses the name of any person claiming any interest in or lien upon the property adverse to the plaintiff, a copy of the summons and complaint and affidavit shall also be served upon such person, if he can be found, in the manner provided by law for the service of a summons in a civil action, other than by publication. Service shall be made during the period of the publication of the summons. A copy of the memorandum provided for in Section 751.07 shall be appended to the copy of the summons served upon any such person.

If such person cannot, with reasonable diligence, be served as provided above within the period of publication of the summons, a copy of the summons, memorandum, complaint, and affidavit shall be mailed, postage prepaid, addressed to him at the address given in the affidavit, or, if no address is given, at his last address known to the plaintiff, or, if none, at the county seat of the county in which the action is brought, forthwith upon the expiration of the period of publication. *(Added by Stats.1953, c. 52, p. 700, § 6. Amended by Stats.1969, c. 1611, p. 3391, § 9, operative July 1, 1970.)*

Research References

Miller and Starr California Real Estate § 11:9, Destruction of Public Records; Proof of Recorded Document.

§ 751.11. Jurisdiction

Upon the completion of the publication and posting of the summons and its service or mailing as provided for in Section 751.10, the court has complete jurisdiction over the plaintiff and the property and the person of everyone having or claiming any estate, right, title, or interest in or to, or lien upon, all or any part of the property, and shall be deemed to have obtained the possession and control of the property for the purposes of the action with complete jurisdiction to render the judgment provided for in this chapter. *(Added by Stats.1953, c. 52, p. 700, § 6. Amended by Stats.1969, c. 1611, p. 3392, § 10, operative July 1, 1970.)*

Research References

Miller and Starr California Real Estate § 11:150, Actions in Which a Lis Pendens May or Must be Recorded.

§ 751.12. Appearance; time; answer

At any time within three months after the first publication of the summons, or such further time not exceeding 30 days as the court for good cause may grant, any person having or claiming any estate, right, title, or interest in or to, or lien upon, all or any part of the property may appear and make himself a party to the action by pleading to the complaint. All answers must be verified and must specifically set forth the estate, right, title, interest, or lien so claimed. *(Added by Stats.1953, c. 52, p. 700, § 6.)*

Research References

Miller and Starr California Real Estate § 11:9, Destruction of Public Records; Proof of Recorded Document.
3 Witkin Cal. Proc. 5th Actions § 985, (S 985) Special Statutes.
3 Witkin Cal. Proc. 5th Actions § 985, (S 985) Special Statutes.
3 Witkin Cal. Proc. 5th Actions § 987, (S 987) Actions Involving Real Property.

§ 751.13. Lis pendens

At the time of filing the complaint the plaintiff, and at the time of filing his or her answer every defendant claiming any affirmative relief, shall record in the office of the recorder of the county in which the property is situated a notice of the pendency of the action containing the object of the action or defense, and a particular description of the property affected by it. The recorder shall record the notice in the same manner as provided in Section 409. *(Added by Stats.1953, c. 52, p. 700, § 6. Amended by Stats.1982, c. 843, p. 3176, § 1.)*

Research References

Miller and Starr California Real Estate § 11:9, Destruction of Public Records; Proof of Recorded Document.
Miller and Starr California Real Estate § 11:149, Procedural and Formal Requirements for a Lis Pendens.
Miller and Starr California Real Estate § 11:150, Actions in Which a Lis Pendens May or Must be Recorded.
Miller and Starr California Real Estate § 19:221, Complaint and Summons.
3 Witkin Cal. Proc. 5th Actions § 381, (S 381) Specific Mandatory Statutes.

§ 751.14. Judgment; default; proof of facts

Judgment in any such action shall not be given by default, but the court must require proof of the facts alleged in the complaint and other pleadings. *(Added by Stats.1953, c. 52, p. 701, § 6.)*

Research References

Miller and Starr California Real Estate § 11:9, Destruction of Public Records; Proof of Recorded Document.
6 Witkin Cal. Proc. 5th Proceedings Without Trial § 137, (S 137) Restrictions on Default Judgments.

§ 751.15. Judgment; scope; effect

The judgment shall determine all estates, rights, titles, interests, and claims in and to such property and every part thereof, whether legal or equitable, present or future, vested or contingent, or whether they consist of mortgages or liens of any description. It shall be conclusive upon every person who at the commencement of the action had or claimed any estate, right, title, or interest in or to all or any part of such property and upon every person claiming under him by title subsequent to the commencement of the action. *(Added by Stats.1953, c. 52, p. 701, § 6.)*

§ 751.16. Judgment and judgment roll; recording

A certified copy of the judgment shall be recorded in the office of the recorder of the county in which the action was commenced. Any party or the successor in interest of any party to the action may file the entire judgment roll for record in the office of the county recorder. *(Added by Stats.1953, c. 52, p. 701, § 6.)*

Research References

Miller and Starr California Real Estate § 11:9, Destruction of Public Records; Proof of Recorded Document.

§ 751.17. Procedure applicable

Except as otherwise provided in this chapter, all rules of law relating to evidence, pleading, practice, new trials, and appeals applicable to other civil actions shall apply to actions authorized by this chapter. *(Added by Stats.1953, c. 52, p. 701, § 6.)*

§ 751.18. Depositions

At any time after the issuance of summons, any party to the action may take depositions in conformity to law upon notice to the adverse party sought to be bound by such depositions and who has appeared in the action and upon notice filed with the clerk. The depositions may be used by any party against any other party giving or receiving the notice, subject to all just exceptions. *(Added by Stats.1953, c. 52, p. 701, § 6.)*

§ 751.19. Actions; numbering; indexing; register

The clerk shall number all actions authorized by this chapter consecutively in a distinct series and shall keep an index and register devoted exclusively to such actions. *(Added by Stats. 1953, c. 52, p. 701, § 6.)*

§ 751.20. Subsequent actions

Whenever judgment in an action authorized by this chapter has been entered as to any real property, no other action relative to all or any part of the same property shall be tried until proof has first been made to the court that all persons who appeared in the first action or their successors in interest have been personally served pursuant to this chapter either within or without the State more than one month before the time to plead expired. *(Added by Stats.1953, c. 52, p. 701, § 6.)*

§ 751.21. Executor, administrator, guardian, conservator, etc. or party

An executor, administrator, guardian, conservator, or other person holding the possession of property in the right of another may maintain as plaintiff, and may appear and defend in, any action provided for by this chapter. *(Added by Stats.1953, c. 52, p. 701, § 6. Amended by Stats.1979, c. 730, § 25, operative Jan. 1, 1981.)*

Section 751.21 is amended to add the reference to a conservator.

§ 751.22. Cumulative remedies

The remedies provided for by this chapter are cumulative and in addition to any other remedy provided by law for quieting or establishing title to real property. *(Added by Stats.1953, c. 52, p. 702, § 6.)*

Research References

Miller and Starr California Real Estate § 11:9, Destruction of Public Records; Proof of Recorded Document.

§ 751.23. Notice of ownership; form

Where the title to real property may be established or quieted pursuant to this chapter, any person who is or claims to be the owner of such real property or of any interest therein or lien thereon, by himself or by his agent duly authorized by letter of attorney theretofore recorded in the office of the county recorder of the county where the property is situated, may sign, verify, and file for record in the office of the county recorder a notice in substantially the following form:

"NOTICE OF OWNERSHIP AND CLAIM TO REAL PROPERTY UNDER THE DESTROYED RECORDS RELIEF LAW

"Notice is hereby given that .... (here insert name of claimant) ...., whose residence is at .... (here insert street and number, city or town, county and state of residence), is the owner of an interest in the real property situated in the .... (here insert name of city if the property be located in a city) ...., county of .... (here insert name of county or city and county in which property is located) ...., State of California, described as follows: .... (here insert a particular description of real property) ....

"The character of the interest in the real property owned by the claimant is .... (here insert description of the character of interest in or lien upon the real property) .... and the interest was obtained from .... (here insert the name of the party from whom the interest was obtained) ...., and at the time and in the manner following .... (here insert time at which and manner in which the interest was acquired) ...." *(Added by Stats.1953, c. 52, p. 702, § 6.)*

Research References

Miller and Starr California Real Estate § 11:6, Instruments Subject to Recording--List of Recordable Documents.
Miller and Starr California Real Estate § 11:9, Destruction of Public Records; Proof of Recorded Document.

§ 751.24. Notice of ownership; signature; verification

The notice shall be signed by the claimant or by his agent and shall be verified by the oath of the party signing it, to the effect that all of the statements therein contained are true to his knowledge. *(Added by Stats.1953, c. 52, p. 702, § 6.)*

Research References

Miller and Starr California Real Estate § 11:6, Instruments Subject to Recording--List of Recordable Documents.

Miller and Starr California Real Estate § 11:9, Destruction of Public Records; Proof of Recorded Document.

§ 751.25. Recordation of notice of ownership

Upon the filing of the notice for recordation the recorder shall record the notice in the same manner as provided in Section 409. *(Added by Stats.1953, c. 52, p. 702, § 6. Amended by Stats.1982, c. 843, p. 3176, § 2.)*

Research References

Miller and Starr California Real Estate § 11:6, Instruments Subject to Recording--List of Recordable Documents.
Miller and Starr California Real Estate § 11:9, Destruction of Public Records; Proof of Recorded Document.

§ 751.26. Notice of ownership; effect of record

After three days after the notice has been filed for record, all persons who may begin actions pursuant to this chapter shall be deemed to have notice of the facts stated in the notice. Neither the filing of the notice for record nor its recordation constitute constructive notice to any other person or for any other purpose. The original of the notice shall be returned to the party requesting the recordation as provided in Section 27321 of the Government Code. *(Added by Stats.1953, c. 52, p. 702, § 6. Amended by Stats.1982, c. 843, p. 3176, § 3.)*

Research References

Miller and Starr California Real Estate § 11:9, Destruction of Public Records; Proof of Recorded Document.

§ 751.27. Parties; claimant in notice of ownership

After three days after the filing of the notice for record, any person who begins an action pursuant to this chapter to perfect or establish his title to the real property described in the notice, or any interest therein, must name, in the affidavit and memorandum appended to the summons, the claimant in the notice, or any person who is a successor in interest of such claimant under a subsequently duly recorded written instrument, judgment, or decree, as a party who claims an interest in or lien upon the property adverse to the plaintiff. He must cause such claimant, or successor in interest, to be served with summons in the action. Otherwise neither the action nor any judgment or decree made therein shall affect the title or interest in the property described in the notice and owned by the claimant at the time of the filing of the notice, or by any such successor in interest prior to the commencement of the action. The failure to name such claimant or successor in interest in the affidavit or memorandum or to serve such claimant or such successor in interest shall not affect the validity of the judgment or decree rendered in such action as to any other persons, but such judgment or decree shall be valid and binding upon all persons except such claimant or successor in interest. *(Added by Stats.1953, c. 52, p. 703, § 6.)*

Research References

Miller and Starr California Real Estate § 11:9, Destruction of Public Records; Proof of Recorded Document.

§ 751.28. Notice of ownership; executor, administrator, guardian, conservator, etc.

An executor, administrator, guardian, conservator, or other person holding the possession of property in the right of another, may make, sign, verify, and file for record the notice and affidavit provided for in this chapter on behalf of the estate or interest which he represents. *(Added by Stats.1953, c. 52, p. 703, § 6. Amended by Stats.1979, c. 730, § 26, operative Jan. 1, 1981.)*

Law Revision Commission Comments

Section 751.28 is amended to add the reference to a conservator.

Research References

Miller and Starr California Real Estate § 11:9, Destruction of Public Records; Proof of Recorded Document.
Miller and Starr California Real Estate § 34:108, Types of Actions for Quiet Title.

CHAPTER 3.6. CULLEN EARTHQUAKE ACT

§ 751.50. Boundaries of land disturbed by earth movements; action to reestablish boundaries and to quiet title

If the boundaries of land owned either by public or by private entities have been disturbed by earth movements such as, but not limited to, slides, subsidence, lateral or vertical displacements or similar disasters caused by man, or by earthquake or other acts of God, so that such lands are in a location different from that at which they were located prior to the disaster, an action in rem may be brought to equitably reestablish boundaries and to quiet title to land within the boundaries so reestablished. *(Added by Stats.1972, c. 936, p. 1691, § 2.)*

Research References

Miller and Starr California Real Estate § 8:70, Water as Property Boundary--Effect of Avulsion, Earth Movement and Subsidence.
Miller and Starr California Real Estate § 34:108, Types of Actions for Quiet Title.
3 Witkin Cal. Proc. 5th Actions § 985, (S 985) Special Statutes.
12 Witkin, California Summary 10th Real Property § 277, Resolving Uncertainties.

§ 751.51. Parties; notice

(a) An action authorized by this chapter may be commenced by:

(1) A county in which lands were affected by a disaster described in Section 751.50 with or without the joinder of a city or cities included in the county and within the area so affected.

(2) A city, if the disaster has affected land in the city.

(3) Any other entity or person owning or having an interest in or lien upon land affected by the disaster if granted permission by the court to bring the action, and if the county in which the land is located is made a party to the action.

(b) In an action authorized by this chapter every entity in actual and peaceable possession of, or having an estate or interest in or lien upon any of the land affected by the action, whose possession or evidence of estate or interest is either recorded or known to the plaintiffs, the city, if the land is within a city, the county in which the land is located, and the State of California must be designated in the complaint of the action, and given notice in the manner required by this chapter.

(c) All unknown entities, including owners, lien or interest claimants, heirs, devisees, legatees or assigns, may be described in the caption and complaint as "all entities claiming any interest in or lien upon, the real property herein described or any part of it." *(Added by Stats.1972, c. 936, p. 1691, § 2.)*

§ 751.52. Separate action for separate portions of disaster area by permissive plaintiff; approval by court

An entity which is a permissive plaintiff under this chapter, may bring a separate action with respect to separate portions of the disaster area of sufficient size to equitably reestablish boundaries without harm to other areas of the common disaster, its decision regarding the desirability of the separate action, and regarding the area to be dealt with in each action to be approved by the court. *(Added by Stats.1972, c. 936, p. 1691, § 2.)*

§ 751.53. Complaint

The complaint shall substantially include:

(a) A statement of the facts which make the provisions of this chapter applicable.

(b) A description of the exterior boundaries of the real property area sought to be affected by the action.

(c) A specification of the estate, title, interest or claim owned, and in the actual possession of the plaintiff or plaintiffs in described parts of the entire real property sought to be affected by the action.

(d) A specification of the estate, title, interest, or claim, so far as they are known to the plaintiffs or either of them, and so far as they are capable of being discovered by reasonably diligent search by the plaintiff or plaintiffs, in each separate part of the entire real property sought to be affected by the action.

(e) A specification of the street areas sought to be vacated or offered by the plaintiff, or plaintiffs, to be vacated in whole or in part for judicial equitable allocation to landowners for the mitigation of the losses inflicted upon the landowners by the particular disaster or disasters to which this chapter is applicable.

(f) A proposed replatting of the entire real property sought to be affected by the action, embodying the land boundaries as fixed by the disaster, except as these boundaries have been equitably and judicially readjusted, or as liberalized by judicially directed use of the vacated lands. *(Added by Stats.1972, c. 936, p. 1691, § 2. Amended by Stats.1984, c. 193, § 10.)*

§ 751.54. Procedures applicable

Summons, publication of notice, posting and related matters and procedures shall be governed by the provisions of Sections 751.05 through 751.10, inclusive, of the Code of Civil Procedure. *(Added by Stats.1972, c. 936, p. 1692, § 2.)*

Research References

3 Witkin Cal. Proc. 5th Actions § 987, (S 987) Actions Involving Real Property.
3 Witkin Cal. Proc. 5th Actions § 1034, Special Statutes.

§ 751.55. Jurisdiction

Upon the completion of the service, publication and posting of the summons, as may be required by this chapter, the court has complete jurisdiction over the parties plaintiff or plaintiffs and the entire real property described in the complaint as intended to be affected by the action, and over every entity having or claiming an estate, right, title or interest in or to, or lien upon, all or any part of the property, and shall be considered to have obtained the possession and control of the property for the purposes of the action with complete jurisdiction to render the judgment provided for in this chapter. *(Added by Stats.1972, c. 936, p. 1691, § 2.)*

§ 751.56. Answer to complaint

(a) An answer to the complaint must be served within 90 days after the first publication of the notice, or such further time not exceeding 30 days, as the court for good cause may grant.

(b) An answer must:

(1) Specifically set out the particulars in which the claimant's estate, right, title, or interest in or to, or lien upon all or any part of the property is different from, or greater than, the interest of the claimant as it is described in the complaint.

(2) Be confined to rights based on events occurring at the time of, or since the time of the disaster.

(c) To whatever extent, if at all, the answering party has rights against anyone whatsoever, based upon facts or events which occurred before the disaster, the claims shall remain unaffected by the action brought under this chapter and shall be assertable subsequent to the conclusion of the action at any time and in any manner permitted by law, notwithstanding the judgment granted in this action, recognizing however the finality of this judgment as to the consequences, with respect to land boundaries as applicable to land in the disaster area. *(Added by Stats.1972, c. 936, p. 1691, § 2.)*

Research References

3 Witkin Cal. Proc. 5th Actions § 985, (S 985) Special Statutes.
3 Witkin Cal. Proc. 5th Actions § 987, (S 987) Actions Involving Real Property.

§ 751.57. Notice of lis pendens

A party to an action authorized by this chapter may file a notice of the pendency of the action in the form and at the place and with the effects specified by law. *(Added by Stats.1972, c. 936, p. 1691, § 2.)*

§ 751.58. Vacation of public ways by voluntary action of governmental agency; acceptance by court

The vacating of streets, highways, or other public ways within or abutting the area affected by the disaster, in whole or in part, by the voluntary action of the governmental agency under whose jurisdiction the streets, highways, or ways are vested, for the purpose of making it possible for the court to mitigate the hardships suffered by entities because of the change in land boundaries caused by the disaster can be accomplished by the affected governmental agency expressing the offer in the proceedings followed by the court's acceptance thereof in an action authorized by this chapter, without complying with any other formalities of law. *(Added by Stats.1972, c. 936, p. 1691, § 2.)*

§ 751.59. Judgment by default; prohibition

In an action of the type authorized by this chapter, judgment shall not be given by default, but the court must require proof of the facts alleged in the complaint and other pleadings. *(Added by Stats.1972, c. 936, p. 1691, § 2.)*

Research References

6 Witkin Cal. Proc. 5th Proceedings Without Trial § 137, (S 137) Restrictions on Default Judgments.

§ 751.60. Judgment; conclusions

The judgment shall:

(a) Determine the land boundaries of each parcel of land located within the entire area of real property sought to be affected by the action, whether owned publicly or privately, as fixed by the disaster, except as these boundaries have been judicially and equitably readjusted and as liberalized by judicial equitable allocation of lands voluntarily vacated by a city, county or the state under this act.

(b) Determine the entity or entities having estates, rights, titles, interests and claims in and to each parcel, whether legal or equitable, present or future, vested or contingent, or whether they consist of mortgages or liens of any description.

(c) Approve and direct the proper filing of an official map covering the entire area of real property sought to be affected by the action, as a substitute for the plat maps previously filed, but rendered inaccurate by the disaster. *(Added by Stats.1972, c. 936, p. 1691, § 2.)*

§ 751.61. Judgment; determination of conclusions

In reaching the conclusions called for by Section 751.60, the court shall give effect to the changes in land boundaries caused by the disaster, mitigated, however, so far as can equitably be done by adjustment of land boundaries and by allocating to contiguous lots parts of the land released by a city, county or the state by its voluntary vacation of areas formerly constituting public ways, which vacatings of streets shall be approved by the judgment. *(Added by Stats.1972, c. 936, p. 1691, § 2.)*

§ 751.62. Conclusiveness of judgment

The judgment shall be conclusive with respect to land boundaries upon every entity who at the commencement of the action had or claimed an estate, right, title or interest in or to or lien upon a part of the entire area of real property described in the complaint as intended to be affected by the action, and upon every entity claiming under any such person by title subsequent to the commencement of the action. *(Added by Stats.1972, c. 936, p. 1691, § 2.)*

§ 751.63. Recordation; certified copy of judgment; effect

A certified copy of the judgment shall be recorded, at the expense of the plaintiff or plaintiffs in the action, in the office of the recorder of the county in which the affected land is situated and shall constitute constructive notice of the findings therein and of the official plat or plats referred to therein, which findings and plats shall supersede and control all prior plats, maps and documents to the extent inconsistent therewith. *(Added by Stats.1972, c. 936, p. 1691, § 2.)*

§ 751.64. Cumulative effect of remedies

The remedies provided for by this chapter are cumulative and in addition to any other remedy provided by law for quieting or establishing title to real property or the boundaries of it. *(Added by Stats.1972, c. 936, p. 1691, § 2.)*

§ 751.65. Short title

This chapter may be cited as the Cullen Earthquake Act. *(Added by Stats.1972, c. 936, p. 1691, § 2.)*

Research References

Miller and Starr California Real Estate § 8:70, Water as Property Boundary--Effect of Avulsion, Earth Movement and Subsidence.
Miller and Starr California Real Estate § 34:108, Types of Actions for Quiet Title.

CHAPTER 4.   QUIET TITLE

ARTICLE 1. GENERAL PROVISIONS

Section

§ 760.010. Definitions

As used in this chapter:

(a) "Claim" includes a legal or equitable right, title, estate, lien, or interest in property or cloud upon title.

(b) "Property" includes real property, and to the extent applicable, personal property. *(Added by Stats.1980, c. 44, p. 109, § 15.)*

Law Revision Commission Comments

Subdivision (a) of Section 760.010 makes clear that the term "claim" as used in this chapter is intended in the broadest possible sense. The definition of "property" in subdivision (b) reflects the fact that title to personal as well as real property may be determined under this chapter. See Section 760.020.

Research References

Rutter, Cal. Practice Guide: Real Prop. Transactions Ch. 11-H, H. Other Remedies.

Miller and Starr California Real Estate § 34:103, Nature of the Remedy.

Miller and Starr California Real Estate § 34:104, Who Can Bring the Action.

3 Witkin Cal. Proc. 5th Actions § 133, Nature of Problem.

2 Witkin Cal. Proc. 5th Jurisdiction § 245, Illustrations.

2 Witkin Cal. Proc. 5th Jurisdiction § 252, Determination of Property Interests of Particular Persons.

5 Witkin Cal. Proc. 5th Pleading § 656, (S 656) Statutory Development.

5 Witkin Cal. Proc. 5th Pleading § 657, (S 657) In General.

5 Witkin Cal. Proc. 5th Pleading § 658, (S 658) Jurisdiction, Venue, and Process.

5 Witkin Cal. Proc. 5th Pleading § 706, (S 706) Action to Quiet Title.

§ 760.020. Action to establish title or interest; agreements to exchange land or establish high-water or low-water marks

(a) An action may be brought under this chapter to establish title against adverse claims to real or personal property or any interest therein.

(b) An action may be brought under this chapter by parties to an agreement entered into pursuant to Section 6307 or 6357 of the Public Resources Code to confirm the validity of the agreement.

(c) Nothing in this section shall be construed to limit the right of members of the public to bring or participate in actions challenging the validity of agreements entered into pursuant to Section 6307 or 6357 of the Public Resources Code. *(Added by Stats.1980, c. 44, p. 109, § 15. Amended by Stats.1989, c. 1045, § 1.)*

Law Revision Commission Comments

Section 760.020 supersedes the first portions of former Sections 738, 749, and 749.1. This chapter does not limit the interests that may be determined or the persons against whom they may be quieted; it is intended to provide the broadest possible forum for clearing title to the fee or any other interest in property.

The ability to quiet title as to both real and personal property may be useful in cases involving land and fixtures, as well as in cases involving personal property alone.

Research References

Rutter, Cal. Practice Guide: Real Prop. Transactions Ch. 11-H, H. Other Remedies.

Miller and Starr California Real Estate § 10:114, Reconveyance When Beneficiary Cannot be Located.

5 Witkin Cal. Proc. 5th Pleading § 657, (S 657) in General.

§ 760.030. Cumulative remedy; resolution of issue establishing or quieting title

(a) The remedy provided in this chapter is cumulative and not exclusive of any other remedy, form or right of action, or proceeding provided by law for establishing or quieting title to property.

(b) In an action or proceeding in which establishing or quieting title to property is in issue the court in its discretion may, upon motion of any party, require that the issue be resolved pursuant to the provisions of this chapter to the extent practicable. *(Added by Stats.1980, c. 44, p. 109, § 15.)*

Law Revision Commission Comments

Subdivision (a) of Section 760.030 continues the substance of the third paragraph of former Section 751 and the first portion of the third paragraph of former Section 751.1. Subdivision (b) is new. Other proceedings that may be available to clear title to property include actions concerning real property titles affected by public improvement assessments (Sections 801.1–801.15), actions under the Destroyed Land Records Relief Law and Cullen Earthquake Act (Sections 751.01–751.28 and 751.50–751.65), partition actions (Sections 872.010–874.240), actions to quiet title to tax-deeded property (Rev. & Tax. Code §§ 3591–3617 and 3950–3972), actions to remove a cloud on title (Civil Code § 3412), and declaratory relief actions (Code Civ.Proc. § 1060). For special actions and proceedings to clear title, see Sections 770.010–770.080 (identity of person in chain of title), 771.010–771.020 (land dedicated for public improvement), and 772.010–772.060 (right of entry or occupation of surface lands under oil or gas lease). See also Civil Code § 794 (quitclaim of expired oil, gas, or mineral lease).

Research References

Rutter, Cal. Practice Guide: Real Prop. Transactions Ch. 11-H, H. Other Remedies.

Miller and Starr California Real Estate § 34:104, Who Can Bring the Action.

5 Witkin Cal. Proc. 5th Pleading § 657, (S 657) in General.

§ 760.040. Jurisdiction; equitable relief

(a) The superior court has jurisdiction of actions under this chapter.

(b) The court has complete jurisdiction over the parties to the action and the property described in the complaint and is deemed to have obtained possession and control of the property for the purposes of the action with complete jurisdiction to render the judgment provided for in this chapter.

(c) Nothing in this chapter limits any authority the court may have to grant such equitable relief as may be proper under the circumstances of the case. *(Added by Stats.1980, c. 44, p. 109, § 15.)*

Law Revision Commission Comments

Subdivision (a) of Section 760.040 is an exception to the rule of Section 86 conferring limited jurisdiction on municipal and justice courts to determine title to personal property. It is consistent with the general rule that determinations involving title to property are within the jurisdiction of the superior court. See, e.g., Sections 872.110 (partition), 1250.010 (Eminent Domain Law).

Subdivision (b) is comparable to Sections 751.11 (Destroyed Land Records Relief Law) and 751.55 (Cullen Earthquake Act).

Subdivision (c) makes clear that the recodification of the quiet title provisions in this chapter does not impair any equitable powers of the court. Cf. 3 B. Witkin, California Procedure Pleading § 534 (2d ed. 1971) (plaintiff's offer to do equity).

Research References

Rutter, Cal. Practice Guide: Real Prop. Transactions Ch. 11-H, H. Other Remedies.

7 Witkin Cal. Proc. 5th Judgment § 24, Quiet Title.

5 Witkin Cal. Proc. 5th Pleading § 658, (S 658) Jurisdiction, Venue, and Process.

§ 760.050. Venue

Subject to the power of the court to transfer actions, the proper county for the trial of an action under this chapter is:

(a) Where the subject of the action is real property or real and personal property, the county in which the real property, or some part thereof, is located.

(b) Where the subject of the action is personal property, the county in which the personal property is principally located at the commencement of the action or in which the defendants, or any of them, reside at the commencement of the action. *(Added by Stats.1980, c. 44, p. 110, § 15.)*

Law Revision Commission Comments

Section 760.050 is consistent with the general venue provisions of Section 392; it is comparable to Section 872.110 (venue in partition). See Section 872.110 and Comment thereto.

Research References

Rutter, Cal. Practice Guide: Real Prop. Transactions Ch. 11-H, H. Other Remedies.

Miller and Starr California Real Estate § 34:105, Requirements of the Complaint.

3 Witkin Cal. Proc. 5th Actions § 796, Quiet Title.

5 Witkin Cal. Proc. 5th Pleading § 658, (S 658) Jurisdiction, Venue, and Process.

§ 760.060. Practice in civil actions; law governing; exceptions

The statutes and rules governing practice in civil actions generally apply to actions under this chapter except where they are inconsistent with the provisions of this chapter. *(Added by Stats.1980, c. 44, p. 110, § 15.)*

Law Revision Commission Comments

Section 760.060 is comparable to Sections 751.17 (Destroyed Land Records Relief Law) and 872.030 (partition).

Research References

Miller and Starr California Real Estate § 34:104, Who Can Bring the Action.

5 Witkin Cal. Proc. 5th Pleading § 657, (S 657) in General.

ARTICLE 2. COMMENCEMENT OF ACTION

Section

761.010.   Complaint; filing; lis pendens.

761.020.   Complaint; verification; contents.

761.030.   Answer; verification; contents.

761.040.   Cross-complaint.

§ 761.010. Complaint; filing; lis pendens

(a) An action under this chapter is commenced by filing a complaint with the court.

(b) Immediately upon commencement of the action, the plaintiff shall file a notice of the pendency of the action in the office of the county recorder of each county in which any real property described in the complaint is located. *(Added by Stats.1980, c. 44, p. 110, § 15.)*

Law Revision Commission Comments

Subdivision (a) of Section 761.010 is comparable to Section 1250.110 (Eminent Domain Law).

Subdivision (b) supersedes the fifth paragraph of former Sections 749 and 749.1, which provided a 10-day period within which to file. The contents of the lis pendens are prescribed in Section 409. Failure to file the lis pendens may result in subsequent bona fide purchasers and encumbrancers of record at the time the judgment is recorded not being bound by the quiet title judgment. See Section 764.040 (persons not bound by judgment).

Research References

Rutter, Cal. Practice Guide: Civ. Pro. Before Trial Ch. 9(I)-J, J. Motion to Expunge Lis Pendens.

Rutter, Cal. Practice Guide: Real Prop. Transactions Ch. 11-H, H. Other Remedies.

Rutter, Cal. Practice Guide: Real Prop. Transactions Ch. 11-I, I. Lis Pendens.

Miller and Starr California Real Estate § 11:150, Actions in Which a Lis Pendens May or Must be Recorded.

Miller and Starr California Real Estate § 34:109, Recordation of Lis Pendens Required.

3 Witkin Cal. Proc. 5th Actions § 381, (S 381) Specific Mandatory Statutes.

5 Witkin Cal. Proc. 5th Pleading § 657, (S 657) in General.

§ 761.020. Complaint; verification; contents

The complaint shall be verified and shall include all of the following:

(a) A description of the property that is the subject of the action. In the case of tangible personal property, the description shall include its usual location. In the case of real property, the description shall include both its legal description and its street address or common designation, if any.

(b) The title of the plaintiff as to which a determination under this chapter is sought and the basis of the title. If the title is based upon adverse possession, the complaint shall allege the specific facts constituting the adverse possession.

(c) The adverse claims to the title of the plaintiff against which a determination is sought.

(d) The date as of which the determination is sought. If the determination is sought as of a date other than the date the complaint is filed, the complaint shall include a statement of the reasons why a determination as of that date is sought.

(e) A prayer for the determination of the title of the plaintiff against the adverse claims. *(Added by Stats.1980, c. 44, p. 110, § 15.)*

Law Revision Commission Comments

Section 761.020 continues the substance of the second sentence of the first paragraph and supersedes a portion of the fourth paragraph of former Sections 749 and 749.1, which required a verified complaint and a statement of facts upon which the plaintiff's title is based.

Under subdivision (a), the description of the property must be sufficiently precise to enable the defendants to identify the property. Nothing in this subdivision precludes the joinder of several properties or of real and personal property in one action, where appropriate.

Subdivision (b) does not require that the plaintiff claim a fee or other freehold interest in the property; any interest is sufficient. This is consistent with former Section 738 and the cases thereunder. See, e.g., 3 B. Witkin, California Procedure Pleading § 522, at 2173 (2d ed. 1971). For provisions relating to title by adverse possession, see Sections 318–328. The 20- and 10-year limitations on establishing title by adverse possession formerly found in Sections 749 and 749.1 are not continued; they are inconsistent with the general adverse possession requirements. See discussion in Willemsen, Improving California's Quiet Title Laws, 21 Hastings L.J. 835, 838–44 (1970).

Subdivision (c) requires the naming of specific adverse claims as to which the plaintiff seeks to quiet title. The plaintiff may also seek to give the quiet title action an in rem effect under this chapter. The plaintiff's title in such a case need not be based on adverse possession as under former Sections 749 and 749.1. This chapter includes special provisions, including pleading provisions, to effectuate the in rem aspects of the quiet title action. See Sections 762.060–762.070 (unknown defendants), 763.010–763.040 (service of process), 764.010–764.050 (judgment).

Subdivision (d) is intended to permit a title determination as of a date prior to the date of the action. This implements suggestions in L. Simes & C. Taylor, The Improvement of Conveyancing by Legislation xxii (1960), and Willemsen, Improving California's Quiet Title Laws, 21 Hastings L.J. 835, 853 (1970).

Research References

Rutter, Cal. Practice Guide: Civ. Pro. Before Trial Ch. 6-B, B. Complaints.

Rutter, Cal. Practice Guide: Real Prop. Transactions Ch. 11-H, H. Other Remedies.

Miller and Starr California Real Estate § 34:104, Who Can Bring the Action.

Miller and Starr California Real Estate § 34:105, Requirements of the Complaint.

4 Witkin Cal. Proc. 5th Pleading § 466, Complaint or Petition.

5 Witkin Cal. Proc. 5th Pleading § 663, (S 663) Statutory Requirements for Complaint.

5 Witkin Cal. Proc. 5th Pleading § 664, in General.

5 Witkin Cal. Proc. 5th Pleading § 665, Title in Fee.

5 Witkin Cal. Proc. 5th Pleading § 668, General Pleading.

§ 761.030. Answer; verification; contents

(a) The answer shall be verified and shall set forth:

(1) Any claim the defendant has.

(2) Any facts tending to controvert such material allegations of the complaint as the defendant does not wish to be taken as true.

(3) A statement of any new matter constituting a defense.

(b) If the defendant disclaims in the answer any claim, or suffers judgment to be taken without answer, the plaintiff shall not recover costs. *(Added by Stats.1980, c. 44, p. 110, § 15.)*

Law Revision Commission Comments

Paragraphs (1) and (2) of subdivision (a) of Section 761.030 are comparable to subdivisions (a) and (b) of Section 872.410 (partition). Paragraph (3) is drawn from Section 431.30(b) (contents of answer in general rules of pleading). See also Section 760.060 (rules of practice in civil actions govern this chapter except where inconsistent). The verification requirement is a specific application of Section 446 (when complaint is verified, answer must be verified).

Subdivision (b) continues the substance of former Section 739. It provides an express exception to Section 1032 (costs in superior court).

Research References

7 Witkin Cal. Proc. 5th Judgment § 110, (S 110) Disclaimer or Default in Quiet Title Action.

7 Witkin Cal. Proc. 5th Judgment § 167, Other Contracts.

2 Witkin Cal. Proc. 5th Jurisdiction § 321, Improper Award or Denial of Costs.

5 Witkin Cal. Proc. 5th Pleading § 661, (S 661) Appearance and Rights of Defendant.

5 Witkin Cal. Proc. 5th Pleading § 1047, in General.

§ 761.040. Cross-complaint

(a) The defendant may by cross-complaint seek affirmative relief in the action.

(b) If the defendant seeks a determination of title as of a date other than the date specified in the complaint, the cross-complaint shall include the date and a statement of the reasons why a determination as of that date is sought. *(Added by Stats.1980, c. 44, p. 111, § 15.)*

Law Revision Commission Comments

Subdivision (a) of Section 761.040 codifies case law permitting a cross-complaint for affirmative relief in a quiet title action. See, e.g., Winter v. McMillan, 87 Cal. 256, 25 P. 407 (1890).

Subdivision (b) is comparable to Section 761.020(d) (complaint).

Research References

5 Witkin Cal. Proc. 5th Pleading § 661, (S 661) Appearance and Rights of Defendant.

ARTICLE 3. DEFENDANTS

Section

762.010. Naming of adverse claimants.

762.020. Names of unknown defendants and parties; unknown, uncertain or contingent claims; statement.

762.030. Joinder of personal representative of required defendant; affidavit and manner of joinder if representative unknown.

762.040. Orders; joinder of additional parties; title report.

762.050. Appearance by any claimant as a defendant.

762.060. Manner of naming persons other than required defendants; naming of persons with adverse claims of record or known to plaintiff; admission of validity of claim.

762.070. Rights of person named and served as unknown defendant.

762.080. Orders; appointment of guardians ad litem.

762.090. State; joinder as party; declaration of existing law.

§ 762.010. Naming of adverse claimants

The plaintiff shall name as defendants in the action the persons having adverse claims to the title of the plaintiff against which a determination is sought. *(Added by Stats.1980, c. 44, p. 111, § 15.)*

Law Revision Commission Comments

Section 762.010 states the rule for joinder of known adverse claimants. Failure to join these persons will result in a judgment that does not bind them. See Sections 764.040 and 764.050. For joinder requirements where the name or interest of the defendant is unknown or the defendant is deceased, see Sections 762.020 and 762.030. For joinder of unknown persons, see Section 762.060.

Research References

Rutter, Cal. Practice Guide: Civ. Pro. Before Trial Ch. 2-C, C. Joinder of Parties.

Rutter, Cal. Practice Guide: Real Prop. Transactions Ch. 11-H, H. Other Remedies.

5 Witkin Cal. Proc. 5th Pleading § 659, (S 659) Necessary Known Defendants.

§ 762.020. Names of unknown defendants and parties; unknown, uncertain or contingent claims; statement

(a) If the name of a person required to be named as a defendant is not known to the plaintiff, the plaintiff shall so state in the complaint and shall name as parties all persons unknown in the manner provided in Section 762.060.

(b) If the claim or the share or quantity of the claim of a person required to be named as a defendant is unknown, uncertain, or contingent, the plaintiff shall so state in the complaint. If the lack of knowledge, uncertainty, or contingency is caused by a transfer to an unborn or unascertained person or class member, or by a transfer in the form of a contingent remainder, vested remainder subject to defeasance, executory interest, or similar disposition, the plaintiff shall also state in the complaint, so far as is known to the plaintiff, the name, age, and legal disability (if any) of the person in being who would be entitled to the claim had the contingency upon which the claim depends occurred prior to the commencement of the action. *(Added by Stats.1980, c. 44, p. 111, § 15.)*

Law Revision Commission Comments

Section 762.020 is comparable to subdivisions (a) and (b) of Section 872.520 (partition).

Research References

Miller and Starr California Real Estate § 34:107, Identification of Defendants.

5 Witkin Cal. Proc. 5th Pleading § 660, (S 660) Defendant or Interest Unknown.

§ 762.030. Joinder of personal representative of required defendant; affidavit and manner of joinder if representative unknown

(a) If a person required to be named as a defendant is dead and the plaintiff knows of a personal representative, the plaintiff shall join the personal representative as a defendant.

(b) If a person required to be named as a defendant is dead, or is believed by the plaintiff to be dead, and the plaintiff knows of no personal representative:

(1) The plaintiff shall state these facts in an affidavit filed with the complaint.

(2) Where it is stated in the affidvit [1] that such person is dead, the plaintiff may join as defendants "the testate and intestate successors of _____ (naming the deceased person), deceased, and all persons claiming by, through, or under such decedent," naming them in that manner.

(3) Where it is stated in the affidavit that such person is believed to be dead, the plaintiff may join the person as a defendant, and may also join "the testate and intestate successors of _____ (naming the person) believed to be deceased, and all persons claiming by, through, or under such person," naming them in that manner. *(Added by Stats.1980, c. 44, p. 111, § 15.)*

[1] So in enrolled bill.

Law Revision Commission Comments

Section 762.030 is comparable to Sections 872.530 (partition) and 1250.220(b) (Eminent Domain Law).

Research References

5 Witkin Cal. Proc. 5th Pleading § 659, (S 659) Necessary Known Defendants.

§ 762.040. Orders; joinder of additional parties; title report

The court upon its own motion may, and upon motion of any party shall, make such orders as appear appropriate:

(a) For joinder of such additional parties as are necessary or proper.

(b) Requiring the plaintiff to procure a title report and designate a place where it shall be kept for inspection, use, and copying by the parties. *(Added by Stats.1980, c. 44, p. 111, § 15.)*

Law Revision Commission Comments

Subdivision (a) of Section 762.040 is comparable to a portion of Section 872.520(c) (partition). Subdivision (d) is drawn from Section 872.220 (partition).

Research References

Miller and Starr California Real Estate § 16:26, Capacity; Quiet Title Action by an Adverse Possessor.

Miller and Starr California Real Estate § 34:107, Identification of Defendants.

5 Witkin Cal. Proc. 5th Pleading § 657, (S 657) in General.

5 Witkin Cal. Proc. 5th Pleading § 659, (S 659) Necessary Known Defendants.

§ 762.050. Appearance by any claimant as a defendant

Any person who has a claim to the property described in the complaint may appear in the proceeding. Whether or not the person is named as a defendant in the complaint, the person shall appear as a defendant. *(Added by Stats.1980, c. 44, p. 112, § 15.)*

Law Revision Commission Comments

Section 762.050 is comparable to Sections 751.12 (Destroyed Land Records Relief Law) and 1250.230 (Eminent Domain Law).

Research References

5 Witkin Cal. Proc. 5th Pleading § 661, (S 661) Appearance and Rights of Defendant.

§ 762.060. Manner of naming persons other than required defendants; naming of persons with adverse claims of record or known to plaintiff; admission of validity of claim

(a) In addition to the persons required to be named as defendants in the action, the plaintiff may name as defendants "all persons unknown, claiming any legal or equitable right, title, estate, lien, or interest in the property described in the complaint adverse to plaintiff's title, or any cloud upon plaintiff's title thereto," naming them in that manner.

(b) In an action under this section, the plaintiff shall name as defendants the persons having adverse claims that are of record or known to the plaintiff or reasonably apparent from an inspection of the property.

(c) If the plaintiff admits the validity of any adverse claim, the complaint shall so state. *(Added by Stats.1980, c. 44, p. 112, § 15.)*

Law Revision Commission Comments

Subdivision (a) of Section 762.060 continues the substance of the last portion of the second paragraph and the third paragraph of former Sections 749 and 749.1. Unlike the former provisions, Section 762.060 does not limit the availability of in rem relief to adverse possessors, but permits joinder of all persons by any plaintiff seeking clear title. See Sections 760.020 and 761.020 and Comments thereto. In addition to unknown persons, the plaintiff must also name known persons pursuant to subdivision (b) and Section 762.010.

Subdivision (b) continues the substance of the first portion of the second paragraph and supersedes a portion of the fourth paragraph of former Sections 749 and 749.1, and extends the joinder requirement to claimants reasonably apparent from an inspection of the property. This provision is drawn from Section 872.510 (partition). For the effect of failure to join holders of interests actually known to the plaintiff or reasonably apparent from an inspection of the property, see Section 764.050.

Subdivision (c) adds express authority to admit by pleadings the validity of an adverse claim, thereby enabling an action to determine title as against all persons, known and unknown, with specified exceptions. This will avoid the need to litigate interests accepted as valid to which the plaintiff's title is subject. See Section 764.010.

Research References

Rutter, Cal. Practice Guide: Civ. Pro. Before Trial Ch. 2-C, C. Joinder of Parties.

Miller and Starr California Real Estate § 34:107, Identification of Defendants.

5 Witkin Cal. Proc. 5th Pleading § 660, (S 660) Defendant or Interest Unknown.

5 Witkin Cal. Proc. 5th Pleading § 663, (S 663) Statutory Requirements for Complaint.

§ 762.070. Rights of person named and served as unknown defendant

A person named and served as an unknown defendant has the same rights as are provided by law in cases of all other defendants named and served, and the action shall proceed against unknown defendants in the same manner as against other defendants named and served, and with the same effect. *(Added by Stats.1980, c. 44, p. 112, § 15.)*

Section 762.070 continues the substance of a portion of former Section 750.

Research References

5 Witkin Cal. Proc. 5th Pleading § 661, (S 661) Appearance and Rights of Defendant.

§ 762.080. Orders; appointment of guardians ad litem

The court upon its own motion may, and upon motion of any party shall, make such orders for appointment of guardians ad litem as appear necessary to protect the interest of any party. *(Added by Stats.1980, c. 44, p. 112, § 15.)*

Section 762.080 is comparable to a portion of Section 872.520(c) (partition). The conditions under which a guardian ad litem should be appointed are prescribed in Sections 372, 373, and 373.5. It should be noted that a judgment in the action binds persons under legal disability. See Section 764.030.

Research References

Miller and Starr California Real Estate § 34:107, Identification of Defendants.
4 Witkin Cal. Proc. 5th Pleading § 70, (S 70) in General.
5 Witkin Cal. Proc. 5th Pleading § 657, (S 657) in General.

§ 762.090. State; joinder as party; declaration of existing law

(a) The state may be joined as a party to an action under this chapter.

(b) This section does not constitute a change in, but is declaratory of, existing law. *(Added by Stats.1980, c. 44, p. 112, § 15.)*

ARTICLE 4. SERVICE OF PROCESS

Section
763.010. Form, content and manner; service by publication, restriction; referee.
763.020. Service by publication; order subject to conditions.
763.030. Service by publication; contents of publication.
763.040. Service by publication; proof of service, etc., of summons and filing of lis pendens.

§ 763.010. Form, content and manner; service by publication, restriction; referee

(a) The form, content, and manner of the service of summons shall be the same as in civil actions generally.

(b) If upon affidavit it appears to the satisfaction of the court that the plaintiff has used reasonable diligence to ascertain the identity and residence of and to serve summons on the persons named as unknown defendants and persons joined as testate or intestate successors of a person known or believed to be dead, the court shall order service by publication pursuant to Section 415.50 and the provisions of this article. The court may, in its discretion, appoint a referee to investigate whether the plaintiff has used reasonable diligence to ascertain the identity and residence of persons sought to be served by publication, and the court may rely on the report of the referee instead of the affidavit of the plaintiff in making the order for service by publication.

(c) Nothing in this section authorizes service by publication upon any person named as an unknown defendant who is in open and actual possession of the property. *(Added by Stats. 1980, c. 44, p. 112, § 15.)*

Subdivision (a) of Section 763.010 supersedes the fourth paragraph of former Sections 749 and 749.1 and the first, third, and fourth paragraphs of former Section 750. The contents of the summons is prescribed in Section 412.20. A description of the property and a statement of the object of the action are not included since the property will already be described and the relief sought will already be stated in the complaint. See Section 761.020. Service on known defendants must be made pursuant to general service provisions; publication as to known defendants is permitted only by court order if it appears upon affidavit that the defendant cannot with reasonable diligence be served in another manner. Section 415.50.

Subdivision (b) makes clear that, where unknown parties or heirs are involved, service on such parties must be by publication. This supersedes the fourth and a portion of the fifth paragraphs of former Section 750. The affidavit contents are drawn from Section 801.9 (real property titles affected by public improvement assessments) and Revenue and Taxation Code Section 3960 (quiet title to tax-deeded property). Subdivision (b) also authorizes the court to appoint a referee to investigate the facts on behalf of the court where service by publication is sought. The authority provided is a specific instance of the general authority contained in Section 638(1). Whether the plaintiff has used reasonable diligence to ascertain the location and identity of known and unknown defendants is a matter to be determined by the trier of fact under the circumstances of the particular case. See, e.g., Gerhard v. Stephens, 68 Cal.2d 864, 908–10, 442 P.2d 692, 725–26, 69 Cal.Rptr. 612, 645–46 (1968).

Subdivision (c) codifies case law. See, e.g., Gerhard v. Stephens, 68 Cal.2d 864, 908, 442 P.2d 692, 725, 69 Cal.Rptr. 612, 645 (1968); Manuel v. Kiser, 94 Cal.App.2d 540, 545, 210 P.2d 918, 921 (1949).

Research References

Rutter, Cal. Practice Guide: Civ. Pro. Before Trial Ch. 2-C, C. Joinder of Parties.
Miller and Starr California Real Estate § 16:26, Capacity; Quiet Title Action by an Adverse Possessor.
Miller and Starr California Real Estate § 34:107, Identification of Defendants.
3 Witkin Cal. Proc. 5th Actions § 987, (S 987) Actions Involving Real Property.
3 Witkin Cal. Proc. 5th Actions § 1034, Special Statutes.
5 Witkin Cal. Proc. 5th Pleading § 658, (S 658) Jurisdiction, Venue, and Process.

§ 763.020. Service by publication; order subject to conditions

Whenever the court orders service by publication, the order is subject to the following conditions:

(a) The plaintiff shall post, not later than 10 days after the date the order is made, a copy of the summons and complaint in a conspicuous place on the real property that is the subject of the action.

(b) The plaintiff shall record, if not already recorded, a notice of the pendency of the action.

(c) The publication shall describe the property that is the subject of the action. In addition to particularly describing the property, the publication shall describe the property by giving its street address, if any, or other common designation, if any; but, if a legal description of the property is given, the validity of the publication shall not be affected by the fact that the street address or other common designation recited is erroneous or that the street address or other common designation is omitted. *(Added by Stats.1980, c. 44, p. 113, § 15.)*

Section 763.020 supersedes the section and a portion of the fifth paragraphs of former Section 750. The manner of service by publication is prescribed in the general provisions of Section 415.50.

Research References

Rutter, Cal. Practice Guide: Civ. Pro. Before Trial Ch. 2-C, C. Joinder of Parties.
Miller and Starr California Real Estate § 16:26, Capacity; Quiet Title Action by an Adverse Possessor.

Miller and Starr California Real Estate § 34:107, Identification of Defendants.

5 Witkin Cal. Proc. 5th Pleading § 658, (S 658) Jurisdiction, Venue, and Process.

§ 763.030. Service by publication; contents of publication

(a) Whenever the court orders service by publication, the publication may:

(1) Name only the defendants to be served thereby.

(2) Describe only the property in which the defendants to be served thereby claim interests.

(b) Judgment against a defendant who fails to appear and answer following service under this section shall be conclusive against the defendant named in respect only to property described in the publication. *(Added by Stats.1980, c. 44, p. 113, § 15.)*

Law Revision Commission Comments

Section 763.030 supersedes the seventh paragraph of former Section 750 and is comparable to Sections 872.330 (partition) and 1250.125 (Eminent Domain Law).

Research References

5 Witkin Cal. Proc. 5th Pleading § 658, (S 658) Jurisdiction, Venue, and Process.

§ 763.040. Service by publication; proof of service, etc., of summons and filing of lis pendens

Whenever the court orders service by publication, the court before hearing the case shall require proof that the summons has been served, posted, published as required, and that the notice of pendency of action has been filed. *(Added by Stats.1980, c. 44, p. 113, § 15.)*

Law Revision Commission Comments

Section 763.040 continues the substance of the second sentence of the first paragraph of former Sections 751 and 751.1.

Research References

3 Witkin Cal. Proc. 5th Actions § 381, (S 381) Specific Mandatory Statutes.

5 Witkin Cal. Proc. 5th Pleading § 658, (S 658) Jurisdiction, Venue, and Process.

ARTICLE 5. JUDGMENT

§ 764.010. Examination into and determination of plaintiff's title; prohibition against default judgment; rendition of judgment

The court shall examine into and determine the plaintiff's title against the claims of all the defendants. The court shall not enter judgment by default but shall in all cases require evidence of plaintiff's title and hear such evidence as may be offered respecting the claims of any of the defendants, other than claims the validity of which is admitted by the plaintiff in the complaint. The court shall render judgment in accordance with the evidence and the law. *(Added by Stats.1980, c. 44, p. 113, § 15.)*

Law Revision Commission Comments

Section 764.010 continues the substance of the first sentence of the first paragraph of former Sections 751 and 751.1. It is consistent with Section 585(3) (default judgment).

Research References

Rutter, Cal. Practice Guide: Civ. Pro. Before Trial Ch. 5-D, D. Default Judgment by Court.

Rutter, Cal. Practice Guide: Civ. Pro. Before Trial Ch. 5-E, E. Limitations on Default Judgments.

Rutter, Cal. Practice Guide: Real Prop. Transactions Ch. 11-H, H. Other Remedies.

Rutter, Cal. Practice Guide: Real Prop. Transactions Gen. Matls., Highlights.

Miller and Starr California Real Estate § 34:105, Requirements of the Complaint.

15 NO. 1 Miller & Starr, California Real Estate Newsalert 15, Remedies.

22 NO. 4 Miller & Starr, California Real Estate Newsalert 36, Judicial Remedies.

23 NO. 1 Miller & Starr, California Real Estate Newsalert 14, Judicial Remedies.

9 Witkin Cal. Proc. 5th Appeal § 572, (S 572) Where No Judgment was Entered.

5 Witkin Cal. Proc. 5th Pleading § 662, (S 662) Trial and Judgment.

6 Witkin Cal. Proc. 5th Proceedings Without Trial § 137, (S 137) Restrictions on Default Judgments.

§ 764.020. Validity or interpretation of gift, devise, bequest or trust under a will; admissibility; determination; effect of probate decree

(a) If in an action under this chapter the validity or interpretation of a gift, devise, bequest, or trust, under a will or instrument purporting to be a will, whether admitted to probate or not, is involved:

(1) The will or instrument purporting to be a will is admissible in evidence.

(2) All questions concerning the validity of the gift, devise, bequest, or trust shall be finally determined in the action.

(3) If the will has been admitted to probate and the gift, devise, bequest, or trust has been interpreted by a final decree of the probate court, the interpretation is conclusive as to the proper construction thereof.

(b) Nothing in this section deprives a party of the right to a jury trial in any case where, by law, the right is now given. *(Added by Stats.1980, c. 44, p. 113, § 15.)*

Law Revision Commission Comments

Section 764.020 continues the substance of the last portion of former Section 738. For determination of title in probate proceedings, see Prob. Code §§ 850–854.

Research References

3 Witkin Cal. Proc. 5th Actions § 133, Nature of Problem.

5 Witkin Cal. Proc. 5th Pleading § 662, (S 662) Trial and Judgment.

§ 764.030. Conclusiveness of judgment

The judgment in the action is binding and conclusive on all of the following persons, regardless of any legal disability:

(a) All persons known and unknown who were parties to the action and who have any claim to the property, whether present or future, vested or contingent, legal or equitable, several or undivided.

(b) Except as provided in Section 764.045, all persons who were not parties to the action and who have any claim to the property which was not of record at the time the lis pendens was filed or, if none was filed, at the time the judgment was recorded. *(Added by Stats.1980, c. 44, p. 114, § 15. Amended by Stats.1984, c. 20, § 1.)*

Law Revision Commission Comments

Section 764.030 supersedes the last portion of the first sentence of the sixth paragraph of former Section 750 and the first portion of the second paragraph of former Sections 751 and 751.1. It is comparable to Sections 751.15 (Destroyed Land Records Relief Law) and 874.210 (partition). Subdivision (b) of Section 764.030 is amended to correct a section reference. Subdivision (c) is deleted because it added nothing to subdivisions (a) and (b) and was inconsistent with Section 764.045 (persons not bound by judgment) in certain cases. [17 Cal.L.Rev.Comm. Reports 947 (1984)].

Research References

Rutter, Cal. Practice Guide: Real Prop. Transactions Ch. 11-H, H. Other Remedies.
Rutter, Cal. Practice Guide: Real Prop. Transactions Ch. 11-I, I. Lis Pendens.
Miller and Starr California Real Estate § 16:26, Capacity; Quiet Title Action by an Adverse Possessor.
Miller and Starr California Real Estate § 11:147, Priority of Judgments and Pending Litigation; in General.
Miller and Starr California Real Estate § 11:150, Actions in Which a Lis Pendens May or Must be Recorded.
Miller and Starr California Real Estate § 34:105, Requirements of the Complaint.
Miller and Starr California Real Estate § 34:111, Effect of Judgment.
22 NO. 6 Miller & Starr, California Real Estate Newsalert 17, Judicial Remedies.
5 Witkin Cal. Proc. 5th Pleading § 662, (S 662) Trial and Judgment.

§ 764.045. Claim in property of person not a party to action; effect of judgment; conditions

Except to the extent provided in Section 1908, the judgment does not affect a claim in the property or part thereof of any person who was not a party to the action if any of the following conditions is satisfied:

(a) The claim was of record at the time the lis pendens was filed or, if none was filed, at the time the judgment was recorded.

(b) The claim was actually known to the plaintiff or would have been reasonably apparent from an inspection of the property at the time the lis pendens was filed or, if none was filed, at the time the judgment was entered. Nothing in this subdivision shall be construed to impair the rights of a bona fide purchaser or encumbrancer for value dealing with the plaintiff or the plaintiff's successors in interest. *(Added by Stats.1984, c. 20, § 3.)*

Law Revision Commission Comments

Subdivision (a) of Section 764.045 continues the substance of former Section 764.040. Subdivision (b) continues the substance of former Section 764.050, with clarifications relating to the time of the plaintiff's knowledge. The introductory portion of Section 764.045 makes clear that notwithstanding the provisions of this section, a claimant may be bound by the proceeding if the claim was acquired from a party after commence-

ment of the proceeding and with actual knowledge of the proceeding. Section 1908(a)(2). [17 Cal.L.Rev.Comm. Reports 947 (1984)].

Research References

Rutter, Cal. Practice Guide: Real Prop. Transactions Ch. 11-H, H. Other Remedies.
Miller and Starr California Real Estate § 16:26, Capacity; Quiet Title Action by an Adverse Possessor.
Miller and Starr California Real Estate § 11:147, Priority of Judgments and Pending Litigation; in General.
Miller and Starr California Real Estate § 11:150, Actions in Which a Lis Pendens May or Must be Recorded.
Miller and Starr California Real Estate § 34:111, Effect of Judgment.
5 Witkin Cal. Proc. 5th Pleading § 662, (S 662) Trial and Judgment.

§ 764.060. Relief granted upon attack on judgment; no effect on rights of purchaser or encumbrancer for value without knowledge of defects or irregularities

The relief granted in an action or proceeding directly or collaterally attacking the judgment in the action, whether based on lack of actual notice to a party or otherwise, shall not impair the rights of a purchaser or encumbrancer for value of the property acting in reliance on the judgment without knowledge of any defects or irregularities in the judgment or the proceedings. *(Added by Stats.1980, c. 44, p. 114, § 15.)*

Law Revision Commission Comments

Section 764.060 is intended to enhance the marketability of property as to which an in rem quiet title decree has been rendered. An action or proceeding directly or collaterally attacking the judgment in the action may not affect the rights of bona fide purchasers of the property; the plaintiff in the action or proceeding may be relegated to a damage remedy. Section 764.060 does not prescribe limitations periods for direct or collateral attack on a quiet title judgment. Such periods are governed by other law. See, e.g., Sections 473, 473.5.

Research References

Rutter, Cal. Practice Guide: Real Prop. Transactions Ch. 11-H, H. Other Remedies.
Miller and Starr California Real Estate § 16:26, Capacity; Quiet Title Action by an Adverse Possessor.
Miller and Starr California Real Estate § 11:147, Priority of Judgments and Pending Litigation; in General.
Miller and Starr California Real Estate § 34:111, Effect of Judgment.
5 Witkin Cal. Proc. 5th Pleading § 662, (S 662) Trial and Judgment.

§ 764.070. State or United States; effect of judgment; exception

Notwithstanding any other provision of this chapter, the judgment in the action is not binding or conclusive on the following:

(a) The state, unless individually joined as a party to the action.

(b) The United States, unless the United States is individually joined as a party to the action and federal law authorizes judgment in the action to be binding or conclusive as to its interests. *(Added by Stats.1980, c. 44, p. 114, § 15. Amended by Stats.1986, c. 271, § 2.)*

Research References

Rutter, Cal. Practice Guide: Real Prop. Transactions Ch. 11-H, H. Other Remedies.
Miller and Starr California Real Estate § 16:26, Capacity; Quiet Title Action by an Adverse Possessor.
Miller and Starr California Real Estate § 34:111, Effect of Judgment.
5 Witkin Cal. Proc. 5th Pleading § 662, (S 662) Trial and Judgment.

§ 764.080. Quiet title actions; agreements to exchange land or establish high-water or low-water marks

(a) In any action brought to quiet title to land that has been subject to an agreement entered into pursuant to Section 6307 or

6357 of the Public Resources Code, at the time set for trial the court shall, at the request of any party, receive evidence on the nature of the agreement. After receiving that evidence, the court shall render a statement of decision. In the case of an agreement pursuant to Section 6357, the statement of decision shall include a recitation of the underlying facts and a determination whether the agreement meets the criteria of Section 6357 and other law applicable to the validity of boundary line agreements. In the case of an agreement pursuant to Section 6307, the statement of decision shall recite the relevant facts and shall contain a determination whether the requirements of Section 6307 of the Public Resources Code, Sections 3 and 4 of Article 10 of the California Constitution, and other applicable law have been met. If the court finds the agreement to be valid, the judgment in the action shall quiet title in the parties named in the agreement in accordance with the agreement. If the judgment is entered prior to the effective date of the agreement, the judgment shall provide that, upon the effective date, title is quieted in the parties in accordance with the agreements. However, no action may be brought pursuant to this section until the State Lands Commission has approved the agreement following a public hearing. All such actions shall be set on the trial calendar within one year from the filing of a memorandum to set, unless the court extends this time for good cause.

(b) Nothing in this section shall be construed to limit the right of members of the public to bring or participate in actions challenging the validity of agreements entered into pursuant to Section 6307 or 6357 of the Public Resources Code. Any action brought by a member of the public shall be set on the trial calendar within one year from the filing of a memorandum to set, unless the court extends this time for good cause. *(Added by Stats.1989, c. 1045, § 2.)*

ARTICLE 6. LIENS AND ENCUMBRANCES

Section
765.010. Petition for hearing.
765.020. Petition contents; affidavit.
765.030. Court order.
765.040. Liability for recording or filing lien or encumbrance in violation of statute.
765.050. Exclusion of claims of encumbrance by financial institution.
765.060. Counsel for public officer or employee who recorded lien or encumbrance in violation of statute.

§ 765.010. Petition for hearing

A public officer or employee whose property is subject to a lien or other encumbrance in violation of Section 6223 of the Government Code may petition the superior court of the county in which the person resides or in which the property is located for an order, which may be granted ex parte, directing the lien or other encumbrance claimant to appear at a hearing before the court and show cause why the lien or other encumbrance should not be stricken and other relief provided by this article should not be granted. The court shall schedule the hearing no earlier than 14 days after the date of the order. The scheduled date of the hearing shall allow adequate time for notice of the hearing. *(Added by Stats.1998, c. 779 (S.B.1759), § 2.)*

Research References

3 Witkin Cal. Proc. 5th Actions § 371, (S 371) Nature and Purpose.
6 Witkin Cal. Proc. 5th Proceedings Without Trial § 58, (S 58) in General.

5 Witkin, California Summary 10th Torts § 527, Filing or Recording to Harass or Influence Public Employee.

§ 765.020. Petition contents; affidavit

A petition under this article shall state the grounds upon which relief is requested, and shall be supported by the affidavit of the petitioner or the petitioner's attorney setting forth a concise statement of the facts upon which the motion is based.

The petition and affidavit shall be in substantially the form prescribed by the Judicial Council. *(Added by Stats.1998, c. 779 (S.B.1759), § 2.)*

§ 765.030. Court order

If the court determines that the lien or other encumbrance is in violation of Section 6223 of the Government Code, the court shall issue an order striking and releasing the lien or other encumbrance and may award costs and reasonable attorney fees to the petitioner to be paid by the lien or other encumbrance claimant. If the court determines that the lien or other encumbrance is valid, the court shall issue an order so stating and may award costs and reasonable attorney fees to the encumbrance claimant to be paid by the petitioner. The court may direct that such an order shall be recorded. *(Added by Stats.1998, c. 779 (S.B.1759), § 2.)*

Research References

Rutter, Cal. Practice Guide: Real Prop. Transactions Ch. 11-I, I. Lis Pendens.
4 Witkin, California Summary 10th Sales § 299, (S 299) Contents.

§ 765.040. Liability for recording or filing lien or encumbrance in violation of statute

Any lien or encumbrance claimant who records or files, or directs another to record or file, a lien or other encumbrance in violation of Section 6223 of the Government Code shall be liable to the owner of the property bound by the lien or other encumbrance for a civil penalty of up to five thousand dollars ($5,000). *(Added by Stats.1998, c. 779 (S.B.1759), § 2.)*

Research References

3 Witkin Cal. Proc. 5th Actions § 371, (S 371) Nature and Purpose.

§ 765.050. Exclusion of claims of encumbrance by financial institution

This article does not apply to a document which acts as a claim of encumbrance by a financial institution, as defined in subdivision (a) of Section 14161 of the Penal Code or Section 481.113 of this code, or a public entity, as defined in Section 481.200 of this code. *(Added by Stats.1998, c. 779 (S.B.1759), § 2.)*

Research References

5 Witkin, California Summary 10th Torts § 527, Filing or Recording to Harass or Influence Public Employee.

§ 765.060. Counsel for public officer or employee who recorded lien or encumbrance in violation of statute

If a lien or other encumbrance is recorded or filed in violation of Section 6223 of the Government Code, the state or local agency that employs the public officer or employee may provide counsel for the public officer or employee in an action brought pursuant to Section 765.010. *(Added by Stats.1998, c. 779 (S.B.1759), § 2.)*

CHAPTER 4.5. SPECIAL ACTIONS AND PROCEEDINGS TO CLEAR TITLE

Civ. Pro.

ARTICLE 1. IDENTITY OF PERSON IN CHAIN OF TITLE

§ 770.010. Definitions

As used in this article:

(a) "Acquired" means received or taken by conveyance, judgment, decree, or otherwise.

(b) "Property" means any right, title, or interest in or lien upon real property or part thereof.

(c) "Subsequent owner" means the person to whom property is transferred whether as owner, part owner, or otherwise, or the successors in interest of the person, and includes a distributee of the estate of a decedent.

(d) "Transfer" means voluntary or involuntary transfer and includes a conveyance, reconveyance, satisfaction of a lien, or divestment by judgment, decree, or otherwise. The probate of the estate of a decedent and entry of the decree of distribution is a transfer within the meaning of this subdivision. *(Added by Stats.1980, c. 44, p. 114, § 16.)*

Law Revision Commission Comments

Section 770.010 is drawn from the first sentence of the first paragraph of former Section 751a for simplicity of drafting.

Research References

Miller and Starr California Real Estate § 8:21, Adjudication of Identity.
Miller and Starr California Real Estate § 11:36, Transfer After Change of Name.
Miller and Starr California Real Estate § 34:108, Types of Actions for Quiet Title.
5 Witkin Cal. Proc. 5th Pleading § 656, (S 656) Statutory Development.
12 Witkin, California Summary 10th Real Property § 265, Adjudication of Identity.

§ 770.020. Transfer of property under name different from name by which property was acquired or recorded; proceeding to determine identity

If property is acquired or stands of record in the name of a person who heretofore or hereafter transfers the property under a name other than or different from the name in which the property is acquired or stands of record, a proceeding is authorized to adjudicate and determine the identity of the person in whose name the property is acquired or stands of record and the person who transfers the property. *(Added by Stats.1980, c. 44, p. 115, § 16.)*

Law Revision Commission Comments

Section 770.020 continues the substance of the first sentence of the first paragraph of former Section 751a. See also Section 770.010 (definitions).

Research References

Miller and Starr California Real Estate § 8:21, Adjudication of Identity.
12 Witkin, California Summary 10th Real Property § 265, Adjudication of Identity.

§ 770.030. Venue

The proceeding shall be brought in the superior court of the county in which the property or any part thereof is situated. *(Added by Stats.1980, c. 44, p. 115, § 16.)*

Law Revision Commission Comments

Section 770.030 continues the substance of the first portion of the first sentence of the second paragraph of former Section 751a.

Research References

Miller and Starr California Real Estate § 8:21, Adjudication of Identity.
12 Witkin, California Summary 10th Real Property § 265, Adjudication of Identity.

§ 770.040. Petition by subsequent owner; answer and denial by any person interested in the property

(a) The proceeding may be brought by a subsequent owner of the property by filing a petition with the court.

(b) At any time before the date fixed for the hearing of the petition, any person interested in the property may answer the petition and deny any of the matters contained therein. *(Added by Stats.1980, c. 44, p. 115, § 16.)*

Law Revision Commission Comments

Subdivision (a) of Section 770.040 continues the substance of the last portion of the first sentence of the first paragraph of former Section 751a. See also Section 770.010 (definitions).

Subdivision (b) continues the substance of the first sentence of the third paragraph of former Section 751a.

Research References

Miller and Starr California Real Estate § 8:21, Adjudication of Identity.
12 Witkin, California Summary 10th Real Property § 265, Adjudication of Identity.

§ 770.050. Petition; verification; form; contents

(a) The petition shall be verified in the manner provided for verification of a complaint.

(b) The petition may be substantially entitled, "In the matter of the determination of the identity of _____" (naming all the persons sought to be identified), and may set forth:

(1) A statement of petitioner's interest in the property as subsequent owner.

(2) A particular description of the property.

(3) The name or names of the person or persons sought to be identified, setting out the name and a reference to the record of the transaction under which the property was acquired or stands of record and the name and a reference to the record of the transaction under which the property was transferred or stands of record, that the names are the names of the same person, and that the transfers affect the petitioner's title to the real property.

(4) A prayer that the identity of such persons be established.

(c) As many persons sought to be identified as appear of record in the chain of title to the property may be joined in one petition or proceeding. *(Added by Stats.1980, c. 44, p. 115, § 16.)*

Law Revision Commission Comments

Subdivision (a) of Section 770.050 continues the substance of the last portion of the first sentence of the second paragraph of former Section 751a.

Subdivision (b) continues the substance of the second sentence of the second paragraph of former Section 751a.

Subdivision (c) continues the substance of the second sentence of the first paragraph of former Section 751a.

Research References

Miller and Starr California Real Estate § 8:21, Adjudication of Identity.
12 Witkin, California Summary 10th Real Property § 265, Adjudication of Identity.

§ 770.060. Hearing; notice; form

(a) Upon the filing of the petition, the clerk shall set the petition for hearing by the court.

(b) The petitioner shall give notice of the hearing by causing notices of the time and place of hearing to be posted at the courthouse of the county where the proceeding is pending and in a conspicuous place on the real property described in the petition, at least 10 days before the hearing.

(c) The special notice shall be substantially in the following form:

(Title of court and cause)

Notice is hereby given that _____ has filed a petition herein claiming to be the owner (or distributee) of the following described lands _____ (description) and praying that the identity of the following-named persons, in former conveyances (or judgments or decrees) to said lands or in decrees of distribution of said lands in probate be determined, to wit: _____ (names as J. Doe and John Doe); and that the time and place of hearing said petition has been set for _____ the _____ day of _____, 19___, at the hour of _____, ___m. of said day at the courtroom of said court in the City of _____, County of _____, State of California.

_____
                                   Clerk

(Added by Stats.1980, c. 44, p. 115, § 16.)

Law Revision Commission Comments

Subdivisions (a) and (b) of Section 770.060 continue the substance of the first sentence of the last portion of the second paragraph of former Section 751a. Subdivision (c) continues the second sentence of the last portion of the second paragraph.

Research References

Miller and Starr California Real Estate § 8:21, Adjudication of Identity.
12 Witkin, California Summary 10th Real Property § 265, Adjudication of Identity.

§ 770.070. Hearing; proofs; decree; appeal

(a) At the time fixed for the hearing or such time thereafter as may be fixed by the court, the court shall hear the proofs offered by the petitioner and by any persons answering the petition, and shall make and enter a decree determining the identity of the person or persons set out in the petition in accordance with the proofs.

(b) An appeal may be taken by any party aggrieved. *(Added by Stats.1980, c. 44, p. 116, § 16.)*

Law Revision Commission Comments

Subdivision (a) of Section 770.070 continues the substance of the second sentence of the third paragraph of former Section 751a.

Subdivision (b) continues the fourth paragraph of former Section 751a.

Research References

Miller and Starr California Real Estate § 8:21, Adjudication of Identity.

12 Witkin, California Summary 10th Real Property § 265, Adjudication of Identity.

§ 770.080. Decree; effect; recordation

(a) After the decree has become final it constitutes prima facie evidence of the matters thereby determined and it is presumed that the identity of the person or persons described in the decree is such as is stated in the decree.

(b) A certified copy of the decree shall be recorded in the office of the county recorder of every county in which any part of the property is situated. *(Added by Stats.1980, c. 44, p. 116, § 16.)*

Law Revision Commission Comments

Subdivision (a) of Section 770.080 continues the substance of the first sentence of the fifth paragraph of former Section 751a.

Subdivision (b) continues the substance of the second sentence of the fifth paragraph of former Section 751a.

Research References

Miller and Starr California Real Estate § 8:21, Adjudication of Identity.
Miller and Starr California Real Estate § 11:36, Transfer After Change of Name.
Miller and Starr California Real Estate § 34:108, Types of Actions for Quiet Title.
12 Witkin, California Summary 10th Real Property § 265, Adjudication of Identity.

ARTICLE 2. LAND DEDICATED FOR PUBLIC IMPROVEMENT

Section
771.010. Proposed dedication; conclusive presumption of nonacceptance; required conditions.
771.020. Action to clear title; law governing; judgment.

§ 771.010. Proposed dedication; conclusive presumption of nonacceptance; required conditions

If a proposal is heretofore or hereafter made to dedicate real property for public improvement, there is a conclusive presumption that the proposed dedication was not accepted if all of the following conditions are satisfied:

(a) The proposal was made by filing a map only.

(b) No acceptance of the dedication was made and recorded within 25 years after the map was filed.

(c) The real property was not used for the purpose for which the dedication was proposed within 25 years after the map was filed.

(d) The real property was sold to a third person after the map was filed and used as if free of the dedication. *(Added by Stats.1980, c. 44, p. 116, § 16.)*

Law Revision Commission Comments

Section 771.010 continues the substance of the first portion of former Section 748.5.

Research References

Miller and Starr California Real Estate § 11:68, Constructive Notice of Interests Barred by the Statute of Limitations--"Ancient Documents" and the Marketable Record Title Act.
Miller and Starr California Real Estate § 26:20, in General; Formal Acceptance.
Miller and Starr California Real Estate § 26:25, Acceptance of the Offer.
Miller and Starr California Real Estate § 26:26, Rejection and Revocation.
Miller and Starr California Real Estate § 26:35, Special Statutory Dedication Procedures.

Miller and Starr California Real Estate § 34:108, Types of Actions for
   Quiet Title.
17 NO. 3 Miller & Starr, California Real Estate Newsalert 5, Dedication.
19 NO. 1 Miller & Starr, California Real Estate Newsalert 8, Dedication.
5 Witkin Cal. Proc. 5th Pleading § 656, (S 656) Statutory Development.
12 Witkin, California Summary 10th Real Property § 246, (S 246)
   Rejection and Revocation.

§ 771.020.   Action to clear title; law governing; judgment

(a) An action is authorized to clear title to real property of a
proposal to dedicate the property for public improvement if
there is a conclusive presumption pursuant to Section 771.010
that the proposed dedication was not accepted.

(b) The action shall be pursuant to Chapter 4 (commencing
with Section 760.010) and shall have the following features:

(1) The public entity to which the dedication was proposed
shall be named as defendant.

(2) The judgment in the action shall clear the title of the
proposed dedication and remove the cloud created by the
proposed dedication. *(Added by Stats.1980, c. 44, p. 116, § 16.)*

Law Revision Commission Comments

Section 771.020 continues the substance of the last portion of former
Section 748.5.

Research References

Miller and Starr California Real Estate § 11:68, Constructive Notice of
   Interests Barred by the Statute of Limitations--"Ancient Documents"
   and the Marketable Record Title Act.
Miller and Starr California Real Estate § 26:20, in General; Formal
   Acceptance.
Miller and Starr California Real Estate § 26:25, Acceptance of the Offer.
Miller and Starr California Real Estate § 26:26, Rejection and Revoca-
   tion.
Miller and Starr California Real Estate § 26:35, Special Statutory
   Dedication Procedures.
Miller and Starr California Real Estate § 34:108, Types of Actions for
   Quiet Title.
12 Witkin, California Summary 10th Real Property § 246, (S 246)
   Rejection and Revocation.

ARTICLE 3.   RIGHT OF ENTRY OR OCCUPATION OF SURFACE LANDS UNDER OIL OR GAS LEASE

Section
772.010. Application of article; cities in Los Angeles and
            Orange counties.
772.020. Definitions.
772.030. Action to terminate right of entry or occupation;
            effect on valid unit or operating agreement.
772.040. Judgment terminating right of entry or occupation;
            conditions; rights of lessee.
772.050. Qualification of judgment; limited easements; relo-
            cation of facilities; costs; setoff; proof of benefit.
772.060. Public policy; waiver of rights.

§ 772.010.   Application of article; cities in Los Angeles and Orange counties

This article applies only to lands within a city in any county
with a population exceeding 4,000,000, or with a population of
more than 700,000 and less than 710,000 as determined by the
1960 Federal Decennial Census. *(Added by Stats.1980, c. 44, p.
117, § 16.)*

Law Revision Commission Comments

Section 772.010 continues the substance of former Section 751.3(g).

Research References

Miller and Starr California Real Estate § 17:24, Minerals--Oil and Gas
   Leases.
Miller and Starr California Real Estate § 34:108, Types of Actions for
   Quiet Title.
5 Witkin Cal. Proc. 5th Pleading § 656, (S 656) Statutory Development.
12 Witkin, California Summary 10th Real Property § 798, (S 798) Right
   to Use Surface.

§ 772.020.   Definitions

As used in this article:

(a) "Surface zone" means the zone which lies above a plane
which is 500 feet below the surface of the land.

(b) "Subject land" means that area occupied by the particular
described surface and surface zone for which plaintiff seeks to
terminate the leasehold right of entry and occupation.

(c) "Lease facilities" means storage tanks, wash tanks, sepa-
rators, heaters, and other facilities reasonably necessary for the
production of oil or gas, including secondary recovery operations. *(Added by Stats.1980, c. 44, p. 117, § 16.)*

Law Revision Commission Comments

Section 772.020 continues the substance of former Section 751.3(e).

§ 772.030.   Action to terminate right of entry or occupation; effect on valid unit or operating agreement

(a) If a mining rights lease, including a community lease,
exists for the production of oil, gas, or other hydrocarbons, and a
right of entry or occupation provided by the lease encumbers all
or part of the surface or surface zone of the leasehold lands, any
person who owns a fee interest in the surface of the leasehold
lands may bring an action in the superior court to terminate the
right of entry or occupation as to all or some described portion
of the surface and surface zone of the leasehold lands in which
the person owns an interest.

(b) No judgment rendered pursuant to this article shall
change or affect the terms or operation of any valid unit
agreement or valid operating agreement which comes within the
provisions of Section 3301 or 3321 of the Public Resources Code.
(Added by Stats.1980, c. 44, p. 117, § 16.)

Law Revision Commission Comments

Subdivision (a) of Section 772.030 continues the substance of former
Section 751.3(a). Subdivision (b) continues the substance of former
Section 751.3(f).

§ 772.040.   Judgment terminating right of entry or occupation; conditions; rights of lessee

The court may render a judgment terminating the lessee's
right of entry or occupation of the surface and surface zone,
subject to such conditions as the court deems fair and equitable,
if the evidence shows each of the following:

(a) The document that created the leasehold interest was
originally executed more than 20 years prior to filing the action
under this article regardless of any amendments to the document. However, if any amendment was entered into expressly
for the purpose of waiving, limiting, or rearranging surface rights
of entry and occupation by the lessee, the 20-year period shall be
computed as if the document were originally executed on the
date of execution of the amendment.

(b) The subject land is not presently occupied by any of the
following:

(1) A producing oil or gas well or well bore.

(2) A well or well bore being utilized for injection of water,
gas, or other substance into geologic substrata as an aid to oil or
gas production or to ameliorating subsidence.

(3) A well or well bore being utilized for the disposal injection of waste oil well brine and byproducts.

(4) A well or well bore being utilized for the production of water for use in oil field injection, waterflood, and pressure maintenance programs.

(c) Termination of the right of entry or occupation within the subject land in the manner requested by the plaintiff, or subject to such conditions as the court may impose pursuant to this section, will not significantly interfere with the right of the lessee, under the lease, to continue to conduct operations for the continued production of oil from leasehold strata beneath the surface zone in a practical and economic manner, utilizing such production techniques as will be appropriate to the leasehold area, consistent with good oilfield practice, and to gather, transport, and market the oil. *(Added by Stats.1980, c. 44, p. 117, § 16.)*

Law Revision Commission Comments

Section 772.040 continues the substance of former Section 751.3(b).

§ 772.050. Qualification of judgment; limited easements; relocation of facilities; costs; setoff; proof of benefit

(a) The court may qualify the judgment terminating the surface and surface zone right of entry or occupation so as to provide for limited surface and surface zone easements that the lessee may continue to enjoy within the subject land.

(b) A judgment may be conditioned upon the relocation of pipelines, roadways, equipment, or lease facilities in such manner as will most effectively free the subject land for surface use while safeguarding continued oil and gas operations in a practical and economic manner. Any such condition of the judgment shall require the plaintiff to pay the costs of the relocation. However, the plaintiff shall be entitled to a setoff against the costs to the extent of any benefit to the lessee resulting from the installation of new equipment or material. The plaintiff has the burden of proving any benefit accruing to the lessee. *(Added by Stats.1980, c. 44, p. 117, § 16.)*

Law Revision Commission Comments

Section 772.050 continues the substance of former Section 751.3(c).

§ 772.060. Public policy; waiver of rights

It is against public policy for any oil or gas lease, at its inception, to provide for the waiver of any rights created by this article, or for such rights to be waived by amendment to any oil or gas lease within 20 years of the date of its execution by a plaintiff or the plaintiff's predecessor in interest. *(Added by Stats.1980, c. 44, p. 117, § 16.)*

Law Revision Commission Comments

Section 772.060 continues the substance of former Section 751.3(d).

Research References

Miller and Starr California Real Estate § 17:24, Minerals--Oil and Gas Leases.

Miller and Starr California Real Estate § 34:108, Types of Actions for Quiet Title.

CHAPTER 4.6. ACTIONS CONCERNING REAL PROPERTY TITLES AFFECTED BY PUBLIC IMPROVEMENT ASSESSMENTS

Law Revision Commission Comments

Former Chapter 4A is redesignated Chapter 4.6 (commencing with Section 801.1) for consistency with the numbering of the other chapters of Title 10.

§ 801.1. Adverse interests, etc., under public improvement assessments or bonds; right of action

An action may be brought to determine adverse interests in, liens or clouds upon title to real property arising out of any public improvement assessment or any bond issued to represent such assessment where the lien of such assessment or bond is presumed to have been extinguished under the provisions of Section 2911 of the Civil Code, or to determine adverse interests in, liens or clouds upon title to real property by reason of any certificate issued on sale made to satisfy any public improvement assessment or bond where such sale was made more than four years prior to the commencement of the action and no deed pursuant thereto has been issued prior to the commencement of the action or prior to January 1, 1951, whichever is the later. *(Added by Stats.1949, c. 1108, p. 2008, § 1.)*

Research References

Miller and Starr California Real Estate § 11:172, Assessment and Bond Liens--Special Tax Liens Under the Mello-Roos Community Facilities Act.

Miller and Starr California Real Estate § 11:174, Assessment and Bond Liens--Action to Remove the Cloud of an Expired Lien.

Miller and Starr California Real Estate § 34:108, Types of Actions for Quiet Title.

§ 801.2. Adverse interests, etc., under public improvement assessments or bonds; joinder of causes

The action may be brought as a separate action or joined as a cause with other causes of action to determine adverse claims to and clouds upon title to real property, but the complaint shall aver the pertinent matters stated in the preceding section and shall be verified. *(Added by Stats.1949, c. 1108, p. 2009, § 2.)*

Research References

Miller and Starr California Real Estate § 11:174, Assessment and Bond Liens--Action to Remove the Cloud of an Expired Lien.

§ 801.3. Adverse interests, etc., under public improvement assessments or bonds; defendants

The complaint shall include as defendants to the action (a) all persons known to the plaintiff owning or claiming an interest under such public improvement assessment, bond or certificate of sale; (b) the payee, as shown by the bond representing the assessment, if any; (c) the owner of the special assessment or certificate of sale, if any, and any person claiming an interest therein, as shown by the records of the treasurer, street superintendent or other public official who is the custodian of the funds to be collected thereon or who issued such certificate of sale, and (d) such treasurer, street superintendent or other public official. If any person owning or claiming an interest under such assessment, bond or certificate of sale is known to be dead, the heirs and devisees of such person may be sued as: "the heirs and devisees of" said person, naming him, or if such person is believed to be dead and such belief is alleged in the complaint on information and belief then the heirs and devisees of such person may also be sued as "the heirs and devisees" of said person, naming him, provided that such person is also named as a defendant. *(Added by Stats.1949, c. 1008, p. 2009, § 3. Amended by Stats.1951, c. 521, p. 1670, § 1.)*

Research References

Miller and Starr California Real Estate § 11:174, Assessment and Bond Liens--Action to Remove the Cloud of an Expired Lien.

§ 801.4. Adverse interests, etc., under public improvement assessments or bonds; unknown persons as defendants

The complaint shall also include, as defendants, unknown persons owning or claiming an interest in such bond, special assessment or certificate of sale and they may be described in the complaint as: "Also the owner or any person claiming an interest (here describe the bond, special assessment or certificate of sale as it is described in the office in which it was issued)." *(Added by Stats.1949, c. 1108, p. 2009, § 4.)*

Research References

Miller and Starr California Real Estate § 11:174, Assessment and Bond Liens--Action to Remove the Cloud of an Expired Lien.

§ 801.5. Adverse interests, etc., under public improvement assessments or bonds; lis pendens

Within ten days after the filing of the complaint, plaintiff shall file or cause to be filed in the office of the recorder of the county where the property is situated, a notice of the pendency of the action, containing the title and object of the action and a description of the property in that county affected thereby. From the time of filing such notice of record only, shall all persons have constructive notice thereof. *(Added by Stats.1949, c. 1108, p. 2009, § 5.)*

Research References

Miller and Starr California Real Estate § 11:150, Actions in Which a Lis Pendens May or Must be Recorded.
Miller and Starr California Real Estate § 11:174, Assessment and Bond Liens--Action to Remove the Cloud of an Expired Lien.

3 Witkin Cal. Proc. 5th Actions § 381, (S 381) Specific Mandatory Statutes.

§ 801.6. Adverse interests, etc., under public improvement assessments or bonds; lis pendens

Within three years after the filing of the complaint, a summons shall be issued which shall contain the matters required by Section 412.20, designating the defendants as in the complaint, and in addition, a description of the property and a statement of the object of the action. *(Added by Stats.1949, c. 1108, p. 2010, § 6. Amended by Stats.1969, c. 1611, p. 3392, § 13, operative July 1, 1970.)*

Research References

Rutter, Cal. Practice Guide: Civ. Pro. Before Trial Ch. 4-C, C. Content of Summons.
Miller and Starr California Real Estate § 11:174, Assessment and Bond Liens--Action to Remove the Cloud of an Expired Lien.
3 Witkin Cal. Proc. 5th Actions § 987, (S 987) Actions Involving Real Property.

§ 801.7. Adverse interests, etc., under public improvement assessments or bonds; posting summons

Within thirty days after the issuance of the summons, the plaintiff shall post, or cause to be posted, a copy thereof in a conspicuous place on the property. *(Added by Stats.1949, c. 1108, p. 2010, § 7.)*

Research References

Miller and Starr California Real Estate § 11:174, Assessment and Bond Liens--Action to Remove the Cloud of an Expired Lien.

§ 801.8. Adverse interests, etc., under public improvement assessments or bonds; service; personal or by publication

All known defendants shall be served in the manner provided by law for the service of a summons in a civil action. All unknown defendants shall be served by publication as provided in Section 750. *(Added by Stats.1949, c. 1108, p. 2010, § 8. Amended by Stats.1969, c. 1611, p. 3393, § 14, operative July 1, 1970.)*

Research References

Miller and Starr California Real Estate § 11:174, Assessment and Bond Liens--Action to Remove the Cloud of an Expired Lien.
3 Witkin Cal. Proc. 5th Actions § 1034, Special Statutes.

§ 801.9. Adverse interests, etc., under public improvement assessments or bonds; diligence to ascertain identity and residence of unknown defendants, heirs and devisees

In addition to the matters required to be set forth in the affidavit by the plaintiff for publication of summons, it shall appear by the affidavit that the plaintiff used reasonable diligence to ascertain the identity and residence of the unknown defendants and of any persons sued as heirs and devisees. *(Added by Stats.1949, c. 1108, p. 2010, § 9. Amended by Stats.1951, c. 521, p. 1671, § 2; Stats.1969, c. 1611, p. 3393, § 15, operative July 1, 1970.)*

Research References

3 Witkin Cal. Proc. 5th Actions § 1034, Special Statutes.

§ 801.10. Adverse interests, etc., under public improvement assessments or bonds; unknown defendants; rights; conclusiveness of judgment

All unknown defendants, including the heirs and devisees designated in the complaint, shall have the same rights as are provided by law for other defendants upon whom summons is served, and the action shall proceed against them in the same manner. Regardless of any legal disability, any unknown defendant, including any heir or devisee designated in the complaint, who has been served, and anyone claiming under him, shall be concluded by a judgment in the action as if the action were brought against and personal service made upon that person by his or her name. *(Added by Stats.1949, c. 1108, p. 2010, § 10. Amended by Stats.1969, c. 1611, p. 3393, § 16, operative July 1, 1970.)*

Research References

Miller and Starr California Real Estate § 11:174, Assessment and Bond Liens--Action to Remove the Cloud of an Expired Lien.

§ 801.11. Adverse interests, etc., under public improvement assessments or bonds; determination of rights; proof; presumptions

On the trial of the action, the court shall determine the rights of all the parties thereto and shall require proof of the facts alleged. Any certificate issued on sale made to satisfy any public improvement assessment or any bond issued to represent such assessment shall be presumed to have been paid and redeemed where no deed pursuant thereto has been issued and such sale was made more than four years prior to the commencement of the action.

The presumption herein mentioned shall become and be conclusive if no deed pursuant to such sale is issued within four years after the date of sale or prior to January 1, 1953, whichever is the later; and no public official shall thereafter execute or issue any deed pursuant to such sale. *(Added by Stats.1949, c. 1108, p. 2010, § 11. Amended by Stats.1951, c. 521, p. 1671, § 3.)*

Research References

Miller and Starr California Real Estate § 11:173, Assessment and Bond Liens--Statute of Limitations for Enforcement of the Lien.
Miller and Starr California Real Estate § 11:174, Assessment and Bond Liens--Action to Remove the Cloud of an Expired Lien.

§ 801.12. Adverse interests, etc., under public improvement assessments or bonds; decree

If the court determines that none of the defendants have any right, title, interest, lien or estate in the property, it shall render its final decree quieting the plaintiff's title. If the court determines that any of the defendants have any right, title, interest, lien or estate in the property, it shall render its decree establishing these rights and may order the sale of the property or partition thereof. The decree shall direct the public officer having the record of the assessment, bond or certificate of sale to cancel the record thereof. *(Added by Stats.1949, c. 1108, p. 2010, § 12.)*

Research References

Miller and Starr California Real Estate § 11:174, Assessment and Bond Liens--Action to Remove the Cloud of an Expired Lien.

§ 801.13. Sale or partition; proceeds

If the court orders a sale of the property or a partition thereof, the same shall be made in accordance with the provisions of Title 10.5 (commencing with Section 872.010) of Part 2, except that proceeds of sale belonging to unknown defendants or defendants whose identities or whereabouts are unascertained shall be paid to the public officer who is the custodian of the funds collected on such public improvement assessments, bonds or certificates of sale, to be held by him as in like instances of collection. *(Added by Stats.1949, c. 1108, p. 2011, § 13. Amended by Stats.1976, c. 73, p. 110, § 5.)*

Law Revision Commission Comments

Former subdivision (a) of Section 801.13 is deleted since the general partition law provides for appointment of a single referee. See Section 873.010.

§ 801.14. Adverse interests, etc., under public improvement assessment or bonds; conclusiveness of decree

The decree, after it has become final, is conclusive against all persons named in the complaint who have been served and all unknown persons and the heirs and devisees of deceased persons designated in the complaint and served as hereinbefore provided. *(Added by Stats.1949, c. 1108, p. 2011, § 14.)*

Research References

Miller and Starr California Real Estate § 11:174, Assessment and Bond Liens--Action to Remove the Cloud of an Expired Lien.

§ 801.15. Adverse interests, etc., under public improvement assessments or bonds; cancellation of assessment, bond or certificate of sale

After the judgment has become final, a certified copy thereof shall be delivered to the public officer having the record of the assessment, bond or certificate of sale in his office and he shall thereupon mark the record of the assessment, bond or certificate of sale as follows: "Canceled by judgment of court, superior court case number (here give number)." *(Added by Stats.1949, c. 1108, p. 2011, § 15.)*

Research References

Miller and Starr California Real Estate § 11:172, Assessment and Bond Liens--Special Tax Liens Under the Mello-Roos Community Facilities Act.
Miller and Starr California Real Estate § 11:174, Assessment and Bond Liens--Action to Remove the Cloud of an Expired Lien.
Miller and Starr California Real Estate § 34:108, Types of Actions for Quiet Title.

CHAPTER 5. ACTIONS FOR THE USURPATION OF AN OFFICE OR A FRANCHISE

Section

§ 802. Scire facias abolished

The writ of *sire facies* [1] is abolished. *(Enacted in 1872. Amended by Code Am.1880, c. 22, p. 11, § 4.)*

[1] Probably should read "scire facias".

Research References

8 Witkin Cal. Proc. 5th Extraordinary Writs § 2, (S 2) Abolition of Common Law Writs.
8 Witkin Cal. Proc. 5th Extraordinary Writs § 27, (S 27) in General.

§ 803. Action by attorney general in name of people

An action may be brought by the attorney-general, in the name of the people of this state, upon his own information, or upon a complaint of a private party, against any person who usurps, intrudes into, or unlawfully holds or exercises any public office, civil or military, or any franchise, or against any corporation, either de jure or de facto, which usurps, intrudes into, or unlawfully holds or exercises any franchise, within this state. And the attorney-general must bring the action, whenever he has reason to believe that any such office or franchise has been usurped, intruded into, or unlawfully held or exercised by any person, or when he is directed to do so by the governor. *(Enacted in 1872. Amended by Stats.1907, c. 324, p. 600, § 1.)*

Research References

8 Witkin Cal. Proc. 5th Extraordinary Writs § 27, (S 27) in General.
8 Witkin Cal. Proc. 5th Extraordinary Writs § 28, (S 28) Action by Attorney General.
4 Witkin Cal. Proc. 5th Pleading § 157, (S 157) Action by Relator.
9 Witkin, California Summary 10th Corporations § 211, Methods of Dissolution.
9 Witkin, California Summary 10th Corporations § 390, (S 390) Examination by Attorney General.
3 Witkin, California Summary 10th Agency and Employment § 16, (S 16) Incompatible Offices.
8 Witkin, California Summary 10th Constitutional Law § 1091, (S 1091) Private Right of Action Rejected.

§ 804. Complaint; alleging name of person entitled to office

Whenever such action is brought, the Attorney General, in addition to the statement of the cause of action, may also set forth in the complaint the name of the person rightly entitled to the office, with a statement of his right thereto. *(Enacted in 1872. Amended by Code Am.1880, c. 22, p. 11, § 5; Stats.1973, c. 20, p. 36, § 10.)*

Law Revision Commission Comments

Section 804, providing for arrest of the defendant in a quo warranto proceeding, is amended to reflect the fact that arrest of a defendant in a civil action is no longer permitted. See Code Civ.Proc. § 478 and Comment thereto. Criminal arrest of the defendant may be available if his taking of public moneys was wrongful. See Penal Code § 424 et seq.

Research References

8 Witkin Cal. Proc. 5th Extraordinary Writs § 28, (S 28) Action by Attorney General.

§ 805. Judgment; determination of rights of defendant and claimant

JUDGMENT MAY DETERMINE THE RIGHTS OF BOTH INCUMBENT AND CLAIMANT. In every such action judgment may be rendered upon the right of the defendant, and also upon the right of the party so alleged to be entitled, or only upon the right of the defendant, as justice may require. *(Enacted in 1872.)*

Research References

8 Witkin Cal. Proc. 5th Extraordinary Writs § 28, (S 28) Action by Attorney General.

§ 806. Judgment for claimant; acquisition of office after qualifying

WHEN RENDERED IN FAVOR OF APPLICANT. If the judgment be rendered upon the right of the person so alleged to be entitled, and the same be in favor of such person, he will be entitled, after taking the oath of office and executing such official bond as may be required by law, to take upon himself the execution of the office. *(Enacted in 1872.)*

Research References

8 Witkin Cal. Proc. 5th Extraordinary Writs § 28, (S 28) Action by Attorney General.

§ 807. Damages; recovery by claimant

DAMAGES MAY BE RECOVERED BY SUCCESSFUL APPLICANT. If judgment be rendered upon the right of the person so alleged to be entitled, in favor of such person, he may recover, by action,

the damages which he may have sustained by reason of the usurpation of the office by the defendant. *(Enacted in 1872.)*

Research References

8 Witkin Cal. Proc. 5th Extraordinary Writs § 28, (S 28) Action by Attorney General.

§ 808. Multiple claimants; single action to determine rights

WHEN SEVERAL PERSONS CLAIM THE SAME OFFICE, ETC. When several persons claim to be entitled to the same office or franchise, one action may be brought against all such persons, in order to try their respective rights to such office or franchise. *(Enacted in 1872.)*

Research References

8 Witkin Cal. Proc. 5th Extraordinary Writs § 28, (S 28) Action by Attorney General.

§ 809. Judgment against defendant; exclusion from office franchise or privilege; costs; fine

IF DEFENDANT FOUND GUILTY, WHAT JUDGMENT TO BE RENDERED AGAINST HIM. When a defendant, against whom such action has been brought, is adjudged guilty of usurping or intruding into, or unlawfully holding any office, franchise, or privilege, judgment must be rendered that such defendant be excluded from the office, franchise, or privilege, and that he pay the costs of the action. The Court may also, in its discretion, impose upon the defendant a fine not exceeding five thousand dollars, which fine, when collected, must be paid into the Treasury of the State. *(Enacted in 1872.)*

Research References

8 Witkin Cal. Proc. 5th Extraordinary Writs § 28, (S 28) Action by Attorney General.

§ 810. Action on information or application of private party; undertaking

When the action is brought upon the information or application of a private party, the Attorney General may require such party to enter into an undertaking, with sureties to be approved by the Attorney General, conditioned that such party or the sureties will pay any judgment for costs or damages recovered against the plaintiff, and all the costs and expenses incurred in the prosecution of the action. *(Added by Code Am.1873–74, c. 383, p. 326, § 103.)*

Research References

8 Witkin Cal. Proc. 5th Extraordinary Writs § 29, (S 29) Action on Application of Private Person.

§ 811. Action by supervisors or by legislative body of municipal corporation

The action provided for in this chapter may be maintained by the board of supervisors of any county or city and county or the legislative body of any municipal corporation, respectively, in the name of such county, city and county or municipal corporation against any person who usurps, intrudes into or unlawfully holds or exercises any franchise, or portion thereof, within the respective territorial limits of such county, city and county or municipal corporation and which is of a kind that is within the jurisdiction of such board or body to grant or withhold. *(Added by Stats.1937, c. 575, p. 1616, § 1.)*

Research References

8 Witkin Cal. Proc. 5th Extraordinary Writs § 30, (S 30) Action by Local Legislative Body.

CHAPTER 8. ACTIONS AGAINST CO–OWNERS OF MINES

Section
850. Nonpayment of proportionate share of taxes; notice by co-owner who paid share.

§ 850. Nonpayment of proportionate share of taxes; notice by co-owner who paid share

Upon the failure of any co-owner of a mine or mining claim to contribute his proportionate share of the taxes which have been levied and assessed upon the mine or claim for the period of five years, any co-owner who has paid such share may at the expiration of the five years serve upon the delinquent co-owner notice thereof. *(Added by Stats.1953, c. 52, p. 704, § 7.)*

§ 851. Service of notice

The notice shall be served in the manner provided by law for the service of a summons in a civil action, but where service is by publication, the publication shall be in a newspaper of general circulation published in the county in which the mine or claim is situated or if there is no such newspaper, in such a newspaper in an adjoining county, and the publication shall be at least once a week for 90 days. *(Added by Stats.1953, c. 52, p. 704, § 7. Amended by Stats.1969, c. 1611, p. 3393, § 17, operative July 1, 1970.)*

§ 852. Nonpayment of proportionate share of taxes after notice; petition

If prior to the expiration of 90 days from the service the delinquent fails or refuses to contribute his proportionate share of the taxes, the co-owner contributing such share may file in the superior court of the county in which the mine or claim is situated a verified petition setting forth the facts and particularly describing the mine or claim. *(Added by Stats.1953, c. 52, p. 704, § 7.)*

§ 853. Venue

If the mine or claim is situated in more than one county, the petition may be filed in the superior court of either county. *(Added by Stats.1953, c. 52, p. 704, § 7.)*

§ 854. Hearing; setting; notice

The clerk shall set the petition for hearing by the court and give notice thereof by causing a notice of the time and place of the hearing to be posted at the county courthouse at least 10 days before the hearing. The court may order such further notice as it deems proper. *(Added by Stats.1953, c. 52, p. 704, § 7.)*

§ 855. Hearing; judgment; vesting title in petitioner

The court shall hear evidence for or against the petition and may order judgment thereon vesting the interest of the delinquent in the mine or claim in the petitioner. *(Added by Stats.1953, c. 52, p. 705, § 7.)*

§ 856. Recording judgment

A certified copy of the decree may be recorded in the office of the recorder of each county in which any part of the mine or claim is situated. *(Added by Stats.1953, c. 52, p. 705, § 7.)*

CHAPTER 9. VALIDATING PROCEEDINGS

§ 860. Authority of public agency; time for proceeding; venue; nature of action

A public agency may upon the existence of any matter which under any other law is authorized to be determined pursuant to this chapter, and for 60 days thereafter, bring an action in the superior court of the county in which the principal office of the public agency is located to determine the validity of such matter. The action shall be in the nature of a proceeding in rem. *(Added by Stats.1961, c. 1479, p. 3331, § 1.)*

Research References

Rutter, Cal. Practice Guide: Civil Appeals & Writs Ch. 1-C, C. Methods and Sequence of Appellate Review.
Rutter, Cal. Practice Guide: Civil Appeals & Writs Ch. 2-B, B. Appealable Judgments and Orders.
Rutter, Cal. Practice Guide: Civil Appeals & Writs Ch. 3-B, B. Filing Deadlines.
Rutter, Cal. Practice Guide: Civ. Pro. Before Trial Ch. 2-A, A. Standing to Sue-"Real Party in Interest" Requirement.
Miller and Starr California Real Estate § 27:33, Public Works Competitive Bidding--Acceptance or Rejection of Public Works Bids.
Miller and Starr California Real Estate § 11:169, Assessment and Bond Liens--Assessment and Lien.
Miller and Starr California Real Estate § 30B:27, Validation Proceedings.
Miller and Starr California Real Estate § 30B:29, Procedural Considerations.
3 Witkin Cal. Proc. 5th Actions § 475, (S 475) Thirty Days.
3 Witkin Cal. Proc. 5th Actions § 476, (S 476) Sixty Days or Two Months.
3 Witkin Cal. Proc. 5th Actions § 506, (S 506) Alternative Remedy With Longer Period.
3 Witkin Cal. Proc. 5th Actions § 862, Nature of Problem.
3 Witkin Cal. Proc. 5th Actions § 988, (S 988) Validating Proceedings.
9 Witkin Cal. Proc. 5th Appeal § 582, (S 582) Special Statutes.
8 Witkin Cal. Proc. 5th Attack Judgment Trial Court § 146, (S 146) When Relief is Not Available.
7 Witkin Cal. Proc. 5th Judgment § 264, (S 264) In General.
7 Witkin Cal. Proc. 5th Judgment § 108A, (New)-Validating Proceeding.
2 Witkin Cal. Proc. 5th Jurisdiction § 245, Illustrations.
4 Witkin Cal. Proc. 5th Pleading § 158, (S 158) Validating Action.
4 Witkin Cal. Proc. 5th Pleading § 216, Other Procedures Compared.
4 Witkin Cal. Proc. 5th Pleading § 342, Statutory Basis.

5 Witkin Cal. Proc. 5th Pleading § 856, (S 856) Special Kind of Declaratory Relief.

§ 861. Jurisdiction; publication of summons; notice

Jurisdiction of all interested parties may be had by publication of summons pursuant to Section 6063 of the Government Code in a newspaper of general circulation designated by the court, published in the county where the action is pending and whenever possible within the boundaries of the public agency, and in such other counties as may be ordered by the court, and if there be no such newspaper in any such county or counties then in some adjoining county. In addition, prior to completion of such publication, the agency shall, to the extent which the court finds reasonably practicable, give notice of the pendency of the proceeding by mail or other means ordered by the court. *(Added by Stats.1961, c. 1479, p. 3331, § 1.)*

Research References

Miller and Starr California Real Estate § 30B:27, Validation Proceedings.
20 NO. 2 Miller & Starr, California Real Estate Newsalert 29, General Validation Procedures, Including Newspaper Publication, Do Not Apply to Actions Contesting Special Assessments Under Municipal Improvement Act.

§ 861.1. Direction of summons; contents; form

The summons shall be directed to "all persons interested in the matter of [specifying the matter]," and shall contain a notice to all persons interested in the matter that they may contest the legality or validity of the matter by appearing and filing a written answer to the complaint not later than the date specified in the summons, which date shall be 10 or more days after the completion of publication of the summons. The summons shall provide a detailed summary of the matter the public agency or other person seeks to validate. The summons shall also state that persons who contest the legality or validity of the matter will not be subject to punitive action, such as wage garnishment or seizure of their real or personal property. Except as otherwise specified in this section the summons shall be in the form prescribed in Section 412.20. *(Added by Stats.1963, c. 1865, p. 3850, § 1. Amended by Stats.1965, c. 894, p. 2498, § 1; Stats.1969, c. 1611, p. 3393, § 18, operative July 1, 1970; Stats.1998, c. 529 (A.B.2049), § 1.)*

Research References

Rutter, Cal. Practice Guide: Civ. Pro. Before Trial Ch. 4-C, C. Content of Summons.
Rutter, Cal. Practice Guide: Civ. Pro. Before Trial Ch. 4-D, D. Service of Summons.
Miller and Starr California Real Estate § 30B:27, Validation Proceedings.
3 Witkin Cal. Proc. 5th Actions § 985, (S 985) Special Statutes.
3 Witkin Cal. Proc. 5th Actions § 988, (S 988) Validating Proceedings.
7 Witkin Cal. Proc. 5th Judgment § 108A, (New)-Validating Proceeding.

§ 862. Completion of jurisdiction; time to appear and contest validity of matter sought to be determined

Jurisdiction shall be complete after the date specified in the summons. Any party interested may, not later than the date specified in the summons, appear and contest the legality or validity of the matter sought to be determined. *(Added by Stats.1961, c. 1479, p. 3331, § 1. Amended by Stats.1965, c. 894, p. 2499, § 2.)*

Research References

3 Witkin Cal. Proc. 5th Actions § 988, (S 988) Validating Proceedings.

§ 863. Action by interested person; time; venue; public agency as defendant

If no proceedings have been brought by the public agency pursuant to this chapter, any interested person may bring an action within the time and in the court specified by Section 860 to determine the validity of such matter. The public agency shall be a defendant and shall be served with the summons and complaint in the action in the manner provided by law for the service of a summons in a civil action. In any such action the summons shall be in the form prescribed in Section 861.1 except that in addition to being directed to "all persons interested in the matter of [specifying the matter]," it shall also be directed to the public agency. If the interested person bringing such action fails to complete the publication and such other notice as may be prescribed by the court in accordance with Section 861 and to file proof thereof in the action within 60 days from the filing of his complaint, the action shall be forthwith dismissed on the motion of the public agency unless good cause for such failure is shown by the interested person. *(Added by Stats.1961, c. 1479, p. 3331, § 1. Amended by Stats.1963, c. 1865, p. 3850, § 2, eff. July 19, 1963; Stats.1969, c. 1611, p. 3393, § 19, operative July 1, 1970.)*

Research References

Rutter, Cal. Practice Guide: Civ. Pro. Before Trial Ch. 2-A, A. Standing to Sue-"Real Party in Interest" Requirement.
Miller and Starr California Real Estate § 30B:27, Validation Proceedings.
Miller and Starr California Real Estate § 30B:29, Procedural Considerations.
20 NO. 2 Miller & Starr, California Real Estate Newsalert 29, General Validation Procedures, Including Newspaper Publication, Do Not Apply to Actions Contesting Special Assessments Under Municipal Improvement Act.
3 Witkin Cal. Proc. 5th Actions § 475, (S 475) Thirty Days.
3 Witkin Cal. Proc. 5th Actions § 476, (S 476) Sixty Days or Two Months.
3 Witkin Cal. Proc. 5th Actions § 506, (S 506) Alternative Remedy With Longer Period.
3 Witkin Cal. Proc. 5th Actions § 988, (S 988) Validating Proceedings.
4 Witkin Cal. Proc. 5th Pleading § 158, (S 158) Validating Action.
5 Witkin Cal. Proc. 5th Pleading § 856, (S 856) Special Kind of Declaratory Relief.

§ 864. Time bonds, warrants, contracts, obligations and evidences of indebtedness deemed authorized and in existence

For purposes of this chapter, bonds, warrants, contracts, obligations, and evidences of indebtedness shall be deemed to be in existence upon their authorization. Bonds and warrants shall be deemed authorized as of the date of adoption by the governing body of the public agency of a resolution or ordinance authorizing their issuance, and contracts shall be deemed authorized as of the date of adoption by the governing body of the public agency of a resolution or ordinance approving the contract and authorizing its execution. *(Added by Stats.1961, c. 1479, p. 3332, § 1.)*

Research References

5 Witkin Cal. Proc. 5th Pleading § 856, (S 856) Special Kind of Declaratory Relief.

§ 865. Consolidation of actions

If more than one action is pending concerning similar contests which may be brought under this chapter, they shall be consolidated for trial. *(Added by Stats.1961, c. 1479, p. 3332, § 1.)*

Research References

4 Witkin Cal. Proc. 5th Pleading § 342, Statutory Basis.

§ 866. Disregard of error, irregularity or omission not affecting substantial rights

The court hearing the action shall disregard any error, irregularity, or omission which does not affect the substantial rights of the parties. *(Added by Stats.1961, c. 1479, p. 3332, § 1.)*

§ 867. Setting for trial; hearing; preference over other actions

Actions brought pursuant to this chapter shall be given preference over all other civil actions before the court in the matter of setting the same for hearing or trial, and in hearing the same, to the end that such actions shall be speedily heard and determined. *(Added by Stats.1961, c. 1479, p. 3332, § 1.)*

§ 867.5. Action by public agency; dismissal after answer; filing of action after dismissal filed

(a) In the event that an action is brought by a public agency pursuant to this chapter, and that public agency later dismisses the action after any party has answered, then, notwithstanding Section 863, the party that answered may file an action pursuant to this chapter within 30 days after the public agency's dismissal was filed by the court.

(b) Subdivision (a) is not applicable to a case in which a public agency has by formal act rescinded the action on the matter subject to validation. *(Added by Stats.2000, c. 723 (A.B.2300), § 2.)*

Research References

3 Witkin Cal. Proc. 5th Actions § 475, (S 475) Thirty Days.
3 Witkin Cal. Proc. 5th Actions § 476, (S 476) Sixty Days or Two Months.
4 Witkin Cal. Proc. 5th Pleading § 158, (S 158) Validating Action.

§ 868. Costs

The costs of any proceeding or action pursuant to this chapter may be allowed and apportioned between the parties or taxed to the losing party in the discretion of the court. *(Added by Stats.1961, c. 1479, p. 3332, § 1.)*

Research References

7 Witkin Cal. Proc. 5th Judgment § 108A, (New)-Validating Proceeding.

§ 869. Exclusive provisions; other remedies

No contest except by the public agency or its officer or agent of any thing or matter under this chapter shall be made other than within the time and the manner herein specified. The availability to any public agency, including any local agency, or to its officers or agents, of the remedy provided by this chapter, shall not be construed to preclude the use by such public agency or its officers or agents, of mandamus or any other remedy to determine the validity of any thing or matter. *(Added by Stats.1961, c. 1479, p. 3332, § 1. Amended by Stats.1963, c. 1865, p. 3850, § 3, eff. July 19, 1963.)*

Research References

3 Witkin Cal. Proc. 5th Actions § 476, (S 476) Sixty Days or Two Months.
3 Witkin Cal. Proc. 5th Actions § 506, (S 506) Alternative Remedy With Longer Period.

§ 870. Conclusiveness of judgment; notice of appeal; issues on appeal

(a) The judgment, if no appeal is taken, or if taken and the judgment is affirmed, shall, notwithstanding any other provision of law including, without limitation, Sections 473 and 473.5, thereupon become and thereafter be forever binding and conclusive, as to all matters therein adjudicated or which at that time could have been adjudicated, against the agency and against all other persons, and the judgment shall permanently enjoin the institution by any person of any action or proceeding raising any issue as to which the judgment is binding and conclusive.

(b) Notwithstanding any other provision of law including, without limitation, Section 901 and any rule of court, no appeal shall be allowed from any judgment entered pursuant to this chapter unless a notice of appeal is filed within 30 days after the notice of entry of the judgment, or, within 30 days after the entry of the judgment if there is no answering party. If there is no answering party, only issues related to the jurisdiction of the court to enter a judgment in the action pursuant to this chapter may be raised on appeal. *(Added by Stats.1961, c. 1479, p. 3332, § 1. Amended by Stats.1963, c. 1865, p. 3851, § 4, eff. July 19, 1963; Stats.1969, c. 1611, p. 3394, § 20, operative July 1, 1970; Stats.1985, c. 229, § 1; Stats.1994, c. 242 (S.B.2107), § 1, eff. July 21, 1994.)*

Research References

Rutter, Cal. Practice Guide: Civil Appeals & Writs Ch. 3-B, B. Filing Deadlines.
Miller and Starr California Real Estate § 27:33, Public Works Competitive Bidding--Acceptance or Rejection of Public Works Bids.
Miller and Starr California Real Estate § 30B:27, Validation Proceedings.
9 Witkin Cal. Proc. 5th Appeal § 575, in General.
9 Witkin Cal. Proc. 5th Appeal § 582, (S 582) Special Statutes.
8 Witkin Cal. Proc. 5th Attack Judgment Trial Court § 146, (S 146) When Relief is Not Available.

§ 870.5. Tax revenues for security obligations; written notice

Any local public agency that pledges sales or retail transaction and use tax revenues received from taxes imposed by another public agency for bond payments or payment of other security obligations shall, in any validation action it files involving those bonds or other obligations, provide written notice thereof to the public agency imposing the taxes pledged as security for the bonds or other obligations at the time it files the validation action. *(Added by Stats.1998, c. 360 (A.B.1964), § 1.)*

Research References

Miller and Starr California Real Estate § 11:169, Assessment and Bond Liens--Assessment and Lien.
Miller and Starr California Real Estate § 30B:29, Procedural Considerations.

CHAPTER 10. GOOD FAITH IMPROVER OF PROPERTY OWNED BY ANOTHER

§ 871.1. Good faith improver defined

As used in this chapter, "good faith improver" means:

(a) A person who makes an improvement to land in good faith and under the erroneous belief, because of a mistake of law or fact, that he is the owner of the land.

(b) A successor in interest of a person described in subdivision (a). *(Added by Stats.1968, c. 150, p. 374, § 3.)*

Law Revision Commission Comments

The definition of "good faith improver" in Section 871.1 is based in part on the language used in Civil Code Section 1013.5 to describe a person who has a right to remove improvements affixed to the land of another. The definition in Section 871.1 is limited, however, to a person who believes he is the owner of the land; unlike Section 1013.5, the definition does not include licensees, tenants, and conditional vendors of chattels. See *Comment*, 27 So.Cal.L.Rev. 89 (1953).

Under this section, a person is not a "good faith improver" as to any improvement made after he becomes aware of facts that preclude him from acting in good faith. For example, a person who builds a house on a lot owned by another may obtain relief under this chapter if he acted in good faith under the erroneous belief, because of a mistake of law or fact, that he was the owner of the land. However, if the same person makes an additional improvement after he has discovered that he is not the owner of the land, he would not be entitled to relief under this chapter with respect to the additional improvement.

As to what constitutes "good faith," see Brown Derby Hollywood Corp. v. Hatton, 61 Cal.2d 855, 858–860, 40 Cal.Rptr. 848, 850–851, 395 P.2d 896, 898–899 (1964) (encroachment case).

Research References

Rutter, Cal. Practice Guide: Civil Trials & Evidence Ch. 2-C, C. Cases in Which Jury Trial May be Demanded.

Miller and Starr California Real Estate § 14:3, Interests Protected.

Miller and Starr California Real Estate § 14:6, Remedies--Balancing of Hardships.

Miller and Starr California Real Estate § 17:44, Where Improver Believes He or She Owns the Improved Property.

Miller and Starr California Real Estate § 11:150, Actions in Which a Lis Pendens May or Must be Recorded.

12 Witkin, California Summary 10th Real Property § 458, (S 458) in General.

12 Witkin, California Summary 10th Real Property § 459, Nature and Scope of Statute.

12 Witkin, California Summary 10th Real Property § 460, Considerations Determining Relief.

12 Witkin, California Summary 10th Real Property § 461, Equitable Lien and Lis Pendens.

12 Witkin, California Summary 10th Real Property § 462, (S 462) Other Relief.

§ 871.2. Person defined

As used in this chapter, "person" includes an unincorporated association. *(Added by Stats.1968, c. 150, p. 374, § 3. Amended by Stats.1971, c. 244, p. 391, § 55, operative July 1, 1972.)*

Law Revision Commission Comments

The definition of "person" in Code of Civil Procedure Section 17 does not clearly include an unincorporated association. Section 871.2 is included to make it clear that an unincorporated association may be a good faith improver.

The amendment of Section 871.2 corrects an obvious technical defect.

Research References

12 Witkin, California Summary 10th Real Property § 459, Nature and Scope of Statute.

§ 871.3. Actions for relief; treatment as unlimited and limited civil cases; cross-complaints for relief; burden on good faith improver

(a) An action for relief under this chapter shall be treated as an unlimited civil case, regardless of the amount in controversy and regardless of whether a defendant cross-complains for relief under this chapter. Any other case in which a defendant cross-complains for relief under this chapter shall be treated as a limited civil case if the cross-complaint is defensive and the case otherwise satisfies the amount in controversy and other requirements of Section 85.

(b) In every case, the burden is on the good faith improver to establish that the good faith improver is entitled to relief under this chapter, and the degree of negligence of the good faith improver should be taken into account by the court in determining whether the improver acted in good faith and in determining the relief, if any, that is consistent with substantial justice to the parties under the circumstances of the particular case. *(Added by Stats.1968, c. 150, p. 374, § 3. Amended by Stats.1971, c. 244, p. 391, § 56, operative July 1, 1972; Stats.1998, c. 931 (S.B.2139), § 99, eff. Sept. 28, 1998; Stats.1999, c. 344 (S.B.210), § 14, eff. Sept. 7, 1999; Stats.2000, c. 688 (A.B.1669), § 7.)*

Law Revision Commission Comments

The amendment of Section 871.3 merely deletes the reference to a "counterclaim." Counterclaims have been abolished; claims that formerly were asserted as counterclaims are now asserted as cross-complaints. See Code of Civil Procedure Section 428.80.

Section 871.3 is amended to accommodate unification of the municipal and superior courts in a county. Cal. Const. art. VI, § 5(e). [28 Cal.L.Rev.Comm. Reports 51 (1998)].

Section 871.3 is amended to reflect relocation of the provisions governing reclassification of a civil case. [29 Cal.L.Rev.Comm. Reports App. 5 (1999)].

Section 871.3 is amended to clarify the jurisdictional classification of a good faith improver claim. This is declarative of existing law.

If a good faith improver claim is asserted by way of complaint, the case is an unlimited civil case regardless of the amount in controversy. This treatment is consistent with the equitable nature of such a claim. See Southern Pac. Transp. Co. v. Superior Court, 58 Cal.App.3d 433, 129 Cal.Rptr. 912 (1976) (no right to jury trial under good faith improver statute); Okuda v. Superior Court, 144 Cal.App.3d 135, 139–41, 192 Cal.Rptr. 388 (1983) (court has "broad equitable jurisdiction" under good faith improver statute). If a defendant in the case cross-complains for relief under this chapter, the case remains an unlimited civil case.

If, however, a good faith improver claim is asserted by way of cross-complaint, and the complaint does not include a good faith improver claim, the proper treatment depends on whether the cross-complaint is defensive and whether the case satisfies the amount in controversy and other requirements for a limited civil case. A case may be transferred from municipal court to superior court if it includes a good faith improver cross-complaint that is not defensive. See Section 396 (court without jurisdiction); see also Cal. Const. art. VI, §10 (original jurisdiction of trial courts); Sections 85 (limited civil cases) & 85.1 (original jurisdiction in limited civil case) & Comments. Likewise, a limited civil case in a unified superior court may be reclassified if it includes a good faith improver cross-complaint that is not defensive. See Section 403.030 (reclassification of limited civil case by cross-complaint); see also Section 403.040 (motion for reclassification). For guidance on whether a cross-complaint is defensive, see Jacobson v. Superior Court, 5 Cal.2d 170, 173, 53 P.2d 756 (1936) (in an action on an insurance policy, cross-complaint seeking cancellation of the policy merely showed plaintiff was in default and not entitled to recover); 2 B. Witkin, California Procedure *Courts* §255, at 330 (4th ed. 1996); see also Section 86(b)(2). For authority to sever a cross-complaint, see Section 1048.

See Section 88 (unlimited civil case). See also Section 32.5 (jurisdictional classification). [30 Cal.L.Rev.Comm.Reports 289 (2000)].

Research References

Rutter, Cal. Practice Guide: Civ. Pro. Before Trial Ch. 3-A, A. Subject Matter Jurisdiction (Competency).

Miller and Starr California Real Estate § 17:44, Where Improver Believes He or She Owns the Improved Property.

7 Witkin Cal. Proc. 5th Trial § 88, (S 88) Legal Issues Not Severable.

12 Witkin, California Summary 10th Real Property § 459, Nature and Scope of Statute.

12 Witkin, California Summary 10th Real Property § 460, Considerations Determining Relief.

12 Witkin, California Summary 10th Real Property § 462, (S 462) Other Relief.

§ 871.4. Grounds for denial of relief; exercise of right of set-off or removal of improvement

The court shall not grant relief under this chapter if the court determines that exercise of the good faith improver's right of setoff under Section 741 of the Code of Civil Procedure or right to remove the improvement under Section 1013.5 of the Civil Code would result in substantial justice to the parties under the circumstances of the particular case. In determining whether removal of the improvement would result in substantial justice to the parties under the circumstances of the particular case, the court shall take into consideration any plans the owner of the land may have for the use or development of the land upon which the improvement was made and his need for the land upon which the improvement was made in connection with the use or development of other property owned by him. *(Added by Stats.1968, c. 150, p. 374, § 3.)*

Research References

Miller and Starr California Real Estate § 17:43, Where Improver Does Not Believe He or She Owns the Improved Property.
Miller and Starr California Real Estate § 17:44, Where Improver Believes He or She Owns the Improved Property.
12 Witkin, California Summary 10th Real Property § 460, Considerations Determining Relief.
12 Witkin, California Summary 10th Real Property § 462, (S 462) Other Relief.

§ 871.5. Adjustment of rights, equities and interests of parties

When an action or cross-complaint is brought pursuant to Section 871.3, the court may, subject to Section 871.4, effect such an adjustment of the rights, equities, and interests of the good faith improver, the owner of the land, and other interested parties (including, but not limited to, lessees, lienholders, and encumbrancers) as is consistent with substantial justice to the parties under the circumstances of the particular case. The relief granted shall protect the owner of the land upon which the improvement was constructed against any pecuniary loss but shall avoid, insofar as possible, enriching him unjustly at the expense of the good faith improver. In protecting the owner of the land against pecuniary loss, the court shall take into consideration the expenses the owner of the land has incurred in the action in which relief under this chapter is sought, including but not limited to reasonable attorney fees. In determining the appropriate form of relief under this section, the court shall take into consideration any plans the owner of the land may have for the use or development of the land upon which the improvement was made and his need for the land upon which the improvement was made in connection with the use or development of other property owned by him. *(Added by Stats.1968, c. 150. p. 374, § 3. Amended by Stats.1971. c. 244, p. 392, § 57, operative July 1, 1972.)*

Law Revision Commission Comments

The amendment of Section 871.5 merely deletes the reference to a "counterclaim." Counterclaims have been abolished; claims that formerly were asserted as counterclaims are now asserted as cross-complaints. See Code of Civil Procedure Section 428.80.

Research References

Miller and Starr California Real Estate § 17:44, Where Improver Believes He or She Owns the Improved Property.
14 NO. 5 Miller & Starr, California Real Estate Newsalert 13, Fixtures.
7 Witkin Cal. Proc. 5th Judgment § 87, (S 87) Distinctions.
7 Witkin Cal. Proc. 5th Judgment § 158, (S 158) Other Types of Fee Awards.
7 Witkin Cal. Proc. 5th Trial § 88, (S 88) Legal Issues Not Severable.
12 Witkin, California Summary 10th Real Property § 460, Considerations Determining Relief.
12 Witkin, California Summary 10th Real Property § 461, Equitable Lien and Lis Pendens.
12 Witkin, California Summary 10th Real Property § 462, (S 462) Other Relief.

§ 871.6. Rules of law governing encroachments not affected

Nothing in this chapter affects the rules of law which determine the relief, if any, to be granted when a person constructs on his own land an improvement which encroaches on adjoining land. *(Added by Stats.1968, c. 150, p. 375, § 3.)*

Law Revision Commission Comments

This chapter has no effect on the law applicable in encroachment cases. There is no necessity for relief under this chapter in such cases since existing law empowers the courts to deal appropriately with such a situation. See Brown Derby Hollywood Corp. v. Hatton, 61 Cal.2d 855, 40 Cal.Rptr. 848, 395 P.2d 896 (1964); Christensen v. Tucker, 114

Cal.App.2d 554, 250 P.2d 660 (1952). See also Recommendation and Study Relating to the Good Faith Improver of Land Owned by Another, 8 Cal.Law Revision Comm'n, Rep., Rec. & Studies 801, 845, n. 101 (1967).

Research References

Miller and Starr California Real Estate § 14:3, Interests Protected.
Miller and Starr California Real Estate § 14:5, Remedies--Injunction.
Miller and Starr California Real Estate § 14:6, Remedies--Balancing of Hardships.
Miller and Starr California Real Estate § 17:43, Where Improver Does Not Believe He or She Owns the Improved Property.
Miller and Starr California Real Estate § 17:44, Where Improver Believes He or She Owns the Improved Property.
12 Witkin, California Summary 10th Real Property § 459, Nature and Scope of Statute.

§ 871.7. Inapplicability of chapter to public land or land appropriated to public use

(a) This chapter does not apply where the improver is a public entity or where the improvement is made to land owned or possessed by a public entity. As used in this section, "public entity" includes the United States, a state, county, city and county, city, district, public authority, public agency, or any other political subdivision or public corporation.

(b) This chapter does not apply where the owner of the land upon which the improvement is constructed has appropriated the land to a public use and could have acquired the land for that use by exercising the power of eminent domain. *(Added by Stats. 1968, c. 150, p. 375. § 3.)*

Research References

Miller and Starr California Real Estate § 14:3, Interests Protected.
Miller and Starr California Real Estate § 14:6, Remedies--Balancing of Hardships.
Miller and Starr California Real Estate § 17:44, Where Improver Believes He or She Owns the Improved Property.
12 Witkin, California Summary 10th Real Property § 459, Nature and Scope of Statute.

Title 10.5

PARTITION OF REAL AND PERSONAL PROPERTY

CHAPTER 1. GENERAL PROVISIONS

ARTICLE 1. PRELIMINARY PROVISIONS

Section

872.040. Compliance with laws, regulations, etc. relating to property.

§ 872.010. Definitions

As used in this title:

(a) "Action" means an action for partition under this title.

(b) "Lien" means a mortgage, deed of trust, or other security interest in property whether arising from contract, statute, common law, or equity.

(c) "Property" includes real and personal property.

(d) "Remainder" includes reversion, reversionary interest, right of entry, and executory interest.

(e) "Title report" includes a preliminary report, guarantee, binder, or policy of title insurance. *(Added by Stats.1976, c. 73, p. 110, § 6. Amended by Stats.1979, c. 730, § 27, operative Jan. 1, 1981.)*

Law Revision Commission Comments

Section 872.010 provides definitions for terms used in this title.

The term "lien" is defined broadly in subdivision (c) to apply to any encumbrance on property, including security interests in personal property.

The term "title report" in subdivision (f) is drawn using the terminology employed in the title insurance industry.

Section 872.010 is amended to delete subdivision (b) ("guardian" includes conservator) as unnecessary. The term "guardian" is used in Sections 873.040 and 873.690, and those sections are amended to include specific references to a conservator. Subdivisions (c) through (f) of Section 872.010 are redesignated as subdivisions (b) through (e), respectively.

Research References

Rutter, Cal. Practice Guide: Real Prop. Transactions Ch. 12-B, B. Agreements Regarding Co-Ownership Rights and Obligations.
Miller and Starr California Real Estate § 12:14, Right of Partition.
Miller and Starr California Real Estate § 12:15, Right of Partition--Procedure in Partition Action.
Miller and Starr California Real Estate § 12:21, Right of Partition--Defenses to Partition; Waiver or Estoppel.
Miller and Starr California Real Estate § 33:28, Actions in Which a Receiver May be Appointed--Partition.
Miller and Starr California Real Estate § 34:124, Partition-In General.
5 Witkin Cal. Proc. 5th Pleading § 679, in General.
5 Witkin Cal. Proc. 5th Pleading § 684, Additional Allegations.
12 Witkin, California Summary 10th Real Property § 66, (S 66) General Provisions.
12 Witkin, California Summary 10th Real Property § 68, Complaint and Lis Pendens.
13 Witkin, California Summary 10th Personal Property § 45, (S 45) Partition of Personal Property.
11 Witkin, California Summary 10th Community Property § 226, Former Law.
11 Witkin, California Summary 10th Community Property § 227, Statutory Revision.
14 Witkin, California Summary 10th Wills and Probate § 738, Partition or Allotment of Property.

§ 872.020. Scope of title

This title governs actions for partition of real property and, except to the extent not applicable, actions for partition of personal property. *(Added by Stats.1976, c. 73, p. 110, § 6.)*

Research References

12 Witkin, California Summary 10th Real Property § 66, (S 66) General Provisions.
12 Witkin, California Summary 10th Real Property § 67, Parties.
13 Witkin, California Summary 10th Personal Property § 45, (S 45) Partition of Personal Property.

§ 872.030. Civil actions; law governing

The statutes and rules governing practice in civil actions generally apply to actions under this title except where they are inconsistent with the provisions of this title. *(Added by Stats. 1976, c. 73, p. 110, § 6.)*

Law Revision Commission Comments

Section 872.030 makes clear that, although partition is nominally a civil action, this title contains some special procedural provisions that apply to partition despite general rules to the contrary. For example, the partition provisions governing referees apply in partition actions notwithstanding any general provisions to the contrary that might be found in Chapter 6 (commencing with Section 638) of Title 8 of Part 2 of the Code of Civil Procedure (references and trials by referees).

Research References

12 Witkin, California Summary 10th Real Property § 66, (S 66) General Provisions.

§ 872.040. Compliance with laws, regulations, etc. relating to property

Nothing in this title excuses compliance with any applicable laws, regulations, or ordinances governing the division, sale, or transfer of property. *(Added by Stats.1976, c. 73, p. 110, § 6.)*

Research References

Miller and Starr California Real Estate § 12:16, Right of Partition--Partition by a Physical Division of the Property.
Miller and Starr California Real Estate § 28:18, Property Included Within the Lien.
12 Witkin, California Summary 10th Real Property § 66, (S 66) General Provisions.

ARTICLE 2. POWERS OF COURT

Section

872.110. Superior court; jurisdiction; venue.
872.120. Motions, reports and accounts; hearing and determination; decrees and orders.
872.130. Restraining orders and injunctions; bonds; purpose.
872.140. Compensatory adjustment among parties; equity.

§ 872.110. Superior court; jurisdiction; venue

(a) The superior court has jurisdiction of actions under this title.

(b) Subject to the power of the court to transfer actions, the proper county for the trial of actions under this title is:

(1) Where the subject of the action is real property or real and personal property, the county in which the real property, or some part thereof, is situated.

(2) Where the subject of the action is personal property, the county in which the personal property is principally located at the commencement of the action or in which the defendants, or any of them, reside at the commencement of the action. *(Added by Stats.1976, c. 73, p. 110, § 6.)*

Research References

Rutter, Cal. Practice Guide: Civ. Pro. Before Trial Ch. 3-D, D. Venue.
Miller and Starr California Real Estate § 12:15, Right of Partition--Procedure in Partition Action.
3 Witkin Cal. Proc. 5th Actions § 798, (S 798) Partition.

12 Witkin, California Summary 10th Real Property § 66, (S 66) General Provisions.

§ 872.120. Motions, reports and accounts; hearing and determination; decrees and orders

In the conduct of the action, the court may hear and determine all motions, reports, and accounts and may make any decrees and orders necessary or incidental to carrying out the purposes of this title and to effectuating its decrees and orders. *(Added by Stats.1976, c. 73, p. 110, § 6.)*

Law Revision Commission Comments

Section 872.120 is new. Generally, its purpose is to give the broadest possible statutory authorization for powers that the court, to a large extent, apparently already had. The succeeding sections of this article elaborate on, but do not exhaust, the court's power in partition actions. While partition actions in California are a creature of statute (Capuccio v. Caire, 207 Cal. 200, 277 P. 475 (1929)), they are nonetheless equitable in nature (Elbert, Ltd. v. Federated Income Properties, 120 Cal.App.2d 194, 261 P.2d 783 (1953)), and the statutory provisions are to be liberally construed in aid of the court's jurisdiction. See Sections 4 and 187.

Research References

12 Witkin, California Summary 10th Real Property § 66, (S 66) General Provisions.

§ 872.130. Restraining orders and injunctions; bonds; purpose

In the conduct of the action, the court may issue temporary restraining orders and injunctions, with or without bond, for the purpose of:

(a) Preventing waste.

(b) Protecting the property or title thereto.

(c) Restraining unlawful interference with a partition of the property ordered by the court. *(Added by Stats.1976, c. 73, p. 110, § 6.)*

Law Revision Commission Comments

Section 872.130 is new. It gives the court authority to take the protective steps described without having to rely either upon its contempt powers or the general provisions as to temporary restraining orders and injunctions.

Research References

Miller and Starr California Real Estate § 12:15, Right of Partition-- Procedure in Partition Action.
6 Witkin Cal. Proc. 5th Provisional Remedies § 291, (S 291) Special Statutes.
12 Witkin, California Summary 10th Real Property § 66, (S 66) General Provisions.

§ 872.140. Compensatory adjustment among parties; equity

The court may, in all cases, order allowance, accounting, contribution, or other compensatory adjustment among the parties according to the principles of equity. *(Added by Stats. 1976, c. 73, p. 110, § 6.)*

Law Revision Commission Comments

Section 872.140 continues the substance of the last sentence of former Section 792. It makes clear the court's authority to order compensatory adjustment for such items as common improvements, unaccounted rents and profits, and other matters for which contribution may be required. See, e.g., Hunter v. Schultz, 240 Cal.App.2d 24, 49 Cal.Rptr. 315 (1966) (equitable adjustment offsetting use value of property against expense of improvements). For a provision for payment of owelty in cases of unequal division, see Section 873.250.

Research References

Miller and Starr California Real Estate § 12:15, Right of Partition-- Procedure in Partition Action.

Miller and Starr California Real Estate § 12:20, Right of Partition-- Compensation for Improvements.
Miller and Starr California Real Estate § 12:21, Right of Partition-- Defenses to Partition; Waiver or Estoppel.
12 Witkin, California Summary 10th Real Property § 66, (S 66) General Provisions.
12 Witkin, California Summary 10th Real Property § 78, (S 78) Division of Property.

CHAPTER 2. COMMENCEMENT OF ACTION

ARTICLE 1. COMPLAINT AND LIS PENDENS

§ 872.210. Persons authorized

(a) A partition action may be commenced and maintained by any of the following persons:

(1) A coowner of personal property.

(2) An owner of an estate of inheritance, an estate for life, or an estate for years in real property where such property or estate therein is owned by several persons concurrently or in successive estates.

(b) Notwithstanding subdivision (a), an action between spouses or putative spouses for partition of their community or quasi-community property or their quasi-marital interest in property may not be commenced or maintained under this title. *(Added by Stats.1976, c. 73, p. 110, § 6.)*

Research References

Miller and Starr California Real Estate § 9:24, Termination; Merger; Partition.
Miller and Starr California Real Estate § 9:31, Remainders--Termination; Court Proceedings.
Miller and Starr California Real Estate § 12:14, Right of Partition.
Miller and Starr California Real Estate § 12:21, Right of Partition-- Defenses to Partition; Waiver or Estoppel.
Miller and Starr California Real Estate § 12:59, Management and Control--Partition of Community Property.
Miller and Starr California Real Estate § 12:60, Disposition on Dissolution.
Miller and Starr California Real Estate § 11:177, Priorities Among State and Local Tax and Assessment Liens--Priority Between Assessment Liens.
20 NO. 6 Miller & Starr, California Real Estate Newsalert 12, Holding Title.
5 Witkin Cal. Proc. 5th Pleading § 680, Ownership of Described Property.
12 Witkin, California Summary 10th Real Property § 67, Parties.
12 Witkin, California Summary 10th Real Property § 72, Determination of Right to Partition.
12 Witkin, California Summary 10th Real Property § 143, (S 143) Against Life Tenant.

§ 872.220. Title report

If it is necessary to have a title report:

(a) The plaintiff may, prior to commencing the action, procure a title report and shall in the complaint indicate this has been done and designate a place where it will be kept for inspection, use, and copying by the parties.

(b) The court may, upon application of a party, authorize the party to procure a title report and shall designate a place where it shall be kept for inspection, use, and copying by the parties. *(Added by Stats.1976, c. 73, p. 110, § 6.)*

Law Revision Commission Comments

Section 872.220 is derived from former Section 799. For a definition of "title report," see Section 872.020(f). Provisions relating to the title report formerly found in Section 800 are omitted as outmoded and inappropriate under modern conditions. For allowance of cost of procuring the title report, see Section 874.010.

Research References

Miller and Starr California Real Estate § 12:19, Right of Partition-- Decree of Partition.
5 Witkin Cal. Proc. 5th Pleading § 684, Additional Allegations.
12 Witkin, California Summary 10th Real Property § 68, Complaint and Lis Pendens.
12 Witkin, California Summary 10th Real Property § 83, (S 83) Costs of Partition.

§ 872.230. Complaint; contents

The complaint shall set forth:

(a) A description of the property that is the subject of the action. In the case of tangible personal property, the description shall include its usual location. In the case of real property, the description shall include both its legal description and its street address or common designation, if any.

(b) All interests the plaintiff has or claims in the property.

(c) All interests of record or actually known to the plaintiff that persons other than the plaintiff have or claim in the property and that the plaintiff reasonably believes will be materially affected by the action, whether the names of such persons are known or unknown to the plaintiff.

(d) The estate as to which partition is sought and a prayer for partition of the interests therein.

(e) Where the plaintiff seeks sale of the property, an allegation of the facts justifying such relief in ordinary and concise language. *(Added by Stats.1976, c. 73, p. 110, § 6.)*

Research References

Miller and Starr California Real Estate § 12:15, Right of Partition-- Procedure in Partition Action.
5 Witkin Cal. Proc. 5th Pleading § 681, Interests of Plaintiff and Defendant.
5 Witkin Cal. Proc. 5th Pleading § 683, Property and Interests Subject to Action.
5 Witkin Cal. Proc. 5th Pleading § 684, Additional Allegations.
12 Witkin, California Summary 10th Real Property § 68, Complaint and Lis Pendens.

§ 872.240. Joinder of property

Real and personal property may be partitioned in one action. *(Added by Stats.1976, c. 73, p. 110, § 6.)*

Law Revision Commission Comments

Section 872.240 continues the last sentence of former Section 752a. Where different parties are interested in real and personal property joined in the action, severance may be appropriate. See Section 1048 (severance and consolidation of issues and causes).

Research References

5 Witkin Cal. Proc. 5th Pleading § 683, Property and Interests Subject to Action.

12 Witkin, California Summary 10th Real Property § 68, Complaint and Lis Pendens.

§ 872.250. Lis pendens; supplemental notice; recordation

(a) Immediately upon filing the complaint, the plaintiff shall record a notice of the pendency of the action in the office of the county recorder of each county in which any real property described in the complaint is located.

(b) If, thereafter, partition of other real property is sought in the same action, the plaintiff or other person seeking such relief shall immediately record a supplemental notice.

(c) If the notice is not recorded, the court, upon its own motion or upon the motion of any party at any time, shall order the plaintiff or person seeking partition of the property, or another party on behalf of the plaintiff or other person, to record the notice and shall stay the action until the notice is recorded. The expense of recordation shall be allowed to the party incurring it.

(d) From the time of filing the notice for record, all persons shall be deemed to have notice of the pendency of the action as to the property described in the notice. *(Added by Stats.1976, c. 73, p. 110, § 6.)*

Law Revision Commission Comments

Subdivisions (a) and (d) of Section 872.250 continue provisions formerly found in Section 755. The detailed listing of the contents of the lis pendens formerly found in Section 755 is omitted since Section 409 covers this matter. The requirement of recording a lis pendens is not jurisdictional. Rutledge v. Rutledge, 119 Cal.App.2d 114, 120, 259 P.2d 79, 82 (1953). Failure to so file, however, may result in subsequent bona fide purchasers and encumbrancers of record at the time the judgment is recorded not being bound by the partition judgment. See Section 874.220 (persons not bound by judgment).

Subdivision (b) is new. The duty under subdivision (b) is upon the person seeking to join additional property to record the lis pendens; this might be either the plaintiff or a cross-complainant.

Subdivision (c) is new. The recording of the lis pendens is an important step in the partition action. Prompt recording enables the court to deal with the title with certainty. The person required to record might be either the plaintiff or a cross-complainant.

Research References

Rutter, Cal. Practice Guide: Civ. Pro. Before Trial Ch. 9(I)-J, J. Motion to Expunge Lis Pendens.
Rutter, Cal. Practice Guide: Real Prop. Transactions Ch. 11-I, I. Lis Pendens.
Miller and Starr California Real Estate § 12:15, Right of Partition-- Procedure in Partition Action.
Miller and Starr California Real Estate § 11:150, Actions in Which a Lis Pendens May or Must be Recorded.
3 Witkin Cal. Proc. 5th Actions § 381, (S 381) Specific Mandatory Statutes.
12 Witkin, California Summary 10th Real Property § 68, Complaint and Lis Pendens.

ARTICLE 2. SUMMONS

Section
872.310. Form, content and service; civil actions; publication.
872.320. Publication; court order; conditions.
872.330. Publication; certain defendants; contents.

§ 872.310. Form, content and service; civil actions; publication

(a) The form, content, and manner of service of summons shall be as in civil actions generally.

(b) Service on persons named as parties pursuant to Sections 872.530(b) and 872.550, and on other persons named as unknown defendants, shall be by publication pursuant to Section 415.50 and the provisions of this article. *(Added by Stats.1976, c. 73, p. 110, § 6.)*

Research References

3 Witkin Cal. Proc. 5th Actions § 987, (S 987) Actions Involving Real Property.
3 Witkin Cal. Proc. 5th Actions § 1034, Special Statutes.
12 Witkin, California Summary 10th Real Property § 69, Summons.

§ 872.320. Publication; court order; conditions

Where the court orders service by publication, such order shall be subject to the following conditions:

(a) The plaintiff shall post, not later than 10 days after the date the order is made, a copy of the summons and complaint on the real property that is the subject of the action.

(b) The plaintiff shall record, if not already recorded, a notice of the pendency of the action.

(c) The publication shall describe the property that is the subject of the action. In addition to particularly describing the property, the publication shall describe the property by giving its street address, if any, or other common designation, if any; but, if a legal description of the property is given, the validity of the publication shall not be affected by the fact that the street address or other common designation recited is erroneous or that the street address or other common designation is omitted. *(Added by Stats.1976, c. 73, p. 110, § 6.)*

Law Revision Commission Comments

Section 872.320 supersedes former Section 757. While publication will be pursuant to Section 415.50, subdivisions (a) and (b) are new requirements that supplement the publication provisions of Section 415.50 in order to increases the likelihood that persons interested in the property will receive notice of the proceeding. Subdivision (c) continues a provision in the last sentence of former Section 757; the language concerning the street address or other common designation is drawn from Section 692 (execution). See also Civil Code § 2924f (sale under deed of trust). Where personal property is involved, an appropriate manner of special service may be ordered. See Section 413.30.

Research References

Miller and Starr California Real Estate § 12:15, Right of Partition-- Procedure in Partition Action.
Miller and Starr California Real Estate § 11:150, Actions in Which a Lis Pendens May or Must be Recorded.
3 Witkin Cal. Proc. 5th Actions § 987, (S 987) Actions Involving Real Property.
12 Witkin, California Summary 10th Real Property § 68, Complaint and Lis Pendens.
12 Witkin, California Summary 10th Real Property § 69, Summons.

§ 872.330. Publication; certain defendants; contents

(a) Where the court orders service by publication, the publication may:

(1) Name only the defendants to be served thereby.

(2) Describe only the property in which the defendants to be served thereby have or claim interests.

(b) Judgment based on failure to appear and answer following service under this section shall be conclusive against the defendants named in respect only to property described in the publication. *(Added by Stats.1976, c. 73, p. 110, § 6.)*

Research References

12 Witkin, California Summary 10th Real Property § 69, Summons.

ARTICLE 3. ANSWER

Section
872.410. Contents.

Section
872.420. Lien claim; date; amount.
872.430. Claim for compensatory adjustment.

§ 872.410. Contents

The answer shall set forth:

(a) Any interest the defendant has or claims in the property.

(b) Any facts tending to controvert such material allegations of the complaint as the defendant does not wish to be taken as true.

(c) Where the defendant seeks sale of the property, an allegation of the facts justifying such relief in ordinary and concise language. *(Added by Stats.1976, c. 73, p. 110, § 6.)*

Law Revision Commission Comments

Section 872.410 continues portions of former Section 758; subdivision (c) is new. The provision of former Section 758 that the defendant's failure to answer within the time allowed by law would result in the allegations of the complaint being taken as true is now contained in Section 431.20. It should be noted that the requirement in subdivision (a) that the defendant list his interest in the property includes liens as well as other interests claimed by the defendant.

Research References

5 Witkin Cal. Proc. 5th Pleading § 1116, (S 1116) Answer in Partition Action.
12 Witkin, California Summary 10th Real Property § 70, Answer.

§ 872.420. Lien claim; date; amount

Where the defendant has or claims a lien on the property, the answer shall set forth the date and character of the lien and the amount remaining due thereon. *(Added by Stats.1976, c. 73, p. 110, § 6.)*

Law Revision Commission Comments

Section 872.420 continues a portion of former Section 758. The provision for waiver for failure to disclose additional security formerly found in Section 758 is omitted because it was unduly harsh. It should be noted that nothing in Section 872.420 precludes the defendant from alleging such additional costs, fees, and expenses related to the lien as he may be entitled to in addition to the amount remaining due on the lien itself.

Research References

5 Witkin Cal. Proc. 5th Pleading § 1116, (S 1116) Answer in Partition Action.
12 Witkin, California Summary 10th Real Property § 70, Answer.

§ 872.430. Claim for compensatory adjustment

The answer may set forth any claim the defendant has for contribution or other compensatory adjustment. *(Added by Stats.1976, c. 73, p. 110, § 6.)*

Research References

Miller and Starr California Real Estate § 12:19, Right of Partition-- Decree of Partition.
5 Witkin Cal. Proc. 5th Pleading § 1116, (S 1116) Answer in Partition Action.
12 Witkin, California Summary 10th Real Property § 70, Answer.

ARTICLE 4. PARTIES

Section
872.510. Joinder of defendants.
872.520. Names and nature of interest unknown; statement in complaint; orders.
872.530. Personal representatives; joinder; affidavits.
872.540. Oil and gas interests.

Civ. Pro.

Section

872.550.   Joinder of all persons unknown claiming any interest.

§ 872.510.   Joinder of defendants

The plaintiff shall join as defendants in the action all persons having or claiming interests of record or actually known to the plaintiff or reasonably apparent from an inspection of the property, in the estate as to which partition is sought. *(Added by Stats.1976, c. 73, p. 110, § 6.)*

Research References

Miller and Starr California Real Estate § 12:14, Right of Partition.
Miller and Starr California Real Estate § 12:15, Right of Partition--Procedure in Partition Action.
5 Witkin Cal. Proc. 5th Pleading § 682, Interests of Other Persons.
12 Witkin, California Summary 10th Real Property § 67, Parties.

§ 872.520.   Names and nature of interest unknown; statement in complaint; orders

(a) If the name of a person described in Section 872.510 is not known to the plaintiff, the plaintiff shall so state in the complaint and shall name as parties all persons unknown in the manner provided in Section 872.550.

(b) If the ownership or the share or quantity of the interest of a person described in Section 872.510 is unknown, uncertain, or contingent, the plaintiff shall so state in the complaint. If the lack of knowledge, uncertainty, or contingency is caused by a transfer to an unborn or unascertained person or class member, or by a transfer in the form of a contingent remainder, vested remainder subject to defeasance, executory interest, or similar disposition, the plaintiff shall also state in the complaint, so far as is known to the plaintiff, the name, age, and legal disability (if any) of the person in being who would be entitled to ownership of the interest had the contingency upon which the right of such person depends occurred prior to the commencement of the action.

(c) The court shall upon its own motion or upon motion of any party make such orders for joinder of additional parties and for appointment of guardians ad litem pursuant to Sections 372, 373, and 373.5 as are necessary or proper. *(Added by Stats.1976, c. 73, p. 110, § 6.)*

Law Revision Commission Comments

Section 872.520 is derived from the last portion of former Section 753. Subdivision (a) incorporates the requirement, formerly found in Section 756, that "all persons unknown" be joined. Subdivision (b) adds the requirement of an indication of possible additional parties, and subdivision (c) provides for joinder of such parties and protection of their interests.

Research References

5 Witkin Cal. Proc. 5th Pleading § 682, Interests of Other Persons.
12 Witkin, California Summary 10th Real Property § 67, Parties.

§ 872.530.   Personal representatives; joinder; affidavits

(a) If a person described in Section 872.510 is dead and the plaintiff knows of a personal representative, the plaintiff shall join such personal representative as a defendant.

(b) If a person described in Section 872.510 is dead, or is believed by the plaintiff to be dead, and the plaintiff knows of no personal representative:

(1) The plaintiff shall state these facts in an affidavit filed with the complaint.

(2) Where it is stated in the affidavit that such person is dead, the plaintiff may join as defendants "the testate and intestate successors of _____ (naming such deceased person), de-

ceased, and all persons claiming by, through, or under said decedent," naming them in that manner.

(3) Where it is stated in the affidavit that such person is believed to be dead, the plaintiff may join such person as a defendant, and he may also join "the testate and intestate successors of _____ (naming such person) believed to be deceased, and all persons claiming by, through, or under such person," naming them in that manner. *(Added by Stats.1976, c. 73, p. 110, § 6.)*

Research References

5 Witkin Cal. Proc. 5th Pleading § 681, Interests of Plaintiff and Defendant.
12 Witkin, California Summary 10th Real Property § 67, Parties.
12 Witkin, California Summary 10th Real Property § 84, (S 84) Judgment.

§ 872.540.   Oil and gas interests

Where property is subject to a lease, community lease, unit agreement, or other pooling arrangement with respect to oil or gas or both, the plaintiff need not join as defendants persons whose only interest in the property is that of a lessee, royalty-owner, lessor-owner of other real property in the community, unit, or pooled area, or working interest owner, or persons claiming under them, and the judgment shall not affect the interests of such persons not joined as defendants. *(Added by Stats.1976, c. 73, p. 110, § 6.)*

Law Revision Commission Comments

Section 872.540 continues the substance of former Section 753.1.

Research References

Miller and Starr California Real Estate § 12:15, Right of Partition--Procedure in Partition Action.
5 Witkin Cal. Proc. 5th Pleading § 682, Interests of Other Persons.
12 Witkin, California Summary 10th Real Property § 67, Parties.

§ 872.550.   Joinder of all persons unknown claiming any interest

Where partition is sought as to all interests in the property, the plaintiff may join as defendants "all persons unknown claiming any interest in the property," naming them in that manner. *(Added by Stats.1976, c. 73, p. 110, § 6.)*

Research References

Miller and Starr California Real Estate § 12:15, Right of Partition--Procedure in Partition Action.
5 Witkin Cal. Proc. 5th Pleading § 682, Interests of Other Persons.
12 Witkin, California Summary 10th Real Property § 67, Parties.
12 Witkin, California Summary 10th Real Property § 84, (S 84) Judgment.

CHAPTER 3.   TRIAL

ARTICLE 1.   DETERMINATION OF INTERESTS OF PARTIES

§ 872.610. Plaintiff and defendant

The interests of the parties, plaintiff as well as defendant, may be put in issue, tried, and determined in the action. *(Added by Stats.1976, c. 73, p. 110, § 6.)*

Law Revision Commission Comments

Section 872.610 continues the substance of the first portion of former Section 759. The section makes clear that the court may resolve any title disputes in the course of the proceeding where placed in issue by answer of a defendant or cross-defendant. See Section 872.410 (answer).

Research References

Miller and Starr California Real Estate § 12:15, Right of Partition--Procedure in Partition Action.
Miller and Starr California Real Estate § 12:19, Right of Partition--Decree of Partition.
12 Witkin, California Summary 10th Real Property § 71, Determination of Interests.

§ 872.620. State of the title; ascertainment

To the extent necessary to grant the relief sought or other appropriate relief, the court shall upon adequate proof ascertain the state of the title to the property. *(Added by Stats.1976, c. 73, p. 110, § 6.)*

Law Revision Commission Comments

Section 872.620 supersedes the portion of former Section 759 that required, where a sale of the premises was necessary, that "the title must be ascertained by proof to the satisfaction of the court." Section 872.620 expands this requirement to any case, sale, division, or appraisal where ascertainment of title appears to be necessary. In contrast with Section 872.610, in cases where it is necessary to know the state of the title, Section 872.620 applies regardless whether a defendant raises the issue in his pleadings.

For special provisions relating to ascertainment of the status of liens, see Section 872.630.

Research References

12 Witkin, California Summary 10th Real Property § 71, Determination of Interests.

§ 872.630. Liens; status and priority

(a) To the extent necessary to grant the relief sought or other appropriate relief, the court shall determine the status and priority of all liens upon the property.

(b) The court may appoint a referee to ascertain the facts necessary for the determination required by this section. Upon application of the referee or a lienholder, the court shall direct the issuance of process to compel attendance of witnesses, the production of books, documents, or things, and the filing of verified claims. The report of the referee thereon shall be made in writing to the court and shall be confirmed, modified, or set aside and a new reference ordered, as the justice of the case may require. *(Added by Stats.1976, c. 73, p. 110, § 6.)*

Law Revision Commission Comments

Section 872.630 supersedes the provisions of former Sections 761 and 762, which applied only to determination of the status of liens of record held by persons not made parties to the action. Section 872.630 extends this requirement to all liens and simplifies the provisions relating to ascertainment of the status of liens by a referee. The provision for ascertainment of other security is omitted. See former Section 772 and Comment thereto.

Research References

12 Witkin, California Summary 10th Real Property § 71, Determination of Interests.

12 Witkin, California Summary 10th Real Property § 76, Appointment.

§ 872.640. Unknown parties; interests

Where two or more parties are unknown, the court may consider their interests together in the action and not as between each other. *(Added by Stats.1976, c. 73, p. 110, § 6.)*

Law Revision Commission Comments

Section 872.640 continues the last portion of former Section 759.

Research References

Miller and Starr California Real Estate § 12:15, Right of Partition--Procedure in Partition Action.
Miller and Starr California Real Estate § 12:19, Right of Partition--Decree of Partition.
12 Witkin, California Summary 10th Real Property § 71, Determination of Interests.
12 Witkin, California Summary 10th Real Property § 78, (S 78) Division of Property.

ARTICLE 2. DETERMINATION OF RIGHT TO PARTITION

Section
872.710. Right of plaintiff to partition; concurrent interests; successive estates.
872.720. Interlocutory judgment.
872.730. Application to partnerships.

§ 872.710. Right of plaintiff to partition; concurrent interests; successive estates

(a) At the trial, the court shall determine whether the plaintiff has the right to partition.

(b) Except as provided in Section 872.730, partition as to concurrent interests in the property shall be as of right unless barred by a valid waiver.

(c) Partition as to successive estates in the property shall be allowed if it is in the best interest of all the parties. The court shall consider whether the possessory interest has become unduly burdensome by reason of taxes or other charges, expense of ordinary or extraordinary repairs, character of the property and change in the character of the property since creation of the estates, circumstances under which the estates were created and change in the circumstances since creation of the estates, and all other factors that would be considered by a court of equity having in mind the intent of the creator of the successive estates and the interests and needs of the successive owners. *(Added by Stats.1976, c. 73, p. 110, § 6.)*

Research References

Miller and Starr California Real Estate § 9:24, Termination; Merger; Partition.
Miller and Starr California Real Estate § 12:14, Right of Partition.
Miller and Starr California Real Estate § 12:21, Right of Partition--Defenses to Partition; Waiver or Estoppel.
12 Witkin, California Summary 10th Real Property § 67, Parties.
12 Witkin, California Summary 10th Real Property § 72, Determination of Right to Partition.

§ 872.720. Interlocutory judgment

(a) If the court finds that the plaintiff is entitled to partition, it shall make an interlocutory judgment that determines the interests of the parties in the property and orders the partition of the property and, unless it is to be later determined, the manner of partition.

(b) If the court determines that it is impracticable or highly inconvenient to make a single interlocutory judgment that determines, in the first instance, the interests of all the parties in the property, the court may first ascertain the interests of the original concurrent or successive owners and thereupon make an interlocutory judgment as if such persons were the sole parties in interest and the only parties to the action. Thereafter, the court may proceed in like manner as between the original concurrent or successive owners and the parties claiming under them or may allow the interests to remain without further partition if the parties so desire. *(Added by Stats.1976, c. 73, p. 110, § 6.)*

Law Revision Commission Comments

Subdivision (a) of Section 872.720 continues the portion of former Section 763 that required a court order of "partition according to the respective rights of the parties as ascertained by the court." Subdivision (b) continues the substance of former Section 760. The interlocutory judgment of partition is appealable. See Section 904.1(i); contrast Emeric v. Alvarado, 64 Cal. 529 (1884).

Research References

Miller and Starr California Real Estate § 12:20, Right of Partition-- Compensation for Improvements.
7 Witkin Cal. Proc. 5th Judgment § 21, Statutory Types.
12 Witkin, California Summary 10th Real Property § 75, Interlocutory Judgment.
12 Witkin, California Summary 10th Real Property § 78, (S 78) Division of Property.

§ 872.730. Application to partnerships

To the extent that the court determines that the provisions of this title are a suitable remedy, such provisions may be applied in a proceeding for partnership accounting and dissolution, or in an action for partition of partnership property, where the rights of unsecured creditors of the partnership will not be prejudiced. *(Added by Stats.1976, c. 73, p. 110, § 6.)*

Research References

Miller and Starr California Real Estate § 12:14, Right of Partition.
12 Witkin, California Summary 10th Real Property § 72, Determination of Right to Partition.

ARTICLE 3. DETERMINATION OF MANNER OF PARTITION

Section
872.810.   Division in accordance with interests.
872.820.   Sale of property; division of proceeds.
872.830.   Partial division and sale.
872.840.   Property subject to express trust; division or sale; duty of trustee.

§ 872.810. Division in accordance with interests

The court shall order that the property be divided among the parties in accordance with their interests in the property as determined in the interlocutory judgment. *(Added by Stats.1976, c. 73, p. 110, § 6.)*

Law Revision Commission Comments

Section 872.810 continues the preference of prior law for partition by division in kind. See former Sections 763, 752 (real property), 752a (personal property). In an appropriate case, the court may order partition by sale (Section 872.820) or appraisal (Chapter 7 (commencing with Section 873.910)).
It should be noted that the provision formerly found in Section 763 for division where the site of an incorporated town or city is included within the exterior boundaries of property has not been continued because it is obsolete.

Research References

Miller and Starr California Real Estate § 9:31, Remainders--Termination; Court Proceedings.

Miller and Starr California Real Estate § 12:15, Right of Partition-- Procedure in Partition Action.
Miller and Starr California Real Estate § 12:17, Right of Partition-- Partition by a Sale of the Property.
Miller and Starr California Real Estate § 12:20, Right of Partition-- Compensation for Improvements.
12 Witkin, California Summary 10th Real Property § 74, Determination of Manner of Partition.
12 Witkin, California Summary 10th Real Property § 78, (S 78) Division of Property.

§ 872.820. Sale of property; division of proceeds

Notwithstanding Section 872.810, the court shall order that the property be sold and the proceeds be divided among the parties in accordance with their interests in the property as determined in the interlocutory judgment in the following situations:

(a) The parties agree to such relief, by their pleadings or otherwise.

(b) The court determines that, under the circumstances, sale and division of the proceeds would be more equitable than division of the property. For the purpose of making the determination, the court may appoint a referee and take into account his report. *(Added by Stats.1976, c. 73, p. 110, § 6.)*

Law Revision Commission Comments

Section 872.820 represents an exception to the rule of partition by division stated in Section 872.810. The court may order a sale under the terms of this section; in addition, partition by appraisal may be available under Chapter 7 (commencing with Section 873.910).
Subdivision (b) changes the standard for allowing a sale of the property from "great prejudice" to "more equitable," thereby enabling sale in cases in which it previously was precluded. See former Sections 763, 752 (real property), 752a (personal property). The reference to a referee for determination whether partition by sale would be more equitable may include a further request for determination whether public or private sale would be more appropriate. See Section 873.520. The portion of former Section 763 requiring sale in the case of a life estate with contingent remainder is not continued.
It should be noted that the provision formerly found in Section 763 which permitted sale where the site of an incorporated town or city was included within the exterior boundaries of the property has not been continued because it is obsolete.

Research References

Miller and Starr California Real Estate § 12:15, Right of Partition-- Procedure in Partition Action.
Miller and Starr California Real Estate § 12:17, Right of Partition-- Partition by a Sale of the Property.
Miller and Starr California Real Estate § 12:20, Right of Partition-- Compensation for Improvements.
5 Witkin Cal. Proc. 5th Pleading § 684, Additional Allegations.
12 Witkin, California Summary 10th Real Property § 74, Determination of Manner of Partition.
12 Witkin, California Summary 10th Real Property § 81, Disposition of Proceeds.

§ 872.830. Partial division and sale

If, in making a determination whether sale would be more equitable than division of the property, the court finds that sale and division of proceeds for part of the property would be more equitable than division of the whole property, the court may order that such part be sold and the remainder divided. *(Added by Stats.1976, c. 73, p. 110, § 6.)*

Law Revision Commission Comments

Section 872.830 makes explicit the authority of the court to order a partial division of the property and a sale and division of proceeds as to the remainder. Provisions of prior law in which such authority was implicit include Sections 763 and 770.

Miller and Starr California Real Estate § 9:31, Remainders--Termination; Court Proceedings.
Miller and Starr California Real Estate § 12:15, Right of Partition--Procedure in Partition Action.
12 Witkin, California Summary 10th Real Property § 74, Determination of Manner of Partition.

§ 872.840. Property subject to express trust; division or sale; duty of trustee

(a) Where the property or an interest therein is subject to an express trust, the court may, in its discretion, order that the property be sold.

(b) Upon division or sale of such property, the property or proceeds of sale allotted to the trustee of the express trust shall be held by him upon the trust therein stated, and no further action by the court pursuant to Section 873.840 is required. *(Added by Stats.1976, c. 73, p. 110, § 6.)*

Law Revision Commission Comments

Section 872.840 continues the substance of the second paragraph of former Section 763.

Research References

Miller and Starr California Real Estate § 12:14, Right of Partition.
12 Witkin, California Summary 10th Real Property § 74, Determination of Manner of Partition.
12 Witkin, California Summary 10th Real Property § 78, (S 78) Division of Property.
12 Witkin, California Summary 10th Real Property § 81, Disposition of Proceeds.

CHAPTER 4. REFEREES

ARTICLE 1. GENERAL PROVISIONS

§ 873.010. Appointment; power and duty of court

(a) The court shall appoint a referee to divide or sell the property as ordered by the court.

(b) The court may:

(1) Determine whether a referee's bond is necessary and fix the amount of the bond.

(2) Instruct the referee.

(3) Fix the reasonable compensation for the services of the referee and provide for payment of the referee's reasonable expenses.

(4) Provide for the date of commencement of the lien of the referee allowed by law.

(5) Require the filing of interim or final accounts of the referee, settle the accounts of the referee, and discharge the referee.

(6) Remove the referee.

(7) Appoint a new referee. *(Added by Stats.1976, c. 73, p. 110, § 6.)*

Research References

Rutter, Cal. Practice Guide: A.D.R. Ch. 6-C, C. Referees.
Miller and Starr California Real Estate § 12:16, Right of Partition--Partition by a Physical Division of the Property.
Miller and Starr California Real Estate § 12:17, Right of Partition--Partition by a Sale of the Property.
Miller and Starr California Real Estate § 33:22, Right to Compensation.
15 NO. 6 Miller & Starr, California Real Estate Newsalert 3, Brokers' Compensation.
2 Witkin Cal. Proc. 5th Courts § 346, (S 346) in General.
6 Witkin Cal. Proc. 5th Proceedings Without Trial § 63, (S 63) Nature and Purpose.
12 Witkin, California Summary 10th Real Property § 76, Appointment.
12 Witkin, California Summary 10th Real Property § 83, (S 83) Costs of Partition.

§ 873.020. Appointment; one or more

The court in its discretion may appoint a referee for sale and a referee for division, or may appoint a single referee for both. *(Added by Stats.1976, c. 73, p. 110, § 6.)*

Law Revision Commission Comments

Section 873.020 is new. It makes clear the court's discretion to appoint referees with different functions where property in an action is to be both divided and sold.

Research References

12 Witkin, California Summary 10th Real Property § 76, Appointment.

§ 873.030. Appointment; three referees

(a) The court may, with the consent of the parties, appoint three referees to divide or sell the property as ordered by the court.

(b) The three referees so appointed shall have all the powers and may perform all the duties required of one referee. *(Added by Stats.1976, c. 73, p. 110, § 6.)*

Law Revision Commission Comments

Section 873.030, providing for court appointment of three referees only with the consent of the parties, replaces provisions of former Section 763 that provided for appointment of three referees as a matter of course.

Research References

12 Witkin, California Summary 10th Real Property § 76, Appointment.

§ 873.040. Consent of all parties; guardian or conservator

(a) The court shall appoint as referee under this title any person or persons to whose appointment all parties have consented.

(b) In the case of a minor party or a party for whom a conservator of the estate has been appointed, the guardian or conservator of the estate of the party may so consent. *(Added by Stats.1976, c. 73, p. 110, § 6. Amended by Stats.1979, c. 730, § 28, operative Jan. 1, 1981.)*

Law Revision Commission Comments

Section 873.040 continues without substantive change a portion of former Section 763. See Section 872.010 (defining guardian). It should be noted that the parties may nominate persons to serve as referee but, absent agreement among the parties, the choice of a referee is in the discretion of the court.

Section 873.040 is amended to substitute a reference to a party for whom a conservator of the estate has been appointed for the former reference to an incompetent. When a person for whom a conservator has been appointed is a party to litigation, he or she must appear by the conservator or by a guardian ad litem. Code Civ.Proc. § 372. When the conservator has made the appearance, the conservator should be the one to take any procedural steps in the litigation, including the giving of consent to the appointment of a referee under Section 873.040.

Research References

12 Witkin, California Summary 10th Real Property § 76, Appointment.

§ 873.050. Ineligible persons

None of the following persons shall be appointed a referee under this title:

(a) A clerk or deputy clerk of the court.

(b) A former or present partner or employee of the judge.

(c) A relative within the third degree of the judge or the judge's spouse or the spouse of such a relative.

(d) An owner of any interest in the property that is the subject of the action. *(Added by Stats.1976, c. 73, p. 110, § 6.)*

Law Revision Commission Comments

Section 873.050 continues provisions formerly found in Section 763.

Research References

12 Witkin, California Summary 10th Real Property § 76, Appointment.

§ 873.060. Authority of referee

The referee may perform any acts necessary to exercise the authority conferred by this title or by order of the court. *(Added by Stats.1976, c. 73, p. 110, § 6.)*

Law Revision Commission Comments

Section 873.060 is new. It makes explicit the referee's general authority to effectuate the partition.

Research References

12 Witkin, California Summary 10th Real Property § 77, Authority of Referee.

§ 873.070. Petition for instructions

The referee or any party may, on noticed motion, petition the court for instructions concerning the referee's duties under this title. *(Added by Stats.1976, c. 73, p. 110, § 6.)*

Law Revision Commission Comments

Section 873.070 is new. It is intended to enable the referee and parties expeditiously to resolve any administrative problems that arise in the execution of the referee's duties.

Research References

Miller and Starr California Real Estate § 12:16, Right of Partition-- Partition by a Physical Division of the Property.
Miller and Starr California Real Estate § 12:17, Right of Partition-- Partition by a Sale of the Property.
12 Witkin, California Summary 10th Real Property § 76, Appointment.
12 Witkin, California Summary 10th Real Property § 77, Authority of Referee.

§ 873.080. Designation of public and private ways

(a) In selling or dividing the property, the referee may, if it will be for the advantage of those interested, designate a portion of the property as a public or private way, road, or street. In connection therewith, the referee may also recommend the closure of any or all other roads on the property and allocation of the portion of the property occupied by such roads to the parties.

(b) Upon making such a designation and recommendation that is adequate to accommodate public and private needs, the referee shall report that fact to the court.

(c) Upon confirmation of the referee's report by the court, subject to any necessary action by the appropriate public entities:

(1) The portion of the property designated as a public way, road, or street shall not be allocated to any of the parties or sold but shall be an open and public way, road, or street.

(2) The property designated as a private way, road, or street shall be a private way for the use of the parties interested.

(3) The roads recommended to be closed shall be deemed abandoned upon the terms stated in the order of confirmation. *(Added by Stats.1976, c. 73, p. 110, § 6.)*

Law Revision Commission Comments

Section 873.080 is new. It makes clear that the actions of the referee in disposing of the property and of the court in confirming the referee's actions must conform to any applicable laws.

Research References

Miller and Starr California Real Estate § 12:16, Right of Partition-- Partition by a Physical Division of the Property.
Miller and Starr California Real Estate § 15:47, Partition.
12 Witkin, California Summary 10th Real Property § 77, Authority of Referee.
12 Witkin, California Summary 10th Real Property § 78, (S 78) Division of Property.

ARTICLE 2. CONTRACTS OF REFEREE

Section

§ 873.110. Services of third persons

Subject to the limitations of this article, the court may:

(a) Authorize or approve contracts of the referee for the services and expenses of surveyors, engineers, appraisers, attorneys, real estate brokers, auctioneers, and others.

(b) Allow and direct payment of or reject claims under such contracts.

(c) Provide for the date of commencement of any lien provided by law or contract for such claims. *(Added by Stats.1976, c. 73, p. 110, § 6.)*

Law Revision Commission Comments

Section 873.110 is new. It recognizes that the court is the supervising entity in carrying out the partition. It removes from the referee, acting alone, the authority to engage the services of third persons for his assistance. It contemplates that the court will authorize or approve contracts of the referees for third-party services and expenses, allow or reject claims thereunder, and in proper cases specify the priority of any lien therefor. See Section 874.120 (lien for costs).

Former Sections 764 and 768 provided only for employment by the referee of surveyors and necessary assistants and allowance of their fees and expenses. For particular provisions relating to employment of third persons, see Sections 873.120 to 873.140.

Section 873.110 is intended to vest the court with broad discretion to approve contracts for services and with the corresponding duty to provide adequate lien protection for persons who render such services. Surveying services, for example, may involve substantial sums. Ability to obtain such services may depend upon assurance of, or security for, payment despite any later settlement by the parties and dismissal of the action.

Similarly, in a particular case, employment of a real estate broker by the referee may be desirable. Under Section 873.110, such employment may be authorized or approved and the terms of the contract prescribed or approved by the court. For the court's authority to fix agents' commissions on a sale, see Section 873.745.

Research References

Miller and Starr California Real Estate § 12:16, Right of Partition-- Partition by a Physical Division of the Property.
12 Witkin, California Summary 10th Real Property § 77, Authority of Referee.
12 Witkin, California Summary 10th Real Property § 83, (S 83) Costs of Partition.

§ 873.120. Attorney

(a) The referee may employ an attorney only with the approval of the court pursuant to Section 873.110.

(b) The application for approval shall be in writing and shall include the name of the attorney whom the referee wishes to employ and the necessity for the employment.

(c) The attorney so employed may not be attorney for, or associated with or employed by an attorney for, any party to the action except with the written consent of all the parties to the action.

(d) Any claim for compensation for the attorney shall detail the services performed by the attorney. *(Added by Stats.1976, c. 73, p. 110, § 6.)*

Law Revision Commission Comments

Section 873.120 is new. It is derived from Rule 528 of the California Rules of Court (employment of an attorney by a receiver).

Research References

12 Witkin, California Summary 10th Real Property § 77, Authority of Referee.

§ 873.130. Surveyor

The referee may, with the approval of the court pursuant to Section 873.110, employ a surveyor with the necessary assistants to aid in making a sale or division of property. *(Added by Stats.1976, c. 73, p. 110, § 6.)*

Law Revision Commission Comments

Section 873.130 continues a portion of former Section 764 with the added requirement for court approval. Court approval is required since the amounts involved may be substantial and means of payment may present a problem.

§ 873.140. Auctioneer

The referee may, with the approval of the court pursuant to Section 873.110, employ an auctioneer, authorized to act as such in the locality, to conduct a public auction and to secure purchasers by such method for any property to be sold at public auction. *(Added by Stats.1976, c. 73, p. 110, § 6.)*

Law Revision Commission Comments

Section 873.140 is new. It is derived from Probate Code Section 760.5 (sale of tangible personal property of estate).

§ 873.150. Interest on unpaid contracts

A contract for the services of an attorney, surveyor, auctioneer, or other third person may provide for the accrual of interest at a rate not in excess of the legal rate for amounts due under the contract that are not paid within three months after the time they become due and payable. *(Added by Stats.1976, c. 73, p. 110, § 6.)*

Law Revision Commission Comments

Section 873.150 is new. It is designed to better enable the referee to obtain competent services where the person rendering the service will not be paid until the conclusion of the action.

Research References

12 Witkin, California Summary 10th Real Property § 77, Authority of Referee.

§ 873.160. Liability of referee

The referee is not personally liable on contracts made, or for expenses incurred, except as such liability is expressly assumed by the referee in writing. *(Added by Stats.1976, c. 73, p. 110, § 6.)*

Law Revision Commission Comments

Section 873.160 is new. The contract itself may provide a means of payment, e.g., the commission of an auctioneer or a real estate broker from the proceeds of sale. In other cases, particularly where the property is divided, the third person will have lien rights. See Section 874.120 (lien for costs).

Research References

Miller and Starr California Real Estate § 12:16, Right of Partition-- Partition by a Physical Division of the Property.
12 Witkin, California Summary 10th Real Property § 77, Authority of Referee.

CHAPTER 5. DIVISION OF THE PROPERTY

§ 873.210. Division by referee

The referee appointed by the court to make a division of the property shall divide the property and allot the several portions to the parties, quality and quantity relatively considered, according to their interests in the property as determined in the interlocutory judgment. *(Added by Stats.1976, c. 73, p. 110, § 6.)*

Law Revision Commission Comments

Section 873.210 continues a portion of former Section 764 with respect to physical division of the property. For provisions relating to sale of the property by the referee, see Chapter 6 (commencing with Section 873.510). See also Section 872.720 (interlocutory judgment).

Research References

Miller and Starr California Real Estate § 12:15, Right of Partition-- Procedure in Partition Action.
Miller and Starr California Real Estate § 12:16, Right of Partition-- Partition by a Physical Division of the Property.
12 Witkin, California Summary 10th Real Property § 78, (S 78) Division of Property.

§ 873.220. Allotment of improvements

As far as practical, and to the extent it can be done without material injury to the rights of the other parties, the property shall be so divided as to allot to a party any portion that embraces improvements made by that party or that party's predecessor in interest. In such division and allotment, the value of such improvements shall be excluded. *(Added by Stats.1976, c. 73, p. 110, § 6.)*

Law Revision Commission Comments

Section 873.220 continues the substance of the last sentence of former Section 764.

This codifies the common law doctrine. See, e.g., Seale v. Soto, 35 Cal. 102 (1868). In the case of sale rather than division of the property, California case law applies a comparable rule. See, e.g., Ventra v. Tiscornia, 23 Cal.App. 598, 138 P. 954 (1913); Mercola v. Chester, 97 Cal.App.2d 140, 217 P.2d 32 (1950).

Research References

Miller and Starr California Real Estate § 12:20, Right of Partition-- Compensation for Improvements.
12 Witkin, California Summary 10th Real Property § 78, (S 78) Division of Property.
12 Witkin, California Summary 10th Real Property § 81, Disposition of Proceeds.

§ 873.230. Allotment of property previously conveyed to purchaser

Where prior to the commencement of the action a party has executed a deed purporting to convey to a purchaser a portion of the property to be divided, to the extent it can be done without material injury to the rights of the other parties, the property shall be so divided as to allot that portion to the purchaser, the purchaser's heirs or assigns, or such other action taken as to make the deed effectual as a conveyance of that portion of the property. *(Added by Stats.1976, p. 73, p. 110, § 6.)*

Law Revision Commission Comments

Section 873.230 continues the substance of the fourth sentence of former Section 764. The provisions of this section apply only to transfers made prior to commencement of the action.

Research References

Miller and Starr California Real Estate § 12:16, Right of Partition-- Partition by a Physical Division of the Property.
12 Witkin, California Summary 10th Real Property § 78, (S 78) Division of Property.

§ 873.240. Division by lots or parcels

Where real property consists of more than one distinct lot or parcel, the property shall be divided by such lots or parcels without other internal division to the extent that it can be done without material injury to the rights of the parties. *(Added by Stats.1976, c. 73, p. 110, § 6.)*

Law Revision Commission Comments

Section 873.240 is new. Cf. former Section 782 (requiring separate sale of "distinct farms or lots"). In order to facilitate division by individual lots, the parties may join additional property whether by complaint or by cross-complaint.

Research References

Miller and Starr California Real Estate § 12:16, Right of Partition-- Partition by a Physical Division of the Property.
12 Witkin, California Summary 10th Real Property § 78, (S 78) Division of Property.

§ 873.250. Owelty

(a) Where division cannot be made equally among the parties according to their interests without prejudice to the rights of some, compensation may be required to be made by one party to another to correct the inequality.

(b) No compensation shall be required to be made to others by unknown owners or by minors unless it appears that a minor has personal property sufficient for that purpose and the minor's interest will be promoted thereby. *(Added by Stats.1976, c. 73, p. 110, § 6.)*

Law Revision Commission Comments

Section 873.250 continues the substance of the first sentence of former Section 792. The bar on requiring owelty of a minor applies to imposition of a lien on the share of the minor as well as to direct payment. The provision in this section for owelty of partition should be distinguished from compensatory adjustments made under the ordinary principles of equity, as for accountings, allowances, and the like, pursuant to Section 872.140.

Research References

Miller and Starr California Real Estate § 12:16, Right of Partition-- Partition by a Physical Division of the Property.
Miller and Starr California Real Estate § 12:19, Right of Partition-- Decree of Partition.
19 NO. 1 Miller & Starr, California Real Estate Newsalert 15, Holding Title.
12 Witkin, California Summary 10th Real Property § 66, (S 66) General Provisions.
12 Witkin, California Summary 10th Real Property § 78, (S 78) Division of Property.

§ 873.260. Lien on undivided interest; charge on allotted share

Where a lien is on an undivided interest of a party, the lien shall, upon division of the property, become a charge only on the share allotted to that party. *(Added by Stats.1976, c. 73, p. 110, § 6.)*

Research References

Miller and Starr California Real Estate § 12:16, Right of Partition-- Partition by a Physical Division of the Property.
12 Witkin, California Summary 10th Real Property § 78, (S 78) Division of Property.

§ 873.270. Combined interests of unknown parties; property remains undivided

Where the court has determined the combined interests of two or more unknown parties, the entire portion of the property allocated to such parties shall remain undivided. *(Added by Stats.1976, c. 73, p. 110, § 6.)*

Law Revision Commission Comments

Section 873.270 continues the portion of former Section 763 that required the court to designate an undivided portion for owners whose interests remain "unknown, or are not ascertained." See Section 872.640 (court authority to consider rights of unknown owners together). If during the action an unknown party becomes known, his interest may be determined and his portion of the undivided property may be allocated to him.

Research References

12 Witkin, California Summary 10th Real Property § 78, (S 78) Division of Property.

§ 873.280. Proceedings of referee; report; notice; contents

(a) The referee shall file with the court a report of the referee's proceedings and give written notice of filing to each party who has appeared in the action.

(b) The report shall include all of the following:

(1) A specification of the manner in which the referee has executed the referee's trust.

(2) A description of the property divided and of the share allotted to each party, along with any recommendation as to owelty.

(3) Any recommendation as to opening and closing public and private ways, roads, streets, and easements. *(Added by Stats. 1976, c. 73, p. 110, § 6.)*

Law Revision Commission Comments

Section 873.280 continues the substance of the first sentence of former Section 765 with the added requirement of any recommendations as to owelty (Section 873.250) and as to public and private ways (Section 873.090). The description required by subdivision (b)(2) must be by metes and bounds, or lots and blocks, or such other method as will enable the precise location of each portion.

Research References

Miller and Starr California Real Estate § 12:16, Right of Partition-- Partition by a Physical Division of the Property.
12 Witkin, California Summary 10th Real Property § 78, (S 78) Division of Property.

§ 873.290. Confirmation, modification or setting aside report; hearing; entry of judgment

(a) Any party, upon notice to the other parties who have appeared, may move the court to confirm, modify, or set aside the report.

(b) At the hearing, the court may either confirm the report as filed or as the court may modify and enter judgment of partition accordingly or set aside the report and order preparation of a new report and, if necessary, appoint a new referee for this purpose.

(c) The division is effective and title vests in accordance therewith upon entry of judgment of partition. *(Added by Stats.1976, c. 73, p. 110, § 6.)*

Law Revision Commission Comments

Subdivision (a) of Section 873.290 continues the substance of the last sentence of former Section 765. See Sections 1005 (time for service of notice) and 1010 (notice must be in writing).

Subdivision (b) supersedes the first sentence of former Section 766.

Subdivision (c) supersedes the second sentence of former Section 766. It makes clear that it is the judgment that gives effect to the referee's report. For persons affected by the judgment, see Chapter 9 (commencing with Section 874.210).

Research References

Miller and Starr California Real Estate § 12:15, Right of Partition-- Procedure in Partition Action.
12 Witkin, California Summary 10th Real Property § 76, Appointment.
12 Witkin, California Summary 10th Real Property § 78, (S 78) Division of Property.

CHAPTER 6. SALE OF THE PROPERTY

ARTICLE 1. MANNER OF SALE

§ 873.510. Sale by referee

The referee appointed by the court to make a sale of the property shall sell the property in the manner and following the procedures provided in this chapter. *(Added by Stats.1976, c. 73, p. 110, § 6.)*

Law Revision Commission Comments

Section 873.510 is new.

Research References

Miller and Starr California Real Estate § 12:15, Right of Partition-- Procedure in Partition Action.
12 Witkin, California Summary 10th Real Property § 79, Procedure.

§ 873.520. Public auction or private sale; determination; report of referee

The property shall be sold at public auction or private sale as the court determines will be more beneficial to the parties. For the purpose of making this determination, the court may refer the matter to the referee and take into account the referee's report. *(Added by Stats.1976, c. 73, p. 110, § 6.)*

Law Revision Commission Comments

Section 873.520 continues a portion of the first sentence of former Section 775, but makes clear that there is no preference for either public or private sale. The reference to a referee for determination whether public or private sale would be more beneficial may be combined with a reference to determine whether partition by sale is more equitable than partition by division. See Section 872.820 and Comment thereto.

Research References

Miller and Starr California Real Estate § 12:17, Right of Partition-- Partition by a Sale of the Property.
12 Witkin, California Summary 10th Real Property § 79, Procedure.

§ 873.530. Public or private sale of part of property

Part of the property may be sold at public auction and part at private sale if it appears that to do so will be more beneficial to the parties. *(Added by Stats.1976, c. 73, p. 110, § 6.)*

Law Revision Commission Comments

Section 873.530 continues the substance of a portion of the first sentence of former Section 775.

Research References

12 Witkin, California Summary 10th Real Property § 79, Procedure.

ARTICLE 2. SALES PROCEDURES

§ 873.600. Order of court; methods and terms; agreement of parties

Notwithstanding any other provision of this title, the court shall order sale by such methods and upon such terms as are expressly agreed to in writing by all the parties to the action. *(Added by Stats.1976, c. 73, p. 110, § 6.)*

Law Revision Commission Comments

Section 873.600 is new. It permits the parties to agree to sales procedures that may vary from the procedures prescribed in this chapter. In order for Section 873.600 to be operative, the consent of all parties is necessary whether or not they have appeared. As a consequence, this section cannot be used where unknown owners are made parties unless a guardian ad litem has been appointed for them. On the other hand, the consent of persons named as parties who are not served and who have not appeared is unnecessary since their interests will not be affected by the judgment in the action.

It should be noted that the court also has authority to prescribe additional sales procedures. See Section 873.610.

Research References

Miller and Starr California Real Estate § 12:17, Right of Partition--Partition by a Sale of the Property.

15 NO. 6 Miller & Starr, California Real Estate Newsalert 3, Brokers' Compensation.

12 Witkin, California Summary 10th Real Property § 79, Procedure.

12 Witkin, California Summary 10th Real Property § 84, (S 84) Judgment.

§ 873.610. Manner, terms and conditions consistent with chapter; recommendations of referee

(a) The court may, at the time of trial or thereafter, prescribe such manner, terms, and conditions of sale not inconsistent with the provisions of this chapter as it deems proper for the particular property or sale.

(b) The court may refer the manner, terms, and conditions of sale to the referee for recommendation but shall not approve the referee's report except following a hearing upon noticed motion. *(Added by Stats.1976, c. 73, p. 110, § 6.)*

Law Revision Commission Comments

Section 873.610 is new; it makes clear the court's authority to control the manner, terms, and conditions of sale. These include, but are not limited to, the following:

(a) Form, manner, and contents of notice of sale. See Sections 873.640–873.650.

(b) Minimum bid and right to reject all bids. For example, if the property is a manufacturing plant which has been shut down and there are few potential buyers, it may be desirable to impose one or more of these conditions. Minimum bids, rejection of all bids, display, or national advertising are tools that are often used in noncourt sales. The use of conditions such as minimum bids in partition sales had not been ruled upon by California appellate courts. Divided views have been expressed in other jurisdictions. See Kemp v. Waters, 165 Md. 521, 170 A. 178 (1934); Schmitt v. Weber, 60 Misc. 361, 113 N.Y.S. 449 (1908); compare Ill.Stats., Ch. 106, § 60 (Smith-Hurd 1952) (requiring sale at two-thirds the property valuation with provision for new valuation if the property cannot be sold at the original "upset" figure).

(c) Terms of credit. See Section 873.630.

(d) Prior estate, charge, or lien to which the property will be subject.

(e) Escrow and title insurance expenses.

(f) Agents' commissions. See Sections 873.740 and 873.745 (permitting the court to make applicable to the confirmation hearing a modified "gross overbidding" procedure and to fix, divide, and limit agents' commissions).

(g) Procedure as to increased offers at court confirmation. See Section 873.740.

(h) Sale of items of personal property individually, in a single lot, or in several lots. See Section 873.620.

Research References

Miller and Starr California Real Estate § 12:17, Right of Partition--Partition by a Sale of the Property.

12 Witkin, California Summary 10th Real Property § 79, Procedure.

§ 873.620. Sale of property separately or as unit

(a) Unless the interests and rights of the parties will be materially prejudiced thereby, the court shall order that distinct lots or parcels of real property be sold separately.

(b) The court may order that the real and personal property or any portion thereof be sold as a unit. *(Added by Stats.1976, c. 73, p. 110, § 6.)*

Law Revision Commission Comments

Subdivision (a) of Section 873.620 supersedes the last portion of former Section 782.

Subdivision (b) is new. Under subdivision (b) where real and personal property are sold as a unit, it is subject to a combined offer or "one bid." See Prob.Code § 754.5.

Research References

Miller and Starr California Real Estate § 12:15, Right of Partition--Procedure in Partition Action.

Miller and Starr California Real Estate § 12:17, Right of Partition--Partition by a Sale of the Property.

12 Witkin, California Summary 10th Real Property § 79, Procedure.

§ 873.630. Credit sales

The court may:

(a) Direct a sale on credit for the property or any part thereof.

(b) Prescribe such terms of credit as may be appropriate.

(c) Approve or prescribe the terms of security to be taken upon the sale, including the manner in which title to the security is to be taken, whether in a single instrument or several instruments, according to the interests of the parties. *(Added by Stats.1976, c. 73, p. 110, § 6.)*

Law Revision Commission Comments

Section 873.630 states the court's authority over purchase money security in general terms. The subject was covered in former Sections 773 and 776, which appeared to divide the authority between the court and referee. The portion of former Section 776 that referred to "unknown owners, infants, or parties out of the state" is deleted as obsolete. Where there are minors or unknown owners, the court may direct that a trustee or other fiduciary hold the security for them and act on their behalf. See Section 873.810.

Under Section 873.630, if the court fails to prescribe the terms of credit, the referee may accept offers which propose varying terms.

Research References

Miller and Starr California Real Estate § 12:17, Right of Partition--Partition by a Sale of the Property.

12 Witkin, California Summary 10th Real Property § 79, Procedure.

§ 873.640. Notice of sale

(a) Notice of the sale of real or personal property shall be given in the manner required for notice of sale of like property upon execution. Such notice shall also be given to every party who has appeared in the action and to such other interested persons as may have in writing requested the referee for special notice.

(b) Where real and personal property are to be sold as a unit, notice of the sale may be in the manner required for notice of sale of real property alone.

(c) The court may order such additional notice as it deems proper.

(d) Where the court orders a new sale of property pursuant to Section 873.730 or Section 873.740, notice of sale shall be as provided in this section. *(Added by Stats.1976, c. 73, p. 110, § 6.)*

Law Revision Commission Comments

Subdivision (a) of Section 873.640 continues the requirement of former Section 775 that real property be sold at public auction "upon notice given in the manner required for the sale of real property on execution." Subdivision (a) extends this provision to personal property and to both public and private sales. For the requirement found in the execution provisions (Section 692) that notice be given to the debtor, subdivision (a) substitutes a requirement that notice be given to parties who have appeared and to other interested persons who have requested notice. This preserves the right of interested persons to receive notice without imposing the burden of widespread notice to persons who may have no interest. It should be noted that inadequate notice of sale to the parties or persons who have requested notice may be a ground for setting aside the sale. See Section 873.730.

Subdivision (b) is new.

Subdivision (c) gives the court discretion to require additional notice. In some types of sales, the court may deem it desirable to order such other types of notice as display or classified advertisement.

Subdivision (d) makes clear that, if at the confirmation hearing the court orders a new sale, full notice of the new sale must be given. This continues a provision of former Section 784.

Research References

Miller and Starr California Real Estate § 12:17, Right of Partition-- Partition by a Sale of the Property.
12 Witkin, California Summary 10th Real Property § 79, Procedure.
12 Witkin, California Summary 10th Real Property § 80, Consummation of Sale.

§ 873.650. Contents of notice of sale

(a) The court shall prescribe the contents of the notice of sale, which shall include a description of the property, the time and place of sale, and a statement of the principal terms of sale. In place of the principal terms of sale, the notice may refer to an order of the court or to a written statement containing such information which may be inspected at the place of business of the referee or the referee's attorney.

(b) A notice of private sale shall state a place where bids or offers will be received and a day on or after which the sale will be made. *(Added by Stats.1976, c. 73, p. 110, § 6.)*

Law Revision Commission Comments

Section 873.650 continues and expands the requirements of former Sections 775 and 782 that the notice of sale contain the principal terms of sale. See Section 873.610 and Comment thereto (court prescribes principal terms, including liens to which the sale is subject).

Subdivision (a) requires a reference to the "time and place of sale." In the case of a private sale (subdivision (b)), the place of sale will normally be the place of business of the referee. For a comparable provision, see Prob.Code § 782.

It should be noted that the court may permit variation from the published terms of sale if to do so will benefit the parties and will not prejudice the rights of other interested persons. See Section 873.730(b).

Research References

Miller and Starr California Real Estate § 12:17, Right of Partition-- Partition by a Sale of the Property.
12 Witkin, California Summary 10th Real Property § 79, Procedure.

§ 873.660. Securities; perishable property; passage of title; proceeds

(a) The court may order securities listed on an established stock or bond exchange, and personal property that is perishable, that will depreciate in value if not promptly disposed of, or that will incur loss or expense by being kept, to be sold upon such notice and conditions as may be appropriate.

(b) Unless otherwise ordered by the court, title to property sold pursuant to this section passes without court confirmation. The referee is responsible for the actual value of the property until, after return and proper showing, the court approves the sale. *(Added by Stats.1976, c. 73, p. 110, § 6.)*

Law Revision Commission Comments

Section 873.660 is new; it is derived from Probate Code Sections 770 and 771. The provisions of Section 873.660 apply notwithstanding the other provisions of this chapter governing sales.

Research References

12 Witkin, California Summary 10th Real Property § 79, Procedure.

§ 873.670. Public auction; location; postponement

(a) A sale at public auction to the highest bidder shall be held in the county in which the action is pending or such other place as may be specified by the court.

(b) Unless otherwise ordered by the court, personal property shall be present at the sale.

(c) The sale may be postponed by the referee by public declaration as provided for sales upon execution. *(Added by Stats.1976, c. 73, p. 110, § 6.)*

Law Revision Commission Comments

Section 873.670, providing procedural detail for sales at public auction, is new. It generally follows execution procedure. See Section 694.

Research References

12 Witkin, California Summary 10th Real Property § 79, Procedure.

§ 873.680. Private sale; time; bids

(a) A sale at private sale shall not be made before the day specified in the notice of sale but shall be made within one year thereafter.

(b) The bids or offers shall be in writing and left at the place designated in the notice at any time after the first publication or, if none, the posting of the notice. *(Added by Stats.1976, c. 73, p. 110, § 6.)*

Law Revision Commission Comments

Section 873.680 continues the substance of the last sentence of former Section 775, which provided for private sale in the manner required in private sales of real property of estates of decedents. Section 873.680 incorporates comparable provisions from Probate Code Sections 782 and 783.

Research References

12 Witkin, California Summary 10th Real Property § 79, Procedure.

§ 873.690. Ineligible purchasers; bona fide purchaser

(a) The following persons shall not purchase property sold in the action directly or indirectly:

(1) The referee.

(2) The attorney of a party.

(3) The guardian or conservator of a party, unless for the benefit of the ward or conservatee.

(b) All sales contrary to this section are void except that a sale to a bona fide purchaser following a sale contrary to this section shall not be disturbed. *(Added by Stats.1976, c. 73, p. 110, § 6. Amended by Stats.1979, c. 730, § 29, operative Jan. 1, 1981.)*

Law Revision Commission Comments

Section 873.690 supersedes former Section 783. Because the parties listed in this section may not purchase the property "directly or indirectly," neither they nor persons for their behalf may purchase the property.

Subdivision (a)(3) expands the coverage of former Section 783, which barred the guardian of an infant in the sale of real property, to bar any guardian in the sale of any property.

It should be noted that Section 873.690 precludes the listed parties only in partition sales. Sales made to enforce the lien of a referee, attorney, or guardian ad litem imposed under this title are sales in which those persons may be interested and may participate.

Section 873.690 is amended to add the reference to conservator and conservatee. This makes no substantive change since formerly Section 872.010 defined "guardian" to include conservator.

Research References

Miller and Starr California Real Estate § 12:17, Right of Partition--
Partition by a Sale of the Property.
12 Witkin, California Summary 10th Real Property § 79, Procedure.

ARTICLE 3.   CONSUMMATION OF SALE

Section
873.710.   Report of sale by referee; contents.
873.720.   Confirmation of or setting aside sale; motion;
notice.
873.730.   Hearing; confirmation of sale; new sale.
873.740.   Hearing; increased offer; action by court.
873.745.   Commissions of agents.
873.750.   Confirmation of sale; duties of referee.
873.760.   Failure of purchaser to pay sale price; liability of
purchaser; relief.
873.770.   Taking setoff from party purchaser.
873.780.   Closing of sale after confirmation; adjustments;
orders.
873.790.   Execution of conveyance or transfer; recordation.

§ 873.710.   Report of sale by referee; contents

(a) Upon making a sale of property, the referee shall report
the sale to the court.

(b) The referee's report shall contain, in addition to such
other information as may be appropriate, all of the following
information:

(1) A description of the property sold to each purchaser.

(2) The name of the purchaser.

(3) The sale price.

(4) The terms and conditions of the sale and the security, if
any, taken.

(5) Any amounts payable to lienholders.

(6) A statement as to contractual or other arrangements or
conditions as to agents' commissions.

(7) Any determination and recommendation as to opening
and closing public and private ways, roads, streets, and easements.

(8) Other material facts relevant to the sale and the confirmation proceeding. *(Added by Stats.1976, c. 73, p. 110, § 6.)*

Law Revision Commission Comments

Section 873.710 continues the substance of the first sentence of former
Section 784 with the added requirements of paragraphs (5)–(8) of
subdivision (b).

Research References

Miller and Starr California Real Estate § 12:16, Right of Partition--
Partition by a Physical Division of the Property.
Miller and Starr California Real Estate § 12:17, Right of Partition--
Partition by a Sale of the Property.
12 Witkin, California Summary 10th Real Property § 80, Consummation
of Sale.

§ 873.720.   Confirmation of or setting aside sale; motion; notice

(a) A purchaser, the referee, or any party may move the court
to confirm or set aside the sale.

(b) The moving party shall give not less than 10 days' notice of
motion to:

(1) The purchaser if the purchaser is not the moving party;
and

(2) All other parties who have appeared in the action.
(Added by Stats.1976, c. 73, p. 110, § 6.)

Law Revision Commission Comments

Section 873.720 continues the substance of the third sentence of former
Section 784.

Research References

Miller and Starr California Real Estate § 12:17, Right of Partition--
Partition by a Sale of the Property.
12 Witkin, California Summary 10th Real Property § 80, Consummation
of Sale.

§ 873.730.   Hearing; confirmation of sale; new sale

(a) At the hearing, the court shall examine the report and
witnesses in relation to the report.

(b) The court may confirm the sale notwithstanding a variance
from the prescribed terms of sale if to do so will be beneficial to
the parties and will not result in substantial prejudice to persons
interested in the sale.

(c) The court may vacate the sale and direct that a new sale be
made if it determines any of the following:

(1) The proceedings were unfair or notice of sale was not
properly given. If there is no finding at the hearing of unfairness
or improper notice, the sale may thereafter not be attacked on
such grounds.

(2) The sale price is disproportionate to the value of the
property.

(3) It appears that a new sale will yield a sum that exceeds the
sale price by at least 10 percent on the first ten thousand dollars
($10,000) and 5 percent on the amount in excess thereof,
determined after a reasonable allowance for the expenses of a
new sale. *(Added by Stats.1976, c. 73, p. 110, § 6.)*

Law Revision Commission Comments

Section 873.730 continues the fourth sentence of former Section 784
with the exceptions noted below. Unlike the former section, subdivision
(b) expressly authorizes confirmation of a sale that varies from the
published terms. Subdivision (c) makes each ground for vacating a sale
independently sufficient. The provision for notice of resale is found in
Section 873.640. The 10-percent formula of former Section 784 is
replaced by a 10–5 percent formula derived from Probate Code Section
785.

Where a credit sale is returned to the court for confirmation, the judge
must determine whether the credit bidder is responsible before confirming
the sale. See Section 873.740 (increased offers by "responsible" bidder).
Agents' commissions on the sale, if any, are fixed by the court. See
Section 873.745.

Research References

Miller and Starr California Real Estate § 12:17, Right of Partition--
Partition by a Sale of the Property.
12 Witkin, California Summary 10th Real Property § 76, Appointment.
12 Witkin, California Summary 10th Real Property § 79, Procedure.
12 Witkin, California Summary 10th Real Property § 80, Consummation
of Sale.

§ 873.740.   Hearing; increased offer; action by court

(a) If at the hearing under Section 873.730 a responsible
bidder makes a written increased offer that exceeds the sale price
by at least 10 percent on the first ten thousand dollars ($10,000)
and 5 percent on the amount in excess thereof, the court in its
discretion may do either of the following:

(1) Vacate the sale and direct that a new sale be made.

(2) Vacate the sale, accept the increased offer, and confirm
the sale to the offerer.

(b) Except as provided in subdivision (c), the amount by
which an increased offer exceeds the sale price is determined on
the basis of the gross amount of the increased offer including any
commission on the increased offer to which an agent may be
entitled.

(c) Where in advance of sale the court has so ordered or the parties have so agreed, if an increased offer is made by a party to the action who is not represented by an agent, the amount by which an increased offer of a nonparty exceeds the sale price is determined on the basis of the net amount of the increased offer excluding any commission on the increased offer to which an agent may be entitled. *(Added by Stats.1976, c. 73, p. 110, § 6.)*

Law Revision Commission Comments

Section 873.740 supersedes the last sentence of former Section 784. The increased offer criterion of subdivision (a) is changed from the straight 10-percent formula of Section 784 to a 10–5 percent formula derived from Probate Code Section 785.

Subdivision (b) is new; the gross overbidding criterion is adopted from the Probate Code.

Subdivision (c) codifies the existing authority of the court sitting as a court of equity to accept increased offers on a "net overbid" basis. See generally Estate of Cole, 124 Cal.App.2d 615, 269 P.2d 73 (1954).

Research References

Miller and Starr California Real Estate § 12:17, Right of Partition-- Partition by a Sale of the Property.
12 Witkin, California Summary 10th Real Property § 76, Appointment.
12 Witkin, California Summary 10th Real Property § 80, Consummation of Sale.

§ 873.745. Commissions of agents

The amount of agents' commissions on the sale, if any, shall be fixed by the court and divided or limited in the manner provided for private sales of real property in decedents' estates. *(Added by Stats.1976, c. 73, p. 110, § 6.)*

Law Revision Commission Comments

Section 873.745 is new; it codifies the court's general authority to fix and, where necessary, limit and divide agents' commissions. See Section 873.110 (services of third persons). For statutory provisions as to agents' commissions in private sales of real property in probate, see Probate Code Sections 760, 761, 761.5, and 785.

Research References

Rutter, Cal. Practice Guide: Real Prop. Transactions Ch. 2-D, D. Broker Compensation.
Rutter, Cal. Practice Guide: Real Prop. Transactions Ch. 2-F, F. Special Rules in Probate Sales.
Miller and Starr California Real Estate § 12:17, Right of Partition-- Partition by a Sale of the Property.
15 NO. 6 Miller & Starr, California Real Estate Newsalert 3, Brokers' Compensation.
12 Witkin, California Summary 10th Real Property § 80, Consummation of Sale.

§ 873.750. Confirmation of sale; duties of referee

(a) Upon confirmation of a sale, the court shall order the referee to execute a conveyance or other instrument of transfer, to collect the proceeds, take security, and perform other acts required to consummate the sale.

(b) The order may direct the referee concerning the distribution, deposit, or securing of sale deposits and sale proceeds. *(Added by Stats.1976, c. 73, p. 110, § 6.)*

Law Revision Commission Comments

Section 873.750 continues the substance of the first two sentences of former Section 785 and supersedes former Section 777. Section 873.750 states the court's authority in broader terms than the former sections, which referred only to "proceeds of sale." These are to be distributed to the person entitled when the court directs or are to be paid into court or deposited therein. However, substantial sums may be held by the referee or others pending a sale. These funds, as well as technical "proceeds of sale," should be subject to the court's order. For provisions concerning the disposition of the proceeds of sale, see Article 4 (commencing with Section 873.810).

Research References

Rutter, Cal. Practice Guide: Civil Appeals & Writs Ch. 2-B, B. Appealable Judgments and Orders.
12 Witkin, California Summary 10th Real Property § 80, Consummation of Sale.
12 Witkin, California Summary 10th Real Property § 84, (S 84) Judgment.

§ 873.760. Failure of purchaser to pay sale price; liability of purchaser; relief

If the purchaser, after the confirmation of the sale, fails to pay the sale price, the purchaser is subject to the court's jurisdiction and to further proceedings in the action. Upon such failure, a party, or the referee, may upon notice move the court to order either of the following forms of relief:

(a) Resale of the property upon notice as provided in this chapter. If any loss is occasioned thereby, the referee may recover the amount of such loss and costs and expenses incurred, including a reasonable attorney's fee, from the purchaser who failed to pay.

(b) Maintenance by the referee of an action against the purchaser for the amount of the sale price. If the referee recovers judgment, the referee shall be awarded a reasonable attorney's fee against the purchaser. *(Added by Stats.1976, c. 73, p. 110, § 6.)*

Law Revision Commission Comments

Section 873.760 continues the substance of the last sentence of former Section 785 with the added requirement of a court order on noticed motion of either a party or the referee and with the addition of express provisions for recovery of a reasonable attorney's fee. To facilitate recovery under this section, the defaulting purchaser remains subject to the jurisdiction of the court.

Research References

Miller and Starr California Real Estate § 12:17, Right of Partition-- Partition by a Sale of the Property.
12 Witkin, California Summary 10th Real Property § 80, Consummation of Sale.

§ 873.770. Taking setoff from party purchaser

Where the purchaser is a party or lienholder entitled to a share of the proceeds of sale, the referee may:

(a) Take the purchaser's receipt for so much of the proceeds of sale as belongs to the purchaser.

(b) Take security, or other arrangement satisfactory to the referee, for payment of amounts which are or may become due from the purchaser on account of the expenses of sale, general costs of the action, and costs of the reference. *(Added by Stats.1976, c. 73, p. 110, § 6.)*

Law Revision Commission Comments

Section 873.770 continues the substance of former Section 786 with the addition of subdivision (b), which provides for assurances of payment of a share of the costs which may not be determined at the time of sale.

Research References

Miller and Starr California Real Estate § 12:17, Right of Partition-- Partition by a Sale of the Property.
12 Witkin, California Summary 10th Real Property § 80, Consummation of Sale.

§ 873.780. Closing of sale after confirmation; adjustments; orders

The court may make orders relating to the closing of a sale after confirmation, including escrow and closing provisions and, if the referee and purchaser so agree and the court upon noticed motion determines it will not result in substantial prejudice to the parties, may make adjustments varying the terms of sale based on after-discovered defects. *(Added by Stats.1976, c. 73, p. 110, § 6.)*

Law Revision Commission Comments

Section 873.780 is new. It recognizes that modern transactions often involve, at closing, minor deviations or adjustments. The court is expressly authorized to make rulings regarding them.

Research References

12 Witkin, California Summary 10th Real Property § 80, Consummation of Sale.

§ 873.790. Execution of conveyance or transfer; recordation

(a) Upon fulfillment of the terms of sale, the referee shall execute a conveyance or other instrument of transfer to the purchaser.

(b) The conveyance or transfer of real property and the order authorizing such conveyance or transfer shall be recorded in each county in which the property is located. *(Added by Stats.1976, c. 73, p. 110, § 6.)*

Law Revision Commission Comments

Subdivision (a) of Section 873.790 is new. Subdivision (b) continues the substance of the first portion of former Section 787.

Research References

12 Witkin, California Summary 10th Real Property § 80, Consummation of Sale.
12 Witkin, California Summary 10th Real Property § 84, (S 84) Judgment.

ARTICLE 4.　DISPOSITION OF PROCEEDS OF SALE

Section
873.810. Court order of disbursement.
873.820. Application of proceeds.
873.830. Setoff in lieu of payment of estate for life or years.
873.840. Treatment of successive estates.
873.850. Continuance of action between parties if proceeds not allocated; determination.

§ 873.810. Court order of disbursement

The court shall order the proceeds of sale and any security therefor to be paid, transferred, deposited in court, placed in trust, or invested in State of California or United States government obligations or interest-bearing accounts in an institution whose accounts are insured by an agency of the federal government, to or for the benefit of the persons in interest entitled thereto, as may be appropriate or as specifically provided in this article. *(Added by Stats.1976, c. 73, p. 110, § 6.)*

Law Revision Commission Comments

Section 873.810 supersedes former Sections 773 and 788. The portion of former Section 773, providing for deposit of proceeds in court if no other direction is given, is not continued. Under Section 873.810, the court must affirmatively specify the disposition of the proceeds, including proceeds for the shares of unknown owners. See former Section 780 (requiring that the court provide for the protection of unknown owners). It should be noted that amounts invested in interest-bearing accounts under this section may exceed the amount insured by an agency of the federal government provided that the accounts are in an institution which carries such insured accounts.

Research References

12 Witkin, California Summary 10th Real Property § 81, Disposition of Proceeds.

§ 873.820. Application of proceeds

The proceeds of sale for any property sold shall be applied in the following order:

(a) Payment of the expenses of sale.

(b) Payment of the other costs of partition in whole or in part or to secure any cost of partition later allowed.

(c) Payment of any liens on the property in their order of priority except liens which under the terms of sale are to remain on the property.

(d) Distribution of the residue among the parties in proportion to their shares as determined by the court. *(Added by Stats.1976, c. 73, p. 110, § 6.)*

Research References

Miller and Starr California Real Estate § 12:19, Right of Partition--Decree of Partition.
12 Witkin, California Summary 10th Real Property § 81, Disposition of Proceeds.
12 Witkin, California Summary 10th Real Property § 83, (S 83) Costs of Partition.

§ 873.830. Setoff in lieu of payment of estate for life or years

Where a part only of the property is sold, a tenant for life or years in an undivided share of the whole property may have his estate equitably set off in any part of the property not sold by way of complete or partial satisfaction of his share of the proceeds. *(Added by Stats.1976, c. 73, p. 110, § 6.)*

Law Revision Commission Comments

Section 873.830 continues the substance of former Section 770.

Research References

12 Witkin, California Summary 10th Real Property § 81, Disposition of Proceeds.

§ 873.840. Treatment of successive estates

(a) The court shall ascertain the proportion of the proceeds of sale that will be a just and reasonable sum for the satisfaction of the estate of a tenant for life or years and shall order such amount distributed to him or held for his benefit.

(b) The court shall ascertain the proportional value of any vested or contingent future right or estate in the property and shall direct such proportion of the proceeds of sale to be distributed, secured, or held in such a manner as to protect the rights and interests of the parties.

(c) Notwithstanding any other provision of this section, in the case of an estate for life or defeasible estate with remainder over, the court may direct that the entire proceeds of sale be placed in trust as provided in this section upon a showing that the establishment of such a trust is economically feasible and will serve the best interests of the parties. The court shall appoint a trustee, upon security satisfactory to the court, who under court supervision shall invest and reinvest the proceeds, pay the income of the investments, if any, to the life tenant or owner of the defeasible interest, and upon termination of the life or defeasible estate, deliver or pay the corpus of the trust estate to the remainderman. The court shall retain jurisdiction over the settlement of the accounts of the trustee and in all matters necessary for the proper administration of the trust and the final distribution of the trust fund. *(Added by Stats.1976, c. 73, p. 110, § 6.)*

Law Revision Commission Comments

Subdivision (a) of Section 873.840 supersedes former Sections 778–780. Particular aspects of the former sections are preserved in other provisions. See Sections 872.520 (protection of interests of unknown owners), 872.640 (interests of unknown owners considered together), 873.820 (proportionate allocation after costs and expenses.) The provision in former Section 778 for prejudgment estimate of the value of a tenancy for life or years which the owner may "consent" to accept is not continued because it is inappropriate under modern conditions.

Subdivision (b) continues the substance of the first portion of former Section 781 and the last portion of former Section 766(2).

Subdivision (c) supersedes the last portion of former Section 781. It makes clear that imposition of a trust under its terms is not mandatory in all cases but is discretionary with the court and then only if the establishment of a trust is both practical and desirable. Contrast Estate of Giacomelos, 192 Cal.App.2d 244, 13 Cal.Rptr 245 (1961) (imposition of trust mandatory). Investment under this subdivision may be by purchase of other property for use of the parties where appropriate. It should be noted that, in the case of successive life or defeasible estates, the court may be required to formulate a more complex formula for investment and distribution than is specified in the statute.

For an exception to the requirements of Section 873.840, see Section 872.840 (disposition of property subject to an express trust).

Research References

Miller and Starr California Real Estate § 9:24, Termination; Merger; Partition.
12 Witkin, California Summary 10th Real Property § 28, (S 28) Conveyance and Partition.
12 Witkin, California Summary 10th Real Property § 81, Disposition of Proceeds.

§ 873.850. Continuance of action between parties if proceeds not allocated; determination

When the proceeds of the sale belonging to persons who are parties to the action, whether known or unknown, have not been allocated among such parties, the action may be continued as between such parties, for the determination of their respective claims thereto, which must be ascertained and adjudged by the court. Further testimony may be taken in court, or by a referee, at the discretion of the court, and the court may, if necessary, require such parties to present the facts or law in controversy, by pleadings, as in an original action. *(Added by Stats.1976, c. 73, p. 110, § 6.)*

Research References

Miller and Starr California Real Estate § 12:15, Right of Partition-- Procedure in Partition Action.
12 Witkin, California Summary 10th Real Property § 81, Disposition of Proceeds.

CHAPTER 7. PARTITION BY APPRAISAL

Section
873.910. Agreement by parties.
873.920. Agreement; contents.
873.930. Agreement; application for approval.
873.940. Referees; appointment; report.
873.950. Motion to confirm, modify or set aside report.
873.960. Hearing; confirmation of report; conditions; judgment.
873.970. Agreement as binding heirs, executors, etc.; default.
873.980. Relation of agreement to other remedies.

§ 873.910. Agreement by parties

When the interests of all parties are undisputed or have been adjudicated, the parties may agree upon a partition by appraisal pursuant to this chapter. *(Added by Stats.1976, c. 73, p. 110, § 6.)*

Law Revision Commission Comments

Section 873.910 and the other sections in this chapter are new. The purpose of this chapter is to provide an alternative method of partition for coowners who agree to use this method. A guardian ad litem may be appointed to represent contingent interests and may agree to the procedure under this chapter on their behalf. A statutory procedure based upon appraisal by referee, with court supervision, may in some situations serve the interests of parties who find themselves in disagreement since an acquisition method does not involve the same tax

consequences as a partition sale. See 3 J. Rabkin & M. Johnson, Federal Income, Gift and Estate Taxation § 43.01 (1975).

Although the same result can be accomplished by an agreement to arbitrate, the authority of the court under this chapter is much broader than in case of arbitration (see Title 9 (commencing with Section 1280) of Part 3 of the Code of Civil Procedure).

Research References

Miller and Starr California Real Estate § 12:14, Right of Partition.
Miller and Starr California Real Estate § 12:15, Right of Partition-- Procedure in Partition Action.
Miller and Starr California Real Estate § 12:18, Right of Partition-- Partition by Appraisal.
12 Witkin, California Summary 10th Real Property § 82, (S 82) Partition by Appraisal.

§ 873.920. Agreement; contents

The agreement shall be in writing filed with the clerk of court and shall include:

(a) A description of the property.

(b) The names of the parties and their interests.

(c) The names of the parties who are willing to acquire the interests.

(d) The name or names of a person or persons to whose appointment as referee or referees the parties consent.

(e) The date or dates as of which the interests to be acquired are to be appraised.

(f) Other terms mutually agreed upon which may include, but are not limited to, provisions relating to abandonment of the action if the appraised value of the interest to be acquired exceeds a stated amount, required deposits on account of purchase price, terms of any credit, title and objections to title, and payment of the expenses of the procedure authorized by this chapter and of costs of the action. *(Added by Stats.1976, c. 73, p. 110, § 6.)*

Law Revision Commission Comments

Section 873.920 is new. It establishes the framework for the agreement of the parties without, however, providing a fixed form of agreement.

Research References

12 Witkin, California Summary 10th Real Property § 82, (S 82) Partition by Appraisal.

§ 873.930. Agreement; application for approval

(a) Any party to the agreement may, upon noticed motion, apply to the court for approval of the agreement.

(b) If the court determines that the agreement complies with Section 873.920 and that the terms and conditions are equitable, it shall approve the agreement and stay any pending division or sale of the property. *(Added by Stats.1976, c. 73, p. 110, § 6.)*

Law Revision Commission Comments

Section 873.930 is new. The court, as a court of equity, may exercise a sound discretion in approving or refusing to approve a particular agreement.

Research References

12 Witkin, California Summary 10th Real Property § 82, (S 82) Partition by Appraisal.

§ 873.940. Referees; appointment; report

The court shall appoint one referee or, if provided in the agreement, three referees to appraise the property and the interests involved. The referee shall report the valuations and other findings to the court in writing filed with the clerk. *(Added by Stats.1976, c. 73, p. 110, § 6.)*

Law Revision Commission Comments

Section 873.940 is new. It follows other partition procedures with respect to the referee's report.

Research References

Miller and Starr California Real Estate § 12:18, Right of Partition--Partition by Appraisal.
12 Witkin, California Summary 10th Real Property § 82, (S 82) Partition by Appraisal.

§ 873.950. Motion to confirm, modify or set aside report

Any party to the agreement or the referee, upon 10 days' notice to the referee if the referee is not the moving party and to the other parties to the agreement, may move the court to confirm, modify, or set aside the report. *(Added by Stats.1976, c. 73, p. 110, § 6.)*

Law Revision Commission Comments

Section 873.950 is new. It follows other partition procedures with respect to a motion for hearing on the referee's report.

Research References

Miller and Starr California Real Estate § 12:18, Right of Partition--Partition by Appraisal.
12 Witkin, California Summary 10th Real Property § 82, (S 82) Partition by Appraisal.

§ 873.960. Hearing; confirmation of report; conditions; judgment

At the hearing, the court shall examine the report and witnesses. If the court determines that the proceedings have been regularly conducted, that transfer of title to the interests may regularly be made, and that no facts appear which would make such transfer inequitable, it shall confirm the report and order the interests transferred to the acquiring parties in proportion to their respective interests, or in such other proportion as is set out in the agreement. The order shall be conditioned upon payment of the amounts fixed as the purchase price and any other amounts required by the agreement, the giving of any required security, and payment by the parties of the expenses of the procedure authorized by this chapter and of the general costs of the partition or an appropriate share thereof. Thereafter the court, upon motion of a party to the agreement or of the referee, made upon not less than 10 days' notice to the parties who have appeared, shall determine whether the conditions have been fulfilled and, if so, shall enter judgment confirming the transfer; otherwise, upon such further proceedings as may be ordered, the action or proceeding shall be ordered terminated. *(Added by Stats.1976, c. 73, p. 110, § 6.)*

Law Revision Commission Comments

Section 873.960 is new. It vests the court with equitable power to refuse to permit consummation of the transaction where it would be inequitable. The parties contract in the light of this power of the court.

Research References

Miller and Starr California Real Estate § 12:18, Right of Partition--Partition by Appraisal.
12 Witkin, California Summary 10th Real Property § 82, (S 82) Partition by Appraisal.
12 Witkin, California Summary 10th Real Property § 84, (S 84) Judgment.

§ 873.970. Agreement as binding heirs, executors, etc.; default

The agreement binds the heirs, executors, administrators, successors, and assigns of the parties. In the event of default, the aggrieved parties may specifically enforce the agreement by further proceedings in the action or may pursue any other remedy they may have at law or in equity. *(Added by Stats.1976, c. 73, p. 110, § 6.)*

Law Revision Commission Comments

Section 873.970 is new. Subject to the provisions of this chapter, the agreement is binding. Even though the subject of the agreement may be personal property, the agreement is specifically enforceable if the innocent party elects this remedy.

Research References

12 Witkin, California Summary 10th Real Property § 82, (S 82) Partition by Appraisal.

§ 873.980. Relation of agreement to other remedies

The provisions of this chapter are cumulative and if, for default or other cause, interests are not transferred and acquired pursuant to this chapter, the parties may pursue their other rights of partition, subject to Section 873.970. *(Added by Stats.1976, c. 73, p. 110, § 6.)*

Law Revision Commission Comments

Section 873.980 is new. It the proceeding aborts or is not carried out, the parties are not prejudiced as to their normal rights of partition except that an innocent party may elect to proceed under the agreement pursuant to Section 873.970.

Research References

Miller and Starr California Real Estate § 12:14, Right of Partition.
Miller and Starr California Real Estate § 12:15, Right of Partition--Procedure in Partition Action.
Miller and Starr California Real Estate § 12:18, Right of Partition--Partition by Appraisal.
12 Witkin, California Summary 10th Real Property § 82, (S 82) Partition by Appraisal.

CHAPTER 8. COSTS OF PARTITION

ARTICLE 1. ALLOWANCE AND APPORTIONMENT OF COSTS OF PARTITION

§ 874.010. Inclusions

The costs of partition include:

(a) Reasonable attorney's fees incurred or paid by a party for the common benefit.

(b) The fee and expenses of the referee.

(c) The compensation provided by contract for services of a surveyor or other person employed by the referee in the action.

(d) The reasonable costs of a title report procured pursuant to Section 872.220 with interest thereon at the legal rate from the time of payment or, if paid before commencement of the action, from the time of commencement of the action.

(e) Other disbursements or expenses determined by the court to have been incurred or paid for the common benefit. *(Added by Stats.1976, c. 73, p. 110, § 6.)*

Law Revision Commission Comments

Section 874.410 is a statement of the "common benefit" rule applicable in partition actions. The listing in this section is illustrative only, and the costs of partition may include other expenses or disbursements, of a like or different kind, found by the court to have been incurred or paid for the common benefit. See subdivision (e). Section 874.010 is supplemented by Section 874.020 (costs incurred in related action).

Subdivision (a) continues the substance of a portion of former Section 796.

Subdivision (b) continues a portion of former Section 768. The reference in the former section to the fee allowed by the court "in its discretion" is not continued since the fee must be a "reasonable sum" pursuant to Section 1023. The expenses of the referee may include attorney's fees where appropriate. See Section 873.120.

Subdivision (c) continues a portion of former Section 768.

Subdivision (d) continues the substance of a portion of former Section 799.

Subdivision (e) is new; it is derived from former Section 796.

Research References

Rutter, Cal. Practice Guide: Civil Trials & Evidence Ch. 17-E, E. Attorney Fees as Costs.
Miller and Starr California Real Estate § 12:10, Right to Contribution; Lien for Repayment.
Miller and Starr California Real Estate § 12:19, Right of Partition-- Decree of Partition.
7 Witkin Cal. Proc. 5th Judgment § 95, (S 95) Prevailing Party in Specified Actions.
7 Witkin Cal. Proc. 5th Judgment § 219, (S 219) Partition Actions.
12 Witkin, California Summary 10th Real Property § 76, Appointment.
12 Witkin, California Summary 10th Real Property § 83, (S 83) Costs of Partition.

§ 874.020. Other actions or proceedings; reasonable expenses

The costs of partition include reasonable expenses, including attorney's fees, necessarily incurred by a party for the common benefit in prosecuting or defending other actions or other proceedings for the protection, confirmation, or perfection of title, setting the boundaries, or making a survey of the property, with interest thereon at the legal rate from the time of making the expenditures. *(Added by Stats.1976, c. 73, p. 110, § 6.)*

Law Revision Commission Comments

Section 874.020 supplements Section 874.010 (costs incurred in partition action). It is derived from a portion of former Section 798. The requirement of the former section that the expenses be pleaded is eliminated; the expenses are presented and allowed just as other costs in the action. The exclusion of recovery of attorney's fees found in the former section is likewise eliminated.

Research References

7 Witkin Cal. Proc. 5th Judgment § 219, (S 219) Partition Actions.
12 Witkin, California Summary 10th Real Property § 83, (S 83) Costs of Partition.

§ 874.030. Interest on disbursements

Where disbursements have been made by a party under the direction of the court, interest at the legal rate shall be allowed thereon from the time of making such disbursements. *(Added by Stats.1976, c. 73, p. 110, § 6.)*

Law Revision Commission Comments

Section 874.030 continues the substance of former Section 801.

Research References

12 Witkin, California Summary 10th Real Property § 83, (S 83) Costs of Partition.

§ 874.040. Apportionment of costs

Except as otherwise provided in this article, the court shall apportion the costs of partition among the parties in proportion to their interests or make such other apportionment as may be equitable. *(Added by Stats.1976, c. 73, p. 110, § 6.)*

Law Revision Commission Comments

Section 874.040 supersedes the first portion of former Section 796. It applies the principle stated in the former section to cases where the property is sold as well as to those where it is divided. The general rule stated in Section 874.040 is qualified by Section 874.050.

Although normally the costs of partition are apportioned in proportion to the interests of the parties, there may be cases in which some other arrangement will be equitable. Where litigation for the common benefit arises among only some of the parties, or where the interests of the parties in all items, lots, or parcels of property are not identical, the court may segregate the costs of partition to the extent practicable and apportion a part among particular parties only. See former Section 796 (last sentence).

Research References

Miller and Starr California Real Estate § 12:10, Right to Contribution; Lien for Repayment.
Miller and Starr California Real Estate § 12:19, Right of Partition-- Decree of Partition.
22 NO. 5 Miller & Starr, California Real Estate Newsalert 11, Holding Title.
7 Witkin Cal. Proc. 5th Judgment § 95, (S 95) Prevailing Party in Specified Actions.
7 Witkin Cal. Proc. 5th Judgment § 219, (S 219) Partition Actions.
12 Witkin, California Summary 10th Real Property § 83, (S 83) Costs of Partition.

§ 874.050. Future interests; apportionment; reimbursement

(a) The court may order that the share of the costs apportioned to a future interest be paid by other parties to the action or by the persons who are then the presumptive owners of the future interest.

(b) Where the court orders payment pursuant to this section, such payment is subject to a right of reimbursement, with interest at the legal rate, secured by a charge upon the future interest. *(Added by Stats.1976, c. 73, p. 110, § 6.)*

Law Revision Commission Comments

Section 874.050 is new. Where a share of the costs is apportioned to a future interest, the amount is discounted based on the present value of the future interest.

Research References

Miller and Starr California Real Estate § 12:19, Right of Partition-- Decree of Partition.
12 Witkin, California Summary 10th Real Property § 83, (S 83) Costs of Partition.

ARTICLE 2. PAYMENT OF COSTS OF PARTITION

§ 874.110. Time; inclusion in judgment

(a) The costs of partition as apportioned by the court may be ordered paid in whole or in part prior to judgment.

(b) Any costs that remain unpaid shall be included and specified in the judgment. *(Added by Stats.1976, c. 73, p. 110, § 6.)*

Research References

Miller and Starr California Real Estate § 12:19, Right of Partition-- Decree of Partition.

12 Witkin, California Summary 10th Real Property § 83, (S 83) Costs of Partition.

§ 874.120. Lien; priority

(a) The costs shall be a lien on the share of the party specified.

(b) A lien imposed by this section has priority over any other lien on the share except those imposed under this section. *(Added by Stats.1976, c. 73, p. 110, § 6.)*

Law Revision Commission Comments

Subdivision (a) of Section 874.120 continues a portion of former Sections 796 and 798. Subdivision (b) is derived from former Section 769.

Research References

Miller and Starr California Real Estate § 12:10, Right to Contribution; Lien for Repayment.
Miller and Starr California Real Estate § 12:19, Right of Partition--Decree of Partition.
12 Witkin, California Summary 10th Real Property § 76, Appointment.
12 Witkin, California Summary 10th Real Property § 78, (S 78) Division of Property.
12 Witkin, California Summary 10th Real Property § 79, Procedure.
12 Witkin, California Summary 10th Real Property § 83, (S 83) Costs of Partition.

§ 874.130. Sale for benefit of lien claimants

Upon application of a person entitled to a lien imposed under this article and upon a showing of good cause, the court may order a sale of all or a portion of the property before or after judgment for the benefit of all such lien claimants without priority among them. *(Added by Stats.1976, c. 73, p. 110, § 6.)*

Law Revision Commission Comments

Section 874.130 is new. Liens imposed under this article have priority over all other liens but have no priority among themselves. The remedies provided in this section and in Section 874.140 are cumulative.

Research References

12 Witkin, California Summary 10th Real Property § 79, Procedure.
12 Witkin, California Summary 10th Real Property § 83, (S 83) Costs of Partition.

§ 874.140. Judgment for unpaid costs; enforcement

A judgment for unpaid costs of partition may be enforced by the person entitled to the costs in the manner provided for enforcement of money judgments generally against the share of the party specified in the judgment or against other property of the party. *(Added by Stats.1976, c. 73, p. 110, § 6. Amended by Stats.1982, c. 497, p. 2164, § 60, operative July 1, 1983.)*

Law Revision Commission Comments

Section 874.140 continues the substance of a portion of former Section 796. See also Section 798. The remedies provided in this section and in Section 874.130 are cumulative.

Section 874.140 is amended to conform to Title 9 (commencing with Section 680.010) of Part 2 (Enforcement of Judgments Law) (15 Cal.L.Rev.Comm. Reports 2001; 82 A.J. 9356).

Research References

Miller and Starr California Real Estate § 12:19, Right of Partition--Decree of Partition.
12 Witkin, California Summary 10th Real Property § 83, (S 83) Costs of Partition.

CHAPTER 9. JUDGMENT

Section
874.210. Persons bound by judgment.

§ 874.210. Persons bound by judgment

The judgment in the action is binding and conclusive on all of the following:

(a) All persons known and unknown who were parties to the action and who have or claim any interest in the property, whether present or future, vested or contingent, legal or beneficial, several or undivided.

(b) All persons not in being or not ascertainable at the time the judgment is entered who have any remainder interest in the property, or any part thereof, after the determination of a particular estate therein and who by any contingency may be entitled to a beneficial interest in the property, provided the judge shall make appropriate provision for the protection of such interests.

(c) Except as provided in Section 874.225, all persons who were not parties to the action and who have or claim any interest in the property which was not of record at the time the lis pendens was filed, or if none was filed, at the time the judgment was recorded. *(Added by Stats.1976, c. 73, p. 110, § 6. Amended by Stats.1984, c. 20, § 5.)*

Law Revision Commission Comments

Subdivision (c) of Section 874.210 is amended to correct a section reference. Subdivision (d) is deleted because it added nothing to subdivisions (a)–(c) and was inconsistent with Section 874.225 (persons not bound by judgment) in certain cases. [17 Cal.L.Rev.Comm. Reports 947 (1984)].

Research References

Rutter, Cal. Practice Guide: Real Prop. Transactions Ch. 11-I, I. Lis Pendens.
Miller and Starr California Real Estate § 12:15, Right of Partition--Procedure in Partition Action.
12 Witkin, California Summary 10th Real Property § 84, (S 84) Judgment.

§ 874.225. Claim in property of person not a party to action; effect of judgment; conditions

Except to the extent provided in Section 1908, the judgment does not affect a claim in the property or part thereof of any person who was not a party to the action if any of the following conditions is satisfied:

(a) The claim was of record at the time the lis pendens was filed or, if none was filed, at the time the judgment was recorded.

(b) The claim was actually known to the plaintiff or would have been reasonably apparent from an inspection of the property at the time the lis pendens was filed or, if none was filed, at the time the judgment was entered. For the purpose of this subdivision, a "claim in the property or part thereof" of any person means the interest of the person in the portion of the property or proceeds of sale thereof allocated to the plaintiff. Nothing in this subdivision shall be construed to impair the rights of a bona fide purchaser or encumbrancer for value dealing with the plaintiff or the plaintiff's successors in interest. *(Added by Stats.1984, c. 20, § 7.)*

Law Revision Commission Comments

Subdivision (a) of Section 874.225 continues the substance of former Section 874.220.

Subdivision (b) continues the substance of former Section 874.230, with clarifications relating to the time of the plaintiff's knowledge. Subdivision (b) is intended to implement the requirement of Section 872.510 that the plaintiff join all persons "actually known" to the plaintiff or "reasonably apparent from an inspection of the property," who have or claim interests in the property or estate as to which partition is sought. Subdivision (b) is an exception to the rule stated in Section 874.210(c) that the judgment binds all persons having unrecorded interests in the property. It should be noted that subdivision (b) makes the judgment not conclusive only with respect to the share of the plaintiff. The portions of the property allocated to other parties in case of a division, or the entire property in case of a sale to a bona fide purchaser, are free of the unrecorded interests.

The introductory portion of Section 874.225 makes clear that notwithstanding the provisions of this section, a claimant may be bound by the proceeding if the claim was acquired from a party after commencement of the proceeding and with actual knowledge of the proceeding. Section 1908 (a)(2). [17 Cal.L.Rev.Comm. Reports 947 (1984)].

Research References

Miller and Starr California Real Estate § 12:15, Right of Partition--Procedure in Partition Action.
12 Witkin, California Summary 10th Real Property § 84, (S 84) Judgment.

§ 874.240. Conveyances or transfers; conclusiveness

A conveyance or transfer pursuant to Sections 873.750 and 873.790 or Section 873.960 is binding and conclusive, in the same manner as a judgment. *(Added by Stats.1976, c. 73, p. 110, § 6.)*

Research References

Miller and Starr California Real Estate § 12:14, Right of Partition.
Miller and Starr California Real Estate § 12:15, Right of Partition--Procedure in Partition Action.
Miller and Starr California Real Estate § 12:21, Right of Partition--Defenses to Partition; Waiver or Estoppel.
Miller and Starr California Real Estate § 33:28, Actions in Which a Receiver May be Appointed--Partition.
Miller and Starr California Real Estate § 34:124, Partition-In General.
12 Witkin, California Summary 10th Real Property § 80, Consummation of Sale.
12 Witkin, California Summary 10th Real Property § 84, (S 84) Judgment.

Title 11

CONTRIBUTION AMONG JOINT JUDGMENT DEBTORS

CHAPTER 1. RELEASES FROM AND CONTRIBUTION AMONG JOINT TORTFEASORS

§ 875. Judgment against two or more defendants; contribution; subrogation by insurer; right of indemnity; satisfaction of judgment in full

(a) Where a money judgment has been rendered jointly against two or more defendants in a tort action there shall be a right of contribution among them as hereinafter provided.

(b) Such right of contribution shall be administered in accordance with the principles of equity.

(c) Such right of contribution may be enforced only after one tortfeasor has, by payment, discharged the joint judgment or has paid more than his pro rata share thereof. It shall be limited to the excess so paid over the pro rata share of the person so paying and in no event shall any tortfeasor be compelled to make contribution beyond his own pro rata share of the entire judgment.

(d) There shall be no right of contribution in favor of any tortfeasor who has intentionally injured the injured person.

(e) A liability insurer who by payment has discharged the liability of a tortfeasor judgment debtor shall be subrogated to his right of contribution.

(f) This title shall not impair any right of indemnity under existing law, and where one tortfeasor judgment debtor is entitled to indemnity from another there shall be no right of contribution between them.

(g) This title shall not impair the right of a plaintiff to satisfy a judgment in full as against any tortfeasor judgment debtor. *(Added by Stats.1957, c. 1700, p. 3076, § 1.)*

Research References

Rutter, Cal. Practice Guide: Civil Appeals & Writs Ch. 2-D, D. Standing to Appeal.
Rutter, Cal. Practice Guide: Insurance Litigation Ch. 9-C, C. Source of Subrogation Right.
Rutter, Cal. Practice Guide: Personal Injury Ch. 4-D, D. Techniques Where Settlement Not Forthcoming.
Rutter, Cal. Practice Guide: Personal Injury Ch. 5-E, E. Selected Pleading Issues.
Miller and Starr California Real Estate § 29:77, Shared Liability When Wrongdoer is Insolvent or Otherwise Unavailable.
3 Witkin Cal. Proc. 5th Actions § 139, (S 139) Distinction.
8 Witkin Cal. Proc. 5th Enforcement of Judgment § 508, (S 508) Joint Obligor: Contribution.
2 Witkin, California Summary 10th Insurance § 4, (S 4) Insurer's Rights of Subrogation, Contribution, and Indemnity.
5 Witkin, California Summary 10th Torts § 74, Application to Alter Ego Liability.
5 Witkin, California Summary 10th Torts § 103, Development of Law.
5 Witkin, California Summary 10th Torts § 105, Contribution Statute.
5 Witkin, California Summary 10th Torts § 106, No Contribution Where Entitlement to Indemnity.
5 Witkin, California Summary 10th Torts § 107, No Contribution to Wilful Wrongdoer.
5 Witkin, California Summary 10th Torts § 108, Necessity of Joint Judgment.
5 Witkin, California Summary 10th Torts § 109, (S 109) Pro Rata Share.
5 Witkin, California Summary 10th Torts § 110, (S 110) Equitable Principles.
6 Witkin, California Summary 10th Torts § 1357, Adoption of Doctrine.
6 Witkin, California Summary 10th Torts § 1360, Where Indemnitor is Strictly Liable.
2 Witkin Cal. Summ. 10th Workers' Compensation § 102, No Right of Contribution Against Employer.

§ 876. Determination of pro rata share

(a) The pro rata share of each tortfeasor judgment debtor shall be determined by dividing the entire judgment equally among all of them.

(b) Where one or more persons are held liable solely for the tort of one of them or of another, as in the case of the liability of a master for the tort of his servant, they shall contribute a single pro rata share, as to which there may be indemnity between them. *(Added by Stats.1957, c. 1700, p. 3077, § 1.)*

Research References

Rutter, Cal. Practice Guide: Personal Injury Ch. 4-D, D. Techniques Where Settlement Not Forthcoming.

Rutter, Cal. Practice Guide: Personal Injury Ch. 5-E, E. Selected Pleading Issues.

8 Witkin Cal. Proc. 5th Enforcement of Judgment § 508, (S 508) Joint Obligor: Contribution.

5 Witkin, California Summary 10th Torts § 109, (S 109) Pro Rata Share.

6 Witkin, California Summary 10th Torts § 1360, Where Indemnitor is Strictly Liable.

§ 877. Release of one or more joint tortfeasors or co-obligors; effect upon liability of others

Where a release, dismissal with or without prejudice, or a covenant not to sue or not to enforce judgment is given in good faith before verdict or judgment to one or more of a number of tortfeasors claimed to be liable for the same tort, or to one or more other co-obligors mutually subject to contribution rights, it shall have the following effect:

(a) It shall not discharge any other such party from liability unless its terms so provide, but it shall reduce the claims against the others in the amount stipulated by the release, the dismissal or the covenant, or in the amount of the consideration paid for it, whichever is the greater.

(b) It shall discharge the party to whom it is given from all liability for any contribution to any other parties.

(c) This section shall not apply to co-obligors who have expressly agreed in writing to an apportionment of liability for losses or claims among themselves.

(d) This section shall not apply to a release, dismissal with or without prejudice, or a covenant not to sue or not to enforce judgment given to a co-obligor on an alleged contract debt where the contract was made prior to January 1, 1988. *(Added by Stats.1957, c. 1700, p. 3077, § 1. Amended by Stats.1987, c. 677, § 2; Stats.2011, c. 296 (A.B.1023), § 39.)*

Research References

Rutter, Cal. Practice Guide: Civil Appeals & Writs Ch. 2-C, C. Nonappealable Orders.

Rutter, Cal. Practice Guide: Civil Appeals & Writs Ch. 2-D, D. Standing to Appeal.

Rutter, Cal. Practice Guide: Civil Appeals & Writs Ch. 8-C, C. Standards of Appellate Review.

Rutter, Cal. Practice Guide: Civil Appeals & Writs Ch. 15-C, C. Statutory Writs.

Rutter, Cal. Practice Guide: Civ. Pro. Before Trial Ch. 12(II)-E, E. Motion to Determine "Good Faith" of "Piecemeal" Settlement (CCP § 877.6).

Rutter, Cal. Practice Guide: Civil Trials & Evidence Ch. 13-B, B. Proper vs. Improper Closing Argument.

Rutter, Cal. Practice Guide: Civil Trials & Evidence Ch. 17-C, C. Entry of Judgment.

Rutter, Cal. Practice Guide: Civil Trials & Evidence Ch. 17-D, D. Costs.

Rutter, Cal. Practice Guide: Civil Trials & Evidence Ch. 17-F, F. Prejudgment Interest.

Rutter, Cal. Practice Guide: Civil Trials & Evidence Ch. 8E-D, D. Other Public Policy Exclusions.

Rutter, Cal. Practice Guide: Enforcing Judgments/Debts Ch. 5-B, B. Overview of Substantive Bankruptcy Law.

Rutter, Cal. Practice Guide: Fed.Civ.Pro. Before Trial Ch. 15-C, C. Settlement Procedures.

Rutter, Cal. Practice Guide: Insurance Litigation Ch. 8-B, B. Contribution Between Insurers.

Rutter, Cal. Practice Guide: Insurance Litigation Ch. 15-H, H. Settlement of Third Party Claims Against Insured.

Rutter, Cal. Practice Guide: Insurance Litigation Ch. 15-K, K. Judgment Creditor's Action to Enforce Judgment Debtor's Liability Insurance (INS.C. § 11580(B)(2)).

Rutter, Cal. Practice Guide: Personal Injury Ch. 4-D, D. Techniques Where Settlement Not Forthcoming.

Rutter, Cal. Practice Guide: Personal Injury Ch. 4-G, G. Concluding and Enforcing Settlement.

Rutter, Cal. Practice Guide: Personal Injury Ch. 5-E, E. Selected Pleading Issues.

Rutter, Cal. Practice Guide: Personal Injury Ch. 9-M, M. Verdicts and Judgment.

Rutter, Cal. Practice Guide: Real Prop. Transactions Ch. 11-E, E. Damages for Fraud.

Miller and Starr California Real Estate § 23:44, Remedies.

Miller and Starr California Real Estate § 29:17, Express and Implied Indemnity.

Miller and Starr California Real Estate § 29:77, Shared Liability When Wrongdoer is Insolvent or Otherwise Unavailable.

18 NO. 5 Miller & Starr, California Real Estate Newsalert 20, Remedies.

18 NO. 4 Miller & Starr, California Real Estate Newsalert 40, Remedies.

20 NO. 6 Miller & Starr, California Real Estate Newsalert 11, Hazardous Substances.

21 NO. 2 Miller & Starr, California Real Estate Newsalert 7, Contracts.

21 NO. 2 Miller & Starr, California Real Estate Newsalert 14, Hazardous Substances.

3 Witkin Cal. Proc. 5th Actions § 157, Conversion or Misappropriation.

7 Witkin Cal. Proc. 5th Judgment § 91, Party Who Obtains Net Monetary Recovery.

7 Witkin Cal. Proc. 5th Judgment § 477, Interests of Justice.

6 Witkin Cal. Proc. 5th Proceedings Without Trial § 105, Amount of Settlement Offset.

1 Witkin Cal. Summ. 10th Contracts § 111, Performance and Discharge.

1 Witkin Cal. Summ. 10th Contracts § 644, (S 644) Collusive Settlement in Joint Tort Action.

5 Witkin, California Summary 10th Torts § 71, in General.

5 Witkin, California Summary 10th Torts § 72, Scope.

5 Witkin, California Summary 10th Torts § 73, Effect of General Release.

5 Witkin, California Summary 10th Torts § 74, Application to Alter Ego Liability.

5 Witkin, California Summary 10th Torts § 76, Time of Settlement.

5 Witkin, California Summary 10th Torts § 77, in General.

5 Witkin, California Summary 10th Torts § 78, Early Cases.

5 Witkin, California Summary 10th Torts § 79, Tech-Bilt Test.

5 Witkin, California Summary 10th Torts § 80, Nonmonetary Consideration for Settlement.

5 Witkin, California Summary 10th Torts § 88, (S 88) General Rule: Bar to Further Claims Against Settling Tortfeasor.

5 Witkin, California Summary 10th Torts § 89, Claims Against Others.

5 Witkin, California Summary 10th Torts § 91, Claims for Contractual or Statutory Indemnity.

5 Witkin, California Summary 10th Torts § 93, Claims of Insurers.

5 Witkin, California Summary 10th Torts § 95, in General.

5 Witkin, California Summary 10th Torts § 96, Valuation of Settlement.

5 Witkin, California Summary 10th Torts § 97, Structured Settlement With Periodic Payments.

5 Witkin, California Summary 10th Torts § 98, Settlement Offsetting Entire Judgment.

5 Witkin, California Summary 10th Torts § 100, (S 100) Nature and Types.

5 Witkin, California Summary 10th Torts § 102, (S 102) Good Faith Requirement.

5 Witkin, California Summary 10th Torts § 105, Contribution Statute.

6 Witkin, California Summary 10th Torts § 1263, (S 1263) Effect of Settlement.

6 Witkin, California Summary 10th Torts § 1357, Adoption of Doctrine.

6 Witkin, California Summary 10th Torts § 1373, (S 1373) Release.

6 Witkin, California Summary 10th Torts § 1641, (S 1641) Uninsured Motorist Proceeds.

13 Witkin, California Summary 10th Equity § 179, (S 179) Nature of Doctrine.

13 Witkin, California Summary 10th Equity § 182, (S 182) Illustrations: Insurance Cases.

§ 877.5. Sliding scale recovery agreement; disclosure to court and jury; service of notice of intent to enter

(a) Where an agreement or covenant is made which provides for a sliding scale recovery agreement between one or more, but not all, alleged defendant tortfeasors and the plaintiff or plaintiffs:

(1) The parties entering into any such agreement or covenant shall promptly inform the court in which the action is pending of the existence of the agreement or covenant and its terms and provisions.

(2) If the action is tried before a jury, and a defendant party to the agreement is called as a witness at trial, the court shall, upon motion of a party, disclose to the jury the existence and content of the agreement or covenant, unless the court finds that this disclosure will create substantial danger of undue prejudice, of confusing the issues, or of misleading the jury.

The jury disclosure herein required shall be no more than necessary to inform the jury of the possibility that the agreement may bias the testimony of the witness.

(b) As used in this section, a "sliding scale recovery agreement" means an agreement or covenant between a plaintiff or plaintiffs and one or more, but not all, alleged tortfeasor defendants, which limits the liability of the agreeing tortfeasor defendants to an amount which is dependent upon the amount of recovery which the plaintiff is able to recover from the nonagreeing defendant or defendants. This includes, but is not limited to, agreements within the scope of Section 877, and agreements in the form of a loan from the agreeing tortfeasor defendant or defendants to the plaintiff or plaintiffs which is repayable in whole or in part from the recovery against the nonagreeing tortfeasor defendant or defendants.

(c) No sliding scale recovery agreement is effective unless, at least 72 hours prior to entering into the agreement, a notice of intent to enter into an agreement has been served on all nonsignatory alleged defendant tortfeasors. However, upon a showing of good cause, the court or a judge thereof may allow a shorter time. The failure to comply with the notice requirements of this subdivision shall not constitute good cause to delay commencement of trial. *(Added by Stats.1977, c. 568, p. 1798, § 1. Amended by Stats.1987, c. 1201, § 3; Stats.1987, c. 1202, § 1; Stats.1990, c. 17 (A.B.366), § 1.)*

Research References

Rutter, Cal. Practice Guide: Civ. Pro. Before Trial Ch. 12(II)-E, E. Motion to Determine "Good Faith" of "Piecemeal" Settlement (CCP § 877.6).

Rutter, Cal. Practice Guide: Civil Trials & Evidence Ch. 8E-D, D. Other Public Policy Exclusions.

Rutter, Cal. Practice Guide: Fed.Civ.Pro. Before Trial Ch. 2D-7, Time for Removal.

Rutter, Cal. Practice Guide: Personal Injury Ch. 4-D, D. Techniques Where Settlement Not Forthcoming.

5 Witkin, California Summary 10th Torts § 81, Settlement With Cross-Defendant.

5 Witkin, California Summary 10th Torts § 100, (S 100) Nature and Types.

5 Witkin, California Summary 10th Torts § 101, (S 101) Notice and Disclosure.

§ 877.6. Determination of good faith of settlement with one or more tortfeasors or co-obligors; review by writ of mandate; tolling of time limitations

(a)(1) Any party to an action in which it is alleged that two or more parties are joint tortfeasors or co-obligors on a contract debt shall be entitled to a hearing on the issue of the good faith of a settlement entered into by the plaintiff or other claimant and one or more alleged tortfeasors or co-obligors, upon giving notice in the manner provided in subdivision (b) of Section 1005. Upon a showing of good cause, the court may shorten the time for giving the required notice to permit the determination of the issue to be made before the commencement of the trial of the

action, or before the verdict or judgment if settlement is made after the trial has commenced.

(2) In the alternative, a settling party may give notice of settlement to all parties and to the court, together with an application for determination of good faith settlement and a proposed order. The application shall indicate the settling parties, and the basis, terms, and amount of the settlement. The notice, application, and proposed order shall be given by certified mail, return receipt requested. Proof of service shall be filed with the court. Within 25 days of the mailing of the notice, application, and proposed order, or within 20 days of personal service, a nonsettling party may file a notice of motion to contest the good faith of the settlement. If none of the nonsettling parties files a motion within 25 days of mailing of the notice, application, and proposed order, or within 20 days of personal service, the court may approve the settlement. The notice by a nonsettling party shall be given in the manner provided in subdivision (b) of Section 1005. However, this paragraph shall not apply to settlements in which a confidentiality agreement has been entered into regarding the case or the terms of the settlement.

(b) The issue of the good faith of a settlement may be determined by the court on the basis of affidavits served with the notice of hearing, and any counteraffidavits filed in response, or the court may, in its discretion, receive other evidence at the hearing.

(c) A determination by the court that the settlement was made in good faith shall bar any other joint tortfeasor or co-obligor from any further claims against the settling tortfeasor or co-obligor for equitable comparative contribution, or partial or comparative indemnity, based on comparative negligence or comparative fault.

(d) The party asserting the lack of good faith shall have the burden of proof on that issue.

(e) When a determination of the good faith or lack of good faith of a settlement is made, any party aggrieved by the determination may petition the proper court to review the determination by writ of mandate. The petition for writ of mandate shall be filed within 20 days after service of written notice of the determination, or within any additional time not exceeding 20 days as the trial court may allow.

(1) The court shall, within 30 days of the receipt of all materials to be filed by the parties, determine whether or not the court will hear the writ and notify the parties of its determination.

(2) If the court grants a hearing on the writ, the hearing shall be given special precedence over all other civil matters on the calendar of the court except those matters to which equal or greater precedence on the calendar is granted by law.

(3) The running of any period of time after which an action would be subject to dismissal pursuant to the applicable provisions of Chapter 1.5 (commencing with Section 583.110) of Title 8 of Part 2 shall be tolled during the period of review of a determination pursuant to this subdivision. *(Added by Stats. 1980, c. 562, p. 1549, § 1. Amended by Stats.1984, c. 311, § 1; Stats.1985, c. 621, § 2; Stats.1987, c. 677, § 3; Stats.1988, c. 128, § 1; Stats.1989, c. 693, § 5; Stats.1992, c. 876 (A.B.3296), § 6; Stats.1995, c. 796 (S.B.45), § 13; Stats.2001, c. 812 (A.B.223), § 7.)*

Research References

Rutter, Cal. Practice Guide: Civil Appeals & Writs Ch. 2-C, C. Nonappealable Orders.

Rutter, Cal. Practice Guide: Civil Appeals & Writs Ch. 5-B, B. Types of Motions, Applications and Requests.

Rutter, Cal. Practice Guide: Civil Appeals & Writs Ch. 8-C, C. Standards of Appellate Review.

Rutter, Cal. Practice Guide: Civil Appeals & Writs Ch. 15-C, C. Statutory Writs.

Rutter, Cal. Practice Guide: Civil Appeals & Writs Ch. 15-E, E. Procedures on Writ Review.

Rutter, Cal. Practice Guide: Civil Appeals & Writs Ch. 2-C, Outline C.

Rutter, Cal. Practice Guide: Civil Appeals & Writs Ch. 15-C, Outline C.

Rutter, Cal. Practice Guide: Civil Appeals & Writs Gen. Matls., Highlights.

Rutter, Cal. Practice Guide: Civ. Pro. Before Trial Ch. 2-E, E. Intervention.

Rutter, Cal. Practice Guide: Civ. Pro. Before Trial Ch. 6-D, D. Cross-Complaint.

Rutter, Cal. Practice Guide: Civ. Pro. Before Trial Ch. 8C-2, "Reasonably Calculated to Lead to Discovery of Admissible Evidence".

Rutter, Cal. Practice Guide: Civ. Pro. Before Trial Ch. 8C-5, Privacy Protection.

Rutter, Cal. Practice Guide: Civ. Pro. Before Trial Ch. 8K-6, Special Statutes and Court Rules.

Rutter, Cal. Practice Guide: Civ. Pro. Before Trial Ch. 7(I)-A, A. Demurrers.

Rutter, Cal. Practice Guide: Civ. Pro. Before Trial Ch. 9(I)-B, B. Preparing and Filing Motions.

Rutter, Cal. Practice Guide: Civ. Pro. Before Trial Ch. 8C-5, Outline 5.

Rutter, Cal. Practice Guide: Civ. Pro. Before Trial Ch. 8K-6, Outline 6.

Rutter, Cal. Practice Guide: Civ. Pro. Before Trial Gen. Matls., Highlights.

Rutter, Cal. Practice Guide: Civ. Pro. Before Trial Ch. 12(II)-E, E. Motion to Determine "Good Faith" of "Piecemeal" Settlement (CCP § 877.6).

Rutter, Cal. Practice Guide: Civil Trials & Evidence Ch. 4-G, G. Motion to Sever or Bifurcate.

Rutter, Cal. Practice Guide: Civil Trials & Evidence Ch. 17-D, D. Costs.

Rutter, Cal. Practice Guide: Fed.Civ.Pro. Before Trial Ch. 1-B, B. Federal vs. State Law.

Rutter, Cal. Practice Guide: Fed.Civ.Pro. Before Trial Ch. 1-D, D. Choosing Between State and Federal Courts.

Rutter, Cal. Practice Guide: Fed.Civ.Pro. Before Trial Ch. 10-C, C. Class Actions.

Rutter, Cal. Practice Guide: Fed.Civ.Pro. Before Trial Ch. 15-C, C. Settlement Procedures.

Rutter, Cal. Practice Guide: Fed.Civ.Pro. Before Trial Gen. Matls., Highlights.

Rutter, Cal. Practice Guide: Insurance Litigation Ch. 8-B, B. Contribution Between Insurers.

Rutter, Cal. Practice Guide: Insurance Litigation Ch. 8-C, C. Primary and Excess Policies.

Rutter, Cal. Practice Guide: Insurance Litigation Ch. 9-D, D. Nature of Subrogation.

Rutter, Cal. Practice Guide: Insurance Litigation Ch. 15-H, H. Settlement of Third Party Claims Against Insured.

Rutter, Cal. Practice Guide: Insurance Litigation Ch. 15-K, K. Judgment Creditor's Action to Enforce Judgment Debtor's Liability Insurance (INS.C. § 11580(B)(2)).

Rutter, Cal. Practice Guide: Insurance Litigation Ch. 7H-E, E. Insuring Clause.

Rutter, Cal. Practice Guide: Insurance Litigation Ch. 12B-B, B. Bad Faith Refusal to Settle.

Rutter, Cal. Practice Guide: Insurance Litigation Ch. 12B-D, D. Refusal to Defend Cases.

Rutter, Cal. Practice Guide: Insurance Litigation Ch. 12D-I, I. Settlement and Release.

Rutter, Cal. Practice Guide: Insurance Litigation Ch. 8-B, Outline B.

Rutter, Cal. Practice Guide: Insurance Litigation Ch. 8-C, Outline C.

Rutter, Cal. Practice Guide: Insurance Litigation Ch. 9-D, Outline D.

Rutter, Cal. Practice Guide: Insurance Litigation Ch. 15-K, Outline K.

Rutter, Cal. Practice Guide: Insurance Litigation Ch. 12B-B, Outline B.

Rutter, Cal. Practice Guide: Insurance Litigation Ch. 12B-D, Outline D.

Rutter, Cal. Practice Guide: Insurance Litigation Ch. 12D-I, Outline I.

Rutter, Cal. Practice Guide: Personal Injury Ch. 4-A, A. General Considerations.

Rutter, Cal. Practice Guide: Personal Injury Ch. 4-D, D. Techniques Where Settlement Not Forthcoming.

Rutter, Cal. Practice Guide: Personal Injury Ch. 4-G, G. Concluding and Enforcing Settlement.

Rutter, Cal. Practice Guide: Personal Injury Ch. 5-E, E. Selected Pleading Issues.

Rutter, Cal. Practice Guide: Personal Injury Ch. 6-A, A. Scope of Discovery and Limitations.

Rutter, Cal. Practice Guide: Personal Injury Form 4:D, Declaration in Support of Application for Determination of Good Faith Settlement (CCP § 877.6(A)(2)).

Rutter, Cal. Practice Guide: Prof. Responsibility Ch. 6-D, D. Professional Liability.

Rutter, Cal. Practice Guide: Prof. Responsibility Ch. 6-D, Outline D.

Miller and Starr California Real Estate § 3:33, Damages Recoverable by the Principal.

Miller and Starr California Real Estate § 23:44, Remedies.

Miller and Starr California Real Estate § 29:17, Express and Implied Indemnity.

Miller and Starr California Real Estate § 29:77, Shared Liability When Wrongdoer is Insolvent or Otherwise Unavailable.

Miller and Starr California Real Estate § 7:208, Settlement and Assignment of the Insured's Claim Against the Insurer.

17 NO. 6 Miller & Starr, California Real Estate Newsalert 5, Defective Construction.

17 NO. 6 Miller & Starr, California Real Estate Newsalert 21, Subject Matter Index.

18 NO. 4 Miller & Starr, California Real Estate Newsalert 40, Remedies.

20 NO. 6 Miller & Starr, California Real Estate Newsalert 11, Hazardous Substances.

21 NO. 2 Miller & Starr, California Real Estate Newsalert 14, Hazardous Substances.

21 NO. 3 Miller & Starr, California Real Estate Newsalert 25, Usury.

Rutter Practice Guide: Fed.Civ.Pro. Bef.Trial(5th Cir) Ch. 1-B, B. Federal vs. State Law.

9 Witkin Cal. Proc. 5th Appeal § 985, (S 985) Frivolous Continuation of Appeal.

2 Witkin Cal. Proc. 5th Courts § 229, (S 229) Ordinary Departments.

7 Witkin Cal. Proc. 5th Judgment § 226, (S 226) Insurance or Indemnity Actions.

7 Witkin Cal. Proc. 5th Judgment § 446, (S 446) Review of Initial Judgment was Not Available.

7 Witkin Cal. Proc. 5th Judgment § 477, Interests of Justice.

2 Witkin Cal. Proc. 5th Jurisdiction § 327, Miscellaneous Unauthorized Orders.

5 Witkin Cal. Proc. 5th Pleading § 1170A, (S 1170A) (New)-Unrestricted Cross-Complaint Against Codefendant.

2 Witkin, California Summary 10th Insurance § 4, (S 4) Insurer's Rights of Subrogation, Contribution, and Indemnity.

2 Witkin, California Summary 10th Insurance § 300, (S 300) Assignment of Cause of Action Against Insurer.

2 Witkin, California Summary 10th Insurance § 305, (S 305) Effect of Stipulated Judgment.

1 Witkin Cal. Summ. 10th Contracts § 111, Performance and Discharge.

5 Witkin, California Summary 10th Torts § 71, in General.

5 Witkin, California Summary 10th Torts § 72, Scope.

5 Witkin, California Summary 10th Torts § 73, Effect of General Release.

5 Witkin, California Summary 10th Torts § 76, Time of Settlement.

5 Witkin, California Summary 10th Torts § 77, in General.

5 Witkin, California Summary 10th Torts § 79, Tech-Bilt Test.

5 Witkin, California Summary 10th Torts § 81, Settlement With Cross-Defendant.

5 Witkin, California Summary 10th Torts § 82, Condition that Settling Tortfeasor Participate in Trial.

5 Witkin, California Summary 10th Torts § 83, Statutory Requirement.

5 Witkin, California Summary 10th Torts § 84, Notice or Application.

5 Witkin, California Summary 10th Torts § 85, Conduct of Hearing.

5 Witkin, California Summary 10th Torts § 86, Review.

5 Witkin, California Summary 10th Torts § 87, Scope of Statute.

5 Witkin, California Summary 10th Torts § 88, (S 88) General Rule: Bar to Further Claims Against Settling Tortfeasor.

5 Witkin, California Summary 10th Torts § 89, Claims Against Others.

5 Witkin, California Summary 10th Torts § 91, Claims for Contractual or Statutory Indemnity.

5 Witkin, California Summary 10th Torts § 92, Claims of Nonparties.

5 Witkin, California Summary 10th Torts § 93, Claims of Insurers.

5 Witkin, California Summary 10th Torts § 94, Claims Not Involving Contribution or Indemnity.

5 Witkin, California Summary 10th Torts § 96, Valuation of Settlement.

5 Witkin, California Summary 10th Torts § 102, (S 102) Good Faith Requirement.

5 Witkin, California Summary 10th Torts § 116, (S 116) Recognition of Comparative Indemnity.

5 Witkin, California Summary 10th Torts § 117, (S 117) Total Indemnity.

5 Witkin, California Summary 10th Torts § 118, (S 118) Implied Contractual Indemnity.

5 Witkin, California Summary 10th Torts § 124, (S 124) Effect of Indemnitee's Settlement of Underlying Claim.

13 Witkin, California Summary 10th Equity § 182, (S 182) Illustrations: Insurance Cases.

2 Witkin Cal. Summ. 10th Workers' Compensation § 73, (S 73) in General.

§ 878. Judgment for contribution; notice of motion; affidavit; contents

Judgment for contribution may be entered by one tortfeasor judgment debtor against other tortfeasor judgment debtors by motion upon notice. Notice of such motion shall be given to all parties in the action, including the plaintiff or plaintiffs, at least 10 days before the hearing thereon. Such notice shall be accompanied by an affidavit setting forth any information which the moving party may have as to the assets of defendants available for satisfaction of the judgment or claim for contribution. *(Added by Stats.1957, c. 1700, p. 3077, § 1.)*

Research References

8 Witkin Cal. Proc. 5th Enforcement of Judgment § 510, (S 510) Procedure to Compel Contribution or Repayment.

5 Witkin, California Summary 10th Torts § 111, Judgment on Notice.

2 Witkin Cal. Summ. 10th Workers' Compensation § 49, (S 49) in General.

§ 879. Partial invalidity

If any provision of this title or the application thereof to any person is held invalid, such invalidity shall not affect other provisions or applications of the title which can be given effect without the invalid provision or application and to this end the provisions of this title are declared to be severable. *(Added by Stats.1957, c. 1700, p. 3077, § 1.)*

§ 880. Effective date

This title shall become effective as to causes of action accruing on or after January 1, 1958. *(Added by Stats.1957, c. 1700, p. 3077, § 1.)*

CHAPTER 2. CONTRIBUTION AMONG OTHER JUDGMENT DEBTORS

Section

881. Application of chapter.

882. Effect of joint liability.

883. Judgment debtor entitled to compel contribution or repayment; application for court order.

§ 881. Application of chapter

This chapter governs contribution among joint judgment debtors other than joint tortfeasors. *(Added by Stats.1982, c. 497, p. 2164, § 63, operative July 1, 1983.)*

Law Revision Commission Comments

Section 881 clarifies the relationship between this chapter and Chapter 1 (commencing with Section 875) which is applicable to contribution among joint tortfeasors (15 Cal.L.Rev.Comm. Reports 2001).

Research References

Rutter, Cal. Practice Guide: Enforcing Judgments/Debts Ch. 6G-12, Enforcement Against Joint Debtors.

Miller and Starr California Real Estate § 32:61, Property Interests Subject to Execution.

8 Witkin Cal. Proc. 5th Enforcement of Judgment § 508, (S 508) Joint Obligor: Contribution.

8 Witkin Cal. Proc. 5th Enforcement of Judgment § 510, (S 510) Procedure to Compel Contribution or Repayment.

5 Witkin, California Summary 10th Torts § 105, Contribution Statute.

13 Witkin, California Summary 10th Equity § 178, Equitable Indemnity: Reimbursement from Principal.

13 Witkin, California Summary 10th Equity § 179, (S 179) Nature of Doctrine.

§ 882. Effect of joint liability

If two or more judgment debtors are jointly liable on a money judgment:

(a) A judgment debtor who has satisfied more than his or her due proportion of the judgment, whether voluntarily or through enforcement procedures, may compel contribution from another judgment debtor who has satisfied less than his or her due proportion of the judgment.

(b) If the judgment is based upon an obligation of one judgment debtor as surety for another and the surety satisfies the judgment or any part thereof, whether voluntarily or through enforcement procedures, the surety may compel repayment from the principal. *(Added by Stats.1982, c. 497, p. 2164, § 63, operative July 1, 1983.)*

Law Revision Commission Comments

Section 882 continues the substance of the first sentence of former Section 709. This section permits contribution where a joint judgment debtor satisfies a disproportionate share of a money judgment, or satisfies the judgment as a surety, whether by voluntary payment or involuntarily through levy upon and sale of property, wage garnishment, examination proceedings, or some other procedure. This section does not determine the proportionate shares of the obligation on a judgment; the joint judgment debtor's share depends on the circumstances of the case. See, e.g., Section 578; Tucker v. Nicholson, 12 Cal.2d 427, 433, 84 P.2d 1045 (1938); Pacific Freight Lines v. Pioneer Express Co., 39 Cal.App.2d 609, 614, 103 P.2d 1056 (1940); Stowers v. Fletcher, 84 Cal.App.2d Supp. 845, 848 190 P.2d 338 (1948) (15 Cal.L.Rev.Comm. Reports 2001).

Research References

Rutter, Cal. Practice Guide: Civil Appeals & Writs Ch. 7-C, C. Stay by Posting Security (Bond or Undertaking).

Rutter, Cal. Practice Guide: Enforcing Judgments/Debts Ch. 6G-12, Enforcement Against Joint Debtors.

Miller and Starr California Real Estate § 10:235, Potentially Liable Persons.

9 Witkin Cal. Proc. 5th Appeal § 266, (S 266) in General.

8 Witkin Cal. Proc. 5th Enforcement of Judgment § 508, (S 508) Joint Obligor: Contribution.

8 Witkin Cal. Proc. 5th Enforcement of Judgment § 509, (S 509) Surety: Repayment.

8 Witkin Cal. Proc. 5th Enforcement of Judgment § 511, (S 511) Assignment of Judgment.

7 Witkin Cal. Proc. 5th Trial § 229, Who May be Sanctioned.

1 Witkin Cal. Summ. 10th Contracts § 113, Contribution.

§ 883. Judgment debtor entitled to compel contribution or repayment; application for court order

(a) A judgment debtor entitled to compel contribution or repayment pursuant to this chapter may apply on noticed motion to the court that entered the judgment for an order determining liability for contribution or repayment. The application shall be made at any time before the judgment is satisfied in full or within 30 days thereafter.

(b) The order determining liability for contribution or repayment entitles the judgment debtor to the benefit of the judgment to enforce the liability, including every remedy that the judgment creditor has against the persons liable, to the extent of the liability.

(c) Nothing in this section limits any other remedy that a judgment debtor entitled to contribution or repayment may have. *(Added by Stats.1982, c. 497, p. 2164, § 63, operative July 1, 1983. Amended by Stats.1998, c. 77 (S.B.1841), § 1.)*

Law Revision Commission Comments

Section 883 supersedes the second sentence of former Section 709. This section codifies the practice under former law of determining the right to contribution only after a hearing on noticed motion. See Stowers v. Fletcher, 84 Cal.App.2d Supp. 845, 848, 190 P.2d 338 (1948); 5 B. Witkin, California Procedure Enforcement of Judgment § 211, at 3564 (2d ed. 1971).

The language in subdivision (b) relating to the entitlement of the judgment debtor to the remedies of the judgment creditor is drawn from Civil Code Section 2848 (right of surety against principal). Under subdivision (b), the judgment debtor receives the priority of any liens created by the judgment creditor.

Subdivision (c) makes clear that Section 883 does not prescribe the exclusive procedure for enforcement of the right to contribution. A joint judgment debtor may take an assignment of the judgment or may bring an action to obtain a judgment for contribution. See e.g., Painter v. Berglund, 31 Cal.App.2d 63, 87 P.2d 360 (1939) (assignment); Tucker v. Nicholson, 12 Cal.2d 427, 431, 84 P.2d 1045 (1938) (action). See also Section 1059 (surety on appeal substituted to rights of judgment creditor) (15 Cal.L.Rev.Comm. Reports 2001).

Research References

Rutter, Cal. Practice Guide: Enforcing Judgments/Debts Ch. 6G-12, Enforcement Against Joint Debtors.
Miller and Starr California Real Estate § 32:61, Property Interests Subject to Execution.
Miller and Starr California Real Estate § 10:235, Potentially Liable Persons.
9 Witkin Cal. Proc. 5th Appeal § 266, (S 266) in General.
8 Witkin Cal. Proc. 5th Enforcement of Judgment § 510, (S 510) Procedure to Compel Contribution or Repayment.
8 Witkin Cal. Proc. 5th Enforcement of Judgment § 511, (S 511) Assignment of Judgment.
7 Witkin Cal. Proc. 5th Trial § 229, Who May be Sanctioned.
9 Witkin, California Summary 10th Partnership § 34, (S 34) Actions Between Partners.

Title 13

APPEALS IN CIVIL ACTIONS

CHAPTER 1. APPEALS IN GENERAL

§ 901. Review of judgment or order; authority of judicial council

A judgment or order in a civil action or proceeding may be reviewed as prescribed in this title. The Judicial Council shall prescribe rules for the practice and procedure on appeal not inconsistent with the provisions of this title. *(Added by Stats. 1968, c. 385, p. 812, § 2.)*

Research References

9 Witkin Cal. Proc. 5th Appeal § 1, (S 1) in General.
9 Witkin Cal. Proc. 5th Appeal § 7, (S 7) Major Developments in Appellate Procedure.
9 Witkin Cal. Proc. 5th Appeal § 8, (S 8) Adoption and Subsequent Amendments.
10 Witkin, California Summary 10th Parent and Child § 704, Miscellaneous Orders.

§ 902. Appeal by party aggrieved; appellant and respondent defined

Any party aggrieved may appeal in the cases prescribed in this title. A party appealing is known as an appellant, and an adverse party as a respondent. *(Added by Stats.1968, c. 385, p. 812, § 2.)*

Research References

Rutter, Cal. Practice Guide: Civil Appeals & Writs Ch. 1-D, D. Access to Appellate Courts and Considerations Impacting Success on Appeal.
Rutter, Cal. Practice Guide: Civil Appeals & Writs Ch. 2-D, D. Standing to Appeal.
Rutter, Cal. Practice Guide: Civil Appeals & Writs Ch. 3-E, E. Filing Steps.
Rutter, Cal. Practice Guide: Civil Appeals & Writs Ch. 9-D, D. Procedural Rules.
Rutter, Cal. Practice Guide: Civil Appeals & Writs Ch. 2-D, Outline D.
Rutter, Cal. Practice Guide: Civil Trials & Evidence Ch. 18-B, B. Motion for New Trial.
9 Witkin Cal. Proc. 5th Appeal § 24, in General.
9 Witkin Cal. Proc. 5th Appeal § 33, (S 33) in General.
9 Witkin Cal. Proc. 5th Appeal § 38, (S 38) Former Attorney Requesting Fees.
9 Witkin Cal. Proc. 5th Appeal § 51, (S 51) No Contest Clause.
9 Witkin Cal. Proc. 5th Appeal § 192, (S 192) Order Granting New Trial.
10 Witkin, California Summary 10th Parent and Child § 700, (S 700) Right to Appeal.
11 Witkin, California Summary 10th Husband and Wife § 332, (S 332) Appeal.

§ 902.1. Entry of judgment; unconstitutional state statute or regulation; appeal after notice

In any case in which a notice was required pursuant to subdivision (e) of Section 664.5, the Attorney General shall have the right to intervene and participate in any appeal taken therefrom. These rights shall apply regardless of whether the Attorney General participated in the case in the trial court. However, the Attorney General has no direct right to appeal. If the Attorney General elects not to intervene and participate in the appeal, he or she shall file a statement with the Legislature and the Judicial Council stating the reason or reasons for the decision not to intervene and participate in the appeal. This statement may be in the form of an annual report to the Legislature and Judicial Council and that report shall be a matter of public record. *(Added by Stats.1997, c. 259 (A.B.380), § 2.)*

Civ. Pro.

Research References

Rutter, Cal. Practice Guide: Civil Appeals & Writs Ch. 2-D, D. Standing to Appeal.
Rutter, Cal. Practice Guide: Civil Appeals & Writs Ch. 9-D, D. Procedural Rules.
9 Witkin Cal. Proc. 5th Appeal § 30, Intervention by Attorney General.

§ 903. Death of person having right of appeal; appeal by attorney or executor or administrator

In the event of the death of any person who would, if still alive, have a right of appeal, either the attorney of record representing the decedent in the court in which the judgment was rendered, or the executor or administrator of the estate of the decedent, may file a notice of appeal therefrom within the time within which the decedent could have filed such a notice if he had survived. *(Added by Stats.1968, c. 385, p. 812, § 2.)*

Research References

Rutter, Cal. Practice Guide: Civil Appeals & Writs Ch. 2-D, D. Standing to Appeal.
Rutter, Cal. Practice Guide: Civil Appeals & Writs Ch. 3-C, C. Extensions of Filing Deadline.
9 Witkin Cal. Proc. 5th Appeal § 49, (S 49) Exercise of Decedent's Right to Appeal.
9 Witkin Cal. Proc. 5th Appeal § 53, Attorney or Representative After Client's Death.
1 Witkin Cal. Proc. 5th Attorneys § 67, Death or Incapacity of Client.
12 Witkin, California Summary 10th Real Property § 774, (S 774) Maintenance of Premises.

§ 904. Authority to take appeal in general

An appeal may be taken in a civil action or proceeding as provided in Sections 904.1, 904.2, 904.3, and 904.5. *(Added by Stats.1968, c. 385, p. 812, § 2. Amended by Stats.2007, c. 263 (A.B.310), § 9.5.)*

Law Revision Commission Comments

Section 904 is amended to delete an obsolete cross-reference. Former Section 904.4, relating to an appeal from a justice court, was repealed by 1976 Cal. Stat. ch. 1288, § 14. [37 Cal.L.Rev.Comm. Reports App.4 (2007)].

§ 904.1. Appealable judgments and orders

(a) An appeal, other than in a limited civil case, is to the court of appeal. An appeal, other than in a limited civil case, may be taken from any of the following:

(1) From a judgment, except (A) an interlocutory judgment, other than as provided in paragraphs (8), (9), and (11), or (B) a judgment of contempt that is made final and conclusive by Section 1222.

(2) From an order made after a judgment made appealable by paragraph (1).

(3) From an order granting a motion to quash service of summons or granting a motion to stay the action on the ground of inconvenient forum, or from a written order of dismissal under Section 581d following an order granting a motion to dismiss the action on the ground of inconvenient forum.

(4) From an order granting a new trial or denying a motion for judgment notwithstanding the verdict.

(5) From an order discharging or refusing to discharge an attachment or granting a right to attach order.

(6) From an order granting or dissolving an injunction, or refusing to grant or dissolve an injunction.

(7) From an order appointing a receiver.

(8) From an interlocutory judgment, order, or decree, hereafter made or entered in an action to redeem real or personal property from a mortgage thereof, or a lien thereon, determining the right to redeem and directing an accounting.

(9) From an interlocutory judgment in an action for partition determining the rights and interests of the respective parties and directing partition to be made.

(10) From an order made appealable by the provisions of the Probate Code or the Family Code.

(11) From an interlocutory judgment directing payment of monetary sanctions by a party or an attorney for a party if the amount exceeds five thousand dollars ($5,000).

(12) From an order directing payment of monetary sanctions by a party or an attorney for a party if the amount exceeds five thousand dollars ($5,000).

(13) From an order granting or denying a special motion to strike under Section 425.16.

(b) Sanction orders or judgments of five thousand dollars ($5,000) or less against a party or an attorney for a party may be reviewed on an appeal by that party after entry of final judgment in the main action, or, at the discretion of the court of appeal, may be reviewed upon petition for an extraordinary writ. *(Added by Stats.1968, c. 385, p. 812, § 2. Amended by Stats.1969, c. 1611, p. 3394, § 21, operative July 1, 1970; Stats.1971, c. 1210, p. 2328, § 8; Stats.1978, c. 395, § 1, eff. July 11, 1978; Stats.1982, c. 931, p. 3387, § 1; Stats.1982, c. 1198, p. 4323, § 63.2, operative July 1, 1983; Stats.1983, c. 1159, § 12, operative July 1, 1984; Stats.1984, c. 29, § 2; Stats.1988, c. 678, § 2; Stats.1988, c. 1199, § 7; Stats.1988, c. 1447, § 1; Stats.1989, c. 1416, § 25; Stats.1992, c. 163 (A.B.2641), § 54, operative Jan. 1, 1994; Stats.1993, c. 456 (A.B.58), § 12; Stats.1998, c. 931 (S.B.2139), § 100, eff. Sept. 28, 1998; Stats.1999, c. 960 (A.B.1675), § 2, eff. Oct. 10, 1999; Stats.2006, c. 567 (A.B.2303), § 8; Stats.2007, c. 43 (S.B.649), § 9.)*

Law Revision Commission Comments

Subdivision (e) of Section 904.1 is amended to make clear that an appeal may be taken from issuance of a right to attach order. See, e.g., Section 484.090 (15 Cal.L.Rev.Comm. Reports 2001).

Subdivision (j) of Section 904.1 is revised to conform to the terminology of the Probate Code. See Prob. Code § 7240 (appealable orders or refusals to make orders). [19 Cal.L.Rev. Comm. Reports 1035 (1988)].

Subdivision (j) of Section 904.1 is amended to substitute a reference to the Family Code for the former reference to the former Family Law Act. The effect of this substitution is to extend the subdivision to include provisions of the Family Code that were not part of the former Family Law Act. [22 Cal.L.Rev.Comm.Reports 1 (1992)].

Section 904.1 is amended to accommodate unification of the municipal and superior courts in a county. Cal. Const. art. VI, § 5(e).

Subdivision (a) implements Constitution Article VI, Section 11(a), as it applies in civil cases (courts of appeal have appellate jurisdiction when superior courts have original jurisdiction in causes of a type within appellate jurisdiction of courts of appeal on June 30, 1995, and in other causes prescribed by statute).

Paragraph (a)(1)(C), which made nonreviewable "a judgment on appeal from a municipal court or a justice court or a small claims court," is deleted as unnecessary, because the introductory clause of Section 904.1 as amended already excludes those matters from its coverage.

Section 904.1 is also amended to reflect elimination of the justice court. Cal. Const. art. VI, §§ 1, 5(b). [28 Cal.L.Rev.Comm. Reports App. 7 (1998)].

Subdivision (a) of Section 904.1 is amended to reflect unification of the municipal and superior courts pursuant to former Section 5(e) of Article VI of the California Constitution. Former Section 904.1(a)(1)(C) is continued in Section 904.3, with revisions to reflect unification. [36 Cal.L.Rev.Comm. Reports 305 (2007)].

Research References

Rutter, Cal. Practice Guide: A.D.R. Ch. 5-G, G. Procedures to Enforce Arbitration.
Rutter, Cal. Practice Guide: A.D.R. Ch. 6-B, B. Temporary Judges.

§ 904.2. Appealable judgments and orders; limited civil case

An appeal of a ruling by a superior court judge or other judicial officer in a limited civil case is to the appellate division of the superior court. An appeal of a ruling by a superior court judge or other judicial officer in a limited civil case may be taken from any of the following:

(a) From a judgment, except (1) an interlocutory judgment, or (2) a judgment of contempt that is made final and conclusive by Section 1222.

(b) From an order made after a judgment made appealable by subdivision (a).

(c) From an order changing or refusing to change the place of trial.

(d) From an order granting a motion to quash service of summons or granting a motion to stay the action on the ground of inconvenient forum, or from a written order of dismissal under Section 581d following an order granting a motion to dismiss the action on the ground of inconvenient forum.

(e) From an order granting a new trial or denying a motion for judgment notwithstanding the verdict.

(f) From an order discharging or refusing to discharge an attachment or granting a right to attach order.

(g) From an order granting or dissolving an injunction, or refusing to grant or dissolve an injunction.

(h) From an order appointing a receiver. *(Added by Stats. 1968, c. 385, p. 813, § 2. Amended by Stats.1969, c. 1611, p. 3395, § 22, operative July 1, 1970; Stats.1976, c. 1288, p. 5764, § 12; Stats.1982, c. 1198, p. 4325, § 64, operative July 1, 1983; Stats.1990, c. 1305 (S.B.2627), § 5; Stats.1998, c. 931 (S.B.2139), § 101, eff. Sept. 28, 1998; Stats.2006, c. 567 (A.B.2303), § 9; Stats.2007, c. 43 (S.B.649), § 10.)*

Law Revision Commission Comments

Subdivision (f) of Section 904.2 is amended to make clear that an appeal may be taken from issuance of a right to attach order. See, e.g., Section 484.090 (15 Cal.L.Rev.Comm. Reports 2001).

Section 904.2 is amended to accommodate unification of the municipal and superior courts in a county. Cal. Const. art. VI, § 5(e). The amendment implements Constitution Article VI, Section 11(b), as it applies in civil cases (appellate division of superior court has appellate jurisdiction in causes prescribed by statute).

For guidance on what constitutes a limited civil case, see Section 85 & Comment.

Subdivision (i) is deleted because review of a judgment of the small claims division is governed by Section 904.5. See also Sections 116.710–116.795.

Section 904.2 is also amended to reflect elimination of the justice court. Cal. Const. art. VI, §§ 1, 5(b). [28 Cal.L.Rev.Comm. Reports App. 7 (1998)].

Section 904.2 is amended to make clear that it governs the appealability of a ruling by a superior court judge or other judicial officer in a limited civil case. For the appealability of a judgment by the appellate division of the superior court on a writ petition in a limited civil case, see Section 904.3. [36 Cal.L.Rev.Comm. Reports 305 (2007)].

Research References

2 Witkin Cal. Proc. 5th Courts § 242, (S 242) Conditions for Limited Civil Cases.

2 Witkin Cal. Proc. 5th Courts § 281, (S 281) in General.

2 Witkin Cal. Proc. 5th Courts § 341, (S 341) Jurisdiction.

2 Witkin Cal. Proc. 5th Jurisdiction § 223, (S 223) Plaintiff's Appeal from Order Granting Motion.

6 Witkin Cal. Proc. 5th Provisional Remedies § 402, (S 402) in General.

6 Witkin Cal. Proc. 5th Provisional Remedies § 449, Motion, Appeal, and Prohibition.

7 Witkin Cal. Proc. 5th Trial § 182, Review.

§ 904.3. Judgments not appealable

An appeal shall not be taken from a judgment of the appellate division of a superior court granting or denying a petition for issuance of a writ of mandamus or prohibition directed to the superior court, or a judge thereof, in a limited civil case or a misdemeanor or infraction case. An appellate court may, in its discretion, upon petition for extraordinary writ, review the judgment. *(Added by Stats.2007, c. 43 (S.B.649), § 11.)*

Law Revision Commission Comments

Section 904.3 continues the substance of former Section 904.1(a)(1)(C), with revisions to reflect unification of the municipal and superior courts pursuant to former Section 5(e) of Article VI of the California Constitution.

Before 1982, if a litigant disagreed with a prejudgment ruling of a municipal or justice court, the litigant could seek an extraordinary writ from the superior court. A judgment on the writ petition could be appealed to the appropriate court of appeal. See Gilbert v. Municipal Court, 73 Cal.App.3d 723, 140 Cal.Rptr. 897 (1977); Burrus v. Municipal Court, 36 Cal.App.3d 233, 111 Cal.Rptr. 539 (1973).

In 1982, the Legislature amended Section 904.1 to preclude an appeal from a superior court judgment on a petition for a writ of mandamus or prohibition directed to a municipal or justice court. See 1982 Cal. Stat. ch. 1198, § 63.2. The language added in 1982, with some modifications, later became former Section 904.1(a)(1)(C). The provision was applicable not just in a civil case, but also when a party to a misdemeanor case sought a petition for a writ of mandamus or prohibition. See Baluyut v. Superior Court, 12 Cal.4th 826, 829 n.3, 911 P.2d 1, 50 Cal.Rptr.2d 101 (1996); Serna v. Superior Court, 40 Cal.3d 239, 245–46 & n.2, 707 P.2d 793, 219 Cal.Rptr. 420 (1985); see also Bermudez v. Municipal Court, 1 Cal.4th 855, 863, 823 P.2d 1210, 4 Cal.Rptr.2d 609 (1992).

In a unified court system, civil cases that used to be adjudicated in the municipal and justice courts are classified as limited civil cases and adjudicated in the superior court. See Section 85 & Comment; *Trial Court Unification: Revision of Codes*, 28 Cal. L. Revision Comm'n Reports 51, 64–65 (1998). Misdemeanor and infraction cases are also adjudicated in superior court. Cal. Const. art. VI, § 10; see also Penal Code § 19.7 (jurisdiction of infraction). If a litigant disagrees with a prejudgment ruling in a limited civil case or a misdemeanor or infraction case, the litigant can seek an extraordinary writ from the appellate division of the superior court. See Cal. Const. art. VI, § 10; see also Sections 1068(b), 1085(b), 1103(b) & Comments.

By precluding an appeal from a judgment of the appellate division on a petition for a writ of mandamus or prohibition directed to the superior court in a limited civil case or a misdemeanor or infraction case, Section 904.3 preserves the intent of former Section 904.1(a)(1)(C). Like former Section 904.1(a)(1)(C), Section 904.3 makes clear that although such a judgment cannot be appealed, a litigant may seek review of the judgment by extraordinary writ.

The clause in former Section 904.1(a)(1)(C) permitting an appellate court to review a sanction order upon petition for an extraordinary writ is not continued. That clause was unnecessary and redundant. See Section 904.1(b) (sanction order of $5,000 or less against party or attorney for party may be reviewed on appeal after entry of final judgment in main action, or, at discretion of court of appeal, reviewed upon petition for extraordinary writ; see also Section 904.1(a)(12) (sanction order exceeding $5,000 is appealable). [36 Cal.L.Rev.Comm. Reports 305 (2007)].

Research References

Rutter, Cal. Practice Guide: Civil Appeals & Writs Ch. 2-B, B. Appealable Judgments and Orders.

Rutter, Cal. Practice Guide: Civil Appeals & Writs Ch. 15-C, C. Statutory Writs.

9 Witkin Cal. Proc. 5th Appeal § 169, Miscellaneous Orders.

9 Witkin Cal. Proc. 5th Appeal § 1005, (S 1005) Nonappealable Judgments and Orders.

2 Witkin Cal. Proc. 5th Courts § 242, (S 242) Conditions for Limited Civil Cases.

8 Witkin Cal. Proc. 5th Extraordinary Writs § 4, (S 4) Constitutional Consolidation of Trial Courts.

8 Witkin Cal. Proc. 5th Extraordinary Writs § 37, (S 37) Other Orders.

8 Witkin Cal. Proc. 5th Extraordinary Writs § 53, Nature of Condition.

8 Witkin Cal. Proc. 5th Extraordinary Writs § 116, Nature of Condition.

8 Witkin Cal. Proc. 5th Extraordinary Writs § 164, (S 164) Jurisdiction and Venue.

8 Witkin Cal. Proc. 5th Extraordinary Writs § 218, No Appeal of Writ in Limited Civil Case.

3 Witkin, California Summary 10th Agency and Employment § 672, in General.

§ 904.5. Small claims division appeals

Appeals from the small claims division of a superior court shall be governed by the Small Claims Act (Chapter 5.5 (commencing with Section 116.110) of Title 1 of Part 1). *(Added by Stats.1968, c. 385, p. 813, § 2. Amended by Stats.1990, c. 1305 (S.B.2627), § 7; Stats.1998, c. 931 (S.B.2139), § 102, eff. Sept. 28, 1998; Stats.2002, c. 784 (S.B.1316), § 70.)*

Law Revision Commission Comments

Section 904.5 is amended to accommodate unification of the municipal and superior courts in a county. Review of a judgment of the small claims division is governed by Sections 116.710–116.795. The section is also amended to reflect elimination of the justice court. Cal. Const. art. VI, §§ 1, 5(b). [28 Cal.L.Rev.Comm. Reports 51 (1998)].

Section 904.5 is amended to reflect unification of the municipal and superior courts pursuant to Article VI, Section 5(e), of the California Constitution. [32 Cal.L.Rev.Comm. Reports 130 (2002)].

Research References

Rutter, Cal. Practice Guide: Enforcing Judgments/Debts Ch. 6E-4, Opposing Claim of Exemption.

2 Witkin Cal. Proc. 5th Courts § 281, (S 281) in General.

§ 906. Powers of reviewing court; matters reviewable

Upon an appeal pursuant to Section 904.1 or 904.2, the reviewing court may review the verdict or decision and any intermediate ruling, proceeding, order or decision which involves the merits or necessarily affects the judgment or order appealed from or which substantially affects the rights of a party, including, on any appeal from the judgment, any order on motion for a new trial, and may affirm, reverse or modify any judgment or order appealed from and may direct the proper judgment or order to be entered, and may, if necessary or proper, direct a new trial or further proceedings to be had. The respondent, or party in whose favor the judgment was given, may, without appealing from such judgment, request the reviewing court to and it may review any of the foregoing matters for the purpose of determining whether or not the appellant was prejudiced by the error or errors upon which he relies for reversal or modification of the judgment from which the appeal is taken. The provisions of this section do not authorize the reviewing court to review any decision or order from which an appeal might have been taken. *(Added by Stats.1968, c. 385, p. 814, § 2. Amended by Stats.1976, c. 1288, p. 5764, § 16).*

Research References

Rutter, Cal. Practice Guide: Civil Appeals & Writs Ch. 2-A, A. Overview.

Rutter, Cal. Practice Guide: Civil Appeals & Writs Ch. 2-C, C. Nonappealable Orders.

Rutter, Cal. Practice Guide: Civil Appeals & Writs Ch. 2-D, D. Standing to Appeal.

Rutter, Cal. Practice Guide: Civil Appeals & Writs Ch. 8-D, D. Limits on Assertion of Issues on Appeal.

Rutter, Cal. Practice Guide: Civil Appeals & Writs Ch. 8-E, E. Limits on Reversal or Modification-"Prejudicial Error" Rule.

Rutter, Cal. Practice Guide: Civil Appeals & Writs Ch. 15-C, C. Statutory Writs.

Rutter, Cal. Practice Guide: Civil Trials & Evidence Ch. 8E-A, A. Privileges.

California Practice Guide: Employment Litigation Ch. 19-D, D. Defendant's Challenges and Responses to Complaint.

Rutter, Cal. Practice Guide: Prof. Responsibility Ch. 4-G, G. Procedural Considerations for Disqualification Based on Conflict of Interest.

9 Witkin Cal. Proc. 5th Appeal § 89, in General.

9 Witkin Cal. Proc. 5th Appeal § 333, to Negate Prejudice from Error Against Appellant.

9 Witkin Cal. Proc. 5th Appeal § 1002, in General.

8 Witkin Cal. Proc. 5th Attack Judgment Trial Court § 138, (S 138) Review on Appeal from Judgment.

6 Witkin Cal. Proc. 5th Proceedings Without Trial § 526, (S 526) Appeal and Review.

§ 907. Frivolous appeal; appeal for delay; damages

When it appears to the reviewing court that the appeal was frivolous or taken solely for delay, it may add to the costs on appeal such damages as may be just. *(Added by Stats.1968, c. 385, p. 814, § 2.)*

Research References

Rutter, Cal. Practice Guide: A.D.R. Ch. 5-J, J. Challenging and Enforcing Arbitrator's Award in Court.

Rutter, Cal. Practice Guide: Civil Appeals & Writs Ch. 2-D, D. Standing to Appeal.

Rutter, Cal. Practice Guide: Civil Appeals & Writs Ch. 3-D, D. Consequences of Lapse of Appeal Deadline; Strategies for Respondents and Appellants.

Rutter, Cal. Practice Guide: Civil Appeals & Writs Ch. 5-D, D. Sanctions for Frivolous Motions.

Rutter, Cal. Practice Guide: Civil Appeals & Writs Ch. 9-B, B. Approaches to Briefwriting.

Rutter, Cal. Practice Guide: Civil Appeals & Writs Ch. 11-D, D. Disposition.

Rutter, Cal. Practice Guide: Civil Appeals & Writs Ch. 11-E, E. Appellate Costs and Sanctions.

Rutter, Cal. Practice Guide: Civil Appeals & Writs Ch. 14-B, B. Recovery of Appellate Costs and Attorney Fees.

Rutter, Cal. Practice Guide: Civ. Pro. Before Trial Ch. 9(III)-A, A. Sources of Sanctions Power.

Rutter, Cal. Practice Guide: Enforcing Judgments/Debts Ch. 1-B, B. Accepting the Collection Case.

Rutter, Cal. Practice Guide: Enforcing Judgments/Debts Ch. 2-C, C. Tort Liability.

Rutter, Cal. Practice Guide: Insurance Litigation Ch. 12C-D, D. Application-Matters Held "Unreasonable".

Rutter, Cal. Practice Guide: Personal Injury Ch. 4-C, C. Effective Settlement Negotiations.

Rutter, Cal. Practice Guide: Prof. Responsibility Ch. 1-A, A. Sources of Regulation of Practice of Law in California-Overview.

Rutter, Cal. Practice Guide: Prof. Responsibility Ch. 8-E, E. Consequences of Improper Advocacy.

9 Witkin Cal. Proc. 5th Appeal § 983, (S 983) Nature of Power.

9 Witkin Cal. Proc. 5th Appeal § 989, (S 989) Objective and Subjective Standards.

9 Witkin Cal. Proc. 5th Appeal § 991, (S 991) in General.

9 Witkin Cal. Proc. 5th Appeal § 998, (S 998) Sanction Over $5,000, But Less Than $100,000.

9 Witkin Cal. Proc. 5th Appeal § 1001, Distinction: No Tort Action for Malicious Appeal.

9 Witkin Cal. Proc. 5th Appeal § 1002, in General.

8 Witkin Cal. Proc. 5th Extraordinary Writs § 215, (S 215) Sanctions for Frivolous Application.

7 Witkin Cal. Proc. 5th Trial § 226, (S 226) in General.

§ 908. Restitution on modification or reversal

When the judgment or order is reversed or modified, the reviewing court may direct that the parties be returned so far as possible to the positions they occupied before the enforcement of or execution on the judgment or order. In doing so, the reviewing court may order restitution on reasonable terms and conditions of all property and rights lost by the erroneous judgment or order, so far as such restitution is consistent with rights of third parties and may direct the entry of a money judgment sufficient to compensate for property or rights not restored. The reviewing court may take evidence and make findings concerning such matters or may, by order, refer such matters to the trial court for determination. *(Added by Stats. 1968, c. 385, p. 814, § 2.)*

Research References

Rutter, Cal. Practice Guide: Civil Appeals & Writs Ch. 14-C, C. Trial Court Proceedings After Reversal.

Rutter, Cal. Practice Guide: Enforcing Judgments/Debts Ch. 6D-7, Sale and Collection of Property Levied Upon.

9 Witkin Cal. Proc. 5th Appeal § 900, (S 900) Nature and Scope of Power.

8 Witkin Cal. Proc. 5th Enforcement of Judgment § 166, (S 166) Restitution After Reversal.

5 Witkin Cal. Proc. 5th Pleading § 1162, Summary Restitution.

§ 909. Factual determinations on appeal; non-jury cases; additional evidence; giving or directing entry of judgment or order; construction of section

In all cases where trial by jury is not a matter of right or where trial by jury has been waived, the reviewing court may make factual determinations contrary to or in addition to those made by the trial court. The factual determinations may be based on the evidence adduced before the trial court either with or without the taking of evidence by the reviewing court. The reviewing court may for the purpose of making the factual determinations or for any other purpose in the interests of justice, take additional evidence of or concerning facts occurring at any time prior to the decision of the appeal, and may give or direct the entry of any judgment or order and may make any further or other order as the case may require. This section shall be liberally construed to the end among others that, where feasible, causes may be finally disposed of by a single appeal and without further proceedings in the trial court except where in the interests of justice a new trial is required on some or all of the issues. *(Added by Stats.1968, c. 385, § 2. Amended by Stats. 1981, c. 900, § 7.)*

Research References

Rutter, Cal. Practice Guide: Civil Appeals & Writs Ch. 4-G, G. Augmentation of the Record.

Rutter, Cal. Practice Guide: Civil Appeals & Writs Ch. 5-B, B. Types of Motions, Applications and Requests.

22 NO. 2 Miller & Starr, California Real Estate Newsalert 11, Easements.

9 Witkin Cal. Proc. 5th Appeal § 309, (S 309) Constitutional and Legislative Development.

9 Witkin Cal. Proc. 5th Appeal § 310, (S 310) Implementing Statute.

9 Witkin Cal. Proc. 5th Appeal § 317, (S 317) Procedure.

9 Witkin Cal. Proc. 5th Appeal § 318, (S 318) in General.

9 Witkin Cal. Proc. 5th Appeal § 321, Lack of Diligence.

8 Witkin Cal. Proc. 5th Attack Judgment Trial Court § 4, Coram Nobis and Coram Vobis.

7 Witkin Cal. Proc. 5th Trial § 386, (S 386) No-Knowledge Affidavit of Attorney and Party.

10 Witkin, California Summary 10th Parent and Child § 356, (S 356) Change in Circumstances Pending Appeal.

10 Witkin, California Summary 10th Parent and Child § 693, Termination of Parental Rights.

§ 911. Transfer of appeal from superior court to court of appeal; grounds; power of reviewing court

A court of appeal may order any case on appeal to a superior court in its district transferred to it for hearing and decision as provided by rules of the Judicial Council when the superior court certifies, or the court of appeal determines, that the transfer appears necessary to secure uniformity of decision or to settle important questions of law.

No case in which there is a right on appeal to a trial anew in the superior court shall be transferred pursuant to this section before a decision in the case becomes final therein.

A court to which any case is transferred pursuant to this section shall have similar power to review any matter and make orders and judgments as the appellate division of the superior court would have in the case, except that if the case was tried anew in the superior court, the court of appeal shall have similar power to review any matter and make orders and judgments as it has in a case appealed pursuant to Section 904.1. *(Added by Stats.1968, c. 385, p. 815, § 2. Amended by Stats.1998, c. 931 (S.B.2139), § 103, eff. Sept. 28, 1998.)*

Law Revision Commission Comments

Section 911 is amended to accommodate unification of the municipal and superior courts in a county. Cal. Const. art. VI, § 5(e). It is also amended to reflect elimination of the justice court. Cal. Const. art. VI, §§ 1, 5(b).

Section 911 applies to appeals taken to the appellate division of the superior court (see Section 904.2 (taking appeal in limited civil case) and to appeals taken to the superior court where the appeal is in the form of a trial de novo (see, e.g., Section 116.770 (small claims appeals)). [28 Cal.L.Rev.Comm. Reports 51 (1998)].

Research References

Rutter, Cal. Practice Guide: Civil Appeals & Writs Ch. 2-B, B. Appealable Judgments and Orders.
Rutter, Cal. Practice Guide: Civil Appeals & Writs Ch. 3-A, A. Necessity of Timely Filing for Appeal.
Rutter, Cal. Practice Guide: Civil Appeals & Writs Ch. 16-K, K. Transfer to Court of Appeal.
9 Witkin Cal. Proc. 5th Appeal § 1002, in General.
9 Witkin Cal. Proc. 5th Appeal § 1020, (S 1020) Nature and Scope of Power.
9 Witkin Cal. Proc. 5th Appeal § 1024, (S 1024) Denial or Grant of Transfer.
2 Witkin Cal. Proc. 5th Courts § 324, Certification to Court of Appeal.
2 Witkin Cal. Proc. 5th Courts § 336, Hearing After Superior Court Appeal.
8 Witkin Cal. Proc. 5th Extraordinary Writs § 128, (S 128) Appeal to Superior Court.

§ 912. Certification of judgment or order and opinion to trial court; filing; attachment to judgment roll; entry of note of judgment

Upon final determination of an appeal by the reviewing court, the clerk of the court shall remit to the trial court a certified copy of the judgment or order of the reviewing court and of its opinion, if any. The clerk of the trial court shall file the certified copy of the judgment and opinion of the reviewing court, shall attach that copy to the judgment roll if the appeal was from a judgment, and shall enter a note of the judgment of the reviewing court stating whether the judgment or order appealed from has been affirmed, reversed or modified, in the margin of the original entry of the judgment or order, and also in the register of actions. *(Added by Stats.1968, c. 385, p. 815, § 2. Amended by Stats.1998, c. 931 (S.B.2139), § 104, eff. Sept. 28, 1998; Stats.2001, c. 44 (S.B.562), § 6; Stats.2002, c. 664 (A.B. 3034), § 49.)*

Law Revision Commission Comments

Section 912 is amended to reflect the elimination of the justice court. Cal. Const. art. VI, §§ 1, 5(b), (e), 10.

The amendment deletes the clause authorizing the judge to substitute for the clerk if there be no clerk. That provision is obsolete because every municipal and superior court has a clerk. Additionally, judges have authority to perform any act that court clerks are allowed to perform. Section 167. [28 Cal.L.Rev.Comm. Reports 51 (1998)].

Section 912 is amended to delete the reference to a "docket," because courts no longer maintain a record denominated a "docket" in civil cases. See former Gov't Code 71614 (1953 Cal. Stat. ch. 206, 1, repealed by 1977

Cal. Stat. ch. 1257, 71) (judge of justice court shall keep a book denominated a "docket"), 71614.5 (1959 Cal. Stat. ch. 671, 2, repealed by 1977 Cal. Stat. ch. 1257, 72) (clerk or judge of justice court shall keep the "docket" and other records of the court). Formerly, justice courts maintained a docket in civil cases, which was a record of actions taken in open court, as well as documents filed and other proceedings in the case. See former Gov't Code 71614 (1953 Cal. Stat. ch. 206, 1, repealed by 1977 Cal. Stat. ch. 1257, 71) (judge of justice court shall keep a book denominated a "docket"), 71614.5 (1959 Cal. Stat. ch. 671, 2, repealed by 1977 Cal. Stat. ch. 1257, 72) (clerk or judge of justice court shall keep the "docket" and other records of the court). Now actions taken in open court are recorded in the minutes of a superior court. Gov't Code 69844; see also Copley Press v. Superior Court, 6 Cal.App.4th 106, 110, 7 Cal.Rptr.2d 841 (1992). Documents filed or lodged and other proceedings in a civil case are recorded in the register of actions. See Gov't Code 69845 (clerk of superior court may keep a register of actions), 69845.5 (alternative to maintaining register of actions in superior court). [30 Cal.L.Rev.Comm. Reports 479 (2000)].

Research References

Rutter, Cal. Practice Guide: Civil Appeals & Writs Ch. 14-A, A. Remittitur.
9 Witkin Cal. Proc. 5th Appeal § 842, (S 842) Procedure.
9 Witkin Cal. Proc. 5th Appeal § 843, (S 843) Proceedings in Which Remittitur Issues.

§ 913. Dismissal; effect

The dismissal of an appeal shall be with prejudice to the right to file another appeal within the time permitted, unless the dismissal is expressly made without prejudice to another appeal. *(Added by Stats.1968, c. 385, p. 816, § 2.)*

Research References

Rutter, Cal. Practice Guide: Civil Appeals & Writs Ch. 5-B, B. Types of Motions, Applications and Requests.
9 Witkin Cal. Proc. 5th Appeal § 739, (S 739) Nature of Power.
9 Witkin Cal. Proc. 5th Appeal § 762, (S 762) Effect of Dismissal.

§ 914. New trial; death or disability of reporter; loss or destruction of notes

When the right to a phonographic report has not been waived and when it shall be impossible to have a phonographic report of the trial transcribed by a stenographic reporter as provided by law or by rule, because of the death or disability of a reporter who participated as a stenographic reporter at the trial or because of the loss or destruction, in whole or in substantial part, of the notes of such reporter, the trial court or a judge thereof, or the reviewing court shall have power to set aside and vacate the judgment, order or decree from which an appeal has been taken or is to be taken and to order a new trial of the action or proceeding. *(Added by Stats.1968, c. 385, p. 816, § 2.)*

Research References

Rutter, Cal. Practice Guide: Civil Appeals & Writs Ch. 4-C, C. Record Preparation Procedure.
Rutter, Cal. Practice Guide: Civil Trials & Evidence Ch. 18-B, B. Motion for New Trial.
Rutter, Cal. Practice Guide: Personal Injury Ch. 10-A, A. Motion for New Trial.
9 Witkin Cal. Proc. 5th Appeal § 673, (S 673) Agreed or Settled Statement.
9 Witkin Cal. Proc. 5th Appeal § 674, in General.
9 Witkin Cal. Proc. 5th Appeal § 675, No Partial New Trial.
9 Witkin Cal. Proc. 5th Appeal § 676, No Reopening of Trial to Recover Lost Testimony.
9 Witkin Cal. Proc. 5th Appeal § 677, Circumstances Justifying Relief.
8 Witkin Cal. Proc. 5th Attack Judgment Trial Court § 45, (S 45) Other Grounds.

12 Witkin, California Summary 10th Real Property § 786, (S 786) Grounds for Termination.

CHAPTER 2.   STAY OF ENFORCEMENT AND OTHER PROCEEDINGS

§ 916.   Stay on perfection of appeal; release from levy; proceeding upon matters not affected by appeal

(a) Except as provided in Sections 917.1 to 917.9, inclusive, and in Section 116.810, the perfecting of an appeal stays proceedings in the trial court upon the judgment or order appealed from or upon the matters embraced therein or affected thereby, including enforcement of the judgment or order, but the trial court may proceed upon any other matter embraced in the action and not affected by the judgment or order.

(b) When there is a stay of proceedings other than the enforcement of the judgment, the trial court shall have jurisdiction of proceedings related to the enforcement of the judgment as well as any other matter embraced in the action and not affected by the judgment or order appealed from. *(Added by Stats.1968, c. 385, p. 816, § 2.   Amended by Stats.1975, c. 266, p. 673, § 5; Stats.1982, c. 497, p. 2165, § 64, operative July 1, 1983; Stats.1990, c. 1305 (S.B.2627), § 8.)*

Law Revision Commission Comments

Subdivision (b) of Section 916 has been deleted as unnecessary in view of Sections 697.040(a) (effect of stay of enforcement on enforcement liens) and 697.050 (release of property). See also Section 917.1 (undertaking required as condition of stay of enforcement of money judgment). Subdivision (a) has been revised to substitute the correct cross-reference (15 Cal.L.Rev.Comm. Reports 2001).

Research References

Rutter, Cal. Practice Guide: Civil Appeals & Writs Ch. 3-A, A. Necessity of Timely Filing for Appeal.

Rutter, Cal. Practice Guide: Civil Appeals & Writs Ch. 7-A, A. Overview.

Rutter, Cal. Practice Guide: Civil Appeals & Writs Ch. 7-B, B. Automatic Stay.

Rutter, Cal. Practice Guide: Civil Appeals & Writs Ch. 7-C, C. Stay by Posting Security (Bond or Undertaking).

Rutter, Cal. Practice Guide: Civil Appeals & Writs Ch. 7-E, E. Stay by Writ of Supersedeas.

Rutter, Cal. Practice Guide: Civil Appeals & Writs Form 7:D, Petition for Writ of Supersedeas or Other Stay Order.

Rutter, Cal. Practice Guide: Civ. Pro. Before Trial Ch. 9(II)-A, A. Injunctions.

Rutter, Cal. Practice Guide: Enforcing Judgments/Debts Ch. 6A-7, Period During Which Judgment Enforceable; Renewal Procedures.

Rutter, Cal. Practice Guide: Enforcing Judgments/Debts Ch. 6E-4, Opposing Claim of Exemption.

Rutter, Cal. Practice Guide: Enforcing Judgments/Debts Ch. 6G-2, Written Interrogatories to Judgment Debtor.

Rutter, Cal. Practice Guide: Enforcing Judgments/Debts Ch. 6G-3, Inspection Demand to Judgment Debtor.

Rutter, Cal. Practice Guide: Insurance Litigation Ch. 6I-B, B. Particular Surety Bond Coverages.

Rutter, Cal. Practice Guide: Real Prop. Transactions Ch. 6-I, I. Real Property Foreclosures and Antideficiency Laws.

Miller and Starr California Real Estate § 16:21, Interruption of Possession--Suit by the Owner.

Miller and Starr California Real Estate § 10:232, Attack on Validity of the Sale.

15 NO. 2 Miller & Starr, California Real Estate Newsalert 3, Commercial Arbitration.

9 Witkin Cal. Proc. 5th Appeal § 17, (S 17) in General.

9 Witkin Cal. Proc. 5th Appeal § 20, (S 20) Jurisdiction Over Collateral Matters.

9 Witkin Cal. Proc. 5th Appeal § 22, Spousal Support.

9 Witkin Cal. Proc. 5th Appeal § 221, (S 221) Methods of Staying Enforcement.

9 Witkin Cal. Proc. 5th Appeal § 222, (S 222) Effect of Stay.

9 Witkin Cal. Proc. 5th Appeal § 269, Theory.

9 Witkin Cal. Proc. 5th Appeal § 270, Illustrations.

9 Witkin Cal. Proc. 5th Appeal § 285, in General.

9 Witkin Cal. Proc. 5th Appeal § 1029, Stay of Proceedings Below.

8 Witkin Cal. Proc. 5th Enforcement of Judgment § 67, (S 67) Duration and Extinguishment.

8 Witkin Cal. Proc. 5th Enforcement of Judgment § 186, (S 186) Disposition of Property During Proceedings.

7 Witkin Cal. Proc. 5th Judgment § 150, (S 150) Fees as Costs.

5 Witkin Cal. Proc. 5th Pleading § 1039, Appeal.

3 Witkin, California Summary 10th Agency and Employment § 670, (S 670) Procedure.

13 Witkin, California Summary 10th Trusts § 323, (S 323) Where No Benefit is Obtained.

§ 917.1.   Appeal from money judgment; undertaking to stay enforcement; subrogation; costs awarded by trial court

(a) Unless an undertaking is given, the perfecting of an appeal shall not stay enforcement of the judgment or order in the trial court if the judgment or order is for any of the following:

(1) Money or the payment of money, whether consisting of a special fund or not, and whether payable by the appellant or another party to the action.

(2) Costs awarded pursuant to Section 998 which otherwise would not have been awarded as costs pursuant to Section 1033.5.

Civ. Pro.

(3) Costs awarded pursuant to Section 1141.21 which otherwise would not have been awarded as costs pursuant to Section 1033.5.

(b) The undertaking shall be on condition that if the judgment or order or any part of it is affirmed or the appeal is withdrawn or dismissed, the party ordered to pay shall pay the amount of the judgment or order, or the part of it as to which the judgment or order is affirmed, as entered after the receipt of the remittitur, together with any interest which may have accrued pending the appeal and entry of the remittitur, and costs which may be awarded against the appellant on appeal. This section shall not apply in cases where the money to be paid is in the actual or constructive custody of the court; and such cases shall be governed, instead, by the provisions of Section 917.2. The undertaking shall be for double the amount of the judgment or order unless given by an admitted surety insurer in which event it shall be for one and one-half times the amount of the judgment or order. The liability on the undertaking may be enforced if the party ordered to pay does not make the payment within 30 days after the filing of the remittitur from the reviewing court.

(c) If a surety on the undertaking pays the judgment, either with or without action, after the judgment is affirmed, the surety is substituted to the rights of the creditor and is entitled to control, enforce, and satisfy the judgment, in all respects as if the surety had recovered the judgment.

(d) Costs awarded by the trial court under Chapter 6 (commencing with Section 1021) of Title 14 shall be included in the amount of the judgment or order for the purpose of applying paragraph (1) of subdivision (a) and subdivision (b). However, no undertaking shall be required pursuant to this section solely for costs awarded under Chapter 6 (commencing with Section 1021) of Title 14. *(Added by Stats.1968, c. 385, p. 816, § 2. Amended by Stats.1972, c. 546, p. 936, § 1; Stats.1981, c. 196, p. 1120, § 1; Stats.1982, c. 517, p. 2354, § 155; Stats.1986, c. 1174, § 1; Stats.1993, c. 456 (A.B.58), § 13.)*

Validity

This section was held preempted by the federal procedural rule prohibiting unsecured stays in the case of Leuzinger v. County of Lake, N.D.Cal.2008, 253 F.R.D. 469.

Law Revision Commission Comments

Section 917.1 is amended to delete provisions duplicated in the Bond and Undertaking Law. See Sections 996.440 (motion to enforce liability), 996.470 (limitation on liability of surety); see also Section 995.120 ("admitted surety insurer" defined). Subdivision (c) continues the substance of former Section 1059 [16 Cal.L.Rev.Comm. Reports 501 (1982)].

Research References

Rutter, Cal. Practice Guide: Civil Appeals & Writs Ch. 7-B, B. Automatic Stay.
Rutter, Cal. Practice Guide: Civil Appeals & Writs Ch. 7-C, C. Stay by Posting Security (Bond or Undertaking).
Rutter, Cal. Practice Guide: Civil Appeals & Writs Ch. 7-E, E. Stay by Writ of Supersedeas.
Rutter, Cal. Practice Guide: Civil Appeals & Writs Ch. 15-D, D. Writ Review of Contempt Orders.
Rutter, Cal. Practice Guide: Civil Appeals & Writs Ch. 7-B, Outline B.
Rutter, Cal. Practice Guide: Civil Appeals & Writs Ch. 7-C, Outline C.
Rutter, Cal. Practice Guide: Civil Trials & Evidence Ch. 18-C, C. Other Post-Trial Motions.
Rutter, Cal. Practice Guide: Enforcing Judgments/Debts Ch. 6A-7, Period During Which Judgment Enforceable; Renewal Procedures.
Rutter, Cal. Practice Guide: Enforcing Judgments/Debts Ch. 6D-6, Debtor's Recourse Against Execution Levy.
Rutter, Cal. Practice Guide: Enforcing Judgments/Debts Ch. 6A-12, Staying Enforcement of Judgment.
Rutter, Cal. Practice Guide: Insurance Litigation Ch. 15-J, J. Appeal.

Rutter, Cal. Practice Guide: Insurance Litigation Ch. 6I-B, B. Particular Surety Bond Coverages.
Rutter, Cal. Practice Guide: Personal Injury Ch. 4-C, C. Effective Settlement Negotiations.
Miller and Starr California Real Estate § 34:81, Recovery of Fees on Appeal.
9 Witkin Cal. Proc. 5th Appeal § 230, Money or Payment of Money.
9 Witkin Cal. Proc. 5th Appeal § 231, Costs Awarded Against Party Rejecting Compromise.
9 Witkin Cal. Proc. 5th Appeal § 232, Costs Awarded Against Party Demanding Trial De Novo After Arbitration.
9 Witkin Cal. Proc. 5th Appeal § 233, Attorneys' Fees Awarded as Sanction.
9 Witkin Cal. Proc. 5th Appeal § 234, in General.
9 Witkin Cal. Proc. 5th Appeal § 235, Judgment for Costs Alone.
9 Witkin Cal. Proc. 5th Appeal § 236, Attorneys' Fees as Costs.
9 Witkin Cal. Proc. 5th Appeal § 237, (S 237) Condition of Undertaking.
9 Witkin Cal. Proc. 5th Appeal § 238, in General.
9 Witkin Cal. Proc. 5th Appeal § 239, Costs.
9 Witkin Cal. Proc. 5th Appeal § 254, (S 254) in General.
9 Witkin Cal. Proc. 5th Appeal § 256, (S 256) Distinction: Changed Circumstances.
9 Witkin Cal. Proc. 5th Appeal § 262, (S 262) Distinction: Valid Partial Undertaking.
9 Witkin Cal. Proc. 5th Appeal § 265, (S 265) Enforcement of Liability.
9 Witkin Cal. Proc. 5th Appeal § 266, (S 266) in General.
9 Witkin Cal. Proc. 5th Appeal § 269, Theory.
9 Witkin Cal. Proc. 5th Appeal § 271, Order or Judgment Under Probate Code.
9 Witkin Cal. Proc. 5th Appeal § 273, Current Statute.
9 Witkin Cal. Proc. 5th Appeal § 1002, in General.
8 Witkin Cal. Proc. 5th Enforcement of Judgment § 446, (S 446) Judgment Not Final and Unconditional.
6 Witkin Cal. Proc. 5th Provisional Remedies § 29, Insufficient Bond in Action or Proceeding.
14 Witkin, California Summary 10th Wills and Probate § 402, Effect of Appeal.

§ 917.15. Appeal from judgment or order to remedy a release or threatened release of hazardous substances; stay of enforcement; exception

The perfecting of an appeal shall not stay enforcement of the judgment or order in the trial court if the judgment or order appealed from, or the administrative order which is the subject of the trial court proceeding, was issued pursuant to either of the following:

(a) Subdivision (a) of Section 25358.3 of the Health and Safety Code and ordered a responsible party to take appropriate removal or remedial actions in response to a release or a threatened release of a hazardous substance.

(b) Section 25181 of the Health and Safety Code and ordered the party to comply with Chapter 6.5 (commencing with Section 25100) of Division 20 of the Health and Safety Code or any rule, regulation, permit, covenant, standard, requirement, or order issued, adopted or executed pursuant to that Chapter 6.5. *(Added by Stats.1985, c. 1492, § 1.)*

Research References

Rutter, Cal. Practice Guide: Civil Appeals & Writs Ch. 7-E, E. Stay by Writ of Supersedeas.
9 Witkin Cal. Proc. 5th Appeal § 277, (S 277) Other Types Not Stayed.
12 Witkin, California Summary 10th Real Property § 905, (S 905) Enforcement.

§ 917.2. Judgment or order directing assignment or delivery of personal property or sale on foreclosure; stay; custody of court officer; undertaking; perishables

The perfecting of an appeal shall not stay enforcement of the judgment or order of the trial court if the judgment or order appealed from directs the assignment or delivery of personal property, including documents, whether by the appellant or another party to the action, or the sale of personal property upon the foreclosure of a mortgage, or other lien thereon, unless an undertaking in a sum and upon conditions fixed by the trial court, is given that the appellant or party ordered to assign or deliver the property will obey and satisfy the order of the reviewing court, and will not commit or suffer to be committed any damage to the property, and that if the judgment or order appealed from is affirmed, or the appeal is withdrawn or dismissed, the appellant shall pay the damage suffered to such property and the value of the use of such property for the period of the delay caused by the appeal. The appellant may cause the property to be placed in the custody of an officer designated by the court to abide the order of the reviewing court, and such fact shall be considered by the court in fixing the amount of the undertaking. If the judgment or order appealed from directs the sale of perishable property the trial court may order such property to be sold and the proceeds thereof to be deposited with the clerk of the trial court to abide the order of the reviewing court; such fact shall be considered by the court in fixing the amount of the undertaking. *(Added by Stats.1968, c. 385, p. 817, § 2. Amended by Stats.1972, c. 546, p. 936, § 2.)*

Research References

Rutter, Cal. Practice Guide: Civil Appeals & Writs Ch. 7-C, C. Stay by Posting Security (Bond or Undertaking).
Rutter, Cal. Practice Guide: Civil Appeals & Writs Ch. 7-C, Outline C.
Rutter, Cal. Practice Guide: Enforcing Judgments/Debts Ch. 6D-6, Debtor's Recourse Against Execution Levy.
9 Witkin Cal. Proc. 5th Appeal § 230, Money or Payment of Money.
9 Witkin Cal. Proc. 5th Appeal § 234, in General.
9 Witkin Cal. Proc. 5th Appeal § 240, (S 240) Application of Statute.
9 Witkin Cal. Proc. 5th Appeal § 241, (S 241) Recovery for Decline in Value.
9 Witkin Cal. Proc. 5th Appeal § 242, (S 242) Exception: Where Appellant is Not in Possession.
9 Witkin Cal. Proc. 5th Appeal § 254, (S 254) in General.
9 Witkin Cal. Proc. 5th Appeal § 277, (S 277) Other Types Not Stayed.
9 Witkin Cal. Proc. 5th Appeal § 288, Where Judgment is Not Stayed by Appeal or Undertaking.
9 Witkin Cal. Proc. 5th Appeal § 306, (S 306) Other Protective Conditions.

§ 917.3. Judgment or order directing execution of instrument; stay on execution and deposit with clerk of court

The perfecting of an appeal shall not stay enforcement of the judgment or order in the trial court if the judgment or order appealed from directs the execution of one or more instruments unless the instrument or instruments are executed and deposited in the office of the clerk of the court where the original judgment or order is entered to abide the order of the reviewing court. *(Added by Stats.1968, c. 385, p. 817, § 2.)*

Research References

Rutter, Cal. Practice Guide: Civil Appeals & Writs Ch. 7-E, E. Stay by Writ of Supersedeas.
Miller and Starr California Real Estate § 16:21, Interruption of Possession--Suit by the Owner.
9 Witkin Cal. Proc. 5th Appeal § 277, (S 277) Other Types Not Stayed.
9 Witkin Cal. Proc. 5th Appeal § 293, (S 293) Failure to Exhaust Other Remedies.
9 Witkin Cal. Proc. 5th Appeal § 306, (S 306) Other Protective Conditions.

§ 917.4. Judgment or order directing sale or delivery of realty; undertaking to stay enforcement; conditions

The perfecting of an appeal shall not stay enforcement of the judgment or order in the trial court if the judgment or order appealed from directs the sale, conveyance or delivery of possession of real property which is in the possession or control of the appellant or the party ordered to sell, convey or deliver possession of the property, unless an undertaking in a sum fixed by the trial court is given that the appellant or party ordered to

sell, convey or deliver possession of the property will not commit or suffer to be committed any waste thereon and that if the judgment or order appealed from is affirmed, or the appeal is withdrawn or dismissed, the appellant shall pay the damage suffered by the waste and the value of the use and occupancy of the property, or the part of it as to which the judgment or order is affirmed, from the time of the taking of the appeal until the delivery of the possession of the property. If the judgment or order directs the sale of mortgaged real property and the payment of any deficiency, the undertaking shall also provide for the payment of any deficiency. *(Added by Stats.1968, c. 385, p. 817, § 2. Amended by Stats.1982, c. 517, p. 2355, § 156.)*

Law Revision Commission Comments

Section 917.4 is amended to delete a provision duplicated in the Bond and Undertaking Law. See Section 996.470 (limitation on liability of surety). The other changes in Section 917.4 are technical [16 Cal.L.Rev. Comm. Reports 501 (1982)].

Research References

Rutter, Cal. Practice Guide: Civil Appeals & Writs Ch. 7-C, C. Stay by Posting Security (Bond or Undertaking).
Rutter, Cal. Practice Guide: Civil Appeals & Writs Ch. 7-D, D. Discretionary Stay by Trial Court.
Rutter, Cal. Practice Guide: Civil Appeals & Writs Ch. 7-C, Outline C.
Rutter, Cal. Practice Guide: Civil Appeals & Writs Ch. 7-D, Outline D.
Rutter, Cal. Practice Guide: Enforcing Judgments/Debts Ch. 6D-6, Debtor's Recourse Against Execution Levy.
Miller and Starr California Real Estate § 16:21, Interruption of Possession--Suit by the Owner.
Miller and Starr California Real Estate § 32:73, Attack on Validity of Sale.
Miller and Starr California Real Estate § 10:232, Attack on Validity of the Sale.
Miller and Starr California Real Estate § 19:230, Trial; Judgment; Stay of Execution.
15 NO. 3 Miller & Starr, California Real Estate Newsalert 4, Deeds of Trust.
16 NO. 2 Miller & Starr, California Real Estate Newsalert 13, Involuntary Liens.
9 Witkin Cal. Proc. 5th Appeal § 243, (S 243) Application of Statute.
9 Witkin Cal. Proc. 5th Appeal § 244, (S 244) Exception: Where Appellant is Not in Possession.
9 Witkin Cal. Proc. 5th Appeal § 245, in General.
9 Witkin Cal. Proc. 5th Appeal § 254, (S 254) in General.
9 Witkin Cal. Proc. 5th Appeal § 255, (S 255) Additional Security is Not Allowable.
8 Witkin Cal. Proc. 5th Enforcement of Judgment § 164, in General.
7 Witkin Cal. Proc. 5th Judgment § 81, in General.

§ 917.5. Judgment or order appointing receiver; undertaking to stay enforcement

The perfecting of an appeal shall not stay enforcement of the judgment or order in the trial court if the judgment or order appealed from appoints a receiver, unless an undertaking in a sum fixed by the trial court is given on condition that if the judgment or order is affirmed or the appeal is withdrawn, or dismissed, the appellant will pay all damages which the respondent may sustain by reason of the stay in the enforcement of the judgment. *(Added by Stats.1968, c. 385, § 2. Amended by Stats.1972, c. 546, § 3; Stats.1982, c. 517, p. 2355, § 156.)*

Law Revision Commission Comments

Section 917.5 is amended to delete a provision duplicated in the Bond and Undertaking Law. See Section 996.470 (limitation on liability of surety). [16 Cal.L.Rev.Comm. Reports 501 (1982)].

Research References

Rutter, Cal. Practice Guide: Civil Appeals & Writs Ch. 7-C, C. Stay by Posting Security (Bond or Undertaking).
Rutter, Cal. Practice Guide: Civil Appeals & Writs Ch. 7-C, Outline C.

Civ. Pro.

Rutter, Cal. Practice Guide: Enforcing Judgments/Debts Ch. 6D-6, Debtor's Recourse Against Execution Levy.
Miller and Starr California Real Estate § 33:8, Appeals, Generally.
9 Witkin Cal. Proc. 5th Appeal § 247, Appointment of Receiver.
9 Witkin Cal. Proc. 5th Appeal § 254, (S 254) In General.

§ 917.6. Judgment or order directing performance of two or more acts specified in sections 917.1 to 917.5; compliance with each section

The perfecting of an appeal shall not stay enforcement of the judgment or order in the trial court if the judgment or order appealed from directs the performance of two or more of the acts specified in Sections 917.1 through 917.5, unless the appellant complies with the requirements of each applicable section. *(Added by Stats.1968, c. 385, p. 818, § 2.)*

Research References

Rutter, Cal. Practice Guide: Civil Appeals & Writs Ch. 7-C, C. Stay by Posting Security (Bond or Undertaking).
Rutter, Cal. Practice Guide: Civil Appeals & Writs Ch. 7-C, Outline C.

§ 917.65. Undertaking; condition

The perfecting of an appeal shall not stay enforcement of a right to attach order unless an undertaking is given. The undertaking shall be in the amount specified in the right to attach order as the amount to be secured by the attachment. The undertaking shall be on condition that if the right to attach order is not reversed and the plaintiff recovers judgment in the action in which the right to attach order was issued, the appellant shall pay the amount of the judgment, together with any interest which may have accrued. The liability on the undertaking may be enforced if the judgment is not paid within 30 days after it becomes final. If a surety on the undertaking pays the judgment, either with or without action, the surety is substituted to the rights of the creditor and is entitled to control, enforce, and satisfy the judgment, in all respects as if the surety had recovered the judgment. *(Added by Stats.1983, c. 155, § 22.5, eff. June 30, 1983, operative July 1, 1983.)*

Research References

Rutter, Cal. Practice Guide: Civil Appeals & Writs Ch. 7-C, C. Stay by Posting Security (Bond or Undertaking).
Rutter, Cal. Practice Guide: Civil Appeals & Writs Ch. 7-C, Outline C.
Rutter, Cal. Practice Guide: Enforcing Judgments/Debts Ch. 4-A, A. Attachment.
Rutter, Cal. Practice Guide: Insurance Litigation Ch. 6I-B, B. Particular Surety Bond Coverages.
9 Witkin Cal. Proc. 5th Appeal § 248, Right to Attach Order.
9 Witkin Cal. Proc. 5th Appeal § 254, (S 254) In General.
9 Witkin Cal. Proc. 5th Appeal § 266, (S 266) In General.

§ 917.7. Appeal; stay of proceedings as to judgment or order affecting custody

The perfecting of an appeal shall not stay proceedings as to those provisions of a judgment or order which award, change, or otherwise affect the custody, including the right of visitation, of a minor child in any civil action, in an action filed under the Juvenile Court Law, or in a special proceeding, or the provisions of a judgment or order for the temporary exclusion of a party from a dwelling, as provided in the Family Code. However, the trial court may in its discretion stay execution of these provisions pending review on appeal or for any other period or periods that it may deem appropriate. Further, in the absence of a writ or order of a reviewing court providing otherwise, the provisions of the judgment or order allowing, or eliminating restrictions against, removal of the minor child from the state are stayed by operation of law for a period of seven calendar days from the entry of the judgment or order by a juvenile court in a dependency hearing, or for a period of 30 calendar days from the entry of judgment or order by any other trial court. The periods during which these provisions allowing, or eliminating restrictions against, removal of the minor child from the state are stayed, are subject to further stays as ordered by the trial court or by the juvenile court pursuant to this section. An order directing the return of a child to a sister state or country, including any order effectuating that return, made in a proceeding brought pursuant to the Uniform Child Custody Jurisdiction and Enforcement Act (Part 3 (commencing with Section 3400) of Division 8 of the Family Code), the Parental Kidnapping Prevention Act of 1980 (28 U.S.C. Sec. 1738A), or the Hague Convention on the Civil Aspects of International Child Abduction (implemented pursuant to the International Child Abduction Remedies Act (42 U.S.C. Secs. 11601–11610)) is not a judgment or order which awards, changes, or otherwise affects the custody of a minor child within the meaning of this section, and therefore is not subject to the automatic stay provisions of this section. *(Added by Stats.1968, c. 385, p. 818, § 2. Amended by Stats.1971, c. 1210, p. 2328, § 9; Stats.1981, c. 714, p. 2596, § 70; Stats.1992, c. 163 (A.B.2641), § 55, operative Jan. 1, 1994; Stats.1993, c. 219 (A.B.1500), § 69.5; Stats.1999, c. 346 (S.B.518), § 1; Stats.2001, c. 48 (S.B.1151), § 1.)*

Law Revision Commission Comments

Section 917.7 is amended to substitute a reference to the Family Code for the reference to former Civil Code Section 4359. A general reference to "a dwelling" has been substituted for the former reference to specific dwellings. This allows the Family Code provisions relating to exclusion from a dwelling to control the details of this type of order. This is not a substantive change, but prevents a conflict from arising in the future where one statute is amended without making a similar revision to the other. For provisions of the Family Code relating to the exclusion of a party from a dwelling, see, e.g., Fam. Code §§ 6321 (ex parte order), 6340 (order after notice and hearing), 6360 (order included in judgment). [23 Cal.L.Rev.Comm. Reports 1 (1993)].

Research References

Rutter, Cal. Practice Guide: Civil Appeals & Writs Ch. 7-B, B. Automatic Stay.
Rutter, Cal. Practice Guide: Civil Appeals & Writs Ch. 7-D, D. Discretionary Stay by Trial Court.
Rutter, Cal. Practice Guide: Family Law Ch. 7-G, G. Removal of Child from Jurisdiction; Wrongful Taking or Withholding of Child.
9 Witkin Cal. Proc. 5th Appeal § 224, (S 224) Statutory Development.
9 Witkin Cal. Proc. 5th Appeal § 225, (S 225) Discretionary Stay by Trial Judge.
9 Witkin Cal. Proc. 5th Appeal § 226, in General.
9 Witkin Cal. Proc. 5th Appeal § 228, Avoidance of Conflicting Rulings by Courts of Concurrent Jurisdiction.
9 Witkin Cal. Proc. 5th Appeal § 229, (S 229) Modification of Custody Order.
10 Witkin, California Summary 10th Parent and Child § 190, (S 190) Appeal.
10 Witkin, California Summary 10th Parent and Child § 192, Other Federal Acts.
10 Witkin, California Summary 10th Parent and Child § 288, Appeal.
10 Witkin, California Summary 10th Parent and Child § 351, (S 351) in General.
10 Witkin, California Summary 10th Parent and Child § 361, Issuance by Appellate Court.
10 Witkin, California Summary 10th Parent and Child § 374, Appellate Court Proceeding.
14 Witkin, California Summary 10th Wills and Probate § 402, Effect of Appeal.

§ 917.8. Circumstances under which the perfecting of an appeal does not stay proceedings to enforce judgments or orders

The perfecting of an appeal does not stay proceedings, in the absence of an order of the trial court providing otherwise or of a writ of supersedeas, under any of the following circumstances:

(a) If a party to the proceeding has been adjudged guilty of usurping, or intruding into, or unlawfully holding a public office, civil or military, within this state.

(b) If the judgment or order directs a corporation, or any of its officers or agents, to give to a person adjudged to be a director, stockholder, or member of that corporation a reasonable opportunity to inspect or make copies of the books, papers, or documents of the corporation as the trial court finds that the director, stockholder, or member is entitled by law to inspect or copy.

(c) If a judgment or order adjudges a building or place to be a nuisance and, as part of that judgment or order, directs the closing or discontinuance of any specific use of the building or place for any period of time.

(d) If a judgment or order, including, but not limited to, a temporary restraining order or preliminary injunction, grants relief in an action brought by a governmental agency under the provisions of Article 2 (commencing with Section 11225) of Chapter 3 of Title 1 of Part 4 of the Penal Code or Article 3 (commencing with Section 11570) of Chapter 10 of Division 10 of the Health and Safety Code. *(Added by Stats.1968, c. 385, p. 818, § 2. Amended by Stats.2003, c. 31 (A.B.1639), § 1.)*

Research References

Rutter, Cal. Practice Guide: Civil Appeals & Writs Ch. 7-C, C. Stay by Posting Security (Bond or Undertaking).
Rutter, Cal. Practice Guide: Civil Appeals & Writs Ch. 7-D, D. Discretionary Stay by Trial Court.
Miller and Starr California Real Estate § 22:28, Actions by Public Entities.
14 NO. 4 Miller & Starr, California Real Estate Newsalert 11, Landowners' Liability.
9 Witkin Cal. Proc. 5th Appeal § 273, Current Statute.
9 Witkin Cal. Proc. 5th Appeal § 277, (S 277) Other Types Not Stayed.
9 Witkin Cal. Proc. 5th Appeal § 292, (S 292) Writ Would Defeat Statutory Purpose.
8 Witkin Cal. Proc. 5th Extraordinary Writs § 219, Stay Pending Appeal.

§ 917.9. Cases not provided for in §§ 917.1 to 917.8; enforcement of judgment or order notwithstanding perfection of appeal; undertaking

(a) The perfecting of an appeal shall not stay enforcement of the judgment or order in cases not provided for in Sections 917.1 to 917.8, inclusive, if the trial court, in its discretion, requires an undertaking and the undertaking is not given, in any of the following cases:

(1) Appellant was found to possess money or other property belonging to respondent.

(2) Appellant is required to perform an act for respondent's benefit pursuant to judgment or order under appeal.

(3) The judgment against appellant is solely for costs awarded to the respondent by the trial court pursuant to Chapter 6 (commencing with Section 1021) of Title 14.

(b) The undertaking shall be in a sum fixed by the court and shall be in an amount sufficient to cover all damages which the respondent may sustain by reason of the stay in the enforcement of the judgment or order.

(c) The undertaking shall be in the sum fixed by the court. The undertaking shall be conditioned upon the performance of the judgment or order appealed from or payment of the sums required by the judgment or order appealed from, if the judgment or order is affirmed or the appeal is withdrawn or dismissed, and it shall provide that if the judgment or order appealed from or any part of it is affirmed, or the appeal is withdrawn or dismissed, the appellant will pay all damages which the respondent may sustain by reason of the stay in the enforcement of the judgment.

(d) For the purpose of this section, "damages" means either of the following:

(1) Reasonable compensation for the loss of use of the money or property.

(2) Payment of the amounts specified in paragraph (3) of subdivision (a). *(Added by Stats.1968, c. 385, p. 819, § 2. Amended by Stats.1972, c. 546, p. 937, § 4; Stats.1982, c. 517, p. 2355, § 158; Stats.1993, c. 456 (A.B.58), § 14; Stats.1994, c. 493 (A.B.651), § 3, eff. Sept. 12, 1994.)*

Law Revision Commission Comments

Section 917.9 is amended to delete a provision duplicated in the Bond and Undertaking Law. See Section 996.470 (limitation on liability of surety). The other changes in Section 917.9 are technical. [16 Cal.L.Rev. Comm. Reports 501 (1982)].

Research References

Rutter, Cal. Practice Guide: Civil Appeals & Writs Ch. 7-B, B. Automatic Stay.
Rutter, Cal. Practice Guide: Civil Appeals & Writs Ch. 7-C, C. Stay by Posting Security (Bond or Undertaking).
Rutter, Cal. Practice Guide: Civil Appeals & Writs Ch. 7-B, Outline B.
Rutter, Cal. Practice Guide: Civil Appeals & Writs Ch. 7-C, Outline C.
Rutter, Cal. Practice Guide: Enforcing Judgments/Debts Ch. 6D-6, Debtor's Recourse Against Execution Levy.
9 Witkin Cal. Proc. 5th Appeal § 230, Money or Payment of Money.
9 Witkin Cal. Proc. 5th Appeal § 272, Background and Former Law.
9 Witkin Cal. Proc. 5th Appeal § 273, Current Statute.
9 Witkin Cal. Proc. 5th Appeal § 289, Cost of Bond is Prohibitive.
6 Witkin Cal. Proc. 5th Provisional Remedies § 219, (S 219) Defendant's Appeal With Undertaking.
14 Witkin, California Summary 10th Wills and Probate § 402, Effect of Appeal.

§ 918. Power of court to stay enforcement of any judgment or order; time limitation; effect of appeal

(a) Subject to subdivision (b), the trial court may stay the enforcement of any judgment or order.

(b) If the enforcement of the judgment or order would be stayed on appeal only by the giving of an undertaking, a trial court shall not have power, without the consent of the adverse party, to stay the enforcement thereof pursuant to this section for a period which extends for more than 10 days beyond the last date on which a notice of appeal could be filed.

(c) This section applies whether or not an appeal will be taken from the judgment or order and whether or not a notice of appeal has been filed. *(Added by Stats.1968, c. 385, p. 819, § 2. Amended by Stats.1982, c. 497, p. 2165, § 65, operative July 1, 1983.)*

Law Revision Commission Comments

Subdivision (c) is added to Section 918 to make clear that, subject to the limitations specified in Section 918, the court is authorized to stay the enforcement of a judgment whether or not an appeal has been or will be taken. In this respect, Section 918 supersedes former Section 681a, which granted the court authority similar to that granted by Section 918 but prescribed limitations that were inconsistent with later enacted Section 918. As to the effect of a stay of enforcement under Section 918 on enforcement liens, see Section 697.040(b) and Section 697.050 (15 Cal.L.Rev.Comm. Reports 2001).

Research References

Rutter, Cal. Practice Guide: Civil Appeals & Writs Ch. 7-A, A. Overview.
Rutter, Cal. Practice Guide: Civil Appeals & Writs Ch. 7-C, C. Stay by Posting Security (Bond or Undertaking).
Rutter, Cal. Practice Guide: Civil Trials & Evidence Ch. 4-B, B. Preliminary Matters Discussed in Final Status Conference or In-Chambers Conference.
Rutter, Cal. Practice Guide: Civil Trials & Evidence Ch. 18-A, A. Motion for Judgment Notwithstanding the Verdict ("JNOV").

Civ. Pro.

Rutter, Cal. Practice Guide: Civil Trials & Evidence Ch. 18-C, C. Other Post-Trial Motions.
Rutter, Cal. Practice Guide: Enforcing Judgments/Debts Ch. 6D-6, Debtor's Recourse Against Execution Levy.
Rutter, Cal. Practice Guide: Enforcing Judgments/Debts Ch. 6A-12, Staying Enforcement of Judgment.
Miller and Starr California Real Estate § 32:67, Stay of Execution Sale.
9 Witkin Cal. Proc. 5th Appeal § 223, (S 223) Stay by Trial Judge.
8 Witkin Cal. Proc. 5th Enforcement of Judgment § 67, (S 67) Duration and Extinguishment.
8 Witkin Cal. Proc. 5th Enforcement of Judgment § 162, (S 162) Stay of Execution.

§ 918.5. Discretion to stay enforcement of judgment or order; considerations

(a) The trial court may, in its discretion, stay the enforcement of a judgment or order if the judgment debtor has another action pending on a disputed claim against the judgment creditor.

(b) In exercising its discretion under this section, the court shall consider all of the following:

(1) The likelihood of the judgment debtor prevailing in the other action.

(2) The amount of the judgment of the judgment creditor as compared to the amount of the probable recovery of the judgment debtor in the action on the disputed claim.

(3) The financial ability of the judgment creditor to satisfy the judgment if a judgment is rendered against the judgment creditor in the action on the disputed claim. *(Added by Stats.1982, c. 497, p. 2165, § 66, operative July 1, 1983.)*

Law Revision Commission Comments

Section 918.5 codifies a judicially developed rule. See Erlich v. Superior Court, 63 Cal.2d 551, 407 P.2d 649, 47 Cal.Rptr. 473 (1965); Airfloor Company of California, Inc. v. The Regents of the University of California, 97 Cal.App.3d 739 (1979). The rationale for the rule is based on equitable principles that not to stay enforcement of the judgment unfairly deprives the judgment debtor not only of the right to offset but also—with an impecunious creditor—of any right to recover at all (15 Cal.L.Rev.Comm. Reports 2001).

Research References

Rutter, Cal. Practice Guide: Civil Appeals & Writs Ch. 7-C, C. Stay by Posting Security (Bond or Undertaking).
Rutter, Cal. Practice Guide: Civil Appeals & Writs Ch. 7-C, Outline C.
Rutter, Cal. Practice Guide: Civil Trials & Evidence Ch. 18-C, C. Other Post-Trial Motions.
Rutter, Cal. Practice Guide: Enforcing Judgments/Debts Ch. 6D-6, Debtor's Recourse Against Execution Levy.
Miller and Starr California Real Estate § 32:67, Stay of Execution Sale.
9 Witkin Cal. Proc. 5th Appeal § 223, (S 223) Stay by Trial Judge.
8 Witkin Cal. Proc. 5th Enforcement of Judgment § 162, (S 162) Stay of Execution.

§ 919. Discretion of court to limit or dispense with required security when appellant executor, administrator, trustee, guardian, etc.

The trial court may, in its discretion, dispense with or limit the security required by any section in this chapter, when the appellant is an executor, administrator, trustee, guardian, conservator or other person acting in another's right. *(Added by Stats.1968, c. 385, p. 819, § 2.)*

Research References

Rutter, Cal. Practice Guide: Civil Appeals & Writs Ch. 7-C, C. Stay by Posting Security (Bond or Undertaking).
Rutter, Cal. Practice Guide: Insurance Litigation Ch. 6I-B, B. Particular Surety Bond Coverages.

9 Witkin Cal. Proc. 5th Appeal § 274, Representatives.

§ 921. Continuance of attachment; undertaking; amount

An appeal by a party who has levied an attachment shall not continue in force the attachment, unless an undertaking is executed and filed on the part of the appellant that the appellant will pay all costs and damages which the respondent may sustain by reason of the attachment, in case the order of the court below is sustained in favor of the respondent; and unless, within five days after written notice of the entry of the order appealed from, the appeal is perfected. The amount of the undertaking on appeal required by this section shall be such amount as is fixed by the trial court on motion of the respondent as provided in Section 489.410 and if no such order has been made, the undertaking shall be in double the amount of the debt claimed by the appellant. If the respondent is not satisfied with the undertaking in double the amount of the debt or the amount fixed by order under Section 489.410, the trial court upon motion of the respondent made within 60 days after perfecting the appeal may order an increase in the amount of the undertaking in such amount as is justified by the detriment reasonably to be anticipated by continuing the attachment. If such an order is made, the attachment shall be discharged and the property released therefrom, unless the undertaking is executed and filed within 10 days after the order is made. *(Added by Stats.1968, c. 385, p. 819, § 2. Amended by Stats.1974, c. 1516, p. 3382, § 20, operative Jan. 1, 1977; Stats.1982, c. 517, p. 2356, § 160.)*

Law Revision Commission Comments

Section 921 is amended for consistency with the Bond and Undertaking Law. See Section 995.910 (objections to undertakings). The other changes in Section 921 are technical. [16 Cal.L.Rev.Comm. Reports 501 (1982)].

Research References

Rutter, Cal. Practice Guide: Civil Appeals & Writs Ch. 3-B, B. Filing Deadlines.
Rutter, Cal. Practice Guide: Civil Appeals & Writs Ch. 7-A, A. Overview.
Rutter, Cal. Practice Guide: Civil Appeals & Writs Ch. 7-C, C. Stay by Posting Security (Bond or Undertaking).
Rutter, Cal. Practice Guide: Civil Appeals & Writs Ch. 7-C, Outline C.
Rutter, Cal. Practice Guide: Enforcing Judgments/Debts Ch. 4-A, A. Attachment.
Miller and Starr California Real Estate § 32:35, Noticed Hearing Procedure.
9 Witkin Cal. Proc. 5th Appeal § 582, (S 582) Special Statutes.
6 Witkin Cal. Proc. 5th Provisional Remedies § 91, (S 91) Undertakings.
6 Witkin Cal. Proc. 5th Provisional Remedies § 215, (S 215) Final Judgment for Defendant.
6 Witkin Cal. Proc. 5th Provisional Remedies § 216, (S 216) Plaintiff's Appeal Without Undertaking.
6 Witkin Cal. Proc. 5th Provisional Remedies § 217, (S 217) Plaintiff's Motion Without Undertaking.
6 Witkin Cal. Proc. 5th Provisional Remedies § 218, (S 218) No Appeal by Defendant.
6 Witkin Cal. Proc. 5th Provisional Remedies § 225, Amount of Recovery.

§ 922. Undertaking; objection; determination of insufficiency; failure to make sufficient; effect

If an undertaking required or permitted by this title is objected to by the respondent and the court determines the undertaking is insufficient and a sufficient undertaking is not given within the time provided by statute, enforcement of the judgment or order appealed from is no longer stayed and property which has been levied upon under execution issued upon such judgment shall not be released from levy. *(Added by Stats.1968, c. 385, p. 820, § 2. Amended by Stats.1982, c. 517, p. 2356, § 161.)*

Law Revision Commission Comments

Section 922 is amended to delete provisions duplicated in the Bond and Undertaking Law. See Sections 995.310 (sureties on undertaking),

995.910–995.960 (objections to undertakings), 996.470 (limitation on liability of surety). [16 Cal.L.Rev.Comm. Reports 501 (1982)].

Research References

Rutter, Cal. Practice Guide: Civil Appeals & Writs Ch. 7-C, C. Stay by Posting Security (Bond or Undertaking).
Rutter, Cal. Practice Guide: Civil Appeals & Writs Ch. 7-E, E. Stay by Writ of Supersedeas.
9 Witkin Cal. Proc. 5th Appeal § 222, (S 222) Effect of Stay.
9 Witkin Cal. Proc. 5th Appeal § 252, (S 252) Provisional Stay.
9 Witkin Cal. Proc. 5th Appeal § 258, (S 258) Execution is Not Stayed.
9 Witkin Cal. Proc. 5th Appeal § 264, (S 264) Failure to Give Sufficient Undertaking.

§ 923. Power of reviewing court to stay proceedings, issue writ of supersedeas, suspend or modify injunction, etc., not limited by chapter provisions

The provisions of this chapter shall not limit the power of a reviewing court or of a judge thereof to stay proceedings during the pendency of an appeal or to issue a writ of supersedeas or to suspend or modify an injunction during the pendency of an appeal or to make any order appropriate to preserve the status quo, the effectiveness of the judgment subsequently to be entered, or otherwise in aid of its jurisdiction. *(Added by Stats.1968, c. 385, p. 820, § 2.)*

Research References

Rutter, Cal. Practice Guide: Civil Appeals & Writs Ch. 2-D, D. Standing to Appeal.
Rutter, Cal. Practice Guide: Civil Appeals & Writs Ch. 7-A, A. Overview.
Rutter, Cal. Practice Guide: Civil Appeals & Writs Ch. 7-B, B. Automatic Stay.
Rutter, Cal. Practice Guide: Civil Appeals & Writs Ch. 7-D, D. Discretionary Stay by Trial Court.
Rutter, Cal. Practice Guide: Civil Appeals & Writs Ch. 7-E, E. Stay by Writ of Supersedeas.
Rutter, Cal. Practice Guide: Enforcing Judgments/Debts Ch. 6E-4, Opposing Claim of Exemption.
3 Witkin Cal. Proc. 5th Actions § 406, (S 406) Deed of Trust as Alternative to Undertaking.
9 Witkin Cal. Proc. 5th Appeal § 279, Nature and Purpose of Writ.
9 Witkin Cal. Proc. 5th Appeal § 288, Where Judgment is Not Stayed by Appeal or Undertaking.
9 Witkin Cal. Proc. 5th Appeal § 289, Cost of Bond is Prohibitive.
9 Witkin Cal. Proc. 5th Appeal § 299, Current Law: Writ Authorized.
10 Witkin, California Summary 10th Parent and Child § 704, Miscellaneous Orders.

§ 936.1. Right to counsel; notice of appeal

An appeal from any judgment or order in any civil commitment or other proceeding wherein the appellant would be entitled to the appointment of counsel on appeal if indigent shall be initiated by the filing of a notice of appeal in conformity with the requirements of Section 1240.1 of the Penal Code. *(Added by Stats.1978, c. 1385, § 1.)*

Title 14

OF MISCELLANEOUS PROVISIONS

CHAPTER 1. PROCEEDINGS AGAINST JOINT DEBTORS

§ 989. Unserved joint debtors; summons to show cause why they should not be bound by judgment

When a judgment is recovered against one or more of several persons, jointly indebted upon an obligation, by proceeding as provided in Section 410.70, those who were not originally served with the summons, and did not appear in the action, may be summoned to appear before the court in which such judgment is entered to show cause why they should not be bound by the judgment, in the same manner as though they had been originally served with the summons. *(Enacted in 1872. Amended by Stats.1933, c. 744, p. 1896, § 170; Stats.1935, c. 722, p. 1965, § 25; Stats.1969, c. 1611, p. 3396, § 24, operative July 1, 1970.)*

Research References

Rutter, Cal. Practice Guide: Civ. Pro. Before Trial Ch. 4-C, C. Content of Summons.
Rutter, Cal. Practice Guide: Civil Trials & Evidence Ch. 18-C, C. Other Post-Trial Motions.
Rutter, Cal. Practice Guide: Enforcing Judgments/Debts Ch. 6D-2, Writ of Execution.
Rutter, Cal. Practice Guide: Enforcing Judgments/Debts Ch. 6G-12, Enforcement Against Joint Debtors.
3 Witkin Cal. Proc. 5th Actions § 990, (S 990) Proceedings Against Unserved Joint Debtors.
8 Witkin Cal. Proc. 5th Enforcement of Judgment § 2, (S 2) in General.
8 Witkin Cal. Proc. 5th Enforcement of Judgment § 398, (S 398) Nature of Remedy.
8 Witkin Cal. Proc. 5th Enforcement of Judgment § 399, (S 399) Affidavit and Summons.
8 Witkin Cal. Proc. 5th Enforcement of Judgment § 401, (S 401) Amendment of Complaint.
8 Witkin Cal. Proc. 5th Enforcement of Judgment § 436, Action on Judgment.
7 Witkin Cal. Proc. 5th Judgment § 39, (S 39) Defendants: Contract Actions.
2 Witkin Cal. Proc. 5th Jurisdiction § 184, (S 184) Jurisdiction Over Joint Debtors.
4 Witkin Cal. Proc. 5th Pleading § 494, Effect of Failure to Amend.
1 Witkin Cal. Summ. 10th Contracts § 112, Action and Judgment.

§ 990. Summons to show cause; issuance; contents; service and return

The summons specified in Section 989 shall be issued by the clerk upon presentation of the affidavit specified in Section 991. The summons must describe the judgment, and require the person summoned to show cause why the person should not be bound by it, and must be served in the same manner, and returnable no later than ninety (90) days after the time specified for the return of the original summons. It is not necessary to file a new complaint. *(Enacted in 1872. Amended by Stats.1935, c. 722, p. 1965, § 26; Stats.1951, c. 1737, p. 4131, § 128, operative*

Jan. 1, 1952; Stats.1957, c. 1195, p. 2484, § 1; Stats.2007, c. 263 (A.B.310), § 10.)

Law Revision Commission Comments

Section 990 is amended to delete unnecessary language authorizing the judge to substitute for the clerk if there is no clerk. See Code Civ. Proc. § 167 (judge may perform any act court clerk may perform); Gov't Code §§ 69840–69848 (duties of clerk of superior court), 71620(b) (executive or administrative officer has authority of clerk of court).

Section 990 is also amended to make stylistic revisions and make the statute gender neutral. [35 Cal.L.Rev.Comm. Reports 219 (2006)].

Research References

Rutter, Cal. Practice Guide: Enforcing Judgments/Debts Ch. 6G-12, Enforcement Against Joint Debtors.

3 Witkin Cal. Proc. 5th Actions § 990, (S 990) Proceedings Against Unserved Joint Debtors.

8 Witkin Cal. Proc. 5th Enforcement of Judgment § 399, (S 399) Affidavit and Summons.

1 Witkin Cal. Summ. 10th Contracts § 112, Action and Judgment.

§ 991. Summons to show cause; affidavit

AFFIDAVIT TO ACCOMPANY SUMMONS. The summons must be accompanied by an affidavit of the plaintiff, his agent, representative, or attorney, that the judgment, or some part thereof, remains unsatisfied, and must specify the amount due thereon. *(Enacted in 1872).*

Research References

Rutter, Cal. Practice Guide: Civ. Pro. Before Trial Ch. 4-C, C. Content of Summons.

Rutter, Cal. Practice Guide: Enforcing Judgments/Debts Ch. 6G-12, Enforcement Against Joint Debtors.

3 Witkin Cal. Proc. 5th Actions § 990, (S 990) Proceedings Against Unserved Joint Debtors.

8 Witkin Cal. Proc. 5th Enforcement of Judgment § 399, (S 399) Affidavit and Summons.

§ 992. Answer

Upon such summons, the defendant may answer within the time specified therein, denying the judgment, or setting up any defense which may have arisen subsequently; or he may deny his liability on the obligation upon which the judgment was recovered, by reason of any defense existing at the commencement of the action. *(Enacted in 1872. Amended by Stats.1907, c. 325, p. 600, § 1.)*

Research References

Rutter, Cal. Practice Guide: Enforcing Judgments/Debts Ch. 6G-12, Enforcement Against Joint Debtors.

8 Witkin Cal. Proc. 5th Enforcement of Judgment § 400, (S 400) Defendant's Answer.

§ 993. Pleading; amendments

If the defendant, in his answer, denies the judgment, or sets up any defense which may have arisen subsequently, the summons, with the affidavit annexed, and the answer, constitute the written allegations in the case; if he denies his liability on the obligation upon which the judgment was recovered, a copy of the original complaint and judgment, the summons, with the affidavit annexed, and the answer, constitute such written allegations, subject to the right of the parties to amend their pleadings as in other cases. *(Enacted in 1872. Amended by Stats.1907, c. 325, p. 600, § 2.)*

Research References

Rutter, Cal. Practice Guide: Enforcing Judgments/Debts Ch. 6G-12, Enforcement Against Joint Debtors.

8 Witkin Cal. Proc. 5th Enforcement of Judgment § 400, (S 400) Defendant's Answer.

8 Witkin Cal. Proc. 5th Enforcement of Judgment § 401, (S 401) Amendment of Complaint.

§ 994. Trial; verdict

ISSUES, HOW TRIED. VERDICT, WHAT TO BE. The issues formed may be tried as in other cases; but when the defendant denies, in his answer, any liability on the obligation upon which the judgment was rendered, if a verdict be found against him, it must be for not exceeding the amount remaining unsatisfied on such original judgment, with interest thereon. *(Enacted in 1872.)*

Research References

Rutter, Cal. Practice Guide: Enforcing Judgments/Debts Ch. 6D-2, Writ of Execution.

Rutter, Cal. Practice Guide: Enforcing Judgments/Debts Ch. 6G-12, Enforcement Against Joint Debtors.

8 Witkin Cal. Proc. 5th Enforcement of Judgment § 400, (S 400) Defendant's Answer.

8 Witkin Cal. Proc. 5th Enforcement of Judgment § 402, (S 402) Trial and Determination.

CHAPTER 2. BONDS AND UNDERTAKINGS

ARTICLE 1. PRELIMINARY PROVISIONS AND DEFINITIONS

§ 995.010.   Short title

This chapter shall be known and may be cited as the Bond and Undertaking Law. *(Added by Stats.1982, c. 998, p. 3659, § 1.)*

Law Revision Commission Comments

Section 995.010 is similar to comparable provisions in recently enacted California law. See, e.g., Sts. & Hy. Code § 8300 (Public Streets, Highways, and Service Easements Vacation Law). [16 Cal.L.Rev.Comm. Reports 501 (1982)].

Research References

Rutter, Cal. Practice Guide: Civil Appeals & Writs Ch. 7-C, C. Stay by Posting Security (Bond or Undertaking).
Rutter, Cal. Practice Guide: Civ. Pro. Before Trial Ch. 1-A, A. Accepting a New Case.
Rutter, Cal. Practice Guide: Civ. Pro. Before Trial Ch. 9(I)-J, J. Motion to Expunge Lis Pendens.
Rutter, Cal. Practice Guide: Enforcing Judgments/Debts Ch. 4-A, A. Attachment.
Rutter, Cal. Practice Guide: Enforcing Judgments/Debts Ch. 6H-7, Statutory Requirements for Undertakings.
Rutter, Cal. Practice Guide: Insurance Litigation Ch. 6I-A, A. Introduction.
Rutter, Cal. Practice Guide: Insurance Litigation Ch. 6I-B, B. Particular Surety Bond Coverages.
Rutter, Cal. Practice Guide: Insurance Litigation Ch. 6I-D, D. Surety's Defenses to Payment of Bond.
Miller and Starr California Real Estate § 28:66, Bond to Release the Lien.
Miller and Starr California Real Estate § 28:90, Release of the Stop Payment Notice.
Miller and Starr California Real Estate § 28:93, Suretyship Terminology and Definitions.
Miller and Starr California Real Estate § 11:154, Expungement of a Lis Pendens--Procedure and Grounds for Expungement.
3 Witkin Cal. Proc. 5th Actions § 364, (S 364) Security.
3 Witkin Cal. Proc. 5th Actions § 369, Hearing, Determination, and Security.
3 Witkin Cal. Proc. 5th Actions § 406, (S 406) Deed of Trust as Alternative to Undertaking.
3 Witkin Cal. Proc. 5th Actions § 420, Security for Costs.
8 Witkin Cal. Proc. 5th Enforcement of Judgment § 366, (S 366) General Rules Governing Undertakings.
6 Witkin Cal. Proc. 5th Provisional Remedies § 8, Enactment of Revised Statute.
6 Witkin Cal. Proc. 5th Provisional Remedies § 9, Scope of Bond and Undertaking Law.
6 Witkin Cal. Proc. 5th Provisional Remedies § 91, (S 91) Undertakings.
2 Witkin, California Summary 10th Insurance § 133, in General.
14 Witkin, California Summary 10th Wills and Probate § 448, in General.
14 Witkin, California Summary 10th Wills and Probate § 983, Requirement.

§ 995.020.　Application of chapter

(a) The provisions of this chapter apply to a bond or undertaking executed, filed, posted, furnished, or otherwise given as security pursuant to any statute of this state, except to the extent the statute prescribes a different rule or is inconsistent.

(b) The provisions of this chapter apply to a bond or undertaking given at any of the following times:

(1) On or after January 1, 1983.

(2) Before January 1, 1983, to the extent another surety is substituted for the original surety on or after January 1, 1983, or to the extent the principal gives a new, additional, or supplemental bond or undertaking on or after January 1, 1983.

Except to the extent provided in this section, the law governing a bond or undertaking given before January 1, 1983, is the law applicable to the bond or undertaking immediately before January 1, 1983, pursuant to Section 414 of Chapter 517 of the Statutes of 1982.

(c) The provisions of this chapter do not apply to a bail bond or an undertaking of bail. *(Added by Stats.1982, c. 998, p. 3660, § 1. Amended by Stats.1983, c. 18, p. 3660, § 18.2, eff. April 21, 1983.)*

Law Revision Commission Comments

Section 995.020 supersedes portions of former Sections 1041 and 1054a through 1059, which applied to statutory bonds and undertakings generally. The provisions of this chapter governing statutory bonds and undertaking are not exclusive, but are supplemented by the general provisions governing all bonds and undertakings, both common-law and statutory. See, e.g., Civil Code §§ 2787–2855 (suretyship). [16 Cal. L.Rev.Comm. Reports 501 (1982)].

Research References

Rutter, Cal. Practice Guide: Enforcing Judgments/Debts Ch. 4-A, A. Attachment.
Rutter, Cal. Practice Guide: Enforcing Judgments/Debts Ch. 6H-7, Statutory Requirements for Undertakings.
Miller and Starr California Real Estate § 28:93, Suretyship Terminology and Definitions.
3 Witkin Cal. Proc. 5th Actions § 406, (S 406) Deed of Trust as Alternative to Undertaking.
6 Witkin Cal. Proc. 5th Provisional Remedies § 9, Scope of Bond and Undertaking Law.

§ 995.030.　Service of notice, etc.

If service of a notice, paper, or other document is required under this chapter, service shall be made in the same manner as service of process in civil actions generally. *(Added by Stats. 1982, c. 998, p. 3660, § 1.)*

Law Revision Commission Comments

Section 995.030 is new. [16 Cal.L.Rev.Comm. Reports 501 (1982)].

Research References

6 Witkin Cal. Proc. 5th Provisional Remedies § 15, Practice and Procedure.

§ 995.040.　Affidavit standards

An affidavit made under this chapter shall conform to the standards prescribed for an affidavit made pursuant to Section 437c. *(Added by Stats.1982, c. 998, p. 3660, § 1.)*

Law Revision Commission Comments

Section 995.040 is drawn from the last sentences of former Sections 1058a (bonds and undertakings) and 535 (injunctions). [16 Cal.L.Rev. Comm. Reports 501 (1982)].

Research References

6 Witkin Cal. Proc. 5th Provisional Remedies § 15, Practice and Procedure.

§ 995.050.　Extension of time

The times provided in this chapter, or in any other statute relating to a bond given in an action or proceeding, may be extended pursuant to Sections 1054 and 1054.1. *(Added by Stats.1982, c. 998, p. 3660, § 1.)*

Law Revision Commission Comments

Section 995.050 continues the substance of provisions formerly found in Sections 1054 and 1054.1 (extensions of time). [16 Cal.L.Rev.Comm. Reports 501 (1982)].

Research References

Rutter, Cal. Practice Guide: Civil Appeals & Writs Ch. 7-C, C. Stay by Posting Security (Bond or Undertaking).
6 Witkin Cal. Proc. 5th Provisional Remedies § 15, Practice and Procedure.

§ 995.110.　Definitions; construction

Unless the provision or context otherwise requires, the definitions in this article govern the construction of this chapter. *(Added by Stats.1982, c. 998, p. 3660, § 1.)*

Law Revision Commission Comments

Section 995.110 makes clear that this article provides definitions applicable only to this chapter. Particular definitions may be applicable to other statutes by their terms or by the context in which they are used. See, e.g., Section 995.120 ("admitted surety insurer" defined). For other definitions and rules of construction applicable to this chapter, see Sections 10–17. [16 Cal.L.Rev.Comm. Reports 501 (1982)].

Research References

6 Witkin Cal. Proc. 5th Provisional Remedies § 11, Definitions of Bond and Undertaking.
6 Witkin Cal. Proc. 5th Provisional Remedies § 12, Other Definitions.

§ 995.120. Admitted surety insurer

(a) "Admitted surety insurer" means a corporate insurer or a reciprocal or interinsurance exchange to which the Insurance Commissioner has issued a certificate of authority to transact surety insurance in this state, as defined in Section 105 of the Insurance Code.

(b) For the purpose of application of this chapter to a bond given pursuant to any statute of this state, the phrases "admitted surety insurer," "authorized surety company," "bonding company," "corporate surety," and comparable phrases used in the statute mean "admitted surety insurer" as defined in this section. *(Added by Stats.1982, c. 998, p. 3660, § 1.)*

Law Revision Commission Comments

Section 995.120 is drawn from the first paragraph of former Section 1056 (bonds and undertakings) and from former Insurance Code Section 1300.5 (reciprocal or interinsurance exchange). [16 Cal.L.Rev.Comm. Reports 501 (1982)].

Research References

Rutter, Cal. Practice Guide: Civil Appeals & Writs Ch. 7-C, C. Stay by Posting Security (Bond or Undertaking).
Rutter, Cal. Practice Guide: Insurance Litigation Ch. 6I-A, A. Introduction.
Miller and Starr California Real Estate § 27:4, Exceptions to Licensing Requirements.
Miller and Starr California Real Estate § 28:74, Duty of Lender to Withhold Funds; Effect of a Bond.
Miller and Starr California Real Estate § 28:81, Release, Bond and Waiver of Stop Payment Notice.
Miller and Starr California Real Estate § 28:93, Suretyship Terminology and Definitions.
6 Witkin Cal. Proc. 5th Provisional Remedies § 12, Other Definitions.
6 Witkin Cal. Proc. 5th Provisional Remedies § 91, (S 91) Undertakings.

§ 995.130. Beneficiary

(a) "Beneficiary" means the person for whose benefit a bond is given, whether executed to, in favor of, in the name of, or payable to the person as an obligee.

(b) If a bond is given for the benefit of the State of California or the people of the state, "beneficiary" means the court, officer, or other person required to determine the sufficiency of the sureties or to approve the bond.

(c) For the purpose of application of this chapter to a bond given pursuant to any statute of this state, the terms "beneficiary," "obligee," and comparable terms used in the statute mean "beneficiary" as defined in this section. *(Added by Stats.1982, c. 998, p. 3660, § 1.)*

Law Revision Commission Comments

Subdivision (a) of Section 995.130 is drawn from former Section 489.020 (attachment).
Subdivision (b) is new. For persons entitled to enforce the liability on a bond or undertaking to the state, see Section 995.850 (enforcement by or for benefit of persons interested). [16 Cal.L.Rev.Comm. Reports 501 (1982)].

Research References

Rutter, Cal. Practice Guide: Insurance Litigation Ch. 6I-A, A. Introduction.
Miller and Starr California Real Estate § 28:93, Suretyship Terminology and Definitions.
6 Witkin Cal. Proc. 5th Provisional Remedies § 12, Other Definitions.

§ 995.140. Bond; in an action or proceeding

(a) "Bond" includes both of the following:

(1) A surety, indemnity, fiduciary, or like bond executed by both the principal and sureties.

(2) A surety, indemnity, fiduciary, or like undertaking executed by the sureties alone.

(b) A bond provided for or given "in an action or proceeding" does not include a bond provided for, or given as, a condition of a license or permit. *(Added by Stats.1982, c. 998, p. 3660, § 1.)*

Law Revision Commission Comments

Section 995.140 is new. The only difference between a bond and undertaking is that a bond is executed by principal as well as sureties. See Section 995.190 ("undertaking" defined). The two instruments are interchangeable if given pursuant to statute. See Section 995.210 (bonds and undertakings interchangeable). For drafting purposes, the term "bond" includes "undertaking." [16 Cal.L.Rev.Comm. Reports 501 (1982)].

Research References

Rutter, Cal. Practice Guide: Civil Appeals & Writs Ch. 7-C, C. Stay by Posting Security (Bond or Undertaking).
Rutter, Cal. Practice Guide: Insurance Litigation Ch. 6I-A, A. Introduction.
Miller and Starr California Real Estate § 33:7, Undertakings, Bonds, Receiver's Oath, and Related Claims.
6 Witkin Cal. Proc. 5th Provisional Remedies § 11, Definitions of Bond and Undertaking.

§ 995.150. Court

"Court" means, if a bond is given in an action or proceeding, the court in which the action or proceeding is pending. *(Added by Stats.1982, c. 998, p. 3661, § 1.)*

Law Revision Commission Comments

Section 995.150 is new. A judge at chambers may approve bonds and undertakings. Code Civ.Proc. § 166 (actions that may be taken in chambers). A court commissioner may take and approve bonds and undertakings and determine objections. Code Civ.Proc. § 259 (court commissioners). [16 Cal.L.Rev.Comm. Reports 501 (1982)].

Research References

6 Witkin Cal. Proc. 5th Provisional Remedies § 12, Other Definitions.

§ 995.160. Officer

"Officer" means the sheriff, marshal, clerk of court, judge or magistrate (if there is no clerk), board, commission, department, or other public official or entity to whom the bond is given or with whom a copy of the bond is filed or who is required to determine the sufficiency of the sureties or to approve the bond. *(Added by Stats.1982, c. 998, p. 3661, § 1. Amended by Stats.1996, c. 872 (A.B.3472), § 19.)*

Law Revision Commission Comments

Section 995.160 is drawn from the introductory portion of former Section 1054a (deposit in lieu of undertaking). It applies not only to bonds and undertakings given in actions and proceedings but to other bonds and undertakings given pursuant to statute as well. [16 Cal.L.Rev. Comm. Reports 501 (1982)].

Research References

6 Witkin Cal. Proc. 5th Provisional Remedies § 12, Other Definitions.

§ 995.170. Principal

(a) "Principal" means the person who gives a bond.

(b) For the purpose of application of this chapter to a bond given pursuant to any statute of this state, the terms "obligor," "principal," and comparable terms used in the statute mean "principal" as defined in this section. *(Added by Stats.1982, c. 998, p. 3661, § 1.)*

Law Revision Commission Comments

Section 995.170 is drawn from former Section 489.020(b) (attachment). [16 Cal.L.Rev.Comm. Reports 501 (1982)].

Research References

Rutter, Cal. Practice Guide: Insurance Litigation Ch. 6I-A, A. Introduction.
Miller and Starr California Real Estate § 28:93, Suretyship Terminology and Definitions.
6 Witkin Cal. Proc. 5th Provisional Remedies § 12, Other Definitions.

§ 995.180. Statute

"Statute" includes administrative regulation promulgated pursuant to statute. *(Added by Stats.1982, c. 998, p. 3661, § 1.)*

Law Revision Commission Comments

Section 995.180 is new. [16 Cal.L.Rev.Comm. Reports 501 (1982)].

Research References

6 Witkin Cal. Proc. 5th Provisional Remedies § 12, Other Definitions.

§ 995.185. Surety

(a) "Surety" has the meaning provided in Section 2787 of the Civil Code and includes personal surety and admitted surety insurer.

(b) For the purpose of application of this chapter to a bond given pursuant to any statute of this state, the terms "bail," "guarantor," "bondsman," "surety," and comparable terms used in the statute mean "surety" as defined in this section. *(Added by Stats.1982, c. 998, p. 3661, § 1.)*

Research References

Rutter, Cal. Practice Guide: Civil Appeals & Writs Ch. 7-C, C. Stay by Posting Security (Bond or Undertaking).
Rutter, Cal. Practice Guide: Insurance Litigation Ch. 6I-A, A. Introduction.
Miller and Starr California Real Estate § 28:93, Suretyship Terminology and Definitions.
6 Witkin Cal. Proc. 5th Provisional Remedies § 12, Other Definitions.

§ 995.190. Undertaking

"Undertaking" means a surety, indemnity, fiduciary, or like undertaking executed by the sureties alone. *(Added by Stats. 1982, c. 998, p. 3661, § 1.)*

Law Revision Commission Comments

Section 995.190 is new. The only difference between a bond and undertaking is that an undertaking is executed by the sureties and not the principal. See Section 995.140 ("bond" defined). The two instruments are interchangeable if given pursuant to statute. See Section 995.210 (bonds and undertakings interchangeable). For drafting purposes, "undertaking" is included in the term "bond." [16 Cal.L.Rev.Comm. Reports 501 (1982)].

Research References

Rutter, Cal. Practice Guide: Civil Appeals & Writs Ch. 7-C, C. Stay by Posting Security (Bond or Undertaking).

Rutter, Cal. Practice Guide: Insurance Litigation Ch. 6I-A, A. Introduction.
Miller and Starr California Real Estate § 33:7, Undertakings, Bonds, Receiver's Oath, and Related Claims.
3 Witkin Cal. Proc. 5th Actions § 406, (S 406) Deed of Trust as Alternative to Undertaking.
6 Witkin Cal. Proc. 5th Provisional Remedies § 11, Definitions of Bond and Undertaking.

ARTICLE 2. GENERAL PROVISIONS

Section

§ 995.210. Bond in lieu of undertaking; undertaking in lieu of bond

Unless the provision or context otherwise requires:

(a) If a statute provides for a bond, an undertaking that otherwise satisfies the requirements for the bond may be given in its place with the same effect as if a bond were given, and references in the statute to the bond shall be deemed to be references to the undertaking.

(b) If a statute provides for an undertaking, a bond that otherwise satisfies the requirements for the undertaking may be given in its place with the same effect as if an undertaking were given, and references in the statute to the undertaking shall be deemed to be references to the bond. *(Added by Stats.1982, c. 998, p. 3661, § 1.)*

Validity

This section was held preempted by the federal procedural rule prohibiting unsecured stays in the case of Leuzinger v. County of Lake, N.D.Cal.2008, 253 F.R.D. 469.

Law Revision Commission Comments

Section 995.210 is new. It recognizes that the terms "bond" and "undertaking" are used interchangeably in both the statutes and cases. See, e.g., Associates Capital Services Corp. v. Security Pac. Nat'l Bank, 91 Cal.App.3d 819, 154 Cal.Rptr. 392 (1979); Alexander v. Superior Court, 91 Cal.App. 312, 266 P. 993 (1928); Connors, Cal. Surety & Fidelity Bond Practice § 21.2, p. 308 (Cal.Cont.Ed. Bar 1969); see also Sections 995.140 ("bond" defined) and 995.190 ("undertaking" defined). While a bond is executed by principal as well as sureties, the signature of the principal provides the beneficiary no additional security. See Section 996.460 (judgment of liability). [16 Cal.L.Rev.Comm. Reports 501 (1982)].

Research References

Rutter, Cal. Practice Guide: Civil Appeals & Writs Ch. 7-C, C. Stay by Posting Security (Bond or Undertaking).
Rutter, Cal. Practice Guide: Civ. Pro. Before Trial Ch. 9(II)-A, A. Injunctions.
Rutter, Cal. Practice Guide: Insurance Litigation Ch. 6I-A, A. Introduction.
Miller and Starr California Real Estate § 11:154, Expungement of a Lis Pendens--Procedure and Grounds for Expungement.
Miller and Starr California Real Estate § 25A:24, Remedies; Attorney's Fees.
6 Witkin Cal. Proc. 5th Provisional Remedies § 9, Scope of Bond and Undertaking Law.

6 Witkin Cal. Proc. 5th Provisional Remedies § 11, Definitions of Bond and Undertaking.

§ 995.220. Bond in action or proceeding; public entities and officers not required to give

Notwithstanding any other statute, if a statute provides for a bond in an action or proceeding, including but not limited to a bond for issuance of a restraining order or injunction, appointment of a receiver, or stay of enforcement of a judgment on appeal, the following public entities and officers are not required to give the bond and shall have the same rights, remedies, and benefits as if the bond were given:

(a) The State of California or the people of the state, a state agency, department, division, commission, board, or other entity of the state, or a state officer in an official capacity or on behalf of the state.

(b) A county, city, or district, or public authority, public agency, or other political subdivision in the state, or an officer of the local public entity in an official capacity or on behalf of the local public entity.

(c) The United States or an instrumentality or agency of the United States, or a federal officer in an official capacity or on behalf of the United States or instrumentality or agency. *(Added by Stats.1982, c. 998, p. 3661, § 1.)*

Validity

This section was held preempted by the federal procedural rule prohibiting unsecured stays in the case of Leuzinger v. County of Lake, N.D.Cal.2008, 253 F.R.D. 469.

Law Revision Commission Comments

Section 995.220 continues the substance of former Section 1058 (bonds and undertakings). [16 Cal.L.Rev.Comm. Reports 501 (1982)].

Research References

Rutter, Cal. Practice Guide: Civil Appeals & Writs Ch. 7-C, C. Stay by Posting Security (Bond or Undertaking).
Rutter, Cal. Practice Guide: Enforcing Judgments/Debts Ch. 6D-6, Debtor's Recourse Against Execution Levy.
Rutter, Cal. Practice Guide: Insurance Litigation Ch. 6I-B, B. Particular Surety Bond Coverages.
Miller and Starr California Real Estate § 33:7, Undertakings, Bonds, Receiver's Oath, and Related Claims.
9 Witkin Cal. Proc. 5th Appeal § 275, Governmental Officers.
6 Witkin Cal. Proc. 5th Provisional Remedies § 13, Reduction, Waiver, or Exemption.
6 Witkin Cal. Proc. 5th Provisional Remedies § 383, (S 383) Exemptions.

§ 995.230. Bond in action or proceeding; consent to lesser amount; waiver

The beneficiary of a bond given in an action or proceeding may in writing consent to the bond in an amount less than the amount required by statute or may waive the bond. *(Added by Stats.1982, c. 998, p. 3662, § 1.)*

Law Revision Commission Comments

Section 995.230 is drawn from a number of provisions of former law. See, e.g., former Sections 489.030 (attachment) and 920 (appeals); Section 1255.250 (eminent domain). [16 Cal.L.Rev.Comm. Reports 501 (1982)].

Research References

Rutter, Cal. Practice Guide: Civil Appeals & Writs Ch. 7-C, C. Stay by Posting Security (Bond or Undertaking).
9 Witkin Cal. Proc. 5th Appeal § 253, (S 253) Waiver or Reduction of Undertaking.

6 Witkin Cal. Proc. 5th Provisional Remedies § 13, Reduction, Waiver, or Exemption.

§ 995.240. Discretion of court; principal indigent or unable to secure sufficient sureties

The court may, in its discretion, waive a provision for a bond in an action or proceeding and make such orders as may be appropriate as if the bond were given, if the court determines that the principal is unable to give the bond because the principal is indigent and is unable to obtain sufficient sureties, whether personal or admitted surety insurers. In exercising its discretion the court shall take into consideration all factors it deems relevant, including but not limited to the character of the action or proceeding, the nature of the beneficiary, whether public or private, and the potential harm to the beneficiary if the provision for the bond is waived. *(Added by Stats.1982, c. 998, p. 3662, § 1.)*

Law Revision Commission Comments

Section 995.240 is drawn from former subdivision (e) of Section 515.020 (claim and delivery). It codifies the common law authority of the courts. See, e.g., Conover v. Hall, 11 Cal.3d 842, 523 P.2d 682, 114 Cal.Rptr. 642 (1974) (waiver of injunction bond because of indigency). [16 Cal.L.Rev. Comm. Reports 501 (1982)].

Research References

Rutter, Cal. Practice Guide: Civil Appeals & Writs Ch. 7-C, C. Stay by Posting Security (Bond or Undertaking).
Rutter, Cal. Practice Guide: Civ. Pro. Before Trial Ch. 9(II)-A, A. Injunctions.
California Practice Guide: Employment Litigation Ch. 11-J, J. Enforcing California Laws Regulating Employee Compensation.
Miller and Starr California Real Estate § 25A:24, Remedies; Attorney's Fees.
3 Witkin Cal. Proc. 5th Actions § 406, (S 406) Deed of Trust as Alternative to Undertaking.
3 Witkin Cal. Proc. 5th Actions § 420, Security for Costs.
6 Witkin Cal. Proc. 5th Provisional Remedies § 13, Reduction, Waiver, or Exemption.

§ 995.250. Costs to include

If a statute allows costs to a party in an action or proceeding, the costs shall include all of the following:

(a) The premium on a bond reasonably paid by the party pursuant to a statute that provides for the bond in the action or proceeding.

(b) The premium on a bond reasonably paid by the party in connection with the action or proceeding, unless the court determines that the bond was unnecessary. *(Added by Stats. 1982, c. 998, p. 3662, § 1.)*

Law Revision Commission Comments

Section 995.250 continues the substance of former Section 1035 (costs). See also provisions formerly found in Sections 1029.5 and 1029.6 (malpractice actions). Contrast Section 1255.240(b) (premium not recoverable if undertaking required because of issue as to title in eminent domain). Subdivision (a) makes clear that the court does not have discretion to deny the cost of a statutory litigation bond. Subdivision (b) continues the rule that costs may be allowed for nonlitigation bonds if procured in connection with litigation. See Acoustics, Inc. v. Trepte Constr. Co., 14 Cal.App.3d 887, 92 Cal.Rptr. 723 (1971). [16 Cal.L.Rev. Comm. Reports 501 (1982)].

Research References

Rutter, Cal. Practice Guide: Civil Appeals & Writs Ch. 7-C, C. Stay by Posting Security (Bond or Undertaking).
Rutter, Cal. Practice Guide: Civil Appeals & Writs Ch. 14-B, B. Recovery of Appellate Costs and Attorney Fees.
Rutter, Cal. Practice Guide: Enforcing Judgments/Debts Ch. 4-A, A. Attachment.

Rutter, Cal. Practice Guide: Insurance Litigation Ch. 6I-C, C. Surety's Obligations and Rights Upon Default by Principal.

9 Witkin Cal. Proc. 5th Appeal § 971, (S 971) in General.

9 Witkin Cal. Proc. 5th Appeal § 972, (S 972) Test of Necessity.

7 Witkin Cal. Proc. 5th Judgment § 128, (S 128) Provisional Remedies.

6 Witkin Cal. Proc. 5th Provisional Remedies § 15, Practice and Procedure.

§ 995.260. Certified copy of record of bond; evidence

If a bond is recorded pursuant to statute, a certified copy of the record of the bond with all affidavits, acknowledgments, endorsements, and attachments may be admitted in evidence in an action or proceeding with the same effect as the original, without further proof. *(Added by Stats.1982, c. 998, p. 3662, § 1.)*

Law Revision Commission Comments

Section 995.260 is drawn from former Civil Code Section 3227 (mechanics' liens and stop notices)[sic] and the last sentence of Government Code Section 8213 (bond of notary public)[sic]. [16 Cal.L.Rev. Comm. Reports 501 (1982)].

Research References

6 Witkin Cal. Proc. 5th Provisional Remedies § 15, Practice and Procedure.

ARTICLE 3. EXECUTION AND FILING

Section

995.310. Sureties necessary.

995.311. Execution of bond required on public works contract; verification of bond.

995.320. Contents of bond; liability of sureties.

995.330. Form of bond or undertaking.

995.340. Place of filing; preservation.

995.350. Entries in register of action; evidence.

995.360. Withdrawal from files; conditions.

995.370. Service of copy of bond; affidavit.

995.380. Defect in bond; continuance of liability of principals and sureties.

§ 995.310. Sureties necessary

Unless the statute providing for the bond requires execution by an admitted surety insurer, a bond shall be executed by two or more sufficient personal sureties or by one sufficient admitted surety insurer or by any combination of sufficient personal sureties and admitted surety insurers. *(Added by Stats.1982, c. 998, p. 3662, § 1.)*

Law Revision Commission Comments

Section 995.310 continues the requirement of two or more personal sureties or one admitted surety insurer found in numerous provisions of former law. See, e.g., former Section 489.040 (attachment); Sections 515.010–515.020 (claim and delivery) and 567 (receivers); former Sections 571 (receivers, referees, commissioners) and 677 (fraudulent conveyances); Sections 682a (deposit account or safe deposit box), 689 and 710c (third-party claims), 922 (appeals), 1029.5–1029.6 (malpractice actions), 1030 (nonresident plaintiff), and 1210 and 1215 (contempt). Cf. River Trails Ranch Co. v. Superior Court, 111 Cal.App.3d 562, 168 Cal.Rptr. 747 (1980). If the statute providing for the bond or undertaking requires execution by personal sureties, the bond or undertaking may be executed by an admitted surety insurer. See also Section 995.610 (admitted surety insurer in lieu of personal sureties). [16 Cal.L.Rev.Comm. Reports 501 (1982)].

Research References

Rutter, Cal. Practice Guide: Civil Appeals & Writs Ch. 7-C, C. Stay by Posting Security (Bond or Undertaking).

Rutter, Cal. Practice Guide: Civ. Pro. Before Trial Ch. 9(II)-A, A. Injunctions.

Rutter, Cal. Practice Guide: Enforcing Judgments/Debts Ch. 4-A, A. Attachment.

Rutter, Cal. Practice Guide: Enforcing Judgments/Debts Ch. 6H-7, Statutory Requirements for Undertakings.

Rutter, Cal. Practice Guide: Insurance Litigation Ch. 6I-A, A. Introduction.

Rutter, Cal. Practice Guide: Insurance Litigation Ch. 6I-B, B. Particular Surety Bond Coverages.

Miller and Starr California Real Estate § 28:93, Suretyship Terminology and Definitions.

Miller and Starr California Real Estate § 11:154, Expungement of a Lis Pendens--Procedure and Grounds for Expungement.

Miller and Starr California Real Estate § 28:120, Payment and Performance Bonds as to Public Projects.

9 Witkin Cal. Proc. 5th Appeal § 251, (S 251) Form and Filing.

7 Witkin Cal. Proc. 5th Judgment § 220, (S 220) Actions Against Surety on Government Construction Bond.

6 Witkin Cal. Proc. 5th Provisional Remedies § 9, Scope of Bond and Undertaking Law.

6 Witkin Cal. Proc. 5th Provisional Remedies § 16, Content, Form, and Execution.

§ 995.311. Execution of bond required on public works contract; verification of bond

(a) Notwithstanding any other provision of law, any bond required on a public works contract, as defined in Section 1101 of the Public Contract Code, shall be executed by an admitted surety insurer. A public agency approving the bond on a public works contract shall have a duty to verify that the bond is being executed by an admitted surety insurer.

(b) A public agency may fulfill its duty under subdivision (a) by verifying the status of the party executing the bond in one of the following ways:

(1) Printing out information from the website of the Department of Insurance confirming the surety is an admitted surety insurer and attaching it to the bond.

(2) Obtaining a certificate from the county clerk that confirms the surety is an admitted insurer and attaching it to the bond. *(Added by Stats.2001, c. 181 (A.B.263), § 1.)*

Research References

Miller and Starr California Real Estate § 28:93, Suretyship Terminology and Definitions.

6 Witkin Cal. Proc. 5th Provisional Remedies § 16, Content, Form, and Execution.

§ 995.320. Contents of bond; liability of sureties

(a) A bond shall be in writing signed by the sureties under oath and shall include all of the following:

(1) A statement that the sureties are jointly and severally liable on the obligations of the statute providing for the bond.

(2) The address at which the principal and sureties may be served with notices, papers, and other documents under this chapter.

(3) If the amount of the bond is based upon the value of property or an interest in property, a description of the property or interest, and the principal's estimate of the value of the property or interest, or if given pursuant to the estimate of the beneficiary or court, the value as so estimated.

(b) The sureties signing the bond are jointly and severally liable on the obligations of the bond, the provisions of this chapter, and the statute providing for the bond. *(Added by Stats.1982, c. 998, p. 3662, § 1.)*

Law Revision Commission Comments

Subdivision (a)(1) of Section 995.320 is drawn from former Section 1041 (undertaking in civil action). Subdivision (a)(2) is drawn from the second sentence of former Section 1058a (security in civil action). Subdivision (a)(3) continues the substance of former Sections 489.050

(attachment) and 677 and 679 (fraudulent conveyances), portions of Section 710c and former Section 712½ (third-party claims), and former Section 1041 (undertaking in civil action). The bond or undertaking may include a stipulation that the liability of a personal surety is limited to the net worth of the surety. See Section 995.520 (affidavit of surety).

Subdivision (b) continues the substance of portions of former Section 1041 (undertaking in civil action) and former Civil Code Section 2781 (obligations of sureties). [16 Cal.L.Rev.Comm. Reports 501 (1982)].

Research References

Rutter, Cal. Practice Guide: Civil Appeals & Writs Ch. 7-C, C. Stay by Posting Security (Bond or Undertaking).
Miller and Starr California Real Estate § 28:94, General Form of the Bond.
Miller and Starr California Real Estate § 28:95, General Conditions of the Bond.
Miller and Starr California Real Estate § 28:96, Interpretation of the Bond.
Miller and Starr California Real Estate § 28:97, Measure of Surety's Liability.
6 Witkin Cal. Proc. 5th Provisional Remedies § 16, Content, Form, and Execution.
6 Witkin Cal. Proc. 5th Provisional Remedies § 35, (S 35) Joint and Several Liability.

§ 995.330. Form of bond or undertaking

A bond or undertaking given in an action or proceeding may be in the following form:

"(Title of court. Title of cause.)

"Whereas the . . . . . . desires to give (a bond) (an undertaking) for (state what) as provided by (state sections of code requiring bond or undertaking); now, therefore, the undersigned (principal and) (sureties) (surety) hereby (obligate ourselves, jointly and severally) (obligates itself) to (name who) under the statutory obligations, in the amount of . . . . . . dollars." *(Added by Stats.1982, c. 998, p. 3663, § 1.)*

Research References

Rutter, Cal. Practice Guide: Civil Appeals & Writs Ch. 7-C, C. Stay by Posting Security (Bond or Undertaking).
Miller and Starr California Real Estate § 28:94, General Form of the Bond.
9 Witkin Cal. Proc. 5th Appeal § 251, (S 251) Form and Filing.
6 Witkin Cal. Proc. 5th Provisional Remedies § 16, Content, Form, and Execution.
6 Witkin Cal. Proc. 5th Provisional Remedies § 384, (S 384) Amount and Form.

§ 995.340. Place of filing; preservation

If a bond is given in an action or proceeding:

(a) The bond shall be filed with the court unless the statute providing for the bond requires that the bond be given to another person.

(b) If the statute providing for the bond requires that the bond be given to an officer, the officer shall file the bond with the court unless the statute providing for the bond otherwise provides.

(c) A bond filed with the court shall be preserved in the office of the clerk of the court. *(Added by Stats.1982, c. 998, p. 3663, § 1.)*

Law Revision Commission Comments

Subdivision (a) of Section 995.340 is drawn from numerous provisions of former law. See, e.g., Sections 515.010–515.020 (claim and delivery) and former Section 677½ (fraudulent conveyances). Contrast Section 682a (bond transmitted by levying officer to financial institution).

Subdivision (b) is new. Specific statutes may provide different rules. See e.g., Rev. & Tax. Code § 2954 (bond filed with tax collector; proof filed with court).

Subdivision (c) is drawn from former Probate Code Section 2332 (guardian or conservator). [16 Cal.L.Rev.Comm. Reports 501 (1982)].

Research References

Rutter, Cal. Practice Guide: Civil Appeals & Writs Ch. 7-C, C. Stay by Posting Security (Bond or Undertaking).
Rutter, Cal. Practice Guide: Enforcing Judgments/Debts Ch. 4-A, A. Attachment.
6 Witkin Cal. Proc. 5th Provisional Remedies § 18, Filing and Service.

§ 995.350. Entries in register of action; evidence

(a) Upon the filing of a bond with the court in an action or proceeding, the clerk shall enter in the register of actions the following information:

(1) The date and amount of the bond.

(2) The names of the sureties on the bond.

(b) In the event of the loss of the bond, the entries in the register of actions are prima facie evidence of the giving of the bond in the manner required by statute. *(Added by Stats.1982, c. 998, p. 3663, § 1.)*

Law Revision Commission Comments

Section 995.350 continues the substance of the second paragraph of former Section 1057 (bonds and undertakings) and the last two sentences of former Probate Code Section 545 (bonds and undertakings under Probate Code). [16 Cal.L.Rev.Comm. Reports 501 (1982)].

Research References

6 Witkin Cal. Proc. 5th Provisional Remedies § 18, Filing and Service.

§ 995.360. Withdrawal from files; conditions

A bond given in an action or proceeding may be withdrawn from the file and returned to the principal on order of the court only if one of the following conditions is satisfied:

(a) The beneficiary so stipulates.

(b) The bond is no longer in force and effect and the time during which the liability on the bond may be enforced has expired. *(Added by Stats.1982, c. 998, p. 3663, § 1.)*

Law Revision Commission Comments

Section 995.360 is drawn from Court Rules 242(c) (Superior Court) and 530(c) (Municipal Court). For the term of the bond or undertaking, see Section 995.430. [16 Cal.L.Rev.Comm. Reports 501 (1982)].

Research References

6 Witkin Cal. Proc. 5th Provisional Remedies § 18, Filing and Service.
6 Witkin Cal. Proc. 5th Provisional Remedies § 33, Release or Substitution of Surety.
6 Witkin Cal. Proc. 5th Provisional Remedies § 45, Enforcement Against Deposit.

§ 995.370. Service of copy of bond; affidavit

At the time a bond is given, the principal shall serve a copy of the bond on the beneficiary. An affidavit of service shall be given and filed with the bond. *(Added by Stats.1982, c. 998, p. 3663, § 1.)*

Law Revision Commission Comments

Section 995.370 is drawn from numerous provisions formerly found in statutes relating to bonds and undertakings. See, e.g., Sections 489.230 (notice of attachment undertaking) and 515.020 (copy of claim and delivery undertaking for redelivery); former Section 677½ (fraudulent conveyances). Contrast Section 514.020 (copy of claim and delivery undertaking delivered or served by levying officer); Civil Code Section 1861.18 (copy of innkeeper's lien undertaking delivered or served by levying officer). [16 Cal.L.Rev.Comm. Reports 501 (1982)].

Research References

Rutter, Cal. Practice Guide: Civil Appeals & Writs Ch. 7-C, C. Stay by Posting Security (Bond or Undertaking).
Rutter, Cal. Practice Guide: Enforcing Judgments/Debts Ch. 4-A, A. Attachment.
6 Witkin Cal. Proc. 5th Provisional Remedies § 18, Filing and Service.

§ 995.380. Defect in bond; continuance of liability of principals and sureties

(a) If a bond does not contain the substantial matter or conditions required by this chapter or by the statute providing for the bond, or if there are any defects in the giving or filing of the bond, the bond is not void so as to release the principal and sureties from liability.

(b) The beneficiary may, in proceedings to enforce the liability on the bond, suggest the defect in the bond, or its giving or filing, and enforce the liability against the principal and the persons who intended to become and were included as sureties on the bond. *(Added by Stats.1982, c. 998, p. 3663, § 1.)*

Law Revision Commission Comments

Section 995.380 is drawn from former Government Code Section 1554 (official bond). The provision of former law relating to "equitable" liability is not continued; the sureties on the bond or undertaking are liable to the extent provided by statute. See Section 995.320 (contents of bond or undertaking); Powers Regulator Co. v. Seaboard Surety Co., 204 Cal.App.2d 338, 22 Cal.Rptr. 373 (1962). [16 Cal.L.Rev.Comm. Reports 501 (1982)].

Research References

Rutter, Cal. Practice Guide: Civil Appeals & Writs Ch. 7-C, C. Stay by Posting Security (Bond or Undertaking).
Rutter, Cal. Practice Guide: Insurance Litigation Ch. 6I-B, B. Particular Surety Bond Coverages.
Miller and Starr California Real Estate § 28:96, Interpretation of the Bond.
Miller and Starr California Real Estate § 28:109, Mistakes, Errors, and Technical Defects in the Bond.
Miller and Starr California Real Estate § 28:110, No Exoneration of the Surety Under Bonds in Favor of Claimants.
6 Witkin Cal. Proc. 5th Provisional Remedies § 35, (S 35) Joint and Several Liability.

ARTICLE 4. APPROVAL AND EFFECT

§ 995.410. Approval or disapproval of bond

(a) A bond becomes effective without approval unless the statute providing for the bond requires that the bond be approved by the court or officer.

(b) If the statute providing for a bond requires that the bond be approved, the court or officer may approve or disapprove the bond on the basis of the affidavit or certificate of the sureties or may require the attendance of witnesses and the production of evidence and may examine the sureties under oath touching their qualifications.

(c) Nothing shall be construed to preclude approval of a bond in an amount greater than that required by statute. *(Added by Stats.1982, c. 998, p. 3664, § 1.)*

Law Revision Commission Comments

Subdivision (a) of Section 995.410 is new. Subdivision (b) continues the substance of numerous provisions of former law. See, e.g., Gov't Code § 1531 (official bonds). If a bond or undertaking is required to be approved by a court, the judge at chambers may approve the bond or undertaking. See Section 166 (actions that may be taken in chambers). Subdivision (c) is drawn from former subdivision (c) of Section 489.060 (attachment). [16 Cal.L.Rev.Comm. Reports 501 (1982)].

Research References

Rutter, Cal. Practice Guide: Civil Appeals & Writs Ch. 7-C, C. Stay by Posting Security (Bond or Undertaking).
6 Witkin Cal. Proc. 5th Provisional Remedies § 9, Scope of Bond and Undertaking Law.
6 Witkin Cal. Proc. 5th Provisional Remedies § 17, Approval.

§ 995.420. Effective date

(a) Unless the statute providing for a bond provides that the bond becomes effective at a different time, a bond is effective at the time it is given or, if the statute requires that the bond be approved, at the time it is approved.

(b) If the statute providing for a bond provides that the bond becomes effective at a time other than the time it is given or approved, the bond is effective at the time provided unless an objection is made to the bond before that time. If an objection is made to a bond before the time provided, the bond becomes effective when the court makes an order determining the sufficiency of the bond. *(Added by Stats.1982, c. 998, p. 3664, § 1.)*

Law Revision Commission Comments

Subdivision (a) of Section 995.420 is drawn from Section 489.060 (attachment).

Subdivision (b) is drawn from former Sections 680 (fraudulent conveyances) and 713½ (third-party claims). For statutes providing different effective dates, see, e.g., Section 710c (third-party claim undertaking effective 10 days after service), Civil Code § 3449 (fraudulent conveyance undertaking effective 10 days after service). [16 Cal.L.Rev.Comm. Reports 501 (1982)].

Research References

Rutter, Cal. Practice Guide: Civil Appeals & Writs Ch. 7-C, C. Stay by Posting Security (Bond or Undertaking).
Miller and Starr California Real Estate § 28:97, Measure of Surety's Liability.
6 Witkin Cal. Proc. 5th Provisional Remedies § 19, Effective Date and Duration.

§ 995.430. Continuation in force and effect

A bond remains in force and effect until the earliest of the following events:

(a) The sureties withdraw from or cancel the bond or a new bond is given in place of the original bond.

(b) The purpose for which the bond was given is satisfied or the purpose is abandoned without any liability having been incurred.

(c) A judgment of liability on the bond that exhausts the amount of the bond is satisfied.

(d) The term of the bond expires. Unless the statute providing for the bond prescribes a fixed term, the bond is continuous. *(Added by Stats.1982, c. 998, p. 3664, § 1.)*

Law Revision Commission Comments

Section 995.430 is drawn from former Insurance Code § 1664 (production agencies). [16 Cal.L.Rev.Comm. Reports 501 (1982)].

Research References

Rutter, Cal. Practice Guide: Insurance Litigation Ch. 6I-C, C. Surety's Obligations and Rights Upon Default by Principal.
Miller and Starr California Real Estate § 28:97, Measure of Surety's Liability.

Civ. Pro.

6 Witkin Cal. Proc. 5th Provisional Remedies § 19, Effective Date and Duration.

§ 995.440. Bond given as condition of license or permit

A bond given as a condition of a license or permit shall be continuous in form, remain in full force and effect, and run concurrently with the license or permit period and any and all renewals, or until cancellation or withdrawal of the surety from the bond. *(Added by Stats.1982, c. 998, p. 3664, § 1.)*

Law Revision Commission Comments

Section 995.440 continues the substance of former Civil Code Section 2852 (bond of licensee or permittee). [16 Cal.L.Rev.Comm. Reports 501 (1982)].

Research References

Miller and Starr California Real Estate § 28:92, Construction-Related Bonds; in General.
Miller and Starr California Real Estate § 28:126, Contractor's License Bond--Who Must File.
6 Witkin Cal. Proc. 5th Provisional Remedies § 19, Effective Date and Duration.

ARTICLE 5. PERSONAL SURETIES

Section
995.510. Sufficiency of sureties; conditions.
995.520. Affidavit of qualifications of each surety.

§ 995.510. Sufficiency of sureties; conditions

(a) A personal surety on a bond is sufficient if all of the following conditions are satisfied:

(1) The surety is a person other than the principal. No officer of the court or member of the State Bar shall act as a surety.

(2) The surety is a resident, and either an owner of real property or householder, within the state.

(3) The surety is worth the amount of the bond in real or personal property, or both, situated in this state, over and above all debts and liabilities, exclusive of property exempt from enforcement of a money judgment.

(b) If the amount of a bond exceeds ten thousand dollars ($10,000) and is executed by more than two personal sureties, the worth of a personal surety may be less than the amount of the bond, so long as the aggregate worth of all sureties executing the bond is twice the amount of the bond. *(Added by Stats.1982, c. 998, p. 3664, § 1.)*

Law Revision Commission Comments

Section 995.510 is drawn from former Section 1057 (bonds and undertakings) and Government Code Sections 1530 and 1531 (official bonds), and from Rules of Court 242(b) (Superior Court) and 530(b) (Municipal Court), with clarifying changes. The substitution of $10,000 for $3,000 is in recognition of the change in value of the dollar since the enactment of the former law. [16 Cal.L.Rev.Comm. Reports 501 (1982)].

Research References

Rutter, Cal. Practice Guide: Civil Appeals & Writs Ch. 7-C, C. Stay by Posting Security (Bond or Undertaking).
Rutter, Cal. Practice Guide: Civ. Pro. Before Trial Ch. 9(I)-J, J. Motion to Expunge Lis Pendens.
Rutter, Cal. Practice Guide: Enforcing Judgments/Debts Ch. 4-A, A. Attachment.
Rutter, Cal. Practice Guide: Enforcing Judgments/Debts Ch. 6H-7, Statutory Requirements for Undertakings.
Rutter, Cal. Practice Guide: Insurance Litigation Ch. 6I-B, B. Particular Surety Bond Coverages.
6 Witkin Cal. Proc. 5th Provisional Remedies § 9, Scope of Bond and Undertaking Law.

6 Witkin Cal. Proc. 5th Provisional Remedies § 20, (S 20) Qualification.

§ 995.520. Affidavit of qualifications of each surety

(a) A bond executed by personal sureties shall be accompanied by an affidavit of qualifications of each surety.

(b) The affidavit shall contain all of the following information:

(1) The name, occupation, residence address, and business address (if any) of the surety.

(2) A statement that the surety is a resident, and either an owner of real property or householder, within the state.

(3) A statement that the surety is worth the amount of the bond in real or personal property, or both, situated in this state, over and above all debts and liabilities, exclusive of property exempt from enforcement of a money judgment.

(c) If the amount of the bond exceeds five thousand dollars ($5,000), the affidavit shall contain, in addition to the information required by subdivision (b), all of the following information:

(1) A description sufficient for identification of real and personal property of the surety situated in this state and the nature of the surety's interest therein that qualifies the surety on the bond.

(2) The surety's best estimate of the fair market value of each item of property.

(3) A statement of any charge or lien and its amount, known to the surety, whether of public record or not, against any item of property.

(4) Any other impediment or cloud known to the surety on the free right of possession, use, benefit, or enjoyment of the property.

(d) If the amount of the bond exceeds ten thousand dollars ($10,000) and is executed by more than two sureties, the affidavit may state that the surety is worth less than the amount of the bond and the bond may stipulate that the liability of the surety is limited to the worth of the surety stated in the affidavit, so long as the aggregate worth of all sureties executing the bond is twice the amount of the bond. *(Added by Stats.1982, c. 998, p. 3665, § 1.)*

Law Revision Commission Comments

Section 995.520 continues the substance of the first sentence of the first paragraph of former Section 1057 (bonds and undertakings) and a portion of former Section 830 (libel and slander). See also Gov't Code §§ 1530, 1531 (official bonds). The substitution of $5,000 for $2,000 and $10,000 for $3,000 is in recognition of the change in value of the dollar since the enactment of the former law. [16 Cal.L.Rev.Comm. Reports 501 (1982)].

Research References

Rutter, Cal. Practice Guide: Civil Appeals & Writs Ch. 7-C, C. Stay by Posting Security (Bond or Undertaking).
Rutter, Cal. Practice Guide: Enforcing Judgments/Debts Ch. 6H-7, Statutory Requirements for Undertakings.
Rutter, Cal. Practice Guide: Insurance Litigation Ch. 6I-B, B. Particular Surety Bond Coverages.
9 Witkin Cal. Proc. 5th Appeal § 251, (S 251) Form and Filing.
6 Witkin Cal. Proc. 5th Provisional Remedies § 21, (S 21) Affidavit.

ARTICLE 6. ADMITTED SURETY INSURERS

Section
995.610. Sole surety; rights and liabilities.
995.620. Executing same or separate bonds; joint and several liability.
995.630. Conditions of acceptance or approval.
995.640. County clerk; review of Department of Insurance Internet Web site; issuance of certificates.
995.650. Objection to sufficiency; certificate; affidavit.

Section

995.660.　　Objection to sufficiency; documents; acceptance or approval.

995.670.　　Public agencies requiring further conditions; prohibition.

995.675.　　Circular 570; admitted surety insurer.

§ 995.610.　Sole surety; rights and liabilities

(a) If a statute provides for a bond with any number of sureties, one sufficient admitted surety insurer may become and shall be accepted as sole surety on the bond.

(b) The admitted surety insurer is subject to all the liabilities and entitled to all the rights of personal sureties. *(Added by Stats.1982, c. 998, p. 3665, § 1.)*

Law Revision Commission Comments

Section 995.610 continues the substance of the first paragraph of former Section 1056 (bonds and undertakings) and former Civil Code Section 3227 (mechanics' liens and stop notices)[sic]. [16 Cal.L.Rev.Comm. Reports 501 (1982)].

Research References

Rutter, Cal. Practice Guide: Civ. Pro. Before Trial Ch. 9(I)-J, J. Motion to Expunge Lis Pendens.

6 Witkin Cal. Proc. 5th Provisional Remedies § 9, Scope of Bond and Undertaking Law.

6 Witkin Cal. Proc. 5th Provisional Remedies § 22, (S 22) in Lieu of Personal Sureties.

§ 995.620.　Executing same or separate bonds; joint and several liability

Two or more admitted surety insurers may be sureties on a bond by executing the same or separate bonds for amounts aggregating the required amount of the bond. Each admitted surety insurer is jointly and severally liable to the extent of the amount of the liability assumed by it. *(Added by Stats.1982, c. 998, p. 3666, § 1.)*

Law Revision Commission Comments

Section 995.620 is drawn from former Insurance Code Section 11698 (worker's compensation). [16 Cal.L.Rev.Comm. Reports 501 (1982)].

Research References

Rutter, Cal. Practice Guide: Civil Appeals & Writs Ch. 7-C, C. Stay by Posting Security (Bond or Undertaking).

6 Witkin Cal. Proc. 5th Provisional Remedies § 22, (S 22) in Lieu of Personal Sureties.

§ 995.630.　Conditions of acceptance or approval

An admitted surety insurer shall be accepted or approved by the court or officer as surety on a bond without further acknowledgment if the bond is executed in the name of the surety insurer under penalty of perjury or the fact of execution of the bond is duly acknowledged before an officer authorized to take and certify acknowledgments, and either one of the following conditions, at the option of the surety insurer, is satisfied:

(a) A copy of the transcript or record of the unrevoked appointment, power of attorney, bylaws, or other instrument, duly certified by the proper authority and attested by the seal of the insurer entitling or authorizing the person who executed the bond to do so for and in behalf of the insurer, is filed in the office of the clerk of the county in which the court or officer is located.

(b) A copy of a power of attorney is attached to the bond. *(Added by Stats.1982, c. 998, p. 3666, § 1. Amended by Stats.1992, c. 380 (S.B.1521), § 1.)*

Law Revision Commission Comments

Section 995.630 is drawn from the second and third paragraphs of former Section 1056 (bonds and undertakings) and from Court Rules 242(a) (Superior Court) and 530(a) (Municipal Court). The requirement that the officer taking an acknowledgment be "of this state" is not continued. See Civil Code § 1189 (acknowledgments outside state). [16 Cal.L.Rev.Comm. Reports 501 (1982)].

Research References

Rutter, Cal. Practice Guide: Civil Appeals & Writs Ch. 7-C, C. Stay by Posting Security (Bond or Undertaking).

6 Witkin Cal. Proc. 5th Provisional Remedies § 23, (S 23) Authentication of Bond.

§ 995.640.　County clerk; review of Department of Insurance Internet Web site; issuance of certificates

Upon review of the Internet Web site of the Department of Insurance, the county clerk of any county shall, upon request of any person, do any of the following:

(a) Issue a certificate stating whether a surety is admitted or if the certificate of authority of an admitted surety insurer issued by the Insurance Commissioner authorizing the insurer to transact surety insurance has been surrendered, revoked, canceled, annulled, or suspended, and, in the event that it has, whether renewed authority has been granted. The county clerk in issuing the certificate shall rely solely upon the information furnished by the Insurance Commissioner pursuant to Article 2 (commencing with Section 12070) of Chapter 1 of Part 4 of Division 2 of the Insurance Code.

(b) Issue a certificate stating whether a copy of the transcript or record of the unrevoked appointment, power of attorney, bylaws, or other instrument, duly certified by the proper authority and attested by the seal of an admitted surety insurer entitling or authorizing the person who executed a bond to do so for and on behalf of the insurer, is filed in the office of the clerk. *(Added by Stats.1982, c. 998, p. 3666, § 1. Amended by Stats.2004, c. 183 (A.B.3082), § 44; Stats.2005, c. 22 (S.B.1108), § 19; Stats.2008, c. 351 (S.B.1279), § 1.)*

Law Revision Commission Comments

Subdivision (a) of Section 995.640 continues the substance of the last two paragraphs of former Section 1057a (bonds and undertakings). Subdivision (b) is new. The fee to be paid by the person requesting the certificate is $3.00 for each certificate issued. See Gov't Code Section 26855.3 (fee for issuing certificate). [16 Cal.L.Rev.Comm. Reports 501 (1982)].

Research References

6 Witkin Cal. Proc. 5th Provisional Remedies § 24, (S 24) Certificate of Authority.

§ 995.650.　Objection to sufficiency; certificate; affidavit

If an objection is made to the sufficiency of an admitted surety insurer, the person making the objection shall attach to and incorporate in the objection one or both of the following:

(a) The certificate of the county clerk of the county in which the court is located stating that the insurer is not listed as an admitted surety insurer on the department's Internet Web site or that the certificate of authority of the insurer has been surrendered, revoked, canceled, annulled, or suspended and has not been renewed.

(b) An affidavit stating facts that establish the insufficiency of the insurer. *(Added by Stats.1982, c. 998, p. 3666, § 1. Amended by Stats.2008, c. 351 (S.B.1279), § 2.)*

Law Revision Commission Comments

Section 995.650 continues the substance of former Section 1057b (justification of admitted surety insurer). For the certificate of the county clerk, see Section 995.640 (certificate of authority). [16 Cal.L.Rev. Comm. Reports 501 (1982)].

§ 995.660. Objection to sufficiency; documents; acceptance or approval

(a) If an objection is made to the sufficiency of an admitted surety insurer on a bond or if the bond is required to be approved, the insurer shall submit to the court or officer the following documents:

(1) The original, or a certified copy, of the unrevoked appointment, power of attorney, bylaws, or other instrument entitling or authorizing the person who executed the bond to do so, within 10 calendar days of the insurer's receipt of a request to submit the instrument.

(2) A certified copy of the certificate of authority of the insurer issued by the Insurance Commissioner, within 10 calendar days of the insurer's receipt of a request to submit the copy.

(3) A certificate from the clerk of the county in which the court or officer is located that the certificate of authority of the insurer has not been surrendered, revoked, canceled, annulled, or suspended or, in the event that it has, that renewed authority has been granted, within 10 calendar days of the insurer's receipt of the certificate.

(4) Copies of the insurer's most recent annual statement and quarterly statement filed with the Department of Insurance pursuant to Article 10 (commencing with Section 900) of Chapter 1 of Part 2 of Division 1 of the Insurance Code, within 10 calendar days of the insurer's receipt of a request to submit the statements.

(b) If the admitted surety insurer complies with subdivision (a), and if it appears that the bond was duly executed, that the insurer is authorized to transact surety insurance in the state, and that its assets exceed its liabilities in an amount equal to or in excess of the amount of the bond, the insurer is sufficient and shall be accepted or approved as surety on the bond, subject to Section 12090 of the Insurance Code. *(Added by Stats.1982, c. 998, p. 3666, § 1. Amended by Stats.1992, c. 379 (S.B.1502), § 1; Stats.1994, c. 487 (A.B.3493), § 1.)*

Law Revision Commission Comments

Section 995.660 continues the substance of the first portion of former Section 1057a (justification of admitted surety insurer). The reference to Insurance Code Section 12090 (admitted surety insurer may not become surety on undertaking in excess of 10% of assets) is new. For the certificate of the county clerk, see Section 995.640. [16 Cal.L.Rev.Comm. Reports 501 (1982)].

§ 995.670. Public agencies requiring further conditions; prohibition

(a) This section applies to a bond executed, filed, posted, furnished, or otherwise given as security pursuant to any statute of this state or any law or ordinance of a public agency.

No public agency shall require an admitted surety insurer to comply with any requirements other than those in Section 995.660 whenever an objection is made to the sufficiency of the admitted surety insurer on the bond or if the bond is required to be approved.

(b) For the purposes of this section, "public agency" means the state, any agency or authority, any city, county, city and county, district, municipal or public corporation, or any instrumentality thereof. *(Added by Stats.1992, c. 997 (A.B.2872), § 1. Amended by Stats.1994, c. 487 (A.B.3493), § 2.)*

§ 995.675. Circular 570; admitted surety insurer

Notwithstanding Sections 995.660 and 995.670, the California Integrated Waste Management Board, the State Water Resources Control Board, and the Department of Toxic Substances Control may require, in order to comply with Subtitle C or Subtitle D of the federal Resource Conservation and Recovery Act of 1976, as amended (42 U.S.C. Sec. 6901 et seq.), an admitted surety insurer to be listed in Circular 570 issued by the United States Treasury. *(Added by Stats.1998, c. 477 (A.B.2353), § 1.)*

ARTICLE 7. DEPOSIT IN LIEU OF BOND

§ 995.710. Deposit; form; amount or value; agreement; terms and conditions; utilization after Jan. 1, 1999

(a) Except as provided in subdivision (e) or to the extent the statute providing for a bond precludes a deposit in lieu of bond or limits the form of deposit, the principal may instead of giving a bond, deposit with the officer any of the following:

(1) Lawful money of the United States. The money shall be maintained by the officer in an interest-bearing trust account.

(2) Bearer bonds or bearer notes of the United States or the State of California.

(3) Certificates of deposit payable to the officer, not exceeding the federally insured amount, issued by banks or savings associations authorized to do business in this state and insured by the Federal Deposit Insurance Corporation.

(4) Savings accounts assigned to the officer, not exceeding the federally insured amount, together with evidence of the deposit in the savings accounts with banks authorized to do business in this state and insured by the Federal Deposit Insurance Corporation.

(5) Investment certificates or share accounts assigned to the officer, not exceeding the federally insured amount, issued by

savings associations authorized to do business in this state and insured by the Federal Deposit Insurance Corporation.

(6) Certificates for funds or share accounts assigned to the officer, not exceeding the guaranteed amount, issued by a credit union, as defined in Section 14002 of the Financial Code, whose share deposits are guaranteed by the National Credit Union Administration or guaranteed by any other agency approved by the Department of Financial Institutions.

(b) The deposit shall be in an amount or have a face value, or in the case of bearer bonds or bearer notes have a market value, equal to or in excess of the amount that would be required to be secured by the bond if the bond were given by an admitted surety insurer. Notwithstanding any other provision of this chapter, in the case of a deposit of bearer bonds or bearer notes other than in an action or proceeding, the officer may, in the officer's discretion, require that the amount of the deposit be determined not by the market value of the bonds or notes but by a formula based on the principal amount of the bonds or notes.

(c) The deposit shall be accompanied by an agreement executed by the principal authorizing the officer to collect, sell, or otherwise apply the deposit to enforce the liability of the principal on the deposit. The agreement shall include the address at which the principal may be served with notices, papers, and other documents under this chapter.

(d) The officer may prescribe terms and conditions to implement this section.

(e) This section may not be utilized after January 1, 1999, for deposits with the Secretary of State. Any principal who made a deposit with the Secretary of State pursuant to this section prior to January 1, 1999, may continue to utilize that deposit in lieu of a bond pursuant to this section and the statute that prescribes a bond; however, the deposit shall not be renewable pursuant to this section. *(Added by Stats.1982, c. 998, p. 3667, § 1. Amended by Stats.1983, c. 18, p. 3667, § 18.5, eff. April 21, 1983; Stats.1996, c. 1064 (A.B.3351), § 6, operative July 1, 1997; Stats.1998, c. 829 (S.B.1652), § 16; Stats.1999, c. 892 (A.B.1672), § 11.)*

Law Revision Commission Comments

Section 995.710 continues the substance of portions of former Section 1054a (deposit in lieu of undertaking) and numerous provisions of other statutes. [16 Cal.L.Rev.Comm. Reports 501 (1982)].

Research References

Rutter, Cal. Practice Guide: Civil Appeals & Writs Ch. 7-C, C. Stay by Posting Security (Bond or Undertaking).
Rutter, Cal. Practice Guide: Civ. Pro. Before Trial Ch. 9(I)-J, J. Motion to Expunge Lis Pendens.
Rutter, Cal. Practice Guide: Civ. Pro. Before Trial Ch. 9(II)-A, A. Injunctions.
Rutter, Cal. Practice Guide: Enforcing Judgments/Debts Ch. 4-A, A. Attachment.
Rutter, Cal. Practice Guide: Enforcing Judgments/Debts Ch. 6H-7, Statutory Requirements for Undertakings.
Rutter, Cal. Practice Guide: Insurance Litigation Ch. 6I-B, B. Particular Surety Bond Coverages.
Miller and Starr California Real Estate § 11:154, Expungement of a Lis Pendens--Procedure and Grounds for Expungement.
9 Witkin Cal. Proc. 5th Appeal § 250, (S 250) Deposit in Lieu of Bond.
6 Witkin Cal. Proc. 5th Provisional Remedies § 9, Scope of Bond and Undertaking Law.
6 Witkin Cal. Proc. 5th Provisional Remedies § 44, in General.
6 Witkin Cal. Proc. 5th Provisional Remedies § 461, Nature of Remedy.
3 Witkin, California Summary 10th Agency and Employment § 433, (S 433) Bond or Deposit.

§ 995.720.　Market value of bearer bonds or bearer notes; stipulation; determination

(a) The market value of bearer bonds or bearer notes shall be agreed upon by stipulation of the principal and beneficiary or, if the bonds or notes are given in an action or proceeding and the principal and beneficiary are unable to agree, the market value shall be determined by court order in the manner prescribed in this section. A certified copy of the stipulation or court order shall be delivered to the officer at the time of the deposit of the bonds or notes.

(b) If the bonds or notes are given in an action or proceeding, the principal may file a written application with the court to determine the market value of the bonds or notes. The application shall be served upon the beneficiary and proof of service shall be filed with the application. The application shall contain all of the following:

(1) A specific description of the bonds or notes.

(2) A statement of the current market value of the bonds or notes as of the date of the filing of the application.

(3) A statement of the amount of the bonds or notes that the principal believes would be equal to the required amount of the deposit.

(c) The application pursuant to subdivision (b) shall be heard by the court not less than five days or more than 10 days after service of the application. If at the time of the hearing no objection is made to the current market value of the bonds or notes alleged in the application, the court shall fix the amount of the bonds or notes on the basis of the market value alleged in the application. If the beneficiary contends that the current market value of the bonds or notes is less than alleged in the application, the principal shall offer evidence in support of the application, and the beneficiary may offer evidence in opposition. At the conclusion of the hearing, the court shall make an order determining the market value of the bonds or notes and shall fix and determine the amount of the bonds or notes to be deposited by the principal. *(Added by Stats.1982, c. 998, p. 3668, § 1.)*

Law Revision Commission Comments

Section 995.720 continues the substance of the portion of former Section 1054a relating to valuation of bearer bonds or bearer notes. [16 Cal.L.Rev.Comm. Reports 501 (1982)].

Research References

Rutter, Cal. Practice Guide: Civil Appeals & Writs Ch. 7-C, C. Stay by Posting Security (Bond or Undertaking).
6 Witkin Cal. Proc. 5th Provisional Remedies § 44, in General.

§ 995.730.　Force and effect of deposit

A deposit given instead of a bond has the same force and effect, is treated the same, and is subject to the same conditions, liability, and statutory provisions, including provisions for increase and decrease of amount, as the bond. *(Added by Stats.1982, c. 998, p. 3669, § 1.)*

Research References

Rutter, Cal. Practice Guide: Civil Appeals & Writs Ch. 7-C, C. Stay by Posting Security (Bond or Undertaking). B, B. Recovery
Rutter, Cal. Practice Guide: Civil Appeals & Writs Ch. of Appellate Costs and Attorney Fees. Gen. Matls., High-
Rutter, Cal. Practice Guide: Civil Appeals & Writs lights. eneral.
9 Witkin Cal. Proc. 5th Appeal § 971, (S 971) in General.
6 Witkin Cal. Proc. 5th Provisional Remedies

§ 995.740.　Interest on deposit

to enforce the liability of the
If no proceedings are pending shall:
principal on the deposit, the hand, any interest on the deposit,
(a) Pay quarterly, once with the terms of the account or when earned in accoal.
certificate, to the pr

(b) Deliver to the principal, on demand, any interest coupons attached to bearer bonds or bearer notes as the interest coupons become due and payable, or pay annually any interest payable on the bonds or notes. *(Added by Stats.1982, c. 998, p. 3669, § 1.)*

Law Revision Commission Comments

Subdivision (a) of Section 995.740 continues the substance of a portion of Harbors and Navigation Code Section 731, with the addition of the provision for payment of interest quarterly, on demand.

Subdivision (b) continues the substance of the fourth paragraph of former Section 1054a (deposit in lieu of undertaking) and former Business and Professions Code Section 9547.4 (cleaning, dyeing, and pressing license). [16 Cal.L.Rev.Comm. Reports 501 (1982)].

Research References

Rutter, Cal. Practice Guide: Civil Appeals & Writs Ch. 7-C, C. Stay by Posting Security (Bond or Undertaking).
6 Witkin Cal. Proc. 5th Provisional Remedies § 44, in General.

§ 995.750. Payment of amount of liability

(a) The principal shall pay the amount of the liability on the deposit within 30 days after the date on which the judgment of liability becomes final.

(b) If the deposit was given to stay enforcement of a judgment on appeal, the principal shall pay the amount of the liability on the deposit, including damages and costs awarded against the principal on appeal, within 30 days after the filing of the remittitur from the appellate court in the court from which the appeal is taken. *(Added by Stats.1982, c. 998, p. 3669, § 1.)*

Law Revision Commission Comments

Section 995.750 is drawn from the third and fifth paragraphs of former Section 1054a (deposit in lieu of undertaking). [16 Cal.L.Rev.Comm. Reports 501 (1982)].

Research References

6 Witkin Cal. Proc. 5th Provisional Remedies § 45, Enforcement Against Deposit.

§ 995.760. Payment of amount of liability; order of court; sale of bearer bonds or notes; distribution

(a) If the principal does not pay the amount of the liability on the deposit within the time prescribed in Section 995.750, the deposit shall be collected, sold, or otherwise applied to the liability upon order of the court that entered the judgment of liability, made upon five days' notice to the parties.

(b) Bearer bonds or bearer notes without a prevailing market price shall be sold at public auction. Notice of sale shall be prd on the principal. Bearer bonds or bearer notes having a lowing market price may be sold at private sale at a price not ... n the prevailing market price.

(c) T. ... eposit shall be distributed in the following order:

(1) First ... tion of the delay the cost of collection, sale, or other applica-

(2) Second, to ... the judgment of liability of the principal on the deposit.

(3) Third, the rema ... principal. *(Added by Star., if any, shall be returned to the ... 82, c. 998, p. 3669, § 1.)*

Law Revision ... ission Comments

Section 995.760 is drawn from the ... of former Section 1054a (bonds and ... ortion of the fourth paragraph drawn from Financial Code Section 12 ... takings). Subdivision (b) is [16 Cal.L.Rev.Comm. Reports 501 (1982)]. ... heck sellers and cashiers).

Research References

6 Witkin Cal. Proc. 5th Provisional Remedies § 45, Enforcement Against Deposit.

§ 995.770. Return of deposit to principal

A deposit given pursuant to this article shall be returned to the principal at the earliest of the following times:

(a) Upon substitution of a sufficient bond for the deposit. The bond shall be in full force and effect for all liabilities incurred, and for acts, omissions, or causes existing or which arose, during the period the deposit was in effect.

(b) The time provided by Section 995.360 for return of a bond.

(c) The time provided by statute for return of the deposit. *(Added by Stats.1982, c. 998, p. 3669, § 1.)*

Law Revision Commission Comments

Section 995.770 is drawn from portions of former Probate Code Sections 541.3 (executor or administrator) and 2331 (guardian or conservator) and of Harbor and Navigation Code Section 731 (broker's license). Statutes may provide a specific time for return of the deposit. See, e.g., Harb. & Nav. Code § 731 (deposit returned in four years); Veh. Code § 11102.1 (deposit returned in three years or earlier upon court order). [16 Cal.L.Rev.Comm. Reports 501 (1982)].

Research References

Rutter, Cal. Practice Guide: Civil Appeals & Writs Ch. 7-C, C. Stay by Posting Security (Bond or Undertaking).
6 Witkin Cal. Proc. 5th Provisional Remedies § 45, Enforcement Against Deposit.

ARTICLE 8. BONDS TO THE STATE OF CALIFORNIA

Section

§ 995.810. Application of article

The provisions of this article apply to a bond executed to, in favor of, in the name of, or payable to the State of California or the people of the state, including but not limited to an official bond. *(Added by Stats.1982, c. 998, p. 3670, § 1.)*

Law Revision Commission Comments

Section 995.810 supersedes former Section 304 (bonds of receivers, executions, and administrators). The other provisions of this chapter also apply to a bond or undertaking under this article. See also Sections 995.130 ("beneficiary" defined) and 996.510 (enforcement lien). [16 Cal.L.Rev.Comm. Reports 501 (1982)].

Research References

6 Witkin Cal. Proc. 5th Provisional Remedies § 9, Scope of Bond and Undertaking Law.
6 Witkin Cal. Proc. 5th Provisional Remedies § 14, Bonds to State of California.
5 Witkin, California Summary 10th Torts § 370, in General.

§ 995.820. Officer of court; discharge of duties and obedience

Except as otherwise provided by statute, a bond given by an officer of the court for the faithful discharge of the officer's duties and obedience to the orders of the court shall be to the State of California. *(Added by Stats.1982, c. 998, p. 3670, § 1.)*

Law Revision Commission Comments

Section 995.820 continues the substance of a portion of former Section 304.1 (bonds or undertaking of trustees, receivers, assignees, officers of court). See also Section 995.840 (court approval of bond or undertaking). [16 Cal.L.Rev.Comm. Reports 501 (1982)].

Research References

6 Witkin Cal. Proc. 5th Provisional Remedies § 14, Bonds to State of California.

§ 995.830. Unspecified beneficiary

If a statute or court order pursuant thereto providing for a bond does not specify the beneficiary of the bond, the bond shall be to the State of California. *(Added by Stats.1982, c. 998, p. 3670, § 1.)*

Law Revision Commission Comments

Section 995.830 is new. [16 Cal.L.Rev.Comm. Reports 501 (1982)].

Research References

6 Witkin Cal. Proc. 5th Provisional Remedies § 14, Bonds to State of California.

§ 995.840. Bond in action or proceeding; approval; objection

If a bond under this article is given in an action or proceeding:

(a) The bond shall be approved by the court.

(b) Any party for whose benefit the bond is given may object to the bond. *(Added by Stats.1982, c. 998, p. 3670, § 1.)*

Law Revision Commission Comments

Section 995.840 continues the substance of numerous provisions of former law. See, e.g., Section 567 (receivers) and former Section 571 (receivers, referees, and commissioners). The judge in chambers may approve a bond or undertaking. Section 166 (actions that may be taken in chambers). [16 Cal.L.Rev.Comm. Reports 501 (1982)].

Research References

Rutter, Cal. Practice Guide: Civil Appeals & Writs Ch. 7-C, C. Stay by Posting Security (Bond or Undertaking).
Miller and Starr California Real Estate § 33:7, Undertakings, Bonds, Receiver's Oath, and Related Claims.
6 Witkin Cal. Proc. 5th Provisional Remedies § 17, Approval.

§ 995.850. Enforcement of liability

(a) The liability on a bond under this article may be enforced by or for the benefit of, and in the name of, any and all persons for whose benefit the bond is given who are damaged by breach of the condition of the bond.

(b) A person described in subdivision (a) may, in addition to any other remedy the person has, enforce the liability on the bond in the person's own name, without assignment of the bond. *(Added by Stats.1982, c. 998, p. 3670, § 1.)*

Law Revision Commission Comments

Section 995.850 continues the substance of numerous provisions of former law. See, e.g., the last portion of former Section 304.1 (bonds of trustees, receivers assignees, or officers of a court). [16 Cal.L.Rev.Comm. Reports 501 (1982)].

Research References

Miller and Starr California Real Estate § 33:7, Undertakings, Bonds, Receiver's Oath, and Related Claims.
Miller and Starr California Real Estate § 33:18, Liabilities of a Receiver.
6 Witkin Cal. Proc. 5th Provisional Remedies § 43, (S 43) Bonds to State of California.

ARTICLE 9. OBJECTIONS TO BONDS

§ 995.910. Application of article

This article governs objections to a bond given in an action or proceeding. *(Added by Stats.1982, c. 998, p. 3670, § 1.)*

Law Revision Commission Comments

Section 995.910 limits the objection procedure to cases where there are adversary parties and a court to resolve disputes. In other situations the officer required to approve a bond or undertaking must do so without the objection procedure. [16 Cal.L.Rev.Comm. Reports 501 (1982)].

Research References

Rutter, Cal. Practice Guide: Civ. Pro. Before Trial Ch. 9(II)-A, A. Injunctions.
Rutter, Cal. Practice Guide: Enforcing Judgments/Debts Ch. 4-A, A. Attachment.
Rutter, Cal. Practice Guide: Enforcing Judgments/Debts Ch. 4-B, B. Claim and Delivery.
Rutter, Cal. Practice Guide: Enforcing Judgments/Debts Ch. 6H-7, Statutory Requirements for Undertakings.
Rutter, Cal. Practice Guide: Insurance Litigation Ch. 6I-B, B. Particular Surety Bond Coverages.
9 Witkin Cal. Proc. 5th Appeal § 257, (S 257) Objections.
6 Witkin Cal. Proc. 5th Provisional Remedies § 9, Scope of Bond and Undertaking Law.
6 Witkin Cal. Proc. 5th Provisional Remedies § 27, Basis for Objection.

§ 995.920. Grounds

The beneficiary may object to a bond on any of the following grounds:

(a) The sureties are insufficient.

(b) The amount of the bond is insufficient.

(c) The bond, from any other cause, is insufficient. *(Added by Stats.1982, c. 998, p. 3670, § 1.)*

Law Revision Commission Comments

Subdivisions (a) and (b) of Section 995.920 are drawn from numerous provisions of former law. See, e.g., former Sections 489.070 (attachment), 678 (fraudulent conveyances), 711½ (third-party claims). Subdivision (c) is intended to cover other defects in the bond or undertaking. For objection to the sufficiency of an admitted surety insurer, see Section 995.650 (objection to sufficiency of surety). [16 Cal.L.Rev.Comm. Reports 501 (1982)].

Research References

Rutter, Cal. Practice Guide: Civil Appeals & Writs Ch. 7-C, C. St⟨ ⟩ Posting Security (Bond or Undertaking). ⟨   ⟩, A.
Rutter, Cal. Practice Guide: Enforcing Judgments/Debts Ch ⟨ ⟩ Attachment. ⟨   ⟩4-B, B.
Rutter, Cal. Practice Guide: Enforcing Judgments/Debt⟨ ⟩ Claim and Delivery. ⟨   ⟩ Ch. 6H-7,
Rutter, Cal. Practice Guide: Enforcing Judgment⟨ ⟩ Statutory Requirements for Undertakings. ⟨ ⟩ertakings, Bonds,
Miller and Starr California Real Estate § 33:7 ⟨ ⟩ Receiver's Oath, and Related Claims. ⟨ ⟩ctions.
9 Witkin Cal. Proc. 5th Appeal § 257, (S 257⟨ ⟩0) Insufficient Bond or
9 Witkin Cal. Proc. 5th Appeal § 260, ⟨ ⟩ Sureties. ⟨   ⟩es § 27, Basis for Objection.
6 Witkin Cal. Proc. 5th Provisional R⟨ ⟩

§ 995.930. Form and proce⟨ ⟩ waiver

(a) An objection shall b⟨ ⟩ writing and shall be made by noticed motion. The n⟨ ⟩ motion shall specify the precise grounds for the objec⟨ ⟩ If a ground for the objection is that the amount of the b⟨ ⟩ insufficient, the notice of motion shall state the reason for the insufficiency and shall include an estimate of the amount that would be sufficient.

(b) The objection shall be made within 10 days after service of a copy of the bond on the beneficiary or such other time as is required by the statute providing for the bond.

(c) If no objection is made within the time required by statute, the beneficiary is deemed to have waived all objections except upon a showing of good cause for failure to make the objection within the time required by statute or of changed circumstances. *(Added by Stats.1982, c. 998, p. 3670, § 1. Amended by Stats.1984, c. 538, § 33.)*

Law Revision Commission Comments

Section 995.930 is drawn from numerous provisions of former law. See, e.g., former Section 489.080 (attachment), Section 515.030 (claim and delivery), former Section 678 (fraudulent conveyances), Section 689 and former Sections 711½ and 712 (third-party claims). Service on the principal of the objection and notice of motion and proof of service are made pursuant to Sections 1010–1013a. [16 Cal.L.Rev.Comm. Reports 501 (1982)].

Subdivision (c) of Section 995.930 is amended to permit an objection to a bond or undertaking after the time for making an objection has expired, upon a showing of good cause for the late objection. Facts constituting good cause might include inadequate time, under the circumstances, to investigate and respond. There is no maximum time limit for making a late objection under this provision. [17 Cal.L.Rev.Comm.Reports 975 (1984)].

Research References

Rutter, Cal. Practice Guide: Civil Appeals & Writs Ch. 7-C, C. Stay by Posting Security (Bond or Undertaking).
Rutter, Cal. Practice Guide: Civ. Pro. Before Trial Ch. 9(II)-A, A. Injunctions.
Rutter, Cal. Practice Guide: Enforcing Judgments/Debts Ch. 4-A, A. Attachment.
Rutter, Cal. Practice Guide: Enforcing Judgments/Debts Ch. 6H-2, Title or Possessory Claims to Real or Personal Property.
Rutter, Cal. Practice Guide: Enforcing Judgments/Debts Ch. 6H-7, Statutory Requirements for Undertakings.
Miller and Starr California Real Estate § 33:7, Undertakings, Bonds, Receiver's Oath, and Related Claims.
9 Witkin Cal. Proc. 5th Appeal § 257, (S 257) Objections.
8 Witkin Cal. Proc. 5th Enforcement of Judgment § 366, (S 366) General Rules Governing Undertakings.
8 Witkin Cal. Proc. 5th Enforcement of Judgment § 386, (S 386) Filing and Service of Undertaking and Release of Property.
6 Witkin Cal. Proc. 5th Provisional Remedies § 28, Procedure.
6 Witkin Cal. Proc. 5th Provisional Remedies § 264, (S 264) Undertaking.
6 Witkin Cal. Proc. 5th Provisional Remedies § 271, (S 271) Defendant's Undertaking to Protect Possession.
6 Witkin Cal. Proc. 5th Provisional Remedies § 386, (S 386) Insufficient Undertaking.

995.940. Insufficient bond; property or interest in property

in a ground for the objection is that the value of property or an excess in property on which the amount of the bond is based

(a) The value estimated in the bond:

market value objection shall state the beneficiary's estimate of the
(b) The pr... f the property or interest in property.

market value al may accept the beneficiary's estimate of the immediately file he property or interest in property and such case, no hea increased bond based on the estimate. In objection, and the be shall be held on that ground for the market value of the prop ary is bound by the estimate of the *Stats.1982, c. 998, p. 3670,* or interest in property. *(Added by*

Law Revision Co... ion Comments

Section 995.940 is drawn from nume... provisions of former law. See, e.g., former Sections 489.080(b) (attac... ances), 711½ (third-party claims). As to st..., 678 (fraudulent convey-...ision (b), see, e.g., former

Section 489.100 (attachment) and the first portions of former Sections 679 (fraudulent conveyance) and 712½ (third-party claims). [16 Cal.L.Rev. Comm. Reports 501 (1982)].

Research References

Rutter, Cal. Practice Guide: Civil Appeals & Writs Ch. 7-C, C. Stay by Posting Security (Bond or Undertaking).
Rutter, Cal. Practice Guide: Enforcing Judgments/Debts Ch. 6H-7, Statutory Requirements for Undertakings.
6 Witkin Cal. Proc. 5th Provisional Remedies § 27, Basis for Objection.

§ 995.950. Hearing; estimate of value of property or interest in property

(a) Unless the parties otherwise agree, the hearing on an objection shall be held not less than two or more than five days after service of the notice of motion.

(b) The hearing shall be conducted in such manner as the court determines is proper. The court may permit witnesses to attend and testify and evidence to be procured and introduced in the same manner as in the trial of a civil case.

(c) If the value of property or an interest in property is a ground for the objection, the court shall estimate its value. The court may appoint one or more disinterested persons to appraise property or an interest in property for the purpose of estimating its value. *(Added by Stats.1982, c. 998, p. 3671, § 1.)*

Law Revision Commission Comments

Section 995.950 is drawn from numerous provisions of former law. See, e.g., former Sections 489.090 (attachment) and 679 (fraudulent conveyances), Section 689 and former Section 712 (third-party claims), and former Civil Code § 3080.13(a) (livestock service liens). It makes uniform the time within which the hearing must be held. [16 Cal.L.Rev. Comm. Reports 501 (1982)].

Research References

Rutter, Cal. Practice Guide: Civil Appeals & Writs Ch. 7-C, C. Stay by Posting Security (Bond or Undertaking).
9 Witkin Cal. Proc. 5th Appeal § 257, (S 257) Objections.
6 Witkin Cal. Proc. 5th Provisional Remedies § 28, Procedure.

§ 995.960. Order of court; determining sufficiency or insufficiency; changed circumstances

(a) Upon the hearing, the court shall make an order determining the sufficiency or insufficiency of the bond.

(b) If the court determines that the bond is insufficient:

(1) The court shall specify in what respect the bond is insufficient and shall order that a bond with sufficient sureties and in a sufficient amount be given within five days. If a sufficient bond is not given within the time required by the court order, all rights obtained by giving the bond immediately cease and the court shall upon ex parte motion so order.

(2) If a bond is in effect, the bond remains in effect until a bond with sufficient sureties and in a sufficient amount is given in its place, or the time in which to give the bond has expired, whichever first occurs. If the time in which to give a sufficient bond expires, the original bond remains in full force and effect for all liabilities incurred before, and for acts, omissions, or causes existing or which arose before, expiration.

(c) If the court determines that a bond is sufficient, no future objection to the bond may be made except upon a showing of changed circumstances. *(Added by Stats.1982, c. 998, p. 3671, § 1.)*

Law Revision Commission Comments

Section 995.960 is drawn from numerous provisions of former law. See, e.g., 489.090(c)–(e) (attachment), 678½ and 679 (fraudulent conveyances), Section 689 and former Sections 712 and 712½ (third-party claims), and former Civil Code Sections 3080.13(b)–(d) (livestock service liens). For the time a bond or undertaking takes effect, see Section 995.420 (time bond or undertaking becomes effective). [16 Cal.L.Rev.Comm. Reports 501 (1982)].

Research References

Rutter, Cal. Practice Guide: Civil Appeals & Writs Ch. 7-C, C. Stay by Posting Security (Bond or Undertaking).
Rutter, Cal. Practice Guide: Civ. Pro. Before Trial Ch. 9(II)-A, A. Injunctions.
Rutter, Cal. Practice Guide: Enforcing Judgments/Debts Ch. 6H-7, Statutory Requirements for Undertakings.
Rutter, Cal. Practice Guide: Insurance Litigation Ch. 6I-B, B. Particular Surety Bond Coverages.
9 Witkin Cal. Proc. 5th Appeal § 252, (S 252) Provisional Stay.
9 Witkin Cal. Proc. 5th Appeal § 261, (S 261) Substitution of Sufficient Undertaking.
9 Witkin Cal. Proc. 5th Appeal § 264, (S 264) Failure to Give Sufficient Undertaking.
6 Witkin Cal. Proc. 5th Provisional Remedies § 28, Procedure.

ARTICLE 10.   INSUFFICIENT AND EXCESSIVE BONDS

Section
996.010.   Bond in action or proceeding; insufficiency; order of court.
996.020.   Bond given in other than action or proceeding; insufficiency; order of officer; rights lost.
996.030.   Reduction of amount of bond; new bond.

§ 996.010.   Bond in action or proceeding; insufficiency; order of court

(a) If a bond is given in an action or proceeding, the court may determine that the bond is or has from any cause become insufficient because the sureties are insufficient or because the amount of the bond is insufficient.

(b) The court determination shall be upon motion supported by affidavit or upon the court's own motion. The motion shall be deemed to be an objection to the bond. The motion shall be heard and notice of motion shall be given in the same manner as an objection to the bond.

(c) Upon the determination the court shall order that a sufficient new, additional, or supplemental bond be given within a reasonable time not less than five days. The court order is subject to any limitations in the statute providing for the bond.

(d) If a sufficient bond is not given within the time required by the court order, all rights obtained by giving the original bond immediately cease and the court shall upon ex parte motion so order. *(Added by Stats.1982, c. 998, p. 3671, § 1.)*

Law Revision Commission Comments

Section 996.010 is drawn from numerous provisions of former law. See, e.g., former Section 1057 (bonds and undertakings) and provisions formerly found in Sections 391.3 (vexatious litigants), 566 (receivers) and 1030 (nonresident plaintiff). [16 Cal.L.Rev.Comm. Reports 501 (1982)].

Research References

Rutter, Cal. Practice Guide: Civil Appeals & Writs Ch. 7-C, C. Stay by Posting Security (Bond or Undertaking).
Rutter, Cal. Practice Guide: Civ. Pro. Before Trial Ch. 9(II)-A, A. Injunctions.
3 Witkin Cal. Proc. 5th Actions § 364, (S 364) Security.
3 Witkin Cal. Proc. 5th Actions § 369, Hearing, Determination, and Security.
9 Witkin Cal. Proc. 5th Appeal § 256, (S 256) Distinction: Changed Circumstances.
8 Witkin Cal. Proc. 5th Enforcement of Judgment § 370, (S 370) Creditor's Undertaking.
8 Witkin Cal. Proc. 5th Enforcement of Judgment § 375, (S 375) Creditor's Undertaking.
6 Witkin Cal. Proc. 5th Provisional Remedies § 9, Scope of Bond and Undertaking Law.

6 Witkin Cal. Proc. 5th Provisional Remedies § 29, Insufficient Bond in Action or Proceeding.

§ 996.020.   Bond given in other than action or proceeding; insufficiency; order of officer; rights lost

(a) If a bond is given other than in an action or proceeding and it is shown by affidavit of a credible witness or it otherwise comes to the attention of the officer that the bond is or has from any cause become insufficient because the sureties are insufficient or because the amount of the bond is insufficient, the officer may serve an order on the principal to appear and show cause why the officer should not make a determination that the bond is insufficient. The order shall name a day not less than three or more than 10 days after service.

(b) If the principal fails to appear or show good cause on the day named why a determination that the bond is insufficient should not be made, the officer may determine that the bond is insufficient and order a sufficient new, additional, or supplemental bond to be given.

(c) If a sufficient bond is not given within 10 days after the order, the officer shall make an order vacating the rights obtained by giving the original bond, including declaring vacant any office and suspending or revoking any license or certificate for which the bond was given. Any office vacated, license suspended or revoked, or any other rights lost, for failure to give a new, additional, or supplemental bond, shall not be reinstated until a new, additional, or supplemental bond is given. *(Added by Stats.1982, c. 998, p. 3672, § 1.)*

Law Revision Commission Comments

Section 996.020 is drawn from numerous provisions of former law. See, e.g., former Gov't Code §§ 1580–1581 and provisions formerly found in Gov't Code § 1582 (official bonds). [16 Cal.L.Rev.Comm. Reports 501 (1982)].

Research References

6 Witkin Cal. Proc. 5th Provisional Remedies § 30, Insufficient Bond Not in Action or Proceeding.

§ 996.030.   Reduction of amount of bond; new bond

(a) The court if a bond is given or ordered in an action or proceeding, or the officer if a bond is given or ordered other than in an action or proceeding, may determine that the amount of the bond is excessive and order the amount reduced to an amount that in the discretion of the court or officer appears proper under the circumstances. The order is subject to any limitations in the statute providing for the bond.

(b) The determination shall be made upon motion or affidavit of the principal in the same manner as a motion or affidavit for a determination under this article that a bond is insufficient. The notice of motion or the order to show cause made pursuant affidavit shall be served on the beneficiary. The determination shall be made in the same manner and pursuant to and is procedures as a determination under this article that insufficient.   reduced

(c) The principal may give a new bond *f* as on the amount. The sureties may be the same s*P. 3672, § 1.* original bond. *(Added by Stats.1982, c.* Amended by Stats.1988, c. 309, § 1.)

Law Revision Commiss~~i~~ons of former law. See,
Section 996.030 is drawn from numer~~~~nts). [16 Cal.L.Rev.Comm. e.g., former Section 391.3 (vexatio~~~~ Reports 501 (1982)].

References
Re~~~~rcing Judgments/Debts Ch. 4-A, A.
Rutter, Cal. Practice Gui~~~~ Attachment.

3 Witkin Cal. Proc. 5th Actions § 364, (S 364) Security.
3 Witkin Cal. Proc. 5th Actions § 369, Hearing, Determination, and
    Security.
6 Witkin Cal. Proc. 5th Provisional Remedies § 31, Excessive Bond.

ARTICLE 11.   RELEASE OR SUBSTITUTION OF SURETIES ON BOND GIVEN IN ACTION OR PROCEEDING

Section
996.110.   Applications; service.
996.120.   Determination and order of court.
996.130.   Liability of substitute surety; order for release of
          original surety.
996.140.   Failure to give sufficient substitute surety.
996.150.   Effect of release of surety.

§ 996.110.   Applications; service

(a) A surety on a bond given in an action or proceeding may at any time apply to the court for an order that the surety be released from liability on the bond.

(b) The principal on a bond may, if a surety applies for release from liability on a bond, apply to the court for an order that another surety be substituted for the original surety.

(c) The applicant shall serve on the principal or surety (other than the applicant) and on the beneficiary a copy of the application and a notice of hearing on the application. Service shall be made not less than 15 days before the date set for hearing. *(Added by Stats.1982, c. 998, p. 3673, § 1.)*

Law Revision Commission Comments

Section 996.110 is drawn from numerous provisions of former law. See, e.g., former Prob. Code §§ 551 and 553.5 (substitution and discharge of sureties). The manner of service is the same as for service of process in civil actions. See Section 995.030. [16 Cal.L.Rev.Comm. Reports 501 (1982)].

Research References

Rutter, Cal. Practice Guide: Civil Appeals & Writs Ch. 7-C, C. Stay by
    Posting Security (Bond or Undertaking).
Rutter, Cal. Practice Guide: Enforcing Judgments/Debts Ch. 4-C, C.
    Receiverships.
Rutter, Cal. Practice Guide: Insurance Litigation Ch. 6I-B, B. Particular
    Surety Bond Coverages.
Rutter, Cal. Practice Guide: Insurance Litigation Ch. 6I-D, D. Surety's
    Defenses to Payment of Bond.
6 Witkin Cal. Proc. 5th Provisional Remedies § 9, Scope of Bond and
    Undertaking Law.
6 Witkin Cal. Proc. 5th Provisional Remedies § 33, Release or Substitu-
    tion of Surety.
12 Witkin, California Summary 10th Real Property § 290, (S 290)
    Liability of Notary and Sureties.

§6.120.   Determination and order of court

wh~~~ the hearing of the application, the court shall determine or re~~jury to the beneficiary would result from substitution would ~f the surety. If the court determines that release sureties b~uce the amount of the bond or the number of the bond, su~ minimum required by the statute providing for the court sha~~on of a sufficient surety is not necessary and determines that ~ the release of the surety. If the court surety, the court sh~~ry would result from substitution of the within such time as a~~~ the substitution of a sufficient surety 998, p. 3673, § 1.) ~~~~reasonable. *(Added by Stats.1982, c.*

Law Revision

Section 996.120 is drawn from n~ssion Comments
e.g., former Prob. Code § 553.6 (subs~ provisions of former law. See,
    ~~ of sureties) and Prob. Code

§ 2335(a) (guardian or conservator); former Gov't Code § 1600 (official bonds). [16 Cal.L.Rev.Comm. Reports 501 (1982)].

Research References

Rutter, Cal. Practice Guide: Civil Appeals & Writs Ch. 7-C, C. Stay by
    Posting Security (Bond or Undertaking).
6 Witkin Cal. Proc. 5th Provisional Remedies § 33, Release or Substitu-
    tion of Surety.

§ 996.130.   Liability of substitute surety; order for release of original surety

(a) If a substitute surety is given, the substitute surety is subject to all the provisions of this chapter, including but not limited to the provisions governing insufficient and excessive bonds.

(b) Upon the substitution of a sufficient surety, the court shall order the release of the original surety from liability on the bond. *(Added by Stats.1982, c. 998, p. 3673, § 1.)*

Law Revision Commission Comments

Section 996.130 is drawn from numerous provisions of former law. See, e.g., former Prob. Code §§ 553 and 553.6 (substitution of sureties). [16 Cal.L.Rev.Comm. Reports 501 (1982)].

Research References

6 Witkin Cal. Proc. 5th Provisional Remedies § 33, Release or Substitu-
    tion of Surety.

§ 996.140.   Failure to give sufficient substitute surety

If the principal does not give a sufficient substitute surety within the time ordered by the court or such longer time as the surety consents to, all rights obtained by giving the original bond immediately cease and the court shall upon ex parte motion so order. *(Added by Stats.1982, c. 998, p. 3673, § 1.)*

Law Revision Commission Comments

Section 996.140 is drawn from numerous provisions of former law. See, e.g., former Prob. Code § 552 (application by surety). [16 Cal.L.Rev. Comm. Reports 501 (1982)].

Research References

Miller and Starr California Real Estate § 11:33, Liability of the Notary's
    Surety.
6 Witkin Cal. Proc. 5th Provisional Remedies § 33, Release or Substitu-
    tion of Surety.

§ 996.150.   Effect of release of surety

If a surety is ordered released from liability on a bond:

(a) The bond remains in full force and effect for all liabilities incurred before, and for acts, omissions, or causes existing or which arose before, the release. Legal proceedings may be had therefor in all respects as though there had been no release.

(b) The surety is not liable for any act, default, or misconduct of the principal or other breach of the condition of the bond that occurs after, or for any liabilities on the bond that arise after, the release.

(c) The release does not affect the bond as to the remaining sureties, or alter or change their liability in any respect. *(Added by Stats.1982, c. 998, p. 3673, § 1.)*

Law Revision Commission Comments

Section 996.150 is drawn from numerous provisions of former law. See, e.g., former Gov't Code §§ 1612–1613 (official bonds) and 8218 (notary public). [16 Cal.L.Rev.Comm. Reports 501 (1982)].

Research References

Rutter, Cal. Practice Guide: Enforcing Judgments/Debts Ch. 4-C, C.
    Receiverships.

Miller and Starr California Real Estate § 11:33, Liability of the Notary's Surety.

Miller and Starr California Real Estate § 28:97, Measure of Surety's Liability.

6 Witkin Cal. Proc. 5th Provisional Remedies § 33, Release or Substitution of Surety.

ARTICLE 12. NEW, ADDITIONAL, AND SUPPLEMENTAL BONDS

Section

996.210. Order of court or officer; withdrawal of surety; cancellation, etc.

996.220. Form; force and effect; additional requirements.

996.230. Applicable provisions.

996.240. New bond; force and effect of original; liability of sureties.

996.250. Additional or supplemental bond; force and effect of original; rights and liabilities of parties.

§ 996.210. Order of court or officer; withdrawal of surety; cancellation, etc.

(a) The principal shall give a new, additional, or supplemental bond if the court or officer orders that a new, additional, or supplemental bond be given.

(b) The principal may give a new bond if a surety withdraws from or cancels the original bond or to obtain the release of sureties from liability on the original bond. *(Added by Stats. 1982, c. 998, p. 3673, § 1.)*

Law Revision Commission Comments

Section 996.210 is drawn from numerous provisions of former law. See, e.g., former Gov't Code §§ 1601 and 1608 (official bonds). [16 Cal. L.Rev.Comm. Reports 501 (1982)].

Research References

6 Witkin Cal. Proc. 5th Provisional Remedies § 9, Scope of Bond and Undertaking Law.

6 Witkin Cal. Proc. 5th Provisional Remedies § 32, New, Additional, or Supplemental Bond.

§ 996.220. Form; force and effect; additional requirements

(a) A new, additional, or supplemental bond shall be in the same form and have the same obligation as the original bond and shall be in all other respects the same as the original bond, and shall be in such amount as is necessary for the purpose for which the new, additional, or supplemental bond is given.

(b) A supplemental bond shall, in addition to any other requirements, recite the names of the remaining original sureties, the name of the new surety, and the amount for which the new surety is liable. The supplemental bond shall be for the amount for which the original surety was liable on the original bond. *(Added by Stats.1982, c. 998, p. 3674, § 1.)*

Law Revision Commission Comments

Section 996.220 is drawn from numerous provisions of former law. As to subdivision (a), see, e.g., former Sections 678½ (fraudulent conveyances) and 712 (third-party claims). As to subdivision (b), see, e.g., former Gov't Code §§ 1608 and 1609 (official bonds). [16 Cal.L.Rev. Comm. Reports 501 (1982)].

Research References

6 Witkin Cal. Proc. 5th Provisional Remedies § 32, New, Additional, or Supplemental Bond.

§ 996.230. Applicable provisions

A new, additional, or supplemental bond is subject to all the provisions applicable to the original bond and to the provisions of this chapter, including but not limited to the provisions

governing giving and objecting to a bond and liabilities and enforcement procedures. *(Added by Stats.1982, c. 998, p. 3674, § 1.)*

Law Revision Commission Comments

Section 996.230 is drawn from numerous provisions of former law. See, e.g., former Sections 678½ (fraudulent conveyances) and 712 (third-party claims); former Gov't Code §§ 1584 and 1602 (official bonds). [16 Cal.L.Rev.Comm. Reports 501 (1982)].

Research References

6 Witkin Cal. Proc. 5th Provisional Remedies § 32, New, Additional, or Supplemental Bond.

§ 996.240. New bond; force and effect of original; liability of sureties

If a new bond is given in place of the original bond:

(a) The original bond remains in full force and effect for all liabilities incurred before, and for acts, omissions, or causes existing or which arose before, the new bond became effective.

(b) The sureties on the original bond are not liable for any act, default, or misconduct of the principal or other breach of the condition of the bond that occurs after or for any liabilities on the bond that arise after, the new bond becomes effective. *(Added by Stats.1982, c. 998, p. 3674, § 1.)*

Law Revision Commission Comments

Section 996.240 is drawn from numerous provisions of former law. See, e.g., Gov't Code §§ 1602 and 1611 (official bonds). For an exception to the rule of Section 996.240, see Business and Professions Code Section 17774 (trading stamp companies). [16 Cal.L.Rev.Comm. Reports 501 (1982)].

Research References

6 Witkin Cal. Proc. 5th Provisional Remedies § 32, New, Additional, or Supplemental Bond.

§ 996.250. Additional or supplemental bond; force and effect of original; rights and liabilities of parties

(a) An additional or supplemental bond does not discharge or affect the original bond. The original bond remains in full force and effect as if the additional or supplemental bond had not been given.

(b) After an additional or supplemental bond is given, the principal and sureties are liable upon either or both bonds for injury caused by breach of any condition of the bonds. Subject to subdivision (c), the beneficiary may enforce the liability on either bond, or may enforce the liability separately on both bonds and recover separate judgments of liability on both

(c) If the beneficiary recovers separate judgments of liability on both bonds for the same cause of action, the beneficiary may enforce both judgments. The beneficiary may enforce execution or otherwise, the costs of both proceedings, the liability and the amount actually awarded to the things, and on the same cause of action in only one of the judgments, no double recovery shall be allowed.   compelled to pay

(d) If the sureties on either bond have b— they are entitled any sum of money on account of the pri— bond a distributive to recover from the sureties on the rem— amounts of the bonds part of the sum paid, in the proportions sums paid. *(Added by* bear one to the other and to *Stats.1982, c. 998, p. 3674, § 1.)*

ssion Comments

Law Revision former Government Code Sections Section 996.250 is draw— Cal.L.Rev.Comm. Reports 501 (1982)]. 1585–1588 (official bonds

Research References

Miller and Starr California Real Estate § 28:97, Measure of Surety's Liability.
6 Witkin Cal. Proc. 5th Provisional Remedies § 32, New, Additional, or Supplemental Bond.

ARTICLE 13.　CANCELLATION OF BOND OR WITHDRAWAL OF SURETIES

Section
996.310.　Application of article.
996.320.　Notice.
996.330.　Effective date.
996.340.　Failure to give new bond; unlicensed or unregistered business; revival of license or registration.
996.350.　Continuation of original bond.
996.360.　Liability of sureties on original bond.

§ 996.310.　Application of article

This article governs cancellation of or withdrawal of a surety from a bond given other than in an action or proceeding. *(Added by Stats.1982, c. 998, p. 3675, § 1.)*

Law Revision Commission Comments

Sections 996.310–996.360 are drawn from numerous provisions of former law. See, e.g., former Civil Code Section 2851 (bond of licensee or permittee). [16 Cal.L.Rev.Comm. Reports 501 (1982)].

Research References

6 Witkin Cal. Proc. 5th Provisional Remedies § 9, Scope of Bond and Undertaking Law.
6 Witkin Cal. Proc. 5th Provisional Remedies § 34, Cancellation or Withdrawal.

§ 996.320.　Notice

A surety may cancel or withdraw from a bond by giving a notice of cancellation or withdrawal to the officer to whom the bond was given in the same manner the bond was given, notwithstanding Section 995.030. The surety shall at the same time mail or deliver a copy of the notice of cancellation or withdrawal to the principal. *(Added by Stats.1982, c. 998, p. 3675, § 1.)*

Law Revision Commission Comments

Sections 996.310–996.360 are drawn from numerous provisions of former law. See, e.g., former Civil Code Section 2851 (bond of licensee or permittee). [16 Cal.L.Rev.Comm. Reports 501 (1982)].

Research References

6 Witkin Cal. Proc. 5th Provisional Remedies § 34, Cancellation or Withdrawal.

330.　Effective date

earl...lation or withdrawal of a surety is effective at the
(a) 'he following times:
given.　...ays after notice of cancellation or withdrawal is
(b) If a ne...
date the substit...ty is substituted for the original surety, the
(c) If a new bo...comes effective.
effective. *(Added by* ...ven, the date the new bond becomes
...982, c. 998, p. 3675, § 1.)*

Law Revisi...

Sections 996.310–996.360 a...mission Comments
former law. See, e.g., former Civ...
or permittee). [16 Cal.L.Rev.Comm...from numerous provisions of
Section 2851 (bond of licensee
...s 501 (1982)].

Research References

6 Witkin Cal. Proc. 5th Provisional Remedies § 34, Cancellation or Withdrawal.

§ 996.340.　Failure to give new bond; unlicensed or unregistered business; revival of license or registration

(a) If the principal does not give a new bond within 30 days after notice of cancellation or withdrawal is given, all rights obtained by giving the original bond immediately cease, any office for which the bond is given is vacant, any commission for which the bond is given is revoked, and any license or registration for which the bond is given is suspended.

(b) A person whose license or registration is suspended shall not operate or carry on business pursuant to the license or registration during the period of suspension. A license or registration that is suspended may be revived only by the giving of a new bond during the license or registration period in which the cancellation or withdrawal occurred. *(Added by Stats.1982, c. 998, p. 3675, § 1. Amended by Stats.1983, c. 18, § 19, eff. April 21, 1983.)*

Law Revision Commission Comments

Sections 996.310–996.360 are drawn from numerous provisions of former law. See, e.g., former Civil Code Section 2851 (bond of licensee or permittee). [16 Cal.L.Rev.Comm. Reports 501 (1982)].

Section 996.340 is amended to continue the substance of a provision formerly found in Business and Professions Code Section 9891.36 (tax preparers). [16 Cal.L.Rev.Comm. Reports 2239 (1982)].

Research References

6 Witkin Cal. Proc. 5th Provisional Remedies § 34, Cancellation or Withdrawal.

§ 996.350.　Continuation of original bond

If the withdrawal of a surety does not reduce the amount of the bond or the number of sureties below the minimum required by the statute providing for the bond, no new bond is required or necessary to maintain the original bond in effect. *(Added by Stats.1982, c. 998, p. 3675, § 1.)*

Law Revision Commission Comments

Section 996.350 is drawn from former Government Code Section 1600 (official bonds). [16 Cal.L.Rev.Comm. Reports 501 (1982)].

Research References

6 Witkin Cal. Proc. 5th Provisional Remedies § 34, Cancellation or Withdrawal.

§ 996.360.　Liability of sureties on original bond

If a surety cancels or withdraws from a bond:

(a) The bond remains in full force and effect for all liabilities incurred before, and for acts, omissions, or causes existing or which arose before, the cancellation or withdrawal. Legal proceedings may be had therefor in all respects as though there had been no cancellation or withdrawal.

(b) The surety is not liable for any act, default, or misconduct of the principal or other breach of the condition of the bond that occurs after, or for any liabilities on the bond that arise after, the cancellation or withdrawal.

(c) The cancellation or withdrawal does not affect the bond as to the remaining sureties, or alter or change their liability in any respect. *(Added by Stats.1982, c. 998, p. 3675, § 1.)*

Law Revision Commission Comments

Sections 996.310–996.360 are drawn from numerous provisions of former law. See, e.g., former Civil Code Section 2851 (bond of licensee or permittee). [16 Cal.L.Rev.Comm. Reports 501 (1982)].

Research References

Rutter, Cal. Practice Guide: Insurance Litigation Ch. 6I-B, B. Particular Surety Bond Coverages.

Miller and Starr California Real Estate § 28:92, Construction-Related Bonds; in General.

6 Witkin Cal. Proc. 5th Provisional Remedies § 34, Cancellation or Withdrawal.

ARTICLE 14. LIABILITY OF PRINCIPAL AND SURETIES

Section

§ 996.410. Enforcement of liability; beneficiary

(a) The beneficiary may enforce the liability on a bond against both the principal and sureties.

(b) If the beneficiary is a class of persons, any person in the class may enforce the liability on a bond in the person's own name, without assignment of the bond. *(Added by Stats.1982, c. 998, p. 3676, § 1.)*

Law Revision Commission Comments

Section 996.410 continues the substance of numerous provisions of former law. For enforcement of liability on a bond to the State of California, see Section 995.850 (enforcement by or for benefit of persons interested).

Subdivision (b) is drawn from former Financial Code Section 12211 (check cashers and sellers) and Health and Safety Code Section 1773 (life care contracts). [16 Cal.L.Rev.Comm. Reports 501 (1982)].

Research References

Rutter, Cal. Practice Guide: Civil Appeals & Writs Ch. 7-C, C. Stay by Posting Security (Bond or Undertaking).

Rutter, Cal. Practice Guide: Insurance Litigation Ch. 6I-B, B. Particular Surety Bond Coverages.

Miller and Starr California Real Estate § 28:97, Measure of Surety's Liability.

Miller and Starr California Real Estate § 28:112, Proper Parties in Suit Against Surety; Necessity of Suit Against or Joinder of the Principal.

9 Witkin Cal. Proc. 5th Appeal § 265, (S 265) Enforcement of Liability.

6 Witkin Cal. Proc. 5th Provisional Remedies § 9, Scope of Bond and Undertaking Law.

6 Witkin Cal. Proc. 5th Provisional Remedies § 37, (S 37) Enforcement by Civil Action.

6 Witkin Cal. Proc. 5th Provisional Remedies § 214, (S 214) Action Against Sureties.

5 Witkin, California Summary 10th Torts § 370, in General.

§ 996.420. Surety submits to jurisdiction; application of section

(a) A surety on a bond given in an action or proceeding submits itself to the jurisdiction of the court in all matters affecting its liability on the bond.

(b) This section does not apply to a bond of a public officer or fiduciary. *(Added by Stats.1982, c. 998, p. 3676, § 1.)*

Law Revision Commission Comments

Section 996.420 continues the substance of the first sentences of former Sections 1058a (bonds and undertakings) and 535 (injunctions). [16 Cal.L.Rev.Comm. Reports 501 (1982)].

Research References

6 Witkin Cal. Proc. 5th Provisional Remedies § 37, (S 37) Enforcement by Civil Action.

§ 996.430. Enforcement of liability; civil action; venue

(a) The liability on a bond may be enforced by civil action. Both the principal and the sureties shall be joined as parties to the action.

(b) If the bond was given in an action or proceeding, the action shall be commenced in the court in which the action or proceeding was pending. If the bond was given other than in an action or proceeding, the action shall be commenced in any court of competent jurisdiction, and the amount of damage claimed in the action, not the amount of the bond, determines the jurisdictional classification of the case.

(c) A cause of action on a bond may be transferred and assigned as other causes of action. *(Added by Stats.1982, c. 998, p. 3676, § 1. Amended by Stats.1998, c. 931 (S.B.2139), § 105, eff. Sept. 28, 1998.)*

Law Revision Commission Comments

Section 996.430 continues the substance of numerous provisions of former law. See, e.g., former Labor Code §§ 1700.42–1700.43 (artists' managers). [16 Cal.L.Rev.Comm. Reports 501 (1982)].

Section 996.430 is amended to accommodate unification of the municipal and superior courts in a county. Cal. Const. art. VI, § 5(e). See Sections 32.5 (jurisdictional classification), 85 (limited civil cases) & Comment. [28 Cal.L.Rev.Comm. Reports 51 (1998)].

Research References

Rutter, Cal. Practice Guide: Civil Appeals & Writs Ch. 7-C, C. Stay by Posting Security (Bond or Undertaking).

Rutter, Cal. Practice Guide: Civ. Pro. Before Trial Ch. 11-A, A. Voluntary Dismissals.

Rutter, Cal. Practice Guide: Enforcing Judgments/Debts Ch. 6H-3, Claim of Security Interest in or Lien on Personal Property or Fixtures.

Rutter, Cal. Practice Guide: Insurance Litigation Ch. 6I-B, B. Particular Surety Bond Coverages.

Miller and Starr California Real Estate § 28:97, Measure of Surety's Liability.

Miller and Starr California Real Estate § 28:112, Proper Parties in Suit Against Surety; Necessity of Suit Against or Joinder of the Principal.

6 Witkin Cal. Proc. 5th Provisional Remedies § 37, (S 37) Enforcement by Civil Action.

6 Witkin Cal. Proc. 5th Provisional Remedies § 38, Nature of Motion.

6 Witkin Cal. Proc. 5th Provisional Remedies § 264, (S 264) Undertaking.

6 Witkin Cal. Proc. 5th Provisional Remedies § 415, Final Termination of Main Action.

§ 996.440. Bond in action or proceeding; motion to enforce; judgment; trial; stay

(a) If a bond is given in an action or proceeding, the liability on the bond may be enforced on motion made without the necessity of an independent action.

(b) The motion shall not be made until after entry of the final judgment in the action or proceeding in which the bond is given and the time for appeal has expired or, if an appeal is taken, until the appeal is finally determined. The motion shall not be made or notice of motion served more than one year after the later of the preceding dates.

(c) Notice of motion shall be served on the principal and sureties at least 30 days before the time set for hearing of the motion. The notice shall state the amount of the claim and shall be supported by affidavits setting forth the facts on which the claim is based. The notice and affidavits shall be served in accordance with any procedure authorized by Chapter 5 (commencing with Section 1010).

(d) Judgment shall be entered against the principal and sureties in accordance with the motion unless the principal or sureties serve and file affidavits in opposition to the motion showing such facts as may be deemed by the judge hearing the motion sufficient to present a triable issue of fact. If such a showing is made, the issues to be tried shall be specified by the court. Trial shall be by the court and shall be set for the earliest date convenient to the court, allowing sufficient time for such discovery proceedings as may be requested.

(e) The principal and sureties shall not obtain a stay of the proceedings pending determination of any conflicting claims among beneficiaries. *(Added by Stats.1982, c. 998, p. 3676, § 1.)*

Law Revision Commission Comments

Section 996.440 continues the substance of former Sections 1058a (bonds and undertakings) and 535 (injunctions), but requires court trial. This requirement should not be construed to deny the right to a jury trial on a bond or undertaking executed pursuant to prior law to the extent constitutionally required. Subdivision (a) also continues the substance of a portion of Probate Code Section 684 (family allowance). Subdivision (b) also continues the substance of a portion of Section 1166a (unlawful detainer) and former Civil Code Section 3080.14(b) (livestock service liens). For the standards for affidavits, see Section 995.040. [16 Cal.L.Rev.Comm. Reports 501 (1982)].

Research References

Rutter, Cal. Practice Guide: Civil Appeals & Writs Ch. 7-C, C. Stay by Posting Security (Bond or Undertaking).
Rutter, Cal. Practice Guide: Civ. Pro. Before Trial Ch. 11-A, A. Voluntary Dismissals.
Rutter, Cal. Practice Guide: Civ. Pro. Before Trial Ch. 9(II)-A, A. Injunctions.
Rutter, Cal. Practice Guide: Enforcing Judgments/Debts Ch. 4-A, A. Attachment.
Rutter, Cal. Practice Guide: Enforcing Judgments/Debts Ch. 6H-3, Claim of Security Interest in or Lien on Personal Property or Fixtures.
Rutter, Cal. Practice Guide: Insurance Litigation Ch. 6I-B, B. Particular Surety Bond Coverages.
Rutter, Cal. Practice Guide: Insurance Litigation Ch. 6I-C, C. Surety's Obligations and Rights Upon Default by Principal.
Miller and Starr California Real Estate § 33:7, Undertakings, Bonds, Receiver's Oath, and Related Claims.
Miller and Starr California Real Estate § 28:81, Release, Bond and Waiver of Stop Payment Notice.
Miller and Starr California Real Estate § 32:39, Statutory Recovery on the Undertaking.
Miller and Starr California Real Estate § 28:112, Proper Parties in Suit Against Surety; Necessity of Suit Against or Joinder of the Principal.
3 Witkin Cal. Proc. 5th Actions § 407, (S 407) Procedure.
3 Witkin Cal. Proc. 5th Actions § 409, Procedure.
9 Witkin Cal. Proc. 5th Appeal § 265, (S 265) Enforcement of Liability.
6 Witkin Cal. Proc. 5th Provisional Remedies § 38, Nature of Motion.
6 Witkin Cal. Proc. 5th Provisional Remedies § 39, Procedure.
Witkin Cal. Proc. 5th Provisional Remedies § 40, (S 40) Statute of Limitations.
6 Cal. Proc. 5th Provisional Remedies § 41, (S 41) Judgment.
6 W.al. Proc. 5th Provisional Remedies § 224, in General.
M. Proc. 5th Provisional Remedies § 264, (S 264) Undertaking.
14 Witk Proc. 5th Provisional Remedies § 415, Final Termination of Particu.
nia Summary 10th Wills and Probate § 514, (S 514)
§ 996.450. s by and Against Personal Representative.
plication of
vision restricting limitation statutes; application in
No provision in a
shorten the period pre
the commencement of valid that attempts by contract to
prescribed by Section 996. by Section 337 or other statute for
This section does not apply on on the bond or the period
a motion to enforce a bond.
principal, beneficiary, and

surety accept a provision for a shorter period in a bond. *(Added by Stats.1982, c. 998, p. 3677, § 1.)*

Law Revision Commission Comments

Section 996.450 is new. For an exception to the rule of Section 996.450, see Food and Agricultural Code § 55435. Although the general statute of limitations for an action on a bond or undertaking is the 4-year statute provided by Section 337, specific statutes may provide different limitation periods. See, e.g., Bus. & Prof. Code §§ 6898 (3 years) and 7071.11 (2 years); Fin. Code §§ 12212, 17205 (2 years); Health and Safety Code §§ 1376 (2 years) and 5021 (6 months); Pub.Util. Code § 4840 (1 year). The time within which a motion to enforce must be made is one year. See Section 996.440(b). [16 Cal.L.Rev.Comm. Reports 501 (1982)].

Research References

Miller and Starr California Real Estate § 28:113, Statute of Limitations--Action by Owner or Obligee.
6 Witkin Cal. Proc. 5th Provisional Remedies § 40, (S 40) Statute of Limitations.

§ 996.460. Judgment; amount; subrogation

(a) Notwithstanding Section 2845 of the Civil Code, a judgment of liability on a bond shall be in favor of the beneficiary and against the principal and sureties and shall obligate each of them jointly and severally.

(b) The judgment shall be in an amount determined by the court.

(c) A judgment that does not exhaust the full amount of the bond decreases the amount of the bond but does not discharge the bond. The liability on the bond may be enforced thereafter from time to time until the amount of the bond is exhausted.

(d) The judgment may be enforced by the beneficiary directly against the sureties. Nothing in this section affects any right of subrogation of a surety against the principal or any right of a surety to compel the principal to satisfy the judgment. *(Added by Stats.1982, c. 998, p. 3677, § 1.)*

Research References

Rutter, Cal. Practice Guide: Enforcing Judgments/Debts Ch. 4-A, A. Attachment.
Miller and Starr California Real Estate § 28:97, Measure of Surety's Liability.
Miller and Starr California Real Estate § 32:39, Statutory Recovery on the Undertaking.
Miller and Starr California Real Estate § 11:155, Expungement of a Lis Pendens--Recovery on an Undertaking.
Miller and Starr California Real Estate § 28:112, Proper Parties in Suit Against Surety; Necessity of Suit Against or Joinder of the Principal.
6 Witkin Cal. Proc. 5th Provisional Remedies § 41, (S 41) Judgment.

§ 996.470. Limitation of liability; amount; stipulation

(a) Notwithstanding any other statute other than Section 996.480, the aggregate liability of a surety to all persons for all breaches of the condition of a bond is limited to the amount of the bond. Except as otherwise provided by statute, the liability of the principal is not limited to the amount of the bond.

(b) If a bond is given in an amount greater than the amount required by statute or by order of the court or officer pursuant to statute, the liability of the surety on the bond is limited to the amount required by statute or by order of the court or officer, unless the amount of the bond has been increased voluntarily or by agreement of the parties to satisfy an objection to the bond made in an action or proceeding.

(c) The liability of a surety is limited to the amount stipulated in any of the following circumstances:

(1) The bond contains a stipulation pursuant to Section 995.520 that the liability of a personal surety is limited to the worth of the surety.

(2) The bond contains a stipulation that the liability of a surety is an amount less than the amount of the bond pursuant to a statute that provides that the liability of sureties in the aggregate need not exceed the amount of the bond. *(Added by Stats.1982, c. 998, p. 3677, § 1. Amended by Stats.1993, c. 527 (A.B.908), § 2.)*

Law Revision Commission Comments

Subdivision (a) of Section 996.470 is drawn from numerous provisions of former law. See, e.g., former Sections 489.110 and 490.030 (attachment) and Sections 917.1, 917.4, 917.5, and 917.9 (appeals). Subdivision (b) is drawn from the last sentence of Section 922 (appeals). Subdivision (c) is drawn from the last paragraph of Section 917.1 (appeals). The liability of a surety may be further limited by the statute providing for the bond or undertaking. See, e.g., Bus. & Prof. Code § 7071.11 (liability on contractor's bond limited to $3,000). [16 Cal.L.Rev.Comm. Reports 501 (1982)].

Research References

Rutter, Cal. Practice Guide: Civil Appeals & Writs Ch. 7-C, C. Stay by Posting Security (Bond or Undertaking).
Rutter, Cal. Practice Guide: Insurance Litigation Ch. 6I-C, C. Surety's Obligations and Rights Upon Default by Principal.
Miller and Starr California Real Estate § 33:7, Undertakings, Bonds, Receiver's Oath, and Related Claims.
Miller and Starr California Real Estate § 28:81, Release, Bond and Waiver of Stop Payment Notice.
Miller and Starr California Real Estate § 28:97, Measure of Surety's Liability.
Miller and Starr California Real Estate § 32:39, Statutory Recovery on the Undertaking.
Miller and Starr California Real Estate § 28:115, Amount of Owner's Recovery--Contract and Tort.
8 Witkin Cal. Proc. 5th Enforcement of Judgment § 375A, (S 375A) (New)-Action on Undertaking.
6 Witkin Cal. Proc. 5th Provisional Remedies § 36, (S 36) Limitation on Liability.
6 Witkin Cal. Proc. 5th Provisional Remedies § 42, (S 42) Payment by Surety.
6 Witkin Cal. Proc. 5th Provisional Remedies § 225, Amount of Recovery.
6 Witkin Cal. Proc. 5th Provisional Remedies § 271, (S 271) Defendant's Undertaking to Protect Possession.

§ 996.475. Liability of sureties not limited

Nothing in this chapter is intended to limit the liability of a surety pursuant to any other statute. This section is declaratory of, and not a change in, existing law. *(Added by Stats.1984, c. 538, § 33.3.)*

Research References

Miller and Starr California Real Estate § 33:7, Undertakings, Bonds, Receiver's Oath, and Related Claims.
6 Witkin Cal. Proc. 5th Provisional Remedies § 36, (S 36) Limitation on Liability.

§ 996.480. Payment on bond; costs, fees and interest; partial payment; right or license affected

(a) If the nature and extent of the liability of the principal is established by final judgment of a court and the time for appeal has expired or, if an appeal is taken, the appeal is finally determined and the judgment is affirmed:

(1) A surety may make payment on a bond without awaiting enforcement of the bond. The amount of the bond is reduced to the extent of any payment made by the surety in good faith.

(2) If the beneficiary makes a claim for payment on a bond given in an action or proceeding after the liability of the principal is so established and the surety fails to make payment, the surety is liable for costs incurred in obtaining a judgment against the surety, including a reasonable attorney's fee, and interest on the judgment from the date of the claim, notwithstanding Section 996.470.

(b) Partial payment of a claim by a surety shall not be considered satisfaction of the claim and the beneficiary may enforce the liability on the bond. If a right is affected or a license is suspended or revoked until payment of a claim, the right continues to be affected and the license continues to be suspended or revoked until the claim is satisfied in full. *(Added by Stats.1982, c. 998, p. 3677, § 1.)*

Law Revision Commission Comments

Subdivisions (a) (1) and (b) of Section 996.480 are drawn from Business and Professions Code Section 7071.11 (contractors). Subdivision (a) (2) is drawn from former Probate Code Section 554 (executor, administrator, guardian, conservator). The provision for a reasonable attorney's fee is intended to ensure prompt payment by the surety where the liability of the principal is established. The reasonableness of the fee should be determined in relationship to the amount of the bond or undertaking. [16 Cal.L.Rev.Comm. Reports 501 (1982)].

Research References

Miller and Starr California Real Estate § 11:33, Liability of the Notary's Surety.
Miller and Starr California Real Estate § 28:66, Bond to Release the Lien.
Miller and Starr California Real Estate § 28:115, Amount of Owner's Recovery--Contract and Tort.
Miller and Starr California Real Estate § 28:116, Interest.
Miller and Starr California Real Estate § 28:118, Action by Claimant to Recover on a Bond as to Private Projects--In General.
6 Witkin Cal. Proc. 5th Provisional Remedies § 36, (S 36) Limitation on Liability.
6 Witkin Cal. Proc. 5th Provisional Remedies § 42, (S 42) Payment by Surety.

§ 996.490. Payment by surety; contribution to cosureties

(a) Payment by a surety of the amount of a bond constitutes a full discharge of all the liability of the surety on the bond.

(b) Each surety is liable to contribution to cosureties who have made payment in proportion to the amount for which each surety is liable. *(Added by Stats.1982, c. 998, p. 3678, § 1.)*

Law Revision Commission Comments

Subdivision (a) of Section 996.490 is drawn from former Insurance Code Section 11711 (worker's compensation). Subdivision (b) is drawn from former Government Code Section 1552 (official bonds). [16 Cal.L.Rev.Comm. Reports 501 (1982)].

Research References

Miller and Starr California Real Estate § 28:97, Measure of Surety's Liability.
6 Witkin Cal. Proc. 5th Provisional Remedies § 42, (S 42) Payment by Surety.

§ 996.495. Enforcement; judgment of liability on bond

A judgment of liability on a bond may be enforced in the sa_ manner and to the same extent as other money judgm_ *(Added by Stats.1982, c. 998, p. 3678, § 1.)*

Law Revision Commission Comments

Section 996.495 is new. For a special enforcement_ Section 996.510 (enforcement lien). [16 Cal.L.Rev.C_ (1982)].

Research References

Rutter, Cal. Practice Guide: Enforcing J_41, (S 41) Judgment. Enforcement of Judgments Law ("Ejl")_
6 Witkin Cal. Proc. 5th Provisional Re_

_MENT LIEN

ARTICLE 15. EN_

Section
996.510. Application o_

Section

996.520. Affidavit; contents.
996.530. Clerk of court; certificate.
996.540. County recorder; duties.
996.550. Real property subject to lien; amount; effective date.
996.560. Agreement to sell real property affected by lien; specific performance; payment.

§ 996.510. Application of article

This article applies to proceedings for the benefit of the state to enforce the liability on a bond executed to, in favor of, or payable to the state or the people of the state, including but not limited to an official bond. *(Added by Stats.1982, c. 998, p. 3678, § 1.)*

Law Revision Commission Comments

Section 996.510 continues the substance of the first portions of former Section 304.2 (bonds to State of California) and former Government Code Section 1555 (official bonds). [16 Cal.L.Rev.Comm. Reports 501 (1982)].

Research References

3 Witkin Cal. Proc. 5th Actions § 380, (S 380) Specific Permissive Statutes.
6 Witkin Cal. Proc. 5th Provisional Remedies § 9, Scope of Bond and Undertaking Law.
6 Witkin Cal. Proc. 5th Provisional Remedies § 43, (S 43) Bonds to State of California.

§ 996.520. Affidavit; contents

The person enforcing the liability may file with the court in the proceedings an affidavit stating the following:

(a) The bond was executed by the defendant or one or more of the defendants (designating whom).

(b) The bond is one to which this article applies.

(c) The defendant or defendants have real property or an interest in real property (designating the county or counties in which the real property is situated).

(d) The liability is being enforced for the benefit of the state. *(Added by Stats.1982, c. 998, p. 3678, § 1.)*

Law Revision Commission Comments

Section 996.520 continues the substance of the first sentence of former Section 304.2 (bonds to State of California) and former Government Code Section 1555 (official bonds). See also Section 995.040 (affidavits). [16 Cal.L.Rev.Comm. Reports 501 (1982)].

Research References

6 Witkin Cal. Proc. 5th Provisional Remedies § 43, (S 43) Bonds to State of California.

§ 996.530. Clerk of court; certificate

The clerk receiving the affidavit shall certify to the recorder of the county in which the real property is situated all of the following:

(b) The names of the parties.

(c) The court in which the proceedings are pending.

(d) The amount claimed.

by Stats.1982, the commencement of the proceedings. *(Added by Stats.1982, c. 998, p. 3678, § 1.)*

Law Revision Commission Comments

Section 996.530 continues the substance of the second sentence of former Section 304.2 (bonds to State of California) and former Government Code Section 1556 (official bonds). [16 Cal.L.Rev.Comm. Reports 501 (1982)].

Research References

6 Witkin Cal. Proc. 5th Provisional Remedies § 43, (S 43) Bonds to State of California.

§ 996.540. County recorder; duties

(a) Upon receiving the certificate the county recorder shall endorse upon it the time of its receipt.

(b) The certificate shall be filed and recorded in the same manner as notice of the pendency of an action affecting real property. *(Added by Stats.1982, c. 998, p. 3678, § 1.)*

Law Revision Commission Comments

Section 996.540 is drawn from former Government Code Section 1557 (official bonds). [16 Cal.L.Rev.Comm. Reports 501 (1982)].

Research References

Miller and Starr California Real Estate § 11:150, Actions in Which a Lis Pendens May or Must be Recorded.
6 Witkin Cal. Proc. 5th Provisional Remedies § 43, (S 43) Bonds to State of California.

§ 996.550. Real property subject to lien; amount; effective date

(a) Any judgment recovered is a lien upon all real property belonging to the defendant situated in any county in which the certificate is filed, from the filing of the certificate.

(b) The lien is for the amount for which the owner of the real property is liable upon the judgment. *(Added by Stats.1982, c. 998, p. 3678, § 1.)*

Law Revision Commission Comments

Section 996.550 is drawn from former Government Code Section 1558 (official bonds). [16 Cal.L.Rev.Comm. Reports 501 (1982)].

Research References

6 Witkin Cal. Proc. 5th Provisional Remedies § 43, (S 43) Bonds to State of California.

§ 996.560. Agreement to sell real property affected by lien; specific performance; payment

If an agreement to sell real property affected by the lien created by the filing of a certificate was made before the filing of the certificate and the purchase price under the agreement was not due until after the filing of the certificate, and the purchaser is otherwise entitled to specific performance of the agreement:

(a) The court in an action to compel specific performance of the agreement shall order the purchaser to pay the purchase price, or so much of the purchase price as may be due, to the State Treasurer, and to take the State Treasurer's receipt for payment.

(b) Upon payment, the purchaser is entitled to enforcement of specific performance of the agreement. The purchaser takes the real property free from the lien created by the filing of the certificate.

(c) The State Treasurer shall hold the payment pending the proceedings referred to in the certificate. The payment is subject to the lien created by the filing of the certificate. *(Added by Stats.1982, c. 998, p. 3678, § 1.)*

Law Revision Commission Comments

Subdivision (a) of Section 996.560 continues the substance of former Government Code Section 1559 (official bonds). Subdivisions (b) and (c) continue the substance of former Government Code Section 1560 (official bonds). [16 Cal.L.Rev.Comm. Reports 501 (1982)].

Research References

Rutter, Cal. Practice Guide: Enforcing Judgments/Debts Ch. 6H-7, Statutory Requirements for Undertakings.

Rutter, Cal. Practice Guide: Insurance Litigation Ch. 6I-A, A. Introduction.

Rutter, Cal. Practice Guide: Insurance Litigation Ch. 6I-B, B. Particular Surety Bond Coverages.

Miller and Starr California Real Estate § 34:24, Mutuality of Remedy; Seller's Defective Title.

Miller and Starr California Real Estate § 28:120, Payment and Performance Bonds as to Public Projects.

6 Witkin Cal. Proc. 5th Provisional Remedies § 43, (S 43) Bonds to State of California.

CHAPTER 3. OFFERS BY A PARTY TO COMPROMISE

Section
998. Withholding or augmenting costs following rejection or acceptance of offer to allow judgment.

§ 998. Withholding or augmenting costs following rejection or acceptance of offer to allow judgment

(a) The costs allowed under Sections 1031 and 1032 shall be withheld or augmented as provided in this section.

(b) Not less than 10 days prior to commencement of trial or arbitration (as provided in Section 1281 or 1295) of a dispute to be resolved by arbitration, any party may serve an offer in writing upon any other party to the action to allow judgment to be taken or an award to be entered in accordance with the terms and conditions stated at that time. The written offer shall include a statement of the offer, containing the terms and conditions of the judgment or award, and a provision that allows the accepting party to indicate acceptance of the offer by signing a statement that the offer is accepted. Any acceptance of the offer, whether made on the document containing the offer or on a separate document of acceptance, shall be in writing and shall be signed by counsel for the accepting party or, if not represented by counsel, by the accepting party.

(1) If the offer is accepted, the offer with proof of acceptance shall be filed and the clerk or the judge shall enter judgment accordingly. In the case of an arbitration, the offer with proof of acceptance shall be filed with the arbitrator or arbitrators who shall promptly render an award accordingly.

(2) If the offer is not accepted prior to trial or arbitration or within 30 days after it is made, whichever occurs first, it shall be deemed withdrawn, and cannot be given in evidence upon the trial or arbitration.

(3) For purposes of this subdivision, a trial or arbitration shall be deemed to be actually commenced at the beginning of the opening statement of the plaintiff or counsel, and if there is no opening statement, then at the time of the administering of the oath or affirmation to the first witness, or the introduction of any evidence.

(c)(1) If an offer made by a defendant is not accepted and the plaintiff fails to obtain a more favorable judgment or award, the plaintiff shall not recover his or her postoffer costs and shall pay the defendant's costs from the time of the offer. In addition, in any action or proceeding other than an eminent domain action, the court or arbitrator, in its discretion, may require the plaintiff to pay a reasonable sum to cover costs of the services of expert witnesses, who are not regular employees of any party, actually incurred and reasonably necessary in either, or both, preparation for trial or arbitration, or during trial or arbitration, of the case by the defendant.

(2)(A) In determining whether the plaintiff obtains a more favorable judgment, the court or arbitrator shall exclude the postoffer costs.

(B) It is the intent of the Legislature in enacting subparagraph (A) to supersede the holding in Encinitas Plaza Real v. Knight, 209 Cal.App.3d 996, that attorney's fees awarded to the prevailing party were not costs for purposes of this section but were part of the judgment.

(d) If an offer made by a plaintiff is not accepted and the defendant fails to obtain a more favorable judgment or award in any action or proceeding other than an eminent domain action, the court or arbitrator, in its discretion, may require the defendant to pay a reasonable sum to cover postoffer costs of the services of expert witnesses, who are not regular employees of any party, actually incurred and reasonably necessary in either, or both, preparation for trial or arbitration, or during trial or arbitration, of the case by the plaintiff, in addition to plaintiff's costs.

(e) If an offer made by a defendant is not accepted and the plaintiff fails to obtain a more favorable judgment or award, the costs under this section, from the time of the offer, shall be deducted from any damages awarded in favor of the plaintiff. If the costs awarded under this section exceed the amount of the damages awarded to the plaintiff the net amount shall be awarded to the defendant and judgment or award shall be entered accordingly.

(f) Police officers shall be deemed to be expert witnesses for the purposes of this section. For purposes of this section, "plaintiff" includes a cross-complainant and "defendant" includes a cross-defendant. Any judgment or award entered pursuant to this section shall be deemed to be a compromise settlement.

(g) This chapter does not apply to either of the following:

(1) An offer that is made by a plaintiff in an eminent domain action.

(2) Any enforcement action brought in the name of the people of the State of California by the Attorney General, a district attorney, or a city attorney, acting as a public prosecutor.

(h) The costs for services of expert witnesses for trial under subdivisions (c) and (d) shall not exceed those specified in Section 68092.5 of the Government Code.

(i) This section shall not apply to labor arbitrations filed pursuant to memoranda of understanding under the Ralph C. Dills Act (Chapter 10.3 (commencing with Section 3512) of Division 4 of Title 1 of the Government Code). *(Added by Stats.1971, c. 1679, p. 3605, § 3. Amended by Stats.1977, c. 458, p. 1513, § 1; Stats.1986, c. 540, § 14; Stats.1987, c. 1080, § 8; Stats.1994, c. 332 (S.B.1324), § 1; Stats.1997, c. 892 (S.B.73), § 1; Stats.1999, c. 353 (S.B.1161), § 1; Stats.2001, c. 153 (A.B.732), § 1; Stats.2005, c. 706 (A.B.1742), § 13.)*

Research References

Rutter, Cal. Practice Guide: A.D.R. Ch. 4-B, B. Judicial Arbitration.

Rutter, Cal. Practice Guide: A.D.R. Ch. 5-H, H. Conduct of Arbi Proceedings.

Rutter, Cal. Practice Guide: A.D.R. Ch. 5-J, J. Challenging an ated Arbitrator's Award in Court.

Rutter, Cal. Practice Guide: A.D.R. Ch. 3B-C, C. Statut ADR.

Rutter, Cal. Practice Guide: A.D.R. Gen. Matls., High

Rutter, Cal. Practice Guide: A.D.R. Ch. 4-B, Outli

Rutter, Cal. Practice Guide: A.D.R. Ch. 5-H, Ou -B, B. Appealable

Rutter, Cal. Practice Guide: A.D.R. Ch. 5-J, O

Rutter, Cal. Practice Guide: Civil Appeals & s Ch. 2-C, C. Nonap- Judgments and Orders.

Rutter, Cal. Practice Guide: Civil App Writs Ch. 2-D, D. Standing pealable Orders.

Rutter, Cal. Practice Guide: Civil als & Writs Ch. 3-E, E. Filing to Appeal.

Rutter, Cal. Practice Guide: Steps.

Civ. Pro.

CHAPTER 3.5.   CONFIDENTIAL SETTLEMENT AGREEMENTS

Section

1002. Confidential settlement agreements; prohibited in certain instances involving felony sex offenses.

§ 1002. Confidential settlement agreements; prohibite~~d~~ certain instances involving felony sex offenses

(a) Notwithstanding any other provision of law, a ~~c~~ivil settlement agreement is prohibited in any civil acti~~e~~ly sex foundation for which establishes a cause of damages for an act that may be prosecuted offense.

(b) Subdivision (a) does not preclude ~~i~~dentifying informing the defendant or any person acting ~~s~~ction 530.5 of the disclosing any medical information o~~r~~ony sex offense or of mation, as defined in subdivision~~~~e relationship between Penal Code, regarding the victim~~~~ crime victim to disclose this any information revealing the crime victim to disclose this the victim and the defend~~~~ construed to limit the ri~~~~ information.

(c) Subdivision (a) does not apply to or affect the ability of the parties to enter into a settlement agreement or stipulated agreement that requires the nondisclosure of the amount of any money paid in a settlement of a claim. *(Added by Stats.2006, c. 151 (A.B.2875), § 1.)*

Research References

Rutter, Cal. Practice Guide: Civ. Pro. Before Trial Ch. 12(II)-H, H. Professional Responsibility Considerations Re Settlements.
Rutter, Cal. Practice Guide: Personal Injury Ch. 4-G, G. Concluding and Enforcing Settlement.

CHAPTER 4. MOTIONS AND ORDERS

Section
1003.   Order and motion defined.
1004.   Motions; court in which made.
1005.   Written notice for motions; service and filing of moving and supporting papers.
1005.5.   Making and pendency of motion.
1006.   Transfer of motion or order to show cause.
1008.   Application to reconsider and modify or revoke prior order; affidavit; noncompliance; revocation of order; contempt; appeal.

§ 1003. Order and motion defined

Every direction of a court or judge, made or entered in writing, and not included in a judgment, is denominated an order. An application for an order is a motion. *(Enacted in 1872. Amended by Stats.1933, c. 744, p. 1897, § 173; Stats.1951, c. 1737, p. 4132, § 131, operative Jan. 1, 1952.)*

Research References

Rutter, Cal. Practice Guide: Civil Appeals & Writs Ch. 2-B, B. Appealable Judgments and Orders.
Rutter, Cal. Practice Guide: Civ. Pro. Before Trial Ch. 9(I)-A, A. Introduction.
Rutter, Cal. Practice Guide: Enforcing Judgments/Debts Ch. 6A-3, "Judgment," "Judgment Debtor" and "Judgment Creditor" Defined.
Miller and Starr California Real Estate § 33:6, Procedures for Appointment.
7 Witkin Cal. Proc. 5th Judgment § 8, (S 8) Order.
7 Witkin Cal. Proc. 5th Judgment § 54, Other Orders.
6 Witkin Cal. Proc. 5th Proceedings Without Trial § 1, (S 1) Application for Order.
6 Witkin Cal. Proc. 5th Proceedings Without Trial § 2, (S 2) Types of Motions.
6 Witkin Cal. Proc. 5th Proceedings Without Trial § 44, (S 44) How Order is Made.

§ 1004. Motions; court in which made

Except as provided in section 166 of this code, motions must be made in the court in which the action is pending. *(Enacted in 1872. Amended by Code Am.1880, c. 23, p. 12, § 1; Stats.1933, c. 44, p. 1897, § 174.)*

Research References

al. Practice Guide: Civil Trials & Evidence Ch. 18-B, B. Motion Trial.
6 Wit ractice Guide: Civil Trials & Evidence Ch. 8C-J, J. Judicial of

§ 1005. 5th Proceedings Without Trial § 3, (S 3) Main Action
moving a

(a) Written nce **for motions; service and filing of** (b) and (c), for the**ing papers**

(1) Notice of Apple given, as prescribed in subdivisions ment under Section 484otions:

d Hearing for Writ of Attach-

(2) Notice of Application and Hearing for Claim and Delivery under Section 512.030.

(3) Notice of Hearing for Claim of Exemption under Section 706.105.

(4) Motion to Quash Summons pursuant to subdivision (b) of Section 418.10.

(5) Motion for Determination of Good Faith Settlement pursuant to Section 877.6.

(6) Hearing for Discovery of Peace Officer Personnel Records pursuant to Section 1043 of the Evidence Code.

(7) Notice of Hearing of Third–Party Claim pursuant to Section 720.320.

(8) Motion for an Order to Attend Deposition more than 150 miles from deponent's residence pursuant to Section 2025.260.

(9) Notice of Hearing of Application for Relief pursuant to Section 946.6 of the Government Code.

(10) Motion to Set Aside Default or Default Judgment and for Leave to Defend Actions pursuant to Section 473.5.

(11) Motion to Expunge Notice of Pendency of Action pursuant to Section 405.30.

(12) Motion to Set Aside Default and for Leave to Amend pursuant to Section 585.5.

(13) Any other proceeding under this code in which notice is required and no other time or method is prescribed by law or by court or judge.

(b) Unless otherwise ordered or specifically provided by law, all moving and supporting papers shall be served and filed at least 16 court days before the hearing. The moving and supporting papers served shall be a copy of the papers filed or to be filed with the court. However, if the notice is served by mail, the required 16–day period of notice before the hearing shall be increased by five calendar days if the place of mailing and the place of address are within the State of California, 10 calendar days if either the place of mailing or the place of address is outside the State of California but within the United States, and 20 calendar days if either the place of mailing or the place of address is outside the United States, and if the notice is served by facsimile transmission, express mail, or another method of delivery providing for overnight delivery, the required 16–day period of notice before the hearing shall be increased by two calendar days. Section 1013, which extends the time within which a right may be exercised or an act may be done, does not apply to a notice of motion, papers opposing a motion, or reply papers governed by this section. All papers opposing a motion so noticed shall be filed with the court and a copy served on each party at least nine court days, and all reply papers at least five court days before the hearing.

The court, or a judge thereof, may prescribe a shorter time.

(c) Notwithstanding any other provision of this section, all papers opposing a motion and all reply papers shall be served by personal delivery, facsimile transmission, express mail, or other means consistent with Sections 1010, 1011, 1012, and 1013, and reasonably calculated to ensure delivery to the other party or parties not later than the close of the next business day after the time the opposing papers or reply papers, as applicable, are filed. This subdivision applies to the service of opposition and reply papers regarding motions for summary judgment or summary adjudication, in addition to the motions listed in subdivision (a).

The court, or a judge thereof, may prescribe a shorter time. *(Enacted in 1872. Amended by Code Am.1880, c. 23, p. 13, § 2; Stats.1907, c. 326, p. 601, § 1; Stats.1919, c. 195, p. 289, § 1; Stats.1933, c. 744, p. 1897, § 175; Stats.1935 c. 658, p. 1816, § 1; Stats.1935, c. 722, p. 1966, § 27; Stats.1951, c. 1737, p. 4132, § 132, operative Jan. 1, 1952; Stats.1963, c. 878, p. 2126, § 3;*

Stats.1980, c. 196, p. 418, § 1; Stats.1981, c. 197, p. 1121, § 1; Stats.1984, c. 352, § 2; Stats.1986, c. 246, § 1; Stats.1989, c. 693, § 6; Stats.1990, c. 1491 (A.B.3765), § 7; Stats.1991, c. 1090 (A.B.1484), § 5; Stats.1992, c. 339 (S.B.1409), § 2; Stats.1993, c. 456 (A.B.58), § 14.5; Stats.1997, c. 571 (A.B.1088), § 1.3; Stats.1998, c. 932 (A.B.1094), § 18; Stats.1999, c. 43 (A.B.1132), § 1; Stats.2002, c. 806 (A.B.3027), § 16; Stats.2004, c. 182 (A.B.3081), § 13; Stats.2004, c. 171 (A.B.3078), § 3; Stats.2005, c. 294 (A.B.333), § 3.)

Law Revision Commission Comments

Subdivision (a) of Section 1005 is amended to reflect nonsubstantive reorganization of the rules governing civil discovery. See 2004 Cal. Stat. ch. 182. [35 Cal.L.Rev.Comm. Reports 77 (2005)].

Research References

Rutter, Cal. Practice Guide: A.D.R. Ch. 6-C, C. Referees.

Rutter, Cal. Practice Guide: Civ. Pro. Before Trial Ch. 1-C, C. Prelawsuit Notices, Claims and Demands.

Rutter, Cal. Practice Guide: Civ. Pro. Before Trial Ch. 3-B, B. Jurisdiction Over Parties-Personal Jurisdiction.

Rutter, Cal. Practice Guide: Civ. Pro. Before Trial Ch. 10-C, C. Procedural Requirements-Moving Party.

Rutter, Cal. Practice Guide: Civ. Pro. Before Trial Ch. 10-D, D. Procedural Requirements-Opposing Party.

Rutter, Cal. Practice Guide: Civ. Pro. Before Trial Ch. 10-E, E. Procedural Requirements-Reply Papers.

Rutter, Cal. Practice Guide: Civ. Pro. Before Trial Ch. 10-J, J. Appellate Review of Summary Judgment and Adjudication Orders.

Rutter, Cal. Practice Guide: Civ. Pro. Before Trial Ch. 11-B, B. Involuntary Dismissals.

Rutter, Cal. Practice Guide: Civ. Pro. Before Trial Ch. 14-C, C. Procedural Issues.

Rutter, Cal. Practice Guide: Civ. Pro. Before Trial Ch. 8C-3, "Not Privileged".

Rutter, Cal. Practice Guide: Civ. Pro. Before Trial Ch. 8E-8, Place of Deposition.

Rutter, Cal. Practice Guide: Civ. Pro. Before Trial Ch. 8F-4, Protective Orders.

Rutter, Cal. Practice Guide: Civ. Pro. Before Trial Ch. 8F-7, Motion to Compel Answers.

Rutter, Cal. Practice Guide: Civ. Pro. Before Trial Ch. 8E-16, Sanctions Re Depositions.

Rutter, Cal. Practice Guide: Civ. Pro. Before Trial Ch. 7(I)-A, A. Demurrers.

Rutter, Cal. Practice Guide: Civ. Pro. Before Trial Ch. 7(I)-B, B. Motions to Strike.

Rutter, Cal. Practice Guide: Civ. Pro. Before Trial Ch. 9(I)-B, B. Preparing and Filing Motions.

Rutter, Cal. Practice Guide: Civ. Pro. Before Trial Ch. 9(I)-C, C. Opposing the Motion-And Rebutting the Opposition.

Rutter, Cal. Practice Guide: Civ. Pro. Before Trial Ch. 9(I)-G, G. Motions Regulating Counsel.

Rutter, Cal. Practice Guide: Civ. Pro. Before Trial Ch. 12(I)-B, B. Case Management ("Fast Track") System.

Rutter, Cal. Practice Guide: Civ. Pro. Before Trial Ch. 12(I)-C, C. Claims for Trial Setting Preference.

Rutter, Cal. Practice Guide: Civ. Pro. Before Trial Ch. 12(I)-E, E. Consolidation, Coordination and Bifurcation.

Rutter, Cal. Practice Guide: Civ. Pro. Before Trial Ch. 9(II)-A, A. Injunctions.

Rutter, Cal. Practice Guide: Civ. Pro. Before Trial Ch. 9(II)-C, C. Writ of Possession ("Claim and Delivery").

Rutter, Cal. Practice Guide: Civ. Pro. Before Trial Ch. 9(II)-D, D. Attachment.

Rutter, Cal. Practice Guide: Civ. Pro. Before Trial Ch. 12(II)-E, E. Motion to Determine "Good Faith" of "Piecemeal" Settlement (CCP § 877.6).

Rutter, Cal. Practice Guide: Civ. Pro. Before Trial Ch. 9(III)-C, C. Sanctions Under CCP § 128.7.

Rutter, Cal. Practice Guide: Civil Trials & Evidence Ch. 2-D, D. Securing Trial by Jury.

Rutter, Cal. Practice Guide: Civil Trials & Evidence Ch. 4-G, G. Motion to Sever or Bifurcate.

Rutter, Cal. Practice Guide: Civil Trials & Evidence Ch. 18-A, A. Motion for Judgment Notwithstanding the Verdict ("JNOV").

Rutter, Cal. Practice Guide: Civil Trials & Evidence Ch. 18-C, C. Other Post-Trial Motions.

Rutter, Cal. Practice Guide: Civil Trials & Evidence Ch. 18-A, Outline a.

Rutter, Cal. Practice Guide: Enforcing Judgments/Debts Ch. 1-B, B. Accepting the Collection Case.

Rutter, Cal. Practice Guide: Enforcing Judgments/Debts Ch. 4-A, A. Attachment.

Rutter, Cal. Practice Guide: Enforcing Judgments/Debts Ch. 4-B, B. Claim and Delivery.

Rutter, Cal. Practice Guide: Enforcing Judgments/Debts Ch. 6F-5, Earnings Exempt from Garnishment.

Rutter, Cal. Practice Guide: Enforcing Judgments/Debts Ch. 6H-4, Hearing on Third Party Claim.

Rutter, Cal. Practice Guide: Fed.Civ.Pro. Before Trial Ch. 1-D, D. Choosing Between State and Federal Courts.

Rutter, Cal. Practice Guide: Personal Injury Ch. 4-D, D. Techniques Where Settlement Not Forthcoming.

Rutter, Cal. Practice Guide: Personal Injury Ch. 5-A, A. Prelawsuit Filings.

Rutter, Cal. Practice Guide: Personal Injury Ch. 6-B, B. Overview of Selected Discovery Procedures.

Rutter, Cal. Practice Guide: Personal Injury Ch. 8-B, B. After Trial Date Set (Three to Four Months Before Trial).

Rutter, Cal. Practice Guide: Personal Injury Ch. 9-E, E. Order of Trial and Proof and Related Matters.

Miller and Starr California Real Estate § 33:6, Procedures for Appointment.

Miller and Starr California Real Estate § 11:154, Expungement of a Lis Pendens--Procedure and Grounds for Expungement.

3 Witkin Cal. Proc. 5th Actions § 304, Filing and Service of Petition.

3 Witkin Cal. Proc. 5th Actions § 391, in General.

8 Witkin Cal. Proc. 5th Attack Judgment Trial Court § 213, (S 213) Notice of Motion.

1 Witkin Cal. Proc. 5th Attorneys § 389, (S 389) Counsel Pro Hac Vice.

2 Witkin Cal. Proc. 5th Courts § 203, Invalid Rules.

2 Witkin Cal. Proc. 5th Courts § 262, Minimum Time Standards.

2 Witkin Cal. Proc. 5th Courts § 289, (S 289) in General.

8 Witkin Cal. Proc. 5th Enforcement of Judgment § 262, (S 262) Notice, Opposition, and Hearing.

8 Witkin Cal. Proc. 5th Enforcement of Judgment § 378, (S 378) Application and Notice.

2 Witkin Cal. Proc. 5th Jurisdiction § 216, General Appearance in Ancillary Proceeding.

4 Witkin Cal. Proc. 5th Pleading § 307, (S 307) Authority for Motion.

5 Witkin Cal. Proc. 5th Pleading § 895, (S 895) Motions.

5 Witkin Cal. Proc. 5th Pleading § 981, (S 981) Hearing.

5 Witkin Cal. Proc. 5th Pleading § 1014, (S 1014) in General.

6 Witkin Cal. Proc. 5th Proceedings Without Trial § 5, (S 5) Time of Motion.

6 Witkin Cal. Proc. 5th Proceedings Without Trial § 12, (S 12) in General.

6 Witkin Cal. Proc. 5th Proceedings Without Trial § 15, (S 15) Required Period Before Hearing.

6 Witkin Cal. Proc. 5th Proceedings Without Trial § 16, (S 16) Shortening Time.

6 Witkin Cal. Proc. 5th Proceedings Without Trial § 17, Statutory Extension Based on Manner of Service.

6 Witkin Cal. Proc. 5th Proceedings Without Trial § 31, Express Limitations.

6 Witkin Cal. Proc. 5th Proceedings Without Trial § 33, (S 33) General Requirements.

6 Witkin Cal. Proc. 5th Proceedings Without Trial § 41, Affidavits and Declarations.

6 Witkin Cal. Proc. 5th Proceedings Without Trial § 146, Filing of Motion Prevents Default.

6 Witkin Cal. Proc. 5th Proceedings Without Trial § 217, (S 217) in General.

6 Witkin Cal. Proc. 5th Proceedings Without Trial § 220, (S 220) Reply.

6 Witkin Cal. Proc. 5th Provisional Remedies § 101, Statutory Requirement.

6 Witkin Cal. Proc. 5th Provisional Remedies § 368, (S 368) in General.

6 Witkin Cal. Proc. 5th Provisional Remedies § 330E, (S 330E) (New)-Hearing, Determination, and Enforcement.

7 Witkin Cal. Proc. 5th Trial § 12, (S 12) Illustrations.

12 Witkin, California Summary 10th Real Property § 78, (S 78) Division of Property.

5 Witkin, California Summary 10th Torts § 84, Notice or Application.

§ 1005.5. Making and pendency of motion

A motion upon all the grounds stated in the written notice thereof is deemed to have been made and to be pending before the court for all purposes, upon the due service and filing of the notice of motion, but this shall not deprive a party of a hearing of the motion to which he is otherwise entitled. Procedure upon a motion for new trial shall be as otherwise provided. (*Added by Stats.1953, c. 909, p. 2265, § 1.*)

Research References

Rutter, Cal. Practice Guide: Civ. Pro. Before Trial Ch. 10-C, C. Procedural Requirements-Moving Party.
Rutter, Cal. Practice Guide: Civ. Pro. Before Trial Ch. 9(I)-A, A. Introduction.
Rutter, Cal. Practice Guide: Civ. Pro. Before Trial Ch. 9(I)-B, B. Preparing and Filing Motions.
Rutter, Cal. Practice Guide: Civil Trials & Evidence Ch. 18-A, A. Motion for Judgment Notwithstanding the Verdict ("JNOV").
8 Witkin Cal. Proc. 5th Attack Judgment Trial Court § 67, in General.
8 Witkin Cal. Proc. 5th Attack Judgment Trial Court § 142, Hearing and Determination.
8 Witkin Cal. Proc. 5th Attack Judgment Trial Court § 175, (S 175) in General.
6 Witkin Cal. Proc. 5th Proceedings Without Trial § 5, (S 5) Time of Motion.
6 Witkin Cal. Proc. 5th Proceedings Without Trial § 38, Making of Motion.
6 Witkin Cal. Proc. 5th Proceedings Without Trial § 214, (S 214) Time After Which Motion May be Made.

§ 1006. Transfer of motion or order to show cause

When a notice of motion is given, or an order to show cause is made returnable before a judge out of court, and at the time fixed for the motion, or on the return day of the order, the judge is unable to hear the parties, the matter may be transferred by his order to some other judge, before whom it might originally have been brought. (*Enacted in 1872. Amended by Stats.1933, c. 744, p. 1897, § 176; Stats.1951, c. 1737, p. 4132, § 133, operative Jan. 1, 1952.*)

Research References

6 Witkin Cal. Proc. 5th Proceedings Without Trial § 36, (S 36) Nature of Hearing.

§ 1008. Application to reconsider and modify or revoke prior order; affidavit; noncompliance; revocation of order; contempt; appeal

(a) When an application for an order has been made to a judge, or to a court, and refused in whole or in part, or granted, or granted conditionally, or on terms, any party affected by the order may, within 10 days after service upon the party of written notice of entry of the order and based upon new or different facts, circumstances, or law, make application to the same judge or court that made the order, to reconsider the matter and modify, amend, or revoke the prior order. The party making the application shall state by affidavit what application was made before, when and to what judge, what order or decisions were made, and what new or different facts, circumstances, or law are claimed to be shown.

(b) A party who originally made an application for an order which was refused in whole or part, or granted conditionally or on terms, may make a subsequent application for the same order upon new or different facts, circumstances, or law, in which case it shall be shown by affidavit what application was made before, when and to what judge, what order or decisions were made, and what new or different facts, circumstances, or law are claimed to be shown. For a failure to comply with this subdivision, any

order made on a subsequent application may be revoked or set aside on ex parte motion.

(c) If a court at any time determines that there has been a change of law that warrants it to reconsider a prior order it entered, it may do so on its own motion and enter a different order.

(d) A violation of this section may be punished as a contempt and with sanctions as allowed by Section 128.7. In addition, an order made contrary to this section may be revoked by the judge or commissioner who made it, or vacated by a judge of the court in which the action or proceeding is pending.

(e) This section specifies the court's jurisdiction with regard to applications for reconsideration of its orders and renewals of previous motions, and applies to all applications to reconsider any order of a judge or court, or for the renewal of a previous motion, whether the order deciding the previous matter or motion is interim or final. No application to reconsider any order or for the renewal of a previous motion may be considered by any judge or court unless made according to this section.

(f) For the purposes of this section, an alleged new or different law shall not include a later enacted statute without a retroactive application.

(g) An order denying a motion for reconsideration made pursuant to subdivision (a) is not separately appealable. However, if the order that was the subject of a motion for reconsideration is appealable, the denial of the motion for reconsideration is reviewable as part of an appeal from that order.

(h) This section applies to all applications for interim orders. (*Added by Stats.1978, c. 631, § 2. Amended by Stats.1992, c. 460 (S.B.1805), § 4; Stats.1998, c. 200 (S.B.1556), § 2; Stats.2011, c. 78 (A.B.1067), § 1.*)

Research References

Rutter, Cal. Practice Guide: A.D.R. Ch. 5-G, G. Procedures to Enforce Arbitration.
Rutter, Cal. Practice Guide: A.D.R. Ch. 6-B, B. Temporary Judges.
Rutter, Cal. Practice Guide: Civil Appeals & Writs Ch. 2-B, B. Appealable Judgments and Orders.
Rutter, Cal. Practice Guide: Civil Appeals & Writs Ch. 2-C, C. Nonappealable Orders.
Rutter, Cal. Practice Guide: Civil Appeals & Writs Ch. 3-C, C. Extensions of Filing Deadline.
Rutter, Cal. Practice Guide: Civil Appeals & Writs Ch. 5-B, B. Types of Motions, Applications and Requests.
Rutter, Cal. Practice Guide: Civil Appeals & Writs Ch. 8-C, C. Standards of Appellate Review.
Rutter, Cal. Practice Guide: Civil Appeals & Writs Ch. 15-A, A. Overview.
Rutter, Cal. Practice Guide: Civil Appeals & Writs Ch. 15-C, C. Statutory Writs.
Rutter, Cal. Practice Guide: Civil Appeals & Writs Ch. 3-C, Outline C.
Rutter, Cal. Practice Guide: Civil Appeals & Writs Form 15:B.2, Sample Return to Writ Petition.
Rutter, Cal. Practice Guide: Civ. Pro. Before Trial Ch. 10-I, I. Challenging Judgment or Order in Trial Court.
Rutter, Cal. Practice Guide: Civ. Pro. Before Trial Ch. 11-B, B. Involuntary Dismissals.
Rutter, Cal. Practice Guide: Civ. Pro. Before Trial Ch. 7(I)-A, A. Demurrers.
Rutter, Cal. Practice Guide: Civ. Pro. Before Trial Ch. 7(I)-C, C. Motion for Judgment on the Pleadings.
Rutter, Cal. Practice Guide: Civ. Pro. Before Trial Ch. 9(I)-D, D. Hearing.
Rutter, Cal. Practice Guide: Civ. Pro. Before Trial Ch. 9(I)-E, E. Posthearing Procedures.
Rutter, Cal. Practice Guide: Civ. Pro. Before Trial Ch. 9(II)-A, A. Injunctions.
Rutter, Cal. Practice Guide: Civ. Pro. Before Trial Ch. 9(II)-D, D. Attachment.
Rutter, Cal. Practice Guide: Civ. Pro. Before Trial Gen. Matls., Highlights.

Rutter, Cal. Practice Guide: Civil Trials & Evidence Ch. 12-B, B. Motion for Nonsuit.

Rutter, Cal. Practice Guide: Civil Trials & Evidence Ch. 16-A, A. General Considerations Re Nonjury Trials.

Rutter, Cal. Practice Guide: Civil Trials & Evidence Ch. 18-A, A. Motion for Judgment Notwithstanding the Verdict ("JNOV").

Rutter, Cal. Practice Guide: Civil Trials & Evidence Ch. 18-B, B. Motion for New Trial.

Rutter, Cal. Practice Guide: Civil Trials & Evidence Ch. 12-B, Outline B.

Rutter, Cal. Practice Guide: Civil Trials & Evidence Ch. 16-A, Outline a.

Rutter, Cal. Practice Guide: Enforcing Judgments/Debts Ch. 4-A, A. Attachment.

Rutter, Cal. Practice Guide: Enforcing Judgments/Debts Ch. 4-A, Outline a.

Rutter, Cal. Practice Guide: Family Law Ch. 7-C, C. Custody Awards, Generally.

Rutter, Cal. Practice Guide: Insurance Litigation Ch. 15-F, F. Pretrial Motions.

Rutter, Cal. Practice Guide: Insurance Litigation Ch. 7B-F, F. Terminating Duty to Defend.

Rutter, Cal. Practice Guide: Personal Injury Ch. 4-D, D. Techniques Where Settlement Not Forthcoming.

Rutter, Cal. Practice Guide: Prof. Responsibility Ch. 11-J, J. Post-Trial Motions.

16 NO. 3 Miller & Starr, California Real Estate Newsalert 3, Commercial Arbitration.

3 Witkin Cal. Proc. 5th Actions § 917, Former Law.

3 Witkin Cal. Proc. 5th Actions § 918, Current Law.

9 Witkin Cal. Proc. 5th Appeal § 165, Order Denying Motion for Reconsideration.

9 Witkin Cal. Proc. 5th Appeal § 600, in General.

9 Witkin Cal. Proc. 5th Appeal § 603, Reconsideration of Appealable Order.

9 Witkin Cal. Proc. 5th Appeal § 1009, Extension After Denial of Motion.

8 Witkin Cal. Proc. 5th Attack Judgment Trial Court § 4, Coram Nobis and Coram Vobis.

8 Witkin Cal. Proc. 5th Attack Judgment Trial Court § 75, (S 75) Time is Jurisdictional.

7 Witkin Cal. Proc. 5th Judgment § 235, (S 235) Statutory Authorization.

2 Witkin Cal. Proc. 5th Jurisdiction § 329, Act in Excess of Jurisdiction.

4 Witkin Cal. Proc. 5th Pleading § 309, (S 309) Necessity of Notice.

4 Witkin Cal. Proc. 5th Pleading § 314, Order and Review of Order.

5 Witkin Cal. Proc. 5th Pleading § 984, Reconsideration.

6 Witkin Cal. Proc. 5th Proceedings Without Trial § 46, (S 46) in General.

6 Witkin Cal. Proc. 5th Proceedings Without Trial § 47, Requirements.

6 Witkin Cal. Proc. 5th Proceedings Without Trial § 48, What Are Not Grounds for Relief.

6 Witkin Cal. Proc. 5th Proceedings Without Trial § 49, in General.

6 Witkin Cal. Proc. 5th Proceedings Without Trial § 50, Inherent Judicial Authority.

6 Witkin Cal. Proc. 5th Proceedings Without Trial § 51, in General.

6 Witkin Cal. Proc. 5th Proceedings Without Trial § 52, Distinction: Court's Authority to Construe as Different Motion.

6 Witkin Cal. Proc. 5th Proceedings Without Trial § 53, (S 53) Reconsideration by Different Judge.

6 Witkin Cal. Proc. 5th Proceedings Without Trial § 53, (S 53) Reconsideration by Different Judge.

6 Witkin Cal. Proc. 5th Proceedings Without Trial § 54, (S 54) Sanctions.

6 Witkin Cal. Proc. 5th Proceedings Without Trial § 55, (S 55) Statutory Authorization.

6 Witkin Cal. Proc. 5th Proceedings Without Trial § 196, (S 196) Renewal of Motion.

6 Witkin Cal. Proc. 5th Proceedings Without Trial § 199, (S 199) Nature and Purpose of Objection.

6 Witkin Cal. Proc. 5th Proceedings Without Trial § 255, (S 255) Challenging Order in Trial Court.

6 Witkin Cal. Proc. 5th Proceedings Without Trial § 566, Confirmation of Award.

6 Witkin Cal. Proc. 5th Provisional Remedies § 110, (S 110) Renewed Application.

7 Witkin Cal. Proc. 5th Trial § 195, (S 195) Deceiving or Taking Advantage of Court.

2 Witkin, California Summary 10th Insurance § 275, Inception and Duration of Duty.

10 Witkin, California Summary 10th Parent and Child § 58, (S 58) Grant or Denial.

10 Witkin, California Summary 10th Parent and Child § 662, Nature and Purpose.

11 Witkin, California Summary 10th Husband and Wife § 207, (S 207) Modification.

11 Witkin, California Summary 10th Husband and Wife § 384, (S 384) Orders After Notice and Hearing.

7 Witkin, California Summary 10th Constitutional Law § 143, (S 143) in General.

CHAPTER 5. NOTICES, AND FILING AND SERVICE OF PAPERS

§ 1010. Notices; writing; contents; supporting papers; service; defaulting party

Notices must be in writing, and the notice of a motion, other than for a new trial, must state when, and the grounds upon which it will be made, and the papers, if any, upon which it is to be based. If any such paper has not previously been served upon the party to be notified and was not filed by him, a copy of such paper must accompany the notice. Notices and other papers may be served upon the party or attorney in the manner prescribed in this chapter, when not otherwise provided by this code. No bill of exceptions, notice of appeal, or other notice or paper, other than amendments to the pleadings, or an amended pleading, need be served upon any party whose default has been duly entered or who has not appeared in the action or proceeding. (*Enacted in 1872. Amended by Stats.1907, c. 327, p. 601, § 1; Stats.1935, c. 722, p. 1966, § 28.*)

Research References

Rutter, Cal. Practice Guide: A.D.R. Ch. 5-G, G. Procedures to Enforce Arbitration.

Rutter, Cal. Practice Guide: A.D.R. Ch. 6-C, C. Referees.

Rutter, Cal. Practice Guide: Civil Appeals & Writs Ch. 9-D, D. Procedural Rules.

Rutter, Cal. Practice Guide: Civ. Pro. Before Trial Ch. 1-C, C. Prelawsuit Notices, Claims and Demands.

Rutter, Cal. Practice Guide: Civ. Pro. Before Trial Ch. 5-B, B. Entry of Default.

Rutter, Cal. Practice Guide: Civ. Pro. Before Trial Ch. 6-D, D. Cross-Complaint.

Rutter, Cal. Practice Guide: Civ. Pro. Before Trial Ch. 6-E, E. Amended and Supplemental Pleadings.

Rutter, Cal. Practice Guide: Civ. Pro. Before Trial Ch. 10-C, C. Procedural Requirements-Moving Party.

§ 1010.5. Filing of papers by facsimile transmission; payment of fees with credit cards

The Judicial Council may adopt rules permitting the filing of papers by facsimile transmission, both directly with the courts and through third parties. Notwithstanding any other provision of law, the rules may provide that the facsimile transmitted document shall constitute an original document, and that notwithstanding Section 6159 of the Government Code or Title 1.3 (commencing with Section 1747) of Part 4 of Division 3 of the Civil Code, any court authorized to accept a credit card as payment pursuant to this section may add a surcharge to the amount of the transaction to be borne by the litigant to cover charges imposed on credit card transactions regarding fax filings between a litigant and the court.

If the Judicial Council adopts rules permitting the filing of papers by facsimile transmission, the consent of the Judicial Council shall not be necessary to permit the use of credit cards to pay fees for the filing of papers by facsimile transmission directly with the court, provided that the court charges a processing fee to the filing party sufficient to cover the cost to the court of processing payment by credit card. *(Added by Stats.1992, c. 339 (S.B.1409), § 3. Amended by Stats.2001, c. 824 (A.B.1700), § 10.)*

Research References

§ 1010.6. Electronic service of documents; local rules for electronic filing; uniform rules

(a) A document may be served electronically in an action filed with the court as provided in this section, in accordance with rules adopted pursuant to subdivision (e).

(1) For purposes of this section:

(A) "Electronic service" means service of a document, on a party or other person, by either electronic transmission or electronic notification. Electronic service may be performed directly by a party, by an agent of a party, including the party's attorney, or through an electronic filing service provider.

(B) "Electronic transmission" means the transmission of a document by electronic means to the electronic service address at or through which a party or other person has authorized electronic service.

(C) "Electronic notification" means the notification of the party or other person that a document is served by sending an electronic message to the electronic address at or through which the party or other person has authorized electronic service, specifying the exact name of the document served, and providing a hyperlink at which the served document may be viewed and downloaded.

(2) If a document may be served by mail, express mail, overnight delivery, or facsimile transmission, electronic service of the document is authorized when a party has agreed to accept service electronically in that action.

(3) In any action in which a party has agreed to accept electronic service under paragraph (2), or in which the court has ordered electronic service under subdivision (c) or (d), the court may electronically serve any document issued by the court that is not required to be personally served in the same manner that parties electronically serve documents. The electronic service of documents by the court shall have the same legal effect as service by mail, except as provided in paragraph (4).

(4) Electronic service of a document is complete at the time of the electronic transmission of the document or at the time that the electronic notification of service of the document is sent. However, any period of notice, or any right or duty to do any act or make any response within any period or on a date certain after the service of the document, which time period or date is prescribed by statute or rule of court, shall be extended after service by electronic means by two court days, but the extension shall not apply to extend the time for filing any of the following:

(A) A notice of intention to move for new trial.

(B) A notice of intention to move to vacate judgment under Section 663a.

(C) A notice of appeal.

This extension applies in the absence of a specific exception provided by any other statute or rule of court.

(b) A trial court may adopt local rules permitting electronic filing of documents, subject to rules adopted pursuant to subdivision (e) and the following conditions:

(1) A document that is filed electronically shall have the same legal effect as an original paper document.

(2)(A) When a document to be filed requires the signature, not under penalty of perjury, of an attorney or a self-represented party, the document shall be deemed to have been signed by that attorney or self-represented party if filed electronically.

(B) When a document to be filed requires the signature, under penalty of perjury, of any person, the document shall be deemed to have been signed by that person if filed electronically and if a printed form of the document has been signed by that person prior to, or on the same day as, the date of filing. The attorney or person filing the document represents, by the act of filing, that the declarant has complied with this section. The attorney or person filing the document shall maintain the printed form of the document bearing the original signature and make it available for review and copying upon the request of the court or any party to the action or proceeding in which it is filed.

(3) Any document that is electronically filed with the court after the close of business on any day shall be deemed to have been filed on the next court day. "Close of business," as used in this paragraph, shall mean 5 p.m. or the time at which the court would not accept filing at the court's filing counter, whichever is earlier.

(4) The court receiving a document filed electronically shall issue a confirmation that the document has been received and filed. The confirmation shall serve as proof that the document has been filed.

(5) Upon electronic filing of a complaint, petition, or other document that must be served with a summons, a trial court, upon request of the party filing the action, shall issue a summons

with the court seal and the case number. The court shall keep the summons in its records and may electronically transmit a copy of the summons to the requesting party. Personal service of a printed form of the electronic summons shall have the same legal effect as personal service of an original summons. If a trial court plans to electronically transmit a summons to the party filing a complaint, the court shall immediately upon receipt of the complaint notify the attorney or party that a summons will be electronically transmitted to the electronic address given by the person filing the complaint.

(6) The court shall permit a party or attorney to file an application for waiver of court fees and costs, in lieu of requiring the payment of the filing fee, as part of the process involving the electronic filing of a document. The court shall consider and determine the application in accordance with Sections 68630 to 68641, inclusive, of the Government Code and shall not require the party or attorney to submit any documentation other than that set forth in Sections 68630 to 68641, inclusive, of the Government Code. Nothing in this section shall require the court to waive a filing fee that is not otherwise waivable.

(c) If a trial court adopts rules conforming to subdivision (b), it may provide by order that all parties to an action file and serve documents electronically in a class action, a consolidated action, or a group of actions, a coordinated action, or an action that is deemed complex under Judicial Council rules, provided that the trial court's order does not cause undue hardship or significant prejudice to any party in the action.

(d)(1) Notwithstanding subdivision (b), the Orange County Superior Court may, by local rule and until July 1, 2014, establish a pilot project to require parties to specified civil actions to electronically file and serve documents, subject to the requirements set forth in paragraphs (1), (2), (4), (5), and (6) of subdivision (b) and rules adopted pursuant to subdivision (e) and the following conditions:

(A) The court shall have the ability to maintain the official court record in electronic format for all cases where electronic filing is required.

(B) The court and the parties shall have access either to more than one electronic filing service provider capable of electronically filing documents with the court, or to electronic filing access directly through the court. Any fees charged by the court shall be for no more than the actual cost of the electronic filing and service of the documents, and shall be waived when deemed appropriate by the court, including, but not limited to, for any party who has received a fee waiver. Any fees charged by an electronic filing service provider shall be reasonable and shall be waived when deemed appropriate by the court, including, but not limited to, for any party who has received a fee waiver.

(C) The court shall have a procedure for the filing of nonelectronic documents in order to prevent the program from causing undue hardship or significant prejudice to any party in an action, including, but not limited to, unrepresented parties.

(D) A court that elects to require electronic filing pursuant to this subdivision may permit documents to be filed electronically until 12 a.m. of the day after the court date that the filing is due, and the filing shall be considered timely. However, if same day service of a document is required, the document shall be electronically filed by 5 p.m. on the court date that the filing is due. Ex parte documents shall be electronically filed on the same date and within the same time period as would be required for the filing of a hard copy of the ex parte documents at the clerk's window in the participating county. Documents filed on or after 12 a.m., or filed upon a noncourt day, will be deemed filed on the soonest court day following the filing.

(2) If a pilot project is established pursuant to paragraph (1), the Judicial Council shall conduct an evaluation of the pilot

project and report to the Legislature, on or before December 31, 2013, on the results of the evaluation. The evaluation shall review, among other things, the cost of the program to participants, cost-effectiveness for the court, effect on unrepresented parties and parties with fee waivers, and ease of use for participants.

(e) The Judicial Council shall adopt uniform rules for the electronic filing and service of documents in the trial courts of the state, which shall include statewide policies on vendor contracts, privacy, and access to public records, and rules relating to the integrity of electronic service. These rules shall conform to the conditions set forth in this section, as amended from time to time.

(f) The Judicial Council shall, on or before July 1, 2014, adopt uniform rules to permit the mandatory electronic filing and service of documents for specified civil actions in the trial courts of the state, which shall be informed by any study performed pursuant to paragraph (2) of subdivision (d) and which shall include statewide policies on vendor contracts, privacy, access to public records, unrepresented parties, parties with fee waivers, hardships, reasonable exceptions to electronic filing, and rules relating to the integrity of electronic service. These rules shall conform to the conditions set forth in this section, as amended from time to time.

(g)(1) Upon the adoption of uniform rules by the Judicial Council for mandatory electronic filing and service of documents for specified civil actions in the trial courts of the state, as specified in subdivision (f), a superior court may, by local rule, require mandatory electronic filing, pursuant to paragraph (2) of this subdivision.

(2) Any superior court that elects to adopt mandatory electronic filing shall do so pursuant to the requirements and conditions set forth in this section, including, but not limited to, paragraphs (1), (2), (4), (5), and (6) of subdivision (b) of this section, and subparagraphs (A), (B), and (C) of paragraph (1) of subdivision (d), and pursuant to the rules adopted by the Judicial Council, as specified in subdivision (f). *(Added by Stats.1999, c. 514 (S.B.367), § 1. Amended by Stats.2001, c. 824 (A.B.1700), § 10.5; Stats.2005, c. 300 (A.B.496), § 5; Stats.2010, c. 156 (S.B.1274), § 1; Stats.2011, c. 296 (A.B.1023), § 40; Stats.2012, c. 320 (A.B.2073), § 1.)*

Research References

Rutter, Cal. Practice Guide: Civil Appeals & Writs Ch. 3-B, B. Filing Deadlines.
Rutter, Cal. Practice Guide: Civil Appeals & Writs Ch. 3-C, C. Extensions of Filing Deadline.
Rutter, Cal. Practice Guide: Civil Appeals & Writs Ch. 16-C, C. Notice of Appeal.
Rutter, Cal. Practice Guide: Civ. Pro. Before Trial Ch. 4-B, B. Issuance of Summons.
Rutter, Cal. Practice Guide: Civ. Pro. Before Trial Ch. 10-C, C. Procedural Requirements-Moving Party.
Rutter, Cal. Practice Guide: Civ. Pro. Before Trial Ch. 8E-4, Notice of Deposition.
Rutter, Cal. Practice Guide: Civ. Pro. Before Trial Ch. 8E-6, Subpoena to Nonparty Deponent or Business Records Custodian.
Rutter, Cal. Practice Guide: Civ. Pro. Before Trial Ch. 8F-5, Responding to Interrogatories.
Rutter, Cal. Practice Guide: Civ. Pro. Before Trial Ch. 8F-7, Motion to Compel Answers.
Rutter, Cal. Practice Guide: Civ. Pro. Before Trial Ch. 8G-5, Responses to Rfas.
Rutter, Cal. Practice Guide: Civ. Pro. Before Trial Ch. 8H-8, Enforcing Demand.
Rutter, Cal. Practice Guide: Civ. Pro. Before Trial Ch. 8J-4, Demand Procedure.
Rutter, Cal. Practice Guide: Civ. Pro. Before Trial Ch. 9(I)-D, D. Hearing.
Rutter, Cal. Practice Guide: Civ. Pro. Before Trial Ch. 7(I)-A, A. Demurrers.
Rutter, Cal. Practice Guide: Civ. Pro. Before Trial Ch. 7(I)-B, B. Motions to Strike.
Rutter, Cal. Practice Guide: Civ. Pro. Before Trial Ch. 7(I)-C, C. Motion for Judgment on the Pleadings.
Rutter, Cal. Practice Guide: Civ. Pro. Before Trial Ch. 9(I)-B, B. Preparing and Filing Motions.
Rutter, Cal. Practice Guide: Civ. Pro. Before Trial Ch. 7(II)-F, F. Procedure.
Rutter, Cal. Practice Guide: Civil Trials & Evidence Ch. 18-B, B. Motion for New Trial.
4 Witkin Cal. Proc. 5th Pleading § 21, (S 21) Nature of Filing Process.
4 Witkin Cal. Proc. 5th Pleading § 22, (S 22) Duties of Courts and Filers.
4 Witkin Cal. Proc. 5th Pleading § 23, (S 23) Court Action on Receipt of Filing.
4 Witkin Cal. Proc. 5th Pleading § 24, (S 24) Electronic Service.
6 Witkin Cal. Proc. 5th Proceedings Without Trial § 27, When Permitted.
6 Witkin Cal. Proc. 5th Proceedings Without Trial § 28, Mechanics of Service.
6 Witkin Cal. Proc. 5th Proceedings Without Trial § 30, Statutory Extension.
6 Witkin Cal. Proc. 5th Proceedings Without Trial § 35, (S 35) Electronic Filing.
7 Witkin Cal. Proc. 5th Trial § 6B, (S 6B) (New)-Pretrial Proceedings.

§ 1011. Personal service; service upon attorney; service at party's residence

The service may be personal, by delivery to the party or attorney on whom the service is required to be made, or it may be as follows:

(a) If upon an attorney, service may be made at the attorney's office, by leaving the notice or other papers in an envelope or package clearly labeled to identify the attorney being served, with a receptionist or with a person having charge thereof. When there is no person in the office with whom the notice or papers may be left for purposes of this subdivision at the time service is to be effected, service may be made by leaving them between the hours of nine in the morning and five in the afternoon, in a conspicuous place in the office, or, if the attorney's office is not open so as to admit of that service, then service may be made by leaving the notice or papers at the attorney's residence, with some person of not less than 18 years of age, if the attorney's residence is in the same county with his or her office, and, if the attorney's residence is not known or is not in the same county with his or her office, or being in the same county it is not open, or a person 18 years of age or older cannot be found at the attorney's residence, then service may be made by putting the notice or papers, enclosed in a sealed envelope, into the post office or a mail box, subpost office, substation, or mail chute or other like facility regularly maintained by the Government of the United States directed to the attorney at his or her office, if known and otherwise to the attorney's residence, if known. If neither the attorney's office nor residence is known, service may be made by delivering the notice or papers to the address of the attorney or party of record as designated on the court papers, or by delivering the notice or papers to the clerk of the court, for the attorney.

(b) If upon a party, service shall be made in the manner specifically provided in particular cases, or, if no specific provision is made, service may be made by leaving the notice or other paper at the party's residence, between the hours of eight in the morning and six in the evening, with some person of not less than 18 years of age. If at the time of attempted service between those hours a person 18 years of age or older cannot be found at the party's residence, the notice or papers may be served by mail. If the party's residence is not known, then service may be made by delivering the notice or papers to the clerk of the court, for that party. *(Enacted in 1872. Amended by Stats.1907, c. 327, p. 602, § 2; Stats.1919, c. 194, p. 289, § 1; Stats.1933, c. 744, p. 1898, § 178; Stats.1949, c. 456, p. 799, § 2;*

Stats.1951, c. 1737, p. 4132, § 135, operative Jan. 1, 1952; Stats.1989, c. 1105, § 8; Stats.1994, c. 467 (S.B.1858), § 1; Stats.2007, c. 263 (A.B.310), § 11.)

Law Revision Commission Comments

Section 1011 is amended to delete unnecessary language authorizing the judge to substitute for the clerk if there is no clerk. See Code Civ. Proc. § 167 (judge may perform any act court clerk may perform); Gov't Code §§ 69840–69848 (duties of clerk of superior court), 71620(b) (executive or administrative officer has authority of clerk of court). [35 Cal.L.Rev. Comm. Reports 219 (2006)].

Research References

Rutter, Cal. Practice Guide: Civ. Pro. Before Trial Ch. 8E-6, Subpoena to Nonparty Deponent or Business Records Custodian.

Rutter, Cal. Practice Guide: Civ. Pro. Before Trial Ch. 9(I)-A, A. Introduction.

Rutter, Cal. Practice Guide: Civ. Pro. Before Trial Ch. 9(I)-B, B. Preparing and Filing Motions.

Rutter, Cal. Practice Guide: Civ. Pro. Before Trial Ch. 9(I)-G, G. Motions Regulating Counsel.

Rutter, Cal. Practice Guide: Civ. Pro. Before Trial Ch. 9(II)-A, A. Injunctions.

Rutter, Cal. Practice Guide: Civil Trials & Evidence Ch. 1-C, C. Marshalling the Evidence.

Rutter, Cal. Practice Guide: Civil Trials & Evidence Ch. 18-B, B. Motion for New Trial.

Rutter, Cal. Practice Guide: Enforcing Judgments/Debts Ch. 6A-10, Service of Writs, Notices and Other Papers in Enforcement Proceedings.

Rutter, Cal. Practice Guide: Prof. Responsibility Ch. 10-B, B. Withdrawal (Termination) by Lawyer.

Miller and Starr California Real Estate § 19:228, Prejudgment Remedies; Attachment and Receivership--Writ of Possession Before Trial.

1 Witkin Cal. Proc. 5th Attorneys § 69, (S 69) Motion to Withdraw.

2 Witkin Cal. Proc. 5th Courts § 366, (S 366) Miscellaneous Duties.

8 Witkin Cal. Proc. 5th Enforcement of Judgment § 26, in General.

6 Witkin Cal. Proc. 5th Proceedings Without Trial § 19, on Attorney or Party.

7 Witkin Cal. Proc. 5th Trial § 6B, (S 6B) (New)-Pretrial Proceedings.

§ 1012. Service by mail; when authorized

Service by mail may be made where the person on whom it is to be made resides or has his office at a place where there is a delivery service by mail, or where the person making the service and the person on whom it is to be made reside or have their offices in different places between which there is a regular communication by mail. *(Enacted in 1872. Amended by Code Am.1873–74, c. 383, p. 343, § 137; Stats.1931, c. 739, p. 1534, § 1.)*

Research References

Rutter, Cal. Practice Guide: Civ. Pro. Before Trial Ch. 1-C, C. Prelawsuit Notices, Claims and Demands.

Rutter, Cal. Practice Guide: Civ. Pro. Before Trial Ch. 8E-6, Subpoena to Nonparty Deponent or Business Records Custodian.

Rutter, Cal. Practice Guide: Civ. Pro. Before Trial Ch. 9(I)-B, B. Preparing and Filing Motions.

Rutter, Cal. Practice Guide: Civil Trials & Evidence Ch. 1-C, C. Marshalling the Evidence.

Rutter, Cal. Practice Guide: Civil Trials & Evidence Ch. 18-B, B. Motion for New Trial.

Rutter, Cal. Practice Guide: Personal Injury Ch. 5-A, A. Prelawsuit Filings.

Rutter, Cal. Practice Guide: Personal Injury Ch. 7-J, J. Arbitration of Uninsured Motorist Claims.

5 Witkin Cal. Proc. 5th Pleading § 1245, Where Defendant Does Not Appear.

6 Witkin Cal. Proc. 5th Proceedings Without Trial § 21, When Permitted.

6 Witkin Cal. Proc. 5th Proceedings Without Trial § 23, Proof of Service.

7 Witkin Cal. Proc. 5th Trial § 6B, (S 6B) (New)-Pretrial Proceedings.

§ 1013. Service by mail, Express Mail or facsimile transmission; procedure; completion of service; extension of time; electronic service permitted

(a) In case of service by mail, the notice or other paper shall be deposited in a post office, mailbox, subpost office, substation, or mail chute, or other like facility regularly maintained by the United States Postal Service, in a sealed envelope, with postage paid, addressed to the person on whom it is to be served, at the office address as last given by that person on any document filed in the cause and served on the party making service by mail; otherwise at that party's place of residence. Service is complete at the time of the deposit, but any period of notice and any right or duty to do any act or make any response within any period or on a date certain after service of the document, which time period or date is prescribed by statute or rule of court, shall be extended five calendar days, upon service by mail, if the place of address and the place of mailing is within the State of California, 10 calendar days if either the place of mailing or the place of address is outside the State of California but within the United States, and 20 calendar days if either the place of mailing or the place of address is outside the United States, but the extension shall not apply to extend the time for filing notice of intention to move for new trial, notice of intention to move to vacate judgment pursuant to Section 663a, or notice of appeal. This extension applies in the absence of a specific exception provided for by this section or other statute or rule of court.

(b) The copy of the notice or other paper served by mail pursuant to this chapter shall bear a notation of the date and place of mailing or be accompanied by an unsigned copy of the affidavit or certificate of mailing.

(c) In case of service by Express Mail, the notice or other paper must be deposited in a post office, mailbox, subpost office, substation, or mail chute, or other like facility regularly maintained by the United States Postal Service for receipt of Express Mail, in a sealed envelope, with Express Mail postage paid, addressed to the person on whom it is to be served, at the office address as last given by that person on any document filed in the cause and served on the party making service by Express Mail; otherwise at that party's place of residence. In case of service by another method of delivery providing for overnight delivery, the notice or other paper must be deposited in a box or other facility regularly maintained by the express service carrier, or delivered to an authorized courier or driver authorized by the express service carrier to receive documents, in an envelope or package designated by the express service carrier with delivery fees paid or provided for, addressed to the person on whom it is to be served, at the office address as last given by that person on any document filed in the cause and served on the party making service; otherwise at that party's place of residence. Service is complete at the time of the deposit, but any period of notice and any right or duty to do any act or make any response within any period or on a date certain after service of the document served by Express Mail or other method of delivery providing for overnight delivery shall be extended by two court days. The extension shall not apply to extend the time for filing notice of intention to move for new trial, notice of intention to move to vacate judgment pursuant to Section 663a, or notice of appeal. This extension applies in the absence of a specific exception provided for by this section or other statute or rule of court.

(d) The copy of the notice or other paper served by Express Mail or another means of delivery providing for overnight delivery pursuant to this chapter shall bear a notation of the date and place of deposit or be accompanied by an unsigned copy of the affidavit or certificate of deposit.

Civ. Pro.

(e) Service by facsimile transmission shall be permitted only where the parties agree and a written confirmation of that agreement is made. The Judicial Council may adopt rules implementing the service of documents by facsimile transmission and may provide a form for the confirmation of the agreement required by this subdivision. In case of service by facsimile transmission, the notice or other paper must be transmitted to a facsimile machine maintained by the person on whom it is served at the facsimile machine telephone number as last given by that person on any document which he or she has filed in the cause and served on the party making the service. Service is complete at the time of transmission, but any period of notice and any right or duty to do any act or make any response within any period or on a date certain after service of the document, which time period or date is prescribed by statute or rule of court, shall be extended, after service by facsimile transmission, by two court days, but the extension shall not apply to extend the time for filing notice of intention to move for new trial, notice of intention to move to vacate judgment pursuant to Section 663a, or notice of appeal. This extension applies in the absence of a specific exception provided for by this section or other statute or rule of court.

(f) The copy of the notice or other paper served by facsimile transmission pursuant to this chapter shall bear a notation of the date and place of transmission and the facsimile telephone number to which transmitted, or to be accompanied by an unsigned copy of the affidavit or certificate of transmission which shall contain the facsimile telephone number to which the notice or other paper was transmitted.

(g) Electronic service shall be permitted pursuant to Section 1010.6 and the rules on electronic service in the California Rules of Court.

(h) Subdivisions (b), (d), and (f) are directory. *(Enacted in 1872. Amended by Code Am.1873–74, c. 383, p. 343, § 138; Stats.1907, c. 327, p. 602, § 3; Stats.1929, c. 480, p. 845, § 1; Stats.1931, c. 739, p. 1534, § 2; Stats.1949, c. 456, p. 800, § 3; Stats.1967, c. 169, p. 1267, § 6; Stats.1968, c. 166, p. 390, § 1; Stats.1974, c. 281, p. 544, § 1; Stats.1974, c. 282, § 1, eff. May 28, 1974; Stats.1974, c. 282, § 2, eff. May 28, 1974, operative Jan. 1, 1975; Stats.1980, c. 196, § 2; Stats.1992, c. 339 (S.B.1409), § 4; Stats.1995, c. 576 (A.B.1225), § 3.8; Stats.2001, c. 812 (A.B.223), § 8; Stats.2010, c. 156 (S.B.1274), § 2.)*

Research References

California Real Estate Forms (Miller & Starr) § 2:17, Office Lease--Mixed Use Building.
California Real Estate Forms (Miller & Starr) § 2:34, Sublease--Shared Office Space.
Rutter, Cal. Practice Guide: A.D.R. Ch. 4-B, B. Judicial Arbitration.
Rutter, Cal. Practice Guide: A.D.R. Ch. 5-G, G. Procedures to Enforce Arbitration.
Rutter, Cal. Practice Guide: A.D.R. Ch. 5-J, J. Challenging and Enforcing Arbitrator's Award in Court.
Rutter, Cal. Practice Guide: Civil Appeals & Writs Ch. 3-B, B. Filing Deadlines.
Rutter, Cal. Practice Guide: Civil Appeals & Writs Ch. 3-C, C. Extensions of Filing Deadline.
Rutter, Cal. Practice Guide: Civil Appeals & Writs Ch. 4-F, F. Extensions of Time and Default.
Rutter, Cal. Practice Guide: Civil Appeals & Writs Ch. 5-B, B. Types of Motions, Applications and Requests.
Rutter, Cal. Practice Guide: Civil Appeals & Writs Ch. 5-C, C. Motion, Application and Request Procedures.
Rutter, Cal. Practice Guide: Civil Appeals & Writs Ch. 7-C, C. Stay by Posting Security (Bond or Undertaking).
Rutter, Cal. Practice Guide: Civil Appeals & Writs Ch. 9-D, D. Procedural Rules.
Rutter, Cal. Practice Guide: Civil Appeals & Writs Ch. 13-B, B. Petition for Review Procedures.

Rutter, Cal. Practice Guide: Civil Appeals & Writs Ch. 14-B, B. Recovery of Appellate Costs and Attorney Fees.
Rutter, Cal. Practice Guide: Civil Appeals & Writs Ch. 15-C, C. Statutory Writs.
Rutter, Cal. Practice Guide: Civil Appeals & Writs Ch. 5-C, Outline C.
Rutter, Cal. Practice Guide: Civil Appeals & Writs Ch. 7-C, Outline C.
Rutter, Cal. Practice Guide: Civil Appeals & Writs Ch. 15-C, Outline C.
Rutter, Cal. Practice Guide: Civ. Pro. Before Trial Ch. 1-C, C. Prelawsuit Notices, Claims and Demands.
Rutter, Cal. Practice Guide: Civ. Pro. Before Trial Ch. 3-B, B. Jurisdiction Over Parties-Personal Jurisdiction.
Rutter, Cal. Practice Guide: Civ. Pro. Before Trial Ch. 4-D, D. Service of Summons.
Rutter, Cal. Practice Guide: Civ. Pro. Before Trial Ch. 10-D, D. Procedural Requirements-Opposing Party.
Rutter, Cal. Practice Guide: Civ. Pro. Before Trial Ch. 10-E, E. Procedural Requirements-Reply Papers.
Rutter, Cal. Practice Guide: Civ. Pro. Before Trial Ch. 11-B, B. Involuntary Dismissals.
Rutter, Cal. Practice Guide: Civ. Pro. Before Trial Ch. 13-E, E. the Arbitration Hearing.
Rutter, Cal. Practice Guide: Civ. Pro. Before Trial Ch. 13-G, G. Trial De Novo.
Rutter, Cal. Practice Guide: Civ. Pro. Before Trial Ch. 8E-4, Notice of Deposition.
Rutter, Cal. Practice Guide: Civ. Pro. Before Trial Ch. 8E-6, Subpoena to Nonparty Deponent or Business Records Custodian.
Rutter, Cal. Practice Guide: Civ. Pro. Before Trial Ch. 8F-5, Responding to Interrogatories.
Rutter, Cal. Practice Guide: Civ. Pro. Before Trial Ch. 8F-7, Motion to Compel Answers.
Rutter, Cal. Practice Guide: Civ. Pro. Before Trial Ch. 8G-5, Responses to Rfas.
Rutter, Cal. Practice Guide: Civ. Pro. Before Trial Ch. 8H-8, Enforcing Demand.
Rutter, Cal. Practice Guide: Civ. Pro. Before Trial Ch. 8J-4, Demand Procedure.
Rutter, Cal. Practice Guide: Civ. Pro. Before Trial Ch. 8L-2, Special Discovery Procedures Permitted.
Rutter, Cal. Practice Guide: Civ. Pro. Before Trial Ch. 7(I)-A, A. Demurrers.
Rutter, Cal. Practice Guide: Civ. Pro. Before Trial Ch. 7(I)-B, B. Motions to Strike.
Rutter, Cal. Practice Guide: Civ. Pro. Before Trial Ch. 7(I)-C, C. Motion for Judgment on the Pleadings.
Rutter, Cal. Practice Guide: Civ. Pro. Before Trial Ch. 9(I)-B, B. Preparing and Filing Motions.
Rutter, Cal. Practice Guide: Civ. Pro. Before Trial Ch. 9(I)-C, C. Opposing the Motion-And Rebutting the Opposition.
Rutter, Cal. Practice Guide: Civ. Pro. Before Trial Ch. 9(I)-D, D. Hearing.
Rutter, Cal. Practice Guide: Civ. Pro. Before Trial Ch. 9(I)-E, E. Posthearing Procedures.
Rutter, Cal. Practice Guide: Civ. Pro. Before Trial Ch. 12(I)-B, B. Case Management ("Fast Track") System.
Rutter, Cal. Practice Guide: Civ. Pro. Before Trial Ch. 7(II)-F, F. Procedure.
Rutter, Cal. Practice Guide: Civ. Pro. Before Trial Ch. 12(II)-C, C. Statutory Offer to Compromise (CCP § 998).
Rutter, Cal. Practice Guide: Civ. Pro. Before Trial Ch. 9(I)-B, Outline B.
Rutter, Cal. Practice Guide: Civil Trials & Evidence Ch. 1-A, A. Importance of Statewide and Local Rules of Court.
Rutter, Cal. Practice Guide: Civil Trials & Evidence Ch. 1-C, C. Marshalling the Evidence.
Rutter, Cal. Practice Guide: Civil Trials & Evidence Ch. 3-A, A. Challenges for Cause.
Rutter, Cal. Practice Guide: Civil Trials & Evidence Ch. 3-B, B. Peremptory Challenge of Judge (CCP § 170.6).
Rutter, Cal. Practice Guide: Civil Trials & Evidence Ch. 16-E, E. Statement of Decision.
Rutter, Cal. Practice Guide: Civil Trials & Evidence Ch. 17-D, D. Costs.
Rutter, Cal. Practice Guide: Civil Trials & Evidence Ch. 18-A, A. Motion for Judgment Notwithstanding the Verdict ("JNOV").
Rutter, Cal. Practice Guide: Civil Trials & Evidence Ch. 18-B, B. Motion for New Trial.
Rutter, Cal. Practice Guide: Civil Trials & Evidence Ch. 18-A, Outline a.

Rutter, Cal. Practice Guide: Enforcing Judgments/Debts Ch. 6A-5, Amount Recoverable Under Judgment.

Rutter, Cal. Practice Guide: Enforcing Judgments/Debts Ch. 6F-3, Issuance and Service of Earnings Withholding Orders.

Rutter, Cal. Practice Guide: Family Law Ch. 6-A, A. Child Support.

Rutter, Cal. Practice Guide: Insurance Litigation Ch. 5-A, A. Cancellation by Insurer.

Rutter, Cal. Practice Guide: Personal Injury Ch. 4-D, D. Techniques Where Settlement Not Forthcoming.

Rutter, Cal. Practice Guide: Personal Injury Ch. 5-A, A. Prelawsuit Filings.

Rutter, Cal. Practice Guide: Personal Injury Ch. 6-B, B. Overview of Selected Discovery Procedures.

Rutter, Cal. Practice Guide: Personal Injury Ch. 6-C, C. Physical and Mental Examinations (CCP § 2032.020 et seq.).

Rutter, Cal. Practice Guide: Personal Injury Ch. 6-D, D. Expert Witness Information Exchanges (CCP § 2034.210 et seq.).

Rutter, Cal. Practice Guide: Personal Injury Ch. 6-E, E. Special Discovery Rules and Procedures in Limited Civil Cases.

Rutter, Cal. Practice Guide: Personal Injury Ch. 7-G, G. Arbitration Hearing.

Rutter, Cal. Practice Guide: Personal Injury Ch. 7-I, I. Trial De Novo After Arbitration Award.

Rutter, Cal. Practice Guide: Personal Injury Ch. 8-B, B. After Trial Date Set (Three to Four Months Before Trial).

Rutter, Cal. Practice Guide: Personal Injury Ch. 9-A, A. Assignment to Trial.

Rutter, Cal. Practice Guide: Personal Injury Ch. 9-M, M. Verdicts and Judgment.

Rutter, Cal. Practice Guide: Personal Injury Ch. 10-A, A. Motion for New Trial.

Rutter, Cal. Practice Guide: Personal Injury Ch. 10-C, C. Motion to Vacate and Enter Different Judgment.

Rutter, Cal. Practice Guide: Personal Injury Ch. 10-A, Outline a.

Rutter, Cal. Practice Guide: Real Prop. Transactions Ch. 10-B, B. Regulation of Real Property Managers and Legal Relationship Between Manager and Owner.

Rutter, Cal. Practice Guide: Prof. Responsibility Ch. 11-H, H. Proceedings Before Trial.

Miller and Starr California Real Estate § 28:28, Statutory Provisions Governing Notice.

Miller and Starr California Real Estate § 28:36, Time and Method for Service of the Preliminary Notice.

Miller and Starr California Real Estate § 19:193, When a Notice is Effective.

Miller and Starr California Real Estate § 19:205, Service of the Notice-- Legal Effect of the Notice; Tenant's Right to Cure a Default.

3 Witkin Cal. Proc. 5th Actions § 688, (S 688) in General.

3 Witkin Cal. Proc. 5th Actions § 727, (S 727) Service of Notice.

3 Witkin Cal. Proc. 5th Actions § 1020, (S 1020) No Extension of Time.

9 Witkin Cal. Proc. 5th Appeal § 552, Policy Considerations.

9 Witkin Cal. Proc. 5th Appeal § 555, (S 555) Jurisdictional Requirement: Filing in Trial Court.

9 Witkin Cal. Proc. 5th Appeal § 586, (S 586) in General.

8 Witkin Cal. Proc. 5th Attack Judgment Trial Court § 54, (S 54) Late Filing is Void.

8 Witkin Cal. Proc. 5th Attack Judgment Trial Court § 62, Commencement and Running of Period.

8 Witkin Cal. Proc. 5th Attack Judgment Trial Court § 74, (S 74) Extensions.

8 Witkin Cal. Proc. 5th Attack Judgment Trial Court § 141, Notice of Motion.

1 Witkin Cal. Proc. 5th Attorneys § 69, (S 69) Motion to Withdraw.

1 Witkin Cal. Proc. 5th Attorneys § 564, (S 564) Pleadings, Papers, and Motions.

2 Witkin Cal. Proc. 5th Courts § 146, Codification.

2 Witkin Cal. Proc. 5th Courts § 150, (S 150) Coordination Judge.

2 Witkin Cal. Proc. 5th Courts § 160, (S 160) Statutory Procedure.

2 Witkin Cal. Proc. 5th Courts § 262, Minimum Time Standards.

2 Witkin Cal. Proc. 5th Courts § 289, (S 289) in General.

8 Witkin Cal. Proc. 5th Enforcement of Judgment § 47, Memorandum of Costs.

8 Witkin Cal. Proc. 5th Enforcement of Judgment § 133, (S 133) Safe Deposit Boxes.

8 Witkin Cal. Proc. 5th Enforcement of Judgment § 267, Issuance by Local Child Support Agency.

8 Witkin Cal. Proc. 5th Enforcement of Judgment § 335, Hearing and Determination.

8 Witkin Cal. Proc. 5th Extraordinary Writs § 305, Shortened Limitations Period.

7 Witkin Cal. Proc. 5th Judgment § 145, (S 145) Service and Filing.

2 Witkin Cal. Proc. 5th Jurisdiction § 224, (S 224) Defendant's Election After Denial.

4 Witkin Cal. Proc. 5th Pleading § 355, (S 355) Peremptory Challenge of Assigned Judge.

5 Witkin Cal. Proc. 5th Pleading § 1033, Procedure.

6 Witkin Cal. Proc. 5th Proceedings Without Trial § 17, Statutory Extension Based on Manner of Service.

6 Witkin Cal. Proc. 5th Proceedings Without Trial § 22, Mechanics of Service.

6 Witkin Cal. Proc. 5th Proceedings Without Trial § 23, Proof of Service.

6 Witkin Cal. Proc. 5th Proceedings Without Trial § 24, When Permitted.

6 Witkin Cal. Proc. 5th Proceedings Without Trial § 25, Mechanics of Service.

6 Witkin Cal. Proc. 5th Proceedings Without Trial § 27, When Permitted.

6 Witkin Cal. Proc. 5th Proceedings Without Trial § 29, Proof of Service.

6 Witkin Cal. Proc. 5th Proceedings Without Trial § 30, Statutory Extension.

6 Witkin Cal. Proc. 5th Proceedings Without Trial § 31, Express Limitations.

6 Witkin Cal. Proc. 5th Proceedings Without Trial § 32, Implied Limitations.

6 Witkin Cal. Proc. 5th Proceedings Without Trial § 44, (S 44) How Order is Made.

6 Witkin Cal. Proc. 5th Proceedings Without Trial § 85, Formal Requirements.

6 Witkin Cal. Proc. 5th Proceedings Without Trial § 94, Offer is Not Revoked by Counteroffer.

6 Witkin Cal. Proc. 5th Proceedings Without Trial § 97, Time.

6 Witkin Cal. Proc. 5th Proceedings Without Trial § 98, Formal Requirements.

6 Witkin Cal. Proc. 5th Proceedings Without Trial § 215, (S 215) Notice of Motion.

6 Witkin Cal. Proc. 5th Proceedings Without Trial § 217, (S 217) in General.

6 Witkin Cal. Proc. 5th Proceedings Without Trial § 220, (S 220) Reply.

6 Witkin Cal. Proc. 5th Proceedings Without Trial § 616, (S 616) Time for Request.

6 Witkin Cal. Proc. 5th Provisional Remedies § 177, Safe Deposit Boxes.

7 Witkin Cal. Proc. 5th Trial § 75, (S 75) Statutory Provisions.

7 Witkin Cal. Proc. 5th Trial § 395, (S 395) Request by Party.

12 Witkin, California Summary 10th Real Property § 521, Identification of Property Owners or Managers.

12 Witkin, California Summary 10th Real Property § 526, (S 526) Changes in Short-Term Leases.

12 Witkin, California Summary 10th Real Property § 680, Periodic Tenancy.

12 Witkin, California Summary 10th Real Property § 727, (S 727) Methods of Service.

12 Witkin, California Summary 10th Real Property § 737, (S 737) Restoration of Possession.

10 Witkin, California Summary 10th Parent and Child § 416, (S 416) Application and Order.

11 Witkin, California Summary 10th Husband and Wife § 107, (S 107) Statement of Decision.

11 Witkin, California Summary 10th Husband and Wife § 251, (S 251) Issuance of Order.

11 Witkin, California Summary 10th Husband and Wife § 270, (S 270) Registration by Local Child Support Agency.

11 Witkin, California Summary 10th Husband and Wife § 272, (S 272) Vacation of Registration.

11 Witkin, California Summary 10th Husband and Wife § 313, (S 313) Payment to County by Court and Referral.

3 Witkin, California Summary 10th Agency and Employment § 319, (S 319) Notice of Appeal.

3 Witkin, California Summary 10th Agency and Employment § 672, in General.

2 Witkin Cal. Summ. 10th Workers' Compensation § 388, Service by Board.

2 Witkin Cal. Summ. 10th Workers' Compensation § 438, Petition, Answer, and Reply.

§ 1013a. Service by mail; proof

Proof of service by mail may be made by one of the following methods:

(1) An affidavit setting forth the exact title of the document served and filed in the cause, showing the name and residence or business address of the person making the service, showing that he or she is a resident of or employed in the county where the mailing occurs, that he or she is over the age of 18 years and not a party to the cause, and showing the date and place of deposit in the mail, the name and address of the person served as shown on the envelope, and also showing that the envelope was sealed and deposited in the mail with the postage thereon fully prepaid.

(2) A certificate setting forth the exact title of the document served and filed in the cause, showing the name and business address of the person making the service, showing that he or she is an active member of the State Bar of California and is not a party to the cause, and showing the date and place of deposit in the mail, the name and address of the person served as shown on the envelope, and also showing that the envelope was sealed and deposited in the mail with the postage thereon fully prepaid.

(3) An affidavit setting forth the exact title of the document served and filed in the cause, showing (A) the name and residence or business address of the person making the service, (B) that he or she is a resident of, or employed in, the county where the mailing occurs, (C) that he or she is over the age of 18 years and not a party to the cause, (D) that he or she is readily familiar with the business' practice for collection and processing of correspondence for mailing with the United States Postal Service, (E) that the correspondence would be deposited with the United States Postal Service that same day in the ordinary course of business, (F) the name and address of the person served as shown on the envelope, and the date and place of business where the correspondence was placed for deposit in the United States Postal Service, and (G) that the envelope was sealed and placed for collection and mailing on that date following ordinary business practices. Service made pursuant to this paragraph, upon motion of a party served, shall be presumed invalid if the postal cancellation date or postage meter date on the envelope is more than one day after the date of deposit for mailing contained in the affidavit.

(4) In case of service by the clerk of a court of record, a certificate by that clerk setting forth the exact title of the document served and filed in the cause, showing the name of the clerk and the name of the court of which he or she is the clerk, and that he or she is not a party to the cause, and showing the date and place of deposit in the mail, the name and address of the person served as shown on the envelope, and also showing that the envelope was sealed and deposited in the mail with the postage thereon fully prepaid. This form of proof is sufficient for service of process in which the clerk or deputy clerk signing the certificate places the document for collection and mailing on the date shown thereon, so as to cause it to be mailed in an envelope so sealed and so addressed on that date following standard court practices. Service made pursuant to this paragraph, upon motion of a party served and a finding of good cause by the court, shall be deemed to have occurred on the date of postage cancellation or postage meter imprint as shown on the envelope if that date is more than one day after the date of deposit for mailing contained in the certificate. *(Added by Stats.1931, c. 739, p. 1534, § 3. Amended by Stats.1953, c. 1110, p. 2606, § 1; Stats.1955, c. 779, p. 1379, § 1; Stats.1959, c. 345, p. 2268, § 1; Stats.1972, c. 601, p. 1065, § 3; Stats.1972, c. 1083, p. 2019, § 1; Stats.1973, c. 302, p. 718, § 1; Stats.1974, c. 282, p. 546, § 3, eff. May 28, 1974; Stats.1980, c. 196, p. 419, § 3;*

Stats.1987, c. 190, § 1; Stats.1988, c. 160, § 18; Stats.1995, c. 576 (A.B.1225), § 4.)

Research References

Rutter, Cal. Practice Guide: Civil Appeals & Writs Ch. 9-D, D. Procedural Rules.

Rutter, Cal. Practice Guide: Civ. Pro. Before Trial Ch. 9(I)-B, B. Preparing and Filing Motions.

Rutter, Cal. Practice Guide: Civil Trials & Evidence Ch. 1-J, J. Notice of Trial.

Rutter, Cal. Practice Guide: Civil Trials & Evidence Ch. 16-E, E. Statement of Decision.

Rutter, Cal. Practice Guide: Enforcing Judgments/Debts Ch. 6A-10, Service of Writs, Notices and Other Papers in Enforcement Proceedings.

Rutter, Cal. Practice Guide: Fed.Civ.Pro. Before Trial Ch. 12-B, B. Preparing and Filing Motions.

Rutter, Cal. Practice Guide: Personal Injury Ch. 5-A, A. Prelawsuit Filings.

Rutter, Cal. Practice Guide: Real Prop. Transactions Ch. 11-I, I. Lis Pendens.

Rutter, Cal. Practice Guide: Prof. Responsibility Ch. 1-B, B. Regulation of Admission to Practice Law.

Rutter, Cal. Practice Guide: Prof. Responsibility Ch. 11-G, G. Commencement of Disciplinary Proceedings.

3 Witkin Cal. Proc. 5th Actions § 262, Manner of Presentation.

3 Witkin Cal. Proc. 5th Actions § 265, Notice of Action Taken.

3 Witkin Cal. Proc. 5th Actions § 385, (S 385) Recordation.

9 Witkin Cal. Proc. 5th Appeal § 12D, (S 12D) (New)-Electronic Service.

8 Witkin Cal. Proc. 5th Enforcement of Judgment § 28, Proof of Service.

4 Witkin Cal. Proc. 5th Pleading § 24, (S 24) Electronic Service.

6 Witkin Cal. Proc. 5th Proceedings Without Trial § 23, Proof of Service.

6 Witkin Cal. Proc. 5th Proceedings Without Trial § 26, Proof of Service.

6 Witkin Cal. Proc. 5th Proceedings Without Trial § 29, Proof of Service.

7 Witkin Cal. Proc. 5th Trial § 75, (S 75) Statutory Provisions.

7 Witkin Cal. Proc. 5th Trial § 395, (S 395) Request by Party.

14 Witkin, California Summary 10th Wills and Probate § 397, Proof of Giving Notice.

§ 1014. Appearance defined; right to notices

A defendant appears in an action when the defendant answers, demurs, files a notice of motion to strike, files a notice of motion to transfer pursuant to Section 396b, moves for reclassification pursuant to Section 403.040, gives the plaintiff written notice of appearance, or when an attorney gives notice of appearance for the defendant. After appearance, a defendant or the defendant's attorney is entitled to notice of all subsequent proceedings of which notice is required to be given. Where a defendant has not appeared, service of notice or papers need not be made upon the defendant. *(Enacted in 1872. Amended by Stats.1955, c. 1452, p. 2644, § 8; Stats.1969, c. 345, p. 725, § 5; Stats.1973, c. 20, p. 36, § 11; Stats.1998, c. 931 (S.B.2139), § 106, eff. Sept. 28, 1998; Stats.1999, c. 344 (S.B.210), § 15, eff. Sept. 7, 1999.)*

Law Revision Commission Comments

Section 1014 is amended to reflect the fact that arrest of a defendant in a civil action is no longer permitted. See Code Civ.Proc. § 478 and Comment thereto.

Section 1014 is amended to accommodate unification of the municipal and superior courts in a county. Cal. Const. art. VI, § 5(e). The amendment reflects the addition of Section 395.9 (misclassification as limited civil case or otherwise), which sets forth a procedure for challenging a caption stating, or failing to state, that an action or proceeding is a limited civil case. See also Sections 85 (limited civil cases) & Comment, 399.5 (reclassification pursuant to Section 395.9), 400 (petition for writ of mandate), 422.30 (caption). [28 Cal.L.Rev.Comm. Reports 51 (1998)].

Section 1014 is amended to reflect relocation of the provisions governing reclassification of a civil case. [29 Cal.L.Rev.Comm. Reports App. 5 (1999)].

Research References

Rutter, Cal. Practice Guide: Civ. Pro. Before Trial Ch. 10-C, C. Procedural Requirements-Moving Party.

Rutter, Cal. Practice Guide: Civ. Pro. Before Trial Ch. 7(I)-A, A. Demurrers.

Rutter, Cal. Practice Guide: Civ. Pro. Before Trial Ch. 7(I)-B, B. Motions to Strike.

Rutter, Cal. Practice Guide: Civ. Pro. Before Trial Ch. 9(I)-B, B. Preparing and Filing Motions.

3 Witkin Cal. Proc. 5th Actions § 924, Time of Notice.

1 Witkin Cal. Proc. 5th Attorneys § 480, Statutory Framework.

2 Witkin Cal. Proc. 5th Jurisdiction § 192, Definition and Scope of Doctrine.

2 Witkin Cal. Proc. 5th Jurisdiction § 200, Personal Appearance Distinguished.

2 Witkin Cal. Proc. 5th Jurisdiction § 208, Notice of Appearance.

2 Witkin Cal. Proc. 5th Jurisdiction § 209, Answer or Demurrer.

2 Witkin Cal. Proc. 5th Jurisdiction § 210, Motions.

2 Witkin Cal. Proc. 5th Jurisdiction § 217, (S 217) in General.

2 Witkin Cal. Proc. 5th Jurisdiction § 232, Attempt to Extend Time to Plead.

5 Witkin Cal. Proc. 5th Pleading § 1245, Where Defendant Does Not Appear.

6 Witkin Cal. Proc. 5th Proceedings Without Trial § 12, (S 12) in General.

6 Witkin Cal. Proc. 5th Proceedings Without Trial § 214, (S 214) Time After Which Motion May be Made.

§ 1015. Service; nonresident party; service on clerk or attorney

When a plaintiff or a defendant, who has appeared, resides out of the state, and has no attorney in the action or proceeding, the service may be made on the clerk of the court, for that party. But in all cases where a party has an attorney in the action or proceeding, the service of papers, when required, must be upon the attorney instead of the party, except service of subpoenas, of writs, and other process issued in the suit, and of papers to bring the party into contempt. If the sole attorney for a party is removed or suspended from practice, then the party has no attorney within the meaning of this section. If the party's sole attorney has no known office in this state, notices and papers may be served by leaving a copy thereof with the clerk of the court, unless the attorney has filed in the cause an address of a place at which notices and papers may be served on the attorney, in which event they may be served at that place. *(Enacted in 1872. Amended by Stats.1907, c. 327, p. 602, § 4; Stats.1933, c. 744, p. 1899, § 179; Stats.1951, c. 1737, p. 4133, § 136, operative Jan. 1, 1952; Stats.2007, c. 263 (A.B.310), § 12.)*

Law Revision Commission Comments

Section 1015 is amended to delete unnecessary language authorizing the judge to substitute for the clerk if there is no clerk. See Code Civ. Proc. § 167 (judge may perform any act court clerk may perform); Gov't Code §§ 69840–69848 (duties of clerk of superior court), 71620(b) (executive or administrative officer has authority of clerk of court).

Section 1015 is also amended to make stylistic revisions and make the statute gender neutral. [35 Cal.L.Rev.Comm. Reports 219 (2006)].

Research References

Rutter, Cal. Practice Guide: Civ. Pro. Before Trial Ch. 8A-8, Discovery in Nonjudicial Proceedings.

Rutter, Cal. Practice Guide: Civ. Pro. Before Trial Ch. 9(I)-A, A. Introduction.

Rutter, Cal. Practice Guide: Civ. Pro. Before Trial Ch. 9(I)-B, B. Preparing and Filing Motions.

Rutter, Cal. Practice Guide: Personal Injury Ch. 7-J, J. Arbitration of Uninsured Motorist Claims.

Rutter, Cal. Practice Guide: Prof. Responsibility Ch. 10-B, B. Withdrawal (Termination) by Lawyer.

2 Witkin Cal. Proc. 5th Courts § 203, Invalid Rules.

2 Witkin Cal. Proc. 5th Courts § 366, (S 366) Miscellaneous Duties.

4 Witkin Cal. Proc. 5th Pleading § 29, (S 29) Service.

6 Witkin Cal. Proc. 5th Proceedings Without Trial § 13, General Rule.

6 Witkin Cal. Proc. 5th Proceedings Without Trial § 14, Exceptions.

2 Witkin Cal. Summ. 10th Workers' Compensation § 353, Appearance and Representation.

§ 1016. Service; process to bring party into contempt; inapplicability of certain sections

PRECEDING PROVISIONS NOT TO APPLY TO PROCEEDING TO BRING PARTY INTO CONTEMPT. The foregoing provisions of this Chapter do not apply to the service of a summons or other process, or of any paper to bring a party into contempt. *(Enacted in 1872.)*

§ 1017. Service; telegraphic copy; return; records; seal

SERVICE BY TELEGRAPH. Any summons, writ, or order in any civil suit or proceeding, and all other papers requiring service, may be transmitted by telegraph for service in any place, and the telegraphic copy of such writ, or order, or paper so transmitted, may be served or executed by the officer or person to whom it is sent for that purpose, and returned by him, if any return be requisite, in the same manner, and with the same force and effect in all respects, as the original thereof might be if delivered to him, and the officer or person serving or executing the same has the same authority, and is subject to the same liabilities, as if the copy were the original. The original, when a writ or order, must also be filed in the Court from which it was issued, and a certified copy thereof must be preserved in the telegraph office from which it was sent. In sending it, either the original or the certified copy may be used by the operator for that purpose. Whenever any document to be sent by telegraph bears a seal, either private or official, it is not necessary for the operator, in sending the same, to telegraph a description of the seal, or any words or device thereon, but the same may be expressed in the telegraphic copy by the letters "L.S.," or by the word "seal." *(Enacted in 1872.)*

Research References

Rutter, Cal. Practice Guide: Civ. Pro. Before Trial Ch. 9(I)-A, A. Introduction.

§ 1019. Size of type

Whenever any notice or publication is required by a provision in this code or any other code or statute of this state to be provided in a specified size of type or printing which is to be measured by points, the size required, unless otherwise specifically defined, shall be determined by the conventional customs and practices of the printing industry and within the tolerances permitted by conventional custom and practice in that industry, except that the provisions of this section shall not be used for purposes of evasion of any requirement for notice or publication. *(Added by Stats.1980, c. 199, p. 421, § 1.)*

Research References

Miller and Starr California Real Estate § 34:38, Liquidated Damages--In Real Property Marketing Contracts.

§ 1019.5. Motions; notice of court's decision

(a) When a motion is granted or denied, unless the court otherwise orders, notice of the court's decision or order shall be given by the prevailing party to all other parties or their attorneys, in the manner provided in this chapter, unless notice is waived by all parties in open court and is entered in the minutes.

(b) When a motion is granted or denied on the court's own motion, notice of the court's order shall be given by the court in the manner provided in this chapter, unless notice is waived by all parties in open court and is entered in the minutes. *(Added by Stats.1982, c. 704, p. 2861, § 10. Amended by Stats.1992, c. 1348 (A.B.2616), § 6.)*

Research References

Rutter, Cal. Practice Guide: Civil Appeals & Writs Ch. 3-B, B. Filing Deadlines.

Rutter, Cal. Practice Guide: Civil Appeals & Writs Gen. Matls., Highlights.

Rutter, Cal. Practice Guide: Civ. Pro. Before Trial Ch. 5-B, B. Entry of Default.

Rutter, Cal. Practice Guide: Civ. Pro. Before Trial Ch. 7(I)-B, B. Motions to Strike.

Rutter, Cal. Practice Guide: Civ. Pro. Before Trial Ch. 9(I)-E, E. Posthearing Procedures.

Rutter, Cal. Practice Guide: Civil Trials & Evidence Ch. 3-B, B. Peremptory Challenge of Judge (CCP § 170.6).

Rutter, Cal. Practice Guide: Civil Trials & Evidence Ch. 18-A, A. Motion for Judgment Notwithstanding the Verdict ("JNOV").

Rutter, Cal. Practice Guide: Family Law Gen. Matls, Highlights.

7 Witkin Cal. Proc. 5th Judgment § 46, Minute Order on Motion.

6 Witkin Cal. Proc. 5th Proceedings Without Trial § 45, (S 45) Notification and Notice.

6 Witkin Cal. Proc. 5th Proceedings Without Trial § 198, (S 198) Further Proceedings Where Leave to Amend is Granted.

§ 1020. Service; registered mail; presumption from return receipt

Any notice required by law, other than those required to be given to a party to an action or to his attorney, the service of which is not governed by the other sections of this chapter and which is not otherwise specifically provided for by law, may be given by sending the same by registered mail with proper postage prepaid addressed to the addressee's last known address with request for return receipt, and the production of a returned receipt purporting to be signed by the addressee shall create a disputable presumption that such notice was received by the person to whom the notice was required to be sent. *(Added by Stats.1939, c. 61, p. 1004, § 1.)*

Research References

Rutter, Cal. Practice Guide: Civil Appeals & Writs Ch. 9-D, D. Procedural Rules.

Rutter, Cal. Practice Guide: Civ. Pro. Before Trial Ch. 9(I)-A, A. Introduction.

Rutter, Cal. Practice Guide: Civil Trials & Evidence Ch. 18-A, A. Motion for Judgment Notwithstanding the Verdict ("JNOV").

Rutter, Cal. Practice Guide: Personal Injury Ch. 5-E, E. Selected Pleading Issues.

2 Witkin Cal. Proc. 5th Courts § 146, Codification.

CHAPTER 6. OF COSTS

§ 1021. Attorney's fees; determination by agreement; right to costs

Except as attorney's fees are specifically provided for by statute, the measure and mode of compensation of attorneys and counselors at law is left to the agreement, express or implied, of the parties; but parties to actions or proceedings are entitled to their costs, as hereinafter provided. *(Enacted in 1872. Amended by Stats.1933, c. 744, p. 1899, § 180; Stats.1986, c. 377, § 2.)*

Research References

California Real Estate Forms (Miller & Starr) § 1:14, Right of First Offer Agreement.

California Real Estate Forms (Miller & Starr) § 1:15, Option Agreement--Long Form.

California Real Estate Forms (Miller & Starr) § 1:16, Option Agreement--Short Form.

§ 1021.4. Attorney's fees; action for damages arising from felony offense

In an action for damages against a defendant based upon that defendant's commission of a felony offense for which that defendant has been convicted, the court may, upon motion, award reasonable attorney's fees to a prevailing plaintiff against the defendant who has been convicted of the felony. *(Added by Stats.1983, c. 938, § 3, eff. Sept. 20, 1983.)*

Research References

§ 1021.5. Attorney fees; important rights affecting public interest; enforcement; public entity award

Upon motion, a court may award attorneys' fees to a successful party against one or more opposing parties in any action which has resulted in the enforcement of an important right affecting the public interest if: (a) a significant benefit, whether pecuniary or nonpecuniary, has been conferred on the general public or a large class of persons, (b) the necessity and financial burden of private enforcement, or of enforcement by one public entity against another public entity, are such as to make the award appropriate, and (c) such fees should not in the interest of justice be paid out of the recovery, if any. With respect to actions involving public entities, this section applies to allowances against, but not in favor of, public entities, and no claim shall be required to be filed therefor, unless one or more successful parties and one or more opposing parties are public entities, in which case no claim shall be required to be filed therefor under Part 3 (commencing with Section 900) of Division 3.6 of Title 1 of the Government Code.

Attorneys' fees awarded to a public entity pursuant to this section shall not be increased or decreased by a multiplier based upon extrinsic circumstances, as discussed in Serrano v. Priest, 20 Cal.3d 25, 49. *(Added by Stats.1977, c. 1197, p. 3979, § 1. Amended by Stats.1993, c. 645 (S.B.764), § 2.)*

Research References

§ 1021.6. Attorneys' fees; implied indemnity; prevailing party; conditions

Upon motion, a court after reviewing the evidence in the principal case may award attorney's fees to a person who prevails on a claim for implied indemnity if the court finds (a) that the indemnitee through the tort of the indemnitor has been required to act in the protection of the indemnitee's interest by bringing an action against or defending an action by a third person and (b) if that indemnitor was properly notified of the demand to bring the action or provide the defense and did not avail itself of the opportunity to do so, and (c) that the trier of fact determined that the indemnitee was without fault in the principal case which is the basis for the action in indemnity or that the indemnitee had a final judgment entered in his or her favor granting a summary judgment, a nonsuit, or a directed verdict. *(Added by Stats.1979, c. 289, § 1. Amended by Stats.1982, c. 1383, p. 5280, § 1.)*

Research References

Rutter, Cal. Practice Guide: Civ. Pro. Before Trial Ch. 12(II)-E, E. Motion to Determine "Good Faith" of "Piecemeal" Settlement (CCP § 877.6).

Rutter, Cal. Practice Guide: Civ. Pro. Before Trial Ch. 9(III)-D, D. Other Sanctions Statutes and Rules.

Rutter, Cal. Practice Guide: Civ. Pro. Before Trial Ch. 9(III)-D, Outline D.

Rutter, Cal. Practice Guide: Civil Trials & Evidence Ch. 17-E, E. Attorney Fees as Costs.

Rutter, Cal. Practice Guide: Insurance Litigation Ch. 7J-D, D. Vendors' Endorsements.

Rutter, Cal. Practice Guide: Personal Injury Ch. 3-A, A. Introduction.

Rutter, Cal. Practice Guide: Personal Injury Ch. 4-D, D. Techniques Where Settlement Not Forthcoming.

Miller and Starr California Real Estate § 29:9, General Principles Concerning Owner's Damages.

Miller and Starr California Real Estate § 3:33, Damages Recoverable by the Principal.

Miller and Starr California Real Estate § 34:76, Recovery of Fees in an Action for Indemnity.

7 Witkin Cal. Proc. 5th Judgment § 226, (S 226) Insurance or Indemnity Actions.

5 Witkin, California Summary 10th Torts § 88, (S 88) General Rule: Bar to Further Claims From Settling Tortfeasor.

3 Witkin, California Summary 10th Agency and Employment § 123, Illustrations: Indemnification Allowed.

§ 1021.7. Attorney fees; actions against peace officers; actions for libel or slander; award to defendant where action not filed in good faith

In any action for damages arising out of the performance of a peace officer's duties, brought against a peace officer, as defined in Chapter 4.5 (commencing with Section 830) of Title 3 of Part 2 of the Penal Code, or against a public entity employing a peace officer or in an action for libel or slander brought pursuant to Section 45 or 46 of the Civil Code, the court may, in its discretion, award reasonable attorney's fees to the defendant or defendants as part of the costs, upon a finding by the court that the action was not filed or maintained in good faith and with reasonable cause. *(Added by Stats.1981, c. 980, p. 3806, § 1.)*

Research References

Rutter, Cal. Practice Guide: Civil Trials & Evidence Ch. 17-E, E. Attorney Fees as Costs.

Rutter, Cal. Practice Guide: Personal Injury Ch. 3-A, A. Introduction.

Rutter, Cal. Practice Guide: Personal Injury Ch. 3-A, Outline a.

7 Witkin Cal. Proc. 5th Judgment § 222, (S 222) Actions in Bad Faith.

5 Witkin, California Summary 10th Torts § 487, (S 487) Public Entity Cannot Sue.

§ 1021.8. Awarding to the Attorney General all costs of investigating and prosecuting enumerated actions

(a) Whenever the Attorney General prevails in a civil action to enforce Section 17537.3, 22445, 22446.5, 22958, 22962, or 22963 of the Business and Professions Code, Section 52, 52.1, 55.1, or 3494 of the Civil Code, the Corporate Securities Law of 1968 (Division 1 (commencing with Section 25000) of Title 4 of the Corporations Code or the California Commodity Law of 1990 (Division 4.5 (commencing with Section 29500) of Title 4 of the Corporations Code), Section 1615, 2014, or 5650.1 of the Fish and Game Code, Section 4458, 12598, 12606, 12607, 12989.3, 16147, 66640, 66641, or 66641.7 of the Government

Code, Section 13009, 13009.1, 19958.5, 25299, 39674, 41513, 42402, 42402.1, 42402.2, 42402.3, 42402.4, 43016, 43017, 43154, 104557, or 118950 of the Health and Safety Code, Section 308.1 or 308.3 of the Penal Code, Section 2774.1, 4601.1, 4603, 4605, 30820, 30821.6, 30822, 42847, or 48023 of the Public Resources Code, Section 30101.7 of the Revenue and Taxation Code, or Section 275, 1052, 1845, 13261, 13262, 13264, 13265, 13268, 13304, 13331, 13350, or 13385 of the Water Code, the court shall award to the Attorney General all costs of investigating and prosecuting the action, including expert fees, reasonable attorney's fees, and costs. Awards under this section shall be paid to the Public Rights Law Enforcement Special Fund established by Section 12530 of the Government Code.

(b) This section applies to any action pending on the effective date of this section and to any action filed thereafter.

(c) The amendments made to this section by Chapter 227 of the Statutes of 2004 shall apply to any action pending on the effective date of these amendments and to any action filed thereafter. *(Added by Stats.2003, c. 159 (A.B.1759), § 4, eff. Aug. 2, 2003. Amended by Stats.2004, c. 183 (A.B.3082), § 45; Stats.2004, c. 227 (S.B.1102), § 12, eff. Aug. 16, 2004; Stats.2004, c. 702 (A.B.2104), § 1, eff. Sept. 23, 2004; Stats.2006, c. 538 (S.B.1852), § 65.)*

Research References

7 Witkin Cal. Proc. 5th Judgment § 95, (S 95) Prevailing Party in Specified Actions.

7 Witkin Cal. Proc. 5th Judgment § 130, (S 130) Investigation.

7 Witkin Cal. Proc. 5th Judgment § 133, (S 133) Fees of Expert Witness.

7 Witkin Cal. Proc. 5th Judgment § 233, (S 233) Other Actions Involving California Statutes.

§ 1021.9. Attorneys' fees; damages from trespass

In any action to recover damages to personal or real property resulting from trespassing on lands either under cultivation or intended or used for the raising of livestock, the prevailing plaintiff shall be entitled to reasonable attorney's fees in addition to other costs, and in addition to any liability for damages imposed by law. *(Added by Stats.1986, c. 1381, § 1.)*

Research References

Rutter, Cal. Practice Guide: Civil Appeals & Writs Ch. 14-B, B. Recovery of Appellate Costs and Attorney Fees.

Rutter, Cal. Practice Guide: Enforcing Judgments/Debts Ch. 4-A, A. Attachment.

Rutter, Cal. Practice Guide: Real Prop. Transactions Ch. 5-D, D. Common Law Environmental Hazards Liability.

Miller and Starr California Real Estate § 22:2, "Nuisance" Defined and Compared With Other Causes of Action.

Miller and Starr California Real Estate § 34:66, Examples of Actions in Which Fees Can be Recovered.

18 NO. 2 Miller & Starr, California Real Estate Newsalert 15, Hazardous Substances.

20 NO. 4 Miller & Starr, California Real Estate Newsalert 34, Judicial Remedies.

7 Witkin Cal. Proc. 5th Judgment § 150, (S 150) Fees as Costs.

7 Witkin Cal. Proc. 5th Judgment § 230, (S 230) Actions Involving Real Property or Environmental Issues.

§ 1021.10. Action for failure to comply with Jenkins Act; award of fees and costs

Notwithstanding any other provision of law, in an action brought in the name of the people of the State of California against any person for failure to comply with Chapter 10A (commencing with Section 375) of Title 15 of the United States Code, otherwise known as the "Jenkins Act," the court, to the extent not expressly prohibited by federal law, shall award fees and costs, including reasonable attorney's fees, to the people if the people succeed on any claim to enforce the Jenkins Act. Any attorney's fees awarded under this section shall be in addition to any other remedies or penalties available under all other laws of this state. *(Added by Stats.2002, c. 686 (S.B.1766), § 2.)*

Research References

7 Witkin Cal. Proc. 5th Judgment § 239, in General.

§ 1022. Multiple actions where defendants could have been joined in one action; disallowance of costs; allowance of disbursements

When several actions are brought on one bond, undertaking, promissory note, bill of exchange, or other instrument in writing, or in any other case for the same cause of action, against several parties who might have been joined as defendants in the same action, no costs can be allowed to the plaintiff in more than one of such actions, which may be at his election, if the party proceeded against in the other actions were, at the commencement of the previous action, openly within this State; but the disbursements of the plaintiff must be allowed to him in each action. *(Formerly § 1023 enacted in 1872. Renumbered § 1022 and amended by Stats.1933, c. 744, p. 1899, § 181.)*

Research References

7 Witkin Cal. Proc. 5th Judgment § 111, (S 111) Unnecessary Additional Trial.

§ 1023. Referees' fees

The fees of referees are such reasonable sum as the court may fix for the time spent in the business of the reference; but the parties may agree, in writing, upon any other rate of compensation, and thereupon such rates shall be allowed. *(Formerly § 1028 enacted in 1872. Renumbered § 1023 and amended by Stats.1933, c. 744, p. 1899, § 182. Amended by Stats.1953, c. 795, p. 2098, § 1.)*

Research References

Rutter, Cal. Practice Guide: A.D.R. Ch. 6-C, C. Referees.
Rutter, Cal. Practice Guide: Civ. Pro. Before Trial Ch. 8K-5, Appointment of Referee in Aid of Discovery.
Rutter, Cal. Practice Guide: Civ. Pro. Before Trial Ch. 8E-12, Conduct of Deposition.
Rutter, Cal. Practice Guide: Civil Trials & Evidence Ch. 16-G, G. Trial by Reference.
Miller and Starr California Real Estate § 33:22, Right to Compensation.
7 Witkin Cal. Proc. 5th Judgment § 123, (S 123) Referee's Fees.
6 Witkin Cal. Proc. 5th Proceedings Without Trial § 77, in General.
12 Witkin, California Summary 10th Real Property § 83, (S 83) Costs of Partition.

§ 1024. Continuance; expenses as condition

When an application is made to the court or referee to postpone a trial, the payment of the expenses occasioned by the postponement may be imposed, in the discretion of the court or referee, as a condition of granting the same. *(Formerly § 1029 enacted in 1872. Renumbered § 1024 and amended by Stats.1933, c. 744, p. 1900, § 183. Amended by Stats.1986, c. 377, § 3.)*

Research References

Rutter, Cal. Practice Guide: Civ. Pro. Before Trial Ch. 12(I)-F, F. Motions to Continue Trial.
Rutter, Cal. Practice Guide: Civil Trials & Evidence Ch. 1-K, K. Continuance Motions.
Rutter, Cal. Practice Guide: Personal Injury Ch. 9-A, A. Assignment to Trial.
Miller and Starr California Real Estate § 34:67, Examples of Actions in Which Fees Cannot be Recovered.
Miller and Starr California Real Estate § 19:215, Nature of the Remedy--Effect of Tenant's Abandonment Before Trial.
6 Witkin Cal. Proc. 5th Proceedings Without Trial § 408, Invalid Order Preventing Matter Going to Trial.
7 Witkin Cal. Proc. 5th Trial § 34, in General.

7 Witkin Cal. Proc. 5th Trial § 35, Improper Expenses.
12 Witkin, California Summary 10th Real Property § 734, Illustrations.

§ 1025. Defendant's tender before action; deposit in court; award of costs

When, in an action for the recovery of money only, the defendant alleges in his answer that before the commencement of the action he tendered to the plaintiff the full amount to which he was entitled, and thereupon deposits in court, for plaintiff, the amount so tendered, and the allegation is found to be true, the plaintiff can not recover costs, but must pay costs to the defendant. *(Formerly § 1030 enacted in 1872. Renumbered § 1025 and amended by Stats.1933, c, 744, p. 1900, § 184.)*

Research References

7 Witkin Cal. Proc. 5th Judgment § 95, (S 95) Prevailing Party in Specified Actions.
6 Witkin Cal. Proc. 5th Proceedings Without Trial § 81, Defendant's Offer Before Action Commenced.
6 Witkin Cal. Proc. 5th Provisional Remedies § 461, Nature of Remedy.

§ 1026. Actions by or against fiduciaries, etc.; payment of costs

(a) Except as provided in subdivision (b), in an action prosecuted or defended by a personal representative, trustee of an express trust, guardian, conservator, or a person expressly authorized by statute, costs may be recovered as in an action by or against a person prosecuting or defending in the person's own right.

(b) Costs allowed under subdivision (a) shall, by the judgment, be made chargeable only upon the estate, fund, or party represented, unless the court directs the costs to be paid by the fiduciary personally for mismanagement or bad faith in the action or defense. *(Formerly § 1031 enacted in 1872. Renumbered § 1026 and amended by Stats.1933, c. 744, p. 1900, § 185. Amended by Stats.1988, c. 1199, § 8, operative July 1, 1989.)*

Law Revision Commission Comments

Section 1026 is subdivided and amended to cover actions prosecuted or defended by a guardian or a conservator. The former reference to an executor or administrator is replaced by a reference to a personal representative. This is a nonsubstantive change. See Prob. Code § 58 ("personal representative" defined). For provisions governing liability for costs in proceedings under the Probate Code, see Prob. Code § 1002 and the Comment thereto. [19 Cal.L.Rev. Comm. Reports 1035 (1988)].

Research References

14 Witkin, California Summary 10th Wills and Probate § 400, (S 400) Costs.

§ 1027. Review other than by appeal; allowance on collection of costs

When the decision of a court of inferior jurisdiction in a special proceeding is brought before a court of higher jurisdiction for a review, in any other way than by appeal, the same costs must be allowed as in cases on appeal, and may be collected in the manner provided for enforcement of money judgments generally, or in such manner as the court may direct, according to the nature of the case. *(Formerly § 1032 enacted in 1872. Renumbered § 1027 and amended by Stats.1933, c. 744, p. 1900, § 186. Amended by Stats.1982, c. 497, p. 2165, § 68, operative July 1, 1983.)*

Law Revision Commission Comments

Section 1027 is amended to conform to Title 9 (commencing with Section 680.010) of Part 2 (Enforcement of Judgments Law) (15 Cal.L.Rev.Comm. Reports 2001).

Research References

8 Witkin Cal. Proc. 5th Extraordinary Writs § 212, Certiorari.
8 Witkin Cal. Proc. 5th Extraordinary Writs § 213, (S 213) Costs in
   Reviewing Court.

§ 1028. Award against state; payment from agency appropriation

Notwithstanding any other provisions of law, when the State is a party, costs shall be awarded against it on the same basis as against any other party and, when awarded, must be paid out of the appropriation for the support of the agency on whose behalf the State appeared. *(Formerly § 1038 enacted in 1872. Renumbered § 1028 and amended by Stats.1933, c. 744, p. 1900, § 187. Amended by Stats.1943, c. 165, p. 1061, § 1.)*

Research References

Rutter, Cal. Practice Guide: Civil Appeals & Writs Ch. 14-B, B. Recovery
   of Appellate Costs and Attorney Fees.
Rutter, Cal. Practice Guide: Civil Trials & Evidence Ch. 17-D, D. Costs.
9 Witkin Cal. Proc. 5th Appeal § 957, (S 957) Award Against Government or Officer.
8 Witkin Cal. Proc. 5th Extraordinary Writs § 212, Certiorari.
7 Witkin Cal. Proc. 5th Judgment § 84, (S 84) Award Against Government.
4 Witkin Cal. Proc. 5th Pleading § 105, as Plaintiffs.
6 Witkin Cal. Proc. 5th Proceedings Without Trial § 110, Offer by
   Defendant.
3 Witkin, California Summary 10th Agency and Employment § 317,
   Prosecution of Actions.

§ 1028.5. Award against state regulatory agency in favor of small business or licensee; action without substantial justification; litigation expenses; short title

(a) In any civil action between a small business or a licensee and a state regulatory agency, involving the regulatory functions of a state agency as applied to a small business or a licensee, if the small business or licensee prevails, and if the court determines that the action of the agency was undertaken without substantial justification, the small business or licensee may, in the discretion of the court, be awarded reasonable litigation expenses in addition to other costs. Funds for such expenses and costs shall be paid from funds in the regular operating budget of the state regulatory agency where the appropriation therefor encompasses the payment of such costs and expenses, and not from unappropriated money in the General Fund.

(b) "Reasonable litigation expenses" means any expenses not in excess of seven thousand five hundred dollars ($7,500) which the judge finds were reasonably incurred in opposing the agency action, including court costs, expenses incurred in administrative proceedings, attorney's fees, witness fees of all necessary witnesses, and such other expenses as were reasonably incurred.

(c) "Small business" means a business activity that is all of the following:

(1) Independently owned and operated.

(2) Not dominant in its field of operation.

(3) Not exceeding the following annual gross receipts or other criteria in the categories of:

(A) Agriculture, one million dollars ($1,000,000).

(B) General construction, nine million five hundred thousand dollars ($9,500,000).

(C) Special trade construction, five million dollars ($5,000,000).

(D) Retail trade, two million dollars ($2,000,000).

(E) Wholesale trade, nine million five hundred thousand dollars ($9,500,000).

(F) Services, two million dollars ($2,000,000).

(G) Transportation and warehousing, one million five hundred thousand dollars ($1,500,000).

(H) A manufacturing enterprise not exceeding 250 employees.

(I) A health care facility not exceeding 150 beds or one million five hundred thousand dollars ($1,500,000) in annual gross receipts.

(J) Generating and transmitting electric power not exceeding 4,500 megawatt hours annually.

(d) "Licensee" means any person licensed by a state agency who does not qualify as a small business, but whose annual gross receipts from the use of such license do not exceed one million dollars ($1,000,000).

(e) A small business or a licensee shall be deemed to prevail in any action in which there is no adjudication, stipulation, or acceptance of liability on the part of the small business or licensee.

(f) A small business or licensee shall not be deemed to have prevailed in actions commenced at the instance of, or on the basis of a complaint filed by, a person who is not an officer, employee, or other agent of the state regulatory agency if the action is dismissed by the agency upon a finding of no cause for the action, or is settled by the agency and small business or licensee without a finding of fault.

(g) Section 800 of the Government Code shall not apply to actions which are subject to the provisions of this section.

(h) Every state regulatory agency against which litigation expenses have been awarded under this section shall, at the time of submission of its proposed budget pursuant to Section 13320 of the Government Code, submit a report to the Department of Finance and the Legislature as to the amount of those expenses awarded and paid during the fiscal year.

(i) This section shall be known and may be cited as the Carpenter-Katz Small Business Equal Access to Justice Act of 1981. *(Added by Stats.1981, c. 814, p. 3159, § 1. Amended by Stats.1983, c. 445, § 1.)*

Research References

21 NO. 5 Miller & Starr, California Real Estate Newsalert 12, Discrimination.
7 Witkin Cal. Proc. 5th Judgment § 225, (S 225) Actions Involving
   Government or Corporate Accountability.
8 Witkin, California Summary 10th Constitutional Law § 956, Damages
   and Penalties.

§ 1029. Award against county, city, district, or other public agencies, etc.; payment

When any county, city, district, or other public agency or entity, or any officer thereof in his official capacity, is a party, costs shall be awarded against it on the same basis as against any other party and, when awarded, must be paid out of the treasury thereof. *(Formerly § 1039, enacted in 1872. Renumbered § 1029 and amended by Stats.1933, c. 744, p. 1900, § 188. Amended by Stats.1945, c. 217, p. 685, § 1.)*

Research References

Rutter, Cal. Practice Guide: Civil Appeals & Writs Ch. 14-B, B. Recovery
   of Appellate Costs and Attorney Fees.
9 Witkin Cal. Proc. 5th Appeal § 957, (S 957) Award Against Government or Officer.
8 Witkin Cal. Proc. 5th Extraordinary Writs § 212, Certiorari.

7 Witkin Cal. Proc. 5th Judgment § 84, (S 84) Award Against Government.

§ 1029.5. Complaint for damages against architect, engineer, etc.; order to file undertaking

(a) Whenever a complaint for damages is filed against any architect, landscape architect, engineer, building designer, or land surveyor, duly licensed as such under the laws of this state, in an action for error, omission, or professional negligence in the creation and preparation of plans, specifications, designs, reports or surveys which are the basis for work performed or agreed to be performed on real property, any such defendant may, within 30 days after service of summons, move the court for an order, upon notice and hearing, requiring the plaintiff to file an undertaking in a sum not to exceed five hundred dollars ($500) as security for the costs of defense as provided in subdivision (d), which may be awarded against the plaintiff. The motion shall be supported by affidavit showing that the claim against the defendant is frivolous.

At the hearing upon the motion, the court shall order the plaintiff to file the undertaking if the defendant shows to the satisfaction of the court that (i) the plaintiff would not suffer undue economic hardship in filing the undertaking, and (ii) there is no reasonable possibility that the plaintiff has a cause of action against each named defendant with respect to whom the plaintiff would otherwise be required to file the undertaking. No appeal shall be taken from any order made pursuant to this subdivision to file or not to file the undertaking.

A determination by the court that the undertaking either shall or shall not be filed or shall be filed as to one or more defendants and not as to others, shall not be deemed a determination of any one or more issues in the action or of the merits thereof. If the court, upon any such motion, makes a determination that an undertaking be filed by the plaintiff as to any one or more defendants, the action shall be dismissed as to the defendant or defendants, unless the undertaking required by the court has been filed within such reasonable time as may be fixed by the court.

(b) This section does not apply to a complaint for bodily injury or for wrongful death, nor to an action commenced in a small claims court.

(c) Whenever more than one such defendant is named, the undertaking shall be increased to the extent of not to exceed five hundred dollars ($500) for each additional defendant in whose favor the undertaking is ordered not to exceed the total of three thousand dollars ($3,000).

(d) In any action requiring an undertaking as provided in this section, upon the dismissal of the action or the award of judgment to the defendant, the court shall require the plaintiff to pay the defendant's costs of defense authorized by law. Any sureties shall be liable for such costs in an amount not to exceed the sum of five hundred dollars ($500) or the amount of the undertaking, whichever is lesser, for each defendant with respect to whom the sureties have executed an undertaking. *(Formerly § 405.7, added by Stats.1967, c. 393, p. 1616, § 1. Renumbered § 1029.5 and amended by Stats.1969, c. 1610, § 6, operative July 1, 1970. Amended by Stats.1980, c. 114, p. 269, § 2; Stats.1982, c. 517, p. 2356, § 162.)*

Law Revision Commission Comments

Subdivisions (a) and (c) of Section 1029.5 are amended to change the flat $500 amount to a maximum amount to conform to the constitutional standard enunciated in Beaudreau v. Superior Court, 14 Cal.3d 448, 460, 535 P.2d 713, 720, 121 Cal.Rptr. 585, 592 (1975). This amendment makes Section 1029.5 consistent in this respect with Section 1029.6.

Section 1029.5 is amended for consistency with the Bond and Undertaking Law. See Sections 995.250 (cost of undertaking recoverable), 995.310 (sureties on undertaking), 995.320 (contents of undertaking), 995.340

(filing required), and 995.710 (deposit in lieu of undertaking). [16 Cal.L.Rev.Comm. Reports 501 (1982)].

Research References

Rutter, Cal. Practice Guide: Civ. Pro. Before Trial Ch. 11-B, B. Involuntary Dismissals.
Miller and Starr California Real Estate § 29:61, Certificates of Merit.
3 Witkin Cal. Proc. 5th Actions § 352, (S 352) Statutory Revision.
3 Witkin Cal. Proc. 5th Actions § 358, Action Against Architect, Engineer, or Related Professional.
3 Witkin Cal. Proc. 5th Actions § 420, Security for Costs.
2 Witkin Cal. Proc. 5th Courts § 289, (S 289) in General.
7 Witkin Cal. Proc. 5th Judgment § 433, Issue was Not Properly Triable.

§ 1029.6. Complaint for damages against medical professionals or hospital; order for undertaking by plaintiff

(a) Whenever a complaint for damages for personal injuries is filed against a physician and surgeon, dentist, registered nurse, dispensing optician, optometrist, pharmacist, registered physical therapist, podiatrist, licensed psychologist, osteopathic physician and surgeon, chiropractor, clinical laboratory bioanalyst, clinical laboratory technologist, or veterinarian, duly licensed as such under the laws of this state, or a licensed hospital as the employer of any such person, in an action for error, omission, or negligence in the performance of professional services, or performance of professional services without consent, any such defendant may, within six months after service of summons, move the court for an order, upon notice to plaintiff and all defendants having appeared in the action, and hearing, requiring the plaintiff to file an undertaking in a sum not to exceed five hundred dollars ($500) as security for the costs of defense as provided in subdivision (d), which may be awarded against the plaintiff. The motion shall be supported by affidavit showing that the claim against the defendant is frivolous. Any defendant having appeared in the action and within 30 days after receipt of notice may join with the moving party requesting an order under this section as to the additional defendant. The failure of any defendant to join with the moving party shall preclude that defendant from subsequently requesting an order under this section.

At the hearing upon the motion, the court shall order the plaintiff to file the undertaking if the defendant shows to the satisfaction of the court that: (i) the plaintiff would not suffer undue economic hardship in filing the undertaking and (ii) there is no reasonable possibility that the plaintiff has a cause of action against each named defendant with respect to whom the plaintiff would otherwise be required to file the undertaking.

A determination by the court that an undertaking either shall or shall not be filed or shall be filed as to one or more defendants and not as to others, shall not be deemed a determination of any one or more issues in the action or of the merits thereof. If the court, upon any such motion, makes a determination that an undertaking be filed by the plaintiff as to any one or more defendants, the action shall be dismissed as to that defendant or defendants, unless the undertaking required by the court shall have been filed within the reasonable time as may be fixed by the court.

(b) This section does not apply to a complaint in an action commenced in a small claims court.

(c) Whenever more than one defendant is named, the undertaking shall be increased to the extent of not to exceed five hundred dollars ($500) for each additional defendant in whose favor the undertaking is ordered, not to exceed the total of one thousand dollars ($1,000).

(d) In any action requiring an undertaking as provided in this section, upon the dismissal of the action or the award of judgment to the defendant, the court shall require the plaintiff to pay the defendant's court costs. Any sureties shall be liable for those costs in an amount not to exceed the sum of five hundred dollars ($500) or the amount of the undertaking, whichever is lesser, for each defendant with respect to whom the sureties have executed an undertaking. If the plaintiff prevails in the action against any defendant with respect to whom an undertaking has been filed, the defendant shall pay the costs to plaintiff incurred in defending the motion for dismissal authorized by this section.

(e) Any defendant filing a motion under this section or joining with a moving party under this section is precluded from subsequently filing a motion for summary judgment.

(f) Any defendant filing a motion for summary judgment is precluded from subsequently filing a motion, or joining with a moving party, under this section. *(Formerly § 405.8, added by Stats.1969, c. 608, p. 1246, § 1. Renumbered § 1029.6 and amended by Stats.1970, c. 910, p. 1652, § 1. Amended by Stats.1972, c. 653, p. 1211, § 1; Stats.1980, c. 114, p. 270, § 3; Stats.1982, c. 517, p. 2357, § 163; Stats.1993, c. 226 (A.B.1987), § 6.)*

Law Revision Commission Comments

Former subdivision (e) has been deleted because it was held unconstitutional in Nork v. Superior Court, 33 Cal.App.3d 997, 1000–01, 109 Cal.Rptr. 428, 430–31 (1973). See also Beaudreau v. Superior Court, 14 Cal.3d 448, 535 P.2d 713, 121 Cal.Rptr. 585 (1975). Former subdivisions (f) and (g) have been renumbered as subdivisions (e) and (f), respectively.

Section 1029.6 is amended for consistency with the Bond and Undertaking Law. See Sections 995.250 (cost of undertaking recoverable), 995.310 (sureties on undertaking), 995.320 (contents of undertaking), 995.340 (filing required), and 995.710 (deposit in lieu of undertaking). [16 Cal.L.Rev.Comm. Reports 501 (1982)].

Research References

Rutter, Cal. Practice Guide: Civ. Pro. Before Trial Ch. 11-B, B. Involuntary Dismissals.
3 Witkin Cal. Proc. 5th Actions § 351, (S 351) Former Statutes Unconstitutional.
3 Witkin Cal. Proc. 5th Actions § 352, (S 352) Statutory Revision.
3 Witkin Cal. Proc. 5th Actions § 359, Action Against Physician or Related Professional.
3 Witkin Cal. Proc. 5th Actions § 420, Security for Costs.
2 Witkin Cal. Proc. 5th Courts § 289, (S 289) in General.
7 Witkin Cal. Proc. 5th Judgment § 433, Issue was Not Properly Triable.

§ 1029.8. Unlicensed persons who cause injury or damage to another person as result of providing goods or performing services for which a license is required; award of treble damages, attorneys fees, and costs; application of section

(a) Any unlicensed person who causes injury or damage to another person as a result of providing goods or performing services for which a license is required under Division 2 (commencing with Section 500) or any initiative act referred to therein, Division 3 (commencing with Section 5000), or Chapter 2 (commencing with Section 18600) or Chapter 3 (commencing with Section 19000) of Division 8, of the Business and Professions Code, or Chapter 2 (commencing with Section 25210) or Chapter 3 (commencing with Section 25230) of Part 3 of Division 1 of Title 4 of the Corporations Code, shall be liable to the injured person for treble the amount of damages assessed in a civil action in any court having proper jurisdiction. The court may, in its discretion, award all costs and attorney's fees to the injured person if that person prevails in the action.

(b) This section shall not be construed to confer an additional cause of action or to affect or limit any other remedy, including, but not limited to, a claim for exemplary damages.

(c) The additional damages provided for in subdivision (a) shall not exceed ten thousand dollars ($10,000).

(d) For the purposes of this section, the term "unlicensed person" shall not apply to any of the following:

(1) Any person, partnership, corporation, or other entity providing goods or services under the good faith belief that they are properly licensed and acting within the proper scope of that licensure.

(2) Any person, partnership, corporation, or other entity whose license has expired for nonpayment of license renewal fees, but who is eligible to renew that license without the necessity of applying and qualifying for an original license.

(3) Any person, partnership, or corporation licensed under Chapter 6 (commencing with Section 2700) or Chapter 6.5 (commencing with Section 2840) of the Business and Professions Code, who provides professional nursing services under an existing license, if the action arises from a claim that the licensee exceeded the scope of practice authorized by his or her license.

(e) This section shall not apply to any action for unfair trade practices brought against an unlicensed person under Chapter 4 (commencing with Section 17000) of Part 2 of Division 7 of the Business and Professions Code, by a person who holds a license that is required, or closely related to the license that is required, to engage in those activities performed by the unlicensed person. *(Added by Stats.1985, c. 895, § 1. Amended by Stats.2004, c. 575 (A.B.2167), § 1.)*

Research References

Rutter, Cal. Practice Guide: Insurance Litigation Ch. 1-A, A. Insurance-In General.
Rutter, Cal. Practice Guide: Real Prop. Transactions Ch. 2-A, A. Preliminary Considerations.
Rutter, Cal. Practice Guide: Prof. Responsibility Ch. 1-D, D. Unauthorized Practice of Law.
Miller and Starr California Real Estate § 27:9, Acting Without a Valid License--Civil Penalties.
Miller and Starr California Real Estate § 29:9, General Principles Concerning Owner's Damages.
Miller and Starr California Real Estate § 6:20, Drafting Documents; Unauthorized Practice of Law.
Miller and Starr California Real Estate § 29:31, Liability for Defective Plans and Specifications; to the Owner.
Miller and Starr California Real Estate § 29:36, Liability to the Owner.
Miller and Starr California Real Estate § 34:99, Punitive Damages--Judicial Review.
Miller and Starr California Real Estate § 27:110, Licensure Requirements; Architects.
23 NO. 3 Miller & Starr, California Real Estate Newsalert 2, Adjoining Landowners.
7 Witkin Cal. Proc. 5th Judgment § 229, (S 229) Actions Involving Personal Injury or Intentional Torts.
1 Witkin Cal. Summ. 10th Contracts § 485, Scope of Rule.
6 Witkin, California Summary 10th Torts § 1570, Treble Damages.

§ 1030. Security for costs and attorney's fees; motion; hearing; undertaking

(a) When the plaintiff in an action or special proceeding resides out of the state, or is a foreign corporation, the defendant may at any time apply to the court by noticed motion for an order requiring the plaintiff to file an undertaking to secure an award of costs and attorney's fees which may be awarded in the action or special proceeding. For the purposes of this section, "attorney's fees" means reasonable attorney's fees a party may be authorized to recover by a statute apart from this section or by contract.

(b) The motion shall be made on the grounds that the plaintiff resides out of the state or is a foreign corporation and that there is a reasonable possibility that the moving defendant will obtain judgment in the action or special proceeding. The motion shall be accompanied by an affidavit in support of the grounds for the motion and by a memorandum of points and authorities. The affidavit shall set forth the nature and amount of the costs and attorney's fees the defendant has incurred and expects to incur by the conclusion of the action or special proceeding.

Civ. Pro.

(c) If the court, after hearing, determines that the grounds for the motion have been established, the court shall order that the plaintiff file the undertaking in an amount specified in the court's order as security for costs and attorney's fees.

(d) The plaintiff shall file the undertaking not later than 30 days after service of the court's order requiring it or within a greater time allowed by the court. If the plaintiff fails to file the undertaking within the time allowed, the plaintiff's action or special proceeding shall be dismissed as to the defendant in whose favor the order requiring the undertaking was made.

(e) If the defendant's motion for an order requiring an undertaking is filed not later than 30 days after service of summons on the defendant, further proceedings may be stayed in the discretion of the court upon application to the court by the defendant by noticed motion for the stay until 10 days after the motion for the undertaking is denied or, if granted, until 10 days after the required undertaking has been filed and the defendant has been served with a copy of the undertaking. The hearing on the application for the stay shall be held not later than 60 days after service of the summons. If the defendant files a motion for an order requiring an undertaking, which is granted but the defendant objects to the undertaking, the court may in its discretion stay the proceedings not longer than 10 days after a sufficient undertaking has been filed and the defendant has been served with a copy of the undertaking.

(f) The determinations of the court under this section have no effect on the determination of any issues on the merits of the action or special proceeding and may not be given in evidence nor referred to in the trial of the action or proceeding.

(g) An order granting or denying a motion for an undertaking under this section is not appealable. *(Formerly § 1036, enacted in 1872. Renumbered § 1030 and amended by Stats.1933, c. 744, p. 1900, § 189. Amended by Stats.1951, c. 1737, p. 4134, § 137, operative Jan. 1, 1952; Stats.1980, c. 114, p. 271, § 4; Stats.1982, c. 517, p. 2358, § 164; Stats.1988, c. 189, § 1.)*

Law Revision Commission Comments

Section 1030 is amended to conform to the constitutional standards enunciated in Beaudreau v. Superior Court, 14 Cal.3d 448, 535 P.2d 713, 121 Cal.Rptr. 585 (1975), and Gonzales v. Fox, 68 Cal.App.3d Supp. 16, 137 Cal.Rptr. 312 (1977).

Subdivision (a) of Section 1030 permits the defendant to require the plaintiff to file an undertaking to secure both costs and allowable attorney's fees whereas Section 1030 formerly referred to "costs and charges." This section does not provide any authority for an award of attorney's fees not otherwise made recoverable by contract or statute. The provision for requiring an undertaking for the probable amount of costs and attorney's fees without limitation supersedes the former provision for an initial undertaking not exceeding $300 with the opportunity to obtain a new or increased undertaking without limitation. See McDermott & Williams, Security for Costs, in 1 California Civil Procedure Before Trial § 14.23, at 477 (Cal.Cont.Ed. Bar 1977).

Since the purpose of this section is to afford security for an award of costs which the defendant might otherwise have difficulty enforcing against a nonresident plaintiff, subdivision (b) permits an undertaking to be required whenever there is a "reasonable possibility" that the defendant will prevail in the action. Cf. Bell v. Burson, 402 U.S. 535, 540 (1971) (State of Georgia may not constitutionally require security for damages from uninsured motorist if there is "no reasonable possibility" of a judgment against motorist).

Subdivisions (b) and (c) provide for a hearing on noticed motion whereas this section formerly provided for a hearing only when the defendant sought a new or additional undertaking. Although the language of subdivision (c) is mandatory, the court has the common law authority to dispense with the undertaking if the plaintiff is indigent. E.g., Conover v. Hall, 11 Cal.3d 842, 523 P.2d 682, 114 Cal.Rptr. 642 (1974). Under Section 1054a, the plaintiff may deposit money or bearer bonds or bearer notes of the United States or California in lieu of an undertaking.

Subdivision (d) continues the substance of a portion of what was formerly the third sentence of Section 1030, and also permits the amount of the undertaking to be decreased.

Subdivision (e) provides for dismissal if the undertaking is not filed within 30 days, as did the former last paragraph of Section 1030, but the 30-day period runs from service of the order on the plaintiff rather than from service of a notice that security is required. Failure to file within the prescribed time is not jurisdictional, and the court may accept a late filing. Boyer v. County of Contra Costa, 235 Cal.App.2d 111, 115–18, 45 Cal.Rptr. 58, 61–63 (1965). If the court authorizes the undertaking to be decreased as provided by subdivision (d), compliance by the plaintiff is optional.

The first sentence of subdivision (f) continues a portion of what was formerly the second sentence of Section 1030. The provision for excepting to the sufficiency of sureties is new. Formerly, sureties could be challenged only by way of a motion for a new or additional undertaking. See Estate of Baker, 176 Cal. 430, 168 P. 881 (1917). See also Sections 1056 (single corporate surety sufficient), 1057 (qualifications of individual surety), 1057a–1057b (qualifications and justification of corporate surety).

Subdivision (g) is a new provision which supersedes the former provision for an indefinite stay and for a stay of 10 days after service on the defendant of notice of the filing of the undertaking.

Subdivision (h) is new and is derived from comparable provisions in cost bond statutes requiring hearings. See, e.g., Code Civ.Proc. §§ 391.2, 1029.5(a), 1029.6(a); Corp. Code § 800(d).

Subdivision (i) codifies existing law. See Horton v. City of Beverly Hills, 261 Cal.App.2d 306, 67 Cal.Rptr. 759 (1968). An order granting or denying a motion for an undertaking may sometimes be reviewed by extraordinary writ. See Beaudreau v. Superior Court, 14 Cal.3d 448, 535 P.2d 713, 121 Cal.Rptr. 585 (1975). A judgment of dismissal following the plaintiff's failure to furnish required security is appealable as a final judgment. Efron v. Kalmanovitz, 185 Cal.App.2d 149, 156–57, 8 Cal. Rptr. 107, 112 (1960).

Section 1030 is amended to delete provisions duplicated by the Bond and Undertaking Law. See Sections 995.310 (sureties on undertaking), 995.320 (contents of undertaking), 995.340 (filing required), 995.370 (service of copy of undertaking), 995.910–995.960 (objections to undertakings), 996.010 (insufficient undertaking), 996.030 (reduced undertaking). [16 Cal.L.Rev.Comm. Reports 501 (1982)].

Research References

Rutter, Cal. Practice Guide: Civil Appeals & Writs Ch. 2-C, C. Nonappealable Orders.

Rutter, Cal. Practice Guide: Civil Appeals & Writs Ch. 15-B, B. Common Law Writs.

Rutter, Cal. Practice Guide: Civ. Pro. Before Trial Ch. 1-A, A. Accepting a New Case.

Rutter, Cal. Practice Guide: Civ. Pro. Before Trial Ch. 11-B, B. Involuntary Dismissals.

Rutter, Cal. Practice Guide: Enforcing Judgments/Debts Ch. 3-A, A. Evaluating the Claim.

3 Witkin Cal. Proc. 5th Actions § 351, (S 351) Former Statutes Unconstitutional.

3 Witkin Cal. Proc. 5th Actions § 352, (S 352) Statutory Revision.

3 Witkin Cal. Proc. 5th Actions § 353, (S 353) in General.

3 Witkin Cal. Proc. 5th Actions § 354, (S 354) Actual Residence.

3 Witkin Cal. Proc. 5th Actions § 355, (S 355) Cross-Complainant Need Not Post Security.

3 Witkin Cal. Proc. 5th Actions § 356, (S 356) Motion and Stay.

3 Witkin Cal. Proc. 5th Actions § 357, (S 357) Hearing, Determination, and Undertaking.

3 Witkin Cal. Proc. 5th Actions § 420, Security for Costs.

9 Witkin Cal. Proc. 5th Appeal § 504, (S 504) Decisions of Sister State Courts.

6 Witkin Cal. Proc. 5th Proceedings Without Trial § 391, When Statute is Not Tolled.

§ 1031. Actions for recovery of wages for labor performed

In actions for the recovery of wages for labor performed, where the amount of the demand, exclusive of interest, does not exceed three hundred dollars ($300), the court shall add, as part of the cost, in any judgment recovered by the plaintiff or cross-complainant, an attorney's fee not exceeding 20 percent of the amount recovered. *(Added by Stats.1933, c. 744, p. 1901, § 190. Amended by Stats.1939, c. 647, p. 2075, § 1; Stats.1945, c. 1149, p. 2189, § 1; Stats.1951, c. 1737, p. 4134, § 138, operative Jan. 1, 1952; Stats.1968, c. 71, p. 219, § 1; Stats.1973, c. 818, p. 1464, § 1; Stats.1986, c. 377, § 4.)*

Research References

Rutter, Cal. Practice Guide: A.D.R. Ch. 5-H, H. Conduct of Arbitration Proceedings.

Rutter, Cal. Practice Guide: Personal Injury Ch. 4-D, D. Techniques Where Settlement Not Forthcoming.

Rutter, Cal. Practice Guide: Personal Injury Ch. 9-M, M. Verdicts and Judgment.

Miller and Starr California Real Estate § 34:77, Recovery of Fees After Judgment in Excess of Rejected Settlement Offer.

7 Witkin Cal. Proc. 5th Judgment § 88, Statutory Development.

7 Witkin Cal. Proc. 5th Judgment § 227, (S 227) Labor and Employment Actions.

6 Witkin Cal. Proc. 5th Proceedings Without Trial § 82, (S 82) in General.

§ 1032. Prevailing party in any action or proceeding; stipulation to alternative procedures

(a) As used in this section, unless the context clearly requires otherwise:

(1) "Complaint" includes a cross-complaint.

(2) "Defendant" includes a cross-defendant or a person against whom a complaint is filed.

(3) "Plaintiff" includes a cross-complainant or a party who files a complaint in intervention.

(4) "Prevailing party" includes the party with a net monetary recovery, a defendant in whose favor a dismissal is entered, a defendant where neither plaintiff nor defendant obtains any relief, and a defendant as against those plaintiffs who do not recover any relief against that defendant. When any party recovers other than monetary relief and in situations other than as specified, the "prevailing party" shall be as determined by the court, and under those circumstances, the court, in its discretion, may allow costs or not and, if allowed may apportion costs between the parties on the same or adverse sides pursuant to rules adopted under Section 1034.

(b) Except as otherwise expressly provided by statute, a prevailing party is entitled as a matter of right to recover costs in any action or proceeding.

(c) Nothing in this section shall prohibit parties from stipulating to alternative procedures for awarding costs in the litigation pursuant to rules adopted under Section 1034. *(Added by Stats.1986, c. 377, § 6.)*

Research References

Rutter, Cal. Practice Guide: A.D.R. Ch. 5-H, H. Conduct of Arbitration Proceedings.

Rutter, Cal. Practice Guide: A.D.R. Ch. 5-I, I. Arbitrator's Award.

Rutter, Cal. Practice Guide: Civil Appeals & Writs Ch. 2-B, B. Appealable Judgments and Orders.

Rutter, Cal. Practice Guide: Civil Appeals & Writs Ch. 3-E, E. Filing Steps.

Rutter, Cal. Practice Guide: Civil Appeals & Writs Ch. 7-C, C. Stay by Posting Security (Bond or Undertaking).

Rutter, Cal. Practice Guide: Civil Appeals & Writs Ch. 8-C, C. Standards of Appellate Review.

Rutter, Cal. Practice Guide: Civ. Pro. Before Trial Ch. 1-A, A. Accepting a New Case.

Rutter, Cal. Practice Guide: Civ. Pro. Before Trial Ch. 11-A, A. Voluntary Dismissals.

Rutter, Cal. Practice Guide: Civ. Pro. Before Trial Ch. 12(II)-C, C. Statutory Offer to Compromise (CCP § 998).

Rutter, Cal. Practice Guide: Civ. Pro. Before Trial Ch. 12(II)-E, E. Motion to Determine "Good Faith" of "Piecemeal" Settlement (CCP § 877.6).

Rutter, Cal. Practice Guide: Civil Trials & Evidence Ch. 15-B, B. Custody and Care of Jurors During Deliberations.

Rutter, Cal. Practice Guide: Civil Trials & Evidence Ch. 17-D, D. Costs.

Rutter, Cal. Practice Guide: Civil Trials & Evidence Ch. 17-E, E. Attorney Fees as Costs.

Rutter, Cal. Practice Guide: Civil Trials & Evidence Gen. Matls., Highlights.

Rutter, Cal. Practice Guide: Civil Trials & Evidence Ch. 17-E, Outline E.

California Practice Guide: Employment Litigation Ch. 11-J, J. Enforcing California Laws Regulating Employee Compensation.

California Practice Guide: Employment Litigation Ch. 17-G, G. Costs.

California Practice Guide: Employment Litigation Ch. 17-H, H. Attorney Fees.

Rutter, Cal. Practice Guide: Enforcing Judgments/Debts Ch. 3-A, A. Evaluating the Claim.

Rutter, Cal. Practice Guide: Enforcing Judgments/Debts Ch. 6A-5, Amount Recoverable Under Judgment.

Rutter, Cal. Practice Guide: Enforcing Judgments/Debts Ch. 6D-6, Debtor's Recourse Against Execution Levy.

Rutter, Cal. Practice Guide: Enforcing Judgments/Debts Ch. 6H-3, Claim of Security Interest in or Lien on Personal Property or Fixtures.

Rutter, Cal. Practice Guide: Enforcing Judgments/Debts Ch. 6K-1, Acknowledgment of Full Satisfaction of Judgment.

Rutter, Cal. Practice Guide: Insurance Litigation Ch. 6G-D, D. Uninsured and Underinsured Motorist Coverages.

Rutter, Cal. Practice Guide: Personal Injury Ch. 4-D, D. Techniques Where Settlement Not Forthcoming.

Rutter, Cal. Practice Guide: Personal Injury Ch. 7-H, H. Arbitration Award and Judgment.

Rutter, Cal. Practice Guide: Personal Injury Ch. 9-M, M. Verdicts and Judgment.

Rutter, Cal. Practice Guide: Real Prop. Transactions Ch. 11-C, C. Seller's Remedies Upon Buyer's Breach-Damages and Specific Performance.

Rutter, Cal. Practice Guide: Real Prop. Transactions Ch. 11-E, E. Damages for Fraud.

Miller and Starr California Real Estate § 22:32, Recovery of Abatement Costs.

Miller and Starr California Real Estate § 30:14, Prejudgment Interest; Attorney Fees; Costs.

Miller and Starr California Real Estate § 34:73, Determining the "Prevailing Party".

Miller and Starr California Real Estate § 34:74, Effect of Dismissal of Action Before Judgment.

Miller and Starr California Real Estate § 34:77, Recovery of Fees After Judgment in Excess of Rejected Settlement Offer.

Miller and Starr California Real Estate § 34:79, Recovery of Fees as an Item of Costs; Procedural Requirements.

Miller and Starr California Real Estate § 19:208, Termination of the Lease; Landlord's Recovery of Rent or Damages--Recovery in an Unlawful Detainer Proceeding.

Miller and Starr California Real Estate § 35:104, Award of Costs and Attorney's Fees in Order Confirming, Correcting, or Vacating an Arbitrator's Award.

17 NO. 5 Miller & Starr, California Real Estate Newsalert 17, Remedies.

18 NO. 1 Miller & Starr, California Real Estate Newsalert 18, Landlord and Tenant.

18 NO. 5 Miller & Starr, California Real Estate Newsalert 20, Remedies.

22 NO. 3 Miller & Starr, California Real Estate Newsalert 4, Common Interest Developments.

22 NO. 4 Miller & Starr, California Real Estate Newsalert 37, Landlord and Tenant.

23 NO. 3 Miller & Starr, California Real Estate Newsalert 3, CEQA.

23 NO. 2 Miller & Starr, California Real Estate Newsalert 13, Judicial Remedies.

3 Witkin Cal. Proc. 5th Actions § 429L, (New)-In General.

9 Witkin Cal. Proc. 5th Appeal § 231, Costs Awarded Against Party Rejecting Compromise.

9 Witkin Cal. Proc. 5th Appeal § 239, Costs.

9 Witkin Cal. Proc. 5th Appeal § 979, (S 979) Right to Recover.

8 Witkin Cal. Proc. 5th Extraordinary Writs § 212, Certiorari.

7 Witkin Cal. Proc. 5th Judgment § 88, Statutory Development.

7 Witkin Cal. Proc. 5th Judgment § 89, Determining Who is Prevailing Party.

7 Witkin Cal. Proc. 5th Judgment § 90, Effect of Cross-Complaint or Complaint in Intervention.

7 Witkin Cal. Proc. 5th Judgment § 91, Party Who Obtains Net Monetary Recovery.

7 Witkin Cal. Proc. 5th Judgment § 92, Defendant Who Obtains Dismissal.

7 Witkin Cal. Proc. 5th Judgment § 93, Defendant Where Neither Party Recovers.

7 Witkin Cal. Proc. 5th Judgment § 94, Defendant Against Whom Plaintiff Recovers Nothing.

7 Witkin Cal. Proc. 5th Judgment § 96, (S 96) Apportionment of Costs Among Multiple Parties.

7 Witkin Cal. Proc. 5th Judgment § 97, (S 97) Prevailing Party Determined by Court.

7 Witkin Cal. Proc. 5th Judgment § 98, Where Party Recovers Something Other Than Money.

7 Witkin Cal. Proc. 5th Judgment § 99, (S 99) General Rule in Superior Court.

7 Witkin Cal. Proc. 5th Judgment § 100, (S 100) Application of Rule in Personal Injury Actions.

7 Witkin Cal. Proc. 5th Judgment § 102, Equitable Actions.

7 Witkin Cal. Proc. 5th Judgment § 108, Action Under Fair Employment and Housing Act.

7 Witkin Cal. Proc. 5th Judgment § 112, Plaintiff Fails to Obtain Judgment More Favorable Than Offer.

7 Witkin Cal. Proc. 5th Judgment § 117, in General.

7 Witkin Cal. Proc. 5th Judgment § 139, (S 139) in General.

7 Witkin Cal. Proc. 5th Judgment § 146, (S 146) Burden of Proof.

7 Witkin Cal. Proc. 5th Judgment § 148, (S 148) Failure to Include Costs.

7 Witkin Cal. Proc. 5th Judgment § 194, Party Recovering Greater Relief.

7 Witkin Cal. Proc. 5th Judgment § 202, (S 202) Distinction: Voluntary Dismissal of Trial De Novo Following Arbitration.

7 Witkin Cal. Proc. 5th Judgment § 203, (S 203) Distinction: Issue of Entitlement to Costs and Attorneys' Fees Expressly Reserved.

7 Witkin Cal. Proc. 5th Judgment § 205, Settlement Under.

7 Witkin Cal. Proc. 5th Judgment § 221, (S 221) Actions to Enforce Equitable Servitude.

7 Witkin Cal. Proc. 5th Judgment § 223, (S 223) Civil Rights Actions.

7 Witkin Cal. Proc. 5th Judgment § 231, (S 231) Taxation Actions.

7 Witkin Cal. Proc. 5th Judgment § 296, (S 296) Fees Based on Contract.

2 Witkin Cal. Proc. 5th Jurisdiction § 29, (S 29) Effect of Puffing.

5 Witkin Cal. Proc. 5th Pleading § 1042, (S 1042) After Dismissal.

6 Witkin Cal. Proc. 5th Proceedings Without Trial § 82, (S 82) in General.

6 Witkin Cal. Proc. 5th Proceedings Without Trial § 99, (S 99) Judgment on Compromise.

6 Witkin Cal. Proc. 5th Proceedings Without Trial § 110, Offer by Defendant.

6 Witkin Cal. Proc. 5th Proceedings Without Trial § 111, Offer by Plaintiff.

6 Witkin Cal. Proc. 5th Proceedings Without Trial § 357, Effect of Dismissal.

6 Witkin Cal. Proc. 5th Proceedings Without Trial § 368, Effect of Dismissal.

6 Witkin Cal. Proc. 5th Proceedings Without Trial § 473, Effect of Dismissal.

6 Witkin Cal. Proc. 5th Provisional Remedies § 36, (S 36) Limitation on Liability.

2 Witkin, California Summary 10th Insurance § 214, (S 214) Award and Review.

12 Witkin, California Summary 10th Real Property § 739, (S 739) Costs and Attorneys' Fees.

4 Witkin, California Summary 10th Sales § 322, (S 322) Costs and Attorneys' Fees.

3 Witkin, California Summary 10th Agency and Employment § 317, Prosecution of Actions.

3 Witkin, California Summary 10th Agency and Employment § 384, (S 384) Judicial Enforcement.

8 Witkin, California Summary 10th Constitutional Law § 1168, Costs and Attorneys' Fees.

2 Witkin Cal. Summ. 10th Workers' Compensation § 80, After Judgment.

§ 1033. Costs; judgment which could have been rendered in limited civil case or small claims division; judicial powers

(a) Costs or any portion of claimed costs shall be as determined by the court in its discretion in a case other than a limited civil case in accordance with Section 1034 where the prevailing party recovers a judgment that could have been rendered in a limited civil case.

(b) When a prevailing plaintiff in a limited civil case recovers less than the amount prescribed by law as the maximum limitation upon the jurisdiction of the small claims court, the following shall apply:

(1) When the party could have brought the action in the small claims division but did not do so, the court may, in its discretion, allow or deny costs to the prevailing party, or may allow costs in part in any amount as it deems proper.

(2) When the party could not have brought the action in the small claims court, costs and necessary disbursements shall be limited to the actual cost of the filing fee, the actual cost of service of process, and, when otherwise specifically allowed by law, reasonable attorneys' fees. However, those costs shall only be awarded to the plaintiff if the court is satisfied that prior to the commencement of the action, the plaintiff informed the defendant in writing of the intended legal action against the defendant and that legal action could result in a judgment against the defendant that would include the costs and necessary disbursements allowed by this paragraph. *(Added by Stats.1986, c. 377, § 11. Amended by Stats.1987, c. 4, § 2, eff. March 17, 1987; Stats.1989, c. 62, § 1; Stats.1998, c. 931 (S.B.2139), § 107, eff. Sept. 28, 1998.)*

Law Revision Commission Comments

Section 1033 is amended to accommodate unification of the municipal and superior courts in a county. Cal. Const. art. VI, § 5(e). It is also amended to reflect elimination of the justice court, Cal. Const. art. VI, §§ 1, 5(b).

For guidance on what constitutes a limited civil case, see Section 85 & Comment. [28 Cal.L.Rev.Comm. Reports App. 7 (1998)].

Research References

Rutter, Cal. Practice Guide: Civ. Pro. Before Trial Ch. 1-B, B. Prelawsuit Investigations, Research and Analysis.

Rutter, Cal. Practice Guide: Civ. Pro. Before Trial Ch. 3-A, A. Subject Matter Jurisdiction (Competency).

Rutter, Cal. Practice Guide: Civil Trials & Evidence Ch. 12-B, B. Motion for Nonsuit.

Rutter, Cal. Practice Guide: Civil Trials & Evidence Ch. 12-C, C. Motion for Directed Verdict.

Rutter, Cal. Practice Guide: Civil Trials & Evidence Ch. 17-D, D. Costs.

Rutter, Cal. Practice Guide: Civil Trials & Evidence Ch. 17-E, E. Attorney Fees as Costs.

California Practice Guide: Employment Litigation Ch. 17-G, G. Costs.

California Practice Guide: Employment Litigation Ch. 17-H, H. Attorney Fees.

Rutter, Cal. Practice Guide: Fed.Civ.Pro. Before Trial Ch. 8-D, D. Complaints.

Rutter, Cal. Practice Guide: Personal Injury Ch. 5-D, D. Classification as Limited or Unlimited Civil Case.

Rutter, Cal. Practice Guide: Personal Injury Ch. 9-M, M. Verdicts and Judgment.

8 Witkin Cal. Proc. 5th Enforcement of Judgment § 43, When Accrual Commences.

7 Witkin Cal. Proc. 5th Judgment § 99, (S 99) General Rule in Superior Court.

7 Witkin Cal. Proc. 5th Judgment § 101, (S 101) Recovery Below Small Claims Maximum.

7 Witkin Cal. Proc. 5th Judgment § 117, in General.

7 Witkin Cal. Proc. 5th Judgment § 142, Premature Service or Filing.

7 Witkin Cal. Proc. 5th Judgment § 217, Standard for Awarding Fees.

2 Witkin Cal. Proc. 5th Jurisdiction § 23, (S 23) Actual Recovery is Not Controlling.

2 Witkin Cal. Proc. 5th Jurisdiction § 29, (S 29) Effect of Puffing.

1 Witkin Cal. Summ. 10th Contracts § 774, (S 774) Excuse of Tender Where Useless.

§ 1033.5. Items allowable

(a) The following items are allowable as costs under Section 1032:

(1) Filing, motion, and jury fees.

(2) Juror food and lodging while they are kept together during trial and after the jury retires for deliberation.

(3) Taking, video recording, and transcribing necessary depositions including an original and one copy of those taken by the claimant and one copy of depositions taken by the party against whom costs are allowed, and travel expenses to attend depositions.

(4) Service of process by a public officer, registered process server, or other means, as follows:

(A) When service is by a public officer, the recoverable cost is the fee authorized by law at the time of service.

(B) If service is by a process server registered pursuant to Chapter 16 (commencing with Section 22350) of Division 8 of the Business and Professions Code, the recoverable cost is the amount actually incurred in effecting service, including, but not limited to, a stakeout or other means employed in locating the person to be served, unless those charges are successfully challenged by a party to the action.

(C) When service is by publication, the recoverable cost is the sum actually incurred in effecting service.

(D) When service is by a means other than that set forth in subparagraph (A), (B), or (C), the recoverable cost is the lesser of the sum actually incurred, or the amount allowed to a public officer in this state for that service, except that the court may allow the sum actually incurred in effecting service upon application pursuant to paragraph (4) of subdivision (c).

(5) Expenses of attachment including keeper's fees.

(6) Premiums on necessary surety bonds.

(7) Ordinary witness fees pursuant to Section 68093 of the Government Code.

(8) Fees of expert witnesses ordered by the court.

(9) Transcripts of court proceedings ordered by the court.

(10) Attorney's fees, when authorized by any of the following:

(A) Contract.

(B) Statute.

(C) Law.

(11) Court reporter fees as established by statute.

(12) Court interpreter fees for a qualified court interpreter authorized by the court for an indigent person represented by a qualified legal services project, as defined in Section 6213 of the Business and Professions Code or a pro bono attorney as defined in Section 8030.4 of the Business and Professions Code.

(13) Models and blowups of exhibits and photocopies of exhibits may be allowed if they were reasonably helpful to aid the trier of fact.

(14) Any other item that is required to be awarded to the prevailing party pursuant to statute as an incident to prevailing in the action at trial or on appeal.

(b) The following items are not allowable as costs, except when expressly authorized by law:

(1) Fees of experts not ordered by the court.

(2) Investigation expenses in preparing the case for trial.

(3) Postage, telephone, and photocopying charges, except for exhibits.

(4) Costs in investigation of jurors or in preparation for voir dire.

(5) Transcripts of court proceedings not ordered by the court.

(c) Any award of costs shall be subject to the following:

(1) Costs are allowable if incurred, whether or not paid.

(2) Allowable costs shall be reasonably necessary to the conduct of the litigation rather than merely convenient or beneficial to its preparation.

(3) Allowable costs shall be reasonable in amount.

(4) Items not mentioned in this section and items assessed upon application may be allowed or denied in the court's discretion.

(5) When any statute of this state refers to the award of "costs and attorney's fees," attorney's fees are an item and component of the costs to be awarded and are allowable as costs pursuant to subparagraph (B) of paragraph (10) of subdivision (a). Any claim not based upon the court's established schedule of attorney's fees for actions on a contract shall bear the burden of proof. Attorney's fees allowable as costs pursuant to subparagraph (B) of paragraph (10) of subdivision (a) may be fixed as follows: (A) upon a noticed motion, (B) at the time a statement of decision is rendered, (C) upon application supported by affidavit made concurrently with a claim for other costs, or (D) upon entry of default judgment. Attorney's fees allowable as costs pursuant to subparagraph (A) or (C) of paragraph (10) of subdivision (a) shall be fixed either upon a noticed motion or upon entry of a default judgment, unless otherwise provided by stipulation of the parties.

Attorney's fees awarded pursuant to Section 1717 of the Civil Code are allowable costs under Section 1032 of this code as authorized by subparagraph (A) of paragraph (10) of subdivision (a). *(Added by Stats.1986, c. 377, § 13. Amended by Stats.1987, c. 1080, § 8.5; Stats.1989, c. 1416, § 26; Stats.1990, c. 804 (A.B.3331), § 1; Stats.1993, c. 456 (A.B.58), § 15; Stats.2009, c. 88 (A.B.176), § 17; Stats.2011, c. 409 (A.B.1403), § 3; Stats. 2012, c. 758 (A.B.2684), § 2.)*

Law Revision Commission Comments

Subdivision (a)(3) of Section 1033.5 is amended to reflect advances in recording technology and for consistency of terminology. For a similar reform, see 2002 Cal. Stat. ch. 1068 (replacing numerous references to "audiotape" in Civil Discovery Act with either "audio technology," "audio recording," or "audio record," as context required). [37 Cal. L. Revision Comm'n Reports 211 (2007)].

Research References

Rutter, Cal. Practice Guide: A.D.R. Ch. 3-A, A. General Considerations.
Rutter, Cal. Practice Guide: A.D.R. Ch. 4-B, B. Judicial Arbitration.
Rutter, Cal. Practice Guide: A.D.R. Ch. 4-C, C. Statutorily-Mandated Court Mediation Programs.
Rutter, Cal. Practice Guide: A.D.R. Ch. 5-H, H. Conduct of Arbitration Proceedings.
Rutter, Cal. Practice Guide: A.D.R. Ch. 5-I, I. Arbitrator's Award.
Rutter, Cal. Practice Guide: A.D.R. Ch. 6-C, C. Referees.
Rutter, Cal. Practice Guide: Civil Appeals & Writs Ch. 2-B, B. Appealable Judgments and Orders.
Rutter, Cal. Practice Guide: Civil Appeals & Writs Ch. 3-E, E. Filing Steps.
Rutter, Cal. Practice Guide: Civil Appeals & Writs Ch. 7-C, C. Stay by Posting Security (Bond or Undertaking).
Rutter, Cal. Practice Guide: Civil Appeals & Writs Ch. 14-B, B. Recovery of Appellate Costs and Attorney Fees.
Rutter, Cal. Practice Guide: Civ. Pro. Before Trial Ch. 1-A, A. Accepting a New Case.
Rutter, Cal. Practice Guide: Civ. Pro. Before Trial Ch. 4-D, D. Service of Summons.
Rutter, Cal. Practice Guide: Civ. Pro. Before Trial Ch. 5-B, B. Entry of Default.
Rutter, Cal. Practice Guide: Civ. Pro. Before Trial Ch. 5-C, C. Default Judgment by Clerk.
Rutter, Cal. Practice Guide: Civ. Pro. Before Trial Ch. 6-B, B. Complaints.
Rutter, Cal. Practice Guide: Civ. Pro. Before Trial Ch. 11-A, A. Voluntary Dismissals.
Rutter, Cal. Practice Guide: Civ. Pro. Before Trial Ch. 13-F, F. Arbitration Award.
Rutter, Cal. Practice Guide: Civ. Pro. Before Trial Ch. 13-G, G. Trial De Novo.
Rutter, Cal. Practice Guide: Civ. Pro. Before Trial Ch. 14-C, C. Procedural Issues.

Civ. Pro.

7 Witkin Cal. Proc. 5th Judgment § 130, (S 130) Investigation.

7 Witkin Cal. Proc. 5th Judgment § 131, (S 131) Exhibits.

7 Witkin Cal. Proc. 5th Judgment § 132, (S 132) Fees of Ordinary Witness.

7 Witkin Cal. Proc. 5th Judgment § 133, (S 133) Fees of Expert Witness.

7 Witkin Cal. Proc. 5th Judgment § 134, (S 134) Mileage.

7 Witkin Cal. Proc. 5th Judgment § 135, (S 135) Reporter's Fees.

7 Witkin Cal. Proc. 5th Judgment § 136, (S 136) Jury Fees and Expenses.

7 Witkin Cal. Proc. 5th Judgment § 138, (S 138) Attorneys' Fees.

7 Witkin Cal. Proc. 5th Judgment § 140, Time Limits.

7 Witkin Cal. Proc. 5th Judgment § 150, (S 150) Fees as Costs.

7 Witkin Cal. Proc. 5th Judgment § 163, (S 163) Nonattorney Representing Himself or Herself.

7 Witkin Cal. Proc. 5th Judgment § 165, (S 165) Nature and Effect.

7 Witkin Cal. Proc. 5th Judgment § 202, (S 202) Distinction: Voluntary Dismissal of Trial De Novo Following Arbitration.

7 Witkin Cal. Proc. 5th Judgment § 295, (S 295) in General.

7 Witkin Cal. Proc. 5th Judgment § 296, (S 296) Fees Based on Contract.

7 Witkin Cal. Proc. 5th Judgment § 297, (S 297) Fees Based on Statute.

7 Witkin Cal. Proc. 5th Judgment § 298, (S 298) Fees Based on Other Grounds.

7 Witkin Cal. Proc. 5th Judgment § 306, Where Contract Does Not Specify Amount.

7 Witkin Cal. Proc. 5th Judgment § 136A, (S 136A) (New)-Interpreter's Fees.

5 Witkin Cal. Proc. 5th Pleading § 1042, (S 1042) After Dismissal.

6 Witkin Cal. Proc. 5th Proceedings Without Trial § 629, (S 629) Items Awarded.

6 Witkin Cal. Proc. 5th Provisional Remedies § 152, Levy by Registered Process Server.

6 Witkin, California Summary 10th Torts § 1654, (S 1654) Arbitration Proceedings.

3 Witkin, California Summary 10th Agency and Employment § 317, Prosecution of Actions.

8 Witkin, California Summary 10th Constitutional Law § 1168, Costs and Attorneys' Fees.

8 Witkin, California Summary 10th Constitutional Law § 1267, Costs.

§ 1034. Prejudgment costs; appeal costs

(a) Prejudgment costs allowable under this chapter shall be claimed and contested in accordance with rules adopted by the Judicial Council.

(b) The Judicial Council shall establish by rule allowable costs on appeal and the procedure for claiming those costs. *(Added by Stats.1986, c. 377, § 15.)*

Research References

Rutter, Cal. Practice Guide: A.D.R. Ch. 6-B, B. Temporary Judges.

Rutter, Cal. Practice Guide: Civil Appeals & Writs Ch. 14-B, B. Recovery of Appellate Costs and Attorney Fees.

Rutter, Cal. Practice Guide: Civil Trials & Evidence Ch. 17-D, D. Costs.

Rutter, Cal. Practice Guide: Personal Injury Ch. 9-M, M. Verdicts and Judgment.

7 Witkin Cal. Proc. 5th Judgment § 97, (S 97) Prevailing Party Determined by Court.

7 Witkin Cal. Proc. 5th Judgment § 99, (S 99) General Rule in Superior Court.

7 Witkin Cal. Proc. 5th Judgment § 139, (S 139) in General.

7 Witkin Cal. Proc. 5th Judgment § 296, (S 296) Fees Based on Contract.

§ 1034.5. Unlawful detainer; request for expenses required for eviction

In unlawful detainer proceedings, the plaintiff who recovers judgment for possession of premises, and who advances or pays to the sheriff or marshal the expenses required for the eviction of any persons in possession or occupancy of the premises and the personal property of such persons, shall, after being advised by the sheriff or marshal of the exact amount necessarily used and expended to effect the eviction, be allowed to file a request for the same pursuant to rules adopted by the Judicial Council. *(Added by Stats.1968, c. 102, p. 223, § 1. Amended by Stats.1970, c. 602, p. 1183, § 3; Stats.1982, c. 497, p. 2166, § 72, operative July 1, 1983; Stats.1986, c. 377, § 16.)*

Law Revision Commission Comments

Section 1034.5 is amended to make clear that a judgment for costs may be enforced by any available means, not only by levy of execution. See Title 9 (commencing with Section 680.010). The other changes are not substantive (15 Cal.L.Rev.Comm. Reports 2001).

Research References

Rutter, Cal. Practice Guide: Civil Trials & Evidence Ch. 17-D, D. Costs.

Rutter, Cal. Practice Guide: Enforcing Judgments/Debts Ch. 6A-5, Amount Recoverable Under Judgment.

Miller and Starr California Real Estate § 19:232, Recovery of Possession; Writ of Possession.

8 Witkin Cal. Proc. 5th Enforcement of Judgment § 46, in General.

8 Witkin Cal. Proc. 5th Enforcement of Judgment § 47, Memorandum of Costs.

7 Witkin Cal. Proc. 5th Judgment § 95, (S 95) Prevailing Party in Specified Actions.

7 Witkin Cal. Proc. 5th Judgment § 137, (S 137) in General.

§ 1036. Inverse condemnation proceeding

In any inverse condemnation proceeding, the court rendering judgment for the plaintiff by awarding compensation, or the attorney representing the public entity who effects a settlement of that proceeding, shall determine and award or allow to the plaintiff, as a part of that judgment or settlement, a sum that will, in the opinion of the court, reimburse the plaintiff's reasonable costs, disbursements, and expenses, including reasonable attorney, appraisal, and engineering fees, actually incurred because of that proceeding in the trial court or in any appellate proceeding in which the plaintiff prevails on any issue in that proceeding. *(Added by Stats.1975, c. 1240, p. 3164, § 8, operative July 1, 1976. Amended by Stats.1995, c. 181 (S.B.51), § 1.)*

Law Revision Commission Comments

Section 1036 continues former Code of Civil Procedure Section 1246.3 without change.

Research References

Rutter, Cal. Practice Guide: Civ. Pro. Before Trial Ch. 1-A, A. Accepting a New Case.

Rutter, Cal. Practice Guide: Civil Trials & Evidence Ch. 17-D, D. Costs.

Rutter, Cal. Practice Guide: Civil Trials & Evidence Ch. 17-E, E. Attorney Fees as Costs.

Rutter, Cal. Practice Guide: Enforcing Judgments/Debts Ch. 6A-5, Amount Recoverable Under Judgment.

Miller and Starr California Real Estate § 30:14, Prejudgment Interest; Attorney Fees; Costs.

Miller and Starr California Real Estate § 30:21, Remedies for Unreasonable Precondemnation Activity.

Miller and Starr California Real Estate § 30:32, Remedies for a Regulatory Taking.

Miller and Starr California Real Estate § 34:35, Rate of Interest; Compound Interest.

Miller and Starr California Real Estate § 34:66, Examples of Actions in Which Fees Can be Recovered.

17 NO. 2 Miller & Starr, California Real Estate Newsalert 10, Easements.

22 NO. 4 Miller & Starr, California Real Estate Newsalert 34, Inverse Condemnation.

7 Witkin Cal. Proc. 5th Judgment § 95, (S 95) Prevailing Party in Specified Actions.

7 Witkin Cal. Proc. 5th Judgment § 230, (S 230) Actions Involving Real Property or Environmental Issues.

6 Witkin Cal. Proc. 5th Proceedings Without Trial § 84, (S 84) Distinction: Inverse Condemnation Actions.

8 Witkin, California Summary 10th Constitutional Law § 1168, Costs and Attorneys' Fees.

§ 1038. Proceedings under Government Claims Act or for indemnity or contribution; motions for summary judgment, judgment before presentation of defense evidence, directed verdict, or nonsuit; good faith; award of defense costs; waiver of malicious prosecution damages

(a) In any civil proceeding under the Government Claims Act (Division 3.6 (commencing with Section 810) of Title 1 of the

Government Code) or for express or implied indemnity or for contribution in any civil action, the court, upon motion of the defendant or cross-defendant, shall, at the time of the granting of any summary judgment, motion for directed verdict, motion for judgment under Section 631.8, or any nonsuit dismissing the moving party other than the plaintiff, petitioner, cross-complainant, or intervenor, or at a later time set forth by rule of the Judicial Council adopted under Section 1034, determine whether or not the plaintiff, petitioner, cross-complainant, or intervenor brought the proceeding with reasonable cause and in the good faith belief that there was a justifiable controversy under the facts and law which warranted the filing of the complaint, petition, cross-complaint, or complaint in intervention. If the court should determine that the proceeding was not brought in good faith and with reasonable cause, an additional issue shall be decided as to the defense costs reasonably and necessarily incurred by the party or parties opposing the proceeding, and the court shall render judgment in favor of that party in the amount of all reasonable and necessary defense costs, in addition to those costs normally awarded to the prevailing party. An award of defense costs under this section shall not be made except on notice contained in a party's papers and an opportunity to be heard.

(b) "Defense costs," as used in this section, shall include reasonable attorneys' fees, expert witness fees, the expense of services of experts, advisers, and consultants in defense of the proceeding, and where reasonably and necessarily incurred in defending the proceeding.

(c) This section shall be applicable only on motion made prior to the discharge of the jury or entry of judgment, and any party requesting the relief pursuant to this section waives any right to seek damages for malicious prosecution. Failure to make the motion shall not be deemed a waiver of the right to pursue a malicious prosecution action.

(d) This section shall only apply if the defendant or cross-defendant has made a motion for summary judgment, judgment under Section 631.8, directed verdict, or nonsuit and the motion is granted. *(Added by Stats.1980, c. 1209, p. 4088, § 1. Amended by Stats.1986, c. 377, § 18; Stats.1989, c. 1416, § 27; Stats.2012, c. 759 (A.B.2690), § 2.)*

Law Revision Commission Comments

Subdivision (a) of Section 1038 is amended to more accurately refer to the content of Division 3.6 (commencing with Section 810) of Title 1 of the Government Code. See City of Stockton v. Superior Court, 42 Cal. 4th 730, 734, 741–42, 171 P.3d 20, 68 Cal. Rptr. 3d 295 (2007); see also Gov't Code § 810 (stating that Division 3.6 of Title 1 of the Government Code may be referred to as "Government Claims Act"). [41 Cal.L.Rev.Comm. Reports 285 (2011)].

Research References

Rutter, Cal. Practice Guide: Civ. Pro. Before Trial Ch. 1-B, B. Prelawsuit Investigations, Research and Analysis.
Rutter, Cal. Practice Guide: Civ. Pro. Before Trial Ch. 10-H, H. Entry of Judgment or Order.
Rutter, Cal. Practice Guide: Civ. Pro. Before Trial Ch. 1-B, Outline B.
Rutter, Cal. Practice Guide: Civ. Pro. Before Trial Ch. 10-H, Outline H.
Rutter, Cal. Practice Guide: Civ. Pro. Before Trial Ch. 9(III)-A, A. Sources of Sanctions Power.
Rutter, Cal. Practice Guide: Civ. Pro. Before Trial Ch. 9(III)-D, D. Other Sanctions Statutes and Rules.
Rutter, Cal. Practice Guide: Civ. Pro. Before Trial Ch. 9(III)-D, Outline D.
Rutter, Cal. Practice Guide: Civil Trials & Evidence Ch. 17-D, D. Costs.
Rutter, Cal. Practice Guide: Enforcing Judgments/Debts Ch. 6A-5, Amount Recoverable Under Judgment.
Rutter, Cal. Practice Guide: Personal Injury Ch. 1-B, B. Initial Evaluation of Case: Decision to Accept or Reject Employment or Undertake Further Evaluation of Claim.
Rutter, Cal. Practice Guide: Personal Injury Ch. 3-A, A. Introduction.

Rutter, Cal. Practice Guide: Personal Injury Ch. 5-A, A. Prelawsuit Filings.
Rutter, Cal. Practice Guide: Personal Injury Ch. 9-M, M. Verdicts and Judgment.
Rutter, Cal. Practice Guide: Personal Injury Ch. 1-B, Outline B.
Rutter, Cal. Practice Guide: Personal Injury Ch. 3-A, Outline a.
Rutter, Cal. Practice Guide: Personal Injury Ch. 9-M, Outline M.
Rutter, Cal. Practice Guide: Prof. Responsibility Ch. 8-E, E. Consequences of Improper Advocacy.
Miller and Starr California Real Estate § 29:9, General Principles Concerning Owner's Damages.
7 Witkin Cal. Proc. 5th Judgment § 95, (S 95) Prevailing Party in Specified Actions.
7 Witkin Cal. Proc. 5th Judgment § 235, (S 235) Statutory Authorization.
7 Witkin Cal. Proc. 5th Judgment § 236, (S 236) Improper Continuation of Action.
7 Witkin Cal. Proc. 5th Judgment § 237, (S 237) What Constitutes "Reasonable Cause.".
7 Witkin Cal. Proc. 5th Judgment § 238, (S 238) Award is Proper Where Plaintiffs Lacked Either Reasonable Cause or Good Faith.
7 Witkin Cal. Proc. 5th Trial § 226, (S 226) in General.
5 Witkin, California Summary 10th Torts § 471, Action as Disfavored.
5 Witkin, California Summary 10th Torts § 486, (S 486) Nature of Tort.
5 Witkin, California Summary 10th Torts § 487, (S 487) Public Entity Cannot Sue.

CHAPTER 7. GENERAL PROVISIONS

§ 1045. Lost pleadings or papers; use of copy

LOST PAPERS, HOW SUPPLIED. If an original pleading or paper be lost, the Court may authorize a copy thereof to be filed and used instead of the original. *(Enacted in 1872.)*

Research References

Rutter, Cal. Practice Guide: Civ. Pro. Before Trial Ch. 5-D, D. Default Judgment by Court.
Rutter, Cal. Practice Guide: Civ. Pro. Before Trial Ch. 10-C, C. Procedural Requirements-Moving Party.
Rutter, Cal. Practice Guide: Civ. Pro. Before Trial Ch. 8C-3, "Not Privileged".
Rutter, Cal. Practice Guide: Civil Trials & Evidence Ch. 8C-B, B. Writings.

§ 1046. Affidavits, notices, etc., without title of action or with defective title; validity

An affidavit, notice, or other paper, without the title of the action or proceeding in which it is made, or with a defective title, is as valid and effectual for any purpose as if duly entitled, if it intelligibly refers to the action or proceeding. *(Enacted in 1872. Amended by Stats.1981, c. 714, p. 2597, § 71.)*

Research References

4 Witkin Cal. Proc. 5th Pleading § 13, in General.

§ 1046a. Public records lost or destroyed in calamity; nunc pro tunc filing; effect

In all cases brought under the provisions of any act providing for the establishment and quieting of title to real property in cases where the public records in the office of the county recorder have been, or shall hereafter be, lost or destroyed, in whole or in any material part by flood, fire or earthquake, all papers filed under order of court nunc pro tunc as of the date when they should have been filed, shall have the same force and effect as if filed on the date when they should have been filed. *(Added by Stats.1909, c. 686, p. 1055, § 1.)*

§ 1047. Successive actions on same contract or transaction

SUCCESSIVE ACTIONS ON THE SAME CONTRACT, ETC. Successive actions may be maintained upon the same contract or transaction, whenever, after the former action, a new cause of action arises therefrom. *(Enacted in 1872.)*

Research References

Miller and Starr California Real Estate § 19:223, Cross-Complaint; Affirmative Defenses.
4 Witkin Cal. Proc. 5th Pleading § 58, Multiple Causes: Continuing Trespass or Nuisance.
4 Witkin Cal. Proc. 5th Pleading § 63, Multiple Causes.

§ 1048. Consolidation of actions; separate trial of any cause of action, or of any separate issues, or causes of action or issues

(a) When actions involving a common question of law or fact are pending before the court, it may order a joint hearing or trial of any or all the matters in issue in the actions; it may order all the actions consolidated and it may make such orders concerning proceedings therein as may tend to avoid unnecessary costs or delay.

(b) The court, in furtherance of convenience or to avoid prejudice, or when separate trials will be conducive to expedition and economy, may order a separate trial of any cause of action, including a cause of action asserted in a cross-complaint, or of any separate issue or of any number of causes of action or issues, preserving the right of trial by jury required by the Constitution or a statute of this state or of the United States. *(Enacted in 1872. Amended by Stats.1927, c. 320, p. 531, § 1; Stats.1971, c. 244, p. 392, § 58, operative July 1, 1972.)*

Research References

Rutter, Cal. Practice Guide: Civil Appeals & Writs Ch. 2-B, B. Appealable Judgments and Orders.
Rutter, Cal. Practice Guide: Civil Appeals & Writs Ch. 8-C, C. Standards of Appellate Review.
Rutter, Cal. Practice Guide: Civ. Pro. Before Trial Ch. 2-C, C. Joinder of Parties.
Rutter, Cal. Practice Guide: Civ. Pro. Before Trial Ch. 6-B, B. Complaints.
Rutter, Cal. Practice Guide: Civ. Pro. Before Trial Ch. 6-D, D. Cross-Complaint.
Rutter, Cal. Practice Guide: Civ. Pro. Before Trial Ch. 7(I)-A, A. Demurrers.
Rutter, Cal. Practice Guide: Civ. Pro. Before Trial Ch. 12(I)-D, D. Demand for Jury Trial and Waiver.
Rutter, Cal. Practice Guide: Civ. Pro. Before Trial Ch. 12(I)-E, E. Consolidation, Coordination and Bifurcation.
Rutter, Cal. Practice Guide: Civil Trials & Evidence Ch. 2-B, B. What Constitutes Jury Trial.
Rutter, Cal. Practice Guide: Civil Trials & Evidence Ch. 2-C, C. Cases in Which Jury Trial May be Demanded.
Rutter, Cal. Practice Guide: Civil Trials & Evidence Ch. 4-G, G. Motion to Sever or Bifurcate.
Rutter, Cal. Practice Guide: Civil Trials & Evidence Ch. 4-H, H. Motions to Consolidate or Coordinate Separate Cases.
Rutter, Cal. Practice Guide: Civil Trials & Evidence Ch. 4-G, Outline G.
Rutter, Cal. Practice Guide: Personal Injury Ch. 5-E, E. Selected Pleading Issues.
Rutter, Cal. Practice Guide: Personal Injury Ch. 9-E, E. Order of Trial and Proof and Related Matters.
Miller and Starr California Real Estate § 28:60, Consolidation of Several Foreclosure Complaints.
Miller and Starr California Real Estate § 30A:50, Parties to the Action.
Miller and Starr California Real Estate § 30A:68, Eminent Domain Trials Generally.
Miller and Starr California Real Estate § 30A:69, Contesting the Right to Take.
3 Witkin Cal. Proc. 5th Actions § 915, Exceptions.
9 Witkin Cal. Proc. 5th Administrative Proceedings § 101, (S 101) Consolidation and Severance.
9 Witkin Cal. Proc. 5th Appeal § 120, (S 120) Appeal in Severed Trial.
4 Witkin Cal. Proc. 5th Pleading § 207, Torts to Person.
4 Witkin Cal. Proc. 5th Pleading § 323, on Court Order: Improper.
4 Witkin Cal. Proc. 5th Pleading § 342, Statutory Basis.
4 Witkin Cal. Proc. 5th Pleading § 344, (S 344) Procedure.
4 Witkin Cal. Proc. 5th Pleading § 345, Discretion of Trial Court.
4 Witkin Cal. Proc. 5th Pleading § 347, Consolidation of Separate Actions for Trial.
4 Witkin Cal. Proc. 5th Pleading § 366, (S 366) Transfer of Noncomplex Actions.
4 Witkin Cal. Proc. 5th Pleading § 375, (S 375) Coordination of Related Cases.
4 Witkin Cal. Proc. 5th Pleading § 377, (S 377) California Statute.
5 Witkin Cal. Proc. 5th Pleading § 1169, in General.
5 Witkin Cal. Proc. 5th Pleading § 1171, Related Causes of Action.
6 Witkin Cal. Proc. 5th Proceedings Without Trial § 409, Consolidated Actions.
7 Witkin Cal. Proc. 5th Trial § 87, (S 87) Distinction: Mutually Exclusive Remedies Sought.
7 Witkin Cal. Proc. 5th Trial § 154, in General.
12 Witkin, California Summary 10th Real Property § 736, Trial.
11 Witkin, California Summary 10th Husband and Wife § 68, in General.
5 Witkin, California Summary 10th Torts § 723, (S 723) Types of Actions.
6 Witkin, California Summary 10th Torts § 1357, Adoption of Doctrine.
8 Witkin, California Summary 10th Constitutional Law § 1219, in General.

§ 1049. Pending action defined

ACTIONS, WHEN DEEMED PENDING. An action is deemed to be pending from the time of its commencement until its final determination upon appeal, or until the time for appeal has passed, unless the judgment is sooner satisfied. *(Enacted in 1872.)*

Validity

This section was held preempted by the Federal Rules of Civil Procedure in the case of Leuzinger v. County of Lake, N.D.Cal.2008, 253 F.R.D. 469.

Research References

Miller and Starr California Real Estate § 35:56, Stay of Litigation Pending Arbitration.
Miller and Starr California Real Estate § 11:149, Procedural and Formal Requirements for a Lis Pendens.
9 Witkin Cal. Proc. 5th Appeal § 1, (S 1) in General.
8 Witkin Cal. Proc. 5th Extraordinary Writs § 163, (S 163) Governing Statutes and Rules.
5 Witkin Cal. Proc. 5th Pleading § 1139, What Constitutes Pendency.
5 Witkin Cal. Proc. 5th Pleading § 1168, (S 1168) Time to File.
11 Witkin, California Summary 10th Husband and Wife § 179, Main Proceeding on Appeal.
6 Witkin, California Summary 10th Torts § 945, Computation of Fee.

§ 1050. Rights of action; determination of adverse claims; surety to compel satisfaction of debt

ACTIONS TO DETERMINE ADVERSE CLAIMS, AND BY SURETIES. An action may be brought by one person against another for the purpose of determining an adverse claim, which the latter makes against the former for money or property upon an alleged obligation; and also against two or more persons, for the purpose of compelling one to satisfy a debt due to the other, for which plaintiff is bound as a surety. *(Enacted in 1872.)*

Research References

5 Witkin Cal. Proc. 5th Pleading § 706, (S 706) Action to Quiet Title.

§ 1053. Referees; meeting; acts by majority

When there are three referees all must meet, but two of them may do any act which might be done by all. *(Enacted in 1872. Amended by Stats.1961, c. 461, p. 1550, § 3.)*

Research References

Rutter, Cal. Practice Guide: A.D.R. Ch. 6-C, C. Referees.
6 Witkin Cal. Proc. 5th Proceedings Without Trial § 69, (S 69) Appointment of Referee.

§ 1054. Extension of time; court order; stipulation

(a) When an act to be done, as provided in this code, relates to the pleadings in the action, or the preparation of bills of exceptions, or of amendments thereto, or to the service of notices other than of appeal and of intention to move for a new trial, the time allowed therefor, unless otherwise expressly provided, may be extended, upon good cause shown, by the judge of the court in which the action is pending, or by the judge who presided at the trial of the action; but the extension so allowed shall not exceed 30 days, without the consent of the adverse party.

(b) In all cases in which the court or judge is authorized by this section to grant an extension of time, the extension of time shall be granted when all attorneys of record of parties who have appeared in the action agree in writing to the extension of time, and any extension of time previously granted by stipulation of all attorneys of record of parties who have appeared in the action shall not be included in the computation of the 30-day limitation upon extensions of time allowed by the court or judge. *(Enacted in 1872. Amended by Code Am.1873–74, c. 383, p. 344, § 140; Code Am. 1880, c. 19, p. 7, § 1; Stats.1889, c. 41, p. 45, § 1; Stats.1895, c. 3, p. 12, § 1; Stats.1906, Ex.Sess., c. 6, p. 9, § 1; Stats.1915, c. 109, p. 203, § 1; Stats.1931, c. 1078, p. 2283, § 2; Stats.1933, c. 282, p. 851, § 2; Stats.1933, c. 744, p. 1903, § 196; Stats.1937, c. 525, p. 1534, § 1; Stats.1945, c. 1512, p. 2824, § 2; Stats.1947, c. 33, p. 519, § 1; Stats.1947, c. 1907, p. 2513, § 1; Stats.1951, c. 1737, p. 4137, § 144, operative Jan. 1, 1952; Stats.1982, c. 517, p. 2360, § 168.)*

Law Revision Commission Comments

The portion of Section 1054 that related to undertakings and sureties is continued in Section 995.050 (extensions of time). [16 Cal.L.Rev.Comm. Reports 501 (1982)].

Research References

Rutter, Cal. Practice Guide: A.D.R. Ch. 4-B, B. Judicial Arbitration.
Rutter, Cal. Practice Guide: Civil Appeals & Writs Ch. 7-C, C. Stay by Posting Security (Bond or Undertaking).
Rutter, Cal. Practice Guide: Civ. Pro. Before Trial Ch. 5-B, B. Entry of Default.
Rutter, Cal. Practice Guide: Civ. Pro. Before Trial Ch. 9(I)-F, F. Ex Parte Motions.
9 Witkin Cal. Proc. 5th Appeal § 586, (S 586) in General.
8 Witkin Cal. Proc. 5th Attack Judgment Trial Court § 54, (S 54) Late Filing is Void.
4 Witkin Cal. Proc. 5th Pleading § 10, Extension to Ordinary Party.
4 Witkin Cal. Proc. 5th Pleading § 12, Procedure.
6 Witkin Cal. Proc. 5th Proceedings Without Trial § 5, (S 5) Time of Motion.
6 Witkin Cal. Proc. 5th Proceedings Without Trial § 18, Extension by Stipulation or Court Order.

6 Witkin Cal. Proc. 5th Proceedings Without Trial § 139, Extension of Time.
6 Witkin Cal. Proc. 5th Provisional Remedies § 15, Practice and Procedure.

§ 1054.1. Extension of time; attorney member of Legislature

(a) When an act to be done in any action or proceeding in any court of this state or before any state administrative agency, as provided by law or rule, relates to the pleadings in the action, or the preparation of bills of exceptions, or of amendments thereto, or to the service of notices (other than of appeal, of intention to move for a new trial, and of intention to move to vacate a judgment), and such act is not a motion for a judgment notwithstanding the verdict, the time allowed therefor, unless otherwise expressly provided, shall be extended to a date certain by the judges of the court or by the agency in which the action or proceeding is pending, or by the judge who presided at the trial of the action, when it appears to the judge of any court or to the agency to whom the application is made that an attorney of record for the party applying for the extension is a Member of the Legislature of this state, and that the Legislature is in session or in recess not exceeding a recess of 40 days or that a legislative committee of which the attorney is a duly appointed member is meeting or is to meet within a period which the court or agency finds does not exceed the time reasonably necessary to enable the member to reach the committee meeting by the ordinary mode of travel. When the Legislature is in session or in recess, extension shall be to a date not less than 30 days next following the final adjournment of the Legislature or the commencement of a recess of more than 40 days. If a date is available during recess, extension shall be to such earlier date. When a legislative committee is meeting or is to meet within a period which the court or agency finds does not exceed the time reasonably necessary to enable the member to reach the committee meeting by the ordinary mode of travel, extension shall be for such period as the court or agency finds will be reasonably necessary to enable the member to perform the act to be done in the action or proceeding, unless the extension would expire when the Legislature is to be in session; and in that case the extension shall be to a date not less than 30 days following the final adjournment of the Legislature or the commencement of a recess of more than 40 days. If the act may be reasonably done by the member within the recess, continuance shall be to such earlier date. However, any postponement granted under the provisions of this section shall suspend for the same period of time as the postponement, the running of any period of time for any ruling or proceeding by a court, board, commission, or officer, or for the performance by any party of any act affected by the postponement.

(b) Extension of time pursuant to this section is mandatory unless the court determines that the extension would defeat or abridge a right to relief pendente lite in a paternity action or a right to invoke a provisional remedy such as pendente lite support in a domestic relations controversy, attachment and sale of perishable goods, receivership of a failing business, and temporary restraining order or preliminary injunction, and that the continuance should not be granted. *(Added by Stats.1947, c. 1097, p. 2514, § 2. Amended by Stats.1951, c. 1737, p. 4137, § 145, operative Jan. 1, 1952; Stats.1959, c. 985, p. 3010, § 1; Stats.1963, c. 1468, p. 3035, § 2; Stats.1965, c. 1989, p. 4517, § 5; Stats.1968, c. 698, p. 1397, § 2; Stats.1982, c. 517, p. 2360, § 169.)*

Law Revision Commission Comments

The portion of Section 1054.1 that related to undertakings and sureties is continued in Section 995.050 (extensions of time). [16 Cal.L.Rev. Comm. Reports 501 (1982)].

Civ. Pro.

Research References

9 Witkin Cal. Proc. 5th Administrative Proceedings § 108, Continuance.

9 Witkin Cal. Proc. 5th Appeal § 586, (S 586) in General.

9 Witkin Cal. Proc. 5th Appeal § 632, (S 632) Time Limitations and Extension.

8 Witkin Cal. Proc. 5th Attack Judgment Trial Court § 62, Commencement and Running of Period.

8 Witkin Cal. Proc. 5th Attack Judgment Trial Court § 141, Notice of Motion.

4 Witkin Cal. Proc. 5th Pleading § 11, Extension to Legislator.

6 Witkin Cal. Proc. 5th Proceedings Without Trial § 5, (S 5) Time of Motion.

6 Witkin Cal. Proc. 5th Proceedings Without Trial § 18, Extension by Stipulation or Court Order.

6 Witkin Cal. Proc. 5th Provisional Remedies § 15, Practice and Procedure.

7 Witkin Cal. Proc. 5th Trial § 26, Persons Entitled.

7 Witkin Cal. Proc. 5th Trial § 29, Exceptions to Mandatory Right.

§ 1055. Action against officer or person holding bond or covenant of indemnity; defense by persons executing bond or covenant; judgment

If an action is brought against any officer or person for an act for the doing of which he had theretofore received any valid bond or covenant of indemnity, and he gives seasonable notice thereof in writing to the persons who executed such bond or covenant, and permits them to conduct the defense of such action, the judgment recovered therein is conclusive evidence against the persons so notified; and the court may, on motion of the defendant, upon notice of five days, and upon proof of such bond or covenant, and of such notice and permission, enter judgment against them for the amount so recovered and costs. *(Enacted in 1872. Amended by Code Am.1880, c. 76, p. 73, § 1; Stats.1907, c. 246, p. 309, § 1.)*

Research References

3 Witkin Cal. Proc. 5th Actions § 214, Steps by Defendant.

CHAPTER 8. DECLARATORY RELIEF

Section

§ 1060. Right of action; actual controversy; scope; effect of declaration

Any person interested under a written instrument, excluding a will or a trust, or under a contract, or who desires a declaration of his or her rights or duties with respect to another, or in respect to, in, over or upon property, or with respect to the location of the natural channel of a watercourse, may, in cases of actual controversy relating to the legal rights and duties of the respective parties, bring an original action or cross-complaint in the superior court for a declaration of his or her rights and duties in the premises, including a determination of any question of construction or validity arising under the instrument or contract. He or she may ask for a declaration of rights or duties, either alone or with other relief; and the court may make a binding declaration of these rights or duties, whether or not further relief is or could be claimed at the time. The declaration may be either affirmative or negative in form and effect, and the declaration shall have the force of a final judgment. The declaration may be had before there has been any breach of the obligation in respect to which said declaration is sought. *(Added by Stats.1921, c. 463, p. 689, § 1. Amended by Stats.1965, c. 959, p. 2579, § 2; Stats.1976, c. 1288, p. 5765, § 18; Stats.1993, c. 1262 (A.B.1272), § 6; Stats.1994, c. 806 (A.B.3686), § 1; Stats. 1998, c. 931 (S.B.2139), § 110, eff. Sept. 28, 1998; Stats.2002, c. 784 (S.B.1316), § 73.)*

Law Revision Commission Comments

Section 1060 is amended to accommodate unification of the municipal and superior courts in a county. Cal. Const. art. VI, § 5(e). It is also amended to reflect the elimination of the justice court. Cal. Const. art. VI, §§ 1, 5(b). [28 Cal.L.Rev.Comm. Reports 51 (1998)].

Section 1060 is amended to reflect unification of the municipal and superior courts pursuant to Article VI, Section 5(e), of the California Constitution. [32 Cal.L.Rev.Comm. Reports 131 (2002)].

Research References

Rutter, Cal. Practice Guide: Civ. Pro. Before Trial Ch. 6-B, B. Complaints.

Rutter, Cal. Practice Guide: Fed.Civ.Pro. Before Trial Ch. 2B-5, The "Well-Pleaded Complaint" Rule.

Rutter, Cal. Practice Guide: Insurance Litigation Ch. 14-B, B. Courts and Regulation.

Rutter, Cal. Practice Guide: Insurance Litigation Ch. 15-B, B. Actions by Insurers.

Rutter, Cal. Practice Guide: Insurance Litigation Ch. 6B-E, E. Conditions.

Rutter, Cal. Practice Guide: Insurance Litigation Ch. 12C-D, D. Application-Matters Held "Unreasonable".

Rutter, Cal. Practice Guide: Real Prop. Transactions Ch. 7-B, B. Sale of Ground Lease Tenant's Interest-Preliminary Concerns Re Assignment and Subletting.

Rutter, Cal. Practice Guide: Real Prop. Transactions Ch. 11-H, H. Other Remedies.

Miller and Starr California Real Estate § 24:25, Rights of Enforcement--Generally.

Miller and Starr California Real Estate § 24:26, Rights of Enforcement--Remedies for Breach.

Miller and Starr California Real Estate § 7:207, Tort Damages for Breach of the Duty to Defend.

Miller and Starr California Real Estate § 11:101, Effect of Foreclosure on Rights of Tenants in Possession.

19 NO. 3 Miller & Starr, California Real Estate Newsalert 25, Subdivisions, Land Use Planning, and Approvals.

3 Witkin Cal. Proc. 5th Actions § 28, (S 28) Declaratory Relief and Agreed Case.

9 Witkin Cal. Proc. 5th Administrative Proceedings § 138, (S 138) in General.

9 Witkin Cal. Proc. 5th Administrative Proceedings § 141, in General.

2 Witkin Cal. Proc. 5th Courts § 249, (S 249) Declaratory Relief.

8 Witkin Cal. Proc. 5th Extraordinary Writs § 270, in General.

8 Witkin Cal. Proc. 5th Extraordinary Writs § 273, Distinction: Decision Applying Invalid Regulation.

8 Witkin Cal. Proc. 5th Extraordinary Writs § 275, (S 275) Purpose of Study.

2 Witkin Cal. Proc. 5th Jurisdiction § 395, (S 395) Controversy Nonjusticiable or Improper for Declaratory Relief.

4 Witkin Cal. Proc. 5th Pleading § 31, Law and Equity.

5 Witkin Cal. Proc. 5th Pleading § 849, (S 849) Statutory Basis.

5 Witkin Cal. Proc. 5th Pleading § 853, (S 853) Requisites of Pleading.

5 Witkin Cal. Proc. 5th Pleading § 854, (S 854) Effect of Mislabeling.

5 Witkin Cal. Proc. 5th Pleading § 855, (S 855) Remedies for Breach With Declaratory Relief.

5 Witkin Cal. Proc. 5th Pleading § 856, (S 856) Special Kind of Declaratory Relief.

5 Witkin Cal. Proc. 5th Pleading § 858, (S 858) Contract.

5 Witkin Cal. Proc. 5th Pleading § 866, in General.

5 Witkin Cal. Proc. 5th Pleading § 872, (S 872) Conflict of Jurisdiction.

5 Witkin Cal. Proc. 5th Pleading § 874, (S 874) Circumvention of Statutory Right.

5 Witkin Cal. Proc. 5th Pleading § 1179, (S 1179) Other Exceptions.

6 Witkin Cal. Proc. 5th Proceedings Without Trial § 274, Declaratory Relief Claim Asserting Issues Disputed in Other Causes of Action.

1 Witkin Cal. Summ. 10th Contracts § 1035, (S 1035) Cases Denying Recovery.
10 Witkin, California Summary 10th Parent and Child § 519, (S 519) Nature of Dependency Proceedings.
10 Witkin, California Summary 10th Parent and Child § 600, (S 600) Petition and Notice of Hearing.
7 Witkin, California Summary 10th Constitutional Law § 100, Declaratory Relief and Quiet Title.

§ 1060.5. Action by one claiming to be nonresident for income tax purposes

Any individual claiming to be a nonresident of the State of California for the purposes of the Personal Income Tax Law may commence an action in the Superior Court in the County of Sacramento, or in the County of Los Angeles, or in the City and County of San Francisco, against the Franchise Tax Board to determine the fact of his or her residence in this state under the conditions and circumstances set forth in Section 19381 of the Revenue and Taxation Code. *(Added by Stats.1955, c. 1555, p. 2834, § 1. Amended by Stats.1996, c. 952 (S.B.715), § 1.)*

Research References

3 Witkin Cal. Proc. 5th Actions § 816, Miscellaneous Local Proceedings.
3 Witkin Cal. Proc. 5th Actions § 862, Nature of Problem.
5 Witkin Cal. Proc. 5th Pleading § 856, (S 856) Special Kind of Declaratory Relief.
9 Witkin, California Summary 10th Taxation § 333, (S 333) Residents and Nonresidents.

§ 1061. Refusal to exercise power

The court may refuse to exercise the power granted by this chapter in any case where its declaration or determination is not necessary or proper at the time under all the circumstances. *(Added by Stats.1921, c. 463, p. 690, § 1.)*

Research References

Rutter, Cal. Practice Guide: Civ. Pro. Before Trial Ch. 6-B, B. Complaints.
Rutter, Cal. Practice Guide: Insurance Litigation Ch. 15-B, B. Actions by Insurers.
Rutter, Cal. Practice Guide: Real Prop. Transactions Ch. 11-H, H. Other Remedies.
Miller and Starr California Real Estate § 19:202, Form and Contents of the Notice; Curable and Noncurable Breaches.
19 NO. 3 Miller & Starr, California Real Estate Newsalert 25, Subdivisions, Land Use Planning, and Approvals.
2 Witkin Cal. Proc. 5th Jurisdiction § 395, (S 395) Controversy Nonjusticiable or Improper for Declaratory Relief.
5 Witkin Cal. Proc. 5th Pleading § 849, (S 849) Statutory Basis.
5 Witkin Cal. Proc. 5th Pleading § 866, in General.
5 Witkin Cal. Proc. 5th Pleading § 873, (S 873) Express Prohibition by Statute.
5 Witkin Cal. Proc. 5th Pleading § 876, (S 876) Other Reasons.
6 Witkin Cal. Proc. 5th Proceedings Without Trial § 205, Actions for Declaratory Relief.
7 Witkin Cal. Proc. 5th Trial § 67, (S 67) Declaratory Relief.

§ 1062. Cumulative remedy

The remedies provided by this chapter are cumulative, and shall not be construed as restricting any remedy, provisional or otherwise, provided by law for the benefit of any party to such action, and no judgment under this chapter shall preclude any party from obtaining additional relief based upon the same facts. *(Added by Stats.1921, c. 463, p. 690, § 1.)*

Research References

Rutter, Cal. Practice Guide: Civ. Pro. Before Trial Ch. 6-B, B. Complaints.
2 Witkin Cal. Proc. 5th Jurisdiction § 53, (S 53) Construction of Complaint as One for Declaratory Relief.
5 Witkin Cal. Proc. 5th Pleading § 849, (S 849) Statutory Basis.

5 Witkin Cal. Proc. 5th Pleading § 868, in General.

§ 1062.3. Setting for trial; precedence

(a) Except as provided in subdivision (b), actions brought under the provisions of this chapter shall be set for trial at the earliest possible date and shall take precedence over all other cases, except older matters of the same character and matters to which special precedence may be given by law.

(b) Any action brought under the provisions of this chapter in which the plaintiff seeks any relief, in addition to a declaration of rights and duties, shall take such precedence only upon noticed motion and a showing that the action requires a speedy trial. *(Formerly § 1062a, added by Stats.1927, c. 321, p. 531, § 1. Amended by Stats.1976, c. 1076, p. 4843, § 1. Renumbered § 1062.3 and amended by Stats.1980, c. 676, p. 1906, § 66.)*

Research References

Rutter, Cal. Practice Guide: Civ. Pro. Before Trial Ch. 6-B, B. Complaints.
Rutter, Cal. Practice Guide: Civ. Pro. Before Trial Ch. 12(I)-C, C. Claims for Trial Setting Preference.
Rutter, Cal. Practice Guide: Civil Trials & Evidence Ch. 1-A, A. Importance of Statewide and Local Rules of Court.
Rutter, Cal. Practice Guide: Insurance Litigation Ch. 15-B, B. Actions by Insurers.
Rutter, Cal. Practice Guide: Insurance Litigation Ch. 12C-D, D. Application-Matters Held "Unreasonable".
5 Witkin Cal. Proc. 5th Pleading § 849, (S 849) Statutory Basis.
7 Witkin Cal. Proc. 5th Trial § 67, (S 67) Declaratory Relief.

§ 1062.5. Professional liability insurance issued to health care provider; action by insurer, provider or aggrieved person; intervention; trial and appeal precedence; declaration by court; remedy

Any insurer who issues policies of professional liability insurance to health care providers for professional negligence, as defined in Chapter 1 as amended by Chapter 2, Statutes of 1975, Second Extraordinary Session, any health care provider covered by such a policy, or any potentially aggrieved person, may bring an action in the superior court for a declaration of its, his, or her rights, duties, and obligations under Chapter 1 as amended by Chapter 2, Statutes of 1975, Second Extraordinary Session.

The court shall permit any of the following persons to intervene in the action:

(1) The Attorney General.

(2) Any other person whose appearance is determined by the court to be essential to a complete determination or settlement of any issues in the action.

The action shall be commenced in the superior court in the county in which the Attorney General is required to reside and keep his office pursuant to Section 1060 of the Government Code.

The action shall be set for trial at the earliest possible date and shall take precedence over all cases other than those in which the state is a party.

The court may make a binding declaration of the rights, duties, and obligations of the insurer, whether or not further relief is or could be claimed at the time. The declaration may be affirmative or negative in form and effect and shall have the force and effect of a final judgment.

If the declaration is appealed, the appeal shall be given precedence in the court of appeal and Supreme Court and placed on the calendar in the order of its date of issue immediately following cases in which the state is a party.

The remedy established by this section is cumulative, and shall not be construed as restricting any remedy established for the benefit of any party to the action by any other provision of law.

No declaration under this section shall preclude any party from obtaining additional relief based upon the same facts. *(Added by Stats.1979, c. 373, § 52.)*

CHAPTER 9. ACTIONS TO ENFORCE REAL PROPERTY AND MOBILEHOME SALES AGREEMENTS

Section
1062.10. Filing or recordation as condition precedent to action to enforce agreement.

§ 1062.10. Filing or recordation as condition precedent to action to enforce agreement

No person or legal entity may maintain an action in any court in this state to enforce the terms of a real property sales contract as defined in Section 2985 of the Civil Code or a conditional sale contract on a mobilehome subject to local property taxation and subject to Division 13 [1] (commencing with Section 18000) of Part 2 of the Health and Safety Code, providing for a change in ownership of real property or of a mobilehome subject to local property taxation until the agreement is duly recorded by the county recorder or the change-in-ownership statement required by Section 480 of the Revenue and Taxation Code is filed as provided in that section.

This section shall apply to the enforcement of those agreements which are alleged to have transferred ownership of real property or of a mobilehome subject to property taxation which are entered into after January 1, 1986. *(Added by Stats.1985, c. 911, § 2. Amended by Stats.1986, c. 62, § 1, eff. April 23, 1986.)*

[1] So in enrolled bill.

CHAPTER 10. COMPUTER ASSISTANCE

Section
1062.20. Pro per court documents; interactive computer systems; specified civil actions; standardized information; fees.

§ 1062.20. Pro per court documents; interactive computer systems; specified civil actions; standardized information; fees

(a) In accordance with rules and policy of the Judicial Council, each court may establish and operate an interactive computer system to enable and assist a pro per litigant to prepare standardized pro per court documents for use in the following civil actions:

(1) Enforcement of court orders, including orders for visitation, child custody, and property division.

(2) Landlord and tenant actions.

(3) Uncontested dissolution of marriage.

(4) Probate of a will.

(b) The computer system may also provide standardized information to users, including, but not limited to, information regarding calculations for child and spousal support payments that meet the requirements described in Section 3830 of the Family Code, court procedures, rights and responsibilities of landlords and tenants, and alternative dispute resolution.

(c) The court may contract with a private entity to establish and operate the program and collect any fees described in subdivision (d).

(d) The court may establish and collect fees from the program not to exceed the reasonable costs to establish and operate the program. *(Added by Stats.1995, c. 507 (A.B.1028), § 1.)*

Part 3

OF SPECIAL PROCEEDINGS OF A CIVIL NATURE

PRELIMINARY PROVISIONS

Section
1063. Parties; designation.
1064. Judgment, motion, and order defined.

§ 1063. Parties; designation

PARTIES, HOW DESIGNATED. The party prosecuting a special proceeding may be known as the plaintiff, and the adverse party as the defendant. *(Enacted in 1872.)*

Research References

Rutter, Cal. Practice Guide: Civil Appeals & Writs Ch. 2-B, B. Appealable Judgments and Orders.
Rutter, Cal. Practice Guide: Civil Appeals & Writs Ch. 7-A, A. Overview.
Rutter, Cal. Practice Guide: Civil Trials & Evidence Ch. 2-C, C. Cases in Which Jury Trial May be Demanded.
3 Witkin Cal. Proc. 5th Actions § 65, (S 65) Statutory Classes.
9 Witkin Cal. Proc. 5th Appeal § 148, (S 148) General Rule: Order Appealable.
8 Witkin Cal. Proc. 5th Extraordinary Writs § 164, (S 164) Jurisdiction and Venue.
8 Witkin Cal. Proc. 5th Extraordinary Writs § 169, in General.
4 Witkin Cal. Proc. 5th Pleading § 67, (S 67) Designation of Parties.
6 Witkin Cal. Proc. 5th Proceedings Without Trial § 283, (S 283) in General.

§ 1064. Judgment, motion, and order defined

JUDGMENT AND ORDER SAME MEANING AS IN CIVIL ACTIONS. A judgment in a special proceeding is the final determination of the rights of the parties therein. The definitions of a motion and an order in a civil action are applicable to similar acts in a special proceeding. *(Enacted in 1872.)*

Research References

Rutter, Cal. Practice Guide: Civil Appeals & Writs Ch. 2-B, B. Appealable Judgments and Orders.
Rutter, Cal. Practice Guide: Enforcing Judgments/Debts Ch. 6A-3, "Judgment," "Judgment Debtor" and "Judgment Creditor" Defined.
8 Witkin Cal. Proc. 5th Extraordinary Writs § 217, Appealable Orders.
7 Witkin Cal. Proc. 5th Judgment § 1, Nature and Classification of Judgment.
6 Witkin Cal. Proc. 5th Proceedings Without Trial § 1, (S 1) Application for Order.

Title 1

OF WRITS OF REVIEW, MANDATE, AND PROHIBITION

CHAPTER 1. WRIT OF REVIEW

§ 1067. Writ of certiorari denominated writ of review

The writ of certiorari may be denominated the writ of review. *(Enacted in 1872. Amended by Code Am.1873–74, c. 383, p. 345, § 142.)*

Research References

Rutter, Cal. Practice Guide: A.D.R. Ch. 6-C, C. Referees.
Rutter, Cal. Practice Guide: Civil Appeals & Writs Ch. 2-B, B. Appealable Judgments and Orders.
Rutter, Cal. Practice Guide: Civil Appeals & Writs Ch. 15-B, B. Common Law Writs.
Rutter, Cal. Practice Guide: Civil Trials & Evidence Ch. 16-G, G. Trial by Reference.
3 Witkin Cal. Proc. 5th Actions § 65, (S 65) Statutory Classes.
8 Witkin Cal. Proc. 5th Extraordinary Writs § 5, (S 5) in General.
8 Witkin Cal. Proc. 5th Extraordinary Writs § 23, (S 23) in General.
8 Witkin Cal. Proc. 5th Extraordinary Writs § 163, (S 163) Governing Statutes and Rules.
8 Witkin Cal. Proc. 5th Extraordinary Writs § 212, Certiorari.
3 Witkin, California Summary 10th Agency and Employment § 586, (S 586) Judicial Review.
3 Witkin, California Summary 10th Agency and Employment § 600, (S 600) Judicial Review.
3 Witkin, California Summary 10th Agency and Employment § 611, (S 611) Judicial Review.
3 Witkin, California Summary 10th Agency and Employment § 671, (S 671) Mediation of Impasse After Certification of Exclusive Representative.

§ 1068. Courts which may grant writ; circumstances authorizing grant

(a) A writ of review may be granted by any court when an inferior tribunal, board, or officer, exercising judicial functions, has exceeded the jurisdiction of such tribunal, board, or officer, and there is no appeal, nor, in the judgment of the court, any plain, speedy, and adequate remedy.

(b) The appellate division of the superior court may grant a writ of review directed to the superior court in a limited civil case or in a misdemeanor or infraction case. Where the appellate division grants a writ of review directed to the superior court, the superior court is an inferior tribunal for purposes of this chapter. *(Enacted in 1872. Amended by Stats.1935, c. 52, p. 386, § 1; Stats.1951, c. 1737, p. 4138, § 147, operative Jan. 1, 1952; Stats.1998, c. 931 (S.B.2139), § 111, eff. Sept. 28, 1998; Stats. 1999, c. 344 (S.B.210), § 16, eff. Sept. 7, 1999; Stats.2002, c. 784 (S.B.1316), § 74.)*

Law Revision Commission Comments

Section 1068 is amended to accommodate unification of the municipal and superior courts in a county. Cal. Const. art. VI, § 5(e). It is also amended to reflect elimination of the justice court. Cal. Const. art. VI, §§ 1, 5(b).

Subdivision (b) implements Constitution Article VI, Section 10. For guidance on what constitutes a limited civil case, see Section 85 & Comment. [28 Cal.L.Rev.Comm. Reports 51 (1998)].

Section 1068 is amended to fully reflect the writ jurisdiction of the appellate division. Cal. Const. art. VI, §§ 10, 11(b). See also Penal Code §§ 691(g) ('misdemeanor or infraction case' defined), 1466 (appeal in misdemeanor or infraction case). [29 Cal.L.Rev.Comm. Reports App. 5 (1999)].

Section 1068 is amended to reflect unification of the municipal and superior courts pursuant to Article VI, Section 5(e), of the California Constitution. [32 Cal.L.Rev.Comm. Reports 132 (2002)].

Research References

Rutter, Cal. Practice Guide: Civil Appeals & Writs Ch. 15-A, A. Overview.
Rutter, Cal. Practice Guide: Civil Appeals & Writs Ch. 15-B, B. Common Law Writs.
California Practice Guide: Employment Litigation Ch. 19-T, T. Appeals.
8 Witkin Cal. Proc. 5th Extraordinary Writs § 4, (S 4) Constitutional Consolidation of Trial Courts.

8 Witkin Cal. Proc. 5th Extraordinary Writs § 5, (S 5) in General.
8 Witkin Cal. Proc. 5th Extraordinary Writs § 41, Lack or Excess of Jurisdiction.
8 Witkin Cal. Proc. 5th Extraordinary Writs § 42, General Rule.
8 Witkin Cal. Proc. 5th Extraordinary Writs § 46, (S 46) Review on Later Appeal.
8 Witkin Cal. Proc. 5th Extraordinary Writs § 47, (S 47) Other Adequate Remedy.

§ 1069. Application; notice; order to show cause

The application must be made on the verified petition of the party beneficially interested, and the court may require a notice of the application to be given to the adverse party, or may grant an order to show cause why it should not be allowed, or may grant the writ without notice. *(Enacted in 1872. Amended by Stats.1907, c. 328, p. 603, § 1.)*

Research References

Rutter, Cal. Practice Guide: Civil Appeals & Writs Ch. 15-A, A. Overview.
Rutter, Cal. Practice Guide: Prof. Responsibility Ch. 6-G, G. Professional Competence in Criminal Cases.
8 Witkin Cal. Proc. 5th Extraordinary Writs § 165, (S 165) Petitioner.
8 Witkin Cal. Proc. 5th Extraordinary Writs § 172, Verification.
8 Witkin Cal. Proc. 5th Extraordinary Writs § 183, (S 183) Service.
8 Witkin Cal. Proc. 5th Extraordinary Writs § 190, (S 190) Service of Writ.
4 Witkin Cal. Proc. 5th Pleading § 67, (S 67) Designation of Parties.
4 Witkin Cal. Proc. 5th Pleading § 466, Complaint or Petition.

§ 1069.1. Applicability of section 1089

The provisions of Section 1089 as to a return by demurrer or answer apply to a proceeding pursuant to this chapter. *(Added by Stats.1971, c. 1475, p. 2914, § 2.)*

Research References

8 Witkin Cal. Proc. 5th Extraordinary Writs § 193, Return as Answer or Demurrer.

§ 1070. Direction of writ; return

THE WRIT TO BE DIRECTED TO THE INFERIOR TRIBUNAL, ETC. The writ may be directed to the inferior tribunal, Board, or officer, or to any other person having the custody of the record or proceedings to be certified. When directed to a tribunal, the Clerk, if there be one, must return the writ with the transcript required. *(Enacted in 1872.)*

Research References

Rutter, Cal. Practice Guide: Civil Appeals & Writs Ch. 15-E, E. Procedures on Writ Review.
2 Witkin Cal. Proc. 5th Courts § 366, (S 366) Miscellaneous Duties.
8 Witkin Cal. Proc. 5th Extraordinary Writs § 168, Certiorari: Custodian of Record.
8 Witkin Cal. Proc. 5th Extraordinary Writs § 188, (S 188) Certiorari.
8 Witkin Cal. Proc. 5th Extraordinary Writs § 192, in General.
8 Witkin Cal. Proc. 5th Extraordinary Writs § 194, Return as Record.

§ 1071. Contents

The writ of review must command the party to whom it is directed to certify fully to the court issuing the writ at a time and place then or thereafter specified by court order a transcript of the record and proceedings (describing or referring to them with convenient certainty), that the same may be reviewed by the court; and requiring the party, in the meantime, to desist from further proceedings in the matter to be reviewed. *(Enacted in 1872. Amended by Stats.1963, c. 461, p. 1309, § 2.)*

Research References

Rutter, Cal. Practice Guide: Civil Appeals & Writs Ch. 15-B, B. Common Law Writs.

Rutter, Cal. Practice Guide: Civil Appeals & Writs Ch. 15-E, E. Procedures on Writ Review.
8 Witkin Cal. Proc. 5th Extraordinary Writs § 188, (S 188) Certiorari.
8 Witkin Cal. Proc. 5th Extraordinary Writs § 191, (S 191) Stay of Pending Proceedings.
8 Witkin Cal. Proc. 5th Extraordinary Writs § 192, in General.
8 Witkin Cal. Proc. 5th Extraordinary Writs § 194, Return as Record.

§ 1072. Stay of proceedings; discretion; effect

PROCEEDINGS IN INFERIOR COURT MAY BE STAYED, OR NOT. If a stay of proceedings be not intended, the words requiring the stay must be omitted from the writ; these words may be inserted or omitted, in the sound discretion of the Court, but if omitted, the power of the inferior Court or officer is not suspended or the proceedings stayed. *(Enacted in 1872.)*

Research References

Rutter, Cal. Practice Guide: Civil Appeals & Writs Ch. 15-E, E. Procedures on Writ Review.
8 Witkin Cal. Proc. 5th Extraordinary Writs § 188, (S 188) Certiorari.
8 Witkin Cal. Proc. 5th Extraordinary Writs § 191, (S 191) Stay of Pending Proceedings.

§ 1073. Service

SERVICE OF THE WRIT. The writ must be served in the same manner as a summons in civil action, except when otherwise expressly directed by the Court. *(Enacted in 1872.)*

Research References

8 Witkin Cal. Proc. 5th Extraordinary Writs § 190, (S 190) Service of Writ.

§ 1074. Scope of review

THE REVIEW UNDER THE WRIT, EXTENT OF. The review upon this writ cannot be extended further than to determine whether the inferior tribunal, Board, or officer has regularly pursued the authority of such tribunal, Board, or officer. *(Enacted in 1872.)*

Research References

8 Witkin Cal. Proc. 5th Extraordinary Writs § 41, Lack or Excess of Jurisdiction.
8 Witkin Cal. Proc. 5th Extraordinary Writs § 199, Scope of Review.

§ 1075. Perfection of defective return; hearing; judgment

A DEFECTIVE RETURN OF THE WRIT MAY BE PERFECTED. HEARING AND JUDGMENT. If the return of the writ be defective, the Court may order a further return to be made. When a full return has been made, the Court must hear the parties, or such of them as may attend for that purpose, and may thereupon give judgment, either affirming or annulling, or modifying the proceedings below. *(Enacted in 1872.)*

Research References

Rutter, Cal. Practice Guide: Civil Appeals & Writs Ch. 15-E, E. Procedures on Writ Review.
8 Witkin Cal. Proc. 5th Extraordinary Writs § 192, in General.
8 Witkin Cal. Proc. 5th Extraordinary Writs § 194, Return as Record.
8 Witkin Cal. Proc. 5th Extraordinary Writs § 199, Scope of Review.
8 Witkin Cal. Proc. 5th Extraordinary Writs § 200, Decision.

§ 1076. Judgment; transmission of copy to inferior tribunal, etc.

COPY OF THE JUDGMENT MUST BE SENT TO THE INFERIOR TRIBUNAL. A copy of the judgment, signed by the Clerk, must be transmitted to the inferior tribunal, Board, or officer having the custody of the record or proceeding certified up. *(Enacted in 1872.)*

Research References

Rutter, Cal. Practice Guide: Civil Appeals & Writs Ch. 15-E, E. Procedures on Writ Review.

8 Witkin Cal. Proc. 5th Extraordinary Writs § 200, Decision.

§ 1077. Judgment roll

JUDGMENT ROLLS. A copy of the judgment, signed by the Clerk, entered upon or attached to the writ and return, constitute the judgment roll. *(Enacted in 1872.)*

Research References

Rutter, Cal. Practice Guide: Civil Appeals & Writs Ch. 15-E, E. Procedures on Writ Review.

9 Witkin Cal. Proc. 5th Appeal § 667, (S 667) Nature of Record.

CHAPTER 2. WRIT OF MANDATE

§ 1084. Writ of mandamus denominated writ of mandate

The writ of mandamus may be denominated a writ of mandate. *(Enacted in 1872. Amended by Code Am.1873–74, c. 383, p. 345, § 143.)*

Research References

Rutter, Cal. Practice Guide: Civil Appeals & Writs Ch. 15-B, B. Common Law Writs.

California Practice Guide: Employment Litigation Ch. 13-H, H. Contesting Citations and Related Orders and Notices.

Miller and Starr California Real Estate § 30:13, Measure of Recoverable Damages.

3 Witkin Cal. Proc. 5th Actions § 65, (S 65) Statutory Classes.

8 Witkin Cal. Proc. 5th Extraordinary Writs § 23, (S 23) in General.

10 Witkin, California Summary 10th Parent and Child § 117, (S 117) Termination of Placement.

§ 1085. Courts which may issue writ; parties to whom issued; purpose of writ

(a) A writ of mandate may be issued by any court to any inferior tribunal, corporation, board, or person, to compel the performance of an act which the law specially enjoins, as a duty resulting from an office, trust, or station, or to compel the admission of a party to the use and enjoyment of a right or office to which the party is entitled, and from which the party is unlawfully precluded by that inferior tribunal, corporation, board, or person.

(b) The appellate division of the superior court may grant a writ of mandate directed to the superior court in a limited civil case or in a misdemeanor or infraction case. Where the appellate division grants a writ of mandate directed to the superior court, the superior court is an inferior tribunal for purposes of this chapter. *(Enacted in 1872. Amended by Stats.1935, c. 52, p. 386, § 2; Stats.1951, c. 1737, p. 4138, § 148, operative Jan. 1, 1952; Stats.1998, c. 931 (S.B.2139), § 112, eff. Sept. 28, 1998; Stats.1999, c. 344 (S.B.210), § 17, eff. Sept. 7, 1999; Stats.2002, c. 784 (S.B.1316), § 75; Stats.2010, c. 212 (A.B.2767), § 2.)*

Law Revision Commission Comments

Section 1085 is amended to accommodate unification of the municipal and superior courts in a county. Cal. Const. art. VI, § 5(e). It is also amended to reflect elimination of the justice court. Cal. Const. art. VI, §§ 1, 5(b).

Subdivision (b) implements Constitution Article VI, Section 10. For guidance on what constitutes a limited civil case, see Section 85 & Comment. [28 Cal.L.Rev.Comm. Reports 51 (1998)].

Section 1085 is amended to fully reflect the writ jurisdiction of the appellate division. Cal. Const. art. VI, §§ 10, 11(b). See also Penal Code §§ 691(g) ('misdemeanor or infraction case' defined), 1466 (appeal in misdemeanor or infraction case). [29 Cal.L.Rev.Comm. Reports App. 5 (1999)].

Section 1085 is amended to reflect unification of the municipal and superior courts pursuant to Article VI, Section 5(e), of the California Constitution. [32 Cal.L.Rev.Comm. Reports 132 (2002)].

Subdivision (a) of Section 1085 is amended to make a stylistic revision.

Subdivision (b) is amended to refer to a writ of mandate instead of a writ of review. [Source: 39 Cal.L.Rev.Comm. Reports 109 (2009)].

Research References

Rutter, Cal. Practice Guide: Civil Appeals & Writs Ch. 15-B, B. Common Law Writs.

Rutter, Cal. Practice Guide: Civil Trials & Evidence Ch. 1-C, C. Marshalling the Evidence.

California Practice Guide: Employment Litigation Ch. 19-T, T. Appeals.

Rutter, Cal. Practice Guide: Insurance Litigation Ch. 14-B, B. Courts and Regulation.

Miller and Starr California Real Estate § 25:9, Judicial Review.

Miller and Starr California Real Estate § 15:80, Abandonment of Public Easements.

Miller and Starr California Real Estate § 25:54, Judicial Review.

Miller and Starr California Real Estate § 25:61, Filing, Approval, and Recordation of the Final Map.

Miller and Starr California Real Estate § 27:18, Department of Industrial Relations--Administrative Powers and Proceedings.

Miller and Starr California Real Estate § 27:19, Civil Wage and Penalty Assessments.

Miller and Starr California Real Estate § 27:35, Public Works Competitive Bidding--Bid Protests and Judicial Review of Award of a Public Contract.

Miller and Starr California Real Estate § 25A:13, Judicial Review When a Negative Declaration is Issued.

Miller and Starr California Real Estate § 25A:21, Judicial Review for Environmental Impact Report.

Miller and Starr California Real Estate § 25A:23, Type of Action; Time to File; Preparation of Administrative Record.

Miller and Starr California Real Estate § 25B:53, Enforcement of the Right to Inspect When the Association is a Nonprofit Mutual Benefit Corporation.

Miller and Starr California Real Estate § 30A:19, Resolution of Necessity.

22 NO. 4 Miller & Starr, California Real Estate Newsalert 42, Subdivisions, Land Use Planning, and Approvals.

3 Witkin Cal. Proc. 5th Actions § 337, (S 337) Distinctions.

3 Witkin Cal. Proc. 5th Actions § 684, (S 684) Mandamus.

9 Witkin Cal. Proc. 5th Administrative Proceedings § 121, (S 121) Forms of Relief.

9 Witkin Cal. Proc. 5th Administrative Proceedings § 138, (S 138) in General.

9 Witkin Cal. Proc. 5th Administrative Proceedings § 140, (S 140) Mandamus.

9 Witkin Cal. Proc. 5th Administrative Proceedings § 152, (S 152) Adjudication by Private Organizations.

9 Witkin Cal. Proc. 5th Administrative Proceedings § 153, (S 153) Permit Decisions Involving Expressive Conduct.

8 Witkin Cal. Proc. 5th Extraordinary Writs § 4, (S 4) Constitutional Consolidation of Trial Courts.

8 Witkin Cal. Proc. 5th Extraordinary Writs § 23, (S 23) in General.

8 Witkin Cal. Proc. 5th Extraordinary Writs § 74, (S 74) in General.

8 Witkin Cal. Proc. 5th Extraordinary Writs § 88, (S 88) Other Local Officials.

8 Witkin Cal. Proc. 5th Extraordinary Writs § 96, Corporations.

8 Witkin Cal. Proc. 5th Extraordinary Writs § 125, (S 125) Remedy by Motion.

8 Witkin Cal. Proc. 5th Extraordinary Writs § 205, Reviewing Court.

8 Witkin Cal. Proc. 5th Extraordinary Writs § 208, (S 208) Procedure.

8 Witkin Cal. Proc. 5th Extraordinary Writs § 265, Private Corporations and Associations.

8 Witkin Cal. Proc. 5th Extraordinary Writs § 273, Distinction: Decision Applying Invalid Regulation.

8 Witkin Cal. Proc. 5th Extraordinary Writs § 275, (S 275) Purpose of Study.

8 Witkin Cal. Proc. 5th Extraordinary Writs § 307, Period and Extensions.

2 Witkin Cal. Proc. 5th Jurisdiction § 405, Subject Matter Jurisdiction is Vested Elsewhere by Statute.

6 Witkin Cal. Proc. 5th Provisional Remedies § 277, Extraordinary Writs Compared.

10 Witkin, California Summary 10th Parent and Child § 117, (S 117) Termination of Placement.

9 Witkin, California Summary 10th Corporations § 337, (S 337) Setting Aside Inspection Demand.

5 Witkin, California Summary 10th Torts § 17, State Constitution.

3 Witkin, California Summary 10th Agency and Employment § 579, Attorneys Employed by County Counsel.

8 Witkin, California Summary 10th Constitutional Law § 1016, (S 1016) Judicial Review.

§ 1085.5. Activities of director of food and agriculture; judicial challenge; procedure for issuing writ of mandate

Notwithstanding this chapter, in any action or proceeding to attack, review, set aside, void, or annul the activity of the Director of Food and Agriculture under Division 4 (commencing with Section 5001) or Division 5 (commencing with Section 9101) of the Food and Agricultural Code, the procedure for issuance of a writ of mandate shall be in accordance with Chapter 1.5 (commencing with Section 5051) of Part 1 of Division 4 of that code. *(Added by Stats.1985, c. 1282, § 1. Amended by Stats.1987, c. 1284, § 1.)*

§ 1086. Circumstances authorizing issuance; petition

The writ must be issued in all cases where there is not a plain, speedy, and adequate remedy, in the ordinary course of law. It must be issued upon the verified petition of the party beneficially interested. *(Enacted in 1872. Amended by Stats.1907, c. 244, p. 307, § 1.)*

Research References

Rutter, Cal. Practice Guide: A.D.R. App. D Form 64, Real Property-Sale-Deposit Receipts, Escrow Instructions, Listing Agreements.

Rutter, Cal. Practice Guide: Civil Appeals & Writs Ch. 2-C, C. Nonappealable Orders.

Rutter, Cal. Practice Guide: Civil Appeals & Writs Ch. 15-A, A. Overview.

Rutter, Cal. Practice Guide: Civil Appeals & Writs Ch. 15-B, B. Common Law Writs.

Rutter, Cal. Practice Guide: Civil Appeals & Writs Ch. 15-C, C. Statutory Writs.

Rutter, Cal. Practice Guide: Civ. Pro. Before Trial Ch. 2-A, A. Standing to Sue-"Real Party in Interest" Requirement.

Rutter, Cal. Practice Guide: Civ. Pro. Before Trial Ch. 6-B, B. Complaints.

Miller and Starr California Real Estate § 25A:22, Challenging CEQA Decisions--Standing; Exhaustion of Administrative Remedies.

22 NO. 5 Miller & Starr, California Real Estate Newsalert 3, CEQA.

22 NO. 1 Miller & Starr, California Real Estate Newsalert 5, CEQA.

9 Witkin Cal. Proc. 5th Administrative Proceedings § 122, (S 122) Standing to Obtain Review.

9 Witkin Cal. Proc. 5th Appeal § 132, Jurisdiction Accepted.

8 Witkin Cal. Proc. 5th Extraordinary Writs § 53, Nature of Condition.

8 Witkin Cal. Proc. 5th Extraordinary Writs § 74, (S 74) in General.

8 Witkin Cal. Proc. 5th Extraordinary Writs § 116, Nature of Condition.

8 Witkin Cal. Proc. 5th Extraordinary Writs § 165, (S 165) Petitioner.

8 Witkin Cal. Proc. 5th Extraordinary Writs § 172, Verification.

4 Witkin Cal. Proc. 5th Pleading § 67, (S 67) Designation of Parties.

4 Witkin Cal. Proc. 5th Pleading § 466, Complaint or Petition.

5 Witkin, California Summary 10th Torts § 124, (S 124) Effect of Indemnitee's Settlement of Underlying Claim.

§ 1087. Contents; alternative writ; peremptory writ

The writ may be either alternative or peremptory. The alternative writ must command the party to whom it is directed immediately after the receipt of the writ, or at some other specified time, to do the act required to be performed, or to show cause before the court at a time and place then or thereafter specified by court order why he has not done so. The peremptory writ must be in a similar form, except that the words requiring the party to show cause why he has not done as commanded must be omitted. *(Enacted in 1872. Amended by Stats.1907, c. 244, p. 307, § 2; Stats.1963, c. 461, p. 1309, § 3.)*

Research References

Rutter, Cal. Practice Guide: Civil Appeals & Writs Ch. 15-B, B. Common Law Writs.

Rutter, Cal. Practice Guide: Civil Appeals & Writs Ch. 15-E, E. Procedures on Writ Review.

8 Witkin Cal. Proc. 5th Extraordinary Writs § 189, (S 189) Prohibition and Mandamus.

8 Witkin Cal. Proc. 5th Extraordinary Writs § 195, in General.

8 Witkin Cal. Proc. 5th Extraordinary Writs § 205, Reviewing Court.

8 Witkin Cal. Proc. 5th Extraordinary Writs § 208, (S 208) Procedure.

8 Witkin Cal. Proc. 5th Extraordinary Writs § 322, Summary Determination.

§ 1088. Issuance of writ in first instance; form; notice; service; hearing required

When the application to the court is made without notice to the adverse party, and the writ is allowed, the alternative must be first issued; but if the application is upon due notice and the writ is allowed, the peremptory may be issued in the first instance. With the alternative writ and also with any notice of an intention to apply for the writ, there must be served on each person against whom the writ is sought a copy of the petition. The notice of the application, when given, must be at least ten days. The writ cannot be granted by default. The case must be heard by the court, whether the adverse party appears or not. *(Enacted in 1872. Amended by Stats.1907, c. 244, p. 308, § 3.)*

Research References

Rutter, Cal. Practice Guide: Civil Appeals & Writs Ch. 15-E, E. Procedures on Writ Review.

8 Witkin Cal. Proc. 5th Extraordinary Writs § 183, (S 183) Service.

8 Witkin Cal. Proc. 5th Extraordinary Writs § 189, (S 189) Prohibition and Mandamus.

8 Witkin Cal. Proc. 5th Extraordinary Writs § 190, (S 190) Service of Writ.

8 Witkin Cal. Proc. 5th Extraordinary Writs § 201, (S 201) Where Demurrer Alone is Filed.

8 Witkin Cal. Proc. 5th Extraordinary Writs § 205, Reviewing Court.

8 Witkin Cal. Proc. 5th Extraordinary Writs § 208, (S 208) Procedure.

8 Witkin Cal. Proc. 5th Extraordinary Writs § 223, in Trial Court.

8 Witkin Cal. Proc. 5th Extraordinary Writs § 224, (S 224) in General.
8 Witkin Cal. Proc. 5th Extraordinary Writs § 227, Current Rule: Where Relief is Obvious or Unusual Circumstances Are Present.
8 Witkin Cal. Proc. 5th Extraordinary Writs § 229, Notice.
8 Witkin Cal. Proc. 5th Extraordinary Writs § 230, No Right to Oral Argument.
6 Witkin Cal. Proc. 5th Proceedings Without Trial § 137, (S 137) Restrictions on Default Judgments.

§ 1088.5. Application; proof of service of petition

In a trial court, if no alternative writ is sought, proof of service of a copy of the petition need not accompany the application for a writ at the time of filing, but proof of service of a copy of the filed petition must be lodged with the court prior to a hearing or any action by the court. *(Added by Stats.1982, c. 193, p. 593, § 1, eff. May 5, 1982. Amended by Stats.1983, c. 818, § 1.)*

Research References

8 Witkin Cal. Proc. 5th Extraordinary Writs § 223, in Trial Court.

§ 1089. Return by demurrer, answer or both; time

On the date for return of the alternative writ, or on which the application for the writ is noticed, or, if the Judicial Council shall adopt rules relating to the return and answer, then at the time provided by those rules, the party upon whom the writ or notice has been served may make a return by demurrer, verified answer or both. If the return is by demurrer alone, the court may allow an answer to be filed within such time as it may designate. Nothing in this section affects rules of the Judicial Council governing original writ proceedings in reviewing courts. *(Enacted in 1872. Amended by Stats.1907, c. 244, p. 308, § 4; Stats.1949, c. 1462, p. 2544, § 1; Stats.1971, c. 1475, p. 2914, § 3.)*

Research References

Rutter, Cal. Practice Guide: Civil Appeals & Writs Ch. 15-E, E. Procedures on Writ Review.
3 Witkin Cal. Proc. 5th Actions § 66, (S 66) General Policy of Uniformity in Procedure.
8 Witkin Cal. Proc. 5th Extraordinary Writs § 193, Return as Answer or Demurrer.
8 Witkin Cal. Proc. 5th Extraordinary Writs § 195, in General.
8 Witkin Cal. Proc. 5th Extraordinary Writs § 196, Demurrer or Motion to Quash.
8 Witkin Cal. Proc. 5th Extraordinary Writs § 201, (S 201) Where Demurrer Alone is Filed.

§ 1089.5. Answer; time

Where a petition for writ of mandate is filed in the trial court pursuant to Section 1088.5, and where a record of the proceedings to be reviewed has been filed with the petition or where no record of a proceeding is required, the respondent shall answer or otherwise respond within 30 days after service of the petition. However, where a record of the proceeding to be reviewed has been requested pursuant to Section 11523 of the Government Code, or otherwise, and has not been filed with the petition, the party upon whom the petition has been served, including any real party in interest, shall answer or otherwise respond within 30 days following receipt of a copy of the record. *(Added by Stats.1982, c. 193, p. 593, § 2, eff. May 5, 1982. Amended by Stats.1983, c. 818, § 2.)*

Research References

8 Witkin Cal. Proc. 5th Extraordinary Writs § 223, in Trial Court.

§ 1090. Jury trial; discretion; order for trial

If a return be made, which raises a question as to a matter of fact essential to the determination of the motion, and affecting the substantial rights of the parties, and upon the supposed truth of the allegation of which the application for the writ is based, the court may, in its discretion, order the question to be tried before a jury, and postpone the argument until such trial can be had, and the verdict certified to the court. The question to be tried must be distinctly stated in the order for trial, and the county must be designated in which the same shall be had. The order may also direct the jury to assess any damages which the applicant may have sustained, in case they find for him. *(Enacted in 1872. Amended by Stats.1971, c. 1475, p. 2914, § 4.)*

Research References

8 Witkin Cal. Proc. 5th Extraordinary Writs § 202, (S 202) Where Answer is Filed.
7 Witkin Cal. Proc. 5th Trial § 31, (S 31) Particular Actions and Proceedings.
7 Witkin Cal. Proc. 5th Trial § 109, (S 109) Where Jury is Not Matter of Right.

§ 1091. Return; objection to sufficiency; countervailing by proof

On the trial, the applicant is not precluded by the return from any valid objection to its sufficiency, and may countervail it by proof either in direct denial or by way of avoidance. *(Enacted in 1872. Amended by Stats.1971, c. 1475, p. 2914, § 5.)*

Research References

8 Witkin Cal. Proc. 5th Extraordinary Writs § 198, Replication.
8 Witkin Cal. Proc. 5th Extraordinary Writs § 202, (S 202) Where Answer is Filed.

§ 1092. Motion for new trial; court in which made

MOTION FOR NEW TRIAL, WHERE MADE. The motion for new trial must be made in the Court in which the issue of fact is tried. *(Enacted in 1872.)*

Research References

8 Witkin Cal. Proc. 5th Attack Judgment Trial Court § 22, in General.
8 Witkin Cal. Proc. 5th Extraordinary Writs § 202, (S 202) Where Answer is Filed.
8 Witkin Cal. Proc. 5th Extraordinary Writs § 216, (S 216) Motion for New Trial.
6 Witkin Cal. Proc. 5th Proceedings Without Trial § 75, (S 75) Review of General Reference.

§ 1093. Transmission of verdict; argument on application; notice

THE CLERK MUST TRANSMIT THE VERDICT TO THE COURT WHERE THE MOTION IS PENDING, AFTER WHICH THE HEARING SHALL BE HAD ON MOTION. If no notice of a motion for a new trial be given, or if given, the motion be denied, the Clerk, within five days after rendition of the verdict or denial of the motion, must transmit to the Court in which the application for the writ is pending, a certified copy of the verdict attached to the order of trial; after which either party may bring on the argument of the application, upon reasonable notice to the adverse party. *(Enacted in 1872.)*

Research References

8 Witkin Cal. Proc. 5th Extraordinary Writs § 202, (S 202) Where Answer is Filed.

§ 1094. Hearing

If no return be made, the case may be heard on the papers of the applicant. If the return raises only questions of law, or puts in issue immaterial statements, not affecting the substantial rights of the parties, the court must proceed to hear or fix a day for hearing the argument of the case.

If a petition for a writ of mandate filed pursuant to Section 1088.5 presents no triable issue of fact or is based solely on an administrative record, the matter may be determined by the court by noticed motion of any party for a judgment on the peremptory writ. *(Enacted in 1872. Amended by Code Am.1873–74, c. 383, p. 345, § 144; Stats.1971, c. 1475, p. 2914, § 6; Stats.1982, c. 193, p. 593, § 3, eff. May 5, 1982.)*

Research References

8 Witkin Cal. Proc. 5th Extraordinary Writs § 201, (S 201) Where Demurrer Alone is Filed.

8 Witkin Cal. Proc. 5th Extraordinary Writs § 223, in Trial Court.

8 Witkin Cal. Proc. 5th Extraordinary Writs § 230, No Right to Oral Argument.

§ 1094.5. Review of administrative orders or decisions; filing record; extent of injury; abuse of discretion; relevant evidence; judgment; stay; disposal of administrative records; application to state employees

(a) Where the writ is issued for the purpose of inquiring into the validity of any final administrative order or decision made as the result of a proceeding in which by law a hearing is required to be given, evidence is required to be taken, and discretion in the determination of facts is vested in the inferior tribunal, corporation, board, or officer, the case shall be heard by the court sitting without a jury. All or part of the record of the proceedings before the inferior tribunal, corporation, board, or officer may be filed with the petition, may be filed with respondent's points and authorities, or may be ordered to be filed by the court. Except when otherwise prescribed by statute, the cost of preparing the record shall be borne by the petitioner. Where the petitioner has proceeded pursuant to Article 6 (commencing with Section 68630) of Chapter 2 of Title 8 of the Government Code and the Rules of Court implementing that section and where the transcript is necessary to a proper review of the administrative proceedings, the cost of preparing the transcript shall be borne by the respondent. Where the party seeking the writ has proceeded pursuant to Section 1088.5, the administrative record shall be filed as expeditiously as possible, and may be filed with the petition, or by the respondent after payment of the costs by the petitioner, where required, or as otherwise directed by the court. If the expense of preparing all or any part of the record has been borne by the prevailing party, the expense shall be taxable as costs.

(b) The inquiry in such a case shall extend to the questions whether the respondent has proceeded without, or in excess of, jurisdiction; whether there was a fair trial; and whether there was any prejudicial abuse of discretion. Abuse of discretion is established if the respondent has not proceeded in the manner required by law, the order or decision is not supported by the findings, or the findings are not supported by the evidence.

(c) Where it is claimed that the findings are not supported by the evidence, in cases in which the court is authorized by law to exercise its independent judgment on the evidence, abuse of discretion is established if the court determines that the findings are not supported by the weight of the evidence. In all other cases, abuse of discretion is established if the court determines that the findings are not supported by substantial evidence in the light of the whole record.

(d) Notwithstanding subdivision (c), in cases arising from private hospital boards or boards of directors of districts organized pursuant to the Local Health Care District Law (Chapter 1 (commencing with Section 32000) of Division 23 of the Health and Safety Code) or governing bodies of municipal hospitals formed pursuant to Article 7 (commencing with Section 37600) or Article 8 (commencing with Section 37650) of Chapter 5 of Part 2 of Division 3 of Title 4 of the Government Code, abuse of discretion is established if the court determines that the findings are not supported by substantial evidence in the light of the whole record. However, in all cases in which the petition alleges discriminatory actions prohibited by Section 1316 of the Health and Safety Code, and the plaintiff makes a preliminary showing of substantial evidence in support of that allegation, the court shall exercise its independent judgment on the evidence and abuse of discretion shall be established if the court determines that the findings are not supported by the weight of the evidence.

(e) Where the court finds that there is relevant evidence that, in the exercise of reasonable diligence, could not have been produced or that was improperly excluded at the hearing before respondent, it may enter judgment as provided in subdivision (f) remanding the case to be reconsidered in the light of that evidence; or, in cases in which the court is authorized by law to exercise its independent judgment on the evidence, the court may admit the evidence at the hearing on the writ without remanding the case.

(f) The court shall enter judgment either commanding respondent to set aside the order or decision, or denying the writ. Where the judgment commands that the order or decision be set aside, it may order the reconsideration of the case in light of the court's opinion and judgment and may order respondent to take such further action as is specially enjoined upon it by law, but the judgment shall not limit or control in any way the discretion legally vested in the respondent.

(g) Except as provided in subdivision (h), the court in which proceedings under this section are instituted may stay the operation of the administrative order or decision pending the judgment of the court, or until the filing of a notice of appeal from the judgment or until the expiration of the time for filing the notice, whichever occurs first. However, no such stay shall be imposed or continued if the court is satisfied that it is against the public interest. The application for the stay shall be accompanied by proof of service of a copy of the application on the respondent. Service shall be made in the manner provided by Title 4.5 (commencing with Section 405) of Part 2 or Chapter 5 (commencing with Section 1010) of Title 14 of Part 2. If an appeal is taken from a denial of the writ, the order or decision of the agency shall not be stayed except upon the order of the court to which the appeal is taken. However, in cases where a stay is in effect at the time of filing the notice of appeal, the stay shall be continued by operation of law for a period of 20 days from the filing of the notice. If an appeal is taken from the granting of the writ, the order or decision of the agency is stayed pending the determination of the appeal unless the court to which the appeal is taken shall otherwise order. Where any final administrative order or decision is the subject of proceedings under this section, if the petition shall have been filed while the penalty imposed is in full force and effect, the determination shall not be considered to have become moot in cases where the penalty imposed by the administrative agency has been completed or complied with during the pendency of the proceedings.

(h)(1) The court in which proceedings under this section are instituted may stay the operation of the administrative order or decision of any licensed hospital or any state agency made after a hearing required by statute to be conducted under the Administrative Procedure Act, as set forth in Chapter 5 (commencing with Section 11500) of Part 1 of Division 3 of Title 2 of the Government Code, conducted by the agency itself or an administrative law judge on the staff of the Office of Administrative Hearings pending the judgment of the court, or until the filing of a notice of appeal from the judgment or until the expiration of the time for filing the notice, whichever occurs first. However, the stay shall not be imposed or continued unless the court is satisfied that the public interest will not suffer and that the licensed hospital or agency is unlikely to prevail ultimately on the merits. The application for the stay shall be accompanied by proof of service of a copy of the application on the respondent. Service shall be made in the manner provided by Title 4.5

(commencing with Section 405) of Part 2 or Chapter 5 (commencing with Section 1010) of Title 14 of Part 2.

(2) The standard set forth in this subdivision for obtaining a stay shall apply to any administrative order or decision of an agency that issues licenses pursuant to Division 2 (commencing with Section 500) of the Business and Professions Code or pursuant to the Osteopathic Initiative Act or the Chiropractic Initiative Act. With respect to orders or decisions of other state agencies, the standard in this subdivision shall apply only when the agency has adopted the proposed decision of the administrative law judge in its entirety or has adopted the proposed decision but reduced the proposed penalty pursuant to subdivision (c) of Section 11517 of the Government Code; otherwise the standard in subdivision (g) shall apply.

(3) If an appeal is taken from a denial of the writ, the order or decision of the hospital or agency shall not be stayed except upon the order of the court to which the appeal is taken. However, in cases where a stay is in effect at the time of filing the notice of appeal, the stay shall be continued by operation of law for a period of 20 days from the filing of the notice. If an appeal is taken from the granting of the writ, the order or decision of the hospital or agency is stayed pending the determination of the appeal unless the court to which the appeal is taken shall otherwise order. Where any final administrative order or decision is the subject of proceedings under this section, if the petition shall have been filed while the penalty imposed is in full force and effect, the determination shall not be considered to have become moot in cases where the penalty imposed by the administrative agency has been completed or complied with during the pendency of the proceedings.

(i) Any administrative record received for filing by the clerk of the court may be disposed of as provided in Sections 1952, 1952.2, and 1952.3.

(j) Effective January 1, 1996, this subdivision shall apply to state employees in State Bargaining Unit 5. For purposes of this section, the court is not authorized to review any disciplinary decisions reached pursuant to Section 19576.1 of the Government Code. *(Added by Stats.1945, c. 868, p. 1636, § 1. Amended by Stats.1949, c. 358, p. 638, § 1; Stats.1974, c. 688, p. 1532, § 1; Stats.1975, 2nd Ex.Sess., c. 1, p. 3973, § 26.5; Stats.1978, c. 1348, § 1; Stats.1979, c. 199, § 1; Stats.1982, c. 193, p. 593, § 4, eff. May 5, 1982; Stats.1982, c. 812, p. 3102, § 3; Stats.1985, c. 324, § 1; Stats.1991, c. 1090 (A.B.1484), § 5.5; Stats.1992, c. 72 (A.B.1525), § 1, eff. May 28, 1992; Stats.1995, c. 768 (S.B.544), § 1, eff. Oct. 12, 1995; Stats.1998, c. 88 (A.B.528), § 5, eff. June 30, 1998; Stats.1998, c. 1024 (A.B.1291), § 5, eff. Sept. 30, 1998; Stats.1999, c. 446 (A.B.1013), § 1, eff. Sept. 21, 1999; Stats.2000, c. 402 (A.B.649), § 1, eff. Sept. 11, 2000; Stats.2008, c. 150 (A.B.3042), § 1; Stats.2011, c. 296 (A.B.1023), § 41.)*

Validity

A prior version of this section was held unconstitutional in the case of State Personnel Bd. v. Department of Personnel Admin. (2005) 36 Cal.Rptr.3d 142, 37 Cal.4th 512, 123 P.3d 169.

Research References

Rutter, Cal. Practice Guide: Civil Appeals & Writs Ch. 2-C, C. Nonappealable Orders.

Rutter, Cal. Practice Guide: Civil Appeals & Writs Ch. 5-B, B. Types of Motions, Applications and Requests.

Rutter, Cal. Practice Guide: Civil Appeals & Writs Ch. 7-B, B. Automatic Stay.

Rutter, Cal. Practice Guide: Civil Appeals & Writs Ch. 7-E, E. Stay by Writ of Supersedeas.

Rutter, Cal. Practice Guide: Civil Appeals & Writs Ch. 8-C, C. Standards of Appellate Review.

Rutter, Cal. Practice Guide: Civil Appeals & Writs Ch. 15-A, A. Overview.

Rutter, Cal. Practice Guide: Civil Appeals & Writs Ch. 15-B, B. Common Law Writs.

Rutter, Cal. Practice Guide: Civ. Pro. Before Trial Ch. 1-F, F. Exhaustion of Other Remedies.

Rutter, Cal. Practice Guide: Civil Trials & Evidence Ch. 17-D, D. Costs.

California Practice Guide: Employment Litigation Ch. 7-A, A. Title VII and the California Fair Employment and Housing Act.

California Practice Guide: Employment Litigation Ch. 16-A, A. Failure to Exhaust Administrative Remedies.

Rutter, Cal. Practice Guide: Family Law Ch. 6-A, A. Child Support.

Rutter, Cal. Practice Guide: Insurance Litigation Ch. 14-A, A. The California Regulator (*).

Rutter, Cal. Practice Guide: Insurance Litigation Ch. 14-B, B. Courts and Regulation.

Miller and Starr California Real Estate § 25:9, Judicial Review.

Miller and Starr California Real Estate § 4:44, Disciplinary Process--Judicial Review.

Miller and Starr California Real Estate § 17:23, Minerals--Oil and Gas.

Miller and Starr California Real Estate § 20:22, California Fair Employment and Housing Act--Administrative Proceedings.

Miller and Starr California Real Estate § 25:45, Payment of Fees in Lieu of Dedication or for Construction of Public Improvements.

Miller and Starr California Real Estate § 25:54, Judicial Review.

Miller and Starr California Real Estate § 25:71, Judicial Review.

Miller and Starr California Real Estate § 25A:1, Environmental Review; Purpose and Objective of the Environmental Impact Report.

Miller and Starr California Real Estate § 27:19, Civil Wage and Penalty Assessments.

Miller and Starr California Real Estate § 30:34, Standards of Judicial Review.

Miller and Starr California Real Estate § 19:104, Enforcement and Remedies--Judicial Review of the Ordinance or the Agency's Decision.

Miller and Starr California Real Estate § 25A:13, Judicial Review When a Negative Declaration is Issued.

Miller and Starr California Real Estate § 25A:21, Judicial Review for Environmental Impact Report.

Miller and Starr California Real Estate § 25A:23, Type of Action; Time to File; Preparation of Administrative Record.

Miller and Starr California Real Estate § 25A:24, Remedies; Attorney's Fees.

Miller and Starr California Real Estate § 25C:45, Violation of the Subdivided Lands Act; Enforcement by the Commissioner.

14 NO. 5 Miller & Starr, California Real Estate Newsalert 9, Discrimination.

17 NO. 4 Miller & Starr, California Real Estate Newsalert 18, Subdivisions.

18 NO. 6 Miller & Starr, California Real Estate Newsalert 4, CEQA.

19 NO. 3 Miller & Starr, California Real Estate Newsalert 25, Subdivisions, Land Use Planning, and Approvals.

19 NO. 4 Miller & Starr, California Real Estate Newsalert 50, Subdivisions, Land Use Planning, and Approvals.

21 NO. 4 Miller & Starr, California Real Estate Newsalert 35, Landowners' Liability.

22 NO. 3 Miller & Starr, California Real Estate Newsalert 22, Subdivisions, Land Use Planning, and Approvals.

22 NO. 4 Miller & Starr, California Real Estate Newsalert 23, CEQA.

22 NO. 4 Miller & Starr, California Real Estate Newsalert 42, Subdivisions, Land Use Planning, and Approvals.

3 Witkin Cal. Proc. 5th Actions § 349, (S 349) Administrative Mandamus Proceeding as Prerequisite to Tort Action.

3 Witkin Cal. Proc. 5th Actions § 419, Costs of Appeal.

3 Witkin Cal. Proc. 5th Actions § 684, (S 684) Mandamus.

3 Witkin Cal. Proc. 5th Actions § 869, Statutory Rule.

3 Witkin Cal. Proc. 5th Actions § 870, Illustrations.

9 Witkin Cal. Proc. 5th Administrative Proceedings § 81, (S 81) Procedure.

9 Witkin Cal. Proc. 5th Administrative Proceedings § 121, (S 121) Forms of Relief.

9 Witkin Cal. Proc. 5th Administrative Proceedings § 124, (S 124) Finality and Ripeness.

9 Witkin Cal. Proc. 5th Administrative Proceedings § 134, (S 134) Determination of Fact.

9 Witkin Cal. Proc. 5th Administrative Proceedings § 140, (S 140) Mandamus.

9 Witkin Cal. Proc. 5th Administrative Proceedings § 147, (S 147) Rulemaking by Private Organizations.

Civ. Pro.

§ 1094.6. Judicial review; decisions of local agencies; petition; filing; time; record; decision and party defined; ordinance or resolution

(a) Judicial review of any decision of a local agency, other than school district, as the term local agency is defined in Section 54951 of the Government Code, or of any commission, board, officer or agent thereof, may be had pursuant to Section 1094.5 of this code only if the petition for writ of mandate pursuant to such section is filed within the time limits specified in this section.

(b) Any such petition shall be filed not later than the 90th day following the date on which the decision becomes final. If there is no provision for reconsideration of the decision, or for a written decision or written findings supporting the decision, in any applicable provision of any statute, charter, or rule, for the purposes of this section, the decision is final on the date it is announced. If the decision is not announced at the close of the hearing, the date, time, and place of the announcement of the decision shall be announced at the hearing. If there is a provision for reconsideration, the decision is final for purposes of this section upon the expiration of the period during which such reconsideration can be sought; provided, that if reconsideration is sought pursuant to any such provision the decision is final for the purposes of this section on the date that reconsideration is rejected. If there is a provision for a written decision or written findings, the decision is final for purposes of this section upon the date it is mailed by first-class mail, postage prepaid, including a copy of the affidavit or certificate of mailing, to the party seeking the writ. Subdivision (a) of Section 1013 does not apply to extend the time, following deposit in the mail of the decision or findings, within which a petition shall be filed.

(c) The complete record of the proceedings shall be prepared by the local agency or its commission, board, officer, or agent which made the decision and shall be delivered to the petitioner within 190 days after he has filed a written request therefor. The local agency may recover from the petitioner its actual costs for transcribing or otherwise preparing the record. Such record shall include the transcript of the proceedings, all pleadings, all notices and orders, any proposed decision by a hearing officer, the final decision, all admitted exhibits, all rejected exhibits in the possession of the local agency or its commission, board, officer, or agent, all written evidence, and any other papers in the case.

(d) If the petitioner files a request for the record as specified in subdivision (c) within 10 days after the date the decision becomes final as provided in subdivision (b), the time within which a petition pursuant to Section 1094.5 may be filed shall be extended to not later than the 30th day following the date on which the record is either personally delivered or mailed to the petitioner or his attorney of record, if he has one.

(e) As used in this section, decision means a decision subject to review pursuant to Section 1094.5, suspending, demoting, or dismissing an officer or employee, revoking, denying an application for a permit, license, or other entitlement, imposing a civil or administrative penalty, fine, charge, or cost, or denying an application for any retirement benefit or allowance.

(f) In making a final decision as defined in subdivision (e), the local agency shall provide notice to the party that the time within which judicial review must be sought is governed by this section.

As used in this subdivision, "party" means an officer or employee who has been suspended, demoted or dismissed; a person whose permit, license, or other entitlement has been revoked or suspended, or whose application for a permit, license, or other entitlement has been denied; or a person whose application for a retirement benefit or allowance has been denied.

(g) This section shall prevail over any conflicting provision in any otherwise applicable law relating to the subject matter, unless the conflicting provision is a state or federal law which provides a shorter statute of limitations, in which case the shorter statute of limitations shall apply. *(Added by Stats.1976, c. 276, p. 581, § 1. Amended by Stats.1983, c. 818, § 3; Stats.1991, c. 1090 (A.B.1484), § 6; Stats.1993, c. 926 (A.B.2205), § 5; Stats.1995, c. 898 (S.B.814), § 1.)*

Research References

Miller and Starr California Real Estate § 25:9, Judicial Review.
Miller and Starr California Real Estate § 25:54, Judicial Review.
Miller and Starr California Real Estate § 30:33, Statute of Limitations.
Miller and Starr California Real Estate § 19:104, Enforcement and Remedies--Judicial Review of the Ordinance or the Agency's Decision.
19 NO. 3 Miller & Starr, California Real Estate Newsalert 25, Subdivisions, Land Use Planning, and Approvals.
22 NO. 5 Miller & Starr, California Real Estate Newsalert 20, Subdivisions, Land Use Planning, and Approvals.
9 Witkin Cal. Proc. 5th Administrative Proceedings § 129, (S 129) Statutes of Limitations.
8 Witkin Cal. Proc. 5th Extraordinary Writs § 305, Shortened Limitations Period.
8 Witkin Cal. Proc. 5th Extraordinary Writs § 306, Period Tolled by Failure to Notify.
8 Witkin Cal. Proc. 5th Extraordinary Writs § 309, (S 309) Content.
8 Witkin Cal. Proc. 5th Extraordinary Writs § 311, (S 311) Obtaining and Filing Record.
8 Witkin Cal. Proc. 5th Extraordinary Writs § 314, in General.
6 Witkin Cal. Proc. 5th Proceedings Without Trial § 31, Express Limitations.

§ 1094.8. Permit proceedings affecting expressive conduct; expedited judicial review

(a) Notwithstanding anything to the contrary in this chapter, an action or proceeding to review the issuance, revocation, suspension, or denial of a permit or other entitlement for expressive conduct protected by the First Amendment to the United States Constitution shall be conducted in accordance with subdivision (d).

(b) For purposes of this section, the following definitions shall apply:

(1) The terms "permit" and "entitlement" are used interchangeably.

(2) The term "permit applicant" means both an applicant for a permit and a permitholder.

(3) The term "public agency" means a city, county, city and county, a joint powers authority or similar public entity formed pursuant to Section 65850.4 of the Government Code, or any other public entity authorized by law to issue permits for expressive conduct protected by the First Amendment to the United States Constitution.

(c) A public agency may, if it so chooses, designate the permits or entitlements to which this section applies by adopting an ordinance or resolution which contains a specific listing or other description of the permits or entitlements issued by the public agency which are eligible for expedited judicial review pursuant to this section because the permits regulate expressive conduct protected by the First Amendment to the United States Constitution.

(d) The procedure set forth in this subdivision, when applicable, shall supersede anything to the contrary set forth in this chapter.

(1) Within five court days after receipt of written notification from a permit applicant that the permit applicant will seek judicial review of a public agency's action on the permit, the public agency shall prepare, certify, and make available the administrative record to the permit applicant.

(2) Either the public agency or the permit applicant may bring an action in accordance with the procedure set forth in this section. If the permit applicant brings the action, the action shall be in the form of a petition for writ of mandate pursuant to Section 1085 or 1094.5, as appropriate.

(3) The party bringing the action pursuant to this section shall file and serve the petition on the respondent no later than 21 calendar days following the public agency's final decision on the permit. The title page of the petition shall contain the following language in 18–point type:

"ATTENTION: THIS MATTER IS ENTITLED TO PRIORITY AND SUBJECT TO THE EXPEDITED HEARING AND REVIEW PROCEDURES CONTAINED IN SECTION 1094.8 OF THE CODE OF CIVIL PROCEDURE."

(4) The clerk of the court shall set a hearing for review of the petition no later than 25 calendar days from the date the petition is filed. Moving, opposition, and reply papers shall be filed as provided in the California Rules of Court. The petitioner shall lodge the administrative record with the court no later than 10 calendar days in advance of the hearing date.

(5) Following the conclusion of the hearing, the court shall render its decision in an expeditious manner consistent with constitutional requirements in view of the particular facts and circumstances. In no event shall the decision be rendered later than 20 calendar days after the matter is submitted or 50 calendar days after the date the petition is filed pursuant to paragraph (4), whichever is earlier.

(e) If the presiding judge of the court in which the action is filed determines that, as a result of either the press of other court business or other factors, the court will be unable to meet any one or more of the deadlines provided within this section, the presiding judge shall request the temporary assignment of a judicial officer to hear the petition and render a decision within the time limits contained herein, pursuant to Section 68543.8 of the Government Code. Given the short time period involved, the request shall be entitled to priority.

(f) In any action challenging the issuance, revocation, suspension, or denial of a permit or entitlement, the parties to the action shall be permitted to jointly waive the time limits provided for herein. *(Added by Stats.1999, c. 49 (S.B.1165), § 1, eff. June 28, 1999.)*

Research References

Rutter, Cal. Practice Guide: Civ. Pro. Before Trial Ch. 12(I)-C, C. Claims for Trial Setting Preference.

Miller and Starr California Real Estate § 22:10, Indecent or Offensive Acts.

Miller and Starr California Real Estate § 22:11, Indecent or Offensive Acts--Adult Entertainment; First Amendment Protection.

Miller and Starr California Real Estate § 25:75, Agency Administration of a Sign Ordinance.

19 NO. 5 Miller & Starr, California Real Estate Newsalert 23, Landowners' Liability.

9 Witkin Cal. Proc. 5th Administrative Proceedings § 153, (S 153) Permit Decisions Involving Expressive Conduct.

8 Witkin Cal. Proc. 5th Extraordinary Writs § 162, (S 162) Procedural Overview.

8 Witkin Cal. Proc. 5th Extraordinary Writs § 300, in General.

7 Witkin, California Summary 10th Constitutional Law § 360, Requirement of License or Permit.

§ 1095. Judgment for applicant; damages; peremptory writ; officer of public entity as respondent

If judgment be given for the applicant, the applicant may recover the damages which the applicant has sustained, as found by the jury, or as may be determined by the court or referee, upon a reference to be ordered, together with costs; and a peremptory mandate must also be awarded without delay. Damages and costs may be enforced in the manner provided for money judgments generally. In all cases where the respondent is an officer of a public entity, all damages and costs, or either, which may be recovered or awarded, shall be recovered and awarded against the public entity represented by the officer, and not against the officer so appearing in the proceeding, and are a proper claim against the public entity for which the officer appeared and shall be paid as other claims against the public entity are paid; but in all such cases, the court shall first determine that the officer appeared and made defense in the proceeding in good faith. For the purpose of this section, "public entity" includes the state, a county, city, district or other public agency or public corporation. For the purpose of this section, "officer" includes officer, agent or employee. *(Enacted in 1872. Amended by Stats.1913, c. 206, p. 359, § 1; Stats.1963, c. 1681, p. 3285, § 3; Stats.1982, c. 497, p. 2167, § 73, operative July 1, 1983.)*

Law Revision Commission Comments

The 1963 amendment makes this section apply to all public entities and to agents and employees as well as officers.

Section 1095 is amended to conform to Title 9 (commencing with Section 680.010) of Part 2 (Enforcement of Judgments Law). The other changes are not substantive (15 Cal.L.Rev.Comm. Reports 2001).

Research References

Rutter, Cal. Practice Guide: Civil Appeals & Writs Ch. 14-B, B. Recovery of Appellate Costs and Attorney Fees.

9 Witkin Cal. Proc. 5th Appeal § 957, (S 957) Award Against Government or Officer.

8 Witkin Cal. Proc. 5th Extraordinary Writs § 201, (S 201) Where Demurrer Alone is Filed.

8 Witkin Cal. Proc. 5th Extraordinary Writs § 204, Superior Court.

8 Witkin Cal. Proc. 5th Extraordinary Writs § 211, Mandamus and Prohibition.

8 Witkin Cal. Proc. 5th Extraordinary Writs § 212, Certiorari.

8 Witkin Cal. Proc. 5th Extraordinary Writs § 213, (S 213) Costs in Reviewing Court.

5 Witkin, California Summary 10th Torts § 229, (S 229) Tort Claims Act Immunities Extend to Liabilities Imposed by Other Statutes.

§ 1096. Service

SERVICE OF THE WRIT. The writ must be served in the same manner as a summons in a civil action, except when otherwise expressly directed by order of the Court. Service upon a majority of the members of any Board or body, is service upon the Board or body, whether at the time of the service the Board or body was in session or not. *(Enacted in 1872).*

Research References

8 Witkin Cal. Proc. 5th Extraordinary Writs § 190, (S 190) Service of Writ.

8 Witkin Cal. Proc. 5th Extraordinary Writs § 205, Reviewing Court.

§ 1097. Refusal or neglect to obey writ; fine; imprisonment

When a peremptory mandate has been issued and directed to any inferior tribunal, corporation, Board, or person, if it appear to the Court that any member of such tribunal, corporation, or Board, or such person upon whom the writ has been personally served, has, without just excuse, refused or neglected to obey the same, the Court may, upon motion, impose a fine not exceeding one thousand dollars. In case of persistence in a refusal of obedience, the Court may order the party to be imprisoned until the writ is obeyed, and may make any orders necessary and proper for the complete enforcement of the writ. *(Enacted in 1872. Amended by Code Am.1873–74, c. 383, p. 345, § 145.)*

Research References

8 Witkin Cal. Proc. 5th Extraordinary Writs § 207, (S 207) Enforcement of Judgment.

8 Witkin Cal. Proc. 5th Extraordinary Writs § 333, Enforcement of Judgment.

CHAPTER 3. WRIT OF PROHIBITION

Section

§ 1102. Definition

The writ of prohibition arrests the proceedings of any tribunal, corporation, board, or person exercising judicial functions, when such proceedings are without or in excess of the jurisdiction of such tribunal, corporation, board, or person. *(Enacted in 1872. Amended by Stats.1881, c. 25, p. 20, § 1; Stats.1919, c. 199, p. 291, § 1; Stats.1955, c. 971, p. 1870, § 1.)*

Research References

Rutter, Cal. Practice Guide: Civil Appeals & Writs Ch. 15-B, B. Common Law Writs.

Rutter, Cal. Practice Guide: Civil Appeals & Writs Form 7:D, Petition for Writ of Supersedeas or Other Stay Order.

California Practice Guide: Employment Litigation Ch. 19-T, T. Appeals.

3 Witkin Cal. Proc. 5th Actions § 65, (S 65) Statutory Classes.

2 Witkin Cal. Proc. 5th Courts § 168, (S 168) Constitutional Jurisdiction Cannot be Curtailed.

8 Witkin Cal. Proc. 5th Extraordinary Writs § 18, (S 18) in General.

8 Witkin Cal. Proc. 5th Extraordinary Writs § 19, Mandamus.

8 Witkin Cal. Proc. 5th Extraordinary Writs § 48, (S 48) Act Must be Judicial.

8 Witkin Cal. Proc. 5th Extraordinary Writs § 49, (S 49) Act Must be Threatened.

6 Witkin Cal. Proc. 5th Provisional Remedies § 277, Extraordinary Writs Compared.

3 Witkin, California Summary 10th Agency and Employment § 66, (S 66) Legislative Response.

§ 1103. Courts which may issue writ; parties to whom issued; petition

(a) A writ of prohibition may be issued by any court to an inferior tribunal or to a corporation, board, or person, in all cases where there is not a plain, speedy, and adequate remedy in the ordinary course of law. It is issued upon the verified petition of the person beneficially interested.

(b) The appellate division of the superior court may grant a writ of prohibition directed to the superior court in a limited civil case or in a misdemeanor or infraction case. Where the appellate division grants a writ of prohibition directed to the superior court, the superior court is an inferior tribunal for purposes of this chapter. *(Enacted in 1872. Amended by Stats.1907, c. 449, p. 838, § 1; Stats.1935, c. 52, p. 386, § 3; Stats.1951, c. 1737, p. 4139, § 149, operative Jan. 1, 1952; Stats.1998, c. 931 (S.B.2139), § 113, eff. Sept. 28, 1998; Stats. 1999, c. 344 (S.B.210), § 18, eff. Sept. 7, 1999; Stats.2002, c. 784 (S.B.1316), § 76; Stats.2010, c. 212 (A.B.2767), § 3.)*

Law Revision Commission Comments

Section 1103 is amended to accommodate unification of the municipal and superior courts in a county. Cal. Const. art. VI, § 5(e). It is also amended to reflect elimination of the justice court. Cal. Const. art. VI, §§ 1, 5(b).

Subdivision (b) implements Constitution Article VI, Section 10. For guidance on what constitutes a limited civil case, see Section 85 & Comment. [Cal.L.Rev.Comm. Reports 51 (1998)].

Section 1103 is amended to fully reflect the writ jurisdiction of the appellate division. Cal. Const. art. VI, §§ 10, 11(b). See also Penal Code §§ 691(g) ('misdemeanor or infraction case' defined), 1466 (appeal in misdemeanor or infraction case). [29 Cal.L.Rev.Comm. Reports App. 5 (1999)].

Section 1103 is amended to reflect unification of the municipal and superior courts pursuant to Article VI, Section 5(e), of the California Constitution. [32 Cal.L.Rev.Comm. Reports 133 (2002)].

Subdivision (b) of Section 1103 is amended to refer to a writ of prohibition instead of a writ of review. [39 Cal.L.Rev.Comm. Reports 109 (2009)].

Research References

Rutter, Cal. Practice Guide: Civil Appeals & Writs Ch. 15-A, A. Overview.

Rutter, Cal. Practice Guide: Civil Appeals & Writs Ch. 15-B, B. Common Law Writs.

8 Witkin Cal. Proc. 5th Extraordinary Writs § 4, (S 4) Constitutional Consolidation of Trial Courts.

8 Witkin Cal. Proc. 5th Extraordinary Writs § 18, (S 18) in General.

8 Witkin Cal. Proc. 5th Extraordinary Writs § 53, Nature of Condition.

8 Witkin Cal. Proc. 5th Extraordinary Writs § 165, (S 165) Petitioner.

8 Witkin Cal. Proc. 5th Extraordinary Writs § 172, Verification.

4 Witkin Cal. Proc. 5th Pleading § 67, (S 67) Designation of Parties.

4 Witkin Cal. Proc. 5th Pleading § 466, Complaint or Petition.

6 Witkin Cal. Proc. 5th Provisional Remedies § 277, Extraordinary Writs Compared.

§ 1104. Contents; alternative writ; peremptory writ

The writ must be either alternative or peremptory. The alternative writ must command the party to whom it is directed to desist or refrain from further proceedings in the action or matter specified therein, until the further order of the court from which it is issued, and to show cause before such court at a time and place then or thereafter specified by court order why such party should not be absolutely restrained from any further proceedings in such action or matter. The peremptory writ must be in a similar form, except that the words requiring the party to show cause why he should not be absolutely restrained must be

omitted. *(Enacted in 1872. Amended by Stats.1907, c. 449, p. 838, § 2; Stats.1963, c. 461, p. 1309, § 4.)*

Research References

Rutter, Cal. Practice Guide: Civil Appeals & Writs Ch. 15-B, B. Common Law Writs.

Rutter, Cal. Practice Guide: Civil Appeals & Writs Ch. 15-E, E. Procedures on Writ Review.

8 Witkin Cal. Proc. 5th Extraordinary Writs § 189, (S 189) Prohibition and Mandamus.

8 Witkin Cal. Proc. 5th Extraordinary Writs § 191, (S 191) Stay of Pending Proceedings.

8 Witkin Cal. Proc. 5th Extraordinary Writs § 195, in General.

8 Witkin Cal. Proc. 5th Extraordinary Writs § 204, Superior Court.

8 Witkin Cal. Proc. 5th Extraordinary Writs § 223, in Trial Court.

§ 1105. Applicability of provisions relating to writ of mandate

CERTAIN PROVISIONS OF THE PRECEDING CHAPTER APPLICABLE. The provisions of the preceding Chapter, except of the first four sections thereof, apply to this proceeding. *(Enacted in 1872.)*

Research References

Rutter, Cal. Practice Guide: Civil Appeals & Writs Ch. 15-E, E. Procedures on Writ Review.

8 Witkin Cal. Proc. 5th Attack Judgment Trial Court § 22, in General.

8 Witkin Cal. Proc. 5th Extraordinary Writs § 19, Mandamus.

8 Witkin Cal. Proc. 5th Extraordinary Writs § 183, (S 183) Service.

8 Witkin Cal. Proc. 5th Extraordinary Writs § 190, (S 190) Service of Writ.

8 Witkin Cal. Proc. 5th Extraordinary Writs § 195, in General.

8 Witkin Cal. Proc. 5th Extraordinary Writs § 198, Replication.

8 Witkin Cal. Proc. 5th Extraordinary Writs § 216, (S 216) Motion for New Trial.

8 Witkin Cal. Proc. 5th Extraordinary Writs § 223, in Trial Court.

6 Witkin Cal. Proc. 5th Proceedings Without Trial § 137, (S 137) Restrictions on Default Judgments.

7 Witkin Cal. Proc. 5th Trial § 109, (S 109) Where Jury is Not Matter of Right.

CHAPTER 4. WRITS OF REVIEW, MANDATE, AND PROHIBITION MAY ISSUE AND BE HEARD

Section

1107. Application for prerogative writ; proof of service; method of service; points and authorities in opposition; ex parte grant; exceptions.

1108. Courts which may issue writs of review, mandate, and prohibition; discretion; return; hearing.

§ 1107. Application for prerogative writ; proof of service; method of service; points and authorities in opposition; ex parte grant; exceptions

When an application is filed for the issuance of any prerogative writ, the application shall be accompanied by proof of service of a copy thereof upon the respondent and the real party in interest named in such application. The provisions of Chapter 5 (commencing with Section 1010) of Title 14 of Part 2 shall apply to the service of the application. However, when a writ of mandate is sought pursuant to the provisions of Section 1088.5, the action may be filed and served in the same manner as an ordinary action under Part 2 (commencing with Section 307). Where the real party in respondent's interest is a board or commission, the service shall be made upon the presiding officer, or upon the secretary, or upon a majority of the members, of the board or commission. Within five days after service and filing of the application, the real party in interest or the respondent or both may serve upon the applicant and file with the court points and authorities in opposition to the granting of the writ.

The court in which the application is filed, in its discretion and for good cause, may grant the application ex parte, without notice or service of the application as herein provided.

The provisions of this section shall not be applicable to applications for the writ of habeas corpus, or to applications for writs of review of the Industrial Accident or Public Utilities Commissions. *(Added by Stats.1941, c. 438, p. 1728, § 1. Amended by Stats.1947, c. 304, p. 864, § 1; Stats.1959, c. 737, p. 2727, § 1; Stats.1982, c. 193, p. 596, § 5, eff. May 5, 1982; Stats.1982, c. 812, p. 3105, § 4.)*

Research References

Rutter, Cal. Practice Guide: Civil Appeals & Writs Ch. 15-E, E. Procedures on Writ Review.
8 Witkin Cal. Proc. 5th Extraordinary Writs § 56, Effect of Alternative Writ.
8 Witkin Cal. Proc. 5th Extraordinary Writs § 166, in General.
8 Witkin Cal. Proc. 5th Extraordinary Writs § 169, in General.
8 Witkin Cal. Proc. 5th Extraordinary Writs § 183, (S 183) Service.
8 Witkin Cal. Proc. 5th Extraordinary Writs § 184, (S 184) Opposing Memorandum.
8 Witkin Cal. Proc. 5th Extraordinary Writs § 223, in Trial Court.
8 Witkin Cal. Proc. 5th Extraordinary Writs § 303, (S 303) in General.
8 Witkin Cal. Proc. 5th Extraordinary Writs § 322, Summary Determination.
4 Witkin Cal. Proc. 5th Pleading § 67, (S 67) Designation of Parties.

§ 1108. Courts which may issue writs of review, mandate, and prohibition; discretion; return; hearing

Writs of review, mandate, and prohibition issued by the Supreme Court, a court of appeal, or a superior court, may, in the discretion of the court issuing the writ, be made returnable, and a hearing thereon be had at any time. *(Enacted in 1872. Amended by Code Am.1873–74, c. 383, p. 346, § 146; Code Am.1880, c. 77, p. 73, § 1; Stats.1935, c. 52, p. 386, § 4; Stats.1967, c. 17, p. 832, § 18.)*

Research References

8 Witkin Cal. Proc. 5th Extraordinary Writs § 192, in General.
8 Witkin Cal. Proc. 5th Extraordinary Writs § 195, in General.

CHAPTER 5. RULES OF PRACTICE AND APPEALS

§ 1109. Applicability of rules governing civil actions; exceptions

CERTAIN PROVISIONS OF PART II APPLICABLE. Except as otherwise provided in this Title, the provisions of Part II of this Code [1] are applicable to and constitute the rules of practice in the proceedings mentioned in this Title. *(Enacted in 1872.)*

[1] Section 307 et seq.

Research References

Miller and Starr California Real Estate § 25A:21, Judicial Review for Environmental Impact Report.
3 Witkin Cal. Proc. 5th Actions § 66, (S 66) General Policy of Uniformity in Procedure.
8 Witkin Cal. Proc. 5th Extraordinary Writs § 163, (S 163) Governing Statutes and Rules.
8 Witkin Cal. Proc. 5th Extraordinary Writs § 170, Allegations.

8 Witkin Cal. Proc. 5th Extraordinary Writs § 193, Return as Answer or Demurrer.
8 Witkin Cal. Proc. 5th Extraordinary Writs § 195, in General.
8 Witkin Cal. Proc. 5th Extraordinary Writs § 196, Demurrer or Motion to Quash.
8 Witkin Cal. Proc. 5th Extraordinary Writs § 198, Replication.
8 Witkin Cal. Proc. 5th Extraordinary Writs § 201, (S 201) Where Demurrer Alone is Filed.
8 Witkin Cal. Proc. 5th Extraordinary Writs § 215, (S 215) Sanctions for Frivolous Application.

§ 1110. Applicability of provisions relative to new trials and appeals; exceptions

SAME. The provisions of Part II of this Code [1] relative to new trials and appeals, except in so far as they are inconsistent with the provisions of this Title, apply to the proceedings mentioned in this Title. *(Enacted in 1872.)*

[1] Code of Civil Procedure § 307 et seq.

Research References

Rutter, Cal. Practice Guide: Civil Appeals & Writs Ch. 7-A, A. Overview.
Rutter, Cal. Practice Guide: Civil Appeals & Writs Ch. 15-A, A. Overview.
Rutter, Cal. Practice Guide: Civil Appeals & Writs Ch. 15-D, D. Writ Review of Contempt Orders.
8 Witkin Cal. Proc. 5th Attack Judgment Trial Court § 22, in General.
8 Witkin Cal. Proc. 5th Extraordinary Writs § 163, (S 163) Governing Statutes and Rules.
8 Witkin Cal. Proc. 5th Extraordinary Writs § 216, (S 216) Motion for New Trial.
8 Witkin Cal. Proc. 5th Extraordinary Writs § 217, Appealable Orders.
8 Witkin Cal. Proc. 5th Extraordinary Writs § 219, Stay Pending Appeal.
8 Witkin Cal. Proc. 5th Extraordinary Writs § 219, Stay Pending Appeal.

§ 1110a. Appeal from mandate commanding delivery of water for irrigation; no stay; bond for expenses

If an appeal be taken from an order or judgment directing the issuance of a writ of mandate commanding a party to deliver water, for irrigation purposes, such appeal shall not stay the operation of the order, judgment or writ as to the delivery of such water, but such water must until the final determination of said appeal be delivered as commanded by said writ; provided, that if any expense is necessary to be incurred by the defendant in connecting the water supply with the land to be irrigated, said defendant shall not be obliged to furnish water unless the plaintiff shall provide a bond in such sum as the court may fix, conditioned that in the event of the judgment being reversed, plaintiff will pay defendant the amount of the expense so incurred not exceeding the amount of said bond. *(Added by Stats.1919, c. 358, p. 754, § 1.)*

Research References

8 Witkin Cal. Proc. 5th Extraordinary Writs § 219, Stay Pending Appeal.

§ 1110b. Appeal from mandate; denial of stay; irreparable damage

If an appeal be taken from an order or judgment granting a writ of mandate the court granting the writ, or the appellate court, may direct that the appeal shall not operate as a stay of execution if it is satisfied upon the showing made by the petitioner that he will suffer irreparable damage in his business or profession if the execution is stayed. *(Added by Stats.1941, c. 330, p. 1561, § 1.)*

Research References

Rutter, Cal. Practice Guide: Civil Appeals & Writs Ch. 7-B, B. Automatic Stay.

8 Witkin Cal. Proc. 5th Extraordinary Writs § 219, Stay Pending Appeal.

Title 3

OF SUMMARY PROCEEDINGS

CHAPTER 1. CONFESSION OF JUDGMENT WITHOUT ACTION

§ 1132. Entry of judgment; obligations for which judgment may be confessed; conditions

(a) A judgment by confession may be entered without action either for money due or to become due, or to secure any person against contingent liability on behalf of the defendant, or both, in the manner prescribed by this chapter. Such judgment may be entered in any superior court.

(b) A judgment by confession shall be entered only if an attorney independently representing the defendant signs a certificate that the attorney has examined the proposed judgment and has advised the defendant with respect to the waiver of rights and defenses under the confession of judgment procedure and has advised the defendant to utilize the confession of judgment procedure. The certificate shall be filed with the filing of the statement required by Section 1133. *(Enacted in 1872. Amended by Stats.1975, c. 304, p. 752, § 1; Stats.1979, c. 568, p. 1795, § 1; Stats.2002, c. 784 (S.B.1316), § 77.)*

Law Revision Commission Comments

Section 1132 of the Code of Civil Procedure is amended to require the certificate of an attorney representing the debtor in any case in which a confession of judgment is filed. This amendment is designed to satisfy the constitutional standards announced in Isbell v. County of Sonoma, 21 Cal.3d 61, 577 P.2d 188, 145 Cal.Rptr. 368 (1978).

Subdivision (a) of Section 1132 is amended to reflect unification of the municipal and superior courts pursuant to Article VI, Section 5(e), of the California Constitution. [32 Cal.L.Rev.Comm. Reports 133 (2002)].

Research References

Rutter, Cal. Practice Guide: Civ. Pro. Before Trial Ch. 4-A, A. Requirements-In General.

Rutter, Cal. Practice Guide: Enforcing Judgments/Debts Ch. 2-B, B. Statutory Liability and Procedures.

Rutter, Cal. Practice Guide: Enforcing Judgments/Debts Ch. 3-B, B. Collection Without Suit.

3 Witkin Cal. Proc. 5th Actions § 65, (S 65) Statutory Classes.

6 Witkin Cal. Proc. 5th Proceedings Without Trial § 128, (S 128) Nature of Proceeding.

6 Witkin Cal. Proc. 5th Proceedings Without Trial § 129, (S 129) Attorney's Advice is Required.

6 Witkin Cal. Proc. 5th Proceedings Without Trial § 130, (S 130) Procedure.

6 Witkin Cal. Proc. 5th Proceedings Without Trial § 132, (S 132) Termination of Parental Rights.

§ 1133. Defendant's written statement; form

STATEMENT IN WRITING AND FORM THEREOF. A statement in writing must be made, signed by the defendant, and verified by his oath, to the following effect:

1. It must authorize the entry of judgment for a specified sum;

2. If it be for money due, or to become due, it must state concisely the facts out of which it arose, and show that the sum confessed therefor is justly due, or to become due;

3. If it be for the purpose of securing the plaintiff against a contingent liability, it must state concisely the facts constituting the liability, and show that the sum confessed therefor does not exceed the same. *(Enacted in 1872.)*

Research References

Rutter, Cal. Practice Guide: Civ. Pro. Before Trial Ch. 4-A, A. Requirements-In General.

Rutter, Cal. Practice Guide: Enforcing Judgments/Debts Ch. 2-B, B. Statutory Liability and Procedures.

Rutter, Cal. Practice Guide: Enforcing Judgments/Debts Ch. 3-B, B. Collection Without Suit.

6 Witkin Cal. Proc. 5th Proceedings Without Trial § 130, (S 130) Procedure.

§ 1134. Defendant's written statement; filing; entry of judgment; costs; judgment roll

(a) The statement required by Section 1133 shall be filed with the clerk of the court in which the judgment is to be entered, who must endorse upon it, and enter a judgment of the court for the amount confessed with the costs provided in subdivision (b).

(b) At the time of filing, the plaintiff shall pay as court costs that shall become a part of the judgment the fee as provided in subdivision (b) of Section 70626 of the Government Code. No fee shall be collected from the defendant.. [1]

(c) The statement and affidavit, with the judgment endorsed thereon, together with the certificate filed pursuant to Section 1132, becomes the judgment roll. *(Enacted in 1872. Amended by Stats.1933, c. 745, p. 1904, § 1; Stats.1951, c. 1737, p. 4139, § 150; Stats.1957, c. 1982, p. 3530, § 1; Stats.1974, c. 1285, p. 2788, § 1; Stats.1975, c. 766, p. 1783, § 1; Stats.1977, c. 1257, p. 4769, § 37, eff. Jan. 3, 1977; Stats.1998, c. 931 (S.B.2139), § 114, eff. Sept. 28, 1998; Stats.2001, c. 812 (A.B.223), § 9; Stats.2005, c. 75 (A.B.145), § 40, eff. July 19, 2005, operative Jan. 1, 2006.)*

[1] So in enrolled bill.

Law Revision Commission Comments

Section 1134 is amended to accommodate unification of the municipal and superior courts in a county. Cal. Const. art. VI, § 5(e). It is also amended to reflect elimination of the justice court. Cal. Const. art. VI, §§ 1, 5(b).

For guidance on what constitutes a limited civil case, see Section 85 & Comment. [28 Cal.L.Rev.Comm. Reports 51 (1998)].

Section 1134 is amended to divide the section into subdivisions and to eliminate the $10 filing fee for a limited civil case. Under this amendment, the filing fee is $15 regardless of the jurisdictional classification of the case.

The reference to "all courts" in subdivision (a) is deleted as obsolete. It derived from an era when a confession of judgment might have been entered in any of several courts, depending on the amount of the judgment and the jurisdiction of the court. Cf. Section 1132(a) ("Such judgment may be entered in any court having jurisdiction for like amounts.").

The attorney's certificate is made part of the judgment roll in subdivision (c). The certificate is a prerequisite to entry of judgment and must be filed with the defendant's written and verified statement. Section 1132(b). [30 Cal.L.Rev.Comm. Reports 443 (2000)].

Research References

Rutter, Cal. Practice Guide: Civ. Pro. Before Trial Ch. 4-A, A. Requirements-In General.
Rutter, Cal. Practice Guide: Enforcing Judgments/Debts Ch. 3-B, B. Collection Without Suit.
9 Witkin Cal. Proc. 5th Appeal § 667, (S 667) Nature of Record.
2 Witkin Cal. Proc. 5th Courts § 364, in General.
6 Witkin Cal. Proc. 5th Proceedings Without Trial § 130, (S 130) Procedure.

CHAPTER 2.   SUBMITTING A CONTROVERSY WITHOUT ACTION

Section
1138.   Submission on agreed statement of facts; actual controversy; hearing; judgment.
1139.   Judgment; entry; costs; judgment roll.
1140.   Judgment; enforcement; appeal.

§ 1138.   Submission on agreed statement of facts; actual controversy; hearing; judgment

CONTROVERSY, HOW SUBMITTED WITHOUT ACTION. Parties to a question in difference, which might be the subject of a civil action, may, without action, agree upon a case containing the facts upon which the controversy depends, and present a submission of the same to any Court which would have jurisdiction if an action had been brought; but it must appear, by affidavit, that the controversy is real and the proceedings in good faith, to determine the rights of the parties. The Court must thereupon hear and determine the case, and render judgment thereon, as if an action were depending. *(Enacted in 1872.)*

Research References

Rutter, Cal. Practice Guide: Insurance Litigation Ch. 6B-E, E. Conditions.
3 Witkin Cal. Proc. 5th Actions § 28, (S 28) Declaratory Relief and Agreed Case.
3 Witkin Cal. Proc. 5th Actions § 29, (S 29) Public Interest in Question.
3 Witkin Cal. Proc. 5th Actions § 65, (S 65) Statutory Classes.
2 Witkin Cal. Proc. 5th Courts § 337, (S 337) Original Jurisdiction.
8 Witkin Cal. Proc. 5th Extraordinary Writs § 79, No Present Duty.
8 Witkin Cal. Proc. 5th Extraordinary Writs § 233, (S 233) Illustrations.
6 Witkin Cal. Proc. 5th Proceedings Without Trial § 79, Agreed Case.

§ 1139.   Judgment; entry; costs; judgment roll

Judgment must be entered as in other cases, but without costs for any proceeding prior to the trial. The case, the submission, and a copy of the judgment constitute the judgment roll. *(Enacted in 1872. Amended by Stats.1933, c. 745, p. 1905, § 3.)*

Research References

9 Witkin Cal. Proc. 5th Appeal § 667, (S 667) Nature of Record.
6 Witkin Cal. Proc. 5th Proceedings Without Trial § 79, Agreed Case.

§ 1140.   Judgment; enforcement; appeal

The judgment may be enforced in the same manner as if it had been rendered in an action of the same jurisdictional classification in the same court, and is in the same manner subject to appeal. *(Enacted in 1872. Amended by Stats.1933, c. 745, p. 1905, § 4; Stats.1998, c. 931 (S.B.2139), § 115, eff. Sept. 28, 1998.)*

Law Revision Commission Comments

Section 1140 is amended to accommodate unification of the municipal and superior courts in a county. Cal. Const. art. VI, § 5(e). See Sections 32.5 (jurisdictional classification), 85 (limited civil cases), 86(a)(8) (enforcement of judgment in limited civil case), 904.1 (taking appeal), 904.2 (taking appeal in limited civil case). See also Section 85 Comment. [28 Cal.L.Rev.Comm. Reports 51 (1998)].

Research References

6 Witkin Cal. Proc. 5th Proceedings Without Trial § 79, Agreed Case.

CHAPTER 2.5.   JUDICIAL ARBITRATION

§ 1141.10.   Legislative findings and declarations and intent

(a) The Legislature finds and declares that litigation involving small civil cases can be so costly and complex that efficiently resolving these civil cases is difficult, and that the resulting delays and expenses may deny parties their right to a timely resolution of minor civil disputes. The Legislature further finds and declares that arbitration has proven to be an efficient and equitable method for resolving small civil cases, and that courts should encourage or require the use of arbitration for those actions whenever possible.

(b) It is the intent of the Legislature that:

(1) Arbitration hearings held pursuant to this chapter shall provide parties with a simplified and economical procedure for obtaining prompt and equitable resolution of their disputes.

(2) Arbitration hearings shall be as informal as possible and shall provide the parties themselves maximum opportunity to participate directly in the resolution of their disputes, and shall be held during nonjudicial hours whenever possible.

(3) Members of the State Bar selected to serve as arbitrators should have experience with cases of the type under dispute and are urged to volunteer their services without compensation whenever possible. *(Added by Stats.1978, c. 743, p. 2303, § 2, operative July 1, 1979. Amended by Stats.2003, c. 449 (A.B.1712), § 9.)*

Research References

Rutter, Cal. Practice Guide: A.D.R. App. A, Selected Statutes Providing for ADR.
Rutter, Cal. Practice Guide: A.D.R. Ch. 4-B, B. Judicial Arbitration.
Rutter, Cal. Practice Guide: A.D.R. Ch. 5-A, A. General Considerations.
Rutter, Cal. Practice Guide: A.D.R. Ch. 7-B, B. Arbitrators.
Rutter, Cal. Practice Guide: A.D.R. Ch. 3A-A, A. Court-Annexed Programs.
Rutter, Cal. Practice Guide: Civil Appeals & Writs Ch. 2-B, B. Appealable Judgments and Orders.
Rutter, Cal. Practice Guide: Civ. Pro. Before Trial Ch. 13-A, A. Introduction.
Rutter, Cal. Practice Guide: Civ. Pro. Before Trial Ch. 13-E, E. the Arbitration Hearing.
Rutter, Cal. Practice Guide: Civ. Pro. Before Trial Ch. 8E-18, Use of Depositions in Judicial Arbitration Hearings.
Rutter, Cal. Practice Guide: Civil Trials & Evidence Ch. 10-D, D. Objectives of Cross-Examination.
Rutter, Cal. Practice Guide: Fed.Civ.Pro. Before Trial Ch. 1-D, D. Choosing Between State and Federal Courts.
Rutter, Cal. Practice Guide: Personal Injury Ch. 3-C, C. Specific Items of Compensatory Damages.
Rutter, Cal. Practice Guide: Personal Injury Ch. 4-G, G. Concluding and Enforcing Settlement.
Rutter, Cal. Practice Guide: Personal Injury Ch. 7-A, A. Introduction-Nature and Purpose of "Judicial Arbitration" in General.
Rutter, Cal. Practice Guide: Personal Injury Ch. 7-G, G. Arbitration Hearing.
Rutter, Cal. Practice Guide: Prof. Responsibility Ch. 8-D, D. Restrictions on Speech and Behavior Outside Courtroom.
Miller and Starr California Real Estate § 27:47, Provisions for Arbitration and Mediation of Disputes--Generally.
Miller and Starr California Real Estate § 35:13, Procedural Aspects of Civil Action Mediation.
Miller and Starr California Real Estate § 35:22, Nature of Arbitration.
21 NO. 6 Miller & Starr, California Real Estate Newsalert 3, Alternative Dispute Resolution.
3 Witkin Cal. Proc. 5th Actions § 65, (S 65) Statutory Classes.
8 Witkin Cal. Proc. 5th Attack Judgment Trial Court § 145, (S 145) When Relief is Available.
1 Witkin Cal. Proc. 5th Attorneys § 252, Stipulating to Binding Arbitration.
6 Witkin Cal. Proc. 5th Proceedings Without Trial § 413, in General.
6 Witkin Cal. Proc. 5th Proceedings Without Trial § 579, in General.
6 Witkin Cal. Proc. 5th Proceedings Without Trial § 588, (S 588) in General.
6 Witkin Cal. Proc. 5th Proceedings Without Trial § 592, (S 592) in General.
6 Witkin Cal. Proc. 5th Proceedings Without Trial § 595, in General.
7 Witkin Cal. Proc. 5th Trial § 5, Trial Practice.
7 Witkin Cal. Proc. 5th Trial § 74, Completion of Discovery.
7 Witkin Cal. Proc. 5th Trial § 227, Scope and Definitions.
2 Witkin, California Summary 10th Insurance § 211, (S 211) Joinder and Consolidation.

§ 1141.11. Nonexempt unlimited civil cases; amount in controversy; submission to arbitration; use of case questionnaires

(a) In each superior court with 18 or more judges, all nonexempt unlimited civil cases shall be submitted to arbitration under this chapter if the amount in controversy, in the opinion of the court, will not exceed fifty thousand dollars ($50,000) for each plaintiff.

(b) In each superior court with fewer than 18 judges, the court may provide by local rule, when it determines that it is in the best interests of justice, that all nonexempt, unlimited civil cases shall be submitted to arbitration under this chapter if the amount in

controversy, in the opinion of the court, will not exceed fifty thousand dollars ($50,000) for each plaintiff.

(c) Each superior court may provide by local rule, when it is determined to be in the best interests of justice, that all nonexempt, limited civil cases shall be submitted to arbitration under this chapter. This section does not apply to any action in small claims court, or to any action maintained pursuant to Section 1781 of the Civil Code or Section 1161.

(d)(1) In each court that has adopted judicial arbitration pursuant to subdivision (c), all limited civil cases that involve a claim for money damages against a single defendant as a result of a motor vehicle collision, except those heard in the small claims division, shall be submitted to arbitration within 120 days of the filing of the defendant's answer to the complaint (except as may be extended by the court for good cause) before an arbitrator selected by the court.

(2) The court may provide by local rule for the voluntary or mandatory use of case questionnaires, established under Section 93, in any proceeding subject to these provisions. Where local rules provide for the use of case questionnaires, the questionnaires shall be exchanged by the parties upon the defendant's answer and completed and returned within 60 days.

(3) For the purposes of this subdivision, the term "single defendant" means any of the following:

(A) An individual defendant, whether a person or an entity.

(B) Two or more persons covered by the same insurance policy applicable to the motor vehicle collision.

(C) Two or more persons residing in the same household when no insurance policy exists that is applicable to the motor vehicle collision.

(4) The naming of one or more cross-defendants, not a plaintiff, shall constitute a multiple-defendant case not subject to the provisions of this subdivision. *(Added by Stats.1978, c. 743, p. 2303, § 2. Amended by Stats.1979, c. 46, p. 118, § 1, eff. May 2, 1979, operative July 1, 1979; Stats.1979, c. 948, p. 3272, § 1, eff. Sept. 22, 1979; Stats.1979, c. 1146, p. 4194, § 2, eff. Sept. 29, 1979; Stats.1981, c. 1110, § 1; Stats.1982, c. 31, p. 55, § 1, eff. Feb. 17, 1982; Stats.1982, c. 921, p. 3362, § 1, eff. Sept. 13, 1982; Stats.1982, c. 1522, p. 5903, § 2; Stats.1983, c. 978, § 1, eff. Sept. 21, 1983; Stats.1985, c. 1383, § 3; Stats.1986, c. 287, § 1; Stats.1987, c. 1201, § 4; Stats.1987, c. 1204, § 1; Stats.1989, c. 894, § 1; Stats.1990, c. 1305 (S.B.2627), § 9; Stats.1998, c. 931 (S.B.2139), § 116, eff. Sept. 28, 1998; Stats.2002, c. 784 (S.B. 1316), § 78; Stats.2003, c. 449 (A.B.1712), § 10.)*

Law Revision Commission Comments

Section 1141.11 is amended to accommodate unification of the municipal and superior courts in a county. Cal. Const. art. VI, § 5(e). *Cf.* Section 85 & Comment (limited civil cases).

Former subdivision (e) is deleted as obsolete. [28 Cal.L.Rev.Comm. Reports 51 (1998)].

Subdivisions (a)-(c) of Section 1141.11 are amended to reflect unification of the municipal and superior courts pursuant to Article VI, Section 5(e), of the California Constitution. [32 Cal.L.Rev.Comm. Reports 134 (2002)].

Research References

Rutter, Cal. Practice Guide: A.D.R. App. A, Selected Statutes Providing for ADR.
Rutter, Cal. Practice Guide: A.D.R. Ch. 4-B, B. Judicial Arbitration.
Rutter, Cal. Practice Guide: A.D.R. Ch. 7-B, B. Arbitrators.
Rutter, Cal. Practice Guide: Civ. Pro. Before Trial Ch. 11-B, B. Involuntary Dismissals.
Rutter, Cal. Practice Guide: Civ. Pro. Before Trial Ch. 13-A, A. Introduction.
Rutter, Cal. Practice Guide: Civ. Pro. Before Trial Ch. 13-C, C. Civil Proceedings Subject to Judicial Arbitration.

Civ. Pro.

Rutter, Cal. Practice Guide: Civ. Pro. Before Trial Ch. 13-G, G. Trial De Novo.

Rutter, Cal. Practice Guide: Civ. Pro. Before Trial Ch. 12(I)-B, B. Case Management ("Fast Track") System.

Rutter, Cal. Practice Guide: Civ. Pro. Before Trial Ch. 12(I)-C, C. Claims for Trial Setting Preference.

Rutter, Cal. Practice Guide: Personal Injury Ch. 6-E, E. Special Discovery Rules and Procedures in Limited Civil Cases.

Rutter, Cal. Practice Guide: Personal Injury Ch. 7-A, A. Introduction-Nature and Purpose of "Judicial Arbitration" in General.

Rutter, Cal. Practice Guide: Personal Injury Ch. 7-C, C. Actions Subject to Judicial Arbitration.

Rutter, Cal. Practice Guide: Personal Injury Ch. 7-D, D. Screening Cases for Judicial Arbitration.

Rutter, Cal. Practice Guide: Personal Injury Ch. 7-E, E. the Arbitrator.

Rutter, Cal. Practice Guide: Personal Injury Ch. 7-G, G. Arbitration Hearing.

Rutter, Cal. Practice Guide: Personal Injury Ch. 8-A, A. Case Management.

Miller and Starr California Real Estate § 27:47, Provisions for Arbitration and Mediation of Disputes--Generally.

Miller and Starr California Real Estate § 35:22, Nature of Arbitration.

6 Witkin Cal. Proc. 5th Proceedings Without Trial § 489, Scope of Pilot Project.

6 Witkin Cal. Proc. 5th Proceedings Without Trial § 553, Commencement and Consolidation.

6 Witkin Cal. Proc. 5th Proceedings Without Trial § 580, Contractual Arbitration Distinguished.

6 Witkin Cal. Proc. 5th Proceedings Without Trial § 582, (S 582) Cases that Must be Arbitrated.

6 Witkin Cal. Proc. 5th Proceedings Without Trial § 583, (S 583) Cases Excluded from Arbitration.

6 Witkin Cal. Proc. 5th Proceedings Without Trial § 585, on Plaintiff's Election to Limit Award.

6 Witkin Cal. Proc. 5th Proceedings Without Trial § 588, (S 588) in General.

6 Witkin Cal. Proc. 5th Proceedings Without Trial § 604, Sanctions for Failure to Participate.

6 Witkin Cal. Proc. 5th Proceedings Without Trial § 606, (S 606) Amount of Damages.

6 Witkin Cal. Proc. 5th Proceedings Without Trial § 615, (S 615) Waiver by Plaintiff Electing Arbitration and Receiving Maximum Award.

6 Witkin Cal. Proc. 5th Proceedings Without Trial § 623, (S 623) Discovery.

6 Witkin Cal. Proc. 5th Proceedings Without Trial § 626, (S 626) in General.

6 Witkin Cal. Proc. 5th Proceedings Without Trial § 627, (S 627) Improper Assignment of Case to Arbitration.

7 Witkin Cal. Proc. 5th Trial § 5, Trial Practice.

7 Witkin Cal. Proc. 5th Trial § 69, (S 69) Party Over Age 70.

§ 1141.12. Uniform system of arbitration; stipulation; election by plaintiff to award limit

In all superior courts, the Judicial Council shall provide by rule for a uniform system of arbitration of the following causes:

(a) Any cause, regardless of the amount in controversy, upon stipulation of the parties.

(b) Upon filing of an election by the plaintiff, any cause in which the plaintiff agrees that the arbitration award shall not exceed the amount in controversy as specified in Section 1141.11. *(Added by Stats.1978, c. 743, p. 2303, § 2, operative July 1, 1979. Amended by Stats.1981, c. 1110, § 2; Stats.1983, c. 123, § 1; Stats.1998, c. 931 (S.B.2139), § 117, eff. Sept. 28, 1998; Stats. 2002, c. 784 (S.B.1316), § 79; Stats.2003, c. 449 (A.B.1712), § 11.)*

Law Revision Commission Comments

Section 1141.12 is amended to reflect the elimination of the justice court. Cal. Const. art. VI, §§ 1, 5(b). [28 Cal.L.Rev.Comm. Reports 51 (1998)].

Subdivision (a) of Section 1141.12 is amended to clarify its application. This is declaratory of existing law.

Subdivision (b) is amended to reflect unification of the municipal and superior courts pursuant to Article VI, Section 5(e), of the California Constitution. [32 Cal.L.Rev.Comm. Reports 135 (2002)].

Research References

Rutter, Cal. Practice Guide: A.D.R. Ch. 4-B, B. Judicial Arbitration.

Rutter, Cal. Practice Guide: Civ. Pro. Before Trial Ch. 13-C, C. Civil Proceedings Subject to Judicial Arbitration.

Rutter, Cal. Practice Guide: Civ. Pro. Before Trial Ch. 13-F, F. Arbitration Award.

Rutter, Cal. Practice Guide: Personal Injury Ch. 7-C, C. Actions Subject to Judicial Arbitration.

Rutter, Cal. Practice Guide: Personal Injury Ch. 7-D, D. Screening Cases for Judicial Arbitration.

Rutter, Cal. Practice Guide: Personal Injury Ch. 7-H, H. Arbitration Award and Judgment.

Miller and Starr California Real Estate § 35:22, Nature of Arbitration.

6 Witkin Cal. Proc. 5th Proceedings Without Trial § 414, Stipulation for Binding Arbitration.

6 Witkin Cal. Proc. 5th Proceedings Without Trial § 580, Contractual Arbitration Distinguished.

6 Witkin Cal. Proc. 5th Proceedings Without Trial § 582, (S 582) Cases that Must be Arbitrated.

6 Witkin Cal. Proc. 5th Proceedings Without Trial § 583, (S 583) Cases Excluded from Arbitration.

6 Witkin Cal. Proc. 5th Proceedings Without Trial § 585, on Plaintiff's Election to Limit Award.

6 Witkin Cal. Proc. 5th Proceedings Without Trial § 588, (S 588) in General.

6 Witkin Cal. Proc. 5th Proceedings Without Trial § 606, (S 606) Amount of Damages.

6 Witkin Cal. Proc. 5th Proceedings Without Trial § 627, (S 627) Improper Assignment of Case to Arbitration.

7 Witkin Cal. Proc. 5th Trial § 5, Trial Practice.

§ 1141.13. Inapplicability of chapter to civil action with prayer for equitable relief; exceptions

This chapter shall not apply to any civil action which includes a prayer for equitable relief, except that if the prayer for equitable relief is frivolous or insubstantial, this chapter shall be applicable. *(Added by Stats.1978, c. 743, p. 2303, § 2, operative July 1, 1979.)*

Research References

Rutter, Cal. Practice Guide: A.D.R. Ch. 4-B, B. Judicial Arbitration.

Rutter, Cal. Practice Guide: Personal Injury Ch. 7-C, C. Actions Subject to Judicial Arbitration.

Rutter, Cal. Practice Guide: Personal Injury Ch. 7-D, D. Screening Cases for Judicial Arbitration.

6 Witkin Cal. Proc. 5th Proceedings Without Trial § 583, (S 583) Cases Excluded from Arbitration.

6 Witkin Cal. Proc. 5th Proceedings Without Trial § 586, on Order of Court.

§ 1141.14. Rules for practice and procedure

Notwithstanding any other provision of law except the provisions of this chapter, the Judicial Council shall provide by rule for practice and procedure for all actions submitted to arbitration under this chapter. The Judicial Council rules shall provide for and conform with the provisions of this chapter. *(Added by Stats.1978, c. 743, p. 2303, § 2, operative July 1, 1979.)*

Research References

Rutter, Cal. Practice Guide: A.D.R. Ch. 4-B, B. Judicial Arbitration.

Rutter, Cal. Practice Guide: Civ. Pro. Before Trial Ch. 13-A, A. Introduction.

Rutter, Cal. Practice Guide: Civil Trials & Evidence Ch. 8D-D, D. Hearsay Exceptions.

Rutter, Cal. Practice Guide: Personal Injury Ch. 7-A, A. Introduction-Nature and Purpose of "Judicial Arbitration" in General.

6 Witkin Cal. Proc. 5th Proceedings Without Trial § 624, (S 624) No Reference to Arbitration.

§ 1141.15. Exceptions for cause to arbitration in § 1141.11; rules

The Judicial Council rules shall provide exceptions for cause to arbitration pursuant to subdivision (a), (b), or (c) of Section 1141.11. In providing for such exceptions, the Judicial Council shall take into consideration whether the civil action might not be amenable to arbitration. *(Added by Stats.1978, c. 743, p. 2303, § 2, operative July 1, 1979.)*

Research References

Rutter, Cal. Practice Guide: A.D.R. Ch. 4-B, B. Judicial Arbitration.
Rutter, Cal. Practice Guide: Personal Injury Ch. 7-C, C. Actions Subject to Judicial Arbitration.

§ 1141.16. Determination of amount in controversy; time to submit to arbitration; discovery order

(a) The determination of the amount in controversy, under subdivision (a) or (b) of Section 1141.11, shall be made by the court and the case referred to arbitration after all named parties have appeared or defaulted. The determination shall be made at a case management conference or based upon review of the written submissions of the parties, as provided in rules adopted by the Judicial Council. The determination shall be based on the total amount of damages, and the judge may not consider questions of liability or comparative negligence or any other defense. At that time the court shall also make a determination whether any prayer for equitable relief is frivolous or insubstantial. The determination of the amount in controversy and whether any prayer for equitable relief is frivolous or insubstantial may not be appealable. No determination pursuant to this section shall be made if all parties stipulate in writing that the amount in controversy exceeds the amount specified in Section 1141.11.

(b) The determination and any stipulation of the amount in controversy shall be without prejudice to any finding on the value of the case by an arbitrator or in a subsequent trial de novo.

(c) Except as provided in this section, the arbitration hearing may not be held until 210 days after the filing of the complaint, or 240 days after the filing of a complaint if the parties have stipulated to a continuance pursuant to subdivision (d) of Section 68616 of the Government Code. A case shall be submitted to arbitration at an earlier time upon any of the following:

(1) The stipulation of the parties to an earlier arbitration hearing.

(2) The written request of all plaintiffs, subject to a motion by a defendant for good cause shown to delay the arbitration hearing.

(3) An order of the court if the parties have stipulated, or the court has ordered under Section 1141.24, that discovery other than that permitted under Chapter 18 (commencing with Section 2034.010) of Title 4 of Part 4 will be permitted after the arbitration award is rendered. *(Added by Stats.1978, c. 743, p. 2303, § 2. Amended by Stats.1979, c. 130, p. 318, § 1; Stats. 1981, c. 181, § 1; Stats.1981, c. 1110, § 3; Stats.1983, c. 123, § 2; Stats.2003, c. 449 (A.B.1712), § 12; Stats.2004, c. 182 (A.B.3081), § 14, operative July 1, 2005.)*

Law Revision Commission Comments

Subdivision (c) of Section 1141.16 is amended to reflect nonsubstantive reorganization of the rules governing civil discovery. [33 Cal.L.Rev. Comm. Reports 996 (2004)].

Research References

Rutter, Cal. Practice Guide: A.D.R. Ch. 4-B, B. Judicial Arbitration.
Rutter, Cal. Practice Guide: A.D.R. Ch. 4-C, C. Statutorily-Mandated Court Mediation Programs.
Rutter, Cal. Practice Guide: Civ. Pro. Before Trial Ch. 13-A, A. Introduction.
Rutter, Cal. Practice Guide: Civ. Pro. Before Trial Ch. 13-C, C. Civil Proceedings Subject to Judicial Arbitration.
Rutter, Cal. Practice Guide: Civ. Pro. Before Trial Ch. 13-E, E. the Arbitration Hearing.
Rutter, Cal. Practice Guide: Civ. Pro. Before Trial Ch. 13-F, F. Arbitration Award.
Rutter, Cal. Practice Guide: Personal Injury Ch. 7-A, A. Introduction-Nature and Purpose of "Judicial Arbitration" in General.
Rutter, Cal. Practice Guide: Personal Injury Ch. 7-C, C. Actions Subject to Judicial Arbitration.
Rutter, Cal. Practice Guide: Personal Injury Ch. 7-D, D. Screening Cases for Judicial Arbitration.
Rutter, Cal. Practice Guide: Personal Injury Ch. 7-G, G. Arbitration Hearing.
Miller and Starr California Real Estate § 35:22, Nature of Arbitration.
6 Witkin Cal. Proc. 5th Proceedings Without Trial § 583, (S 583) Cases Excluded from Arbitration.
6 Witkin Cal. Proc. 5th Proceedings Without Trial § 586, on Order of Court.
6 Witkin Cal. Proc. 5th Proceedings Without Trial § 587, Effect of Submission.
6 Witkin Cal. Proc. 5th Proceedings Without Trial § 606, (S 606) Amount of Damages.
6 Witkin Cal. Proc. 5th Proceedings Without Trial § 615, (S 615) Waiver by Plaintiff Electing Arbitration and Receiving Maximum Award.
6 Witkin Cal. Proc. 5th Proceedings Without Trial § 627, (S 627) Improper Assignment of Case to Arbitration.

§ 1141.17. Suspension of running of limitations; exception

(a) Submission of an action to arbitration pursuant to this chapter shall not suspend the running of the time periods specified in Chapter 1.5 (commencing with Section 583.110) of Title 8 of Part 2, except as provided in this section.

(b) If an action is or remains submitted to arbitration pursuant to this chapter more than four years and six months after the plaintiff has filed the action, then the time beginning on the date four years and six months after the plaintiff has filed the action and ending on the date on which a request for a de novo trial is filed under Section 1141.20 shall not be included in computing the five-year period specified in Section 583.310. *(Added by Stats.1978, c. 743, p. 2303, § 2, operative July 1, 1979. Amended by Stats.1983, c. 123, § 3; Stats.1984, c. 1705, § 6.)*

Research References

Rutter, Cal. Practice Guide: A.D.R. Ch. 4-B, B. Judicial Arbitration.
Rutter, Cal. Practice Guide: Civ. Pro. Before Trial Ch. 11-B, B. Involuntary Dismissals.
Rutter, Cal. Practice Guide: Civ. Pro. Before Trial Ch. 13-G, G. Trial De Novo.
Rutter, Cal. Practice Guide: Personal Injury Ch. 7-I, I. Trial De Novo After Arbitration Award.
6 Witkin Cal. Proc. 5th Proceedings Without Trial § 413, in General.
6 Witkin Cal. Proc. 5th Proceedings Without Trial § 414, Stipulation for Binding Arbitration.
6 Witkin Cal. Proc. 5th Proceedings Without Trial § 416, Plaintiff's Duty to Monitor Resetting.
6 Witkin Cal. Proc. 5th Proceedings Without Trial § 417, Impracticability and Diligence.
6 Witkin Cal. Proc. 5th Proceedings Without Trial § 423, Extension Where Less Than 6 Months Remain.
6 Witkin Cal. Proc. 5th Proceedings Without Trial § 457, Effect of Judicial Arbitration.
6 Witkin Cal. Proc. 5th Proceedings Without Trial § 587, Effect of Submission.

§ 1141.18. Arbitrators; qualifications; compensation; selection; disqualification

(a) Arbitrators shall be retired judges, retired court commissioners who were licensed to practice law prior to their appointment as a commissioner, or members of the State Bar, and shall sit individually. A judge may also serve as an arbitrator without compensation. People who are not attorneys may serve as arbitrators upon the stipulation of all parties.

(b) The Judicial Council rules shall provide for the compensation, if any, of arbitrators. Compensation for arbitrators may not be less than one hundred fifty dollars ($150) per case, or one hundred fifty dollars ($150) per day, whichever is greater. A superior court may set a higher level of compensation for that court. Arbitrators may waive compensation in whole or in part. No compensation shall be paid before the filing of the award by the arbitrator, or before the settlement of the case by the parties.

(c) In cases submitted to arbitration under Section 1141.11 or 1141.12, an arbitrator shall be assigned within 30 days from the time of submission to arbitration.

(d) Any party may request the disqualification of the arbitrator selected for his or her case on the grounds and by the procedures specified in Section 170.1 or 170.6. A request for disqualification of an arbitrator on grounds specified in Section 170.6 shall be made within five days of the naming of the arbitrator. An arbitrator shall disqualify himself or herself, upon demand of any party to the arbitration made before the conclusion of the arbitration proceedings on any of the grounds specified in Section 170.1. *(Added by Stats.1978, c. 743, p. 2303, § 2. Amended by Stats.1981, c. 1110, § 3.5; Stats.1993, c. 768 (S.B.252), § 2; Stats.1995, c. 576 (A.B.1225), § 5; Stats.2003, c. 449 (A.B.1712), § 13.)*

Research References

Rutter, Cal. Practice Guide: A.D.R. Ch. 4-B, B. Judicial Arbitration.
Rutter, Cal. Practice Guide: Civ. Pro. Before Trial Ch. 13-B, B. Judicial Arbitration Distinguished from Contract Arbitration.
Rutter, Cal. Practice Guide: Civ. Pro. Before Trial Ch. 13-D, D. the Arbitrator.
Rutter, Cal. Practice Guide: Personal Injury Ch. 7-E, E. the Arbitrator.
Miller and Starr California Real Estate § 35:22, Nature of Arbitration.
6 Witkin Cal. Proc. 5th Proceedings Without Trial § 588, (S 588) in General.
6 Witkin Cal. Proc. 5th Proceedings Without Trial § 591, Disqualification.
6 Witkin Cal. Proc. 5th Proceedings Without Trial § 592, (S 592) in General.

§ 1141.19. Arbitrators; powers

Arbitrators approved pursuant to this chapter shall have the powers necessary to perform duties pursuant to this chapter as prescribed by the Judicial Council. *(Added by Stats.1978, c. 743, p. 2303, § 2, operative July 1, 1979.)*

Research References

6 Witkin Cal. Proc. 5th Proceedings Without Trial § 595, in General.

§ 1141.19.5. Arbitration; limitation on production of evidence

In any arbitration proceeding under this chapter, no party may require the production of evidence specified in subdivision (a) of Section 3295 of the Civil Code at the arbitration, unless the court enters an order permitting pretrial discovery of that evidence pursuant to subdivision (c) of Section 3295 of the Civil Code. *(Added by Stats.1993, c. 768 (S.B.252), § 3. Amended by Stats.1994, c. 327 (S.B.140), § 1.)*

Research References

Rutter, Cal. Practice Guide: A.D.R. Ch. 4-B, B. Judicial Arbitration.
Rutter, Cal. Practice Guide: Civ. Pro. Before Trial Ch. 13-E, E. the Arbitration Hearing.
Rutter, Cal. Practice Guide: Personal Injury Ch. 3-E, E. Punitive Damages.
Rutter, Cal. Practice Guide: Personal Injury Ch. 6-A, A. Scope of Discovery and Limitations.

6 Witkin Cal. Proc. 5th Proceedings Without Trial § 600, (S 600) in General.

§ 1141.20. Finality of award; de novo trial; request; limitation; calendar

(a) An arbitration award shall be final unless a request for a de novo trial or a request for dismissal in the form required by the Judicial Council is filed within 60 days after the date the arbitrator files the award with the court.

(b) Any party may elect to have a de novo trial, by court or jury, both as to law and facts. Such trial shall be calendared, insofar as possible, so that the trial shall be given the same place on the active list as it had prior to arbitration, or shall receive civil priority on the next setting calendar. *(Added by Stats.1978, c. 743, p. 2303, § 2, operative July 1, 1979. Amended by Stats.1984, c. 1249, § 2; Stats.2011, c. 49 (S.B.731), § 3.)*

Research References

Rutter, Cal. Practice Guide: A.D.R. Ch. 4-B, B. Judicial Arbitration.
Rutter, Cal. Practice Guide: A.D.R. Ch. 5-A, A. General Considerations.
Rutter, Cal. Practice Guide: Civil Appeals & Writs Ch. 2-B, B. Appealable Judgments and Orders.
Rutter, Cal. Practice Guide: Civ. Pro. Before Trial Ch. 11-A, A. Voluntary Dismissals.
Rutter, Cal. Practice Guide: Civ. Pro. Before Trial Ch. 11-B, B. Involuntary Dismissals.
Rutter, Cal. Practice Guide: Civ. Pro. Before Trial Ch. 13-A, A. Introduction.
Rutter, Cal. Practice Guide: Civ. Pro. Before Trial Ch. 13-B, B. Judicial Arbitration Distinguished from Contract Arbitration.
Rutter, Cal. Practice Guide: Civ. Pro. Before Trial Ch. 13-F, F. Arbitration Award.
Rutter, Cal. Practice Guide: Civ. Pro. Before Trial Ch. 13-G, G. Trial De Novo.
Rutter, Cal. Practice Guide: Civ. Pro. Before Trial Ch. 12(I)-C, C. Claims for Trial Setting Preference.
Rutter, Cal. Practice Guide: Civ. Pro. Before Trial Gen. Matls., Highlights.
Rutter, Cal. Practice Guide: Civil Trials & Evidence Ch. 1-A, A. Importance of Statewide and Local Rules of Court.
Rutter, Cal. Practice Guide: Personal Injury Ch. 7-A, A. Introduction-Nature and Purpose of "Judicial Arbitration" in General.
Rutter, Cal. Practice Guide: Personal Injury Ch. 7-H, H. Arbitration Award and Judgment.
Rutter, Cal. Practice Guide: Personal Injury Ch. 7-I, I. Trial De Novo After Arbitration Award.
Rutter, Cal. Practice Guide: Personal Injury Ch. 8-A, A. Case Management.
Rutter, Cal. Practice Guide: Personal Injury Gen. Matls., Highlights.
Miller and Starr California Real Estate § 35:22, Nature of Arbitration.
21 NO. 6 Miller & Starr, California Real Estate Newsalert 3, Alternative Dispute Resolution.
2 Witkin Cal. Proc. 5th Courts § 203, Invalid Rules.
6 Witkin Cal. Proc. 5th Proceedings Without Trial § 413, in General.
6 Witkin Cal. Proc. 5th Proceedings Without Trial § 415, Tolling Until New Trial Date.
6 Witkin Cal. Proc. 5th Proceedings Without Trial § 416, Plaintiff's Duty to Monitor Resetting.
6 Witkin Cal. Proc. 5th Proceedings Without Trial § 604, Sanctions for Failure to Participate.
6 Witkin Cal. Proc. 5th Proceedings Without Trial § 614, (S 614) in General.
6 Witkin Cal. Proc. 5th Proceedings Without Trial § 615, (S 615) Waiver by Plaintiff Electing Arbitration and Receiving Maximum Award.
6 Witkin Cal. Proc. 5th Proceedings Without Trial § 616, (S 616) Time for Request.
6 Witkin Cal. Proc. 5th Proceedings Without Trial § 619, (S 619) Request by One of Several Coparties.
6 Witkin Cal. Proc. 5th Proceedings Without Trial § 621, (S 621) Subsequent Withdrawal of Request.
6 Witkin Cal. Proc. 5th Proceedings Without Trial § 622, (S 622) Calendaring.

7 Witkin Cal. Proc. 5th Trial § 72, (S 72) Miscellaneous Statutes.

§ 1141.21. Judgment on trial de novo equal to or less favorable than arbitration award for party electing; payment of nonrefundable costs and fees

(a)(1) If the judgment upon the trial de novo is not more favorable in either the amount of damages awarded or the type of relief granted for the party electing the trial de novo than the arbitration award, the court shall order that party to pay the following nonrefundable costs and fees, unless the court finds in writing and upon motion that the imposition of these costs and fees would create such a substantial economic hardship as not to be in the interest of justice:

(A) To the court, the compensation actually paid to the arbitrator, less any amount paid pursuant to subparagraph (D).

(B) To the other party or parties, all costs specified in Section 1033.5, and the party electing the trial de novo shall not recover his or her costs.

(C) To the other party or parties, the reasonable costs of the services of expert witnesses, who are not regular employees of any party, actually incurred or reasonably necessary in the preparation or trial of the case.

(D) To the other party or parties, the compensation paid by the other party or parties to the arbitrator, pursuant to subdivision (b) of Section 1141.28.

(2) Those costs and fees, other than the compensation of the arbitrator, shall include only those incurred from the time of election of the trial de novo.

(b) If the party electing the trial de novo has proceeded in the action in forma pauperis and has failed to obtain a more favorable judgment, the costs and fees under subparagraphs (B) and (C) of paragraph (1) of subdivision (a) shall be imposed only as an offset against any damages awarded in favor of that party.

(c) If the party electing the trial de novo has proceeded in the action in forma pauperis and has failed to obtain a more favorable judgment, the costs under subparagraph (A) of paragraph (1) of subdivision (a) shall be imposed only to the extent that there remains a sufficient amount in the judgment after the amount offset under subdivision (b) has been deducted from the judgment. *(Added by Stats.1978, c. 743, p. 2303, § 2, operative July 1, 1979. Amended by Stats.1982, c. 1354, p. 5052, § 4; Stats.1982, c. 1408, p. 5364, § 1; Stats.1986, c. 377, § 20; Stats.2005, c. 706 (A.B.1742), § 14; Stats.2006, c. 538 (S.B.1852), § 66.)*

Research References

Rutter, Cal. Practice Guide: A.D.R. Ch. 4-B, B. Judicial Arbitration.
Rutter, Cal. Practice Guide: Civil Appeals & Writs Ch. 7-C, C. Stay by Posting Security (Bond or Undertaking).
Rutter, Cal. Practice Guide: Civil Appeals & Writs Ch. 7 App., Appendix: Methods of Obtaining Stay for Particular Judgments and Orders.
Rutter, Cal. Practice Guide: Civ. Pro. Before Trial Ch. 13-D, D. the Arbitrator.
Rutter, Cal. Practice Guide: Civ. Pro. Before Trial Ch. 13-G, G. Trial De Novo.
Rutter, Cal. Practice Guide: Civil Trials & Evidence Ch. 17-D, D. Costs.
Rutter, Cal. Practice Guide: Enforcing Judgments/Debts Ch. 6D-6, Debtor's Recourse Against Execution Levy.
Rutter, Cal. Practice Guide: Personal Injury Ch. 7-E, E. the Arbitrator.
Rutter, Cal. Practice Guide: Personal Injury Ch. 7-F, F. Preparing for Arbitration.
Rutter, Cal. Practice Guide: Personal Injury Ch. 7-I, I. Trial De Novo After Arbitration Award.
Rutter, Cal. Practice Guide: Personal Injury Ch. 9-M, M. Verdicts and Judgment.
Miller and Starr California Real Estate § 35:22, Nature of Arbitration.
9 Witkin Cal. Proc. 5th Administrative Proceedings § 85, (S 85) Judicial Review of Award.
9 Witkin Cal. Proc. 5th Appeal § 232, Costs Awarded Against Party Demanding Trial De Novo After Arbitration.
9 Witkin Cal. Proc. 5th Appeal § 239, Costs.
7 Witkin Cal. Proc. 5th Judgment § 111, (S 111) Unnecessary Additional Trial.
6 Witkin Cal. Proc. 5th Proceedings Without Trial § 579, in General.
6 Witkin Cal. Proc. 5th Proceedings Without Trial § 581, Administration.
6 Witkin Cal. Proc. 5th Proceedings Without Trial § 593, (S 593) Source of Payment.
6 Witkin Cal. Proc. 5th Proceedings Without Trial § 625, (S 625) Adoption of Arbitrator's Findings is Improper.
6 Witkin Cal. Proc. 5th Proceedings Without Trial § 626, (S 626) in General.
6 Witkin Cal. Proc. 5th Proceedings Without Trial § 627, (S 627) Improper Assignment of Case to Arbitration.
6 Witkin Cal. Proc. 5th Proceedings Without Trial § 628, (S 628) Effect of Rejection of Statutory Offer to Compromise.
6 Witkin Cal. Proc. 5th Proceedings Without Trial § 629, (S 629) Items Awarded.
2 Witkin Cal. Summ. 10th Workers' Compensation § 80, After Judgment.

§ 1141.22. Grounds for correction, modification or vacation of award

The Judicial Council rules shall specify the grounds upon which the arbitrator or the court, or both, may correct, modify or vacate an award. *(Added by Stats.1978, c. 743, p. 2303, § 2, operative July 1, 1979.)*

Research References

6 Witkin Cal. Proc. 5th Proceedings Without Trial § 612, Vacation.

§ 1141.23. Award; writing, signature and filing; entry in judgment book; force and effect

The arbitration award shall be in writing, signed by the arbitrator and filed in the court in which the action is pending. If there is no request for a de novo trial or a request for dismissal in the form required by the Judicial Council and the award is not vacated, the award shall be entered in the judgment book in the amount of the award. Such award shall have the same force and effect as a judgment in any civil action or proceeding, except that it is not subject to appeal and it may not be attacked or set aside except as provided by Section 473, 1286.2, or Judicial Council rule. *(Added by Stats.1978, c. 743, p. 2303, § 2, operative July 1, 1979. Amended by Stats.1982, c. 621, p. 2612, § 1; Stats.2011, c. 49 (S.B.731), § 4.)*

Research References

Rutter, Cal. Practice Guide: A.D.R. Ch. 4-B, B. Judicial Arbitration.
Rutter, Cal. Practice Guide: Civil Appeals & Writs Ch. 2-B, B. Appealable Judgments and Orders.
Rutter, Cal. Practice Guide: Civ. Pro. Before Trial Ch. 13-F, F. Arbitration Award.
Rutter, Cal. Practice Guide: Personal Injury Ch. 7-H, H. Arbitration Award and Judgment.
Rutter, Cal. Practice Guide: Personal Injury Gen. Matls., Highlights.
Miller and Starr California Real Estate § 35:22, Nature of Arbitration.
9 Witkin Cal. Proc. 5th Appeal § 198, (S 198) No Effective Appeal from Judgment.
8 Witkin Cal. Proc. 5th Attack Judgment Trial Court § 145, (S 145) When Relief is Available.
6 Witkin Cal. Proc. 5th Proceedings Without Trial § 605, (S 605) in General.
6 Witkin Cal. Proc. 5th Proceedings Without Trial § 607, (S 607) Award of Costs.
6 Witkin Cal. Proc. 5th Proceedings Without Trial § 608, Filing.
6 Witkin Cal. Proc. 5th Proceedings Without Trial § 610, Effect.
6 Witkin Cal. Proc. 5th Proceedings Without Trial § 611, Appealability.
6 Witkin Cal. Proc. 5th Proceedings Without Trial § 612, Vacation.

§ 1141.24. Post-award discovery restrictions

In cases ordered to arbitration pursuant to Section 1141.11, no discovery other than that permitted by Chapter 18 (commencing with Section 2034.010) of Title 4 of Part 4 is permissible after an arbitration award except by stipulation of the parties or by leave of court upon a showing of good cause. *(Added by Stats.1978, c. 743, p. 2303, § 2, operative July 1, 1979. Amended by Stats.1985, c. 94, § 1; Stats.1990, c. 1491 (A.B.3765), § 8; Stats.2003, c. 449 (A.B.1712), § 14; Stats.2004, c. 182 (A.B.3081), § 15, operative July 1, 2005.)*

Law Revision Commission Comments

Section 1141.24 is amended to correct a section reference. Although new Section 2034 includes matters covered by former Sections 2037.1 to 2037.9 as well as by former Section 2037, the reference to former Section 2037 apparently was also intended to incorporate those related sections. [20 Cal.L.Rev.Comm. Reports 2297 (1990)].

Section 1141.24 is amended to reflect nonsubstantive reorganization of the rules governing civil discovery. [33 Cal.L.Rev.Comm. Reports 997 (2004)].

Research References

Rutter, Cal. Practice Guide: A.D.R. Ch. 4-B, B. Judicial Arbitration.
Rutter, Cal. Practice Guide: Civ. Pro. Before Trial Ch. 13-A, A. Introduction.
Rutter, Cal. Practice Guide: Civ. Pro. Before Trial Ch. 13-E, E. the Arbitration Hearing.
Rutter, Cal. Practice Guide: Civ. Pro. Before Trial Ch. 13-G, G. Trial De Novo.
Rutter, Cal. Practice Guide: Civ. Pro. Before Trial Ch. 8B-3, Limitations on Right to Discovery.
Rutter, Cal. Practice Guide: Civ. Pro. Before Trial Ch. 8E-2, When Depositions May be Taken.
Rutter, Cal. Practice Guide: Civil Trials & Evidence Ch. 1-A, A. Importance of Statewide and Local Rules of Court.
Rutter, Cal. Practice Guide: Personal Injury Ch. 7-C, C. Actions Subject to Judicial Arbitration.
Rutter, Cal. Practice Guide: Personal Injury Ch. 7-F, F. Preparing for Arbitration.
6 Witkin Cal. Proc. 5th Proceedings Without Trial § 623, (S 623) Discovery.
7 Witkin Cal. Proc. 5th Trial § 74, Completion of Discovery.

§ 1141.25. Reference to arbitration proceedings or award during trial; grounds for new trial

Any reference to the arbitration proceedings or arbitration award during any subsequent trial shall constitute an irregularity in the proceedings of the trial for the purposes of Section 657. *(Added by Stats.1978, c. 743, p. 2303, § 2, operative July 1, 1979.)*

Research References

Rutter, Cal. Practice Guide: A.D.R. Ch. 4-B, B. Judicial Arbitration.
Rutter, Cal. Practice Guide: Civ. Pro. Before Trial Ch. 13-G, G. Trial De Novo.
Rutter, Cal. Practice Guide: Personal Injury Ch. 7-I, I. Trial De Novo After Arbitration Award.

§ 1141.26. Award in excess of § 1141.11 amount; validity; exemption from § 1141.21

Nothing in this act shall prohibit an arbitration award in excess of the amount in controversy as specified in Section 1141.11. No party electing a trial de novo after such award shall be subject to the provisions of Section 1141.21 if the judgment upon the trial de novo is in excess of the amount in controversy as specified in Section 1141.11. *(Added by Stats.1978, c. 743, p. 2303, § 2, operative July 1, 1979. Amended by Stats.1981, c. 1110, § 4.)*

Research References

Rutter, Cal. Practice Guide: A.D.R. Ch. 4-B, B. Judicial Arbitration.
Rutter, Cal. Practice Guide: Civ. Pro. Before Trial Ch. 13-F, F. Arbitration Award.
Rutter, Cal. Practice Guide: Civ. Pro. Before Trial Ch. 13-G, G. Trial De Novo.
Rutter, Cal. Practice Guide: Personal Injury Ch. 7-H, H. Arbitration Award and Judgment.

Rutter, Cal. Practice Guide: Personal Injury Ch. 7-I, I. Trial De Novo After Arbitration Award.
6 Witkin Cal. Proc. 5th Proceedings Without Trial § 606, (S 606) Amount of Damages.
6 Witkin Cal. Proc. 5th Proceedings Without Trial § 615, (S 615) Waiver by Plaintiff Electing Arbitration and Receiving Maximum Award.
6 Witkin Cal. Proc. 5th Proceedings Without Trial § 626, (S 626) in General.
6 Witkin Cal. Proc. 5th Proceedings Without Trial § 627, (S 627) Improper Assignment of Case to Arbitration.

§ 1141.27. Application of chapter to actions with public agency or entity as party

This chapter shall apply to any civil action otherwise within the scope of this chapter in which a party to the action is a public agency or public entity. *(Added by Stats.1978, c. 743, p. 2303, § 2, operative July 1, 1979.)*

Research References

Rutter, Cal. Practice Guide: A.D.R. Ch. 4-B, B. Judicial Arbitration.

§ 1141.28. Administrative costs; compensation of arbitrators; payment

(a) All administrative costs of arbitration, including compensation of arbitrators, shall be paid for by the court in which the arbitration costs are incurred, except as otherwise provided in subdivision (b) and in Section 1141.21.

(b) The actual costs of compensation of arbitrators in any proceeding which would not otherwise be subject to the provisions of this chapter but in which arbitration is conducted pursuant to this chapter solely because of the stipulation of the parties, shall be paid for in equal shares by the parties. If the imposition of these costs would create such a substantial economic hardship for any party as not to be in the interest of justice, as determined by the arbitrator, that party's share of costs shall be paid for by the court in which the arbitration costs are incurred. The determination as to substantial economic hardship may be reviewed by the court. *(Added by Stats.1978, c. 743, p. 2303, § 2, operative July 1, 1979. Amended by Stats.1982, c. 1408, p. 5365, § 2; Stats.2000, c. 447 (S.B.1533), § 3.)*

Research References

Rutter, Cal. Practice Guide: A.D.R. Ch. 4-B, B. Judicial Arbitration.
Rutter, Cal. Practice Guide: A.D.R. Ch. 4-C, C. Statutorily-Mandated Court Mediation Programs.
Rutter, Cal. Practice Guide: Civ. Pro. Before Trial Ch. 13-A, A. Introduction.
Rutter, Cal. Practice Guide: Civ. Pro. Before Trial Ch. 13-D, D. the Arbitrator.
Rutter, Cal. Practice Guide: Personal Injury Ch. 7-E, E. the Arbitrator.
6 Witkin Cal. Proc. 5th Proceedings Without Trial § 581, Administration.
6 Witkin Cal. Proc. 5th Proceedings Without Trial § 593, (S 593) Source of Payment.

§ 1141.30. Construction of chapter in relation to provisions in title on arbitration

This chapter shall not be construed in derogation of Title 9 (commencing with Section 1280) of Part 3, and, to that extent, this chapter and that title, other than Section 1280.1, are mutually exclusive and independent of each other. *(Added by Stats.1978, c. 743, § 2, operative July 1, 1979. Amended by Stats.1985, c. 709, § 2; Stats.1990, c. 817 (S.B.1951), § 1.)*

Research References

Rutter, Cal. Practice Guide: Civ. Pro. Before Trial Ch. 13-B, B. Judicial Arbitration Distinguished from Contract Arbitration.

Civ. Pro.

6 Witkin Cal. Proc. 5th Proceedings Without Trial § 580, Contractual Arbitration Distinguished.

§ 1141.31. Operative date of chapter; date of adoption of arbitration rules

The provisions of this chapter shall become operative July 1, 1979, except that the Judicial Council shall adopt the arbitration rules for practice and procedures on or before March 31, 1979. *(Added by Stats.1978, c. 743, p. 2303, § 2, operative July 1, 1979.)*

Research References

Miller and Starr California Real Estate § 27:47, Provisions for Arbitration and Mediation of Disputes--Generally.

CHAPTER 4. SUMMARY PROCEEDINGS FOR OBTAINING POSSESSION OF REAL PROPERTY IN CERTAIN CASES

§ 1159. Forcible entry; party in possession

Every person is guilty of a forcible entry who either:

1. By breaking open doors, windows, or other parts of a house, or by any kind of violence or circumstance of terror enters upon or into any real property; or,

2. Who, after entering peaceably upon real property, turns out by force, threats, or menacing conduct, the party in possession.

The "party in possession" means any person who hires real property and includes a boarder or lodger, except those persons whose occupancy is described in subdivision (b) of Section 1940 of the Civil Code. *(Enacted in 1872. Amended by Stats.1976, c. 712, p. 1728, § 2.)*

Research References

California Real Estate Forms (Miller & Starr) § 3:55, Subordination, Nondisturbance, and Attornment Agreement.
Rutter, Cal. Practice Guide: Enforcing Judgments/Debts Ch. 6I-3, Enforcement of Judgment for Possession of Real Property.
Rutter, Cal. Practice Guide: Real Prop. Transactions Ch. 7-B, B. Sale of Ground Lease Tenant's Interest-Preliminary Concerns Re Assignment and Subletting.
Miller and Starr California Real Estate § 19:7, Other Interests Distinguished--Eviction of a Guest or Lodger.
Miller and Starr California Real Estate § 19:161, Nature of the Offense.
Miller and Starr California Real Estate § 19:162, Elements of the Offense--Forcible Entry.
Miller and Starr California Real Estate § 19:167, Defenses.
3 Witkin Cal. Proc. 5th Actions § 65, (S 65) Statutory Classes.
2 Witkin Cal. Proc. 5th Courts § 251, Nature and Scope of Statute.
8 Witkin Cal. Proc. 5th Enforcement of Judgment § 335, Hearing and Determination.
4 Witkin Cal. Proc. 5th Pleading § 10, Extension to Ordinary Party.
5 Witkin Cal. Proc. 5th Pleading § 649, in General.
5 Witkin Cal. Proc. 5th Pleading § 651, Defendant's Forcible Entry.
7 Witkin Cal. Proc. 5th Trial § 74, Completion of Discovery.
12 Witkin, California Summary 10th Real Property § 514, Statutory Rights of Lodger.

12 Witkin, California Summary 10th Real Property § 559, (S 559) Remedies for Transfer in Violation of Restriction.

12 Witkin, California Summary 10th Real Property § 577, Due Process and Related Challenges.

12 Witkin, California Summary 10th Real Property § 599, Other Acts and Powers of Entity Are Not Affected.

12 Witkin, California Summary 10th Real Property § 703, (S 703) Nature of Remedy.

12 Witkin, California Summary 10th Real Property § 757, in General.

12 Witkin, California Summary 10th Real Property § 759, Where Landlord Has Lien.

12 Witkin, California Summary 10th Real Property § 781, (S 781) Purchaser's Acceptance of Rental Agreement.

12 Witkin, California Summary 10th Real Property § 784, (S 784) in General.

1 Witkin Cal. Summ. 10th Contracts § 683, Waivers by Tenants.

5 Witkin, California Summary 10th Torts § 421, (S 421) No Privilege for Forcible Entry.

§ 1160. Forcible detainer defined

FORCIBLE DETAINER DEFINED. Every person is guilty of a forcible detainer who either:

1. By force, or by menaces and threats of violence, unlawfully holds and keeps the possession of any real property, whether the same was acquired peaceably or otherwise; or,

2. Who, in the night-time, or during the absence of the occupant of any lands, unlawfully enters upon real property, and who, after demand made for the surrender thereof, for the period of five days, refuses to surrender the same to such former occupant.

The occupant of real property, within the meaning of this subdivision, is one who, within five days preceding such unlawful entry, was in the peaceable and undisturbed possession of such lands. *(Enacted in 1872.)*

Research References

Miller and Starr California Real Estate § 19:163, Elements of the Offense--Forcible Detainer.

Miller and Starr California Real Estate § 19:164, Demand for Return of Possession.

5 Witkin Cal. Proc. 5th Pleading § 653, (S 653) Recovery of Possession: Forcible Detainer.

12 Witkin, California Summary 10th Real Property § 759, Where Landlord Has Lien.

§ 1161. Unlawful detainer defined

A tenant of real property, for a term less than life, or the executor or administrator of his or her estate heretofore qualified and now acting or hereafter to be qualified and act, is guilty of unlawful detainer:

1. When he or she continues in possession, in person or by subtenant, of the property, or any part thereof, after the expiration of the term for which it is let to him or her; provided the expiration is of a nondefault nature however brought about without the permission of his or her landlord, or the successor in estate of his or her landlord, if applicable; including the case where the person to be removed became the occupant of the premises as a servant, employee, agent, or licensee and the relation of master and servant, or employer and employee, or principal and agent, or licensor and licensee, has been lawfully terminated or the time fixed for occupancy by the agreement between the parties has expired; but nothing in this subdivision shall be construed as preventing the removal of the occupant in any other lawful manner; but in case of a tenancy at will, it must first be terminated by notice, as prescribed in the Civil Code.

2. When he or she continues in possession, in person or by subtenant, without the permission of his or her landlord, or the successor in estate of his or her landlord, if applicable, after default in the payment of rent, pursuant to the lease or

agreement under which the property is held, and three days' notice, in writing, requiring its payment, stating the amount which is due, the name, telephone number, and address of the person to whom the rent payment shall be made, and, if payment may be made personally, the usual days and hours that person will be available to receive the payment (provided that, if the address does not allow for personal delivery, then it shall be conclusively presumed that upon the mailing of any rent or notice to the owner by the tenant to the name and address provided, the notice or rent is deemed received by the owner on the date posted, if the tenant can show proof of mailing to the name and address provided by the owner), or the number of an account in a financial institution into which the rental payment may be made, and the name and street address of the institution (provided that the institution is located within five miles of the rental property), or if an electronic funds transfer procedure has been previously established, that payment may be made pursuant to that procedure, or possession of the property, shall have been served upon him or her and if there is a subtenant in actual occupation of the premises, also upon the subtenant.

The notice may be served at any time within one year after the rent becomes due. In all cases of tenancy upon agricultural lands, where the tenant has held over and retained possession for more than 60 days after the expiration of the term without any demand of possession or notice to quit by the landlord or the successor in estate of his or her landlord, if applicable, he or she shall be deemed to be holding by permission of the landlord or successor in estate of his or her landlord, if applicable, and shall be entitled to hold under the terms of the lease for another full year, and shall not be guilty of an unlawful detainer during that year, and the holding over for that period shall be taken and construed as a consent on the part of a tenant to hold for another year.

3. When he or she continues in possession, in person or by subtenant, after a neglect or failure to perform other conditions or covenants of the lease or agreement under which the property is held, including any covenant not to assign or sublet, than the one for the payment of rent, and three days' notice, in writing, requiring the performance of such conditions or covenants, or the possession of the property, shall have been served upon him or her, and if there is a subtenant in actual occupation of the premises, also, upon the subtenant. Within three days after the service of the notice, the tenant, or any subtenant in actual occupation of the premises, or any mortgagee of the term, or other person interested in its continuance, may perform the conditions or covenants of the lease or pay the stipulated rent, as the case may be, and thereby save the lease from forfeiture; provided, if the conditions and covenants of the lease, violated by the lessee, cannot afterward be performed, then no notice, as last prescribed herein, need be given to the lessee or his or her subtenant, demanding the performance of the violated conditions or covenants of the lease.

A tenant may take proceedings, similar to those prescribed in this chapter, to obtain possession of the premises let to a subtenant or held by a servant, employee, agent, or licensee, in case of his or her unlawful detention of the premises underlet to him or her or held by him or her.

4. Any tenant, subtenant, or executor or administrator of his or her estate heretofore qualified and now acting, or hereafter to be qualified and act, assigning or subletting or committing waste upon the demised premises, contrary to the conditions or covenants of his or her lease, or maintaining, committing, or permitting the maintenance or commission of a nuisance upon the demised premises or using the premises for an unlawful purpose, thereby terminates the lease, and the landlord, or his or her successor in estate, shall upon service of three days' notice to quit upon the person or persons in possession, be entitled to

restitution of possession of the demised premises under this chapter. For purposes of this subdivision, a person who commits or maintains a public nuisance as described in Section 3482.8 of the Civil Code, or who commits an offense described in subdivision (c) of Section 3485 of the Civil Code, or subdivision (c) of Section 3486 of the Civil Code, or uses the premises to further the purpose of that offense shall be deemed to have committed a nuisance upon the premises.

5. When he or she gives written notice as provided in Section 1946 of the Civil Code of his or her intention to terminate the hiring of the real property, or makes a written offer to surrender which is accepted in writing by the landlord, but fails to deliver possession at the time specified in that written notice, without the permission of his or her landlord, or the successor in estate of the landlord, if applicable.

As used in this section, tenant includes any person who hires real property except those persons whose occupancy is described in subdivision (b) of Section 1940 of the Civil Code.

This section shall become operative on January 1, 2012. *(Added by Stats.2008, c. 440 (A.B.2052), § 3, eff. Sept. 27, 2008, operative Jan. 1, 2012. Amended by Stats.2009, c. 244 (A.B.530), § 5, operative Jan. 1, 2012; Stats.2011, c. 128 (S.B.426), § 2.)*

Research References

California Real Estate Forms (Miller & Starr) § 2:16, Office Lease-- Multistory Office Building.

California Real Estate Forms (Miller & Starr) § 2:17, Office Lease-- Mixed Use Building.

California Real Estate Forms (Miller & Starr) § 2:18, Office Lease-- Office/Warehouse Building With Four or Fewer Tenants.

California Real Estate Forms (Miller & Starr) § 2:19, Retail Lease-- Power Shopping Center.

California Real Estate Forms (Miller & Starr) § 2:20, Retail Lease-- Shopping Center With for Profit Parking Garage.

California Real Estate Forms (Miller & Starr) § 2:21, Retail Lease-- 15,000 RSF to 30,000 RSF (Tenant Oriented).

California Real Estate Forms (Miller & Starr) § 2:22, Retail Lease-- Regional Shopping Center.

California Real Estate Forms (Miller & Starr) § 2:23, Retail Lease--Small Strip-Shopping Center.

California Real Estate Forms (Miller & Starr) § 2:24, Retail Lease-- Restaurant.

California Real Estate Forms (Miller & Starr) § 2:25, Industrial Lease.

California Real Estate Forms (Miller & Starr) § 2:26, Triple Net Lease-- Industrial Build-To-Suit Lease.

California Real Estate Forms (Miller & Starr) § 2:27, Ground Lease.

California Real Estate Forms (Miller & Starr) § 2:28, Triple Net Lease-- Stand-Alone Building.

California Real Estate Forms (Miller & Starr) § 2:29, Parking Garage Lease.

California Real Estate Forms (Miller & Starr) § 2:30, Storage Lease-- Office Building.

California Real Estate Forms (Miller & Starr) § 2:31, Rental Agree- ment--Self Storage.

California Real Estate Forms (Miller & Starr) § 2:32, Gross Lease--Small Commercial Property.

California Real Estate Forms (Miller & Starr) § 2:33, Sublease-- With Consent of Master Landlord.

California Real Estate Forms (Miller & Starr) § 2:34, Sublease--Shared Office Space.

California Real Estate Forms (Miller & Starr) § 2:62, Standard Industri- al/Commercial Multi-Tenant Lease--Net.

California Real Estate Forms (Miller & Starr) § 2:63, Standard Industri- al/Commercial Multi-Tenant Lease--Gross.

California Real Estate Forms (Miller & Starr) § 2:65, Residential Lease.

California Real Estate Forms (Miller & Starr) § 2:66, Residential Lease With Purchase Option.

California Real Estate Forms (Miller & Starr) § 2:80, Defaults--Default by Tenant.

California Real Estate Forms (Miller & Starr) § 2:92, Mediation; Arbitration.

California Real Estate Forms (Miller & Starr) § 2:18.50, Management Office License Agreement.

Rutter, Cal. Practice Guide: A.D.R. Ch. 4-B, B. Judicial Arbitration.

Rutter, Cal. Practice Guide: Landlord-Tenant Form 2:A, Residential Rental Agreement.

Rutter, Cal. Practice Guide: Landlord-Tenant Form 2:C, Office Lease.

Rutter, Cal. Practice Guide: Real Prop. Transactions Ch. 7-C, C. Representing the Purchasing Tenant.

Miller and Starr California Real Estate § 19:7, Other Interests Distin- guished--Eviction of a Guest or Lodger.

Miller and Starr California Real Estate § 22:8, Conditions Dangerous to Health and Safety; Noise and Emissions.

Miller and Starr California Real Estate § 22:9, Sale of Alcohol or Drugs.

Miller and Starr California Real Estate § 19:11, Apartment House Manager as an Employee--Occupation by an Employee or Agent.

Miller and Starr California Real Estate § 19:32, Tenancy at Sufferance.

Miller and Starr California Real Estate § 19:45, Presumption of Nature of Holdover Tenancy--Agricultural Lands.

Miller and Starr California Real Estate § 19:48, Covenants and Condi- tions Distinguished.

Miller and Starr California Real Estate § 19:67, Liability of the Parties-- Between Tenant-Sublessor and Subtenant.

Miller and Starr California Real Estate § 19:74, Landlord's Remedies for Tenant's Breach of the Restriction.

Miller and Starr California Real Estate § 19:77, Nature of and Obligation to Pay Rent.

Miller and Starr California Real Estate § 19:82, Modification of the Rent.

Miller and Starr California Real Estate § 22:17, Landlord and Tenant.

Miller and Starr California Real Estate § 33:40, Secured Creditor Actions--Unlawful Detainer After Foreclosure.

Miller and Starr California Real Estate § 19:111, Specification or Restriction of Use.

Miller and Starr California Real Estate § 19:130, Landlord's Remedies.

Miller and Starr California Real Estate § 19:167, Defenses.

Miller and Starr California Real Estate § 19:188, Notice Required by Statute.

Miller and Starr California Real Estate § 19:196, Surrender.

Miller and Starr California Real Estate § 19:200, Termination for Cause or Default.

Miller and Starr California Real Estate § 19:201, Landlord's Alternative Remedies for Tenant's Breach; When Notice is Required.

Miller and Starr California Real Estate § 19:202, Form and Contents of the Notice; Curable and Noncurable Breaches.

Miller and Starr California Real Estate § 19:204, Service of the Notice.

Miller and Starr California Real Estate § 19:205, Service of the Notice-- Legal Effect of the Notice; Tenant's Right to Cure a Default.

Miller and Starr California Real Estate § 19:208, Termination of the Lease; Landlord's Recovery of Rent or Damages--Recovery in an Unlawful Detainer Proceeding.

Miller and Starr California Real Estate § 19:214, Nature of the Remedy.

Miller and Starr California Real Estate § 19:218, Required Relationship of the Parties.

Miller and Starr California Real Estate § 19:220, Parties.

Miller and Starr California Real Estate § 19:224, Cross-Complaint; Affirmative Defenses--Breach of the Warranty of Habitability.

18 NO. 4 Miller & Starr, California Real Estate Newsalert 16, Landlord and Tenant.

18 NO. 4 Miller & Starr, California Real Estate Newsalert 45, Table of Statutes (Newsalert Vol 18).

19 NO. 1 Miller & Starr, California Real Estate Newsalert 1, The Perata Foreclosure Bill (SB 1137): New Rights for Defaulting Borrowers and Tenants; New Complications for Foreclosing Lenders.

19 NO. 4 Miller & Starr, California Real Estate Newsalert 19, Landlord and Tenant.

19 NO. 5 Miller & Starr, California Real Estate Newsalert 22, Landlord and Tenant.

20 NO. 2 Miller & Starr, California Real Estate Newsalert 2, Landlord and Tenant.

20 NO. 4 Miller & Starr, California Real Estate Newsalert 13, Landlord and Tenant.

21 NO. 3 Miller & Starr, California Real Estate Newsalert 10, Deeds of Trust.

21 NO. 4 Miller & Starr, California Real Estate Newsalert 14, Landlord and Tenant.

22 NO. 4 Miller & Starr, California Real Estate Newsalert 15, Landlord and Tenant.

3 Witkin Cal. Proc. 5th Actions § 216, Landlord's Proceeding Against Tenant.

4 Witkin Cal. Proc. 5th Pleading § 472, Limited Civil Cases.

5 Witkin Cal. Proc. 5th Pleading § 640, (S 640) Procedure.

5 Witkin Cal. Proc. 5th Pleading § 641, (S 641) Relationship and Possession.

5 Witkin Cal. Proc. 5th Pleading § 642, in General.

5 Witkin Cal. Proc. 5th Pleading § 643, Lessee Holding Over.

5 Witkin Cal. Proc. 5th Pleading § 644, Lessee's Default or Breach.

6 Witkin Cal. Proc. 5th Proceedings Without Trial § 32, Implied Limitations.

12 Witkin, California Summary 10th Real Property § 503, Statutory Framework.

12 Witkin, California Summary 10th Real Property § 545, (S 545) Lease Provisions Are Not Incorporated.

12 Witkin, California Summary 10th Real Property § 620, Tenant's Remedies.

12 Witkin, California Summary 10th Real Property § 667, in General.

12 Witkin, California Summary 10th Real Property § 668, Construction of Forfeiture Clause.

12 Witkin, California Summary 10th Real Property § 674, (S 674) Illegal Use of Premises.

12 Witkin, California Summary 10th Real Property § 679, Tenancy at Will.

12 Witkin, California Summary 10th Real Property § 695, Proof of Abandonment.

12 Witkin, California Summary 10th Real Property § 703, (S 703) Nature of Remedy.

12 Witkin, California Summary 10th Real Property § 706, Nature of Defense.

12 Witkin, California Summary 10th Real Property § 720, (S 720) Necessity and Effect of Notice.

12 Witkin, California Summary 10th Real Property § 721, (S 721) Where No Notice is Necessary.

12 Witkin, California Summary 10th Real Property § 722, (S 722) Commercial Tenant's Tender of Rent in Response.

12 Witkin, California Summary 10th Real Property § 723, Notice to Perform or Quit.

12 Witkin, California Summary 10th Real Property § 724, Statement of Amount Due.

12 Witkin, California Summary 10th Real Property § 725, Statement of Payment Options.

12 Witkin, California Summary 10th Real Property § 726, Notice to Quit.

12 Witkin, California Summary 10th Real Property § 727, (S 727) Methods of Service.

12 Witkin, California Summary 10th Real Property § 730, Pleadings.

1 Witkin Cal. Summ. 10th Contracts § 423, (S 423) General Rule and Theory.

1 Witkin Cal. Summ. 10th Contracts § 523, Statutory Regulation: Tenant's Right to Initial Inspection by Landlord.

1 Witkin Cal. Summ. 10th Contracts § 525, Disposition of Security.

13 Witkin, California Summary 10th Equity § 150, Other Statutes.

§ 1161.1. Commercial real property after default in payment of rent; application of section 1161; estimate of amount due; partial payment; presumption

With respect to application of Section 1161 in cases of possession of commercial real property after default in the payment of rent:

(a) If the amount stated in the notice provided to the tenant pursuant to subdivision (2) of Section 1161 is clearly identified by the notice as an estimate and the amount claimed is not in fact correct, but it is determined upon the trial or other judicial determination that rent was owing, and the amount claimed in the notice was reasonably estimated, the tenant shall be subject to judgment for possession and the actual amount of rent and other sums found to be due. However, if (1) upon receipt of such a notice claiming an amount identified by the notice as an estimate, the tenant tenders to the landlord within the time for payment required by the notice, the amount which the tenant has reasonably estimated to be due and (2) if at trial it is determined that the amount of rent then due was the amount tendered by the tenant or a lesser amount, the tenant shall be deemed the prevailing party for all purposes. If the court determines that the amount so tendered by the tenant was less than the amount due, but was reasonably estimated, the tenant shall retain the right to possession if the tenant pays to the landlord within five days of the effective date of the judgment (1) the amount previously tendered if it had not been previously accepted, (2) the difference between the amount tendered and the amount determined by the court to be due, and (3) any other sums as ordered by the court.

(b) If the landlord accepts a partial payment of rent, including any payment pursuant to subdivision (a), after serving notice pursuant to Section 1161, the landlord, without any further notice to the tenant, may commence and pursue an action under this chapter to recover the difference between the amount demanded in that notice and the payment actually received, and this shall be specified in the complaint.

(c) If the landlord accepts a partial payment of rent after filing the complaint pursuant to Section 1166, the landlord's acceptance of the partial payment is evidence only of that payment, without waiver of any rights or defenses of any of the parties. The landlord shall be entitled to amend the complaint to reflect the partial payment without creating a necessity for the filing of an additional answer or other responsive pleading by the tenant, and without prior leave of court, and such an amendment shall not delay the matter from proceeding. However, this subdivision shall apply only if the landlord provides actual notice to the tenant that acceptance of the partial rent payment does not constitute a waiver of any rights, including any right the landlord may have to recover possession of the property.

(d) "Commercial real property" as used in this section, means all real property in this state except dwelling units made subject to Chapter 2 (commencing with Section 1940) of Title 5 of Part 4 of Division 3 of the Civil Code, mobilehomes as defined in Section 798.3 of the Civil Code, or recreational vehicles as defined in Section 799.24 of the Civil Code.

(e) For the purposes of this section, there is a presumption affecting the burden of proof that the amount of rent claimed or tendered is reasonably estimated if, in relation to the amount determined to be due upon the trial or other judicial determination of that issue, the amount claimed or tendered was no more than 20 percent more or less than the amount determined to be due. However, if the rent due is contingent upon information primarily within the knowledge of the one party to the lease and that information has not been furnished to, or has not accurately been furnished to, the other party, the court shall consider that fact in determining the reasonableness of the amount of rent claimed or tendered pursuant to subdivision (a). *(Added by Stats.1990, c. 890 (S.B.2498), § 1.)*

Research References

California Real Estate Forms (Miller & Starr) § 2:16, Office Lease-- Multistory Office Building.

California Real Estate Forms (Miller & Starr) § 2:17, Office Lease-- Mixed Use Building.

California Real Estate Forms (Miller & Starr) § 2:18, Office Lease-- Office/Warehouse Building With Four or Fewer Tenants.

California Real Estate Forms (Miller & Starr) § 2:19, Retail Lease--Power Shopping Center.

California Real Estate Forms (Miller & Starr) § 2:20, Retail Lease--Shopping Center With for Profit Parking Garage.

California Real Estate Forms (Miller & Starr) § 2:22, Retail Lease--Regional Shopping Center.

California Real Estate Forms (Miller & Starr) § 2:23, Retail Lease--Small Strip-Shopping Center.

California Real Estate Forms (Miller & Starr) § 2:24, Retail Lease--Restaurant.

California Real Estate Forms (Miller & Starr) § 2:25, Industrial Lease.

California Real Estate Forms (Miller & Starr) § 2:26, Triple Net Lease--Industrial Build-To-Suit Lease.

California Real Estate Forms (Miller & Starr) § 2:27, Ground Lease.

California Real Estate Forms (Miller & Starr) § 2:28, Triple Net Lease--Stand-Alone Building.

California Real Estate Forms (Miller & Starr) § 2:29, Parking Garage Lease.

California Real Estate Forms (Miller & Starr) § 2:32, Gross Lease--Small Commercial Property.

California Real Estate Forms (Miller & Starr) § 2:62, Standard Industrial/Commercial Multi-Tenant Lease--Net.

California Real Estate Forms (Miller & Starr) § 2:63, Standard Industrial/Commercial Multi-Tenant Lease--Gross.

Miller and Starr California Real Estate § 19:203, Form and Contents of the Notice; Curable and Noncurable Breaches--Commercial Premises.

12 Witkin, California Summary 10th Real Property § 722, (S 722) Commercial Tenant's Tender of Rent in Response.

12 Witkin, California Summary 10th Real Property § 724, Statement of Amount Due.

12 Witkin, California Summary 10th Real Property § 730, Pleadings.

§ 1161.2. Case court records; public access; defendant notice; filing fee; mobilehome park tenancy

(a) The clerk may allow access to limited civil case records filed under this chapter, including the court file, index, and register of actions, only as follows:

(1) To a party to the action, including a party's attorney.

(2) To any person who provides the clerk with the names of at least one plaintiff and one defendant and the address of the premises, including the apartment or unit number, if any.

(3) To a resident of the premises who provides the clerk with the name of one of the parties or the case number and shows proof of residency.

(4) To any person by order of the court, which may be granted ex parte, on a showing of good cause.

(5) Except as provided in paragraph (6), to any other person 60 days after the complaint has been filed, unless a defendant prevails in the action within 60 days of the filing of the complaint, in which case the clerk may not allow access to any court records in the action, except as provided in paragraphs (1) to (4), inclusive.

(6) In the case of a complaint involving residential property based on Section 1161a as indicated in the caption of the complaint, as required in subdivision (c) of Section 1166, to any other person, if 60 days have elapsed since the complaint was filed with the court, and, as of that date, judgment against all defendants has been entered for the plaintiff, after a trial. If judgment is not entered under the conditions described in this paragraph, the clerk shall not allow access to any court records in the action, except as provided in paragraphs (1) to (4), inclusive.

(b) For purposes of this section, "good cause" includes, but is not limited to, the gathering of newsworthy facts by a person described in Section 1070 of the Evidence Code. It is the intent of the Legislature that a simple procedure be established to request the ex parte order described in subdivision (a).

(c) Upon the filing of any case so restricted, the court clerk shall mail notice to each defendant named in the action. The notice shall be mailed to the address provided in the complaint. The notice shall contain a statement that an unlawful detainer complaint (eviction action) has been filed naming that party as a defendant, and that access to the court file will be delayed for 60 days except to a party, an attorney for one of the parties, or any other person who (1) provides to the clerk the names of at least one plaintiff and one defendant in the action and provides to the clerk the address, including any applicable apartment, unit, or space number, of the subject premises, or (2) provides to the clerk the name of one of the parties in the action or the case number and can establish through proper identification that he or she lives at the subject premises. The notice shall also contain a statement that access to the court index, register of actions, or other records is not permitted until 60 days after the complaint is filed, except pursuant to an order upon a showing of good cause therefor. The notice shall contain on its face the following information:

(1) The name and telephone number of the county bar association.

(2) The name and telephone number of any entity that requests inclusion on the notice and demonstrates to the satisfaction of the court that it has been certified by the State Bar as a lawyer referral service and maintains a panel of attorneys qualified in the practice of landlord-tenant law pursuant to the minimum standards for a lawyer referral service established by the State Bar and Section 6155 of the Business and Professions Code.

(3) The following statement:

"The State Bar of California certifies lawyer referral services in California and publishes a list of certified lawyer referral services organized by county. To locate a lawyer referral service in your county, go to the State Bar's website at www.calbar.ca.gov or call 1–866–442–2529."

(4) The name and telephone number of an office or offices funded by the federal Legal Services Corporation or qualified legal services projects that receive funds distributed pursuant to Section 6216 of the Business and Professions Code that provide legal services to low-income persons in the county in which the action is filed. The notice shall state that these numbers may be called for legal advice regarding the case. The notice shall be issued between 24 and 48 hours of the filing of the complaint, excluding weekends and holidays. One copy of the notice shall be addressed to "all occupants" and mailed separately to the subject premises. The notice shall not constitute service of the summons and complaint.

(d) Notwithstanding any other provision of law, the court shall charge an additional fee of fifteen dollars ($15) for filing a first appearance by the plaintiff. This fee shall be added to the uniform filing fee for actions filed under this chapter.

(e) This section does not apply to a case that seeks to terminate a mobilehome park tenancy if the statement of the character of the proceeding in the caption of the complaint clearly indicates that the complaint seeks termination of a mobilehome park tenancy. (*Added by Stats.1991, c. 1007*

(S.B.892), § 3. Amended by Stats.1992, c. 666 (A.B.3453), § 2; Stats.1992, c. 876 (A.B.3296), § 7; Stats.1993, c. 1191 (S.B.236), § 3; Stats.1994, c. 587 (A.B.3600), § 7.5; Stats.1998, c. 931 (S.B.2139), § 118, eff. Sept. 28, 1998; Stats.2001, c. 824 (A.B. 1700), § 11; Stats.2003, c. 449 (A.B.1712), § 15; Stats.2003, c. 787 (S.B.345), § 2; Stats.2004, c. 568 (S.B.1145), § 6; Stats.2005, c. 75 (A.B.145), § 41, eff. July 19, 2005, operative Jan. 1, 2006; Stats.2005, c. 610 (A.B.664), § 2; Stats.2010, c. 641 (S.B.1149), § 1; Stats.2012, c. 241 (A.B.1865), § 1.)

Law Revision Commission Comments

Section 1161.2 is amended to accommodate unification of the municipal and superior courts in a county. Cal. Const. art. VI, § 5(e). Formerly, each county had one or more municipal courts and a superior court, and subdivision (a) referred to an unlawful detainer case filed in a municipal court. A limited civil case is equivalent to a matter within the original jurisdiction of the municipal court under former law, so Section 1161.2 as amended continues the effect of former law. See Section 85 (limited civil cases) & Comment.

For guidance in applying subdivision (e), see Section 38 (judicial districts) & Comment. [28 Cal.L.Rev.Comm. Reports 51 (1998)].

Research References

Rutter, Cal. Practice Guide: Civ. Pro. Before Trial Ch. 3-A, A. Subject Matter Jurisdiction (Competency).
Miller and Starr California Real Estate § 19:188, Notice Required by Statute.
Miller and Starr California Real Estate § 19:217, Restrictions on Access and Reporting of Unlawful Detainer Actions.
15 NO. 4 Miller & Starr, California Real Estate Newsalert 12, Landlord and Tenant.
21 NO. 4 Miller & Starr, California Real Estate Newsalert 14, Landlord and Tenant.
2 Witkin Cal. Proc. 5th Courts § 370, (S 370) in General.
4 Witkin Cal. Proc. 5th Pleading § 26, Additional Fees.
12 Witkin, California Summary 10th Real Property § 731, Restricted Access to Files.

§ 1161.3. Termination of lease prohibited based upon acts of domestic violence, sexual assault, stalking, human trafficking, or abuse of elder or dependent adult; exceptions; limitation of landlord liability to other tenants; definition; forms

(a) Except as provided in subdivision (b), a landlord shall not terminate a tenancy or fail to renew a tenancy based upon an act or acts against a tenant or a tenant's household member that constitute domestic violence as defined in Section 6211 of the Family Code, sexual assault as defined in Section 1219, stalking as defined in Section 1708.7 of the Civil Code or Section 646.9 of the Penal Code, human trafficking as defined in Section 236.1 of the Penal Code, or abuse of an elder or a dependent adult as defined in Section 15610.07 of the Welfare and Institutions Code, if both of the following apply:

(1) The act or acts of domestic violence, sexual assault, stalking, human trafficking, or abuse of an elder or a dependent adult have been documented by one of the following:

(A) A temporary restraining order, emergency protective order, or protective order lawfully issued within the last 180 days pursuant to Section 527.6, Part 3 (commencing with Section 6240), Part 4 (commencing with Section 6300), or Part 5 (commencing with Section 6400) of Division 10 of the Family Code, Section 136.2 of the Penal Code, or Section 213.5 or 15657.03 of the Welfare and Institutions Code that protects the tenant or household member from domestic violence, sexual assault, stalking, human trafficking, or abuse of an elder or a dependent adult.

(B) A copy of a written report, written within the last 180 days, by a peace officer employed by a state or local law enforcement agency acting in his or her official capacity, stating that the tenant or household member has filed a report alleging that he or she or the household member is a victim of domestic violence, sexual assault, stalking, human trafficking, or abuse of an elder or a dependent adult.

(2) The person against whom the protection order has been issued or who was named in the police report of the act or acts of domestic violence, sexual assault, stalking, human trafficking, or abuse of an elder or dependent adult is not a tenant of the same dwelling unit as the tenant or household member.

(b) A landlord may terminate or decline to renew a tenancy after the tenant has availed himself or herself of the protections afforded by subdivision (a) if both of the following apply:

(1) Either of the following:

(A) The tenant allows the person against whom the protection order has been issued or who was named in the police report of the act or acts of domestic violence, sexual assault, stalking, human trafficking, or abuse of an elder or a dependent adult to visit the property.

(B) The landlord reasonably believes that the presence of the person against whom the protection order has been issued or who was named in the police report of the act or acts of domestic violence, sexual assault, stalking, human trafficking, or abuse of an elder or dependent adult poses a physical threat to other tenants, guests, invitees, or licensees, or to a tenant's right to quiet possession pursuant to Section 1927 of the Civil Code.

(2) The landlord previously gave at least three days' notice to the tenant to correct a violation of paragraph (1).

(c) Notwithstanding any provision in the lease to the contrary, the landlord shall not be liable to any other tenants for any action that arises due to the landlord's compliance with this section.

(d) For the purposes of this section, "tenant" means tenant, subtenant, lessee, or sublessee.

(e) The Judicial Council shall, on or before July 1, 2014, develop a new form or revise an existing form that may be used by a party to assert in the responsive pleading the grounds set forth in this section as an affirmative defense to an unlawful detainer action. *(Added by Stats.2010, c. 626 (S.B.782), § 4. Amended by Stats.2012, c. 516 (S.B.1403), § 2; Stats.2013, c. 130 (S.B.612), § 3.)*

Research References

Miller and Starr California Real Estate § 19:86, Termination of the Obligation to Pay Rent.
21 NO. 4 Miller & Starr, California Real Estate Newsalert 14, Landlord and Tenant.
12 Witkin, California Summary 10th Real Property § 683A, (New)-Domestic Violence or Sexual Assault Against Tenant.

§ 1161.5. Notice stating lessor or landlord may elect to declare forfeiture of lease or rental agreement; nullification; performance by lessee or tenant

When the notice required by Section 1161 states that the lessor or the landlord may elect to declare the forfeiture of the lease or rental agreement, that declaration shall be nullified and the lease or rental agreement shall remain in effect if the lessee or tenant performs within three days after service of the notice or if the breach is waived by the lessor or the landlord after service of the notice. *(Added by Stats.1984, c. 174, § 1.)*

Research References

Miller and Starr California Real Estate § 19:201, Landlord's Alternative Remedies for Tenant's Breach; When Notice is Required.
Miller and Starr California Real Estate § 19:202, Form and Contents of the Notice; Curable and Noncurable Breaches.
Miller and Starr California Real Estate § 19:205, Service of the Notice-- Legal Effect of the Notice; Tenant's Right to Cure a Default.

12 Witkin, California Summary 10th Real Property § 720, (S 720) Necessity and Effect of Notice.

§ 1161a. Sale of manufactured home, mobilehome, floating home or real property; removal of person holding over after notice

(a) As used in this section:

(1) "Manufactured home" has the same meaning as provided in Section 18007 of the Health and Safety Code.

(2) "Mobilehome" has the same meaning as provided in Section 18008 of the Health and Safety Code.

(3) "Floating home" has the same meaning as provided in subdivision (d) of Section 18075.55 of the Health and Safety Code.

(b) In any of the following cases, a person who holds over and continues in possession of a manufactured home, mobilehome, floating home, or real property after a three-day written notice to quit the property has been served upon the person, or if there is a subtenant in actual occupation of the premises, also upon such subtenant, as prescribed in Section 1162, may be removed therefrom as prescribed in this chapter.

(1) Where the property has been sold pursuant to a writ of execution against such person, or a person under whom such person claims, and the title under the sale has been duly perfected.

(2) Where the property has been sold pursuant to a writ of sale, upon the foreclosure by proceedings taken as prescribed in this code of a mortgage, or under an express power of sale contained therein, executed by such person, or a person under whom such person claims, and the title under the foreclosure has been duly perfected.

(3) Where the property has been sold in accordance with Section 2924 of the Civil Code, under a power of sale contained in a deed of trust executed by such person, or a person under whom such person claims, and the title under the sale has been duly perfected.

(4) Where the property has been sold by such person, or a person under whom such person claims, and the title under the sale has been duly perfected.

(5) Where the property has been sold in accordance with Section 18037.5 of the Health and Safety Code under the default provisions of a conditional sale contract or security agreement executed by such person, or a person under whom such person claims, and the title under the sale has been duly perfected.

(c) Notwithstanding the provisions of subdivision (b), a tenant or subtenant in possession of a rental housing unit which has been sold by reason of any of the causes enumerated in subdivision (b), who rents or leases the rental housing unit either on a periodic basis from week to week, month to month, or other interval, or for a fixed period of time, shall be given written notice to quit pursuant to Section 1162, at least as long as the term of hiring itself but not exceeding 30 days, before the tenant or subtenant may be removed therefrom as prescribed in this chapter.

(d) For the purpose of subdivision (c), "rental housing unit" means any structure or any part thereof which is rented or offered for rent for residential occupancy in this state. *(Added by Stats.1929, c. 393, p. 719, § 1. Amended by Stats.1941, c. 1095, p. 2789, § 1; Stats.1982, c. 497, p. 2167, § 74, operative July 1, 1983; Stats.1983, c. 346, § 1; Stats.1983, c. 1124, § 11, operative July 1, 1984; Stats.1991, c. 942 (A.B.628), § 11.)*

Law Revision Commission Comments

Section 1161a is amended to conform to the Enforcement of Judgments Law. See Sections 701.510–701.680 (sale under writ of execution),

716.020 (sale under writ of sale). The other changes are not substantive (15 Cal.L.Rev.Comm. Reports 2001).

Research References

Miller and Starr California Real Estate § 33:40, Secured Creditor Actions--Unlawful Detainer After Foreclosure.

Miller and Starr California Real Estate § 10:220, Possession and Rents After Trustee's Sale.

Miller and Starr California Real Estate § 11:101, Effect of Foreclosure on Rights of Tenants in Possession.

Miller and Starr California Real Estate § 19:188, Notice Required by Statute.

Miller and Starr California Real Estate § 19:218, Required Relationship of the Parties.

Miller and Starr California Real Estate § 19:220, Parties.

Miller and Starr California Real Estate § 19:223, Cross-Complaint; Affirmative Defenses.

Miller and Starr California Real Estate § 19:231, Trial; Judgment; Stay of Execution--Res Judicata Effect of an Unlawful Detainer Judgment.

Miller and Starr California Real Estate § 19:233, Tenant's Personal Property.

19 NO. 1 Miller & Starr, California Real Estate Newsalert 1, The Perata Foreclosure Bill (SB 1137): New Rights for Defaulting Borrowers and Tenants; New Complications for Foreclosing Lenders.

21 NO. 4 Miller & Starr, California Real Estate Newsalert 14, Landlord and Tenant.

2 Witkin Cal. Proc. 5th Courts § 370, (S 370) in General.

7 Witkin Cal. Proc. 5th Judgment § 431, (S 431) Unlawful Detainer.

5 Witkin Cal. Proc. 5th Pleading § 640, (S 640) Procedure.

5 Witkin Cal. Proc. 5th Pleading § 648, Action by Purchaser at Judicial Sale.

5 Witkin Cal. Proc. 5th Pleading § 1114, (S 1114) Action by Purchaser.

5 Witkin Cal. Proc. 5th Pleading § 1160, (S 1160) Pleading is Not Permitted.

6 Witkin Cal. Proc. 5th Provisional Remedies § 433, (S 433) Unlawful Detainer.

12 Witkin, California Summary 10th Real Property § 703, (S 703) Nature of Remedy.

12 Witkin, California Summary 10th Real Property § 730, Pleadings.

12 Witkin, California Summary 10th Real Property § 731, Restricted Access to Files.

4 Witkin, California Summary 10th Security Transactions in Real Property § 171, in General.

4 Witkin, California Summary 10th Security Transactions in Real Property § 172, (S 172) Validity of Sale.

4 Witkin, California Summary 10th Security Transactions in Real Property § 173, (S 173) Fraud in Acquisition of Title.

§ 1161b. Tenants in possession of rental housing units during foreclosure sale; notice to vacate; rights of possession; repeal

(a) Notwithstanding Section 1161a, a tenant or subtenant in possession of a rental housing unit under a month-to-month lease or periodic tenancy at the time the property is sold in foreclosure shall be given 90 days' written notice to quit pursuant to Section 1162 before the tenant or subtenant may be removed from the property as prescribed in this chapter.

(b) In addition to the rights set forth in subdivision (a), tenants or subtenants holding possession of a rental housing unit under a fixed-term residential lease entered into before transfer of title at the foreclosure sale shall have the right to possession until the end of the lease term, and all rights and obligations under the lease shall survive foreclosure, except that the tenancy may be terminated upon 90 days' written notice to quit pursuant to subdivision (a) if any of the following conditions apply:

(1) The purchaser or successor in interest will occupy the housing unit as a primary residence.

(2) The lessee is the mortgagor or the child, spouse, or parent of the mortgagor.

(3) The lease was not the result of an arms' length transaction.

(4) The lease requires the receipt of rent that is substantially less than fair market rent for the property, except when rent is

reduced or subsidized due to a federal, state, or local subsidy or law.

(c) The purchaser or successor in interest shall bear the burden of proof in establishing that a fixed-term residential lease is not entitled to protection under subdivision (b).

(d) This section shall not apply if any party to the note remains in the property as a tenant, subtenant, or occupant.

(e) Nothing in this section is intended to affect any local just cause eviction ordinance. This section does not, and shall not be construed to, affect the authority of a public entity that otherwise exists to regulate or monitor the basis for eviction.

(f) This section shall remain in effect only until December 31, 2019, and as of that date is repealed, unless a later enacted statute, that is enacted before December 31, 2019, deletes or extends that date. *(Added by Stats.2008, c. 69 (S.B.1137), § 6, eff. July 8, 2008. Amended by Stats.2012, c. 562 (A.B.2610), § 3.)*

Repeal

For repeal of this section, see its terms.

Research References

Miller and Starr California Real Estate § 10:220, Possession and Rents After Trustee's Sale.

Miller and Starr California Real Estate § 10:230, Possession and Rents During the Redemption Period.

Miller and Starr California Real Estate § 11:101, Effect of Foreclosure on Rights of Tenants in Possession.

Miller and Starr California Real Estate § 19:218, Required Relationship of the Parties.

Miller and Starr California Real Estate § 19:59.10, Termination of Residential Tenancy Following Foreclosure of Landlord's Interest.

19 NO. 1 Miller & Starr, California Real Estate Newsalert 1, The Perata Foreclosure Bill (SB 1137): New Rights for Defaulting Borrowers and Tenants; New Complications for Foreclosing Lenders.

19 NO. 4 Miller & Starr, California Real Estate Newsalert 10, Deeds of Trust.

§ 1161c. Cover sheet; form

(a) In the case of any foreclosure on a residential property, the immediate successor in interest in the property pursuant to the foreclosure shall attach a cover sheet, in the form as set forth in subdivision (b), to any notice of termination of tenancy served on a tenant of that property within the first year after the foreclosure sale. This notice shall not be required if any of the following apply:

(1) The tenancy is terminated pursuant to Section 1161.

(2) The successor in interest and the tenant have executed a written rental agreement or lease or a written acknowledgment of a preexisting rental agreement or lease.

(3) The tenant receiving the notice was not a tenant at the time of the foreclosure.

(b) The cover sheet shall consist of the following notice, in at least 12–point type:

Notice to Any Renters Living At

[street address of the unit]

The attached notice means that your home was recently sold in foreclosure and the new owner plans to evict you.

You should talk to a lawyer NOW to see what your rights are. You may receive court papers in a few days. If your name is on the papers it may hurt your credit if you do not respond and simply move out.

Also, if you do not respond within five days of receiving the papers, even if you are not named in the papers, you will likely lose any rights you may have. In some cases, you can respond without hurting your credit. You should ask a lawyer about it.

You may have the right to stay in your home for 90 days or longer, regardless of any deadlines stated on any attached papers. In some cases and in some cities with a "just cause for eviction law," you may not have to move at all. But you must take the proper legal steps in order to protect your rights.

How to Get Legal Help

If you cannot afford an attorney, you may be eligible for free legal services from a nonprofit legal services program. You can locate these nonprofit groups at the California Legal Services Internet Web site (www.lawhelpca.org), the California Courts Online Self–Help Center (www.courtinfo.ca.gov/selfhelp), or by contacting your local court or county bar association.

(c) If the notice to quit specifies an effective date of at least 90 days after the notice is served, without qualification, no cover sheet shall be required, provided that the notice incorporates the text of the cover sheet, as set forth in subdivision (b) in at least 10–point type. The incorporated text shall omit the caption and the first paragraph of the cover sheet and the fourth paragraph of the cover sheet shall be replaced by the following language:

You may have the right to stay in your home for longer than 90 days. If you have a lease that ends more than 90 days from now, the new owner must honor the lease under many circumstances. Also, in some cases and in some cities with a "just cause for eviction law," you may not have to move at all. But you must take the proper legal steps in order to protect your rights.

(d) This section shall remain in effect only until December 31, 2019, and as of that date is repealed, unless a later enacted statute, that is enacted before December 31, 2019, deletes or extends that date. *(Added by Stats.2010, c. 641 (S.B.1149), § 2. Amended by Stats.2012, c. 210 (S.B.825), § 1.)*

Repeal

For repeal of this section, see its terms.

Research References

Miller and Starr California Real Estate § 19:188, Notice Required by Statute.

21 NO. 4 Miller & Starr, California Real Estate Newsalert 14, Landlord and Tenant.

12 Witkin, California Summary 10th Real Property § 680, Periodic Tenancy.

4 Witkin, California Summary 10th Security Transactions in Real Property § 171, in General.

§ 1162. Notice; methods of service; service upon commercial tenants

(a) Except as provided in subdivision (b), the notices required by Sections 1161 and 1161a may be served by any of the following methods:

(1) By delivering a copy to the tenant personally.

(2) If he or she is absent from his or her place of residence, and from his or her usual place of business, by leaving a copy with some person of suitable age and discretion at either place, and sending a copy through the mail addressed to the tenant at his or her place of residence.

(3) If such place of residence and business cannot be ascertained, or a person of suitable age or discretion there can not be found, then by affixing a copy in a conspicuous place on the property, and also delivering a copy to a person there residing, if

such person can be found; and also sending a copy through the mail addressed to the tenant at the place where the property is situated. Service upon a subtenant may be made in the same manner.

(b) The notices required by Section 1161 may be served upon a commercial tenant by any of the following methods:

(1) By delivering a copy to the tenant personally.

(2) If he or she is absent from the commercial rental property, by leaving a copy with some person of suitable age and discretion at the property, and sending a copy through the mail addressed to the tenant at the address where the property is situated.

(3) If, at the time of attempted service, a person of suitable age or discretion is not found at the rental property through the exercise of reasonable diligence, then by affixing a copy in a conspicuous place on the property, and also sending a copy through the mail addressed to the tenant at the address where the property is situated. Service upon a subtenant may be made in the same manner.

(c) For purposes of subdivision (b), "commercial tenant" means a person or entity that hires any real property in this state that is not a dwelling unit, as defined in subdivision (c) of Section 1940 of the Civil Code, or a mobilehome, as defined in Section 798.3 of the Civil Code. *(Enacted in 1872. Amended by Code Am.1873–74, c. 383, p. 347, § 148; Stats.1935, c. 52, p. 386, § 5; Stats.2002, c. 664 (A.B.3034), § 49.5; Stats.2010, c. 144 (A.B. 1263), § 1.)*

Research References

California Real Estate Forms (Miller & Starr) § 2:16, Office Lease--Multistory Office Building.

California Real Estate Forms (Miller & Starr) § 2:17, Office Lease--Mixed Use Building.

California Real Estate Forms (Miller & Starr) § 2:18, Office Lease--Office/Warehouse Building With Four or Fewer Tenants.

California Real Estate Forms (Miller & Starr) § 2:19, Retail Lease--Power Shopping Center.

California Real Estate Forms (Miller & Starr) § 2:20, Retail Lease--Shopping Center With for Profit Parking Garage.

California Real Estate Forms (Miller & Starr) § 2:21;, Retail Lease--15,000 RSF to 30,000 RSF (Tenant Oriented).

California Real Estate Forms (Miller & Starr) § 2:22, Retail Lease--Regional Shopping Center.

California Real Estate Forms (Miller & Starr) § 2:23, Retail Lease--Small Strip-Shopping Center.

California Real Estate Forms (Miller & Starr) § 2:24, Retail Lease--Restaurant.

California Real Estate Forms (Miller & Starr) § 2:25, Industrial Lease.

California Real Estate Forms (Miller & Starr) § 2:26, Triple Net Lease--Industrial Build-To-Suit Lease.

California Real Estate Forms (Miller & Starr) § 2:27, Ground Lease.

California Real Estate Forms (Miller & Starr) § 2:28, Triple Net Lease--Stand-Alone Building.

California Real Estate Forms (Miller & Starr) § 2:29, Parking Garage Lease.

California Real Estate Forms (Miller & Starr) § 2:30, Storage Lease--Office Building.

California Real Estate Forms (Miller & Starr) § 2:31, Rental Agreement--Self Storage.

California Real Estate Forms (Miller & Starr) § 2:32, Gross Lease--Small Commercial Property.

California Real Estate Forms (Miller & Starr) § 2:33, Sublease-- With Consent of Master Landlord.

California Real Estate Forms (Miller & Starr) § 2:34, Sublease--Shared Office Space.

California Real Estate Forms (Miller & Starr) § 2:18.50, Management Office License Agreement.

Rutter, Cal. Practice Guide: Landlord-Tenant Form 2:A, Residential Rental Agreement.

Miller and Starr California Real Estate § 19:7, Other Interests Distinguished--Eviction of a Guest or Lodger.

Miller and Starr California Real Estate § 19:55, Requirements for Modification of Lease Terms.

Miller and Starr California Real Estate § 19:82, Modification of the Rent.

Miller and Starr California Real Estate § 31:32, Termination of Tenancies--Mobilehomes.

Miller and Starr California Real Estate § 10:220, Possession and Rents After Trustee's Sale.

Miller and Starr California Real Estate § 10:230, Possession and Rents During the Redemption Period.

Miller and Starr California Real Estate § 19:192, Timing and Service of a Notice of Termination.

Miller and Starr California Real Estate § 19:201, Landlord's Alternative Remedies for Tenant's Breach; When Notice is Required.

Miller and Starr California Real Estate § 19:204, Service of the Notice.

Miller and Starr California Real Estate § 19:217, Restrictions on Access and Reporting of Unlawful Detainer Actions.

Miller and Starr California Real Estate § 19:220, Parties.

19 NO. 1 Miller & Starr, California Real Estate Newsalert 1, The Perata Foreclosure Bill (SB 1137): New Rights for Defaulting Borrowers and Tenants; New Complications for Foreclosing Lenders.

21 NO. 4 Miller & Starr, California Real Estate Newsalert 14, Landlord and Tenant.

12 Witkin, California Summary 10th Real Property § 514, Statutory Rights of Lodger.

12 Witkin, California Summary 10th Real Property § 526, (S 526) Changes in Short-Term Leases.

12 Witkin, California Summary 10th Real Property § 668, Construction of Forfeiture Clause.

12 Witkin, California Summary 10th Real Property § 679, Tenancy at Will.

12 Witkin, California Summary 10th Real Property § 680, Periodic Tenancy.

12 Witkin, California Summary 10th Real Property § 695, Proof of Abandonment.

12 Witkin, California Summary 10th Real Property § 727, (S 727) Methods of Service.

12 Witkin, California Summary 10th Real Property § 759, Where Landlord Has Lien.

12 Witkin, California Summary 10th Real Property § 785, (S 785) Notice of Termination.

§ 1162a. Receiver's or levying officer's deed; exhibition; service of copy

In any case in which service or exhibition of a receiver's or levying officer's deed is required, in lieu thereof service of a copy or copies of the deed may be made as provided in Section 1162. *(Added by Stats.1939, c. 519, p. 1905, § 1. Amended by Stats.1982, c. 497, p. 2167, § 75, operative July 1, 1983.)*

Law Revision Commission Comments

Section 1162a is amended to conform to the Enforcement of Judgments Law. See Sections 701.660 (deed of sale of real property), 712.060 (receiver to enforce judgment for sale of real property), 716.020 (sale under writ of sale) (15 Cal.L.Rev.Comm. Reports 2001).

§ 1164. Necessary parties defendant; joinder; judgment; subtenants after notice to tenant; persons bound by judgment

No person other than the tenant of the premises and subtenant, if there be one, in the actual occupation of the premises when the complaint is filed, need be made parties defendant in the proceeding, nor shall any proceeding abate, nor the plaintiff be nonsuited for the nonjoinder of any person who might have been made party defendant, but when it appears that any of the parties served with process, or appearing in the proceeding, are guilty of the offense charged, judgment must be rendered against him or her. In case a defendant has become a subtenant of the premises in controversy, after the service of the notice provided for by subdivision 2 of Section 1161 of this code, upon the tenant of the premises, the fact that such notice was not served on each subtenant shall constitute no defense to the action. All persons who enter the premises under the tenant, after the commencement of the suit, shall be bound by the judgment, the same as if he or they had been made party to the action. *(Enacted in 1872. Amended by Code Am.1873–74, c. 383, p. 348, § 149; Stats.1885, c. 139, p. 129, § 1; Stats.1975, c. 1241, p. 3191, § 8.)*

Research References

Rutter, Cal. Practice Guide: Enforcing Judgments/Debts Ch. 6I-3, Enforcement of Judgment for Possession of Real Property.
Miller and Starr California Real Estate § 19:220, Parties.
8 Witkin Cal. Proc. 5th Enforcement of Judgment § 336, (S 336) Failure to Vacate Property.
12 Witkin, California Summary 10th Real Property § 721, (S 721) Where No Notice is Necessary.
12 Witkin, California Summary 10th Real Property § 729, Parties.

§ 1165. Parties; sections applicable

PARTIES GENERALLY. Except as provided in the preceding section, the provisions of Part II of this Code,[1] relating to parties to civil actions, are applicable to this proceeding. *(Enacted in 1872.)*

[1] Sections 307 to 1062a.

Research References

Miller and Starr California Real Estate § 19:220, Parties.
12 Witkin, California Summary 10th Real Property § 729, Parties.

§ 1166. Complaint; verification; allegations; caption; attachments to complaint; summons

(a) The complaint shall:

(1) Be verified and include the typed or printed name of the person verifying the complaint.

(2) Set forth the facts on which the plaintiff seeks to recover.

(3) Describe the premises with reasonable certainty.

(4) If the action is based on paragraph (2) of Section 1161, state the amount of rent in default.

(5) State specifically the method used to serve the defendant with the notice or notices of termination upon which the complaint is based. This requirement may be satisfied by using and completing all items relating to service of the notice or notices in an appropriate Judicial Council form complaint, or by attaching a proof of service of the notice or notices of termination served on the defendant.

(b) The complaint may set forth any circumstances of fraud, force, or violence that may have accompanied the alleged forcible entry or forcible or unlawful detainer, and claim damages therefor.

(c) In an action regarding residential real property based on Section 1161a, the plaintiff shall state in the caption of the complaint "Action based on Code of Civil Procedure Section 1161a."

(d)(1) In an action regarding residential property, the plaintiff shall attach to the complaint the following:

(A) A copy of the notice or notices of termination served on the defendant upon which the complaint is based.

(B) A copy of any written lease or rental agreement regarding the premises. Any addenda or attachments to the lease or written agreement that form the basis of the complaint shall also be attached. The documents required by this subparagraph are not required to be attached if the complaint alleges any of the following:

(i) The lease or rental agreement is oral.

(ii) A written lease or rental agreement regarding the premises is not in the possession of the landlord or any agent or employee of the landlord.

(iii) An action based solely on subdivision (2) of Section 1161.

(2) If the plaintiff fails to attach the documents required by this subdivision, the court shall grant leave to amend the complaint for a five-day period in order to include the required attachments.

(e) Upon filing the complaint, a summons shall be issued thereon. *(Added by Stats.2003, c. 787 (S.B.345), § 4, operative Jan. 1, 2005. Amended by Stats.2010, c. 641 (S.B.1149), § 3.)*

Research References

Rutter, Cal. Practice Guide: Civ. Pro. Before Trial Ch. 6-B, B. Complaints.
Miller and Starr California Real Estate § 11:150, Actions in Which a Lis Pendens May or Must be Recorded.
Miller and Starr California Real Estate § 19:166, Jurisdiction, Venue, Summons and Complaint.
Miller and Starr California Real Estate § 19:188, Notice Required by Statute.
Miller and Starr California Real Estate § 19:221, Complaint and Summons.
14 NO. 4 Miller & Starr, California Real Estate Newsalert 10, Landlord and Tenant.
21 NO. 4 Miller & Starr, California Real Estate Newsalert 14, Landlord and Tenant.
4 Witkin Cal. Proc. 5th Pleading § 466, Complaint or Petition.
4 Witkin Cal. Proc. 5th Pleading § 471, Superior Court.
5 Witkin Cal. Proc. 5th Pleading § 641, (S 641) Relationship and Possession.
5 Witkin Cal. Proc. 5th Pleading § 642, in General.
5 Witkin Cal. Proc. 5th Pleading § 644, Lessee's Default or Breach.
5 Witkin Cal. Proc. 5th Pleading § 645, (S 645) Damages.
5 Witkin Cal. Proc. 5th Pleading § 648, Action by Purchaser at Judicial Sale.
5 Witkin Cal. Proc. 5th Pleading § 649, in General.
5 Witkin Cal. Proc. 5th Pleading § 652, Defendant's Withholding and Damage.
5 Witkin Cal. Proc. 5th Pleading § 653, (S 653) Recovery of Possession: Forcible Detainer.
12 Witkin, California Summary 10th Real Property § 730, Pleadings.

§ 1166a. Writ of possession; issuance and directions; grounds; undertaking; findings; order for immediate possession

(a) Upon filing the complaint, the plaintiff may, upon motion, have immediate possession of the premises by a writ of possession of a manufactured home, mobilehome, or real property issued by the court and directed to the sheriff of the county or marshal, for execution, where it appears to the satisfaction of the court, after a hearing on the motion, from the verified complaint and from any affidavits filed or oral testimony given by or on behalf of the parties, that the defendant resides out of state, has departed from the state, cannot, after due diligence, be found within the state, or has concealed himself or herself to avoid the service of summons. The motion shall indicate that the writ applies to all tenants, subtenants, if any, named claimants, if any, and any other occupants of the premises.

(b) Written notice of the hearing on the motion shall be served on the defendant by the plaintiff in accordance with the provisions of Section 1011, and shall inform the defendant as follows: "You may file affidavits on your own behalf with the court and may appear and present testimony on your own behalf.

However, if you fail to appear, the plaintiff will apply to the court for a writ of possession of a manufactured home, mobilehome, or real property."

(c) The plaintiff shall file an undertaking in a sum that shall be fixed and determined by the judge, to the effect that, if the plaintiff fails to recover judgment against the defendant for the possession of the premises or if the suit is dismissed, the plaintiff will pay to the defendant those damages, not to exceed the amount fixed in the undertaking, as may be sustained by the defendant by reason of that dispossession under the writ of possession of a manufactured home, mobilehome, or real property.

(d) If, at the hearing on the motion, the findings of the court are in favor of the plaintiff and against the defendant, an order shall be entered for the immediate possession of the premises.

(e) The order for the immediate possession of the premises may be enforced as provided in Division 3 (commencing with Section 712.010) of Title 9 of Part 2.

(f) For the purposes of this section, references in Division 3 (commencing with Section 712.010) of Title 9 of Part 2 and in subdivisions (e) to (m), inclusive, of Section 1174, to the "judgment debtor" shall be deemed references to the defendant, to the "judgment creditor" shall be deemed references to the plaintiff, and to the "judgment of possession or sale of property" shall be deemed references to an order for the immediate possession of the premises. *(Added by Stats.1939, c. 751, p. 2282, § 2. Amended by Stats.1941, c. 1095, § 1; Stats.1949, c. 372, p. 653, § 1; Stats.1951, c. 1737, p. 4140, § 157, operative Jan. 1, 1952; Stats.1969, c. 903, p. 1809, § 1; Stats.1970, c. 1165, p. 2070, § 1; Stats.1982, c. 517, p. 2361, § 178; Stats.1982, c. 497, p. 2167, § 75.5, operative July 1, 1983; Stats.1983, c. 18, § 20, eff. April 21, 1983, operative July 1, 1983; Stats.1983, c. 1124, § 12, operative July 1, 1984; Stats.1990, c. 1535 (S.B.2508), § 2; Stats.1996, c. 872 (A.B.3472), § 20.)*

Law Revision Commission Comments

Section 1166a is amended for consistency with the Bond and Undertaking Law. See Sections 995.910 (objections to undertakings) and 996.410 (enforcement of liability on undertaking). [16 Cal.L.Rev.Comm. Reports 2239 (1982)].

Research References

Rutter, Cal. Practice Guide: Civil Appeals & Writs Ch. 15-A, A. Overview.
Miller and Starr California Real Estate § 10:230, Possession and Rents During the Redemption Period.
Miller and Starr California Real Estate § 19:226, Cross-Complaint; Affirmative Defenses--Action by Petroleum Distributor.
Miller and Starr California Real Estate § 19:228, Prejudgment Remedies; Attachment and Receivership--Writ of Possession Before Trial.
5 Witkin Cal. Proc. 5th Pleading § 646, (S 646) Facts Justifying Immediate Possession.
12 Witkin, California Summary 10th Real Property § 718, (S 718) Distinction: Termination of Gasoline Dealer's Lease.
12 Witkin, California Summary 10th Real Property § 732, (S 732) Immediate Possession.

§ 1167. Summons; form; issuance; service and return

The summons shall be in the form specified in Section 412.20 except that when the defendant is served, the defendant's response shall be filed within five days, including Saturdays and Sundays but excluding all other judicial holidays, after the complaint is served upon him or her. If the last day for filing the response falls on a Saturday or Sunday, the response period shall be extended to and including the next court day.

In all other respects the summons shall be issued and served and returned in the same manner as a summons in a civil action. *(Enacted in 1872. Amended by Code Am.1873–74, c. 383, p. 349, § 151; Code Am.1880, c. 20, p. 8, § 3; Stats.1905, c. 357, p. 428,*

§ 1; Stats.1907, c. 257, p. 323, § 2; Stats.1969, c. 1611, p. 3396, § 25, operative July 1, 1970; Stats.1971, c. 849, p. 1683, § 1; Stats.1971, c. 1127, p. 2141, § 1; Stats.1989, c. 873, § 1.)

Research References

Rutter, Cal. Practice Guide: Civ. Pro. Before Trial Ch. 4-C, C. Content of Summons.
Rutter, Cal. Practice Guide: Civ. Pro. Before Trial Ch. 5-B, B. Entry of Default.
Rutter, Cal. Practice Guide: Civ. Pro. Before Trial Ch. 6-C, C. Answer.
Miller and Starr California Real Estate § 19:166, Jurisdiction, Venue, Summons and Complaint.
Miller and Starr California Real Estate § 19:218, Required Relationship of the Parties.
Miller and Starr California Real Estate § 19:221, Complaint and Summons.
3 Witkin Cal. Proc. 5th Actions § 985, (S 985) Special Statutes.
3 Witkin Cal. Proc. 5th Actions § 987, (S 987) Actions Involving Real Property.
2 Witkin Cal. Proc. 5th Jurisdiction § 31, (S 31) Insufficiency of Allegations.
12 Witkin, California Summary 10th Real Property § 730, Pleadings.

§ 1167.3. Answer or amendment; time allowed

In any action under this chapter, unless otherwise ordered by the court for good cause shown, the time allowed the defendant to answer the complaint, answer the complaint, if amended, or amend the answer under paragraph (2), (3), (5), (6), or (7) of subdivision (a) of Section 586 shall not exceed five days. *(Added by Stats.1971, c. 849, p. 1684, § 2.5. Amended by Stats.1974, c. 430, p. 1041, § 1; Stats.1984, c. 572, § 3; Stats.1999, c. 83 (S.B.966), § 25; Stats.1999, c. 344 (S.B.210), § 19, eff. Sept. 7, 1999.)*

Law Revision Commission Comments

Section 1167.3 is amended to correct cross-references. [29 Cal.L.Rev. Comm. Reports App. 5 (1999)].

Research References

Rutter, Cal. Practice Guide: Civ. Pro. Before Trial Ch. 5-B, B. Entry of Default.
Rutter, Cal. Practice Guide: Civ. Pro. Before Trial Ch. 6-C, C. Answer.
Rutter, Cal. Practice Guide: Civ. Pro. Before Trial Ch. 6-E, E. Amended and Supplemental Pleadings.
Miller and Starr California Real Estate § 19:221, Complaint and Summons.
Miller and Starr California Real Estate § 19:222, Complaint and Summons--Service of the Summons and Complaint; Claim to Right of Possession.
3 Witkin Cal. Proc. 5th Actions § 985, (S 985) Special Statutes.
3 Witkin Cal. Proc. 5th Actions § 987, (S 987) Actions Involving Real Property.
12 Witkin, California Summary 10th Real Property § 730, Pleadings.

§ 1167.4. Motion to quash service or stay or dismiss action; time

Notwithstanding any other provision of law, in any action under this chapter:

(a) Where the defendant files a notice of motion as provided for in subdivision (a) of Section 418.10, the time for making the motion shall be not less than three days nor more than seven days after the filing of the notice.

(b) The service and filing of a notice of motion under subdivision (a) shall extend the defendant's time to plead until five days after service upon him of the written notice of entry of an order denying his motion, except that for good cause shown the court may extend the defendant's time to plead for an additional period not exceeding 15 days. *(Added by Stats.1971, c. 1332, p. 2634, § 1.)*

Research References

Rutter, Cal. Practice Guide: Civ. Pro. Before Trial Ch. 3-B, B. Jurisdiction Over Parties-Personal Jurisdiction.

Miller and Starr California Real Estate § 19:223, Cross-Complaint; Affirmative Defenses.

2 Witkin Cal. Proc. 5th Jurisdiction § 218, (S 218) Time and Form.

2 Witkin Cal. Proc. 5th Jurisdiction § 225, (S 225) Extension of Time to Plead.

12 Witkin, California Summary 10th Real Property § 730, Pleadings.

§ 1167.5. Extension of time; consent of adverse party

Unless otherwise ordered by the court for good cause shown, no extension of time allowed in any action under this chapter for the causes specified in Section 1054 shall exceed 10 days without the consent of the adverse party. *(Added by Stats.1971, c. 849, p. 1684, § 3.)*

Research References

Miller and Starr California Real Estate § 19:222, Complaint and Summons--Service of the Summons and Complaint; Claim to Right of Possession.

4 Witkin Cal. Proc. 5th Pleading § 10, Extension to Ordinary Party.

12 Witkin, California Summary 10th Real Property § 730, Pleadings.

§ 1169. Entry of default; application for relief

If, at the time appointed, any defendant served with a summons does not appear and defend, the clerk, upon written application of the plaintiff and proof of the service of summons and complaint, shall enter the default of any defendant so served, and, if requested by the plaintiff, immediately shall enter judgment for restitution of the premises and shall issue a writ of execution thereon. The application for default judgment and the default judgment shall include a place to indicate that the judgment includes tenants, subtenants, if any, named claimants, if any, and any other occupants of the premises. Thereafter, the plaintiff may apply to the court for any other relief demanded in the complaint, including the costs, against the defendant, or defendants, or against one or more of the defendants. *(Enacted in 1872. Amended by Stats.1933, c. 745, p. 1906, § 10; Stats. 1951, c. 1737, p. 4140, § 159, operative Jan. 1, 1952; Stats.1982, c. 1620, p. 6482, § 1; Stats.1986, c. 953, § 5; Stats.1987, c. 768, § 1; Stats.1990, c. 1535 (S.B.2508), § 2.6; Stats.1991, c. 57 (S.B.323), § 5, eff. June 17, 1991; Stats.2007, c. 263 (A.B.310), § 13.)*

Law Revision Commission Comments

Section 1169 is amended to delete unnecessary language authorizing the judge to substitute for the clerk if there is no clerk. See Code Civ. Proc. § 167 (judge may perform any act court clerk may perform); Gov't Code §§ 69840–69848 (duties of clerk of superior court), 71620(b) (executive or administrative officer has authority of clerk of court). [35 Cal.L.Rev. Comm. Reports 219 (2006)].

Research References

Rutter, Cal. Practice Guide: Civ. Pro. Before Trial Ch. 5-C, C. Default Judgment by Clerk.

Rutter, Cal. Practice Guide: Enforcing Judgments/Debts Ch. 6I-3, Enforcement of Judgment for Possession of Real Property.

Miller and Starr California Real Estate § 19:222, Complaint and Summons--Service of the Summons and Complaint; Claim to Right of Possession.

Miller and Starr California Real Estate § 19:228, Prejudgment Remedies; Attachment and Receivership--Writ of Possession Before Trial.

Miller and Starr California Real Estate § 19:229, Trial Setting and Hearing Preference; Discovery.

6 Witkin Cal. Proc. 5th Proceedings Without Trial § 137, (S 137) Restrictions on Default Judgments.

6 Witkin Cal. Proc. 5th Proceedings Without Trial § 165, When Clerk May Act.

12 Witkin, California Summary 10th Real Property § 735, (S 735) Judgment by Default and Summary Judgment.

§ 1170. Appearance; answer or demurrer

DEFENDANT MAY APPEAR, ETC. On or before the day fixed for his appearance, the defendant may appear and answer or demur. *(Enacted in 1872.)*

Research References

Rutter, Cal. Practice Guide: Civ. Pro. Before Trial Ch. 7(I)-A, A. Demurrers.

Miller and Starr California Real Estate § 19:222, Complaint and Summons--Service of the Summons and Complaint; Claim to Right of Possession.

Miller and Starr California Real Estate § 19:223, Cross-Complaint; Affirmative Defenses.

12 Witkin, California Summary 10th Real Property § 730, Pleadings.

§ 1170.5. Time of trial; extension; trial not within time; order of payment; amount of damages

(a) If the defendant appears pursuant to Section 1170, trial of the proceeding shall be held not later than the 20th day following the date that the request to set the time of the trial is made. Judgment shall be entered thereon and, if the plaintiff prevails, a writ of execution shall be issued immediately by the court upon the request of the plaintiff.

(b) The court may extend the period for trial upon the agreement of all of the parties. No other extension of the time for trial of an action under this chapter may be granted unless the court, upon its own motion or on motion of any party, holds a hearing and renders a decision thereon as specified in subdivision (c).

(c) If trial is not held within the time specified in this section, the court, upon finding that there is a reasonable probability that the plaintiff will prevail in the action, shall determine the amount of damages, if any, to be suffered by the plaintiff by reason of the extension, and shall issue an order requiring the defendant to pay that amount into court as the rent would have otherwise become due and payable or into an escrow designated by the court for so long as the defendant remains in possession pending the termination of the action.

The determination of the amount of the payment shall be based on the plaintiff's verified statement of the contract rent for rental payment, any verified objection thereto filed by the defendant, and the oral or demonstrative evidence presented at the hearing. The court's determination of the amount of damages shall include consideration of any evidence, presented by the parties, embracing the issue of diminution of value or any set off permitted by law.

(d) If the defendant fails to make a payment ordered by the court, trial of the action shall be held within 15 days of the date payment was due.

(e) Any cost for administration of an escrow account pursuant to this section shall be recoverable by the prevailing party as part of any recoverable cost in the action.

(f) After trial of the action, the court shall determine the distribution of the payment made into court or the escrow designated by the court.

(g) Where payments into court or the escrow designated by the court are made pursuant to this section, the court may order that the payments be invested in an insured interest-bearing account. Interest on the account shall be allocated to the parties in the same proportions as the original funds are allocated.

(h) If any provision of this section or the application thereof to any person or circumstances is held invalid, such invalidity shall not affect other provisions or applications of the section which can be given effect without the invalid provision or application, and to this end the provisions of this section are severable.

(i) Nothing in this section shall be construed to abrogate or interfere with the precedence given to the trial of criminal cases over the trial of civil matters by Section 1050 of the Penal Code. *(Added by Stats.1982, c. 1620, p. 6483, § 2.)*

Research References

Rutter, Cal. Practice Guide: Civ. Pro. Before Trial Ch. 12(I)-C, C. Claims for Trial Setting Preference.
Rutter, Cal. Practice Guide: Enforcing Judgments/Debts Ch. 6I-1, Writ of Possession or Sale.
Miller and Starr California Real Estate § 19:229, Trial Setting and Hearing Preference; Discovery.
6 Witkin Cal. Proc. 5th Proceedings Without Trial § 204, Actions for Unlawful Detainer and Forcible Entry.
12 Witkin, California Summary 10th Real Property § 734, Illustrations.
12 Witkin, California Summary 10th Real Property § 736, Trial.

§ 1170.7. Summary judgment; motion; grant or denial

A motion for summary judgment may be made at any time after the answer is filed upon giving five days notice. Summary judgment shall be granted or denied on the same basis as a motion under Section 437c. *(Added by Stats.1982, c. 1620, p. 6484, § 3.)*

Research References

Rutter, Cal. Practice Guide: Civ. Pro. Before Trial Ch. 10-C, C. Procedural Requirements-Moving Party.
Miller and Starr California Real Estate § 19:229, Trial Setting and Hearing Preference; Discovery.
6 Witkin Cal. Proc. 5th Proceedings Without Trial § 204, Actions for Unlawful Detainer and Forcible Entry.
12 Witkin, California Summary 10th Real Property § 735, (S 735) Judgment by Default and Summary Judgment.

§ 1170.8. Discovery; motion

In any action under this chapter, a discovery motion may be made at any time upon giving five days' notice. *(Added by Stats.2007, c. 113 (A.B.1126), § 1.)*

Law Revision Commission Comments

Section 1170.8 is new. The section provides for an expedited hearing on a discovery motion in a forcible entry or forcible or unlawful detainer case, consistent with the precedence for such cases expressed in Section 1179a. The section is modeled on Section 1170.7 (five days notice required for summary judgment motion in action under this chapter). [36 Cal.L.Rev. Comm. Reports 271 (2006)].

Research References

12 Witkin, California Summary 10th Real Property § 736, Trial.

§ 1170.9. Time for filing opposition and reply papers

The Judicial Council shall adopt rules, not inconsistent with statute, prescribing the time for filing and serving opposition and reply papers, if any, relating to a motion under Section 1167.4, 1170.7, or 1170.8. *(Added by Stats.2007, c. 113 (A.B.1126), § 2.)*

Law Revision Commission Comments

Section 1170.9 is new. To prevent confusion and disputes, it directs the Judicial Council to establish briefing schedules for a motion to quash, summary judgment motion, and discovery motion in a summary proceeding for possession of real property. For general guidance on means of service, including service by overnight delivery, see Sections 1010–1020; see also Cal. R. Ct. 2.200–2.306. [36 Cal.L.Rev.Comm. Reports 271 (2006)].

§ 1171. Jury trial

Whenever an issue of fact is presented by the pleadings, it must be tried by a jury, unless such jury be waived as in other cases. The jury shall be formed in the same manner as other

trial juries in an action of the same jurisdictional classification in the Court in which the action is pending. *(Enacted in 1872. Amended by Code Am.1873–74, c. 383, p. 349, § 152; Code Am.1880, c. 20, p. 9, § 5; Stats.1998, c. 931 (S.B.2139), § 120, eff. Sept. 28, 1998.)*

Law Revision Commission Comments

Section 1171 is amended to accommodate unification of the municipal and superior courts in a county. Cal. Const. art. VI, § 5(e). See Sections 32.5 (jurisdictional classification), 85 (limited civil cases) & Comment. [28 Cal.L.Rev.Comm. Reports 51 (1998)].

Research References

Rutter, Cal. Practice Guide: Civ. Pro. Before Trial Ch. 12(I)-D, D. Demand for Jury Trial and Waiver.
Rutter, Cal. Practice Guide: Civil Trials & Evidence Ch. 2-C, C. Cases in Which Jury Trial May be Demanded.
Miller and Starr California Real Estate § 19:230, Trial; Judgment; Stay of Execution.
2 Witkin Cal. Proc. 5th Courts § 318, No Right to Jury Trial.
7 Witkin Cal. Proc. 5th Trial § 86, (S 86) Legal Issues Severable.
12 Witkin, California Summary 10th Real Property § 736, Trial.

§ 1172. Prima facie case; defense

SHOWING REQUIRED OF PLAINTIFF IN FORCIBLE ENTRY OR DETAINER. On the trial of any proceeding for any forcible entry or forcible detainer, the plaintiff shall only be required to show, in addition to the forcible entry or forcible detainer complained of, that he was peaceably in the actual possession at the time of the forcible entry, or was entitled to the possession at the time of the forcible detainer. The defendant may show in his defense that he or his ancestors, or those whose interest in such premises he claims, have been in the quiet possession thereof for the space of one whole year together next before the commencement of the proceedings, and that his interest therein is not then ended or determined; and such showing is a bar to the proceedings. *(Enacted in 1872.)*

Research References

Miller and Starr California Real Estate § 19:162, Elements of the Offense--Forcible Entry.
Miller and Starr California Real Estate § 19:163, Elements of the Offense--Forcible Detainer.
Miller and Starr California Real Estate § 19:167, Defenses.
Miller and Starr California Real Estate § 19:174, Remedies for Wrongful Eviction.
5 Witkin Cal. Proc. 5th Pleading § 653, (S 653) Recovery of Possession: Forcible Detainer.

§ 1173. Amendment of complaint to conform to proof; terms; continuance

When, upon the trial of any proceeding under this chapter, it appears from the evidence that the defendant has been guilty of either a forcible entry or a forcible or unlawful detainer, and other than the offense charged in the complaint, the Judge must order that such complaint be forthwith amended to conform to such proofs; such amendment must be made without any imposition of terms. No continuance shall be permitted upon account of such amendment unless the defendant, by affidavit filed, shows to the satisfaction of the Court good cause therefor. *(Enacted in 1872. Amended by Stats.1885, c. 121, p. 102, § 1.)*

Research References

Miller and Starr California Real Estate § 19:166, Jurisdiction, Venue, Summons and Complaint.
5 Witkin Cal. Proc. 5th Pleading § 1211, (S 1211) Liberal Allowance of Amendment.

7 Witkin Cal. Proc. 5th Trial § 31, (S 31) Particular Actions and Proceedings.

§ 1174. Judgment for possession of premises; forfeiture of lease or agreement; rental payments; damages; enforcement; personal property; notice; storage; release; disposal; liability

(a) If upon the trial, the verdict of the jury, or, if the case be tried without a jury, the findings of the court be in favor of the plaintiff and against the defendant, judgment shall be entered for the possession of the premises; and if the proceedings be for an unlawful detainer after neglect, or failure to perform the conditions or covenants of the lease or agreement under which the property is held, or after default in the payment of rent, the judgment shall also declare the forfeiture of that lease or agreement if the notice required by Section 1161 states the election of the landlord to declare the forfeiture thereof, but if that notice does not so state that election, the lease or agreement shall not be forfeited.

Except as provided in Section 1166a, in any action for unlawful detainer brought by a petroleum distributor against a gasoline dealer, possession shall not be restored to the petroleum distributor unless the court in the unlawful detainer action determines that the petroleum distributor had good cause under Section 20999.1 of the Business and Professions Code to terminate, cancel, or refuse to renew the franchise of the gasoline dealer.

In any action for unlawful detainer brought by a petroleum distributor against the gasoline dealer, the court may, at the time of request of either party, require the tenant to make rental payments into the court, for the lessor, at the contract rate, pending the resolution of the action.

(b) The jury or the court, if the proceedings be tried without a jury, shall also assess the damages occasioned to the plaintiff by any forcible entry, or by any forcible or unlawful detainer, alleged in the complaint and proved on the trial, and find the amount of any rent due, if the alleged unlawful detainer be after default in the payment of rent. If the defendant is found guilty of forcible entry, or forcible or unlawful detainer, and malice is shown, the plaintiff may be awarded statutory damages of up to six hundred dollars ($600), in addition to actual damages, including rent found due. The trier of fact shall determine whether actual damages, statutory damages, or both, shall be awarded, and judgment shall be entered accordingly.

(c) When the proceeding is for an unlawful detainer after default in the payment of rent, and the lease or agreement under which the rent is payable has not by its terms expired, and the notice required by Section 1161 has not stated the election of the landlord to declare the forfeiture thereof, the court may, and, if the lease or agreement is in writing, is for a term of more than one year, and does not contain a forfeiture clause, shall order that a writ shall not be issued to enforce the judgment until the expiration of five days after the entry of the judgment, within which time the tenant, or any subtenant, or any mortgagee of the term, or any other party interested in its continuance, may pay into the court, for the landlord, the amount found due as rent, with interest thereon, and the amount of the damages found by the jury or the court for the unlawful detainer, and the costs of the proceedings, and thereupon the judgment shall be satisfied and the tenant be restored to the tenant's estate. If payment as provided in this subdivision is not made within five days, the judgment may be enforced for its full amount and for the possession of the premises. In all other cases the judgment may be enforced immediately.

(d) Subject to subdivision (c), the judgment for possession of the premises may be enforced as provided in Division 3 (commencing with Section 712.010) of Title 9 of Part 2.

(e) Personal property remaining on the premises which the landlord reasonably believes to have been lost shall be disposed of pursuant to Article 1 (commencing with Section 2080) of Chapter 4 of Title 6 of Part 4 of Division 3 of the Civil Code. The landlord is not liable to the owner of any property which is disposed of in this manner. If the appropriate police or sheriff's department refuses to accept that property, it shall be deemed not to have been lost for the purposes of this subdivision.

(f) The landlord shall give notice pursuant to Section 1983 of the Civil Code to any person (other than the tenant) reasonably believed by the landlord to be the owner of personal property remaining on the premises unless the procedure for surrender of property under Section 1965 of the Civil Code has been initiated or completed.

(g) The landlord shall store the personal property in a place of safekeeping until it is either released pursuant to subdivision (h) or disposed of pursuant to subdivision (i).

(h) The landlord shall release the personal property pursuant to Section 1965 of the Civil Code or shall release it to the tenant or, at the landlord's option, to a person reasonably believed by the landlord to be its owner if the tenant or other person pays the costs of storage as provided in Section 1990 of the Civil Code and claims the property not later than the date specified in the writ of possession before which the tenant must make his or her claim or the date specified in the notice before which a person other than the tenant must make his or her claim.

(i) Personal property not released pursuant to subdivision (h) shall be disposed of pursuant to Section 1988 of the Civil Code.

(j) Where the landlord releases personal property to the tenant pursuant to subdivision (h), the landlord is not liable with respect to that property to any person.

(k) Where the landlord releases personal property pursuant to subdivision (h) to a person (other than the tenant) reasonably believed by the landlord to be its owner, the landlord is not liable with respect to that property to:

(1) The tenant or to any person to whom notice was given pursuant to subdivision (f); or

(2) Any other person, unless that person proves that, prior to releasing the property, the landlord believed or reasonably should have believed that the person had an interest in the property and also that the landlord knew or should have known upon reasonable investigation the address of that person.

(l) Where personal property is disposed of pursuant to Section 1988 of the Civil Code, the landlord is not liable with respect to that property to:

(1) The tenant or to any person to whom notice was given pursuant to subdivision (f); or

(2) Any other person, unless that person proves that, prior to disposing of the property pursuant to Section 1988 of the Civil Code, the landlord believed or reasonably should have believed that the person had an interest in the property and also that the landlord knew or should have known upon reasonable investigation the address of that person.

(m) For the purposes of subdivisions (e), (f), (h), (k), and (l), the terms "owner," "premises," and "reasonable belief" have the same meaning as provided in Section 1980 of the Civil Code. (*Enacted in 1872. Amended by Code Am.1873–74, c. 383, p. 349, § 153; Stats.1907, c. 37, p. 55, § 1; Stats.1931, c. 259, p. 447, § 1; Stats.1933, c. 741, p. 1803, § 1; Stats.1939, c. 717, p. 2237, § 1; Stats.1945, c. 593, p. 1126, § 1; Stats.1967, c. 1600, p. 3830, § 2; Stats.1968, c. 102, p. 315, § 2; Stats.1969, c. 480, p. 1042, § 1; Stats.1970, c. 654, p. 1277, § 1; Stats.1971, c. 1658, p. 3572, § 1; Stats.1974, c. 331, p. 658, § 3; Stats.1974, c. 1516, p. 3383, § 21, operative Jan. 1, 1977; Stats.1977, c. 372, p. 1355, § 1; Stats.1982,*) *c. 497, p. 2168, § 76, operative July 1, 1983; Stats.1988, c. 797, § 3; Stats.1993, c. 755 (S.B.444), § 2.)*

Law Revision Commission Comments

Section 1174 is amended to conform generally to the provisions of Civil Code Sections 1980 to 1991 relating to the disposition of personal property remaining on the premises at the termination of a tenancy. The procedure for disposition of property under Section 1174 differs from the Civil Code procedure to the extent that the notice to the tenant is given in the writ of restitution, and the time allowed the tenant for making a claim is always 15 days after restitution of the premises. Compare subdivision (d) of Section 1174 with Civil Code Section 1983. The procedure for giving notice to a person reasonably believed by the landlord to be an owner of the property is the same in both procedures. The form of notice to the owner (other than the tenant) provided in Civil Code Section 1985 satisfies the requirement of subdivision (f). Property which is not released is to be sold (or may be retained by the landlord if worth less than $100) as provided in Civil Code Section 1988. The limitations on the landlord's liability provided in subdivisions (j) to (*l*) are substantively identical to those provided in Civil Code Section 1989. See Comment to Civil Code Section 1989.

The provisions that allowed the landlord to apply the proceeds of the sale of the tenant's personal property to his judgment and required the tenant to satisfy the landlord's judgment before property left on the premises could be reclaimed have been deleted from Section 1174. These provisions were held unconstitutional in Gray v. Whitmore, 17 Cal.App.3d 1, 94 Cal.Rptr. 904 (1971). Finding a denial of substantive and procedural due process and equal protection of the laws, the court pointed out in Gray v. Whitmore that the deleted provisions resulted in circumvention of the execution statutes and prevented a tenant from asserting his claim for exemption, that they deprived the tenant of the opportunity to dispute the landlord's claim that his money judgment be satisfied out of the tenant's property in the landlord's possession, and that they resulted in an invidious discrimination between debtors without a compelling interest or a necessity furthering the statutory purpose. Gray v. Whitmore was cited with approval in Love v. Keays, 6 Cal.3d 339, 491 P.2d 395, 98 Cal.Rptr. 811 (1971).

Research References

Rutter, Cal. Practice Guide: Civil Appeals & Writs Ch. 15-A, A. Overview.

Rutter, Cal. Practice Guide: Civ. Pro. Before Trial Ch. 7(I)-B, B. Motions to Strike.

Rutter, Cal. Practice Guide: Enforcing Judgments/Debts Ch. 6I-1, Writ of Possession or Sale.

Rutter, Cal. Practice Guide: Enforcing Judgments/Debts Ch. 6I-3, Enforcement of Judgment for Possession of Real Property.

Rutter, Cal. Practice Guide: Landlord-Tenant Form 2:A, Residential Rental Agreement.

Rutter, Cal. Practice Guide: Landlord-Tenant Form 2:C, Office Lease.

Miller and Starr California Real Estate § 19:46, Liability of Holdover Tenant.

Miller and Starr California Real Estate § 19:168, Judgment; Damages.

Miller and Starr California Real Estate § 19:202, Form and Contents of the Notice; Curable and Noncurable Breaches.

Miller and Starr California Real Estate § 19:207, Termination of the Lease; Landlord's Recovery of Rent or Damages.

Miller and Starr California Real Estate § 19:208, Termination of the Lease; Landlord's Recovery of Rent or Damages--Recovery in an Unlawful Detainer Proceeding.

Miller and Starr California Real Estate § 19:226, Cross-Complaint; Affirmative Defenses--Action by Petroleum Distributor.

Miller and Starr California Real Estate § 19:230, Trial; Judgment; Stay of Execution.

Miller and Starr California Real Estate § 19:232, Recovery of Possession; Writ of Possession.

Miller and Starr California Real Estate § 19:233, Tenant's Personal Property.

Miller and Starr California Real Estate § 19:240, Relief from Forfeiture.

2 Witkin Cal. Proc. 5th Courts § 303, (S 303) Enforcement and Stay.

8 Witkin Cal. Proc. 5th Enforcement of Judgment § 162, (S 162) Stay of Execution.

8 Witkin Cal. Proc. 5th Enforcement of Judgment § 332, (S 332) in General.

8 Witkin Cal. Proc. 5th Enforcement of Judgment § 337, (S 337) Disposition of Personal Property.

7 Witkin Cal. Proc. 5th Judgment § 33, (S 33) Unlawful Detainer.

5 Witkin Cal. Proc. 5th Pleading § 645, (S 645) Damages.

5 Witkin Cal. Proc. 5th Pleading § 652, Defendant's Withholding and Damage.

6 Witkin Cal. Proc. 5th Provisional Remedies § 461, Nature of Remedy.

12 Witkin, California Summary 10th Real Property § 670, Relief from Forfeiture.

12 Witkin, California Summary 10th Real Property § 718, (S 718) Distinction: Termination of Gasoline Dealer's Lease.

12 Witkin, California Summary 10th Real Property § 737, (S 737) Restoration of Possession.

12 Witkin, California Summary 10th Real Property § 738, (S 738) Rent and Damages.

12 Witkin, California Summary 10th Real Property § 741, (S 741) in General.

12 Witkin, California Summary 10th Real Property § 742, (S 742) Storage of Tenant's Property.

12 Witkin, California Summary 10th Real Property § 749, Nature of Statute.

12 Witkin, California Summary 10th Real Property § 754, Alternative Procedure on Tenant's Request.

6 Witkin, California Summary 10th Torts § 1570, Treble Damages.

§ 1174.2. Affirmative defense of breach of landlord's obligations or warranty of habitability; determination of substantial breach; judgment for tenant; judgment for landlord, on failure to pay rent to date of trial

(a) In an unlawful detainer proceeding involving residential premises after default in payment of rent and in which the tenant has raised as an affirmative defense a breach of the landlord's obligations under Section 1941 of the Civil Code or of any warranty of habitability, the court shall determine whether a substantial breach of these obligations has occurred. If the court finds that a substantial breach has occurred, the court (1) shall determine the reasonable rental value of the premises in its untenantable state to the date of trial, (2) shall deny possession to the landlord and adjudge the tenant to be the prevailing party, conditioned upon the payment by the tenant of the rent that has accrued to the date of the trial as adjusted pursuant to this subdivision within a reasonable period of time not exceeding five days, from the date of the court's judgment or, if service of the court's judgment is made by mail, the payment shall be made within the time set forth in Section 1013, (3) may order the landlord to make repairs and correct the conditions which constitute a breach of the landlord's obligations, (4) shall order that the monthly rent be limited to the reasonable rental value of the premises as determined pursuant to this subdivision until repairs are completed, and (5) except as otherwise provided in subdivision (b), shall award the tenant costs and attorneys' fees if provided by, and pursuant to, any statute or the contract of the parties. If the court orders repairs or corrections, or both, pursuant to paragraph (3), the court's jurisdiction continues over the matter for the purpose of ensuring compliance. The court shall, however, award possession of the premises to the landlord if the tenant fails to pay all rent accrued to the date of trial, as determined due in the judgment, within the period prescribed by the court pursuant to this subdivision. The tenant shall, however, retain any rights conferred by Section 1174.

(b) If the court determines that there has been no substantial breach of Section 1941 of the Civil Code or of any warranty of habitability by the landlord or if the tenant fails to pay all rent accrued to the date of trial, as required by the court pursuant to subdivision (a), then judgment shall be entered in favor of the landlord, and the landlord shall be the prevailing party for the purposes of awarding costs or attorneys' fees pursuant to any statute or the contract of the parties.

(c) As used in this section, "substantial breach" means the failure of the landlord to comply with applicable building and housing code standards which materially affect health and safety.

(d) Nothing in this section is intended to deny the tenant the right to a trial by jury. Nothing in this section shall limit or supersede any provision of Chapter 12.75 (commencing with Section 7060) of Division 7 of Title 1 of the Government Code. *(Added by Stats.1986, c. 805, § 1. Amended by Stats.1988, c. 1405, § 3; Stats.1992, c. 488 (A.B.2574), § 2; Stats.1993, c. 589 (A.B.2211), § 28.)*

Research References

Rutter, Cal. Practice Guide: Civil Trials & Evidence Ch. 17-D, D. Costs.

Miller and Starr California Real Estate § 19:119, Tenant's Right to Repair and Deduct.

Miller and Starr California Real Estate § 19:208, Termination of the Lease; Landlord's Recovery of Rent or Damages--Recovery in an Unlawful Detainer Proceeding.

Miller and Starr California Real Estate § 19:224, Cross-Complaint; Affirmative Defenses--Breach of the Warranty of Habitability.

Miller and Starr California Real Estate § 19:230, Trial; Judgment; Stay of Execution.

16 NO. 3 Miller & Starr, California Real Estate Newsalert 11, Landlord and Tenant.

19 NO. 4 Miller & Starr, California Real Estate Newsalert 44, Landlord and Tenant.

7 Witkin Cal. Proc. 5th Judgment § 95, (S 95) Prevailing Party in Specified Actions.

12 Witkin, California Summary 10th Real Property § 737, (S 737) Restoration of Possession.

12 Witkin, California Summary 10th Real Property § 739, (S 739) Costs and Attorneys' Fees.

§ 1174.21.   Landlords in violation of section 1942.4; attorneys' fees and costs

A landlord who institutes an unlawful detainer proceeding based upon a tenant's nonpayment of rent, and who is liable for a violation of Section 1942.4 of the Civil Code, shall be liable to the tenant or lessee for reasonable attorneys' fees and costs of the suit, in an amount to be fixed by the court. *(Added by Stats.2003, c. 109 (A.B.647), § 2.)*

Research References

14 NO. 4 Miller & Starr, California Real Estate Newsalert 10, Landlord and Tenant.

7 Witkin Cal. Proc. 5th Judgment § 228, (S 228) Landlord and Tenant Actions.

12 Witkin, California Summary 10th Real Property § 739, (S 739) Costs and Attorneys' Fees.

§ 1174.25.   Occupant filing prejudgment claim of right to possession; time to file; appearance; claimant as unlawful detainer defendant

(a) Any occupant who is served with a prejudgment claim of right to possession in accordance with Section 415.46 may file a claim as prescribed in Section 415.46, with the court within 10 days of the date of service of the prejudgment claim to right of possession as shown on the return of service, which period shall include Saturday and Sunday but excluding all other judicial holidays. If the last day for filing the claim falls on a Saturday or Sunday, the filing period shall be extended to and including the next court day. Filing the prejudgment claim of right to possession shall constitute a general appearance for which a fee shall be collected as provided in Section 70614 of the Government Code. Section 68511.3 of the Government Code applies to the prejudgment claim of right to possession.

(b) At the time of filing, the claimant shall be added as a defendant in the action for unlawful detainer and the clerk shall notify the plaintiff that the claimant has been added as a defendant in the action by mailing a copy of the claim filed with the court to the plaintiff with a notation so indicating. The claimant shall answer or otherwise respond to the summons and complaint within five days, including Saturdays and Sundays but excluding all other judicial holidays, after filing the prejudgment

claim of possession. Thereafter, the name of the claimant shall be added to any pleading, filing or form filed in the action for unlawful detainer. *(Added by Stats.1990, c. 1535 (S.B.2508), § 2.8. Amended by Stats.1991, c. 57 (S.B.323), § 6, eff. June 17, 1991; Stats.2005, c. 75 (A.B.145), § 42, eff. July 19, 2005, operative Jan. 1, 2006.)*

Research References

Miller and Starr California Real Estate § 19:222, Complaint and Summons--Service of the Summons and Complaint; Claim to Right of Possession.

12 Witkin, California Summary 10th Real Property § 729, Parties.

§ 1174.3.   Occupants not named in judgment for possession; claim of right to possession; filing; hearing; further proceedings; form

(a) Unless a prejudgment claim of right to possession has been served upon occupants in accordance with Section 415.46, any occupant not named in the judgment for possession who occupied the premises on the date of the filing of the action may object to enforcement of the judgment against that occupant by filing a claim of right to possession as prescribed in this section. A claim of right to possession may be filed at any time after service or posting of the writ of possession pursuant to subdivision (a) or (b) of Section 715.020, up to and including the time at which the levying officer returns to effect the eviction of those named in the judgment of possession. Filing the claim of right to possession shall constitute a general appearance for which a fee shall be collected as provided in Section 70614 of the Government Code. Section 68511.3 of the Government Code applies to the claim of right to possession. An occupant or tenant who is named in the action shall not be required to file a claim of right to possession to protect that occupant's right to possession of the premises.

(b) The court issuing the writ of possession of real property shall set a date or dates when the court will hold a hearing to determine the validity of objections to enforcement of the judgment specified in subdivision (a). An occupant of the real property for which the writ is issued may make an objection to eviction to the levying officer at the office of the levying officer or at the premises at the time of the eviction.

If a claim of right to possession is completed and presented to the sheriff, marshal, or other levying officer, the officer shall forthwith (1) stop the eviction of occupants at the premises, and (2) provide a receipt or copy of the completed claim of right of possession to the claimant indicating the date and time the completed form was received, and (3) deliver the original completed claim of right to possession to the court issuing the writ of possession of real property.

(c) A claim of right to possession is effected by any of the following:

(1) Presenting a completed claim form in person with identification to the sheriff, marshal, or other levying officer as prescribed in this section, and delivering to the court within two court days after its presentation, an amount equal to 15 days' rent together with the appropriate fee or form for proceeding in forma pauperis. Upon receipt of a claim of right to possession, the sheriff, marshal, or other levying officer shall indicate thereon the date and time of its receipt and forthwith deliver the original to the issuing court and a receipt or copy of the claim to the claimant and notify the plaintiff of that fact. Immediately upon receipt of an amount equal to 15 days' rent and the appropriate fee or form for proceeding in forma pauperis, the court shall file the claim of right to possession and serve an endorsed copy with the notice of the hearing date on the plaintiff and the claimant by first-class mail. The court issuing the writ of

possession shall set and hold a hearing on the claim not less than five nor more than 15 days after the claim is filed with the court.

(2) Presenting a completed claim form in person with identification to the sheriff, marshal, or other levying officer as prescribed in this section, and delivering to the court within two court days after its presentation, the appropriate fee or form for proceeding in forma pauperis without delivering the amount equivalent to 15 days' rent. In this case, the court shall immediately set a hearing on the claim to be held on the fifth day after the filing is completed. The court shall notify the claimant of the hearing date at the time the claimant completes the filing by delivering to the court the appropriate fee or form for proceeding in forma pauperis, and shall notify the plaintiff of the hearing date by first-class mail. Upon receipt of a claim of right to possession, the sheriff, marshal, or other levying officer shall indicate thereon the date and time of its receipt and forthwith deliver the original to the issuing court and a receipt or copy of the claim to the claimant and notify the plaintiff of that fact.

(d) At the hearing, the court shall determine whether there is a valid claim of possession by the claimant who filed the claim, and the court shall consider all evidence produced at the hearing, including, but not limited to, the information set forth in the claim. The court may determine the claim to be valid or invalid based upon the evidence presented at the hearing. The court shall determine the claim to be invalid if the court determines that the claimant is an invitee, licensee, guest, or trespasser. If the court determines the claim is invalid, the court shall order the return to the claimant of the amount of the 15 days' rent paid by the claimant, if that amount was paid pursuant to paragraph (1) or (3) of subdivision (c), less a pro rata amount for each day that enforcement of the judgment was delayed by reason of making the claim of right to possession, which pro rata amount shall be paid to the landlord. If the court determines the claim is valid, the amount equal to 15 days' rent paid by the claimant shall be returned immediately to the claimant.

(e) If, upon hearing, the court determines that the claim is valid, then the court shall order further proceedings as follows:

(1) If the unlawful detainer is based upon a curable breach, and the claimant was not previously served with a proper notice, if any notice is required, then the required notice may at the plaintiff's discretion be served on the claimant at the hearing or

thereafter. If the claimant does not cure the breach within the required time, then a supplemental complaint may be filed and served on the claimant as defendant if the plaintiff proceeds against the claimant in the same action. For the purposes of this section only, service of the required notice, if any notice is required, and of the supplemental complaint may be made by first-class mail addressed to the claimant at the subject premises or upon his or her attorney of record and, in either case, Section 1013 shall otherwise apply. Further proceedings on the merits of the claimant's continued right to possession after service of the Summons and Supplemental Complaint as prescribed by this subdivision shall be conducted pursuant to this chapter.

(2) In all other cases, the court shall deem the unlawful detainer Summons and Complaint to be amended on their faces to include the claimant as defendant, service of the Summons and Complaint, as thus amended, may at the plaintiff's discretion be made at the hearing or thereafter, and the claimant thus named and served as a defendant in the action shall answer or otherwise respond within five days thereafter.

(f) If a claim is made without delivery to the court of the appropriate filing fee or a form for proceeding in forma pauperis, as prescribed in this section, the claim shall be immediately deemed denied and the court shall so order. Upon the denial of the claim, the court shall immediately deliver an endorsed copy of the order to the levying officer and shall serve an endorsed copy of the order on the plaintiff and claimant by first-class mail.

(g) If the claim of right to possession is denied pursuant to subdivision (f), or if the claimant fails to appear at the hearing or, upon hearing, if the court determines that there are no valid claims, or if the claimant does not prevail at a trial on the merits of the unlawful detainer action, the court shall order the levying officer to proceed with enforcement of the original writ of possession of real property as deemed amended to include the claimant, which shall be effected within a reasonable time not to exceed five days. Upon receipt of the court's order, the levying officer shall enforce the writ of possession of real property against any occupant or occupants.

(h) The claim of right to possession shall be made on the following form:

CLAIMANT OR CLAIMANT'S ATTORNEY   TELEPHONE NO.   FOR COURT USE ONLY
(Name and Address):

ATTORNEY FOR (Name):

NAME OF COURT:
  STREET ADDRESS:
  MAILING ADDRESS:
  CITY AND ZIP CODE:
  BRANCH NAME:

PLAINTIFF:

DEFENDANT:

CLAIM OF RIGHT TO POSSESSION
AND NOTICE OF HEARING

CASE NUMBER:

(For levying officer use only)
Completed form was received on

Date: _____ Time: _____
By: _____

Complete this form only if ALL of these statements are true:
1. You are NOT named in the accompanying form called Writ of Possession.
2. You occupied the premises on or before the date the unlawful detainer
   (eviction) action was filed.
   (The date is in the accompanying Writ of Possession.)
3. You still occupy the premises.

I DECLARE THE FOLLOWING UNDER PENALTY OF PERJURY:
1. My name is (specify):
2. I reside at (street address, unit no., city and ZIP Code):
3. The address of "the premises" subject to this claim is (address):
4. On (insert date): [_____] , the landlord or the landlord's
   authorized agent filed a complaint to recover possession of the premises.
   (This date is in the accompanying Writ of Possession.)
5. I occupied the premises on the date the complaint was filed (the date in
   item 4). I have continued to occupy the premises ever since.
6. I was at least 18 years of age on the date the complaint was filed (the date in
   item 4).
7. I claim a right to possession of the premises because I occupied the
   premises on the date the complaint was filed (the date in item 4).

CLAIM OF RIGHT TO POSSESSION AND NOTICE OF HEARING

8. I was not named in the Writ of Possession.

9. I understand that if I make this claim of possession, a court hearing will be held to decide whether my claim will be granted.

10. (Filing fee) To obtain a court hearing on my claim, I understand that after I present this form to the levying officer I must go to the court and pay a filing fee of $ or file with the court "Application for Waiver of Court Fees and Costs." I understand that if I don't pay the filing fee or file the form for waiver of court fees within 2 court days, the court will immediately deny my claim.

11. (Immediate court hearing unless you deposit 15 days' rent) To obtain a court hearing on my claim, I understand I must also present a copy of this completed complaint form or a receipt from the levying officer. I also understand the date of my hearing will be set immediately if I do not deliver to the court an amount equal to 15 days' rent.

I am filing my claim in the following manner (check the box that shows how you are filing your claim. Note that you must deliver to the court a copy of the claim form or a levying officer's receipt):

     a. ☐ I presented this claim form to the sheriff, marshal, or other levying officer, and within two court days I shall deliver to the court the following: (1) a copy of this completed claim form or a receipt, (2) the court filing fee or form for proceeding in forma pauperis, and (3) an amount equal to 15 days' rent; or

     b. ☐ I presented this claim form to the sheriff, marshal, or other levying officer, and within two court days I shall deliver to the court (1) a copy of this completed claim form or a receipt, and (2) the court filing fee or form for proceeding in forma pauperis.

IMPORTANT: Do not take a copy of this claim form to the court unless you have first given the form to the sheriff, marshal, or other levying officer.

(To be completed by the court.)

Date of Hearing: Time: Dept. or Div.:   Room:

Address of court:

NOTICE: If you fail to appear at this hearing you will be evicted without further hearing.

CLAIM OF RIGHT TO POSSESSION AND NOTICE OF HEARING

12. Rental agreement. I have (check all that apply to you):

    a. ☐ an oral rental agreement with the landlord.

    b. ☐ a written rental agreement with the landlord.

    c. ☐ an oral rental agreement with a person other than the landlord.

    d. ☐ a written rental agreement with a person other than the landlord.

    e. ☐ other (explain):

I declare under penalty of perjury under the laws of the State of California that the foregoing is true and correct.

> WARNING: Perjury is a felony punishable by imprisonment in the state prison.

Date:

.... ▶ _____

  (TYPE OR PRINT NAME)   (SIGNATURE OF CLAIMANT)

> NOTICE: If your claim to possession is found to be valid, the unlawful detainer action against you will be determined at trial. At trial, you may be found liable for rent, costs, and, in some cases, treble damages.

NOTICE TO OCCUPANTS

YOU MUST ACT AT ONCE IF ALL THE FOLLOWING ARE TRUE:

(1) You are not named, in the accompanying form called Writ of Possession;

(2) You occupied the premises on or before the date the unlawful detainer (eviction) action was filed; and

(3) You still occupy the premises.

You can complete and SUBMIT THIS CLAIM FORM

(1) Before the date of eviction at the sheriff's or marshal's office located at: (address)

(2) OR at the premises at the time of the eviction. (Give this form to the officer who comes to evict you.)

If you do not complete and submit this form (and pay a filing fee or file the form for proceeding in forma pauperis if you cannot pay the fee), YOU WILL BE EVICTED along with the parties named in the writ.

After this form is properly filed, A HEARING WILL BE HELD to decide your claim. If you do not appear at the hearing, you will be evicted without further hearing.

CLAIM OF RIGHT TO POSSESSION AND NOTICE OF HEARING

(Added by Stats.1986, c. 1220, § 2. Amended by Stats.1987, c. 720, § 1; Stats.1988, c. 1405, § 4; Stats.1989, c. 12, § 3, eff. April 28, 1989, operative May 1, 1989; Stats.1990, c. 1535 (S.B.2508), § 3; Stats.1991, c. 57 (S.B.323), § 7, eff. June 17, 1991; Stats. 1995, c. 196 (S.B.832), § 10, eff. July 31, 1995; Stats.2001, c. 115 (S.B.153), § 5; Stats.2002, c. 664 (A.B.3034), § 50; Stats.2005, c. 75 (A.B.145), § 43, eff. July 19, 2005, operative Jan. 1, 2006.)

Law Revision Commission Comments

Subdivision (a) of Section 1174.3 is amended to delete an obsolete reference to former Section 1167.25. [30 Cal.L.Rev.Comm. Reports 327 (2000)].

Research References

Rutter, Cal. Practice Guide: Civil Appeals & Writs Ch. 15-A, A. Overview.

Rutter, Cal. Practice Guide: Enforcing Judgments/Debts Ch. 6I-1, Writ of Possession or Sale.

Rutter, Cal. Practice Guide: Enforcing Judgments/Debts Ch. 6I-3, Enforcement of Judgment for Possession of Real Property.

Miller and Starr California Real Estate § 19:220, Parties.

Miller and Starr California Real Estate § 19:222, Complaint and Summons--Service of the Summons and Complaint; Claim to Right of Possession.

Miller and Starr California Real Estate § 19:232, Recovery of Possession; Writ of Possession.

8 Witkin Cal. Proc. 5th Enforcement of Judgment § 332, (S 332) in General.

8 Witkin Cal. Proc. 5th Enforcement of Judgment § 334, in General.

8 Witkin Cal. Proc. 5th Enforcement of Judgment § 335, Hearing and Determination.

12 Witkin, California Summary 10th Real Property § 741, (S 741) in General.

§ 1174.5. Recovery of unpaid rent; effect of judgment on liability of lessee

A judgment in unlawful detainer declaring the forfeiture of the lease or agreement under which real property is held shall not relieve the lessee from liability pursuant to Section 1951.2 of the Civil Code. *(Added by Stats.1982, c. 488, p. 2105, § 1.)*

Research References

Miller and Starr California Real Estate § 19:207, Termination of the Lease; Landlord's Recovery of Rent or Damages.

Miller and Starr California Real Estate § 19:209, Termination of the Lease; Landlord's Recovery of Rent or Damages--Recovery in a Separate Action.

Miller and Starr California Real Estate § 19:210, Continuation of the Lease; Landlord's Recovery of Rent or Damages.

Miller and Starr California Real Estate § 19:214, Nature of the Remedy.

Miller and Starr California Real Estate § 19:215, Nature of the Remedy--Effect of Tenant's Abandonment Before Trial.

Miller and Starr California Real Estate § 19:223, Cross-Complaint; Affirmative Defenses.

Miller and Starr California Real Estate § 19:230, Trial; Judgment; Stay of Execution.

Miller and Starr California Real Estate § 19:232, Recovery of Possession; Writ of Possession.

§ 1176. Stay on appeal; petition for extraordinary writ; conditions of stay; reasonable rental value; new cause of action for rental of real property

(a) An appeal taken by the defendant shall not automatically stay proceedings upon the judgment. Petition for stay of the judgment pending appeal shall first be directed to the judge before whom it was rendered. Stay of judgment shall be granted when the court finds that the moving party will suffer extreme hardship in the absence of a stay and that the nonmoving party will not be irreparably injured by its issuance. If the stay is denied by the trial court, the defendant may forthwith file a petition for an extraordinary writ with the appropriate appeals court. If the trial or appellate court stays enforcement of the judgment, the court may condition the stay on whatever conditions the court deems just, but in any case it shall order the payment of the reasonable monthly rental value to the court monthly in advance as rent would otherwise become due as a condition of issuing the stay of enforcement. As used in this subdivision, "reasonable rental value" means the contract rent unless the rental value has been modified by the trial court in which case that modified rental value shall be used.

(b) A new cause of action on the same agreement for the rental of real property shall not be barred because of an appeal by any party. *(Enacted in 1872. Amended by Code Am.1880, c. 20, p. 9, § 6; Stats.1951, c. 1737, p. 4140, § 160; Stats.1979, c. 958, p. 3299, § 2; Stats.1985, c. 1279, § 3.)*

Research References

Rutter, Cal. Practice Guide: Civil Appeals & Writs Ch. 7-A, A. Overview.

Rutter, Cal. Practice Guide: Civil Appeals & Writs Ch. 7-B, B. Automatic Stay.

Rutter, Cal. Practice Guide: Civil Appeals & Writs Ch. 7-C, C. Stay by Posting Security (Bond or Undertaking).

Rutter, Cal. Practice Guide: Civil Appeals & Writs Ch. 7-D, D. Discretionary Stay by Trial Court.

Rutter, Cal. Practice Guide: Civil Appeals & Writs Ch. 15-C, C. Statutory Writs.

Rutter, Cal. Practice Guide: Insurance Litigation Ch. 6I-B, B. Particular Surety Bond Coverages.

Miller and Starr California Real Estate § 19:210, Continuation of the Lease; Landlord's Recovery of Rent or Damages.

Miller and Starr California Real Estate § 19:214, Nature of the Remedy.

Miller and Starr California Real Estate § 19:215, Nature of the Remedy--Effect of Tenant's Abandonment Before Trial.

Miller and Starr California Real Estate § 19:223, Cross-Complaint; Affirmative Defenses.

Miller and Starr California Real Estate § 19:230, Trial; Judgment; Stay of Execution.

9 Witkin Cal. Proc. 5th Appeal § 21, in General.

9 Witkin Cal. Proc. 5th Appeal § 245, in General.

9 Witkin Cal. Proc. 5th Appeal § 246, Attorneys' Fees.

8 Witkin Cal. Proc. 5th Extraordinary Writs § 62, No Practical Stay.

5 Witkin Cal. Proc. 5th Pleading § 639, (S 639) Successive Actions.

12 Witkin, California Summary 10th Real Property § 740, (S 740) Res Judicata and Collateral Estoppel.

4 Witkin, California Summary 10th Security Transactions in Real Property § 173, (S 173) Fraud in Acquisition of Title.

§ 1177. Applicable rules of practice

RULES OF PRACTICE. Except as otherwise provided in this Chapter the provisions of Part II of this Code [1] are applicable to, and constitute the rules of practice in the proceedings mentioned in this Chapter. *(Enacted in 1872.)*

[1] Code of Civil Procedure §§ 307 to 1062.5.

Research References

3 Witkin Cal. Proc. 5th Actions § 66, (S 66) General Policy of Uniformity in Procedure.

§ 1178. New trials and appeals; applicable provisions

The provisions of Part 2 of this code,[1] relative to new trials and appeals, except insofar as they are inconsistent with the provisions of this chapter or with rules adopted by the Judicial Council, apply to the proceedings mentioned in this chapter. *(Enacted in 1872. Amended by Stats.1945, c. 40, p. 357, § 5.)*

[1] Code of Civil Procedure §§ 307 to 1062.5.

Research References

8 Witkin Cal. Proc. 5th Attack Judgment Trial Court § 22, in General.

§ 1179. Relief against a forfeiture of a lease or rental agreement

The court may relieve a tenant against a forfeiture of a lease or rental agreement, whether written or oral, and whether or not the tenancy has terminated, and restore him or her to his or her former estate or tenancy, in case of hardship, as provided in Section 1174. The court has the discretion to relieve any person against forfeiture on its own motion.

An application for relief against forfeiture may be made at any time prior to restoration of the premises to the landlord. The application may be made by a tenant or subtenant, or a mortgagee of the term, or any person interested in the continuance of the term. It must be made upon petition, setting forth the facts upon which the relief is sought, and be verified by the applicant. Notice of the application, with a copy of the petition, must be served at least five days prior to the hearing on the plaintiff in the judgment, who may appear and contest the application. Alternatively, a person appearing without an attorney may make the application orally, if the plaintiff either is present and has an opportunity to contest the application, or has been given ex parte notice of the hearing and the purpose of the oral application. In no case shall the application or motion be granted except on condition that full payment of rent due, or full performance of conditions or covenants stipulated, so far as the same is practicable, be made. *(Added by Code Am.1873–74, c. 383, p. 350, § 154. Amended by Code Am.1880, c. 20, p. 9, § 7; Stats.2002, c. 301 (S.B.1403), § 4.)*

Research References

California Real Estate Forms (Miller & Starr) § 2:20, Retail Lease--Shopping Center With for Profit Parking Garage.
Miller and Starr California Real Estate § 10:16, Property Interests that Are Lienable.
Miller and Starr California Real Estate § 19:37, Option to Extend or Renew Lease Term--Requirements for Exercise of the Option.
Miller and Starr California Real Estate § 19:167, Defenses.
Miller and Starr California Real Estate § 19:232, Recovery of Possession; Writ of Possession.
Miller and Starr California Real Estate § 19:240, Relief from Forfeiture.
13 NO. 4 Miller & Starr, California Real Estate Newsalert 14, Landlord and Tenant.
16 NO. 5 Miller & Starr, California Real Estate Newsalert 15, Landlord and Tenant.
7 Witkin Cal. Proc. 5th Judgment § 79, (S 79) Statutory Authority to Modify Judgment.
2 Witkin Cal. Proc. 5th Jurisdiction § 76, Bankruptcy Cases and Proceedings.
2 Witkin Cal. Proc. 5th Jurisdiction § 428, (S 428) in General.
12 Witkin, California Summary 10th Real Property § 670, Relief from Forfeiture.
12 Witkin, California Summary 10th Real Property § 740, (S 740) Res Judicata and Collateral Estoppel.
12 Witkin, California Summary 10th Real Property § 746, Termination of Lessee's Right of Possession.
13 Witkin, California Summary 10th Equity § 21, Illustrations.

§ 1179a. Precedence

In all proceedings brought to recover the possession of real property pursuant to the provisions of this chapter all courts, wherein such actions are or may hereafter be pending, shall give such actions precedence over all other civil actions therein, except actions to which special precedence is given by law, in the matter of the setting the same for hearing or trial, and in hearing the same, to the end that all such actions shall be quickly heard and determined. *(Added by Stats.1931, c. 885, p. 1899, § 1.)*

Research References

Rutter, Cal. Practice Guide: Civil Appeals & Writs Ch. 5-B, B. Types of Motions, Applications and Requests.
Rutter, Cal. Practice Guide: Civ. Pro. Before Trial Ch. 12(I)-C, C. Claims for Trial Setting Preference.
Miller and Starr California Real Estate § 33:29, Actions in Which a Receiver May be Appointed--Unlawful Detainer.
Miller and Starr California Real Estate § 19:229, Trial Setting and Hearing Preference; Discovery.
9 Witkin Cal. Proc. 5th Appeal § 764, Statutory Preferences and Advancement.
7 Witkin Cal. Proc. 5th Trial § 68, (S 68) Unlawful Detainer.
12 Witkin, California Summary 10th Real Property § 736, Trial.

Title 4

OF THE ENFORCEMENT OF LIENS

CHAPTER 1. LIENS IN GENERAL

Section
1180. Lien defined.

§ 1180. Lien defined

DEFINITION OF LIEN. A lien is a charge imposed upon specific property, by which it is made security for the performance of an act. *(Enacted in 1872.)*

Research References

Rutter, Cal. Practice Guide: Insurance Litigation Ch. 6H-B, B. Types of Policies and Services Provided by Title Insurers.
Rutter, Cal. Practice Guide: Real Prop. Transactions Ch. 3-C, C. Types of Title Insurance Policies.
Miller and Starr California Real Estate § 2:23, Liens and Encumbrances.
Miller and Starr California Real Estate § 7:48, Indemnity for Defects, Liens, and Encumbrances.
3 Witkin Cal. Proc. 5th Actions § 65, (S 65) Statutory Classes.

CHAPTER 2.5. OIL AND GAS LIENS

§ 1203.50. Short title

This chapter shall be known and may be cited as the Oil and Gas Lien Act. *(Added by Stats.1959, c. 2020, p. 4660, § 1.)*

Research References

3 Witkin Cal. Proc. 5th Actions § 65, (S 65) Statutory Classes.
13 Witkin, California Summary 10th Personal Property § 233, (S 233) Statutory List.

§ 1203.51. Definitions

Unless the context otherwise requires, the definitions set forth in this section shall govern the construction of this chapter.

(a) "Person" means an individual, corporation, firm, partnership, limited liability company, or association.

(b) "Owner" means a person holding any interest in the legal or equitable title or both to any leasehold for oil or gas purposes, or his or her agent and shall include purchasers under executory contract, receivers, and trustees.

(c) "Contract" means a contract, written or oral, express or implied, or partly express and partly implied, or executory or executed, or partly executory and partly executed.

(d) "Material" means any material, machinery, appliances, buildings, structures, casing, tanks, pipelines, tools, bits, or other equipment or supplies but does not include rigs or hoists or their integral component parts except wire lines.

(e) "Labor" means work performed in return for wages.

(f) "Services" means work performed exclusive of labor, including the hauling of material, whether or not involving the furnishing of material.

(g) "Furnish" means sell or rent.

(h) "Drilling" means drilling, digging, shooting, torpedoing, perforating, fracturing, testing, logging, acidizing, cementing, completing or repairing.

(i) "Operating" means all operations conducted on the lease in connection with or necessary to the production of oil or gas, either in the development thereof or in working thereon by the subtractive process.

(j) "Construction" means construction, maintenance, operation, or repair, either in the development thereof or in working thereon by the subtractive process.

(k) "Original contractor" means any person for whose benefit a lien is prescribed under Section 1203.52. *(Added by Stats.1959, c. 2020, p. 4660, § 1. Amended by Stats.1994, c. 1010 (S.B.2053), § 62.)*

§ 1203.52. Lien for labor, materials or services

Any person who shall, under contract with the owner of any leasehold for oil or gas purposes perform any labor or furnish any material or services used or employed, or furnished to be used or employed in the drilling or operating of any oil or gas well upon such leasehold, or in the constructing, putting together, or repairing of any material so used or employed, or furnished to be so used or employed, shall be entitled to a lien under this chapter, whether or not a producing well is obtained and whether or not such material is incorporated in or becomes a part of the completed oil or gas well, for the amount due him for any such labor performed, or materials or services furnished, within six months prior to the date of recording the statement of lien as provided in Section 1203.58, including, without limitation, shipping and mileage charges connected therewith, and interest from the date the same was due. *(Added by Stats.1959, c. 2020, p. 4661, § 1.)*

§ 1203.53. Extent of lien

Liens created under Section 1203.52 shall extend to:

(a) The leasehold for oil or gas purposes to which the materials or services were furnished, or for which the labor was performed, and the appurtenances thereunto belonging, exclusive of any and all royalty interest, overriding interests and production payments created by an instrument recorded prior to the date such materials or services were first furnished or such labor was first performed for which lien is claimed; and

(b) All materials and fixtures owned by the owner or owners of such leasehold and used or employed, or furnished to be used or employed in the drilling or operating of any oil or gas well located thereon; and

(c) All oil or gas wells located on such leasehold, and the oil or gas produced therefrom, and the proceeds thereof, except the interest therein owned by the owners of royalty interests, overriding royalty interests and production payments created by an instrument recorded prior to the date such materials or services were first furnished or such labor was first performed for which the lien is claimed. *(Added by Stats.1959, c. 2020, p. 4661, § 1.)*

§ 1203.54. Subcontractor's lien; extent

Any person who shall, under contract, perform any labor or furnish any material or services as a subcontractor under an original contractor or for or to an original contractor or a subcontractor under an original contractor, shall be entitled to a lien upon all the property upon which the lien of an original contractor may attach to the same extent as an original contractor, and the lien provided for in this section shall further extend and attach to all materials and fixtures owned by such original contractor or subcontractor to or for whom the labor is performed or material or services furnished and used or employed, or furnished to be used or employed in the drilling or operating of such oil or gas wells. *(Added by Stats.1959, c. 2020, p. 4662. § 1.)*

§ 1203.55. Leasehold estate; effect of forfeiture on lien; interests subject to condition subsequent; effect of failure of interests on lien

When a lien provided for in this chapter shall have attached to a leasehold estate, forfeiture of such estate shall not impair any lien as to material, appurtenances and fixtures located thereon and to which such lien has attached prior to forfeiture. If a lien provided for in this chapter attaches to an equitable interest or to a legal interest contingent upon the happening of a condition subsequent, failure of such interest to ripen into legal title or such condition subsequent to be fulfilled, shall not impair any such lien as to material, appurtenances and fixtures located thereon and to which said lien had attached prior to such failure. *(Added by Stats.1959, c. 2020, p. 4662, § 1.)*

§ 1203.56. Date of lien; preference

The lien provided for in this chapter arises on the date of the furnishing of the first item of material or services or the date of performance of the first labor for which a lien is claimed under the provisions of this chapter. Upon compliance with the provisions of Section 1203.58, such lien shall be preferred to all other titles, charges, liens or encumbrances which may attach to or upon any of the property upon which a lien is given by this chapter subsequent to the date the lien herein provided for arises. *(Added by Stats.1959, c. 2020, p. 4662, § 1.)*

§ 1203.57. Liens upon same property; equal standings; preference of liens for labor

All liens arising by virtue of this chapter upon the same property shall be of equal standing except that liens of persons for the performance of labor shall be preferred to all other liens arising by virtue of this chapter. *(Added by Stats.1959, c. 2020, p. 4662, § 1.)*

§ 1203.58. Recordation of verified statement; contents; date of recordation

Every person claiming a lien under this chapter, shall record in the office of the county recorder for the county in which such leasehold, or some part thereof, is situated, a verified statement setting forth the amount claimed and the items thereof, the dates on which labor was performed or material or services furnished, the name of the owner of the leasehold, if known, the name of the claimant and his mailing address, a description of the leasehold, and if the claimant be a claimant under Section 1203.54, the name of the person for whom the labor was immediately performed or the material or services were immediately furnished. The statement of lien must be recorded within six months after the date on which the claimant's labor was performed or his materials or services were furnished to be effective as to such labor, materials, or services. *(Added by Stats.1959, c. 2020, p. 4662, § 1.)*

§ 1203.59. Notice of claim; delivery; contents; withholding payments; payment of lien judgment; notice of payment

Anything in this chapter to the contrary notwithstanding, any lien claimed by virtue of this chapter, insofar as it may extend to oil or gas or the proceeds of the sale of oil or gas, shall not be effective against any purchaser of such oil or gas until written notice of such claim has been delivered to such purchaser. Such notice shall state the name of the claimant, his address, the amount for which the lien is claimed, and a description of the leasehold upon which the lien is claimed. Such notice shall be delivered personally to the purchaser or by registered letter or certified mail. Upon receipt of such notice the purchaser shall withhold payments for such oil or gas runs to the extent of the lien amount claimed until delivery of notice in writing that the claim has been paid. The funds so withheld by the purchaser shall be used in payment of the lien judgment upon foreclosure. The lien claimant shall within 10 days give notice in writing that the claim has been paid. *(Added by Stats.1959, c. 2020, p. 4663, § 1.)*

§ 1203.60. Recordation of bond; contents; amount; execution; suit on bond

(a) Whenever any lien or liens shall be claimed or recorded under the provisions of this chapter then the lessor or owner of the property on which the lien or liens are claimed or the contractor or subcontractor through whom such lien or liens are claimed, or either of them, may record a bond with the county recorder of the county in which the property is located as herein provided. Such bond shall describe the property on which lien or liens are claimed, shall refer to the lien or liens claimed in manner sufficient to identify them and shall be in an amount equal to 150 percent of the amount of the claimed lien or liens referred to and shall be payable to the party or parties claiming same. Such bond shall be executed by the party recording same as principal and by a corporate surety authorized to execute such bonds as surety and shall be conditioned substantially that the principal and surety will pay to the obligees named or their assigns the amounts of the liens so claimed by them with all costs in the event same shall be proven to be liens on such property.

(b) Such bond, when recorded, shall take the place of the property against which any claim for lien referred to in such bond is asserted. At any time within the period of time provided in Section 1203.61, any person claiming such lien may sue upon such bond but no action shall be brought upon such bond after the expiration of such period. One action upon such bond shall not exhaust the remedies thereon but each obligee or assignee of an obligee named therein may maintain a separate suit thereon in any court having jurisdiction. *(Added by Stats.1959, c. 2020, p. 4663, § 1.)*

§ 1203.61. Enforcement of lien; dismissal; cancellation; notice of credit, extension of lien or time to enforce lien

(a) Any lien provided for by this chapter shall be enforced in the same manner as provided in Chapter 4 (commencing with Section 8400)of Title 2 of Part 6 of Division 4 of the Civil Code. The action shall be filed within 180 days from the time of the recording of the lien. If a credit is given and notice of the fact and terms of the credit is filed in the office of the county recorder subsequent to the filing of the lien and prior to the expiration of the 180–day period, then the lien continues in force until 180 days after the expiration of the credit, but no lien continues in force by reason of any agreement to give credit for a longer time than one year from the time the work is completed. If the proceedings to enforce the lien are not prosecuted to trial within two years after commencement, the court may in its discretion dismiss the action for want of prosecution, and in all cases the dismissal of the action (unless it is expressly stated that it is without prejudice) or a judgment in the action that no lien exists is equivalent to the cancellation and removal from the record of the lien.

(b) As against any purchaser or encumbrancer for value and in good faith whose rights are acquired subsequent to the expiration of the 180–day period following the filing of the lien, no giving of credit or extension of the lien or time to enforce the lien shall be effective unless evidenced by a notice or agreement filed for record in the office of the county recorder prior to the acquisition of the rights of the purchaser or encumbrancer. *(Added by Stats.1959, c. 2020, p. 4664, § 1. Amended by Stats.1969, c. 1362, p. 2781, § 4, operative Jan. 1, 1971; Stats. 2010, c. 697 (S.B.189), § 24, operative July 1, 2012.)*

Law Revision Commission Comments

Section 1203.61 is amended to correct a cross-reference and make stylistic revisions. [37 Cal.L.Rev.Comm. Reports 527 (2007)].

§ 1203.62. Personal action

Nothing in this chapter shall be construed to impair or affect the right of any person to whom any debt may be due for work performed or materials or services furnished to maintain a personal action against the person liable for such debt. *(Added by Stats.1959, c. 2020, p. 4664, § 1.)*

§ 1203.63. Additional security; waiver of lien; agreement

The taking of any note or any additional security by any person given a lien by this chapter shall not constitute a waiver of the lien given by this chapter unless made a waiver by express agreement of the parties in writing. The claiming of a lien under this chapter shall not constitute a waiver of any other right or security held by the claimant unless made a waiver by express agreement of the parties in writing. *(Added by Stats.1959, c. 2020, p. 4664, § 1.)*

§ 1203.64. Assignment of claims for liens

All claims for liens and likewise all actions to recover therefor under this chapter shall be assignable upon compliance with the provisions of Section 1203.58 so as to vest in the assignee all rights and remedies herein given subject to all defenses thereto that might be raised if such assignments had not been made. *(Added by Stats.1959, c. 2020, p. 4664, § 1.)*

§ 1203.65. Perfection and enforcement; effective date of chapter

All liens granted by this chapter shall be perfected and enforced in accordance with the provisions hereof whether such liens arise before or after the effective date of this chapter; provided, however, that any unperfected lien granted under any statute in effect prior to the effective date of this chapter and which could be subsequently perfected in accordance with such prior statute were it not for the existence of this chapter may be perfected and enforced in accordance with the provisions of this chapter if the statement of lien required to be recorded under Section 1203.58 is recorded within the time therein required or within two months after the effective date of this chapter, whichever period is longer; and provided further, that the validity of any lien perfected prior to the effective date of this chapter in accordance with the requirements of any statute in effect prior to such effective date shall be determined on the basis of such prior statute but the enforcement thereof shall insofar as possible be governed by the provisions of this chapter. *(Added by Stats.1959, c. 2020, p. 4664, § 1.)*

§ 1203.66. Liberal construction

This chapter shall be given liberal construction in favor of all persons entitled to any lien under it. *(Added by Stats.1959, c. 2020, p. 4665, § 1.)*

CHAPTER 3. CERTAIN LIENS AND PRIORITIES FOR SALARIES, WAGES AND CONSUMER DEPOSITS

§ 1204. Assignments for benefit of creditors; preferred labor claims; payments; pro rata distribution; presentation of claims; disputed claims; receivership actions

When any assignment, whether voluntary or involuntary, and whether formal or informal, is made for the benefit of creditors of the assignor, or results from any proceeding in insolvency or receivership commenced against him or her, or when any property is turned over to the creditors of a person, firm, association or corporation, or to a receiver or trustee for the benefit of creditors, the following claims have priority in the following order:

(a) Allowed unsecured claims, but only to the extent of four thousand three hundred dollars ($4,300) for each individual or corporation, as the case may be, earned within 90 days before the date of the making of such assignment or the taking over of the property or the commencement of the court proceeding or the date of the cessation of the debtor's business, whichever occurs first, for either of the following:

(1) Wages, salaries, or commissions, including vacation, severance and sick leave pay earned by an individual.

(2) Sales commissions earned by an individual, or by a corporation with only one employee, acting as an independent contractor in the sale of goods or services of the debtor in the ordinary course of the debtor's business if, and only if, during the 12 months preceding the date of the making of the assignment or the taking over of the property or the commencement of the proceeding or the date of the cessation of the debtor's business, whichever occurs first, at least 75 percent of the amount that the individual or corporation earned by acting as an independent contractor in the sale of goods or services was earned from the debtor.

(b) Allowed unsecured claims for contributions to employee benefit plans arising from services rendered within 180 days before the date of the making of the assignment or the taking over of the property or the commencement of the court proceeding or the date of the cessation of the debtor's business,

whichever occurs first; but only for each employee benefit plan, to the extent of the number of employees covered by the plan multiplied by four thousand three hundred dollars ($4,300), less the aggregate amount paid to the employees under subdivision (a), plus the aggregate amount paid by the estate on behalf of the employees to any other employee benefit plan.

(c) The above claims shall be paid by the trustee, assignee or receiver before the claim of any other creditor of the assignor, insolvent, or debtor whose property is so turned over, and shall be paid as soon as the money with which to pay same becomes available. If there is insufficient money to pay all the labor claims in full, the money available shall be distributed among the claimants in proportion to the amount of their respective claims. The trustee, receiver or assignee for the benefit of creditors shall have the right to require sworn claims to be presented and shall have the right to refuse to pay any such preferred claim, either in whole or in part, if he or she has reasonable cause to believe that a claim is not valid but shall pay any part thereof that is not disputed, without prejudice to the claimant's rights, as to the balance of his or her claim, and withhold sufficient money to cover the disputed portion until the claimant in question has a reasonable opportunity to establish the validity of his or her claim by court action, either in his or her own name or through an assignee.

(d) This section is binding upon all the courts of this state and in all receivership actions the court shall order the receiver to pay promptly out of the first receipts and earnings of the receivership, after paying the current operating expenses, such preferred labor claims. *(Added by Stats.1907, c. 256, p. 321, § 1. Amended by Stats.1931, c. 820, p. 1699, § 1; Stats.1933, c. 175, p. 621, § 1; Stats.1945, c. 1192, p. 2244, § 1; Stats.1951, c. 476, p. 1613, § 1; Stats.1961, c. 1082, p. 2813, § 1; Stats.1979, c. 394, p. 1465, § 3, eff. July 27, 1979, operative Oct. 1, 1979; Stats.1999, c. 202 (S.B.219), § 1.)*

Research References

California Practice Guide: Employment Litigation Ch. 11-J, J. Enforcing California Laws Regulating Employee Compensation.
Rutter, Cal. Practice Guide: Enforcing Judgments/Debts Ch. 5-D, D. Involuntary Bankruptcy.
Miller and Starr California Real Estate § 11:164, Personal Property Tax Liens.
Miller and Starr California Real Estate § 11:167, State Tax Liens-- Unemployment Insurance Contribution Liens.
9 Witkin, California Summary 10th Taxation § 370, Lien and Priority.
3 Witkin, California Summary 10th Agency and Employment § 317, Prosecution of Actions.
3 Witkin, California Summary 10th Agency and Employment § 403, (S 403) Nature of Funds.

§ 1204.5. Assignments for benefit of creditors; priority of deposits for the purchase or lease of realty or purchase of services

In any general assignment for the benefit of creditors, the following claims shall have priority, subordinate to the priorities for labor claims under Section 1204, but prior to all other unsecured claims: allowed unsecured claims of individuals, to the extent of nine hundred dollars ($900) for each such individual, arising from the deposit, before the commencement of the case, of money in connection with the purchase, lease, or rental of property, or the purchase of services, for the personal, family, or household use of such individuals, that were not delivered or provided. The priority granted by this section shall be subordinate to that granted by Sections 18933 and 26312 of the Revenue and Taxation Code. *(Added by Stats.1979, c. 394, p. 1466, § 4, eff. July 27, 1979, operative Oct. 1, 1979. Amended by Stats.1980, c. 135, § 5.)*

Law Revision Commission Comments

Section 1204.5 is amended to delete the distinction between general assignments at common law "or otherwise." Former Civil Code Sections 3448 through 3473, which prescribed a general assignment other than at common law, are not continued. See Comment thereto.

§ 1205. Sale or transfer of business or stock in trade, in bulk, not in regular course of business; preferred wage claims

Upon the sale or transfer of any business or the stock in trade, in bulk, or a substantial part thereof, not in the ordinary and regular course of business or trade, unpaid wages of employees of the seller or transferor earned within ninety (90) days prior to the sale, transfer, or opening of an escrow for the sale thereof, shall constitute preferred claims and liens thereon as between creditors of the seller or transferor and must be paid first from the proceeds of the sale or transfer. *(Added by Stats.1961, c. 1083, p. 2814, § 1.)*

Research References

4 Witkin, California Summary 10th Sales § 226, Sales Through Escrow.

§ 1206. Writ of attachment or execution; preferred labor claims; verification; filing; notation on writ of execution or abstract of judgment; inclusion of claims in execution; payment; disputed claims; costs; hearing; appeal; retention of proceeds

(a) Upon the levy under a writ of attachment or execution not founded upon a claim for labor, any miner, mechanic, salesman, servant, clerk, laborer or other person who has performed work or rendered personal services for the defendant within 90 days prior to the levy may file a verified statement of the claim with the officer executing the writ, file a copy with the court that issued the writ, and give copies, containing his or her address, to the plaintiff and the defendant, or any attorney, clerk or agent representing them, or mail copies to them by registered mail at their last known address, return of which by the post office undelivered shall be deemed a sufficient service if no better address is available, and that claim, not exceeding nine hundred dollars ($900), unless disputed, shall be paid by the officer, immediately upon the expiration of the time for dispute of the claim as prescribed in Section 1207, from the proceeds of the levy remaining in the officer's hands at the time of the filing of the statement or collectible by the officer on the basis of the writ.

(b) The court issuing the writ shall make a notation in the register of actions of every preferred labor claim of which it receives a copy and shall endorse on any writ of execution or abstract of judgment issued subsequently in the case that it is issued subject to the rights of a preferred labor claimant or claimants and giving the names and amounts of all preferred labor claims of which it has notice. In levying under any writ of execution the officer making the levy shall include in the amount due under the execution all preferred labor claims that have been filed in the action and of which the officer has notice, except any claims that may have been finally disallowed by the court under this procedure and of which disallowance the officer has actual notice. The amount due on preferred labor claims that have not been finally disallowed by the court shall be considered a part of the sum due under any writ of attachment or execution in augmentation of that amount and any person, firm, association, or corporation on whom a writ of attachment or execution is levied shall immediately pay to the levying officer the amount of the preferred labor claims, out of any money belonging to the defendant in the action, before paying the principal sum called for in the writ.

(c) If any claim is disputed within the time, and in the manner prescribed in Section 1207, and a copy of the dispute is mailed by registered mail to the claimant or the claimant's attorney at the address given in the statement of claim and the registry receipt is attached to the original of the dispute when it is filed with the levying officer, or is handed to the claimant or the claimant's attorney, the claimant, or the claimant's assignee, must within 10 days after the copy is deposited in the mail or is handed to the claimant or the claimant's attorney, petition the court having jurisdiction of the action on which the claim is based, for a hearing before it to determine the claim for priority, or the claim to priority is barred. If more than one attachment or execution is involved, the petition shall be filed in the court having jurisdiction over the senior attachment or execution. The hearing shall be held within 20 days from the filing of the petition, unless the court continues it for good cause. Ten days' notice of the hearing shall be given by the petitioner to the plaintiff, the defendant, and all parties claiming an interest in the property, or their attorneys. The notice may be informal and need specify only the name of the court, the names of the principal parties to the senior attachment or execution, and the name of the wage claimant or claimants on whose behalf it is filed but shall specify that the hearing is for the purpose of determining the claim for priority. The plaintiff, the defendant, or any other party claiming an interest may contest the amount or validity of the claim in spite of any confession of judgment or failure to appear or to contest the claim on the part of any other person.

(d) There shall be no cost for filing or hearing the petition. The hearing on the petition shall be informal but all parties testifying shall be sworn. Any claimant may appear on the claimant's own behalf at the hearing and may call and examine witnesses to substantiate his or her claim. An appeal may be taken from a judgment in a proceeding under this section in the manner provided for appeals from judgments of the court where the proceeding occurred, in an action of the same jurisdictional classification.

(e) The officer shall keep, until the determination of the claim for priority, any amount of the proceeds of the writ necessary to satisfy the claim. If the claim for priority is allowed, the officer shall pay the amount due, including the claimant's cost of suit, from those proceeds, immediately after the order allowing the claim becomes final. *(Added by Stats.1907, c. 256, p. 321, § 1. Amended by Stats.1929, c. 230, p. 432, § 1; Stats.1931, c. 822, p. 1702, § 1; Stats.1935, c. 557, p. 1644, § 1; Stats.1951, c. 476, p. 1613, § 2; Stats.1961, c. 1085, p. 2815, § 1; Stats.1982, c. 497, p. 2171, § 77, operative July 1, 1983; Stats.1998, c. 931 (S.B.2139), § 121, eff. Sept. 28, 1998; Stats.2001, c. 44 (S.B.562), § 7; Stats.2002, c. 664 (A.B.3034), § 51.)*

Law Revision Commission Comments

Section 1206 is amended to delete references to garnishment which is not a separate remedy. The other changes are not substantive (15 Cal.L.Rev.Comm. Reports 2001).

Section 1206 is amended to accommodate unification of the municipal and superior courts in a county. Cal. Const. art. VI, § 5(e). See Sections 32.5 (jurisdictional classification), 85 (limited civil cases), 904.1 (taking appeal), 904.2 (taking appeal in limited civil case). See also Section 85 Comment. [28 Cal.L.Rev.Comm. Reports 51 (1998)].

Section 1206 is amended to replace the term "docket" with "register of actions," because courts no longer maintain a record denominated a "docket" in civil cases. Formerly, justice courts maintained a docket in civil cases, which was a record of actions taken in open court, as well as documents filed and other proceedings in the case. See former Gov't Code 71614 (1953 Cal. Stat. ch. 206, 1, repealed by 1977 Cal. Stat. ch. 1257, 71) (judge of justice court shall keep a book denominated a "docket"), 71614.5 (1959 Cal. Stat. ch. 671, 2, repealed by 1977 Cal. Stat. ch. 1257, 72) (clerk or judge of justice court shall keep the "docket" and other records of the court). Now actions taken in open court are recorded in the minutes of a superior court. Gov't Code 69844; see also Copley Press v. Superior Court, 6 Cal.App.4th 106, 110, 7 Cal.Rptr.2d 841 (1992). Documents filed or lodged and other proceedings in a civil case are recorded in the register of actions. See Gov't Code 69845 (clerk of superior court may keep a register of actions), 69845.5 (alternative to maintaining register of actions in superior court).

Technical changes are also made for conformity with preferred drafting style. [30 Cal.L.Rev.Comm. Reports 479 (2000)].

Research References

Rutter, Cal. Practice Guide: Civ. Pro. Before Trial Ch. 9(II)-D, D. Attachment.

California Practice Guide: Employment Litigation Ch. 11-J, J. Enforcing California Laws Regulating Employee Compensation.

Rutter, Cal. Practice Guide: Enforcing Judgments/Debts Ch. 4-A, A. Attachment.

Rutter, Cal. Practice Guide: Enforcing Judgments/Debts Ch. 6D-7, Sale and Collection of Property Levied Upon.

Miller and Starr California Real Estate § 32:17, Unsecured Obligation.

Miller and Starr California Real Estate § 11:164, Personal Property Tax Liens.

Miller and Starr California Real Estate § 11:167, State Tax Liens-- Unemployment Insurance Contribution Liens.

8 Witkin Cal. Proc. 5th Enforcement of Judgment § 153, in General.

8 Witkin Cal. Proc. 5th Enforcement of Judgment § 158, (S 158) Order of Distribution.

6 Witkin Cal. Proc. 5th Provisional Remedies § 179, Securities.

6 Witkin Cal. Proc. 5th Provisional Remedies § 186, (S 186) Other Rules of Priority.

9 Witkin, California Summary 10th Taxation § 370, Lien and Priority.

§ 1207.　Disputed claims; admission of part of claim; costs

Within five days after receiving a copy of the statement provided for in the next preceding section, either the plaintiff or the defendant in the action in which the writ issued may file with the officer a sworn statement denying that any part of such claim is due for services rendered within ninety days next preceding the levy of the writ, or denying that any part of such claim, beyond a sum specified, is so due. Such sworn statement can not be made on information and belief unless the party swearing to same has actual information and belief that the wage claim, or the portion thereof that is contested, is not justly due, and in such case the nature and source of the information must be given. If a part of the claim is admitted to be due, and the claimant nevertheless files a petition for hearing and the court does not allow more than the amount so admitted, he can not recover costs but the costs must be adjudged against him, and the amount thereof deducted from the sum found due him. *(Added by Stats.1907, c. 256, p. 322, § 1. Amended by Stats.1931, c. 822, p. 1703, § 2; Stats.1935, c. 557, p. 1645, § 2.)*

§ 1208.　Pro rata distribution of proceeds of writ; costs; proceedings by claimants against property levied upon; notice of intention to release

If the claims presented under Section 1206 and not disputed, or, if disputed, established by judgment, exceed the proceeds of the writ not disposed of before their presentation, such proceeds shall be distributed among the claimants in proportion to the amount of their respective claims after the costs incurred by the senior attaching plaintiff or judgment creditor in such action have first been taken care of.

If sufficient money to pay in full all preferred labor claims filed under an attachment or execution does not become available immediately upon the expiration of the time for dispute of such claims under Section 1207, any of the claimants, or their assignees, have the right to proceed directly against the money or other property levied on in individual or joint actions by themselves or their assignees against the defendant, and the attachment or execution under which the preferred claims were filed shall be considered set aside as far as such claimants, or their assignees, are concerned so as to enable them, or any of them, or any of their assignees, to proceed directly against any or all of the money or other property in question by means of their own attachments or executions; provided, however, that any money collected on behalf of any such labor claimant, or his or her assignee, on the basis of such new attachment or execution

shall be shared in by the other preferred labor claimants who have filed claims that have not been disputed, or, if disputed, established by judgment, in proportion to the amount of their respective claims, deducting only the costs in the action brought by the said labor claimant, or his or her assignee, and the costs in the original action brought by the senior attaching plaintiff or judgment creditor.

If such senior attaching plaintiff or judgment creditor requests a release of his or her original attachment or execution, and the preferred labor claims filed under same are not released, the officer who levied the writ must first mail notices of such request to release to each of the labor claimants who have filed claims, or their attorneys, which notices must specify that unless the claimants bring attachment actions of their own and levy on the money or property in question within five days from the date thereof the money or property will be released from the attachment or execution; provided, however, that such officer may instead collect sufficient money on the basis of the original writ to pay off the preferred labor claims in full and then release the attachment or execution, but in no case shall the officer release the attachment or execution without first taking care of the labor claims until the five-day period has expired, unless the officer's costs, keepers' fees or storage charges have not been immediately taken care of by some of the parties involved. In any case it shall be lawful for a garnishee to pay over to the officer levying the writ any money held by the garnishee without waiting for execution to be levied and the officer's receipt for the money shall be a sufficient quittance, and the officer shall collect such money and immediately pay off the established preferred labor claims in all cases where it is possible to do so without additional court proceedings on the officer's part. *(Added by Stats.1907, c. 256, p. 322, § 1. Amended by Stats.1931, c. 822, p. 1703, § 3; Stats.1982, c. 497, p. 2172, § 78, operative July 1, 1983.)*

Law Revision Commission Comments

Section 1208 is amended to delete references to garnishment which is not a separate remedy. The other changes are not substantive (15 Cal.L.Rev.Comm. Reports 2001).

Research References

Rutter, Cal. Practice Guide: Enforcing Judgments/Debts Ch. 6D-7, Sale and Collection of Property Levied Upon.

Miller and Starr California Real Estate § 32:17, Unsecured Obligation.

CHAPTER 4.　CERTAIN LIENS UPON ANIMALS

Section

1208.5.　Satisfaction of liens for acts in prevention of cruelty to animals; action; sale; notice; proceeds.

§ 1208.5.　Satisfaction of liens for acts in prevention of cruelty to animals; action; sale; notice; proceeds

Any person having a lien upon any animal or animals under the provisions of Section 597a or 597f of the Penal Code may satisfy the lien as follows: If the lien is not discharged and satisfied, by the person responsible, within three days after the obligation becomes due, then the person holding the lien may resort to the proper court to satisfy the claim; or may, three days after the charges against the property become due, sell the property, or an undivided fraction thereof as may become necessary, to defray the amount due and costs of sale, by giving three days' notice of the sale by advertising in some newspaper published in the county, or city and county, in which the lien has attached to the property; or, if there is no newspaper published in the county, then by posting notices of the sale in three of the most public places in the town or county for three days previous to the sale. The notices shall contain an accurate description of the property to be sold, together with the terms of sale, which must be for cash, payable on the consummation of the sale. The proceeds of the sale shall be applied to the discharge of the lien and the costs of sale; the remainder, if any, shall be paid over to the owner, if known, and if not known shall be paid into the treasury of the humane society of the county, or city and county, wherein the sale takes place; if no humane society exists in the county, then the remainder shall be paid into the county treasury. *(Formerly § 1208, added by Stats.1905, c. 472, p. 632, § 1. Amended by Stats.1935, c. 104, p. 457, § 1. Renumbered § 1208.5 and amended by Stats.1943, c. 913, p. 2770, § 1. Amended by Stats.1951, c. 1737, p. 4141, § 161, operative Jan. 1, 1952; Stats.1980, c. 676, § 67; Stats.2002, c. 784 (S.B.1316), § 81; Stats.2003, c. 62 (S.B.600), § 25.)*

Law Revision Commission Comments

Section 1208.5 is amended to reflect unification of the municipal and superior courts pursuant to Article VI, Section 5(e), of the California Constitution. See Section 38 (judicial district). [32 Cal.L.Rev.Comm. Reports 136 (2002)].

CHAPTER 5. LIENS ON AIRCRAFT

§ 1208.61.   Persons entitled to lien; possession

Subject to the limitations set forth in this chapter, every person has a lien dependent upon possession for the compensation to which he is legally entitled for making repairs or performing labor upon, and furnishing supplies or materials for, and for the storage, repair, or safekeeping of, any aircraft, also for reasonable charges for the use of any landing aid furnished such aircraft and reasonable landing fees. *(Added by Stats.1953, c. 52, p. 705, § 8.)*

Research References

13 Witkin, California Summary 10th Personal Property § 233, (S 233) Statutory List.
13 Witkin, California Summary 10th Personal Property § 243, Aircraft Keeper's or Repairer's Lien.

§ 1208.62.   Amount of lien; notice to and consent of legal owner and mortgagee

That portion of such lien in excess of two hundred fifty dollars ($250) for work or services rendered or performed at the request of any person other than the holder of the legal title is invalid, unless prior to commencing such work or service the person claiming the lien gives actual notice to the legal owner and the mortgagee, if any, of the aircraft, and the written consent of the legal owner and the mortgagee of the aircraft is obtained before such work or services are performed. For the purposes of this chapter the person named in the federal aircraft registration certificate issued by the Administrator of Civil Aeronautics shall be deemed to be the legal owner. *(Added by Stats.1953, c. 52, p. 705, § 8.)*

Research References

13 Witkin, California Summary 10th Personal Property § 243, Aircraft Keeper's or Repairer's Lien.

§ 1208.63.   Assignment; delivery of possession; notice

Any lien for labor or materials provided for in this chapter may be assigned by written instrument accompanied by delivery of possession of the aircraft subject to the lien and the assignee may exercise the rights of a lienholder pursuant to this chapter. Any lienholder assigning a lien shall at the time of the assignment give written notice, either by personal delivery or by registered mail with return receipt requested, to the legal owner of the property covered by the lien, including the name and address of the person to whom the lien is assigned. *(Added by Stats.1953, c. 52, p. 705, § 8.)*

Research References

13 Witkin, California Summary 10th Personal Property § 243, Aircraft Keeper's or Repairer's Lien.

§ 1208.64.   Loss of possession; revival on repossession; priorities

Whenever the lien upon any aircraft is lost by reason of the loss of possession through trick, fraud, or device, the repossession of such aircraft by the lienholder revives the lien, but the lien so revived is subordinate to any right, title, or interest of any person under any sale, transfer, encumbrance, lien, or other interest acquired or secured in good faith and for value between the time of the loss of possession and the time of repossession. *(Added by Stats.1953, c. 52, p. 705, § 8.)*

Research References

13 Witkin, California Summary 10th Personal Property § 243, Aircraft Keeper's or Repairer's Lien.

§ 1208.65.   Sale to satisfy lien

If the lienholder is not paid the amount due within 10 days after it becomes due, the lienholder may proceed to sell the property, or so much thereof as is necessary to satisfy the lien and costs of sale, at public auction. *(Added by Stats.1953, c. 52, p. 705, § 8.)*

Validity

This section was held unconstitutional as a violation of procedural due process in the decision of Martin v. Heady (Cal.App., 1980), 163 Cal.Rptr. 117, 103 Cal.App.3d 580.

Research References

13 Witkin, California Summary 10th Personal Property § 243, Aircraft Keeper's or Repairer's Lien.

§ 1208.66.   Notice of sale

Prior to any such sale the lienholder shall publish a notice of the sale pursuant to Section 6062 of the Government Code in a newspaper published in the county in which the aircraft is situated, or if there is no such newspaper, by posting notice of sale in three of the most public places in the city or place where such aircraft is to be sold for 10 days previous to the date of the sale. Prior to the sale of any aircraft to satisfy any such lien, 20 days' notice by registered mail shall be given to the legal owner as it appears in the registration certificate. *(Added by Stats.1953, c. 52, p. 705, § 8. Amended by Stats.1957, c. 452, p. 1304, § 1.)*

Validity

This section was held unconstitutional as a violation of procedural due process in the decision of Martin v. Heady (Cal.App., 1980), 163 Cal.Rptr. 117, 103 Cal.App.3d 580.

§ 1208.67. Proceeds of sale

The proceeds of the sale must be applied to the discharge of the lien and the cost of keeping and selling the property. The remainder, if any, shall be paid to the legal owner. *(Added by Stats.1953, c. 52, p. 706, § 8.)*

Validity

This section was held unconstitutional as a violation of procedural due process in the decision of Martin v. Heady (Cal.App., 1980), 163 Cal.Rptr. 117, 103 Cal.App.3d 580.

§ 1208.68. Redemption after sale

Within 20 days after the sale, the legal owner may redeem the aircraft so sold upon the payment of the amount of the lien, all costs and expenses of sale, and interest on such sum at the rate of 12 percent a year from the date it became due or the date when the amounts were advanced until the repayment. *(Added by Stats.1953, c. 52, p. 706, § 8.)*

Validity

This section was held unconstitutional as a violation of procedural due process in the decision of Martin v. Heady (Cal.App., 1980), 163 Cal.Rptr. 117, 103 Cal.App.3d 580.

§ 1208.69. Aircraft subject to lien; improperly obtaining possession; offense

It is a misdemeanor for any person to obtain possession of all or any part of any aircraft subject to a lien under this chapter through surreptitious removal or by trick, fraud, or device perpetrated upon the lienholder. *(Added by Stats.1953, c. 52, p. 706, § 8.)*

§ 1208.70. Exclusions from chapter

This chapter shall not apply to aircraft operated exclusively by an air carrier or a foreign air carrier, as defined in subdivisions (2) and (19) of Section 1 of Chapter 601 of the Statutes of the Seventy-fifth United States Congress, Second Session (1938), engaged in air transportation as defined in subdivision (10) of the same section while there is in force a certificate by, or a foreign air carrier permit of, the Civil Aeronautics Board of the United States, or its successor, authorizing such air carrier to engage in such transportation. *(Added by Stats.1953, c. 52, p. 706, § 8.)*

Research References

13 Witkin, California Summary 10th Personal Property § 243, Aircraft Keeper's or Repairer's Lien.

Title 5

OF CONTEMPTS

§ 1209. Acts or omissions constituting; stay of sentence pending appeal

(a) The following acts or omissions in respect to a court of justice, or proceedings therein, are contempts of the authority of the court:

(1) Disorderly, contemptuous, or insolent behavior toward the judge while holding the court, tending to interrupt the due course of a trial or other judicial proceeding.

(2) A breach of the peace, boisterous conduct, or violent disturbance, tending to interrupt the due course of a trial or other judicial proceeding.

(3) Misbehavior in office, or other willful neglect or violation of duty by an attorney, counsel, clerk, sheriff, coroner, or other person, appointed or elected to perform a judicial or ministerial service.

(4) Abuse of the process or proceedings of the court, or falsely pretending to act under authority of an order or process of the court.

(5) Disobedience of any lawful judgment, order, or process of the court.

(6) Willful disobedience by a juror of a court admonishment related to the prohibition on any form of communication or research about the case, including all forms of electronic or wireless communication or research.

(7) Rescuing any person or property in the custody of an officer by virtue of an order or process of that court.

(8) Unlawfully detaining a witness or party to an action while going to, remaining at, or returning from the court where the action is on the calendar for trial.

(9) Any other unlawful interference with the process or proceedings of a court.

(10) Disobedience of a subpoena duly served, or refusing to be sworn or answer as a witness.

(11) When summoned as a juror in a court, neglecting to attend or serve as a juror, or improperly conversing with a party to an action to be tried at the court, or with any other person, in relation to the merits of the action, or receiving a communication

from a party or other person in respect to the action, without immediately disclosing the communication to the court.

(12) Disobedience by an inferior tribunal or judicial officer of the lawful judgment, order, or process of a superior court, or proceeding in an action or special proceeding contrary to law, after the action or special proceeding is removed from the jurisdiction of the inferior tribunal or judicial officer.

(b) A speech or publication reflecting upon or concerning a court or an officer thereof shall not be treated or punished as a contempt of the court unless made in the immediate presence of the court while in session and in such a manner as to actually interfere with its proceedings.

(c) Notwithstanding Section 1211 or any other law, if an order of contempt is made affecting an attorney, his or her agent, investigator, or any person acting under the attorney's direction, in the preparation and conduct of an action or proceeding, the execution of any sentence shall be stayed pending the filing within three judicial days of a petition for extraordinary relief testing the lawfulness of the court's order, the violation of which is the basis of the contempt, except for conduct proscribed by subdivision (b) of Section 6068 of the Business and Professions Code, relating to an attorney's duty to maintain respect due to the courts and judicial officers.

(d) Notwithstanding Section 1211 or any other law, if an order of contempt is made affecting a public safety employee acting within the scope of employment for reason of the employee's failure to comply with a duly issued subpoena or subpoena duces tecum, the execution of any sentence shall be stayed pending the filing within three judicial days of a petition for extraordinary relief testing the lawfulness of the court's order, a violation of which is the basis for the contempt.

As used in this subdivision, "public safety employee" includes any peace officer, firefighter, paramedic, or any other employee of a public law enforcement agency whose duty is either to maintain official records or to analyze or present evidence for investigative or prosecutorial purposes. *(Enacted in 1872. Amended by Stats.1891, c. 9, p. 6, § 1; Stats.1907, c. 255, p. 319, § 1; Stats.1939, c. 979, p. 2731, § 1; Stats.1975, c. 836, p. 1896, § 2; Stats.1982, c. 510, p. 2286, § 2; Stats.2011, c. 181 (A.B.141), § 3.)*

Research References

Rutter, Cal. Practice Guide: Civil Appeals & Writs Ch. 15-D, D. Writ Review of Contempt Orders.

Rutter, Cal. Practice Guide: Civ. Pro. Before Trial Ch. 4-D, D. Service of Summons.

Rutter, Cal. Practice Guide: Civ. Pro. Before Trial Ch. 8E-6, Subpoena to Nonparty Deponent or Business Records Custodian.

Rutter, Cal. Practice Guide: Civ. Pro. Before Trial Ch. 9(II)-A, A. Injunctions.

Rutter, Cal. Practice Guide: Civil Trials & Evidence Ch. 4-F, F. Motions in Limine.

Rutter, Cal. Practice Guide: Civil Trials & Evidence Ch. 6-E, E. Remedies for Misconduct During Opening Statement.

Rutter, Cal. Practice Guide: Civil Trials & Evidence Ch. 7-B, B. Explanations, Admonitions and Preinstructions.

Rutter, Cal. Practice Guide: Civil Trials & Evidence Ch. 7-F, F. Juror Misconduct During Trial.

Rutter, Cal. Practice Guide: Civil Trials & Evidence Ch. 10-A, A. Preliminary Considerations.

Rutter, Cal. Practice Guide: Civil Trials & Evidence Ch. 12-A, A. Motion for Mistrial.

Rutter, Cal. Practice Guide: Civil Trials & Evidence Ch. 12-E, E. Contempt Proceedings.

Rutter, Cal. Practice Guide: Civil Trials & Evidence Ch. 13-B, B. Proper vs. Improper Closing Argument.

Rutter, Cal. Practice Guide: Civil Trials & Evidence Ch. 13-C, C. Challenging Improper Argument.

Rutter, Cal. Practice Guide: Civil Trials & Evidence Ch. 15-F, F. Juror Misconduct During Deliberations.

Rutter, Cal. Practice Guide: Civil Trials & Evidence Gen. Matls., Highlights.

Rutter, Cal. Practice Guide: Enforcing Judgments/Debts Ch. 6G-1, Examination of Judgment Debtor and Third Parties.

Rutter, Cal. Practice Guide: Enforcing Judgments/Debts Ch. 6G-4, Creditor's Suit.

Rutter, Cal. Practice Guide: Enforcing Judgments/Debts Ch. 6G-5, Assignment Order.

Rutter, Cal. Practice Guide: Prof. Responsibility Ch. 2-A, A. Regulations Generally.

Rutter, Cal. Practice Guide: Prof. Responsibility Ch. 8-C, C. Restrictions on Advocacy in Court Proceedings.

Rutter, Cal. Practice Guide: Prof. Responsibility Ch. 8-E, E. Consequences of Improper Advocacy.

3 Witkin Cal. Proc. 5th Actions § 65, (S 65) Statutory Classes.

3 Witkin Cal. Proc. 5th Actions § 69, (S 69) Contempt.

1 Witkin Cal. Proc. 5th Attorneys § 498, Disobedience of Order.

1 Witkin Cal. Proc. 5th Attorneys § 500, (S 500) Conduct Subject to Discipline.

1 Witkin Cal. Proc. 5th Attorneys § 556, (S 556) Other Measures.

2 Witkin Cal. Proc. 5th Courts § 61, (S 61) Sanctions for Violation.

2 Witkin Cal. Proc. 5th Courts § 362, (S 362) Control by Court.

8 Witkin Cal. Proc. 5th Enforcement of Judgment § 288, (S 288) Failure to Appear for Examination.

8 Witkin Cal. Proc. 5th Enforcement of Judgment § 340, Nature and Scope of Power.

8 Witkin Cal. Proc. 5th Enforcement of Judgment § 341, Action by District Attorney.

7 Witkin Cal. Proc. 5th Trial § 116, Adoption of Uniform System.

7 Witkin Cal. Proc. 5th Trial § 169, Any Judicial Tribunal.

7 Witkin Cal. Proc. 5th Trial § 171, (S 171) Statutory Framework.

7 Witkin Cal. Proc. 5th Trial § 172, (S 172) Legislative Regulation.

7 Witkin Cal. Proc. 5th Trial § 186, (S 186) Right Under State Constitution.

7 Witkin Cal. Proc. 5th Trial § 189, (S 189) Disrespectful or Offensive Behavior.

7 Witkin Cal. Proc. 5th Trial § 190, Conduct Constituting Contempt.

7 Witkin Cal. Proc. 5th Trial § 195, (S 195) Deceiving or Taking Advantage of Court.

7 Witkin Cal. Proc. 5th Trial § 199, (S 199) Assisting Witness to Evade Subpena.

7 Witkin Cal. Proc. 5th Trial § 200, in General.

10 Witkin, California Summary 10th Parent and Child § 437, (S 437) Contempt Proceedings.

8 Witkin, California Summary 10th Constitutional Law § 895, Hate Crimes, Intimidation, and Threats of Violence.

13 Witkin, California Summary 10th Equity § 149, (S 149) Decision and Order.

2 Witkin Cal. Summ. 10th Workers' Compensation § 14, Powers.

§ 1209.5. Noncompliance with order for care or support of child

When a court of competent jurisdiction makes an order compelling a parent to furnish support or necessary food, clothing, shelter, medical attendance, or other remedial care for his or her child, proof that the order was made, filed, and served on the parent or proof that the parent was present in court at the time the order was pronounced and proof that the parent did not comply with the order is prima facie evidence of a contempt of court. *(Added by Stats.1955, c. 1359, p. 2444, § 1. Amended by Stats.1961, c. 1307, p. 3087, § 1, eff. July 10, 1961; Stats.1992, c. 163 (A.B.2641), § 57, operative Jan. 1, 1994.)*

Law Revision Commission Comments

Section 1209.5 is amended to make clear that it applies to an order directed to a mother as well as to a father. This is not a substantive change. See Code Civ.Proc. § 17 (masculine gender includes the feminine). [22 Cal.L.Rev.Comm.Reports 1 (1992)].

Research References

8 Witkin Cal. Proc. 5th Enforcement of Judgment § 343, in General.

8 Witkin Cal. Proc. 5th Enforcement of Judgment § 350, No Notice or Knowledge.

2 Witkin Cal. Proc. 5th Jurisdiction § 450, (S 450) Support: Dissolution Court and Other Court.

6 Witkin Cal. Proc. 5th Proceedings Without Trial § 131, (S 131) Paternity and Support Judgments.

7 Witkin Cal. Proc. 5th Trial § 171, (S 171) Statutory Framework.

10 Witkin, California Summary 10th Parent and Child § 437, (S 437) Contempt Proceedings.

§ 1210. Re-entry after ejectment; alias process after conviction; undertaking for appeal

Every person dispossessed or ejected from any any real property by the judgment or process of any court of competent jurisdiction, who, not having right so to do, reenters into or upon or takes possession of the real property, or induces or procures any person not having right so to do, or aids or abets such a person therein, is guilty of a contempt of the court by which the judgment was rendered or from which the process issued. Upon a conviction for contempt the court must immediately issue an alias process, directed to the proper officer, and requiring the officer to restore possession to the party entitled under the original judgment or process, or to the party's lessee, grantee, or successor in interest. No appeal from the order directing the issuance of an alias writ of possession stays the execution of the writ, unless an undertaking is executed on the part of the appellant to the effect that the appellant will not commit or suffer to be committed any waste on the property, and if the order is affirmed, or the appeal dismissed, the appellant will pay the value of the use and occupation of the property from the time of the unlawful reentry until the delivery of the possession of the property, pursuant to the judgment or order, not exceeding a sum to be fixed by the judge of the court by which the order for the alias writ was made. *(Enacted in 1872. Amended by Stats.1893, c. 198, p. 281, § 1; Stats.1907, c. 255, p. 320, § 2; Stats.1982, c. 517, p. 2362, § 179.)*

Law Revision Commission Comments

Section 1210 is amended to delete provisions duplicated in the Bond and Undertaking Law. See Sections 995.310 (sureties on undertaking) and 995.320 (contents of undertaking). The other changes in Section 1210 are technical. [16 Cal.L.Rev.Comm. Reports 501 (1982)].

Research References

Miller and Starr California Real Estate § 19:228, Prejudgment Remedies; Attachment and Receivership--Writ of Possession Before Trial.

Miller and Starr California Real Estate § 19:230, Trial; Judgment; Stay of Execution.

7 Witkin Cal. Proc. 5th Trial § 171, (S 171) Statutory Framework.

§ 1211. Summary punishment; order; affidavit or statement of facts; compliance by filing of form

(a) When a contempt is committed in the immediate view and presence of the court, or of the judge at chambers, it may be punished summarily; for which an order must be made, reciting the facts as occurring in such immediate view and presence, adjudging that the person proceeded against is thereby guilty of a contempt, and that he or she be punished as therein prescribed.

When the contempt is not committed in the immediate view and presence of the court, or of the judge at chambers, an affidavit shall be presented to the court or judge of the facts constituting the contempt, or a statement of the facts by the referees or arbitrators, or other judicial officers.

(b) In family law matters, filing of the Judicial Council form entitled "Order to Show Cause and Affidavit for Contempt (Family Law)" shall constitute compliance with this section. *(Enacted in 1872. Amended by Stats.1933, c. 745, p. 1906, § 11; Stats.1951, c. 1737, p. 4141, § 162, operative Jan. 1, 1952; Stats.1995, c. 904 (A.B.965), § 1; Stats.2001, c. 754 (A.B.1697), § 1.)*

Research References

Rutter, Cal. Practice Guide: A.D.R. Ch. 6-B, B. Temporary Judges.

Rutter, Cal. Practice Guide: Civil Appeals & Writs Ch. 15-D, D. Writ Review of Contempt Orders.

Rutter, Cal. Practice Guide: Civ. Pro. Before Trial Ch. 9(II)-A, A. Injunctions.

Rutter, Cal. Practice Guide: Civil Trials & Evidence Ch. 6-E, E. Remedies for Misconduct During Opening Statement.

Rutter, Cal. Practice Guide: Civil Trials & Evidence Ch. 12-E, E. Contempt Proceedings.

Rutter, Cal. Practice Guide: Enforcing Judgments/Debts Ch. 6G-1, Examination of Judgment Debtor and Third Parties.

Rutter, Cal. Practice Guide: Prof. Responsibility Ch. 8-E, E. Consequences of Improper Advocacy.

8 Witkin Cal. Proc. 5th Enforcement of Judgment § 343, in General.

7 Witkin Cal. Proc. 5th Trial § 175, Hearing.

7 Witkin Cal. Proc. 5th Trial § 177, Summary Punishment.

7 Witkin Cal. Proc. 5th Trial § 183, (S 183) Distinguishing Direct from Indirect Contempt.

7 Witkin Cal. Proc. 5th Trial § 184, (S 184) Order Affecting County Government.

7 Witkin Cal. Proc. 5th Trial § 203, Victim of Domestic Violence.

§ 1211.5. Affidavit or statement of facts; rules for construction, amendment and review

At all stages of all proceedings, the affidavit or statement of facts, as the case may be, required by Section 1211 shall be construed, amended, and reviewed according to the followings[1] rules:

(a) If no objection is made to the sufficiency of such affidavit or statement during the hearing on the charges contained therein, jurisdiction of the subject matter shall not depend on the averments of such affidavit or statement, but may be established by the facts found by the trial court to have been proved at such hearing, and the court shall cause the affidavit or statement to be amended to conform to proof.

(b) The court may order or permit amendment of such affidavit or statement for any defect or insufficiency at any stage of the proceedings, and the trial of the person accused of contempt shall continue as if the affidavit or statement had been originally filed as amended, unless substantial rights of such person accused would be prejudiced thereby, in which event a reasonable postponement, not longer than the ends of justice require, may be granted.

(c) No such affidavit or statement is insufficient, nor can the trial, order, judgment, or other proceeding thereon be affected by reason of any defect or imperfection in matter of form which does not prejudice a substantial right of the person accused on the merits. No order or judgment of conviction of contempt shall be set aside, nor new trial granted, for any error as to any matter of pleading in such affidavit or statement, unless, after an examination of the entire cause, including the evidence, the court shall be of the opinion that the error complained of has resulted in a miscarriage of justice. *(Added by Stats.1970, c. 1264, p. 2282, § 1.)*

[1] So in chaptered copy.

Research References

Rutter, Cal. Practice Guide: Civ. Pro. Before Trial Ch. 9(II)-A, A. Injunctions.

Rutter, Cal. Practice Guide: Civil Trials & Evidence Ch. 12-E, E. Contempt Proceedings.

8 Witkin Cal. Proc. 5th Enforcement of Judgment § 345, Construction, Amendment, and Review.

2 Witkin Cal. Proc. 5th Jurisdiction § 290, (S 290) Procedural Error or Omission.

7 Witkin Cal. Proc. 5th Trial § 176, Review.

§ 1212. Warrant of attachment; issuance; order to show cause; warrant of commitment

When the contempt is not committed in the immediate view and presence of the court or judge, a warrant of attachment may be issued to bring the person charged to answer, or, without a previous arrest, a warrant of commitment may, upon notice, or upon an order to show cause, be granted; and no warrant of commitment can be issued without such previous attachment to answer, or such notice or order to show cause. *(Enacted in 1872. Amended by Stats.1933, c. 745, p. 1906, § 12; Stats.1951, c. 1737, p. 4141, § 163, operative Jan. 1, 1952.)*

Research References

Rutter, Cal. Practice Guide: Civ. Pro. Before Trial Ch. 9(II)-A, A. Injunctions.
Rutter, Cal. Practice Guide: Civil Trials & Evidence Ch. 12-E, E. Contempt Proceedings.
Rutter, Cal. Practice Guide: Enforcing Judgments/Debts Ch. 6G-1, Examination of Judgment Debtor and Third Parties.
8 Witkin Cal. Proc. 5th Enforcement of Judgment § 346, in General.
6 Witkin Cal. Proc. 5th Proceedings Without Trial § 61, When Order is Used.

§ 1213. Warrant of attachment; endorsement for undertaking

Whenever a warrant of attachment is issued pursuant to this title the court or judge must direct, by an endorsement on the warrant, that the person charged may give an undertaking for the person's appearance in an amount to be specified in such endorsement. *(Enacted in 1872. Amended by Stats.1933, c. 745, p. 1906, § 13; Stats.1951, c. 1737, p. 4142, § 164, operative Jan. 1, 1952; Stats.1982, c. 517, p. 2362, § 179.5.)*

Law Revision Commission Comments

Section 1213 is amended to substitute the more accurate reference to an undertaking for the misleading reference to "bail." The other changes in Section 1213 are technical. [16 Cal.L.Rev.Comm. Reports 501 (1982)].

§ 1214. Warrant of attachment; execution

Upon executing the warrant of attachment, the officer executing the warrant must keep the person in custody, bring him before the court or judge, and detain him until an order be made in the premises, unless the person arrested entitle himself to be discharged, as provided in the next section. *(Enacted in 1872. Amended by Stats.1933, c. 745, p. 1906, § 14; Stats.1951, c. 1737, p. 4142, § 165, operative Jan. 1, 1952.)*

Research References

Miller and Starr California Real Estate § 11:147, Priority of Judgments and Pending Litigation; in General.

§ 1215. Discharge on undertaking

The person arrested must be discharged from the arrest upon executing and delivering to the officer, at any time before the return day of the warrant, an undertaking to the effect that the person arrested will appear on the return of the warrant and abide the order of the court or judge thereupon. *(Enacted in 1872. Amended by Stats.1933, c. 745, p. 1907, § 15; Stats.1951, c. 1737, p. 4142, § 166, operative Jan. 1, 1952; Stats.1982, c. 517, p. 2362, § 180.)*

Law Revision Commission Comments

Section 1215 is amended to delete the reference to "bail" and to delete provisions duplicated in the Bond and Undertaking Law. See Sections 995.310 (sureties on undertaking) and 995.320 (contents of undertaking). [16 Cal.L.Rev.Comm. Reports 501 (1982)].

§ 1216. Warrant of attachment; undertaking; return

OFFICER MUST RETURN WARRANT AND UNDERTAKING, IF ANY. The officer must return the warrant of arrest and undertaking, if any, received by him from the person arrested, by the return day specified therein. *(Enacted in 1872.)*

Research References

Rutter, Cal. Practice Guide: Civil Trials & Evidence Ch. 12-E, E. Contempt Proceedings.

§ 1217. Trial

When the person arrested has been brought up or appeared, the court or judge must proceed to investigate the charge, and must hear any answer which the person arrested may make to the same, and may examine witnesses for or against him, for which an adjournment may be had from time to time if necessary. *(Enacted in 1872. Amended by Stats.1933, c. 745, p. 1907, § 16; Stats.1951, c. 1737, p. 4142, § 167, operative Jan. 1, 1952).*

Research References

Rutter, Cal. Practice Guide: Civ. Pro. Before Trial Ch. 9(II)-A, A. Injunctions.
Rutter, Cal. Practice Guide: Civil Trials & Evidence Ch. 12-E, E. Contempt Proceedings.
8 Witkin Cal. Proc. 5th Enforcement of Judgment § 348, (S 348) Hearing.
7 Witkin Cal. Proc. 5th Trial § 31, (S 31) Particular Actions and Proceedings.

§ 1218. Determination of guilt; punishment; restrictions on enforcement of orders by party in contempt; action for contempt of domestic violence prevention order

(a) Upon the answer and evidence taken, the court or judge shall determine whether the person proceeded against is guilty of the contempt charged, and if it be adjudged that he or she is guilty of the contempt, a fine may be imposed on him or her not exceeding one thousand dollars ($1,000), payable to the court, or he or she may be imprisoned not exceeding five days, or both. In addition, a person who is subject to a court order as a party to the action, or any agent of this person, who is adjudged guilty of contempt for violating that court order may be ordered to pay to the party initiating the contempt proceeding the reasonable attorney's fees and costs incurred by this party in connection with the contempt proceeding.

(b) Any party, who is in contempt of a court order or judgment in a dissolution of marriage, dissolution of domestic partnership, or legal separation action, shall not be permitted to enforce such an order or judgment, by way of execution or otherwise, either in the same action or by way of a separate action, against the other party. This restriction shall not affect nor apply to the enforcement of child or spousal support orders.

(c) In any court action in which a party is found in contempt of court for failure to comply with a court order pursuant to the Family Code, the court shall order the following:

(1) Upon a first finding of contempt, the court shall order the contemner to perform community service of up to 120 hours, or to be imprisoned up to 120 hours, for each count of contempt.

(2) Upon the second finding of contempt, the court shall order the contemner to perform community service of up to 120 hours, in addition to ordering imprisonment of the contemner up to 120 hours, for each count of contempt.

(3) Upon the third or any subsequent finding of contempt, the court shall order both of the following:

(A) The court shall order the contemner to serve a term of imprisonment of up to 240 hours, and to perform community service of up to 240 hours, for each count of contempt.

(B) The court shall order the contemner to pay an administrative fee, not to exceed the actual cost of the contemner's administration and supervision, while assigned to a community service program pursuant to this paragraph.

(4) The court shall take parties' employment schedules into consideration when ordering either community service or imprisonment, or both.

(d) Pursuant to Section 1211 and this section, a district attorney or city attorney may initiate and pursue a court action for contempt against a party for failing to comply with a court order entered pursuant to the Domestic Violence Protection Act (Division 10 (commencing with Section 6200) of the Family Code). Any attorney's fees and costs ordered by the court pursuant to subdivision (a) against a party who is adjudged guilty of contempt under this subdivision shall be paid to the * * * Office of Emergency Services' account established for the purpose of funding domestic violence shelter service providers pursuant to subdivision (f) of Section 13823.15 of the Penal Code. *(Enacted in 1872. Amended by Stats.1933, c. 745, p. 1907, § 17; Stats.1951, c. 1737, p. 4142, § 168, operative Jan. 1, 1952; Stats.1968, c. 938, p. 1788, § 2; Stats.1977, c. 1257, p. 4770, § 39, eff. Jan. 3, 1977; Stats.1983, c. 1092, § 72, eff. Sept. 27, 1983, operative Jan. 1, 1984; Stats.1988, c. 969, § 2; Stats.1993, c. 745 (S.B.788), § 1; Stats.1993, c. 746 (A.B.934), § 1; Stats.1994, c. 368 (A.B.2911), § 1; Stats.1994, c. 1269 (A.B.2208), § 3.3; Stats.1995, c. 576 (A.B.1225), § 5.5; Stats.2000, c. 808 (A.B. 1358), § 20, eff. Sept. 28, 2000; Stats.2005, c. 75 (A.B.145), § 44, eff. July 19, 2005, operative Jan. 1, 2006; Stats.2005, c. 631 (S.B.720), § 1; Stats.2010, c. 618 (A.B.2791), § 3; Stats.2013, c. 352 (A.B.1317), § 56, eff. Sept. 26, 2013, operative July 1, 2013.)*

Research References

Rutter, Cal. Practice Guide: Civil Appeals & Writs Ch. 15-D, D. Writ Review of Contempt Orders.

Rutter, Cal. Practice Guide: Civ. Pro. Before Trial Ch. 8E-6, Subpoena to Nonparty Deponent or Business Records Custodian.

Rutter, Cal. Practice Guide: Civ. Pro. Before Trial Ch. 8E-16, Sanctions Re Depositions.

Rutter, Cal. Practice Guide: Civ. Pro. Before Trial Ch. 9(II)-A, A. Injunctions.

Rutter, Cal. Practice Guide: Civ. Pro. Before Trial Ch. 9(III)-A, A. Sources of Sanctions Power.

Rutter, Cal. Practice Guide: Civil Trials & Evidence Ch. 4-F, F. Motions in Limine.

Rutter, Cal. Practice Guide: Civil Trials & Evidence Ch. 12-E, E. Contempt Proceedings.

Rutter, Cal. Practice Guide: Civil Trials & Evidence Ch. 17-E, E. Attorney Fees as Costs.

Rutter, Cal. Practice Guide: Enforcing Judgments/Debts Ch. 6G-1, Examination of Judgment Debtor and Third Parties.

Rutter, Cal. Practice Guide: Real Prop. Transactions Ch. 12-B, B. Agreements Regarding Co-Ownership Rights and Obligations.

Rutter, Cal. Practice Guide: Prof. Responsibility Ch. 1-D, D. Unauthorized Practice of Law.

Rutter, Cal. Practice Guide: Prof. Responsibility Ch. 8-B, B. Accepting or Rejecting Employment.

Rutter, Cal. Practice Guide: Prof. Responsibility Ch. 8-E, E. Consequences of Improper Advocacy.

8 Witkin Cal. Proc. 5th Enforcement of Judgment § 341, Action by District Attorney.

8 Witkin Cal. Proc. 5th Enforcement of Judgment § 354, (S 354) Contempt Order.

8 Witkin Cal. Proc. 5th Enforcement of Judgment § 355, in General.

8 Witkin Cal. Proc. 5th Enforcement of Judgment § 356, (S 356) in General.

8 Witkin Cal. Proc. 5th Enforcement of Judgment § 357, (S 357) Necessity for Coercive Purpose.

8 Witkin Cal. Proc. 5th Enforcement of Judgment § 358, Denial of Litigation Rights.

8 Witkin Cal. Proc. 5th Enforcement of Judgment § 360, No Compensatory Damages.

8 Witkin Cal. Proc. 5th Enforcement of Judgment § 361, Multiple Punishment for Separate Acts.

2 Witkin Cal. Proc. 5th Jurisdiction § 327, Miscellaneous Unauthorized Orders.

2 Witkin Cal. Proc. 5th Jurisdiction § 394, Contempt of Prior Judgment or Order.

7 Witkin Cal. Proc. 5th Trial § 59, (S 59) Judicial Council Rules.

7 Witkin Cal. Proc. 5th Trial § 178, Jailing Attorney in Midtrial.

7 Witkin Cal. Proc. 5th Trial § 186, (S 186) Right Under State Constitution.

7 Witkin Cal. Proc. 5th Trial § 188, (S 188) Limitations on Punishment.

10 Witkin, California Summary 10th Parent and Child § 285, (S 285) in General.

10 Witkin, California Summary 10th Parent and Child § 417, (S 417) Provision and Termination of Coverage.

11 Witkin, California Summary 10th Husband and Wife § 205, Contempt.

11 Witkin, California Summary 10th Husband and Wife § 253, (S 253) Rights and Obligations of Employer.

11 Witkin, California Summary 10th Husband and Wife § 258, (S 258) Nature of Remedy.

11 Witkin, California Summary 10th Husband and Wife § 343, (S 343) CalWORKs Aid.

11 Witkin, California Summary 10th Husband and Wife § 362, Integrated Agreement.

11 Witkin, California Summary 10th Husband and Wife § 373, (S 373) in General.

13 Witkin, California Summary 10th Equity § 149, (S 149) Decision and Order.

§ 1218.5. Child, family, or spousal support; contempt for failure to pay; separate counts; limitation of actions

(a) If the contempt alleged is for failure to pay child, family, or spousal support, each month for which payment has not been made in full may be alleged as a separate count of contempt and punishment imposed for each count proven.

(b) If the contempt alleged is the failure to pay child, family, or spousal support, the period of limitations for commencing a contempt action is three years from the date that the payment was due. If the action before the court is enforcement of another order under the Family Code, the period of limitations for commencing a contempt action is two years from the time that the alleged contempt occurred. *(Added by Stats.1994, c. 1269 (A.B.2208), § 3.5.)*

Research References

8 Witkin Cal. Proc. 5th Enforcement of Judgment § 340, Nature and Scope of Power.

8 Witkin Cal. Proc. 5th Enforcement of Judgment § 361, Multiple Punishment for Separate Acts.

10 Witkin, California Summary 10th Parent and Child § 285, (S 285) in General.

11 Witkin, California Summary 10th Husband and Wife § 205, Contempt.

11 Witkin, California Summary 10th Husband and Wife § 258, (S 258) Nature of Remedy.

11 Witkin, California Summary 10th Husband and Wife § 259, (S 259) Procedure.

§ 1219. Imprisonment to compel performance of acts; exemption of sexual assault and domestic violence victims who refuse to testify; confidential communications between victim and counselor; definitions

(a) Except as provided in subdivision (b), when the contempt consists of the omission to perform an act which is yet in the power of the person to perform, he or she may be imprisoned until he or she has performed it, and in that case the act shall be specified in the warrant of commitment.

(b) Notwithstanding any other law, no court may imprison or otherwise confine or place in custody the victim of a sexual assault or domestic violence crime for contempt when the contempt consists of refusing to testify concerning that sexual assault or domestic violence crime. Before finding a victim of a domestic violence crime in contempt as described in this section, the court may refer the victim for consultation with a domestic violence counselor. All communications between the victim and the domestic violence counselor that occur as a result of that referral shall remain confidential under Section 1037.2 of the Evidence Code.

(c) As used in this section, the following terms have the following meanings:

(1) "Sexual assault" means any act made punishable by Section 261, 262, 264.1, 285, 286, 288, 288a, or 289 of the Penal Code.

(2) "Domestic violence" means "domestic violence" as defined in Section 6211 of the Family Code.

(3) "Domestic violence counselor" means "domestic violence counselor" as defined in subdivision (a) of Section 1037.1 of the Evidence Code. *(Enacted in 1872. Amended by Stats.1980, c. 676, § 68; Stats.1984, c. 1644, § 2; Stats.1991, c. 866 (A.B.363), § 4; Stats.1992, c. 163 (A.B.2641), § 58, operative Jan. 1, 1994; Stats.1993, c. 219 (A.B.1500), § 69.7; Stats.2008, c. 49 (S.B.1356), § 1; Stats.2009, c. 35 (S.B.174), § 3; Stats.2012, c. 510 (A.B. 2051), § 1.)*

Law Revision Commission Comments

Subdivision (d)(2) of Section 1219 is amended to substitute a reference to the Family Code provision defining "domestic violence." The Family Code definition is the same as the definition formerly included in this provision, except that the Family Code provision applies to children. See Fam. Code § 6211 ("domestic violence" defined) & Comment. For the special provisions applicable to child witnesses, see Code Civ. Proc. 1219.5 (referral to probation officer where minor in contempt); Penal Code §§ 1346–1348.5 (examination of child victims of abuse). [23 Cal.L.Rev. Comm. Reports 1 (1993)].

Research References

Rutter, Cal. Practice Guide: Civ. Pro. Before Trial Ch. 8E-16, Sanctions Re Depositions.
Rutter, Cal. Practice Guide: Civ. Pro. Before Trial Ch. 9(II)-A, A. Injunctions.
Rutter, Cal. Practice Guide: Civil Trials & Evidence Ch. 12-E, E. Contempt Proceedings.
Rutter, Cal. Practice Guide: Enforcing Judgments/Debts Ch. 6G-1, Examination of Judgment Debtor and Third Parties.
3 Witkin Cal. Proc. 5th Actions § 69, (S 69) Contempt.
8 Witkin Cal. Proc. 5th Enforcement of Judgment § 354, (S 354) Contempt Order.
8 Witkin Cal. Proc. 5th Enforcement of Judgment § 356, (S 356) in General.
7 Witkin Cal. Proc. 5th Trial § 188, (S 188) Limitations on Punishment.
7 Witkin Cal. Proc. 5th Trial § 200, in General.
7 Witkin Cal. Proc. 5th Trial § 202, Victim of Sexual Assault.
7 Witkin Cal. Proc. 5th Trial § 203, Victim of Domestic Violence.

§ 1219.5. Minors under 16 years of age; refusal to take oath; referral to probation officer; meeting with victim advocate; placement outside minor's home; sanctions

(a) Except as provided in subdivision (d), in any case in which a contempt consists of the refusal of a minor under 16 years of age to take the oath or to testify, before imposing any sanction for the contempt, the court shall first refer the matter to the probation officer in charge of matters coming before the juvenile court for a report and recommendation as to the appropriateness of the imposition of a sanction. The probation officer shall prepare and file the report and recommendation within the time directed by the court. In making the report and recommendation, the probation officer shall consider factors such as the maturity of the minor, the reasons for the minor's refusal to take the oath or to testify, the probability that available sanctions will affect the decision of the minor not to take the oath or not to testify, the potential impact on the minor of his or her testimony, the potential impact on the pending litigation of the minor's unavailability as a witness, and the appropriateness of the various available sanctions in the minor's case. The court shall consider the report and recommendation in imposing a sanction in the case.

(b) A victim of a sex crime who is subject to subdivision (a) shall meet with a victim advocate, as defined in Section 679.04 of the Penal Code, unless the court, for good cause, finds that it is not in the best interest of the victim.

(c) In any case in which the court orders the minor to be placed outside of his or her home, the placement shall be in the least restrictive setting available. Except as provided in subdivision (e), the court shall not order the minor to be placed in a secure facility unless other placements have been made and the minor has fled the custody and control of the person under the control of whom he or she has been placed or has persistently refused to obey the reasonable and proper orders or directions of the person under the control of whom he or she has been placed.

(d) The court may impose a sanction for contempt prior to receipt of the report and recommendation required by subdivision (a) if the court enters a finding, supported by specific facts stated on the record, that the minor would be likely to flee if released before the receipt of the report and recommendation.

(e) The court may order the minor placed in a secure facility without first attempting the nonsecure placement required by subdivision (c) if the court enters a finding, supported by specific facts stated on the record, that the minor would be likely to flee if released to nonsecure placement as a prerequisite to secure confinement. *(Added by Stats.1984, c. 1643, § 1. Amended by Stats.2012, c. 223 (S.B.1248), § 1.)*

Research References

7 Witkin Cal. Proc. 5th Trial § 201, Minor Under Age 16.
10 Witkin, California Summary 10th Parent and Child § 284, Trial.

§ 1220. Nonappearance; alias warrant; enforcement of undertaking; damages

When the warrant of arrest has been returned served, if the person arrested does not appear on the return day, the court or judge may issue another warrant of arrest or may order the undertaking to be enforced, or both. If the undertaking is enforced, the measure of damages is the extent of the loss or injury sustained by the aggrieved party by reason of the misconduct for which the warrant was issued. *(Enacted in 1872. Amended by Stats.1933, c. 745, p. 1907, § 18; Stats.1951, c. 1737, p. 2143, § 169, operative Jan. 1, 1952; Stats.1982, c. 517, p. 2362, § 181.)*

Law Revision Commission Comments

Section 1220 is amended to delete a provision duplicated in the Bond and Undertaking Law and for consistency with the provisions of the Law. See Sections 996.410–996.495 (liability of principal and sureties) and 996.460 (judgment of liability). [16 Cal.L.Rev.Comm. Reports 501 (1982)].

§ 1221. Illness for excuse for not bringing in prisoner; unnecessary restraint

Whenever, by the provisions of this title, an officer is required to keep a person arrested on a warrant of attachment in custody, and to bring him before a court or judge, the inability, from illness or otherwise, of the person to attend, is a sufficient excuse for not bringing him up; and the officer must not confine a person arrested upon the warrant in a prison, or otherwise restrain him of personal liberty, except so far as may be necessary to secure his personal attendance. *(Enacted in 1872. Amended by Stats.1933, c. 745, p. 1907, § 19; Stats.1951, c. 1737, p. 4143, § 170, operative Jan. 1, 1952.)*

§ 1222. Conclusiveness of judgments and orders

The judgment and orders of the court or judge, made in cases of contempt, are final and conclusive. *(Enacted in 1872. Amended by Stats.1933, c. 745, p. 1908, § 20; Stats.1951, c. 1737, p. 4143, § 171, operative Jan. 1, 1952.)*

Civ. Pro.

Research References

Rutter, Cal. Practice Guide: Civil Appeals & Writs Ch. 2-B, B. Appealable Judgments and Orders.

Rutter, Cal. Practice Guide: Civil Appeals & Writs Ch. 15-B, B. Common Law Writs.

Rutter, Cal. Practice Guide: Civ. Pro. Before Trial Ch. 9(II)-A, A. Injunctions.

Rutter, Cal. Practice Guide: Civil Trials & Evidence Ch. 12-E, E. Contempt Proceedings.

Rutter, Cal. Practice Guide: Enforcing Judgments/Debts Ch. 6G-1, Examination of Judgment Debtor and Third Parties.

Rutter, Cal. Practice Guide: Enforcing Judgments/Debts Ch. 6G-4, Creditor's Suit.

9 Witkin Cal. Proc. 5th Appeal § 95, (S 95) Appeal from Judgment.

9 Witkin Cal. Proc. 5th Appeal § 147, Contempt.

9 Witkin Cal. Proc. 5th Appeal § 149, (S 149) Judgment Directed at Superior Court.

9 Witkin Cal. Proc. 5th Appeal § 1004, (S 1004) Appealable Judgments and Orders.

8 Witkin Cal. Proc. 5th Enforcement of Judgment § 362, (S 362) Review by Certiorari or Habeas Corpus.

8 Witkin Cal. Proc. 5th Extraordinary Writs § 35, (S 35) Contempt Orders.

7 Witkin Cal. Proc. 5th Trial § 177, Summary Punishment.

7 Witkin Cal. Proc. 5th Trial § 182, Review.

Title 7

EMINENT DOMAIN LAW

CHAPTER 1. GENERAL PROVISIONS

§ 1230.010. Short title

This title shall be known and may be cited as the Eminent Domain Law. *(Added by Stats.1975, c. 1275, p. 3410, § 2, operative July 1, 1976.)*

Law Revision Commission Comments

Section 1230.010 is similar to comparable sections in recently enacted California laws. E.g., Civil Code § 4000 (The Family Law Act).

Research References

Rutter, Cal. Practice Guide: Real Prop. Transactions Ch. 7-C, C. Representing the Purchasing Tenant.

Miller and Starr California Real Estate § 30:1, Basis for Inverse Condemnation.

Miller and Starr California Real Estate § 30A:1, Introduction.

Miller and Starr California Real Estate § 30A:3, California Eminent Domain Law.

Miller and Starr California Real Estate § 30B:2, Sources and Validity of Redevelopment Law.

Miller and Starr California Real Estate § 30B:21, Application of Eminent Domain Law.

3 Witkin Cal. Proc. 5th Actions § 65, (S 65) Statutory Classes.

3 Witkin Cal. Proc. 5th Actions § 378, (S 378) Condemnation Action.

5 Witkin Cal. Proc. 5th Pleading § 1170, Exceptions.

6 Witkin Cal. Proc. 5th Proceedings Without Trial § 84, (S 84) Distinction: Inverse Condemnation Actions.

7 Witkin Cal. Proc. 5th Trial § 74, Completion of Discovery.

13 Witkin, California Summary 10th Personal Property § 27, (S 27) in General.

8 Witkin, California Summary 10th Constitutional Law § 1112, (S 1112) Nature of Power.

8 Witkin, California Summary 10th Constitutional Law § 1170, Nature, Organization, and Scope.

8 Witkin, California Summary 10th Constitutional Law § 1174, Jurisdiction of Public Utilities Commission.

§ 1230.020. Exercise of power

Except as otherwise specifically provided by statute, the power of eminent domain may be exercised only as provided in this title. *(Added by Stats.1975, c. 1275, p. 3410, § 2, operative July 1, 1976.)*

Law Revision Commission Comments

Section 1230.020 is the same in substance as the second sentence of former Section 1237. See also former Section 1258. The provisions of the Eminent Domain Law govern all acquisitions by eminent domain except to the extent that specific provision is otherwise made by statute. Instances of specific provisions otherwise are (1) where the Public Utilities Commission may determine just compensation (see Pub.Util.Code §§ 1206–1218 and 1401–1421) and (2) where the state has expressly provided that federal law controls (see, e.g., County of Marin v. Superior Court, 53 Cal.2d 633, 349 P.2d 526, 2 Cal.Rptr. 758 (1960)). In addition, there may be specific provisions in other statutes that are preserved even though they may impose restrictions beyond those of the Eminent Domain Law. See, e.g., Fish and Game Code § 1348 (condemnation only with consent of board of supervisors in county where property is situated); Pub.Res.Code § 5542 (limitations on acquisition of property already appropriated to public use).

The provisions of the Eminent Domain Law are intended to supply rules only for eminent domain proceedings. The law of inverse condemnation is left for determination by judicial development. *Cf.* Section 1263.010 and Comment thereto (right to compensation).

Research References

Miller and Starr California Real Estate § 30A:3, California Eminent Domain Law.

Miller and Starr California Real Estate § 19:149, Valuation and Apportionment of the Award.

8 Witkin, California Summary 10th Constitutional Law § 1170, Nature, Organization, and Scope.

§ 1230.030. Acquisition of property; purchase, eminent domain or other means

Nothing in this title requires that the power of eminent domain be exercised to acquire property necessary for public use. Whether property necessary for public use is to be acquired by purchase or other means or by eminent domain is a decision left to the discretion of the person authorized to acquire the property. *(Added by Stats.1975, c. 1275, p. 3410, § 2, operative July 1, 1976.)*

Law Revision Commission Comments

Section 1230.030 makes clear that whether property is to be acquired by purchase or other means, or by exercise of the power of eminent domain, is a discretionary decision. Nothing in this title requires that the power of eminent domain be exercised; but, if the decision is that the power of eminent domain is to be used to acquire property for public use, the provisions of this title apply except as otherwise specifically provided by statute. See Section 1230.020. Compare Govt.Code § 15854 (property acquired pursuant to Property Acquisition Law).

Research References

Miller and Starr California Real Estate § 30A:3, California Eminent Domain Law.
8 Witkin, California Summary 10th Constitutional Law § 1170, Nature, Organization, and Scope.

§ 1230.040. Rules of practice

Except as otherwise provided in this title, the rules of practice that govern civil actions generally are the rules of practice for eminent domain proceedings. *(Added by Stats.1975, c. 1275, p. 3410, § 2, operative July 1, 1976.)*

Research References

Miller and Starr California Real Estate § 30A:3, California Eminent Domain Law.
Miller and Starr California Real Estate § 30A:47, Introduction to the Eminent Domain Action.
3 Witkin Cal. Proc. 5th Actions § 66, (S 66) General Policy of Uniformity in Procedure.
8 Witkin, California Summary 10th Constitutional Law § 1172, Rules of Practice.
8 Witkin, California Summary 10th Constitutional Law § 1219, in General.

§ 1230.050. Powers of court

The court in which a proceeding in eminent domain is brought has the power to:

(a) Determine the right to possession of the property, as between the plaintiff and the defendant, in accordance with this title.

(b) Enforce any of its orders for possession by appropriate process. The plaintiff is entitled to enforcement of an order for possession as a matter of right. *(Added by Stats.1975, c. 1275, p. 3410, § 2, operative July 1, 1976.)*

Law Revision Commission Comments

Section 1230.050 is new. In general, the section codifies judicial decisions which hold that, after an eminent domain proceeding is begun, the court in which that proceeding is pending has the exclusive power to determine the respective rights of the plaintiff and of the defendant to possession and to enforce its determinations. See, e.g., Neale v. Superior Court, 77 U.S. 28, 18 P. 790 (1888); In re Bryan, 65 Cal. 375, 4 P. 304 (1884); San Bernardino Valley Municipal Water Dist. v. Gage Canal Co., 226 Ca.App.2d 206, 37 Cal.Rptr. 856 (1964). In addition to the writs of possession or writs of assistance which the court may issue and enforce in exercise of its general jurisdiction (see Marblehead Land Co. v. County of Los Angeles, 276 Fed. 305 (S.D.Cal.1921); 3 B. Witkin, California Procedure Enforcement of Judgment § 64 (1954)), orders for possession contemplated by the section include those made under Article 3 (commencing with Section 1255.410) of Chapter 6 and Article 3 (commencing with Section 1268.210) of Chapter 11.

Research References

8 Witkin, California Summary 10th Constitutional Law § 1216, (S 1216) Application and Order.
8 Witkin, California Summary 10th Constitutional Law § 1257, Possession After Judgment.

§ 1230.060. Public utilities commission; effect on jurisdiction

Nothing in this title affects any other statute granting jurisdiction over any issue in eminent domain proceedings to the Public Utilities Commission. *(Added by Stats.1975, c. 1275, p. 3410, § 2, operative July 1, 1976.)*

Law Revision Commission Comments

Section 1230.060 preserves such jurisdiction as the Public Utilities Commission may have over issues in eminent domain proceedings. It supersedes the portion of former Section 1243 of the Code of Civil Procedure which provided that the jurisdiction of the Public Utilities Commission to ascertain just compensation was not affected by eminent domain law.

The Public Utilities Commission has concurrent jurisdiction over certain eminent domain proceedings. See, e.g., Pub.Util.Code § 1401 et seq. (local public entities may petition Public Utilities Commission to acquire public utility property by eminent domain) and Pub.Util.Code, § 1351 (Public Utilities Commission may ascertain value of public utility property in such proceeding). Cf. Cal.Const., Art. XII, § 23a (legislative power to grant Public Utilities Commission jurisdiction to ascertain just compensation).

The Public Utilities Commission has exclusive jurisdiction over railroad crossing. See, e.g., Pub.Util.Code § 1201 et seq. and Northwestern Pac. R.R. v. Superior Court, 34 Cal.2d 454, 211 P.2d 571 (1949) (Public Utilities Commission jurisdiction over crossings extends to eminent domain proceedings in superior court); cf. Cal.Const., Art. XII, § 23 (legislative power to grant Public Utilities Commission control of public utilities) and Pub.Util.Code § 7537 (farm and private crossings). In addition, there may be specific grants of jurisdiction to the Public Utilities Commission over certain issues involved in particular eminent domain acquisitions. See, e.g., Pub.Util.Code §§ 861 (Public Utilities Commission jurisdiction over controversies concerning relocation of utility improvements), 30503 (Public Utilities Commission review of acquisition of railroad property by Southern California Rapid Transit District), and 102243 (Public Utilities Commission jurisdiction in proceedings of Sacramento Regional Transit District). Whether the Public Utilities Commission has jurisdiction over the place and manner of relocation of utility property generally is not clear. Compare Pub.Util.Code § 851 (Public Utilities Commission approval required before utility property may be disposed of) with People v. City of Fresno, 254 Cal.App.2d 76, 62 Cal.Rptr. 79 (1967) (Section 851 not applicable in condemnation of public utility property). See also Govt.Code §§ 55300–55367 (joint project for construction of conduit or line).

Research References

8 Witkin, California Summary 10th Constitutional Law § 1174, Jurisdiction of Public Utilities Commission.
8 Witkin, California Summary 10th Constitutional Law § 1204, Jurisdiction and Venue.

§ 1230.065. Operative date; commencement of proceedings application; law applicable to appeal or motion

(a) This title becomes operative July 1, 1976.

(b) This title does not apply to an eminent domain proceeding commenced prior to January 1, 1976. Subject to subdivisions (c) and (d), in the case of an eminent domain proceeding which is commenced on or after January 1, 1976, but prior to the operative date, this title upon the operative date applies to the proceeding to the fullest extent practicable with respect to issues to be tried or retried.

(c) Chapter 3 (commencing with Section 1240.010), Chapter 4 (commencing with Section 1245.010), and Chapter 5 (commencing with Section 1250.010) do not apply to a proceeding commenced prior to the operative date.

(d) If, on the operative date, an appeal, motion to modify or vacate the verdict or judgment, or motion for new trial is pending, the law applicable thereto prior to the operative date governs the determination of the appeal or motion. *(Added by Stats.1975, c. 1275, p. 3416, § 2, operative July 1, 1976.)*

§ 1230.070. Effect of judgment rendered prior to July 1, 1976

No judgment rendered prior to the operative date of this title in a proceeding to enforce the right of eminent domain is affected by the enactment of this title and the repeal of former

Title 7 of this part. (*Added by Stats.1975, c. 1275, p. 3410, § 2, operative July 1, 1976.*)

Law Revision Commission Comments

Section 1230.070 is new. It makes clear that the repeal of the former eminent domain title of this code and the enactment of new provisions of the Eminent Domain Law in no way affect the validity of judgments rendered prior thereto.

CHAPTER 2. PRINCIPLES OF CONSTRUCTION; DEFINITIONS

ARTICLE 1. CONSTRUCTION

§ 1235.010. Construction of title

Unless the provision or context otherwise requires, these preliminary provisions and rules of construction shall govern the construction of this title. (*Added by Stats.1975, c. 1275, p. 3411, § 2, operative July 1, 1976.*)

Law Revision Commission Comments

Section 1235.010 is a standard provision in the various California codes. E.g., Evid.Code § 4; Veh.Code § 6. Unless otherwise provided in this title, the preliminary provisions of the Code of Civil Procedure are applicable. See, e.g., Code Civ.Proc. § 17 ("words used in the masculine gender include the feminine and neuter; the singular number includes the plural and the plural the singular"). See also Code Civ.Proc. § 5 (construction of provisions as continuation of existing statutes). See also Govt.Code § 9604.

Research References

8 Witkin, California Summary 10th Constitutional Law § 1170, Nature, Organization, and Scope.

§ 1235.020. Headings, effect

Chapter, article, and section headings do not in any manner affect the scope, meaning, or intent of the provisions of this title. (*Added by Stats.1975, c. 1275, p. 3411, § 2, operative July 1, 1976.*)

Law Revision Commission Comments

Provisions similar to Section 1235.020 appear in almost all of the existing California codes. E.g., Evid.Code § 5; Veh.Code § 7.

§ 1235.030. Application to amendments and additions

Whenever any reference is made to any portion of this title or to any other statute, such reference shall apply to all amendments and additions heretofore or hereafter made. (*Added by Stats.1975, c. 1275, p. 3411, § 2, operative July 1, 1976.*)

Law Revision Commission Comments

Section 1235.030 is a standard provision in various California codes. E.g., Evid.Code § 6; Veh.Code § 10.

§ 1235.040. Definitions

Unless otherwise expressly stated:

(a) "Chapter" means a chapter of this title.

(b) "Article" means an article of the chapter in which that term occurs.

(c) "Section" means a section of this code.

(d) "Subdivision" means a subdivision of the section in which that term occurs.

(e) "Paragraph" means a paragraph of the subdivision in which that term occurs. (*Added by Stats.1975, c. 1275, p. 3411, § 2, operative July 1, 1976.*)

Law Revision Commission Comments

Section 1235.040 is similar to Evidence Code Section 7. Compare Code Civ.Proc. § 17(8).

§ 1235.050. Tenses

The present tense includes the past and future tenses; and the future, the present. (*Added by Stats.1975, c. 1275, p. 3411, § 2, operative July 1, 1976.*)

Law Revision Commission Comments

Section 1235.050 is a standard provision in various California codes. E.g., Evid.Code § 8; Veh.Code § 12. Compare Code Civ.Proc. § 17.

§ 1235.060. Shall; may

"Shall" is mandatory and "may" is permissive. (*Added by Stats.1975, c. 1275, p. 3411, § 2, operative July 1, 1976.*)

Law Revision Commission Comments

Section 1235.060 is a standard provision in various California codes. E.g., Evid.Code § 11; Veh.Code § 15.

§ 1235.070. Severability

If any provision or clause of this title or application thereof to any person or circumstances is held invalid, the invalidity does not affect other provisions or applications of the title that can be given effect without the invalid provision or application, and to this end the provisions of this title are severable. (*Added by Stats.1975, c. 1275, p. 3411, § 2, operative July 1, 1976.*)

Law Revision Commission Comments

Section 1235.070 is the same in substance as Section 3 of the Evidence Code and Section 1108 of the Commercial Code.

ARTICLE 2. WORDS AND PHRASES DEFINED

§ 1235.110. Construction of title

Unless the provision or context otherwise requires, these definitions govern the construction of this title. (*Added by Stats.1975, c. 1275, p. 3411, § 2, operative July 1, 1976.*)

Law Revision Commission Comments

Section 1235.110 is a standard provision found in the definitional portion of recently enacted California codes. See, e.g., Evid.Code § 100; Veh.Code § 100. Unless otherwise provided in this title, the definitions in the preliminary portion of the Code of Civil Procedure are applicable. See, e.g. Code Civ.Proc. § 17.

Research References

8 Witkin, California Summary 10th Constitutional Law § 1170, Nature, Organization, and Scope.
8 Witkin, California Summary 10th Constitutional Law § 1171, Definitions.

§ 1235.120. Final judgment

"Final judgment" means a judgment with respect to which all possibility of direct attack by way of appeal, motion for a new trial, or motion under Section 663 to vacate the judgment has been exhausted. *(Added by Stats.1975, c. 1275, p. 3411, § 2, operative July 1, 1976.)*

Law Revision Commission Comments

Section 1235.120 continues the substance of the second sentence of former Section 1264.7. Unlike the former section, Section 1235.120 makes clear that the motion to vacate must be one made under Section 663, thus excluding, for example, a motion for relief from a default under Section 473. This clarification is consistent with the construction given the language of the former section by the courts. E.g., Southern Pac. Util. Dist. v. Silva, 47 Cal.2d 163, 301 P.2d 841 (1956).

Research References

Miller and Starr California Real Estate § 30A:5, Definitions; Eminent Domain Terminology.
7 Witkin Cal. Proc. 5th Judgment § 1, Nature and Classification of Judgment.
8 Witkin, California Summary 10th Constitutional Law § 1171, Definitions.
8 Witkin, California Summary 10th Constitutional Law § 1254, Payment and Final Order.

§ 1235.125. Interest

When used with reference to property, "interest" includes any right, title, or estate in property. *(Added by Stats.1975, c. 1275, p. 3411, § 2, operative July 1, 1976.)*

Law Revision Commission Comments

Section 1235.125 defines the term "interest" as used with relation to property and not as used with relation to the rate of return on money. It is broadly defined to include all interests in property of whatever character or extent.

Research References

Miller and Starr California Real Estate § 26:31, Fee or Easement.
Miller and Starr California Real Estate § 30A:5, Definitions; Eminent Domain Terminology.
5 Witkin Cal. Proc. 5th Pleading § 688, Map and Description of Land.
8 Witkin, California Summary 10th Constitutional Law § 1171, Definitions.

§ 1235.130. Judgment

"Judgment" means the judgment determining the right to take the property by eminent domain and fixing the amount of compensation to be paid by the plaintiff. *(Added by Stats.1975, c. 1275, p. 3411, § 2, operative July 1, 1976.)*

Law Revision Commission Comments

Section 1235.130 continues the substance of the first sentence of former Section 1264.7.

Research References

7 Witkin Cal. Proc. 5th Judgment § 1, Nature and Classification of Judgment.

7 Witkin Cal. Proc. 5th Judgment § 35, (S 35) Condemnation.
8 Witkin, California Summary 10th Constitutional Law § 1171, Definitions.

§ 1235.140. Litigation expenses

"Litigation expenses" includes both of the following:

(a) All expenses reasonably and necessarily incurred in the proceeding in preparing for trial, during trial, and in any subsequent judicial proceedings.

(b) Reasonable attorney's fees, appraisal fees, and fees for the services of other experts where such fees were reasonably and necessarily incurred to protect the defendant's interests in the proceeding in preparing for trial, during trial, and in any subsequent judicial proceedings whether such fees were incurred for services rendered before or after the filing of the complaint. *(Added by Stats.1975, c. 1275, p. 3411, § 2, operative July 1, 1976.)*

Law Revision Commission Comments

The definition provided in Section 1235.140 is the same in substance as the second sentence of former Section 1255a(c). It is used in Sections 1245.060 (entry for survey or examination), 1250.325 (disclaimer), 1250.340 (amendment of pleadings), 1250.410 (settlement offers), 1255.030 (increase or decrease in amount of deposit), 1258.290 (exchange of valuation data), 1260.120 (conditional dismissal on objection to right to take), and 1268.610 (expenses on dismissal or defeat of right to take).

Research References

Rutter, Cal. Practice Guide: Civil Trials & Evidence Ch. 17-D, D. Costs.
Miller and Starr California Real Estate § 30A:5, Definitions; Eminent Domain Terminology.
Miller and Starr California Real Estate § 30A:78, Litigation Expenses.
1 Witkin Cal. Proc. 5th Attorneys § 167, (S 167) Statutory Liens.
7 Witkin Cal. Proc. 5th Judgment § 95, (S 95) Prevailing Party in Specified Actions.
7 Witkin Cal. Proc. 5th Judgment § 124, (S 124) Condemnation Expert.
7 Witkin Cal. Proc. 5th Judgment § 234, in General.
8 Witkin, California Summary 10th Constitutional Law § 1171, Definitions.
8 Witkin, California Summary 10th Constitutional Law § 1209, (S 1209) Award of Litigation Expenses.
8 Witkin, California Summary 10th Constitutional Law § 1265, (S 1265) Litigation Expenses.
8 Witkin, California Summary 10th Constitutional Law § 1267, Costs.

§ 1235.150. Local public entity

"Local public entity" means any public entity other than the state. *(Added by Stats.1975, c. 1275, p. 3412, § 2, operative July 1, 1976.)*

Research References

Miller and Starr California Real Estate § 30A:5, Definitions; Eminent Domain Terminology.
8 Witkin, California Summary 10th Constitutional Law § 1171, Definitions.

§ 1235.155. Nonprofit, special use property

"Nonprofit, special use property" means property which is operated for a special nonprofit, tax-exempt use such as a school, church, cemetery, hospital, or similar property. "Nonprofit, special use property" does not include property owned by a public entity. *(Added by Stats.1992, c. 7 (S.B.821), § 1.)*

Research References

Miller and Starr California Real Estate § 30A:5, Definitions; Eminent Domain Terminology.
8 Witkin, California Summary 10th Constitutional Law § 1171, Definitions.

8 Witkin, California Summary 10th Constitutional Law § 1175, in General.

§ 1235.160. Person

"Person" includes any public entity, individual, association, organization, partnership, trust, limited liability company, or corporation. *(Added by Stats.1975, c. 1275, p. 3412, § 2, operative July 1, 1976. Amended by Stats.1994, c. 1010 (S.B. 2053), § 63.)*

Law Revision Commission Comments

Section 1235.160 provides a broad definition of "person." Compare Code Civ.Proc. § 17.

Research References

Miller and Starr California Real Estate § 30A:3, California Eminent Domain Law.

Miller and Starr California Real Estate § 30A:7, Taking for a Public Use Only.

8 Witkin, California Summary 10th Constitutional Law § 1171, Definitions.

§ 1235.165. Proceeding

"Proceeding" means an eminent domain proceeding under this title. *(Added by Stats.1975, c. 1275, p. 3412, § 2, operative July 1, 1976.)*

Law Revision Commission Comments

Section 1235.165 makes clear that, where the term "proceeding" is used in this title, it refers only to proceedings under the Eminent Domain Law and not, for example, to eminent domain matters before the Public Utilities Commission.

Research References

8 Witkin, California Summary 10th Constitutional Law § 1171, Definitions.

§ 1235.170. Property

"Property" includes real and personal property and any interest therein. *(Added by Stats.1975, c. 1275, p. 3412, § 2, operative July 1, 1976.)*

Law Revision Commission Comments

Section 1235.170 is intended to provide the broadest possible definition of property and to include any type of right, title, or interest in property that may be required for public use. See Section 1235.125 ("interest" defined). If the property authorized to be taken is limited by the statutory grant of condemnation authority to property of a certain type, an attempt to take property other than the type designated in the grant of condemnation authority is precluded by Section 1240.020. See Section 1240.020 and Comment thereto.

Section 1235.170 eliminates the need for duplicative listings of property types and interests subject to condemnation. Cf., e.g., former Section 1240 (real property, tide and submerged lands, franchises for any public utility, rights of way and any and all structures and improvements thereon) and former Section 1238(3) ("ponds, lakes, canals, aqueducts, reservoirs, tunnels, flumes, ditches, or pipes, lands, water system plants, buildings, rights of any nature in water, and any other character of property necessary" for certain purposes. For the authority of an authorized condemnor to acquire property of any type necessary for public use, see Section 1240.110 (right to acquire any necessary interest in property).

Research References

Miller and Starr California Real Estate § 26:31, Fee or Easement.

Miller and Starr California Real Estate § 30A:5, Definitions; Eminent Domain Terminology.

Miller and Starr California Real Estate § 19:148, Termination of the Lease Upon Condemnation.

5 Witkin Cal. Proc. 5th Pleading § 688, Map and Description of Land.

8 Witkin, California Summary 10th Constitutional Law § 1171, Definitions.

8 Witkin, California Summary 10th Constitutional Law § 1176, Condemnation of Sport Franchise.

§ 1235.180. Property appropriated to public use

"Property appropriated to public use" means property either already in use for a public purpose or set aside for a specific public purpose with the intention of using it for such purpose within a reasonable time. *(Added by Stats.1975, c. 1275, p. 3412, § 2, operative July 1, 1976.)*

Law Revision Commission Comments

Section 1235.180 defines "property appropriated to public use" in accordance with prior California decisions. See East Bay Mun. Util. Dist. v. Lodi, 120 Cal.App. 740, 750–758, 8 P.2d 532, 536–539 (1932). The general concept of "public use" is discussed in connection with Section 1240.010. See Section 1240.010 and Comment thereto.

It should be noted that appropriation to a public use does not require actual physical use, but may be satisfied by formal dedication or facts indicating a reasonable prospect of use within a reasonable time. See, e.g., Woodland School Dist. v. Woodland Cemetery Ass'n, 174 Cal.App.2d 243, 344 P.2d 326 (1959) (property formally dedicated but not yet used by corporation for cemetery purposes); City of Los Angeles v. Los Angeles Pac. Co., 31 Cal.App. 100, 159 P. 992 (1916) (property assembled by electric railway for planned subway). Moreover, property may be appropriated to public use even though it is owned by a private individual or corporation. E.g., Woodland School Dist. v. Woodland Cemetery Ass'n, supra; City of Los Angeles v. Los Angeles Pac. Co., supra. Conversely, property may be owned by a public entity but not be appropriated to public use. Deseret Water, Oil & Irr. Co. v. State, 167 Cal. 147, 138 P. 981 (1914), rev'd on other grounds, 243 U.S. 415, and 176 Cal. 745, 171 P. 287 (1917). The term defined in Section 1235.180 is used primarily in Article 6 (commencing with Section 1240.510) and Article 7 (commencing with Section 1240.610) of Chapter 3. These articles relate to a taking for a compatible use or for a more necessary public use.

Research References

Miller and Starr California Real Estate § 30A:5, Definitions; Eminent Domain Terminology.

8 Witkin, California Summary 10th Constitutional Law § 1171, Definitions.

§ 1235.190. Public entity

"Public entity" includes the state, a county, city, district, public authority, public agency, and any other political subdivision in the state. *(Added by Stats.1975, c. 1275, p. 3412, § 2, operative July 1, 1976.)*

Research References

Miller and Starr California Real Estate § 30A:5, Definitions; Eminent Domain Terminology.

8 Witkin, California Summary 10th Constitutional Law § 1171, Definitions.

§ 1235.193. Electric, gas, or water public utility property

"Electric, gas, or water public utility property" means property appropriated to a public use by a public utility, as defined in Section 218, 222, or 241 of the Public Utilities Code. *(Added by Stats.1992, c. 812 (S.B.1757), § 1.)*

Research References

8 Witkin, California Summary 10th Constitutional Law § 1171, Definitions.

§ 1235.195. Resolution

"Resolution" includes ordinance. *(Added by Stats.1975, c. 1275, p. 3412, § 2, operative July 1, 1976.)*

Law Revision Commission Comments

Section 1235.195, which applies primarily to the resolution of necessity, is intended to cover the situation of particular local public entities which act by ordinance rather than by resolution.

Research References

8 Witkin, California Summary 10th Constitutional Law § 1171, Definitions.

§ 1235.200. State

"State" means the State of California and includes the Regents of the University of California. *(Added by Stats.1975, c. 1275, p. 3412, § 2, operative July 1, 1976.)*

Research References

8 Witkin, California Summary 10th Constitutional Law § 1171, Definitions.

§ 1235.210. Statute

"Statute" means a constitutional provision or statute, but does not include a charter provision or ordinance. *(Added by Stats.1975, c. 1275, p. 3412, § 2, operative July 1, 1976.)*

Research References

8 Witkin, California Summary 10th Constitutional Law § 1171, Definitions.

CHAPTER 3. THE RIGHT TO TAKE

ARTICLE 1. GENERAL LIMITATIONS ON EXERCISE OF POWER OF EMINENT DOMAIN

§ 1240.010. Exercise of power for public use

The power of eminent domain may be exercised to acquire property only for a public use. Where the Legislature provides by statute that a use, purpose, object, or function is one for which the power of eminent domain may be exercised, such action is deemed to be a declaration by the Legislature that such use, purpose, object, or function is a public use. *(Added by Stats. 1975, c. 1275, p. 3412, § 2, operative July 1, 1976.)*

Law Revision Commission Comments

The first sentence of Section 1240.010 reiterates the basic constitutional limitation that property may be acquired by eminent domain only for "public use." Cal.Const., Art. I, § 19; U.S.Const., Amend. XIV.

The second sentence is included in Section 1240.010 to avoid the need to state in each condemnation authorization statute that the taking by eminent domain under that statute is a taking for public use. For example, Section 104 of the Streets and Highways Code authorizes the acquisition of property by eminent domain for state highway purposes. Section 1240.010 provides that such legislative action is also deemed to be a legislative declaration that use for state highway purposes constitutes a public use. Section 1240.010 supersedes former Section 1238 of the Code of Civil Procedure, which purported to declare the public uses for which property might be taken by eminent domain.

The scheme of the Eminent Domain Law renders a listing of public uses in the general condemnation statute, as under former Section 1238, unnecessary. Under this scheme, every public entity that would be authorized to condemn for a use listed in former Section 1238 may still condemn for that use. The state (Govt.Code § 15853), cities (Govt.Code § 37350.5), counties (Govt.Code § 25350.5), and school districts (Educ. Code § 1047) may exercise the power of eminent domain to acquire property necessary for any of their powers or functions. These general authorizations to condemn for proper state, city, county, and school district functions often overlap more specific authorizations to condemn or simply to acquire property for particular public uses. On occasion, a statute authorizes a public entity to undertake a public use but specifically denies the right of eminent domain for that use. See, e.g., Govt.Code § 37353(c) (existing golf course may not be acquired by city by eminent domain). In such a case, the specific provision controls over the general authorization. Special districts may condemn only for those specific public uses for which they have expressly been granted the power of eminent domain. The great majority of special districts have, by virtue of their enabling statutes, general authority to condemn all property necessary to carry out any powers of the district. A few districts, such as soil conservation districts (Pub.Res.Code §§ 9074–9953) and the City of Marysville Levee District (Cal.Stats.1875–76, Ch. 134), have limited condemnation authority or none at all.

The fact that Section 1240.010 declares that a particular use for which the power of eminent domain may be exercised is a public use does not preclude judicial review to determine whether the proposed use in the particular case is actually a public use. E.g., City & County of San Francisco v. Ross, 44 Cal.2d 52, 279 P.2d 529 (1955). Nevertheless, the Legislature's declaration that the particular use is a public use will be accepted as controlling unless clearly erroneous and without reasonable foundation. E.g., People v. Superior Court, 68 Cal.2d 206, 210, 436 P.2d 342, 345, 65 Cal.Rptr. 342, 345 (1968); Housing Authority v. Dockweiler, 14 Cal.2d 437, 449–450, 94 P.2d 794, 801 (1939); County of Los Angeles v. Anthony, 224 Cal.App.2d 103, 36 Cal.Rptr. 308, cert. denied, 376 U.S. 963 (1964); Redevelopment Agency v. Hayes, 122 Cal.App.2d 777, 266 P.2d 105, cert. denied, 348 U.S. 897 (1954). Doubts are resolved in favor of the legislative declaration. University of So. Cal. v. Robbins, 1 Cal. App.2d 523, 525–526, 37 P.2d 163, 164 (1934). A legislatively authorized taking will be upheld if the taking is for a "use which concerns the whole community or promotes the general interest in its relation to any legitimate object of government." Bauer v. County of Ventura, 45 Cal.2d 276, 284, 289 P.2d 1, 6 (1955).

Research References

Miller and Starr California Real Estate § 26:31, Fee or Easement.
Miller and Starr California Real Estate § 30A:7, Taking for a Public Use Only.
8 Witkin, California Summary 10th Constitutional Law § 1112, (S 1112) Nature of Power.
8 Witkin, California Summary 10th Constitutional Law § 1118, in General.
8 Witkin, California Summary 10th Constitutional Law § 1175, in General.
8 Witkin, California Summary 10th Constitutional Law § 1187, Future Use.

§ 1240.020. Authority

The power of eminent domain may be exercised to acquire property for a particular use only by a person authorized by statute to exercise the power of eminent domain to acquire such property for that use. *(Added by Stats.1975, c. 1275, p. 3416, § 2, operative July 1, 1976.)*

Research References

Miller and Starr California Real Estate § 30A:2, Constitutional Authority.
Miller and Starr California Real Estate § 30A:6, Public Agencies and Other Entities With the Power of Eminent Domain.
Miller and Starr California Real Estate § 30A:7, Taking for a Public Use Only.
Miller and Starr California Real Estate § 30A:50, Parties to the Action.

8 Witkin, California Summary 10th Constitutional Law § 1114, in General.

8 Witkin, California Summary 10th Constitutional Law § 1177, in General.

§ 1240.030. Requirements

The power of eminent domain may be exercised to acquire property for a proposed project only if all of the following are established:

(a) The public interest and necessity require the project.

(b) The project is planned or located in the manner that will be most compatible with the greatest public good and the least private injury.

(c) The property sought to be acquired is necessary for the project. *(Added by Stats.1975, c. 1275, p. 3412, § 2, operative July 1, 1976.)*

Research References

Miller and Starr California Real Estate § 15:44, Condemnation.

Miller and Starr California Real Estate § 30A:8, Necessity of the Project and the Property; Location and Planning.

Miller and Starr California Real Estate § 30A:19, Resolution of Necessity.

Miller and Starr California Real Estate § 30B:20, Challenges to Public Use or Purpose of Agency's Exercise of Eminent Domain Power.

Miller and Starr California Real Estate § 30B:23, Disposition and Development Agreements.

14 NO. 5 Miller & Starr, California Real Estate Newsalert 11, Eminent Domain.

15 NO. 2 Miller & Starr, California Real Estate Newsalert 7, Easements.

15 NO. 2 Miller & Starr, California Real Estate Newsalert 8, Eminent Domain.

5 Witkin Cal. Proc. 5th Pleading § 687, Right to Condemn.

8 Witkin, California Summary 10th Constitutional Law § 1178, Private Person's Utility Easement.

8 Witkin, California Summary 10th Constitutional Law § 1180, (S 1180) Public Necessity Required.

8 Witkin, California Summary 10th Constitutional Law § 1181, (S 1181) Extraterritorial Condemnation.

8 Witkin, California Summary 10th Constitutional Law § 1203, (S 1203) Consent to Proceeding by Quasi-Public Entity.

§ 1240.040. Resolution of necessity

A public entity may exercise the power of eminent domain only if it has adopted a resolution of necessity that meets the requirements of Article 2 (commencing with Section 1245.210) of Chapter 4. *(Added by Stats.1975, c. 1275, p. 3413, § 2, operative July 1, 1976.)*

Law Revision Commission Comments

A public entity may not take property by eminent domain unless its governing body has adopted a resolution of necessity that meets the requirements of Section 1245.210 et seq. If the public entity fails to adopt such a resolution, or adopts a defective resolution, it may not condemn property.

Section 1240.040 generalizes the provisions, previously applicable to some but not all public entities, that a resolution of necessity is a condition precedent to condemnation. See, e.g., former Water Code § 8594 and former Govt.Code § 15855 (resolution required).

As to the effect of the resolution of necessity on matters of proof in eminent domain proceedings, see Section 1245.250 and Comment thereto.

Research References

Miller and Starr California Real Estate § 30A:8, Necessity of the Project and the Property; Location and Planning.

Miller and Starr California Real Estate § 30B:20, Challenges to Public Use or Purpose of Agency's Exercise of Eminent Domain Power.

Miller and Starr California Real Estate § 30B:23, Disposition and Development Agreements.

8 Witkin, California Summary 10th Constitutional Law § 1180, (S 1180) Public Necessity Required.

§ 1240.050. Property within territorial limits; acquisition; exception

A local public entity may acquire by eminent domain only property within its territorial limits except where the power to acquire by eminent domain property outside its limits is expressly granted by statute or necessarily implied as an incident of one of its other statutory powers. *(Added by Stats.1975, c. 1275, p. 3413, § 2, operative July 1, 1976.)*

Research References

Miller and Starr California Real Estate § 30A:6, Public Agencies and Other Entities With the Power of Eminent Domain.

Miller and Starr California Real Estate § 30A:9, Condemnation Outside Agency's Territorial Limits.

8 Witkin, California Summary 10th Constitutional Law § 1176, Condemnation of Sport Franchise.

8 Witkin, California Summary 10th Constitutional Law § 1181, (S 1181) Extraterritorial Condemnation.

§ 1240.055. Acquisition of property subject to conservation easement by eminent domain; authority; proceedings; compensation; exceptions

(a) As used in this section, the following terms have the following meanings:

(1) "Conservation easement" means a conservation easement as defined in Section 815.1 of the Civil Code and recorded as required by Section 815.5 of the Civil Code.

(2) "Holder of a conservation easement" means the entity or organization that holds the conservation easement on the property that is proposed for acquisition and that is authorized to acquire and hold conservation easements pursuant to Section 815.3 of the Civil Code.

(3) "Property appropriated to public use," as used in Article 6 (commencing with Section 1240.510) and Article 7 (commencing with Section 1240.610), includes a conservation easement if any of the following applies:

(A) The conservation easement is held by a public entity.

(B) A public entity provided funds, not including the value of a charitable contribution for federal or state income tax purposes but including the California Natural Heritage Preservation Tax Credit, for the acquisition of that easement.

(C) A public entity imposed conditions on approval or permitting of a project that were satisfied, in whole or in part, by the conservation easement.

(b) A person authorized to acquire property for public use by eminent domain shall exercise the power of eminent domain to acquire property that is subject to a conservation easement only as provided in this section.

(c) Not later than 105 days prior to the hearing held pursuant to Section 1245.235, or at the time of the offer made to the owner or owners of record pursuant to Section 7267.2 of the Government Code, whichever occurs earlier, the person seeking to acquire property subject to a conservation easement shall give notice to the holder of the conservation easement as provided in this subdivision. If the person is not required to hold a hearing pursuant to Section 1245.235, then the notice shall be given 105 days prior to the time of the offer made to the owner or owners of record pursuant to Section 7267.2 of the Government Code.

(1) The notice required by subdivision (c) shall be sent by first-class mail and shall state all of the following:

(A) A general description, in text or by diagram, of the property subject to a conservation easement that the person proposes to acquire by eminent domain.

(B) A description of the public use or improvement that the person is considering for the property subject to a conservation easement.

(C) That written comments on the acquisition may be submitted in accordance with paragraph (3) no later than 45 days from the date the person seeking to acquire the property mailed the notice to the holder of the conservation easement.

(D) That the holder of the conservation easement, within 15 days of receipt of the notice required by subdivision (c), is required, under certain circumstances, to do all of the following:

(i) Send a copy of the notice by first-class mail to each public entity that provided funds for the purchase of the easement or that imposed conditions on approval or permitting of a project that were satisfied, in whole or in part, by the creation of the conservation easement.

(ii) Inform the public entity that written comments on the acquisition may be submitted in accordance with paragraph (3).

(iii) Notify the person seeking to acquire the property of the name and address of any public entity that was sent a copy of the notice pursuant to this paragraph.

(2)(A) The holder of the conservation easement, within 15 days of receipt of the notice required by subdivision (c), shall do all of the following:

(i) Send a copy of the notice by first-class mail to each public entity that provided funds for the purchase of the easement or that imposed conditions on approval or permitting of a project that were satisfied, in whole or in part, by the creation of the conservation easement.

(ii) Inform the public entity that written comments on the acquisition may be submitted in accordance with paragraph (3).

(iii) Notify the person seeking to acquire the property of the name and address of any public entity that was sent a copy of the notice pursuant to this paragraph.

(B) Subparagraph (A) shall apply only if one of the following applies:

(i) The holder of the easement is the original grantee of the conservation easement and there is a public entity as described in subparagraph (A).

(ii) The holder of the easement has actual knowledge of a public entity as described in subparagraph (A).

(iii) Recorded documents evidence the identity of a public entity as described in subparagraph (A).

(3) The holder of the conservation easement or the public entity receiving notice, or both, may provide to the person seeking to acquire the property written comments on the acquisition, including identifying any potential conflict between the public use proposed for the property and the purposes and terms of the conservation easement. Written comments on the acquisition may be submitted no later than 45 days from the date the person seeking to acquire the property mailed the notice to the holder of the conservation easement.

(d) The person seeking to acquire the property subject to a conservation easement, within 30 days after receipt of written comments from the holder of the conservation easement or from a public entity described in paragraph (2) of subdivision (c), shall respond in writing to the comments. The response to the comments shall be mailed by first-class mail to each easement holder or public entity that filed comments.

(e) The notice of the hearing on the resolution of necessity, pursuant to Section 1245.235, shall be sent by first-class mail to the holder of any conservation easement and to any public entity whose name and address are provided as described in paragraph (2) of subdivision (c) and shall state that they have the right to appear and be heard on the matters referred to in Sections 1240.030, 1240.510, and 1240.610. The notice shall state that, pursuant to paragraph (3) of subdivision (b) of Section 1245.235, failure to file a written request to appear and be heard within 15 days after the notice was mailed will result in waiver of the right to appear and be heard. The resolution of necessity to acquire property subject to a conservation easement shall refer specifically either to Section 1240.510 or 1240.610 as authority for the acquisition of the property.

(f) In any eminent domain proceeding to acquire property subject to a conservation easement, the holder of the conservation easement:

(1) Shall be named as a defendant, as set forth in Section 1250.220.

(2) May appear in the proceedings, as set forth in Section 1250.230.

(3) Shall have all the same rights and obligations as any other defendant in the eminent domain proceeding.

(g)(1) The holder of the conservation easement is an owner of property entitled to compensation determined pursuant to Section 1260.220 and Chapter 9 (commencing with Section 1263.010) and in accordance with all of the following:

(A) The total compensation for the acquisition of all interests in property encumbered by a conservation easement shall not be less than, and shall not exceed, the fair market value of the fee simple interest of the property as if it were not encumbered by the conservation easement.

(B) If the acquisition does not damage the conservation easement, the total compensation shall be assessed by determining the value of all interests in the property as encumbered by the conservation easement.

(C) If the acquisition damages the conservation easement in whole or in part, compensation shall be determined consistent with Section 1260.220 and the value of the fee simple interest of the property shall be assessed as if it were not encumbered by the conservation easement.

(2) This subdivision shall not apply if the requirements of Section 10261 of the Public Resources Code apply.

(h) This section shall not apply if the requirements of Section 1348.3 of the Fish and Game Code apply. *(Added by Stats.2011, c. 589 (S.B.328), § 2.)*

Research References

22 NO. 4 Miller & Starr, California Real Estate Newsalert 13, Eminent Domain.

8 Witkin, California Summary 10th Constitutional Law § 1113, (S 1113) Property that May be Taken.

8 Witkin, California Summary 10th Constitutional Law § 1175, in General.

ARTICLE 2.   RIGHTS INCLUDED IN GRANT OF EMINENT DOMAIN AUTHORITY

Section

1240.150.   Acquisition of whole parcel where remainder valueless or subject to claim for damages.

1240.160.   Construction of articles; separate authority.

§ 1240.110. Acquisition of certain interests in property; enumeration; restriction

(a) Except to the extent limited by statute, any person authorized to acquire property for a particular use by eminent domain may exercise the power of eminent domain to acquire any interest in property necessary for that use including, but not limited to, submerged lands, rights of any nature in water, subsurface rights, airspace rights, flowage or flooding easements, aircraft noise or operation easements, right of temporary occupancy, public utility facilities and franchises, and franchises to collect tolls on a bridge or highway.

(b) Where a statute authorizes the acquisition by eminent domain only of specified interests in or types of property, this section does not expand the scope of the authority so granted. *(Added by Stats.1975, c. 1275, p. 3413, § 2, operative July 1, 1976.)*

Law Revision Commission Comments

Section 1240.110 is both an authorization and a limitation on the power of condemnation. It provides that a person authorized to condemn may take any type of property and any interest in such property but limits this grant only to property that is necessary for the purpose for which the condemnation is authorized. See Sections 1235.170 ("property" includes any interest in property) and 1240.030 (necessity to acquire particular property must be established). It should be noted that the resolution of necessity of a public entity may be conclusive evidence of the necessity for the acquisition of the particular property and interest therein. See Section 1245.250 and Comment thereto.

The authorization to take any interest is generally consistent with the former law that permitted a public entity to take a fee rather than merely an easement. See former Code Civ.Proc. § 1239(4) (local public entities). However, under former law, most privately owned public utilities and some local public entities were permitted to acquire only an easement except in certain circumstances. See former Code Civ.Proc. § 1239. Moreover, under former law, the distinction generally made was between taking a fee or an easement. See generally Taylor, The Right to Take—The Right to Take a Fee or Any Lesser Interest, 1 Pac.L.J. 555 (1970). Section 1240.110 permits taking of the fee or any other interest in property. See Sections 1235.125 (defining "interest") and 1235.170 (defining "property").

Subdivision (b) of Section 1240.110 recognizes that, if the interest in property authorized to be taken is limited by the statutory grant (as, for example, where the statute authorizes acquisition of only an easement), an attempt to take an interest in the property other than that permitted by the statute is precluded. Also, if the statutory grant to the particular entity is specifically limited to "real property," Section 1240.110 does not extend that grant to include personal property. On the other hand, if the statutory grant of condemnation authority is to acquire any "property" necessary for a particular use, Section 1240.110 makes clear that this includes authority to condemn both real and personal property of any type.

The authorization to take any interest in property necessary for a particular use supersedes former Code of Civil Procedure Section 1240 which attempted to list the various types of property interests that might be taken. The broad authorization in Section 1240.110 codifies cases holding that inherent in the right to condemn property is the right to take all interests and all rights appurtenant. See e.g., City of Los Angeles v. Hughes, 202 Cal. 731, 262 P. 737 (1927) (nursery plants and trees); People v. Superior Court, 208 Cal.App.2d 659, 25 Cal.Rptr. 363 (1962) (dredger tailings); County of Kern v. Galatas, 200 Cal.App.2d 353, 19 Cal.Rptr. 348 (1962) (oil, gas, mineral rights); Northern Light etc. Co. v. Stacher, 13 Cal.App. 404, 109 P. 896 (1910) (water). It should be noted, however, that money is not subject to the power of eminent domain. Emery v. San Francisco Gas Co., 28 Cal. 346 (1865).

The initial proviso to subdivision (a) recognizes that other statutes may make certain property exempt from condemnation. For example, an existing golf course may not be acquired by a city for golf course purposes. Govt.Code § 37353(c). Cemetery land may not be taken for rights of way. Health & Saf.Code §§ 8134, 8560, 8560.5; see Eden Memorial Park

Ass'n v. Superior Court, 189 Cal.App.2d 421, 11 Cal.Rptr. 189 (1961). Property within the Aptos Forest is not subject to eminent domain except by specific permission of the Legislature. Pub.Res.Code § 5006.2. Certain land in the public domain may not be taken at all. Pub.Res.Code § 8030. An existing airport owned by a local entity cannot be taken by the Department of Transportation without consent. Pub.Util.Code § 21632. See generally Article 6 (commencing with Section 1240.510) and Article 7 (commencing with Section 1240.610) (limitations on the acquisition of property appropriated to public use).

It should be noted that the listing of types of property or property interests in subdivision (a) is intended for the sole purpose of illustrating the breadth of scope of a condemnor's acquisition authority. The illustrative listing is not intended as complete; a condemnor may acquire, for example, rights to limit the use or development of property in order to preserve land in an open or natural condition. Nor is the listing intended to create compensable interests in inverse condemnation actions that are not otherwise compensable under Article I, Section 19, of the Constitution.

Research References

Miller and Starr California Real Estate § 15:87, Condemnation.

Miller and Starr California Real Estate § 26:31, Fee or Easement.

Miller and Starr California Real Estate § 19:148, Termination of the Lease Upon Condemnation.

Miller and Starr California Real Estate § 19:149, Valuation and Apportionment of the Award.

Miller and Starr California Real Estate § 30A:13, Types of Property Interests Which May be Acquired.

Miller and Starr California Real Estate § 30A:29, Easements.

Miller and Starr California Real Estate § 30A:33, Leaseholds--Apportionment Between Landlord and Tenant.

5 Witkin Cal. Proc. 5th Pleading § 688, Map and Description of Land.

8 Witkin, California Summary 10th Constitutional Law § 1113, (S 1113) Property that May be Taken.

8 Witkin, California Summary 10th Constitutional Law § 1171, Definitions.

8 Witkin, California Summary 10th Constitutional Law § 1175, in General.

8 Witkin, California Summary 10th Constitutional Law § 1182, (S 1182) Necessary Interests in Property.

§ 1240.120. Acquisition of property for principal purpose; intent to sell, lease, etc. acquired property

(a) Subject to any other statute relating to the acquisition of property, any person authorized to acquire property for a particular use by eminent domain may exercise the power of eminent domain to acquire property necessary to carry out and make effective the principal purpose involved including but not limited to property to be used for the protection or preservation of the attractiveness, safety, and usefulness of the project.

(b) Subject to any applicable procedures governing the disposition of property, a person may acquire property under subdivision (a) with the intent to sell, lease, exchange, or otherwise dispose of the property, or an interest therein, subject to such reservations or restrictions as are necessary to protect or preserve the attractiveness, safety, and usefulness of the project. *(Added by Stats.1975, c. 1275, p. 3413, § 2, operative July 1, 1976.)*

Law Revision Commission Comments

Subdivision (a) of Section 1240.120 codifies the rule that, absent any express limitation imposed by the Legislature, the power to condemn property for a particular purpose includes the power to condemn property necessary to carry out and make effective the principal purpose involved. See City of Santa Barbara v. Cloer, 216 Cal.App.2d 127, 30 Cal.Rptr. 743 (1963). See also University of So. Cal. v. Robbins, 1 Cal.App.2d 523, 37 P.2d 163 (1934). *Cf.* Flood Control & Water Conservation Dist. v. Hughes, 201 Cal.App.2d 197, 20 Cal.Rptr. 252 (1962).

Section 1240.120 permits a condemnor to protect the attractiveness, safety, or usefulness of a public work or improvement from deleterious conditions or uses by condemning a fee or any lesser interest necessary for protective purposes. See Section 1235.170 (defining "property" to include any interest). A taking for this purpose is a public use. E.g., People v. Lagiss, 223 Cal.App.2d 23, 35 Cal.Rptr. 554 (1963); Flood

Control & Water Conservation Dist. v. Hughes, *supra*. See also United States v. Bowman, 367 F.2d 768, 770 (1966). See Capron, Excess Condemnation in California—A Further Expansion of the Right to Take, 20 Hastings L.J. 571, 589–591 (1969).

Where it is necessary to protect a public work or improvement from detrimental uses on adjoining property, the condemnor has the option either (1) to acquire an easement-like interest in the adjoining property that will preclude the detrimental use or (2) to acquire the fee or some other interest and then—if the condemnor desires—lease, sell, exchange, or otherwise dispose of the property to some other public entity or a private person subject to carefully specified permitted uses.

If a condemnor has the power of eminent domain to condemn property for a particular improvement, Section 1240.120 is sufficient authority to condemn such additional property as is necessary to preserve or protect the attractiveness, safety, and usefulness of the improvement. No additional statutory authority is required, and some of the former specific grants of protective condemnation authority have been repealed as unnecessary. E.g., former Code Civ.Proc. § 1238(18) (trees along highways). Not all such specific authorizations have been repealed. E.g., Sts. & Hwys.Code § 104(f) (trees along highways), (g) (highway drainage), (h) (maintenance of unobstructed view along highway). Except to the extent that these specific authorizations contain restrictions on protective condemnation for particular types of projects (see Govt.Code §§ 7000–7001), they do not limit the general protective condemnation authority granted by Section 1240.120.

In the case of a public entity, the resolution of necessity is conclusive on the necessity of taking the property or interest therein for protective purposes. See Section 1245.250 and Comment thereto. However, the resolution does not preclude the condemnee from raising the question whether the condemnor actually intends to use the property for protective purposes. If the property is claimed to be needed for protective purposes but is not actually to be used for that purposes, the taking can be defeated on that ground. See Section 1250.360 and Comment thereto. See People v. Lagiss, 223 Cal.App.2d 23, 33–44, 35 Cal.Rptr. 554, 560–567 (1963).

Section 1240.120 is derived from and supersedes former Government Code Sections 190–196, Streets and Highways Code Section 104.3, and Water Code Section 256.

Research References

Miller and Starr California Real Estate § 30A:16, Additional Property Which May be Acquired for the Project.
8 Witkin, California Summary 10th Constitutional Law § 1183, (S 1183) Property to Make Principal Use Effective.

§ 1240.125. Property outside territorial limits for water, gas, electrical supply, etc.

Except as otherwise expressly provided by statute and subject to any limitations imposed by statute, a local public entity may acquire property by eminent domain outside its territorial limits for water, gas, or electric supply purposes or for airports, drainage or sewer purposes if it is authorized to acquire property by eminent domain for the purposes for which the property is to be acquired. *(Added by Stats.1975, c. 1275, p. 3413, § 2, operative July 1, 1976.)*

Research References

Miller and Starr California Real Estate § 30A:6, Public Agencies and Other Entities With the Power of Eminent Domain.
Miller and Starr California Real Estate § 30A:9, Condemnation Outside Agency's Territorial Limits.
Miller and Starr California Real Estate § 30A:14, Restrictions on Types of Property Being Condemned.
8 Witkin, California Summary 10th Constitutional Law § 1115, Municipal Corporation.
8 Witkin, California Summary 10th Constitutional Law § 1181, (S 1181) Extraterritorial Condemnation.

§ 1240.130. Acquisition by grant, purchase, lease, etc.

Subject to any other statute relating to the acquisition of property, any public entity authorized to acquire property for a particular use by eminent domain may also acquire such property for such use by grant, purchase, lease, gift, devise, contract, or other means. *(Added by Stats.1975, c. 1275, p. 3413, § 2, operative July 1, 1976.)*

Law Revision Commission Comments

Section 1240.130 makes clear that a public entity is authorized to acquire property by negotiation or other means in any case in which it may condemn property. See also Govt.Code § 7267.1(a) (public entity shall make every reasonable effort to acquire real property by negotiation). This general authority is, of course, subject to any limitations that may be imposed by statute. See, e.g., Govt. Code § 15854 (acquisition under the Property Acquisition Law must be by condemnation except in certain circumstances).

Section 1240.130 makes unnecessary the detailed listing of various types of property that may be acquired under specific statutes authorizing acquisition by eminent domain and other means. See Sections 1235.170 ("property" defined), 1235.125 ("interest" in property defined), and 1240.110 (right to acquire any necessary property or interest therein). Section 1240.130 supersedes former Code of Civil Procedure Section 1266.1 (gift or purchase authorized for certain purposes).

Research References

Miller and Starr California Real Estate § 30A:13, Types of Property Interests Which May be Acquired.
8 Witkin, California Summary 10th Constitutional Law § 1186, (S 1186) Acquisition by Gift, Purchase, Lease, or Other Means.

§ 1240.140. Public agencies; joint exercise of powers; law governing

(a) As used in this section, "public agencies" includes all those agencies included within the definition of "public agency" in Section 6500 of the Government Code.

(b) Two or more public agencies may enter into an agreement for the joint exercise of their respective powers of eminent domain, whether or not possessed in common, for the acquisition of property as a single parcel. Such agreement shall be entered into and performed pursuant to the provisions of Chapter 5 (commencing with Section 6500) of Division 7 of Title 1 of the Government Code. *(Added by Stats.1975, c. 1275, p. 3414, § 2, operative July 1, 1976.)*

Law Revision Commission Comments

Section 1240.140 authorizes several public agencies to acquire a particular parcel under the Joint Powers Agreements Act, not only where the particular parcel is needed for a joint project but also where each of the agencies requires a portion of the parcel for its own purposes. The section is based on former Education Code Section 15007.5. Section 15007.5, however, applied only where a school district was a party to the joint powers agreement, and Section 1240.140 is not so restricted. As to how title is to be held, see Govt.Code § 6508. *Cf.* Govt.Code § 55004 (joint sanitation projects).

Research References

Miller and Starr California Real Estate § 30A:6, Public Agencies and Other Entities With the Power of Eminent Domain.
8 Witkin, California Summary 10th Constitutional Law § 1185, (S 1185) Joint Exercise of Power.

§ 1240.150. Acquisition of whole parcel where remainder valueless or subject to claim for damages

Whenever a part of a larger parcel of property is to be acquired by a public entity for public use and the remainder, or a portion of the remainder, will be left in such size, shape, or condition as to be of little value to its owner or to give rise to a claim for severance or other damages, the public entity may acquire the remainder, or portion of the remainder, by any means (including eminent domain) expressly consented to by the owner. *(Added by Stats.1975, c. 1275, p. 3414, § 2, operative July 1, 1976.)*

Law Revision Commission Comments

Section 1240.150 provides a broad authorization for public entities to acquire remainders of property by a voluntary transaction or a condemnation proceeding initiated with the consent of the owner. *Cf.* Govt.Code § 7267.7 ("If the acquisition of only a portion of a property would leave the remaining portion in such a shape or condition as to constitute an uneconomic remnant, the public entity shall offer to and may acquire the entire property if the owner so desires."). See also former Code Civ.Proc. § 1266.1 (cities and counties may acquire excess property by purchase or gift). Compare Article 5 (commencing with Section 1240.410) and the Comments to the sections in that article (condemnation of remnants). *Cf.* Section 1240.240 (acquisition for future use with owner's consent).

The language of Section 1240.150 is similar to that contained in former Sections 104.1 and 943.1 of the Streets and Highways Code and former Sections 254, 8590.1, 11575.2, and 43533 of the Water Code. Inasmuch as exercise of the authority conferred by this section depends upon the consent and concurrence of the property owner, the language of the section is broadly drawn to authorize acquisition whenever the remainder would have little value to its owner (rather than little market value or value to another owner). Compare Dep't of Public Works v. Superior Court, 68 Cal.2d 206, 436 P.2d 342, 65 Cal.Rptr. 342 (1968); La Mesa v. Tweed & Gambrell Planing Mill, 146 Cal.App.2d 762, 304 P.2d 803 (1956).

Where property is needed for public use and a structure is located partly on the property to be acquired and partly on other property, Section 1240.150 permits the public entity to acquire the entire structure by agreement with the owner or by a condemnation proceeding initiated with the consent of the owner. Where a structure is located partly on property needed for a public use and partly on other property, there are a number of alternatives available to the parties which may be less costly or more convenient than taking only part of the structure and paying severance damages on this basis. In some cases, severance may so destroy a structure that total demolition in one operation is the only economically or practically feasible alternative. Pursuant to Section 1240.150, the parties may agree that the public entity will acquire the entire structure and demolish it, leaving the property owner with the remainder in a cleared condition. Section 1240.150 also permits the parties to agree that the public entity will purchase the structure to relocate it. For authority to condemn the structure where the parties are unable to agree, see Section 1263.270 (court order that entire improvement be acquired). For other possibilities, see Section 1263.610 (condemnor may relocate structure or perform other work for owner); Section 1240.410 (excess condemnation). See also the Comments to the cited sections.

Research References

Miller and Starr California Real Estate § 30A:16, Additional Property Which May be Acquired for the Project.
8 Witkin, California Summary 10th Constitutional Law § 1184, (S 1184) Acquisition of Remainder With Consent.

§ 1240.160. Construction of articles; separate authority

(a) None of the provisions of this article is intended to limit, or shall limit, any other provision of this article, each of which is a distinct and separate authorization.

(b) None of the provisions of Article 2 (commencing with Section 1240.110), Article 3 (commencing with Section 1240.210), Article 4 (commencing with Section 1240.310), Article 5 (commencing with Section 1240.410), Article 6 (commencing with Section 1240.510), or Article 7 (commencing with Section 1240.610) is intended to limit, or shall limit, the provisions of any other of the articles, each of which articles is a distinct and separate authorization. *(Added by Stats.1975, c. 1275, p. 3414, § 2, operative July 1, 1976.)*

Law Revision Commission Comments

Section 1240.160 makes clear that the various articles contained in this chapter are distinct and separate authorizations. For example, the authority granted by Article 6 (condemnation for compatible use) is independent of the authority contained in Article 7 (more necessary public use) and is not limited in any way by the rules set forth therein. Likewise, condemnation of property appropriated to a public use may be accomplished under Article 7 independently of any authority stated in

Article 6. Section 1240.160 is based on former Section 104.7 of the Streets and Highways Code.

Research References

8 Witkin, California Summary 10th Constitutional Law § 1175, in General.

ARTICLE 3. FUTURE USE

Section
1240.210. Date of use.
1240.220. Authority; probability of use within seven years; estimated date of use.
1240.230. Burden of proof.
1240.240. Acquisition by any means with consent of owner.
1240.250. Taking pursuant to federal highway act.

§ 1240.210. Date of use

For the purposes of this article, the "date of use" of property taken for public use is the date when the property is devoted to that use or when construction is started on the project for which the property is taken with the intent to complete the project within a reasonable time. In determining the "date of use," periods of delay caused by extraordinary litigation or by failure to obtain from any public entity any agreement or permit necessary for construction shall not be included. *(Added by Stats.1975, c. 1275, p. 3414, § 2, operative July 1, 1976.)*

Law Revision Commission Comments

See the Comment to Section 1240.220.

Research References

Miller and Starr California Real Estate § 30A:12, Condemnation for a Future Public Use.
8 Witkin, California Summary 10th Constitutional Law § 1175, in General.
8 Witkin, California Summary 10th Constitutional Law § 1187, Future Use.

§ 1240.220. Authority; probability of use within seven years; estimated date of use

(a) Any person authorized to acquire property for a particular use by eminent domain may exercise the power of eminent domain to acquire property to be used in the future for that use, but property may be taken for future use only if there is a reasonable probability that its date of use will be within seven years from the date the complaint is filed or within such longer period as is reasonable.

(b) Unless the plaintiff plans that the date of use of property taken will be within seven years from the date the complaint is filed, the complaint, and the resolution of necessity if one is required, shall refer specifically to this section and shall state the estimated date of use. *(Added by Stats.1975, c. 1275, p. 3414, § 2, operative July 1, 1976.)*

Law Revision Commission Comments

Section 1240.220 continues prior case law and makes clear that statutory grants of condemnation power carry with them the power to condemn property in anticipation of the condemnor's future needs. See, e.g., Central Pac. Ry. v. Feldman, 152 Cal. 303, 309, 92 P. 849, 852 (1907); City of Los Angeles v. Pomeroy, 124 Cal. 597, 616, 57 P. 585, 591 (1899); Pacific Gas & Elec. Co. v. Parachini, 29 Cal.App.3d 159, 105 Cal.Rptr. 477 (1972); San Diego Gas & Elec. Co. v. Lux Land Co., 194 Cal.App.2d 472, 480–481, 14 Cal.Rptr. 899, 904–905 (1961). Section 1240.220 may be duplicated in part by specific statutory grants of the power to condemn for future use. See, e.g., Sts. & Hwys.Code § 104.6 (Department of Transportation authorized to acquire real property for future highway needs); Water Code § 258 (Department of Water Resources authorized to acquire real property for future state dam and water purposes). These specific statutory grants are subject to the general provisions of Section 1240.220.

The basic substantive test that determines when condemnation for future needs is permitted is stated in subdivision (a). If the date of use of property will be within seven years from the date the complaint is filed, the taking is permitted. (The date of use is that date when property is actually devoted to the use for which taken or when construction on the project is commenced in good faith. See Section 1240.210.) If the date of use will not be within the seven-year period, the taking is permitted only if there is a reasonable probability that the date of use will be within a "reasonable time." What constitutes a reasonable time depends upon all the circumstances of the particular case: Is there a reasonable probability that funds for the construction of the project will become available? Have plans been drawn and adopted? Is the project a logical extension of existing improvements? Is future growth likely, and should the condemnor anticipate and provide for that growth? However, it should be noted that periods of delay caused by litigation (other than the normal resolution of valuation issues) or by difficulty in obtaining an agreement or permit necessary for construction from a public entity (such as freeway route agreements from local public entities) are not to be included in determining date of use. See Section 1240.210.

Subdivision (b) specifies an additional requirement for the complaint and, if the plaintiff is a public entity, for the resolution of necessity. If the plaintiff does not plan to use the property for the public use within seven years from the date the complaint is filed, it must so state in the complaint and resolution. The required information in the complaint will put the defendant on notice that there is a potential issue whether the plaintiff is authorized to take the property under this section.

Research References

Miller and Starr California Real Estate § 30A:12, Condemnation for a Future Public Use.

8 Witkin, California Summary 10th Constitutional Law § 1187, Future Use.

§ 1240.230. Burden of proof

(a) If the defendant objects to a taking for future use, the burden of proof is as prescribed in this section.

(b) Unless the complaint states an estimated date of use that is not within seven years from the date the complaint is filed, the defendant has the burden of proof that there is no reasonable probability that the date of use will be within seven years from the date the complaint is filed.

(c) If the defendant proves that there is no reasonable probability that the date of use will be within seven years from the date the complaint is filed, or if the complaint states an estimated date of use that is not within seven years from the date the complaint is filed, the plaintiff has the burden of proof that a taking for future use satisfies the requirements of this article. *(Added by Stats.1975, c. 1275, p. 3415, § 2, operative July 1, 1976.)*

Law Revision Commission Comments

Section 1240.230 states the rules governing the burden of proof where the defendant objects to a taking for future use. A defendant who desires to contest the taking of his property on the ground that the taking is for a future use and is not authorized under Section 1240.220 must plead this defense. See Sections 430.30, 1250.350, and 1250.360.

If the defendant does contest the taking, the court must first find that there is no reasonable probability that date of use will be within the seven-year period. Unless the court so finds, the taking cannot be defeated on the ground that it is not authorized under Section 1240.220. Except where the complaint indicates that the date of use will not be within the seven-year period, the defendant has the burden of proof to establish that there is no reasonable probability that his property will be used for the public use within that period. When the plaintiff estimates that the date of use will not be within the seven-year period or when it is established by proof that there is no reasonable probability that the property will be used for the designated use within such period, the burden shifts to the plaintiff to prove that there is a reasonable probability that the property will actually be devoted to the public use within a "reasonable time." See discussion in Comment to Section 1240.220.

Section 1240.230 makes a significant change in former practice. Under prior law, as under Section 1240.230, condemnation for future use was permitted only if there was a reasonable probability that the property would be devoted to the public use within a reasonable time. See, e.g., San Diego Gas & Elec. Co. v. Lux Land Co., 194 Cal.App.2d 472, 480–481, 14 Cal.Rptr. 899, 904–905 (1961). See also East Bay Mun. Util. Dist. v. City of Lodi, 120 Cal.App. 740, 750–755, 8 P.2d 532, 536–538 (1932). However, under prior law, this issue—whether there was a reasonable probability of use within a reasonable time—was ordinarily nonjusticiable. The issue was regarded as an issue of necessity. The resolution of necessity was conclusive on issues of necessity in the great majority of takings; hence, the issue could be raised only in those few cases where the resolution was not conclusive. Compare Anaheim Union High School Dist. v. Vieira, 241 Cal.App.2d 169, 51 Cal.Rptr. 94 (1966) (resolution conclusive), and County of San Mateo v. Bartole, 184 Cal.App.2d 422, 7 Cal.Rptr. 569 (1960) (resolution conclusive), with San Diego Gas & Elec. Co. v. Lux Land Co., *supra* (justiciable issue). This aspect of the prior law has not been continued. The resolution of necessity is not conclusive on the issue of whether a taking is authorized under this article. But see Pub.Res.Code § 25531 (decision of State Energy Resources Conservation and Development Commission conclusive on issue whether property will be devoted to the public use within a "reasonable time").

Research References

Miller and Starr California Real Estate § 30A:12, Condemnation for a Future Public Use.

8 Witkin, California Summary 10th Constitutional Law § 1187, Future Use.

§ 1240.240. Acquisition by any means with consent of owner

Notwithstanding any other provision of this article, any public entity authorized to acquire property for a particular use by eminent domain may acquire property to be used in the future for that use by any means (including eminent domain) expressly consented to by its owner. *(Added by Stats.1975, c. 1275, p. 3415, § 2, operative July 1, 1976.)*

Law Revision Commission Comments

Section 1240.240 makes clear that a public entity may take property for future use, regardless of the restrictions on takings for future use imposed by this article, in any case where the owner of the property consents to the taking.

Research References

8 Witkin, California Summary 10th Constitutional Law § 1184, (S 1184) Acquisition of Remainder With Consent.

8 Witkin, California Summary 10th Constitutional Law § 1187, Future Use.

§ 1240.250. Taking pursuant to federal highway act

Notwithstanding any other provision of this article, where property is taken pursuant to the Federal Aid Highway Act of 1973 [1]:

(a) A date of use within 10 years from the date the complaint is filed shall be deemed reasonable.

(b) The resolution of necessity and the complaint shall indicate that the taking is pursuant to the Federal Aid Highway Act of 1973 [1] and shall state the estimated date of use.

(c) If the defendant objects to the taking, the defendant has the burden of proof that there is no reasonable probability that the date of use will be within 10 years from the date the complaint is filed. If the defendant proves that there is no reasonable probability that the date of use will be within 10 years from the date the complaint is filed, the plaintiff has the burden of proof that the taking satisfies the requirements of this article. *(Added by Stats.1975, c. 1275, p. 3415, § 2, operative July 1, 1976.)*

[1] 23 U.S.C.A. § 101 et seq.

Research References

Miller and Starr California Real Estate § 30A:12, Condemnation for a Future Public Use.

8 Witkin, California Summary 10th Constitutional Law § 1181, (S 1181) Extraterritorial Condemnation.

8 Witkin, California Summary 10th Constitutional Law § 1187, Future Use.

ARTICLE 4. SUBSTITUTE CONDEMNATION

Section

§ 1240.310. Necessary and substitute property

As used in this article:

(a) "Necessary property" means property to be used for a public use for which the public entity is authorized to acquire property by eminent domain.

(b) "Substitute property" means property to be exchanged for necessary property. *(Added by Stats.1975, c. 1275, p. 3415, § 2, operative July 1, 1976.)*

Law Revision Commission Comments

Section 1240.310 provides definitions useful in applying the "substitute condemnation" provisions contained in this chapter. Briefly stated, "substitute condemnation" involves the following type of situation: The potential condemnor determines that it needs certain property (the "necessary property") for its use. It agrees to compensate the owner of the necessary property in whole or in part by other property (the "substitute property") rather than money. It then condemns the "substitute property" and exchanges it for the "necessary property." See generally Note, Substitute Condemnation, 54 Cal.L.Rev. 1097 (1966).

Research References

Miller and Starr California Real Estate § 30A:15, Substitute Condemnation.

8 Witkin, California Summary 10th Constitutional Law § 1175, in General.

8 Witkin, California Summary 10th Constitutional Law § 1188, (S 1188) in General.

§ 1240.320. Authority; substitute property; requirements

(a) Any public entity authorized to exercise the power of eminent domain to acquire property for a particular use may exercise the power of eminent domain to acquire for that use substitute property if all of the following are established:

(1) The owner of the necessary property has agreed in writing to the exchange.

(2) The necessary property is devoted to or held for some public use and the substitute property will be devoted to or held for the same public use by the owner of the necessary property.

(3) The owner of the necessary property is authorized to exercise the power of eminent domain to acquire the substitute property for such use.

(b) Where property is sought to be acquired pursuant to this section, the resolution of necessity and the complaint filed pursuant to such resolution shall specifically refer to this section and shall include a statement that the property is necessary for the purpose specified in this section. The determination in the resolution that the taking of the substitute property is necessary has the effect prescribed in Section 1245.250. *(Added by Stats.1975, c. 1275, p. 3415, § 2, operative July 1, 1976.)*

Research References

Miller and Starr California Real Estate § 30A:15, Substitute Condemnation.

8 Witkin, California Summary 10th Constitutional Law § 1188, (S 1188) in General.

8 Witkin, California Summary 10th Constitutional Law § 1189, (S 1189) to Relocate Public Use.

§ 1240.330. Conveyance of substitute property to owner of necessary property; requirements

(a) Where necessary property is devoted to public use, any public entity authorized to exercise the power of eminent domain to acquire such property for a particular use may exercise the power of eminent domain to acquire substitute property in its own name, relocate on such substitute property the public use to which necessary property is devoted, and thereafter convey the substitute property to the owner of the necessary property if all of the following are established:

(1) The public entity is required by court order or judgment in an eminent domain proceeding, or by agreement with the owner of the necessary property, to relocate the public use to which the necessary property is devoted and thereafter to convey the property upon which the public use has been relocated to the owner of the necessary property.

(2) The substitute property is necessary for compliance with the court order or judgment or agreement.

(3) The owner of the necessary property will devote the substitute property to the public use being displaced from the necessary property.

(b) Where property is sought to be acquired pursuant to this section, the resolution of necessity and the complaint filed pursuant to such resolution shall specifically refer to this section and shall include a statement that the property is necessary for the purpose specified in this section. The determination in the resolution that the taking of the substitute property is necessary has the effect prescribed in Section 1245.250. *(Added by Stats.1975, c. 1275, p. 3416, § 2, operative July 1, 1976.)*

Law Revision Commission Comments

Section 1240.330 provides general authority for substitute condemnation where a public entity is required by a court order or judgment or by agreement to relocate a public use. It should be noted that condemnation of property devoted to public use may be accomplished only in certain circumstances and the relocation of improvements in an eminent domain proceeding may be ordered only upon express statutory authority. See, e.g., Section 1240.530 (compatible use); Pub.Util.Code § 7557; Orange County Water District Act, § 39 (Cal.Stats.1933, Ch. 924); San Bernardino County Flood Control District Act, § 25 (Cal.Stats.1939, Ch. 73); Ventura County Flood Control District Act, § 29 (Cal.Stats.1944, 4th Ex.Sess., Ch. 44). Unlike Section 1240.320 (which applies where the owner of the necessary property is the one who will relocate the public use), Section 1240.330 applies where the public entity seeks to acquire substitute property in its own name so that it may itself relocate the public use and then convey the property as improved to the owner of the necessary property. Subdivision (b) specifies an additional requirement for the resolution of necessity and complaint. The second sentence of subdivision (b) makes clear that the determination in the resolution authorizing the taking that the property is necessary for the purposes of this section is conclusive unless a local public entity is acquiring property outside its territorial limits. See Section 1245.250 and Comment thereto (effect of resolution of necessity).

Section 1240.330 is derived from and supersedes numerous special provisions providing such authority to particular public entities. See, e.g., Alameda County Flood Control and Water Conservation District Act, § 28 (Cal.Stats.1949, Ch. 1275); Alpine County Water Agency Act, § 19 (Cal.Stats.1961, Ch. 1896); Amador County Water Agency Act, § 4.9 (Cal.Stats.1959, Ch. 2137); Contra Costa County Flood Control and Water Conservation District Act, § 29 (Cal.Stats.1951, Ch. 1617); Del Norte County Flood Control District Act, § 30 (Cal.Stats.1955, Ch. 166); El Dorado County Water Agency Act, § 20 (Cal.Stats.1959, Ch. 2139); Humboldt County Flood Control District Act, § 30 (Cal.Stats.1945, Ch. 939); Kern County Water Agency Act, § 4.9 (Cal.Stats.1961, Ch. 1003); Lake County Flood Control and Water Conservation District Act (Cal.Stats.1951, Ch. 1544), § 33 (added Cal.Stats.1954, 1st Ex.Sess., Ch.

Civ. Pro.

62, § 48); Madera County Flood Control and Water Conservation Agency Act, § 651 (Cal.Stats.1969, Ch. 916); Marin County Flood Control and Water Conservation District Act, § 28 (Cal.Stats.1953, Ch. 666); Mariposa County Water Agency Act, § 4.9 (Cal.Stats.1959, Ch. 2036); Monterey County Flood Control and Water Conservation District Act, § 29 (Cal.Stats.1947, Ch. 699); Napa County Flood Control and Water Conservation District Act, § 29 (Cal.Stats.1951, Ch. 1449); Nevada County Water Agency Act, § 19 (Cal.Stats.1959, Ch. 2122); Orange County Water District Act, § 39 (Cal.Stats.1933, Ch. 924); Placer County Water Agency Act, § 4.9 (Cal.Stats.1957, Ch. 1234); Riverside County Flood Control and Water Conservation District Act, § 35 (Cal.Stats.1945, Ch. 1122); Sacramento County Water Agency Act, § 4.9 (Cal.Stats.1952, 1st Ex.Sess., Ch. 10); San Benito County Water Conservation and Flood Control District Act, § 33 (Cal.Stats.1953, Ch. 1598); San Bernardino County Flood Control District Act, § 33 (Cal.Stats.1953, Ch. 73); San Diego Flood Control District Act, § 39 (Cal.Stats.1966, 1st Ex.Sess., Ch. 55); San Joaquin County Flood Control and Water Conservation District Act, § 33 (Cal.Stats.1956, 1st Ex.Sess., Ch. 46); San Luis Obispo County Flood Control and Water Conservation District Act, § 29 (Cal.Stats.1945, Ch. 1294); San Mateo County Flood Control District Act, § 31 (Cal.Stats.1959, Ch. 2108); Santa Barbara County Flood Control and Water Conservation District Act, § 30 (Cal.Stats.1955, Ch. 1057); Santa Barbara County Water Agency Act, § 4.9 (Cal.Stats.1945, Ch. 1501); Santa Clara Valley Water District Act, § 29 (Cal.Stats.1951, Ch. 1405); Shasta County Water Agency Act, § 58 (Cal.Stats.1957, Ch. 1512); Solano County Flood Control and Water Conservation District Act, § 4.8 (Cal.Stats.1951, Ch. 1656); Sutter County Water Agency Act, § 4.9 (Cal.Stats.1959, Ch. 2088); Tulare County Flood Control District Act, § 32 (Cal.Stats.1969, Ch. 1149); Tuolumne County Water Agency Act, § 20 (Cal.Stats.1969, Ch. 1236); Ventura County Flood Control District Act, § 29 (Cal.Stats.1944, 4th Ex.Sess., Ch. 44); Yuba-Bear River Basin Authority Act, § 19 (Cal.Stats.1959, Ch. 2131); Yuba County Water Agency Act, § 4.9 (Cal.Stats.1959, Ch. 788).

Public Utilities Code Section 861 grants the Public Utilities Commission jurisdiction in certain controversies that may arise under Section 1240.330 where the public entity is a special law water district.

It should be noted that property may be acquired for the purpose specified in Section 1240.330 by gift, purchase, on other means. See Section 1240.130.

Research References

Miller and Starr California Real Estate § 30A:15, Substitute Condemnation.
8 Witkin, California Summary 10th Constitutional Law § 1189, (S 1189) to Relocate Public Use.

§ 1240.350. Additional property to provide utility service or road access to property cut off by public acquisition

(a) Whenever a public entity acquires property for a public use and exercises or could have exercised the power of eminent domain to acquire such property for such use, the public entity may exercise the power of eminent domain to acquire such additional property as appears reasonably necessary and appropriate (after taking into account any hardship to the owner of the additional property) to provide utility service to, or access to a public road from, any property that is not acquired for such public use but which is cut off from utility service or access to a public road as a result of the acquisition by the public entity.

(b) Where property is sought to be acquired pursuant to this section, the resolution of necessity and the complaint filed pursuant to such resolution shall specifically refer to this section and shall include a statement that the property is necessary for the purpose specified in this section. The determination in the resolution that the taking of the substitute property is necessary has the effect prescribed in Section 1245.250. *(Added by Stats.1975, c. 1275, p. 3416, § 2, operative July 1, 1976.)*

Research References

Miller and Starr California Real Estate § 15:44, Condemnation.
Miller and Starr California Real Estate § 30A:15, Substitute Condemnation.
23 NO. 2 Miller & Starr, California Real Estate Newsalert 10, Eminent Domain.

8 Witkin, California Summary 10th Constitutional Law § 1190, (S 1190) to Provide Utility Service or Access to Road.

ARTICLE 5. EXCESS CONDEMNATION

Section
1240.410. Remnant; authority; acquisition.
1240.420. Resolution and complaint; reference; presumption.
1240.430. Disposition of property taken; use of proceeds.

§ 1240.410. Remnant; authority; acquisition

(a) As used in this section, "remnant" means a remainder or portion thereof that will be left in such size, shape, or condition as to be of little market value.

(b) Whenever the acquisition by a public entity by eminent domain of part of a larger parcel of property will leave a remnant, the public entity may exercise the power of eminent domain to acquire the remnant in accordance with this article.

(c) Property may not be acquired under this section if the defendant proves that the public entity has a reasonable, practicable, and economically sound means to prevent the property from becoming a remnant. *(Added by Stats.1975, c. 1275, p. 3417, § 2, operative July 1, 1976.)*

Law Revision Commission Comments

Section 1240.410 states the test to be applied by the court in determining whether a remainder or portion thereof is a remnant that may be taken by eminent domain. With respect to physical remnants, see Kern County High School Dist. v. McDonald, 180 Cal. 7, 179 P. 180 (1919); People v. Thomas, 108 Cal.App.2d 832, 239 P.2d 914 (1952). As to the concept of "financial remnants," see Dep't of Public Works v. Superior Court, 68 Cal.2d 206, 436 P.2d 342, 65 Cal.Rptr. 342 (1968).

The test is essentially that stated in Dep't of Public Works v. Superior Court, *supra*, except that the confusing concept of "excessive" damages is not used. The remainder or a portion thereof may be taken if it would be left in "such size, shape, or condition as to be of little market value." The "of little market value" concept is a flexible one; whether the excess property may be taken is to be determined in light of the circumstances of the particular case. Thus, the project may result in the excess property having relatively little market value in situations such as, for example, where (1) it will be totally "landlocked" and no physical solution will be practical, (2) it will be reduced below the minimum zoning limits for building purposes and it is not reasonably probable that there will be a zoning change, (3) it will be of significant value to only one or few persons (such as adjoining landowners), or (4) it will be landlocked and have primarily a speculative value dependent upon access being provided when adjacent land is developed and the time when the adjacent land will be developed is a matter of speculation. See, e.g., Dep't of Public Works v. Superior Court, *supra*; State v. Buck, 94 N.J.S. 84, 226 A.2d 840 (1967). The test is the objective one of marketability and market value generally of the excess property. Compare Section 1240.150 (purchase of remnants). *Cf.* Govt.Code § 7267.7 ("If the acquisition of only a portion of a property would leave the remaining portion in such a shape or condition as to constitute an uneconomic remnant, the public entity shall offer to and may acquire the entire property if the owner so desires.").

On the other hand, a usable and generally salable piece of property is neither a physical nor financial remnant even though its "highest and best use" has been downgraded by its severance or a serious controversy exists as to its best use and value after severance. See, e.g., La Mesa v. Tweed & Gambrell Planing Mill, 146 Cal.App.2d 762, 304 P.2d 803 (1956); State Highway Comm'n v. Chapman, 152 Mont. 79, 446 P.2d 709 (1968). Likewise, Section 1240.410 does not authorize a taking of excess property (1) to avoid the cost and inconvenience of litigating the issue of damages, (2) to preclude the payment of damages, including damages substantial in amount in appropriate cases, (3) to coerce the condemnee to accept whatever price the condemnor offers for the property actually needed for the public project, or (4) to afford the condemnor an opportunity to "recoup" damages or unrecognized benefits by speculating as to the future market for the property not actually devoted to the public project. See Dep't of Public Works v. Superior Court, *supra*.

A remnant may be a portion of a remainder where the taking affecting a parcel leaves more than one piece (e.g., the severance of a ranch by a highway so as to leave pieces on both sides of the highway). In certain cases, only one piece might be a remnant.

Subdivision (c) permits the condemnee to contest a taking under Section 1240.410 upon the ground that a "physical solution" could be provided by the condemnor as an alternative to either a total taking or a partial taking that would leave an unusable or unmarketable remainder. The condemnee may be able to demonstrate that, given construction of the public improvement in the manner proposed, the public entity is able to provide substitute access or take other steps that would be equitable under the circumstances of the particular case. If he can do so, subdivision (c) prevents acquisition of the excess property. In most cases, some physical solution would be possible; but subdivision (c) requires that the solution also be "reasonable, practicable, and economically sound." To be "economically sound," the proposed solution must, at a minimum, reduce the overall cost to the condemnor of the taking. Thus, the total of the cost of the solution, the compensation paid for the part taken, and the damages to the remainder must be less than the amount that would be required to be paid if the entire parcel were taken. The court should, moreover, consider questions of maintenance, hardship to third persons, potential dangers, risk of tort liability, and similar matters in determining whether the solution is also "reasonable and practicable." If the physical solution might interfere with or impair the public project, it would not be "reasonable."

If the court determines that a taking is not permitted under Section 1240.410 because a physical solution is "reasonable, practicable, and economically sound," the damages to the remainder must be computed taking into account the extent to which any physical solution that will be provided avoids or reduces such damages. See Section 1263.450 and the Comment thereto.

Section 1240.410 supersedes Section 1266 of the Code of Civil Procedure, Sections 100130.5 and 102241 of the Public Utilities Code, Sections 104.1 and 943.1 of the Streets and Highways Code, Sections 254, 8590.1, 11575.2, and 43533 of the Water Code, and various provisions of uncodified special district acts.

Research References

Miller and Starr California Real Estate § 30A:16, Additional Property Which May be Acquired for the Project.

13 NO. 3 Miller & Starr, California Real Estate Newsalert 10, Eminent Domain.

8 Witkin, California Summary 10th Constitutional Law § 1175, in General.

8 Witkin, California Summary 10th Constitutional Law § 1190, (S 1190) to Provide Utility Service or Access to Road.

8 Witkin, California Summary 10th Constitutional Law § 1191, Excess Condemnation.

8 Witkin, California Summary 10th Constitutional Law § 1220, Contesting Right to Take.

8 Witkin, California Summary 10th Constitutional Law § 1264, Abandonment and Dismissal.

§ 1240.420. Resolution and complaint; reference; presumption

When property is sought to be acquired pursuant to Section 1240.410, the resolution of necessity and the complaint filed pursuant to such resolution shall specifically refer to that section. It shall be presumed from the adoption of the resolution that the taking of the property is authorized under Section 1240.410. This presumption is a presumption affecting the burden of producing evidence. *(Added by Stats.1975, c. 1275, p. 3417, § 2, operative July 1, 1976.)*

Law Revision Commission Comments

Section 1240.420 requires a specific reference in both the resolution and the complaint to the section that is the statutory basis for the proposed taking; it does not require either the recitation or the pleading of the facts that may bring the case within the purview of the section. See People v. Jarvis, 274 Cal.App.2d 217, 79 Cal.Rptr. 175 (1969). A resolution that refers to Section 1240.410 gives rise to a presumption that the taking is authorized under that section. Thus, in the absence of a contest of that issue, Section 1240.420 permits a finding and judgment that the "excess" property may be taken. However, the presumption is specified to be one

affecting the burden of producing evidence (see Evid.Code §§ 603, 604) rather than one affecting the burden of proof (see Evid.Code §§ 605, 606). Accordingly, the burden of proving the facts that bring the case within Section 1240.410 is on the plaintiff. See People v. Van Gorden, 226 Cal.App.2d 634, 38 Cal.Rptr. 265 (1964); People v. O'Connell Bros., 204 Cal.App.2d 34, 21 Cal.Rptr. 890 (1962). In this respect, Section 1240.420 eliminates any greater effect that might be attributed to the resolution (compare People v. Chevalier, 52 Cal.2d 299, 340 P.2d 598 (1959)) or that might be drawn from a legislative (see County of Los Angeles v. Anthony, 224 Cal.App.2d 103, 36 Cal.Rptr. 308 (1964)) or administrative (see County of San Mateo v. Bartole, 184 Cal.App.2d 422, 7 Cal.Rptr. 569 (1960)) determination or declaration as to "public use." Compare former Section 1266.

As to the manner of raising the issue whether a taking is authorized under Section 1240.410, see Sections 1250.350 and 1250.360(f).

Research References

8 Witkin, California Summary 10th Constitutional Law § 1191, Excess Condemnation.

§ 1240.430. Disposition of property taken; use of proceeds

A public entity may sell, lease, exchange, or otherwise dispose of property taken under this article and may credit the proceeds to the fund or funds available for acquisition of the property being acquired for the public work or improvement. Nothing in this section relieves a public entity from complying with any applicable statutory procedures governing the disposition of property. *(Added by Stats.1975, c. 1275, p. 3417, § 2, operative July 1, 1976.)*

Law Revision Commission Comments

Section 1240.430 authorizes the entity to dispose of property acquired under this article.

Research References

Miller and Starr California Real Estate § 30A:16, Additional Property Which May be Acquired for the Project.

8 Witkin, California Summary 10th Constitutional Law § 1191, Excess Condemnation.

ARTICLE 6. CONDEMNATION FOR COMPATIBLE USE

Section
1240.510. Authority; reference in complaint and resolution.
1240.520. Burden of proof.
1240.530. Agreement; terms and conditions; determination by court.

§ 1240.510. Authority; reference in complaint and resolution

Any person authorized to acquire property for a particular use by eminent domain may exercise the power of eminent domain to acquire for that use property appropriated to public use if the proposed use will not unreasonably interfere with or impair the continuance of the public use as it then exists or may reasonably be expected to exist in the future. Where property is sought to be acquired pursuant to this section, the complaint, and the resolution of necessity if one is required, shall refer specifically to this section. *(Added by Stats.1975, c. 1275, p. 3417, § 2, operative July 1, 1976.)*

Law Revision Commission Comments

Section 1240.510 makes clear that the authority to condemn property includes the general authority to condemn for compatible joint use property already devoted to public use. See Section 1235.180 ("property appropriated to public use" defined). Section 1240.510 does not contemplate displacement of the existing use by the second use; rather it authorizes common enjoyment of the property where the second use does not unreasonably interfere with the existing use.

The authority granted by Section 1240.510 is independent of the authority contained in Article 7 ("more necessary public use") and is not limited in any way by the rules set forth therein. Likewise, condemnation of property appropriated to a public use may be accomplished under Article 7 independent of any authority stated in Article 6. See Section 1240.160. It should be noted, however, that, where property is taken under more necessary use authority, the defendant may be entitled to continue joint use of the property. See Section 1240.630.

The requirement that the proposed use be compatible with the existing use continues prior law that permitted condemnation for consistent uses. See former Code Civ.Proc. § 1240(3), (4), (6). The term "consistent" was necessarily imprecise because of the variety of circumstances it embraced. See, e.g., City of San Diego v. Cuyamaca Water Co., 209 Cal. 152, 287 P. 496 (1930), cert. denied, 282 U.S. 863 (1930) (abundant water for use of both parties) (alternate holding); Reclamation Dist. No. 551 v. Superior Court, 151 Cal. 263, 90 P. 545 (1907) (railroad right of way sought on top of reclamation district levee); City of Pasadena v. Stimson, 91 Cal. 238, 27 P. 604 (1891) (sewer line in highway right of way); City of Los Angeles v. Lon Angeles Pac. Co., 31 Cal.App. 100, 159 P. 992 (1916) (railway company's electric transmission lines and subway on property taken for city park).

Section 1240.510 continues the basic principle of consistency by requiring that the proposed use not unreasonably interfere with or impair the continuance of the existing use or such future use as may reasonably be anticipated for the purpose for which the property is already appropriated. See San Bernardino County Flood Control Dist. v. Superior Court, 269 Cal.App.2d 514, 75 Cal.Rptr. 24 (1969); Reclamation Dist. No. 551 v. Superior Court, supra. See generally 1 P. Nichols, Eminent Domain § 2.2[8], at 235–238 (3d ed. 1964). Section 1240.510 does not grant authority to displace or interfere substantially with a prior use; the power to displace an existing use is dealt with in Article 7 (commencing with Section 1240.610).

Section 1240.510 authorizes any condemnor able to satisfy the requirement that its proposed use will be compatible with the existing one to condemn the property of any person. Former law was uncertain. See San Bernardino County Flood Control Dist. v. Superior Court, 269 Cal.App.2d 514, 523–524 n. 10, 75 Cal.Rptr. 24, 32 n. 10 (1969). Subdivision 3 of former Code of Civil Procedure Section 1240 referred only to property "appropriated to a public use or purpose, by any person, firm or private corporation," thereby implying that property appropriated to public use by a public entity could not be subjected to imposition of a consistent use. Subdivision 4 of former Section 1240 also dealt with joint use, but the subdivision was limited to property appropriated to public use by an irrigation district. However, subdivision 6 of former Section 1240 authorized the imposition of "rights of way" on property appropriated to public use with no limitation as to the person who had appropriated the property to public use. In view of the limited nature of the authority granted and the desirability of encouraging common use, Section 1240.510 adopts the latter approach and is applicable to all condemnors and all condemnees.

It should be noted that Section 1240.510 had no effect on the respective rights of the owner of the underlying fee and any easement holders to compensation for the additional burdens imposed by a condemnor exercising the authority granted by this section. In such a situation, if the plaintiff does not make the owner of the underlying fee or easement holder a party to the eminent domain proceeding, the owner or easement holder may either appear as a defendant in the eminent domain proceeding or bring a separate inverse action. See Section 1250.230 (appearance as defendant in eminent domain proceeding) and People v. Schultz Co., 123 Cal.App.2d 925, 268 P.2d 117 (1954) (possibility of subsequent action).

Section 1240.510 requires the plaintiff to refer specifically to this section in its complaint where it seeks to exercise the authority granted here. If the plaintiff is a public entity, it also must refer to this section in its resolution of necessity.

In certain situations, a plaintiff may be uncertain of its authority to condemn under Article 7 and may, therefore, proceed under both that article and Section 1240.510. Such inconsistent allegations are proper. See Section 1250.310 and Comment thereto.

The authority granted by Section 1240.510 does not permit condemnation of property made exempt from condemnation by statute. See Section 1240.110 and Comment thereto.

Research References

Miller and Starr California Real Estate § 30A:10, Condemnation of Public Property for Compatible Use.

8 Witkin, California Summary 10th Constitutional Law § 1113, (S 1113) Property that May be Taken.

8 Witkin, California Summary 10th Constitutional Law § 1171, Definitions.

8 Witkin, California Summary 10th Constitutional Law § 1175, in General.

8 Witkin, California Summary 10th Constitutional Law § 1192, Nature of Power.

8 Witkin, California Summary 10th Constitutional Law § 1193, Terms and Conditions of Joint Use.

8 Witkin, California Summary 10th Constitutional Law § 1219, in General.

§ 1240.520. Burden of proof

If the defendant objects to a taking under Section 1240.510, the defendant has the burden of proof that his property is appropriated to public use. If it is established that the property is appropriated to public use, the plaintiff has the burden of proof that its proposed use satisfies the requirements of Section 1240.510. *(Added by Stats.1975, c. 1275, p. 3417, § 2, operative July 1, 1976.)*

Law Revision Commission Comments

Section 1240.520 states the rules governing the burden of proof where the defendant objects to a taking for compatible use. As to the manner of raising the objection that a taking is not authorized under Section 1240.510 because the proposed use will be incompatible with the public use to which the property is appropriated, see Sections 1250.350 and 1250.360(f). If the taking is contested, the court must first determine whether the property is in fact already appropriated to a public use, and the defendant bears the burden of proof on this issue. *Cf.* City of Los Angeles v. Los Angeles Pac. Co., 31 Cal.App. 100, 159 P. 992 (1916). Where this fact is established, the plaintiff must then show that the taking is authorized under this article.

Research References

Miller and Starr California Real Estate § 30A:10, Condemnation of Public Property for Compatible Use.

8 Witkin, California Summary 10th Constitutional Law § 1192, Nature of Power.

§ 1240.530. Agreement; terms and conditions; determination by court

(a) Where property is taken under Section 1240.510, the parties shall make an agreement determining the terms and conditions upon which the property is taken and the manner and extent of its use by each of the parties. Except as otherwise provided by statute, if the parties are unable to agree, the court shall fix the terms and conditions upon which the property is taken and the manner and extent of its use by each of the parties.

(b) If the court determines that the use in the manner proposed by the plaintiff would not satisfy the requirements of Section 1240.510, the court shall further determine whether the requirements of Section 1240.510 could be satisfied by fixing terms and conditions upon which the property may be taken. If the court determines that the requirements of Section 1240.510 could be so satisfied, the court shall permit the plaintiff to take the property upon such terms and conditions and shall prescribe the manner and extent of its use by each of the parties.

(c) Where property is taken under this article, the court may order any necessary removal or relocation of structures or improvements if such removal or relocation would not require any significant alteration of the use to which the property is appropriated. Unless otherwise provided by statute, all costs and damages that result from the relocation or removal shall be paid by the plaintiff. *(Added by Stats.1975, c. 1275, p. 3418, § 2, operative July 1, 1976.)*

Law Revision Commission Comments

Subdivision (a) of Section 1240.530 requires that, in granting the plaintiff the right to use property appropriated to public use, the court may regulate the manner in which the proposed and prior uses will be enjoyed. This continues the substance of portions of former Code of Civil Procedure Sections 1240(3), 1247(1), 1247a.

The introductory clause of the second sentence of subdivision (a) recognizes that exceptions to its provisions may be found in other statutes. E.g., the Public Utilities Commission has exclusive jurisdiction to determine and regulate crossings involving railroads (Pub.Util.Code §§ 1201 and 1202), and issues involving street and highway crossings may not be subject to judicial review. (*Cf.* Sts. & Hwys.Code § 100.2.)

If the parties agree as to the terms and conditions upon which the property is taken and the manner and extent of its use by each of the parties, the agreement avoids the need for the court to act under subdivisions (a) and (b).

The terms and conditions referred to in subdivision (a) would include a provision specifying how any liability arising out of the compatible use is to be borne.

Subdivision (b) requires that, before a court refuses to allow a taking for joint use because the taking does not satisfy the requirements of Section 1240.510, the court must determine whether terms and conditions could be imposed on the proposed taking so that it would satisfy the requirements of Section 1240.510. If the court refuses to approve the joint use as proposed because of a particular feature of the joint use, the court must specify in what respect the joint use as proposed fails to satisfy the requirements of Section 1240.510 and, where possible, specify the modifications in the use as proposed that are necessary in order to satisfy the requirements of Section 1240.510. Under prior law, decisions could be found which implied that the court could not review the proposed joint use or indicate what changes would be required in the proposed joint use so that the taking would be permitted. E.g., San Bernardino County Flood Control Dist. v. Superior Court, 269 Cal.App.2d 514, 75 Cal.Rptr. 24 (1969).

Under subdivision (c), the court may require any necessary removal or relocation of structures or improvements if such removal or relocation would not require any significant alteration of the existing use. A similar provision was found in former Code of Civil Procedure Sections 1240(3) and 1247a. See County of Marin v. Superior Court, 53 Cal.2d 633, 349 P.2d 526, 2 Cal.Rptr. 758 (1960). Subdivision (c) provides that the plaintiff will normally bear the cost of such relocation although, in some cases, specific statutory provisions may allocate all or part of such cost otherwise. For a listing and discussion of statutes dealing with the cost of relocation of facilities of franchise holders, see A Study Relating to Sovereign Immunity, 5 Cal.L.Revision Comm'n Reports 1, 186–190 (1963); California Inverse Condemnation Law, 10 Cal.L.Revision Comm'n Reports 1, 353–358 (1971). See also Note, Cost Allocation in Public Utility Relocation in California, 23 Hastings L.J. 848 (1972).

Research References

Miller and Starr California Real Estate § 30A:10, Condemnation of Public Property for Compatible Use.

8 Witkin, California Summary 10th Constitutional Law § 1193, Terms and Conditions of Joint Use.

ARTICLE 7. CONDEMNATION FOR MORE NECESSARY PUBLIC USE

§ 1240.610. Authority; reference in complaint and resolution

Any person authorized to acquire property for a particular use by eminent domain may exercise the power of eminent domain to acquire for that use property appropriated to public use if the use for which the property is sought to be taken is a more necessary public use than the use to which the property is appropriated. Where property is sought to be acquired pursuant to this section, the complaint, and the resolution of necessity if one is required, shall refer specifically to this section. (*Added by Stats.1975, c. 1275, p. 3418, § 2, operative July 1, 1976.*)

Law Revision Commission Comments

Section 1240.610 permits a plaintiff to exercise the power of eminent domain to displace an existing public use. (For the definition of "property appropriated to public use," see Section 1235.180.) The plaintiff may do so only if the proposed use is "more necessary" than the existing use. It should be noted, however, that the defendant may be permitted to continue joint use of the property under authority granted in Section 1240.630.

The authority to take property appropriated to public use for a more necessary use continues prior law. See former Code of Civil Procedure Sections 1240(3), (5) and 1241(3) and numerous repetitions of the rule in other provisions. The authority to take property for a "more necessary" public use makes unnecessary the authority formerly granted to a number of condemnors to take property "whether the property is already devoted to the same use or otherwise." See, e.g., Harb. & Nav.Code § 6296; Pub.Res.Code § 5542; Pub.Util.Code § 16404; Sts. & Hwys.Code § 27166; Water Code § 71693. The meaning of "more necessary public use" is given greater specificity in the succeeding sections in this article as well as numerous provisions in other codes. See, e.g., Sts. & Hwys.Code §§ 30402 (use by Toll Bridge Authority a more necessary use than any other use except railroad uses), 31001 (use by Folsom Lake Bridge Authority a more necessary use than any other use), 31201 (use by El Dorado County Toll Tunnel Authority a more necessary use than any other use).

Prior law apparently required a plaintiff seeking to condemn property already appropriated to a public use to alleged facts showing that its proposed use was a more necessary public use than that to which the property was already appropriated. See Woodland School Dist. v. Woodland Cemetery Ass'n, 174 Cal.App.2d 243, 344 P.2d 326 (1959). Section 1240.610 eliminates this pleading requirement, but Section 1240.620 continues the rule that the condemnor has the burden of proving that the proposed use is a more necessary public use.

The authority granted by Section 1240.610 does not permit condemnation of property made exempt from condemnation by statute. See Section 1240.110 and Comment thereto.

Research References

Miller and Starr California Real Estate § 30A:10, Condemnation of Public Property for Compatible Use.

Miller and Starr California Real Estate § 30A:11, Condemnation of Public Property for More Necessary Public Use.

Miller and Starr California Real Estate § 30A:68, Eminent Domain Trials Generally.

8 Witkin, California Summary 10th Constitutional Law § 1105, Right to Abandon Operation.

8 Witkin, California Summary 10th Constitutional Law § 1113, (S 1113) Property that May be Taken.

8 Witkin, California Summary 10th Constitutional Law § 1171, Definitions.

8 Witkin, California Summary 10th Constitutional Law § 1175, in General.

8 Witkin, California Summary 10th Constitutional Law § 1192, Nature of Power.

8 Witkin, California Summary 10th Constitutional Law § 1194, Nature of Power.

8 Witkin, California Summary 10th Constitutional Law § 1219, in General.

§ 1240.620. Burden of proof

If the defendant objects to a taking under Section 1240.610, the defendant has the burden of proof that his property is appropriated to public use. If it is established that the property is appropriated to public use, the plaintiff has the burden of proof that its use satisfies the requirements of Section 1240.610. *(Added by Stats.1975, c. 1275, p. 3418, § 2, operative July 1, 1976.)*

Law Revision Commission Comments

Section 1240.620 states the rules governing the burden of proof where the defendant objects to a taking for a more necessary public use. As to the manner of raising the objection that a taking is not authorized under Section 1240.610 because the proposed use is not more necessary than the public use to which the property is appropriated, see Sections 1250.350 and 1250.360(f). If the taking is contested, the court must first determine whether the property is in fact already appropriated to public use, the defendant bearing the burden of proof on this issue. *Cf.* City of Los Angeles v. Los Angeles Pac. Co., 31 Cal.App. 100, 159 P. 992 (1916). Where this fact is proved or otherwise established, the plaintiff must then show that its use is a more necessary public use than the existing use.

Research References

Miller and Starr California Real Estate § 30A:11, Condemnation of Public Property for More Necessary Public Use.
8 Witkin, California Summary 10th Constitutional Law § 1194, Nature of Power.

§ 1240.630. Continuation of public use; determination by court; agreement

(a) Where property is sought to be taken under Section 1240.610, the defendant is entitled to continue the public use to which the property is appropriated if the continuance of such use will not unreasonably interfere with or impair, or require a significant alteration of, the more necessary public use as it is then planned or exists or may reasonably be expected to exist in the future.

(b) If the defendant objects to a taking under this article on the ground that he is entitled under subdivision (a) to continue the public use to which the property is appropriated, upon motion of either party, the court shall determine whether the defendant is entitled under subdivision (a) to continue the use to which the property is appropriated; and, if the court determines that the defendant is so entitled, the parties shall make an agreement determining the terms and conditions upon which the defendant may continue the public use to which the property is appropriated, the terms and conditions upon which the property taken by the plaintiff is acquired, and the manner and extent of the use of the property by each of the parties. Except as otherwise provided by statute, if the parties are unable to agree, the court shall fix such terms and conditions and the manner and extent of the use of the property by each of the parties. *(Added by Stats.1975, c. 1275, p. 3418, § 2, operative July 1, 1976.)*

Law Revision Commission Comments

Section 1240.630 provides a right new to California law; where property appropriated to public use is taken for a more necessary public use, the prior user may continue his use jointly with the more necessary use if the continuance will not unreasonably interfere with or impair, or require a significant alteration of, the more necessary use.

Subdivision (a). The test for whether the defendant may continue to jointly use the property is comparable to that defining compatible uses. *Cf.* Sections 1240.510 and 1240.530 and Comments thereto.

Subdivision (b). In order to have a determination of the right to joint use under subdivision (a), the defendant must raise the issue. As to the manner of raising the issue, see Sections 1250.350 and 1250.360(g).

If the defendant objects to the taking on the ground that he is entitled under subdivision (a) to continue the prior use as a joint use, the court must determine whether the defendant is entitled to continue use of the

property and must consider possible alterations that would enable joint use and, at the same time, not require significant alteration of the more necessary use or unreasonably impair or interfere with it.

Research References

Miller and Starr California Real Estate § 30A:11, Condemnation of Public Property for More Necessary Public Use.
8 Witkin, California Summary 10th Constitutional Law § 1194, Nature of Power.

§ 1240.640. Use by state as more necessary than use by other person; presumption

(a) Where property has been appropriated to public use by any person other than the state, the use thereof by the state for the same use or any other public use is presumed to be a more necessary use than the use to which such property has already been appropriated.

(b) Where property has been appropriated to public use by the state, the use thereof by the state is presumed to be a more necessary use than any use to which such property might be put by any other person.

(c) The presumptions established by this section are presumptions affecting the burden of proof. *(Added by Stats.1975, c. 1275, p. 3419, § 2, operative July 1, 1976.)*

Research References

Miller and Starr California Real Estate § 30A:11, Condemnation of Public Property for More Necessary Public Use.
8 Witkin, California Summary 10th Constitutional Law § 1195, Uses Presumed to be More Necessary.

§ 1240.650. Use by public entity as more necessary than use by other person; rebuttable presumption for electric, gas, or water public utility property

(a) Where property has been appropriated to public use by any person other than a public entity, the use thereof by a public entity for the same use or any other public use is a more necessary use than the use to which such property has already been appropriated.

(b) Where property has been appropriated to public use by a public entity, the use thereof by the public entity is a more necessary use than any use to which such property might be put by any person other than a public entity.

(c) Where property which has been appropriated to a public use is electric, gas, or water public utility property which the public entity intends to put to the same use, the presumption of a more necessary use established by subdivision (a) is a rebuttable presumption affecting the burden of proof, unless the acquiring public entity is a sanitary district exercising the powers of a county water district pursuant to Section 6512.7 of the Health and Safety Code. *(Added by Stats.1975, c. 1275, p. 3419, § 2, operative July 1, 1976. Amended by Stats.1992, c. 812 (S.B.1757), § 2.)*

Law Revision Commission Comments

Section 1240.650 is similar in substance to former Code of Civil Procedure Section 1240(3) except that Section 1240.650 embraces all public entities. Thus, for example, Section 1240.650 includes school districts which formerly were not included.

The preference under Section 1240.650 is not merely one of public ownership over private ownership for the same use but includes any use. Thus, for example, a public entity may condemn the easement of a privately owned public utility not merely to perpetuate the utility use in public ownership but also to provide some separate and distinct use. Specific exceptions to the rule of public supremacy may be legislatively declared elsewhere.

Property appropriated to public use by a public entity may always be taken for common use by any other person where compatible pursuant to Section 1240.510 et seq.

Research References

Miller and Starr California Real Estate § 30A:11, Condemnation of Public Property for More Necessary Public Use.

8 Witkin, California Summary 10th Constitutional Law § 1105, Right to Abandon Operation.

8 Witkin, California Summary 10th Constitutional Law § 1195, Uses Presumed to be More Necessary.

§ 1240.660. Use by local public entity as more necessary than use by other local public entity; presumption

Where property has been appropriated to public use by a local public entity, the use thereof by the local public entity is presumed to be a more necessary use than any use to which such property might be put by any other local public entity. The presumption established by this section is a presumption affecting the burden of proof. *(Added by Stats.1975, c. 1275, p. 3419, § 2, operative July 1, 1976.)*

Research References

8 Witkin, California Summary 10th Constitutional Law § 1195, Uses Presumed to be More Necessary.

§ 1240.670. Presumption that property appropriated for best and most necessary use; requirements

(a) Subject to Section 1240.690, notwithstanding any other provision of law, property is presumed to have been appropriated for the best and most necessary public use if all of the following are established:

(1) The property is owned by a nonprofit organization contributions to which are deductible for state and federal income tax purposes under the laws of this state and of the United States and having the primary purpose of preserving areas in their natural condition.

(2) The property is open to the public subject to reasonable restrictions and is appropriated, and used exclusively, for the preservation of native plants or native animals including, but not limited to, mammals, birds, and marine life, or biotic communities, or geological or geographical formations of scientific or educational interest.

(3) The property is irrevocably dedicated to such uses so that, upon liquidation, dissolution, or abandonment of or by the owner, such property will be distributed only to a fund, foundation, or corporation whose property is likewise irrevocably dedicated to such uses, or to a governmental agency holding land for such uses.

(b) The presumption established by this section is a presumption affecting the burden of proof. *(Added by Stats.1975, c. 1275, p. 3419, § 2, operative July 1, 1976.)*

Law Revision Commission Comments

Section 1240.670 continues without substantive change the provisions of subdivision (a) of former Section 1241.9 of the Code of Civil Procedure. For special procedural limitations where the property described is sought to be taken for state highway purposes, see Section 1240.690.

Research References

Miller and Starr California Real Estate § 30A:11, Condemnation of Public Property for More Necessary Public Use.

8 Witkin, California Summary 10th Constitutional Law § 1195, Uses Presumed to be More Necessary.

§ 1240.680. Park, open space, recreation, etc. areas; presumption

(a) Subject to Sections 1240.690 and 1240.700, notwithstanding any other provision of law, property is presumed to have been appropriated for the best and most necessary public use if the property is appropriated to public use as any of the following:

(1) A state, regional, county, or city park, open space, or recreation area.

(2) A wildlife or waterfowl management area established by the Department of Fish and Game pursuant to Section 1525 of the Fish and Game Code.

(3) A historic site included in the National Register of Historic Places or state-registered landmarks.

(4) An ecological reserve as provided for in Article 4 (commencing with Section 1580) of Chapter 5 of Division 2 of the Fish and Game Code.

(b) The presumption established by this section is a presumption affecting the burden of proof. *(Added by Stats.1975, c. 1275, p. 3419, § 3, operative July 1, 1976.)*

Law Revision Commission Comments

Section 1240.680 continues without substantive change the provisions of subdivision (a) of former Section 1241.7 of the Code of Civil Procedure and subdivision (a) of former Section 5542.5 of the Public Resources Code. The portion of Section 5542.5(a) which described the property ("whether owned in fee or lesser title interest, leased, or operated under a license, management agreement, or otherwise") has been omitted in view of the broad definition of "property" in Section 1235.170. See also Section 1235.180 (defining "property appropriated to public use"). For special procedural limitations where the property described is sought to be taken for state highway purposes, see Section 1240.690. For special procedural limitations where the property described is sought to be taken for city or county road, street, or highway purposes, see Section 1240.700.

Research References

Miller and Starr California Real Estate § 30A:11, Condemnation of Public Property for More Necessary Public Use.

12 Witkin, California Summary 10th Real Property § 253, Public Entity's Dedication of Its Own Property.

8 Witkin, California Summary 10th Constitutional Law § 1195, Uses Presumed to be More Necessary.

§ 1240.690. Declaratory relief against state highway use; procedure

(a) When property described in Section 1240.670 or 1240.680 is sought to be acquired for state highway purposes, and the property was dedicated or devoted to a use described in those sections prior to the initiation of highway route location studies, an action for declaratory relief may be brought by the public entity or nonprofit organization owning the property in the superior court to determine the question of which public use is the best and most necessary public use for the property.

(b) The action for declaratory relief shall be filed and served within 120 days after the California Transportation Commission has published in a newspaper of general circulation pursuant to Section 6061 of the Government Code, and delivered to the public entity or nonprofit organization owning the property a written notice that a proposed route or an adopted route includes the property. In the case of nonprofit organizations, the written notice need only be given to nonprofit organizations that are on file with the Registrar of Charitable Trusts of this state.

(c) In the declaratory relief action, the resolution of the California Transportation Commission is not conclusive evidence of the matters set forth in Section 1240.030.

(d) With respect to property described in Section 1240.670 or 1240.680 which is sought to be acquired for state highway purposes:

(1) If an action for declaratory relief is not filed and served within the 120-day period established by subdivision (b), the right to bring the action is waived and Sections 1240.670 and 1240.680 do not apply.

(2) When a declaratory relief action may not be brought pursuant to this section, Sections 1240.670 and 1240.680 do not apply. *(Added by Stats.1975, c. 1275, p. 3420, § 2, operative July 1, 1976. Amended by Stats.1982, c. 681, p. 2784, § 2.)*

Law Revision Commission Comments

Section 1240.690 continues without substantive change the provisions of subdivision (b) of former Sections 1241.7 and 1241.9 of the Code of Civil Procedure except for portions that have been omitted as unnecessary. The portion of subdivision (b) that related to trial preference duplicates Code of Civil Procedure Section 1062a (trial preference for declaratory relief actions generally). The portions of former Section 1241.7 relating to takings for public utility purposes are unnecessary because use by a public entity is more necessary than use by a public utility. See Section 1240.650.

Research References

Miller and Starr California Real Estate § 30A:11, Condemnation of Public Property for More Necessary Public Use.
5 Witkin Cal. Proc. 5th Pleading § 856, (S 856) Special Kind of Declaratory Relief.
12 Witkin, California Summary 10th Real Property § 882, Parks and Recreation Areas.
12 Witkin, California Summary 10th Real Property § 883, Wilderness Areas.
8 Witkin, California Summary 10th Constitutional Law § 1195, Uses Presumed to be More Necessary.

§ 1240.700. Declaratory relief against road, street and highway use

(a) When property described in Section 1240.680 is sought to be acquired for city or county road, street, or highway purposes, and such property was dedicated or devoted to regional park, recreational, or open-space purposes prior to the initiation of road, street, or highway route location studies, an action for declaratory relief may be brought in the superior court by the regional park district which operates the park, recreational, or open-space area to determine the question of which public use is the best and most necessary public use for such property.

(b) The action for declaratory relief shall be filed and served within 120 days after the city or county, as the case may be, has published in a newspaper of general circulation pursuant to Section 6061 of the Government Code, and delivered to the regional park district, a written notice that a proposed route or site or an adopted route includes such property.

(c) With respect to property dedicated or devoted to regional park, recreational, or open-space purposes which is sought to be acquired for city or county road, street, or highway purposes:

(1) If an action for declaratory relief is not filed and served within the 120-day period established by subdivision (b), the right to bring such action is waived and the provisions of Section 1240.680 do not apply.

(2) When a declaratory relief action may not be brought pursuant to this section, the provisions of Section 1240.680 do not apply. *(Added by Stats.1975, c. 1275, p. 3421, § 4, operative July 1, 1976.)*

Law Revision Commission Comments

Section 1240.700 continues without substantive change the provisions of subdivision (b) of former Section 5542.5 of the Public Resources Code except that the portion of Section 5542.5 relating to trial preference has been omitted as unnecessary. See Code Civ.Proc. § 1062a (trial preference for declaratory relief actions generally).

Research References

Miller and Starr California Real Estate § 30A:11, Condemnation of Public Property for More Necessary Public Use.
5 Witkin Cal. Proc. 5th Pleading § 856, (S 856) Special Kind of Declaratory Relief.

8 Witkin, California Summary 10th Constitutional Law § 1195, Uses Presumed to be More Necessary.

CHAPTER 4. PRECONDEMNATION ACTIVITIES

ARTICLE 1. PRELIMINARY LOCATION, SURVEY, AND TESTS

§ 1245.010. Authority

Subject to requirements of this article, any person authorized to acquire property for a particular use by eminent domain may enter upon property to make photographs, studies, surveys, examinations, tests, soundings, borings, samplings, or appraisals or to engage in similar activities reasonably related to acquisition or use of the property for that use. *(Added by Stats.1975, c. 1275, p. 3421, § 2, operative July 1, 1976.)*

Law Revision Commission Comments

Section 1245.010 continues without substantive change the provisions of subdivision (b) of former Section 1242.

No time limitation upon entry is prescribed. Although appraisal and suitability studies generally precede the commencement of the eminent domain proceeding, Section 1245.010 does not preclude such studies after the proceeding to acquire the property has been commenced.

Research References

Miller and Starr California Real Estate § 30A:17, Government Access to the Property Prior to Filing of Condemnation Action.
5 Witkin, California Summary 10th Torts § 340, (S 340) Condemnor's Entry to Survey Land.
8 Witkin, California Summary 10th Constitutional Law § 1196, (S 1196) Right to Enter.

§ 1245.020. Prerequisites to entry and activities

In any case in which the entry and activities mentioned in Section 1245.010 will subject the person having the power of eminent domain to liability under Section 1245.060, before making such entry and undertaking such activities, the person shall secure:

(a) The written consent of the owner to enter upon his property and to undertake such activities; or

(b) An order for entry from the superior court in accordance with Section 1245.030. *(Added by Stats.1975, c. 1275, p. 3421, § 2, operative July 1, 1976.)*

Law Revision Commission Comments

Section 1245.020 continues without substantive change the provisions of subdivision (a) of former Section 1242.5.

Section 1245.020 requires a person desiring to make an entry upon property to secure either the permission of the landowner or an order of the court before making an entry that would subject it to liability under subdivision (a) of Section 1245.060. In many cases, the entry and activities upon the property will involve no more than trivial injuries to the property and inconsequential interference with the owner's possession and use. In such cases, neither the owner's permission nor the court order is required. See Comment to Section 1245.060. However, where there will be compensable damage, Section 1245.020 applies.

Research References

Miller and Starr California Real Estate § 30A:17, Government Access to the Property Prior to Filing of Condemnation Action.
8 Witkin, California Summary 10th Constitutional Law § 1196, (S 1196) Right to Enter.

§ 1245.030. Court order permitting entry; petition; notice

(a) The person seeking to enter upon the property may petition the court for an order permitting the entry and shall give such prior notice to the owner of the property as the court determines is appropriate under the circumstances of the particular case.

(b) Upon such petition and after such notice has been given, the court shall determine the purpose for the entry, the nature and scope of the activities reasonably necessary to accomplish such purpose, and the probable amount of compensation to be paid to the owner of the property for the actual damage to the property and interference with its possession and use.

(c) After such determination, the court may issue its order permitting the entry. The order shall prescribe the purpose for the entry and the nature and scope of the activities to be undertaken and shall require the person seeking to enter to deposit with the court the probable amount of compensation. *(Added by Stats.1975, c. 1275, p. 3422, § 2, operative July 1, 1976.)*

Law Revision Commission Comments

Section 1245.030 continues without substantive change the provisions of subdivision (b) of former Section 1242.5.

Under Section 1245.030, the court should examine the purpose of the entry and determine the nature and scope of the activities reasonably necessary to accomplish the purpose. Its order should provide suitable limitations by way of time, area, and type of activity to strike the best possible balance between the needs of the condemnor and the interests of the property owner. The order also must require the condemnor to deposit an amount sufficient to reimburse the owner for the probable damage to his property and interference with its use.

Research References

Miller and Starr California Real Estate § 30A:17, Government Access to the Property Prior to Filing of Condemnation Action.
9 Witkin Cal. Proc. 5th Appeal § 169, Miscellaneous Orders.
8 Witkin, California Summary 10th Constitutional Law § 1197, (S 1197) Entry Under Court Order.

§ 1245.040. Court order; modification; deposit

(a) The court, after notice and hearing, may modify any of the provisions of an order made under Section 1245.030.

(b) If the amount required to be deposited is increased by an order of modification, the court shall specify the time within which the additional amount shall be deposited and may direct that any further entry or that specified activities under the order as modified be stayed until the additional amount has been deposited. *(Added by Stats.1975, c. 1275, p. 3422, § 2, operative July 1, 1976.)*

Law Revision Commission Comments

Section 1245.040 is derived from Section 304 of the Uniform Eminent Domain Code.

If it appears after an order has been made that the activities must either be extended to accomplish the purpose or curtailed to prevent unwarranted damage or interference, or that greater or lesser damage to the property will occur, the owner or the condemnor may apply to the court for a redetermination and appropriate changes in the previous order.

To insure the effectiveness of the deposit requirement, a stay of proceedings may be imposed until the additional amount is deposited. The stay, however, is not automatic but is discretionary with the court in light of the circumstances. For example, if the condemnor is solvent, or if the probable damages up to the date for the additional deposit are covered by the amount of the original deposit, or if crews and equipment on the property pursuant to the original order would have to be withdrawn under a stay order, a stay might not be appropriate.

In some circumstances, a modification order may properly decrease the amount of the required deposit; in such an event, the court (pursuant to subdivision (a) of Section 1245.050) can order that the excess be disbursed at once to the person who made the deposit.

Subdivision (a) of Section 1245.040 continues the substance of subdivision (c) of former Section 1242.5. Subdivision (b) of Section 1245.040 is new to California.

Research References

Miller and Starr California Real Estate § 30A:17, Government Access to the Property Prior to Filing of Condemnation Action.
8 Witkin, California Summary 10th Constitutional Law § 1197, (S 1197) Entry Under Court Order.

§ 1245.050. Retention of deposit by court; time; deposit in treasury

(a) Unless sooner disbursed by court order, the amount deposited under this article shall be retained on deposit for six months following the termination of the entry. The period of retention may be extended by the court for good cause.

(b) The deposit shall be made in the Condemnation Deposits Fund in the State Treasury or, upon written request of the plaintiff filed with the deposit, in the county treasury. If made in the State Treasury, the deposit shall be held, invested, deposited, and disbursed in accordance with Article 10 (commencing with Section 16429) of Chapter 2 of Part 2 of Division 4 of Title 2 of the Government Code. *(Added by Stats.1975, c. 1275, p. 3422, § 2, operative July 1, 1976.)*

Law Revision Commission Comments

Section 1245.050 continues the substance of subdivision (d) of former Section 1242.5. Unlike the former provision, Section 1245.050 provides that the period of retention may be extended by the court for good cause.

Research References

Miller and Starr California Real Estate § 30A:17, Government Access to the Property Prior to Filing of Condemnation Action.
8 Witkin, California Summary 10th Constitutional Law § 1197, (S 1197) Entry Under Court Order.

§ 1245.060. Civil action for damages or interference with possession or use of property; costs and litigation expenses

(a) If the entry and activities upon property cause actual damage to or substantial interference with the possession or use of the property, whether or not a claim has been presented in compliance with Part 3 (commencing with Section 900) of Division 3.6 of Title 1 of the Government Code, the owner may recover for such damage or interference in a civil action or by application to the court under subdivision (c).

(b) The prevailing claimant in an action or proceeding under this section shall be awarded his costs and, if the court finds that any of the following occurred, his litigation expenses incurred in proceedings under this article:

(1) The entry was unlawful.

(2) The entry was lawful but the activities upon the property were abusive or lacking in due regard for the interests of the owner.

(3) There was a failure substantially to comply with the terms of an order made under Section 1245.030 or 1245.040.

(c) If funds are on deposit under this article, upon application of the owner, the court shall determine and award the amount the owner is entitled to recover under this section and shall order such amount paid out of the funds on deposit. If the funds on deposit are insufficient to pay the full amount of the award, the court shall enter judgment for the unpaid portion.

(d) Nothing in this section affects the availability of any other remedy the owner may have for the damaging of his property. *(Added by Stats.1975, c. 1275, p. 3422, § 2, operative July 1, 1976.)*

Law Revision Commission Comments

Section 1245.060 is derived from Section 305 of the Uniform Eminent Domain Code.

Subdivision (a) provides the substantive basis for the condemnor's liability for damages arising out of an entry to make suitability studies. Damages provided by this subdivision do not depend upon the issuance of a court order; there may also be liability for a lawful entry made without judicial assistance under Section 1245.010 as well as for an unlawful entry. No claim need be failed against the state or a local public entity under Part 3 (commencing with Section 900) of Division 3.6 of Title 1 of the Government Code. *Cf.* Code Civ.Proc. § 426.70.

The terms "actual damages" and "substantial interference" under subdivision (a) require a common sense interpretation. See, e.g., Onorato Bros. v. Massachusetts Turnpike Authority, 336 Mass. 54, 142 N.E.2d 389 (1957); Wood v. Mississippi Power Co., 245 Miss. 103, 146 So.2d 546 (1962). The term "actual damages," for example, is intended to preclude recovery of merely nominal or "constructive" damages not based on physical injury to property. Similarly, the term "substantial interference" excludes liability for minimal annoyance or interference that does not seriously impinge upon or impair possession and use of the property. See Jacobsen v. Superior Court, 192 Cal. 319, 219 P. 986 (1923). The standard of liability stated in subdivision (a) continues the substance of subdivisions (c) and (d) of former Code of Civil Procedure Section 1242 and of former Government Code Section 816.

It is important to note that, if an eminent domain proceeding eventually is failed to take the property, or a portion of it, a defendant in the eminent domain proceeding may recover only by a cross-complaint in the eminent domain proceeding. See Code Civ.Proc. § 426.70 and Comment thereto.

Subdivision (b) requires the court to award costs to the prevailing claimant in an action or proceeding for damages under this section. In addition, this subdivision requires an award of litigation expenses incurred in the proceedings under this article if the condemnor entered unlawfully, abused the right of lawful entry, or violated the terms of an order permitting entry. The prospect of such an award is an inducement to condemnors to adhere to the requirements of this article. "Litigation expenses" is defined in Section 1235.140 to include not only a reasonable attorney's fee but also any appraisal and engineering fees necessarily incurred by the claimant. Under subdivision (e) of former Section 1242.5, reasonable attorney's fees—but not other litigation expenses—were required to be awarded in any case where the owner recovered judgment.

Subdivision (c) provides a simple and expeditious method, in lieu of a civil action, for adjudication of a claim for damages and expenses where a deposit has been made and the funds deposited have not been disbursed. Similar provision was made in subdivision (e) of former Section 1242.5.

Subdivision (d), which is not included in the Uniform Code section, continues the last sentence of former Section 1242.5.

Research References

Miller and Starr California Real Estate § 30A:17, Government Access to the Property Prior to Filing of Condemnation Action.
5 Witkin, California Summary 10th Torts § 224, (S 224) Liability Under Statutes and Constitution.
5 Witkin, California Summary 10th Torts § 340, (S 340) Condemnor's Entry to Survey Land.
8 Witkin, California Summary 10th Constitutional Law § 1196, (S 1196) Right to Enter.
8 Witkin, California Summary 10th Constitutional Law § 1198, (S 1198) Owner's Action for Damages.

ARTICLE 2. RESOLUTION OF NECESSITY

Section

Section

§ 1245.210. Governing body

As used in this article, "governing body" means:

(a) In the case of a taking by a local public entity, the legislative body of the local public entity.

(b) In the case of a taking by the Sacramento and San Joaquin Drainage District, the State Reclamation Board.

(c) In the case of a taking by the State Public Works Board pursuant to the Property Acquisition Law (Part 11 (commencing with Section 15850) of Division 3 of Title 2 of the Government Code), the State Public Works Board.

(d) In the case of a taking by the Department of Fish and Game pursuant to Section 1348 of the Fish and Game Code, the Wildlife Conservation Board.

(e) In the case of a taking by the Department of Transportation (other than a taking pursuant to Section 21633 of the Public Utilities Code or Section 30100 of the Streets and Highways Code), the California Transportation Commission.

(f) In the case of a taking by the Department of Transportation pursuant to Section 21633 of the Public Utilities Code, the California Transportation Commission.

(g) In the case of a taking by the Department of Transportation pursuant to Section 30100 of the Streets and Highways Code, the California Transportation Commission.

(h) In the case of a taking by the Department of Water Resources, the California Water Commission.

(i) In the case of a taking by the University of California, the Regents of the University of California.

(j) In the case of a taking by the State Lands Commission, the State Lands Commission.

(k) In the case of a taking by Hastings College of Law, the board of directors of that college. *(Added by Stats.1975, c. 1275, p. 3423, § 2, operative July 1, 1976. Amended by Stats.1982, c. 681, p. 2784, § 3.)*

Research References

Miller and Starr California Real Estate § 30A:7, Taking for a Public Use Only.
Miller and Starr California Real Estate § 30A:19, Resolution of Necessity.
Miller and Starr California Real Estate § 30A:30, Fixtures, Equipment, and Improvements.
5 Witkin Cal. Proc. 5th Pleading § 1195, Imposition of Conditions.
8 Witkin, California Summary 10th Constitutional Law § 1180, (S 1180) Public Necessity Required.
8 Witkin, California Summary 10th Constitutional Law § 1199, (S 1199) Requirement.

8 Witkin, California Summary 10th Constitutional Law § 1206, Pleading.

§ 1245.220.　Necessary adoption of resolution

A public entity may not commence an eminent domain proceeding until its governing body has adopted a resolution of necessity that meets the requirements of this article. *(Added by Stats.1975, c. 1275, p. 3423, § 2, operative July 1, 1976.)*

Research References

Miller and Starr California Real Estate § 30A:19, Resolution of Necessity.

8 Witkin, California Summary 10th Constitutional Law § 1124, (S 1124) Public Necessity.

8 Witkin, California Summary 10th Constitutional Law § 1199, (S 1199) Requirement.

§ 1245.230.　Resolution; contents

In addition to other requirements imposed by law, the resolution of necessity shall contain all of the following:

(a) A general statement of the public use for which the property is to be taken and a reference to the statute that authorizes the public entity to acquire the property by eminent domain.

(b) A description of the general location and extent of the property to be taken, with sufficient detail for reasonable identification.

(c) A declaration that the governing body of the public entity has found and determined each of the following:

(1) The public interest and necessity require the proposed project.

(2) The proposed project is planned or located in the manner that will be most compatible with the greatest public good and the least private injury.

(3) The property described in the resolution is necessary for the proposed project.

(4) That either the offer required by Section 7267.2 of the Government Code has been made to the owner or owners of record, or the offer has not been made because the owner cannot be located with reasonable diligence.

If at the time the governing body of a public entity is requested to adopt a resolution of necessity and the project for which the property is needed has been determined by the public entity to be an emergency project, which project is necessary either to protect or preserve health, safety, welfare, or property, the requirements of Section 7267.2 of the Government Code need not be a prerequisite to the adoption of an authorizing resolution at the time. However, in those cases the provisions of Section 7267.2 of the Government Code shall be implemented by the public entity within a reasonable time thereafter but in any event, not later than 90 days after adoption of the resolution of necessity. *(Added by Stats.1975, c. 1275, p. 3423, § 2, operative July 1, 1976. Amended by Stats.1982, c. 1059, p. 3833, § 1; Stats.1983, c. 1079, § 1.)*

Law Revision Commission Comments

Section 1245.230 prescribes the contents of the resolution of necessity by a public entity. The resolution is an administrative determination that the statutory prerequisites for taking particular property have been met. Section 1245.230 supersedes various provisions that required a resolution of necessity by different public entities.

Subdivision (a). The resolution of necessity must contain a general statement of the public use. A statement, for example, that the public use is an "elementary school and grounds" or "right of way for a freeway" or "open space to be maintained in its natural condition" would satisfy this requirement.

The resolution also must make reference to the statute authorizing the acquisition of the property by eminent domain. Only persons authorized by statute to condemn for a particular public use can condemn for that use. Section 1240.020. Such authorizing statutes may be of several types. The state, the University of California, cities, counties, and school districts, for example, may condemn any property necessary to carry out any of their powers or functions. See, e.g., Educ.Code §§ 1047 (school districts), 23151 (Regents of the University of California); Govt.Code §§ 15853 (Public Works Board), 25350.5 (counties), 37350.5 (cities). Many special districts have similar broad authority, but some may condemn only for limited or special purposes. Additionally, if the condemnor is acquiring property under authority of certain general public uses, it must specify that authority. E.g., Sections 1240.220 (taking for future use), 1240.320 to 1240.350 (condemnation for exchange purposes), 1240.420 (excess condemnation), 1240.510 (taking for compatible use), and 1240.610 (taking for more necessary public use).

Subdivision (b). The resolution of necessity must contain a description of the property to be taken. The description must be sufficiently precise to enable the owner to determine the physical extent of the taking and the interest sought. See Sections 1235.170 (defining "property") and 1235.125 (defining "interest" in property).

Subdivision (c). The resolution of necessity must contain a declaration that the governing body of the public entity has found and determined the existence of each of the three elements of public necessity required by Section 1240.030 to be established for a taking. See Section 1240.030 and Comment thereto. This provision is modeled after similar provisions formerly applicable to various condemnors. See, e.g., former Code Civ.Proc. § 1241(2), former Sts. & Hwys.Code § 25052, former Water Code § 8595.

Research References

Miller and Starr California Real Estate § 30A:19, Resolution of Necessity.

Miller and Starr California Real Estate § 30A:28, Fee Interests.

16 NO. 1 Miller & Starr, California Real Estate Newsalert 1, a Takings Trifecta: the Supreme Court's Lingle, San Remo & Kelo Decisions.

19 NO. 5 Miller & Starr, California Real Estate Newsalert 16, Eminent Domain.

8 Witkin, California Summary 10th Constitutional Law § 1186, (S 1186) Acquisition by Gift, Purchase, Lease, or Other Means.

8 Witkin, California Summary 10th Constitutional Law § 1199, (S 1199) Requirement.

§ 1245.235.　Notice and hearing; contents; conduct

(a) The governing body of the public entity may adopt a resolution of necessity only after the governing body has given each person whose property is to be acquired by eminent domain and whose name and address appears on the last equalized county assessment roll notice and a reasonable opportunity to appear and be heard on the matters referred to in Section 1240.030.

(b) The notice required by subdivision (a) shall be sent by first-class mail to each person described in subdivision (a) and shall state all of the following:

(1) The intent of the governing body to adopt the resolution.

(2) The right of such person to appear and be heard on the matters referred to in Section 1240.030.

(3) Failure to file a written request to appear and be heard within 15 days after the notice was mailed will result in waiver of the right to appear and be heard.

(c) The governing body, or a committee of not less than 11 members thereof designated by the governing body if the governing body has more than 40 members, shall hold a hearing at which all persons described in subdivision (a) who filed a written request within the time specified in the notice may appear and be heard on the matters referred to in Section 1240.030. Such a committee shall be reasonably representative of the various geographical areas within the public entity's jurisdiction. The governing body need not give an opportunity to appear and be heard to any person who fails to so file a written request within the time specified in the notice. If a committee is designated by the governing body pursuant to this subdivision to hold the hearing, the committee, subsequent to the hearing, shall provide the governing body and any person described in subdivision (a) who has appeared before the committee with a written summary of the hearing and a written recommendation as to whether to adopt the resolution of necessity. Any person described in subdivision (a) who has appeared before the committee shall also be given an opportunity to appear and be heard before the governing body on the matters referred to in Section 1240.030.

(d) Notwithstanding subdivision (b), the governing body may satisfy the requirements of this section through any other procedure that has given each person described in subdivision (a) reasonable written personal notice and a reasonable opportunity to appear and be heard on the matters referred to in Section 1240.030. *(Added by Stats.1975, c. 1275, p. 3424, § 2, operative July 1, 1976. Amended by Stats.1986, c. 358, § 1.)*

Research References

Miller and Starr California Real Estate § 30:17, Precondemnation Activity by a Public Agency.
Miller and Starr California Real Estate § 30A:8, Necessity of the Project and the Property; Location and Planning.
Miller and Starr California Real Estate § 30A:19, Resolution of Necessity.
13 NO. 3 Miller & Starr, California Real Estate Newsalert 10, Eminent Domain.
8 Witkin, California Summary 10th Constitutional Law § 1199, (S 1199) Requirement.

§ 1245.240.   Vote required for adoption

Unless a greater vote is required by statute, charter, or ordinance, the resolution shall be adopted by a vote of two-thirds of all the members of the governing body of the public entity. *(Added by Stats.1975, c. 1275, p. 3424, § 2, operative July 1, 1976.)*

Research References

Miller and Starr California Real Estate § 30A:19, Resolution of Necessity.
8 Witkin, California Summary 10th Constitutional Law § 1199, (S 1199) Requirement.

§ 1245.245.   Resolution adopting different use of acquired property; resolution reauthorizing existing use of property; failure to adopt resolution; sale of property

(a) Property acquired by a public entity by any means set forth in subdivision (e) that is subject to a resolution of necessity adopted pursuant to this article shall only be used for the public use stated in the resolution unless the governing body of the public entity adopts a resolution authorizing a different use of the property by a vote of at least two-thirds of all members of the governing body of the public entity, or a greater vote as required by statute, charter, or ordinance. The resolution shall contain all of the following:

(1) A general statement of the new public use that is proposed for the property and a reference to the statute that would have authorized the public entity to acquire the property by eminent domain for that use.

(2) A description of the general location and extent of the property proposed to be used for the new use, with sufficient detail for reasonable identification.

(3) A declaration that the governing body has found and determined each of the following:

(A) The public interest and necessity require the proposed use.

(B) The proposed use is planned and located in the manner that will be most compatible with the greatest public good and least private injury.

(C) The property described in the resolution is necessary for the proposed use.

(b) Property acquired by a public entity by any means set forth in subdivision (e) that is subject to a resolution of necessity pursuant to this article, and is not used for the public use stated in the resolution of necessity within 10 years of the adoption of the resolution of necessity, shall be sold in accordance with the terms of subdivisions (f) and (g), unless the governing body adopts a resolution according to the terms of subdivision (a) or a resolution according to the terms of this subdivision reauthorizing the existing stated public use of the property by a vote of at least two-thirds of all members of the governing body of the public entity or a greater vote as required by statute, charter, or ordinance. A reauthorization resolution under this subdivision shall contain all of the following:

(1) A general statement of the public use that is proposed to be reauthorized for the property and a reference to the statute that authorized the public entity to acquire the property by eminent domain for that use.

(2) A description of the general location and extent of the property proposed to be used for the public use, but not yet in use for the public use, with sufficient detail for reasonable identification.

(3) A declaration that the governing body has found and determined each of the following:

(A) The public interest and necessity require the proposed use.

(B) The proposed use is planned and located in the manner that will be most compatible with the greatest public good and least private injury.

(C) The property described in the resolution is necessary for the proposed use.

(c) In addition to any notice required by law, the notice required for a new or reauthorization resolution sought pursuant to subdivision (a) or (b) shall comply with Section 1245.235 and shall be sent to each person who was given notice required by Section 1245.235 in connection with the original acquisition of the property by the public entity.

(d) Judicial review of an action pursuant to subdivision (a) or (b) may be obtained by a person who had an interest in the property described in the resolution at the time that the property was acquired by the public entity, and shall be governed by Section 1085.

(e) The following property acquisitions are subject to the requirements of this section:

(1) Any acquisition by a public entity pursuant to eminent domain.

(2) Any acquisition by a public entity following adoption of a resolution of necessity pursuant to this article for the property.

(3) Any acquisition by a public entity prior to the adoption of a resolution of necessity pursuant to this article for the property, but subsequent to a written notice that the public entity may take the property by eminent domain.

(f) If the public entity fails to adopt either a new resolution pursuant to subdivision (a) or a reauthorization resolution pursuant to subdivision (b), as required by this section, and that property was not used for the public use stated in a resolution of necessity adopted pursuant to this article or a resolution adopted pursuant to subdivision (a) or (b) between the time of its acquisition and the time of the public entity's failure to adopt a resolution pursuant to subdivision (a) or (b), the public entity shall offer the person or persons from whom the property was acquired the right of first refusal to purchase the property pursuant to this section, as follows:

(1) At the present market value, as determined by independent licensed appraisers.

(2) For property that was a single-family residence at the time of acquisition, at an affordable price, which price shall not be greater than the price paid by the agency for the original acquisition, adjusted for inflation, and shall not be greater than fair market value, if the following requirements are met:

(A) The person or persons from whom the property was acquired certify their income to the public entity as persons or families of low or moderate income.

(B) If the single-family residence is offered at a price that is less than fair market value, the public entity may verify the certifications of income in accordance with procedures used for verification of incomes of purchasers and occupants of housing financed by the California Housing Finance Agency.

(C) If the single-family residence is offered at a price that is less than fair market value, the public entity shall impose terms, conditions, and restrictions to ensure that the residence will either:

(i) Remain owner-occupied by the person or persons from whom the property was acquired for at least five years.

(ii) Remain available to persons or families of low or moderate income and households with incomes no greater than the incomes of the present occupants in proportion to the area median income for the longest feasible time, but for not less than 55 years for rental units and 45 years for home ownership units.

(D) The Department of Housing and Community Development shall provide to the public entity recommendations of standards and criteria for those prices, terms, conditions, and restrictions.

(g) If after a diligent effort the public entity is unable to locate the person from whom the property was acquired, if the person from whom the property was acquired does not choose to purchase the property as provided in subdivision (f), or if the public entity fails to adopt a resolution as required pursuant to subdivision (a) or (b) but is not required to offer a right of first refusal pursuant to subdivision (f), the public entity shall sell the property as surplus property pursuant to Article 8 (commencing with Section 54220) of Chapter 5 of Part 1 of Division 2 of Title 5 of the Government Code.

(h) If residential property acquired by a public entity by any means set forth in subdivision (e) is sold as surplus property pursuant to subdivision (g), and that property was not used for the public use stated in a resolution of necessity adopted pursuant to this article or a resolution adopted pursuant to subdivision (a) or (b) between the time of its acquisition and the time of its sale as surplus property, the public entity shall pay to the person or persons from whom the public entity acquired the property the sum of any financial gain between the original acquisition price, adjusted for inflation, and the final sale price.

(i) Upon completion of any acquisition described in subdivision (e) or upon the adoption of a resolution of necessity pursuant to this section, whichever is later, the public entity shall give written notice to the person or persons from whom the property was acquired as described in subdivision (e) stating that the notice, right of first refusal, and return of financial gain rights discussed in this section may accrue.

(j) At least 60 days before selling the property pursuant to subdivision (g), the public entity shall make a diligent effort to locate the person from whom the property was acquired. At any time before the proposed sale, the person from whom the property was acquired may exercise the rights provided by this section. As used in this section, "diligent effort" means that the public entity has done all of the following:

(1) Mailed the notice of the proposed sale by certified mail, return receipt requested, to the last known address of the person from whom the property was acquired.

(2) Mailed the notice of the proposed sale by certified mail, return receipt requested, to each person with the same name as the person from whom the property was acquired at any other address on the last equalized assessment roll.

(3) Published the notice of the proposed sale pursuant to Section 6061 of the Government Code in at least one newspaper of general circulation within the city or county in which the property is located.

(4) Posted the notice of the proposed sale in at least three public places within the city or county in which the property is located.

(5) Posted the notice of the proposed sale on the property proposed to be sold.

(k) For purposes of this section, "adjusted for inflation" means the original acquisition price increased to reflect the proportional increase in the Consumer Price Index for all items for the State of California, as determined by the United States Bureau of Labor Statistics, for the period from the date of acquisition to the date the property is offered for sale. *(Added by Stats.2006, c. 602 (S.B.1650), § 1. Amended by Stats.2007, c. 130 (A.B.299), § 36.)*

Research References

Miller and Starr California Real Estate § 30A:19, Resolution of Necessity.

17 NO. 4 Miller & Starr, California Real Estate Newsalert 1, Redevelopment Redefined: State Legislative Responses to the Kelo Decision.

17 NO. 4 Miller & Starr, California Real Estate Newsalert 2, Statutory Update:.

17 NO. 6 Miller & Starr, California Real Estate Newsalert 20, Table of Statutes (Newsalert Vol 17).

8 Witkin, California Summary 10th Constitutional Law § 1121A, (New)-New Resolution for Change of Use.

§ 1245.250. Conclusive effect of resolution; rebuttable presumption for electric, gas, or water public utility property; presumption; Sacramento and San Joaquin Drainage District

(a) Except as otherwise provided by statute, a resolution of necessity adopted by the governing body of the public entity pursuant to this article conclusively establishes the matters referred to in Section 1240.030.

(b) If the taking is by a local public entity, other than a sanitary district exercising the powers of a county water district pursuant to Section 6512.7 of the Health and Safety Code, and the property is electric, gas, or water public utility property, the resolution of necessity creates a rebuttable presumption that the matters referred to in Section 1240.030 are true. This presumption is a presumption affecting the burden of proof.

(c) If the taking is by a local public entity and the property described in the resolution is not located entirely within the boundaries of the local public entity, the resolution of necessity creates a presumption that the matters referred to in Section 1240.030 are true. This presumption is a presumption affecting the burden of producing evidence.

(d) For the purposes of subdivision (b), a taking by the State Reclamation Board for the Sacramento and San Joaquin Drainage District is not a taking by a local public entity. *(Added by Stats.1975, c. 1275, p. 3424, § 2, operative July 1, 1976. Amended by Stats.1992, c. 812 (S.B.1757), § 3.)*

Research References

Miller and Starr California Real Estate § 30A:19, Resolution of Necessity.

8 Witkin, California Summary 10th Constitutional Law § 1181, (S 1181) Extraterritorial Condemnation.

8 Witkin, California Summary 10th Constitutional Law § 1182, (S 1182) Necessary Interests in Property.

8 Witkin, California Summary 10th Constitutional Law § 1188, (S 1188) in General.

8 Witkin, California Summary 10th Constitutional Law § 1189, (S 1189) to Relocate Public Use.

8 Witkin, California Summary 10th Constitutional Law § 1190, (S 1190) to Provide Utility Service or Access to Road.

8 Witkin, California Summary 10th Constitutional Law § 1200, (S 1200) Effect of Resolution.

8 Witkin, California Summary 10th Constitutional Law § 1203, (S 1203) Consent to Proceeding by Quasi-Public Entity.

§ 1245.255. Judicial review of validity; abuse of discretion; rescission and adoption of new resolution

(a) A person having an interest in the property described in a resolution of necessity adopted by the governing body of the public entity pursuant to this article may obtain judicial review of the validity of the resolution:

(1) Before the commencement of the eminent domain proceeding, by petition for a writ of mandate pursuant to Section 1085. The court having jurisdiction of the writ of mandate action, upon motion of any party, shall order the writ of mandate action dismissed without prejudice upon commencement of the eminent domain proceeding unless the court determines that dismissal will not be in the interest of justice.

(2) After the commencement of the eminent domain proceeding, by objection to the right to take pursuant to this title.

(b) A resolution of necessity does not have the effect prescribed in Section 1245.250 to the extent that its adoption or contents were influenced or affected by gross abuse of discretion by the governing body.

(c) Nothing in this section precludes a public entity from rescinding a resolution of necessity and adopting a new resolution as to the same property subject, after the commencement of an eminent domain proceeding, to the same consequences as a conditional dismissal of the proceeding under Section 1260.120. (Added by Stats.1975, c. 1275, p. 3425, § 2, operative July 1, 1976. Amended by Stats.1978, c. 286, p. 578, § 1.)

Research References

Miller and Starr California Real Estate § 30A:19, Resolution of Necessity.

23 NO. 2 Miller & Starr, California Real Estate Newsalert 10, Eminent Domain.

8 Witkin Cal. Proc. 5th Extraordinary Writs § 88, (S 88) Other Local Officials.

8 Witkin, California Summary 10th Constitutional Law § 1200, (S 1200) Effect of Resolution.

8 Witkin, California Summary 10th Constitutional Law § 1201, (S 1201) Judicial Review.

8 Witkin, California Summary 10th Constitutional Law § 1220, Contesting Right to Take.

§ 1245.260. Inverse condemnation; alternatives; limitations; mandate

(a) If a public entity has adopted a resolution of necessity but has not commenced an eminent domain proceeding to acquire the property within six months after the date of adoption of the resolution, or has commenced such proceeding but has not within six months after the commencement of such proceeding attempted diligently to serve the complaint and the summons relating to such proceeding, the property owner may, by an action in inverse condemnation, do either or both of the following:

(1) Require the public entity to take the property and pay compensation therefor.

(2) Recover damages from the public entity for any interference with the possession and use of the property resulting from adoption of the resolution.

Service by mail pursuant to Section 415.30 shall constitute a diligent attempt at service within the meaning of this section.

(b) No claim need be presented against a public entity under Part 3 (commencing with Section 900) of Division 3.6 of Title 1 of the Government Code as a prerequisite to commencement or maintenance of an action under subdivision (a), but any such action shall be commenced within one year and six months after the date the public entity adopted the resolution of necessity.

(c) A public entity may commence an eminent domain proceeding or rescind a resolution of necessity as a matter of right at any time before the property owner commences an action under this section. If the public entity commences an eminent domain proceeding or rescinds the resolution of necessity before the property owner commences an action under this section, the property owner may not thereafter bring an action under this section.

(d) After a property owner has commenced an action under this section, the public entity may rescind the resolution of necessity and abandon the taking of the property only under the same circumstances and subject to the same conditions and consequences as abandonment of an eminent domain proceeding.

(e) Commencement of an action under this section does not affect any authority a public entity may have to commence an eminent domain proceeding, take possession of the property pursuant to Article 3 (commencing with Section 1255.410) of Chapter 6, or abandon the eminent domain proceeding.

(f) In lieu of bringing an action under subdivision (a) or if the limitations period provided in subdivision (b) has run, the property owner may obtain a writ of mandate to compel the public entity, within such time as the court deems appropriate, to rescind the resolution of necessity or to commence an eminent domain proceeding to acquire the property. (Added by Stats. 1975, c. 1275, p. 3425, § 2, operative July 1, 1976. Amended by Stats.1978, c. 411, p. 1304, § 1.)

Law Revision Commission Comments

Section 1245.260 continues the substance of former Section 1243.1 but makes a number of clarifying changes:

(1) Subdivision (a) of Section 1245.260 makes clear that the owner of the property may bring an inverse condemnation action seeking the various types of relief specified. In addition, subdivision (f) provides for relief by way of a writ of mandate as an alternative to bringing an inverse condemnation action. Former Section 1243.1 was unclear as to the nature of the relief that might be obtained in an inverse condemnation action and did not contain any provision relating to relief by way of a writ of mandate.

(2) Subdivision (b) eliminates the claims presentation requirement and specifies a statute of limitations that is comparable to the time within which a claim would have had to be presented to the public entity, assuming that the cause of action accrued upon the expiration of six months from the adoption of the resolution of necessity. See Govt.Code §§ 901 (date of accrual of cause of action), 911.2 (time for presentation of claims). Under former Section 1243.1, it was not clear whether a claim was required to be presented to the public entity.

It should be noted that the statute of limitations provided in subdivision (b) applies only to commencement of an inverse condemnation action under subdivision (a). The provision for a writ of mandate in subdivision (f) remains operative despite the expiration of the limitations period.

(3) Subdivision (c) makes clear that the public entity can commence an eminent domain proceeding or rescind the resolution of necessity at any time prior to the commencement of the action and thereby avoid liability under subdivision (a). This provision does not, however, affect the owner's right to bring an inverse condemnation action based on Article I, Section 19, of the California Constitution. See Klopping v. City of Whittier, 8 Cal.3d 39, 500 P.2d 1345, 104 Cal.Rptr. 1 (1972). Former

Section 1243.1 was silent on the consequences of the public entity's commencing an eminent domain proceeding or rescinding the resolution.

(4) Subdivision (d) makes clear that the public entity may rescind the resolution and abandon the taking after commencement of an action under this section only under the circumstances and subject to the same conditions and consequences as abandonment of an eminent domain proceeding. For the circumstances under which a plaintiff may abandon, see Section 1268.510. For conditions and consequences of abandonment, see also Sections 1268.610 and 1268.620. Former Section 1243.1 did not deal with these matters.

Research References

Miller and Starr California Real Estate § 30:19, Announcement of Intent to Condemn or Adoption of Resolution of Necessity.
Miller and Starr California Real Estate § 30:21, Remedies for Unreasonable Precondemnation Activity.
Miller and Starr California Real Estate § 30A:19, Resolution of Necessity.
15 NO. 6 Miller & Starr, California Real Estate Newsalert 10, Eminent Domain.
8 Witkin, California Summary 10th Constitutional Law § 1169, Action Prior to Taking or Damage.
8 Witkin, California Summary 10th Constitutional Law § 1202, (S 1202) Remedies If Proceeding is Not Promptly Commenced.

§ 1245.270. Failure of resolution to meet requirements of this article; bribery; proof

(a) A resolution of necessity does not meet the requirements of this article if the defendant establishes by a preponderance of the evidence both of the following:

(1) A member of the governing body who voted in favor of the resolution received or agreed to receive a bribe (as that term is defined in subdivision 6 of Section 7 of the Penal Code) involving adoption of the resolution.

(2) But for the conduct described in paragraph (1), the resolution would not otherwise have been adopted.

(b) Where there has been a prior criminal prosecution of the member for the conduct described in paragraph (1) of subdivision (a), proof of conviction shall be conclusive evidence that the requirement of paragraph (1) of subdivision (a) is satisfied, and proof of acquittal or other dismissal of the prosecution shall be conclusive evidence that the requirement of paragraph (1) of subdivision (a) is not satisfied. Where there is a pending criminal prosecution of the member for the conduct described in paragraph (1) of subdivision (a), the court may take such action as is just under the circumstances of the case.

(c) Nothing in this section precludes a public entity from rescinding a resolution of necessity and adopting a new resolution as to the same property, subject to the same consequences as a conditional dismissal of the proceeding under Section 1260.120. *(Added by Stats.1975, c. 1275, p. 3426, § 2, operative July 1, 1976.)*

Research References

Miller and Starr California Real Estate § 30A:19, Resolution of Necessity.
8 Witkin, California Summary 10th Constitutional Law § 1200, (S 1200) Effect of Resolution.

ARTICLE 3. RESOLUTION CONSENTING
TO EMINENT DOMAIN PROCEEDING
BY QUASI–PUBLIC ENTITY

§ 1245.310. Legislative body

As used in this article, "legislative body" means both of the following:

(a) The legislative body of each city within whose boundaries property sought to be taken by the quasi-public entity by eminent domain is located.

(b) If property sought to be taken by the quasi-public entity is not located within city boundaries, the legislative body of each county within whose boundaries such property is located. *(Added by Stats.1975, c. 1275, p. 3426, § 2, operative July 1, 1976.)*

Research References

Miller and Starr California Real Estate § 14:22, Lateral Support--Depth of an Excavation.
Miller and Starr California Real Estate § 25:42, Construction of Public Improvements.
Miller and Starr California Real Estate § 30A:6, Public Agencies and Other Entities With the Power of Eminent Domain.
8 Witkin, California Summary 10th Constitutional Law § 1203, (S 1203) Consent to Proceeding by Quasi-Public Entity.

§ 1245.320. Quasi-public entity

As used in this article, "quasi-public entity" means:

(a) An educational institution of collegiate grade not conducted for profit that seeks to take property by eminent domain under Section 94500 of the Education Code.

(b) A nonprofit hospital that seeks to take property by eminent domain under Section 1260 of the Health and Safety Code.

(c) A cemetery authority that seeks to take property by eminent domain under Section 8501 of the Health and Safety Code.

(d) A limited-dividend housing corporation that seeks to take property by eminent domain under Section 34874 of the Health and Safety Code.

(e) A land-chest corporation that seeks to take property by eminent domain under former Section 35167 of the Health and Safety Code.

(f) A mutual water company that seeks to take property by eminent domain under Section 2729 of the Public Utilities Code. *(Added by Stats.1975, c. 1275, p. 3426, § 2, operative July 1, 1976. Amended by Stats.2006, c. 538 (S.B.1852), § 67.)*

Research References

Miller and Starr California Real Estate § 30A:6, Public Agencies and Other Entities With the Power of Eminent Domain.
8 Witkin, California Summary 10th Constitutional Law § 1203, (S 1203) Consent to Proceeding by Quasi-Public Entity.

§ 1245.325. Appurtenant easement; acquisition by private owner for utility service

Where an owner of real property seeks to acquire an appurtenant easement by eminent domain pursuant to Section 1001 of the Civil Code:

(a) The person seeking to exercise the power of eminent domain shall be deemed to be a "quasi-public entity" for the purposes of this article.

(b) In lieu of the requirements of subdivision (c) of Section 1245.340, the resolution required by this article shall contain a declaration that the legislative body has found and determined each of the following:

(1) There is a great necessity for the taking.

(2) The location of the easement affords the most reasonable service to the property to which it is appurtenant, consistent with the least damage to the burdened property.

(3) The hardship to the owner of the appurtenant property, if the taking is not permitted, clearly outweighs any hardship to the owner of the burdened property. *(Added by Stats.1976, c. 994, p. 2362, § 2.)*

Law Revision Commission Comments

Subdivision (a) of Section 1245.325 makes clear that acquisitions pursuant to Civil Code Section 1001 are subject to the requirements of this article. Subdivision (b) replaces the findings required in Section 1245.340(c) with findings necessitated by the special provisions of Civil Code Section [1001(c)].

Research References

Miller and Starr California Real Estate § 15:44, Condemnation.
Miller and Starr California Real Estate § 15:87, Condemnation.
Miller and Starr California Real Estate § 30A:6, Public Agencies and Other Entities With the Power of Eminent Domain.
Miller and Starr California Real Estate § 30A:29, Easements.
8 Witkin, California Summary 10th Constitutional Law § 1178, Private Person's Utility Easement.
8 Witkin, California Summary 10th Constitutional Law § 1203, (S 1203) Consent to Proceeding by Quasi-Public Entity.

§ 1245.326. Temporary right to enter adjacent or nearby property; eminent domain by private property owner; quasi-public entity; resolution

Where an owner of real property seeks to acquire by eminent domain a temporary right of entry pursuant to Section 1002 of the Civil Code:

(a) The person seeking to exercise the power of eminent domain shall be deemed to be a "quasi-public entity" for the purposes of this article.

(b) In lieu of the requirements of subdivision (c) of Section 1245.340, the resolution required by this article shall contain a declaration that the legislative body has found and determined that each of the conditions required by Section 1002 of the Civil Code appears to exist. *(Added by Stats.1982, c. 1239, p. 4565, § 2.)*

Research References

Miller and Starr California Real Estate § 30A:6, Public Agencies and Other Entities With the Power of Eminent Domain.
8 Witkin, California Summary 10th Constitutional Law § 1203, (S 1203) Consent to Proceeding by Quasi-Public Entity.

§ 1245.330. Necessity of resolution before commencement of proceeding by entity

Notwithstanding any other provision of law, a quasi-public entity may not commence an eminent domain proceeding to acquire any property until the legislative body has adopted a resolution consenting to the acquisition of such property by eminent domain. *(Added by Stats.1975, c. 1275, p. 3427, § 2, operative July 1, 1976.)*

Research References

8 Witkin, California Summary 10th Constitutional Law § 1203, (S 1203) Consent to Proceeding by Quasi-Public Entity.

§ 1245.340. Resolution; contents

The resolution required by this article shall contain all of the following:

(a) A general statement of the public use for which the property is to be taken and a reference to the statute that authorizes the quasi-public entity to acquire the property by eminent domain.

(b) A description of the general location and extent of the property to be taken, with sufficient detail for reasonable identification.

(c) A declaration that the legislative body has found and determined each of the following:

(1) The public interest and necessity require the proposed project.

(2) The proposed project is planned or located in the manner that will be most compatible with the greatest good and least private injury.

(3) The property described in the resolution is necessary for the proposed project.

(4) The hardship to the quasi-public entity if the acquisition of the property by eminent domain is not permitted outweighs any hardship to the owners of such property. *(Added by Stats.1975, c. 1275, p. 3427, § 2, operative July 1, 1976.)*

Research References

Miller and Starr California Real Estate § 30A:6, Public Agencies and Other Entities With the Power of Eminent Domain.
Miller and Starr California Real Estate § 30A:7, Taking for a Public Use Only.
8 Witkin, California Summary 10th Constitutional Law § 1203, (S 1203) Consent to Proceeding by Quasi-Public Entity.

§ 1245.350. Resolution; adoption; hearing; notice

(a) The legislative body may refuse to consent to the acquisition with or without a hearing, but it may adopt the resolution required by this article only after the legislative body has held a hearing at which persons whose property is to be acquired by eminent domain have had a reasonable opportunity to appear and be heard.

(b) Notice of the hearing shall be sent by first-class mail to each person whose property is to be acquired by eminent domain if the name and address of the person appears on the last equalized county assessment roll (including the roll of state-assessed property). The notice shall state the time, place, and subject of the hearing and shall be mailed at least 15 days prior to the date of the hearing. *(Added by Stats.1975, c. 1275, p. 3427, § 2, operative July 1, 1976.)*

Research References

Miller and Starr California Real Estate § 30A:19, Resolution of Necessity.

§ 1245.360. Vote required for adoption

The resolution required by this article shall be adopted by a vote of two-thirds of all the members of the legislative body. *(Added by Stats.1975, c. 1275, p. 3427, § 2, operative July 1, 1976.)*

Research References

Miller and Starr California Real Estate § 30A:19, Resolution of Necessity.

8 Witkin, California Summary 10th Constitutional Law § 1203, (S 1203) Consent to Proceeding by Quasi-Public Entity.

§ 1245.370. Costs; security

The legislative body may require that the quasi-public entity pay all of the costs reasonably incurred by the legislative body under this article. The legislative body may require that such costs be secured by payment or deposit or other satisfactory security in advance of any action by the legislative body under this article. *(Added by Stats.1975, c. 1275, p. 3427, § 2, operative July 1, 1976.)*

Research References

8 Witkin, California Summary 10th Constitutional Law § 1203, (S 1203) Consent to Proceeding by Quasi-Public Entity.

§ 1245.380. Requirements; effect of this article

The requirement of this article is in addition to any other requirements imposed by law. Nothing in this article relieves the quasi-public entity from satisfying the requirements of Section 1240.030 or any other requirements imposed by law. *(Added by Stats.1975, c. 1275, p. 3428, § 2, operative July 1, 1976.)*

Research References

8 Witkin, California Summary 10th Constitutional Law § 1203, (S 1203) Consent to Proceeding by Quasi-Public Entity.

§ 1245.390. Liability of city and county

The adoption of a resolution pursuant to this article does not make the city or county liable for any damages caused by the acquisition of the property or by the project for which it is acquired. *(Added by Stats.1975, c. 1275, p. 3428, § 2, operative July 1, 1976.)*

Research References

Miller and Starr California Real Estate § 25:42, Construction of Public Improvements.
Miller and Starr California Real Estate § 30A:19, Resolution of Necessity.
8 Witkin, California Summary 10th Constitutional Law § 1203, (S 1203) Consent to Proceeding by Quasi-Public Entity.

CHAPTER 5. COMMENCEMENT OF PROCEEDING

ARTICLE 1. JURISDICTION AND VENUE

§ 1250.010. Jurisdiction

Except as otherwise provided in Section 1230.060 and in Chapter 12 (commencing with Section 1273.010), all eminent domain proceedings shall be commenced and prosecuted in the superior court. *(Added by Stats.1975, c. 1275, p. 3428, § 2, operative July 1, 1976.)*

Law Revision Commission Comments

Section 1250.010 declares the basic rule that eminent domain proceedings are to be conducted in the superior court. This declaration continues prior law. See former Section 1243. For demurrer based on lack of jurisdiction, see Section 430.10.

However, the jurisdiction of the superior court is not exclusive. The issue of just compensation may be submitted to arbitration. See Chapter 12. Moreover, Section 1230.060 preserves such jurisdiction as the Public Utilities Commission may have over issues in eminent domain proceedings. See Section 1230.060 and Comment thereto.

Research References

Rutter, Cal. Practice Guide: Civ. Pro. Before Trial Ch. 3-A, A. Subject Matter Jurisdiction (Competency).
Miller and Starr California Real Estate § 30A:49, Jurisdiction and Venue.
8 Witkin, California Summary 10th Constitutional Law § 1204, Jurisdiction and Venue.

§ 1250.020. Venue; county of location of property

(a) Except as provided in subdivision (b), the proceeding shall be commenced in the county in which the property sought to be taken is located.

(b) When property sought to be taken is situated in more than one county, the plaintiff may commence the proceeding in any one of such counties. *(Added by Stats.1975, c. 1275, p. 3428, § 2, operative July 1, 1976.)*

Law Revision Commission Comments

Section 1250.020 specifies where an eminent domain proceeding must be brought. Failure to bring the proceeding in the proper county is a failure to vest the necessary jurisdiction in the court. For provisions authorizing transfer of the proceedings for trial, see Section 1250.040. For demurrer on ground of lack of jurisdiction, see Section 430.10. See also Section 1250.345 (waiver of objections to complaint).

Section 1250.020 does not authorize a condemnor to condemn property beyond its territorial limits. *Cf.* Section 1240.050 and Comment thereto. For authority to separate property in a complaint for trial, see Section 1048.

Section 1250.020 recodifies the substance of the venue provisions of former Section 1243.

Subdivision (a). Generally speaking, the only place an eminent domain proceeding may be brought is the county in which the property sought to be acquired lies.

Subdivision (b). Where property straddles a county line, the plaintiff has the option to bring suit on either side of the line, and the county so chosen is the proper place of trial for all the property even though a portion is not located in the county. See Section 1250.030. Under former law, where property situated in more than one county was sought to be acquired, the plaintiff could elect to bring separate proceedings relating to separate portions of the property in the county where such portion was situated. See former Section 1243. Subdivision (b), however, requires the plaintiff in this situation to make an election and bring the proceeding in one of the counties in which the tract is situated. In certain situations, relief from the plaintiff's choice of county may be obtained pursuant to Section 1250.040. See Section 1250.040 and Comment thereto.

Research References

Rutter, Cal. Practice Guide: Civ. Pro. Before Trial Ch. 3-D, D. Venue.
Miller and Starr California Real Estate § 30A:49, Jurisdiction and Venue.
3 Witkin Cal. Proc. 5th Actions § 800, (S 800) Condemnation.
8 Witkin, California Summary 10th Constitutional Law § 1204, Jurisdiction and Venue.

§ 1250.030. Venue; county for trial

(a) Except as provided in subdivision (b), the county in which the proceeding is commenced pursuant to Section 1250.020 is the proper county for trial of the proceeding.

(b) Where the court changes the place of trial pursuant to Section 1250.040, the county to which the proceeding is transferred is the proper county for trial of the proceeding. *(Added by Stats.1975, c. 1275, p. 3428, § 2, operative July 1, 1976.)*

Law Revision Commission Comments

Section 1250.030 continues the substance of a portion of former Section 1243.

Research References

8 Witkin, California Summary 10th Constitutional Law § 1204, Jurisdiction and Venue.

§ 1250.040. Venue; law governing change of place of trial

The provisions of the Code of Civil Procedure for the change of place of trial of actions apply to eminent domain proceedings. *(Added by Stats.1975, c. 1275, p. 3428, § 2, operative July 1, 1976.)*

Law Revision Commission Comments

Section 1250.040 makes clear that the rules of practice for civil actions generally govern venue change in eminent domain proceedings. This continues prior law. See former Section 1243 and City of Long Beach v. Lakewood Park, 118 Cal.App.2d 596, 258 P.2d 538 (1953). See also Section 1230.040 and Yolo Water & Power Co. v. Superior Court, 28 Cal.App. 589, 153 P. 394 (1915). Contrast City of Santa Rosa v. Fountain Water Co., 138 Cal. 579, 581, 71 P. 1123, 1124 (1903).

Included in the provisions incorporated by Section 1250.040 is Section 394. Under the applicable portions of Section 394, if a local public entity commences an eminent domain proceeding in a county in which it is situated against a defendant who is not situated, doing business, or residing in such county, either party may move to have the proceeding transferred for trial to another county. Alternatively, if a local public entity commences an eminent domain proceeding in a county in which it is not situated, either the entity or any defendant who is not situated, doing business, or residing in such county may move to have the proceeding transferred for trial to another county. Upon such motion, the court is obligated to transfer the trial to as nearly a neutral county as possible. The county to which the proceeding may be transferred includes the county (1) upon which the parties agree, (2) in which, as nearly as possible, no party is situated, doing business, or residing, or (3) in which, as nearly as possible, all parties are situated, doing business, or residing. Where the property is located in a neutral county to begin with, the court need not transfer the proceeding even though a motion to transfer would be authorized under Section 394. See City of Stockton v. Wilson, 79 Cal.App. 422, 249 P. 835 (1926). See also City of Los Angeles v. Pacific Tel. & Tel. Co., 164 Cal.App.2d 253, 330 P.2d 888 (1958).

Section 394 applies to proceedings commenced by any public entity other than the state. See Section 394(3). See also People v. Spring Valley Co., 109 Cal.App.2d 656, 241 P.2d 1069 (1952) (Section 394 not applicable in action by state); Riverside etc. Dist. v. Joseph W. Wolfskill Co., 147 Cal.App.2d 714, 306 P.2d 22 (1957) (Section 394 not applicable in action by state agency); Georgetown Divide Pub. Util. Dist. v. Bacchi, 204 Cal.App.2d 194, 22 Cal.Rptr. 27 (1962) (Section 394 applicable in action by special district having status of local public entity); Garrett v. Superior Court, 11 Cal.3d 245, 520 P.2d 968, 113 Cal.Rptr. 152 (1974) (Section 394 applicable in action by flood control district).

Section 394 applies to any defendant regardless of the interest the defendant claims in the property sought to be taken. See Georgetown Divide Pub. Util. Dist. v. Bacchi, *supra* (joint owners may take advantage of Section 394); City of Oakland v. Darbee, 102 Cal.App.2d 493, 227 P.2d 909 (1951) (separate owners may take advantage of Section 394); City of Long Beach v. Lakewood Park, *supra* (owners of oil exploration and development rights may take advantage of Section 394). The mere fact that the proceeding is a "mixed action," one in which only some of the defendants fall within the terms of this section, does not preclude its applicability. See Georgetown Divide Pub. Util. Dist. v. Bacchi, *supra*; 1 J. Chadbourn, H. Grossman, A. Van Alstyne, California Pleading § 367 (1961). See also People v. Ocean Shore R.R., 24 Cal.App.2d 420, 75 P.2d 560 (1938) (order changing venue on motion by but one of several defendants on grounds of impossibility of impartial trial affirmed).

The term "doing business" as used in Section 394 is intended to mean conducting some substantial activity, e.g., holding one's self out to others as engaged in the selling of goods or services. See City of Los Angeles v. Pacific Tel. & Tel. Co., *supra*.

Research References

Rutter, Cal. Practice Guide: Civ. Pro. Before Trial Ch. 3-D, D. Venue.
Miller and Starr California Real Estate § 30A:49, Jurisdiction and Venue.
3 Witkin Cal. Proc. 5th Actions § 879, Condemnation.

8 Witkin, California Summary 10th Constitutional Law § 1204, Jurisdiction and Venue.

ARTICLE 2. COMMENCEMENT OF PROCEEDING GENERALLY

Section
1250.110.   Complaint; filing.
1250.120.   Summons; form and content.
1250.125.   Service by publication; summons; default judgment; effect.
1250.130.   Service by publication; court order; duties of plaintiff.
1250.140.   Service on attorney general.
1250.150.   Lis pendens.

§ 1250.110. Complaint; filing

An eminent domain proceeding is commenced by filing a complaint with the court. *(Added by Stats.1975, c. 1275, p. 3428, § 2, operative July 1, 1976.)*

Law Revision Commission Comments

Section 1250.110 supersedes a portion of former Section 1243 which provided that eminent domain proceedings were commenced by filing a complaint and issuing summons. Section 1250.110 makes clear that the filing of a complaint alone is sufficient to commence an eminent domain proceeding and confers subject matter jurisdiction on the court. See Harrington v. Superior Court, 194 Cal. 185, 228 P. 15 (1924); Bayle-Lacoste & Co. v. Superior Court, 46 Cal.App.2d 636, 116 P.2d 458 (1941).

Section 1250.110 is comparable to Section 411.10 which provides that "a civil action is commenced by filing a complaint with the court."

Research References

Miller and Starr California Real Estate § 30A:48, The Complaint.
8 Witkin, California Summary 10th Constitutional Law § 1206, Pleading.

§ 1250.120. Summons; form and content

(a) Except as provided in subdivision (b), the form and contents of the summons shall be as in civil actions generally.

(b) Where process is served by publication, in addition to the summons, the publication shall describe the property sought to be taken in a manner reasonably calculated to give persons with an interest in the property actual notice of the pending proceeding. *(Added by Stats.1975, c. 1275, p. 3428, § 2, operative July 1, 1976.)*

Law Revision Commission Comments

Section 1250.120, which prescribes the contents of the summons, supersedes former Section 1245. Sections 412.20 and 412.30 specify the matters to be included in the summons.

Since the summons does not contain a description of the property (which formerly was required), the defendant must refer to the complaint for this information. However, where service of the summons is by publication, a copy of the complaint is not published. To assure that a person served by publication will be able to determine if he has an interest in the property, subdivision (b) requires the publication to contain a description of the property where process is served by publication. *Cf.* Section 413.10 (service required in a manner "reasonably calculated to give actual notice").

Research References

Rutter, Cal. Practice Guide: Civ. Pro. Before Trial Ch. 4-C, C. Content of Summons.
Miller and Starr California Real Estate § 30A:48, The Complaint.
3 Witkin Cal. Proc. 5th Actions § 987, (S 987) Actions Involving Real Property.
3 Witkin Cal. Proc. 5th Actions § 1034, Special Statutes.

8 Witkin, California Summary 10th Constitutional Law § 1207, Process.

§ 1250.125. Service by publication; summons; default judgment; effect

(a) Where summons is served by publication, the publication may name only the defendants to be served thereby and describe only the property in which the defendants to be served thereby have or claim interests.

(b) Judgment based on failure to appear and answer following service under this section shall be conclusive against the defendants named in respect only to property described in the publication.

(c) Notwithstanding subdivision (b), a defendant who did not receive the offer required by Section 7267.2 of the Government Code because the owner could not be located with reasonable diligence, who was served by publication, and who failed to appear, may contest the amount of compensation within one year of the judgment and for good cause shown, whereupon that issue shall be litigated according to the provisions of this title. *(Added by Stats.1975, c. 1275, p. 3428, § 2, operative July 1, 1976. Amended by Stats.1983, c. 1079, p. 3907, § 2.)*

Law Revision Commission Comments

Section 1250.125 continues the substance of former Section 1245.2.

Research References

Miller and Starr California Real Estate § 30A:48, The Complaint.
12 Witkin, California Summary 10th Real Property § 69, Summons.
8 Witkin, California Summary 10th Constitutional Law § 1207, Process.

§ 1250.130. Service by publication; court order; duties of plaintiff

Where the court orders service by publication, it shall also order the plaintiff (1) to post a copy of the summons and complaint on the property sought to be taken and (2), if not already recorded, to record a notice of the pendency of the proceeding in the manner provided by Section 1250.150. Such posting and recording shall be done not later than 10 days after the date the order is made. *(Added by Stats.1975, c. 1275, p. 3429, § 2, operative July 1, 1976.)*

Law Revision Commission Comments

Section 1250.130 provides additional requirements where service is by publication. The manner of service generally in an eminent domain proceeding is provided by Sections 415.10–415.50. See Section 1230.040 (rules of practice in eminent domain proceeding).

Due process requires that the rights of a person may be adjudicated only if that person is served with process in a manner reasonably calculated to give him actual notice and an opportunity to be heard. See, e.g., Milliken v. Meyer, 311 U.S. 457 (1940); Title & Document Restoration Co. v. Kerrigan, 150 Cal. 289, 88 P. 356 (1906). If a person cannot, after reasonable diligence, be served personally or by mail, the court may order service by publication. Section 415.50. This may occur either because the whereabouts of a named defendant are unknown or because the identity of the defendant is unknown (as where there are heirs and devisees or all persons unknown are named as defendants pursuant to Section 1250.220). However, where service by publication is ordered pursuant to Section 415.50, Section 1250.130 requires that the court also order the plaintiff to post a copy of the summons and complaint on the property and record a lis pendens within 10 days after the making of the order. This provision is designed to increase the likelihood that interested parties will receive actual notice of the proceeding. *Cf.* Title & Document Restoration Co. v. Kerrigan, *supra.* The court should give appropriate directions as to the manner of posting, e.g., location and number of copies. See Section 413.30.

Section 1250.130 supersedes a portion of the second sentence of former Section 1245.3 relating to service on heirs and devisees, persons unknown, and others. Section 1250.130 extends the posting requirement to the case where any defendant is served by publication. As to the requirement of recording, compare Sections 749, 749.1 (lis pendens must be filed in quiet title action against unknown claimants).

Although generally service statutes are liberally construed (*cf.* Sections 4 and 187), the due process considerations involved in service by publication demand strict compliance with the statute. See Stanford v. Worn, 27 Cal. 171 (1865). See also City of Los Angeles v. Glassell, 203 Cal. 44, 262 P. 1084 (1928).

Research References

Rutter, Cal. Practice Guide: Civ. Pro. Before Trial Ch. 9(I)-J, J. Motion to Expunge Lis Pendens.
Rutter, Cal. Practice Guide: Real Prop. Transactions Ch. 11-I, I. Lis Pendens.
Miller and Starr California Real Estate § 11:150, Actions in Which a Lis Pendens May or Must be Recorded.
Miller and Starr California Real Estate § 30A:48, The Complaint.
8 Witkin, California Summary 10th Constitutional Law § 1207, Process.

§ 1250.140. Service on attorney general

Where the state is a defendant, the summons and the complaint shall be served on the Attorney General. *(Added by Stats.1975, c. 1275, p. 3429, § 2, operative July 1, 1976.)*

Law Revision Commission Comments

Section 1250.140 requires service on the Attorney General when property belonging to the state is sought to be taken. This continues a requirement of subdivision 8 of former Section 1240 which also required service on the Governor and the State Lands Commission. In a special provision relating to the condemnation of a "square," former Section 1245.4 required service on the Director of General Services. These additional service requirements are eliminated. The Attorney General is charged with the responsibility for seeing that the proper agency of the state receives notice of the proceeding.

Research References

Miller and Starr California Real Estate § 30A:48, The Complaint.
8 Witkin, California Summary 10th Constitutional Law § 1207, Process.

§ 1250.150. Lis pendens

The plaintiff, at the time of the commencement of the proceeding, shall record a notice of the pendency of the proceeding in the office of the county recorder of any county in which property described in the complaint is located. A copy of the notice shall be served with the summons and complaint. *(Added by Stats.1975, c. 1275, p. 3429, § 2, operative July 1, 1976. Amended by Stats.1983, c. 78, § 2.)*

Research References

Rutter, Cal. Practice Guide: Civ. Pro. Before Trial Ch. 9(I)-J, J. Motion to Expunge Lis Pendens.
Rutter, Cal. Practice Guide: Real Prop. Transactions Ch. 11-I, I. Lis Pendens.
Miller and Starr California Real Estate § 11:149, Procedural and Formal Requirements for a Lis Pendens.
Miller and Starr California Real Estate § 11:150, Actions in Which a Lis Pendens May or Must be Recorded.
Miller and Starr California Real Estate § 30A:48, The Complaint.
3 Witkin Cal. Proc. 5th Actions § 378, (S 378) Condemnation Action.
3 Witkin Cal. Proc. 5th Actions § 381, (S 381) Specific Mandatory Statutes.
8 Witkin, California Summary 10th Constitutional Law § 1207, Process.

ARTICLE 3. PARTIES; JOINDER OF PROPERTY

Civ. Pro.

Section
1250.250. Liens for ad valorem taxes or special assessments; defendants; certification in lieu of answer.

§ 1250.210. Plaintiff; person seeking to take property

Each person seeking to take property by eminent domain shall be named as a plaintiff. *(Added by Stats.1975, c. 1275, p. 3429, § 2, operative July 1, 1976.)*

Research References

Miller and Starr California Real Estate § 30A:50, Parties to the Action.
5 Witkin Cal. Proc. 5th Pleading § 686, Parties.
8 Witkin, California Summary 10th Constitutional Law § 1205, Parties.

§ 1250.220. Defendants; persons of record or known to have interest in property; heirs and devisees; effect of judgment

(a) The plaintiff shall name as defendants, by their real names, those persons who appear of record or are known by the plaintiff to have or claim an interest in the property described in the complaint.

(b) If a person described in subdivision (a) is dead and the plaintiff knows of a duly qualified and acting personal representative of the estate of such person, the plaintiff shall name such personal representative as a defendant. If a person described in subdivision (a) is dead or is believed by the plaintiff to be dead and if plaintiff knows of no duly qualified and acting personal representative of the estate of such person and states these facts in an affidavit filed with the complaint, plaintiff may name as defendants "the heirs and devisees of _____ (naming such deceased person), deceased, and all persons claiming by, through, or under said decedent," naming them in that manner and, where it is stated in the affidavit that such person is believed by the plaintiff to be dead, such person also may be named as a defendant.

(c) In addition to those persons described in subdivision (a), the plaintiff may name as defendants "all persons unknown claiming an interest in the property," naming them in that manner.

(d) A judgment rendered in a proceeding under this title is binding and conclusive upon all persons named as defendants as provided in this section and properly served. *(Added by Stats.1975, c. 1275, p. 3429, § 2, operative July 1, 1976.)*

Law Revision Commission Comments

Section 1250.220 supersedes portions of former Sections 1244 and 1245.3. Subdivision (a) is substantively the same as paragraph 2 of former Section 1244. Subdivisions (b) and (c) are substantively the same as the first sentence of former Section 1245.3. See also paragraph 2 of former Section 1244. Subdivision (d) is substantively same as the last paragraph of former Section 1245.3. See also Section 1250.130 and Comment thereto (posting where service is by publication).

The naming of defendants is basically within the control of the plaintiff—People v. Shasta Pipe etc. Co., 264 Cal.App.2d 520, 537, 70 Cal.Rptr. 618, 629 (1968)—but failure to join a proper party to the proceeding leaves his interest unimpaired. Wilson v. Beville, 47 Cal.2d 852, 306 P.2d 789 (1957). Nevertheless, a person not named as a defendant who claims an interest in the property sought to be acquired may participate in the proceeding. Section 1250.230.

Subdivision (a). Subdivision (a) reenacts the requirement found in paragraph 2 of former Section 1244 that the names of all owners and claimants of the property must be listed in the complaint. This includes occupants of the property who claim a possessory interest in the property. The form of subdivision (a) has been adapted from former Section 1245.3.

Subdivision (b). Subdivision (b) specifies the requirements for naming defendants where one of the claimants to the property is deceased. The basic rule is that the personal representative of the estate of the decedent must be named as defendant in the decedent's place. This codifies prior law. See Monterey County v. Cushing, 83 Cal. 507, 23 P. 700 (1890) (decided under former Code of Civil Procedure Section 1582, predecessor of Probate Code Section 573).

Where there is no duly qualified and acting personal representative known to the plaintiff, the plaintiff need not await the appointment and qualification of one but may proceed with the suit naming as defendants the heirs and devisees of the deceased person and, if such person is believed to be but not known to be dead, the plaintiff may also name such person as a defendant.

Subdivision (c). Subdivision (c) enables the plaintiff to name unknown holders of interests in the property. A plaintiff may also proceed pursuant to Section 474 by fictitiously naming defendants who claim an interest but whose names are not known. See Bayle-Lacoste & Co. v. Superior Court, 46 Cal.App.2d 636, 116 P.2d 458 (1941). When the fictitiously named party's real name is discovered, the pleading must be amended accordingly. Alameda County v. Crocker, 125 Cal. 101, 57 P. 766 (1899).

Subdivision (d). Subdivision (d) assures that persons properly named under this section and served in compliance with the general provisions governing service—Chapter 4 (commencing with Section 413.10) of Title 5 of Part 2—and the requirements for service provided by this title (Sections 1250.120 and 1250.130) are bound by the judgment in the proceeding.

Research References

Miller and Starr California Real Estate § 30A:50, Parties to the Action.
5 Witkin Cal. Proc. 5th Pleading § 686, Parties.
12 Witkin, California Summary 10th Real Property § 67, Parties.
8 Witkin, California Summary 10th Constitutional Law § 1205, Parties.
8 Witkin, California Summary 10th Constitutional Law § 1220, Contesting Right to Take.

§ 1250.230. Person claiming legal or equitable interest; defendant

Any person who claims a legal or equitable interest in the property described in the complaint may appear in the proceeding. Whether or not such person is named as a defendant in the complaint, he shall appear as a defendant. *(Added by Stats.1975, c. 1275, p. 3429, § 2, operative July 1, 1976.)*

Research References

Rutter, Cal. Practice Guide: Civ. Pro. Before Trial Ch. 2-E, E. Intervention.
Miller and Starr California Real Estate § 30A:50, Parties to the Action.
4 Witkin Cal. Proc. 5th Pleading § 215, Special Statutes.
5 Witkin Cal. Proc. 5th Pleading § 686, Parties.
8 Witkin, California Summary 10th Constitutional Law § 1205, Parties.

§ 1250.240. Joinder of all property within county in one complaint

The plaintiff may join in one complaint all property located within the same county which is sought to be acquired for the same project. *(Added by Stats.1975, c. 1275, p. 3429, § 2, operative July 1, 1976.)*

Law Revision Commission Comments

Section 1250.240, which reenacts the substance of a portion of subdivision 5 of former Section 1244, permits the plaintiff at his option to join an unlimited number of parcels belonging to different defendants in the same eminent domain proceeding provided that the property joined lies wholly or partially in the same county (see Section 1250.020) and it is to be used for the same project. See County of Sacramento v. Glann, 14 Cal.App. 780, 788–790, 113 P. 360, 363–364 (1910). The contents of the complaint must, of course, be complete as to all property joined. See Section 1250.310 and Comment thereto.

Section 1250.240 provides simply for joinder in the initial pleading; it in no way limits the authority of the court to order separate trials where appropriate. See Section 1048.

Research References

Miller and Starr California Real Estate § 30A:50, Parties to the Action.

8 Witkin, California Summary 10th Constitutional Law § 1206, Pleading.

§ 1250.250. Liens for ad valorem taxes or special assessments; defendants; certification in lieu of answer

(a) If the only interest of the county or other taxing agency in the property described in the complaint is a lien for ad valorem taxes, the county or other taxing agency need not be named as a defendant.

(b) The holder of a lien that secures a special assessment or a bond representing the special assessment shall be named as a defendant, regardless of the nature of the special assessment and the manner of collection of the special assessment. The holder of the lien may, instead of an answer, certify to the court within 30 days after service of the summons and complaint on the holder all of the following information:

(1) A complete description of the lien.

(2) A description of the property encumbered by the lien.

(3) The amount remaining due on the lien as of the date of the certificate.

(4) The date upon which each installment payable on the lien is due and the amount of each installment.

(c) A copy of the certification shall be sent by first-class mail to all parties to the proceeding at the time it is provided to the court. The filing of the certification or answer shall be considered as a general appearance. *(Added by Stats.1979, c. 31, p. 88, § 1. Amended by Stats.1980, c. 122, § 1; Stats.1981, c. 139, § 1.)*

Law Revision Commission Comments

Section 1250.250 continues the substance of the first portion of former Revenue and Taxation Code Section 4986.9(c). In the case of exempt property, the lien for ad valorem taxes is extinguished and transfers and attaches to the proceeds constituting the award pursuant to Section 5083 of the Revenue and Taxation Code.

Subdivision (b) is added to Section 1250.250 to ensure that special assessment and bond lienholders are included in the eminent domain proceeding, just as general lienholders are. A special assessment lienholder must be joined even though the lien may secure a special annual assessment and may be collectible with ad valorem taxes by the county tax collector. Failure to join a lienholder leaves the lien unimpaired. This codifies existing law. See Section 1250.220 and Comment thereto. The names and addresses of persons upon whom service may be made in the name of special assessment lienholders may be obtained from the "Roster of Public Agencies." See Govt.Code § 53051.

The procedure in subdivision (b) for certification of relevant information to the court in lieu of an answer is comparable to the procedure for tax liens. See Section 1260.250.

For payment of special assessment liens, see Section 1265.250.

Research References

Miller and Starr California Real Estate § 30A:50, Parties to the Action.
8 Witkin, California Summary 10th Constitutional Law § 1205, Parties.
8 Witkin, California Summary 10th Constitutional Law § 1260, (S 1260) Liability, Proration, and Payment.
8 Witkin, California Summary 10th Constitutional Law § 1263, Special Assessment Liens.

ARTICLE 4. PLEADINGS

§ 1250.310. Complaint; contents

The complaint shall contain all of the following:

(a) The names of all plaintiffs and defendants.

(b) A description of the property sought to be taken. The description may, but is not required to, indicate the nature or extent of the interest of the defendant in the property.

(c) If the plaintiff claims an interest in the property sought to be taken, the nature and extent of such interest.

(d) A statement of the right of the plaintiff to take by eminent domain the property described in the complaint. The statement shall include:

(1) A general statement of the public use for which the property is to be taken.

(2) An allegation of the necessity for the taking as required by Section 1240.030; where the plaintiff is a public entity, a reference to its resolution of necessity; where the plaintiff is a quasi-public entity within the meaning of Section 1245.320, a reference to the resolution adopted pursuant to Article 3 (commencing with Section 1245.310) of Chapter 4; where the plaintiff is a nonprofit hospital, a reference to the certificate required by Section 1260 of the Health and Safety Code; where the plaintiff is a public utility and relies on a certification of the State Energy Resources Conservation and Development Commission or a requirement of that commission that development rights be acquired, a reference to such certification or requirement.

(3) A reference to the statute that authorizes the plaintiff to acquire the property by eminent domain. Specification of the statutory authority may be in the alternative and may be inconsistent.

(e) A map or diagram portraying as far as practicable the property described in the complaint and showing its location in relation to the project for which it is to be taken. *(Added by Stats.1975, c. 1275, p. 3430, § 2, operative July 1, 1976.)*

Research References

Miller and Starr California Real Estate § 30A:48, The Complaint.
4 Witkin Cal. Proc. 5th Pleading § 387, Allegations of Ultimate Facts.
5 Witkin Cal. Proc. 5th Pleading § 685, in General.
5 Witkin Cal. Proc. 5th Pleading § 686, Parties.
5 Witkin Cal. Proc. 5th Pleading § 687, Right to Condemn.
5 Witkin Cal. Proc. 5th Pleading § 688, Map and Description of Land.
8 Witkin, California Summary 10th Constitutional Law § 1206, Pleading.

§ 1250.320. Answer; statement of nature and extent of interest

(a) The answer shall include a statement of the nature and extent of the interest the defendant claims in the property described in the complaint.

(b) Where the defendant seeks compensation provided in Article 6 (commencing with Section 1263.510) (goodwill) of Chapter 9, the answer shall include a statement that the defendant claims compensation under Section 1263.510, but the answer need not specify the amount of such compensation. *(Added by Stats.1975, c. 1275, p. 3430, § 2, operative July 1, 1976.)*

Research References

Miller and Starr California Real Estate § 30A:58, Answer.
5 Witkin Cal. Proc. 5th Pleading § 1115, (S 1115) Answer in Condemnation Action.
8 Witkin, California Summary 10th Constitutional Law § 1206, Pleading.

§ 1250.325. Disclaimer by defendant; effect

(a) A defendant may file a disclaimer at any time, whether or not he is in default, and the disclaimer supersedes an answer previously filed by the defendant. The disclaimer need not be in any particular form. It shall contain a statement that the defendant claims no interest in the property or in the compensation that may be awarded. Notwithstanding Section 1250.330, the disclaimer shall be signed by the defendant.

(b) Subject to subdivision (c), a defendant who has filed a disclaimer has no right to participate in further proceedings or to share in the compensation awarded.

(c) The court may implement the disclaimer by appropriate orders including, where justified, awarding costs and litigation expenses. *(Added by Stats.1975, c. 1275, p. 3430, § 2, operative July 1, 1976.)*

Law Revision Commission Comments

Section 1250.325 provides a simplified method for a defendant to disclaim any interest in the property or compensation awarded in the proceeding. The disclaimer may be an informal document which merely states that the defendant claims no interest in either the property or the award. A defendant wishing to make only a partial disclaimer may do so by filing an answer describing only the limited interest claimed by him. See Section 1250.320. A disclaimer to be filed "at any time," even after an answer has been filed or after the defendant's right to respond has been terminated by his default. The disclaimer supersedes any earlier response.

The disclaimer, in effect, removes the defendant from the proceeding and may result in a dismissal as to him. The power to implement a disclaimer, as provided in subdivision (c), is intended to assure that the court has full authority to enter a dismissal, with award of costs and litigation expenses where appropriate or to enter other implementing orders calculated to facilitate use of the disclaimer as an aid to settlement. See Section 1235.140 (defining "litigation expenses"). Adequate flexibility in this regard may be particularly useful, for example, in disposing of claims having relatively slight value.

Research References

Miller and Starr California Real Estate § 30A:57, Disclaimer.
5 Witkin Cal. Proc. 5th Pleading § 1115, (S 1115) Answer in Condemnation Action.
8 Witkin, California Summary 10th Constitutional Law § 1206, Pleading.

§ 1250.330. Signature of attorney

Where a party is represented by an attorney, his pleading need not be verified but shall be signed by the attorney for the party. The signature of the attorney constitutes a certificate by him that he has read the pleading and that to the best of his knowledge, information, and belief there is ground to support it. If the pleading is not signed or is signed with intent to defeat the purposes of this section, it may be stricken. *(Added by Stats. 1975, c. 1275, p. 3431, § 2, operative July 1, 1976.)*

Law Revision Commission Comments

Section 1250.330 requires all pleadings to be signed by the attorney where the party in an eminent domain proceeding is represented by an attorney. The effect of signature by the attorney is substantially the same as that under Rule 11 of the Federal Rules of Civil Procedure. For a willful violation of this section, an attorney is subject to appropriate disciplinary action. See Rules 1, 13, 17 of the Rules of Professional Conduct of the State Bar of California. See Also Bus. & Prof.Code § 6076.

It should be noted that Section 1250.330 requires both the attorney for the plaintiff and the attorney for the defendant to sign their respective pleadings. The plaintiff may also verify, if it chooses, but such verification will not require verification by the defendant if he is represented by an attorney. Compare Section 446 (verification by defendant generally required where plaintiff is a public entity or where complaint is verified).

Research References

Miller and Starr California Real Estate § 30A:58, Answer.
4 Witkin Cal. Proc. 5th Pleading § 466, Complaint or Petition.

8 Witkin, California Summary 10th Constitutional Law § 1206, Pleading.

§ 1250.340. Amendment or supplement to pleading; terms and conditions; law governing

(a) Subject to subdivisions (b) and (c), the court may allow upon such terms and conditions as may be just an amendment or supplement to any pleading. In the case of an amendment or supplement to the complaint, such terms and conditions may include a change in the applicable date of valuation for the proceeding and an award of costs and litigation expenses which would not have been incurred had the proceeding as originally commenced been the same as the proceeding following such amendment or supplement.

(b) A public entity may add to the property sought to be taken only if it has adopted a resolution of necessity that satisfies the requirements of Article 2 (commencing with Section 1245.210) of Chapter 4 for the property to be added.

(c) Property previously sought to be taken may be deleted from the complaint only if the plaintiff has followed the procedure for partial abandonment of the proceeding as to that property. *(Added by Stats.1975, c. 1275, p. 3431, § 2, operative July 1, 1976.)*

Law Revision Commission Comments

Section 1250.340 supplements the liberal rules applicable to amendments and supplements provided by Sections 464 and 473. Subdivision (a) makes clear that the terms and conditions which may be imposed by the court include a change in the date of valuation for either all or a portion of the property sought to be taken in the proceeding and payment of costs and litigation expenses which would not have been incurred but for the amendment. See Section 1235.140 ("litigation expenses" defined).

Subdivision (b) makes clear that, in order to add property to the complaint a public entity must adopt a valid resolution of necessity for the property to be added.

Subdivision (c) makes clear that, in order to delete property from the complaint, the plaintiff must follow the procedures and pay the price for abandonment. See Sections 1268.510, 1268.610–1268.620. This provision continues prior law as to "partial abandonment". See, e.g., County of Kern v. Galatas, 200 Cal.App.2d 353, 19 Cal.Rptr. 348 (1962); Metropolitan Water Dist. v. Adams, 23 Cal.2d 770, 147 P.2d 6 (1944); Merced Irr. Dist. v. Woolstenhulme, 4 Cal.3d 478, 483 P.2d 1, 93 Cal.Rptr. 833 (1971).

Research References

5 Witkin Cal. Proc. 5th Pleading § 1195, Imposition of Conditions.
5 Witkin Cal. Proc. 5th Pleading § 1246, (S 1246) Nature of Supplemental Pleadings.
8 Witkin, California Summary 10th Constitutional Law § 1206, Pleading.

§ 1250.345. Failure of defendant to object; waiver

Subject to the power of the court to permit an amendment of the answer, if the defendant fails to object to the complaint, either by demurrer or answer, he is deemed to have waived the objection. *(Added by Stats.1975, c. 1275, p. 3431, § 2, operative July 1, 1976.)*

Research References

Miller and Starr California Real Estate § 30A:59, Objection to Complaint by Demurrer or Answer.
8 Witkin, California Summary 10th Constitutional Law § 1206, Pleading.

ARTICLE 5. OBJECTIONS TO RIGHT TO TAKE

Section

§ 1250.350. Demurrer or answer; statement of grounds or facts

A defendant may object to the plaintiff's right to take, by demurrer or answer as provided in Section 430.30, on any ground authorized by Section 1250.360 or Section 1250.370. The demurrer or answer shall state the specific ground upon which the objection is taken and, if the objection is taken by answer, the specific facts upon which the objection is based. An objection may be taken on more than one ground, and the grounds may be inconsistent. *(Added by Stats.1975, c. 1275, p. 3431, § 2, operative July 1, 1976.)*

Law Revision Commission Comments

Section 1250.350 makes clear the rules governing the pleading of subjections to the right to take. See Sections 1250.360 and 1250.370 (listing grounds upon which objection may be taken). The general rules that determine whether the objection may be taken by demurrer or answer (see Section 430.30) apply to pleading an objection to the right to take.

The facts supporting each objection to the right to take must be specifically stated in the answer. This requirement is generally consistent with former law that, for example, required the defendant to allege specific facts indicating an abuse of discretion such as an intention not to use the property as resolved. See, e.g., County of San Mateo v. Bartole, 184 Cal.App.2d 422, 433, 7 Cal.Rptr. 569, 576 (1960). See also People v. Chevalier, 52 Cal.2d 299, 340 P.2d 598 (1959); People v. Nahabedian, 171 Cal.App.2d 302, 340 P.2d 1053 (1959); People v. Olsen, 109 Cal.App. 523, 293 P. 645 (1930).

Section 1250.345, relating to waiver of objections to the complaint, applies to objections to the right to take.

Research References

Miller and Starr California Real Estate § 30A:7, Taking for a Public Use Only.
Miller and Starr California Real Estate § 30A:59, Objection to Complaint by Demurrer or Answer.
5 Witkin Cal. Proc. 5th Pleading § 1115, (S 1115) Answer in Condemnation Action.
8 Witkin, California Summary 10th Constitutional Law § 1120, Review of Legislative Determination.
8 Witkin, California Summary 10th Constitutional Law § 1206, Pleading.
8 Witkin, California Summary 10th Constitutional Law § 1220, Contesting Right to Take.

§ 1250.360. Grounds; inclusions

Grounds for objection to the right to take, regardless of whether the plaintiff has adopted a resolution of necessity that satisfies the requirements of Article 2 (commencing with Section 1245.210) of Chapter 4, include:

(a) The plaintiff is not authorized by statute to exercise the power of eminent domain for the purpose stated in the complaint.

(b) The stated purpose is not a public use.

(c) The plaintiff does not intend to devote the property described in the complaint to the stated purpose.

(d) There is no reasonable probability that the plaintiff will devote the described property to the stated purpose within (1) seven years, or (2) 10 years where the property is taken pursuant to the Federal Aid Highway Act of 1973 [1], or (3) such longer period as is reasonable.

(e) The described property is not subject to acquisition by the power of eminent domain for the stated purpose.

(f) The described property is sought to be acquired pursuant to Section 1240.410 (excess condemnation), 1240.510 (condemnation for compatible use), or 1240.610 (condemnation for more necessary public use), but the acquisition does not satisfy the requirements of those provisions.

(g) The described property is sought to be acquired pursuant to Section 1240.610 (condemnation for more necessary public use), but the defendant has the right under Section 1240.630 to continue the public use to which the property is appropriated as a joint use.

(h) Any other ground provided by law. *(Added by Stats.1975, c. 1275, p. 3431, § 2, operative July 1, 1976.)*

[1] 23 U.S.C.A. § 101 et seq.

Research References

Miller and Starr California Real Estate § 30A:59, Objection to Complaint by Demurrer or Answer.
5 Witkin Cal. Proc. 5th Pleading § 1115, (S 1115) Answer in Condemnation Action.
8 Witkin, California Summary 10th Constitutional Law § 1187, Future Use.
8 Witkin, California Summary 10th Constitutional Law § 1206, Pleading.
8 Witkin, California Summary 10th Constitutional Law § 1220, Contesting Right to Take.

§ 1250.370. Grounds if resolution of necessity not adopted

In addition to the grounds listed in Section 1250.360, grounds for objection to the right to take where the plaintiff has not adopted a resolution of necessity that conclusively establishes the matters referred to in Section 1240.030 include:

(a) The plaintiff is a public entity and has not adopted a resolution of necessity that satisfies the requirements of Article 2 (commencing with Section 1245.210) of Chapter 4.

(b) The public interest and necessity do not require the proposed project.

(c) The proposed project is not planned or located in the manner that will be most compatible with the greatest public good and the least private injury.

(d) The property described in the complaint is not necessary for the proposed project.

(e) The plaintiff is a quasi-public entity within the meaning of Section 1245.320 and has not satisfied the requirements of Article 3 (commencing with Section 1245.310) of Chapter 4. *(Added by Stats.1975, c. 1275, p. 3432, § 2, operative July 1, 1976.)*

Research References

Miller and Starr California Real Estate § 30A:7, Taking for a Public Use Only.
Miller and Starr California Real Estate § 30A:59, Objection to Complaint by Demurrer or Answer.
5 Witkin Cal. Proc. 5th Pleading § 1115, (S 1115) Answer in Condemnation Action.
8 Witkin, California Summary 10th Constitutional Law § 1206, Pleading.

ARTICLE 6. SETTLEMENT OFFERS AND ALTERNATIVE DISPUTE RESOLUTION

Section
1250.410. Final offer and demand; reasonableness; costs; litigation expenses.
1250.420. Alternative dispute resolution; methods.
1250.430. Postponement of trial date for a period to enable resolution of a dispute; conditions.

§ 1250.410. Final offer and demand; reasonableness; costs; litigation expenses

(a) At least 20 days prior to the date of the trial on issues relating to compensation, the plaintiff shall file with the court and serve on the defendant its final offer of compensation in the proceeding and the defendant shall file and serve on the plaintiff its final demand for compensation in the proceeding. The offer and the demand shall include all compensation required pursuant to this title, including compensation for loss of goodwill, if any, and shall state whether interest and costs are included. These offers and demands shall be the only offers and demands considered by the court in determining the entitlement, if any, to litigation expenses. Service shall be in the manner prescribed by Chapter 5 (commencing with Section 1010) of Title 14 of Part 2.

(b) If the court, on motion of the defendant made within 30 days after entry of judgment, finds that the offer of the plaintiff was unreasonable and that the demand of the defendant was reasonable viewed in the light of the evidence admitted and the compensation awarded in the proceeding, the costs allowed pursuant to Section 1268.710 shall include the defendant's litigation expenses.

(c) In determining the amount of litigation expenses allowed under this section, the court shall consider the offer required to be made by the plaintiff pursuant to Section 7267.2 of the Government Code, any deposit made by the plaintiff pursuant to Chapter 6 (commencing with Section 1255.010), and any other written offers and demands filed and served before or during the trial.

(d) If timely made, the offers and demands as provided in subdivision (a) shall be considered by the court on the issue of determining an entitlement to litigation expenses.

(e) As used in this section, "litigation expenses" means the party's reasonable attorney's fees and costs, including reasonable expert witness and appraiser fees. *(Added by Stats.1975, c. 1275, p. 3432, § 2, operative July 1, 1976. Amended by Stats.1982, c. 1059, p. 3833, § 2; Stats.1999, c. 102 (S.B.634), § 1; Stats.2001, c. 428 (A.B.237), § 2; Stats.2002, c. 295 (A.B.1770), § 1; Stats.2006, c. 594 (S.B.1210), § 1.)*

Law Revision Commission Comments

Subdivision (a) of Section 1250.410 is amended to counteract dictum in cases to the effect that the provision is not intended to require the offer and demand to cover items other than the value of the part taken and damage, if any, to the remainder. See, e.g., Coachella Valley County Water Dist. v. Dreyfuss, 91 Cal.App.3d 949, 154 Cal.Rptr. 467 (1979); People ex rel. Dep't of Transp. v. Gardella Square, 200 Cal.App.3d 559, 246 Cal.Rptr. 139 (1988). [30 Cal.L.Rev.Comm. Reports 567 (2000)].

Section 1250.410 is amended to make clear that the matters considered by the court in determining the amount of litigation expenses that may be allowed include any deposit by the plaintiff of probable compensation in the proceeding. The other changes in Section 1250.410 are technical [31 Cal.L.Rev.Comm. Reports 119 (2002)].l.

Research References

Rutter, Cal. Practice Guide: Civ. Pro. Before Trial Ch. 12(II)-C, C. Statutory Offer to Compromise (CCP § 998).
Rutter, Cal. Practice Guide: Civil Trials & Evidence Ch. 17-D, D. Costs.
Rutter, Cal. Practice Guide: Civil Trials & Evidence Ch. 17-E, E. Attorney Fees as Costs.
Miller and Starr California Real Estate § 34:66, Examples of Actions in Which Fees Can be Recovered.
Miller and Starr California Real Estate § 30A:66, Procedure for Final Offers and Demands.
Miller and Starr California Real Estate § 30A:78, Litigation Expenses.
13 NO. 4 Miller & Starr, California Real Estate Newsalert 9, Eminent Domain.
14 NO. 2 Miller & Starr, California Real Estate Newsalert 9, Eminent Domain.
14 NO. 2 Miller & Starr, California Real Estate Newsalert 18, Remedies.
16 NO. 1 Miller & Starr, California Real Estate Newsalert 15, Eminent Domain.
17 NO. 4 Miller & Starr, California Real Estate Newsalert 1, Redevelopment Redefined: State Legislative Responses to the Kelo Decision.
17 NO. 4 Miller & Starr, California Real Estate Newsalert 2, Statutory Update:.
17 NO. 2 Miller & Starr, California Real Estate Newsalert 10, Easements.
17 NO. 6 Miller & Starr, California Real Estate Newsalert 20, Table of Statutes (Newsalert Vol 17).
18 NO. 5 Miller & Starr, California Real Estate Newsalert 13, Eminent Domain.

18 NO. 4 Miller & Starr, California Real Estate Newsalert 33, Eminent Domain.
20 NO. 3 Miller & Starr, California Real Estate Newsalert 13, Eminent Domain.
21 NO. 3 Miller & Starr, California Real Estate Newsalert 14, Eminent Domain.
22 NO. 5 Miller & Starr, California Real Estate Newsalert 9, Eminent Domain.
8 Witkin, California Summary 10th Constitutional Law § 1186, (S 1186) Acquisition by Gift, Purchase, Lease, or Other Means.
8 Witkin, California Summary 10th Constitutional Law § 1208, (S 1208) in General.
8 Witkin, California Summary 10th Constitutional Law § 1209, (S 1209) Award of Litigation Expenses.
8 Witkin, California Summary 10th Constitutional Law § 1267, Costs.

§ 1250.420.   Alternative dispute resolution; methods

The parties may by agreement refer a dispute that is the subject of an eminent domain proceeding for resolution by any of the following means:

(a) Mediation by a neutral mediator.

(b) Binding arbitration by a neutral arbitrator. The arbitration is subject to Chapter 12 (commencing with Section 1273.010).

(c) Nonbinding arbitration by a neutral arbitrator. The arbitrator's decision in a nonbinding arbitration is final unless within 30 days after service of the arbitrator's decision a party moves the court for a trial of the eminent domain proceeding. If the judgment in the eminent domain proceeding is not more favorable to the moving party, the court shall order that party to pay to the other parties the following nonrefundable costs and fees, unless the court finds in writing and on motion that the imposition of costs and fees would create such a substantial economic hardship as not to be in the interest of justice:

(1) All costs specified in Section 1033.5, limited to those incurred from the time of election of the trial de novo. Nothing in this subdivision affects the right of a defendant to recover costs otherwise allowable pursuant to Section 1268.710, incurred before election of a trial de novo, except that a defendant may recover the costs of determining the apportionment of the award made pursuant to subdivision (b) of Section 1260.220 whenever incurred.

(2) The reasonable costs of the services of expert witnesses who are not regular employees of any party, actually incurred and reasonably necessary in the preparation or trial of the case, limited to those incurred from the time of election of the trial de novo.

(3) The compensation paid by the parties to the arbitrator. *(Added by Stats.2001, c. 428 (A.B.237), § 3.)*

Law Revision Commission Comments

Section 1250.420 is drawn from Government Code Section 11420.10 (ADR authorized in administrative adjudication). The section is intended to remove any question about the authority of a public entity to refer an eminent domain dispute for alternative dispute resolution. Alternative dispute resolution pursuant to this section is optional, applicable only on agreement of the parties. Nothing in this section limits any authority of parties in any other type of action or proceeding by agreement to refer a dispute that is the subject of the action or proceeding for resolution by alternative dispute resolution.

Under subdivision (a), the mediator may use any mediation technique. Subdivision (c) parallels the procedure applicable in judicial arbitration. See Sections 1141.20–1141.21. A defendant who elects a trial de novo under this procedure may be subject to assessment of costs and litigation expenses; this is in effect a waiver of the defendant's general protection against assessment of costs and litigation expenses in an eminent domain proceeding. See, e.g., Section 1268.710 (court costs).

Standard protections of confidentiality of communications made in alternative dispute resolution apply to alternative dispute resolution pursuant to this section. See, e.g., Evid. Code 1115–1128 (mediation),

703.5 (testimony by arbitrator or mediator). [31 Cal.L.Rev.Comm. Reports 81 (2001)].

Research References

Rutter, Cal. Practice Guide: A.D.R. App. A, Selected Statutes Providing for ADR.

Miller and Starr California Real Estate § 30A:1, Introduction.

Miller and Starr California Real Estate § 35:15, Statutory Provisions for Mediations (And Arbitration) of Real Property Disputes.

Miller and Starr California Real Estate § 30A:67, Agreements to Mediate or Arbitrate.

6 Witkin Cal. Proc. 5th Proceedings Without Trial § 482, (S 482) Programs and Legislation.

8 Witkin, California Summary 10th Constitutional Law § 1210, Alternative Dispute Resolution.

§ 1250.430. Postponement of trial date for a period to enable resolution of a dispute; conditions

Notwithstanding any other statute or rule of court governing the date of trial of an eminent domain proceeding, on motion of a party the court may postpone the date of trial for a period that appears adequate to enable resolution of a dispute pursuant to alternative resolution procedures, if it is demonstrated to the satisfaction of the court that all of the following conditions are satisfied:

(a) The parties are actively engaged in alternative resolution of the dispute pursuant to Section 1250.420.

(b) The parties appear to be making progress toward resolution of the dispute without the need for a trial of the matter.

(c) The parties agree that additional time for the purpose of alternative dispute resolution is desirable. *(Added by Stats.2001, c. 428 (A.B.237), § 4.)*

Law Revision Commission Comments

Section 1250.430 is intended to allow waiver of trial court delay reduction programs and other case processing requirements in order to facilitate productive alternative dispute resolution. This provision may be applied to foster resolution of some or all of the issues between the parties. Nothing in this section limits any authority of the court in any other type of action or proceeding to postpone the date of trial to enable resolution of a dispute by alternative dispute resolution. [31 Cal.L.Rev. Comm. Reports 82 (2001)].

Research References

Miller and Starr California Real Estate § 35:15, Statutory Provisions for Mediations (And Arbitration) of Real Property Disputes.

Miller and Starr California Real Estate § 30A:67, Agreements to Mediate or Arbitrate.

8 Witkin, California Summary 10th Constitutional Law § 1210, Alternative Dispute Resolution.

CHAPTER 6. DEPOSIT AND WITHDRAWAL OF PROBABLE COMPENSATION; POSSESSION PRIOR TO JUDGMENT

ARTICLE 1. DEPOSIT OF PROBABLE COMPENSATION

§ 1255.010. Deposit by plaintiff; appraisal; affidavit

(a) At any time before entry of judgment, the plaintiff may deposit with the State Treasury the probable amount of compensation, based on an appraisal, that will be awarded in the proceeding. The appraisal upon which the deposit is based shall be one that satisfies the requirements of subdivision (b). The deposit may be made whether or not the plaintiff applies for an order for possession or intends to do so.

(b) Before making a deposit under this section, the plaintiff shall have an expert qualified to express an opinion as to the value of the property (1) make an appraisal of the property and (2) prepare a written statement of, or summary of the basis for, the appraisal. The statement or summary shall contain detail sufficient to indicate clearly the basis for the appraisal, including, but not limited to, all of the following information:

(A) The date of valuation, highest and best use, and applicable zoning of the property.

(B) The principal transactions, reproduction or replacement cost analysis, or capitalization analysis, supporting the appraisal.

(C) If the appraisal includes compensation for damages to the remainder, the compensation for the property and for damages to the remainder separately stated, and the calculations and a narrative explanation supporting the compensation, including any offsetting benefits.

(c) On noticed motion, or upon ex parte application in an emergency, the court may permit the plaintiff to make a deposit without prior compliance with subdivision (b) if the plaintiff presents facts by affidavit showing that (1) good cause exists for permitting an immediate deposit to be made, (2) an adequate appraisal has not been completed and cannot reasonably be prepared before making the deposit, and (3) the amount of the deposit to be made is not less than the probable amount of compensation that the plaintiff, in good faith, estimates will be awarded in the proceeding. In its order, the court shall require that the plaintiff comply with subdivision (b) within a reasonable time, to be specified in the order, and also that any additional amount of compensation shown by the appraisal required by subdivision (b) be deposited within that time. *(Added by Stats.1975, c. 1275, p. 3433, § 2, operative July 1, 1976. Amended by Stats.1990, c. 1491 (A.B.3765), § 9; Stats.2001, c. 428 (A.B. 237), § 5.)*

Law Revision Commission Comments

Section 1255.010 is new. In contrast with subdivision (a) of former Section 1243.5, (1) the deposit may be made without obtaining the court's order therefor and without regard to an order for possession and (2) the amount of the initial deposit is determined by an appraisal obtained by the plaintiff rather than by the court upon ex parte application of the plaintiff. Under Section 1255.030, however, the amount deposited may be determined or redetermined by the court on motion of any interested party.

Under subdivision (a), where there are several properties joined in the proceeding (see Section 1250.240), the plaintiff may make a deposit as to any of the properties and need not make a deposit as to all the properties.

The appraisal and the statement or summary required by subdivision (b) may be made either by a member of the condemnor's appraisal staff or by an independent appraiser. The statement or summary is necessary to enable the plaintiff to comply with Section 1255.020 which requires the notice of the deposit to be accompanied by the statement or summary which justifies the amount of the deposit.

The making of a deposit by the plaintiff, and any subsequent possession of the property by the plaintiff, does not waive its right to appeal in the proceeding. See Sections 1255.080 and 1255.470. *Cf.* Section 1268.170.

Under emergency circumstances, it may be possible to make only a rough, preliminary estimate of the probable amount of compensation that will be awarded in the proceeding. In such cases, subdivision (c) permits the court to make an order allowing the plaintiff to make a deposit without prior compliance with subdivision (b).

Upon entry of judgment, a deposit made pursuant to this article is deemed to be a deposit made pursuant to Section 1268.110 (postjudgment deposit of award). See Section 1268.010.

Subdivision (b) of Section 1255.010 is amended to prescribe the contents of the written statement or summary of the basis for the deposit appraisal. The detail prescribed is the same as that prescribed for the moving party under Section 1255.030 (increase or decrease in amount of deposit) and for the written statement and summary under Government Code Section 7267.2 (precondemnation offer). The requirement in subdivision (b)(3) that the statement or summary include detail relating to damages to the remainder applies equally in a situation where no compensation for damages to the remainder is provided due to a complete offset by benefits to the remainder. [31 Cal.L.Rev.Comm.Reports 82 (2001)].

Research References

Miller and Starr California Real Estate § 19:149, Valuation and Apportionment of the Award.
Miller and Starr California Real Estate § 30A:53, Deposit of Probable Compensation.
16 NO. 4 Miller & Starr, California Real Estate Newsalert 27, Eminent Domain.
8 Witkin, California Summary 10th Constitutional Law § 1209, (S 1209) Award of Litigation Expenses.
8 Witkin, California Summary 10th Constitutional Law § 1212, (S 1212) in General.
8 Witkin, California Summary 10th Constitutional Law § 1213, (S 1213) Procedure.
8 Witkin, California Summary 10th Constitutional Law § 1216, (S 1216) Application and Order.
8 Witkin, California Summary 10th Constitutional Law § 1224, Date of Valuation.
8 Witkin, California Summary 10th Constitutional Law § 1255, (S 1255) Deposit After Judgment.
8 Witkin, California Summary 10th Constitutional Law § 1257, Possession After Judgment.
8 Witkin, California Summary 10th Constitutional Law § 1259, (S 1259) Market Rate of Interest.

§ 1255.020. Notice of deposit; service; written statement or summary

(a) On making a deposit pursuant to Section 1255.010, the plaintiff shall serve a notice of deposit on all parties who have appeared in the proceeding and file with the court a proof of service together with the notice of deposit. The plaintiff shall so serve parties who appear thereafter on their appearance. The notice of deposit shall state that a deposit has been made and the date and the amount of the deposit. Service of the notice of deposit shall be made in the manner provided in Section 1255.450 for service of an order for possession.

(b) The notice of deposit shall be accompanied by a written statement or summary of the basis for the appraisal referred to in Section 1255.010.

(c) If the plaintiff has obtained an order under Section 1255.010 deferring completion of the written statement or summary, the plaintiff:

(1) On making the deposit, shall comply with subdivision (a) and include with the notice a copy of all affidavits on which the order was based.

(2) Upon completion of the written statement or summary, shall comply with subdivision (b). *(Added by Stats.1975, c. 1275, p. 3433, § 2, operative July 1, 1976. Amended by Stats.1990, c. 1491 (A.B.3765), § 10.)*

Law Revision Commission Comments

Section 1255.020 is new. It requires that notice of the deposit be given in all cases to facilitate motions to change the amount of the deposit (Section 1255.030) or applications to withdraw the funds deposited (Section 1255.210 et seq.).

Research References

Miller and Starr California Real Estate § 30A:53, Deposit of Probable Compensation.
8 Witkin, California Summary 10th Constitutional Law § 1213, (S 1213) Procedure.
8 Witkin, California Summary 10th Constitutional Law § 1214, (S 1214) Deposit on Demand of Homeowner or Lessor.

§ 1255.030. Determination or redetermination of amount deposited; increase or decrease

(a) At any time after a deposit has been made pursuant to this article, the court shall, upon motion of the plaintiff or of any party having an interest in the property for which the deposit was made, determine or redetermine whether the amount deposited is the probable amount of compensation that will be awarded in the proceeding. The motion shall be supported with detail sufficient to indicate clearly the basis for the motion, including, but not limited to, the following information to the extent relevant to the motion:

(1) The date of valuation, highest and best use, and applicable zoning of the property.

(2) The principal transactions, reproduction or replacement cost analysis, or capitalization analysis, supporting the motion.

(3) The compensation for the property and for damages to the remainder separately stated, and the calculations and a narrative explanation supporting the compensation, including any offsetting benefits.

(b) If the plaintiff has not taken possession of the property and the court determines that the probable amount of compensation exceeds the amount deposited, the court may order the plaintiff to increase the deposit or may deny the plaintiff possession of the property until the amount deposited has been increased to the amount specified in the order.

(c) If the plaintiff has taken possession of the property and the court determines that the probable amount of compensation exceeds the amount deposited, the court shall order the amount deposited to be increased to the amount determined to be the probable amount of compensation. If the amount on deposit is not increased accordingly within 30 days from the date of the court's order, or any longer time as the court may have allowed at the time of making the order, the defendant may serve on the plaintiff a notice of election to treat that failure as an abandonment of the proceeding. If the plaintiff does not cure its failure within 10 days after receipt of such notice, the court shall, upon motion of the defendant, enter judgment dismissing the proceeding and awarding the defendant his or her litigation expenses and damages as provided in Sections 1268.610 and 1268.620.

(d) After any amount deposited pursuant to this article has been withdrawn by a defendant, the court may not determine or redetermine the probable amount of compensation to be less than the total amount already withdrawn. Nothing in this subdivision precludes the court from making a determination or redetermination that probable compensation is greater than the amount withdrawn.

(e) If the court determines that the amount deposited exceeds the probable amount of compensation, it may permit the plaintiff to withdraw the excess not already withdrawn by the defendant.

(f) The plaintiff may at any time increase the amount deposited without making a motion under this section. In that case, notice of the increase shall be served as provided in subdivision (a) of Section 1255.020. *(Added by Stats.1975, c. 1275, p. 3434, § 2, operative July 1, 1976. Amended by Stats.2001, c. 428 (A.B.237), § 6.)*

Law Revision Commission Comments

Section 1255.030 is new. It supersedes subdivision (d) of former Section 1243.5, which provided for redetermination of the amount of probable compensation.

Subdivisions (b) and (c) require that the plaintiff increase the amount of the deposit in accordance with the court's order. Failure to so increase the deposit while in possession may result in an abandonment with attendant litigation expenses and damages. See Sections 1268.610 and 1268.620. *Cf.* Section 1263.110 (effect on date of valuation of failure to increase deposit).

Section 1255.280 provides for recovery of any excessive withdrawal after final determination of amounts in the eminent domain proceeding. No provision is made for recovery, prior to such final determination, of any amount withdrawn. Accordingly, subdivision (d) prevents determination or redetermination of the amount of probable compensation to be less than the total sum withdrawn.

Subdivision (f) is included to make clear that the deposit may be increased without the need for a court determination under this section.

Section 1255.030 is amended to prescribe the supporting data that may be required for a motion to increase or decrease the amount of the deposit. The detail prescribed is the same as that prescribed for the written statement or summary under Section 1255.010 (deposit of probable compensation) and for the written statement and summary under Government Code Section 7267.2 (precondemnation offer). It should be noted that the information provided by the moving party under this section is protected from use at trial to the same extent as other evidence related to the deposit or withdrawal. See Section 1255.060 (limitations on use of evidence in connection with deposit). [31 Cal. L.Rev.Comm. Reports 82 (2001)].

Research References

Rutter, Cal. Practice Guide: Civil Appeals & Writs Ch. 7-A, A. Overview.
Miller and Starr California Real Estate § 30A:53, Deposit of Probable Compensation.
Miller and Starr California Real Estate § 30A:54, Withdrawal of Deposit.
8 Witkin, California Summary 10th Constitutional Law § 1213, (S 1213) Procedure.
8 Witkin, California Summary 10th Constitutional Law § 1215, (S 1215) Withdrawal of Deposit.

§ 1255.040. Residence of defendant; notice requiring deposit by defendant; possession; interest

(a) If the plaintiff has not made a deposit that satisfies the requirements of this article and the property includes a dwelling containing not more than two residential units and the dwelling or one of its units is occupied as his or her residence by a defendant, the defendant may serve notice on the plaintiff requiring a deposit of the probable amount of compensation that will be awarded in the proceeding. The notice shall specify the date by which the defendant desires the deposit to be made. The date shall not be earlier than 30 days after the date service of the notice and may be any later date.

(b) If the plaintiff deposits the probable amount of ⸮⸮⸮ tion, determined or redetermined as provided in ⸮⸮⸮ or before the date specified by the defendant ⸮date ⸮⸮ obtain an order for possession that autho⸮⸮ date as the take possession of the property 30 day⸮ deposit specified by the defendant ⸮⸮⸮ plaintiff may request.

(c) Notwithstanding Section 1268.310, if the deposit is not made on or before the date specified by the defendant or such later date as the court specifies on motion and good cause shown by the plaintiff, the compensation awarded to the defendant in the proceeding shall draw legal interest from that date. The defendant is entitled to the full amount of such interest without offset for rents or other income received by him or her or the value of his or her continued possession of the property.

(d) If the proceeding is abandoned by the plaintiff, the interest under subdivision (c) may be recovered as costs in the proceeding in the manner provided for the recovery of litigation expenses under Section 1268.610. If, in the proceeding, the court or a jury verdict eventually determines the compensation that would have been awarded to the defendant, then the interest shall be computed on the amount of the award. If no determination is ever made, then the interest shall be computed on the probable amount of compensation as determined by the court.

(e) The serving of a notice pursuant to this section constitutes a waiver by operation of law, conditioned upon subsequent deposit by the plaintiff of the probable amount of compensation, of all claims and defenses in favor of the defendant except his or her claim for greater compensation.

(f) Notice of a deposit made under this section shall be served as provided by subdivision (a) of Section 1255.020. The defendant may withdraw the deposit as provided in Article 2 (commencing with Section 1255.210).

(g) No notice may be served by a defendant under subdivision (a) after entry of judgment unless the judgment is reversed, vacated, or set aside and no other judgment has been entered at the time the notice is served. *(Added by Stats.1975, c. 1275, p. 3435, § 2, operative July 1, 1976. Amended by Stats.2006, c. 594 (S.B.1210), § 2.)*

Law Revision Commission Comments

Section 1255.040 is new. Section 1255.040 makes available a procedure by which a homeowner can demand that a deposit be made and specifies the consequences if the deposit is not made.

Except as provided in Sections 1255.040 and 1255.050, the depositing of probable compensation pursuant to this article or the taking of possession pursuant to this chapter is optional with the plaintiff; if a deposit is not made and possession is not taken, a defendant is not entitled to be paid until 30 days after final judgment. Section 1268.010.

Subdivision (a) limits the application of Section 1255.040 to an owner-occupied dwelling containing no more than two residential units.

Subdivision (b) provides that the timely making of a deposit under this section entitles the plaintiff to an order for possession effective 30 days after the date for the making of the deposit specified in the notice served by the defendant.

Subdivision (c) provides a special rule governing the time interest commences to accrue. If the required deposit is made on or before the date specified by the defendant, interest on the amount deposited does not accrue. If the deposit is not made on or before the date specified by the defendant or by the court on motion and showing of good cause by the plaintiff, interest commences to accrue on that date. If a deposit is thereafter made, subdivision (a) of Section 1268.320 provides that interest ceases to accrue on the date such amount is withdrawn by the person entitled thereto.

Under subdivision (d), abandonment by the plaintiff entitles the defendant to recover interest in the manner provided for recovery of litigation expenses upon abandonment. The plaintiff may not abandon, however, if the defendant, to his detriment, has substantially changed his position in justifiable reliance upon the proceeding. Section 1268.510.

Research References

Miller and Starr California Real Estate § 30A:53, Deposit of Probable Compensation.
17 NO. 4 Miller & Starr, California Real Estate Newsalert 2, Statutory Update:.

17 NO. 6 Miller & Starr, California Real Estate Newsalert 20, Table of
    Statutes (Newsalert Vol 17).
8 Witkin, California Summary 10th Constitutional Law § 1214, (S 1214)
    Deposit on Demand of Homeowner or Lessor.

§ 1255.050. Leasehold interest; notice requiring deposit by plaintiff; interest offset by net rentals

If the property to be taken is subject to a leasehold interest
and the plaintiff has not made a deposit that satisfies the
requirements of this article, the lessor may serve notice on the
plaintiff requiring a deposit of the probable amount of compensation that will be awarded in the proceeding in the same manner
and subject to the same procedures and conditions as a motion
pursuant to Section 1255.040 except that, if the plaintiff fails to
make the deposit, the interest awarded shall be offset by the
lessor's net rental profits on the property. *(Added by Stats.1975,
c. 1275, p. 3435, § 2, operative July 1, 1976.)*

Law Revision Commission Comments

Section 1255.050 is new to California law. Section 1255.050 provides
for recovery of damages (interest less net rental profits) only where the
lessor has required a deposit prior to judgment and the plaintiff fails to
comply. Only damages after the date specified in the notice for
depositing the probable compensation are recoverable under Section
1255.050. Compare Klopping v. City of Whittier, 8 Cal.3d 39, 500 P.2d
1345, 104 Cal.Rptr. 1 (1972) (rental losses may be recovered in cases of
unreasonable delay in instituting the eminent domain proceeding or other
unreasonable conduct by plaintiff). Nothing in Section 1255.050 limits
the application of Klopping.

Section 1255.050 incorporates the procedures and conditions of the
deposit under Section 1255.040 (deposit for homeowner). Under the
latter section, the sanction for failure to comply is accrual of interest;
Section 1255.050 incorporates this sanction but provides for offset of net
rental profits in case of failure to comply.

Research References

Miller and Starr California Real Estate § 19:149, Valuation and Appor-
    tionment of the Award.
Miller and Starr California Real Estate § 30A:53, Deposit of Probable
    Compensation.
8 Witkin, California Summary 10th Constitutional Law § 1214, (S 1214)
    Deposit on Demand of Homeowner or Lessor.

§ 1255.060. Amount deposited or withdrawn; admissibility and reference at trial; witnesses

(a) The amount deposited or withdrawn pursuant to this
chapter may not be given in evidence or referred to in the trial of
the issue of compensation.

(b) In the trial of the issue of compensation, an appraisal
report, written statement and summary of an appraisal, or other
statement made in connection with a deposit or withdrawal
pursuant to this chapter may not be considered to be an
admission of any party.

(c) Upon objection of the party at whose request an appraisal
report, written statement and summary of the appraisal, or other
statement was made in connection with a deposit or withdrawal
pursuant to this chapter, the person who made the report or
statement and summary or other statement may not be called at
the trial on the issue of compensation by any other party to give
an opinion as to compensation. If the person who prepared the
report, statement and summary, or other statement is called at
trial to give an opinion as to compensation, the report, statement
and summary, or other statement may be used for impeachment
of the witness. *(Added by Stats.1975, c. 1275, p. 3436, § 2,
operative July 1, 1976. Amended by Stats.2002, c. 295 (A.B.1770),
§ 2.)*

Law Revision Commission Comments

Subdivision (a) of Section 1255.060 restates the substance of subdivision
(e) of former Section 1243.5. Subdivisions (b) and (c) are new. Like

subdivision (a), the purpose of subdivisions (b) and (c) is to encourage the
plaintiff to make an adequate deposit by protecting the plaintiff from the
defendant's use of the evidence upon which the deposit is based in the
trial on the issue of compensation. If such evidence could be so used, it is
likely that the plaintiff would make an inadequate deposit in order to
protect itself against the use at the trial of evidence submitted in
connection with the deposit. Subdivisions (b) and (c) apply, of course, to
witnesses for the defendants as well as to those for the plaintiff.
Subdivision (b) precludes impeachment of a witness at the trial by
reference to appraisal reports, written statement or summary of the
appraisal, or other statements made in connection with the deposit and
notice thereof and proceedings to determine or redetermine the amount
of the deposit. The subdivision also precludes such reports or statements
being considered to be admissions of the party on whose behalf they were
made. See Evidence Code Sections 813 and 822. Subdivision (c) is
intended to prevent a party from circumventing subdivision (b) by calling
another party's appraiser as his own witness. It thus expressly overrules
People v. Cowan, 1 Cal.App.3d 1001, 81 Cal.Rptr. 713 (1969), and People
v. Douglas, 15 Cal.App.3d 814, 96 Cal.Rptr. 644 (1971).

Section 1255.060 is amended to allow impeachment of a valuation
witness who prepared an appraisal report, written statement and summary
of an appraisal, or other statement made in connection with a deposit or
withdrawal pursuant to this chapter. This codifies existing law. County of
Contra Costa v. Pinole Point Properties, Inc., 27 Cal.App.4th 1105, 33
Cal.Rptr.2d 38 (1994). [31 Cal.L.Rev.Comm. Reports 120 (2002)].

It should be noted that Section 1255.060 protects an appraisal statement
made by or on behalf of a property owner in connection with a deposit or
withdrawal under this chapter to the same extent as one made by or on
behalf of the condemnor.

Research References

Miller and Starr California Real Estate § 30A:53, Deposit of Probable
    Compensation.
13 NO. 4 Miller & Starr, California Real Estate Newsalert 9, Eminent
    Domain.
8 Witkin, California Summary 10th Constitutional Law § 1212, (S 1212) in
    General.
8 Witkin, California Summary 10th Constitutional Law § 1219, in
    General.

§ 1255.070. Deposit in treasury; investment; law governing; increments earned

In lieu of depositing the money with the State Treasury as
provided in Section 1255.010, upon written request of the
plaintiff, the court shall order the money be deposited in the
county treasury. If money is deposited in the State Treasury
pursuant to Section 1255.010, it shall be held, invested, deposited, and disbursed in the manner specified in Article 10 (commencing with Section 16429) of Chapter 2 of Part 2 of Division 4
of Title 2 of the Government Code, and interest earned or other
increment derived from its investment shall be apportioned and
disbursed in the manner specified in that article. As between
the parties to the proceeding, money deposited pursuant to this
article shall remain at the risk of the plaintiff until paid or made
payable to the defendant by order of the court. *(Added by
Stats.1975, c. 1275, p. 3436, § 2, operative July 1, 1976. Amended
by Stats.1990, c. 1491 (A.B.3765), § 11.)*

Law Revision Commission Comments

The first two sentences of Section 1255.070 are the same in substance as
former Section 1243.6. The last sentence is based on the first two
sentences of subdivision (h) of former Section 1254. For a comparable
provision, see Section 1268.150.

Research References

8 Witkin, California Real Estate § 30A:53, Deposit of Probable
    Procedure.

Miller and Starr California Summary 10th Constitutional Law § 1213, (S 1213)

8 Witkin, California Summary 10th Constitutional Law § 1255, (S 1255) Deposit After Judgment.

§ 1255.075. Investment of deposit for benefit of defendant; motion; hearing

(a) Prior to entry of judgment, a defendant who has an interest in the property for which a deposit has been made under this chapter may, upon notice to the other parties to the proceeding, move the court to have all of such deposit invested for the benefit of the defendants.

(b) At the hearing on the motion, the court shall consider the interests of the parties and the effect that investment would have upon them. The court may, in its discretion, if it finds that the interests of justice will be served, grant the motion subject to such terms and conditions as are appropriate under the circumstances of the case.

(c) An investment under this section shall be specified by the court and shall be limited to United States government obligations or interest-bearing accounts in an institution whose accounts are insured by an agency of the federal government.

(d) The investment of the deposit has the same consequences as if the deposit has been withdrawn under this chapter. *(Added by Stats.1975, c. 1275, p. 3436, § 2, operative July 1, 1976.)*

Law Revision Commission Comments

Section 1255.075 provides a method whereby a defendant may have a prejudgment deposit invested for the benefit of all defendants. For a comparable postjudgment provision, see Section 1268.150. The primary use for this section is to supply an expeditious means for the defendants to obtain interest on the deposit in cases where the plaintiff has not taken possession or to obtain a higher rate of interest than the legal rate in cases where the plaintiff has taken possession without the need for a hearing on the respective rights of the parties.

Under subdivision (a), one defendant may require the whole deposit invested. The return on the investment, however, is for the benefit of all defendants and will be apportioned according to their interests as finally determined in the eminent domain proceeding.

Subdivision (b) makes clear that the granting of a motion under this section is in the discretion of the court. The court should determine whether any of the parties would be prejudiced by the investment. Factors that might be taken into consideration include the interest of a defendant who is an occupant of the property because investment of the deposit will subject him to dispossession under Section 1255.460, or the interest of a defendant who has a bona fide objection to the right to take that would be waived under Section 1255.260.

Under subdivision (b), the court must tailor its order for investment to fit the circumstances of the particular case. Factors the court might take into consideration in making its order include length of commitment of investment, e.g., in certificates of deposit in anticipation of either lengthy or speedy conclusion of trial, or provision for withdrawal by individual defendants from the lump-sum investment where necessary for relocation, and the like. Likewise, the court may impose the risk of loss on the defendant requesting the investment in an appropriate case.

Under subdivision (c), the lump sum may be invested in amounts greater than are insured by an agency of the federal government so long as the institution in which it is invested does carry such insured accounts.

Subdivision (d) makes clear that investment under this section carries with it the same consequences as a withdrawal of a prejudgment deposit. Among these consequences are waiver of defenses (Section 1255.2ᵉˢᵗ) subjection to possession (Section 1255.460), and cessation of i (Section 1268.320).

Research References   of Probable

Miller and Starr California Real Estate § 30A:53ₛ 1213, (S 1213) Compensation.
8 Witkin, California Summary 10th Constitut. Procedure.

8 Witkin, California Summary 10th Constitutional Law § 1259, (S 1259) Market Rate of Interest.

§ 1255.080. Deposit of probable compensation; effect on rights of plaintiff

By depositing the probable compensation pursuant to this article, the plaintiff does not waive the right to appeal from the judgment, the right to move to abandon, or the right to request a new trial. *(Added by Stats.1975, c. 1275, p. 3437, § 2, operative July 1, 1976.)*

Law Revision Commission Comments

Section 1255.080 is new. For comparable provisions, see Sections 1255.470 (possession prior to judgment) and 1268.170 (deposit of amount of award after judgment).

Research References

Miller and Starr California Real Estate § 30A:53, Deposit of Probable Compensation.
8 Witkin, California Summary 10th Constitutional Law § 1212, (S 1212) in General.

ARTICLE 2. WITHDRAWAL OF DEPOSIT

§ 1255.210. Application

Prior to entry of judgment, any defendant may apply to the court for the withdrawal of all or any portion of the amount deposited. The application shall be verified, set forth the applicant's interest in the property, and request withdrawal of a stated amount. The applicant shall serve a copy of the application on the plaintiff. *(Added by Stats.1975, c. 1275, p. 3437, § 2, operative July 1, 1976.)*

Law Revision Commission Comments

Section 1255.210 is derived from subdivisions (a) and (c) of former Section 1243.7. After entry of judgment, deposits made under this chapter may be withdrawn pursuant to Section 1268.140. See Section 1268.010 (upon entry of judgment deposit made pursuant to this chapter deemed to be deposit made pursuant to Section 1268.110).

Research References

Miller and Starr California Real Estate § 30A:54, Withdrawal of Deposit.
8 Witkin, California Summary 10th Constitutional Law § 1215, (S 1215) Withdrawal of Deposit.
8 Witkin, California Summary 10th Constitutional Law § 1256, (S 1256) Withdrawal Deposit.

§ 1255.220 Court order; payment to applicant

Subject to the requirements of this article, the court shall order the amount requested in the application, or such portion of that amount as the applicant is entitled to receive, to be paid to the applicant. *(Added by Stats.1975, c. 1275, p. 3437, § 2, operative July 1, 1976.)*

Law Revision Commission Comments

Section 1255.220 continues the substance of the second sentence of subdivision (a) of former Section 1243.7.

Research References

8 Witkin, California Summary 10th Constitutional Law § 1215, (S 1215)
    Withdrawal of Deposit.

§ 1255.230. Withdrawal; objections; grounds

(a) No withdrawal may be ordered until 20 days after service on the plaintiff of a copy of the application or until the time for all objections has expired, whichever is later.

(b) Within the 20-day period, the plaintiff may file objections to withdrawal on any one or more of the following grounds:

(1) Other parties to the proceeding are known or believed to have interests in the property.

(2) An undertaking should be filed by the applicant as provided in Section 1255.240 or 1255.250.

(3) The amount of an undertaking filed by the applicant under this chapter or the sureties thereon are insufficient.

(c) If an objection is filed on the ground that other parties are known or believed to have interests in the property, the plaintiff shall serve or attempt to serve on such other parties a notice that they may appear within 10 days after such service and object to the withdrawal. The notice shall advise such parties that their failure to object will result in waiver of any rights against the plaintiff to the extent of the amount withdrawn. The notice shall be served in the manner provided in Section 1255.450 for service of an order for possession. The plaintiff shall file, and serve on the applicant, a report setting forth (1) the names of the parties upon whom the notice was served and the dates of service and (2) the names and last known addresses of the other parties who are known or believed to have interests in the property but who were not so served. The applicant may serve parties whom the plaintiff has been unable to serve. Parties served in the manner provided in Section 1255.450 shall have no claim against the plaintiff for compensation to the extent of the amount withdrawn by all applicants. The plaintiff shall remain liable to parties having an interest of record who are not so served but, if such liability is enforced, the plaintiff shall be subrogated to the rights of such parties under Section 1255.280.

(d) If any party objects to the withdrawal, or if the plaintiff so requests, the court shall determine, upon hearing, the amounts to be withdrawn, if any, and by whom. *(Added by Stats.1975, c. 1275, p. 3437, § 2, operative July 1, 1976.)*

Research References

Miller and Starr California Real Estate § 30A:54, Withdrawal of Deposit.
22 NO. 3 Miller & Starr, California Real Estate Newsalert 12, Eminent
    Domain.
8 Witkin, California Summary 10th Constitutional Law § 1215, (S 1215)
    Withdrawal of Deposit.

§ 1255.240. Withdrawal; court determination; undertaking; recovery of premium

(a) If the court determines that an applicant is entitled to withdraw any portion of a deposit that other parties claims or to which another person may be entitled, the court may require the applicant, before withdrawing such portion, file an undertaking. The undertaking shall secure payment such party or person of any amount withdrawn that exceeds amount to which the applicant is entitled as finally determined in proceeding, together with interest as provided in Section 1255.280. If withdrawal is permitted notwithstanding the lack of personal service of the application for withdrawal upon any party to the proceeding, the court may also require that the undertaking indemnify the plaintiff against any liability it may incur under Section 1255.230. The undertaking shall be in such amount as is fixed by the court, but if executed by an admitted surety insurer the amount shall not exceed the portion claimed by the adverse claimant or appearing to belong to another person. If executed

by two or more sufficient sureties, the amount shall not exceed double such portion.

(b) If the undertaking is required primarily because of an issue as to title between the applicant and another party or person, the applicant filing the undertaking is not entitled to recover the premium reasonably paid for the undertaking as a part of the recoverable costs in the eminent domain proceeding. *(Added by Stats.1975, c. 1275, p. 3438, § 2, operative July 1, 1976. Amended by Stats.1982, c. 517, p. 2363, § 182.)*

Law Revision Commission Comments

Section 1255.240 continues the substance of subdivision (f) of former Section 1243.7. Subdivision (a) of Section 1255.240 permits the court to exercise its discretion whether to require an undertaking in cases where there are conflicting claims to the amount to be withdrawn.

Subdivision (b) permits recovery of the bond premium as costs in the proceeding unless the necessity for the undertaking arises primarily from an issue of title. For use of the same distinction in assessing the costs of apportionment proceedings, see Section 1268.710 and People v. Nogarr, 181 Cal.App.2d 312, 5 Cal.Rptr. 247 (1960).

Subdivision (a) of Section 1255.240 is amended for consistency with the Bond and Undertaking Law. See Sections 995.310 (sureties on undertaking) and 995.910 (objections to undertakings). Subdivision (b) is an exception to the rule of Section 995.250 (cost of undertaking recoverable). [16 Cal.L.Rev.Comm. Reports 501 (1982)].

Research References

Miller and Starr California Real Estate § 30A:54, Withdrawal of Deposit.
8 Witkin, California Summary 10th Constitutional Law § 1215, (S 1215)
    Withdrawal of Deposit.
8 Witkin, California Summary 10th Constitutional Law § 1256, (S 1256)
    Withdrawal of Deposit.

§ 1255.250. Withdrawal in excess of original deposit; undertaking

(a) If the amount originally deposited is increased pursuant to Section 1255.030 and the total amount sought to be withdrawn exceeds the amount of the original deposit, the applicant, or each applicant if there are two or more, shall file an undertaking. The undertaking shall be in favor of the plaintiff and shall secure repayment of any amount withdrawn that exceeds the amount to which the applicant is entitled as finally determined in the eminent domain proceeding, together with interest as provided in Section 1255.280. If the undertaking is executed by an admitted surety insurer, the undertaking shall be in the amount by which the total amount to be withdrawn exceeds the amount originally deposited. If the undertaking is executed by two or more sufficient sureties, the undertaking shall be in double such amount, but the maximum amount that may be recovered from such sureties is the amount by which the total amount to be withdrawn exceeds the amount originally deposited.

(b) If there are two or more applicants, the applicants, in lieu of filing separate undertakings, may jointly file a single undertaking in the amount required by subdivision (a). *(Added by Stats.1975, c. 1275, p. 3438, § 2, operative July 1, 1976. Amended by Stats.1982, c. 517, p. 2363, § 183.)*

Law Revision Commission Comments

Section 1255.250 is the same in substance as subdivision (b) of former Code of Civil Procedure Section 1243.7 except that the former two-percent limitation of the amount recoverable for a premium on an undertaking has been replaced by the "reasonably paid" limitation. Withdrawal by one or more defendants of an amount in excess of the original deposit is possible if the deposit has been increased as provided Section 1255.030.

Section 1255.250 is amended to delete provisions duplicated in the Bond and Undertaking Law. See Sections 995.230 (waiver or reduction by beneficiary) (sureties on undertakings) 995.250 (cost of undertaking recoverable), 995.310 undertaking). See also Section 995.910 (objections to undertaking). Cal.L.Rev.Comm. Reports 501 (1982)].

Research References

Miller and Starr California Real Estate § 30A:54, Withdrawal of Deposit.
8 Witkin, California Summary 10th Constitutional Law § 1215, (S 1215)
  Withdrawal of Deposit.

§ 1255.260. Withdrawal; effect; waiver of claims and defenses

If any portion of the money deposited pursuant to this chapter is withdrawn, the receipt of any such money shall constitute a waiver by operation of law of all claims and defenses in favor of the persons receiving such payment except a claim for greater compensation. *(Added by Stats.1975, c. 1275, p. 3439, § 2, operative July 1, 1976.)*

Law Revision Commission Comments

Section 1255.260 restates the substance of subdivision (g) of former Section 1243.7. In addition to the defendant's waiving claims and defenses other than the claim to greater compensation, withdrawal of the deposit may also entitle the plaintiff to an order for possession. See Section 1255.460. *Cf.* People v. Gutierrez, 207 Cal.App.2d 759, 24 Cal.Rptr. 781 (1962). Any amount withdrawn is credited upon the judgment in the eminent domain proceeding. See Section 1268.010.

Research References

Miller and Starr California Real Estate § 30A:54, Withdrawal of Deposit.
15 NO. 5 Miller & Starr, California Real Estate Newsalert 9, Eminent Domain.
17 NO. 5 Miller & Starr, California Real Estate Newsalert 6, Eminent Domain.
22 NO. 3 Miller & Starr, California Real Estate Newsalert 12, Eminent Domain.
3 Witkin Cal. Proc. 5th Actions § 879, Condemnation.
8 Witkin, California Summary 10th Constitutional Law § 1215, (S 1215)
  Withdrawal of Deposit.

§ 1255.280. Withdrawal of excess amount; judgment; interest

(a) Any amount withdrawn by a party pursuant to this article in excess of the amount to which he is entitled as finally determined in the eminent domain proceeding shall be paid to the parties entitled thereto. The court shall enter judgment accordingly.

(b) The judgment so entered shall not include interest except in the following cases:

(1) Any amount that is to be paid to a defendant shall include legal interest from the date of its withdrawal by another defendant.

(2) If the amount originally deposited by a plaintiff was increased pursuant to Section 1255.030 on motion of a party obligated to pay under this section, any amount that is attributable to such increase and that is to be repaid to the plaintiff shall include legal interest from the date of its withdrawal.

(c) If the judgment so entered is not paid within 30 days after its entry, the court may, on motion, enter judgment against the sureties, if any, for the amount of such judgment.

(d) The court may, in its discretion and with such security, if any, as it deems appropriate, grant a party obligated to pay under this section a stay of execution for any amount to be paid to a plaintiff. Such stay of execution shall not exceed one year following entry of judgment under this section. *(Added by Stats.1975, c. 1275, p. 3439, § 2, operative July 1, 1976.)*

Law Revision Commission Comments

Section 1255.280 supersedes subdivision (h) of former Section 1243.7. Unlike former Section 1243.7, which required the payment of interest upon the return of excess amounts withdrawn, Section 1255.280 requires payment of interest only where the excess is to be redistributed among defendants or where the excess is to be repaid to a plaintiff to the extent the excess was procured upon motion for increased deposit by a defendant.

Section 1255.280 also provides for a stay of execution on the return of the excess for a period of up to one year. See subdivision (d). The stay may be conditioned upon appropriate security, which may be simply recordation of an abstract of judgment. It should be noted, however, that the stay is available only as against amounts to be repaid to a plaintiff. Moreover, because execution has been stayed, interest will accrue during the period of the stay regardless of the means by which the excess was obtained. *Cf.* Bellflower City School Dist. v. Skaggs, 52 Cal.2d 278, 282, 339 P.2d 848, 851 (1959).

Section 1255.280 requires repayment of excess amounts withdrawn only after the judgment in an eminent domain proceeding is final. See also Section 1255.330(d) (court may not redetermine probable compensation to be less than amount withdrawn). For a comparable provision, see Section 1268.160.

Research References

Miller and Starr California Real Estate § 30A:54, Withdrawal of Deposit.
8 Witkin, California Summary 10th Constitutional Law § 1213, (S 1213)
  Procedure.
8 Witkin, California Summary 10th Constitutional Law § 1215, (S 1215)
  Withdrawal of Deposit.

ARTICLE 3. POSSESSION PRIOR TO JUDGMENT

Section

§ 1255.410. Motion for order for possession; contents; service of notice; issuance

(a) At the time of filing the complaint or at any time after filing the complaint and prior to entry of judgment, the plaintiff may move the court for an order for possession under this article, demonstrating that the plaintiff is entitled to take the property by eminent domain and has deposited pursuant to Article 1 (commencing with Section 1255.010) an amount that satisfies the requirements of that article.

The motion shall describe the property of which the plaintiff is seeking to take possession, which description may be by reference to the complaint, and shall state the date after which the plaintiff is seeking to take possession of the property. The motion shall include a statement substantially in the following form: "You have the right to oppose this motion for an order of possession of your property. If you oppose this motion you must serve the plaintiff and file with the court a written opposition to the motion within 30 days from the date you were served with this motion." If the written opposition asserts a hardship, it shall be supported by a declaration signed under penalty of perjury stating facts supporting the hardship.

(b) The plaintiff shall serve a copy of the motion on the record owner of the property and on the occupants, if any. The plaintiff shall set the court hearing on the motion not less than 60 days after service of the notice of motion on the record owner of unoccupied property. If the property is lawfully occupied by a person dwelling thereon or by a farm or business operation, service of the notice of motion shall be made not less than 90 days prior to the hearing on the motion.

(c) Not later than 30 days after service of the plaintiff's motion seeking to take possession of the property, any defendant or occupant of the property may oppose the motion in writing by serving the plaintiff and filing with the court the opposition. If the written opposition asserts a hardship, it shall be supported by a declaration signed under penalty of perjury stating facts supporting the hardship. The plaintiff shall serve and file any reply to the opposition not less than 15 days before the hearing.

(d)(1) If the motion is not opposed within 30 days of service on each defendant and occupant of the property, the court shall make an order for possession of the property if the court finds each of the following:

(A) The plaintiff is entitled to take the property by eminent domain.

(B) The plaintiff has deposited pursuant to Article 1 (commencing with Section 1255.010) an amount that satisfies the requirements of that article.

(2) If the motion is opposed by a defendant or occupant within 30 days of service, the court may make an order for possession of the property upon consideration of the relevant facts and any opposition, and upon completion of a hearing on the motion, if the court finds each of the following:

(A) The plaintiff is entitled to take the property by eminent domain.

(B) The plaintiff has deposited pursuant to Article 1 (commencing with Section 1255.010) an amount that satisfies the requirements of that article.

(C) There is an overriding need for the plaintiff to possess the property prior to the issuance of final judgment in the case, and the plaintiff will suffer a substantial hardship if the application for possession is denied or limited.

(D) The hardship that the plaintiff will suffer if possession is denied or limited outweighs any hardship on the defendant or occupant that would be caused by the granting of the order of possession.

(e)(1) Notwithstanding the time limits for notice prescribed by this section and Section 1255.450, a court may issue an order of possession upon an ex parte application by a water, wastewater, gas, electric, or telephone utility, as the court deems appropriate under the circumstances of the case, if the court finds each of the following:

(A) An emergency exists and as a consequence the utility has an urgent need for possession of the property. For purposes of this section, an emergency is defined to include, but is not limited to, a utility's urgent need to protect the public's health and safety or the reliability of utility service.

(B) An emergency order of possession will not displace or unreasonably affect any person in actual and lawful possession of the property to be taken or the larger parcel of which it is a part.

(2) Not later than 30 days after service of the order authorizing the plaintiff to take possession of the property, any defendant or occupant of the property may move for relief from an emergency order of possession that has been issued under this subdivision. The court may modify, stay, or vacate the order upon consideration of the relevant facts and any objections raised, and upon completion of a hearing if requested. *(Added by Stats.1975, c. 1275, p. 3439, § 2, operative July 1, 1976. Amended by Stats.2006, c. 594 (S.B.1210), § 3; Stats.2007, c. 436 (S.B.698), § 1.)*

Research References

Rutter, Cal. Practice Guide: Civil Appeals & Writs Ch. 2-C, C. Nonappealable Orders.
Miller and Starr California Real Estate § 30A:55, Motion for Order of Prejudgment Possession.
Miller and Starr California Real Estate § 30A:79, Possession After Judgment.
17 NO. 4 Miller & Starr, California Real Estate Newsalert 1, Redevelopment Redefined: State Legislative Responses to the Kelo Decision.
17 NO. 4 Miller & Starr, California Real Estate Newsalert 2, Statutory Update:.
17 NO. 6 Miller & Starr, California Real Estate Newsalert 20, Table of Statutes (Newsalert Vol 17).
18 NO. 4 Miller & Starr, California Real Estate Newsalert 9, Eminent Domain.
18 NO. 4 Miller & Starr, California Real Estate Newsalert 45, Table of Statutes (Newsalert Vol 18).
8 Witkin, California Summary 10th Constitutional Law § 1216, (S 1216) Application and Order.
8 Witkin, California Summary 10th Constitutional Law § 1217, (S 1217) Service of Order.
8 Witkin, California Summary 10th Constitutional Law § 1218, (S 1218) Stay and Vacation of Order.
8 Witkin, California Summary 10th Constitutional Law § 1257, Possession After Judgment.
8 Witkin, California Summary 10th Constitutional Law § 1259, (S 1259) Market Rate of Interest.

§ 1255.440.   Vacation of order of possession

If an order has been made under Section 1255.410 authorizing the plaintiff to take possession of property and the court subsequently determines that the conditions specified in Section 1255.410 for issuance of the order are not satisfied, the court shall vacate the order. *(Added by Stats.1975, c. 1275, p. 3440, § 2, operative July 1, 1976.)*

Law Revision Commission Comments

Because the order for possession is issued following an ex parte application by the plaintiff, Section 1255.440 expressly authorizes the court to vacate the order for possession if it subsequently determines, whether upon motion of the defendant or upon its own motion, that the requirements of Section 1255.410 are not satisfied.

Research References

Miller and Starr California Real Estate § 30A:55, Motion for Order of Prejudgment Possession.
8 Witkin, California Summary 10th Constitutional Law § 1218, (S 1218) Stay and Vacation of Order.

§ 1255.450.   Record owner; service

(a) As used in this section, "record owner" means the owner of the legal or equitable title to the fee or any lesser interest in property as shown by recorded deeds or other recorded instruments.

(b) The plaintiff shall serve a copy of the order for possession issued under Section 1255.410 on the record owner of the property and on the occupants, if any. If the property is lawfully occupied by a person dwelling thereon or by a farm or business operation, service shall be made not less than 30 days prior to the time possession is to be taken pursuant to the order. In all other cases, service shall be made not less than 10 days prior to the time possession is to be taken pursuant to the order. Service may be made with or following service of summons.

(c) At least 30 days prior to the time possession is taken pursuant to an order for possession made pursuant to Section 1255.040, 1255.050, or 1255.460, the plaintiff shall serve a copy of the order on the record owner of the property and on the occupants, if any.

(d) Service of the order shall be made by personal service except that:

(1) If the person on whom service is to be made has previously appeared in the proceeding or been served with summons in the proceeding, service of the order may be made by mail upon that person and his or her attorney of record, if any.

(2) If the person on whom service is to be made resides out of the state, or has departed from the state or cannot with due diligence be found within the state, service of the order may be made by registered or certified mail addressed to that person at his or her last known address.

(e) When the record owner cannot be located, the court may, for good cause shown on ex parte application, authorize the plaintiff to take possession of unoccupied property without serving a copy of the order for possession upon a record owner.

(f) A single service upon or mailing to one of several persons having a common business or residence address is sufficient. *(Added by Stats.1975, c. 1275, p. 3440, § 2, operative July 1, 1976. Amended by Stats.2006, c. 594 (S.B.1210), § 6.)*

Research References

Miller and Starr California Real Estate § 30A:55, Motion for Order of Prejudgment Possession.

17 NO. 4 Miller & Starr, California Real Estate Newsalert 2, Statutory Update:.

17 NO. 6 Miller & Starr, California Real Estate Newsalert 20, Table of Statutes (Newsalert Vol 17).

8 Witkin, California Summary 10th Constitutional Law § 1216, (S 1216) Application and Order.

8 Witkin, California Summary 10th Constitutional Law § 1217, (S 1217) Service of Order.

§ 1255.460. Order for possession; contents

An order for possession issued pursuant to Section 1255.410 shall:

(a) Recite that it has been made under this section.

(b) Describe the property to be acquired, which description may be by reference to the complaint.

(c) State the date after which plaintiff is authorized to take possession of the property. *(Added by Stats.1975, c. 1275, p. 3441, § 2, operative July 1, 1976. Amended by Stats.2006, c. 594 (S.B.1210), § 7.)*

Law Revision Commission Comments

Section 1255.460 is new. Article 1 (commencing with Section 1255.010) permits the plaintiff to deposit probable compensation whether or not it obtains an order for possession. This section makes applicable to withdrawal of a deposit made prior to judgment the analogous rule that applies when a deposit made after judgment is withdrawn. *Cf.* People v. Gutierrez, 207 Cal.App.2d 759, 24 Cal.Rptr. 781 (1962). It also permits the plaintiff to take possession of the property after each of the defendants entitled to possession has in writing expressed his willingness to surrender it on or after a date certain. Service of the order for possession is required by subdivision (c) of Section 1255.450.

Research References

Miller and Starr California Real Estate § 30A:55, Motion for Order of Prejudgment Possession.

17 NO. 4 Miller & Starr, California Real Estate Newsalert 2, Statutory Update:.

17 NO. 6 Miller & Starr, California Real Estate Newsalert 20, Table of Statutes (Newsalert Vol 17).

8 Witkin, California Summary 10th Constitutional Law § 1216, (S 1216) Application and Order.

§ 1255.470. Rights of plaintiff

By taking possession pursuant to this chapter, the plaintiff does not waive the right to appeal from the judgment, the right to move to abandon, or the right to request a new trial. *(Added by Stats.1975, c. 1275, p. 3441, § 2, operative July 1, 1976.)*

Law Revision Commission Comments

Section 1255.470 is the same in substance as subdivision (f) of former Section 1243.5. The language has been changed to preclude implied waiver of appeal, right to move to abandon, or right to new trial by taking possession pursuant to any order obtained under this chapter, including orders under Sections 1255.040 and 1255.050. Under Section 1255.260, the defendant also retains his right to appeal or to request a new trial upon the issue of compensation even though he withdraws the deposit made by the plaintiff. However, such withdrawal does waive all claims and defenses other than the claim to compensation. For a comparable provision, see Section 1268.230.

Research References

Rutter, Cal. Practice Guide: Civil Appeals & Writs Ch. 2-D, D. Standing to Appeal.

Miller and Starr California Real Estate § 30A:55, Motion for Order of Prejudgment Possession.

9 Witkin Cal. Proc. 5th Appeal § 75, (S 75) Statute or Agreement Preserving Right to Appeal.

8 Witkin, California Summary 10th Constitutional Law § 1216, (S 1216) Application and Order.

8 Witkin, California Summary 10th Constitutional Law § 1257, Possession After Judgment.

§ 1255.480. Police power; exercise by public entity

Nothing in this article limits the right of a public entity to exercise its police power in emergency situations. *(Added by Stats.1975, c. 1275, p. 3441, § 2, operative July 1, 1976.)*

Law Revision Commission Comments

Section 1255.480 is new. It makes clear that the requirements of this article—such as obtaining and serving an order for possession—do not limit the exercise of the police power. See Surocco v. Geary, 3 Cal. 69 (1853). See generally Van Alstyne, Statutory Modification of Inverse Condemnation: Deliberately Inflicted Injury or Destruction, 20 Stan. L. Rev. 617 (1968), reprinted in Van Alstyne, California Inverse Condemnation Law, 10 Cal.L.Revision Comm'n Reports 111 (1971). For a comparable provision, see Section 1268.240.

Research References

Miller and Starr California Real Estate § 30A:55, Motion for Order of Prejudgment Possession.

8 Witkin, California Summary 10th Constitutional Law § 1216, (S 1216) Application and Order.

8 Witkin, California Summary 10th Constitutional Law § 1257, Possession After Judgment.

CHAPTER 7. DISCOVERY; EXCHANGE OF VALUATION DATA

ARTICLE 1. DISCOVERY

§ 1258.010. Use of discovery procedures

The provisions of this chapter supplement but do not replace, restrict, or prevent the use of discovery procedures or limit the matters that are discoverable in eminent domain proceedings. *(Added by Stats.1975, c. 1275, p. 3442, § 2, operative July 1, 1976.)*

Law Revision Commission Comments

Section 1258.010 supersedes former Section 1272.08 and makes clear that the special provisions of this chapter relating to exchange of valuation data (Article 2) and further discovery following exchange (Section 1258.020) do not limit the availability of discovery generally in eminent domain. See Section 1230.040 and Comment thereto (rules of practice in eminent domain proceedings).

Research References

Rutter, Cal. Practice Guide: Civ. Pro. Before Trial Ch. 8J-1, Who May Make Demand.

Rutter, Cal. Practice Guide: Civ. Pro. Before Trial Ch. 8K-3, Exchange of Valuation Data and Expert Witness Lists in Condemnation Actions.

Miller and Starr California Real Estate § 30A:3, California Eminent Domain Law.

Miller and Starr California Real Estate § 30A:61, Special Discovery Rules in Eminent Domain Actions.

8 Witkin, California Summary 10th Constitutional Law § 1211, Discovery and Exchange of Valuation Data.

§ 1258.020. Authority; exchange of lists and statements; order protecting person from annoyance, etc.

(a) Notwithstanding any other statute or any court rule relating to discovery, proceedings pursuant to subdivision (b) may be had without requirement of court order and may proceed until not later than 20 days prior to the day set for trial of the issue of compensation.

(b) A party to an exchange of lists of expert witnesses and statements of valuation data pursuant to Article 2 (commencing with Section 1258.210) or pursuant to court rule as provided in Section 1258.300 may after the time of the exchange obtain discovery from the other party to the exchange and from any person listed by him as an expert witness.

(c) The court, upon noticed motion by the person subjected to discovery pursuant to subdivision (b), may make any order that justice requires to protect such person from annoyance, embarrassment, or oppression. *(Added by Stats.1975, c. 1275, p. 3442, § 2, operative July 1, 1976. Amended by Stats.1992, c. 876 (A.B.3296), § 8.)*

Law Revision Commission Comments

Section 1258.020 is new. It permits discovery of experts who will testify at trial, notwithstanding any implications to the contrary in the "work product" exception of Section 2016, without requirement of a court order. The section, however, provides for court relief of any person to protect him from annoyance, embarrassment, or oppression. Section 1258.020 permits discovery proceedings to within 20 days prior to trial despite the general provision of Rule 222 of the California Rules of Court limiting discovery within 30 days of trial. The liberal discovery provisions of Section 1258.020 apply only after an exchange pursuant to Article 2 or a comparable exchange of valuation data and lists of experts has taken place. Section 1258.020 does not, however, preclude use of the ordinary discovery procedures prior to the exchange. See Section 1258.010.

The expenses of an expert deposed under this section may be compensable. See Govt.Code § 68092.5.

Research References

Rutter, Cal. Practice Guide: Civ. Pro. Before Trial Ch. 8E-2, When Depositions May be Taken.

Miller and Starr California Real Estate § 30A:61, Special Discovery Rules in Eminent Domain Actions.

§ 1258.030. Admissibility of evidence

Nothing in this chapter makes admissible any evidence that is not otherwise admissible or permits a witness to base an opinion on any matter that is not a proper basis for such an opinion. *(Added by Stats.1975, c. 1275, p. 3442, § 2, operative July 1, 1976.)*

Law Revision Commission Comments

Section 1258.030 is the same as former Section 1272.09 but makes clear that not only the exchange provisions of Article 2 but also the discovery provisions of Article 1 do not affect or alter the rules on admissibility of evidence. The admission of evidence in eminent domain proceedings is governed by the Evidence Code.

Research References

Miller and Starr California Real Estate § 30A:61, Special Discovery Rules in Eminent Domain Actions.

ARTICLE 2.   EXCHANGE OF VALUATION DATA

Section

Section

§ 1258.210.   Demand for exchange, contents

(a) Not later than the 10th day after the trial date is selected, any party may file and serve on any other party a demand to exchange lists of expert witnesses and statements of valuation data. Thereafter, the court may, upon noticed motion and a showing of good cause, permit any party to serve such a demand upon any other party.

(b) The demand shall:

(1) Describe the property to which it relates, which description may be by reference to the complaint.

(2) Include a statement in substantially the following form: "You are required to serve and deposit with the clerk of court a list of expert witnesses and statements of valuation data in compliance with Article 2 (commencing with Section 1258.210) of Chapter 7 of Title 7 of Part 3 of the Code of Civil Procedure not later than the date of exchange to be set in accordance with that article. Except as otherwise provided in that article, your failure to do so will constitute a waiver of your right to call unlisted expert witnesses during your case in chief and of your right to introduce on direct examination during your case in chief any matter that is required to be, but is not, set forth in your statements of valuation data." *(Added by Stats.1975, c. 1275, p. 3442, § 2, operative July 1, 1976.)*

Law Revision Commission Comments

Section 1258.210 supersedes subdivisions (a)–(c) of former Section 1272.01. The simplified procedure provided by this article for exchanging valuation information is not mandatory in all cases; it applies only if invoked by a party to the proceeding. Moreover, the procedure provided by this article is not applicable in counties which provide an adequate substitute. See Section 1258.300.

Subdivision (a) of Section 1258.210 changes the time for making a demand to exchange from 50 days prior to trial to not later than the tenth day after the date at which a trial date is selected with provision for a later demand where good cause is shown. This change will enable an earlier exchange, thereby permitting additional discovery, if necessary, based on information exchanged. See Section 1258.020 (further discovery following exchange). It will also remove the uncertainty of the 50-day time limit prior to trial in cases where the trial date is known only 30 days prior to trial.

Where a party makes a demand to exchange data, that party must himself provide his own data to the party on whom the demand was served. See Section 1258.230(a).

Subdivision (b) of Section 1258.210 is the same in substance as former Section 1272.01(c).

Subdivision (b) of the former section—permitting cross-demands within 40 days prior to trial—is deleted because it gave rise to confusion that a person serving a demand need not exchange his own data unless a cross-demand is served on him. The deleted provision is unnecessary in light of the provision in subdivision (a) for relief from the time limits for serving a demand upon a showing of good cause.

Research References

Rutter, Cal. Practice Guide: Civ. Pro. Before Trial Ch. 8D-5, Selecting Proper Discovery Tools.
Rutter, Cal. Practice Guide: Civ. Pro. Before Trial Ch. 8K-3, Exchange of Valuation Data and Expert Witness Lists in Condemnation Actions.
Miller and Starr California Real Estate § 30A:63, Exchange of Expert Discovery.

§ 1258.220. Date of exchange

(a) For the purposes of this article, the "date of exchange" is the date agreed to for the exchange of their lists of expert witnesses and statements of valuation data by the party who served a demand and the party on whom the demand was served or, failing agreement, a date 90 days prior to commencement of the trial on the issue of compensation or the date set by the court on noticed motion of either party establishing good cause therefor.

(b) Notwithstanding subdivision (a), unless otherwise agreed to by the parties, the date of exchange shall not be earlier than nine months after the date of commencement of the proceeding. *(Added by Stats.1975, c. 1275, p. 3442, § 2, operative July 1, 1976. Amended by Stats.1999, c. 102 (S.B.634), § 2; Stats.2001, c. 428 (A.B.237), § 7.)*

Law Revision Commission Comments

Section 1258.220, defining the date of exchange, supersedes the exchange date—20 days prior to trial—prescribed by former Section 1272.01(d). The exchange date is to be the date selected by the parties to the exchange or, failing agreement, either 40 days prior to trial or such other date selected by the court. This earlier exchange date will enable subsequent discovery. See Section 1258.020 (further discovery following exchange).

Section 1258.220 is amended to make the exchange date 90, rather than 60, days before trial on the issue of compensation (but not earlier than nine months after the case was filed). As used in subdivision (b), "months" refers to calendar months. See Section 17(4).

The statutory exchange date of 90, rather than 60, days before trial remains subject to the authority of the court to provide relief on motion of a party and showing of good cause. The practicalities of preparing sufficiently to enable a fair exchange within the prescribed period may, in the circumstances of a particular case, constitute good cause for a later exchange date. The need to commence trial within one year in order to preserve the date of valuation may, in the circumstances of a particular case (such as where the date of valuation is not otherwise established by a deposit of probable compensation), constitute good cause for an exchange date less than 90 days before commencement of trial on the issue of compensation. *Cf.* Sections 1263.110 (date of valuation fixed by deposit), 1263.120 (trial within one year). [31 Cal.L.Rev.Comm. Reports 82 (2001)].

Research References

Rutter, Cal. Practice Guide: Civ. Pro. Before Trial Ch. 8K-3, Exchange of Valuation Data and Expert Witness Lists in Condemnation Actions.
Miller and Starr California Real Estate § 30A:63, Exchange of Expert Discovery.

§ 1258.230. Service and deposit of list and statements; duties of clerk

(a) Not later than the date of exchange:

(1) Each party who served a demand and each party upon whom a demand was served shall deposit with the clerk of the court a list of expert witnesses and statements of valuation data.

(2) A party who served a demand shall serve his list and statements upon each party on whom he served his demand.

(3) Each party on whom a demand was served shall serve his list and statements upon the party who served the demand.

(b) The clerk of the court shall make an entry in the register of actions for each list of expert witnesses and statement of valuation data deposited with him pursuant to this article. The lists and statements shall not be filed in the proceeding, but the clerk shall make them available to the court at the commencement of the trial for the limited purpose of enabling the court to apply the provisions of this article. Unless the court otherwise orders, the clerk shall, at the conclusion of the trial, return all lists and statements to the attorneys for the parties who deposited them. Lists or statements ordered by the court to be retained may thereafter be destroyed or otherwise disposed of in accordance with the provisions of law governing the destruction or disposition of exhibits introduced in the trial. *(Added by Stats.1975, c. 1275, p. 3443, § 2, operative July 1, 1976.)*

Law Revision Commission Comments

Section 1258.230 is the same in substance as former Section 1272.01(d)–(e).

Subdivision (b) requires that deposits with the clerk of lists and statements be entered in the register of actions. With respect to maintenance of the register, see Govt.Code § 69845. Such entries will permit the court to determine whether a list and statements have been deposited in compliance with this article. However, the statements or appraisal reports used as statements (see Section 1258.260) will not necessarily be in the form prescribed by court rules for papers to be filed. Also, the copies deposited with the clerk serve the limited purpose of enabling the trial court to rule under Section 1258.280. Hence, the subdivision does not require or permit the filing of list and statements but instead requires the clerk to maintain custody of them and make them available to the trial court at the commencement of the trial. In the usual case, the copies furnished to the court will have served their only purpose at the conclusion of evidence. The subdivision therefore permits them to be returned to the attorneys. For those instances in which the copies might be of significance in connection with an appeal or posttrial motion, the court, on its own initiative or on request of a party, may order them retained. In this event, the copies retained may thereafter be disposed of in the manner of exhibits introduced in the trial.

Research References

Miller and Starr California Real Estate § 30A:63, Exchange of Expert Discovery.

§ 1258.240. List of witnesses; contents

The list of expert witnesses shall include the name, business or residence address, and business, occupation, or profession of each person intended to be called as an expert witness by the party and a statement of the subject matter to which his testimony relates. *(Added by Stats.1975, c. 1275, p. 3443, § 2, operative July 1, 1976.)*

Law Revision Commission Comments

Section 1258.240 is the same as former Section 1272.03. It requires inclusion of all persons to be called as experts, not merely those to be called as valuation experts. See Evid.Code §§ 813(b), 814. In addition to naming each proposed expert witness, the list must identify the subject matter of his testimony, e.g., "valuation testimony," "existence of oil on subject property," and the like. This further information is necessary to apprise the adverse party of the range and general nature of the expert testimony to be presented at the trial.

Unlike Section 1258.260 (contents of statement of valuation data), this section does not require that the particulars of the expert opinion be stated or that the supporting factual data be set forth. In such case, normal discovery techniques can be used to obtain the particulars of the opinion and supporting factual data. See Section 1258.020 (further discovery after exchange) and Government Code Section 68092.5 (costs of deposition of expert witness). See also Section 1258.010 (use of discovery procedures).

Research References

Rutter, Cal. Practice Guide: Civ. Pro. Before Trial Ch. 8K-3, Exchange of Valuation Data and Expert Witness Lists in Condemnation Actions.

Miller and Starr California Real Estate § 30A:64, Expert Witness Lists and Statements of Valuation Data.

§ 1258.250. Statement of valuation data; persons from whom exchanged; contents

A statement of valuation data shall be exchanged for each person the party intends to call as a witness to testify to his opinion as to any of the following matters:

(a) The value of the property being taken.

(b) The amount of the damage, if any, to the remainder of the larger parcel from which such property is taken.

(c) The amount of the benefit, if any, to the remainder of the larger parcel from which such property is taken.

(d) The amount of any other compensation required to be paid by Chapter 9 (commencing with Section 1263.010) or Chapter 10 (commencing with Section 1265.010). *(Added by Stats.1975, c. 1275, p. 3443, § 2, operative July 1, 1976.)*

Law Revision Commission Comments

Section 1258.250 is the same in substance as subdivision (a) of former Section 1272.02 with conforming changes made to reflect the compensation provisions of Chapters 9 (commencing with Section 1263.010) and 10 (commencing with Section 1265.010).

Section 1258.250 requires that a statement of valuation data be provided for each person who is to testify to his opinion as to one or more of the matters listed in the section whether or not that person is to qualify as an expert. For example, a statement must be provided for the owner of the property if he is to testify concerning value, damages, benefits, or other items of compensation.

Research References

Rutter, Cal. Practice Guide: Civil Trials & Evidence Ch. 8C-H, H. Opinion Evidence.

Miller and Starr California Real Estate § 30A:63, Exchange of Expert Discovery.

Miller and Starr California Real Estate § 30A:64, Expert Witness Lists and Statements of Valuation Data.

§ 1258.260. Statement of valuation data; opinion evidence

(a) The statement of valuation data shall give the name and business or residence address of the witness and shall include a statement whether the witness will testify to an opinion as to any of the matters listed in Section 1258.250 and, as to each matter upon which the witness will give an opinion, what that opinion is and the following items to the extent that the opinion is based on them:

(1) The interest being valued.

(2) The date of valuation used by the witness.

(3) The highest and best use of the property.

(4) The applicable zoning and the opinion of the witness as to the probability of any change in zoning.

(5) The sales, contracts to sell and purchase, and leases supporting the opinion.

(6) The cost of reproduction or replacement of the existing improvements on the property, the depreciation or obsolescence the improvements have suffered, and the method of calculation used to determine depreciation.

(7) The gross income from the property, the deductions from gross income, and the resulting net income; the reasonable net rental value attributable to the land and existing improvements, and the estimated gross rental income and deductions upon which the reasonable net rental value is computed; the rate of capitalization used; and the value indicated by the capitalization.

(8) If the property is a portion of a larger parcel, a description of the larger parcel and its value.

(9) If the opinion concerns loss of goodwill, the method used to determine the loss, and a summary of the data supporting the opinion.

(b) With respect to each sale, contract, or lease listed under paragraph (5) of subdivision (a), the statement of valuation data shall give:

(1) The names and business or residence addresses, if known, of the parties to the transaction.

(2) The location of the property subject to the transaction.

(3) The date of the transaction.

(4) If recorded, the date of recording and the volume and page or other identification of the record of the transaction.

(5) The price and other terms and circumstances of the transaction. In lieu of stating the terms contained in any contract, lease, or other document, the statement may, if the document is available for inspection by the adverse party, state the place where and the times when it is available for inspection.

(6) The total area and shape of the property subject to the transaction.

(c) If any opinion referred to in Section 1258.250 is based in whole or in substantial part upon the opinion of another person, the statement of valuation data shall include the name and business or residence address of that other person, his business, occupation, or profession, and a statement as to the subject matter to which his or her opinion relates.

(d) Except when an appraisal report is used as a statement of valuation data as permitted by subdivision (e), the statement of valuation data shall include a statement, signed by the witness, that the witness has read the statement of valuation data and that it fairly and correctly states his or her opinions and knowledge as to the matters therein stated.

(e) An appraisal report that has been prepared by the witness which includes the information required to be included in a statement of valuation data may be used as a statement of valuation data under this article. *(Added by Stats.1975, c. 1275, p. 3443, § 2, operative July 1, 1976. Amended by Stats.1978, c. 342, p. 723, § 1; Stats.2001, c. 428 (A.B.237), § 8.)*

Law Revision Commission Comments

Section 1258.260 is the same in substance as former Section 1272.02(b)–(f).

Subdivision (a) requires the setting forth of the specified data to the extent that any opinion is based thereof. *Cf.* Evid. Code §§ 814–821. It does not require that the specified data be set forth if the witness' opinion is not based thereon even though such data may have been compiled or ascertained by the witness. Also, the supporting data required by subdivision (a) commonly will pertain to the witness' opinion as to value, and the same data will be considered by the witness to support his opinion as to damages and benefits. In this case, the statement or appraisal report may simply recite that the opinion as to damages or benefits is supported by the same data as the opinion as to value. Where the required information, however, is not identical with respect to all opinions of the witness, subdivision (a) requires that the item of supporting data be separately stated with respect to each opinion of the witness.

Subdivision (c) requires that each valuation statement give information regarding any person who will not be called as a witness but upon whose opinion the testimony of the valuation witness will be based in whole or substantial part. This information is needed by the adverse party not only for the general purpose of properly preparing for trial but also to enable him to utilize his right under Section 804 of the Evidence Code to call the other expert and examine him as an adverse witness concerning his opinion. The subdivision also requires a statement of the subject matter of the supporting opinion. As to this requirement, and the parallel requirement under Section 1258.240, see the Comment to Section 1258.240.

Paragraph (9) is added to Section 1258.260(a) to make clear that the basis for an opinion as to loss of goodwill is to be included in the exchange of valuation data. This codifies the rule in *City of Fresno v. Harrison*, 154 Cal.App.3d 296, 201 Cal.Rptr. 219 (1984).

Technical revisions are also made for consistency with contemporary statutory drafting techniques. [30 Cal.L.Rev.Comm. Reports 567 (2000)].

Research References

Rutter, Cal. Practice Guide: Civ. Pro. Before Trial Ch. 8K-3, Exchange of Valuation Data and Expert Witness Lists in Condemnation Actions.
Miller and Starr California Real Estate § 30A:64, Expert Witness Lists and Statements of Valuation Data.

§ 1258.270. Additional witnesses and data; notice to persons upon whom list and statements served

(a) A party who is required to exchange lists of expert witnesses and statements of valuation data shall diligently give notice to the parties upon whom his list and statements were served if, after service of his list and statements, he:

(1) Determines to call an expert witness not included in his list of expert witnesses to testify on direct examination during his case in chief;

(2) Determines to have a witness called by him testify on direct examination during his case in chief to any opinion or data required to be listed in the statement of valuation data for that witness but which was not so listed; or

(3) Discovers any data required to be listed in a statement of valuation data but which was not so listed.

(b) The notice required by subdivision (a) shall include the information specified in Sections 1258.240 and 1258.260 and shall be in writing; but such notice is not required to be in writing if it is given after the commencement of the trial. *(Added by Stats.1975, c. 1275, p. 3445, § 2, operative July 1, 1976.)*

Law Revision Commission Comments

Section 1258.270 is the same in substance as former Section 1272.04. Although Section 1258.270 requires supplementation of lists and statements exchanged, compliance with the section does not insure that the party will be permitted to call the witness or have a witness testify as to the opinion or data. See Sections 1258.280 and 1258.290.

Research References

Miller and Starr California Real Estate § 30A:64, Expert Witness Lists and Statements of Valuation Data.

§ 1258.280. Limitations upon calling witnesses and testimony by witnesses

Except as provided in Section 1258.290, upon objection of a party who has served his list of expert witnesses and statements of valuation data in compliance with Section 1258.230:

(a) No party required to serve a list of expert witnesses on the objecting party may call an expert witness to testify on direct examination during his case in chief unless the information required by Section 1258.240 for such witness is included in the list served.

(b) No party required to serve statements of valuation data on the objecting party may call a witness to testify on direct examination during his case in chief to his opinion on any matter listed in Section 1258.250 unless a statement of valuation data for such witness was served.

(c) No witness called by a party required to serve statements of valuation data on the objecting party may testify on direct examination during the case in chief of the party who called him to any opinion or data required to be listed in the statement of valuation data for such witness unless such opinion or data is listed in the statement served except that testimony that is merely an explanation or elaboration of data so listed is not inadmissible under this subdivision. *(Added by Stats.1975, c. 1275, p. 3445, § 2, operative July 1, 1976.)*

Law Revision Commission Comments

Section 1258.280 is the same in substance as former Section 1272.05. Section 1258.280 provides a sanction calculated to insure that the parties make a good faith exchange of lists of expert witnesses and essential valuation data. For applications of the same sanction to other required pretrial disclosures, see Sections 454 (copies of accounts) and 2032 (physicians' statements). Although the furnishing of a list of expert witnesses and statements of valuation data is analogous to responding to interrogatories or a request for admissions, the consequences specified by Section 2034 for failure or refusal to make discovery are not made applicable to a failure to comply with the requirements of this article. Existence of the sanction provided by Section 1258.280 does not, of course, prevent those consequences from attaching to a failure to make discovery when regular discovery techniques are invoked in the proceeding. The sanction for failure to exchange valuation data applies to all persons intended to be called as valuation witnesses, including the owner of the property. See Section 1258.250 and Comment thereto (persons for whom statements of valuation data must be exchanged).

Under exceptional circumstances, the court is authorized to permit the use of a witness or of valuation data not included in the list or statements. See Section 1258.290 and the Comment to that section.

Section 1258.280 limits only the calling of a witness, or the presentation of testimony, during the case in chief of the party calling the witness or presenting the testimony. The section does not preclude a party from calling a witness in rebuttal or having a witness give rebuttal testimony that is otherwise proper. See *City & County of San Francisco v. Tillman Estate Co.*, 205 Cal. 651, 272 P. 585 (1928); *State v. Loop*, 127 Cal.App.2d 786, 274 P.2d 885 (1954). The section also does not preclude a party from bringing out additional data on redirect examination where it is necessary to meet matters brought out on the cross-examination of his witness. However, the court should take care to confine a party's rebuttal case and his redirect examination of his witnesses to their purpose of meeting matters brought out during the adverse party's case or cross-examination of his witnesses. A party should not be permitted to defeat the purpose of this article by reserving witnesses and valuation data for use in rebuttal where such witnesses should have been called and such valuation data presented on the direct examination during the case in chief.

Application of the concept of "case in chief" to the presentation of evidence by the plaintiff requires particular attention. The defendant presents his case in chief first in the order of the trial. Therefore, the following presentation by the plaintiff may include evidence of two kinds; i.e., evidence comprising the case in chief of the plaintiff and evidence in rebuttal of evidence previously presented by the defendants. If the evidence offered in rebuttal is proper as such, this section does not prevent its presentation at that time.

Research References

Rutter, Cal. Practice Guide: Civ. Pro. Before Trial Ch. 8K-3, Exchange of Valuation Data and Expert Witness Lists in Condemnation Actions.
Rutter, Cal. Practice Guide: Civil Trials & Evidence Ch. 8C-H, H. Opinion Evidence.
Miller and Starr California Real Estate § 30A:64, Expert Witness Lists and Statements of Valuation Data.
15 NO. 6 Miller & Starr, California Real Estate Newsalert 10, Eminent Domain.

§ 1258.290. Grounds for court authority to call witnesses or permit testimony by witness

(a) The court may, upon such terms as may be just (including but not limited to continuing the trial for a reasonable period of time and awarding costs and litigation expenses), permit a party to call a witness, or permit a witness called by a party to testify to an opinion or data on direct examination, during the party's case in chief where such witness, opinion, or data is required to be, but is not, included in such party's list of expert witnesses or statements of valuation data if the court finds that such party has made a good faith effort to comply with Sections 1258.210 to 1258.260, inclusive, that he has complied with Section 1258.270, and that by the date of exchange he:

(1) Would not in the exercise of reasonable diligence have determined to call such witness or discovered or listed such opinion or data; or

(2) Failed to determine to call such witness or to discover or list such opinion or data through mistake, inadvertence, surprise, or excusable neglect.

(b) In making a determination under this section, the court shall take into account the extent to which the opposing party has relied upon the list of expert witnesses and statements of valuation data and will be prejudiced if the witness is called or the testimony concerning such opinion or data is given. (*Added by Stats.1975, c. 1275, p. 3445, § 2, operative July 1, 1976.*)

Law Revision Commission Comments

Section 1258.290 is the same in substance as former Section 1272.06 and allows the court to permit a party who has made a good faith effort to comply with this article to call a witness or use valuation data that was not included in his list of expert witnesses or statements of valuation data. The standards set out in Section 1258.290 are similar to those applied under Section 657 (granting a new trial upon newly discovered evidence) and Section 473 (relieving a party from default). The court should apply the same standards in making determinations under this section. The consideration listed in subdivision (b) is important but is not necessarily the only consideration to be taken into account in making determinations under this section. See Section 1235.140 for the definition of "litigation expenses."

Research References

Rutter, Cal. Practice Guide: Civ. Pro. Before Trial Ch. 8K-3, Exchange of Valuation Data and Expert Witness Lists in Condemnation Actions.
Miller and Starr California Real Estate § 30A:64, Expert Witness Lists and Statements of Valuation Data.
18 NO. 4 Miller & Starr, California Real Estate Newsalert 33, Eminent Domain.

§ 1258.300. Procedure for exchange of valuation data; court rule

The superior court in any county may provide by court rule a procedure for the exchange of valuation data which shall be used in lieu of the procedure provided by this article if the Judicial Council finds that such procedure serves the same purpose and is an adequate substitute for the procedure provided by this article. (*Added by Stats.1975, c. 1275, p. 3446, § 2, operative July 1, 1976.*)

Law Revision Commission Comments

Section 1258.300 supersedes former Section 1272.07, which provided that the statutory exchange provisions did not apply to an eminent domain proceeding in Los Angeles County. Section 1258.300 supplants the special provision relating to Los Angeles County by the general principle that any county that has adopted adequate rules that are approved by the Judicial Council is exempt from the provisions of this article. Under this general standard, a system for disclosing valuation data under judicial supervision such as that in Los Angeles County would qualify for approval by the Judicial Council. See Policy Memorandum, Eminent Domain (Including Inverse Condemnation), Superior Court, County of Los Angeles (dated February 7, 1973); Swartzman v. Superior Court, 231 Cal.App.2d 195, 41 Cal.Rptr. 721 (1964).

CHAPTER 8. PROCEDURES FOR DETERMINING RIGHT TO TAKE AND COMPENSATION

ARTICLE 1. GENERAL PROVISIONS

§ 1260.010. Precedence over other civil actions

Proceedings under this title take precedence over all other civil actions in the matter of setting the same for hearing or trial in order that such proceedings shall be quickly heard and determined. (*Added by Stats.1975, c. 1275, p. 3446, § 2, operative July 1, 1976.*)

Law Revision Commission Comments

Section 1260.010 reenacts the substance of former Section 1264.

Research References

Rutter, Cal. Practice Guide: Civil Appeals & Writs Ch. 5-B, B. Types of Motions, Applications and Requests.
Rutter, Cal. Practice Guide: Civ. Pro. Before Trial Ch. 12(I)-C, C. Claims for Trial Setting Preference.
Miller and Starr California Real Estate § 30A:68, Eminent Domain Trials Generally.
9 Witkin Cal. Proc. 5th Appeal § 764, Statutory Preferences and Advancement.
7 Witkin Cal. Proc. 5th Trial § 72, (S 72) Miscellaneous Statutes.
8 Witkin, California Summary 10th Constitutional Law § 1219, in General.

§ 1260.020. Consolidated proceedings; compatibility; apportionment of payment; incompatibility; necessary use

(a) If proceedings to acquire the same property are consolidated, the court shall first determine whether the public uses for which the property is sought are compatible within the meaning of Article 6 (commencing with Section 1240.510) of Chapter 3. If the court determines that the uses are compatible, it shall permit the proceeding to continue with the plaintiffs acting jointly. The court shall apportion the obligation to pay any award in the proceeding in proportion to the use, damage, and benefits attributable to each plaintiff.

(b) If the court determines pursuant to subdivision (a) that the uses are not all compatible, it shall further determine which of the uses is the more necessary public use within the meaning of Article 7 (commencing with Section 1240.610) of Chapter 3. The court shall permit the plaintiff alleging the more necessary public use, along with any other plaintiffs alleging compatible public uses under subdivision (a), to continue the proceeding. The court shall dismiss the proceeding as to the other plaintiffs. (*Added by Stats.1975, c. 1275, p. 3446, § 2, operative July 1, 1976.*)

Law Revision Commission Comments

Section 1260.020 deals with the issues of compatibility and more necessary public use where two proceedings to acquire the same property are consolidated pursuant to Section 1048. Section 1260.020 does not deal with whether consolidation is proper; that is a matter dealt with by Section 1048. Moreover, nothing in this section is intended to limit the authority of the court to consolidate proceedings or sever issues for trial under the latter section. However, where consolidation of two proceedings to acquire the same property is ordered, subdivision (a) requires the court to determine first whether the public uses for which the property is sought are compatible and, if so, to take the action indicated. Under subdivision (b), if the public uses are not all compatible, the court must determine which are "more necessary" and again take the appropriate action. For reimbursement of expenses and damages on dismissal, see Sections 1268.610 and 1268.620.

Research References

Miller and Starr California Real Estate § 30A:68, Eminent Domain Trials Generally.

8 Witkin, California Summary 10th Constitutional Law § 1219, in General.

8 Witkin, California Summary 10th Constitutional Law § 1265, (S 1265) Litigation Expenses.

§ 1260.030. Improvements pertaining to realty; determination

(a) If there is a dispute between plaintiff and defendant whether particular property is an improvement pertaining to the realty, either party may, not later than 30 days prior to the date specified in an order for possession of the property, move the court for a determination whether the property is an improvement pertaining to the realty.

(b) A motion under this section shall be heard not sooner than 10 days and not later than 20 days after service of notice of the motion. At the hearing, the court may consider any relevant evidence, including a view of the premises and property, in making its determinations. *(Added by Stats.1975, c. 1275, p. 3446, § 2, operative July 1, 1976.)*

Law Revision Commission Comments

Section 1260.030 is new; it is designed to enable the parties to obtain a prompt resolution of disputes concerning the character of improvements so that, when possession is transferred, the parties will know their rights with respect to the property. See Section 1263.205 et seq. (improvements).

Research References

Miller and Starr California Real Estate § 30A:55, Motion for Order of Prejudgment Possession.

8 Witkin, California Summary 10th Constitutional Law § 1219, in General.

§ 1260.040. Compensation determinations; evidentiary or other legal issue disputes affecting determinations

(a) If there is a dispute between plaintiff and defendant over an evidentiary or other legal issue affecting the determination of compensation, either party may move the court for a ruling on the issue. The motion shall be made not later than 60 days before commencement of trial on the issue of compensation. The motion shall be heard by the judge assigned for trial of the case.

(b) Notwithstanding any other statute or rule of court governing the date of final offers and demands of the parties and the date of trial of an eminent domain proceeding, the court may postpone those dates for a period sufficient to enable the parties to engage in further proceedings before trial in response to its ruling on the motion.

(c) This section supplements, and does not replace any other pretrial or trial procedure otherwise available to resolve an evidentiary or other legal issue affecting the determination of compensation. *(Added by Stats.2001, c. 428 (A.B.237), § 9.)*

Law Revision Commission Comments

Section 1260.040 is intended to provide a mechanism by which a party may obtain early resolution of an *in limine* motion or other dispute affecting valuation. It should be noted that the procedure provided in this section is limited to resolution of legal issues that may affect compensation; it may not be used to ascertain just compensation. *Cf.* Cal. Const. art. I, 19 (just compensation ascertained by jury unless waived).

Nothing in this section precludes the use of other procedures for the same purpose, including, without limitation, bifurcation of issues and control of the order of proof pursuant to statute, or other pretrial procedure pursuant to court rule. [31 Cal.L.Rev.Comm. Reports 83 (2001)].

Research References

Miller and Starr California Real Estate § 30:1, Basis for Inverse Condemnation.

Miller and Starr California Real Estate § 30A:65, Motions Regarding Evidentiary or Legal Disputes.

18 NO. 1 Miller & Starr, California Real Estate Newsalert 13, Eminent Domain.

18 NO. 1 Miller & Starr, California Real Estate Newsalert 17, Inverse Condemnation.

18 NO. 1 Miller & Starr, California Real Estate Newsalert 19, Landowners' Liability.

8 Witkin, California Summary 10th Constitutional Law § 1164, in General.

8 Witkin, California Summary 10th Constitutional Law § 1221, (S 1221) in General.

ARTICLE 2. CONTESTING RIGHT TO TAKE

Section

1260.110.   Objections; determination; trial.

1260.120.   Authority and duty of court; order.

§ 1260.110. Objections; determination; trial

(a) Where objections to the right to take are raised, unless the court orders otherwise, they shall be heard and determined prior to the determination of the issue of compensation.

(b) The court may, on motion of any party, after notice and hearing, specially set such objections for trial. *(Added by Stats.1975, c. 1275, p. 3447, § 2, operative July 1, 1976.)*

Law Revision Commission Comments

Section 1260.110 makes provision for bringing to trial the objections, if any, that have been raised against the plaintiff's right to take. See Sections 1250.350–1250.370. Under subdivision (a), disposition of the right to take is generally a prerequisite to trial of the issue of just compensation. However, this does not preclude such activities as depositions and other discovery, and the court may order a different order of trial. See also Section 1048. *Cf.* City of Los Angeles v. Keck, 14 Cal.App.3d 920, 92 Cal.Rptr. 599 (1971) (parties stipulated to determination of compensation and tried only issues of public use and necessity).

Subdivision (b) makes clear that the determination of the objections to the right to take may be specially set for trial. See Rule 225 of the California Rules of Court and Swartzman v. Superior Court, 231 Cal.App.2d 195, 198–199, 41 Cal.Rptr. 721, 724–725 (1964).

Research References

Miller and Starr California Real Estate § 30A:69, Contesting the Right to Take.

8 Witkin, California Summary 10th Constitutional Law § 1218, (S 1218) Stay and Vacation of Order.

8 Witkin, California Summary 10th Constitutional Law § 1220, Contesting Right to Take.

§ 1260.120. Authority and duty of court; order

(a) The court shall hear and determine all objections to the right to take.

(b) If the court determines that the plaintiff has the right to acquire by eminent domain the property described in the complaint, the court shall so order.

(c) If the court determines that the plaintiff does not have the right to acquire by eminent domain any property described in the complaint, it shall order either of the following:

(1) Immediate dismissal of the proceeding as to that property.

(2) Conditional dismissal of the proceeding as to that property unless such corrective and remedial action as the court may prescribe has been taken within the period prescribed by the court in the order. An order made under this paragraph may impose such limitations and conditions as the court determines to be just under the circumstances of the particular case

including the requirement that the plaintiff pay to the defendant all or part of the reasonable litigation expenses necessarily incurred by the defendant because of the plaintiff's failure or omission which constituted the basis of the objection to the right to take. *(Added by Stats.1975, c. 1275, p. 3447, § 2, operative July 1, 1976.)*

Law Revision Commission Comments

Subdivision (a) of Section 1260.120 provides for a court determination of right to take issues (see Sections 1250.350–1250.370). This is consistent with the California Constitution and with prior law. See Comment to Section 1230.040 (rules of practice in eminent domain proceedings: trial).

The form of review of a determination that the plaintiff may condemn the defendant's property is governed by the rules of procedure generally. See Section 904.1 (appeal); Harden v. Superior Court, 44 Cal.2d 630, 284 P.2d 9 (1955) (review by writ).

A determination that the plaintiff has no right to condemn the defendant's property ordinarily requires an order of dismissal. Paragraph (1) of subdivision (c). However, where the complaint alleges alternative grounds for condemnation, a finding which would require dismissal as to one ground does not preclude a finding of right to take on another ground, and the proceeding may continue to be prosecuted on that basis. As to whether an order of dismissal is appealable, see Section 904.1. See also People v. Rodoni, 243 Cal.App.2d 771, 52 Cal.Rptr. 857 (1966). As to the recovery of litigation expenses following dismissal, see Section 1268.610.

Paragraph (2) of subdivision (c) is designed to ameliorate the all-or-nothing effect of paragraph (1). The court is authorized in its discretion to dispose of an objection in a just and equitable manner. This authority does not permit the court to create a right to acquire where none exists, but it does authorize the court to grant leave to the plaintiff to amend pleadings or take other corrective action that is just in light of all of the circumstances of the case. The court may frame its order in whatever manner may be desirable, and subdivision (c) makes clear that the order may include the awarding of reasonable litigation expenses to the defendant. See Section 1235.140 (defining "litigation expenses"). For example, if the resolution of necessity was not properly adopted, the court may, where appropriate, order that such a resolution be properly adopted within such time as is specified by the court and that, if a proper resolution has not been adopted within the time specified, the proceeding is dismissed. The plaintiff is not required to comply with an order made under paragraph (2), but a failure to comply results in a dismissal of the proceeding as to that property which the court has determined the plaintiff lacks the right to acquire.

Research References

Miller and Starr California Real Estate § 30A:19, Resolution of Necessity.

Miller and Starr California Real Estate § 30A:69, Contesting the Right to Take.

19 NO. 5 Miller & Starr, California Real Estate Newsalert 16, Eminent Domain.

8 Witkin, California Summary 10th Constitutional Law § 1200, (S 1200) Effect of Resolution.

8 Witkin, California Summary 10th Constitutional Law § 1220, Contesting Right to Take.

ARTICLE 3. PROCEDURES RELATING TO DETERMINATION OF COMPENSATION

Section

§ 1260.210. Presentation of evidence and argument by defendant; burden of proof

(a) The defendant shall present his evidence on the issue of compensation first and shall commence and conclude the argument.

(b) Except as otherwise provided by statute, neither the plaintiff nor the defendant has the burden of proof on the issue of compensation. *(Added by Stats.1975, c. 1275, p. 3447, § 2, operative July 1, 1976.)*

Law Revision Commission Comments

Subdivision (a) of Section 1260.210 requires the defendant to present his evidence on the issue of compensation first and to commence and conclude the argument. This continues former law. See former Section 1256.1 ("the defendant shall commence and conclude the argument"); City & County of San Francisco v. Tillman Estate Co., 205 Cal. 651, 272 P. 585 (1928) (order of proof).

The rule as to burden of proof provided by subdivision (b) changes former law. Compare City & County of San Francisco v. Tillman Estate Co., *supra*. Assignment of the burden of proof in the context of an eminent domain proceeding is not appropriate. The trier of fact generally is presented with conflicting opinions of value and supporting data and is required to fix value based on the weight it gives to the opinions and supporting data. See, e.g., City of Pleasant Hill v. First Baptist Church, 1 Cal.App.3d 384, 408–410, 82 Cal.Rptr. 1, 16–18 (1969); People v. Jarvis, 274 Cal.App.2d 217, 79 Cal.Rptr. 175 (1969). See also State v. 45,621 Square Feet of Land, 475 P.2d 553 (Alaska 1970); State v. Amunsis, 61 Wash.2d 160, 377 P.2d 462 (1963). Absent the production of evidence by one party, the trier of fact will determine compensation solely from the other party's evidence, but neither party should be made to appear to bear some greater burden of persuasion than the other. Subdivision (b) therefore so provides.

For an exception to the rule stated in subdivision (b), see Section 1263.510 (loss of goodwill).

Research References

Rutter, Cal. Practice Guide: Civil Trials & Evidence Ch. 6-B, B. Order of Presentation of Opening Statements.

Rutter, Cal. Practice Guide: Civil Trials & Evidence Ch. 13-A, A. Procedural Considerations Re Closing Argument.

Rutter, Cal. Practice Guide: Civil Trials & Evidence Ch. 8G-D, D. Burdens and Standards of Proof.

Miller and Starr California Real Estate § 30A:46, Valuation of Goodwill Loss.

Miller and Starr California Real Estate § 30A:47, Introduction to the Eminent Domain Action.

Miller and Starr California Real Estate § 30A:68, Eminent Domain Trials Generally.

Miller and Starr California Real Estate § 30A:71, Burden of Proof and Order of Proceedings.

16 NO. 4 Miller & Starr, California Real Estate Newsalert 27, Eminent Domain.

18 NO. 1 Miller & Starr, California Real Estate Newsalert 13, Eminent Domain.

7 Witkin Cal. Proc. 5th Trial § 162, (S 162) Trial by Jury.

8 Witkin, California Summary 10th Constitutional Law § 1219, in General.

8 Witkin, California Summary 10th Constitutional Law § 1221, (S 1221) in General.

8 Witkin, California Summary 10th Constitutional Law § 1246, (S 1246) Valuation and Proof of Loss.

§ 1260.220. Valuation of each interest and injury to remainder; separate assessments; apportionment of award

(a) Except as provided in subdivision (b), where there are divided interests in property acquired by eminent domain, the value of each interest and the injury, if any, to the remainder of such interest shall be separately assessed and compensation awarded therefor.

(b) The plaintiff may require that the amount of compensation be first determined as between plaintiff and all defendants claiming an interest in the property. Thereafter, in the same proceeding, the trier of fact shall determine the respective rights of the defendants in and to the amount of compensation awarded and shall apportion the award accordingly. Nothing in this subdivision limits the right of a defendant to present during the first stage of the proceeding evidence of the value of, or injury to, the property or the defendant's interest in the property; and the right of a defendant to present evidence during the second stage of the proceeding is not affected by the failure to exercise the right to present evidence during the first stage of the proceeding. *(Added by Stats.1975, c. 1275, p. 3447, § 2, operative July 1, 1976. Amended by Stats.1978, c. 294, p. 614, § 1.)*

Law Revision Commission Comments

Section 1260.220 retains the existing California scheme of permitting a plaintiff the option of having the interests in property valued separately or as a whole. Subdivision (a) retains the procedure formerly provided by Section 1248(1)–(3). Subdivision (b) retains the procedure formerly provided by the first sentence of Section 1246.1. It is intended as procedural only. It does not for example, affect the rule that, where the plaintiff elects the two-stage proceeding, the value of the property includes any enhanced value created by the existence of a favorable lease on the property. See People v. Lynbar, Inc., 253 Cal.App.2d 870, 62 Cal.Rptr. 320 (1967). See also Section 1263.310 (compensation for property taken).

The last sentence of subdivision (b) is an elaboration of the introductory clause of former Section 1248.

Subdivision (b) of Section 1260.220 is amended to make clear the right of a defendant, whether or not a fee owner, to present evidence of the value of the whole property in order to assure an adequate award for purposes of apportionment.

Research References

Miller and Starr California Real Estate § 19:149, Valuation and Apportionment of the Award.
Miller and Starr California Real Estate § 30A:33, Leaseholds--Apportionment Between Landlord and Tenant.
Miller and Starr California Real Estate § 30A:67, Agreements to Mediate or Arbitrate.
Miller and Starr California Real Estate § 30A:73, Apportionment of Compensation Award.
8 Witkin, California Summary 10th Constitutional Law § 1222, (S 1222) Valuation of Divided Interests.
8 Witkin, California Summary 10th Constitutional Law § 1250, Leases.

§ 1260.230. Separate assessments

As far as practicable, the trier of fact shall assess separately each of the following:

(a) Compensation for the property taken as required by Article 4 (commencing with Section 1263.310) of Chapter 9.

(b) Where the property acquired is part of a larger parcel:

(1) The amount of the damage, if any, to the remainder as required by Article 5 (commencing with Section 1263.410) of Chapter 9.

(2) The amount of the benefit, if any, to the remainder as required by Article 5 (commencing with Section 1263.410) of Chapter 9.

(c) Compensation for loss of goodwill, if any, as required by Article 6 (commencing with Section 1263.510) of Chapter 9. *(Added by Stats.1975, c. 1275, p. 3448, § 2, operative July 1, 1976.)*

Law Revision Commission Comments

Section 1260.230 continues the separate assessment requirement of subdivisions 1–3 and 7 of former Section 1248. The section does not affect the right of a party to request special interrogatories to the jury on these issues or on any other issues, including those where a separate finding on an element of compensation not listed in Section 1260.230 would be useful. For example, a party may desire a special finding on the amount of compensation required under Section 1263.620 for performance of work to protect the public from injury from a partially completed improvement.

Research References

Miller and Starr California Real Estate § 30A:73, Apportionment of Compensation Award.
8 Witkin, California Summary 10th Constitutional Law § 1220, Contesting Right to Take.

§ 1260.240. Unknown or deceased persons and heirs and devisees of deceased as defendants; failure to appear; determination of interests and compensation by court

Where any persons unknown or any deceased persons or the heirs and devisees of any deceased persons have been properly joined as defendants but have not appeared either personally or by a personal representative, the court shall determine the extent of the interests of such defendants in the property taken or in the remainder if the property taken is part of a larger parcel and the compensation to be awarded for such interests. The court may determine the extent and value of the interests of all such defendants in the aggregate without apportionment between the respective defendants. In any event, in the case of deceased persons, the court shall determine only the extent and value of the interest of the decedent and shall not determine the extent and value of the separate interests of the heirs and devisees in such decedent's interest. *(Added by Stats.1975, c. 1275, p. 3448, § 2, operative July 1, 1976.)*

Law Revision Commission Comments

Section 1260.240 is based on a portion of former Section 1245.3 which provided for the court determination of the compensation to be awarded deceased and unknown persons; however, Section 1260.240 authorizes the court to make a lump sum award where such persons have not appeared. Former law was not clear on this point. For provisions authorizing joinder of deceased persons and persons unknown, see Section 1250.220.

Research References

Miller and Starr California Real Estate § 30A:73, Apportionment of Compensation Award.
8 Witkin, California Summary 10th Constitutional Law § 1220, Contesting Right to Take.

§ 1260.250. Certification by auditor or tax collector; court order; judgment

(a) In a county where both the auditor and the tax collector are elected officials, the court shall by order give the auditor or tax collector the legal description of the property sought to be taken and direct the auditor or tax collector to certify to the court the information required by subdivision (c), and the auditor or tax collector shall promptly certify the required information to the court. In all other counties, the court shall by order give the tax collector the legal description of the property sought to be taken and direct the tax collector to certify to the court the information required by subdivision (c), and the tax collector shall promptly certify the required information to the court.

(b) The court order shall be made on or before the earliest of the following dates:

(1) The date the court makes an order for possession.

(2) The date set for trial.

(3) The date of entry of judgment.

(c) The court order shall require certification of the following information:

(1) The current assessed value of the property together with its assessed identification number.

(2) All unpaid taxes on the property, and any penalties and costs that have accrued thereon while on the secured roll, levied for prior tax years that constitute a lien on the property.

(3) All unpaid taxes on the property, and any penalties and costs that have accrued thereon while on the secured roll, levied for the current tax year that constitute a lien on the property prorated to, but not including, the date of apportionment determined pursuant to Section 5082 of the Revenue and Taxation Code or the date of trial, whichever is earlier. If the amount of the current taxes is not ascertainable at the time of proration, the amount shall be estimated and computed based on the assessed value for the current assessment year and the tax rate levied on the property for the immediately prior tax year.

(4) The actual or estimated amount of taxes on the property that are or will become a lien on the property in the next succeeding tax year prorated to, but not including, the date of apportionment determined pursuant to Section 5082 of the Revenue and Taxation Code or the date of trial, whichever is earlier. Any estimated amount of taxes shall be computed based on the assessed value of the property for the current assessment year and the tax rate levied on the property for the current tax year.

(5) The amount of the taxes, penalties, and costs allocable to one day of the current tax year, and where applicable, the amount allocable to one day of the next succeeding tax year, hereinafter referred to as the "daily prorate."

(6) The total of paragraphs (2), (3), and (4).

(d) If the property sought to be taken does not have a separate valuation on the assessment roll, the information required by this section shall be for the larger parcel of which the property is a part.

(e) The court, as part of the judgment, shall separately state the amount certified pursuant to this section and order that the amount be paid to the tax collector from the award. If the amount so certified is prorated to the date of trial, the order shall include, in addition to the amount so certified, an amount equal to the applicable daily prorate multiplied by the number of days commencing on the date of trial and ending on and including the day before the date of apportionment determined pursuant to Section 5082 of the Revenue and Taxation Code.

(f) Notwithstanding any other provision of this section, if the board of supervisors provides the procedure set forth in Section 5087 of the Revenue and Taxation Code, the court shall make no award of taxes in the judgment. *(Added by Stats.1979, c. 31, p. 88, § 2. Amended by Stats.1999, c. 892 (A.B.1672), § 12.)*

Law Revision Commission Comments

Subdivision (a) to (c), and (e) of Section 1260.250 continue the substance of subdivisions (a) and (b) of former Revenue and Taxation Code Section 4986.9. Subdivision (b)(3) is added in recognition of the fact that judgment may be entered without a trial. Subdivision (d) is added so that, in a partial taking, the award is security for taxes due on the whole parcel. See subdivision (e). Subdivision (f) continues the second sentence of subdivision (b) of former Section 4986.1.

Taxes on exempt property not paid from the award pursuant to subdivision (e) may be transferred to the unsecured roll for collection. See Rev. & Tax.Code §§ 5084(b), 5086(a), 5087. For the rules governing reimbursement for taxes subject to cancellation, and liability for taxes after the date of apportionment, see Article 5 (commencing with Section 1268.410) of Chapter 11.

Research References

8 Witkin, California Summary 10th Constitutional Law § 1260, (S 1260) Liability, Proration, and Payment.

CHAPTER 9. COMPENSATION

ARTICLE 1. GENERAL PROVISIONS

§ 1263.010. Rights of property owner; single payment for loss

(a) The owner of property acquired by eminent domain is entitled to compensation as provided in this chapter.

(b) Nothing in this chapter affects any rights the owner of property acquired by eminent domain may have under any other statute. In any case where two or more statutes provide compensation for the same loss, the person entitled to compensation may be paid only once for that loss. *(Added by Stats.1975, c. 1275, p. 3448, § 2, operative July 1, 1976.)*

Law Revision Commission Comments

This chapter, relating to compensation, supersedes various provisions formerly found in the eminent domain title of the Code of Civil Procedure. The elements of compensation provided in this chapter include compensation for property taken (Section 1263.310), injury to the remainder (Section 1263.410), and loss of goodwill (Section 1263.510). In connection with compensation, see also Chapter 10 (commencing with Section 1265.010) (divided interests), Section 1268.610 (litigation expenses). See also Section 1235.170 (defining "property" to include any interest in property), Section 1235.125 (defining "interest" in property), and Section 1235.140 (defining "litigation expenses"). For related provisions, see Article 1 (commencing with Section 1245.010) of Chapter 4 (damages from preliminary location, survey, and tests) and Section 1268.620 (damages caused by possession when proceeding dismissed or right to take defeated). See also Section 1250.410 (pretrial settlement offers).

Subdivision (b) of Section 1263.010 makes clear that this chapter does not affect any statute providing for additional compensation such as compensation for relocation of public utility facilities. See discussion in A Study Relating to Sovereign Immunity, 5 Cal.L.Revision Comm'n Reports 1, 78–96 (1963). See also Govt.Code § 7260 et seq. (relocation assistance).

Likewise, this chapter in no way limits compensation that may be required by Article I, Section 19, the "just compensation" clause of the California Constitution. On the other hand, the "just compensation" clause does not limit the compensation required by this chapter. This chapter is intended to provide rules of compensation for eminent domain proceedings; the law of inverse condemnation is left for determination by judicial development. See Section 1230.020 and Comment thereto (law governing exercise of eminent domain power).

The second sentence of subdivision (b), prohibiting double payment for the same loss, applies only to statutes that purport to compensate for the same loss. Thus, for example, a person who suffers a business loss would not be entitled to compensation for that loss under both Section 1263.510 (loss of goodwill) and Government Code Section 7262(c) (relocation or in-lieu payment). This prohibition on double recovery in no way limits compensation under different statutes for separate and distinct losses such as the fair market value of property taken, injury to the remainder, moving expense, court costs, and the like.

Research References

Rutter, Cal. Practice Guide: Real Prop. Transactions Ch. 7-C, C. Representing the Purchasing Tenant.

Miller and Starr California Real Estate § 17:62, Condemnors.

Miller and Starr California Real Estate § 19:150, Valuation and Apportionment of the Award--Compensation for Tenant's Personal Property, Improvements, and Fixtures.

Miller and Starr California Real Estate § 30A:30, Fixtures, Equipment, and Improvements.

16 NO. 1 Miller & Starr, California Real Estate Newsalert 15, Eminent Domain.

13 Witkin, California Summary 10th Personal Property § 109, Fixtures Condemned as Real Property.

8 Witkin, California Summary 10th Constitutional Law § 1225, (S 1225) in General.

§ 1263.210. Determination; rights of tenants

(a) Except as otherwise provided by statute, all improvements pertaining to the realty shall be taken into account in determining compensation.

(b) Subdivision (a) applies notwithstanding the right or obligation of a tenant, as against the owner of any other interest in real property, to remove such improvement at the expiration of his term. *(Added by Stats.1975, c. 1275, p. 3450, § 2, operative July 1, 1976.)*

Law Revision Commission Comments

Section 1263.210 continues the substance of portions of former Sections 1248(1) (compensation shall be awarded for the property taken "and all improvements thereon pertaining to the realty") and 1249.1 ("All improvements pertaining to the realty that are on the property at the time of the service of summons and which affect its value shall be considered in the assessment of compensation . . . ."). For exceptions to the rule provided in Section 1263.210, see Sections 1263.230 (improvements removed or destroyed) and 1263.240 (improvements made after service of summons). *Cf.* Section 1263.250 (growing crops).

Subdivision (a) requires that the property taken by eminent domain be valued as it stands improved. If the improvements serve to enhance the value of the property over its unimproved condition, the property receives the enhanced value; if the improvements serve to decrease the value of the property below its unimproved condition, the property suffers the decreased value. See, e.g., City of Los Angeles v. Sabatasso, 3 Cal.App.3d 973, 83 Cal.Rptr. 898 (1970) (lessee may recover severance damages for reduction in value of equipment used in place on remainder).

Subdivision (b) of Section 1263.210, which adopts the language of Section 302(b)(1) of the Uniform Relocation Assistance and Real Property Acquisition Policies Act of 1970, 42 U.S.C. § 4652(b)(1) (1971), continues prior California law. See People v. Klopstock, 24 Cal.2d 897, 151 P.2d 641 (1944); Concrete Service Co. v. State, 274 Cal.App.2d 142, 78 Cal.Rptr. 923 (1969). *Cf.* City of Los Angeles v. Klinker, 219 Cal. 198, 25 P.2d 826 (1933).

Research References

Miller and Starr California Real Estate § 17:62, Condemnors.

Miller and Starr California Real Estate § 30:12, Who May Recover Damages.

Miller and Starr California Real Estate § 30:13, Measure of Recoverable Damages.

Miller and Starr California Real Estate § 19:150, Valuation and Apportionment of the Award--Compensation for Tenant's Personal Property, Improvements, and Fixtures.

Miller and Starr California Real Estate § 30A:30, Fixtures, Equipment, and Improvements.

16 NO. 1 Miller & Starr, California Real Estate Newsalert 15, Eminent Domain.

8 Witkin, California Summary 10th Constitutional Law § 1209, (S 1209) Award of Litigation Expenses.

8 Witkin, California Summary 10th Constitutional Law § 1225, (S 1225) in General.

§ 1263.230. Removal or destruction; time; determination of compensation

(a) Improvements pertaining to the realty shall not be taken into account in determining compensation to the extent that they are removed or destroyed before the earliest of the following times:

(1) The time the plaintiff takes title to the property.

(2) The time the plaintiff takes possession of the property.

(3) If the defendant moves from the property in compliance with an order for possession, the date specified in the order; except that, if the defendant so moves prior to such date and gives the plaintiff written notice thereof, the date 24 hours after such notice is received by the plaintiff.

(b) Where improvements pertaining to the realty are removed or destroyed by the defendant at any time, such improvements shall not be taken into account in determining compensation. Where such removal or destruction damages the remaining property, such damage shall be taken into account in determining compensation to the extent it reduces the value of the remaining property. *(Added by Stats.1975, c. 1275, p. 3450, § 2, operative July 1, 1976.)*

Law Revision Commission Comments

Subdivision (a) of Section 1263.230 continues the substance of former Section 1249.1. See also Redevelopment Agency v. Maxwell, 193 Cal.App.2d 414, 14 Cal.Rptr. 170 (1961). See also Section 1268.030 (title to property acquired by eminent domain passes upon the date that a certified copy of the final order of condemnation is recorded. *Cf.* Klopping v. City of Whittier, 8 Cal.3d 39, 46, 500 P.2d 1345, 1351, 104 Cal.Rptr. 1, 7 (1972) (dictum) (risk of loss in inverse condemnation). Subdivision (a) also provides that, where a defendant moves from property in compliance with an order for possession prior to the date specified in the order, he may shift the risk of loss to the plaintiff by serving notice that he has moved; such notice may be served prior to the time he moves. The risk of loss does not shift to the plaintiff until 24 hours after the plaintiff receives such notice. As to the authority of the Department of Transportation to secure fire insurance in cases in which property acquired is leased to the former owner, see Government Code Section 11007.1. If removal or destruction serves to decrease the value of the property below its improved condition, the property is valued accordingly; if removal or destruction serves to increase the value of the property over its improved condition, the property receives the increased value.

Subdivision (b) makes clear that, where the defendant removes or destroys improvements even after the time the risk of loss shifts to the plaintiff, compensation is not awarded for the improvements. Subdivision (b) does not authorize the defendant to remove property or preclude the plaintiff from bringing an independent action against the defendant for conversion where such removal or destruction occurs after valuation of the property.

Where removal or destruction of improvements damages the remaining property, such as a structure in which the improvements were installed, subdivision (b) makes clear that such damage is included in the determination of property value. It should be noted that the defendant may be able to remove improvements without suffering the damage to the structure caused by the removal under Section 1263.260.

Research References

Rutter, Cal. Practice Guide: Real Prop. Transactions Ch. 7-C, C. Representing the Purchasing Tenant.

Miller and Starr California Real Estate § 17:62, Condemnors.

Miller and Starr California Real Estate § 19:150, Valuation and Apportionment of the Award--Compensation for Tenant's Personal Property, Improvements, and Fixtures.

Miller and Starr California Real Estate § 19:151, Valuation and Apportionment of the Award--Costs of Relocation.

Miller and Starr California Real Estate § 30A:30, Fixtures, Equipment, and Improvements.

Miller and Starr California Real Estate § 30A:31, Business Inventory and Other Personal Property.

Miller and Starr California Real Estate § 30A:40, Damage to Improvements.

8 Witkin, California Summary 10th Constitutional Law § 1226, (S 1226) Improvements Removed or Destroyed.

§ 1263.240. Improvements after service of summons

Improvements pertaining to the realty made subsequent to the date of service of summons shall not be taken into account in determining compensation unless one of the following is established:

(a) The improvement is one required to be made by a public utility to its utility system.

(b) The improvement is one made with the written consent of the plaintiff.

(c) The improvement is one authorized to be made by a court order issued after a noticed hearing and upon a finding by the court that the hardship to the defendant of not permitting the improvement outweighs the hardship to the plaintiff of permitting the improvement. The court may, at the time it makes an order under this subdivision authorizing the improvement to be made, limit the extent to which the improvement shall be taken into account in determining compensation. *(Added by Stats. 1975, c. 1275, p. 3450, § 2, operative July 1, 1976.)*

Research References

Miller and Starr California Real Estate § 30:13, Measure of Recoverable Damages.
Miller and Starr California Real Estate § 19:150, Valuation and Apportionment of the Award--Compensation for Tenant's Personal Property, Improvements, and Fixtures.
Miller and Starr California Real Estate § 30A:30, Fixtures, Equipment, and Improvements.
14 NO. 6 Miller & Starr, California Real Estate Newsalert 11, Inverse Condemnation.
8 Witkin, California Summary 10th Constitutional Law § 1227, (S 1227) Improvements Made After Summons is Served.

§ 1263.250. Harvesting and marketing of crops

(a) The acquisition of property by eminent domain shall not prevent the defendant from harvesting and marketing crops planted before or after the service of summons. If the plaintiff takes possession of the property at a time that prevents the defendant from harvesting and marketing the crops, the fair market value of the crops in place at the date the plaintiff is authorized to take possession of the property shall be included in the compensation awarded for the property taken.

(b) Notwithstanding subdivision (a), the plaintiff may obtain a court order precluding the defendant from planting crops after service of summons, in which case the compensation awarded for the property taken shall include an amount sufficient to compensate for loss caused by the limitation on the defendant's right to use the property. *(Added by Stats.1975, c. 1275, p. 3450, § 2, operative July 1, 1976.)*

Law Revision Commission Comments

Section 1263.250 supersedes former Section 1249.2. Despite the contrary implication of former Section 1249.2, subdivision (a) makes clear that the defendant has the right to grow and harvest crops and to retain the profit for his own benefit up to the time the property is actually taken. Where possession is taken and the defendant is prevented from realizing the value of his crops, he is entitled to the fair market value of the crops as of the date the plaintiff is authorized to take possession. The plaintiff may preclude the defendant from planting after service of summons but must pay the loss of use value. Subdivision (b).

Research References

Miller and Starr California Real Estate § 19:150, Valuation and Apportionment of the Award--Compensation for Tenant's Personal Property, Improvements, and Fixtures.
Miller and Starr California Real Estate § 30A:32, Crops, Trees and Vegetation.

8 Witkin, California Summary 10th Constitutional Law § 1228, Compensation for Crops.

§ 1263.260. Election to remove improvements; notice

Notwithstanding Section 1263.210, the owner of improvements pertaining to the realty may elect to remove any or all such improvements by serving on the plaintiff within 60 days after service of summons written notice of such election. If the plaintiff fails within 30 days thereafter to serve on the owner written notice of refusal to allow removal of such improvements, the owner may remove such improvements and shall be compensated for their reasonable removal and relocation cost not to exceed the market value of the improvements. Where such removal will cause damage to the structure in which the improvements are located, the defendant shall cause no more damage to the structure than is reasonably necessary in removing the improvements, and the structure shall be valued as if the removal had caused no damage to the structure. *(Added by Stats.1975, c. 1275, p. 3451, § 2, operative July 1, 1976.)*

Law Revision Commission Comments

Section 1263.260 is new. It provides a means whereby the defendant may convert improvements pertaining to the realty to personalty and receive the moving cost for such personalty. *Cf.* Govt.Code § 7262 (moving expense of personal property). Where the owner of improvements pertaining to the realty makes the election provided in this section, compensation is not awarded for the property removed. See Section 1263.230 (improvements removed or destroyed). For a comparable provision, see Pennsylvania Eminent Domain Code § 1–607 (1964).

Research References

Miller and Starr California Real Estate § 19:150, Valuation and Apportionment of the Award--Compensation for Tenant's Personal Property, Improvements, and Fixtures.
Miller and Starr California Real Estate § 19:151, Valuation and Apportionment of the Award--Costs of Relocation.
Miller and Starr California Real Estate § 30A:30, Fixtures, Equipment, and Improvements.
8 Witkin, California Summary 10th Constitutional Law § 1226, (S 1226) Improvements Removed or Destroyed.

§ 1263.270. Location of improvement on property not taken; order to acquire entire improvement

Where an improvement pertaining to the realty is located in part upon property taken and in part upon property not taken, the court may, on motion of any party and a determination that justice so requires, direct the plaintiff to acquire the entire improvement, including the part located on property not taken, together with an easement or other interest reasonably necessary for the demolition, removal, or relocation of the improvement. *(Added by Stats.1975, c. 1275, p. 3451, § 2, operative July 1, 1976.)*

Law Revision Commission Comments

Section 1263.270 is comparable to Section 1011 of the Uniform Eminent Domain Code and supersedes Section 16¾ of the Los Angeles County Flood Control Act (Cal.Stats.1915, Ch. 755). It authorizes the court, on motion, to direct the plaintiff to take and pay compensation for improvements located in part on property not taken in the proceeding. *Cf.* Section 1240.150 (acquisition of all or portion of remainder with owner's consent). See the Comment to Section 1240.150.

Research References

Miller and Starr California Real Estate § 19:150, Valuation and Apportionment of the Award--Compensation for Tenant's Personal Property, Improvements, and Fixtures.
Miller and Starr California Real Estate § 30A:30, Fixtures, Equipment, and Improvements.
Miller and Starr California Real Estate § 30A:40, Damage to Improvements.
8 Witkin, California Summary 10th Constitutional Law § 1184, (S 1184) Acquisition of Remainder With Consent.

8 Witkin, California Summary 10th Constitutional Law § 1225, (S 1225) in General.

ARTICLE 4. MEASURE OF COMPENSATION FOR PROPERTY TAKEN

Section
1263.310.   Mandatory compensation; measure.
1263.320.   Fair market value.
1263.321.   Nonprofit, special use property; determination of value.
1263.330.   Exclusions from fair market value.

§ 1263.310. Mandatory compensation; measure

Compensation shall be awarded for the property taken. The measure of this compensation is the fair market value of the property taken. *(Added by Stats.1975, c. 1275, p. 3451, § 2, operative July 1, 1976.)*

Law Revision Commission Comments

Section 1263.310 provides the basic rule that compensation for property taken by eminent domain is the fair market value of the property. Compensation for the property taken, however, is only one element of the damages to which a property owner may be entitled under this chapter. See Section 1263.010 and the Comment thereto (right to compensation). See also Section 1263.410 (injury to remainder) and Section 1263.510 (goodwill).

Research References

Rutter, Cal. Practice Guide: Civil Trials & Evidence Ch. 8B-B, B. Particular Types of Evidence.
Rutter, Cal. Practice Guide: Real Prop. Transactions Ch. 7-C, C. Representing the Purchasing Tenant.
Miller and Starr California Real Estate § 30:13, Measure of Recoverable Damages.
Miller and Starr California Real Estate § 30A:5, Definitions; Eminent Domain Terminology.
Miller and Starr California Real Estate § 19:149, Valuation and Apportionment of the Award.
Miller and Starr California Real Estate § 30A:21, Principles of Just Compensation.
Miller and Starr California Real Estate § 30A:22, Fair Market Value Defined.
21 NO. 1 Miller & Starr, California Real Estate Newsalert 12, Eminent Domain.
21 NO. 2 Miller & Starr, California Real Estate Newsalert 13, Eminent Domain.
8 Witkin, California Summary 10th Constitutional Law § 1220, Contesting Right to Take.
8 Witkin, California Summary 10th Constitutional Law § 1229, in General.

§ 1263.320. Fair market value

(a) The fair market value of the property taken is the highest price on the date of valuation that would be agreed to by a seller, being willing to sell but under no particular or urgent necessity for so doing, nor obliged to sell, and a buyer, being ready, willing, and able to buy but under no particular necessity for so doing, each dealing with the other with full knowledge of all the uses and purposes for which the property is reasonably adaptable and available.

(b) The fair market value of property taken for which there is no relevant, comparable market is its value on the date of valuation as determined by any method of valuation that is just and equitable. *(Added by Stats.1975, c. 1275, p. 3451, § 2, operative July 1, 1976. Amended by Stats.1992, c. 7 (S.B.821), § 2.)*

Research References

Miller and Starr California Real Estate § 30:13, Measure of Recoverable Damages.

Miller and Starr California Real Estate § 30:21, Remedies for Unreasonable Precondemnation Activity.
Miller and Starr California Real Estate § 30A:5, Definitions; Eminent Domain Terminology.
Miller and Starr California Real Estate § 19:149, Valuation and Apportionment of the Award.
Miller and Starr California Real Estate § 30A:22, Fair Market Value Defined.
Miller and Starr California Real Estate § 30A:25, Determining Highest and Best Use.
Miller and Starr California Real Estate § 30A:26, Appraisal Methods of Determining Fair Market Value.
16 NO. 4 Miller & Starr, California Real Estate Newsalert 27, Eminent Domain.
18 NO. 5 Miller & Starr, California Real Estate Newsalert 16, Inverse Condemnation.
8 Witkin, California Summary 10th Constitutional Law § 1230, Determining Market Value.
8 Witkin, California Summary 10th Constitutional Law § 1231, Admissible Matters.
8 Witkin, California Summary 10th Constitutional Law § 1240, Unity of Use.

§ 1263.321. Nonprofit, special use property; determination of value

A just and equitable method of determining the value of nonprofit, special use property for which there is no relevant, comparable market is as set forth in Section 824 of the Evidence Code, but subject to the exceptions set forth in subdivision (c) of Section 824 of the Evidence Code. *(Added by Stats.1992, c. 7 (S.B.821), § 3.)*

Research References

Miller and Starr California Real Estate § 30A:22, Fair Market Value Defined.
Miller and Starr California Real Estate § 30A:26, Appraisal Methods of Determining Fair Market Value.
8 Witkin, California Summary 10th Constitutional Law § 1230, Determining Market Value.

§ 1263.330. Exclusions from fair market value

The fair market value of the property taken shall not include any increase or decrease in the value of the property that is attributable to any of the following:

(a) The project for which the property is taken.

(b) The eminent domain proceeding in which the property is taken.

(c) Any preliminary actions of the plaintiff relating to the taking of the property. *(Added by Stats.1975, c. 1275, p. 3451, § 2, operative July 1, 1976.)*

Law Revision Commission Comments

Section 1263.330 is an adjustment to the basic definition of fair market value in Section 1263.320 and requires that the compensation for property taken by eminent domain be determined as if there had been no enhancement or diminution in the value of property due to the imminence of the eminent domain proceeding or the project for which the property is taken. For related provisions of state and federal law that apply to offers for voluntary acquisition of property, see Government Code Section 7267.2 and Uniform Relocation Assistance and Real Property Acquisition Policies Act of 1970, 42 U.S.C. § 4651(3) (1971) (excluding from consideration the effect of the "public improvement" for which the property is acquired).

Prior case law held that, in general, increases in the value of the property caused by the project may not be included in the compensation. See, e.g., County of San Luis Obispo v. Bailey, 4 Cal.3d 518, 483 P.2d 27, 93 Cal.Rptr. 859 (1971). The effect of Section 1263.330(a) is to codify this rule. It should be noted that Merced Irr. Dist. v. Woolstenhulme, 4 Cal.3d 478, 483 P.2d 1, 93 Cal.Rptr. 833 (1971), stated an exception to the rule of exclusion of enhancement from market value where the property was not originally included within the scope of the project; this exception is discussed below under the "scope of the project" rule.

Civ. Pro.

Prior case law was uncertain respecting the treatment of any decrease in value due to such factors as general knowledge of the pendency of the public project. Several decisions indicated that the rules respecting enhancement and diminution were not parallel and that value was to be determined as of the date of valuation notwithstanding that such value reflects a decrease due to general knowledge of the pendency of the public project. See City of Oakland v. Partridge, 214 Cal.App.2d 196, 29 Cal.Rptr. 388 (1963); People v. Lucas, 155 Cal.App.2d 1, 317 P.2d 104 (1957); and Atchison, T. & S.F.R.R. v. Southern Pac. Co., 13 Cal.App.2d 505, 57 P.2d 575 (1936). Seemingly to the contrary were People v. Lillard, 219 Cal.App.2d 368, 33 Cal.Rptr. 189 (1963), and Buena Park School Dist. v. Metrim Corp., 176 Cal.App.2d 255, 1 Cal.Rptr. 250 (1959). The Supreme Court case of Klopping v. City of Whittier, 8 Cal.3d 39, 500 P.2d 1345, 104 Cal.Rptr. 1 (1972), cited the Lillard and Metrim approach while disapproving the Partridge, Lucas, and Atchison approach in the inverse condemnation context. The Klopping case, however, does not make clear the approach the court would take in a direct condemnation case. See 8 Cal.3d at 45 n. 1, 51 n. 3, 500 P.2d at 1350 n. 1, 1354 n. 3, 104 Cal.Rptr. at 6 n. 1, 10 n. 3; cf. Merced Irr. Dist. v. Woolstenhulme, 4 Cal.3d at 483 n. 1, 483 P.2d at 3 n. 1, 93 Cal.Rptr. at 835 n. 1. Section 1263.330(a) is intended to make the rules respecting appreciation and depreciation parallel by codifying the views expressed in the Lillard and Metrim decisions. See Anderson, Consequences of Anticipated Eminent Domain Proceedings—Is Loss of Value a Factor?, 5 Santa Clara Lawyer 35 (1964).

Subdivision (a) of Section 1263.330 is also intended to codify the proposition that any increase or decrease in value resulting from the use which the condemnor is to make of the property must be eliminated in determining compensable market value. See Merced Irr. Dist. v. Woolstenhulme, 4 Cal.3d at 490–491, 483 P.2d at 12–14, 93 Cal.Rptr. at 841–842. If, however, the condemnor's proposed use is one of the highest and best uses of the property, the adaptability of the property for that purpose may be shown by the property owner. See San Diego Land & Town Co. v. Neale, 78 Cal. 63, 20 P. 372 (1888).

While Section 1263.330(a) provides that changes in value caused by the project for which the property is taken may not be included in the compensation, this exclusionary provision is not intended to apply to value changes that are beyond the scope of the "project." Thus, where changes in value are caused by a project other than the one for which the property is taken, even though the two projects may be related, the property owner may enjoy the benefit or suffer the detriment caused by the other project. See, e.g., People v. Cramer, 14 Cal.App.3d 513, 92 Cal.Rptr. 401 (1971). Likewise, if property is affected by a project but is not to be taken for that project and subsequently the scope of the project is changed or expanded and the property is acquired for the changed or expanded project, the property should be valued as affected by the original project up to the change in scope. See, e.g., People v. Miller, 21 Cal.App.3d 467, 98 Cal.Rptr. 539 (1971), and Merced Irr. Dist. v. Woolstenhulme, supra ("increases in value, attributable to a project but reflecting a reasonable expectation that property will not be taken for the improvement, should properly be considered in determining 'just compensation.'" (4 Cal.3d at 495, 483 P.2d at 12, 93 Cal.Rptr. at 844); cf. United States v. Miller, 317 U.S. 369 (1943), and Annot., 14 A.L.R.Fed. 806 (1973).

Subdivision (b) of Section 1263.330 requires that value changes caused by the fact that the property will be taken by eminent domain must be excluded from fair market value. Changes based on conjecture of a favorable or unfavorable award are not a proper element of compensation. See Merced Irr. Dist. v. Woolstenhulme, 4 Cal.3d at 491–492, 483 P.2d at 9, 93 Cal.Rptr. at 841–842.

Subdivision (c) of Section 1263.330 requires that preliminary actions on the part of the condemnor related to the taking of the property should not be allowed to affect the compensation. See Buena Park School Dist. v. Metrim Corp., *supra.*

Research References

Miller and Starr California Real Estate § 30:13, Measure of Recoverable Damages.

Miller and Starr California Real Estate § 30A:24, Impact of the Project on Property Value.

15 NO. 6 Miller & Starr, California Real Estate Newsalert 10, Eminent Domain.

8 Witkin, California Summary 10th Constitutional Law § 1234, Project Enhancement.

8 Witkin, California Summary 10th Constitutional Law § 1235, Condemnation Blight.

8 Witkin, California Summary 10th Constitutional Law § 1236, (S 1236) Right to Compensation.

ARTICLE 5. COMPENSATION FOR INJURY TO REMAINDER

Section

1263.410.   Mandatory compensation; amount.

1263.420.   Damage to remainder; severance; construction and use of project.

1263.430.   Benefit to remainder; construction and use of project.

1263.440.   Amount as reflecting delay in time of realization of damage or benefit.

1263.450.   Basis on project as proposed; mitigation.

§ 1263.410. Mandatory compensation; amount

(a) Where the property acquired is part of a larger parcel, in addition to the compensation awarded pursuant to Article 4 (commencing with Section 1263.310) for the part taken, compensation shall be awarded for the injury, if any, to the remainder.

(b) Compensation for injury to the remainder is the amount of the damage to the remainder reduced by the amount of the benefit to the remainder. If the amount of the benefit to the remainder equals or exceeds the amount of the damage to the remainder, no compensation shall be awarded under this article. If the amount of the benefit to the remainder exceeds the amount of damage to the remainder, such excess shall be deducted from the compensation provided in Section 1263.510, if any, but shall not be deducted from the compensation required to be awarded for the property taken or from the other compensation required by this chapter. *(Added by Stats.1975, c. 1275, p. 3452, § 2, operative July 1, 1976.)*

Law Revision Commission Comments

Section 1263.410 provides the measure of compensation for injury to the remainder in a partial taking. It supersedes subdivisions 2 and 3 of former Section 1248. The phrase "damage to the remainder" is defined in Section 1263.420; "benefit to the remainder" is defined in Section 1263.430.

It should be noted that the term "larger parcel" is not defined in the Eminent Domain Law, just as it was not defined in the former eminent domain provisions of the Code of Civil Procedure. The legal definition of the larger parcel is in the process of judicial development. See, e.g., City of Los Angeles v. Wolfe, 6 Cal.3d 326, 491 P.2d 813, 99 Cal.Rptr. 21 (1971) (contiguilty not essential). Leaving the larger parcel definition uncodified permits continued judicial development of the concept.

Research References

Rutter, Cal. Practice Guide: Civil Trials & Evidence Ch. 8B-B, B. Particular Types of Evidence.

Miller and Starr California Real Estate § 30A:5, Definitions; Eminent Domain Terminology.

Miller and Starr California Real Estate § 30A:36, Severance Damages in General.

Miller and Starr California Real Estate § 30A:37, Condemnation of Part of a Larger Parcel.

Miller and Starr California Real Estate § 30A:44, Offsetting Benefits of Project.

8 Witkin, California Summary 10th Constitutional Law § 1220, Contesting Right to Take.

8 Witkin, California Summary 10th Constitutional Law § 1236, (S 1236) Right to Compensation.

8 Witkin, California Summary 10th Constitutional Law § 1244, When Offset is Improper.

§ 1263.420. Damage to remainder; severance; construction and use of project

Damage to the remainder is the damage, if any, caused to the remainder by either or both of the following:

(a) The severance of the remainder from the part taken.

(b) The construction and use of the project for which the property is taken in the manner proposed by the plaintiff whether or not the damage is caused by a portion of the project located on the part taken. *(Added by Stats.1975, c. 1275, p. 3452, § 2, operative July 1, 1976.)*

Law Revision Commission Comments

Section 1263.420 continues prior law as to the damage to the remainder compensable in an eminent domain proceeding. See former Section 1248(2). Section 1263.420 does not abrogate any court-developed rules relating to the compensability of specific elements of damage, nor does it impair the ability of the courts to continue to develop the law in this area. See Eachus v. Los Angeles Consol. Elec. Ry., 103 Cal. 614, 37 P. 750 (1894) (damage that causes "mere inconvenience" not compensable); City of Berkeley v. Von Adelung, 214 Cal.App.2d 791, 29 Cal.Rptr. 802 (1963) ("general" damage not compensable); People v. Volunteers of America, 21 Cal.App.3d 111, 98 Cal.Rptr. 423 (1971) (test of compensability is whether the condemnee is obligated to bear more than his "proper share" of the burden of the public improvement).

Prior law was not clear whether damage to the remainder caused by the construction and use of the project were recoverable if the damage-causing portion of the project was not located on the property from which the remainder was severed. Compare People v. Symons, 54 Cal.2d 855, 357 P.2d 451, 9 Cal.Rptr. 363 (1960), with People v. Ramos, 1 Cal.3d 261, 460 P.2d 992, 81 Cal.Rptr. 792 (1969), and People v. Volunteers of America, 21 Cal.App.3d 111, 98 Cal.Rptr. 423 (1971). Subdivision (b) abrogates the rule in Symons by allowing recovery for damages to the remainder caused by the project regardless of the precise location of the damage-causing portion of the project if the damages are otherwise compensable.

It should be noted that the cost to cure may be a proper measure of severance damages in appropriate cases. See discussion in Condemnation Practice in California, Matteoni, Severance Damages § 5.11 (Cal. Cont.Ed.Bar 1973).

Research References

Rutter, Cal. Practice Guide: Civil Trials & Evidence Ch. 8B-B, B. Particular Types of Evidence.
Miller and Starr California Real Estate § 30A:36, Severance Damages in General.
Miller and Starr California Real Estate § 30A:38, Valuing Severance Damage.
Miller and Starr California Real Estate § 30A:41, Valuation of Damage When Project Ongoing.
15 NO. 5 Miller & Starr, California Real Estate Newsalert 11, Inverse Condemnation.
8 Witkin, California Summary 10th Constitutional Law § 1237, in General.
8 Witkin, California Summary 10th Constitutional Law § 1243, When Offset is Proper.

§ 1263.430. Benefit to remainder; construction and use of project

Benefit to the remainder is the benefit, if any, caused by the construction and use of the project for which the property is taken in the manner proposed by the plaintiff whether or not the benefit is caused by a portion of the project located on the part taken. *(Added by Stats.1975, c. 1275, p. 3452, § 2, operative July 1, 1976.)*

Law Revision Commission Comments

Section 1263.430 codifies prior law by defining the benefit to the remainder that may be offset against damage to the remainder in an eminent domain proceeding. See former Section 1248(3). Section 1263.430 does not abrogate any court-developed rules relating to the offset of benefits nor does it impair the ability of the courts to continue to develop the law in this area. See Beveridge v. Lewis, 137 Cal. 619, 70 P. 1083 (1902) (only "special" benefits may be offset); People v. Giumarra Farms, Inc., 22 Cal.App.3d 98, 99 Cal.Rptr. 272 (1971) (increased, traffic a special benefit); but see People v. Ayon, 54 Cal.2d 217, 352 P.2d 519, 5 Cal.Rptr. 151 (1960) (increased or decreased traffic not a proper item of damage).

As with damage to the remainder (Section 1263.420 and Comment thereto), benefits created by the construction and use of the project need not be derived from the portion of the project located on property from which the remainder was severed. This continues existing law. See People v. Hurd, 205 Cal.App.2d 16, 23 Cal.Rptr. 67 (1962).

Research References

Miller and Starr California Real Estate § 30:13, Measure of Recoverable Damages.
Miller and Starr California Real Estate § 30A:44, Offsetting Benefits of Project.
8 Witkin, California Summary 10th Constitutional Law § 1243, When Offset is Proper.

§ 1263.440. Amount as reflecting delay in time of realization of damage or benefit

(a) The amount of any damage to the remainder and any benefit to the remainder shall reflect any delay in the time when the damage or benefit caused by the construction and use of the project in the manner proposed by the plaintiff will actually be realized.

(b) The value of the remainder on the date of valuation, excluding prior changes in value as prescribed in Section 1263.330, shall serve as the base from which the amount of any damage and the amount of any benefit to the remainder shall be determined. *(Added by Stats.1975, c. 1275, p. 3452, § 2, operative July 1, 1976.)*

Law Revision Commission Comments

Section 1263.440 embodies two rules for computing the damage and benefit to the remainder that represent departures from prior law. It has been held that damage and benefit must be based on the assumption that the improvement is completed. See, e.g., People v. Schultz Co., 123 Cal.App.2d 925, 268 P.2d 117 (1954). Subdivision (a) alters this rule and requires that compensation for damage to the remainder (and the amount of benefit offset) be computed in a manner that will take into account any delay in the accrual of the damage and benefit under the project as proposed. If there is a subsequent change in plans so that the damage and benefit do not occur as the plaintiff proposed, the property owner may recover any additional damage in a subsequent action. See People v. Adamson, 118 Cal.App.2d 714, 722, 258 P.2d 1020, 1025 (1953).

Whether changes in the value of the remainder caused by imminence of the project prior to the date of valuation should be included in the computation of damage and benefit to the remainder was unclear under prior law. Subdivision (b) adopts the position that it is the value of the remainder in the before condition, unaffected by any enhancement or blight, that is to be used as a basis in computing damages and benefits that will be caused by the project. See Section 1263.330 and the Comment thereto.

Research References

Miller and Starr California Real Estate § 30A:38, Valuing Severance Damage.
Miller and Starr California Real Estate § 30A:41, Valuation of Damage When Project Ongoing.
Miller and Starr California Real Estate § 30A:44, Offsetting Benefits of Project.
8 Witkin, California Summary 10th Constitutional Law § 1236, (S 1236) Right to Compensation.

§ 1263.450. Basis on project as proposed; mitigation

Compensation for injury to the remainder shall be based on the project as proposed. Any features of the project which mitigate the damage or provide benefit to the remainder, including but not limited to easements, crossings, underpasses, access roads, fencing, drainage facilities, and cattle guards, shall be taken into account in determining the compensation for injury to the remainder. *(Added by Stats.1975, c. 1275, p. 3452, § 2, operative July 1, 1976.)*

Civ. Pro.

Section 1263.450 makes clear that any "physical solutions" provided by the plaintiff to mitigate damages are to be considered in the assessment of damages.

Section 1263.450 supersedes former Section 1248(5), relating to the cost of fencing, cattle guards, and crossings. The cost of fencing, cattle guards, and crossings is an element of damage only if lack of fencing, cattle guards, or crossings would damage the remainder; if the fencing, cattle guards, or crossings are to be supplied by the plaintiff as part of its project as designed, this fact should be taken into consideration in determining the damage, if any, to the remainder. *Cf.* former Section 1251 (plaintiff may elect to build fencing, cattle guards, and crossings in lieu of payment of damages).

If the plaintiff has no specific proposal for the manner of construction and use of the project, damages will be assessed on the basis of the most injurious lawful use reasonably possible. People v. Schultz Co., 123 Cal.App.2d 925, 268 P.2d 117 (1954).

Research References

Miller and Starr California Real Estate § 30A:5, Definitions; Eminent Domain Terminology.
Miller and Starr California Real Estate § 30A:41, Valuation of Damage When Project Ongoing.
8 Witkin, California Summary 10th Constitutional Law § 1190, (S 1190) to Provide Utility Service or Access to Road.
8 Witkin, California Summary 10th Constitutional Law § 1236, (S 1236) Right to Compensation.

ARTICLE 6. COMPENSATION FOR LOSS OF GOODWILL

Section
1263.510. Mandatory compensation; proof required; lease-back agreement.
1263.520. State tax returns; availability; confidentiality.
1263.530. Inverse condemnation.

§ 1263.510. Mandatory compensation; proof required; lease-back agreement

(a) The owner of a business conducted on the property taken, or on the remainder if the property is part of a larger parcel, shall be compensated for loss of goodwill if the owner proves all of the following:

(1) The loss is caused by the taking of the property or the injury to the remainder.

(2) The loss cannot reasonably be prevented by a relocation of the business or by taking steps and adopting procedures that a reasonably prudent person would take and adopt in preserving the goodwill.

(3) Compensation for the loss will not be included in payments under Section 7262 of the Government Code.

(4) Compensation for the loss will not be duplicated in the compensation otherwise awarded to the owner.

(b) Within the meaning of this article, "goodwill" consists of the benefits that accrue to a business as a result of its location, reputation for dependability, skill or quality, and any other circumstances resulting in probable retention of old or acquisition of new patronage.

(c) If the public entity and the owner enter into a leaseback agreement pursuant to Section 1263.615, the following shall apply:

(1) No additional goodwill shall accrue during the lease.

(2) The entering of a leaseback agreement shall not be a factor in determining goodwill. Any liability for goodwill shall be established and paid at the time of acquisition of the property by eminent domain or subsequent to notice that the property may be taken by eminent domain. *(Added by Stats.1975, c. 1275,*

p. 3453, § 2, operative July 1, 1976. Amended by Stats.2006, c. 602 (S.B.1650), § 2.)

Section 1263.510, which is the same in substance as Section 1016 of the Uniform Eminent Domain Code, is new to California eminent domain law. Under prior court decisions, compensation for business losses in eminent domain was not allowed. See, e.g., City of Oakland v. Pacific Coast Lumber & Mill Co., 171 Cal. 392, 153 P. 705 (1915); but see Community Redevelopment Agency v. Abrams, (hearing granted by Supreme Court 1974). Section 1263.510 provides compensation for loss of goodwill in both a whole or a partial taking. Goodwill loss is recoverable under Section 1263.510 only to the extent it cannot reasonably be prevented by relocation or other efforts by the owner to mitigate.

The determination of loss of goodwill is governed by the rules of evidence generally applicable to such a determination and not by the special rules relating to valuation in eminent domain contained in Article 2 (commencing with Section 810) of Chapter 1 of Division 7 of the Evidence Code. See Evid.Code § 811 and Comment thereto. Thus, the provisions of Evidence Code Sections 817 and 819 that restrict admissibility of income from a business for the determination of value, damage, and benefit in no way limit admissibility of income from a business for the determination of loss of goodwill. Notwithstanding Section 1260.210, the burden of proof is on the property owner under this section.

Section 1263.510 compensates for goodwill loss only to the extent such loss is not compensated by Government Code Section 7262 (moving expense and moving losses for relocated business or farm operations; in lieu payments for business or farm operation that cannot be relocated without a substantial loss of patronage). See also Sections 1263.010 (no double recovery), 1263.410 (offset against benefits to remainder).

Research References

Rutter, Cal. Practice Guide: Civil Trials & Evidence Ch. 8C-H, H. Opinion Evidence.
Rutter, Cal. Practice Guide: Real Prop. Transactions Ch. 7-C, C. Representing the Purchasing Tenant.
Miller and Starr California Real Estate § 30:1, Basis for Inverse Condemnation.
Miller and Starr California Real Estate § 30:3, Temporary Use, Occupation, or Interference.
Miller and Starr California Real Estate § 30:13, Measure of Recoverable Damages.
Miller and Starr California Real Estate § 30A:5, Definitions; Eminent Domain Terminology.
Miller and Starr California Real Estate § 19:148, Termination of the Lease Upon Condemnation.
Miller and Starr California Real Estate § 19:152, Tenant's Goodwill.
Miller and Starr California Real Estate § 30A:20, Relocation Assistance.
Miller and Starr California Real Estate § 30A:45, Entitlement to Compensation for Lost Business Goodwill.
Miller and Starr California Real Estate § 30A:46, Valuation of Goodwill Loss.
Miller and Starr California Real Estate § 30A:56, Property Owner's Leaseback Rights.
Miller and Starr California Real Estate § 30A:58, Answer.
15 NO. 3 Miller & Starr, California Real Estate Newsalert 10, Inverse Condemnation.
16 NO. 5 Miller & Starr, California Real Estate Newsalert 10, Eminent Domain.
17 NO. 4 Miller & Starr, California Real Estate Newsalert 1, Redevelopment Redefined: State Legislative Responses to the Kelo Decision.
17 NO. 4 Miller & Starr, California Real Estate Newsalert 2, Statutory Update:.
17 NO. 6 Miller & Starr, California Real Estate Newsalert 20, Table of Statutes (Newsalert Vol 17).
18 NO. 2 Miller & Starr, California Real Estate Newsalert 14, Eminent Domain.
19 NO. 4 Miller & Starr, California Real Estate Newsalert 37, Eminent Domain.
20 NO. 1 Miller & Starr, California Real Estate Newsalert 11, Eminent Domain.
20 NO. 3 Miller & Starr, California Real Estate Newsalert 13, Eminent Domain.
22 NO. 1 Miller & Starr, California Real Estate Newsalert 15, Eminent Domain.

5 Witkin Cal. Proc. 5th Pleading § 1115, (S 1115) Answer in Condemnation Action.

8 Witkin, California Summary 10th Constitutional Law § 1145, Recovery for Loss of Goodwill.

8 Witkin, California Summary 10th Constitutional Law § 1206, Pleading.

8 Witkin, California Summary 10th Constitutional Law § 1220, Contesting Right to Take.

8 Witkin, California Summary 10th Constitutional Law § 1223, Right to Compensation.

8 Witkin, California Summary 10th Constitutional Law § 1244, When Offset is Improper.

8 Witkin, California Summary 10th Constitutional Law § 1245, (S 1245) in General.

8 Witkin, California Summary 10th Constitutional Law § 1246, (S 1246) Valuation and Proof of Loss.

§ 1263.520. State tax returns; availability; confidentiality

The owner of a business who claims compensation under this article shall make available to the court, and the court shall, upon such terms and conditions as will preserve their confidentiality, make available to the plaintiff, the state tax returns of the business for audit for confidential use solely for the purpose of determining the amount of compensation under this article. Nothing in this section affects any right a party may otherwise have to discovery or to require the production of documents, papers, books, and accounts. (*Added by Stats.1975, c. 1275, p. 3453, § 2, operative July 1, 1976.*)

Research References

Miller and Starr California Real Estate § 19:152, Tenant's Goodwill.

Miller and Starr California Real Estate § 30A:62, Special Discovery Rules for Goodwill Claims.

8 Witkin, California Summary 10th Constitutional Law § 1246, (S 1246) Valuation and Proof of Loss.

§ 1263.530. Inverse condemnation

Nothing in this article is intended to deal with compensation for inverse condemnation claims for temporary interference with or interruption of business. (*Added by Stats.1975, c. 1275, p. 3453, § 2, operative July 1, 1976.*)

Research References

Miller and Starr California Real Estate § 30A:46, Valuation of Goodwill Loss.

8 Witkin, California Summary 10th Constitutional Law § 1245, (S 1245) in General.

ARTICLE 7. MISCELLANEOUS PROVISIONS

Section
1263.610. Agreement by plaintiff to relocate structure or work on property not taken; reduction in compensation otherwise payable.
1263.615. Leaseback agreement; conditions; renewal of leaseback agreement.
1263.620. Cessation of construction or installation upon service of summons; compensation of owner.

§ 1263.610. Agreement by plaintiff to relocate structure or work on property not taken; reduction in compensation otherwise payable

A public entity and the owner of property to be acquired for public use may make an agreement that the public entity will:

(a) Relocate for the owner any structure if such relocation is likely to reduce the amount of compensation otherwise payable to the owner by an amount equal to or greater than the cost of such relocation.

(b) Carry out for the owner any work on property not taken, including work on any structure, if the performance of the work is likely to reduce the amount of compensation otherwise payable to the owner by an amount equal to or greater than the cost of the work. (*Added by Stats.1975, c. 1275, p. 3453, § 2, operative July 1, 1976.*)

Law Revision Commission Comments

Section 1263.610 generalizes former Section 970 of the Streets and Highways Code, which related to certain types of work in connection with an acquisition for opening or widening a county highway. As to the authority of the Department of Transportation to contract for relocation of structures outside the State Contract Act (Govt.Code §§ 14250–14424), see Sts. & Hwys.Code §§ 135 and 136.5.

The phrase "any work" is used without qualification so as to have the broadest possible meaning. It would include any physical or structural operation whatsoever. Thus, it would cover such things as screening off roads or canals or sound-proofing buildings adjacent to highways as well as constructing rights of way, fences, driveways, sidewalks, retaining walls, and drainage or utility connections, all of which latter operations were specifically listed in former Section 970.

Nothing in Section 1263.610 precludes the public entity from including features in the design of the public project that will have the effect of mitigating damages. See Section 1263.450.

Research References

8 Witkin, California Summary 10th Constitutional Law § 1248, Mitigation Work by Condemnor.

§ 1263.615. Leaseback agreement; conditions; renewal of leaseback agreement

(a) A public entity shall offer a one-year leaseback agreement to the owner of a property to be acquired by any method set forth in subdivision (b) for that property owner's continued use of the property upon acquisition, subject to the property owner's payment of fair market rents and compliance with other conditions set forth in subdivision (c), unless the public entity states in writing that the development, redevelopment, or use of the property for its stated public use is scheduled to begin within two years of its acquisition. This section shall not apply if the public entity states in writing that a leaseback of the property would create or allow the continuation of a public nuisance to the surrounding community.

(b) The following property acquisitions are subject to the requirements of this section:

(1) Any acquisition by a public entity pursuant to eminent domain.

(2) Any acquisition by a public entity following adoption of a resolution of necessity pursuant to Article 2 (commencing with Section 1245.210) of Chapter 4 for the property.

(3) Any acquisition by a public entity prior to the adoption of a resolution of necessity pursuant to Article 2 (commencing with Section 1245.210) of Chapter 4 for the property, but subsequent to a written notice that the public entity may take the property by eminent domain.

(c) The following conditions shall apply to any leaseback offered pursuant to this section:

(1) The lessee shall be responsible for any additional waste or nuisance on the property, and for any other liability arising from the continued use of the property.

(2) The lessor may demand a security deposit to cover any potential liability arising from the leaseback. The security deposit shall be reasonable in light of the use of the leased property.

(3) The lessor shall be indemnified from any legal liability and attorney's fees resulting from any lawsuit against the lessee or lessor, arising from the operation of the lessee's business or use of the property.

(4) The lessor shall require the lessee to carry adequate insurance to cover potential liabilities arising from the lease and

use of the property, and shall require that insurance to name the lessor as an additional insured.

(5) Additional goodwill shall not accrue during any lease.

(6) The lessee shall be subject to unlawful detainer proceedings as provided by law.

(d) A public entity shall offer to renew a leaseback agreement for one-year terms, subject to any rent adjustment to reflect inflation and upon compliance with other conditions set forth in subdivision (c), unless the public entity states in writing that the development, redevelopment, or use of the property for its stated public use is scheduled to begin within two years of the termination date of the lease. At least 60 days prior to the lease termination date, the public entity lessor shall either offer a one-year renewal of the lease or send a statement declaring that the lease will not be renewed because the development, redevelopment, or use of the property is scheduled to begin within two years of the lease termination date. The lessee shall either accept or reject a lease renewal offer at least 30 days prior to the lease termination date. The lessee's failure to accept a renewal offer in a timely manner shall constitute a rejection of the renewal offer. A lessor's failure to offer a renewal or give the notice as required shall extend the lease term for 60–day increments until an offer or notice is made, and if a notice of termination is given after the lease termination date, the lessee shall have no less than 60 days to vacate the property. A lessee's failure to accept within 30 days a renewal offer made subsequent to the lease termination date shall constitute a rejection of the offer.

(e) A party who holds over after expiration of the lease shall be subject to unlawful detainer proceedings and shall also be subject to the lessor for holdover damages.

(f) A leaseback entered into pursuant to this section shall not affect the amount of compensation otherwise payable to the property owner for the property to be acquired. *(Added by Stats.2006, c. 602 (S.B.1650), § 3.)*

Research References

Miller and Starr California Real Estate § 19:148, Termination of the Lease Upon Condemnation.
Miller and Starr California Real Estate § 30A:18, Precondemnation Appraisal and Offer.
Miller and Starr California Real Estate § 30A:33, Leaseholds--Apportionment Between Landlord and Tenant.
Miller and Starr California Real Estate § 30A:56, Property Owner's Leaseback Rights.
17 NO. 4 Miller & Starr, California Real Estate Newsalert 1, Redevelopment Redefined: State Legislative Responses to the Kelo Decision.
17 NO. 4 Miller & Starr, California Real Estate Newsalert 2, Statutory Update:.
17 NO. 6 Miller & Starr, California Real Estate Newsalert 20, Table of Statutes (Newsalert Vol 17).
8 Witkin, California Summary 10th Constitutional Law § 1218A, (S 1218A) (New)-Owner's Right to Leaseback.

§ 1263.620. Cessation of construction or installation upon service of summons; compensation of owner

(a) Where summons is served during construction of an improvement or installation of machinery or equipment on the property taken or on the remainder if such property is part of a larger parcel, and the owner of the property ceases the construction or installation due to such service, the owner shall be compensated for his expenses reasonably incurred for work necessary for either of the following purposes:

(1) To protect against the risk of injury to persons or to other property created by the uncompleted improvement.

(2) To protect the partially installed machinery or equipment from damage, deterioration, or vandalism.

(b) The compensation provided in this section is recoverable only if the work was preceded by notice to the plaintiff except in the case of an emergency. The plaintiff may agree with the owner (1) that the plaintiff will perform work necessary for the purposes of this section or (2) as to the amount of compensation payable under this section. *(Added by Stats.1975, c. 1275, p. 3453, § 2, operative July 1, 1976.)*

Law Revision Commission Comments

Section 1263.620 provides compensation for expenses "reasonably incurred" for work necessary to protect the public or partially installed machinery or equipment from injury. It is available only if the work is preceded by notice to the plaintiff unless emergency conditions preclude prior notice. Should the plaintiff, upon receipt of notice, object to the necessity or reasonableness of the expenses to be incurred, this fact should be taken into consideration by the court in determining the amount of compensation to be awarded under this section. On the other hand, the failure of the plaintiff to object does not prejudice its right subsequently to show that the work was not necessary or that the expense was not reasonable.

The amount, if any, by which the work performed enhances the value of the property is not the measure of value and is not considered in determining compensation under Section 1263.620. If compensation is sought on the basis of the enhanced value of the property, the improvement must be one that may be taken into account under Section 1263.240.

Research References

8 Witkin, California Summary 10th Constitutional Law § 1227, (S 1227) Improvements Made After Summons is Served.
8 Witkin, California Summary 10th Constitutional Law § 1249, Protective Work by Owner.

ARTICLE 8. REMEDIATION OF HAZARDOUS MATERIALS ON PROPERTY TO BE ACQUIRED BY SCHOOL DISTRICTS

Section

§ 1263.710. Definitions

(a) As used in this article, "remedial action" and "removal" shall have the meanings accorded to those terms in Sections 25322 and 25323, respectively, of the Health and Safety Code.

(b) As used in this article, "required action" means any removal or other remedial action with regard to hazardous materials that is necessary to comply with any requirement of federal, state, or local law. *(Added by Stats.1995, c. 247 (S.B.231), § 2.)*

Research References

Miller and Starr California Real Estate § 30A:52, Hazardous Substances on Property Being Acquired by School Districts.

§ 1263.711. "Hazardous material"

As used in this article, "hazardous material" shall have the same meaning as that term is defined in Section 25260 of the Health and Safety Code, except that under no circumstances shall petroleum which is naturally occurring on a site be considered a hazardous material. *(Added by Stats.1995, c. 247 (S.B.231), § 2.)*

Research References

Miller and Starr California Real Estate § 30A:52, Hazardous Substances on Property Being Acquired by School Districts.

§ 1263.720. Hearings; actions of court; trustees; costs

(a) Upon petition of any party to the proceeding, the court in which the proceeding is brought shall specially set for hearing the issue of whether any hazardous material is present within the property to be taken.

(b) If the court determines that any hazardous material is present within the property to be taken, the court shall do all of the following:

(1) Identify those measures constituting the required action with regard to the hazardous material, the probable cost of the required action, and the party that shall be designated by the court to cause the required action to be performed.

(2) Designate a trustee to monitor the completion of the required action and to hold funds, deducted from amounts that are otherwise to be paid to the defendant pursuant to this title, to defray the probable cost of the required action.

(3) Transfer to the trustee funds necessary to defray the probable cost of the required action from amounts deposited with the court pursuant to Article 1 (commencing with Section 1255.010) of Chapter 6 or pursuant to Section 1268.110. In the case of any payment to be made directly to the defendant pursuant to Section 1268.010, the plaintiff shall first pay to the trustee the amount necessary to defray the probable cost of the required action, as identified by the court, and shall pay the remainder of the judgment to the defendant. The total amount transferred or paid to the trustee pursuant to this paragraph shall not exceed an amount equal to 75 percent of the following, as applicable:

(A) Prior to entry of judgment, the amount deposited as the probable amount of compensation pursuant to Article 1 (commencing with Section 1255.010) of Chapter 6.

(B) Subsequent to entry of judgment, the fair market value of the property taken, as determined pursuant to Article 4 (commencing with Section 1263.310). If the amount determined as fair market value pursuant to that article exceeds the amount deposited pursuant to Article 1 (commencing with Section 1255.010) of Chapter 6, that excess shall be available, subject to the 75 percent limit set forth in this paragraph, for transfer to the trustee for the purposes of this paragraph or for reimbursement of the plaintiff for payments made to the trustee pursuant to this paragraph. If the amount determined as fair market value pursuant to Article 4 (commencing with Section 1263.310) is less than the amount deposited pursuant to Article 1 (commencing with Section 1255.010) of Chapter 6, the plaintiff shall be entitled to a return of amounts thereby deposited, a judgment against the defendant, or both, as necessary to ensure that the total amount transferred or paid to the trustee pursuant to this paragraph not exceed an amount equal to 75 percent of the fair market value of the property taken, as determined pursuant to Article 4 (commencing with Section 1263.310).

(4) Establish a procedure by which the trustee shall make one or more payments from the funds it receives pursuant to paragraph (3) to the party causing the required action to be performed, upon completion of all or specified portions of the required action. Any amount of those funds that remains following the completion of all of the required action shall be applied in accordance with the provisions of this title that govern the disposition of the deposit amounts referred to in paragraph (3).

(c) The actual and reasonable costs of the trustee incurred pursuant to this section shall be paid by the plaintiff. *(Added by Stats.1995, c. 247 (S.B.231), § 2.)*

Research References

Miller and Starr California Real Estate § 30A:27, Valuing Contaminated Property.

Miller and Starr California Real Estate § 30A:52, Hazardous Substances on Property Being Acquired by School Districts.

§ 1263.730. Funds available to trustee; additional costs

Where the required action is caused to be performed by the plaintiff, and the amount available to the trustee under this article is insufficient to meet the actual cost incurred by the plaintiff to complete the required action, the plaintiff may either apply to the court for a new hearing regarding identification of the probable cost, or complete the required action at its own expense and bring an action against the defendant to recover the additional costs. *(Added by Stats.1995, c. 247 (S.B.231), § 2.)*

Research References

Miller and Starr California Real Estate § 30A:52, Hazardous Substances on Property Being Acquired by School Districts.

§ 1263.740. Appraisal of property

The presence of any hazardous material within a property shall not be considered in appraising the property, for purposes of Section 1263.720, pursuant to Article 1 (commencing with Section 1255.010) of Chapter 6, or pursuant to Article 4 (commencing with Section 1263.310). *(Added by Stats.1995, c. 247 (S.B.231), § 2.)*

Research References

Miller and Starr California Real Estate § 30A:27, Valuing Contaminated Property.

§ 1263.750. Other remedies; abandonment of proceeding; compensation for benefit; liens

(a) Notwithstanding any action taken pursuant to this article, the plaintiff shall have available all remedies in law that are available to a purchaser of real property with respect to any cost, loss, or liability for which the plaintiff is not reimbursed under this article.

(b) If the plaintiff abandons the proceeding at any time, the plaintiff shall be entitled to compensation for the benefit, if any, conferred on the property by reason of the remedial action performed pursuant to this article. That benefit shall be applied as an offset to the amount of any entitlement to damages on the part of the defendant pursuant to Section 1268.620 or, if it exceeds the amount of those damages, shall constitute a lien upon the property, to the extent of that excess, when recorded with the county recorder in the county in which the real property is located. The lien shall contain the legal description of the real property, the assessor's parcel number, and the name of the owner of record as shown on the latest equalized assessment roll. The lien shall be enforceable upon the transfer or sale of the property, and the priority of the lien shall be as of the date of recording. In determining the amount of the benefit, if any, neither party shall have the burden of proof.

For the purposes of this subdivision, "benefit" means the extent to which the remedial action has enhanced the fair market value of the property. *(Added by Stats.1995, c. 247 (S.B.231), § 2.)*

Research References

Miller and Starr California Real Estate § 30A:52, Hazardous Substances on Property Being Acquired by School Districts.

§ 1263.760. Offer by plaintiff to purchase property

An offer by the plaintiff to purchase the property subject to this article shall be deemed to satisfy the requirements of Section

7267.2 of the Government Code. *(Added by Stats.1995, c. 247 (S.B.231), § 2.)*

§ 1263.770. Application of article

This article shall only apply to the acquisition of property by school districts. *(Added by Stats.1995, c. 247 (S.B.231), § 2.)*

Research References

Miller and Starr California Real Estate § 30A:27, Valuing Contaminated Property.

CHAPTER 10. DIVIDED INTERESTS

ARTICLE 1. GENERAL PROVISIONS

§ 1265.010. Compensation for particular interests; other interests not affected

Although this chapter provides rules governing compensation for particular interests in property, it does not otherwise limit or affect the right to compensation for any other interest in property. *(Added by Stats.1975, c. 1275, p. 3454, § 2, operative July 1, 1976.)*

ARTICLE 2. LEASES

§ 1265.110. Termination; all of leased property acquired

Where all the property subject to a lease is acquired for public use, the lease terminates. *(Added by Stats.1975, c. 1275, p. 3454, § 2, operative July 1, 1976.)*

Law Revision Commission Comments

Section 1265.110 codifies the rule that the taking of the entire demised premises for public use by eminent domain or agreement operates to release the tenant from liability for subsequently accruing rent. See City of Pasadena v. Porter, 201 Cal. 381, 387, 257 P. 526, 528 (1927); Carlstrom v. Lyon Van & Storage Co., 152 Cal.App.2d 625, 313 P.2d 645 (1957). This section does not affect the right of a lessee, if any, to compensation for the impairment of his leasehold interest. See Section 1265.150. Nor does this section apply where there is a valid provision to the contrary in the lease. See Section 1265.160.

Research References

California Real Estate Forms (Miller & Starr) § 2:21, Retail Lease--15,000 RSF to 30,000 RSF (Tenant Oriented).
Rutter, Cal. Practice Guide: Real Prop. Transactions Ch. 7-C, C. Representing the Purchasing Tenant.

Miller and Starr California Real Estate § 19:148, Termination of the Lease Upon Condemnation.
Miller and Starr California Real Estate § 30A:33, Leaseholds--Apportionment Between Landlord and Tenant.
8 Witkin, California Summary 10th Constitutional Law § 1143, Nature of Action.
8 Witkin, California Summary 10th Constitutional Law § 1250, Leases.

§ 1265.120. Partial termination; part of leased property acquired; rent

Except as provided in Section 1265.130, where part of the property subject to a lease is acquired for public use, the lease terminates as to the part taken and remains in force as to the remainder, and the rent reserved in the lease that is allocable to the part taken is extinguished. *(Added by Stats.1975, c. 1275, p. 3454, § 2, operative July 1, 1976.)*

Law Revision Commission Comments

Section 1265.120 abrogates the rule in City of Pasadena v. Porter, 201 Cal. 381, 257 P. 526 (1927), and numerous cases following it that required continuation of the lessee's full rental obligation for the duration of the lease in cases of a partial taking of property subject to a lease. Section 1265.120 requires a pro rata abatement of the rental obligation. For a comparable provision, see W.Va.Code § 37-6-29 (1966). The requirements of Section 1265.120 do not apply where there is a valid provision to the contrary in the lease. See Section 1265.160. Nor does this section affect the right of a lessee, if any, to compensation for the impairment of his leasehold interest. See Section 1265.150.

Research References

California Real Estate Forms (Miller & Starr) § 2:17, Office Lease--Mixed Use Building.
Rutter, Cal. Practice Guide: Real Prop. Transactions Ch. 7-C, C. Representing the Purchasing Tenant.
Miller and Starr California Real Estate § 19:148, Termination of the Lease Upon Condemnation.
Miller and Starr California Real Estate § 30A:33, Leaseholds--Apportionment Between Landlord and Tenant.
12 Witkin, California Summary 10th Real Property § 656, Condemnation.
8 Witkin, California Summary 10th Constitutional Law § 1250, Leases.

§ 1265.130. Termination; court order; essential part of property taken or remainder not suitable for purposes of lease

Where part of the property subject to a lease is acquired for public use, the court may, upon petition of any party to the lease, terminate the lease if the court determines that an essential part of the property subject to the lease is taken or that the remainder of the property subject to the lease is no longer suitable for the purposes of the lease. *(Added by Stats.1975, c. 1275, p. 3454, § 2, operative July 1, 1976.)*

Law Revision Commission Comments

Section 1265.130 is new to California law. It provides for termination of a lease in a partial taking case where the taking in effect destroys the value or utility of the lease for either of the parties. Section 1265.130 is not applicable in cases where there is a valid provision in the lease covering the situation. See Section 1265.160.

Research References

California Real Estate Forms (Miller & Starr) § 2:17, Office Lease--Mixed Use Building.
California Real Estate Forms (Miller & Starr) § 2:19, Retail Lease--Power Shopping Center.
California Real Estate Forms (Miller & Starr) § 2:22, Retail Lease--Regional Shopping Center.
Rutter, Cal. Practice Guide: Landlord-Tenant Form 2:C, Office Lease.
Rutter, Cal. Practice Guide: Real Prop. Transactions Ch. 7-C, C. Representing the Purchasing Tenant.
Miller and Starr California Real Estate § 19:148, Termination of the Lease Upon Condemnation.

Miller and Starr California Real Estate § 30A:33, Leaseholds--Apportionment Between Landlord and Tenant.

12 Witkin, California Summary 10th Real Property § 656, Condemnation.

8 Witkin, California Summary 10th Constitutional Law § 1250, Leases.

§ 1265.140. Time of termination

The termination or partial termination of a lease pursuant to this article shall be at the earlier of the following times:

(a) The time title to the property is taken by the person who will put it to the public use.

(b) The time the plaintiff is authorized to take possession of the property as stated in an order for possession. *(Added by Stats.1975, c. 1275, p. 3454, § 2, operative July 1, 1976.)*

Law Revision Commission Comments

Section 1265.140 makes clear the time of partial termination (Section 1265.120) or termination (Sections 1265.110 and 1265.130) of a lease.

Research References

Rutter, Cal. Practice Guide: Real Prop. Transactions Ch. 7-C, C. Representing the Purchasing Tenant.

Miller and Starr California Real Estate § 19:148, Termination of the Lease Upon Condemnation.

Miller and Starr California Real Estate § 30A:33, Leaseholds--Apportionment Between Landlord and Tenant.

8 Witkin, California Summary 10th Constitutional Law § 1250, Leases.

§ 1265.150. Rights of lessee

Nothing in this article affects or impairs any right a lessee may have to compensation for the taking of his lease in whole or in part or for the taking of any other property in which he has an interest. *(Added by Stats.1975, c. 1275, p. 3454, § 2, operative July 1, 1976.)*

Law Revision Commission Comments

Section 1265.150 is added to assure that partial termination or termination of a lease pursuant to this article does not preclude a lessee's recovery of compensation for the value of his leasehold interest, if any, and any of his property taken in the eminent domain proceeding. See Sections 1263.010 (right of owner of property to compensation), 1263.210 (improvements pertaining to realty), and 1263.510 (compensation for loss of goodwill); *cf.* Section 1265.220 (procedure where there are divided interests).

Research References

Rutter, Cal. Practice Guide: Real Prop. Transactions Ch. 7-C, C. Representing the Purchasing Tenant.

Miller and Starr California Real Estate § 19:148, Termination of the Lease Upon Condemnation.

Miller and Starr California Real Estate § 30A:33, Leaseholds--Apportionment Between Landlord and Tenant.

16 NO. 5 Miller & Starr, California Real Estate Newsalert 10, Eminent Domain.

8 Witkin, California Summary 10th Constitutional Law § 1250, Leases.

§ 1265.160. Rights and obligations of parties to lease

Nothing in this article affects or impairs the rights and obligations of the parties to a lease to the extent that the lease provides for such rights and obligations in the event of the acquisition of all or a portion of the property for public use. *(Added by Stats.1975, c. 1275, p. 3455, § 2, operative July 1, 1976.)*

Law Revision Commission Comments

While this article provides rules that govern the rights of parties to a lease of property taken by eminent domain, Section 1265.160 makes clear that these rules apply only absent a valid provision in the lease covering the situation.

Research References

Rutter, Cal. Practice Guide: Real Prop. Transactions Ch. 7-C, C. Representing the Purchasing Tenant.

Miller and Starr California Real Estate § 19:148, Termination of the Lease Upon Condemnation.

Miller and Starr California Real Estate § 30A:33, Leaseholds--Apportionment Between Landlord and Tenant.

8 Witkin, California Summary 10th Constitutional Law § 1250, Leases.

ARTICLE 3. ENCUMBRANCES

Section

1265.210. Lien.

1265.220. Indebtedness not yet due.

1265.225. Partial taking of encumbered property; lienholder share in award; agreement.

1265.230. Senior and junior liens; allocation.

1265.240. Penalty for prepayment.

1265.250. Eminent domain; fixed lien special assessments; special annual assessments.

§ 1265.210. Lien

As used in this article, "lien" means a mortgage, deed of trust, or other security interest in property whether arising from contract, statute, common law, or equity. *(Added by Stats.1975, c. 1275, p. 3455, § 2, operative July 1, 1976.)*

Law Revision Commission Comments

The definition of "lien" provided in Section 1265.210 is new. It is intended to include security interests of all types, not merely types similar to the specifically mentioned mortgage and deed of trust. As used in this article, the definition of "lien" thus may expand the coverage of former Sections 1248(8), 1248(9), and 1246.2, which are continued as Sections 1265.220–1265.240. The former provisions may have been limited to a mortgage, deed of trust, contract of sale, and liens similar thereto.

Research References

Miller and Starr California Real Estate § 30A:34, Deeds of Trust, Taxes and Other Monetary Liens.

4 Witkin, California Summary 10th Security Transactions in Real Property § 81, Right to Condemnation Award.

8 Witkin, California Summary 10th Constitutional Law § 1251, Encumbrances.

§ 1265.220. Indebtedness not yet due

Where property acquired by eminent domain is encumbered by a lien and the indebtedness secured thereby is not due at the time of the entry of judgment, the amount of such indebtedness may be, at the option of the plaintiff, deducted from the judgment and the lien shall be continued until such indebtedness is paid; but the amount for which, as between the plaintiff and the defendant, the plaintiff is liable under Article 5 (commencing with Section 1268.410) of Chapter 11 may not be deducted from the judgment. *(Added by Stats.1975, c. 1275, p. 3455, § 2, operative July 1, 1976.)*

Law Revision Commission Comments

Section 1265.220 is the same in substance as former Section 1248(8). But see the Comment to Section 1265.210 (defining "lien").

Research References

Miller and Starr California Real Estate § 10:69, Condemnation of the Property Security.

Miller and Starr California Real Estate § 11:179, Priorities Among State and Local Tax and Assessment Liens--Effect of Acquisition of Property by a Public Entity.

Miller and Starr California Real Estate § 30A:34, Deeds of Trust, Taxes and Other Monetary Liens.

4 Witkin, California Summary 10th Security Transactions in Real Property § 81, Right to Condemnation Award.

8 Witkin, California Summary 10th Constitutional Law § 1251, Encumbrances.

Civ. Pro.

8 Witkin, California Summary 10th Constitutional Law § 1263, Special Assessment Liens.

§ 1265.225. Partial taking of encumbered property; lienholder share in award; agreement

(a) Where there is a partial taking of property encumbered by a lien, the lienholder may share in the award only to the extent determined by the court to be necessary to prevent an impairment of the security, and the lien shall continue upon the part of the property not taken as security for the unpaid portion of the indebtedness.

(b) Notwithstanding subdivision (a), the lienholder and the property owner may at any time after commencement of the proceeding agree that some or all of the award shall be apportioned to the lienholder on the indebtedness. *(Added by Stats.1975, c. 1275, p. 3455, § 2, operative July 1, 1976.)*

Law Revision Commission Comments

Section 1265.225 is new; it codifies the case law principle that a lienholder is entitled to share in the award only to the extent of the impairment of his security notwithstanding any agreement to the contrary entered into at the time of the creation of the indebtedness on which the lien is based. See, e.g., Milstein v. Security Pac. Nat'l Bank, 27 Cal.App.3d 482, 103 Cal.Rptr. 16 (1972); Sacramento & San Joaquin Drainage Dist. v. Truslow, 125 Cal.App.2d 478, 270 P.2d 928 (1954). Subdivision (b) makes clear, however, that the parties may by subsequent agreement provide that the lienholder is to take a specified portion of the award even if there is no impairment of security. This may be advantageous, for example, in situations where the award will be sufficient to discharge the indebtedness on which the lien is based.

Section 1265.225 determines the amount of the award that will be available to the lienholders. For allocation of that amount among junior and senior lienholders, see Section 1265.230.

Research References

California Real Estate Forms (Miller & Starr) § 3:8, Deed of Trust, Security Agreement, and Fixture Filing With Assignment of Rents and Agreements.

California Real Estate Forms (Miller & Starr) § 3:14, Construction Deed of Trust, Security Agreement, and Fixture Filing With Assignment of Rents and Agreements.

Rutter, Cal. Practice Guide: Real Prop. Transactions Ch. 6-H, H. Security for Promissory Note.

Miller and Starr California Real Estate § 10:69, Condemnation of the Property Security.

Miller and Starr California Real Estate § 11:179, Priorities Among State and Local Tax and Assessment Liens--Effect of Acquisition of Property by a Public Entity.

Miller and Starr California Real Estate § 30A:34, Deeds of Trust, Taxes and Other Monetary Liens.

4 Witkin, California Summary 10th Security Transactions in Real Property § 81, Right to Condemnation Award.

8 Witkin, California Summary 10th Constitutional Law § 1251, Encumbrances.

§ 1265.230. Senior and junior liens; allocation

(a) This section applies only where there is a partial taking of property encumbered by a lien and the part taken or some portion of it is also encumbered by a junior lien that extends to only a portion of the property encumbered by the senior lien. This section provides only for allocation of the portion of the award, if any, that will be available for payment to the junior and senior lienholders and does not provide for determination of the amount of such portion.

(b) As used in this section, "impairment of security" means the security of the lienholder remaining after the taking, if any, is of less value in proportion to the remaining indebtedness than the value of the security before the taking was in proportion to the indebtedness secured thereby.

(c) The portion of the award that will be available for payment to the senior and junior lienholders shall be allocated first to the senior lien up to the full amount of the indebtedness secured thereby and the remainder, if any, to the junior lien.

(d) If the allocation under subdivision (c) would result in an impairment of the junior lienholder's security, the allocation to the junior lien shall be adjusted so as to preserve the junior lienholder's security to the extent that the remaining amount allocated to the senior lien, if paid to the senior lienholder, would not result in an impairment of the senior lienholder's security.

(e) The amounts allocated to the senior and junior liens by this section are the amounts of indebtedness owing to such senior and junior lienholders that are secured by their respective liens on the property taken, and any other indebtedness owing to the senior or junior lienholders shall not be considered as secured by the property taken. If the plaintiff makes the election provided in Section 1265.220, the indebtedness that is deducted from the judgment is the indebtedness so determined, and the lien shall continue until that amount of indebtedness is paid. *(Added by Stats.1975, c. 1275, p. 3455, § 2, operative July 1, 1976.)*

Law Revision Commission Comments

Section 1265.230 continues the substance of former Section 1248(9) which was designed to meet the problems that arise when a parcel is encumbered with a first trust deed, or other senior lien, and a portion is encumbered with a subordinate lien as well. In this situation, condemnation of all or part of the smaller portion may result in an award inadequate to satisfy both liens. Section 1265.230 prescribes a procedure for allocating eminent domain awards between senior and junior lienholders of condemned property. The scope of former Section 1248(9) may be somewhat expanded by the broad definition of "lien" in Section 1265.210. See the Comment to that section.

The allocation procedure of Section 1265.230 is designed to allow adjustment of the portion of the condemnation award available to the lienholders so that both the senior and junior lienholders will retain security interests proportionate to those existing before the taking. If the amount is not sufficient to pay both in full, it will be initially allocated to pay the full amount of the senior lien with any balance to the junior. At that time, the court will determine the adequacy of the remaining property to secure the junior lien. If it determines that the junior lienholder's security is disproportionately low, the court may make adjustments as to the initial allocation to place the junior in the same relative position as before the taking. The adjustment, made by reducing the allocation to the senior and adding to that of the junior, is permissible only if it preserves the proportional security of the senior lienholder.

Section 1265.230 is not intended to affect the rule precluding recovery by a lienholder of any part of the award where there is no impairment of security. See Section 1265.225. Section 1265.230 merely specifies rules for apportionment of the amount allocated to lienholders under Section 1265.255.

Research References

Miller and Starr California Real Estate § 10:69, Condemnation of the Property Security.

Miller and Starr California Real Estate § 30A:34, Deeds of Trust, Taxes and Other Monetary Liens.

4 Witkin, California Summary 10th Security Transactions in Real Property § 81, Right to Condemnation Award.

8 Witkin, California Summary 10th Constitutional Law § 1251, Encumbrances.

8 Witkin, California Summary 10th Constitutional Law § 1252, Partial Taking and Impairment of Security.

§ 1265.240. Penalty for prepayment

Where the property acquired for public use is encumbered by a lien, the amount payable to the lienholder shall not include any penalty for prepayment. *(Added by Stats.1975, c. 1275, p. 3456, § 2, operative July 1, 1976.)*

Law Revision Commission Comments

Section 1265.240 continues the substance of former Section 1246.2. Section 1265.240 is intended to apply to penalties for prepayment of liens of all kinds (see Section 1265.210 defining "lien") including but not limited to prepayment penalties under mortgages, deeds of trust, contracts of sale, and redemption premiums under Streets and Highways Code Sections 6447 and 6464.

Research References

Miller and Starr California Real Estate § 9:21, Rights and Powers.
Miller and Starr California Real Estate § 10:69, Condemnation of the Property Security.
Miller and Starr California Real Estate § 10:97, Prepayment Fee-- Obligation for Payment.
Miller and Starr California Real Estate § 30A:34, Deeds of Trust, Taxes and Other Monetary Liens.
4 Witkin, California Summary 10th Security Transactions in Real Property § 81, Right to Condemnation Award.
8 Witkin, California Summary 10th Constitutional Law § 1251, Encumbrances.

§ 1265.250. Eminent domain; fixed lien special assessments; special annual assessments

(a) As used in this section:

(1) "Fixed lien special assessment" means a nonrecurring assessment levied on property in a fixed amount by a local public entity for the capital expenditure for a specific improvement, whether collectible in a lump sum or in installments.

(2) "Special annual assessment" means a recurring assessment levied on property annually in an indeterminate amount by a local public entity, whether for the capital expenditure for a specific improvement or for other purposes.

(b) If property acquired by eminent domain is encumbered by the lien of a fixed lien special assessment or of a bond representing the fixed lien special assessment:

(1) The amount of the lien shall be paid to the lienholder from the award or withheld from the award for payment pursuant to Section 1265.220.

(2) Where there is a partial taking of the property, the amount of the lien prescribed in Section 1265.225 shall be paid to the lienholder from the award, or at the option of the lienholder the applicable statutory procedure, if any, for segregation and apportionment of the lien may be invoked and the amount apportioned to the part taken shall be paid to the lienholder from the award.

(c) If property acquired by eminent domain is encumbered by the lien of a special annual assessment:

(1) The amount of the lien prorated to, but not including, the date of apportionment determined pursuant to Section 5082 of the Revenue and Taxation Code, shall be paid to the lienholder from the award. As between the plaintiff and defendant, the plaintiff is liable for the amount of the lien prorated from and including the date of apportionment determined pursuant to Section 5082 of the Revenue and Taxation Code.

(2) Where there is a partial taking of the property, the amount of the lien, reduced by the amount for which the plaintiff is liable pursuant to this paragraph, shall be paid to the lienholder from the award. As between the plaintiff and defendant, the plaintiff is liable for the amount of the lien allocable to the part taken for the current assessment year, determined to the extent practicable in the same manner and by the same method as the amount of the assessment on the property for the current assessment year was determined, prorated from and including the date of apportionment determined pursuant to Section 5082 of the Revenue and Taxation Code. (*Added by Stats.1980, c. 122, § 2.*)

Law Revision Commission Comments

Section 1265.250 clarifies the rules for payment of special assessment liens on property acquired by eminent domain, regardless whether the assessments or bonds secured by the liens are collected by the county tax collector along with ad valorem taxes or in some other manner. *Cf.* Section 1260.250 (determination and payment of property taxes). The lienholder must be made a party to the proceeding. See Section 1250.250. Priority of special assessment liens is governed by Sections 53930–53937 of the Government Code.

Subdivision (b) governs fixed lien special assessments, which are levied for the cost of acquisition and installation of a particular local improvement, and are the responsibility of the property owner. Under subdivision (b)(1) the amount of the lien must be either paid wholly from the award or at the plaintiff's option deducted from the award and paid by the plaintiff as the obligation comes due. This codifies existing law. See Sections 1260.220 and 1265.220; Redevelopment Agency v. Penzner, 8 Cal.App.3d 417, 87 Cal.Rptr. 183 (1970); City of Los Angeles v. Superior Court, 2 Cal.2d 138, 39 P.2d 401 (1934); People v. Cheda, 154 Cal.App.2d 531, 317 P.2d 145 (1957). In case of a partial taking, the lien is paid from the award only to the extent necessary to prevent an impairment of the security, and the obligation of the lien remains on the property owner. This also codifies existing law. See Section 1265.225. A provision is added to subdivision (b)(2) to permit a lienholder to invoke any applicable statutory procedure for segregation and apportionment of the lien. See, e.g., Sts. & Hy.Code §§ 6580–6488 (Improvement Act of 1911), 8730– 8734 (Improvement Bond Act of 1915), 8740–8740.5 (Improvement Bond Act of 1915).

Subdivision (c) governs special annual assessments, which are levied for maintenance of improvements and other general purposes of the assessing entity as well as capital expenditures. These assessments are comparable to taxes, and their obligation is apportioned between property owner and condemnor in the same manner as taxes. *Cf.* Sections 1260.250 (determination and payment of property taxes) and 1268.410 (liability for taxes). The amount apportioned to the condemnor under subdivision (c) may or may not be subject to cancellation, just as property taxes may or may not be subject to cancellation, depending upon the particular condemnor and the statute governing imposition of the assessment. See Recommendation Relating to Special Assessment Liens on Property Acquired for Public Use, 15 Cal.L.Revision Comm'n Reports 1101 (1980).

Research References

Miller and Starr California Real Estate § 11:179, Priorities Among State and Local Tax and Assessment Liens--Effect of Acquisition of Property by a Public Entity.
Miller and Starr California Real Estate § 30A:34, Deeds of Trust, Taxes and Other Monetary Liens.
8 Witkin, California Summary 10th Constitutional Law § 1263, Special Assessment Liens.

ARTICLE 4. FUTURE INTERESTS

§ 1265.410. Violation of use restriction coupled with contingent right of possession; compensation

(a) Where the acquisition of property for public use violates a use restriction coupled with a contingent future interest granting a right to possession of the property upon violation of the use restriction:

(1) If violation of the use restriction was otherwise reasonably imminent, the owner of the contingent future interest is entitled to compensation for its value, if any.

(2) If violation of the use restriction was not otherwise reasonably imminent but the benefit of the use restriction was appurtenant to other property, the owner of the contingent future interest is entitled to compensation to the extent that the failure to comply with the use restriction damages the dominant premises to which the restriction was appurtenant and of which he was the owner.

(b) Where the acquisition of property for public use violates a use restriction coupled with a contingent future interest granting a right to possession of the property upon violation of the use restriction but the contingent future interest is not compensable under subdivision (a), if the use restriction is that the property be devoted to a particular charitable or public use, the compensation for the property shall be devoted to the same or similar use coupled with the same contingent future interest. (*Added by Stats.1975, c. 1275, p. 3456, § 2, operative July 1, 1976.*)

Law Revision Commission Comments

Section 1265.410 makes clear that, where there are contingent future interests in property acquired by eminent domain, such interests may be entitled to compensation despite any implications to the contrary in such cases as Romero v. Department of Public Works, 17 Cal.2d 189, 109 P.2d 662 (1941); People v. City of Fresno, 210 Cal.App.2d 500, 26 Cal.Rptr. 853 (1962); People v. City of Los Angeles, 179 Cal.App.2d 558, 4 Cal.Rptr. 531 (1960); City of Santa Monica v. Jones, 104 Cal.App.2d 463, 232 P.2d 55 (1951). Since the value of the fee owner's interest in the property is diminished to the extent of the value of the contingent future interest, the award for the value of the property must be so apportioned. See Section 1260.220 (procedure where there are divided interests).

The test stated in subdivision (a)—"reasonably imminent"—is derived from 1 RESTATEMENT OF PROPERTY § 53(c) (1936). The reference to "public use" in subdivision (b) is intended to include all uses, including public utility purposes, for which the power of eminent domain might be exercised. See Section 1240.010 (public use limitation).

Research References

Miller and Starr California Real Estate § 9:4, Fee Simple Defeasible--In General.
Miller and Starr California Real Estate § 30A:35, Condemnation of Non-Monetary Encumbrances.
8 Witkin, California Summary 10th Constitutional Law § 1253, Future Interests.

§ 1265.420. Life tenancy

Where property acquired for public use is subject to a life tenancy, upon petition of the life tenant or any other person having an interest in the property, the court may order any of the following:

(a) An apportionment and distribution of the award based on the value of the interest of life tenant and remainderman.

(b) The compensation to be used to purchase comparable property to be held subject to the life tenancy.

(c) The compensation to be held in trust and invested and the income (and, to the extent the instrument that created the life tenancy permits, principal) to be distributed to the life tenant for the remainder of the tenancy.

(d) Such other arrangement as will be equitable under the circumstances. (*Added by Stats.1975, c. 1275, p. 3456, § 2, operative July 1, 1976.*)

Law Revision Commission Comments

Section 1265.420 provides the court express statutory authority to devise an equitable solution where property subject to a life tenancy is taken and an outright division of the award would not result in substantial justice under the circumstances of the particular case. See Estate of Giacomelos, 192 Cal.App.2d 244, 13 Cal.Rptr. 245 (1961) (trust imposed on proceeds).

Eminent domain law. 13 Cal.L.Rev.Comm.Reports 1001 (1975).

Research References

Miller and Starr California Real Estate § 30A:35, Condemnation of Non-Monetary Encumbrances.
12 Witkin, California Summary 10th Real Property § 26, (S 26) Insurance and Condemnation Award.

8 Witkin, California Summary 10th Constitutional Law § 1253, Future Interests.

CHAPTER 11. POSTJUDGMENT PROCEDURE

ARTICLE 1. PAYMENT OF JUDGMENT; FINAL ORDER OF CONDEMNATION

§ 1268.010. Payment of judgment; methods

(a) Not later than 30 days after final judgment, or 30 days after the conclusion of any other court proceedings, including any federal court proceedings, commenced by the defendant challenging the judgment or any of the condemnation proceedings, whichever date is later, the plaintiff shall pay the full amount required by the judgment.

(b) Payment shall be made by either or both of the following methods:

(1) Payment of money directly to the defendant. Any amount which the defendant has previously withdrawn pursuant to Article 2 (commencing with Section 1255.210) of Chapter 6 shall be credited as a payment to him on the judgment.

(2) Deposit of money with the court pursuant to Section 1268.110. Upon entry of judgment, a deposit made pursuant to Article 1 (commencing with Section 1255.010) of Chapter 6 is deemed to be a deposit made pursuant to Section 1268.110 if the full amount required by the judgment is deposited or paid. (*Added by Stats.1975, c. 1275, p. 3457, § 2, operative July 1, 1976. Amended by Stats.1981, c. 831, § 1.*)

Law Revision Commission Comments

Section 1268.010 retains the rule under former Section 1251 that the plaintiff must pay the full amount of the judgment not later than 30 days after final judgment. See Section 1235.120 (defining "final judgment"). See also Section 1268.110 (deposit of full amount of award, together with interest when due thereon, less amounts previously paid or deposited). Section 1268.010 omits the provision of former Section 1251 that extended the 30-day time by one year where necessary to permit bonds to be issued and sold.

Subdivision (b) of Section 1268.010 specifies the manner in which payment may be made and supersedes the first sentence of former Section 1252. The payment can be made directly to the defendant or defendants, or the plaintiff may pay the money into court as provided in Article 2 (commencing with Section 1268.110). See the Comment to Section 1268.110. The provision that amounts previously withdrawn are credited as payment is derived from former Section 1243.7(g).

Research References

Miller and Starr California Real Estate § 30A:74, Judgment.
8 Witkin Cal. Proc. 5th Enforcement of Judgment § 431, Payment Obligation.

8 Witkin, California Summary 10th Constitutional Law § 1254, Payment and Final Order.

§ 1268.020. Failure to pay judgment; enforcement; dismissal of proceeding; requirements

(a) If the plaintiff fails to pay the full amount required by the judgment within the time specified in Section 1268.010, the defendant may:

(1) If the plaintiff is a public entity, enforce the judgment as provided in Division 3.6 (commencing with Section 810) of Title 1 of the Government Code.

(2) If the plaintiff is not a public entity, enforce the judgment as in a civil case.

(b) Upon noticed motion of the defendant, the court shall enter judgment dismissing the eminent domain proceeding if all of the following are established:

(1) The plaintiff failed to pay the full amount required by the judgment within the time specified in Section 1268.010.

(2) The defendant has filed in court and served upon the plaintiff, by registered or certified mail, a written notice of the plaintiff's failure to pay the full amount required by the judgment within the time specified in Section 1268.010.

(3) The plaintiff has failed for 20 days after service of the notice under paragraph (2) to pay the full amount required by the judgment in the manner provided in subdivision (b) of Section 1268.010.

(c) The defendant may elect to exercise the remedy provided by subdivision (b) without attempting to use the remedy provided by subdivision (a).

(d) As used in this section, "public entity" does not include the Regents of the University of California. *(Added by Stats. 1975, c. 1275, p. 3457, § 2, operative July 1, 1976. Amended by Stats.1980, c. 215, § 1.)*

Law Revision Commission Comments

Section 1268.020, which generally continues the substance of portions of former Sections 1252 and 1255a, provides remedies for the defendant if the plaintiff does not pay the judgment as required; the defendant may enforce the plaintiff's obligation to pay by execution or, at the defendant's election, may obtain a dismissal of the proceeding with its attendant award of litigation expenses. See Section 1268.610. Under former Section 1252, these remedies were provided, but the section required that the defendant resort first to execution and, if unsuccessful, he could have the proceeding dismissed. However, former Section 1255a, a later enactment, provided that failure to pay the judgment within the required time constituted an implied abandonment of the proceeding. The two sections were construed together to give the defendant the option of resorting to execution or to having the proceeding dismissed as impliedly abandoned. See, e.g., County of Los Angeles v. Bartlett, 223 Cal.App.2d 353, 36 Cal.Rptr. 193 (1963). Under the former law, it was possible that an inadvertent failure to pay the judgment within the time specified might result in an implied abandonment even though the plaintiff did not intend to abandon the proceeding. See, e.g., County of Los Angeles v. Bartlett, *supra*. To protect the plaintiff against this possibility, Section 1268.020 requires that notice of the failure to pay the judgment within the time specified be given to the plaintiff and that he be given 20 days to pay the judgment before the proceeding can be dismissed upon motion of the defendant.

Section 1268.020 is amended to make clear that the eminent domain judgment is enforced against a public entity under the Government Code provisions relating to payment of judgments against public entities. See Gov't Code §§ 965–965.9 (judgment against the state), 970–971.2 (judgment against local public entity). The judgment is not enforceable against a public entity by execution or other remedies provided a judgment creditor under the Code of Civil Procedure. See Gov't Code §§ 965.5(b) (state), 970.1(b) (local public entity). See also Gov't Code §§ 965.7, 965.8, 970.2 (writ of mandate to compel payment of money judgment). The Regents of the University of California is not subject to the applicable provisions of Division 3.6 (see Gov't Code § 965.9). Hence, the

judgment is enforceable under paragraph (2) of subdivision (a) if the plaintiff is the Regents of the University of California.

Research References

Rutter, Cal. Practice Guide: Enforcing Judgments/Debts Ch. 6A-6, Payment of Final Judgments Against Public Entities.
Miller and Starr California Real Estate § 30A:74, Judgment.
8 Witkin Cal. Proc. 5th Attack Judgment Trial Court § 2, in Trial Court.
8 Witkin Cal. Proc. 5th Enforcement of Judgment § 61, (S 61) Governmental Property.
8 Witkin Cal. Proc. 5th Enforcement of Judgment § 431, Payment Obligation.
8 Witkin Cal. Proc. 5th Extraordinary Writs § 125, (S 125) Remedy by Motion.
8 Witkin, California Summary 10th Constitutional Law § 1254, Payment and Final Order.

§ 1268.030. Final order of condemnation; contents

(a) Upon application of any party, the court shall make a final order of condemnation if the full amount of the judgment has been paid as required by Section 1268.010 or satisfied pursuant to Section 1268.020.

(b) The final order of condemnation shall describe the property taken and identify the judgment authorizing the taking.

(c) The party upon whose application the order was made shall serve notice of the making of the order on all other parties affected thereby. Any party affected by the order may thereafter record a certified copy of the order in the office of the recorder of the county in which the property is located and shall serve notice of recordation upon all other parties affected thereby. Title to the property vests in the plaintiff upon the date of recordation. *(Added by Stats.1975, c. 1275, p. 3457, § 2, operative July 1, 1976.)*

Research References

Miller and Starr California Real Estate § 30A:75, Post Judgment Procedures.
Miller and Starr California Real Estate § 30A:80, Final Order of Condemnation.
7 Witkin Cal. Proc. 5th Judgment § 35, (S 35) Condemnation.
9 Witkin, California Summary 10th Taxation § 320, Documentary Transfer Tax.
8 Witkin, California Summary 10th Constitutional Law § 1254, Payment and Final Order.

ARTICLE 2. DEPOSIT AND WITHDRAWAL OF AWARD

Section

§ 1268.110. Deposit of award and interest less previous payment

(a) Except as provided in subdivision (b), the plaintiff may, at any time after entry of judgment, deposit with the court for the persons entitled thereto the full amount of the award, together with interest then due thereon, less any amounts previously paid directly to the defendants or deposited pursuant to Article 1 (commencing with Section 1255.010) of Chapter 6.

(b) A deposit may be made under this section notwithstanding an appeal, a motion for a new trial, or a motion to vacate or set aside the judgment but may not be made after the judgment has been reversed, vacated, or set aside.

(c) Any amount deposited pursuant to this article on a judgment that is later reversed, vacated, or set aside shall be deemed to be an amount deposited pursuant to Article 1 (commencing with Section 1255.010) of Chapter 6. *(Added by Stats.1975, c. 1275, p. 3458, § 2, operative July 1, 1976.)*

Law Revision Commission Comments

This article (commencing with Section 1268.110) provides a uniform scheme for postjudgment deposits, superseding portions of former Sections 1245.3, 1252, and 1254.

Subdivision (a) of Section 1268.110 is similar to subdivision (a) of former Section 1254. However, the deposit provided for in this subdivision consists only of the amount of the judgment and accrued interest (less amounts previously deposited or paid to defendants); the former provision for an additional sum to secure payment of further compensation and costs is superseded by Section 1268.130. In addition, a deposit may be made under this section without regard to whether an order for possession is sought.

In case the judgment is reversed, vacated, or set aside, there is no longer a judgment for deposit and possession purposes; subsequent proceedings are under the provisions relating to deposit and possession prior to judgment. See Chapter 6 (commencing with Section 1255.010). Any amount deposited under Section 1268.110 or Section 1268.130 is deemed to be an amount deposited under Chapter 6 if the judgment is reversed, vacated, or set aside; after the judgment is reversed, vacated, or set aside, the procedure for increasing or decreasing the amount of the deposit and withdrawal of the deposit is governed by the provisions of Chapter 6. See subdivision (c) and Section 1268.140(d).

Research References

6 Witkin Cal. Proc. 5th Provisional Remedies § 461, Nature of Remedy.
8 Witkin, California Summary 10th Constitutional Law § 1254, Payment and Final Order.
8 Witkin, California Summary 10th Constitutional Law § 1255, (S 1255) Deposit After Judgment.
8 Witkin, California Summary 10th Constitutional Law § 1256, (S 1256) Withdrawal of Deposit.
8 Witkin, California Summary 10th Constitutional Law § 1257, Possession After Judgment.

§ 1268.120. Notice of deposit; service

If the deposit is made under Section 1268.110 prior to apportionment of the award, the plaintiff shall serve a notice that the deposit has been made on all of the parties who have appeared in the proceeding. If the deposit is made after apportionment of the award, the plaintiff shall serve a notice that the deposit has been made on all of the parties to the proceeding determined by the order apportioning the award to have an interest in the money deposited. The notice of deposit shall state that a deposit has been made and the date and the amount of the deposit. Service of the notice shall be made in the manner provided in Section 1268.220 for the service of an order for possession. Service of an order for possession under Section 1268.220 is sufficient compliance with this section. *(Added by Stats.1975, c. 1275, p. 3458, § 2, operative July 1, 1976.)*

Law Revision Commission Comments

Section 1268.120 is new. In requiring that notice of the deposit be given, it parallels Section 1255.020 which requires that notice of a prejudgment deposit be sent to the parties having an interest in the property for which the deposit is made. Under former Section 1254, the defendant received notice that the deposit had been made only when served with an order for possession.

Research References

8 Witkin, California Summary 10th Constitutional Law § 1255, (S 1255) Deposit After Judgment.

§ 1268.130. Deposit of additional amount; court order; withdrawal

At any time after the plaintiff has made a deposit upon the award pursuant to Section 1268.110, the court may, upon motion of any defendant, order the plaintiff to deposit such additional amount as the court determines to be necessary to secure payment of any further compensation, costs, or interest that may be recovered in the proceeding. After the making of such an order, the court may, on motion of any party, order an increase or a decrease in such additional amount. A defendant may withdraw the amount deposited under this section or a portion thereof only if it is determined that he is entitled to recover such amount in the proceeding. *(Added by Stats.1975, c. 1275, p. 3458, § 2, operative July 1, 1976.)*

Law Revision Commission Comments

Section 1268.130 supersedes subdivisions (a) and (d) of former Section 1254. The additional amount referred to in Section 1268.130 is the amount determined by the court to be necessary, in addition to the amount of the judgment and the interest then due thereon, to secure payment of any further compensation, costs, or interest that may be recovered in the proceeding. Deposit of the amount of the award itself after entry of judgment is provided for by Section 1268.110.

Former Section 1254 was construed to make the amount, if any, to be deposited in addition to the award discretionary with the trial court. Orange County Water Dist. v. Bennett, 156 Cal.App.2d 745, 320 P.2d 536 (1958). This construction is continued under Section 1268.130.

Research References

8 Witkin, California Summary 10th Constitutional Law § 1255, (S 1255) Deposit After Judgment.

§ 1268.140. Application of defendant for payment; filing; notice; undertaking

(a) After entry of judgment, any defendant who has an interest in the property for which a deposit has been made may apply for and obtain a court order that he be paid from the deposit the amount to which he is entitled upon his filing either of the following:

(1) A satisfaction of the judgment.

(2) A receipt for the money which shall constitute a waiver by operation of law of all claims and defenses except a claim for greater compensation.

(b) If the award has not been apportioned at the time the application is made, the applicant shall give notice of the application to all the other defendants who have appeared in the proceeding and who have an interest in the property. If the award has been apportioned at the time the application is made, the applicant shall give such notice to the other defendants as the court may require.

(c) Upon objection to the withdrawal made by any party to the proceeding, the court, in its discretion, may require the applicant to file an undertaking in the same manner and upon the conditions prescribed in Section 1255.240 for withdrawal of a deposit prior to entry of judgment.

(d) If the judgment is reversed, vacated, or set aside, a defendant may withdraw a deposit only pursuant to Article 2 (commencing with Section 1255.210) of Chapter 6. *(Added by Stats.1975, c. 1275, p. 3458, § 2, operative July 1, 1976.)*

Law Revision Commission Comments

Section 1268.140 is based on subdivision (f) of former Section 1254 but provides notice requirements to protect the other defendants where money is to be withdrawn. Section 1268.140 is the only provision for withdrawal of a deposit after entry of judgment regardless whether the deposit was made before or after judgment.

Former Section 1254 was construed to permit the defendant to withdraw any amount paid into court upon the judgment whether or not the plaintiff applied for or obtained an order for possession. See People v. Gutierrez, 207 Cap.App.2d 759, 24 Cal.Rptr. 781 (1962); San Francisco Bay Area Rapid Transit Dist. v. Fremont Meadows, Inc., 20 Cal.App.3d 797, 97 Cal.Rptr. 898 (1971). That construction is continued in effect by Section 1268.140.

For purposes of withdrawal of deposits, a judgment that is reversed, vacated, or set aside has no effect; withdrawal may be made only under the procedures provided for withdrawing deposits prior to entry of judgment. This is made clear by subdivision (d).

Under Section 1268.140, the defendant may retain his right to appeal or to request a new trial upon the issue of compensation even though he withdraws the deposit. This may be accomplished by filing a receipt which constitutes a waiver of all claims and defenses except the claim to greater compensation. See subdivision (a). Cf. People v. Gutierrez, 207 Cal.App.2d 759, 24 Cal.Rptr. 781 (1962).

Research References

Miller and Starr California Real Estate § 30A:75, Post Judgment Procedures.
8 Witkin, California Summary 10th Constitutional Law § 1215, (S 1215) Withdrawal of Deposit.
8 Witkin, California Summary 10th Constitutional Law § 1256, (S 1256) Withdrawal of Deposit.

§ 1268.150. Deposit of award in treasury; investment; disposition of increments

(a) Except as provided in subdivision (b), when money is deposited as provided in this article, the court shall order the money to be deposited in the State Treasury or, upon written request of the plaintiff filed with the deposit, in the county treasury. If the money is deposited in the State Treasury pursuant to this subdivision, it shall be held, invested, deposited, and disbursed in the manner specified in Article 10 (commencing with Section 16429) of Chapter 2 of Part 2 of Division 4 of Title 2 of the Government Code, and interest earned or other increment derived from its investment shall be apportioned and disbursed in the manner specified in that article. As between the parties to the proceeding, money deposited pursuant to this subdivision shall remain at the risk of the plaintiff until paid or made payable to the defendant by order of the court.

(b) If after entry of judgment but prior to apportionment of the award the defendants are unable to agree as to the withdrawal of all or a portion of any amount deposited, the court shall upon motion of any defendant order that the amount deposited be invested in United States government obligations or interest-bearing accounts in an institution whose accounts are insured by an agency of the federal government for the benefit of the defendants who shall be entitled to the interest earned on the investments in proportion to the amount of the award they receive when the award is apportioned. (Added by Stats.1975, c. 1275, p. 3459, § 2, operative July 1, 1976.)

Law Revision Commission Comments

Subdivision (a) of Section 1268.150 is the same in substance as former Section 1243.6 and a portion of subdivision (h) of former Section 1254. For a comparable section, see Section 1255.070.

Subdivision (b) is new. It provides a means whereby a defendant may avoid the loss of interest earnings on amounts held on deposit pending resolution of an apportionment dispute. Cf. Section 1268.320 (interest ceases to accrue on judgment upon deposit). Subdivision (b) does not preclude a voluntary agreement among all defendants to draw down the award and place it in an interest-bearing trust fund pending resolution of apportionment issues. It should be noted that subdivision (b) permits investments in amounts in excess of insurance coverage. For a comparable provision, see Section 1255.075 (investment of deposit).

Research References

Miller and Starr California Real Estate § 30A:75, Post Judgment Procedures.
8 Witkin, California Summary 10th Constitutional Law § 1255, (S 1255) Deposit After Judgment.

§ 1268.160. Withdrawal of amount in excess of entitlement; judgment; interest; stay of execution

(a) Any amount withdrawn by a party pursuant to this article in excess of the amount to which he is entitled as finally determined in the eminent domain proceeding shall be paid to the parties entitled thereto. The court shall enter judgment accordingly.

(b) The judgment so entered shall not include interest except that any amount that is to be paid to a defendant shall include legal interest from the date of its withdrawal by another defendant.

(c) If the judgment so entered is not paid within 30 days after its entry, the court may, on motion, enter judgment against the sureties, if any, for the amount of such judgment.

(d) The court may, in its discretion and with such security as it deems appropriate, grant a party obligated to pay under this section a stay of execution for any amount to be paid to a plaintiff. Such stay of execution shall not exceed one year following entry of judgment under this section. (Added by Stats.1975, c. 1275, p. 3459, § 2, operative July 1, 1976.)

Law Revision Commission Comments

Section 1268.160 supersedes subdivision (g) of former Section 1254. Unlike Section 1254, which did not require the payment of interest where excess amounts were withdrawn, Section 1268.160 requires payment of interest where the excess is to be redistributed among defendants but not where the excess is to be paid to the plaintiff. For a comparable provision, see Section 1255.280. It should be noted, however, that where execution is stayed under subdivision (d), interest will accrue during the stay.

Research References

8 Witkin, California Summary 10th Constitutional Law § 1256, (S 1256) Withdrawal of Deposit.

§ 1268.170. Deposit by plaintiff; effect on right to appeal, abandon or request new trial

By making a deposit pursuant to this article, the plaintiff does not waive the right to appeal from the judgment, the right to move to abandon, or the right to request a new trial. (Added by Stats.1975, c. 1275, p. 3460, § 2, operative July 1, 1976.)

Law Revision Commission Comments

Section 1268.170 continues the substance of a portion of subdivision (e) of former Section 1254. For a comparable provision permitting the defendant to withdraw the deposit without waiving his right to seek greater compensation, see Section 1268.140(a).

Research References

8 Witkin, California Summary 10th Constitutional Law § 1255, (S 1255) Deposit After Judgment.

ARTICLE 3. POSSESSION AFTER JUDGMENT

Section

§ 1268.210. Application; court order for possession; requirements

(a) If the plaintiff is not in possession of the property to be taken, the plaintiff may, at any time after entry of judgment, apply ex parte to the court for an order for possession, and the court shall authorize the plaintiff to take possession of the property pending conclusion of the litigation if:

(1) The judgment determines that the plaintiff is entitled to take the property; and

(2) The plaintiff has paid to or deposited for the defendants, pursuant to Article 1 (commencing with Section 1255.010) of Chapter 6 or Article 2 (commencing with Section 1268.110), an amount not less than the amount of the award, together with the interest then due thereon.

(b) The court's order shall state the date after which the plaintiff is authorized to take possession of the property. Where deposit is made, the order shall state such fact and the date and the amount of the deposit.

(c) Where the judgment is reversed, vacated, or set aside, the plaintiff may obtain possession of the property only pursuant to Article 3 (commencing with Section 1255.410) of Chapter 6. (Added by Stats.1975, c. 1275, p. 3460, § 2, operative July 1, 1976.)

Law Revision Commission Comments

Section 1268.210 restates the substance of portions of subdivisions (a) and (b) of former Section 1254. Where the requirements of subdivision (a) are satisfied, the court must grant the order of possession. See Pacific Gas & Elec. Co. v. Superior Court, 33 Cal.App.3d 321, 109 Cal.Rptr. 10 (1973). The time for possession is lengthened, however, from 10 to 30 days after the order for possession where the property is occupied. See Section 1268.220. For purposes of possession, a judgment that is reversed, vacated, or set aside has no effect; the plaintiff must utilize procedures for obtaining possession prior to entry of judgment.

Research References

Rutter, Cal. Practice Guide: Civil Appeals & Writs Ch. 7-A, A. Overview.
Miller and Starr California Real Estate § 30A:79, Possession After Judgment.
8 Witkin, California Summary 10th Constitutional Law § 1257, Possession After Judgment.

§ 1268.220. Copy of order; service

(a) The plaintiff shall serve a copy of the order for possession upon each defendant and his attorney, either personally or by mail:

(1) At least 30 days prior to the date possession is to be taken of property lawfully occupied by a person dwelling thereon or by a farm or business operation.

(2) At least 10 days prior to the date possession is to be taken in any case not covered by paragraph (1).

(b) A single service upon or mailing to one of several persons having a common business or residence address is sufficient. (Added by Stats.1975, c. 1275, p. 3460, § 2, operative July 1, 1976.)

Law Revision Commission Comments

Section 1268.220 is the same in substance as subdivisions (b) and (c) of former Section 1254 except that the 10-day notice period is lengthened to 30 days where the property is occupied. With respect to subdivision (b), see the Comment to Section 1255.450.

Research References

Miller and Starr California Real Estate § 30A:79, Possession After Judgment.
8 Witkin, California Summary 10th Constitutional Law § 1255, (S 1255) Deposit After Judgment.

8 Witkin, California Summary 10th Constitutional Law § 1257, Possession After Judgment.

§ 1268.230. Possession by plaintiff; effect on right to appeal, abandon, or request new trial

By taking possession pursuant to this article, the plaintiff does not waive the right to appeal from the judgment, the right to move to abandon, or the right to request a new trial. (Added by Stats.1975, c. 1275, p. 3460, § 2, operative July 1, 1976.)

Law Revision Commission Comments

Section 1268.230 is the same in substance as a portion of subdivision (e) of former Section 1254. For a comparable provision, see Section 1255.470.

Research References

Miller and Starr California Real Estate § 30A:79, Possession After Judgment.
8 Witkin, California Summary 10th Constitutional Law § 1257, Possession After Judgment.

§ 1268.240. Emergencies; exercise of police powers

Nothing in this article limits the right of a public entity to exercise its police power in emergency situations. (Added by Stats.1975, c. 1275, p. 3460, § 2, operative July 1, 1976.)

Law Revision Commission Comments

Section 1268.240 is new. It makes clear that the requirements of this article—such as obtaining and serving an order for possession—do not limit the exercise of the police power. See Surocco v. Geary, 3 Cal. 69 (1853). See generally Van Alstyne, Statutory Modification of Inverse Condemnation: Deliberately Inflicted Injury or Destruction, 20 Stan. L. Rev 617 (1968), reprinted in Van Alstyne, California Inverse Condemnation Law, 10 Cal.L.Revision Comm'n Reports 111 (1971). See also Section 1255.480.

Research References

Miller and Starr California Real Estate § 30A:79, Possession After Judgment.
8 Witkin, California Summary 10th Constitutional Law § 1257, Possession After Judgment.

ARTICLE 4. INTEREST

Section

§ 1268.310. Inclusion in compensation; earliest accrual date

The compensation awarded in the proceeding shall draw interest, computed as prescribed by Section 1268.350, from the earliest of the following dates:

(a) The date of entry of judgment.

(b) The date the plaintiff takes possession of the property.

(c) The date after which the plaintiff is authorized to take possession of the property as stated in an order for possession. (Added by Stats.1975, c. 1275, p. 3461, § 2, operative July 1, 1976. Amended by Stats.1986, c. 1372, § 1.)

Law Revision Commission Comments

Section 1268.310 is the same in substance as subdivision (a) of former Section 1255b except that the phrase "or damage [to the property] occurs" has been deleted from subdivision (2). The deleted phrase was inadvertently included in the 1961 revision of Section 1255b. See Recommendation and Study Relating to Taking Possession and Passage of Title in Eminent Domain Proceedings, 3 Cal.L.Revision Comm'n Reports B–1, B–9, B–20 (1961). The 1961 revision was not intended to and has not been construed to require computation of interest on severance damages from a date prior to the earliest date stated in Section 1268.310. The deletion of this phrase is not intended to affect any rules relating to the time of accrual of interest on a cause of action based on inverse condemnation, whether raised in a separate action or by cross-complaint in the eminent domain proceeding. See, e.g., Youngblood v. Los Angeles County Flood Control Dist., 56 Cal.2d 603, 364 P.2d 840, 15 Cal.Rptr. 904 (1961); Heimann v. City of Los Angeles, 30 Cal.2d 746, 185 P.2d 597 (1947). For exceptions to the rules stated in Section 1268.310, see Sections 1255.040 and 1255.050 (deposit on notice of certain defendants).

Research References

Rutter, Cal. Practice Guide: Civil Trials & Evidence Ch. 17-F, F. Prejudgment Interest.
Miller and Starr California Real Estate § 30:19, Announcement of Intent to Condemn or Adoption of Resolution of Necessity.
Miller and Starr California Real Estate § 19:149, Valuation and Apportionment of the Award.
Miller and Starr California Real Estate § 30A:77, Interest.
8 Witkin, California Summary 10th Constitutional Law § 1167, Interest.
8 Witkin, California Summary 10th Constitutional Law § 1258, (S 1258) in General.
8 Witkin, California Summary 10th Constitutional Law § 1259, (S 1259) Market Rate of Interest.

§ 1268.311. Inverse condemnation proceeding

In any inverse condemnation proceeding in which interest is awarded, the interest shall be computed as prescribed by Section 1268.350. *(Added by Stats.1986, c. 1372, § 2.)*

Research References

Miller and Starr California Real Estate § 30:14, Prejudgment Interest; Attorney Fees; Costs.
Miller and Starr California Real Estate § 30:21, Remedies for Unreasonable Precondemnation Activity.
Miller and Starr California Real Estate § 30A:77, Interest.
8 Witkin, California Summary 10th Constitutional Law § 1167, Interest.

§ 1268.320. Inclusion in compensation; earliest cessation date

The compensation awarded in the proceeding shall cease to draw interest at the earliest of the following dates:

(a) As to any amount deposited pursuant to Article 1 (commencing with Section 1255.010) of Chapter 6 (deposit of probable compensation prior to judgment), the date such amount is withdrawn by the person entitled thereto.

(b) As to the amount deposited in accordance with Article 2 (commencing with Section 1268.110) (deposit of amount of award), the date of such deposit.

(c) As to any amount paid to the person entitled thereto, the date of such payment. *(Added by Stats.1975, c. 1275, p. 3461, § 2, operative July 1, 1976.)*

Law Revision Commission Comments

Section 1268.320 continues the substance of subdivision (c) of former Section 1255b. For an exception to the rule stated in subdivision (a), see Sections 1255.040 and 1255.050 (deposit on notice of certain defendants). Subdivision (b) of Section 1268.320 supersedes paragraphs (2) and (4) of subdivision (c) of former Section 1255b. Unlike the former law, there is now only one procedure for payments into court after entry of judgment. See Section 1268.110 and Comment thereto.

It should be noted that, if a prejudgment deposit is made and the deposit is not withdrawn, interest does not cease to accrue upon entry of judgment unless the amount of the deposit is in the full amount required by the judgment. See subdivision (b) and Section 1268.010(b)(2) (such a deposit deemed a post-judgment deposit on entry of judgment). Where the amount of the prejudgment deposit is not in the full amount required by the judgment, interest does not cease to accrue until an amount sufficient to bring it up to the full amount of the judgment is added. See

subdivision (b) and Section 1268.110(a) (postjudgment deposit must be in full amount of judgment less amounts previously deposited).

Research References

Miller and Starr California Real Estate § 30A:77, Interest.
8 Witkin, California Summary 10th Constitutional Law § 1258, (S 1258) in General.

§ 1268.330. Offsets against interest accrual; value of defendant's possession and rents

If, after the date that interest begins to accrue, the defendant:

(a) Continues in actual possession of the property, the value of that possession shall be offset against the interest. For the purpose of this section, the value of possession of the property shall be presumed to be the rate of interest calculated as prescribed by Section 1268.350 on the compensation awarded. This presumption is one affecting the burden of proof.

(b) Receives rents or other income from the property attributable to the period after interest begins to accrue, the net amount of these rents and other income shall be offset against the interest. *(Added by Stats.1975, c. 1275, p. 3461, § 2, operative July 1, 1976. Amended by Stats.1986, c. 1372, § 3.)*

Law Revision Commission Comments

Section 1268.330 supersedes subdivision (b) of former Section 1255b. Revisions have been made to clarify the meaning of the former language. See also Govt.Code § 7267.4 ("If the public entity permits an owner or tenant to occupy the real property acquired on a rental basis for a short term, or for a period subject to termination by the public entity on short notice, the amount of rent required shall not exceed the fair rental value of the property to a short-term occupier.") For an exception to the rule stated in Section 1268.330, see Section 1255.040 (deposit on notice of homeowner). See also Section 1255.050 (deposit on notice of owner of rental property).

Research References

Miller and Starr California Real Estate § 19:149, Valuation and Apportionment of the Award.
Miller and Starr California Real Estate § 30A:77, Interest.
8 Witkin, California Summary 10th Constitutional Law § 1258, (S 1258) in General.

§ 1268.340. Assessment of interest by court

Interest, including interest accrued due to possession of property by the plaintiff prior to judgment, and any offset against interest as provided in Section 1268.330, shall be assessed by the court rather than by jury. *(Added by Stats.1975, c. 1275, p. 3461, § 2, operative July 1, 1976.)*

Law Revision Commission Comments

Section 1268.340 is new. It clarifies former law by specifying that the court, rather than the jury, shall assess interest, including interest required to satisfy the defendant's constitutional right to compensation for possession of his property prior to conclusion of the eminent domain proceeding. See Metropolitan Water Dist. v. Adams, 16 Cal.2d 676, 107 P.2d 618 (1940); People v. Johnson, 203 Cal.App.2d 712, 22 Cal.Rptr. 149 (1962); City of San Rafael v. Wood, 144 Cal.App.2d 604, 301 P.2d 421 (1956). Section 1268.340 also resolves a further uncertainty by specifying that the amount of the offset against interest provided by Section 1268.330 is likewise assessed by the court, thus requiring that any evidence on that issue is to be heard by the court rather than the jury. Compare People v. McCoy, 248 Cal.App.2d 27, 56 Cal.Rptr. 352 (1967), with People v. Giumarra Vineyards Corp., 245 Cal.App.2d 309, 53 Cal.Rptr. 902 (1966).

Research References

Miller and Starr California Real Estate § 30A:77, Interest.

8 Witkin, California Summary 10th Constitutional Law § 1258, (S 1258) in General.

§ 1268.350. Rate of interest as apportionment rate; definitions

(a) As used in this section, "apportionment rate" means the apportionment rate calculated by the Controller as the rate of earnings by the Surplus Money Investment Fund for each calendar quarter.

(b) The rate of interest payable under this article for each calendar quarter, or fraction thereof, for which interest is due, shall be the apportionment rate for the immediately preceding calendar quarter.

(c) Each district office of the Department of Transportation shall quote the apportionment rate to any person upon request. *(Added by Stats.1986, c. 1372, § 4. Amended by Stats.2006, c. 311 (S.B.1586), § 1.)*

Research References

Rutter, Cal. Practice Guide: Civil Trials & Evidence Ch. 17-F, F. Prejudgment Interest.
Miller and Starr California Real Estate § 30:14, Prejudgment Interest; Attorney Fees; Costs.
Miller and Starr California Real Estate § 30:19, Announcement of Intent to Condemn or Adoption of Resolution of Necessity.
Miller and Starr California Real Estate § 30:21, Remedies for Unreasonable Precondemnation Activity.
Miller and Starr California Real Estate § 30A:77, Interest.
17 NO. 4 Miller & Starr, California Real Estate Newsalert 2, Statutory Update:.
17 NO. 6 Miller & Starr, California Real Estate Newsalert 20, Table of Statutes (Newsalert Vol 17).
8 Witkin, California Summary 10th Constitutional Law § 1167, Interest.
8 Witkin, California Summary 10th Constitutional Law § 1258, (S 1258) in General.
8 Witkin, California Summary 10th Constitutional Law § 1259, (S 1259) Market Rate of Interest.

§ 1268.360. Interest compounded quarterly

The interest payable for each calendar quarter shall draw interest, computed as prescribed by Section 1268.350, in each succeeding calendar quarter for which interest is due. *(Added by Stats.1986, c. 1372, § 5. Amended by Stats.2006, c. 311 (S.B. 1586), § 2.)*

Research References

Miller and Starr California Real Estate § 30:14, Prejudgment Interest; Attorney Fees; Costs.
Miller and Starr California Real Estate § 30A:77, Interest.
17 NO. 4 Miller & Starr, California Real Estate Newsalert 2, Statutory Update:.
17 NO. 6 Miller & Starr, California Real Estate Newsalert 20, Table of Statutes (Newsalert Vol 17).
8 Witkin, California Summary 10th Constitutional Law § 1259, (S 1259) Market Rate of Interest.

ARTICLE 5. PRORATION OF PROPERTY TAXES

Section

§ 1268.410. Liability of plaintiff for ad valorem taxes, penalties and costs

As between the plaintiff and defendant, the plaintiff is liable for any ad valorem taxes, penalties, and costs upon property acquired by eminent domain prorated from and including the date of apportionment determined pursuant to Section 5082 of the Revenue and Taxation Code. *(Added by Stats.1975, c. 1275, p. 3461, § 2, operative July 1, 1976. Amended by Stats.1979, c. 31, p. 89, § 3.)*

Law Revision Commission Comments

Section 1268.410 is the same in substance as the first paragraph of former Section 1252.1.

Section 1268.410 is amended for clarity. The proration under this section applies whether or not the property becomes exempt from taxation, but affects only the relationship between plaintiff and defendant. Collection and cancellation of taxes is not governed by Section 1268.410 but by the relevant provisions of the Revenue and Taxation Code. See, e.g., Rev. & Tax.Code § 5090. See also Section 1268.420 (tax collection moratorium).

Research References

Miller and Starr California Real Estate § 30A:34, Deeds of Trust, Taxes and Other Monetary Liens.
9 Witkin, California Summary 10th Taxation § 284, Cancellation of Assessment or Tax.
8 Witkin, California Summary 10th Constitutional Law § 1260, (S 1260) Liability, Proration, and Payment.
8 Witkin, California Summary 10th Constitutional Law § 1261, (S 1261) Exempt Property.

§ 1268.420. Collection of ad valorem taxes, penalties and costs; exempt property; dismissal of proceedings

(a) Except as provided in subdivision (b):

(1) If the acquisition of property by eminent domain will make the property exempt property as defined in Section 5081 of the Revenue and Taxation Code, any ad valorem taxes, penalties, or costs on the property for which the plaintiff is liable pursuant to Section 1268.410 are not collectible.

(2) If the acquisition of property by eminent domain will not make the property exempt property as defined in Section 5081 of the Revenue and Taxation Code, the plaintiff shall be deemed to be the assessee for the purposes of collection of any ad valorem taxes, penalties, and costs on the property for which the plaintiff is liable pursuant to Section 1268.410.

(b) To the extent there is a dismissal or partial dismissal of the eminent domain proceeding, the amount of any unpaid ad valorem taxes, penalties, and costs on the property for which the plaintiff would be liable pursuant to Section 1268.410 until the entry of judgment of dismissal shall be awarded to the defendant. The amount awarded shall be paid to the tax collector from the award or, if unpaid for any reason, are collectible from the defendant. *(Added by Stats.1979, c. 31, p. 90, § 5.)*

Law Revision Commission Comments

The substance of former Section 1268.420 is continued in Section 1268.450.

Subdivision (a)(1) of Section 1268.420 places a moratorium on collection of taxes on property that it appears will become exempt from taxation by virtue of acquisition by a public entity. *Cf.* Rev. & Tax.Code § 5091 (notice of proposed acquisition of property that will become exempt). If the eminent domain proceeding is ultimately abandoned or otherwise dismissed, the moratorium ends and collection may thereafter be made from the award or from the defendant. See subdivision (b).

Subdivision (a)(2) makes clear that taxes on property that will not become exempt by virtue of acquisition by a public entity are collectible from the plaintiff as of the date of apportionment. See Section 1268.410. The taxes are collectible notwithstanding the fact that the final order of condemnation vesting title in the plaintiff has not yet been made or recorded. For cancellation and refund of taxes collected on property that becomes exempt by virtue of a claimed exemption, see Revenue and Taxation Code Section 272. In the case of abandonment or other dismissal, unpaid taxes for which the plaintiff is liable must be awarded to the defendant, and are collectible either from the award or from the defendant. See subdivision (b).

In the case of a partial taking, a separate valuation may be necessary in order to make taxes, penalties, and costs collectible, whether on the part taken or on the remainder. *Cf.* Section 1268.450 (application for separate valuation of property).

Research References

Miller and Starr California Real Estate § 30A:34, Deeds of Trust, Taxes and Other Monetary Liens.
8 Witkin, California Summary 10th Constitutional Law § 1261, (S 1261) Exempt Property.

§ 1268.430. Payment by defendant of amount of plaintiff's liability; claim by defendant; time

(a) If the defendant has paid any amount for which, as between the plaintiff and defendant, the plaintiff is liable under this article, the plaintiff shall pay to the defendant a sum equal to such amount.

(b) The amount the defendant is entitled to be paid under this section shall be claimed in the manner provided for claiming costs and at the following times:

(1) If the plaintiff took possession of the property prior to judgment, at the time provided for claiming costs.

(2) If the plaintiff did not take possession of the property prior to judgment, not later than 30 days after the plaintiff took title to the property. *(Added by Stats.1975, c. 1275, p. 3462, § 2, operative July 1, 1976.)*

Law Revision Commission Comments

Section 1268.430 is the same in substance as the final two paragraphs of former Section 1252.1.

Research References

Miller and Starr California Real Estate § 30A:34, Deeds of Trust, Taxes and Other Monetary Liens.
8 Witkin, California Summary 10th Constitutional Law § 1260, (S 1260) Liability, Proration, and Payment.
8 Witkin, California Summary 10th Constitutional Law § 1261, (S 1261) Exempt Property.

§ 1268.440. Refunds; exempt property; taxes subject to cancellation

(a) If taxes have been paid on property that is exempt property as defined in Section 5081 of the Revenue and Taxation Code, the amount of the taxes that, if unpaid, would have been subject to cancellation under Article 5 (commencing with Section 5081) of Chapter 4 of Part 9 of Division 1 of the Revenue and Taxation Code shall be deemed to be erroneously collected and shall be refunded in the manner provided in Article 1 (commencing with Section 5096) of Chapter 5 of Part 9 of Division 1 of the Revenue and Taxation Code to the person who paid the taxes.

(b) The public entity shall be deemed to be the person who paid the taxes if the public entity reimbursed the defendant for the taxes under a cost bill filed in the eminent domain proceeding pursuant to Section 1268.430. A claim for refund of taxes filed by a public entity pursuant to this section shall contain a copy of the cost bill under which taxes were reimbursed or a declaration under penalty of perjury by the public entity that the taxes were reimbursed under a cost bill.

(c) Taxes paid on either the secured or unsecured roll may be refunded pursuant to this section. *(Added by Stats.1979, c. 31, p. 90, § 6.)*

Law Revision Commission Comments

Section 1268.440 continues the substance of former Section 5096.3 of the Revenue and Taxation Code. Refund of taxes on exempt property other than that defined in Revenue and Taxation Code Section 5081 is governed by Revenue and Taxation Code Section 272. The terms "secured roll" and "unsecured roll" are defined in Revenue and Taxation Code Section 109.

Research References

Miller and Starr California Real Estate § 30A:34, Deeds of Trust, Taxes and Other Monetary Liens.
9 Witkin, California Summary 10th Taxation § 285, Claim for Refund of Tax.
8 Witkin, California Summary 10th Constitutional Law § 1261, (S 1261) Exempt Property.

§ 1268.450. Separate valuation on assessment roll; application

If property acquired by eminent domain does not have a separate valuation on the assessment roll, any party to the eminent domain proceeding may, at any time after the taxes on the property are subject to cancellation under Article 5 (commencing with Section 5081) of Chapter 4 of Part 9 of Division 1 of the Revenue and Taxation Code, apply to the tax collector for a separate valuation of the property in accordance with Article 3 (commencing with Section 2821) of Chapter 3 of Part 5 of Division 1 of the Revenue and Taxation Code notwithstanding any provision in that article to the contrary. *(Added by Stats.1979, c. 31, p. 90, § 7.)*

Law Revision Commission Comments

Section 1268.450 continues the substance of former Section 1268.420. It is revised to reflect the enactment of Article 5 (commencing with Section 5081) of Chapter 4 of Part 9 of Division 1 of the Revenue and Taxation Code relating to cancellation of taxes on exempt property.

Research References

Miller and Starr California Real Estate § 30A:34, Deeds of Trust, Taxes and Other Monetary Liens.
8 Witkin, California Summary 10th Constitutional Law § 1261, (S 1261) Exempt Property.

ARTICLE 6. ABANDONMENT

Section
1268.510. Notice by plaintiff; filing; actions by court.

§ 1268.510. Notice by plaintiff; filing; actions by court

(a) At any time after the filing of the complaint and before the expiration of 30 days after final judgment, the plaintiff may wholly or partially abandon the proceeding by serving on the defendant and filing in court a written notice of such abandonment.

(b) The court may, upon motion made within 30 days after the filing of such notice, set the abandonment aside if it determines that the position of the moving party has been substantially changed to his detriment in justifiable reliance upon the proceeding and such party cannot be restored to substantially the same position as if the proceeding had not been commenced.

(c) Upon denial of a motion to set aside such abandonment or, if no such motion is filed, upon the expiration of the time for filing such a motion, the court shall, on motion of any party, enter judgment wholly or partially dismissing the proceeding. *(Added by Stats.1975, c. 1275, p. 3462, § 2, operative July 1, 1976.)*

Law Revision Commission Comments

Section 1268.510 is the same in substance as portions of former Section 1255a: subdivision (a) is the same in substance as the first sentence of former Section 1255a; subdivision (b) is the same in substance as subdivision (b) of former Section 1255a; subdivision (c) is the same in substance as the first sentence of subdivision (c) of former Section 1255a. For recovery of litigation expenses and damages on dismissal, see Sections 1268.610 and 1268.620.

Research References

Miller and Starr California Real Estate § 30A:82, Abandonment.
1 Witkin Cal. Proc. 5th Attorneys § 167, (S 167) Statutory Liens.
7 Witkin Cal. Proc. 5th Judgment § 21, Statutory Types.
6 Witkin Cal. Proc. 5th Proceedings Without Trial § 280, in General.
8 Witkin, California Summary 10th Constitutional Law § 1202, (S 1202) Remedies If Proceeding is Not Promptly Commenced.
8 Witkin, California Summary 10th Constitutional Law § 1264, Abandonment and Dismissal.

ARTICLE 7. LITIGATION EXPENSES AND DAMAGES UPON DISMISSAL OR DEFEAT OF RIGHT TO TAKE

Section

1268.610.   Award of litigation expenses to defendant; dismissal and final judgment conditions; notice of abandonment.

1268.620.   Dismissal or final judgment that plaintiff cannot acquire property after defendant moved from property; delivery of possession and damages to persons entitled.

§ 1268.610. Award of litigation expenses to defendant; dismissal and final judgment conditions; notice of abandonment

(a) Subject to subdivisions (b) and (c), the court shall award the defendant his or her litigation expenses whenever:

(1) The proceeding is wholly or partly dismissed for any reason.

(2) Final judgment in the proceeding is that the plaintiff cannot acquire property it sought to acquire in the proceeding.

(b) Where there is a partial dismissal or a final judgment that the plaintiff cannot acquire a portion of the property originally sought to be acquired, or a dismissal of one or more plaintiffs pursuant to Section 1260.020, the court shall award the defendant only those litigation expenses, or portion thereof, that would not have been incurred had the property sought to be acquired following the dismissal or judgment been the property originally sought to be acquired.

(c) If the plaintiff files a notice of abandonment as to a particular defendant, or a request for dismissal of a particular defendant, and the court determines that the defendant did not own or have any interest in the property that the plaintiff sought to acquire in the proceeding, the court shall award that defendant only those litigation expenses incurred up to the time of filing the notice of abandonment or request for dismissal.

(d) Litigation expenses under this section shall be claimed in and by a cost bill to be prepared, served, filed, and taxed as in a civil action. If the proceeding is dismissed upon motion of the plaintiff, the cost bill shall be filed within 30 days after notice of entry of judgment. *(Added by Stats.1975, c. 1275, p. 3462, § 2, operative July 1, 1976. Amended by Stats.2001, c. 192 (A.B.1463), § 1.)*

Law Revision Commission Comments

Section 1268.610 deals with the litigation expenses that a defendant may recover when an eminent domain proceeding is dismissed for any reason or there is a final judgment that the plaintiff does not have the right to take. The section is based primarily on former Section 1255a but expands the scope of protection afforded the defendant to cover dismissal for any reason. Compare Alta Bates Hosp. v. Mertle, 31 Cal.App.3d 349, 107 Cal.Rptr. 277 (1973).

To a large extent, Section 1268.610 continues provisions of former Section 1255a. Thus, as formerly was the rule under Section 1255a, the plaintiff must reimburse the defendant:

(1) When the plaintiff voluntarily abandons the proceeding. See also Section 1268.510.

(2) When there is an implied abandonment of the proceeding such as abandonment resulting from failure to pay the judgment. See Section 1268.020. See County of Los Angeles v. Bartlett, 223 Cal.App.2d 353, 36 Cal.Rptr. 193 (1963); Capistrano Union High School Dist. v. Capistrano Beach Acreage Co., 188 Cal.App.2d 612, 10 Cal.Rptr. 750 (1961).

(3) When there is a "partial abandonment" of the proceeding (see Section 1250.340) by an amendment of the complaint to significantly reduce the property or property interest being taken. (Reimbursement of defendant's litigation expenses when the complaint is amended to add additional property is not covered by Section 1268.610; this is covered by Section 1250.340.)

Section 1268.610 also continues the rule under former Section 1246.4 that public-entity plaintiffs must reimburse the defendant when there is a final judgment that the plaintiff does not have a right to take the property sought to be acquired and expands this rule to apply to nonpublic-entity plaintiffs. See also federal Uniform Relocation Assistance and Real Property Acquisition Policies Act of 1970, 42 U.S.C. § 4654 (1971).

Section 1268.610 also changes prior law to require reimbursement of the defendant where the eminent domain proceeding is dismissed for failure to prosecute. Under prior law, the defendant was not entitled to reimbursement upon such failure. See City of Industry v. Gordon, 29 Cal.App.3d 90, 105 Cal.Rptr. 206 (1972); Bell v. American States Water Service Co., 10 Cal.App.2d 604, 52 P.2d 503 (1935). But see Alta Bates Hosp. v. Mertle, *supra*.

The term "litigation expenses" used in subdivision (a) is defined in Section 1235.140.

The "partial dismissal" provision of subdivision (b) continues the rule that litigation expenses do not include any items that would have been incurred notwithstanding a partial abandonment. See the third sentence of former Section 1255a(c). Subdivision (b) expands this rule to make it applicable where a final judgment determines that the plaintiff does not have the right to take a portion of the property it originally sought to acquire in the eminent domain proceeding and where there is a dismissal of one or more plaintiffs pursuant to Section 1260.020 (determination of more necessary public use where separate proceedings are consolidated).

Subdivision (c) is the same in substance as the fourth and fifth sentences of former Section 1255a(c).

Research References

Miller and Starr California Real Estate § 30:21, Remedies for Unreasonable Precondemnation Activity.
Miller and Starr California Real Estate § 30A:53, Deposit of Probable Compensation.
Miller and Starr California Real Estate § 30A:78, Litigation Expenses.
17 NO. 5 Miller & Starr, California Real Estate Newsalert 6, Eminent Domain.
1 Witkin Cal. Proc. 5th Attorneys § 167, (S 167) Statutory Liens.
7 Witkin Cal. Proc. 5th Judgment § 95, (S 95) Prevailing Party in Specified Actions.
7 Witkin Cal. Proc. 5th Judgment § 124, (S 124) Condemnation Expert.
7 Witkin Cal. Proc. 5th Judgment § 139, (S 139) in General.
7 Witkin Cal. Proc. 5th Judgment § 140, Time Limits.
7 Witkin Cal. Proc. 5th Judgment § 234, in General.
6 Witkin Cal. Proc. 5th Proceedings Without Trial § 280, in General.
8 Witkin, California Summary 10th Constitutional Law § 1213, (S 1213) Procedure.
8 Witkin, California Summary 10th Constitutional Law § 1265, (S 1265) Litigation Expenses.
8 Witkin, California Summary 10th Constitutional Law § 1267, Costs.

§ 1268.620. Dismissal or final judgment that plaintiff cannot acquire property after defendant moved from property; delivery of possession and damages to persons entitled

If, after the defendant moves from property in compliance with an order or agreement for possession or in reasonable contemplation of its taking by the plaintiff, the proceeding is dismissed with regard to that property for any reason or there is a final judgment that the plaintiff cannot acquire that property, the court shall:

(a) Order the plaintiff to deliver possession of the property to the persons entitled to it; and

(b) Make such provision as shall be just for the payment of all damages proximately caused by the proceeding and its dismissal as to that property. *(Added by Stats.1975, c. 1275, p. 3463, § 2, operative July 1, 1976.)*

Law Revision Commission Comments

Section 1268.620 provides for restoration of possession of the property and damages where the defendant was dispossessed from property prior to a dismissal or a final judgment that the plaintiff cannot acquire the property. Section 1268.620 is not intended to limit any remedies the defendant may have on an inverse condemnation theory for damage to the property during litigation.

The provision on restoration of possession of the property supersedes the final portion of the second sentence of former Section 1252 and a portion of subdivision (d) of former Section 1255a. Whereas the prior provisions required possession to be restored to the defendants when the plaintiff failed to deposit the award in a condemnation proceeding, abandoned the proceeding, or because the right to take was defeated, Section 1268.620 requires restoration in any case where the proceeding is dismissed or there is a final judgment that the plaintiff cannot take the property, thus covering, for example, a case where the proceeding is dismissed for delay in bringing it to trial.

The provision relating to the payment of damages supersedes subdivision (d) of former Section 1255a. Whereas the prior provision required payment of damages when the plaintiff abandoned or the right to take was defeated, subdivision (b) makes clear that this rule applies as well where the proceeding is dismissed, e.g., because the plaintiff fails to prosecute.

In addition, subdivision (b) requires payment of all damages proximately caused by the proceeding. Such damages would include, for example, damages for temporary interference with the operation of a business even though such damages might not have been compensable had the proceeding not been abandoned. Compare People v. Ayon, 54 Cal.2d 217, 228, 5 Cal.Rptr. 151, 157 (1960) (general inconvenience and annoyance not compensable), with Heimann v. City of Los Angeles, 30 Cal.2d 746, 754, 185 P.2d 597, 603 (1947) (substantial unnecessary interference compensable). Where there is a partial dismissal, only those damages allocable to the property subject to the dismissal may be recovered.

Research References

Miller and Starr California Real Estate § 30A:53, Deposit of Probable Compensation.
Miller and Starr California Real Estate § 30A:78, Litigation Expenses.
8 Witkin, California Summary 10th Constitutional Law § 1213, (S 1213) Procedure.
8 Witkin, California Summary 10th Constitutional Law § 1266, (S 1266) Damages Caused by Dispossession.

ARTICLE 8. COSTS

Section
1268.710. Allowance to defendants; apportionment of award; exception.
1268.720. Allowance of defendants costs on appeal; exception.

§ 1268.710. Allowance to defendants; apportionment of award; exception

The defendants shall be allowed their costs, including the costs of determining the apportionment of the award made pursuant to subdivision (b) of Section 1260.220, except that the costs of determining any issue as to title between two or more defendants shall be borne by the defendants in such proportion as the court may direct. *(Added by Stats.1975, c. 1275, p. 3463, § 2, operative July 1, 1976.)*

Research References

Rutter, Cal. Practice Guide: Civil Trials & Evidence Ch. 17-D, D. Costs.
Miller and Starr California Real Estate § 30:14, Prejudgment Interest; Attorney Fees; Costs.

Miller and Starr California Real Estate § 30A:76, Costs.
7 Witkin Cal. Proc. 5th Judgment § 95, (S 95) Prevailing Party in Specified Actions.
8 Witkin, California Summary 10th Constitutional Law § 1209, (S 1209) Award of Litigation Expenses.
8 Witkin, California Summary 10th Constitutional Law § 1267, Costs.

§ 1268.720. Allowance of defendants costs on appeal; exception

Unless the court otherwise orders, whether or not he is the prevailing party, the defendant in the proceeding shall be allowed his costs on appeal. This section does not apply to an appeal involving issues between defendants. *(Added by Stats. 1975, c. 1275, p. 3463, § 2, operative July 1, 1976.)*

Law Revision Commission Comments

Section 1268.720 states the basic rule that the defendant is allowed his costs on appeal in an eminent domain case. This basic rule is an exception to the rule that the prevailing party is entitled to his costs on appeal. Compare Cal.R.Ct. 26 (costs on appeal). The basic rule continues case law that the general constitutional principle of "just compensation" requires that the plaintiff-condemnor bear the costs of all parties to the action in case of an appeal. See, e.g., Sacramento & San Joaquin Drainage Dist. v. Reed, 217 Cal.App.2d 611, 31 Cal.Rptr. 754 (1963) (defendant entitled to costs on plaintiff's appeal even if the plaintiff prevails); Regents of Univ. of Cal. v. Morris, 12 Cal.App.2d 679, 90 Cal.Rptr. 816 (1970) (defendant entitled to costs on defendant's appeal where defendant prevails).

Where the defendant is the appellant and loses, the former law was not clear. The trend in recent years was to award the defendant-appellant his costs whether or not he prevailed. See City of Baldwin Park v. Stoskus, 8 Cal.2d 563, 743a, 503 P.2d 1333, 1338, 105 Cal.Rptr. 325, 330 (1972); Klopping v. City of Whittier, 8 Cal.3d 39, 59, 500 P.2d 1345, 1360, 104 Cal.Rptr. 1, 16 (1972); People v. International Tel. & Tel. Corp., 26 Cal.App.3d 549, 103 Cal.Rptr. 63 (1972). See also In re Redevelopment Plan for Bunker Hill, 61 Cal.2d 21, 68–71, 389 P.2d 538, 568–570, 37 Cal.Rptr. 74, 104–106 (1964). However, such action apparently was discretionary with the reviewing court. See City of Oakland v. Pacific Coast Lumber & Mill Co., 172 Cal. 332, 156 P. 468 (1916) (not unconstitutional to award costs to plaintiff-respondent where he is the prevailing party). See also Stafford v. County of Los Angeles, 219 Cal.App.2d 770, 33 Cal.Rptr. 475 (1963) (plaintiff in inverse condemnation case taxed costs for frivolous appeal). Moreover, the defendant was not entitled to costs where the issue involved title as between two or more defendants. See former Section 1246.1; Section 1268.710(b) and Comment thereto.

Section 1268.720 preserves the rule allowing defendant costs and makes clear that this rule applies in the event of an appeal by the defendant that fails. The section authorizes the court to deviate from this principle.

It should be noted that Section 1268.720 is limited to an appeal involving the plaintiff. Where the appeal is between defendants, whether or not an issue of title is involved, the general rules governing costs on appeal prevail.

Research References

Rutter, Cal. Practice Guide: Civil Appeals & Writs Ch. 14-B, B. Recovery of Appellate Costs and Attorney Fees.
Miller and Starr California Real Estate § 30:14, Prejudgment Interest; Attorney Fees; Costs.
Miller and Starr California Real Estate § 30A:76, Costs.
8 Witkin, California Summary 10th Constitutional Law § 1267, Costs.

CHAPTER 12. ARBITRATION OF COMPENSATION IN ACQUISITIONS OF PROPERTY FOR PUBLIC USE

Section
1273.010. Authority of person to enter arbitration agreement.
1273.020. Expenses and fees payable by party acquiring property; fees of any other party payable by agreement; source of funds.
1273.030. Applicability of Title 9; exceptions.

Section

1273.040. Abandonment of proceedings; time; expenses; attorney fees.

1273.050. Agreements acknowledged, recorded and rerecorded; notice; memorandum.

Law Revision Commission Comments

Chapter 12 (commencing with Section 1273.010) continues without substantive change the provisions of former Chapter 3 (commencing with Section 1273.01) of Title 7 of Part 3 of the Code of Civil Procedure. For background, see Recommendation Relating to Arbitration of Just Compensation, 9 Cal.L.Revision Comm. Reports 123 (1969). Nothing in this chapter precludes the defendants from entering into an agreement to arbitrate any issue between themselves under the general arbitration statute. See Title 9 (commencing with Section 1280) of Part 3 of the Code of Civil Procedure.

§ 1273.010. Authority of person to enter arbitration agreement

(a) Any person authorized to acquire property for public use may enter into an agreement to arbitrate any controversy as to the compensation to be made in connection with the acquisition of the property.

(b) Where property is already appropriated to a public use, the person authorized to compromise or settle the claim arising from a taking or damaging of such property for another public use may enter into an agreement to arbitrate any controversy as to the compensation to be made in connection with such taking or damaging.

(c) For the purposes of this section, in the case of a public entity, "person" refers to the particular department, officer, commission, board, or governing body authorized to acquire property on behalf of the public entity or to compromise or settle a claim arising from the taking or damaging of the entity's property. (Added by Stats.1975, c. 1275, p. 3463, § 2, operative July 1, 1976.)

Law Revision Commission Comments

Section 1273.010, which supersedes former Section 1273.02, authorizes arbitration in connection with the acquisition of property for public use.

The phrase "compensation to be made in connection with the acquisition of the property" is intended to encompass any amounts that may be assessed or awarded in a condemnation proceeding and, specifically, to include compensation for injury to the remainder and compensation for loss of goodwill.

The term "controversy" is defined, for purposes of arbitration, in subdivision (c) of Section 1280.

The enactment of this chapter does not imply that public entities authorized to purchase, but not to condemn, property are not authorized to agree to arbitration. See Section 1273.030(d).

This chapter contains no provisions comparable to Sections 1250.220, 1250.230, and 1260.220, which require that all persons having an interest in the property be named as defendants in the condemnation complaint permit any unnamed interest holder to appear as a defendant in the proceeding, and provide for allocation of the award among holders of various interests. The chapter assumes that prudence on the part of the acquiring agency will assure that it agrees to arbitrate with the person who owns the interest it seeks to acquire. Also, the interests of persons other than parties to the arbitration would be unaffected by the arbitration agreement or the carrying out of that agreement. In short, an arbitration agreement and award operates only as a contract and conveyance between the parties to the particular agreement.

Subdivision (a). Subdivision (a) authorizes any acquirer of property for public use to agree to arbitrate the question of compensation and to act in accordance with the agreement. The subdivision does not imply that the public entity must have complied with the formalities (such as the adoption of a formal condemnation resolution) prescribed as conditions precedent to the commencement of an eminent domain proceeding. Rather, the subdivision contemplates that the question of compensation may be submitted to arbitration whenever acquisition has been authorized in the manner required of the particular entity or agency. As the arbitration agreement ordinarily would commit the public entity to purchase the property at the amount of the award (see Section 1273.040), the agreement should be approved and executed in the same manner as a contract to purchase property. Cf. Santa Monica Unified School Dist. v. Persh, 5 Cal.App.3d 945, 85 Cal.Rptr. 463 (1970).

Subdivision (b). Subdivision (b) authorizes "persons" who own, hold, or control public property that may be taken by eminent domain proceedings to agree to arbitrate the amount of compensation. Public property may be taken by eminent domain proceedings whether or not it is already "appropriated to a public use" (see Sections 1240.510 and 1240.610), and condemnation by one public entity of property already devoted to a public use by another public entity is a fairly common occurrence.

Research References

Rutter, Cal. Practice Guide: A.D.R. App. D Form 65, Real Property-Eminent Domain-Arbitration of Compensation in Acquisitions of Property for Public Use.

Miller and Starr California Real Estate § 30A:1, Introduction.

Miller and Starr California Real Estate § 35:23, Public Policy in Favor of Arbitration.

Miller and Starr California Real Estate § 30A:67, Agreements to Mediate or Arbitrate.

8 Witkin, California Summary 10th Constitutional Law § 1204, Jurisdiction and Venue.

8 Witkin, California Summary 10th Constitutional Law § 1210, Alternative Dispute Resolution.

8 Witkin, California Summary 10th Constitutional Law § 1268, in General.

§ 1273.020. Expenses and fees payable by party acquiring property; fees of any other party payable by agreement; source of funds

(a) Notwithstanding Sections 1283.2 and 1284.2, the party acquiring the property shall pay all of the expenses and fees of the neutral arbitrator and the statutory fees and mileage of all witnesses subpoenaed in the arbitration, together with other expenses of the arbitration incurred or approved by the neutral arbitrator, not including attorney's fees or expert witness fees or other expenses incurred by other parties for their own benefit.

(b) An agreement authorized by this chapter may require that the party acquiring the property pay reasonable attorney's fees or expert witness fees, or both, to any other party to the arbitration. If the agreement requires the payment of such fees, the amount of the fees is a matter to be determined in the arbitration proceeding unless the agreement prescribes otherwise.

(c) The party acquiring the property may pay the expenses and fees referred to in subdivisions (a) and (b) from funds available for the acquisition of the property or other funds available for the purpose. (Added by Stats.1975, c. 1275, p. 3463, § 2, operative July 1, 1976.)

Law Revision Commission Comments

Section 1273.020 supersedes former Section 1273.03. Subdivision (a) of Section 1273.020 is consistent with the rule applicable to eminent domain proceedings that the condemnee is entitled to recover all "court costs." See Section 1268.710 and Comment thereto. Subdivision (a) precludes the parties by agreement from imposing costs of this nature on the party from whom the property is being acquired.

Subdivision (b), on the other hand, does permit the parties to provide in the arbitration agreement that the party acquiring the property will pay reasonable attorney's fees or expert witness fees incurred by other parties to the agreement. Absent such provision in the agreement, the party from whom the property is being acquired must pay his own attorney's fees and expert witness fees.

Research References

Rutter, Cal. Practice Guide: A.D.R. App. D Form 65, Real Property-Eminent Domain-Arbitration of Compensation in Acquisitions of Property for Public Use.

Miller and Starr California Real Estate § 30A:67, Agreements to Mediate or Arbitrate.

8 Witkin, California Summary 10th Constitutional Law § 1269, Effect and Enforcement of Agreement.

§ 1273.030. Applicability of Title 9; exceptions

(a) Except as specifically provided in this chapter, agreements authorized by this chapter are subject to Title 9 (commencing with Section 1280) of this part.

(b) An agreement authorized by this chapter may be made whether or not an eminent domain proceeding has been commenced to acquire the property. If a proceeding has been commenced or is commenced, any petition or response relating to the arbitration shall be filed and determined in the proceeding.

(c) Notwithstanding Section 1281.4, an agreement authorized by this chapter does not waive or restrict the power of any person to commence and prosecute an eminent domain proceeding, including the taking of possession prior to judgment, except that, upon motion of a party to the proceeding, the court shall stay the determination of compensation until any petition for an order to arbitrate is determined and, if arbitration is ordered, until arbitration is had in accordance with the order.

(d) The effect and enforceability of an agreement authorized by this chapter is not defeated or impaired by contention or proof by any party to the agreement that the party acquiring the property pursuant to the agreement lacks the power or capacity to take the property by eminent domain.

(e) Notwithstanding the rules as to venue provided by Sections 1292 and 1292.2, any petition relating to arbitration authorized by this chapter shall be filed in the superior court in the county in which the property, or any portion of the property, is located. *(Added by Stats.1975, c. 1275, p. 3464, § 2, operative July 1, 1976.)*

Law Revision Commission Comments

Section 1273.030 supersedes former Section 1273.04. Although Section 1273.030 provides that arbitration under this chapter is governed by the general arbitration statute (Sections 1280–1294.2), a few minor modifications in the procedure provided by the general statute are desirable when arbitration is used to determine the compensation property acquired for public use.

Subdivision (a). Subdivision (a) makes clear that, in general, agreements to arbitrate under this chapter are subject to the general arbitration statute. See, in particular, Sections 1285–1288.8 (enforcement of the award) and 1290–1294.2 (judicial proceedings relating to the arbitration or the award).

Subdivision (b). Subdivision (b) makes clear that it is not necessary to commence an eminent domain proceeding in order to arbitrate under this chapter and also provides a special rule concerning the court in which any petition or response relating to the arbitration shall be filed and determined when an eminent domain proceeding is pending.

Subdivision (c). Subdivision (c) makes clear that an eminent domain proceeding may be begun and prosecuted notwithstanding an agreement to arbitrate the question of compensation and that such an agreement does not impair the condemnor's power to take possession prior to judgment. There is, of course, nothing to preclude the parties from including a provision in the arbitration agreement that prohibits the condemnor from taking possession of the property prior to the award in the arbitration proceeding. Subdivision (c) also provides for staying the determination of compensation in an eminent domain proceeding pending an agreed arbitration—a practice provided for as to other arbitrations by Section 1281.4.

Subdivision (d). Subdivision (d) makes clear that an agreement to arbitrate and to purchase and sell at the amount of the award does not require, and is not impaired by the acquirer's lack of, power to take the property by eminent domain.

Subdivision (e). Subdivision (e) requires that petitions relating to arbitration be filed in the county in which the property lies. The venue provided by this subdivision corresponds with the rule as to venue for eminent domain proceedings. See Section 1250.020.

Research References

Miller and Starr California Real Estate § 30A:67, Agreements to Mediate or Arbitrate.

8 Witkin, California Summary 10th Constitutional Law § 1268, in General.

8 Witkin, California Summary 10th Constitutional Law § 1269, Effect and Enforcement of Agreement.

§ 1273.040. Abandonment of proceedings; time; expenses; attorney fees

(a) Except as provided in subdivision (b), an agreement authorized by this chapter may specify the terms and conditions under which the party acquiring the property may abandon the acquisition, the arbitration proceeding, and any eminent domain proceeding that may have been, or may be, filed. Unless the agreement provides that the acquisition may not be abandoned, the party acquiring the property may abandon the acquisition, the arbitration proceeding, and any eminent domain proceeding at any time not later than the time for filing and serving a petition or response to vacate an arbitration award under Sections 1288, 1288.2, and 1290.6.

(b) If the proceeding to acquire the property is abandoned after the arbitration agreement is executed, the party from whom the property was to be acquired is entitled to recover (1) all expenses reasonably and necessarily incurred (i) in preparing for the arbitration proceeding and for any judicial proceedings in connection with the acquisition of the property, (ii) during the arbitration proceeding and during any judicial proceedings in connection with the acquisition, and (iii) in any subsequent judicial proceedings in connection with the acquisition and (2) reasonable attorney's fees, appraisal fees, and fees for the services of other experts where such fees were reasonably and necessarily incurred to protect his interests in connection with the acquisition of the property. Unless the agreement otherwise provides, the amount of such expenses and fees shall be determined by arbitration in accordance with the agreement. *(Added by Stats.1975, c. 1275, p. 3464, § 2, operative July 1, 1976.)*

Law Revision Commission Comments

Subdivision (a) of Section 1273.040 supersedes former Section 1273.05. It permits the parties to the agreement to provide whether and under what conditions the acquirer may abandon the acquisition. If the agreement does not so provide, the party who was to have acquired the property may abandon the acquisition within the time within which a petition or response to vacate an arbitration award may be filed and served. This period is generally 100 days after service of the award (Sections 1288–1288.2) but is further limited by Section 1290.6 which limits the time for response to a petition. See Coordinated Constr., Inc. v. Canoga Big "A," Inc., 238 Cal.App.2d 313, 47 Cal.Rptr. 749 (1965).

Subdivision (b) makes clear that the right of the "condemnee" to recover certain expenses in the event of abandonment is not subject to modification under the arbitration agreement but the amount of such expenses is to be determined by arbitration unless the agreement otherwise provides. This subdivision is consistent with Section 1268.610 (rules governing litigation expenses upon dismissal of judicial condemnation proceeding).

Research References

Miller and Starr California Real Estate § 30A:67, Agreements to Mediate or Arbitrate.

8 Witkin, California Summary 10th Constitutional Law § 1270, Abandonment of Acquisition.

§ 1273.050. Agreements acknowledged, recorded and rerecorded; notice; memorandum

(a) An agreement authorized by this chapter may be acknowledged and recorded, and rerecorded, in the same manner and with the same effect as a conveyance of real property except that two years after the date the agreement is recorded, or rerecorded, the record ceases to be notice to any person for any purpose.

(b) In lieu of recording the agreement, there may be recorded a memorandum thereof, executed by the parties to the agreement, containing at least the following information: the names of the parties to the agreement, a description of the property, and a statement that an arbitration agreement affecting such property has been entered into pursuant to this chapter. Such memorandum when acknowledged and recorded, or rerecorded, in the same manner as a conveyance of real property has the same effect as if the agreement itself were recorded or rerecorded. *(Added by Stats.1975, c. 1275, p. 3465, § 2, operative July 1, 1976.)*

Law Revision Commission Comments

Section 1273.050 supersedes former Section 1273.06. Section 1273.050 permits an agreement authorized by this chapter, or a memorandum thereof, to be acknowledged and recorded to afford "constructive notice" to subsequent purchasers and lienors. Arbitration rules may provide for the escrowing of an instrument of transfer (see, e.g., Sections 1, 44, and 45 of the Eminent Domain Arbitration Rules of the American Arbitration Association (June 1, 1968)), but such an escrow would not, of itself, protect the "condemnor" against subsequent transferees. Section 1273.050 provides a means for obtaining such protection (see Civil Code Sections 1213–1220) and is calculated to make unnecessary the filing of an eminent domain proceeding solely to obtain the effect of a lis pendens.

Research References

Rutter, Cal. Practice Guide: A.D.R. App. D Form 65, Real Property-Eminent Domain-Arbitration of Compensation in Acquisitions of Property for Public Use.
Miller and Starr California Real Estate § 30A:3, California Eminent Domain Law.
Miller and Starr California Real Estate § 30A:67, Agreements to Mediate or Arbitrate.
8 Witkin, California Summary 10th Constitutional Law § 1268, in General.

Title 8

CHANGE OF NAMES

§ 1275. Jurisdiction

Applications for change of names must be determined by the Superior Courts. *(Enacted in 1872. Amended by Code Am.1880, c. 113, p. 117, § 1; Stats.1983, c. 486, § 1.)*

Research References

Miller and Starr California Real Estate § 8:19, Change in Name.
3 Witkin Cal. Proc. 5th Actions § 65, (S 65) Statutory Classes.
2 Witkin Cal. Proc. 5th Courts § 203, Invalid Rules.
10 Witkin, California Summary 10th Parent and Child § 46, in General.
13 Witkin, California Summary 10th Personal Property § 24, Right to Change Name.

13 Witkin, California Summary 10th Personal Property § 25A, (New)-Right to Maintain or Change Name Following Marriage or Domestic Partnership Registration.
11 Witkin, California Summary 10th Husband and Wife § 20, After Judgment of Dissolution or Nullity.

§ 1276. Application or petition; venue; contents

(a) All applications for change of names shall be made to the superior court of the county where the person whose name is proposed to be changed resides, except as specified in subdivision (e), either (1) by petition signed by the person or, if the person is under 18 years of age, either by one of the person's parents, or by any guardian of the person, or if both parents are dead and there is no guardian of the person, then by some near relative or friend of the person or (2) as provided in Section 7638 of the Family Code.

The petition or pleading shall specify the place of birth and residence of the person, his or her present name, the name proposed, and the reason for the change of name.

(b) In a proceeding for a change of name commenced by the filing of a petition, if the person whose name is to be changed is under 18 years of age, the petition shall, if neither parent of the person has signed the petition, name, as far as known to the person proposing the name change, the parents of the person and their place of residence, if living, or if neither parent is living, near relatives of the person, and their place of residence.

(c) In a proceeding for a change of name commenced by the filing of a petition, if the person whose name is proposed to be changed is under 18 years of age and the petition is signed by only one parent, the petition shall specify the address, if known, of the other parent if living. If the petition is signed by a guardian, the petition shall specify the name and address, if known, of the parent or parents, if living, or the grandparents, if the addresses of both parents are unknown or if both parents are deceased, of the person whose name is proposed to be changed.

(d) In a proceeding for a change of name commenced by the filing of a petition, if the person whose name is proposed to be changed is 12 years of age or older, has been relinquished to an adoption agency by his or her parent or parents, and has not been legally adopted, the petition shall be signed by the person and the adoption agency to which the person was relinquished. The near relatives of the person and their place of residence shall not be included in the petition unless they are known to the person whose name is proposed to be changed.

(e) All petitions for the change of the name of a minor submitted by a guardian appointed by the juvenile court or the probate court shall be made in the appointing court.

(f) If the petition is signed by a guardian, the petition shall specify relevant information regarding the guardianship, the likelihood that the child will remain under the guardian's care until the child reaches the age of majority, and information suggesting that the child will not likely be returned to the custody of his or her parents. *(Enacted in 1872. Amended by Code Am.1877–78, c. 413, p. 110, § 1; Code Am.1880, c. 113, p. 117, § 2; Stats.1885, c. 128, p. 112, § 1; Stats.1929, c. 710, p. 1260, § 1; Stats.1945, c. 842, p. 1540, § 1; Stats.1961, c. 1817, p. 3864, § 1; Stats.1970, c. 651, p. 1276, § 1; Stats.1971, c. 1748, p. 3748, § 30; Stats.1975, c. 1241, p. 3192, § 9; Stats.1989, c. 1105, § 9; Stats.1992, c. 163 (A.B.2641), § 59, operative Jan. 1, 1994; Stats.2000, c. 111 (A.B.2155), § 1; Stats.2006, c. 567 (A.B.2303), § 10.)*

Law Revision Commission Comments

Section 1276 is amended to substitute a reference to the Family Code provision that replaced former Civil Code Section 7007(d). [22 Cal.L.Rev.Comm.Reports 1 (1992)].

Research References

3 Witkin Cal. Proc. 5th Actions § 816, Miscellaneous Local Proceedings.

10 Witkin, California Summary 10th Parent and Child § 109, (S 109) in General.

10 Witkin, California Summary 10th Parent and Child § 292, Common Law Rule Against Change.

13 Witkin, California Summary 10th Personal Property § 24, Right to Change Name.

§ 1277. Orders to show cause; publication or posting; petitions for minors; exemptions; service of notice

Section operative until July 1, 2014. See, also, section operative July 1, 2014.

(a) If a proceeding for a change of name is commenced by the filing of a petition, except as provided in subdivisions (b), (c), and (e), the court shall thereupon make an order reciting the filing of the petition, the name of the person by whom it is filed, and the name proposed. The order shall direct all persons interested in the matter to appear before the court at a time and place specified, which shall be not less than six nor more than 12 weeks from the time of making the order, unless the court orders a different time, to show cause why the application for change of name should not be granted. The order shall direct all persons interested in the matter to make known any objection that they may have to the granting of the petition for change of name by filing a written objection, which includes the reasons for the objection, with the court at least two court days before the matter is scheduled to be heard and by appearing in court at the hearing to show cause why the petition for change of name should not be granted. The order shall state that, if no written objection is timely filed, the court may grant the petition without a hearing.

A copy of the order to show cause shall be published pursuant to Section 6064 of the Government Code in a newspaper of general circulation to be designated in the order published in the county. If no newspaper of general circulation is published in the county, a copy of the order to show cause shall be posted by the clerk of the court in three of the most public places in the county in which the court is located, for a like period. Proof shall be made to the satisfaction of the court of this publication or posting, at the time of the hearing of the application.

Four weekly publications shall be sufficient publication of the order to show cause. If the order is published in a daily newspaper, publication once a week for four successive weeks shall be sufficient.

If a petition has been filed for a minor by a parent and the other parent, if living, does not join in consenting thereto, the petitioner shall cause, not less than 30 days prior to the hearing, to be served notice of the time and place of the hearing or a copy of the order to show cause on the other parent pursuant to Section 413.10, 414.10, 415.10, or 415.40. If notice of the hearing cannot reasonably be accomplished pursuant to Section 415.10 or 415.40, the court may order that notice be given in a manner that the court determines is reasonably calculated to give actual notice to the nonconsenting parent. In that case, if the court determines that notice by publication is reasonably calculated to give actual notice to the nonconsenting parent, the court may determine that publication of the order to show cause pursuant to this subdivision is sufficient notice to the nonconsenting parent.

(b)(1) If the petition for a change of name alleges a reason or circumstance described in paragraph (2), and the petitioner is a participant in the address confidentiality program created pursuant to Chapter 3.1 (commencing with Section 6205) of Division 7 of Title 1 of the Government Code, the action for a change of name is exempt from the requirement for publication of the order to show cause under subdivision (a), and the petition and the order of the court shall, in lieu of reciting the proposed name, indicate that the proposed name is confidential and will be on file with the Secretary of State pursuant to the provisions of the address confidentiality program.

(2) The procedure described in paragraph (1) applies to petitions alleging any of the following reasons or circumstances:

(A) To avoid domestic violence, as defined in Section 6211 of the Family Code.

(B) To avoid stalking, as defined in Section 646.9 of the Penal Code.

(C) The petitioner is, or is filing on behalf of, a victim of sexual assault, as defined in Section 1036.2 of the Evidence Code.

(3) For any petition under this subdivision, the current legal name of the petitioner shall be kept confidential by the court and shall not be published or posted in the court's calendars, indexes, or register of actions, as required by Article 7 (commencing with Section 69840) of Chapter 5 of Title 8 of the Government Code, or by any means or in any public forum, including a hardcopy or an electronic copy, or any other type of public media or display.

(4)(A) A petitioner may request that the court file the petition and any other papers associated with the proceeding under seal. The court may consider the request at the same time as the petition for name change, and may grant the request in any case in which the court finds that all of the following factors apply:

(i) There exists an overriding interest that overcomes the right of public access to the record.

(ii) The overriding interest supports sealing the record.

(iii) A substantial probability exists that the overriding interest will be prejudiced if the record is not sealed.

(iv) The proposed order to seal the records is narrowly tailored.

(v) No less restrictive means exist to achieve the overriding interest.

(B) On or before January 1, 2010, the Judicial Council shall develop rules of court and forms consistent with the requirements of this paragraph.

(c) A proceeding for a change of name for a witness participating in the state Witness Protection Program established by Title 7.5 (commencing with Section 14020) of Part 4 of the Penal Code who has been approved for the change of name by the program is exempt from the requirement for publication of the order to show cause under subdivision (a).

(d) If application for change of name is brought as part of an action under the Uniform Parentage Act (Part 3 (commencing with Section 7600) of Division 12 of the Family Code), whether as part of a petition or cross-complaint or as a separate order to show cause in a pending action thereunder, service of the application shall be made upon all other parties to the action in a like manner as prescribed for the service of a summons, as is set forth in Article 3 (commencing with Section 415.10) of Chapter 4 of Title 5 of Part 2. Upon the setting of a hearing on the issue, notice of the hearing shall be given to all parties in the action in a like manner and within the time limits prescribed generally for the type of hearing (whether trial or order to show cause) at which the issue of the change of name is to be decided.

(e) If a guardian files a petition to change the name of his or her minor ward pursuant to Section 1276:

(1) The guardian shall provide notice of the hearing to any living parent of the minor by personal service at least 30 days prior to the hearing.

(2) If either or both parents are deceased or cannot be located, the guardian shall cause, not less than 30 days prior to the hearing, to be served a notice of the time and place of the hearing or a copy of the order to show cause on the child's grandparents, if living, pursuant to Section 413.10, 414.10, 415.10, or 415.40.

(f) This section shall remain in effect only until July 1, 2014, and as of that date is repealed, unless a later enacted statute, that is enacted before July 1, 2014, deletes or extends that date. (Enacted in 1872. Amended by Stats.1905, c. 45, p. 40, § 1; Stats.1929, c. 710, p. 1260, § 2; Stats.1945, c. 854, p. 1565, § 1; Stats.1951, c. 45, p. 169, § 1; Stats.1961, c. 1817, p. 3865, § 2; Stats.1989, c. 1105, § 10; Stats.1990, c. 411 (A.B.3973), § 6, eff. July 25, 1990; Stats.1992, c. 163 (A.B.2641), § 60, operative Jan. 1, 1994; Stats.2000, c. 33 (A.B.205), § 1.5; Stats.2000, c. 111 (A.B.2155), § 4; Stats.2000, c. 688 (A.B.1669), § 8.3; Stats.2006, c. 567 (A.B.2303), § 11; Stats.2006, c. 689 (S.B.1743), § 1.5; Stats.2007, c. 130 (A.B.299), § 37; Stats.2008, c. 586 (A.B.2304), § 1; Stats.2013, c. 651 (A.B.1121), § 1.)

Repeal

For repeal of this section, see its terms.

Law Revision Commission Comments

Subdivision (b) of Section 1277 is amended to substitute the new reference to the Uniform Parentage Act in the Family Code. [22 Cal.L.Rev.Comm.Reports 1 (1992)].

Research References

10 Witkin, California Summary 10th Parent and Child § 46, in General.

§ 1277. Orders to show cause; publication or posting; petitions for minors; exemptions; service of notice

Section operative July 1, 2014. See, also, section operative until July 1, 2014.

(a)(1) If a proceeding for a change of name is commenced by the filing of a petition, except as provided in subdivisions (b), (c), and (e), the court shall thereupon make an order reciting the filing of the petition, the name of the person by whom it is filed, and the name proposed. The order shall direct all persons interested in the matter to appear before the court at a time and place specified, which shall be not less than six nor more than 12 weeks from the time of making the order, unless the court orders a different time, to show cause why the application for change of name should not be granted. The order shall direct all persons interested in the matter to make known any objection that they may have to the granting of the petition for change of name by filing a written objection, which includes the reasons for the objection, with the court at least two court days before the matter is scheduled to be heard and by appearing in court at the hearing to show cause why the petition for change of name should not be granted. The order shall state that, if no written objection is timely filed, the court may grant the petition without a hearing. If the petition seeks to conform the petitioner's name to his or her gender identity and no objection is timely filed, the court shall grant the petition without a hearing.

(2) A copy of the order to show cause shall be published pursuant to Section 6064 of the Government Code in a newspaper of general circulation to be designated in the order published in the county. If no newspaper of general circulation is published in the county, a copy of the order to show cause shall be posted by the clerk of the court in three of the most public places in the county in which the court is located, for a like period. Proof shall be made to the satisfaction of the court of this publication or posting, at the time of the hearing of the application.

(3) Four weekly publications shall be sufficient publication of the order to show cause. If the order is published in a daily newspaper, publication once a week for four successive weeks shall be sufficient.

(4) If a petition has been filed for a minor by a parent and the other parent, if living, does not join in consenting thereto, the petitioner shall cause, not less than 30 days prior to the hearing, to be served notice of the time and place of the hearing or a copy of the order to show cause on the other parent pursuant to Section 413.10, 414.10, 415.10, or 415.40. If notice of the hearing cannot reasonably be accomplished pursuant to Section 415.10 or 415.40, the court may order that notice be given in a manner that the court determines is reasonably calculated to give actual notice to the nonconsenting parent. In that case, if the court determines that notice by publication is reasonably calculated to give actual notice to the nonconsenting parent, the court may determine that publication of the order to show cause pursuant to this subdivision is sufficient notice to the nonconsenting parent.

(5) If the petition for a change of name is sought in order to conform the petitioner's name to his or her gender identity, the action for a change of name is exempt from the requirement for publication of the order to show cause under this subdivision.

(b)(1) If the petition for a change of name alleges a reason or circumstance described in paragraph (2), and the petitioner is a participant in the address confidentiality program created pursuant to Chapter 3.1 (commencing with Section 6205) of Division 7 of Title 1 of the Government Code, the action for a change of name is exempt from the requirement for publication of the order to show cause under subdivision (a), and the petition and the order of the court shall, in lieu of reciting the proposed name, indicate that the proposed name is confidential and will be on file with the Secretary of State pursuant to the provisions of the address confidentiality program.

(2) The procedure described in paragraph (1) applies to petitions alleging any of the following reasons or circumstances:

(A) To avoid domestic violence, as defined in Section 6211 of the Family Code.

(B) To avoid stalking, as defined in Section 646.9 of the Penal Code.

(C) The petitioner is, or is filing on behalf of, a victim of sexual assault, as defined in Section 1036.2 of the Evidence Code.

(3) For any petition under this subdivision, the current legal name of the petitioner shall be kept confidential by the court and shall not be published or posted in the court's calendars, indexes, or register of actions, as required by Article 7 (commencing with Section 69840) of Chapter 5 of Title 8 of the Government Code, or by any means or in any public forum, including a hardcopy or an electronic copy, or any other type of public media or display.

(4) Notwithstanding paragraph (3), the court may, at the request of the petitioner, issue an order reciting the name of the petitioner at the time of the filing of the petition and the new legal name of the petitioner as a result of the court's granting of the petition.

(5) A petitioner may request that the court file the petition and any other papers associated with the proceeding under seal. The court may consider the request at the same time as the petition for name change, and may grant the request in any case in which the court finds that all of the following factors apply:

(A) There exists an overriding interest that overcomes the right of public access to the record.

(B) The overriding interest supports sealing the record.

(C) A substantial probability exists that the overriding interest will be prejudiced if the record is not sealed.

(D) The proposed order to seal the records is narrowly tailored.

(E) No less restrictive means exist to achieve the overriding interest.

(c) A proceeding for a change of name for a witness participating in the state Witness Protection Program established by Title 7.5 (commencing with Section 14020) of Part 4 of the Penal Code who has been approved for the change of name by the program is exempt from the requirement for publication of the order to show cause under subdivision (a).

(d) If application for change of name is brought as part of an action under the Uniform Parentage Act (Part 3 (commencing with Section 7600) of Division 12 of the Family Code), whether as part of a petition or cross-complaint or as a separate order to show cause in a pending action thereunder, service of the application shall be made upon all other parties to the action in a like manner as prescribed for the service of a summons, as is set forth in Article 3 (commencing with Section 415.10) of Chapter 4 of Title 5 of Part 2. Upon the setting of a hearing on the issue, notice of the hearing shall be given to all parties in the action in a like manner and within the time limits prescribed generally for the type of hearing (whether trial or order to show cause) at which the issue of the change of name is to be decided.

(e) If a guardian files a petition to change the name of his or her minor ward pursuant to Section 1276:

(1) The guardian shall provide notice of the hearing to any living parent of the minor by personal service at least 30 days prior to the hearing.

(2) If either or both parents are deceased or cannot be located, the guardian shall cause, not less than 30 days prior to the hearing, to be served a notice of the time and place of the hearing or a copy of the order to show cause on the child's grandparents, if living, pursuant to Section 413.10, 414.10, 415.10, or 415.40.

(f) This section shall become operative on July 1, 2014. *(Added by Stats.2013, c. 651 (A.B.1121), § 2, operative July 1, 2014.)*

§ 1278. Hearings; orders without hearings

Section operative until July 1, 2014. See, also, section operative July 1, 2014.

(a) Except as provided in subdivisions (c) and (d), the petition or application shall be heard at the time designated by the court, only if objections are filed by any person who can, in those objections, show to the court good reason against the change of name. At the hearing, the court may examine on oath any of the petitioners, remonstrants, or other persons * * * touching the petition or application, and may make an order changing the name, or dismissing the petition or application, as to the court may seem right and proper.

If no objection is filed at least two court days before the date set for hearing, the court may, without hearing, enter the order that the change of name is granted.

(b) If the provisions of subdivision (b) of Section 1277 apply, the court shall not disclose the proposed name unless the court finds by clear and convincing evidence that the allegations of domestic violence or stalking * * * are false.

(c) If the application for a change of name is brought as part of an action under the Uniform Parentage Act (Part 3 (commencing with Section 7600) of Division 12 of the Family Code), the hearing on the issue of the change of name shall be conducted pursuant to statutes and rules of court governing

those proceedings, whether the hearing is conducted upon an order to show cause or upon trial.

(d) If the petition for a change of name is filed by a guardian on behalf of a minor ward, the court shall first find that the ward is likely to remain in the guardian's care until the age of majority and that the ward is not likely to be returned to the custody of his or her parents. Upon making those findings, the court shall consider the petition and may grant the petition only if it finds that the proposed name change is in the best interest of the child.

(e) This section shall remain in effect only until July 1, 2014, and as of that date is repealed, unless a later enacted statute, that is enacted before July 1, 2014, deletes or extends that date. *(Enacted in 1872. Amended by Code Am.1880, c. 113, p. 117, § 3; Stats.1905, c. 103, p. 99, § 1; Stats.1915, c. 85, p. 108, § 1; Stats.1929, c. 710, p. 1261, § 3; Stats.1983, c. 486, § 2; Stats. 1989, c. 1105, § 11; Stats.1992, c. 163 (A.B.2641), § 61, operative Jan. 1, 1994; Stats.2000, c. 33 (A.B.205), § 2.5; Stats.2000, c. 111 (A.B.2155), § 7; Stats.2006, c. 567 (A.B.2303), § 12; Stats.2013, c. 651 (A.B.1121), § 3.)*

Repeal

For repeal of this section, see its terms.

Law Revision Commission Comments

Subdivision (b) of Section 1278 is amended to substitute the new reference to the Uniform Parentage Act in the Family Code. [22 Cal.L.Rev.Comm.Reports 1 (1992)].

Research References

10 Witkin, California Summary 10th Parent and Child § 46, in General.

§ 1278. Hearings; orders without hearings

Section operative July 1, 2014. See, also, section operative until July 1, 2014.

(a)(1) Except as provided in subdivisions (c) and (d), the petition or application shall be heard at the time designated by the court, only if objections are filed by a person who can, in those objections, show to the court good reason against the change of name. At the hearing, the court may examine on oath any of the petitioners, remonstrants, or other persons touching the petition or application, and may make an order changing the name, or dismissing the petition or application, as the court may seem right and proper.

(2) If no objection is filed at least two court days before the date set for hearing, the court may, without hearing, enter the order that the change of name is granted. If the petition seeks to conform the petitioner's name to his or her gender identity and no objection is timely filed, the court shall grant the petition without a hearing.

(b) If the provisions of subdivision (b) of Section 1277 apply, the court shall not disclose the proposed name unless the court finds by clear and convincing evidence that the allegations of domestic violence, stalking, sexual assault, or gender identity in the petition are false.

(c) If the application for a change of name is brought as part of an action under the Uniform Parentage Act (Part 3 (commencing with Section 7600) of Division 12 of the Family Code), the hearing on the issue of the change of name shall be conducted pursuant to statutes and rules of court governing those proceedings, whether the hearing is conducted upon an order to show cause or upon trial.

(d) If the petition for a change of name is filed by a guardian on behalf of a minor ward, the court shall first find that the ward is likely to remain in the guardian's care until the age of majority and that the ward is not likely to be returned to the custody of his or her parents. Upon making those findings, the court shall consider the petition and may grant the petition only if it finds that the proposed name change is in the best interest of the child.

(e) This section shall become operative on July 1, 2014. *(Added by Stats.2013, c. 651 (A.B.1121), § 4, operative July 1, 2014.)*

§ 1278.5. Petitions relating to minors; absence of consent of both parents

In any proceeding pursuant to this title in which a petition has been filed to change the name of a minor, and both parents, if living, do not join in consent, the court may deny the petition in whole or in part if it finds that any portion of the proposed name change is not in the best interest of the child. *(Added by Stats.1996, c. 1061 (S.B.1033), § 2. Amended by Stats.2006, c. 567 (A.B.2303), § 13.)*

Research References

Miller and Starr California Real Estate § 8:19, Change in Name.

§ 1279.5. Name change; common law right; state prisoners, parolees and probationers; registered sex offenders

(a) Except as provided in subdivision (b), (c), (d), or (e), nothing in this title shall be construed to abrogate the common law right of any person to change his or her name.

(b) Notwithstanding any other law, no person imprisoned in the state prison and under the jurisdiction of the Director of Corrections shall be allowed to file a petition for change of name pursuant to Section 1276, except as permitted at the discretion of the Director of Corrections.

(c) A court shall deny a petition for a name change pursuant to Section 1276 made by a person who is under the jurisdiction of the Department of Corrections, unless that person's parole agent or probation officer grants prior written approval. Before granting that approval, the parole agent or probation officer shall determine that the name change will not pose a security risk to the community.

(d) Notwithstanding any other law, a court shall deny a petition for a name change pursuant to Section 1276 made by a person who is required to register as a sex offender under Section 290 of the Penal Code, unless the court determines that it is in the best interest of justice to grant the petition and that doing so will not adversely affect the public safety. If a petition for a name change is granted for an individual required to register as a sex offender, the individual shall, within five working days, notify the chief of police of the city in which he or she is domiciled, or the sheriff of the county if he or she is domiciled in an unincorporated area, and additionally with the chief of police of a campus of a University of California or California State University if he or she is domiciled upon the campus or in any of its facilities.

(e) For the purpose of this section, the court shall use the California Law Enforcement Telecommunications System (CLETS) and Criminal Justice Information System (CJIS) to determine whether or not an applicant for a name change is under the jurisdiction of the Department of Corrections or is required to register as a sex offender pursuant to Section 290 of the Penal Code. Each person applying for a name change shall declare under penalty of perjury that he or she is not under the jurisdiction of the Department of Corrections or is required to register as a sex offender pursuant to Section 290 of the Penal Code. If a court is not equipped with CLETS or CJIS, the clerk of the court shall contact an appropriate local law enforcement agency, which shall determine whether or not the petitioner is under the jurisdiction of the Department of Corrections or is required to register as a sex offender pursuant to Section 290 of

the Penal Code. *(Added by Stats.1974, c. 1235, p. 2681, § 3. Amended by Stats.1975, c. 1070, p. 2616, § 3; Stats.1992, c. 163 (A.B.2641), § 62, operative Jan. 1, 1994; Stats.1994, c. 557 (A.B.2782), § 1; Stats.1996, c. 730 (A.B.2359), § 1; Stats.1997, c. 821 (A.B.290), § 1, eff. Oct. 9, 1997; Stats.2006, c. 567 (A.B. 2303), § 14.)*

Law Revision Commission Comments

Former subdivision (b) of Section 1279.5 is continued in Section 1279.6 without substantive change. [22 Cal.L.Rev.Comm.Reports 1 (1992)].

Research References

Miller and Starr California Real Estate § 8:19, Change in Name.
13 Witkin, California Summary 10th Personal Property § 24, Right to Change Name.

§ 1279.6. Trade or business; doing business or providing services; prohibitions

No person engaged in a trade or business of any kind or in the provision of a service of any kind shall do any of the following:

(a) Refuse to do business with a person, or refuse to provide the service to a person, regardless of the person's marital status, because he or she has chosen to use or regularly uses his or her birth name, former name, or name adopted upon solemnization of marriage or registration of domestic partnership.

(b) Impose, as a condition of doing business with a person, or as a condition of providing the service to a person, a requirement that the person, regardless of his or her marital status, use a name other than his or her birth name, former name, or name adopted upon solemnization of marriage or registration of domestic partnership, if the person has chosen to use or regularly uses that name. *(Added by Stats.1992, c. 163 (A.B.2641), § 63, operative Jan. 1, 1994. Amended by Stats.2007, c. 567 (A.B.102), § 3.)*

Law Revision Commission Comments

Section 1279.6 continues without substantive change former subdivision (b) of Code of Civil Procedure Section 1279.5, former Civil Code Section 4362(d), and former Civil Code Section 4457(d). [22 Cal.L.Rev.Comm.Reports 1 (1992)].

Research References

13 Witkin, California Summary 10th Personal Property § 23, in General.
11 Witkin, California Summary 10th Husband and Wife § 21, in Business Transactions.
11 Witkin, California Summary 10th Husband and Wife § 33, Other Rights.

Title 9

ARBITRATION

CHAPTER 1. GENERAL PROVISIONS

§ 1280. Definitions

As used in this title:

(a) "Agreement" includes but is not limited to agreements providing for valuations, appraisals and similar proceedings and agreements between employers and employees or between their respective representatives.

(b) "Award" includes but is not limited to an award made pursuant to an agreement not in writing.

(c) "Controversy" means any question arising between parties to an agreement whether such question is one of law or of fact or both.

(d) "Neutral arbitrator" means an arbitrator who is (1) selected jointly by the parties or by the arbitrators selected by the parties or (2) appointed by the court when the parties or the arbitrators selected by the parties fail to select an arbitrator who was to be selected jointly by them.

(e) "Party to the arbitration" means a party to the arbitration agreement:

(1) Who seeks to arbitrate a controversy pursuant to the agreement;

(2) Against whom such arbitration is sought pursuant to the agreement; or

(3) Who is made a party to such arbitration by order of the neutral arbitrator upon such party's application, upon the application of any other party to the arbitration or upon the neutral arbitrator's own determination.

(f) "Written agreement" shall be deemed to include a written agreement which has been extended or renewed by an oral or implied agreement. *(Added by Stats.1961, c. 461, p. 1540, § 2.)*

Research References

California Real Estate Forms (Miller & Starr) § 4:6, Construction Contract--Fixed Price--Commercial Project.
Rutter, Cal. Practice Guide: A.D.R. App. A, Selected Statutes Providing for ADR.
Rutter, Cal. Practice Guide: A.D.R. Ch. 1-E, E. Enforcing ADR Settlements.
Rutter, Cal. Practice Guide: A.D.R. Ch. 4-B, B. Judicial Arbitration.
Rutter, Cal. Practice Guide: A.D.R. Ch. 5-A, A. General Considerations.
Rutter, Cal. Practice Guide: A.D.R. Ch. 5-B, B. Federal vs. State Law Governing.
Rutter, Cal. Practice Guide: A.D.R. Ch. 5-C, C. Enforceability of Arbitration Agreements-In General.
Rutter, Cal. Practice Guide: A.D.R. Ch. 5-D, D. Defenses to Enforcement.
Rutter, Cal. Practice Guide: A.D.R. Ch. 5-G, G. Procedures to Enforce Arbitration.
Rutter, Cal. Practice Guide: A.D.R. Ch. 5-H, H. Conduct of Arbitration Proceedings.
Rutter, Cal. Practice Guide: A.D.R. Ch. 5-J, J. Challenging and Enforcing Arbitrator's Award in Court.
Rutter, Cal. Practice Guide: A.D.R. Ch. 7-B, B. Arbitrators.
Rutter, Cal. Practice Guide: A.D.R. Ch. 8-D, D. Drafting Considerations-In General.
Rutter, Cal. Practice Guide: A.D.R. Ch. 3B-C, C. Statutorily-Mandated ADR.
Rutter, Cal. Practice Guide: A.D.R. App. D Form 29, Governing Law Clauses.
Rutter, Cal. Practice Guide: A.D.R. App. D Form 30, Nonadministered (Ad Hoc) Arbitration Clause.
Rutter, Cal. Practice Guide: A.D.R. App. D Form 65, Real Property-Eminent Domain-Arbitration of Compensation in Acquisitions of Property for Public Use.
Rutter, Cal. Practice Guide: A.D.R. App. D Form 67, Lease Provision for Arbitration of Disputes Re Disputes Re Habitability.
Rutter, Cal. Practice Guide: A.D.R. App. D Form 71, Probate Disputes.
Rutter, Cal. Practice Guide: A.D.R. App. D Form 78, Attorney Retainer or Contingent Fee Agreements.

Rutter, Cal. Practice Guide: A.D.R. Ch. 5-B, Outline B.
Rutter, Cal. Practice Guide: A.D.R. App. D Form Intro. 4, Practice and Procedure Forms-Arbitration.
Rutter, Cal. Practice Guide: Civ. Pro. Before Trial Ch. 13-A, A. Introduction.
Rutter, Cal. Practice Guide: Civ. Pro. Before Trial Ch. 13-B, B. Judicial Arbitration Distinguished from Contract Arbitration.
Rutter, Cal. Practice Guide: Civ. Pro. Before Trial Ch. 13-C, C. Civil Proceedings Subject to Judicial Arbitration.
California Practice Guide: Employment Litigation Ch. 18-C, C. Contractual Arbitration.
California Practice Guide: Employment Litigation Ch. 18-C, Outline C.
Rutter, Cal. Practice Guide: Enforcing Judgments/Debts Ch. 3-A, A. Evaluating the Claim.
Rutter, Cal. Practice Guide: Insurance Litigation Ch. 15-C, C. Arbitration/Appraisal/Mediation.
Rutter, Cal. Practice Guide: Insurance Litigation Ch. 6G-D, D. Uninsured and Underinsured Motorist Coverages.
Rutter, Cal. Practice Guide: Personal Injury Ch. 4-G, G. Concluding and Enforcing Settlement.
Rutter, Cal. Practice Guide: Personal Injury Ch. 5-B, B. When to Sue-Statute of Limitations.
Rutter, Cal. Practice Guide: Personal Injury Ch. 7-A, A. Introduction-Nature and Purpose of "Judicial Arbitration" in General.
Rutter, Cal. Practice Guide: Personal Injury Ch. 7-J, J. Arbitration of Uninsured Motorist Claims.
Rutter, Cal. Practice Guide: Real Prop. Transactions Ch. 1-C, C. Attorney Fees and Costs Agreements.
Rutter, Cal. Practice Guide: Prof. Responsibility Ch. 1-K, K. Additional Regulations Affecting Lawyer Conduct.
Rutter, Cal. Practice Guide: Prof. Responsibility Ch. 5-K, K. Fee Recovery/Enforcing Fee Agreements.
Miller and Starr California Real Estate § 1:65, Provisions Applicable to Real Estate Transactions.
Miller and Starr California Real Estate § 27:47, Provisions for Arbitration and Mediation of Disputes--Generally.
Miller and Starr California Real Estate § 35:22, Nature of Arbitration.
Miller and Starr California Real Estate § 35:23, Public Policy in Favor of Arbitration.
Miller and Starr California Real Estate § 35:25, Written Agreement Required.
Miller and Starr California Real Estate § 35:30, Parties Subject to the Arbitration Agreement.
Miller and Starr California Real Estate § 35:31, Parties Who Did Not Sign the Agreement.
Miller and Starr California Real Estate § 35:38, Issues Subject to Arbitration--Examples.
Miller and Starr California Real Estate § 35:65, Appointment and Removal of an Arbitrator.
Miller and Starr California Real Estate § 35:80, Time to Render the Award.
13 NO. 6 Miller & Starr, California Real Estate Newsalert 1, Using Basura to Make Construction Defect Claims Arbitrable, or Woodside to Send Them to a Referee.
14 NO. 3 Miller & Starr, California Real Estate Newsalert 4, Commercial Arbitration.
3 Witkin Cal. Proc. 5th Actions § 65, (S 65) Statutory Classes.
9 Witkin Cal. Proc. 5th Appeal § 142, Orders After Arbitration: Appealable.
1 Witkin Cal. Proc. 5th Attorneys § 220, Methods Available.
1 Witkin Cal. Proc. 5th Attorneys § 221, Nature and Purpose of Arbitration Program.
1 Witkin Cal. Proc. 5th Attorneys § 224, Scope of Jurisdiction.
7 Witkin Cal. Proc. 5th Judgment § 478, Following Arbitration.
6 Witkin Cal. Proc. 5th Proceedings Without Trial § 122, Agreement Made in Arbitration.
6 Witkin Cal. Proc. 5th Proceedings Without Trial § 499, Definition and Nature.
6 Witkin Cal. Proc. 5th Proceedings Without Trial § 500, Public Policy Considerations.
6 Witkin Cal. Proc. 5th Proceedings Without Trial § 502, General Statute.
6 Witkin Cal. Proc. 5th Proceedings Without Trial § 511, Effect of Choice-Of-Law Provision.
6 Witkin Cal. Proc. 5th Proceedings Without Trial § 512, Agreement is Enforceable.
6 Witkin Cal. Proc. 5th Proceedings Without Trial § 514, (S 514) Oral Agreement.

§ 1280.2. Reference to statutes

Whenever reference is made in this title to any portion of the title or of any other law of this State, the reference applies to all amendments and additions thereto now or hereafter made. *(Added by Stats.1961, c. 461, p. 1541, § 2.)*

Research References

Miller and Starr California Real Estate § 35:52, Potential for Conflicting Decisions in Other Tribunals.

CHAPTER 2. ENFORCEMENT OF ARBITRATION AGREEMENTS

§ 1281. Validity, enforceability and irrevocability of agreements

A written agreement to submit to arbitration an existing controversy or a controversy thereafter arising is valid, enforceable and irrevocable, save upon such grounds as exist for the revocation of any contract. *(Added by Stats.1961, c. 461, p. 1541, § 2.)*

Research References

Rutter, Cal. Practice Guide: A.D.R. Ch. 5-A, A. General Considerations.

Rutter, Cal. Practice Guide: A.D.R. Ch. 5-C, C. Enforceability of Arbitration Agreements-In General.

Rutter, Cal. Practice Guide: A.D.R. Ch. 5-D, D. Defenses to Enforcement.

Rutter, Cal. Practice Guide: A.D.R. App. D Form 95, Notice of Motion to Stay Action Pending Arbitration.

Rutter, Cal. Practice Guide: Civ. Pro. Before Trial Ch. 1-F, F. Exhaustion of Other Remedies.

Rutter, Cal. Practice Guide: Civ. Pro. Before Trial Ch. 12(I)-D, D. Demand for Jury Trial and Waiver.

Rutter, Cal. Practice Guide: Civil Trials & Evidence Ch. 2-E, E. Waiver of Jury Trial.

California Practice Guide: Employment Litigation Ch. 18-C, C. Contractual Arbitration.

Rutter, Cal. Practice Guide: Insurance Litigation Ch. 15-C, C. Arbitration/Appraisal/Mediation.

Rutter, Cal. Practice Guide: Insurance Litigation Ch. 6G-D, D. Uninsured and Underinsured Motorist Coverages.

Rutter, Cal. Practice Guide: Personal Injury Ch. 7-G, G. Arbitration Hearing.

Rutter, Cal. Practice Guide: Real Prop. Transactions Ch. 4-E, E. Drafting the Purchase and Sale Agreement-Terms and Conditions.

Miller and Starr California Real Estate § 4:49, Persons Who Qualify for Payment from the Recovery Account--Judgment Based on Fraud, Conversion, or Restitution.

Miller and Starr California Real Estate § 35:19, Contract Provisions and Enforceability.

Miller and Starr California Real Estate § 35:24, Federal Arbitration Act.

Miller and Starr California Real Estate § 35:25, Written Agreement Required.

Miller and Starr California Real Estate § 35:30, Parties Subject to the Arbitration Agreement.

Miller and Starr California Real Estate § 35:38, Issues Subject to Arbitration--Examples.

Miller and Starr California Real Estate § 35:40, Modification, Rescission, and Revocation of the Arbitration Agreement.

Miller and Starr California Real Estate § 35:42, Enforceability of Arbitration Agreements; Necessity for Petition to Compel.

Miller and Starr California Real Estate § 35:51, Fraud or Mistake.

Miller and Starr California Real Estate § 35:53, Unconscionability.

14 NO. 1 Miller & Starr, California Real Estate Newsalert 2, Commercial Arbitration.

18 NO. 4 Miller & Starr, California Real Estate Newsalert 27, Commercial Arbitration.

21 NO. 1 Miller & Starr, California Real Estate Newsalert 1, is an Arbitration Provision in Recorded CC&RS Ever Enforceable by the Developer?

22 NO. 4 Miller & Starr, California Real Estate Newsalert 22, Alternative Dispute Resolution.

1 Witkin Cal. Proc. 5th Attorneys § 220, Methods Available.

1 Witkin Cal. Proc. 5th Attorneys § 224, Scope of Jurisdiction.

6 Witkin Cal. Proc. 5th Proceedings Without Trial § 83, (S 83) Scope of Statute.
6 Witkin Cal. Proc. 5th Proceedings Without Trial § 502, General Statute.
6 Witkin Cal. Proc. 5th Proceedings Without Trial § 512, Agreement is Enforceable.
6 Witkin Cal. Proc. 5th Proceedings Without Trial § 514, (S 514) Oral Agreement.
6 Witkin Cal. Proc. 5th Proceedings Without Trial § 531, in General.
6 Witkin Cal. Proc. 5th Proceedings Without Trial § 538, (S 538) Unconscionable Contract or Term.
1 Witkin Cal. Summ. 10th Contracts § 400, (S 400) Miscellaneous Provisions.
6 Witkin, California Summary 10th Torts § 950, Retroactive Agreements.
6 Witkin, California Summary 10th Torts § 1654, (S 1654) Arbitration Proceedings.
3 Witkin, California Summary 10th Agency and Employment § 384, (S 384) Judicial Enforcement.
13 Witkin, California Summary 10th Equity § 36, (S 36) Arbitration Agreement.

§ 1281.1. Requests to arbitrate

For the purposes of this article, any request to arbitrate made pursuant to subdivision (a) of Section 1299.4 shall be considered as made pursuant to a written agreement to submit a controversy to arbitration. *(Added by Stats.2000, c. 906 (S.B.402), § 1.)*

Research References

California Practice Guide: Employment Litigation Ch. 19-B, B. Defendant's Challenges to Forum Plaintiff Selects.
Miller and Starr California Real Estate § 35:45, Contents of the Petition.
3 Witkin, California Summary 10th Agency and Employment § 567, (S 567) Statutory Framework.

§ 1281.12. Tolling arbitration time period

If an arbitration agreement requires that arbitration of a controversy be demanded or initiated by a party to the arbitration agreement within a period of time, the commencement of a civil action by that party based upon that controversy, within that period of time, shall toll the applicable time limitations contained in the arbitration agreement with respect to that controversy, from the date the civil action is commenced until 30 days after a final determination by the court that the party is required to arbitrate the controversy, or 30 days after the final termination of the civil action that was commenced and initiated the tolling, whichever date occurs first. *(Added by Stats.2006, c. 266 (A.B.1553), § 1.)*

Research References

Rutter, Cal. Practice Guide: A.D.R. Ch. 5-D, D. Defenses to Enforcement.
Rutter, Cal. Practice Guide: A.D.R. Ch. 5-I, I. Arbitrator's Award.
California Practice Guide: Employment Litigation Ch. 16-D, D. Failure to Exhaust Contractual Dispute Resolution Procedures (Arbitration, Mediation, etc.).
California Practice Guide: Employment Litigation Ch. 18-C, C. Contractual Arbitration.
17 NO. 4 Miller & Starr, California Real Estate Newsalert 2, Statutory Update:.
17 NO. 6 Miller & Starr, California Real Estate Newsalert 20, Table of Statutes (Newsalert Vol 17).
6 Witkin Cal. Proc. 5th Proceedings Without Trial § 546, (S 546) Delay in Demanding Arbitration.
6 Witkin Cal. Proc. 5th Proceedings Without Trial § 578, (S 578) Exceptions to Finality Rule.

§ 1281.2. Order to arbitrate controversy; petition; determination of court

On petition of a party to an arbitration agreement alleging the existence of a written agreement to arbitrate a controversy and that a party thereto refuses to arbitrate such controversy, the court shall order the petitioner and the respondent to arbitrate the controversy if it determines that an agreement to arbitrate the controversy exists, unless it determines that:

(a) The right to compel arbitration has been waived by the petitioner; or

(b) Grounds exist for the revocation of the agreement.

(c) A party to the arbitration agreement is also a party to a pending court action or special proceeding with a third party, arising out of the same transaction or series of related transactions and there is a possibility of conflicting rulings on a common issue of law or fact. For purposes of this section, a pending court action or special proceeding includes an action or proceeding initiated by the party refusing to arbitrate after the petition to compel arbitration has been filed, but on or before the date of the hearing on the petition. This subdivision shall not be applicable to an agreement to arbitrate disputes as to the professional negligence of a health care provider made pursuant to Section 1295.

If the court determines that a written agreement to arbitrate a controversy exists, an order to arbitrate such controversy may not be refused on the ground that the petitioner's contentions lack substantive merit.

If the court determines that there are other issues between the petitioner and the respondent which are not subject to arbitration and which are the subject of a pending action or special proceeding between the petitioner and the respondent and that a determination of such issues may make the arbitration unnecessary, the court may delay its order to arbitrate until the determination of such other issues or until such earlier time as the court specifies.

If the court determines that a party to the arbitration is also a party to litigation in a pending court action or special proceeding with a third party as set forth under subdivision (c) herein, the court (1) may refuse to enforce the arbitration agreement and may order intervention or joinder of all parties in a single action or special proceeding; (2) may order intervention or joinder as to all or only certain issues; (3) may order arbitration among the parties who have agreed to arbitration and stay the pending court action or special proceeding pending the outcome of the arbitration proceeding; or (4) may stay arbitration pending the outcome of the court action or special proceeding. *(Added by Stats.1961, c. 461, p. 1541, § 2. Amended by Stats.1978, c. 260, p. 543, § 1.)*

Research References

Rutter, Cal. Practice Guide: A.D.R. Ch. 4-B, B. Judicial Arbitration.
Rutter, Cal. Practice Guide: A.D.R. Ch. 5-B, B. Federal vs. State Law Governing.
Rutter, Cal. Practice Guide: A.D.R. Ch. 5-D, D. Defenses to Enforcement.
Rutter, Cal. Practice Guide: A.D.R. Ch. 5-E, E. Claims Subject to Arbitration (Arbitrability).
Rutter, Cal. Practice Guide: A.D.R. Ch. 5-F, F. Arbitration by and Against Nonsignatories.
Rutter, Cal. Practice Guide: A.D.R. Ch. 5-G, G. Procedures to Enforce Arbitration.
Rutter, Cal. Practice Guide: A.D.R. Ch. 5-I, I. Arbitrator's Award.
Rutter, Cal. Practice Guide: A.D.R. Ch. 5-K, K. Arbitration of International Commercial Disputes.
Rutter, Cal. Practice Guide: A.D.R. Ch. 3B-B, B. ADR Options in Construction Disputes.
Rutter, Cal. Practice Guide: A.D.R. Gen. Matls., Highlights.
Rutter, Cal. Practice Guide: A.D.R. App. D Form 64, Real Property-Sale-Deposit Receipts, Escrow Instructions, Listing Agreements.
Rutter, Cal. Practice Guide: A.D.R. App. D Form 92, Response to Petition for Arbitration Seeking Denial Because of Third Party Action Pending.
Rutter, Cal. Practice Guide: Civil Appeals & Writs Ch. 2-B, B. Appealable Judgments and Orders.

Rutter, Cal. Practice Guide: Civil Appeals & Writs Ch. 8-C, C. Standards of Appellate Review.

Rutter, Cal. Practice Guide: Civ. Pro. Before Trial Ch. 9(I)-H, H. Motions Relating to Contractual Arbitration.

Rutter, Cal. Practice Guide: Civ. Pro. Before Trial Ch. 12(I)-E, E. Consolidation, Coordination and Bifurcation.

California Practice Guide: Employment Litigation Ch. 15-C, C. Labor Management Relations Act Preemption (Including Nlra).

California Practice Guide: Employment Litigation Ch. 18-C, C. Contractual Arbitration.

California Practice Guide: Employment Litigation Ch. 18-G, G. Drafting Dispute Resolution Clauses and Creating Dispute Resolution Systems.

Rutter, Cal. Practice Guide: Insurance Litigation Ch. 15-C, C. Arbitration/Appraisal/Mediation.

Rutter, Cal. Practice Guide: Insurance Litigation Ch. 15-E, E. Pleadings.

Rutter, Cal. Practice Guide: Insurance Litigation Ch. 15-F, F. Pretrial Motions.

Rutter, Cal. Practice Guide: Insurance Litigation Ch. 6G-D, D. Uninsured and Underinsured Motorist Coverages.

Rutter, Cal. Practice Guide: Personal Injury Ch. 5-B, B. When to Sue-Statute of Limitations.

Rutter, Cal. Practice Guide: Personal Injury Ch. 7-J, J. Arbitration of Uninsured Motorist Claims.

Miller and Starr California Real Estate § 35:24, Federal Arbitration Act.

Miller and Starr California Real Estate § 35:25, Written Agreement Required.

Miller and Starr California Real Estate § 35:31, Parties Who Did Not Sign the Agreement.

Miller and Starr California Real Estate § 35:42, Enforceability of Arbitration Agreements; Necessity for Petition to Compel.

Miller and Starr California Real Estate § 35:44, Petition to Compel Arbitration.

Miller and Starr California Real Estate § 35:45, Contents of the Petition.

Miller and Starr California Real Estate § 35:47, Statutes of Limitation.

Miller and Starr California Real Estate § 35:48, Hearing and Order on the Petition.

Miller and Starr California Real Estate § 35:49, Issues Decided by the Court Addressing Motion to Compel.

Miller and Starr California Real Estate § 35:50, Defenses to Petition to Compel Arbitration--In General.

Miller and Starr California Real Estate § 35:51, Fraud or Mistake.

Miller and Starr California Real Estate § 35:52, Potential for Conflicting Decisions in Other Tribunals.

Miller and Starr California Real Estate § 35:54, Review of Order Granting or Denying Petition to Compel Arbitration.

Miller and Starr California Real Estate § 35:56, Stay of Litigation Pending Arbitration.

Miller and Starr California Real Estate § 35:57, Stay of Arbitration Pending Litigation.

Miller and Starr California Real Estate § 35:59, Loss of Right to Arbitrate by Waiver, Estoppel, or Forfeiture.

Miller and Starr California Real Estate § 35:63, Waiver by Participation in Litigation.

Miller and Starr California Real Estate § 11:148, Nature and Effect of a Lis Pendens.

13 NO. 3 Miller & Starr, California Real Estate Newsalert 4, Commercial Arbitration.

14 NO. 6 Miller & Starr, California Real Estate Newsalert 3, Commercial Arbitration.

15 NO. 6 Miller & Starr, California Real Estate Newsalert 1, Refuse to Mediate and (Under Some Contracts) Wave Goodbye to Your Attorney's Fees.

15 NO. 5 Miller & Starr, California Real Estate Newsalert 2, Commercial Arbitration.

15 NO. 2 Miller & Starr, California Real Estate Newsalert 3, Commercial Arbitration.

16 NO. 5 Miller & Starr, California Real Estate Newsalert 4, Commercial Arbitration.

17 NO. 3 Miller & Starr, California Real Estate Newsalert 2, Commercial Arbitration.

18 NO. 5 Miller & Starr, California Real Estate Newsalert 3, Commercial Arbitration.

18 NO. 6 Miller & Starr, California Real Estate Newsalert 3, Alternative Dispute Resolution.

18 NO. 1 Miller & Starr, California Real Estate Newsalert 4, Commercial Arbitration.

18 NO. 2 Miller & Starr, California Real Estate Newsalert 4, Commercial Arbitration.

19 NO. 6 Miller & Starr, California Real Estate Newsalert 18, Recording and Priorities.

21 NO. 1 Miller & Starr, California Real Estate Newsalert 1, is an Arbitration Provision in Recorded CC&RS Ever Enforceable by the Developer?

21 NO. 1 Miller & Starr, California Real Estate Newsalert 2, Alternative Dispute Resolution.

21 NO. 2 Miller & Starr, California Real Estate Newsalert 2, Alternative Dispute Resolution.

21 NO. 6 Miller & Starr, California Real Estate Newsalert 3, Alternative Dispute Resolution.

21 NO. 3 Miller & Starr, California Real Estate Newsalert 4, Alternative Dispute Resolution.

22 NO. 5 Miller & Starr, California Real Estate Newsalert 2, Alternative Dispute Resolution.

22 NO. 1 Miller & Starr, California Real Estate Newsalert 4, Alternative Dispute Resolution.

22 NO. 6 Miller & Starr, California Real Estate Newsalert 5, Alternative Dispute Resolution.

22 NO. 4 Miller & Starr, California Real Estate Newsalert 22, Alternative Dispute Resolution.

23 NO. 2 Miller & Starr, California Real Estate Newsalert 4, Alternative Dispute Resolution.

23 NO. 1 Miller & Starr, California Real Estate Newsalert 14, Judicial Remedies.

8 Witkin Cal. Proc. 5th Extraordinary Writs § 125, (S 125) Remedy by Motion.

6 Witkin Cal. Proc. 5th Proceedings Without Trial § 381, (S 381) Stipulation to Binding Arbitration.

6 Witkin Cal. Proc. 5th Proceedings Without Trial § 509, (S 509) Distinctions.

6 Witkin Cal. Proc. 5th Proceedings Without Trial § 509, (S 509) Distinctions.

6 Witkin Cal. Proc. 5th Proceedings Without Trial § 510, (S 510) Illustrations.

6 Witkin Cal. Proc. 5th Proceedings Without Trial § 511, Effect of Choice-Of-Law Provision.

6 Witkin Cal. Proc. 5th Proceedings Without Trial § 514, (S 514) Oral Agreement.

6 Witkin Cal. Proc. 5th Proceedings Without Trial § 524, (S 524) in General.

6 Witkin Cal. Proc. 5th Proceedings Without Trial § 526, (S 526) Appeal and Review.

6 Witkin Cal. Proc. 5th Proceedings Without Trial § 527, Consolidation With Pending Litigation.

6 Witkin Cal. Proc. 5th Proceedings Without Trial § 531, in General.

6 Witkin Cal. Proc. 5th Proceedings Without Trial § 533, (S 533) in General.

6 Witkin Cal. Proc. 5th Proceedings Without Trial § 536, Pending Litigation.

6 Witkin Cal. Proc. 5th Proceedings Without Trial § 541, (S 541) When Issue is Determined by Arbitrator.

6 Witkin Cal. Proc. 5th Proceedings Without Trial § 542, Fraud Directed to Arbitration Provision.

6 Witkin Cal. Proc. 5th Proceedings Without Trial § 543, Fraud in Inception of Contract.

6 Witkin Cal. Proc. 5th Proceedings Without Trial § 545, (S 545) Nature of Defense.

6 Witkin Cal. Proc. 5th Proceedings Without Trial § 551, Failure to Inform Insured of Remedy.

6 Witkin Cal. Proc. 5th Proceedings Without Trial § 552, Requirement of Bad Faith Conduct.

2 Witkin, California Summary 10th Insurance § 207, (S 207) Action to Compel Arbitration.

2 Witkin, California Summary 10th Insurance § 211, (S 211) Joinder and Consolidation.

7 Witkin, California Summary 10th Constitutional Law § 21, United States Supreme Court.

§ 1281.3. Consolidation of separate arbitration proceedings; petition; grounds; procedure

A party to an arbitration agreement may petition the court to consolidate separate arbitration proceedings, and the court may order consolidation of separate arbitration proceedings when:

(1) Separate arbitration agreements or proceedings exist between the same parties; or one party is a party to a separate arbitration agreement or proceeding with a third party; and

(2) The disputes arise from the same transactions or series of related transactions; and

(3) There is common issue or issues of law or fact creating the possibility of conflicting rulings by more than one arbitrator or panel of arbitrators.

If all of the applicable arbitration agreements name the same arbitrator, arbitration panel, or arbitration tribunal, the court, if it orders consolidation, shall order all matters to be heard before the arbitrator, panel, or tribunal agreed to by the parties. If the applicable arbitration agreements name separate arbitrators, panels, or tribunals, the court, if it orders consolidation, shall, in the absence of an agreed method of selection by all parties to the consolidated arbitration, appoint an arbitrator in accord with the procedures set forth in Section 1281.6.

In the event that the arbitration agreements in consolidated proceedings contain inconsistent provisions, the court shall resolve such conflicts and determine the rights and duties of the various parties to achieve substantial justice under all the circumstances.

The court may exercise its discretion under this section to deny consolidation of separate arbitration proceedings or to consolidate separate arbitration proceedings only as to certain issues, leaving other issues to be resolved in separate proceedings.

This section shall not be applicable to an agreement to arbitrate disputes as to the professional negligence of a health care provider made pursuant to Section 1295. *(Added by Stats.1978, c. 260, p. 549, § 2.)*

Research References

Rutter, Cal. Practice Guide: A.D.R. Ch. 5-G, G. Procedures to Enforce Arbitration.
Rutter, Cal. Practice Guide: A.D.R. Ch. 3B-B, B. ADR Options in Construction Disputes.
Rutter, Cal. Practice Guide: A.D.R. App. D Form 40, Consolidation.
Rutter, Cal. Practice Guide: Civ. Pro. Before Trial Ch. 9(I)-H, H. Motions Relating to Contractual Arbitration.
Rutter, Cal. Practice Guide: Civ. Pro. Before Trial Ch. 12(I)-E, E. Consolidation, Coordination and Bifurcation.
California Practice Guide: Employment Litigation Ch. 18-C, C. Contractual Arbitration.
Rutter, Cal. Practice Guide: Personal Injury Ch. 7-J, J. Arbitration of Uninsured Motorist Claims.
Miller and Starr California Real Estate § 35:33, Classwide Arbitrations.
Miller and Starr California Real Estate § 35:55, Consolidation of Arbitration Proceedings.
Miller and Starr California Real Estate § 35:65, Appointment and Removal of an Arbitrator.
15 NO. 5 Miller & Starr, California Real Estate Newsalert 2, Commercial Arbitration.
15 NO. 2 Miller & Starr, California Real Estate Newsalert 3, Commercial Arbitration.
16 NO. 3 Miller & Starr, California Real Estate Newsalert 3, Commercial Arbitration.
6 Witkin Cal. Proc. 5th Proceedings Without Trial § 553, Commencement and Consolidation.
2 Witkin, California Summary 10th Insurance § 211, (S 211) Joinder and Consolidation.

§ 1281.4. Stay of pending actions or proceedings

If a court of competent jurisdiction, whether in this State or not, has ordered arbitration of a controversy which is an issue involved in an action or proceeding pending before a court of this State, the court in which such action or proceeding is pending shall, upon motion of a party to such action or proceeding, stay the action or proceeding until an arbitration is

had in accordance with the order to arbitrate or until such earlier time as the court specifies.

If an application has been made to a court of competent jurisdiction, whether in this State or not, for an order to arbitrate a controversy which is an issue involved in an action or proceeding pending before a court of this State and such application is undetermined, the court in which such action or proceeding is pending shall, upon motion of a party to such action or proceeding, stay the action or proceeding until the application for an order to arbitrate is determined and, if arbitration of such controversy is ordered, until an arbitration is had in accordance with the order to arbitrate or until such earlier time as the court specifies.

If the issue which is the controversy subject to arbitration is severable, the stay may be with respect to that issue only. *(Added by Stats.1961, c. 461, p. 1541, § 2.)*

Research References

Rutter, Cal. Practice Guide: A.D.R. Ch. 4-B, B. Judicial Arbitration.
Rutter, Cal. Practice Guide: A.D.R. Ch. 5-G, G. Procedures to Enforce Arbitration.
Rutter, Cal. Practice Guide: A.D.R. Ch. 3B-B, B. ADR Options in Construction Disputes.
Rutter, Cal. Practice Guide: A.D.R. App. D Form 95, Notice of Motion to Stay Action Pending Arbitration.
Rutter, Cal. Practice Guide: A.D.R. App. D Form 98, Notice of Motion to Stay Proceedings Until Application for Arbitration is Determined.
Rutter, Cal. Practice Guide: Civ. Pro. Before Trial Ch. 9(I)-H, H. Motions Relating to Contractual Arbitration.
Rutter, Cal. Practice Guide: Civ. Pro. Before Trial Ch. 12(I)-G, G. Stays Caused by Other Proceedings.
California Practice Guide: Employment Litigation Ch. 18-C, C. Contractual Arbitration.
California Practice Guide: Employment Litigation Ch. 19-B, B. Defendant's Challenges to Forum Plaintiff Selects.
Rutter, Cal. Practice Guide: Insurance Litigation Ch. 15-F, F. Pretrial Motions.
Rutter, Cal. Practice Guide: Insurance Litigation Ch. 6G-D, D. Uninsured and Underinsured Motorist Coverages.
Miller and Starr California Real Estate § 28:2, Alternative (Cumulative) Remedies of the Claimant.
Miller and Starr California Real Estate § 35:27, Construction Contracts.
Miller and Starr California Real Estate § 35:39, Issues Which Cannot be the Subject of Arbitration.
Miller and Starr California Real Estate § 35:48, Hearing and Order on the Petition.
Miller and Starr California Real Estate § 35:53, Unconscionability.
Miller and Starr California Real Estate § 35:56, Stay of Litigation Pending Arbitration.
Miller and Starr California Real Estate § 35:57, Stay of Arbitration Pending Litigation.
Miller and Starr California Real Estate § 35:83, Authority of the Arbitrators; Issues and Remedies.
21 NO. 4 Miller & Starr, California Real Estate Newsalert 19, Alternative Dispute Resolution.
6 Witkin Cal. Proc. 5th Proceedings Without Trial § 511, Effect of Choice-Of-Law Provision.
6 Witkin Cal. Proc. 5th Proceedings Without Trial § 528, Stay of Pending Litigation.
6 Witkin Cal. Proc. 5th Proceedings Without Trial § 547, No Waiver by Mere Filing or Limited Participation.
7 Witkin Cal. Proc. 5th Trial § 41, Notice of Settlement or Stay.

§ 1281.5. Waiver of right to arbitration; actions to enforce liens on works of improvement; notice of motion and motion to stay actions pending arbitration

(a) Any person who proceeds to record and enforce a claim of lien by commencement of an action pursuant to Chapter 4 (commencing with Section 8400) of Title 2 of Part 6 of Division 4 of the Civil Code, does not thereby waive any right of arbitration the person may have pursuant to a written agreement to arbitrate, if, in filing an action to enforce the claim of lien, the claimant does either of the following:

(1) Includes an allegation in the complaint that the claimant does not intend to waive any right of arbitration, and intends to move the court, within 30 days after service of the summons and complaint, for an order to stay further proceedings in the action.

(2) At the same time that the complaint is filed, the claimant files an application that the action be stayed pending the arbitration of any issue, question, or dispute that is claimed to be arbitrable under the agreement and that is relevant to the action to enforce the claim of lien.

(b) Within 30 days after service of the summons and complaint, the claimant shall file and serve a motion and notice of motion pursuant to Section 1281.4 to stay the action pending the arbitration of any issue, question, or dispute that is claimed to be arbitrable under the agreement and that is relevant to the action to enforce the claim of lien. The failure of a claimant to comply with this subdivision is a waiver of the claimant's right to compel arbitration.

(c) The failure of a defendant to file a petition pursuant to Section 1281.2 at or before the time the defendant answers the complaint filed pursuant to subdivision (a) is a waiver of the defendant's right to compel arbitration. *(Added by Stats.1977, c. 135, p. 571, § 1. Amended by Stats.1989, c. 470, § 1; Stats.1998, c. 931 (S.B.2139), § 122, eff. Sept. 28, 1998; Stats.2002, c. 784 (S.B.1316), § 82; Stats.2003, c. 22 (S.B.113), § 1; Stats.2010, c. 697 (S.B.189), § 25, operative July 1, 2012.)*

Law Revision Commission Comments

Section 1281.5 is amended to accommodate unification of the municipal and superior courts in a county. Cal. Const. art. VI, § 5(e). See Section 85 (limited civil cases) & Comment. [28 Cal.L.Rev.Comm. Reports 51 (1998)].

Subdivision (a) of Section 1281.5 is amended to reflect unification of the municipal and superior courts pursuant to Article VI, Section 5(e), of the California Constitution. [32 Cal.L.Rev.Comm. Reports 137 (2002)].

Subdivision (a) of Section 1281.5 is amended to add an alternative to the requirement that an application for a stay be made when the action is filed. In lieu of preparing a separate application for a stay, the lien claimant may include appropriate allegations in the complaint.

Subdivision (b) is added to require the lien claimant to file a motion for a stay order within 30 days after service of the summons and complaint. This is generally consistent with case law, but provides concrete guidance implementing the "reasonable time" requirement recognized by the courts. See Kaneko Ford Design v. Citipark, Inc., 202 Cal.App.3d 1220, 1227, 249 Cal.Rptr. 544 (1988).

Subdivision (c) (former subdivision (b)) is amended to make technical changes.

Section 1281.5 is amended to correct a cross-reference. [37 Cal.L.Rev. Comm. Reports 527 (2007)].

Research References

Rutter, Cal. Practice Guide: A.D.R. Ch. 5-D, D. Defenses to Enforcement.

Rutter, Cal. Practice Guide: A.D.R. Ch. 3B-B, B. ADR Options in Construction Disputes.

Miller and Starr California Real Estate § 28:2, Alternative (Cumulative) Remedies of the Claimant.

Miller and Starr California Real Estate § 28:84, Recovery of Attorney's Fees.

Miller and Starr California Real Estate § 35:23, Public Policy in Favor of Arbitration.

Miller and Starr California Real Estate § 35:27, Construction Contracts.

Miller and Starr California Real Estate § 35:63, Waiver by Participation in Litigation.

14 NO. 4 Miller & Starr, California Real Estate Newsalert 2, Commercial Arbitration.

14 NO. 4 Miller & Starr, California Real Estate Newsalert 12, Mechanic's Liens.

3 Witkin Cal. Proc. 5th Actions § 201, (S 201) Statutory or Contractual Provisions.

8 Witkin Cal. Proc. 5th Extraordinary Writs § 125, (S 125) Remedy by Motion.

6 Witkin Cal. Proc. 5th Proceedings Without Trial § 547, No Waiver by Mere Filing or Limited Participation.

§ 1281.6. Appointment of arbitrator

If the arbitration agreement provides a method of appointing an arbitrator, that method shall be followed. If the arbitration agreement does not provide a method for appointing an arbitrator, the parties to the agreement who seek arbitration and against whom arbitration is sought may agree on a method of appointing an arbitrator and that method shall be followed. In the absence of an agreed method, or if the agreed method fails or for any reason cannot be followed, or when an arbitrator appointed fails to act and his or her successor has not been appointed, the court, on petition of a party to the arbitration agreement, shall appoint the arbitrator.

When a petition is made to the court to appoint a neutral arbitrator, the court shall nominate five persons from lists of persons supplied jointly by the parties to the arbitration or obtained from a governmental agency concerned with arbitration or private disinterested association concerned with arbitration. The parties to the agreement who seek arbitration and against whom arbitration is sought may within five days of receipt of notice of the nominees from the court jointly select the arbitrator whether or not the arbitrator is among the nominees. If the parties fail to select an arbitrator within the five-day period, the court shall appoint the arbitrator from the nominees. *(Added by Stats.1961, c. 461, p. 1542, § 2. Amended by Stats.1994, c. 587 (A.B.3600), § 8; Stats.1997, c. 445 (A.B.1093), § 1; Stats.2001, c. 362 (S.B.475), § 3.)*

Research References

Rutter, Cal. Practice Guide: A.D.R. Ch. 5-A, A. General Considerations.

Rutter, Cal. Practice Guide: A.D.R. Ch. 5-G, G. Procedures to Enforce Arbitration.

Rutter, Cal. Practice Guide: A.D.R. Ch. 5-H, H. Conduct of Arbitration Proceedings.

Rutter, Cal. Practice Guide: A.D.R. Ch. 7-B, B. Arbitrators.

Rutter, Cal. Practice Guide: A.D.R. Ch. 8-D, D. Drafting Considerations-In General.

Rutter, Cal. Practice Guide: A.D.R. App. D Form 28, Arbitrator Qualification Clauses.

Rutter, Cal. Practice Guide: A.D.R. App. D Form 89, Petition to Compel Arbitration and Appoint Neutral Arbitrator.

Rutter, Cal. Practice Guide: A.D.R. App. D Form 102, Petition for Appointment of Neutral Arbitrator.

Rutter, Cal. Practice Guide: Civ. Pro. Before Trial Ch. 13-B, B. Judicial Arbitration Distinguished from Contract Arbitration.

Rutter, Cal. Practice Guide: Civ. Pro. Before Trial Ch. 9(I)-H, H. Motions Relating to Contractual Arbitration.

California Practice Guide: Employment Litigation Ch. 18-C, C. Contractual Arbitration.

Rutter, Cal. Practice Guide: Personal Injury Ch. 7-J, J. Arbitration of Uninsured Motorist Claims.

Miller and Starr California Real Estate § 35:53, Unconscionability.

Miller and Starr California Real Estate § 35:65, Appointment and Removal of an Arbitrator.

18 NO. 5 Miller & Starr, California Real Estate Newsalert 3, Commercial Arbitration.

6 Witkin Cal. Proc. 5th Proceedings Without Trial § 554, (S 554) Selection and Appointment.

6 Witkin Cal. Proc. 5th Proceedings Without Trial § 557, Statutory Requirements.

2 Witkin, California Summary 10th Insurance § 208, (S 208) Requirement.

1 Witkin Cal. Summ. 10th Contracts § 334, Promotor's Contract With Artist.

§ 1281.7. Petition in lieu of answer

A petition pursuant to Section 1281.2 may be filed in lieu of filing an answer to a complaint. The petitioning defendant shall have 15 days after any denial of the petition to plead to the complaint. *(Added by Stats.1987, c. 1080, § 9.)*

Research References

Rutter, Cal. Practice Guide: A.D.R. Ch. 5-G, G. Procedures to Enforce Arbitration.

Rutter, Cal. Practice Guide: A.D.R. App. D Form 88, Motion for Order Compelling Arbitration and for Stay (Pending Lawsuit).

Rutter, Cal. Practice Guide: Civ. Pro. Before Trial Ch. 5-B, B. Entry of Default.

Rutter, Cal. Practice Guide: Civ. Pro. Before Trial Ch. 6-C, C. Answer.

California Practice Guide: Employment Litigation Ch. 19-B, B. Defendant's Challenges to Forum Plaintiff Selects.

Rutter, Cal. Practice Guide: Insurance Litigation Ch. 15-E, E. Pleadings.

Miller and Starr California Real Estate § 35:44, Petition to Compel Arbitration.

6 Witkin Cal. Proc. 5th Proceedings Without Trial § 139, Extension of Time.

6 Witkin Cal. Proc. 5th Proceedings Without Trial § 524, (S 524) in General.

§ 1281.8. Provisional remedies; attachment, temporary protective or restraining order, writ of possession, preliminary injunction, or receiver

(a) As used in this section, "provisional remedy" includes the following:

(1) Attachments and temporary protective orders issued pursuant to Title 6.5 (commencing with Section 481.010) of Part 2.

(2) Writs of possession issued pursuant to Article 2 (commencing with Section 512.010) of Chapter 2 of Title 7 of Part 2.

(3) Preliminary injunctions and temporary restraining orders issued pursuant to Section 527.

(4) Receivers appointed pursuant to Section 564.

(b) A party to an arbitration agreement may file in the court in the county in which an arbitration proceeding is pending, or if an arbitration proceeding has not commenced, in any proper court, an application for a provisional remedy in connection with an arbitrable controversy, but only upon the ground that the award to which the applicant may be entitled may be rendered ineffectual without provisional relief. The application shall be accompanied by a complaint or by copies of the demand for arbitration and any response thereto. If accompanied by a complaint, the application shall also be accompanied by a statement stating whether the party is or is not reserving the party's right to arbitration.

(c) A claim by the party opposing issuance of a provisional remedy, that the controversy is not subject to arbitration, shall not be grounds for denial of any provisional remedy.

(d) An application for a provisional remedy under subdivision (b) shall not operate to waive any right of arbitration which the applicant may have pursuant to a written agreement to arbitrate, if, at the same time as the application for a provisional remedy is presented, the applicant also presents to the court an application that all other proceedings in the action be stayed pending the arbitration of any issue, question, or dispute which is claimed to be arbitrable under the agreement and which is relevant to the action pursuant to which the provisional remedy is sought. *(Added by Stats.1989, c. 470, § 2.)*

Research References

Rutter, Cal. Practice Guide: A.D.R. Ch. 5-D, D. Defenses to Enforcement.

Rutter, Cal. Practice Guide: A.D.R. Ch. 5-G, G. Procedures to Enforce Arbitration.

Rutter, Cal. Practice Guide: A.D.R. Ch. 5-J, J. Challenging and Enforcing Arbitrator's Award in Court.

Rutter, Cal. Practice Guide: A.D.R. Ch. 3B-B, B. ADR Options in Construction Disputes.

Rutter, Cal. Practice Guide: Enforcing Judgments/Debts Ch. 4-A, A. Attachment.

Rutter, Cal. Practice Guide: Enforcing Judgments/Debts Ch. 4-B, B. Claim and Delivery.

Rutter, Cal. Practice Guide: Enforcing Judgments/Debts Ch. 4-C, C. Receiverships.

Miller and Starr California Real Estate § 33:4, Standards for Appointment.

Miller and Starr California Real Estate § 33:8, Appeals, Generally.

Miller and Starr California Real Estate § 33:23, Actions in Which a Receiver May be Appointed--In General.

Miller and Starr California Real Estate § 35:58, Provisional Remedies While Arbitration Pending.

Miller and Starr California Real Estate § 35:63, Waiver by Participation in Litigation.

14 NO. 1 Miller & Starr, California Real Estate Newsalert 2, Commercial Arbitration.

15 NO. 6 Miller & Starr, California Real Estate Newsalert 1, Refuse to Mediate and (Under Some Contracts) Wave Goodbye to Your Attorney's Fees.

21 NO. 5 Miller & Starr, California Real Estate Newsalert 3, Alternative Dispute Resolution.

22 NO. 1 Miller & Starr, California Real Estate Newsalert 4, Alternative Dispute Resolution.

6 Witkin Cal. Proc. 5th Proceedings Without Trial § 529, (S 529) in General.

6 Witkin Cal. Proc. 5th Proceedings Without Trial § 530, (S 530) Injunctive Relief.

6 Witkin Cal. Proc. 5th Provisional Remedies § 74, (S 74) Attachment Despite Arbitration Provision.

6 Witkin Cal. Proc. 5th Provisional Remedies § 334, Arbitration Proceeding.

6 Witkin Cal. Proc. 5th Provisional Remedies § 423, Specific Statutory Enumeration.

6 Witkin Cal. Proc. 5th Provisional Remedies § 440, (S 440) Other Actions or Proceedings.

§ 1281.85. Ethical standards applicable to neutral arbitrators

(a) Beginning July 1, 2002, a person serving as a neutral arbitrator pursuant to an arbitration agreement shall comply with the ethics standards for arbitrators adopted by the Judicial Council pursuant to this section. The Judicial Council shall adopt ethical standards for all neutral arbitrators effective July 1, 2002. These standards shall be consistent with the standards established for arbitrators in the judicial arbitration program and may expand but may not limit the disclosure and disqualification requirements established by this chapter. The standards shall address the disclosure of interests, relationships, or affiliations that may constitute conflicts of interest, including prior service as an arbitrator or other dispute resolution neutral entity, disqualifications, acceptance of gifts, and establishment of future professional relationships.

(b) Subdivision (a) does not apply to an arbitration conducted pursuant to the terms of a public or private sector collective bargaining agreement.

(c) The ethics requirements and standards of this chapter are nonnegotiable and shall not be waived. *(Added by Stats.2001, c. 362 (S.B.475), § 4. Amended by Stats.2002, c. 176 (S.B.1707), § 1; Stats.2009, c. 133 (A.B.1090), § 1.)*

Research References

Rutter, Cal. Practice Guide: A.D.R. Ch. 5-J, J. Challenging and Enforcing Arbitrator's Award in Court.

Rutter, Cal. Practice Guide: A.D.R. Ch. 7-B, B. Arbitrators.

Rutter, Cal. Practice Guide: Personal Injury Ch. 7-J, J. Arbitration of Uninsured Motorist Claims.

Miller and Starr California Real Estate § 35:24, Federal Arbitration Act.

Miller and Starr California Real Estate § 35:35, Member of an Organization.

16 NO. 1 Miller & Starr, California Real Estate Newsalert 7. for Arbitration Administered by the National Association of Securities Dealers, The Federal Securities Exchange Act Preempts Both the California Ethics Standards Established by the Judicial Council for Persons Serving...

20 NO. 4 Miller & Starr, California Real Estate Newsalert 3, Alternative Dispute Resolution.

2 Witkin Cal. Proc. 5th Courts § 198, (S 198) Additional Elements.

6 Witkin Cal. Proc. 5th Proceedings Without Trial § 558, Ethics Standards for Neutral Arbitrators.

§ 1281.9. Neutral arbitrators; disclosure of information; disqualification; waiver

(a) In any arbitration pursuant to an arbitration agreement, when a person is to serve as a neutral arbitrator, the proposed neutral arbitrator shall disclose all matters that could cause a person aware of the facts to reasonably entertain a doubt that the proposed neutral arbitrator would be able to be impartial, including all of the following:

(1) The existence of any ground specified in Section 170.1 for disqualification of a judge. For purposes of paragraph (8) of subdivision (a) of Section 170.1, the proposed neutral arbitrator shall disclose whether or not he or she has a current arrangement concerning prospective employment or other compensated service as a dispute resolution neutral or is participating in, or, within the last two years, has participated in, discussions regarding such prospective employment or service with a party to the proceeding.

(2) Any matters required to be disclosed by the ethics standards for neutral arbitrators adopted by the Judicial Council pursuant to this chapter.

(3) The names of the parties to all prior or pending noncollective bargaining cases in which the proposed neutral arbitrator served or is serving as a party arbitrator for any party to the arbitration proceeding or for a lawyer for a party and the results of each case arbitrated to conclusion, including the date of the arbitration award, identification of the prevailing party, the names of the parties' attorneys and the amount of monetary damages awarded, if any. In order to preserve confidentiality, it shall be sufficient to give the name of any party who is not a party to the pending arbitration as "claimant" or "respondent" if the party is an individual and not a business or corporate entity.

(4) The names of the parties to all prior or pending noncollective bargaining cases involving any party to the arbitration or lawyer for a party for which the proposed neutral arbitrator served or is serving as neutral arbitrator, and the results of each case arbitrated to conclusion, including the date of the arbitration award, identification of the prevailing party, the names of the parties' attorneys and the amount of monetary damages awarded, if any. In order to preserve confidentiality, it shall be sufficient to give the name of any party not a party to the pending arbitration as "claimant" or "respondent" if the party is an individual and not a business or corporate entity.

(5) Any attorney-client relationship the proposed neutral arbitrator has or had with any party or lawyer for a party to the arbitration proceeding.

(6) Any professional or significant personal relationship the proposed neutral arbitrator or his or her spouse or minor child living in the household has or has had with any party to the arbitration proceeding or lawyer for a party.

(b) Subject only to the disclosure requirements of law, the proposed neutral arbitrator shall disclose all matters required to be disclosed pursuant to this section to all parties in writing within 10 calendar days of service of notice of the proposed nomination or appointment.

(c) For purposes of this section, "lawyer for a party" includes any lawyer or law firm currently associated in the practice of law with the lawyer hired to represent a party.

(d) For purposes of this section, "prior cases" means noncollective bargaining cases in which an arbitration award was rendered within five years prior to the date of the proposed nomination or appointment.

(e) For purposes of this section, "any arbitration" does not include an arbitration conducted pursuant to the terms of a public or private sector collective bargaining agreement. *(Added by Stats.1994, c. 1202 (S.B.1638), § 1. Amended by Stats.1997, c. 445 (A.B.1093), § 2; Stats.2001, c. 362 (S.B.475), § 5; Stats. 2002, c. 1094 (A.B.2504), § 2.)*

Research References

Rutter, Cal. Practice Guide: A.D.R. Ch. 3-D, D. "Classic" (Facilitative) Mediation.
Rutter, Cal. Practice Guide: A.D.R. Ch. 5-D, D. Defenses to Enforcement.
Rutter, Cal. Practice Guide: A.D.R. Ch. 5-G, G. Procedures to Enforce Arbitration.
Rutter, Cal. Practice Guide: A.D.R. Ch. 5-J, J. Challenging and Enforcing Arbitrator's Award in Court.
Rutter, Cal. Practice Guide: A.D.R. Ch. 5-K, K. Arbitration of International Commercial Disputes.
Rutter, Cal. Practice Guide: A.D.R. Ch. 7-B, B. Arbitrators.
Rutter, Cal. Practice Guide: A.D.R. Ch. 8-E, E. Special Drafting Considerations Re Arbitration Agreements.
Rutter, Cal. Practice Guide: A.D.R. Ch. 5-G, Outline G.
Rutter, Cal. Practice Guide: A.D.R. Ch. 7-B, Outline B.
Rutter, Cal. Practice Guide: Civil Appeals & Writs Ch. 8-A, A. Overview.
California Practice Guide: Employment Litigation Ch. 18-F, F. Selecting the Neutral.
Rutter, Cal. Practice Guide: Insurance Litigation Ch. 15-C, C. Arbitration/Appraisal/Mediation.
Rutter, Cal. Practice Guide: Prof. Responsibility Ch. 5-K, K. Fee Recovery/Enforcing Fee Agreements.
Miller and Starr California Real Estate § 35:22, Nature of Arbitration.
Miller and Starr California Real Estate § 35:39, Issues Which Cannot be the Subject of Arbitration.
Miller and Starr California Real Estate § 35:68, Bias or Impartiality of an Arbitrator.
Miller and Starr California Real Estate § 35:69, Arbitrator's Duty of Written Disclosure.
Miller and Starr California Real Estate § 35:70, Disqualification of the Arbitrator.
Miller and Starr California Real Estate § 35:94, Grounds for Vacating an Award.
18 NO. 5 Miller & Starr, California Real Estate Newsalert 3, Commercial Arbitration.
18 NO. 6 Miller & Starr, California Real Estate Newsalert 3, Alternative Dispute Resolution.
20 NO. 5 Miller & Starr, California Real Estate Newsalert 3, Alternative Dispute Resolution.
21 NO. 3 Miller & Starr, California Real Estate Newsalert 4, Alternative Dispute Resolution.
22 NO. 1 Miller & Starr, California Real Estate Newsalert 4, Alternative Dispute Resolution.
23 NO. 2 Miller & Starr, California Real Estate Newsalert 4, Alternative Dispute Resolution.
6 Witkin Cal. Proc. 5th Proceedings Without Trial § 557, Statutory Requirements.
6 Witkin Cal. Proc. 5th Proceedings Without Trial § 569, (S 569) in General.
6 Witkin Cal. Proc. 5th Proceedings Without Trial § 572, (S 572) Arbitrator's Failure to Disclose.

§ 1281.91. Disqualification of neutral arbitrator

(a) A proposed neutral arbitrator shall be disqualified if he or she fails to comply with Section 1281.9 and any party entitled to receive the disclosure serves a notice of disqualification within 15 calendar days after the proposed nominee or appointee fails to comply with Section 1281.9.

(b)(1) If the proposed neutral arbitrator complies with Section 1281.9, the proposed neutral arbitrator shall be disqualified on the basis of the disclosure statement after any party entitled to receive the disclosure serves a notice of disqualification within 15 calendar days after service of the disclosure statement.

(2) A party shall have the right to disqualify one court-appointed arbitrator without cause in any single arbitration, and

may petition the court to disqualify a subsequent appointee only upon a showing of cause.

(c) The right of a party to disqualify a proposed neutral arbitrator pursuant to this section shall be waived if the party fails to serve the notice pursuant to the times set forth in this section, unless the proposed nominee or appointee makes a material omission or material misrepresentation in his or her disclosure. Except as provided in subdivision (d), in no event may a notice of disqualification be given after a hearing of any contested issue of fact relating to the merits of the claim or after any ruling by the arbitrator regarding any contested matter. Nothing in this subdivision shall limit the right of a party to vacate an award pursuant to Section 1286.2, or to disqualify an arbitrator pursuant to any other law or statute.

(d) If any ground specified in Section 170.1 exists, a neutral arbitrator shall disqualify himself or herself upon the demand of any party made before the conclusion of the arbitration proceeding. However, this subdivision does not apply to arbitration proceedings conducted under a collective bargaining agreement between employers and employees or their respective representatives. *(Added by Stats.2001, c. 362 (S.B.475), § 6.)*

Research References

Rutter, Cal. Practice Guide: A.D.R. Ch. 5-D, D. Defenses to Enforcement.
Rutter, Cal. Practice Guide: A.D.R. Ch. 5-J, J. Challenging and Enforcing Arbitrator's Award in Court.
Rutter, Cal. Practice Guide: A.D.R. Ch. 5-K, K. Arbitration of International Commercial Disputes.
Rutter, Cal. Practice Guide: A.D.R. Ch. 7-B, B. Arbitrators.
Rutter, Cal. Practice Guide: A.D.R. Ch. 8-E, E. Special Drafting Considerations Re Arbitration Agreements.
Rutter, Cal. Practice Guide: Civ. Pro. Before Trial Ch. 9(I)-H, H. Motions Relating to Contractual Arbitration.
California Practice Guide: Employment Litigation Ch. 18-F, F. Selecting the Neutral.
Miller and Starr California Real Estate § 35:39, Issues Which Cannot be the Subject of Arbitration.
Miller and Starr California Real Estate § 35:65, Appointment and Removal of an Arbitrator.
Miller and Starr California Real Estate § 35:68, Bias or Impartiality of an Arbitrator.
Miller and Starr California Real Estate § 35:70, Disqualification of the Arbitrator.
Miller and Starr California Real Estate § 35:94, Grounds for Vacating an Award.
15 NO. 2 Miller & Starr, California Real Estate Newsalert 3, Commercial Arbitration.
16 NO. 3 Miller & Starr, California Real Estate Newsalert 3, Commercial Arbitration.
6 Witkin Cal. Proc. 5th Proceedings Without Trial § 557, Statutory Requirements.
6 Witkin Cal. Proc. 5th Proceedings Without Trial § 569, (S 569) in General.
6 Witkin Cal. Proc. 5th Proceedings Without Trial § 572, (S 572) Arbitrator's Failure to Disclose.

§ 1281.92. Restrictions against private arbitration company from administering consumer arbitration or related services

(a) No private arbitration company may administer a consumer arbitration, or provide any other services related to a consumer arbitration, if the company has, or within the preceding year has had, a financial interest, as defined in Section 170.5, in any party or attorney for a party.

(b) No private arbitration company may administer a consumer arbitration, or provide any other services related to a consumer arbitration, if any party or attorney for a party has, or within the preceding year has had, any type of financial interest in the private arbitration company.

(c) This section shall operate only prospectively so as not to prohibit the administration of consumer arbitrations on the basis of financial interests held prior to January 1, 2003.

(d) This section applies to all consumer arbitration agreements subject to this article, and to all consumer arbitration proceedings conducted in California.

(e) This section shall become operative on January 1, 2003. *(Added by Stats.2002, c. 952 (A.B.2574), § 1, operative Jan. 1, 2003.)*

Research References

Rutter, Cal. Practice Guide: A.D.R. Ch. 7-B, B. Arbitrators.
6 Witkin Cal. Proc. 5th Proceedings Without Trial § 557, Statutory Requirements.

§ 1281.95. Residential construction or improvements; arbitrator disclosures; disqualification

(a) In a binding arbitration of any claim for more than three thousand dollars ($3,000) pursuant to a contract for the construction or improvement of residential property consisting of one to four units, the arbitrator shall, within 10 days following his or her appointment, provide to each party a written declaration under penalty of perjury. This declaration shall disclose (1) whether the arbitrator or his or her employer or arbitration service had or has a personal or professional affiliation with either party, and (2) whether the arbitrator or his or her employer or arbitration service has been selected or designated as an arbitrator by either party in another transaction.

(b) If the arbitrator discloses an affiliation with either party, discloses that the arbitrator has been selected or designated as an arbitrator by either party in another arbitration, or fails to comply with this section, he or she may be disqualified from the arbitration by either party.

(c) A notice of disqualification shall be served within 15 days after the arbitrator makes the required disclosures or fails to comply. The right of a party to disqualify an arbitrator shall be waived if the party fails to serve the notice of disqualification pursuant to this subdivision unless the arbitration makes a material omission or material misrepresentation in his or her disclosure. Nothing in this section shall limit the right of a party to vacate an award pursuant to Section 1286.2, or to disqualify an arbitrator pursuant to any other law or statute. *(Added by Stats.1994, c. 804 (A.B.3436), § 1. Amended by Stats.2002, c. 1008 (A.B.3028), § 5.)*

Research References

Rutter, Cal. Practice Guide: A.D.R. Ch. 7-B, B. Arbitrators.
Rutter, Cal. Practice Guide: A.D.R. Ch. 7-B, Outline B.
Miller and Starr California Real Estate § 35:69, Arbitrator's Duty of Written Disclosure.
6 Witkin Cal. Proc. 5th Proceedings Without Trial § 557, Statutory Requirements.

§ 1281.96. Private arbitration companies; quarterly or biannual publication of consumer arbitration information; liability

(a) Except as provided in paragraph (2) of subdivision (b), any private arbitration company that administers or is otherwise involved in, a consumer arbitration, shall collect, publish at least quarterly, and make available to the public in a computer-searchable format, which shall be accessible at the Internet Web site of the private arbitration company, if any, and on paper upon request, all of the following information regarding each consumer arbitration within the preceding five years:

(1) The name of the nonconsumer party, if the nonconsumer party is a corporation or other business entity.

(2) The type of dispute involved, including goods, banking, insurance, health care, employment, and, if it involves employment, the amount of the employee's annual wage divided into the following ranges: less than one hundred thousand dollars ($100,000), one hundred thousand dollars ($100,000) to two hundred fifty thousand dollars ($250,000), inclusive, and over two hundred fifty thousand dollars ($250,000).

(3) Whether the consumer or nonconsumer party was the prevailing party.

(4) On how many occasions, if any, the nonconsumer party has previously been a party in an arbitration or mediation administered by the private arbitration company.

(5) Whether the consumer party was represented by an attorney.

(6) The date the private arbitration company received the demand for arbitration, the date the arbitrator was appointed, and the date of disposition by the arbitrator or private arbitration company.

(7) The type of disposition of the dispute, if known, including withdrawal, abandonment, settlement, award after hearing, award without hearing, default, or dismissal without hearing.

(8) The amount of the claim, the amount of the award, and any other relief granted, if any.

(9) The name of the arbitrator, his or her total fee for the case, and the percentage of the arbitrator's fee allocated to each party.

(b)(1) If the information required by subdivision (a) is provided by the private arbitration company in a computer-searchable format at the company's Internet Web site and may be downloaded without any fee, the company may charge the actual cost of copying to any person who requests the information on paper. If the information required by subdivision (a) is not accessible by the Internet, the company shall provide that information without charge to any person who requests the information on paper.

(2) Notwithstanding paragraph (1), a private arbitration company that receives funding pursuant to Chapter 8 (commencing with Section 465) of Division 1 of the Business and Professions Code, and that administers or conducts fewer than 50 consumer arbitrations per year may collect and publish the information required by subdivision (a) semiannually, provide the information only on paper, and charge the actual cost of copying.

(c) This section shall apply to any consumer arbitration commenced on or after January 1, 2003.

(d) No private arbitration company shall have any liability for collecting, publishing, or distributing the information required by this section. *(Added by Stats.2002, c. 1158 (A.B.2656), § 1.)*

Research References

Rutter, Cal. Practice Guide: A.D.R. Ch. 5-H, H. Conduct of Arbitration Proceedings.
Rutter, Cal. Practice Guide: A.D.R. Ch. 7-B, B. Arbitrators.
13 NO. 4 Miller & Starr, California Real Estate Newsalert 3, Commercial Arbitration.
6 Witkin Cal. Proc. 5th Proceedings Without Trial § 557, Statutory Requirements.

CHAPTER 3. CONDUCT OF ARBITRATION PROCEEDINGS

§ 1282. Exercise of powers and duties of neutral arbitrator

Unless the arbitration agreement otherwise provides, or unless the parties to the arbitration otherwise provide by an agreement which is not contrary to the arbitration agreement as made or as modified by all of the parties thereto:

(a) The arbitration shall be by a single neutral arbitrator.

(b) If there is more than one arbitrator, the powers and duties of the arbitrators, other than the powers and duties of a neutral arbitrator, may be exercised by a majority of them if reasonable notice of all proceedings has been given to all arbitrators.

(c) If there is more than one neutral arbitrator:

(1) The powers and duties of a neutral arbitrator may be exercised by a majority of the neutral arbitrators.

(2) By unanimous agreement of the neutral arbitrators, the powers and duties may be delegated to one of their number but the power to make or correct the award may not be so delegated.

(d) If there is no neutral arbitrator, the powers and duties of a neutral arbitrator may be exercised by a majority of the arbitrators. *(Added by Stats.1961, c. 461, p. 1542, § 2. Amended by Stats.1993, c. 768 (S.B.252), § 4; Stats.1997, c. 445 (A.B.1093), § 3.)*

Research References

California Real Estate Forms (Miller & Starr) § 2:92, Mediation; Arbitration.
Rutter, Cal. Practice Guide: A.D.R. App. D Form 39, Arbitrator's Powers.
Rutter, Cal. Practice Guide: Civ. Pro. Before Trial Ch. 13-B, B. Judicial Arbitration Distinguished from Contract Arbitration.
Rutter, Cal. Practice Guide: Real Prop. Transactions Ch. 4-E, E. Drafting the Purchase and Sale Agreement-Terms and Conditions.
Miller and Starr California Real Estate § 35:65, Appointment and Removal of an Arbitrator.
Miller and Starr California Real Estate § 35:69, Arbitrator's Duty of Written Disclosure.
Miller and Starr California Real Estate § 35:74, Hearing Procedures; Control Over Conduct of the Hearing.
13 NO. 6 Miller & Starr, California Real Estate Newsalert 1, Using Basura to Make Construction Defect Claims Arbitrable, or Woodside to Send Them to a Referee.
6 Witkin Cal. Proc. 5th Proceedings Without Trial § 502, General Statute.
6 Witkin Cal. Proc. 5th Proceedings Without Trial § 554, (S 554) Selection and Appointment.

1 Witkin Cal. Summ. 10th Contracts § 334, Promotor's Contract With Artist.

§ 1282.2. Hearing; time and place; witness lists; adjournment or postponement; conduct; evidence; procedure

Unless the arbitration agreement otherwise provides, or unless the parties to the arbitration otherwise provide by an agreement which is not contrary to the arbitration agreement as made or as modified by all the parties thereto:

(a)(1) The neutral arbitrator shall appoint a time and place for the hearing and cause notice thereof to be served personally or by registered or certified mail on the parties to the arbitration and on the other arbitrators not less than seven days before the hearing. Appearance at the hearing waives the right to notice.

(2) With the exception of matters arising out of collective-bargaining agreements, those described in Section 1283.05, actions involving personal injury or death, or as provided in the parties' agreement to arbitrate, in the event the aggregate amount in controversy exceeds fifty thousand dollars ($50,000) and the arbitrator is informed thereof by any party in writing by personal service, registered or certified mail, prior to designating a time and place of hearing pursuant to paragraph (1), the neutral arbitrator by the means prescribed in paragraph (1) shall appoint a time and place for hearing not less than 60 days before the hearing, and the following provisions shall apply:

(A) Either party shall within 15 days of receipt of the notice of hearing have the right to demand in writing, served personally or by registered or certified mail, that the other party provide a list of witnesses it intends to call designating which witnesses will be called as expert witnesses and a list of documents it intends to introduce at the hearing provided that the demanding party provides such lists at the time of its demand. A copy of such demand and the demanding party's lists shall be served on the arbitrator.

(B) Such lists shall be served personally or by registered or certified mail on the requesting party 15 days thereafter. Copies thereof shall be served on the arbitrator.

(C) Listed documents shall be made available for inspection and copying at reasonable times prior to the hearing.

(D) Time limits provided herein may be waived by mutual agreement of the parties if approved by the arbitrator.

(E) The failure to list a witness or a document shall not bar the testimony of an unlisted witness or the introduction of an undesignated document at the hearing, provided that good cause for omission from the requirements of subparagraph (A) is shown, as determined by the arbitrator.

(F) The authority of the arbitrator to administer and enforce this paragraph shall be as provided in subdivisions (b) to (e), inclusive, of Section 1283.05.

(b) The neutral arbitrator may adjourn the hearing from time to time as necessary. On request of a party to the arbitration for good cause, or upon his own determination, the neutral arbitrator may postpone the hearing to a time not later than the date fixed by the agreement for making the award, or to a later date if the parties to the arbitration consent thereto.

(c) The neutral arbitrator shall preside at the hearing, shall rule on the admission and exclusion of evidence and on questions of hearing procedure and shall exercise all powers relating to the conduct of the hearing.

(d) The parties to the arbitration are entitled to be heard, to present evidence and to cross-examine witnesses appearing at the hearing, but rules of evidence and rules of judicial procedure need not be observed. On request of any party to the arbitration, the testimony of witnesses shall be given under oath.

(e) If a court has ordered a person to arbitrate a controversy, the arbitrators may hear and determine the controversy upon the evidence produced notwithstanding the failure of a party ordered to arbitrate, who has been duly notified, to appear.

(f) If an arbitrator, who has been duly notified, for any reason fails to participate in the arbitration, the arbitration shall continue but only the remaining neutral arbitrator or neutral arbitrators may make the award.

(g) If a neutral arbitrator intends to base an award upon information not obtained at the hearing, he shall disclose the information to all parties to the arbitration and give the parties an opportunity to meet it. *(Added by Stats.1961, c. 461, p. 1542, § 2. Amended by Stats.1979, c. 948, p. 3273, § 2, eff. Sept. 22, 1979; Stats.1981, c. 714, § 72.)*

Research References

Rutter, Cal. Practice Guide: A.D.R. Ch. 4-B, B. Judicial Arbitration.
Rutter, Cal. Practice Guide: A.D.R. Ch. 5-H, H. Conduct of Arbitration Proceedings.
Rutter, Cal. Practice Guide: A.D.R. Ch. 7-B, B. Arbitrators.
Rutter, Cal. Practice Guide: A.D.R. Ch. 3B-B, B. ADR Options in Construction Disputes.
Rutter, Cal. Practice Guide: A.D.R. App. D Form 106, Arbitrator's Notice of Time and Place of Hearing.
Rutter, Cal. Practice Guide: A.D.R. App. D Form 107, Discovery-Demand for List of Witnesses and Documents.
Rutter, Cal. Practice Guide: A.D.R. App. D Form 108, Discovery-List of Witnesses and Documents.
Rutter, Cal. Practice Guide: Civ. Pro. Before Trial Ch. 13-B, B. Judicial Arbitration Distinguished from Contract Arbitration.
California Practice Guide: Employment Litigation Ch. 18-C, C. Contractual Arbitration.
Rutter, Cal. Practice Guide: Insurance Litigation Ch. 6G-D, D. Uninsured and Underinsured Motorist Coverages.
Rutter, Cal. Practice Guide: Personal Injury Ch. 7-J, J. Arbitration of Uninsured Motorist Claims.
Miller and Starr California Real Estate § 35:22, Nature of Arbitration.
Miller and Starr California Real Estate § 35:73, Notice of the Hearing.
Miller and Starr California Real Estate § 35:74, Hearing Procedures; Control Over Conduct of the Hearing.
Miller and Starr California Real Estate § 35:75, Evidence; Burden of Proof.
Miller and Starr California Real Estate § 35:77, Production and Testimony of a Witness.
Miller and Starr California Real Estate § 35:81, Basis for the Award.
21 NO. 4 Miller & Starr, California Real Estate Newsalert 19, Alternative Dispute Resolution.
6 Witkin Cal. Proc. 5th Proceedings Without Trial § 559, (S 559) Powers.
6 Witkin Cal. Proc. 5th Proceedings Without Trial § 560, Discovery and Subpenas.
6 Witkin Cal. Proc. 5th Proceedings Without Trial § 561, Hearing.
6 Witkin Cal. Proc. 5th Proceedings Without Trial § 580, Contractual Arbitration Distinguished.

§ 1282.4. Representation by counsel

(a) A party to the arbitration has the right to be represented by an attorney at any proceeding or hearing in arbitration under this title. A waiver of this right may be revoked; but if a party revokes that waiver, the other party is entitled to a reasonable continuance for the purpose of procuring an attorney.

(b) Notwithstanding any other * * * law, including Section 6125 of the Business and Professions Code, an attorney admitted to the bar of any other state may represent the parties in the course of, or in connection with, an arbitration proceeding in this state, provided that the attorney, if not admitted to the State Bar of California, satisfies all of the following:

(1) He or she timely serves the certificate described in subdivision (c).

(2) The attorney's appearance is approved in writing on that certificate by the arbitrator, the arbitrators, or the arbitral forum.

(3) The certificate bearing approval of the attorney's appearance is filed with the State Bar of California and served on the parties as described in this section.

(c) Within a reasonable period of time after the attorney described in subdivision (b) indicates an intention to appear in the arbitration, the attorney shall serve a certificate in a form prescribed by the State Bar of California on the arbitrator, arbitrators, or arbitral forum, the State Bar of California, and all other parties and counsel in the arbitration whose addresses are known to the attorney. The certificate shall state all of the following:

(1) The case name and number, and the name of the arbitrator, arbitrators, or arbitral forum assigned to the proceeding in which the attorney seeks to appear.

(2) The attorney's residence and office address.

(3) The courts before which the attorney has been admitted to practice and the dates of admission.

(4) That the attorney is currently a member in good standing of, and eligible to practice law before, the bar of those courts.

(5) That the attorney is not currently on suspension or disbarred from the practice of law before the bar of any court.

(6) That the attorney is not a resident of the State of California.

(7) That the attorney is not regularly employed in the State of California.

(8) That the attorney is not regularly engaged in substantial business, professional, or other activities in the State of California.

(9) That the attorney agrees to be subject to the jurisdiction of the courts of this state with respect to the law of this state governing the conduct of attorneys to the same extent as a member of the State Bar of California.

(10) The title of the court and the cause in which the attorney has filed an application to appear as counsel pro hac vice in this state or filed a certificate pursuant to this section in the preceding two years, the date of each application or certificate, and whether or not it was granted. If the attorney has made repeated appearances, the certificate shall reflect the special circumstances that warrant the approval of the attorney's appearance in the arbitration.

(11) The name, address, and telephone number of the active member of the State Bar of California who is the attorney of record.

(d) The arbitrator, arbitrators, or arbitral forum may approve the attorney's appearance if the attorney has complied with subdivision (c). Failure to timely file and serve the certificate described in subdivision (c) shall be grounds for disapproval of the appearance and disqualification from serving as an attorney in the arbitration in which the certificate was filed. In the absence of special circumstances, repeated appearances shall be grounds for disapproval of the appearance and disqualification from serving as an attorney in the arbitration in which the certificate was filed.

(e) Within a reasonable period of time after the arbitrator, arbitrators, or arbitral forum approves the certificate, the attorney shall file the certificate with the State Bar of California and serve the certificate as described in Section 1013a on all parties and counsel in the arbitration whose * * * <u>addresses are</u> known to the attorney.

(f) An attorney who fails to file or serve the certificate required by this section or files or serves a certificate containing false information or who otherwise fails to comply with the standards of professional conduct required of members of the State Bar of California shall be subject to the disciplinary

jurisdiction of the State Bar with respect to that certificate or any of his or her acts occurring in the course of the arbitration.

(g) Notwithstanding any other * * * law, including Section 6125 of the Business and Professions Code, an attorney who is a member in good standing of the bar of any state may represent the parties in connection with rendering legal services in this state in the course of and in connection with an arbitration pending in another state.

(h) Notwithstanding any other * * * law, including Section 6125 of the Business and Professions Code, any party to an arbitration arising under collective bargaining agreements in industries and provisions subject to either state or federal law may be represented in the course of, and in connection with, those proceedings by any person, regardless of whether that person is licensed to practice law in this state.

(i) Nothing in this section shall apply to Division 4 (commencing with Section 3201) of the Labor Code.

(j)(1) In enacting the amendments to this section made by Assembly Bill 2086 of the 1997–98 Regular Session, it is the intent of the Legislature to respond to the holding in Birbrower v. Superior Court (1998) 17 Cal.4th <u>119</u>, as modified at 17 Cal.4th 643a (hereafter Birbrower), to provide a procedure for nonresident attorneys who are not licensed in this state to appear in California arbitration proceedings.

(2) In enacting subdivision (h), it is the intent of the Legislature to make clear that any party to an arbitration arising under a collective bargaining agreement governed by the laws of this state may be represented in the course of and in connection with those proceedings by any person regardless of whether that person is licensed to practice law in this state.

(3) Except as otherwise specifically provided in this section, in enacting the amendments to this section made by Assembly Bill 2086 of the 1997–98 Regular Session, it is the Legislature's intent that nothing in this section is intended to expand or restrict the ability of a party prior to the decision in Birbrower to elect to be represented by any person in a nonjudicial arbitration proceeding, to the extent those rights or abilities existed prior to that decision. To the extent that Birbrower is interpreted to expand or restrict that right or ability pursuant to the laws of this state, it is hereby abrogated except as specifically provided in this section.

(4) In enacting subdivision (i), it is the intent of the Legislature to make clear that nothing in this section shall affect those provisions of law governing the right of injured workers to elect to be represented by any person, regardless of whether that person is licensed to practice law in this state, as set forth in Division 4 (commencing with Section 3200) of the Labor Code. *(Added by Stats.1961, c. 461, p. 1543, § 2. Amended by Stats.1998, c. 915 (A.B.2086), § 1; Stats.2000, c. 1011 (S.B.2153), § 2; Stats.2005, c. 607 (A.B.415), § 1, eff. Oct. 6, 2005; Stats. 2006, c. 357 (A.B.2482), § 1; Stats.2010, c. 277 (S.B.877), § 1; Stats.2012, c. 53 (A.B.1631), § 1; Stats.2013, c. 76 (A.B.383), § 24.)*

Research References

Rutter, Cal. Practice Guide: A.D.R. Ch. 5-H, H. Conduct of Arbitration Proceedings.

Rutter, Cal. Practice Guide: Prof. Responsibility Ch. 1-A, A. Sources of Regulation of Practice of Law in California-Overview.

Rutter, Cal. Practice Guide: Prof. Responsibility Ch. 1-B, B. Regulation of Admission to Practice Law.

Rutter, Cal. Practice Guide: Prof. Responsibility Ch. 1-D, D. Unauthorized Practice of Law.

Miller and Starr California Real Estate § 35:78, Right to Counsel.

1 Witkin Cal. Proc. 5th Attorneys § 387, (S 387) in General.

6 Witkin Cal. Proc. 5th Proceedings Without Trial § 561, Hearing.

§ 1282.6. Issuance of subpoenas

(a) A subpoena requiring the attendance of witnesses, and a subpoena duces tecum for the production of books, records, documents and other evidence, at an arbitration proceeding or a deposition under Section 1283, and if Section 1283.05 is applicable, for the purposes of discovery, shall be issued as provided in this section. In addition, the neutral arbitrator upon his own determination may issue subpoenas for the attendance of witnesses and subpoenas duces tecum for the production of books, records, documents and other evidence.

(b) Subpoenas shall be issued, as of course, signed but otherwise in blank, to the party requesting them, by a neutral association, organization, governmental agency, or office if the arbitration agreement provides for administration of the arbitration proceedings by, or under the rules of, a neutral association, organization, governmental agency or office or by the neutral arbitrator.

(c) The party serving the subpoena shall fill it in before service. Subpoenas [1] shall be served and enforced in accordance with Chapter 2 (commencing with Section 1985) of Title 3 of Part 4 of this code. *(Added by Stats.1961, c. 461, p. 1543, § 2. Amended by Stats.1982, c. 108, p. 325, § 1.)*

[1] So in chaptered copy.

Research References

Rutter, Cal. Practice Guide: A.D.R. Ch. 5-H, H. Conduct of Arbitration Proceedings.
Rutter, Cal. Practice Guide: A.D.R. Ch. 3-B-B, B. ADR Options in Construction Disputes.
Rutter, Cal. Practice Guide: A.D.R. App. D Form 111, Discovery-Arbitrator's Subpoena Re Deposition (CCP § 1282.6).
Rutter, Cal. Practice Guide: A.D.R. App. D Form 112, Application for Arbitrator's Subpoena.
Rutter, Cal. Practice Guide: A.D.R. App. D Form 114, Arbitrator's Subpoena Duces Tecum.
Miller and Starr California Real Estate § 35:76, Depositions and Discovery.
Miller and Starr California Real Estate § 35:77, Production and Testimony of a Witness.
6 Witkin Cal. Proc. 5th Proceedings Without Trial § 559, (S 559) Powers.
6 Witkin Cal. Proc. 5th Proceedings Without Trial § 560, Discovery and Subpenas.
6 Witkin Cal. Proc. 5th Proceedings Without Trial § 596, Subpenas.

§ 1282.8. Administration of oaths

The neutral arbitrator may administer oaths. *(Added by Stats.1961, c. 461, p. 1543, § 2.)*

Research References

Miller and Starr California Real Estate § 35:74, Hearing Procedures; Control Over Conduct of the Hearing.
6 Witkin Cal. Proc. 5th Proceedings Without Trial § 559, (S 559) Powers.

§ 1283. Depositions

On application of a party to the arbitration, the neutral arbitrator may order the deposition of a witness to be taken for use as evidence and not for discovery if the witness cannot be compelled to attend the hearing or if exceptional circumstances exist as to make it desirable, in the interest of justice and with due regard to the importance of presenting the testimony of witnesses orally at the hearing, to allow the deposition to be taken. The deposition shall be taken in the manner prescribed by law for the taking of depositions in civil actions. If the neutral arbitrator orders the taking of the deposition of a witness who resides outside the state, the party who applied for the taking of the deposition shall obtain a commission, letters rogatory, or a letter of request therefor from the superior court in accordance with Chapter 10 (commencing with Section

2026.010) of Title 4 of Part 4. *(Added by Stats.1970, c. 1045, p. 1867, § 1. Amended by Stats.2005, c. 294 (A.B.333), § 4.)*

Law Revision Commission Comments

Section 1283 is amended to reflect revision and relocation of the civil discovery provisions referenced in it. As enacted in 1970, the section referred to Sections 2024–2028. 1970 Cal. Stat. ch. 1045, § 1. That cross-reference is obsolete. See 1986 Cal. Stat. ch. 1334, § 1 (repealing former Sections 2024–2025); 1961 Cal. Stat. ch. 192, §§ 8–10 (repealing former Sections 2026–2028). The modern provisions governing an out-of-state deposition are Sections 2026.010 (oral deposition in another state or territory of the United States) and 2027.010 (oral deposition in a foreign nation).

Section 1283 is also amended to make clear that letters rogatory or a letter of request are to be obtained, when necessary, for a deposition taken in arbitration.

Section 1283 is further amended to delete surplusage.

Research References

Rutter, Cal. Practice Guide: A.D.R. Ch. 5-H, H. Conduct of Arbitration Proceedings.
Rutter, Cal. Practice Guide: A.D.R. App. D Form 111, Discovery-Arbitrator's Subpoena Re Deposition (CCP § 1282.6).
California Practice Guide: Employment Litigation Ch. 18-C, C. Contractual Arbitration.
Rutter, Cal. Practice Guide: Real Prop. Transactions Ch. 4-E, E. Drafting the Purchase and Sale Agreement-Terms and Conditions.
Miller and Starr California Real Estate § 35:22, Nature of Arbitration.
Miller and Starr California Real Estate § 35:74, Hearing Procedures; Control Over Conduct of the Hearing.
Miller and Starr California Real Estate § 35:77, Production and Testimony of a Witness.
6 Witkin Cal. Proc. 5th Proceedings Without Trial § 559, (S 559) Powers.
6 Witkin Cal. Proc. 5th Proceedings Without Trial § 560, Discovery and Subpenas.

§ 1283.05. Manner of taking deposition

To the extent provided in Section 1283.1 depositions may be taken and discovery obtained in arbitration proceedings as follows:

(a) After the appointment of the arbitrator or arbitrators, the parties to the arbitration shall have the right to take depositions and to obtain discovery regarding the subject matter of the arbitration, and, to that end, to use and exercise all of the same rights, remedies, and procedures, and be subject to all of the same duties, liabilities, and obligations in the arbitration with respect to the subject matter thereof, as provided in Chapter 2 (commencing with Section 1985) of Title 3 of Part 4, and in Title 4 (commencing with Section 2016.010) of Part 4, as if the subject matter of the arbitration were pending before a superior court of this state in a civil action other than a limited civil case, subject to the limitations as to depositions set forth in subdivision (e) of this section.

(b) The arbitrator or arbitrators themselves shall have power, in addition to the power of determining the merits of the arbitration, to enforce the rights, remedies, procedures, duties, liabilities, and obligations of discovery by the imposition of the same terms, conditions, consequences, liabilities, sanctions, and penalties as can be or may be imposed in like circumstances in a civil action by a superior court of this state under the provisions of this code, except the power to order the arrest or imprisonment of a person.

(c) The arbitrator or arbitrators may consider, determine, and make such orders imposing such terms, conditions, consequences, liabilities, sanctions, and penalties, whenever necessary or appropriate at any time or stage in the course of the arbitration, and such orders shall be as conclusive, final, and enforceable as an arbitration award on the merits, if the making of any such order that is equivalent to an award or correction of an award is subject to the same conditions, if any, as are applicable to the making of an award or correction of an award.

(d) For the purpose of enforcing the duty to make discovery, to produce evidence or information, including books and records, and to produce persons to testify at a deposition or at a hearing, and to impose terms, conditions, consequences, liabilities, sanctions, and penalties upon a party for violation of any such duty, such party shall be deemed to include every affiliate of such party as defined in this section. For such purpose:

(1) The personnel of every such affiliate shall be deemed to be the officers, directors, managing agents, agents, and employees of such party to the same degree as each of them, respectively, bears such status to such affiliate; and

(2) The files, books, and records of every such affiliate shall be deemed to be in the possession and control of, and capable of production by, such party. As used in this section, "affiliate" of the party to the arbitration means and includes any party or person for whose immediate benefit the action or proceeding is prosecuted or defended, or an officer, director, superintendent, member, agent, employee, or managing agent of such party or person.

(e) Depositions for discovery shall not be taken unless leave to do so is first granted by the arbitrator or arbitrators. *(Formerly § 1283, added by Stats.1970, c. 581, p. 1157, § 2. Renumbered § 1283.05 and amended by Stats.1970, c. 1045, p. 1868, § 2. Amended by Stats.1976, c. 1185, p. 5318, § 91.5; Stats.1998, c. 931 (S.B.2139), § 123, eff. Sept. 28, 1998; Stats. 2004, c. 182 (A.B.3081), § 16, operative July 1, 2005.)*

Law Revision Commission Comments

Section 1283.05 is amended to accommodate unification of the municipal and superior courts in a county. Cal. Const. art. VI, § 5(e). See Section 85 (limited civil cases) & Comment. [28 Cal.L.Rev.Comm. Reports 51 (1998)].

Subdivision (a) of Section 1283.05 is amended to reflect nonsubstantive reorganization of the rules governing civil discovery. [33 Cal.L.Rev. Comm. Reports 997 (2004)].

Research References

California Real Estate Forms (Miller & Starr) § 1:22, Agreement of Purchase and Sale--Multi-Property.
California Real Estate Forms (Miller & Starr) § 1:26, Purchase and Sale Agreement--Seller-Oriented Short Form.
Rutter, Cal. Practice Guide: A.D.R. Ch. 4-B, B. Judicial Arbitration.
Rutter, Cal. Practice Guide: A.D.R. Ch. 5-H, H. Conduct of Arbitration Proceedings.
Rutter, Cal. Practice Guide: A.D.R. Ch. 5-I, I. Arbitrator's Award.
Rutter, Cal. Practice Guide: A.D.R. Ch. 8-E, E. Special Drafting Considerations Re Arbitration Agreements.
Rutter, Cal. Practice Guide: A.D.R. App. D Form 29, Governing Law Clauses.
Rutter, Cal. Practice Guide: A.D.R. App. D Form 33, Discovery (As Provided by Statute).
Rutter, Cal. Practice Guide: A.D.R. App. D Form 111, Discovery-Arbitrator's Subpoena Re Deposition (CCP § 1282.6).
Rutter, Cal. Practice Guide: Civ. Pro. Before Trial Ch. 13-B, B. Judicial Arbitration Distinguished from Contract Arbitration.
Rutter, Cal. Practice Guide: Civ. Pro. Before Trial Ch. 8A-8, Discovery in Nonjudicial Proceedings.
California Practice Guide: Employment Litigation Ch. 18-C, C. Contractual Arbitration.
Rutter, Cal. Practice Guide: Real Prop. Transactions Ch. 4-E, E. Drafting the Purchase and Sale Agreement-Terms and Conditions.
Miller and Starr California Real Estate § 35:74, Hearing Procedures; Control Over Conduct of the Hearing.
Miller and Starr California Real Estate § 35:76, Depositions and Discovery.
17 NO. 1 Miller & Starr, California Real Estate Newsalert 2, Commercial Arbitration.

19 NO. 1 Miller & Starr, California Real Estate Newsalert 3, Alternative Dispute Resolution.
6 Witkin Cal. Proc. 5th Proceedings Without Trial § 559, (S 559) Powers.
6 Witkin Cal. Proc. 5th Proceedings Without Trial § 560, Discovery and Subpenas.

§ 1283.1. Incorporation of § 1283.05 in arbitration agreements

(a) All of the provisions of Section 1283.05 shall be conclusively deemed to be incorporated into, made a part of, and shall be applicable to, every agreement to arbitrate any dispute, controversy, or issue arising out of or resulting from any injury to, or death of, a person caused by the wrongful act or neglect of another.

(b) Only if the parties by their agreement so provide, may the provisions of Section 1283.05 be incorporated into, made a part of, or made applicable to, any other arbitration agreement. *(Added by Stats.1970, c. 581, p. 1158, § 3. Amended by Stats.1970, c. 1045, p. 1869, § 3.)*

Research References

Rutter, Cal. Practice Guide: A.D.R. Ch. 4-B, B. Judicial Arbitration.
Rutter, Cal. Practice Guide: A.D.R. Ch. 5-H, H. Conduct of Arbitration Proceedings.
Rutter, Cal. Practice Guide: A.D.R. Ch. 8-E, E. Special Drafting Considerations Re Arbitration Agreements.
Rutter, Cal. Practice Guide: A.D.R. App. D Form 111, Discovery-Arbitrator's Subpoena Re Deposition (CCP § 1282.6).
Rutter, Cal. Practice Guide: Civ. Pro. Before Trial Ch. 13-B, B. Judicial Arbitration Distinguished from Contract Arbitration.
Rutter, Cal. Practice Guide: Civ. Pro. Before Trial Ch. 8A-8, Discovery in Nonjudicial Proceedings.
California Practice Guide: Employment Litigation Ch. 18-C, C. Contractual Arbitration.
Miller and Starr California Real Estate § 35:22, Nature of Arbitration.
Miller and Starr California Real Estate § 35:74, Hearing Procedures; Control Over Conduct of the Hearing.
Miller and Starr California Real Estate § 35:76, Depositions and Discovery.
17 NO. 1 Miller & Starr, California Real Estate Newsalert 2, Commercial Arbitration.
19 NO. 1 Miller & Starr, California Real Estate Newsalert 3, Alternative Dispute Resolution.
6 Witkin Cal. Proc. 5th Proceedings Without Trial § 560, Discovery and Subpenas.
6 Witkin Cal. Proc. 5th Proceedings Without Trial § 580, Contractual Arbitration Distinguished.

§ 1283.2. Witnesses; fees and mileage; payment

Except for the parties to the arbitration and their agents, officers and employees, all witnesses appearing pursuant to subpoena are entitled to receive fees and mileage in the same amount and under the same circumstances as prescribed by law for witnesses in civil actions in the superior court. The fee and mileage of a witness subpoenaed upon the application of a party to the arbitration shall be paid by such party. The fee and mileage of a witness subpoenaed solely upon the determination of the neutral arbitrator shall be paid in the manner provided for the payment of the neutral arbitrator's expenses. *(Added by Stats.1961, c. 461, p. 1544, § 2.)*

Research References

Rutter, Cal. Practice Guide: A.D.R. Ch. 5-H, H. Conduct of Arbitration Proceedings.
Miller and Starr California Real Estate § 35:77, Production and Testimony of a Witness.

§ 1283.4. Form and contents of award

The award shall be in writing and signed by the arbitrators concurring therein. It shall include a determination of all the questions submitted to the arbitrators the decision of which is necessary in order to determine the controversy. *(Added by Stats.1961, c. 461, p. 1544, § 2.)*

Research References

Rutter, Cal. Practice Guide: A.D.R. Ch. 5-I, I. Arbitrator's Award.

Rutter, Cal. Practice Guide: A.D.R. Ch. 5-J, J. Challenging and Enforcing Arbitrator's Award in Court.

California Practice Guide: Employment Litigation Ch. 18-C, C. Contractual Arbitration.

Miller and Starr California Real Estate § 35:82, Form and Contents of the Award.

Miller and Starr California Real Estate § 35:97, Arbitrators Exceeded Their Powers.

Miller and Starr California Real Estate § 35:98, Arbitrators Decided Issue Not Submitted.

Miller and Starr California Real Estate § 35:99, Arbitrators Failed to Decide Submitted Issues.

17 NO. 5 Miller & Starr, California Real Estate Newsalert 3, Commercial Arbitration.

6 Witkin Cal. Proc. 5th Proceedings Without Trial § 559, (S 559) Powers.

6 Witkin Cal. Proc. 5th Proceedings Without Trial § 562, in General.

§ 1283.6.   Service of award

The neutral arbitrator shall serve a signed copy of the award on each party to the arbitration personally or by registered or certified mail or as provided in the agreement. *(Added by Stats.1961, c. 461, p. 1544, § 2.)*

Research References

Rutter, Cal. Practice Guide: A.D.R. Ch. 5-I, I. Arbitrator's Award.

Rutter, Cal. Practice Guide: A.D.R. App. D Form 115, Arbitration Award.

Rutter, Cal. Practice Guide: Personal Injury Ch. 7-J, J. Arbitration of Uninsured Motorist Claims.

Miller and Starr California Real Estate § 35:86, Service and Legal Effect of the Award.

6 Witkin Cal. Proc. 5th Proceedings Without Trial § 562, in General.

§ 1283.8.   Time for making award

The award shall be made within the time fixed therefor by the agreement or, if not so fixed, within such time as the court orders on petition of a party to the arbitration. The parties to the arbitration may extend the time either before or after the expiration thereof. A party to the arbitration waives the objection that an award was not made within the time required unless he gives the arbitrators written notice of his objection prior to the service of a signed copy of the award on him. *(Added by Stats.1961, c. 461, p. 1544, § 2.)*

Research References

Rutter, Cal. Practice Guide: A.D.R. Ch. 5-G, G. Procedures to Enforce Arbitration.

Rutter, Cal. Practice Guide: A.D.R. Ch. 5-I, I. Arbitrator's Award.

California Practice Guide: Employment Litigation Ch. 18-C, C. Contractual Arbitration.

Rutter, Cal. Practice Guide: Personal Injury Ch. 7-J, J. Arbitration of Uninsured Motorist Claims.

Miller and Starr California Real Estate § 35:48, Hearing and Order on the Petition.

Miller and Starr California Real Estate § 35:62, Effect of Five-Year Period to Bring Litigation to Trial.

Miller and Starr California Real Estate § 35:65, Appointment and Removal of an Arbitrator.

Miller and Starr California Real Estate § 35:80, Time to Render the Award.

6 Witkin Cal. Proc. 5th Proceedings Without Trial § 562, in General.

2 Witkin, California Summary 10th Insurance § 208, (S 208) Requirement.

§ 1284.   Correction of award; application; objections; action by arbitrators; service of copy of denial or correction

The arbitrators, upon written application of a party to the arbitration, may correct the award upon any of the grounds set forth in subdivisions (a) and (c) of Section 1286.6 not later than 30 days after service of a signed copy of the award on the applicant.

Application for such correction shall be made not later than 10 days after service of a signed copy of the award on the applicant. Upon or before making such application, the applicant shall deliver or mail a copy of the application to all of the other parties to the arbitration.

Any party to the arbitration may make written objection to such application. The objection shall be made not later than 10 days after the application is delivered or mailed to the objector. Upon or before making such objection, the objector shall deliver or mail a copy of the objection to the applicant and all the other parties to the arbitration.

The arbitrators shall either deny the application or correct the award. The denial of the application or the correction of the award shall be in writing and signed by the arbitrators concurring therein, and the neutral arbitrator shall serve a signed copy of such denial or correction on each party to the arbitration personally or by registered or certified mail or as provided in the agreement. If no denial of the application or correction of the award is served within the 30-day period provided in this section, the application for correction shall be deemed denied on the last day thereof. *(Added by Stats.1961, c. 461, p. 1544, § 2.)*

Research References

Rutter, Cal. Practice Guide: A.D.R. Ch. 5-I, I. Arbitrator's Award.

Rutter, Cal. Practice Guide: A.D.R. Ch. 5-J, J. Challenging and Enforcing Arbitrator's Award in Court.

Rutter, Cal. Practice Guide: A.D.R. App. D Form 116, Application to Arbitrator(S) for Correction of Award.

Rutter, Cal. Practice Guide: A.D.R. App. D Form 117, Objection to Application for Correction of Arbitration Award.

Rutter, Cal. Practice Guide: A.D.R. App. D Form 118, Arbitrator's Denial or Grant of Application to Correct Award.

Rutter, Cal. Practice Guide: Personal Injury Ch. 7-J, J. Arbitration of Uninsured Motorist Claims.

Miller and Starr California Real Estate § 4:49, Persons Who Qualify for Payment from the Recovery Account--Judgment Based on Fraud, Conversion, or Restitution.

Miller and Starr California Real Estate § 32:49, Real Property Subject to the Judgment Lien.

Miller and Starr California Real Estate § 35:67, Qualifications and Compensation of an Arbitrator.

Miller and Starr California Real Estate § 35:83, Authority of the Arbitrators; Issues and Remedies.

Miller and Starr California Real Estate § 35:87, Correction of the Award by the Arbitrators.

17 NO. 5 Miller & Starr, California Real Estate Newsalert 3, Commercial Arbitration.

6 Witkin Cal. Proc. 5th Proceedings Without Trial § 502, General Statute.

6 Witkin Cal. Proc. 5th Proceedings Without Trial § 559, (S 559) Powers.

6 Witkin Cal. Proc. 5th Proceedings Without Trial § 567, Correction of Award.

6 Witkin Cal. Proc. 5th Proceedings Without Trial § 568, Amendment of Award.

6 Witkin Cal. Proc. 5th Proceedings Without Trial § 573, Procedure to Correct or Vacate Award.

§ 1284.2.   Payment of expenses

Unless the arbitration agreement otherwise provides or the parties to the arbitration otherwise agree, each party to the arbitration shall pay his pro rata share of the expenses and fees of the neutral arbitrator, together with other expenses of the arbitration incurred or approved by the neutral arbitrator, not including counsel fees or witness fees or other expenses incurred by a party for his own benefit. *(Added by Stats.1961, c. 461, p. 1545, § 2.)*

Research References

Rutter, Cal. Practice Guide: A.D.R. Ch. 5-B, B. Federal vs. State Law Governing.
Rutter, Cal. Practice Guide: A.D.R. Ch. 5-H, H. Conduct of Arbitration Proceedings.
Rutter, Cal. Practice Guide: A.D.R. Ch. 5-I, I. Arbitrator's Award.
California Practice Guide: Employment Litigation Ch. 18-C, C. Contractual Arbitration.
Rutter, Cal. Practice Guide: Insurance Litigation Ch. 6G-D, D. Uninsured and Underinsured Motorist Coverages.
Rutter, Cal. Practice Guide: Personal Injury Ch. 7-J, J. Arbitration of Uninsured Motorist Claims.
Miller and Starr California Real Estate § 35:35, Member of an Organization.
Miller and Starr California Real Estate § 35:67, Qualifications and Compensation of an Arbitrator.
Miller and Starr California Real Estate § 35:84, Ancillary Remedies.
Miller and Starr California Real Estate § 35:104, Award of Costs and Attorney's Fees in Order Confirming, Correcting, or Vacating an Arbitrator's Award.
14 NO. 6 Miller & Starr, California Real Estate Newsalert 3, Commercial Arbitration.
7 Witkin Cal. Proc. 5th Judgment § 224, (S 224) Consumer Protection Actions.
6 Witkin Cal. Proc. 5th Proceedings Without Trial § 513, (S 513) in General.
6 Witkin Cal. Proc. 5th Proceedings Without Trial § 564, (S 564) in General.

§ 1284.3. Consumer arbitrations; agreements or rules requiring a nonprevailing consumer party to pay fees and costs incurred by the opposing party; waiver of fees and costs for indigent consumers; application of section

(a) No neutral arbitrator or private arbitration company shall administer a consumer arbitration under any agreement or rule requiring that a consumer who is a party to the arbitration pay the fees and costs incurred by an opposing party if the consumer does not prevail in the arbitration, including, but not limited to, the fees and costs of the arbitrator, provider organization, attorney, or witnesses.

(b)(1) All fees and costs charged to or assessed upon a consumer party by a private arbitration company in a consumer arbitration, exclusive of arbitrator fees, shall be waived for an indigent consumer. For the purposes of this section, "indigent consumer" means a person having a gross monthly income that is less than 300 percent of the federal poverty guidelines. Nothing in this section shall affect the ability of a private arbitration company to shift fees that would otherwise be charged or assessed upon a consumer party to a nonconsumer party.

(2) Prior to requesting or obtaining any fee, a private arbitration company shall provide written notice of the right to obtain a waiver of fees to a consumer or prospective consumer in a manner calculated to bring the matter to the attention of a reasonable consumer, including, but not limited to, prominently placing a notice in its first written communication to the consumer and in any invoice, bill, submission form, fee schedule, rules, or code of procedure.

(3) Any consumer requesting a waiver of fees or costs may establish his or her eligibility by making a declaration under oath on a form provided to the consumer by the private arbitration company for signature stating his or her monthly income and the number of persons living in his or her household. No private arbitration company may require a consumer to provide any further statement or evidence of indigence.

(4) Any information obtained by a private arbitration company about a consumer's identity, financial condition, income, wealth, or fee waiver request shall be kept confidential and may not be disclosed to any adverse party or any nonparty to the arbitration, except a private arbitration company may not keep confidential the number of waiver requests received or granted, or the total amount of fees waived.

(c) This section applies to all consumer arbitration agreements subject to this article, and to all consumer arbitration proceedings conducted in California. *(Added by Stats.2002, c. 1101 (A.B.2915), § 1.)*

Research References

Rutter, Cal. Practice Guide: A.D.R. Ch. 5-H, H. Conduct of Arbitration Proceedings.
Rutter, Cal. Practice Guide: A.D.R. Ch. 5-I, I. Arbitrator's Award.
Rutter, Cal. Practice Guide: A.D.R. Ch. 7-B, B. Arbitrators.
Rutter, Cal. Practice Guide: Real Prop. Transactions Ch. 4-E, E. Drafting the Purchase and Sale Agreement-Terms and Conditions.
Miller and Starr California Real Estate § 35:26, Form and Contents of the Arbitration Agreement.
6 Witkin Cal. Proc. 5th Proceedings Without Trial § 554, (S 554) Selection and Appointment.

CHAPTER 4. ENFORCEMENT OF THE AWARD

ARTICLE 1. CONFIRMATION, CORRECTION OR VACATION OF THE AWARD

§ 1285. Petition; parties

Any party to an arbitration in which an award has been made may petition the court to confirm, correct or vacate the award. The petition shall name as respondents all parties to the arbitration and may name as respondents any other persons bound by the arbitration award. *(Added by Stats.1961, c. 461, p. 1545, § 2.)*

Research References

Rutter, Cal. Practice Guide: A.D.R. Ch. 5-A, A. General Considerations.
Rutter, Cal. Practice Guide: A.D.R. Ch. 5-J, J. Challenging and Enforcing Arbitrator's Award in Court.
Rutter, Cal. Practice Guide: A.D.R. Ch. 3B-C, C. Statutorily-Mandated ADR.
Rutter, Cal. Practice Guide: A.D.R. App. D Form 123, Notice of Motion for Order to Confirm, Vacate or Correct Award.
Rutter, Cal. Practice Guide: Civil Appeals & Writs Ch. 2-E, E. Appealability of Private Judge Decisions.
Rutter, Cal. Practice Guide: Civ. Pro. Before Trial Ch. 13-B, B. Judicial Arbitration Distinguished from Contract Arbitration.
California Practice Guide: Employment Litigation Ch. 18-C, C. Contractual Arbitration.

Rutter, Cal. Practice Guide: Insurance Litigation Ch. 15-C, C. Arbitration/Appraisal/Mediation.

Rutter, Cal. Practice Guide: Personal Injury Ch. 7-J, J. Arbitration of Uninsured Motorist Claims.

Rutter, Cal. Practice Guide: Prof. Responsibility Ch. 5-K, K. Fee Recovery/Enforcing Fee Agreements.

Miller and Starr California Real Estate § 27:49, Provisions for Arbitration and Mediation of Disputes--Public Works.

Miller and Starr California Real Estate § 35:25, Written Agreement Required.

Miller and Starr California Real Estate § 35:90, Petition to Confirm an Award.

Miller and Starr California Real Estate § 35:92, Petition to Correct an Arbitrator's Award.

Miller and Starr California Real Estate § 35:93, Petition to Vacate an Arbitration Award.

Miller and Starr California Real Estate § 35:103, Order of Confirmation; Judgment; Court's Award of Costs.

15 NO. 6 Miller & Starr, California Real Estate Newsalert 4, Commercial Arbitration.

22 NO. 2 Miller & Starr, California Real Estate Newsalert 4, Alternative Dispute Resolution.

9 Witkin Cal. Proc. 5th Administrative Proceedings § 85, (S 85) Judicial Review of Award.

1 Witkin Cal. Proc. 5th Attorneys § 230, Arbitration Award.

6 Witkin Cal. Proc. 5th Proceedings Without Trial § 502, General Statute.

6 Witkin Cal. Proc. 5th Proceedings Without Trial § 523, Self-Executing Agreement.

6 Witkin Cal. Proc. 5th Proceedings Without Trial § 566, Confirmation of Award.

6 Witkin Cal. Proc. 5th Proceedings Without Trial § 573, Procedure to Correct or Vacate Award.

6 Witkin Cal. Proc. 5th Proceedings Without Trial § 580, Contractual Arbitration Distinguished.

§ 1285.2. Response to petition

A response to a petition under this chapter may request the court to dismiss the petition or to confirm, correct or vacate the award. *(Added by Stats.1961, c. 461, p. 1545, § 2.)*

Research References

Miller and Starr California Real Estate § 35:90, Petition to Confirm an Award.

Miller and Starr California Real Estate § 35:92, Petition to Correct an Arbitrator's Award.

Miller and Starr California Real Estate § 35:93, Petition to Vacate an Arbitration Award.

6 Witkin Cal. Proc. 5th Proceedings Without Trial § 523, Self-Executing Agreement.

6 Witkin Cal. Proc. 5th Proceedings Without Trial § 566, Confirmation of Award.

6 Witkin Cal. Proc. 5th Proceedings Without Trial § 573, Procedure to Correct or Vacate Award.

§ 1285.4. Contents of petition

A petition under this chapter shall:

(a) Set forth the substance of or have attached a copy of the agreement to arbitrate unless the petitioner denies the existence of such an agreement.

(b) Set forth the names of the arbitrators.

(c) Set forth or have attached a copy of the award and the written opinion of the arbitrators, if any. *(Added by Stats.1961, c. 461, p. 1545, § 2.)*

Research References

Rutter, Cal. Practice Guide: A.D.R. Ch. 5-J, J. Challenging and Enforcing Arbitrator's Award in Court.

Miller and Starr California Real Estate § 35:90, Petition to Confirm an Award.

20 NO. 3 Miller & Starr, California Real Estate Newsalert 7, Alternative Dispute Resolution.

6 Witkin Cal. Proc. 5th Proceedings Without Trial § 566, Confirmation of Award.

6 Witkin Cal. Proc. 5th Proceedings Without Trial § 573, Procedure to Correct or Vacate Award.

§ 1285.6. Contents of response to petition

Unless a copy thereof is set forth in or attached to the petition, a response to a petition under this chapter shall:

(a) Set forth the substance of or have attached a copy of the agreement to arbitrate unless the respondent denies the existence of such an agreement.

(b) Set forth the names of the arbitrators.

(c) Set forth or have attached a copy of the award and the written opinion of the arbitrators, if any. *(Added by Stats.1961, c. 461, p. 1545, § 2.)*

Research References

Rutter, Cal. Practice Guide: A.D.R. Ch. 5-J, J. Challenging and Enforcing Arbitrator's Award in Court.

Miller and Starr California Real Estate § 35:90, Petition to Confirm an Award.

20 NO. 3 Miller & Starr, California Real Estate Newsalert 7, Alternative Dispute Resolution.

§ 1285.8. Grounds for relief

A petition to correct or vacate an award, or a response requesting such relief, shall set forth the grounds on which the request for such relief is based. *(Added by Stats.1961, c. 461, p. 1545, § 2.)*

Research References

Rutter, Cal. Practice Guide: A.D.R. Ch. 5-J, J. Challenging and Enforcing Arbitrator's Award in Court.

Miller and Starr California Real Estate § 35:92, Petition to Correct an Arbitrator's Award.

6 Witkin Cal. Proc. 5th Proceedings Without Trial § 573, Procedure to Correct or Vacate Award.

§ 1286. Powers of court

If a petition or response under this chapter is duly served and filed, the court shall confirm the award as made, whether rendered in this state or another state, unless in accordance with this chapter it corrects the award and confirms it as corrected, vacates the award or dismisses the proceeding. *(Added by Stats.1961, c. 461, p. 1546, § 2. Amended by Stats.1978, c. 260, p. 545, § 3.)*

Research References

Rutter, Cal. Practice Guide: A.D.R. Ch. 5-G, G. Procedures to Enforce Arbitration.

Rutter, Cal. Practice Guide: A.D.R. Ch. 5-I, I. Arbitrator's Award.

Rutter, Cal. Practice Guide: A.D.R. Ch. 5-J, J. Challenging and Enforcing Arbitrator's Award in Court.

Rutter, Cal. Practice Guide: Civil Appeals & Writs Ch. 2-B, B. Appealable Judgments and Orders.

Rutter, Cal. Practice Guide: Prof. Responsibility Ch. 5-K, K. Fee Recovery/Enforcing Fee Agreements.

Miller and Starr California Real Estate § 35:25, Written Agreement Required.

Miller and Starr California Real Estate § 35:83, Authority of the Arbitrators; Issues and Remedies.

Miller and Starr California Real Estate § 35:88, Limitations on Judicial Review of Arbitrators' Awards.

Miller and Starr California Real Estate § 35:90, Petition to Confirm an Award.

Miller and Starr California Real Estate § 35:91, Defenses to Confirmation.

20 NO. 2 Miller & Starr, California Real Estate Newsalert 3, Alternative Dispute Resolution.

6 Witkin Cal. Proc. 5th Proceedings Without Trial § 566, Confirmation of Award.

6 Witkin Cal. Proc. 5th Proceedings Without Trial § 575, (S 575) Illustrations of Finality Rule.

§ 1286.2. Grounds for vacation of award

(a) Subject to Section 1286.4, the court shall vacate the award if the court determines any of the following:

(1) The award was procured by corruption, fraud or other undue means.

(2) There was corruption in any of the arbitrators.

(3) The rights of the party were substantially prejudiced by misconduct of a neutral arbitrator.

(4) The arbitrators exceeded their powers and the award cannot be corrected without affecting the merits of the decision upon the controversy submitted.

(5) The rights of the party were substantially prejudiced by the refusal of the arbitrators to postpone the hearing upon sufficient cause being shown therefor or by the refusal of the arbitrators to hear evidence material to the controversy or by other conduct of the arbitrators contrary to the provisions of this title.

(6) An arbitrator making the award either: (A) failed to disclose within the time required for disclosure a ground for disqualification of which the arbitrator was then aware; or (B) was subject to disqualification upon grounds specified in Section 1281.91 but failed upon receipt of timely demand to disqualify himself or herself as required by that provision. However, this subdivision does not apply to arbitration proceedings conducted under a collective bargaining agreement between employers and employees or between their respective representatives.

(b) Petitions to vacate an arbitration award pursuant to Section 1285 are subject to the provisions of Section 128.7. (Added by Stats.1961, c. 461, p. 1546, § 2. Amended by Stats.1993, c. 768 (S.B.252), § 5; Stats.1997, c. 445 (A.B.1093), § 4; Stats.2001, c. 362 (S.B.475), § 7.)

Validity

For validity of this section, see Mayo v. Dean Witter Reynolds, Inc., N.D.Cal.2003, 258 F.Supp.2d 1097, amended 260 F.Supp.2d 979.

Research References

Rutter, Cal. Practice Guide: A.D.R. App. A, Selected Statutes Providing for ADR.
Rutter, Cal. Practice Guide: A.D.R. Ch. 4-B, B. Judicial Arbitration.
Rutter, Cal. Practice Guide: A.D.R. Ch. 5-A, A. General Considerations.
Rutter, Cal. Practice Guide: A.D.R. Ch. 5-B, B. Federal vs. State Law Governing.
Rutter, Cal. Practice Guide: A.D.R. Ch. 5-H, H. Conduct of Arbitration Proceedings.
Rutter, Cal. Practice Guide: A.D.R. Ch. 5-J, J. Challenging and Enforcing Arbitrator's Award in Court.
Rutter, Cal. Practice Guide: A.D.R. Ch. 5-K, K. Arbitration of International Commercial Disputes.
Rutter, Cal. Practice Guide: A.D.R. Ch. 7-B, B. Arbitrators.
Rutter, Cal. Practice Guide: A.D.R. Ch. 8-E, E. Special Drafting Considerations Re Arbitration Agreements.
Rutter, Cal. Practice Guide: Civil Appeals & Writs Ch. 2-E, E. Appealability of Private Judge Decisions.
Rutter, Cal. Practice Guide: Civil Appeals & Writs Ch. 8-C, C. Standards of Appellate Review.
Rutter, Cal. Practice Guide: Civ. Pro. Before Trial Ch. 3-A, A. Subject Matter Jurisdiction (Competency).
Rutter, Cal. Practice Guide: Civ. Pro. Before Trial Ch. 13-F, F. Arbitration Award.
Rutter, Cal. Practice Guide: Civ. Pro. Before Trial Ch. 9(I)-H, H. Motions Relating to Contractual Arbitration.
Rutter, Cal. Practice Guide: Civ. Pro. Before Trial Ch. 13-F, Outline F.
California Practice Guide: Employment Litigation Ch. 18-C, C. Contractual Arbitration.
California Practice Guide: Employment Litigation Ch. 18-F, F. Selecting the Neutral.

Rutter, Cal. Practice Guide: Insurance Litigation Ch. 15-C, C. Arbitration/Appraisal/Mediation.
Rutter, Cal. Practice Guide: Insurance Litigation Ch. 6G-D, D. Uninsured and Underinsured Motorist Coverages.
Rutter, Cal. Practice Guide: Personal Injury Ch. 3-F, F. MICRA Provisions Affecting Damages.
Rutter, Cal. Practice Guide: Personal Injury Ch. 7-H, H. Arbitration Award and Judgment.
Rutter, Cal. Practice Guide: Personal Injury Ch. 7-J, J. Arbitration of Uninsured Motorist Claims.
Rutter, Cal. Practice Guide: Real Prop. Transactions Ch. 4-E, E. Drafting the Purchase and Sale Agreement-Terms and Conditions.
Rutter, Cal. Practice Guide: Prof. Responsibility Ch. 5-K, K. Fee Recovery/Enforcing Fee Agreements.
Miller and Starr California Real Estate § 20:22, California Fair Employment and Housing Act--Administrative Proceedings.
Miller and Starr California Real Estate § 34:92, Punitive Damages--Constitutional Validity and Limits.
Miller and Starr California Real Estate § 35:24, Federal Arbitration Act.
Miller and Starr California Real Estate § 35:25, Written Agreement Required.
Miller and Starr California Real Estate § 35:42, Enforceability of Arbitration Agreements; Necessity for Petition to Compel.
Miller and Starr California Real Estate § 35:69, Arbitrator's Duty of Written Disclosure.
Miller and Starr California Real Estate § 35:70, Disqualification of the Arbitrator.
Miller and Starr California Real Estate § 35:71, Vacating of an Award Based Upon Arbitrator's Bias.
Miller and Starr California Real Estate § 35:74, Hearing Procedures; Control Over Conduct of the Hearing.
Miller and Starr California Real Estate § 35:75, Evidence; Burden of Proof.
Miller and Starr California Real Estate § 35:83, Authority of the Arbitrators; Issues and Remedies.
Miller and Starr California Real Estate § 35:89, No Review for Mistake of Fact or Law by the Arbitrators.
Miller and Starr California Real Estate § 35:93, Petition to Vacate an Arbitration Award.
Miller and Starr California Real Estate § 35:94, Grounds for Vacating an Award.
Miller and Starr California Real Estate § 35:95, Award Obtained by Fraud, Corruption, or Undue Means.
Miller and Starr California Real Estate § 35:96, Misconduct or Conduct Contrary to Statute by a Neutral Arbitrator.
Miller and Starr California Real Estate § 35:97, Arbitrators Exceeded Their Powers.
Miller and Starr California Real Estate § 35:98, Arbitrators Decided Issue Not Submitted.
Miller and Starr California Real Estate § 35:99, Arbitrators Failed to Decide Submitted Issues.
Miller and Starr California Real Estate § 35:100, Refusal to Postpone the Hearing.
Miller and Starr California Real Estate § 35:101, Refusal to Hear Material Evidence.
13 NO. 6 Miller & Starr, California Real Estate Newsalert 3, Commercial Arbitration.
13 NO. 4 Miller & Starr, California Real Estate Newsalert 20, Commercial Arbitration.
14 NO. 3 Miller & Starr, California Real Estate Newsalert 4, Commercial Arbitration.
16 NO. 3 Miller & Starr, California Real Estate Newsalert 3, Commercial Arbitration.
17 NO. 1 Miller & Starr, California Real Estate Newsalert 2, Commercial Arbitration.
17 NO. 2 Miller & Starr, California Real Estate Newsalert 4, Commercial Arbitration.
19 NO. 1 Miller & Starr, California Real Estate Newsalert 3, Alternative Dispute Resolution.
20 NO. 2 Miller & Starr, California Real Estate Newsalert 3, Alternative Dispute Resolution.
20 NO. 5 Miller & Starr, California Real Estate Newsalert 3, Alternative Dispute Resolution.
20 NO. 3 Miller & Starr, California Real Estate Newsalert 7, Alternative Dispute Resolution.
21 NO. 2 Miller & Starr, California Real Estate Newsalert 2, Alternative Dispute Resolution.

21 NO. 3 Miller & Starr, California Real Estate Newsalert 4, Alternative Dispute Resolution.

21 NO. 4 Miller & Starr, California Real Estate Newsalert 19, Alternative Dispute Resolution.

22 NO. 1 Miller & Starr, California Real Estate Newsalert 4, Alternative Dispute Resolution.

8 Witkin Cal. Proc. 5th Attack Judgment Trial Court § 242, (S 242) Illustrations.

6 Witkin Cal. Proc. 5th Proceedings Without Trial § 510, (S 510) Illustrations.

6 Witkin Cal. Proc. 5th Proceedings Without Trial § 557, Statutory Requirements.

6 Witkin Cal. Proc. 5th Proceedings Without Trial § 561, Hearing.

6 Witkin Cal. Proc. 5th Proceedings Without Trial § 569, (S 569) in General.

6 Witkin Cal. Proc. 5th Proceedings Without Trial § 570, (S 570) Corruption, Fraud, or Undue Means.

6 Witkin Cal. Proc. 5th Proceedings Without Trial § 571, (S 571) Arbitrator Exceeded Powers.

6 Witkin Cal. Proc. 5th Proceedings Without Trial § 572, (S 572) Arbitrator's Failure to Disclose.

6 Witkin Cal. Proc. 5th Proceedings Without Trial § 573, Procedure to Correct or Vacate Award.

6 Witkin Cal. Proc. 5th Proceedings Without Trial § 574, (S 574) General Rule of Finality.

6 Witkin Cal. Proc. 5th Proceedings Without Trial § 575, (S 575) Illustrations of Finality Rule.

6 Witkin Cal. Proc. 5th Proceedings Without Trial § 576, (S 576) Effect of Agreement Extending Scope of Review.

6 Witkin Cal. Proc. 5th Proceedings Without Trial § 578, (S 578) Exceptions to Finality Rule.

6 Witkin Cal. Proc. 5th Proceedings Without Trial § 610, Effect.

6 Witkin Cal. Proc. 5th Proceedings Without Trial § 612, Vacation.

2 Witkin, California Summary 10th Insurance § 208, (S 208) Requirement.

2 Witkin, California Summary 10th Insurance § 214, (S 214) Award and Review.

12 Witkin, California Summary 10th Real Property § 418, in General.

3 Witkin, California Summary 10th Agency and Employment § 588, (S 588) Nature and Scope of Act.

3 Witkin, California Summary 10th Agency and Employment § 671, (S 671) Mediation of Impasse After Certification of Exclusive Representative.

§ 1286.4. Conditions to vacation of award

The court may not vacate an award unless:

(a) A petition or response requesting that the award be vacated has been duly served and filed; or

(b) A petition or response requesting that the award be corrected has been duly served and filed and:

(1) All petitioners and respondents are before the court; or

(2) All petitioners and respondents have been given reasonable notice that the court will be requested at the hearing to vacate the award or that the court on its own motion has determined to vacate the award and all petitioners and respondents have been given an opportunity to show why the award should not be vacated. (*Added by Stats.1961, c. 461, p. 1546, § 2.*)

Research References

Rutter, Cal. Practice Guide: A.D.R. Ch. 5-J, J. Challenging and Enforcing Arbitrator's Award in Court.

Miller and Starr California Real Estate § 35:93, Petition to Vacate an Arbitration Award.

§ 1286.6. Grounds for correction of award

Subject to Section 1286.8, the court, unless it vacates the award pursuant to Section 1286.2, shall correct the award and confirm it as corrected if the court determines that:

(a) There was an evident miscalculation of figures or an evident mistake in the description of any person, thing or property referred to in the award;

(b) The arbitrators exceeded their powers but the award may be corrected without affecting the merits of the decision upon the controversy submitted; or

(c) The award is imperfect in a matter of form, not affecting the merits of the controversy. (*Added by Stats.1961, c. 461, p. 1546, § 2.*)

Research References

Rutter, Cal. Practice Guide: A.D.R. Ch. 5-H, H. Conduct of Arbitration Proceedings.

Rutter, Cal. Practice Guide: A.D.R. Ch. 5-J, J. Challenging and Enforcing Arbitrator's Award in Court.

Rutter, Cal. Practice Guide: Civ. Pro. Before Trial Ch. 1-A, A. Accepting a New Case.

Rutter, Cal. Practice Guide: Personal Injury Ch. 3-F, F. MICRA Provisions Affecting Damages.

Rutter, Cal. Practice Guide: Personal Injury Ch. 7-J, J. Arbitration of Uninsured Motorist Claims.

Rutter, Cal. Practice Guide: Prof. Responsibility Ch. 5-K, K. Fee Recovery/Enforcing Fee Agreements.

Miller and Starr California Real Estate § 32:49, Real Property Subject to the Judgment Lien.

Miller and Starr California Real Estate § 34:92, Punitive Damages-- Constitutional Validity and Limits.

Miller and Starr California Real Estate § 35:67, Qualifications and Compensation of an Arbitrator.

Miller and Starr California Real Estate § 35:87, Correction of the Award by the Arbitrators.

Miller and Starr California Real Estate § 35:89, No Review for Mistake of Fact or Law by the Arbitrators.

Miller and Starr California Real Estate § 35:92, Petition to Correct an Arbitrator's Award.

Miller and Starr California Real Estate § 35:94, Grounds for Vacating an Award.

13 NO. 6 Miller & Starr, California Real Estate Newsalert 3, Commercial Arbitration.

13 NO. 4 Miller & Starr, California Real Estate Newsalert 20, Commercial Arbitration.

17 NO. 1 Miller & Starr, California Real Estate Newsalert 2, Commercial Arbitration.

20 NO. 2 Miller & Starr, California Real Estate Newsalert 3, Alternative Dispute Resolution.

21 NO. 6 Miller & Starr, California Real Estate Newsalert 3, Alternative Dispute Resolution.

6 Witkin Cal. Proc. 5th Proceedings Without Trial § 567, Correction of Award.

6 Witkin Cal. Proc. 5th Proceedings Without Trial § 568, Amendment of Award.

6 Witkin Cal. Proc. 5th Proceedings Without Trial § 574, (S 574) General Rule of Finality.

6 Witkin Cal. Proc. 5th Proceedings Without Trial § 575, (S 575) Illustrations of Finality Rule.

6 Witkin Cal. Proc. 5th Proceedings Without Trial § 576, (S 576) Effect of Agreement Extending Scope of Review.

6 Witkin Cal. Proc. 5th Proceedings Without Trial § 578, (S 578) Exceptions to Finality Rule.

2 Witkin, California Summary 10th Insurance § 214, (S 214) Award and Review.

12 Witkin, California Summary 10th Real Property § 418, in General.

§ 1286.8. Conditions to correction of award

The court may not correct an award unless:

(a) A petition or response requesting that the award be corrected has been duly served and filed; or

(b) A petition or response requesting that the award be vacated has been duly served and filed and:

(1) All petitioners and respondents are before the court; or

(2) All petitioners and respondents have been given reasonable notice that the court will be requested at the hearing to correct the award or that the court on its own motion has determined to correct the award and all petitioners and respondents have been given an opportunity to show why the award

Civ. Pro.

should not be corrected.　*(Added by Stats.1961, c. 461, p. 1546, § 2.)*

Research References

Rutter, Cal. Practice Guide: A.D.R. Ch. 5-J, J. Challenging and Enforcing Arbitrator's Award in Court.

Miller and Starr California Real Estate § 35:92, Petition to Correct an Arbitrator's Award.

§ 1287.　Rehearing

If the award is vacated, the court may order a rehearing before new arbitrators.　If the award is vacated on the grounds set forth in paragraph (4) or (5) of subdivision (a) of Section 1286.2, the court with the consent of the parties to the court proceeding may order a rehearing before the original arbitrators.

If the arbitration agreement requires that the award be made within a specified period of time, the rehearing may nevertheless be held and the award made within an equal period of time beginning with the date of the order for rehearing but only if the court determines that the purpose of the time limit agreed upon by the parties to the arbitration agreement will not be frustrated by the application of this provision.　*(Added by Stats.1961, c. 461, p. 1547, § 2.　Amended by Stats.2012, c. 162 (S.B.1171), § 15.)*

Research References

Rutter, Cal. Practice Guide: A.D.R. Ch. 5-J, J. Challenging and Enforcing Arbitrator's Award in Court.

Miller and Starr California Real Estate § 35:102, Rehearing After Order Vacating an Award.

15 NO. 6 Miller & Starr, California Real Estate Newsalert 4, Commercial Arbitration.

§ 1287.2.　Dismissal of proceeding as to person not bound by award and not party to arbitration

The court shall dismiss the proceeding under this chapter as to any person named as a respondent if the court determines that such person was not bound by the arbitration award and was not a party to the arbitration.　*(Added by Stats.1961, c. 461, p. 1547, § 2.)*

Research References

Rutter, Cal. Practice Guide: A.D.R. Ch. 5-J, J. Challenging and Enforcing Arbitrator's Award in Court.

Miller and Starr California Real Estate § 35:94, Grounds for Vacating an Award.

§ 1287.4.　Entry of judgment on confirmation of award; force and effect; enforcement

If an award is confirmed, judgment shall be entered in conformity therewith.　The judgment so entered has the same force and effect as, and is subject to all the provisions of law relating to, a judgment in a civil action of the same jurisdictional classification; and it may be enforced like any other judgment of the court in which it is entered, in an action of the same jurisdictional classification.　*(Added by Stats.1961, c. 461, p. 1547, § 2.　Amended by Stats.1998, c. 931 (S.B.2139), § 124, eff. Sept. 28, 1998.)*

Law Revision Commission Comments

Section 1287.4 is amended to accommodate unification of the municipal and superior courts in a county. Cal. Const. art. VI, § 5(e). See Sections 32.5 (jurisdictional classification), 85 (limited civil cases), 86(a)(8) (enforcement of judgment in limited civil case), 86(a)(10)(A) (arbitration-related limited civil cases). See also Section 85 Comment.　[28 Cal.L.Rev. Comm. Reports 51 (1998)].

Research References

Rutter, Cal. Practice Guide: A.D.R. Ch. 4-B, B. Judicial Arbitration.

Rutter, Cal. Practice Guide: A.D.R. Ch. 5-A, A. General Considerations.

Rutter, Cal. Practice Guide: A.D.R. Ch. 5-J, J. Challenging and Enforcing Arbitrator's Award in Court.

Rutter, Cal. Practice Guide: Civ. Pro. Before Trial Ch. 13-B, B. Judicial Arbitration Distinguished from Contract Arbitration.

Rutter, Cal. Practice Guide: Enforcing Judgments/Debts Ch. 6A-2, Enforcement of Judgments Law ("Ejl")-Background.

Rutter, Cal. Practice Guide: Insurance Litigation Ch. 15-C, C. Arbitration/Appraisal/Mediation.

Rutter, Cal. Practice Guide: Personal Injury Ch. 7-J, J. Arbitration of Uninsured Motorist Claims.

Rutter, Cal. Practice Guide: Real Prop. Transactions Ch. 2-C, C. Broker's Relationship and Obligations to Principal and Third Parties.

Rutter, Cal. Practice Guide: Prof. Responsibility Ch. 5-K, K. Fee Recovery/Enforcing Fee Agreements.

Miller and Starr California Real Estate § 4:49, Persons Who Qualify for Payment from the Recovery Account--Judgment Based on Fraud, Conversion, or Restitution.

Miller and Starr California Real Estate § 35:84, Ancillary Remedies.

Miller and Starr California Real Estate § 35:86, Service and Legal Effect of the Award.

Miller and Starr California Real Estate § 35:103, Order of Confirmation; Judgment; Court's Award of Costs.

Miller and Starr California Real Estate § 35:105, Appeal of Judgment Based on Confirmation, or Order Denying Confirmation or Vacating an Arbitration Award.

3 Witkin Cal. Proc. 5th Actions § 687, (S 687) Petition to Vacate or Correct Arbitration Award.

9 Witkin Cal. Proc. 5th Appeal § 96, in General.

6 Witkin Cal. Proc. 5th Proceedings Without Trial § 566, Confirmation of Award.

§ 1287.6.　Force and effect of unconfirmed or vacated award

An award that has not been confirmed or vacated has the same force and effect as a contract in writing between the parties to the arbitration.　*(Added by Stats.1961, c. 461, p. 1547, § 2.)*

Research References

Rutter, Cal. Practice Guide: A.D.R. Ch. 5-J, J. Challenging and Enforcing Arbitrator's Award in Court.

California Practice Guide: Employment Litigation Ch. 18-C, C. Contractual Arbitration.

Rutter, Cal. Practice Guide: Insurance Litigation Ch. 15-C, C. Arbitration/Appraisal/Mediation.

Rutter, Cal. Practice Guide: Personal Injury Ch. 7-J, J. Arbitration of Uninsured Motorist Claims.

Rutter, Cal. Practice Guide: Prof. Responsibility Ch. 5-K, K. Fee Recovery/Enforcing Fee Agreements.

Miller and Starr California Real Estate § 35:86, Service and Legal Effect of the Award.

6 Witkin Cal. Proc. 5th Proceedings Without Trial § 562, in General.

6 Witkin Cal. Proc. 5th Proceedings Without Trial § 566, Confirmation of Award.

1 Witkin Cal. Summ. 10th Contracts § 49, Parent's Agreement to Arbitrate.

1 Witkin Cal. Summ. 10th Contracts § 1011, Unconfirmed Arbitration Award.

ARTICLE 2.　LIMITATIONS OF TIME

§ 1288.　Petition; time for service and filing

A petition to confirm an award shall be served and filed not later than four years after the date of service of a signed copy of the award on the petitioner.　A petition to vacate an award or to correct an award shall be served and filed not later than 100 days after the date of the service of a signed copy of the award on the petitioner. *(Added by Stats.1961, c. 461, p. 1547, § 2.)*

Research References

Rutter, Cal. Practice Guide: A.D.R. Ch. 5-A, A. General Considerations.
Rutter, Cal. Practice Guide: A.D.R. Ch. 5-J, J. Challenging and Enforcing Arbitrator's Award in Court.
Rutter, Cal. Practice Guide: Civil Appeals & Writs Ch. 2-B, B. Appealable Judgments and Orders.
Rutter, Cal. Practice Guide: Civ. Pro. Before Trial Ch. 9(I)-H, H. Motions Relating to Contractual Arbitration.
Rutter, Cal. Practice Guide: Insurance Litigation Ch. 6G-D, D. Uninsured and Underinsured Motorist Coverages.
Rutter, Cal. Practice Guide: Personal Injury Ch. 7-J, J. Arbitration of Uninsured Motorist Claims.
Miller and Starr California Real Estate § 32:49, Real Property Subject to the Judgment Lien.
Miller and Starr California Real Estate § 35:87, Correction of the Award by the Arbitrators.
Miller and Starr California Real Estate § 35:90, Petition to Confirm an Award.
Miller and Starr California Real Estate § 35:92, Petition to Correct an Arbitrator's Award.
Miller and Starr California Real Estate § 35:93, Petition to Vacate an Arbitration Award.
Miller and Starr California Real Estate § 30A:67, Agreements to Mediate or Arbitrate.
18 NO. 1 Miller & Starr, California Real Estate Newsalert 4, Commercial Arbitration.
20 NO. 5 Miller & Starr, California Real Estate Newsalert 3, Alternative Dispute Resolution.
3 Witkin Cal. Proc. 5th Actions § 478, (S 478) One Hundred Days.
3 Witkin Cal. Proc. 5th Actions § 484, (S 484) Four Years.
3 Witkin Cal. Proc. 5th Actions § 687, (S 687) Petition to Vacate or Correct Arbitration Award.
6 Witkin Cal. Proc. 5th Proceedings Without Trial § 566, Confirmation of Award.
6 Witkin Cal. Proc. 5th Proceedings Without Trial § 573, Procedure to Correct or Vacate Award.

§ 1288.2. Response; time for service and filing

A response requesting that an award be vacated or that an award be corrected shall be served and filed not later than 100 days after the date of service of a signed copy of the award upon:

(a) The respondent if he was a party to the arbitration; or

(b) The respondent's representative if the respondent was not a party to the arbitration. *(Added by Stats.1961, c. 461, p. 1547, § 2.)*

Research References

Rutter, Cal. Practice Guide: A.D.R. Ch. 5-A, A. General Considerations.
Rutter, Cal. Practice Guide: A.D.R. Ch. 5-J, J. Challenging and Enforcing Arbitrator's Award in Court.
Rutter, Cal. Practice Guide: A.D.R. App. D Form 120, Response to Petition to Confirm Award of Arbitrators.
Rutter, Cal. Practice Guide: Personal Injury Ch. 7-J, J. Arbitration of Uninsured Motorist Claims.
Miller and Starr California Real Estate § 35:93, Petition to Vacate an Arbitration Award.
Miller and Starr California Real Estate § 30A:67, Agreements to Mediate or Arbitrate.
6 Witkin Cal. Proc. 5th Proceedings Without Trial § 573, Procedure to Correct or Vacate Award.

§ 1288.4. Petition; service and filing at least ten days after service of copy of award

No petition may be served and filed under this chapter until at least 10 days after service of the signed copy of the award upon the petitioner. *(Added by Stats.1961, c. 461, p. 1547, § 2.)*

Research References

Rutter, Cal. Practice Guide: A.D.R. Ch. 5-J, J. Challenging and Enforcing Arbitrator's Award in Court.
Rutter, Cal. Practice Guide: Personal Injury Ch. 7-J, J. Arbitration of Uninsured Motorist Claims.
Miller and Starr California Real Estate § 35:90, Petition to Confirm an Award.
Miller and Starr California Real Estate § 35:92, Petition to Correct an Arbitrator's Award.
Miller and Starr California Real Estate § 35:93, Petition to Vacate an Arbitration Award.
6 Witkin Cal. Proc. 5th Proceedings Without Trial § 566, Confirmation of Award.
6 Witkin Cal. Proc. 5th Proceedings Without Trial § 573, Procedure to Correct or Vacate Award.

§ 1288.6. Application for correction of award; service and filing of petition after determination by arbitrators

If an application is made to the arbitrators for correction of the award, a petition may not be served and filed under this chapter until the determination of that application. *(Added by Stats.1961, c. 461, p. 1547, § 2.)*

Research References

Rutter, Cal. Practice Guide: A.D.R. Ch. 5-J, J. Challenging and Enforcing Arbitrator's Award in Court.
Rutter, Cal. Practice Guide: Personal Injury Ch. 7-J, J. Arbitration of Uninsured Motorist Claims.
Miller and Starr California Real Estate § 35:87, Correction of the Award by the Arbitrators.
Miller and Starr California Real Estate § 35:90, Petition to Confirm an Award.
Miller and Starr California Real Estate § 35:93, Petition to Vacate an Arbitration Award.

§ 1288.8. Application for correction of award; date of service of award

If an application is made to the arbitrators for correction of the award, the date of the service of the award for the purposes of this article shall be deemed to be whichever of the following dates is the earlier:

(a) The date of service upon the petitioner of a signed copy of the correction of the award or of the denial of the application.

(b) The date that such application is deemed to be denied under Section 1284. *(Added by Stats.1961, c. 461, p. 1548, § 2.)*

Research References

Rutter, Cal. Practice Guide: A.D.R. Ch. 5-J, J. Challenging and Enforcing Arbitrator's Award in Court.
Rutter, Cal. Practice Guide: A.D.R. Ch. 3B-C, C. Statutorily-Mandated ADR.
Rutter, Cal. Practice Guide: Personal Injury Ch. 7-J, J. Arbitration of Uninsured Motorist Claims.
Miller and Starr California Real Estate § 27:49, Provisions for Arbitration and Mediation of Disputes--Public Works.
Miller and Starr California Real Estate § 35:87, Correction of the Award by the Arbitrators.

CHAPTER 5. GENERAL PROVISIONS RELATING TO JUDICIAL PROCEEDINGS

ARTICLE 1. PETITIONS AND RESPONSES

Section

§ 1290. Commencement of proceedings by filing petition; response; allegations

A proceeding under this title in the courts of this State is commenced by filing a petition. Any person named as a respondent in a petition may file a response thereto. The allegations of a petition are deemed to be admitted by a respondent duly served therewith unless a response is duly served and filed. The allegations of a response are deemed controverted or avoided. *(Added by Stats.1961, c. 461, p. 1548, § 2.)*

Research References

Rutter, Cal. Practice Guide: A.D.R. Ch. 5-G, G. Procedures to Enforce Arbitration.
Miller and Starr California Real Estate § 35:46, Venue and Service of the Petition and Response.
Miller and Starr California Real Estate § 35:90, Petition to Confirm an Award.
Miller and Starr California Real Estate § 35:92, Petition to Correct an Arbitrator's Award.
Miller and Starr California Real Estate § 35:93, Petition to Vacate an Arbitration Award.
6 Witkin Cal. Proc. 5th Proceedings Without Trial § 502, General Statute.
6 Witkin Cal. Proc. 5th Proceedings Without Trial § 524, (S 524) in General.
6 Witkin Cal. Proc. 5th Proceedings Without Trial § 566, Confirmation of Award.
6 Witkin Cal. Proc. 5th Proceedings Without Trial § 573, Procedure to Correct or Vacate Award.
6 Witkin Cal. Proc. 5th Proceedings Without Trial § 580, Contractual Arbitration Distinguished.

§ 1290.2. Summary hearing; notice

A petition under this title shall be heard in a summary way in the manner and upon the notice provided by law for the making and hearing of motions, except that not less than 10 days' notice of the date set for the hearing on the petition shall be given. *(Added by Stats.1961, c. 461, p. 1548, § 2.)*

Research References

Rutter, Cal. Practice Guide: A.D.R. Ch. 5-D, D. Defenses to Enforcement.
Rutter, Cal. Practice Guide: A.D.R. Ch. 5-E, E. Claims Subject to Arbitration (Arbitrability).
Rutter, Cal. Practice Guide: A.D.R. Ch. 5-G, G. Procedures to Enforce Arbitration.
California Practice Guide: Employment Litigation Ch. 18-C, C. Contractual Arbitration.
Miller and Starr California Real Estate § 35:48, Hearing and Order on the Petition.
Miller and Starr California Real Estate § 35:90, Petition to Confirm an Award.
21 NO. 1 Miller & Starr, California Real Estate Newsalert 2, Alternative Dispute Resolution.
6 Witkin Cal. Proc. 5th Proceedings Without Trial § 509, (S 509) Distinctions.

6 Witkin Cal. Proc. 5th Proceedings Without Trial § 525, (S 525) Hearing.

§ 1290.4. Service of copy of petition and notice of hearing

(a) A copy of the petition and a written notice of the time and place of the hearing thereof and any other papers upon which the petition is based shall be served in the manner provided in the arbitration agreement for the service of such petition and notice.

(b) If the arbitration agreement does not provide the manner in which such service shall be made and the person upon whom service is to be made has not previously appeared in the proceeding and has not previously been served in accordance with this subdivision:

(1) Service within this State shall be made in the manner provided by law for the service of summons in an action.

(2) Service outside this State shall be made by mailing the copy of the petition and notice and other papers by registered or certified mail. Personal service is the equivalent of such service by mail. Proof of service by mail shall be made by affidavit showing such mailing together with the return receipt of the United States Post Office bearing the signature of the person on whom service was made. Notwithstanding any other provision of this title, if service is made in the manner provided in this paragraph, the petition may not be heard until at least 30 days after the date of such service.

(c) If the arbitration agreement does not provide the manner in which such service shall be made and the person on whom service is to be made has previously appeared in the proceeding or has previously been served in accordance with subdivision (b) of this section, service shall be made in the manner provided in Chapter 5 (commencing with Section 1010) of Title 14 of Part 2 of this code. *(Added by Stats.1961, c. 461, p. 1548, § 2.)*

Research References

Rutter, Cal. Practice Guide: A.D.R. Ch. 5-G, G. Procedures to Enforce Arbitration.
Miller and Starr California Real Estate § 35:46, Venue and Service of the Petition and Response.
Miller and Starr California Real Estate § 35:90, Petition to Confirm an Award.
Miller and Starr California Real Estate § 35:93, Petition to Vacate an Arbitration Award.
6 Witkin Cal. Proc. 5th Proceedings Without Trial § 524, (S 524) in General.
6 Witkin Cal. Proc. 5th Proceedings Without Trial § 525, (S 525) Hearing.
6 Witkin Cal. Proc. 5th Proceedings Without Trial § 573, Procedure to Correct or Vacate Award.

§ 1290.6. Time for service and filing of response; extension

A response shall be served and filed within 10 days after service of the petition except that if the petition is served in the manner provided in paragraph (2) of subdivision (b) of Section 1290.4, the response shall be served and filed within 30 days after service of the petition. The time provided in this section for serving and filing a response may be extended by an agreement in writing between the parties to the court proceeding or, for good cause, by order of the court. *(Added by Stats.1961, c. 461, p. 1549, § 2.)*

Research References

Rutter, Cal. Practice Guide: A.D.R. Ch. 5-G, G. Procedures to Enforce Arbitration.
Rutter, Cal. Practice Guide: A.D.R. Ch. 5-J, J. Challenging and Enforcing Arbitrator's Award in Court.
Rutter, Cal. Practice Guide: A.D.R. App. D Form 120, Response to Petition to Confirm Award of Arbitrators.
Rutter, Cal. Practice Guide: A.D.R. App. D Form 123, Notice of Motion for Order to Confirm, Vacate or Correct Award.

Miller and Starr California Real Estate § 35:90, Petition to Confirm an Award.

Miller and Starr California Real Estate § 35:92, Petition to Correct an Arbitrator's Award.

Miller and Starr California Real Estate § 35:93, Petition to Vacate an Arbitration Award.

Miller and Starr California Real Estate § 30A:67, Agreements to Mediate or Arbitrate.

20 NO. 2 Miller & Starr, California Real Estate Newsalert 3, Alternative Dispute Resolution.

20 NO. 5 Miller & Starr, California Real Estate Newsalert 3, Alternative Dispute Resolution.

6 Witkin Cal. Proc. 5th Proceedings Without Trial § 524, (S 524) in General.

6 Witkin Cal. Proc. 5th Proceedings Without Trial § 566, Confirmation of Award.

6 Witkin Cal. Proc. 5th Proceedings Without Trial § 573, Procedure to Correct or Vacate Award.

§ 1290.8. Manner of serving response

A response shall be served as provided in Chapter 5 (commencing with Section 1010) of Title 14 of Part 2 of this code. *(Added by Stats.1961, c. 461, p. 1549, § 2.)*

Research References

Miller and Starr California Real Estate § 35:46, Venue and Service of the Petition and Response.

Miller and Starr California Real Estate § 35:90, Petition to Confirm an Award.

§ 1291. Statement of decision

A statement of decision shall be made by the court, if requested pursuant to Section 632, whenever an order or judgment, except a special order after final judgment, is made that is appealable under this title. *(Added by Stats.1961, c. 461, p. 1549, § 2. Amended by Stats.1983, c. 302, § 2.)*

Research References

Rutter, Cal. Practice Guide: A.D.R. Ch. 5-G, G. Procedures to Enforce Arbitration.

Rutter, Cal. Practice Guide: A.D.R. Ch. 7-B, B. Arbitrators.

Rutter, Cal. Practice Guide: Civil Appeals & Writs Ch. 8-E, E. Limits on Reversal or Modification-"Prejudicial Error" Rule.

Rutter, Cal. Practice Guide: Civil Appeals & Writs Gen. Matls., Highlights.

Rutter, Cal. Practice Guide: Civ. Pro. Before Trial Ch. 9(I)-E, E. Posthearing Procedures.

Rutter, Cal. Practice Guide: Civil Trials & Evidence Ch. 16-E, E. Statement of Decision.

Miller and Starr California Real Estate § 35:54, Review of Order Granting or Denying Petition to Compel Arbitration.

Miller and Starr California Real Estate § 35:57, Stay of Arbitration Pending Litigation.

Miller and Starr California Real Estate § 35:90, Petition to Confirm an Award.

Miller and Starr California Real Estate § 35:92, Petition to Correct an Arbitrator's Award.

Miller and Starr California Real Estate § 35:103, Order of Confirmation; Judgment; Court's Award of Costs.

Miller and Starr California Real Estate § 35:105, Appeal of Judgment Based on Confirmation, or Order Denying Confirmation or Vacating an Arbitration Award.

§ 1291.2. Setting for hearing; hearing; preference

In all proceedings brought under the provisions of this title, all courts wherein such proceedings are pending shall give such proceedings preference over all other civil actions or proceedings, except older matters of the same character and matters to which special precedence may be given by law, in the matter of setting the same for hearing and in hearing the same to the end that all such proceedings shall be quickly heard and determined. *(Added by Stats.1961, c. 461, p. 1549, § 2.)*

Research References

Rutter, Cal. Practice Guide: A.D.R. Ch. 5-G, G. Procedures to Enforce Arbitration.

Rutter, Cal. Practice Guide: Civil Appeals & Writs Ch. 5-B, B. Types of Motions, Applications and Requests.

Rutter, Cal. Practice Guide: Civ. Pro. Before Trial Ch. 12(I)-C, C. Claims for Trial Setting Preference.

Miller and Starr California Real Estate § 35:48, Hearing and Order on the Petition.

Miller and Starr California Real Estate § 35:90, Petition to Confirm an Award.

ARTICLE 2. VENUE, JURISDICTION AND COSTS

§ 1292. Petition made prior to commencement of arbitration; place of filing

Except as otherwise provided in this article, any petition made prior to the commencement of arbitration shall be filed in a court having jurisdiction in:

(a) The county where the agreement is to be performed or was made.

(b) If the agreement does not specify a county where the agreement is to be performed and the agreement was not made in any county in this state, the county where any party to the court proceeding resides or has a place of business.

(c) In any case not covered by subdivision (a) or (b) of this section, in any county in this state. *(Added by Stats.1961, c. 461, p. 1549, § 2. Amended by Stats.1993, c. 1261 (S.B.401), § 2.)*

Research References

Rutter, Cal. Practice Guide: A.D.R. Ch. 5-G, G. Procedures to Enforce Arbitration.

Rutter, Cal. Practice Guide: A.D.R. Ch. 5-J, J. Challenging and Enforcing Arbitrator's Award in Court.

Miller and Starr California Real Estate § 35:46, Venue and Service of the Petition and Response.

Miller and Starr California Real Estate § 35:56, Stay of Litigation Pending Arbitration.

2 Witkin Cal. Proc. 5th Courts § 243, (S 243) in General.

6 Witkin Cal. Proc. 5th Proceedings Without Trial § 524, (S 524) in General.

§ 1292.2. Petition made after commencement or completion of arbitration; place of filing

Except as otherwise provided in this article, any petition made after the commencement or completion of arbitration shall be filed in a court having jurisdiction in the county where the arbitration is being or has been held, or, if not held exclusively in any one county of this state, or if held outside of this state, then the petition shall be filed as provided in Section 1292. *(Added by Stats.1961, c. 461, p. 1549, § 2. Amended by Stats.1978, c. 260, p. 543, § 4; Stats.1993, c. 1261 (S.B.401), § 3.)*

Research References

Rutter, Cal. Practice Guide: A.D.R. Ch. 5-J, J. Challenging and Enforcing Arbitrator's Award in Court.

Miller and Starr California Real Estate § 35:90, Petition to Confirm an Award.

Miller and Starr California Real Estate § 35:92, Petition to Correct an Arbitrator's Award.

Miller and Starr California Real Estate § 35:93, Petition to Vacate an Arbitration Award.

3 Witkin Cal. Proc. 5th Actions § 786, (S 786) Distinctions and Exceptions.

§ 1292.4. Order to arbitrate; filing in pending action or proceeding

If a controversy referable to arbitration under an alleged agreement is involved in an action or proceeding pending in a superior court, a petition for an order to arbitrate shall be filed in such action or proceeding. *(Added by Stats.1961, c. 461, p. 1549, § 2.)*

Research References

Rutter, Cal. Practice Guide: A.D.R. Ch. 5-G, G. Procedures to Enforce Arbitration.

6 Witkin Cal. Proc. 5th Proceedings Without Trial § 524, (S 524) in General.

§ 1292.6. Continuing jurisdiction

After a petition has been filed under this title, the court in which such petition was filed retains jurisdiction to determine any subsequent petition involving the same agreement to arbitrate and the same controversy, and any such subsequent petition shall be filed in the same proceeding. *(Added by Stats.1961, c. 461, p. 1549, § 2.)*

Research References

Rutter, Cal. Practice Guide: A.D.R. Ch. 5-G, G. Procedures to Enforce Arbitration.

Rutter, Cal. Practice Guide: Civ. Pro. Before Trial Ch. 9(I)-H, H. Motions Relating to Contractual Arbitration.

Miller and Starr California Real Estate § 35:48, Hearing and Order on the Petition.

Miller and Starr California Real Estate § 35:90, Petition to Confirm an Award.

2 Witkin Cal. Proc. 5th Jurisdiction § 423, (S 423) Other Examples.

5 Witkin Cal. Proc. 5th Pleading § 1139, What Constitutes Pendency.

§ 1292.8. Motion for stay of action

A motion for a stay of an action on the ground that an issue therein is subject to arbitration shall be made in the court where the action is pending. *(Added by Stats.1961, c. 461, p. 1550, § 2.)*

Research References

Rutter, Cal. Practice Guide: A.D.R. Ch. 5-G, G. Procedures to Enforce Arbitration.

§ 1293. Making of agreement as consent to jurisdiction of state courts

The making of an agreement in this State providing for arbitration to be had within this State shall be deemed a consent of the parties thereto to the jurisdiction of the courts of this State to enforce such agreement by the making of any orders provided for in this title and by entering of judgment on an award under the agreement. *(Added by Stats.1961, c. 461, p. 1550, § 2.)*

Research References

Rutter, Cal. Practice Guide: A.D.R. Ch. 5-G, G. Procedures to Enforce Arbitration.

Rutter, Cal. Practice Guide: A.D.R. Ch. 5-J, J. Challenging and Enforcing Arbitrator's Award in Court.

Miller and Starr California Real Estate § 35:46, Venue and Service of the Petition and Response.

9 Witkin Cal. Proc. 5th Appeal § 142, Orders After Arbitration: Appealable.

2 Witkin Cal. Proc. 5th Jurisdiction § 188, Provision for Arbitration.

§ 1293.2. Costs

The court shall award costs upon any judicial proceeding under this title as provided in Chapter 6 (commencing with Section 1021) of Title 14 of Part 2 of this code. *(Added by Stats.1961, c. 461, p. 1550, § 2.)*

Research References

Rutter, Cal. Practice Guide: A.D.R. Ch. 5-I, I. Arbitrator's Award.

Rutter, Cal. Practice Guide: A.D.R. Ch. 5-J, J. Challenging and Enforcing Arbitrator's Award in Court.

California Practice Guide: Employment Litigation Ch. 18-C, C. Contractual Arbitration.

Rutter, Cal. Practice Guide: Insurance Litigation Ch. 6G-D, D. Uninsured and Underinsured Motorist Coverages.

Miller and Starr California Real Estate § 35:56, Stay of Litigation Pending Arbitration.

Miller and Starr California Real Estate § 35:104, Award of Costs and Attorney's Fees in Order Confirming, Correcting, or Vacating an Arbitrator's Award.

15 NO. 6 Miller & Starr, California Real Estate Newsalert 4, Commercial Arbitration.

6 Witkin Cal. Proc. 5th Proceedings Without Trial § 565, (S 565) Proceeding to Confirm Award.

ARTICLE 3. APPEALS

Section

1294.   Appealable orders.

1294.2.   Manner of taking appeal; scope of review.

§ 1294. Appealable orders

An aggrieved party may appeal from:

(a) An order dismissing or denying a petition to compel arbitration.

(b) An order dismissing a petition to confirm, correct or vacate an award.

(c) An order vacating an award unless a rehearing in arbitration is ordered.

(d) A judgment entered pursuant to this title.

(e) A special order after final judgment. *(Added by Stats. 1961, c. 461, p. 1550, § 2.)*

Research References

Rutter, Cal. Practice Guide: A.D.R. Ch. 5-G, G. Procedures to Enforce Arbitration.

Rutter, Cal. Practice Guide: A.D.R. Ch. 5-J, J. Challenging and Enforcing Arbitrator's Award in Court.

Rutter, Cal. Practice Guide: A.D.R. Gen. Matls., Highlights.

Rutter, Cal. Practice Guide: Civil Appeals & Writs Ch. 2-B, B. Appealable Judgments and Orders.

Rutter, Cal. Practice Guide: Civil Appeals & Writs Ch. 2-E, E. Appealability of Private Judge Decisions.

Rutter, Cal. Practice Guide: Civil Appeals & Writs Ch. 15-B, B. Common Law Writs.

Rutter, Cal. Practice Guide: Personal Injury Ch. 7-J, J. Arbitration of Uninsured Motorist Claims.

Miller and Starr California Real Estate § 35:54, Review of Order Granting or Denying Petition to Compel Arbitration.

Miller and Starr California Real Estate § 35:105, Appeal of Judgment Based on Confirmation, or Order Denying Confirmation or Vacating an Arbitration Award.

14 NO. 3 Miller & Starr, California Real Estate Newsalert 1, Court of Appeal Finds Title Insurance Arbitration Provision Enforceable, Without Reaching "Unconscionability" Analysis.

15 NO. 6 Miller & Starr, California Real Estate Newsalert 4, Commercial Arbitration.

16 NO. 1 Miller & Starr, California Real Estate Newsalert 7. for Arbitration Administered by the National Association of Securities Dealers, The Federal Securities Exchange Act Preempts Both the California Ethics Standards Established by the Judicial Council for Persons Serving...

21 NO. 1 Miller & Starr, California Real Estate Newsalert 1, is an Arbitration Provision in Recorded CC&RS Ever Enforceable by the Developer?

9 Witkin Cal. Proc. 5th Appeal § 140, Order Directing Arbitration: Not Appealable.

9 Witkin Cal. Proc. 5th Appeal § 141, Order Denying Arbitration: Appealable.

9 Witkin Cal. Proc. 5th Appeal § 142, Orders After Arbitration: Appealable.

8 Witkin Cal. Proc. 5th Extraordinary Writs § 37, (S 37) Other Orders.

6 Witkin Cal. Proc. 5th Proceedings Without Trial § 526, (S 526) Appeal and Review.

6 Witkin Cal. Proc. 5th Proceedings Without Trial § 566, Confirmation of Award.

6 Witkin Cal. Proc. 5th Proceedings Without Trial § 573, Procedure to Correct or Vacate Award.

§ 1294.2. Manner of taking appeal; scope of review

The appeal shall be taken in the same manner as an appeal from an order or judgment in a civil action. Upon an appeal from any order or judgment under this title, the court may review the decision and any intermediate ruling, proceeding, order or decision which involves the merits or necessarily affects the order or judgment appealed from, or which substantially affects the rights of a party. The court may also on such appeal review any order on motion for a new trial. The respondent on the appeal, or party in whose favor the judgment or order was given, may, without appealing from such judgment, request the court to and it may review any of the foregoing matters for the purpose of determining whether or not the appellant was prejudiced by the error or errors upon which he relies for reversal or modification of the judgment or order from which the appeal is taken. The provisions of this section do not authorize the court to review any decision or order from which an appeal might have been taken. *(Added by Stats.1961, c. 461, p. 1550, § 2.)*

Research References

Rutter, Cal. Practice Guide: Civil Appeals & Writs Ch. 2-B, B. Appealable Judgments and Orders.

Rutter, Cal. Practice Guide: Civ. Pro. Before Trial Ch. 13-B, B. Judicial Arbitration Distinguished from Contract Arbitration.

Rutter, Cal. Practice Guide: Personal Injury Ch. 7-J, J. Arbitration of Uninsured Motorist Claims.

Miller and Starr California Real Estate § 35:54, Review of Order Granting or Denying Petition to Compel Arbitration.

Miller and Starr California Real Estate § 35:105, Appeal of Judgment Based on Confirmation, or Order Denying Confirmation or Vacating an Arbitration Award.

9 Witkin Cal. Proc. 5th Appeal § 140, Order Directing Arbitration: Not Appealable.

9 Witkin Cal. Proc. 5th Appeal § 141, Order Denying Arbitration: Appealable.

Title 9.1

ARBITRATION OF MEDICAL MALPRACTICE

Section

1295. Contract for medical services; mandatory provision; waiver of right to sue; form of notice; nature of contract.

§ 1295. Contract for medical services; mandatory provision; waiver of right to sue; form of notice; nature of contract

(a) Any contract for medical services which contains a provision for arbitration of any dispute as to professional negligence of a health care provider shall have such provision as the first article of the contract and shall be expressed in the following language: "It is understood that any dispute as to medical malpractice, that is as to whether any medical services rendered under this contract were unnecessary or unauthorized or were improperly, negligently or incompetently rendered, will be determined by submission to arbitration as provided by California law, and not by a lawsuit or resort to court process except as California law provides for judicial review of arbitration proceedings. Both parties to this contract, by entering into it, are giving up their constitutional right to have any such dispute decided in a court of law before a jury, and instead are accepting the use of arbitration."

(b) Immediately before the signature line provided for the individual contracting for the medical services must appear the following in at least 10-point bold red type:

"NOTICE: BY SIGNING THIS CONTRACT YOU ARE AGREEING TO HAVE ANY ISSUE OF MEDICAL MAL-PRACTICE DECIDED BY NEUTRAL ARBITRATION AND YOU ARE GIVING UP YOUR RIGHT TO A JURY OR COURT TRIAL. SEE ARTICLE 1 OF THIS CON-TRACT."

(c) Once signed, such a contract governs all subsequent open-book account transactions for medical services for which the contract was signed until or unless rescinded by written notice within 30 days of signature. Written notice of such rescission may be given by a guardian or conservator of the patient if the patient is incapacitated or a minor.

(d) Where the contract is one for medical services to a minor, it shall not be subject to disaffirmance if signed by the minor's parent or legal guardian.

(e) Such a contract is not a contract of adhesion, nor unconscionable nor otherwise improper, where it complies with subdivisions (a), (b) and (c) of this section.

(f) Subdivisions (a), (b), and (c) shall not apply to any health care service plan contract offered by an organization registered pursuant to Article 2.5 (commencing with Section 12530) of Division 3 of Title 2 of the Government Code, or licensed pursuant to Chapter 2.2 (commencing with Section 1340) of Division 2 of the Health and Safety Code, which contains an arbitration agreement if the plan complies with paragraph (10) of subdivision (a) of Section 1363 of the Health and Safety Code, or otherwise has a procedure for notifying prospective subscribers of the fact that the plan has an arbitration provision, and the plan contracts conform to subdivision (h) of Section 1373 of the Health and Safety Code.

(g) For the purposes of this section:

(1) "Health care provider" means any person licensed or certified pursuant to Division 2 (commencing with Section 500) of the Business and Professions Code, or licensed pursuant to the Osteopathic Initiative Act, or the Chiropractic Initiative Act, or licensed pursuant to Chapter 2.5 (commencing with Section 1440) of Division 2 of the Health and Safety Code; and any clinic, health dispensary, or health facility, licensed pursuant to Division 2 (commencing with Section 1200) of the Health and Safety Code. "Health care provider" includes the legal representatives of a health care provider;

(2) "Professional negligence" means a negligent act or omission to act by a health care provider in the rendering of professional services, which act or omission is the proximate cause of a personal injury or wrongful death, provided that such services are within the scope of services for which the provider is licensed and which are not within any restriction imposed by the licensing agency or licensed hospital. *(Added by Stats.1975, 2nd Ex.Sess., c. 1, p. 3975, § 26.6. Amended by Stats.1975, 2nd Ex.Sess., c. 2, p. 3994, § 1.195, eff. Dec. 12, 1975; Stats.1975, 2nd*

Ex.Sess., c. 2, p. 3996, § 1.196, eff. Sept. 24, 1975, operative July 1, 1976; Stats.1976, c. 1079, p. 4853, § 5; Stats.1976, c. 1185, p. 5320, § 92.)

Research References

Rutter, Cal. Practice Guide: A.D.R. Ch. 5-A, A. General Considerations.

Rutter, Cal. Practice Guide: A.D.R. Ch. 5-D, D. Defenses to Enforcement.

Rutter, Cal. Practice Guide: A.D.R. Ch. 5-F, F. Arbitration by and Against Nonsignatories.

Rutter, Cal. Practice Guide: A.D.R. Ch. 5-G, G. Procedures to Enforce Arbitration.

Rutter, Cal. Practice Guide: A.D.R. Ch. 5-H, H. Conduct of Arbitration Proceedings.

Rutter, Cal. Practice Guide: A.D.R. Ch. 8-E, E. Special Drafting Considerations Re Arbitration Agreements.

Rutter, Cal. Practice Guide: A.D.R. App. D Form 72, Health Care Providers.

Rutter, Cal. Practice Guide: A.D.R. App. D Form 74, Health Care Providers (Arbitration Clause Between Hospital and Patient to be Included in Hospital Admission Agreement).

Rutter, Cal. Practice Guide: Civ. Pro. Before Trial Ch. 1-A, A. Accepting a New Case.

Rutter, Cal. Practice Guide: Civil Trials & Evidence Ch. 2-E, E. Waiver of Jury Trial.

Rutter, Cal. Practice Guide: Insurance Litigation Ch. 6E-B, B. Basic Limitations.

Rutter, Cal. Practice Guide: Personal Injury Ch. 3-G, G. Independent Damages Claims.

Rutter, Cal. Practice Guide: Personal Injury Ch. 4-D, D. Techniques Where Settlement Not Forthcoming.

Rutter, Cal. Practice Guide: Personal Injury Ch. 7-A, A. Introduction-Nature and Purpose of "Judicial Arbitration" in General.

Rutter, Cal. Practice Guide: Personal Injury Ch. 7-G, G. Arbitration Hearing.

Rutter, Cal. Practice Guide: Real Prop. Transactions Ch. 1-C, C. Attorney Fees and Costs Agreements.

Rutter, Cal. Practice Guide: Prof. Responsibility Ch. 5-F, F. Formalizing Fee Agreements.

Miller and Starr California Real Estate § 35:26, Form and Contents of the Arbitration Agreement.

Miller and Starr California Real Estate § 35:30, Parties Subject to the Arbitration Agreement.

Miller and Starr California Real Estate § 35:55, Consolidation of Arbitration Proceedings.

22 NO. 1 Miller & Starr, California Real Estate Newsalert 4, Alternative Dispute Resolution.

23 NO. 2 Miller & Starr, California Real Estate Newsalert 4, Alternative Dispute Resolution.

1 Witkin Cal. Proc. 5th Attorneys § 331, (S 331) Arbitration Agreement.

6 Witkin Cal. Proc. 5th Proceedings Without Trial § 83, (S 83) Scope of Statute.

6 Witkin Cal. Proc. 5th Proceedings Without Trial § 503, (S 503) in General.

6 Witkin Cal. Proc. 5th Proceedings Without Trial § 504, (S 504) Medical Malpractice and Health Care Plans.

6 Witkin Cal. Proc. 5th Proceedings Without Trial § 513, (S 513) in General.

6 Witkin Cal. Proc. 5th Proceedings Without Trial § 532, Controversy is Not Within Scope of Arbitration Agreement.

7 Witkin Cal. Proc. 5th Trial § 103, Predispute Agreement.

1 Witkin Cal. Summ. 10th Contracts § 39, Unwed Pregnant Minors.

1 Witkin Cal. Summ. 10th Contracts § 328, (S 328) Statutory Compulsory Agreement.

6 Witkin, California Summary 10th Torts § 946, in General.

6 Witkin, California Summary 10th Torts § 947, Subsequent Medical Services.

6 Witkin, California Summary 10th Torts § 948, Persons Who Did Not Sign: in General.

6 Witkin, California Summary 10th Torts § 950, Retroactive Agreements.

6 Witkin, California Summary 10th Torts § 951, Intentional Torts.

6 Witkin, California Summary 10th Torts § 952, Punitive Damages.

6 Witkin, California Summary 10th Torts § 965, Intentional Torts.

6 Witkin, California Summary 10th Torts § 1654, (S 1654) Arbitration Proceedings.

Title 9.2

PUBLIC CONSTRUCTION CONTRACT ARBITRATION

Section
1296.   Award to be supported by law and substantial evidence; agreement in writing; review.

§ 1296.   Award to be supported by law and substantial evidence; agreement in writing; review

The parties to a construction contract with a public agency may expressly agree in writing that in any arbitration to resolve a dispute relating to the contract, the arbitrator's award shall be supported by law and substantial evidence. If the agreement so provides, a court shall, subject to Section 1286.4, vacate the award if after review of the award it determines either that the award is not supported by substantial evidence or that it is based on an error of law. *(Added by Stats.1979, c. 46, p. 119, § 2, eff. May 2, 1979.)*

Research References

Rutter, Cal. Practice Guide: A.D.R. Ch. 5-H, H. Conduct of Arbitration Proceedings.

Miller and Starr California Real Estate § 27:49, Provisions for Arbitration and Mediation of Disputes--Public Works.

Miller and Starr California Real Estate § 35:23, Public Policy in Favor of Arbitration.

Miller and Starr California Real Estate § 35:89, No Review for Mistake of Fact or Law by the Arbitrators.

6 Witkin Cal. Proc. 5th Proceedings Without Trial § 503, (S 503) in General.

6 Witkin Cal. Proc. 5th Proceedings Without Trial § 576, (S 576) Effect of Agreement Extending Scope of Review.

Title 9.3

ARBITRATION AND CONCILIATION OF INTERNATIONAL COMMERCIAL DISPUTES

CHAPTER 1.   APPLICATION AND INTERPRETATION

ARTICLE 1. SCOPE OF APPLICATION

Section

§ 1297.11.   Application of title; subject to certain agreements

This title applies to international commercial arbitration and conciliation, subject to any agreement which is in force between the United States and any other state or states. *(Added by Stats.1988, c. 23, § 1, eff. March 7, 1988.)*

Research References

Rutter, Cal. Practice Guide: A.D.R. Ch. 5-H, H. Conduct of Arbitration Proceedings.
Rutter, Cal. Practice Guide: A.D.R. Ch. 5-K, K. Arbitration of International Commercial Disputes.
Rutter, Cal. Practice Guide: A.D.R. Ch. 7-B, B. Arbitrators.
6 Witkin Cal. Proc. 5th Proceedings Without Trial § 503, (S 503) in General.

§ 1297.12.   Application of title; California as place of arbitration or conciliation

This title, except Article 2 (commencing with Section 1297.81) of Chapter 2 and Article 3 (commencing with Section 1297.91) of Chapter 2, applies only if the place of arbitration or conciliation is in the State of California. *(Added by Stats.1988, c. 23, § 1, eff. March 7, 1988.)*

Research References

Rutter, Cal. Practice Guide: A.D.R. Ch. 5-K, K. Arbitration of International Commercial Disputes.

§ 1297.13.   International status of agreement; requirements

An arbitration or conciliation agreement is international if any of the following applies:

(a) The parties to an arbitration or conciliation agreement have, at the time of the conclusion of that agreement, their places of business in different states.

(b) One of the following places is situated outside the state in which the parties have their places of business:

(i) The place of arbitration or conciliation if determined in, or pursuant to, the arbitration or conciliation agreement.

(ii) Any place where a substantial part of the obligations of the commercial relationship is to be performed.

(iii) The place with which the subject matter of the dispute is most closely connected.

(c) The parties have expressly agreed that the subject matter of the arbitration or conciliation agreement relates to commercial interests in more than one state.

(d) The subject matter of the arbitration or conciliation agreement is otherwise related to commercial interests in more than one state. *(Added by Stats.1988, c. 23, § 1, eff. March 7, 1988.)*

Research References

Rutter, Cal. Practice Guide: A.D.R. Ch. 5-K, K. Arbitration of International Commercial Disputes.

§ 1297.14.   Place of business; habitual residence

For the purposes of Section 1297.13, if a party has more than one place of business, the place of business is that which has the closest relationship to the arbitration agreement, and if a party does not have a place of business, reference is to be made to his habitual residence. *(Added by Stats.1988, c. 23, § 1, eff. March 7, 1988.)*

§ 1297.15.   One state; United States and District of Columbia

For the purposes of Section 1297.13, the states of the United States, including the District of Columbia, shall be considered one state. *(Added by Stats.1988, c. 23, § 1, eff. March 7, 1988.)*

§ 1297.16.   Commercial agreements; nature of relationships

An arbitration or conciliation agreement is commercial if it arises out of a relationship of a commercial nature including, but not limited to, any of the following:

(a) A transaction for the supply or exchange of goods or services.

(b) A distribution agreement.

(c) A commercial representation or agency.

(d) An exploitation agreement or concession.

(e) A joint venture or other, related form of industrial or business cooperation.

(f) The carriage of goods or passengers by air, sea, rail, or road.

(g) Construction.

(h) Insurance.

(i) Licensing.

(j) Factoring.

(k) Leasing.

(*l*) Consulting.

(m) Engineering.

(n) Financing.

(*o*) Banking.

(p) The transfer of data or technology.

(q) Intellectual or industrial property, including trademarks, patents, copyrights and software programs.

(r) Professional services. *(Added by Stats.1988, c. 23, § 1, eff. March 7, 1988.)*

§ 1297.17.   Effect on other laws; supersession

This title shall not affect any other law in force in California by virtue of which certain disputes may not be submitted to arbitration or may be submitted to arbitration only in accordance with provisions other than those of this title. Notwithstanding the foregoing, this title supersedes Sections 1280 to 1284.2, inclusive, with respect to international commercial arbitration and conciliation. *(Added by Stats.1988, c. 23, § 1, eff. March 7, 1988.)*

Research References

Rutter, Cal. Practice Guide: A.D.R. Ch. 5-H, H. Conduct of Arbitration Proceedings.

Civ. Pro.

Rutter, Cal. Practice Guide: A.D.R. Ch. 5-K, K. Arbitration of International Commercial Disputes.

ARTICLE 2. INTERPRETATION

Section
1297.21. Definitions.
1297.22. Freedom of parties to determine issue; third party.
1297.23. Agreement of parties as including arbitration or conciliation rules.
1297.24. Claim; counterclaim; defense.

§ 1297.21. Definitions

For the purposes of this title:

(a) "Arbitral award" means any decision of the arbitral tribunal on the substance of the dispute submitted to it and includes an interim, interlocutory, or partial arbitral award.

(b) "Arbitral tribunal" means a sole arbitrator or a panel of arbitrators.

(c) "Arbitration" means any arbitration whether or not administered by a permanent arbitral institution.

(d) "Conciliation" means any conciliation whether or not administered by a permanent conciliation institution.

(e) "Chief Justice" means the Chief Justice of California or his or her designee.

(f) "Court" means a body or an organ of the judicial system of a state.

(g) "Party" means a party to an arbitration or conciliation agreement.

(h) "Superior court" means the superior court in the county in this state selected pursuant to Section 1297.61.

(i) "Supreme Court" means the Supreme Court of California. (Added by Stats.1988, c. 23, § 1, eff. March 7, 1988.)

§ 1297.22. Freedom of parties to determine issue; third party

Where a provision of this title, except Article 1 (commencing with Section 1297.281) of Chapter 6, leaves the parties free to determine a certain issue, such freedom includes the right of the parties to authorize a third party, including an institution, to make that determination. (Added by Stats.1988, c. 23, § 1, eff. March 7, 1988.)

Research References

Rutter, Cal. Practice Guide: A.D.R. Ch. 5-K, K. Arbitration of International Commercial Disputes.

§ 1297.23. Agreement of parties as including arbitration or conciliation rules

Where a provision of this title refers to the fact that the parties have agreed or that they may agree, or in any other way refers to an agreement of the parties, such agreement shall be deemed to include any arbitration or conciliation rules referred to in that agreement. (Added by Stats.1988, c. 23, § 1, eff. March 7, 1988.)

Research References

Rutter, Cal. Practice Guide: A.D.R. Ch. 5-K, K. Arbitration of International Commercial Disputes.

§ 1297.24. Claim; counterclaim; defense

Where this title, other than Article 8 (commencing with Section 1297.251) of Chapter 5, Article 5 (commencing with Section 1297.321) of Chapter 6, or subdivision (a) of Section 1297.322, refers to a claim, it also applies to a counterclaim, and where it refers to a defense, it also applies to a defense to that counterclaim. (Added by Stats.1988, c. 23, § 1, eff. March 7, 1988.)

ARTICLE 3. RECEIPT OF WRITTEN COMMUNICATIONS

Section
1297.31. Receipt if delivered to addressee personally, at place of business, habitual residence or mailing address on day of delivery.
1297.32. Receipt if delivered to last known address if not found after reasonable inquiry.
1297.33. Court proceedings; inapplicability of this article to written communications.

§ 1297.31. Receipt if delivered to addressee personally, at place of business, habitual residence or mailing address on day of delivery

Unless otherwise agreed by the parties, any written communication is deemed to have been received if it is delivered to the addressee personally or if it is delivered at his place of business, habitual residence, or mailing address, and the communication is deemed to have been received on the day it is so delivered. (Added by Stats.1988, c. 23, § 1, eff. March 7, 1988.)

§ 1297.32. Receipt if delivered to last known address if not found after reasonable inquiry

If none of the places referred to in Section 1297.31 can be found after making a reasonable inquiry, a written communication is deemed to have been received if it is sent to the addressee's last known place of business, habitual residence, or mailing address by registered mail or by any other means which provides a record of the attempt to deliver it. (Added by Stats.1988, c. 23, § 1, eff. March 7, 1988.)

§ 1297.33. Court proceedings; inapplicability of this article to written communications

This article does not apply to written communications in respect of court proceedings. (Added by Stats.1988, c. 23, § 1, eff. March 7, 1988.)

ARTICLE 4. WAIVER OF RIGHT TO OBJECT

Section
1297.41. Failure to state objection without delay; waiver.
1297.42. Any provision of this title, defined.

§ 1297.41. Failure to state objection without delay; waiver

A party who knows that any provision of this title, or any requirement under the arbitration agreement, has not been complied with and yet proceeds with the arbitration without stating his or her objection to noncompliance without undue delay or, if a time limit is provided for stating that objection, within that period of time, shall be deemed to have waived his right to object. (Added by Stats.1988, c. 23, § 1, eff. March 7, 1988.)

Research References

Rutter, Cal. Practice Guide: A.D.R. Ch. 5-K, K. Arbitration of International Commercial Disputes.

§ 1297.42. Any provision of this title, defined

For purposes of Section 1297.41, "any provision of this title" means any provision of this title in respect of which the parties may otherwise agree. (Added by Stats.1988, c. 23, § 1, eff. March 7, 1988.)

ARTICLE 5. EXTENT OF JUDICIAL INTERVENTION

Section
1297.51. Prohibition against intervention unless provided for in title or federal law.

§ 1297.51. Prohibition against intervention unless provided for in title or federal law

In matters governed by this title, no court shall intervene except where so provided in this title, or applicable federal law. *(Added by Stats.1988, c. 23, § 1, eff. March 7, 1988.)*

ARTICLE 6. FUNCTIONS

Section
1297.61. Superior court; performance of duties.

§ 1297.61. Superior court; performance of duties

The functions referred to in Sections 1297.114, 1297.115, 1297.116, 1297.134, 1297.135, 1297.136, 1297.165, 1297.166, and 1297.167 shall be performed by the superior court of the county in which the place of arbitration is located. The functions referred to in Section 1297.81 shall be performed by the superior court selected pursuant to Article 2 (commencing with Section 1292) of Chapter 5 of Title 9. *(Added by Stats.1988, c. 23, § 1, eff. March 7, 1988.)*

CHAPTER 2. ARBITRATION AGREEMENTS AND JUDICIAL MEASURES IN AID OF ARBITRATION

ARTICLE 1. DEFINITION AND FORM OF ARBITRATION AGREEMENTS

Section
1297.71. Arbitration agreement, defined; form.
1297.72. Writing; signed document, exchange of communications, statements of claim and defense or reference in contract.

§ 1297.71. Arbitration agreement, defined; form

An "arbitration agreement" is an agreement by the parties to submit to arbitration all or certain disputes which have arisen or which may arise between them in respect of a defined legal relationship, whether contractual or not. An arbitration agreement may be in the form of an arbitration clause in a contract or in the form of a separate agreement. *(Added by Stats.1988, c. 23, § 1, eff. March 7, 1988.)*

§ 1297.72. Writing; signed document, exchange of communications, statements of claim and defense or reference in contract

An arbitration agreement shall be in writing. An agreement is in writing if it is contained in a document signed by the parties or in an exchange of letters, telex, telegrams, or other means of telecommunication which provide a record of this agreement, or in an exchange of statements of claim and defense in which the existence of an agreement is alleged by one party and not denied by another. The reference in a contract to a document containing an arbitration clause constitutes an arbitration agreement provided that the contract is in writing and the reference is such as to make that clause part of the contract. *(Added by Stats.1988, c. 23, § 1, eff. March 7, 1988.)*

ARTICLE 2. STAY OF PROCEEDINGS

Section
1297.81. Commencement of judicial proceedings by one party; right of other party to stay proceedings and compel arbitration.
1297.82. Timely request; grant.

§ 1297.81. Commencement of judicial proceedings by one party; right of other party to stay proceedings and compel arbitration

When a party to an international commercial arbitration agreement as defined in this title commences judicial proceedings seeking relief with respect to a matter covered by the agreement to arbitrate, any other party to the agreement may apply to the superior court for an order to stay the proceedings and to compel arbitration. *(Added by Stats.1988, c. 23, § 1, eff. March 7, 1988.)*

Research References

Rutter, Cal. Practice Guide: A.D.R. Ch. 5-K, K. Arbitration of International Commercial Disputes.

§ 1297.82. Timely request; grant

A timely request for a stay of judicial proceedings made under Section 1297.81 shall be granted. *(Added by Stats.1988, c. 23, § 1, eff. March 7, 1988.)*

ARTICLE 3. INTERIM MEASURES

Section
1297.91. Request for interim protection; incompatibility with arbitration agreement.
1297.92. Tribunal's award to take interim measure of protection, request to superior court for enforcement.
1297.93. Measures which court may grant.
1297.94. Considerations by court on request for interim relief; public policy.
1297.95. Absence of ruling by tribunal to objection to its jurisdiction; independent finding by court; effect.

§ 1297.91. Request for interim protection; incompatibility with arbitration agreement

It is not incompatible with an arbitration agreement for a party to request from a superior court, before or during arbitral proceedings, an interim measure of protection, or for the court to grant such a measure. *(Added by Stats.1988, c. 23, § 1, eff. March 7, 1988.)*

Research References

Rutter, Cal. Practice Guide: A.D.R. Ch. 5-K, K. Arbitration of International Commercial Disputes.

§ 1297.92. Tribunal's award to take interim measure of protection, request to superior court for enforcement

Any party to an arbitration governed by this title may request from the superior court enforcement of an award of an arbitral tribunal to take any interim measure of protection of an arbitral tribunal pursuant to Article 2 (commencing with Section 1297.171) of Chapter 4. Enforcement shall be granted pursuant to the law applicable to the granting of the type of interim relief requested. *(Added by Stats.1988, c. 23, § 1, eff. March 7, 1988.)*

§ 1297.93.　Measures which court may grant

Measures which the court may grant in connection with a pending arbitration include, but are not limited to:

(a) An order of attachment issued to assure that the award to which applicant may be entitled is not rendered ineffectual by the dissipation of party assets.

(b) A preliminary injunction granted in order to protect trade secrets or to conserve goods which are the subject matter of the arbitral dispute. *(Added by Stats.1988, c. 23, § 1, eff. March 7, 1988.)*

§ 1297.94.　Considerations by court on request for interim relief; public policy

In considering a request for interim relief, the court shall give preclusive effect to any and all findings of fact of the arbitral tribunal including the probable validity of the claim which is the subject of the award for interim relief and which the arbitral tribunal has previously granted in the proceeding in question, provided that such interim award is consistent with public policy. *(Added by Stats.1988, c. 23, § 1, eff. March 7, 1988.)*

§ 1297.95.　Absence of ruling by tribunal to objection to its jurisdiction; independent finding by court; effect

Where the arbitral tribunal has not ruled on an objection to its jurisdiction, the court shall not grant preclusive effect to the tribunal's findings until the court has made an independent finding as to the jurisdiction of the arbitral tribunal.　If the court rules that the arbitral tribunal did not have jurisdiction, the application for interim measures of relief shall be denied.　Such a ruling by the court that the arbitral tribunal lacks jurisdiction is not binding on the arbitral tribunal or subsequent judicial proceeding. *(Added by Stats.1988, c. 23, § 1, eff. March 7, 1988.)*

Research References

Rutter, Cal. Practice Guide: A.D.R. Ch. 5-K, K. Arbitration of International Commercial Disputes.

CHAPTER 3.　COMPOSITION OF ARBITRAL TRIBUNALS

ARTICLE 1.　NUMBER OF ARBITRATORS

§ 1297.101.　Agreement by parties if more than one arbitrator

The parties may agree on the number of arbitrators.　Otherwise, there shall be one arbitrator. *(Added by Stats.1988, c. 23, § 1, eff. March 7, 1988.)*

Research References

Rutter, Cal. Practice Guide: A.D.R. Ch. 5-K, K. Arbitration of International Commercial Disputes.

ARTICLE 2.　APPOINTMENT OF ARBITRATORS

§ 1297.111.　Nationality of arbitrator

A person of any nationality may be an arbitrator. *(Added by Stats.1988, c. 23, § 1, eff. March 7, 1988.)*

§ 1297.112.　Procedure

Subject to Sections 1297.115 and 1297.116, the parties may agree on a procedure for appointing the arbitral tribunal. *(Added by Stats.1988, c. 23, § 1, eff. March 7, 1988.)*

§ 1297.113.　Appointment of third arbitrator by two party-appointed arbitrators

Failing such agreement referred to in Section 1297.112, in an arbitration with three arbitrators and two parties, each party shall appoint one arbitrator, and the two appointed arbitrators shall appoint the third arbitrator. *(Added by Stats.1988, c. 23, § 1, eff. March 7, 1988.)*

Research References

Rutter, Cal. Practice Guide: A.D.R. Ch. 5-K, K. Arbitration of International Commercial Disputes.

§ 1297.114.　Three arbitrator tribunal; failure to appoint arbitrator; appointment by court

If the appointment procedure in Section 1297.113 applies and either a party fails to appoint an arbitrator within 30 days after receipt of a request to do so from the other party, or the two appointed arbitrators fail to agree on the third arbitrator within 30 days after their appointment, the appointment shall be made, upon request of a party, by the superior court. *(Added by Stats.1988, c. 23, § 1, eff. March 7, 1988.)*

Research References

Rutter, Cal. Practice Guide: A.D.R. Ch. 5-K, K. Arbitration of International Commercial Disputes.

§ 1297.115.　Sole arbitrator tribunal; failure of agreement; appointment by court

Failing any agreement referred to in Section 1297.112, in an arbitration with a sole arbitrator, if the parties fail to agree on the arbitrator, the appointment shall be made, upon request of a party, by the superior court. *(Added by Stats.1988, c. 23, § 1, eff. March 7, 1988.)*

Research References

Rutter, Cal. Practice Guide: A.D.R. Ch. 5-K, K. Arbitration of International Commercial Disputes.

§ 1297.116.　Measures to be taken by court to secure appointment

The superior court, upon the request of a party, may take the necessary measures, unless the agreement on the appointment procedure provides other means for securing the appointment, where, under an appointment procedure agreed upon by the parties, any of the following occurs:

(a) A party fails to act as required under that procedure.

(b) The parties, or two appointed arbitrators, fail to reach an agreement expected of them under that procedure.

(c) A third party, including an institution, fails to perform any function entrusted to it under that procedure. *(Added by Stats.1988, c. 23, § 1, eff. March 7, 1988.)*

§ 1297.117. Decision by court; finality; not subject to appeal

A decision on a matter entrusted to the superior court pursuant to Sections 1297.114, 127.115,[1] and 1297.116 is final and is not subject to appeal. *(Added by Stats.1988, c. 23, § 1, eff. March 7, 1988.)*

[1] So in chaptered copy. Code of Civil Procedure § 1297.115 is probably intended.

§ 1297.118. Superior court; considerations in appointing arbitrators

The superior court, in appointing an arbitrator, shall have due regard to all of the following:

(a) Any qualifications required of the arbitrator by the agreement of the parties.

(b) Other considerations as are likely to secure the appointment of an independent and impartial arbitrator.

(c) In the case of a sole or third arbitrator, the advisability of appointing an arbitrator of a nationality other than those of the parties. *(Added by Stats.1988, c. 23, § 1, eff. March 7, 1988.)*

§ 1297.119. Immunity; civil liability

An arbitrator has the immunity of a judicial officer from civil liability when acting in the capacity of arbitrator under any statute or contract.

The immunity afforded by this section shall supplement, and not supplant, any otherwise applicable common law or statutory immunity. *(Added by Stats.1994, c. 228 (S.B.1660), § 1.)*

Research References

Rutter, Cal. Practice Guide: A.D.R. Ch. 5-A, A. General Considerations.

ARTICLE 3. GROUNDS FOR CHALLENGE

Section

§ 1297.121. Disclosure of information questioning impartiality; circumstances

Except as otherwise provided in this title, all persons whose names have been submitted for consideration for appointment or designation as arbitrators or conciliators, or who have been appointed or designated as such, shall, within 15 days, make a disclosure to the parties of any information which might cause their impartiality to be questioned including, but not limited to, any of the following instances:

(a) The person has a personal bias or prejudice concerning a party, or personal knowledge of disputed evidentiary facts concerning the proceeding.

(b) The person served as a lawyer in the matter in controversy, or the person is or has been associated with another who has participated in the matter during such association, or he or she has been a material witness concerning it.

(c) The person served as an arbitrator or conciliator in another proceeding involving one or more of the parties to the proceeding.

(d) The person, individually or a fiduciary, or such person's spouse or minor child residing in such person's household, has a financial interest in the subject matter in controversy or in a party to the proceeding, or any other interest that could be substantially affected by the outcome of the proceeding.

(e) The person, his or her spouse, or a person within the third degree of relationship to either of them, or the spouse of such a person meets any of the following conditions:

(i) The person is or has been a party to the proceeding, or an officer, director, or trustee of a party.

(ii) The person is acting or has acted as a lawyer in the proceeding.

(iii) The person is known to have an interest that could be substantially affected by the outcome of the proceeding.

(iv) The person is likely to be a material witness in the proceeding.

(f) The person has a close personal or professional relationship with a person who meets any of the following conditions:

(i) The person is or has been a party to the proceeding, or an officer, director, or trustee of a party.

(ii) The person is acting or has acted as a lawyer or representative in the proceeding.

(iii) The person is or expects to be nominated as an arbitrator or conciliator in the proceedings.

(iv) The person is known to have an interest that could be substantially affected by the outcome of the proceeding.

(v) The person is likely to be a material witness in the proceeding. *(Added by Stats.1988, c. 23, § 1, eff. March 7, 1988.)*

Research References

Rutter, Cal. Practice Guide: A.D.R. Ch. 5-K, K. Arbitration of International Commercial Disputes.

Rutter, Cal. Practice Guide: A.D.R. Ch. 7-B, B. Arbitrators.

Rutter, Cal. Practice Guide: A.D.R. Ch. 8-E, E. Special Drafting Considerations Re Arbitration Agreements.

Miller and Starr California Real Estate § 35:69, Arbitrator's Duty of Written Disclosure.

Miller and Starr California Real Estate § 25B:113, Arbitration or Other Resolution of Disputes With the Subdivider.

§ 1297.122. Mandatory obligation to disclose information; waiver

The obligation to disclose information set forth in Section 1297.121 is mandatory and cannot be waived as to the parties with respect to persons serving either as the sole arbitrator or sole conciliator or as the chief or prevailing arbitrator or conciliator. The parties may otherwise agree to waive such disclosure. *(Added by Stats.1988, c. 23, § 1, eff. March 7, 1988.)*

§ 1297.123. Disclosure by arbitrator of circumstances not previously disclosed; time

From the time of appointment and throughout the arbitral proceedings, an arbitrator, shall, without delay, disclose to the parties any circumstances referred to in Section 1297.121 which were not previously disclosed. *(Added by Stats.1988, c. 23, § 1, eff. March 7, 1988.)*

§ 1297.124. Challenge for doubts as to independence, impartiality or qualifications

Unless otherwise agreed by the parties or the rules governing the arbitration, an arbitrator may be challenged only if circumstances exist that give rise to justifiable doubts as to his or her independence or impartiality, or as to his or her possession of the qualifications upon which the parties have agreed. *(Added by Stats.1988, c. 23, § 1, eff. March 7, 1988.)*

Research References

Rutter, Cal. Practice Guide: A.D.R. Ch. 5-K, K. Arbitration of International Commercial Disputes.

Rutter, Cal. Practice Guide: A.D.R. Ch. 8-E, E. Special Drafting Considerations Re Arbitration Agreements.

Miller and Starr California Real Estate § 25B:113, Arbitration or Other Resolution of Disputes With the Subdivider.

§ 1297.125. Challenge only for reasons aware of after appointment

A party may challenge an arbitrator appointed by it, or in whose appointment it has participated, only for reasons of which it becomes aware after the appointment has been made. *(Added by Stats.1988, c. 23, § 1, eff. March 7, 1988.)*

Research References

Rutter, Cal. Practice Guide: A.D.R. Ch. 5-K, K. Arbitration of International Commercial Disputes.

ARTICLE 4. CHALLENGE PROCEDURE

Section
1297.131.   Agreement on procedure; finality of decision.
1297.132.   Reasons for challenge; statement to tribunal; time.
1297.133.   Decision by tribunal.
1297.134.   Unsuccessful challenge; superior court; decision on challenge; sustaining challenge.
1297.135.   Finality of superior court decision; no appeal.
1297.136.   Continuation of arbitral proceedings while court request pending.

§ 1297.131. Agreement on procedure; finality of decision

The parties may agree on a procedure for challenging an arbitrator and the decision reached pursuant to that procedure shall be final. *(Added by Stats.1988, c. 23, § 1, eff. March 7, 1988.)*

§ 1297.132. Reasons for challenge; statement to tribunal; time

Failing any agreement referred to in Section 1297.131, a party which intends to challenge an arbitrator shall, within 15 days after becoming aware of the constitution of the arbitral tribunal or after becoming aware of any circumstances referred to in Sections 1297.124 and 1297.125, whichever shall be later, send a written statement of the reasons for the challenge to the arbitral tribunal. *(Added by Stats.1988, c. 23, § 1, eff. March 7, 1988.)*

Research References

Rutter, Cal. Practice Guide: A.D.R. Ch. 5-K, K. Arbitration of International Commercial Disputes.

§ 1297.133. Decision by tribunal

Unless the arbitrator challenged under Section 1297.132 withdraws from his or her office or the other party agrees to the challenge, the arbitral tribunal shall decide on the challenge. *(Added by Stats.1988, c. 23, § 1, eff. March 7, 1988.)*

§ 1297.134. Unsuccessful challenge; superior court; decision on challenge; sustaining challenge

If a challenge following the procedure under Section 1297.133 is not successful, the challenging party may request the superior court, within 30 days after having received notice of the decision rejecting the challenge, to decide on the challenge. If a challenge is based upon the grounds set forth in Section 1297.121, and the superior court determines that the facts support a finding that such ground or grounds fairly exist, then the challenge should be sustained. *(Added by Stats.1988, c. 23, § 1, eff. March 7, 1988.)*

§ 1297.135. Finality of superior court decision; no appeal

The decision of the superior court under Section 1297.134 is final and is not subject to appeal. *(Added by Stats.1988, c. 23, § 1, eff. March 7, 1988.)*

Research References

Rutter, Cal. Practice Guide: A.D.R. Ch. 5-K, K. Arbitration of International Commercial Disputes.

§ 1297.136. Continuation of arbitral proceedings while court request pending

While a request under Section 1297.134 is pending, the arbitral tribunal, including the challenged arbitrator, may continue with the arbitral proceedings and make an arbitral award. *(Added by Stats.1988, c. 23, § 1, eff. March 7, 1988.)*

ARTICLE 5. FAILURE OR IMPOSSIBILITY TO ACT

Section
1297.141.   Termination of arbitrator's mandate; circumstances.
1297.142.   Remaining controversy; decision by superior court; request of party.
1297.143.   Decision of superior court not appealable.
1297.144.   Withdrawal of arbitrator or termination of mandate; effect on validity of grounds for challenge.

§ 1297.141. Termination of arbitrator's mandate; circumstances

The mandate of an arbitrator terminates if he becomes de jure or de facto unable to perform his or her functions or for other reasons fails to act without undue delay, and he withdraws from his or her office or the parties agree to the termination of his or her mandate. *(Added by Stats.1988, c. 23, § 1, eff. March 7, 1988.)*

§ 1297.142. Remaining controversy; decision by superior court; request of party

If a controversy remains concerning any of the grounds referred to in Section 1297.141, a party may request the superior court to decide on the termination of the mandate. *(Added by Stats.1988, c. 23, § 1, eff. March 7, 1988.)*

§ 1297.143. Decision of superior court not appealable

A decision of the superior court under Section 1297.142 is not subject to appeal. *(Added by Stats.1988, c. 23, § 1, eff. March 7, 1988.)*

§ 1297.144. Withdrawal of arbitrator or termination of mandate; effect on validity of grounds for challenge.

If, under this section or Section 1297.132, an arbitrator withdraws from office or a party agrees to the termination of the mandate of an arbitrator, this does not imply acceptance of the validity of any ground referred to in Section 1297.132. *(Added by Stats.1988, c. 23, § 1, eff. March 7, 1988.)*

ARTICLE 6. TERMINATION OF MANDATE AND SUBSTITUTION OF ARBITRATORS

§ 1297.151. Withdrawal of arbitrator from office or by agreement of parties

In addition to the circumstances referred to under Article 4 (commencing with Section 1297.131) and Article 5 (commencing with Section 1297.141) of this chapter, the mandate of an arbitrator terminates upon his or her withdrawal from office for any reason, or by or pursuant to agreement of the parties. *(Added by Stats.1988, c. 23, § 1, eff. March 7, 1988.)*

§ 1297.152. Substitute arbitrator; appointment

Where the mandate of an arbitrator terminates, a substitute arbitrator shall be appointed according to the rules that were applicable to the appointment of the arbitrator being replaced. *(Added by Stats.1988, c. 23, § 1, eff. March 7, 1988.)*

§ 1297.153. Repetition of previous hearings; agreement of parties or discretion of tribunal

Unless otherwise agreed by the parties:

(a) Where the sole or presiding arbitrator is replaced, any hearings previously held shall be repeated.

(b) Where an arbitrator other than the sole or presiding arbitrator is replaced, any hearings previously held may be repeated at the discretion of the arbitral tribunal. *(Added by Stats.1988, c. 23, § 1, eff. March 7, 1988.)*

§ 1297.154. Order or ruling of tribunal prior to replacement of arbitrator; effect

Unless otherwise agreed by the parties, an order or ruling of the arbitral tribunal made prior to the replacement of an arbitrator under this section is not invalid because there has been a change in the composition of the tribunal. *(Added by Stats.1988, c. 23, § 1, eff. March 7, 1988.)*

CHAPTER 4. JURISDICTION OF ARBITRAL TRIBUNALS

ARTICLE 1. COMPETENCE OF AN ARBITRAL TRIBUNAL TO RULE ON ITS JURISDICTION

§ 1297.161. Authority to rule on jurisdiction and arbitration agreement; treatment and effect of arbitration clause

The arbitral tribunal may rule on its own jurisdiction, including ruling on any objections with respect to the existence or validity of the arbitration agreement, and for that purpose, an arbitration clause which forms part of a contract shall be treated as an agreement independent of the other terms of the contract, and a decision by the arbitral tribunal that the contract is null and void shall not entail ipso jure the invalidity of the arbitration clause. *(Added by Stats.1988, c. 23, § 1, eff. March 7, 1988.)*

Research References

Rutter, Cal. Practice Guide: A.D.R. Ch. 5-K, K. Arbitration of International Commercial Disputes.

§ 1297.162. Plea of lack of jurisdiction; effect if party participated in appointment of arbitrator

A plea that the arbitral tribunal does not have jurisdiction shall be raised not later than the submission of the statement of defense. However, a party is not precluded from raising such a plea by the fact that he or she has appointed, or participated in the appointment of, an arbitrator. *(Added by Stats.1988, c. 23, § 1, eff. March 7, 1988.)*

Research References

Rutter, Cal. Practice Guide: A.D.R. Ch. 5-K, K. Arbitration of International Commercial Disputes.

§ 1297.163. Plea of exceeding scope of authority; time

A plea that the arbitral tribunal is exceeding the scope of its authority shall be raised as soon as the matter alleged to be beyond the scope of its authority is raised during the arbitral proceedings. *(Added by Stats.1988, c. 23, § 1, eff. March 7, 1988.)*

Research References

Rutter, Cal. Practice Guide: A.D.R. Ch. 5-K, K. Arbitration of International Commercial Disputes.

§ 1297.164. Admission of later plea if delay justified

The arbitral tribunal may, in either of the cases referred to in Sections 1297.162 and 1297.163, admit a later plea if it considers the delay justified. *(Added by Stats.1988, c. 23, § 1, eff. March 7, 1988.)*

§ 1297.165. Ruling on plea as a preliminary question or in award on merits

The arbitral tribunal may rule on a plea referred to in Sections 1297.162 and 1297.163 either as a preliminary question or in an award on the merits. *(Added by Stats.1988, c. 23, § 1, eff. March 7, 1988.)*

§ 1297.166. Ruling on plea as a preliminary question; request to superior court; waiver

If the arbitral tribunal rules as a preliminary question that it has jurisdiction, any party shall request the superior court, within

30 days after having received notice of that ruling, to decide the matter or shall be deemed to have waived objection to such finding. *(Added by Stats.1988, c. 23, § 1, eff. March 7, 1988.)*

Research References

Rutter, Cal. Practice Guide: A.D.R. Ch. 5-K, K. Arbitration of International Commercial Disputes.

§ 1297.167. Continuation of arbitral proceedings while court request pending

While a request under Section 1297.166 is pending, the arbitral tribunal may continue with the arbitral proceedings and make an arbitral award. *(Added by Stats.1988, c. 23, § 1, eff. March 7, 1988.)*

Research References

Rutter, Cal. Practice Guide: A.D.R. Ch. 5-K, K. Arbitration of International Commercial Disputes.

ARTICLE 2. INTERIM MEASURES ORDERED BY ARBITRAL TRIBUNALS

Section
1297.171.   Interim measure of protection; order by tribunal.
1297.172.   Requiring party to provide security.

§ 1297.171. Interim measure of protection; order by tribunal

Unless otherwise agreed by the parties, the arbitral tribunal may, at the request of a party, order a party to take any interim measure of protection as the arbitral tribunal may consider necessary in respect of the subject matter of the dispute. *(Added by Stats.1988, c. 23, § 1, eff. March 7, 1988.)*

Research References

Rutter, Cal. Practice Guide: A.D.R. Ch. 5-K, K. Arbitration of International Commercial Disputes.

§ 1297.172. Requiring party to provide security

The arbitral tribunal may require a party to provide appropriate security in connection with a measure ordered under Section 1297.171. *(Added by Stats.1988, c. 23, § 1, eff. March 7, 1988.)*

Research References

Rutter, Cal. Practice Guide: A.D.R. Ch. 5-K, K. Arbitration of International Commercial Disputes.

CHAPTER 5. MANNER AND CONDUCT OF ARBITRATION

ARTICLE 1. EQUAL TREATMENT OF PARTIES

Section
1297.181.   Equal treatment and opportunity to present case.

§ 1297.181. Equal treatment and opportunity to present case

The parties shall be treated with equality and each party shall be given a full opportunity to present his or her case. *(Added by Stats.1988, c. 23, § 1, eff. March 7, 1988.)*

Research References

Rutter, Cal. Practice Guide: A.D.R. Ch. 5-K, K. Arbitration of International Commercial Disputes.

ARTICLE 2. DETERMINATION OF RULES OF PROCEDURE

Section
1297.191.   Agreement of parties.
1297.192.   Conduct of arbitration by tribunal.
1297.193.   Evidentiary questions; determination by tribunal.

§ 1297.191. Agreement of parties

Subject to this title, the parties may agree on the procedure to be followed by the arbitral tribunal in conducting the proceedings. *(Added by Stats.1988, c. 23, § 1, eff. March 7, 1988.)*

§ 1297.192. Conduct of arbitration by tribunal

Failing any agreement referred to in Section 1297.191, the arbitral tribunal may, subject to this title, conduct the arbitration in the manner it considers appropriate. *(Added by Stats.1988, c. 23, § 1, eff. March 7, 1988.)*

§ 1297.193. Evidentiary questions; determination by tribunal

The power of the arbitral tribunal under Section 1297.192 includes the power to determine the admissibility, relevance, materiality, and weight of any evidence. *(Added by Stats.1988, c. 23, § 1, eff. March 7, 1988.)*

ARTICLE 3. PLACE OF ARBITRATION

Section
1297.201.   Agreement of parties.
1297.202.   Determination by tribunal upon failure of parties to agree.
1297.203.   Meetings at place tribunal considers appropriate.

§ 1297.201. Agreement of parties

The parties may agree on the place of arbitration. *(Added by Stats.1988, c. 23, § 1, eff. March 7, 1988.)*

§ 1297.202. Determination by tribunal upon failure of parties to agree

Failing any agreement referred to in Section 1297.201, the place of arbitration shall be determined by the arbitral tribunal having regard to the circumstances of the case, including the convenience of the parties. *(Added by Stats.1988, c. 23, § 1, eff. March 7, 1988.)*

Research References

Rutter, Cal. Practice Guide: A.D.R. Ch. 5-K, K. Arbitration of International Commercial Disputes.

§ 1297.203. Meetings at place tribunal considers appropriate

Notwithstanding Section 1297.201, the arbitral tribunal may, unless otherwise agreed by the parties, meet at any place it considers appropriate for consultation among its members, for hearing witnesses, experts, or the parties, or for inspection of documents, goods, or other property. *(Added by Stats.1988, c. 23, § 1, eff. March 7, 1988.)*

ARTICLE 4.   COMMENCEMENT OF ARBITRAL PROCEEDINGS

Section
1297.211.   Date on which arbitration referral received by respondent.

§ 1297.211.   Date on which arbitration referral received by respondent

Unless otherwise agreed by the parties, the arbitral proceedings in respect of a particular dispute commence on the date on which a request for that dispute to be referred to arbitration is received by the respondent. *(Added by Stats.1988, c. 23, § 1, eff. March 7, 1988.)*

ARTICLE 5.   LANGUAGE

Section
1297.221.   Agreement by parties.
1297.222.   Determination by tribunal.
1297.223.   Application of agreement of parties or determination by tribunal.
1297.224.   Documentary evidence; accompaniment by translation; order by tribunal.

§ 1297.221.   Agreement by parties

The parties may agree upon the language or languages to be used in the arbitral proceedings. *(Added by Stats.1988, c. 23, § 1, eff. March 7, 1988.)*

§ 1297.222.   Determination by tribunal

Failing any agreement referred to in Section 1297.221, the arbitral tribunal shall determine the language or languages to be used in the arbitral proceedings. *(Added by Stats.1988, c. 23, § 1, eff. March 7, 1988.)*

Research References

Rutter, Cal. Practice Guide: A.D.R. Ch. 5-K, K. Arbitration of International Commercial Disputes.

§ 1297.223.   Application of agreement of parties or determination by tribunal

The agreement or determination, unless otherwise specified, shall apply to any written statement by a party, any hearing, and any arbitral award, decision, or other communication by the arbitral tribunal. *(Added by Stats.1988, c. 23, § 1, eff. March 7, 1988.)*

§ 1297.224.   Documentary evidence; accompaniment by translation; order by tribunal

The arbitral tribunal may order that any documentary evidence shall be accompanied by a translation into the language or languages agreed upon by the parties or determined by the arbitral tribunal. *(Added by Stats.1988, c. 23, § 1, eff. March 7, 1988.)*

ARTICLE 6.   STATEMENTS OF CLAIM AND DEFENSE

Section
1297.231.   Statement of claim by claimant; statement of defense by respondent; time.
1297.232.   Submission of documents with statement.
1297.233.   Amendment or supplement to claim or defense; exception.

§ 1297.231.   Statement of claim by claimant; statement of defense by respondent; time

Within the period of time agreed upon by the parties or determined by the arbitral tribunal, the claimant shall state the facts supporting his or her claim, the points at issue, and the relief or remedy sought, and the respondent shall state his or her defense in respect of these particulars, unless the parties have otherwise agreed as to the required elements of those statements. *(Added by Stats.1988, c. 23, § 1, eff. March 7, 1988.)*

§ 1297.232.   Submission of documents with statement

The parties may submit with their statements all documents they consider to be relevant or may add a reference to the documents or other evidence they will submit. *(Added by Stats.1988, c. 23, § 1, eff. March 7, 1988.)*

§ 1297.233.   Amendment or supplement to claim or defense; exception

Unless otherwise agreed by the parties, either party may amend or supplement his or her claim or defense during the course of the arbitral proceedings, unless the arbitral tribunal considers it inappropriate to allow the amendment or supplement having regard to the delay in making it. *(Added by Stats.1988, c. 23, § 1, eff. March 7, 1988.)*

ARTICLE 7.   HEARINGS AND WRITTEN PROCEEDINGS

Section
1297.241.   Oral or written presentation of evidence; agreement or decision.
1297.242.   Oral hearings.
1297.243.   Notice of hearings and meetings.
1297.244.   Statements, documents, etc. by one party to tribunal; communication to other party.
1297.245.   Oral hearings and meetings in camera.

§ 1297.241.   Oral or written presentation of evidence; agreement or decision

Unless otherwise agreed by the parties, the arbitral tribunal shall decide whether to hold oral hearings for the presentation of evidence or for oral argument, or whether the proceedings shall be conducted on the basis of documents and other materials. *(Added by Stats.1988, c. 23, § 1, eff. March 7, 1988.)*

§ 1297.242.   Oral hearings

Unless the parties have agreed that no oral hearings shall be held, the arbitral tribunal shall hold oral hearings at an appropriate state of the proceedings, if so requested by a party. *(Added by Stats.1988, c. 23, § 1, eff. March 7, 1988.)*

Research References

Rutter, Cal. Practice Guide: A.D.R. Ch. 5-K, K. Arbitration of International Commercial Disputes.

§ 1297.243.   Notice of hearings and meetings

The parties shall be given sufficient advance notice of any hearing and of any meeting of the arbitral tribunal for the purpose of inspection of documents, goods, or other property. *(Added by Stats.1988, c. 23, § 1, eff. March 7, 1988.)*

§ 1297.244.   Statements, documents, etc. by one party to tribunal; communication to other party

All statements, documents, or other information supplied to, or applications made to, the arbitral tribunal by one party shall be communicated to the other party, and any expert report or evidentiary document on which the arbitral tribunal may rely in making its decision shall be communicated to the parties. *(Added by Stats.1988, c. 23, § 1, eff. March 7, 1988.)*

§ 1297.245. Oral hearings and meetings in camera

Unless otherwise agreed by the parties, all oral hearings and meetings in arbitral proceedings shall be held in camera. *(Added by Stats.1988, c. 23, § 1, eff. March 7, 1988.)*

Research References

Rutter, Cal. Practice Guide: A.D.R. Ch. 5-K, K. Arbitration of International Commercial Disputes.

ARTICLE 8. DEFAULT OF A PARTY

Section
1297.251.   Claimant's failure to communicate statement of claim; termination of proceedings.
1297.252.   Respondent's failure to communicate statement of defense; continuance of proceedings.
1297.253.   Failure to appear at hearing or produce evidence.

§ 1297.251. Claimant's failure to communicate statement of claim; termination of proceedings

Unless otherwise agreed by the parties, where, without showing sufficient cause, the claimant fails to communicate his or her statement of claim in accordance with Sections 1297.231 and 1297.232, the arbitral tribunal shall terminate the proceedings. *(Added by Stats.1988, c. 23, § 1, eff. March 7, 1988.)*

§ 1297.252. Respondent's failure to communicate statement of defense; continuance of proceedings

Unless otherwise agreed by the parties, where, without showing sufficient cause, the respondent fails to communicate his or her statement of defense in accordance with Sections 1297.231 and 1297.232, the arbitral tribunal shall continue the proceedings without treating that failure in itself as an admission of the claimant's allegations. *(Added by Stats.1988, c. 23, § 1, eff. March 7, 1988.)*

§ 1297.253. Failure to appear at hearing or produce evidence

Unless otherwise agreed by the parties, where, without showing sufficient cause, a party fails to appear at an oral hearing or to produce documentary evidence, the arbitral tribunal may continue with the proceedings and make the arbitral award on the evidence before it. *(Added by Stats.1988, c. 23, § 1, eff. March 7, 1988.)*

ARTICLE 9. EXPERT APPOINTED BY ARBITRAL TRIBUNAL

Section
1297.261.   Appointment of expert; requirement of party to furnish information, documents, etc.
1297.262.   Participation of expert in oral hearing.

§ 1297.261. Appointment of expert; requirement of party to furnish information, documents, etc.

Unless otherwise agreed by the parties, the arbitral tribunal may appoint one or more experts to report to it on specific issues to be determined by the arbitral tribunal, and require a party to give the expert any relevant information or to produce, or to provide access to, any relevant documents, goods, or other property for his or her inspection. *(Added by Stats.1988, c. 23, § 1, eff. March 7, 1988.)*

Research References

Rutter, Cal. Practice Guide: A.D.R. Ch. 5-K, K. Arbitration of International Commercial Disputes.

§ 1297.262. Participation of expert in oral hearing

Unless otherwise agreed by the parties, if a party so requests or if the arbitral tribunal considers it necessary, the expert shall, after delivery of his or her written or oral report, participate in an oral hearing where the parties have the opportunity to question the expert and to present expert witnesses on the points at issue. *(Added by Stats.1988, c. 23, § 1, eff. March 7, 1988.)*

ARTICLE 10. COURT ASSISTANCE IN TAKING EVIDENCE AND CONSOLIDATING ARBITRATIONS

Section
1297.271.   Request of superior court for assistance on taking evidence; subpoena, witness compensation.
1297.272.   Consolidations of arbitrations; actions of superior court.
1297.273.   Consolidations of arbitrations; agreement of parties.

§ 1297.271. Request of superior court for assistance on taking evidence; subpoena, witness compensation

The arbitral tribunal, or a party with the approval of the arbitral tribunal, may request from the superior court assistance in taking evidence and the court may execute the request within its competence and according to its rules on taking evidence. In addition, a subpoena may issue as provided in Section 1282.6, in which case the witness compensation provisions of Section 1283.2 shall apply. *(Added by Stats.1988, c. 23, § 1, eff. March 7, 1988.)*

§ 1297.272. Consolidations of arbitrations; actions of superior court

Where the parties to two or more arbitration agreements have agreed, in their respective arbitration agreements or otherwise, to consolidate the arbitrations arising out of those arbitration agreements, the superior court may, on application by one party with the consent of all the other parties to those arbitration agreements, do one or more of the following:

(a) Order the arbitrations to be consolidated on terms the court considers just and necessary.

(b) Where all the parties cannot agree on an arbitral tribunal for the consolidated arbitration, appoint an arbitral tribunal in accordance with Section 1297.118.

(c) Where all the parties cannot agree on any other matter necessary to conduct the consolidated arbitration, make any other order it considers necessary. *(Added by Stats.1988, c. 23, § 1, eff. March 7, 1988.)*

§ 1297.273. Consolidations of arbitrations; agreement of parties

Nothing in this article shall be construed to prevent the parties to two or more arbitrations from agreeing to consolidate those arbitrations and taking any steps that are necessary to effect that consolidation. *(Added by Stats.1988, c. 23, § 1, eff. March 7, 1988.)*

CHAPTER 6. MAKING OF ARBITRAL AWARD AND TERMINATION OF PROCEEDINGS

ARTICLE 1. RULES APPLICABLE TO SUBSTANCE OF DISPUTE

Section
1297.281. Rules of law designated by parties.
1297.282. Designation by parties of substantive and not conflict of law rules.
1297.283. Application of appropriate law by tribunal if parties fail to designate law.
1297.284. Decision ex aequo et bono or as amiable compositeur if authorized.
1297.285. Decision of tribunal in accord with terms of contract and usages of trade.

§ 1297.281. Rules of law designated by parties

The arbitral tribunal shall decide the dispute in accordance with the rules of law designated by the parties as applicable to the substance of the dispute. *(Added by Stats.1988, c. 23, § 1, eff. March 7, 1988.)*

Research References

Rutter, Cal. Practice Guide: A.D.R. Ch. 5-K, K. Arbitration of International Commercial Disputes.

§ 1297.282. Designation by parties of substantive and not conflict of law rules

Any designation by the parties of the law or legal system of a given state shall be construed, unless otherwise expressed, as directly referring to the substantive law of that state and not to its conflict of laws rules. *(Added by Stats.1988, c. 23, § 1, eff. March 7, 1988.)*

§ 1297.283. Application of appropriate law by tribunal if parties fail to designate law

Failing any designation of the law under Section 1297.282 by the parties, the arbitral tribunal shall apply the rules of law it considers to be appropriate given all the circumstances surrounding the dispute. *(Added by Stats.1988, c. 23, § 1, eff. March 7, 1988.)*

Research References

Rutter, Cal. Practice Guide: A.D.R. Ch. 5-K, K. Arbitration of International Commercial Disputes.

§ 1297.284. Decision ex aequo et bono or as amiable compositeur if authorized

The arbitral tribunal shall decide ex aequo et bono or as amiable compositeur, if the parties have expressly authorized it to do so. *(Added by Stats.1988, c. 23, § 1, eff. March 7, 1988.)*

§ 1297.285. Decision of tribunal in accord with terms of contract and usages of trade

In all cases, the arbitral tribunal shall decide in accordance with the terms of the contract and shall take into account the usages of the trade applicable to the transaction. *(Added by Stats.1988, c. 23, § 1, eff. March 7, 1988.)*

Research References

Rutter, Cal. Practice Guide: A.D.R. Ch. 5-K, K. Arbitration of International Commercial Disputes.

ARTICLE 2. DECISIONMAKING BY PANEL OF ARBITRATORS

Section
1297.291. Majority vote in proceedings with more than one arbitrator; decisions on procedural questions by presiding arbitrator.

§ 1297.291. Majority vote in proceedings with more than one arbitrator; decisions on procedural questions by presiding arbitrator

Unless otherwise agreed by the parties, in arbitral proceedings with more than one arbitrator, any decision of the arbitral tribunal shall be made by a majority of all of its members.

Notwithstanding this section, if authorized by the parties or all the members of the arbitral tribunal, questions of procedure may be decided by a presiding arbitrator. *(Added by Stats.1988, c. 23, § 1, eff. March 7, 1988.)*

ARTICLE 3. SETTLEMENT

Section
1297.301. Encouragement of settlement; mediation, conciliation, etc.
1297.302. Termination of proceedings; record of award.
1297.303. Arbitral award on agreed terms; law governing.
1297.304. Arbitral award on agreed terms; status and effect.

§ 1297.301. Encouragement of settlement; mediation, conciliation, etc.

It is not incompatible with an arbitration agreement for an arbitral tribunal to encourage settlement of the dispute and, with the agreement of the parties, the arbitral tribunal may use mediation, conciliation, or other procedures at any time during the arbitral proceedings to encourage settlement. *(Added by Stats.1988, c. 23, § 1, eff. March 7, 1988.)*

§ 1297.302. Termination of proceedings; record of award

If, during arbitral proceedings, the parties settle the dispute, the arbitral tribunal shall terminate the proceedings and, if requested by the parties and not objected to by the arbitral tribunal, record the settlement in the form of an arbitral award on agreed terms. *(Added by Stats.1988, c. 23, § 1, eff. March 7, 1988.)*

§ 1297.303. Arbitral award on agreed terms; law governing

An arbitral award on agreed terms shall be made in accordance with Article 4 (commencing with Section 1297.311) of this chapter and shall state that it is an arbitral award. *(Added by Stats.1988, c. 23, § 1, eff. March 7, 1988.)*

§ 1297.304. Arbitral award on agreed terms; status and effect

An arbitral award on agreed terms has the same status and effect as any other arbitral award on the substance of the dispute. *(Added by Stats.1988, c. 23, § 1, eff. March 7, 1988.)*

ARTICLE 4. FORM AND CONTENT OF ARBITRAL AWARD

Section
1297.311. Award in writing; signatures.

§ 1297.311. Award in writing; signatures

An arbitral award shall be made in writing and shall be signed by the members of the arbitral tribunal. *(Added by Stats.1988, c. 23, § 1, eff. March 7, 1988.)*

Research References

Rutter, Cal. Practice Guide: A.D.R. Ch. 5-K, K. Arbitration of International Commercial Disputes.

§ 1297.312. Signatures; majority of members; reasons for omitted signatures

For the purposes of Section 1297.311, in arbitral proceedings with more than one arbitrator, the signatures of the majority of all the members of the arbitral tribunal shall be sufficient so long as the reason for any omitted signature is stated. *(Added by Stats.1988, c. 23, § 1, eff. March 7, 1988.)*

§ 1297.313. Basis for award; statement of reasons; exceptions

The arbitral award shall state the reasons upon which it is based, unless the parties have agreed that no reasons are to be given, or the award is an arbitral award on agreed terms under Article 3 (commencing with Section 1297.301) of this chapter. *(Added by Stats.1988, c. 23, § 1, eff. March 7, 1988.)*

Research References

Rutter, Cal. Practice Guide: A.D.R. Ch. 5-K, K. Arbitration of International Commercial Disputes.

§ 1297.314. Date of award and place of arbitration

The arbitral award shall state its date and the place of arbitration as determined in accordance with Article 3 (commencing with Section 1297.201) of Chapter 5 and the award shall be deemed to have been made at that place. *(Added by Stats.1988, c. 23, § 1, eff. March 7, 1988.)*

§ 1297.315. Signed copy; delivery to each party

After the arbitral award is made, a signed copy shall be delivered to each party. *(Added by Stats.1988, c. 23, § 1, eff. March 7, 1988.)*

§ 1297.316. Interim award; enforcement

The arbitral tribunal may, at any time during the arbitral proceedings, make an interim arbitral award on any matter with respect to which it may make a final arbitral award. The interim award may be enforced in the same manner as a final arbitral award. *(Added by Stats.1988, c. 23, § 1, eff. March 7, 1988.)*

§ 1297.317. Interest

Unless otherwise agreed by the parties, the arbitral tribunal may award interest. *(Added by Stats.1988, c. 23, § 1, eff. March 7, 1988.)*

§ 1297.318. Costs; inclusions

(a) Unless otherwise agreed by the parties, the costs of an arbitration shall be at the discretion of the arbitral tribunal.

(b) In making an order for costs, the arbitral tribunal may include as costs any of the following:

(1) The fees and expenses of the arbitrators and expert witnesses.

(2) Legal fees and expenses.

(3) Any administration fees of the institution supervising the arbitration, if any.

(4) Any other expenses incurred in connection with the arbitral proceedings.

(c) In making an order for costs, the arbitral tribunal may specify any of the following:

(1) The party entitled to costs.

(2) The party who shall pay the costs.

(3) The amount of costs or method of determining that amount.

(4) The manner in which the costs shall be paid. *(Added by Stats.1988, c. 23, § 1, eff. March 7, 1988.)*

Research References

Rutter, Cal. Practice Guide: A.D.R. Ch. 5-K, K. Arbitration of International Commercial Disputes.

ARTICLE 5. TERMINATION OF PROCEEDINGS

§ 1297.321. Means; finality of award

The arbitral proceedings are terminated by the final arbitral award or by an order of the arbitral tribunal under Section 1297.322. The award shall be final upon the expiration of the applicable periods in Article 6 (commencing with Section 1297.331) of this chapter. *(Added by Stats.1988, c. 23, § 1, eff. March 7, 1988.)*

§ 1297.322. Order for termination; circumstances

The arbitral tribunal shall issue an order for the termination of the arbitral proceedings where any of the following occurs:

(a) The claimant withdraws his or her claim, unless the respondent objects to the order and the arbitral tribunal recognizes a legitimate interest on the respondent's part in obtaining a final settlement of the dispute.

(b) The parties agree on the termination of the proceedings.

(c) The arbitral tribunal finds that the continuation of the proceedings has for any other reason become unnecessary or impossible. *(Added by Stats.1988, c. 23, § 1, eff. March 7, 1988.)*

§ 1297.323. Mandate of tribunal; termination

Subject to Article 6 (commencing with Section 1297.331) of this chapter, the mandate of the arbitral tribunal terminates with the termination of the arbitral proceedings. *(Added by Stats. 1988, c. 23, § 1, eff. March 7, 1988.)*

ARTICLE 6. CORRECTION AND INTERPRETATION OF AWARDS AND ADDITIONAL AWARDS

§ 1297.331.   Correction of errors; interpretations; time

Within 30 days after receipt of the arbitral award, unless another period of time has been agreed upon by the parties:

(a) A party may request the arbitral tribunal to correct in the arbitral award any computation errors, any clerical or typographical errors, or any other errors of a similar nature.

(b) A party may, if agreed by the parties, request the arbitral tribunal to give an interpretation of a specific point or part of the arbitral award. *(Added by Stats.1988, c. 23, § 1, eff. March 7, 1988.)*

Research References

Rutter, Cal. Practice Guide: A.D.R. Ch. 5-K, K. Arbitration of International Commercial Disputes.

§ 1297.332.   Duty of tribunal to correct or interpret award; time

If the arbitral tribunal considers any request made under Section 1297.331 to be justified, it shall make the correction or give the interpretation within 30 days after receipt of the request and the interpretation shall form part of the arbitral award. *(Added by Stats.1988, c. 23, § 1, eff. March 7, 1988.)*

§ 1297.333.   Correction of errors by tribunal on its own initiative; time

The arbitral tribunal may correct any error of the type referred to in subdivision (a) of Section 1297.331, on its own initiative, within 30 days after the date of the arbitral award. *(Added by Stats.1988, c. 23, § 1, eff. March 7, 1988.)*

§ 1297.334.   Request for additional award; time

Unless otherwise agreed by the parties, a party may request, within 30 days after receipt of the arbitral award, the arbitral tribunal to make an additional arbitral award as to the claims presented in the arbitral proceedings but omitted from the arbitral award. *(Added by Stats.1988, c. 23, § 1, eff. March 7, 1988.)*

§ 1297.335.   Additional award; time

If the arbitral tribunal considers any request made under Section 1297.334 to be justified, it shall make the additional arbitral award within 60 days after receipt of the request. *(Added by Stats.1988, c. 23, § 1, eff. March 7, 1988.)*

§ 1297.336.   Extension of time for tribunal action under this article

The arbitral tribunal may extend, if necessary, the period of time within which it shall make a correction, give an interpretation, or make an additional arbitral award under Section 1297.331 or 1297.334. *(Added by Stats.1988, c. 23, § 1, eff. March 7, 1988.)*

§ 1297.337.   Construction with other laws

Article 4 (commencing with Section 1297.311) of this chapter applies to a correction or interpretation of the arbitral award or to an additional arbitral award made under this section. *(Added by Stats.1988, c. 23, § 1, eff. March 7, 1988.)*

Research References

Rutter, Cal. Practice Guide: A.D.R. Ch. 5-K, K. Arbitration of International Commercial Disputes.

CHAPTER 7.   CONCILIATION

ARTICLE 1.   APPOINTMENT OF CONCILIATORS

§ 1297.341.   State policy; resolution of disputes by conciliation

It is the policy of the State of California to encourage parties to an international commercial agreement or transaction which qualifies for arbitration or conciliation pursuant to Section 1297.13, to resolve disputes arising from such agreements or transactions through conciliation. The parties may select or permit an arbitral tribunal or other third party to select one or more persons to serve as the conciliator or conciliators who shall assist the parties in an independent and impartial manner in their attempt to reach an amicable settlement of their dispute. *(Added by Stats.1988, c. 23, § 1, eff. March 7, 1988.)*

§ 1297.342.   Principles, rights, obligations, etc. or guides for conciliators

The conciliator or conciliators shall be guided by principles of objectivity, fairness, and justice, giving consideration to, among other things, the rights and obligations of the parties, the usages of the trade concerned and the circumstances surrounding the dispute, including any previous practices between the parties. *(Added by Stats.1988, c. 23, § 1, eff. March 7, 1988.)*

§ 1297.343.   Conduct of proceedings; criteria; other codes

The conciliator or conciliators may conduct the conciliation proceedings in such a manner as they consider appropriate, taking into account the circumstances of the case, the wishes of the parties, and the desirability of a speedy settlement of the dispute. Except as otherwise provided in this title, other provisions of this code, the Evidence Code, or the California Rules of Court, shall not apply to conciliation proceedings brought under this title. *(Added by Stats.1988, c. 23, § 1, eff. March 7, 1988.)*

ARTICLE 2.   REPRESENTATION AND ASSISTANCE

§ 1297.351.   Choice of parties; qualification

The parties may appear in person or be represented or assisted by any person of their choice. A person assisting or representing a party need not be a member of the legal profession or licensed to practice law in California. *(Added by Stats.1988, c. 23, § 1, eff. March 7, 1988.)*

Research References

Rutter, Cal. Practice Guide: A.D.R. Ch. 5-H, H. Conduct of Arbitration Proceedings.

Rutter, Cal. Practice Guide: A.D.R. Ch. 5-K, K. Arbitration of International Commercial Disputes.

Rutter, Cal. Practice Guide: Prof. Responsibility Ch. 1-D, D. Unauthorized Practice of Law.

ARTICLE 3.   REPORT OF CONCILIATORS

Section
1297.361.   Draft conciliation settlement; contents; copies.
1297.362.   Acceptance of settlement not required.

§ 1297.361.   Draft conciliation settlement; contents; copies

At any time during the proceedings, the conciliator or conciliators may prepare a draft conciliation settlement which may include the assessment and apportionment of costs between the parties, and send copies to the parties, specifying the time within which they must signify their approval. *(Added by Stats.1988, c. 23, § 1, eff. March 7, 1988.)*

§ 1297.362.   Acceptance of settlement not required

No party may be required to accept any settlement proposed by the conciliator or conciliators. *(Added by Stats.1988, c. 23, § 1, eff. March 7, 1988.)*

ARTICLE 4.   CONFIDENTIALITY

Section
1297.371.   Admissibility of evidence; nondisclosure; exception.

§ 1297.371.   Admissibility of evidence; nondisclosure; exception

When persons agree to participate in conciliation under this title:

(a) Evidence of anything said or of any admission made in the course of the conciliation is not admissible in evidence, and disclosure of any such evidence shall not be compelled, in any civil action in which, pursuant to law, testimony may be compelled to be given. However, this subdivision does not limit the admissibility of evidence if all parties participating in conciliation consent to its disclosure.

(b) In the event that any such evidence is offered in contravention of this section, the arbitration tribunal or the court shall make any order which it considers to be appropriate to deal with the matter, including, without limitation, orders restricting the introduction of evidence, or dismissing the case without prejudice.

(c) Unless the document otherwise provides, no document prepared for the purpose of, or in the course of, or pursuant to, the conciliation, or any copy thereof, is admissible in evidence, and disclosure of any such document shall not be compelled, in any arbitration or civil action in which, pursuant to law, testimony may be compelled to be given. *(Added by Stats.1988, c. 23, § 1, eff. March 7, 1988.)*

ARTICLE 5.   STAY OF ARBITRATION AND RESORT TO OTHER PROCEEDINGS

Section
1297.381.   Agreement to stay judicial or arbitral proceedings; time period.
1297.382.   Limitations; tolling.

§ 1297.381.   Agreement to stay judicial or arbitral proceedings; time period

The agreement of the parties to submit a dispute to conciliation shall be deemed an agreement between or among those parties to stay all judicial or arbitral proceedings from the commencement of conciliation until the termination of conciliation proceedings. *(Added by Stats.1988, c. 23, § 1, eff. March 7, 1988.)*

§ 1297.382.   Limitations; tolling

All applicable limitation periods including periods of prescription shall be tolled or extended upon the commencement of conciliation proceedings to conciliate a dispute under this title and all limitation periods shall remain tolled and periods of prescription extended as to all parties to the conciliation proceedings until the 10th day following the termination of conciliation proceedings. For purposes of this article, conciliation proceedings are deemed to have commenced as soon as (a) a party has requested conciliation of a particular dispute or disputes, and (b) the other party or parties agree to participate in the conciliation proceeding. *(Added by Stats.1988, c. 23, § 1, eff. March 7, 1988.)*

ARTICLE 6.   TERMINATION

Section
1297.391.   Circumstances.
1297.392.   Particular parties.
1297.393.   Conciliator as arbitrator; ineligibility for appointment; exception.
1297.394.   Nonwaiver of rights or remedies by submission to conciliation.

§ 1297.391.   Circumstances

The conciliation proceedings may be terminated as to all parties by any of the following:

(a) A written declaration of the conciliator or conciliators, after consultation with the parties, to the effect that further efforts at conciliation are no longer justified, on the date of the declaration.

(b) A written declaration of the parties addressed to the conciliator or conciliators to the effect that the conciliation proceedings are terminated, on the date of the declaration.

(c) The signing of a settlement agreement by all of the parties, on the date of the agreement. *(Added by Stats.1988, c. 23, § 1, eff. March 7, 1988.)*

§ 1297.392.   Particular parties

The conciliation proceedings may be terminated as to particular parties by either of the following:

(a) A written declaration of a party to the other party and the conciliator or conciliators, if appointed, to the effect that the conciliation proceedings shall be terminated as to that particular party, on the date of the declaration.

(b) The signing of a settlement agreement by some of the parties, on the date of the agreement. *(Added by Stats.1988, c. 23, § 1, eff. March 7, 1988.)*

§ 1297.393. Conciliator as arbitrator; ineligibility for appointment; exception

No person who has served as conciliator may be appointed as an arbitrator for, or take part in any arbitral or judicial proceedings in, the same dispute unless all parties manifest their consent to such participation or the rules adopted for conciliation or arbitration otherwise provide. *(Added by Stats.1988, c. 23, § 1, eff. March 7, 1988.)*

§ 1297.394. Nonwaiver of rights or remedies by submission to conciliation

By submitting to conciliation, no party shall be deemed to have waived any rights or remedies which that party would have had if conciliation had not been initiated, other than those set forth in any settlement agreement which results from the conciliation. *(Added by Stats.1988, c. 23, § 1, eff. March 7, 1988.)*

ARTICLE 7. ENFORCEABILITY OF DECREE

Section
1297.401. Written conciliation agreement as arbitration award; effect.

§ 1297.401. Written conciliation agreement as arbitration award; effect

If the conciliation succeeds in settling the dispute, and the result of the conciliation is reduced to writing and signed by the conciliator or conciliators and the parties or their representatives, the written agreement shall be treated as an arbitral award rendered by an arbitral tribunal duly constituted in and pursuant to the laws of this state, and shall have the same force and effect as a final award in arbitration. *(Added by Stats.1988, c. 23, § 1, eff. March 7, 1988.)*

ARTICLE 8. COSTS

Section
1297.411. Costs; inclusions.
1297.412. Equality of costs among parties; expenses.

§ 1297.411. Costs; inclusions

Upon termination of the conciliation proceedings, the conciliator shall fix the costs of the conciliation and give written notice thereof to the parties. As used in this article, "costs" includes only the following:

(a) A reasonable fee to be paid to the conciliator or conciliators.

(b) The travel and other reasonable expenses of the conciliator or conciliators.

(c) The travel and other reasonable expenses of witnesses requested by the conciliator or conciliators with the consent of the parties.

(d) The cost of any expert advice requested by the conciliator or conciliators with the consent of the parties.

(e) The cost of any court. *(Added by Stats.1988, c. 23, § 1, eff. March 7, 1988.)*

§ 1297.412. Equality of costs among parties; expenses

These costs shall be borne equally by the parties unless the settlement agreement provides for a different apportionment. All other expenses incurred by a party shall be borne by that party. *(Added by Stats.1988, c. 23, § 1, eff. March 7, 1988.)*

ARTICLE 9. EFFECT ON JURISDICTION

Section
1297.421. No consent to court jurisdiction upon failure of conciliation.

§ 1297.421. No consent to court jurisdiction upon failure of conciliation

Neither the request for conciliation, the consent to participate in the conciliation proceedings, the participation in such proceedings, nor the entering into a conciliation agreement or settlement shall be deemed as consent to the jurisdiction of any court in this state in the event conciliation fails. *(Added by Stats.1988, c. 23, § 1, eff. March 7, 1988.)*

ARTICLE 10. IMMUNITY OF CONCILIATORS AND PARTIES

Section
1297.431. Service of process; immunity of participants in conciliation.
1297.432. Action for damages; nonliability of conciliators.

§ 1297.431. Service of process; immunity of participants in conciliation

Neither the conciliator or conciliators, the parties, nor their representatives shall be subject to service of process on any civil matter while they are present in this state for the purpose of arranging for or participating in conciliation pursuant to this title. *(Added by Stats.1988, c. 23, § 1, eff. March 7, 1988.)*

§ 1297.432. Action for damages; nonliability of conciliators

No person who serves as a conciliator shall be held liable in an action for damages resulting from any act or omission in the performance of his or her role as a conciliator in any proceeding subject to this title. *(Added by Stats.1988, c. 23, § 1, eff. March 7, 1988.)*

Research References

Rutter, Cal. Practice Guide: A.D.R. Ch. 3-B, B. Commencing Mediation Process.

Title 9.4

REAL ESTATE CONTRACT ARBITRATION

Section
1298. Contracts; provision title; print type; notice provision; jurisdiction of court; escrowholder's right to interpleader.
1298.5. Recording notice of pending action; waiver of arbitration.
1298.7. Actions for bodily injury, wrongful death, or actions under §§ 337.1, 337.15.
1298.8. Operative date; application of title.

§ 1298. Contracts; provision title; print type; notice provision; jurisdiction of court; escrowholder's right to interpleader

(a) Whenever any contract to convey real property, or contemplated to convey real property in the future, including marketing contracts, deposit receipts, real property sales contracts as defined in Section 2985 of the Civil Code, leases together with options to purchase, or ground leases coupled with improvements, but not including powers of sale contained in deeds of trust or mortgages, contains a provision for binding arbitration of any dispute between the principals in the transaction, the contract shall have that provision clearly titled "ARBITRATION OF DISPUTES."

If a provision for binding arbitration is included in a printed contract, it shall be set out in at least 8–point bold type or in contrasting red in at least 8–point type, and if the provision is included in a typed contract, it shall be set out in capital letters.

(b) Whenever any contract or agreement between principals and agents in real property sales transactions, including listing agreements, as defined in Section 1086 of the Civil Code, contains a provision requiring binding arbitration of any dispute between the principals and agents in the transaction, the contract or agreement shall have that provision clearly titled "ARBITRATION OF DISPUTES."

If a provision for binding arbitration is included in a printed contract, it shall be set out in at least 8–point bold type or in contrasting red in at least 8–point type, and if the provision is included in a typed contract, it shall be set out in capital letters.

(c) Immediately before the line or space provided for the parties to indicate their assent or nonassent to the arbitration provision described in subdivision (a) or (b), and immediately following that arbitration provision, the following shall appear:

"NOTICE: BY INITIALLING IN THE SPACE BELOW YOU ARE AGREEING TO HAVE ANY DISPUTE ARISING OUT OF THE MATTERS INCLUDED IN THE 'ARBITRATION OF DISPUTES' PROVISION DECIDED BY NEUTRAL ARBITRATION AS PROVIDED BY CALIFORNIA LAW AND YOU ARE GIVING UP ANY RIGHTS YOU MIGHT POSSESS TO HAVE THE DISPUTE LITIGATED IN A COURT OR JURY TRIAL. BY INITIALLING IN THE SPACE BELOW YOU ARE GIVING UP YOUR JUDICIAL RIGHTS TO DISCOVERY AND APPEAL, UNLESS THOSE RIGHTS ARE SPECIFICALLY INCLUDED IN THE 'ARBITRATION OF DISPUTES' PROVISION. IF YOU REFUSE TO SUBMIT TO ARBITRATION AFTER AGREEING TO THIS PROVISION, YOU MAY BE COMPELLED TO ARBITRATE UNDER THE AUTHORITY OF THE CALIFORNIA CODE OF CIVIL PROCEDURE. YOUR AGREEMENT TO THIS ARBITRATION PROVISION IS VOLUNTARY."

"WE HAVE READ AND UNDERSTAND THE FOREGOING AND AGREE TO SUBMIT DISPUTES ARISING OUT OF THE MATTERS INCLUDED IN THE 'ARBITRATION OF DISPUTES' PROVISION TO NEUTRAL ARBITRATION."

If the above provision is included in a printed contract, it shall be set out either in at least 10–point bold type or in contrasting red print in at least 8–point bold type, and if the provision is included in a typed contract, it shall be set out in capital letters.

(d) Nothing in this section shall be construed to diminish the authority of any court of competent jurisdiction with respect to real property transactions in areas involving court supervision or jurisdiction, including, but not limited to, probate, marital dissolution, foreclosure of liens, unlawful detainer, or eminent domain.

(e) In the event an arbitration provision is contained in an escrow instruction, it shall not preclude the right of an escrow-holder to institute an interpleader action. *(Added by Stats.1988, c. 881, § 1, operative July 1, 1989. Amended by Stats.1989, c. 22, § 1, eff. May 25, 1989, operative July 1, 1989.)*

Validity

This section was held to be preempted by federal law, the United States Arbitration Act, in Westra v. Marcus &

Millichap Real Estate Inv. Brokerage Co., Inc. (App. 1 Dist. 2005) 28 Cal.Rptr.3d 752, 129 Cal.App.4th 759.

Research References

California Real Estate Forms (Miller & Starr) § 1:22, Agreement of Purchase and Sale--Multi-Property.

California Real Estate Forms (Miller & Starr) § 1:30, Planned Development Deposit Receipt and Agreement of Sale..

California Real Estate Forms (Miller & Starr) § 1:31, Condominium Deposit Receipt and Agreement of Sale.

California Real Estate Forms (Miller & Starr) § 1:33, Real Estate Purchase Contract and Receipt for Deposit--Income Property.

California Real Estate Forms (Miller & Starr) § 1:76, Standard Offer, Agreement and Escrow Instructions for Purchase of Real Estate.

Rutter, Cal. Practice Guide: A.D.R. Ch. 5-A, A. General Considerations.

Rutter, Cal. Practice Guide: A.D.R. Ch. 5-B, B. Federal vs. State Law Governing.

Rutter, Cal. Practice Guide: A.D.R. Ch. 5-D, D. Defenses to Enforcement.

Rutter, Cal. Practice Guide: A.D.R. Ch. 5-H, H. Conduct of Arbitration Proceedings.

Rutter, Cal. Practice Guide: A.D.R. App. D Form 64, Real Property-Sale-Deposit Receipts, Escrow Instructions, Listing Agreements.

Rutter, Cal. Practice Guide: A.D.R. Ch. 5-D, Outline D.

Rutter, Cal. Practice Guide: Civil Trials & Evidence Ch. 2-E, E. Waiver of Jury Trial.

Rutter, Cal. Practice Guide: Real Prop. Transactions Ch. 2-E, E. Listing Agreements.

Rutter, Cal. Practice Guide: Real Prop. Transactions Ch. 4-E, E. Drafting the Purchase and Sale Agreement-Terms and Conditions.

Miller and Starr California Real Estate § 3:4, "Broker" Defined; Broker as an Agent.

Miller and Starr California Real Estate § 3:7, Agent's Authority by Common Law.

Miller and Starr California Real Estate § 24:2, Definition and Explanation of Covenants that "Run With the Land".

Miller and Starr California Real Estate § 5:36, Required Terms of a Listing.

Miller and Starr California Real Estate § 24:24, Nature of the Right to Enforce Restrictions; Appurtenant to Benefited Property.

Miller and Starr California Real Estate § 24:26, Rights of Enforcement--Remedies for Breach.

Miller and Starr California Real Estate § 35:23, Public Policy in Favor of Arbitration.

Miller and Starr California Real Estate § 35:26, Form and Contents of the Arbitration Agreement.

Miller and Starr California Real Estate § 35:28, Real Estate Contracts and Listing Agreements.

Miller and Starr California Real Estate § 35:38, Issues Subject to Arbitration--Examples.

Miller and Starr California Real Estate § 25B:113, Arbitration or Other Resolution of Disputes With the Subdivider.

13 NO. 6 Miller & Starr, California Real Estate Newsalert 1, Using Basura to Make Construction Defect Claims Arbitrable, or Woodside to Send Them to a Referee.

16 NO. 3 Miller & Starr, California Real Estate Newsalert 3, Commercial Arbitration.

16 NO. 1 Miller & Starr, California Real Estate Newsalert 7. for Arbitration Administered by the National Association of Securities Dealers, The Federal Securities Exchange Act Preempts Both the California Ethics Standards Established by the Judicial Council for Persons Serving...

19 NO. 5 Miller & Starr, California Real Estate Newsalert 4, Alternative Dispute Resolution.

19 NO. 5 Miller & Starr, California Real Estate Newsalert 27, Specific Contracts.

21 NO. 2 Miller & Starr, California Real Estate Newsalert 2, Alternative Dispute Resolution.

21 NO. 4 Miller & Starr, California Real Estate Newsalert 19, Alternative Dispute Resolution.

22 NO. 1 Miller & Starr, California Real Estate Newsalert 4, Alternative Dispute Resolution.

6 Witkin Cal. Proc. 5th Proceedings Without Trial § 503, (S 503) in General.

6 Witkin Cal. Proc. 5th Proceedings Without Trial § 505, (S 505) Real Estate Contracts.

6 Witkin Cal. Proc. 5th Proceedings Without Trial § 510, (S 510) Illustrations.

6 Witkin Cal. Proc. 5th Proceedings Without Trial § 513, (S 513) in General.

6 Witkin Cal. Proc. 5th Proceedings Without Trial § 515, (S 515) Illustrations.

12 Witkin, California Summary 10th Real Property § 502, Arbitration Provision in Real Property Sales Contract.

1 Witkin Cal. Summ. 10th Contracts § 14, Applicability.

1 Witkin Cal. Summ. 10th Contracts § 335, Purchase Subject to Covenants, Conditions, and Restrictions.

§ 1298.5. Recording notice of pending action; waiver of arbitration

Any party to an action who proceeds to record a notice of pending action pursuant to Section 409 shall not thereby waive any right of arbitration which that person may have pursuant to a written agreement to arbitrate, nor any right to petition the court to compel arbitration pursuant to Section 1281.2, if, in filing an action to record that notice, the party at the same time presents to the court an application that the action be stayed pending the arbitration of any dispute which is claimed to be arbitrable and which is relevant to the action. *(Added by Stats.1988, c. 881, § 1, operative July 1, 1989.)*

Research References

California Real Estate Forms (Miller & Starr) § 1:94, California Residential Purchase Agreement and Joint Escrow Instructions.

Rutter, Cal. Practice Guide: A.D.R. Ch. 5-D, D. Defenses to Enforcement.

Rutter, Cal. Practice Guide: A.D.R. App. D Form 64, Real Property-Sale-Deposit Receipts, Escrow Instructions, Listing Agreements.

Miller and Starr California Real Estate § 35:63, Waiver by Participation in Litigation.

Miller and Starr California Real Estate § 35:83, Authority of the Arbitrators; Issues and Remedies.

Miller and Starr California Real Estate § 11:148, Nature and Effect of a Lis Pendens.

19 NO. 6 Miller & Starr, California Real Estate Newsalert 18, Recording and Priorities.

§ 1298.7. Actions for bodily injury, wrongful death, or actions under §§ 337.1, 337.15

In the event an arbitration provision is included in a contract or agreement covered by this title, it shall not preclude or limit any right of action for bodily injury or wrongful death, or any right of action to which Section 337.1 or 337.15 is applicable. *(Added by Stats.1988, c. 881, § 1, operative July 1, 1989.)*

Validity

This section was held to be preempted by the Federal Arbitration Act in the decision of Shepard v. Edward Mackay Enterprises, Inc. (App. 3 Dist. 2007) 56 Cal. Rptr.3d 326, 148 Cal.App.4th 1092.

Research References

Rutter, Cal. Practice Guide: A.D.R. Ch. 5-B, B. Federal vs. State Law Governing.

Rutter, Cal. Practice Guide: A.D.R. Ch. 5-C, C. Enforceability of Arbitration Agreements-In General.

Rutter, Cal. Practice Guide: A.D.R. Ch. 5-D, D. Defenses to Enforcement.

Rutter, Cal. Practice Guide: A.D.R. Ch. 6-C, C. Referees.

Rutter, Cal. Practice Guide: A.D.R. App. D Form 64, Real Property-Sale-Deposit Receipts, Escrow Instructions, Listing Agreements.

Rutter, Cal. Practice Guide: Real Prop. Transactions Ch. 4-E, E. Drafting the Purchase and Sale Agreement-Terms and Conditions.

Rutter, Cal. Practice Guide: Real Prop. Transactions Ch. 4-E Outline, Outline E.

Miller and Starr California Real Estate § 27:47, Provisions for Arbitration and Mediation of Disputes--Generally.

Miller and Starr California Real Estate § 35:19, Contract Provisions and Enforceability.

Miller and Starr California Real Estate § 35:24, Federal Arbitration Act.

Miller and Starr California Real Estate § 35:28, Real Estate Contracts and Listing Agreements.

Miller and Starr California Real Estate § 35:38, Issues Subject to Arbitration--Examples.

Miller and Starr California Real Estate § 25B:113, Arbitration or Other Resolution of Disputes With the Subdivider.

13 NO. 6 Miller & Starr, California Real Estate Newsalert 1, Using Basura to Make Construction Defect Claims Arbitrable, or Woodside to Send Them to a Referee.

16 NO. 2 Miller & Starr, California Real Estate Newsalert 4, Commercial Arbitration.

17 NO. 3 Miller & Starr, California Real Estate Newsalert 2, Commercial Arbitration.

17 NO. 6 Miller & Starr, California Real Estate Newsalert 2, Commercial Arbitration.

23 NO. 2 Miller & Starr, California Real Estate Newsalert 4, Alternative Dispute Resolution.

1 Witkin Cal. Summ. 10th Contracts § 335, Purchase Subject to Covenants, Conditions, and Restrictions.

§ 1298.8. Operative date; application of title

This title shall become operative on July 1, 1989, and shall only apply to contracts or agreements entered into on or after that date. *(Added by Stats.1988, c. 881, § 1, operative July 1, 1989.)*

Research References

13 NO. 6 Miller & Starr, California Real Estate Newsalert 1, Using Basura to Make Construction Defect Claims Arbitrable, or Woodside to Send Them to a Referee.

1 Witkin Cal. Summ. 10th Contracts § 335, Purchase Subject to Covenants, Conditions, and Restrictions.

Title 9.5

ARBITRATION OF FIREFIGHTER AND LAW ENFORCEMENT OFFICER LABOR DISPUTES

Section

§ 1299. Legislative findings, declarations, and intent

The Legislature hereby finds and declares that strikes taken by firefighters and law enforcement officers against public employers are a matter of statewide concern, are a predictable consequence of labor strife and poor morale that is often the outgrowth of substandard wages and benefits, and are not in the public interest. The Legislature further finds and declares that the dispute resolution procedures contained in this title provide the appropriate method for resolving public sector labor disputes that could otherwise lead to strikes by firefighters or law enforcement officers.

It is the intent of the Legislature to protect the health and welfare of the public by providing impasse remedies necessary to afford public employers the opportunity to safely alleviate the effects of labor strife that would otherwise lead to strikes by firefighters and law enforcement officers. It is further the intent of the Legislature that, in order to effectuate its predominant purpose, this title be construed to apply broadly to all public employers, including, but not limited to, charter cities, counties, and cities and counties in this state.

It is not the intent of the Legislature to alter the scope of issues subject to collective bargaining between public employers and employee organizations representing firefighters or law enforcement officers.

The provisions of this title are intended by the Legislature to govern the resolution of impasses reached in collective bargaining between public employers and employee organizations representing firefighters and law enforcement officers over economic issues that remain in dispute over their respective interests. However, the provisions of this title are not intended by the Legislature to be used as a procedure to determine the rights of any firefighter or law enforcement officer in any grievance initiated as a result of a disciplinary action taken by any public employer. The Legislature further intends that this title shall not apply to any law enforcement policy that pertains to how law enforcement officers interact with members of the public or pertains to police-community relations, such as policies on the use of police powers, enforcement priorities and practices, or supervision, oversight, and accountability covering officer behavior toward members of the public, to any community-oriented policing policy or to any process employed by an employer to investigate firefighter or law enforcement officer behavior that could lead to discipline against any firefighter or law enforcement officer, nor to contravene any provision of a charter that governs an employer that is a city, county, or city and county, which provision prescribes a procedure for the imposition of any disciplinary action taken against a firefighter or law enforcement officer. *(Added by Stats.2000, c. 906 (S.B.402), § 2.)*

Validity

Stats.2000, c. 906 (S.B.402), which enacted this Title 9.5, consisting of Code of Civil Procedure §§ 1299 to 1299.9, was declared invalidly infringing on counties' constitutional rights, in County of Riverside v. Superior Court (2003) 132 Cal.Rptr.2d 713, 30 Cal.4th 278, 66 P.3d 718. Portions of Title 9.5 were subsequently amended by Stats.2003, c. 877 (S.B.440). For legislative intent relating to the 2003 amending legislation, see Historical and Statutory Notes under Code of Civil Procedure § 1299.7.

Research References

Rutter, Cal. Practice Guide: A.D.R. App. A, Selected Statutes Providing for ADR.

Miller and Starr California Real Estate § 35:23, Public Policy in Favor of Arbitration.

3 Witkin, California Summary 10th Agency and Employment § 567, (S 567) Statutory Framework.

§ 1299.2. Application of title

This title shall apply to all employers of firefighters and law enforcement officers. *(Added by Stats.2000, c. 906 (S.B.402), § 2.)*

Validity

Stats.2000, c. 906 (S.B.402), which enacted this Title 9.5, consisting of Code of Civil Procedure §§ 1299 to 1299.9, was declared invalidly infringing on counties'

constitutional rights, in County of Riverside v. Superior Court (2003) 132 Cal.Rptr.2d 713, 30 Cal.4th 278, 66 P.3d 718. Portions of Title 9.5 were subsequently amended by Stats.2003, c. 877 (S.B.440). For legislative intent relating to the 2003 amending legislation, see Historical and Statutory Notes under Code of Civil Procedure § 1299.7.

§ 1299.3. Definitions

As used in this title:

(a) "Employee" means any firefighter or law enforcement officer represented by an employee organization, as defined in subdivision (b).

(b) "Employee organization" means any organization recognized by the employer for the purpose of representing firefighters or law enforcement officers in matters relating to wages, hours, and other terms and conditions of employment within the scope of arbitration.

(c) "Employer" means any local agency employing employees, as defined in subdivision (a), or any entity, except the State of California, acting as an agent of any local agency, either directly or indirectly.

(d) "Firefighter" means any person who is employed to perform firefighting, fire prevention, fire training, hazardous materials response, emergency medical services, fire or arson investigation, or any related duties, without respect to the rank, job title, or job assignment of that person.

(e) "Law enforcement officer" means any person who is a peace officer, as defined in Section 830.1 of, subdivisions (b) and (d) of Section 830.31 of, subdivisions (a), (b), and (c) of Section 830.32 of, subdivisions (a), (b), and (d) of Section 830.33 of, subdivisions (a) and (b) of Section 830.35 of, subdivision (a) of Section 830.5 of, and subdivision (a) of Section 830.55 of, the Penal Code, without respect to the rank, job title, or job assignment of that person.

(f) "Local agency" means any governmental subdivision, district, public and quasi-public corporation, joint powers agency, public agency or public service corporation, town, city, county, city and county, or municipal corporation, whether incorporated or not or whether chartered or not.

(g) "Scope of arbitration" means economic issues, including salaries, wages and overtime pay, health and pension benefits, vacation and other leave, reimbursements, incentives, differentials, and all other forms of remuneration. The scope of arbitration shall not include any issue that is protected by what is commonly referred to as the "management rights" clause contained in Section 3504 of the Government Code. Notwithstanding the foregoing, any employer that is not exempt under Section 1299.9 may supersede this subdivision by adoption of an ordinance that establishes a broader definition of "scope of arbitration." *(Added by Stats.2000, c. 906 (S.B.402), § 2. Amended by Stats.2002, c. 664 (A.B.3034), § 52.)*

Validity

Stats.2000, c. 906 (S.B.402), which enacted this Title 9.5, consisting of Code of Civil Procedure §§ 1299 to 1299.9, was declared invalidly infringing on counties' constitutional rights, in County of Riverside v. Superior Court (2003) 132 Cal.Rptr.2d 713, 30 Cal.4th 278, 66 P.3d 718. Portions of Title 9.5 were subsequently amended by Stats.2003, c. 877 (S.B.440). For legislative intent relating to the 2003 amending legislation, see Historical and Statutory Notes under Code of Civil Procedure § 1299.7.

§ 1299.4. Submission to arbitration

(a) If an impasse has been declared after the parties have exhausted their mutual efforts to reach agreement over matters within the scope of arbitration, and the parties are unable to agree to the appointment of a mediator, or if a mediator agreed to by the parties is unable to effect settlement of a dispute between the parties after his or her appointment, the employee organization may, by written notification to the employer, request that their differences be submitted to an arbitration panel.

(b) Within three days after receipt of the written notification, each party shall designate a person to serve as its member of an arbitration panel. Within five days thereafter, or within additional periods to which they mutually agree, the two members of the arbitration panel appointed by the parties shall designate an impartial person with experience in labor and management dispute resolution to act as chairperson of the arbitration panel .

(c) In the event that the parties are unable or unwilling to agree upon a third person to serve as chairperson, the two members of the arbitration panel shall jointly request from the American Arbitration Association a list of seven impartial and experienced persons who are familiar with matters of employer-employee relations. The two panel members may as an alternative, jointly request a list of seven names from the California State Mediation and Conciliation Service, or a list from either entity containing more or less than seven names, so long as the number requested is an odd number. If after five days of receipt of the list, the two panel members cannot agree on which of the listed persons shall serve as chairperson, they shall, within two days, alternately strike names from the list, with the first panel member to strike names being determined by lot. The last person whose name remains on the list shall be chairperson.

(d) Employees as defined by this chapter shall not be permitted to engage in strikes that endanger public safety.

(e) No employer shall interfere with, intimidate, restrain, coerce, or discriminate against an employee organization or employee because of an exercise of rights under this title.

(f) No employer shall refuse to meet and confer or condition agreement upon a memorandum of understanding based upon an employee organization's exercise of rights under this title. *(Added by Stats.2000, c. 906 (S.B.402), § 2.)*

Validity

This section was held unconstitutional as an improper delegation of municipal functions in the decision of County of Sonoma v. Superior Court (App. 1 Dist. 2009) 93 Cal.Rptr.3d 39, 173 Cal.App.4th 322, review denied.

Stats.2000, c. 906 (S.B.402), which enacted this Title 9.5, consisting of Code of Civil Procedure §§ 1299 to 1299.9, was declared invalidly infringing on counties' constitutional rights, in County of Riverside v. Superior Court (2003) 132 Cal.Rptr.2d 713, 30 Cal.4th 278, 66 P.3d 718. Portions of Title 9.5 were subsequently amended by Stats.2003, c. 877 (S.B.440). For legislative intent relating to the 2003 amending legislation, see Historical and Statutory Notes under Code of Civil Procedure § 1299.7.

Research References

Rutter, Cal. Practice Guide: A.D.R. App. A, Selected Statutes Providing for ADR.

§ 1299.5. Procedure

(a) The arbitration panel shall, within 10 days after its establishment or any additional periods to which the parties agree, meet with the parties or their representatives, either jointly or separately, make inquiries and investigations, hold hearings, and take any other action including further mediation, that the arbitration panel deems appropriate.

(b) For the purpose of its hearings, investigations, or inquiries, the arbitration panel may subpoena witnesses, administer oaths, take the testimony of any person, and issue subpoenas duces tecum to require the production and examination of any employer's or employee organization's records, books, or papers relating to any subject matter before the panel. *(Added by Stats.2000, c. 906 (S.B.402), § 2.)*

Validity

Stats.2000, c. 906 (S.B.402), which enacted this Title 9.5, consisting of Code of Civil Procedure §§ 1299 to 1299.9, was declared invalidly infringing on counties' constitutional rights, in County of Riverside v. Superior Court (2003) 132 Cal.Rptr.2d 713, 30 Cal.4th 278, 66 P.3d 718. Portions of Title 9.5 were subsequently amended by Stats.2003, c. 877 (S.B.440). For legislative intent relating to the 2003 amending legislation, see Historical and Statutory Notes under Code of Civil Procedure § 1299.7.

§ 1299.6. Decision

(a) The arbitration panel shall direct that five days prior to the commencement of its hearings, each of the parties shall submit the last best offer of settlement as to each of the issues within the scope of arbitration, as defined in this title, made in bargaining as a proposal or counterproposal and not previously agreed to by the parties prior to any arbitration request made pursuant to subdivision (a) of Section 1299.4. The arbitration panel, within 30 days after the conclusion of the hearing, or any additional period to which the parties agree, shall separately decide on each of the disputed issues submitted by selecting, without modification, the last best offer that most nearly complies with the applicable factors described in subdivision (c). This subdivision shall be applicable except as otherwise provided in subdivision (b).

(b) Notwithstanding the terms of subdivision (a), the parties by mutual agreement may elect to submit as a package the last best offer of settlement made in bargaining as a proposal or counterproposal on those issues within the scope of arbitration, as defined in this title, not previously agreed to by the parties prior to any arbitration request made pursuant to subdivision (a) of Section 1299.4. The arbitration panel, within 30 days after the conclusion of the hearing, or any additional period to which the parties agree, shall decide on the disputed issues submitted by selecting, without modification, the last best offer package that most nearly complies with the applicable factors described in subdivision (c).

(c) The arbitration panel, unless otherwise agreed to by the parties, shall limit its findings to issues within the scope of arbitration and shall base its findings, opinions, and decisions upon those factors traditionally taken into consideration in the determination of those matters within the scope of arbitration, including but not limited to the following factors, as applicable:

(1) The stipulations of the parties.

(2) The interest and welfare of the public.

(3) The financial condition of the employer and its ability to meet the costs of the award.

(4) The availability and sources of funds to defray the cost of any changes in matters within the scope of arbitration.

(5) Comparison of matters within the scope of arbitration of other employees performing similar services in corresponding fire or law enforcement employment.

(6) The average consumer prices for goods and services, commonly known as the Consumer Price Index.

(7) The peculiarity of requirements of employment, including, but not limited to, mental, physical, and educational qualifications; job training and skills; and hazards of employment.

(8) Changes in any of the foregoing that are traditionally taken into consideration in the determination of matters within the scope of arbitration. *(Added by Stats.2000, c. 906 (S.B.402), § 2.)*

Validity

This section was held unconstitutional as an improper delegation of municipal functions in the decision of County of Sonoma v. Superior Court (App. 1 Dist. 2009) 93 Cal.Rptr.3d 39, 173 Cal.App.4th 322, review denied.

Stats.2000, c. 906 (S.B.402), which enacted this Title 9.5, consisting of Code of Civil Procedure §§ 1299 to 1299.9, was declared invalidly infringing on counties' constitutional rights, in County of Riverside v. Superior Court (2003) 132 Cal.Rptr.2d 713, 30 Cal.4th 278, 66 P.3d 718. Portions of Title 9.5 were subsequently amended by Stats.2003, c. 877 (S.B.440). For legislative intent relating to the 2003 amending legislation, see Historical and Statutory Notes under Code of Civil Procedure § 1299.7.

§ 1299.7. Amendment or modification of decision; disclosure; binding effect

(a) The arbitration panel shall mail or otherwise deliver a copy of the decision to the parties. However, the decision of the arbitration panel shall not be publicly disclosed, and shall not be binding, for a period of five days after service to the parties. During that five-day period, the parties may meet privately, attempt to resolve their differences and, by mutual agreement, amend or modify the decision of the arbitration panel.

(b) At the conclusion of the five-day period, which may be extended by the parties, the arbitration panel's decision, as may be amended or modified by the parties pursuant to subdivision (a), shall be publicly disclosed and, unless the governing body acts in accordance with subdivision (c), shall be binding on all parties, and, if specified by the arbitration panel, be incorporated into and made a part of any existing memorandum of understanding as defined in Section 3505.1 of the Government Code.

(c) The employer may by unanimous vote of all the members of the governing body reject the decision of the arbitration panel, except as specifically provided to the contrary in a city, county, or city and county charter with respect to the rejection of an arbitration award. *(Added by Stats.2000, c. 906 (S.B.402), § 2. Amended by Stats.2003, c. 877 (S.B.440), § 1.)*

Validity

This section was held unconstitutional as an improper delegation of municipal functions in the decision of County of Sonoma v. Superior Court (App. 1 Dist. 2009) 93 Cal.Rptr.3d 39, 173 Cal.App.4th 322, review denied.

Stats.2000, c. 906 (S.B.402), which enacted this Title 9.5, consisting of Code of Civil Procedure §§ 1299 to 1299.9, was declared invalidly infringing on counties' constitutional rights, in County of Riverside v. Superior Court (2003) 132 Cal.Rptr.2d 713, 30 Cal.4th 278, 66 P.3d 718. Portions of Title 9.5 were subsequently amended by Stats.2003, c. 877 (S.B.440). For legislative intent relating to the 2003 amending legislation, see Historical and Statutory Notes under Code of Civil Procedure § 1299.7.

Research References

Rutter, Cal. Practice Guide: A.D.R. App. A, Selected Statutes Providing for ADR.

§ 1299.8. Application of Title 9

Unless otherwise provided in this title, Title 9 (commencing with Section 1280) shall be applicable to any arbitration proceeding undertaken pursuant to this title. *(Added by Stats.2000, c. 906 (S.B.402), § 2.)*

Validity

Stats.2000, c. 906 (S.B.402), which enacted this Title 9.5, consisting of Code of Civil Procedure §§ 1299 to 1299.9, was declared invalidly infringing on counties' constitutional rights, in County of Riverside v. Superior Court (2003) 132 Cal.Rptr.2d 713, 30 Cal.4th 278, 66 P.3d 718. Portions of Title 9.5 were subsequently amended by Stats.2003, c. 877 (S.B.440). For legislative intent relating to the 2003 amending legislation, see Historical and Statutory Notes under Code of Civil Procedure § 1299.7.

§ 1299.9. Application to cities and counties with arbitration procedures; costs

(a) The provisions of this title shall not apply to any employer that is a city, county, or city and county, governed by a charter that was amended prior to January 1, 2004, to incorporate a procedure requiring the submission of all unresolved disputes relating to wages, hours, and other terms and conditions of employment within the scope of arbitration to an impartial and experienced neutral person or panel for final and binding determination, provided however that the charter amendment is not subsequently repealed or amended in a form that would no longer require the submission of all unresolved disputes relating to wages, hours, and other terms and conditions of employment within the scope of arbitration to an impartial and experienced neutral person or panel, for final and binding determination.

(b) Unless otherwise agreed to by the parties, the costs of the arbitration proceeding and the expenses of the arbitration panel, except those of the employer representative, shall be borne by the employee organization. *(Added by Stats.2000, c. 906 (S.B. 402), § 2. Amended by Stats.2003, c. 877 (S.B.440), § 2.)*

Validity

Stats.2000, c. 906 (S.B.402), which enacted this Title 9.5, consisting of Code of Civil Procedure §§ 1299 to 1299.9, was declared invalidly infringing on counties' constitutional rights, in County of Riverside v. Superior Court (2003) 132 Cal.Rptr.2d 713, 30 Cal.4th 278, 66 P.3d 718. Portions of Title 9.5 were subsequently amended by Stats.2003, c. 877 (S.B.440). For legislative intent relating to the 2003 amending legislation, see Historical and Statutory Notes under Code of Civil Procedure § 1299.7.

Research References

Miller and Starr California Real Estate § 35:23, Public Policy in Favor of Arbitration.

Title 10

UNCLAIMED PROPERTY

CHAPTER 1. GENERAL PROVISIONS

ARTICLE 1. DEFINITIONS

§ 1300. Definitions

For the purposes of this title, the following definitions shall apply:

(a) "Property," unless specifically qualified, includes all classes of property, real, personal and mixed.

(b) "Unclaimed property," unless specifically qualified, means all property (1) which is unclaimed, abandoned, escheated, permanently escheated, or distributed to the state, or (2) which, under any provision of law, will become unclaimed, abandoned, escheated, permanently escheated, or distributed to the state, or (3) to the possession of which the state is or will become entitled, if not claimed by the person or persons entitled thereto within the time allowed by law, whether or not there has been a judicial determination that such property is unclaimed, abandoned, escheated, permanently escheated, or distributed to the state.

(c) "Escheat," unless specifically qualified, means the vesting in the state of title to property the whereabouts of whose owner is unknown or whose owner is unknown or which a known owner has refused to accept, whether by judicial determination or by operation of law, subject to the right of claimants to appear and claim the escheated property or any portion thereof. When used in reference to the law of another state, "escheat" includes the transfer to the state of the right to the custody of such property.

(d) "Permanent escheat" means the absolute vesting in the state of title to property the whereabouts of whose owner is unknown or whose owner is unknown or which a known owner has refused to accept, pursuant to judicial determination, pursuant to a proceeding of escheat as provided by Chapter 5 (commencing with Section 1410) of this title, or pursuant to operation of law, and the barring of all claims to the property by the former owner thereof or his successors.

(e) "Controller" means the State Controller.

(f) "Treasurer" means the State Treasurer.

(g) "Domicile," in the case of a corporation, refers to the place where the corporation is incorporated. *(Added by Stats. 1951, c. 1708, p. 3934, § 5. Amended by Stats.1968, c. 356, p. 738, § 1, operative Jan. 1, 1969.)*

Law Revision Commission Comments

Section 1300 is amended to permit more convenient use of the defined terms in Chapter 7 (commencing with Section 1500) of this title.

The term "presumptively abandoned" has been deleted from subdivision (b) because it is no longer used, as it formerly was, in the substantive provisions relating to the escheat of abandoned property. The reference to the initiative act approved in 1920 has been deleted from subdivision

(b) because it is obsolete. The act referred to was declared unconstitutional (Sei Fujii v. State, 38 Cal.2d 718, 242 P.2d 617 (1952)) and has been repealed (Cal.Stats.1955, Ch. 316, §§ 1–2, p. 767; Cal.Stats.1957, p. cxxxvii).

The definitions in subdivisions (c) and (d) have been broadened to include escheats under the law of other states. The change is important because the right of California to escheat certain intangible property depends on whether such property is subject to escheat under the law of another state. See subdivision (c) of Section 1510. Under the laws of some states, the right to the custody of abandoned property vests in the state after the property has remained unclaimed for a specified period of time, but the state never acquires the technical title to the property. The revised definition in subdivision (c) makes it clear that this acquisition of the right to custody is included in the term "escheat."

In *Texas v. New Jersey*, 379 U.S. 674 (1965), the Supreme Court referred to the state of incorporation as a corporation's domicile. Subdivision (g) codifies this rule to facilitate reference to it in Chapter 7 (commencing with Section 1500).

Research References

Miller and Starr California Real Estate § 18:3, Property of Decedent Not Leaving a Will or Heirs.

Miller and Starr California Real Estate § 18:6, Permanent Escheat.

Miller and Starr California Real Estate § 18:7, The Unclaimed Property Law--Property Unclaimed or Abandoned.

Miller and Starr California Real Estate § 18:8, The Unclaimed Property Law--Property Exempt.

Miller and Starr California Real Estate § 4:33, Handling of Trust Funds.

Miller and Starr California Real Estate § 6:16, Funds Held in Trust; Restrictions on Disbursement.

Miller and Starr California Real Estate § 18:10, The Unclaimed Property Law--Duties of the State.

19 NO. 1 Miller & Starr, California Real Estate Newsalert 13, Escheat.

3 Witkin Cal. Proc. 5th Actions § 65, (S 65) Statutory Classes.

3 Witkin Cal. Proc. 5th Actions § 71, (S 71) Escheat Proceedings.

13 Witkin, California Summary 10th Personal Property § 27, (S 27) in General.

13 Witkin, California Summary 10th Personal Property § 36, (S 36) Former Law.

13 Witkin, California Summary 10th Personal Property § 39, (S 39) Other Statutes Dealing With Unclaimed Property.

13 Witkin, California Summary 10th Personal Property § 41, Exemptions.

14 Witkin, California Summary 10th Wills and Probate § 99, (S 99) Nature and Scope of Statute.

14 Witkin, California Summary 10th Wills and Probate § 421, Deposit of Money of Estate.

14 Witkin, California Summary 10th Wills and Probate § 737, Distribution to State.

§ 1301. References to other sections, articles, and chapters

For the purposes of this title, unless otherwise specified, (1) a reference to a section refers to a section of this code; (2) a reference to an article refers to an article of the chapter of this title in which such reference is made; and (3) a reference to a chapter refers to a chapter of this title. *(Added by Stats.1951, c. 1708, p. 3935, § 5.)*

ARTICLE 2. PURPOSE AND SCOPE

§ 1305. Purpose

It is the purpose of this title to provide for the receipt, custody, investment, management, disposal, escheat and permanent escheat of various classes of unclaimed property, to the possession of which the State is, or may become, entitled under the provisions of this title or under other provision of law. *(Added by Stats.1951, c. 1708, p. 3935, § 5.)*

§ 1306. Scope

The provisions of this title do not apply to money or other property held by the State or any officer thereof as trustee or bailee under the terms of an express contract to which the State or any officer thereof is a party. *(Added by Stats.1951, c. 1708, p. 3935, § 5.)*

CHAPTER 2.   RECEIPT AND EXPENDITURE OF FUNDS

ARTICLE 1.   DEPOSIT OF UNCLAIMED PROPERTY

§ 1310. Transmittal of money to state treasurer and of property to controller

Whenever, under the provisions of this title or under any other provision of law, unclaimed money or other unclaimed property is payable into the State Treasury, the person responsible for making such payment shall, if it is cash, transmit it to the Treasurer, and if it is personal property other than cash, transmit it to the Controller for deposit in the State Treasury. *(Added by Stats.1951, c. 1708, p. 3935, § 5.)*

Research References

3 Witkin Cal. Proc. 5th Actions § 71, (S 71) Escheat Proceedings.

§ 1311. Transmittal; notice

Any person transmitting money or other property to the Treasurer or Controller under the provisions of this title shall, at the time of such transmittal, furnish written notice thereof to the Controller, setting forth the amount of cash transmitted, the nature and description of the personal property other than cash transmitted, the name and last known address of the person entitled to such property or for whose benefit such property is transmitted, a reference to the specific statutory provision under which such property is transmitted, and if such property represents the proceeds of an estate of a decedent, or an unclaimed amount payable pursuant to an allowed and approved claim

against such an estate, the name of the decedent, the county and court in which probate or escheat proceedings, if any, were held, the number of the action, if any; and, in the case of all classes of property so transmitted, such other identifying information available from the records of the person making such transmittal, as the Controller may require. *(Added by Stats.1951, c. 1708, p. 3935, § 5.)*

Research References

14 Witkin, California Summary 10th Wills and Probate § 424, (S 424) Procedure.

§ 1312. Transmittal; certified copy of court order or decree

Whenever money or other property is paid to the State or any officer or employee thereof under the provisions of this title, and such money or other property has been covered by a decree of distribution in a decedent's estate, or by an order or decree of a court ordering such payment or adjudging that title to such property has vested in the State, the person transmitting such money or other property to the Treasurer or Controller shall, at the time of such transmittal, furnish to the Controller a certified copy of each court order or decree, and of each court order correcting or amending the same, covering such money or other property. *(Added by Stats.1951, c. 1708, p. 3936, § 5.)*

§ 1313. Unclaimed property fund; creation; deposits

A fund is hereby created in the State Treasury, to be known as the Unclaimed Property Fund.

All money, except permanently escheated money, paid to the state or any officer or employee thereof for deposit in the State Treasury under the provisions of this title shall, on order of the Controller, be deposited in the Unclaimed Property Fund.

All property other than money, including the proceeds from the sale or other disposition thereof, except permanently escheated property received by, or coming into the possession of, the state or any officer or employee thereof under the provisions of this title shall, on order of the Controller, be deposited in the State Treasury to be held in the Unclaimed Property Fund. *(Added by Stats.1951, c. 1708, p. 3936, § 5. Amended by Stats.1953, c. 218, p. 1358, § 1; Stats.1978, c. 1183, p. 3823, § 1.)*

§ 1314. Unclaimed property fund; separate accounts; accounting for, and holding property in name of fund

The Controller shall maintain a separate account in the Unclaimed Property Fund covering the accountability for money deposited in the Unclaimed Property Fund under each article of Chapter 6. All real and personal property distributed to the State or delivered into the possession of the State or any officer or employee thereof under the provisions of this title, shall be accounted for by the Controller in the name of the account in the Unclaimed Property Fund to which the proceeds thereof, if converted into cash, would be credited under the provisions of this title. All personal property deposited in the State Treasury under the provisions of this title shall be held by the Treasurer in the name of the same account in the Unclaimed Property Fund for which such property is accounted by the Controller, as herein provided. *(Added by Stats.1951, c. 1708, p. 3936, § 5.)*

§ 1315. Unclaimed property fund; recordation of money or property received from or through an estate

If unclaimed money or other property in an estate of a deceased person, or if any unclaimed amount payable pursuant to an allowed and approved claim against such an estate, is received by the State or any officer or employee thereof and deposited in the State Treasury under the provisions of this title, it shall be recorded on the books of the Controller to the credit, or in the name, of such estate, for the benefit of the person entitled thereto or his successors in interest. *(Added by Stats. 1951, c. 1708, p. 3936, § 5.)*

§ 1316. Unclaimed property fund; recordation of money or property deposited for benefit of known heirs, creditors, claimants, payees, etc.

If unclaimed money or other property is received by the State or any officer or employee thereof and deposited in the State Treasury under the provisions of this title for the benefit of known heirs, devisees, legatees or creditors of an estate of a deceased person, or for the benefit of known claimants, payees, or other persons entitled thereto, it shall be recorded on the books of the Controller to the credit, or in the name, of such heirs, devisees, legatees, creditors, claimants, payees, or other persons entitled thereto. *(Added by Stats.1951, c. 1708, p. 3937, § 5.)*

§ 1317. Unclaimed property fund; cancelled warrants; transfer of amount to general fund

The amount of each canceled warrant credited to the Unclaimed Property Fund under the provisions of Section 17072 of the Government Code shall, on order of the Controller, be transferred to the General Fund. *(Added by Stats.1951, c. 1708, p. 3937, § 5. Amended by Stats.1978, c. 1183, p. 3823, § 3.)*

§ 1318. Unclaimed property fund; interest and income from investments; deposit in general fund

All interest received and other income derived from the investment of moneys in the Unclaimed Property Fund, as provided in Section 13470 of the Government Code, shall, on order of the Controller, be deposited in the General Fund. *(Added by Stats.1951, c. 1708, p. 3937, § 5. Amended by Stats.1978, c. 1183, p. 3823, § 4.)*

§ 1319. Unclaimed property fund; rents, interest, dividends, etc.; deposits; accounts credited; claims

Except as otherwise provided in Section 1318, all rents, interest, dividends or other income or increment derived from real or personal property received and held by the State in the name of the Unclaimed Property Fund under the provisions of this title shall, on order of the Controller, be deposited in the Unclaimed Property Fund, and shall be credited by the Controller to the account maintained by him, in the name of which such property is accounted, as provided in Chapter 2. Any moneys deposited in the Unclaimed Property Fund under the provisions of this section shall be held for the benefit of the person or persons entitled to the property from which such moneys were derived, or their successors in interest; and shall be subject to claim in the same manner as such property may be claimed; but the period in which such moneys shall be available for claim by and payment to the person or persons entitled thereto shall not extend beyond the period in which the property from which such moneys were derived is available for claim and payment under the provisions of this title. *(Added by Stats.1951, c. 1708, p. 3937, § 5.)*

§ 1320. Unclaimed property fund; rents, interest, dividends, etc. from permanently escheated property; deposit in general fund; presumption

Except as otherwise provided in Section 1318, all rents, interest, dividends or other income or increment derived from real or personal property that has permanently escheated to the state, shall, on order of the Controller, be deposited in the General Fund.

All moneys deposited in the General Fund under the provisions of this section shall be deemed to have permanently escheated to the state as of the date of permanent escheat of the property from which such moneys were derived. *(Added by*

Stats.1951, c. 1708, p. 3937, § 5. Amended by Stats.1978, c. 1183, p. 3823, § 5.)

§ 1321. Protection of person delivering money or property to treasurer or controller; termination of right to interest; definitions

Any person delivering money or other property to the Treasurer or Controller under the provisions of this title shall, upon such delivery, be relieved and held harmless by the State from all or any claim or claims which exist at that time with reference to such money or other property, or which may thereafter be made, or which may come into existence, on account of, or in respect to, such money or other property.

No action shall be maintained against any person who is the holder of such money or other property, nor against any officer as agent thereof, for:

(a) The recovery of such money or other property delivered to the Treasurer or Controller pursuant to this title, or for interest thereon subsequent to the date of the report thereof, if any, to the Controller; or

(b) Damages alleged to have resulted from such delivery to the Treasurer or Controller.

No owner of money or other property shall be entitled to receive interest thereon or with respect thereto from and after the date on which a report of such money or other property is made to the Controller pursuant to any provision of this title, whether or not he was entitled to such interest prior to such report.

As used in this section, "person" and "holder" have the respective meanings set forth in Section 1461 of this code. *(Added by Stats.1953, c. 279, p. 1429, § 1.)*

ARTICLE 2. APPROPRIATION

Section
1325. Unclaimed property fund; continuous appropriation; purposes.

§ 1325. Unclaimed property fund; continuous appropriation; purposes

Notwithstanding Section 13340 of the Government Code, all money in the Unclaimed Property Fund is hereby continuously appropriated to the Controller, without regard to fiscal years, for expenditure for any of the following purposes:

(a) For refund, to the person making such deposit, of amounts, including overpayments, deposited in error in such fund.

(b) For payment of the cost of title searches and appraisals incurred by the Controller covering real or personal property held in the name of an account in such fund.

(c) For payment of the cost incurred by the Controller covering indemnity bonds required in order to have duplicate certificates of ownership issued in order to replace lost certificates, covering personal property held in the name of an account in such fund.

(d) For payment of amounts required to be paid by the state as trustee, bailee, or successor in interest to the preceding owner, pursuant to the provisions of trust deeds, mortgages, or other liens on real property held in the name of an account in such fund.

(e) For payment of costs incurred by the Controller for the repair, maintenance and upkeep of real and personal property held in the name of an account in such fund.

(f) For payment of costs of official advertising in connection with the sale of real or personal property held in the name of an account in such fund.

(g) For payment to taxing agencies of the amounts deducted by the Controller from allowed and approved claims, in accordance with the provisions of subdivision (c) of Section 4986.5 of the Revenue and Taxation Code.

(h) For transfer to the Inheritance Tax Fund, on order of the Controller, of the amount of any inheritance taxes determined to be due and payable to the state by any claimant, with respect to any real or personal property, including cash, claimed by that person under the provisions of this title.

(i) For payment and delivery to claimants of money or other property held to the credit, or in the name, of an account in such fund, under the provisions of this title.

(j) For transfer to the General Fund, on order of the Controller, of any money or other property in the Unclaimed Property Fund which becomes permanently escheated to the state under the provisions of this title.

Any expenditure made by the Controller pursuant to the provisions of this section shall be charged against any balance credited to the particular account in the Unclaimed Property Fund, in the name of which is held the real or personal property for which the expenditure is made; and if sufficient balance is not available in such account, the expenditure may be made from any appropriation from the General Fund for the support of the Controller, or, in the case of official advertising, from any appropriation available therefor, to be reimbursed from the proceeds of any subsequent sale of the property for which such expenditure is made. *(Added by Stats.1951, c. 1708, p. 3938, § 5. Amended by Stats.1951, c. 122, p. 378, § 5; Stats.1953, c. 1705, p. 3453, § 1; Stats.1963, c. 1762, p. 3517, § 2; Stats.1978, c. 1183, p. 3824, § 6; Stats.1993, c. 692 (A.B.1854), § 1.)*

CHAPTER 3. PAYMENT OF CLAIMS

ARTICLE 1. GENERAL

§ 1335. Payment or delivery to claimant as bar to further actions

When payment or delivery of money or other property has been made to any claimant under the provisions of this chapter, no suit shall thereafter be maintained by any other claimant against the State or any officer thereof for or on account of such property. *(Added by Stats.1951, c. 1708, p. 3939, § 5.)*

Research References

14 Witkin, California Summary 10th Wills and Probate § 736, Deposit With County Treasurer.

ARTICLE 2. REFUND OF ERRONEOUS RECEIPTS

§ 1345. Unclaimed property fund; refund; order of controller; approval

If any person has erroneously delivered any unclaimed moneys or other unclaimed property to the state or any officer or employee thereof, and the moneys or other property is deposited in the Unclaimed Property Fund or is held by the Controller or Treasurer in the name of any account in that fund pursuant to this title, the moneys or other property delivered in error may be refunded or returned to that person on order of the Controller, with the approval of the California Victim Compensation and Government Claims Board. *(Added by Stats.1951, c. 1708, p. 3939, § 5. Amended by Stats.2006, c. 538 (S.B.1852), § 68.)*

§ 1346. General fund; transfer to unclaimed property fund; adjustment of records; refund

If any person has erroneously delivered any unclaimed moneys or other unclaimed property to the state or any officer or employee thereof, and the moneys or other property is deposited in, or transferred to, the General Fund, or is held by the Controller or Treasurer in the name of that fund, pursuant to this title, the moneys or other property delivered in error, if cash, shall on order of the Controller, be transferred from the General Fund to the Unclaimed Property Fund, and, if other than cash, the records of the Controller and Treasurer shall be adjusted to show that it is held in the name of the proper account in the Unclaimed Property Fund; and the moneys or other property may be refunded or returned to that person on order of the Controller, with the approval of the California Victim Compensation and Government Claims Board. *(Added by Stats.1951, c. 1708, p. 3939, § 5. Amended by Stats.1978, c. 1183, p. 3825, § 9; Stats.2006, c. 538 (S.B.1852), § 69.)*

§ 1347. General fund; money or property not permanently escheated; retransfer to unclaimed property fund; adjustment of records

Whenever money deposited in the Unclaimed Property Fund is transferred to the General Fund under the provisions of this title, and whenever the records of the Controller and Treasurer covering property other than money held in the name of any account in the Unclaimed Property Fund are adjusted to record such property as held in the name of the General Fund, as permanently escheated property under the provisions of this title, if it is subsequently determined that such money or other property is not, in fact, permanently escheated, such money or other property, if cash, shall, on order of the Controller, be retransferred from the General Fund to the Unclaimed Property Fund; and, if the property is other than money, the records of the Controller and Treasurer shall be adjusted to show that it is held in the name and for the benefit of the proper account in the Unclaimed Property Fund. *(Added by Stats.1951, c. 1708, p. 3939, § 5. Amended by Stats.1978, c. 1183, p. 3025, § 10.)*

ARTICLE 3. CLAIMS

§ 1350. Right; time

Unless otherwise provided in this title, all money or other property deposited in the State Treasury under the provisions of this title may be claimed by the person entitled thereto at any time prior to the date on which such money or other property has become permanently escheated, as provided by this title. *(Added by Stats.1951, c. 1708, p. 3940, § 5.)*

§ 1351. Escheat for failure to claim; establishment of state's title

Unless otherwise provided in this title, all money or other property deposited in the State Treasury under the provisions of this title, if not claimed by the person entitled thereto within five years from the date of such deposit, shall become the property of the State by escheat; and upon request by the Controller, the Attorney General shall commence a proceeding under the provisions of Section 1410, or, in lieu of such proceeding, the Controller may take action as provided by Article 2 of Chapter 5[1], to have it adjudged, determined or established that the title to such money or other property has vested in the State. *(Added by Stats.1951, c. 1708, p. 3940, § 5.)*

[1] Section 1451.

§ 1352. Persons authorized to present claim; form; appeal of decision

(a) Whenever unclaimed money or other property is deposited in the State Treasury under this title, and, except as otherwise provided by law, whenever there is in the possession of the state or its officers any money or other property which is held for third persons or the title to which has vested in the state subject to the rights of third persons, and the period during which it may be claimed by a person entitled thereto has not terminated, the period and person being prescribed by law, if the value of the money or other property to which the claimant is entitled is less than sixty thousand dollars ($60,000), any such person may present his or her claim for it to the Controller.

The claim shall be made in the form prescribed by the Controller, which shall set forth the information required by Section 1355 or any other information that the Controller may deem necessary to establish right or title to the money or other property in the claimant.

(b) Property assigned or distributed to a name distributee may be claimed by the distributee himself or herself or his or her legal guardian or conservator, as provided in subdivision (a) regardless of the amount. This subdivision does not apply to the heirs or estate of a distributee, or to property distributed to the state for lack of known heirs.

(c) Any person aggrieved by a decision of the Controller may commence an action, naming the Controller as a defendant, to establish his or her claim in the superior court in any county or city and county in which the Attorney General has an office pursuant to Section 1541. *(Added by Stats.1951, c. 1708, p. 3940, § 5. Amended by Stats.1970, c. 811, p. 1533, § 1; Stats.1990, c. 450 (S.B.57), § 1, eff. July 31, 1990.)*

Research References

Miller and Starr California Real Estate § 18:10, The Unclaimed Property Law--Duties of the State.

§ 1353. Jurisdiction to determine title; petition, filing, verification, form; certificate of right or title; payment

Except as otherwise provided in Sections 401 or 1352, whenever money or other property is deposited in the State Treasury under the provisions of this title, and, except as otherwise provided by law, when there is in the possession of the State or its officers any money or other property which is to be held for third persons or the title to which has vested in the State subject to the rights of third persons, the Superior Court of the County of Sacramento shall have full and exclusive jurisdiction to determine the title to such money or other property and all claims thereto.

If the period in which such money or other property may be claimed by a person entitled thereto has not terminated, such period and person being prescribed by law, any such person may file a petition in the Superior Court of the County of Sacramento, or as provided in Section 401, showing his claim or right to the money or other property or the proceeds thereof, or any portion thereof.

The petition shall be verified, and, among other things, must, insofar as they are applicable or material to the matters at issue, state the facts required to be stated in a petition filed under Section 1355. If the money or other property at issue did not come into the possession of the State or its officers in connection with estates of deceased persons, the petition shall, in addition to the foregoing facts, state any material facts necessary to establish a prima facie right or title in the petitioner. Upon the filing of the petition, the same proceedings shall be had as are required in Section 1355.

If, upon trial of the issues, the court is satisfied of the claimant's right or title to the money or other property claimed, it shall grant him a certificate to that effect under its seal. Upon presentation of such certificate, the Controller shall draw his warrant on the Treasurer for the amount of money covered thereby; and if the certificate covers any property other than money, a certified copy of the certificate filed with the officer of the State having possession of the property shall serve as sufficient authority to the officer for the delivery of such property to the claimant. *(Added by Stats.1951, c. 1708, p. 3940, § 5.)*

Research References

Miller and Starr California Real Estate § 18:10, The Unclaimed Property Law--Duties of the State.
3 Witkin Cal. Proc. 5th Actions § 66, (S 66) General Policy of Uniformity in Procedure.

§ 1354. Petition or claim by representative of estate, etc.; evidence required; allowance of creditors' claims; application of section

Whenever any claim is made or petition filed by the representative of an estate or other person, under the provisions of this chapter, or under any other provision of law, to recover money or other property deposited in the State Treasury or held by the State or any officer thereof to the credit, or in the name, of any account in the Unclaimed Property Fund, no recovery will be allowed unless it affirmatively appears that there are heirs or legatees who will receive such money or other property or creditors of the deceased owner of the claim whose claims are valid and are not barred, and whose claims were in existence prior to the death of such deceased owner of the claim. Where only creditors exist, and there are no heirs or legatees, said claims shall be allowed only to the extent necessary to pay such claims and the reasonable costs of administration of the estate, including court costs, administrator's fees and attorney's fees. This section shall apply to all claims which are pending at the time that this section goes into effect as well as to claims arising hereafter. *(Added by Stats.1951, c. 1708, p. 3940, § 5.)*

§ 1355. Petition for escheated property; parties authorized; filing; verification; contents; service; lis pendens; trial; court order; bar for nonappearance, etc.

Within five years after date of entry of judgment in any proceeding had under the provisions of Chapter 5,[1] or within five years after completion of notice by publication in an escheat action taken under the provisions of Section 1415, a person not a party or privy to such proceeding or action, if not otherwise barred, may file a petition in the Superior Court of the County of Sacramento, or as provided in Section 401, showing his claim or right to the money or other property, or the proceeds thereof.

Said petition shall be verified; and, in a proceeding for the recovery by the petitioner as heir, devisee, or legatee, or the successor in interest of an heir, devisee or legatee, of money or other property received by the State from the estate of a decedent under the provisions of Article 1 of Chapter 6,[2] such petition, among other things must state:

The full name, and the place and date of birth of the decedent whose estate, or any part thereof, is claimed.

The full name of such decedent's father and the maiden name of his mother, the places and dates of their respective births, the place and date of their marriage, the full names of all children the issue of such marriage, with the date of birth of each, and the place and date of death of all children of such marriage who have died unmarried and without issue.

Whether or not such decedent was ever married, and if so, where, when and to whom.

How, when and where such marriage, if any, was dissolved.

Whether or not said decedent was ever remarried, and, if so, where, when and to whom.

The full names, and the dates and places of birth of all lineal descendants, if any, of said decedent; the dates and places of death of any thereof who died prior to the filing of such petition; and the places of residence of all who are then surviving, with the degree of relationship of each of such survivors to said decedent.

Whether any of the brothers or sisters of such decedent ever married, and, if so, where, when and whom.

The full names, and the places and dates of birth of all children who are the issue of the marriage of any such brother or sister of the decedent, and the date and place of death of all deceased nephews and nieces of said decedent.

Whether or not said decedent, if of foreign birth, ever became a naturalized citizen of the United States, and, if so, when, where, and by what court citizenship was conferred.

The post-office names of the cities, towns or other places, each in its appropriate connection, wherein are preserved the records of the births, marriages and deaths hereinbefore enumerated, and, if known, the title of the public official or other person having custody of such records.

The nationality of each of the heirs of the decedent.

The street address of each of the heirs of the decedent.

If, for any reason, the petitioner is unable to set forth any of the matters or things hereinbefore required, he shall clearly state such reason in his petition.

At least 20 days before the hearing of the petition, a copy of the petition and notice of hearing must be served on the Attorney General and on the Controller, and the Attorney General may answer the same at his discretion.

If such claim includes a claim to real property or any interest therein, the petitioner shall record in the office of the county recorder of the county in which the real property is situated, a notice of the pendency of the petition containing the object of the action and a description of the property in the county affected thereby. From the time of filing such notice for record only, shall a purchaser or encumbrancer of the property be deemed to have constructive notice of the pendency of the action, and only of its pendency against parties designated by their real names.

The court must thereupon try the issue as issues are tried in civil actions; and if it is determined that such person is entitled to the money or other property or the proceeds thereof, it must order the property, if it has not been sold, to be delivered to him, or if it has been sold and the proceeds thereof paid into the State Treasury, it must order the Controller to draw his warrant on the Treasurer for the payment of the same, but without interest or cost to the State. A copy of such order, under the seal of the court, shall be a sufficient voucher for drawing such warrant.

All persons who fail to appear and file their petitions within the time limited are forever barred; saving, however, to infants and persons of unsound mind, the right to appear and file their petitions at any time within the time limited, or within one year after their respective disabilities cease. *(Added by Stats.1951, c. 1708, p. 3940, § 5. Amended by Stats.1951, c. 1738, p. 4145, § 1.)*

[1] Code of Civil Procedure § 1410 et seq.
[2] Code of Civil Procedure § 1440 et seq.

Research References

Rutter, Cal. Practice Guide: Civ. Pro. Before Trial Ch. 9(I)-J, J. Motion to Expunge Lis Pendens.
Rutter, Cal. Practice Guide: Real Prop. Transactions Ch. 11-I, I. Lis Pendens.
Miller and Starr California Real Estate § 18:4, Necessity of a Judicial Action Before Decedent's Property Escheats; Claims to Escheated Property.
Miller and Starr California Real Estate § 18:6, Permanent Escheat.
Miller and Starr California Real Estate § 11:150, Actions in Which a Lis Pendens May or Must be Recorded.
3 Witkin Cal. Proc. 5th Actions § 381, (S 381) Specific Mandatory Statutes.
3 Witkin Cal. Proc. 5th Actions § 485, (S 485) Five Years.
3 Witkin Cal. Proc. 5th Actions § 695, (S 695) in General.
8 Witkin Cal. Proc. 5th Attack Judgment Trial Court § 228, (S 228) Nonfiduciary Cases.
4 Witkin Cal. Proc. 5th Pleading § 466, Complaint or Petition.
14 Witkin, California Summary 10th Wills and Probate § 736, Deposit With County Treasurer.

CHAPTER 4. MANAGEMENT OF UNCLAIMED PROPERTY

ARTICLE 1. GENERAL PROVISIONS

§ 1360. Definitions

For the purposes of this chapter, the following definitions shall apply:

Civ. Pro.

(a) "Personal property" means personal property falling within the definition of "unclaimed property" under the provisions of this title;

(b) "Real property" means real property falling within the definition of "unclaimed property" under the provisions of this title;

(c) "Securities" includes stocks, bonds, notes, debentures, certificates of deposit, shares, and all other evidences of ownership or indebtedness, and all forms of chose in action and the interests in property represented thereby, falling within the definition of unclaimed property under the provisions of this title. *(Added by Stats.1951, c. 1708, p. 3943, § 5.)*

§ 1361. Care, custody, and responsibility

The care and custody of all property delivered to the Treasurer or Controller pursuant to this title is assumed by the State for the benefit of those entitled thereto, and the State is responsible for the payment of all claims established thereto pursuant to law, less any lawful deductions. *(Added by Stats. 1951, c. 1708, p. 3943, § 5.)*

ARTICLE 2. POWERS OF THE CONTROLLER

Section
1365. Powers of Controller.

§ 1365. Powers of Controller

In connection with all unclaimed property, the Controller has all of the powers necessary in order to safeguard and conserve the interests of all parties, including the State, having any vested or expectant interest in such unclaimed property. His powers include, but are not limited to, the authority to incur obligations the payment of which is authorized by the provisions of Section 1325. *(Added by Stats.1951, c. 1708, p. 3943, § 5.)*

ARTICLE 3. SALE OR DISPOSAL OF PROPERTY

Section
1370. Personal property; sale or lease; authority; approval.
1371. Personal property; securities; choses in action; authority to sell, cash, redeem, exchange, compromise, etc.; approval.
1372. Controller's right to sign, endorse, or authenticate documents; effect.
1373. Real estate; lease or sale at auction; notice; cost of publication.
1374. Rejection of bids.
1375. Real estate; private sale or lease without notice; approval.
1376. Execution of deed, bill of sale, or lease by Controller.
1377. Transactions creating additional obligations prohibited.
1378. Transactions under chapter; bar of suits against state.
1379. Destruction of valueless personal property; approval; nonliability.
1380. Sales, exchanges, etc.; approval of department of finance not required.
1381. Conclusiveness of sales, leases or other transactions.
1382. Sales of real property; applicability of article; exclusion of tax-deeded lands.

§ 1370. Personal property; sale or lease; authority; approval

The Controller, with the prior approval of the California Victim Compensation and Government Claims Board, may sell or lease personal property at any time, and in any manner, and may execute those leases on behalf and in the name of the State of California. *(Added by Stats.1951, c. 1708, p. 3944, § 5. Amended by Stats.2006, c. 538 (S.B.1852), § 70.)*

§ 1371. Personal property; securities; choses in action; authority to sell, cash, redeem, exchange, compromise, etc.; approval

The Controller, with the prior approval of the California Victim Compensation and Government Claims Board, may sell, cash, redeem, exchange, or otherwise dispose of any securities and all other classes of personal property, and may sell, cash, redeem, exchange, compromise, adjust, settle, or otherwise dispose of any accounts, debts, contractual rights, or other choses in action if, in his or her opinion, that action on his or her part is necessary or will tend to safeguard and conserve the interests of all parties, including the state, having any vested or expectant interest in the property. *(Added by Stats.1951, c. 1708, p. 3944, § 5. Amended by Stats.2006, c. 538 (S.B.1852), § 71.)*

§ 1372. Controller's right to sign, endorse, or authenticate documents; effect

The Controller may sign, endorse, or otherwise authenticate, in the name and on behalf of the State, subscribing his name, as Controller, under such writing, any securities, bills of sale, documents, or other instruments required, under customary business practice, for the consummation of the transactions authorized by this chapter. For all purposes, such endorsement is conclusive and binding against the State and the heirs, devisees, legatees, or other claimants of the property covered by such endorsement. *(Added by Stats.1951, c. 1708, p. 3944, § 5.)*

§ 1373. Real estate; lease or sale at auction; notice; cost of publication

The Controller may lease or sell any real property for cash at public auction to the highest bidder.

Before such sale or lease, notice thereof shall be published pursuant to Government Code Section 6063 in a newspaper published in the county in which the real property is situated, or in an adjoining county, if there is no newspaper published in such county. The notice is sufficient for all the purposes of such lease or sale if the real property is described sufficiently to identify it. The cost of publication shall be a charge against the proceeds of the lease or sale, or, if the lease or sale is not consummated, such cost shall be a legal charge against the appropriation for official advertising.

If the value of the property to be sold does not appear to exceed one thousand dollars ($1,000) in the determination of the Controller, notice of sale thereof may be published pursuant to Government Code Section 6061. *(Added by Stats.1951, c. 1708, p. 3944, § 5. Amended by Stats.1953, c. 281, p. 1431, § 1.5; Stats.1963, c. 752, p. 1766, § 1.)*

§ 1374. Rejection of bids

The Controller may reject any and all bids made at sales or public auctions held under the provisions of this chapter. *(Added by Stats.1951, c. 1708, p. 3944, § 5.)*

§ 1375. Real estate; private sale or lease without notice; approval

With the approval of the California Victim Compensation and Government Claims Board, any real property may be sold or leased by the Controller at private sale without published notice. *(Added by Stats.1951, c. 1708, p. 3944, § 5. Amended by Stats.2006, c. 538 (S.B.1852), § 72.)*

§ 1376. Execution of deed, bill of sale, or lease by Controller

Upon receipt of the proceeds of any sale made pursuant to this chapter, the Controller shall execute, in the name and on behalf of the State of California, a deed covering the real property, and a bill of sale covering the personal property, sold. He may execute leases for real or personal property in the name and on behalf of the State of California. *(Added by Stats.1951, c. 1708, p. 3944, § 5.)*

§ 1377. Transactions creating additional obligations prohibited

The Controller shall not enter into any transaction which shall create or impose upon the owners, heirs, devisees, legatees, or other claimants of the property involved, any obligation under an executory contract, the performance of which is not already an obligation of such owners, heirs, devisees, legatees, or other claimants prior to the consummation of the transactions authorized by this chapter. *(Added by Stats.1951, c. 1708, p. 3944, § 5.)*

§ 1378. Transactions under chapter; bar of suits against state

No suit shall be maintained by any person against the State or any officer thereof, for or on account of any transaction entered into by the Controller pursuant to this chapter. *(Added by Stats.1951, c. 1708, p. 3945, § 5.)*

§ 1379. Destruction of valueless personal property; approval; nonliability

With the prior approval of the California Victim Compensation and Government Claims Board, the Controller may destroy or otherwise dispose of any personal property other than cash deposited in the State Treasury under this title, if that property is determined by him or her to be valueless or of such little value that the costs of conducting a sale would probably exceed the amount that would be realized from the sale, and neither the Treasurer nor Controller shall be held to respond in damages at the suit of any person claiming loss by reason of that destruction or disposition. *(Added by Stats.1951, c. 1708, p. 3945, § 5. Amended by Stats.2006, c. 538 (S.B.1852), § 73.)*

§ 1380. Sales, exchanges, etc.; approval of department of finance not required

All sales, exchanges, or other transactions entered into by the Controller pursuant to this chapter are exempt from the provisions of Section 11009 of the Government Code. *(Added by Stats.1951, c. 1708, p. 3945, § 5.)*

§ 1381. Conclusiveness of sales, leases or other transactions

All sales, leases or other transactions entered into by the Controller pursuant to this chapter shall be conclusive against everyone, except a purchaser or encumbrancer who in good faith and for a valuable consideration acquires a title or interest by an instrument in writing that is first duly recorded. *(Added by Stats.1951, c. 1738, p. 4149, § 6.)*

§ 1382. Sales of real property; applicability of article; exclusion of tax-deeded lands

Any provision of this article which authorizes the Controller to sell real property applies to any real property distributed or escheated to, or the title to which has vested in, the State of California by court order or decree of distribution, if such real property is held in the name of the Unclaimed Property Fund under the provisions of this title, whether or not such real property has permanently escheated to the State.

This section does not apply to the disposition of tax-deeded lands under Chapter 7,[1] 8 [2] or 9 [3] of Part 6 of Division 1 of the Revenue and Taxation Code. *(Added by Stats.1953, c. 281, p. 1431, § 1.)*

[1] Revenue and Taxation Code § 3691 et seq.

[2] Revenue and Taxation Code § 3771 et seq.

[3] Revenue and Taxation Code § 3900 et seq. (repealed).

ARTICLE 4. DISPOSAL OF PROCEEDS OF SALE OR LEASE

§ 1390. Property not permanently escheated; deposit in unclaimed property fund; beneficiaries

The Controller shall deliver to the Treasurer the proceeds of any sale or lease of property, other than permanently escheated property, made pursuant to this chapter; and, on order of the Controller, the amount thereof shall be deposited in the Unclaimed Property Fund. Such amount shall be credited by the Controller to the account in said fund, in the name of which the property sold or leased was held. All moneys deposited in the Unclaimed Property Fund under the provisions of this section shall be held for the benefit of those entitled to claim the property sold or leased; but the period in which such moneys shall be available for claim by and payment to the persons entitled thereto shall not extend beyond the period in which such property is available for claim and payment under the provisions of this title. *(Added by Stats.1951, c. 1708, p. 3945, § 5.)*

§ 1391. Permanently escheated property; deposit in general fund; presumption

The Controller shall deliver to the Treasurer the proceeds of any sale or lease of permanently escheated property made pursuant to this chapter; and, on order of the Controller, the amount thereof shall be deposited in the General Fund. All moneys deposited in the General Fund under the provisions of this section shall be deemed to have permanently escheated to the state as of the date of permanent escheat of the property from which such moneys were derived. *(Added by Stats.1951, c. 1708, p. 3945, § 5. Amended by Stats.1978, c. 1183, p. 3825, § 12.)*

§ 1392. Property from estates; credit to estate from which property received or to general fund

The proceeds of any transaction by the Controller under the provisions of this chapter in connection with property received and held by the state under the provisions of Article 1 (commencing with Section 1440) of Chapter 6 of this title shall be credited by the Controller to the estate from which the property affected by the transaction was received; or, if such property has permanently escheated to the state, to the account in the General Fund to which the permanently escheated cash derived from estates of deceased persons is credited. *(Added by Stats.1951, c. 1708, p. 3945, § 5. Amended by Stats.1978, c. 1183, p. 3826, § 13.)*

§ 1393. Property from estates; credit to unlocated heirs, devisees, or legatees or to general fund

The proceeds of any transaction by the Controller under the provisions of this chapter, in connection with property received and held by the state under the provisions of Article 1 (commencing with Section 1440) of Chapter 6 of this title, for the benefit of unlocated heirs, devisees or legatees of estates of deceased persons, shall be credited by the Controller to such heirs, devisees or legatees of the property affected by such transaction; or, if such property has permanently escheated to the state, to the account in the General Fund to which the permanently escheated cash derived from estates of deceased persons is credited. *(Added by Stats.1951, c. 1708, p. 3946, § 5. Amended by Stats.1978, c. 1183, p. 3826, § 14.)*

§ 1394. Property for benefit of known persons; credit to such persons or general fund

The proceeds of any transaction by the Controller under the provisions of this chapter in connection with property received and held by the state under the provisions of this title, for the benefit of the persons entitled thereto, shall be credited by the Controller to such persons; or, if the property affected by such transaction has permanently escheated to the state, to the account in the General Fund in the name of which such permanently escheated property was recorded. *(Added by Stats.1951, c. 1708, p. 3946, § 5. Amended by Stats.1978, c. 1183, p. 3826, § 15.)*

CHAPTER 5. ESCHEAT PROCEEDINGS

ARTICLE 1. ESCHEAT PROCEEDINGS ON UNCLAIMED PROPERTY

§ 1410. Action to establish title of state by escheat; jurisdiction and venue; commencement; lis pendens; order to show cause; service; publication; judgment; costs

The Attorney General shall, from time to time, commence actions on behalf of the state for the purpose of having it adjudged that title to unclaimed property to which the state has become entitled by escheat has vested in the state, and for the purpose of having it adjudged that property has been actually abandoned or that the owner thereof has died and there is no person entitled thereto and the same has escheated and vested in the state. Such actions shall be brought in the Superior Court for the County of Sacramento; except that if any real property covered by the petition is not situated in the County of Sacramento, an action respecting the real property shall be commenced in the superior court for the county in which such real property or any part thereof is situated. The Attorney General shall cause to be recorded in the office of the county recorder of the county in which the real property is situated, a notice of the pendency of the petition containing the names of the parties, and the object of the action and a description of the property in the county affected thereby. From the time of filing such notice for record only, shall a purchaser or encumbrancer of the property affected thereby be deemed to have constructive notice of the pendency of the action, and only of the pendency against parties designated by their real names.

Such action shall be commenced by filing a petition. The provisions of Section 1420, relating to the facts to be set forth in the petition, joinder of parties and causes of action, and the provisions of Section 1423, relating to appearances and pleadings, shall be applicable to any proceeding had under this section.

Upon the filing of the petition, the court shall make an order requiring all persons interested in the property or estate to appear on a day not more than 90 days nor less than 60 days from the date of the order and show cause, if any they have, why title to the property should not vest in the State of California.

Service of process in such actions shall be made by delivery of a copy of the order, together with a copy of the petition, to each person who claims title to any property covered by the petition and who is known to the Attorney General or the Controller or who has theretofore filed in the office of the Controller a written request for such service of process, stating his name and address, including street number, or post-office box number, if any, and by publishing the order at least once a week for two consecutive weeks in a newspaper published in the county in which the action is filed, the last publication to be at least 10 days prior to the date set for the hearing.

Upon completion of the service of process, as provided in this section, the court shall have full and complete jurisdiction over the estate, the property, and the person of everyone having or claiming any interest in the property, and shall have full and complete jursidiction [1] to hear and determine the issues therein, and to render an appropriate judgment.

In addition to the foregoing publication of the order, a notice shall be given by publication, at least once a week for two successive weeks in a newspaper published in the county from which the property was forwarded to the State Treasury or is situated, of each estate and item of property from such county or situated in such county in excess of one thousand dollars ($1,000). Such notice shall state that a petition has been filed and an order made as hereinbefore provided and shall list each estate and item in excess of one thousand dollars ($1,000) and show the amount of the property, if money, or a description thereof, if other than money, and the name of the owner or claimant and his last known address. Any omission or defect in the giving of such additional notice shall not affect the jurisdiction of the court.

If it appears from the facts found or admitted that the state is entitled to the property or any part thereof mentioned in the petition, judgment shall be rendered that title to such property or part thereof, as the case may be, has vested in the state by escheat.

No costs of suit shall be allowed against any party in any action or proceeding had under this section. *(Added by Stats.1951, c. 1708, p. 3946, § 5. Amended by Stats.1951, c. 1738, p. 4146, § 2; Stats.1965, c. 2066, p. 4810, § 2; Stats.1972, c. 856, p. 1521, § 1, operative Jan. 1, 1973; Stats.1984, c. 268, § 1, eff. June 30, 1984.)*

[1] So in chaptered copy.

Research References

Rutter, Cal. Practice Guide: Civ. Pro. Before Trial Ch. 9(I)-J, J. Motion to Expunge Lis Pendens.
Rutter, Cal. Practice Guide: Real Prop. Transactions Ch. 11-I, I. Lis Pendens.
Miller and Starr California Real Estate § 18:2, Escheat Proceedings by the State.
Miller and Starr California Real Estate § 18:6, Permanent Escheat.
Miller and Starr California Real Estate § 11:150, Actions in Which a Lis Pendens May or Must be Recorded.
3 Witkin Cal. Proc. 5th Actions § 71, (S 71) Escheat Proceedings.
3 Witkin Cal. Proc. 5th Actions § 381, (S 381) Specific Mandatory Statutes.
3 Witkin, California Summary 10th Agency and Employment § 403, (S 403) Nature of Funds.

ARTICLE 2. ESCHEAT BY NOTICE AND PUBLICATION

Section

display of notice on return; publication; time to claim property.

§ 1415. Money or personal property valued at $1,000 or less; alternative escheat proceedings; return of controller; display of notice on return; publication; time to claim property

Whenever any money or other personal property of a value of one thousand dollars ($1,000) or less has heretofore been, or is hereafter, deposited in the State Treasury and the same is subject to being declared escheated to the state or being declared vested in the state as abandoned property, or otherwise, under any laws of this state, in lieu of the procedure provided for elsewhere in this chapter, the Controller may, from time to time, prepare a return listing such property and give notice thereof in the manner hereinafter provided. Such return shall list each item and show (1) the amount of the property, if money, or a description thereof if other than money; (2) the name of the owner or claimant and his last known address, if known; (3) the name and address of the person delivering the property to the State Treasury, if known but where the property is received from an estate, only the name of the decedent together with the name of the county and the number of the proceeding need be given; (4) the facts and circumstances by virtue of which it is claimed the property has escheated or vested in the state; and (5) such other information as the Controller may desire to include to assist in identifying each item.

When such return has been completed, the Controller shall prepare, date, and attach thereto a notice that the property listed in the return has escheated or vested in the state. Copies of such return and notice shall then be displayed and be open to public inspection during business hours in at least three offices of the Controller, one in the City of Sacramento, one in the City and County of San Francisco, and one in the City of Los Angeles.

The Controller shall then cause notice to be given by publication in one newspaper of general circulation published in the City of Sacramento, and also by publication in one newspaper of general circulation published in the City and County of San Francisco, and also by publication in one newspaper of general circulation published in the City of Los Angeles, at least once each calendar week for two consecutive weeks, that said return and notice that the property listed in the return has escheated or vested in the state has been prepared and is on display and open to public inspection during business hours, giving the addresses and room numbers of the locations where the same may be inspected.

Such publication shall be made within 90 days after attaching the notice to the return. Notice by such publication shall be deemed completed 120 days after attaching the notice to the return.

Within five years after such notice by publication is completed, any person entitled to such property may claim it in the manner provided in Chapter 3 [1] of this title. All persons who fail to make such claim within the time limited are forever barred; saving, however, to infants and persons of unsound mind, the right to appear and claim such property at any time within the time limited, or within one year after their respective disabilities cease. *(Added by Stats.1951, c. 1708, p. 3947, § 5. Amended by Stats.1965, c. 1350, p. 3237, § 1; Stats.1984, c. 268, § 2, eff. June 30, 1984.)*

[1] Code of Civil Procedure § 1335 et seq.

Research References

Miller and Starr California Real Estate § 18:3, Property of Decedent Not Leaving a Will or Heirs.

Miller and Starr California Real Estate § 18:4, Necessity of a Judicial Action Before Decedent's Property Escheats; Claims to Escheated Property.

Miller and Starr California Real Estate § 18:5, Escheat Procedure for Money or Personal Property Valued at $1,000 or Less.

ARTICLE 3. ESCHEAT PROCEEDINGS IN DECEDENTS' ESTATES

§ 1420. Action by state; court; commencement of action; petition; order to show cause; publication; jurisdiction; probate distribution; joinder of parties and causes of action; direction for administration by public administrator

(a) At any time after two years after the death of any decedent who leaves property to which the state is entitled by reason of it having escheated to the state, the Attorney General shall commence a proceeding on behalf of the state in the Superior Court for the County of Sacramento to have it adjudged that the state is so entitled. The action shall be commenced by filing a petition, which shall be treated as the information elsewhere referred to in this title.

(b) The petition shall set forth a description of the property, the name of the person last in possession thereof, the name of the person, if any, claiming the property, or portion thereof, and the facts and circumstances by virtue of which it is claimed the property has escheated.

(c) Upon the filing of the petition, the court shall make an order requiring all persons interested in the estate to appear and show cause, if any, within 60 days from the date of the order, why the estate should not vest in the state. The order must be published at least once a week for four consecutive weeks in a newspaper published in the County of Sacramento, the last publication to be at least 10 days prior to the date set for the hearing. Upon the completion of the publication of the order, the court shall have full and complete jurisdiction over the estate, the property, and the person of everyone having or claiming any interest in the property, and shall have full and complete jurisdiction to hear and determine the issues therein, and render the appropriate judgment thereon.

(d) If proceedings for the administration of the estate have been instituted, a copy of the order must be filed with the papers in the estate. If proceedings for the administration of any estate of the decedent have been instituted and none of the persons entitled to succeed thereto have appeared and made claim to the property, or any portion thereof, before the decree of final distribution therein is made, or before the commencement of a proceeding by the Attorney General, or if the court shall find that the persons as have appeared are not entitled to the property of the estate, or any portion thereof, the court shall, upon final settlement of the proceedings for the administration of the estate, after the payment of all debts and expenses of administration, distribute all moneys and other property remaining to the State of California.

In any proceeding brought by the Attorney General under this chapter, any two or more parties and any two or more causes of action may be joined in the same proceedings and in the same petition without being separately stated, and it shall be sufficient to allege in the petition that the decedent left no heirs to take the estate and the failure of heirs to appear and set up their claims in any proceeding, or in any proceedings for the administration of the estate, shall be sufficient proof upon which to base the judgment in any proceeding or decree of distribution.

(e) If proceedings for the administration of any estate have not been commenced within six months from the death of any decedent the Attorney General may direct the public administrator to commence the same forthwith. *(Added by Stats.1951, c. 1708, p. 3949, § 5. Amended by Stats.2002, c. 784 (S.B.1316), § 83; Stats.2003, c. 62 (S.B.600), § 26.)*

Law Revision Commission Comments

Section 1420 is amended to reflect elimination of the county clerk's role as ex officio clerk of the superior court. See former Gov't Code § 26800 (county clerk acting as clerk of superior court). The powers, duties, and responsibilities formerly exercised by the county clerk as ex officio clerk of the court are delegated to the court administrator or executive officer, and the county clerk is relieved of those powers, duties, and responsibilities. See Gov't Code §§ 69840 (powers, duties, and responsibilities of clerk of court and deputy clerk of court), 71620 (trial court personnel). [32 Cal.L.Rev.Comm. Reports 138 (2002)].

Research References

Miller and Starr California Real Estate § 18:3, Property of Decedent Not Leaving a Will or Heirs.

Miller and Starr California Real Estate § 18:4, Necessity of a Judicial Action Before Decedent's Property Escheats; Claims to Escheated Property.

Miller and Starr California Real Estate § 18:6, Permanent Escheat.

14 Witkin, California Summary 10th Wills and Probate § 99, (S 99) Nature and Scope of Statute.

§ 1421. Attorney general; authority to commence action or to intervene; application for order for deposit of money and property in state treasury

Whenever the Attorney General is informed that any estate has escheated or is about to escheat to the state, or that the property involved in any action or special proceeding has escheated or is about to escheat to the state, the Attorney General may commence an action on behalf of the state to determine its rights to the property or may intervene on its behalf in any action or special proceeding affecting the estate and contest the rights of any claimant or claimants thereto. The Attorney General may also apply to the superior court or any judge thereof for an order directing the county treasurer to deposit in the State Treasury all money, and to deliver to the Controller for deposit in the State Treasury, all other personal property, in the possession of the county treasurer, which may become payable to the State Treasury pursuant to Section 7643 of the Probate Code. *(Added by Stats.1951, c. 1708, p. 3950, § 5. Amended by Stats.1988, c. 1199, § 9, operative July 1, 1989.)*

Law Revision Commission Comments

Section 1421 is amended to correct a section reference and to make other technical changes. [19 Cal.L.Rev.Comm. Reports 1036 (1988)].

Research References

Miller and Starr California Real Estate § 18:2, Escheat Proceedings by the State.

4 Witkin Cal. Proc. 5th Pleading § 215, Special Statutes.

§ 1422. Receiver of estate, etc.; appointment

The court, upon the information being filed, and upon application of the Attorney General, either before or after answer, upon notice to the party claiming the estate, if known, may, upon sufficient cause therefor being shown, appoint a receiver to take charge of such estate, or any part thereof, or to receive the rents, income and profits of the same until the title of such estate is finally settled. *(Added by Stats.1951, c. 1708, p. 3950, § 5.)*

Research References

Miller and Starr California Real Estate § 18:2, Escheat Proceedings by the State.

Miller and Starr California Real Estate § 33:1, Nature of Receiverships; in General.

Miller and Starr California Real Estate § 33:23, Actions in Which a Receiver May be Appointed--In General.

6 Witkin Cal. Proc. 5th Provisional Remedies § 423, Specific Statutory Enumeration.

6 Witkin Cal. Proc. 5th Provisional Remedies § 440, (S 440) Other Actions or Proceedings.

§ 1423. Appearances; answer; added parties; default judgment; trial; judgment; sale; confirmation of sale; costs

All persons named in the information may appear and answer, and may traverse or deny the facts stated therein at any time before the time for answering expires, and any other person claiming an interest in such estate may appear and be made a defendant, by motion for that purpose in open court within the time allowed for answering, and if no such person appears and answers within the time, then judgment must be rendered that the State is the owner of the property in such information claimed.

If any person appears and denies the title set up by the State, or traverses any material fact set forth in the information, the issue of fact must be tried as issues of fact are tried in civil actions.

If, after the issues are tried, it appears from the facts found or admitted that the State has good title to the property in the information mentioned, or any part thereof, judgment must be rendered that the State is the owner and entitled to the possession thereof, and that it recover costs of suit against the defendants who have appeared and answered.

In any judgment rendered, or that has heretofore been rendered by any court escheating property to the State, on motion of the Attorney General, the court must make an order that such property, unless it consists of money, be sold by the sheriff of the county where it is situate, at public sale, for cash, after giving notice of the time and place of sale, as may be prescribed by the court in such order; that the sheriff, within five days after such sale, make a report thereof to the court, and upon the hearing of such report, the court may examine the report and witnesses in relation thereto, and if the proceedings were unfair, or if the sum bid disproportionate to the value, or if it appears that a sum exceeding said bid, exclusive of the expense of a new sale, may be obtained, the court may vacate the sale, and direct another to be had, of which notice must be given, and the sale in all respects conducted as if no previous sale had taken place. If an offer greater in amount than that named in the report is made to the court in writing by a responsible person, the court may, in its discretion, accept such offer and confirm the sale to such person, or order a new sale.

If it appears to the court that the sale was legally made and fairly conducted and that the sum bid is not disproportionate to the value of the property sold, and that a sum exceeding such bid, exclusive of the expense of a new sale, cannot be obtained, or if the increased bid above mentioned is made and accepted by the court, the court must make an order confirming the sale and directing the sheriff, in the name of the State, to execute to the purchaser or purchasers a conveyance of said property sold; and said conveyance vests in the purchaser or purchasers all the right and title of the State therein.

The sheriff shall, out of the proceeds of such sale, pay the cost of said proceedings incurred on behalf of the State, including the expenses of making such sale, and also an attorney's fee, if additional counsel was employed in said proceedings, to be fixed by the court, not exceeding 10 percent on the amount of such sale; and the residue thereof shall be paid by said sheriff into the State Treasury. *(Added by Stats.1951, c. 1708, p. 3950, § 5.)*

Research References

7 Witkin Cal. Proc. 5th Judgment § 232, (S 232) Probate and Trust Actions.

§ 1424. Judgment vesting unclaimed property in state and creating trust vests legal and equitable titles; claimants' rights

If, in any proceeding had under this title, the judgment or decree distributes or vests unclaimed property or any portion thereof to or in the State of California, and the distributing or vesting clause contains words otherwise creating a trust in favor of certain unknown or unidentified persons as a class, such judgment or decree shall vest in the State of California both legal and equitable title to such property; saving, however, the right of claimants to appear and claim the property, as provided in this title. *(Added by Stats.1951, c. 1708, p. 3950, § 5.)*

ARTICLE 4. PERMANENT ESCHEAT

Section
1430. Permanent escheat; time; rights of persons under disability; presumption; named beneficiaries or their blood relatives.
1431. Unclaimed property fund; transfer of permanently escheated money or property to general fund.

§ 1430. Permanent escheat; time; rights of persons under disability; presumption; named beneficiaries or their blood relatives

(a) Upon the expiration of five years after the date of entry of judgment in any proceeding pursuant to this chapter, or upon the expiration of five years after completion of notice by publication in an escheat action taken pursuant to Section 1415, the property covered by that proceeding or action shall permanently escheat to the state, except as provided in subdivision (b).

(b) Infants and persons of unsound mind shall have the right to appear and claim such property as provided in this title if born before the expiration of the five-year period; but it shall be presumed that there are no infants nor persons of unsound mind who are or will be entitled to claim this property unless and until they appear and claim the property as provided in this title. This presumption shall be conclusive in favor of any purchaser in good faith and for a valuable consideration from the state and everyone subsequently claiming under him or her, saving however, to infants and persons of unsound mind the right of recourse to the proceeds of any sale or other disposition of any such property by the state and as herein provided.

(c) Except as otherwise provided in this subdivision, a named beneficiary of property that escheats pursuant to this title or, if the beneficiary is deceased or a court renders a judgment that the beneficiary is dead, a blood relative of the named beneficiary may claim property described in subdivision (a) at any time within five years after the date of entry of judgment in any

proceeding under this chapter. The named beneficiary or, if a court has rendered a judgment that the named beneficiary is dead, the blood relative of the named beneficiary shall be entitled to immediate payment upon this claim. If a court has not rendered a judgment that the named beneficiary is dead, payment of the claim of a blood relative of the named beneficiary shall be made on the day before the expiration of the five-year period described in this section. This subdivision shall not apply to authorize a claim by any person, including any issue or blood relative of that person, whose interest or inheritance was specifically restricted or barred by a provision in the donating or transferring instrument. *(Added by Stats.1951, c. 1708, p. 3951, § 5. Amended by Stats.1951, c. 1738, p. 4148, § 3; Stats.1997, c. 671 (S.B.999), § 1.)*

Research References

Miller and Starr California Real Estate § 18:3, Property of Decedent Not Leaving a Will or Heirs.
Miller and Starr California Real Estate § 18:4, Necessity of a Judicial Action Before Decedent's Property Escheats; Claims to Escheated Property.
Miller and Starr California Real Estate § 18:6, Permanent Escheat.
3 Witkin Cal. Proc. 5th Actions § 485, (S 485) Five Years.

§ 1431. Unclaimed property fund; transfer of permanently escheated money or property to general fund

When money in the Unclaimed Property Fund has become permanently escheated to the state, the amount thereof shall, on order of the Controller, be transferred to the General Fund. When property other than money held by the Controller or Treasurer in the name of any account in the Unclaimed Property Fund has become permanently escheated to the state, the records of the Controller and Treasurer shall be adjusted to show that such property is held in the name of the General Fund. *(Added by Stats.1951, c. 1708, p. 3952, § 5. Amended by Stats.1978, c. 1183, p. 3826, § 16; Stats.1980, c. 676, § 69.)*

CHAPTER 6. DISPOSITION OF UNCLAIMED PROPERTY

ARTICLE 1. ESTATES OF DECEASED PERSONS

Section

1447.   Money or property of person who died while confined in state mental institution; delivery to state; presumption.

1448.   Money or property of person who died while confined in state youth institution; delivery to state; presumption.

1449.   Presumption of payment or delivery under article; transmittal, receipt, accounting, and disposal.

§ 1440. Payment to state of unclaimed property from decedent's estate; presumption of payment under article

Whenever, under the provisions of this title or under any other provision of law, any unclaimed money or other property in an estate of a deceased person, or any unclaimed amount payable pursuant to an allowed and approved claim against such an estate, is paid to the State or any officer or employee thereof for deposit in the State Treasury, it shall be deemed to have been so paid under the provisions of this article. *(Added by Stats.1951, c. 1708, p. 3952, § 5.)*

Research References

3 Witkin Cal. Proc. 5th Actions § 71, (S 71) Escheat Proceedings.

14 Witkin, California Summary 10th Wills and Probate § 421, Deposit of Money of Estate.

14 Witkin, California Summary 10th Wills and Probate § 653, Deposit for Missing Creditor.

§ 1441. Money or property distributed to state; permanent escheat for failure to claim; rights of persons under disability; presumption in favor of bona fide purchasers

Money or other property distributed to the state under Chapter 6 (commencing with Section 11900) of Part 10 of Division 7 of the Probate Code, if not claimed within five years from the date of the order for distribution, as provided in Chapter 3 [1], is permanently escheated to the state without further proceeding; saving, however, to infants and persons of unsound mind, the right to appear and file their claims within the time limited pursuant to Section 1430, or within one year after their respective disabilities cease; provided, however, that any such property shall be conclusively presumed to be permanently escheated to the state as to all persons in favor of a purchaser in good faith and for a valuable consideration from the state and anyone subsequently claiming under that purchaser, saving however, to infants and persons of unsound mind the right of recourse to the proceeds of any sale or other disposition of that property by the state and as herein provided. *(Added by Stats.1951, c. 1708, p. 3952, § 5. Amended by Stats.1951, c. 1738, p. 4148, § 4; Stats.1988, c. 1199, § 10, operative July 1, 1989; Stats.1995, c. 105 (S.B.481), § 1.)*

[1] Code of Civil Procedure § 1335 et seq.

Law Revision Commission Comments

Section 1441 is amended to reflect the repeal of Probate Code Section 1144 and its replacement, in part, by Probate Code Section 7663 (distribution of property), which provides for escheat to the county, and to reflect the repeal of Probate Code Section 1027 and its replacement, in part, by Probate Code Section 11900 (distribution to State of California). [19 Cal.L.Rev.Comm. Reports 1036 (1988)].

Research References

Miller and Starr California Real Estate § 18:3, Property of Decedent Not Leaving a Will or Heirs.

Miller and Starr California Real Estate § 18:6, Permanent Escheat.

§ 1442. Right to claim; exception

Except as otherwise provided in Section 1441, any money or other property paid into the State Treasury under the provisions of this article may be claimed by the person entitled thereto, as provided in Chapter 3.[1] *(Added by Stats.1951, c. 1708, p. 3952, § 5.)*

[1] Code of Civil Procedure § 1335 et seq.

§ 1443. Payment to state; presumption as to applicable law

Notwithstanding any other provision of law, all money or other property paid or delivered to the state or any officer or employee thereof under the provisions of Section 7643 or 11428, Chapter 6 (commencing with Section 11900) of Part 10 of Division 7, or Section 6800, of the Probate Code, or under any other section of the Probate Code, or any amendment thereof adopted after the effective date of this section, shall be deemed to be paid or delivered for deposit in the State Treasury under the provisions of this article, and shall be transmitted, received, accounted for, and disposed of, as provided in this title. *(Added by Stats.1951, c. 1708, p. 3952, § 5. Amended by Stats.1953, c. 1758, p. 3517, § 3; Stats.1983, c. 842, § 13, operative Jan. 1, 1985; Stats.1988, c. 1199, § 11, operative July 1, 1989.)*

Law Revision Commission Comments

Section 1443 is amended to substitute a reference to the provision that supersedes former Section 231 which was formerly referred to in Section 1443. [16 Cal.L.Rev.Comm. Reports 183 (1982)].

Section 1443 is amended to reflect the repeal of Probate Code Section 738 and its replacement by Probate Code Section 11428 (deposit for missing creditor), the repeal of Probate Code Section 1027 and its replacement, in part, by Probate Code Section 11900 (distribution to State of California), the repeal of Probate Code Section 1148 and its replacement by Probate Code Section 7643 (deposit with county treasurer), and the repeal of Probate Code Section 1144 and its replacement, in part, by Probate Code Section 7663 (distribution of property), which provides for escheat to the county. [19 Cal.L.Rev.Comm. Reports 1202 (1988)].

Research References

3 Witkin Cal. Proc. 5th Actions § 71, (S 71) Escheat Proceedings.

§ 1444. Money or property deposited in county treasury for known heirs, etc.; payment to state treasurer or controller

At the time of the next county settlement following the expiration of one year from the date of its deposit in the county treasury, all money or other property distributed in the administration of an estate of a deceased person and heretofore or hereafter deposited in the county treasury to the credit of known heirs, legatees, or devisees, and any money or other property remaining on deposit to the credit of an estate after final distribution to such known heirs, legatees or devisees, shall be paid to the Treasurer or Controller as provided in Chapter 2.[1] *(Added by Stats.1951, c. 1708, p. 3952, § 5.)*

[1] Code of Civil Procedure § 1310 et seq.

Research References

14 Witkin, California Summary 10th Wills and Probate § 653, Deposit for Missing Creditor.

§ 1444.5. Money on deposit with county treasurer received from public administrator or coroner

Notwithstanding any other provision of law, any money on deposit with the county treasurer of a county received from a public administrator of the county in trust and to the account of the estate of a deceased person or the creditor of a deceased person, in an amount of fifty dollars ($50) or less as to any one estate or creditor, and not covered by a decree of distribution, which was received or remained on hand after the final accounting in such deceased person's estate and the discharge of such public administrator as representative of the estate, and where the money has so remained on deposit in trust for a period of 15 years or more unclaimed by any heir, devisee or legatee of such deceased person, or by any creditor having an allowed and approved claim against the deceased person's estate remaining

Civ. Pro.

unpaid, shall be deemed permanently escheated to the State of California. The total of any such moneys so held in trust unclaimed for such period may be paid in a lump sum by the county treasurer, from such funds as he may have on hand for the purpose, to the State Treasurer, at the time of the next county settlement after the effective date of this section, or at any county settlement thereafter. Such lump sum payment may be made by designating it to have been made under this section, without the necessity of any further report or statement of the estates or claimants concerned, without the necessity of any order of court, and without being subject to the provisions of Section 1311 or 1312. Upon receipt by the State Treasurer, any permanently escheated money received by him under this section shall forthwith be deposited in the School Land Fund, subject only to the rights of minors and persons of unsound mind saved to them by Section 1430.

This section shall also apply in all respects to any money on deposit with a county treasurer received from the coroner of the county in trust and to the account of a deceased person, and any such money shall be held, deemed permanently escheated, reported and paid over in like manner as hereinabove set forth. *(Added by Stats.1957, c. 1375, p. 2708 § 1.)*

§ 1445. Undistributed money or property of estate; county treasurer's petition to pay into state treasury; order; payment

If money or other property is deposited in a county treasury, and if the deposits belong (1) to known decedents' estates on which letters testamentary or letters of administration have never been issued or (2) to known decedents' estates on which letters testamentary or letters of administration have been issued but no decree of distribution has been rendered, due to the absence of any parties interested in the estate or the failure of such parties diligently to protect their interests by taking reasonable steps for the purpose of securing a distribution of the estate, the county treasurer shall, within one year following the expiration of five years from the date of such deposit, file a petition in the superior court of the county in which the deposit is held, setting forth the fact that the money or other personal property has remained in the county treasury under such circumstances for such five-year period, and petitioning the court for an order directing him to pay such money or other property into the State Treasury.

At the time of the next county settlement following the date of the making of the order by the court, unless earlier payment is required by the Controller, the county treasurer shall pay such money or other property to the Treasurer or Controller as provided in Chapter 2. *(Added by Stats.1951, c. 1708, p. 3953, § 5.)*

§ 1446. Money or property of person who died while confined in state penal institution; delivery to state; presumption

Notwithstanding any other provision of law, all unclaimed money or other property belonging to any person who dies while confined in any state institution subject to the jurisdiction of the Director of Corrections, which is paid or delivered to the State or any officer or employee thereof under the provisions of Section 5061 of the Penal Code, or under any amendment thereof adopted after the effective date of this section, shall be deemed to be paid or delivered for deposit in the State Treasury under the provisions of this article, and shall be transmitted, received, accounted for, and disposed of, as provided in this part. *(Added by Stats.1951, c. 1708, p. 3953, § 5.)*

Research References

3 Witkin Cal. Proc. 5th Actions § 71, (S 71) Escheat Proceedings.

§ 1447. Money or property of person who died while confined in state mental institution; delivery to state; presumption

Notwithstanding any other provision of law, all unclaimed money or other property belonging to any person who dies while confined in any state institution subject to the jurisdiction of the Department of Mental Hygiene, which is paid or delivered to the State or any officer or employee thereof under the provisions of Section 166 of the Welfare and Institutions Code, or under any amendment thereof adopted after the effective date of this section, shall be deemed to be paid or delivered for deposit in the State Treasury under the provisions of this article, and shall be transmitted, received, accounted for, and disposed of, as provided in this part. *(Added by Stats.1951, c. 1708, p. 3953, § 5.)*

§ 1448. Money or property of person who died while confined in state youth institution; delivery to state; presumption

Notwithstanding any other provision of law, all unclaimed money or other property belonging to any person who dies while confined in any state institution subject to the jurisdiction of the Youth Authority, which is paid or delivered to the State or any officer thereof under the provisions of Section 1015 of the Welfare and Institutions Code or under any amendment thereof adopted after the effective date of this section, shall be deemed to be paid or delivered for deposit in the State Treasury under the provisions of this article, and shall be transmitted, received, accounted for, and disposed of, as provided in this part. *(Added by Stats.1951, c. 1708, p. 3953, § 5.)*

§ 1449. Presumption of payment or delivery under article; transmittal, receipt, accounting, and disposal

Notwithstanding any other provision of law, all presumptively abandoned money or other property paid or delivered to the Treasurer or Controller under the provisions of Section 7644 of the Probate Code shall be deemed to be paid or delivered for deposit in the State Treasury under the provisions of this article, and shall be transmitted, received, accounted for, and disposed of as provided in this title. *(Added by Stats.1953, c. 219, p. 1360, § 2. Amended by Stats.1988, c. 1199, § 12, operative July 1, 1989.)*

Law Revision Commission Comments

Section 1449 is amended to reflect the repeal of Probate Code Section 1147.5 and its replacement by Probate Code Section 7644 (deposit unclaimed in financial institution). [19 Cal.L.Rev.Comm. Reports 1036 (1988)].

ARTICLE 2. ABANDONED PROPERTY

Section
1476.　Limitation of actions; inapplicability.

§ 1476. Limitation of actions; inapplicability

The expiration of any period of time specified by law, during which an action or proceeding may be commenced or enforced to secure payment of a claim for money or recovery of property, shall not prevent any such money or other property from being deemed abandoned property, nor affect any duty to file a report required by this title or to deliver to the Treasurer or Controller any such abandoned property; and shall not serve as a defense in any action or proceeding brought under the provisions of this article to compel the filing of any report or the delivery of any abandoned property required by this article or to enforce or collect any penalty provided by this article. *(Added by Stats. 1951, c. 1708, p. 3958, § 5.)*

Research References

Miller and Starr California Real Estate § 18:7, The Unclaimed Property Law--Property Unclaimed or Abandoned.

3 Witkin Cal. Proc. 5th Actions § 489, Express Statutory Provisions.

CHAPTER 7. UNCLAIMED PROPERTY LAW

ARTICLE 1. SHORT TITLE; DEFINITIONS; APPLICATION

§ 1500. Short title

This chapter may be cited as the Unclaimed Property Law. *(Added by Stats.1959, c. 1809, p. 4296, § 2. Amended by Stats.1968, c. 356, p. 739, § 4, operative Jan. 1, 1969.)*

Law Revision Commission Comments

The short title of the chapter has been revised to reflect the fact that the chapter is no longer substantially the same as the Uniform Disposition of Unclaimed Property Act promulgated by the National Conference of Commissioners on Uniform State Laws.

The second sentence of this section has been recodified as subdivision (c) [now, subd. (b)] of Section 1502.

Research References

Miller and Starr California Real Estate § 18:7, The Unclaimed Property Law--Property Unclaimed or Abandoned.
Miller and Starr California Real Estate § 1:144, Duty of Seller of Real Property to Disclose--Statutory Duty of Disclosure.
Miller and Starr California Real Estate § 31:43, Sale of a Mobilehome by a Tenant.
Miller and Starr California Real Estate § 33:21, Duties of a Receiver--To Account and Secure Discharge.
Miller and Starr California Real Estate § 10:113, Reconveyance When Trustee Fails to Reconvey.
3 Witkin Cal. Proc. 5th Actions § 65, (S 65) Statutory Classes.
3 Witkin Cal. Proc. 5th Actions § 71, (S 71) Escheat Proceedings.
3 Witkin Cal. Proc. 5th Actions § 489, Express Statutory Provisions.
3 Witkin Cal. Proc. 5th Actions § 664, (S 664) in General.
2 Witkin, California Summary 10th Insurance § 72A, (New)-Manner of Payment of Life Insurance Proceeds.
12 Witkin, California Summary 10th Real Property § 481, (S 481) Excluded Transfers.
13 Witkin, California Summary 10th Personal Property § 37, Purpose of Revision.
9 Witkin, California Summary 10th Corporations § 235, (S 235) Dissolution of Corporation.

§ 1501. Definitions

As used in this chapter, unless the context otherwise requires:

(a) "Apparent owner" means the person who appears from the records of the holder to be entitled to property held by the holder.

(b) "Banking organization" means any national or state bank, trust company, banking company, land bank, savings bank, safe-deposit company, private banker, or any similar organization.

(c) "Business association" means any private corporation, joint stock company, business trust, partnership, or any association for business purposes of two or more individuals, whether or not for profit, including, but not by way of limitation, a banking organization, financial organization, life insurance corporation, and utility.

(d) "Financial organization" means any federal or state savings and loan association, building and loan association, credit union, investment company, or any similar organization.

(e) "Holder" means any person in possession of property subject to this chapter belonging to another, or who is trustee in case of a trust, or is indebted to another on an obligation subject to this chapter.

(f) "Life insurance corporation" means any association or corporation transacting the business of insurance on the lives of persons or insurance appertaining thereto, including, but not by way of limitation, endowments, and annuities.

(g) "Owner" means a depositor in case of a deposit, a beneficiary in case of a trust, or creditor, claimant, or payee in case of other choses in action, or any person having a legal or equitable interest in property subject to this chapter, or his or her legal representative.

(h) "Person" means any individual, business association, government or governmental subdivision or agency, two or more persons having a joint or common interest, or any other legal or commercial entity, whether that person is acting in his or her own right or in a representative or fiduciary capacity.

(i) "Employee benefit plan distribution" means any money, life insurance, endowment or annuity policy or proceeds thereof, securities or other intangible property, or any tangible property, distributable to a participant, former participant, or the beneficiary or estate or heirs of a participant or former participant or beneficiary, from a trust or custodial fund established under a plan to provide health and welfare, pension, vacation, severance, retirement benefit, death benefit, stock purchase, profit sharing, employee savings, supplemental unemployment insurance benefits or similar benefits, or which is established under a plan by a business association functioning as or in conjunction with a labor union which receives for distribution residuals on behalf of employees working under collective-bargaining agreements.

(j) "Residuals" means payments pursuant to a collective bargaining agreement of additional compensation for domestic and foreign uses of recorded materials. *(Added by Stats.1959, c. 1809, p. 4296, § 2. Amended by Stats.1968, c. 356, p. 739, § 5, operative Jan. 1, 1969; Stats.1972, c. 856, p. 1523, § 2, operative Jan. 1, 1973; Stats.1976, c. 582, p. 1421, § 1; Stats.1977, c. 579, p. 1843, § 36; Stats.1982, c. 786, p. 3046, § 1; Stats.1984, c. 899, § 1; Stats.1990, c. 450 (S.B.57), § 2, eff. July 31, 1990.)*

Law Revision Commission Comments

The definitions in Section 1501 have been revised to reflect the fact that the revised chapter applies to persons in other states who are holding property belonging to another. All of the definitions have been revised, therefore, to eliminate any requirement that such persons be engaged in business in California.

Subdivision (a) has been added to facilitate reference to the person who appears from the holder's records to be the person entitled to the property. The right of this state to escheat unclaimed property depends on the information the holder has concerning the apparent owner identified on its records. That he may have transferred his interest to another person without notice to the holder is of no consequence for escheat purposes. Of course, nothing in this statute prevents the actual owner from recovering the property from the holder or the State Controller. See Sections 1540, 1560.

The listing of certain additional organizations in subdivision (b) is clarifying and eliminates whatever doubts there may have been that those organizations are covered by the subdivision.

A "utility" is included under the definition of "business association" in subdivision (c). Utilities formerly were excluded in this definition, but such exclusion is no longer necessary since the exemption for utilities is now provided by subdivision (b) of Section 1502. The other revisions of subdivision (c) are clarifying changes. The substitution of "private corporation" for "corporation (other than a public corporation . . . .)" makes no substantive change. See 3 Witkin, Summary of California Law, Corporations § 13 at 2312 (1960).

The words "federal or state" have been added to subdivision (d) to eliminate any uncertainty concerning whether all such organizations are covered by the chapter.

Subdivision (e) excludes the federal government and its agencies from the operation of this statute because the escheat of property in federal custody is governed by Sections 1600 et seq.

The reference to "utility" has been deleted from subdivision (i) as unnecessary in the light of Section 1502. Public corporations formerly were specifically excluded from the term "person," which is defined in subdivision (i). This exclusion has been deleted. It is apparent that the exclusion was a technical defect since, under former Code of Civil Procedure Section 1507, certain property held by public corporations was presumed abandoned if unclaimed for seven years, but the procedural provisions of the former statute dealing with reporting and delivery of abandoned property applied only to "persons." It should be noted, however, that certain property in the custody of certain governmental entities is exempted from this chapter by Section 1502 and that certain other property in the custody of governmental entities is not subject to this chapter because its disposition is governed by special statutes such as those listed in the Comment to Section 1519. The other revisions of subdivision (i) are nonsubstantive, clarifying changes.

Subdivision (j) has been revised to limit the definition to utilities whose rates are regulated by public agencies.

Research References

Miller and Starr California Real Estate § 18:7, The Unclaimed Property Law--Property Unclaimed or Abandoned.
13 Witkin, California Summary 10th Personal Property § 40, Escheat of Unclaimed Personal Property.
3 Witkin, California Summary 10th Agency and Employment § 403, (S 403) Nature of Funds.

§ 1501.5. Permanency of escheat; legislative findings and declarations and intent

(a) Notwithstanding any provision of law to the contrary, property received by the state under this chapter shall not permanently escheat to the state.

(b) The Legislature finds and declares that this section is declaratory of the existing law and sets forth the intent of the Legislature regarding the Uniform Disposition of Unclaimed Property Act (Chapter 1809, Statutes of 1959) and all amendments thereto and revisions thereof. Any opinions, rulings, orders, judgments, or other statements to the contrary by any court are erroneous and inconsistent with the intent of the Legislature.

(c) It is the intent of the Legislature that property owners be reunited with their property. In making changes to the unclaimed property program in conjunction with the Budget Act of 2007, the Legislature intends to adopt a more expansive notification program that will provide all of the following:

(1) Notification by the state to all owners of unclaimed property prior to escheatment.

(2) A more expansive postescheatment policy that takes action to identify those owners of unclaimed property.

(3) A waiting period of not less than 18 months from delivery of property to the state prior to disposal of any unclaimed property deemed to have no commercial value. *(Added by Stats.1988, c. 286, § 1. Amended by Stats.2007, c. 179 (S.B.86), § 1, eff. Aug. 24, 2007.)*

Research References

Miller and Starr California Real Estate § 18:7, The Unclaimed Property Law--Property Unclaimed or Abandoned.
18 NO. 4 Miller & Starr, California Real Estate Newsalert 45, Table of Statutes (Newsalert Vol 18).

§ 1502. Exemptions from chapter

(a) This chapter does not apply to any of the following:

(1) Any property in the official custody of a municipal utility district.

(2) Any property in the official custody of a local agency if such property may be transferred to the general fund of such agency under the provisions of Sections 50050–50053 of the Government Code.

(3) Any property in the official custody of a court if the property may be transferred to the Trial Court Operations Fund under Section 68084.1 of the Government Code.

(b) None of the provisions of this chapter applies to any type of property received by the state under the provisions of Chapter 1 (commencing with Section 1300) to Chapter 6 (commencing with Section 1440), inclusive, of this title. *(Formerly § 1526, added by Stats.1959, c. 1809, p. 4307, § 2. Renumbered § 1502 and amended by Stats.1968, c. 356, p. 740, § 6, operative Jan. 1, 1969. Amended by Stats.1976, c. 582, p. 1422, § 2; Stats.2004, c. 227 (S.B.1102), § 13, eff. Aug. 16, 2004; Stats.2007, c. 738 (A.B.1248), § 6.)*

Research References

Miller and Starr California Real Estate § 18:7, The Unclaimed Property Law--Property Unclaimed or Abandoned.
Miller and Starr California Real Estate § 18:8, The Unclaimed Property Law--Property Exempt.
13 Witkin, California Summary 10th Personal Property § 40, Escheat of Unclaimed Personal Property.
13 Witkin, California Summary 10th Personal Property § 41, Exemptions.

§ 1503. Filing report or payment or delivery of property not subject to old act; action barred prior to Jan. 1, 1969; property held less than escheat period

(a) As used in this section:

(1) "Old act" means this chapter as it existed prior to January 1, 1969.

(2) "New act" means this chapter as it exists on and after January 1, 1969.

(3) "Property not subject to the old act" means property that was not presumed abandoned under the old act and would never have been presumed abandoned under the old act had the old act continued in existence on and after January 1, 1969, without change.

(b) The holder is not required to file a report concerning, or to pay or deliver to the Controller, any property not subject to the old act if an action by the owner against the holder to recover that property was barred by an applicable statute of limitations prior to January 1, 1969.

(c) The holder is not required to file a report concerning, or to pay or deliver to the Controller, any property not subject to the old act, or any property that was not required to be reported under the old act, unless on January 1, 1969, the property has been held by the holder for less than the escheat period. "Escheat period" means the period referred to in Sections 1513 to 1521, inclusive, of the new act, whichever is applicable to the particular property. *(Added by Stats.1968, c. 356, p. 741, § 7, operative Jan. 1, 1969. Amended by Stats.1990, c. 450 (S.B.57), § 3, eff. July 31, 1990.)*

Research References

Miller and Starr California Real Estate § 18:8, The Unclaimed Property Law--Property Exempt.
13 Witkin, California Summary 10th Personal Property § 41, Exemptions.
13 Witkin, California Summary 10th Personal Property § 42, Procedure in Escheating Property.

§ 1504. Payment or delivery of property not subject to old act; escheat of property under laws of another state

(a) As used in this section:

(1) "Old act" means this chapter as it existed prior to January 1, 1969.

(2) "New act" means this chapter as it exists on and after January 1, 1969.

(3) "Property not subject to the old act" means property that was not presumed abandoned under the old act and would never have been presumed abandoned under the old act had the old act continued in existence on and after January 1, 1969, without change.

(b) This chapter does not apply to any property that was escheated under the laws of another state prior to September 18, 1959.

(c) This chapter does not require the holder to pay or deliver any property not subject to the old act to this state if that property was escheated under the laws of another state prior to January 1, 1969, and was delivered to the custody of that state prior to January 1, 1970, in compliance with the laws of that state. Nothing in this subdivision affects or limits the right of the State Controller to recover such property from the other state. *(Added by Stats.1968, c. 356, p. 741, § 8, operative Jan. 1, 1969.)*

Law Revision Commission Comments

Subdivision (b) of Section 1504 continues without substantive change that portion of former Section 1526 which provided that this chapter did not apply to "any property that has been presumed abandoned or escheated under the laws of another state prior to the effective date of this chapter [September 18, 1959]."

Subdivision (c) relieves the holder of the duty to pay to California property that (1) was not subject to this chapter as it existed prior to January 1, 1969, (2) was escheated by another state prior to January 1, 1969, and (3) was delivered to the custody of the other state prior to January 1, 1970. The subdivision reflects the same policy as subdivision (b). Subdivision (c) will minimize the transitional problems that will arise with respect to property not subject to the chapter as it existed prior to January 1, 1969, but escheated under the chapter as it existed on and after January 1, 1969. Subdivision (c) has no effect on property which was presumed abandoned—escheated—after September 18, 1959, and prior to January 1, 1969, under this chapter as it existed prior to January 1, 1969. See Section 1505.

Subdivision (c) has no effect on the right of the State Controller to claim for California property that has been escheated by and paid to another state. For example, where unclaimed intangible personal property has been paid to another state which is the state of the holder's domicile, California may recover the property from the other state if the last known address of the owner as shown by the records of the holder is in California or if the actual last known address of the owner is in California. See Texas v. New Jersey, 379 U.S. 674 (1965). In this connection, it should be noted that subdivision (c) does not relieve the holder of the duty to make such reports to the State Controller as may be necessary in order that California may establish its claim to the property paid to the other state.

Research References

Miller and Starr California Real Estate § 18:8, The Unclaimed Property Law--Property Exempt.
13 Witkin, California Summary 10th Personal Property § 41, Exemptions.

§ 1505. Duty to file report or to pay or deliver property arising prior to Jan. 1, 1969; enforcement by controller; penalties

This chapter does not affect any duty to file a report with the State Controller or to pay or deliver any property to him that arose prior to January 1, 1969, under the provisions of this chapter as it existed prior to January 1, 1969. Such duties may be enforced by the State Controller, and the penalties for failure to perform such duties may be imposed, under the provisions of this chapter as it existed prior to January 1, 1969. The provisions of this chapter as it existed prior to January 1, 1969, are continued in existence for the purposes of this section. *(Added by Stats.1968, c. 356, p. 742, § 9, operative Jan. 1, 1969.)*

Law Revision Commission Comments

Section 1505 makes it clear that the amendments, additions, and repeals made in this chapter in 1968 have no effect on certain duties that arose under this chapter prior to January 1, 1969—the operative date of the 1968 legislation. Such duties may be enforced under the prior law just as if the 1968 legislation had not been enacted. After January 1, 1969, however, the procedure for handling and disposing of property escheated under this chapter is governed by by 1968 legislation. For example, the procedure provided in the 1968 legislation applies to claims by the holder, the owner, or another state to recover property escheated under this chapter, whether or not the property escheated prior to January 1, 1969.

§ 1506. Construction of chapter; restatement and continuation of provisions

The provisions of this chapter as it exists on and after January 1, 1969, insofar as they are substantially the same as the provisions of this chapter as it existed prior to January 1, 1969, relating to the same subject matter, shall be construed as restatements and continuations thereof and not as new enactments. *(Added by Stats.1968, c. 356, p. 742, § 10, operative Jan. 1, 1969.)*

Law Revision Commission Comments

The 1968 legislation which added, amended, and repealed sections in this chapter was largely a restatement and continuation of the former law. Section 1506 is included to make it clear that the provisions of this chapter, insofar as they are substantially the same as the former law relating to the same subject matter, shall be construed as restatements and continuations thereof and not as new enactments.

The inclusion of Section 1506 makes it clear, for example, that the mere fact that the owner's claim against the holder is barred by the statute of limitations prior to January 1, 1969, does not relieve the holder from the obligation of paying escheated property to the State Controller. For example, assume that the holder is doing business in California and that the statute of limitations ran on a contract obligation of the holder on November 1, 1968. The fact that the statute of limitations ran before January 1, 1969, does not relieve the holder from the obligation of paying the escheated funds to the state in any case where the sum payable by the holder on this obligation would have been presumed abandoned in the course of time under the former law. So far as these escheated funds are concerned, the chapter merely continues the prior law. See Section 1570 and the *Comment* thereto. Compare Section 1503(b) and the *Comment* thereto.

Research References

13 Witkin, California Summary 10th Personal Property § 38, Nature of Law.

ARTICLE 2. ESCHEAT OF UNCLAIMED PERSONAL PROPERTY

Section
1510.   Escheat of intangible personal property.

§ 1510.   Escheat of intangible personal property

Unless otherwise provided by statute of this state, intangible personal property escheats to this state under this chapter if the conditions for escheat stated in Sections 1513 through 1521 exist, and if:

(a) The last known address, as shown on the records of the holder, of the apparent owner is in this state.

(b) No address of the apparent owner appears on the records of the holder and:

(1) The last known address of the apparent owner is in this state; or

(2) The holder is domiciled in this state and has not previously paid the property to the state of the last known address of the apparent owner; or

(3) The holder is a government or governmental subdivision or agency of this state and has not previously paid the property to the state of the last known address of the apparent owner.

(c) The last known address, as shown on the records of the holder, of the apparent owner is in a state that does not provide by law for the escheat of such property and the holder is (1) domiciled in this state or (2) a government or governmental subdivision or agency of this state.

(d) The last known address, as shown on the records of the holder, of the apparent owner is in a foreign nation and the holder is (1) domiciled in this state or (2) a government or governmental subdivision or agency of this state. *(Added by Stats.1968, c. 356, p. 742, § 11, operative Jan. 1, 1969. Amended*

by Stats.1972, c. 856, p. 1524, § 3, operative Jan. 1, 1973; Stats.1978, c. 1183, p. 3826, § 17.)

Research References

Miller and Starr California Real Estate § 18:7, The Unclaimed Property Law--Property Unclaimed or Abandoned.

2 Witkin Cal. Proc. 5th Jurisdiction § 261, (S 261) Escheat.

13 Witkin, California Summary 10th Personal Property § 37, Purpose of Revision.

13 Witkin, California Summary 10th Personal Property § 38, Nature of Law.

13 Witkin, California Summary 10th Personal Property § 39, (S 39) Other Statutes Dealing With Unclaimed Property.

13 Witkin, California Summary 10th Personal Property § 40, Escheat of Unclaimed Personal Property.

3 Witkin, California Summary 10th Agency and Employment § 403, (S 403) Nature of Funds.

§ 1511.   Escheat of money orders, travelers checks, etc.; conditions

(a) Any sum payable on a money order, travelers check, or other similar written instrument (other than a third-party bank check) on which a business association is directly liable escheats to this state under this chapter if the conditions for escheat stated in Section 1513 exist and if:

(1) The books and records of such business association show that such money order, travelers check, or similar written instrument was purchased in this state;

(2) The business association has its principal place of business in this state and the books and records of the business association do not show the state in which such money order, travelers check, or similar written instrument was purchased; or

(3) The business association has its principal place of business in this state, the books and records of the business association show the state in which such money order, travelers check, or similar written instrument was purchased, and the laws of the state of purchase do not provide for the escheat of the sum payable on such instrument.

(b) Notwithstanding any other provision of this chapter, this section applies to sums payable on money orders, travelers checks, and similar written instruments deemed abandoned on or after February 1, 1965, except to the extent that such sums have been paid over to a state prior to January 1, 1974. For the purposes of this subdivision, the words "deemed abandoned" have the same meaning as those words have as used in Section 604 of Public Law Number 93–495 (October 28, 1974), 88th Statutes at Large 1500.[1] *(Added by Stats.1975, c. 25, p. 45, § 2.)*

[1] 12 U.S.C.A. § 2501 note.

Law Revision Commission Comments

Section 1511 is replaced by new Section 1511 which conforms the California law to federal law. Pub.L. No. 93–495, §§ 601–604 (Oct. 28, 1974), 88 Stat. 1525–1526. See the Comment to new Section 1511.

Section 1511 adopts the rules provided in federal legislation which determines which state is entitled to escheat sums payable on money orders, travelers checks, and similar written instruments. See Pub.L. No. 93–495, §§ 603, 604 (Oct. 28, 1974), 88 Stat. 1525–1526. See also Recommendation Relating to Escheat of Amounts Payable on Travelers Checks, Money Orders, and Similar Instruments, 12 Cal.L.Revision Comm'n Reports 609 (1974).

Research References

Miller and Starr California Real Estate § 18:7, The Unclaimed Property Law--Property Unclaimed or Abandoned.

13 Witkin, California Summary 10th Personal Property § 38, Nature of Law.

§ 1513. Property held by banking or financial organizations or business associations

(a) Subject to Sections 1510 and 1511, the following property held or owing by a business association escheats to this state:

(1)(A) Except as provided in paragraph (6), any demand, savings, or matured time deposit, or account subject to a negotiable order of withdrawal, made with a banking organization, together with any interest or dividends thereon, excluding, from demand deposits and accounts subject to a negotiable order of withdrawal only, any reasonable service charges that may lawfully be withheld and that do not (where made in this state) exceed those set forth in schedules filed by the banking organization from time to time with the Controller, when the owner, for more than three years, has not done any of the following:

(i) Increased or decreased the amount of the deposit, cashed an interest check, or presented the passbook or other similar evidence of the deposit for the crediting of interest.

(ii) Corresponded electronically or in writing with the banking organization concerning the deposit.

(iii) Otherwise indicated an interest in the deposit as evidenced by a memorandum or other record on file with the banking organization.

(B) A deposit or account shall not, however, escheat to the state if, during the previous three years, the owner has owned another deposit or account with the banking organization or the owner has owned an individual retirement account or funds held by the banking organization under a retirement plan for self-employed individuals or a similar account or plan established pursuant to the internal revenue laws of the United States or the laws of this state, as described in paragraph (6), and, with respect to that deposit, account, or plan, the owner has done any of the acts described in clause (i), (ii), or (iii) of subparagraph (A), and the banking organization has communicated electronically or in writing with the owner, at the address to which communications regarding that deposit, account, or plan are regularly sent, with regard to the deposit or account that would otherwise escheat under subparagraph (A). For purposes of this subparagraph, "communications" includes account statements or statements required under the internal revenue laws of the United States.

(C) No banking organization may discontinue any interest or dividends on any savings deposit because of the inactivity contemplated by this section.

(2)(A) Except as provided in paragraph (6), any demand, savings, or matured time deposit, or matured investment certificate, or account subject to a negotiable order of withdrawal, or other interest in a financial organization or any deposit made therewith, and any interest or dividends thereon, excluding, from demand deposits and accounts subject to a negotiable order of withdrawal only, any reasonable service charges that may lawfully be withheld and that do not (where made in this state) exceed those set forth in schedules filed by the financial organization from time to time with the Controller, when the owner, for more than three years, has not done any of the following:

(i) Increased or decreased the amount of the funds or deposit, cashed an interest check, or presented an appropriate record for the crediting of interest or dividends.

(ii) Corresponded electronically or in writing with the financial organization concerning the funds or deposit.

(iii) Otherwise indicated an interest in the funds or deposit as evidenced by a memorandum or other record on file with the financial organization.

(B) A deposit or account shall not, however, escheat to the state if, during the previous three years, the owner has owned another deposit or account with the financial organization or the owner has owned an individual retirement account or funds held by the financial organization under a retirement plan for self-employed individuals or a similar account or plan established pursuant to the internal revenue laws of the United States or the laws of this state, as described in paragraph (6), and, with respect to that deposit, account, or plan, the owner has done any of the acts described in clause (i), (ii), or (iii) of subparagraph (A), and the financial organization has communicated electronically or in writing with the owner, at the address to which communications regarding that deposit, account, or plan are regularly sent, with regard to the deposit or account that would otherwise escheat under subparagraph (A). For purposes of this subparagraph, "communications" includes account statements or statements required under the internal revenue laws of the United States.

(C) No financial organization may discontinue any interest or dividends on any funds paid toward purchase of shares or other interest, or on any deposit, because of the inactivity contemplated by this section.

(3) Any sum payable on a traveler's check issued by a business association that has been outstanding for more than 15 years from the date of its issuance, when the owner, for more than 15 years, has not corresponded in writing with the business association concerning it, or otherwise indicated an interest as evidenced by a memorandum or other record on file with the association.

(4) Any sum payable on any other written instrument on which a banking or financial organization is directly liable, including, by way of illustration but not of limitation, any draft, cashier's check, teller's check, or certified check, that has been outstanding for more than three years from the date it was payable, or from the date of its issuance if payable on demand, when the owner, for more than three years, has not corresponded electronically or in writing with the banking or financial organization concerning it, or otherwise indicated an interest as evidenced by a memorandum or other record on file with the banking or financial organization.

(5) Any sum payable on a money order issued by a business association (including a banking or financial organization), that has been outstanding for more than seven years from the date it was payable, or from the date of its issuance if payable on demand, excluding any reasonable service charges that may lawfully be withheld and that do not, when made in this state, exceed those set forth in schedules filed by the business association from time to time with the Controller, when the owner, for more than seven years, has not corresponded electronically or in writing with the business association, banking, or financial organization concerning it, or otherwise indicated an interest as evidenced by a memorandum or other record on file with the business association. For the purposes of this subdivision, "reasonable service charge" means a service charge that meets all of the following requirements:

(A) It is uniformly applied to all of the issuer's money orders.

(B) It is clearly disclosed to the purchaser at the time of purchase and to the recipient of the money order.

(C) It does not begin to accrue until three years after the purchase date, and it stops accruing after the value of the money order escheats.

(D) It is permitted by contract between the issuer and the purchaser.

(E) It does not exceed 25 cents ($0.25) per month or the aggregate amount of twenty-one dollars ($21).

(6)(A) Any funds held by a business association in an individual retirement account or under a retirement plan for self-employed individuals or similar account or plan established pursuant to the internal revenue laws of the United States or of this state, when the owner, for more than three years after the funds become payable or distributable, has not done any of the following:

(i) Increased or decreased the principal.

(ii) Accepted payment of principal or income.

(iii) Corresponded electronically or in writing concerning the property or otherwise indicated an interest.

(B) Funds held by a business association in an individual retirement account or under a retirement plan for self-employed individuals or a similar account or plan created pursuant to the internal revenue laws of the United States or the laws of this state shall not escheat to the state if, during the previous three years, the owner has owned another such account, plan, or any other deposit or account with the business association and, with respect to that deposit, account, or plan, the owner has done any of the acts described in clause (i), (ii), or (iii) of subparagraph (A), and the business association has communicated electronically or in writing with the owner, at the address to which communications regarding that deposit, account, or plan are regularly sent, with regard to the account or plan that would otherwise escheat under subparagraph (A). For purposes of this subparagraph, "communications" includes account statements or statements required under the internal revenue laws of the United States.

(C) These funds are not payable or distributable within the meaning of this subdivision unless either of the following is true:

(i) Under the terms of the account or plan, distribution of all or a part of the funds would then be mandatory.

(ii) For an account or plan not subject to mandatory distribution requirement under the internal revenue laws of the United States or the laws of this state, the owner has attained 70 ½ years of age.

(7) Any wages or salaries that remained unclaimed by the owner for more than one year after the wages or salaries become payable.

(b) For purposes of this section "service charges" means service charges imposed because of the inactivity contemplated by this section. *(Formerly § 1502, added by Stats.1959, c. 1809, p. 4297, § 2. Amended by Stats.1961, c. 1904, p. 4011, § 1. Renumbered § 1513 and amended by Stats.1968, c. 356, p. 743, § 12, operative Jan. 1, 1969. Amended by Stats.1975, c. 578, p. 1157, § 1; Stats.1976, c. 648, p. 1599, § 1; Stats.1976, c. 1214, p. 5515, § 1; Stats.1978, c. 1183, p. 3827, § 17.5; Stats.1981, c. 831, § 1.5; Stats.1982, c. 786, p. 3047, § 2; Stats.1983, c. 104, § 1; Stats.1988, c. 286, § 2; Stats.1990, c. 450 (S.B.57), § 4, eff. July 31, 1990; Stats.1990, c. 1069 (S.B.1186), § 1, eff. Sept. 20, 1990; Stats.1999, c. 835 (A.B.777), § 1; Stats.2003, c. 304 (A.B.378), § 1; Stats.2009, c. 522 (A.B.1291), § 1; Stats.2011, c. 305 (S.B.495), § 1.)*

Research References

Miller and Starr California Real Estate § 18:7, The Unclaimed Property Law--Property Unclaimed or Abandoned.

13 Witkin, California Summary 10th Personal Property § 40, Escheat of Unclaimed Personal Property.

§ 1513.5. Notice of escheat by banking or financial organization

(a) Except as provided in subdivision (c), if the holder has in its records an address for the apparent owner, which the holder's records do not disclose to be inaccurate, every banking or financial organization shall make reasonable efforts to notify any owner by mail or, if the owner has consented to electronic notice, electronically, that the owner's deposit, account, shares, or other interest in the banking or financial organization will escheat to the state pursuant to clause (i), (ii), or (iii) of subparagraph (A) of paragraph (1), (2), or (6) of subdivision (a) of Section 1513. The holder shall give notice either:

(1) Not less than two years nor more than two and one-half years after the date of last activity by, or communication with, the owner with respect to the account, deposit, shares, or other interest, as shown on the record of the banking or financial organization.

(2) Not less than 6 nor more than 12 months before the time the account, deposit, shares, or other interest becomes reportable to the Controller in accordance with this chapter.

(b) The notice required by this section shall specify the time that the deposit, account, shares, or other interest will escheat and the effects of escheat, including the necessity for filing a claim for the return of the deposit, account, shares, or other interest. The face of the notice shall contain a heading at the top that reads as follows: "THE STATE OF CALIFORNIA REQUIRES US TO NOTIFY YOU THAT YOUR UN-CLAIMED PROPERTY MAY BE TRANSFERRED TO THE STATE IF YOU DO NOT CONTACT US," or substantially similar language. The notice required by this section shall, in boldface type or in a font a minimum of two points larger than the rest of the notice, exclusive of the heading, (1) specify that since the date of last activity, or for the last two years, there has been no owner activity on the deposit, account, shares, or other interest; (2) identify the deposit, account, shares, or other interest by number or identifier, which need not exceed four digits; (3) indicate that the deposit, account, shares, or other interest is in danger of escheating to the state; and (4) specify that the Unclaimed Property Law requires banking and financial organizations to transfer funds of a deposit, account, shares, or other interest if it has been inactive for three years. It shall also include a form, as prescribed by the Controller, by which the owner may declare an intention to maintain the deposit, account, shares, or other interest. If that form is filled out, signed by the owner, and returned to the banking or financial organization, it shall satisfy the requirement of clause (iii) of subparagraph (A) of paragraph (1), clause (iii) of subparagraph (A) of paragraph (2), or clause (iii) of subparagraph (A) of paragraph (6) of subdivision (a) of Section 1513. In lieu of returning the form, the banking or financial organization may provide a telephone number or other electronic means to enable the owner to contact that organization. The contact, as evidenced by a memorandum or other record on file with the banking or financial organization, shall satisfy the requirement of clause (iii) of subparagraph (A) of paragraph (1), clause (iii) of subparagraph (A) of paragraph (2), or clause (iii) of subparagraph (A) of paragraph (6) of subdivision (a) of Section 1513. <u>If the deposit, account, shares, or other interest has a value greater than two dollars ($2), the</u> banking or financial organization may impose a service charge on the deposit, account, shares, or other interest for this notice in an amount not to exceed the administrative cost of mailing or electronically sending the notice and form and in no case to exceed two dollars ($2).

(c) Notice as provided by subdivisions (a) and (b) shall not be required for deposits, accounts, shares, or other interests of less than fifty dollars ($50), and, <u>except as provided in subdivision (b),</u> no service charge may be made for notice on these items.

(d) In addition to the notices required pursuant to subdivision (a), the holder may give additional notice as described in subdivision (b) at any time between the date of last activity by, or communication with, the owner and the date the holder transfers the deposit, account, shares, or other interest to the Controller.

(e) At the time a new account is opened with a banking or financial organization, the organization shall provide a written notice to the person opening the account informing the person that his or her property may be transferred to the appropriate state if no activity occurs in the account within the time period specified by state law. If the person opening the account has consented to electronic notice, that notice may be provided electronically. * * * (*Added by Stats.1976, c. 1214, p. 5516, § 2. Amended by Stats.1981, c. 831, § 2; Stats.1988, c. 286, § 3; Stats.1990, c. 450 (S.B.57), § 5, eff. July 31, 1990; Stats.1990, c. 1069 (S.B.1186), § 2, eff. Sept. 20, 1990; Stats.1993, c. 692 (A.B.1854), § 2; Stats.1994, c. 587 (A.B.3600), § 8.5; Stats.1996, c. 762 (S.B.2014), § 3; Stats.2002, c. 813 (A.B.1772), § 1, operative Jan. 1, 2004; Stats.2009, c. 522 (A.B.1291), § 2; Stats.2011, c. 305 (S.B.495), § 2; Stats.2013, c. 362 (A.B.212), § 1.*)

Research References

Miller and Starr California Real Estate § 18:7, The Unclaimed Property Law--Property Unclaimed or Abandoned.
13 Witkin, California Summary 10th Personal Property § 40, Escheat of Unclaimed Personal Property.

§ 1514. Safe deposit box or other safekeeping depository, contents or proceeds of sale of contents; notice of escheat to state; default by owner

(a) The contents of, or the proceeds of sale of the contents of, any safe deposit box or any other safekeeping repository, held in this state by a business association, escheat to this state if unclaimed by the owner for more than three years from the date on which the lease or rental period on the box or other repository expired, or from the date of termination of any agreement because of which the box or other repository was furnished to the owner without cost, whichever last occurs.

(b) If a business association has in its records an address for an apparent owner of the contents of, or the proceeds of sale of the contents of, a safe deposit box or other safekeeping repository described in subdivision (a), and the records of the business association do not disclose the address to be inaccurate, the business association shall make reasonable efforts to notify the owner by mail, or, if the owner has consented to electronic notice, electronically, that the owner's contents, or the proceeds of the sale of the contents, will escheat to the state pursuant to this section. The business association shall give notice not less than 6 months and not more than 12 months before the time the contents, or the proceeds of the sale of the contents, become reportable to the Controller in accordance with this chapter.

(c) The face of the notice shall contain a heading at the top that reads as follows: "THE STATE OF CALIFORNIA REQUIRES US TO NOTIFY YOU THAT YOUR UNCLAIMED PROPERTY MAY BE TRANSFERRED TO THE STATE IF YOU DO NOT CONTACT US," or substantially similar language. The notice required by this subdivision shall specify the date that the property will escheat and the effects of escheat, including the necessity for filing a claim for the return of the property. The notice required by this section shall, in boldface type or in a font a minimum of two points larger than the rest of the notice, exclusive of the heading, do all of the following:

(1) Identify the safe deposit box or other safekeeping repository by number or identifier.

(2) State that the lease or rental period on the box or repository has expired or the agreement has terminated.

(3) Indicate that the contents of, or the proceeds of sale of the contents of, the safe deposit box or other safekeeping repository will escheat to the state unless the owner requests the contents or their proceeds.

(4) Specify that the Unclaimed Property Law requires business associations to transfer the contents of, or the proceeds of sale of the contents of, a safe deposit box or other safekeeping repository to the Controller if they remain unclaimed for more than three years.

(5) Advise the owner to make arrangements with the business association to either obtain possession of the contents of, or the proceeds of sale of the contents of, the safe deposit box or other safekeeping repository, or enter into a new agreement with the business association to establish a leasing or rental arrangement. If an owner fails to establish such an arrangement prior to the end of the period described in subdivision (a), the contents or proceeds shall escheat to this state.

(d) In addition to the notice required pursuant to subdivision (b), the business association may give additional notice in accordance with subdivision (c) at any time between the date on which the lease or rental period for the safe deposit box or repository expired, or from the date of the termination of any agreement, through which the box or other repository was furnished to the owner without cost, whichever is earlier, and the date the business association transfers the contents of, or the proceeds of sale of the contents of, the safe deposit box or other safekeeping repository to the Controller.

(e) The contents of, or the proceeds of sale of the contents of, a safe deposit box or other safekeeping repository shall not escheat to the state if, as of June 30 or the fiscal yearend next preceding the date on which a report is required to be filed under Section 1530, the owner has owned, with a banking organization providing the safe deposit box or other safekeeping repository, any demand, savings, or matured time deposit, or account subject to a negotiable order of withdrawal, which has not escheated under Section 1513 and is not reportable under subdivision (d) of Section 1530.

(f) The contents of, or the proceeds of sale of the contents of, a safe deposit box or other safekeeping repository shall not escheat to the state if, as of June 30 or the fiscal yearend next preceding the date on which a report is required to be filed under Section 1530, the owner has owned, with a financial organization providing the safe deposit box or other safekeeping repository, any demand, savings, or matured time deposit, or matured investment certificate, or account subject to a negotiable order of withdrawal, or other interest in a financial organization or any deposit made therewith, and any interest or dividends thereon, which has not escheated under Section 1513 and is not reportable under subdivision (d) of Section 1530.

(g) The contents of, or the proceeds of sale of the contents of, a safe deposit box or other safekeeping repository shall not escheat to the state if, as of June 30 or the fiscal yearend next preceding the date on which a report is required to be filed under Section 1530, the owner has owned, with a banking or financial organization providing the safe deposit box or other safekeeping repository, any funds in an individual retirement account or under a retirement plan for self-employed individuals or similar account or plan pursuant to the internal revenue laws of the United States or the income tax laws of this state, which has not escheated under Section 1513 and is not reportable under subdivision (d) of Section 1530.

(h) In the event the owner is in default under the safe deposit box or other safekeeping repository agreement and the owner has owned any demand, savings, or matured time deposit, account, or plan described in subdivision (e), (f), or (g), the banking or financial organization may pay or deliver the contents of, or the proceeds of sale of the contents of, the safe deposit box or other safekeeping repository to the owner after deducting any amount due and payable from those proceeds under that agreement. Upon making that payment or delivery under this subdivision, the banking or financial organization shall be relieved of all liability to the extent of the value of those contents or proceeds.

(i) For new accounts opened for a safe deposit box or other safekeeping repository with a business association on and after January 1, 2011, the business association shall provide a written notice to the person leasing the safe deposit box or safekeeping repository informing the person that his or her property, or the proceeds of sale of the property, may be transferred to the appropriate state upon running of the time period specified by state law from the date the lease or rental period on the safe deposit box or repository expired, or from the date of termination of any agreement because of which the box or other repository was furnished to the owner without cost, whichever is earlier.

(j) A business association may directly escheat the contents of a safe deposit box or other safekeeping repository without exercising its rights under Article 2 (commencing with Section 1630) of Chapter 17 of Division 1 of the Financial Code. *(Added by Stats.1968, c. 356, p. 744, § 13, operative Jan. 1, 1969. Amended by Stats.1979, c. 761, p. 2624, § 1; Stats.1988, c. 286, § 4; Stats.1990, c. 450 (S.B.57), § 6, eff. July 31, 1990; Stats. 2009, c. 522 (A.B.1291), § 3; Stats.2011, c. 305 (S.B.495), § 3; Stats.2012, c. 162 (S.B.1171), § 16.)*

Law Revision Commission Comments

Section 1514 is substantially the same as subdivision (e) of former Section 1502 except that "contents" has been substituted for "any funds or other personal property, tangible or intangible."

Under Section 1533, the State Controller may reject tangible personal property that escheats under Section 1514 if he determines that the state's interest would not be served by accepting it.

Research References

Miller and Starr California Real Estate § 18:7, The Unclaimed Property Law--Property Unclaimed or Abandoned.

13 Witkin, California Summary 10th Personal Property § 40, Escheat of Unclaimed Personal Property.

13 Witkin, California Summary 10th Personal Property § 42, Procedure in Escheating Property.

§ 1515. Funds held or owing by life insurance corporations

(a) Subject to Section 1510, funds held or owing by a life insurance corporation under any life or endowment insurance policy or annuity contract which has matured or terminated escheat to this state if unclaimed and unpaid for more than three years after the funds became due and payable as established from the records of the corporation.

(b) If a person other than the insured or annuitant is entitled to the funds and no address of that person is known to the corporation or if it is not definite and certain from the records of the corporation what person is entitled to the funds, it is presumed that the last known address of the person entitled to the funds is the same as the last known address of the insured or annuitant according to the records of the corporation. This presumption is a presumption affecting the burden of proof.

(c) A life insurance policy not matured by actual proof of the death of the insured according to the records of the corporation is deemed to be matured and the proceeds due and payable if:

(1) The insured has attained, or would have attained if he or she were living, the limiting age under the mortality table on which the reserve is based.

(2) The policy was in force at the time the insured attained, or would have attained, the limiting age specified in paragraph (1).

(3) Neither the insured nor any other person appearing to have an interest in the policy has, within the preceding three years, according to the records of the corporation (i) assigned, readjusted, or paid premiums on the policy, (ii) subjected the

policy to loan, or (iii) corresponded in writing with the life insurance corporation concerning the policy.

(d) Any funds otherwise payable according to the records of the corporation are deemed due and payable although the policy or contract has not been surrendered as required. *(Added by Stats.1968, c. 356, p. 744, § 15, operative Jan. 1, 1969. Amended by Stats.1988, c. 286, § 5; Stats.1990, c. 450 (S.B.57), § 7, eff. July 31, 1990; Stats.1993, c. 692 (A.B.1854), § 3.)*

Research References

Miller and Starr California Real Estate § 18:7, The Unclaimed Property Law--Property Unclaimed or Abandoned.

13 Witkin, California Summary 10th Personal Property § 40, Escheat of Unclaimed Personal Property.

§ 1515.5. Determination of abandonment of property distributable in course of demutualization or related reorganization of insurance company

Property distributable in the course of a demutualization or related reorganization of an insurance company is deemed abandoned as follows:

(a) On the date of the demutualization or reorganization, if the instruments or statements reflecting the distribution are not mailed to the owner because the address on the books and records for the holder is known to be incorrect.

(b) Two years after the date of the demutualization or reorganization, if instruments or statements reflecting the distribution are mailed to the owner and returned by the post office as undeliverable and the owner has done neither of the following:

(1) Communicated in writing with the holder or its agent regarding the property.

(2) Otherwise communicated with the holder or its agent regarding the property as evidenced by a memorandum or other record on file with the holder or its agent.

(c) Three years after the date of the demutualization or reorganization, if instruments or statements reflecting the distribution are mailed to the owner and not returned by the post office as undeliverable and the owner has done neither of the following:

(1) Communicated in writing with the holder or its agent regarding the property.

(2) Otherwise communicated with the holder or its agent regarding the property as evidenced by a memorandum or other record on file with the holder or its agent. *(Added by Stats.2003, c. 304 (A.B.378), § 2.)*

Research References

13 Witkin, California Summary 10th Personal Property § 40, Escheat of Unclaimed Personal Property.

§ 1516. Undistributed dividends and distributions of business associations; notice of escheat; form

(a) Subject to Section 1510, any dividend, profit, distribution, interest, payment on principal, or other sum held or owing by a business association for or to its shareholder, certificate holder, member, bondholder, or other security holder, or a participating patron of a cooperative, who has not claimed it, or corresponded in writing with the business association concerning it, within three years after the date prescribed for payment or delivery, escheats to this state.

(b) Subject to Section 1510, any intangible interest in a business association, as evidenced by the stock records or membership records of the association, escheats to this state if (1) the interest in the association is owned by a person who for more than three years has neither claimed a dividend or other sum referred to in subdivision (a) nor corresponded in writing with the association or otherwise indicated an interest as evidenced by a memorandum or other record on file with the association, and (2) the association does not know the location of the owner at the end of the three-year period. With respect to the interest, the business association shall be deemed the holder.

(c) Subject to Section 1510, any dividends or other distributions held for or owing to a person at the time the stock or other security to which they attach escheats to this state also escheat to this state as of the same time.

(d) If the business association has in its records an address for the apparent owner, which the business association's records do not disclose to be inaccurate, with respect to any interest that may escheat pursuant to subdivision (b), the business association shall make reasonable efforts to notify the owner by mail or, if the owner has consented to electronic notice, electronically, that the owner's interest in the business association will escheat to the state. The notice shall be given not less than 6 nor more than 12 months before the time the interest in the business association becomes reportable to the Controller in accordance with this chapter. The face of the notice shall contain a heading at the top that reads as follows: "THE STATE OF CALIFORNIA REQUIRES US TO NOTIFY YOU THAT YOUR UN-CLAIMED PROPERTY MAY BE TRANSFERRED TO THE STATE IF YOU DO NOT CONTACT US." or substantially similar language. The notice required by this subdivision shall specify the time that the interest will escheat and the effects of escheat, including the necessity for filing a claim for the return of the interest. The notice required by this section shall, in boldface type or in a font a minimum of two points larger than the rest of the notice, exclusive of the heading, (1) specify that since the date of last activity, or for the last two years, there has been no owner activity on the deposit, account, shares, or other interest; (2) identify the deposit, account, shares, or other interest by number or identifier, which need not exceed four digits; (3) indicate that the deposit, account, shares, or other interest is in danger of escheating to the state; and (4) specify that the Unclaimed Property Law requires business associations to transfer funds of a deposit, account, shares, or other interest if it has been inactive for three years. It shall also include a form, as prescribed by the Controller, by which the owner may confirm the owner's current address. If that form is filled out, signed by the owner, and returned to the holder, it shall be deemed that the business association knows the location of the owner. In lieu of returning the form, the business association may provide a telephone number or other electronic means to enable the owner to contact the association. With that contact, as evidenced by a memorandum or other record on file with the business association, the business association shall be deemed to know the location of the owner. The business association may impose a service charge on the deposit, account, shares, or other interest for this notice and form in an amount not to exceed the administrative cost of mailing or electronically sending the notice and form, and in no case to exceed two dollars ($2).

(e) In addition to the notice required pursuant to subdivision (d), the holder may give additional notice as described in subdivision (d) at any time between the date of last activity by, or communication with, the owner and the date the holder transfers the deposit, shares, or other interest to the Controller. *(Former-ly § 1504, added by Stats.1959, c. 1809, p. 4299, § 2. Amended by Stats.1961, c. 1904, p. 4012, § 2. Renumbered § 1516 and amended by Stats.1968, c. 356, p. 745, § 16, operative Jan. 1, 1969. Amended by Stats.1975, c. 578, p. 1159, § 1.5; Stats.1988, c. 286, § 6; Stats.1990, c. 450 (S.B.57), § 8, eff. July 31, 1990; Stats. 1993, c. 692 (A.B.1854), § 4; Stats.2002, c. 813 (A.B.1772), § 2, operative Jan. 1, 2004; Stats.2009, c. 522 (A.B.1291), § 4; Stats.2011, c. 305 (S.B.495), § 4.)*

Research References

Miller and Starr California Real Estate § 18:7, The Unclaimed Property Law--Property Unclaimed or Abandoned.

19 NO. 1 Miller & Starr, California Real Estate Newsalert 13, Escheat.

13 Witkin, California Summary 10th Personal Property § 40, Escheat of Unclaimed Personal Property.

13 Witkin, California Summary 10th Personal Property § 42, Procedure in Escheating Property.

§ 1517. Property distributable in course of voluntary or involuntary dissolution or liquidation; business associations; insurers

(a) All property distributable in the course of a voluntary or involuntary dissolution or liquidation of a business association that is unclaimed by the owner within six months after the date of final distribution or liquidation escheats to this state.

(b) All property distributable in the course of voluntary or involuntary dissolution or liquidation of an insurer or other person brought under Article 14 (commencing with Section 1010) of Chapter 1 of Part 2 of Division 1 of the Insurance Code, that is unclaimed by the owner after six months of the date of final distribution, shall be transferred to the Department of Insurance, with any proceeds of sale of property and other funds to be deposited in the Insurance Fund for expenditure as provided in Section 12937 of the Insurance Code.

(c) This section applies to all tangible personal property located in this state and, subject to Section 1510, to all intangible personal property. *(Added by Stats.1968, c. 356, p. 745, § 18, operative Jan. 1, 1969. Amended by Stats.1996, c. 187 (A.B.3137), § 1, eff. July 19, 1996.)*

Law Revision Commission Comments

Section 1517 is similar to former Section 1505. Unlike the former section, however, Section 1517 applies to tangible personal property located in this state as well as to intangible personal property. Section 1517 also extends the state's claim to such property even though the business association may not have been organized under the laws of this state. Section 1517 provides that the property escheats six months after final distribution or liquidation. The former section specified two years. Since property escheated under Section 1517 remains subject to the owner's claim, there appears to be no reason to delay transfer of custody to the state.

Under Section 1533, the State Controller may reject tangible personal property that escheats under Section 1517 if he determines that the state's interest would not be served by accepting it.

This section does not supersede or impliedly repeal special statutes that provide for a particular disposition of unclaimed property under circumstances similar to those described in Section 1517. See, e.g., Code Civ.Proc. § 570 (receiver); Corp.Code §§ 5009–5011 (dissolving or winding up corporation); Fin.Code §§ 3121, 3160–3162 (liquidation of bank or trust corporation); Ins.Code § 1056.5 (liquidated insurer).

Research References

Miller and Starr California Real Estate § 18:7, The Unclaimed Property Law--Property Unclaimed or Abandoned.

13 Witkin, California Summary 10th Personal Property § 40, Escheat of Unclaimed Personal Property.

9 Witkin, California Summary 10th Corporations § 219, Distribution to Shareholders.

§ 1518. Property held by fiduciaries

(a)(1) All tangible personal property located in this state and, subject to Section 1510, all intangible personal property, including intangible personal property maintained in a deposit or account, and the income or increment on such tangible or intangible property, held in a fiduciary capacity for the benefit of another person escheats to this state if for more than three years after it becomes payable or distributable, the owner has not done any of the following:

(A) Increased or decreased the principal.

Civ. Pro.

(B) Accepted payment of principal or income.

(C) Corresponded in writing concerning the property.

(D) Otherwise indicated an interest in the property as evidenced by a memorandum or other record on file with the fiduciary.

(2) Notwithstanding paragraph (1), tangible or intangible property, and the income or increment on the tangible or intangible property, held in a fiduciary capacity for another person shall not escheat to the state if the requirements of subparagraphs (A) and (B) are satisfied.

(A) During the previous three years, the fiduciary took one of the following actions:

(i) Held another deposit or account for the benefit of the owner.

(ii) Maintained a deposit or account on behalf of the owner in an individual retirement account.

(iii) Held funds or other property under a retirement plan for a self-employed individual, or similar account or plan, established pursuant to the internal revenue laws of the United States or the laws of this state.

(B) During the previous three years, the owner has done any of the acts described in subparagraph (A), (B), (C), or (D) of paragraph (1) with respect to the deposit, account, or plan described in subparagraph (A), and the fiduciary has communicated electronically or in writing with the owner at the address to which communications regarding that deposit, account, or plan are regularly sent, with regard to the deposit, account, or plan that would otherwise escheat under this subdivision. "Communications," for purposes of this subparagraph, includes account statements or statements required under the internal revenue laws of the United States.

(b) Funds in an individual retirement account or a retirement plan for self-employed individuals or similar account or plan established pursuant to the internal revenue laws of the United States or of this state are not payable or distributable within the meaning of subdivision (a) unless either of the following is true:

(1) Under the terms of the account or plan, distribution of all or part of the funds would then be mandatory.

(2) For an account or plan not subject to mandatory distribution requirement under the internal revenue laws of the United States or the laws of this state, the owner has attained 70 ½ years of age.

(c) For the purpose of this section, when a person holds property as an agent for a business association, he or she is deemed to hold the property in a fiduciary capacity for the business association alone, unless the agreement between him or her and the business association clearly provides the contrary. For the purposes of this chapter, if a person holds property in a fiduciary capacity for a business association alone, he or she is the holder of the property only insofar as the interest of the business association in the property is concerned and the association is deemed to be the holder of the property insofar as the interest of any other person in the property is concerned. *(Formerly § 1506, added by Stats.1959, c. 1809, p. 4300, § 2. Amended by Stats.1961, c. 1904, p. 4013, § 3. Renumbered § 1518 and amended by Stats.1968, c. 356, p. 746, § 19, operative Jan. 1, 1969. Amended by Stats.1976, c. 49, p. 80, § 1; Stats.1982, c. 786, p. 3049, § 3; Stats.1988, c. 286, § 7; Stats.1990, c. 450 (S.B.57), § 9, eff. July 31, 1990; Stats.2011, c. 305 (S.B.495), § 5.)*

Research References

Rutter, Cal. Practice Guide: Prof. Responsibility Ch. 9-B, B. Establishing and Maintaining Client Trust Accounts.
Miller and Starr California Real Estate § 18:7, The Unclaimed Property Law--Property Unclaimed or Abandoned.

Miller and Starr California Real Estate § 4:33, Handling of Trust Funds.
Miller and Starr California Real Estate § 6:16, Funds Held in Trust; Restrictions on Disbursement.
13 Witkin, California Summary 10th Personal Property § 40, Escheat of Unclaimed Personal Property.

§ 1519. Property held for owner by government, governmental subdivision or agency

All tangible personal property located in this state, and, subject to Section 1510, all intangible personal property, held for the owner by any government or governmental subdivision or agency, that has remained unclaimed by the owner for more than three years escheats to this state. *(Formerly § 1507, added by Stats.1959, c. 1809, p. 4300, § 2. Renumbered § 1519 and amended by Stats.1968, c. 356, p. 746, § 20, operative Jan. 1, 1969. Amended by Stats.1988, c. 286, § 8; Stats.1990, c. 450 (S.B.57), § 10, eff. July 31, 1990.)*

Law Revision Commission Comments

Section 1519 is substantially the same as former Section 1507. The section has been modified to make it apply to tangible, as well as intangible, property and to intangible property wherever the holder of the property may be located.

Under Section 1533, the State Controller may reject tangible personal property that escheats under Section 1519 if he determines that the state's interest would not be served by accepting it.

This chapter does not apply to certain property in the custody of certain governmental entities. See Section 1502. Nor does this section supersede or impliedly repeal special statutes which provide for a particular disposition of unclaimed property held by governmental subdivisions or agencies. See, e.g., Agric.Code § 4702 (citrus fruit fair); Civil Code §§ 1873, 2080.4–2080.6 (police or sheriff), §§ 1874, 2080.8 (University of California), §§ 1875, 2080.9 (state colleges); Educ.Code § 24002 (state colleges); Govt.Code §§ 16373–16374 (money deposited by state agency in state treasury trust fund); Harb. & Nav.Code §§ 513–521 (proceeds from sheriff's sale of perishable cargo from stranded vessel), § 522 (watercraft abandoned upon tidelands of public entity); Penal Code § 1411 (stolen or embezzled property in custody of county), § 1418 (exhibits from criminal trials), §§ 1420–1422 (money held by district attorney in criminal proceeding), §§ 5061–5066 (unclaimed property of inmates held by Director of Corrections); Pub.Res.Code §§ 2268–2271 [repealed] (stolen ores), § 5561.5 (unclaimed property in possession of regional park district); Veh.Code §§ 22660, 22705, 22707 (abandoned motor vehicles), §§ 2414–2415 (property, other than vehicles, held by Department of Motor Vehicles); Welf. & Inst.Code § 516 (bicycles and toys held by sheriff), § 4126 (property of deceased patient in Department of Mental Hygiene institution).

Research References

Miller and Starr California Real Estate § 18:7, The Unclaimed Property Law--Property Unclaimed or Abandoned.
13 Witkin, California Summary 10th Personal Property § 39, (S 39) Other Statutes Dealing With Unclaimed Property.
13 Witkin, California Summary 10th Personal Property § 40, Escheat of Unclaimed Personal Property.

§ 1519.5. Money ordered by court or public agency to be refunded by a business association; retroactive effect; legislative intent

Subject to Section 1510, any sums held by a business association that have been ordered to be refunded by a court or an administrative agency including, but not limited to, the Public Utilities Commission, which have remained unclaimed by the owner for more than one year after becoming payable in accordance with the final determination or order providing for the refund, whether or not the final determination or order requires any person entitled to a refund to make a claim for it, escheats to this state.

It is the intent of the Legislature that the provisions of this section shall apply retroactively to all funds held by business associations on or after January 1, 1977, and which remain undistributed by the business association as of the effective date of this act.

Further, it is the intent of the Legislature that nothing in this section shall be construed to change the authority of a court or administrative agency to order equitable remedies. *(Added by Stats.1984, c. 1096, § 1.)*

Research References

1 Witkin Cal. Summ. 10th Contracts § 528, Payment of Unreturnable Deposits to Tenants' Union.
13 Witkin, California Summary 10th Personal Property § 40, Escheat of Unclaimed Personal Property.

§ 1520. Other personal property held for another person in ordinary course of holder's business; notice of potential escheat

(a) All tangible personal property located in this state and, subject to Section 1510, all intangible personal property, except property of the classes mentioned in Sections 1511, 1513, 1514, 1515, 1515.5, 1516, 1517, 1518, 1519, and 1521, including any income or increment thereon and deducting any lawful charges, that is held or owing in the ordinary course of the holder's business and has remained unclaimed by the owner for more than three years after it became payable or distributable escheats to this state.

(b) Except as provided in subdivision (a) of Section 1513.5, subdivision (b) of Section 1514, and subdivision (d) of Section 1516, if the holder has in its records an address for the apparent owner of property valued at fifty dollars ($50) or more, which the holder's records do not disclose to be inaccurate, the holder shall make reasonable efforts to notify the owner by mail or, if the owner has consented to electronic notice, electronically, that the owner's property will escheat to the state pursuant to this chapter. The notice shall be mailed not less than 6 nor more than 12 months before the time when the owner's property held by the business becomes reportable to the Controller in accordance with this chapter. The face of the notice shall contain a heading at the top that reads as follows: "THE STATE OF CALIFORNIA REQUIRES US TO NOTIFY YOU THAT YOUR UNCLAIMED PROPERTY MAY BE TRANSFERRED TO THE STATE IF YOU DO NOT CONTACT US," or substantially similar language. The notice required by this subdivision shall specify the time when the property will escheat and the effects of escheat, including the need to file a claim in order for the owner's property to be returned to the owner. The notice required by this section shall, in boldface type or in a font a minimum of two points larger than the rest of the notice, exclusive of the heading, (1) specify that since the date of last activity, or for the last two years, there has been no owner activity on the deposit, account, shares, or other interest; (2) identify the deposit, account, shares, or other interest by number or identifier, which need not exceed four digits; (3) indicate that the deposit, account, shares, or other interest is in danger of escheating to the state; and (4) specify that the Unclaimed Property Law requires holders to transfer funds of a deposit, account, shares, or other interest if it has been inactive for three years. It shall also include a form, as prescribed by the Controller, by which the owner may confirm the owner's current address. If that form is filled out, signed by the owner, and returned to the holder, it shall be deemed that the account, or other device in which the owner's property is being held, remains currently active and recommences the escheat period. In lieu of returning the form, the holder may provide a telephone number or other electronic means to enable the owner to contact the holder. With that contact, as evidenced by a memorandum or other record on file with the holder, the account or other device in which the owner's property is being held shall be deemed to remain currently active and shall recommence the escheat

period. The holder may impose a service charge on the deposit, account, shares, or other interest for this notice in an amount not to exceed the administrative cost of mailing or electronically sending the notice and form, and in no case to exceed two dollars ($2).

(c) In addition to the notice required pursuant to subdivision (b), the holder may give additional notice as described in subdivision (b) at any time between the date of last activity by, or communication with, the owner and the date the holder transfers the property to the Controller.

(d) For purposes of this section, "lawful charges" means charges which are specifically authorized by statute, other than the Unclaimed Property Law, or by a valid, enforceable contract. *(Formerly § 1508, added by Stats.1959, c. 1809, p. 4300, § 2. Renumbered § 1520 and amended by Stats.1968, c. 356, p. 746, § 21, operative Jan. 1, 1969. Amended by Stats.1975, c. 578, p. 1159, § 2; Stats.1978, c. 1183, p. 3828, § 18; Stats.1988, c. 286, § 9; Stats.1990, c. 450 (S.B.57), § 11, eff. July 31, 1990; Stats.1996, c. 762 (S.B.2014), § 4; Stats.2002, c. 813 (A.B.1772), § 3, operative Jan. 1, 2004; Stats.2003, c. 304 (A.B.378), § 3; Stats.2009, c. 522 (A.B.1291), § 5; Stats.2011, c. 305 (S.B.495), § 6.)*

Law Revision Commission Comments

Section 1520 is substantially the same as former Section 1508. The section has been modified to make it apply to tangible, as well as intangible, property and to intangible property wherever the holder of the property may be located.

Under Section 1533, the State Controller may reject tangible personal property that escheats under Section 1520 if he determines that the state's interest would not be served by accepting it.

This section does not supersede or impliedly repeal special statutes which provide for a particular disposition of unclaimed property. See examples cited in the Comments to Sections 1510, 1517, and 1519. See also Civil Code §§ 1861, 1861a, 1862 (unclaimed property held by keeper of hotel, boarding house, apartment, and the like), § 1862.5 (unclaimed property in hospital), § 3072 (excess proceeds from sale of motor vehicle by lienholder).

Research References

Miller and Starr California Real Estate § 18:7, The Unclaimed Property Law--Property Unclaimed or Abandoned.
21 NO. 4 Miller & Starr, California Real Estate Newsalert 29, Escheat.
13 Witkin, California Summary 10th Personal Property § 40, Escheat of Unclaimed Personal Property.

§ 1520.5. Application of § 1520

Section 1520 does not apply to gift certificates subject to Title 1.4A (commencing with Section 1749.45) of Part 4 of Division 3 of the Civil Code. However, Section 1520 applies to any gift certificate that has an expiration date and that is given in exchange for money or any other thing of value. *(Added by Stats.1996, c. 933 (A.B.2466), § 2. Amended by Stats.1997, c. 472 (A.B.1054), § 2; Stats.2003, c. 116 (A.B.1092), § 3.)*

Research References

13 Witkin, California Summary 10th Personal Property § 40, Escheat of Unclaimed Personal Property.

§ 1521. Employee benefit plan distributions, income and other increments; conditions; exception; claim for residuals

(a) Except as provided in subdivision (b), and subject to Section 1510, all employee benefit plan distributions and any income or other increment thereon escheats to the state if the owner has not, within three years after it becomes payable or distributable, accepted the distribution, corresponded in writing concerning the distribution, or otherwise indicated an interest as evidenced by a memorandum or other record on file with the fiduciary of the trust or custodial fund or administrator of the plan under which the trust or fund is established. As used in this section, "fiduciary" means any person exercising any power, authority, or responsibility of management or disposition with respect to any money or other property of a retirement system or plan, and "administrator" means the person specifically so designated by the plan, trust agreement, contract, or other instrument under which the retirement system or plan is operated, or if none is designated, the employer.

(b) Except as provided in subdivision (c), an employee benefit plan distribution and any income or other increment thereon shall not escheat to this state if, at the time the distribution shall become payable to a participant in an employee benefit plan, the plan contains a provision for forfeiture or expressly authorizes the administrator to declare a forfeiture of a distribution to a beneficiary thereof who cannot be found after a period of time specified in the plan, and the trust or fund established under the plan has not terminated prior to the date on which the distribution would become forfeitable in accordance with the provision.

(c) A participant entitled to an employee benefit plan distribution in the form of residuals shall be relieved from a forfeiture declared under subdivision (b) upon the making of a claim therefor. *(Added by Stats.1972, c. 856, p. 1524, § 4, operative Jan. 1, 1973. Amended by Stats.1982, c. 786, p. 3050, § 4; Stats.1984, c. 899, § 2; Stats.1988, c. 286, § 10; Stats.1990, c. 450 (S.B.57), § 12, eff. July 31, 1990.)*

Research References

Miller and Starr California Real Estate § 18:7, The Unclaimed Property Law--Property Unclaimed or Abandoned.
13 Witkin, California Summary 10th Personal Property § 40, Escheat of Unclaimed Personal Property.
3 Witkin, California Summary 10th Agency and Employment § 403, (S 403) Nature of Funds.
14 Witkin, California Summary 10th Wills and Probate § 102, (S 102) Benefits Distributable from Certain Trusts.

§ 1522.   Service, maintenance or other charge or fee; deduction

No service, handling, maintenance or other charge or fee of any kind which is imposed because of the inactive or unclaimed status contemplated by this chapter, may be deducted or withheld from any property subject to escheat under this chapter, unless specifically permitted by this chapter.

Even when specifically permitted by this chapter, such charges or fees may not be excluded, withheld or deducted from property subject to this chapter if, under its policy or procedure, the holder would not have excluded, withheld or deducted such charges or fees in the event the property had been claimed by the owner prior to being reported or remitted to the Controller. *(Added by Stats.1975, c. 578, p. 1159, § 3. Amended by Stats.1981, c. 831, § 3.)*

Research References

Miller and Starr California Real Estate § 18:7, The Unclaimed Property Law--Property Unclaimed or Abandoned.
13 Witkin, California Summary 10th Personal Property § 40, Escheat of Unclaimed Personal Property.

§ 1523.   Insurers; Proposition 103 rebates; unlocatable policyholders; use of escheated funds

If an insurer, after a good faith effort to locate and deliver to a policyholder a Proposition 103 rebate ordered or negotiated pursuant to Section 1861.01 of the Insurance Code, determines that a policyholder cannot be located, all funds attributable to that rebate escheat to the state and shall be delivered to the Controller. The funds subject to escheat on or after July 1, 1997, shall be transferred by the Controller to the Department of

Insurance for deposit in the Insurance Fund in the following amounts and for the following purposes:

(a) Up to the amount that will repay principal and interest on the General Fund loan authorized by Item 0845–001–0001 of the Budget Act of 1996 for expenditure as provided in Section 12936 of the Insurance Code.

(b) The sum of four million dollars ($4,000,000) for expenditure during the 1998–1999 fiscal year as provided in Section 12967 of the Insurance Code. *(Added by Stats.1996, c. 187 (A.B.3137), § 2, eff. July 19, 1996. Amended by Stats.1997, c. 239 (S.B.18), § 1, eff. Aug. 6, 1997; Stats.1998, c. 963 (S.B.1530), § 1, eff. Sept. 29, 1998.)*

Research References

Miller and Starr California Real Estate § 18:7, The Unclaimed Property Law--Property Unclaimed or Abandoned.
13 Witkin, California Summary 10th Personal Property § 40, Escheat of Unclaimed Personal Property.

§ 1528.   Funds held by domestic fraternal benefit society; use

This chapter does not apply to unclaimed funds held by a life insurance corporation which is organized or admitted as a domestic fraternal benefit society under Chapter 10 (commencing with Section 10970) of Part 2 of Division 2 of the Insurance Code, so long as such funds are used for scholarship funds, exclusive of costs of administration thereof. *(Added by Stats. 1974, c. 1050, p. 2267, § 1.)*

Research References

Miller and Starr California Real Estate § 18:7, The Unclaimed Property Law--Property Unclaimed or Abandoned.
Miller and Starr California Real Estate § 18:8, The Unclaimed Property Law--Property Exempt.
13 Witkin, California Summary 10th Personal Property § 41, Exemptions.

ARTICLE 3.   IDENTIFICATION OF ESCHEATED PROPERTY

Section
1530.   Report of escheated property.
1531.   Notice and publication of lists of escheated property.
1531.5.   Notification program for possible owners of escheated property.
1532.   Payment or delivery of escheated property.
1532.1.   Payment or delivery of property escheated to state.
1533.   Exclusion of certain tangible personal property from notice requirement and escheat.

§ 1530.   Report of escheated property

(a) Every person holding funds or other property escheated to this state under this chapter shall report to the Controller as provided in this section.

(b) The report shall be on a form prescribed or approved by the Controller and shall include:

(1) Except with respect to traveler's checks and money orders, the name, if known, and last known address, if any, of each person appearing from the records of the holder to be the owner of any property of value of at least fifty dollars ($50) escheated under this chapter. <u>This paragraph shall become inoperative on July 1, 2014.</u>

(2) <u>Except with respect to traveler's checks and money orders, the name, if known, and last known address, if any, of each person appearing from the records of the holder to be the owner of any property of value of at least twenty-five dollars ($25) escheated under this chapter. This paragraph shall become operative on July 1, 2014.</u>

(3) In the case of escheated funds of life insurance corporations, the full name of the insured or annuitant, and his or her last known address, according to the life insurance corporation's records.

(4) In the case of the contents of a safe deposit box or other safekeeping repository or in the case of other tangible property, a description of the property and the place where it is held and may be inspected by the Controller. The report shall set forth any amounts owing to the holder for unpaid rent or storage charges and for the cost of opening the safe deposit box or other safekeeping repository, if any, in which the property was contained.

(5) The nature and identifying number, if any, or description of any intangible property and the amount appearing from the records to be due, except that items of value under * * * twenty five dollars ($25) each may be reported in aggregate.

(6) Except for any property reported in the aggregate, the date when the property became payable, demandable, or returnable, and the date of the last transaction with the owner with respect to the property.

(7) Other information which the Controller prescribes by rule as necessary for the administration of this chapter.

(c) If the holder is a successor to other persons who previously held the property for the owner, or if the holder has changed his or her name while holding the property, he or she shall file with his or her report all prior known names and addresses of each holder of the property.

(d) The report shall be filed before November 1 of each year as of June 30 or fiscal yearend next preceding, but the report of life insurance corporations, and the report of all insurance corporation demutualization proceeds subject to Section 1515.5, shall be filed before May 1 of each year as of December 31 next preceding. The initial report for property subject to Section 1515.5 shall be filed on or before May 1, 2004, with respect to conditions in effect on December 31, 2003, and all property shall be determined to be reportable under Section 1515.5 as if that section were in effect on the date of the insurance company demutualization or related reorganization. The Controller may postpone the reporting date upon his or her own motion or upon written request by any person required to file a report.

(e) The report, if made by an individual, shall be verified by the individual; if made by a partnership, by a partner; if made by an unincorporated association or private corporation, by an officer; and if made by a public corporation, by its chief fiscal officer or other employee authorized by the holder. *(Formerly § 1510, added by Stats.1959, c. 1809, p. 4301, § 2. Amended by Stats.1961, c. 1904, p. 4014, § 4. Renumbered § 1530 and amended by Stats.1968, c. 356, p. 746, § 24, operative Jan. 1, 1969. Amended by Stats.1990, c. 1069 (S.B.1186), § 3, eff. Sept. 20, 1990; Stats.1993, c. 692 (A.B.1854), § 5; Stats.1996, c. 762 (S.B.2014), § 5; Stats.2003, c. 304 (A.B.378), § 4; Stats.2013, c. 362 (A.B.212), § 2.)*

Research References

Miller and Starr California Real Estate § 18:9, The Unclaimed Property Law--Duties of Persons Holding Funds.

Miller and Starr California Real Estate § 4:33, Handling of Trust Funds.

Miller and Starr California Real Estate § 6:16, Funds Held in Trust; Restrictions on Disbursement.

Miller and Starr California Real Estate § 18:10, The Unclaimed Property Law--Duties of the State.

Miller and Starr California Real Estate § 10:113, Reconveyance When Trustee Fails to Reconvey.

15 NO. 5 Miller & Starr, California Real Estate Newsalert 5, Deeds of Trust.

1 Witkin Cal. Summ. 10th Contracts § 603, Parens Patriae Action.

13 Witkin, California Summary 10th Personal Property § 42, Procedure in Escheating Property.

§ 1531. Notice and publication of lists of escheated property

(a) Within one year after payment or delivery of escheated property as required by Section 1532, the Controller shall cause a notice to be published, in a newspaper of general circulation which the Controller determines is most likely to give notice to the apparent owner of the property.

(b) Each published notice shall be entitled "notice to owners of unclaimed property."

(c) Each published notice shall also contain a statement that information concerning the amount or description of the property may be obtained by any persons possessing an interest in the property by addressing any inquiry to the Controller.

(d) Within 165 days after the final date for filing the report required by Section 1530, the Controller shall mail a notice to each person having an address listed in the report who appears to be entitled to property of the value of fifty dollars ($50) or more escheated under this chapter. If the report filed pursuant to Section 1530 includes a social security number, the Controller shall request the Franchise Tax Board to provide a current address for the apparent owner on the basis of that number. The Controller shall mail the notice to the apparent owner for whom a current address is obtained if the address is different from the address previously reported to the Controller. If the Franchise Tax Board does not provide an address or a different address, then the Controller shall mail the notice to the address listed in the report required by Section 1530.

(e) The mailed notice shall contain all of the following:

(1) A statement that, according to a report filed with the Controller, property is being held to which the addressee appears entitled.

(2) The name and address of the person holding the property and any necessary information regarding changes of name and address of the holder.

(3) A statement that, if satisfactory proof of claim is not presented by the owner to the holder by the date specified in the notice, the property will be placed in the custody of the Controller and may be sold or destroyed pursuant to this chapter, and all further claims concerning the property or, if sold, the net proceeds of its sale, must be directed to the Controller.

(f) This section is intended to inform owners about the possible existence of unclaimed property identified pursuant to this chapter. *(Formerly § 1511, added by Stats.1959, c. 1809, § 2. Renumbered § 1531 and amended by Stats.1968, c. 356, p. 748, § 25, operative Jan. 1, 1969. Amended by Stats.1975, c. 25, p. 46, § 3; Stats.1978, c. 1183, p. 3829, § 19; Stats.1978, c. 1184, p. 3832, § 1; Stats.1979, c. 761, p. 2625, § 2; Stats.1983, c. 323, § 1, eff. July 21, 1983; Stats.1990, c. 450 (S.B.57), § 13, eff. July 30, 1990; Stats.1996, c. 762 (S.B.2014), § 6; Stats.2007, c. 179 (S.B.86), § 2, eff. Aug. 24, 2007.)*

Law Revision Commission Comments

Section 1531 is substantially the same as former Section 1511.

Subdivision (b) has been revised to indicate more clearly the names to be contained in the notice.

Subdivision (g) incorporates the substance of a change made by the National Conference of Commissioners on Uniform State Laws in the Uniform Disposition of Unclaimed Property Act. See 26 Suggested State Legislation D–31 (1967).

The time limits in subdivision (c)(2) have been changed to conform to the change made in the time for remitting escheated property to the State Controller under Section 1532. See the Comment to that section.

Subdivision (e) has been revised to require that notice be given to the apparent owner within 120 days from the final date for filing the report.

Civ. Pro.

This change conforms subdivision (e) to subdivision (a) and will avoid mechanical and processing difficulties in mailing the notice to the owner.

Research References

Miller and Starr California Real Estate § 18:10, The Unclaimed Property Law--Duties of the State.
18 NO. 4 Miller & Starr, California Real Estate Newsalert 45, Table of Statutes (Newsalert Vol 18).
13 Witkin, California Summary 10th Personal Property § 42, Procedure in Escheating Property.

§ 1531.5. Notification program for possible owners of escheated property

(a) The Controller shall establish and conduct a notification program designed to inform owners about the possible existence of unclaimed property received pursuant to this chapter.

(b) Any notice sent pursuant to this section shall not contain a photograph or likeness of an elected official.

(c)(1) Notwithstanding any other law, upon the request of the Controller, a state or local governmental agency may furnish to the Controller from its records the address or other identification or location information that could reasonably be used to locate an owner of unclaimed property.

(2) If the address or other identification or location information requested by the Controller is deemed confidential under any laws or regulations of this state, it shall nevertheless be furnished to the Controller. However, neither the Controller nor any officer, agent, or employee of the Controller shall use or disclose that information except as may be necessary in attempting to locate the owner of unclaimed property.

(3) This subdivision shall not be construed to require disclosure of information in violation of federal law.

(4) If a fee or charge is customarily made for the information requested by the Controller, the Controller shall pay that customary fee or charge.

(d) Costs for administering this section shall be subject to the level of appropriation in the annual Budget Act. *(Added by Stats.2007, c. 179 (S.B.86), § 3, eff. Aug. 24, 2007.)*

Research References

18 NO. 4 Miller & Starr, California Real Estate Newsalert 10, Escheat.
18 NO. 4 Miller & Starr, California Real Estate Newsalert 45, Table of Statutes (Newsalert Vol 18).
13 Witkin, California Summary 10th Personal Property § 42, Procedure in Escheating Property.

§ 1532. Payment or delivery of escheated property

(a) Every person filing a report as provided by Section 1530 shall, no sooner than seven months and no later than seven months and 15 days after the final date for filing the report, pay or deliver to the Controller all escheated property specified in the report. Any payment of unclaimed cash in an amount of at least twenty thousand dollars ($20,000) shall be made by electronic funds transfer pursuant to regulations adopted by the Controller. The Controller may postpone the date for payment or delivery of the property, and the date for any report required by subdivision (b), upon his or her own motion or upon written request by any person required to pay or deliver the property or file a report as required by this section.

(b) If a person establishes his or her right to receive any property specified in the report to the satisfaction of the holder before that property has been delivered to the Controller, or it appears that, for any other reason, the property may not be subject to escheat under this chapter, the holder shall not pay or deliver the property to the Controller but shall instead file a report with the Controller, on a form and in a format prescribed or approved by the Controller, containing information pertaining to the property subject to escheat.

(c) Any property not paid or delivered pursuant to subdivision (b) that is later determined by the holder to be subject to escheat under this chapter shall not be subject to the interest provision of Section 1577.

(d) The holder of any interest under subdivision (b) of Section 1516 shall deliver a duplicate certificate to the Controller or shall register the securities in uncertificated form in the name of the Controller. Upon delivering a duplicate certificate or providing evidence of registration of the securities in uncertificated form to the Controller, the holder, any transfer agent, registrar, or other person acting for or on behalf of the holder in executing or delivering the duplicate certificate or registering the uncertificated securities, shall be relieved from all liability of every kind to any person including, but not limited to, any person acquiring the original certificate or the duplicate of the certificate issued to the Controller for any losses or damages resulting to that person by the issuance and delivery to the Controller of the duplicate certificate or the registration of the uncertificated securities to the Controller.

(e) Payment of any intangible property to the Controller shall be made at the office of the Controller in Sacramento or at another location as the Controller by regulation may designate. Except as otherwise agreed by the Controller and the holder, tangible personal property shall be delivered to the Controller at the place where it is held.

(f) Payment is deemed complete on the date the electronic funds transfer is initiated if the settlement to the state's demand account occurs on or before the banking day following the date the transfer is initiated. If the settlement to the state's demand account does not occur on or before the banking day following the date the transfer is initiated, payment is deemed to occur on the date settlement occurs.

(g) Any person required to pay cash by electronic funds transfer who makes the payment by means other than an authorized electronic funds transfer shall be liable for a civil penalty of 2 percent of the amount of the payment that is due pursuant to this section, in addition to any other penalty provided by law. Penalties are due at the time of payment. If the Controller finds that a holder's failure to make payment by an appropriate electronic funds transfer in accordance with the Controller's procedures is due to reasonable cause and circumstances beyond the holder's control, and occurred notwithstanding the exercise of ordinary care and in the absence of willful neglect, that holder shall be relieved of the penalties.

(h) An electronic funds transfer shall be accomplished by an automated clearinghouse debit, an automated clearinghouse credit, a Federal Reserve Wire Transfer (Fedwire), or by an international funds transfer. Banking costs incurred for the automated clearinghouse debit transaction by the holder shall be paid by the state. Banking costs incurred by the state for the automated clearinghouse credit transaction may be paid by the holder originating the credit. Banking costs incurred for the Fedwire transaction charged to the holder and the state shall be paid by the person originating the transaction. Banking costs charged to the holder and to the state for an international funds transfer may be charged to the holder.

(i) For purposes of this section:

(1) "Electronic funds transfer" means any transfer of funds, other than a transaction originated by check, draft, or similar paper instrument, that is initiated through an electronic terminal, telephonic instrument, modem, computer, or magnetic tape, so as to order, instruct, or authorize a financial institution to credit or debit an account.

(2) "Automated clearinghouse" means any federal reserve bank, or an organization established by agreement with the National Automated Clearing House Association or any similar organization, that operates as a clearinghouse for transmitting or receiving entries between banks or bank accounts and that authorizes an electronic transfer of funds between those banks or bank accounts.

(3) "Automated clearinghouse debit" means a transaction in which the state, through its designated depository bank, originates an automated clearinghouse transaction debiting the holder's bank account and crediting the state's bank account for the amount of payment.

(4) "Automated clearinghouse credit" means an automated clearinghouse transaction in which the holder, through its own bank, originates an entry crediting the state's bank account and debiting the holder's bank account.

(5) "Fedwire" means any transaction originated by the holder and utilizing the national electronic payment system to transfer funds through federal reserve banks, pursuant to which the holder debits its own bank account and credits the state's bank account.

(6) "International funds transfer" means any transaction originated by the holder and utilizing the international electronic payment system to transfer funds, pursuant to which the holder debits its own bank account, and credits the funds to a United States bank that credits the Unclaimed Property Fund. *(Formerly § 1512, added by Stats.1959, c. 1809, p. 4303, § 2. Amended by Stats.1961, c. 1904, p. 4015, § 5. Renumbered § 1532 and amended by Stats.1968, c. 356, p. 749, § 26, operative Jan. 1, 1969. Amended by Stats.1978, c. 1183, p. 3830, § 20; Stats.1990, c. 450 (S.B.57), § 14, eff. July 31, 1990; Stats.1996, c. 762 (S.B.2014), § 7; Stats.2003, c. 228 (A.B.1756), § 7, eff. Aug. 11, 2003; Stats.2004, c. 520 (A.B.2530), § 2; Stats.2007, c. 179 (S.B.86), § 4, eff. Aug. 24, 2007; Stats.2009, c. 522 (A.B.1291), § 6; Stats.2011, c. 305 (S.B.495), § 7.)*

Law Revision Commission Comments

Subdivisions (a), (b), and (d) of Section 1532 are substantially the same as former Section 1512. The time period for remitting escheated property to the State Controller has been shortened from seven to six months from the final date for filing reports so that the property may be received by the Controller in some month other than the last month of the fiscal year.

Subdivision (c) incorporates the substance of an amendment made by the National Conference of Commissioners, on Uniform State Laws to the Uniform Disposition of the Unclaimed Property Act. See 26 Suggested State Legislation D–31 (1967).

Subdivision (e) has been added to prevent the holder's having to bear the expense of shipping tangible property to the Controller in Sacramento. By agreement, the Controller and the holder may provide that the holder shall bear the expense of such shipment. This might be done, for example, in return for the Controller's agreement to relieve the holder of the further responsibility for various kinds of worthless unclaimed property.

Research References

Miller and Starr California Real Estate § 18:9, The Unclaimed Property Law--Duties of Persons Holding Funds.

Miller and Starr California Real Estate § 4:33, Handling of Trust Funds.

Miller and Starr California Real Estate § 6:16, Funds Held in Trust; Restrictions on Disbursement.

Miller and Starr California Real Estate § 10:113, Reconveyance When Trustee Fails to Reconvey.

15 NO. 5 Miller & Starr, California Real Estate Newsalert 5, Deeds of Trust.

17 NO. 2 Miller & Starr, California Real Estate Newsalert 12, Escheat.

18 NO. 4 Miller & Starr, California Real Estate Newsalert 45, Table of Statutes (Newsalert Vol 18).

20 NO. 1 Miller & Starr, California Real Estate Newsalert 12, Escheat.

13 Witkin, California Summary 10th Personal Property § 42, Procedure in Escheating Property.

§ 1532.1. Payment or delivery of property escheated to state

Notwithstanding Sections 1531 and 1532, property that escheats to the state pursuant to Section 1514 shall not be paid or delivered to the state until the earlier of (a) the time when the holder is requested to do so by the Controller or (b) within one year after the final date for filing the report required by Section 1530 as specified in subdivision (d) of Section 1530. Within one year after receipt of property as provided by this section, the Controller shall cause a notice to be published as provided in Section 1531. *(Added by Stats.1990, c. 450 (S.B.57), § 15, eff. July 31, 1990. Amended by Stats.1990, c. 1069 (S.B.1186), § 4, eff. Sept. 20, 1990; Stats.1996, c. 762 (S.B.2014), § 8.)*

Research References

13 Witkin, California Summary 10th Personal Property § 42, Procedure in Escheating Property.

§ 1533. Exclusion of certain tangible personal property from notice requirement and escheat

Tangible personal property may be excluded from the notices required by Section 1531, shall not be delivered to the State Controller, and shall not escheat to the state, if the State Controller, in his discretion, determines that it is not in the interest of the state to take custody of the property and notifies the holder in writing, within 120 days from receipt of the report required by Section 1530, of his determination not to take custody of the property. *(Added by Stats.1968, c. 356, p. 750, § 27, operative Jan. 1, 1969.)*

Research References

13 Witkin, California Summary 10th Personal Property § 42, Procedure in Escheating Property.

ARTICLE 4. PAYMENT OF CLAIMS

Section

1540. Filing of claim; form; consideration; interest; "owner" defined.
1541. Judicial action on determinations.
1542. Recovery of property by another state; grounds.

§ 1540. Filing of claim; form; consideration; interest; "owner" defined

(a) Any person, excluding another state, who claims * * * to have been the owner, as defined in subdivision (d), of property paid or delivered to the Controller under this chapter may file a claim to the property or to the net proceeds from its sale. The claim shall be on a form prescribed by the Controller and shall be verified by the claimant.

(b) The Controller shall consider each claim within 180 days after it is filed to determine if the claimant is the owner, as defined in subdivision (d), and may hold a hearing and receive evidence. The Controller shall give written notice to the claimant if he or she denies the claim in whole or in part. The notice may be given by mailing it to the address, if any, stated in the claim as the address to which notices are to be sent. If no address is stated in the claim, the notice may be mailed to the address, if any, of the claimant as stated in the claim. A notice of denial need not be given if the claim fails to state either an address to which notices are to be sent or an address of the claimant.

(c) * * * Interest shall not be payable on any claim paid under this chapter.

(d) * * * Notwithstanding subdivision (g) of Section 1501, for purposes of filing a claim pursuant to this section, "owner" means the person who had legal right to the property prior to its escheat, his or her heirs or estate representative, his or her * * * guardian or conservator, or a public administrator acting pursuant to the authority granted in Sections 7660 and 7661 of the Probate Code. Only an owner, as defined in this subdivision, may file a claim with the Controller pursuant to this article.

(e) Following a public hearing, the Controller shall adopt guidelines and forms that shall provide specific instructions to assist owners in filing claims pursuant to this article. *(Added by States.1968, c. 356, p. 750, § 28, operative Jan. 1, 1969. Amended by Stats.1976, c. 49, p. 80, § 2; Stats.1976, c. 1151, p. 5212, § 1; Stats.1978, c. 815, p. 2602, § 1; Stats.1998, c. 1029 (A.B.698), § 1; Stats.2002, c. 1124 (A.B.3000), § 3, eff. Sept. 30, 2002; Stats.2003, c. 228 (A.B.1756), § 8, eff. Aug. 11, 2003; Stats.2005, c. 706 (A.B.1742), § 15; Stats.2013, c. 128 (A.B.1275), § 1.)*

Law Revision Commission Comments

Section 1540 repeats in substance the provisions of former Section 1518 and 1519. Although the time limit specified in subdivision (b) was not contained in either of the superseded sections, it was contained, in effect, in former Section 1520 (renumbered as Section 1541).

Section 1540 does not continue the requirement of the former law that the Controller make a written finding and decision if he holds a hearing. A written finding and decision formerly was not required if no hearing was held. As any further proceedings in court are tried in the same manner whether or not there is such a finding and decision, there appears to be no reason for requiring a written finding and decision if there is a hearing. [8 Cal. L.Rev.Comm. Reports 1001 (1967)].

Research References

Miller and Starr California Real Estate § 18:10, The Unclaimed Property Law--Duties of the State.
19 NO. 3 Miller & Starr, California Real Estate Newsalert 14, Escheat.
20 NO. 2 Miller & Starr, California Real Estate Newsalert 14, Escheat.
1 Witkin Cal. Summ. 10th Contracts § 603, Parens Patriae Action.
13 Witkin, California Summary 10th Personal Property § 43, Claim by Owner of Interest.

§ 1541. Judicial action on determinations

Any person aggrieved by a decision of the Controller or as to whose claim the Controller has failed to make a decision within 180 days after the filing of the claim, may commence an action, naming the Controller as a defendant, to establish his or her claim in the superior court in any county or city and county in which the Attorney General has an office. The action shall be brought within 90 days after the decision of the Controller or within 270 days from the filing of the claim if the Controller fails to make a decision. The summons and a copy of the complaint shall be served upon the Controller and the Attorney General and the Controller shall have 60 days within which to respond by answer. The action shall be tried without a jury. *(Formerly § 1520, added by Stats.1959, c. 1809, p. 4305, § 2. Renumbered § 1541 and amended by Stats.1968, c. 356, p. 750, § 31, operative Jan. 1, 1969. Amended by Stats.1978, c. 1183, p. 3831, § 21; Stats.2003, c. 228 (A.B.1756), § 9, eff. Aug. 11, 2003.)*

Law Revision Commission Comments

Section 1541 is substantially the same as former Section 1520. The former section did not specify the time within which the Attorney General must answer. The revised section does so. The sentence authorizing his filing of a statement of noninterest has been deleted as unnecessary. The last sentence has been deleted to make applicable the normal rules that govern costs in civil proceedings. [8 Cal. L.Rev.Comm. Reports 1001 (1967)].

Research References

Miller and Starr California Real Estate § 18:10, The Unclaimed Property Law--Duties of the State.

13 Witkin, California Summary 10th Personal Property § 43, Claim by Owner of Interest.

§ 1542. Recovery of property by another state; grounds

(a) At any time after property has been paid or delivered to the Controller under this chapter, another state is entitled to recover the property if:

(1) The property escheated to this state under subdivision (b) of Section 1510 because no address of the apparent owner of the property appeared on the records of the holder when the property was escheated under this chapter, the last known address of the apparent owner was in fact in that other state, and, under the laws of that state, the property escheated to that state.

(2) The last known address of the apparent owner of the property appearing on the records of the holder is in that other state and, under the laws of that state, the property has escheated to that state.

(3) The property is the sum payable on a travelers check, money order, or other similar instrument that escheated to this state under Section 1511, the travelers check, money order, or other similar instrument was in fact purchased in that other state, and, under the laws of that state, the property escheated to that state.

(4) The property is funds held or owing by a life insurance corporation that escheated to this state by application of the presumption provided by subdivision (b) of Section 1515, the last known address of the person entitled to the funds was in fact in that other state, and, under the laws of that state, the property escheated to that state.

(b) The claim of another state to recover escheated property under this section shall be presented in writing to the Controller, who shall consider the claim within 180 days after it is presented. The Controller may hold a hearing and receive evidence. The Controller shall allow the claim upon determination that the other state is entitled to the escheated property.

(c) Paragraphs (1) and (2) of subdivision (a) do not apply to property described in paragraph (3) or (4) of that subdivision. *(Added by Stats.1968, c. 356, p. 751, § 32, operative Jan. 1, 1969. Amended by Stats.1975, c. 25, p. 47, § 4; Stats.1978, c. 1183, p. 3831, § 22; Stats.2003, c. 228 (A.B.1756), § 10, eff. Aug. 11, 2003.)*

Law Revision Commission Comments

Section 1542 is new. It is necessary to provide a procedural means for complying with Texas v. New Jersey, 379 U.S. 674 (1965). That decision holds that property escheated by one state (under the conditions now specified by subdivisions (b) and (c) of Section 1510) may be claimed by another state under the circumstances stated in paragraphs (1) and (2) of subdivision (a) of this section.

It should be noted that the presumption created by Section 1511 operates to permit another state to escheat the sum payable on a travelers check or money order even though the holder of the instrument is domiciled in California if the check or order was purchased in the other state. Such sums therefore may be recovered under subdivision (a)(2) of this section. Of course, such sums escheat to the other state only if that state has a statute which so provides.

For a comparable provision, see N.H.Rev.Stats. § 471–A:24 (1965 Supp.), enacted by N.H.Stats.1965, Ch. 214, § 1, eff. Jan. 1, 1966.

Section 1542(a)(3) is amended to conform to the rules stated in Section 1511. Subdivision (c), a clarifying provision, makes no substantive change.

Research References

13 Witkin, California Summary 10th Personal Property § 44, Claim by Another State.

ARTICLE 5. ADMINISTRATION OF UNCLAIMED PROPERTY

Section

1560. Relief from liability by payment or delivery; payment to others; reimbursement; reclamation of property.
1561. Defense of payee against claims of others; indemnification; mistake of law or fact; refund or redelivery of property.
1562. Income accruing after payment or delivery.
1563. Sale of escheated property.
1564. Deposit of funds.
1565. Destruction or disposition of property having no commercial value.
1566. Suits against state or officer or employee.
1567. Use of property by department of parks and recreation.

§ 1560. Relief from liability by payment or delivery; payment to others; reimbursement; reclamation of property

(a) Upon the payment or delivery of escheated property to the Controller, the state shall assume custody and shall be responsible for the safekeeping of the property. Any person who pays or delivers escheated property to the Controller under this chapter and who, prior to escheat, if the person's records contain an address for the apparent owner, which the holder's records do not disclose to be inaccurate, has made reasonable efforts to notify the owner by mail or, if the owner has consented to electronic notice, electronically, in substantial compliance with Sections 1513.5, 1514, 1516, and 1520, that the owner's property, deposit, account, shares, or other interest will escheat to the state, is relieved of all liability to the extent of the value of the property so paid or delivered for any claim which then exists or which thereafter may arise or be made in respect to the property. Property removed from a safe deposit box or other safekeeping repository shall be received by the Controller subject to any valid lien of the holder for rent and other charges, such rent and other charges to be paid out of the proceeds remaining after the Controller has deducted therefrom his or her selling cost.

(b) Any holder who has paid moneys to the State Controller pursuant to this chapter may make payment to any person appearing to such holder to be entitled thereto, and upon filing proof of such payment and proof that the payee was entitled thereto, the Controller shall forthwith reimburse the holder for the payment without deduction of any fee or other charges. Where reimbursement is sought for a payment made on a negotiable instrument (including a traveler's check or money order), the holder shall be reimbursed under this subdivision upon filing proof that the instrument was duly presented to him or her and that payment was made thereon to a person who appeared to the holder to be entitled to payment.

(c) The holder shall be reimbursed under this section even if he made the payment to a person whose claim against him was barred because of the expiration of any such period of time as those described in Section 1570.

(d) Any holder who has delivered personal property, including a certificate of any interest in a business association, to the Controller pursuant to this chapter may reclaim such personal property if still in the possession of the Controller without payment of any fee or other charges upon filing proof that the owner thereof has claimed such personal property from such holder. The Controller may, in his or her discretion, accept an affidavit of the holder stating the facts that entitle the holder to reimbursement under this subdivision as sufficient proof for the

purposes of this subdivision. *(Formerly § 1513, added by Stats. 1959, c. 1809, p. 4302, § 2. Amended by Stats.1961, c. 1904, p. 4016, § 6. Renumbered § 1560 and amended by Stats.1968, c. 356, p. 752, § 34, operative Jan. 1, 1969. Amended by Stats.2009, c. 522 (A.B.1291), § 7.)*

Law Revision Commission Comments

Section 1560 is substantially the same as former Section 1513.

The provision in subdivision (b) requiring reimbursement to be "without deduction of any fee or other charges" has been added to conform this subdivision with the policy reflected in subdivision (d). Subdivision (b) also has been revised to specify the proof required to be filed by a holder to obtain reimbursement for payment of a negotiable instrument.

Subdivision (c) has been added to make it clear that the holder may obtain reimbursement for a payment made on a claim barred by the statute of limitations.

The last sentence of subdivision (d) is new and reflects the practice followed by the State Controller under former Section 1513.

Research References

Miller and Starr California Real Estate § 18:9, The Unclaimed Property Law--Duties of Persons Holding Funds.
Miller and Starr California Real Estate § 6:16, Funds Held in Trust; Restrictions on Disbursement.
13 Witkin, California Summary 10th Personal Property § 42, Procedure in Escheating Property.
13 Witkin, California Summary 10th Personal Property § 44, Claim by Another State.

§ 1561. Defense of payee against claims of others; indemnification; mistake of law or fact; refund or redelivery of property

(a) If the holder pays or delivers escheated property to the State Controller in accordance with this chapter and thereafter any person claims the property from the holder or another state claims the property from the holder under that state's laws relating to escheat, the State Controller shall, upon written notice of such claim, defend the holder against the claim and indemnify him against any liability on the claim.

(b) If any holder, because of mistake of law or fact, pays or delivers any property to the State Controller that has not escheated under this chapter and thereafter claims the property from the State Controller, the State Controller shall, if he has not disposed of the property in accordance with this chapter, refund or redeliver the property to the holder without deduction for any fee or other charge.

(c) As used in this section, "escheated property" means property which this chapter provides escheats to this state, whether or not it is determined that another state had a superior right to escheat such property at the time it was paid or delivered to the State Controller or at some time thereafter. *(Added by Stats.1968, c. 356, p. 752, § 35, operative Jan. 1, 1969.)*

Law Revision Commission Comments

Under Section 1510, certain property may escheat to this state but later escheat to another state. In other cases, the owner of property may claim it from the holder after it has escheated and been delivered to this state. To protect a holder who has delivered escheated property to this state from the necessity to defend either the owner's claim or another state's claim of escheat, subdivision (a) requires the State Controller to defend the claim and to indemnify the holder against liability. If the owner or the other state is entitled to the property, the Controller may deliver the property to the claimant as provided in Section 1540 or 1542.

Subdivision (a), like Section 1560, applies only in cases in which *escheated* property has been paid or delivered to the Controller. If the holder mistakenly delivers to the Controller property that has not escheated, this section does not require the Controller to defend the claim of the owner or indemnify the holder. Of course, under subdivision (b), the holder may recover any property mistakenly delivered to the Controller.

Research References

Miller and Starr California Real Estate § 18:9, The Unclaimed Property Law--Duties of Persons Holding Funds.

Miller and Starr California Real Estate § 6:16, Funds Held in Trust; Restrictions on Disbursement.

13 Witkin, California Summary 10th Personal Property § 42, Procedure in Escheating Property.

§ 1562. Income accruing after payment or delivery

When property other than money is delivered to the State Controller under this chapter, any dividends, interest or other increments realized or accruing on such property at or prior to liquidation or conversion thereof into money, shall upon receipt be credited to the owner's account by the State Controller. Except for amounts so credited the owner is not entitled to receive income or other increments on money or other property paid or delivered to the State Controller under this chapter. All interest received and other income derived from the investment of moneys deposited in the Unclaimed Property Fund under the provisions of this chapter shall, on order of the State Controller, be transferred to the General Fund. *(Formerly § 1514, added by Stats.1959, c. 1809, p. 4304, § 2. Amended by Stats.1961, c. 1904, p. 4016, § 7. Renumbered § 1562 and amended by Stats.1968, c. 356, p. 753, § 36, operative Jan. 1, 1969.)*

Research References

Miller and Starr California Real Estate § 18:10, The Unclaimed Property Law--Duties of the State.

13 Witkin, California Summary 10th Personal Property § 42, Procedure in Escheating Property.

§ 1563. Sale of escheated property

(a) Except as provided in subdivisions (b) and (c), all escheated property delivered to the Controller under this chapter shall be sold by the Controller to the highest bidder at public sale in whatever city in the state affords in his or her judgment the most favorable market for the property involved, or the Controller may conduct the sale by electronic media, including, but not limited to, the Internet, if in his or her judgment it is cost effective to conduct the sale of the property involved in that manner. However, no sale shall be made pursuant to this subdivision until 18 months after the final date for filing the report required by Section 1530. The Controller may decline the highest bid and reoffer the property for sale if he or she considers the price bid insufficient. The Controller need not offer any property for sale if, in his or her opinion, the probable cost of sale exceeds the value of the property. Any sale of escheated property held under this section shall be preceded by a single publication of notice thereof, at least one week in advance of sale, in an English language newspaper of general circulation in the county where the property is to be sold.

(b) Securities listed on an established stock exchange shall be sold at the prevailing prices on that exchange. Other securities may be sold over the counter at prevailing prices or, with prior approval of the California Victim Compensation and Government Claims Board, by any other method that the Controller may determine to be advisable. These securities shall be sold by the Controller no sooner than 18 months, but no later than 20 months, after the final date for filing the report required by Section 1530. If securities delivered to the Controller by a holder of the securities remain in the custody of the Controller, a person making a valid claim for those securities under this chapter shall be entitled to receive the securities from the Controller. If the securities have been sold, the person shall be entitled to receive the net proceeds received by the Controller from the sale of the securities. United States government savings bonds and United States war bonds shall be presented to the United States for payment. Subdivision (a) does not apply to the property described in this subdivision.

(c)(1) All escheated property consisting of military awards, decorations, equipment, artifacts, memorabilia, documents, photographs, films, literature, and any other item relating to the military history of California and Californians that is delivered to the Controller is exempt from subdivision (a) and shall be held in trust for the Controller at the California State Military Museum and Resource Center. All escheated property held in trust pursuant to this subdivision is subject to the applicable regulations of the United States Army governing Army museum activities as described in Section 179 of the Military and Veterans Code. Any person claiming an interest in the escheated property may file a claim to the property pursuant to Article 4 (commencing with Section 1540).

(2) The California State Military Museum and Resource Center shall be responsible for the costs of storage and maintenance of escheated property delivered by the Controller under this subdivision.

(d) The purchaser at any sale conducted by the Controller pursuant to this chapter shall receive title to the property purchased, free from all claims of the owner or prior holder thereof and of all persons claiming through or under them. The Controller shall execute all documents necessary to complete the transfer of title. *(Formerly § 1516, added by Stats.1959, c. 1809, p. 4304, § 2. Amended by Stats.1963, c. 669, p. 1657, § 1. Renumbered § 1563 and amended by Stats.1968, c. 356, p. 753, § 37, operative Jan. 1, 1969. Amended by Stats.1972, c. 1165, p. 2290, § 1; Stats.1993, c. 692 (A.B.1854), § 6; Stats.1996, c. 762 (S.B.2014), § 9; Stats.2000, c. 16 (A.B.938), § 2, eff. May 5, 2000; Stats.2000, c. 924 (A.B.2935), § 2; Stats.2003, c. 265 (A.B.542), § 2; Stats.2004, c. 183 (A.B.3082), § 46; Stats.2007, c. 179 (S.B.86), § 5, eff. Aug. 24, 2007.)*

Law Revision Commission Comments

Section 1563 is substantially the same as former Section 1516.

Because United States Savings Bonds and United States War Bonds are not subject to sale, provisions relating to these bonds have been added to subdivision (b) to authorize their presentation to the United States for payment.

Former subdivision (d) has been deleted as unnecessary in light of the broader provisions of Section 1566.

Research References

Miller and Starr California Real Estate § 18:10, The Unclaimed Property Law--Duties of the State.

18 NO. 4 Miller & Starr, California Real Estate Newsalert 45, Table of Statutes (Newsalert Vol 18).

13 Witkin, California Summary 10th Personal Property § 42, Procedure in Escheating Property.

§ 1564. Deposit of funds

(a) All money received under this chapter, including the proceeds from the sale of property under Section 1563, shall be deposited in the Unclaimed Property Fund in an account titled "Abandoned Property."

(b) Notwithstanding Section 13340 of the Government Code, all money in the Abandoned Property Account in the Unclaimed Property Fund is hereby continuously appropriated to the Controller, without regard to fiscal years, for expenditure in accordance with law in carrying out and enforcing the provisions of this chapter, including, but not limited to, the following purposes:

(1) For payment of claims allowed by the Controller under the provisions of this chapter.

(2) For refund, to the person making such deposit, of amounts, including overpayments, deposited in error in such fund.

(3) For payment of the cost of appraisals incurred by the Controller covering property held in the name of an account in such fund.

(4) For payment of the cost incurred by the Controller for the purchase of lost instrument indemnity bonds, or for payment to the person entitled thereto, for any unpaid lawful charges or costs which arose from holding any specific property or any specific funds which were delivered or paid to the Controller, or which arose from complying with this chapter with respect to such property or funds.

(5) For payment of amounts required to be paid by the state as trustee, bailee, or successor in interest to the preceding owner.

(6) For payment of costs incurred by the Controller for the repair, maintenance, and upkeep of property held in the name of an account in such fund.

(7) For payment of costs of official advertising in connection with the sale of property held in the name of an account in such fund.

(8) For transfer to the General Fund as provided in subdivision (c).

(9) For transfer to the Inheritance Tax Fund of the amount of any inheritance taxes determined to be due and payable to the state by any claimant with respect to any property claimed by him or her under the provisions of this chapter.

(c) At the end of each month, or more often if he or she deems it advisable, the Controller shall transfer all money in the Abandoned Property Account in excess of fifty thousand dollars ($50,000) to the General Fund. Before making this transfer, the Controller shall record the name and last known address of each person appearing from the holders' report to be entitled to the escheated property and the name and last known address of each insured person or annuitant, and with respect to each policy or contract listed in the report of a life insurance corporation, its number, and the name of the corporation. The record shall be available for public inspection at all reasonable business hours. *(Formerly § 1517, added by Stats.1959, c. 1809, p. 4304, § 2. Renumbered § 1564 and amended by Stats.1968, c. 356, p. 754, § 38, operative Jan. 1, 1969. Amended by Stats.1980, c. 676, § 70; Stats.1993, c. 692 (A.B.1854), § 7.)*

Research References

Miller and Starr California Real Estate § 18:10, The Unclaimed Property Law--Duties of the State.

13 Witkin, California Summary 10th Personal Property § 42, Procedure in Escheating Property.

§ 1565. Destruction or disposition of property having no commercial value

Any property delivered to the Controller pursuant to this chapter that has no apparent commercial value shall be retained by the Controller for a period of not less than seven years from the date the property is delivered to the Controller. If the Controller determines that any property delivered to him or her pursuant to this chapter has no apparent commercial value, he or she may at any time thereafter destroy or otherwise dispose of the property, and in that event no action or proceeding shall be brought or maintained against the state or any officer thereof, or against the holder for, or on account of any action taken by, the Controller pursuant to this chapter with respect to the property. *(Formerly § 1521, added by Stats.1959, c. 1809, p. 4306, § 2. Amended by Stats.1961, c. 1904, p. 4016, § 8. Renumbered § 1565 and amended by Stats.1968, c. 356, p. 755, § 39, operative Jan. 1, 1969. Amended by Stats.2007, c. 179 (S.B.86), § 6, eff. Aug. 24, 2007; Stats.2011, c. 305 (S.B.495), § 8.)*

Research References

Miller and Starr California Real Estate § 18:10, The Unclaimed Property Law--Duties of the State.

18 NO. 4 Miller & Starr, California Real Estate Newsalert 45, Table of Statutes (Newsalert Vol 18).

13 Witkin, California Summary 10th Personal Property § 42, Procedure in Escheating Property.

§ 1566. Suits against state or officer or employee

(a) When payment or delivery of money or other property has been made to any claimant under the provisions of this chapter, no suit shall thereafter be maintained by any other claimant against the state or any officer or employee thereof for or on account of such property.

(b) Except as provided in Section 1541, no suit shall be maintained by any person against the state or any officer or employee thereof for or on account of any transaction entered into by the State Controller pursuant to this chapter. *(Added by Stats.1968, c. 356, p. 755, § 40, operative Jan. 1, 1969.)*

Law Revision Commission Comments

Subdivision (a) is substantially the same as Code of Civil Procedure Section 1335; subdivision (b) is substantially the same as Code of Civil Procedure Section 1378.

Section 1566 is similar to subdivision (d) of former Section 1516. The provision has been broadened to exonerate the state if, despite compliance with all requirements of this chapter, a state officer or employee erroneously pays or delivers property to one claimant and it is ultimately determined that another is entitled to the property. This section does not affect the right of a person entitled to the property to recover it from the person to whom it was erroneously paid.

Research References

Miller and Starr California Real Estate § 18:10, The Unclaimed Property Law--Duties of the State.

13 Witkin, California Summary 10th Personal Property § 43, Claim by Owner of Interest.

5 Witkin, California Summary 10th Torts § 348, Nature of Immunities and Defenses.

§ 1567. Use of property by department of parks and recreation

The Director of Parks and Recreation may examine any tangible personal property delivered to the Controller under this chapter for purposes of determining whether such property would be useful under the provisions of Section 512 of the Public Resources Code. If the director makes such a determination with respect to the property, the Controller may deliver the property to the director for use in carrying out the purposes of Section 512 of the Public Resources Code. Upon the termination of any such use, the director shall return the property to the Controller. *(Added by Stats.1969, c. 838, p. 1670, § 1. Amended by Stats.1981, c. 714, § 73.)*

ARTICLE 6. COMPLIANCE AND ENFORCEMENT

Section

1577.   Failure to report, pay or deliver property; interest; substantial compliance of report, limitation on interest.

1577.5.   Amnesty program.

§ 1570. Limitations as not preventing money or property from being escheated; duty to file report or to pay or deliver escheated property

The expiration of any period of time specified by statute or court order, during which an action or proceeding may be commenced or enforced to obtain payment of a claim for money or recovery of property from the holder, does not prevent the money or property from being escheated, nor affect any duty to file a report required by this chapter or to pay or deliver escheated property to the State Controller. *(Formerly § 1515, added by Stats.1959, c. 1809, p. 4304, § 2. Renumbered § 1570 and amended by Stats.1968, c. 356, p. 755, § 42, operative Jan. 1, 1969.)*

Law Revision Commission Comments

Section 1570 is the same in substance as former Section 1515.

This chapter was originally enacted in 1959 and took effect on September 18, 1959. In Douglas Aircraft Co. v. Cranston, 58 Cal.2d 462, 24 Cal.Rptr. 851, 374 P.2d 819 (1962), the court held, as a matter of statutory construction, that former Section 1515 (now Section 1570) was not "retroactive" and, therefore, applied only to claims on which the statute of limitations had not run prior to September 18, 1959. Thus, if the period of limitations applicable to the owner's claim against the holder had expired prior to that date, the holder had no duty to report or to pay or deliver the property even though the property was "presumed abandoned" as of that date under former Section 1510(g). Conversely, under the *Douglas Aircraft* decision, if the statute of limitations did not bar the owner's claim against the holder until after September 17, 1959, the holder was required to report and to pay or deliver the property, whether the presumption of abandonment arose before or after that date. The 1968 amendments, repeals, and additions to this chapter have no effect on the rule applied in the *Douglas Aircraft* case. See Section 1506 and the *Comment* to that section.

For a discussion of the effect of the statute of limitations having run prior to January 1, 1969 (the effective date of the 1968 amendments, additions, and repeals in this chapter), see Sections 1503(b) and 1506 and the *Comments* to those provisions.

The rules that determine when a claim against the holder is barred by lapse of time are not provided by this chapter but by the statutes of limitation and related judicial decisions. Significantly, there are several types of claims that never become barred by lapse of time alone. See Bank of America v. Cranston, 252 Cal.App.2d 208, 60 Cal.Rptr. 336 (1967) (hearing denied by Supreme Court).

Research References

Miller and Starr California Real Estate § 18:10, The Unclaimed Property Law--Duties of the State.

3 Witkin Cal. Proc. 5th Actions § 489, Express Statutory Provisions.

3 Witkin Cal. Proc. 5th Actions § 664, (S 664) in General.

13 Witkin, California Summary 10th Personal Property § 42, Procedure in Escheating Property.

§ 1571. Examination of records

(a) The Controller may at reasonable times and upon reasonable notice examine the records of any person if the Controller has reason to believe that the person is a holder who has failed to report property that should have been reported pursuant to this chapter.

(b) When requested by the Controller, the examination shall be conducted by any licensing or regulating agency otherwise empowered by the laws of this state to examine the records of the holder. For the purpose of determining compliance with this chapter, the Commissioner of Financial Institutions is vested with full authority to examine the records of any banking organization and any savings association doing business within

this state but not organized under the laws of or created in this state.

(c) Following a public hearing, the Controller shall adopt guidelines as to the policies and procedures governing the activity of third-party auditors who are hired by the Controller.

(d) Following a public hearing, the Controller shall adopt guidelines, on or before July 1, 1999, establishing forms, policies, and procedures to enable a person to dispute or appeal the results of any record examination conducted pursuant to this section. *(Formerly § 1522, added by Stats.1959, c. 1809, p. 4306, § 2. Renumbered § 1571 and amended by Stats.1968, c. 356, p. 756, § 43, operative Jan. 1, 1969. Amended by Stats.1996, c. 1064 (A.B.3351), § 7, operative July 1, 1997; Stats.1998, c. 1029 (A.B.698), § 2.)*

Research References

13 Witkin, California Summary 10th Personal Property § 42, Procedure in Escheating Property.

§ 1572. Action by state controller; purposes

(a) The State Controller may bring an action in a court of appropriate jurisdiction, as specified in this section, for any of the following purposes:

(1) To enforce the duty of any person under this chapter to permit the examination of the records of such person.

(2) For a judicial determination that particular property is subject to escheat by this state pursuant to this chapter.

(3) To enforce the delivery of any property to the State Controller as required under this chapter.

(b) The State Controller may bring an action under this chapter in any court of this state of appropriate jurisdiction in any of the following cases:

(1) Where the holder is any person domiciled in this state, or is a government or governmental subdivision or agency of this state.

(2) Where the holder is any person engaged in or transacting business in this state, although not domiciled in this state.

(3) Where the property is tangible personal property and is held in this state.

(c) In any case where no court of this state can obtain jurisdiction over the holder, the State Controller may bring an action in any federal or state court with jurisdiction over the holder. *(Added by Stats.1968, c. 356, p. 756, § 45, operative Jan. 1, 1969.)*

Law Revision Commission Comments

Section 1572 clarifies the circumstances under which the Controller may sue in the courts of this state or another state or in the federal courts to enforce the provisions of this chapter. In general, the section requires the Controller to proceed in the courts of California unless the California courts cannot obtain jurisdiction over the holder.

Research References

Miller and Starr California Real Estate § 18:10, The Unclaimed Property Law--Duties of the State.

13 Witkin, California Summary 10th Personal Property § 42, Procedure in Escheating Property.

§ 1573. Agreements by state controller with other states to furnish information; reporting of information to controller; regulations

The State Controller may enter into an agreement to provide information needed to enable another state to determine unclaimed property it may be entitled to escheat if such other state or an official thereof agrees to provide this state with information needed to enable this state to determine unclaimed property it may be entitled to escheat. The State Controller may, by regulation, require the reporting of information needed to enable him to comply with agreements made pursuant to this section and may, by regulation, prescribe the form, including verification, of the information to be reported and the times for filing the reports. *(Added by Stats.1968, c. 356, p. 756, § 46, operative Jan. 1, 1969.)*

Law Revision Commission Comments

Section 1573 is new. Persons domiciled in this state may hold property that has escheated to another state, but that state may be unable to obtain jurisdiction over the holder to compel his reporting and delivery of the property. Conversely, persons domiciled in other states may hold property that has escheated to California, yet California may have no means to compel the reporting and delivery of the property.

Section 1573 permits the Controller to agree with other states that he and they will furnish information obtained from holders within their jurisdictions as to property that may have escheated to the other state.

The section also authorizes the Controller, by regulation, to require reports from California holders so that he can furnish the information required by the agreements with officials of the other states. By making the information available to other states, the Controller can enable them to assert their claims directly against the holder or to request this state to enforce their claims under Section 1574. Through reciprocal cooperation, this state may obtain escheated property from holders in other states either by proceeding directly or by requesting the assistance of other states pursuant to Section 1575.

Research References

13 Witkin, California Summary 10th Personal Property § 38, Nature of Law.

§ 1574. Action by Attorney General, in name of other state, to enforce unclaimed property laws of other state

At the request of another state, the Attorney General of this state may bring an action in the name of the other state, in any court of appropriate jurisdiction of this state or federal court within this state, to enforce the unclaimed property laws of the other state against a holder in this state of property subject to escheat by the other state, if:

(a) The courts of the other state cannot obtain jurisdiction over the holder;

(b) The other state has agreed to bring actions in the name of this state at the request of the Attorney General of this state to enforce the provisions of this chapter against any person in the other state believed by the State Controller to hold property subject to escheat under this chapter, where the courts of this state cannot obtain jurisdiction over such person; and

(c) The other state has agreed to pay reasonable costs incurred by the Attorney General in bringing the action. *(Added by Stats.1968, c. 356, p. 757, § 47, operative Jan. 1, 1969.)*

Law Revision Commission Comments

Section 1574 authorizes the Attorney General of this state to sue in this state to compel compliance with the unclaimed property laws of another state. Under the section, however, the Attorney General may do so only if the other state will act similarly to enforce the unclaimed property laws of California against holders of unclaimed property in that state. For a similar provision, see N.H.Rev.Stats. 1965 Supp.) § 471–A:15, enacted by N.H.Stats. 1965, Ch. 214, § 1, eff. Jan. 1, 1966.

Research References

13 Witkin, California Summary 10th Personal Property § 38, Nature of Law.

§ 1575. Request by State Controller to bring action in name of state to enforce provisions of this chapter in another state; costs and rewards

(a) If the State Controller believes that a person in another state holds property subject to escheat under this chapter and the courts of this state cannot obtain jurisdiction over that person, the Attorney General of this state may request an officer of the other state to bring an action in the name of this state to enforce the provisions of this chapter against such person.

(b) This state shall pay all reasonable costs incurred by the other state in any action brought under the authority of this section. The State Controller may agree to pay to any state bringing such an action a reward not to exceed fifteen percent of the value, after deducting reasonable costs, of any property recovered for this state as a direct or indirect result of such action. Any costs or rewards paid pursuant to this section shall be paid from the Abandoned Property Account in the Unclaimed Property Fund and shall not be deducted from the amount that is subject to be claimed by the owner in accordance with this chapter. *(Added by Stats.1968, c. 356, p. 757, § 48, operative Jan. 1, 1969.)*

Law Revision Commission Comments

Section 1575 authorizes this state to request the officials of another state to bring an action to recover property escheated to California. To provide an incentive for the recovery of such property, the section authorizes payment of a reward of not more than 15 percent of the value of the property. The reward is not paid from the escheated property itself. Because California's claim is made for the benefit of the state rather than the owner, it would be inappropriate to charge the owner of the property with the reward if he should later recover the property.

For a similar provision, see N.H.Rev.Stats. 1965 Supp.) § 471–A:15, enacted by N.H.Stats. 1965, Ch. 214, § 1, eff. Jan. 1, 1966.

Research References

13 Witkin, California Summary 10th Personal Property § 38, Nature of Law.

§ 1576. Penalties

(a) Any person who willfully fails to render any report or perform other duties, including use of the report format described in Section 1530, required under this chapter shall be punished by a fine of one hundred dollars ($100) for each day such report is withheld or such duty is not performed, but not more than ten thousand dollars ($10,000).

(b) Any person who willfully refuses to pay or deliver escheated property to the Controller as required under this chapter shall be punished by a fine of not less than five thousand dollars ($5,000) nor more than fifty thousand dollars ($50,000).

(c) No person shall be considered to have willfully failed to report, pay, or deliver escheated property, or perform other duties unless he or she has failed to respond within a reasonable time after notification by certified mail by the Controller's office of his or her failure to act. *(Formerly § 1524, added by Stats.1959, c. 1809, p. 4307, § 2. Renumbered § 1576 and amended by Stats.1968, c. 356, p. 757, § 49, operative Jan. 1, 1969. Amended by Stats.1983, c. 1092, § 73, eff. Sept. 27, 1983, operative Jan. 1, 1984; Stats.1996, c. 762 (S.B.2014), § 10.)*

Research References

Miller and Starr California Real Estate § 18:9, The Unclaimed Property Law--Duties of Persons Holding Funds.
Miller and Starr California Real Estate § 4:33, Handling of Trust Funds.
Miller and Starr California Real Estate § 6:16, Funds Held in Trust; Restrictions on Disbursement.
13 Witkin, California Summary 10th Personal Property § 42, Procedure in Escheating Property.

§ 1577. Failure to report, pay or deliver property; interest; substantial compliance of report, limitation on interest

In addition to any damages, penalties, or fines for which a person may be liable under other provisions of law, any person who fails to report, pay, or deliver unclaimed property within the time prescribed by this chapter, unless that failure is due to reasonable cause, shall pay to the Controller interest at the rate of 12 percent per annum on that property or value thereof from the date the property should have been reported, paid, or delivered. If a holder pays or delivers unclaimed property in a timely manner, but files a report that is not in substantial compliance with the requirements of Section 1530, the interest payable shall not exceed ten thousand dollars ($10,000). The holder shall not be subject to any interest payment if the holder's failure to report in substantial compliance with the requirements of Section 1530 is due to reasonable cause. *(Added by Stats. 1976, c. 49, p. 81, § 3. Amended by Stats.2003, c. 304 (A.B.378), § 5; Stats.2009, c. 522 (A.B.1291), § 8.)*

Research References

Miller and Starr California Real Estate § 18:9, The Unclaimed Property Law--Duties of Persons Holding Funds.
13 Witkin, California Summary 10th Personal Property § 42, Procedure in Escheating Property.

§ 1577.5. Amnesty program

(a) Section 1577 does not apply to, and interest may not be imposed upon, any escheated property paid or delivered to the Controller at any time on or before December 31, 2002.

(b) Subdivision (a) shall apply only if the following requirements are met:

(1) On or before January 1, 2003, the holder of the property was not the subject of an investigation by the Attorney General or a party to litigation with the Controller, relating to the property. "Investigation by the Attorney General" means an investigation being conducted under any law authorizing the investigation, including, but not limited to, investigations authorized by or conducted pursuant to Article 2 (commencing with Section 11180) of Chapter 2 of Part 1 of Division 3 of Title 2 of the Government Code by the office of the Attorney General relating to the escheat of property subject to subdivision (a).

(2) On or before January 3, 2000, the holder of the property was not the subject of an audit by the Controller relating to the property. "Audit by the Controller" means a formal field audit of the propertyholder's books and records by audit personnel of the Controller's office for the purpose of determining compliance with this chapter.

(3) The property was required to be reported on or before November 1, 1999.

(4) The property is surrendered directly to the state or its authorized agent.

(5) Reports respecting the property are reported by electronic media satisfactory to the Controller, provided that paper reports shall be permitted with respect to holders reporting fewer than 50 accounts or other items.

(6) All property reported after the effective date of this act shall be reported on a report separate from property currently reportable, and may not be reported with property not eligible for the amnesty program.

(7) The property is paid or delivered to the Controller at the time the report is made.

(8) Securities are remitted in accordance with Section 1532.

(9) Records shall be maintained in a manner satisfactory to the Controller, to permit verification and compliance audits.

(c) Nothing in subdivision (a) shall create an entitlement to a refund of interest paid to the Controller prior to the effective date of this section.

(d) The Controller shall conduct an outreach and publicity program regarding the provisions of this section.

(e) The Controller shall submit a report to the Legislature on the amnesty program. The report shall include a comprehensive accounting of all unclaimed property surrendered under the amnesty program, the date the property was surrendered, and the identities of the holders of surrendered unclaimed property. The report shall be published no later than July 31, 2003.

(f) Nothing in this section shall preclude liability pursuant to Article 9 (commencing with Section 12650) of Chapter 6 of Title 2 of Division 3 of the Government Code regarding false claims. Reporting or filing extensions shall not be granted for property under this section. *(Added by Stats.2000, c. 267 (A.B.1888), § 1. Amended by Stats.2002, c. 22 (A.B.227), § 1, eff. April 17, 2002.)*

Research References

13 NO. 4 Miller & Starr, California Real Estate Newsalert 10, Escheat.
14 NO. 5 Miller & Starr, California Real Estate Newsalert 12, Escheat.
13 Witkin, California Summary 10th Personal Property § 42, Procedure in Escheating Property.

ARTICLE 7. MISCELLANEOUS

Section

§ 1580. Rules and regulations

The State Controller is hereby authorized to make necessary rules and regulations to carry out the provisions of this chapter. *(Formerly § 1525, added by Stats.1959, c. 1809, p. 4307, § 2. Renumbered § 1580 and amended by Stats.1968, c. 356, p. 758, § 51, operative Jan. 1, 1969. Amended by Stats.1978, c. 1183, p. 3832, § 23.)*

Law Revision Commission Comments

Subdivision (a) of Section 1580 is the same as former Section 1525. Subdivision (b) has been added to provide holders with a source of information for determining the property that escheats to this state under Section 1510 and Texas v. New Jersey, 379 U.S. 674 (1965).

Research References

Miller and Starr California Real Estate § 18:9, The Unclaimed Property Law--Duties of Persons Holding Funds.

§ 1581. Record of sales of travelers checks, money orders, etc.; civil penalty

(a) Any business association that sells in this state its travelers checks, money orders, or other similar written instruments (other than third-party bank checks) on which such business association is directly liable, or that provides such travelers checks, money orders, or similar written instruments to others for sale in this state, shall maintain a record indicating those travelers checks, money orders, or similar written instruments that are purchased from it in this state.

(b) The record required by this section may be destroyed after it has been retained for such reasonable time as the State Controller shall designate by regulation.

(c) Any business association that willfully fails to comply with this section is liable to the state for a civil penalty of five hundred dollars ($500) for each day of such failure to comply, which penalty may be recovered in an action brought by the State Controller. *(Added by Stats.1968, c. 356, p. 758, § 52, operative Jan. 1, 1969. Amended by Stats.1975, c. 25, p. 48, § 5.)*

Research References

13 Witkin, California Summary 10th Personal Property § 38, Nature of Law.

§ 1582. Agreements to locate, deliver or recover property; time; validity; availability of records for public inspection or copying

No agreement to locate, deliver, recover, or assist in the recovery of property reported under Section 1530, entered into between the date a report is filed under subdivision (d) of Section 1530 and the date of publication of notice under Section 1531 is valid. Such an agreement made after publication of notice is valid if the fee or compensation agreed upon is not in excess of 10 percent of the recoverable property and the agreement is in writing and signed by the owner after disclosure in the agreement of the nature and value of the property and the name and address of the person or entity in possession of the property. Nothing in this section shall be construed to prevent an owner from asserting, at any time, that any agreement to locate property is based upon an excessive or unjust consideration.

Notwithstanding any other provision of law, records of the Controller's office pertaining to unclaimed property are not available for public inspection or copying until after publication of notice of the property or, if publication of notice of the property is not required, until one year after delivery of the property to the Controller. *(Formerly § 1527, added by Stats. 1959, c. 1809, p. 4307, § 2. Renumbered § 1582 and amended by Stats.1968, c. 356, p. 759, § 53, operative Jan. 1, 1969. Amended by Stats.1978, c. 815, p. 2603, § 2; Stats.1990, c. 450 (S.B.57), § 16, eff. July 31, 1990.)*

Research References

Miller and Starr California Real Estate § 18:7, The Unclaimed Property Law--Property Unclaimed or Abandoned.

Miller and Starr California Real Estate § 18:11, Heir Locators.

13 Witkin, California Summary 10th Personal Property § 38, Nature of Law.

CHAPTER 8. PROPERTY IN CUSTODY OF FEDERAL OFFICERS, AGENCIES, AND DEPARTMENTS

§ 1600. State policy

It is the policy of this State:

(a) To discover property in the custody of officers, departments, and agencies of the United States, which property is unclaimed by owners whose addresses are known or presumed to be in this State;

(b) To provide a procedure for judicial determination of the right of the State to receive custody of such unclaimed property; and

(c) To authorize expenditure of state funds to pay the proportionate cost of the State in discovering such unclaimed property and to hold the United States harmless against claims concerning such property when delivered to the custody of the State in accordance with this chapter. *(Added by Stats.1959, c. 1801, p. 4283, § 1.)*

Research References

3 Witkin Cal. Proc. 5th Actions § 65, (S 65) Statutory Classes.

3 Witkin Cal. Proc. 5th Actions § 71, (S 71) Escheat Proceedings.

§ 1601. Definitions

As used in this chapter:

(a) "Unclaimed property" means any tangible personal property or intangible personal property, including choses in action in amounts certain, and all debts owed or entrusted funds or other property held by any federal agency or any officer or employee thereof, whether occasioned by contract or operation of law or otherwise, except bonuses and gratuities, which has remained unclaimed by the owner for:

(1) Twenty years from the date of maturity or call for payment, if arising from transactions under the public debt; or

(2) Twenty years after the last transaction concerning principal or interest, if deposits in the postal savings system; or

(3) Five years after the property first became payable, demandable, or returnable, if arising from any other transaction.

(b) "Owner" means any person, including his or her legal representative, who has or had a legal or equitable interest in unclaimed property. The owner shall be conclusively presumed to be the person to whom unclaimed property was or is payable or returnable according to the records of the United States Government. If two or more persons are interested in the property, and the extent of their respective interests is unknown, it shall be presumed that their interests in such property are equal.

(c) "Person" includes any individual, partnership, corporation, limited liability company, unincorporated association, or other legal entity. *(Added by Stats.1959, c. 1801, p. 4283, § 1. Amended by Stats.1994, c. 1010 (S.B.2053), § 64.)*

§ 1602. Agreements for payment of state's proportionate share of costs

The Controller is authorized to enter into agreements establishing the time and manner for payments of this State's proportionate share of the actual and necessary cost incurred by the United States in examining records and reporting information to this State as such share of such cost shall be determined pursuant to federal law. Said agreements may provide for single payments at stated times over a period of years. The State Controller shall make all payments at the time and in the manner provided in said agreements. *(Added by Stats.1959, c. 1801, p. 4284, § 1.)*

§ 1603. Property in custody of state; claims against United States; intervention; consent by state to suit; defenses

The State hereby undertakes to hold the United States harmless against any claim concerning property delivered to the custody of the State in accordance with the provisions of this chapter. In the event an action or proceeding on such claim is brought against the United States the Attorney General shall intervene therein. The State consents to suit by such claimant in such contingency and any defense in favor of the United States shall be available to and urged by the State. *(Added by Stats.1959, c. 1801, p. 4284, § 1.)*

§ 1604. Unclaimed property subject to delivery to state; situs; presumptions

(a) All unclaimed intangible property, together with all interest and other increments accruing thereto, is subject to delivery to this state if the last known address of the owner is in this state. If the last known address of an owner is in this state, any other owner's address which is unknown shall be presumed to be in this state. If the last known addresses of owners are in this state and in one or more other states, the addresses of other owners whose addresses are unknown shall be presumed to be within this state if the federal agency having custody of the unclaimed property initially acquired possession in this state. If the records of the United States do not disclose the address of any owner of unclaimed property, such address shall be presumed to be within this state if the federal agency having custody of such property initially acquired possession in this state. All addresses presumed to be within this state are presumed to be within the County of Sacramento. For the purposes of this chapter, it shall be presumed that the situs of unclaimed intangible property is in this state if the last known or presumed address of the owner is in this state.

(b) All unclaimed tangible property is subject to delivery to this state if the federal agency having custody of the unclaimed property initially acquired possession in this state. *(Added by Stats.1959, c. 1801, p. 4284, § 1. Amended by Stats.1968, c. 356, p. 759, § 54, operative Jan. 1, 1969.)*

Law Revision Commission Comments

Section 1604 has been modified to accord with the rules stated in Texas v. New Jersey, 379 U.S. 674 (1965). In accordance with that decision, subdivision (a) provides for delivery of intangible property to this state if the last known address of the owner is in this state. Subdivision (b) is new and is based on the suggestion in Texas v. New Jersey, *supra*, that tangible property is subject to escheat to the state where the property is located.

§ 1605. Certification by Governor

The Governor shall certify to the Comptroller General or other proper officer of the United States that the law of this State provides effective means whereby the United States shall be compensated at reasonable times for this State's proportionate share of the actual and necessary cost of examining records and for reporting information and whereby the United States shall be held harmless in the event of claim for property delivered to this State in accordance with the provisions of this chapter.

Such certification shall be made on the thirtieth day of June next following the effective date of any federal statute requiring such certification. *(Added by Stats.1959, c. 1801, p. 4284, § 1.)*

§ 1606. Request for unreported information relating to unclaimed property

On the thirtieth day of June next following the date of certification by the Governor, and annually thereafter, the Controller shall request the Comptroller General or other proper officer of the United States to report all previously unreported information relating to unclaimed property as determined by that officer pursuant to federal law. *(Added by Stats.1959, c. 1801, p. 4285, § 1.)*

§ 1607. Forwarding copies of reports to county clerks; posting; election to claim against United States

When a report is received from the Comptroller General or other proper officer of the United States, the Controller shall prepare and forward a copy thereof to the clerk of the superior court of each county within this state and the clerk shall post a copy at the courthouse for a period of 60 days. Any person asserting an interest in property mentioned in the report may elect to claim against the United States under the laws of the United States, in which event and within 90 days following the date of initial posting by the clerk the person shall notify the Controller of the asserted interest and intention to so claim. The Controller shall omit the property from any claim by the state until such time as the asserted interest may be finally determined against the claimant. The interest may not thereafter be asserted against the state. *(Added by Stats.1959, c. 1801, p. 4285, § 1. Amended by Stats.2002, c. 784 (S.B.1316), § 84; Stats.2003, c. 62 (S.B.600), § 27.)*

Law Revision Commission Comments

Section 1607 is amended to reflect elimination of the county clerk's role as ex officio clerk of the superior court. See former Gov't Code § 26800 (county clerk acting as clerk of superior court). The powers, duties, and responsibilities formerly exercised by the county clerk as ex officio clerk of the court are delegated to the court administrative or executive officer, and the county clerk is relieved of those powers, duties, and responsibilities. See Gov't Code §§ 69840 (powers, duties, and responsibilities of clerk of court and deputy clerk of court), 71620 (trial court personnel). [32 Cal.L.Rev.Comm. Reports 139 (2002)].

§ 1608. Limitations as affecting right of state to acquire possession of unclaimed property

The expiration of any period of time specified by statute or court order, during which an action or proceeding may be commenced or enforced to obtain payment of a claim for funds or delivery of property shall not affect the right of this State to acquire possession of unclaimed property in accordance with the provisions of this chapter. *(Added by Stats.1959, c. 1801, p. 4285, § 1.)*

§ 1609. Proceeding to determine state's right to unclaimed property; commencement; venue; petition; contents; parties; joinder

Within 120 days following the date of initial posting by the clerk of the superior court, the Attorney General shall commence a proceeding by filing a petition to determine the state's right to custody of all property mentioned in such report and unclaimed within the time and in the manner provided by Section 1607. The proceeding shall be commenced and heard in the superior court in the County of Sacramento and venue shall not be affected by the provisions of Section 401, Code of Civil Procedure.

The petition shall name as respondents all persons known to have been interested and "all persons unknown claiming any title or interest in or to the property described or referred to in the petition." If the records of the United States fail to disclose with reasonable certainty the identity or number of owners or claimants of specific funds or other personal property, or the extent of their interests therein, such persons may be designated and described as a class, to wit, as "all unknown owners or claimants to the funds or property mentioned in or affected by _____," and, as the case may be, the petition shall identify and set forth the court actions or proceedings to the credit of which such funds or other property are held, or the accounts or other identifying references under which they are carried upon the records of the United States. The petition shall describe or refer to the property, and may include one or more items, as the Attorney General may be advised, without prejudice to his right to commence subsequent proceedings relating to other items not included. The petition shall also state the name of the owner and his last address as known or as presumed under this chapter, and shall set forth the facts and circumstances by virtue of which it is claimed that such funds or property are subject to custody by the state. Any number of respondents may be joined whether they reside in the same or different counties, and any number of causes of action may be joined and need not be separately stated. *(Added by Stats.1959, c. 1801, p. 4285, § 1. Amended by Stats.2002, c. 784 (S.B.1316), § 85.)*

Law Revision Commission Comments

Section 1609 is amended to reflect elimination of the county clerk's role as ex officio clerk of the superior court. See former Gov't Code § 26800 (county clerk acting as clerk of superior court). The powers, duties, and responsibilities formerly exercised by the county clerk as ex officio clerk of the court are delegated to the court administrative or executive officer, and the county clerk is relieved of those powers, duties, and responsibilities. See Gov't Code §§ 69840 (powers, duties, and responsibilities of clerk of court and deputy clerk of court), 71620 (trial court personnel). [32 Cal.L.Rev.Comm. Reports 140 (2002)].

§ 1610. Necessity of summons or process; publication of notice; contents; posting; completion; jurisdiction of court

No summons or other process shall issue to direct the appearance and answer of a respondent. Commencing within five days after filing petition, notice of the proceeding shall be published once each week for three consecutive weeks in a newspaper of general circulation published within the County of Sacramento. At the time the notice is first published, a copy of the petition and notice shall be posted at the courthouse in the county where each defendant was last known or presumed to have had an address. Such petition and such notice shall remain posted for 45 days. The notice of proceeding shall advise that the State seeks custody of unclaimed property held by the United States. The names but not the addresses of the respondents shall be contained in the notice with a statement that such persons are believed to live or to have lived within the State and are believed to be or to have been owners of the unclaimed property. The notice shall not contain a description of the unclaimed property but shall advise that such description together with the last known or presumed addresses of owners may be determined by examining the petition filed in the proceeding. The petition and its place of filing shall be sufficiently identified and described. The notice shall advise that persons claiming an interest must answer the petition within the time prescribed by law, which time shall be stated, if they elect to pursue their claims against the United States, otherwise their rights to property shall be preserved subject to delayed delivery as provided by law. The notice shall advise that Section 1611, Code of Civil Procedure, should be consulted for the time, form, and costs of an answer.

The notice shall be deemed completed 45 days after the date of first publication, whereupon the court shall have full and complete jurisdiction over the property described in the petition and not claimed within the time or in the manner provided in Section 1611, and shall have full and complete jurisdiction to determine the right of the State to custody and to render an appropriate judgment therefor. *(Added by Stats.1959, c. 1801, p. 4286, § 1.)*

§ 1611. Answer; deposit of costs; dismissal as to property described in answer

Any person, whether or not named in the petition, may within 15 days after completion of notice respond to the petition by answer describing the property, asserting an interest as owner or successor, and declaring an intention to claim the same from the United States under the laws of the United States. Such answer shall not be filed unless accompanied by the sum of ten dollars ($10) for deposit in court, and no other answer or response shall be filed by or on behalf of a claimant. The court shall strike from the petition and dismiss from the proceeding all property described in the answer. The funds on deposit shall be transmitted by the court to the Controller and shall be received for deposit in the abandoned property account in the Unclaimed Property Fund as total reimbursement for costs and services expended on behalf of the claimant. Such dismissal shall be without prejudice to a subsequent petition should it appear that the claimant is not entitled to the property, and the interest asserted in said answer shall not thereafter be asserted against the State. *(Added by Stats.1959, c. 1801, p. 4286, § 1.)*

§ 1612. Application for judgment as to property not claimed by answer; finding and order of court

Within 20 days following expiration of time for filing answer under Section 1611, the Attorney General shall apply to the court for a judgment relating to all property set forth in the petition and not claimed by answer. The court shall find that such property appears to be or to have been owned by persons residing within this State and remains unclaimed by such persons. The court shall declare that the property, which shall be described, is subject to custody of the State and shall be delivered to and received by the State of California to be retained until such time as it may be claimed pursuant to law. *(Added by Stats.1959, c. 1801, p. 4287, § 1.)*

§ 1613. Request for delivery or payment of property described in judgment; receipts

The Controller shall request delivery or payment of all unclaimed property described in the judgment declaring the right of the State to receive custody of such property. The request shall be accompanied by a certified copy of said judgment and shall be directed to such officer, agency, or department of the United States as may be designated for such purposes by federal law. The Controller shall furnish receipts for all property delivered or paid. *(Added by Stats.1959, c. 1801, p. 4287, § 1.)*

§ 1614. Deposit or sale of property as though received under Unclaimed Property Law

Property received under this chapter shall be deposited or sold by the State Controller as though received under Chapter 7 (commencing with Section 1500) of this title. Property received under this chapter shall not be subject to claim within two years following the date upon which it is paid to or received by the state. Thereafter, claims shall be made in the manner provided in Chapter 7 (commencing with Section 1500) of this title. *(Added by Stats.1959, c. 1801, p. 4287, § 1. Amended by Stats.1968, c. 356, p. 759, § 55, operative Jan. 1, 1969.)*

§ 1615. Appropriation; purposes

All money in the abandoned property account in the Unclaimed Property Fund is hereby continuously appropriated to the State Controller without regard to fiscal years, for expenditure in accordance with this chapter for the following purposes:

(a) For payment of the proportionate costs of this State pursuant to the terms of any contract entered with the United States;

(b) For payment of sums necessary to indemnify the United States for losses occasioned by claims to property delivered to the custody of this State. *(Added by Stats.1959, c. 1801, p. 4287, § 1.)*

Title 11

SISTER STATE AND FOREIGN MONEY-JUDGMENTS

CHAPTER 1. SISTER STATE MONEY-JUDGMENTS

§ 1710.10. Definitions

As used in this chapter:

(a) "Judgment creditor" means the person or persons who can bring an action to enforce a sister state judgment.

(b) "Judgment debtor" means the person or persons against whom an action to enforce a sister state judgment can be brought.

(c) "Sister state judgment" means that part of any judgment, decree, or order of a court of a state of the United States, other than California, which requires the payment of money, but does not include a support order as defined in Section 155 of the Family Code. *(Added by Stats.1974, c. 211, p. 405, § 3. Amended by Stats.1992, c. 163 (A.B.2641), § 64, operative Jan. 1, 1994.)*

Law Revision Commission Comments

Subdivisions (a) and (b) of Section 1710.10 incorporate the general law determining the persons who may enforce a judgment and against whom a judgment may be enforced. See, e.g., Title 3 (commencing with Section 367) of Part 2 and Sections 578 and 579 of this code.

Subdivision (c) is based on Section 1 of the revised Uniform Enforcement of Foreign Judgments Act of 1964. 9A Uniform Laws Ann. 488 (1965). However, unlike the Uniform Act which applies to all state and federal judgments entitled to full faith and credit, Section 1710.10(c) applies only to judgments of sister state courts which require the payment of money. Moreover, support orders as defined in Section 1653(k) are excluded from the coverage of this chapter since they are enforceable under the Revised Uniform Reciprocal Enforcement of Support Act of 1968, Title 10a (commencing with Section 1650). It should be noted that

"sister state judgment" is defined as that part of a judgment requiring the payment of money. Hence, for example, if a judgment of a sister state court requires both the payment of money and the performance of some other act, such as the conveyance of land, only the part requiring the payment of money is considered a "sister state judgment" enforceable under this chapter. The part requiring the performance of some other act may be enforced, if at all, only by a separate action. See Section 1710.65.

Subdivision (c) of Section 1710.10 is amended to substitute a reference to the Family Code for the reference to the former Civil Code section. [22 Cal.L.Rev.Comm.Reports 1 (1992)].

Research References

Rutter, Cal. Practice Guide: Enforcing Judgments/Debts Ch. 6A-2, Enforcement of Judgments Law ("Ejl")-Background.

Rutter, Cal. Practice Guide: Enforcing Judgments/Debts Ch. 6D-2, Writ of Execution.

Rutter, Cal. Practice Guide: Enforcing Judgments/Debts Ch. 6J-2, Enforcing Sister State Judgments in California.

Miller and Starr California Real Estate § 11:125, Recordation of the Abstract of Judgment.

3 Witkin Cal. Proc. 5th Actions § 54, (S 54) Modern Approach.

8 Witkin Cal. Proc. 5th Enforcement of Judgment § 23, Enforcement of Particular Judgments.

8 Witkin Cal. Proc. 5th Enforcement of Judgment § 35, (S 35) Right to Renew.

8 Witkin Cal. Proc. 5th Enforcement of Judgment § 68, (S 68) Relation Back and Priorities.

8 Witkin Cal. Proc. 5th Enforcement of Judgment § 445, When Action May be Brought.

8 Witkin Cal. Proc. 5th Enforcement of Judgment § 449, (S 449) Nature and Purpose.

8 Witkin Cal. Proc. 5th Enforcement of Judgment § 450, (S 450) Scope.

8 Witkin Cal. Proc. 5th Enforcement of Judgment § 454, (S 454) Who May File.

8 Witkin Cal. Proc. 5th Enforcement of Judgment § 462, Former Law: Uniform Foreign Money Judgments Recognition Act.

8 Witkin Cal. Proc. 5th Enforcement of Judgment § 476, Enforcement of Judgment Rendered in Another Jurisdiction.

7 Witkin Cal. Proc. 5th Judgment § 368, (S 368) Judgments in Different States.

§ 1710.15. Application for entry; statement; contents

(a) A judgment creditor may apply for the entry of a judgment based on a sister state judgment by filing an application pursuant to Section 1710.20.

(b) The application shall be executed under oath and shall include all of the following:

(1) A statement that an action in this state on the sister state judgment is not barred by the applicable statute of limitations.

(2) A statement, based on the applicant's information and belief, that no stay of enforcement of the sister state judgment is currently in effect in the sister state.

(3) A statement of the amount remaining unpaid under the sister state judgment and, if accrued interest on the sister state judgment is to be included in the California judgment, a statement of the amount of interest accrued on the sister state judgment (computed at the rate of interest applicable to the judgment under the law of the sister state), a statement of the rate of interest applicable to the judgment under the law of the sister state, and a citation to the law of the sister state establishing the rate of interest.

(4) A statement that no action based on the sister state judgment is currently pending in any court in this state and that no judgment based on the sister state judgment has previously been entered in any proceeding in this state.

(5) Where the judgment debtor is an individual, a statement setting forth the name and last known residence address of the judgment debtor. Where the judgment debtor is a corporation, a statement of the corporation's name, place of incorporation, and whether the corporation, if foreign, has qualified to do

business in this state under the provisions of Chapter 21 (commencing with Section 2100) of Division 1 of Title 1 of the Corporations Code. Where the judgment debtor is a partnership, a statement of the name of the partnership, whether it is a foreign partnership, and, if it is a foreign partnership, whether it has filed a statement pursuant to Section 15800 of the Corporations Code designating an agent for service of process. Except for facts which are matters of public record in this state, the statements required by this paragraph may be made on the basis of the judgment creditor's information and belief.

(6) A statement setting forth the name and address of the judgment creditor.

(c) A properly authenticated copy of the sister state judgment shall be attached to the application. *(Added by Stats.1974, c. 211, p. 406, § 3. Amended by Stats.1977, c. 232, p. 1029, § 1; Stats.1982, c. 150, p. 495, § 4; Stats.1984, c. 311, § 2; Stats.1985, c. 106, § 11.)*

Law Revision Commission Comments

Section 1710.15 states the requirements for the appelication for entry of judgment and requires that the application be filed with a superior court regardless of the amount of the judgment. See also Section 1710.20 (venue).

Paragraph (1) of subdivision (b) adopts the statute of limitations applicable to bringing an action in this state on the sister state judgment. The limitations period is determined by Title 2 (commencing with Section 312) of Part 2 of this code. Subdivision 3 of Section 337.5 prescribes a basic 10-year period for commencement of an action upon a sister state judgment. However, the 10-year period is tolled while the judgment debtor is absent from the state. See Code Civ.Proc. § 351; Cvecich v. Giardino, 37 Cal.App.2d 394, 99 P.2d 573 (1940). On the other hand, a lesser period as provided by the law of the sister state may be applicable under the borrowing provision of Section 361. E.g., Biewind v. Biewind, 17 Cal.2d 108, 109 P.2d 701 (1941); Parhm v. Parhm, 2 Cal.App.3d 311, 82 Cal.Rptr. 570 (1969); but *cf.* Mark v. Safren, 227 Cal.App.2d 151, 38 Cal.Rptr. 500 (1964). For a good discussion of the problems of applying a borrowing statute like Section 361, see Juneau Spruce Corp. v. International Longshoremen's & Warehousemen's Union, 128 F.Supp. 697 (D.Hawaii 1955). If the judgment is made payable in installments, the statute of limitations for each installment runs from the time each payment falls due. Biewind v. Biewind, *supra*; DeUprey v. DeUprey, 23 Cal. 352 (1863); Mark v. Safren, *supra*. It should be noted that the bar of the statute of limitations is also a ground for vacating a judgment entered pursuant to this chapter. See Section 1710.40 and Comment.

Paragraph (2) of subdivision (b) reflects the substantive requirement of subdivision (a) of Section 1710.55. See also Section 1710.50(a)(2). Paragraph (3) is designed to prevent double recovery. Where the sister state judgment is payable in installments, the "amount remaining unpaid" will be the total amount of the judgment less amounts which have been paid. Of course, only the installments which have fallen due and remain unpaid may be enforced by execution. Paragraph (4) reflects the substantive requirement of subdivisions (b) and (c) of Section 1710.55. The statement required by paragraph (5) of subdivision (b) will provide information necessary to determine whether a writ of execution may issue before notice of entry is given the judgment debtor. See Section 1710.45(b) and Comment.

Subdivision (c) requires that a properly authenticated copy of the sister state judgment be attached to the application. Section 1738 of Title 28 of the United States Code requires that full faith and credit be given to judgments authenticated in the manner there set forth and thereby provides certain maximum restrictions. For California provisions relating to authentication of judgments, see, e.g., Evid.Code §§ 1452, 1453, 1530(a).

Section 1710.15 is amended to reflect the change in the rate of interest on a judgment from seven to 10 percent and to delete the seven percent limit on the rate at which interest accrues on a sister state judgment. See Section 685.010. [15 Cal.L.Rev.Comm. Reports 7 (1980)].

Research References

Rutter, Cal. Practice Guide: Enforcing Judgments/Debts Ch. 6A-5, Amount Recoverable Under Judgment.
Rutter, Cal. Practice Guide: Enforcing Judgments/Debts Ch. 6J-2, Enforcing Sister State Judgments in California.

Miller and Starr California Real Estate § 32:48, Nature and Creation.
8 Witkin Cal. Proc. 5th Enforcement of Judgment § 453, (S 453) Jurisdiction and Venue.
8 Witkin Cal. Proc. 5th Enforcement of Judgment § 454, (S 454) Who May File.
8 Witkin Cal. Proc. 5th Enforcement of Judgment § 455, (S 455) Form and Content.
7 Witkin Cal. Proc. 5th Judgment § 327, Rate of Interest.

§ 1710.20. Filing of application; place

(a) An application for entry of a judgment based on a sister state judgment shall be filed in a superior court.

(b) Subject to the power of the court to transfer proceedings under this chapter pursuant to Title 4 (commencing with Section 392) of Part 2, the proper county for the filing of an application is any of the following:

(1) The county in which any judgment debtor resides.

(2) If no judgment debtor is a resident, any county in this state.

(c) A case in which the sister state judgment amounts to twenty-five thousand dollars ($25,000) or less is a limited civil case. *(Added by Stats.1974, c. 211, p. 406, § 3. Amended by Stats.1984, c. 311, § 3; Stats.1988, c. 54, § 1; Stats.1998, c. 931 (S.B.2139), § 125, eff. Sept. 28, 1998; Stats.2002, c. 784 (S.B. 1316), § 86.)*

Law Revision Commission Comments

Section 1710.20 states the venue requirements for proceedings under this chapter. Where a judgment creditor errs in his application, the judgment debtor may request a transfer of the proceedings under the general provisions relating to transfer of venue. A transfer will not, however, affect the validity of actions already taken.

Section 1710.20 is amended to accommodate unification of the municipal and superior courts in a county. Cal. Const. art. VI, § 5(e). It is also amended to reflect elimination of the justice court. Cal. Const. art. VI, §§ 1, 5(b).

See Section 85 (limited civil cases) & Comment. [28 Cal.L.Rev.Comm. Reports 51 (1998)].

Subdivision (a) of Section 1710.20 is amended to reflect unification of the municipal and superior courts pursuant to Article VI, Section 5(e), of the California Constitution. [32 Cal.L.Rev.Comm. Reports 141 (2002)].

Research References

Rutter, Cal. Practice Guide: Enforcing Judgments/Debts Ch. 6J-2, Enforcing Sister State Judgments in California.
8 Witkin Cal. Proc. 5th Enforcement of Judgment § 453, (S 453) Jurisdiction and Venue.
7 Witkin Cal. Proc. 5th Judgment § 327, Rate of Interest.

§ 1710.25. Entry of judgment; accrued interest

(a) Upon the filing of the application, the clerk shall enter a judgment based upon the application for the total of the following amounts as shown therein:

(1) The amount remaining unpaid under the sister state judgment.

(2) The amount of interest accrued on the sister state judgment (computed at the rate of interest applicable to the judgment under the law of the sister state).

(3) The amount of the fee for filing the application for entry of the sister state judgment.

(b) Entry shall be made in the same manner as entry of an original judgment of the court. From the time of entry, interest shall accrue on the judgment so entered at the rate of interest applicable to a judgment entered in this state. *(Added by Stats.1974, c. 211, p. 406, § 3. Amended by Stats.1977, c. 232, p. 1030, § 2; Stats.1982, c. 150, p. 495, § 5; Stats.1984, c. 311, § 4.)*

Law Revision Commission Comments

Section 1710.25 is similar to Section 2 of the revised Uniform Enforcement of Foreign Judgments Act of 1964 which requires the clerk to file a sister state judgment and treat it in the same manner as a judgment of his state. 9A Uniform Laws Ann. 488 (1965). Section 1710.25 accomplishes the same end by requiring entry of a judgment on the basis of the judgment creditor's application. See Section 1710.15. An authenticated copy of the sister state judgment is attached to the application. Where the sister state judgment is payable in installments, the clerk enters judgment in installment form for the amount remaining unpaid. Execution may issue only as to unpaid installments which have accrued.

Section 1710.25 is amended to reflect the change in the rate of interest on a judgment from seven to 10 percent and to conform to the change made in Section 1710.15. See Section 685.010. [15 Cal.L.Rev.Comm. Reports 7 (1980)].

Research References

Rutter, Cal. Practice Guide: Enforcing Judgments/Debts Ch. 6A-5, Amount Recoverable Under Judgment.
Rutter, Cal. Practice Guide: Enforcing Judgments/Debts Ch. 6J-2, Enforcing Sister State Judgments in California.
Miller and Starr California Real Estate § 32:48, Nature and Creation.
8 Witkin Cal. Proc. 5th Enforcement of Judgment § 455, (S 455) Form and Content.
8 Witkin Cal. Proc. 5th Enforcement of Judgment § 456, (S 456) Entry of Judgment.
7 Witkin Cal. Proc. 5th Judgment § 327, Rate of Interest.

§ 1710.30.   Notice of entry; procedure; fee

(a) Notice of entry of judgment shall be served promptly by the judgment creditor upon the judgment debtor in the manner provided for service of summons by Article 3 (commencing with Section 415.10) of Chapter 4 of Title 5 of Part 2. Notice shall be in a form prescribed by the Judicial Council and shall inform the judgment debtor that the judgment debtor has 30 days within which to make a motion to vacate the judgment.

(b) The fee for service of the notice of entry of judgment under this section is an item of costs recoverable in the same manner as statutory fees for service of a writ as provided in Chapter 5 (commencing with Section 685.010) of Division 1 of Title 9 of Part 2, but such fee may not exceed the amount allowed to a public officer or employee in this state for such service. *(Added by Stats.1974, c. 211, p. 406, § 3. Amended by Stats.1977, c. 232, p. 1030, § 3; Stats.1982, c. 497, p. 2173, § 79, operative July 1, 1983.)*

Law Revision Commission Comments

Section 1710.30 requires the judgment creditor to serve notice of entry of judgment promptly. In proceedings under this chapter, the court clerk does not send notice of entry of judgment as provided in Section 664.5.

Ordinarily, service of notice of entry of judgment must be made at least 30 days before a writ of execution may issue. See Section 1710.45(a) and Comment. However, in certain circumstances, the judgment debtor may be served with a writ of execution before he is served with notice of entry of judgment. See Section 1710.45(b), (c), and Comment. See also Code Civ.Proc. § 682.1 (service of writ on judgment debtor).

Subdivision (b) is added to Section 1710.30 to provide the manner of recovering the cost of serving the notice of entry of judgment on the judgment debtor. This cost is recovered in the same manner as, for example, the statutory fees for the service of a writ of execution under Section 1033.7. See Govt.Code § 26721 (basic fee for service of a notice).

Section 1710.30 is amended to correct a cross-reference. See Sections 685.050 (costs satisfied under writ), 685.070 (memorandum of costs). (15 Cal.L.Rev.Comm. Reports 2001).

Research References

Rutter, Cal. Practice Guide: Enforcing Judgments/Debts Ch. 6J-2, Enforcing Sister State Judgments in California.

8 Witkin Cal. Proc. 5th Enforcement of Judgment § 457, (S 457) Notice of Entry.

§ 1710.35.   Effect of entry; enforcement

Except as otherwise provided in this chapter, a judgment entered pursuant to this chapter shall have the same effect as an original money judgment of the court and may be enforced or satisfied in like manner. *(Added by Stats.1974, c. 211, p. 407, § 3. Amended by Stats.1984, c. 311, § 5.)*

Law Revision Commission Comments

Section 1710.35 provides that a judgment entered pursuant to this chapter is to be treated as a judgment of the superior court for purposes of enforcement. Hence, for example, the provisions of this code regarding judgment liens (Section 674), execution (Sections 681–713½), and supplemental proceedings (Sections 714–723) apply to the judgment. However, some variations exist between the enforcement procedures of this chapter and those generally applicable. See, e.g., Section 1710.45. A judgment entered pursuant to this chapter may be enforced after 10 years as provided by Section 685. Likewise, an action may be brought upon a judgment entered pursuant to this chapter. *Cf.* Thomas v. Thomas, 14 Cal.2d 355, 94 P.2d 810 (1939); Atkinson v. Adkins, 92 Cal.App. 424, 268 P. 461 (1928). However, the same sister state judgment may not serve as the basis for entry of more than one California judgment. See Section 1710.55(b), (c), 1710.60, and the Comments thereto.

Research References

Rutter, Cal. Practice Guide: Enforcing Judgments/Debts Ch. 6A-2, Enforcement of Judgments Law ("Ejl")-Background.
Rutter, Cal. Practice Guide: Enforcing Judgments/Debts Ch. 6J-2, Enforcing Sister State Judgments in California.
Miller and Starr California Real Estate § 32:48, Nature and Creation.
Miller and Starr California Real Estate § 10:127, Conflict of Laws.
Miller and Starr California Real Estate § 11:125, Recordation of the Abstract of Judgment.
8 Witkin Cal. Proc. 5th Enforcement of Judgment § 452, (S 452) Effect of Judgment.

§ 1710.40.   Vacation of judgment; motion; entry of another and different judgment; filing

(a) A judgment entered pursuant to this chapter may be vacated on any ground which would be a defense to an action in this state on the sister state judgment, including the ground that the amount of interest accrued on the sister state judgment and included in the judgment entered pursuant to this chapter is incorrect.

(b) Not later than 30 days after service of notice of entry of judgment pursuant to Section 1710.30, proof of which has been made in the manner provided by Article 5 (commencing with Section 417.10) of Chapter 4 of Title 5 of Part 2, the judgment debtor, on written notice to the judgment creditor, may make a motion to vacate the judgment under this section.

(c) Upon the hearing of the motion to vacate the judgment under this section, the judgment may be vacated upon any ground provided in subdivision (a) and another and different judgment entered, including, but not limited to, another and different judgment for the judgment creditor if the decision of the court is that the judgment creditor is entitled to such different judgment. The decision of the court on the motion to vacate the judgment shall be given and filed with the clerk of court in the manner provided in Sections 632, 634, and 635, except that the court is not required to make any written findings and conclusions if the amount of the judgment as entered under Section 1710.25 does not exceed one thousand dollars ($1,000). *(Added by Stats.1974, c. 211, p. 407, § 3. Amended by Stats.1977, c. 232, p. 1031, § 4.)*

Law Revision Commission Comments

Section 1710.40 allows the judgment debtor to make a noticed motion to vacate the entry of judgment on any ground which would be a defense to an action in this state on the sister state judgment. Common defenses to enforcement of a sister state judgment include the following: the judgment is not final and unconditional (where finality means that no further action by the court rendering the judgment is necessary to resolve the matter litigated); the judgment was obtained by extrinsic fraud; the judgment was rendered in excess of jurisdiction; the judgment is not enforceable in the state of rendition; the plaintiff is guilty of misconduct; the judgment has already been paid; suit on the judgment is barred by the statute of limitations in the state where enforcement is sought. See 5B Witkin, California Procedure Enforcement of Judgment §§ 194–195 at 3549–3550 (2d ed. 1971); Restatement (Second) of Conflict of Laws §§ 103–121 (1971).

Where it appears that a writ of execution may be issued or levied before the 10-day notice of motion period specified in Section 1005 has run, the court may either shorten the time of notice under Section 1005 or grant a stay of enforcement under Section 1710.50 in order to prevent execution before the judgment debtor's motion can be heard. Equitable relief from the judgment may be available in certain circumstances after the time for making a motion to vacate has expired. See 5 B. Witkin, California Procedure Attack on Judgment in Trial Court § 175 at 3744–3745 (2d ed. 1971); Restatement of Judgments §§ 112–130 (1942).

Research References

Rutter, Cal. Practice Guide: Enforcing Judgments/Debts Ch. 6J-2, Enforcing Sister State Judgments in California.
Miller and Starr California Real Estate § 32:48, Nature and Creation.
Miller and Starr California Real Estate § 10:127, Conflict of Laws.
3 Witkin Cal. Proc. 5th Actions § 54, (S 54) Modern Approach.
8 Witkin Cal. Proc. 5th Attack Judgment Trial Court § 226, (S 226) in General.
8 Witkin Cal. Proc. 5th Enforcement of Judgment § 449, (S 449) Nature and Purpose.
8 Witkin Cal. Proc. 5th Enforcement of Judgment § 457, (S 457) Notice of Entry.
8 Witkin Cal. Proc. 5th Enforcement of Judgment § 458, (S 458) in General.
8 Witkin Cal. Proc. 5th Enforcement of Judgment § 459, (S 459) Grounds.
8 Witkin Cal. Proc. 5th Enforcement of Judgment § 461, (S 461) Stay of Enforcement.

§ 1710.45. Writ of execution or enforcement; resident and nonresident debtors; sale or distribution of property

(a) Except as otherwise provided in this section, a writ of execution on a judgment entered pursuant to this chapter shall not issue, nor may the judgment be enforced by other means, until at least 30 days after the judgment creditor serves notice of entry of the judgment upon the judgment debtor, proof of which has been made in the manner provided by Article 5 (commencing with Section 417.10) of Chapter 4 of Title 5 of Part 2.

(b) A writ of execution may be issued, or other enforcement sought, before service of the notice of entry of judgment if the judgment debtor is any of the following:

(1) An individual who does not reside in this state.

(2) A foreign corporation not qualified to do business in this state under the provisions of Chapter 21 (commencing with Section 2100) of Division 1 of Title 1 of the Corporations Code.

(3) A foreign partnership which has not filed a statement pursuant to Section 15700 of the Corporations Code designating an agent for service of process.

(c) The court may order that a writ of execution be issued, or may permit enforcement by other means, before service of the notice of entry of judgment if the court finds upon an ex parte showing that great or irreparable injury would result to the judgment creditor if issuance of the writ or enforcement were delayed as provided in subdivision (a).

(d) Property levied upon pursuant to a writ issued under subdivision (b) or (c) or otherwise sought to be applied to the satisfaction of the judgment shall not be sold or distributed before 30 days after the judgment creditor serves notice of entry of the judgment upon the judgment debtor, proof of which has been made in the manner provided by Article 5 (commencing with Section 417.10) of Chapter 4 of Title 5 of Part 2. However, if property levied upon is perishable, it may be sold in order to prevent its destruction or loss of value, but the proceeds of the sale shall not be distributed to the judgment creditor before the date sale of nonperishable property is permissible. *(Added by Stats.1974, c. 211, p. 407, § 3. Amended by Stats.1976, c. 641, p. 1508, § 1.2, eff. Jan. 1, 1977; Stats.1982, c. 497, p. 2174, § 80, operative July 1, 1983.)*

Law Revision Commission Comments

Subdivision (a) of Section 1710.45 states the general rule which requires service of the notice of entry of judgment at least 30 days before a writ of execution may be issued. A writ of execution may not be issued under subdivision (a) unless proof of service has been filed which shows that the 30-day requirement has been satisfied. Exceptions to subdivision (a) are stated in subdivisions (b) and (c).

Subdivision (b) permits the issuance and levy of a writ of execution before notice against the assets of three types of nonresident debtors. Subdivision (c) permits issuance of a writ upon an ex parte showing that great or irreparable injury would result if the judgment creditor were required to give notice before obtaining a writ of execution. Although the clerk may issue writs of execution against the debtors described in subdivision (b), the creditor must obtain a court order before a writ of execution may issue under subdivision (c). The clerk may rely on the information in the creditor's application in deciding whether a writ of execution may be issued under subdivision (b). See Section 1710.15(b)(5).

Subdivision (d) provides a special 30-day delay period which gives the judgment debtor an opportunity to make a motion to vacate the judgment before his property is sold or distributed. See Section 1710.40. Section 1710.45 does not otherwise affect the general execution procedures.

Research References

Rutter, Cal. Practice Guide: Enforcing Judgments/Debts Ch. 6J-2, Enforcing Sister State Judgments in California.
8 Witkin Cal. Proc. 5th Enforcement of Judgment § 457, (S 457) Notice of Entry.
8 Witkin Cal. Proc. 5th Enforcement of Judgment § 460, (S 460) 30-Day Delay.

§ 1710.50. Stay of enforcement

(a) The court shall grant a stay of enforcement where:

(1) An appeal from the sister state judgment is pending or may be taken in the state which originally rendered the judgment. Under this paragraph, enforcement shall be stayed until the proceedings on appeal have been concluded or the time for appeal has expired.

(2) A stay of enforcement of the sister state judgment has been granted in the sister state. Under this paragraph, enforcement shall be stayed until the sister state stay of enforcement expires or is vacated.

(3) The judgment debtor has made a motion to vacate pursuant to Section 1710.40. Under this paragraph, enforcement shall be stayed until the judgment debtor's motion to vacate is determined.

(4) Any other circumstance exists where the interests of justice require a stay of enforcement.

(b) The court may grant a stay of enforcement under this section on its own motion, on ex parte motion, or on noticed motion.

(c) The court shall grant a stay of enforcement under this section on such terms and conditions as are just including but not limited to the following:

(1) The court may require an undertaking in an amount it determines to be just, but the amount of the undertaking shall not exceed double the amount of the judgment creditor's claim.

(2) If a writ of execution has been issued, the court may order that it remain in effect.

(3) If property of the judgment debtor has been levied upon under a writ of execution, the court may order the levying officer to retain possession of the property capable of physical possession and to maintain the levy on other property. *(Added by Stats.1974, c. 211, p. 408, § 3.)*

Law Revision Commission Comments

Section 1710.50 gives broad discretion to the court to grant a stay of enforcement in the interests of justice. Where the court has adequate information, it may grant the stay on its own motion. Otherwise, the burden is on the judgment debtor to show a need for the stay on ex parte or noticed motion. Subdivision (c) gives the court broad discretion in fashioning the terms of the stay in order to adequately protect the interests of both the judgment creditor and the judgment debtor. Whether an undertaking is to be required, and the amount of the undertaking if one is required, is left to the discretion of the court which may consider factors such as whether (1) a successful defense is probable, (2) it is likely that the debtor will conceal or transfer his assets, (3) the debtor has already given a bond on appeal in the sister state, and (4) the debtor prefers having his property held subject to levy rather than giving an undertaking.

Research References

Rutter, Cal. Practice Guide: Enforcing Judgments/Debts Ch. 6J-2, Enforcing Sister State Judgments in California.

Miller and Starr California Real Estate § 32:58, Satisfaction or Release of the Judgment Lien.

8 Witkin Cal. Proc. 5th Enforcement of Judgment § 67, (S 67) Duration and Extinguishment.

8 Witkin Cal. Proc. 5th Enforcement of Judgment § 446, (S 446) Judgment Not Final and Unconditional.

8 Witkin Cal. Proc. 5th Enforcement of Judgment § 458, (S 458) in General.

8 Witkin Cal. Proc. 5th Enforcement of Judgment § 461, (S 461) Stay of Enforcement.

§ 1710.55. Restrictions on entry of judgment

No judgment based on a sister state judgment may be entered pursuant to this chapter in any of the following cases:

(a) A stay of enforcement of the sister state judgment is currently in effect in the sister state.

(b) An action based on the sister state judgment is currently pending in any court in this state.

(c) A judgment based on the sister state judgment has previously been entered in any proceeding in this state. *(Added by Stats.1974, c. 211, p. 408, § 3.)*

Law Revision Commission Comments

Subdivision (a) of Section 1710.55 prevents the judgment creditor from using the procedures of this chapter to obtain the entry of a judgment based on a sister state judgment where enforcement has been stayed in the sister state. If entry of judgment is obtained in this state before the stay of enforcement of the sister state judgment is granted in the sister state, the judgment debtor may seek to stay enforcement of the California judgment under Section 1710.50(a)(2).

Subdivisions (b) and of Section 1710.55, together with subdivision (b) of Section 1710.60, preclude a judgment creditor from using his sister state judgment as defined in Section 1710.10(c) as the basis for more than one California judgment.

Research References

Rutter, Cal. Practice Guide: Enforcing Judgments/Debts Ch. 6J-2, Enforcing Sister State Judgments in California.

8 Witkin Cal. Proc. 5th Enforcement of Judgment § 451, (S 451) Restrictions on Entry of Judgment.

8 Witkin Cal. Proc. 5th Enforcement of Judgment § 455, (S 455) Form and Content.

§ 1710.60. Right of action to enforce judgment; exception

(a) Except as provided in subdivision (b), nothing in this chapter affects any right a judgment creditor may have to bring an action to enforce a sister state judgment.

(b) No action to enforce a sister state judgment may be brought where a judgment based on such sister state judgment has previously been entered pursuant to this chapter. *(Added by Stats.1974, c. 211, p. 408, § 3.)*

Law Revision Commission Comments

Subdivision (a) of Section 1710.60 is similar to Section 6 of the revised Uniform Enforcement of Foreign Judgments Act of 1964. 9A Uniform Laws Ann. 489 (1965). The enactment of this chapter is not intended to restrict the traditional method of enforcing a sister state money judgment which requires the judgment creditor to bring an independent action in this state. See 5 B. Witkin, California Procedure Enforcement of Judgment § 193 at 3548–3549 (2d ed. 1970); Restatement (Second) of Conflict of Laws §§ 99, 100, Comment b (1971); Restatement of Judgments § 47, Comment e (1942). However, subdivision (b) makes clear that the judgment creditor must choose between the methods of enforcement offered. He may not obtain two money judgments in this state based on one sister state judgment as defined in Section 1710.10(c) by using the two different procedures. See also Section 1710.55(b).

Research References

Rutter, Cal. Practice Guide: Enforcing Judgments/Debts Ch. 6J-2, Enforcing Sister State Judgments in California.

8 Witkin Cal. Proc. 5th Enforcement of Judgment § 451, (S 451) Restrictions on Entry of Judgment.

§ 1710.65. Right of action for other than payment of money

The entry of a judgment based on a sister state judgment pursuant to this chapter does not limit the right of the judgment creditor to bring an action based on the part of a judgment of a sister state which does not require the payment of money, nor does the bringing of such an action limit the right of the judgment creditor to obtain entry of judgment based on the sister state judgment pursuant to this chapter. *(Added by Stats.1974, c. 211, p. 408, § 3.)*

Law Revision Commission Comments

Section 1710.65 makes it clear that the enforcement of the part of a judgment of a sister state ordering the payment of money pursuant to this chapter is independent of any action on the part of such judgment awarding some other relief and that use of the two separate procedures is not to be regarded as splitting a single cause of action.

Research References

Rutter, Cal. Practice Guide: Enforcing Judgments/Debts Ch. 6J-2, Enforcing Sister State Judgments in California.

Miller and Starr California Real Estate § 11:125, Recordation of the Abstract of Judgment.

8 Witkin Cal. Proc. 5th Enforcement of Judgment § 445, When Action May be Brought.

8 Witkin Cal. Proc. 5th Enforcement of Judgment § 450, (S 450) Scope.

8 Witkin Cal. Proc. 5th Enforcement of Judgment § 451, (S 451) Restrictions on Entry of Judgment.

CHAPTER 2 . FOREIGN–COUNTRY MONEY JUDGMENTS

Section

Section

§ 1713.   Short title

This chapter may be cited as the Uniform Foreign–Country Money Judgments Recognition Act. *(Added by Stats.2007, c. 212 (S.B.639), § 2.)*

Research References

Rutter, Cal. Practice Guide: Enforcing Judgments/Debts Ch. 6A-9, Restrictions on Enforcement of Judgments Involving Indian Tribes.
Rutter, Cal. Practice Guide: Enforcing Judgments/Debts Ch. 6J-4, Enforcing Foreign Country Money Judgments-Uniform Foreign-Country Money Judgments Recognition Act.
Miller and Starr California Real Estate § 11:125, Recordation of the Abstract of Judgment.
8 Witkin Cal. Proc. 5th Enforcement of Judgment § 23, Enforcement of Particular Judgments.
8 Witkin Cal. Proc. 5th Enforcement of Judgment § 462, Former Law: Uniform Foreign Money Judgments Recognition Act.
8 Witkin Cal. Proc. 5th Enforcement of Judgment § 463, Current Law: Uniform Foreign-Country Money Judgments Recognition Act.
7 Witkin Cal. Proc. 5th Judgment § 356, (S 356) Foreign Courts.
14 Witkin, California Summary 10th Wills and Probate § 67, Will Previously Admitted to Probate.

§ 1714.   Definitions

As used in this chapter:

(a) "Foreign country" means a government other than any of the following:

(1) The United States.

(2) A state, district, commonwealth, territory, or insular possession of the United States.

(3) Any other government with regard to which the decision in this state as to whether to recognize a judgment of that government's courts is initially subject to determination under the Full Faith and Credit Clause of the United States Constitution.

(b) "Foreign-country judgment" means a judgment of a court of a foreign country. "Foreign-country judgment" includes a judgment by any Indian tribe recognized by the government of the United States. *(Added by Stats.2007, c. 212 (S.B.639), § 2.)*

Research References

Rutter, Cal. Practice Guide: Enforcing Judgments/Debts Ch. 6A-9, Restrictions on Enforcement of Judgments Involving Indian Tribes.
Rutter, Cal. Practice Guide: Enforcing Judgments/Debts Ch. 6J-4, Enforcing Foreign Country Money Judgments-Uniform Foreign-Country Money Judgments Recognition Act.
8 Witkin Cal. Proc. 5th Enforcement of Judgment § 463, Current Law: Uniform Foreign-Country Money Judgments Recognition Act.

§ 1715.   Applicability

(a) Except as otherwise provided in subdivision (b), this chapter applies to a foreign-country judgment to the extent that the judgment both:

(1) Grants or denies recovery of a sum of money.

(2) Under the law of the foreign country where rendered, is final, conclusive, and enforceable.

(b) This chapter does not apply to a foreign-country judgment, even if the judgment grants or denies recovery of a sum of money, to the extent that the judgment is any of the following:

(1) A judgment for taxes.

(2) A fine or other penalty.

(3)(A) A judgment for divorce, support, or maintenance, or other judgment rendered in connection with domestic relations.

(B) A judgment for divorce, support, or maintenance, or other judgment rendered in connection with domestic relations may be recognized by a court of this state pursuant to Section 1723.

(c) A party seeking recognition of a foreign-country judgment has the burden of establishing that the foreign-country judgment is entitled to recognition under this chapter. *(Added by Stats. 2007, c. 212 (S.B.639), § 2.)*

Research References

Rutter, Cal. Practice Guide: Enforcing Judgments/Debts Ch. 6J-4, Enforcing Foreign Country Money Judgments-Uniform Foreign-Country Money Judgments Recognition Act.
8 Witkin Cal. Proc. 5th Enforcement of Judgment § 464, Scope of Act.
8 Witkin Cal. Proc. 5th Enforcement of Judgment § 466, Procedure for Recognition.

§ 1716.   Standards for recognition; mandatory and permissible reasons for refusal

(a) Except as otherwise provided in subdivisions (b) and (c), a court of this state shall recognize a foreign-country judgment to which this chapter applies.

(b) A court of this state shall not recognize a foreign-country judgment if any of the following apply:

(1) The judgment was rendered under a judicial system that does not provide impartial tribunals or procedures compatible with the requirements of due process of law.

(2) The foreign court did not have personal jurisdiction over the defendant.

(3) The foreign court did not have jurisdiction over the subject matter.

(c) A court of this state is not required to recognize a foreign-country judgment if any of the following apply:

(1) The defendant in the proceeding in the foreign court did not receive notice of the proceeding in sufficient time to enable the defendant to defend.

(2) The judgment was obtained by fraud that deprived the losing party of an adequate opportunity to present its case.

(3) The judgment or the cause of action or claim for relief on which the judgment is based is repugnant to the public policy of this state or of the United States.

(4) The judgment conflicts with another final and conclusive judgment.

(5) The proceeding in the foreign court was contrary to an agreement between the parties under which the dispute in question was to be determined otherwise than by proceedings in that foreign court.

(6) In the case of jurisdiction based only on personal service, the foreign court was a seriously inconvenient forum for the trial of the action.

(7) The judgment was rendered in circumstances that raise substantial doubt about the integrity of the rendering court with respect to the judgment.

(8) The specific proceeding in the foreign court leading to the judgment was not compatible with the requirements of due process of law.

(9) The judgment includes recovery for a claim of defamation unless the court determines that the defamation law applied by the foreign court provided at least as much protection for freedom of speech and the press as provided by both the United States and California Constitutions.

(d) If the party seeking recognition of a foreign-country judgment has met its burden of establishing recognition of the foreign-country judgment pursuant to subdivision (c) of Section 1715, a party resisting recognition of a foreign-country judgment has the burden of establishing that a ground for nonrecognition stated in subdivision (b) or (c) exists. *(Added by Stats.2007, c. 212 (S.B.639), § 2. Amended by Stats.2009, c. 579 (S.B.320), § 1.)*

Research References

Rutter, Cal. Practice Guide: Enforcing Judgments/Debts Ch. 6J-4, Enforcing Foreign Country Money Judgments-Uniform Foreign-Country Money Judgments Recognition Act.
8 Witkin Cal. Proc. 5th Enforcement of Judgment § 465, Standards for Recognition.
8 Witkin Cal. Proc. 5th Enforcement of Judgment § 466, Procedure for Recognition.
14 Witkin, California Summary 10th Wills and Probate § 67, Will Previously Admitted to Probate.

§ 1717. Refusal for lack of personal jurisdiction; permissible reasons; defamation proceedings

(a) A foreign-country judgment shall not be refused recognition for lack of personal jurisdiction if any of the following apply:

(1) The defendant was served with process personally in the foreign country.

(2) The defendant voluntarily appeared in the proceeding, other than for the purpose of protecting property seized or threatened with seizure in the proceeding or of contesting the jurisdiction of the court over the defendant.

(3) The defendant, before the commencement of the proceeding, had agreed to submit to the jurisdiction of the foreign court with respect to the subject matter involved.

(4) The defendant was domiciled in the foreign country when the proceeding was instituted or was a corporation or other form of business organization that had its principal place of business in, or was organized under the laws of, the foreign country.

(5) The defendant had a business office in the foreign country and the proceeding in the foreign court involved a cause of action or claim for relief arising out of business done by the defendant through that office in the foreign country.

(6) The defendant operated a motor vehicle or airplane in the foreign country and the proceeding involved a cause of action or claim for relief arising out of that operation.

(b) The list of bases for personal jurisdiction in subdivision (a) is not exclusive. The courts of this state may recognize bases of personal jurisdiction other than those listed in subdivision (a) as sufficient to support a foreign-country judgment.

(c) If a judgment was rendered in an action for defamation in a foreign country against a person who is a resident of California or a person or entity amenable to jurisdiction in California, and declaratory relief with respect to liability for the judgment or a determination that the judgment is not recognizable in California under Section 1716 is sought, a court has jurisdiction to determine the declaratory relief action as well as personal jurisdiction over the person or entity who obtained the foreign-country judgment if both of the following apply:

(1) The publication at issue was published in California.

(2) The person who is a resident, or the person or entity who is amenable to jurisdiction in California, either (A) has assets in California that might be subject to an enforcement proceeding to satisfy the foreign-country defamation judgment, or (B) may have to take actions in California to comply with the foreign-country defamation judgment.

This subdivision shall apply to persons who obtained judgments in defamation proceedings in a foreign country both prior to and after January 1, 2010. *(Added by Stats.2007, c. 212 (S.B.639), § 2. Amended by Stats.2009, c. 579 (S.B.320), § 2.)*

Research References

Rutter, Cal. Practice Guide: Enforcing Judgments/Debts Ch. 6J-4, Enforcing Foreign Country Money Judgments-Uniform Foreign-Country Money Judgments Recognition Act.
Miller and Starr California Real Estate § 34:73, Determining the "Prevailing Party".
Miller and Starr California Real Estate § 34:74, Effect of Dismissal of Action Before Judgment.
Miller and Starr California Real Estate § 34:77, Recovery of Fees After Judgment in Excess of Rejected Settlement Offer.
Miller and Starr California Real Estate § 34:79, Recovery of Fees as an Item of Costs; Procedural Requirements.
Miller and Starr California Real Estate § 35:84, Ancillary Remedies.
8 Witkin Cal. Proc. 5th Enforcement of Judgment § 465, Standards for Recognition.

§ 1718. Procedure for recognition of foreign-country judgment

(a) If recognition of a foreign-country judgment is sought as an original matter, the issue of recognition shall be raised by filing an action seeking recognition of the foreign-country judgment.

(b) If recognition of a foreign-country judgment is sought in a pending action, the issue of recognition may be raised by counterclaim, cross-claim, or affirmative defense. *(Added by Stats.2007, c. 212 (S.B.639), § 2.)*

Research References

Rutter, Cal. Practice Guide: Enforcing Judgments/Debts Ch. 6J-4, Enforcing Foreign Country Money Judgments-Uniform Foreign-Country Money Judgments Recognition Act.
8 Witkin Cal. Proc. 5th Enforcement of Judgment § 466, Procedure for Recognition.

§ 1719. Effect of recognition of foreign-country judgment

If the court in a proceeding under Section 1718 finds that the foreign-country judgment is entitled to recognition under this chapter then, to the extent that the foreign-country judgment grants or denies recovery of a sum of money, the foreign-country judgment is both of the following:

(a) Conclusive between the parties to the same extent as the judgment of a sister state entitled to full faith and credit in this state would be conclusive.

(b) Enforceable in the same manner and to the same extent as a judgment rendered in this state. *(Added by Stats.2007, c. 212 (S.B.639), § 2.)*

Research References

Rutter, Cal. Practice Guide: Enforcing Judgments/Debts Ch. 6J-4, Enforcing Foreign Country Money Judgments-Uniform Foreign-Country Money Judgments Recognition Act.
8 Witkin Cal. Proc. 5th Enforcement of Judgment § 467, Effect of Recognition.

§ 1720. Stay of proceedings pending appeal of foreign-county judgment

If a party establishes that an appeal from a foreign-country judgment is pending or will be taken in the foreign country, the court may stay any proceedings with regard to the foreign-country judgment until the appeal is concluded, the time for appeal expires, or the appellant has had sufficient time to prosecute the appeal and has failed to do so. *(Added by Stats.2007, c. 212 (S.B.639), § 2.)*

Research References

Rutter, Cal. Practice Guide: Enforcing Judgments/Debts Ch. 6J-4, Enforcing Foreign Country Money Judgments-Uniform Foreign-Country Money Judgments Recognition Act.

8 Witkin Cal. Proc. 5th Enforcement of Judgment § 446, (S 446) Judgment Not Final and Unconditional.

8 Witkin Cal. Proc. 5th Enforcement of Judgment § 466, Procedure for Recognition.

§ 1721. Statute of limitations

An action to recognize a foreign-country judgment shall be commenced within the earlier of the time during which the foreign-country judgment is effective in the foreign country or 10 years from the date that the foreign-country judgment became effective in the foreign country. *(Added by Stats.2007, c. 212 (S.B.639), § 2.)*

Research References

Rutter, Cal. Practice Guide: Enforcing Judgments/Debts Ch. 6J-4, Enforcing Foreign Country Money Judgments-Uniform Foreign-Country Money Judgments Recognition Act.

8 Witkin Cal. Proc. 5th Enforcement of Judgment § 466, Procedure for Recognition.

§ 1722. Uniformity of interpretation

In applying and construing this uniform act, consideration shall be given to the need to promote uniformity of the law with respect to its subject matter among states that enact it. *(Added by Stats.2007, c. 212 (S.B.639), § 2.)*

Research References

Rutter, Cal. Practice Guide: Enforcing Judgments/Debts Ch. 6J-4, Enforcing Foreign Country Money Judgments-Uniform Foreign-Country Money Judgments Recognition Act.

8 Witkin Cal. Proc. 5th Enforcement of Judgment § 463, Current Law: Uniform Foreign-Country Money Judgments Recognition Act.

§ 1723. Saving clause

This chapter does not prevent the recognition under principles of comity or otherwise of a foreign-country judgment not within the scope of this chapter. *(Added by Stats.2007, c. 212 (S.B.639), § 2.)*

Research References

Rutter, Cal. Practice Guide: Enforcing Judgments/Debts Ch. 6J-4, Enforcing Foreign Country Money Judgments-Uniform Foreign-Country Money Judgments Recognition Act.

8 Witkin Cal. Proc. 5th Enforcement of Judgment § 464, Scope of Act.

8 Witkin Cal. Proc. 5th Enforcement of Judgment § 465, Standards for Recognition.

§ 1724. Effective date; continuing application of former law

(a) This chapter applies to all actions commenced on or after the effective date of this chapter in which the issue of recognition of a foreign-country judgment is raised.

(b) The former Uniform Foreign Money–Judgments Recognition Act (Chapter 2 (commencing with Section 1713) of Title 11 of Part 3) applies to all actions commenced before the effective date of this chapter in which the issue of recognition of a foreign-country judgment is raised. *(Added by Stats.2007, c. 212 (S.B.639), § 2.)*

Research References

Rutter, Cal. Practice Guide: Enforcing Judgments/Debts Ch. 6A-9, Restrictions on Enforcement of Judgments Involving Indian Tribes.

Rutter, Cal. Practice Guide: Enforcing Judgments/Debts Ch. 6J-4, Enforcing Foreign Country Money Judgments-Uniform Foreign-Country Money Judgments Recognition Act.

8 Witkin Cal. Proc. 5th Enforcement of Judgment § 462, Former Law: Uniform Foreign Money Judgments Recognition Act.

8 Witkin Cal. Proc. 5th Enforcement of Judgment § 464, Scope of Act.

Title 11.6

CIVIL ACTION MEDIATION

§ 1775. Findings and declarations

The Legislature finds and declares that:

(a) The peaceful resolution of disputes in a fair, timely, appropriate, and cost-effective manner is an essential function of the judicial branch of state government under Article VI of the California Constitution.

(b) In the case of many disputes, litigation culminating in a trial is costly, time consuming, and stressful for the parties involved. Many disputes can be resolved in a fair and equitable manner through less formal processes.

(c) Alternative processes for reducing the cost, time, and stress of dispute resolution, such as mediation, have been effectively used in California and elsewhere. In appropriate cases mediation provides parties with a simplified and economical procedure for obtaining prompt and equitable resolution of their disputes and a greater opportunity to participate directly in resolving these disputes. Mediation may also assist to reduce the backlog of cases burdening the judicial system. It is in the public interest for mediation to be encouraged and used where appropriate by the courts.

(d) Mediation and similar alternative processes can have the greatest benefit for the parties in a civil action when used early, before substantial discovery and other litigation costs have been incurred. Where appropriate, participants in disputes should be encouraged to utilize mediation and other alternatives to trial for resolving their differences in the early stages of a civil action.

(e) As a pilot project in Los Angeles County and in other counties which elect to apply this title, courts should be able to refer cases to appropriate dispute resolution processes such as judicial arbitration and mediation as an alternative to trial, consistent with the parties' right to obtain a trial if a dispute is not resolved through an alternative process.

(f) The purpose of this title is to encourage the use of court-annexed alternative dispute resolution methods in general, and mediation in particular. It is estimated that the average cost to the court for processing a civil case of the kind described in Section 1775.3 through judgment is three thousand nine hundred forty-three dollars ($3,943) for each judge day, and that a substantial portion of this cost can be saved if these cases are resolved before trial.

The Judicial Council, through the Administrative Office of the Courts, shall conduct a survey to determine the number of cases resolved by alternative dispute resolution authorized by this title, and shall estimate the resulting savings realized by the courts and the parties. The results of the survey shall be included in the report submitted pursuant to Section 1775.14. The programs authorized by this title shall be deemed successful if they result in estimated savings of at least two hundred fifty thousand dollars ($250,000) to the courts and corresponding savings to the parties. *(Added by Stats.1993, c. 1261 (S.B.401), § 4.)*

Research References

Rutter, Cal. Practice Guide: A.D.R. App. A, Selected Statutes Providing for ADR.
Rutter, Cal. Practice Guide: A.D.R. Ch. 4-C, C. Statutorily-Mandated Court Mediation Programs.
Rutter, Cal. Practice Guide: Civ. Pro. Before Trial Ch. 11-B, B. Involuntary Dismissals.
Rutter, Cal. Practice Guide: Civ. Pro. Before Trial Ch. 13-A, A. Introduction.
Rutter, Cal. Practice Guide: Personal Injury Ch. 4-F, F. Court-Conducted Settlement Proceedings.
Rutter, Cal. Practice Guide: Personal Injury Ch. 7-A, A. Introduction-Nature and Purpose of "Judicial Arbitration" in General.
Miller and Starr California Real Estate § 35:5, --Voluntary Participation and Self Determination in Mediations.
Miller and Starr California Real Estate § 35:13, Procedural Aspects of Civil Action Mediation.
Miller and Starr California Real Estate § 35:22, Nature of Arbitration.
15 NO. 6 Miller & Starr, California Real Estate Newsalert 1, Refuse to Mediate and (Under Some Contracts) Wave Goodbye to Your Attorney's Fees.
6 Witkin Cal. Proc. 5th Proceedings Without Trial § 488, (S 488) Regulation of Mediation.
6 Witkin Cal. Proc. 5th Proceedings Without Trial § 489, Scope of Pilot Project.

§ 1775.1. Definitions

(a) As used in this title, "mediation" means a process in which a neutral person or persons facilitate communication between the disputants to assist them in reaching a mutually acceptable agreement.

(b) Unless otherwise specified in this title or ordered by the court, any act to be performed by a party may also be performed by his or her counsel of record. *(Added by Stats.1993, c. 1261 (S.B.401), § 4. Amended by Stats.1998, c. 931 (S.B.2139), § 126, eff. Sept. 28, 1998; Stats.2002, c. 784 (S.B.1316), § 87.)*

Law Revision Commission Comments

Section 1775.1 is amended to reflect the elimination of the justice court. Cal. Const. art. VI, §§ 1, 5(b). [28 Cal.L.Rev.Comm. Reports 51 (1998)].

Section 1775.1 is amended to reflect unification of the municipal and superior courts pursuant to Article VI, Section 5(e), of the California Constitution. [32 Cal.L.Rev.Comm. Reports 142 (2002)].

Research References

Rutter, Cal. Practice Guide: Personal Injury Ch. 7-A, A. Introduction-Nature and Purpose of "Judicial Arbitration" in General.
Miller and Starr California Real Estate § 35:22, Nature of Arbitration.

6 Witkin Cal. Proc. 5th Proceedings Without Trial § 486, (S 486) in General.

§ 1775.2. Application of title

(a) This title shall apply to the courts of the County of Los Angeles.

(b) A court of any county, at the option of the presiding judge, may elect whether or not to apply this title to eligible actions filed in that court, and this title shall not apply in any court which has not so elected. An election under this subdivision may be revoked by the court at any time.

(c) Courts are authorized to apply this title to all civil actions pending or commenced on or after January 1, 1994. *(Added by Stats.1993, c. 1261 (S.B.401), § 4.)*

Research References

Rutter, Cal. Practice Guide: A.D.R. Ch. 4-C, C. Statutorily-Mandated Court Mediation Programs.
Rutter, Cal. Practice Guide: Civ. Pro. Before Trial Ch. 13-A, A. Introduction.
Rutter, Cal. Practice Guide: Personal Injury Ch. 7-A, A. Introduction-Nature and Purpose of "Judicial Arbitration" in General.
Miller and Starr California Real Estate § 35:13, Procedural Aspects of Civil Action Mediation.
6 Witkin Cal. Proc. 5th Proceedings Without Trial § 489, Scope of Pilot Project.

§ 1775.3. At-issue civil actions; actions with public agency or public entity as party

(a) In the courts of the County of Los Angeles and in other courts that elect to apply this title, all at-issue civil actions in which arbitration is otherwise required pursuant to Section 1141.11, whether or not the action includes a prayer for equitable relief, may be submitted to mediation by the presiding judge or the judge designated under this title as an alternative to judicial arbitration pursuant to Chapter 2.5 (commencing with Section 1141.10) of Title 3.

(b) Any civil action otherwise within the scope of this title in which a party to the action is a public agency or public entity may be submitted to mediation pursuant to subdivision (a). *(Added by Stats.1993, c. 1261 (S.B.401), § 4.)*

Research References

Rutter, Cal. Practice Guide: A.D.R. Ch. 4-B, B. Judicial Arbitration.
Rutter, Cal. Practice Guide: A.D.R. Ch. 4-C, C. Statutorily-Mandated Court Mediation Programs.
Rutter, Cal. Practice Guide: Civ. Pro. Before Trial Ch. 13-A, A. Introduction.
Rutter, Cal. Practice Guide: Personal Injury Ch. 7-A, A. Introduction-Nature and Purpose of "Judicial Arbitration" in General.
Miller and Starr California Real Estate § 35:13, Procedural Aspects of Civil Action Mediation.
6 Witkin Cal. Proc. 5th Proceedings Without Trial § 489, Scope of Pilot Project.

§ 1775.4. Actions ordered into arbitration; actions ordered into mediation

An action that has been ordered into arbitration pursuant to Section 1141.11 or 1141.12 may not be ordered into mediation under this title, and an action that has been ordered into mediation pursuant to Section 1775.3 may not be ordered into arbitration pursuant to Section 1141.11. *(Added by Stats.1993, c. 1261 (S.B.401), § 4.)*

Research References

Rutter, Cal. Practice Guide: A.D.R. Ch. 4-C, C. Statutorily-Mandated Court Mediation Programs.
Rutter, Cal. Practice Guide: Civ. Pro. Before Trial Ch. 13-A, A. Introduction.

Rutter, Cal. Practice Guide: Personal Injury Ch. 7-A, A. Introduction-Nature and Purpose of "Judicial Arbitration" in General.

Miller and Starr California Real Estate § 35:13, Procedural Aspects of Civil Action Mediation.

6 Witkin Cal. Proc. 5th Proceedings Without Trial § 489, Scope of Pilot Project.

§ 1775.5. Cases ordered into mediation; limitation on amount in controversy

The court shall not order a case into mediation where the amount in controversy exceeds fifty thousand dollars ($50,000). The determination of the amount in controversy shall be made in the same manner as provided in Section 1141.16 and, in making this determination, the court shall not consider the merits of questions of liability, defenses, or comparative negligence. *(Added by Stats.1993, c. 1261 (S.B.401), § 4.)*

Research References

Rutter, Cal. Practice Guide: A.D.R. Ch. 4-C, C. Statutorily-Mandated Court Mediation Programs.

Rutter, Cal. Practice Guide: Civ. Pro. Before Trial Ch. 13-A, A. Introduction.

Rutter, Cal. Practice Guide: Personal Injury Ch. 7-A, A. Introduction-Nature and Purpose of "Judicial Arbitration" in General.

Miller and Starr California Real Estate § 35:13, Procedural Aspects of Civil Action Mediation.

6 Witkin Cal. Proc. 5th Proceedings Without Trial § 489, Scope of Pilot Project.

§ 1775.6. Selection of mediator; time limitations

In actions submitted to mediation pursuant to Section 1775.3, a mediator shall be selected for the action within 30 days of its submission to mediation. The method of selection and qualification of the mediator shall be as the parties determine. If the parties are unable to agree on a mediator within 15 days of the date of submission of the action to mediation, the court may select a mediator pursuant to standards adopted by the Judicial Council. *(Added by Stats.1993, c. 1261 (S.B.401), § 4.)*

Research References

Rutter, Cal. Practice Guide: A.D.R. Ch. 4-C, C. Statutorily-Mandated Court Mediation Programs.

Rutter, Cal. Practice Guide: Civ. Pro. Before Trial Ch. 13-A, A. Introduction.

Rutter, Cal. Practice Guide: Personal Injury Ch. 7-A, A. Introduction-Nature and Purpose of "Judicial Arbitration" in General.

Miller and Starr California Real Estate § 35:13, Procedural Aspects of Civil Action Mediation.

6 Witkin Cal. Proc. 5th Proceedings Without Trial § 491, Procedure.

§ 1775.7. Running of time limitations

(a) Submission of an action to mediation pursuant to this title shall not suspend the running of the time periods specified in Chapter 1.5 (commencing with Section 583.110) of Title 8 of Part 2, except as provided in this section.

(b) If an action is or remains submitted to mediation pursuant to this title more than four years and six months after the plaintiff has filed the action, then the time beginning on the date four years and six months after the plaintiff has filed the action and ending on the date on which a statement of nonagreement is filed pursuant to Section 1775.9 shall not be included in computing the five-year period specified in Section 583.310. *(Added by Stats.1993, c. 1261 (S.B.401), § 4.)*

Research References

Rutter, Cal. Practice Guide: A.D.R. Ch. 4-C, C. Statutorily-Mandated Court Mediation Programs.

Rutter, Cal. Practice Guide: Civ. Pro. Before Trial Ch. 11-B, B. Involuntary Dismissals.

Rutter, Cal. Practice Guide: Civ. Pro. Before Trial Ch. 13-A, A. Introduction.

Rutter, Cal. Practice Guide: Personal Injury Ch. 7-A, A. Introduction-Nature and Purpose of "Judicial Arbitration" in General.

Miller and Starr California Real Estate § 35:13, Procedural Aspects of Civil Action Mediation.

6 Witkin Cal. Proc. 5th Proceedings Without Trial § 490, Time for Mediation.

§ 1775.8. Compensation of court-appointed mediators; administrative costs

(a) The compensation of court-appointed mediators shall be the same as the compensation of arbitrators pursuant to Section 1141.18, except that no compensation shall be paid prior to the filing of a statement of nonagreement by the mediator pursuant to Section 1775.9 or prior to settlement of the action by the parties.

(b) All administrative costs of mediation, including compensation of mediators, shall be paid in the same manner as for arbitration pursuant to Section 1141.28. Funds allocated for the payment of arbitrators under the judicial arbitration program shall be equally available for the payment of mediators under this title. *(Added by Stats.1993, c. 1261 (S.B.401), § 4.)*

Research References

Rutter, Cal. Practice Guide: A.D.R. Ch. 3-A, A. General Considerations.

Rutter, Cal. Practice Guide: A.D.R. Ch. 4-C, C. Statutorily-Mandated Court Mediation Programs.

Rutter, Cal. Practice Guide: Civ. Pro. Before Trial Ch. 13-A, A. Introduction.

Miller and Starr California Real Estate § 35:13, Procedural Aspects of Civil Action Mediation.

§ 1775.9. Termination of mediation; statement of nonagreement

(a) In the event that the parties to mediation are unable to reach a mutually acceptable agreement and any party to the mediation wishes to terminate the mediation, then the mediator shall file a statement of nonagreement. This statement shall be in a form to be developed by the Judicial Council.

(b) Upon the filing of a statement of nonagreement, the matter shall be calendared for trial, by court or jury, both as to law and fact, insofar as possible, so that the trial shall be given the same place on the active list as it had prior to mediation, or shall receive civil priority on the next setting calendar. *(Added by Stats.1993, c. 1261 (S.B.401), § 4.)*

Research References

Rutter, Cal. Practice Guide: A.D.R. Ch. 4-C, C. Statutorily-Mandated Court Mediation Programs.

Rutter, Cal. Practice Guide: Civ. Pro. Before Trial Ch. 11-B, B. Involuntary Dismissals.

Rutter, Cal. Practice Guide: Civ. Pro. Before Trial Ch. 13-A, A. Introduction.

Rutter, Cal. Practice Guide: Personal Injury Ch. 7-A, A. Introduction-Nature and Purpose of "Judicial Arbitration" in General.

Miller and Starr California Real Estate § 35:13, Procedural Aspects of Civil Action Mediation.

6 Witkin Cal. Proc. 5th Proceedings Without Trial § 490, Time for Mediation.

6 Witkin Cal. Proc. 5th Proceedings Without Trial § 491, Procedure.

§ 1775.10. Statements made during mediation; evidence

All statements made by the parties during the mediation shall be subject to Sections 703.5 and 1152, and Chapter 2 (commencing with Section 1115) of Division 9, of the Evidence Code. *(Added by Stats.1993, c. 1261 (S.B.401), § 4. Amended by Stats.1997, c. 772 (A.B.939), § 2.)*

Law Revision Commission Comments

Section 1775.10 is amended to reflect the relocation of former Evidence Code Section 1152.5 and the addition of new Evidence Code provisions governing mediation confidentiality. See Evid. Code §§ 703.5 (testimony by a judge, arbitrator, or mediator), 1115–1128 (mediation). [1997–98 Annual Report, 27 Cal.L.Rev.Comm. Reports App. 5 (1997)].

Research References

Rutter, Cal. Practice Guide: A.D.R. Ch. 4-C, C. Statutorily-Mandated Court Mediation Programs.

Rutter, Cal. Practice Guide: Civ. Pro. Before Trial Ch. 13-A, A. Introduction.

Rutter, Cal. Practice Guide: Personal Injury Ch. 7-A, A. Introduction-Nature and Purpose of "Judicial Arbitration" in General.

Rutter, Cal. Practice Guide: Prof. Responsibility Ch. 6-D, D. Professional Liability.

Miller and Starr California Real Estate § 35:13, Procedural Aspects of Civil Action Mediation.

6 Witkin Cal. Proc. 5th Proceedings Without Trial § 491, Procedure.

§ 1775.11. Discovery

Any party who participates in mediation pursuant to Section 1775.3 shall retain the right to obtain discovery to the extent available under the Civil Discovery Act, Title 4 (commencing with Section 2016.010) of Part 4. *(Added by Stats.1993, c. 1261 (S.B.401), § 4. Amended by Stats.2004, c. 182 (A.B.3081), § 17, operative July 1, 2005.)*

Law Revision Commission Comments

Section 1775.11 is amended to reflect nonsubstantive reorganization of the rules governing civil discovery. [33 Cal.L.Rev.Comm. Reports 999 (2004)].

Research References

Rutter, Cal. Practice Guide: A.D.R. Ch. 4-C, C. Statutorily-Mandated Court Mediation Programs.

Rutter, Cal. Practice Guide: Civ. Pro. Before Trial Ch. 13-A, A. Introduction.

Rutter, Cal. Practice Guide: Personal Injury Ch. 7-A, A. Introduction-Nature and Purpose of "Judicial Arbitration" in General.

Miller and Starr California Real Estate § 35:13, Procedural Aspects of Civil Action Mediation.

6 Witkin Cal. Proc. 5th Proceedings Without Trial § 491, Procedure.

§ 1775.12. Reference to mediation or statement of nonagreement at subsequent trial

Any reference to the mediation or the statement of nonagreement filed pursuant to Section 1775.9 during any subsequent trial shall constitute an irregularity in the proceedings of the trial for the purposes of Section 657. *(Added by Stats.1993, c. 1261 (S.B.401), § 4.)*

Research References

Rutter, Cal. Practice Guide: Civ. Pro. Before Trial Ch. 13-A, A. Introduction.

Rutter, Cal. Practice Guide: Civil Trials & Evidence Ch. 18-B, B. Motion for New Trial.

Rutter, Cal. Practice Guide: Personal Injury Ch. 7-A, A. Introduction-Nature and Purpose of "Judicial Arbitration" in General.

Miller and Starr California Real Estate § 35:13, Procedural Aspects of Civil Action Mediation.

6 Witkin Cal. Proc. 5th Proceedings Without Trial § 491, Procedure.

§ 1775.13. Legislative intent

It is the intent of the Legislature that nothing in this title be construed to preempt other current or future alternative dispute resolution programs operating in the trial courts. *(Added by Stats.1993, c. 1261 (S.B.401), § 4.)*

Research References

Rutter, Cal. Practice Guide: A.D.R. Ch. 4-C, C. Statutorily-Mandated Court Mediation Programs.

Rutter, Cal. Practice Guide: Civ. Pro. Before Trial Ch. 13-A, A. Introduction.

6 Witkin Cal. Proc. 5th Proceedings Without Trial § 489, Scope of Pilot Project.

§ 1775.14. Report to Legislature

(a) On or before January 1, 1998, the Judicial Council shall submit a report to the Legislature concerning court alternative dispute resolution programs. This report shall include, but not be limited to, a review of programs operated in Los Angeles County and other courts that have elected to apply this title, and shall examine, among other things, the effect of this title on the judicial arbitration programs of courts that have participated in that program.

(b) The Judicial Council shall, by rule, require that each court applying this title file with the Judicial Council data that will enable the Judicial Council to submit the report required by subdivision (a). *(Added by Stats.1993, c. 1261 (S.B.401), § 4. Amended by Stats.2006, c. 538 (S.B.1852), § 74.)*

§ 1775.15. Rules provided by Judicial Council

Notwithstanding any other provision of law except the provisions of this title, the Judicial Council shall provide by rule for all of the following:

(a) The procedures to be followed in submitting actions to mediation under this act.

(b) Coordination of the procedures and processes under this act with those under the trial Court Delay Reduction Act, Article 5 (commencing with Section 68600) of Chapter 2 of Title 8 of the Government Code.

(c) Exceptions for cause from provisions of this title. In providing for exceptions, the Judicial Council shall take into consideration whether the civil action might not be amenable to mediation. *(Added by Stats.1993, c. 1261 (S.B.401), § 4.)*

Research References

Rutter, Cal. Practice Guide: A.D.R. App. A, Selected Statutes Providing for ADR.

Rutter, Cal. Practice Guide: A.D.R. Ch. 4-C, C. Statutorily-Mandated Court Mediation Programs.

Rutter, Cal. Practice Guide: Civ. Pro. Before Trial Ch. 13-A, A. Introduction.

Rutter, Cal. Practice Guide: Personal Injury Ch. 7-A, A. Introduction-Nature and Purpose of "Judicial Arbitration" in General.

Title 11.7

RECOVERY OF PREFERENCES AND EXEMPT PROPERTY IN AN ASSIGNMENT FOR THE BENEFIT OF CREDITORS

§ 1800. Recovery of preferences

(a) As used in this section, the following terms have the following meanings:

(1) "Insolvent" means:

(A) With reference to a person other than a partnership, a financial condition such that the sum of the person's debts is greater than all of the person's property, at a fair valuation, exclusive of both of the following:

(i) Property transferred, concealed, or removed with intent to hinder, delay, or defraud the person's creditors.

(ii) Property that is exempt from property of the estate pursuant to the election of the person made pursuant to Section 1801.

(B) With reference to a partnership, financial condition such that the sum of the partnership's debts are greater than the aggregate of, at a fair valuation, both of the following:

(i) All of the partnership's property, exclusive of property of the kind specified in clause (i) of subparagraph (A).

(ii) The sum of the excess of the value of each general partner's separate property, exclusive of property of the kind specified in clause (ii) of subparagraph (A), over the partner's separate debts.

(2) "Inventory" means personal property leased or furnished, held for sale or lease, or to be furnished under a contract for service, raw materials, work in process, or materials used or consumed in a business, including farm products such as crops or livestock, held for sale or lease.

(3) "Insider" means:

(A) If the assignor is an individual, any of the following:

(i) A relative of the assignor or of a general partner of the assignor.

(ii) A partnership in which the assignor is a general partner.

(iii) A general partner of the assignor.

(iv) A corporation of which the assignor is a director, officer, or person in control.

(B) If the assignor is a corporation, any of the following:

(i) A director of the assignor.

(ii) An officer of the assignor.

(iii) A person in control of the assignor.

(iv) A partnership in which the assignor is a general partner.

(v) A general partner of the assignor.

(vi) A relative of a general partner, director, officer, or person in control of the assignor.

(C) If the assignor is a partnership, any of the following:

(i) A general partner in the assignor.

(ii) A relative of a general partner in, general partner of, or person in control of the assignor.

(iii) A partnership in which the assignor is a general partner.

(iv) A general partner of the assignor.

(v) A person in control of the assignor.

(D) An affiliate of the assignor or an insider of an affiliate as if the affiliate were the assignor.

(E) A managing agent of the assignor.

As used in this paragraph, the following terms have the following meanings:

"Relative" means an individual related by affinity or consanguinity within the third degree as determined by the common law, or an individual in a step or adoptive relationship within the third degree.

An "affiliate" means a person that directly or indirectly owns, controls, or holds, with power to vote, 20 percent or more of the outstanding voting securities of the assignor, or 20 percent or more of whose outstanding voting securities are directly or indirectly owned, controlled, or held with power to vote by the assignor, excluding securities held in a fiduciary or agency capacity without sole discretionary power to vote, or held solely to secure a debt if the holder has not in fact exercised the power to vote, or a person who operates the business of the assignor under a lease or operating agreement or whose business is operated by the assignor under a lease or operating agreement.

(4) "Judicial lien" means a lien obtained by judgment, levy, sequestration, or other legal or equitable process or proceeding.

(5) "New value" means money or money's worth in goods, services, or new credit, or release by a transferee of property previously transferred to the transferee in a transaction that is neither void nor voidable by the assignor or the assignee under any applicable law, but does not include an obligation substituted for an existing obligation.

(6) "Receivable" means a right to payment, whether or not the right has been earned by performance.

(7) "Security agreement" means an agreement that creates or provides for a security interest.

(8) "Security interest" means a lien created by an agreement.

(9) "Statutory lien" means a lien arising solely by force of a statute on specified circumstances or conditions, or lien of distress for rent, whether or not statutory, but does not include a security interest or judicial lien, whether or not the interest or lien is provided by or is dependent on a statute and whether or not the interest or lien is made fully effective by statute.

(10) "Transfer" means every mode, direct or indirect, absolute or conditional, voluntary or involuntary, or disposing of or parting with property or with an interest in property, including retention of title as a security interest.

(b) Except as provided in subdivision (c), the assignee of any general assignment for the benefit of creditors, as defined in Section 493.010, may recover any transfer of property of the assignor that is all of the following:

(1) To or for the benefit of a creditor.

(2) For or on account of an antecedent debt owed by the assignor before the transfer was made.

(3) Made while the assignor was insolvent.

(4) Made on or within 90 days before the date of the making of the assignment or made between 90 days and one year before the date of making the assignment if the creditor, at the time of the transfer, was an insider and had reasonable cause to believe the debtor was insolvent at the time of the transfer.

(5) Enables the creditor to receive more than another creditor of the same class.

(c) The assignee may not recover under this section a transfer as follows:

(1) To the extent that the transfer was both of the following:

(A) Intended by the assignor and the creditor to or for whose benefit the transfer was made to be a contemporaneous exchange for new value given to the assignor.

(B) In fact a substantially contemporaneous exchange.

(2) To the extent that the transfer was all of the following:

(A) In payment of a debt incurred in the ordinary course of business or financial affairs of the assignor and the transferee.

(B) Made in the ordinary course of business or financial affairs of the assignor and the transferee.

(C) Made according to ordinary business terms.

(3) Of a security interest in property acquired by the assignor that meets both of the following:

(A) To the extent the security interest secures new value that was all of the following:

(i) Given at or after the signing of a security agreement that contains a description of the property as collateral.

(ii) Given by or on behalf of the secured party under the agreement.

(iii) Given to enable the assignor to acquire the property.

(iv) In fact used by the assignor to acquire the property.

(B) That is perfected within 20 days after the security interest attaches.

(4) To or for the benefit of a creditor, to the extent that, after the transfer, the creditor gave new value to or for the benefit of the assignor that meets both of the following:

(A) Not secured by an otherwise unavoidable security interest.

(B) On account of which new value the assignor did not make an otherwise unavoidable transfer to or for the benefit of the creditor.

(5) Of a perfected security interest in inventory or a receivable or the proceeds of either, except to the extent that the aggregate of all the transfers to the transferee caused a reduction, as of the date of the making of the assignment and to the prejudice of other creditors holding unsecured claims, of any amount by which the debt secured by the security interest exceeded the value of all security interest for the debt on the later of the following:

(A) Ninety days before the date of the making of the assignment.

(B) The date on which new value was first given under the security agreement creating the security interest.

(6) That is the fixing of a statutory lien.

(7) That is payment to a claimant, as defined in Section 8004 of the Civil Code, in exchange for the claimant's waiver or release of any potential or asserted claim of lien, stop payment notice, or right to recover on a payment bond, or any combination thereof.

(8) To the extent that the transfer was a bona fide payment of a debt to a spouse, former spouse, or child of the debtor, for alimony to, maintenance for, or support of, the spouse or child, in connection with a separation agreement, divorce decree, or other order of a court of record, or a determination made in accordance with state or territorial law by a governmental unit, or property settlement agreement; but not to the extent that either of the following occurs:

(A) The debt is assigned to another entity voluntarily, by operation of law or otherwise, in which case the assignee may not recover that portion of the transfer that is assigned to the state or any political subdivision of the state pursuant to Part D of Title IV of the Social Security Act (42 U.S.C. Sec. 601 et seq.) and passed on to the spouse, former spouse, or child of the debtor.

(B) The debt includes a liability designated as alimony, maintenance, or support, unless the liability is actually in the nature of alimony, maintenance, or support.

(d) An assignee of any general assignment for the benefit of creditors, as defined in Section 493.010, may avoid a transfer of property of the assignor transferred to secure reimbursement of a surety that furnished a bond or other obligation to dissolve a judicial lien that would have been avoidable by the assignee under subdivision (b). The liability of the surety under the bond or obligation shall be discharged to the extent of the value of the property recovered by the assignee or the amount paid to the assignee.

(e)(1) For the purposes of this section:

(A) A transfer of real property other than fixtures, but including the interest of a seller or purchaser under a contract for the sale of real property, is perfected when a bona fide purchaser of the property from the debtor, against whom applicable law permits the transfer to be perfected, cannot acquire an interest that is superior to the interest of the transferee.

(B) A transfer of a fixture or property other than real property is perfected when a creditor on a simple contract cannot acquire a judicial lien that is superior to the interest of the transferee.

(2) For the purposes of this section, except as provided in paragraph (3), a transfer is made at any of the following times:

(A) At the time the transfer takes effect between the transferor and the transferee, if the transfer is perfected at, or within 10 days after, the time, except as provided in subparagraph (B) of paragraph (3) of subdivision (c).

(B) At the time the transfer is perfected, if the transfer is perfected after the 10 days.

(C) Immediately before the date of making the assignment if the transfer is not perfected at the later of:

(i) The making of the assignment.

(ii) Ten days after the transfer takes effect between the transferor and the transferee.

(3) For the purposes of this section, a transfer is not made until the assignor has acquired rights in the property transferred.

(f) For the purposes of this section, the assignor is presumed to have been insolvent on and during the 90 days immediately preceding the date of making the assignment.

(g) An action by an assignee under this section must be commenced within one year after making the assignment. (Added by Stats.1979, c. 394, p. 1467, § 5, eff. July 27, 1979, operative Oct. 1, 1979. Amended by Stats.1980, c. 135, § 6; Stats.1982, c. 35, p. 64, § 3, eff. Feb. 17, 1982; Stats.1982, c. 497, p. 2175, § 81.5, operative July 1, 1983; Stats.1992, c. 1348 (A.B.2616), § 7; Stats.1995, c. 152 (A.B.1156), § 1; Stats.1999, c. 202 (S.B.219), § 2; Stats.2006, c. 538 (S.B.1852), § 75; Stats. 2010, c. 697 (S.B.189), § 26, operative July 1, 2012.)

Law Revision Commission Comments

Section 1800 is amended to delete the distinction between general assignments at common law "or otherwise." Former Civil Code Sections 3448 through 3473, which prescribed a general assignment other than at common law, are not continued. See Comment thereto. [15 Cal.L.Rev. Comm. Reports (1980)].

Section 1800 is amended to correct a cross-reference and terminology. [37 Cal.L.Rev.Comm. Reports 527 (2007)].

Research References

Rutter, Cal. Practice Guide: Enforcing Judgments/Debts Ch. 5-D, D. Involuntary Bankruptcy.

Miller and Starr California Real Estate § 28:67, Payment, Release, and Waiver of the Lien.

8 Witkin Cal. Proc. 5th Enforcement of Judgment § 480, (S 480) Distinctions.

8 Witkin Cal. Proc. 5th Enforcement of Judgment § 505, (S 505) Avoidance of Preferential Transfers by Assignee for Benefit of Creditors.

1 Witkin Cal. Summ. 10th Contracts § 711, (S 711) Conformity With Federal Statutes.

§ 1801. Assignments for benefit of creditors; exempt property

In any general assignment for the benefit of creditors (as defined in Section 493.010), the assignor, if an individual, may choose to retain as exempt property either the property which is otherwise exempt under Chapter 4 (commencing with Section 703.010) of Division 2 of Title 9 of Part 2 or, in the alternative, the following property:

(a) The assignor's aggregate interest, not to exceed seven thousand five hundred dollars ($7,500) in value, in real property or personal property that the assignor or a dependent of the assignor uses as a residence, in a cooperative that owns property that the assignor or a dependent of the assignor uses as a residence, or in a burial plot for the assignor or a dependent of the assignor.

(b) The assignor's interest, not to exceed one thousand two hundred dollars ($1,200) in value, in one motor vehicle.

(c) The assignor's interest, not to exceed two hundred dollars ($200) in value in any particular item, in household furnishings, household goods, wearing apparel, appliances, books, animals, crops, or musical instruments, that are held primarily for the personal, family, or household use of the assignor or a dependent of the assignor.

(d) The assignor's aggregate interest, not to exceed five hundred dollars ($500) in value, in jewelry held primarily for the personal, family, or household use of the assignor or a dependent of the assignor.

(e) The assignor's aggregate interest, not to exceed in value four hundred dollars ($400) plus any unused amount of the exemption provided under subdivision (a), in any property.

(f) The assignor's aggregate interest, not to exceed seven hundred fifty dollars ($750) in value, in any implements, professional books, or tools, of the trade of the assignor or the trade of a dependent of the assignor.

(g) Any unmatured life insurance contract owned by the assignor, other than a credit life insurance contract.

(h) The assignor's aggregate interest, not to exceed in value four thousand dollars ($4,000) in any accrued dividend or interest under, or loan value of, any unmatured life insurance contract owned by the assignor under which the insured is the assignor or an individual of whom the assignor is a dependent.

(i) Professionally prescribed health aids for the assignor or a dependent of the assignor.

(j) The assignor's right to receive any of the following:

(1) A social security benefit, unemployment compensation, or a local public assistance benefit except that this paragraph does not preclude the application of Section 1255.7 of the Unemployment Insurance Code.

(2) A veterans' benefit.

(3) A disability, illness, or unemployment benefit except that this paragraph does not preclude the application of Section 1255.7 of the Unemployment Insurance Code.

(4) Alimony, support, or separate maintenance, to the extent reasonably necessary for the support of the assignor and any dependent of the assignor.

(5) A payment under a stock bonus, pension, profit sharing, annuity, or similar plan or contract on account of illness, disability, death, age, or length of service, to the extent reasonably necessary for the support of the assignor and any dependent of the assignor, unless:

(i) The plan or contract was established by or under the auspices of an employer of which the assignor was a partner, officer, director or controlling person at the time the assignor's rights under the plan or contract arose;

(ii) The payment is on account of age or length of service; and

(iii) Such plan or contract does not qualify under Section 401(a), 403(a), 403(b), 408, or 409 of the Internal Revenue Code of 1954 (26 U.S.C. 401(a), 403(a), 403(b), 408, or 409).[1]

(k) The assignor's right to receive, or property that is traceable to any of the following:

(1) An award under a crime victim's reparation law.

(2) A payment on account of the wrongful death of an individual of whom the assignor was a dependent, to the extent reasonably necessary for the support of the assignor and any dependent of the assignor.

(3) A payment under a life insurance contract that insured the life of an individual of whom the assignor was a dependent on the date of such individual's death, to the extent reasonably necessary for the support of the assignor and any dependent of the assignor.

(4) A payment, not to exceed seven thousand five hundred dollars ($7,500), on account of personal bodily injury, as compensation for pain and suffering or actual pecuniary loss (other than loss of future earnings), of the assignor or an individual of whom the assignor is a dependent.

(5) A payment in compensation of loss of future earnings of the assignor or an individual of whom the assignor is or was a dependent, to the extent reasonably necessary for the support of the assignor and any dependent of the assignor.

In this section, "dependent" includes spouse, whether or not actually dependent, "assignor" means each spouse, if the assignment is made by a married couple, and "value" means fair market value as of the date of the making of the assignment. *(Added by Stats.1982, c. 497, p. 2178, § 82, operative July 1, 1983. Amended by Stats.1983, c. 155, § 23, eff. June 30, 1983, operative July 1, 1983.)*

[1] 26 U.S.C.A. §§ 401(a), 403(a), 403(b), 408, 409.

Law Revision Commission Comments

Section 1801 continues former Section 690.60 without substantive change (15 Cal.L.Rev.Comm. Reports 2001).

Research References

8 Witkin Cal. Proc. 5th Enforcement of Judgment § 170, (S 170) Persons Entitled to Exemptions.

8 Witkin Cal. Proc. 5th Enforcement of Judgment § 505, (S 505) Avoidance of Preferential Transfers by Assignee for Benefit of Creditors.

§ 1802. Notice of assignment to parties in interest; claims filing deadline; list of parties in interest

(a) In any general assignment for the benefit of creditors, as defined in Section 493.010, the assignee shall, within 30 days after the assignment has been accepted in writing, give written notice of the assignment to the assignor's creditors, equityholders, and other parties in interest as set forth on the list provided by the assignor pursuant to subdivision (c).

(b) In the notice given pursuant to subdivision (a), the assignee shall establish a date by which creditors must file their claims to be able to share in the distribution of proceeds of the liquidation of the assignor's assets. That date shall be not less than 150 days and not greater than 180 days after the date of the first giving of the written notice to creditors and parties in interest.

(c) The assignor shall provide to the assignee at the time of the making of the assignment a list of creditors, equityholders, and other parties in interest, signed under penalty of perjury, which shall include the names, addresses, cities, states, and ZIP Codes for each person together with the amount of that person's anticipated claim in the assignment proceedings. *(Added by Stats.1992, c. 1348 (A.B.2616), § 8.)*

Research References

8 Witkin Cal. Proc. 5th Enforcement of Judgment § 505, (S 505) Avoidance of Preferential Transfers by Assignee for Benefit of Creditors.

6 Witkin Cal. Proc. 5th Provisional Remedies § 179, Securities.

6 Witkin Cal. Proc. 5th Provisional Remedies § 188, (S 188) in General.

Title 12

TRIBAL INJUNCTIONS

Section

§ 1811. Violation of designated tribal compact; authority to seek relief; appeals

(a) Following the issuance of the bonds as specified in Section 63048.65 of the Government Code and during the term of the bonds, if it reasonably appears that the exclusive right of an Indian tribe with a designated tribal compact, as defined in subdivision (b) of Section 63048.6 of the Government Code, pursuant to Section 3.2(a) of that compact has been violated, the tribe may seek a preliminary and permanent injunction against that gaming or the authorization of that gaming as a substantial impairment of the rights specified in Section 3.2(a), in order to afford the tribe stability in its gaming operation and to maintain the bargained-for source of payment and security of the bonds. However, no remedy other than an injunction shall be available against the state or any of its political subdivisions for a violation of Section 3.2(a). The Legislature hereby finds and declares that any such violation of the exclusive right to gaming under Section 3.2(a) is a substantial impairment of the rights specified in that section and will cause irreparable harm that cannot be adequately remedied by damages. No undertaking shall be required on the part of the tribes in connection with any action to seek the preliminary or permanent injunction.

(b) Notwithstanding any other provision of law, the parties to an action brought pursuant to subdivision (a) may petition the Supreme Court for a writ of mandate from any order granting or denying a preliminary injunction. Any such petition shall be filed within 15 days following the notice of entry of the superior court order, and no extension of that period shall be allowed. In any case in which a petition has been filed within the time allowed therefor, the Supreme Court shall make any orders, as it may deem proper in the circumstances. *(Added by Stats.2004, c. 91 (A.B.687), § 2, eff. July 1, 2004.)*

Research References

6 Witkin Cal. Proc. 5th Provisional Remedies § 291, (S 291) Special Statutes.
11 Witkin, California Summary 10th Community Property § 14, (S 14) Separate Property Acquired During Marriage.

Title 13

INSPECTION WARRANTS

Section

§ 1822.50. Definition

An inspection warrant is an order, in writing, in the name of the people, signed by a judge of a court of record, directed to a state or local official, commanding him to conduct any inspection required or authorized by state or local law or regulation relating to building, fire, safety, plumbing, electrical, health, labor, or zoning. *(Added by Stats.1968, c. 1097, p. 2105, § 1. Amended by Stats.1980, c. 230, § 1.)*

Research References

California Practice Guide: Employment Litigation Ch. 13-E, E. Division Investigations and Inspections.
12 Witkin, California Summary 10th Real Property § 899, in General.

§ 1822.51. Requirements for issue

An inspection warrant shall be issued upon cause, unless some other provision of state or federal law makes another standard applicable. An inspection warrant shall be supported by an affidavit, particularly describing the place, dwelling, structure, premises, or vehicle to be inspected and the purpose for which the inspection is made. In addition, the affidavit shall contain either a statement that consent to inspect has been sought and refused or facts or circumstances reasonably justifying the failure to seek such consent. *(Added by Stats.1968, c. 1097, p. 2105, § 1. Amended by Stats.1970, c. 241, p. 501, § 2; Stats.1971, c. 438, p. 861 § 20; Stats.1984, c. 476, § 2.)*

§ 1822.52. Cause

Cause shall be deemed to exist if either reasonable legislative or administrative standards for conducting a routine or area inspection are satisfied with respect to the particular place, dwelling, structure, premises, or vehicle, or there is reason to believe that a condition of nonconformity exists with respect to the particular place, dwelling, structure, premises, or vehicle. *(Added by Stats.1968, c. 1097, p. 2105, § 1.)*

Research References

California Practice Guide: Employment Litigation Ch. 13-E, E. Division Investigations and Inspections.

§ 1822.53. Examination of applicant

Before issuing an inspection warrant, the judge may examine on oath the applicant and any other witness, and shall satisfy himself of the existence of grounds for granting such application. *(Added by Stats.1968, c. 1097, p. 2105, § 1.)*

§ 1822.54. Issue; contents

If the judge is satisfied that the proper standard for issuance of the warrant has been met, he or she shall issue the warrant particularly describing each place, dwelling, structure, premises, or vehicle to be inspected and designating on the warrant the purpose and limitations of the inspection, including the limitations required by this title. *(Added by Stats.1968, c. 1097, p. 2105, § 1. Amended by Stats.1984, c. 476, § 3.)*

Research References

California Practice Guide: Employment Litigation Ch. 13-E, E. Division Investigations and Inspections.

§ 1822.55. Duration

An inspection warrant shall be effective for the time specified therein, but not for a period of more than 14 days, unless extended or renewed by the judge who signed and issued the original warrant, upon satisfying himself that such extension or renewal is in the public interest. Such inspection warrant must be executed and returned to the judge by whom it was issued within the time specified in the warrant or within the extended or renewed time. After the expiration of such time, the warrant, unless executed, is void. *(Added by Stats.1968, c. 1097, p. 2105, § 1.)*

Research References

California Practice Guide: Employment Litigation Ch. 13-E, E. Division Investigations and Inspections.

§ 1822.56. Conduct of inspection; notice

An inspection pursuant to this warrant may not be made between 6:00 p.m. of any day and 8:00 a.m. of the succeeding day, nor in the absence of an owner or occupant of the particular place, dwelling, structure, premises, or vehicle unless specifically authorized by the judge upon a showing that such authority is reasonably necessary to effectuate the purpose of the regulation being enforced. An inspection pursuant to a warrant shall not be made by means of forcible entry, except that the judge may expressly authorize a forcible entry where facts are shown sufficient to create a reasonable suspicion of a violation of a state or local law or regulation relating to building, fire, safety, plumbing, electrical, health, labor, or zoning, which, if such violation existed, would be an immediate threat to health or safety, or where facts are shown establishing that reasonable attempts to serve a previous warrant have been unsuccessful. Where prior consent has been sought and refused, notice that a warrant has been issued must be given at least 24 hours before the warrant is executed, unless the judge finds that immediate execution is reasonably necessary in the circumstances shown. *(Added by Stats.1968, c. 1097, p. 2106, § 1. Amended by Stats.1980, c. 230, § 2.)*

Research References

California Practice Guide: Employment Litigation Ch. 13-E, E. Division Investigations and Inspections.

§ 1822.57. Refusal to permit authorized inspection; offense

Any person who willfully refuses to permit an inspection lawfully authorized by warrant issued pursuant to this title is guilty of a misdemeanor. *(Added by Stats.1968, c. 1097, p. 2106, § 1.)*

§ 1822.58. Aquaculture; locations where fish, amphibia, or aquatic plants are held or stored

A warrant may be issued under the requirements of this title to authorize personnel of the Department of Fish and Game to conduct inspections of locations where fish, amphibia, or aquatic plants are held or stored under Division 12 (commencing with Section 15000) of the Fish and Game Code. *(Added by Stats.1982, c. 1486, p. 5715, § 1.)*

§ 1822.59. Issuance of warrants; animal or plant pest or disease eradication efforts

(a) Notwithstanding the provisions of Section 1822.54, for purposes of an animal or plant pest or disease eradication effort pursuant to Division 4 (commencing with Section 5001) or Division 5 (commencing with Section 9101) of the Food and Agricultural Code, the judge may issue a warrant under the requirements of this title describing a specified geographic area to be inspected by authorized personnel of the Department of Food and Agriculture.

(b) A warrant issued pursuant to this section may only authorize the inspection of the exterior of places, dwellings, structures, premises or vehicles, and only in areas urban in character. The warrant shall state the geographical area which it covers and the purpose of and limitations on the inspection.

(c) A warrant may be issued pursuant to this section whether or not the property owners in the area have refused to consent to the inspection. A peace officer may use reasonable force to enter a property to be inspected if so authorized by the warrant. *(Added by Stats.1984, c. 476, § 4.)*

§ 1822.60. Department of Justice personnel; inspections under Business and Professions Code § 19827

A warrant may be issued under the requirements of this title to authorize personnel of the Department of Justice to conduct inspections as provided in subdivision (a) of Section 19827 of the Business and Professions Code. *(Added by Stats.1997, c. 867 (S.B.8), § 53. Amended by Stats.2004, c. 183 (A.B.3082), § 47; Stats.2007, c. 176 (S.B.82), § 51, eff. Aug. 24, 2007.)*

Part 4

MISCELLANEOUS PROVISIONS

Title 1

OF THE GENERAL PRINCIPLES OF EVIDENCE

§ 1855. Map lost, injured, destroyed, or stolen; recording copy

When any map which has been recorded in the office of the recorder of any county is injured, destroyed, lost, or stolen, any person interested may file in the superior court of the county in which the map was originally filed or recorded a verified petition in writing alleging that the map has been injured, destroyed, lost, or stolen without fault of the person making the application, and that the petitioner has a true and correct copy of the original map which he or she offers for record in the place of the original map. The petition shall be accompanied by a copy of the true copy offered for recording.

Upon the filing of the petition the clerk shall set it for hearing by the court, and give notice of the hearing by causing notice of the time and place of the hearing to be posted at the courthouse in the county where the court is held at least 10 days prior to the hearing. A copy of the petition and a copy of the true copy offered for record shall be served upon the recorder of the county in which the proceedings are brought at least 10 days prior to the hearing. The court may order any further notice to be given as it deems proper. At the time set for the hearing the court shall take evidence for and against the petition, and if it appears to the court from the evidence presented that the copy of the map submitted is a true copy of the original map, it shall decree that the copy is a true copy of the original map, and order the copy placed of record in the office of the recorder in the place of the original map.

A certified copy of the decree shall accompany the true copy of the map for record. When presented to the county recorder for record, he or she shall place of record the copy of the map in the place of the original map.

When placed of record the copy shall have the same effect as the original map, and conveyances of property referring to the original map shall have the same effect as though the original map had not been injured, destroyed, lost, or stolen, and conveyances thereafter made referring to the copy of the original map shall be deemed to refer also to the original map. *(Formerly § 1855b, added by Stats.1953, c. 52, p. 711, § 12. Renumbered § 1855 and amended by Stats.1987, c. 56, § 23.)*

Law Revision Commission Comments

The following comments of the Law Revision Commission are contained in 16 Cal.L.Rev.Comm.Reports 1 to 394 (1965).

Section 1855 is superseded by Evidence Code Sections 1500–1510.

§ 1856. Terms in writing intended as final expression of agreement; exclusion of parol evidence; exceptions

(a) Terms set forth in a writing intended by the parties as a final expression of their agreement with respect to the terms * * * included therein may not be contradicted by evidence of a prior agreement or of a contemporaneous oral agreement.

(b) The terms set forth in a writing described in subdivision (a) may be explained or supplemented by evidence of consistent additional terms unless the writing is intended also as a complete and exclusive statement of the terms of the agreement.

(c) The terms set forth in a writing described in subdivision (a) may be explained or supplemented by course of dealing or usage of trade or by course of performance.

(d) The court shall determine whether the writing is intended by the parties as a final expression of their agreement with respect to the terms * * * included therein and whether the writing is intended also as a complete and exclusive statement of the terms of the agreement.

(e) Where a mistake or imperfection of the writing is put in issue by the pleadings, this section does not exclude evidence relevant to that issue.

(f) Where the validity of the agreement is the fact in dispute, this section does not exclude evidence relevant to that issue.

(g) This section does not exclude other evidence of the circumstances under which the agreement was made or to which

it relates, as defined in Section 1860, or to explain an extrinsic ambiguity or otherwise interpret the terms of the agreement, or to establish illegality or fraud.

(h) As used in this section, * * * "agreement" includes trust instruments, deeds, wills, * * * and contracts between parties. *(Enacted in 1872. Amended by Stats.1978, c. 150, p. 374, § 1; Stats.2013, c. 81 (A.B.824), § 1.)*

Law Revision Commission Comments

Section 1856 is amended to restate the substance of the parol evidence rule for contracts and other written instruments. Its application to other written instruments is subject to express statutory provisions relating to admissibility of extrinsic evidence. See, e.g., Probate Code § 105 (excluding oral declarations of testator); Estate of Russell, 69 Cal.2d 200, 212, 444 P.2d 353, 361, 70 Cal.Rptr. 561, 569 (1968). For the law applicable to contracts for the sale of goods, see Commercial Code Section 2202. Section 1856 governs the admissibility of parol evidence notwithstanding any implications to the contrary in Civil Code Sections 1625, 1638, and 1639 (creation and interpretation of contracts). Nothing in Section 1856 is intended to affect any statute requiring the terms of a contract to be in writing. See, e.g., Civil Code §§ 1624 (statute of frauds), 1803.1–1803.8 (retail installment contracts), 1812.52 (dance studio contracts).

Subdivisions (a) and (b) make inadmissible parol evidence in a few limited cases. These cases are discussed below.

If the written instrument is intended by the parties as the final embodiment of the terms contained in it, subdivision (a) makes parol evidence inadmissible to contradict those terms. Subdivision (a) is comparable to the introductory portion of Commercial Code Section 2202 and codifies prior law. See, e.g., American Nat'l Ins. Co. v. Continental Parking Corp., 42 Cal.App.3d 260, 116 Cal.Rptr. 801 (1974) (hearing denied). The issue of the finality of the terms of the agreement is a matter for court determination under subdivision (d). This also codifies prior law. See, e.g., Brawthen v. H & R Block, Inc., 28 Cal.App.3d 131, 104 Cal.Rptr. 486 (1972). Subdivision (a) does not make inadmissible evidence of a contemporaneous written agreement that contradicts the terms of the main written agreement even though final. Cf. Civil Code § 1642 (several contracts relating to the same matters, between the same parties, and made as parts of substantially one transaction are to be taken together).

As a general rule, evidence of consistent additional terms is admissible to explain or supplement the terms of an agreement notwithstanding the finality of the terms of the agreement. Because a writing has been worked out which is final on some matters, it is not to be taken as including all the matters agreed upon unless it is also a complete and exclusive statement of all the terms. Subdivision (b) makes inadmissible evidence of consistent additional terms, whether or not reduced to writing, if the written instrument was intended by both parties as a complete and exclusive statement of all the terms. Subdivision (b) is comparable to subdivision (b) of Commercial Code Section 2202 and codifies prior law. See, e.g., Masterson v. Sine, 68 Cal.2d 222, 436 P.2d 561, 65 Cal.Rptr. 545 (1968). The issues of completeness and exclusivity are matters for court determination under subdivision (d). This also codifies prior law. See, e.g., Brawthen v. H & R Block, Inc., 28 Cal.App.3d 131, 104 Cal.Rptr. 486 (1972). One indication of the completeness and exclusivity of the writing is whether the additional term is such that, if agreed upon, it would certainly have been included in the writing.

The foregoing discussion of subdivisions (a) and (b) indicates the extent of the limitations imposed by Section 1856. Except to the extent indicated in that discussion, the section does not make inadmissible evidence offered to explain or supplement the terms of a written agreement. Subdivision (c) makes clear that the parol evidence rule does not make inadmissible evidence of course of dealing, usage of trade, and course of performance to explain or supplement the terms of a writing stating the agreement of the parties, in order that the true understanding of the parties as to the agreement may be reached. Such writings are to be read on the assumption that the course of prior dealings between the parties and the usages of trade were taken for granted when the document was phrased. Unless carefully negated, they have become an element of the meaning of the words used. Similarly, the course of actual performance by the parties is considered the best indication of what the parties intended the writing to mean. Subdivision (c) thus definitely rejects (1) the premise that the language used has the meaning attributable to such language by rules of construction existing in the law rather than the meaning which arises out of the context in which it was used and (2) the requirement that a condition precedent to the admissibility of the type of evidence specified in the subdivision is an original determination that the language used is ambiguous. Subdivision (c) is comparable to subdivision (a) of Commercial Code Section 2202 and codifies prior law. See discussions in 1 California Commercial Law §§ 7.39–7.41, at 335–37 (Cal.Cont.Ed.Bar 1966); 1 B. Witkin, Summary of California Law Contracts §§ 527, 534 at 449–50, 455–56 (8th ed. 1973). It is expected that the courts will look to the definitions in Commercial Code Sections 1205 and 2208 for guidance in interpreting the meaning of the terms "course of dealing," "usage of trade," and "course of performance."

Section 1856 does not make inadmissible extrinsic evidence, other than that made inadmissible by subdivisions (a) and (b), offered to interpret or explain the meaning of the terms of a written agreement, regardless whether the writing is intended by the parties as a final, complete, and exclusive statement of those terms. See subdivision (g). Evidence offered to interpret or explain the meaning of the terms of a written agreement is subject to the normal rules of admissibility and construction of instruments, including the rule that the "test of admissibility of extrinsic evidence to explain the meaning of a written instrument is not whether it appears to the court to be plain and unambiguous on its face, but whether the offered evidence is relevant to prove a meaning to which the language of the instrument is reasonably susceptible." Pacific Gas & Elec. Co. v. G. W. Thomas Drayage & Rigging Co., 69 Cal.2d 33, 37, 442 P.2d 641, 644, 69 Cal.Rptr. 561, 564 (1968). [14 Cal.L.Rev.Comm.Reports 143 (1978)].

Research References

Rutter, Cal. Practice Guide: Civil Trials & Evidence Ch. 4-B, B. Preliminary Matters Discussed in Final Status Conference or In-Chambers Conference.
Rutter, Cal. Practice Guide: Civil Trials & Evidence Ch. 8E-G, G. Parol Evidence Rule.
California Practice Guide: Employment Litigation Ch. 4-B, B. Agreements Limiting At-Will Termination.
Rutter, Cal. Practice Guide: Insurance Litigation Ch. 4-B, B. "Plain Meaning" vs. Ambiguity.
Rutter, Cal. Practice Guide: Insurance Litigation Ch. 15-I, I. Trial.
Rutter, Cal. Practice Guide: Real Prop. Transactions Ch. 4-E, E. Drafting the Purchase and Sale Agreement-Terms and Conditions.
Miller and Starr California Real Estate § 1:19, Conditions Precedent to a Binding Agreement.
Miller and Starr California Real Estate § 1:60, Parol Evidence; Extrinsic Evidence Rules.
Miller and Starr California Real Estate § 1:73, Parol Evidence Rule Distinguished.
21 NO. 1 Miller & Starr, California Real Estate Newsalert 18, Landlord and Tenant.
21 NO. 4 Miller & Starr, California Real Estate Newsalert 23, Contracts.
22 NO. 3 Miller & Starr, California Real Estate Newsalert 3, Alternative Dispute Resolution.
22 NO. 3 Miller & Starr, California Real Estate Newsalert 6, Contracts.
22 NO. 2 Miller & Starr, California Real Estate Newsalert 15, Judicial Remedies.
4 Witkin, California Summary 10th Sales § 33, Parol Evidence.
5 Witkin, California Summary 10th Torts § 783, (S 783) Oral Promise Unenforceable in Contract Action.
3 Witkin, California Summary 10th Agency and Employment § 234, Parol Evidence Rule and Express Terms Doctrine.
14 Witkin, California Summary 10th Wills and Probate § 185, Surrounding Circumstances.

§ 1857. Language of writing; interpretation according to meaning in place of execution; exception

CONSTRUCTION OF LANGUAGE RELATES TO PLACE WHERE USED. The language of a writing is to be interpreted according to the meaning it bears in the place of its execution, unless the parties have reference to a different place. *(Enacted in 1872.)*

Research References

California Practice Guide: Employment Litigation Ch. 19-A, A. Plaintiff's Forum Selection.
Rutter, Cal. Practice Guide: Insurance Litigation Ch. 15-D, D. Filing Considerations.

1 Witkin Cal. Summ. 10th Contracts § 90, (S 90) California Cases and Statutes.

§ 1858. Construction of statutes or instruments; duty of judge

CONSTRUCTION OF STATUTES AND INSTRUMENTS, GENERAL RULE. In the construction of a statute or instrument, the office of the Judge is simply to ascertain and declare what is in terms or in substance contained therein, not to insert what has been omitted, or to omit what has been inserted; and where there are several provisions or particulars, such a construction is, if possible, to be adopted as will give effect to all. *(Enacted in 1872.)*

Research References

2 Witkin, California Summary 10th Insurance § 64, (S 64) in General.
1 Witkin Cal. Summ. 10th Contracts § 746, Single Writing.
5 Witkin, California Summary 10th Torts § 13, Legislative Intent Approach.

§ 1859. Construction of statutes or instruments; intent

THE INTENTION OF THE LEGISLATURE OR PARTIES. In the construction of a statute the intention of the Legislature, and in the construction of the instrument the intention of the parties, is to be pursued, if possible; and when a general and particular provision are inconsistent, the latter is paramount to the former. So a particular intent will control a general one that is inconsistent with it. *(Enacted in 1872.)*

Research References

Miller and Starr California Real Estate § 34:42, Comparison of "Marketing" and "Security" Contracts.
18 NO. 6 Miller & Starr, California Real Estate Newsalert 1, Does the Density Bonus Law (Gov. Code § 65915) Require Local Government to Approve Mixed Use and Housing Projects Where Local Zoning Does Not Allow Housing at All?
20 NO. 2 Miller & Starr, California Real Estate Newsalert 9, Covenants, Conditions, and Restrictions.
1 Witkin Cal. Summ. 10th Contracts § 754, (S 754) Inconsistency Between Parts of Contract.

§ 1860. Construction of instruments; consideration of circumstances

THE CIRCUMSTANCES TO BE CONSIDERED. For the proper construction of an instrument, the circumstances under which it was made, including the situation of the subject of the instrument, and of the parties to it, may also be shown, so that the Judge be placed in the position of those whose language he is to interpret. *(Enacted in 1872.)*

Research References

Rutter, Cal. Practice Guide: Civil Trials & Evidence Ch. 8E-G, G. Parol Evidence Rule.
Miller and Starr California Real Estate § 1:60, Parol Evidence; Extrinsic Evidence Rules.
1 Witkin Cal. Summ. 10th Contracts § 748, (S 748) Surrounding Circumstances.

§ 1861. Terms of writing; presumption as to use; evidence of local, technical or other signification

TERMS TO BE CONSTRUED IN THEIR GENERAL ACCEPTATION. The terms of a writing are presumed to have been used in their primary and general acceptation, but evidence is nevertheless admissible that they have a local, technical, or otherwise peculiar signification, and were so used and understood in the particular instance, in which case the agreement must be construed accordingly. *(Enacted in 1872.)*

Civ. Pro.

Research References

1 Witkin Cal. Summ. 10th Contracts § 745, (S 745) Ordinary Words and Technical Language.

§ 1862. Written words on printed form; control

WRITTEN WORDS CONTROL THOSE PRINTED IN A BLANK FORM. When an instrument consists partly of written words and partly of a printed form, and the two are inconsistent, the former controls the latter. *(Enacted in 1872.)*

Research References

Miller and Starr California Real Estate § 6:30, Requirement of a Contract.
Miller and Starr California Real Estate § 27:50, Rules of Contract Interpretation.
1 Witkin Cal. Summ. 10th Contracts § 754, (S 754) Inconsistency Between Parts of Contract.

§ 1864. Two permissible constructions; preference

OF TWO CONSTRUCTIONS, WHICH PREFERRED. When the terms of an agreement have been intended in a different sense by the different parties to it, that sense is to prevail against either party in which he supposed the other understood it, and when different constructions of a provision are otherwise equally proper, that is to be taken which is most favorable to the party in whose favor the provision was made. *(Enacted in 1872.)*

Research References

Rutter, Cal. Practice Guide: Real Prop. Transactions Ch. 4-E, E. Drafting the Purchase and Sale Agreement-Terms and Conditions.
Miller and Starr California Real Estate § 1:60, Parol Evidence; Extrinsic Evidence Rules.
Miller and Starr California Real Estate § 15:16, Rules of Construction.
Miller and Starr California Real Estate § 19:47, Rules of Interpretation.
12 Witkin, California Summary 10th Real Property § 530, (S 530) First Right of Refusal.
1 Witkin Cal. Summ. 10th Contracts § 744, (S 744) Intention of Parties: Objective Test.

§ 1865. Written notice; construction according to ordinary acceptation of terms; notice of protest of bill or note

A WRITTEN INSTRUMENT CONSTRUED AS UNDERSTOOD BY PARTIES. A written notice, as well as every other writing, is to be construed according to the ordinary acceptation of its terms. Thus a notice to the drawers or indorsers of a bill of exchange or promissory note, that it has been protested for want of acceptance or payment, must be held to import that the same has been duly presented for acceptance or payment and the same refused, and that the holder looks for payment to the person to whom the notice is given. *(Enacted in 1872.)*

§ 1866. Two permissible interpretations; construction in favor of natural right

CONSTRUCTION IN FAVOR OF NATURAL RIGHT PREFERRED. When a statute or instrument is equally susceptible of two interpretations, one in favor of natural right, and the other against it, the former is to be adopted. *(Enacted in 1872.)*

Title 2

OF THE KINDS AND DEGREES OF EVIDENCE

CHAPTER 2. WITNESSES

§ 1878. Witness defined

WITNESSES DEFINED. A witness is a person whose declaration under oath is received as evidence for any purpose, whether such declaration be made on oral examination, or by deposition or affidavit. *(Enacted in 1872.)*

CHAPTER 3. WRITINGS

ARTICLE 2. PUBLIC WRITINGS

§ 1895. Laws; kinds

LAWS WRITTEN OR UNWRITTEN. Laws, whether organic or ordinary, are either written or unwritten. *(Enacted in 1872.)*

§ 1896. Written laws defined

WRITTEN LAWS DEFINED. A written law is that which is promulgated in writing, and of which a record is in existence. *(Enacted in 1872.)*

§ 1897. Written laws; constitution; statutes

CONSTITUTION AND STATUTES. The organic law is the constitution of government, and is altogether written. Other written laws are denominated statutes. The written law of this State is therefore contained in its Constitution and statutes, and in the Constitution and statutes of the United States. *(Enacted in 1872.)*

§ 1898. Public and private statutes defined

PUBLIC AND PRIVATE STATUTES DEFINED. Statutes are public or private. A private statute is one which concerns only certain designated individuals, and affects only their private rights. All other statutes are public, in which are included statutes creating or affecting corporations. *(Enacted in 1872.)*

§ 1899.   Unwritten law defined

UNWRITTEN LAW DEFINED. Unwritten law is the law not promulgated and recorded, as mentioned in Section 1896, but which is, nevertheless, observed and administered in the courts of the country. It has no certain repository, but is collected from the reports of the decisions of the courts, and the treatises of learned men. *(Enacted in 1872.)*

§ 1904.   Judicial record defined

JUDICIAL RECORD DEFINED. A judicial record is the record or official entry of the proceedings in a Court of justice, or of the official act of a judicial officer, in an action or special proceeding. *(Enacted in 1872.)*

§ 1908.   Judgment or final order; effect; conclusiveness; non-party

(a) The effect of a judgment or final order in an action or special proceeding before a court or judge of this state, or of the United States, having jurisdiction to pronounce the judgment or order, is as follows:

(1) In case of a judgment or order against a specific thing, or in respect to the probate of a will, or the administration of the estate of a decedent, or in respect to the personal, political, or legal condition or relation of a particular person, the judgment or order is conclusive upon the title to the thing, the will, or administration, or the condition or relation of the person.

(2) In other cases, the judgment or order is, in respect to the matter directly adjudged, conclusive between the parties and their successors in interest by title subsequent to the commencement of the action or special proceeding, litigating for the same thing under the same title and in the same capacity, provided they have notice, actual or constructive, of the pendency of the action or proceeding.

(b) A person who is not a party but who controls an action, individually or in cooperation with others, is bound by the adjudications of litigated matters as if he were a party if he has a proprietary or financial interest in the judgment or in the determination of a question of fact or of a question of law with reference to the same subject matter or transaction; if the other party has notice of his participation, the other party is equally bound.

At any time prior to a final judgment, as defined in Section 577, a determination of whether the judgment, verdict upon which it was entered, or a finding upon which it was entered is to be binding upon a nonparty pursuant to this subdivision or whether such nonparty is entitled to the benefit of this subdivision may, on the noticed motion of any party or any nonparty that may be affected by this subdivision, be made in the court in which the action was tried or in which the action is pending on appeal. If no such motion is made before the judgment becomes final, the determination may be made in a separate action. If appropriate, a judgment may be entered or ordered to be entered pursuant to such determination. *(Enacted in 1872. Amended by Code Am.1873–74, c. 383, p. 382, § 222; Stats.1975, c. 225, p. 607, § 1.)*

Research References

Rutter, Cal. Practice Guide: Civ. Pro. Before Trial Ch. 6-B, B. Complaints.
Rutter, Cal. Practice Guide: Civ. Pro. Before Trial Ch. 14-D, D. Representative Suits.
Rutter, Cal. Practice Guide: Civ. Pro. Before Trial Ch. 9(I)-J, J. Motion to Expunge Lis Pendens.
Rutter, Cal. Practice Guide: Enforcing Judgments/Debts Ch. 6A-3, "Judgment," "Judgment Debtor" and "Judgment Creditor" Defined.
Rutter, Cal. Practice Guide: Real Prop. Transactions Ch. 11-D, D. Buyer's Remedies Upon Seller's Breach-Damages and Specific Performance.

Rutter, Cal. Practice Guide: Real Prop. Transactions Ch. 11-I, I. Lis Pendens.
Miller and Starr California Real Estate § 11:147, Priority of Judgments and Pending Litigation; in General.
Miller and Starr California Real Estate § 11:149, Procedural and Formal Requirements for a Lis Pendens.
Miller and Starr California Real Estate § 11:152, Effect of Lis Pendens on Prior Interests.
7 Witkin Cal. Proc. 5th Judgment § 334, (S 334) Nature of Doctrine.
7 Witkin Cal. Proc. 5th Judgment § 350, (S 350) in General.
7 Witkin Cal. Proc. 5th Judgment § 355, (S 355) Federal Courts.
7 Witkin Cal. Proc. 5th Judgment § 385, (S 385) Judgment Affecting Status.
7 Witkin Cal. Proc. 5th Judgment § 454, Parties in Representative Capacity.
7 Witkin Cal. Proc. 5th Judgment § 460, (S 460) Successor in Interest.
7 Witkin Cal. Proc. 5th Judgment § 461, (S 461) Interest Previously Acquired.
7 Witkin Cal. Proc. 5th Judgment § 465, (S 465) Nature and Scope of Rule.
12 Witkin, California Summary 10th Real Property § 84, (S 84) Judgment.
13 Witkin, California Summary 10th Equity § 193, (S 193) Distinctions.

§ 1908.5.   Allegation of conclusive judgment or order in pleadings; use as evidence

When a judgment or order of a court is conclusive, the judgment or order must be alleged in the pleadings if there be an opportunity to do so; if there be no such opportunity, the judgment or order may be used as evidence. *(Added by Stats.1965, c. 299, p. 1361, § 74, operative Jan. 1, 1967.)*

Law Revision Commission Comments

Section 1908.5 recodifies the rule of pleading stated in subdivision 6 of Section 1962 of the Code of Civil Procedure. See the Law Revision Commission's Comment to that section. [7 Cal.L.Rev.Comm. Reports 1305 (1965)].

Research References

7 Witkin Cal. Proc. 5th Judgment § 334, (S 334) Nature of Doctrine.
7 Witkin Cal. Proc. 5th Judgment § 348, Waiver and Estoppel.
5 Witkin Cal. Proc. 5th Pleading § 1127, (S 1127) Requirement of Special Pleading.

§ 1909.   Judicial orders; disputable presumption

EFFECT OF OTHER JUDICIAL ORDERS, WHEN CONCLUSIVE. Other judicial orders of a Court or Judge of this State, or of the United States, create a disputable presumption, according to the matter directly determined, between the same parties and their representatives and successors in interest by title subsequent to the commencement of the action or special proceeding, litigating for the same thing under the same title and in the same capacity. *(Enacted in 1872.)*

§ 1910.   Parties; when deemed to be the same

WHERE PARTIES ARE TO BE DEEMED THE SAME. The parties are deemed to be the same when those between whom the evidence is offered were on opposite sides in the former case, and a judgment or other determination could in that case have been made between them alone, though other parties were joined with both or either. *(Enacted in 1872.)*

Research References

7 Witkin Cal. Proc. 5th Judgment § 452, Substantial Identity.
7 Witkin Cal. Proc. 5th Judgment § 453, Nonadversary Parties.

§ 1911.   Judgment; items adjudged

WHAT DEEMED ADJUDGED IN A JUDGMENT. That only is deemed to have been adjudged in a former judgment which appears upon its face to have been so adjudged, or which was actually and necessarily included therein or necessary thereto. *(Enacted in 1872.)*

Research References

7 Witkin Cal. Proc. 5th Judgment § 334, (S 334) Nature of Doctrine.
7 Witkin Cal. Proc. 5th Judgment § 415, (S 415) in General.

§ 1912. Principal bound when surety bound

WHERE SURETIES BOUND, PRINCIPAL IS ALSO. Whenever, pursuant to the last four sections, a party is bound by a record, and such party stands in the relation of a surety for another, the latter is also bound from the time that he has notice of the action or proceeding, and an opportunity at the surety's request to join in the defense. *(Enacted in 1872.)*

Research References

Rutter, Cal. Practice Guide: Insurance Litigation Ch. 6I-C, C. Surety's Obligations and Rights Upon Default by Principal.
Rutter, Cal. Practice Guide: Insurance Litigation Ch. 6I-D, D. Surety's Defenses to Payment of Bond.
Miller and Starr California Real Estate § 28:66, Bond to Release the Lien.
Miller and Starr California Real Estate § 28:112, Proper Parties in Suit Against Surety; Necessity of Suit Against or Joinder of the Principal.
7 Witkin Cal. Proc. 5th Judgment § 465, (S 465) Nature and Scope of Rule.

§ 1913. Judicial record; foreign state; effect; enforcement; authority of guardian, etc.

(a) Subject to subdivision (b), the effect of a judicial record of a sister state is the same in this state as in the state where it was made, except that it can only be enforced in this state by an action or special proceeding.

(b) The authority of a guardian, conservator, or committee, or of a personal representative, does not extend beyond the jurisdiction of the government under which that person was invested with authority, except to the extent expressly authorized by statute. *(Enacted in 1872. Amended by Stats.1979, c. 730, p. 2482, § 34, operative Jan. 1, 1981; Stats.1988, c. 1199, § 13, operative July 1, 1989.)*

Law Revision Commission Comments

Section 1913 is amended to add the reference to a conservator. [14 Cal.L.Rev. Comm.Reports 501 (1978)].

Section 1913 is divided into subdivisions and subdivision (b) is amended to recognize that a specific statute may provide for limited authority in California of a sister state personal representative. See Prob. Code §§ 12570–12573 (collection of personal property of small estate without ancillary administration). [19 Cal.L.Rev. Comm. Reports 1036 (1988)].

Research References

Rutter, Cal. Practice Guide: Enforcing Judgments/Debts Ch. 6J-2, Enforcing Sister State Judgments in California.
8 Witkin Cal. Proc. 5th Enforcement of Judgment § 445, When Action May be Brought.
8 Witkin Cal. Proc. 5th Enforcement of Judgment § 446, (S 446) Judgment Not Final and Unconditional.
7 Witkin Cal. Proc. 5th Judgment § 353, Sister State Judgment in State Action.
4 Witkin Cal. Proc. 5th Pleading § 113, (S 113) Foreign Representatives.
14 Witkin, California Summary 10th Wills and Probate § 63, Actions by or Against Representative.
14 Witkin, California Summary 10th Wills and Probate § 69, Collection of Personal Property.

§ 1914. Judicial record; foreign country; admiralty court; effect

RECORD OF A COURT OF ADMIRALTY. The effect of the judicial record of a Court of admiralty of a foreign country is the same as if it were the record of a court of admiralty of the United States. *(Enacted in 1872.)*

§ 1916. Judicial record; impeachment

MANNER OF IMPEACHING A RECORD. Any judicial record may be impeached by evidence of a want of jurisdiction in the Court or judicial officer, of collusion between the parties, or of fraud in the party offering the record, in respect to the proceedings. *(Enacted in 1872.)*

Research References

9 Witkin Cal. Proc. 5th Appeal § 663, No Settlement by Reviewing Court.

§ 1917. Judgment; jurisdiction necessary

THE JURISDICTION NECESSARY IN A JUDGMENT. The jurisdiction sufficient to sustain a record is jurisdiction over the cause, over the parties, and over the thing, when a specific thing is the subject of the judgment. *(Enacted in 1872.)*

Research References

Miller and Starr California Real Estate § 21:35, Who is Liable for Usury Penalties--Other Exemptions.
2 Witkin Cal. Proc. 5th Jurisdiction § 1, (S 1) in General.
2 Witkin Cal. Proc. 5th Jurisdiction § 106, Traditional Analysis.

ARTICLE 3. PRIVATE WRITINGS

Section	
1929.	Kinds.
1930.	"Seal" defined.
1931.	Public seal, defined, method of affixing; private seal, method of making; recognition of seal made in foreign state or country.
1932.	Distinction between sealed and unsealed instruments abolished.
1933.	"Execution of instrument" defined.
1934.	Unsealed agreement for compromise or settlement of debt; validity.
1935.	"Subscribing witness" defined.
1950.	Public records; removal on court order.
1952.	Retention or return of exhibits, depositions, or administrative records; destruction or disposition; notice; request for preservation.
1952.2.	Return of exhibits, depositions, and administrative records.
1952.3.	Destruction or other disposition of exhibits, depositions, or administrative records; notice requesting preservation; sealed files.

§ 1929. Kinds

PRIVATE WRITINGS CLASSIFIED. Private writings are either:

1. Sealed; or,

2. Unsealed. *(Enacted in 1872).*

§ 1930. "Seal" defined

SEAL DEFINED. A seal is a particular sign, made to attest, in the most formal manner, the execution of an instrument. *(Enacted in 1872).*

§ 1931. Public seal, defined, method of affixing; private seal, method of making; recognition of seal made in foreign state or country

A public seal in this State is a stamp or impression made by a public officer with an instrument provided by law, to attest the execution of an official or public document, upon the paper, or upon any substance attached to the paper, which is capable of receiving a visible impression. A private seal may be made in the same manner by any instrument, or it may be made by the scroll of a pen, or by writing the word "seal" against the signature of the writer. A scroll or other sign, made in a sister

State or foreign country, and there recognized as a seal, must be so regarded in this State. *(Enacted in 1872. Amended Code Am.1873–74, c. 383, p. 385, § 228.)*

Research References

Rutter, Cal. Practice Guide: Civil Trials & Evidence Ch. 8C-B, B. Writings.
Rutter, Cal. Practice Guide: Civil Trials & Evidence Ch. 8D-D, D. Hearsay Exceptions.

§ 1932. Distinction between sealed and unsealed instruments abolished

There shall be no difference hereafter, in this State, between sealed and unsealed writings. A writing under seal may therefore be changed, or altogether discharged by a writing not under seal. *(Enacted in 1872. Amended Code Am.1873–74, c. 383, p. 386, § 229.)*

Research References

Miller and Starr California Real Estate § 1:7, Sealed and Unsealed Contracts.
Miller and Starr California Real Estate § 8:3, Requirements; Form and Content.
12 Witkin, California Summary 10th Real Property § 254, (S 254) Requisites of Deed.
1 Witkin Cal. Summ. 10th Contracts § 3, in General.

§ 1933. "Execution of instrument" defined

EXECUTION OF AN INSTRUMENT DEFINED. The execution of an instrument is the subscribing and delivering it, with or without affixing a seal. *(Enacted in 1872.)*

Research References

Rutter, Cal. Practice Guide: Civil Trials & Evidence Ch. 8C-B, B. Writings.
Miller and Starr California Real Estate § 8:3, Requirements; Form and Content.
Miller and Starr California Real Estate § 8:41, "Delivery" Defined.
Miller and Starr California Real Estate § 13:32, Execution and Acknowledgment.
12 Witkin, California Summary 10th Real Property § 520, Execution and Delivery.

§ 1934. Unsealed agreement for compromise or settlement of debt; validity

COMPROMISE OF A DEBT WITHOUT SEAL GOOD. An agreement, in writing, without a seal, for the compromise or settlement of a debt, is as obligatory as if a seal were affixed. *(Enacted in 1872.)*

§ 1935. "Subscribing" witness defined

SUBSCRIBING WITNESS DEFINED. A subscribing witness is one who sees a writing executed or hears it acknowledged, and at the request of the party thereupon signs his name as a witness. *(Enacted in 1872.)*

§ 1950. Public records; removal on court order

The record of a conveyance of real property, or any other record, a transcript of which is admissible in evidence, must not be removed from the office where it is kept, except upon the order of a Court, in cases where the inspection of the record is shown to be essential to the just determination of the cause or proceeding pending, or where the Court is held in the same building with such office. *(Enacted in 1872. Amended Code Am.1873–74, c. 383, p. 387, § 236.)*

§ 1952. Retention or return of exhibits, depositions, or administrative records; destruction or disposition; notice; request for preservation

(a) The clerk shall retain in his or her custody any exhibit, deposition, or administrative record introduced in the trial of a civil action or proceeding or filed in the action or proceeding until the final determination thereof or the dismissal of the action or proceeding, except that the court may order the exhibit, deposition, or administrative record returned to the respective party or parties at any time upon oral stipulation in open court or by written stipulation by the parties or for good cause shown.

(b) No exhibit or deposition shall be ordered destroyed or otherwise disposed of pursuant to this section where a party to the action or proceeding files a written notice with the court requesting the preservation of any exhibit, deposition, or administrative record for a stated time, but not to exceed one year.

(c) Upon the conclusion of the trial of a civil action or proceeding at which any exhibit or deposition has been introduced, the court shall order that the exhibit or deposition be destroyed or otherwise disposed of by the clerk. The operative destruction or disposition date shall be 60 days following final determination of the action or proceeding. Final determination includes final determination on appeal. Written notice of the order shall be sent by first-class mail to the parties by the clerk.

(d) Upon the conclusion of any posttrial hearing at which any exhibit, deposition, or administrative record has been introduced, the court shall order that the exhibit or deposition be destroyed or otherwise disposed of by the clerk. The operative date of destruction or disposition shall be 60 days following the conclusion of the hearing, or if an appeal is taken, upon final determination of the appeal. Written notice of the order shall be sent by first-class mail to the parties by the clerk. *(Added by Stats.1984, c. 27, § 2. Amended by Stats.1990, c. 382 (A.B.3408), § 1; Stats.1991, c. 1090 (A.B.1484), § 7.)*

Research References

Rutter, Cal. Practice Guide: Civil Appeals & Writs Ch. 4-H, H. Transmittal of Exhibits.
Rutter, Cal. Practice Guide: Civ. Pro. Before Trial Ch. 8E-14, Deposition Transcript.
2 Witkin Cal. Proc. 5th Courts § 373, Destruction.
8 Witkin Cal. Proc. 5th Extraordinary Writs § 311, (S 311) Obtaining and Filing Record.

§ 1952.2. Return of exhibits, depositions, and administrative records

Notwithstanding any other provisions of law, upon a judgment becoming final, at the expiration of the appeal period, unless an appeal is pending, the court, in its discretion, and on its own motion by a written order signed by the judge, filed in the action, and an entry thereof made in the register of actions, may order the clerk to return all of the exhibits, depositions, and administrative records introduced or filed in the trial of a civil action or proceeding to the attorneys for the parties introducing or filing the same. *(Added by Stats.1959, c. 343, p. 2267, § 1. Amended by Stats.1969, c. 44, p. 156, § 1; Stats.1984, c. 27, § 3; Stats.1991, c. 1090 (A.B.1484), § 8.)*

Research References

8 Witkin Cal. Proc. 5th Extraordinary Writs § 311, (S 311) Obtaining and Filing Record.

§ 1952.3. Destruction or other disposition of exhibits, depositions, or administrative records; notice requesting preservation; sealed files

Notwithstanding any other provision of the law, the court, on its own motion, may order the destruction or other disposition of any exhibit, deposition, or administrative record introduced in the trial or posttrial hearing of a civil action or proceeding or filed in the action or proceeding that, if appeal has not been taken from the decision of the court in the action or proceeding, remains in the custody of the court or clerk five years after time for appeal has expired, or, if appeal has been taken, remains in the custody of the court or clerk five years after final determination thereof, or that remains in the custody of the court or clerk for a period of five years after any of the following:

(a) A motion for a new trial has been granted and a memorandum to set the case for trial has not been filed, or a motion to set for trial has not been made within five years.

(b) The dismissal of the action or proceeding.

In addition, the court on its own motion, may order the destruction or other disposition of any exhibit, deposition, or administrative record that remains in the custody of the court or clerk for a period of 10 years after the introduction or filing of the action or proceeding if, in the discretion of the court, the exhibit, deposition, or administrative record should be disposed of or destroyed.

The order shall be entered in the register of actions of each case in which the order is made.

No exhibit, deposition, or administrative record shall be ordered destroyed or otherwise disposed of pursuant to this section if a party to the action or proceeding files a written notice with the court requesting the preservation of any exhibit, deposition, or administrative record for a stated time, but not to exceed one year.

Any sealed file shall be retained for at least two years after the date on which destruction would otherwise be authorized pursuant to this section. *(Added by Stats.1984, c. 250, § 3. Amended by Stats.1985, c. 875, § 1; Stats.1990, c. 382 (A.B.3408), § 2; Stats.1991, c. 1090 (A.B.1484), § 9.)*

Research References

2 Witkin Cal. Proc. 5th Courts § 373, Destruction.
8 Witkin Cal. Proc. 5th Extraordinary Writs § 311, (S 311) Obtaining and Filing Record.

ARTICLE 4.　RECORDS DESTROYED IN FIRE OR CALAMITY

§ 1953.　"Record" defined

As used in this article "record" includes all or any part of any judgment, decree, order, document, paper, process, or file. *(Added by Stats.1953, c. 52, p. 712, § 14.)*

§ 1953.01.　Certified copy; petition to substitute for original

Whenever in any action or special proceeding, civil or criminal, in any court of this State any record is lost, injured, or destroyed by reason of conflagration or other public calamity, any person interested therein may apply by a duly verified petition in writing to the court for an order authorizing such defect to be supplied by a duly certified copy of the original, where such copy can be obtained. *(Added by Stats.1953, c. 52, § 712, § 14.)*

§ 1953.02.　Certified copy; order giving effect of original; notices

Upon notice given pursuant to Sections 1010 to 1020, inclusive, of this code, and its being shown to the satisfaction of the court that the record has been so lost, injured, or destroyed, the court shall make an order that the certified copy shall thereafter have the same effect in all respects as the original would have had. *(Added by Stats.1953, c. 52, p. 713, § 14.)*

§ 1953.03.　Application to supply record; notices

Whenever in any action or special proceeding, civil or criminal, in any court of this State any record is lost, injured, or destroyed by reason of conflagration or other public calamity, and a certified copy of the original cannot be supplied, any person interested therein may make written application to the court, verified by affidavit, showing such loss, injury, or destruction, and that a certified copy of the record cannot be obtained by the person making the application, and that such loss, injury, or destruction occurred by conflagration, or other calamity, without the fault or neglect of the person making the application, and that such loss, injury, or destruction, unless supplied or remedied may result in damage to the person making the application. Thereupon the court shall cause notice of the application to be given pursuant to Sections 1010 to 1020, inclusive, of this code. *(Added by Stats.1953, c. 52, p. 713, § 14.)*

§ 1953.04.　Hearing; order reciting substance of record; effect

Upon the hearing if the court is satisfied that the statements contained in the written application are true, it shall make an order reciting the substance and effect of the lost, injured, or destroyed record. The order shall have the same effect that the original would have had if it had not been lost, injured, or destroyed, so far as concerns the person making the application, and the persons who have been notified, pursuant to Section 1953.03. *(Added by Stats.1953, c. 52, p. 713, § 14.)*

§ 1953.05.　Restoration of record in proceedings in rem; procedure; effect

The record in all cases where the proceeding is in rem, including probate, guardianship, conservatorship, and insolvency proceedings, may be supplied in like manner upon like notice to all persons who have appeared therein, and upon notice by publication or postings for not less than 10 days, as the court may order, to all persons who have not appeared. When restored the record shall have the same effect as the original upon all persons who have been personally served with notice of the application, and as to all other persons it shall be prima facie evidence of the contents of the original. *(Added by Stats.1953, c. 52, p. 713, § 14. Amended by Stats.1979, c. 730, p. 2483, § 35, operative Jan. 1, 1981.)*

Law Revision Commission Comments

Section 1953.05 is amended to add the reference to conservatorship. [14 Cal.L.Rev. Comm. Reports 501 (1978)].

§ 1953.06.　Transcript on appeal; substitution for destroyed trial court record

If an appeal to a reviewing court has been taken in any action or special proceeding in any trial court in which the record has been subsequently lost or destroyed by conflagration or other public calamity and a transcript of such record has been filed in the reviewing court, any person interested in the action or special proceeding may obtain a certified copy of all or any portion of the transcript from the clerk of the reviewing court and may file such certified copy in the office of the clerk of the court from which the appeal was taken. Thereupon the certified copy may be made the basis of any further proceedings or processes in the trial court in such action or special proceeding to all intents and purposes as if the original record were on file. *(Added by Stats.1953, c. 52, p. 713, § 14. Amended by Stats.1967, c. 17, p. 833, § 21.)*

ARTICLE 4.5. PRIVATE RECORDS DESTROYED IN DISASTER OR CALAMITY

Section
1953.10. Petition for order establishing existence, genuineness or authenticity.
1953.11. Notice and hearing.
1953.12. Evidence; contents of order.
1953.13. Reference to documents in order; order in lieu of original; effect.

§ 1953.10. Petition for order establishing existence, genuineness or authenticity

Any person, corporation, copartnership, organization, institution, business, member of profession or calling interested in establishing the existence, substance, genuineness, or authenticity of any memorandum, book, map, chart, manuscript, writing, account, entry, record, print, document, representation, or combination thereof that has been damaged, rendered wholly or partially illegible, destroyed in whole or in part or lost by explosion, conflagration, earthquake, disaster or other public calamity, may apply by duly verified petition to the court for an order establishing, reciting, or declaring the existence, substance, genuineness or authenticity of the same. *(Added by Stats.1961, c. 1311, p. 3090, § 1.)*

Research References

Rutter, Cal. Practice Guide: Civil Trials & Evidence Ch. 8C-B, B. Writings.
Rutter, Cal. Practice Guide: Insurance Litigation Ch. 15-I, I. Trial.
3 Witkin Cal. Proc. 5th Actions § 65, (S 65) Statutory Classes.
7 Witkin Cal. Proc. 5th Trial § 94, Special Proceedings.

§ 1953.11. Notice and hearing

Notice of the filing of the petition and of the time and place of the hearing thereof shall be given to such persons, if any, as the court shall designate by its order. Such order shall specify how such notice shall be given and may be by publication, posting, personal service or otherwise as the court shall direct. Upon the hearing of the petition proof shall be submitted to the court that notice has been given as prescribed in such order. *(Added by Stats.1961, c. 1311, p. 3091, § 1.)*

§ 1953.12. Evidence; contents of order

Upon the hearing the court shall receive such evidence as may be required and if the court is satisfied that the statements contained in the petition are true, it shall make an order reciting the existence, substance, genuineness or authenticity of the destroyed or lost memorandum, book, map, chart, manuscript, writing, account, entry, print, document, representation or combination thereof. *(Added by Stats.1961, c. 1311, p. 3091, § 1.)*

Research References

Rutter, Cal. Practice Guide: Civil Trials & Evidence Ch. 2-B, B. What Constitutes Jury Trial.

§ 1953.13. Reference to documents in order; order in lieu of original; effect

The order of court made upon such hearing shall refer to the memorandum, book, map, chart, manuscript, writing, account, entry, record, print, document, representation or combination thereof which is the subject of said petition and such court order shall be deemed in lieu of the original and have the same effect as if the original had not been damaged, destroyed or otherwise rendered wholly or partially illegible. *(Added by Stats.1961, c. 1311, p. 3091, § 1.)*

CHAPTER 6. INDISPENSABLE EVIDENCE

Section
1971. Creation of interest in real property.
1972. Effect of § 1971; power of court; creation of trust.
1974. Representation as to credit of third person; writing.

§ 1971. Creation of interest in real property

No estate or interest in real property, other than for leases for a term not exceeding one year, nor any power over or concerning it, or in any manner relating thereto, can be created, granted, assigned, surrendered, or declared, otherwise than by operation of law, or a conveyance or other instrument in writing, subscribed by the party creating, granting, assigning, surrendering, or declaring the same, or by the party's lawful agent thereunto authorized by writing. *(Enacted in 1872. Amended by Stats. 1986, c. 820, § 19, operative July 1, 1987.)*

Law Revision Commission Comments

Section 1971 is amended to reflect the enactment of Probate Code Section 15206 which retains the Statute of Frauds as applied to trusts. This amendment of Section 1971 is not substantive. [18 Cal.L.Rev. Comm. Reports 501 (1986)].

Research References

Rutter, Cal. Practice Guide: Real Prop. Transactions Ch. 4-B, B. Interests to be Conveyed.
Rutter, Cal. Practice Guide: Real Prop. Transactions Ch. 4-D, D. Selecting the Form of Written Agreement.
Miller and Starr California Real Estate § 8:1, Definitions and Terminology.
Miller and Starr California Real Estate § 8:3, Requirements; Form and Content.
Miller and Starr California Real Estate § 1:65, Provisions Applicable to Real Estate Transactions.
Miller and Starr California Real Estate § 1:67, Agreement that Will Not be Performed Within One Year from the Date it is Made--Oral Leases.
Miller and Starr California Real Estate § 1:69, Contract for the Sale, Gift, or Financing of Real Property.
Miller and Starr California Real Estate § 1:71, Contract for the Sale, Gift, or Financing of Real Property--Exception: Part Performance by the Buyer or Lessee.
Miller and Starr California Real Estate § 1:72, Effect When Statute of Frauds Not Satisfied.
Miller and Starr California Real Estate § 1:81, Written Authority Required; the Equal Dignities Rule.
Miller and Starr California Real Estate § 5:16, Exception: Estoppel to Raise Statute of Frauds as a Defense.
Miller and Starr California Real Estate § 5:21, Property Management Employment Agreements.
Miller and Starr California Real Estate § 8:28, Insertion of Name After Execution by the Grantor.
Miller and Starr California Real Estate § 8:29, Requirements of Grantor's Signature.
Miller and Starr California Real Estate § 8:30, Execution by an Agent or Attorney-In-Fact.
Miller and Starr California Real Estate § 9:20, Creation.
Miller and Starr California Real Estate § 19:21, Lease as a Contract and Conveyance--Application of the Statute of Frauds/Translation of Leases Into Other Languages.
Miller and Starr California Real Estate § 19:196, Surrender.
15 NO. 6 Miller & Starr, California Real Estate Newsalert 1, Refuse to Mediate and (Under Some Contracts) Wave Goodbye to Your Attorney's Fees.
1 Witkin Cal. Summ. 10th Contracts § 385, Scope of Statute.

1 Witkin Cal. Summ. 10th Contracts § 402, Scope of Exception.

§ 1972. Effect of § 1971; power of court; creation of trust

(a) Section 1971 shall not be construed to abridge the power of any court to compel the specific performance of an agreement, in case of part performance thereof.

(b) Section 1971 does not affect the creation of a trust under Division 9 (commencing with Section 15000) of the Probate Code nor prevent any trust from arising or being extinguished by implication or operation of law. *(Enacted in 1872. Amended by Stats.1986, c. 820, § 20, operative July 1, 1987.)*

Law Revision Commission Comments

Section 1972 is amended to reflect the enactment of Probate Code Section 15206 which provides the Statute of Frauds as applied to trusts. This amendment of Section 1972 is not substantive. Section 1972 is also amended to delete the reference to the impact of the Statute of Frauds on a testamentary disposition of real property. Oral wills are no longer permitted; all wills, whether disposing of real or personal property, must be in writing. Prob.Code §§ 6110–6111. [18 Cal.L.Rev.Comm. Reports 501 (1986)].

Research References

Rutter, Cal. Practice Guide: Real Prop. Transactions Ch. 4-D, D. Selecting the Form of Written Agreement.
Miller and Starr California Real Estate § 1:71, Contract for the Sale, Gift, or Financing of Real Property--Exception: Part Performance by the Buyer or Lessee.
Miller and Starr California Real Estate § 9:20, Creation.
1 Witkin Cal. Summ. 10th Contracts § 402, Scope of Exception.

§ 1974. Representation as to credit of third person; writing

No evidence is admissible to charge a person upon a representation as to the credit of a third person, unless such representation, or some memorandum thereof, be in writing, and either subscribed by or in the handwriting of the party to be charged. This section is a Statute of Frauds provision and is to be applied in a manner that is consistent with the manner in which subdivision 2 of Section 1624 of the Civil Code is applied. *(Enacted in 1872. Amended by Stats.1965, c. 299, p. 1363, § 114, operative Jan. 1, 1967; Stats.1970, c. 720, p. 1347, § 1.)*

Research References

Miller and Starr California Real Estate § 1:65, Provisions Applicable to Real Estate Transactions.
Miller and Starr California Real Estate § 36:15, Liability for Fraud.
5 Witkin Cal. Proc. 5th Pleading § 710, Elements of Action for Deceit.
1 Witkin Cal. Summ. 10th Contracts § 343, California Codes.
5 Witkin, California Summary 10th Torts § 788, Representations Concerning Credit.

Title 3

OF THE PRODUCTION OF EVIDENCE

CHAPTER 2. MEANS OF PRODUCTION

§ 1985. Subpoena defined; affidavit for subpoena duces tecum; issuance of subpoena in blank

(a) The process by which the attendance of a witness is required is the subpoena. It is a writ or order directed to a person and requiring the person's attendance at a particular time and place to testify as a witness. It may also require a witness to bring any books, documents, electronically stored information, or other things under the witness's control which the witness is bound by law to produce in evidence. When a county recorder is using the microfilm system for recording, and a witness is subpoenaed to present a record, the witness shall be deemed to have complied with the subpoena if the witness produces a certified copy thereof.

(b) A copy of an affidavit shall be served with a subpoena duces tecum issued before trial, showing good cause for the production of the matters and things described in the subpoena, specifying the exact matters or things desired to be produced, setting forth in full detail the materiality thereof to the issues involved in the case, and stating that the witness has the desired matters or things in his or her possession or under his or her control.

(c) The clerk, or a judge, shall issue a subpoena or subpoena duces tecum signed and sealed but otherwise in blank to a party requesting it, who shall fill it in before service. An attorney at law who is the attorney of record in an action or proceeding, may sign and issue a subpoena to require attendance before the court in which the action or proceeding is pending or at the trial of an issue therein, or upon the taking of a deposition in an action or proceeding pending therein; the subpoena in such a case need not be sealed. An attorney at law who is the attorney of record in an action or proceeding, may sign and issue a subpoena duces tecum to require production of the matters or things described in the subpoena. *(Enacted in 1872. Amended by Stats.1933, c. 567, p. 1479, § 1; Stats.1961, c. 496, p. 1590, § 1; Stats.1967, c. 431, p. 1645, § 1; Stats.1968, c. 95, p. 305, § 1; Stats.1979, c. 458, p. 1607, § 1; Stats.1982, c. 452, § 1; Stats.1986, c. 603, § 3; Stats.1990, c. 511 (S.B.163), § 1, eff. Aug. 13, 1990; Stats.2012, c. 72 (S.B.1574), § 1.)*

Research References

Rutter, Cal. Practice Guide: A.D.R. Ch. 4-B, B. Judicial Arbitration.
Rutter, Cal. Practice Guide: A.D.R. Ch. 5-H, H. Conduct of Arbitration Proceedings.
Rutter, Cal. Practice Guide: A.D.R. App. D Form 111, Discovery-Arbitrator's Subpoena Re Deposition (CCP § 1282.6).
Rutter, Cal. Practice Guide: A.D.R. App. D Form 114, Arbitrator's Subpoena Duces Tecum.
Rutter, Cal. Practice Guide: A.D.R. App. D Form 127, ADR Clause (Conduct of Reference Proceeding).
Rutter, Cal. Practice Guide: Civ. Pro. Before Trial Ch. 13-E, E. the Arbitration Hearing.
Rutter, Cal. Practice Guide: Civ. Pro. Before Trial Ch. 8E-1, When Prior Court Order Required.
Rutter, Cal. Practice Guide: Civ. Pro. Before Trial Ch. 8E-6, Subpoena to Nonparty Deponent or Business Records Custodian.
Rutter, Cal. Practice Guide: Civ. Pro. Before Trial Ch. 8E-1, Outline 1.
Rutter, Cal. Practice Guide: Civil Trials & Evidence Ch. 1-C, C. Marshalling the Evidence.
California Practice Guide: Employment Litigation Ch. 13-H, H. Contesting Citations and Related Orders and Notices.
Rutter, Cal. Practice Guide: Personal Injury Ch. 6-B, B. Overview of Selected Discovery Procedures.
Rutter, Cal. Practice Guide: Personal Injury Ch. 7-F, F. Preparing for Arbitration.
Rutter, Cal. Practice Guide: Personal Injury Ch. 8-C, C. Two Months Before Trial.
Rutter, Cal. Practice Guide: Prof. Responsibility Ch. 11-H, H. Proceedings Before Trial.
9 Witkin Cal. Proc. 5th Administrative Proceedings § 89, (S 89) Subpenas.
10 Witkin, California Summary 10th Parent and Child § 566, (S 566) Notices, Citations, Warrants, and Subpenas.
2 Witkin Cal. Summ. 10th Workers' Compensation § 95, Employer is Party.

§ 1985.1. Agreement to appear at time other than specified in subpoena

Any person who is subpoenaed to appear at a session of court, or at the trial of an issue therein, may, in lieu of appearance at the time specified in the subpoena, agree with the party at whose request the subpoena was issued to appear at another time or upon such notice as may be agreed upon. Any failure to appear pursuant to such agreement may be punished as a contempt by the court issuing the subpoena. The facts establishing or disproving such agreement and the failure to appear may be proved by an affidavit of any person having personal knowledge of the facts. *(Added by Stats.1969, c. 140, p. 385, § 1.)*

§ 1985.2. Subpoenas; civil trials, attendance of witnesses; notice

Any subpoena which requires the attendance of a witness at any civil trial shall contain the following notice in a type face designed to call attention to the notice:

Contact the attorney requesting this subpoena, listed above, before the date on which you are required to be in court, if you have any question about the time or date for you to appear, or if you want to be certain that your presence in court is required. *(Added by Stats.1978, c. 431, p. 1494, § 1, operative July 1, 1979.)*

§ 1985.3. Subpoena duces tecum; personal records of consumer

(a) For purposes of this section, the following definitions apply:

(1) "Personal records" means the original, any copy of books, documents, other writings, or electronically stored information pertaining to a consumer and which are maintained by any "witness" which is a physician, dentist, ophthalmologist, optometrist, chiropractor, physical therapist, acupuncturist, podiatrist, veterinarian, veterinary hospital, veterinary clinic, pharmacist, pharmacy, hospital, medical center, clinic, radiology or MRI center, clinical or diagnostic laboratory, state or national bank, state or federal association (as defined in Section 5102 of the Financial Code), state or federal credit union, trust company, anyone authorized by this state to make or arrange loans that are secured by real property, security brokerage firm, insurance company, title insurance company, underwritten title company, escrow agent licensed pursuant to Division 6 (commencing with Section 17000) of the Financial Code or exempt from licensure pursuant to Section 17006 of the Financial Code, attorney, accountant, institution of the Farm Credit System, as specified in Section 2002 of Title 12 of the United States Code, or telephone corporation which is a public utility, as defined in Section 216 of the Public Utilities Code, or psychotherapist, as defined in Section 1010 of the Evidence Code, or a private or public preschool, elementary school, secondary school, or postsecondary school as described in Section 76244 of the Education Code.

(2) "Consumer" means any individual, partnership of five or fewer persons, association, or trust which has transacted business with, or has used the services of, the witness or for whom the witness has acted as agent or fiduciary.

(3) "Subpoenaing party" means the person or persons causing a subpoena duces tecum to be issued or served in connection with any civil action or proceeding pursuant to this code, but shall not include the state or local agencies described in Section 7465 of the Government Code, or any entity provided for under Article VI of the California Constitution in any proceeding maintained before an adjudicative body of that entity pursuant to Chapter 4 (commencing with Section 6000) of Division 3 of the Business and Professions Code.

(4) "Deposition officer" means a person who meets the qualifications specified in Section 2020.420.

(b) Prior to the date called for in the subpoena duces tecum for the production of personal records, the subpoenaing party shall serve or cause to be served on the consumer whose records are being sought a copy of the subpoena duces tecum, of the affidavit supporting the issuance of the subpoena, if any, and of the notice described in subdivision (e), and proof of service as indicated in paragraph (1) of subdivision (c). This service shall be made as follows:

(1) To the consumer personally, or at his or her last known address, or in accordance with Chapter 5 (commencing with Section 1010) of Title 14 of Part 3, or, if he or she is a party, to his or her attorney of record. If the consumer is a minor, service shall be made on the minor's parent, guardian, conservator, or similar fiduciary, or if one of them cannot be located with reasonable diligence, then service shall be made on any person having the care or control of the minor or with whom the minor resides or by whom the minor is employed, and on the minor if the minor is at least 12 years of age.

(2) Not less than 10 days prior to the date for production specified in the subpoena duces tecum, plus the additional time provided by Section 1013 if service is by mail.

(3) At least five days prior to service upon the custodian of the records, plus the additional time provided by Section 1013 if service is by mail.

(c) Prior to the production of the records, the subpoenaing party shall do either of the following:

(1) Serve or cause to be served upon the witness a proof of personal service or of service by mail attesting to compliance with subdivision (b).

(2) Furnish the witness a written authorization to release the records signed by the consumer or by his or her attorney of record. The witness may presume that any attorney purporting to sign the authorization on behalf of the consumer acted with the consent of the consumer, and that any objection to release of records is waived.

(d) A subpoena duces tecum for the production of personal records shall be served in sufficient time to allow the witness a reasonable time, as provided in Section 2020.410, to locate and produce the records or copies thereof.

(e) Every copy of the subpoena duces tecum and affidavit, if any, served on a consumer or his or her attorney in accordance with subdivision (b) shall be accompanied by a notice, in a typeface designed to call attention to the notice, indicating that (1) records about the consumer are being sought from the witness named on the subpoena; (2) if the consumer objects to the witness furnishing the records to the party seeking the records, the consumer must file papers with the court or serve a written objection as provided in subdivision (g) prior to the date specified for production on the subpoena; and (3) if the party who is seeking the records will not agree in writing to cancel or limit the subpoena, an attorney should be consulted about the consumer's interest in protecting his or her rights of privacy. If a notice of taking of deposition is also served, that other notice may be set forth in a single document with the notice required by this subdivision.

(f) A subpoena duces tecum for personal records maintained by a telephone corporation which is a public utility, as defined in Section 216 of the Public Utilities Code, shall not be valid or effective unless it includes a consent to release, signed by the consumer whose records are requested, as required by Section 2891 of the Public Utilities Code.

(g) Any consumer whose personal records are sought by a subpoena duces tecum and who is a party to the civil action in which this subpoena duces tecum is served may, prior to the date for production, bring a motion under Section 1987.1 to quash or modify the subpoena duces tecum. Notice of the bringing of that motion shall be given to the witness and deposition officer at least five days prior to production. The failure to provide notice to the deposition officer shall not invalidate the motion to quash

or modify the subpoena duces tecum but may be raised by the deposition officer as an affirmative defense in any action for liability for improper release of records.

Any other consumer or nonparty whose personal records are sought by a subpoena duces tecum may, prior to the date of production, serve on the subpoenaing party, the witness, and the deposition officer, a written objection that cites the specific grounds on which production of the personal records should be prohibited.

No witness or deposition officer shall be required to produce personal records after receipt of notice that the motion has been brought by a consumer, or after receipt of a written objection from a nonparty consumer, except upon order of the court in which the action is pending or by agreement of the parties, witnesses, and consumers affected.

The party requesting a consumer's personal records may bring a motion under Section 1987.1 to enforce the subpoena within 20 days of service of the written objection. The motion shall be accompanied by a declaration showing a reasonable and good faith attempt at informal resolution of the dispute between the party requesting the personal records and the consumer or the consumer's attorney.

(h) Upon good cause shown and provided that the rights of witnesses and consumers are preserved, a subpoenaing party shall be entitled to obtain an order shortening the time for service of a subpoena duces tecum or waiving the requirements of subdivision (b) where due diligence by the subpoenaing party has been shown.

(i) Nothing contained in this section shall be construed to apply to any subpoena duces tecum which does not request the records of any particular consumer or consumers and which requires a custodian of records to delete all information which would in any way identify any consumer whose records are to be produced.

(j) This section shall not apply to proceedings conducted under Division 1 (commencing with Section 50), Division 4 (commencing with Section 3200), Division 4.5 (commencing with Section 6100), or Division 4.7 (commencing with Section 6200), of the Labor Code.

(k) Failure to comply with this section shall be sufficient basis for the witness to refuse to produce the personal records sought by a subpoena duces tecum.

(*l*) If the subpoenaing party is the consumer, and the consumer is the only subject of the subpoenaed records, notice to the consumer, and delivery of the other documents specified in subdivision (b) to the consumer, is not required under this section. (Added by Stats.1980, c. 976, p. 3101, § 1, operative July 1, 1981. Amended by Stats.1981, c. 227, p. 1152, § 1, eff. July 20, 1981, operative July 1, 1981; Stats.1981, c. 1014, p. 3912, § 1; Stats.1982, c. 666, § 1; Stats.1984, c. 603, § 1; Stats.1985, c. 983, § 1, eff. Sept. 26, 1985; Stats.1986, c. 248, § 21; Stats.1986, c. 605, § 1; Stats.1986, c. 1209, § 2; Stats.1987, c. 20, § 1; Stats.1987, c. 149, § 1, eff. July 10, 1987; Stats.1987, c. 1080, § 10; Stats.1987, c. 1492, § 2; Stats.1988, c. 184, § 1; Stats.1990, c. 1220 (A.B.2980), § 1; Stats.1996, c. 679 (S.B.1821), § 1; Stats.1997, c. 442 (A.B.758), § 10; Stats.1998, c. 932 (A.B.1094), § 19; Stats.1999, c. 444 (A.B.794), § 1; Stats.2004, c. 182 (A.B.3081), § 18, operative July 1, 2005; Stats.2005, c. 300 (A.B.496), § 6; Stats.2012, c. 72 (S.B.1574), § 2.)

Law Revision Commission Comments

Subdivisions (a) and (d) of Section 1985.3 are amended to reflect nonsubstantive reorganization of the rules governing civil discovery. [33 Cal.L.Rev.Comm. Reports 1000 (2004)].

Research References

Rutter, Cal. Practice Guide: Civ. Pro. Before Trial Ch. 8C-5, Privacy Protection.

Rutter, Cal. Practice Guide: Civ. Pro. Before Trial Ch. 8E-5, Subpoena Not Necessary for Party or "Party-Affiliated" Witnesses.

Rutter, Cal. Practice Guide: Civ. Pro. Before Trial Ch. 8E-6, Subpoena to Nonparty Deponent or Business Records Custodian.

Rutter, Cal. Practice Guide: Civ. Pro. Before Trial Ch. 8E-6, Outline 6.

Rutter, Cal. Practice Guide: Civil Trials & Evidence Ch. 1-C, C. Marshalling the Evidence.

Rutter, Cal. Practice Guide: Civil Trials & Evidence Section 8E-A, A. Privileges.

Rutter, Cal. Practice Guide: Civil Trials & Evidence Ch. 8E-C, C. Right of Privacy.

Rutter, Cal. Practice Guide: Enforcing Judgments/Debts Ch. 6G-1, Examination of Judgment Debtor and Third Parties.

Rutter, Cal. Practice Guide: Fed.Civ.Pro. Before Trial Ch. 11(IV)-A, A. Depositions.

Rutter, Cal. Practice Guide: Fed.Civ.Pro. Before Trial Ch. 11(III)-B, B. Scope of Discovery.

Rutter, Cal. Practice Guide: Personal Injury Ch. 6-A, A. Scope of Discovery and Limitations.

Rutter, Cal. Practice Guide: Personal Injury Ch. 6-B, B. Overview of Selected Discovery Procedures.

Rutter, Cal. Practice Guide: Personal Injury Ch. 8-B, B. After Trial Date Set (Three to Four Months Before Trial).

Rutter, Cal. Practice Guide: Personal Injury Ch. 8-C, C. Two Months Before Trial.

Rutter, Cal. Practice Guide: Prof. Responsibility Ch. 7-B, B. Duty to Maintain Client Confidence and Secrets Under State Bar Act.

Rutter, Cal. Practice Guide: Prof. Responsibility Ch. 11-H, H. Proceedings Before Trial.

5 Witkin, California Summary 10th Torts § 455, Privilege.

5 Witkin, California Summary 10th Torts § 567, in General.

5 Witkin, California Summary 10th Torts § 686, (S 686) Privileges.

§ 1985.4. Application of procedures in § 1985.3; subpoena duces tecum for records exempt from public disclosure under Public Records Act and maintained by state or local agency

The procedures set forth in Section 1985.3 are applicable to a subpoena duces tecum for records containing "personal information," as defined in Section 1798.3 of the Civil Code which are otherwise exempt from public disclosure under Section 6254 of the Government Code which are maintained by a state or local agency as defined in Section 6252 of the Government Code. For the purposes of this section, "witness" means a state or local agency as defined in Section 6252 of the Government Code and "consumer" means any employee of any state or local agency as defined in Section 6252 of the Government Code, or any other natural person. Nothing in this section shall pertain to personnel records as defined in Section 832.8 of the Penal Code. *(Added by Stats.1984, c. 437, § 1. Amended by Stats.1988, c. 441, § 1.)*

Research References

Rutter, Cal. Practice Guide: Civ. Pro. Before Trial Ch. 8E-6, Subpoena to Nonparty Deponent or Business Records Custodian.

Rutter, Cal. Practice Guide: Civil Trials & Evidence Ch. 1-C, C. Marshalling the Evidence.

California Practice Guide: Employment Litigation Ch. 13-H, H. Contesting Citations and Related Orders and Notices.

§ 1985.5. Subpena for attendance before officer or commissioner out of court; alternative requirement

If a subpena requires the attendance of a witness before an officer or commissioner out of court, it shall, for a refusal to be sworn, or to answer as a witness, or to subscribe an affidavit or deposition when required, also require the witness to attend a session of the court issuing the subpena at a time and place thereof to be fixed by said officer or commissioner. *(Added by Stats.1941, c. 405, p. 1690, § 1.)*

§ 1985.6. Employment records; subpoena duces tecum or production of records; notice and service; motion to quash or modify subpoena

(a) For purposes of this section, the following terms have the following meanings:

(1) "Deposition officer" means a person who meets the qualifications specified in Section 2020.420.

(2) "Employee" means any individual who is or has been employed by a witness subject to a subpoena duces tecum. "Employee" also means any individual who is or has been represented by a labor organization that is a witness subject to a subpoena duces tecum.

(3) "Employment records" means the original or any copy of books, documents, other writings, or electronically stored information pertaining to the employment of any employee maintained by the current or former employer of the employee, or by any labor organization that has represented or currently represents the employee.

(4) "Labor organization" has the meaning set forth in Section 1117 of the Labor Code.

(5) "Subpoenaing party" means the person or persons causing a subpoena duces tecum to be issued or served in connection with any civil action or proceeding, but does not include the state or local agencies described in Section 7465 of the Government Code, or any entity provided for under Article VI of the California Constitution in any proceeding maintained before an adjudicative body of that entity pursuant to Chapter 4 (commencing with Section 6000) of Division 3 of the Business and Professions Code.

(b) Prior to the date called for in the subpoena duces tecum of the production of employment records, the subpoenaing party shall serve or cause to be served on the employee whose records are being sought a copy of: the subpoena duces tecum; the affidavit supporting the issuance of the subpoena, if any; the notice described in subdivision (e); and proof of service as provided in paragraph (1) of subdivision (c). This service shall be made as follows:

(1) To the employee personally, or at his or her last known address, or in accordance with Chapter 5 (commencing with Section 1010) of Title 14 of Part 2, or, if he or she is a party, to his or her attorney of record. If the employee is a minor, service shall be made on the minor's parent, guardian, conservator, or similar fiduciary, or if one of them cannot be located with reasonable diligence, then service shall be made on any person having the care or control of the minor, or with whom the minor resides, and on the minor if the minor is at least 12 years of age.

(2) Not less than 10 days prior to the date for production specified in the subpoena duces tecum, plus the additional time provided by Section 1013 if service is by mail.

(3) At least five days prior to service upon the custodian of the employment records, plus the additional time provided by Section 1013 if service is by mail.

(c) Prior to the production of the records, the subpoenaing party shall either:

(1) Serve or cause to be served upon the witness a proof of personal service or of service by mail attesting to compliance with subdivision (b).

(2) Furnish the witness a written authorization to release the records signed by the employee or by his or her attorney of record. The witness may presume that the attorney purporting to sign the authorization on behalf of the employee acted with the consent of the employee, and that any objection to the release of records is waived.

(d) A subpoena duces tecum for the production of employment records shall be served in sufficient time to allow the witness a reasonable time, as provided in Section 2020.410, to locate and produce the records or copies thereof.

(e) Every copy of the subpoena duces tecum and affidavit served on an employee or his or her attorney in accordance with subdivision (b) shall be accompanied by a notice, in a typeface designed to call attention to the notice, indicating that (1) employment records about the employee are being sought from the witness named on the subpoena; (2) the employment records may be protected by a right of privacy; (3) if the employee objects to the witness furnishing the records to the party seeking the records, the employee shall file papers with the court prior to the date specified for production on the subpoena; and (4) if the subpoenaing party does not agree in writing to cancel or limit the subpoena, an attorney should be consulted about the employee's interest in protecting his or her rights of privacy. If a notice of taking of deposition is also served, that other notice may be set forth in a single document with the notice required by this subdivision.

(f)(1) Any employee whose employment records are sought by a subpoena duces tecum may, prior to the date for production, bring a motion under Section 1987.1 to quash or modify the subpoena duces tecum. Notice of the bringing of that motion shall be given to the witness and the deposition officer at least five days prior to production. The failure to provide notice to the deposition officer does not invalidate the motion to quash or modify the subpoena duces tecum but may be raised by the deposition officer as an affirmative defense in any action for liability for improper release of records.

(2) Any nonparty employee whose employment records are sought by a subpoena duces tecum may, prior to the date of production, serve on the subpoenaing party, the deposition officer, and the witness a written objection that cites the specific grounds on which production of the employment records should be prohibited.

(3) No witness or deposition officer shall be required to produce employment records after receipt of notice that the motion has been brought by an employee, or after receipt of a written objection from a nonparty employee, except upon order of the court in which the action is pending or by agreement of the parties, witnesses, and employees affected.

(4) The party requesting an employee's employment records may bring a motion under subdivision (c) of Section 1987 to enforce the subpoena within 20 days of service of the written objection. The motion shall be accompanied by a declaration showing a reasonable and good faith attempt at informal resolution of the dispute between the party requesting the employment records and the employee or the employee's attorney.

(g) Upon good cause shown and provided that the rights of witnesses and employees are preserved, a subpoenaing party shall be entitled to obtain an order shortening the time for service of a subpoena duces tecum or waiving the requirements of subdivision (b) if due diligence by the subpoenaing party has been shown.

(h) This section may not be construed to apply to any subpoena duces tecum that does not request the records of any particular employee or employees and that requires a custodian of records to delete all information that would in any way identify any employee whose records are to be produced.

(i) This section does not apply to proceedings conducted under Division 1 (commencing with Section 50), Division 4 (commencing with Section 3200), Division 4.5 (commencing with Section 6100), or Division 4.7 (commencing with Section 6200), of the Labor Code.

(j) Failure to comply with this section shall be sufficient basis for the witness to refuse to produce the employment records sought by subpoena duces tecum.

(k) If the subpoenaing party is the employee, and the employee is the only subject of the subpoenaed records, notice to the employee, and delivery of the other documents specified in subdivision (b) to the employee, are not required under this section. *(Added by Stats.1995, c. 299 (A.B.617), § 1. Amended by Stats.1996, c. 679 (S.B.1821), § 2; Stats.1997, c. 442 (A.B.758), § 11; Stats.1998, c. 932 (A.B.1094), § 20; Stats.1999, c. 444 (A.B.794), § 2; Stats.2004, c. 182 (A.B.3081), § 19, operative July 1, 2005; Stats.2004, c. 101 (S.B.1465), § 1; Stats.2005, c. 22 (S.B.1108), § 20; Stats.2005, c. 294 (A.B.333), § 5; Stats.2005, c. 300 (A.B.496), § 7.5; Stats.2006, c. 538 (S.B.1852), § 76; Stats. 2012, c. 72 (S.B.1574), § 3.)*

Law Revision Commission Comments

Subdivisions (a) and (d) of Section 1985.6 are amended to reflect nonsubstantive reorganization of the rules governing civil discovery. See 2004 Cal. Stat. ch. 182. Subdivision (b) is amended to correct a cross-reference. Subdivision (f) is amended to make a grammatical correction.

Research References

Rutter, Cal. Practice Guide: Civ. Pro. Before Trial Ch. 8C-5, Privacy Protection.
Rutter, Cal. Practice Guide: Civ. Pro. Before Trial Ch. 8E-6, Subpoena to Nonparty Deponent or Business Records Custodian.
Rutter, Cal. Practice Guide: Civ. Pro. Before Trial Ch. 8E-6, Outline 6.
Rutter, Cal. Practice Guide: Civil Trials & Evidence Ch. 1-C, C. Marshalling the Evidence.
Rutter, Cal. Practice Guide: Civil Trials & Evidence Ch. 8E-C, C. Right of Privacy.
Rutter, Cal. Practice Guide: Civil Trials & Evidence Ch. 1-C, Outline C.
California Practice Guide: Employment Litigation Ch. 19-F, F. Discovery.
Rutter, Cal. Practice Guide: Enforcing Judgments/Debts Ch. 6G-1, Examination of Judgment Debtor and Third Parties.
Rutter, Cal. Practice Guide: Fed.Civ.Pro. Before Trial Ch. 11(IV)-A, A. Depositions.
Rutter, Cal. Practice Guide: Fed.Civ.Pro. Before Trial Ch. 11(III)-B, B. Scope of Discovery.
Rutter, Cal. Practice Guide: Personal Injury Ch. 6-B, B. Overview of Selected Discovery Procedures.
Rutter, Cal. Practice Guide: Personal Injury Ch. 8-B, B. After Trial Date Set (Three to Four Months Before Trial).
Rutter, Cal. Practice Guide: Personal Injury Ch. 8-C, C. Two Months Before Trial.
Rutter, Cal. Practice Guide: Prof. Responsibility Ch. 11-H, H. Proceedings Before Trial.

§ 1985.7. Medical records; failure to produce; order to show cause

When a medical provider fails to comply with Section 1158 of the Evidence Code, in addition to any other available remedy, the demanding party may apply to the court for an order to show cause why the records should not be produced.

Any order to show cause issued pursuant to this section shall be served upon respondent in the same manner as a summons. It shall be returnable no sooner than 20 days after issuance unless ordered otherwise upon a showing of substantial hardship. The court shall impose monetary sanctions pursuant to Section 1158 of the Evidence Code unless it finds that the person subject to the sanction acted with substantial justification or that other circumstances make the imposition of the sanction unjust. *(Added by Stats.1996, c. 1159 (A.B.3471), § 12.)*

Research References

Rutter, Cal. Practice Guide: Civ. Pro. Before Trial Ch. 1-C, C. Prelawsuit Notices, Claims and Demands.
Rutter, Cal. Practice Guide: Civ. Pro. Before Trial Ch. 8C-5, Privacy Protection.

Rutter, Cal. Practice Guide: Civ. Pro. Before Trial Ch. 8K-6, Special Statutes and Court Rules.

§ 1985.8. Electronically stored information; form of production; objection to form of production; undue burden or expense; limits on discovery

(a)(1) A subpoena in a civil proceeding may require that electronically stored information, as defined in Section 2016.020, be produced and that the party serving the subpoena, or someone acting on the party's request, be permitted to inspect, copy, test, or sample the information.

(2) Any subpoena seeking electronically stored information shall comply with the requirements of this chapter.

(b) A party serving a subpoena requiring production of electronically stored information may specify the form or forms in which each type of information is to be produced.

(c) If a person responding to a subpoena for production of electronically stored information objects to the specified form or forms for producing the information, the subpoenaed person may provide an objection stating the form or forms in which it intends to produce each type of information.

(d) Unless the subpoenaing party and the subpoenaed person otherwise agree or the court otherwise orders, the following shall apply:

(1) If a subpoena requiring production of electronically stored information does not specify a form or forms for producing a type of electronically stored information, the person subpoenaed shall produce the information in the form or forms in which it is ordinarily maintained or in a form that is reasonably usable.

(2) A subpoenaed person need not produce the same electronically stored information in more than one form.

(e) The subpoenaed person opposing the production, inspection, copying, testing, or sampling of electronically stored information on the basis that information is from a source that is not reasonably accessible because of undue burden or expense shall bear the burden of demonstrating that the information is from a source that is not reasonably accessible because of undue burden or expense.

(f) If the person from whom discovery of electronically stored information is subpoenaed establishes that the information is from a source that is not reasonably accessible because of undue burden or expense, the court may nonetheless order discovery if the subpoenaing party shows good cause, subject to any limitations imposed under subdivision (i).

(g) If the court finds good cause for the production of electronically stored information from a source that is not reasonably accessible, the court may set conditions for the discovery of the electronically stored information, including allocation of the expense of discovery.

(h) If necessary, the subpoenaed person, at the reasonable expense of the subpoenaing party, shall, through detection devices, translate any data compilations included in the subpoena into a reasonably usable form.

(i) The court shall limit the frequency or extent of discovery of electronically stored information, even from a source that is reasonably accessible, if the court determines that any of the following conditions exists:

(1) It is possible to obtain the information from some other source that is more convenient, less burdensome, or less expensive.

(2) The discovery sought is unreasonably cumulative or duplicative.

(3) The party seeking discovery has had ample opportunity by discovery in the action to obtain the information sought.

(4) The likely burden or expense of the proposed discovery outweighs the likely benefit, taking into account the amount in controversy, the resources of the parties, the importance of the issues in the litigation, and the importance of the requested discovery in resolving the issues.

(j) If a subpoenaed person notifies the subpoenaing party that electronically stored information produced pursuant to a subpoena is subject to a claim of privilege or of protection as attorney work product, as described in Section 2031.285, the provisions of Section 2031.285 shall apply.

(k) A party serving a subpoena requiring the production of electronically stored information shall take reasonable steps to avoid imposing undue burden or expense on a person subject to the subpoena.

(*l*) An order of the court requiring compliance with a subpoena issued under this section shall protect a person who is neither a party nor a party's officer from undue burden or expense resulting from compliance.

(m)(1) Absent exceptional circumstances, the court shall not impose sanctions on a subpoenaed person or any attorney of a subpoenaed person for failure to provide electronically stored information that has been lost, damaged, altered, or overwritten as the result of the routine, good faith operation of an electronic information system.

(2) This subdivision shall not be construed to alter any obligation to preserve discoverable information. *(Added by Stats.2009, c. 5 (A.B.5), § 2, eff. June 29, 2009. Amended by Stats.2012, c. 72 (S.B.1574), § 4.)*

Research References

Rutter, Cal. Practice Guide: Civ. Pro. Before Trial Ch. 8A-3, Civil Discovery Act.

Rutter, Cal. Practice Guide: Civ. Pro. Before Trial Ch. 8A-7, Duty to Preserve Evidence Before Discovery Request?

Rutter, Cal. Practice Guide: Civ. Pro. Before Trial Ch. 8E-5, Subpoena Not Necessary for Party or "Party-Affiliated" Witnesses.

Rutter, Cal. Practice Guide: Civ. Pro. Before Trial Ch. 8E-6, Subpoena to Nonparty Deponent or Business Records Custodian.

Rutter, Cal. Practice Guide: Personal Injury Ch. 6-B, B. Overview of Selected Discovery Procedures.

§ 1986. Subpoena; obtainable

A subpoena is obtainable as follows:

(a) To require attendance before a court, or at the trial of an issue therein, or upon the taking of a deposition in an action or proceeding pending therein, it is obtainable from the clerk of the court in which the action or proceeding is pending.

(b) To require attendance before a commissioner appointed to take testimony by a court of a foreign country, or of the United States, or of any other state in the United States, or before any officer or officers empowered by the laws of the United States to take testimony, it may be obtained from the clerk of the superior court of the county in which the witness is to be examined.

(c) To require attendance out of court, in cases not provided for in subdivision (a), before a judge, justice, or other officer authorized to administer oaths or take testimony in any matter under the laws of this state, it is obtainable from the judge, justice, or other officer before whom the attendance is required.

If the subpoena is to require attendance before a court, or at the trial of an issue therein, it is obtainable from the clerk, as of course, upon the application of the party desiring it. If it is obtained to require attendance before a commissioner or other officer upon the taking of a deposition, it must be obtained, as of course, from the clerk of the superior court of the county wherein the attendance is required upon the application of the party requiring it. *(Enacted in 1872. Amended by Stats.1907, c. 391, p. 730, § 1; Stats.1929, c. 110, p. 197, § 1; Stats.1957, c. 1904, p. 3321, § 2, operative Jan. 1, 1958; Stats.1979, c. 458, p. 1607, § 2; Stats.2007, c. 263 (A.B.310), § 14.)*

Law Revision Commission Comments

Section 1986 is amended to delete unnecessary language authorizing the judge to substitute for the clerk if there is no clerk. See Code Civ. Proc. § 167 (judge may perform any act court clerk may perform); Gov't Code §§ 69840–69848 (duties of clerk of superior court), 71620(b) (executive or administrative officer has authority of clerk of court). [35 Cal.L.Rev. Comm. Reports 219 (2007)].

Research References

2 Witkin Cal. Proc. 5th Courts § 363, (S 363) Process and Notices.

§ 1986.1. Testimony given by journalist under subpoena; immunity rights; notice

(a) No testimony or other evidence given by a journalist under subpoena in a civil or criminal proceeding may be construed as a waiver of the immunity rights provided by subdivision (b) of Section 2 of Article I of the California Constitution.

(b)(1) Because important constitutional rights of a third-party witness are adjudicated when rights under subdivision (b) of Section 2 of Article I of the California Constitution are asserted, except in * * * circumstances <u>that pose a clear and substantial threat to the integrity of the criminal investigation or present an imminent risk of death or serious bodily harm,</u> a journalist who is subpoenaed in any civil or criminal proceeding shall be given at least five days' notice by the party issuing the subpoena that his or her appearance will be required.

<u>(2) To protect against the inadvertent disclosure by a third party of information protected by Section 2 of Article I of the California Constitution, a party issuing a subpoena in any civil or criminal proceeding to a third party that seeks the records of a journalist shall, except in circumstances that pose a clear and substantial threat to the integrity of the criminal investigation or present an imminent risk of death or serious bodily harm, provide notice of the subpoena to the journalist and the publisher of the newspaper, magazine, or other publication or station operations manager of the broadcast station that employs or contracts with the journalist, as applicable, at least five days prior to issuing the subpoena.</u> The party issuing the subpoena shall include in the notice, at a minimum, an explanation of why the requested records will be of material assistance to the party seeking them and why alternate sources of information are not sufficient to avoid the need for the subpoena.

(c) If a trial court holds a journalist in contempt of court in a criminal proceeding notwithstanding subdivision (b) of Section 2 of Article I of the California Constitution, the court shall set forth findings, either in writing or on the record, stating at a minimum, why the information will be of material assistance to the party seeking the evidence, and why alternate sources of information are not sufficient to satisfy the defendant's right to a fair trial under the Sixth Amendment to the United States Constitution and Section 15 of Article I of the California Constitution.

(d) As used in this section, "journalist" means the persons specified in subdivision (b) of Section 2 of Article I of the California Constitution. *(Added by Stats.2000, c. 377 (A.B.1860), § 1. Amended by Stats.2013, c. 519 (S.B.558), § 1.)*

Research References

Rutter, Cal. Practice Guide: Civ. Pro. Before Trial Ch. 8C-6, Protection for News Media.
Rutter, Cal. Practice Guide: Civ. Pro. Before Trial Ch. 8E-6, Subpoena to Nonparty Deponent or Business Records Custodian.

Rutter, Cal. Practice Guide: Civil Trials & Evidence Ch. 1-C, C. Marshalling the Evidence.
Rutter, Cal. Practice Guide: Civil Trials & Evidence Ch. 8E-A, A. Privileges.
Rutter, Cal. Practice Guide: Personal Injury Ch. 6-A, A. Scope of Discovery and Limitations.

§ 1986.5. Witness fees and mileage for persons required to give depositions; fees for production of business records

Any person who is subpoenaed and required to give a deposition shall be entitled to receive the same witness fees and mileage as if the subpoena required him or her to attend and testify before a court in which the action or proceeding is pending. Notwithstanding this requirement, the only fees owed to a witness who is required to produce business records under Section 1560 of the Evidence Code pursuant to a subpoena duces tecum, but who is not required to personally attend a deposition away from his or her place of business, shall be those prescribed in Section 1563 of the Evidence Code. *(Added by Stats.1961, c. 1386, p. 3159, § 1. Amended by Stats.1986, c. 603, § 4.)*

Research References

Rutter, Cal. Practice Guide: Civ. Pro. Before Trial Ch. 8E-6, Subpoena to Nonparty Deponent or Business Records Custodian.
Rutter, Cal. Practice Guide: Personal Injury Ch. 6-B, B. Overview of Selected Discovery Procedures.

§ 1987. Subpoena; notice to produce party or agent; method of service; production of books, documents, and electronically stored information

(a) Except as provided in Sections 68097.1 to 68097.8, inclusive, of the Government Code, the service of a subpoena is made by delivering a copy, or a ticket containing its substance, to the witness personally, giving or offering to the witness at the same time, if demanded by him or her, the fees to which he or she is entitled for travel to and from the place designated, and one day's attendance there. The service shall be made so as to allow the witness a reasonable time for preparation and travel to the place of attendance. The service may be made by any person. If service is to be made on a minor, service shall be made on the minor's parent, guardian, conservator, or similar fiduciary, or if one of those persons cannot be located with reasonable diligence, service shall be made on any person having the care or control of the minor or with whom the minor resides or by whom the minor is employed, and on the minor if the minor is 12 years of age or older. If the minor is alleged to come within the description of Section 300, 601, or 602 of the Welfare and Institutions Code and the minor is not in the custody of a parent or guardian, regardless of the age of the minor, service also shall be made upon the designated agent for service of process at the county child welfare department or the probation department under whose jurisdiction the minor has been placed.

(b) In the case of the production of a party to the record of any civil action or proceeding or of a person for whose immediate benefit an action or proceeding is prosecuted or defended or of anyone who is an officer, director, or managing agent of any such party or person, the service of a subpoena upon any such witness is not required if written notice requesting the witness to attend before a court, or at a trial of an issue therein, with the time and place thereof, is served upon the attorney of that party or person. The notice shall be served at least 10 days before the time required for attendance unless the court prescribes a shorter time. If entitled thereto, the witness, upon demand, shall be paid witness fees and mileage before being required to testify. The giving of the notice shall have the same effect as service of a subpoena on the witness, and the parties shall have those rights and the court may make those orders, including the imposition of sanctions, as in the case of a subpoena for attendance before the court.

(c) If the notice specified in subdivision (b) is served at least 20 days before the time required for attendance, or within any shorter period of time as the court may order, it may include a request that the party or person bring with him or her books, documents, electronically stored information, or other things. The notice shall state the exact materials or things desired and that the party or person has them in his or her possession or under his or her control. Within five days thereafter, or any other time period as the court may allow, the party or person of whom the request is made may serve written objections to the request or any part thereof, with a statement of grounds. Thereafter, upon noticed motion of the requesting party, accompanied by a showing of good cause and of materiality of the items to the issues, the court may order production of items to which objection was made, unless the objecting party or person establishes good cause for nonproduction or production under limitations or conditions. The procedure of this subdivision is alternative to the procedure provided by Sections 1985 and 1987.5 in the cases herein provided for, and no subpoena duces tecum shall be required.

Subject to this subdivision, the notice provided in this subdivision shall have the same effect as is provided in subdivision (b) as to a notice for attendance of that party or person. *(Enacted in 1872. Amended by Stats.1963, c. 1485, p. 3049, § 3; Stats.1968, c. 933, p. 1783, § 1; Stats.1969, c. 311, p. 678, § 1; Stats.1969, c. 1034, p. 2013, § 1.5; Stats.1981, c. 184, p. 1105, § 2; Stats.1986, c. 605, § 2; Stats.1989, c. 1416, § 28; Stats.2002, c. 1008 (A.B.3028), § 6; Stats.2012, c. 72 (S.B.1574), § 5.)*

Research References

Rutter, Cal. Practice Guide: Civ. Pro. Before Trial Ch. 2-B, B. Capacity to Sue or Defend.

Rutter, Cal. Practice Guide: Civ. Pro. Before Trial Ch. 8E-1, When Prior Court Order Required.

Rutter, Cal. Practice Guide: Civ. Pro. Before Trial Ch. 8E-6, Subpoena to Nonparty Deponent or Business Records Custodian.

Rutter, Cal. Practice Guide: Civ. Pro. Before Trial Ch. 8E-1, Outline 1.

Rutter, Cal. Practice Guide: Civil Trials & Evidence Ch. 1-C, C. Marshalling the Evidence.

Rutter, Cal. Practice Guide: Civil Trials & Evidence Ch. 9-A, A. Preliminary Considerations.

Rutter, Cal. Practice Guide: Civil Trials & Evidence Ch. 9-C, C. Direct Examination of Adverse Witness (EV.C. § 776).

Rutter, Cal. Practice Guide: Civil Trials & Evidence Ch. 8C-B, B. Writings.

California Practice Guide: Employment Litigation Ch. 13-H, H. Contesting Citations and Related Orders and Notices.

Rutter, Cal. Practice Guide: Enforcing Judgments/Debts Ch. 6G-1, Examination of Judgment Debtor and Third Parties.

Rutter, Cal. Practice Guide: Personal Injury Ch. 8-C, C. Two Months Before Trial.

Rutter, Cal. Practice Guide: Prof. Responsibility Ch. 11-F, F. Investigation Stage.

Rutter, Cal. Practice Guide: Prof. Responsibility Ch. 11-H, H. Proceedings Before Trial.

9 Witkin Cal. Proc. 5th Administrative Proceedings § 89, (S 89) Subpenas.

§ 1987.1. Subpoena; motion and order to quash; other orders

(a) If a subpoena requires the attendance of a witness or the production of books, documents, electronically stored information, or other things before a court, or at the trial of an issue therein, or at the taking of a deposition, the court, upon motion reasonably made by any person described in subdivision (b), or upon the court's own motion after giving counsel notice and an opportunity to be heard, may make an order quashing the subpoena entirely, modifying it, or directing compliance with it upon those terms or conditions as the court shall declare, including protective orders. In addition, the court may make any other order as may be appropriate to protect the person from unreasonable or oppressive demands, including unreasonable violations of the right of privacy of the person.

(b) The following persons may make a motion pursuant to subdivision (a):

(1) A party.

(2) A witness.

(3) A consumer described in Section 1985.3.

(4) An employee described in Section 1985.6.

(5) A person whose personally identifying information, as defined in subdivision (b) of Section 1798.79.8 of the Civil Code, is sought in connection with an underlying action involving that person's exercise of free speech rights.

(c) Nothing in this section shall require any person to move to quash, modify, or condition any subpoena duces tecum of personal records of any consumer served under paragraph (1) of subdivision (b) of Section 1985.3 or employment records of any employee served under paragraph (1) of subdivision (b) of Section 1985.6. *(Added by Stats.1976, c. 1168, p. 5249, § 1. Amended by Stats.1980, c. 976, p. 3102, § 2, operative July 1, 1981; Stats.1997, c. 442 (A.B.758), § 12; Stats.2007, c. 113 (A.B.1126), § 3; Stats.2008, c. 742 (A.B.2433), § 1; Stats.2012, c. 72 (S.B.1574), § 6.)*

Law Revision Commission Comments

Section 1987.1 is amended to clarify its application when employment records of an employee are subpoenaed under Section 1985.6. [36 Cal.L.Rev.Comm. Reports 271 (2007)].

Research References

Rutter, Cal. Practice Guide: A.D.R. Ch. 5-H, H. Conduct of Arbitration Proceedings.

Rutter, Cal. Practice Guide: Civ. Pro. Before Trial Ch. 8E-5, Subpoena Not Necessary for Party or "Party-Affiliated" Witnesses.

Rutter, Cal. Practice Guide: Civ. Pro. Before Trial Ch. 8E-6, Subpoena to Nonparty Deponent or Business Records Custodian.

Rutter, Cal. Practice Guide: Civil Trials & Evidence Ch. 1-C, C. Marshalling the Evidence.

Rutter, Cal. Practice Guide: Civil Trials & Evidence Ch. 8E-C, C. Right of Privacy.

Rutter, Cal. Practice Guide: Enforcing Judgments/Debts Ch. 6G-1, Examination of Judgment Debtor and Third Parties.

§ 1987.2. Award of reasonable expenses and reasonable attorney's fees incurred in making or opposing motion; failure to provide lost, damaged, altered, or overwritten electronically stored information; award of reasonable expenses and attorney's fees in making a motion in an action arising from free speech rights on the Internet

(a) Except as specified in subdivision (c), in making an order pursuant to motion made under subdivision (c) of Section 1987 or under Section 1987.1, the court may in its discretion award the amount of the reasonable expenses incurred in making or opposing the motion, including reasonable attorney's fees, if the court finds the motion was made or opposed in bad faith or without substantial justification or that one or more of the requirements of the subpoena was oppressive.

(b)(1) Notwithstanding subdivision (a), absent exceptional circumstances, the court shall not impose sanctions on a subpoenaed person or the attorney of a subpoenaed person for failure to provide electronically stored information that has been lost, damaged, altered, or overwritten as the result of the routine, good faith operation of an electronic information system.

(2) This subdivision shall not be construed to alter any obligation to preserve discoverable information.

(c) If a motion is filed under Section 1987.1 for an order to quash or modify a subpoena from a court of this state for personally identifying information, as defined in subdivision (b) of Section 1798.79.8 of the Civil Code, for use in an action pending in another state, territory, or district of the United States, or in a foreign nation, and that subpoena has been served on any Internet service provider, or on the provider of any other interactive computer service, as defined in Section 230(f)(2) of Title 47 of the United States Code, if the moving party prevails, and if the underlying action arises from the moving party's exercise of free speech rights on the Internet and the respondent has failed to make a prima facie showing of a cause of action, the court shall award the amount of the reasonable expenses incurred in making the motion, including reasonable attorney's fees. *(Added by Stats.1976, c. 1168, p. 5249, § 2. Amended by Stats.2008, c. 742 (A.B.2433), § 2; Stats.2012, c. 72 (S.B.1574), § 7.)*

Research References

Rutter, Cal. Practice Guide: Civ. Pro. Before Trial Ch. 8C-3, "Not Privileged".
Rutter, Cal. Practice Guide: Civ. Pro. Before Trial Ch. 8E-6, Subpoena to Nonparty Deponent or Business Records Custodian.
Rutter, Cal. Practice Guide: Civ. Pro. Before Trial Ch. 8E-16, Sanctions Re Depositions.
Rutter, Cal. Practice Guide: Civil Trials & Evidence Ch. 1-C, C. Marshalling the Evidence.

§ 1987.3. Service of subpoena duces tecum upon custodian of records or other qualified witness under Evidence Code section 1560

When a subpoena duces tecum is served upon a custodian of records or other qualified witness as provided in Article 4 (commencing with Section 1560) of Chapter 2 of Division 11 of the Evidence Code, and his personal attendance is not required by the terms of the subpoena, Section 1989 shall not apply. *(Added by Stats.1970, c. 590, p. 1171, § 1.)*

Research References

Rutter, Cal. Practice Guide: Civil Trials & Evidence Ch. 1-C, C. Marshalling the Evidence.
Rutter, Cal. Practice Guide: Enforcing Judgments/Debts Ch. 6G-1, Examination of Judgment Debtor and Third Parties.

§ 1987.5. Subpoena duces tecum; conditions to validity; original affidavit; deposition subpoenas for production of business records

The service of a subpoena duces tecum is invalid unless at the time of such service a copy of the affidavit upon which the subpoena is based is served on the person served with the subpoena. In the case of a subpoena duces tecum which requires appearance and the production of matters and things at the taking of a deposition, the subpoena shall not be valid unless a copy of the affidavit upon which the subpoena is based and the designation of the materials to be produced, as set forth in the subpoena, is attached to the notice of taking the deposition served upon each party or its attorney as provided in Chapter 3 (commencing with Section 2002) and in Title 4 (commencing with Section 2016.010). If matters and things are produced pursuant to a subpoena duces tecum in violation of this section, any other party to the action may file a motion for, and the court may grant, an order providing appropriate relief, including, but not limited to, exclusion of the evidence affected by the violation, a retaking of the deposition notwithstanding any other limitation on discovery proceedings, or a continuance. The party causing the subpoena to be served shall retain the original affidavit until final judgment in the action, and shall file the affidavit with the court only upon reasonable request by any party or witness affected thereby. This section does not apply to deposition subpoenas commanding only the production of business records for copying under Article 4 (commencing with Section 2020.410) of Chapter 6 of Title 4. *(Added by Stats.1951, c. 1413, p. 3368,*

§ 1. Amended by Stats.1968, c. 95, p. 1783, § 2; Stats.1981, c. 189, p. 1114, § 1; Stats.1982, c. 452, § 2; Stats.1985, c. 1239, § 1; Stats.1993, c. 926 (A.B.2205), § 7; Stats.2004, c. 182 (A.B.3081), § 20, operative July 1, 2005.)

Law Revision Commission Comments

Section 1987.5 is amended to reflect nonsubstantive reorganization of the rules governing civil discovery. [33 Cal.L.Rev.Comm. Reports 1008 (2004)].

Research References

Rutter, Cal. Practice Guide: Civ. Pro. Before Trial Ch. 8E-6, Subpoena to Nonparty Deponent or Business Records Custodian.
Rutter, Cal. Practice Guide: Civil Trials & Evidence Ch. 1-C, C. Marshalling the Evidence.
Rutter, Cal. Practice Guide: Personal Injury Ch. 6-B, B. Overview of Selected Discovery Procedures.

§ 1988. Subpoena; service; witness concealed

If a witness is concealed in a building or vessel, so as to prevent the service of a subpoena upon him, any Court or Judge, or any officer issuing the subpoena, may, upon proof by affidavit of the concealment, and of the materiality of the witness, make an order that the Sheriff of the county serve the subpoena; and the Sheriff must serve it accordingly, and for that purpose may break into the building or vessel where the witness is concealed. *(Enacted in 1872.)*

Research References

Rutter, Cal. Practice Guide: Civil Trials & Evidence Ch. 1-C, C. Marshalling the Evidence.
California Practice Guide: Employment Litigation Ch. 13-H, H. Contesting Citations and Related Orders and Notices.
9 Witkin Cal. Proc. 5th Administrative Proceedings § 89, (S 89) Subpenas.

§ 1989. Residency requirements for attendance of witnesses

A witness, including a witness specified in subdivision (b) of Section 1987, is not obliged to attend as a witness before any court, judge, justice or any other officer, unless the witness is a resident within the state at the time of service. *(Enacted in 1872. Amended by Stats.1915, c. 162, p. 330, § 1; Stats.1935, c. 257, p. 942, § 1; Stats.1957, c. 1560, p. 2918, § 1; Stats.1980, c. 591, p. 1603, § 1; Stats.1981, c. 184, p. 1106, § 3.)*

Research References

Rutter, Cal. Practice Guide: Civ. Pro. Before Trial Ch. 8E-8, Place of Deposition.
Rutter, Cal. Practice Guide: Civ. Pro. Before Trial Ch. 8E-6, Subpoena to Nonparty Deponent or Business Records Custodian.
Rutter, Cal. Practice Guide: Civ. Pro. Before Trial Gen. Matls., Highlights.
Rutter, Cal. Practice Guide: Civil Trials & Evidence Ch. 1-C, C. Marshalling the Evidence.
Rutter, Cal. Practice Guide: Civil Trials & Evidence Ch. 8D-C, C. General Parameters Re Admissibility of Hearsay Evidence.
Rutter, Cal. Practice Guide: Enforcing Judgments/Debts Ch. 6G-1, Examination of Judgment Debtor and Third Parties.
Rutter, Cal. Practice Guide: Personal Injury Ch. 6-B, B. Overview of Selected Discovery Procedures.
Rutter, Cal. Practice Guide: Personal Injury Ch. 8-C, C. Two Months Before Trial.
Rutter, Cal. Practice Guide: Personal Injury Gen. Matls., Highlights.

§ 1990. Person present; compelling to testify

A person present in Court, or before a judicial officer, may be required to testify in the same manner as if he were in attendance upon a subpoena issued by such Court or officer. *(Enacted in 1872.)*

Research References

Rutter, Cal. Practice Guide: Civil Trials & Evidence Ch. 1-C, C. Marshalling the Evidence.

§ 1991. Disobedience to subpoena; refusal to be sworn, to answer as witness, or to subscribe affidavit or deposition; contempt; report of disobedience

Disobedience to a subpoena, or a refusal to be sworn, or to answer as a witness, or to subscribe an affidavit or deposition when required, may be punished as a contempt by the court issuing the subpoena.

When the subpoena, in any such case, requires the attendance of the witness before an officer or commissioner out of court, it is the duty of the officer or commissioner to report any disobedience or refusal to be sworn or to answer a question or to subscribe an affidavit or deposition when required, to the court issuing the subpoena. The witness shall not be punished for any refusal to be sworn or to answer a question or to subscribe an affidavit or deposition, unless, after a hearing upon notice, the court orders the witness to be sworn, or to so answer or subscribe and then only for disobedience to the order.

Any judge, justice, or other officer mentioned in subdivision (c) of Section 1986, may report any disobedience or refusal to be sworn or to answer a question or to subscribe an affidavit or deposition when required to the superior court of the county in which attendance was required; and the court thereupon has power, upon notice, to order the witness to perform the omitted act, and any refusal or neglect to comply with the order may be punished as a contempt of court.

In lieu of the reporting of the refusal as hereinabove provided, the party seeking to obtain the deposition or to have the deposition or affidavit signed, at the time of the refusal may request the officer or commissioner to notify the witness that at a time stated, not less than five days nor more than 20 days from the date of the refusal, he or she will report the refusal of the witness to the court and that the party will, at that time, or as soon thereafter as he or she may be heard, apply to the court for an order directing the witness to be sworn, or to answer as a witness, or subscribe the deposition or affidavit, as the case may be, and that the witness is required to attend that session of the court.

The officer or commissioner shall enter in the record of the proceedings an exact transcription of the request made of him or her that he or she notify the witness that the party will apply for an order directing the witness to be sworn or to answer as a witness or subscribe the deposition or affidavit, and of his or her notice to the witness, and the transcription shall be attached to his or her report to the court of the refusal of the witness. The report shall be filed by the officer with the clerk of the court issuing the subpoena, and the witness shall attend that session of the court, and for failure or refusal to do so may be punished for contempt.

At the time so specified by the officer, or at a subsequent time to which the court may have continued the matter, if the officer has theretofore filed a report showing the refusal of the witness, the court shall hear the matter, and without further notice to the witness, may order the witness to be sworn or to answer as a witness or subscribe the deposition or affidavit, as the case may be, and may in the order specify the time and place at which compliance shall be made or to which the taking of the deposition is continued. Thereafter if the witness refuses to comply with the order he or she may be punished for contempt. *(Enacted in 1872. Amended by Stats.1907, c. 391, p. 731, § 2; Stats.1941, c. 406, p. 1690, § 1; Stats.1987, c. 56, § 24.)*

Research References

Rutter, Cal. Practice Guide: Civ. Pro. Before Trial Ch. 8E-6, Subpoena to Nonparty Deponent or Business Records Custodian.
Rutter, Cal. Practice Guide: Civil Trials & Evidence Ch. 1-C, C. Marshalling the Evidence.
Rutter, Cal. Practice Guide: Civil Trials & Evidence Ch. 12-E, E. Contempt Proceedings.
7 Witkin Cal. Proc. 5th Trial § 171, (S 171) Statutory Framework.
7 Witkin Cal. Proc. 5th Trial § 199, (S 199) Assisting Witness to Evade Subpena.
7 Witkin Cal. Proc. 5th Trial § 200, in General.
11 Witkin, California Summary 10th Husband and Wife § 291, (S 291) Discovery.

§ 1991.1. Depositions; disobedience to subpoena or refusal to be sworn; punishment

Disobedience to a subpoena requiring attendance of a witness before an officer out of court in a deposition taken pursuant to Title 4 (commencing with Section 2016.010), or refusal to be sworn as a witness at that deposition, may be punished as contempt, as provided in subdivision (e) of Section 2023.030, without the necessity of a prior order of court directing compliance by the witness. *(Added by Stats.1959, c. 1590, p. 3933, § 13. Amended by Stats.1996, c. 124 (A.B.3470), § 15.5; Stats.2004, c. 182 (A.B.3081), § 21, operative July 1, 2005.)*

Law Revision Commission Comments

Section 1991.1 is amended to reflect nonsubstantive reorganization of the rules governing civil discovery. [33 Cal.L.Rev.Comm. Reports 1009 (2004)].

Research References

Rutter, Cal. Practice Guide: Civ. Pro. Before Trial Ch. 8E-6, Subpoena to Nonparty Deponent or Business Records Custodian.
Rutter, Cal. Practice Guide: Civ. Pro. Before Trial Ch. 8E-16, Sanctions Re Depositions.
7 Witkin Cal. Proc. 5th Trial § 171, (S 171) Statutory Framework.
11 Witkin, California Summary 10th Husband and Wife § 291, (S 291) Discovery.

§ 1991.2. Depositions; applicability of section 1991

The provisions of Section 1991 do not apply to any act or omission occurring in a deposition taken pursuant to Title 4 (commencing with Section 2016.010). The provisions of Chapter 7 (commencing with Section 2023.010) of Title 4 are exclusively applicable. *(Added by Stats.1959, c. 1590, p. 3934, § 14. Amended by Stats.2005, c. 294 (A.B.333), § 6.)*

Law Revision Commission Comments

Section 1991.2 is amended to delete obsolete language, correct the cross-references, and conform to modern drafting conventions. For the text of former Section 2034, see 1959 Cal. Stat. ch. 1590, § 12. Former Section 2034 was repealed in 1986 and its substance relocated to Section 2023, which was in turn repealed and recodified in 2004, as part of a nonsubstantive reorganization of the Civil Discovery Act. 1986 Cal. Stat. ch. 1334, §§ 1, 2; 2004 Cal. Stat. ch. 182, §§ 22, 23, 23.5, 61, 62; see *Civil Discovery: Nonsubstantive Reform*, 33 Cal. L. Revision Comm'n Reports 789 (2003).

Research References

11 Witkin, California Summary 10th Husband and Wife § 291, (S 291) Discovery.

§ 1992. Disobedience to subpoena; forfeiture; damages

A person failing to appear pursuant to a subpoena or a court order also forfeits to the party aggrieved the sum of five hundred dollars ($500), and all damages that he or she may sustain by the failure of the person to appear pursuant to the subpoena or court order, which forfeiture and damages may be recovered in a civil action. *(Enacted in 1872. Amended by Stats.1978, c. 479, p. 1606, § 1; Stats.2005, c. 474 (A.B.1150), § 1.)*

Research References

Rutter, Cal. Practice Guide: Civ. Pro. Before Trial Ch. 8C-6, Protection for News Media.
Rutter, Cal. Practice Guide: Civ. Pro. Before Trial Ch. 8E-6, Subpoena to Nonparty Deponent or Business Records Custodian.
Rutter, Cal. Practice Guide: Civ. Pro. Before Trial Ch. 8E-16, Sanctions Re Depositions.
Rutter, Cal. Practice Guide: Civil Trials & Evidence Ch. 1-C, C. Marshalling the Evidence.
Rutter, Cal. Practice Guide: Civil Trials & Evidence Ch. 8E-A, A. Privileges.
Rutter, Cal. Practice Guide: Personal Injury Ch. 6-A, A. Scope of Discovery and Limitations.
11 Witkin, California Summary 10th Husband and Wife § 291, (S 291) Discovery.

§ 1993. Warrant for absent witness

(a)(1) As an alternative to issuing a warrant for contempt pursuant to paragraph (5) or (9) of subdivision (a) of Section 1209, the court may issue a warrant for the arrest of a witness who failed to appear pursuant to a subpoena or a person who failed to appear pursuant to a court order. The court, upon proof of the service of the subpoena or order, may issue a warrant to the sheriff of the county in which the witness or person may be located and the sheriff shall, upon payment of fees as provided in Section 26744.5 of the Government Code, arrest the witness or person and bring him or her before the court.

(2) Before issuing a warrant for a failure to appear pursuant to a subpoena pursuant to this section, the court shall issue a "failure to appear" notice informing the person subject to the subpoena that a failure to appear in response to the notice may result in the issuance of a warrant. This notice requirement may be omitted only upon a showing that the appearance of the person subject to the subpoena is material to the case and that urgency dictates the person's immediate appearance.

(b) The warrant shall contain all of the following:

(1) The title and case number of the action.

(2) The name and physical description of the person to be arrested.

(3) The last known address of the person to be arrested.

(4) The date of issuance and county in which it is issued.

(5) The signature or name of the judicial officer issuing the warrant, the title of his or her office, and the name of the court.

(6) A command to arrest the person for failing to appear pursuant to the subpoena or court order, and specifying the date of service of the subpoena or court order.

(7) A command to bring the person to be arrested before the issuing court, or the nearest court if in session, for the setting of bail in the amount of the warrant or to release on the person's own recognizance. Any person so arrested shall be released from custody if he or she cannot be brought before the court within 12 hours of arrest, and the person shall not be arrested if the court will not be in session during the 12–hour period following the arrest.

(8) A statement indicating the expiration date of the warrant as determined by the court.

(9) The amount of bail.

(10) An endorsement for nighttime service if good cause is shown, as provided in Section 840 of the Penal Code.

(11) A statement indicating whether the person may be released upon a promise to appear, as provided by Section 1993.1. The court shall permit release upon a promise to appear, unless it makes a written finding that the urgency and materiality of the person's appearance in court precludes use of the promise to appear process.

(12) The date and time to appear in court if arrested and released pursuant to paragraph (11). *(Added by Stats.2005, c. 474 (A.B.1150), § 3. Amended by Stats.2006, c. 277 (A.B.2369), § 3; Stats.2010, c. 680 (A.B.2394), § 15.)*

Research References

Rutter, Cal. Practice Guide: Civ. Pro. Before Trial Ch. 8E-6, Subpoena to Nonparty Deponent or Business Records Custodian.
Rutter, Cal. Practice Guide: Civil Trials & Evidence Ch. 1-C, C. Marshalling the Evidence.
Rutter, Cal. Practice Guide: Enforcing Judgments/Debts Ch. 4-A, A. Attachment.
Rutter, Cal. Practice Guide: Enforcing Judgments/Debts Ch. 6G-1, Examination of Judgment Debtor and Third Parties.
Miller and Starr California Real Estate § 11:156, Effect of an Expungement or Withdrawal; Appellate Review.
8 Witkin Cal. Proc. 5th Enforcement of Judgment § 288, (S 288) Failure to Appear for Examination.
6 Witkin Cal. Proc. 5th Provisional Remedies § 197, (S 197) Order to Appear.
11 Witkin, California Summary 10th Husband and Wife § 291, (S 291) Discovery.

§ 1993.1. Release of arrested witness upon promise to appear

(a) If authorized by the court as provided by paragraph (11) of subdivision (b) of Section 1993, the sheriff may release the person arrested upon his or her promise to appear as provided in this section.

(b) The sheriff shall prepare in duplicate a written notice to appear in court, containing the title of the case, case number, name and address of the person, the offense charged, and the time when, and place where, the person shall appear in court. In addition, the notice shall advise the person arrested of the provisions of Section 1992.

(c) The date and time specified in the notice to appear in court shall be that determined by the issuing court pursuant to paragraph (12) of subdivision (b) of Section 1993.

(d) The sheriff shall deliver one copy of the notice to appear to the arrested person, and the arrested person, in order to secure release, shall give his or her written promise to appear in court as specified in the notice by signing the duplicate notice, which shall be retained by the sheriff, and the sheriff may require the arrested person, if he or she has no satisfactory identification, to place a right thumbprint, or a left thumbprint or fingerprint if the person has a missing or disfigured right thumb, on the notice to appear. Except for law enforcement purposes relating to the identity of the arrestee, no person or entity may sell, give away, allow the distribution of, include in a database, or create a database with, this print. Upon the signing of the duplicate notice, the arresting officer shall immediately release the person arrested from custody.

(e) The sheriff shall, as soon as practicable, file the original notice with the issuing court. The notice may be electronically transmitted to the court.

(f) The person arrested shall be released unless one of the following is a reason for nonrelease, in which case the arresting officer either may release the person or shall indicate, on a form to be established by his or her employing law enforcement agency, which of the following was a reason for the nonrelease:

(1) The person arrested was so intoxicated that he or she could have been a danger to himself or herself or to others.

(2) The person arrested required medical examination or medical care or was otherwise unable to care for his or her own safety.

(3) There were one or more additional outstanding arrest warrants for the person.

(4) The person arrested demanded to be taken before a magistrate or refused to sign the notice to appear. *(Added by Stats.2005, c. 474 (A.B.1150), § 4.)*

§ 1993.2. Failure of released witness to appear as promised

If a person arrested on a civil bench warrant issued pursuant to Section 1993 fails to appear after being released on a promise to appear, the court may issue another warrant to bring the person before the court or assess a civil assessment in the amount of not more than one thousand dollars ($1,000), which shall be collected as follows:

(a) The assessment shall not become effective until at least 10 calendar days after the court mails a warning notice to the person by first-class mail to the address shown on the promise to appear or to the person's last known address. If the person appears within the time specified in the notice and shows good cause for the failure to appear or for the failure to pay a fine, the court shall vacate the assessment.

(b) The assessment imposed under subdivision (a) may be enforced in the same manner as a money judgment in a limited civil case, and shall be subject to the due process requirements governing defense of actions and collection of civil money judgments generally. *(Added by Stats.2005, c. 474 (A.B.1150), § 5.)*

Research References

Rutter, Cal. Practice Guide: Civ. Pro. Before Trial Ch. 8E-6, Subpoena to Nonparty Deponent or Business Records Custodian.

§ 1994. Warrants; contents; direction; execution

Every warrant of commitment, issued by a court or officer pursuant to this chapter, shall specify therein, particularly, the cause of the commitment, and if it be for refusing to answer a question, that question shall be stated in the warrant. *(Enacted in 1872. Amended Code Am.1880, c. 111, p. 115, § 1; Stats.2005, c. 474 (A.B.1150), § 6.)*

Research References

Rutter, Cal. Practice Guide: Civil Trials & Evidence Ch. 12-E, E. Contempt Proceedings.

§ 1995. Witness a prisoner; deposition; production before court; courts authorized to order production

If the witness be a prisoner, confined in a jail within this state, an order for his examination in the jail upon deposition, or for his temporary removal and production before a court or officer may be made as follows:

1. By the court itself in which the action or special proceeding is pending, unless it be a small claims court.

2. By a justice of the Supreme Court, or a judge of the superior court of the county where the action or proceeding is pending, if pending before a small claims court, or before a judge or other person out of court. *(Enacted in 1872. Amended by Code Am.1880, c. 111, p. 115, § 2; Stats.1941, c. 802, p. 2350, § 6; Stats.1951, c. 1737, p. 4143, § 172, operative Jan. 1, 1952; Stats.1977, c. 1257, p. 4770, § 40, eff. Jan. 3, 1977.)*

Research References

Rutter, Cal. Practice Guide: Civ. Pro. Before Trial Ch. 8E-1, When Prior Court Order Required.
Rutter, Cal. Practice Guide: Civ. Pro. Before Trial Ch. 8E-3, Whose Deposition May be Taken.

Rutter, Cal. Practice Guide: Personal Injury Ch. 8-C, C. Two Months Before Trial.

§ 1996. Witness a prisoner; order for production before court; motion; supporting affidavit

Such order can only be made on the motion of a party, upon affidavit showing the nature of the action or proceeding, the testimony expected from the witness, and its materiality. *(Enacted in 1872.)*

Research References

Rutter, Cal. Practice Guide: Civ. Pro. Before Trial Ch. 8E-3, Whose Deposition May be Taken.

§ 1997. Witness a prisoner; production before court in county of imprisonment; deposition

If the witness be imprisoned in a jail in the county where the action or proceeding is pending, his production may be required. In all other cases his examination, when allowed, must be taken upon deposition. *(Enacted in 1872. Amended by Stats.1941, c. 802, p. 2350, § 7.)*

Research References

Rutter, Cal. Practice Guide: A.D.R. Ch. 5-H, H. Conduct of Arbitration Proceedings.
Rutter, Cal. Practice Guide: Civ. Pro. Before Trial Ch. 8E-1, When Prior Court Order Required.
Rutter, Cal. Practice Guide: Civ. Pro. Before Trial Ch. 8E-3, Whose Deposition May be Taken.
Rutter, Cal. Practice Guide: Personal Injury Ch. 8-C, C. Two Months Before Trial.

CHAPTER 3. MANNER OF PRODUCTION

ARTICLE 1. MODE OF TAKING THE TESTIMONY OF WITNESSES

§ 2002. Modes in which testimony may be taken

The testimony of witnesses is taken in three modes:

1. By affidavit;

2. By deposition;

3. By oral examination. *(Enacted in 1872.)*

Research References

6 Witkin Cal. Proc. 5th Proceedings Without Trial § 594, (S 594) Discovery.

§ 2003. "Affidavit" defined

An affidavit is a written declaration under oath, made without notice to the adverse party. *(Enacted in 1872.)*

§ 2004. "Deposition" defined; default as waiver of notice of deposition proceedings

A deposition is a written declaration, under oath, made upon notice to the adverse party, for the purpose of enabling him to attend and cross-examine. In all actions and proceedings where the default of the defendant has been duly entered, and in all proceedings to obtain letters of administration, or for the probate of wills and the issuance of letters testamentary thereon, where, after due and legal notice, those entitled to contest the application have failed to appear, the entry of said defaults, and the failure of said persons to appear after notice, shall be deemed to be a waiver of the right to any further notice of any application or proceeding to take testimony by deposition in such action or proceeding. *(Enacted in 1872. Amended by Stats.1907, c. 527, p. 981, § 1.)*

§ 2005. "Oral examination" defined

An oral examination is an examination in presence of the jury or tribunal which is to decide the fact or act upon it, the testimony being heard by the jury or tribunal from the lips of the witness. *(Enacted in 1872.)*

ARTICLE 2. AFFIDAVITS

§ 2009. Use

An affidavit may be used to verify a pleading or a paper in a special proceeding, to prove the service of a summons, notice, or other paper in an action or special proceeding, to obtain a provisional remedy, the examination of a witness, or a stay of proceedings, and in uncontested proceedings to establish a record of birth, or upon a motion, and in any other case expressly permitted by statute. *(Enacted in 1872. Amended by Stats.1927, c. 242, p. 433, § 1; Stats.1929, c. 493, p. 856, § 1; Stats.1943, c. 11, p. 119, § 1, eff. Feb. 5, 1943; Stats.1943, c. 821, p. 2619, § 2, eff. May 28, 1943; Stats.1965, c. 299, p. 1363, § 124, operative Jan. 1, 1967.)*

Law Revision Commission Comments

Section 2009 has been amended to reflect the fact that statutes in other codes may also authorize the use of affidavits. See, e.g., Prob.Code §§ 630, 705. [7 Cal.L.Rev.Comm. Reports 1001 to 1337 (1965)].

§ 2010. Evidence of publication

Evidence of the publication of a document or notice required by law, or by an order of a Court or Judge, to be published in a newspaper, may be given by the affidavit of the printer of the newspaper, or his foreman or principal clerk, annexed to a copy of the document or notice, specifying the times when, and the paper in which, the publication was made. *(Enacted in 1872.)*

§ 2011. Evidence of publication; filing; original or certified copy as prima facie evidence

If such affidavit be made in an action or special proceeding pending in a Court, it may be filed with the Court or a Clerk thereof. If not so made, it may be filed with the Clerk of the county where the newspaper is printed. In either case the original affidavit, or a copy thereof, certified by the Judge of the Court or Clerk having it in custody, is prima facie evidence of the facts stated therein. *(Enacted in 1872. Amended by Code Am.1873–74, c. 383, p. 388, § 240.)*

§ 2012. Officers before whom taken

An affidavit to be used before any court, judge, or officer of this state may be taken before any officer authorized to administer oaths. *(Enacted in 1872. Amended by Stats.1907, c. 393, p. 734, § 1.)*

§ 2013. Made in foreign state; before whom taken

An affidavit taken in another State of the United States, to be used in this State, may be taken before a Commissioner appointed by the Governor of this State to take affidavits and depositions in such other State, or before any Notary Public in another State, or before any Judge or Clerk of a Court of record having a seal. *(Enacted in 1872. Amended by Stats.1873–74, c. 383, p. 389, § 241.)*

§ 2014. Made in foreign country; before whom taken

An affidavit taken in a foreign country to be used in this State, may be taken before an Embassador,[1] Minister, Consul, Vice Consul, or Consular Agent of the United States, or before any Judge of a Court of record having a seal in such foreign country. *(Enacted in 1872. Amended by Code Am.1873–74, c. 383, p. 389, § 242.)*

[1] So in chaptered copy.

§ 2015. Made in foreign state or country before judge or court; clerk's certificate; seal of court

When an affidavit is taken before a Judge or a Court in another State, or in a foreign country, the genuineness of the signature of the Judge, the existence of the Court, and the fact that such Judge is a member thereof, must be certified by the Clerk of the Court, under the seal thereof. *(Enacted in 1872.)*

§ 2015.3. Certificate of sheriff, marshal, or court clerk; force and effect

The certificate of a sheriff, marshal, or the clerk of the superior court, has the same force and effect as his or her affidavit. *(Added by Stats.1969, c. 1611, p. 3398, § 28, operative*

July 1, 1970. Amended by Stats.1982, c. 834, § 1; Stats.1996, c. 872 (A.B.3472), § 21; Stats.1998, c. 931 (S.B.2139), § 127, eff. Sept. 28, 1998; Stats.2002, c. 784 (S.B.1316), § 88.)

Law Revision Commission Comments

Section 2015.3 is amended to reflect the elimination of the justice court. Cal. Const. art. VI, §§ 1, 5(b). [28 Cal.L.Rev.Comm. Reports 51 (1998)].

Section 2015.3 is amended to reflect unification of the municipal and superior courts pursuant to Article VI, Section 5(e), of the California Constitution. [32 Cal.L.Rev.Comm. Reports 143 (2002)].

§ 2015.5.   Certification or declaration under penalty of perjury

Whenever, under any law of this state or under any rule, regulation, order or requirement made pursuant to the law of this state, any matter is required or permitted to be supported, evidenced, established, or proved by the sworn statement, declaration, verification, certificate, oath, or affidavit, in writing of the person making the same (other than a deposition, or an oath of office, or an oath required to be taken before a specified official other than a notary public), such matter may with like force and effect be supported, evidenced, established or proved by the unsworn statement, declaration, verification, or certificate, in writing of such person which recites that it is certified or declared by him or her to be true under penalty of perjury, is subscribed by him or her, and (1), if executed within this state, states the date and place of execution, or (2), if executed at any place, within or without this state, states the date of execution and that it is so certified or declared under the laws of the State of California. The certification or declaration may be in substantially the following form:

(a) If executed within this state:

"I certify (or declare) under penalty of perjury that the foregoing is true and correct":

_____   _____
(Date and Place)   (Signature)

(b) If executed at any place, within or without this state:

"I certify (or declare) under penalty of perjury under the laws of the State of California that the foregoing is true and correct":

_____   _____
(Date)   (Signature)

(Added by Stats.1957, c. 1612, p. 2959, § 1. Amended by Stats.1961, c. 495, p. 1589, § 1; Stats.1963, c. 2080, p. 4346, § 1; Stats.1975, c. 666, p. 1456, § 1, operative Jan. 1, 1977; Stats.1980, c. 889, p. 2789, § 1, operative July 1, 1981.)

Research References

Rutter, Cal. Practice Guide: Civil Appeals & Writs Ch. 5-C, C. Motion, Application and Request Procedures.
Rutter, Cal. Practice Guide: Civ. Pro. Before Trial Ch. 5-G, G. Relief from Default.
Rutter, Cal. Practice Guide: Civ. Pro. Before Trial Ch. 6-B, B. Complaints.
Rutter, Cal. Practice Guide: Civ. Pro. Before Trial Ch. 10-C, C. Procedural Requirements-Moving Party.
Rutter, Cal. Practice Guide: Civ. Pro. Before Trial Ch. 8F-5, Responding to Interrogatories.
Rutter, Cal. Practice Guide: Civ. Pro. Before Trial Ch. 9(I)-B, B. Preparing and Filing Motions.
Rutter, Cal. Practice Guide: Civ. Pro. Before Trial Ch. 9(II)-A, A. Injunctions.
Rutter, Cal. Practice Guide: Civil Trials & Evidence Ch. 18-B, B. Motion for New Trial.
Rutter, Cal. Practice Guide: Enforcing Judgments/Debts Ch. 4-A, A. Attachment.
Rutter, Cal. Practice Guide: Enforcing Judgments/Debts Ch. 4-B, B. Claim and Delivery.

Rutter, Cal. Practice Guide: Enforcing Judgments/Debts Ch. 6A-5, Amount Recoverable Under Judgment.
Rutter, Cal. Practice Guide: Family Law Ch. 5-D, D. Notice of Motion/OSC and Stipulation Procedures.
Rutter, Cal. Practice Guide: Personal Injury Ch. 5-A, A. Prelawsuit Filings.
Rutter, Cal. Practice Guide: Personal Injury Ch. 10-A, A. Motion for New Trial.
Miller and Starr California Real Estate § 25C:15, Application, Notice of Intention, and Questionnaire.
Miller and Starr California Real Estate § 25C:68, Procedure for Registering Time-Share Plans and Issuance of Public Reports.
16 NO. 1 Miller & Starr, California Real Estate Newsalert 10, Covenants, Conditions, and Restrictions.
8 Witkin Cal. Proc. 5th Attack Judgment Trial Court § 65, (S 65) Affidavits and Counteraffidavits.
4 Witkin Cal. Proc. 5th Pleading § 459, (S 459) Nature of Verification.
4 Witkin Cal. Proc. 5th Pleading § 462, Affidavit or Declaration.
6 Witkin Cal. Proc. 5th Proceedings Without Trial § 41, Affidavits and Declarations.
6 Witkin Cal. Proc. 5th Proceedings Without Trial § 224, General Requirements.
6 Witkin Cal. Proc. 5th Provisional Remedies § 3, (S 3) Use of Declaration.

§ 2015.6.   Affirmation in lieu of oath

Whenever, under any law of this State or under any rule, regulation, order or requirement made pursuant to law, an oath is required to be taken by a person appointed to discharge specific duties in a particular action, proceeding or matter, whether or not pending in court, including but not limited to a person appointed as executor, administrator, guardian, conservator, appraiser, receiver, or elisor, an unsworn written affirmation may be made and executed, in lieu of such oath. Such affirmation shall commence "I solemnly affirm," shall state the substance of the other matter required by the oath, the date and place of execution and shall be subscribed by him. *(Added by Stats.1961, c. 1364, p. 3140, § 1.)*

Research References

8 Witkin Cal. Proc. 5th Attack Judgment Trial Court § 65, (S 65) Affidavits and Counteraffidavits.
6 Witkin Cal. Proc. 5th Proceedings Without Trial § 41, Affidavits and Declarations.
6 Witkin Cal. Proc. 5th Provisional Remedies § 444, Qualification and Undertaking.
14 Witkin, California Summary 10th Wills and Probate § 446, (S 446) Letters and Oath.
14 Witkin, California Summary 10th Wills and Probate § 982, (S 982) Oath and Letters.

Title 4

CIVIL DISCOVERY ACT

Disposition of Existing Law

Note. In 2004, California's Civil Discovery Act was reorganized on recommendation of the Law Revision Commission. In connection with that reform, the Commission prepared a disposition table, showing the disposition of each provision, which is set out below. See also *Civil Discovery: Nonsubstantive Reform*, 33 Cal. L. Revision Comm'n Reports 789, 1073–1087 (2003). This table shows the disposition of Article 3 (commencing with Section 2016) of Chapter 3 of Title 3 of Part 4 of the Code of Civil Procedure. Unless otherwise indicated, all dispositions are to the Code of Civil Procedure.

Existing Provision	Corresponding New Provision
2016(a)	2016.010
2016(b)	2016.020
2016(c)	2016.070
2017(a)	2017.010
2017(b)	2017.210
2017(c), 1st ¶	2017.020(a)
2017(c), 2d ¶	2017.020(b)
2017(d), 1st ¶	2017.220(a)
2017(d), 2d ¶	2017.220(b)
2017(e)(1), 1st snt.	2017.730(a)
2017(e)(1), 2d snt.	2017.730(b)
2017(e)(2)	2017.730(c)
2017(e)(3), 1st & 2d snt.	2017.730(d)
2017(e)(3), 3d snt.	2017.730(e)
2017(e)(4)	2017.720(a)
2017(e)(5), 1st–4th snt.	2017.740(a)
2017(e)(5), 5th–7th snt.	2017.740(b)
2017(e)(6)	2017.710
2017(e)(7)	2017.720(b)
2017(e)(8)	2017.720(c)
2018(a)	2018.020
2018(b)	2018.030(b)
2018(c)	2018.030(a)
2018(d), 1st & 2d snt.	2018.040
2018(d), 3d snt.	2018.050
2018(d), 4th snt.	2018.060
2018(e), 1st snt.	2018.070(a)-(b)
2018(e), 2d snt.	2018.070(c)
2018(f), 1st ¶	2018.080
2018(f), 2d ¶	2018.010
2019(a)	2019.010
2019(b), intro. clause	2019.030(a), intro. clause
2019(b)(1)	2019.030(a)(1)
2019(b)(2)	2019.030(a)(2)
2019(b), next-to-last ¶	2019.030(b)
2019(b), last ¶	2019.030(c)
2019(c), 1st snt.	2019.020(a)
2019(c), 2d snt.	2019.020(b)
2019(d)	2019.210
2019(e)	2016.050
2020(a), 1st snt.	2020.010(a)
2020(a), 2d snt.	2020.010(b)

Existing Provision	Corresponding New Provision
2020(a), 3d snt. (including items (1)-(3))	2020.020
2020(a), last ¶	2020.030
2020(b), 1st snt.	2020.210(a)
2020(b), 2d snt.	2020.210(b)
2020(c)	2020.310
2020(d)(1), 1st snt.	2020.410(a)-(b)
2020(d)(1), 2d–4th snt.	2020.410(c)
2020(d)(2)	2020.410(d)
2020(d)(3)	2020.420
2020(d)(4), 1st snt.	2020.430(a), (e)
2020(d)(4), 2d snt.	2020.430(b)
2020(d)(4), 3d & 4th snt.	2020.430(c)
2020(d)(4), 5th & 6th snt.	2020.430(d)
2020(d)(5)	2020.440
2020(d)(6)	2020.430(f)
2020(e), 1st snt.	2020.510(a)
2020(e), 2d snt.	2020.510(b)
2020(e), 2d ¶	2020.510(c)
2020(f), 1st snt.	2020.220(a)
2020(f), 2d snt.	2020.220(b)
2020(f), 2d ¶	2020.230(a)
2020(f), 3d ¶	2020.230(b)
2020(g)	2020.220(c)
2020(h)	2020.240
2021	2016.030
2023(a)(1)-(8) & (9), 1st snt.	2023.010
2023(a)(9), 2d snt.	2023.020
2023(b), intro. clause	2023.030, intro. clause
2023(b)(1)	2023.030(a)
2023(b)(2)	2023.030(b)
2023(b)(3)	2023.030(c)
2023(b)(4)	2023.030(d)
2023(b)(5)	2023.030(e)
2023(c)	2023.040
2024(a), 1st snt.	2024.020(a) Not continued (redundant).
2024(a), 2d snt.	See 2016.060
2024(a), 3d snt.	2024.010
2024(a), 4th snt.	2024.020(b)
2024(b)	2024.040(a)
2024(c)	2024.040(b)
2024(d)	2024.030
2024(e), 1st ¶	2024.050(a)
2024(e), 2d ¶ (including items (1)-(4))	2024.050(b)
2024(e), last ¶	2024.050(c)
2024(f)	2024.060
2024(g)	2016.060
2025(a)	2025.010
2025(b)	2025.210
2025(c), 1st snt.	2025.220(a), intro. clause
2025(c), 2d snt.	2025.220(b)
2025(c), 3d & 4th snt.	2025.240(a)
2025(c), 2d ¶	2025.240(b)
2025(d), intro. clause	2025.220(a), intro. clause
2025(d)(1)	2025.220(a)(1)
2025(d)(2)	2025.220(a)(2)
2025(d)(3)	2025.220(a)(3)
2025(d)(4)	2025.220(a)(4)
2025(d)(5)	2025.220(a)(5)
2025(d)(6), 1st ¶	2025.220(a)(6)
2025(d)(6), 2d ¶, 1st snt.	2025.230
2025(d)(6), 2d ¶, 2d snt.	Not continued (redundant). See 2020.310(e), 2020.510(a)(1).
2025(d)(6), 3d ¶	2025.240(c)

Existing Provision	Corresponding New Provision
2025(e)(1)	2025.250(a)
2025(e)(2), 1st snt.	2025.250(b)
2025(e)(2), 2d & 3d snt.	2025.250(c)
2025(e)(3), 1st ¶	2025.260(a)
2025(e)(3), 2d ¶ (including items (A)-(F))	2025.260(b)
2025(e)(3), next-to-last ¶	2025.260(c)
2025(e)(3), last ¶	2025.260(d)
2025(f), 1st & 2d snt.	2025.270(a)
2025(f), 3d snt.	2025.270(b)
2025(f), 2d ¶	2025.270(c)
2025(g), 1st snt.	2025.410(a)
2025(g), 2d & 3d snt.	2025.410(b)
2025(g), 2d ¶	2025.410(c)
2025(g), 3d ¶	2025.410(d)
2025(h)(1)	2025.280(a)
2025(h)(2)	2025.280(b)
2025(h)(3), 1st snt.	2025.310(a)
2025(h)(3), 2d & 3d snt.	2025.310(b)
2025(h)(3), 4th snt.	2025.310(c)
2025(i), 1st ¶	2025.420(a)
2025(i), 2d ¶ (including items (1)-(15))	2025.420(b)
2025(i), next-to-last ¶	2025.420(c)
2025(i), last ¶	2025.420(d)
2025(j)(1)	2025.430
2025(j)(2), 1st ¶	2025.440(a)
2025(j)(2), 2d ¶	2025.440(b)
2025(j)(3), 1st snt.	2025.450(a)
2025(j)(3), 2d snt.	2025.450(b)
2025(j)(3), 3d & 4th snt.	2025.450(c)
2025(j)(3), 2d ¶	2025.450(d)
2025(k), intro. clause	2025.320, intro. clause
2025(k)(1)	2025.320(a)
2025(k)(2)	2025.320(b)
2025(k)(3)	2025.320(c)
2025(k)(4)	2025.320(d)
2025(k)(5)	2025.320(e)
2025(l)(1), 1st snt.	2025.330(a)
2025(l)(1), 2d snt.	2025.330(b)
2025(l)(1), 3d–5th snt.	2025.330(c)
2025(l)(1), 6th snt.	2025.330(d)
2025(l)(2), intro. clause	2025.340, intro. clause
2025(l)(2)(A)	2025.340(a)
2025(l)(2)(B), 1st & 2d snt.	2025.340(b)
2025(l)(2)(B), 3d snt.	2025.340(c)
2025(l)(2)(B), 4th–6th snt.	2025.340(d)
2025(l)(2)(B), 7th & 8th snt.	2025.340(e)
2025(l)(2)(B), 9th & 10th snt.	2025.340(f)
2025(l)(2)(C)	2025.340(g)
2025(l)(2)(D)	2025.340(h)
2025(l)(2)(E)	2025.340(i)
2025(l)(2)(F)	2025.340(j)
2025(l)(2)(G)	2025.340(k)
2025(l)(2)(H)	2025.340(l)
2025(l)(2)(I)	2025.340(m)
2025(l)(3)	2025.330(e)
2025(m)(1)	2025.460(a)
2025(m)(2)	2025.460(b)
2025(m)(3)	2025.460(c)
2025(m)(4)	2025.460(d)
2025(n), 1st & 2d snt.	2025.470
2025(n), 3d & 4th snt.	2025.420(b)(16)
2025(n), 2d ¶	2025.470
2025(o), 1st snt.	2025.480(a)
2025(o), 2d snt.	2025.480(b)
2025(o), 3d & 4th snt.	2025.480(c)

Existing Provision	Corresponding New Provision
2025(o), 5th & 6th snt.	2025.480(d)
2025(o), 7th snt.	2025.480(e)
2025(o), 2d ¶	2025.480(f)
2025(o), 3d ¶	2025.480(g)
2025(p), 1st snt.	2025.510(a)
2025(p), 2d snt.	2025.510(b)
2025(p), 3d snt.	2025.510(c)
2025(p), 4th snt.	2025.510(d)
2025(p), 5th & 6th snt.	2025.510(e)
2025(p), 7th snt.	2025.510(f)
2025(p), 2d ¶	2025.510(g)
2025(q)(1), 1st snt.	2025.520(a)
2025(q)(1), 2d snt.	2025.520(b)
2025(q)(1), 2d ¶, 1st & 2d snt.	2025.520(c)
2025(q)(1), 2d ¶, 3d snt.	2025.520(d)
2025(q)(1), 3d ¶, 1st & 2d snt.	2025.520(e)
2025(q)(1), 3d ¶, 3d snt.	2025.520(f)
2025(q)(1), 3d ¶, 4th snt.	2025.520(g)
2025(q)(1), 4th ¶	2025.520(h)
2025(q)(2), 1st snt.	2025.530(a)
2025(q)(2), 2d snt.	2025.530(b)
2025(q)(2), 2d ¶, 1st snt.	2025.530(c)
2025(q)(2), 2d ¶, 2d snt.	2025.530(d)
2025(q)(2), 2d ¶, 3d snt.	2025.530(e)
2025(q)(2), 3d ¶	2025.530(f)
2025(r)(1)	2025.540(a)
2025(r)(2)	2025.540(b)
2025(s)(1), 1st ¶	2025.550(a)
2025(s)(1), 2d ¶	2025.550(b)
2025(s)(2), 1st ¶	2025.560(a)
2025(s)(2), 2d ¶	2025.560(b)
2025(s)(2), 3d ¶	2025.560(c)
2025(t), 1st snt.	2025.610(a)
2025(t), 2d snt.	2025.610(b)
2025(t), 3d snt.	2025.610(c)
2025(t), 4th snt.	2025.610(d)
2025(u), intro. clause	2025.620, intro. clause
2025(u)(1)	2025.620(a)
2025(u)(2)	2025.620(b)
2025(u)(3)	2025.620(c)
2025(u)(4)	2025.620(d)
2025(u)(5)	2025.620(e)
2025(u)(6)	2025.620(f)
2025(u)(7)	2025.620(g)
2025(v)	2025.320(f)
2025.5(a)	2025.570(a)
2025.5(b), 1st snt.	2025.570(b)
2025.5(b), 2d snt.	2025.570(c)
2025.5(c)	2025.570(d)
2026(a)	2026.010(a)
2026(b)(1)	2026.010(b)
2026(b)(2)	2026.010(c)
2026(c), 1st snt.	2026.010(d)
2026(c), 2d snt.	2026.010(e)
2026(c), 3d–7th snt.	2026.010(f)
2027(a)	2027.010(a)
2027(b)(1)	2027.010(b)
2027(b)(2)	2027.010(c)
2027(c), 1st ¶	2027.010(d)
2027(c), 2d ¶	2027.010(e)
2028(a)	2028.010
2028(b)	2028.020
2028(c), 1st ¶	2028.030(a)
2028(c), 2d ¶	2028.030(b)
2028(c), 3d ¶	2028.030(c)
2028(c), 4th ¶	2028.030(d)
2028(c), 5th ¶	2028.030(e)

Existing Provision	Corresponding New Provision
2028(d)(1), 1st & 2d snt.	2028.040(a)
2028(d)(1), 3d–5th snt.	2028.040(b)
2028(d)(1), 2d ¶	2028.040(c)
2028(d)(2), 1st & 2d snt.	2028.050(a)
2028(d)(2), 3d–5th snt.	2028.050(b)
2028(d)(2), 2d ¶	2028.050(c)
2028(e), 1st snt.	2028.060(a)
2028(e), 2d snt.	2028.060(b)
2028(f)	2028.070
2028(g)	2028.080
2029	2029.010
2030(a)	2030.010(a)
2030(b), 1st snt.	2030.020(a)
2030(b), 2d snt.	2030.020(b)
2030(b), 3d snt.	2030.020(c)
2030(c)(1), 1st snt.	2030.030(a)
2030(c)(1), 2d & 3d snt.	2030.030(b)
2030(c)(1), 4th snt.	2030.030(c)
2030(c)(2), 1st ¶ (including items (A)-(C))	2030.040(a)
2030(c)(2), last ¶	2030.040(b)
2030(c)(3)	2030.050
2030(c)(4), 1st snt.	2030.060(a)
2030(c)(4), 2d snt.	2030.060(b)
2030(c)(4), 3d snt.	2030.060(c)
2030(c)(5), 1st & 2d snt.	2030.060(d)
2030(c)(5), 3d snt.	2030.060(e)
2030(c)(5), 4th snt.	2030.060(f)
2030(c)(6)	2030.010(b)
2030(c)(7)	2030.060(g)
2030(c)(8), 1st snt.	2030.070(a)-(b)
2030(c)(8), 2d snt.	2030.070(c)
2030(d)	2030.080
2030(e), 1st ¶	2030.090(a)
2030(e), 2d ¶ (including items (1)-(7))	2030.090(b)
2030(e), next-to-last ¶	2030.090(c)
2030(e), last ¶	2030.090(d)
2030(f), 1st snt.	2030.210(a)
2030(f), 2d snt.	2030.210(b)
2030(f), 3d snt.	2030.210(c)
2030(f)(1), 1st snt.	2030.220(a)
2030(f)(1), 2d snt.	2030.220(b)
2030(f)(1), 3d snt.	2030.220(c)
2030(f)(2)	2030.230
2030(f)(3), 1st snt.	2030.240(a)
2030(f)(3), 2d–4th snt.	2030.240(b)
2030(g), 1st snt.	2030.250(a)
2030(g), 2d & 3d snt.	2030.250(b)
2030(g), 4th snt.	2030.250(c)
2030(h), 1st & 2d snt.	2030.260(a)
2030(h), 3d snt.	2030.260(b)
2030(i), 1st snt.	2030.270(a)
2030(i), 2d snt.	2030.270(b)
2030(i), 3d snt.	2030.270(c)
2030(j), 1st snt.	2030.280(a)
2030(j), 2d & 3d snt.	2030.280(b)
2030(k), 1st ¶	2030.290(a)
2030(k), 2d ¶, 1st snt.	2030.290(b)
2030(k), 2d ¶, 2d–4th snt.	2030.290(c)
2030(*l*), 1st snt.	2030.300(a)
2030(*l*), 2d snt.	2030.300(b)
2030(*l*), 2d ¶	2030.300(c)
2030(*l*), 3d ¶	2030.300(d)
2030(*l*), 4th ¶	2030.300(e)
2030(m), 1st ¶	2030.310(a)
2030(m), 2d ¶, 1st & 2d snt.	2030.310(b)

Existing Provision	Corresponding New Provision
2030(m), 2d ¶, 3d snt.	2030.310(c)
2030(m), 3d ¶	2030.310(d)
2030(n)	2030.410
2031(a), intro. ¶	2031.010(a)
2031(a)(1)	2031.010(b)
2031(a)(2)	2031.010(c)
2031(a)(3)	2031.010(d)
2031(b), 1st snt.	2031.020(a)
2031(b), 2d snt.	2031.020(b)
2031(b), 3d snt.	2031.020(c)
2031(c), 1st snt.	2031.030(a)
2031(c), 2d snt.	2031.030(b)
2031(c), 3d snt. (including items (1)-(4))	2031.030(c)
2031(d)	2031.040
2031(e), 1st snt.	2031.050(a)-(b)
2031(e), 2d snt.	2031.050(c)
2031(f), 1st ¶	2031.060(a)
2031(f), 2d ¶ (including items (1)-(6))	2031.060(b)
2031(f), next-to-last ¶	2031.060(c)
2031(f), last ¶	2031.060(d)
2031(g), 1st ¶	2031.210(a)
2031(g), 2d ¶, 1st snt.	2031.210(b)
2031(g), 2d ¶, 2d snt.	2031.210(c)
2031(g)(1), 1st ¶	2031.220
2031(g)(1), 2d ¶, 1st snt.	2031.280(a)
2031(g)(1), 2d ¶, 2d snt.	2031.280(b)
2031(g)(2)	2031.230
2031(g)(3), 1st snt.	2031.240(a)
2031(g)(3), 2d–4th snt.	2031.240(b)
2031(h), 1st snt.	2031.250(a)
2031(h), 2d & 3d snt.	2031.250(b)
2031(h), 4th snt.	2031.250(c)
2031(i)	2031.260
2031(j), 1st snt.	2031.270(a)
2031(j), 2d snt.	2031.270(b)
2031(j), 3d snt.	2031.270(c)
2031(k), 1st snt.	2031.290(a)
2031(k), 2d & 3d snt.	2031.290(b)
2031(*l*), 1st ¶	2031.300, intro. cl. & (a)
2031(*l*), 2d ¶, 1st snt.	2031.300(b)
2031(*l*), 2d ¶, 2d–4th snt.	2031.300(c)
2031(m), 1st snt.	2031.310(a)
2031(m), 2d snt.	2031.310(b)
2031(m), 2d ¶	2031.310(c)
2031(m), 3d ¶	2031.310(d)
2031(m), 4th ¶	2031.310(e)
2031(n), 1st ¶	2031.320(a)
2031(n), 2d ¶	2031.320(b)
2031(n), 3d ¶	2031.320(c)
2031.1	2017.310
2031.2	2017.320
2031.5, 1st snt.	2031.510(a)
2031.5, 2d & 3d snt.	2031.510(b)
2032(a)	2032.020(a)
2032(b), 1st snt.	2032.020(b)
2032(b), 2d snt.	2032.020(c)
2032(b), 3d snt.	2032.010(a)
2032(c)(1)	2032.210
2032(c)(2), 1st snt.	2032.220(a)
2032(c)(2), 2d snt.	2032.220(b)
2032(c)(2), 3d snt.	2032.220(c)
2032(c)(3)	2032.220(d)
2032(c)(4)	2032.220(e)
2032(c)(5), 1st snt.	2032.230(a)
2032(c)(5), 2d snt.	2032.230(b)

Existing Provision	Corresponding New Provision
2032(c)(6), 1st ¶	2032.240(a)
2032(c)(6), 2d ¶, 1st snt.	2032.240(b)
2032(c)(6), 2d ¶, 2d snt.	2032.240(c)
2032(c)(6), 3d ¶	2032.240(d)
2032(c)(7), 1st ¶	2032.250(a)
2032(c)(7), 2d ¶	2032.250(b)
2032(c)(8), 1st snt.	2032.260(a)
2032(c)(8), 2d snt.	2032.260(b)
2032(d), 1st snt.	2032.310(a)
2032(d), 2d & 3d snt.	2032.310(b)
2032(d), 4th snt.	2032.310(c)
2032(d), 2d ¶, 1st snt.	2032.320(a)
2032(d), 2d ¶, 2d snt.	2032.320(b)-(c)
2032(d), 2d ¶, 3d snt.	2032.320(d)
2032(d), 2d ¶, 4th snt.	2032.320(e)
	Not continued (redundant).
2032(e)	See 2016.030.
2032(f), 1st ¶	2032.410
2032(f), 2d ¶	2032.420
2032(g)(1), 1st snt.	2032.510(a)
2032(g)(1), 2d snt.	2032.510(b)
2032(g)(1), 3d snt.	2032.510(c)
2032(g)(1), 2d ¶, 1st snt.	2032.510(d)
2032(g)(1), 2d ¶, 2d snt.	2032.510(e)
2032(g)(1), 3d ¶	2032.510(f)
2032(g)(1), 4th ¶	2032.520
2032(g)(2), 1st snt.	2032.530(a)
2032(g)(2), 2d snt.	2032.530(b)
2032(h), 1st snt.	2032.610(a)
2032(h), 2d snt.	2032.610(b)
2032(h), 3d snt.	2032.610(c)
2032(h), 2d ¶	2032.620(a)
2032(h), 3d ¶	2032.620(b)
2032(h), 4th ¶	2032.620(c)
2032(i)	2032.630
2032(j), 1st ¶	2032.640
2032(j), 2d ¶	2032.650(a)
2032(j), 3d ¶	2032.650(b)
2032(j), 4th ¶	2032.650(c)
2032(k)	2032.010(b)
2033(a)	2033.010
2033(b), 1st snt.	2033.020(a)
2033(b), 2d snt.	2033.020(b)
2033(b), 3d snt.	2033.020(c)
2033(c)(1), 1st snt.	2033.030(a)
2033(c)(1), 2d snt.	2033.030(b)
2033(c)(1), 2d ¶	2033.030(c)
2033(c)(2), 1st ¶	2033.040(a)
2033(c)(2), 2d ¶	2033.040(b)
2033(c)(3)	2033.050
2033(c)(4), 1st snt.	2033.060(a)
2033(c)(4), 2d snt.	2033.060(b)
2033(c)(4), 3d snt.	2033.060(c)
2033(c)(5), 1st & 2d snt.	2033.060(d)
2033(c)(5), 3d snt.	2033.060(e)
2033(c)(5), 4th snt.	2033.060(f)
2033(c)(6)	2033.060(g)
2033(c)(7)	2033.060(h)
2033(d)	2033.070
2033(e), 1st ¶	2033.080(a)
2033(e), 2d ¶ (including items (1)-(5))	2033.080(b)
2033(e), next-to-last ¶	2033.080(c)
2033(e), last ¶	2033.080(d)
2033(f), intro. ¶, 1st snt.	2033.210(a)
2033(f), intro. ¶, 2d snt.	2033.210(b)
2033(f), intro. ¶, 3d snt.	2033.210(c)

Existing Provision	Corresponding New Provision
2033(f), intro. ¶, 4th snt.	2033.210(d)
2033(f)(1), 1st snt.	2033.220(a)
2033(f)(1), 2d snt.	2033.220(b)
2033(f)(1), 3d snt.	2033.220(c)
2033(f)(2), 1st snt.	2033.230(a)
2033(f)(2), 2d–4th snt.	2033.230(b)
2033(g), 1st snt.	2033.240(a)
2033(g), 2d & 3d snt.	2033.240(b)
2033(g), 4th snt.	2033.240(c)
2033(h)	2033.250
2033(i), 1st snt.	2033.260(a)
2033(i), 2d snt.	2033.260(b)
2033(i), 3d snt.	2033.260(c)
2033(i), 4th snt.	2033.260(d)
2033(j), 1st snt.	2033.270(a)
2033(j), 2d & 3d snt.	2033.270(b)
2033(k), 1st ¶	2033.280(a)
2033(k), 2d ¶, 1st snt.	2033.280(b)
2033(k), 2d ¶, 2d & 3d snt.	2033.280(c)
2033(*l*), 1st snt.	2033.290(a)
2033(*l*), 2d snt.	2033.290(b)
2033(*l*), 2d ¶	2033.290(c)
2033(*l*), 3d ¶	2033.290(d)
2033(*l*), 4th ¶	2033.290(e)
2033(m), 1st snt.	2033.300(a)
2033(m), 2d snt.	2033.300(b)
2033(m), 3d snt.	2033.300(c)
2033(n), 1st snt.	2033.410(a)
2033(n), 2d & 3d snt.	2033.410(b)
2033(o), 1st snt.	2033.420(a)
2033(o), 2d snt.	2033.420(b)
2033.5(a), 1st snt.	2033.710
2033.5(a), 2d snt.	2033.740(a)
2033.5(b), 1st snt.	2033.730(a)
2033.5(b), 2d snt., 1st clause	2033.730(b)
2033.5(b), 2d snt., 2d clause	2033.740(b)
2033.5(c)	2033.740(c)
2033.5(d)	2033.720(a)
2033.5(e)	2033.720(b)
2033.5(f)	Not continued (obsolete)
2034(a), intro. clause	2034.210, intro. clause
2034(a)(1)	2034.210(a)
2034(a)(2)	2034.210(b)
2034(a)(3)	2034.210(c)
2034(a), last ¶	2034.010
2034(b)	2034.220
2034(c), 1st ¶	2034.230(a)
2034(c), 2d ¶	2034.230(b)
2034(d)	2034.240
2034(e), 1st ¶	2034.250(a)
2034(e), 2d ¶ (including items (1)-(6))	2034.250(b)
2034(e), next-to-last ¶	2034.250(c)
2034(e), last ¶	2034.250(d)
2034(f), intro. ¶	2034.260(a)
2034(f)(1) (including items (A) and (B))	2034.260(b)
2034(f)(2) (including items (A)-(E))	2034.260(c)
2034(g)	2034.270
2034(h), 1st snt.	2034.280(a)
2034(h), 2d snt.	2034.280(b)
2034(h), 3d snt.	2034.280(c)
2034(i), intro. ¶	2034.410
2034(i)(1)	2034.420
2034(i)(2), 1st ¶, 1st snt.	2034.430(a)-(b)
2034(i)(2), 1st ¶, 2d snt.	2034.430(c)

Existing Provision	Corresponding New Provision
2034(i)(2), 1st ¶ , 3d snt.	2034.430(d)
2034(i)(2), 1st ¶ , 4th snt.	2034.430(e)
2034(i)(2), 1st ¶ , 5th snt.	2034.430(f)
2034(i)(2), 2d ¶ , 1st snt.	2034.450(a)
2034(i)(2), 2d ¶ , 2d snt.	2034.450(b)
2034(i)(2), 2d ¶ , 3d snt.	2034.450(c)
2034(i)(2), 2d ¶ , 4th snt.	2034.440
2034(i)(3), 1st snt.	2034.460(a)
2034(i)(3), 2d snt.	2034.460(b)
2034(i)(4), 1st ¶ , 1st & 3d snt.	2034.470(a)
2034(i)(4), 1st ¶ , 2d & 4th snt.	2034.470(b)
2034(i)(4), 2d ¶ , 1st & 2d snt.	2034.470(c)-(d)
2034(i)(4), 2d ¶ , 3d snt.	2034.470(e)
2034(i)(4), 3d ¶	2034.470(f)
2034(i)(4), 4th ¶	2034.470(g)
2034(j)	2034.300
2034(k), 1st ¶ , 1st snt.	2034.610(a)
2034(k), 1st ¶ , 2d & 3d snt.	2034.610(b)
2034(k), 1st ¶ , 4th snt.	2034.610(c)
2034(k), 1st ¶ , 5th snt.	2034.290(c)
2034(k), 1st ¶ , 6th snt.	2034.620, intro. cl. & (a)-(c)
2034(k), 1st ¶ , 7th snt.	2034.620(d)
2034(k), 2d ¶	2034.630
2034(l), 1st snt.	2034.710(a)
2034(l), 2d & 3d snt.	2034.710(b)
2034(l), 4th snt.	2034.710(c)
2034(l), 2d ¶ , 1st snt.	2034.720, intro. cl. & (a)-(c)
2034(l), 2d ¶ , 2d snt.	2034.720(d)
2034(l), 3d ¶	2034.730
2034(m)	2034.310
2034(n), 1st snt.	2034.290(a)
2034(n), 2d & 3d snt.	2034.290(b)
2035(a), 1st snt.	2035.010(a)
2035(a), 2d snt.	2035.010(b)
2035(b)	2035.020
2035(c)	2035.030(a)
2035(d), 1st ¶ (including items (1)-(9))	2035.030(b)
2035(d), last ¶	2035.030(c)
2035(e), 1st & 2d snt.	2035.040(a)
2035(e), 3d & 4th snt.	2035.040(b)
2035(e), 5th snt.	2035.040(c)
2035(e), 2d ¶ , 1st snt.	2035.040(d)
2035(e), 2d ¶ , 2d & 3d snt.	2035.040(e)
2035(f), 1st snt.	2035.050(a)
2035(f), 2d snt.	2035.050(b)
2035(f), 3d snt.	2035.050(c)
2035(g)	2035.060
2036(a)	2036.010
2036(b)	2036.020
2036(c)	2036.030(a)
2036(d)	2036.030(b)
2036(e), 1st snt.	2036.040(a)
2036(e), 2d snt.	2036.040(b)
2036(e), 3d snt.	2036.040(c)
2036(f)	2036.050

DERIVATION TABLE

This table shows the derivation by section number of the subject matter of Part 4, added by Stats.2004, c. 182 (A.B.3081), § 23, operative July 1, 2005. This part was derived from Article 3 (commencing with Code of Civil Procedure § 2016) of Chapter 3 of Title 3 of Part 4 of the Code of Civil Procedure. Section references are to the Code of Civil Procedure.

New	Old
2016.010	2016(a)
2016.020	2016(b)
2016.030	2021
2016.040	(none)
2016.050	2019(e)
2016.060	2024(g)
2016.070	2016(c)
2017.010	2017(a)
2017.020	2017(c)
2017.210	2017(b)
2017.220	2017(d)
2017.310	2031.1
2017.320	2031.2
2017.710	2017(e)(6)
2017.720	2017(e)(4), (e)(7), (e)(8)
2017.730	2017(e)(1), (e)(2), (e)(3)
2017.740	2017(e)(5)
2018.010	2018(f)
2018.020	2018(a)
2018.030	2018(b), (c)
2018.040	2018(d)
2018.050	2018(d)
2018.060	2018(d)
2018.070	2018(e)
2018.080	2018(f)
2019.010	2019(a)
2019.020	2019(c)
2019.030	2019(b)
2019.210	2019(d)
2020.010	2020(a)
2020.020	2020(a)
2020.030	2020(a)
2020.210	2020(b)
2020.220	2020(f), (g)
2020.230	2020(f)
2020.240	2020(h)
2020.310	2020(c)
2020.410	2020(d)(1), (d)(2)
2020.420	2020(d)(3)
2020.430	2020(d)(4), (d)(6)
2020.440	2020(d)(5)
2020.510	2020(e)
2023.010	2023(a)
2023.020	2023(a)
2023.030	2023(b)
2023.040	2023(c)
2024.010	2024(a)
2024.020	2024(a)
2024.030	2024(d)
2024.040	2024(b), (c)
2024.050	2024(e)
2024.060	2024(f)
2025.010	2025(a)
2025.210	2025(b)
2025.220	2025(c), (d)
2025.230	2025(d)
2025.240	2025(c), (d)
2025.250	2025(e)(1), (e)(2)
2025.260	2025(e)(3)
2025.270	2025(f)
2025.280	2025(h)(1), (h)(2)
2025.310	2025(h)(3)
2025.320	2025(k)(v)
2025.330	2025(l)(1), (l)(3)
2025.340	2025(l)(2)
2025.410	2025(g)
2025.420	2025(i), (n)
2025.430	2025(j)(1)
2025.440	2025(j)(2)
2025.450	2025(j)(3)
2025.460	2025(m)

New	Old
2025.470	2025(n)
2025.480	2025(o)
2025.510	2025(p)
2025.520	2025(q)(1)
2025.530	2025(q)(2)
2025.540	2025(r)
2025.550	2025(s)(1)
2025.560	2025(s)(2)
2025.570	2025.5
2025.610	2025(t)
2025.620	2025(u)
2026.010	2026
2027.010	2027
2028.010	2028(a)
2028.020	2028(b)
2028.030	2028(c)
2028.040	2028(d)(1)
2028.050	2028(d)(2)
2028.060	2028(e)
2028.070	2028(f)
2028.080	2028(g)
2029.010	2029
2030.010	2030(a), (c)(b)
2030.020	2030(b)
2030.030	2030(c)(1)
2030.040	2030(c)(2)
2030.050	2030(c)(3)
2030.060	2030(c)(4), (c)(5), (c)(7)
2030.070	2030(c)(8)
2030.080	2030(d)
2030.090	2030(e)
2030.210	2030(f)
2030.220	2030(f)(1)
2030.230	2030(f)(2)
2030.240	2030(f)(3)
2030.250	2030(g)
2030.260	2030(h)
2030.270	2030(i)
2030.280	2030(j)
2030.290	2030(k)
2030.300	2030(l)
2030.310	2030(m)
2030.410	2030(n)
2031.010	2031(a)
2031.020	2031(b)
2031.030	2031(c)
2031.040	2031(d)
2031.050	2031(e)
2031.060	2031(f)
2031.210	2031(g)
2031.220	2031(g)(1)
2031.230	2031(g)(2)
2031.240	2031(g)(3)
2031.250	2031(h)
2031.260	2031(i)
2031.270	2031(j)
2031.280	2031(g)(1)
2031.290	2031(k)
2031.300	2031(l)
2031.310	2031(m)
2031.320	2031(n)
2031.510	2031.5
2032.010	2032(b), (k)
2032.020	2032(a), (b)
2032.210	2032(c)(1)
2032.220	2032(c)(2) to (c)(4)
2032.230	2032(c)(5)
2032.240	2032(c)(6)
2032.250	2032(c)(7)
2032.260	2032(c)(8)
2032.310	2032(d)
2032.320	2032(d)
2032.410	2032(f)
2032.420	2032(f)
2032.510	2032(g)(1)
2032.520	2032(g)(1)
2032.530	2032(g)(2)
2032.610	2032(h)
2032.620	2032(h)
2032.630	2032(i)
2032.640	2032(j)
2032.650	2032(j)
2033.010	2033(a)
2033.020	2033(b)
2033.030	2033(c)(1)
2033.040	2033(c)(2)
2033.050	2033(c)(3)
2033.060	2033(c)(4) to (c)(7)
2033.070	2033(d)
2033.080	2033(e)
2033.210	2033(f)
2033.220	2033(f)(1)
2033.230	2033(f)(2)
2033.240	2033(g)
2033.250	2033(h)
2033.260	2033(i)
2033.270	2033(j)
2033.280	2033(k)
2033.290	2033(l)
2033.300	2033(m)
2033.410	2033(n)
2033.420	2033(o)
2033.710	2033.5(a)
2033.720	2033.5(d), (e)
2033.730	2033.5(b)
2033.740	2033.5(a) to (c)
2034.010	2034(a)
2034.210	2034(a)
2034.220	2034(b)
2034.230	2034(c)
2034.240	2034(d)
2034.250	2034(e)
2034.260	2034(f)
2034.270	2034(g)
2034.280	2034(h)
2034.290	2034(k), (n)
2034.300	2034(j)
2034.310	2034(m)
2034.410	2034(i)
2034.420	2034(i)(1)
2034.430	2034(i)(2)
2034.440	2034(i)(2)
2034.450	2034(i)(2)
2034.460	2034(i)(3)
2034.470	2034(i)(4)
2034.610	2034(k)
2034.620	2034(k)
2034.630	2034(k)
2034.710	2034(l)
2034.720	2034(l)
2034.730	2034(l)
2035.010	2035(a)
2035.020	2035(b)
2035.030	2035(c), (d)
2035.040	2035(e)
2035.050	2035(f)

CHAPTER 1. GENERAL PROVISIONS

§ 2016.010. Short title

This title may be cited as the "Civil Discovery Act." *(Added by Stats.2004, c. 182 (A.B.3081), § 23, operative July 1, 2005.)*

Law Revision Commission Comments

Section 2016.010 continues former Section 2016(a) without substantive change. [33 Cal.L.Rev.Comm. Reports 809 (2004)].

Research References

Rutter, Cal. Practice Guide: A.D.R. App. D Form 127, ADR Clause (Conduct of Reference Proceeding).
Rutter, Cal. Practice Guide: Civ. Pro. Before Trial Ch. 12(I)-B, B. Case Management ("Fast Track") System.
Rutter, Cal. Practice Guide: Enforcing Judgments/Debts Ch. 4-A, A. Attachment.
Rutter, Cal. Practice Guide: Fed.Civ.Pro. Before Trial Ch. 11(I)-A, A. Introduction.
1 Witkin Cal. Proc. 5th Attorneys § 584, in General.
2 Witkin Cal. Proc. 5th Courts § 262, Minimum Time Standards.
6 Witkin Cal. Proc. 5th Provisional Remedies § 90, (S 90) Discovery.
7 Witkin Cal. Proc. 5th Trial § 293, (S 293) Depositions and Interrogatories.
2 Witkin, California Summary 10th Insurance § 210, (S 210) Notice and Hearing.
11 Witkin, California Summary 10th Husband and Wife § 291, (S 291) Discovery.

§ 2016.020. Definitions

As used in this title:

(a) "Action" includes a civil action and a special proceeding of a civil nature.

(b) "Court" means the trial court in which the action is pending, unless otherwise specified.

(c) "Document" and "writing" mean a writing, as defined in Section 250 of the Evidence Code.

(d) "Electronic" means relating to technology having electrical, digital, magnetic, wireless, optical, electromagnetic, or similar capabilities.

(e) "Electronically stored information" means information that is stored in an electronic medium. *(Added by Stats.2004, c. 182 (A.B.3081), § 23, operative July 1, 2005. Amended by Stats.2009, c. 5 (A.B.5), § 3, eff. June 29, 2009.)*

Law Revision Commission Comments

Section 2016.020 continues former Section 2016(b) without substantive change. [33 Cal.L.Rev.Comm. Reports 809 (2004)].

Research References

Rutter, Cal. Practice Guide: Civ. Pro. Before Trial Ch. 8C-4, Attorney Work Product Protection.
Rutter, Cal. Practice Guide: Civ. Pro. Before Trial Ch. 8E-6, Subpoena to Nonparty Deponent or Business Records Custodian.
Rutter, Cal. Practice Guide: Civ. Pro. Before Trial Ch. 8H-2, What May be Inspected.
Rutter, Cal. Practice Guide: Insurance Litigation Ch. 12D-G, G. Insurer's Reliance on Advice of Counsel.
Rutter, Cal. Practice Guide: Personal Injury Ch. 6-B, B. Overview of Selected Discovery Procedures.
3 Witkin Cal. Proc. 5th Actions § 66, (S 66) General Policy of Uniformity in Procedure.

§ 2016.030. Stipulation to modify discovery; requirements

Unless the court orders otherwise, the parties may by written stipulation modify the procedures provided by this title for any method of discovery permitted under Section 2019.010. *(Added by Stats.2004, c. 182 (A.B.3081), § 23, operative July 1, 2005.)*

Law Revision Commission Comments

Section 2016.030 continues former Section 2021 without substantive change. [33 Cal.L.Rev.Comm. Reports 810 (2004)].

Research References

Rutter, Cal. Practice Guide: Civ. Pro. Before Trial Ch. 8B-3, Limitations on Right to Discovery.
Rutter, Cal. Practice Guide: Civ. Pro. Before Trial Ch. 8E-4, Notice of Deposition.
Rutter, Cal. Practice Guide: Civ. Pro. Before Trial Ch. 8E-8, Place of Deposition.
Rutter, Cal. Practice Guide: Civ. Pro. Before Trial Ch. 8F-3, Propounding Interrogatories.
Rutter, Cal. Practice Guide: Civ. Pro. Before Trial Ch. 8I-1, Examinations by Stipulation.
Rutter, Cal. Practice Guide: Civ. Pro. Before Trial Ch. 8J-7, Deposing Opposing Experts.
Rutter, Cal. Practice Guide: Civ. Pro. Before Trial Ch. 8E-12, Conduct of Deposition.
Rutter, Cal. Practice Guide: Civ. Pro. Before Trial Ch. 8E-14, Deposition Transcript.
Rutter, Cal. Practice Guide: Civil Trials & Evidence Ch. 4-B, B. Preliminary Matters Discussed in Final Status Conference or In-Chambers Conference.
Rutter, Cal. Practice Guide: Personal Injury Ch. 6-B, B. Overview of Selected Discovery Procedures.
Rutter, Cal. Practice Guide: Personal Injury Ch. 6-C, C. Physical and Mental Examinations (CCP § 2032.020 et seq.).

§ 2016.040. Meet and confer declaration; requirements

A meet and confer declaration in support of a motion shall state facts showing a reasonable and good faith attempt at an informal resolution of each issue presented by the motion. *(Added by Stats.2004, c. 182 (A.B.3081), § 23, operative July 1, 2005.)*

Law Revision Commission Comments

Section 2016.040 is added for drafting convenience. The language is drawn from numerous provisions. See former Sections 2017(c)-(d), 2019(b), 2024(e), 2025(e), (g), (i), (j), (n), (o), (q), 2028(d), 2030(e), (l), (m), 2031(f), (m), 2032(c), (d), (h), (j), 2033(e), (l), 2034(e), (i), (k), (l). To eliminate redundancy, these have been revised to refer to Section 2016.040. See Sections 2017.020(a), 2017.220(a), 2019.030(b), 2024.050(a), 2025.260(a), 2025.410(c), 2025.420(a), 2025.450(b)(2), 2025.480(b), 2025.520(g), 2025.530(e), 2028.040(b), 2028.050(b), 2030.090(a), 2030.300(b), 2030.310(b), 2031.060(a), 2031.310(b), 2032.250(a), 2032.310(b), 2032.620(a), 2032.650(a), 2033.080(a), 2033.290(b), 2034.250(a), 2034.470(b), 2034.610(c), 2034.710(c). [33 Cal.L.Rev. Comm. Reports 810 (2004)].

Research References

Rutter, Cal. Practice Guide: Civ. Pro. Before Trial Ch. 8A-3, Civil Discovery Act.

Rutter, Cal. Practice Guide: Civ. Pro. Before Trial Ch. 8F-3, Propounding Interrogatories.

Rutter, Cal. Practice Guide: Civ. Pro. Before Trial Ch. 8F-5, Responding to Interrogatories.

Rutter, Cal. Practice Guide: Civ. Pro. Before Trial Ch. 8F-7, Motion to Compel Answers.

Rutter, Cal. Practice Guide: Civ. Pro. Before Trial Ch. 8G-4, Protective Orders.

Rutter, Cal. Practice Guide: Civ. Pro. Before Trial Ch. 8H-5, Protective Orders.

Rutter, Cal. Practice Guide: Civ. Pro. Before Trial Ch. 8H-8, Enforcing Demand.

Rutter, Cal. Practice Guide: Civ. Pro. Before Trial Ch. 8I-2, Physical Examination by Demand in Personal Injury Cases.

Rutter, Cal. Practice Guide: Civ. Pro. Before Trial Ch. 8I-5, Exchange of Medical Reports; Waiver of Privilege.

Rutter, Cal. Practice Guide: Civ. Pro. Before Trial Ch. 8J-5, Protective Orders.

Rutter, Cal. Practice Guide: Civ. Pro. Before Trial Ch. 8J-7, Deposing Opposing Experts.

Rutter, Cal. Practice Guide: Civ. Pro. Before Trial Ch. 8J-10, Relief from Exclusion Sanction.

Rutter, Cal. Practice Guide: Civil Trials & Evidence Ch. 11-A, A. Direct Examination of Expert Witnesses.

Rutter, Cal. Practice Guide: Personal Injury Ch. 6-C, C. Physical and Mental Examinations (CCP § 2032.020 et seq.).

Rutter, Cal. Practice Guide: Personal Injury Ch. 6-D, D. Expert Witness Information Exchanges (CCP § 2034.210 et seq.).

Rutter, Cal. Practice Guide: Personal Injury Ch. 8-B, B. After Trial Date Set (Three to Four Months Before Trial).

Rutter, Cal. Practice Guide: Personal Injury Ch. 8-C, C. Two Months Before Trial.

§ 2016.050. Service of notice or other papers; allowed methods

Section 1013 applies to any method of discovery or service of a motion provided for in this title. *(Added by Stats.2004, c. 182 (A.B.3081), § 23, operative July 1, 2005.)*

Law Revision Commission Comments

Section 2016.050 continues former Section 2019(e) but broadens the language to clearly encompass a motion for a protective order, as well as a motion for discovery. [33 Cal.L.Rev.Comm. Reports 810 (2004)].

Research References

Rutter, Cal. Practice Guide: Civ. Pro. Before Trial Ch. 8E-4, Notice of Deposition.

Rutter, Cal. Practice Guide: Civ. Pro. Before Trial Ch. 8E-6, Subpoena to Nonparty Deponent or Business Records Custodian.

Rutter, Cal. Practice Guide: Civ. Pro. Before Trial Ch. 8F-5, Responding to Interrogatories.

Rutter, Cal. Practice Guide: Civ. Pro. Before Trial Ch. 8G-5, Responses to Rfas.

Rutter, Cal. Practice Guide: Civ. Pro. Before Trial Ch. 8G-7, Motion to Compel Further Answers.

Rutter, Cal. Practice Guide: Civ. Pro. Before Trial Ch. 8H-4, Demand Procedure.

Rutter, Cal. Practice Guide: Civ. Pro. Before Trial Ch. 8H-6, Responding to Demand.

Rutter, Cal. Practice Guide: Civ. Pro. Before Trial Ch. 8H-8, Enforcing Demand.

Rutter, Cal. Practice Guide: Civ. Pro. Before Trial Ch. 8I-2, Physical Examination by Demand in Personal Injury Cases.

Rutter, Cal. Practice Guide: Civ. Pro. Before Trial Ch. 8E-13, Compare-Depositions on Written Questions.

Rutter, Cal. Practice Guide: Enforcing Judgments/Debts Ch. 6G-2, Written Interrogatories to Judgment Debtor.

Rutter, Cal. Practice Guide: Enforcing Judgments/Debts Ch. 6G-3, Inspection Demand to Judgment Debtor.

Rutter, Cal. Practice Guide: Personal Injury Ch. 6-B, B. Overview of Selected Discovery Procedures.

Rutter, Cal. Practice Guide: Personal Injury Ch. 6-C, C. Physical and Mental Examinations (CCP § 2032.020 et seq.).

Rutter, Cal. Practice Guide: Personal Injury Ch. 8-B, B. After Trial Date Set (Three to Four Months Before Trial).

§ 2016.060. Saturday, Sunday or holiday as last day to act

When the last day to perform or complete any act provided for in this title falls on a Saturday, Sunday, or holiday as specified in Section 10, the time limit is extended until the next court day closer to the trial date. *(Added by Stats.2004, c. 182 (A.B.3081), § 23.5, operative July 1, 2005.)*

Law Revision Commission Comments

Section 2016.060 continues former Section 2024(g) (as amended by 2004 Cal. Stat. ch. 171, § 5) without change, except to replace article with title. [33 Cal.L.Rev.Comm. Reports 811 (2004)].

Research References

Rutter, Cal. Practice Guide: Civ. Pro. Before Trial Ch. 8E-2, When Depositions May be Taken.

Rutter, Cal. Practice Guide: Civ. Pro. Before Trial Ch. 8F-1, When Interrogatories May be Served.

Rutter, Cal. Practice Guide: Civ. Pro. Before Trial Ch. 8F-5, Responding to Interrogatories.

Rutter, Cal. Practice Guide: Civ. Pro. Before Trial Ch. 8G-5, Responses to Rfas.

Rutter, Cal. Practice Guide: Civ. Pro. Before Trial Ch. 8H-6, Responding to Demand.

Rutter, Cal. Practice Guide: Civ. Pro. Before Trial Ch. 8I-2, Physical Examination by Demand in Personal Injury Cases.

Rutter, Cal. Practice Guide: Civ. Pro. Before Trial Ch. 8J-3, Deadline for Demand.

Rutter, Cal. Practice Guide: Civil Trials & Evidence Ch. 11-A, A. Direct Examination of Expert Witnesses.

Rutter, Cal. Practice Guide: Personal Injury Ch. 6-B, B. Overview of Selected Discovery Procedures.

Rutter, Cal. Practice Guide: Personal Injury Ch. 6-C, C. Physical and Mental Examinations (CCP § 2032.020 et seq.).

Rutter, Cal. Practice Guide: Personal Injury Ch. 6-D, D. Expert Witness Information Exchanges (CCP § 2034.210 et seq.).

Rutter, Cal. Practice Guide: Personal Injury Ch. 8-B, B. After Trial Date Set (Three to Four Months Before Trial).

7 Witkin Cal. Proc. 5th Trial § 74, Completion of Discovery.

§ 2016.070. Application to enforcement of money judgments

This title applies to discovery in aid of enforcement of a money judgment only to the extent provided in Article 1 (commencing with Section 708.010) of Chapter 6 of Title 9 of Part 2. *(Added by Stats.2004, c. 182 (A.B.3081), § 23, operative July 1, 2005.)*

Law Revision Commission Comments

Section 2016.070 continues former Section 2016(c) without change, except to replace article with title. [33 Cal.L.Rev.Comm. Reports 811 (2004)].

Research References

Rutter, Cal. Practice Guide: Enforcing Judgments/Debts Ch. 6G-2, Written Interrogatories to Judgment Debtor.

Rutter, Cal. Practice Guide: Enforcing Judgments/Debts Ch. 6G-3, Inspection Demand to Judgment Debtor.

8 Witkin Cal. Proc. 5th Enforcement of Judgment § 381, (S 381) Proceedings and Determination.

CHAPTER 2. SCOPE OF DISCOVERY

ARTICLE 1.   GENERAL PROVISIONS

Section

2017.010.   Persons entitled to discovery; matters discoverable.

2017.020.   Judicial limits upon discovery; order; sanctions; exceptions.

§ 2017.010.   Persons entitled to discovery; matters discoverable

Unless otherwise limited by order of the court in accordance with this title, any party may obtain discovery regarding any matter, not privileged, that is relevant to the subject matter involved in the pending action or to the determination of any motion made in that action, if the matter either is itself admissible in evidence or appears reasonably calculated to lead to the discovery of admissible evidence. Discovery may relate to the claim or defense of the party seeking discovery or of any other party to the action. Discovery may be obtained of the identity and location of persons having knowledge of any discoverable matter, as well as of the existence, description, nature, custody, condition, and location of any document, electronically stored information, tangible thing, or land or other property. *(Added by Stats.2004, c. 182 (A.B.3081), § 23, operative July 1, 2005.   Amended by Stats.2012, c. 72 (S.B.1574), § 8.)*

Law Revision Commission Comments

Section 2017.010 continues former Section 2017(a) without change, except to replace article with title.   [33 Cal.L.Rev.Comm. Reports 811 (2004)].

Research References

Rutter, Cal. Practice Guide: Civ. Pro. Before Trial Ch. 8A-3, Civil Discovery Act.

Rutter, Cal. Practice Guide: Civ. Pro. Before Trial Ch. 8B-3, Limitations on Right to Discovery.

Rutter, Cal. Practice Guide: Civ. Pro. Before Trial Ch. 8C-1, "Relevant to Subject Matter".

Rutter, Cal. Practice Guide: Civ. Pro. Before Trial Ch. 8C-2, "Reasonably Calculated to Lead to Discovery of Admissible Evidence".

Rutter, Cal. Practice Guide: Civ. Pro. Before Trial Ch. 8C-3, "Not Privileged".

Rutter, Cal. Practice Guide: Civ. Pro. Before Trial Ch. 8F-3, Propounding Interrogatories.

Rutter, Cal. Practice Guide: Civ. Pro. Before Trial Ch. 8E-12, Conduct of Deposition.

Rutter, Cal. Practice Guide: Civil Trials & Evidence Ch. 8E-D, D. Other Public Policy Exclusions.

Rutter, Cal. Practice Guide: Enforcing Judgments/Debts Ch. 4-A, A. Attachment.

Rutter, Cal. Practice Guide: Fed.Civ.Pro. Before Trial Ch. 11(III)-B, B. Scope of Discovery.

Rutter, Cal. Practice Guide: Insurance Litigation Ch. 15-G, G. Discovery.

Rutter, Cal. Practice Guide: Personal Injury Ch. 4-C, C. Effective Settlement Negotiations.

Rutter, Cal. Practice Guide: Personal Injury Ch. 6-A, A. Scope of Discovery and Limitations.

Rutter, Cal. Practice Guide: Personal Injury Ch. 6-B, B. Overview of Selected Discovery Procedures.

Rutter, Cal. Practice Guide: Personal Injury Gen. Matls., Highlights.

7 Witkin, California Summary 10th Constitutional Law § 581, (S 581) Discovery of Medical Patient's Records.

§ 2017.020.   Judicial limits upon discovery; order; sanctions; exceptions

(a) The court shall limit the scope of discovery if it determines that the burden, expense, or intrusiveness of that discovery clearly outweighs the likelihood that the information sought will lead to the discovery of admissible evidence. The court may make this determination pursuant to a motion for protective order by a party or other affected person. This motion shall be accompanied by a meet and confer declaration under Section 2016.040.

(b) The court shall impose a monetary sanction under Chapter 7 (commencing with Section 2023.010) against any party, person, or attorney who unsuccessfully makes or opposes a motion for a protective order, unless it finds that the one subject to the sanction acted with substantial justification or that other circumstances make the imposition of the sanction unjust.

(c)(1) Notwithstanding subdivision (b), or any other section of this title, absent exceptional circumstances, the court shall not impose sanctions on a party or any attorney of a party for failure to provide electronically stored information that has been lost, damaged, altered, or overwritten as the result of the routine, good faith operation of an electronic information system.

(2) This subdivision shall not be construed to alter any obligation to preserve discoverable information. *(Added by Stats.2004, c. 182 (A.B.3081), § 23, operative July 1, 2005. Amended by Stats.2012, c. 72 (S.B.1574), § 9.)*

Law Revision Commission Comments

Subdivision (a) of Section 2017.020 continues the first paragraph of former Section 2017(c) without substantive change.

Subdivision (b) continues the second paragraph of former Section 2017(c) without change, except to conform the cross-reference.   [33 Cal.L.Rev.Comm. Reports 812 (2004)].

Research References

Rutter, Cal. Practice Guide: Civ. Pro. Before Trial Ch. 8B-3, Limitations on Right to Discovery.

Rutter, Cal. Practice Guide: Civ. Pro. Before Trial Ch. 8C-2, "Reasonably Calculated to Lead to Discovery of Admissible Evidence".

Rutter, Cal. Practice Guide: Civ. Pro. Before Trial Ch. 8F-4, Protective Orders.

Rutter, Cal. Practice Guide: Civ. Pro. Before Trial Ch. 8E-11, Protective Orders.

Rutter, Cal. Practice Guide: Personal Injury Ch. 6-A, A. Scope of Discovery and Limitations.

ARTICLE 2.   SCOPE OF DISCOVERY IN SPECIFIC CONTEXTS

Section

2017.210.   Insurance carriers; nature, limits or disputes regarding coverage.

2017.220.   Sexual harassment, assault or battery allegations; monetary sanctions.

§ 2017.210.   Insurance carriers; nature, limits or disputes regarding coverage

A party may obtain discovery of the existence and contents of any agreement under which any insurance carrier may be liable to satisfy in whole or in part a judgment that may be entered in the action or to indemnify or reimburse for payments made to satisfy the judgment. This discovery may include the identity of the carrier and the nature and limits of the coverage. A party may also obtain discovery as to whether that insurance carrier is disputing the agreement's coverage of the claim involved in the action, but not as to the nature and substance of that dispute. Information concerning the insurance agreement is not by reason of disclosure admissible in evidence at trial. *(Added by Stats.2004, c. 182 (A.B.3081), § 23, operative July 1, 2005.)*

Law Revision Commission Comments

Section 2017.210 continues former Section 2017(b) without change.   [33 Cal.L.Rev.Comm. Reports 812 (2004)].

Research References

Rutter, Cal. Practice Guide: Civ. Pro. Before Trial Ch. 8C-2, "Reasonably Calculated to Lead to Discovery of Admissible Evidence".

California Practice Guide: Employment Litigation Ch. 3-B, B. Liability Insurance-General Considerations.

§ 2017.220. Sexual harassment, assault or battery allegations; monetary sanctions

(a) In any civil action alleging conduct that constitutes sexual harassment, sexual assault, or sexual battery, any party seeking discovery concerning the plaintiff's sexual conduct with individuals other than the alleged perpetrator shall establish specific facts showing that there is good cause for that discovery, and that the matter sought to be discovered is relevant to the subject matter of the action and reasonably calculated to lead to the discovery of admissible evidence. This showing shall be made by a noticed motion, accompanied by a meet and confer declaration under Section 2016.040, and shall not be made or considered by the court at an ex parte hearing.

(b) The court shall impose a monetary sanction under Chapter 7 (commencing with Section 2023.010) against any party, person, or attorney who unsuccessfully makes or opposes a motion for discovery under subdivision (a), unless it finds that the one subject to the sanction acted with substantial justification or that other circumstances make the imposition of the sanction unjust. *(Added by Stats.2004, c. 182 (A.B.3081), § 23, operative July 1, 2005.)*

Law Revision Commission Comments

Subdivision (a) of Section 2017.220 continues the first paragraph of former Section 2017(d) without substantive change.

Subdivision (b) continues the second paragraph of former Section 2017(d) without substantive change. [33 Cal.L.Rev.Comm. Reports 813 (2004)].

Research References

ARTICLE 3. VIOLATION OF THE ELDER ABUSE AND DEPENDENT ADULT CIVIL PROTECTION ACT

§ 2017.310. Confidential settlement agreements; recognition or enforcement by court; sealing or redacting defendant's name; enforcement of nondisclosure provisions

(a) Notwithstanding any other provision of law, it is the policy of the State of California that confidential settlement agreements are disfavored in any civil action the factual foundation for which establishes a cause of action for a violation of the Elder Abuse and Dependent Adult Civil Protection Act (Chapter 11(commencing with Section 15600) of Part 3 of Division 9 of the Welfare and Institutions Code).

(b) Provisions of a confidential settlement agreement described in subdivision (a) may not be recognized or enforced by the court absent a showing of any of the following:

(1) The information is privileged under existing law.

(2) The information is not evidence of abuse of an elder or dependent adult, as described in Sections 15610.30, 15610.57, and 15610.63 of the Welfare and Institutions Code.

(3) The party seeking to uphold the confidentiality of the information has demonstrated that there is a substantial probability that prejudice will result from the disclosure and that the party's interest in the information cannot be adequately protected through redaction.

(c) Nothing in paragraph (1), (2), or (3) of subdivision (b) permits the sealing or redacting of a defendant's name in any information made available to the public.

(d) Except as expressly provided in this section, nothing in this section is intended to alter, modify, or amend existing law.

(e) Nothing in this section may be deemed to prohibit the entry or enforcement of that part of a confidentiality agreement, settlement agreement, or stipulated agreement between the parties that requires the nondisclosure of the amount of any money paid in a settlement of a claim.

(f) Nothing in this section applies to or affects an action for professional negligence against a health care provider. *(Added by Stats.2004, c. 182 (A.B.3081), § 23, operative July 1, 2005.)*

Law Revision Commission Comments

Section 2017.310 continues former Section 2031.1 without change. [33 Cal.L.Rev.Comm. Reports 814 (2004)].

Research References

§ 2017.320. Evidence subject to pre-existing protective order; evidence of abuse excluded from protection; use in subsequent proceedings; standard of proof; judicial authority to seal or redact

(a) In any civil action the factual foundation for which establishes a cause of action for a violation of the Elder Abuse and Dependent Adult Civil Protection Act (Chapter 11 (commencing with Section 15600) of Part 3 of Division 9 of the Welfare and Institutions Code), any information that is acquired through discovery and is protected from disclosure by a stipulated protective order shall remain subject to the protective order, except for information that is evidence of abuse of an elder or dependent adult as described in Sections 15610.30, 15610.57, and 15610.63 of the Welfare and Institutions Code.

(b) In that instance, after redacting information in the document that is not evidence of abuse of an elder or dependent adult as described in Sections 15610.30, 15610.57, and 15610.63 of the Welfare and Institutions Code, a party may file that particularized information with the court. The party proposing to file the information shall offer to meet and confer with the party from whom the information was obtained at least one week prior to filing that information with the court.

(c) The filing party shall give concurrent notice of the filing with the court and its basis to the party from whom the information was obtained.

(d) Any filed information submitted to the court shall remain confidential under any protective order for 30 days after the filing and shall be part of the public court record thereafter, unless an affected party petitions the court and shows good cause for a court protective order.

(e) The burden of showing good cause shall be on the party seeking the court protective order.

(f) A stipulated protective order may not be recognized or enforced by the court to prevent disclosure of information filed with the court pursuant to subdivision (b), absent a showing of any of the following:

(1) The information is privileged under existing law.

(2) The information is not evidence of abuse of an elder or dependent adult as described in Sections 15610.30, 15610.57, and 15610.63 of the Welfare and Institutions Code.

(3) The party seeking to uphold the confidentiality of the information has demonstrated that there is a substantial probability that prejudice will result from the disclosure and that the party's interest in the information cannot be adequately protected through redaction.

(g) If the court denies the petition for a court protective order, it shall redact any part of the filed information it finds is not evidence of abuse of an elder or dependent adult, as described in Sections 15610.30, 15610.57, and 15610.63 of the Welfare and Institutions Code. Nothing in this subdivision or in paragraph (1), (2), or (3) of subdivision (f) permits the sealing or redacting of a defendant's name in any information made available to the public.

(h) Nothing in this section applies to or affects an action for professional negligence against a health care provider. *(Added by Stats.2004, c. 182 (A.B.3081), § 23, operative July 1, 2005.)*

Law Revision Commission Comments

Section 2017.320 continues former Section 2031.2 without substantive change. [33 Cal.L.Rev.Comm. Reports 815 (2004)].

Research References

Rutter, Cal. Practice Guide: Civ. Pro. Before Trial Ch. 8B-3, Limitations on Right to Discovery.
Rutter, Cal. Practice Guide: Personal Injury Ch. 6-A, A. Scope of Discovery and Limitations.
5 Witkin, California Summary 10th Torts § 149, (S 149) Confidentiality and Disclosure.

CHAPTER 4.   ATTORNEY WORK PRODUCT

§ 2018.010.   "Client" defined

For purposes of this chapter, "client" means a "client" as defined in Section 951 of the Evidence Code. *(Added by Stats.2004, c. 182 (A.B.3081), § 23, operative July 1, 2005.)*

Law Revision Commission Comments

Section 2018.010 continues the second paragraph of former Section 2018(f) without substantive change. [33 Cal.L.Rev.Comm. Reports 820 (2004)].

Research References

Rutter, Cal. Practice Guide: Civ. Pro. Before Trial Ch. 8A-3, Civil Discovery Act.
Rutter, Cal. Practice Guide: Civ. Pro. Before Trial Ch. 8C-4, Attorney Work Product Protection.
Rutter, Cal. Practice Guide: Civil Trials & Evidence Ch. 4-B, B. Preliminary Matters Discussed in Final Status Conference or In-Chambers Conference.
Rutter, Cal. Practice Guide: Civil Trials & Evidence Ch. 8E-A, A. Privileges.
Rutter, Cal. Practice Guide: Civil Trials & Evidence Ch. 8E-B, B. Attorney Work Product Doctrine.

§ 2018.020.   Policy of the state

It is the policy of the state to do both of the following:

(a) Preserve the rights of attorneys to prepare cases for trial with that degree of privacy necessary to encourage them to prepare their cases thoroughly and to investigate not only the favorable but the unfavorable aspects of those cases.

(b) Prevent attorneys from taking undue advantage of their adversary's industry and efforts. *(Added by Stats.2004, c. 182 (A.B.3081), § 23, operative July 1, 2005.)*

Law Revision Commission Comments

Section 2018.020 continues former Section 2018(a) without substantive change. [33 Cal.L.Rev.Comm. Reports 820 (2004)].

Research References

Rutter, Cal. Practice Guide: Civ. Pro. Before Trial Ch. 8C-4, Attorney Work Product Protection.
Rutter, Cal. Practice Guide: Civil Trials & Evidence Ch. 8E-B, B. Attorney Work Product Doctrine.
Rutter, Cal. Practice Guide: Personal Injury Ch. 6-A, A. Scope of Discovery and Limitations.

§ 2018.030.   Writings and written documentation

(a) A writing that reflects an attorney's impressions, conclusions, opinions, or legal research or theories is not discoverable under any circumstances.

(b) The work product of an attorney, other than a writing described in subdivision (a), is not discoverable unless the court determines that denial of discovery will unfairly prejudice the party seeking discovery in preparing that party's claim or defense or will result in an injustice. *(Added by Stats.2004, c. 182 (A.B.3081), § 23, operative July 1, 2005.)*

Law Revision Commission Comments

Subdivision (a) of Section 2018.030 continues former Section 2018(c) without substantive change.
Subdivision (b) continues former Section 2018(b) without substantive change. [33 Cal.L.Rev.Comm. Reports 821 (2004)].

Research References

Rutter, Cal. Practice Guide: A.D.R. Ch. 3-C, C. Confidentiality.
Rutter, Cal. Practice Guide: Civ. Pro. Before Trial Ch. 1-B, B. Prelawsuit Investigations, Research and Analysis.
Rutter, Cal. Practice Guide: Civ. Pro. Before Trial Ch. 1-D, D. Prelawsuit Consultation Requirement in Certain Professional Negligence Actions.

Rutter, Cal. Practice Guide: Civ. Pro. Before Trial Ch. 8C-4, Attorney Work Product Protection.

Rutter, Cal. Practice Guide: Civ. Pro. Before Trial Ch. 8H-8, Enforcing Demand.

Rutter, Cal. Practice Guide: Civ. Pro. Before Trial Ch. 8E-12, Conduct of Deposition.

Rutter, Cal. Practice Guide: Civ. Pro. Before Trial Ch. 12(I)-B, B. Case Management ("Fast Track") System.

Rutter, Cal. Practice Guide: Civil Trials & Evidence Ch. 5-E, E. Preparation for Attorney Voir Dire.

Rutter, Cal. Practice Guide: Civil Trials & Evidence Ch. 8E-B, B. Attorney Work Product Doctrine.

Rutter, Cal. Practice Guide: Civil Trials & Evidence Ch. 8E-D, D. Other Public Policy Exclusions.

Rutter, Cal. Practice Guide: Civil Trials & Evidence Gen. Matls., Highlights.

Rutter, Cal. Practice Guide: Insurance Litigation Ch. 15-G, G. Discovery.

Rutter, Cal. Practice Guide: Personal Injury Ch. 6-A, A. Scope of Discovery and Limitations.

Rutter, Cal. Practice Guide: Personal Injury Ch. 6-B, B. Overview of Selected Discovery Procedures.

Rutter, Cal. Practice Guide: Prof. Responsibility Ch. 7-D, D. Attorney Work Product Doctrine.

Rutter, Cal. Practice Guide: Prof. Responsibility Ch. 10-F, F. Attorney Obligations Upon Termination of Representation.

Rutter, Cal. Practice Guide: Prof. Responsibility Gen. Matls., Highlights.

§ 2018.040. Restatement of existing law

This chapter is intended to be a restatement of existing law relating to protection of work product. It is not intended to expand or reduce the extent to which work product is discoverable under existing law in any action. *(Added by Stats.2004, c. 182 (A.B.3081), § 23, operative July 1, 2005.)*

Law Revision Commission Comments

Section 2018.040 continues the first and second sentences of former Section 2018(d) without change, except to replace section with chapter. [33 Cal.L.Rev.Comm. Reports 821 (2004)].

§ 2018.050. Participation in crime or fraud

Notwithstanding Section 2018.040, when a lawyer is suspected of knowingly participating in a crime or fraud, there is no protection of work product under this chapter in any official investigation by a law enforcement agency or proceeding or action brought by a public prosecutor in the name of the people of the State of California if the services of the lawyer were sought or obtained to enable or aid anyone to commit or plan to commit a crime or fraud. *(Added by Stats.2004, c. 182 (A.B. 3081), § 23, operative July 1, 2005.)*

Law Revision Commission Comments

Section 2018.050 continues the third sentence of former Section 2018(d) without substantive change. [33 Cal.L.Rev.Comm. Reports 821 (2004)].

Research References

Rutter, Cal. Practice Guide: Civ. Pro. Before Trial Ch. 8C-4, Attorney Work Product Protection.

Rutter, Cal. Practice Guide: Civil Trials & Evidence Ch. 8E-B, B. Attorney Work Product Doctrine.

Rutter, Cal. Practice Guide: Personal Injury Ch. 6-A, A. Scope of Discovery and Limitations.

Rutter, Cal. Practice Guide: Prof. Responsibility Ch. 7-D, D. Attorney Work Product Doctrine.

1 Witkin Cal. Proc. 5th Attorneys § 584, in General.

§ 2018.060. In camera hearings

Nothing in this chapter is intended to limit an attorney's ability to request an in camera hearing as provided for in People v. Superior Court (Laff) (2001) 25 Cal.4th 703 [1]. *(Added by Stats.2004, c. 182 (A.B.3081), § 23, operative July 1, 2005.)*

[1] 107 Cal.Rptr.2d 328.

Law Revision Commission Comments

Section 2018.060 continues the fourth sentence of former Section 2018(d) without change, except to replace section with chapter. [33 Cal.L.Rev.Comm. Reports 822 (2004)].

§ 2018.070. Disciplinary proceedings

(a) The State Bar may discover the work product of an attorney against whom disciplinary charges are pending when it is relevant to issues of breach of duty by the lawyer and requisite client approval has been granted.

(b) Where requested and for good cause, discovery under this section shall be subject to a protective order to ensure the confidentiality of the work product except for its use by the State Bar in disciplinary investigations and its consideration under seal in State Bar Court proceedings.

(c) For purposes of this chapter, whenever a client has initiated a complaint against an attorney, the requisite client approval shall be deemed to have been granted. *(Added by Stats.2004, c. 182 (A.B.3081), § 23, operative July 1, 2005.)*

Law Revision Commission Comments

Subdivisions (a) and (b) of Section 2018.070 continue the first sentence of former Section 2018(e) without substantive change.

Subdivision (c) continues the second sentence of former Section 2018(e) without change, except to replace section with chapter. [33 Cal.L.Rev.Comm. Reports 822 (2004)].

Research References

Rutter, Cal. Practice Guide: Civ. Pro. Before Trial Ch. 1-A, A. Accepting a New Case.

Rutter, Cal. Practice Guide: Civ. Pro. Before Trial Ch. 1-B, B. Prelawsuit Investigations, Research and Analysis.

Rutter, Cal. Practice Guide: Civ. Pro. Before Trial Ch. 8C-4, Attorney Work Product Protection.

Rutter, Cal. Practice Guide: Personal Injury Ch. 6-A, A. Scope of Discovery and Limitations.

Rutter, Cal. Practice Guide: Prof. Responsibility Ch. 7-D, D. Attorney Work Product Doctrine.

Rutter, Cal. Practice Guide: Prof. Responsibility Ch. 11-E, E. Receiving Complaints of Attorney Misconduct.

1 Witkin Cal. Proc. 5th Attorneys § 584, in General.

§ 2018.080. Breach of duty; actions against attorney by client or former client

In an action between an attorney and a client or a former client of the attorney, no work product privilege under this chapter exists if the work product is relevant to an issue of breach by the attorney of a duty to the client arising out of the attorney-client relationship. *(Added by Stats.2004, c. 182 (A.B. 3081), § 23, operative July 1, 2005.)*

Law Revision Commission Comments

Section 2018.080 continues the first paragraph of former Section 2018(f) without substantive change. [33 Cal.L.Rev.Comm. Reports 822 (2004)].

Research References

Rutter, Cal. Practice Guide: Civ. Pro. Before Trial Ch. 1-A, A. Accepting a New Case.

Rutter, Cal. Practice Guide: Civ. Pro. Before Trial Ch. 8C-4, Attorney Work Product Protection.

Rutter, Cal. Practice Guide: Personal Injury Ch. 6-A, A. Scope of Discovery and Limitations.

Rutter, Cal. Practice Guide: Prof. Responsibility Ch. 7-D, D. Attorney Work Product Doctrine.

Rutter, Cal. Practice Guide: Prof. Responsibility Ch. 10-F, F. Attorney Obligations Upon Termination of Representation.

CHAPTER 5. METHODS AND SEQUENCE OF DISCOVERY

ARTICLE 1. GENERAL PROVISIONS

§ 2019.010. Approved methods

Any party may obtain discovery by one or more of the following methods:

(a) Oral and written depositions.

(b) Interrogatories to a party.

(c) Inspections of documents, things, and places.

(d) Physical and mental examinations.

(e) Requests for admissions.

(f) Simultaneous exchanges of expert trial witness information. *(Added by Stats.2004, c. 182 (A.B.3081), § 23, operative July 1, 2005.)*

Law Revision Commission Comments

Section 2019.010 continues former Section 2019(a) without change. [33 Cal.L.Rev.Comm. Reports 823 (2004)].

Research References

Rutter, Cal. Practice Guide: Civ. Pro. Before Trial Ch. 8A-8, Discovery in Nonjudicial Proceedings.
Rutter, Cal. Practice Guide: Civ. Pro. Before Trial Ch. 8D-5, Selecting Proper Discovery Tools.
Rutter, Cal. Practice Guide: Civ. Pro. Before Trial Ch. 8G-1, When RFAs May be Served.
Rutter, Cal. Practice Guide: Civ. Pro. Before Trial Ch. 8G-3, Propounding Requests.
2 Witkin Cal. Proc. 5th Courts § 289, (S 289) in General.
2 Witkin Cal. Proc. 5th Courts § 316, in General.

§ 2019.020. Sequence and timing; discretion of parties; court order

(a) Except as otherwise provided by a rule of the Judicial Council, a local court rule, or a local uniform written policy, the methods of discovery may be used in any sequence, and the fact that a party is conducting discovery, whether by deposition or another method, shall not operate to delay the discovery of any other party.

(b) Notwithstanding subdivision (a), on motion and for good cause shown, the court may establish the sequence and timing of discovery for the convenience of parties and witnesses and in the interests of justice. *(Added by Stats.2004, c. 182 (A.B.3081), § 23, operative July 1, 2005.)*

Law Revision Commission Comments

Subdivision (a) of Section 2019.020 continues the first sentence of former Section 2019(c) without substantive change.

Subdivision (b) continues the second sentence of former Section 2019(c) without substantive change. [33 Cal.L.Rev.Comm. Reports 823 (2004)].

Research References

Rutter, Cal. Practice Guide: Civ. Pro. Before Trial Ch. 8B-3, Limitations on Right to Discovery.
Rutter, Cal. Practice Guide: Civ. Pro. Before Trial Ch. 8E-4, Notice of Deposition.

§ 2019.030. Court–imposed restrictions; motion; monetary sanction

(a) The court shall restrict the frequency or extent of use of a discovery method provided in Section 2019.010 if it determines either of the following:

(1) The discovery sought is unreasonably cumulative or duplicative, or is obtainable from some other source that is more convenient, less burdensome, or less expensive.

(2) The selected method of discovery is unduly burdensome or expensive, taking into account the needs of the case, the amount in controversy, and the importance of the issues at stake in the litigation.

(b) The court may make these determinations pursuant to a motion for a protective order by a party or other affected person. This motion shall be accompanied by a meet and confer declaration under Section 2016.040.

(c) The court shall impose a monetary sanction under Chapter 7 (commencing with Section 2023.010) against any party, person, or attorney who unsuccessfully makes or opposes a motion for a protective order, unless it finds that the one subject to the sanction acted with substantial justification or that other circumstances make the imposition of the sanction unjust. *(Added by Stats.2004, c. 182 (A.B.3081), § 23, operative July 1, 2005.)*

Law Revision Commission Comments

The introductory clause of subdivision (a) of Section 2019.030 continues the introductory clause of former Section 2019(b) without substantive change. Subdivision (a)(1) continues former Section 2019(b)(1) without change. Subdivision (a)(2) continues former Section 2019(b)(2) without change.

Subdivision (b) continues the next-to-last paragraph of former Section 2019(b) without substantive change.

Subdivision (c) continues the last paragraph of former Section 2019(b) without change, except to conform the cross-reference. [33 Cal.L.Rev. Comm. Reports 824 (2004)].

Research References

Rutter, Cal. Practice Guide: Civ. Pro. Before Trial Ch. 8A-3, Civil Discovery Act.
Rutter, Cal. Practice Guide: Civ. Pro. Before Trial Ch. 8B-3, Limitations on Right to Discovery.
Rutter, Cal. Practice Guide: Civ. Pro. Before Trial Ch. 8F-4, Protective Orders.
Rutter, Cal. Practice Guide: Civ. Pro. Before Trial Ch. 8E-11, Protective Orders.
Rutter, Cal. Practice Guide: Personal Injury Ch. 6-B, B. Overview of Selected Discovery Procedures.
Rutter, Cal. Practice Guide: Personal Injury Ch. 6-C, C. Physical and Mental Examinations (CCP § 2032.020 et seq.).
Rutter, Cal. Practice Guide: Personal Injury Ch. 8-B, B. After Trial Date Set (Three to Four Months Before Trial).

§ 2019.040. Application of discovery methods and procedures to electronically stored information

(a) When any method of discovery permits the production, inspection, copying, testing, or sampling of documents or tangible things, that method shall also permit the production, inspection, copying, testing, or sampling of electronically stored information.

(b) All procedures available under this title to compel, prevent, or limit the production, inspection, copying, testing, or sampling of documents or tangible things shall be available to compel, prevent, or limit the production, inspection, copying, testing, or sampling of electronically stored information. *(Added by Stats.2012, c. 72 (S.B.1574), § 14.)*

ARTICLE 2. METHODS AND SEQUENCE OF DISCOVERY IN SPECIFIC CONTEXTS

Section
2019.210. Misappropriation of trade secrets.

§ 2019.210. Misappropriation of trade secrets

In any action alleging the misappropriation of a trade secret under the Uniform Trade Secrets Act (Title 5 (commencing with Section 3426) of Part 1 of Division 4 of the Civil Code), before commencing discovery relating to the trade secret, the party alleging the misappropriation shall identify the trade secret with reasonable particularity subject to any orders that may be appropriate under Section 3426.5 of the Civil Code. *(Added by Stats.2004, c. 182 (A.B.3081), § 23, operative July 1, 2005.)*

Law Revision Commission Comments

Section 2019.210 continues former Section 2019(d) without change. [33 Cal.L.Rev.Comm. Reports 825 (2004)].

Research References

Rutter, Cal. Practice Guide: Civil Appeals & Writs Ch. 8-C, C. Standards of Appellate Review.
Rutter, Cal. Practice Guide: Civ. Pro. Before Trial Ch. 8B-4, Status of Pleadings Affecting Right to Discovery.
Rutter, Cal. Practice Guide: Fed.Civ.Pro. Before Trial Ch. 11(III)-A, A. Limitations on Right to Discovery.
13 Witkin, California Summary 10th Equity § 92, (S 92) Orders to Preserve Secrecy.

CHAPTER 6. NONPARTY DISCOVERY

ARTICLE 1. GENERAL PROVISIONS

Section
2020.010. Persons within the state; approved methods.
2020.020. Deposition subpoena; scope of authority.
2020.030. Application of Evidence Code provisions to deposition subpoena.

§ 2020.010. Persons within the state; approved methods

(a) Any of the following methods may be used to obtain discovery within the state from a person who is not a party to the action in which the discovery is sought:

(1) An oral deposition under Chapter 9 (commencing with Section 2025.010).

(2) A written deposition under Chapter 11 (commencing with Section 2028.010).

(3) A deposition for production of business records and things under Article 4 (commencing with Section 2020.410) or Article 5 (commencing with Section 2020.510).

(b) Except as provided in subdivision (a) of Section 2025.280, the process by which a nonparty is required to provide discovery is a deposition subpoena. *(Added by Stats.2004, c. 182 (A.B. 3081), § 23, operative July 1, 2005.)*

Law Revision Commission Comments

Subdivision (a) of Section 2020.010 continues the first sentence of former Section 2020(a) without substantive change.

Subdivision (b) continues the second sentence of former Section 2020(a) without change, except to conform the cross-reference. [33 Cal.L.Rev.Comm. Reports 825 (2004)].

Research References

Rutter, Cal. Practice Guide: Civ. Pro. Before Trial Ch. 8A-3, Civil Discovery Act.
Rutter, Cal. Practice Guide: Civ. Pro. Before Trial Ch. 8E-1, When Prior Court Order Required.
Rutter, Cal. Practice Guide: Civ. Pro. Before Trial Ch. 8E-3, Whose Deposition May be Taken.
Rutter, Cal. Practice Guide: Civ. Pro. Before Trial Ch. 8E-6, Subpoena to Nonparty Deponent or Business Records Custodian.
Rutter, Cal. Practice Guide: Civ. Pro. Before Trial Ch. 8E-16, Sanctions Re Depositions.
Rutter, Cal. Practice Guide: Civ. Pro. Before Trial Ch. 8E-1, Outline 1.
Rutter, Cal. Practice Guide: Personal Injury Ch. 6-B, B. Overview of Selected Discovery Procedures.
10 Witkin, California Summary 10th Parent and Child § 58, (S 58) Grant or Denial.
14 Witkin, California Summary 10th Wills and Probate § 597, Powers of Probate Referee.

§ 2020.020. Deposition subpoena; scope of authority

A deposition subpoena may command any of the following:

(a) Only the attendance and the testimony of the deponent, under Article 3 (commencing with Section 2020.310).

(b) Only the production of business records for copying, under Article 4 (commencing with Section 2020.410).

(c) The attendance and the testimony of the deponent, as well as the production of business records, other documents, electronically stored information, and tangible things, under Article 5 (commencing with Section 2020.510). *(Added by Stats.2004, c. 182 (A.B.3081), § 23, operative July 1, 2005. Amended by Stats.2012, c. 72 (S.B.1574), § 15.)*

Law Revision Commission Comments

Section 2020.020 continues the third sentence (including items (1)-(3)) of former Section 2020(a) without substantive change. [33 Cal.L.Rev. Comm. Reports 826 (2004)].

Research References

Rutter, Cal. Practice Guide: Civ. Pro. Before Trial Ch. 8A-3, Civil Discovery Act.
Rutter, Cal. Practice Guide: Civ. Pro. Before Trial Ch. 8E-4, Notice of Deposition.
Rutter, Cal. Practice Guide: Civ. Pro. Before Trial Ch. 8E-6, Subpoena to Nonparty Deponent or Business Records Custodian.
Rutter, Cal. Practice Guide: Civ. Pro. Before Trial Ch. 8H-1, on Whom Demand May be Served.

Rutter, Cal. Practice Guide: Personal Injury Ch. 6-B, B. Overview of Selected Discovery Procedures.

§ 2020.030. Application of Evidence Code provisions to deposition subpoena

Except as modified in this chapter, the provisions of Chapter 2 (commencing with Section 1985) of Title 3 of Part 4 of this code, and of Article 4 (commencing with Section 1560) of Chapter 2 of Division 11 of the Evidence Code, apply to a deposition subpoena. *(Added by Stats.2004, c. 182 (A.B.3081), § 23, operative July 1, 2005.)*

Law Revision Commission Comments

Section 2020.030 continues the last paragraph of former Section 2020(a) without substantive change. [33 Cal.L.Rev.Comm. Reports 826 (2004)].

Research References

Rutter, Cal. Practice Guide: Civ. Pro. Before Trial Ch. 8E-3, Whose Deposition May be Taken.

Rutter, Cal. Practice Guide: Civ. Pro. Before Trial Ch. 8E-6, Subpoena to Nonparty Deponent or Business Records Custodian.

Rutter, Cal. Practice Guide: Personal Injury Ch. 6-B, B. Overview of Selected Discovery Procedures.

ARTICLE 2. PROCEDURES APPLICABLE TO ALL TYPES OF DEPOSITION SUBPOENAS

Section

2020.210. Issuance by court clerk; alternative method of issuance.

2020.220. Service of deposition subpoena; timing; persons authorized to serve; scope of subpoena authority; subpoena of electronically stored information.

2020.230. Personal attendance of deponent; witness and mileage fees; custodian of records.

2020.240. Failure to obey subpoena; contempt; punishment; compliance.

§ 2020.210. Issuance by court clerk; alternative method of issuance

(a) The clerk of the court in which the action is pending shall issue a deposition subpoena signed and sealed, but otherwise in blank, to a party requesting it, who shall fill it in before service.

(b) Instead of a court-issued deposition subpoena, an attorney of record for any party may sign and issue a deposition subpoena. A deposition subpoena issued under this subdivision need not be sealed. A copy may be served on the nonparty, and the attorney may retain the original. *(Added by Stats.2004, c. 182 (A.B.3081), § 23, operative July 1, 2005.)*

Law Revision Commission Comments

Subdivision (a) of Section 2020.210 continues the first sentence of former Section 2020(b) without substantive change.

Subdivision (b) continues the second sentence of former Section 2020(b) without substantive change. [33 Cal.L.Rev.Comm. Reports 826 (2004)].

Research References

Rutter, Cal. Practice Guide: Civ. Pro. Before Trial Ch. 8E-6, Subpoena to Nonparty Deponent or Business Records Custodian.

§ 2020.220. Service of deposition subpoena; timing; persons authorized to serve; scope of subpoena authority; subpoena of electronically stored information

(a) Subject to subdivision (c) of Section 2020.410, service of a deposition subpoena shall be effected a sufficient time in advance of the deposition to provide the deponent a reasonable opportunity to locate and produce any designated business records, documents, electronically stored information, and tangible things, as described in Article 4 (commencing with Section 2020.410), and, where personal attendance is commanded, a reasonable time to travel to the place of deposition.

(b) Any person may serve the subpoena by personal delivery of a copy of it as follows:

(1) If the deponent is a natural person, to that person.

(2) If the deponent is an organization, to any officer, director, custodian of records, or to any agent or employee authorized by the organization to accept service of a subpoena.

(c) Personal service of any deposition subpoena is effective to require all of the following of any deponent who is a resident of California at the time of service:

(1) Personal attendance and testimony, if the subpoena so specifies.

(2) Any specified production, inspection, testing, and sampling.

(3) The deponent's attendance at a court session to consider any issue arising out of the deponent's refusal to be sworn, or to answer any question, or to produce specified items, or to permit inspection or photocopying, if the subpoena so specifies, or specified testing and sampling of the items produced.

(d) Unless the subpoenaing party and the subpoenaed person otherwise agree or the court otherwise orders, the following shall apply:

(1) If a subpoena requiring production of electronically stored information does not specify a form or forms for producing a type of electronically stored information, the person subpoenaed shall produce the information in the form or forms in which it is ordinarily maintained or in a form that is reasonably usable.

(2) A subpoenaed person need not produce the same electronically stored information in more than one form.

(e) The subpoenaed person opposing the production, inspection, copying, testing, or sampling of electronically stored information on the basis that the information is from a source that is not reasonably accessible because of undue burden or expense shall bear the burden of demonstrating that the information is from a source that is not reasonably accessible because of undue burden or expense.

(f) If the person from whom discovery of electronically stored information is subpoenaed establishes that the information is from a source that is not reasonably accessible because of undue burden or expense, the court may nonetheless order discovery if the subpoenaing party shows good cause, subject to any limitations imposed under subdivision (i).

(g) If the court finds good cause for the production of electronically stored information from a source that is not reasonably accessible, the court may set conditions for the discovery of the electronically stored information, including allocation of the expense of discovery.

(h) If necessary, the subpoenaed person, at the reasonable expense of the subpoenaing party, shall, through detection devices, translate any data compilations included in the subpoena into a reasonably usable form.

(i) The court shall limit the frequency or extent of discovery of electronically stored information, even from a source that is reasonably accessible, if the court determines that any of the following conditions exists:

(1) It is possible to obtain the information from some other source that is more convenient, less burdensome, or less expensive.

(2) The discovery sought is unreasonably cumulative or duplicative.

(3) The party seeking discovery has had ample opportunity by discovery in the action to obtain the information sought.

(4) The likely burden or expense of the proposed discovery outweighs the likely benefit, taking into account the amount in controversy, the resources of the parties, the importance of the issues in the litigation, and the importance of the requested discovery in resolving the issues.

(j) If a subpoenaed person notifies the subpoenaing party that electronically stored information produced pursuant to a subpoena is subject to a claim of privilege or of protection as attorney work product, as described in Section 2031.285, the provisions of Section 2031.285 shall apply.

(k) A party serving a subpoena requiring the production of electronically stored information shall take reasonable steps to avoid imposing undue burden or expense on a person subject to the subpoena.

(*l*) An order of the court requiring compliance with a subpoena issued under this section shall protect a person who is neither a party nor a party's officer from undue burden or expense resulting from compliance.

(m)(1) Absent exceptional circumstances, the court shall not impose sanctions on a subpoenaed person or any attorney of a subpoenaed person for failure to provide electronically stored information that has been lost, damaged, altered, or overwritten as the result of the routine, good faith operation of an electronic information system.

(2) The subdivision shall not be construed to alter any obligation to preserve discoverable information. (*Added by Stats.2004, c. 182 (A.B.3081), § 23, operative July 1, 2005. Amended by Stats.2012, c. 72 (S.B.1574), § 16.*)

Law Revision Commission Comments

Subdivision (a) of Section 2020.220 continues the first sentence of former Section 2020(f) without change, except to conform the cross-references.

Subdivision (b) continues the second sentence of former Section 2020(f) without substantive change.

Subdivision (c) continues former Section 2020(g) without substantive change. [33 Cal.L.Rev.Comm. Reports 827 (2004)].

Research References

Rutter, Cal. Practice Guide: Civ. Pro. Before Trial Ch. 8E-6, Subpoena to Nonparty Deponent or Business Records Custodian.
Rutter, Cal. Practice Guide: Personal Injury Ch. 6-B, B. Overview of Selected Discovery Procedures.
Rutter, Cal. Practice Guide: Personal Injury Ch. 8-B, B. After Trial Date Set (Three to Four Months Before Trial).

§ 2020.230. Personal attendance of deponent; witness and mileage fees; custodian of records

(a) If a deposition subpoena requires the personal attendance of the deponent, under Article 3 (commencing with Section 2020.310) or Article 5 (commencing with Section 2020.510), the party noticing the deposition shall pay to the deponent in cash or by check the same witness fee and mileage required by Chapter 1 (commencing with Section 68070) of Title 8 of the Government Code for attendance and testimony before the court in which the action is pending. This payment, whether or not demanded by the deponent, shall be made, at the option of the party noticing the deposition, either at the time of service of the deposition subpoena, or at the time the deponent attends for the taking of testimony.

(b) Service of a deposition subpoena that does not require the personal attendance of a custodian of records or other qualified person, under Article 4 (commencing with Section 2020.410),

shall be accompanied, whether or not demanded by the deponent, by a payment in cash or by check of the witness fee required by paragraph (6) of subdivision (b) of Section 1563 of the Evidence Code. (*Added by Stats.2004, c. 182 (A.B.3081), § 23, operative July 1, 2005.*)

Law Revision Commission Comments

Subdivision (a) of Section 2020.230 continues the second paragraph of former Section 2020(f) without change, except to conform cross-references.

Subdivision (b) continues the third paragraph of former Section 2020(f) without change, except to conform a cross-reference. [33 Cal.L.Rev. Comm. Reports 828 (2004)].

Research References

Rutter, Cal. Practice Guide: Civ. Pro. Before Trial Ch. 8E-6, Subpoena to Nonparty Deponent or Business Records Custodian.
Rutter, Cal. Practice Guide: Civil Trials & Evidence Ch. 1-C, C. Marshalling the Evidence.
Rutter, Cal. Practice Guide: Personal Injury Ch. 6-B, B. Overview of Selected Discovery Procedures.
Rutter, Cal. Practice Guide: Personal Injury Ch. 8-B, B. After Trial Date Set (Three to Four Months Before Trial).

§ 2020.240. Failure to obey subpoena; contempt; punishment; compliance

A deponent who disobeys a deposition subpoena in any manner described in subdivision (c) of Section 2020.220 may be punished for contempt under Chapter 7 (commencing with Section 2023.010) without the necessity of a prior order of court directing compliance by the witness. The deponent is also subject to the forfeiture and the payment of damages set forth in Section 1992. (*Added by Stats.2004, c. 182 (A.B.3081), § 23, operative July 1, 2005.*)

Law Revision Commission Comments

Section 2020.240 continues former Section 2020(h) without substantive change. [33 Cal.L.Rev.Comm. Reports 829 (2004)].

Research References

Rutter, Cal. Practice Guide: Civ. Pro. Before Trial Ch. 8E-6, Subpoena to Nonparty Deponent or Business Records Custodian.
Rutter, Cal. Practice Guide: Civ. Pro. Before Trial Ch. 8E-16, Sanctions Re Depositions.

ARTICLE 3. SUBPOENA COMMANDING ONLY ATTENDANCE AND TESTIMONY OF THE DEPONENT

Section
2020.310. Contents of subpoena; summarization of enumerated topics; recordation at hearing; visual displays; necessity of attendance by agents or employees of deponent.

§ 2020.310. Contents of subpoena; summarization of enumerated topics; recordation at hearing; visual displays; necessity of attendance by agents or employees of deponent

The following rules apply to a deposition subpoena that commands only the attendance and the testimony of the deponent:

(a) The subpoena shall specify the time when and the place where the deponent is commanded to attend the deposition.

(b) The subpoena shall set forth a summary of all of the following:

(1) The nature of a deposition.

(2) The rights and duties of the deponent.

(3) The penalties for disobedience of a deposition subpoena, as described in Section 2020.240.

(c) If the deposition will be recorded using audio or video technology by, or at the direction of, the noticing party under Section 2025.340, the subpoena shall state that it will be recorded in that manner.

(d) If the deposition testimony will be conducted using instant visual display, the subpoena shall state that it will be conducted in that manner.

(e) If the deponent is an organization, the subpoena shall describe with reasonable particularity the matters on which examination is requested. The subpoena shall also advise the organization of its duty to make the designation of employees or agents who will attend the deposition, as described in Section 2025.230. *(Added by Stats.2004, c. 182 (A.B.3081), § 23, operative July 1, 2005.)*

Law Revision Commission Comments

Section 2020.310 continues former Section 2020(c) without substantive change. [33 Cal.L.Rev.Comm. Reports 829 (2004)].

Research References

Rutter, Cal. Practice Guide: Civ. Pro. Before Trial Ch. 8E-6, Subpoena to Nonparty Deponent or Business Records Custodian.
Rutter, Cal. Practice Guide: Civ. Pro. Before Trial Ch. 8E-10, Preservation of Testimony.
Rutter, Cal. Practice Guide: Civ. Pro. Before Trial Ch. 8E-17, Use of Depositions at Trial.
Rutter, Cal. Practice Guide: Civil Trials & Evidence Ch. 8C-E, E. Audio or Visual Recordings.
Rutter, Cal. Practice Guide: Civil Trials & Evidence Ch. 8C-I, I. Depositions and Discovery.
Rutter, Cal. Practice Guide: Personal Injury Ch. 6-B, B. Overview of Selected Discovery Procedures.

ARTICLE 4.   SUBPOENA COMMANDING ONLY PRODUCTION OF BUSINESS RECORDS FOR COPYING

Section
2020.410.   Specificity of requests; production of business records and electronically stored information; certification by custodian; personal records pertaining to consumers.
2020.420.   Professional photocopier services; qualifications; objections.
2020.430.   Delivery for copying; requirements; time to deliver; application of Evidence Code concerning inspection of records.
2020.440.   Distribution of copies to parties; deposition officer duties; additional copies.

§ 2020.410.   Specificity of requests; production of business records and electronically stored information; certification by custodian; personal records pertaining to consumers

(a) A deposition subpoena that commands only the production of business records for copying shall designate the business records to be produced either by specifically describing each individual item or by reasonably particularizing each category of item, and shall specify the form in which any electronically stored information is to be produced, if a particular form is desired.

(b) Notwithstanding subdivision (a), specific information identifiable only to the deponent's records system, like a policy number or the date when a consumer interacted with the witness, is not required.

(c) A deposition subpoena that commands only the production of business records for copying need not be accompanied by an affidavit or declaration showing good cause for the production of the business records designated in it. It shall be directed to the custodian of those records or another person qualified to certify the records. It shall command compliance in accordance with Section 2020.430 on a date that is no earlier than 20 days after the issuance, or 15 days after the service, of the deposition subpoena, whichever date is later.

(d) If, under Section 1985.3 or 1985.6, the one to whom the deposition subpoena is directed is a witness, and the business records described in the deposition subpoena are personal records pertaining to a consumer, the service of the deposition subpoena shall be accompanied either by a copy of the proof of service of the notice to the consumer described in subdivision (e) of Section 1985.3, or subdivision (b) of Section 1985.6, as applicable, or by the consumer's written authorization to release personal records described in paragraph (2) of subdivision (c) of Section 1985.3, or paragraph (2) of subdivision (c) of Section 1985.6, as applicable. *(Added by Stats.2004, c. 182 (A.B.3081), § 23, operative July 1, 2005.   Amended by Stats.2012, c. 72 (S.B.1574), § 17.)*

Law Revision Commission Comments

Subdivisions (a) and (b) of Section 2020.410 continue the first sentence of former Section 2020(d)(1) without substantive change.

Subdivision (c) continues the second, third, and fourth sentences of former Section 2020(d)(1) without substantive change.

Subdivision (d) continues former Section 2020(d)(2) without change. [33 Cal.L.Rev.Comm. Reports 830 (2004)].

Research References

Rutter, Cal. Practice Guide: A.D.R. Ch. 5-H, H. Conduct of Arbitration Proceedings.
Rutter, Cal. Practice Guide: Civ. Pro. Before Trial Ch. 8D-5, Selecting Proper Discovery Tools.
Rutter, Cal. Practice Guide: Civ. Pro. Before Trial Ch. 8E-3, Whose Deposition May be Taken.
Rutter, Cal. Practice Guide: Civ. Pro. Before Trial Ch. 8E-6, Subpoena to Nonparty Deponent or Business Records Custodian.
Rutter, Cal. Practice Guide: Civ. Pro. Before Trial Ch. 8L-1, Limitations on Existing Discovery Procedures.
Rutter, Cal. Practice Guide: Civ. Pro. Before Trial Ch. 8D-5, Outline 5.
Rutter, Cal. Practice Guide: Civil Trials & Evidence Ch. 1-C, C. Marshalling the Evidence.
Rutter, Cal. Practice Guide: Personal Injury Ch. 6-B, B. Overview of Selected Discovery Procedures.

§ 2020.420.   Professional photocopier services; qualifications; objections

The officer for a deposition seeking discovery only of business records for copying under this article shall be a professional photocopier registered under Chapter 20 (commencing with Section 22450) of Division 8 of the Business and Professions Code, or a person exempted from the registration requirements of that chapter under Section 22451 of the Business and Professions Code. This deposition officer shall not be financially interested in the action, or a relative or employee of any attorney of the parties. Any objection to the qualifications of the deposition officer is waived unless made before the date of production or as soon thereafter as the ground for that objection becomes known or could be discovered by reasonable diligence. *(Added by Stats.2004, c. 182 (A.B.3081), § 23, operative July 1, 2005.)*

Law Revision Commission Comments

Section 2020.420 continues former Section 2020(d)(3) without change, except to replace subdivision with article. [33 Cal.L.Rev.Comm. Reports 831 (2004)].

Research References

Rutter, Cal. Practice Guide: Civ. Pro. Before Trial Ch. 8E-6, Subpoena to Nonparty Deponent or Business Records Custodian.

§ 2020.430. Delivery for copying; requirements; time to deliver; application of Evidence Code concerning inspection of records

(a) Except as provided in subdivision (e), if a deposition subpoena commands only the production of business records for copying, the custodian of the records or other qualified person shall, in person, by messenger, or by mail, deliver both of the following only to the deposition officer specified in the subpoena:

(1) A true, legible, and durable copy of the records.

(2) An affidavit in compliance with Section 1561 of the Evidence Code.

(b) If the delivery required by subdivision (a) is made to the office of the deposition officer, the records shall be enclosed, sealed, and directed as described in subdivision (c) of Section 1560 of the Evidence Code.

(c) If the delivery required by subdivision (a) is made at the office of the business whose records are the subject of the deposition subpoena, the custodian of those records or other qualified person shall do one of the following:

(1) Permit the deposition officer specified in the deposition subpoena to make a copy of the originals of the designated business records during normal business hours, as defined in subdivision (e) of Section 1560 of the Evidence Code.

(2) Deliver to the deposition officer a true, legible, and durable copy of the records on receipt of payment in cash or by check, by or on behalf of the party serving the deposition subpoena, of the reasonable costs of preparing that copy, together with an itemized statement of the cost of preparation, as determined under subdivision (b) of Section 1563 of the Evidence Code. This copy need not be delivered in a sealed envelope.

(d) Unless the parties, and if the records are those of a consumer as defined in Section 1985.3 or 1985.6, the consumer, stipulate to an earlier date, the custodian of the records shall not deliver to the deposition officer the records that are the subject of the deposition subpoena prior to the date and time specified in the deposition subpoena. The following legend shall appear in boldface type on the deposition subpoena immediately following the date and time specified for production: "Do not release the requested records to the deposition officer prior to the date and time stated above."

(e) This section does not apply if the subpoena directs the deponent to make the records available for inspection or copying by the subpoenaing party's attorney or a representative of that attorney at the witness' business address under subdivision (e) of Section 1560 of the Evidence Code.

(f) The provisions of Section 1562 of the Evidence Code concerning the admissibility of the affidavit of the custodian or other qualified person apply to a deposition subpoena served under this article. *(Added by Stats.2004, c. 182 (A.B.3081), § 23, operative July 1, 2005.)*

Law Revision Commission Comments

Subdivisions (a) and (e) of Section 2020.430 continue the first sentence of former Section 2020(d)(4) without substantive change.

Subdivision (b) continues the second sentence of former Section 2020(d)(4) without substantive change.

Subdivision (c) continues the third and fourth sentences of former Section 2020(d)(4) without substantive change.

Subdivision (d) continues the fifth and sixth sentences of former Section 2020(d)(4) without change.

Subdivision (f) continues former Section 2020(d)(6) without change, except to replace subdivision with article. [33 Cal.L.Rev.Comm. Reports 832 (2004)].

Research References

Rutter, Cal. Practice Guide: Civ. Pro. Before Trial Ch. 8E-6, Subpoena to Nonparty Deponent or Business Records Custodian.
Rutter, Cal. Practice Guide: Civil Trials & Evidence Ch. 1-C, C. Marshalling the Evidence.

§ 2020.440. Distribution of copies to parties; deposition officer duties; additional copies

Promptly on or after the deposition date and after the receipt or the making of a copy of business records under this article, the deposition officer shall provide that copy to the party at whose instance the deposition subpoena was served, and a copy of those records to any other party to the action who then or subsequently, within a period of six months following the settlement of the case, notifies the deposition officer that the party desires to purchase a copy of those records. *(Added by Stats.2004, c. 182 (A.B.3081), § 23, operative July 1, 2005.)*

Law Revision Commission Comments

Section 2020.440 continues former Section 2020(d)(5) without change, except to replace subdivision with article. [33 Cal.L.Rev.Comm. Reports 833 (2004)].

Research References

Rutter, Cal. Practice Guide: Civ. Pro. Before Trial Ch. 8E-6, Subpoena to Nonparty Deponent or Business Records Custodian.

ARTICLE 5. SUBPOENA COMMANDING BOTH PRODUCTION OF BUSINESS RECORDS AND ATTENDANCE AND TESTIMONY OF THE DEPONENT

Section
2020.510. Contents of subpoena; necessity of affidavit or declaration showing good cause; personal records pertaining to consumers; employment records pertaining to employees.

§ 2020.510. Contents of subpoena; necessity of affidavit or declaration showing good cause; personal records pertaining to consumers; employment records pertaining to employees

(a) A deposition subpoena that commands the attendance and the testimony of the deponent, as well as the production of business records, documents, electronically stored information, and tangible things, shall:

(1) Comply with the requirements of Section 2020.310.

(2) Designate the business records, documents, electronically stored information, and tangible things to be produced either by specifically describing each individual item or by reasonably particularizing each category of item.

(3) Specify any testing or sampling that is being sought.

(4) Specify the form in which any electronically stored information is to be produced, if a particular form is desired.

(b) A deposition subpoena under subdivision (a) need not be accompanied by an affidavit or declaration showing good cause for the production of the documents and things designated.

(c) If, as described in Section 1985.3, the person to whom the deposition subpoena is directed is a witness, and the business records described in the deposition subpoena are personal records pertaining to a consumer, the service of the deposition subpoena shall be accompanied either by a copy of the proof of service of the notice to the consumer described in subdivision (e) of Section 1985.3, or by the consumer's written authorization to release personal records described in paragraph (2) of subdivision (c) of Section 1985.3.

(d) If, as described in Section 1985.6, the person to whom the deposition subpoena is directed is a witness and the business records described in the deposition subpoena are employment records pertaining to an employee, the service of the deposition subpoena shall be accompanied either by a copy of the proof of service of the notice to the employee described in subdivision (e) of Section 1985.6, or by the employee's written authorization to release personal records described in paragraph (2) of subdivision (c) of Section 1985.6. *(Added by Stats.2004, c. 182 (A.B.3081), § 23, operative July 1, 2005. Amended by Stats.2007, c. 113 (A.B.1126), § 4; Stats.2012, c. 72 (S.B.1574), § 18.)*

Law Revision Commission Comments

Subdivision (a) of Section 2020.510 continues the first sentence of former Section 2020(e) without substantive change.

Subdivision (b) continues the second sentence of former Section 2020(e) without substantive change.

Subdivision (c) continues the second paragraph of former Section 2020(e) without change. [33 Cal.L.Rev.Comm. Reports 834 (2004)].

Section 2020.510 is amended to clarify its application when employment records of an employee are subpoenaed under Section 1985.6. [36 Cal.L.Rev.Comm. Reports 271 (2007)].

Research References

Rutter, Cal. Practice Guide: Civ. Pro. Before Trial Ch. 8D-5, Selecting Proper Discovery Tools.
Rutter, Cal. Practice Guide: Civ. Pro. Before Trial Ch. 8E-6, Subpoena to Nonparty Deponent or Business Records Custodian.
Rutter, Cal. Practice Guide: Civ. Pro. Before Trial Ch. 8D-5, Outline 5.
Rutter, Cal. Practice Guide: Civ. Pro. Before Trial Ch. 8E-6, Outline 6.
Rutter, Cal. Practice Guide: Personal Injury Ch. 6-B, B. Overview of Selected Discovery Procedures.

CHAPTER 7. SANCTIONS

Section

§ 2023.010. Conduct subject to sanctions

Misuses of the discovery process include, but are not limited to, the following:

(a) Persisting, over objection and without substantial justification, in an attempt to obtain information or materials that are outside the scope of permissible discovery.

(b) Using a discovery method in a manner that does not comply with its specified procedures.

(c) Employing a discovery method in a manner or to an extent that causes unwarranted annoyance, embarrassment, or oppression, or undue burden and expense.

(d) Failing to respond or to submit to an authorized method of discovery.

(e) Making, without substantial justification, an unmeritorious objection to discovery.

(f) Making an evasive response to discovery.

(g) Disobeying a court order to provide discovery.

(h) Making or opposing, unsuccessfully and without substantial justification, a motion to compel or to limit discovery.

(i) Failing to confer in person, by telephone, or by letter with an opposing party or attorney in a reasonable and good faith attempt to resolve informally any dispute concerning discovery, if the section governing a particular discovery motion requires the filing of a declaration stating facts showing that an attempt at informal resolution has been made. *(Added by Stats.2004, c. 182 (A.B.3081), § 23, operative July 1, 2005.)*

Law Revision Commission Comments

Section 2023.010 continues former Section 2023(a)(1)-(8) and the first sentence of former Section 2023(a)(9) without substantive change. [33 Cal.L.Rev.Comm. Reports 835 (2004)].

Research References

Rutter, Cal. Practice Guide: Civ. Pro. Before Trial Ch. 1-C, C. Prelawsuit Notices, Claims and Demands.
Rutter, Cal. Practice Guide: Civ. Pro. Before Trial Ch. 8A-3, Civil Discovery Act.
Rutter, Cal. Practice Guide: Civ. Pro. Before Trial Ch. 8E-3, Whose Deposition May be Taken.
Rutter, Cal. Practice Guide: Civ. Pro. Before Trial Ch. 8E-4, Notice of Deposition.
Rutter, Cal. Practice Guide: Civ. Pro. Before Trial Ch. 8E-6, Subpoena to Nonparty Deponent or Business Records Custodian.
Rutter, Cal. Practice Guide: Civ. Pro. Before Trial Ch. 8F-3, Propounding Interrogatories.
Rutter, Cal. Practice Guide: Civ. Pro. Before Trial Ch. 8F-5, Responding to Interrogatories.
Rutter, Cal. Practice Guide: Civ. Pro. Before Trial Ch. 8F-7, Motion to Compel Answers.
Rutter, Cal. Practice Guide: Civ. Pro. Before Trial Ch. 8F-8, Sanctions in Enforcing Discovery.
Rutter, Cal. Practice Guide: Civ. Pro. Before Trial Ch. 8H-2, What May be Inspected.
Rutter, Cal. Practice Guide: Civ. Pro. Before Trial Ch. 8H-6, Responding to Demand.
Rutter, Cal. Practice Guide: Civ. Pro. Before Trial Ch. 8I-2, Physical Examination by Demand in Personal Injury Cases.
Rutter, Cal. Practice Guide: Civ. Pro. Before Trial Ch. 8J-6, Exchange Required.
Rutter, Cal. Practice Guide: Civ. Pro. Before Trial Ch. 8K-1, Request for Statement of Damages (Personal Injury or Death Cases).
Rutter, Cal. Practice Guide: Civ. Pro. Before Trial Ch. 8K-5, Appointment of Referee in Aid of Discovery.
Rutter, Cal. Practice Guide: Civ. Pro. Before Trial Ch. 8L-2, Special Discovery Procedures Permitted.
Rutter, Cal. Practice Guide: Civ. Pro. Before Trial Ch. 8E-12, Conduct of Deposition.
Rutter, Cal. Practice Guide: Civ. Pro. Before Trial Ch. 8E-16, Sanctions Re Depositions.
Rutter, Cal. Practice Guide: Civ. Pro. Before Trial Ch. 9(I)-A, A. Introduction.
Rutter, Cal. Practice Guide: Civ. Pro. Before Trial Ch. 9(III)-A, A. Sources of Sanctions Power.
Rutter, Cal. Practice Guide: Civil Trials & Evidence Ch. 17-E, E. Attorney Fees as Costs.
Rutter, Cal. Practice Guide: Insurance Litigation Ch. 11-J, J. Other Torts Not Necessarily Related to Insurer "Bad Faith".
Rutter, Cal. Practice Guide: Personal Injury Ch. 6-D, D. Expert Witness Information Exchanges (CCP § 2034.210 et seq.).
Rutter, Cal. Practice Guide: Personal Injury Ch. 8-B, B. After Trial Date Set (Three to Four Months Before Trial).
Rutter, Cal. Practice Guide: Prof. Responsibility Ch. 3-D, D. Authority of Client vs. Authority of Attorney.
Rutter, Cal. Practice Guide: Prof. Responsibility Ch. 8-E, E. Consequences of Improper Advocacy.
2 Witkin Cal. Proc. 5th Courts § 252, Pleadings and Motions.
6 Witkin Cal. Proc. 5th Proceedings Without Trial § 55, (S 55) Statutory Authorization.
7 Witkin Cal. Proc. 5th Trial § 226, (S 226) in General.
7 Witkin Cal. Proc. 5th Trial § 237, Nature and Scope.

§ 2023.020. Monetary sanctions for failure to confer

Notwithstanding the outcome of the particular discovery motion, the court shall impose a monetary sanction ordering that any party or attorney who fails to confer as required pay the reasonable expenses, including attorney's fees, incurred by anyone as a result of that conduct. *(Added by Stats.2004, c. 182 (A.B.3081), § 23, operative July 1, 2005.)*

Law Revision Commission Comments

Section 2023.020 continues the second sentence of former Section 2023(a)(9) without change. [33 Cal.L.Rev.Comm. Reports 836 (2004)].

Research References

Rutter, Cal. Practice Guide: Civ. Pro. Before Trial Ch. 8A-3, Civil Discovery Act.

Rutter, Cal. Practice Guide: Civ. Pro. Before Trial Ch. 8F-7, Motion to Compel Answers.

Rutter, Cal. Practice Guide: Civ. Pro. Before Trial Ch. 8F-8, Sanctions in Enforcing Discovery.

Rutter, Cal. Practice Guide: Personal Injury Ch. 8-B, B. After Trial Date Set (Three to Four Months Before Trial).

§ 2023.030. Monetary sanctions; issue sanctions; evidence sanctions; terminating sanctions; contempt sanctions; electronically stored information sanctions

To the extent authorized by the chapter governing any particular discovery method or any other provision of this title, the court, after notice to any affected party, person, or attorney, and after opportunity for hearing, may impose the following sanctions against anyone engaging in conduct that is a misuse of the discovery process:

(a) The court may impose a monetary sanction ordering that one engaging in the misuse of the discovery process, or any attorney advising that conduct, or both pay the reasonable expenses, including attorney's fees, incurred by anyone as a result of that conduct. The court may also impose this sanction on one unsuccessfully asserting that another has engaged in the misuse of the discovery process, or on any attorney who advised that assertion, or on both. If a monetary sanction is authorized by any provision of this title, the court shall impose that sanction unless it finds that the one subject to the sanction acted with substantial justification or that other circumstances make the imposition of the sanction unjust.

(b) The court may impose an issue sanction ordering that designated facts shall be taken as established in the action in accordance with the claim of the party adversely affected by the misuse of the discovery process. The court may also impose an issue sanction by an order prohibiting any party engaging in the misuse of the discovery process from supporting or opposing designated claims or defenses.

(c) The court may impose an evidence sanction by an order prohibiting any party engaging in the misuse of the discovery process from introducing designated matters in evidence.

(d) The court may impose a terminating sanction by one of the following orders:

(1) An order striking out the pleadings or parts of the pleadings of any party engaging in the misuse of the discovery process.

(2) An order staying further proceedings by that party until an order for discovery is obeyed.

(3) An order dismissing the action, or any part of the action, of that party.

(4) An order rendering a judgment by default against that party.

(e) The court may impose a contempt sanction by an order treating the misuse of the discovery process as a contempt of court.

(f)(1) Notwithstanding subdivision (a), or any other section of this title, absent exceptional circumstances, the court shall not impose sanctions on a party or any attorney of a party for failure to provide electronically stored information that has been lost, damaged, altered, or overwritten as the result of the routine, good faith operation of an electronic information system.

(2) This subdivision shall not be construed to alter any obligation to preserve discoverable information. *(Added by Stats.2004, c. 182 (A.B.3081), § 23, operative July 1, 2005. Amended by Stats.2012, c. 72 (S.B.1574), § 19.)*

Law Revision Commission Comments

The introductory clause of Section 2023.030 continues the introductory clause of former Section 2023(b) without substantive change.

Subdivision (a) continues former Section 2023(b)(1) without change, except to replace article with title.

Subdivision (b) continues former Section 2023(b)(2) without change.

Subdivision (c) continues former Section 2023(b)(3) without change.

Subdivision (d) continues former Section 2023(b)(4) without change.

Subdivision (e) continues former Section 2023(b)(5) without change. [33 Cal.L.Rev.Comm. Reports 836 (2004)].

Research References

Rutter, Cal. Practice Guide: Civ. Pro. Before Trial Ch. 2-B, B. Capacity to Sue or Defend.

Rutter, Cal. Practice Guide: Civ. Pro. Before Trial Ch. 5-A, A. General.

Rutter, Cal. Practice Guide: Civ. Pro. Before Trial Ch. 5-B, B. Entry of Default.

Rutter, Cal. Practice Guide: Civ. Pro. Before Trial Ch. 11-B, B. Involuntary Dismissals.

Rutter, Cal. Practice Guide: Civ. Pro. Before Trial Ch. 8A-3, Civil Discovery Act.

Rutter, Cal. Practice Guide: Civ. Pro. Before Trial Ch. 8A-7, Duty to Preserve Evidence Before Discovery Request?

Rutter, Cal. Practice Guide: Civ. Pro. Before Trial Ch. 8E-6, Subpoena to Nonparty Deponent or Business Records Custodian.

Rutter, Cal. Practice Guide: Civ. Pro. Before Trial Ch. 8F-7, Motion to Compel Answers.

Rutter, Cal. Practice Guide: Civ. Pro. Before Trial Ch. 8F-8, Sanctions in Enforcing Discovery.

Rutter, Cal. Practice Guide: Civ. Pro. Before Trial Ch. 8H-8, Enforcing Demand.

Rutter, Cal. Practice Guide: Civ. Pro. Before Trial Ch. 8I-5, Exchange of Medical Reports; Waiver of Privilege.

Rutter, Cal. Practice Guide: Civ. Pro. Before Trial Ch. 8E-15, Motion to Compel Answers.

Rutter, Cal. Practice Guide: Civ. Pro. Before Trial Ch. 8E-16, Sanctions Re Depositions.

Rutter, Cal. Practice Guide: Civ. Pro. Before Trial Ch. 8G-10, Sanctions in Enforcing Rfas.

Rutter, Cal. Practice Guide: Civ. Pro. Before Trial Ch. 8A-3, Outline 3.

Rutter, Cal. Practice Guide: Civ. Pro. Before Trial Ch. 9(III)-D, D. Other Sanctions Statutes and Rules.

Rutter, Cal. Practice Guide: Civil Trials & Evidence Ch. 4-F, F. Motions in Limine.

Rutter, Cal. Practice Guide: Enforcing Judgments/Debts Ch. 6G-2, Written Interrogatories to Judgment Debtor.

Rutter, Cal. Practice Guide: Enforcing Judgments/Debts Ch. 6G-3, Inspection Demand to Judgment Debtor.

Rutter, Cal. Practice Guide: Personal Injury Ch. 6-B, B. Overview of Selected Discovery Procedures.

Rutter, Cal. Practice Guide: Personal Injury Ch. 6-C, C. Physical and Mental Examinations (CCP § 2032.020 et seq.).

Rutter, Cal. Practice Guide: Personal Injury Ch. 6-D, D. Expert Witness Information Exchanges (CCP § 2034.210 et seq.).

Rutter, Cal. Practice Guide: Personal Injury Ch. 6-E, E. Special Discovery Rules and Procedures in Limited Civil Cases.

Rutter, Cal. Practice Guide: Personal Injury Ch. 8-B, B. After Trial Date Set (Three to Four Months Before Trial).

Rutter, Cal. Practice Guide: Personal Injury Ch. 8-C, C. Two Months Before Trial.

Rutter, Cal. Practice Guide: Prof. Responsibility Ch. 6-D, D. Professional Liability.

1 Witkin Cal. Proc. 5th Attorneys § 584, in General.

7 Witkin Cal. Proc. 5th Judgment § 380, (S 380) Refusal to Comply With Discovery Order.

Civ. Pro.

6 Witkin Cal. Proc. 5th Proceedings Without Trial § 133, (S 133) Nature and Effect.

6 Witkin Cal. Proc. 5th Proceedings Without Trial § 140, Types of Actions.

6 Witkin Cal. Proc. 5th Proceedings Without Trial § 151, Default Entered as Discovery Sanction.

6 Witkin Cal. Proc. 5th Proceedings Without Trial § 474, in General.

7 Witkin Cal. Proc. 5th Trial § 58, (S 58) in General.

7 Witkin Cal. Proc. 5th Trial § 171, (S 171) Statutory Framework.

7 Witkin Cal. Proc. 5th Trial § 200, in General.

§ 2023.040. Requests for sanctions; form and supporting documents

A request for a sanction shall, in the notice of motion, identify every person, party, and attorney against whom the sanction is sought, and specify the type of sanction sought. The notice of motion shall be supported by a memorandum of points and authorities, and accompanied by a declaration setting forth facts supporting the amount of any monetary sanction sought. *(Added by Stats.2004, c. 182 (A.B.3081), § 23, operative July 1, 2005.)*

Law Revision Commission Comments

Section 2023.040 continues former Section 2023(c) without change. [33 Cal.L.Rev.Comm. Reports 838 (2004)].

Research References

Rutter, Cal. Practice Guide: Civ. Pro. Before Trial Ch. 8F-8, Sanctions in Enforcing Discovery.

Rutter, Cal. Practice Guide: Civ. Pro. Before Trial Ch. 8E-16, Sanctions Re Depositions.

Rutter, Cal. Practice Guide: Civ. Pro. Before Trial Ch. 8G-10, Sanctions in Enforcing Rfas.

Rutter, Cal. Practice Guide: Personal Injury Ch. 8-B, B. After Trial Date Set (Three to Four Months Before Trial).

CHAPTER 8. TIME FOR COMPLETION OF DISCOVERY

Section

2024.010. Completion date.
2024.020. Discovery cutoff.
2024.030. Expert witnesses; time to complete discovery; motions prior to trial.
2024.040. Application to arbitration proceedings; application to summary proceedings to obtain possession of real property or eminent domain.
2024.050. Motions to complete discovery closer to initial trial date; reopening of discovery; discretion of court; monetary sanctions.
2024.060. Agreements to extend time or reopen discovery; written agreement.

§ 2024.010. Completion date

As used in this chapter, discovery is considered completed on the day a response is due or on the day a deposition begins. *(Added by Stats.2004, c. 182 (A.B.3081), § 23, operative July 1, 2005.)*

Law Revision Commission Comments

Section 2024.010 continues the third sentence of former Section 2024(a) without change, except to replace section with chapter. [33 Cal.L.Rev. Comm. Reports 838 (2004)].

Research References

Rutter, Cal. Practice Guide: Civ. Pro. Before Trial Ch. 8E-2, When Depositions May be Taken.

Rutter, Cal. Practice Guide: Civ. Pro. Before Trial Ch. 8F-1, When Interrogatories May be Served.

Rutter, Cal. Practice Guide: Civ. Pro. Before Trial Ch. 8H-3, When Demand for Inspection May be Made.

Rutter, Cal. Practice Guide: Personal Injury Ch. 6-B, B. Overview of Selected Discovery Procedures.

7 Witkin Cal. Proc. 5th Trial § 74, Completion of Discovery.

§ 2024.020. Discovery cutoff

(a) Except as otherwise provided in this chapter, any party shall be entitled as a matter of right to complete discovery proceedings on or before the 30th day, and to have motions concerning discovery heard on or before the 15th day, before the date initially set for the trial of the action.

(b) Except as provided in Section 2024.050, a continuance or postponement of the trial date does not operate to reopen discovery proceedings. *(Added by Stats.2004, c. 182 (A.B.3081), § 23, operative July 1, 2005.)*

Law Revision Commission Comments

Subdivision (a) of Section 2024.020 continues the first sentence of former Section 2024(a) without change, except to replace section with chapter. For computation of the discovery cutoff when the last day falls on a Saturday, Sunday, or holiday, see Section 2016.060.

Subdivision (b) continues the fourth sentence of former Section 2024(a) without change, except to conform the cross-reference. [33 Cal.L.Rev. Comm. Reports 838 (2004)].

Research References

Rutter, Cal. Practice Guide: A.D.R. Ch. 4-D, D. Mandatory Settlement Conferences.

Rutter, Cal. Practice Guide: Civil Appeals & Writs Ch. 14-C, C. Trial Court Proceedings After Reversal.

Rutter, Cal. Practice Guide: Civ. Pro. Before Trial Ch. 10-C, C. Procedural Requirements-Moving Party.

Rutter, Cal. Practice Guide: Civ. Pro. Before Trial Ch. 13-E, E. the Arbitration Hearing.

Rutter, Cal. Practice Guide: Civ. Pro. Before Trial Ch. 8B-3, Limitations on Right to Discovery.

Rutter, Cal. Practice Guide: Civ. Pro. Before Trial Ch. 8D-7, Proper Scheduling of Discovery.

Rutter, Cal. Practice Guide: Civ. Pro. Before Trial Ch. 8E-1, When Prior Court Order Required.

Rutter, Cal. Practice Guide: Civ. Pro. Before Trial Ch. 8E-2, When Depositions May be Taken.

Rutter, Cal. Practice Guide: Civ. Pro. Before Trial Ch. 8F-1, When Interrogatories May be Served.

Rutter, Cal. Practice Guide: Civ. Pro. Before Trial Ch. 8F-7, Motion to Compel Answers.

Rutter, Cal. Practice Guide: Civ. Pro. Before Trial Ch. 8G-1, When RFAs May be Served.

Rutter, Cal. Practice Guide: Civ. Pro. Before Trial Ch. 8H-3, When Demand for Inspection May be Made.

Rutter, Cal. Practice Guide: Civ. Pro. Before Trial Ch. 9(I)-B, B. Preparing and Filing Motions.

Rutter, Cal. Practice Guide: Civil Trials & Evidence Ch. 1-A, A. Importance of Statewide and Local Rules of Court.

Rutter, Cal. Practice Guide: Civil Trials & Evidence Ch. 11-A, A. Direct Examination of Expert Witnesses.

Rutter, Cal. Practice Guide: Personal Injury Ch. 6-B, B. Overview of Selected Discovery Procedures.

Rutter, Cal. Practice Guide: Personal Injury Ch. 6-D, D. Expert Witness Information Exchanges (CCP § 2034.210 et seq.).

Rutter, Cal. Practice Guide: Personal Injury Ch. 8-A, A. Case Management.

Rutter, Cal. Practice Guide: Personal Injury Ch. 8-B, B. After Trial Date Set (Three to Four Months Before Trial).

Rutter, Cal. Practice Guide: Personal Injury Ch. 8-C, C. Two Months Before Trial.

Rutter, Cal. Practice Guide; Personal Injury Ch. 8-B, Outline B.

6 Witkin Cal. Proc. 5th Proceedings Without Trial § 594, (S 594) Discovery.

7 Witkin Cal. Proc. 5th Trial § 74, Completion of Discovery.

§ 2024.030. Expert witnesses; time to complete discovery; motions prior to trial

Any party shall be entitled as a matter of right to complete discovery proceedings pertaining to a witness identified under

Chapter 18 (commencing with Section 2034.010) on or before the 15th day, and to have motions concerning that discovery heard on or before the 10th day, before the date initially set for the trial of the action. *(Added by Stats.2004, c. 182 (A.B.3081), § 23, operative July 1, 2005.)*

Law Revision Commission Comments

Section 2024.030 continues former Section 2024(d) (as amended by 2004 Cal. Stat. ch. 171, § 5) without change, except to conform the cross-reference and delete the second sentence as surplusage. See Section 2016.060 (computation of time when last day falls on Saturday, Sunday, or holiday). [33 Cal.L.Rev.Comm. Reports 839 (2004)].

Research References

Rutter, Cal. Practice Guide: Civ. Pro. Before Trial Ch. 8E-2, When Depositions May be Taken.

Rutter, Cal. Practice Guide: Civ. Pro. Before Trial Ch. 8J-7, Deposing Opposing Experts.

Rutter, Cal. Practice Guide: Civ. Pro. Before Trial Ch. 8J-10, Relief from Exclusion Sanction.

Rutter, Cal. Practice Guide: Civil Trials & Evidence Ch. 1-A, A. Importance of Statewide and Local Rules of Court.

Rutter, Cal. Practice Guide: Civil Trials & Evidence Ch. 1-C, C. Marshalling the Evidence.

Rutter, Cal. Practice Guide: Civil Trials & Evidence Ch. 11-A, A. Direct Examination of Expert Witnesses.

Rutter, Cal. Practice Guide: Personal Injury Ch. 6-B, B. Overview of Selected Discovery Procedures.

Rutter, Cal. Practice Guide: Personal Injury Ch. 6-D, D. Expert Witness Information Exchanges (CCP § 2034.210 et seq.).

Rutter, Cal. Practice Guide: Personal Injury Ch. 8-B, B. After Trial Date Set (Three to Four Months Before Trial).

Rutter, Cal. Practice Guide: Personal Injury Ch. 8-C, C. Two Months Before Trial.

7 Witkin Cal. Proc. 5th Trial § 74, Completion of Discovery.

§ 2024.040. Application to arbitration proceedings; application to summary proceedings to obtain possession of real property or eminent domain

(a) The time limit on completing discovery in an action to be arbitrated under Chapter 2.5 (commencing with Section 1141.10) of Title 3 of Part 3 is subject to Judicial Council Rule. After an award in a case ordered to judicial arbitration, completion of discovery is limited by Section 1141.24.

(b) This chapter does not apply to either of the following:

(1) Summary proceedings for obtaining possession of real property governed by Chapter 4 (commencing with Section 1159) of Title 3 of Part 3. Except as provided in Sections 2024.050 and 2024.060, discovery in these proceedings shall be completed on or before the fifth day before the date set for trial.

(2) Eminent domain proceedings governed by Title 7 (commencing with Section 1230.010) of Part 3. *(Added by Stats.2004, c. 182 (A.B.3081), § 23, operative July 1, 2005. Amended by Stats.2012, c. 162 (S.B.1171), § 17.)*

Law Revision Commission Comments

Subdivision (a) of Section 2024.040 continues former Section 2024(b) without change.

Subdivision (b) continues former Section 2024(c) without substantive change. [33 Cal.L.Rev.Comm. Reports 839 (2004)].

Research References

Rutter, Cal. Practice Guide: Civ. Pro. Before Trial Ch. 8E-2, When Depositions May be Taken.

Rutter, Cal. Practice Guide: Civ. Pro. Before Trial Ch. 8F-1, When Interrogatories May be Served.

Rutter, Cal. Practice Guide: Civ. Pro. Before Trial Ch. 8H-3, When Demand for Inspection May be Made.

Rutter, Cal. Practice Guide: Personal Injury Ch. 6-B, B. Overview of Selected Discovery Procedures.

6 Witkin Cal. Proc. 5th Proceedings Without Trial § 594, (S 594) Discovery.

7 Witkin Cal. Proc. 5th Trial § 74, Completion of Discovery.

§ 2024.050. Motions to complete discovery closer to initial trial date; reopening of discovery; discretion of court; monetary sanctions

(a) On motion of any party, the court may grant leave to complete discovery proceedings, or to have a motion concerning discovery heard, closer to the initial trial date, or to reopen discovery after a new trial date has been set. This motion shall be accompanied by a meet and confer declaration under Section 2016.040.

(b) In exercising its discretion to grant or deny this motion, the court shall take into consideration any matter relevant to the leave requested, including, but not limited to, the following:

(1) The necessity and the reasons for the discovery.

(2) The diligence or lack of diligence of the party seeking the discovery or the hearing of a discovery motion, and the reasons that the discovery was not completed or that the discovery motion was not heard earlier.

(3) Any likelihood that permitting the discovery or hearing the discovery motion will prevent the case from going to trial on the date set, or otherwise interfere with the trial calendar, or result in prejudice to any other party.

(4) The length of time that has elapsed between any date previously set, and the date presently set, for the trial of the action.

(c) The court shall impose a monetary sanction under Chapter 7 (commencing with Section 2023.010) against any party, person, or attorney who unsuccessfully makes or opposes a motion to extend or to reopen discovery, unless it finds that the one subject to the sanction acted with substantial justification or that other circumstances make the imposition of the sanction unjust. *(Added by Stats.2004, c. 182 (A.B.3081), § 23, operative July 1, 2005.)*

Law Revision Commission Comments

Subdivision (a) of Section 2024.050 continues the first paragraph of former Section 2024(e) without substantive change.

Subdivision (b) continues the second paragraph (including items (1)-(4)) of former Section 2024(e) without change.

Subdivision (c) continues the last paragraph of former Section 2024(e) without change, except to conform the cross-reference. [33 Cal.L.Rev. Comm. Reports 840 (2004)].

Research References

Rutter, Cal. Practice Guide: Civ. Pro. Before Trial Ch. 8E-1, When Prior Court Order Required.

Rutter, Cal. Practice Guide: Civ. Pro. Before Trial Ch. 8E-2, When Depositions May be Taken.

Rutter, Cal. Practice Guide: Civ. Pro. Before Trial Ch. 8F-1, When Interrogatories May be Served.

Rutter, Cal. Practice Guide: Civ. Pro. Before Trial Ch. 8G-1, When RFAs May be Served.

Rutter, Cal. Practice Guide: Civ. Pro. Before Trial Ch. 9(I)-F, F. Ex Parte Motions.

Rutter, Cal. Practice Guide: Civil Trials & Evidence Ch. 1-A, A. Importance of Statewide and Local Rules of Court.

Rutter, Cal. Practice Guide: Personal Injury Ch. 6-B, B. Overview of Selected Discovery Procedures.

Rutter, Cal. Practice Guide: Personal Injury Ch. 7-F, F. Preparing for Arbitration.

Rutter, Cal. Practice Guide: Personal Injury Ch. 8-B, B. After Trial Date Set (Three to Four Months Before Trial).

7 Witkin Cal. Proc. 5th Trial § 74, Completion of Discovery.

§ 2024.060. Agreements to extend time or reopen discovery; written agreement

Parties to an action may, with the consent of any party affected by it, enter into an agreement to extend the time for the completion of discovery proceedings or for the hearing of motions concerning discovery, or to reopen discovery after a new date for trial of the action has been set. This agreement may be informal, but it shall be confirmed in a writing that specifies the extended date. In no event shall this agreement require a court to grant a continuance or postponement of the trial of the action. *(Added by Stats.2004, c. 182 (A.B.3081), § 23, operative July 1, 2005.)*

Law Revision Commission Comments

Section 2024.060 continues former Section 2024(f) without substantive change. [33 Cal.L.Rev.Comm. Reports 841 (2004)].

Research References

Rutter, Cal. Practice Guide: Civ. Pro. Before Trial Ch. 8E-2, When Depositions May be Taken.
Rutter, Cal. Practice Guide: Civ. Pro. Before Trial Ch. 8F-1, When Interrogatories May be Served.
Rutter, Cal. Practice Guide: Personal Injury Ch. 6-B, B. Overview of Selected Discovery Procedures.
7 Witkin Cal. Proc. 5th Trial § 74, Completion of Discovery.

CHAPTER 9. ORAL DEPOSITION INSIDE CALIFORNIA

ARTICLE 1. GENERAL PROVISIONS

§ 2025.010. Persons and entities within the state subject to deposition

Any party may obtain discovery within the scope delimited by Chapter 2 (commencing with Section 2017.010) and Chapter 3 (commencing with Section 2017.710), and subject to the restrictions set forth in Chapter 5 (commencing with Section 2019.010), by taking in California the oral deposition of any person, including any party to the action. The person deposed may be a natural person, an organization such as a public or private corporation, a partnership, an association, or a governmental agency. *(Added by Stats.2004, c. 182 (A.B.3081), § 23, operative July 1, 2005.)*

Law Revision Commission Comments

Section 2025.010 continues former Section 2025(a) without change, except to conform the cross-references. [33 Cal.L.Rev.Comm. Reports 841 (2004)].

Research References

Rutter, Cal. Practice Guide: Civ. Pro. Before Trial Ch. 8A-3, Civil Discovery Act.

Rutter, Cal. Practice Guide: Civ. Pro. Before Trial Ch. 8D-5, Selecting Proper Discovery Tools.
Rutter, Cal. Practice Guide: Civ. Pro. Before Trial Ch. 8E-1, When Prior Court Order Required.
Rutter, Cal. Practice Guide: Civ. Pro. Before Trial Ch. 8E-3, Whose Deposition May be Taken.
Rutter, Cal. Practice Guide: Civ. Pro. Before Trial Ch. 8E-1, Outline 1.
California Practice Guide: Employment Litigation Ch. 13-H, H. Contesting Citations and Related Orders and Notices.
Rutter, Cal. Practice Guide: Personal Injury Ch. 6-B, B. Overview of Selected Discovery Procedures.
Rutter, Cal. Practice Guide: Personal Injury Ch. 8-C, C. Two Months Before Trial.
7 Witkin Cal. Proc. 5th Trial § 31, (S 31) Particular Actions and Proceedings.

ARTICLE 2. DEPOSITION NOTICE

§ 2025.210. Service of notice; time allowed

Subject to Sections 2025.270 and 2025.610, an oral deposition may be taken as follows:

(a) The defendant may serve a deposition notice without leave of court at any time after that defendant has been served or has appeared in the action, whichever occurs first.

(b) The plaintiff may serve a deposition notice without leave of court on any date that is 20 days after the service of the summons on, or appearance by, any defendant. On motion with or without notice, the court, for good cause shown, may grant to a plaintiff leave to serve a deposition notice on an earlier date. *(Added by Stats.2004, c. 182 (A.B.3081), § 23, operative July 1, 2005.)*

Law Revision Commission Comments

Section 2025.210 continues former Section 2025(b) without substantive change. For the consequences of noncompliance with the requirements of a deposition notice, see Section 2025.410. [33 Cal.L.Rev.Comm. Reports 842 (2004)].

Research References

Rutter, Cal. Practice Guide: Civ. Pro. Before Trial Ch. 4-A, A. Requirements-In General.
Rutter, Cal. Practice Guide: Civ. Pro. Before Trial Ch. 8B-3, Limitations on Right to Discovery.
Rutter, Cal. Practice Guide: Civ. Pro. Before Trial Ch. 8E-1, When Prior Court Order Required.
Rutter, Cal. Practice Guide: Civ. Pro. Before Trial Ch. 8E-2, When Depositions May be Taken.
Rutter, Cal. Practice Guide: Civ. Pro. Before Trial Ch. 9(I)-F, F. Ex Parte Motions.
California Practice Guide: Employment Litigation Ch. 19-F, F. Discovery.
Rutter, Cal. Practice Guide: Personal Injury Ch. 4-A, A. General Considerations.

Rutter, Cal. Practice Guide: Personal Injury Ch. 6-B, B. Overview of Selected Discovery Procedures.

§ 2025.220. Contents of deposition notice; copy of deposition subpoena as notice of deposition

(a) A party desiring to take the oral deposition of any person shall give notice in writing. The deposition notice shall state all of the following:

(1) The address where the deposition will be taken.

(2) The date of the deposition, selected under Section 2025.270, and the time it will commence.

(3) The name of each deponent, and the address and telephone number, if known, of any deponent who is not a party to the action. If the name of the deponent is not known, the deposition notice shall set forth instead a general description sufficient to identify the person or particular class to which the person belongs.

(4) The specification with reasonable particularity of any materials or category of materials, including any electronically stored information, to be produced by the deponent.

(5) Any intention by the party noticing the deposition to record the testimony by audio or video technology, in addition to recording the testimony by the stenographic method as required by Section 2025.330 and any intention to record the testimony by stenographic method through the instant visual display of the testimony. If the deposition will be conducted using instant visual display, a copy of the deposition notice shall also be given to the deposition officer. Any offer to provide the instant visual display of the testimony or to provide rough draft transcripts to any party which is accepted prior to, or offered at, the deposition shall also be made by the deposition officer at the deposition to all parties in attendance. Any party or attorney requesting the provision of the instant visual display of the testimony, or rough draft transcripts, shall pay the reasonable cost of those services, which may be no greater than the costs charged to any other party or attorney.

(6) Any intention to reserve the right to use at trial a video recording of the deposition testimony of a treating or consulting physician or of any expert witness under subdivision (d) of Section 2025.620. In this event, the operator of the video camera shall be a person who is authorized to administer an oath, and shall not be financially interested in the action or be a relative or employee of any attorney of any of the parties.

(7) The form in which any electronically stored information is to be produced, if a particular form is desired.

(b) Notwithstanding subdivision (a), where under Article 4 (commencing with Section 2020.410) only the production by a nonparty of business records for copying is desired, a copy of the deposition subpoena shall serve as the notice of deposition. *(Added by Stats.2004, c. 182 (A.B.3081), § 23, operative July 1, 2005. Amended by Stats.2012, c. 72 (S.B.1574), § 20.)*

Law Revision Commission Comments

The introductory clause of subdivision (a) of Section 2025.220 continues the first sentence of former Section 2025(c) and the introductory clause of former Section 2025(d) without substantive change. Subdivision (a)(1) continues former Section 2025(d)(1) without change. Subdivision (a)(2) continues former Section 2025(d)(2) without change, except to conform the cross-reference. Subdivision (a)(3) continues former Section 2025(d)(3) without change. Subdivision (a)(4) continues former Section 2025(d)(4) without change. Subdivision (a)(5) continues former Section 2025(d)(5) without change, except to conform the cross-reference. Subdivision (a)(6) continues the first paragraph of former Section 2025(d)(6) without change, except to conform the cross-reference.

Subdivision (b) continues the second sentence of former Section 2025(c) without substantive change.

For the consequences of noncompliance with the requirements of a deposition notice, see Section 2025.410. [33 Cal.L.Rev.Comm. Reports 842 (2004)].

Research References

Rutter, Cal. Practice Guide: Civ. Pro. Before Trial Ch. 8E-4, Notice of Deposition.

Rutter, Cal. Practice Guide: Civ. Pro. Before Trial Ch. 8E-5, Subpoena Not Necessary for Party or "Party-Affiliated" Witnesses.

Rutter, Cal. Practice Guide: Civ. Pro. Before Trial Ch. 8E-6, Subpoena to Nonparty Deponent or Business Records Custodian.

Rutter, Cal. Practice Guide: Civ. Pro. Before Trial Ch. 8E-10, Preservation of Testimony.

Rutter, Cal. Practice Guide: Civ. Pro. Before Trial Ch. 8E-17, Use of Depositions at Trial.

Rutter, Cal. Practice Guide: Civil Trials & Evidence Ch. 4-B, B. Preliminary Matters Discussed in Final Status Conference or In-Chambers Conference.

Rutter, Cal. Practice Guide: Civil Trials & Evidence Ch. 8C-E, E. Audio or Visual Recordings.

Rutter, Cal. Practice Guide: Civil Trials & Evidence Ch. 8C-I, I. Depositions and Discovery.

California Practice Guide: Employment Litigation Ch. 19-F, F. Discovery.

Rutter, Cal. Practice Guide: Personal Injury Ch. 6-B, B. Overview of Selected Discovery Procedures.

Rutter, Cal. Practice Guide: Personal Injury Ch. 8-C, C. Two Months Before Trial.

Rutter, Cal. Practice Guide: Prof. Responsibility Ch. 11-F, F. Investigation Stage.

§ 2025.230. Contents of deposition notice; deponent not a natural person

If the deponent named is not a natural person, the deposition notice shall describe with reasonable particularity the matters on which examination is requested. In that event, the deponent shall designate and produce at the deposition those of its officers, directors, managing agents, employees, or agents who are most qualified to testify on its behalf as to those matters to the extent of any information known or reasonably available to the deponent. *(Added by Stats.2004, c. 182 (A.B.3081), § 23, operative July 1, 2005.)*

Law Revision Commission Comments

Section 2025.230 continues the first sentence of the second paragraph of former Section 2025(d)(6) without change. For the consequences of noncompliance with the requirements of a deposition notice, see Section 2025.410. [33 Cal.L.Rev.Comm. Reports 844 (2004)].

Research References

Rutter, Cal. Practice Guide: Civ. Pro. Before Trial Ch. 8E-3, Whose Deposition May be Taken.

Rutter, Cal. Practice Guide: Civ. Pro. Before Trial Ch. 8E-4, Notice of Deposition.

Rutter, Cal. Practice Guide: Civ. Pro. Before Trial Ch. 8L-1, Limitations on Existing Discovery Procedures.

Rutter, Cal. Practice Guide: Civil Trials & Evidence Ch. 1-C, C. Marshalling the Evidence.

Rutter, Cal. Practice Guide: Personal Injury Ch. 6-B, B. Overview of Selected Discovery Procedures.

Rutter, Cal. Practice Guide: Personal Injury Ch. 9-H, H. Introduction of Discovered Evidence.

§ 2025.240. Notice to parties to the action; subpoenaing party duties; consumer or employee records

(a) The party who prepares a notice of deposition shall give the notice to every other party who has appeared in the action. The deposition notice, or the accompanying proof of service, shall list all the parties or attorneys for parties on whom it is served.

(b) If, as defined in subdivision (a) of Section 1985.3 or subdivision (a) of Section 1985.6, the party giving notice of the deposition is a subpoenaing party, and the deponent is a witness commanded by a deposition subpoena to produce personal records of a consumer or employment records of an employee, the subpoenaing party shall serve on that consumer or employee all of the following:

(1) A notice of the deposition.

(2) The notice of privacy rights specified in subdivision (e) of Section 1985.3 or in subdivision (e) of Section 1985.6.

(3) A copy of the deposition subpoena.

(c) If the attendance of the deponent is to be compelled by service of a deposition subpoena under Chapter 6 (commencing with Section 2020.010), an identical copy of that subpoena shall be served with the deposition notice. *(Added by Stats.2004, c. 182 (A.B.3081), § 23, operative July 1, 2005. Amended by Stats.2007, c. 113 (A.B.1126), § 5.)*

Law Revision Commission Comments

Subdivision (a) of Section 2025.240 continues the third and fourth sentences of former Section 2025(c) without substantive change.

Subdivision (b) continues the second paragraph of former Section 2025(c) without substantive change.

Subdivision (c) continues the third paragraph of former Section 2025(d)(6) without change, except to conform the cross-reference.

For the consequences of noncompliance with the requirements of a deposition notice, see Section 2025.410. [33 Cal.L.Rev.Comm. Reports 844 (2004)].

Section 2025.240 is amended to clarify its application when employment records of an employee are subpoenaed under Section 1985.6. [36 Cal.L.Rev.Comm. Reports 271 (2007)].

Research References

Rutter, Cal. Practice Guide: Civ. Pro. Before Trial Ch. 2-B, B. Capacity to Sue or Defend.
Rutter, Cal. Practice Guide: Civ. Pro. Before Trial Ch. 8E-4, Notice of Deposition.
Rutter, Cal. Practice Guide: Civ. Pro. Before Trial Ch. 8E-6, Subpoena to Nonparty Deponent or Business Records Custodian.
Rutter, Cal. Practice Guide: Civil Trials & Evidence Ch. 1-C, C. Marshalling the Evidence.
Rutter, Cal. Practice Guide: Personal Injury Ch. 6-B, B. Overview of Selected Discovery Procedures.

§ 2025.250. Location of deposition; mileage restrictions

(a) Unless the court orders otherwise under Section 2025.260, the deposition of a natural person, whether or not a party to the action, shall be taken at a place that is, at the option of the party giving notice of the deposition, either within 75 miles of the deponent's residence, or within the county where the action is pending and within 150 miles of the deponent's residence.

(b) The deposition of an organization that is a party to the action shall be taken at a place that is, at the option of the party giving notice of the deposition, either within 75 miles of the organization's principal executive or business office in California, or within the county where the action is pending and within 150 miles of that office.

(c) Unless the organization consents to a more distant place, the deposition of any other organization shall be taken within 75 miles of the organization's principal executive or business office in California.

(d) If an organization has not designated a principal executive or business office in California, the deposition shall be taken at a place that is, at the option of the party giving notice of the deposition, either within the county where the action is pending, or within 75 miles of any executive or business office in California of the organization. *(Added by Stats.2004, c. 182 (A.B.3081), § 23, operative July 1, 2005. Amended by Stats.2005, c. 294 (A.B.333), § 7.)*

Law Revision Commission Comments

Subdivision (a) of Section 2025.250 continues former Section 2025(e)(1) without substantive change.

Subdivision (b) continues the first sentence of former Section 2025(e)(2) without change.

Subdivision (c) continues the second and third sentences of former Section 2025(e)(2) without substantive change.

For the consequences of noncompliance with the requirements of a deposition notice, see Section 2025.410. [33 Cal.L.Rev.Comm. Reports 845 (2004)].

Section 2025.250 is amended to make clear that the rule regarding where to depose an organization that has not designated a principal executive or business office in California applies regardless of whether the organization is a party or a nonparty. This is not a substantive change.

Research References

Rutter, Cal. Practice Guide: Civ. Pro. Before Trial Ch. 8B-3, Limitations on Right to Discovery.
Rutter, Cal. Practice Guide: Civ. Pro. Before Trial Ch. 8E-1, When Prior Court Order Required.
Rutter, Cal. Practice Guide: Civ. Pro. Before Trial Ch. 8E-6, Subpoena to Nonparty Deponent or Business Records Custodian.
Rutter, Cal. Practice Guide: Civ. Pro. Before Trial Ch. 8E-8, Place of Deposition.
Rutter, Cal. Practice Guide: Civ. Pro. Before Trial Ch. 8J-7, Deposing Opposing Experts.
Rutter, Cal. Practice Guide: Personal Injury Ch. 6-B, B. Overview of Selected Discovery Procedures.

§ 2025.260. Location of deposition; exemption from mileage restrictions; order of court

(a) A party desiring to take the deposition of a natural person who is a party to the action or an officer, director, managing agent, or employee of a party may make a motion for an order that the deponent attend for deposition at a place that is more distant than that permitted under Section 2025.250. This motion shall be accompanied by a meet and confer declaration under Section 2016.040.

(b) In exercising its discretion to grant or deny this motion, the court shall take into consideration any factor tending to show whether the interests of justice will be served by requiring the deponent's attendance at that more distant place, including, but not limited to, the following:

(1) Whether the moving party selected the forum.

(2) Whether the deponent will be present to testify at the trial of the action.

(3) The convenience of the deponent.

(4) The feasibility of conducting the deposition by written questions under Chapter 11 (commencing with Section 2028.010), or of using a discovery method other than a deposition.

(5) The number of depositions sought to be taken at a place more distant than that permitted under Section 2025.250.

(6) The expense to the parties of requiring the deposition to be taken within the distance permitted under Section 2025.250.

(7) The whereabouts of the deponent at the time for which the deposition is scheduled.

(c) The order may be conditioned on the advancement by the moving party of the reasonable expenses and costs to the deponent for travel to the place of deposition.

(d) The court shall impose a monetary sanction under Chapter 7 (commencing with Section 2023.010) against any party, person, or attorney who unsuccessfully makes or opposes a motion to increase the travel limits for a party deponent, unless it finds that the one subject to the sanction acted with substantial justification or that other circumstances make the imposition of the sanction unjust. *(Added by Stats.2004, c. 182 (A.B.3081), § 23, operative July 1, 2005.)*

Law Revision Commission Comments

Subdivision (a) of Section 2025.260 continues the first paragraph of former Section 2025(e)(3) without substantive change.

Subdivision (b) continues the second paragraph of former Section 2025(e)(3) (including items (A)-(F)) without change, except to conform the cross-references.

Subdivision (c) continues the next-to-last paragraph of former Section 2025(e)(3) without change.

Subdivision (d) continues the last paragraph of former Section 2025(e)(3) without substantive change.

For the consequences of noncompliance with the requirements of a deposition notice, see Section 2025.410. [33 Cal.L.Rev.Comm. Reports 846 (2004)].

Research References

Rutter, Cal. Practice Guide: Civ. Pro. Before Trial Ch. 8E-8, Place of Deposition.
Rutter, Cal. Practice Guide: Civ. Pro. Before Trial Gen. Matls., Highlights.
Rutter, Cal. Practice Guide: Civil Trials & Evidence Ch. 1-C, C. Marshalling the Evidence.
Rutter, Cal. Practice Guide: Personal Injury Ch. 6-B, B. Overview of Selected Discovery Procedures.
Rutter, Cal. Practice Guide: Personal Injury Ch. 7-J, J. Arbitration of Uninsured Motorist Claims.

§ 2025.270.   Date of deposition

(a) An oral deposition shall be scheduled for a date at least 10 days after service of the deposition notice.

(b) Notwithstanding subdivision (a), in an unlawful detainer action or other proceeding under Chapter 4 (commencing with Section 1159) of Title 3 of Part 3, an oral deposition shall be scheduled for a date at least five days after service of the deposition notice, but not later than five days before trial.

(c) Notwithstanding subdivisions (a) and (b), if, as defined in Section 1985.3 or 1985.6, the party giving notice of the deposition is a subpoenaing party, and the deponent is a witness commanded by a deposition subpoena to produce personal records of a consumer or employment records of an employee, the deposition shall be scheduled for a date at least 20 days after issuance of that subpoena.

(d) On motion or ex parte application of any party or deponent, for good cause shown, the court may shorten or extend the time for scheduling a deposition, or may stay its taking until the determination of a motion for a protective order under Section 2025.420. *(Added by Stats.2004, c. 182 (A.B.3081), § 23, operative July 1, 2005. Amended by Stats.2007, c. 113 (A.B.1126), § 6.)*

Law Revision Commission Comments

Subdivision (a) of Section 2025.270 continues the first and second sentences of former Section 2025(f) without change.

Subdivision (b) continues the third sentence of former Section 2025(f) without substantive change.

Subdivision (c) continues the second paragraph of former Section 2025(f) without change, except to conform the cross-reference.

For the consequences of noncompliance with the requirements of a deposition notice, see Section 2025.410. [33 Cal.L.Rev.Comm. Reports 847 (2004)].

Section 2025.270 is amended to clarify its application when personal records of a consumer are subpoenaed in an unlawful detainer case. The provision is also amended to clarify its application when employment records of an employee are subpoenaed. Further, the amendment makes clear that the special notice requirement for an unlawful detainer case also applies to a proceeding for forcible entry (see Section 1159) or forcible detainer (see Section 1160).

Under subdivision (c), a litigant must give twenty days notice when subpoenaing personal records of a consumer or employment records of an employee. This rule applies even in an unlawful detainer case or other summary proceeding for possession of real property.

Under subdivision (d), a court may adjust the notice period for good cause shown. Likewise, on a showing of good cause, a court may shorten the time limits for serving a consumer or a custodian of records under Section 1985.3, provided that the rights of witnesses and consumers are preserved. See Section 1985.3(h). Similarly, on a showing of good cause, a court may shorten the time limits for serving an employee or a custodian of records under Section 1985.6, provided that the rights of witnesses and employees are preserved. See Section 1985.6(g). In addition, under specified circumstances, a court may continue the trial date or extend other time limits in an unlawful detainer case or other summary proceeding for possession of real property. See Sections 1167.3, 1167.5, 1170.5; see also Deal v. Municipal Court, 157 Cal.App.3d 991, 997–98, 204 Cal.Rptr. 79 (1984). [36 Cal.L.Rev.Comm. Reports 271 (2007)].

Research References

Rutter, Cal. Practice Guide: Civ. Pro. Before Trial Ch. 8B-3, Limitations on Right to Discovery.
Rutter, Cal. Practice Guide: Civ. Pro. Before Trial Ch. 8E-2, When Depositions May be Taken.
Rutter, Cal. Practice Guide: Civ. Pro. Before Trial Ch. 8E-4, Notice of Deposition.
Rutter, Cal. Practice Guide: Civ. Pro. Before Trial Ch. 8E-6, Subpoena to Nonparty Deponent or Business Records Custodian.
Rutter, Cal. Practice Guide: Civ. Pro. Before Trial Ch. 9(I)-F, F. Ex Parte Motions.
Rutter, Cal. Practice Guide: Personal Injury Ch. 6-B, B. Overview of Selected Discovery Procedures.
Rutter, Cal. Practice Guide: Personal Injury Ch. 8-B, B. After Trial Date Set (Three to Four Months Before Trial).
12 Witkin, California Summary 10th Real Property § 736, Trial.

§ 2025.280.   Service of notice upon party deponents; production of documents and electronically stored information for inspection and copying

(a) The service of a deposition notice under Section 2025.240 is effective to require any deponent who is a party to the action or an officer, director, managing agent, or employee of a party to attend and to testify, as well as to produce any document, electronically stored information, or tangible thing for inspection and copying.

(b) The attendance and testimony of any other deponent, as well as the production by the deponent of any document, electronically stored information, or tangible thing for inspection and copying, requires the service on the deponent of a deposition subpoena under Chapter 6 (commencing with Section 2020.010). *(Added by Stats.2004, c. 182 (A.B.3081), § 23, operative July 1, 2005. Amended by Stats.2012, c. 72 (S.B.1574), § 21.)*

Law Revision Commission Comments

Subdivision (a) of Section 2025.280 continues former Section 2025(h)(1) without change, except to conform the cross-reference.

Subdivision (b) continues former Section 2025(h)(2) without change, except to conform the cross-reference.

For the consequences of noncompliance with the requirements of a deposition notice, see Section 2025.410. [33 Cal.L.Rev.Comm. Reports 848 (2004)].

Research References

Rutter, Cal. Practice Guide: Civ. Pro. Before Trial Ch. 8E-4, Notice of Deposition.
Rutter, Cal. Practice Guide: Civ. Pro. Before Trial Ch. 8E-5, Subpoena Not Necessary for Party or "Party-Affiliated" Witnesses.
Rutter, Cal. Practice Guide: Civ. Pro. Before Trial Ch. 8E-6, Subpoena to Nonparty Deponent or Business Records Custodian.
Rutter, Cal. Practice Guide: Civ. Pro. Before Trial Ch. 8H-1, on Whom Demand May be Served.
Rutter, Cal. Practice Guide: Personal Injury Ch. 6-B, B. Overview of Selected Discovery Procedures.

Civ. Pro.

Rutter, Cal. Practice Guide: Personal Injury Ch. 7-J, J. Arbitration of Uninsured Motorist Claims.

§ 2025.290. Time limits of depositions

(a) Except as provided in subdivision (b), or by any court order, including a case management order, a deposition examination of the witness by all counsel, other than the witness' counsel of record, shall be limited to seven hours of total testimony. The court shall allow additional time, beyond any limits imposed by this section, if needed to fairly examine the deponent or if the deponent, another person, or any other circumstance impedes or delays the examination.

(b) This section shall not apply under any of the following circumstances:

(1) If the parties have stipulated that this section will not apply to a specific deposition or to the entire proceeding.

(2) To any deposition of a witness designated as an expert pursuant to Sections 2034.210 to 2034.310, inclusive.

(3) To any case designated as complex by the court pursuant to Rule 3.400 of the California Rules of Court, unless a licensed physician attests in a declaration served on the parties that the deponent suffers from an illness or condition that raises substantial medical doubt of survival of the deponent beyond six months, in which case the deposition examination of the witness by all counsel, other than the witness' counsel of record, shall be limited to two days of no more than seven hours of total testimony each day, or 14 hours of total testimony.

(4) To any case brought by an employee or applicant for employment against an employer for acts or omissions arising out of or relating to the employment relationship.

(5) To any deposition of a person who is designated as the most qualified person to be deposed under Section 2025.230.

(6) To any party who appeared in the action after the deposition has concluded, in which case the new party may notice another deposition subject to the requirements of this section.

(c) It is the intent of the Legislature that any exclusions made by this section shall not be construed to create any presumption or any substantive change to existing law relating to the appropriate time limit for depositions falling within the exclusion. Nothing in this section shall be construed to affect the existing right of any party to move for a protective order or the court's discretion to make any order that justice requires to limit a deposition in order to protect any party, deponent, or other natural person or organization from unwarranted annoyance, embarrassment, oppression, undue burden, or expense. *(Added by Stats.2012, c. 346 (A.B.1875), § 1.)*

Research References

California Practice Guide: Employment Litigation Ch. 19-F, F. Discovery.
California Practice Guide: Employment Litigation Gen. Matls, Highlights.

ARTICLE 3. CONDUCT OF DEPOSITION

§ 2025.310. Use of telephone or other remote electronic means

(a) A person may take, and any person other than the deponent may attend, a deposition by telephone or other remote electronic means.

(b) The court may expressly provide that a nonparty deponent may appear at the deposition by telephone if it finds there is good cause and no prejudice to any party. A party deponent shall appear at the deposition in person and be in the presence of the deposition officer.

(c) The procedures to implement this section shall be established by court order in the specific action or proceeding or by the California Rules of Court. *(Added by Stats.2004, c. 182 (A.B.3081), § 23, operative July 1, 2005.)*

Law Revision Commission Comments

Subdivision (a) of Section 2025.310 continues the first sentence of former Section 2025(h)(3) without change.

Subdivision (b) continues the second and third sentences of former Section 2025(h)(3) without substantive change.

Subdivision (c) continues the fourth sentence of former Section 2025(h)(3) without substantive change. [33 Cal.L.Rev.Comm. Reports 849 (2004)].

Research References

Rutter, Cal. Practice Guide: Civ. Pro. Before Trial Ch. 8E-8, Place of Deposition.
Rutter, Cal. Practice Guide: Personal Injury Ch. 6-B, B. Overview of Selected Discovery Procedures.

§ 2025.320. Deposition officers; officer qualifications and requirements; conflict of interest; objections; civil penalty for violations

Except as provided in Section 2020.420, the deposition shall be conducted under the supervision of an officer who is authorized to administer an oath and is subject to all of the following requirements:

(a) The officer shall not be financially interested in the action and shall not be a relative or employee of any attorney of the parties, or of any of the parties.

(b) Services and products offered or provided by the deposition officer or the entity providing the services of the deposition officer to any party or to any party's attorney or third party who is financing all or part of the action shall be offered to all parties or their attorneys attending the deposition. No service or product may be offered or provided by the deposition officer or by the entity providing the services of the deposition officer to any party or any party's attorney or third party who is financing all or part of the action unless the service or product is offered or provided to all parties or their attorneys attending the deposition. All services and products offered or provided shall be made available at the same time to all parties or their attorneys.

(c) The deposition officer or the entity providing the services of the deposition officer shall not provide to any party or any party's attorney or third party who is financing all or part of the action any service or product consisting of the deposition officer's notations or comments regarding the demeanor of any witness, attorney, or party present at the deposition. The deposition officer or entity providing the services of the deposition officer shall not collect any personal identifying information about the witness as a service or product to be provided to any party or third party who is financing all or part of the action.

(d) Upon the request of any party or any party's attorney attending a deposition, any party or any party's attorney attending the deposition shall enter in the record of the deposition all services and products made available to that party or party's attorney or third party who is financing all or part of the action by the deposition officer or by the entity providing the services of the deposition officer. A party in the action who is not represented by an attorney shall be informed by the noticing party or the party's attorney that the unrepresented party may request this statement.

(e) Any objection to the qualifications of the deposition officer is waived unless made before the deposition begins or as soon thereafter as the ground for that objection becomes known or could be discovered by reasonable diligence.

(f) Violation of this section by any person may result in a civil penalty of up to five thousand dollars ($5,000) imposed by a court of competent jurisdiction. *(Added by Stats.2004, c. 182 (A.B.3081), § 23, operative July 1, 2005.)*

Law Revision Commission Comments

The introductory clause of Section 2025.320 continues the introductory clause of former Section 2025(k) without change, except to conform the cross-reference.

Subdivision (a) continues former Section 2025(k)(1) without change.
Subdivision (b) continues former Section 2025(k)(2) without change.
Subdivision (c) continues former Section 2025(k)(3) without change.
Subdivision (d) continues former Section 2025(k)(4) without change.
Subdivision (e) continues former Section 2025(k)(5) without substantive change.

Subdivision (f) continues former Section 2025(v) without substantive change. [33 Cal.L.Rev.Comm. Reports 849 (2004)].

Research References

Rutter, Cal. Practice Guide: Civ. Pro. Before Trial Ch. 8E-9, Deposition Officer.
Rutter, Cal. Practice Guide: Civ. Pro. Before Trial Ch. 8E-10, Preservation of Testimony.
Rutter, Cal. Practice Guide: Civ. Pro. Before Trial Ch. 8E-14, Deposition Transcript.
Rutter, Cal. Practice Guide: Personal Injury Ch. 6-B, B. Overview of Selected Discovery Procedures.

§ 2025.330. Oath or affirmation; stenographic record; electronic recording; examination subject to Evidence Code provisions; questions submitted to deposition officer for answer by deponent in lieu of party participation

(a) The deposition officer shall put the deponent under oath or affirmation.

(b) Unless the parties agree or the court orders otherwise, the testimony, as well as any stated objections, shall be taken stenographically. If taken stenographically, it shall be by a person certified pursuant to Article 3 (commencing with Section 8020) of Chapter 13 of Division 3 of the Business and Professions Code.

(c) The party noticing the deposition may also record the testimony by audio or video technology if the notice of deposition stated an intention also to record the testimony by either of those methods, or if all the parties agree that the testimony may also be recorded by either of those methods. Any other party, at that party's expense, may make an audio or video record of the deposition, provided that the other party promptly, and in no event less than three calendar days before the date for which the deposition is scheduled, serves a written notice of this intention to make an audio or video record of the deposition testimony on the party or attorney who noticed the deposition, on all other parties or attorneys on whom the deposition notice was served under Section 2025.240, and on any deponent whose attendance is being compelled by a deposition subpoena under Chapter 6

(commencing with Section 2020.010). If this notice is given three calendar days before the deposition date, it shall be made by personal service under Section 1011.

(d) Examination and cross-examination of the deponent shall proceed as permitted at trial under the provisions of the Evidence Code.

(e) In lieu of participating in the oral examination, parties may transmit written questions in a sealed envelope to the party taking the deposition for delivery to the deposition officer, who shall unseal the envelope and propound them to the deponent after the oral examination has been completed. *(Added by Stats.2004, c. 182 (A.B.3081), § 23, operative July 1, 2005. Amended by Stats.2005, c. 294 (A.B.333), § 8.)*

Law Revision Commission Comments

Subdivision (a) of Section 2025.330 continues the first sentence of former Section 2025(l)(1) without change.

Subdivision (b) continues the second sentence of former Section 2025(l)(1) without change.

Subdivision (c) continues the third, fourth, and fifth sentences of former Section 2025(l)(1) without change, except to conform the cross-references.

Subdivision (d) continues the sixth sentence of former Section 2025(l)(1) without change. [33 Cal.L.Rev.Comm. Reports 851 (2004)].

Subdivision (e) continues former Section 2025(l)(3) without change.

Subdivision (c) of Section 2025.330 is amended to make clear that the right of a non-deposing party to make an audio or video record of deposition testimony is not dependent on the method of recording used by the party noticing the deposition.

Research References

Rutter, Cal. Practice Guide: Civ. Pro. Before Trial Ch. 8A-4, Use of Technology in Discovery.
Rutter, Cal. Practice Guide: Civ. Pro. Before Trial Ch. 8E-10, Preservation of Testimony.
Rutter, Cal. Practice Guide: Civ. Pro. Before Trial Ch. 8E-12, Conduct of Deposition.
California Practice Guide: Employment Litigation Ch. 19-F, F. Discovery.
Rutter, Cal. Practice Guide: Personal Injury Ch. 6-B, B. Overview of Selected Discovery Procedures.
Rutter, Cal. Practice Guide: Personal Injury Ch. 8-C, C. Two Months Before Trial.
7 Witkin Cal. Proc. 5th Trial § 5, Trial Practice.

§ 2025.340. Recordation by audio or video technology; procedural requirements; submission at hearing with stenographic transcript

If a deposition is being recorded by means of audio or video technology by, or at the direction of, any party, the following procedure shall be observed:

(a) The area used for recording the deponent's oral testimony shall be suitably large, adequately lighted, and reasonably quiet.

(b) The operator of the recording equipment shall be competent to set up, operate, and monitor the equipment in the manner prescribed in this section. Except as provided in subdivision (c), the operator may be an employee of the attorney taking the deposition unless the operator is also the deposition officer.

(c) If a video recording of deposition testimony is to be used under subdivision (d) of Section 2025.620, the operator of the recording equipment shall be a person who is authorized to administer an oath, and shall not be financially interested in the action or be a relative or employee of any attorney of any of the parties, unless all parties attending the deposition agree on the record to waive these qualifications and restrictions.

(d) Services and products offered or provided by the deposition officer or the entity providing the services of the deposition officer to any party or to any party's attorney or third party who is financing all or part of the action shall be offered or provided to all parties or their attorneys attending the deposition. No service or product may be offered or provided by the deposition officer or by the entity providing the services of the deposition officer to any party or any party's attorney or third party who is financing all or part of the action unless the service or product is offered or provided to all parties or their attorneys attending the deposition. All services and products offered or provided shall be made available at the same time to all parties or their attorneys.

(e) The deposition officer or the entity providing the services of the deposition officer shall not provide to any party or any other person or entity any service or product consisting of the deposition officer's notations or comments regarding the demeanor of any witness, attorney, or party present at the deposition. The deposition officer or the entity providing the services of the deposition officer shall not collect any personal identifying information about the witness as a service or product to be provided to any party or third party who is financing all or part of the action.

(f) Upon the request of any party or any party's attorney attending a deposition, any party or any party's attorney attending the deposition shall enter in the record of the deposition all services and products made available to that party or party's attorney or third party who is financing all or part of the action by the deposition officer or by the entity providing the services of the deposition officer. A party in the action who is not represented by an attorney shall be informed by the noticing party that the unrepresented party may request this statement.

(g) The operator shall not distort the appearance or the demeanor of participants in the deposition by the use of camera or sound recording techniques.

(h) The deposition shall begin with an oral or written statement on camera or on the audio recording that includes the operator's name and business address, the name and business address of the operator's employer, the date, time, and place of the deposition, the caption of the case, the name of the deponent, a specification of the party on whose behalf the deposition is being taken, and any stipulations by the parties.

(i) Counsel for the parties shall identify themselves on camera or on the audio recording.

(j) The oath shall be administered to the deponent on camera or on the audio recording.

(k) If the length of a deposition requires the use of more than one unit of tape or electronic storage, the end of each unit and the beginning of each succeeding unit shall be announced on camera or on the audio recording.

(*l*) At the conclusion of a deposition, a statement shall be made on camera or on the audio recording that the deposition is ended and shall set forth any stipulations made by counsel concerning the custody of the audio or video recording and the exhibits, or concerning other pertinent matters.

(m) A party intending to offer an audio or video recording of a deposition in evidence under Section 2025.620 shall notify the court and all parties in writing of that intent and of the parts of the deposition to be offered. That notice shall be given within sufficient time for objections to be made and ruled on by the judge to whom the case is assigned for trial or hearing, and for any editing of the recording. Objections to all or part of the deposition shall be made in writing. The court may permit further designations of testimony and objections as justice may require. With respect to those portions of an audio or video record of deposition testimony that are not designated by any party or that are ruled to be objectionable, the court may order that the party offering the recording of the deposition at the trial or hearing suppress those portions, or that an edited version of the deposition recording be prepared for use at the trial or

hearing. The original audio or video record of the deposition shall be preserved unaltered. If no stenographic record of the deposition testimony has previously been made, the party offering an audio or video recording of that testimony under Section 2025.620 shall accompany that offer with a stenographic transcript prepared from that recording. (*Added by Stats.2004, c. 182 (A.B.3081), § 23, operative July 1, 2005.*)

Law Revision Commission Comments

The introductory clause of Section 2025.340 continues the introductory clause of former Section 2025(*l*)(2) without substantive change.

Subdivision (a) continues former Section 2025(*l*)(2)(A) without change.

Subdivision (b) continues the first and second sentences of former Section 2025(*l*)(2)(B) without substantive change.

Subdivision (c) continues the third sentence of former Section 2025(*l*)(2)(B) without substantive change.

Subdivision (d) continues the fourth, fifth, and sixth sentences of former Section 2025(*l*)(2)(B) without change.

Subdivision (e) continues the seventh and eighth sentences of former Section 2025(*l*)(2)(B) without change.

Subdivision (f) continues the ninth and tenth sentences of former Section 2025(*l*)(2)(B) without change.

Subdivision (g) continues former Section 2025(*l*)(2)(C) without change.

Subdivision (h) continues former Section 2025(*l*)(2)(D) without change.

Subdivision (i) continues former Section 2025(*l*)(2)(E) without change.

Subdivision (j) continues former Section 2025(*l*)(2)(F) without change.

Subdivision (k) continues former Section 2025(*l*)(2)(G) without change.

Subdivision (*l*) continues former Section 2025(*l*)(2)(H) with revisions to encompass all types of audio and video technology, not just audiotape and videotape.

Subdivision (m) continues former Section 2025(*l*)(2)(I) with revisions to conform cross-references and to encompass all types of audio and video technology in the last sentence, not just audiotape and videotape. [33 Cal.L.Rev.Comm. Reports 852 (2004)].

Research References

Rutter, Cal. Practice Guide: Civ. Pro. Before Trial Ch. 8E-10, Preservation of Testimony.

Rutter, Cal. Practice Guide: Civ. Pro. Before Trial Ch. 8E-17, Use of Depositions at Trial.

Rutter, Cal. Practice Guide: Civil Trials & Evidence Ch. 4-B, B. Preliminary Matters Discussed in Final Status Conference or In-Chambers Conference.

Rutter, Cal. Practice Guide: Civil Trials & Evidence Ch. 8C-E, E. Audio or Visual Recordings.

Rutter, Cal. Practice Guide: Civil Trials & Evidence Ch. 8C-I, I. Depositions and Discovery.

Rutter, Cal. Practice Guide: Personal Injury Ch. 6-A, A. Scope of Discovery and Limitations.

Rutter, Cal. Practice Guide: Personal Injury Ch. 6-B, B. Overview of Selected Discovery Procedures.

Rutter, Cal. Practice Guide: Personal Injury Ch. 8-C, C. Two Months Before Trial.

Rutter, Cal. Practice Guide: Personal Injury Ch. 9-B, B. In-Chambers Conference Before Commencement of Trial.

ARTICLE 4. OBJECTIONS, SANCTIONS, PROTECTIVE ORDERS, MOTIONS TO COMPEL, AND SUSPENSION OF DEPOSITIONS

§ 2025.410. Defective notice; time to object; waiver; motion to stay; meet and confer declaration; monetary sanctions; electronically stored information sanctions

(a) Any party served with a deposition notice that does not comply with Article 2 (commencing with Section 2025.210) waives any error or irregularity unless that party promptly serves a written objection specifying that error or irregularity at least three calendar days prior to the date for which the deposition is scheduled, on the party seeking to take the deposition and any other attorney or party on whom the deposition notice was served.

(b) If an objection is made three calendar days before the deposition date, the objecting party shall make personal service of that objection pursuant to Section 1011 on the party who gave notice of the deposition. Any deposition taken after the service of a written objection shall not be used against the objecting party under Section 2025.620 if the party did not attend the deposition and if the court determines that the objection was a valid one.

(c) In addition to serving this written objection, a party may also move for an order staying the taking of the deposition and quashing the deposition notice. This motion shall be accompanied by a meet and confer declaration under Section 2016.040. The taking of the deposition is stayed pending the determination of this motion.

(d) The court shall impose a monetary sanction under Chapter 7 (commencing with Section 2023.010) against any party, person, or attorney who unsuccessfully makes or opposes a motion to quash a deposition notice, unless it finds that the one subject to the sanction acted with substantial justification or that other circumstances make the imposition of the sanction unjust.

(e)(1) Notwithstanding subdivision (d), absent exceptional circumstances, the court shall not impose sanctions on any party, person, or attorney for failure to provide electronically stored information that has been lost, damaged, altered, or overwritten as the result of the routine, good faith operation of an electronic information system.

(2) This subdivision shall not be construed to alter any obligation to preserve discoverable information. *(Added by*

Stats.2004, c. 182 (A.B.3081), § 23, operative July 1, 2005. Amended by Stats.2012, c. 72 (S.B.1574), § 22.)

Law Revision Commission Comments

Subdivision (a) of Section 2025.410 continues the first sentence of former Section 2025(g) without change, except to conform the cross-references.

Subdivision (b) continues the second and third sentences of former Section 2025(g) without change, except to conform a cross-reference.

Subdivision (c) continues the second paragraph of former Section 2025(g) without substantive change.

Subdivision (d) continues the third paragraph of former Section 2025(g) without change, except to conform the cross-reference. [33 Cal.L.Rev. Comm. Reports 856 (2004)].

Research References

Rutter, Cal. Practice Guide: Civ. Pro. Before Trial Ch. 13-E, E. the Arbitration Hearing.

Rutter, Cal. Practice Guide: Civ. Pro. Before Trial Ch. 8E-4, Notice of Deposition.

Rutter, Cal. Practice Guide: Civ. Pro. Before Trial Ch. 8E-5, Subpoena Not Necessary for Party or "Party-Affiliated" Witnesses.

Rutter, Cal. Practice Guide: Civil Trials & Evidence Ch. 4-B, B. Preliminary Matters Discussed in Final Status Conference or In-Chambers Conference.

Rutter, Cal. Practice Guide: Personal Injury Ch. 7-G, G. Arbitration Hearing.

Rutter, Cal. Practice Guide: Personal Injury Ch. 8-B, B. After Trial Date Set (Three to Four Months Before Trial).

6 Witkin Cal. Proc. 5th Proceedings Without Trial § 603, (S 603) Depositions.

§ 2025.420. Protective orders; authority and action by court; burden of demonstrating inaccessibility of information; court order and conditions for discovery; monetary sanctions; electronically stored information sanctions

(a) Before, during, or after a deposition, any party, any deponent, or any other affected natural person or organization may promptly move for a protective order. The motion shall be accompanied by a meet and confer declaration under Section 2016.040.

(b) The court, for good cause shown, may make any order that justice requires to protect any party, deponent, or other natural person or organization from unwarranted annoyance, embarrassment, or oppression, or undue burden and expense. This protective order may include, but is not limited to, one or more of the following directions:

(1) That the deposition not be taken at all.

(2) That the deposition be taken at a different time.

(3) That a video recording of the deposition testimony of a treating or consulting physician or of any expert witness, intended for possible use at trial under subdivision (d) of Section 2025.620, be postponed until the moving party has had an adequate opportunity to prepare, by discovery deposition of the deponent, or other means, for cross-examination.

(4) That the deposition be taken at a place other than that specified in the deposition notice, if it is within a distance permitted by Sections 2025.250 and 2025.260.

(5) That the deposition be taken only on certain specified terms and conditions.

(6) That the deponent's testimony be taken by written, instead of oral, examination.

(7) That the method of discovery be interrogatories to a party instead of an oral deposition.

(8) That the testimony be recorded in a manner different from that specified in the deposition notice.

(9) That certain matters not be inquired into.

(10) That the scope of the examination be limited to certain matters.

(11) That all or certain of the writings or tangible things designated in the deposition notice not be produced, inspected, copied, tested, or sampled, or that conditions be set for the production of electronically stored information designated in the deposition notice.

(12) That designated persons, other than the parties to the action and their officers and counsel, be excluded from attending the deposition.

(13) That a trade secret or other confidential research, development, or commercial information not be disclosed or be disclosed only to specified persons or only in a specified way.

(14) That the parties simultaneously file specified documents enclosed in sealed envelopes to be opened as directed by the court.

(15) That the deposition be sealed and thereafter opened only on order of the court.

(16) That examination of the deponent be terminated. If an order terminates the examination, the deposition shall not thereafter be resumed, except on order of the court.

(c) The party, deponent, or any other affected natural person or organization that seeks a protective order regarding the production, inspection, copying, testing, or sampling of electronically stored information on the basis that the information is from a source that is not reasonably accessible because of undue burden or expense shall bear the burden of demonstrating that the information is from a source that is not reasonably accessible because of undue burden or expense.

(d) If the party or affected person from whom discovery of electronically stored information is sought establishes that the information is from a source that is not reasonably accessible because of undue burden or expense, the court may nonetheless order discovery if the demanding party shows good cause, subject to any limitations imposed under subdivision (f).

(e) If the court finds good cause for the production of electronically stored information from a source that is not reasonably accessible, the court may set conditions for the discovery of the electronically stored information, including allocation of the expense of discovery.

(f) The court shall limit the frequency or extent of discovery of electronically stored information, even from a source that is reasonably accessible, if the court determines that any of the following conditions exist:

(1) It is possible to obtain the information from some other source that is more convenient, less burdensome, or less expensive.

(2) The discovery sought is unreasonably cumulative or duplicative.

(3) The party seeking discovery has had ample opportunity by discovery in the action to obtain the information sought.

(4) The likely burden or expense of the proposed discovery outweighs the likely benefit, taking into account the amount in controversy, the resources of the parties, the importance of the issues in the litigation, and the importance of the requested discovery in resolving the issues.

(g) If the motion for a protective order is denied in whole or in part, the court may order that the deponent provide or permit the discovery against which protection was sought on those terms and conditions that are just.

(h) The court shall impose a monetary sanction under Chapter 7 (commencing with Section 2023.010) against any party, person, or attorney who unsuccessfully makes or opposes a motion for a protective order, unless it finds that the one subject to the sanction acted with substantial justification or that other circumstances make the imposition of the sanction unjust.

(i)(1) Notwithstanding subdivision (h), absent exceptional circumstances, the court shall not impose sanctions on any party, deponent, or other affected natural person or organization or any of their attorneys for failure to provide electronically stored information that has been lost, damaged, altered, or overwritten as the result of the routine, good faith operation of an electronic information system.

(2) This subdivision shall not be construed to alter any obligation to preserve discoverable information. *(Added by Stats.2004, c. 182 (A.B.3081), § 23, operative July 1, 2005. Amended by Stats.2012, c. 72 (S.B.1574), § 23.)*

Law Revision Commission Comments

Subdivision (a) of Section 2025.420 continues the first paragraph of former Section 2025(i) without substantive change.

Subdivision (b) continues the second paragraph (including items (1)-(15)) of former Section 2025(i) without change, except to conform the cross-references. Subdivision (b)(16) continues the third and fourth sentences of former Section 2025(n) without substantive change.

Subdivision (c) continues the next-to-last paragraph of former Section 2025(i) without change.

Subdivision (d) continues the last paragraph of former Section 2025(i) without change, except to conform the cross-reference. [33 Cal.L.Rev. Comm. Reports 857 (2004)].

Research References

Rutter, Cal. Practice Guide: Civil Appeals & Writs Ch. 2-B, B. Appealable Judgments and Orders.

Rutter, Cal. Practice Guide: Civil Appeals & Writs Ch. 2-D, D. Standing to Appeal.

Rutter, Cal. Practice Guide: Civ. Pro. Before Trial Ch. 2-E, E. Intervention.

Rutter, Cal. Practice Guide: Civ. Pro. Before Trial Ch. 8B-3, Limitations on Right to Discovery.

Rutter, Cal. Practice Guide: Civ. Pro. Before Trial Ch. 8E-4, Notice of Deposition.

Rutter, Cal. Practice Guide: Civ. Pro. Before Trial Ch. 8E-5, Subpoena Not Necessary for Party or "Party-Affiliated" Witnesses.

Rutter, Cal. Practice Guide: Civ. Pro. Before Trial Ch. 8E-8, Place of Deposition.

Rutter, Cal. Practice Guide: Civ. Pro. Before Trial Ch. 8E-11, Protective Orders.

Rutter, Cal. Practice Guide: Civ. Pro. Before Trial Ch. 8E-12, Conduct of Deposition.

Rutter, Cal. Practice Guide: Civ. Pro. Before Trial Ch. 8E-13, Compare-Depositions on Written Questions.

Rutter, Cal. Practice Guide: Civ. Pro. Before Trial Ch. 8E-14, Deposition Transcript.

Rutter, Cal. Practice Guide: Personal Injury Ch. 6-B, B. Overview of Selected Discovery Procedures.

Rutter, Cal. Practice Guide: Personal Injury Ch. 8-B, B. After Trial Date Set (Three to Four Months Before Trial).

Rutter, Cal. Practice Guide: Personal Injury Ch. 8-C, C. Two Months Before Trial.

6 Witkin Cal. Proc. 5th Provisional Remedies § 382, (S 382) in General.

§ 2025.430. Failure to attend by party giving notice; sanctions; exceptions

If the party giving notice of a deposition fails to attend or proceed with it, the court shall impose a monetary sanction under Chapter 7 (commencing with Section 2023.010) against that party, or the attorney for that party, or both, and in favor of any party attending in person or by attorney, unless it finds that the one subject to the sanction acted with substantial justification or that other circumstances make the imposition of the sanction unjust. *(Added by Stats.2004, c. 182 (A.B.3081), § 23, operative July 1, 2005.)*

Law Revision Commission Comments

Section 2025.430 continues former Section 2025(j)(1) without change, except to conform the cross-reference. [33 Cal.L.Rev.Comm. Reports 859 (2004)].

Research References

Rutter, Cal. Practice Guide: Civ. Pro. Before Trial Ch. 8E-16, Sanctions Re Depositions.

Rutter, Cal. Practice Guide: Personal Injury Ch. 8-B, B. After Trial Date Set (Three to Four Months Before Trial).

§ 2025.440. Failure to attend by deponent; defective service; monetary sanctions; sanction where service is effective; refusal to give oath

(a) If a deponent does not appear for a deposition because the party giving notice of the deposition failed to serve a required deposition subpoena, the court shall impose a monetary sanction under Chapter 7 (commencing with Section 2023.010) against that party, or the attorney for that party, or both, in favor of any other party who, in person or by attorney, attended at the time and place specified in the deposition notice in the expectation that the deponent's testimony would be taken, unless the court finds that the one subject to the sanction acted with substantial justification or that other circumstances make the imposition of the sanction unjust.

(b) If a deponent on whom a deposition subpoena has been served fails to attend a deposition or refuses to be sworn as a witness, the court may impose on the deponent the sanctions described in Section 2020.240. *(Added by Stats.2004, c. 182 (A.B.3081), § 23, operative July 1, 2005.)*

Law Revision Commission Comments

Subdivision (a) of Section 2025.440 continues the first paragraph of former Section 2025(j)(2) without change, except to conform the cross-reference.

Subdivision (b) continues the second paragraph of former Section 2025(j)(2) without change, except to conform the cross-reference. [33 Cal.L.Rev.Comm. Reports 860 (2004)].

Research References

Rutter, Cal. Practice Guide: Civ. Pro. Before Trial Ch. 8E-16, Sanctions Re Depositions.

Rutter, Cal. Practice Guide: Personal Injury Ch. 8-B, B. After Trial Date Set (Three to Four Months Before Trial).

§ 2025.450. Failure of party deponent to appear or produce documents, electronically stored information, or items; contents of motion to compel; burden of demonstrating inaccessibility of electronic information; court order and conditions for discovery; monetary sanctions; issue, evidence, or terminating sanction; electronically stored information sanctions

(a) If, after service of a deposition notice, a party to the action or an officer, director, managing agent, or employee of a party, or a person designated by an organization that is a party under Section 2025.230, without having served a valid objection under Section 2025.410, fails to appear for examination, or to proceed with it, or to produce for inspection any document, electronically stored information, or tangible thing described in the deposition notice, the party giving the notice may move for an order compelling the deponent's attendance and testimony, and the production for inspection of any document, electronically stored information, or tangible thing described in the deposition notice.

(b) A motion under subdivision (a) shall comply with both of the following:

(1) The motion shall set forth specific facts showing good cause justifying the production for inspection of any document, electronically stored information, or tangible thing described in the deposition notice.

(2) The motion shall be accompanied by a meet and confer declaration under Section 2016.040, or, when the deponent fails to attend the deposition and produce the documents, electronically stored information, or things described in the deposition notice, by a declaration stating that the petitioner has contacted the deponent to inquire about the nonappearance.

(c) In a motion under subdivision (a) relating to the production of electronically stored information, the party or party-affiliated deponent objecting to or opposing the production, inspection, copying, testing, or sampling of electronically stored information on the basis that the information is from a source that is not reasonably accessible because of the undue burden or expense shall bear the burden of demonstrating that the information is from a source that is not reasonably accessible because of undue burden or expense.

(d) If the party or party-affiliated deponent from whom discovery of electronically stored information is sought establishes that the information is from a source that is not reasonably accessible because of the undue burden or expense, the court may nonetheless order discovery if the demanding party shows good cause, subject to any limitations imposed under subdivision (f).

(e) If the court finds good cause for the production of electronically stored information from a source that is not reasonably accessible, the court may set conditions for the discovery of the electronically stored information, including allocation of the expense of discovery.

(f) The court shall limit the frequency or extent of discovery of electronically stored information, even from a source that is reasonably accessible, if the court determines that any of the following conditions exists:

(1) It is possible to obtain the information from some other source that is more convenient, less burdensome, or less expensive.

(2) The discovery sought is unreasonably cumulative or duplicative.

(3) The party seeking discovery has had ample opportunity by discovery in the action to obtain the information sought.

(4) The likely burden or expense of the proposed discovery outweighs the likely benefit, taking into account the amount in controversy, the resources of the parties, the importance of the issues in the litigation, and the importance of the requested discovery in resolving the issues.

(g)(1) If a motion under subdivision (a) is granted, the court shall impose a monetary sanction under Chapter 7 (commencing with Section 2023.010) in favor of the party who noticed the deposition and against the deponent or the party with whom the deponent is affiliated, unless the court finds that the one subject to the sanction acted with substantial justification or that other circumstances make the imposition of the sanction unjust.

(2) On motion of any other party who, in person or by attorney, attended at the time and place specified in the deposition notice in the expectation that the deponent's testimony would be taken, the court shall impose a monetary sanction under Chapter 7 (commencing with Section 2023.010) in favor of that party and against the deponent or the party with whom the deponent is affiliated, unless the court finds that the one subject to the sanction acted with substantial justification or that other circumstances make the imposition of the sanction unjust.

(h) If that party or party-affiliated deponent then fails to obey an order compelling attendance, testimony, and production, the court may make those orders that are just, including the imposition of an issue sanction, an evidence sanction, or a terminating sanction under Chapter 7 (commencing with Section 2023.010) against that party deponent or against the party with whom the deponent is affiliated. In lieu of, or in addition to, this sanction, the court may impose a monetary sanction under Chapter 7 (commencing with Section 2023.010) against that deponent or against the party with whom that party deponent is affiliated, and in favor of any party who, in person or by attorney, attended in the expectation that the deponent's testimony would be taken pursuant to that order.

(i)(1) Notwithstanding subdivisions (g) and (h), absent exceptional circumstances, the court shall not impose sanctions on a party or any attorney of a party for failure to provide electronically stored information that has been lost, damaged, altered, or overwritten as the result of the routine, good faith operation of an electronic information system.

(2) This subdivision shall not be construed to alter any obligation to preserve discoverable information. *(Added by Stats.2004, c. 182 (A.B.3081), § 23, operative July 1, 2005. Amended by Stats.2012, c. 72 (S.B.1574), § 24.)*

Law Revision Commission Comments

Subdivision (a) of Section 2025.450 continues the first sentence of former Section 2025(j)(3) without change, except to conform the cross-references.

Subdivision (b) continues the second sentence of former Section 2025(j)(3) without substantive change.

Subdivision (c) continues the third and fourth sentences of former Section 2025(j)(3) without substantive change.

Subdivision (d) continues the second paragraph of former Section 2025(j)(3) without change, except to conform the cross-references. [33 Cal.L.Rev.Comm. Reports 860 (2004)].

Research References

Rutter, Cal. Practice Guide: Civ. Pro. Before Trial Ch. 8A-3, Civil Discovery Act.
Rutter, Cal. Practice Guide: Civ. Pro. Before Trial Ch. 8E-5, Subpoena Not Necessary for Party or "Party-Affiliated" Witnesses.
Rutter, Cal. Practice Guide: Civ. Pro. Before Trial Ch. 8E-6, Subpoena to Nonparty Deponent or Business Records Custodian.
Rutter, Cal. Practice Guide: Civ. Pro. Before Trial Ch. 8E-15, Motion to Compel Answers.
Rutter, Cal. Practice Guide: Civ. Pro. Before Trial Ch. 8E-16, Sanctions Re Depositions.
Rutter, Cal. Practice Guide: Personal Injury Ch. 8-B, B. After Trial Date Set (Three to Four Months Before Trial).

§ 2025.460. Privileged or protected information; objection to disclosure; waiver; identification of inaccessible electronically stored information; adjournment

(a) The protection of information from discovery on the ground that it is privileged or that it is a protected work product under Chapter 4 (commencing with Section 2018.010) is waived unless a specific objection to its disclosure is timely made during the deposition.

(b) Errors and irregularities of any kind occurring at the oral examination that might be cured if promptly presented are waived unless a specific objection to them is timely made during the deposition. These errors and irregularities include, but are not limited to, those relating to the manner of taking the deposition, to the oath or affirmation administered, to the conduct of a party, attorney, deponent, or deposition officer, or to the form of any question or answer. Unless the objecting party demands that the taking of the deposition be suspended to permit a motion for a protective order under Sections 2025.420 and 2025.470, the deposition shall proceed subject to the objection.

(c) Objections to the competency of the deponent, or to the relevancy, materiality, or admissibility at trial of the testimony or of the materials produced are unnecessary and are not waived by failure to make them before or during the deposition.

(d) If a deponent objects to the production of electronically stored information on the grounds that it is from a source that is not reasonably accessible because of undue burden or expense and that the deponent will not search the source in the absence of an agreement with the deposing party or court order, the deponent shall identify in its objection the types or categories of sources of electronically stored information that it asserts are not reasonably accessible. By objecting and identifying information of a type or category of source or sources that are not reasonably accessible, the deponent preserves any objections it may have relating to that electronically stored information.

(e) If a deponent fails to answer any question or to produce any document, electronically stored information, or tangible thing under the deponent's control that is specified in the deposition notice or a deposition subpoena, the party seeking that answer or production may adjourn the deposition or complete the examination on other matters without waiving the right at a later time to move for an order compelling that answer or production under Section 2025.480.

(f) Notwithstanding subdivision (a), if a deponent notifies the party that took a deposition that electronically stored information produced pursuant to the deposition notice or subpoena is subject to a claim of privilege or of protection as attorney work product, as described in Section 2031.285, the provisions of Section 2031.285 shall apply. *(Added by Stats.2004, c. 182 (A.B.3081), § 23, operative July 1, 2005. Amended by Stats.2012, c. 72 (S.B.1574), § 25.)*

Law Revision Commission Comments

Subdivision (a) of Section 2025.460 continues former Section 2025(m)(1) without change, except to conform the cross-reference.

Subdivision (b) continues former Section 2025(m)(2) without change, except to conform the cross-reference.

Subdivision (c) continues former Section 2025(m)(3) without change.

Subdivision (d) continues former Section 2025(m)(4) without change, except to conform the cross-reference. [33 Cal.L.Rev.Comm. Reports 862 (2004)].

Research References

Rutter, Cal. Practice Guide: Civ. Pro. Before Trial Ch. 8C-3, "Not Privileged".
Rutter, Cal. Practice Guide: Civ. Pro. Before Trial Ch. 8E-12, Conduct of Deposition.
Rutter, Cal. Practice Guide: Civil Trials & Evidence Ch. 4-B, B. Preliminary Matters Discussed in Final Status Conference or In-Chambers Conference.
Rutter, Cal. Practice Guide: Civil Trials & Evidence Ch. 8E-A, A. Privileges.
Rutter, Cal. Practice Guide: Personal Injury Ch. 9-H, H. Introduction of Discovered Evidence.

§ 2025.470. Suspension of testimony; authority of deposition officer

The deposition officer may not suspend the taking of testimony without the stipulation of all parties present unless any party attending the deposition, including the deponent, demands that the deposition officer suspend taking the testimony to enable that party or deponent to move for a protective order under Section 2025.420 on the ground that the examination is being conducted in bad faith or in a manner that unreasonably annoys, embarrasses, or oppresses that deponent or party. *(Added by Stats.2004, c. 182 (A.B.3081), § 23, operative July 1, 2005.)*

Law Revision Commission Comments

Section 2025.470 continues the first sentence of former Section 2025(n) without substantive change. By incorporating the requirements of Section 2025.420, Section 2025.470 also continues the second sentence of former Section 2025(n) and the second paragraph of that provision without substantive change. See Sections 2025.420(a) (motion for protective order shall be accompanied by meet and confer declaration), 2025.420(d) (monetary sanction against party, person, or attorney who unsuccessfully makes or opposes motion for protective order). [33 Cal.L.Rev.Comm. Reports 863 (2004)].

Research References

Rutter, Cal. Practice Guide: Civ. Pro. Before Trial Ch. 8J-7, Deposing Opposing Experts.

Rutter, Cal. Practice Guide: Civ. Pro. Before Trial Ch. 8E-12, Conduct of Deposition.

§ 2025.480. Motion to compel answers or produce documents, electronically stored information, or items; procedural requirements; burden of demonstrating inaccessibility of electronic information; court order and conditions of discovery; monetary sanctions; contempt of court; electronically stored information sanctions

(a) If a deponent fails to answer any question or to produce any document, electronically stored information, or tangible thing under the deponent's control that is specified in the deposition notice or a deposition subpoena, the party seeking discovery may move the court for an order compelling that answer or production.

(b) This motion shall be made no later than 60 days after the completion of the record of the deposition, and shall be accompanied by a meet and confer declaration under Section 2016.040.

(c) Notice of this motion shall be given to all parties and to the deponent either orally at the examination, or by subsequent service in writing. If the notice of the motion is given orally, the deposition officer shall direct the deponent to attend a session of the court at the time specified in the notice.

(d) In a motion under subdivision (a) relating to the production of electronically stored information, the deponent objecting to or opposing the production, inspection, copying, testing, or sampling of electronically stored information on the basis that the information is from a source that is not reasonably accessible because of the undue burden or expense shall bear the burden of demonstrating that the information is from a source that is not reasonably accessible because of undue burden or expense.

(e) If the deponent from whom discovery of electronically stored information is sought establishes that the information is from a source that is not reasonably accessible because of the undue burden or expense, the court may nonetheless order discovery if the deposing party shows good cause, subject to any limitations imposed under subdivision (g).

(f) If the court finds good cause for the production of electronically stored information from a source that is not reasonably accessible, the court may set conditions for the discovery of the electronically stored information, including allocation of the expense of discovery.

(g) The court shall limit the frequency or extent of discovery of electronically stored information, even from a source that is reasonably accessible, if the court determines that any of the following conditions exists:

(1) It is possible to obtain the information from some other source that is more convenient, less burdensome, or less expensive.

(2) The discovery sought is unreasonably cumulative or duplicative.

(3) The party seeking discovery has had ample opportunity by discovery in the action to obtain the information sought.

(4) The likely burden or expense of the proposed discovery outweighs the likely benefit, taking into account the amount in controversy, the resources of the parties, the importance of the issues in the litigation, and the importance of the requested discovery in resolving the issues.

(h) Not less than five days prior to the hearing on this motion, the moving party shall lodge with the court a certified copy of any parts of the stenographic transcript of the deposition that are relevant to the motion. If a deposition is recorded by audio or video technology, the moving party is required to lodge a certified copy of a transcript of any parts of the deposition that are relevant to the motion.

(i) If the court determines that the answer or production sought is subject to discovery, it shall order that the answer be given or the production be made on the resumption of the deposition.

(j) The court shall impose a monetary sanction under Chapter 7 (commencing with Section 2023.010) against any party, person, or attorney who unsuccessfully makes or opposes a motion to compel an answer or production, unless it finds that the one subject to the sanction acted with substantial justification or that other circumstances make the imposition of the sanction unjust.

(k) If a deponent fails to obey an order entered under this section, the failure may be considered a contempt of court. In addition, if the disobedient deponent is a party to the action or an officer, director, managing agent, or employee of a party, the court may make those orders that are just against the disobedient party, or against the party with whom the disobedient deponent is affiliated, including the imposition of an issue sanction, an evidence sanction, or a terminating sanction under Chapter 7 (commencing with Section 2023.010). In lieu of or in addition to this sanction, the court may impose a monetary sanction under Chapter 7 (commencing with Section 2023.010) against that party deponent or against any party with whom the deponent is affiliated.

(*l*)(1) Notwithstanding subdivisions (j) and (k), absent exceptional circumstances, the court shall not impose sanctions on a deponent or any attorney of a deponent for failure to provide electronically stored information that has been lost, damaged, altered, or overwritten as the result of the routine, good faith operation of an electronic information system.

(2) This subdivision shall not be construed to alter any obligation to preserve discoverable information. *(Added by Stats.2004, c. 182 (A.B.3081), § 23, operative July 1, 2005. Amended by Stats.2005, c. 22 (S.B.1108), § 21; Stats.2012, c. 72 (S.B.1574), § 26.)*

Law Revision Commission Comments

Subdivision (a) of Section 2025.480 continues the first sentence of former Section 2025(*o*) without change.

Subdivision (b) continues the second sentence of former Section 2025(*o*) without substantive change.

Subdivision (c) continues the third and fourth sentences of former Section 2025(*o*) without change.

Subdivision (d) continues the fifth and sixth sentences of former Section 2025(*o*) without change.

Subdivision (e) continues the seventh sentence of former Section 2025(*o*) without change.

Subdivision (f) continues the second paragraph of former Section 2025(*o*) without change, except to conform the cross-reference.

Subdivision (g) continues the third paragraph of former Section 2025(*o*) without change, except to replace subdivision with section and to conform the cross-references. [33 Cal.L.Rev.Comm. Reports 864 (2004)].

Research References

Rutter, Cal. Practice Guide: Civ. Pro. Before Trial Ch. 8E-6, Subpoena to Nonparty Deponent or Business Records Custodian.

Rutter, Cal. Practice Guide: Civ. Pro. Before Trial Ch. 8F-8, Sanctions in Enforcing Discovery.

Rutter, Cal. Practice Guide: Civ. Pro. Before Trial Ch. 8E-12, Conduct of Deposition.

Rutter, Cal. Practice Guide: Civ. Pro. Before Trial Ch. 8E-15, Motion to Compel Answers.

Rutter, Cal. Practice Guide: Civ. Pro. Before Trial Ch. 8E-16, Sanctions Re Depositions.
Rutter, Cal. Practice Guide: Civ. Pro. Before Trial Ch. 9(III)-F, F. Appellate Review of Sanctions.
Rutter, Cal. Practice Guide: Civil Trials & Evidence Ch. 8C-D, D. Demonstrative Evidence.
Rutter, Cal. Practice Guide: Personal Injury Ch. 8-B, B. After Trial Date Set (Three to Four Months Before Trial).

ARTICLE 5. TRANSCRIPT OR RECORDING

Section

2025.510.   Transcription of testimony; payment of cost; distribution of original and copies; record retention; audio or video recordings; official record.

2025.520.   Reading and correction of transcript; signed approval; change of form or substance of an answer; waiver; suppression motions.

2025.530.   Depositions without stenographic transcription; review of recording; change of form or substance of an answer; signed approval; suppression motions.

2025.540.   Certification of deposition record; rough draft transcripts.

2025.550.   Original certified transcript; transmittal and custody; record retention.

2025.560.   Audio or video recording of deposition; transmittal and custody of electronic media; distribution of copies; recording retention.

2025.570.   Third–party request where original in possession of deposition officer; availability; notice to parties and deponent; protective orders.

§ 2025.510. Transcription of testimony; payment of cost; distribution of original and copies; record retention; audio or video recordings; official record

(a) Unless the parties agree otherwise, the testimony at any deposition recorded by stenographic means shall be transcribed.

(b) The party noticing the deposition shall bear the cost of that transcription, unless the court, on motion and for good cause shown, orders that the cost be borne or shared by another party.

(c) Notwithstanding subdivision (b) of Section 2025.320, any other party or the deponent, at the expense of that party or deponent, may obtain a copy of the transcript.

(d) If the deposition officer receives a request from a party for an original or a copy of the deposition transcript, or any portion thereof, and the full or partial transcript will be available to that party prior to the time the original or copy would be available to any other party, the deposition officer shall immediately notify all other parties attending the deposition of the request, and shall, upon request by any party other than the party making the original request, make that copy of the full or partial deposition transcript available to all parties at the same time.

(e) Stenographic notes of depositions shall be retained by the reporter for a period of not less than eight years from the date of the deposition, where no transcript is produced, and not less than one year from the date on which the transcript is produced. Those notes may be either on paper or electronic media, as long as it allows for satisfactory production of a transcript at any time during the periods specified.

(f) At the request of any other party to the action, including a party who did not attend the taking of the deposition testimony, any party who records or causes the recording of that testimony by means of audio or video technology shall promptly do both of the following:

(1) Permit that other party to hear the audio recording or to view the video recording.

(2) Furnish a copy of the audio or video recording to that other party on receipt of payment of the reasonable cost of making that copy of the recording.

(g) If the testimony at the deposition is recorded both stenographically, and by audio or video technology, the stenographic transcript is the official record of that testimony for the purpose of the trial and any subsequent hearing or appeal.

(h)(1) The requesting attorney or party appearing in propria persona shall timely pay the deposition officer or the entity providing the services of the deposition officer for the transcription or copy of the transcription described in subdivision (b) or (c), and any other deposition products or services that are requested either orally or in writing.

(2) This subdivision shall apply unless responsibility for the payment is otherwise provided by law or unless the deposition officer or entity is notified in writing at the time the services or products are requested that the party or another identified person will be responsible for payment.

(3) This subdivision does not prohibit or supersede an agreement between an attorney and a party allocating responsibility for the payment of deposition costs to the party.

(4) The requesting attorney or party appearing in propria persona, upon the written request of a deposition officer who has obtained a final judgment for payment of services provided pursuant to this subdivision, shall provide to the deposition officer an address that can be used to effectuate service for the purpose of Section 708.110 in the manner specified in Section 415.10.

(i) For purposes of this section, "deposition product or service" means any product or service provided in connection with a deposition that qualifies as shorthand reporting, as described in Section 8017 of the Business and Professions Code, and any product or service derived from that shorthand reporting. *(Added by Stats.2004, c. 182 (A.B.3081), § 23, operative July 1, 2005. Amended by Stats.2007, c. 115 (A.B.1211), § 1; Stats. 2012, c. 125 (A.B.2372), § 1.)*

Law Revision Commission Comments

Subdivision (a) of Section 2025.510 continues the first sentence of former Section 2025(p) without change.

Subdivision (b) continues the second sentence of former Section 2025(p) without change.

Subdivision (c) continues the third sentence of former Section 2025(p) without substantive change.

Subdivision (d) continues the fourth sentence of former Section 2025(p) without change.

Subdivision (e) continues the fifth and sixth sentences of former Section 2025(p) without change.

Subdivision (f) continues the seventh sentence of former Section 2025(p) without substantive change.

Subdivision (g) continues the second paragraph of former Section 2025(p) without change. [33 Cal.L.Rev.Comm. Reports 866 (2004)].

Research References

Rutter, Cal. Practice Guide: Civ. Pro. Before Trial Ch. 8E-10, Preservation of Testimony.
Rutter, Cal. Practice Guide: Civ. Pro. Before Trial Ch. 8E-14, Deposition Transcript.
Rutter, Cal. Practice Guide: Personal Injury Ch. 6-B, B. Overview of Selected Discovery Procedures.

§ 2025.520. Reading and correction of transcript; signed approval; change of form or substance of an answer; waiver; suppression motions

(a) If the deposition testimony is stenographically recorded, the deposition officer shall send written notice to the deponent and to all parties attending the deposition when the original transcript of the testimony for each session of the deposition is available for reading, correcting, and signing, unless the deponent and the attending parties agree on the record that the reading, correcting, and signing of the transcript of the testimony will be waived or that the reading, correcting, and signing of a transcript of the testimony will take place after the entire deposition has been concluded or at some other specific time.

(b) For 30 days following each notice under subdivision (a), unless the attending parties and the deponent agree on the record or otherwise in writing to a longer or shorter time period, the deponent may change the form or the substance of the answer to a question, and may either approve the transcript of the deposition by signing it, or refuse to approve the transcript by not signing it.

(c) Alternatively, within this same period, the deponent may change the form or the substance of the answer to any question and may approve or refuse to approve the transcript by means of a letter to the deposition officer signed by the deponent which is mailed by certified or registered mail with return receipt requested. A copy of that letter shall be sent by first-class mail to all parties attending the deposition.

(d) For good cause shown, the court may shorten the 30–day period for making changes, approving, or refusing to approve the transcript.

(e) The deposition officer shall indicate on the original of the transcript, if the deponent has not already done so at the office of the deposition officer, any action taken by the deponent and indicate on the original of the transcript, the deponent's approval of, or failure or refusal to approve, the transcript. The deposition officer shall also notify in writing the parties attending the deposition of any changes which the deponent timely made in person.

(f) If the deponent fails or refuses to approve the transcript within the allotted period, the deposition shall be given the same effect as though it had been approved, subject to any changes timely made by the deponent.

(g) Notwithstanding subdivision (f), on a seasonable motion to suppress the deposition, accompanied by a meet and confer declaration under Section 2016.040, the court may determine that the reasons given for the failure or refusal to approve the transcript require rejection of the deposition in whole or in part.

(h) The court shall impose a monetary sanction under Chapter 7 (commencing with Section 2023.010) against any party, person, or attorney who unsuccessfully makes or opposes a motion to suppress a deposition under this section, unless the court finds that the one subject to the sanction acted with substantial justification or that other circumstances make the imposition of the sanction unjust. *(Added by Stats.2004, c. 182 (A.B.3081), § 23, operative July 1, 2005.)*

Law Revision Commission Comments

Subdivision (a) of Section 2025.520 continues the first sentence of former Section 2025(q)(1) without change.

Subdivision (b) continues the second sentence of former Section 2025(q)(1) without substantive change.

Subdivision (c) continues the first and second sentences of the second paragraph of former Section 2025(q)(1) without change.

Subdivision (d) continues the third sentence of the second paragraph of former Section 2025(q)(1) without change.

Subdivision (e) continues the first and second sentences of the third paragraph of former Section 2025(q)(1) without change.

Subdivision (f) continues the third sentence of the third paragraph of former Section 2025(q)(1) without change.

Subdivision (g) continues the fourth sentence of the third paragraph of former Section 2025(q)(1) without substantive change.

Subdivision (h) continues the fourth paragraph of former Section 2025(q)(1) without substantive change. [33 Cal.L.Rev.Comm. Reports 867 (2004)].

Research References

Rutter, Cal. Practice Guide: Civ. Pro. Before Trial Ch. 8E-12, Conduct of Deposition.

Rutter, Cal. Practice Guide: Civ. Pro. Before Trial Ch. 8E-14, Deposition Transcript.

Rutter, Cal. Practice Guide: Civil Trials & Evidence Ch. 1-K, K. Continuance Motions.

Rutter, Cal. Practice Guide: Civil Trials & Evidence Ch. 4-B, B. Preliminary Matters Discussed in Final Status Conference or In-Chambers Conference.

Rutter, Cal. Practice Guide: Civil Trials & Evidence Ch. 10-E, E. Preparing for Cross-Examination-A Checklist.

Rutter, Cal. Practice Guide: Personal Injury Ch. 6-B, B. Overview of Selected Discovery Procedures.

Rutter, Cal. Practice Guide: Personal Injury Ch. 8-B, B. After Trial Date Set (Three to Four Months Before Trial).

Rutter, Cal. Practice Guide: Personal Injury Ch. 9-H, H. Introduction of Discovered Evidence.

§ 2025.530. Depositions without stenographic transcription; review of recording; change of form or substance of an answer; signed approval; suppression motions

(a) If there is no stenographic transcription of the deposition, the deposition officer shall send written notice to the deponent and to all parties attending the deposition that the audio or video recording made by, or at the direction of, any party, is available for review, unless the deponent and all these parties agree on the record to waive the hearing or viewing of the audio or video recording of the testimony.

(b) For 30 days following a notice under subdivision (a), the deponent, either in person or by signed letter to the deposition officer, may change the substance of the answer to any question.

(c) The deposition officer shall set forth in a writing to accompany the recording any changes made by the deponent, as well as either the deponent's signature identifying the deposition as the deponent's own, or a statement of the deponent's failure to supply the signature, or to contact the officer within the period prescribed by subdivision (b).

(d) When a deponent fails to contact the officer within the period prescribed by subdivision (b), or expressly refuses by a signature to identify the deposition as the deponent's own, the deposition shall be given the same effect as though signed.

(e) Notwithstanding subdivision (d), on a reasonable motion to suppress the deposition, accompanied by a meet and confer declaration under Section 2016.040, the court may determine that the reasons given for the refusal to sign require rejection of the deposition in whole or in part.

(f) The court shall impose a monetary sanction under Chapter 7 (commencing with Section 2023.010) against any party, person, or attorney who unsuccessfully makes or opposes a motion to suppress a deposition under this section, unless it finds that the one subject to the sanction acted with substantial justification or that other circumstances make the imposition of the sanction unjust. *(Added by Stats.2004, c. 182 (A.B.3081), § 23, operative July 1, 2005.)*

Law Revision Commission Comments

Subdivision (a) of Section 2025.530 continues the first sentence of former Section 2025(q)(2) without change.

Subdivision (b) continues the second sentence of former Section 2025(q)(2) without substantive change.

Subdivision (c) continues the first sentence of the second paragraph of former Section 2025(q)(2) without substantive change.

Subdivision (d) continues the second sentence of the second paragraph of former Section 2025(q)(2) without substantive change.

Subdivision (e) continues the third sentence of the second paragraph of former Section 2025(q)(2) without substantive change.

Subdivision (f) continues the third paragraph of former Section 2025(q)(2) without substantive change. [33 Cal.L.Rev.Comm. Reports 869 (2004)].

Research References

Rutter, Cal. Practice Guide: Civ. Pro. Before Trial Ch. 8E-14, Deposition Transcript.

Rutter, Cal. Practice Guide: Personal Injury Ch. 6-B, B. Overview of Selected Discovery Procedures.

§ 2025.540. Certification of deposition record; rough draft transcripts

(a) The deposition officer shall certify on the transcript of the deposition, or in a writing accompanying an audio or video record of deposition testimony, as described in Section 2025.530, that the deponent was duly sworn and that the transcript or recording is a true record of the testimony given.

(b) When prepared as a rough draft transcript, the transcript of the deposition may not be certified and may not be used, cited, or transcribed as the certified transcript of the deposition proceedings. The rough draft transcript may not be cited or used in any way or at any time to rebut or contradict the certified transcript of deposition proceedings as provided by the deposition officer. *(Added by Stats.2004, c. 182 (A.B.3081), § 23, operative July 1, 2005.)*

Law Revision Commission Comments

Subdivision (a) of Section 2025.540 continues former Section 2025(r)(1) without change, except to conform the cross-reference.

Subdivision (b) continues former Section 2025(r)(2) without change. [33 Cal.L.Rev.Comm. Reports 871 (2004)].

Research References

Rutter, Cal. Practice Guide: Civ. Pro. Before Trial Ch. 8E-14, Deposition Transcript.

Rutter, Cal. Practice Guide: Civ. Pro. Before Trial Ch. 8E-15, Motion to Compel Answers.

Rutter, Cal. Practice Guide: Personal Injury Ch. 6-B, B. Overview of Selected Discovery Procedures.

§ 2025.550. Original certified transcript; transmittal and custody; record retention

(a) The certified transcript of a deposition shall not be filed with the court. Instead, the deposition officer shall securely seal that transcript in an envelope or package endorsed with the title of the action and marked: "Deposition of (here insert name of deponent)," and shall promptly transmit it to the attorney for the party who noticed the deposition. This attorney shall store it under conditions that will protect it against loss, destruction, or tampering.

(b) The attorney to whom the transcript of a deposition is transmitted shall retain custody of it until six months after final disposition of the action. At that time, the transcript may be destroyed, unless the court, on motion of any party and for good cause shown, orders that the transcript be preserved for a longer period. *(Added by Stats.2004, c. 182 (A.B.3081), § 23, operative July 1, 2005.)*

Law Revision Commission Comments

Subdivision (a) of Section 2025.550 continues the first paragraph of former Section 2025(s)(1) without change.

Subdivision (b) continues the second paragraph of former Section 2025(s)(1) without change. [33 Cal.L.Rev.Comm. Reports 871 (2004)].

Research References

Rutter, Cal. Practice Guide: Civ. Pro. Before Trial Ch. 8E-14, Deposition Transcript.

Rutter, Cal. Practice Guide: Civ. Pro. Before Trial Ch. 9(I)-B, B. Preparing and Filing Motions.

Rutter, Cal. Practice Guide: Civil Trials & Evidence Ch. 1-C, C. Marshalling the Evidence.

Rutter, Cal. Practice Guide: Civil Trials & Evidence Ch. 4-B, B. Preliminary Matters Discussed in Final Status Conference or In-Chambers Conference.

Rutter, Cal. Practice Guide: Personal Injury Ch. 8-C, C. Two Months Before Trial.

Rutter, Cal. Practice Guide: Personal Injury Ch. 9-B, B. In-Chambers Conference Before Commencement of Trial.

2 Witkin Cal. Proc. 5th Courts § 372, Custody.

6 Witkin Cal. Proc. 5th Proceedings Without Trial § 42, Other Documentary Evidence.

§ 2025.560. Audio or video recording of deposition; transmittal and custody of electronic media; distribution of copies; recording retention

(a) An audio or video recording of deposition testimony made by, or at the direction of, any party, including a certified recording made by an operator qualified under subdivisions (b) to (f), inclusive, of Section 2025.340, shall not be filed with the court. Instead, the operator shall retain custody of that recording and shall store it under conditions that will protect it against loss, destruction, or tampering, and preserve as far as practicable the quality of the recording and the integrity of the testimony and images it contains.

(b) At the request of any party to the action, including a party who did not attend the taking of the deposition testimony, or at the request of the deponent, that operator shall promptly do both of the following:

(1) Permit the one making the request to hear or to view the recording on receipt of payment of a reasonable charge for providing the facilities for hearing or viewing the recording.

(2) Furnish a copy of the audio or video recording to the one making the request on receipt of payment of the reasonable cost of making that copy of the recording.

(c) The attorney or operator who has custody of an audio or video recording of deposition testimony made by, or at the direction of, any party, shall retain custody of it until six months after final disposition of the action. At that time, the audio or video recording may be destroyed or erased, unless the court, on motion of any party and for good cause shown, orders that the recording be preserved for a longer period. *(Added by Stats. 2004, c. 182 (A.B.3081), § 23, operative July 1, 2005. Amended by Stats.2009, c. 88 (A.B.176), § 18.)*

Law Revision Commission Comments

Subdivision (a) of Section 2025.560 continues the first paragraph of former Section 2025(s)(2) without change, except to conform the cross-reference.

Subdivision (b) continues the second paragraph of former Section 2025(s)(2) without substantive change.

Subdivision (c) continues the third paragraph of former Section 2025(s)(2) without change. [33 Cal.L.Rev.Comm. Reports 872 (2004)].

Section 2025.560 is amended to reflect advances in recording technology and for consistency of terminology. For a similar reform, see 2002 Cal. Stat. ch. 1068 (replacing numerous references to "audiotape" in Civil Discovery Act with either "audio technology," "audio recording," or "audio record," as context required). [37 Cal. L. Revision Comm'n Reports 211 (2007)].

Research References

Rutter, Cal. Practice Guide: Civ. Pro. Before Trial Ch. 8E-14, Deposition Transcript.

2 Witkin Cal. Proc. 5th Courts § 372, Custody.

6 Witkin Cal. Proc. 5th Proceedings Without Trial § 42, Other Documentary Evidence.

§ 2025.570. Third–party request where original in possession of deposition officer; availability; notice to parties and deponent; protective orders

(a) Notwithstanding subdivision (b) of Section 2025.320, unless the court issues an order to the contrary, a copy of the transcript of the deposition testimony made by, or at the direction of, any party, or an audio or video recording of the deposition testimony, if still in the possession of the deposition officer, shall be made available by the deposition officer to any person requesting a copy, on payment of a reasonable charge set by the deposition officer.

(b) If a copy is requested from the deposition officer, the deposition officer shall mail a notice to all parties attending the deposition and to the deponent at the deponent's last known address advising them of all of the following:

(1) The copy is being sought.

(2) The name of the person requesting the copy.

(3) The right to seek a protective order under Section 2025.420.

(c) If a protective order is not served on the deposition officer within 30 days of the mailing of the notice, the deposition officer shall make the copy available to the person requesting the copy.

(d) This section shall apply only to recorded testimony taken at depositions occurring on or after January 1, 1998. *(Added by Stats.2004, c. 182 (A.B.3081), § 23, operative July 1, 1995.)*

Law Revision Commission Comments

Subdivision (a) of Section 2025.570 continues former Section 2025.5(a) without substantive change.

Subdivision (b) continues the first sentence of former Section 2025.5(b) without substantive change.

Subdivision (c) continues the second sentence of former Section 2025.5(b) without change.

Subdivision (d) continues former Section 2025.5(c) without change. [33 Cal.L.Rev.Comm. Reports 873 (2004)].

Research References

Rutter, Cal. Practice Guide; Civ. Pro. Before Trial Ch. 8K-6, Special Statutes and Court Rules.

Rutter, Cal. Practice Guide: Civ. Pro. Before Trial Ch. 8E-14, Deposition Transcript.

ARTICLE 6. POST–DEPOSITION PROCEDURES

Section
2025.610.   Subsequent deposition of deponents; restrictions; exceptions.
2025.620.   Use of deposition at trial or other hearings; procedural requirements; permitted uses; submission of total or partial testimony.

§ 2025.610. Subsequent deposition of deponents; restrictions; exceptions

(a) Once any party has taken the deposition of any natural person, including that of a party to the action, neither the party who gave, nor any other party who has been served with a deposition notice pursuant to Section 2025.240 may take a subsequent deposition of that deponent.

(b) Notwithstanding subdivision (a), for good cause shown, the court may grant leave to take a subsequent deposition, and the parties, with the consent of any deponent who is not a party, may stipulate that a subsequent deposition be taken.

(c) This section does not preclude taking one subsequent deposition of a natural person who has previously been examined under either or both of the following circumstances:

(1) The person was examined as a result of that person's designation to testify on behalf of an organization under Section 2025.230.

(2) The person was examined pursuant to a court order under Section 485.230, for the limited purpose of discovering pursuant to Section 485.230 the identity, location, and value of property in which the deponent has an interest.

(d) This section does not authorize the taking of more than one subsequent deposition for the limited purpose of Section 485.230. *(Added by Stats.2004, c. 182 (A.B.3081), § 23, operative July 1, 2005.)*

Law Revision Commission Comments

Subdivision (a) of Section 2025.610 continues the first sentence of former Section 2025(t) without change, except to conform the cross-reference.

Subdivision (b) continues the second sentence of former Section 2025(t) without substantive change.

Subdivision (c) continues the third sentence of former Section 2025(t) without substantive change.

Subdivision (d) continues the fourth sentence of former Section 2025(t) without change, except to replace subdivision with section. [33 Cal.L.Rev. Comm. Reports 874 (2004)].

Research References

Rutter, Cal. Practice Guide: Civ. Pro. Before Trial Ch. 8E-1, When Prior Court Order Required.

Rutter, Cal. Practice Guide: Civ. Pro. Before Trial Ch. 8E-2, When Depositions May be Taken.

Rutter, Cal. Practice Guide: Civ. Pro. Before Trial Ch. 8E-3, Whose Deposition May be Taken.

Rutter, Cal. Practice Guide: Civ. Pro. Before Trial Ch. 8L-1, Limitations on Existing Discovery Procedures.

Rutter, Cal. Practice Guide: Civ. Pro. Before Trial Ch. 8E-12, Conduct of Deposition.

Rutter, Cal. Practice Guide: Fed.Civ.Pro. Before Trial Ch. 1-D, D. Choosing Between State and Federal Courts.

Rutter, Cal. Practice Guide: Personal Injury Ch. 6-B, B. Overview of Selected Discovery Procedures.

§ 2025.620. Use of deposition at trial or other hearings; procedural requirements; permitted uses; submission of total or partial testimony

At the trial or any other hearing in the action, any part or all of a deposition may be used against any party who was present or represented at the taking of the deposition, or who had due notice of the deposition and did not serve a valid objection under Section 2025.410, so far as admissible under the rules of evidence applied as though the deponent were then present and testifying as a witness, in accordance with the following provisions:

(a) Any party may use a deposition for the purpose of contradicting or impeaching the testimony of the deponent as a witness, or for any other purpose permitted by the Evidence Code.

(b) An adverse party may use for any purpose, a deposition of a party to the action, or of anyone who at the time of taking the deposition was an officer, director, managing agent, employee, agent, or designee under Section 2025.230 of a party. It is not ground for objection to the use of a deposition of a party under this subdivision by an adverse party that the deponent is available to testify, has testified, or will testify at the trial or other hearing.

(c) Any party may use for any purpose the deposition of any person or organization, including that of any party to the action, if the court finds any of the following:

(1) The deponent resides more than 150 miles from the place of the trial or other hearing.

(2) The deponent, without the procurement or wrongdoing of the proponent of the deposition for the purpose of preventing testimony in open court, is any of the following:

(A) Exempted or precluded on the ground of privilege from testifying concerning the matter to which the deponent's testimony is relevant.

(B) Disqualified from testifying.

(C) Dead or unable to attend or testify because of existing physical or mental illness or infirmity.

(D) Absent from the trial or other hearing and the court is unable to compel the deponent's attendance by its process.

(E) Absent from the trial or other hearing and the proponent of the deposition has exercised reasonable diligence but has been unable to procure the deponent's attendance by the court's process.

(3) Exceptional circumstances exist that make it desirable to allow the use of any deposition in the interests of justice and with due regard to the importance of presenting the testimony of witnesses orally in open court.

(d) Any party may use a video recording of the deposition testimony of a treating or consulting physician or of any expert witness even though the deponent is available to testify if the deposition notice under Section 2025.220 reserved the right to use the deposition at trial, and if that party has complied with subdivision (m) of Section 2025.340.

(e) Subject to the requirements of this chapter, a party may offer in evidence all or any part of a deposition, and if the party introduces only part of the deposition, any other party may introduce any other parts that are relevant to the parts introduced.

(f) Substitution of parties does not affect the right to use depositions previously taken.

(g) When an action has been brought in any court of the United States or of any state, and another action involving the same subject matter is subsequently brought between the same parties or their representatives or successors in interest, all depositions lawfully taken and duly filed in the initial action may be used in the subsequent action as if originally taken in that subsequent action. A deposition previously taken may also be used as permitted by the Evidence Code. *(Added by Stats.2004, c. 182 (A.B.3081), § 23, operative July 1, 2005.)*

Law Revision Commission Comments

The introductory clause of Section 2025.620 continues the introductory clause of former Section 2025(u) without change, except to conform the cross-reference.

Subdivision (a) continues former Section 2025(u)(1) without change.

Subdivision (b) continues former Section 2025(u)(2) without change, except to replace paragraph with subdivision and to conform the cross-reference.

Subdivision (c) continues former Section 2025(u)(3) without substantive change.

Subdivision (d) continues former Section 2025(u)(4) without change, except to conform the cross-references.

Subdivision (e) continues former Section 2025(u)(5) without change, except to replace section with chapter.

Subdivision (f) continues former Section 2025(u)(6) without change.

Subdivision (g) continues former Section 2025(u)(7) without change. [33 Cal.L.Rev.Comm. Reports 875 (2004)].

Research References

Rutter, Cal. Practice Guide: A.D.R. Ch. 4-B, B. Judicial Arbitration.
Rutter, Cal. Practice Guide: Civ. Pro. Before Trial Ch. 5-D, D. Default Judgment by Court.

Rutter, Cal. Practice Guide: Civ. Pro. Before Trial Ch. 13-E, E. the Arbitration Hearing.
Rutter, Cal. Practice Guide: Civ. Pro. Before Trial Ch. 8E-4, Notice of Deposition.
Rutter, Cal. Practice Guide: Civ. Pro. Before Trial Ch. 8E-10, Preservation of Testimony.
Rutter, Cal. Practice Guide: Civ. Pro. Before Trial Ch. 8E-11, Protective Orders.
Rutter, Cal. Practice Guide: Civ. Pro. Before Trial Ch. 8E-17, Use of Depositions at Trial.
Rutter, Cal. Practice Guide: Civ. Pro. Before Trial Ch. 8E-18, Use of Depositions in Judicial Arbitration Hearings.
Rutter, Cal. Practice Guide: Civil Trials & Evidence Ch. 1-C, C. Marshalling the Evidence.
Rutter, Cal. Practice Guide: Civil Trials & Evidence Ch. 1-K, K. Continuance Motions.
Rutter, Cal. Practice Guide: Civil Trials & Evidence Ch. 4-B, B. Preliminary Matters Discussed in Final Status Conference or In-Chambers Conference.
Rutter, Cal. Practice Guide: Civil Trials & Evidence Ch. 10-D, D. Objectives of Cross-Examination.
Rutter, Cal. Practice Guide: Civil Trials & Evidence Ch. 13-E, E. Presentation of Closing Argument.
Rutter, Cal. Practice Guide: Civil Trials & Evidence Ch. 8C-E, E. Audio or Visual Recordings.
Rutter, Cal. Practice Guide: Civil Trials & Evidence Ch. 8C-I, I. Depositions and Discovery.
Rutter, Cal. Practice Guide: Civil Trials & Evidence Ch. 8D-C, C. General Parameters Re Admissibility of Hearsay Evidence.
Rutter, Cal. Practice Guide: Civil Trials & Evidence Ch. 8D-D, D. Hearsay Exceptions.
Rutter, Cal. Practice Guide: Personal Injury Ch. 6-B, B. Overview of Selected Discovery Procedures.
Rutter, Cal. Practice Guide: Personal Injury Ch. 7-G, G. Arbitration Hearing.
Rutter, Cal. Practice Guide: Personal Injury Ch. 8-C, C. Two Months Before Trial.
Rutter, Cal. Practice Guide: Personal Injury Ch. 9-H, H. Introduction of Discovered Evidence.
Rutter, Cal. Practice Guide: Prof. Responsibility Ch. 11-F, F. Investigation Stage.
6 Witkin Cal. Proc. 5th Proceedings Without Trial § 42, Other Documentary Evidence.
6 Witkin Cal. Proc. 5th Proceedings Without Trial § 603, (S 603) Depositions.
7 Witkin Cal. Proc. 5th Trial § 166, Reopening Case After Submission.

CHAPTER 10. ORAL DEPOSITION OUTSIDE CALIFORNIA

Section

§ 2026.010.   Depositions in another state of the United States

(a) Any party may obtain discovery by taking an oral deposition, as described in Section 2025.010, in another state of the United States, or in a territory or an insular possession subject to its jurisdiction. Except as modified in this section, the procedures for taking oral depositions in California set forth in Chapter 9 (commencing with Section 2025.010) apply to an oral deposition taken in another state of the United States, or in a territory or an insular possession subject to its jurisdiction.

(b) If a deponent is a party to the action or an officer, director, managing agent, or employee of a party, the service of the deposition notice is effective to compel that deponent to attend and to testify, as well as to produce any document, electronically stored information, or tangible thing for inspection, copying, testing, or sampling. The deposition notice shall specify a place in the state, territory, or insular possession of the United States that is within 75 miles of the residence or a business office of a deponent.

(c) If the deponent is not a party to the action or an officer, director, managing agent, or employee of a party, a party serving a deposition notice under this section shall use any process and procedures required and available under the laws of the state, territory, or insular possession where the deposition is to be taken to compel the deponent to attend and to testify, as well as to produce any document, electronically stored information, or tangible thing for inspection, copying, testing, sampling, and any related activity.

(d) A deposition taken under this section shall be conducted in either of the following ways:

(1) Under the supervision of a person who is authorized to administer oaths by the laws of the United States or those of the place where the examination is to be held, and who is not otherwise disqualified under Section 2025.320 and subdivisions (b) to (f), inclusive, of Section 2025.340.

(2) Before a person appointed by the court.

(e) An appointment under subdivision (d) is effective to authorize that person to administer oaths and to take testimony.

(f) On request, the clerk of the court shall issue a commission authorizing the deposition in another state or place. The commission shall request that process issue in the place where the examination is to be held, requiring attendance and enforcing the obligations of the deponents to produce documents and electronically stored information and answer questions. The commission shall be issued by the clerk to any party in any action pending in its venue without a noticed motion or court order. The commission may contain terms that are required by the foreign jurisdiction to initiate the process. If a court order is required by the foreign jurisdiction, an order for a commission may be obtained by ex parte application. *(Added by Stats.2004, c. 182 (A.B.3081), § 23, operative July 1, 2005. Amended by Stats.2012, c. 72 (S.B.1574), § 27.)*

Law Revision Commission Comments

Subdivision (a) of Section 2026.010 continues former Section 2026(a) without change, except to conform the cross-references.

Subdivision (b) continues former Section 2026(b)(1) without change.

Subdivision (c) continues former Section 2026(b)(2) without change.

Subdivision (d) continues the first sentence of former Section 2026(c) without substantive change.

Subdivision (e) continues the second sentence of former Section 2026(c) without substantive change.

Subdivision (f) continues the third, fourth, fifth, sixth, and seventh sentences of former Section 2026(c) without substantive change. [33 Cal.L.Rev.Comm. Reports 877 (2004)].

Research References

Rutter, Cal. Practice Guide: Civ. Pro. Before Trial Ch. 8E-1, When Prior Court Order Required.
Rutter, Cal. Practice Guide: Civ. Pro. Before Trial Ch. 8E-8, Place of Deposition.
Rutter, Cal. Practice Guide: Civ. Pro. Before Trial Ch. 8E-1, Outline 1.
Rutter, Cal. Practice Guide: Personal Injury Ch. 6-B, B. Overview of Selected Discovery Procedures.

§ 2027.010. Depositions in a foreign nation

(a) Any party may obtain discovery by taking an oral deposition, as described in Section 2025.010, in a foreign nation. Except as modified in this section, the procedures for taking oral depositions in California set forth in Chapter 9 (commencing with Section 2025.010) apply to an oral deposition taken in a foreign nation.

(b) If a deponent is a party to the action or an officer, director, managing agent, or employee of a party, the service of the deposition notice is effective to compel the deponent to attend and to testify, as well as to produce any document,

electronically stored information, or tangible thing for inspection, copying, testing, or sampling.

(c) If a deponent is not a party to the action or an officer, director, managing agent or employee of a party, a party serving a deposition notice under this section shall use any process and procedures required and available under the laws of the foreign nation where the deposition is to be taken to compel the deponent to attend and to testify, as well as to produce any document, electronically stored information, or tangible thing for inspection, copying, testing, sampling, and any related activity.

(d) A deposition taken under this section shall be conducted under the supervision of any of the following:

(1) A person who is authorized to administer oaths or their equivalent by the laws of the United States or of the foreign nation, and who is not otherwise disqualified under Section 2025.320 and subdivisions (b) to (f), inclusive, of Section 2025.340.

(2) A person or officer appointed by commission or under letters rogatory.

(3) Any person agreed to by all the parties.

(e) On motion of the party seeking to take an oral deposition in a foreign nation, the court in which the action is pending shall issue a commission, letters rogatory, or a letter of request, if it determines that one is necessary or convenient. The commission, letters rogatory, or letter of request may include any terms and directions that are just and appropriate. The deposition officer may be designated by name or by descriptive title in the deposition notice and in the commission. Letters rogatory or a letter of request may be addressed: "To the Appropriate Judicial Authority in [name of foreign nation]." *(Added by Stats.2004, c. 182 (A.B.3081), § 23, operative July 1, 2005. Amended by Stats.2012, c. 72 (S.B.1574), § 28.)*

Law Revision Commission Comments

Subdivision (a) of Section 2027.010 continues former Section 2027(a) without change, except to conform the cross-references.

Subdivision (b) continues former Section 2027(b)(1) without change.

Subdivision (c) continues former Section 2027(b)(2) without change.

Subdivision (d) continues the first paragraph of former Section 2027(c) without substantive change.

Subdivision (e) continues the second paragraph of former Section 2027(c) without change. [33 Cal.L.Rev.Comm. Reports 879 (2004)].

Research References

Rutter, Cal. Practice Guide: Civ. Pro. Before Trial Ch. 8E-1, When Prior Court Order Required.
Rutter, Cal. Practice Guide: Civ. Pro. Before Trial Ch. 8E-8, Place of Deposition.
Rutter, Cal. Practice Guide: Civ. Pro. Before Trial Ch. 8E-1, Outline 1.

CHAPTER 11. DEPOSITION BY WRITTEN QUESTIONS

Section

2028.070.   Orders for protection of parties and deponents; additional court remedies.

2028.080.   Duty of officer before whom deposition is taken.

§ 2028.010. Procedures applicable

Any party may obtain discovery by taking a deposition by written questions instead of by oral examination. Except as modified in this chapter, the procedures for taking oral depositions set forth in Chapters 9 (commencing with Section 2025.010) and 10 (commencing with Section 2026.010) apply to written depositions. *(Added by Stats.2004, c. 182 (A.B.3081), § 23, operative July 1, 2005.)*

Law Revision Commission Comments

Section 2028.010 continues former Section 2028(a) without change, except to replace section with chapter and to conform the cross-references. [33 Cal.L.Rev.Comm. Reports 880 (2004)].

Research References

Rutter, Cal. Practice Guide: Civ. Pro. Before Trial Ch. 8D-5, Selecting Proper Discovery Tools.

Rutter, Cal. Practice Guide: Civ. Pro. Before Trial Ch. 8E-1, When Prior Court Order Required.

Rutter, Cal. Practice Guide: Civ. Pro. Before Trial Ch. 8E-3, Whose Deposition May be Taken.

Rutter, Cal. Practice Guide: Civ. Pro. Before Trial Ch. 8F-1, When Interrogatories May be Served.

Rutter, Cal. Practice Guide: Civ. Pro. Before Trial Ch. 8E-13, Compare-Depositions on Written Questions.

Rutter, Cal. Practice Guide: Civ. Pro. Before Trial Ch. 8E-1, Outline 1.

§ 2028.020. Notice requirements

The notice of a written deposition shall comply with Sections 2025.220 and 2025.230, and with subdivision (c) of Section 2020.240 [1], except as follows:

(a) The name or descriptive title, as well as the address, of the deposition officer shall be stated.

(b) The date, time, and place for commencement of the deposition may be left to future determination by the deposition officer. *(Added by Stats.2004, c. 182 (A.B.3081), § 23, operative July 1, 2005.)*

[1] So in chaptered copy; probably should refer to Section 2025.240.

Law Revision Commission Comments

Section 2028.020 continues former Section 2028(b) without substantive change. [33 Cal.L.Rev.Comm. Reports 881 (2004)].

Research References

Rutter, Cal. Practice Guide: Civ. Pro. Before Trial Ch. 8E-13, Compare-Depositions on Written Questions.

§ 2028.030. Attachment of questions to notice; cross questions; redirect and recross questions

(a) The questions to be propounded to the deponent by direct examination shall accompany the notice of a written deposition.

(b) Within 30 days after the deposition notice and questions are served, a party shall serve any cross questions on all other parties entitled to notice of the deposition.

(c) Within 15 days after being served with cross questions, a party shall serve any redirect questions on all other parties entitled to notice of the deposition.

(d) Within 15 days after being served with redirect questions, a party shall serve any recross questions on all other parties entitled to notice of the deposition.

(e) The court may, for good cause shown, extend or shorten the time periods for the interchange of cross, redirect, and recross questions. *(Added by Stats.2004, c. 182 (A.B.3081), § 23, operative July 1, 2005.)*

Law Revision Commission Comments

Subdivision (a) of Section 2028.030 continues the first paragraph of former Section 2028(c) without change.

Subdivision (b) continues the second paragraph of former Section 2028(c) without change.

Subdivision (c) continues the third paragraph of former Section 2028(c) without change.

Subdivision (d) continues the fourth paragraph of former Section 2028(c) without change.

Subdivision (e) continues the fifth paragraph of former Section 2028(c) without change. [33 Cal.L.Rev.Comm. Reports 881 (2004)].

Research References

Rutter, Cal. Practice Guide: Civ. Pro. Before Trial Ch. 8E-13, Compare-Depositions on Written Questions.

§ 2028.040. Objection to form of question; service; time to serve; meet and confer declaration; court action

(a) A party who objects to the form of any question shall serve a specific objection to that question on all parties entitled to notice of the deposition within 15 days after service of the question. A party who fails to timely serve an objection to the form of a question waives it.

(b) The objecting party shall promptly move the court to sustain the objection. This motion shall be accompanied by a meet and confer declaration under Section 2016.040. Unless the court has sustained that objection, the deposition officer shall propound to the deponent that question subject to that objection as to its form.

(c) The court shall impose a monetary sanction under Chapter 7 (commencing with Section 2023.010) against any party, person, or attorney who unsuccessfully makes or opposes a motion to sustain an objection, unless it finds that the one subject to the sanction acted with substantial justification or that other circumstances make the imposition of the sanction unjust. *(Added by Stats.2004, c. 182 (A.B.3081), § 23, operative July 1, 2005.)*

Law Revision Commission Comments

Subdivision (a) of Section 2028.040 continues the first and second sentences of former Section 2028(d)(1) without change.

Subdivision (b) continues the third, fourth, and fifth sentences of former Section 2028(d)(1) without substantive change.

Subdivision (c) continues the second paragraph of former Section 2028(d)(1) without change, except to conform the cross-reference. [33 Cal.L.Rev.Comm. Reports 882 (2004)].

Research References

Rutter, Cal. Practice Guide: Civ. Pro. Before Trial Ch. 8E-13, Compare-Depositions on Written Questions.

§ 2028.050. Protection of privileged or attorney work product; time to object; meet and confer declaration; court action

(a) A party who objects to any question on the ground that it calls for information that is privileged or is protected work product under Chapter 4 (commencing with Section 2018.010) shall serve a specific objection to that question on all parties entitled to notice of the deposition within 15 days after service of the question. A party who fails to timely serve that objection waives it.

(b) The party propounding any question to which an objection is made on those grounds may then move the court for an order overruling that objection. This motion shall be accompanied by a meet and confer declaration under Section 2016.040. The deposition officer shall not propound to the deponent any question to which a written objection on those grounds has been served unless the court has overruled that objection.

(c) The court shall impose a monetary sanction under Chapter 7 (commencing with Section 2023.010) against any party, person, or attorney who unsuccessfully makes or opposes a motion to overrule an objection, unless it finds that the one subject to the sanction acted with substantial justification or that other circumstances make the imposition of the sanction unjust. *(Added by Stats.2004, c. 182 (A.B.3081), § 23, operative July 1, 2005.)*

Law Revision Commission Comments

Subdivision (a) of Section 2028.050 continues the first and second sentences of former Section 2028(d)(2) without change, except to conform the cross-reference.

Subdivision (b) continues the third, fourth, and fifth sentences of former Section 2028(d)(2) without substantive change.

Subdivision (c) continues the second paragraph of former Section 2028(d)(2) without change, except to conform the cross-reference. [33 Cal.L.Rev.Comm. Reports 882 (2004)].

Research References

Rutter, Cal. Practice Guide: Civ. Pro. Before Trial Ch. 8E-13, Compare-Depositions on Written Questions.

§ 2028.060. Questions on direct examination; copy for prior study by deponent

(a) The party taking a written deposition may forward to the deponent a copy of the questions on direct examination for study prior to the deposition.

(b) No party or attorney shall permit the deponent to preview the form or the substance of any cross, redirect, or recross questions. *(Added by Stats.2004, c. 182 (A.B.3081), § 23, operative July 1, 2005.)*

Law Revision Commission Comments

Subdivision (a) of Section 2028.060 continues the first sentence of former Section 2028(e) without change.

Subdivision (b) continues the second sentence of former Section 2028(e) without change. [33 Cal.L.Rev.Comm. Reports 883 (2004)].

Research References

Rutter, Cal. Practice Guide: Civ. Pro. Before Trial Ch. 8A-3, Civil Discovery Act.

Rutter, Cal. Practice Guide: Civ. Pro. Before Trial Ch. 8E-13, Compare-Depositions on Written Questions.

§ 2028.070. Orders for protection of parties and deponents; additional court remedies

In addition to any appropriate order listed in Section 2025.420, the court may order any of the following:

(a) That the deponent's testimony be taken by oral, instead of written, examination.

(b) That one or more of the parties receiving notice of the written deposition be permitted to attend in person or by attorney and to propound questions to the deponent by oral examination.

(c) That objections under Sections 2028.040 and 2028.050 be sustained or overruled.

(d) That the deposition be taken before an officer other than the one named or described in the deposition notice. *(Added by Stats.2004, c. 182 (A.B.3081), § 23, operative July 1, 2005.)*

Law Revision Commission Comments

Section 2028.070 continues former Section 2028(f) without change, except to conform the cross-reference. [33 Cal.L.Rev.Comm. Reports 884 (2004)].

Research References

Rutter, Cal. Practice Guide: Civ. Pro. Before Trial Ch. 8E-13, Compare-Depositions on Written Questions.

§ 2028.080. Duty of officer before whom deposition is taken

The party taking a written deposition shall deliver to the officer designated in the deposition notice a copy of that notice and of all questions served under Section 2028.030. The deposition officer shall proceed promptly to propound the questions and to take and record the testimony of the deponent in response to the questions. *(Added by Stats.2004, c. 182 (A.B.3081), § 23, operative July 1, 2005.)*

Law Revision Commission Comments

Section 2028.080 continues former Section 2028(g) without substantive change. [33 Cal.L.Rev.Comm. Reports 884 (2004)].

Research References

Rutter, Cal. Practice Guide: Civ. Pro. Before Trial Ch. 8E-13, Compare-Depositions on Written Questions.

Rutter, Cal. Practice Guide: Personal Injury Ch. 8-C, C. Two Months Before Trial.

CHAPTER 12. DISCOVERY IN ACTION PENDING OUTSIDE CALIFORNIA

Law Revision Commission Comments

The heading of Chapter 12 is amended to make a grammatical correction.

To improve clarity, the heading of Chapter 12 is amended to replace the reference to "Deposition" with a reference to "Discovery." This change helps to emphasize that the chapter applies not only to an oral deposition, but also to other forms of discovery. For example, the chapter applies to a deposition solely for the production of business records (see Sections 2020.010(a)(3), 2020.410–2020.440), yet in some jurisdictions such a procedure might not be referred to as a "deposition." [37 Cal.L.Rev. Comm. Reports 99 (2007)].

ARTICLE 1. INTERSTATE AND INTERNATIONAL DEPOSITIONS AND DISCOVERY ACT

Operative Effect

For operative effect of this Article, see Code
of Civil Procedure § 2029.900.

§ 2029.100. Short title

This article may be cited as the Interstate and International Depositions and Discovery Act. *(Added by Stats.2008, c. 231 (A.B.2193), § 3, operative Jan. 1, 2010.)*

Operative Effect

For operative effect of this Article, see Code
of Civil Procedure § 2029.900.

Law Revision Commission Comments

Section 2029.100 is similar to Section 1 of the Uniform Interstate Depositions and Discovery Act (2007) ("UIDDA"). This article differs in two significant respects from UIDDA: (1) it addresses procedural details not addressed in UIDDA (see Sections 2029.300, 2029.350, 2029.390, 2029.600, 2029.610, 2029.620, 2029.630, 2029.640, 2029.650), and (2) it governs discovery for purposes of an action pending in a foreign nation, not just discovery for purposes of an action pending in another jurisdiction of the United States (see Section 2029.200(a)(2) & Comment).

The entire article may be referred to as the "Interstate and International Depositions and Discovery Act." The portions of the article that are drawn from the Uniform Interstate Depositions and Discovery Act may collectively be referred to as the "California version of the Uniform Interstate Depositions and Discovery Act." See Section 2029.700 (uniformity of application and construction). [37 Cal.L.Rev.Comm. Reports 99 (2007)].

Research References

Rutter, Cal. Practice Guide: Civ. Pro. Before Trial Ch. 8E-1, When Prior Court Order Required.
Rutter, Cal. Practice Guide: Civ. Pro. Before Trial Ch. 8E-7, Foreign Subpoenas.
Rutter, Cal. Practice Guide: Civ. Pro. Before Trial Ch. 8E-8, Place of Deposition.

§ 2029.200. Definitions

In this article:

(a) "Foreign jurisdiction" means either of the following:

(1) A state other than this state.

(2) A foreign nation.

(b) "Foreign subpoena" means a subpoena issued under authority of a court of record of a foreign jurisdiction.

(c) "Person" means an individual, corporation, business trust, estate, trust, partnership, limited liability company, association, joint venture, public corporation, government, or governmental subdivision, agency, or instrumentality, or any other legal or commercial entity.

(d) "State" means a state of the United States, the District of Columbia, Puerto Rico, the Virgin Islands, a federally recognized Indian tribe, or any territory or insular possession subject to the jurisdiction of the United States.

(e) "Subpoena" means a document, however denominated, issued under authority of a court of record requiring a person to do any of the following:

(1) Attend and give testimony at a deposition.

(2) Produce and permit inspection, copying, testing, or sampling of designated books, documents, records, electronically stored information, or tangible things in the possession, custody, or control of the person.

(3) Permit inspection of premises under the control of the person. *(Added by Stats.2008, c. 231 (A.B.2193), § 3, operative Jan. 1, 2010. Amended by Stats.2012, c. 72 (S.B.1574), § 29.)*

Operative Effect

For operative effect of this Article, see Code
of Civil Procedure § 2029.900.

Law Revision Commission Comments

Section 2029.200 is the same as Section 2 of the Uniform Interstate Depositions and Discovery Act (2007), except that (1) the definition of "foreign jurisdiction" in subdivision (a) includes a foreign nation, not just a state other than California, and (2) the term "Virgin Islands" is substituted for "United States Virgin Islands" in subdivision (d), because "Virgin Islands" is the official name for the entity in question.

Subdivision (c) defines "person" broadly. This is consistent with the general code-wide definition in Section 17 ("the word 'person' includes a corporation as well as a natural person"). For guidance on interpreting other provisions of this code referring to a "person," see Hassan v. Mercy American River Hospital, 31 Cal.4th 709, 715,18, 74 P.3d 726, 3 Cal.Rptr.3d 623 (2003) (whether "person" as used in particular section of Code of Civil Procedure includes corporation or non-corporate entity "is ultimately a question of legislative intent"); Diamond View Limited v. Herz, 180 Cal.App.3d 612, 616-19, 225 Cal.Rptr. 651 (1986) ("[T]he preliminary definition contained in section 17 is superseded when it obviously conflicts with the Legislature's subsequent use of the term in a different statute."); Oil Workers Int'l Union v. Superior Court, 103 Cal.App.2d 512, 570,71, 230 P.2d 71 (1951) (unincorporated association is "person" for purpose of statutes in Code of Civil Procedure governing contempt).

To facilitate discovery under this article, subdivision (e) defines "subpoena" broadly. The term includes not only a document denominated a "subpoena," but also a mandate, writ, letters rogatory, letter of request, commission, or other court document that requires a person to testify at a deposition, produce documents or other items, or permit inspection of property.

Background from Uniform Act

The term "Subpoena" includes a subpoena duces tecum. The description of a subpoena in the Act is based on the language of Rule 45 of the Federal Rules of Civil Procedure.

The term "Subpoena" does not include a subpoena for the inspection of a person (subdivision (e)(3) is limited to inspection of premises). Medical examinations in a personal injury case, for example, are separately controlled by state discovery rules (the corresponding federal rule is Rule 35 of the Federal Rules of Civil Procedure). Since the plaintiff is already subject to the jurisdiction of the trial state, a subpoena is never necessary.

The term "Court of Record" was chosen to exclude non-court of record proceedings from the ambit of the Act. Extending the Act to such proceedings as arbitrations would be a significant expansion that might generate resistance to the Act. A "Court of Record" includes anyone who is authorized to issue a subpoena under the laws of that state, which usually includes an attorney of record for a party in the proceeding. [Adapted from UIDDA § 2 comment & § 3 comment.] [37 Cal. L.Rev.Comm. Reports 99 (2007)].

Research References

Rutter, Cal. Practice Guide: Civ. Pro. Before Trial Ch. 8E-7, Foreign Subpoenas.
Rutter, Cal. Practice Guide: Civ. Pro. Before Trial Ch. 8E-8, Place of Deposition.

§ 2029.300. Issuance of subpoena

(a) To request issuance of a subpoena under this section, a party shall submit the original or a true and correct copy of a foreign subpoena to the clerk of the superior court in the county in which discovery is sought to be conducted in this state. A request for the issuance of a subpoena under this section does not constitute making an appearance in the courts of this state.

(b) In addition to submitting a foreign subpoena under subdivision (a), a party seeking discovery shall do both of the following:

(1) Submit an application requesting that the superior court issue a subpoena with the same terms as the foreign subpoena. The application shall be on a form prescribed by the Judicial Council pursuant to Section 2029.390. No civil case cover sheet is required.

(2) Pay the fee specified in Section 70626 of the Government Code.

(c) When a party submits a foreign subpoena to the clerk of the superior court in accordance with subdivision (a), and satisfies the requirements of subdivision (b), the clerk shall promptly issue a subpoena for service upon the person to which the foreign subpoena is directed.

(d) A subpoena issued under this section shall satisfy all of the following conditions:

(1) It shall incorporate the terms used in the foreign subpoena.

(2) It shall contain or be accompanied by the names, addresses, and telephone numbers of all counsel of record in the proceeding to which the subpoena relates and of any party not represented by counsel.

(3) It shall bear the caption and case number of the out-of-state case to which it relates.

(4) It shall state the name of the court that issues it.

(5) It shall be on a form prescribed by the Judicial Council pursuant to Section 2029.390. *(Added by Stats.2008, c. 231 (A.B.2193), § 3, operative Jan. 1, 2010.)*

Operative Effect

For operative effect of this Article, see Code of Civil Procedure § 2029.900.

Law Revision Commission Comments

Section 2029.300 is added to clarify the procedure for obtaining a California subpoena to obtain discovery from a witness in this state for use in a proceeding pending in another jurisdiction. For the benefit of the party seeking the subpoena and the court issuing it, the procedure is designed to be simple and expeditious.

Subdivisions (a), (c), and (d)(1)–(2) are similar to Section 3 of the Uniform Interstate Depositions and Discovery Act (2007). Subdivisions (b) and (d)(3)–(5) address additional procedural details.

To obtain a subpoena under this section, a party must submit the original or a true and correct copy of a "foreign subpoena." For definitions of "foreign subpoena" and "subpoena," see Section 2029.200 (definitions). The definition of "subpoena" is broad, encompassing not only a document denominated a "subpoena," but also a mandate, writ, letters rogatory, letter of request, commission, or other court document that requires a person to testify at a deposition, produce documents or other items, or permit inspection of property.

Subdivision (a) makes clear that requesting and obtaining a subpoena under this section does not constitute making an appearance in the California courts. For further guidance on avoiding unauthorized practice of law, see Bus. & Prof. Code § 6125; Cal.R.Ct. 9.40, 9.47; Report of the California Supreme Court Multijurisdictional Practice Implementation Committee: Final Report and Proposed Rules (March 10, 2004); California Supreme Court Advisory Task Force on Multijurisdictional Practice, Final Report and Recommendations (Jan. 7, 2002). In general, a party to out-of-state litigation may take a deposition in California without retaining local counsel if the party is self-represented or represented by an attorney duly admitted to practice in another jurisdiction of the United States. Birbrower v. Superior Court, 17 Cal.4th 119, 127, 949 P.2d 1, 70 Cal.Rptr.2d 304 (1998) ("[P]ersons may represent themselves and their own interests regardless of State Bar membership..."); Cal.R.Ct. 9.47; Final Report and Recommendations, *supra*, at 24. Different considerations may apply, however, if a discovery dispute arises in connection with such a deposition and a party to out-of-state litigation wants to appear in a California court with respect to the dispute.

See also Sections 2029.350 (issuance of subpoena by local counsel), 2029.640 (discovery on notice or agreement).

Background from Uniform Act

The term "Submitted" to a clerk of court includes delivering to or filing. Presenting a subpoena to the clerk of court in the discovery state, so that a subpoena is then issued in the name of the discovery state, is the necessary act that invokes the jurisdiction of the discovery state, which in turn makes the newly issued subpoena both enforceable and challengeable in the discovery state.

The committee envisions the standard procedure under this section will become as follows, using as an example a case filed in Kansas (the trial state) where the witness to be deposed lives in California (the discovery state): A lawyer of record for a party in the action pending in Kansas will issue a subpoena in Kansas (the same way lawyers in Kansas routinely issue subpoenas in pending actions). That lawyer will then check with the clerk's office, in the California county in which the witness to be deposed lives, to obtain a copy of its subpoena form (the clerk's office will usually have a Web page explaining its forms and procedures). The lawyer will then prepare a California subpoena so that it has the same terms as the Kansas subpoena. The lawyer will then hire a process server (or local counsel) in California, who will take the completed and executed Kansas subpoena and the completed but not yet executed California subpoena to the clerk's office in California. The clerk of court, upon being given the Kansas subpoena, will then issue the identical California subpoena. The process server (or other agent of the party) will pay any necessary filing fees, and then serve the California subpoena on the deponent in accordance with California law (which includes any applicable local rules).

The advantages of this process are readily apparent. The act of the clerk of court is ministerial, yet is sufficient to invoke the jurisdiction of the discovery state over the deponent. The only documents that need to be presented to the clerk of court in the discovery state are the subpoena issued in the trial state and the draft subpoena of the discovery state. [Note: In California, an application form would also be required.] There is no need to hire local counsel to have the subpoena issued in the discovery state, and there is no need to present the matter to a judge in the discovery state before the subpoena can be issued. In effect, the clerk of court in the discovery state simply reissues the subpoena of the trial state, and the new subpoena is then served on the deponent in accordance with the laws of the discovery state. The process is simple and efficient, costs are kept to a minimum, and local counsel and judicial participation are unnecessary to have the subpoena issued and served in the discovery state.

The Act will not change or repeal the law in those states that still require a commission or letters rogatory to take a deposition in a foreign jurisdiction. The Act does, however, repeal the law in those discovery states that still require a commission or letter rogatory from a trial state before a deposition can be taken in those states. It is the hope of the Conference that this Act will encourage states that still require the use of commissions or letters rogatory to repeal those laws.

The Act requires that, when the subpoena is served, it contain or be accompanied by the names, addresses, and telephone numbers of all counsel of record and of any party not represented by counsel. The committee believes that this requirement imposes no significant burden on the lawyer issuing the subpoena, given that the lawyer already has the obligation to send a notice of deposition to every counsel of record and any unrepresented parties. The benefits in the discovery state, by contrast, are significant. This requirement makes it easy for the deponent (or, as will frequently be the case, the deponent's lawyer) to learn the names of and contact the other lawyers in the case. This requirement can easily be met, since the subpoena will contain or be accompanied by the names, addresses, and telephone numbers of all counsel of record and of any party not represented by counsel (which is the same information that will ordinarily be contained on a notice of deposition and proof of service).

[Adapted from UIDDA § 3 comment.] [37 Cal.L.Rev.Comm. Reports 99 (2007)].

Research References

Rutter, Cal. Practice Guide: Civ. Pro. Before Trial Ch. 8A-3, Civil Discovery Act.

Rutter, Cal. Practice Guide: Civ. Pro. Before Trial Ch. 8E-7, Foreign Subpoenas.

§ 2029.350. Foreign subpoenas; issuance of subpoena under this article

(a) Notwithstanding Sections 1986 and 2029.300, if a party to a proceeding pending in a foreign jurisdiction retains an attorney licensed to practice in this state, who is an active member of the State Bar, and that attorney receives the original or a true and correct copy of a foreign subpoena, the attorney may issue a subpoena under this article.

(b) A subpoena issued under this section shall satisfy all of the following conditions:

(1) It shall incorporate the terms used in the foreign subpoena.

(2) It shall contain or be accompanied by the names, addresses, and telephone numbers of all counsel of record in the proceeding to which the subpoena relates and of any party not represented by counsel.

(3) It shall bear the caption and case number of the out-of-state case to which it relates.

(4) It shall state the name of the superior court of the county in which the discovery is to be conducted.

(5) It shall be on a form prescribed by the Judicial Council pursuant to Section 2029.390. *(Added by Stats.2008, c. 231 (A.B.2193), § 3, operative Jan. 1, 2010.)*

Operative Effect

For operative effect of this Article, see Code of Civil Procedure § 2029.900.

Law Revision Commission Comments

Section 2029.350 is added to make clear that if certain conditions are satisfied, local counsel may issue process compelling a California witness to appear at a deposition for an action pending in another jurisdiction.

To issue a subpoena under this section, a California attorney acting as local counsel must receive the original or a true and correct copy of a "foreign subpoena." For definitions of "foreign subpoena" and "subpoena," see Section 2029.200 (definitions). The definition of 'subpoena' is broad, encompassing not only a document denominated a "subpoena," but also a mandate, writ, letters rogatory, letter of request, commission, or other court document that requires a person to testify at a deposition, produce documents or other items, or permit inspection of property.

This section does not make retention of local counsel mandatory. For guidance on that point, see Section 2029.300(a); Bus. & Prof. Code § 6125; Cal.R.Ct. 9.40, 9.47; Report of the California Supreme Court Multijurisdictional Practice Implementation Committee: Final Report and Proposed Rules (March 10, 2004); California Supreme Court Advisory Task Force on Multijurisdictional Practice, Final Report and Recommendations (Jan. 7, 2002). In general, a party to out-of-state litigation may take a deposition in California without retaining local counsel if the party is self-represented or represented by an attorney duly admitted to practice in another jurisdiction of the United States. Birbrower v. Superior Court, 17 Cal.4th 119, 127, 949 P.2d 1, 70 Cal.Rptr.2d 304 (1998) ("[P]ersons may represent themselves and their own interests regardless of State Bar membership..."); Cal.R.Ct. 9.47; Final Report and Recommendations, *supra*, at 24. Different considerations may apply, however, if a discovery dispute arises in connection with such a deposition and a party to out-of-state litigation wants to appear in a California court with respect to the dispute.

See also Sections 2029.300 (issuance of subpoena by clerk of court), 2029.640 (discovery on notice or agreement). [37 Cal.L.Rev.Comm. Reports 99 (2007)].

Research References

Rutter, Cal. Practice Guide: Civ. Pro. Before Trial Ch. 8E-7, Foreign Subpoenas.

§ 2029.390.   Judicial Council; development of forms

On or before January 1, 2010, the Judicial Council shall do all of the following:

(a) Prepare an application form to be used for purposes of Section 2029.300.

(b) Prepare one or more new subpoena forms that include clear instructions for use in issuance of a subpoena under Section 2029.300 or 2029.350. Alternatively, the Judicial Council may modify one or more existing subpoena forms to include clear instructions for use in issuance of a subpoena under Section 2029.300 or 2029.350. *(Added by Stats.2008, c. 231 (A.B.2193), § 3.)*

Operative Effect

For operative effect of this Article, see Code of Civil Procedure § 2029.900.

Law Revision Commission Comments

Section 2029.390 is new. The Judicial Council is to prepare forms to facilitate compliance with this article. [37 Cal.L.Rev.Comm. Reports 99 (2007)].

Research References

Rutter, Cal. Practice Guide: Civ. Pro. Before Trial Ch. 8E-7, Foreign Subpoenas.

§ 2029.400.   Service of subpoena

A subpoena issued under this article shall be personally served in compliance with the law of this state, including, without limitation, Section 1985. *(Added by Stats.2008, c. 231 (A.B. 2193), § 3, operative Jan. 1, 2010.)*

Operative Effect

For operative effect of this Article, see Code of Civil Procedure § 2029.900.

Law Revision Commission Comments

Section 2029.400 is similar to Section 4 of the Uniform Interstate Depositions and Discovery Act (2007). Section 2029.400 applies not only to a subpoena issued by a clerk of court under Section 2029.300, but also to a subpoena issued by local counsel under Section 2029.350. [37 Cal.L.Rev.Comm. Reports 99 (2007)].

Research References

Rutter, Cal. Practice Guide: Civ. Pro. Before Trial Ch. 8E-7, Foreign Subpoenas.

§ 2029.500.   Deposition, production, and inspection; applicable laws and rules

Titles 3 (commencing with Section 1985) and 4 (commencing with Section 2016.010) of Part 4, and any other law or court rule of this state governing a deposition, a production of documents or other tangible items, or an inspection of premises, including any law or court rule governing payment of court costs or sanctions, apply to discovery under this article. *(Added by Stats.2008, c. 231 (A.B.2193), § 3, operative Jan. 1, 2010.)*

Operative Effect

For operative effect of this Article, see Code of Civil Procedure § 2029.900.

Law Revision Commission Comments

Section 2029.500 is similar to Section 5 of the Uniform Interstate Depositions and Discovery Act (2007). Section 2029.500 applies not only to a subpoena issued by a clerk of court under Section 2029.300, but also to a subpoena issued by local counsel under Section 2029.350 and to discovery taken in this state pursuant to properly issued notice or by agreement.

Background from Uniform Act

The Act requires that the discovery permitted by this section must comply with the laws of the discovery state. The discovery state has a significant interest in these cases in protecting its residents who become non-party witnesses in an action pending in a foreign jurisdiction from any unreasonable or unduly burdensome discovery request. Therefore, the committee believes that the discovery procedure must be the same as it would be if the case had originally been filed in the discovery state.

[Adapted from UIDDA § 5 comment.] [37 Cal.L.Rev.Comm. Reports 99 (2008)].

Research References

Rutter, Cal. Practice Guide: Civ. Pro. Before Trial Ch. 8E-7, Foreign Subpoenas.

§ 2029.600. Application to court

(a) If a dispute arises relating to discovery under this article, any request for a protective order or to enforce, quash, or modify a subpoena, or for other relief may be filed in the superior court in the county in which discovery is to be conducted and, if so filed, shall comply with the applicable rules or statutes of this state.

(b) A request for relief pursuant to this section shall be referred to as a petition notwithstanding any statute under which a request for the same relief would be referred to as a motion or by another term if it was brought in a proceeding pending in this state.

(c) A petition for relief pursuant to this section shall be accompanied by a civil case cover sheet. *(Added by Stats.2008, c. 231 (A.B.2193), § 3, operative Jan. 1, 2010.)*

Operative Effect

For operative effect of this Article, see Code of Civil Procedure § 2029.900.

Law Revision Commission Comments

Section 2029.600 is similar to Section 6 of the Uniform Interstate Depositions and Discovery Act (2007). It serves to clarify the procedure for using a California court to resolve a dispute relating to discovery conducted in this state for purposes of a proceeding pending in another jurisdiction.

The objective of subdivision (a) is to ensure that if a dispute arises relating to discovery under this article, California is able to protect its policy interests and the interests of persons located in the state. In particular, the state must be able to protect its residents from unreasonable or unduly burdensome discovery requests. A court should interpret the provision with this objective in mind.

Subdivision (b) makes clear that a request for relief pursuant to this section is properly denominated a "petition," not a "motion." For example, suppose a party to an out-of-state proceeding subpoenas personal records of a nonparty consumer under Section 1985.3 and the nonparty consumer serves a written objection to production as authorized by the statute. To obtain production, the subpoenaing party would have to file a "petition" to enforce the subpoena, not a "motion" as Section 1985.3(g) prescribes for a case pending in California.

See also Sections 2029.610 (fees and format of papers relating to discovery dispute), 2029.620 (subsequent discovery dispute in same case and county), 2029.630 (hearing date and briefing schedule), 2029.640 (discovery on notice or agreement), 2029.650 (writ petition). [37 Cal.L.Rev.Comm. Reports 99 (2007)].

Research References

Rutter, Cal. Practice Guide: Civ. Pro. Before Trial Ch. 8E-7, Foreign Subpoenas.

§ 2029.610. Fees; assignment of case number; requirements for filed documents

(a) On filing a petition under Section 2029.600, a petitioner who is a party to the out-of-state proceeding shall pay a first appearance fee as specified in Section 70611 of the Government Code. A petitioner who is not a party to the out-of-state proceeding shall pay the fee specified in subdivision (c) of Section 70626 of the Government Code.

(b) The court in which the petition is filed shall assign it a case number.

(c) On responding to a petition under Section 2029.600, a party to the out-of-state proceeding shall pay a first appearance fee as specified in Section 70612 of the Government Code. A person who is not a party to the out-of-state proceeding may file a response without paying a fee.

(d) Any petition, response, or other document filed under this section shall satisfy all of the following conditions:

(1) It shall bear the caption and case number of the out-of-state case to which it relates.

(2) The first page shall state the name of the court in which the document is filed.

(3) The first page shall state the case number assigned by the court under subdivision (b).

(4) The first page shall state whether or not the person filing the document is a party to the out-of-state case. *(Added by Stats.2008, c. 231 (A.B.2193), § 3, operative Jan. 1, 2010. Amended by Stats.2011, c. 308 (S.B.647), § 4.)*

Operative Effect

For operative effect of this Article, see Code of Civil Procedure § 2029.900.

Law Revision Commission Comments

Section 2029.610 is added to clarify procedural details for resolution of a dispute relating to discovery under this article.

See also Sections 2029.600 (discovery dispute), 2029.620 (subsequent discovery dispute in same case and county), 2029.630 (hearing date and briefing schedule), 2029.640 (discovery on notice or agreement), 2029.650 (writ petition). [37 Cal.L.Rev.Comm. Reports 99 (2007)].

§ 2029.620. Subsequent petitions

(a) If a petition has been filed under Section 2029.600 and another dispute later arises relating to discovery being conducted in the same county for purposes of the same out-of-state proceeding, the deponent or other disputant may file a petition for appropriate relief in the same superior court as the previous petition.

(b) The first page of the petition shall clearly indicate that it is not the first petition filed in that court that relates to the out-of-state case.

(c)(1) If the petitioner in the new dispute is a party to the out-of-state case who previously paid a first appearance fee under this article, the petitioner shall pay a motion fee as specified in subdivision (a) of Section 70617 of the Government Code. If the petitioner in the new dispute is a party to the out-of-state case but has not previously paid a first appearance fee under this article, the petitioner shall pay a first appearance fee as specified in Section 70611 of the Government Code.

(2) If the petitioner in the new dispute is not a party to the out-of-state case, the petitioner shall pay the fee specified in subdivision (c) of Section 70626 of the Government Code, unless the petitioner previously paid that fee. If the petitioner previously paid the fee specified in subdivision (c) of Section 70626 of the Government Code, the petitioner shall pay a motion fee as specified in subdivision (a) of Section 70617 of the Government Code.

(d) If a person responding to the new petition is not a party to the out-of-state case, or is a party who previously paid a first appearance fee under this article, that person does not have to pay a fee for responding. If a person responding to the new petition is a party to the out-of-state case but has not previously paid a first appearance fee under this article, that person shall pay a first appearance fee as specified in Section 70612 of the Government Code.

(e) Any petition, response, or other document filed under this section shall satisfy all of the following conditions:

(1) It shall bear the caption and case number of the out-of-state case to which it relates.

(2) The first page shall state the name of the court in which the document is filed.

(3) The first page shall state the same case number that the court assigned to the first petition relating to the out-of-state case.

(4) The first page shall state whether or not the person filing the document is a party to the out-of-state case.

(f) A petition for relief pursuant to this section shall be accompanied by a civil case cover sheet. *(Added by Stats.2008, c. 231 (A.B.2193), § 3, operative Jan. 1, 2010. Amended by Stats.2011, c. 308 (S.B.647), § 5.)*

Operative Effect

For operative effect of this Article, see Code of Civil Procedure § 2029.900.

Law Revision Commission Comments

Section 2029.620 is added to clarify the procedure that applies when two or more discovery disputes relating to the same out-of-state proceeding arise in the same county. To promote efficiency and fairness and minimize inconsistent results, all documents relating to the same out-of-state case are to be filed together, bearing the same California case number.

In addition, subdivision (b) requires the first page of a subsequent petition to clearly indicate that it is not the first petition filed in the court relating to the out-of-state case. If the petitioner does not know the history of the case, the petitioner has a duty to determine whether a previous petition has been filed. That duty should not be difficult to satisfy, because the petitioner has an obligation to meet and confer with the other disputant before seeking relief in court.

Section 2029.620 does not apply when discovery disputes relate to the same out-of-state case but arise in different counties. In that situation, each petition for relief must be filed in the superior court of the county in which the deposition is being taken. See Section 2029.600. In appropriate circumstances, a petition may be transferred and consolidated with a petition pending in another county. See Sections 403 (transfer), 1048(a) (consolidation); see also Gov't Code § 70618 (transfer fees). In determining whether to order a transfer, a court should consider factors such as convenience of the deponent and similarity of issues.

See also Sections 2029.600 (discovery dispute), 2029.610 (fees and format of papers relating to discovery dispute), 2029.630 (hearing date and briefing schedule), 2029.640 (discovery on notice or agreement), 2029.650 (writ petition). [37 Cal.L.Rev.Comm. Reports 99 (2007)].

§ 2029.630. Application of requirements of Code of Civil Procedure § 1005

A petition under Section 2029.600 or Section 2029.620 is subject to the requirements of Section 1005 relating to notice and to filing and service of papers. *(Added by Stats.2008, c. 231 (A.B.2193), § 3, operative Jan. 1, 2010.)*

Operative Effect

For operative effect of this Article, see Code of Civil Procedure § 2029.900.

Law Revision Commission Comments

Section 2029.630 is added to clarify the proper hearing date and briefing schedule for a petition under Section 2029.600 or 2029.620. The petition is to be treated in the same manner as a discovery motion in a case pending within the state. [37 Cal.L.Rev.Comm. Reports 99 (2007)].

§ 2029.640. Witnesses in state; necessity of subpoena

If a party to a proceeding pending in a foreign jurisdiction seeks discovery from a witness in this state by properly issued notice or by agreement, it is not necessary for that party to obtain a subpoena under this article to be able to seek relief under Section 2029.600 or 2029.620. The deponent or any other party may also seek relief under Section 2029.600 or 2029.620 in those circumstances, regardless of whether the deponent was subpoenaed under this article. *(Added by Stats.2008, c. 231 (A.B.2193), § 3, operative Jan. 1, 2010.)*

Operative Effect

For operative effect of this Article, see Code of Civil Procedure § 2029.900.

Law Revision Commission Comments

Section 2029.640 is added to clarify how this article applies when a party to a proceeding pending in another jurisdiction seeks discovery from a witness in this state by properly issued notice or by agreement. See also Section 2029.500 (deposition, production, and inspection). [37 Cal.L.Rev. Comm. Reports 99 (2007)].

§ 2029.650. Writ petition

(a) If a superior court issues an order granting, denying, or otherwise resolving a petition under Section 2029.600 or 2029.620, a person aggrieved by the order may petition the appropriate court of appeal for an extraordinary writ. No order or other action of a court under this article is appealable in this state.

(b) Pending its decision on the writ petition, the court of appeal may stay the order of the superior court, the discovery that is the subject of that order, or both. *(Added by Stats.2008, c. 231 (A.B.2193), § 3, operative Jan. 1, 2010.)*

Operative Effect

For operative effect of this Article, see Code of Civil Procedure § 2029.900.

Law Revision Commission Comments

Section 2029.650 is added to clarify the procedure for reviewing a decision of a superior court on a dispute arising in connection with discovery under this article. For further guidance on that procedure, see in particular Cal.R.Ct. 8.264(a)(1) (when relevant, clerk of court of appeal shall promptly send court of appeal's opinion or order to lower court), 8.272(b) (transmittal of remittitur and opinion or order to lower court), 8.490(k) (notice to trial court with regard to writ), 8.490(f)(1) (writ petition shall be served on respondent superior court). [37 Cal.L.Rev. Comm. Reports 99 (2007)].

§ 2029.700. Uniformity of application and construction

(a) Sections 2029.100, 2029.200, 2029.300, 2029.400, 2029.500, 2029.600, 2029.800, 2029.900, and this section, collectively, constitute and may be referred to as the "California version of the Uniform Interstate Depositions and Discovery Act."

(b) In applying and construing this uniform act, consideration shall be given to the need to promote uniformity of the law with respect to its subject matter among the states that enact it. *(Added by Stats.2008, c. 231 (A.B.2193), § 3, operative Jan. 1, 2010.)*

Operative Effect

For operative effect of this Article, see Code of Civil Procedure § 2029.900.

Law Revision Commission Comments

Subdivision (a) of Section 2029.700 provides a convenient means of referring to the sections within this article that are drawn from the Uniform Interstate Depositions and Discovery Act (2007). The entire article may be referred to as the "Interstate and International Depositions and Discovery Act." See Section 2029.100 & Comment.

Subdivision (b) is similar to Section 7 of the Uniform Interstate Depositions and Discovery Act. [37 Cal.L.Rev.Comm. Reports 99 (2007)].

§ 2029.800. Application to pending actions

This article applies to requests for discovery in cases pending on or after the operative date of this section. *(Added by Stats.2008, c. 231 (A.B.2193), § 3, operative Jan. 1, 2010.)*

Operative Effect

For operative effect of this Article, see Code of Civil Procedure § 2029.900.

Law Revision Commission Comments

Section 2029.800 is the same as Section 8 of the Uniform Interstate Depositions and Discovery Act (2007), except "or after" is inserted to improve clarity and "operative date" is substituted for "effective date."

In California, "effective date" refers to the date on which a statute is recognized as constituting California law. In contrast, "operative date" refers to the date on which the statute actually becomes operative. See, e.g., People v. Palomar, 171 Cal.App.3d 131, 134 (1985) ("The 'enactment is a law on its effective date only in the sense that it cannot be changed except by legislative process; the rights of individuals under its provisions are not substantially affected until the provision operates as law.'").

The effective date of this article is January 1 of the year following its enactment. See Cal. Const. art. IV, § 8(c)(1); Gov't Code § 9600(a). Usually, the operative date of a statute is the same as the effective date. People v. Henderson, 107 Cal.App.3d 475, 488 (1980). In some instances, a statute may specify a different operative date. Cline v. Lewis, 175 Cal. 315, 318; Johnston v. Alexis, 153 Cal.App.3d 33, 40 (1984). Here, the operative date for this article (except for Section 2029.390) is delayed to allow time for the Judicial Council to prepare forms pursuant to Section 2029.390. See Section 2029.900. [37 Cal.L.Rev.Comm. Reports 99 (2007)].

§ 2029.900. Operative date

Section 2029.390 is operative on January 1, 2009. The remainder of this article is operative on January 1, 2010. *(Added by Stats.2008, c. 231 (A.B.2193), § 3, operative Jan. 1, 2010.)*

Law Revision Commission Comments

Section 2029.900 is similar to Section 9 of the Uniform Interstate Depositions and Discovery Act (2007), except that "operative date" is substituted for "effective date" and the operative date for the article (except for Section 2029.390) is delayed to allow time for the Judicial Council to prepare forms pursuant to Section 2029.390. For an explanation of the distinction between "effective date" and "operative date" in California, see Section 2029.800 Comment. [37 Cal.L.Rev.Comm. Reports 99 (2007)].

CHAPTER 13. WRITTEN INTERROGATORIES

ARTICLE 1. PROPOUNDING INTERROGATORIES

§ 2030.010. Scope of discovery; restrictions

(a) Any party may obtain discovery within the scope delimited by Chapters 2 (commencing with Section 2017.010) and 3 (commencing with Section 2017.710), and subject to the restrictions set forth in Chapter 5 (commencing with Section 2019.010), by propounding to any other party to the action written interrogatories to be answered under oath.

(b) An interrogatory may relate to whether another party is making a certain contention, or to the facts, witnesses, and writings on which a contention is based. An interrogatory is not objectionable because an answer to it involves an opinion or contention that relates to fact or the application of law to fact, or would be based on information obtained or legal theories developed in anticipation of litigation or in preparation for trial. *(Added by Stats.2004, c. 182 (A.B.3081), § 23, operative July 1, 2005.)*

Law Revision Commission Comments

Subdivision (a) of Section 2030.010 continues former Section 2030(a) without change, except to conform the cross-references.

Subdivision (b) continues former Section 2030(c)(6) without change. [33 Cal.L.Rev.Comm. Reports 885 (2004)].

Research References

Rutter, Cal. Practice Guide: Civ. Pro. Before Trial Ch. 8F-5, Responding to Interrogatories.
Rutter, Cal. Practice Guide: Civ. Pro. Before Trial Ch. 8A-3, Civil Discovery Act.
Rutter, Cal. Practice Guide: Civ. Pro. Before Trial Ch. 8C-2, "Reasonably Calculated to Lead to Discovery of Admissible Evidence".
Rutter, Cal. Practice Guide: Civ. Pro. Before Trial Ch. 8D-5, Selecting Proper Discovery Tools.
Rutter, Cal. Practice Guide: Civ. Pro. Before Trial Ch. 8F-1, When Interrogatories May be Served.
Rutter, Cal. Practice Guide: Civ. Pro. Before Trial Ch. 8F-2, to Whom Interrogatories May be Sent.
Rutter, Cal. Practice Guide: Civ. Pro. Before Trial Ch. 8F-3, Propounding Interrogatories.
Rutter, Cal. Practice Guide: Civ. Pro. Before Trial Ch. 8D-5, Outline 5.
Rutter, Cal. Practice Guide: Enforcing Judgments/Debts Ch. 6G-2, Written Interrogatories to Judgment Debtor.
Rutter, Cal. Practice Guide: Insurance Litigation Ch. 15-G, G. Discovery.
Rutter, Cal. Practice Guide: Personal Injury Ch. 6-B, B. Overview of Selected Discovery Procedures.
2 Witkin Cal. Proc. 5th Courts § 253, Discovery.
8 Witkin Cal. Proc. 5th Enforcement of Judgment § 275, Written Interrogatories to Judgment Debtor.
7 Witkin Cal. Proc. 5th Trial § 293, (S 293) Depositions and Interrogatories.

§ 2030.020. Time to submit interrogatories; motion to submit at earlier time

(a) A defendant may propound interrogatories to a party to the action without leave of court at any time.

(b) A plaintiff may propound interrogatories to a party without leave of court at any time that is 10 days after the service of the summons on, or appearance by, that party, whichever occurs first.

(c) Notwithstanding subdivision (b), in an unlawful detainer action or other proceeding under Chapter 4 (commencing with Section 1159) of Title 3 of Part 3, a plaintiff may propound interrogatories to a party without leave of court at any time that is five days after service of the summons on, or appearance by, that party, whichever occurs first.

(d) Notwithstanding subdivisions (b) and (c), on motion with or without notice, the court, for good cause shown, may grant leave to a plaintiff to propound interrogatories at an earlier time. *(Added by Stats.2004, c. 182 (A.B.3081), § 23, operative July 1, 2005. Amended by Stats.2007, c. 113 (A.B.1126), § 7.)*

Law Revision Commission Comments

Subdivision (a) of Section 2030.020 continues the first sentence of former Section 2030(b) without change.

Subdivision (b) continues the second sentence of former Section 2030(b) without change.

Subdivision (c) continues the third sentence of former Section 2030(b) without substantive change. [33 Cal.L.Rev.Comm. Reports 885 (2004)].

Section 2030.020 is amended to improve clarity by separately stating the special hold period for an unlawful detainer case. The amendment also makes clear that the special hold period applies to a proceeding for forcible entry (see Section 1159) or forcible detainer (see Section 1160), as well as to an unlawful detainer case. [36 Cal.L.Rev.Comm. Reports 271 (2007)].

Research References

Rutter, Cal. Practice Guide: Civ. Pro. Before Trial Ch. 8F-1, When Interrogatories May be Served.

Rutter, Cal. Practice Guide: Civ. Pro. Before Trial Ch. 9(I)-F, F. Ex Parte Motions.

Rutter, Cal. Practice Guide: Personal Injury Ch. 4-A, A. General Considerations.

Rutter, Cal. Practice Guide: Personal Injury Ch. 6-B, B. Overview of Selected Discovery Procedures.

12 Witkin, California Summary 10th Real Property § 736, Trial.

§ 2030.030. Special interrogatories; official form interrogatories; restriction on number allowed; numbers in excess of amount allowed

(a) A party may propound to another party either or both of the following:

(1) Thirty-five specially prepared interrogatories that are relevant to the subject matter of the pending action.

(2) Any additional number of official form interrogatories, as described in Chapter 17 (commencing with Section 2033.710), that are relevant to the subject matter of the pending action.

(b) Except as provided in Section 2030.070, no party shall, as a matter of right, propound to any other party more than 35 specially prepared interrogatories. If the initial set of interrogatories does not exhaust this limit, the balance may be propounded in subsequent sets.

(c) Unless a declaration as described in Section 2030.050 has been made, a party need only respond to the first 35 specially prepared interrogatories served, if that party states an objection to the balance, under Section 2030.240, on the ground that the limit has been exceeded. *(Added by Stats.2004, c. 182 (A.B. 3081), § 23, operative July 1, 2005.)*

Law Revision Commission Comments

Subdivision (a) of Section 2030.030 continues the first sentence of former Section 2030(c)(1) without substantive change.

Subdivision (b) continues the second and third sentences of former Section 2030(c)(1) without change, except to conform the cross-reference.

Subdivision (c) continues the fourth sentence of former Section 2030(c)(1) without change, except to conform the cross-references. [33 Cal.L.Rev.Comm. Reports 886 (2004)].

Research References

Rutter, Cal. Practice Guide: Civ. Pro. Before Trial Ch. 8E-2, When Depositions May be Taken.

Rutter, Cal. Practice Guide: Civ. Pro. Before Trial Ch. 8F-3, Propounding Interrogatories.

Rutter, Cal. Practice Guide: Civ. Pro. Before Trial Ch. 8L-1, Limitations on Existing Discovery Procedures.

Rutter, Cal. Practice Guide: Civ. Pro. Before Trial Ch. 8E-16, Sanctions Re Depositions.

California Practice Guide: Employment Litigation Ch. 19-F, F. Discovery.

Rutter, Cal. Practice Guide: Enforcing Judgments/Debts Ch. 6G-2, Written Interrogatories to Judgment Debtor.

Rutter, Cal. Practice Guide: Fed.Civ.Pro. Before Trial Ch. 1-D, D. Choosing Between State and Federal Courts.

Rutter, Cal. Practice Guide: Insurance Litigation Ch. 15-G, G. Discovery.

Rutter, Cal. Practice Guide: Personal Injury Ch. 6-B, B. Overview of Selected Discovery Procedures.

Rutter, Cal. Practice Guide: Personal Injury Ch. 8-B, B. After Trial Date Set (Three to Four Months Before Trial).

8 Witkin Cal. Proc. 5th Enforcement of Judgment § 275, Written Interrogatories to Judgment Debtor.

§ 2030.040. Special interrogatories with supporting declaration; exception to number restrictions; burden of proof; protective order

(a) Subject to the right of the responding party to seek a protective order under Section 2030.090, any party who attaches a supporting declaration as described in Section 2030.050 may propound a greater number of specially prepared interrogatories to another party if this greater number is warranted because of any of the following:

(1) The complexity or the quantity of the existing and potential issues in the particular case.

(2) The financial burden on a party entailed in conducting the discovery by oral deposition.

(3) The expedience of using this method of discovery to provide to the responding party the opportunity to conduct an inquiry, investigation, or search of files or records to supply the information sought.

(b) If the responding party seeks a protective order on the ground that the number of specially prepared interrogatories is unwarranted, the propounding party shall have the burden of justifying the number of these interrogatories. *(Added by Stats.2004, c. 182 (A.B.3081), § 23, operative July 1, 2005.)*

Law Revision Commission Comments

Subdivision (a) of Section 2030.040 continues the first paragraph of former Section 2030(c)(2) (including items (A)-(C)) without change, except to conform the cross-references.

Subdivision (b) continues the last paragraph of former Section 2030(c)(2) without change. [33 Cal.L.Rev.Comm. Reports 887 (2004)].

Research References

Rutter, Cal. Practice Guide: Civ. Pro. Before Trial Ch. 8F-3, Propounding Interrogatories.

Rutter, Cal. Practice Guide: Civ. Pro. Before Trial Ch. 8F-4, Protective Orders.

Rutter, Cal. Practice Guide: Civ. Pro. Before Trial Ch. 8F-5, Responding to Interrogatories.

Rutter, Cal. Practice Guide: Personal Injury Ch. 6-B, B. Overview of Selected Discovery Procedures.

§ 2030.050. Special interrogatories exceeding numeric restriction; Declaration for Additional Discovery; form and contents

Any party who is propounding or has propounded more than 35 specially prepared interrogatories to any other party shall attach to each set of those interrogatories a declaration containing substantially the following:

DECLARATION FOR ADDITIONAL DISCOVERY

I, _____, declare:

1. I am (a party to this action or proceeding appearing in propria persona) (presently the attorney for _____, a party to this action or proceeding).

2. I am propounding to _____ the attached set of interrogatories.

3. This set of interrogatories will cause the total number of specially prepared interrogatories propounded to the party to whom they are directed to exceed the number of specially prepared interrogatories permitted by Section 2030.030 of the Code of Civil Procedure.

4. I have previously propounded a total of _____ interrogatories to this party, of which _____ interrogatories were not official form interrogatories.

5. This set of interrogatories contains a total of _____ specially prepared interrogatories.

6. I am familiar with the issues and the previous discovery conducted by all of the parties in the case.

7. I have personally examined each of the questions in this set of interrogatories.

8. This number of questions is warranted under Section 2030.040 of the Code of Civil Procedure because _____. (Here state each factor described in Section 2030.040 that is relied on, as well as the reasons why any factor relied on is applicable to the instant lawsuit.)

9. None of the questions in this set of interrogatories is being propounded for any improper purpose, such as to harass the party, or the attorney for the party, to whom it is directed, or to cause unnecessary delay or needless increase in the cost of litigation.

I declare under penalty of perjury under the laws of California that the foregoing is true and correct, and that this declaration was executed on _____.

_____

(Signature)

Attorney for _____

(Added by Stats.2004, c. 182 (A.B.3081), § 23, operative July 1, 2005. Amended by Stats.2005, c. 22 (S.B.1108), § 22.)

Law Revision Commission Comments

Section 2030.050 continues former Section 2030(c)(3) without change, except to conform the cross-references. [33 Cal.L.Rev.Comm. Reports 887 (2004)].

Research References

Rutter, Cal. Practice Guide: Civ. Pro. Before Trial Ch. 8F-3, Propounding Interrogatories.
Rutter, Cal. Practice Guide: Civ. Pro. Before Trial Ch. 8F-5, Responding to Interrogatories.
Rutter, Cal. Practice Guide: Enforcing Judgments/Debts Ch. 6G-2, Written Interrogatories to Judgment Debtor.
Rutter, Cal. Practice Guide: Personal Injury Ch. 6-B, B. Overview of Selected Discovery Procedures.
Rutter, Cal. Practice Guide: Personal Injury Ch. 8-B, B. After Trial Date Set (Three to Four Months Before Trial).

§ 2030.060. Form of interrogatories; content requirements

(a) A party propounding interrogatories shall number each set of interrogatories consecutively.

(b) In the first paragraph immediately below the title of the case, there shall appear the identity of the propounding party, the set number, and the identity of the responding party.

(c) Each interrogatory in a set shall be separately set forth and identified by number or letter.

(d) Each interrogatory shall be full and complete in and of itself. No preface or instruction shall be included with a set of interrogatories unless it has been approved under Chapter 17 (commencing with Section 2033.710).

(e) Any term specially defined in a set of interrogatories shall be typed with all letters capitalized wherever that term appears.

(f) No specially prepared interrogatory shall contain subparts, or a compound, conjunctive, or disjunctive question.

(g) An interrogatory may not be made a continuing one so as to impose on the party responding to it a duty to supplement an answer to it that was initially correct and complete with later acquired information. *(Added by Stats.2004, c. 182 (A.B.3081), § 23, operative July 1, 2005.)*

Law Revision Commission Comments

Subdivision (a) of Section 2030.060 continues the first sentence of former Section 2030(c)(4) without change.

Subdivision (b) continues the second sentence of former Section 2030(c)(4) without change.

Subdivision (c) continues the third sentence of former Section 2030(c)(4) without change.

Subdivision (d) continues the first and second sentences of former Section 2030(c)(5) without change, except to conform the cross-reference.

Subdivision (e) continues the third sentence of former Section 2030(c)(5) without change.

Subdivision (f) continues the fourth sentence of former Section 2030(c)(5) without change.

Subdivision (g) continues former Section 2030(c)(7) without change. [33 Cal.L.Rev.Comm. Reports 889 (2004)].

Research References

Rutter, Cal. Practice Guide: Civ. Pro. Before Trial Ch. 8E-6, Subpoena to Nonparty Deponent or Business Records Custodian.
Rutter, Cal. Practice Guide: Civ. Pro. Before Trial Ch. 8F-3, Propounding Interrogatories.
Rutter, Cal. Practice Guide: Civ. Pro. Before Trial Ch. 8F-5, Responding to Interrogatories.
Rutter, Cal. Practice Guide: Enforcing Judgments/Debts Ch. 6G-2, Written Interrogatories to Judgment Debtor.
Rutter, Cal. Practice Guide: Personal Injury Ch. 6-B, B. Overview of Selected Discovery Procedures.
12 Witkin, California Summary 10th Real Property § 736, Trial.

§ 2030.070. Supplemental interrogatories; restriction on number permitted; exception

(a) In addition to the number of interrogatories permitted by Sections 2030.030 and 2030.040, a party may propound a supplemental interrogatory to elicit any later acquired information bearing on all answers previously made by any party in response to interrogatories.

(b) A party may propound a supplemental interrogatory twice before the initial setting of a trial date, and, subject to the time limits on discovery proceedings and motions provided in Chapter 8 (commencing with Section 2024.010), once after the initial setting of a trial date.

(c) Notwithstanding subdivisions (a) and (b), on motion, for good cause shown, the court may grant leave to a party to propound an additional number of supplemental interrogatories. *(Added by Stats.2004, c. 182 (A.B.3081), § 23, operative July 1, 2005.)*

Law Revision Commission Comments

Subdivisions (a) and (b) of Section 2030.070 continue the first sentence of former Section 2030(c)(8) without substantive change.

Subdivision (c) continues the second sentence of former Section 2030(c)(8) without substantive change. [33 Cal.L.Rev.Comm. Reports 890 (2004)].

Research References

Rutter, Cal. Practice Guide: Civ. Pro. Before Trial Ch. 8F-3, Propounding Interrogatories.
Rutter, Cal. Practice Guide: Civ. Pro. Before Trial Ch. 8F-5, Responding to Interrogatories.
Rutter, Cal. Practice Guide: Civil Trials & Evidence Ch. 1-A, A. Importance of Statewide and Local Rules of Court.
Rutter, Cal. Practice Guide: Enforcing Judgments/Debts Ch. 6G-2, Written Interrogatories to Judgment Debtor.
Rutter, Cal. Practice Guide: Personal Injury Ch. 6-B, B. Overview of Selected Discovery Procedures.

Civ. Pro.

Rutter, Cal. Practice Guide: Personal Injury Ch. 8-B, B. After Trial Date Set (Three to Four Months Before Trial).

§ 2030.080. Service of documents

(a) The party propounding interrogatories shall serve a copy of them on the party to whom the interrogatories are directed.

(b) The propounding party shall also serve a copy of the interrogatories on all other parties who have appeared in the action. On motion, with or without notice, the court may relieve the party from this requirement on its determination that service on all other parties would be unduly expensive or burdensome. *(Added by Stats.2004, c. 182 (A.B.3081), § 23, operative July 1, 2005.)*

Law Revision Commission Comments

Section 2030.080 continues former Section 2030(d) without substantive change. [33 Cal.L.Rev.Comm. Reports 890 (2004)].

Research References

Rutter, Cal. Practice Guide: Civ. Pro. Before Trial Ch. 8F-3, Propounding Interrogatories.
Rutter, Cal. Practice Guide: Personal Injury Ch. 6-B, B. Overview of Selected Discovery Procedures.

§ 2030.090. Protective orders; persons entitled to protection; time to file; meet and confer; authorized court action; monetary sanctions

(a) When interrogatories have been propounded, the responding party, and any other party or affected natural person or organization may promptly move for a protective order. This motion shall be accompanied by a meet and confer declaration under Section 2016.040.

(b) The court, for good cause shown, may make any order that justice requires to protect any party or other natural person or organization from unwarranted annoyance, embarrassment, or oppression, or undue burden and expense. This protective order may include, but is not limited to, one or more of the following directions:

(1) That the set of interrogatories, or particular interrogatories in the set, need not be answered.

(2) That, contrary to the representations made in a declaration submitted under Section 2030.050, the number of specially prepared interrogatories is unwarranted.

(3) That the time specified in Section 2030.260 to respond to the set of interrogatories, or to particular interrogatories in the set, be extended.

(4) That the response be made only on specified terms and conditions.

(5) That the method of discovery be an oral deposition instead of interrogatories to a party.

(6) That a trade secret or other confidential research, development, or commercial information not be disclosed or be disclosed only in a certain way.

(7) That some or all of the answers to interrogatories be sealed and thereafter opened only on order of the court.

(c) If the motion for a protective order is denied in whole or in part, the court may order that the party provide or permit the discovery against which protection was sought on terms and conditions that are just.

(d) The court shall impose a monetary sanction under Chapter 7 (commencing with Section 2023.010) against any party, person, or attorney who unsuccessfully makes or opposes a motion for a protective order under this section, unless it finds that the one subject to the sanction acted with substantial justification or that other circumstances make the imposition of the sanction unjust. *(Added by Stats.2004, c. 182 (A.B.3081), § 23, operative July 1, 2005.)*

Law Revision Commission Comments

Subdivision (a) of Section 2030.090 continues the first paragraph of former Section 2030(e) without substantive change.

Subdivision (b) continues the second paragraph of former Section 2030(e) (including items (1)-(7)) without change, except to conform the cross-references.

Subdivision (c) continues the next-to-last paragraph of former Section 2030(e) without change.

Subdivision (d) continues the last paragraph of former Section 2030(e) without substantive change. [33 Cal.L.Rev.Comm. Reports 891 (2004)].

Research References

Rutter, Cal. Practice Guide: Civ. Pro. Before Trial Ch. 8F-3, Propounding Interrogatories.
Rutter, Cal. Practice Guide: Civ. Pro. Before Trial Ch. 8F-4, Protective Orders.
Rutter, Cal. Practice Guide: Civ. Pro. Before Trial Ch. 8F-5, Responding to Interrogatories.
Rutter, Cal. Practice Guide: Civ. Pro. Before Trial Ch. 8F-9, Use of Interrogatories at Trial.
California Practice Guide: Employment Litigation Ch. 19-F, F. Discovery.
Rutter, Cal. Practice Guide: Personal Injury Ch. 6-B, B. Overview of Selected Discovery Procedures.
Rutter, Cal. Practice Guide: Personal Injury Ch. 8-B, B. After Trial Date Set (Three to Four Months Before Trial).
8 Witkin Cal. Proc. 5th Enforcement of Judgment § 275, Written Interrogatories to Judgment Debtor.

ARTICLE 2. RESPONSE TO INTERROGATORIES

§ 2030.210. Mode of response; required contents

(a) The party to whom interrogatories have been propounded shall respond in writing under oath separately to each interrogatory by any of the following:

(1) An answer containing the information sought to be discovered.

(2) An exercise of the party's option to produce writings.

(3) An objection to the particular interrogatory.

(b) In the first paragraph of the response immediately below the title of the case, there shall appear the identity of the responding party, the set number, and the identity of the propounding party.

(c) Each answer, exercise of option, or objection in the response shall bear the same identifying number or letter and be in the same sequence as the corresponding interrogatory, but the text of that interrogatory need not be repeated. *(Added by Stats.2004, c. 182 (A.B.3081), § 23, operative July 1, 2005.)*

Law Revision Commission Comments

Subdivision (a) of Section 2030.210 continues the first sentence of former Section 2030(f) without substantive change.

Subdivision (b) continues the second sentence of former Section 2030(f) without change.

Subdivision (c) continues the third sentence of former Section 2030(f) without change. [33 Cal.L.Rev.Comm. Reports 892 (2004)].

Research References

Rutter, Cal. Practice Guide: Civ. Pro. Before Trial Ch. 8F-5, Responding to Interrogatories.
Rutter, Cal. Practice Guide: Personal Injury Ch. 6-B, B. Overview of Selected Discovery Procedures.
Rutter, Cal. Practice Guide: Personal Injury Ch. 8-B, B. After Trial Date Set (Three to Four Months Before Trial).

§ 2030.220. Answers in response; contents and form; obligations of responding party

(a) Each answer in a response to interrogatories shall be as complete and straightforward as the information reasonably available to the responding party permits.

(b) If an interrogatory cannot be answered completely, it shall be answered to the extent possible.

(c) If the responding party does not have personal knowledge sufficient to respond fully to an interrogatory, that party shall so state, but shall make a reasonable and good faith effort to obtain the information by inquiry to other natural persons or organizations, except where the information is equally available to the propounding party. *(Added by Stats.2004, c. 182 (A.B.3081), § 23, operative July 1, 2005.)*

Law Revision Commission Comments

Subdivision (a) of Section 2030.220 continues the first sentence of former Section 2030(f)(1) without substantive change.

Subdivision (b) continues the second sentence of former Section 2030(f)(1) without change.

Subdivision (c) continues the third sentence of former Section 2030(f)(1) without change. [33 Cal.L.Rev.Comm. Reports 893 (2004)].

Research References

Rutter, Cal. Practice Guide: Civ. Pro. Before Trial Ch. 8F-5, Responding to Interrogatories.
Rutter, Cal. Practice Guide: Insurance Litigation Ch. 15-G, G. Discovery.
Rutter, Cal. Practice Guide: Personal Injury Ch. 6-B, B. Overview of Selected Discovery Procedures.

§ 2030.230. Answers supplemented by attached documents; specificity of references to attachments; examination and inspection by responding party

If the answer to an interrogatory would necessitate the preparation or the making of a compilation, abstract, audit, or summary of or from the documents of the party to whom the interrogatory is directed, and if the burden or expense of preparing or making it would be substantially the same for the party propounding the interrogatory as for the responding party, it is a sufficient answer to that interrogatory to refer to this section and to specify the writings from which the answer may be derived or ascertained. This specification shall be in sufficient detail to permit the propounding party to locate and to identify, as readily as the responding party can, the documents from which the answer may be ascertained. The responding party

shall then afford to the propounding party a reasonable opportunity to examine, audit, or inspect these documents and to make copies, compilations, abstracts, or summaries of them. *(Added by Stats.2004, c. 182 (A.B.3081), § 23, operative July 1, 2005.)*

Law Revision Commission Comments

Section 2030.230 continues former Section 2030(f)(2) without change, except to replace subdivision with section. [33 Cal.L.Rev.Comm. Reports 893 (2004)].

Research References

Rutter, Cal. Practice Guide: Civ. Pro. Before Trial Ch. 8F-5, Responding to Interrogatories.
Rutter, Cal. Practice Guide: Civ. Pro. Before Trial Ch. 8F-5, Outline 5.
Rutter, Cal. Practice Guide: Personal Injury Ch. 6-B, B. Overview of Selected Discovery Procedures.

§ 2030.240. Partial objection to form of interrogatory; response; statement of claim of privilege or work product

(a) If only a part of an interrogatory is objectionable, the remainder of the interrogatory shall be answered.

(b) If an objection is made to an interrogatory or to a part of an interrogatory, the specific ground for the objection shall be set forth clearly in the response. If an objection is based on a claim of privilege, the particular privilege invoked shall be clearly stated. If an objection is based on a claim that the information sought is protected work product under Chapter 4 (commencing with Section 2018.010), that claim shall be expressly asserted. *(Added by Stats.2004, c. 182 (A.B.3081), § 23, operative July 1, 2005.)*

Law Revision Commission Comments

Subdivision (a) of Section 2030.240 continues the first sentence of former Section 2030(f)(3) without change.

Subdivision (b) continues the second, third, and fourth sentences of former Section 2030(f)(3) without change, except to conform the cross-reference. [33 Cal.L.Rev.Comm. Reports 894 (2004)].

Research References

Rutter, Cal. Practice Guide: Civ. Pro. Before Trial Ch. 8F-3, Propounding Interrogatories.
Rutter, Cal. Practice Guide: Civ. Pro. Before Trial Ch. 8F-8, Sanctions in Enforcing Discovery.
Rutter, Cal. Practice Guide: Personal Injury Ch. 6-B, B. Overview of Selected Discovery Procedures.
Rutter, Cal. Practice Guide: Personal Injury Ch. 8-B, B. After Trial Date Set (Three to Four Months Before Trial).

§ 2030.250. Signature upon response; oath; officers or agents of an entity; responses containing objections

(a) The party to whom the interrogatories are directed shall sign the response under oath unless the response contains only objections.

(b) If that party is a public or private corporation, or a partnership, association, or governmental agency, one of its officers or agents shall sign the response under oath on behalf of that party. If the officer or agent signing the response on behalf of that party is an attorney acting in that capacity for the party, that party waives any lawyer-client privilege and any protection for work product under Chapter 4 (commencing with Section 2018.010) during any subsequent discovery from that attorney concerning the identity of the sources of the information contained in the response.

(c) The attorney for the responding party shall sign any responses that contain an objection. *(Added by Stats.2004, c. 182 (A.B.3081), § 23, operative July 1, 2005.)*

Law Revision Commission Comments

Subdivision (a) of Section 2030.250 continues the first sentence of former Section 2030(g) without change.

Subdivision (b) continues the second and third sentences of former Section 2030(g) without change, except to conform the cross-reference.

Subdivision (c) continues the fourth sentence of former Section 2030(g) without change. [33 Cal.L.Rev.Comm. Reports 895 (2004)].

Research References

Rutter, Cal. Practice Guide: Civ. Pro. Before Trial Ch. 8F-5, Responding to Interrogatories.

Rutter, Cal. Practice Guide: Personal Injury Ch. 6-B, B. Overview of Selected Discovery Procedures.

§ 2030.260. Time to respond; shortening of time; copies to all parties

(a) Within 30 days after service of interrogatories, the party to whom the interrogatories are propounded shall serve the original of the response to them on the propounding party, unless on motion of the propounding party the court has shortened the time for response, or unless on motion of the responding party the court has extended the time for response.

(b) Notwithstanding subdivision (a), in an unlawful detainer action or other proceeding under Chapter 4 (commencing with Section 1159) of Title 3 of Part 3, the party to whom the interrogatories are propounded shall have five days from the date of service to respond, unless on motion of the propounding party the court has shortened the time for response, or unless on motion of the responding party the court has extended the time for response.

(c) The party to whom the interrogatories are propounded shall also serve a copy of the response on all other parties who have appeared in the action. On motion, with or without notice, the court may relieve the party from this requirement on its determination that service on all other parties would be unduly expensive or burdensome. *(Added by Stats.2004, c. 182 (A.B. 3081), § 23, operative July 1, 2005. Amended by Stats.2007, c. 113 (A.B.1126), § 8.)*

Law Revision Commission Comments

Subdivision (a) of Section 2030.260 continues the first and second sentences of former Section 2030(h) without change.

Subdivision (b) continues the third sentence of former Section 2030(h) without substantive change. [33 Cal.L.Rev.Comm. Reports 895 (2004)].

Section 2030.260 is amended to improve clarity by separately stating the special deadline for an unlawful detainer case. The amendment also makes clear that the special deadline applies to a proceeding for forcible entry (see Section 1159) or forcible detainer (see Section 1160), as well as to an unlawful detainer case. In addition, the amendment eliminates an ambiguity by clearly permitting a court to extend, as well as shorten, the time to respond to interrogatories in an unlawful detainer case. [36 Cal.L.Rev.Comm. Reports 271 (2007)].

Research References

Rutter, Cal. Practice Guide: Civ. Pro. Before Trial Ch. 8F-4, Protective Orders.

Rutter, Cal. Practice Guide: Civ. Pro. Before Trial Ch. 8F-5, Responding to Interrogatories.

Rutter, Cal. Practice Guide: Civ. Pro. Before Trial Ch. 9(I)-F, F. Ex Parte Motions.

Rutter, Cal. Practice Guide: Enforcing Judgments/Debts Ch. 6G-2, Written Interrogatories to Judgment Debtor.

Rutter, Cal. Practice Guide: Personal Injury Ch. 6-B, B. Overview of Selected Discovery Procedures.

Rutter, Cal. Practice Guide: Personal Injury Ch. 8-B, B. After Trial Date Set (Three to Four Months Before Trial).

§ 2030.270. Time to respond; extension of time by agreement

(a) The party propounding interrogatories and the responding party may agree to extend the time for service of a response to a set of interrogatories, or to particular interrogatories in a set, to a date beyond that provided in Section 2030.260.

(b) This agreement may be informal, but it shall be confirmed in a writing that specifies the extended date for service of a response.

(c) Unless this agreement expressly states otherwise, it is effective to preserve to the responding party the right to respond to any interrogatory to which the agreement applies in any manner specified in Sections 2030.210, 2030.220, 2030.230, and 2030.240. *(Added by Stats.2004, c. 182 (A.B.3081), § 23, operative July 1, 2005.)*

Law Revision Commission Comments

Subdivision (a) of Section 2030.270 continues the first sentence of former Section 2030(i) without change, except to conform the cross-reference.

Subdivision (b) continues the second sentence of former Section 2030(i) without change.

Subdivision (c) continues the third sentence of former Section 2030(i) without change, except to conform the cross-reference. [33 Cal.L.Rev. Comm. Reports 896 (2004)].

Research References

Rutter, Cal. Practice Guide: Civ. Pro. Before Trial Ch. 8F-5, Responding to Interrogatories.

Rutter, Cal. Practice Guide: Personal Injury Ch. 6-B, B. Overview of Selected Discovery Procedures.

§ 2030.280. Custody of interrogatories, responses and supporting documents; originals; record retention

(a) The interrogatories and the response thereto shall not be filed with the court.

(b) The propounding party shall retain both the original of the interrogatories, with the original proof of service affixed to them, and the original of the sworn response until six months after final disposition of the action. At that time, both originals may be destroyed, unless the court on motion of any party and for good cause shown orders that the originals be preserved for a longer period. *(Added by Stats.2004, c. 182 (A.B.3081), § 23, operative July 1, 2005.)*

Law Revision Commission Comments

Subdivision (a) of Section 2030.280 continues the first sentence of former Section 2030(j) without change.

Subdivision (b) continues the second and third sentences of former Section 2030(j) without change. [33 Cal.L.Rev.Comm. Reports 896 (2004)].

Research References

Rutter, Cal. Practice Guide: Civ. Pro. Before Trial Ch. 8F-6, Custody of Interrogatories and Responses.

Rutter, Cal. Practice Guide: Civ. Pro. Before Trial Ch. 9(I)-B, B. Preparing and Filing Motions.

Rutter, Cal. Practice Guide: Personal Injury Ch. 6-B, B. Overview of Selected Discovery Procedures.

6 Witkin Cal. Proc. 5th Proceedings Without Trial § 42, Other Documentary Evidence.

§ 2030.290. Untimely responses; waiver of rights; exception; motions to compel; monetary sanctions

If a party to whom interrogatories are directed fails to serve a timely response, the following rules apply:

(a) The party to whom the interrogatories are directed waives any right to exercise the option to produce writings under Section 2030.230, as well as any objection to the interrogatories, including one based on privilege or on the protection for work product under Chapter 4 (commencing with Section 2018.010). The court, on motion, may relieve that party from this waiver on its determination that both of the following conditions are satisfied:

(1) The party has subsequently served a response that is in substantial compliance with Sections 2030.210, 2030.220, 2030.230, and 2030.240.

(2) The party's failure to serve a timely response was the result of mistake, inadvertence, or excusable neglect.

(b) The party propounding the interrogatories may move for an order compelling response to the interrogatories.

(c) The court shall impose a monetary sanction under Chapter 7 (commencing with Section 2023.010) against any party, person, or attorney who unsuccessfully makes or opposes a motion to compel a response to interrogatories, unless it finds that the one subject to the sanction acted with substantial justification or that other circumstances make the imposition of the sanction unjust. If a party then fails to obey an order compelling answers, the court may make those orders that are just, including the imposition of an issue sanction, an evidence sanction, or a terminating sanction under Chapter 7 (commencing with Section 2023.010). In lieu of or in addition to that sanction, the court may impose a monetary sanction under Chapter 7 (commencing with Section 2023.010). *(Added by Stats.2004, c. 182 (A.B.3081), § 23, operative July 1, 2005.)*

Law Revision Commission Comments

Subdivision (a) of Section 2030.290 continues the first paragraph of former Section 2030(k) without substantive change.

Subdivision (b) continues the first sentence of the second paragraph of former Section 2030(k) without change.

Subdivision (c) continues the second, third, and fourth sentences of the second paragraph of former Section 2030(k) without change, except to conform the cross-references. [33 Cal.L.Rev.Comm. Reports 897 (2004)].

Research References

Rutter, Cal. Practice Guide: Civ. Pro. Before Trial Ch. 8A-3, Civil Discovery Act.

Rutter, Cal. Practice Guide: Civ. Pro. Before Trial Ch. 8C-3, "Not Privileged".

Rutter, Cal. Practice Guide: Civ. Pro. Before Trial Ch. 8C-5, Privacy Protection.

Rutter, Cal. Practice Guide: Civ. Pro. Before Trial Ch. 8F-5, Responding to Interrogatories.

Rutter, Cal. Practice Guide: Civ. Pro. Before Trial Ch. 8F-7, Motion to Compel Answers.

Rutter, Cal. Practice Guide: Civ. Pro. Before Trial Ch. 8F-8, Sanctions in Enforcing Discovery.

Rutter, Cal. Practice Guide: Civil Trials & Evidence Ch. 8E-A, A. Privileges.

Rutter, Cal. Practice Guide: Civil Trials & Evidence Ch. 8E-B, B. Attorney Work Product Doctrine.

California Practice Guide: Employment Litigation Ch. 19-F, F. Discovery.

Rutter, Cal. Practice Guide: Enforcing Judgments/Debts Ch. 6G-2, Written Interrogatories to Judgment Debtor.

Rutter, Cal. Practice Guide: Personal Injury Ch. 6-B, B. Overview of Selected Discovery Procedures.

Rutter, Cal. Practice Guide: Personal Injury Ch. 8-B, B. After Trial Date Set (Three to Four Months Before Trial).

§ 2030.300. Motion to compel further response; meet and confer declaration; time to serve motion; monetary sanctions; failure to obey court order

(a) On receipt of a response to interrogatories, the propounding party may move for an order compelling a further response if the propounding party deems that any of the following apply:

(1) An answer to a particular interrogatory is evasive or incomplete.

(2) An exercise of the option to produce documents under Section 2030.230 is unwarranted or the required specification of those documents is inadequate.

(3) An objection to an interrogatory is without merit or too general.

(b) A motion under subdivision (a) shall be accompanied by a meet and confer declaration under Section 2016.040.

(c) Unless notice of this motion is given within 45 days of the service of the verified response, or any supplemental verified response, or on or before any specific later date to which the propounding party and the responding party have agreed in writing, the propounding party waives any right to compel a further response to the interrogatories.

(d) The court shall impose a monetary sanction under Chapter 7 (commencing with Section 2023.010) against any party, person, or attorney who unsuccessfully makes or opposes a motion to compel a further response to interrogatories, unless it finds that the one subject to the sanction acted with substantial justification or that other circumstances make the imposition of the sanction unjust.

(e) If a party then fails to obey an order compelling further response to interrogatories, the court may make those orders that are just, including the imposition of an issue sanction, an evidence sanction, or a terminating sanction under Chapter 7 (commencing with Section 2023.010). In lieu of, or in addition to, that sanction, the court may impose a monetary sanction under Chapter 7 (commencing with Section 2023.010). *(Added by Stats.2004, c. 182 (A.B.3081), § 23, operative July 1, 2005. Amended by Stats.2013, c. 18 (A.B.1183), § 1.)*

Law Revision Commission Comments

Subdivision (a) of Section 2030.300 continues the first sentence of former Section 2030(l) without substantive change.

Subdivision (b) continues the second sentence of former Section 2030(l) without substantive change.

Subdivision (c) continues the second paragraph of former Section 2030(l) without change.

Subdivision (d) continues the third paragraph of former Section 2030(l) without change, except to conform the cross-reference.

Subdivision (e) continues the fourth paragraph of former Section 2030(l) without change, except to conform the cross-references. [33 Cal.L.Rev.Comm. Reports 898 (2004)].

Research References

Rutter, Cal. Practice Guide: Civ. Pro. Before Trial Ch. 8F-5, Responding to Interrogatories.

Rutter, Cal. Practice Guide: Civ. Pro. Before Trial Ch. 8F-7, Motion to Compel Answers.

Rutter, Cal. Practice Guide: Civ. Pro. Before Trial Ch. 8F-8, Sanctions in Enforcing Discovery.

Rutter, Cal. Practice Guide: Enforcing Judgments/Debts Ch. 6G-2, Written Interrogatories to Judgment Debtor.

Rutter, Cal. Practice Guide: Personal Injury Ch. 8-B, B. After Trial Date Set (Three to Four Months Before Trial).

§ 2030.310. Amended answers to interrogatories; use at trial; motion to bind original answer; meet and confer; court order; monetary sanctions

(a) Without leave of court, a party may serve an amended answer to any interrogatory that contains information subsequently discovered, inadvertently omitted, or mistakenly stated in the initial interrogatory. At the trial of the action, the propounding party or any other party may use the initial answer under Section 2030.410, and the responding party may then use the amended answer.

(b) The party who propounded an interrogatory to which an amended answer has been served may move for an order that the initial answer to that interrogatory be deemed binding on the responding party for the purpose of the pending action. This motion shall be accompanied by a meet and confer declaration under Section 2016.040.

(c) The court shall grant a motion under subdivision (b) if it determines that all of the following conditions are satisfied:

(1) The initial failure of the responding party to answer the interrogatory correctly has substantially prejudiced the party who propounded the interrogatory.

(2) The responding party has failed to show substantial justification for the initial answer to that interrogatory.

(3) The prejudice to the propounding party cannot be cured either by a continuance to permit further discovery or by the use of the initial answer under Section 2030.410.

(d) The court shall impose a monetary sanction under Chapter 7 (commencing with Section 2023.010) against any party, person, or attorney who unsuccessfully makes or opposes a motion to deem binding an initial answer to an interrogatory, unless it finds that the one subject to the sanction acted with substantial justification or that other circumstances make the imposition of the sanction unjust. *(Added by Stats.2004, c. 182 (A.B.3081), § 23, operative July 1, 2005.)*

Law Revision Commission Comments

Subdivision (a) of Section 2030.310 continues the first paragraph of former Section 2030(m) without change, except to conform the cross-reference.

Subdivision (b) continues the first and second sentences of the second paragraph of former Section 2030(m) without substantive change.

Subdivision (c) continues the third sentence of the second paragraph of former Section 2030(m) without substantive change.

Subdivision (d) continues the third paragraph of former Section 2030(m) without change, except to conform the cross-reference. [33 Cal.L.Rev.Comm. Reports 899 (2004)].

Research References

Rutter, Cal. Practice Guide: Civ. Pro. Before Trial Ch. 10-C, C. Procedural Requirements-Moving Party.

Rutter, Cal. Practice Guide: Civ. Pro. Before Trial Ch. 8F-5, Responding to Interrogatories.

Rutter, Cal. Practice Guide: Civ. Pro. Before Trial Ch. 8F-9, Use of Interrogatories at Trial.

Rutter, Cal. Practice Guide: Personal Injury Ch. 6-B, B. Overview of Selected Discovery Procedures.

Rutter, Cal. Practice Guide: Personal Injury Ch. 6-C, C. Physical and Mental Examinations (CCP § 2032.020 et seq.).

Rutter, Cal. Practice Guide: Personal Injury Ch. 8-B, B. After Trial Date Set (Three to Four Months Before Trial).

ARTICLE 3. USE OF INTERROGATORY ANSWER

Section
2030.410. Trial or hearing in which respondent is a party.

§ 2030.410. Trial or hearing in which respondent is a party

At the trial or any other hearing in the action, so far as admissible under the rules of evidence, the propounding party or any party other than the responding party may use any answer or part of an answer to an interrogatory only against the responding party. It is not ground for objection to the use of an answer to an interrogatory that the responding party is available to testify, has testified, or will testify at the trial or other hearing. *(Added by Stats.2004, c. 182 (A.B.3081), § 23, operative July 1, 2005.)*

Law Revision Commission Comments

Section 2030.410 continues former Section 2030(n) without change. [33 Cal.L.Rev.Comm. Reports 901 (2004)].

Research References

Rutter, Cal. Practice Guide: Civ. Pro. Before Trial Ch. 8F-9, Use of Interrogatories at Trial.

Rutter, Cal. Practice Guide: Civil Trials & Evidence Ch. 1-C, C. Marshalling the Evidence.

Rutter, Cal. Practice Guide: Civil Trials & Evidence Ch. 4-B, B. Preliminary Matters Discussed in Final Status Conference or In-Chambers Conference.

Rutter, Cal. Practice Guide: Civil Trials & Evidence Ch. 8C-I, I. Depositions and Discovery.

Rutter, Cal. Practice Guide: Civil Trials & Evidence Ch. 8D-D, D. Hearsay Exceptions.

Rutter, Cal. Practice Guide: Personal Injury Ch. 9-H, H. Introduction of Discovered Evidence.

6 Witkin Cal. Proc. 5th Proceedings Without Trial § 42, Other Documentary Evidence.

CHAPTER 14. INSPECTION, COPYING, TESTING, SAMPLING, AND PRODUCTION OF DOCUMENTS, ELECTRONICALLY STORED INFORMATION, TANGIBLE THINGS, LAND, AND OTHER PROPERTY

ARTICLE 1. INSPECTION DEMAND

§ 2031.010. Persons subject to demand; scope of demand; entrance on land or property; electronically stored information

(a) Any party may obtain discovery within the scope delimited by Chapters 2 (commencing with Section 2017.010) and 3 (commencing with Section 2017.710), and subject to the restrictions set forth in Chapter 5 (commencing with Section 2019.010), by inspecting, copying, testing, or sampling documents, tangible things, land or other property, and electronically stored information in the possession, custody, or control of any other party to the action.

(b) A party may demand that any other party produce and permit the party making the demand, or someone acting on that party's behalf, to inspect and to copy a document that is in the possession, custody, or control of the party on whom the demand is made.

(c) A party may demand that any other party produce and permit the party making the demand, or someone acting on that party's behalf, to inspect and to photograph, test, or sample any tangible things that are in the possession, custody, or control of the party on whom the demand is made.

(d) A party may demand that any other party allow the party making the demand, or someone acting on that party's behalf, to enter on any land or other property that is in the possession, custody, or control of the party on whom the demand is made, and to inspect and to measure, survey, photograph, test, or sample the land or other property, or any designated object or operation on it.

(e) A party may demand that any other party produce and permit the party making the demand, or someone acting on that party's behalf, to inspect, copy, test, or sample electronically stored information in the possession, custody, or control of the party on whom demand is made. *(Added by Stats.2004, c. 182 (A.B.3081), § 23, operative July 1, 2005. Amended by Stats.2009, c. 5 (A.B.5), § 4, eff. June 29, 2009.)*

Law Revision Commission Comments

Subdivision (a) of Section 2031.010 continues the introductory paragraph of former Section 2031(a) without change, except to conform the cross-references.

Subdivision (b) continues former Section 2031(a)(1) without change.
Subdivision (c) continues former Section 2031(a)(2) without change.
Subdivision (d) continues former Section 2031(a)(3) without change. [33 Cal.L.Rev.Comm. Reports 901 (2004)].

Research References

Rutter, Cal. Practice Guide: Civ. Pro. Before Trial Ch. 8A-7, Duty to Preserve Evidence Before Discovery Request?
Rutter, Cal. Practice Guide: Civ. Pro. Before Trial Ch. 10-C, C. Procedural Requirements-Moving Party.
Rutter, Cal. Practice Guide: Civ. Pro. Before Trial Ch. 8A-3, Civil Discovery Act.
Rutter, Cal. Practice Guide: Civ. Pro. Before Trial Ch. 8C-2, "Reasonably Calculated to Lead to Discovery of Admissible Evidence".
Rutter, Cal. Practice Guide: Civ. Pro. Before Trial Ch. 8C-3, "Not Privileged".
Rutter, Cal. Practice Guide: Civ. Pro. Before Trial Ch. 8C-4, Attorney Work Product Protection.
Rutter, Cal. Practice Guide: Civ. Pro. Before Trial Ch. 8D-5, Selecting Proper Discovery Tools.
Rutter, Cal. Practice Guide: Civ. Pro. Before Trial Ch. 8E-1, When Prior Court Order Required.
Rutter, Cal. Practice Guide: Civ. Pro. Before Trial Ch. 8E-3, Whose Deposition May be Taken.
Rutter, Cal. Practice Guide: Civ. Pro. Before Trial Ch. 8E-5, Subpoena Not Necessary for Party or "Party-Affiliated" Witnesses.
Rutter, Cal. Practice Guide: Civ. Pro. Before Trial Ch. 8E-6, Subpoena to Nonparty Deponent or Business Records Custodian.
Rutter, Cal. Practice Guide: Civ. Pro. Before Trial Ch. 8F-3, Propounding Interrogatories.
Rutter, Cal. Practice Guide: Civ. Pro. Before Trial Ch. 8F-5, Responding to Interrogatories.
Rutter, Cal. Practice Guide: Civ. Pro. Before Trial Ch. 8F-8, Sanctions in Enforcing Discovery.
Rutter, Cal. Practice Guide: Civ. Pro. Before Trial Ch. 8G-5, Responses to Rfas.
Rutter, Cal. Practice Guide: Civ. Pro. Before Trial Ch. 8H-1, on Whom Demand May be Served.
Rutter, Cal. Practice Guide: Civ. Pro. Before Trial Ch. 8H-2, What May be Inspected.
Rutter, Cal. Practice Guide: Civ. Pro. Before Trial Ch. 8H-3, When Demand for Inspection May be Made.
Rutter, Cal. Practice Guide: Civ. Pro. Before Trial Ch. 8H-4, Demand Procedure.
Rutter, Cal. Practice Guide: Civ. Pro. Before Trial Ch. 8H-6, Responding to Demand.
Rutter, Cal. Practice Guide: Civ. Pro. Before Trial Ch. 8H-8, Enforcing Demand.
Rutter, Cal. Practice Guide: Civ. Pro. Before Trial Ch. 8I-2, Physical Examination by Demand in Personal Injury Cases.
Rutter, Cal. Practice Guide: Civ. Pro. Before Trial Ch. 8L-1, Limitations on Existing Discovery Procedures.
Rutter, Cal. Practice Guide: Civ. Pro. Before Trial Ch. 8E-16, Sanctions Re Depositions.
Rutter, Cal. Practice Guide: Civ. Pro. Before Trial Ch. 8D-5, Outline 5.
Rutter, Cal. Practice Guide: Civil Trials & Evidence Ch. 1-C, C. Marshalling the Evidence.
California Practice Guide: Employment Litigation Ch. 19-F, F. Discovery.
Rutter, Cal. Practice Guide: Enforcing Judgments/Debts Ch. 6G-3, Inspection Demand to Judgment Debtor.

Rutter, Cal. Practice Guide: Insurance Litigation Ch. 15-G, G. Discovery.
Rutter, Cal. Practice Guide: Personal Injury Ch. 6-A, A. Scope of Discovery and Limitations.
Rutter, Cal. Practice Guide: Personal Injury Ch. 6-B, B. Overview of Selected Discovery Procedures.
2 Witkin Cal. Proc. 5th Courts § 253, Discovery.
8 Witkin Cal. Proc. 5th Enforcement of Judgment § 276, Demand for Inspection of Documents.
5 Witkin, California Summary 10th Torts § 563, Scope of Privilege.

§ 2031.020. Time to make demand; inspection, copying, testing, or sampling prior to time allowed

(a) A defendant may make a demand for inspection, copying, testing, or sampling without leave of court at any time.

(b) A plaintiff may make a demand for inspection, copying, testing, or sampling without leave of court at any time that is 10 days after the service of the summons on, or appearance by, the party to whom the demand is directed, whichever occurs first.

(c) Notwithstanding subdivision (b), in an unlawful detainer action or other proceeding under Chapter 4 (commencing with Section 1159) of Title 3 of Part 3, a plaintiff may make a demand for inspection, copying, testing, or sampling without leave of court at any time that is five days after service of the summons on, or appearance by, the party to whom the demand is directed, whichever occurs first.

(d) Notwithstanding subdivisions (b) and (c), on motion with or without notice, the court, for good cause shown, may grant leave to a plaintiff to make a demand for inspection, copying, testing, or sampling at an earlier time. *(Added by Stats.2004, c. 182 (A.B.3081), § 23, operative July 1, 2005. Amended by Stats.2007, c. 113 (A.B.1126), § 9; Stats.2009, c. 5 (A.B.5), § 5, eff. June 29, 2009.)*

Law Revision Commission Comments

Subdivision (a) of Section 2031.020 continues the first sentence of former Section 2031(b) without change.

Subdivision (b) of Section 2031.020 continues the second sentence of former Section 2031(b) without change.

Subdivision (c) continues the third sentence of former Section 2031(b) without substantive change. [33 Cal.L.Rev.Comm. Reports 902 (2004)].

Section 2031.020 is amended to improve clarity by separately stating the special hold period for an unlawful detainer case. The amendment also makes clear that the special hold period applies to a proceeding for forcible entry (see Section 1159) or forcible detainer (see Section 1160), as well as to an unlawful detainer case. [36 Cal.L.Rev.Comm. Reports 271 (2007)].

Research References

Rutter, Cal. Practice Guide: Civ. Pro. Before Trial Ch. 8H-3, When Demand for Inspection May be Made.
Rutter, Cal. Practice Guide: Personal Injury Ch. 4-A, A. General Considerations.
Rutter, Cal. Practice Guide: Personal Injury Ch. 6-B, B. Overview of Selected Discovery Procedures.

§ 2031.030. Form and content of demand

(a)(1) A party demanding inspection, copying, testing, or sampling shall number each set of demands consecutively.

(2) A party demanding inspection, copying, testing, or sampling of electronically stored information may specify the form or forms in which each type of electronically stored information is to be produced.

(b) In the first paragraph immediately below the title of the case, there shall appear the identity of the demanding party, the set number, and the identity of the responding party.

(c) Each demand in a set shall be separately set forth, identified by number or letter, and shall do all of the following:

(1) Designate the documents, tangible things, land or other property, or electronically stored information to be inspected, copied, tested, or sampled either by specifically describing each individual item or by reasonably particularizing each category of item.

(2) Specify a reasonable time for the inspection, copying, testing, or sampling that is at least 30 days after service of the demand, unless the court for good cause shown has granted leave to specify an earlier date. In an unlawful detainer action or other proceeding under Chapter 4 (commencing with Section 1159) of Title 3 of Part 3, the demand shall specify a reasonable time for the inspection, copying, testing, or sampling that is at least five days after service of the demand, unless the court, for good cause shown, has granted leave to specify an earlier date.

(3) Specify a reasonable place for making the inspection, copying, testing, or sampling, and performing any related activity.

(4) Specify any inspection, copying, testing, sampling, or related activity that is being demanded, as well as the manner in which that activity will be performed, and whether that activity will permanently alter or destroy the item involved. *(Added by Stats.2004, c. 182 (A.B.3081), § 23, operative July 1, 2005. Amended by Stats.2007, c. 113 (A.B.1126), § 10; Stats.2009, c. 5 (A.B.5), § 6, eff. June 29, 2009.)*

Law Revision Commission Comments

Subdivision (a) of Section 2031.030 continues the first sentence of former Section 2031(c) without change.

Subdivision (b) continues the second sentence of former Section 2031(c) without change.

Subdivision (c) continues the third sentence of former Section 2031(c) (including items (1)-(4)) without change. [33 Cal.L.Rev.Comm. Reports 903 (2004)].

Subdivision (c) of Section 2031.030 is amended to improve clarity by separately stating the special time requirement for an unlawful detainer case. The amendment also makes clear that the special time requirement applies to a proceeding for forcible entry (see Section 1159) or forcible detainer (see Section 1160), as well as to an unlawful detainer case. [36 Cal.L.Rev.Comm. Reports 271 (2007)].

Research References

Rutter, Cal. Practice Guide: Civ. Pro. Before Trial Ch. 8H-4, Demand Procedure.
Rutter, Cal. Practice Guide: Civ. Pro. Before Trial Ch. 8H-6, Responding to Demand.
Rutter, Cal. Practice Guide: Civil Trials & Evidence Ch. 1-C, C. Marshalling the Evidence.
Rutter, Cal. Practice Guide: Personal Injury Ch. 6-B, B. Overview of Selected Discovery Procedures.
12 Witkin, California Summary 10th Real Property § 736, Trial.

§ 2031.040. Service of documents

The party making a demand for inspection, copying, testing, or sampling shall serve a copy of the demand on the party to whom it is directed and on all other parties who have appeared in the action. *(Added by Stats.2004, c. 182 (A.B.3081), § 23, operative July 1, 2005. Amended by Stats.2009, c. 5 (A.B.5), § 7, eff. June 29, 2009.)*

Law Revision Commission Comments

Section 2031.040 continues former Section 2031(d) without change. [33 Cal.L.Rev.Comm. Reports 903 (2004)].

Research References

Rutter, Cal. Practice Guide: Civ. Pro. Before Trial Ch. 8H-4, Demand Procedure.

Rutter, Cal. Practice Guide: Personal Injury Ch. 6-B, B. Overview of Selected Discovery Procedures.

§ 2031.050. Supplemental demands; limitations and restrictions; court order

(a) In addition to the demands for inspection, copying, testing, or sampling permitted by this chapter, a party may propound a supplemental demand to inspect, copy, test, or sample any later acquired or discovered documents, tangible things, land or other property, or electronically stored information in the possession, custody, or control of the party on whom the demand is made.

(b) A party may propound a supplemental demand for inspection, copying, testing, or sampling twice before the initial setting of a trial date, and, subject to the time limits on discovery proceedings and motions provided in Chapter 8 (commencing with Section 2024.010), once after the initial setting of a trial date.

(c) Notwithstanding subdivisions (a) and (b), on motion, for good cause shown, the court may grant leave to a party to propound an additional number of supplemental demands for inspection, copying, testing, or sampling. *(Added by Stats.2004, c. 182 (A.B.3081), § 23, operative July 1, 2005. Amended by Stats.2009, c. 5 (A.B.5), § 8, eff. June 29, 2009.)*

Law Revision Commission Comments

Subdivisions (a) and (b) of Section 2031.050 continue the first sentence of former Section 2031(e) without substantive change.

Subdivision (c) continues the second sentence of former Section 2031(e) without substantive change. [33 Cal.L.Rev.Comm. Reports 904 (2004)].

Research References

Rutter, Cal. Practice Guide: Civ. Pro. Before Trial Ch. 8H-3, When Demand for Inspection May be Made.
Rutter, Cal. Practice Guide: Civ. Pro. Before Trial Ch. 8H-4, Demand Procedure.
Rutter, Cal. Practice Guide: Civil Trials & Evidence Ch. 1-A, A. Importance of Statewide and Local Rules of Court.
Rutter, Cal. Practice Guide: Personal Injury Ch. 6-B, B. Overview of Selected Discovery Procedures.

§ 2031.060. Protective order; time to demand; meet and confer; authorized court action; electronically stored information; monetary sanctions

(a) When an inspection, copying, testing, or sampling of documents, tangible things, places, or electronically stored information has been demanded, the party to whom the demand has been directed, and any other party or affected person, may promptly move for a protective order. This motion shall be accompanied by a meet and confer declaration under Section 2016.040.

(b) The court, for good cause shown, may make any order that justice requires to protect any party or other person from unwarranted annoyance, embarrassment, or oppression, or undue burden and expense. This protective order may include, but is not limited to, one or more of the following directions:

(1) That all or some of the items or categories of items in the demand need not be produced or made available at all.

(2) That the time specified in Section 2030.260 to respond to the set of demands, or to a particular item or category in the set, be extended.

(3) That the place of production be other than that specified in the demand.

(4) That the inspection, copying, testing, or sampling be made only on specified terms and conditions.

(5) That a trade secret or other confidential research, development, or commercial information not be disclosed, or be disclosed only to specified persons or only in a specified way.

(6) That the items produced be sealed and thereafter opened only on order of the court.

(c) The party or affected person who seeks a protective order regarding the production, inspection, copying, testing, or sampling of electronically stored information on the basis that the information is from a source that is not reasonably accessible because of undue burden or expense shall bear the burden of demonstrating that the information is from a source that is not reasonably accessible because of undue burden or expense.

(d) If the party or affected person from whom discovery of electronically stored information is sought establishes that the information is from a source that is not reasonably accessible because of undue burden or expense, the court may nonetheless order discovery if the demanding party shows good cause, subject to any limitations imposed under subdivision (f).

(e) If the court finds good cause for the production of electronically stored information from a source that is not reasonably accessible, the court may set conditions for the discovery of the electronically stored information, including allocation of the expense of discovery.

(f) The court shall limit the frequency or extent of discovery of electronically stored information, even from a source that is reasonably accessible, if the court determines that any of the following conditions exist:

(1) It is possible to obtain the information from some other source that is more convenient, less burdensome, or less expensive.

(2) The discovery sought is unreasonably cumulative or duplicative.

(3) The party seeking discovery has had ample opportunity by discovery in the action to obtain the information sought.

(4) The likely burden or expense of the proposed discovery outweighs the likely benefit, taking into account the amount in controversy, the resources of the parties, the importance of the issues in the litigation, and the importance of the requested discovery in resolving the issues.

(g) If the motion for a protective order is denied in whole or in part, the court may order that the party to whom the demand was directed provide or permit the discovery against which protection was sought on terms and conditions that are just.

(h) Except as provided in subdivision (i), the court shall impose a monetary sanction under Chapter 7 (commencing with Section 2023.010) against any party, person, or attorney who unsuccessfully makes or opposes a motion for a protective order, unless it finds that the one subject to the sanction acted with substantial justification or that other circumstances make the imposition of the sanction unjust.

(i)(1) Notwithstanding subdivision (h), absent exceptional circumstances, the court shall not impose sanctions on a party or any attorney of a party for failure to provide electronically stored information that has been lost, damaged, altered, or overwritten as the result of the routine, good faith operation of an electronic information system.

(2) This subdivision shall not be construed to alter any obligation to preserve discoverable information. *(Added by Stats.2004, c. 182 (A.B.3081), § 23, operative July 1, 2005. Amended by Stats.2009, c. 5 (A.B.5), § 9, eff. June 29, 2009.)*

Law Revision Commission Comments

Subdivision (a) of Section 2031.060 continues the first paragraph of former Section 2031(f) without substantive change.

Subdivision (b) continues the second paragraph of former Section 2031(f) (including items (1)-(6)) without change, except to conform the cross-reference.

Subdivision (c) continues the next-to-last paragraph of former Section 2031(f) without change.

Subdivision (d) continues the last paragraph of former Section 2031(f) without change, except to conform the cross-reference. [33 Cal.L.Rev. Comm. Reports 904 (2004)].

Research References

Rutter, Cal. Practice Guide: Civ. Pro. Before Trial Ch. 8A-7, Duty to Preserve Evidence Before Discovery Request?

Rutter, Cal. Practice Guide: Civ. Pro. Before Trial Ch. 8H-4, Demand Procedure.

Rutter, Cal. Practice Guide: Civ. Pro. Before Trial Ch. 8H-5, Protective Orders.

Rutter, Cal. Practice Guide: Civ. Pro. Before Trial Ch. 8H-6, Responding to Demand.

Rutter, Cal. Practice Guide: Civ. Pro. Before Trial Ch. 8H-8, Enforcing Demand.

Rutter, Cal. Practice Guide: Family Law Ch. 6-A, A. Child Support.

Rutter, Cal. Practice Guide: Insurance Litigation Ch. 15-G, G. Discovery.

Rutter, Cal. Practice Guide: Personal Injury Ch. 6-B, B. Overview of Selected Discovery Procedures.

Rutter, Cal. Practice Guide: Personal Injury Ch. 8-B, B. After Trial Date Set (Three to Four Months Before Trial).

ARTICLE 2.   RESPONSE TO INSPECTION DEMAND

Section

§ 2031.210.   Content and form of response

(a) The party to whom a demand for inspection, copying, testing, or sampling has been directed shall respond separately to each item or category of item by any of the following:

(1) A statement that the party will comply with the particular demand for inspection, copying, testing, or sampling by the date set for the inspection, copying, testing, or sampling pursuant to paragraph (2) of subdivision (c) of Section 2031.030 and any related activities.

(2) A representation that the party lacks the ability to comply with the demand for inspection, copying, testing, or sampling of a particular item or category of item.

(3) An objection to the particular demand for inspection, copying, testing, or sampling.

(b) In the first paragraph of the response immediately below the title of the case, there shall appear the identity of the responding party, the set number, and the identity of the demanding party.

(c) Each statement of compliance, each representation, and each objection in the response shall bear the same number and be in the same sequence as the corresponding item or category in the demand, but the text of that item or category need not be repeated.

(d) If a party objects to the discovery of electronically stored information on the grounds that it is from a source that is not reasonably accessible because of undue burden or expense and that the responding party will not search the source in the absence of an agreement with the demanding party or court order, the responding party shall identify in its response the types or categories of sources of electronically stored information that it asserts are not reasonably accessible. By objecting and identifying information of a type or category of source or sources that are not reasonably accessible, the responding party preserves any objections it may have relating to that electronically stored information. *(Added by Stats.2004, c. 182 (A.B.3081), § 23, operative July 1, 2005. Amended by Stats.2007, c. 738 (A.B.1248), § 7; Stats.2009, c. 5 (A.B.5), § 10, eff. June 29, 2009.)*

Law Revision Commission Comments

Subdivision (a) of Section 2031.210 continues the first paragraph of former Section 2031(g) without substantive change.

Subdivision (b) continues the first sentence of the second paragraph of former Section 2031(g) without change.

Subdivision (c) continues the second sentence of the second paragraph of former Section 2031(g) without change. [33 Cal.L.Rev.Comm. Reports 906 (2004)].

Research References

Rutter, Cal. Practice Guide: Civ. Pro. Before Trial Ch. 8H-6, Responding to Demand.

Rutter, Cal. Practice Guide: Personal Injury Ch. 6-B, B. Overview of Selected Discovery Procedures.

Rutter, Cal. Practice Guide: Personal Injury Ch. 8-B, B. After Trial Date Set (Three to Four Months Before Trial).

§ 2031.220.   Statement of compliance in full or in part

A statement that the party to whom a demand for inspection, copying, testing, or sampling has been directed will comply with the particular demand shall state that the production, inspection, copying, testing, or sampling, and related activity demanded, will be allowed either in whole or in part, and that all documents or things in the demanded category that are in the possession, custody, or control of that party and to which no objection is being made will be included in the production. *(Added by Stats.2004, c. 182 (A.B.3081), § 23, operative July 1, 2005. Amended by Stats.2009, c. 5 (A.B.5), § 11, eff. June 29, 2009.)*

Law Revision Commission Comments

Section 2031.220 continues the first paragraph of former Section 2031(g)(1) without change. [33 Cal.L.Rev.Comm. Reports 907 (2004)].

Research References

Rutter, Cal. Practice Guide: Civ. Pro. Before Trial Ch. 8H-6, Responding to Demand.

Rutter, Cal. Practice Guide: Personal Injury Ch. 6-B, B. Overview of Selected Discovery Procedures.

§ 2031.230.   Statement of inability to comply; contents

A representation of inability to comply with the particular demand for inspection, copying, testing, or sampling shall affirm that a diligent search and a reasonable inquiry has been made in an effort to comply with that demand. This statement shall also specify whether the inability to comply is because the particular item or category has never existed, has been destroyed, has been lost, misplaced, or stolen, or has never been, or is no longer, in the possession, custody, or control of the responding party. The statement shall set forth the name and address of any natural person or organization known or believed by that party to have possession, custody, or control of that item or category of item. *(Added by Stats.2004, c. 182 (A.B.3081), § 23, operative July 1, 2005. Amended by Stats.2009, c. 5 (A.B.5), § 12, eff. June 29, 2009.)*

Law Revision Commission Comments

Section 2031.230 continues former Section 2031(g)(2) without change. [33 Cal.L.Rev.Comm. Reports 907 (2004)].

Research References

Rutter, Cal. Practice Guide: Civ. Pro. Before Trial Ch. 8H-6, Responding to Demand.

Rutter, Cal. Practice Guide: Personal Injury Ch. 6-B, B. Overview of Selected Discovery Procedures.

§ 2031.240.   Partial objection to demand; statement of compliance or representation of inability to comply; privilege log

(a) If only part of an item or category of item in a demand for inspection, copying, testing, or sampling is objectionable, the response shall contain a statement of compliance, or a representation of inability to comply with respect to the remainder of that item or category.

(b) If the responding party objects to the demand for inspection, copying, testing, or sampling of an item or category of item, the response shall do both of the following:

(1) Identify with particularity any document, tangible thing, land, or electronically stored information falling within any category of item in the demand to which an objection is being made.

(2) Set forth clearly the extent of, and the specific ground for, the objection. If an objection is based on a claim of privilege, the particular privilege invoked shall be stated. If an objection is based on a claim that the information sought is protected work product under Chapter 4 (commencing with Section 2018.010), that claim shall be expressly asserted.

(c)(1) If an objection is based on a claim of privilege or a claim that the information sought is protected work product, the response shall provide sufficient factual information for other parties to evaluate the merits of that claim, including, if necessary, a privilege log.

(2) It is the intent of the Legislature to codify the concept of a privilege log as that term is used in California case law. Nothing in this subdivision shall be construed to constitute a substantive change in case law. *(Added by Stats.2004, c. 182 (A.B.3081), § 23, operative July 1, 2005. Amended by Stats.2009, c. 5 (A.B.5), § 13, eff. June 29, 2009; Stats.2012, c. 232 (A.B.1354), § 1.)*

Law Revision Commission Comments

Subdivision (a) of Section 2031.240 continues the first sentence of former Section 2031(g)(3) without change.

Subdivision (b) continues the second, third, and fourth sentences of former Section 2031(g)(3) without substantive change. [33 Cal.L.Rev.Comm. Reports 907 (2004)].

Research References

Rutter, Cal. Practice Guide: Civ. Pro. Before Trial Ch. 8H-6, Responding to Demand.

Rutter, Cal. Practice Guide: Civ. Pro. Before Trial Ch. 8H-8, Enforcing Demand.

California Practice Guide: Employment Litigation Ch. 19-F, F. Discovery.

Rutter, Cal. Practice Guide: Personal Injury Ch. 6-B, B. Overview of Selected Discovery Procedures.

Rutter, Cal. Practice Guide: Personal Injury Ch. 8-B, B. After Trial Date Set (Three to Four Months Before Trial).

§ 2031.250. Signatures; oath; officers or agents; responses with objections

(a) The party to whom the demand for inspection, copying, testing, or sampling is directed shall sign the response under oath unless the response contains only objections.

(b) If that party is a public or private corporation or a partnership or association or governmental agency, one of its officers or agents shall sign the response under oath on behalf of that party. If the officer or agent signing the response on behalf of that party is an attorney acting in that capacity for a party, that party waives any lawyer-client privilege and any protection for work product under Chapter 4 (commencing with Section 2018.010) during any subsequent discovery from that attorney concerning the identity of the sources of the information contained in the response.

(c) The attorney for the responding party shall sign any responses that contain an objection. *(Added by Stats.2004, c. 182 (A.B.3081), § 23, operative July 1, 2005. Amended by Stats.2009, c. 5 (A.B.5), § 14, eff. June 29, 2009.)*

Law Revision Commission Comments

Subdivision (a) of Section 2031.250 continues the first sentence of former Section 2031(h) without change.

Subdivision (b) continues the second and third sentences of former Section 2031(h) without change, except to conform the cross-reference.

Subdivision (c) continues the fourth sentence of former Section 2031(h) without change. [33 Cal.L.Rev.Comm. Reports 908 (2004)].

Research References

Rutter, Cal. Practice Guide: Civ. Pro. Before Trial Ch. 8H-6, Responding to Demand.

Rutter, Cal. Practice Guide: Personal Injury Ch. 6-B, B. Overview of Selected Discovery Procedures.

§ 2031.260. Time to respond

(a) Within 30 days after service of a demand for inspection, copying, testing, or sampling, the party to whom the demand is directed shall serve the original of the response to it on the party making the demand, and a copy of the response on all other parties who have appeared in the action, unless on motion of the party making the demand, the court has shortened the time for response, or unless on motion of the party to whom the demand has been directed, the court has extended the time for response.

(b) Notwithstanding subdivision (a), in an unlawful detainer action or other proceeding under Chapter 4 (commencing with Section 1159) of Title 3 of Part 3, the party to whom a demand for inspection, copying, testing, or sampling is directed shall have at least five days from the date of service of the demand to respond, unless on motion of the party making the demand, the court has shortened the time for the response, or unless on motion of the party to whom the demand has been directed, the court has extended the time for response. *(Added by Stats.2004, c. 182 (A.B.3081), § 23, operative July 1, 2005. Amended by Stats.2007, c. 113 (A.B.1126), § 11; Stats.2009, c. 5 (A.B.5), § 15, eff. June 29, 2009.)*

Law Revision Commission Comments

Section 2031.260 continues former Section 2031(i) without change. [33 Cal.L.Rev.Comm. Reports 909 (2004)].

Section 2031.260 is amended to improve clarity by separately stating the special deadline for an unlawful detainer case. The amendment also makes clear that the special deadline applies to a proceeding for forcible entry (see Section 1159) or forcible detainer (see Section 1160), as well as to an unlawful detainer case. In addition, the amendment eliminates an

ambiguity by clearly permitting a court to extend, as well as shorten, the time to respond to an inspection demand in an unlawful detainer case.

Section 2031.260 is further amended to make stylistic revisions. [36 Cal.L.Rev.Comm. Reports 271 (2007)].

Research References

Rutter, Cal. Practice Guide: Civ. Pro. Before Trial Ch. 8H-4, Demand Procedure.

Rutter, Cal. Practice Guide: Civ. Pro. Before Trial Ch. 8H-6, Responding to Demand.

Rutter, Cal. Practice Guide: Civ. Pro. Before Trial Ch. 9(I)-F, F. Ex Parte Motions.

Rutter, Cal. Practice Guide: Enforcing Judgments/Debts Ch. 6G-3, Inspection Demand to Judgment Debtor.

Rutter, Cal. Practice Guide: Personal Injury Ch. 6-B, B. Overview of Selected Discovery Procedures.

Rutter, Cal. Practice Guide: Personal Injury Ch. 8-B, B. After Trial Date Set (Three to Four Months Before Trial).

12 Witkin, California Summary 10th Real Property § 736, Trial.

§ 2031.270. Extension of time to respond; agreement of the parties

(a) The party demanding inspection, copying, testing, or sampling and the responding party may agree to extend the date for the inspection, copying, testing, or sampling or the time for service of a response to a set of demands, or to particular items or categories of items in a set, to a date or dates beyond those provided in Sections 2031.030, 2031.210, 2031.260, and 2031.280.

(b) This agreement may be informal, but it shall be confirmed in a writing that specifies the extended date for inspection, copying, testing, or sampling, or for the service of a response.

(c) Unless this agreement expressly states otherwise, it is effective to preserve to the responding party the right to respond to any item or category of item in the demand to which the agreement applies in any manner specified in Sections 2031.210, 2031.220, 2031.230, 2031.240, and 2031.280. *(Added by Stats. 2004, c. 182 (A.B.3081), § 23, operative July 1, 2005. Amended by Stats.2007, c. 738 (A.B.1248), § 8; Stats.2009, c. 5 (A.B.5), § 16, eff. June 29, 2009.)*

Law Revision Commission Comments

Subdivision (a) of Section 2031.270 continues the first sentence of former Section 2031(j) without change, except to conform the cross-reference.

Subdivision (b) continues the second sentence of former Section 2031(j) without change.

Subdivision (c) continues the third sentence of former Section 2031(j) without change, except to conform the cross-reference. [33 Cal.L.Rev. Comm. Reports 909 (2004)].

Research References

Rutter, Cal. Practice Guide: Civ. Pro. Before Trial Ch. 8H-6, Responding to Demand.

Rutter, Cal. Practice Guide: Personal Injury Ch. 8-B, B. After Trial Date Set (Three to Four Months Before Trial).

§ 2031.280. Production of documents; form; data translation

(a) Any documents produced in response to a demand for inspection, copying, testing, or sampling shall either be produced as they are kept in the usual course of business, or be organized and labeled to correspond with the categories in the demand.

(b) The documents shall be produced on the date specified in the demand pursuant to paragraph (2) of subdivision (c) of Section 2031.030, unless an objection has been made to that date. If the date for inspection has been extended pursuant to Section 2031.270, the documents shall be produced on the date agreed to pursuant to that section.

(c) If a party responding to a demand for production of electronically stored information objects to a specified form for producing the information, or if no form is specified in the demand, the responding party shall state in its response the form in which it intends to produce each type of information.

(d) Unless the parties otherwise agree or the court otherwise orders, the following shall apply:

(1) If a demand for production does not specify a form or forms for producing a type of electronically stored information, the responding party shall produce the information in the form or forms in which it is ordinarily maintained or in a form that is reasonably usable.

(2) A party need not produce the same electronically stored information in more than one form.

(e) If necessary, the responding party at the reasonable expense of the demanding party shall, through detection devices, translate any data compilations included in the demand into reasonably usable form. *(Added by Stats.2004, c. 182 (A.B.3081), § 23, operative July 1, 2005. Amended by Stats.2007, c. 738 (A.B.1248), § 9; Stats.2009, c. 5 (A.B.5), § 17, eff. June 29, 2009.)*

Law Revision Commission Comments

Subdivision (a) of Section 2031.280 continues the first sentence of the second paragraph of former Section 2031(g)(1) without substantive change.

Subdivision (b) continues the second sentence of the second paragraph of former Section 2031(g)(1) without change. [33 Cal.L.Rev.Comm. Reports 910 (2004)].

Research References

Rutter, Cal. Practice Guide: Civ. Pro. Before Trial Ch. 8E-5, Subpoena Not Necessary for Party or "Party-Affiliated" Witnesses.
Rutter, Cal. Practice Guide: Civ. Pro. Before Trial Ch. 8H-4, Demand Procedure.
Rutter, Cal. Practice Guide: Civ. Pro. Before Trial Ch. 8H-6, Responding to Demand.
Rutter, Cal. Practice Guide: Personal Injury Ch. 6-B, B. Overview of Selected Discovery Procedures.

§ 2031.285. Electronically stored information; privileged information or attorney work product

(a) If electronically stored information produced in discovery is subject to a claim of privilege or of protection as attorney work product, the party making the claim may notify any party that received the information of the claim and the basis for the claim.

(b) After being notified of a claim of privilege or of protection under subdivision (a), a party that received the information shall immediately sequester the information and either return the specified information and any copies that may exist or present the information to the court conditionally under seal for a determination of the claim.

(c)(1) Prior to the resolution of the motion brought under subdivision (d), a party shall be precluded from using or disclosing the specified information until the claim of privilege is resolved.

(2) A party who received and disclosed the information before being notified of a claim of privilege or of protection under subdivision (a) shall, after that notification, immediately take reasonable steps to retrieve the information.

(d)(1) If the receiving party contests the legitimacy of a claim of privilege or protection, he or she may seek a determination of the claim from the court by making a motion within 30 days of receiving the claim and presenting the information to the court conditionally under seal.

(2) Until the legitimacy of the claim of privilege or protection is resolved, the receiving party shall preserve the information and keep it confidential and shall be precluded from using the information in any manner. *(Added by Stats.2009, c. 5 (A.B.5), § 18, eff. June 29, 2009.)*

Research References

Rutter, Cal. Practice Guide: Civ. Pro. Before Trial Ch. 8E-6, Subpoena to Nonparty Deponent or Business Records Custodian.
Rutter, Cal. Practice Guide: Civ. Pro. Before Trial Ch. 8H-7, "Clawback" Procedure Where Privileged Information Produced in Esi.

§ 2031.290. Original demand, response and service documents; custody of documents; record retention

(a) The demand for inspection, copying, testing, or sampling, and the response to it, shall not be filed with the court.

(b) The party demanding an inspection, copying, testing, or sampling shall retain both the original of the demand, with the original proof of service affixed to it, and the original of the sworn response until six months after final disposition of the action. At that time, both originals may be destroyed, unless the court, on motion of any party and for good cause shown, orders that the originals be preserved for a longer period. *(Added by Stats.2004, c. 182 (A.B.3081), § 23, operative July 1, 2005. Amended by Stats.2009, c. 5 (A.B.5), § 19, eff. June 29, 2009.)*

Law Revision Commission Comments

Subdivision (a) of Section 2031.290 continues the first sentence of former Section 2031(k) without change.

Subdivision (b) continues the second and third sentences of former Section 2031(k) without change. [33 Cal.L.Rev.Comm. Reports 910 (2004)].

Research References

Rutter, Cal. Practice Guide: Civ. Pro. Before Trial Ch. 8H-6, Responding to Demand.
Rutter, Cal. Practice Guide: Personal Injury Ch. 6-B, B. Overview of Selected Discovery Procedures.

§ 2031.300. Untimely responses; waiver; motion to compel response; monetary sanctions

If a party to whom a demand for inspection, copying, testing, or sampling is directed fails to serve a timely response to it, the following rules shall apply:

(a) The party to whom the demand for inspection, copying, testing, or sampling is directed waives any objection to the demand, including one based on privilege or on the protection for work product under Chapter 4 (commencing with Section 2018.010). The court, on motion, may relieve that party from this waiver on its determination that both of the following conditions are satisfied:

(1) The party has subsequently served a response that is in substantial compliance with Sections 2031.210, 2031.220, 2031.230, 2031.240, and 2031.280.

(2) The party's failure to serve a timely response was the result of mistake, inadvertence, or excusable neglect.

(b) The party making the demand may move for an order compelling response to the demand.

(c) Except as provided in subdivision (d), the court shall impose a monetary sanction under Chapter 7 (commencing with Section 2023.010) against any party, person, or attorney who unsuccessfully makes or opposes a motion to compel a response to a demand for inspection, copying, testing, or sampling, unless it finds that the one subject to the sanction acted with substantial justification or that other circumstances make the imposition of the sanction unjust. If a party then fails to obey the order compelling a response, the court may make those orders that are just, including the imposition of an issue sanction, an evidence sanction, or a terminating sanction under Chapter 7 (commencing with Section 2023.010). In lieu of or in addition to this sanction, the court may impose a monetary sanction under Chapter 7 (commencing with Section 2023.010).

(d)(1) Notwithstanding subdivision (c), absent exceptional circumstances, the court shall not impose sanctions on a party or any attorney of a party for failure to provide electronically stored information that has been lost, damaged, altered, or overwritten as a result of the routine, good faith operation of an electronic information system.

(2) This subdivision shall not be construed to alter any obligation to preserve discoverable information. *(Added by Stats.2004, c. 182 (A.B.3081), § 23, operative July 1, 2005. Amended by Stats.2005, c. 22 (S.B.1108), § 23; Stats.2009, c. 5 (A.B.5), § 20, eff. June 29, 2009.)*

Law Revision Commission Comments

The introductory clause and subdivision (a) of Section 2031.300 continue the first paragraph of former Section 2031(*l*) without substantive change.

Subdivision (b) continues the first sentence of the second paragraph of former Section 2031(*l*) without change.

Subdivision (c) continues the second, third, and fourth sentences of the second paragraph of former Section 2030(*l*) without change, except to conform the cross-references. [33 Cal.L.Rev.Comm. Reports 911 (2004)].

Research References

Rutter, Cal. Practice Guide: Civ. Pro. Before Trial Ch. 8A-3, Civil Discovery Act.
Rutter, Cal. Practice Guide: Civ. Pro. Before Trial Ch. 8C-3, "Not Privileged".
Rutter, Cal. Practice Guide: Civ. Pro. Before Trial Ch. 8H-5, Protective Orders.
Rutter, Cal. Practice Guide: Civ. Pro. Before Trial Ch. 8H-6, Responding to Demand.
Rutter, Cal. Practice Guide: Civ. Pro. Before Trial Ch. 8H-8, Enforcing Demand.
Rutter, Cal. Practice Guide: Civil Trials & Evidence Ch. 8E-A, A. Privileges.
Rutter, Cal. Practice Guide: Enforcing Judgments/Debts Ch. 6G-3, Inspection Demand to Judgment Debtor.
Rutter, Cal. Practice Guide: Family Law Ch. 6-A, A. Child Support.
Rutter, Cal. Practice Guide: Insurance Litigation Ch. 15-G, G. Discovery.
Rutter, Cal. Practice Guide: Personal Injury Ch. 6-B, B. Overview of Selected Discovery Procedures.
Rutter, Cal. Practice Guide: Personal Injury Ch. 8-B, B. After Trial Date Set (Three to Four Months Before Trial).
Rutter, Cal. Practice Guide: Prof. Responsibility Ch. 7-C, C. Attorney-Client Privilege.

§ 2031.310. Motion to compel further response; form and content; time to bring motion; electronically stored information; monetary sanctions; failure to obey court order

(a) On receipt of a response to a demand for inspection, copying, testing, or sampling, the demanding party may move for an order compelling further response to the demand if the demanding party deems that any of the following apply:

(1) A statement of compliance with the demand is incomplete.

(2) A representation of inability to comply is inadequate, incomplete, or evasive.

(3) An objection in the response is without merit or too general.

(b) A motion under subdivision (a) shall comply with both of the following:

(1) The motion shall set forth specific facts showing good cause justifying the discovery sought by the demand.

(2) The motion shall be accompanied by a meet and confer declaration under Section 2016.040.

(c) Unless notice of this motion is given within 45 days of the service of the verified response, or any supplemental verified response, or on or before any specific later date to which the demanding party and the responding party have agreed in writing, the demanding party waives any right to compel a further response to the demand.

(d) In a motion under subdivision (a) relating to the production of electronically stored information, the party or affected person objecting to or opposing the production, inspection, copying, testing, or sampling of electronically stored information on the basis that the information is from a source that is not reasonably accessible because of the undue burden or expense shall bear the burden of demonstrating that the information is from a source that is not reasonably accessible because of undue burden or expense.

(e) If the party or affected person from whom discovery of electronically stored information is sought establishes that the information is from a source that is not reasonably accessible because of the undue burden or expense, the court may nonetheless order discovery if the demanding party shows good cause, subject to any limitations imposed under subdivision (g).

(f) If the court finds good cause for the production of electronically stored information from a source that is not reasonably accessible, the court may set conditions for the discovery of the electronically stored information, including allocation of the expense of discovery.

(g) The court shall limit the frequency or extent of discovery of electronically stored information, even from a source that is reasonably accessible, if the court determines that any of the following conditions exists:

(1) It is possible to obtain the information from some other source that is more convenient, less burdensome, or less expensive.

(2) The discovery sought is unreasonably cumulative or duplicative.

(3) The party seeking discovery has had ample opportunity by discovery in the action to obtain the information sought.

(4) The likely burden or expense of the proposed discovery outweighs the likely benefit, taking into account the amount in controversy, the resources of the parties, the importance of the issues in the litigation, and the importance of the requested discovery in resolving the issues.

(h) Except as provided in subdivision (j), the court shall impose a monetary sanction under Chapter 7 (commencing with Section 2023.010) against any party, person, or attorney who unsuccessfully makes or opposes a motion to compel further response to a demand, unless it finds that the one subject to the sanction acted with substantial justification or that other circumstances make the imposition of the sanction unjust.

(i) Except as provided in subdivision (j), if a party fails to obey an order compelling further response, the court may make those orders that are just, including the imposition of an issue sanction, an evidence sanction, or a terminating sanction under Chapter 7 (commencing with Section 2023.010). In lieu of, or in addition to, that sanction, the court may impose a monetary sanction under Chapter 7 (commencing with Section 2023.010).

(j)(1) Notwithstanding subdivisions (h) and (i), absent exceptional circumstances, the court shall not impose sanctions on a party or any attorney of a party for failure to provide electronically stored information that has been lost, damaged, altered, or overwritten as the result of the routine, good faith operation of an electronic information system.

(2) This subdivision shall not be construed to alter any obligation to preserve discoverable information. *(Added by Stats.2004, c. 182 (A.B.3081), § 23, operative July 1, 2005. Amended by Stats.2009, c. 5 (A.B.5), § 21, eff. June 29, 2009; Stats.2013, c. 18 (A.B.1183), § 2.)*

Subdivision (a) of Section 2031.310 continues the first sentence of former Section 2031(m) without substantive change.

Subdivision (b) continues the second sentence of former Section 2031(m) without substantive change.

Subdivision (c) continues the second paragraph of former Section 2031(m) without change.

Subdivision (d) continues the third paragraph of former Section 2031(m) without change, except to conform the cross-reference.

Subdivision (e) continues the fourth paragraph of former Section 2031(m) without change, except to conform the cross-references. [33 Cal.L.Rev.Comm. Reports 912 (2004)].

Research References

Rutter, Cal. Practice Guide: Civ. Pro. Before Trial Ch. 8H-5, Protective Orders.
Rutter, Cal. Practice Guide: Civ. Pro. Before Trial Ch. 8H-6, Responding to Demand.
Rutter, Cal. Practice Guide: Civ. Pro. Before Trial Ch. 8H-8, Enforcing Demand.
Rutter, Cal. Practice Guide: Civ. Pro. Before Trial Ch. 9(I)-C, C. Opposing the Motion-And Rebutting the Opposition.
Rutter, Cal. Practice Guide: Enforcing Judgments/Debts Ch. 6G-3, Inspection Demand to Judgment Debtor.
Rutter, Cal. Practice Guide: Family Law Ch. 6-A, A. Child Support.
Rutter, Cal. Practice Guide: Personal Injury Ch. 4-G, G. Concluding and Enforcing Settlement.
Rutter, Cal. Practice Guide: Personal Injury Ch. 6-A, A. Scope of Discovery and Limitations.
Rutter, Cal. Practice Guide: Personal Injury Ch. 8-B, B. After Trial Date Set (Three to Four Months Before Trial).
Rutter, Cal. Practice Guide: Personal Injury Ch. 6-A, Outline a.

§ 2031.320. Failure to produce items for inspection, copying, testing, or sampling; order compelling compliance; monetary sanctions; failure to obey court order

(a) If a party filing a response to a demand for inspection, copying, testing, or sampling under Sections 2031.210, 2031.220, 2031.230, 2031.240, and 2031.280 thereafter fails to permit the inspection, copying, testing, or sampling in accordance with that party's statement of compliance, the demanding party may move for an order compelling compliance.

(b) Except as provided in subdivision (d), the court shall impose a monetary sanction under Chapter 7 (commencing with Section 2023.010) against any party, person, or attorney who unsuccessfully makes or opposes a motion to compel compliance with a demand, unless it finds that the one subject to the sanction acted with substantial justification or that other circumstances make the imposition of the sanction unjust.

(c) Except as provided in subdivision (d), if a party then fails to obey an order compelling inspection, copying, testing, or sampling, the court may make those orders that are just, including the imposition of an issue sanction, an evidence sanction, or a terminating sanction under Chapter 7 (commencing with Section 2023.010). In lieu of or in addition to that sanction, the court may impose a monetary sanction under Chapter 7 (commencing with Section 2023.010).

(d)(1) Notwithstanding subdivisions (b) and (c), absent exceptional circumstances, the court shall not impose sanctions on a party or any attorney of a party for failure to provide electronically stored information that has been lost, damaged, altered, or overwritten as the result of the routine, good faith operation of an electronic information system.

(2) This subdivision shall not be construed to alter any obligation to preserve discoverable information. (Added by Stats.2004, c. 182 (A.B.3081), § 23, operative July 1, 2005. Amended by Stats.2009, c. 5 (A.B.5), § 22, eff. June 29, 2009.)

Subdivision (a) of Section 2031.320 continues the first paragraph of former Section 2031(n) without change, except to conform the cross-reference.

Subdivision (b) continues the second paragraph of former Section 2031(n) without change, except to conform the cross-reference.

Subdivision (c) continues the third paragraph of former Section 2031(n) without change, except to conform the cross-references. [33 Cal.L.Rev. Comm. Reports 913 (2004)].

Research References

Rutter, Cal. Practice Guide: Civ. Pro. Before Trial Ch. 8F-8, Sanctions in Enforcing Discovery.
Rutter, Cal. Practice Guide: Civ. Pro. Before Trial Ch. 8H-8, Enforcing Demand.
Rutter, Cal. Practice Guide: Family Law Ch. 6-A, A. Child Support.
Rutter, Cal. Practice Guide: Personal Injury Ch. 8-B, B. After Trial Date Set (Three to Four Months Before Trial).

ARTICLE 3.　INSPECTION AND PRODUCTION OF DOCUMENTS AND OTHER PROPERTY IN SPECIFIC CONTEXTS

Section
2031.510.　Land patented or granted by the state; time to disclose.

§ 2031.510. Land patented or granted by the state; time to disclose

(a) In any action, regardless of who is the moving party, where the boundary of land patented or otherwise granted by the state is in dispute, or the validity of any state patent or grant dated before 1950 is in dispute, all parties shall have the duty to disclose to all opposing parties all nonprivileged relevant written evidence then known and available, including evidence against interest, relating to the above issues.

(b) This evidence shall be disclosed within 120 days after the filing with the court of proof of service upon all named defendants. Thereafter, the parties shall have the continuing duty to make all subsequently discovered relevant and nonprivileged written evidence available to the opposing parties. (Added by Stats.2004, c. 182 (A.B.3081), § 23, operative July 1, 2005.)

Subdivision (a) of Section 2031.510 continues the first sentence of former Section 2031.5 without substantive change.

Subdivision (b) continues the second and third sentences of former Section 2031.5 without change. [33 Cal.L.Rev.Comm. Reports 914 (2004)].

Research References

12 Witkin, California Summary 10th Real Property § 277, Resolving Uncertainties.

CHAPTER 15. PHYSICAL OR MENTAL EXAMINATION

ARTICLE 1.　GENERAL PROVISIONS

Section

2032.010.　Application to paternity blood test statutes;　disclosure of certifying experts in professional negligence actions.

2032.020.　Persons subject to discovery;　restrictions;　qualifications of examining physicians and psychologists.

§ 2032.010.　Application to paternity blood test statutes;　disclosure of certifying experts in professional negligence actions

(a) Nothing in this chapter affects tests under the Uniform Act on Blood Tests to Determine Paternity (Chapter 2 (commencing with Section 7550) of Part 2 of Division 12 of the Family Code).

(b) Nothing in this chapter requires the disclosure of the identity of an expert consulted by an attorney in order to make the certification required in an action for professional negligence under Sections 411.30 and 411.35. *(Added by Stats.2004, c. 182 (A.B.3081), § 23, operative July 1, 2005.)*

Law Revision Commission Comments

Subdivision (a) of Section 2032.010 continues the third sentence of former Section 2032(b) without change, except to replace section with chapter.

Subdivision (b) continues former Section 2032(k) without substantive change. [33 Cal.L.Rev.Comm. Reports 915 (2004)].

Research References

Rutter, Cal. Practice Guide: Civ. Pro. Before Trial Ch. 8A-3, Civil Discovery Act.

Rutter, Cal. Practice Guide: Civ. Pro. Before Trial Ch. 8C-5, Privacy Protection.

Rutter, Cal. Practice Guide: Civ. Pro. Before Trial Ch. 8D-5, Selecting Proper Discovery Tools.

Rutter, Cal. Practice Guide: Civ. Pro. Before Trial Ch. 8I-1, Examinations by Stipulation.

Rutter, Cal. Practice Guide: Civ. Pro. Before Trial Ch. 8I-2, Physical Examination by Demand in Personal Injury Cases.

Rutter, Cal. Practice Guide: Civ. Pro. Before Trial Ch. 8L-1, Limitations on Existing Discovery Procedures.

California Practice Guide: Employment Litigation Ch. 17-C, C. Extracontractual Compensatory Damages (Tort and Statutory).

1 Witkin Cal. Proc. 5th Attorneys § 585, Physical and Mental Examinations.

2 Witkin Cal. Proc. 5th Courts § 253, Discovery.

11 Witkin, California Summary 10th Husband and Wife § 245, Examination by Vocational Training Counselor.

§ 2032.020.　Persons subject to discovery;　restrictions;　qualifications of examining physicians and psychologists

(a) Any party may obtain discovery, subject to the restrictions set forth in Chapter 5 (commencing with Section 2019.010), by means of a physical or mental examination of (1) a party to the action, (2) an agent of any party, or (3) a natural person in the custody or under the legal control of a party, in any action in which the mental or physical condition (including the blood group) of that party or other person is in controversy in the action.

(b) A physical examination conducted under this chapter shall be performed only by a licensed physician or other appropriate licensed health care practitioner.

(c) A mental examination conducted under this chapter shall be performed only by a licensed physician, or by a licensed clinical psychologist who holds a doctoral degree in psychology and has had at least five years of postgraduate experience in the diagnosis of emotional and mental disorders. *(Added by Stats. 2004, c. 182 (A.B.3081), § 23, operative July 1, 2005.)*

Law Revision Commission Comments

Subdivision (a) of Section 2032.020 continues former Section 2032(a) without change, except to conform the cross-reference.

Subdivision (b) continues the first sentence of former Section 2032(b) without change, except to replace section with chapter.

Subdivision (c) continues the second sentence of former Section 2032(b) without change, except to replace section with chapter. [33 Cal.L.Rev.Comm. Reports 915 (2004)].

Research References

Rutter, Cal. Practice Guide: Civ. Pro. Before Trial Ch. 8I-2, Physical Examination by Demand in Personal Injury Cases.

Rutter, Cal. Practice Guide: Civ. Pro. Before Trial Ch. 8I-3, Examination Upon Court Order.

Rutter, Cal. Practice Guide: Civil Trials & Evidence Ch. 8E-A, A. Privileges.

Rutter, Cal. Practice Guide: Civil Trials & Evidence Ch. 8E-C, C. Right of Privacy.

California Practice Guide: Employment Litigation Ch. 10-F, F. Discovery Issues.

California Practice Guide: Employment Litigation Ch. 19-F, F. Discovery.

Rutter, Cal. Practice Guide: Personal Injury Ch. 3-C, C. Specific Items of Compensatory Damages.

Rutter, Cal. Practice Guide: Personal Injury Ch. 4-C, C. Effective Settlement Negotiations.

Rutter, Cal. Practice Guide: Personal Injury Ch. 6-B, B. Overview of Selected Discovery Procedures.

Rutter, Cal. Practice Guide: Personal Injury Ch. 6-C, C. Physical and Mental Examinations (CCP § 2032.020 et seq.).

Rutter, Cal. Practice Guide: Personal Injury Ch. 6-E, E. Special Discovery Rules and Procedures in Limited Civil Cases.

10 Witkin, California Summary 10th Parent and Child § 284, Trial.

ARTICLE 2.　PHYSICAL EXAMINATION OF PERSONAL INJURY PLAINTIFF

Section

2032.210.　Definitions.

2032.220.　Number of examinations;　conditions upon examination;　time to demand;　form and content of demand;　service upon parties.

2032.230.　Statement of compliance, partial compliance or refusal to comply;　time to respond;　shortened or extended time by court.

2032.240.　Untimely response to demand;　waiver;　order compelling response and compliance;　monetary sanctions;　failure to obey court order.

2032.250.　Motion to compel compliance;　meet and confer declaration;　monetary sanctions.

2032.260.　Original demand, response and service documents;　custody;　record retention.

§ 2032.210.　Definitions

As used in this article, "plaintiff" includes a cross-complainant, and "defendant" includes a cross-defendant. *(Added by Stats.2004, c. 182 (A.B.3081), § 23, operative July 1, 2005.)*

Law Revision Commission Comments

Section 2032.210 continues former Section 2032(c)(1) without substantive change. [33 Cal.L.Rev.Comm. Reports 916 (2004)].

Research References

Rutter, Cal. Practice Guide: Civ. Pro. Before Trial Ch. 8I-2, Physical Examination by Demand in Personal Injury Cases.

§ 2032.220.　Number of examinations;　conditions upon examination;　time to demand;　form and content of demand;　service upon parties

(a) In any case in which a plaintiff is seeking recovery for personal injuries, any defendant may demand one physical examination of the plaintiff, if both of the following conditions are satisfied:

(1) The examination does not include any diagnostic test or procedure that is painful, protracted, or intrusive.

(2) The examination is conducted at a location within 75 miles of the residence of the examinee.

(b) A defendant may make a demand under this article without leave of court after that defendant has been served or has appeared in the action, whichever occurs first.

(c) A demand under subdivision (a) shall specify the time, place, manner, conditions, scope, and nature of the examination, as well as the identity and the specialty, if any, of the physician who will perform the examination.

(d) A physical examination demanded under subdivision (a) shall be scheduled for a date that is at least 30 days after service of the demand. On motion of the party demanding the examination, the court may shorten this time.

(e) The defendant shall serve a copy of the demand under subdivision (a) on the plaintiff and on all other parties who have appeared in the action. *(Added by Stats.2004, c. 182 (A.B.3081), § 23, operative July 1, 2005.)*

Law Revision Commission Comments

Subdivision (a) of Section 2032.220 continues the first sentence of former Section 2032(c)(2) without substantive change.

Subdivision (b) continues the second sentence of former Section 2032(c)(2) without substantive change.

Subdivision (c) continues the third sentence of former Section 2032(c)(2) without substantive change.

Subdivision (d) continues former Section 2032(c)(3) without substantive change.

Subdivision (e) continues former Section 2032(c)(4) without substantive change. [33 Cal.L.Rev.Comm. Reports 916 (2004)].

Research References

Rutter, Cal. Practice Guide: Civ. Pro. Before Trial Ch. 8B-1, Leave of Court Generally Not Required.

Rutter, Cal. Practice Guide: Civ. Pro. Before Trial Ch. 8I-2, Physical Examination by Demand in Personal Injury Cases.

Rutter, Cal. Practice Guide: Civ. Pro. Before Trial Ch. 8I-3, Examination Upon Court Order.

California Practice Guide: Employment Litigation Ch. 19-F, F. Discovery.

Rutter, Cal. Practice Guide: Personal Injury Ch. 4-C, C. Effective Settlement Negotiations.

Rutter, Cal. Practice Guide: Personal Injury Ch. 6-A, A. Scope of Discovery and Limitations.

Rutter, Cal. Practice Guide: Personal Injury Ch. 6-C, C. Physical and Mental Examinations (CCP § 2032.020 et seq.).

Rutter, Cal. Practice Guide: Personal Injury Ch. 8-B, B. After Trial Date Set (Three to Four Months Before Trial).

Rutter, Cal. Practice Guide: Personal Injury Ch. 8-C, C. Two Months Before Trial.

Rutter, Cal. Practice Guide: Personal Injury Ch. 6-A, Outline a.

§ 2032.230. Statement of compliance, partial compliance or refusal to comply; time to respond; shortened or extended time by court

(a) The plaintiff to whom a demand for a physical examination under this article is directed shall respond to the demand by a written statement that the examinee will comply with the demand as stated, will comply with the demand as specifically modified by the plaintiff, or will refuse, for reasons specified in the response, to submit to the demanded physical examination.

(b) Within 20 days after service of the demand the plaintiff to whom the demand is directed shall serve the original of the response to it on the defendant making the demand, and a copy of the response on all other parties who have appeared in the action. On motion of the defendant making the demand, the court may shorten the time for response. On motion of the

plaintiff to whom the demand is directed, the court may extend the time for response. *(Added by Stats.2004, c. 182 (A.B.3081), § 23, operative July 1, 2005.)*

Law Revision Commission Comments

Subdivision (a) of Section 2032.230 continues the first sentence of former Section 2032(c)(5) without substantive change.

Subdivision (b) continues the second sentence of former Section 2032(c)(5) without substantive change. [33 Cal.L.Rev.Comm. Reports 917 (2004)].

Research References

Rutter, Cal. Practice Guide: Civ. Pro. Before Trial Ch. 8I-2, Physical Examination by Demand in Personal Injury Cases.

Rutter, Cal. Practice Guide: Personal Injury Ch. 6-C, C. Physical and Mental Examinations (CCP § 2032.020 et seq.).

Rutter, Cal. Practice Guide: Personal Injury Ch. 8-B, B. After Trial Date Set (Three to Four Months Before Trial).

§ 2032.240. Untimely response to demand; waiver; order compelling response and compliance; monetary sanctions; failure to obey court order

(a) If a plaintiff to whom a demand for a physical examination under this article is directed fails to serve a timely response to it, that plaintiff waives any objection to the demand. The court, on motion, may relieve that plaintiff from this waiver on its determination that both of the following conditions are satisfied:

(1) The plaintiff has subsequently served a response that is in substantial compliance with Section 2032.230.

(2) The plaintiff's failure to serve a timely response was the result of mistake, inadvertence, or excusable neglect.

(b) The defendant may move for an order compelling response and compliance with a demand for a physical examination.

(c) The court shall impose a monetary sanction under Chapter 7 (commencing with Section 2023.010) against any party, person, or attorney who unsuccessfully makes or opposes a motion to compel response and compliance with a demand for a physical examination, unless it finds that the one subject to the sanction acted with substantial justification or that other circumstances make the imposition of the sanction unjust.

(d) If a plaintiff then fails to obey the order compelling response and compliance, the court may make those orders that are just, including the imposition of an issue sanction, an evidence sanction, or a terminating sanction under Chapter 7 (commencing with Section 2023.010). In lieu of or in addition to that sanction the court may impose a monetary sanction under Chapter 7 (commencing with Section 2023.010). *(Added by Stats.2004, c. 182 (A.B.3081), § 23, operative July 1, 2005.)*

Law Revision Commission Comments

Subdivision (a) of Section 2032.240 continues the first paragraph of former Section 2032(c)(6) without substantive change.

Subdivision (b) continues the first sentence of the second paragraph of former Section 2032(c)(6) without change.

Subdivision (c) continues the second sentence of the second paragraph of former Section 2032(c)(6) without change, except to conform the cross-reference.

Subdivision (d) continues the third paragraph of former Section 2032(c)(6) without change, except to conform the cross-references. [33 Cal.L.Rev.Comm. Reports 918 (2004)].

Research References

Rutter, Cal. Practice Guide: Civ. Pro. Before Trial Ch. 8I-2, Physical Examination by Demand in Personal Injury Cases.

Rutter, Cal. Practice Guide: Personal Injury Ch. 6-C, C. Physical and Mental Examinations (CCP § 2032.020 et seq.).

Rutter, Cal. Practice Guide: Personal Injury Ch. 8-B, B. After Trial Date Set (Three to Four Months Before Trial).

§ 2032.250. Motion to compel compliance; meet and confer declaration; monetary sanctions

(a) If a defendant who has demanded a physical examination under this article, on receipt of the plaintiff's response to that demand, deems that any modification of the demand, or any refusal to submit to the physical examination is unwarranted, that defendant may move for an order compelling compliance with the demand. This motion shall be accompanied by a meet and confer declaration under Section 2016.040.

(b) The court shall impose a monetary sanction under Chapter 7 (commencing with Section 2023.010) against any party, person, or attorney who unsuccessfully makes or opposes a motion to compel compliance with a demand for a physical examination, unless it finds that the one subject to the sanction acted with substantial justification or that other circumstances make the imposition of the sanction unjust. *(Added by Stats. 2004, c. 182 (A.B.3081), § 23, operative July 1, 2005.)*

Law Revision Commission Comments

Subdivision (a) of Section 2032.250 continues the first paragraph of former Section 2032(c)(7) without substantive change.

Subdivision (b) continues the second paragraph of former Section 2032(c)(7) without change, except to conform the cross-reference. [33 Cal.L.Rev.Comm. Reports 919 (2004)].

Research References

Rutter, Cal. Practice Guide: Civ. Pro. Before Trial Ch. 8I-2, Physical Examination by Demand in Personal Injury Cases.
Rutter, Cal. Practice Guide: Civ. Pro. Before Trial Ch. 8I-4, Sanctions.
Rutter, Cal. Practice Guide: Personal Injury Ch. 6-C, C. Physical and Mental Examinations (CCP § 2032.020 et seq.).
Rutter, Cal. Practice Guide: Personal Injury Ch. 8-B, B. After Trial Date Set (Three to Four Months Before Trial).

§ 2032.260. Original demand, response and service documents; custody; record retention

(a) The demand for a physical examination under this article and the response to it shall not be filed with the court.

(b) The defendant shall retain both the original of the demand, with the original proof of service affixed to it, and the original response until six months after final disposition of the action. At that time, the original may be destroyed, unless the court, on motion of any party and for good cause shown, orders that the originals be preserved for a longer period. *(Added by Stats.2004, c. 182 (A.B.3081), § 23, operative July 1, 2005.)*

Law Revision Commission Comments

Subdivision (a) of Section 2032.260 continues the first sentence of former Section 2032(c)(8) without substantive change.

Subdivision (b) continues the second sentence of former Section 2032(c)(8) without change. [33 Cal.L.Rev.Comm. Reports 920 (2004)].

Research References

Rutter, Cal. Practice Guide: Civ. Pro. Before Trial Ch. 8I-2, Physical Examination by Demand in Personal Injury Cases.
Rutter, Cal. Practice Guide: Personal Injury Ch. 6-C, C. Physical and Mental Examinations (CCP § 2032.020 et seq.).

ARTICLE 3. MOTION FOR PHYSICAL OR MENTAL EXAMINATION

Section
2032.310. Other forms of examination by leave of court; form and contents of notice of motion; parties served.

Section
2032.320. Standard of proof; exceptional circumstances; stipulation of parties; form and content of order; mileage limitations.

§ 2032.310. Other forms of examination by leave of court; form and contents of notice of motion; parties served

(a) If any party desires to obtain discovery by a physical examination other than that described in Article 2 (commencing with Section 2032.210), or by a mental examination, the party shall obtain leave of court.

(b) A motion for an examination under subdivision (a) shall specify the time, place, manner, conditions, scope, and nature of the examination, as well as the identity and the specialty, if any, of the person or persons who will perform the examination. The motion shall be accompanied by a meet and confer declaration under Section 2016.040.

(c) Notice of the motion shall be served on the person to be examined and on all parties who have appeared in the action. *(Added by Stats.2004, c. 182 (A.B.3081), § 23, operative July 1, 2005.)*

Law Revision Commission Comments

Subdivision (a) of Section 2032.310 continues the first sentence of former Section 2032(d) without change, except to conform the cross-reference.

Subdivision (b) continues the second and third sentences of former Section 2032(d) without substantive change.

Subdivision (c) continues the fourth sentence of former Section 2032(d) without change. [33 Cal.L.Rev.Comm. Reports 920 (2004)].

Research References

Rutter, Cal. Practice Guide: Civ. Pro. Before Trial Ch. 8B-1, Leave of Court Generally Not Required.
Rutter, Cal. Practice Guide: Civ. Pro. Before Trial Ch. 8I-3, Examination Upon Court Order.
Rutter, Cal. Practice Guide: Civil Trials & Evidence Ch. 1-A, A. Importance of Statewide and Local Rules of Court.
California Practice Guide: Employment Litigation Ch. 5-B, B. Intentional Infliction of Emotional Distress.
California Practice Guide: Employment Litigation Ch. 19-F, F. Discovery.
Rutter, Cal. Practice Guide: Family Law Ch. 6-B, B. Spousal Support.
Rutter, Cal. Practice Guide: Family Law Ch. 7-B, B. Contested Custody Proceedings, Generally.
Rutter, Cal. Practice Guide: Personal Injury Ch. 6-C, C. Physical and Mental Examinations (CCP § 2032.020 et seq.).
Rutter, Cal. Practice Guide: Personal Injury Ch. 8-B, B. After Trial Date Set (Three to Four Months Before Trial).

§ 2032.320. Standard of proof; exceptional circumstances; stipulation of parties; form and content of order; mileage limitations

(a) The court shall grant a motion for a physical or mental examination under Section 2032.310 only for good cause shown.

(b) If a party stipulates as provided in subdivision (c), the court shall not order a mental examination of a person for whose personal injuries a recovery is being sought except on a showing of exceptional circumstances.

(c) A stipulation by a party under this subdivision shall include both of the following:

(1) A stipulation that no claim is being made for mental and emotional distress over and above that usually associated with the physical injuries claimed.

(2) A stipulation that no expert testimony regarding this usual mental and emotional distress will be presented at trial in support of the claim for damages.

(d) An order granting a physical or mental examination shall specify the person or persons who may perform the examination,

Civ. Pro.

as well as the time, place, manner, diagnostic tests and procedures, conditions, scope, and nature of the examination.

(e) If the place of the examination is more than 75 miles from the residence of the person to be examined, an order to submit to it shall be entered only if both of the following conditions are satisfied:

(1) The court determines that there is good cause for the travel involved.

(2) The order is conditioned on the advancement by the moving party of the reasonable expenses and costs to the examinee for travel to the place of examination. *(Added by Stats.2004, c. 182 (A.B.3081), § 23, operative July 1, 2005.)*

Law Revision Commission Comments

Subdivision (a) of Section 2032.320 continues the first sentence of the second paragraph of former Section 2032(d) without substantive change.

Subdivisions (b) and (c) continue the second sentence of the second paragraph of former Section 2032(d) without substantive change.

Subdivision (d) continues the third sentence of the second paragraph of former Section 2032(d) without substantive change.

Subdivision (e) continues the fourth sentence of the second paragraph of former Section 2032(d) without substantive change. [33 Cal.L.Rev. Comm. Reports 921 (2004)].

Research References

Rutter, Cal. Practice Guide: Civ. Pro. Before Trial Ch. 8I-3, Examination Upon Court Order.
California Practice Guide: Employment Litigation Ch. 19-F, F. Discovery.
Rutter, Cal. Practice Guide: Family Law Ch. 6-B, B. Spousal Support.
Rutter, Cal. Practice Guide: Personal Injury Ch. 4-C, C. Effective Settlement Negotiations.
Rutter, Cal. Practice Guide: Personal Injury Ch. 6-C, C. Physical and Mental Examinations (CCP § 2032.020 et seq.).
Rutter, Cal. Practice Guide: Personal Injury Ch. 8-B, B. After Trial Date Set (Three to Four Months Before Trial).

ARTICLE 4.　FAILURE TO SUBMIT TO OR PRODUCE ANOTHER FOR PHYSICAL OR MENTAL EXAMINATION

Section
2032.410.　Failure of party to submit to examination; availability of sanctions.
2032.420.　Failure of nonparty to submit to examination; availability of sanctions.

§ 2032.410.　Failure of party to submit to examination; availability of sanctions

If a party is required to submit to a physical or mental examination under Articles 2 (commencing with Section 2032.210) or 3 (commencing with Section 2032.310), or under Section 2016.030, but fails to do so, the court, on motion of the party entitled to the examination, may make those orders that are just, including the imposition of an issue sanction, an evidence sanction, or a terminating sanction under Chapter 7 (commencing with Section 2023.010). In lieu of or in addition to that sanction, the court may, on motion of the party, impose a monetary sanction under Chapter 7 (commencing with Section 2023.010). *(Added by Stats.2004, c. 182 (A.B.3081), § 23, operative July 1, 2005.)*

Law Revision Commission Comments

Section 2032.410 continues the first paragraph of former Section 2032(f) without substantive change. [33 Cal.L.Rev.Comm. Reports 922 (2004)].

Research References

Rutter, Cal. Practice Guide: Civ. Pro. Before Trial Ch. 8I-2, Physical Examination by Demand in Personal Injury Cases.

Rutter, Cal. Practice Guide: Civ. Pro. Before Trial Ch. 8I-4, Sanctions.
Rutter, Cal. Practice Guide: Family Law Ch. 6-B, B. Spousal Support.
Rutter, Cal. Practice Guide: Personal Injury Ch. 6-C, C. Physical and Mental Examinations (CCP § 2032.020 et seq.).

§ 2032.420.　Failure of nonparty to submit to examination; availability of sanctions

If a party is required to produce another for a physical or mental examination under Articles 2 (commencing with Section 2032.210) or 3 (commencing with Section 2032.310), or under Section 2032.030, but fails to do so, the court, on motion of the party entitled to the examination, may make those orders that are just, including the imposition of an issue sanction, an evidence sanction, or a terminating sanction under Chapter 7 (commencing with Section 2023.010), unless the party failing to comply demonstrates an inability to produce that person for examination. In lieu of or in addition to that sanction, the court may impose a monetary sanction under Chapter 7 (commencing with Section 2023.010). *(Added by Stats.2004, c. 182 (A.B.3081), § 23, operative July 1, 2005.)*

Law Revision Commission Comments

Section 2032.420 continues the second paragraph of former Section 2032(f) without substantive change. [33 Cal.L.Rev.Comm. Reports 922 (2004)].

Research References

Rutter, Cal. Practice Guide: Civ. Pro. Before Trial Ch. 8I-4, Sanctions.
Rutter, Cal. Practice Guide: Personal Injury Ch. 6-C, C. Physical and Mental Examinations (CCP § 2032.020 et seq.).

ARTICLE 5.　CONDUCT OF EXAMINATION

Section
2032.510.　Attendance of attorney or attorney's representative at examination; use of stenographic or audio technology recording; rights of attendee to monitor; authorization of attorney's representative; suspension of examination; monetary sanctions.
2032.520.　X-ray examinations.
2032.530.　Recording mental examination by audio technology.

§ 2032.510.　Attendance of attorney or attorney's representative at examination; use of stenographic or audio technology recording; rights of attendee to monitor; authorization of attorney's representative; suspension of examination; monetary sanctions

(a) The attorney for the examinee or for a party producing the examinee, or that attorney's representative, shall be permitted to attend and observe any physical examination conducted for discovery purposes, and to record stenographically or by audio technology any words spoken to or by the examinee during any phase of the examination.

(b) The observer under subdivision (a) may monitor the examination, but shall not participate in or disrupt it.

(c) If an attorney's representative is to serve as the observer, the representative shall be authorized to so act by a writing subscribed by the attorney which identifies the representative.

(d) If in the judgment of the observer the examiner becomes abusive to the examinee or undertakes to engage in unauthorized diagnostic tests and procedures, the observer may suspend it to enable the party being examined or producing the examinee to make a motion for a protective order.

(e) If the observer begins to participate in or disrupt the examination, the person conducting the physical examination may suspend the examination to enable the party at whose instance it is being conducted to move for a protective order.

(f) The court shall impose a monetary sanction under Chapter 7 (commencing with Section 2023.010) against any party, person, or attorney who unsuccessfully makes or opposes a motion for a protective order under this section, unless it finds that the one subject to the sanction acted with substantial justification or that other circumstances make the imposition of the sanction unjust. *(Added by Stats.2004, c. 182 (A.B.3081), § 23, operative July 1, 2005. Amended by Stats.2005, c. 294 (A.B.333), § 10.)*

Law Revision Commission Comments

Subdivision (a) of Section 2032.510 continues the first sentence of former Section 2032(g)(1) without change.

Subdivision (b) continues the second sentence of former Section 2032(g)(1) without substantive change.

Subdivision (c) continues the third sentence of the first paragraph of former Section 2032(g)(1) without change.

Subdivision (d) continues the first sentence of the second paragraph of former Section 2032(g)(1) without change.

Subdivision (e) continues the second sentence of the second paragraph of former Section 2032(g)(1) without change.

Subdivision (f) continues the third paragraph of former Section 2032(g)(1) without substantive change. [33 Cal.L.Rev.Comm. Reports 923 (2004)].

Subdivision (a) of Section 2032.510 is amended to reflect advances in technology and for consistency of terminology throughout the Civil Discovery Act. See 2002 Cal. Stat. ch. 1068 (replacing numerous references to "audiotape" in the Civil Discovery Act with either "audio technology," "audio recording," or "audio record," as the context required).

Research References

Rutter, Cal. Practice Guide: Civ. Pro. Before Trial Ch. 8I-2, Physical Examination by Demand in Personal Injury Cases.
Rutter, Cal. Practice Guide: Civ. Pro. Before Trial Ch. 8I-3, Examination Upon Court Order.
Rutter, Cal. Practice Guide: Personal Injury Ch. 6-C, C. Physical and Mental Examinations (CCP § 2032.020 et seq.).
Rutter, Cal. Practice Guide: Personal Injury Ch. 8-B, B. After Trial Date Set (Three to Four Months Before Trial).

§ 2032.520. X-ray examinations

If an examinee submits or authorizes access to X-rays of any area of his or her body for inspection by the examining physician, no additional X-rays of that area may be taken by the examining physician except with consent of the examinee or on order of the court for good cause shown. *(Added by Stats.2004, c. 182 (A.B.3081), § 23, operative July 1, 2005.)*

Law Revision Commission Comments

Section 2032.520 continues the fourth paragraph of former Section 2032(g)(1) without substantive change. [33 Cal.L.Rev.Comm. Reports 924 (2004)].

Research References

Rutter, Cal. Practice Guide: Civ. Pro. Before Trial Ch. 8I-3, Examination Upon Court Order.
Rutter, Cal. Practice Guide: Personal Injury Ch. 6-C, C. Physical and Mental Examinations (CCP § 2032.020 et seq.).

§ 2032.530. Recording mental examination by audio technology

(a) The examiner and examinee shall have the right to record a mental examination by audio technology.

(b) Nothing in this title shall be construed to alter, amend, or affect existing case law with respect to the presence of the attorney for the examinee or other persons during the examination by agreement or court order. *(Added by Stats.2004, c. 182*

(A.B.3081), § 23, operative July 1, 2005. Amended by Stats.2005, c. 294 (A.B.333), § 11.)

Law Revision Commission Comments

Subdivision (a) of Section 2032.530 continues the first sentence of former Section 2032(g)(2) without substantive change.

Subdivision (b) continues the second sentence of former Section 2032(g)(2) without substantive change. [33 Cal.L.Rev.Comm. Reports 924 (2004)].

Subdivision (a) of Section 2032.530 is amended to reflect advances in technology and for consistency of terminology throughout the Civil Discovery Act. See 2002 Cal. Stat. ch. 1068 (replacing numerous references to "audiotape" in the Civil Discovery Act with either "audio technology," "audio recording," or "audio record," as the context required).

Research References

Rutter, Cal. Practice Guide: Civ. Pro. Before Trial Ch. 8I-3, Examination Upon Court Order.
Rutter, Cal. Practice Guide: Personal Injury Ch. 6-C, C. Physical and Mental Examinations (CCP § 2032.020 et seq.).

ARTICLE 6. REPORTS OF EXAMINATION

Section
2032.610. Demand for copy of examination records; right to demand; time to deliver documents; waiver of work product protection.
2032.620. Untimely delivery of requested documents; motion to compel; meet and confer declaration; monetary sanction; failure to obey court order.
2032.630. Waiver of work product privilege in pending and subsequent actions.
2032.640. Exchange of documents and reports related to condition; exchange of follow–up or late reports.
2032.650. Failure to deliver or exchange reports; motion to compel delivery; meet and confer; monetary sanctions; failure to obey court order.

§ 2032.610. Demand for copy of examination records; right to demand; time to deliver documents; waiver of work product protection

(a) If a party submits to, or produces another for, a physical or mental examination in compliance with a demand under Article 2 (commencing with Section 2032.210), an order of court under Article 3 (commencing with Section 2032.310), or an agreement under Section 2016.030, that party has the option of making a written demand that the party at whose instance the examination was made deliver both of the following to the demanding party:

(1) A copy of a detailed written report setting out the history, examinations, findings, including the results of all tests made, diagnoses, prognoses, and conclusions of the examiner.

(2) A copy of reports of all earlier examinations of the same condition of the examinee made by that or any other examiner.

(b) If the option under subdivision (a) is exercised, a copy of the requested reports shall be delivered within 30 days after service of the demand, or within 15 days of trial, whichever is earlier.

(c) In the circumstances described in subdivision (a), the protection for work product under Chapter 4 (commencing with Section 2018.010) is waived, both for the examiner's writings and reports and to the taking of the examiner's testimony. *(Added by Stats.2004, c. 182 (A.B.3081), § 23, operative July 1, 2005.)*

Law Revision Commission Comments

Subdivision (a) of Section 2032.610 continues the first sentence of former Section 2032(h) without substantive change.

Subdivision (b) continues the second sentence of former Section 2032(h) without substantive change.

Subdivision (c) continues the third sentence of former Section 2032(h) without substantive change.   [33 Cal.L.Rev.Comm. Reports 925 (2004)].

Research References

Rutter, Cal. Practice Guide: Civ. Pro. Before Trial Ch. 8I-1, Examinations by Stipulation.

Rutter, Cal. Practice Guide: Civ. Pro. Before Trial Ch. 8I-5, Exchange of Medical Reports; Waiver of Privilege.

Rutter, Cal. Practice Guide: Personal Injury Ch. 4-C, C. Effective Settlement Negotiations.

Rutter, Cal. Practice Guide: Personal Injury Ch. 6-A, A. Scope of Discovery and Limitations.

Rutter, Cal. Practice Guide: Personal Injury Ch. 6-C, C. Physical and Mental Examinations (CCP § 2032.020 et seq.).

Rutter, Cal. Practice Guide: Personal Injury Ch. 8-B, B. After Trial Date Set (Three to Four Months Before Trial).

Rutter, Cal. Practice Guide: Personal Injury Ch. 8-C, C. Two Months Before Trial.

§ 2032.620. Untimely delivery of requested documents; motion to compel; meet and confer declaration; monetary sanction; failure to obey court order

(a) If the party at whose instance an examination was made fails to make a timely delivery of the reports demanded under Section 2032.610, the demanding party may move for an order compelling their delivery. This motion shall be accompanied by a meet and confer declaration under Section 2016.040.

(b) The court shall impose a monetary sanction under Chapter 7 (commencing with Section 2023.010) against any party, person, or attorney who unsuccessfully makes or opposes a motion to compel delivery of medical reports under this section, unless it finds that the one subject to the sanction acted with substantial justification or that other circumstances make the imposition of the sanction unjust.

(c) If a party then fails to obey an order compelling delivery of demanded medical reports, the court may make those orders that are just, including the imposition of an issue sanction, an evidence sanction, or a terminating sanction under Chapter 7 (commencing with Section 2023.010). In lieu of or in addition to those sanctions, the court may impose a monetary sanction under Chapter 7 (commencing with Section 2023.010). The court shall exclude at trial the testimony of any examiner whose report has not been provided by a party. *(Added by Stats.2004, c. 182 (A.B.3081), § 23, operative July 1, 2005.)*

Law Revision Commission Comments

Subdivision (a) of Section 2032.620 continues the second paragraph of former Section 2032(h) without substantive change.

Subdivision (b) continues the third paragraph of former Section 2032(h) without substantive change.

Subdivision (c) continues the fourth paragraph of former Section 2032(h) without change, except to conform the cross-references. [33 Cal.L.Rev.Comm. Reports 926 (2004)].

Research References

Rutter, Cal. Practice Guide: Civ. Pro. Before Trial Ch. 8I-5, Exchange of Medical Reports; Waiver of Privilege.

Rutter, Cal. Practice Guide: Personal Injury Ch. 4-C, C. Effective Settlement Negotiations.

Rutter, Cal. Practice Guide: Personal Injury Ch. 6-C, C. Physical and Mental Examinations (CCP § 2032.020 et seq.).

Rutter, Cal. Practice Guide: Personal Injury Ch. 8-B, B. After Trial Date Set (Three to Four Months Before Trial).

§ 2032.630. Waiver of work product privilege in pending and subsequent actions

By demanding and obtaining a report of a physical or mental examination under Section 2032.610 or 2032.620, or by taking the deposition of the examiner, other than under Article 3

(commencing with Section 2034.410) of Chapter 18, the party who submitted to, or produced another for, a physical or mental examination waives in the pending action, and in any other action involving the same controversy, any privilege, as well as any protection for work product under Chapter 4 (commencing with Section 2018.010), that the party or other examinee may have regarding reports and writings as well as the testimony of every other physician, psychologist, or licensed health care practitioner who has examined or may thereafter examine the party or other examinee in respect of the same physical or mental condition. *(Added by Stats.2004, c. 182 (A.B.3081), § 23, operative July 1, 2005.)*

Law Revision Commission Comments

Section 2032.630 continues former Section 2032(i) without change, except to conform the cross-references. [33 Cal.L.Rev.Comm. Reports 927 (2004)].

Research References

Rutter, Cal. Practice Guide: Civ. Pro. Before Trial Ch. 8C-4, Attorney Work Product Protection.

Rutter, Cal. Practice Guide: Civ. Pro. Before Trial Ch. 8I-5, Exchange of Medical Reports; Waiver of Privilege.

Rutter, Cal. Practice Guide: Personal Injury Ch. 4-C, C. Effective Settlement Negotiations.

Rutter, Cal. Practice Guide: Personal Injury Ch. 6-C, C. Physical and Mental Examinations (CCP § 2032.020 et seq.).

Rutter, Cal. Practice Guide: Personal Injury Ch. 8-B, B. After Trial Date Set (Three to Four Months Before Trial).

Rutter, Cal. Practice Guide: Personal Injury Ch. 8-C, C. Two Months Before Trial.

§ 2032.640. Exchange of documents and reports related to condition; exchange of follow–up or late reports

A party receiving a demand for a report under Section 2032.610 is entitled at the time of compliance to receive in exchange a copy of any existing written report of any examination of the same condition by any other physician, psychologist, or licensed health care practitioner. In addition, that party is entitled to receive promptly any later report of any previous or subsequent examination of the same condition, by any physician, psychologist, or licensed health care practitioner. *(Added by Stats.2004, c. 182 (A.B.3081), § 23, operative July 1, 2005.)*

Law Revision Commission Comments

Section 2032.640 continues the first paragraph of former Section 2032(j) without change, except to conform the cross-reference. [33 Cal.L.Rev.Comm. Reports 927 (2004)].

Research References

Rutter, Cal. Practice Guide: Civ. Pro. Before Trial Ch. 8I-5, Exchange of Medical Reports; Waiver of Privilege.

Rutter, Cal. Practice Guide: Personal Injury Ch. 6-A, A. Scope of Discovery and Limitations.

Rutter, Cal. Practice Guide: Personal Injury Ch. 6-C, C. Physical and Mental Examinations (CCP § 2032.020 et seq.).

Rutter, Cal. Practice Guide: Personal Injury Ch. 8-B, B. After Trial Date Set (Three to Four Months Before Trial).

§ 2032.650. Failure to deliver or exchange reports; motion to compel delivery; meet and confer; monetary sanctions; failure to obey court order

(a) If a party who has demanded and received delivery of medical reports under Section 2032.610 fails to deliver existing or later reports of previous or subsequent examinations under Section 2032.640, a party who has complied with Section 2032.610 may move for an order compelling delivery of medical reports. This motion shall be accompanied by a meet and confer declaration under Section 2016.040.

(b) The court shall impose a monetary sanction under Chapter 7 (commencing with Section 2023.010) against any party, person, or attorney who unsuccessfully makes or opposes a motion to compel delivery of medical reports under this section, unless it finds that the one subject to the sanction acted with substantial justification or that other circumstances make the imposition of the sanction unjust.

(c) If a party then fails to obey an order compelling delivery of medical reports, the court may make those orders that are just, including the imposition of an issue sanction, an evidence sanction, or a terminating sanction under Chapter 7 (commencing with Section 2023.010). In lieu of or in addition to the sanction, the court may impose a monetary sanction under Chapter 7 (commencing with Section 2023.010). The court shall exclude at trial the testimony of any health care practitioner whose report has not been provided by a party ordered to do so by the court. *(Added by Stats.2004, c. 182 (A.B.3081), § 23, operative July 1, 2005.)*

Law Revision Commission Comments

Subdivision (a) of Section 2032.650 continues the second paragraph of former Section 2032(j) without substantive change.

Subdivision (b) continues the third paragraph of former Section 2032(j) without substantive change.

Subdivision (c) continues the fourth paragraph of former Section 2032(j) without change, except to conform the cross-references. [33 Cal.L.Rev.Comm. Reports 927 (2004)].

Research References

Rutter, Cal. Practice Guide: Civ. Pro. Before Trial Ch. 8I-5, Exchange of Medical Reports; Waiver of Privilege.

Rutter, Cal. Practice Guide: Personal Injury Ch. 6-C, C. Physical and Mental Examinations (CCP § 2032.020 et seq.).

Rutter, Cal. Practice Guide: Personal Injury Ch. 8-B, B. After Trial Date Set (Three to Four Months Before Trial).

CHAPTER 16. REQUESTS FOR ADMISSION

ARTICLE 1. REQUESTS FOR ADMISSION

§ 2033.010. Persons subject to admission requests; restrictions; scope of requests

Any party may obtain discovery within the scope delimited by Chapters 2 (commencing with Section 2017.010) and 3 (commencing with Section 2017.710), and subject to the restrictions set forth in Chapter 5 (commencing with Section 2019.010), by a written request that any other party to the action admit the genuineness of specified documents, or the truth of specified matters of fact, opinion relating to fact, or application of law to fact. A request for admission may relate to a matter that is in controversy between the parties. *(Added by Stats.2004, c. 182 (A.B.3081), § 23, operative July 1, 2005.)*

Law Revision Commission Comments

Section 2033.010 continues former Section 2033(a) without change, except to conform the cross-references. [33 Cal.L.Rev.Comm. Reports 929 (2004)].

Research References

Rutter, Cal. Practice Guide: Civ. Pro. Before Trial Ch. 8A-3, Civil Discovery Act.

Rutter, Cal. Practice Guide: Civ. Pro. Before Trial Ch. 8C-2, "Reasonably Calculated to Lead to Discovery of Admissible Evidence".

Rutter, Cal. Practice Guide: Civ. Pro. Before Trial Ch. 8D-5, Selecting Proper Discovery Tools.

Rutter, Cal. Practice Guide: Civ. Pro. Before Trial Ch. 8G-1, When RFAs May be Served.

Rutter, Cal. Practice Guide: Civ. Pro. Before Trial Ch. 8G-2, on Whom RFAs May be Served.

Rutter, Cal. Practice Guide: Civ. Pro. Before Trial Ch. 8G-3, Propounding Requests.

Rutter, Cal. Practice Guide: Civ. Pro. Before Trial Ch. 8D-5, Outline 5.

Rutter, Cal. Practice Guide: Civil Trials & Evidence Ch. 1-A, A. Importance of Statewide and Local Rules of Court.

Rutter, Cal. Practice Guide: Civil Trials & Evidence Ch. 1-C, C. Marshalling the Evidence.

Rutter, Cal. Practice Guide: Civil Trials & Evidence Ch. 8C-B, B. Writings.

Rutter, Cal. Practice Guide: Civil Trials & Evidence Ch. 8C-C, C. Material Objects ("Real Evidence").

Rutter, Cal. Practice Guide: Insurance Litigation Ch. 15-G, G. Discovery.

Rutter, Cal. Practice Guide: Personal Injury Ch. 6-B, B. Overview of Selected Discovery Procedures.

2 Witkin Cal. Proc. 5th Courts § 253, Discovery.

4 Witkin Cal. Proc. 5th Pleading § 460, (S 460) Former Requirement of Denial of Instrument.

6 Witkin Cal. Proc. 5th Proceedings Without Trial § 229, (S 229) Evidence Obtained by Discovery.

6 Witkin Cal. Proc. 5th Proceedings Without Trial § 298, (S 298) Default on Request for Admissions.

2 Witkin, California Summary 10th Insurance § 210, (S 210) Notice and Hearing.

§ 2033.020. Admissions without leave of court; time to request; earlier requests with leave of court

(a) A defendant may make requests for admission by a party without leave of court at any time.

(b) A plaintiff may make requests for admission by a party without leave of court at any time that is 10 days after the service of the summons on, or appearance by, that party, whichever occurs first.

(c) Notwithstanding subdivision (b), in an unlawful detainer action or other proceeding under Chapter 4 (commencing with Section 1159) of Title 3 of Part 3, a plaintiff may make requests for admission by a party without leave of court at any time that is five days after service of the summons on, or appearance by, that party, whichever occurs first.

(d) Notwithstanding subdivisions (b) and (c), on motion with or without notice, the court, for good cause shown, may grant leave to a plaintiff to make requests for admission at an earlier time. *(Added by Stats.2004, c. 182 (A.B.3081), § 23, operative July 1, 2005. Amended by Stats.2007, c. 113 (A.B.1126), § 12.)*

Law Revision Commission Comments

Subdivision (a) of Section 2033.020 continues the first sentence of former Section 2033(b) without change.

Subdivision (b) continues the second sentence of former Section 2033(b) without change.

Subdivision (c) continues the third sentence of former Section 2033(b) without substantive change. [33 Cal.L.Rev.Comm. Reports 929 (2004)].

Section 2033.020 is amended to improve clarity by separately stating the special hold period for an unlawful detainer case. The amendment also makes clear that the special hold period applies to a proceeding for forcible entry (see Section 1159) or forcible detainer (see Section 1160), as well as to an unlawful detainer case. [36 Cal.L.Rev.Comm. Reports 271 (2007)].

Research References

Rutter, Cal. Practice Guide: Civ. Pro. Before Trial Ch. 8G-1, When RFAs May be Served.

Rutter, Cal. Practice Guide: Personal Injury Ch. 4-A, A. General Considerations.

Rutter, Cal. Practice Guide: Personal Injury Ch. 6-B, B. Overview of Selected Discovery Procedures.

§ 2033.030. Number of admission requests; limitations; requests exceeding numeric limitation; exception

(a) No party shall request, as a matter of right, that any other party admit more than 35 matters that do not relate to the genuineness of documents. If the initial set of admission requests does not exhaust this limit, the balance may be requested in subsequent sets.

(b) Unless a declaration as described in Section 2033.050 has been made, a party need only respond to the first 35 admission requests served that do not relate to the genuineness of documents, if that party states an objection to the balance under Section 2033.230 on the ground that the limit has been exceeded.

(c) The number of requests for admission of the genuineness of documents is not limited except as justice requires to protect the responding party from unwarranted annoyance, embarrassment, oppression, or undue burden and expense. *(Added by Stats.2004, c. 182 (A.B.3081), § 23, operative July 1, 2005.)*

Law Revision Commission Comments

Subdivision (a) of Section 2033.030 continues the first sentence of former Section 2033(c)(1) without change.

Subdivision (b) continues the second sentence of former Section 2033(c)(1) without change, except to conform the cross-references.

Subdivision (c) continues the second paragraph of former Section 2033(c)(1) without change. [33 Cal.L.Rev.Comm. Reports 930 (2004)].

Research References

Rutter, Cal. Practice Guide: Civ. Pro. Before Trial Ch. 8E-2, When Depositions May be Taken.

Rutter, Cal. Practice Guide: Civ. Pro. Before Trial Ch. 8G-3, Propounding Requests.

Rutter, Cal. Practice Guide: Civ. Pro. Before Trial Ch. 8G-5, Responses to Rfas.

Rutter, Cal. Practice Guide: Personal Injury Ch. 6-B, B. Overview of Selected Discovery Procedures.

§ 2033.040. Exemption from numeric limitations; nature and complexity of issues; protective order; burden of proof

(a) Subject to the right of the responding party to seek a protective order under Section 2033.080, any party who attaches a supporting declaration as described in Section 2033.050 may request a greater number of admissions by another party if the greater number is warranted by the complexity or the quantity of the existing and potential issues in the particular case.

(b) If the responding party seeks a protective order on the ground that the number of requests for admission is unwarranted, the propounding party shall have the burden of justifying the number of requests for admission. *(Added by Stats.2004, c. 182 (A.B.3081), § 23, operative July 1, 2005.)*

Law Revision Commission Comments

Subdivision (a) of Section 2033.040 continues the first paragraph of former Section 2033(c)(2) without change, except to conform the cross-references.

Subdivision (b) continues the second paragraph of former Section 2033(c)(2) without change. [33 Cal.L.Rev.Comm. Reports 930 (2004)].

Research References

Rutter, Cal. Practice Guide: Civ. Pro. Before Trial Ch. 8G-3, Propounding Requests.

Rutter, Cal. Practice Guide: Civ. Pro. Before Trial Ch. 8G-4, Protective Orders.

Rutter, Cal. Practice Guide: Civ. Pro. Before Trial Ch. 8G-5, Responses to Rfas.

§ 2033.050. Admissions exceeding numeric restrictions; Declaration for Additional Discovery; form and content

Any party who is requesting or who has already requested more than 35 admissions not relating to the genuineness of documents by any other party shall attach to each set of requests for admissions a declaration containing substantially the following words:

DECLARATION FOR ADDITIONAL DISCOVERY

I, _____, declare:

1. I am (a party to this action or proceeding appearing in propria persona) (presently the attorney for _____, a party to this action or proceeding).

2. I am propounding to _____ the attached set of requests for admission.

3. This set of requests for admission will cause the total number of requests propounded to the party to whom they are directed to exceed the number of requests permitted by Section 2033.030 of the Code of Civil Procedure.

4. I have previously propounded a total of _____ requests for admission to this party.

5. This set of requests for admission contains a total of _____ requests.

6. I am familiar with the issues and the previous discovery conducted by all of the parties in this case.

7. I have personally examined each of the requests in this set of requests for admission.

8. This number of requests for admission is warranted under Section 2033.040 of the Code of Civil Procedure because _____. (Here state the reasons why the complexity or the quantity of issues in the instant lawsuit warrant this number of requests for admission.)

9. None of the requests in this set of requests is being propounded for any improper purpose, such as to harass the party, or the attorney for the party, to whom it is directed, or to cause unnecessary delay or needless increase in the cost of litigation.

I declare under penalty of perjury under the laws of California that the foregoing is true and correct, and that this declaration was executed on _____.

_____
(Signature)

Attorney for _____

(Added by Stats.2004, c. 182 (A.B.3081), § 23, operative July 1, 2005.)

Civ. Pro.

Section 2033.050 continues former Section 2033(c)(3) without change, except to conform the cross-references. [33 Cal.L.Rev.Comm. Reports 931 (2004)].

Research References

Rutter, Cal. Practice Guide: Civ. Pro. Before Trial Ch. 8G-5, Responses to Rfas.

§ 2033.060. Form and content of request for admissions

(a) A party requesting admissions shall number each set of requests consecutively.

(b) In the first paragraph immediately below the title of the case, there shall appear the identity of the party requesting the admissions, the set number, and the identity of the responding party.

(c) Each request for admission in a set shall be separately set forth and identified by letter or number.

(d) Each request for admission shall be full and complete in and of itself. No preface or instruction shall be included with a set of admission requests unless it has been approved under Chapter 17 (commencing with Section 2033.710).

(e) Any term specially defined in a request for admission shall be typed with all letters capitalized whenever the term appears.

(f) No request for admission shall contain subparts, or a compound, conjunctive, or disjunctive request unless it has been approved under Chapter 17 (commencing with Section 2033.710).

(g) A party requesting an admission of the genuineness of any documents shall attach copies of those documents to the requests, and shall make the original of those documents available for inspection on demand by the party to whom the requests for admission are directed.

(h) No party shall combine in a single document requests for admission with any other method of discovery. *(Added by Stats.2004, c. 182 (A.B.3081), § 23, operative July 1, 2005.)*

Law Revision Commission Comments

Subdivision (a) of Section 2033.060 continues the first sentence of former Section 2033(c)(4) without change.

Subdivision (b) continues the second sentence of former Section 2033(c)(4) without substantive change.

Subdivision (c) continues the third sentence of former Section 2033(c)(4) without change.

Subdivision (d) continues the first and second sentences of former Section 2033(c)(5) without change, except to conform the cross-reference.

Subdivision (e) continues the third sentence of former Section 2033(c)(5) without change.

Subdivision (f) continues the fourth sentence of former Section 2033(c)(5) without change, except to conform the cross-reference.

Subdivision (g) continues former Section 2033(c)(6) without change.

Subdivision (h) continues former Section 2033(c)(7) without change. [33 Cal.L.Rev.Comm. Reports 932 (2004)].

Research References

Rutter, Cal. Practice Guide: Civ. Pro. Before Trial Ch. 8F-3, Propounding Interrogatories.

Rutter, Cal. Practice Guide: Civ. Pro. Before Trial Ch. 8G-3, Propounding Requests.

Rutter, Cal. Practice Guide: Civ. Pro. Before Trial Ch. 8G-5, Responses to Rfas.

Rutter, Cal. Practice Guide: Personal Injury Ch. 6-B, B. Overview of Selected Discovery Procedures.

§ 2033.070. Service of documents

The party requesting admissions shall serve a copy of them on the party to whom they are directed and on all other parties who have appeared in the action. *(Added by Stats.2004, c. 182 (A.B.3081), § 23, operative July 1, 2005.)*

Law Revision Commission Comments

Section 2033.070 continues former Section 2033(d) without change. [33 Cal.L.Rev.Comm. Reports 933 (2004)].

Research References

Rutter, Cal. Practice Guide: Civ. Pro. Before Trial Ch. 8G-3, Propounding Requests.

Rutter, Cal. Practice Guide: Personal Injury Ch. 6-B, B. Overview of Selected Discovery Procedures.

§ 2033.080. Motion for protective order; meet and confer declaration; standard of proof; scope of order; monetary sanctions

(a) When requests for admission have been made, the responding party may promptly move for a protective order. This motion shall be accompanied by a meet and confer declaration under Section 2016.040.

(b) The court, for good cause shown, may make any order that justice requires to protect any party from unwarranted annoyance, embarrassment, oppression, or undue burden and expense. This protective order may include, but is not limited to, one or more of the following directions:

(1) That the set of admission requests, or particular requests in the set, need not be answered at all.

(2) That, contrary to the representations made in a declaration submitted under Section 2033.050, the number of admission requests is unwarranted.

(3) That the time specified in Section 2033.250 to respond to the set of admission requests, or to particular requests in the set, be extended.

(4) That a trade secret or other confidential research, development, or commercial information not be admitted or be admitted only in a certain way.

(5) That some or all of the answers to requests for admission be sealed and thereafter opened only on order of the court.

(c) If the motion for a protective order is denied in whole or in part, the court may order that the responding party provide or permit the discovery against which protection was sought on terms and conditions that are just.

(d) The court shall impose a monetary sanction under Chapter 7 (commencing with Section 2023.010) against any party, person, or attorney who unsuccessfully makes or opposes a motion for a protective order under this section, unless it finds that the one subject to the sanction acted with substantial justification or that other circumstances make the imposition of the sanction unjust. *(Added by Stats.2004, c. 182 (A.B.3081), § 23, operative July 1, 2005.)*

Law Revision Commission Comments

Subdivision (a) of Section 2033.080 continues the first paragraph of former Section 2033(e) without substantive change.

Subdivision (b) continues the second paragraph of former Section 2033(e) (including items (1)-(5)) without change, except to conform the cross references.

Subdivision (c) continues the next-to-last paragraph of former Section 2033(e) without change.

Subdivision (d) continues the last paragraph of former Section 2033(e) without substantive change. [33 Cal.L.Rev.Comm. Reports 933 (2004)].

Research References

Rutter, Cal. Practice Guide: A.D.R. Ch. 6-B, B. Temporary Judges.

Rutter, Cal. Practice Guide: Civ. Pro. Before Trial Ch. 8G-4, Protective Orders.

Rutter, Cal. Practice Guide: Personal Injury Ch. 6-B, B. Overview of Selected Discovery Procedures.

Rutter, Cal. Practice Guide: Personal Injury Ch. 8-B, B. After Trial Date Set (Three to Four Months Before Trial).

ARTICLE 2.   RESPONSE TO REQUESTS FOR ADMISSION

Section

2033.210.   Written response; oath; form and contents.

2033.220.   Scope of response; statement of reasonable inquiry into matters where respondent lacks information or knowledge.

2033.230.   Partial objection to requested admission; grounds for objection.

2033.240.   Signatures; oath; employees or agents; responses that contain objections.

2033.250.   Time to respond.

2033.260.   Extension of time by agreement; writing; notice to all parties.

2033.270.   Original requests, admissions and proof of service; custody; document retention.

2033.280.   Untimely response; waiver; relief from waiver; motion for court order; monetary sanctions.

2033.290.   Motion to compel further response; meet and confer declaration; time to bring motion; monetary sanctions; failure to obey court order.

2033.300.   Withdrawal of or amendment to admission; authority and discretion of court.

§ 2033.210.   Written response; oath; form and contents

(a) The party to whom requests for admission have been directed shall respond in writing under oath separately to each request.

(b) Each response shall answer the substance of the requested admission, or set forth an objection to the particular request.

(c) In the first paragraph of the response immediately below the title of the case, there shall appear the identity of the responding party, the set number, and the identity of the requesting party.

(d) Each answer or objection in the response shall bear the same identifying number or letter and be in the same sequence as the corresponding request, but the text of the particular request need not be repeated. *(Added by Stats.2004, c. 182 (A.B.3081), § 23, operative July 1, 2005.)*

Law Revision Commission Comments

Subdivision (a) of Section 2033.210 continues the first sentence of the introductory paragraph of former Section 2033(f) without change.

Subdivision (b) continues the second sentence of the introductory paragraph of former Section 2033(f) without change.

Subdivision (c) continues the third sentence of the introductory paragraph of former Section 2033(f) without change.

Subdivision (d) continues the fourth sentence of the introductory paragraph of former Section 2033(f) without change. [33 Cal.L.Rev. Comm. Reports 935 (2004)].

Research References

Rutter, Cal. Practice Guide: Civ. Pro. Before Trial Ch. 8G-5, Responses to Rfas.

Rutter, Cal. Practice Guide: Personal Injury Ch. 6-B, B. Overview of Selected Discovery Procedures.

§ 2033.220.   Scope of response; statement of reasonable inquiry into matters where respondent lacks information or knowledge

(a) Each answer in a response to requests for admission shall be as complete and straightforward as the information reasonably available to the responding party permits.

(b) Each answer shall:

(1) Admit so much of the matter involved in the request as is true, either as expressed in the request itself or as reasonably and clearly qualified by the responding party.

(2) Deny so much of the matter involved in the request as is untrue.

(3) Specify so much of the matter involved in the request as to the truth of which the responding party lacks sufficient information or knowledge.

(c) If a responding party gives lack of information or knowledge as a reason for a failure to admit all or part of a request for admission, that party shall state in the answer that a reasonable inquiry concerning the matter in the particular request has been made, and that the information known or readily obtainable is insufficient to enable that party to admit the matter. *(Added by Stats.2004, c. 182 (A.B.3081), § 23, operative July 1, 2005. Amended by Stats.2005, c. 22 (S.B.1108), § 24.)*

Law Revision Commission Comments

Subdivision (a) of Section 2033.220 continues the first sentence of former Section 2033(f)(1) without substantive change.

Subdivision (b) continues the second sentence of former Section 2033(f)(1) without substantive change.

Subdivision (c) continues the third sentence of former Section 2033(f)(1) without change. [33 Cal.L.Rev.Comm. Reports 935 (2004)].

Research References

Rutter, Cal. Practice Guide: Civ. Pro. Before Trial Ch. 8G-5, Responses to Rfas.

Rutter, Cal. Practice Guide: Personal Injury Ch. 6-B, B. Overview of Selected Discovery Procedures.

§ 2033.230.   Partial objection to requested admission; grounds for objection

(a) If only a part of a request for admission is objectionable, the remainder of the request shall be answered.

(b) If an objection is made to a request or to a part of a request, the specific ground for the objection shall be set forth clearly in the response. If an objection is based on a claim of privilege, the particular privilege invoked shall be clearly stated. If an objection is based on a claim that the matter as to which an admission is requested is protected work product under Chapter 4 (commencing with Section 2018.010), that claim shall be expressly asserted. *(Added by Stats.2004, c. 182 (A.B.3081), § 23, operative July 1, 2005.)*

Law Revision Commission Comments

Subdivision (a) of Section 2033.230 continues the first sentence of former Section 2033(f)(2) without change.

Subdivision (b) continues the second, third, and fourth sentences of former Section 2033(f)(2) without change, except to conform the cross-reference. [33 Cal.L.Rev.Comm. Reports 936 (2004)].

Research References

Rutter, Cal. Practice Guide: Civ. Pro. Before Trial Ch. 8G-5, Responses to Rfas.

Rutter, Cal. Practice Guide: Personal Injury Ch. 6-B, B. Overview of Selected Discovery Procedures.

§ 2033.240.   Signatures; oath; employees or agents; responses that contain objections

(a) The party to whom the requests for admission are directed shall sign the response under oath, unless the response contains only objections.

(b) If that party is a public or private corporation, or a partnership or association or governmental agency, one of its officers or agents shall sign the response under oath on behalf of that party. If the officer or agent signing the response on behalf of that party is an attorney acting in that capacity for the party, that party waives any lawyer-client privilege and any protection for work product under Chapter 4 (commencing with Section 2018.010) during any subsequent discovery from that attorney concerning the identity of the sources of the information contained in the response.

(c) The attorney for the responding party shall sign any response that contains an objection. *(Added by Stats.2004, c. 182 (A.B.3081), § 23, operative July 1, 2005.)*

Law Revision Commission Comments

Subdivision (a) of Section 2033.240 continues the first sentence of former Section 2033(g) without change.

Subdivision (b) continues the second and third sentences of former Section 2033(g) without change, except to conform the cross-reference.

Subdivision (c) continues the fourth sentence of former Section 2033(g) without change. [33 Cal.L.Rev.Comm. Reports 937 (2004)].

Research References

Rutter, Cal. Practice Guide: Civ. Pro. Before Trial Ch. 8G-5, Responses to Rfas.

Rutter, Cal. Practice Guide: Personal Injury Ch. 6-B, B. Overview of Selected Discovery Procedures.

§ 2033.250. Time to respond

(a) Within 30 days after service of requests for admission, the party to whom the requests are directed shall serve the original of the response to them on the requesting party, and a copy of the response on all other parties who have appeared, unless on motion of the requesting party the court has shortened the time for response, or unless on motion of the responding party the court has extended the time for response.

(b) Notwithstanding subdivision (a), in an unlawful detainer action or other proceeding under Chapter 4 (commencing with Section 1159) of Title 3 of Part 3, the party to whom the request is directed shall have at least five days from the date of service to respond, unless on motion of the requesting party the court has shortened the time for response, or unless on motion of the responding party the court has extended the time for response. *(Added by Stats.2004, c. 182 (A.B.3081), § 23, operative July 1, 2005. Amended by Stats.2007, c. 113 (A.B.1126), § 13.)*

Law Revision Commission Comments

Section 2033.250 continues former Section 2033(h) without change. [33 Cal.L.Rev.Comm. Reports 937 (2004)].

Section 2033.250 is amended to improve clarity by separately stating the special deadline for an unlawful detainer case. The amendment also makes clear that the special deadline applies to a proceeding for forcible entry (see Section 1159) or forcible detainer (see Section 1160), as well as to an unlawful detainer case. In addition, the amendment eliminates an ambiguity by clearly permitting a court to extend, as well as shorten, the time to respond to requests for admission in an unlawful detainer case.

Section 2033.250 is further amended to make a stylistic revision. [36 Cal.L.Rev.Comm. Reports 271 (2007)].

Research References

Rutter, Cal. Practice Guide: Civ. Pro. Before Trial Ch. 8G-5, Responses to Rfas.

Rutter, Cal. Practice Guide: Civ. Pro. Before Trial Ch. 9(I)-F, F. Ex Parte Motions.

Rutter, Cal. Practice Guide: Personal Injury Ch. 6-B, B. Overview of Selected Discovery Procedures.

Rutter, Cal. Practice Guide: Personal Injury Ch. 8-B, B. After Trial Date Set (Three to Four Months Before Trial).

12 Witkin, California Summary 10th Real Property § 736, Trial.

§ 2033.260. Extension of time by agreement; writing; notice to all parties

(a) The party requesting admissions and the responding party may agree to extend the time for service of a response to a set of admission requests, or to particular requests in a set, to a date beyond that provided in Section 2033.250.

(b) This agreement may be informal, but it shall be confirmed in a writing that specifies the extended date for service of a response.

(c) Unless this agreement expressly states otherwise, it is effective to preserve to the responding party the right to respond to any request for admission to which the agreement applies in any manner specified in Sections 2033.210, 2033.220, and 2033.230.

(d) Notice of this agreement shall be given by the responding party to all other parties who were served with a copy of the request. *(Added by Stats.2004, c. 182 (A.B.3081), § 23, operative July 1, 2005.)*

Law Revision Commission Comments

Subdivision (a) of Section 2033.260 continues the first sentence of former Section 2033(i) without change, except to conform the cross-reference.

Subdivision (b) continues the second sentence of former Section 2033(i) without change.

Subdivision (c) continues the third sentence of former Section 2033(i) without change, except to conform the cross-reference.

Subdivision (d) continues the fourth sentence of former Section 2033(i) without change. [33 Cal.L.Rev.Comm. Reports 938 (2004)].

Research References

Rutter, Cal. Practice Guide: Civ. Pro. Before Trial Ch. 8G-5, Responses to Rfas.

Rutter, Cal. Practice Guide: Personal Injury Ch. 8-B, B. After Trial Date Set (Three to Four Months Before Trial).

§ 2033.270. Original requests, admissions and proof of service; custody; document retention

(a) The requests for admission and the response to them shall not be filed with the court.

(b) The party requesting admissions shall retain both the original of the requests for admission, with the original proof of service affixed to them, and the original of the sworn response until six months after final disposition of the action. At that time, both originals may be destroyed, unless the court, on motion of any party and for good cause shown, orders that the originals be preserved for a longer period. *(Added by Stats.2004, c. 182 (A.B.3081), § 23, operative July 1, 2005.)*

Law Revision Commission Comments

Subdivision (a) of Section 2033.270 continues the first sentence of former Section 2033(j) without change.

Subdivision (b) continues the second and third sentences of former Section 2033(j) without change. [33 Cal.L.Rev.Comm. Reports 939 (2004)].

Research References

Rutter, Cal. Practice Guide: Civ. Pro. Before Trial Ch. 8G-5, Responses to Rfas.

Rutter, Cal. Practice Guide: Civ. Pro. Before Trial Ch. 9(I)-B, B. Preparing and Filing Motions.

Rutter, Cal. Practice Guide: Personal Injury Ch. 6-B, B. Overview of Selected Discovery Procedures.

6 Witkin Cal. Proc. 5th Proceedings Without Trial § 42, Other Documentary Evidence.

§ 2033.280. Untimely response; waiver; relief from waiver; motion for court order; monetary sanctions

If a party to whom requests for admission are directed fails to serve a timely response, the following rules apply:

(a) The party to whom the requests for admission are directed waives any objection to the requests, including one based on privilege or on the protection for work product under Chapter 4 (commencing with Section 2018.010). The court, on motion, may relieve that party from this waiver on its determination that both of the following conditions are satisfied:

(1) The party has subsequently served a response that is in substantial compliance with Sections 2033.210, 2033.220, and 2033.230.

(2) The party's failure to serve a timely response was the result of mistake, inadvertence, or excusable neglect.

(b) The requesting party may move for an order that the genuineness of any documents and the truth of any matters specified in the requests be deemed admitted, as well as for a monetary sanction under Chapter 7 (commencing with Section 2023.010).

(c) The court shall make this order, unless it finds that the party to whom the requests for admission have been directed has served, before the hearing on the motion, a proposed response to the requests for admission that is in substantial compliance with Section 2033.220. It is mandatory that the court impose a monetary sanction under Chapter 7 (commencing with Section 2023.010) on the party or attorney, or both, whose failure to serve a timely response to requests for admission necessitated this motion. *(Added by Stats.2004, c. 182 (A.B.3081), § 23, operative July 1, 2005. Amended by Stats.2005, c. 294 (A.B.333), § 12.)*

Law Revision Commission Comments

Subdivision (a) of Section 2033.280 continues the first paragraph of former Section 2033(k) without substantive change.

Subdivision (b) continues the first sentence of the second paragraph of former Section 2033(k) without change, except to conform the cross-reference.

Subdivision (c) continues the second and third sentences of the second paragraph of former Section 2033(k) without change, except to conform the cross-references. [33 Cal.L.Rev.Comm. Reports 939 (2004)].

Subdivision (c) of Section 2033.280 is amended to correct a cross-reference.

Research References

Rutter, Cal. Practice Guide: Civ. Pro. Before Trial Ch. 8A-3, Civil Discovery Act.
Rutter, Cal. Practice Guide: Civ. Pro. Before Trial Ch. 8C-3, "Not Privileged".
Rutter, Cal. Practice Guide: Civ. Pro. Before Trial Ch. 8G-4, Protective Orders.
Rutter, Cal. Practice Guide: Civ. Pro. Before Trial Ch. 8G-6, Effect of Delay or Failure to Respond to Rfas.
Rutter, Cal. Practice Guide: Civ. Pro. Before Trial Ch. 8H-6, Responding to Demand.
Rutter, Cal. Practice Guide: Civil Trials & Evidence Ch. 8D-D, D. Hearsay Exceptions.
Rutter, Cal. Practice Guide: Civil Trials & Evidence Ch. 8E-A, A. Privileges.
Rutter, Cal. Practice Guide: Personal Injury Ch. 6-B, B. Overview of Selected Discovery Procedures.
Rutter, Cal. Practice Guide: Personal Injury Ch. 8-B, B. After Trial Date Set (Three to Four Months Before Trial).

§ 2033.290. Motion to compel further response; meet and confer declaration; time to bring motion; monetary sanctions; failure to obey court order

(a) On receipt of a response to requests for admissions, the party requesting admissions may move for an order compelling a further response if that party deems that either or both of the following apply:

(1) An answer to a particular request is evasive or incomplete.

(2) An objection to a particular request is without merit or too general.

(b) A motion under subdivision (a) shall be accompanied by a meet and confer declaration under Section 2016.040.

(c) Unless notice of this motion is given within 45 days of the service of the verified response, or any supplemental verified response, or any specific later date to which the requesting party and the responding party have agreed in writing, the requesting party waives any right to compel further response to the requests for admission.

(d) The court shall impose a monetary sanction under Chapter 7 (commencing with Section 2023.010) against any party, person, or attorney who unsuccessfully makes or opposes a motion to compel further response, unless it finds that the one subject to the sanction acted with substantial justification or that other circumstances make the imposition of the sanction unjust.

(e) If a party then fails to obey an order compelling further response to requests for admission, the court may order that the matters involved in the requests be deemed admitted. In lieu of, or in addition to, this order, the court may impose a monetary sanction under Chapter 7 (commencing with Section 2023.010). *(Added by Stats.2004, c. 182 (A.B.3081), § 23, operative July 1, 2005. Amended by Stats.2013, c. 18 (A.B.1183), § 3.)*

Law Revision Commission Comments

Subdivision (a) of Section 2033.290 continues the first sentence of former Section 2033(*l*) without substantive change.

Subdivision (b) continues the second sentence of former Section 2033(*l*) without substantive change.

Subdivision (c) continues the second paragraph of former Section 2033(*l*) without change.

Subdivision (d) continues the third paragraph of former Section 2033(*l*) without change, except to conform the cross-reference.

Subdivision (e) continues the fourth paragraph of former Section 2033(*l*) without change, except to conform the cross-reference. [33 Cal.L.Rev.Comm. Reports 940 (2004)].

Research References

Rutter, Cal. Practice Guide: Civ. Pro. Before Trial Ch. 8G-7, Motion to Compel Further Answers.
Rutter, Cal. Practice Guide: Civ. Pro. Before Trial Ch. 8G-10, Sanctions in Enforcing Rfas.
Rutter, Cal. Practice Guide: Personal Injury Ch. 8-B, B. After Trial Date Set (Three to Four Months Before Trial).

§ 2033.300. Withdrawal of or amendment to admission; authority and discretion of court

(a) A party may withdraw or amend an admission made in response to a request for admission only on leave of court granted after notice to all parties.

(b) The court may permit withdrawal or amendment of an admission only if it determines that the admission was the result of mistake, inadvertence, or excusable neglect, and that the party who obtained the admission will not be substantially prejudiced in maintaining that party's action or defense on the merits.

(c) The court may impose conditions on the granting of the motion that are just, including, but not limited to, the following:

(1) An order that the party who obtained the admission be permitted to pursue additional discovery related to the matter involved in the withdrawn or amended admission.

(2) An order that the costs of any additional discovery be borne in whole or in part by the party withdrawing or amending the admission. *(Added by Stats.2004, c. 182 (A.B.3081), § 23, operative July 1, 2005.)*

Law Revision Commission Comments

Subdivision (a) of Section 2033.300 continues the first sentence of former Section 2033(m) without change.

Subdivision (b) continues the second sentence of former Section 2033(m) without change.

Subdivision (c) continues the third sentence of former Section 2033(m) without substantive change. [33 Cal.L.Rev.Comm. Reports 941 (2004)].

Research References

Rutter, Cal. Practice Guide: Civ. Pro. Before Trial Ch. 10-C, C. Procedural Requirements-Moving Party.
Rutter, Cal. Practice Guide: Civ. Pro. Before Trial Ch. 8A-3, Civil Discovery Act.
Rutter, Cal. Practice Guide: Civ. Pro. Before Trial Ch. 8G-6, Effect of Delay or Failure to Respond to Rfas.
Rutter, Cal. Practice Guide: Civ. Pro. Before Trial Ch. 8G-8, Amending or Withdrawing Admissions.
Rutter, Cal. Practice Guide: Civ. Pro. Before Trial Ch. 8G-9, Evidentiary Effect of Admissions.
Rutter, Cal. Practice Guide: Civil Trials & Evidence Ch. 8D-D, D. Hearsay Exceptions.
Rutter, Cal. Practice Guide: Personal Injury Ch. 6-B, B. Overview of Selected Discovery Procedures.
Rutter, Cal. Practice Guide: Personal Injury Ch. 8-B, B. After Trial Date Set (Three to Four Months Before Trial).
Rutter, Cal. Practice Guide: Personal Injury Ch. 9-H, H. Introduction of Discovered Evidence.

ARTICLE 3.   EFFECT OF ADMISSION

Section

§ 2033.410.   Conclusiveness of admission; application to other proceedings

(a) Any matter admitted in response to a request for admission is conclusively established against the party making the admission in the pending action, unless the court has permitted withdrawal or amendment of that admission under Section 2033.300.

(b) Notwithstanding subdivision (a), any admission made by a party under this section is binding only on that party and is made for the purpose of the pending action only. It is not an admission by that party for any other purpose, and it shall not be used in any manner against that party in any other proceeding. *(Added by Stats.2004, c. 182 (A.B.3081), § 23, operative July 1, 2005.)*

Law Revision Commission Comments

Subdivision (a) of Section 2033.410 continues the first sentence of former Section 2033(n) without change, except to conform the cross-reference.

Subdivision (b) continues the second and third sentences of former Section 2033(n) without substantive change. [33 Cal.L.Rev.Comm. Reports 942 (2004)].

Research References

Rutter, Cal. Practice Guide: Civ. Pro. Before Trial Ch. 10-C, C. Procedural Requirements-Moving Party.
Rutter, Cal. Practice Guide: Civ. Pro. Before Trial Ch. 11-A, A. Voluntary Dismissals.
Rutter, Cal. Practice Guide: Civ. Pro. Before Trial Ch. 8G-9, Evidentiary Effect of Admissions.
Rutter, Cal. Practice Guide: Civil Trials & Evidence Ch. 1-C, C. Marshalling the Evidence.
Rutter, Cal. Practice Guide: Civil Trials & Evidence Ch. 4-B, B. Preliminary Matters Discussed in Final Status Conference or In-Chambers Conference.
Rutter, Cal. Practice Guide: Civil Trials & Evidence Ch. 8C-B, B. Writings.
Rutter, Cal. Practice Guide: Civil Trials & Evidence Ch. 8C-I, I. Depositions and Discovery.
Rutter, Cal. Practice Guide: Civil Trials & Evidence Ch. 8D-D, D. Hearsay Exceptions.
Rutter, Cal. Practice Guide: Personal Injury Ch. 6-B, B. Overview of Selected Discovery Procedures.

6 Witkin Cal. Proc. 5th Proceedings Without Trial § 42, Other Documentary Evidence.

§ 2033.420.   Failure to admit genuineness of document or truth of any matter; binding effect; reasonable expenses and attorneys fees

(a) If a party fails to admit the genuineness of any document or the truth of any matter when requested to do so under this chapter, and if the party requesting that admission thereafter proves the genuineness of that document or the truth of that matter, the party requesting the admission may move the court for an order requiring the party to whom the request was directed to pay the reasonable expenses incurred in making that proof, including reasonable attorney's fees.

(b) The court shall make this order unless it finds any of the following:

(1) An objection to the request was sustained or a response to it was waived under Section 2033.290.

(2) The admission sought was of no substantial importance.

(3) The party failing to make the admission had reasonable ground to believe that that party would prevail on the matter.

(4) There was other good reason for the failure to admit. *(Added by Stats.2004, c. 182 (A.B.3081), § 23, operative July 1, 2005.)*

Law Revision Commission Comments

Subdivision (a) of Section 2033.420 continues the first sentence of former Section 2033(*o*) without change, except to replace section with chapter.

Subdivision (b) continues the second sentence of former Section 2033(*o*) without substantive change. [33 Cal.L.Rev.Comm. Reports 943 (2004)].

Research References

Rutter, Cal. Practice Guide: Civil Appeals & Writs Ch. 2-B, B. Appealable Judgments and Orders.
Rutter, Cal. Practice Guide: Civ. Pro. Before Trial Ch. 10-A, A. Introduction.
Rutter, Cal. Practice Guide: Civ. Pro. Before Trial Ch. 10-H, H. Entry of Judgment or Order.
Rutter, Cal. Practice Guide: Civ. Pro. Before Trial Ch. 8G-5, Responses to Rfas.
Rutter, Cal. Practice Guide: Civ. Pro. Before Trial Ch. 8G-10, Sanctions in Enforcing Rfas.
Rutter, Cal. Practice Guide: Civil Trials & Evidence Ch. 1-C, C. Marshalling the Evidence.
Rutter, Cal. Practice Guide: Civil Trials & Evidence Ch. 17-E, E. Attorney Fees as Costs.
Rutter, Cal. Practice Guide: Personal Injury Ch. 6-B, B. Overview of Selected Discovery Procedures.
9 Witkin Cal. Proc. 5th Appeal § 182, When Order Affects Judgment or Relates to Enforcement.
9 Witkin Cal. Proc. 5th Appeal § 183, (S 183) Order Must Raise Different Issues.

CHAPTER 17.   FORM INTERROGATORIES AND REQUESTS FOR ADMISSION

Section

§ 2033.710. Interrogatories and requests for admission of the genuineness of documents or truths; Judicial Council official forms

The Judicial Council shall develop and approve official form interrogatories and requests for admission of the genuineness of any relevant documents or of the truth of any relevant matters of fact for use in any civil action in a state court based on personal injury, property damage, wrongful death, unlawful detainer, breach of contract, family law, or fraud and for any other civil actions the Judicial Council deems appropriate. *(Added by Stats.2004, c. 182 (A.B.3081), § 23, operative July 1, 2005.)*

Law Revision Commission Comments

Section 2033.710 continues the first sentence of former Section 2033.5(a) without change. [33 Cal.L.Rev.Comm. Reports 943 (2004)].

Research References

Rutter, Cal. Practice Guide: Civ. Pro. Before Trial Ch. 8F-3, Propounding Interrogatories.
Rutter, Cal. Practice Guide: Civ. Pro. Before Trial Ch. 8G-3, Propounding Requests.
Rutter, Cal. Practice Guide: Civ. Pro. Before Trial Ch. 8L-1, Limitations on Existing Discovery Procedures.
California Practice Guide: Employment Litigation Ch. 19-F, F. Discovery.

§ 2033.720. Interrogatories for use by a victim who has not received complete payment under certain restitution orders; Judicial Council official forms

(a) The Judicial Council shall develop and approve official form interrogatories for use by a victim who has not received complete payment of a restitution order made pursuant to Section 1202.4 of the Penal Code.

(b) Notwithstanding whether a victim initiates or maintains an action to satisfy the unpaid restitution order, a victim may propound the form interrogatories approved pursuant to this section once each calendar year. The defendant subject to the restitution order shall, in responding to the interrogatories propounded, provide current information regarding the nature, extent, and location of any assets, income, and liabilities in which the defendant claims a present or future interest. *(Added by Stats.2004, c. 182 (A.B.3081), § 23, operative July 1, 2005.)*

Law Revision Commission Comments

Subdivision (a) of Section 2033.720 continues former Section 2033.5(d) without change.
Subdivision (b) continues former Section 2033.5(e) without change. [33 Cal.L.Rev.Comm. Reports 944 (2004)].

§ 2033.730. Advisory committee to assist with form development; use of nontechnical language

(a) In developing the form interrogatories and requests for admission required by Sections 2033.710 and 2033.720, the Judicial Council shall consult with a representative advisory committee which shall include, but not be limited to, representatives of all of the following:

(1) The plaintiff's bar.

(2) The defense bar.

(3) The public interest bar.

(4) Court administrators.

(5) The public.

(b) The form interrogatories and requests for admission shall be drafted in nontechnical language. *(Added by Stats.2004, c. 182 (A.B.3081), § 23, operative July 1, 2005.)*

Law Revision Commission Comments

Subdivision (a) of Section 2033.730 continues the first sentence of former Section 2033.5(b) without substantive change.

Subdivision (b) continues the first clause of the second sentence of former Section 2033.5(b) without substantive change. [33 Cal.L.Rev. Comm. Reports 944 (2004)].

§ 2033.740. Optional use of forms; rules and regulations

(a) Use of the form interrogatories and requests for admission approved by the Judicial Council shall be optional.

(b) The form interrogatories and requests for admission shall be made available through the office of the clerk of the appropriate trial court.

(c) The Judicial Council shall promulgate any necessary rules to govern the use of the form interrogatories and requests for admission. *(Added by Stats.2004, c. 182 (A.B.3081), § 23, operative July 1, 2005.)*

Law Revision Commission Comments

Subdivision (a) of Section 2033.740 continues the second sentence of former Section 2033.5(a) without substantive change.
Subdivision (b) continues the second clause of the second sentence of former Section 2033.5(b) without substantive change.
Subdivision (c) continues former Section 2033.5(c) without substantive change. [33 Cal.L.Rev.Comm. Reports 945 (2004)].

Research References

Rutter, Cal. Practice Guide: Civ. Pro. Before Trial Ch. 8F-3, Propounding Interrogatories.

CHAPTER 18. SIMULTANEOUS EXCHANGE OF EXPERT WITNESS INFORMATION

ARTICLE 1. GENERAL PROVISIONS

§ 2034.010. Application to eminent domain proceedings

This chapter does not apply to exchanges of lists of experts and valuation data in eminent domain proceedings under Chapter 7 (commencing with Section 1258.010) of Title 7 of Part 3. *(Added by Stats.2004, c. 182 (A.B.3081), § 23, operative July 1, 2005.)*

Law Revision Commission Comments

Section 2034.010 continues the last paragraph of former Section 2034(a) without change, except to replace section with chapter. [33 Cal.L.Rev.Comm. Reports 945 (2004)].

Research References

Rutter, Cal. Practice Guide: Civ. Pro. Before Trial Ch. 10-C, C. Procedural Requirements-Moving Party.
Rutter, Cal. Practice Guide: Civ. Pro. Before Trial Ch. 10-D, D. Procedural Requirements-Opposing Party.
Rutter, Cal. Practice Guide: Civ. Pro. Before Trial Ch. 10-F, F. Burden of Proof on Motion.
Rutter, Cal. Practice Guide: Civ. Pro. Before Trial Ch. 8A-3, Civil Discovery Act.
Rutter, Cal. Practice Guide: Civ. Pro. Before Trial Ch. 8C-2, "Reasonably Calculated to Lead to Discovery of Admissible Evidence".

Rutter, Cal. Practice Guide: Civ. Pro. Before Trial Ch. 8C-3, "Not Privileged".

Rutter, Cal. Practice Guide: Civ. Pro. Before Trial Ch. 8C-4, Attorney Work Product Protection.

Rutter, Cal. Practice Guide: Civ. Pro. Before Trial Ch. 8D-5, Selecting Proper Discovery Tools.

Rutter, Cal. Practice Guide: Civ. Pro. Before Trial Ch. 8E-2, When Depositions May be Taken.

Rutter, Cal. Practice Guide: Civ. Pro. Before Trial Ch. 8E-3, Whose Deposition May be Taken.

Rutter, Cal. Practice Guide: Civ. Pro. Before Trial Ch. 8E-6, Subpoena to Nonparty Deponent or Business Records Custodian.

Rutter, Cal. Practice Guide: Civ. Pro. Before Trial Ch. 8I-5, Exchange of Medical Reports; Waiver of Privilege.

Rutter, Cal. Practice Guide: Civ. Pro. Before Trial Ch. 8J-1, Who May Make Demand.

Rutter, Cal. Practice Guide: Civ. Pro. Before Trial Ch. 8J-6, Exchange Required.

Rutter, Cal. Practice Guide: Civ. Pro. Before Trial Ch. 8K-3, Exchange of Valuation Data and Expert Witness Lists in Condemnation Actions.

Rutter, Cal. Practice Guide: Civ. Pro. Before Trial Ch. 8L-1, Limitations on Existing Discovery Procedures.

Rutter, Cal. Practice Guide: Civ. Pro. Before Trial Ch. 8J-10, Relief from Exclusion Sanction.

Rutter, Cal. Practice Guide: Civ. Pro. Before Trial Ch. 8D-5, Outline 5.

Rutter, Cal. Practice Guide: Civ. Pro. Before Trial Ch. 8E-6, Outline 6.

Rutter, Cal. Practice Guide: Civ. Pro. Before Trial Ch. 8K-3, Outline 3.

Rutter, Cal. Practice Guide: Civil Trials & Evidence Ch. 1-C, C. Marshalling the Evidence.

Rutter, Cal. Practice Guide: Personal Injury Ch. 6-D, D. Expert Witness Information Exchanges (CCP § 2034.210 et seq.).

2 Witkin Cal. Proc. 5th Courts § 253, Discovery.

6 Witkin Cal. Proc. 5th Proceedings Without Trial § 623, (S 623) Discovery.

7 Witkin Cal. Proc. 5th Trial § 74, Completion of Discovery.

ARTICLE 2.   DEMAND FOR EXCHANGE OF EXPERT WITNESS INFORMATION

§ 2034.210. Simultaneous exchange of information; time to issue demand; discoverable reports and writings supporting opinion

After the setting of the initial trial date for the action, any party may obtain discovery by demanding that all parties simultaneously exchange information concerning each other's expert trial witnesses to the following extent:

(a) Any party may demand a mutual and simultaneous exchange by all parties of a list containing the name and address of any natural person, including one who is a party, whose oral or deposition testimony in the form of an expert opinion any party expects to offer in evidence at the trial.

(b) If any expert designated by a party under subdivision (a) is a party or an employee of a party, or has been retained by a party for the purpose of forming and expressing an opinion in anticipation of the litigation or in preparation for the trial of the action, the designation of that witness shall include or be accompanied by an expert witness declaration under Section 2034.260.

(c) Any party may also include a demand for the mutual and simultaneous production for inspection and copying of all discoverable reports and writings, if any, made by any expert described in subdivision (b) in the course of preparing that expert's opinion. *(Added by Stats.2004, c. 182 (A.B.3081), § 23, operative July 1, 2005.)*

Law Revision Commission Comments

The introductory clause of Section 2034.210 continues the introductory clause of former Section 2034(a) without change.

Subdivision (a) continues former Section 2034(a)(1) without change.

Subdivision (b) continues former Section 2034(a)(2) without change, except to conform the cross-references.

Subdivision (c) continues former Section 2034(a)(3) without change, except to conform the cross-reference. [33 Cal.L.Rev.Comm. Reports 946 (2004)].

Research References

Rutter, Cal. Practice Guide: A.D.R. Ch. 4-B, B. Judicial Arbitration.

Rutter, Cal. Practice Guide: A.D.R. App. D Form 127, ADR Clause (Conduct of Reference Proceeding).

Rutter, Cal. Practice Guide: Civ. Pro. Before Trial Ch. 10-D, D. Procedural Requirements-Opposing Party.

Rutter, Cal. Practice Guide: Civ. Pro. Before Trial Ch. 13-A, A. Introduction.

Rutter, Cal. Practice Guide: Civ. Pro. Before Trial Ch. 13-G, G. Trial De Novo.

Rutter, Cal. Practice Guide: Civ. Pro. Before Trial Ch. 8B-3, Limitations on Right to Discovery.

Rutter, Cal. Practice Guide: Civ. Pro. Before Trial Ch. 8C-3, "Not Privileged".

Rutter, Cal. Practice Guide: Civ. Pro. Before Trial Ch. 8I-5, Exchange of Medical Reports; Waiver of Privilege.

Rutter, Cal. Practice Guide: Civ. Pro. Before Trial Ch. 8J-1, Who May Make Demand.

Rutter, Cal. Practice Guide: Civ. Pro. Before Trial Ch. 8J-2, Who Must Exchange.

Rutter, Cal. Practice Guide: Civ. Pro. Before Trial Ch. 8J-3, Deadline for Demand.

Rutter, Cal. Practice Guide: Civ. Pro. Before Trial Ch. 8J-4, Demand Procedure.

Rutter, Cal. Practice Guide: Civ. Pro. Before Trial Ch. 8J-6, Exchange Required.

Rutter, Cal. Practice Guide: Civ. Pro. Before Trial Ch. 8J-7, Deposing Opposing Experts.

Rutter, Cal. Practice Guide: Civil Trials & Evidence Ch. 1-C, C. Marshalling the Evidence.

Rutter, Cal. Practice Guide: Civil Trials & Evidence Ch. 4-F, F. Motions in Limine.

Rutter, Cal. Practice Guide: Civil Trials & Evidence Ch. 11-A, A. Direct Examination of Expert Witnesses.

Rutter, Cal. Practice Guide: Civil Trials & Evidence Ch. 4-F, Outline F.

Rutter, Cal. Practice Guide: Civil Trials & Evidence Gen. Matls., Highlights.

Rutter, Cal. Practice Guide: Fed.Civ.Pro. Before Trial Ch. 1-D, D. Choosing Between State and Federal Courts.

Rutter, Cal. Practice Guide: Personal Injury Ch. 3-C, C. Specific Items of Compensatory Damages.

Rutter, Cal. Practice Guide: Personal Injury Ch. 4-F, F. Court-Conducted Settlement Proceedings.

Rutter, Cal. Practice Guide: Personal Injury Ch. 6-A, A. Scope of Discovery and Limitations.

Rutter, Cal. Practice Guide: Personal Injury Ch. 6-B, B. Overview of Selected Discovery Procedures.

Rutter, Cal. Practice Guide: Personal Injury Ch. 6-D, D. Expert Witness Information Exchanges (CCP § 2034.210 et seq.).

Rutter, Cal. Practice Guide: Personal Injury Ch. 7-C, C. Actions Subject to Judicial Arbitration.

Rutter, Cal. Practice Guide: Personal Injury Ch. 7-F, F. Preparing for Arbitration.

Rutter, Cal. Practice Guide: Personal Injury Ch. 7-G, G. Arbitration Hearing.

Rutter, Cal. Practice Guide: Personal Injury Ch. 8-B, B. After Trial Date Set (Three to Four Months Before Trial).

Rutter, Cal. Practice Guide: Personal Injury Ch. 8-C, C. Two Months Before Trial.

Rutter, Cal. Practice Guide: Personal Injury Ch. 9-G, G. Expert Witnesses.

Rutter, Cal. Practice Guide: Personal Injury Ch. 4-F, Outline F.

Rutter, Cal. Practice Guide: Personal Injury Ch. 6-D, Outline D.

Rutter, Cal. Practice Guide: Prof. Responsibility Ch. 4-C, C. Conflicts Between Present and Former Clients (Successive Representation).

7 Witkin Cal. Proc. 5th Judgment § 133, (S 133) Fees of Expert Witness.

§ 2034.220. Persons authorized to issue demand; time to make demand

Any party may make a demand for an exchange of information concerning expert trial witnesses without leave of court. A party shall make this demand no later than the 10th day after the initial trial date has been set, or 70 days before that trial date, whichever is closer to the trial date. *(Added by Stats.2004, c. 182 (A.B.3081), § 23, operative July 1, 2005.)*

Law Revision Commission Comments

Section 2034.220 continues former Section 2034(b) (as amended by 2004 Cal. Stat. ch. 171, § 6) without change, except to delete the third sentence as surplusage. See Section 2016.060 (computation of time when last day falls on Saturday, Sunday, or holiday). [33 Cal.L.Rev.Comm. Reports 947 (2004)].

Research References

Rutter, Cal. Practice Guide: Civ. Pro. Before Trial Ch. 8F-5, Responding to Interrogatories.

Rutter, Cal. Practice Guide: Civ. Pro. Before Trial Ch. 8J-3, Deadline for Demand.

Rutter, Cal. Practice Guide: Civ. Pro. Before Trial Ch. 8J-5, Protective Orders.

Rutter, Cal. Practice Guide: Civil Trials & Evidence Ch. 1-A, A. Importance of Statewide and Local Rules of Court.

Rutter, Cal. Practice Guide: Civil Trials & Evidence Ch. 1-C, C. Marshalling the Evidence.

Rutter, Cal. Practice Guide: Civil Trials & Evidence Ch. 11-A, A. Direct Examination of Expert Witnesses.

Rutter, Cal. Practice Guide: Personal Injury Ch. 6-D, D. Expert Witness Information Exchanges (CCP § 2034.210 et seq.).

Rutter, Cal. Practice Guide: Personal Injury Ch. 8-B, B. After Trial Date Set (Three to Four Months Before Trial).

§ 2034.230. Written demand; form and contents of demand

(a) A demand for an exchange of information concerning expert trial witnesses shall be in writing and shall identify, below the title of the case, the party making the demand. The demand shall state that it is being made under this chapter.

(b) The demand shall specify the date for the exchange of lists of expert trial witnesses, expert witness declarations, and any demanded production of writings. The specified date of exchange shall be 50 days before the initial trial date, or 20 days after service of the demand, whichever is closer to the trial date, unless the court, on motion and a showing of good cause, orders an earlier or later date of exchange. *(Added by Stats.2004, c. 182 (A.B.3081), § 23, operative July 1, 2005.)*

Law Revision Commission Comments

Subdivision (a) of Section 2034.230 continues the first paragraph of former Section 2034(c) without change, except to replace section with chapter.

Subdivision (b) continues the second paragraph of former Section 2034(c) (as amended by 2004 Cal. Stat. ch. 171, § 6) without change, except to delete the third sentence as surplusage. See Section 2016.060 (computation of time when last day falls on Saturday, Sunday, or holiday). [33 Cal.L.Rev.Comm. Reports 947 (2004)].

Research References

Rutter, Cal. Practice Guide: Civ. Pro. Before Trial Ch. 8J-3, Deadline for Demand.

Rutter, Cal. Practice Guide: Civ. Pro. Before Trial Ch. 8J-4, Demand Procedure.

Rutter, Cal. Practice Guide: Civ. Pro. Before Trial Ch. 8J-6, Exchange Required.

Rutter, Cal. Practice Guide: Civil Trials & Evidence Ch. 11-A, A. Direct Examination of Expert Witnesses.

Rutter, Cal. Practice Guide: Personal Injury Ch. 6-D, D. Expert Witness Information Exchanges (CCP § 2034.210 et seq.).

Rutter, Cal. Practice Guide: Personal Injury Ch. 8-C, C. Two Months Before Trial.

§ 2034.240. Service of documents

The party demanding an exchange of information concerning expert trial witnesses shall serve the demand on all parties who have appeared in the action. *(Added by Stats.2004, c. 182 (A.B.3081), § 23, operative July 1, 2005.)*

Law Revision Commission Comments

Section 2034.240 continues former Section 2034(d) without change. [33 Cal.L.Rev.Comm. Reports 947 (2004)].

Research References

Rutter, Cal. Practice Guide: Civ. Pro. Before Trial Ch. 8J-4, Demand Procedure.

Rutter, Cal. Practice Guide: Civil Trials & Evidence Ch. 11-A, A. Direct Examination of Expert Witnesses.

Rutter, Cal. Practice Guide: Personal Injury Ch. 6-D, D. Expert Witness Information Exchanges (CCP § 2034.210 et seq.).

§ 2034.250. Protective orders; motion; meet and confer declaration; standard of proof; scope of order; monetary sanctions

(a) A party who has been served with a demand to exchange information concerning expert trial witnesses may promptly move for a protective order. This motion shall be accompanied by a meet and confer declaration under Section 2016.040.

(b) The court, for good cause shown, may make any order that justice requires to protect any party from unwarranted annoyance, embarrassment, oppression, or undue burden and expense. The protective order may include, but is not limited to, one or more of the following directions:

(1) That the demand be quashed because it was not timely served.

(2) That the date of exchange be earlier or later than that specified in the demand.

(3) That the exchange be made only on specified terms and conditions.

(4) That the production and exchange of any reports and writings of experts be made at a different place or at a different time than specified in the demand.

(5) That some or all of the parties be divided into sides on the basis of their identity of interest in the issues in the action, and that the designation of any experts as described in subdivision (b) of Section 2034.210 be made by any side so created.

(6) That a party or a side reduce the list of employed or retained experts designated by that party or side under subdivision (b) of Section 2034.210.

(c) If the motion for a protective order is denied in whole or in part, the court may order that the parties against whom the motion is brought, provide or permit the discovery against which the protection was sought on those terms and conditions that are just.

(d) The court shall impose a monetary sanction under Chapter 7 (commencing with Section 2023.010) against any party, person, or attorney who unsuccessfully makes or opposes a motion for a protective order under this section, unless it finds that the one subject to the sanction acted with substantial justification or that other circumstances make the imposition of the sanction unjust. *(Added by Stats.2004, c. 182 (A.B.3081), § 23, operative July 1, 2005.)*

Law Revision Commission Comments

Subdivision (a) of Section 2034.250 continues the first paragraph of former Section 2034(e) without substantive change.

Subdivision (b) continues the second paragraph of former Section 2034(e) (including items (1)-(6)) without change, except to conform the cross-references.

Subdivision (c) continues the next-to-last paragraph of former Section 2034(e) without change.

Subdivision (d) continues the last paragraph of former Section 2034(e) without substantive change. [33 Cal.L.Rev.Comm. Reports 948 (2004)].

Research References

Rutter, Cal. Practice Guide: Civ. Pro. Before Trial Ch. 8J-5, Protective Orders.
Rutter, Cal. Practice Guide: Civ. Pro. Before Trial Ch. 8J-7, Deposing Opposing Experts.
Rutter, Cal. Practice Guide: Civil Trials & Evidence Ch. 11-A, A. Direct Examination of Expert Witnesses.
Rutter, Cal. Practice Guide: Personal Injury Ch. 6-D, D. Expert Witness Information Exchanges (CCP § 2034.210 et seq.).
Rutter, Cal. Practice Guide: Personal Injury Ch. 8-B, B. After Trial Date Set (Three to Four Months Before Trial).

§ 2034.260. Method of exchange; form and contents; expert witness declaration; form and contents

(a) All parties who have appeared in the action shall exchange information concerning expert witnesses in writing on or before the date of exchange specified in the demand. The exchange of information may occur at a meeting of the attorneys for the parties involved or by a mailing on or before the date of exchange.

(b) The exchange of expert witness information shall include either of the following:

(1) A list setting forth the name and address of any person whose expert opinion that party expects to offer in evidence at the trial.

(2) A statement that the party does not presently intend to offer the testimony of any expert witness.

(c) If any witness on the list is an expert as described in subdivision (b) of Section 2034.210, the exchange shall also include or be accompanied by an expert witness declaration signed only by the attorney for the party designating the expert, or by that party if that party has no attorney. This declaration shall be under penalty of perjury and shall contain:

(1) A brief narrative statement of the qualifications of each expert.

(2) A brief narrative statement of the general substance of the testimony that the expert is expected to give.

(3) A representation that the expert has agreed to testify at the trial.

(4) A representation that the expert will be sufficiently familiar with the pending action to submit to a meaningful oral deposition concerning the specific testimony, including any opinion and its basis, that the expert is expected to give at trial.

(5) A statement of the expert's hourly and daily fee for providing deposition testimony and for consulting with the retaining attorney. *(Added by Stats.2004, c. 182 (A.B.3081), § 23, operative July 1, 2005.)*

Law Revision Commission Comments

Subdivision (a) of Section 2034.260 continues the introductory paragraph of former Section 2034(f) without change.

Subdivision (b) continues former Section 2034(f)(1) (including items (A) and (B)) without change.

Subdivision (c) continues former Section 2034(f)(2) (including items (A)-(E)) without change, except to conform the cross-reference. [33 Cal.L.Rev.Comm. Reports 949 (2004)].

Research References

Rutter, Cal. Practice Guide: Civ. Pro. Before Trial Ch. 8C-4, Attorney Work Product Protection.
Rutter, Cal. Practice Guide: Civ. Pro. Before Trial Ch. 8J-6, Exchange Required.
Rutter, Cal. Practice Guide: Civ. Pro. Before Trial Ch. 8J-7, Deposing Opposing Experts.
Rutter, Cal. Practice Guide: Civ. Pro. Before Trial Ch. 8J-8, Exclusion of Expert Testimony as Sanction for Failure to Comply.
Rutter, Cal. Practice Guide: Civ. Pro. Before Trial Ch. 8J-10, Relief from Exclusion Sanction.
Rutter, Cal. Practice Guide: Civil Trials & Evidence Ch. 1-C, C. Marshalling the Evidence.
Rutter, Cal. Practice Guide: Civil Trials & Evidence Ch. 11-A, A. Direct Examination of Expert Witnesses.
Rutter, Cal. Practice Guide: Civil Trials & Evidence Ch. 11-B, B. Procedures to Challenge Admissibility of Expert Witness Testimony.
Rutter, Cal. Practice Guide: Civil Trials & Evidence Ch. 11-E, E. Impeachment Evidence from Other Witnesses.
Rutter, Cal. Practice Guide: Personal Injury Ch. 6-D, D. Expert Witness Information Exchanges (CCP § 2034.210 et seq.).
Rutter, Cal. Practice Guide: Personal Injury Ch. 8-C, C. Two Months Before Trial.

§ 2034.270. Production of reports and writings; time and place to exchange

If a demand for an exchange of information concerning expert trial witnesses includes a demand for production of reports and writings as described in subdivision (c) of Section 2034.210, all parties shall produce and exchange, at the place and on the date specified in the demand, all discoverable reports and writings, if any, made by any designated expert described in subdivision (b) of Section 2034.210. *(Added by Stats.2004, c. 182 (A.B.3081), § 23, operative July 1, 2005.)*

Law Revision Commission Comments

Section 2034.270 continues former Section 2034(g) without change, except to conform the cross-references. [33 Cal.L.Rev.Comm. Reports 950 (2004)].

Research References

Rutter, Cal. Practice Guide: Civ. Pro. Before Trial Ch. 8J-6, Exchange Required.
Rutter, Cal. Practice Guide: Civil Trials & Evidence Ch. 1-C, C. Marshalling the Evidence.
Rutter, Cal. Practice Guide: Personal Injury Ch. 6-D, D. Expert Witness Information Exchanges (CCP § 2034.210 et seq.).
Rutter, Cal. Practice Guide: Personal Injury Ch. 8-C, C. Two Months Before Trial.

§ 2034.280. Supplemental expert witness lists

(a) Within 20 days after the exchange described in Section 2034.260, any party who engaged in the exchange may submit a supplemental expert witness list containing the name and address of any experts who will express an opinion on a subject to be covered by an expert designated by an adverse party to the exchange, if the party supplementing an expert witness list has not previously retained an expert to testify on that subject.

(b) This supplemental list shall be accompanied by an expert witness declaration under subdivision (c) of Section 2034.260 concerning those additional experts, and by all discoverable reports and writings, if any, made by those additional experts.

(c) The party shall also make those experts available immediately for a deposition under Article 3 (commencing with Section 2034.410), which deposition may be taken even though the time limit for discovery under Chapter 8 (commencing with Section 2024.010) has expired. *(Added by Stats.2004, c. 182 (A.B.3081), § 23, operative July 1, 2005.)*

Law Revision Commission Comments

Subdivision (a) of Section 2034.280 continues the first sentence of former Section 2034(h) without change, except to conform the cross-reference.

Subdivision (b) continues the second sentence of former Section 2034(h) without change, except to conform the cross-reference.

Subdivision (c) continues the third sentence of former Section 2034(h) without change, except to conform the cross-references. [33 Cal.L.Rev. Comm. Reports 951 (2004)].

Research References

Rutter, Cal. Practice Guide: Civ. Pro. Before Trial Ch. 8J-6, Exchange Required.

Rutter, Cal. Practice Guide: Civ. Pro. Before Trial Ch. 8J-7, Deposing Opposing Experts.

Rutter, Cal. Practice Guide: Civ. Pro. Before Trial Ch. 8J-8, Exclusion of Expert Testimony as Sanction for Failure to Comply.

Rutter, Cal. Practice Guide: Civil Trials & Evidence Ch. 11-A, A. Direct Examination of Expert Witnesses.

Rutter, Cal. Practice Guide: Personal Injury Ch. 6-B, B. Overview of Selected Discovery Procedures.

Rutter, Cal. Practice Guide: Personal Injury Ch. 6-D, D. Expert Witness Information Exchanges (CCP § 2034.210 et seq.).

Rutter, Cal. Practice Guide: Personal Injury Ch. 8-C, C. Two Months Before Trial.

§ 2034.290. Original demand for exchange of information, responses and proof of service; custody of documents; record retention; time to file with court

(a) A demand for an exchange of information concerning expert trial witnesses, and any expert witness lists and declarations exchanged shall not be filed with the court.

(b) The party demanding the exchange shall retain both the original of the demand, with the original proof of service affixed, and the original of all expert witness lists and declarations exchanged in response to the demand until six months after final disposition of the action. At that time, all originals may be destroyed unless the court, on motion of any party and for good cause shown, orders that the originals be preserved for a longer period.

(c) Notwithstanding subdivisions (a) and (b), a demand for exchange of information concerning expert trial witnesses, and all expert witness lists and declarations exchanged in response to it, shall be lodged with the court when their contents become relevant to an issue in any pending matter in the action. *(Added by Stats.2004, c. 182 (A.B.3081), § 23, operative July 1, 2005.)*

Law Revision Commission Comments

Subdivision (a) of Section 2034.290 continues the first sentence of former Section 2034(n) without substantive change.

Subdivision (b) continues the second and third sentences of former Section 2034(n) without change.

Subdivision (c) continues the fifth sentence of the first paragraph of former Section 2034(k) without substantive change. [33 Cal.L.Rev. Comm. Reports 951 (2004)].

Research References

Rutter, Cal. Practice Guide: Civ. Pro. Before Trial Ch. 8J-4, Demand Procedure.

Rutter, Cal. Practice Guide: Personal Injury Ch. 6-D, D. Expert Witness Information Exchanges (CCP § 2034.210 et seq.).

§ 2034.300. Exclusion of expert opinions; failure of party to comply with certain conditions

Except as provided in Section 2034.310 and in Articles 4 (commencing with Section 2034.610) and 5 (commencing with Section 2034.710), on objection of any party who has made a complete and timely compliance with Section 2034.260, the trial court shall exclude from evidence the expert opinion of any witness that is offered by any party who has unreasonably failed to do any of the following:

(a) List that witness as an expert under Section 2034.260.

(b) Submit an expert witness declaration.

(c) Produce reports and writings of expert witnesses under Section 2034.270.

(d) Make that expert available for a deposition under Article 3 (commencing with Section 2034.410). *(Added by Stats.2004, c. 182 (A.B.3081), § 23, operative July 1, 2005.)*

Law Revision Commission Comments

Section 2034.300 continues former Section 2034(j) without change, except to conform the cross-references. [33 Cal.L.Rev.Comm. Reports 952 (2004)].

Research References

Rutter, Cal. Practice Guide: Civ. Pro. Before Trial Ch. 8J-6, Exchange Required.

Rutter, Cal. Practice Guide: Civ. Pro. Before Trial Ch. 8J-7, Deposing Opposing Experts.

Rutter, Cal. Practice Guide: Civ. Pro. Before Trial Ch. 8J-8, Exclusion of Expert Testimony as Sanction for Failure to Comply.

Rutter, Cal. Practice Guide: Civ. Pro. Before Trial Ch. 8J-9, Exceptions to Exclusion Sanction.

Rutter, Cal. Practice Guide: Civil Trials & Evidence Ch. 4-F, F. Motions in Limine.

Rutter, Cal. Practice Guide: Civil Trials & Evidence Ch. 11-A, A. Direct Examination of Expert Witnesses.

Rutter, Cal. Practice Guide: Civil Trials & Evidence Ch. 11-B, B. Procedures to Challenge Admissibility of Expert Witness Testimony.

Rutter, Cal. Practice Guide: Personal Injury Ch. 6-D, D. Expert Witness Information Exchanges (CCP § 2034.210 et seq.).

Rutter, Cal. Practice Guide: Personal Injury Ch. 8-C, C. Two Months Before Trial.

Rutter, Cal. Practice Guide: Personal Injury Ch. 9-B, B. In-Chambers Conference Before Commencement of Trial.

Rutter, Cal. Practice Guide: Personal Injury Ch. 9-G, G. Expert Witnesses.

§ 2034.310. Experts not designated on party's list; testimony at trial; permissible conditions

A party may call as a witness at trial an expert not previously designated by that party if either of the following conditions is satisfied:

(a) That expert has been designated by another party and has thereafter been deposed under Article 3 (commencing with Section 2034.410).

(b) That expert is called as a witness to impeach the testimony of an expert witness offered by any other party at the trial. This impeachment may include testimony to the falsity or nonexistence of any fact used as the foundation for any opinion by any other party's expert witness, but may not include testimony that contradicts the opinion. *(Added by Stats.2004, c. 182 (A.B.3081), § 23, operative July 1, 2005.)*

Law Revision Commission Comments

Section 2034.310 continues former Section 2034(m) without substantive change. [33 Cal.L.Rev.Comm. Reports 953 (2004)].

Research References

Rutter, Cal. Practice Guide: Civ. Pro. Before Trial Ch. 10-D, D. Procedural Requirements-Opposing Party.

Rutter, Cal. Practice Guide: Civ. Pro. Before Trial Ch. 8J-6, Exchange Required.

Rutter, Cal. Practice Guide: Civ. Pro. Before Trial Ch. 8J-9, Exceptions to Exclusion Sanction.

Rutter, Cal. Practice Guide: Civ. Pro. Before Trial Ch. 8K-3, Exchange of Valuation Data and Expert Witness Lists in Condemnation Actions.

Rutter, Cal. Practice Guide: Civil Trials & Evidence Ch. 1-C, C. Marshalling the Evidence.

Rutter, Cal. Practice Guide: Civil Trials & Evidence Ch. 4-F, F. Motions in Limine.

Rutter, Cal. Practice Guide: Civil Trials & Evidence Ch. 9-H, H. Rebuttal and Surrebuttal.

Rutter, Cal. Practice Guide: Civil Trials & Evidence Ch. 11-A, A. Direct Examination of Expert Witnesses.

Rutter, Cal. Practice Guide: Civil Trials & Evidence Gen. Matls., Highlights.

Rutter, Cal. Practice Guide: Personal Injury Ch. 6-D, D. Expert Witness Information Exchanges (CCP § 2034.210 et seq.).

Rutter, Cal. Practice Guide: Personal Injury Ch. 9-G, G. Expert Witnesses.

ARTICLE 3.   DEPOSITION OF EXPERT WITNESS

Section

2034.410. Persons permitted to depose experts; procedural requirements.

2034.420. Location of deposition; mileage limitations; exception.

2034.430. Application of section to certain designated experts; payment of fees; fees for delay caused by tardy counsel; daily fee; application to certain worker compensation claims.

2034.440. Fees for preparation and travel.

2034.450. Tender of fees; deposition conducted beyond anticipated length of time; time to tender additional fee amount.

2034.460. Production of expert at deposition; proper service of notice and prepayment of fees; proper service without tender of fees.

2034.470. Reasonableness of expert fees; order setting compensation of expert; service of notice; meet and confer declaration; determination by court; monetary sanctions.

§ 2034.410.   Persons permitted to depose experts; procedural requirements

On receipt of an expert witness list from a party, any other party may take the deposition of any person on the list. The procedures for taking oral and written depositions set forth in Chapters 9 (commencing with Section 2025.010), 10 (commencing with Section 2026.010), and 11 (commencing with Section 2028.010) apply to a deposition of a listed trial expert witness except as provided in this article. *(Added by Stats.2004, c. 182 (A.B.3081), § 23, operative July 1, 2005.)*

Law Revision Commission Comments

Section 2034.410 continues the introductory paragraph of former Section 2034(i) without substantive change. [33 Cal.L.Rev.Comm. Reports 953 (2004)].

Research References

Rutter, Cal. Practice Guide: Civil Appeals & Writs Ch. 8-C, C. Standards of Appellate Review.

Rutter, Cal. Practice Guide: Civ. Pro. Before Trial Ch. 8J-7, Deposing Opposing Experts.

Rutter, Cal. Practice Guide: Civ. Pro. Before Trial Ch. 8J-9, Exceptions to Exclusion Sanction.

Rutter, Cal. Practice Guide: Civil Trials & Evidence Ch. 11-A, A. Direct Examination of Expert Witnesses.

Rutter, Cal. Practice Guide: Personal Injury Ch. 6-D, D. Expert Witness Information Exchanges (CCP § 2034.210 et seq.).

Rutter, Cal. Practice Guide: Personal Injury Ch. 8-C, C. Two Months Before Trial.

Rutter, Cal. Practice Guide: Personal Injury Ch. 9-M, M. Verdicts and Judgment.

9 Witkin Cal. Proc. 5th Appeal § 32, Res Judicata Effect on Nonparty.

9 Witkin Cal. Proc. 5th Appeal § 107, (S 107) Discovery Cases.

§ 2034.420.   Location of deposition; mileage limitations; exception

The deposition of any expert described in subdivision (b) of Section 2034.210 shall be taken at a place that is within 75 miles of the courthouse where the action is pending. On motion for a protective order by the party designating an expert witness, and on a showing of exceptional hardship, the court may order that the deposition be taken at a more distant place from the courthouse. *(Added by Stats.2004, c. 182 (A.B.3081), § 23, operative July 1, 2005. Amended by Stats.2008, c. 303 (A.B.2619), § 1.)*

Law Revision Commission Comments

Section 2034.420 continues former Section 2034(i)(1) without substantive change. [33 Cal.L.Rev.Comm. Reports 953 (2004)].

Research References

Rutter, Cal. Practice Guide: Civ. Pro. Before Trial Ch. 8J-7, Deposing Opposing Experts.

Rutter, Cal. Practice Guide: Personal Injury Ch. 8-C, C. Two Months Before Trial.

§ 2034.430.   Application of section to certain designated experts; payment of fees; fees for delay caused by tardy counsel; daily fee; application to certain worker compensation claims

(a) Except as provided in subdivision (f), this section applies to an expert witness, other than a party or an employee of a party, who is any of the following:

(1) An expert described in subdivision (b) of Section 2034.210.

(2) A treating physician and surgeon or other treating health care practitioner who is to be asked during the deposition to express opinion testimony, including opinion or factual testimony regarding the past or present diagnosis or prognosis made by the practitioner or the reasons for a particular treatment decision made by the practitioner, but not including testimony requiring only the reading of words and symbols contained in the relevant medical record or, if those words and symbols are not legible to the deponent, the approximation by the deponent of what those words or symbols are.

(3) An architect, professional engineer, or licensed land surveyor who was involved with the original project design or survey for which that person is asked to express an opinion within the person's expertise and relevant to the action or proceeding.

(b) A party desiring to depose an expert witness described in subdivision (a) shall pay the expert's reasonable and customary hourly or daily fee for any time spent at the deposition from the time noticed in the deposition subpoena, or from the time of the arrival of the expert witness should that time be later than the time noticed in the deposition subpoena, until the time the expert witness is dismissed from the deposition, regardless of whether the expert is actually deposed by any party attending the deposition.

(c) If any counsel representing the expert or a nonnoticing party is late to the deposition, the expert's reasonable and customary hourly or daily fee for the time period determined from the time noticed in the deposition subpoena until the counsel's late arrival, shall be paid by that tardy counsel.

(d) Notwithstanding subdivision (c), the hourly or daily fee charged to the tardy counsel shall not exceed the fee charged to the party who retained the expert, except where the expert donated services to a charitable or other nonprofit organization.

(e) A daily fee shall only be charged for a full day of attendance at a deposition or where the expert was required by the deposing party to be available for a full day and the expert necessarily had to forgo all business that the expert would otherwise have conducted that day but for the request that the expert be available all day for the scheduled deposition.

(f) In a worker's compensation case arising under Division 4 (commencing with Section 3201) or Division 4.5 (commencing with Section 6100) of the Labor Code, a party desiring to depose any expert on another party's expert witness list shall pay the fee under this section. *(Added by Stats.2004, c. 182 (A.B.3081), § 23, operative July 1, 2005. Amended by Stats.2008, c. 303 (A.B.2619), § 2.)*

Law Revision Commission Comments

Subdivisions (a) and (b) of Section 2034.430 continue the first sentence of the first paragraph of former Section 2034(i)(2) without substantive change.

Subdivision (c) continues the second sentence of the first paragraph of former Section 2034(i)(2) without change.

Subdivision (d) continues the third sentence of the first paragraph of former Section 2034(i)(2) without substantive change.

Subdivision (e) continues the fourth sentence of the first paragraph of former Section 2034(i)(2) without substantive change.

Subdivision (f) continues the fifth sentence of the first paragraph of former Section 2034(i)(2) without substantive change. [33 Cal.L.Rev. Comm. Reports 954 (2004)].

Research References

Rutter, Cal. Practice Guide: Civil Appeals & Writs Ch. 2-B, B. Appealable Judgments and Orders.
Rutter, Cal. Practice Guide: Civ. Pro. Before Trial Ch. 8E-6, Subpoena to Nonparty Deponent or Business Records Custodian.
Rutter, Cal. Practice Guide: Civ. Pro. Before Trial Ch. 8J-6, Exchange Required.
Rutter, Cal. Practice Guide: Civ. Pro. Before Trial Ch. 8J-7, Deposing Opposing Experts.
Rutter, Cal. Practice Guide: Civ. Pro. Before Trial Ch. 8J-10, Relief from Exclusion Sanction.
Rutter, Cal. Practice Guide: Civil Trials & Evidence Ch. 17-D, D. Costs.
Rutter, Cal. Practice Guide: Personal Injury Ch. 6-B, B. Overview of Selected Discovery Procedures.
Rutter, Cal. Practice Guide: Personal Injury Ch. 8-B, B. After Trial Date Set (Three to Four Months Before Trial).
Rutter, Cal. Practice Guide: Personal Injury Ch. 8-C, C. Two Months Before Trial.
7 Witkin Cal. Proc. 5th Judgment § 133, (S 133) Fees of Expert Witness.

§ 2034.440.   Fees for preparation and travel

The party designating an expert is responsible for any fee charged by the expert for preparing for a deposition and for traveling to the place of the deposition, as well as for any travel expenses of the expert. *(Added by Stats.2004, c. 182 (A.B.3081), § 23, operative July 1, 2005.)*

Law Revision Commission Comments

Section 2034.440 continues the fourth sentence of the second paragraph of former Section 2034(i)(2) without substantive change. [33 Cal.L.Rev. Comm. Reports 956 (2004)].

Research References

Rutter, Cal. Practice Guide: Civ. Pro. Before Trial Ch. 8J-7, Deposing Opposing Experts.
Rutter, Cal. Practice Guide: Personal Injury Ch. 8-C, C. Two Months Before Trial.

§ 2034.450.   Tender of fees; deposition conducted beyond anticipated length of time; time to tender additional fee amount

(a) The party taking the deposition of an expert witness shall either accompany the service of the deposition notice with a tender of the expert's fee based on the anticipated length of the deposition, or tender that fee at the commencement of the deposition.

(b) The expert's fee shall be delivered to the attorney for the party designating the expert.

(c) If the deposition of the expert takes longer than anticipated, the party giving notice of the deposition shall pay the balance of the expert's fee within five days of receipt of an itemized statement from the expert. *(Added by Stats.2004, c. 182 (A.B.3081), § 23, operative July 1, 2005.)*

Law Revision Commission Comments

Subdivision (a) of Section 2034.450 continues the first sentence of the second paragraph of former Section 2034(i)(2) without substantive change.

Subdivision (b) continues the second sentence of the second paragraph of former Section 2034(i)(2) without change.

Subdivision (c) continues the third sentence of the second paragraph of former Section 2034(i)(2) without change. [33 Cal.L.Rev.Comm. Reports 956 (2004)].

Research References

Rutter, Cal. Practice Guide: Civ. Pro. Before Trial Ch. 8E-6, Subpoena to Nonparty Deponent or Business Records Custodian.
Rutter, Cal. Practice Guide: Civ. Pro. Before Trial Ch. 8J-7, Deposing Opposing Experts.
Rutter, Cal. Practice Guide: Personal Injury Ch. 8-C, C. Two Months Before Trial.

§ 2034.460.   Production of expert at deposition; proper service of notice and prepayment of fees; proper service without tender of fees

(a) The service of a proper deposition notice accompanied by the tender of the expert witness fee described in Section 2034.430 is effective to require the party employing or retaining the expert to produce the expert for the deposition.

(b) If the party noticing the deposition fails to tender the expert's fee under Section 2034.430, the expert shall not be deposed at that time unless the parties stipulate otherwise. *(Added by Stats.2004, c. 182 (A.B.3081), § 23, operative July 1, 2005.)*

Law Revision Commission Comments

Subdivision (a) of Section 2034.460 continues the first sentence of former Section 2034(i)(3) without change, except to conform the cross-reference.

Subdivision (b) continues the second sentence of former Section 2034(i)(3) without change, except to conform the cross-reference. [33 Cal.L.Rev.Comm. Reports 956 (2004)].

Research References

Rutter, Cal. Practice Guide: Civ. Pro. Before Trial Ch. 8E-6, Subpoena to Nonparty Deponent or Business Records Custodian.

Rutter, Cal. Practice Guide: Civ. Pro. Before Trial Ch. 8J-7, Deposing Opposing Experts.

Rutter, Cal. Practice Guide: Personal Injury Ch. 6-B, B. Overview of Selected Discovery Procedures.

Rutter, Cal. Practice Guide: Personal Injury Ch. 8-C, C. Two Months Before Trial.

§ 2034.470. Reasonableness of expert fees; order setting compensation of expert; service of notice; meet and confer declaration; determination by court; monetary sanctions

(a) If a party desiring to take the deposition of an expert witness under this article deems that the hourly or daily fee of that expert for providing deposition testimony is unreasonable, that party may move for an order setting the compensation of that expert. Notice of this motion shall also be given to the expert.

(b) A motion under subdivision (a) shall be accompanied by a meet and confer declaration under Section 2016.040. In any attempt at an informal resolution under Section 2016.040, either the party or the expert shall provide the other with all of the following:

(1) Proof of the ordinary and customary fee actually charged and received by that expert for similar services provided outside the subject litigation.

(2) The total number of times the presently demanded fee has ever been charged and received by that expert.

(3) The frequency and regularity with which the presently demanded fee has been charged and received by that expert within the two-year period preceding the hearing on the motion.

(c) In addition to any other facts or evidence, the expert or the party designating the expert shall provide, and the court's determination as to the reasonableness of the fee shall be based on, proof of the ordinary and customary fee actually charged and received by that expert for similar services provided outside the subject litigation.

(d) In an action filed after January 1, 1994, the expert or the party designating the expert shall also provide, and the court's determination as to the reasonableness of the fee shall also be based on, both of the following:

(1) The total number of times the presently demanded fee has ever been charged and received by that expert.

(2) The frequency and regularity with which the presently demanded fee has been charged and received by that expert within the two-year period preceding the hearing on the motion.

(e) The court may also consider the ordinary and customary fees charged by similar experts for similar services within the relevant community and any other factors the court deems necessary or appropriate to make its determination.

(f) Upon a determination that the fee demanded by that expert is unreasonable, and based upon the evidence and factors considered, the court shall set the fee of the expert providing testimony.

(g) The court shall impose a monetary sanction under Chapter 7 (commencing with Section 2023.010) against any party, person, or attorney who unsuccessfully makes or opposes a motion to set the expert witness fee, unless it finds that the one subject to the sanction acted with substantial justification or that other circumstances make the imposition of the sanction unjust. *(Added by Stats.2004, c. 182 (A.B.3081), § 23, operative July 1, 2005.)*

Law Revision Commission Comments

Subdivision (a) of Section 2034.470 continues the first and third sentences of the first paragraph of former Section 2034(i)(4) without change, except to replace subdivision with article.

Subdivision (b) continues the second and fourth sentences of the first paragraph of former Section 2034(i)(4) without substantive change.

Subdivisions (c) and (d) continue the first and second sentences of the second paragraph of former Section 2034(i)(4) without substantive change.

Subdivision (e) continues the third sentence of the second paragraph of former Section 2034(i)(4) without change.

Subdivision (f) continues the third paragraph of former Section 2034(i)(4) without change.

Subdivision (g) continues the fourth paragraph of former Section 2034(i)(4) without change, except to conform the cross-reference. [33 Cal.L.Rev.Comm. Reports 957 (2004)].

Research References

Rutter, Cal. Practice Guide: Civ. Pro. Before Trial Ch. 8J-7, Deposing Opposing Experts.

Rutter, Cal. Practice Guide: Civ. Pro. Before Trial Ch. 8J-9, Exceptions to Exclusion Sanction.

Rutter, Cal. Practice Guide: Personal Injury Ch. 8-B, B. After Trial Date Set (Three to Four Months Before Trial).

Rutter, Cal. Practice Guide: Personal Injury Ch. 8-C, C. Two Months Before Trial.

ARTICLE 4. MOTION TO AUGMENT OR AMEND EXPERT WITNESS LIST OR DECLARATION

Section

2034.610. Scope of judicial authority where exchange of information was timely; time to complete additional discovery; meet and confer declaration.

2034.620. Expert witness lists; court authority upon satisfaction of certain conditions.

2034.630. Monetary sanctions; exception.

§ 2034.610. Scope of judicial authority where exchange of information was timely; time to complete additional discovery; meet and confer declaration

(a) On motion of any party who has engaged in a timely exchange of expert witness information, the court may grant leave to do either or both of the following:

(1) Augment that party's expert witness list and declaration by adding the name and address of any expert witness whom that party has subsequently retained.

(2) Amend that party's expert witness declaration with respect to the general substance of the testimony that an expert previously designated is expected to give.

(b) A motion under subdivision (a) shall be made at a sufficient time in advance of the time limit for the completion of discovery under Chapter 8 (commencing with Section 2024.010) to permit the deposition of any expert to whom the motion relates to be taken within that time limit. Under exceptional circumstances, the court may permit the motion to be made at a later time.

(c) The motion shall be accompanied by a meet and confer declaration under Section 2016.040. *(Added by Stats.2004, c. 182 (A.B.3081), § 23, operative July 1, 2005.)*

Law Revision Commission Comments

Subdivision (a) of Section 2034.610 continues the first sentence of the first paragraph of former Section 2034(k) without substantive change.

Subdivision (b) continues the second and third sentences of the first paragraph of former Section 2034(k) without substantive change.

Subdivision (c) continues the fourth sentence of the first paragraph of former Section 2034(k) without substantive change. [33 Cal.L.Rev. Comm. Reports 959 (2004)].

Research References

Rutter, Cal. Practice Guide: Civ. Pro. Before Trial Ch. 10-F, F. Burden of Proof on Motion.

Rutter, Cal. Practice Guide: Civ. Pro. Before Trial Ch. 8J-8, Exclusion of Expert Testimony as Sanction for Failure to Comply.

Rutter, Cal. Practice Guide: Civ. Pro. Before Trial Ch. 8J-10, Relief from Exclusion Sanction.

Rutter, Cal. Practice Guide: Civil Trials & Evidence Ch. 4-F, F. Motions in Limine.

Rutter, Cal. Practice Guide: Civil Trials & Evidence Ch. 11-A, A. Direct Examination of Expert Witnesses.

Rutter, Cal. Practice Guide: Personal Injury Ch. 6-D, D. Expert Witness Information Exchanges (CCP § 2034.210 et seq.).

Rutter, Cal. Practice Guide: Personal Injury Ch. 8-B, B. After Trial Date Set (Three to Four Months Before Trial).

Rutter, Cal. Practice Guide: Personal Injury Ch. 9-G, G. Expert Witnesses.

§ 2034.620. Expert witness lists; court authority upon satisfaction of certain conditions

The court shall grant leave to augment or amend an expert witness list or declaration only if all of the following conditions are satisfied:

(a) The court has taken into account the extent to which the opposing party has relied on the list of expert witnesses.

(b) The court has determined that any party opposing the motion will not be prejudiced in maintaining that party's action or defense on the merits.

(c) The court has determined either of the following:

(1) The moving party would not in the exercise of reasonable diligence have determined to call that expert witness or have decided to offer the different or additional testimony of that expert witness.

(2) The moving party failed to determine to call that expert witness, or to offer the different or additional testimony of that expert witness as a result of mistake, inadvertence, surprise, or excusable neglect, and the moving party has done both of the following:

(A) Sought leave to augment or amend promptly after deciding to call the expert witness or to offer the different or additional testimony.

(B) Promptly thereafter served a copy of the proposed expert witness information concerning the expert or the testimony described in Section 2034.260 on all other parties who have appeared in the action.

(d) Leave to augment or amend is conditioned on the moving party making the expert available immediately for a deposition under Article 3 (commencing with Section 2034.410), and on any other terms as may be just, including, but not limited to, leave to any party opposing the motion to designate additional expert witnesses or to elicit additional opinions from those previously designated, a continuance of the trial for a reasonable period of time, and the awarding of costs and litigation expenses to any party opposing the motion. *(Added by Stats.2004, c. 182 (A.B.3081), § 23, operative July 1, 2005.)*

Law Revision Commission Comments

The introductory clause and subdivisions (a), (b), and (c) of Section 2034.620 continue the sixth sentence of the first paragraph of former Section 2034(k) without substantive change.

Subdivision (d) continues the seventh sentence of the first paragraph of former Section 2034(k) without substantive change. [33 Cal.L.Rev. Comm. Reports 960 (2004)].

Research References

Rutter, Cal. Practice Guide: Civ. Pro. Before Trial Ch. 8J-10, Relief from Exclusion Sanction.

Rutter, Cal. Practice Guide: Civil Trials & Evidence Ch. 4-F, F. Motions in Limine.

Rutter, Cal. Practice Guide: Civil Trials & Evidence Ch. 11-A, A. Direct Examination of Expert Witnesses.

Rutter, Cal. Practice Guide: Personal Injury Ch. 6-D, D. Expert Witness Information Exchanges (CCP § 2034.210 et seq.).

8 Witkin Cal. Proc. 5th Attack Judgment Trial Court § 148, (S 148) Relief from Discovery Default.

§ 2034.630. Monetary sanctions; exception

The court shall impose a monetary sanction under Chapter 7 (commencing with Section 2023.010) against any party, person, or attorney who unsuccessfully makes or opposes a motion to augment or amend expert witness information, unless it finds that the one subject to the sanction acted with substantial justification or that other circumstances make the imposition of the sanction unjust. *(Added by Stats.2004, c. 182 (A.B.3081), § 23, operative July 1, 2005.)*

Law Revision Commission Comments

Section 2034.630 continues the second paragraph of former Section 2034(k) without change, except to conform the cross-reference. [33 Cal.L.Rev.Comm. Reports 961 (2004)].

Research References

Rutter, Cal. Practice Guide: Civ. Pro. Before Trial Ch. 8J-8, Exclusion of Expert Testimony as Sanction for Failure to Comply.

Rutter, Cal. Practice Guide: Civ. Pro. Before Trial Ch. 8J-10, Relief from Exclusion Sanction.

Rutter, Cal. Practice Guide: Civil Trials & Evidence Ch. 4-F, F. Motions in Limine.

Rutter, Cal. Practice Guide: Civil Trials & Evidence Ch. 11-A, A. Direct Examination of Expert Witnesses.

Rutter, Cal. Practice Guide: Personal Injury Ch. 6-D, D. Expert Witness Information Exchanges (CCP § 2034.210 et seq.).

Rutter, Cal. Practice Guide: Personal Injury Ch. 8-B, B. After Trial Date Set (Three to Four Months Before Trial).

ARTICLE 5. MOTION TO SUBMIT TARDY EXPERT WITNESS INFORMATION

Section

§ 2034.710. Untimely response to demand for witness information; court authority to extend time; time to complete discovery; meet and confer declaration

(a) On motion of any party who has failed to submit expert witness information on the date specified in a demand for that exchange, the court may grant leave to submit that information on a later date.

(b) A motion under subdivision (a) shall be made a sufficient time in advance of the time limit for the completion of discovery under Chapter 8 (commencing with Section 2024.010) to permit the deposition of any expert to whom the motion relates to be taken within that time limit. Under exceptional circumstances, the court may permit the motion to be made at a later time.

(c) The motion shall be accompanied by a meet and confer declaration under Section 2016.040. *(Added by Stats.2004, c. 182 (A.B.3081), § 23, operative July 1, 2005.)*

Law Revision Commission Comments

Subdivision (a) of Section 2034.710 continues the first sentence of former Section 2034(l) without change.

Subdivision (b) continues the second and third sentences of former Section 2034(l) without substantive change.

Subdivision (c) continues the fourth sentence of former Section 2034(*l*) without substantive change. [33 Cal.L.Rev.Comm. Reports 961 (2004)].

Research References

Rutter, Cal. Practice Guide: Civ. Pro. Before Trial Ch. 8J-10, Relief from Exclusion Sanction.
Rutter, Cal. Practice Guide: Civil Trials & Evidence Ch. 4-F, F. Motions in Limine.
Rutter, Cal. Practice Guide: Civil Trials & Evidence Ch. 11-A, A. Direct Examination of Expert Witnesses.
Rutter, Cal. Practice Guide: Personal Injury Ch. 6-D, D. Expert Witness Information Exchanges (CCP § 2034.210 et seq.).
Rutter, Cal. Practice Guide: Personal Injury Ch. 8-B, B. After Trial Date Set (Three to Four Months Before Trial).
Rutter, Cal. Practice Guide: Personal Injury Ch. 9-G, G. Expert Witnesses.

§ 2034.720. Scope of judicial authority to grant tardy filing of list; satisfaction of certain conditions

The court shall grant leave to submit tardy expert witness information only if all of the following conditions are satisfied:

(a) The court has taken into account the extent to which the opposing party has relied on the absence of a list of expert witnesses.

(b) The court has determined that any party opposing the motion will not be prejudiced in maintaining that party's action or defense on the merits.

(c) The court has determined that the moving party did all of the following:

(1) Failed to submit the information as the result of mistake, inadvertence, surprise, or excusable neglect.

(2) Sought leave to submit the information promptly after learning of the mistake, inadvertence, surprise, or excusable neglect.

(3) Promptly thereafter served a copy of the proposed expert witness information described in Section 2034.260 on all other parties who have appeared in the action.

(d) The order is conditioned on the moving party making the expert available immediately for a deposition under Article 3 (commencing with Section 2034.410), and on any other terms as may be just, including, but not limited to, leave to any party opposing the motion to designate additional expert witnesses or to elicit additional opinions from those previously designated, a continuance of the trial for a reasonable period of time, and the awarding of costs and litigation expenses to any party opposing the motion. (*Added by Stats.2004, c. 182 (A.B.3081), § 23, operative July 1, 2005.*)

Law Revision Commission Comments

The introductory clause and subdivisions (a), (b), and (c) of Section 2034.720 continue the first sentence of the second paragraph of former Section 2034(*l*) without substantive change.

Subdivision (d) continues the second sentence of the second paragraph of former Section 2034(*l*) without substantive change. [33 Cal.L.Rev. Comm. Reports 962 (2004)].

Research References

Rutter, Cal. Practice Guide: Civ. Pro. Before Trial Ch. 8J-10, Relief from Exclusion Sanction.
Rutter, Cal. Practice Guide: Civil Trials & Evidence Ch. 4-F, F. Motions in Limine.
Rutter, Cal. Practice Guide: Civil Trials & Evidence Ch. 11-A, A. Direct Examination of Expert Witnesses.
Rutter, Cal. Practice Guide: Personal Injury Ch. 6-D, D. Expert Witness Information Exchanges (CCP § 2034.210 et seq.).

Rutter, Cal. Practice Guide: Personal Injury Ch. 8-B, B. After Trial Date Set (Three to Four Months Before Trial).

§ 2034.730. Monetary sanctions; exception

The court shall impose a monetary sanction under Chapter 7 (commencing with Section 2023.010) against any party, person, or attorney who unsuccessfully makes or opposes a motion to submit tardy expert witness information, unless it finds that the one subject to the sanction acted with substantial justification or that other circumstances make the imposition of the sanction unjust. (*Added by Stats.2004, c. 182 (A.B.3081), § 23, operative July 1, 2005.*)

Law Revision Commission Comments

Section 2034.730 continues the third paragraph of former Section 2034(*l*) without change, except to conform the cross-reference. [33 Cal.L.Rev.Comm. Reports 963 (2004)].

Research References

Rutter, Cal. Practice Guide: Civ. Pro. Before Trial Ch. 8J-10, Relief from Exclusion Sanction.
Rutter, Cal. Practice Guide: Personal Injury Ch. 6-D, D. Expert Witness Information Exchanges (CCP § 2034.210 et seq.).
Rutter, Cal. Practice Guide: Personal Injury Ch. 8-B, B. After Trial Date Set (Three to Four Months Before Trial).

CHAPTER 19. PERPETUATION OF TESTIMONY OR PRESERVATION OF EVIDENCE BEFORE FILING ACTION

§ 2035.010. Persons permitted to obtain discovery; restrictions

(a) One who expects to be a party or expects a successor in interest to be a party to any action that may be cognizable in any court of the State of California, whether as a plaintiff, or as a defendant, or in any other capacity, may obtain discovery within the scope delimited by Chapters 2 (commencing with Section 2017.010) and 3 (commencing with Section 2017.710), and subject to the restrictions set forth in Chapter 5 (commencing with Section 2019.010), for the purpose of perpetuating that person's own testimony or that of another natural person or organization, or of preserving evidence for use in the event an action is subsequently filed.

(b) One shall not employ the procedures of this chapter for the purpose either of ascertaining the possible existence of a cause of action or a defense to it, or of identifying those who might be made parties to an action not yet filed. (*Added by Stats.2004, c. 182 (A.B.3081), § 23, operative July 1, 2005. Amended by Stats.2005, c. 294 (A.B.333), § 13.*)

Law Revision Commission Comments

Subdivision (a) of Section 2035.010 continues the first sentence of former Section 2035(a) without change, except to conform the cross-references.

Subdivision (b) continues the second sentence of former Section 2035(a) without change, except to replace section with chapter. [33 Cal.L.Rev.Comm. Reports 963 (2004)].

Section 2035.010 is amended to permit a person to take presuit discovery on behalf of a successor in interest (i.e., in anticipation of a suit by the person's successor in interest), so long as the statutory requirements for such discovery are satisfied. For similar provisions, see Ohio R. Civ. Proc. 27; Okla. Stat. Ann., tit. 12, § 3227; Or. R. Civ. Proc. 37; 1959 Unif. Perpetuation of Testimony Act, § 1(a) & Comment.

In connection with this reform, several new safeguards have been added to ensure that presuit discovery is conducted only when it is warranted. Under Section 2035.030(b)(2), when a petitioner seeks presuit discovery on behalf of a successor in interest, presuit discovery is permissible only if both the petitioner and the petitioner's successor in interest are unable to bring suit. This requirement is drawn from Section 1(a) of the 1959 Uniform Perpetuation of Testimony Act. Under Section 2035.030(b)(3), a petition for presuit discovery must include a copy of any written instrument connected with the subject matter of the discovery. This requirement is drawn from Section 1(b) of the 1959 Uniform Perpetuation of Testimony Act. Under Section 2035.050(a), when a petitioner seeks presuit discovery on behalf of a successor in interest, the court must consider, in addition to other appropriate factors, whether the requested discovery could be conducted by the successor in interest, instead of by the petitioner. This factor is significant but not necessarily determinative.

Research References

Rutter, Cal. Practice Guide: Civ. Pro. Before Trial Ch. 6-B, B. Complaints.

Rutter, Cal. Practice Guide: Civ. Pro. Before Trial Ch. 8E-1, When Prior Court Order Required.

Rutter, Cal. Practice Guide: Civ. Pro. Before Trial Ch. 8E-1, Outline 1.

Rutter, Cal. Practice Guide: Personal Injury Ch. 4-A, A. General Considerations.

Rutter, Cal. Practice Guide: Personal Injury Ch. 5-A, A. Prelawsuit Filings.

3 Witkin Cal. Proc. 5th Actions § 689, Scope and Accrual.

§ 2035.020. Methods available

The methods available for discovery conducted for the purposes set forth in Section 2035.010 are all of the following:

(a) Oral and written depositions.

(b) Inspections of documents, things, and places.

(c) Physical and mental examinations. *(Added by Stats.2004, c. 182 (A.B.3081), § 23, operative July 1, 2005.)*

Law Revision Commission Comments

Section 2035.020 continues former Section 2035(b) without substantive change. [33 Cal.L.Rev.Comm. Reports 964 (2004)].

Research References

Rutter, Cal. Practice Guide: Civ. Pro. Before Trial Ch. 8E-1, When Prior Court Order Required.

§ 2035.030. Filing of verified petition; content and form of petition; court order

(a) One who desires to perpetuate testimony or preserve evidence for the purposes set forth in Section 2035.010 shall file a verified petition in the superior court of the county of the residence of at least one expected adverse party, or, if no expected adverse party is a resident of the State of California, in the superior court of a county where the action or proceeding may be filed.

(b) The petition shall be titled in the name of the one who desires the perpetuation of testimony or the preservation of evidence. The petition shall set forth all of the following:

(1) The expectation that the petitioner or the petitioner's successor in interest will be a party to an action cognizable in a court of the State of California.

(2) The present inability of the petitioner and, if applicable, the petitioner's successor in interest either to bring that action or to cause it to be brought.

(3) The subject matter of the expected action and the petitioner's involvement. A copy of any written instrument the validity or construction of which may be called into question, or which is connected with the subject matter of the proposed discovery, shall be attached to the petition.

(4) The particular discovery methods described in Section 2035.020 that the petitioner desires to employ.

(5) The facts that the petitioner desires to establish by the proposed discovery.

(6) The reasons for desiring to perpetuate or preserve these facts before an action has been filed.

(7) The name or a description of those whom the petitioner expects to be adverse parties so far as known.

(8) The name and address of those from whom the discovery is to be sought.

(9) The substance of the information expected to be elicited from each of those from whom discovery is being sought.

(c) The petition shall request the court to enter an order authorizing the petitioner to engage in discovery by the described methods for the purpose of perpetuating the described testimony or preserving the described evidence. *(Added by Stats.2004, c. 182 (A.B.3081), § 23, operative July 1, 2005. Amended by Stats.2005, c. 294 (A.B.333), § 14.)*

Law Revision Commission Comments

Subdivision (a) of Section 2035.030 continues former Section 2035(c) without change, except to conform the cross-reference.

Subdivision (b) continues the first paragraph (including items (1)-(9)) of former Section 2035(d) without change, except to conform the cross-reference.

Subdivision (c) continues the last paragraph of former Section 2035(d) without change. [33 Cal.L.Rev.Comm. Reports 964 (2004)].

Subdivision (b)(1) of Section 2035.030 is amended to reflect the rule that a person may take presuit discovery on behalf of a successor in interest (i.e., in anticipation of a suit by the person's successor in interest), so long as the statutory requirements for such discovery are satisfied. See Section 2035.010 (perpetuation of testimony or preservation of evidence before filing action).

Subdivision (b)(2) is amended to ensure that if a person seeks presuit discovery on behalf of a successor in interest, a court may authorize such discovery only if both the petitioner and the petitioner's successor in interest are unable to bring suit. This requirement is drawn from Section 1(a) of the 1959 Uniform Perpetuation of Testimony Act.

Subdivision (b)(3) is amended to add the requirement that a petition for presuit discovery include a copy of any written instrument connected with the subject matter of the discovery. This requirement is drawn from Section 1(b) of the 1959 Uniform Perpetuation of Testimony Act.

For an additional safeguard relating to presuit discovery on behalf of a successor in interest, see Section 2035.050(a) (in deciding whether to permit petitioner to take presuit discovery on behalf of successor in interest, court must consider whether requested discovery could instead be conducted by successor in interest).

Research References

Rutter, Cal. Practice Guide: Civ. Pro. Before Trial Ch. 8E-1, When Prior Court Order Required.

§ 2035.040. Service of notice; form and contents; time; service by publication; appointment of counsel for absent party; payment of attorney's fees

(a) The petitioner shall cause service of a notice of the petition under Section 2035.030 to be made on each natural person or organization named in the petition as an expected adverse party. This service shall be made in the same manner provided for the service of a summons.

(b) The service of the notice shall be accompanied by a copy of the petition. The notice shall state that the petitioner will apply to the court at a time and place specified in the notice for the order requested in the petition.

(c) This service shall be effected at least 20 days prior to the date specified in the notice for the hearing on the petition.

(d) If after the exercise of due diligence, the petitioner is unable to cause service to be made on any expected adverse party named in the petition, the court in which the petition is filed shall make an order for service by publication.

(e) If any expected adverse party served by publication does not appear at the hearing, the court shall appoint an attorney to represent that party for all purposes, including the cross-examination of any person whose testimony is taken by deposition. The court shall order that the petitioner pay the reasonable fees and expenses of any attorney so appointed. *(Added by Stats.2004, c. 182 (A.B.3081), § 23, operative July 1, 2005.)*

Law Revision Commission Comments

Subdivision (a) of Section 2035.040 continues the first and second sentences of former Section 2035(e) without substantive change.

Subdivision (b) continues the third and fourth sentences of former Section 2035(e) without change.

Subdivision (c) continues the fifth sentence of former Section 2035(e) without change.

Subdivision (d) continues the first sentence of the second paragraph of former Section 2035(e) without change.

Subdivision (e) continues the second and third sentences of the second paragraph of former Section 2035(e) without change. [33 Cal.L.Rev. Comm. Reports 965 (2004)].

Research References

Rutter, Cal. Practice Guide: Civ. Pro. Before Trial Ch. 8E-1, When Prior Court Order Required.

§ 2035.050. Authority to issue order; considerations; contents of order

(a) If the court determines that all or part of the discovery requested under this chapter may prevent a failure or delay of justice, it shall make an order authorizing that discovery. In determining whether to authorize discovery by a petitioner who expects a successor in interest to be a party to an action, the court shall consider, in addition to other appropriate factors, whether the requested discovery could be conducted by the petitioner's successor in interest, instead of by the petitioner.

(b) The order shall identify any witness whose deposition may be taken, and any documents, things, or places that may be inspected, and any person whose physical or mental condition may be examined.

(c) Any authorized depositions, inspections, and physical or mental examinations shall then be conducted in accordance with the provisions of this title relating to those methods of discovery in actions that have been filed. *(Added by Stats.2004, c. 182 (A.B.3081), § 23, operative July 1, 2005. Amended by Stats.2005, c. 294 (A.B.333), § 15.)*

Law Revision Commission Comments

Subdivision (a) of Section 2035.050 continues the first sentence of former Section 2035(f) without substantive change.

Subdivision (b) continues the second sentence of former Section 2035(f) without change.

Subdivision (c) continues the third sentence of former Section 2035(f) without change, except to replace article with title. [33 Cal.L.Rev.Comm. Reports 966 (2004)].

Subdivision (a) of Section 2035.050 is amended to make clear that when a petitioner seeks presuit discovery on behalf of a successor in interest (i.e., in the expectation that a successor in interest will be a party to an action), the court must consider, in addition to other appropriate factors,

whether the requested discovery could be conducted by the successor in interest, instead of by the petitioner. This factor is significant but not necessarily determinative.

For the provision authorizing presuit discovery on behalf of a successor in interest, see Section 2035.010 (perpetuation of testimony or preservation of evidence before filing action). For other safeguards applicable to such discovery, see Section 2035.030 (petition) & Comment.

Research References

Rutter, Cal. Practice Guide: Civ. Pro. Before Trial Ch. 8E-1, When Prior Court Order Required.

§ 2035.060. Use of deposition to perpetuate testimony in subsequent actions; requirements

If a deposition to perpetuate testimony has been taken either under the provisions of this chapter, or under comparable provisions of the laws of the state in which it was taken, or the federal courts, or a foreign nation in which it was taken, that deposition may be used, in any action involving the same subject matter that is brought in a court of the State of California, in accordance with Section 2025.620 against any party, or the successor in interest of any party, named in the petition as an expected adverse party. *(Added by Stats.2004, c. 182 (A.B.3081), § 23, operative July 1, 2005. Amended by Stats.2005, c. 294 (A.B.333), § 16.)*

Law Revision Commission Comments

Section 2035.060 continues former Section 2035(g) without change, except to replace section with chapter and to conform the cross-reference. [33 Cal.L.Rev.Comm. Reports 967 (2004)].

Section 2035.060 is amended to make clear that a deposition to perpetuate testimony may be used in California only if it was taken under this section or under a comparable provision of the federal courts or of the jurisdiction in which it was taken.

Research References

Rutter, Cal. Practice Guide: Civ. Pro. Before Trial Ch. 8E-1, When Prior Court Order Required.

CHAPTER 20. PERPETUATION OF TESTIMONY OR PRESERVATION OF INFORMATION PENDING APPEAL

§ 2036.010. Persons permitted to obtain discovery; scope of use

If an appeal has been taken from a judgment entered by any court of the State of California, or if the time for taking an appeal has not expired, a party may obtain discovery within the scope delimited by Chapters 2 (commencing with Section 2017.010) and 3 (commencing with Section 2017.710), and subject to the restrictions set forth in Chapter 5 (commencing with Section 2019.010), for the purpose of perpetuating testimony or preserving information for use in the event of further proceedings in that court. *(Added by Stats.2004, c. 182 (A.B. 3081), § 23, operative July 1, 2005.)*

Law Revision Commission Comments

Section 2036.010 continues former Section 2036(a) without change, except to conform the cross-references. [33 Cal.L.Rev.Comm. Reports 967 (2004)].

Research References

Rutter, Cal. Practice Guide: Civ. Pro. Before Trial Ch. 8E-1, When Prior Court Order Required.

Rutter, Cal. Practice Guide: Civ. Pro. Before Trial Ch. 8E-1, Outline 1.

9 Witkin Cal. Proc. 5th Appeal § 20, (S 20) Jurisdiction Over Collateral Matters.

§ 2036.020. Methods available

The methods available for discovery for the purpose set forth in Section 2036.010 are all of the following:

(a) Oral and written depositions.

(b) Inspections of documents, things, and places.

(c) Physical and mental examinations. *(Added by Stats.2004, c. 182 (A.B.3081), § 23, operative July 1, 2005.)*

Law Revision Commission Comments

Section 2036.020 continues former Section 2036(b) without substantive change. [33 Cal.L.Rev.Comm. Reports 968 (2004)].

Research References

Rutter, Cal. Practice Guide: Civ. Pro. Before Trial Ch. 8E-1, When Prior Court Order Required.

§ 2036.030. Motion to obtain discovery; notice and service of motion; form and contents

(a) A party who desires to obtain discovery pending appeal shall obtain leave of the court that entered the judgment. This motion shall be made on the same notice to and service of parties as is required for discovery sought in an action pending in that court.

(b) The motion for leave to conduct discovery pending appeal shall set forth all of the following:

(1) The names and addresses of the natural persons or organizations from whom the discovery is being sought.

(2) The particular discovery methods described in Section 2036.020 for which authorization is being sought.

(3) The reasons for perpetuating testimony or preserving evidence. *(Added by Stats.2004, c. 182 (A.B.3081), § 23, operative July 1, 2005.)*

Law Revision Commission Comments

Subdivision (a) of Section 2036.030 continues former Section 2036(c) without change.

Subdivision (b) continues former Section 2036(d) without substantive change. [33 Cal.L.Rev.Comm. Reports 968 (2004)].

Research References

Rutter, Cal. Practice Guide: Civ. Pro. Before Trial Ch. 8E-1, When Prior Court Order Required.

§ 2036.040. Determination of necessity in the event of further proceedings; order; contents; compliance with discovery provisions

(a) If the court determines that all or part of the discovery requested under this chapter may prevent a failure or delay of justice in the event of further proceedings in the action in that court, it shall make an order authorizing that discovery.

(b) The order shall identify any witness whose deposition may be taken, and any documents, things, or places that may be inspected, and any person whose physical or mental condition may be examined.

(c) Any authorized depositions, inspections, and physical and mental examinations shall then be conducted in accordance with the provisions of this title relating to these methods of discovery in a pending action. *(Added by Stats.2004, c. 182 (A.B.3081), § 23, operative July 1, 2005.)*

Law Revision Commission Comments

Subdivision (a) of Section 2036.040 continues the first sentence of former Section 2036(e) without substantive change.

Subdivision (b) continues the second sentence of former Section 2036(e) without change.

Subdivision (c) continues the third sentence of former Section 2036(e) without change, except to replace article with title. [33 Cal.L.Rev.Comm. Reports 969 (2004)].

§ 2036.050. Use of deposition at subsequent proceedings; scope of use

If a deposition to perpetuate testimony has been taken under the provisions of this chapter, it may be used in any later proceeding in accordance with Section 2025.620. *(Added by Stats.2004, c. 182 (A.B.3081), § 23, operative July 1, 2005.)*

Law Revision Commission Comments

Section 2036.050 continues former Section 2036(f) without change, except to replace section with chapter and to conform the cross-reference. [33 Cal.L.Rev.Comm. Reports 969 (2004)].

Title 5

OF THE RIGHTS AND DUTIES OF WITNESSES

Section
2064. Subpoenaed witness; attendance; answering questions.
2065. Fees and mileage; notice of entitlement.

§ 2064. Subpoenaed witness; attendance; answering questions

A witness, served with a subpoena, must attend at the time appointed, with any papers under his control lawfully required by the subpoena, and answer all pertinent and legal questions; and, unless sooner discharged, must remain until the testimony is closed. *(Enacted in 1872. Amended by Stats.1907, c. 395, p. 735, § 1.)*

§ 2065. Fees and mileage; notice of entitlement

Any witness who is subpoenaed in any civil or administrative action or proceeding shall be given written notice on the subpoena that the witness may be entitled to receive fees and mileage. Such notice shall indicate generally the manner in which the request for fees and mileage should be made. *(Added by Stats.1979, c. 67, p. 171, § 1, operative July 1, 1980.)*

Title 6

OF EVIDENCE IN PARTICULAR CASES, AND MISCELLANEOUS AND GENERAL PROVISIONS

CHAPTER 1. EVIDENCE IN PARTICULAR CASES

Section

2074. Rejected offer as equivalent to production and tender of money, instrument, or property.
2075. Right to receipt for payment or delivery.
2076. Objections to tender; time; specification.
2077. Real estate descriptions; rules for construing.

§ 2074. Rejected offer as equivalent to production and tender of money, instrument, or property

An offer in writing to pay a particular sum of money, or to deliver a written instrument or specific personal property, is, if not accepted, equivalent to the actual production and tender of the money, instrument, or property. *(Enacted in 1872.)*

Research References

Miller and Starr California Real Estate § 1:163, Conditions Concurrent--Performance; Requirements for an Effective Tender.
1 Witkin Cal. Summ. 10th Contracts § 771, Requisites of Tender.

§ 2075. Right to receipt for payment or delivery

Whoever pays money, or delivers an instrument or property, is entitled to a receipt therefor from the person to whom the payment or delivery is made, and may demand a proper signature to such receipt as a condition of the payment or delivery. *(Enacted in 1872.)*

§ 2076. Objections to tender; time; specification

The person to whom a tender is made must, at the time, specify any objection he may have to the money, instrument, or property, or he must be deemed to have waived it; and if the objection be to the amount of money, the terms of the instrument, or the amount or kind of property, he must specify the amount, terms, or kind which he requires, or be precluded from objecting afterwards. *(Enacted in 1872.)*

Research References

Miller and Starr California Real Estate § 1:55, Performance of a Legal Obligation.
Miller and Starr California Real Estate § 1:100, Modification of Written Agreement by Subsequent Oral Agreement.
Miller and Starr California Real Estate § 1:112, Accord and Satisfaction--Acceptance of Satisfaction by a Creditor.
Miller and Starr California Real Estate § 1:163, Conditions Concurrent--Performance; Requirements for an Effective Tender.
Miller and Starr California Real Estate § 19:78, Time and Place of Payment; Late Charges.
16 NO. 4 Miller & Starr, California Real Estate Newsalert 26, Deeds of Trust.
21 NO. 6 Miller & Starr, California Real Estate Newsalert 15, Landlord and Tenant.
22 NO. 1 Miller & Starr, California Real Estate Newsalert 20, Landlord and Tenant.
1 Witkin Cal. Summ. 10th Contracts § 277, (S 277) Waiver of Right.
1 Witkin Cal. Summ. 10th Contracts § 772, in General.
1 Witkin Cal. Summ. 10th Contracts § 773, Timely Correction of Mistake.

§ 2077. Real estate descriptions; rules for construing

The following are the rules for construing the descriptive part of a conveyance of real property, when the construction is doubtful and there are no other sufficient circumstances to determine it:

One—Where there are certain definite and ascertained particulars in the description, the addition of others which are indefinite, unknown, or false, does not frustrate the conveyance, but it is to be construed by the first mentioned particulars.

Two—When permanent and visible or ascertained boundaries or monuments are inconsistent with the measurement, either of lines, angles, or surfaces, the boundaries or monuments are paramount.

Three—Between different measurements which are inconsistent with each other, that of angles is paramount to that of surfaces, and that of lines paramount to both.

Four—When a road, or stream of water not navigable, is the boundary, the rights of the grantor to the middle of the road or the thread of the stream are included in the conveyance, except where the road or thread of the stream is held under another title.

Five—When tide water is the boundary, the rights of the grantor to ordinary high-water mark are included in the conveyance. When a navigable lake, where there is no tide, is the boundary, the rights of the grantor to low-water mark are included in the conveyance.

Six—When the description refers to a map, and that reference is inconsistent with other particulars, it controls them if it appear that the parties acted with reference to the map; otherwise the map is subordinate to other definite and ascertained particulars. *(Enacted in 1872. Amended by Code Am.1873–74, c. 383, p. 390, § 244.)*

Research References

Miller and Starr California Real Estate § 8:62, Description of the Property--Rules of Construction; Ambiguities, Conflicting Calls, Monuments and Surveys.
Miller and Starr California Real Estate § 8:63, Description of the Property--Description by Metes and Bounds or Prior Conveyances.
Miller and Starr California Real Estate § 8:65, Road, Street or Highway as Property Boundary.
Miller and Starr California Real Estate § 8:66, Water as Property Boundary--In General.
Miller and Starr California Real Estate § 8:67, Water as Property Boundary--Where Adjacent to Tidewaters.
Miller and Starr California Real Estate § 8:68, Water as Property Boundary--Where Adjacent to Nontidal Waters.
Miller and Starr California Real Estate § 15:45, Estoppel; Executed Oral Conveyance; Irrevocable License.
Miller and Starr California Real Estate § 26:31, Fee or Easement.
12 Witkin, California Summary 10th Real Property § 272, Presumption of Ownership to Center Line.
12 Witkin, California Summary 10th Real Property § 275, (S 275) General Rule.
12 Witkin, California Summary 10th Real Property § 277, Resolving Uncertainties.
12 Witkin, California Summary 10th Real Property § 367, (S 367) Waiver of Conditions.

CHAPTER 3. ADMINISTRATION OF OATHS AND AFFIRMATIONS

Section

2093. Officers authorized to administer oaths or affirmations.
2094. Oath, affirmation, or declaration; form.

§ 2093. Officers authorized to administer oaths or affirmations

(a) Every court, every judge, or clerk of any court, every justice, and every notary public, and every officer or person authorized to take testimony in any action or proceeding, or to decide upon evidence, has the power to administer oaths or affirmations.

(b)(1) Every shorthand reporter certified pursuant to Article 3 (commencing with Section 8020) of Chapter 13 of Division 3 of the Business and Professions Code has the power to administer oaths or affirmations and may perform the duties of the deposition officer pursuant to Chapter 9 (commencing with Section 2025.010) of Title 4. The certified shorthand reporter shall be entitled to receive fees for services rendered during a deposition, including fees for deposition services, as specified in subdivision (c) of Section 8211 of the Government Code.

(2) This subdivision shall also apply to depositions taken by telephone or other remote electronic means as specified in Chapter 2 (commencing with Section 2017.010), Chapter 3 (commencing with Section 2017.710), and Chapter 9 (commencing with Section 2025.010) of Title 4.

(c) A former judge or justice of a court of record in this state who retired or resigned from office, other than a judge or justice who was retired by the Supreme Court for disability, shall have the power to administer oaths or affirmations, if the former judge or justice requests and receives a certification from the Commission on Judicial Performance that there was no formal disciplinary proceeding pending at the time of retirement or resignation. Where no formal disciplinary proceeding was pending at the time of retirement or resignation, the Commission on Judicial Performance shall issue the certification.

No law, rule, or regulation regarding the confidentiality of proceedings of the Commission on Judicial Performance shall be construed to prohibit the Commission on Judicial Performance from issuing a certificate as provided for in this section. *(Enacted in 1872. Amended by Stats.1986, c. 1417, § 3; Stats. 1986, c. 1418, § 1.3; Stats.1988, c. 1032, § 1; Stats.2001, c. 812 (A.B.223), § 12; Stats.2004, c. 182 (A.B.3081), § 24, operative July 1, 2005.)*

Law Revision Commission Comments

Subdivision (b) of Section 2093 is amended to reflect nonsubstantive reorganization of the rules governing civil discovery. [33 Cal.L.Rev. Comm. Reports 1010 (2004)].

Research References

Rutter, Cal. Practice Guide: A.D.R. Ch. 6-B, B. Temporary Judges.
Rutter, Cal. Practice Guide: Civ. Pro. Before Trial Ch. 8E-8, Place of Deposition.
Rutter, Cal. Practice Guide: Civ. Pro. Before Trial Ch. 8E-9, Deposition Officer.
Rutter, Cal. Practice Guide: Personal Injury Ch. 6-B, B. Overview of Selected Discovery Procedures.
Rutter, Cal. Practice Guide: Personal Injury Ch. 9-F, F. Examination of Witnesses.
2 Witkin Cal. Proc. 5th Courts § 344, (S 344) Statutory Duties.
2 Witkin Cal. Proc. 5th Courts § 366, (S 366) Miscellaneous Duties.

§ 2094. Oath, affirmation, or declaration; form

(a) An oath, affirmation, or declaration in an action or a proceeding, may be administered by obtaining an affirmative response to one of the following questions:

(1) "Do you solemnly state that the evidence you shall give in this issue (or matter) shall be the truth, the whole truth, and nothing but the truth, so help you God?"

(2) "Do you solemnly state, under penalty of perjury, that the evidence that you shall give in this issue (or matter) shall be the truth, the whole truth, and nothing but the truth?"

(b) In the alternative to the forms prescribed in subdivision (a), the court may administer an oath, affirmation, or declaration in an action or a proceeding in a manner that is calculated to awaken the person's conscience and impress the person's mind with the duty to tell the truth. The court shall satisfy itself that the person testifying understands that his or her testimony is being given under penalty of perjury. *(Enacted in 1872. Amended Code Am.1873–74, c. 383, p. 394, § 250. Amended by Stats.2000, c. 688 (A.B.1669), § 13; Stats.2002, c. 806 (A.B.3027), § 17.)*

Research References

Rutter, Cal. Practice Guide: Civ. Pro. Before Trial Ch. 8E-10, Preservation of Testimony.

Rutter, Cal. Practice Guide: Civil Trials & Evidence Ch. 9-E, E. Conduct of Direct Examination.
Rutter, Cal. Practice Guide: Civil Trials & Evidence Ch. 8C-A, A. Testimony.
Rutter, Cal. Practice Guide: Personal Injury Ch. 9-F, F. Examination of Witnesses.

Title 7

UNIFORM FEDERAL LIEN REGISTRATION ACT

Section
2100.   Application of title.
2101.   Notices and certificates; place of filing.
2102.   Certification.
2103.   Duties of officer with whom filing made.
2104.   Fee; billing.
2105.   Filings initiated before January 1, 1968.
2106.   Uniformity of construction.
2106.5.   Construction of title; transmission and recording of notices; electronic or magnetic means.
2107.   Short title.

§ 2100. Application of title

This title applies only to federal tax liens and to other federal liens notices of which under any Act of Congress or any regulation adopted pursuant thereto are required or permitted to be filed in the same manner as notices of federal tax liens. *(Added by Stats.1979, c. 330, p. 1185, § 1.)*

Research References

Miller and Starr California Real Estate § 11:180, Priority of Federal Tax Liens--In General.
12 Witkin, California Summary 10th Real Property § 2, Uniform Laws and Model Acts.
12 Witkin, California Summary 10th Real Property § 318, (S 318) Unusual Instruments.
4 Witkin, California Summary 10th Security Transactions in Real Property § 65, Uniform Federal Lien Registration Act.

§ 2101. Notices and certificates; place of filing

(a) Notices of liens, certificates, and other notices affecting federal tax liens or other federal liens must be filed in accordance with this title.

(b) Notices of liens upon real property for obligations payable to the United States and certificates and notices affecting the liens shall be filed for record in the office of the recorder of the county in which the real property subject to the liens is situated.

(c) Notices of federal liens upon personal property, whether tangible or intangible, for obligations payable to the United States and certificates and notices affecting the liens shall be filed as follows:

(1) If the person against whose interest the lien applies is a corporation, a limited liability company, or a partnership whose principal executive office is in this state, as these entities are defined in the internal revenue laws of the United States, in the office of the Secretary of State.

(2) If the person against whose interest the lien applies is a trust that is not covered by paragraph (1), in the office of the Secretary of State.

(3) If the person against whose interest the lien applies is the estate of a decedent, in the office of the Secretary of State.

(4) In all other cases, in the office of the recorder of the county where the person against whose interest the lien applies resides at the time of filing of the notice of lien. *(Added by*

Stats.1979, c. 330, p. 1185, § 1. Amended by Stats.1991, c. 932 (A.B.1646), § 2; Stats.1997, c. 892 (S.B.73), § 2.)

Research References

Miller and Starr California Real Estate § 11:6, Instruments Subject to Recording--List of Recordable Documents.

Miller and Starr California Real Estate § 11:180, Priority of Federal Tax Liens--In General.

4 Witkin, California Summary 10th Security Transactions in Real Property § 65, Uniform Federal Lien Registration Act.

§ 2102. Certification

Certification of notices of liens, certificates, or other notices affecting federal liens by the Secretary of the Treasury of the United States or his or her delegate, or by any official or entity of the United States responsible for filing or certifying of notice of any other lien, entitles them to be filed and no other attestation, certification, or acknowledgment is necessary. *(Added by Stats. 1979, c. 330, p. 1185, § 1.)*

Research References

Miller and Starr California Real Estate § 11:180, Priority of Federal Tax Liens--In General.

4 Witkin, California Summary 10th Security Transactions in Real Property § 65, Uniform Federal Lien Registration Act.

§ 2103. Duties of officer with whom filing made

(a) If a notice of federal lien, a refiling of a notice of federal lien, or a notice of revocation of any certificate described in subdivision (b) is presented to a filing officer who is:

(1) The Secretary of State, he or she shall cause the notice to be filed, indexed, and marked in accordance with the provisions of Sections 9515, 9516, and 9522 of the Commercial Code as if the notice were a financing statement within the meaning of that code; or

(2) A county recorder, he or she shall accept for filing, file for record in the manner set forth in Section 27320 of the Government Code, and index the document by the name of the person against whose interest the lien applies in the general index.

(b) If a certificate of release, nonattachment, discharge, or subordination of any lien is presented to the Secretary of State for filing he or she shall:

(1) Cause a certificate of release or nonattachment to be filed, indexed, and marked as if the certificate were a termination statement within the meaning of the Commercial Code.

(2) Cause a certificate of discharge or subordination to be filed, indexed, and marked as if the certificate were a release of collateral within the meaning of the Commercial Code.

(c) If a refiled notice of federal lien referred to in subdivision (a) or any of the certificates or notices referred to in subdivision (b) is presented for filing to a county recorder, he or she shall accept for filing, file for record in the manner set forth in Section 27320 of the Government Code, and index the document by the name of the person against whose interest the lien applies in the general index.

(d) Upon request of any person, the filing officer shall issue his or her certificate showing whether there is on file, on the date and hour stated therein, any notice of lien or certificate or notice affecting any lien filed after January 1, 1968, under this title or former Chapter 14 (commencing with Section 7200) of Division 7 of Title 1 of the Government Code, naming a particular person, and if a notice or certificate is on file, giving the date and hour of filing of each notice or certificate. Upon request, the filing officer shall furnish a copy of any notice of federal lien, or notice or certificate affecting a federal lien. If the filing officer is a county recorder, the fee for a certificate for each name searched shall be set by the filing officer in an amount that covers actual costs, and the fee for copies shall be in accordance with Section 27366 of the Government Code. If the filing officer is the Secretary of State, the certificate shall be issued as part of a combined certificate pursuant to Section 9528 of the Commercial Code, and the fee for the certificate and copies shall be in accordance with that section. *(Added by Stats.1979, c. 330, p. 1185, § 1. Amended by Stats.1982, c. 865, § 1; Stats.1988, c. 393, § 10; Stats.1999, c. 991 (S.B.45), § 25.5, operative July 1, 2001; Stats.2009, c. 606 (S.B.676), § 1; Stats.2012, c. 494 (S.B.1532), § 2.)*

Research References

Miller and Starr California Real Estate § 11:6, Instruments Subject to Recording--List of Recordable Documents.

Miller and Starr California Real Estate § 10:200, Special Notice to the Internal Revenue Service.

Miller and Starr California Real Estate § 11:180, Priority of Federal Tax Liens--In General.

4 Witkin, California Summary 10th Security Transactions in Real Property § 65, Uniform Federal Lien Registration Act.

4 Witkin, California Summary 10th Secured Transactions in Personal Property § 93, (S 93) Acknowledgments and Responses to Requests.

§ 2104. Fee; billing

The fee charged for recording and indexing each notice of lien or certificate or notice affecting the lien filed with the county recorder shall be the same as those established by Article 5 (commencing with Section 27360) of Chapter 6 of Part 3 of Division 2 of Title 3 of the Government Code for the recording and indexing of documents.

The fee for filing and indexing each notice of lien or certificate or notice affecting the lien with the office of the Secretary of State is set forth in subdivision (a) of Section 12194 of the Government Code.

The officer shall bill the district directors of internal revenue or other appropriate federal officials on a monthly basis for fees for documents recorded or filed by the county recorder or the Secretary of State. *(Added by Stats.1995, c. 656 (S.B.888), § 3.5, operative Jan. 1, 2000. Amended by Stats.1999, c. 1000 (S.B.284), § 13.)*

Research References

12 Witkin, California Summary 10th Real Property § 320, Fees.

4 Witkin, California Summary 10th Security Transactions in Real Property § 65, Uniform Federal Lien Registration Act.

§ 2105. Filings initiated before January 1, 1968

Filing officers with whom notices of federal tax liens, certificates and notices affecting such liens have been filed on or before January 1, 1968, shall, after that date, continue to maintain a file labeled "federal tax lien notices filed prior to January 2, 1968" containing notices and certificates filed in numerical order of receipt. If a notice of lien was filed on or before January 1, 1968, any certificate or notice affecting the lien shall be filed in the same office. *(Added by Stats.1979, c. 330, p. 1185, § 1.)*

Research References

4 Witkin, California Summary 10th Security Transactions in Real Property § 65, Uniform Federal Lien Registration Act.

§ 2106. Uniformity of construction

This title shall be applied and construed to effectuate its general purpose to make uniform the law with respect to the subject of this title among states enacting it. *(Added by Stats.1979, c. 330, p. 1185, § 1.)*

§ 2106.5. Construction of title; transmission and recording of notices; electronic or magnetic means

This title shall be applied and construed to permit the transmission, filing, recording, and indexing of notices of federal tax liens and all certificates that relate to or affect those liens, including, but not limited to, certificates of release, discharge, subordination, and nonattachment, by electronic or magnetic means, using computerized data processing, telecommunications, and other similar information technologies available to the filing offices. *(Added by Stats.1998, c. 463 (A.B.1906), § 1.)*

§ 2107. Short title

This title may be cited as the Uniform Federal Lien Registration Act. *(Added by Stats.1979, c. 330, p. 1185, § 1.)*

EVIDENCE CODE

Division 1

PRELIMINARY PROVISIONS AND CONSTRUCTION

§ 1. Short title

This code shall be known as the Evidence Code. *(Stats.1965, c. 299, § 2, operative Jan. 1, 1967.)*

Law Revision Commission Comments

This section is similar to comparable sections in recently enacted California codes. *E.g.,* Vehicle Code § 1. See also Code Civ.Proc. §§ 1, 19. [7 Cal.L.Rev.Comm. Reports 1 (1965)].

Research References

Rutter, Cal. Practice Guide: Civil Trials & Evidence Ch. 4-C, C. Jury Matters.

Rutter, Cal. Practice Guide: Civil Trials & Evidence Ch. 8E-A, A. Privileges.

Rutter, Cal. Practice Guide: Civil Trials & Evidence Ch. 8F-C, C. Procedural Considerations.

Rutter, Cal. Practice Guide: Personal Injury Ch. 9-F, F. Examination of Witnesses.

9 Witkin Cal. Proc. 5th Appeal § 683, Nature of Remedy.

1 Witkin Cal. Proc. 5th Attorneys § 592, (S 592) in General.

7 Witkin Cal. Proc. 5th Judgment § 439, Judgment on Offer to Compromise.

6 Witkin Cal. Proc. 5th Proceedings Without Trial § 99, (S 99) Judgment on Compromise.

6 Witkin Cal. Proc. 5th Proceedings Without Trial § 603, (S 603) Depositions.

7 Witkin Cal. Proc. 5th Trial § 432, (S 432) Evidence from Examination of Adverse Party.

2 Witkin, California Summary 10th Insurance § 297, Action Defended by Insured.

1 Witkin Cal. Summ. 10th Contracts § 80, (S 80) Where Applicable Law Not Ascertainable.

1 Witkin Cal. Summ. 10th Contracts § 426, Loan to Gambler.

10 Witkin, California Summary 10th Parent and Child § 248, Supreme Court Decisions Resolving Conflict.

11 Witkin, California Summary 10th Husband and Wife § 53, (S 53) in General.

11 Witkin, California Summary 10th Husband and Wife § 54, (S 54) Presumption of Valid Marriage from Proof of Solemnization.

5 Witkin, California Summary 10th Torts § 611, Standard of Proof.

6 Witkin, California Summary 10th Torts § 1064, (S 1064) Distinction: Medical Proctor.

9 Witkin, California Summary 10th Partnership § 10, (S 10) Proof of Oral Agreement.

§ 2. Abrogation of common law rule of strict construction; liberal construction

The rule of the common law, that statutes in derogation thereof are to be strictly construed, has no application to this code. This code establishes the law of this state respecting the subject to which it relates, and its provisions are to be liberally construed with a view to effecting its objects and promoting justice. *(Stats.1965, c. 299, § 2, operative Jan. 1, 1967.)*

Law Revision Commission Comments

This section is substantially the same as Section 4 of the Code of Civil Procedure. [7 Cal.L.Rev.Comm. Reports 1 (1965)].

Research References

Rutter, Cal. Practice Guide: Civil Trials & Evidence Ch. 8E-A, A. Privileges.

12 Witkin, California Summary 10th Real Property § 283, Nature of Requirement.

1 Witkin Cal. Summ. 10th Contracts § 45, Minor Needing Mental Health Treatment.

11 Witkin, California Summary 10th Husband and Wife § 16, (S 16) Licensing of Marriage and Family Therapists.

11 Witkin, California Summary 10th Husband and Wife § 371, (S 371) Civil Remedies.

§ 3. Severability

If any provision or clause of this code or application thereof to any person or circumstances is held invalid, such invalidity shall not affect other provisions or applications of the code which can be given effect without the invalid provision or application, and to this end the provisions of this code are declared to be severable. *(Stats.1965, c. 299, § 2, operative Jan. 1, 1967.)*

Law Revision Commission Comments

Section 3 is the same as Section 1108 of the Commercial Code. See also, *e.g.,* Vehicle Code § 5. This general "severability" provision permits the repeal of comparable provisions applicable to specific sections formerly compiled in the Code of Civil Procedure that are now compiled in the Evidence Code and makes it unnecessary to include similar provisions in future amendments to this code. See Code Civ.Proc. § 1928.4 (superseded by the Evidence Code). [7 Cal.L.Rev.Comm. Reports 1 (1965)].

Research References

Rutter, Cal. Practice Guide: Civil Trials & Evidence Ch. 8E-A, A. Privileges.
8 Witkin, California Summary 10th Constitutional Law § 1012, (S 1012) Nature and Scope.

§ 4. Construction of code

Unless the provision or context otherwise requires, these preliminary provisions and rules of construction shall govern the construction of this code. *(Stats.1965, c. 299, § 2, operative Jan. 1, 1967.)*

Law Revision Commission Comments

This is a standard provision in various California codes. *E.g.,* Vehicle Code § 6. [7 Cal.L.Rev.Comm. Reports 1 (1965)].

Research References

Rutter, Cal. Practice Guide: Civil Trials & Evidence Ch. 8E-A, A. Privileges.

§ 5. Construction of headings

Division, chapter, article, and section headings do not in any manner affect the scope, meaning, or intent of the provisions of this code. *(Stats.1965, c. 299, § 2, operative Jan. 1, 1967.)*

Law Revision Commission Comments

Similar provisions appear in all the existing California codes except the Civil Code, the Commercial Code, and the Code of Civil Procedure. *E.g.,* Vehicle Code § 7. [7 Cal.L.Rev.Comm. Reports 1 (1965)].

§ 6. References to statutes; application

Whenever any reference is made to any portion of this code or of any other statute, such reference shall apply to all amendments and additions heretofore or hereafter made. *(Stats.1965, c. 299, § 2, operative Jan. 1, 1967.)*

Law Revision Commission Comments

This is a standard provision in various California codes. *E.g.,* Vehicle Code § 10. [7 Cal.L.Rev.Comm. Reports 1 (1965)].

§ 7. Definitions

Unless otherwise expressly stated:

(a) "Division" means a division of this code.

(b) "Chapter" means a chapter of the division in which that term occurs.

(c) "Article" means an article of the chapter in which that term occurs.

(d) "Section" means a section of this code.

(e) "Subdivision" means a subdivision of the section in which that term occurs.

(f) "Paragraph" means a paragraph of the subdivision in which that term occurs. *(Stats.1965, c. 299, § 2, operative Jan. 1, 1967.)*

Law Revision Commission Comments

Somewhat similar provisions appear in various California codes. *E.g.,* Vehicle Code § 11. See also Code Civ.Proc. § 17(8). [7 Cal.L.Rev. Comm. Reports 1 (1965)].

§ 8. Construction of tenses

The present tense includes the past and future tenses; and the future, the present. *(Stats.1965, c. 299, § 2, operative Jan. 1, 1967.)*

Law Revision Commission Comments

This is a standard provision in various California codes. *E.g.,* Vehicle Code § 12. See also Code Civ.Proc. § 17. [7 Cal.L.Rev.Comm. Reports 1 (1965)].

§ 9. Construction of gender references

The masculine gender includes the feminine and neuter. *(Stats.1965, c. 299, § 2, operative Jan. 1, 1967.)*

Law Revision Commission Comments

This is a standard provision in various California codes. *E.g.,* Vehicle Code § 13. See also Code Civ.Proc. § 17. [7 Cal.L.Rev.Comm. Reports 1 (1965)].

§ 10. Construction of singular and plural

The singular number includes the plural; and the plural, the singular. *(Stats.1965, c. 299, § 2, operative Jan. 1, 1967.)*

Law Revision Commission Comments

This is a standard provision in various California codes. *E.g.,* Vehicle Code § 14. See also Code Civ.Proc. § 17. [7 Cal.L.Rev.Comm. Reports 1 (1965)].

§ 11. "Shall" and "may"

"Shall" is mandatory and "may" is permissive. *(Stats.1965, c. 299, § 2, operative Jan. 1, 1967.)*

Law Revision Commission Comments

This is a standard provision in various California codes. *E.g.,* Vehicle Code § 15. [7 Cal.L.Rev.Comm. Reports 1 (1965)].

§ 12. Operative date of code; effect on pending proceedings

(a) This code shall become operative on January 1, 1967, and shall govern proceedings in actions brought on or after that date and, except as provided in subdivision (b), further proceedings in actions pending on that date.

(b) Subject to subdivision (c), a trial commenced before January 1, 1967, shall not be governed by this code. For the purpose of this subdivision:

(1) A trial is commenced when the first witness is sworn or the first exhibit is admitted into evidence and is terminated when the issue upon which such evidence is received is submitted to the trier of fact. A new trial, or a separate trial of a different issue, commenced on or after January 1, 1967, shall be governed by this code.

(2) If an appeal is taken from a ruling made at a trial commenced before January 1, 1967, the appellate court shall apply the law applicable at the time of the commencement of the trial.

(c) The provisions of Division 8 (commencing with Section 900) relating to privileges shall govern any claim of privilege made after December 31, 1966. *(Stats.1965, c. 299, § 2, operative Jan. 1, 1967.)*

Division 2

WORDS AND PHRASES DEFINED

Law Revision Commission Comments

Division 2 contains definitions of general application only. Words and phrases that have special significance only to a particular division or article are defined in the division or article in which the defined term is used. For example, Sections 900–905 define terms that are used only in Division 8 (Privileges), and Sections 950–953 define terms that are used in the article relating to the lawyer-client privilege. Some additional sections of general application that are of a definitional nature include Sections 7–11 in Division 1. [7 Cal.L.Rev.Comm. Reports 1 (1965)].

§ 100. Application of definitions

Unless the provision or context otherwise requires, these definitions govern the construction of this code. *(Stats.1965, c. 299, § 2, operative Jan. 1, 1967.)*

Law Revision Commission Comments

Section 100 is a standard provision found in the definitional portion of recently enacted California codes. See, *e.g.,* Vehicle Code § 100. [7 Cal.L.Rev.Comm. Reports 1 (1965)].

§ 105. Action

"Action" includes a civil action and a criminal action. *(Stats. 1965, c. 299, § 2, operative Jan. 1, 1967.)*

Law Revision Commission Comments

Defining the word "action" to include both a civil action or proceeding and a criminal action or proceeding eliminates the necessity of repeating "civil action and criminal action" in numerous code sections. [7 Cal.L.Rev.Comm. Reports 1 (1965)].

§ 110. Burden of producing evidence

"Burden of producing evidence" means the obligation of a party to introduce evidence sufficient to avoid a ruling against him on the issue. *(Stats.1965, c. 299, § 2, operative Jan. 1, 1967.)*

Research References

Rutter, Cal. Practice Guide: Civil Trials & Evidence Ch. 8G-C, C. Presumptions.
Rutter, Cal. Practice Guide: Civil Trials & Evidence Ch. 8G-D, D. Burdens and Standards of Proof.
California Practice Guide: Employment Litigation Ch. 7-A, A. Title VII and the California Fair Employment and Housing Act.
Rutter, Cal. Practice Guide: Personal Injury Ch. 9-E, E. Order of Trial and Proof and Related Matters.

§ 115. Burden of proof

"Burden of proof" means the obligation of a party to establish by evidence a requisite degree of belief concerning a fact in the mind of the trier of fact or the court. The burden of proof may require a party to raise a reasonable doubt concerning the existence or nonexistence of a fact or that he establish the existence or nonexistence of a fact by a preponderance of the evidence, by clear and convincing proof, or by proof beyond a reasonable doubt.

Except as otherwise provided by law, the burden of proof requires proof by a preponderance of the evidence. *(Stats.1965, c. 299, § 2, operative Jan. 1, 1967.)*

Research References

Rutter, Cal. Practice Guide: Civil Trials & Evidence Ch. 5-I, I. Challenging Prospective Jurors.
Rutter, Cal. Practice Guide: Civil Trials & Evidence Ch. 8G-B, B. Procedures on Objection.
Rutter, Cal. Practice Guide: Civil Trials & Evidence Ch. 8G-C, C. Presumptions.
Rutter, Cal. Practice Guide: Civil Trials & Evidence Ch. 8G-D, D. Burdens and Standards of Proof.
California Practice Guide: Employment Litigation Ch. 7-A, A. Title VII and the California Fair Employment and Housing Act.
California Practice Guide: Employment Litigation Ch. 19-O, O. Burdens and Standards of Proof.
Rutter, Cal. Practice Guide: Family Law Ch. 8-B, B. Property Characterization.
Rutter, Cal. Practice Guide: Family Law Ch. 20-A, A. Nonmarital "Marvin" Cohabitation Relationships.
Rutter, Cal. Practice Guide: Insurance Litigation Ch. 13-C, C. Punitive Damages.
Rutter, Cal. Practice Guide: Personal Injury Ch. 9-E, E. Order of Trial and Proof and Related Matters.
Miller and Starr California Real Estate § 1:100, Modification of Written Agreement by Subsequent Oral Agreement.
Miller and Starr California Real Estate § 1:124, Definitions; Burden of Proof.
Miller and Starr California Real Estate § 12:41, Basic Rules for Determining Character of Property; Definitions--Presumptions, Generally.
17 NO. 2 Miller & Starr, California Real Estate Newsalert 16, Holding Title.
18 NO. 1 Miller & Starr, California Real Estate Newsalert 16, Holding Title.
3 Witkin Cal. Proc. 5th Actions § 394, Burden and Degree of Proof.
3 Witkin Cal. Proc. 5th Actions § 593, (S 593) Statutory Rule.
9 Witkin Cal. Proc. 5th Administrative Proceedings § 111, Evidence.
10 Witkin, California Summary 10th Parent and Child § 345, (S 345) Clear and Convincing Evidence is Required.
10 Witkin, California Summary 10th Parent and Child § 679, (S 679) Eighteen-Month Review.

Evidence

10 Witkin, California Summary 10th Parent and Child § 741, (S 741) Duty to Suspend Proceedings and Certify to Juvenile Court.

11 Witkin, California Summary 10th Community Property § 11, (S 11) Valuation Based on Date of Separation.

5 Witkin, California Summary 10th Torts § 611, Standard of Proof.

5 Witkin, California Summary 10th Torts § 769, (S 769) Standard of Proof.

9 Witkin, California Summary 10th Partnership § 10, (S 10) Proof of Oral Agreement.

14 Witkin, California Summary 10th Wills and Probate § 996, (S 996) Removal of Life Support.

§ 120. Civil action

"Civil action" includes civil proceedings. *(Stats.1965, c. 299, § 2, operative Jan. 1, 1967.)*

Law Revision Commission Comments

Defining "civil action" to include civil proceedings eliminates the necessity of repeating "civil action or proceeding" in numerous code sections, and, together with the definition of "criminal action" in Section 130, it assures the applicability of the Evidence Code to all actions and proceedings. See Evidence Code § 300. [7 Cal.L.Rev.Comm. Reports 1 (1965)].

§ 125. Conduct

"Conduct" includes all active and passive behavior, both verbal and nonverbal. *(Stats.1965, c. 299, § 2, operative Jan. 1, 1967.)*

Law Revision Commission Comments

This broad definition of "conduct" is self-explanatory. [7 Cal.L.Rev. Comm. Reports 1 (1965)].

§ 130. Criminal action

"Criminal action" includes criminal proceedings. *(Stats.1965, c. 299, § 2, operative Jan. 1, 1967.)*

Law Revision Commission Comments

See the Comment to Section 120. [7 Cal.L.Rev.Comm. Reports 1 (1965)].

§ 135. Declarant

"Declarant" is a person who makes a statement. *(Stats.1965, c. 299, § 2, operative Jan. 1, 1967.)*

Law Revision Commission Comments

Ordinarily, the word "declarant" is used in the Evidence Code to refer to a person who makes a hearsay statement as distinguished from the witness who testifies to the content of the statement. See Evidence Code § 1200 and the Comment thereto. [7 Cal.L.Rev.Comm. Reports 1 (1965)].

Research References

Rutter, Cal. Practice Guide: Civil Trials & Evidence Ch. 8D-B, B. Hearsay vs. Nonhearsay.

§ 140. Evidence

"Evidence" means testimony, writings, material objects, or other things presented to the senses that are offered to prove the existence or nonexistence of a fact. *(Stats.1965, c. 299, § 2, operative Jan. 1, 1967.)*

Law Revision Commission Comments

"Evidence" is defined broadly to include the testimony of witnesses, tangible objects, sights (such as a jury view or the appearance of a person exhibited to a jury), sounds (such as the sound of a voice demonstrated for a jury), and any other thing that may be presented as a basis of proof. The definition includes anything offered in evidence whether or not it is technically inadmissible and whether or not it is received. For example, Division 10 (commencing with Section 1200) uses "evidence" to refer to hearsay which may be excluded as inadmissible but which may be admitted

if no proper objection is made. Thus, when inadmissible hearsay or opinion testimony is admitted without objection, this definition makes it clear that it constitutes evidence that may be considered by the trier of fact.

Section 140 is a better statement of existing law than Code of Civil Procedure Section 1823, which is superseded by Section 140. Although Section 1823 by its terms restricts "judicial evidence" to that "sanctioned by law," the general principle is well established that matter which is technically inadmissible under an exclusionary rule is nonetheless evidence and may be considered in support of a judgment if it is offered and received in evidence without proper objection or motion to strike. *E.g.,* People v. Alexander, 212 Cal.App.2d 84, 98, 27 Cal.Rptr. 720, 727 (1963) ("illustrations of this principle are numerous and cover a wide range of evidentiary topics such as incompetent hearsay, secondary evidence violating the best evidence rule, inadmissible opinions, lack of foundation, incompetent, privileged or unqualified witnesses, and violations of the parol evidence rule"). See Witkin, California Evidence §§ 723–724 (1958).

Under this definition, a presumption is not evidence. See also Evidence Code § 600 and the Comment thereto. [7 Cal.L.Rev.Comm. Reports 1 (1965)].

Research References

Rutter, Cal. Practice Guide: Civil Trials & Evidence Ch. 8A-A, A. Types of Evidence.

Rutter, Cal. Practice Guide: Civil Trials & Evidence Ch. 8C-A, A. Testimony.

Rutter, Cal. Practice Guide: Civil Trials & Evidence Ch. 8C-B, B. Writings.

Rutter, Cal. Practice Guide: Civil Trials & Evidence Ch. 8C-C, C. Material Objects ("Real Evidence").

Rutter, Cal. Practice Guide: Civil Trials & Evidence Ch. 8F-C, C. Procedural Considerations.

Rutter, Cal. Practice Guide: Civil Trials & Evidence Ch. 8G-A, A. Objections and Motions Challenging Admissibility.

Rutter, Cal. Practice Guide: Civil Trials & Evidence Ch. 8G-B, B. Procedures on Objection.

§ 145. The hearing

"The hearing" means the hearing at which a question under this code arises, and not some earlier or later hearing. *(Stats. 1965, c. 299, § 2, operative Jan. 1, 1967.)*

Law Revision Commission Comments

"The hearing" is defined to mean the hearing at which the particular question under the Evidence Code arises, and, unless a particular provision or its context otherwise indicates, not some earlier or later hearing. This definition is much broader than would be a reference to the trial itself; the definition includes, for example, preliminary hearings and post-trial proceedings. [7 Cal.L.Rev.Comm. Reports 1 (1965)].

§ 150. Hearsay evidence

"Hearsay evidence" is defined in Section 1200. *(Stats.1965, c. 299, § 2, operative Jan. 1, 1967.)*

Law Revision Commission Comments

Because of its special significance to Division 10, the substantive definition of "hearsay evidence" is contained in Section 1200. See the Comment to Section 1200. [7 Cal.L.Rev.Comm. Reports 1 (1965)].

§ 160. Law

"Law" includes constitutional, statutory, and decisional law. *(Stats.1965, c. 299, § 2, operative Jan. 1, 1967.)*

Law Revision Commission Comments

This definition makes it clear that a reference to "law" includes the law established by judicial decisions as well as by constitutional and statutory provisions. [7 Cal.L.Rev.Comm. Reports 1 (1965)].

Research References

Rutter, Cal. Practice Guide: Civil Trials & Evidence Ch. 8D-C, C. General Parameters Re Admissibility of Hearsay Evidence.

Rutter, Cal. Practice Guide: Civil Trials & Evidence Ch. 8G-C, C. Presumptions.

Rutter, Cal. Practice Guide: Civil Trials & Evidence Ch. 8G-D, D. Burdens and Standards of Proof.

§ 165. Oath

"Oath" includes affirmation or declaration under penalty of perjury. *(Stats.1965, c. 299, § 2, operative Jan. 1, 1967.)*

Law Revision Commission Comments

Similar definitions are found in other California codes. *E.g.,* Vehicle Code § 16. [7 Cal.L.Rev.Comm. Reports 1 (1965)].

Research References

Rutter, Cal. Practice Guide: Civil Trials & Evidence Ch. 8C-A, A. Testimony.

§ 170. Perceive

"Perceive" means to acquire knowledge through one's senses. *(Stats.1965, c. 299, § 2, operative Jan. 1, 1967.)*

Law Revision Commission Comments

This definition is self-explanatory. [7 Cal.L.Rev.Comm. Reports 1 (1965)].

Research References

Rutter, Cal. Practice Guide: Civil Trials & Evidence Ch. 8C-A, A. Testimony.

Rutter, Cal. Practice Guide: Civil Trials & Evidence Ch. 8C-H, H. Opinion Evidence.

§ 175. Person

"Person" includes a natural person, firm, association, organization, partnership, business trust, corporation, limited liability company, or public entity. *(Stats.1965, c. 299, § 2, operative Jan. 1, 1967. Amended by Stats.1994, c. 1010 (S.B.2053), § 103.)*

Law Revision Commission Comments

This broad definition is similar to definitions found in other codes. *E.g.,* Govt.Code § 17; Vehicle Code § 470. See also Code Civ.Proc. § 17. [7 Cal.L.Rev.Comm. Reports 1 (1965)].

Research References

Rutter, Cal. Practice Guide: Civil Trials & Evidence Ch. 8E-A, A. Privileges.

Rutter, Cal. Practice Guide: Personal Injury Ch. 6-A, A. Scope of Discovery and Limitations.

Rutter, Cal. Practice Guide: Prof. Responsibility Ch. 7-C, C. Attorney-Client Privilege.

§ 177. Dependent person

"Dependent person" means any person who has a physical or mental impairment that substantially restricts his or her ability to carry out normal activities or to protect his or her rights, including, but not limited to, persons who have physical or developmental disabilities or whose physical or mental abilities have significantly diminished because of age. "Dependent person" includes any person who is admitted as an inpatient to a 24–hour health facility, as defined in Sections 1250, 1250.2, and 1250.3 of the Health and Safety Code. *(Added by Stats.2004, c. 823 (A.B.20), § 2.)*

§ 180. Personal property

"Personal property" includes money, goods, chattels, things in action, and evidences of debt. *(Stats.1965, c. 299, § 2, operative Jan. 1, 1967.)*

Law Revision Commission Comments

This definition is the same as the definition of "personal property" in Section 17(3) of the Code of Civil Procedure. [7 Cal.L.Rev.Comm. Reports 1 (1965)].

§ 185. Property

"Property" includes both real and personal property. *(Stats. 1965, c. 299, § 2, operative Jan. 1, 1967.)*

Law Revision Commission Comments

This definition is the same as the definition of "property" in Section 17(1) of the Code of Civil Procedure. [7 Cal.L.Rev.Comm. Reports 1 (1965)].

§ 190. Proof

"Proof" is the establishment by evidence of a requisite degree of belief concerning a fact in the mind of the trier of fact or the court. *(Stats.1965, c. 299, § 2, operative Jan. 1, 1967.)*

Law Revision Commission Comments

This definition is more accurate than the definition of "proof" in Code of Civil Procedure Section 1824, which is superseded by Section 190. The disjunctive reference to "the trier of fact or the court" is needed because, even when the jury is the trier of fact, the court is required to determine preliminary questions of fact on the basis of proof. [7 Cal.L.Rev.Comm. Reports 1 (1965)].

Research References

Rutter, Cal. Practice Guide: Civ. Pro. Before Trial Ch. 8G-10, Sanctions in Enforcing Rfas.

Rutter, Cal. Practice Guide: Civil Trials & Evidence Ch. 8G-D, D. Burdens and Standards of Proof.

§ 195. Public employee

"Public employee" means an officer, agent, or employee of a public entity. *(Stats.1965, c. 299, § 2, operative Jan. 1, 1967.)*

Law Revision Commission Comments

This definition specifically includes public officers and agents, thereby eliminating any distinction between employees and officers and making it unnecessary to repeat the phrase "officer, agent, or employee" in numerous code sections. [7 Cal.L.Rev.Comm. Reports 1 (1965)].

Research References

Rutter, Cal. Practice Guide: Civil Trials & Evidence Ch. 8D-D, D. Hearsay Exceptions.

§ 200. Public entity

"Public entity" includes a nation, state, county, city and county, city, district, public authority, public agency, or any other political subdivision or public corporation, whether foreign or domestic. *(Stats.1965, c. 299, § 2, operative Jan. 1, 1967.)*

Law Revision Commission Comments

The broad definition of "public entity" includes every form of public authority, both foreign and domestic. Occasionally, "public entity" is used in the Evidence Code with limiting language to refer specifically to entities within this State or the United States. *E.g.,* Evidence Code § 452(b). *Cf.* Evidence Code § 452(f). [7 Cal.L.Rev.Comm. Reports 1 (1965)].

Research References

Rutter, Cal. Practice Guide: Civ. Pro. Before Trial Ch. 7(I)-A, A. Demurrers.

6 Witkin, California Summary 10th Torts § 877, (S 877) Agency Manual is Not Regulation.

§ 205. Real property

"Real property" includes lands, tenements, and hereditaments. *(Stats.1965, c. 299, § 2, operative Jan. 1, 1967.)*

Evidence

Law Revision Commission Comments

This definition is substantially the same as the definition of "real property" in Section 17(2) of the Code of Civil Procedure. [7 Cal.L.Rev. Comm. Reports 1 (1965)].

§ 210. Relevant evidence

"Relevant evidence" means evidence, including evidence relevant to the credibility of a witness or hearsay declarant, having any tendency in reason to prove or disprove any disputed fact that is of consequence to the determination of the action. *(Stats.1965, c. 299, § 2, operative Jan. 1, 1967.)*

Law Revision Commission Comments

This definition restates existing law. *E.g.,* Larson v. Solbakken, 221 Cal.App.2d 410, 419, 34 Cal.Rptr. 450, 455 (1963); People v. Lint, 182 Cal.App.2d 402, 415, 6 Cal.Rptr. 95, 102–103 (1960). Thus, under Section 210, "relevant evidence" includes not only evidence of the ultimate facts actually in dispute but also evidence of other facts from which such ultimate facts may be presumed or inferred. This retains existing law as found in subdivisions 1 and 15 of Code of Civil Procedure Section 1870, which are superseded by the Evidence Code. In addition, Section 210 makes it clear that evidence relating to the credibility of witnesses and hearsay declarants is "relevant evidence." This restates existing law. See Code Civ.Proc. §§ 1868, 1870(16) (credibility of witnesses), which are superseded by the Evidence Code, and Tentative Recommendation and a Study Relating to the Uniform Rules of Evidence (Article VIII. Hearsay Evidence), 6 Cal.Law Revision Comm'n, Rep., Rec. & Studies Appendix at 339–340, 569–575 (1964) (credibility of hearsay declarants). [7 Cal.L.Rev.Comm. Reports 1 (1965)].

Research References

Rutter, Cal. Practice Guide: Civ. Pro. Before Trial Ch. 10-C, C. Procedural Requirements-Moving Party.
Rutter, Cal. Practice Guide: Civil Trials & Evidence Ch. 4-B, B. Preliminary Matters Discussed in Final Status Conference or In-Chambers Conference.
Rutter, Cal. Practice Guide: Civil Trials & Evidence Ch. 8B-A, A. General Considerations.
Rutter, Cal. Practice Guide: Civil Trials & Evidence Ch. 8C-K, K. Stipulations.
Rutter, Cal. Practice Guide: Civil Trials & Evidence Ch. 8D-B, B. Hearsay vs. Nonhearsay.
Rutter, Cal. Practice Guide: Civil Trials & Evidence Ch. 8E-G, G. Parol Evidence Rule.
Rutter, Cal. Practice Guide: Insurance Litigation Ch. 15-I, I. Trial.
Rutter, Cal. Practice Guide: Personal Injury Ch. 9-E, E. Order of Trial and Proof and Related Matters.
Rutter, Cal. Practice Guide: Personal Injury Ch. 9-I, I. Use of Writings, Exhibits and Demonstrative Evidence.

§ 220. State

"State" means the State of California, unless applied to the different parts of the United States. In the latter case, it includes any state, district, commonwealth, territory, or insular possession of the United States. *(Stats.1965, c. 299, § 2, operative Jan. 1, 1967.)*

Law Revision Commission Comments

This definition is more precise than the comparable definition found in Section 17(7) of the Code of Civil Procedure. For example, Section 220 makes it clear that "state" includes Puerto Rico, even though Puerto Rico is now a "commonwealth" rather than a "territory." [7 Cal.L.Rev.Comm. Reports 1 (1965)].

§ 225. Statement

"Statement" means (a) oral or written verbal expression or (b) nonverbal conduct of a person intended by him as a substitute for oral or written verbal expression. *(Stats.1965, c. 299, § 2, operative Jan. 1, 1967.)*

Law Revision Commission Comments

The significance of this definition is explained in the Comment to Evidence Code Section 1200. [7 Cal.L.Rev.Comm. Reports 1 (1965)].

Research References

Rutter, Cal. Practice Guide: Civil Trials & Evidence Ch. 8D-B, B. Hearsay vs. Nonhearsay.

§ 230. Statute

"Statute" includes a treaty and a constitutional provision. *(Stats.1965, c. 299, § 2, operative Jan. 1, 1967.)*

Law Revision Commission Comments

In the Evidence Code, "statute" includes a constitutional provision. Thus, for example, when a particular section in subject to any exceptions "otherwise provided by statute," exceptions provided by the Constitution also are applicable. [7 Cal.L.Rev.Comm. Reports 1 (1965)].

Research References

Rutter, Cal. Practice Guide: Civil Trials & Evidence Ch. 8B-A, A. General Considerations.

§ 235. Trier of fact

"Trier of fact" includes (a) the jury and (b) the court when the court is trying an issue of fact other than one relating to the admissibility of evidence. *(Stats.1965, c. 299, § 2, operative Jan. 1, 1967.)*

Law Revision Commission Comments

"Trier of fact" is defined to include not only the jury but also the court when it is trying an issue of fact without a jury. The definition is not exclusive; a referee, court commissioner, or other officer conducting proceedings governed by the Evidence Code may be a trier of fact. See Evidence Code § 300. [7 Cal.L.Rev.Comm. Reports 1 (1965)].

§ 240. Unavailable as a witness

(a) Except as otherwise provided in subdivision (b), "unavailable as a witness" means that the declarant is any of the following:

(1) Exempted or precluded on the ground of privilege from testifying concerning the matter to which his or her statement is relevant.

(2) Disqualified from testifying to the matter.

(3) Dead or unable to attend or to testify at the hearing because of then-existing physical or mental illness or infirmity.

(4) Absent from the hearing and the court is unable to compel his or her attendance by its process.

(5) Absent from the hearing and the proponent of his or her statement has exercised reasonable diligence but has been unable to procure his or her attendance by the court's process.

(6) Persistent in refusing to testify concerning the subject matter of the declarant's statement despite having been found in contempt for refusal to testify.

(b) A declarant is not unavailable as a witness if the exemption, preclusion, disqualification, death, inability, or absence of the declarant was brought about by the procurement or wrongdoing of the proponent of his or her statement for the purpose of preventing the declarant from attending or testifying.

(c) Expert testimony that establishes that physical or mental trauma resulting from an alleged crime has caused harm to a witness of sufficient severity that the witness is physically unable to testify or is unable to testify without suffering substantial trauma may constitute a sufficient showing of unavailability pursuant to paragraph (3) of subdivision (a). As used in this section, the term "expert" means a physician and surgeon, including a psychiatrist, or any person described by subdivision (b), (c), or (e) of Section 1010.

The introduction of evidence to establish the unavailability of a witness under this subdivision shall not be deemed procurement of unavailability, in absence of proof to the contrary. *(Stats.1965, c. 299, § 2, operative Jan. 1, 1967. Amended by Stats.1984, c. 401, § 1; Stats.1988, c. 485, § 1; Stats.2010, c. 537 (A.B.1723), § 1.)*

Research References

Rutter, Cal. Practice Guide: Civ. Pro. Before Trial Ch. 8E-17, Use of Depositions at Trial.

Rutter, Cal. Practice Guide: Civil Trials & Evidence Ch. 4-B, B. Preliminary Matters Discussed in Final Status Conference or In-Chambers Conference.

Rutter, Cal. Practice Guide: Civil Trials & Evidence Ch. 11-E, E. Impeachment Evidence from Other Witnesses.

Rutter, Cal. Practice Guide: Civil Trials & Evidence Ch. 8C-A, A. Testimony.

Rutter, Cal. Practice Guide: Civil Trials & Evidence Ch. 8C-I, I. Depositions and Discovery.

Rutter, Cal. Practice Guide: Civil Trials & Evidence Ch. 8D-C, C. General Parameters Re Admissibility of Hearsay Evidence.

Rutter, Cal. Practice Guide: Civil Trials & Evidence Ch. 8D-D, D. Hearsay Exceptions.

Rutter, Cal. Practice Guide: Family Law Ch. 13-B, B. Contested Family Law Trial.

Rutter, Cal. Practice Guide: Personal Injury Ch. 9-H, H. Introduction of Discovered Evidence.

6 Witkin Cal. Proc. 5th Proceedings Without Trial § 603, (S 603) Depositions.

10 Witkin, California Summary 10th Parent and Child § 578, (S 578) Confrontation and Cross-Examination.

14 Witkin, California Summary 10th Wills and Probate § 545, Proof by Subscribing Witness.

§ 250. Writing

"Writing" means handwriting, typewriting, printing, photostating, photographing, photocopying, transmitting by electronic mail or facsimile, and every other means of recording upon any tangible thing, any form of communication or representation, including letters, words, pictures, sounds, or symbols, or combinations thereof, and any record thereby created, regardless of the manner in which the record has been stored. *(Stats.1965, c. 299, § 2, operative Jan. 1, 1967. Amended by Stats.2002, c. 945 (A.B.1962), § 1.)*

Law Revision Commission Comments

"Writing" is defined very broadly to include all forms of tangible expression, including pictures and sound recordings. [7 Cal.L.Rev. Comm. Reports 1 (1965)].

Research References

Rutter, Cal. Practice Guide: A.D.R. Ch. 2-F, F. Wrapping Up Settlement.

Rutter, Cal. Practice Guide: A.D.R. Ch. 3-C, C. Confidentiality.

Rutter, Cal. Practice Guide: Civ. Pro. Before Trial Ch. 13-A, A. Introduction.

Rutter, Cal. Practice Guide: Civ. Pro. Before Trial Ch. 8C-4, Attorney Work Product Protection.

Rutter, Cal. Practice Guide: Civ. Pro. Before Trial Ch. 8F-3, Propounding Interrogatories.

Rutter, Cal. Practice Guide: Civ. Pro. Before Trial Ch. 8H-2, What May be Inspected.

Rutter, Cal. Practice Guide: Civ. Pro. Before Trial Ch. 9(I)-B, B. Preparing and Filing Motions.

Rutter, Cal. Practice Guide: Civ. Pro. Before Trial Ch. 12(II)-F, F. Motion to Enforce Settlement (CCP §§ 664.6, 664.7).

Rutter, Cal. Practice Guide: Civil Trials & Evidence Ch. 8C-B, B. Writings.

Rutter, Cal. Practice Guide: Civil Trials & Evidence Ch. 8D-D, D. Hearsay Exceptions.

Rutter, Cal. Practice Guide: Civil Trials & Evidence Ch. 8E-D, D. Other Public Policy Exclusions.

California Practice Guide: Employment Litigation Ch. 18-E, E. Confidentiality of ADR Processes.

Rutter, Cal. Practice Guide: Personal Injury Ch. 6-B, B. Overview of Selected Discovery Procedures.

Rutter, Cal. Practice Guide: Personal Injury Ch. 7-A, A. Introduction-Nature and Purpose of "Judicial Arbitration" in General.

Rutter, Cal. Practice Guide: Prof. Responsibility Ch. 4-A, A. General Considerations.

Rutter, Cal. Practice Guide: Prof. Responsibility Ch. 1 App., California Rules of Professional Conduct.

1 Witkin Cal. Proc. 5th Attorneys § 438, (S 438) in General.

5 Witkin, California Summary 10th Torts § 563, Scope of Privilege.

§ 255. Original

"Original" means the writing itself or any counterpart intended to have the same effect by a person executing or issuing it. An "original" of a photograph includes the negative or any print therefrom. If data are stored in a computer or similar device, any printout or other output readable by sight, shown to reflect the data accurately, is an "original." *(Added by Stats.1977, c. 708, p. 2268, § 1.)*

Research References

Rutter, Cal. Practice Guide: Civil Trials & Evidence Ch. 8C-B, B. Writings.

Rutter, Cal. Practice Guide: Insurance Litigation Ch. 15-I, I. Trial.

§ 260. Duplicate

A "duplicate" is a counterpart produced by the same impression as the original, or from the same matrix, or by means of photography, including enlargements and miniatures, or by mechanical or electronic rerecording, or by chemical reproduction, or by other equivalent technique which accurately reproduces the original. *(Added by Stats.1977, c. 708, p. 2268, § 2.)*

Research References

Rutter, Cal. Practice Guide: Civ. Pro. Before Trial Ch. 10-C, C. Procedural Requirements-Moving Party.

Rutter, Cal. Practice Guide: Civil Trials & Evidence Ch. 8C-B, B. Writings.

Rutter, Cal. Practice Guide: Civil Trials & Evidence Ch. 8C-E, E. Audio or Visual Recordings.

Rutter, Cal. Practice Guide: Enforcing Judgments/Debts Ch. 4-A, A. Attachment.

Rutter, Cal. Practice Guide: Insurance Litigation Ch. 15-I, I. Trial.

Division 3

GENERAL PROVISIONS

CHAPTER 1. APPLICABILITY OF CODE

§ 300. Applicability of code

Except as otherwise provided by statute, this code applies in every action before the Supreme Court or a court of appeal or superior court, including proceedings in such actions conducted by a referee, court commissioner, or similar officer, but does not apply in grand jury proceedings. *(Stats.1965, c. 299, § 2, operative Jan. 1, 1967. Amended by Stats.1967, c. 17, p. 836, § 35; Stats.1998, c. 931 (S.B.2139), § 141, eff. Sept. 28, 1998; Stats. 2002, c. 784 (S.B.1316), § 101.)*

Law Revision Commission Comments

Section 300 makes the Evidence Code applicable to all proceedings conducted by California courts except those court proceedings to which it is made inapplicable by statute. The provisions of the code do not apply in administrative proceedings, legislative hearings, or any other proceedings unless some statute so provides or the agency concerned chooses to apply them.

Various code sections—in the Evidence Code as well as in other codes—make the provisions of the Evidence Code applicable to a certain extent in proceedings other than court proceedings. *E.g.,* Govt.Code § 11513 (a finding in a proceeding conducted under the Administrative Procedure Act may not be based on hearsay evidence unless the evidence would be admissible over objection in a civil action); Penal Code § 939.6 (a grand jury, in investigating a charge, may receive only evidence admissible over objection in a criminal action); Evidence Code § 910 (provisions of the Evidence Code relating to privileges are applicable in all proceedings of every kind in which testimony can be compelled to be given); and Evidence Code § 1566 (Sections 1560–1565 are applicable in nonjudicial proceedings).

Section 300 does not affect any other statute relaxing rules of evidence for specified purposes. See, *e.g.,* Code Civ.Proc. § 117g (judge of small claims court may make informal investigation either in or out of court), § 1768 (hearing of conciliation proceeding to be conducted informally), § 2016(b) (inadmissibility of testimony at trial is not ground for objection to testimony sought from a deponent, provided that such testimony is reasonably calculated to lead to the discovery of admissible evidence); Penal Code § 1203 (judge must consider probation officer's investigative report on question of probation); Welf. & Inst. Code § 706 (juvenile court must consider probation officer's social study in determining disposition to be made of ward or dependent child). [7 Cal.L.Rev.Comm. Reports 1 (1965)].

Section 300 is amended to reflect elimination of the justice court. Cal. Const. art. VI, §§ 1, 5(b). [28 Cal.L.Rev.Comm. Reports 51 (1998)].

Section 300 is amended to reflect unification of the municipal and superior courts pursuant to Article VI, Section 5(e), of the California Constitution. [32 Cal.L.Rev.Comm. Reports 157 (2002)].

Research References

Rutter, Cal. Practice Guide: A.D.R. Ch. 6-B, B. Temporary Judges.
Rutter, Cal. Practice Guide: A.D.R. Ch. 6-C, C. Referees.
Rutter, Cal. Practice Guide: Civil Trials & Evidence Ch. 16-G, G. Trial by Reference.
Rutter, Cal. Practice Guide: Civil Trials & Evidence Ch. 8D-C, C. General Parameters Re Admissibility of Hearsay Evidence.
Miller and Starr California Real Estate § 35:20, The Reference Procedure.
6 Witkin Cal. Proc. 5th Proceedings Without Trial § 73, (S 73) Hearing.
6 Witkin Cal. Proc. 5th Proceedings Without Trial § 498, (S 498) Procedure.
10 Witkin, California Summary 10th Parent and Child § 303, in General.
10 Witkin, California Summary 10th Parent and Child § 679, (S 679) Eighteen-Month Review.

CHAPTER 2. PROVINCE OF COURT AND JURY

Section

§ 310. Questions of law for court

(a) All questions of law (including but not limited to questions concerning the construction of statutes and other writings, the admissibility of evidence, and other rules of evidence) are to be decided by the court. Determination of issues of fact preliminary to the admission of evidence are to be decided by the court as provided in Article 2 (commencing with Section 400) of Chapter 4.

(b) Determination of the law of an organization of nations or of the law of a foreign nation or a public entity in a foreign nation is a question of law to be determined in the manner provided in Division 4 (commencing with Section 450). *(Stats. 1965, c. 299, § 2, operative Jan. 1, 1967.)*

Research References

Rutter, Cal. Practice Guide: Civil Trials & Evidence Ch. 2-B, B. What Constitutes Jury Trial.
Rutter, Cal. Practice Guide: Insurance Litigation Ch. 4-A, A. "General Rules" of Policy Interpretation.
Rutter, Cal. Practice Guide: Personal Injury Ch. 3-C, C. Specific Items of Compensatory Damages.
7 Witkin Cal. Proc. 5th Trial § 81, Jury Tries Issues of Fact Only.
7 Witkin Cal. Proc. 5th Trial § 256, (S 256) Nature of Instruction.

§ 311. Foreign law applicable; law undetermined; procedures

If the law of an organization of nations, a foreign nation or a state other than this state, or a public entity in a foreign nation or a state other than this state, is applicable and such law cannot be determined, the court may, as the ends of justice require, either:

(a) Apply the law of this state if the court can do so consistently with the Constitution of the United States and the Constitution of this state; or

(b) Dismiss the action without prejudice or, in the case of a reviewing court, remand the case to the trial court with directions to dismiss the action without prejudice. *(Stats.1965, c. 299, § 2, operative Jan. 1, 1967.)*

Research References

1 Witkin Cal. Summ. 10th Contracts § 80, (S 80) Where Applicable Law Not Ascertainable.

§ 312. Jury as trier of fact

Except as otherwise provided by law, where the trial is by jury:

(a) All questions of fact are to be decided by the jury.

(b) Subject to the control of the court, the jury is to determine the effect and value of the evidence addressed to it, including the credibility of witnesses and hearsay declarants. *(Stats.1965, c. 299, § 2, operative Jan. 1, 1967.)*

Law Revision Commission Comments

Section 312 restates the substance of and supersedes Section 2101 and the first sentence of Section 2061 of the Code of Civil Procedure. The rule stated in Section 312 is subject to such exceptions as are otherwise provided by statutory or decisional law. See, *e.g.,* Evidence Code §§ 310, 311, 457. [7 Cal.L.Rev.Comm. Reports 1 (1965)].

Research References

Rutter, Cal. Practice Guide: Civil Trials & Evidence Ch. 2-B, B. What Constitutes Jury Trial.
Rutter, Cal. Practice Guide: Civil Trials & Evidence Ch. 16-B, B. Judge's Role as Trier of Fact.
7 Witkin Cal. Proc. 5th Trial § 81, Jury Tries Issues of Fact Only.
7 Witkin Cal. Proc. 5th Trial § 256, (S 256) Nature of Instruction.

7 Witkin Cal. Proc. 5th Trial § 289, (S 289) Power to Instruct.

CHAPTER 3.   ORDER OF PROOF

Section
320.   Power of court to regulate order of proof.

§ 320.   Power of court to regulate order of proof

Except as otherwise provided by law, the court in its discretion shall regulate the order of proof.   *(Stats.1965, c. 299, § 2, operative Jan. 1, 1967.)*

Law Revision Commission Comments

Section 320 restates the substance of and supersedes the first sentence of Section 2042 of the Code of Civil Procedure.   Under Section 320, as under existing law, the trial judge has wide discretion to determine the order of proof.   See California Civil Procedure During Trial, Parrish, Order of Proof, 205 (Cal.Cont.Ed.Bar 1960).   Of course, the order of proof ordinarily should be as prescribed in Code of Civil Procedure Section 607 or 631.7 (added in this recommendation [Chapter 299, Statutes of 1965]) or in Penal Code Sections 1093 and 1094.

Directions of the trial judge which control the order of proof should be distinguished from those which actually exclude evidence.   Obviously, it is not permissible, through repeated directions of the order of proof, to prevent a party from presenting relevant evidence on a disputed fact.   Foster v. Keating, 120 Cal.App.2d 435, 261 P.2d 529 (1953);   California Civil Procedure During Trial, Parrish, Order of Proof, 205, 210 (Cal. Cont.Ed.Bar 1960).   See also Murry v. Manley, 170 Cal.App.2d 364, 338 P.2d 976 (1959).   [7 Cal.L.Rev.Comm. Reports 1 (1965)].

Research References

Rutter, Cal. Practice Guide: Civil Trials & Evidence Ch. 1-M, M. Order of Proceedings.
Rutter, Cal. Practice Guide: Civil Trials & Evidence Ch. 2-C, C. Cases in Which Jury Trial May be Demanded.
Rutter, Cal. Practice Guide: Civil Trials & Evidence Ch. 4-B, B. Preliminary Matters Discussed in Final Status Conference or In-Chambers Conference.
Rutter, Cal. Practice Guide: Civil Trials & Evidence Ch. 4-G, G. Motion to Sever or Bifurcate.
Rutter, Cal. Practice Guide: Civil Trials & Evidence Ch. 4-I, I. Other Motions at Final Status Conference.
Rutter, Cal. Practice Guide: Civil Trials & Evidence Ch. 12-D, D. Other Motions During Trial.
Rutter, Cal. Practice Guide: Civil Trials & Evidence Ch. 16-A, A. General Considerations Re Nonjury Trials.
Rutter, Cal. Practice Guide: Civil Trials & Evidence Ch. 8G-A, A. Objections and Motions Challenging Admissibility.
Rutter, Cal. Practice Guide: Personal Injury Ch. 9-E, E. Order of Trial and Proof and Related Matters.
6 Witkin Cal. Proc. 5th Proceedings Without Trial § 210, Trial of Special Defenses.
7 Witkin Cal. Proc. 5th Trial § 149, (S 149) Order of Proof: in General.
7 Witkin Cal. Proc. 5th Trial § 154, in General.

CHAPTER 4.   ADMITTING AND EXCLUDING EVIDENCE

ARTICLE 1.   GENERAL PROVISIONS

§ 350.   Only relevant evidence admissible

No evidence is admissible except relevant evidence.   *(Stats. 1965, c. 299, § 2, operative Jan. 1, 1967.)*

Law Revision Commission Comments

Section 350 restates and supersedes that portion of Code of Civil Procedure Section 1868 requiring the exclusion of irrelevant evidence.   [7 Cal.L.Rev.Comm. Reports 1 (1965)].

Research References

Rutter, Cal. Practice Guide: Civ. Pro. Before Trial Ch. 6-A, A. Introduction.
Rutter, Cal. Practice Guide: Civil Trials & Evidence Ch. 4-B, B. Preliminary Matters Discussed in Final Status Conference or In-Chambers Conference.
Rutter, Cal. Practice Guide: Civil Trials & Evidence Ch. 4-F, F. Motions in Limine.
Rutter, Cal. Practice Guide: Civil Trials & Evidence Ch. 6-C, C. Improper Conduct During Opening Statement.
Rutter, Cal. Practice Guide: Civil Trials & Evidence Ch. 11-B, B. Procedures to Challenge Admissibility of Expert Witness Testimony.
Rutter, Cal. Practice Guide: Civil Trials & Evidence Ch. 8A-C, C. Analytic Approach.
Rutter, Cal. Practice Guide: Civil Trials & Evidence Ch. 8B-A, A. General Considerations.
Rutter, Cal. Practice Guide: Civil Trials & Evidence Ch. 8C-K, K. Stipulations.
Rutter, Cal. Practice Guide: Civil Trials & Evidence Ch. 8D-B, B. Hearsay vs. Nonhearsay.
Rutter, Cal. Practice Guide: Civil Trials & Evidence Ch. 8D-D, D. Hearsay Exceptions.
Rutter, Cal. Practice Guide: Civil Trials & Evidence Ch. 8E-E, E. Limitations on Character Evidence.
California Practice Guide: Employment Litigation Ch. 19-J, J. Motions in Limine.
Rutter, Cal. Practice Guide: Insurance Litigation Ch. 15-I, I. Trial.

§ 351.   Admissibility of relevant evidence

Except as otherwise provided by statute, all relevant evidence is admissible.   *(Stats.1965, c. 299, § 2, operative Jan. 1, 1967.)*

Law Revision Commission Comments

Section 351 abolishes all limitations on the admissibility of relevant evidence except those that are based on a statute, including a constitutional provision.   See Evidence Code § 230.   The Evidence Code contains a number of provisions that exclude relevant evidence either for reasons of public policy or because the evidence is too unreliable to be presented to the trier of fact.   See, *e.g.,* Evidence Code § 352 (cumulative, unduly prejudicial, etc. evidence), §§ 900–1070 (privileges), §§ 1100–1156 (extrinsic policies), § 1200 (hearsay).   Other codes also contain provisions that may in some cases result in the exclusion of relevant evidence.   See, *e.g.,* Civil Code §§ 79.06, 79.09, 227; Code Civ.Proc. § 1747; Educ.Code § 14026; Fin.Code § 8754; Fish and Game Code § 7923; Govt.Code §§ 15619, 18573, 18934, 18952, 20134, 31532; Health & Saf.Code §§ 211.5, 410; Ins.Code §§ 735, 855, 10381.5; Labor Code § 6319; Penal Code §§ 290, 938.1, 3046, 3107, 11105; Pub.Res.Code § 3234; Rev. & Tax.Code §§ 16563, 19282–19289; Unempl.Ins.Code §§ 1094, 2111, 2714; Vehicle Code §§ 1808, 16005, 20012–20015, 40803, 40804, 40832, 40833; Water Code § 12516; Welf. & Inst.Code §§ 118, 827.   [7 Cal.L.Rev.Comm.Reports 1 (1965)].

Evidence

Research References

Rutter, Cal. Practice Guide: Civil Trials & Evidence Ch. 4-B, B. Preliminary Matters Discussed in Final Status Conference or In-Chambers Conference.

Rutter, Cal. Practice Guide: Civil Trials & Evidence Ch. 8B-A, A. General Considerations.

Rutter, Cal. Practice Guide: Civil Trials & Evidence Ch. 8D-B, B. Hearsay vs. Nonhearsay.

Rutter, Cal. Practice Guide: Civil Trials & Evidence Ch. 8E-D, D. Other Public Policy Exclusions.

Rutter, Cal. Practice Guide: Civil Trials & Evidence Ch. 8F-A, A. General Considerations.

California Practice Guide: Employment Litigation Ch. 19-N, N. Evidence Issues.

Rutter, Cal. Practice Guide: Personal Injury Ch. 9-E, E. Order of Trial and Proof and Related Matters.

Rutter, Cal. Practice Guide: Personal Injury Ch. 9-F, F. Examination of Witnesses.

Rutter, Cal. Practice Guide: Personal Injury Ch. 9-I, I. Use of Writings, Exhibits and Demonstrative Evidence.

22 NO. 6 Miller & Starr, California Real Estate Newsalert 13, Eminent Domain.

6 Witkin, California Summary 10th Torts § 1692, Earnings of Husband and Father.

§ 351.1. Polygraph examinations; results, opinion of examiner or reference; exclusion

(a) Notwithstanding any other provision of law, the results of a polygraph examination, the opinion of a polygraph examiner, or any reference to an offer to take, failure to take, or taking of a polygraph examination, shall not be admitted into evidence in any criminal proceeding, including pretrial and post conviction motions and hearings, or in any trial or hearing of a juvenile for a criminal offense, whether heard in juvenile or adult court, unless all parties stipulate to the admission of such results.

(b) Nothing in this section is intended to exclude from evidence statements made during a polygraph examination which are otherwise admissible. *(Added by Stats.1983, c. 202, § 1, eff. July 12, 1983.)*

Research References

Rutter, Cal. Practice Guide: Civil Trials & Evidence Ch. 8C-G, G. Scientific Evidence.

Rutter, Cal. Practice Guide: Civil Trials & Evidence Ch. 8C-K, K. Stipulations.

10 Witkin, California Summary 10th Parent and Child § 617, (S 617) in General.

10 Witkin, California Summary 10th Parent and Child § 872, (S 872) in General.

§ 352. Discretion of court to exclude evidence

The court in its discretion may exclude evidence if its probative value is substantially outweighed by the probability that its admission will (a) necessitate undue consumption of time or (b) create substantial danger of undue prejudice, of confusing the issues, or of misleading the jury. *(Stats.1965, c. 299, § 2, operative Jan. 1, 1967.)*

Law Revision Commission Comments

Section 352 expresses a rule recognized by statute and in several California decisions. Code Civ. Proc. §§ 1868, 2044 (superseded by the Evidence Code); Adkins v. Brett, 184 Cal. 252, 258, 193 Pac. 251, 254 (1920) ("the matter [of excluding prejudicial evidence] is largely one of discretion on the part of the trial judge"); Moody v. Peirano, 4 Cal.App. 411, 418, 88 Pac. 380, 382 (1906) ("a wide discretion is left to the trial judge in determining whether [evidence of a collateral nature] is admissible or not"). [7 Cal.L.Rev.Comm.Reports 1 (1965)].

Research References

Rutter, Cal. Practice Guide: Civil Appeals & Writs Ch. 1-D, D. Access to Appellate Courts and Considerations Impacting Success on Appeal.

Rutter, Cal. Practice Guide: Civil Appeals & Writs Ch. 8-C, C. Standards of Appellate Review.

Rutter, Cal. Practice Guide: Civil Appeals & Writs Ch. 9-B, B. Approaches to Briefwriting.

Rutter, Cal. Practice Guide: Civ. Pro. Before Trial Ch. 3-A, A. Subject Matter Jurisdiction (Competency).

Rutter, Cal. Practice Guide: Civ. Pro. Before Trial Ch. 8F-9, Use of Interrogatories at Trial.

Rutter, Cal. Practice Guide: Civil Trials & Evidence Ch. 1-C, C. Marshalling the Evidence.

Rutter, Cal. Practice Guide: Civil Trials & Evidence Ch. 4-B, B. Preliminary Matters Discussed in Final Status Conference or In-Chambers Conference.

Rutter, Cal. Practice Guide: Civil Trials & Evidence Ch. 4-C, C. Jury Matters.

Rutter, Cal. Practice Guide: Civil Trials & Evidence Ch. 4-F, F. Motions in Limine.

Rutter, Cal. Practice Guide: Civil Trials & Evidence Ch. 5-G, G. Scope of Permissible Voir Dire-Proper vs. Improper Questions.

Rutter, Cal. Practice Guide: Civil Trials & Evidence Ch. 9-B, B. Form of Questions.

Rutter, Cal. Practice Guide: Civil Trials & Evidence Ch. 10-B, B. Scope of Permissible Cross-Examination.

Rutter, Cal. Practice Guide: Civil Trials & Evidence Ch. 10-C, C. Form of Questions.

Rutter, Cal. Practice Guide: Civil Trials & Evidence Ch. 10-D, D. Objectives of Cross-Examination.

Rutter, Cal. Practice Guide: Civil Trials & Evidence Ch. 11-A, A. Direct Examination of Expert Witnesses.

Rutter, Cal. Practice Guide: Civil Trials & Evidence Ch. 11-B, B. Procedures to Challenge Admissibility of Expert Witness Testimony.

Rutter, Cal. Practice Guide: Civil Trials & Evidence Ch. 11-D, D. Cross-Examination of Expert Witnesses.

Rutter, Cal. Practice Guide: Civil Trials & Evidence Ch. 12-A, A. Motion for Mistrial.

Rutter, Cal. Practice Guide: Civil Trials & Evidence Ch. 15-C, C. Matters Allowed in Jury Room During Deliberations.

Rutter, Cal. Practice Guide: Civil Trials & Evidence Ch. 8A-C, C. Analytic Approach.

Rutter, Cal. Practice Guide: Civil Trials & Evidence Ch. 8B-A, A. General Considerations.

Rutter, Cal. Practice Guide: Civil Trials & Evidence Ch. 8B-B, B. Particular Types of Evidence.

Rutter, Cal. Practice Guide: Civil Trials & Evidence Ch. 8B-C, C. Procedural Considerations.

Rutter, Cal. Practice Guide: Civil Trials & Evidence Ch. 8C-C, C. Material Objects ("Real Evidence").

Rutter, Cal. Practice Guide: Civil Trials & Evidence Ch. 8C-D, D. Demonstrative Evidence.

Rutter, Cal. Practice Guide: Civil Trials & Evidence Ch. 8C-E, E. Audio or Visual Recordings.

Rutter, Cal. Practice Guide: Civil Trials & Evidence Ch. 8C-H, H. Opinion Evidence.

Rutter, Cal. Practice Guide: Civil Trials & Evidence Ch. 8C-J, J. Judicial Notice.

Rutter, Cal. Practice Guide: Civil Trials & Evidence Ch. 8D-B, B. Hearsay vs. Nonhearsay.

Rutter, Cal. Practice Guide: Civil Trials & Evidence Ch. 8D-D, D. Hearsay Exceptions.

Rutter, Cal. Practice Guide: Civil Trials & Evidence Ch. 8E-D, D. Other Public Policy Exclusions.

Rutter, Cal. Practice Guide: Civil Trials & Evidence Ch. 8E-E, E. Limitations on Character Evidence.

Rutter, Cal. Practice Guide: Civil Trials & Evidence Ch. 8E-F, F. Limitations on Impeachment and Rehabilitation.

Rutter, Cal. Practice Guide: Civil Trials & Evidence Ch. 8E-G, G. Parol Evidence Rule.

Rutter, Cal. Practice Guide: Civil Trials & Evidence Ch. 8F-A, A. General Considerations.

Rutter, Cal. Practice Guide: Civil Trials & Evidence Ch. 8F-B, B. Particular Grounds.

Rutter, Cal. Practice Guide: Civil Trials & Evidence Ch. 8F-C, C. Procedural Considerations.

Rutter, Cal. Practice Guide: Civil Trials & Evidence Ch. 8G-B, B. Procedures on Objection.

Rutter, Cal. Practice Guide: Civil Trials & Evidence Ch. 4-F, Outline F.

Rutter, Cal. Practice Guide: Civil Trials & Evidence Ch. 10-B, Outline B.

Rutter, Cal. Practice Guide: Civil Trials & Evidence Ch. 10-D, Outline D.
Rutter, Cal. Practice Guide: Civil Trials & Evidence Ch. 11-D, Outline D.
Rutter, Cal. Practice Guide: Civil Trials & Evidence Ch. 8C-D, Outline D.
Rutter, Cal. Practice Guide: Civil Trials & Evidence Ch. 8C-E, Outline E.
Rutter, Cal. Practice Guide: Civil Trials & Evidence Ch. 8C-H, Outline H.
Rutter, Cal. Practice Guide: Civil Trials & Evidence Ch. 8E-E, Outline E.
California Practice Guide: Employment Litigation Ch. 7-A, A. Title VII and the California Fair Employment and Housing Act.
California Practice Guide: Employment Litigation Ch. 10-D, D. Employer Liability for Workplace Harassment.
California Practice Guide: Employment Litigation Ch. 19-J, J. Motions in Limine.
California Practice Guide: Employment Litigation Ch. 19-N, N. Evidence Issues.
Rutter, Cal. Practice Guide: Family Law Ch. 7-B, B. Contested Custody Proceedings, Generally.
Rutter, Cal. Practice Guide: Family Law Ch. 13-B, B. Contested Family Law Trial.
Rutter, Cal. Practice Guide: Insurance Litigation Ch. 13-C, C. Punitive Damages.
Rutter, Cal. Practice Guide: Insurance Litigation Ch. 7A-G, G. Intentional Acts Limitation.
Rutter, Cal. Practice Guide: Insurance Litigation Ch. 12C-D, D. Application-Matters Held "Unreasonable".
Rutter, Cal. Practice Guide: Landlord-Tenant Ch. 9-D, D. Assignment to Trial.
Rutter, Cal. Practice Guide: Personal Injury Ch. 3-C, C. Specific Items of Compensatory Damages.
Rutter, Cal. Practice Guide: Personal Injury Ch. 4-D, D. Techniques Where Settlement Not Forthcoming.
Rutter, Cal. Practice Guide: Personal Injury Ch. 8-C, C. Two Months Before Trial.
Rutter, Cal. Practice Guide: Personal Injury Ch. 9-B, B. In-Chambers Conference Before Commencement of Trial.
Rutter, Cal. Practice Guide: Personal Injury Ch. 9-E, E. Order of Trial and Proof and Related Matters.
Rutter, Cal. Practice Guide: Personal Injury Ch. 9-F, F. Examination of Witnesses.
Rutter, Cal. Practice Guide: Personal Injury Ch. 9-H, H. Introduction of Discovered Evidence.
Rutter, Cal. Practice Guide: Personal Injury Ch. 9-I, I. Use of Writings, Exhibits and Demonstrative Evidence.
Rutter, Cal. Practice Guide: Personal Injury Ch. 3-C, Outline C.
Rutter, Cal. Practice Guide: Personal Injury Ch. 4-D, Outline D.
Rutter, Cal. Practice Guide: Personal Injury Ch. 2(I)-C, C. Special Considerations Re Product Liability Investigations.
22 NO. 6 Miller & Starr, California Real Estate Newsalert 7, Common Interest Developments.
2 Witkin Cal. Proc. 5th Courts § 301, (S 301) Admission and Exclusion of Evidence.
7 Witkin Cal. Proc. 5th Trial § 219, (S 219) Evidence Relevant on Issue.
1 Witkin Cal. Summ. 10th Contracts § 923, (S 923) Distinction: Deduction for Tax Benefits.
10 Witkin, California Summary 10th Parent and Child § 30, Blood Test Disproving Paternity.
10 Witkin, California Summary 10th Parent and Child § 540, in General.
10 Witkin, California Summary 10th Parent and Child § 887, in General.
8 Witkin, California Summary 10th Constitutional Law § 926, Discrimination Based on Pregnancy.

§ 352.1. Criminal sex acts; victim's address and telephone number

In any criminal proceeding under Section 261, 262, or 264.1, subdivision (d) of Section 286, or subdivision (d) of Section 288a of the Penal Code, or in any criminal proceeding under subdivision (c) of Section 286 or subdivision (c) of Section 288a of the Penal Code in which the defendant is alleged to have compelled the participation of the victim by force, violence, duress, menace, or threat of great bodily harm, the district attorney may, upon written motion with notice to the defendant or the defendant's attorney, if he or she is represented by an attorney, within a reasonable time prior to any hearing, move to exclude from evidence the current address and telephone number of any victim at the hearing.

The court may order that evidence of the victim's current address and telephone number be excluded from any hearings conducted pursuant to the criminal proceeding if the court finds that the probative value of the evidence is outweighed by the creation of substantial danger to the victim.

Nothing in this section shall abridge or limit the defendant's right to discover or investigate the information. *(Added by Stats.1985, c. 335, § 3. Amended by Stats.1996, c. 1075 (S.B. 1444), § 5.)*

§ 353. Erroneous admission of evidence; effect

A verdict or finding shall not be set aside, nor shall the judgment or decision based thereon be reversed, by reason of the erroneous admission of evidence unless:

(a) There appears of record an objection to or a motion to exclude or to strike the evidence that was timely made and so stated as to make clear the specific ground of the objection or motion; and

(b) The court which passes upon the effect of the error or errors is of the opinion that the admitted evidence should have been excluded on the ground stated and that the error or errors complained of resulted in a miscarriage of justice. *(Stats.1965, c. 299, § 2, operative Jan. 1, 1967.)*

Research References

Rutter, Cal. Practice Guide: Civil Appeals & Writs Ch. 8-D, D. Limits on Assertion of Issues on Appeal.
Rutter, Cal. Practice Guide: Civil Appeals & Writs Ch. 8-E, E. Limits on Reversal or Modification-"Prejudicial Error" Rule.
Rutter, Cal. Practice Guide: Civ. Pro. Before Trial Ch. 11-B, B. Involuntary Dismissals.
Rutter, Cal. Practice Guide: Civ. Pro. Before Trial Ch. 8F-9, Use of Interrogatories at Trial.
Rutter, Cal. Practice Guide: Civ. Pro. Before Trial Ch. 8E-12, Conduct of Deposition.
Rutter, Cal. Practice Guide: Civ. Pro. Before Trial Ch. 9(I)-B, B. Preparing and Filing Motions.
Rutter, Cal. Practice Guide: Civil Trials & Evidence Ch. 4-F, F. Motions in Limine.
Rutter, Cal. Practice Guide: Civil Trials & Evidence Ch. 5-H, H. Challenging Improper Questions.
Rutter, Cal. Practice Guide: Civil Trials & Evidence Ch. 6-D, D. Objecting to Improper Opening Statement.
Rutter, Cal. Practice Guide: Civil Trials & Evidence Ch. 11-A, A. Direct Examination of Expert Witnesses.
Rutter, Cal. Practice Guide: Civil Trials & Evidence Ch. 11-B, B. Procedures to Challenge Admissibility of Expert Witness Testimony.
Rutter, Cal. Practice Guide: Civil Trials & Evidence Ch. 12-A, A. Motion for Mistrial.
Rutter, Cal. Practice Guide: Civil Trials & Evidence Ch. 8B-C, C. Procedural Considerations.
Rutter, Cal. Practice Guide: Civil Trials & Evidence Ch. 8C-A, A. Testimony.
Rutter, Cal. Practice Guide: Civil Trials & Evidence Ch. 8C-B, B. Writings.
Rutter, Cal. Practice Guide: Civil Trials & Evidence Ch. 8C-H, H. Opinion Evidence.
Rutter, Cal. Practice Guide: Civil Trials & Evidence Ch. 8D-D, D. Hearsay Exceptions.
Rutter, Cal. Practice Guide: Civil Trials & Evidence Ch. 8E-G, G. Parol Evidence Rule.
Rutter, Cal. Practice Guide: Civil Trials & Evidence Ch. 8F-C, C. Procedural Considerations.
Rutter, Cal. Practice Guide: Civil Trials & Evidence Ch. 8G-A, A. Objections and Motions Challenging Admissibility.
Rutter, Cal. Practice Guide: Family Law Ch. 16-B, B. Challenge by Appeal.
Rutter, Cal. Practice Guide: Family Law Ch. 18-B, B. Enforcement Remedies and Procedures.
Rutter, Cal. Practice Guide: Personal Injury Ch. 9-E, E. Order of Trial and Proof and Related Matters.
22 NO. 5 Miller & Starr, California Real Estate Newsalert 8, Easements.

Evidence

9 Witkin Cal. Proc. 5th Appeal § 1019, (S 1019) Rehearing.

§ 354. Erroneous exclusion of evidence; effect

A verdict or finding shall not be set aside, nor shall the judgment or decision based thereon be reversed, by reason of the erroneous exclusion of evidence unless the court which passes upon the effect of the error or errors is of the opinion that the error or errors complained of resulted in a miscarriage of justice and it appears of record that:

(a) The substance, purpose, and relevance of the excluded evidence was made known to the court by the questions asked, an offer of proof, or by any other means;

(b) The rulings of the court made compliance with subdivision (a) futile; or

(c) The evidence was sought by questions asked during cross-examination or recross-examination. *(Stats.1965, c. 299, § 2, operative Jan. 1, 1967.)*

Law Revision Commission Comments

Section 354, like Section 353, reiterates the requirement of the California Constitution that a judgment may not be reversed, nor may a new trial be granted, because of an error unless the error is prejudicial. Cal.Const., Art. VI, § 4½.

The provisions of Section 354 that require an offer of proof or other disclosure of the evidence improperly excluded reflect existing law. See Witkin, California Evidence § 713 (1958). The exceptions to this requirement that are stated in Section 354 also reflect existing law. Thus, an offer of proof is unnecessary where the judge has limited the issues so that an offer to prove matters related to excluded issues would be futile. Lawless v. Calaway, 24 Cal.2d 81, 91, 147 P.2d 604, 609 (1944). An offer of proof is also unnecessary when an objection is improperly sustained to a question on cross-examination. Tossman v. Newman, 37 Cal.2d 522, 525–526, 233 P.2d 1, 3 (1951) ("no offer of proof is necessary in order to obtain a review of rulings on cross-examination"); People v. Jones, 160 Cal. 358, 117 Pac. 176 (1911). [7 Cal.L.Rev.Comm.Reports 1 (1965)].

Research References

Rutter, Cal. Practice Guide: Civil Appeals & Writs Ch. 8-D, D. Limits on Assertion of Issues on Appeal.

Rutter, Cal. Practice Guide: Civil Appeals & Writs Ch. 8-E, E. Limits on Reversal or Modification-"Prejudicial Error" Rule.

Rutter, Cal. Practice Guide: Civ. Pro. Before Trial Ch. 11-B, B. Involuntary Dismissals.

Rutter, Cal. Practice Guide: Civil Trials & Evidence Ch. 4-F, F. Motions in Limine.

Rutter, Cal. Practice Guide: Civil Trials & Evidence Ch. 8B-C, C. Procedural Considerations.

Rutter, Cal. Practice Guide: Civil Trials & Evidence Ch. 8C-H, H. Opinion Evidence.

Rutter, Cal. Practice Guide: Civil Trials & Evidence Ch. 8E-D, D. Other Public Policy Exclusions.

Rutter, Cal. Practice Guide: Civil Trials & Evidence Ch. 8F-C, C. Procedural Considerations.

Rutter, Cal. Practice Guide: Civil Trials & Evidence Ch. 8G-B, B. Procedures on Objection.

Rutter, Cal. Practice Guide: Family Law Ch. 5-D, D. Notice of Motion/OSC and Stipulation Procedures.

Rutter, Cal. Practice Guide: Family Law Ch. 16-B, B. Challenge by Appeal.

Rutter, Cal. Practice Guide: Personal Injury Ch. 9-E, E. Order of Trial and Proof and Related Matters.

§ 355. Limited admissibility

When evidence is admissible as to one party or for one purpose and is inadmissible as to another party or for another purpose, the court upon request shall restrict the evidence to its proper scope and instruct the jury accordingly. *(Stats.1965, c. 299, § 2, operative Jan. 1, 1967.)*

Law Revision Commission Comments

Section 355 codifies existing law which requires the court to instruct the jury as to the limited purpose for which evidence may be considered when

such evidence is admissible for one purpose and inadmissible for another. See Adkins v. Brett, 184 Cal. 252, 193 Pac. 251 (1920).

Under Section 352, as under existing law, the judge is permitted to exclude such evidence if he deems it so prejudicial that a limiting instruction would not protect a party adequately and the matter in question can be proved sufficiently by other evidence. See discussion in Adkins v. Brett, 184 Cal. 252, 258, 193 Pac. 251, 254 (1920); Tentative Recommendation and a Study Relating to the Uniform Rules of Evidence (Article VI. Extrinsic Policies Affecting Admissibility), 6 Cal.Law Revision Comm'n, Rep., Rec. & Studies 601, 612, 639–640 (1964). [7 Cal.L.Rev. Comm. Reports 1 (1965)].

Research References

Rutter, Cal. Practice Guide: Civil Trials & Evidence Ch. 4-F, F. Motions in Limine.

Rutter, Cal. Practice Guide: Civil Trials & Evidence Ch. 15-C, C. Matters Allowed in Jury Room During Deliberations.

Rutter, Cal. Practice Guide: Civil Trials & Evidence Ch. 8B-C, C. Procedural Considerations.

Rutter, Cal. Practice Guide: Civil Trials & Evidence Ch. 8E-D, D. Other Public Policy Exclusions.

Rutter, Cal. Practice Guide: Civil Trials & Evidence Ch. 8G-B, B. Procedures on Objection.

7 Witkin Cal. Proc. 5th Trial § 296, Limited Admission.

§ 356. Entire act, declaration, conversation, or writing to elucidate part offered

Where part of an act, declaration, conversation, or writing is given in evidence by one party, the whole on the same subject may be inquired into by an adverse party; when a letter is read, the answer may be given; and when a detached act, declaration, conversation, or writing is given in evidence, any other act, declaration, conversation, or writing which is necessary to make it understood may also be given in evidence. *(Stats.1965, c. 299, § 2, operative Jan. 1, 1967.)*

Research References

Rutter, Cal. Practice Guide: Civil Trials & Evidence Ch. 10-B, B. Scope of Permissible Cross-Examination.

Rutter, Cal. Practice Guide: Civil Trials & Evidence Ch. 10-D, D. Objectives of Cross-Examination.

Rutter, Cal. Practice Guide: Civil Trials & Evidence Ch. 8B-A, A. General Considerations.

Rutter, Cal. Practice Guide: Personal Injury Ch. 9-I, I. Use of Writings, Exhibits and Demonstrative Evidence.

ARTICLE 2. PRELIMINARY DETERMINATIONS ON ADMISSIBILITY OF EVIDENCE

Section

§ 400. "Preliminary fact" defined

As used in this article, "preliminary fact" means a fact upon the existence or nonexistence of which depends the admissibility or inadmissibility of evidence. The phrase "the admissibility or inadmissibility of evidence" includes the qualification or disqualification of a person to be a witness and the existence or nonexistence of a privilege. *(Stats.1965, c. 299, § 2, operative Jan. 1, 1967.)*

Law Revision Commission Comments

"Preliminary fact" is defined to distinguish those facts upon which the admissibility of evidence depends from those facts sought to be proved by that evidence. [7 Cal.L.Rev.Comm. Reports 1 (1965)].

Research References

Rutter, Cal. Practice Guide: Civil Trials & Evidence Ch. 8C-B, B. Writings.

Rutter, Cal. Practice Guide: Civil Trials & Evidence Ch. 8E-A, A. Privileges.

Rutter, Cal. Practice Guide: Civil Trials & Evidence Ch. 8E-D, D. Other Public Policy Exclusions.

Rutter, Cal. Practice Guide: Civil Trials & Evidence Ch. 8G-B, B. Procedures on Objection.

Rutter, Cal. Practice Guide: Family Law Ch. 13-B, B. Contested Family Law Trial.

Rutter, Cal. Practice Guide: Personal Injury Ch. 9-E, E. Order of Trial and Proof and Related Matters.

10 Witkin, California Summary 10th Parent and Child § 617, (S 617) in General.

§ 401. "Proffered evidence" defined

As used in this article, "proffered evidence" means evidence, the admissibility or inadmissibility of which is dependent upon the existence or nonexistence of a preliminary fact. *(Stats.1965, c. 299, § 2, operative Jan. 1, 1967.)*

Law Revision Commission Comments

"Proffered evidence" is defined to avoid confusion between evidence whose admissibility is in question and evidence offered on the preliminary fact issue. "Proffered evidence" includes such matters as the testimony to be elicited from a witness who is claimed to be disqualified, testimony or tangible evidence claimed to be privileged, and any other evidence to which objection is made. [7 Cal.L.Rev.Comm. Reports 1 (1965)].

Research References

Rutter, Cal. Practice Guide: Civil Trials & Evidence Ch. 8G-B, B. Procedures on Objection.

§ 402. Procedure for determining foundational and other preliminary facts

(a) When the existence of a preliminary fact is disputed, its existence or nonexistence shall be determined as provided in this article.

(b) The court may hear and determine the question of the admissibility of evidence out of the presence or hearing of the jury; but in a criminal action, the court shall hear and determine the question of the admissibility of a confession or admission of the defendant out of the presence and hearing of the jury if any party so requests.

(c) A ruling on the admissibility of evidence implies whatever finding of fact is prerequisite thereto; a separate or formal finding is unnecessary unless required by statute. *(Stats.1965, c. 299, § 2, operative Jan. 1, 1967.)*

Research References

Rutter, Cal. Practice Guide: Civ. Pro. Before Trial Ch. 8C-3, "Not Privileged".

Rutter, Cal. Practice Guide: Civil Trials & Evidence Ch. 2-B, B. What Constitutes Jury Trial.

Rutter, Cal. Practice Guide: Civil Trials & Evidence Ch. 4-A, A. General Considerations.

Rutter, Cal. Practice Guide: Civil Trials & Evidence Ch. 4-F, F. Motions in Limine.

Rutter, Cal. Practice Guide: Civil Trials & Evidence Ch. 10-A, A. Preliminary Considerations.

Rutter, Cal. Practice Guide: Civil Trials & Evidence Ch. 11-A, A. Direct Examination of Expert Witnesses.

Rutter, Cal. Practice Guide: Civil Trials & Evidence Ch. 11-B, B. Procedures to Challenge Admissibility of Expert Witness Testimony.

Rutter, Cal. Practice Guide: Civil Trials & Evidence Ch. 8C-G, G. Scientific Evidence.

Rutter, Cal. Practice Guide: Civil Trials & Evidence Ch. 8D-C, C. General Parameters Re Admissibility of Hearsay Evidence.

Rutter, Cal. Practice Guide: Civil Trials & Evidence Ch. 8E-A, A. Privileges.

Rutter, Cal. Practice Guide: Civil Trials & Evidence Ch. 8F-C, C. Procedural Considerations.

Rutter, Cal. Practice Guide: Civil Trials & Evidence Ch. 8G-B, B. Procedures on Objection.

Rutter, Cal. Practice Guide: Civil Trials & Evidence Ch. 8G-B, Outline B.

Rutter, Cal. Practice Guide: Personal Injury Ch. 9-E, E. Order of Trial and Proof and Related Matters.

22 NO. 6 Miller & Starr, California Real Estate Newsalert 8, Construction Law and Contracting.

§ 403. Determination of foundational and other preliminary facts where relevancy, personal knowledge, or authenticity is disputed

(a) The proponent of the proffered evidence has the burden of producing evidence as to the existence of the preliminary fact, and the proffered evidence is inadmissible unless the court finds that there is evidence sufficient to sustain a finding of the existence of the preliminary fact, when:

(1) The relevance of the proffered evidence depends on the existence of the preliminary fact;

(2) The preliminary fact is the personal knowledge of a witness concerning the subject matter of his testimony;

(3) The preliminary fact is the authenticity of a writing; or

(4) The proffered evidence is of a statement or other conduct of a particular person and the preliminary fact is whether that person made the statement or so conducted himself.

(b) Subject to Section 702, the court may admit conditionally the proffered evidence under this section, subject to evidence of the preliminary fact being supplied later in the course of the trial.

(c) If the court admits the proffered evidence under this section, the court:

(1) May, and on request shall, instruct the jury to determine whether the preliminary fact exists and to disregard the proffered evidence unless the jury finds that the preliminary fact does exist.

(2) Shall instruct the jury to disregard the proffered evidence if the court subsequently determines that a jury could not reasonably find that the preliminary fact exists. *(Stats.1965, c. 299, § 2, operative Jan. 1, 1967.)*

Research References

Rutter, Cal. Practice Guide: Civil Trials & Evidence Ch. 4-B, B. Preliminary Matters Discussed in Final Status Conference or In-Chambers Conference.

Rutter, Cal. Practice Guide: Civil Trials & Evidence Ch. 9-A, A. Preliminary Considerations.

Rutter, Cal. Practice Guide: Civil Trials & Evidence Ch. 11-A, A. Direct Examination of Expert Witnesses.

Rutter, Cal. Practice Guide: Civil Trials & Evidence Ch. 11-B, B. Procedures to Challenge Admissibility of Expert Witness Testimony.

Rutter, Cal. Practice Guide: Civil Trials & Evidence Ch. 8B-C, C. Procedural Considerations.

Rutter, Cal. Practice Guide: Civil Trials & Evidence Ch. 8C-A, A. Testimony.

Rutter, Cal. Practice Guide: Civil Trials & Evidence Ch. 8C-B, B. Writings.

Rutter, Cal. Practice Guide: Civil Trials & Evidence Ch. 8C-C, C. Material Objects ("Real Evidence").

Rutter, Cal. Practice Guide: Civil Trials & Evidence Ch. 8D-C, C. General Parameters Re Admissibility of Hearsay Evidence.

Rutter, Cal. Practice Guide: Civil Trials & Evidence Ch. 8D-D, D. Hearsay Exceptions.

Rutter, Cal. Practice Guide: Civil Trials & Evidence Ch. 8G-A, A. Objections and Motions Challenging Admissibility.

Rutter, Cal. Practice Guide: Civil Trials & Evidence Ch. 8G-B, B. Procedures on Objection.

Rutter, Cal. Practice Guide: Civil Trials & Evidence Ch. 8C-B, Outline B.

Rutter, Cal. Practice Guide: Personal Injury Ch. 9-E, E. Order of Trial and Proof and Related Matters.

Rutter, Cal. Practice Guide: Personal Injury Ch. 9-F, F. Examination of Witnesses.

Rutter, Cal. Practice Guide: Personal Injury Ch. 9-E, Outline E.

§ 404. Determination of whether proffered evidence is incriminatory

Whenever the proffered evidence is claimed to be privileged under Section 940, the person claiming the privilege has the burden of showing that the proffered evidence might tend to incriminate him; and the proffered evidence is inadmissible unless it clearly appears to the court that the proffered evidence cannot possibly have a tendency to incriminate the person claiming the privilege. *(Stats.1965, c. 299, § 2, operative Jan. 1, 1967.)*

Law Revision Commission Comments

Section 404 provides a special procedure to be followed by the judge when an objection is made in reliance upon the privilege against self-incrimination. Under Section 404, the objecting party has the burden of showing that the testimony sought might incriminate him. However, the party is not required to produce evidence as such. In addition to considering evidence, the judge must consider the matters disclosed in argument, the implications of the question, the setting in which it is asked, the applicable statute of limitations, and all other relevant factors. See Cohen v. Superior Court, 173 Cal.App.2d 61, 70, 343 P.2d 286, 291 (1959). Nonetheless, the burden is on the objector to present to the judge information of this sort sufficient to indicate that the proffered evidence might incriminate him. If he presents information of this sort, Section 404 requires the judge to sustain the claim of privilege unless it clearly appears that the proffered evidence cannot possibly have a tendency to incriminate the person claiming the privilege.

Section 404 is consistent with existing law: The party claiming the privilege "has the burden of showing that the testimony which was being required might be used in a prosecution to help establish his guilt"; the court may require testimony to be given only if it clearly appears to the court that the claim of privilege is mistaken and that any answer " '*cannot possibly*' " have a tendency to incriminate the witness. Cohen v. Superior Court, 173 Cal.App.2d 61, 68, 70–72, 343 P.2d 286, 290, 291–292 (1959) (italics in original). [7 Cal.L.Rev.Comm. Reports 1 (1965)].

Research References

Rutter, Cal. Practice Guide: Civil Trials & Evidence Ch. 8E-A, A. Privileges.

Rutter, Cal. Practice Guide: Civil Trials & Evidence Ch. 8G-B, B. Procedures on Objection.

Rutter, Cal. Practice Guide: Personal Injury Ch. 9-E, E. Order of Trial and Proof and Related Matters.

Rutter, Cal. Practice Guide: Personal Injury Ch. 9-E, Outline E.

§ 405. Determination of foundational and other preliminary facts in other cases

With respect to preliminary fact determinations not governed by Section 403 or 404:

(a) When the existence of a preliminary fact is disputed, the court shall indicate which party has the burden of producing evidence and the burden of proof on the issue as implied by the rule of law under which the question arises. The court shall determine the existence or nonexistence of the preliminary fact and shall admit or exclude the proffered evidence as required by the rule of law under which the question arises.

(b) If a preliminary fact is also a fact in issue in the action:

(1) The jury shall not be informed of the court's determination as to the existence or nonexistence of the preliminary fact.

(2) If the proffered evidence is admitted, the jury shall not be instructed to disregard the evidence if its determination of the

fact differs from the court's determination of the preliminary fact. *(Stats.1965, c. 299, § 2, operative Jan. 1, 1967.)*

Research References

Rutter, Cal. Practice Guide: Civ. Pro. Before Trial Ch. 8C-3, "Not Privileged".

Rutter, Cal. Practice Guide: Civil Trials & Evidence Ch. 9-A, A. Preliminary Considerations.

Rutter, Cal. Practice Guide: Civil Trials & Evidence Ch. 10-A, A. Preliminary Considerations.

Rutter, Cal. Practice Guide: Civil Trials & Evidence Ch. 11-C, C. Ruling on Admissibility of Expert Opinion Testimony.

Rutter, Cal. Practice Guide: Civil Trials & Evidence Ch. 8C-A, A. Testimony.

Rutter, Cal. Practice Guide: Civil Trials & Evidence Ch. 8C-H, H. Opinion Evidence.

Rutter, Cal. Practice Guide: Civil Trials & Evidence Ch. 8D-C, C. General Parameters Re Admissibility of Hearsay Evidence.

Rutter, Cal. Practice Guide: Civil Trials & Evidence Ch. 8D-D, D. Hearsay Exceptions.

Rutter, Cal. Practice Guide: Civil Trials & Evidence Ch. 8E-A, A. Privileges.

Rutter, Cal. Practice Guide: Civil Trials & Evidence Ch. 8E-G, G. Parol Evidence Rule.

Rutter, Cal. Practice Guide: Civil Trials & Evidence Ch. 8F-C, C. Procedural Considerations.

Rutter, Cal. Practice Guide: Civil Trials & Evidence Ch. 8G-B, B. Procedures on Objection.

Rutter, Cal. Practice Guide: Family Law Ch. 13-B, B. Contested Family Law Trial.

Rutter, Cal. Practice Guide: Personal Injury Ch. 9-E, E. Order of Trial and Proof and Related Matters.

Rutter, Cal. Practice Guide: Personal Injury Ch. 9-F, F. Examination of Witnesses.

Rutter, Cal. Practice Guide: Personal Injury Ch. 9-G, G. Expert Witnesses.

Rutter, Cal. Practice Guide: Personal Injury Ch. 9-H, H. Introduction of Discovered Evidence.

Rutter, Cal. Practice Guide: Personal Injury Ch. 9-E, Outline E.

§ 406. Evidence affecting weight or credibility

This article does not limit the right of a party to introduce before the trier of fact evidence relevant to weight or credibility. *(Stats.1965, c. 299, § 2, operative Jan. 1, 1967.)*

Law Revision Commission Comments

Other sections in this article provide that the judge determines whether proffered evidence is admissible, *i.e.*, whether it may be considered by the trier of fact. Section 406 simply makes it clear that the judge's decision on a question of admissibility does not preclude the parties from introducing before the trier of fact evidence relevant to weight and credibility. [7 Cal.L.Rev.Comm. Reports 1 (1965)].

CHAPTER 5. WEIGHT OF EVIDENCE GENERALLY

§ 410. "Direct evidence" defined

As used in this chapter, "direct evidence" means evidence that directly proves a fact, without an inference or presumption, and which in itself, if true, conclusively establishes that fact. *(Stats. 1965, c. 299, § 2, operative Jan. 1, 1967.)*

Law Revision Commission Comments

Section 410 restates the substance of and supersedes Section 1831 of the Code of Civil Procedure. [7 Cal.L.Rev.Comm. Reports 1 (1965)].

Evidence

Research References

Rutter, Cal. Practice Guide: Civil Trials & Evidence Ch. 8A-A, A. Types of Evidence.

Rutter, Cal. Practice Guide: Civil Trials & Evidence Ch. 8C-C, C. Material Objects ("Real Evidence").

7 Witkin Cal. Proc. 5th Trial § 291, (S 291) Direct and Circumstantial.

§ 411. Direct evidence of one witness sufficient

Except where additional evidence is required by statute, the direct evidence of one witness who is entitled to full credit is sufficient for proof of any fact. *(Stats.1965, c. 299, § 2, operative Jan. 1, 1967.)*

Law Revision Commission Comments

Section 411 restates the substance of and supersedes Section 1844 of the Code of Civil Procedure. The phrase "except where additional evidence is required by statute" has been substituted for the phrase "except perjury and treason" in Section 1844 because the "perjury and treason" exception to Section 1844 is too limited: Corroboration is required by Section 20 of Article I of the California Constitution (treason) and by Penal Code Sections 653f (solicitation to commit felonies), 1103a (perjury), 1108 (abortion and prostitution cases), 1110 (obtaining property by oral false pretenses), and 1111 (testimony of accomplices); in addition, Civil Code Section 130 provides that divorces cannot be granted on the uncorroborated testimony of the parties. [7 Cal.L.Rev.Comm. Reports 1 (1965)].

Research References

Rutter, Cal. Practice Guide: Civil Trials & Evidence Ch. 8C-A, A. Testimony.

Rutter, Cal. Practice Guide: Insurance Litigation Ch. 15-I, I. Trial.

§ 412. Party having power to produce better evidence

If weaker and less satisfactory evidence is offered when it was within the power of the party to produce stronger and more satisfactory evidence, the evidence offered should be viewed with distrust. *(Stats.1965, c. 299, § 2, operative Jan. 1, 1967.)*

Law Revision Commission Comments

Section 412 restates the substance of and supersedes subdivisions 6 and 7 of Section 2061 of the Code of Civil Procedure.

Section 413, taken together with Section 412, restates in substance the meaning that has been given to the presumptions appearing in subdivisions 5 and 6 of Code of Civil Procedure Section 1963.

Evidence Code Section 913 provides that "no presumption shall arise because of the exercise of [a] privilege, and the trier of fact may not draw any inference therefrom," and the trial judge is required to give such an instruction if he is requested to do so. However, there is no inconsistency between Section 913 and Sections 412 and 413. Section 913 deals only with the inferences that may be drawn from the exercise of a privilege; it does not purport to deal with the inferences that may be drawn from the evidence in the case. Sections 412 and 413, on the other hand, deal with the inferences to be drawn from the evidence in the case; and the fact that

a privilege has been relied on is irrelevant to the application of these sections. *Cf.* People v. Adamson, 27 Cal.2d 478, 165 P.2d 3 (1946). [7 Cal.L.Rev.Comm. Reports 1 (1965)].

Research References

Rutter, Cal. Practice Guide: Civil Trials & Evidence Ch. 13-B, B. Proper vs. Improper Closing Argument.

Rutter, Cal. Practice Guide: Civil Trials & Evidence Ch. 13-D, D. Preparing for Closing Argument.

Rutter, Cal. Practice Guide: Civil Trials & Evidence Ch. 8C-B, B. Writings.

Rutter, Cal. Practice Guide: Personal Injury Ch. 3-C, C. Specific Items of Compensatory Damages.

Rutter, Cal. Practice Guide: Personal Injury Ch. 2(I)-C, C. Special Considerations Re Product Liability Investigations.

7 Witkin Cal. Proc. 5th Trial § 302, (S 302) Suppressed or Weaker Evidence.

5 Witkin, California Summary 10th Torts § 503, (S 503) Failure to Make Discovery.

§ 413. Party's failure to explain or deny evidence

In determining what inferences to draw from the evidence or facts in the case against a party, the trier of fact may consider, among other things, the party's failure to explain or to deny by his testimony such evidence or facts in the case against him, or his willful suppression of evidence relating thereto, if such be the case. *(Stats.1965, c. 299, § 2, operative Jan. 1, 1967.)*

Law Revision Commission Comments

See the Comment to Section 412. [7 Cal.L.Rev.Comm. Reports 1 (1965)].

Research References

Rutter, Cal. Practice Guide: Civil Trials & Evidence Ch. 13-B, B. Proper vs. Improper Closing Argument.

Rutter, Cal. Practice Guide: Civil Trials & Evidence Ch. 13-D, D. Preparing for Closing Argument.

California Practice Guide: Employment Litigation Ch. 19-N, N. Evidence Issues.

Rutter, Cal. Practice Guide: Insurance Litigation Ch. 11-J, J. Other Torts Not Necessarily Related to Insurer "Bad Faith".

Rutter, Cal. Practice Guide: Personal Injury Ch. 3-E, E. Punitive Damages.

Rutter, Cal. Practice Guide: Personal Injury Ch. 8-B, B. After Trial Date Set (Three to Four Months Before Trial).

Rutter, Cal. Practice Guide: Personal Injury Ch. 9-K, K. Submission of Case to Jury.

2 Witkin Cal. Proc. 5th Courts § 86, Evidence.

7 Witkin Cal. Proc. 5th Trial § 302, (S 302) Suppressed or Weaker Evidence.

5 Witkin, California Summary 10th Torts § 503, (S 503) Failure to Make Discovery.

Division 4

JUDICIAL NOTICE

Law Revision Commission Comments

The statutory scheme in Division 4 is based on Article 2 (Rules 9–12) of the Uniform Rules of Evidence. The court is required to take judicial notice of the matters listed in Section 451. It may take judicial notice of the matters listed in Section 452 even when not requested to do so; it is required to notice them, however, if a party requests it and satisfies the requirements of Section 453.

There is some overlap between the matters listed in the mandatory notice provisions of Section 451 and the matters listed in the permissive-unless-a-request-is-made provisions of Section 452. Thus, when a matter falls within Section 451, judicial notice is mandatory even though the matter would otherwise fall within Section 452. The introductory clause of Section 452 makes this clear. For example, public statutory law is required to be noticed under subdivision (a) of Section 451 even though it would also be included under official acts of the legislative department under subdivision (c) of Section 452. Certain regulations are required to be noticed under subdivision (b) of Section 451 even though they might also be included under subdivisions (b) and (c) of Section 452. And indisputable matters of universal knowledge are required to be noticed under subdivision (f) of Section 451 even though such matters might be included under subdivisions (g) and (h) of Section 452.

There is also some overlap between the various categories listed in Section 452. However, this overlap will cause no difficulty because all of the matters listed in Section 452 are treated alike. [7 Cal.L.Rev.Comm. Reports 1 (1965)].

§ 450. Judicial notice may be taken only as authorized by law

Judicial notice may not be taken of any matter unless authorized or required by law. *(Stats.1965, c. 299, § 2, operative Jan. 1, 1967.)*

Law Revision Commission Comments

Section 450 provides that judicial notice may not be taken of any matter unless authorized or required by law. See Evidence Code § 160, defining "law." Sections 451 and 452 state a number of matters which must or may be judicially noticed. Judicial notice of other matters is authorized or required by other statutes or by decisional law. *E.g.,* Civil Code § 53; Corp.Code § 6602. In this respect, the Evidence Code is consistent with existing law, for the principal judicial notice provision found in existing law—Code of Civil Procedure Section 1875 (superseded by this division of the Evidence Code)—does not limit judicial notice to those matters specified by statute. Judicial notice has been taken of various matters not so specified, principally of those matters of common knowledge which are certain and indisputable. Witkin, California Evidence §§ 50–52 (1958).

Under the Evidence Code, as under existing law, courts may consider whatever materials are appropriate in construing statutes, determining constitutional issues, and formulating rules of law. That a court may consider legislative history, discussions by learned writers in treatises and law reviews, materials that contain controversial economic and social facts or findings or that indicate contemporary opinion, and similar materials is inherent in the requirement that it take judicial notice of the law. In many cases, the meaning and validity of statutes, the precise nature of a common law rule, or the correct interpretation of a constitutional provision can be determined only with the help of such extrinsic aids. *Cf.* People v. Sterling Refining Co., 86 Cal.App. 558, 564, 261 Pac. 1080, 1083 (1927) (statutory authority to notice "public and private acts" of legislature held to authorize examination of legislative history of certain acts). See also Perez v. Sharp, 32 Cal.2d 711, 198 P.2d 17 (1948) (texts and authorities used by court in opinions determining constitutionality of statute prohibiting interracial marriages). Section 450 will neither broaden nor limit the extent to which a court may resort to extrinsic aids in determining the rules of law that it is required to notice. Nor will Section 450 broaden or limit the extent to which a court may take judicial notice of any other matter not specified in Section 451 or 452. [7 Cal.L.Rev.Comm. Reports 1 (1965)].

Research References

Rutter, Cal. Practice Guide: Civil Trials & Evidence Ch. 11-E, E. Impeachment Evidence from Other Witnesses.
Rutter, Cal. Practice Guide: Civil Trials & Evidence Ch. 8C-J, J. Judicial Notice.
Rutter, Cal. Practice Guide: Insurance Litigation Ch. 15-I, I. Trial.
Rutter, Cal. Practice Guide: Landlord-Tenant Ch. 9-C, C. Final Preparation for Trial.
Rutter, Cal. Practice Guide: Personal Injury Ch. 8-C, C. Two Months Before Trial.

§ 451. Matters which must be judicially noticed

Judicial notice shall be taken of the following:

(a) The decisional, constitutional, and public statutory law of this state and of the United States and the provisions of any charter described in Section 3, 4, or 5 of Article XI of the California Constitution.

(b) Any matter made a subject of judicial notice by Section 11343.6, 11344.6, or 18576 of the Government Code or by Section 1507 of Title 44 of the United States Code.

(c) Rules of professional conduct for members of the bar adopted pursuant to Section 6076 of the Business and Professions Code and rules of practice and procedure for the courts of this state adopted by the Judicial Council.

(d) Rules of pleading, practice, and procedure prescribed by the United States Supreme Court, such as the Rules of the United States Supreme Court, the Federal Rules of Civil Procedure, the Federal Rules of Criminal Procedure, the Admiralty Rules, the Rules of the Court of Claims, the Rules of the Customs Court, and the General Orders and Forms in Bankruptcy.

(e) The true signification of all English words and phrases and of all legal expressions.

(f) Facts and propositions of generalized knowledge that are so universally known that they cannot reasonably be the subject of dispute. *(Stats.1965, c. 299, § 2, operative Jan. 1, 1967. Amended by Stats.1971, c. 438, p. 881, § 88; Stats.1972, c. 764, p. 1373, § 1; Stats.1982, c. 454, p. 1835, § 20; Stats.1985, c. 106, § 32; Stats.1986, c. 248, § 43.)*

Research References

Rutter, Cal. Practice Guide: Civil Appeals & Writs Ch. 5-B, B. Types of Motions, Applications and Requests.
Rutter, Cal. Practice Guide: Civ. Pro. Before Trial Ch. 10-C, C. Procedural Requirements-Moving Party.
Rutter, Cal. Practice Guide: Civ. Pro. Before Trial Ch. 7(I)-A, A. Demurrers.
Rutter, Cal. Practice Guide: Civil Trials & Evidence Ch. 1-C, C. Marshalling the Evidence.
Rutter, Cal. Practice Guide: Civil Trials & Evidence Ch. 11-D, D. Cross-Examination of Expert Witnesses.
Rutter, Cal. Practice Guide: Civil Trials & Evidence Ch. 11-E, E. Impeachment Evidence from Other Witnesses.
Rutter, Cal. Practice Guide: Civil Trials & Evidence Ch. 13-B, B. Proper vs. Improper Closing Argument.
Rutter, Cal. Practice Guide: Civil Trials & Evidence Ch. 8C-B, B. Writings.
Rutter, Cal. Practice Guide: Civil Trials & Evidence Ch. 8C-J, J. Judicial Notice.
Rutter, Cal. Practice Guide: Civil Trials & Evidence Ch. 8C-J, Outline J.
California Practice Guide: Employment Litigation Ch. 13-H, H. Contesting Citations and Related Orders and Notices.
Rutter, Cal. Practice Guide: Family Law Ch. 8-E, E. Division of Community Estate Upon Dissolution, Legal Separation or Nullity.
Rutter, Cal. Practice Guide: Landlord-Tenant Ch. 8-C, C. Defendant's Preanswer Responsive Pleadings.
Rutter, Cal. Practice Guide: Landlord-Tenant Ch. 9-C, C. Final Preparation for Trial.
Rutter, Cal. Practice Guide: Personal Injury Ch. 8-C, C. Two Months Before Trial.
Rutter, Cal. Practice Guide: Prof. Responsibility Ch. 6-D, D. Professional Liability.
6 Witkin Cal. Proc. 5th Proceedings Without Trial § 43, Judicial Notice.
6 Witkin Cal. Proc. 5th Proceedings Without Trial § 232, (S 232) Judicial Notice.

§ 452. Matters which may be judicially noticed

Judicial notice may be taken of the following matters to the extent that they are not embraced within Section 451:

(a) The decisional, constitutional, and statutory law of any state of the United States and the resolutions and private acts of the Congress of the United States and of the Legislature of this state.

(b) Regulations and legislative enactments issued by or under the authority of the United States or any public entity in the United States.

(c) Official acts of the legislative, executive, and judicial departments of the United States and of any state of the United States.

(d) Records of (1) any court of this state or (2) any court of record of the United States or of any state of the United States.

(e) Rules of court of (1) any court of this state or (2) any court of record of the United States or of any state of the United States.

(f) The law of an organization of nations and of foreign nations and public entities in foreign nations.

(g) Facts and propositions that are of such common knowledge within the territorial jurisdiction of the court that they cannot reasonably be the subject of dispute.

(h) Facts and propositions that are not reasonably subject to dispute and are capable of immediate and accurate determination by resort to sources of reasonably indisputable accuracy. *(Stats.1965, c. 299, § 2, operative Jan. 1, 1967.)*

Research References

Rutter, Cal. Practice Guide: Civil Appeals & Writs Ch. 4-D, D. Record on Multiple and Later Appeals.

Rutter, Cal. Practice Guide: Civil Appeals & Writs Ch. 5-B, B. Types of Motions, Applications and Requests.

Rutter, Cal. Practice Guide: Civil Appeals & Writs Ch. 8-C, C. Standards of Appellate Review.

Rutter, Cal. Practice Guide: Civ. Pro. Before Trial Ch. 10-C, C. Procedural Requirements-Moving Party.

Rutter, Cal. Practice Guide: Civ. Pro. Before Trial Ch. 7(I)-A, A. Demurrers.

Rutter, Cal. Practice Guide: Civ. Pro. Before Trial Ch. 7(I)-C, C. Motion for Judgment on the Pleadings.

Rutter, Cal. Practice Guide: Civ. Pro. Before Trial Ch. 9(I)-B, B. Preparing and Filing Motions.

Rutter, Cal. Practice Guide: Civil Trials & Evidence Ch. 1-C, C. Marshalling the Evidence.

Rutter, Cal. Practice Guide: Civil Trials & Evidence Ch. 11-D, D. Cross-Examination of Expert Witnesses.

Rutter, Cal. Practice Guide: Civil Trials & Evidence Ch. 11-E, E. Impeachment Evidence from Other Witnesses.

Rutter, Cal. Practice Guide: Civil Trials & Evidence Ch. 8C-B, B. Writings.

Rutter, Cal. Practice Guide: Civil Trials & Evidence Ch. 8C-J, J. Judicial Notice.

Rutter, Cal. Practice Guide: Civil Trials & Evidence Ch. 8D-D, D. Hearsay Exceptions.

Rutter, Cal. Practice Guide: Civil Trials & Evidence Ch. 8C-J, Outline J.

California Practice Guide: Employment Litigation Ch. 13-H, H. Contesting Citations and Related Orders and Notices.

Rutter, Cal. Practice Guide: Family Law Ch. 8-E, E. Division of Community Estate Upon Dissolution, Legal Separation or Nullity.

Rutter, Cal. Practice Guide: Insurance Litigation Ch. 15-F, F. Pretrial Motions.

Rutter, Cal. Practice Guide: Landlord-Tenant Ch. 8-C, C. Defendant's Preanswer Responsive Pleadings.

Rutter, Cal. Practice Guide: Landlord-Tenant Ch. 9-C, C. Final Preparation for Trial.

Rutter, Cal. Practice Guide: Personal Injury Ch. 3-C, C. Specific Items of Compensatory Damages.

Rutter, Cal. Practice Guide: Personal Injury Ch. 8-C, C. Two Months Before Trial.

9 Witkin Cal. Proc. 5th Appeal § 323, (S 323) Illustrations.

7 Witkin Cal. Proc. 5th Judgment § 349, Methods of Proof.

6 Witkin Cal. Proc. 5th Proceedings Without Trial § 43, Judicial Notice.

6 Witkin Cal. Proc. 5th Proceedings Without Trial § 189, (S 189) Statutory Requirements.

6 Witkin Cal. Proc. 5th Proceedings Without Trial § 232, (S 232) Judicial Notice.

10 Witkin, California Summary 10th Parent and Child § 531, Determining Adequacy of Notice.

§ 452.5. Criminal conviction records; computer-generated records and electronically digitized copies; admissibility

(a) The official acts and records specified in subdivisions (c) and (d) of Section 452 include any computer-generated official court records, as specified by the Judicial Council which relate to criminal convictions, when the record is certified by a clerk of the superior court pursuant to Section 69844.5 of the Government Code at the time of computer entry.

(b)(1) An official record of conviction certified in accordance with subdivision (a) of Section 1530, or an electronically digitized copy thereof, is admissible * * * under Section 1280 to prove the commission, attempted commission, or solicitation of a criminal offense, prior conviction, service of a prison term, or other act, condition, or event recorded by the record.

(2) For purposes of this subdivision, "electronically digitized copy" means a copy that is made by scanning, photographing, or otherwise exactly reproducing a document, is stored or maintained in a digitized format, and bears an electronic signature or watermark unique to the entity responsible for certifying the document. *(Added by Stats.1996, c. 642 (A.B.1387), § 3. Amended by Stats.2002, c. 784 (S.B.1316), § 102; Stats.2013, c. 150 (S.B.378), § 1.)*

Law Revision Commission Comments

Subdivision (a) of Section 452.5 is amended to reflect unification of the municipal and superior courts pursuant to Article VI, Section 5(e), of the California Constitution. The reference to former Government Code Section 71280.5 is deleted, because that provision concerned certification and submission of municipal court records relating to criminal convictions. Government Code Section 69844.5 is the comparable superior court provision. [32 Cal.L.Rev.Comm. Reports 158 (2002)].

Research References

Rutter, Cal. Practice Guide: Civil Trials & Evidence Ch. 8C-B, B. Writings.

Rutter, Cal. Practice Guide: Civil Trials & Evidence Ch. 8C-J, J. Judicial Notice.

Rutter, Cal. Practice Guide: Civil Trials & Evidence Ch. 8D-D, D. Hearsay Exceptions.

Rutter, Cal. Practice Guide: Civil Trials & Evidence Ch. 8G-C, C. Presumptions.

§ 453. Compulsory judicial notice upon request

The trial court shall take judicial notice of any matter specified in Section 452 if a party requests it and:

(a) Gives each adverse party sufficient notice of the request, through the pleadings or otherwise, to enable such adverse party to prepare to meet the request; and

(b) Furnishes the court with sufficient information to enable it to take judicial notice of the matter. *(Stats.1965, c. 299, § 2, operative Jan. 1, 1967.)*

Law Revision Commission Comments

Section 453 provides that the court must take judicial notice of any matter specified in Section 452 if a party requests that such notice be taken, furnishes the court with sufficient information to enable it to take judicial notice of the matter, and gives each adverse party sufficient notice of the request to prepare to meet it.

Section 453 is intended as a safeguard and not as a rigid limitation on the court's power to take judicial notice. The section does not affect the discretionary power of the court to take judicial notice under Section 452 where the party requesting that judicial notice be taken fails to give the requisite notice to each adverse party or fails to furnish sufficient information as to the propriety of taking judicial notice or as to the tenor of the matter to be noticed. Hence, when he considers it appropriate, the judge may take judicial notice under Section 452 and may consult and use any source of pertinent information, whether or not furnished by the parties. However, where the matter noticed under Section 452 is one that is of substantial consequence to the action—even though the court may take judicial notice under Section 452 when the requirements of Section 453 have not been satisfied—the party adversely affected must be given a reasonable opportunity to present information as to the propriety of taking judicial notice and as to the tenor of the matter to be noticed. See Evidence Code § 455 and the Comment thereto.

The "notice" requirement. The party requesting the court to judicially notice a matter under Section 453 must give each adverse party sufficient notice, through the pleadings or otherwise, to enable him to prepare to meet the request. In cases where the notice given does not satisfy this requirement, the court may decline to take judicial notice. A somewhat similar notice to the adverse parties is required under subdivision 4 of Section 1875 of the Code of Civil Procedure when a request for judicial notice of the law of a foreign country is made. Section 453 broadens this existing requirement to cover all matters specified in Section 452.

The notice requirement is an important one since judicial notice is binding on the jury under Section 457. Accordingly, the adverse parties should be given ample notice so that they will have an opportunity to prepare to oppose the taking of judicial notice and to obtain information relevant to the tenor of the matter to be noticed.

Since Section 452 relates to a wide variety of facts and law, the notice requirement should be administered with flexibility in order to insure that the policy behind the judicial notice rules is properly implemented. In many cases, it will be reasonable to expect the notice to be given at or before the time of the pretrial conference. In other cases, matters of fact or law of which the court should take judicial notice may come up at the trial. Section 453 merely requires reasonable notice, and the reasonableness of the notice given will depend upon the circumstances of the particular case.

The "sufficient information" requirement. Under Section 453, the court is not required to resort to any sources of information not provided by the parties. If the party requesting that judicial notice be taken under Section 453 fails to provide the court with "sufficient information," the judge may decline to take judicial notice. For example, if the party requests the court to take judicial notice of the specific gravity of gold, the party requesting that notice be taken must furnish the judge with definitive information as to the specific gravity of gold. The judge is not required to undertake the necessary research to determine the fact, though, of course, he is not precluded from doing such research if he so desires.

Section 453 does not define "sufficient information"; this will necessarily vary from case to case. While the parties will understandably use the best evidence they can produce under the circumstances, mechanical requirements that are ill-suited to the individual case should be avoided. The court justifiably might require that the party requesting that judicial notice be taken provide expert testimony to clarify especially difficult problems.

Burden on party requesting that judicial notice be taken. Where a request is made to take judicial notice under Section 453, the court may decline to take judicial notice unless the party requesting that notice be taken persuades the judge that the matter is one that properly may be noticed under Section 452 and also persuades the judge as to tenor of the matter to be noticed. The degree of the judge's persuasion regarding a particular matter is determined by the subdivision of Section 452 which authorizes judicial notice of the matter. For example, if the matter is claimed to be a fact of common knowledge under paragraph (g) of Section 452, the party must persuade the judge that the fact is of such common knowledge within the territorial jurisdiction of the court that it cannot reasonably be subject to dispute, i.e., that no reasonable person having the same information as is available to the judge could rationally disbelieve the fact. On the other hand, if the matter to be noticed is a city ordinance under paragraph (b) of Section 452, the party must persuade the judge that a valid ordinance exists and also as to its tenor; but the judge need not believe that no reasonable person could conclude otherwise.

Without regard to the evidence supplied by the party requesting that judicial notice be taken, the judge's determination to take judicial notice of a matter specified in Section 452 will be upheld on appeal if the matter was properly noticed. The reviewing court may resort to any information, whether or not available at the trial, in order to sustain the proper taking of judicial notice. See Evidence Code § 459. On the other hand, even though a party requested that judicial notice be taken under Section 453 and gave notice to each adverse party in compliance with subdivision (a) of Section 453, the decision of the judge not to take judicial notice will be upheld on appeal unless the reviewing court determines that the party furnished information to the judge that was so persuasive that no

reasonable judge would have refused to take judicial notice of the matter. [7 Cal.L.Rev.Comm. Reports 1 (1965)].

Research References

Rutter, Cal. Practice Guide: Civil Appeals & Writs Ch. 8-C, C. Standards of Appellate Review.
Rutter, Cal. Practice Guide: Civ. Pro. Before Trial Ch. 10-C, C. Procedural Requirements-Moving Party.
Rutter, Cal. Practice Guide: Civ. Pro. Before Trial Ch. 7(I)-A, A. Demurrers.
Rutter, Cal. Practice Guide: Civ. Pro. Before Trial Ch. 7(I)-C, C. Motion for Judgment on the Pleadings.
Rutter, Cal. Practice Guide: Civ. Pro. Before Trial Ch. 9(I)-B, B. Preparing and Filing Motions.
Rutter, Cal. Practice Guide: Civil Trials & Evidence Ch. 1-C, C. Marshalling the Evidence.
Rutter, Cal. Practice Guide: Civil Trials & Evidence Ch. 8C-J, J. Judicial Notice.
Rutter, Cal. Practice Guide: Family Law Ch. 8-E, E. Division of Community Estate Upon Dissolution, Legal Separation or Nullity.
Rutter, Cal. Practice Guide: Landlord-Tenant Ch. 9-C, C. Final Preparation for Trial.
Rutter, Cal. Practice Guide: Personal Injury Ch. 8-C, C. Two Months Before Trial.
6 Witkin Cal. Proc. 5th Proceedings Without Trial § 43, Judicial Notice.
6 Witkin Cal. Proc. 5th Proceedings Without Trial § 189, (S 189) Statutory Requirements.

§ 454. Information that may be used in taking judicial notice

(a) In determining the propriety of taking judicial notice of a matter, or the tenor thereof:

(1) Any source of pertinent information, including the advice of persons learned in the subject matter, may be consulted or used, whether or not furnished by a party.

(2) Exclusionary rules of evidence do not apply except for Section 352 and the rules of privilege.

(b) Where the subject of judicial notice is the law of an organization of nations, a foreign nation, or a public entity in a foreign nation and the court resorts to the advice of persons learned in the subject matter, such advice, if not received in open court, shall be in writing. (Stats.1965, c. 299, § 2, operative Jan. 1, 1967.)

Research References

Rutter, Cal. Practice Guide: Civil Appeals & Writs Ch. 5-B, B. Types of Motions, Applications and Requests.
Rutter, Cal. Practice Guide: Civil Trials & Evidence Ch. 8C-J, J. Judicial Notice.

§ 455. Opportunity to present information to court

With respect to any matter specified in Section 452 or in subdivision (f) of Section 451 that is of substantial consequence to the determination of the action:

(a) If the trial court has been requested to take or has taken or proposes to take judicial notice of such matter, the court shall afford each party reasonable opportunity, before the jury is instructed or before the cause is submitted for decision by the court, to present to the court information relevant to (1) the propriety of taking judicial notice of the matter and (2) the tenor of the matter to be noticed.

(b) If the trial court resorts to any source of information not received in open court, including the advice of persons learned in the subject matter, such information and its source shall be made a part of the record in the action and the court shall afford each party reasonable opportunity to meet such information before judicial notice of the matter may be taken. (Stats.1965, c. 299, § 2, operative Jan. 1, 1967.)

Law Revision Commission Comments

Section 455 provides procedural safeguards designed to afford the parties reasonable opportunity to be heard both as to the propriety of taking judicial notice of a matter and as to the tenor of the matter to be noticed.

Subdivision (a). This subdivision guarantees to the parties a reasonable opportunity to present information to the court as to the propriety of taking judicial notice and as to the tenor of the matter to be noticed. In a jury case, the subdivision provides the parties with an opportunity to present their information to the judge before a jury instruction based on a matter judicially noticed is given. Where the matter subject to judicial notice relates to a cause tried by the court, the subdivision guarantees the parties an opportunity to dispute the taking of judicial notice of the matter before the cause is submitted for decision. If the judge does not discover that a matter should be judicially noticed until after the cause is submitted for decision, he may, of course, order the cause to be reopened for the purpose of permitting the parties to provide him with information concerning the matter.

Subdivision (a) is limited in its application to those matters specified in subdivision (f) of Section 451 or in Section 452 that are of substantial consequence to the determination of the action, for it would not be practicable to make the subdivision applicable to the other matters listed in Section 451 or to matters that are of inconsequential significance.

What constitutes a "reasonable opportunity" to "present . . . information" will depend upon the complexity of the matter and its importance to the case. For example, in a case where there is no dispute as to the existence and validity of a city ordinance, no formal hearing would be necessary to determine the propriety of taking judicial notice of the ordinance and of its tenor. But, where there is a complex question as to the tenor of foreign law applicable to the case, the granting of a hearing under subdivision (a) would be mandatory. The New York courts have so construed their judicial notice statute, saying that an opportunity for a litigant to know what the deciding tribunal is considering and to be heard with respect to both law and fact is guaranteed by due process of law. Arams v. Arams, 182 Misc. 328, 182 Misc. 336, 45 N.Y.S.2d 251 (Sup.Ct.1943).

Subdivision (b). If the court resorts to sources of information not previously known to the parties, this subdivision requires that such information and its source be made a part of the record when it relates to taking judicial notice of a matter specified in subdivision (f) of Section 451 or in Section 452 that is of substantial consequence to the determination of the action. This requirement is based on a somewhat similar requirement found in Code of Civil Procedure Section 1875 regarding the law of a foreign nation. Making the information and its source a part of the record assures its availability for examination by the parties and by a reviewing court. In addition, subdivision (b) requires the court to give the parties a reasonable opportunity to meet such additional information before judicial notice of the matter may be taken. [7 Cal.L.Rev.Comm. Report 1 (1965)].

Research References

Rutter, Cal. Practice Guide: Civil Appeals & Writs Ch. 5-B, B. Types of Motions, Applications and Requests.
Rutter, Cal. Practice Guide: Civil Trials & Evidence Ch. 8C-J, J. Judicial Notice.

§ 456. Noting denial of request to take judicial notice

If the trial court denies a request to take judicial notice of any matter, the court shall at the earliest practicable time so advise the parties and indicate for the record that it has denied the request. *(Stats.1965, c. 299, § 2, operative Jan. 1, 1967.)*

Law Revision Commission Comments

Section 456 requires the judge to advise the parties and indicate for the record at the earliest practicable time any denial of a request to take judicial notice of a matter. The requirement is imposed in order to provide the parties with an adequate opportunity to submit evidence on any matter as to which judicial notice was anticipated but not taken. No comparable requirement is found in existing law. Compare Evidence Code § 455 and the Comment thereto. [7 Cal.L.Rev.Comm. Reports 1 (1965)].

Research References

Rutter, Cal. Practice Guide: Civil Trials & Evidence Ch. 8C-J, J. Judicial Notice.
Rutter, Cal. Practice Guide: Family Law Ch. 8-E, E. Division of Community Estate Upon Dissolution, Legal Separation or Nullity.

§ 457. Instructing jury on matter judicially noticed

If a matter judicially noticed is a matter which would otherwise have been for determination by the jury, the trial court may, and upon request shall, instruct the jury to accept as a fact the matter so noticed. *(Stats.1965, c. 299, § 2, operative Jan. 1, 1967.)*

Law Revision Commission Comments

Section 457 makes matters judicially noticed binding on the jury and thereby eliminates any possibility of presenting to the jury evidence disputing the fact as noticed by the court. The section is limited to instruction on a matter that would otherwise have been for determination by the jury; instruction of juries on matters of law is not a matter of evidence and is covered by the general provisions of law governing instruction of juries. The section states the substance of the existing law as found in Code of Civil Procedure Section 2102. See People v. Mayes, 113 Cal. 618, 625–626, 45 Pac. 860, 862 (1896); Gallegos v. Union-Tribune Publishing Co., 195 Cal.App.2d 791, 797–798, 16 Cal.Rptr. 185, 189–190 (1961). [7 Cal.L.Rev.Comm. Reports 1 (1965)].

Research References

Rutter, Cal. Practice Guide: Civil Trials & Evidence Ch. 8C-J, J. Judicial Notice.

§ 458. Judicial notice by trial court in subsequent proceedings

The failure or refusal of the trial court to take judicial notice of a matter, or to instruct the jury with respect to the matter, does not preclude the trial court in subsequent proceedings in the action from taking judicial notice of the matter in accordance with the procedure specified in this division. *(Stats.1965, c. 299, § 2, operative Jan. 1, 1967.)*

Law Revision Commission Comments

This section provides that the failure or even the refusal of the court to take judicial notice of a matter at the trial does not bar the trial judge, or another trial judge, from taking judicial notice of that matter in a subsequent proceeding, such as a hearing on a motion for new trial or the like. Although no California case in point has been found, it seems safe to assume that the trial judge has the power to take judicial notice of a matter in subsequent proceedings, since the appellate court can properly take judicial notice of any matter that the trial court could properly notice. See People v. Tossetti, 107 Cal.App. 7, 12, 289 Pac. 881, 883 (1930). [7 Cal.L.Rev.Comm. Reports 1 (1965)].

§ 459. Judicial notice by reviewing court

(a) The reviewing court shall take judicial notice of (1) each matter properly noticed by the trial court and (2) each matter that the trial court was required to notice under Section 451 or 453. The reviewing court may take judicial notice of any matter specified in Section 452. The reviewing court may take judicial notice of a matter in a tenor different from that noticed by the trial court.

(b) In determining the propriety of taking judicial notice of a matter, or the tenor thereof, the reviewing court has the same power as the trial court under Section 454.

(c) When taking judicial notice under this section of a matter specified in Section 452 or in subdivision (f) of Section 451 that is of substantial consequence to the determination of the action, the reviewing court shall comply with the provisions of subdivision (a) of Section 455 if the matter was not theretofore judicially noticed in the action.

(d) In determining the propriety of taking judicial notice of a matter specified in Section 452 or in subdivision (f) of Section 451 that is of substantial consequence to the determination of the action, or the tenor thereof, if the reviewing court resorts to any source of information not received in open court or not included in the record of the action, including the advice of persons learned in the subject matter, the reviewing court shall afford each party reasonable opportunity to meet such information before judicial notice of the matter may be taken. *(Stats. 1965, c. 299, § 2, operative Jan. 1, 1967.)*

Law Revision Commission Comments

Section 459 sets forth a separate set of rules for the taking of judicial notice by a reviewing court.

Subdivision (a). Subdivision (a) requires that a reviewing court take judicial notice of any matter that the trial court properly noticed or was obliged to notice. This means that the matters specified in Section 451 must be judicially noticed by the reviewing court even though the trial court failed to take judicial notice of such matters. A matter specified in Section 452 also must be judicially noticed by the reviewing court if such matter was properly noticed by the trial court in the exercise of its discretion or an appropriate request was made at the trial level and the party making the request satisfied the conditions specified in Section 453. However, if the trial court erred, the reviewing court is not bound by the tenor of the notice taken by the trial court.

Having taken judicial notice of such a matter, the reviewing court may or may not apply it in the particular case on appeal. The effect to be given to matters judicially noticed on appeal, where the question was not been raised below, depends on factors that are not evidentiary in character and are not mentioned in this code. For example, the appellate court is required to notice the matters of law mentioned in Section 451, but it may hold that an error which the appellant has "invited" is not reversible error or that points not urged in the trial court may not be advanced on appeal, and refuse, therefore, to apply the law to the pending case. These principles do not mean that the appellate court does not take judicial notice of the applicable law; they merely mean that, for reasons of policy governing appellate review, the appellate court may refuse to apply the law to the case before it.

In addition to requiring the reviewing court to judicially notice those matters which the trial court properly noticed or was required to notice, the subdivision also provides authority for the reviewing court to exercise the same discretionary power to take judicial notice as is possessed by the trial court.

Subdivision (b). The reviewing court may consult any source of pertinent information for the purpose of determining the propriety of taking judicial notice or the tenor of the matter to be noticed. This includes, of course, the power to consult such sources for the purpose of sustaining or reversing the taking of judicial notice by the trial court. As to the rights of the parties when the reviewing court consults such materials, see subdivision (d) and the Comment thereto.

Subdivision (c). This subdivision provides the parties with the same procedural protection when judicial notice is taken by the reviewing court as is provided by Section 455(a).

Subdivision (d). This subdivision assures the parties the same procedural safeguard at the appellate level that they have in the trial court: If the appellate court resorts to sources of information not included in the record in the action or proceeding, or not received in open court at the appellate level, either to sustain the tenor of the notice taken by the trial court or to notice a matter in a tenor different from that noticed by the trial court, the parties must be given a reasonable opportunity to meet such additional information before judicial notice of the matter may be taken. See Evidence Code § 455(b) and the Comment thereto. [7 Cal.L.Rev.Comm. Reports 1 (1965)].

Research References

Rutter, Cal. Practice Guide: Civil Appeals & Writs Ch. 4-D, D. Record on Multiple and Later Appeals.

Rutter, Cal. Practice Guide: Civil Appeals & Writs Ch. 5-B, B. Types of Motions, Applications and Requests.

Rutter, Cal. Practice Guide: Civil Trials & Evidence Ch. 8C-J, J. Judicial Notice.

Rutter, Cal. Practice Guide: Family Law Ch. 16-B, B. Challenge by Appeal.

Miller and Starr California Real Estate § 11:8, Evidentiary Effect of Recording.

9 Witkin Cal. Proc. 5th Appeal § 683, Nature of Remedy.

§ 460. Appointment of expert by court

Where the advice of persons learned in the subject matter is required in order to enable the court to take judicial notice of a matter, the court on its own motion or on motion of any party may appoint one or more such persons to provide such advice. If the court determines to appoint such a person, he shall be appointed and compensated in the manner provided in Article 2 (commencing with Section 730) of Chapter 3 of Division 6. *(Stats.1965, c. 299, § 2, operative Jan. 1, 1967.)*

Research References

Rutter, Cal. Practice Guide: Family Law Ch. 8-E, E. Division of Community Estate Upon Dissolution, Legal Separation or Nullity.

Rutter, Cal. Practice Guide: Landlord-Tenant Ch. 9-C, C. Final Preparation for Trial.

Rutter, Cal. Practice Guide: Personal Injury Ch. 8-C, C. Two Months Before Trial.

Division 5

BURDEN OF PROOF; BURDEN OF PRODUCING EVIDENCE; PRESUMPTIONS AND INFERENCES

CHAPTER 1. BURDEN OF PROOF

ARTICLE 1. GENERAL

§ 500. Party who has the burden of proof

Except as otherwise provided by law, a party has the burden of proof as to each fact the existence or nonexistence of which is essential to the claim for relief or defense that he is asserting. *(Stats.1965, c. 299, § 2, operative Jan. 1, 1967.)*

Law Revision Commission Comments

As used in Section 500, the burden of proof means the obligation of a party to produce a particular state of conviction in the mind of the trier of fact as to the existence or nonexistence of a fact. See Evidence Code §§ 115, 190. If this requisite degree of conviction is not achieved as to the existence of a particular fact, the trier of fact must assume that the fact does not exist. Morgan, Basic Problems of Evidence 19 (1957); 9

Wigmore, Evidence § 2485 (3d ed. 1940). Usually, the burden of proof requires a party to convince the trier of fact that the existence of a particular fact is more probable than its nonexistence—a degree of proof usually described as proof by a preponderance of the evidence. Evidence Code § 115; Witkin, California Evidence § 59 (1958). However, in some instances, the burden of proof requires a party to produce a substantially greater degree of belief in the mind of the trier of fact concerning the existence of the fact—a burden usually described by stating that the party must introduce clear and convincing proof (Witkin, California Evidence § 60 (1958)) or, with respect to the prosecution in a criminal case, proof beyond a reasonable doubt (Penal Code § 1096).

The defendant in a criminal case sometimes has the burden of proof in regard to a fact essential to negate his guilt. However, in such cases, he usually is not required to persuade that trier of fact as to the existence of such fact; he is merely required to raise a reasonable doubt in the mind of the trier of fact as to his guilty. Evidence Code § 501; People v. Bushton, 80 Cal. 160, 22 Pac. 127 (1889). If the defendant produces no evidence concerning the fact, there is no issue on the matter to be decided by the jury; hence, the jury may be instructed that the nonexistence of the fact must be assumed. See, *e.g.,* People v. Harmon, 89 Cal.App.2d 55, 58, 200 P.2d 32, 34 (1948) (prosecution for narcotics possession; jury instructed "that the burden of proof is upon the defendant that he possessed a written prescription and that in the absence of such evidence it must be assumed that he had no such prescription"). See also People v. Boo Doo Hong, 122 Cal. 606, 607, 55 Pac. 402, 403 (1898).

Section 1981 of the Code of Civil Procedure (superseded by Evidence Code Section 500) provides that the party holding the affirmative of the issue must produce the evidence to prove it and that the burden of proof lies on the party who would be defeated if no evidence were given on either side. This section has been criticized as establishing a meaningless standard:

The "affirmative of the issue" lacks any substantial objective meaning, and the allocation of the burden actually requires the application of several rules of practice and policy, not entirely consistent and not wholly reliable. [Witkin, California Evidence § 56 at 72–73 (1958)].

That the burden is on the party having the affirmative [or] that a party is not required to prove a negative . . . is no more than a play on words, since practically any proposition may be stated in either affirmative or negative form. Thus a plaintiff's exercise of ordinary care equals absence of contributory negligence, in the minority of jurisdictions which place this element in plaintiff's case. In any event, the proposition seems simply not to be so. [Cleary, Presuming and Pleading: An Essay on Juristic Immaturity, 12 Stan. L. Rev 5, 11 (1959)].

"The basic rule, which covers most situations, is that whatever facts a party must affirmatively plead he also has the burden of proving." Witkin, California Evidence § 56 at 73 (1958). Section 500 follows this basic rule. However, Section 500 is broader, applying to issues not necessarily raised in the pleadings.

Under Section 500, the burden of proof as to a particular fact is normally on the party to whose case the fact is essential. "[W]hen a party seeks relief the burden is upon him to prove his case, and he cannot depend wholly upon the failure of the defendant to prove his defenses." Cal. Employment Comm'n v. Malm, 59 Cal.App.2d 322, 323, 138 P.2d 744, 745 (1943). And, "as a general rule, the burden is on the defendant to prove new matter alleged as a defense . . ., even though it requires the proof of a negative." Wilson v. California Cent. R.R., 94 Cal. 166, 172, 29 Pac. 861, 864 (1892).

Section 500 does not attempt to indicate what facts may be essential to a particular party's claim for relief or defense. The facts that must be shown to establish a cause of action or a defense are determined by the substantive law, not the law of evidence.

The general rule allocating the burden of proof applies "except as otherwise provided by law." The exception is included in recognition of the fact that the burden of proof is sometimes allocated in a manner that is at variance with the general rule. In determining whether the normal allocation of the burden of proof should be altered, the courts consider a number of factors: the knowledge of the parties concerning the particular fact, the availability of the evidence to the parties, the most desirable result in terms of public policy in the absence of proof of the particular fact, and the probability of the existence or nonexistence of the fact. In determining the incidence of the burden of proof, "the truth is that there is not and cannot be any one general solvent for all cases. It is merely a question of policy and fairness based on experience in the different situations." 9 Wigmore, Evidence § 2486 at 275 (3d ed. 1940).

Under existing California law, certain matters have been called "presumptions" even though they do not fall within the definition contained in Code of Civil Procedure Section 1959 (superseded by Evidence Code Section 600). Both Section 1959 and Evidence Code Section 600 define a presumption to be an assumption or conclusion of fact that the law requires to be drawn from the proof or establishment of some other fact. Despite the statutory definition, subdivisions 1 and 4 of Code of Civil Procedure Section 1963 (superseded by Sections 520 and 521 of the Evidence Code) provide presumptions that a person is innocent of crime or wrong and that a person exercises ordinary care for his own concerns. Similarly, some cases refer to a presumption of sanity. It is apparent that these so-called presumptions do not arise from the establishment or proof of a fact in the action. In fact, they are not presumptions at all but are preliminary allocations of the burden of proof in regard to the particular issue. This preliminary allocation of the burden of proof may be satisfied in particular cases by proof of a fact giving rise to a presumption that does affect the burden of proof. For example, the initial burden of proving negligence may be satisfied in a particular case by proof that undamaged goods were delivered to a bailee and that such goods were lost or damaged while in the bailee's possession. Upon such proof, the bailee would have the burden of proof as to his lack of negligence. George v. Bekins Van & Storage Co., 33 Cal.2d 834, 205 P.2d 1037 (1949). *Cf.* Com. Code § 7403.

Because the assumptions referred to above do not meet the definition of a presumption contained in Section 600, they are not continued in this code as presumptions. Instead, they appear in the next article in several sections allocating the burden of proof on specific issues. See Article 2 (Sections 520–522). [7 Cal.L.Rev.Comm. Reports 1 (1965)].

Research References

Rutter, Cal. Practice Guide: Civ. Pro. Before Trial Ch. 10-F, F. Burden of Proof on Motion.

Rutter, Cal. Practice Guide: Civ. Pro. Before Trial Ch. 8E-16, Sanctions Re Depositions.

Rutter, Cal. Practice Guide: Civ. Pro. Before Trial Ch. 9(I)-J, J. Motion to Expunge Lis Pendens.

Rutter, Cal. Practice Guide: Civil Trials & Evidence Ch. 8G-D, D. Burdens and Standards of Proof.

California Practice Guide: Employment Litigation Ch. 3-A, A. Employer's Obligation to Indemnify Employees.

California Practice Guide: Employment Litigation Ch. 9-C, C. California Fair Employment and Housing Act (FEHA).

Rutter, Cal. Practice Guide: Family Law Ch. 9-C, C. Premarital Agreements.

Rutter, Cal. Practice Guide: Insurance Litigation Ch. 13-C, C. Punitive Damages.

Rutter, Cal. Practice Guide: Insurance Litigation Ch. 15-B, B. Actions by Insurers.

Rutter, Cal. Practice Guide: Insurance Litigation Ch. 15-I, I. Trial.

Rutter, Cal. Practice Guide: Insurance Litigation Ch. 7B-K, K. Insurer's Duty to Provide Independent Counsel When Conflict of Interest Arises.

Rutter, Cal. Practice Guide: Insurance Litigation Ch. 7H-I, I. Key Exclusions.

Rutter, Cal. Practice Guide: Landlord-Tenant Ch. 7-D, D. Limitation Against "Retaliatory Evictions".

Rutter, Cal. Practice Guide: Landlord-Tenant Ch. 8-D, D. Answer to Unlawful Detainer Complaint.

Rutter, Cal. Practice Guide: Personal Injury Ch. 3-E, E. Punitive Damages.

Rutter, Cal. Practice Guide: Personal Injury Ch. 2(I)-C, C. Special Considerations Re Product Liability Investigations.

Miller and Starr California Real Estate § 7:37, General Rules of Construction.

Miller and Starr California Real Estate § 10:71, Payment or Performance of the Secured Obligation.

Miller and Starr California Real Estate § 11:154, Expungement of a Lis Pendens--Procedure and Grounds for Expungement.

Miller and Starr California Real Estate § 19:171, Right to Evict for Occupancy by the Landlord.

Miller and Starr California Real Estate § 19:225, Cross-Complaint; Affirmative Defenses--Retaliatory Eviction.

16 NO. 5 Miller & Starr, California Real Estate Newsalert 11, Fixtures.

19 NO. 5 Miller & Starr, California Real Estate Newsalert 22, Landlord and Tenant.

3 Witkin Cal. Proc. 5th Actions § 394, Burden and Degree of Proof.

3 Witkin Cal. Proc. 5th Actions § 407, (S 407) Procedure.

3 Witkin Cal. Proc. 5th Actions § 630, Alternative Periods.

8 Witkin Cal. Proc. 5th Extraordinary Writs § 287, in General.

5 Witkin Cal. Proc. 5th Pleading § 1027, Illustrations.

2 Witkin, California Summary 10th Insurance § 297, Action Defended by Insured.

2 Witkin, California Summary 10th Insurance § 293A, (S 293A) (New)-Reimbursement on Determination that Insurer Had No Duty to Defend.

12 Witkin, California Summary 10th Real Property § 573, (S 573) in General.

12 Witkin, California Summary 10th Real Property § 714, Burden of Proof.

10 Witkin, California Summary 10th Parent and Child § 741, (S 741) Duty to Suspend Proceedings and Certify to Juvenile Court.

6 Witkin, California Summary 10th Torts § 1619, (S 1619) Introduction of Evidence is Essential.

6 Witkin, California Summary 10th Torts § 1648, (S 1648) Verdict for Personal Injury and Other Damages.

3 Witkin, California Summary 10th Agency and Employment § 476, (S 476) Parental Responsibilities.

§ 501. Criminal actions; statutory assignment of burden of proof; controlling section

Insofar as any statute, except Section 522, assigns the burden of proof in a criminal action, such statute is subject to Penal Code Section 1096. *(Stats.1965, c. 299, § 2, operative Jan. 1, 1967.)*

Law Revision Commission Comments

A statute assigning the burden of proof may require the party to whom the burden is assigned to raise a reasonable doubt in the mind of the trier of fact or to persuade the trier of fact by a preponderance of evidence, by clear and convincing proof, or by proof beyond a reasonable doubt. See Evidence Code § 115.

Sections 520–522 (Which assign the burden of proof on specific issues) may, at times, assign the burden of proof to the defendant in a criminal action. Elsewhere in the codes are other sections that either specifically allocate the burden of proof to the defendant in a criminal action or have been construed to allocate the burden of proof to the defense. For example, Health and Safety Code Section 11721 provides specifically that, in a prosecution for the use of narcotics, it is the burden of the defense to show that the narcotics were administered by or under the direction of a person licensed to prescribe and administer narcotics. Health and Safety Code Section 11500, on the other hand, prohibits the possession of narcotics but provides an exception for narcotics possessed pursuant to a prescription. The courts have construed this section to place the burden of proof on the defense to show that the exception applies and that the narcotics were possessed pursuant to a prescription. People v. Marschalk, 206 Cal.App.2d 346, 23 Cal.Rptr. 743 (1962); People v. Bill, 140 Cal.App. 389, 392–394, 35 P.2d 645, 647–648 (1934).

Section 501 is intended to make it clear that the statutory allocations of the burden of proof appearing in this chapter and elsewhere in the codes are subject to Penal Code Section 1096, which requires that a criminal defendant be proved guilty beyond a reasonable doubt, *i.e.*, that the statutory allocations do not (except on the issue of insanity) require the defendant to persuade the trier of fact of his innocence. Under Evidence Code Section 522, as under existing law, the defendant must prove his insanity by a preponderance of the evidence. People v. Daugherty, 40 Cal.2d 876, 256 P.2d 911 (1953). However, where a statute allocates the burden of proof to the defendant on any other issue relating to the defendant's guilt, the defendant's burden, as under existing law, is merely to raise a reasonable doubt as to his guilt. People v. Bushton, 80 Cal. 160, 22 Pac. 127 (1889). Section 501 also makes it clear that, when a statute assigns the burden of proof to the prosecution in a criminal action, the prosecution must discharge that burden by proof beyond a reasonable doubt. [7 Cal.L.Rev.Comm. Reports 1 (1965)].

Research References

Rutter, Cal. Practice Guide: Civil Trials & Evidence Ch. 8G-D, D. Burdens and Standards of Proof.

§ 502. Instructions on burden of proof

The court on all proper occasions shall instruct the jury as to which party bears the burden of proof on each issue and as to whether that burden requires that a party raise a reasonable doubt concerning the existence or nonexistence of a fact or that

he establish the existence or nonexistence of a fact by a preponderance of the evidence, by clear and convincing proof, or by proof beyond a reasonable doubt. *(Stats.1965, c. 299, § 2, operative Jan. 1, 1967.)*

Law Revision Commission Comments

Section 502 supersedes subdivision 5 of Code of Civil Procedure Section 2061. [7 Cal.L.Rev.Comm. Reports 1 (1965)].

Research References

Rutter, Cal. Practice Guide: Civil Trials & Evidence Ch. 13-D, D. Preparing for Closing Argument.

Rutter, Cal. Practice Guide: Civil Trials & Evidence Ch. 14-A, A. General Considerations.

Rutter, Cal. Practice Guide: Civil Trials & Evidence Ch. 8G-D, D. Burdens and Standards of Proof.

Rutter, Cal. Practice Guide: Insurance Litigation Ch. 13-C, C. Punitive Damages.

Miller and Starr California Real Estate § 19:225, Cross-Complaint; Affirmative Defenses--Retaliatory Eviction.

7 Witkin Cal. Proc. 5th Trial § 294, (S 294) Proper Instructions.

ARTICLE 2. BURDEN OF PROOF ON SPECIFIC ISSUES

Section
520. Claim that person is guilty of crime or wrongdoing.
521. Claim that person did not exercise care.
522. Claim that person is or was insane.
523. Historic locations of water; claims involving state land patents or grants.
524. Burden of proof in cases involving State Board of Equalization; unreasonable search or access to records prohibited; taxpayer defined.

§ 520. Claim that person is guilty of crime or wrongdoing

The party claiming that a person is guilty of crime or wrongdoing has the burden of proof on that issue. *(Stats.1965, c. 299, § 2, operative Jan. 1, 1967.)*

Law Revision Commission Comments

Section 520 restates the substance of and supersedes subdivision 1 of Code of Civil Procedure Section 1963. [7 Cal.L.Rev.Comm. Reports 1 (1965)].

Research References

Rutter, Cal. Practice Guide: Civil Trials & Evidence Ch. 8G-D, D. Burdens and Standards of Proof.

Miller and Starr California Real Estate § 1:124, Definitions; Burden of Proof.

12 Witkin, California Summary 10th Real Property § 714, Burden of Proof.

1 Witkin Cal. Summ. 10th Contracts § 426, Loan to Gambler.

5 Witkin, California Summary 10th Torts § 769, (S 769) Standard of Proof.

§ 521. Claim that person did not exercise care

The party claiming that a person did not exercise a requisite degree of care has the burden of proof on that issue. *(Stats. 1965, c. 299, § 2, operative Jan. 1, 1967.)*

Law Revision Commission Comments

Section 521 supersedes the presumption in subdivision 4 of Code of Civil Procedure Section 1963. Under existing law, the presumption is considered "evidence"; while under the Evidence Code, it is not. See Evidence Code § 600 and the Comment thereto. [7 Cal.L.Rev.Comm. Reports 1 (1965)].

Rutter, Cal. Practice Guide: Civil Trials & Evidence Ch. 8G-D, D. Burdens and Standards of Proof.

§ 522. Claim that person is or was insane

The party claiming that any person, including himself, is or was insane has the burden of proof on that issue. *(Stats.1965, c. 299, § 2, operative Jan. 1, 1967.)*

Law Revision Commission Comments

Section 522 codifies an allocation of the burden of proof that is frequently referred to in the cases as a presumption. See, *e.g.,* People v. Daugherty, 40 Cal.2d 876, 899, 256 P.2d 911, 925–926 (1953). [7 Cal.L.Rev.Comm. Reports 1 (1965)].

Research References

Rutter, Cal. Practice Guide: Civil Trials & Evidence Ch. 8G-D, D. Burdens and Standards of Proof.
1 Witkin Cal. Summ. 10th Contracts § 52, Insanity Without Adjudication.
14 Witkin, California Summary 10th Wills and Probate § 123, Burden of Proof.

§ 523. Historic locations of water; claims involving state land patents or grants

In any action where the state is a party, regardless of who is the moving party, where (a) the boundary of land patented or otherwise granted by the state is in dispute, or (b) the validity of any state patent or grant dated prior to 1950 is in dispute, the state shall have the burden of proof on all issues relating to the historic locations of rivers, streams, and other water bodies and the authority of the state in issuing the patent or grant.

This section is not intended to nor shall it be construed to supersede existing statutes governing disputes where the state is a party and regarding title to real property. *(Added by Stats. 1994, c. 128 (S.B.1429), § 2.)*

Research References

Rutter, Cal. Practice Guide: Civil Trials & Evidence Ch. 8G-D, D. Burdens and Standards of Proof.
Miller and Starr California Real Estate § 8:62, Description of the Property--Rules of Construction; Ambiguities, Conflicting Calls, Monuments and Surveys.
Miller and Starr California Real Estate § 8:66, Water as Property Boundary--In General.
12 Witkin, California Summary 10th Real Property § 275, (S 275) General Rule.
12 Witkin, California Summary 10th Real Property § 277, Resolving Uncertainties.

§ 524. Burden of proof in cases involving State Board of Equalization; unreasonable search or access to records prohibited; taxpayer defined

(a) Notwithstanding any other provision of law, in a civil proceeding to which the State Board of Equalization is a party, that board shall have the burden of proof by clear and convincing evidence in sustaining its assertion of a penalty for intent to evade or fraud against a taxpayer, with respect to any factual issue relevant to ascertaining the liability of a taxpayer.

(b) Nothing in this section shall be construed to override any requirement for a taxpayer to substantiate any item on a return or claim filed with the State Board of Equalization.

(c) Nothing in this section shall subject a taxpayer to unreasonable search or access to records in violation of the United States Constitution, the California Constitution, or any other law.

(d) For purposes of this section, "taxpayer" includes a person on whom fees administered by the State Board of Equalization are imposed. *(Added by Stats.2010, c. 168 (A.B.2195), § 1.)*

CHAPTER 2. BURDEN OF PRODUCING EVIDENCE

Section
550. Party who has the burden of producing evidence.

§ 550. Party who has the burden of producing evidence

(a) The burden of producing evidence as to a particular fact is on the party against whom a finding on that fact would be required in the absence of further evidence.

(b) The burden of producing evidence as to a particular fact is initially on the party with the burden of proof as to that fact. *(Stats.1965, c. 299, § 2, operative Jan. 1, 1967.)*

Law Revision Commission Comments

Section 550 deals with the allocation of the burden of producing evidence. At the outset of the case, this burden will coincide with the burden of proof. 9 Wigmore, Evidence § 2487 at 279 (3d ed. 1940). However, during the course of the trial, the burden may shift from one party to another, irrespective of the incidence of the burden of proof. For example, if the party with the initial burden of producing evidence establishes a fact giving rise to a presumption, the burden of producing evidence will shift to the other party, whether or not the presumption is one that affects the burden of proof. In addition, a party may introduce evidence of such overwhelming probative force that no person could reasonably disbelieve it in the absence of countervailing evidence, in which case the burden of producing evidence would shift to the opposing party to produce some evidence. These principles are in accord with well-settled California law. See Discussion in Witkin, California Evidence §§ 53–56 (1958). See also 9 Wigmore, Evidence § 2487 (3d ed. 1940). [7 Cal.L.Rev.Comm. Reports 1 (1965)].

Research References

Rutter, Cal. Practice Guide: Civil Trials & Evidence Ch. 8G-D, D. Burdens and Standards of Proof.
Rutter, Cal. Practice Guide: Insurance Litigation Ch. 15-I, I. Trial.
Rutter, Cal. Practice Guide: Landlord-Tenant Ch. 7-D, D. Limitation Against "Retaliatory Evictions".
Rutter, Cal. Practice Guide: Personal Injury Ch. 4-D, D. Techniques Where Settlement Not Forthcoming.
Miller and Starr California Real Estate § 11:154, Expungement of a Lis Pendens--Procedure and Grounds for Expungement.
3 Witkin Cal. Proc. 5th Actions § 394, Burden and Degree of Proof.
3 Witkin Cal. Proc. 5th Actions § 407, (S 407) Procedure.
10 Witkin, California Summary 10th Parent and Child § 741, (S 741) Duty to Suspend Proceedings and Certify to Juvenile Court.

CHAPTER 3. PRESUMPTIONS AND INFERENCES

ARTICLE 1. GENERAL

§ 600. "Presumption" and "inference" defined

(a) A presumption is an assumption of fact that the law requires to be made from another fact or group of facts found or otherwise established in the action. A presumption is not evidence.

(b) An inference is a deduction of fact that may logically and reasonably be drawn from another fact or group of facts found or otherwise established in the action. *(Stats.1965, c. 299, § 2, operative Jan. 1, 1967.)*

Research References

Rutter, Cal. Practice Guide: Civil Trials & Evidence Ch. 13-B, B. Proper vs. Improper Closing Argument.

Rutter, Cal. Practice Guide: Civil Trials & Evidence Ch. 8A-A, A. Types of Evidence.

Rutter, Cal. Practice Guide: Civil Trials & Evidence Ch. 8B-A, A. General Considerations.

Rutter, Cal. Practice Guide: Civil Trials & Evidence Ch. 8G-C, C. Presumptions.

Rutter, Cal. Practice Guide: Civil Trials & Evidence Ch. 8G-D, D. Burdens and Standards of Proof.

Rutter, Cal. Practice Guide: Insurance Litigation Ch. 15-I, I. Trial.

Miller and Starr California Real Estate § 8:42, Presumptions and Proof-- Generally.

Miller and Starr California Real Estate § 1:126, Negligent Misrepresentation (Negligent Fraud).

9 Witkin Cal. Proc. 5th Administrative Proceedings § 72, (S 72) Statement of Factual Basis.

1 Witkin Cal. Proc. 5th Attorneys § 95, Showing to Overcome Presumption.

7 Witkin Cal. Proc. 5th Trial § 291, (S 291) Direct and Circumstantial.

7 Witkin Cal. Proc. 5th Trial § 300, (S 300) Presumptions and Conflicting Testimony.

7 Witkin Cal. Proc. 5th Trial § 410, in General.

1 Witkin Cal. Summ. 10th Contracts § 426, Loan to Gambler.

14 Witkin, California Summary 10th Wills and Probate § 123, Burden of Proof.

§ 601. Classification of presumptions

A presumption is either conclusive or rebuttable. Every rebuttable presumption is either (a) a presumption affecting the burden of producing evidence or (b) a presumption affecting the burden of proof. *(Stats.1965, c. 299, § 2, operative Jan. 1, 1967.)*

Law Revision Commission Comments

Under existing law, some presumptions are conclusive. The court or jury is required to find the existence of the presumed fact regardless of the strength of the opposing evidence. The conclusive presumptions are specified in Section 1962 of the Code of Civil Procedure (superseded by Article 2 (Sections 620–624) of this chapter).

Under existing law, too, all presumptions that are not conclusive are rebuttable presumptions. Code Civ.Proc. § 1961 (superseded by Evidence Code § 601). However, the existing statutes make no attempt to classify the rebuttable presumptions.

For several decades, courts and legal scholars have wrangled over the purpose and function of presumptions. The view espoused by Professors Thayer (Thayer, Preliminary Treatise on Evidence 313–352 (1898)) and Wigmore (9 Wigmore, Evidence §§ 2485–2491 (3d ed. 1940)), accepted by most courts (see Morgan, Presumptions, 10 Rutgers L.Rev. 512, 516 (1956)), and adopted by the American Law Institute's Model Code of Evidence, is that a presumption is a preliminary assumption of fact that disappears from the case upon the introduction of evidence sufficient to sustain a finding of the nonexistence of the presumed fact. In Professor Thayer's view, a presumption merely reflects the judicial determination that the same conclusionary fact exists so frequently when the preliminary fact exists that, once the preliminary fact is established, proof of the conclusionary fact may be dispensed with unless there is actually some contrary evidence:

> Many facts and groups of facts often recur, and when a body of men with a continuous tradition has carried on for some length of time this process of reasoning upon facts that often repeat themselves, they cut short the process and lay down a rule. To such facts they affix, by a general declaration, the

character and operation which common experience has assigned to them. [Thayer, Preliminary Treatise on Evidence 326 (1898)].

Professors Morgan and McCormick argue that a presumption should shift the burden of proof to the adverse party. Morgan, Some Problems of Proof 81 (1956); McCormick, Evidence § 317 at 671–672 (1954). They believe that presumptions are created for reasons of policy and argue that, if the policy underlying a presumption is of sufficient weight to require a finding of the presumed fact when there is no contrary evidence, it should be of sufficient weight to require a finding when the mind of the trier of fact is in equilibrium, and, *a fortiori*, it should be of sufficient weight to require a finding if the trier of fact does not believe the contrary evidence.

The classification of presumptions in the Evidence Code is based on a third view suggested by Professor Bohlen in 1920. Bohlen, The Effect of Rebuttable Presumptions of Law Upon the Burden of Proof, 68 U.Pa. L.Rev. 307 (1920). Underlying the presumptions provisions of the Evidence Code is the conclusion that the Thayer view is correct as to some presumptions, but that the Morgan view is right as to others. The fact is that presumptions are created for a variety of reasons, and no single theory or rationale of presumptions can deal adequately with all of them. Hence, the Evidence Code classifies all rebuttable presumptions as either (1) presumptions affecting the burden of producing evidence (essentially Thayer presumptions), or (2) presumptions affecting the burden of proof (essentially Morgan presumptions).

Sections 603 and 605 set forth the criteria by which the two classes of rebuttable presumptions may be distinguished, and Sections 604, 606, and 607 prescribe their effect. Articles 3 and 4 (Sections 630–668) classify many presumptions found in California law; but many other presumptions, both statutory and common law, must await classification by the courts in accordance with the criteria contained in Sections 603 and 605.

The classification scheme contained in the Evidence Code follows a distinction that appears in the California cases. Thus, for example, the courts have at times held that presumptions do not affect the burden of proof. Estate of Eakle, 33 Cal.App.2d 379, 91 P.2d 954 (1939) (presumption of undue influence); Valentine v. Provident Mut. Life Ins. Co., 12 Cal.App.2d 616, 55 P.2d 1243 (1936) (presumption of death from seven years' absence). And at other times the courts have held that certain presumptions do affect the burden of proof. Estate of Nickson, 187 Cal. 603, 203 Pac. 106 (1921) ("clear and convincing proof" required to overcome presumption of community property); Estate of Walker, 180 Cal. 478, 181 Pac. 792 (1919) ("clear and satisfactory proof" required to overcome presumption of legitimacy). The cases have not, however, explicitly recognized the distinction, nor have they applied it consistently. Compare Estate of Eakle, *supra* (presumption of undue influence does not affect burden of proof), *with* Estate of Witt, 198 Cal. 407, 245 Pac. 197 (1926) (presumption of undue influence must be overcome with "the clearest and most satisfactory evidence"). The Evidence Code clarifies the law relating to presumptions by identifying the distinguishing factors, and it provides a measure of certainty by classifying a number of specific presumptions. [7 Cal.L.Rev.Comm. Reports 1 (1965)].

Research References

Rutter, Cal. Practice Guide: Civil Trials & Evidence Ch. 8G-C, C. Presumptions.

§ 602. Statute making one fact prima facie evidence of another fact

A statute providing that a fact or group of facts is prima facie evidence of another fact establishes a rebuttable presumption. *(Stats.1965, c. 299, § 2, operative Jan. 1, 1967.)*

Law Revision Commission Comments

Section 602 indicates the construction to be given to the large number of statutes scattered through the codes that state that one fact or group of facts is prima facie evidence of another fact. See, *e.g.,* Agric.Code § 18, Com.Code § 1202, Rev. & Tax.Code § 6714. In some instances, these statutes have been enacted for reasons of public policy that require them to be treated as presumptions affecting the burden of proof. See People v. Schwartz, 31 Cal.2d 59, 63, 187 P.2d 12, 14 (1947); People v. Mahoney, 13 Cal.2d 729, 732–733, 91 P.2d 1029, 1030–1031 (1939). It seems likely, however, that in many instances such statutes are not intended to affect the burden of proof but only the burden of producing evidence. Section 602 provides that these statutes are to be regarded as rebuttable presumptions. Hence, unless some specific language applicable to the particular statute in question indicates whether it affects the burden of proof or only the burden of producing evidence, the courts will be required to classify these statutes as presumptions affecting the burden of proof or the burden of producing evidence in accordance with the criteria set forth in Sections 603 and 605. [7 Cal.L.Rev.Comm. Reports 1 (1965)].

Research References

Rutter, Cal. Practice Guide: Civil Trials & Evidence Ch. 8G-C, C. Presumptions.

Miller and Starr California Real Estate § 10:26, Evidence of the Parties' Intentions.

Miller and Starr California Real Estate § 34:37, Liquidated Damages--Generally.

Miller and Starr California Real Estate § 10:211, Presumption of Validity.

§ 603. "Presumption affecting the burden of producing evidence" defined

A presumption affecting the burden of producing evidence is a presumption established to implement no public policy other than to facilitate the determination of the particular action in which the presumption is applied. *(Stats.1965, c. 299, § 2, operative Jan. 1, 1967.)*

Law Revision Commission Comments

Sections 603 and 605 set forth the criteria for determining whether a particular presumption is a presumption affecting the burden of producing evidence or a presumption affecting the burden of proof. Many presumptions are classified in Articles 3 and 4 (Sections 630–668) of this chapter. In the absence of specific statutory classification, the courts may determine whether a presumption is a presumption affecting the burden of producing evidence or a presumption affecting the burden of proof by applying the standards contained in Sections 603 and 605.

Section 603 describes those presumptions that are not based on any public policy extrinsic to the action in which they are invoked. These presumptions are designed to dispense with unnecessary proof of facts that are likely to be true if not disputed. Typically, such presumptions are based on an underlying logical inference. In some cases, the presumed fact is so likely to be true and so little likely to be disputed that the law requires it to be assumed in the absence of contrary evidence. In other cases, evidence of the nonexistence of the presumed fact, if there is any, is so much more readily available to the party against whom the presumption operates that he is not permitted to argue that the presumed fact does not exist unless he is willing to produce such evidence. In still other cases, there may be no direct evidence of the existence or nonexistence of the presumed fact; but, because the case must be decided, the law requires a determination that the presumed fact exists in light of common experience indicating that it usually exists in such cases. *Cf.* Bohlen, Studies in the Law of Torts 644 (1926). Typical of such presumptions are the presumption that a mailed letter was received (Section 641) and presumptions relating to the authenticity of documents (Sections 643–645).

The presumptions described in Section 603 are not expressions of policy; they are expressions of experience. They are intended solely to eliminate the need for the trier of fact to reason from the proven or established fact to the presumed fact and to forestall argument over the existence of the presumed fact when there is no evidence tending to prove the nonexistence of the presumed fact. [7 Cal.L.Rev.Comm. Reports 1 (1965)].

Research References

Rutter, Cal. Practice Guide: Civ. Pro. Before Trial Ch. 10-F, F. Burden of Proof on Motion.

Rutter, Cal. Practice Guide: Civil Trials & Evidence Ch. 8G-C, C. Presumptions.

Rutter, Cal. Practice Guide: Civil Trials & Evidence Ch. 8G-C, Outline C.

Miller and Starr California Real Estate § 8:42, Presumptions and Proof--Generally.

7 Witkin Cal. Proc. 5th Trial § 300, (S 300) Presumptions and Conflicting Testimony.

§ 604. Effect of presumption affecting burden of producing evidence

The effect of a presumption affecting the burden of producing evidence is to require the trier of fact to assume the existence of the presumed fact unless and until evidence is introduced which

would support a finding of its nonexistence, in which case the trier of fact shall determine the existence or nonexistence of the presumed fact from the evidence and without regard to the presumption. Nothing in this section shall be construed to prevent the drawing of any inference that may be appropriate. *(Stats.1965, c. 299, § 2, operative Jan. 1, 1967.)*

Research References

Rutter, Cal. Practice Guide: Civ. Pro. Before Trial Ch. 10-C, C. Procedural Requirements-Moving Party.

Rutter, Cal. Practice Guide: Civil Trials & Evidence Ch. 8G-C, C. Presumptions.

Rutter, Cal. Practice Guide: Landlord-Tenant Ch. 3-C, C. Establishing Breach of Warranty.

Rutter, Cal. Practice Guide: Landlord-Tenant Ch. 3-D, D. Tenant Remedies.

Rutter, Cal. Practice Guide: Personal Injury Ch. 2(II)-G, G. Inability to Prove Negligence or Causation-Res Ipsa Loquitur, "Alternative Liability" and "Market Share Liability".

Miller and Starr California Real Estate § 1:126, Negligent Misrepresentation (Negligent Fraud).

22 NO. 4 Miller & Starr, California Real Estate Newsalert 29, Deeds of Trust.

§ 605. "Presumption affecting the burden of proof" defined

A presumption affecting the burden of proof is a presumption established to implement some public policy other than to facilitate the determination of the particular action in which the presumption is applied, such as the policy in favor of establishment of a parent and child relationship, the validity of marriage, the stability of titles to property, or the security of those who entrust themselves or their property to the administration of others. *(Stats.1965, c. 299, § 2, operative Jan. 1, 1967. Amended by Stats.1975, c. 1244, p. 3201, § 12.)*

Law Revision Commission Comments

Section 605 describes a presumption affecting the burden of proof. Such presumptions are established in order to carry out or to effectuate some public policy other than or in addition to the policy of facilitating the trial of actions.

Frequently, presumptions affecting the burden of proof are designed to facilitate determination of the action in which they are applied. Superficially, therefore, such presumptions may appear merely to be presumptions affecting the burden of producing evidence. What makes a presumption one affecting the burden of proof is the fact that there is always some further reason of policy for the establishment of the presumption. It is the existence of this further basis in policy that distinguishes a presumption affecting the burden of proof from a presumption affecting the burden of producing evidence. For example, the presumption of death from seven years' absence (Section 667) exists in part to facilitate the disposition of actions by supplying a rule of thumb to govern certain cases in which there is likely to be no direct evidence of the presumed fact. But the policy in favor of distributing estates, of settling titles, and of permitting life to proceed normally at some time prior to the expiration of the absentee's normal life expectancy (perhaps 30 or 40 years) that underlies the presumption indicates that it should be a presumption affecting the burden of proof.

Frequently, too, a presumption affecting the burden of proof will have an underlying basis in probability and logical inference. For example, the presumption of the validity of a ceremonial marriage may be based in part on the probability that most marriages are valid. However, an underlying logical inference is not essential. In fact, the lack of an underlying inference is a strong indication that the presumption affects the burden of proof. Only the needs of public policy can justify the direction of a particular assumption that is not warranted by the application of probability and common experience to the known facts. Thus, the total lack of any inference underlying the presumption of the negligence of an employer that arises from his failure to secure the payment of workmen's compensation (Labor Code § 3708) is a clear indication that the presumption is based on public policy and affects the burden of proof. Similarly, the fact that the presumption of death from seven years' absence may conflict directly with the logical inference that life continues for its normal expectancy is an indication that the presumption is based on public policy and, hence, affects the burden of proof. [7 Cal.L.Rev. Comm. Reports 1 (1965)].

Research References

Rutter, Cal. Practice Guide: Civ. Pro. Before Trial Ch. 10-C, C. Procedural Requirements-Moving Party.

Rutter, Cal. Practice Guide: Civil Trials & Evidence Ch. 8G-C, C. Presumptions.

Rutter, Cal. Practice Guide: Civil Trials & Evidence Ch. 8G-C, Outline C.

California Practice Guide: Employment Litigation Ch. 4-A, A. Employment Presumed at Will.

Rutter, Cal. Practice Guide: Insurance Litigation Ch. 15-K, K. Judgment Creditor's Action to Enforce Judgment Debtor's Liability Insurance (INS.C. § 11580(B)(2)).

Rutter, Cal. Practice Guide: Prof. Responsibility Ch. 2-A, A. Regulations Generally.

Rutter, Cal. Practice Guide: Prof. Responsibility Ch. 1 App., California Rules of Professional Conduct.

1 Witkin Cal. Proc. 5th Attorneys § 95, Showing to Overcome Presumption.

1 Witkin Cal. Proc. 5th Attorneys § 418, (S 418) State Bar Standards.

7 Witkin Cal. Proc. 5th Trial § 300, (S 300) Presumptions and Conflicting Testimony.

13 Witkin, California Summary 10th Trusts § 257, Transfer of Real Property.

§ 606.   Effect of presumption affecting burden of proof

The effect of a presumption affecting the burden of proof is to impose upon the party against whom it operates the burden of proof as to the nonexistence of the presumed fact. *(Stats.1965, c. 299, § 2, operative Jan. 1, 1967.)*

Research References

Rutter, Cal. Practice Guide: Civil Trials & Evidence Ch. 8G-C, C. Presumptions.

Rutter, Cal. Practice Guide: Civil Trials & Evidence Ch. 8G-D, D. Burdens and Standards of Proof.

Rutter, Cal. Practice Guide: Prof. Responsibility Ch. 2-A, A. Regulations Generally.

Rutter, Cal. Practice Guide: Prof. Responsibility Ch. 1 App., California Rules of Professional Conduct.

Miller and Starr California Real Estate § 8:42, Presumptions and Proof--Generally.

22 NO. 4 Miller & Starr, California Real Estate Newsalert 29, Deeds of Trust.

1 Witkin Cal. Proc. 5th Attorneys § 418, (S 418) State Bar Standards.

§ 607.   Effect of certain presumptions in a criminal action

When a presumption affecting the burden of proof operates in a criminal action to establish presumptively any fact that is essential to the defendant's guilt, the presumption operates only if the facts that give rise to the presumption have been found or otherwise established beyond a reasonable doubt and, in such case, the defendant need only raise a reasonable doubt as to the existence of the presumed fact. *(Stats.1965, c. 299, § 2, operative Jan. 1, 1967.)*

Research References

Rutter, Cal. Practice Guide: Civil Trials & Evidence Ch. 8G-C, C. Presumptions.

ARTICLE 2.   CONCLUSIVE PRESUMPTIONS

Section

§ 620.   Conclusive presumptions

The presumptions established by this article, and all other presumptions declared by law to be conclusive, are conclusive presumptions. *(Stats.1965, c. 299, § 2, operative Jan. 1, 1967.)*

Law Revision Commission Comments

This article supersedes and continues in effect without substantive change the provisions of subdivisions 2, 3, 4, and 5 of Section 1962 of the Code of Civil Procedure. Other statutes not listed in this article also provide conclusive presumptions. See, *e.g.,* Civil Code § 3440. There may also be a few nonstatutory conclusive presumptions. See Witkin, California Evidence § 63 (1958).

Conclusive presumptions are not evidentiary rules so much as they are rules of substantive law. Hence, the Commission has not recommended any substantive revision of the conclusive presumptions contained in this article. [7 Cal.L.Rev.Comm. Reports 1 (1965)].

Research References

Rutter, Cal. Practice Guide: Civil Trials & Evidence Ch. 8G-C, C. Presumptions.

§ 622.   Facts recited in written instrument

The facts recited in a written instrument are conclusively presumed to be true as between the parties thereto, or their successors in interest; but this rule does not apply to the recital of a consideration. *(Stats.1965, c. 299, § 2, operative Jan. 1, 1967.)*

Law Revision Commission Comments

Section 622 restates and supersedes subdivision 2 of Code of Civil Procedure Section 1962. [7 Cal.L.Rev.Comm. Reports 1 (1965)].

Research References

Rutter, Cal. Practice Guide: Civil Trials & Evidence Ch. 8E-G, G. Parol Evidence Rule.

Rutter, Cal. Practice Guide: Civil Trials & Evidence Ch. 8G-C, C. Presumptions.

Rutter, Cal. Practice Guide: Personal Injury Ch. 4-D, D. Techniques Where Settlement Not Forthcoming.

Rutter, Cal. Practice Guide: Real Prop. Transactions Ch. 4-E, E. Drafting the Purchase and Sale Agreement-Terms and Conditions.

Rutter, Cal. Practice Guide: Real Prop. Transactions Ch. 7-C, C. Representing the Purchasing Tenant.

Miller and Starr California Real Estate § 1:53, "Consideration" Defined.

Miller and Starr California Real Estate § 1:59, Rules of Contract Interpretation.

Miller and Starr California Real Estate § 19:59, Transfer of the Reversion.

Miller and Starr California Real Estate § 21:28, Mistake and Reformation.

Miller and Starr California Real Estate § 21:34, Who is Liable for Usury Penalties--Loans "Made or Arranged" by a Licensed Real Estate Broker.

14 NO. 5 Miller & Starr, California Real Estate Newsalert 16, Landlord and Tenant.

18 NO. 2 Miller & Starr, California Real Estate Newsalert 25, Usury.

1 Witkin Cal. Summ. 10th Contracts § 206, (S 206) Presumption of Consideration.

1 Witkin Cal. Summ. 10th Contracts § 207, (S 207) Recital of Consideration.

5 Witkin, California Summary 10th Torts § 400, in General.

13 Witkin, California Summary 10th Equity § 193, (S 193) Distinctions.

§ 623.   Estoppel by own statement or conduct

Whenever a party has, by his own statement or conduct, intentionally and deliberately led another to believe a particular thing true and to act upon such belief, he is not, in any litigation arising out of such statement or conduct, permitted to contradict it. *(Stats.1965, c. 299, § 2, operative Jan. 1, 1967.)*

Law Revision Commission Comments

Section 623 restates and supersedes subdivision 3 of Code of Civil Procedure Section 1962. [7 Cal.L.Rev.Comm. Reports 1 (1965)].

Research References

Rutter, Cal. Practice Guide: Civil Trials & Evidence Ch. 8G-C, C. Presumptions.

Rutter, Cal. Practice Guide: Insurance Litigation Ch. 6A-F, F. Waiver, Estoppel and Forfeiture of Policy Defenses.

Rutter, Cal. Practice Guide: Landlord-Tenant Ch. 2B-7, Enforcing Rental Agreement.

Rutter, Cal. Practice Guide: Personal Injury Ch. 5-B, B. When to Sue-Statute of Limitations.

Rutter, Cal. Practice Guide: Real Prop. Transactions Ch. 4-E, E. Drafting the Purchase and Sale Agreement-Terms and Conditions.

Rutter, Cal. Practice Guide: Prof. Responsibility Ch. 6-D, D. Professional Liability.

Miller and Starr California Real Estate § 1:76, Waiver--Exception: Estoppel to Assert the Statute of Frauds.

Miller and Starr California Real Estate § 8:28, Insertion of Name After Execution by the Grantor.

Miller and Starr California Real Estate § 8:73, After-Acquired Title.

Miller and Starr California Real Estate § 1:166, Excuse or Waiver of Conditions.

Miller and Starr California Real Estate § 19:239, Waiver and Estoppel.

14 NO. 2 Miller & Starr, California Real Estate Newsalert 1, "The Outer Limit": The California Supreme Court Reigns in the 10-Year Statute of Repose for Construction Defects.

23 NO. 3 Miller & Starr, California Real Estate Newsalert 5, Construction Law and Contracting.

13 Witkin, California Summary 10th Equity § 190, (S 190) Nature of Doctrine.

§ 624. Estoppel of tenant to deny title of landlord

A tenant is not permitted to deny the title of his landlord at the time of the commencement of the relation. *(Stats.1965, c. 299, § 2, operative Jan. 1, 1967.)*

Law Revision Commission Comments

Section 624 restates and supersedes subdivision 4 of Code of Civil Procedure Section 1962. [7 Cal.L.Rev.Comm. Reports 1 (1965)].

Research References

Rutter, Cal. Practice Guide: Civil Trials & Evidence Ch. 8G-C, C. Presumptions.

Miller and Starr California Real Estate § 19:57, Estoppel of Tenant to Deny Landlord's Title.

12 Witkin, California Summary 10th Real Property § 607, (S 607) Estoppel to Deny Landlord's Title.

ARTICLE 3. PRESUMPTIONS AFFECTING THE BURDEN OF PRODUCING EVIDENCE

§ 630. Presumptions affecting the burden of producing evidence

The presumptions established by this article, and all other rebuttable presumptions established by law that fall within the criteria of Section 603, are presumptions affecting the burden of producing evidence. *(Stats.1965, c. 299, § 2, operative Jan. 1, 1967.)*

Law Revision Commission Comments

Article 3 sets forth a list of presumptions, recognized in existing law, that are classified here as presumptions affecting the burden of producing evidence. The list is not exhaustive. Other presumptions affecting the burden of producing evidence may be found in other codes. Others will be found in the common law. Specific statutes will classify some of these, but some must await classification by the courts. The list here, however, will eliminate any uncertainty as to the proper classification for the presumptions in this article. [7 Cal.L.Rev.Comm. Reports 1 (1965)].

Research References

Miller and Starr California Real Estate § 34:110, Burden of Proof.

§ 631. Money delivered by one to another

Money delivered by one to another is presumed to have been due to the latter. *(Stats.1965, c. 299, § 2, operative Jan. 1, 1967.)*

Law Revision Commission Comments

Section 631 restates and supersedes the presumption in subdivision 7 of Code of Civil Procedure Section 1963. [7 Cal.L.Rev.Comm. Reports 1 (1965)].

Research References

Rutter, Cal. Practice Guide: Civil Trials & Evidence Ch. 8G-C, C. Presumptions.

§ 632. Thing delivered by one to another

A thing delivered by one to another is presumed to have belonged to the latter. *(Stats.1965, c. 299, § 2, operative Jan. 1, 1967.)*

Law Revision Commission Comments

Section 632 restates and supersedes the presumption in subdivision 8 of Code of Civil Procedure Section 1963. [7 Cal.L.Rev.Comm. Reports 1 (1965)].

Research References

Rutter, Cal. Practice Guide: Civil Trials & Evidence Ch. 8G-C, C. Presumptions.

§ 633. Obligation delivered up to the debtor

An obligation delivered up to the debtor is presumed to have been paid. *(Stats.1965, c. 299, § 2, operative Jan. 1, 1967.)*

Law Revision Commission Comments

Section 633 restates and supersedes the presumption in subdivision 9 of Code of Civil Procedure Section 1963. [7 Cal.L.Rev.Comm. Reports 1 (1965)].

Research References

Rutter, Cal. Practice Guide: Civil Trials & Evidence Ch. 8G-C, C. Presumptions.

§ 634. Person in possession of order on self

A person in possession of an order on himself for the payment of money, or delivery of a thing, is presumed to have paid the money or delivered the thing accordingly. *(Stats.1965, c. 299, § 2, operative Jan. 1, 1967.)*

Law Revision Commission Comments

Section 634 restates and supersedes the presumption found in subdivision 13 of Code of Civil Procedure Section 1963. [7 Cal.L.Rev.Comm. Reports 1 (1965)].

Research References

Rutter, Cal. Practice Guide: Civil Trials & Evidence Ch. 8G-C, C. Presumptions.

§ 635. Obligation possessed by creditor

An obligation possessed by the creditor is presumed not to have been paid. *(Stats.1965, c. 299, § 2, operative Jan. 1, 1967.)*

Law Revision Commission Comments

The presumption in Section 635 is a common law presumption recognized in the California cases. *E.g.,* Light v. Stevens, 159 Cal. 288, 113 Pac. 659 (1911). [7 Cal.L.Rev.Comm. Reports 1 (1965)].

Research References

Rutter, Cal. Practice Guide: Civil Trials & Evidence Ch. 8G-C, C. Presumptions.

§ 636. Payment of earlier rent or installments

The payment of earlier rent or installments is presumed from a receipt for later rent or installments. *(Stats.1965, c. 299, § 2, operative Jan. 1, 1967.)*

Law Revision Commission Comments

Section 636 restates and supersedes the presumption in subdivision 10 of Code of Civil Procedure Section 1963. [7 Cal.L.Rev.Comm. Reports 1 (1965)].

Research References

Rutter, Cal. Practice Guide: Civil Trials & Evidence Ch. 8G-C, C. Presumptions.

§ 637. Ownership of things possessed

The things which a person possesses are presumed to be owned by him. *(Stats.1965, c. 299, § 2, operative Jan. 1, 1967.)*

Law Revision Commission Comments

Section 637 restates and supersedes the presumption found in subdivision 11 of Code of Civil Procedure Section 1963. [7 Cal.L.Rev.Comm. Reports 1 (1965)].

Research References

Rutter, Cal. Practice Guide: Civil Trials & Evidence Ch. 8G-C, C. Presumptions.
12 Witkin, California Summary 10th Real Property § 208, (S 208) Possession as Evidence of Title.

§ 638. Property ownership acts

A person who exercises acts of ownership over property is presumed to be the owner of it. *(Stats.1965, c. 299, § 2, operative Jan. 1, 1967.)*

Law Revision Commission Comments

Section 638 restates and supersedes the presumption found in subdivision 12 of Code of Civil Procedure Section 1963. Subdivision 12 of Code of Civil Procedure Section 1963 provides that a presumption of ownership arises from common reputation of ownership. This is inaccurate, however, for common reputation is not admissible to prove private title to property. Berniaud v. Beecher, 76 Cal. 394, 18 Pac. 598 (1888); Simons v. Inyo Cerro Gordo Co., 48 Cal.App. 524, 192 Pac. 144 (1920). [7 Cal.L.Rev.Comm. Reports 1 (1965)].

Research References

Rutter, Cal. Practice Guide: Civil Trials & Evidence Ch. 8G-C, C. Presumptions.
12 Witkin, California Summary 10th Real Property § 208, (S 208) Possession as Evidence of Title.

§ 639. Judgment correctly determines rights of parties

A judgment, when not conclusive, is presumed to correctly determine or set forth the rights of the parties, but there is no presumption that the facts essential to the judgment have been correctly determined. *(Stats.1965, c. 299, § 2, operative Jan. 1, 1967.)*

Law Revision Commission Comments

Section 639 restates and supersedes the presumption found in subdivision 17 of Code of Civil Procedure Section 1963. The presumption involved here is that the judgment correctly determines that one party owes another money, or that the parties are divorced, or their marriage has been annulled, or any similar rights of the parties. The presumption does not apply to the facts underlying the judgment. For example, a judgment of annulment is presumed to determine correctly that the marriage is void. Clark v. City of Los Angeles, 187 Cal.App.2d 792, 9 Cal.Rptr. 913 (1960). However, the judgment may not be used to establish presumptively that one of the parties was guilty of fraud as against some third party who is not bound by the judgment.

In a few cases, a judgment may be used as evidence of the facts necessarily determined by the judgment. See, *e.g.,* Evidence Code §§ 1300–1302. But, even in those cases, the judgments do not presumptively establish the facts determined; they are merely evidence. [7 Cal.L.Rev.Comm. Reports 1 (1965)].

Research References

Rutter, Cal. Practice Guide: Civil Trials & Evidence Ch. 8G-C, C. Presumptions.

§ 640. Writing truly dated

A writing is presumed to have been truly dated. *(Stats.1965, c. 299, § 2, operative Jan. 1, 1967.)*

Law Revision Commission Comments

Section 640 restates and supersedes the presumption in subdivision 23 of Code of Civil Procedure Section 1963. [7 Cal.L.Rev.Comm. Reports 1 (1965)].

Research References

Rutter, Cal. Practice Guide: Civil Trials & Evidence Ch. 8G-C, C. Presumptions.

§ 641. Letter received in ordinary course of mail

A letter correctly addressed and properly mailed is presumed to have been received in the ordinary course of mail. *(Stats. 1965, c. 299, § 2, operative Jan. 1, 1967.)*

Law Revision Commission Comments

Section 641 restates and supersedes the presumption in subdivision 24 of Code of Civil Procedure Section 1963. [7 Cal.L.Rev.Comm. Reports 1 (1965)].

Research References

Rutter, Cal. Practice Guide: Civ. Pro. Before Trial Ch. 9(I)-B, B. Preparing and Filing Motions.
Rutter, Cal. Practice Guide: Civil Trials & Evidence Ch. 8G-C, C. Presumptions.
Rutter, Cal. Practice Guide: Landlord-Tenant Ch. 8-D, D. Answer to Unlawful Detainer Complaint.
Rutter, Cal. Practice Guide: Landlord-Tenant Ch. 9-E, E. Trial of the Case-Selected Evidentiary Issues.
Rutter, Cal. Practice Guide: Real Prop. Transactions Ch. 4-E, E. Drafting the Purchase and Sale Agreement-Terms and Conditions.
Rutter, Cal. Practice Guide: Real Prop. Transactions Ch. 6-H, H. Security for Promissory Note.
9 Witkin Cal. Proc. 5th Appeal § 586, (S 586) in General.

6 Witkin Cal. Proc. 5th Proceedings Without Trial § 23, Proof of Service.

6 Witkin Cal. Proc. 5th Proceedings Without Trial § 261, (S 261) Mandamus.

10 Witkin, California Summary 10th Parent and Child § 610, (S 610) Notice of Hearing.

§ 642. Conveyance by person having duty to convey real property

A trustee or other person, whose duty it was to convey real property to a particular person, is presumed to have actually conveyed to him when such presumption is necessary to perfect title of such person or his successor in interest. *(Stats.1965, c. 299, § 2, operative Jan. 1, 1967.)*

Law Revision Commission Comments

Section 642 restates and supersedes the presumption in subdivision 37 of Code of Civil Procedure Section 1963. [7 Cal.L.Rev.Comm. Reports 1 (1965)].

Research References

Rutter, Cal. Practice Guide: Civil Trials & Evidence Ch. 8G-C, C. Presumptions.

§ 643. Authenticity of ancient document

A deed or will or other writing purporting to create, terminate, or affect an interest in real or personal property is presumed to be authentic if it:

(a) Is at least 30 years old;

(b) Is in such condition as to create no suspicion concerning its authenticity;

(c) Was kept, or if found was found, in a place where such writing, if authentic, would be likely to be kept or found; and

(d) Has been generally acted upon as authentic by persons having an interest in the matter. *(Stats.1965, c. 299, § 2, operative Jan. 1, 1967.)*

Law Revision Commission Comments

Section 643 restates and supersedes the presumption found in subdivision 34 of Code of Civil Procedure Section 1963. Although the statement of the ancient documents rule in Section 1963 requires the document to have been acted upon as if genuine before the presumption applies, some recent cases have not insisted upon this requirement. Estate of Nidever, 181 Cal.App.2d 367, 5 Cal.Rptr. 343 (1960); Kirkpatrick v. Tapo Oil Co., 144 Cal.App.2d 404, 301 P.2d 274 (1956). The requirement that the document be acted upon as genuine is, in substance, a requirement of the possession of property by those persons who would be entitled to such possession under the document if it were genuine. See 7 Wigmore, Evidence §§ 2141, 2146 (3d ed. 1940); Tentative Recommendation and a Study Relating to the Uniform Rules of Evidence (Article IX. Authentication and Content of Writings), 6 Cal. Law Revision Comm'n, Rep., Rec. & Studies 101, 135–137 (1964). Giving the ancient documents rule a presumptive effect—*i.e., requiring* a finding of the authenticity of an ancient document—seems justified when it is a dispositive instrument and the persons interested in the matter have acted upon the instrument for a period of at least 30 years as if it were genuine. Evidence which is not of this strength may be sufficient in particular cases to warrant an inference of genuineness and thus justify the admission of the document into evidence, but the presumption should be confined to those cases where the evidence of genuineness is not likely to be disputed. See 7 Wigmore, Evidence § 2146 (3d ed. 1940). Accordingly, Section 643 limits the presumptive application of the ancient documents rule to dispositive instruments. [7 Cal.L.Rev.Comm. Reports 1 (1965)].

Research References

Rutter, Cal. Practice Guide: Civil Trials & Evidence Ch. 8C-B, B. Writings.

Rutter, Cal. Practice Guide: Civil Trials & Evidence Ch. 8G-C, C. Presumptions.

§ 644. Book purporting to be published by public authority

A book, purporting to be printed or published by public authority, is presumed to have been so printed or published. *(Stats.1965, c. 299, § 2, operative Jan. 1, 1967.)*

Law Revision Commission Comments

Section 644 restates and supersedes the presumption in subdivision 35 of Code of Civil Procedure Section 1963. [7 Cal.L.Rev.Comm. Reports 1 (1965)].

Research References

Rutter, Cal. Practice Guide: Civil Trials & Evidence Ch. 8G-C, C. Presumptions.

§ 645. Book purporting to contain reports of cases

A book, purporting to contain reports of cases adjudged in the tribunals of the state or nation where the book is published, is presumed to contain correct reports of such cases. *(Stats.1965, c. 299, § 2, operative Jan. 1, 1967.)*

Law Revision Commission Comments

Section 645 restates and supersedes the presumption found in subdivision 36 of Code of Civil Procedure Section 1963. [7 Cal.L.Rev.Comm. Reports 1 (1965)].

Research References

Rutter, Cal. Practice Guide: Civil Trials & Evidence Ch. 8G-C, C. Presumptions.

§ 645.1. Printed materials purporting to be particular newspaper or periodical

Printed materials, purporting to be a particular newspaper or periodical, are presumed to be that newspaper or periodical if regularly issued at average intervals not exceeding three months. *(Added by Stats.1986, c. 330, § 1.)*

Research References

Rutter, Cal. Practice Guide: Civil Trials & Evidence Ch. 8C-B, B. Writings.

Rutter, Cal. Practice Guide: Civil Trials & Evidence Ch. 8G-C, C. Presumptions.

§ 646. Res ipsa loquitur; instruction

(a) As used in this section, "defendant" includes any party against whom the res ipsa loquitur presumption operates.

(b) The judicial doctrine of res ipsa loquitur is a presumption affecting the burden of producing evidence.

(c) If the evidence, or facts otherwise established, would support a res ipsa loquitur presumption and the defendant has introduced evidence which would support a finding that he was not negligent or that any negligence on his part was not a proximate cause of the occurrence, the court may, and upon request shall, instruct the jury to the effect that:

(1) If the facts which would give rise to a res ipsa loquitur presumption are found or otherwise established, the jury may draw the inference from such facts that a proximate cause of the occurrence was some negligent conduct on the part of the defendant; and

(2) The jury shall not find that a proximate cause of the occurrence was some negligent conduct on the part of the defendant unless the jury believes, after weighing all the evidence in the case and drawing such inferences therefrom as the jury believes are warranted, that it is more probable than not that the occurrence was caused by some negligent conduct on the part of the defendant. *(Added by Stats.1970, c. 69, p. 83, § 1.)*

Evidence

Law Revision Commission Comments

Section 646 is designed to clarify the manner in which the doctrine of res ipsa loquitur functions under the provisions of the Evidence Code relating to presumptions.

The doctrine of res ipsa loquitur, as developed by the California courts, is applicable in an action to recover damages for negligence when the plaintiff establishes three conditions:

First, that it is the kind of [accident] [injury] which ordinarily does not occur in the absence of someone's negligence;

Second, that it was caused by an agency or instrumentality in the exclusive control of the defendant [originally, and which was not mishandled or otherwise changed after defendant relinquished control]; and

Third, that the [accident] [injury] was not due to any voluntary action or contribution on the part of the plaintiff which was the responsible cause of his injury [BAJI (5th ed.1969) No. 4.00 (brackets in original)].

This section provides that the doctrine of res ipsa loquitur is a presumption affecting the burden of producing evidence. Therefore, when the plaintiff has established the three conditions that give rise to the doctrine, the jury is required to find that the accident resulted from the defendant's negligence unless the defendant comes forward with evidence that would support a contrary finding. EVIDENCE CODE 604. If evidence is produced that would support a finding that the defendant was not negligent or that any negligence on his part was not a proximate cause of the accident, the presumptive effect of the doctrine vanishes. However, the jury may still be able to draw an inference that the accident was caused by the defendant's lack of due care from the facts that gave rise to the presumption. See EVIDENCE CODE § 604 and the Comment thereto. In rare cases, the defendant may produce such conclusive evidence that the inference of negligence is dispelled as a matter of law. See, e.g., Leonard v. Watsonville Community Hosp., 47 Cal.2d 509, 305 P.2d 36 (1956). But, except in such a case, the facts giving rise to the doctrine will support an inference of negligence even after its presumptive effect has disappeared.

To assist the jury in the performance of its factfinding function, the court may instruct that the facts that give rise to res ipsa loquitur are themselves circumstantial evidence from which the jury can infer that the accident resulted from the defendant's failure to exercise due care. This section requires the court to give such an instruction when a party so requests. Whether the jury should so find will depend on whether the jury believes that the probative force of the circumstantial and other evidence of the defendant's negligence exceeds the probative force of the contrary evidence and, therefore, that it is more probable than not that the accident resulted from the defendant's negligence.

At times the doctrine of res ipsa loquitur will coincide in a particular case with another presumption or with another rule of law that requires the defendant to discharge the burden of proof on the issue. See Prosser, Res Ipsa Loquitur in California, 37 Cal.L.Rev. 183 (1949). In such cases the defendant will have the burden of proof on issues where res ipsa loquitur appears to apply. But because of the allocation of the burden of proof to the defendant, the doctrine of res ipsa loquitur will serve no function in the disposition of the case. However, the facts that would give rise to the doctrine may nevertheless be used as circumstantial evidence tending to rebut the evidence produced by the party with the burden of proof.

For example, a bailee who has received undamaged goods and returns damaged goods has the burden of proving that the damage was not caused by his negligence unless the damage resulted from a fire. See discussion in Redfoot v. J. T. Jenkins Co., 138 Cal.App.2d 108, 112, 291 P.2d 134, 135 (1955). See Com. Code § 7403(1)(b). When the defendant has produced evidence of his exercise of care in regard to the bailed goods, the facts that would give rise to the doctrine of res ipsa loquitur may be weighed against the evidence produced by the defendant in determining whether it is more likely than not that the goods were damaged without fault on the part of the bailee. But because the bailee has both the burden of producing evidence and the burden of proving that the damage was not caused by his negligence, the presumption of negligence arising from res ipsa loquitur cannot have any effect on the proceeding.

Effect of the Failure of the Plaintiff to Establish All the Preliminary Facts That Give Rise to the Presumption. The fact that the plaintiff fails to establish all of the facts giving rise to the res ipsa presumption does not necessarily mean that he has not produced sufficient evidence of negligence to sustain a jury finding in his favor. The requirements of res ipsa loquitur are merely those that must be met to give rise to a compelled conclusion (or presumption) of negligence in the absence of contrary evidence. An inference of negligence may well be warranted from all of the evidence in the case even though the plaintiff fails to establish all the elements of res ipsa loquitur. See Prosser, Res Ipsa Loquitur: A Reply to Professor Carpenter, 10 So.Cal.L.Rev. 459 (1937). In appropriate cases, therefore, the jury may be instructed that, even though it does not find that the facts giving rise to the presumption have been proved by a preponderance of the evidence, it may nevertheless find the defendant negligent if it concludes from a consideration of all the evidence that it is more probable than not that the defendant was negligent. Such an instruction would be appropriate, for example, in a case where there was evidence of the defendant's negligence apart from the evidence going to the elements of the res ipsa loquitur doctrine.

Examples of Operation of Res Ipsa Loquitur Presumption. The doctrine of res ipsa loquitur may be applicable to a case under four varying sets of circumstances:

(1) Where the facts giving rise to the doctrine are established as a matter of law (by the pleadings by stipulation, by pretrial order, or by some other means) and there is no evidence sufficient to sustain a finding either that the accident resulted from some cause other than the defendant's negligence or that he exercised due care in all possible respects wherein he might have been negligent.

(2) Where the facts giving rise to the doctrine are established as a matter of law, but the defendant has introduced evidence sufficient to sustain a finding either of his due care or of some cause for the accident other than his negligence.

(3) Where the defendant introduces evidence tending to show the nonexistence of the essential conditions of the doctrine but does not introduce evidence to rebut the presumption.

(4) Where the defendant introduces evidence to contest both the conditions of the doctrine and the conclusion that his negligence caused the accident.

Set forth below is an explanation of the manner in which this section functions in each of these situations.

Basic facts established as a matter of law; no rebuttal evidence. If the basic facts that give rise to the presumption are established as a matter of law (by the pleadings, by stipulation, by pretrial order, etc.), the presumption requires that the jury find that the defendant's negligence was the proximate cause of the accident unless evidence is introduced sufficient to sustain a finding either that the accident resulted from some cause other than the defendant's negligence or that he exercised due care in all possible respects wherein he might have been negligent. When the defendant fails to introduce such evidence, the court must simply instruct the jury that it is required to find that the accident was caused by the defendant's negligence.

For example, if a plaintiff automobile passenger sues the driver for injuries sustained in an accident, the defendant may determine not to contest the fact that the accident was of a type that ordinarily does not occur unless the driver was negligent. Moreover, the defendant may introduce no evidence that he exercised due care in the driving of the automobile. Instead, the defendant may rest his defense solely on the ground that the plaintiff was a guest and not a paying passenger. In this case, the court should instruct the jury that it must assume that the defendant was negligent. Cf. Phillips v. Noble, 50 Cal.2d 163, 323 P.2d 385 (1958); Fiske v. Wilkie, 67 Cal.App.2d 440, 154 P.2d 725 (1945).

Basic facts established as matter of law; evidence introduced to rebut presumption. Where the facts giving rise to the doctrine are established as a matter of law but the defendant has introduced evidence sufficient to sustain a finding either of his due care or of a cause for the accident other than his negligence, the presumptive effect of the doctrine vanishes. Except in those rare cases where the inference is dispelled as a matter of law, the court may instruct the jury that it may infer from the established facts that negligence on the part of the defendant was a proximate cause of the accident. The court is required to give such an instruction when requested. The instruction should make it clear, however, that the jury should not find that a proximate cause of the occurrence was some negligent conduct on the part of the defendant unless the jury believes, after weighing all the evidence in the case, that it is more probable than not that the accident was caused by the defendant's negligence.

Basic facts contested; no rebuttal evidence. The defendant may attack only the elements of the doctrine. His purpose in doing so would be to prevent the application of the doctrine. In this situation, the court cannot determine whether the doctrine is applicable or not because the basic facts that give rise to the doctrine must be determined by the jury. Therefore, the court must give an instruction on what has become known as conditional res ipsa loquitur.

Where the basic facts contested by evidence, but there is no rebuttal evidence, the court should instruct the jury that, if it finds that the basic facts have been established by a preponderance of the evidence, then it must also find that the accident was caused by some negligent conduct on the part of the defendant.

Basic facts contested; evidence introduced to rebut presumption. The defendant may introduce evidence that both attacks the basic facts that underlie the doctrine of res ipsa loquitur and tends to show that the accident was not caused by his failure to exercise due care. Because of the evidence contesting the presumed conclusion of negligence, the presumptive effect of the doctrine vanishes, and the greatest effect the doctrine can have in the case is to support an inference that the accident resulted from the defendant's negligence.

In this situation, the court should instruct the jury that, if it finds that the basic facts have been established by a preponderance of the evidence, then it may infer from those facts that the accident was caused because the defendant was negligent. But the court shall also instruct the jury that it should not find that a proximate cause of the accident was some negligent conduct on the part of the defendant unless it believes, after weighing all of the evidence, that it is more probable than not that the defendant was negligent and that the accident resulted from his negligence. Other Appropriate Instructions.

The jury instructions referred to in Section 646 do not preclude the judge from giving the jury any additional instructions on res ipsa loquitur that are appropriate to the particular case. [9 Cal.L.Rev.Comm. Reports 137 (1970)].

Research References

Rutter, Cal. Practice Guide: Civil Trials & Evidence Ch. 8G-C, C. Presumptions.
Rutter, Cal. Practice Guide: Civil Trials & Evidence Ch. 8G-D, D. Burdens and Standards of Proof.
Rutter, Cal. Practice Guide: Personal Injury Ch. 2(II)-G, G. Inability to Prove Negligence or Causation-Res Ipsa Loquitur, "Alternative Liability" and "Market Share Liability".
Miller and Starr California Real Estate § 22:45, Business Owner's Knowledge of a Dangerous Condition.
21 NO. 3 Miller & Starr, California Real Estate Newsalert 20, Landowners' Liability.
7 Witkin Cal. Proc. 5th Trial § 300, (S 300) Presumptions and Conflicting Testimony.

§ 647. Return of process served by registered process server

The return of a process server registered pursuant to Chapter 16 (commencing with Section 22350) of Division 8 of the Business and Professions Code upon process or notice establishes a presumption, affecting the burden of producing evidence, of the facts stated in the return. *(Added by Stats.1978, c. 528, p. 1687, § 1.)*

Research References

Rutter, Cal. Practice Guide: Civil Trials & Evidence Ch. 8G-C, C. Presumptions.
Rutter, Cal. Practice Guide: Landlord-Tenant Ch. 9-E, E. Trial of the Case-Selected Evidentiary Issues.
3 Witkin Cal. Proc. 5th Actions § 1066, (S 1066) Sufficiency of Return.
12 Witkin, California Summary 10th Real Property § 727, (S 727) Methods of Service.

ARTICLE 4. PRESUMPTIONS AFFECTING THE BURDEN OF PROOF

Section
660.   Presumptions affecting the burden of proof.
662.   Owner of legal title to property is owner of beneficial title.
663.   Ceremonial marriage.
664.   Official duty regularly performed.
665.   Ordinary consequences of voluntary act.
666.   Judicial action in lawful exercise of jurisdiction.
667.   Death of person not heard from in five years.
668.   Unlawful intent.
669.   Due care; failure to exercise.

Section
669.1.   Standards of conduct for public employees; presumption of failure to exercise due care.
669.5.   Ordinances limiting building permits or development of buildable lots for residential purposes; impact on supply of residential units; actions challenging validity.
670.   Payments by check.

§ 660. Presumptions affecting the burden of proof

The presumptions established by this article, and all other rebuttable presumptions established by law that fall within the criteria of Section 605, are presumptions affecting the burden of proof. *(Stats.1965, c. 299, § 2, operative Jan. 1, 1967.)*

Law Revision Commission Comments

In some cases it may be difficult to determine whether a particular presumption is a presumption affecting the burden of proof or a presumption affecting the burden of producing evidence. To avoid uncertainty, it is desirable to classify as many presumptions as possible. Article 4 (§§ 660–668), therefore, lists several presumptions that are to be regarded as presumptions affecting the burden of proof. The list is not exclusive. Other statutory and common law presumptions that affect the burden of proof must await classification by the courts. [7 Cal.L.Rev. Comm. Reports 1 (1965)].

Research References

Rutter, Cal. Practice Guide: Civil Trials & Evidence Ch. 5-I, I. Challenging Prospective Jurors.
Rutter, Cal. Practice Guide: Insurance Litigation Ch. 6C-A, A. Life Insurance.
8 Witkin Cal. Proc. 5th Attack Judgment Trial Court § 16, Court of Limited or Special Jurisdiction.

§ 662. Owner of legal title to property is owner of beneficial title

The owner of the legal title to property is presumed to be the owner of the full beneficial title. This presumption may be rebutted only by clear and convincing proof. *(Stats.1965, c. 299, § 2, operative Jan. 1, 1967.)*

Law Revision Commission Comments

Section 662 codifies a common law presumption recognized in the California cases. The presumption may be overcome only by clear and convincing proof. Olson v. Olson, 4 Cal.2d 434, 437, 49 P.2d 827, 828 (1935); Rench v. McMullen, 82 Cal.App.2d 872, 187 P.2d 111 (1947). [7 Cal.L.Rev.Comm. Reports 1 (1965)].

Research References

Rutter, Cal. Practice Guide: Civil Trials & Evidence Ch. 8G-C, C. Presumptions.
Rutter, Cal. Practice Guide: Civil Trials & Evidence Ch. 8G-D, D. Burdens and Standards of Proof.
Rutter, Cal. Practice Guide: Civil Trials & Evidence Ch. 8G-C, Outline C.
Rutter, Cal. Practice Guide: Family Law Ch. 8-B, B. Property Characterization.
Rutter, Cal. Practice Guide: Family Law Ch. 9-B, B. General Drafting and Analytical Considerations.
Rutter, Cal. Practice Guide: Family Law Ch. 9-D, D. Marital Agreements.
Rutter, Cal. Practice Guide: Family Law Ch. 20-A, A. Nonmarital "Marvin" Cohabitation Relationships.
Rutter, Cal. Practice Guide: Family Law Ch. 8-B, Outline B.
Rutter, Cal. Practice Guide: Family Law Ch. 9-D, Outline D.
Rutter, Cal. Practice Guide: Real Prop. Transactions Ch. 4-C, C. Parties to the Purchase Agreement.
Rutter, Cal. Practice Guide: Real Prop. Transactions Ch. 12-B, B. Agreements Regarding Co-Ownership Rights and Obligations.
Miller and Starr California Real Estate § 1:70, Contract for the Sale, Gift, or Financing of Real Property--Exception: Partnerships and Joint Ventures.
Miller and Starr California Real Estate § 11:7, Presumption of Record Title.

Evidence

Miller and Starr California Real Estate § 8:59, Property Interest Transferred; Presumptions.

Miller and Starr California Real Estate § 10:26, Evidence of the Parties' Intentions.

Miller and Starr California Real Estate § 10:27, Enforcement Against a Purchaser from the Creditor or Other Third Person.

Miller and Starr California Real Estate § 12:41, Basic Rules for Determining Character of Property; Definitions--Presumptions, Generally.

Miller and Starr California Real Estate § 12:42, Basic Rules for Determining Character of Property; Definitions--Presumption from Joint Title.

Miller and Starr California Real Estate § 12:50, Management and Control, in General.

Miller and Starr California Real Estate § 12:61, Disposition on Death of a Spouse.

Miller and Starr California Real Estate § 34:110, Burden of Proof.

14 NO. 4 Miller & Starr, California Real Estate Newsalert 23, Holding Title.

19 NO. 4 Miller & Starr, California Real Estate Newsalert 41, Holding Title.

21 NO. 3 Miller & Starr, California Real Estate Newsalert 17, Holding Title.

22 NO. 6 Miller & Starr, California Real Estate Newsalert 16, Homesteads.

9 Witkin Cal. Proc. 5th Appeal § 406, Exceptions to Requirement.

11 Witkin, California Summary 10th Community Property § 20, Abolition of Presumption.

11 Witkin, California Summary 10th Community Property § 275, Nature of Relief.

13 Witkin, California Summary 10th Trusts § 324, in General.

13 Witkin, California Summary 10th Trusts § 326, (S 326) Promise to Reconvey to Transferor.

§ 663. Ceremonial marriage

A ceremonial marriage is presumed to be valid. *(Stats.1965, c. 299, § 2, operative Jan. 1, 1967.)*

Law Revision Commission Comments

Section 663 codifies a common law presumption recognized in the California cases. Estate of Hughson, 173 Cal. 448, 160 Pac. 548 (1916); Wilcox v. Wilcox, 171 Cal. 770, 155 Pac. 95 (1916); Freeman S.S. Co. v. Pillsbury, 172 F.2d 321 (9th Cir.1949). [7 Cal.L.Rev.Comm. Reports 1 (1965)].

Research References

Rutter, Cal. Practice Guide: Civil Trials & Evidence Ch. 8G-C, C. Presumptions.

Rutter, Cal. Practice Guide: Family Law Ch. 19-A, A. Validity of Marriage.

11 Witkin, California Summary 10th Husband and Wife § 54, (S 54) Presumption of Valid Marriage from Proof of Solemnization.

§ 664. Official duty regularly performed

It is presumed that official duty has been regularly performed. This presumption does not apply on an issue as to the lawfulness of an arrest if it is found or otherwise established that the arrest was made without a warrant. *(Stats.1965, c. 299, § 2, operative Jan. 1, 1967.)*

Research References

Rutter, Cal. Practice Guide: Civ. Pro. Before Trial Ch. 6-B, B. Complaints.

Rutter, Cal. Practice Guide: Civil Trials & Evidence Ch. 5-I, I. Challenging Prospective Jurors.

Rutter, Cal. Practice Guide: Civil Trials & Evidence Ch. 8C-B, B. Writings.

Rutter, Cal. Practice Guide: Civil Trials & Evidence Ch. 8D-D, D. Hearsay Exceptions.

Rutter, Cal. Practice Guide: Civil Trials & Evidence Ch. 8G-C, C. Presumptions.

Miller and Starr California Real Estate § 25:9, Judicial Review.

Miller and Starr California Real Estate § 4:44, Disciplinary Process--Judicial Review.

Miller and Starr California Real Estate § 25A:15, Procedures for Preparing an Environmental Impact Report.

2 Witkin Cal. Proc. 5th Courts § 361, (S 361) Ministerial Functions.

10 Witkin, California Summary 10th Parent and Child § 248, Supreme Court Decisions Resolving Conflict.

10 Witkin, California Summary 10th Parent and Child § 531, Determining Adequacy of Notice.

10 Witkin, California Summary 10th Parent and Child § 960, (S 960) in General.

3 Witkin, California Summary 10th Agency and Employment § 581, Emergency Exception.

§ 665. Ordinary consequences of voluntary act

A person is presumed to intend the ordinary consequences of his voluntary act. This presumption is inapplicable in a criminal action to establish the specific intent of the defendant where specific intent is an element of the crime charged. *(Stats.1965, c. 299, § 2, operative Jan. 1, 1967.)*

Research References

Rutter, Cal. Practice Guide: Civil Trials & Evidence Ch. 8G-C, C. Presumptions.

§ 666. Judicial action in lawful exercise of jurisdiction

Any court of this state or the United States, or any court of general jurisdiction in any other state or nation, or any judge of such a court, acting as such, is presumed to have acted in the lawful exercise of its jurisdiction. This presumption applies only when the act of the court or judge is under collateral attack. *(Stats.1965, c. 299, § 2, operative Jan. 1, 1967.)*

Research References

Rutter, Cal. Practice Guide: Civil Trials & Evidence Ch. 8G-C, C. Presumptions.

8 Witkin Cal. Proc. 5th Attack Judgment Trial Court § 16, Court of Limited or Special Jurisdiction.

2 Witkin Cal. Proc. 5th Courts § 162, (S 162) Courts of Record.

§ 667. Death of person not heard from in five years

A person not heard from in five years is presumed to be dead. *(Stats.1965, c. 299, § 2, operative Jan. 1, 1967. Amended by Stats.1983, c. 201, § 1.)*

Law Revision Commission Comments

Section 667 restates and supersedes the presumption in subdivision 26 of Code of Civil Procedure Section 1963. [7 Cal.L.Rev.Comm. Reports 1 (1965)].

Section 667 is amended to adopt a five-year missing period. This period is consistent with Probate Code Section 1301 (administration of estates of persons missing five years) and Civil Code Sections 4401(2), 4425(b) (five-year absence in bigamy situations). Except for the change in the duration of the missing period from seven to five years, the amendment of Section 667 has no effect on the case law interpreting this section. [16 Cal.L.Rev.Comm. Reports 105 (1982)].

Research References

Rutter, Cal. Practice Guide: Civil Trials & Evidence Ch. 8G-C, C. Presumptions.

Rutter, Cal. Practice Guide: Insurance Litigation Ch. 6C-A, A. Life Insurance.

Rutter, Cal. Practice Guide: Insurance Litigation Ch. 6C-B, B. Accidental Death Insurance.

14 Witkin, California Summary 10th Wills and Probate § 369, Presumption and Order.

§ 668. Unlawful intent

An unlawful intent is presumed from the doing of an unlawful act. This presumption is inapplicable in a criminal action to establish the specific intent of the defendant where specific intent is an element of the crime charged. *(Stats.1965, c. 299, § 2, operative Jan. 1, 1967.)*

Research References

Rutter, Cal. Practice Guide: Civil Trials & Evidence Ch. 8G-C, C. Presumptions.

Miller and Starr California Real Estate § 21:27, Intent to Violate the Usury Law.

§ 669. Due care; failure to exercise

(a) The failure of a person to exercise due care is presumed if:

(1) He violated a statute, ordinance, or regulation of a public entity;

(2) The violation proximately caused death or injury to person or property;

(3) The death or injury resulted from an occurrence of the nature which the statute, ordinance, or regulation was designed to prevent; and

(4) The person suffering the death or the injury to his person or property was one of the class of persons for whose protection the statute, ordinance, or regulation was adopted.

(b) This presumption may be rebutted by proof that:

(1) The person violating the statute, ordinance, or regulation did what might reasonably be expected of a person of ordinary prudence, acting under similar circumstances, who desired to comply with the law; or

(2) The person violating the statute, ordinance, or regulation was a child and exercised the degree of care ordinarily exercised by persons of his maturity, intelligence, and capacity under similar circumstances, but the presumption may not be rebutted by such proof if the violation occurred in the course of an activity normally engaged in only by adults and requiring adult qualifications. *(Added by Stats.1967, c. 650, p. 2004, § 1.)*

Law Revision Commission Comments

Section 669 codifies a common law presumption that is frequently applied in the California cases. See Alarid v. Vanier, 50 Cal.2d 617, 327 P.2d 897 (1958). The presumption may be used to establish a plaintiff's contributory negligence as well as a defendant's negligence. Nevis v. Pacific Gas & Elec. Co., 43 Cal.2d 626, 275 P.2d 761 (1954).

If the conditions listed in subdivision (a) are established, a presumption of negligence arises which may be rebutted by proof of the facts specified in subdivision (b). The presumption is one of simple negligence only, not gross negligence. Taylor v. Cockrell, 116 Cal.App. 596, 3 P.2d 16 (1931).

Section 669 appears in Article 4 (beginning with Section 660), Chapter 3, of Division 5 of the Evidence Code and, therefore, is a presumption affecting the burden of proof. Evidence Code § 660. Thus, if it is established that a person violated a statute under the conditions specified in subdivision (a), the opponent of the presumption is required to prove to the trier of fact that it is more probable than not that the violation of the statute was reasonable and justifiable under the circumstances. See Evidence Code § 606 and the *Comment* thereto. Since the ultimate question is whether the opponent of the presumption was negligent rather than whether he violated the statute, proof of justification or excuse under subdivision (b) negates the existence of negligence instead of merely establishing an excuse for negligent conduct. Therefore, if the presumption is rebutted by proof of justification or excuse under subdivision (b), the trier of fact is required to find that the violation of the statute was not negligent.

Violations by children. Section 669 applies to the violation of a statute, ordinance, or regulation by a child as well as by an adult. But in the case of a violation by a child, the presumption may be rebutted by a showing that the child, in spite of the violation, exercised the care that children of his maturity, intelligence, and capacity ordinarily exercise under similar circumstances. Daun v. Truax, 56 Cal.2d 647, 16 Cal.Rptr. 351, 365 P.2d 407 (1961). However, if a child engages in an activity normally engaged in only by adults and requiring adult qualifications, the "reasonable" behavior he must show to establish justification or excuse under subdivision (b) must meet the standard of conduct established primarily for adults. Cf. Prichard v. Veterans Cab Co., 63 Cal.2d 727, 47 Cal.Rptr. 904, 408 P.2d 360 (1965) (minor operating a motorcycle).

Failure to establish conditions of presumption. Even though a party fails to establish that a violation occurred or that a proven violation meets all the requirements of subdivision (a), it is still possible for the party to recover by proving negligence apart from any statutory violation. Nunneley v. Edgar Hotel, 36 Cal.2d 493, 225 P.2d 497 (1950) (plaintiff permitted to recover even though her injury was not of the type to be prevented by statute).

If a case is tried without a jury, the judge is responsible for deciding both questions of law and questions of fact arising under Section 669. However, in a case tried by a jury, there is an allocation between the judge and jury of the responsibility for determining the existence or nonexistence of the elements underlying the presumption and the existence of excuse or justification.

Subdivision (a), paragraph (3) and (4). Whether the death or injury involved in an action resulted from an occurrence of the nature which the statute, ordinance, or regulation was designed to prevent (paragraph (3) of subdivision (a)) and whether the plaintiff was one of the class of persons for whose protection the statute, ordinance, or regulation was adopted (paragraph (4) of subdivision (a)) are questions of law. Nunneley v. Edgar Hotel, 36 Cal.2d 493, 225 P.2d 497 (1950) (statute requiring parapet of particular height at roofline of vent shaft designed to protect against walking into shaft, not against falling into shaft while sitting on parapet). If a party were relying solely on the violation of a statute to establish the other party's negligence or contributory negligence, his opponent would be entitled to a directed verdict on the issue if the judge failed to find either of the above elements of the presumption. See Nunneley v. Edgar Hotel, 36 Cal.2d 493, 225 P.2d 497 (1950) (by implication).

Subdivision (a), paragraphs (1) and (2). Whether or not a party to an action has violated a statute, ordinance, or regulation (paragraph (1) of subdivision (a)) is generally a question of fact. However, if a party admits the violation or if the evidence of the violation is undisputed, it is appropriate for the judge to instruct the jury that a violation of the statute, ordinance, or regulation has been established as a matter of law. Alarid v. Vanier, 50 Cal.2d 617, 327 P.2d 897 (1958) (undisputed evidence of driving with faulty brakes).

The question of whether the violation has proximately caused or contributed to the plaintiff's death or injury (paragraph (2) of subdivision (a)) is normally a question for the jury. Satterlee v. Orange Glenn School Dist., 29 Cal.2d 581, 177 P.2d 279 (1947). However, the existence or nonexistence of proximate cause becomes a question of law to be decided by the judge if reasonable men can draw but one inference from the facts. Satterlee v. Orange Glenn School Dist., 29 Cal.2d 581, 177 P.2d 279 (1947). See also Alarid v. Vanier, 50 Cal.2d 617, 327 P.2d 897 (1958) (defendant's admission establishes proximate cause); Moon v. Payne, 97 Cal.App.2d 717, 218 P.2d 550 (1950) (failure to obtain permit to burn weeds not proximate cause of child's burns).

Subdivision (b). Normally, the question of justification or excuse is a jury question. Fuentes v. Panella, 120 Cal.App.2d 175, 260 P.2d 853 (1953). The jury should be instructed on the issue of justification or excuse whether the excuse or justification appears from the circumstances surrounding the violation itself or appears from evidence offered specifically to show justification. Fuentes v. Panella, 120 Cal.App.2d 175, 260 P.2d 853 (1953) (instruction on justification proper in light of conflicting testimony concerning violation itself and surrounding circumstances). However, an instruction on the issue of excuse or justification should not be given if there is no evidence that would sustain a finding by the jury that the violation was excused. McCaughan v. Hansen Pac. Lumber Co., 176 Cal.App.2d 827, 833–834, 1 Cal.Rptr. 796, 800 (1959) (evidence went to contributory negligence, not to excuse); Fuentes v. Panella, 120 Cal.App.2d 175, 260 P.2d 853 (1953) (dictum). [8 Cal.L.Rev.Comm. Reports 101 (1967)].

Research References

Rutter, Cal. Practice Guide: Civ. Pro. Before Trial Ch. 6-B, B. Complaints.

Rutter, Cal. Practice Guide: Civil Trials & Evidence Ch. 8G-C, C. Presumptions.

Rutter, Cal. Practice Guide: Civil Trials & Evidence Ch. 8G-D, D. Burdens and Standards of Proof.

California Practice Guide: Employment Litigation Ch. 13-I, I. Collateral (Non-Osh) Actions Relating to Occupational Safety and Health.

Rutter, Cal. Practice Guide: Landlord-Tenant Ch. 3-D, D. Tenant Remedies.

Rutter, Cal. Practice Guide: Personal Injury Ch. 3-D, D. Mitigating Factors in Reduction of Damages.

Rutter, Cal. Practice Guide: Personal Injury Ch. 2(II)-H, H. Negligence Predicated on Statutory Violation ("Negligence Per Se").

Rutter, Cal. Practice Guide: Real Prop. Transactions Ch. 5-D, D. Common Law Environmental Hazards Liability.

Miller and Starr California Real Estate § 22:77, Owner's Defenses.

Miller and Starr California Real Estate § 23:70, Negligence.

Miller and Starr California Real Estate § 29:31, Liability for Defective Plans and Specifications; to the Owner.

Miller and Starr California Real Estate § 29:36, Liability to the Owner.

19 NO. 2 Miller & Starr, California Real Estate Newsalert 19, Landowners' Liability.

21 NO. 5 Miller & Starr, California Real Estate Newsalert 20, Landowners' Liability.

3 Witkin Cal. Proc. 5th Actions § 150, Breach of Warranty of Habitability.

5 Witkin, California Summary 10th Torts § 13, Legislative Intent Approach.

5 Witkin, California Summary 10th Torts § 245, Statutory Rule of Liability.

6 Witkin, California Summary 10th Torts § 866, (S 866) Due Care and Causation Are Questions of Fact.

6 Witkin, California Summary 10th Torts § 873, Codification of Doctrine.

6 Witkin, California Summary 10th Torts § 874, Illustrations.

6 Witkin, California Summary 10th Torts § 875, (S 875) Statute or Ordinance.

6 Witkin, California Summary 10th Torts § 877, (S 877) Agency Manual is Not Regulation.

6 Witkin, California Summary 10th Torts § 890, in General.

6 Witkin, California Summary 10th Torts § 892, Class of Persons.

6 Witkin, California Summary 10th Torts § 893, Type of Harm.

6 Witkin, California Summary 10th Torts § 895, (S 895) Proximate Cause.

6 Witkin, California Summary 10th Torts § 896, (S 896) Doctrine is Inapplicable to Immature Children.

6 Witkin, California Summary 10th Torts § 972, (S 972) Diagnosis of Battered Child Syndrome.

6 Witkin, California Summary 10th Torts § 1000, (S 1000) Child Vehicle Driver.

6 Witkin, California Summary 10th Torts § 1055, Care Facility for Elderly.

6 Witkin, California Summary 10th Torts § 1067, Liability to Third Person.

6 Witkin, California Summary 10th Torts § 1248, Work Under Public License.

6 Witkin, California Summary 10th Torts § 1323, Exposure to Electrical Shock.

6 Witkin, California Summary 10th Torts § 1340, (S 1340) Extension to Noncompetitive Recreational Activity.

6 Witkin, California Summary 10th Torts § 1349, (S 1349) Skiing and Snowboarding.

§ 669.1. Standards of conduct for public employees; presumption of failure to exercise due care

A rule, policy, manual, or guideline of state or local government setting forth standards of conduct or guidelines for its employees in the conduct of their public employment shall not be considered a statute, ordinance, or regulation of that public entity within the meaning of Section 669, unless the rule, manual, policy, or guideline has been formally adopted as a statute, as an ordinance of a local governmental entity in this state empowered to adopt ordinances, or as a regulation by an agency of the state pursuant to the Administrative Procedure Act (Chapter 3.5 (commencing with Section 11340) of Division 3 of Title 2 of the Government Code), or by an agency of the United States government pursuant to the federal Administrative Procedure Act (Chapter 5 (commencing with Section 5001) of Title 5 of the United States Code). This section affects only the presumption set forth in Section 669, and is not otherwise intended to affect the admissibility or inadmissibility of the rule, policy, manual, or guideline under other provisions of law. *(Added by Stats.1987, c. 1201, § 13; Stats.1987, c. 1207, § 2.)*

Research References

Rutter, Cal. Practice Guide: Civil Trials & Evidence Ch. 8G-C, C. Presumptions.

Rutter, Cal. Practice Guide: Personal Injury Ch. 2(III)-B, B. Immunity from Liability for Government Employee Conduct.

Rutter, Cal. Practice Guide: Personal Injury Ch. 2(III)-C, C. Liability for Failure to Perform "Mandatory Duty".

6 Witkin, California Summary 10th Torts § 877, (S 877) Agency Manual is Not Regulation.

§ 669.5. Ordinances limiting building permits or development of buildable lots for residential purposes; impact on supply of residential units; actions challenging validity

(a) Any ordinance enacted by the governing body of a city, county, or city and county which (1) directly limits, by number, the building permits that may be issued for residential construction or the buildable lots which may be developed for residential purposes, or (2) changes the standards of residential development on vacant land so that the governing body's zoning is rendered in violation of Section 65913.1 of the Government Code is presumed to have an impact on the supply of residential units available in an area which includes territory outside the jurisdiction of the city, county, or city and county.

(b) With respect to any action which challenges the validity of an ordinance specified in subdivision (a) the city, county, or city and county enacting the ordinance shall bear the burden of proof that the ordinance is necessary for the protection of the public health, safety, or welfare of the population of the city, county, or city and county.

(c) This section does not apply to state and federal building code requirements or local ordinances which (1) impose a moratorium, to protect the public health and safety, on residential construction for a specified period of time, if, under the terms of the ordinance, the moratorium will cease when the public health or safety is no longer jeopardized by the construction, (2) create agricultural preserves under Chapter 7 (commencing with Section 51200) of Part 1 of Division 1 of Title 5 of the Government Code, or (3) restrict the number of buildable parcels or designate lands within a zone for nonresidential uses in order to protect agricultural uses as defined in subdivision (b) of Section 51201 of the Government Code or open-space land as defined in subdivision (b) of Section 65560 of the Government Code.

(d) This section shall not apply to a voter approved ordinance adopted by referendum or initiative prior to the effective date of this section which (1) requires the city, county, or city and county to establish a population growth limit which represents its fair share of each year's statewide population growth, or (2) which sets a growth rate of no more than the average population growth rate experienced by the state as a whole. Paragraph (2) of subdivision (a) does not apply to a voter-approved ordinance adopted by referendum or initiative which exempts housing affordable to persons and families of low or moderate income, as defined in Section 50093 of the Health and Safety Code, or which otherwise provides low- and moderate-income housing sites equivalent to such an exemption. *(Added by Stats.1980, c. 1144, p. 3703, § 2. Amended by Stats.1988, c. 541, § 1.)*

Research References

Rutter, Cal. Practice Guide: Civil Trials & Evidence Ch. 8G-C, C. Presumptions.

Miller and Starr California Real Estate § 25:6, Provisions Regarding the Housing Element.

Miller and Starr California Real Estate § 30:28, Effect of Zoning.

9 Witkin Cal. Proc. 5th Appeal § 46, Consent Given to Facilitate Appeal.

8 Witkin, California Summary 10th Constitutional Law § 1012, (S 1012) Nature and Scope.

§ 670. Payments by check

(a) In any dispute concerning payment by means of a check, a copy of the check produced in accordance with Section 1550 of the Evidence Code, together with the original bank statement that reflects payment of the check by the bank on which it was drawn or a copy thereof produced in the same manner, creates a presumption that the check has been paid.

(b) As used in this section:

(1) "Bank" means any person engaged in the business of banking and includes, in addition to a commercial bank, a savings and loan association, savings bank, or credit union.

(2) "Check" means a draft, other than a documentary draft, payable on demand and drawn on a bank, even though it is described by another term, such as "share draft" or "negotiable order of withdrawal." *(Added by Stats.1992, c. 914 (S.B.833), § 51. Amended by Stats.2001, c. 854 (S.B.205), § 3.)*

Research References

Rutter, Cal. Practice Guide: Civil Trials & Evidence Ch. 8G-C, C. Presumptions.
4 Witkin, California Summary 10th Negotiable Instruments § 3, (S 3) Division 3.

Division 6

WITNESSES

CHAPTER 1. COMPETENCY

§ 700. General rule as to competency

Except as otherwise provided by statute, every person, irrespective of age, is qualified to be a witness and no person is disqualified to testify to any matter. *(Stats.1965, c. 299, § 2, operative Jan. 1, 1967. Amended by Stats.1985, c. 884, § 1.)*

Law Revision Commission Comments

Section 700 makes it clear that all grounds for disqualification of witnesses must be based on statute. There can be no nonstatutory grounds for disqualification. The section is similar to and supersedes Section 1879 of the Code of Civil Procedure, which provides that "all persons . . . who, having organs of sense, can perceive, and perceiving, can make known their perceptions to others, may be witnesses."

Just as Code of Civil Procedure Section 1879 is limited by various statutory restrictions on the competency of witnesses, the broad rule stated in Section 700 is also substantially qualified by statutory restrictions appearing in the Evidence Code and in other California codes. See, *e.g.,* Evidence Code § 701 (mental or physical capacity to be a witness), § 702 (requirement of personal knowledge), § 703 (judge as a witness), § 704 (juror as a witness), §§ 900–1070 (privileges), § 1150 (continuing existing law limiting use of juror's evidence concerning jury misconduct); Vehicle Code § 40804 (speed trap evidence). [7 Cal.L.Rev.Comm. Reports 1 (1965)].

Research References

Rutter, Cal. Practice Guide: Civil Trials & Evidence Ch. 4-B, B. Preliminary Matters Discussed in Final Status Conference or In-Chambers Conference.
Rutter, Cal. Practice Guide: Civil Trials & Evidence Ch. 9-A, A. Preliminary Considerations.
Rutter, Cal. Practice Guide: Civil Trials & Evidence Ch. 8C-A, A. Testimony.
Rutter, Cal. Practice Guide: Enforcing Judgments/Debts Ch. 4-A, A. Attachment.

Rutter, Cal. Practice Guide: Enforcing Judgments/Debts Ch. 4-B, B. Claim and Delivery.
Rutter, Cal. Practice Guide: Family Law Ch. 11-F, F. Preparing Client and Witnesses for Trial.
Rutter, Cal. Practice Guide: Personal Injury Ch. 9-F, F. Examination of Witnesses.
10 Witkin, California Summary 10th Parent and Child § 284, Trial.

§ 701. Disqualification of witness

(a) A person is disqualified to be a witness if he or she is:

(1) Incapable of expressing himself or herself concerning the matter so as to be understood, either directly or through interpretation by one who can understand him; or

(2) Incapable of understanding the duty of a witness to tell the truth.

(b) In any proceeding held outside the presence of a jury, the court may reserve challenges to the competency of a witness until the conclusion of the direct examination of that witness. *(Stats.1965, c. 299, § 2, operative Jan. 1, 1967. Amended by Stats.1985, c. 884, § 2.)*

Law Revision Commission Comments

Under existing law, the competency of a person to be a witness is a question to be determined by the court and depends upon his capacity to understand the oath and to perceive, recollect, and communicate that which he is offered to relate. "Whether he did perceive accurately, does recollect, and is communicating accurately and truthfully are questions of credibility to be resolved by the trier of fact." People v. McCaughan, 49 Cal.2d 409, 420, 317 P.2d 974, 981 (1957).

Under the Evidence Code, too, the competency of a person to be a witness is a question to be determined by the court. See Evidence Code § 405 and the Comment thereto. However, Section 701 requires the court to determine only the prospective witness' capacity to communicate and his understanding of the duty to tell the truth. The missing qualifications—the capacity to perceive and to recollect—are determined in a different manner. Because a witness, qualified under Section 701, must have personal knowledge of the facts to which he testifies (Section 702), he must, of course, have the capacity to perceive and to recollect those facts. But the court may exclude the testimony of a witness for lack of personal knowledge only if no jury could reasonably find that he has such knowledge. See Evidence Code § 403 and the Comment thereto. Thus, the Evidence Code has made a person's capacity to perceive and to recollect a condition for the admission of his testimony concerning a particular matter instead of a condition for his competency to be a witness. And, under the Evidence Code, if there is evidence that the witness has those capacities, the determination whether he in fact perceived and does recollect is left to the trier of fact. See Evidence Code §§ 403 and 702 and the Comments thereto.

Although Section 701 modifies the existing law with respect to determining the competency of witnesses, it seems unlikely that the change will have much practical significance. Theoretically, Section 701 may permit children and persons suffering from mental impairment to testify in some instances where they are now disqualified from testifying; in practice, however, the California courts have permitted children of very tender years and persons with mental impairment to testify. See Witkin,

California Evidence §§ 389, 390 (1958). See also Bradburn v. Peacock, 135 Cal.App.2d 161, 164–165, 286 P.2d 972, 974 (1955) (reversible error to preclude a child from testifying without conducting a *voir dire* examination to determine his competency: "We cannot say that *no* child of 3 years and 3 months is capable of receiving just impressions of the facts that a man whom he knows in a truck which he knows ran over his little sister. Nor can we say that *no* child of 3 years and 3 months would remember such facts and be able to relate them truly at the age of 5." (Emphasis in original.)); People v. McCaughan, 49 Cal.2d 409, 317 P.2d 974 (1957) (indicating that committed mental patients may be competent witnesses. For further discussion, see Tentative Recommendation and a Study Relating to the Uniform Rules of Evidence (Article IV. Witnesses), 6 Cal. Law Revision Comm'n, Rep., Rec. & Studies 701, 709–710 (1964). [7 Cal.L.Rev.Comm. Reports 1 (1965)].

Research References

Rutter, Cal. Practice Guide: Civil Trials & Evidence Ch. 9-A, A. Preliminary Considerations.

Rutter, Cal. Practice Guide: Civil Trials & Evidence Ch. 10-D, D. Objectives of Cross-Examination.

Rutter, Cal. Practice Guide: Civil Trials & Evidence Ch. 8C-A, A. Testimony.

Rutter, Cal. Practice Guide: Civil Trials & Evidence Ch. 8D-D, D. Hearsay Exceptions.

Rutter, Cal. Practice Guide: Family Law Ch. 11-F, F. Preparing Client and Witnesses for Trial.

Rutter, Cal. Practice Guide: Personal Injury Ch. 9-F, F. Examination of Witnesses.

10 Witkin, California Summary 10th Parent and Child § 284, Trial.

§ 702. Personal knowledge of witness

(a) Subject to Section 801, the testimony of a witness concerning a particular matter is inadmissible unless he has personal knowledge of the matter. Against the objection of a party, such personal knowledge must be shown before the witness may testify concerning the matter.

(b) A witness' personal knowledge of a matter may be shown by any otherwise admissible evidence, including his own testimony. *(Stats.1965, c. 299, § 2, operative Jan. 1, 1967.)*

Law Revision Commission Comments

Section 702 states the general requirement that a witness must have personal knowledge of the facts to which he testifies. "Personal knowledge" means a present recollection of an impression derived from the exercise of the witness' own senses. 2 Wigmore, Evidence § 657 at 762 (3d ed. 1940). *Cf.* Evidence Code § 170, defining "perceive." Section 702 restates the substance of and supersedes Code of Civil Procedure Section 1845.

Except to the extent that experts may give opinion testimony not based on personal knowledge (see Evidence Code § 801), the requirement of Section 702 is applicable to all witnesses, whether expert or not. Certain additional qualifications that an expert witness must possess are set forth in Article 1 (commencing with Section 720) of Chapter 3.

Under existing law, as under Section 702, an objection must be made to the testimony of a witness who does not have personal knowledge; but, if there is no reasonable opportunity to object before the testimony is given, a motion to strike is appropriate after lack of knowledge has been shown. Fildew v. Shattuck & Nimmo Warehouse Co., 39 Cal.App. 42, 46, 177 Pac. 866, 867 (1918) (objection to question properly sustained when foundational showing of personal knowledge was not made); Sneed v. Marysville Gas & Elec. Co., 149 Cal. 704, 709, 87 Pac. 376, 378 (1906) (error to overrule motion to strike testimony after lack of knowledge shown on cross-examination); Parker v. Smith, 4 Cal. 105 (1854) (testimony properly stricken by court when lack of knowledge shown on cross-examination).

If a timely objection is made that a witness lacks personal knowledge, the court may not receive his testimony subject to the condition that evidence of personal knowledge be supplied later in the trial. Section 702 thus limits the ordinary power of the court with respect to the order of proof. See Evidence Code § 403(b). See also Evidence Code § 320. [7 Cal.L.Rev.Comm. Reports 1 (1965)].

Research References

Rutter, Cal. Practice Guide: Civ. Pro. Before Trial Ch. 10-C, C. Procedural Requirements-Moving Party.

Rutter, Cal. Practice Guide: Civ. Pro. Before Trial Ch. 9(I)-B, B. Preparing and Filing Motions.

Rutter, Cal. Practice Guide: Civil Trials & Evidence Ch. 9-A, A. Preliminary Considerations.

Rutter, Cal. Practice Guide: Civil Trials & Evidence Ch. 10-A, A. Preliminary Considerations.

Rutter, Cal. Practice Guide: Civil Trials & Evidence Ch. 8C-A, A. Testimony.

Rutter, Cal. Practice Guide: Civil Trials & Evidence Ch. 8D-D, D. Hearsay Exceptions.

Rutter, Cal. Practice Guide: Civil Trials & Evidence Ch. 8E-F, F. Limitations on Impeachment and Rehabilitation.

Rutter, Cal. Practice Guide: Civil Trials & Evidence Ch. 8G-B, B. Procedures on Objection.

Rutter, Cal. Practice Guide: Civil Trials & Evidence Gen. Matls., Highlights.

Rutter, Cal. Practice Guide: Family Law Ch. 11-F, F. Preparing Client and Witnesses for Trial.

Rutter, Cal. Practice Guide: Insurance Litigation Ch. 13-B, B. Extracontractual Compensatory Damages.

Rutter, Cal. Practice Guide: Personal Injury Ch. 8-D, D. Final Preparation (One Month Before Trial).

Rutter, Cal. Practice Guide: Personal Injury Ch. 9-E, E. Order of Trial and Proof and Related Matters.

Rutter, Cal. Practice Guide: Personal Injury Ch. 9-F, F. Examination of Witnesses.

22 NO. 4 Miller & Starr, California Real Estate Newsalert 36, Judicial Remedies.

5 Witkin Cal. Proc. 5th Pleading § 1035, (S 1035) Affidavit on Information and Belief.

§ 703. Judge as witness

(a) Before the judge presiding at the trial of an action may be called to testify in that trial as a witness, he shall, in proceedings held out of the presence and hearing of the jury, inform the parties of the information he has concerning any fact or matter about which he will be called to testify.

(b) Against the objection of a party, the judge presiding at the trial of an action may not testify in that trial as a witness. Upon such objection, the judge shall declare a mistrial and order the action assigned for trial before another judge.

(c) The calling of the judge presiding at a trial to testify in that trial as a witness shall be deemed a consent to the granting of a motion for mistrial, and an objection to such calling of a judge shall be deemed a motion for mistrial.

(d) In the absence of objection by a party, the judge presiding at the trial of an action may testify in that trial as a witness. *(Stats.1965, c. 299, § 2, operative Jan. 1, 1967.)*

Research References

Rutter, Cal. Practice Guide: Civil Trials & Evidence Ch. 9-A, A. Preliminary Considerations.

Rutter, Cal. Practice Guide: Civil Trials & Evidence Ch. 12-A, A. Motion for Mistrial.

Rutter, Cal. Practice Guide: Civil Trials & Evidence Ch. 8C-A, A. Testimony.

Rutter, Cal. Practice Guide: Personal Injury Ch. 9-L, L. Motions to Terminate Trial Before Verdict.

7 Witkin Cal. Proc. 5th Trial § 167, Mistrial.

§ 703.5. Judges, arbitrators or mediators as witnesses; subsequent civil proceeding

No person presiding at any judicial or quasi-judicial proceeding, and no arbitrator or mediator, shall be competent to testify, in any subsequent civil proceeding, as to any statement, conduct, decision, or ruling, occurring at or in conjunction with the prior proceeding, except as to a statement or conduct that could (a) give rise to civil or criminal contempt, (b) constitute a crime, (c) be the subject of investigation by the State Bar or Commission on Judicial Performance, or (d) give rise to disqualification proceedings under paragraph (1) or (6) of subdivision (a) of Section 170.1 of the Code of Civil Procedure. However, this section does not apply to a mediator with regard to any mediation under Chapter 11 (commencing with Section 3160) of Part 2 of Division 8 of the Family Code. *(Added by Stats.1979, c. 205, p. 449, § 1. Amended by Stats.1980, c. 290, p. 617, § 1; Stats.1988, c. 281, § 1; Stats.1990, c. 1491 (A.B.3765), § 13; Stats.1993, c. 114 (A.B.1757), § 1; Stats.1993, c. 1261 (S.B.401), § 5; Stats.1994, c. 1269 (A.B.2208), § 7.)*

Law Revision Commission Comments

Section 703.5 is amended to correct the cross-reference to former Family Code Section 3155 to reflect the reorganization of those sections in 1993 Cal. Stat. ch. 219. This is a technical, nonsubstantive change. [24 Cal.L.Rev.Comm. Reports 621 (1994)].

Research References

Rutter, Cal. Practice Guide: A.D.R. Ch. 3-A, A. General Considerations.
Rutter, Cal. Practice Guide: A.D.R. Ch. 3-C, C. Confidentiality.
Rutter, Cal. Practice Guide: A.D.R. Ch. 4-B, B. Judicial Arbitration.
Rutter, Cal. Practice Guide: A.D.R. Ch. 4-C, C. Statutorily-Mandated Court Mediation Programs.
Rutter, Cal. Practice Guide: A.D.R. Ch. 5-A, A. General Considerations.
Rutter, Cal. Practice Guide: A.D.R. Ch. 5-J, J. Challenging and Enforcing Arbitrator's Award in Court.
Rutter, Cal. Practice Guide: A.D.R. Ch. 7-B, B, Arbitrators.
Rutter, Cal. Practice Guide: A.D.R. Ch. 3B-B, B. ADR Options in Construction Disputes.
Rutter, Cal. Practice Guide: A.D.R. App. D Form 9, Mediation Agreement (Comprehensive Form).
Rutter, Cal. Practice Guide: A.D.R. App. D Form 10, Mini-Trial Agreement.
Rutter, Cal. Practice Guide: A.D.R. App. D Form 12, Confidentiality Provision.
Rutter, Cal. Practice Guide: Civ. Pro. Before Trial Ch. 13-A, A. Introduction.
Rutter, Cal. Practice Guide: Civ. Pro. Before Trial Ch. 13-D, D. the Arbitrator.
Rutter, Cal. Practice Guide: Civ. Pro. Before Trial Ch. 13-E, E. the Arbitration Hearing.
Rutter, Cal. Practice Guide: Civil Trials & Evidence Ch. 9-A, A. Preliminary Considerations.
Rutter, Cal. Practice Guide: Civil Trials & Evidence Ch. 8C-A, A. Testimony.
California Practice Guide: Employment Litigation Ch. 18-B, B. Nonbinding ADR Procedures.
California Practice Guide: Employment Litigation Ch. 18-E, E. Confidentiality of ADR Processes.
Rutter, Cal. Practice Guide: Family Law Ch. 7-B, B. Contested Custody Proceedings, Generally.
Rutter, Cal. Practice Guide: Personal Injury Ch. 4-F, F. Court-Conducted Settlement Proceedings.
Rutter, Cal. Practice Guide: Personal Injury Ch. 4-G, G. Concluding and Enforcing Settlement.
Rutter, Cal. Practice Guide: Personal Injury Ch. 7-A, A. Introduction-Nature and Purpose of "Judicial Arbitration" in General.
Miller and Starr California Real Estate § 35:6, --Confidentiality in Mediation.
Miller and Starr California Real Estate § 35:17, Efficacy of the Mediation Process; Enforceability.
Miller and Starr California Real Estate § 35:94, Grounds for Vacating an Award.
Miller and Starr California Real Estate § 35:96, Misconduct or Conduct Contrary to Statute by a Neutral Arbitrator.
22 NO. 1 Miller & Starr, California Real Estate Newsalert 4, Alternative Dispute Resolution.
9 Witkin Cal. Proc. 5th Administrative Proceedings § 86, (S 86) Protection of Communications.
6 Witkin Cal. Proc. 5th Proceedings Without Trial § 487, (S 487) Confidentiality.

6 Witkin Cal. Proc. 5th Proceedings Without Trial § 488, (S 488) Regulation of Mediation.

§ 704. Juror as witness

(a) Before a juror sworn and impaneled in the trial of an action may be called to testify before the jury in that trial as a witness, he shall, in proceedings conducted by the court out of the presence and hearing of the remaining jurors, inform the parties of the information he has concerning any fact or matter about which he will be called to testify.

(b) Against the objection of a party, a juror sworn and impaneled in the trial of an action may not testify before the jury in that trial as a witness. Upon such objection, the court shall declare a mistrial and order the action assigned for trial before another jury.

(c) The calling of a juror to testify before the jury as a witness shall be deemed a consent to the granting of a motion for mistrial, and an objection to such calling of a juror shall be deemed a motion for mistrial.

(d) In the absence of objection by a party, a juror sworn and impaneled in the trial of an action may be compelled to testify in that trial as a witness. *(Stats.1965, c. 299, § 2, operative Jan. 1, 1967.)*

Research References

Rutter, Cal. Practice Guide: Civil Trials & Evidence Ch. 4-B, B. Preliminary Matters Discussed in Final Status Conference or In-Chambers Conference.
Rutter, Cal. Practice Guide: Civil Trials & Evidence Ch. 5-I, I. Challenging Prospective Jurors.
Rutter, Cal. Practice Guide: Civil Trials & Evidence Ch. 9-A, A. Preliminary Considerations.
Rutter, Cal. Practice Guide: Civil Trials & Evidence Ch. 12-A, A. Motion for Mistrial.
Rutter, Cal. Practice Guide: Civil Trials & Evidence Ch. 8C-A, A. Testimony.
Rutter, Cal. Practice Guide: Personal Injury Ch. 9-L, L. Motions to Terminate Trial Before Verdict.
7 Witkin Cal. Proc. 5th Trial § 167, Mistrial.

CHAPTER 2. OATH AND CONFRONTATION

Section
710. Oath required.
711. Confrontation.
712. Blood samples; technique in taking; affidavits in criminal actions; service; objections.

§ 710. Oath required

Every witness before testifying shall take an oath or make an affirmation or declaration in the form provided by law, except that a child under the age of 10 or a dependent person with a substantial cognitive impairment, in the court's discretion, may be required only to promise to tell the truth. *(Stats.1965, c. 299, § 2, operative Jan. 1, 1967. Amended by Stats.1988, c. 486, § 1; Stats.2004, c. 823 (A.B.20), § 3.)*

Law Revision Commission Comments

Sections 710 and 711 restate the substance of and supersede Section 1846 of the Code of Civil Procedure. [7 Cal.L.Rev.Comm. Reports 1 (1965)].

Research References

Rutter, Cal. Practice Guide: Civil Trials & Evidence Ch. 8C-A, A. Testimony.
Rutter, Cal. Practice Guide: Family Law Ch. 11-F, F. Preparing Client and Witnesses for Trial.
Rutter, Cal. Practice Guide: Personal Injury Ch. 9-F, F. Examination of Witnesses.

10 Witkin, California Summary 10th Parent and Child § 303, in General.

§ 711. Confrontation

At the trial of an action, a witness can be heard only in the presence and subject to the examination of all the parties to the action, if they choose to attend and examine. *(Stats.1965, c. 299, § 2, operative Jan. 1, 1967.)*

Law Revision Commission Comments

See the Comment to Section 710. [7 Cal.L.Rev.Comm. Reports 1 (1965)].

Research References

Rutter, Cal. Practice Guide: Civil Trials & Evidence Ch. 10-A, A. Preliminary Considerations.

§ 712. Blood samples; technique in taking; affidavits in criminal actions; service; objections

Notwithstanding Sections 711 and 1200, at the trial of a criminal action, evidence of the technique used in taking blood samples may be given by a registered nurse, licensed vocational nurse, or licensed clinical laboratory technologist or clinical laboratory bioanalyst, by means of an affidavit. The affidavit shall be admissible, provided the party offering the affidavit as evidence has served all other parties to the action, or their counsel, with a copy of the affidavit no less than 10 days prior to trial. Nothing in this section shall preclude any party or his counsel from objecting to the introduction of the affidavit at any time, and requiring the attendance of the affiant, or compelling attendance by subpoena. *(Added by Stats.1978, c. 93, p. 256, § 1, eff. April 14, 1978.)*

CHAPTER 3. EXPERT WITNESSES

ARTICLE 1. EXPERT WITNESSES GENERALLY

§ 720. Qualification as an expert witness

(a) A person is qualified to testify as an expert if he has special knowledge, skill, experience, training, or education sufficient to qualify him as an expert on the subject to which his testimony relates. Against the objection of a party, such special knowledge, skill, experience, training, or education must be shown before the witness may testify as an expert.

(b) A witness' special knowledge, skill, experience, training, or education may be shown by any otherwise admissible evidence, including his own testimony. *(Stats.1965, c. 299, § 2, operative Jan. 1, 1967.)*

Law Revision Commission Comments

This section states existing law as declared in subdivision 9 (last clause) of Code of Civil Procedure Section 1870, which is superseded by Sections 720 and 801.

The judge must be satisfied that the proposed witness is an expert. People v. Haeussler, 41 Cal.2d 252, 260 P.2d 8 (1953); Pfingsten v. Westenhaver, 39 Cal.2d 12, 244 P.2d 395 (1952); Bossert v. Southern Pac. Co., 172 Cal. 504, 157 Pac. 597 (1916); People v. Pacific Gas & Elec. Co., 27 Cal.App.2d 725, 81 P.2d 584 (1938).

Against the objection of a party, the special qualifications of the proposed witness must be shown as a prerequisite to his testimony as an expert. With the consent of the parties, the judge may receive a witness' testimony conditionally, subject to the necessary foundation being supplied later in the trial. See Evidence Code § 320. Unless the foundation is subsequently supplied, however, the judge should grant a motion to strike or should order the testimony stricken from the record on his own motion.

The judge's determination that a witness qualifies as an expert witness is binding on the trier of fact, but the trier of fact may consider the witness' qualifications as an expert in determining the weight to be given his testimony. Pfingsten v. Westenhaver, 39 Cal.2d 12, 244 P.2d 395 (1952); Howland v. Oakland Consol. St. Ry., 110 Cal. 513, 42 Pac. 983 (1895); Estate of Johnson, 100 Cal.App.2d 73, 223 P.2d 105 (1950). See Evidence Code §§ 405 and 406 and the Comments thereto. [7 Cal.L.Rev.Comm. Reports 1 (1965)].

Research References

Rutter, Cal. Practice Guide: Civil Appeals & Writs Ch. 8-C, C. Standards of Appellate Review.
Rutter, Cal. Practice Guide: Civ. Pro. Before Trial Ch. 10-C, C. Procedural Requirements-Moving Party.
Rutter, Cal. Practice Guide: Civil Trials & Evidence Ch. 1-C, C. Marshalling the Evidence.
Rutter, Cal. Practice Guide: Civil Trials & Evidence Ch. 9-A, A. Preliminary Considerations.
Rutter, Cal. Practice Guide: Civil Trials & Evidence Ch. 11-A, A. Direct Examination of Expert Witnesses.
Rutter, Cal. Practice Guide: Civil Trials & Evidence Ch. 11-B, B. Procedures to Challenge Admissibility of Expert Witness Testimony.
Rutter, Cal. Practice Guide: Civil Trials & Evidence Ch. 8C-A, A. Testimony.
Rutter, Cal. Practice Guide: Civil Trials & Evidence Ch. 8C-G, G. Scientific Evidence.
Rutter, Cal. Practice Guide: Civil Trials & Evidence Ch. 8C-H, H. Opinion Evidence.
Rutter, Cal. Practice Guide: Civil Trials & Evidence Ch. 8G-B, B. Procedures on Objection.
Rutter, Cal. Practice Guide: Family Law Ch. 6-B, B. Spousal Support.
Rutter, Cal. Practice Guide: Family Law Ch. 8-E, E. Division of Community Estate Upon Dissolution, Legal Separation or Nullity.
Rutter, Cal. Practice Guide: Family Law Ch. 13-B, B. Contested Family Law Trial.
Rutter, Cal. Practice Guide: Insurance Litigation Ch. 15-I, I. Trial.
Rutter, Cal. Practice Guide: Personal Injury Ch. 3-C, C. Specific Items of Compensatory Damages.
Rutter, Cal. Practice Guide: Personal Injury Ch. 9-G, G. Expert Witnesses.
Rutter, Cal. Practice Guide: Personal Injury Ch. 2(I)-D, D. Employment of Experts.
7 Witkin Cal. Proc. 5th Trial § 292, (S 292) Expert.

§ 721. Cross-examination of expert witness

(a) Subject to subdivision (b), a witness testifying as an expert may be cross-examined to the same extent as any other witness and, in addition, may be fully cross-examined as to (1) his or her qualifications, (2) the subject to which his or her expert testimony relates, and (3) the matter upon which his or her opinion is based and the reasons for his or her opinion.

(b) If a witness testifying as an expert testifies in the form of an opinion, he or she may not be cross-examined in regard to the content or tenor of any scientific, technical, or professional text, treatise, journal, or similar publication unless any of the following occurs:

(1) The witness referred to, considered, or relied upon such publication in arriving at or forming his or her opinion.

(2) The publication has been admitted in evidence.

(3) The publication has been established as a reliable authority by the testimony or admission of the witness or by other expert testimony or by judicial notice.

If admitted, relevant portions of the publication may be read into evidence but may not be received as exhibits. *(Stats.1965, c.*

299, § 2, operative Jan. 1, 1967. Amended by Stats.1997, c. 892 (S.B.73), § 11.)

Law Revision Commission Comments

Under Section 721, a witness who testifies as an expert may, of course, be cross-examined to the same extent as any other witness. See Chapter 5 (commencing with Section 760). But, under subdivision (a) of Section 721, as under existing law, the expert witness is also subject to a somewhat broader cross-examination: "Once an expert offers his opinion, however, he exposes himself to the kind of inquiry which ordinarily would have no place in the cross-examination of a factual witness. The expert invites investigation into the extent of his knowledge, the reasons for his opinion including facts and other matters upon which it is based (Code Civ.Proc., § 1872), and which he took into consideration; and he may be 'subjected to the most rigid cross examination' concerning his qualifications, and his opinion and its sources [citation omitted]." Hope v. Arrowhead & Puritas Waters, Inc., 174 Cal.App.2d 222, 230, 344 P.2d 428, 433 (1959). The cross-examination rule stated in subdivision (a) is based in part on the last clause of Code of Civil Procedure Section 1872.

Subdivision (b) clarifies a matter concerning which there is considerable confusion in the California decisions. It is at least clear under existing law that an expert witness may be cross-examined in regard to those books on which he relied in forming or arriving at his opinion. Lewis v. Johnson, 12 Cal.2d 558, 86 P.2d 99 (1939); People v. Hooper, 10 Cal.App.2d 332, 51 P.2d 1131 (1935). Dicta in some decisions indicate that the cross-examiner is strictly limited to the books relied on by the expert witness. See, *e.g.*, Baily v. Kreutzmann, 141 Cal. 519, 75 Pac. 104 (1904). Other cases, however, suggest that an expert witness may be cross-examined in regard to any book of the same character as the books on which he relied in forming his opinion. Griffith v. Los Angeles Pac. Co., 14 Cal.App. 145, 111 Pac. 107 (1910). See Salgo v. Leland Stanford etc. Bd. Trustees, 154 Cal.App.2d 560, 317 P.2d 170 (1957); Gluckstein v. Lipsett, 93 Cal. App.2d 391, 209 P.2d 98 (1949) (reviewing California authorities). (Possibly, the cross-examiner is restricted under this view to the use of such books as "are not in harmony with the testimony of the witness." Griffith v. Los Angeles Pac. Co., *supra*.) Language in several earlier cases indicated that the cross-examiner could use books to test the competency of an expert witness, whether or not the expert relied on books in forming his opinion. Fisher v. Southern Pac. R.R., 89 Cal. 399, 26 Pac. 894 (1891); People v. Hooper, 10 Cal.App.2d 332, 51 P.2d 1131 (1935). More recent decisions indicate, however, that the opinion of an expert witness must be based either generally or specifically on books before the expert can be cross-examined concerning them. Lewis v. Johnson, 12 Cal.2d 558, 86 P.2d 99 (1939); Salgo v. Leland Stanford etc. Bd. Trustees, 154 Cal.App.2d 560, 317 P.2d 170 (1957); Gluckstein v. Lipsett, 93 Cal. App.2d 391, 209 P.2d 98 (1949). The conflicting California cases are gathered in Annot., 60 A.L.R.2d 77 (1958).

If an expert witness has relied on a particular publication in forming his opinion, it is necessary to permit cross-examination in regard to that publication in order to show whether the expert correctly read, interpreted, and applied the portions he relied on. Similarly, it is important to permit an expert witness to be cross-examined concerning those publications referred to or considered by him even though not specifically relied on by him in forming his opinion. An expert's reasons for not relying on particular publications that were referred to or considered by him while forming his opinion may reveal important information bearing upon the credibility of his testimony. However, a rule permitting cross-examination on technical treatises not considered by the expert witness would permit the cross-examiner to utilize this opportunity not for its ostensible purpose—to test the expert's opinion—but to bring before the trier of fact the opinions of absentee authors without the safeguard of cross-examination. Although the court would be required upon request to caution the jury that the statements read are not to be considered evidence of the truth of the propositions stated, there is a danger that at least some jurors might rely on the author's statements for this purpose. Yet, the statements in the text might be based on inadequate background research, might be subject to unexpressed qualifications that would be applicable to the case before the court, or might be unreliable for some other reason that could be revealed if the author were subject to cross-examination. Therefore, subdivision (b) does not permit cross-examination of an expert witness on scientific, technical, or professional works not referred to, considered, or relied on by him.

If a particular publication has already been admitted in evidence, however, the reason for subdivision (b)—to prevent inadmissible evidence from being brought before the jury—is inapplicable. Hence, the subdivision permits an expert witness to be examined concerning such a publication without regard to whether he referred to, considered, or relied on it in forming his opinion. *Cf.* Laird v. T. W. Mather, Inc., 51 Cal.2d 210, 331 P.2d 617 (1958).

The rule state in subdivision (b) thus provides a fair and workable solution to this conflict of competing interests with respect to the permissible use of scientific, technical, or professional publications by the cross-examiner. [7 Cal.L.Rev.Comm. Reports 1 (1965)].

Research References

Rutter, Cal. Practice Guide: Civil Trials & Evidence Ch. 10-B, B. Scope of Permissible Cross-Examination.

Rutter, Cal. Practice Guide: Civil Trials & Evidence Ch. 11-D, D. Cross-Examination of Expert Witnesses.

Rutter, Cal. Practice Guide: Civil Trials & Evidence Ch. 8D-D, D. Hearsay Exceptions.

Rutter, Cal. Practice Guide: Fed.Civ.Pro. Before Trial Ch. 1-D, D. Choosing Between State and Federal Courts.

Rutter, Cal. Practice Guide: Personal Injury Ch. 9-G, G. Expert Witnesses.

§ 722. Credibility of expert witness

(a) The fact of the appointment of an expert witness by the court may be revealed to the trier of fact.

(b) The compensation and expenses paid or to be paid to an expert witness by the party calling him is a proper subject of inquiry by any adverse party as relevant to the credibility of the witness and the weight of his testimony. *(Stats.1965, c. 299, § 2, operative Jan. 1, 1967.)*

Law Revision Commission Comments

Subdivision (a) of Section 722 codifies a rule recognized in the California decisions. People v. Cornell, 203 Cal. 144, 263 Pac. 216 (1928); People v. Strong, 114 Cal.App. 522, 300 Pac. 84 (1931).

Subdivision (b) of Section 722 restates the substance of Section 1256.2 of the Code of Civil Procedure. Section 1256.2, however, applies only in condemnation cases, while Section 722 is not so limited. It is uncertain whether the California law in other fields of litigation is as stated in Section 722. At least one California case has held that an expert could be asked whether he was being compensated but that he could not be asked the amount of the compensation. People v. Tomalty, 14 Cal.App. 224, 111 Pac. 513 (1910). However, the decision may have been based on the discretionary right of the trial judge to curtail collateral inquiry.

In any event, the rule enunciated in Section 722 is a desirable rule. The tendency of some experts to become advocates for the party employing them has been recognized. 2 Wigmore, Evidence § 563 (3d ed. 1940); Friedenthal, Discovery and Use of an Adverse Party's Expert Information, 14 Stan. L. Rev 455, 485–486 (1962). The jury can better appraise the extent to which bias may have influenced an expert's opinion if it is informed of the amount of his fee—and, hence, the extent of his possible feeling of obligation to the party calling him. [7 Cal.L.Rev.Comm. Reports 1 (1965)].

Research References

Rutter, Cal. Practice Guide: Civil Trials & Evidence Ch. 1-E, E. Preparing Witnesses to Testify.

Rutter, Cal. Practice Guide: Civil Trials & Evidence Ch. 10-B, B. Scope of Permissible Cross-Examination.

Rutter, Cal. Practice Guide: Civil Trials & Evidence Ch. 10-D, D. Objectives of Cross-Examination.

Rutter, Cal. Practice Guide: Civil Trials & Evidence Ch. 11-D, D. Cross-Examination of Expert Witnesses.

Rutter, Cal. Practice Guide: Civil Trials & Evidence Ch. 8E-F, F. Limitations on Impeachment and Rehabilitation.

Rutter, Cal. Practice Guide: Family Law Ch. 11-F, F. Preparing Client and Witnesses for Trial.

Rutter, Cal. Practice Guide: Family Law Ch. 13-B, B. Contested Family Law Trial.

Rutter, Cal. Practice Guide: Personal Injury Ch. 8-D, D. Final Preparation (One Month Before Trial).

Evidence

Rutter, Cal. Practice Guide: Personal Injury Ch. 9-G, G. Expert Witnesses.

§ 723. Limit on number of expert witnesses

The court may, at any time before or during the trial of an action, limit the number of expert witnesses to be called by any party. *(Stats.1965, c. 299, § 2, operative Jan. 1, 1967.)*

Law Revision Commission Comments

Section 723 restates the substance of and supersedes that last sentence of Section 1871 of the Code of Civil Procedure. [7 Cal.L.Rev.Comm. Reports 1 (1965)].

Research References

Rutter, Cal. Practice Guide: Civ. Pro. Before Trial Ch. 8J-6, Exchange Required.

Rutter, Cal. Practice Guide: Civil Trials & Evidence Ch. 1-C, C. Marshalling the Evidence.

Rutter, Cal. Practice Guide: Personal Injury Ch. 9-G, G. Expert Witnesses.

Miller and Starr California Real Estate § 30A:72, Valuation Testimony.

ARTICLE 2. APPOINTMENT OF EXPERT WITNESS BY COURT

Section
730. Appointment of expert by court.
731. Payment of court-appointed expert.
732. Calling and examining court-appointed expert.
733. Right to produce other expert evidence.

§ 730. Appointment of expert by court

When it appears to the court, at any time before or during the trial of an action, that expert evidence is or may be required by the court or by any party to the action, the court on its own motion or on motion of any party may appoint one or more experts to investigate, to render a report as may be ordered by the court, and to testify as an expert at the trial of the action relative to the fact or matter as to which the expert evidence is or may be required. The court may fix the compensation for these services, if any, rendered by any person appointed under this section, in addition to any service as a witness, at the amount as seems reasonable to the court.

Nothing in this section shall be construed to permit a person to perform any act for which a license is required unless the person holds the appropriate license to lawfully perform that act. *(Added by Stats.1979, c. 746, p. 2592, § 3, operative Jan. 1, 1983. Amended by Stats.1990, c. 295 (A.B.3371), § 1.)*

Research References

Rutter, Cal. Practice Guide: A.D.R. Ch. 3-G, G. Other Dispute Resolution Methods Using Neutral Advisor.

Rutter, Cal. Practice Guide: Civ. Pro. Before Trial Ch. 8H-6, Responding to Demand.

Rutter, Cal. Practice Guide: Civil Trials & Evidence Ch. 1-C, C. Marshalling the Evidence.

Rutter, Cal. Practice Guide: Civil Trials & Evidence Ch. 17-D, D. Costs.

Rutter, Cal. Practice Guide: Civil Trials & Evidence Ch. 8C-G, G. Scientific Evidence.

Rutter, Cal. Practice Guide: Civil Trials & Evidence Ch. 8C-H, H. Opinion Evidence.

Rutter, Cal. Practice Guide: Civil Trials & Evidence Ch. 8C-J, J. Judicial Notice.

Rutter, Cal. Practice Guide: Family Law Ch. 7-B, B. Contested Custody Proceedings, Generally.

Rutter, Cal. Practice Guide: Family Law Ch. 7-C, C. Custody Awards, Generally.

Rutter, Cal. Practice Guide: Family Law Ch. 7-G, G. Removal of Child from Jurisdiction; Wrongful Taking or Withholding of Child.

Rutter, Cal. Practice Guide: Family Law Ch. 8-E, E. Division of Community Estate Upon Dissolution, Legal Separation or Nullity.

Rutter, Cal. Practice Guide: Family Law Ch. 13-B, B. Contested Family Law Trial.

10 Witkin, California Summary 10th Parent and Child § 208, (S 208) Child's Preference.

10 Witkin, California Summary 10th Parent and Child § 275, (S 275) in General.

10 Witkin, California Summary 10th Parent and Child § 284, Trial.

10 Witkin, California Summary 10th Parent and Child § 617, (S 617) in General.

11 Witkin, California Summary 10th Husband and Wife § 94, (S 94) Participation in Domestic Violence Programs.

11 Witkin, California Summary 10th Husband and Wife § 381, Criminal Background Search.

§ 731. Payment of court-appointed expert

(a)(1) In all criminal actions and juvenile court proceedings, the compensation fixed under Section 730 shall be a charge against the county in which the action or proceeding is pending and shall be paid out of the treasury of that county on order of the court.

(2) Notwithstanding paragraph (1), if the expert is appointed for the court's needs, the compensation shall be a charge against the court.

(b) In any county in which the superior court so provides, the compensation fixed under Section 730 for medical experts appointed for the court's needs in civil actions shall be a charge against the court. In any county in which the board of supervisors so provides, the compensation fixed under Section 730 for medical experts appointed in civil actions, for purposes other than the court's needs, shall be a charge against and paid out of the treasury of that county on order of the court.

(c) Except as otherwise provided in this section, in all civil actions, the compensation fixed under Section 730 shall, in the first instance, be apportioned and charged to the several parties in a proportion as the court may determine and may thereafter be taxed and allowed in like manner as other costs. *(Added by Stats.1979, c. 746, § 5, operative Jan. 1, 1983. Amended by Stats.2012, c. 470 (A.B.1529), § 8.)*

Law Revision Commission Comments

Subdivisions (a) and (b) of Section 731 are amended to reflect the enactment of the Lockyer–Isenberg Trial Court Funding Act, 1997 Cal. Stat. ch. 850 (see generally Gov't Code §§ 77000–77655). See, e.g., Gov't Code §§ 77001 (local trial court management), 77003 ("court operations" defined), 77200 (state funding of "court operations"); see also Cal. R. Ct. 10.810(d), Functions 4 (court interpreters) & 10 (referring to "court-appointed expert witness fees (for the court's needs)").

Subdivisions (a), (b), and (c) are also amended to make stylistic revisions. [39 Cal.L.Rev.Comm. Reports 109 (2009)].

Research References

Rutter, Cal. Practice Guide: Civ. Pro. Before Trial Ch. 8H-6, Responding to Demand.

Rutter, Cal. Practice Guide: Civil Trials & Evidence Ch. 9-F, F. Witnesses Needing Assistance in Testifying.

Rutter, Cal. Practice Guide: Civil Trials & Evidence Ch. 8C-H, H. Opinion Evidence.

7 Witkin Cal. Proc. 5th Judgment § 133, (S 133) Fees of Expert Witness.

10 Witkin, California Summary 10th Parent and Child § 284, Trial.

§ 732. Calling and examining court-appointed expert

Any expert appointed by the court under Section 730 may be called and examined by the court or by any party to the action. When such witness is called and examined by the court, the parties have the same right as is expressed in Section 775 to cross-examine the witness and to object to the questions asked and the evidence adduced. *(Stats.1965, c. 299, § 2, operative Jan. 1, 1967.)*

Section 732 restates the substance of and supersedes the fourth paragraph of Section 1871 of the Code of Civil Procedure. Section 732 refers to Section 775, which is based on language originally contained in Section 1871. Section 775 permits each party to the action to object to questions asked and evidence adduced and, also, to cross-examine any person called by the court as a witness to the same extent as if such person were called as a witness by an adverse party. [7 Cal.L.Rev.Comm. Reports 1 (1965)].

§ 733. Right to produce other expert evidence

Nothing contained in this article shall be deemed or construed to prevent any party to any action from producing other expert evidence on the same fact or matter mentioned in Section 730; but, where other expert witnesses are called by a party to the action, their fees shall be paid by the party calling them and only ordinary witness fees shall be taxed as costs in the action. *(Stats.1965, c. 299, § 2, operative Jan. 1, 1967.)*

Section 733 restates the substance of and supersedes the third paragraph of Section 1871 of the Code of Civil Procedure. [7 Cal.L.Rev. Comm. Reports 1 (1965)].

Rutter, Cal. Practice Guide: Civil Trials & Evidence Ch. 8C-H, H. Opinion Evidence.
Rutter, Cal. Practice Guide: Family Law Ch. 7-B, B. Contested Custody Proceedings, Generally.

CHAPTER 4. INTERPRETERS AND TRANSLATORS

Section

§ 750. Rules relating to witnesses apply to interpreters and translators

A person who serves as an interpreter or translator in any action is subject to all the rules of law relating to witnesses. *(Stats.1965, c. 299, § 2, operative Jan. 1, 1967.)*

Section 750 codifies existing law. *E.g.,* People v. Lem Deo, 132 Cal. 199, 201, 64 Pac. 265, 266 (1901) (interpreter); People v. Bardin, 148 Cal.App.2d 776, 307 P.2d 384 (1957) (translator). [7 Cal.L.Rev.Comm. Reports 1 (1965)].

2 Witkin Cal. Proc. 5th Courts § 387, Interpreters and Translators.
10 Witkin, California Summary 10th Parent and Child § 303, in General.

§ 751. Oath required of interpreters and translators

(a) An interpreter shall take an oath that he or she will make a true interpretation to the witness in a language that the witness understands and that he or she will make a true interpretation of the witness' answers to questions to counsel, court, or jury, in the English language, with his or her best skill and judgment.

(b) In any proceeding in which a deaf or hard-of-hearing person is testifying under oath, the interpreter certified pursuant to subdivision (f) of Section 754 shall advise the court whenever he or she is unable to comply with his or her oath taken pursuant to subdivision (a).

(c) A translator shall take an oath that he or she will make a true translation in the English language of any writing he or she is to decipher or translate.

(d) An interpreter regularly employed by the court and certified or registered in accordance with Article 4 (commencing with Section 68560) of Chapter 2 of Title 8 of the Government Code, or a translator regularly employed by the court, may file an oath as prescribed by this section with the clerk of the court. The filed oath shall serve for all subsequent court proceedings until the appointment is revoked by the court. *(Stats.1965, c. 299, § 2, operative Jan. 1, 1967. Amended by Stats.1984, c. 30, § 1, eff. March 7, 1984; Stats.1990, c. 1450 (S.B.2046), § 1; Stats.1997, c. 376 (A.B.1445), § 1.)*

Section 751 is based on language presently contained in subdivision (c) of Section 1885 of the Code of Civil Procedure. [7 Cal.L.Rev.Comm. Reports 1 (1965)].

10 Witkin, California Summary 10th Parent and Child § 303, in General.

§ 752. Interpreters for witnesses; compensation

(a) When a witness is incapable of understanding the English language or is incapable of expressing himself or herself in the English language so as to be understood directly by counsel, court, and jury, an interpreter whom the witness can understand and who can understand the witness shall be sworn to interpret for the witness.

(b) The record shall identify the interpreter, who may be appointed and compensated as provided in Article 2 (commencing with Section 730) of Chapter 3, with that compensation charged as follows:

(1) In all criminal actions and juvenile court proceedings, the compensation for an interpreter under this section shall be a charge against the court.

(2) In all civil actions, the compensation for an interpreter under this section shall, in the first instance, be apportioned and charged to the several parties in a proportion as the court may determine and may thereafter be taxed and allowed in a like manner as other costs. *(Stats.1965, c. 299, § 2, operative Jan. 1, 1967. Amended by Stats.1984, c. 30, § 2, eff. March 7, 1984; Stats.1984, c. 768, § 1; Stats.2012, c. 470 (A.B.1529), § 9.)*

Section 752 restates the substance of and supersedes Section 1884 of the Code of Civil Procedure. It is drawn broadly enough to authorize the use of an interpreter for a person whose inability to be understood directly stems from physical disability as well as from lack of understanding of the English language. See discussion in People v. Walker, 69 Cal.App. 475, 231 Pac. 572 (1924). Under Section 752, as under existing law, whether an interpreter should be appointed is largely within the discretion of the trial judge. People v. Holtzclaw, 76 Cal.App. 168, 243 Pac. 894 (1926).

Subdivision (b) of Section 752 substitutes for the detailed language in Code of Civil Procedure Section 1884 a reference to the general authority of a court to appoint expert witnesses, since interpreters are treated as expert witnesses and subject to the same rules of competency and examination as are experts generally. The existing procedure provided by Code of Civil Procedure Section 1884 does not insure that an interpreter who is required to testify will be paid reasonable compensation for his

Evidence

services. Section 752 corrects this deficiency in the existing law. [7 Cal.L.Rev.Comm. Reports 1 (1965)].

Subdivision (a) of Section 752 is amended to make stylistic revisions.

Subdivision (b) is amended to reflect enactment of the Lockyer–Isenberg Trial Court Funding Act, 1997 Cal. Stat. ch. 850 (see generally Gov't Code §§ 77000–77655). See, e.g., Gov't Code §§ 77001 (local trial court management), 77003 ("court operations" defined), 77200 (state funding of "court operations"); see also Cal. R. Ct. 10.810(d), Function 4 (court interpreters).

Subdivision (b) is also amended to make a stylistic revision.

The purpose of the revisions in the act that amended this section is to remove material made obsolete by trial court restructuring. See Gov't Code § 71674. The act should not be construed as a re-evaluation of the extent to which interpretation or translation should be provided in court proceedings, or who should bear the expense of interpretation or translation. [39 Cal.L.Rev.Comm. Reports 109 (2009)].

Research References

Rutter, Cal. Practice Guide: Civil Trials & Evidence Ch. 6-G, G. Preparing Opening Statement.
Rutter, Cal. Practice Guide: Civil Trials & Evidence Ch. 9-F, F. Witnesses Needing Assistance in Testifying.
Rutter, Cal. Practice Guide: Personal Injury Ch. 9-F, F. Examination of Witnesses.
3 Witkin Cal. Proc. 5th Actions § 422, (S 422) No Right to Interpreter.
10 Witkin, California Summary 10th Parent and Child § 303, in General.

§ 753. Translators of writings; compensation

(a) When the written characters in a writing offered in evidence are incapable of being deciphered or understood directly, a translator who can decipher the characters or understand the language shall be sworn to decipher or translate the writing.

(b) The record shall identify the translator, who may be appointed and compensated as provided in Article 2 (commencing with Section 730) of Chapter 3, with that compensation charged as follows:

(1) In all criminal actions and juvenile court proceedings, the compensation for a translator under this section shall be a charge against the court.

(2) In all civil actions, the compensation for a translator under this section shall, in the first instance, be apportioned and charged to the several parties in a proportion as the court may determine and may thereafter be taxed and allowed in like manner as other costs. *(Stats.1965, c. 299, § 2, operative Jan. 1, 1967. Amended by Stats.1984, c. 30, § 3, eff. March 7, 1984; Stats.2012, c. 470 (A.B.1529), § 10.)*

Law Revision Commission Comments

Section 753 restates the substance of and supersedes Section 1863 of the Code of Civil Procedure, but the language of Section 753 is new. The same principles that require the appointment of an interpreter for a witness who is incapable of expressing himself so as to be understood directly apply with equal force to documentary evidence. See Evidence Code § 752 and the Comment thereto. [7 Cal.L.Rev.Comm. Reports 1 (1965)].

Subdivision (b) is amended to reflect enactment of the Lockyer–Isenberg Trial Court Funding Act, 1997 Cal. Stat. ch. 850 (see generally Gov't Code §§ 77000–77655). See, e.g., Gov't Code §§ 77001 (local trial court management), 77003 ("court operations" defined), 77200 (state funding of "court operations"); see also Cal. R. Ct. 10.810(d), Function 4 (court interpreters).

Subdivision (b) is also amended to make a stylistic revision.

The purpose of the revisions in the act that amended this section is to remove material made obsolete by trial court restructuring. See Gov't Code § 71674. The act should not be construed as a re-evaluation of the extent to which interpretation or translation should be provided in court proceedings, or who should bear the expense of interpretation or translation. [39 Cal.L.Rev.Comm. Reports 109 (2009)].

§ 754. Deaf or hearing impaired persons; interpreters; qualifications; guidelines; compensation; questioning; use of statements

(a) As used in this section, "individual who is deaf or hearing impaired" means an individual with a hearing loss so great as to prevent his or her understanding language spoken in a normal tone, but does not include an individual who is hearing impaired provided with, and able to fully participate in the proceedings through the use of, an assistive listening system or computer-aided transcription equipment provided pursuant to Section 54.8 of the Civil Code.

(b) In any civil or criminal action, including, but not limited to, any action involving a traffic or other infraction, any small claims court proceeding, any juvenile court proceeding, any family court proceeding or service, or any proceeding to determine the mental competency of a person, in any court-ordered or court-provided alternative dispute resolution, including mediation and arbitration, or any administrative hearing, where a party or witness is an individual who is deaf or hearing impaired and the individual who is deaf or hearing impaired is present and participating, the proceedings shall be interpreted in a language that the individual who is deaf or hearing impaired understands by a qualified interpreter appointed by the court or other appointing authority, or as agreed upon.

(c) For purposes of this section, "appointing authority" means a court, department, board, commission, agency, licensing or legislative body, or other body for proceedings requiring a qualified interpreter.

(d) For the purposes of this section, "interpreter" includes, but is not limited to, an oral interpreter, a sign language interpreter, or a deaf-blind interpreter, depending upon the needs of the individual who is deaf or hearing impaired.

(e) For purposes of this section, "intermediary interpreter" means an individual who is deaf or hearing impaired, or a hearing individual who is able to assist in providing an accurate interpretation between spoken English and sign language or between variants of sign language or between American Sign Language and other foreign languages by acting as an intermediary between the individual who is deaf or hearing impaired and the qualified interpreter.

(f) For purposes of this section, "qualified interpreter" means an interpreter who has been certified as competent to interpret court proceedings by a testing organization, agency, or educational institution approved by the Judicial Council as qualified to administer tests to court interpreters for individuals who are deaf or hearing impaired.

(g) In the event that the appointed interpreter is not familiar with the use of particular signs by the individual who is deaf or hearing impaired or his or her particular variant of sign language, the court or other appointing authority shall, in consultation with the individual who is deaf or hearing impaired or his or her representative, appoint an intermediary interpreter.

(h) Prior to July 1, 1992, the Judicial Council shall conduct a study to establish the guidelines pursuant to which it shall determine which testing organizations, agencies, or educational institutions will be approved to administer tests for certification of court interpreters for individuals who are deaf or hearing impaired. It is the intent of the Legislature that the study obtain the widest possible input from the public, including, but not limited to, educational institutions, the judiciary, linguists, members of the State Bar, court interpreters, members of professional interpreting organizations, and members of the deaf and hearing-impaired communities. After obtaining public comment and completing its study, the Judicial Council shall publish these guidelines. By January 1, 1997, the Judicial Council shall approve one or more entities to administer testing for court interpreters for individuals who are deaf or hearing impaired. Testing entities may include educational institutions, testing organizations, joint powers agencies, or public agencies.

Commencing July 1, 1997, court interpreters for individuals who are deaf or hearing impaired shall meet the qualifications specified in subdivision (f).

(i) Persons appointed to serve as interpreters under this section shall be paid, in addition to actual travel costs, the prevailing rate paid to persons employed by the court to provide other interpreter services unless such service is considered to be a part of the person's regular duties as an employee of the state, county, or other political subdivision of the state. Except as provided in subdivision (j), payment of the interpreter's fee shall be a charge against the court. Payment of the interpreter's fee in administrative proceedings shall be a charge against the appointing board or authority.

(j) Whenever a peace officer or any other person having a law enforcement or prosecutorial function in any criminal or quasi-criminal investigation or non-court proceeding questions or otherwise interviews an alleged victim or witness who demonstrates or alleges deafness or hearing impairment, a good faith effort to secure the services of an interpreter shall be made, without any unnecessary delay unless either the individual who is deaf or hearing impaired affirmatively indicates that he or she does not need or cannot use an interpreter, or an interpreter is not otherwise required by Title II of the Americans with Disabilities Act of 1990 (Public Law 101–336)[1] and federal regulations adopted thereunder. Payment of the interpreter's fee shall be a charge against the county, or other political subdivision of the state, in which the action is pending.

(k) No statement, written or oral, made by an individual who the court finds is deaf or hearing impaired in reply to a question of a peace officer, or any other person having a law enforcement or prosecutorial function in any criminal or quasi-criminal investigation or proceeding, may be used against that individual who is deaf or hearing impaired unless the question was accurately interpreted and the statement was made knowingly, voluntarily, and intelligently and was accurately interpreted, or the court makes special findings that either the individual could not have used an interpreter or an interpreter was not otherwise required by Title II of the Americans with Disabilities Act of 1990 (Public Law 101–336) and federal regulations adopted thereunder and that the statement was made knowingly, voluntarily, and intelligently.

(*l*) In obtaining services of an interpreter for purposes of subdivision (j) or (k), priority shall be given to first obtaining a qualified interpreter.

(m) Nothing in subdivision (j) or (k) shall be deemed to supersede the requirement of subdivision (b) for use of a qualified interpreter for individuals who are deaf or hearing impaired participating as parties or witnesses in a trial or hearing.

(n) In any action or proceeding in which an individual who is deaf or hearing impaired is a participant, the appointing authority shall not commence proceedings until the appointed interpreter is in full view of and spatially situated to assure proper communication with the participating individual who is deaf or hearing impaired.

(*o*) Each superior court shall maintain a current roster of qualified interpreters certified pursuant to subdivision (f). *(Stats.1965, c. 299, § 2, operative Jan. 1, 1967. Amended by Stats.1977, c. 1182, p. 3873, § 1; Stats.1984, c. 768, § 2; Stats.1989, c. 1002, § 2; Stats.1990, c. 1450 (S.B.2046), § 2; Stats.1991, c. 883 (S.B.585), § 1; Stats.1992, c. 118 (S.B.16), § 1, eff. July 7, 1992; Stats.1992, c. 913 (A.B.1077), § 14; Stats.1995,*

c. 143 (A.B.1833), § 1, eff. July 18, 1995; Stats.2012, c. 470 (A.B.1529), § 11.)

1 42 U.S.C.A. §12101 et seq.

Law Revision Commission Comments

Section 754 restates the substance of and supersedes Section 1885 of the Code of Civil Procedure. Subdivision (c) of Section 1885 is not continued in Section 754 but is restated in substance in Section 751.

The phrase "with or without a hearing aid" has been deleted from the definition of "deaf person" as unnecessary. The court's inquiry should be directed towards the ability of the person to hear; the court should not be concerned with the means by which he might be enabled to hear. [7 Cal.L.Rev.Comm. Reports 1 (1965)].

Subdivisions (i) and (j) of Section 754 are amended to reflect enactment of the Lockyer–Isenberg Trial Court Funding Act, 1997 Cal. Stat. ch. 850 (see generally Gov't Code §§ 77000–77655). See, e.g., Gov't Code §§ 77003 ("court operations" defined), 77200 (state funding of "court operations"); see also Cal. R. Ct. 10.810(d), Function 4 (court interpreters). [39 Cal.L.Rev.Comm. Reports 157 (2009)].

Research References

Rutter, Cal. Practice Guide: Civil Trials & Evidence Ch. 6-G, G. Preparing Opening Statement.
Rutter, Cal. Practice Guide: Civil Trials & Evidence Ch. 9-F, F. Witnesses Needing Assistance in Testifying.
9 Witkin Cal. Proc. 5th Administrative Proceedings § 77, Language Assistance.

§ 754.5. Privileged statements; deaf or hearing impaired persons; use of interpreter

Whenever an otherwise valid privilege exists between an individual who is deaf or hearing impaired and another person, that privilege is not waived merely because an interpreter was used to facilitate their communication. *(Added by Stats.1990, c. 1450 (S.B.2046), § 3. Amended by Stats.1992, c. 913 (A.B.1077), § 15.)*

Research References

Rutter, Cal. Practice Guide: Civil Trials & Evidence Ch. 8E-A, A. Privileges.

§ 755. Hearings or proceedings related to domestic violence; party not proficient in English; interpreters; fees

(a) In any action or proceeding under Division 10 (commencing with Section 6200) of the Family Code, and in any action or proceeding under the Uniform Parentage Act (Part 3 (commencing with Section 7600) of Division 12 of the Family Code) or for dissolution or nullity of marriage or legal separation of the parties in which a protective order has been granted or is being sought pursuant to Section 6221 of the Family Code, in which a party does not proficiently speak or understand the English language, and that party is present, an interpreter, as provided in this section, shall be present to interpret the proceedings in a language that the party understands, and to assist communication between the party and his or her attorney. Notwithstanding this requirement, a court may issue an ex parte order pursuant to Sections 2045 and 7710 of, and Article 1 (commencing with Section 6320) of Chapter 2 of Part 4 of Division 10 of the Family Code, without the presence of an interpreter. The interpreter selected shall be certified pursuant to Article 4 (commencing with Section 68560) of Chapter 2 of Title 8 of the Government Code, unless the court in its discretion appoints an interpreter who is not certified.

(b) The fees of interpreters utilized under this section shall be paid as provided in subdivision (b) of Section 68092 of the Government Code. However, the fees of an interpreter shall be waived for a party who needs an interpreter and appears in forma pauperis pursuant to Section 68511.3 of the Government Code. The Judicial Council shall amend subdivision (i) of

California Rule of Court 985 and revise its forms accordingly by July 1, 1996.

(c) In any civil action in which an interpreter is required under this section, the court shall not commence proceedings until the appointed interpreter is present and situated near the party and his or her attorney. However, this section shall not prohibit the court from doing any of the following:

(1) Issuing an order when the necessity for the order out-weighs the necessity for an interpreter.

(2) Extending the duration of a previously issued temporary order if an interpreter is not readily available.

(3) Issuing a permanent order where a party who requires an interpreter fails to make appropriate arrangements for an interpreter after receiving proper notice of the hearing with information about obtaining an interpreter.

(d) This section does not prohibit the presence of any other person to assist a party.

(e) A local public entity may, and the Judicial Council shall, apply to the appropriate state agency that receives federal funds authorized pursuant to the federal Violence Against Women Act (P.L. 103–322) for these federal funds or for funds from sources other than the state to implement this section. A local public entity and the Judicial Council shall comply with the require-ments of this section only to the extent that any of these funds are made available.

(f) The Judicial Council shall draft rules and modify forms necessary to implement this section, including those for the petition for a temporary restraining order and related forms, to inform both parties of their right to an interpreter pursuant to this section. *(Added by Stats.1995, c. 888 (S.B.982), § 1.)*

Research References

Rutter, Cal. Practice Guide: Civil Trials & Evidence Ch. 9-A, A. Preliminary Considerations.
Rutter, Cal. Practice Guide: Civil Trials & Evidence Ch. 9-F, F. Witnesses Needing Assistance in Testifying.
Rutter, Cal. Practice Guide: Family Law Ch. 5-D, D. Notice of Mo-tion/OSC and Stipulation Procedures.
Rutter, Cal. Practice Guide: Family Law Ch. 13-B, B. Contested Family Law Trial.

§ 755.5. Medical examinations; parties not proficient in En-glish language; interpreters; fees; admissibility of record

(a) During any medical examination, requested by an insurer or by the defendant, of a person who is a party to a civil action and who does not proficiently speak or understand the English language, conducted for the purpose of determining damages in a civil action, an interpreter shall be present to interpret the examination in a language that the person understands. The interpreter shall be certified pursuant to Article 8 (commencing with Section 11435.05) of Chapter 4.5 of Part 1 of Division 3 of Title 2 of the Government Code.

(b) The fees of interpreters used under subdivision (a) shall be paid by the insurer or defendant requesting the medical examination.

(c) The record of, or testimony concerning, any medical examination conducted in violation of subdivision (a) shall be inadmissible in the civil action for which it was conducted or any other civil action.

(d) This section does not prohibit the presence of any other person to assist a party.

(e) In the event that interpreters certified pursuant to Article 8 (commencing with Section 11435.05) of Chapter 4.5 of Part 1 of Division 3 of Title 2 of the Government Code cannot be present at the medical examination, upon stipulation of the parties the requester specified in subdivision (a) shall have the

discretionary authority to provisionally qualify and use other interpreters. *(Added by Stats.1992, c. 1302 (A.B.3107), § 5, eff. Sept. 30, 1992. Amended by Stats.1995, c. 938 (S.B.523), § 8, operative July 1, 1997.)*

Law Revision Commission Comments

Section 755.5 is amended to correct references to the Administrative Procedure Act. The former reference in subdivision (a) to January 1, 1994, is deleted as obsolete. [25 Cal.L.Rev.Comm. Reports 55 (1995)].

Research References

Rutter, Cal. Practice Guide: Civ. Pro. Before Trial Ch. 8I-3, Examination Upon Court Order.
Rutter, Cal. Practice Guide: Civil Trials & Evidence Ch. 4-F, F. Motions in Limine.
Rutter, Cal. Practice Guide: Civil Trials & Evidence Ch. 4-F, Outline F.
Rutter, Cal. Practice Guide: Personal Injury Ch. 6-C, C. Physical and Mental Examinations (CCP § 2032.020 et seq.).

CHAPTER 5. METHOD AND SCOPE OF EXAMINATION

ARTICLE 1. DEFINITIONS

§ 760. Direct examination

"Direct examination" is the first examination of a witness upon a matter that is not within the scope of a previous examination of the witness. *(Stats.1965, c. 299, § 2, operative Jan. 1, 1967.)*

Law Revision Commission Comments

Section 760 restates the substance of and supersedes the first clause of Code of Civil Procedure Section 2045 and the last clause of Code of Civil Procedure Section 2048. Under Section 760, an examination of a witness called by another party is direct examination if the examination relates to a matter that is not within the scope of the previous examination of the witness. [7 Cal.L.Rev.Comm. Reports 1 (1965)].

Research References

Rutter, Cal. Practice Guide: Civil Trials & Evidence Ch. 9-A, A. Preliminary Considerations.
Rutter, Cal. Practice Guide: Civil Trials & Evidence Ch. 10-B, B. Scope of Permissible Cross-Examination.
Rutter, Cal. Practice Guide: Personal Injury Ch. 9-F, F. Examination of Witnesses.

§ 761. Cross-examination

"Cross-examination" is the examination of a witness by a party other than the direct examiner upon a matter that is within the scope of the direct examination of the witness. *(Stats.1965, c. 299, § 2, operative Jan. 1, 1967.)*

Law Revision Commission Comments

Section 761 restates the substance of and supersedes the definition of "cross-examination" found in Section 2045 of the Code of Civil Proce-dure. In accordance with existing law, it limits cross-examination of a witness to the scope of the witness' direct examination. See generally Witkin, California Evidence §§ 622–638 (1958).

Section 761, together with Section 773, retains the cross-examination rule now applicable to a defendant in a criminal action who testifies as a witness in that action. See People v. McCarthy, 88 Cal.App.2d 883, 200 P.2d 69 (1948). See also People v. Arrighini, 122 Cal. 121, 54 Pac. 591 (1898); People v. O'Brien, 66 Cal. 602, 6 Pac. 695 (1885); Witkin, California Evidence § 629 (1958). See also Evidence Code § 772(d). [7 Cal.L.Rev.Comm. Reports 1 (1965)].

Research References

Rutter, Cal. Practice Guide: Civil Trials & Evidence Ch. 10-A, A. Preliminary Considerations.
Rutter, Cal. Practice Guide: Civil Trials & Evidence Ch. 10-B, B. Scope of Permissible Cross-Examination.
Rutter, Cal. Practice Guide: Personal Injury Ch. 9-F, F. Examination of Witnesses.

§ 762. Redirect examination

"Redirect examination" is an examination of a witness by the direct examiner subsequent to the cross-examination of the witness. *(Stats.1965, c. 299, § 2, operative Jan. 1, 1967.)*

Law Revision Commission Comments

"Redirect examination" and "recross-examination" are not defined in existing statutes, but the terms are recognized in practice. See Witkin, California Evidence §§ 697, 698 (1958). The scope of redirect and recross-examination is limited by Section 774.

The definition of "redirect examination" embraces not only the examination immediately following cross-examination of the witness but also any subsequent re-examination of the witness by the direct examiner. [7 Cal.L.Rev.Comm. Reports 1 (1965)].

Research References

Rutter, Cal. Practice Guide: Civil Trials & Evidence Ch. 9-G, G. Redirect Examination.
Rutter, Cal. Practice Guide: Civil Trials & Evidence Ch. 10-I, I. Recross Examination.
Rutter, Cal. Practice Guide: Personal Injury Ch. 9-F, F. Examination of Witnesses.

§ 763. Recross-examination

"Recross-examination" is an examination of a witness by a cross-examiner subsequent to a redirect examination of the witness. *(Stats.1965, c. 299, § 2, operative Jan. 1, 1967.)*

Law Revision Commission Comments

See the Comment to Section 762. The definition of "recross-examination" embraces not only the examination immediately following the first redirect examination of the witness but also any subsequent re-examination of the witness by a cross-examiner. [7 Cal.L.Rev.Comm. Reports 1 (1965)].

Research References

Rutter, Cal. Practice Guide: Civil Trials & Evidence Ch. 10-I, I. Recross Examination.
Rutter, Cal. Practice Guide: Personal Injury Ch. 9-F, F. Examination of Witnesses.

§ 764. Leading question

A "leading question" is a question that suggests to the witness the answer that the examining party desires. *(Stats.1965, c. 299, § 2, operative Jan. 1, 1967.)*

Law Revision Commission Comments

Section 764 restates the substance of and supersedes the first sentence of Section 2046 of the Code of Civil Procedure. For restrictions on the use of leading questions in the examination of a witness, see Evidence Code § 767 and the Comment thereto. [7 Cal.L.Rev.Comm. Reports 1 (1965)].

Research References

Rutter, Cal. Practice Guide: Civil Trials & Evidence Ch. 9-B, B. Form of Questions.

Rutter, Cal. Practice Guide: Personal Injury Ch. 9-F, F. Examination of Witnesses.

ARTICLE 2. EXAMINATION OF WITNESSES

§ 765. Court to control mode of interrogation

(a) The court shall exercise reasonable control over the mode of interrogation of a witness so as to make interrogation as rapid, as distinct, and as effective for the ascertainment of the truth, as may be, and to protect the witness from undue harassment or embarrassment.

(b) With a witness under the age of 14 or a dependent person with a substantial cognitive impairment, the court shall take special care to protect him or her from undue harassment or embarrassment, and to restrict the unnecessary repetition of questions. The court shall also take special care to ensure that questions are stated in a form which is appropriate to the age or cognitive level of the witness. The court may, in the interests of justice, on objection by a party, forbid the asking of a question which is in a form that is not reasonably likely to be understood by a person of the age or cognitive level of the witness. *(Stats.1965, c. 299, § 2, operative Jan. 1, 1967. Amended by Stats.1985, c. 884, § 3; Stats.1986, c. 1051, § 1; Stats.2004, c. 823 (A.B.20), § 4.)*

Law Revision Commission Comments

Section 765 restates the substance of and supersedes Section 2044 of the Code of Civil Procedure. As to the latitude permitted the judge in controlling the examination of witnesses under existing law, which is continued in effect by Section 765, see Commercial Union Assur. Co. v. Pacific Gas & Elec. Co., 220 Cal. 515, 31 P.2d 793 (1934). See also People v. Davis, 6 Cal.App. 229, 91 Pac. 810 (1907). [7 Cal.L.Rev.Comm. Reports 1 (1965)].

Research References

Rutter, Cal. Practice Guide: Civil Trials & Evidence Ch. 9-B, B. Form of Questions.
Rutter, Cal. Practice Guide: Civil Trials & Evidence Ch. 9-C, C. Direct Examination of Adverse Witness (EV.C. § 776).
Rutter, Cal. Practice Guide: Civil Trials & Evidence Ch. 9-F, F. Witnesses Needing Assistance in Testifying.
Rutter, Cal. Practice Guide: Civil Trials & Evidence Ch. 9-G, G. Redirect Examination.
Rutter, Cal. Practice Guide: Civil Trials & Evidence Ch. 10-A, A. Preliminary Considerations.
Rutter, Cal. Practice Guide: Civil Trials & Evidence Ch. 10-C, C. Form of Questions.
Rutter, Cal. Practice Guide: Civil Trials & Evidence Ch. 10-H, H. Cross-Examining "Problem" Witnesses.
Rutter, Cal. Practice Guide: Civil Trials & Evidence Ch. 12-A, A. Motion for Mistrial.

Rutter, Cal. Practice Guide: Civil Trials & Evidence Ch. 8C-A, A. Testimony.

Rutter, Cal. Practice Guide: Family Law Ch. 5-D, D. Notice of Motion/OSC and Stipulation Procedures.

Rutter, Cal. Practice Guide: Family Law Ch. 7-C, C. Custody Awards, Generally.

Rutter, Cal. Practice Guide: Family Law Ch. 11-F, F. Preparing Client and Witnesses for Trial.

Rutter, Cal. Practice Guide: Family Law Ch. 13-B, B. Contested Family Law Trial.

Rutter, Cal. Practice Guide: Family Law Gen. Matls, Highlights.

Rutter, Cal. Practice Guide: Personal Injury Ch. 9-F, F. Examination of Witnesses.

Rutter, Cal. Practice Guide: Prof. Responsibility Ch. 8-C, C. Restrictions on Advocacy in Court Proceedings.

10 Witkin, California Summary 10th Parent and Child § 284, Trial.

11 Witkin, California Summary 10th Husband and Wife § 5, Generally Applicable Procedures.

§ 766. Responsive answers

A witness must give responsive answers to questions, and answers that are not responsive shall be stricken on motion of any party. *(Stats.1965, c. 299, § 2, operative Jan. 1, 1967.)*

Law Revision Commission Comments

Section 766 restates the substance of and supersedes Section 2056 of the Code of Civil Procedure. [7 Cal.L.Rev.Comm. Reports 1 (1965)].

Research References

Rutter, Cal. Practice Guide: Civil Trials & Evidence Ch. 10-H, H. Cross-Examining "Problem" Witnesses.

Rutter, Cal. Practice Guide: Family Law Ch. 13-B, B. Contested Family Law Trial.

§ 767. Leading questions

(a) Except under special circumstances where the interests of justice otherwise require:

(1) A leading question may not be asked of a witness on direct or redirect examination.

(2) A leading question may be asked of a witness on cross-examination or recross-examination.

(b) The court may, in the interests of justice permit a leading question to be asked of a child under 10 years of age or a dependent person with a substantial cognitive impairment in a case involving a prosecution under Section 273a, 273d, 288.5, 368, or any of the acts described in Section 11165.1 or 11165.2 of the Penal Code. *(Stats.1965, c. 299, § 2, operative Jan. 1, 1967. Amended by Stats.1984, c. 1423, § 1, eff. Sept. 26, 1984; Stats. 1995, c. 87 (A.B.355), § 1; Stats.2004, c. 823 (A.B.20), § 5.)*

Research References

Rutter, Cal. Practice Guide: Civil Trials & Evidence Ch. 9-B, B. Form of Questions.

Rutter, Cal. Practice Guide: Civil Trials & Evidence Ch. 9-C, C. Direct Examination of Adverse Witness (EV.C. § 776).

Rutter, Cal. Practice Guide: Civil Trials & Evidence Ch. 9-F, F. Witnesses Needing Assistance in Testifying.

Rutter, Cal. Practice Guide: Civil Trials & Evidence Ch. 10-C, C. Form of Questions.

Rutter, Cal. Practice Guide: Civil Trials & Evidence Ch. 11-A, A. Direct Examination of Expert Witnesses.

Rutter, Cal. Practice Guide: Family Law Ch. 13-B, B. Contested Family Law Trial.

Rutter, Cal. Practice Guide: Personal Injury Ch. 9-F, F. Examination of Witnesses.

§ 768. Writings

(a) In examining a witness concerning a writing, it is not necessary to show, read, or disclose to him any part of the writing.

(b) If a writing is shown to a witness, all parties to the action must be given an opportunity to inspect it before any question concerning it may be asked of the witness. *(Stats.1965, c. 299, § 2, operative Jan. 1, 1967.)*

Research References

Rutter, Cal. Practice Guide: Civil Trials & Evidence Ch. 4-B, B. Preliminary Matters Discussed in Final Status Conference or In-Chambers Conference.

Rutter, Cal. Practice Guide: Civil Trials & Evidence Ch. 10-D, D. Objectives of Cross-Examination.

Rutter, Cal. Practice Guide: Family Law Ch. 13-B, B. Contested Family Law Trial.

Rutter, Cal. Practice Guide: Personal Injury Ch. 9-H, H. Introduction of Discovered Evidence.

Rutter, Cal. Practice Guide: Personal Injury Ch. 9-I, I. Use of Writings, Exhibits and Demonstrative Evidence.

§ 769. Inconsistent statement or conduct

In examining a witness concerning a statement or other conduct by him that is inconsistent with any part of his testimony at the hearing, it is not necessary to disclose to him any information concerning the statement or other conduct. *(Stats. 1965, c. 299, § 2, operative Jan. 1, 1967.)*

Research References

Rutter, Cal. Practice Guide: Civil Trials & Evidence Ch. 10-D, D. Objectives of Cross-Examination.

Rutter, Cal. Practice Guide: Civil Trials & Evidence Ch. 8D-D, D. Hearsay Exceptions.

Rutter, Cal. Practice Guide: Personal Injury Ch. 9-H, H. Introduction of Discovered Evidence.

§ 770. Evidence of inconsistent statement of witness; exclusion; exceptions

Unless the interests of justice otherwise require, extrinsic evidence of a statement made by a witness that is inconsistent with any part of his testimony at the hearing shall be excluded unless:

(a) The witness was so examined while testifying as to give him an opportunity to explain or to deny the statement; or

(b) The witness has not been excused from giving further testimony in the action. *(Stats.1965, c. 299, § 2, operative Jan. 1, 1967.)*

Law Revision Commission Comments

Under Section 2052 of the Code of Civil Procedure, extrinsic evidence of a witness' inconsistent statement may be admitted only if the witness was given the opportunity, while testifying, to explain or deny the contradictory statement. Permitting a witness to explain or deny an alleged inconsistent statement is desirable, but there is no compelling reason to provide the opportunity for explanation *before* the inconsistent statement is introduced in evidence. Accordingly, unless the interests of justice otherwise require, Section 770 permits the judge to exclude evidence of an inconsistent statement only if the witness during his examination was not given an opportunity to explain or deny the statement *and* he has been unconditionally excused and is not subject to being recalled as a witness. Among other things, Section 770 will permit more effective cross-examination and impeachment of several collusive witnesses, since there need be no disclosure of prior inconsistency before all such witnesses have been examined.

Where the interests of justice require it, the court may permit extrinsic evidence of an inconsistent statement to be admitted even though the witness has been excused and has had no opportunity to explain or deny the statement. An absolute rule forbidding introduction of such evidence where the specified conditions are not met may cause hardship in some cases. For example, the party seeking to introduce the statement may not have learned of its existence until after the witness has left the court and is no longer available to testify. For the foundational requirements for the admission of a hearsay declarant's inconsistent statement, see Evidence Code § 1202 and the Comment thereto. [7 Cal.L.Rev.Comm.Reports 1 (1965)].

Research References

Rutter, Cal. Practice Guide: Civ. Pro. Before Trial Ch. 8E-17, Use of Depositions at Trial.
Rutter, Cal. Practice Guide: Civil Trials & Evidence Ch. 4-B, B. Preliminary Matters Discussed in Final Status Conference or In-Chambers Conference.
Rutter, Cal. Practice Guide: Civil Trials & Evidence Ch. 10-D, D. Objectives of Cross-Examination.
Rutter, Cal. Practice Guide: Civil Trials & Evidence Ch. 8C-I, I. Depositions and Discovery.
Rutter, Cal. Practice Guide: Civil Trials & Evidence Ch. 8D-D, D. Hearsay Exceptions.
Rutter, Cal. Practice Guide: Civil Trials & Evidence Ch. 8E-F, F. Limitations on Impeachment and Rehabilitation.
Rutter, Cal. Practice Guide: Family Law Ch. 13-B, B. Contested Family Law Trial.
Rutter, Cal. Practice Guide: Personal Injury Ch. 9-F, F. Examination of Witnesses.
Rutter, Cal. Practice Guide: Personal Injury Ch. 9-H, H. Introduction of Discovered Evidence.

§ 771. Production of writing used to refresh memory

(a) Subject to subdivision (c), if a witness, either while testifying or prior thereto, uses a writing to refresh his memory with respect to any matter about which he testifies, such writing must be produced at the hearing at the request of an adverse party and, unless the writing is so produced, the testimony of the witness concerning such matter shall be stricken.

(b) If the writing is produced at the hearing, the adverse party may, if he chooses, inspect the writing, cross-examine the witness concerning it, and introduce in evidence such portion of it as may be pertinent to the testimony of the witness.

(c) Production of the writing is excused, and the testimony of the witness shall not be stricken, if the writing:

(1) Is not in the possession or control of the witness or the party who produced his testimony concerning the matter; and

(2) Was not reasonably procurable by such party through the use of the court's process or other available means. (Stats.1965, c. 299, § 2, operative Jan. 1, 1967.)

Research References

Rutter, Cal. Practice Guide: Civ. Pro. Before Trial Ch. 8E-12, Conduct of Deposition.
Rutter, Cal. Practice Guide: Civil Trials & Evidence Ch. 1-E, E. Preparing Witnesses to Testify.
Rutter, Cal. Practice Guide: Civil Trials & Evidence Ch. 9-F, F. Witnesses Needing Assistance in Testifying.
Rutter, Cal. Practice Guide: Civil Trials & Evidence Ch. 10-H, H. Cross-Examining "Problem" Witnesses.
Rutter, Cal. Practice Guide: Civil Trials & Evidence Ch. 8C-B, B. Writings.
Rutter, Cal. Practice Guide: Civil Trials & Evidence Ch. 8D-D, D. Hearsay Exceptions.
Rutter, Cal. Practice Guide: Civil Trials & Evidence Ch. 8E-A, A. Privileges.
Rutter, Cal. Practice Guide: Family Law Ch. 13-B, B. Contested Family Law Trial.
Rutter, Cal. Practice Guide: Personal Injury Ch. 3-C, C. Specific Items of Compensatory Damages.
Rutter, Cal. Practice Guide: Personal Injury Ch. 9-H, H. Introduction of Discovered Evidence.
Rutter, Cal. Practice Guide: Personal Injury Ch. 9-I, I. Use of Writings, Exhibits and Demonstrative Evidence.

§ 772. Order of examination

(a) The examination of a witness shall proceed in the following phases: direct examination, cross-examination, redirect examination, recross-examination, and continuing thereafter by redirect and recross-examination.

(b) Unless for good cause the court otherwise directs, each phase of the examination of a witness must be concluded before the succeeding phase begins.

(c) Subject to subdivision (d), a party may, in the discretion of the court, interrupt his cross-examination, redirect examination, or recross-examination of a witness, in order to examine the witness upon a matter not within the scope of a previous examination of the witness.

(d) If the witness is the defendant in a criminal action, the witness may not, without his consent, be examined under direct examination by another party. (Stats.1965, c. 299, § 2, operative Jan. 1, 1967.)

Research References

Rutter, Cal. Practice Guide: Civil Trials & Evidence Ch. 4-I, I. Other Motions at Final Status Conference.
Rutter, Cal. Practice Guide: Civil Trials & Evidence Ch. 9-G, G. Redirect Examination.
Rutter, Cal. Practice Guide: Civil Trials & Evidence Ch. 10-A, A. Preliminary Considerations.
Rutter, Cal. Practice Guide: Civil Trials & Evidence Ch. 10-B, B. Scope of Permissible Cross-Examination.
Rutter, Cal. Practice Guide: Civil Trials & Evidence Ch. 10-I, I. Recross Examination.
Rutter, Cal. Practice Guide: Personal Injury Ch. 9-E, E. Order of Trial and Proof and Related Matters.
Rutter, Cal. Practice Guide: Personal Injury Ch. 9-F, F. Examination of Witnesses.

§ 773. Cross-examination

(a) A witness examined by one party may be cross-examined upon any matter within the scope of the direct examination by each other party to the action in such order as the court directs.

(b) The cross-examination of a witness by any party whose interest is not adverse to the party calling him is subject to the same rules that are applicable to the direct examination. (Stats.1965, c. 299, § 2, operative Jan. 1, 1967.)

Law Revision Commission Comments

Subdivision (a) restates the substance of Sections 2045 (part) and 2048 of the Code of Civil Procedure and Section 1323 of the Penal Code.

Subdivision (b) is based on the holding in Atchison, T. & S.F. Ry. v. Southern Pac. Co., 13 Cal.App.2d 505, 57 P.2d 575 (1936). That case held that a party not adverse to the direct examiner of a witness did not have the right to cross-examine the witness. Under subdivision (a), such a party would have the right to cross-examine the witness upon any matter within the scope of the direct examination, but he would be prohibited by Section 767 from asking leading questions during such examination. If the witness testifies on direct examination to matters that are, in fact, antagonistic to a party's position, he may be permitted to cross-examine with leading questions even though from a technical point of view the interest of the cross-examiner is not adverse to that of the direct examiner. Cf. McCarthy v. Mobile Cranes, Inc., 199 Cal.App.2d 500, 18 Cal.Rptr. 750 (1962). [7 Cal.L.Rev.Comm. Reports 1 (1965)].

Research References

Rutter, Cal. Practice Guide: Civil Trials & Evidence Ch. 10-A, A. Preliminary Considerations.
Rutter, Cal. Practice Guide: Civil Trials & Evidence Ch. 10-B, B. Scope of Permissible Cross-Examination.
Rutter, Cal. Practice Guide: Civil Trials & Evidence Ch. 10-C, C. Form of Questions.
Rutter, Cal. Practice Guide: Personal Injury Ch. 9-F, F. Examination of Witnesses.

§ 774. Re-examination

A witness once examined cannot be reexamined as to the same matter without leave of the court, but he may be reexamined as to any new matter upon which he has been examined by another party to the action. Leave may be granted or withheld in the court's discretion. *(Stats.1965, c. 299, § 2, operative Jan. 1, 1967.)*

Law Revision Commission Comments

Section 774 is based on and supersedes the first and third sentences of Section 2050 of the Code of Civil Procedure. The nature of a re-examination is to be determined in accordance with the definitions in Sections 760–763. [7 Cal.L.Rev.Comm. Reports 1 (1965)].

Research References

Rutter, Cal. Practice Guide: Personal Injury Ch. 9-F, F. Examination of Witnesses.

§ 775. Court may call witnesses

The court, on its own motion or on the motion of any party, may call witnesses and interrogate them the same as if they had been produced by a party to the action, and the parties may object to the questions asked and the evidence adduced the same as if such witnesses were called and examined by an adverse party. Such witnesses may be cross-examined by all parties to the action in such order as the court directs. *(Stats.1965, c. 299, § 2, operative Jan. 1, 1967.)*

Research References

Rutter, Cal. Practice Guide: Civil Trials & Evidence Ch. 9-E, E. Conduct of Direct Examination.

Rutter, Cal. Practice Guide: Civil Trials & Evidence Ch. 10-A, A. Preliminary Considerations.

Rutter, Cal. Practice Guide: Civil Trials & Evidence Ch. 12-A, A. Motion for Mistrial.

Rutter, Cal. Practice Guide: Personal Injury Ch. 9-F, F. Examination of Witnesses.

§ 776. Examination of adverse party or person identified with adverse party

(a) A party to the record of any civil action, or a person identified with such a party, may be called and examined as if under cross-examination by any adverse party at any time during the presentation of evidence by the party calling the witness.

(b) A witness examined by a party under this section may be cross-examined by all other parties to the action in such order as the court directs; but, subject to subdivision (e), the witness may be examined only as if under redirect examination by:

(1) In the case of a witness who is a party, his own counsel and counsel for a party who is not adverse to the witness.

(2) In the case of a witness who is not a party, counsel for the party with whom the witness is identified and counsel for a party who is not adverse to the party with whom the witness is identified.

(c) For the purpose of this section, parties represented by the same counsel are deemed to be a single party.

(d) For the purpose of this section, a person is identified with a party if he is:

(1) A person for whose immediate benefit the action is prosecuted or defended by the party.

(2) A director, officer, superintendent, member, agent, employee, or managing agent of the party or of a person specified in paragraph (1), or any public employee of a public entity when such public entity is the party.

(3) A person who was in any of the relationships specified in paragraph (2) at the time of the act or omission giving rise to the cause of action.

(4) A person who was in any of the relationships specified in paragraph (2) at the time he obtained knowledge of the matter concerning which he is sought to be examined under this section.

(e) Paragraph (2) of subdivision (b) does not require counsel for the party with whom the witness is identified and counsel for a party who is not adverse to the party with whom the witness is identified to examine the witness as if under redirect examination if the party who called the witness for examination under this section:

(1) Is also a person identified with the same party with whom the witness is identified.

(2) Is the personal representative, heir, successor, or assignee of a person identified with the same party with whom the witness is identified. *(Stats.1965, c. 299, § 2, operative Jan. 1, 1967. Amended by Stats.1967, c. 650, p. 2005, § 2.)*

Law Revision Commission Comments

Section 776 restates the substance of Code of Civil Procedure Section 2055 as it has been interpreted by the courts. See Witkin, California Evidence §§ 607–613 (1958), and pertinent cases cited and discussed therein.

Subdivision (a). Subdivision (a) restates the provisions of Section 2055 that permit a party to call and examine as if under cross-examination an adverse party and certain adverse witnesses. However, Section 776 substitutes the phrase "or a person identified with such a party" for the confusing enumeration of persons listed in the first sentence of Section 2055. This phrase is defined in subdivision (d) of Section 776 to include all of the persons presently named in Section 2055. See the Comment to subdivision (d), *infra*.

Subdivision (b). Subdivision (b) is based in part on similar provisions contained in Code of Civil Procedure Section 2055. Unlike Section 2055, however, this subdivision is drafted in recognition of the problems involved in multiple party litigation. Thus, the introductory portion of subdivision (b) states the general rule that a witness examined under this section may be cross-examined by all other parties to the action in such order as the court directs. For example, a party whose interest in the action is identical with that of the party who called the witness for examination under this section has a right to cross-examine the witness fully because he, too, has the right to call the witness for examination under this section. Similarly, a party whose interest in the action is adverse to the party who calls the witness for examination under this section has the right to cross-examine the witness fully unless he is identified with the witness as described in paragraphs (1) and (2) of this subdivision. Paragraphs (1) and (2) restrict the nature of the cross-examination permitted of a witness by a party with whom the witness is identified and by parties whose interest in the action is not adverse to the party with whom the witness is identified. These parties are limited to examination of the witness as if under redirect examination. In essence, this means that leading questions cannot be asked of the witness by these parties. See Evidence Code § 767. Although the examination must proceed as if it were a redirect examination, under Section 761 it is in fact a cross-examination and limited to the scope of the direct. See also Evidence Code §§ 760, 773.

Subdivision (c). Subdivision (c) codifies a principle that has been recognized in the California cases even though not explicitly stated in Code of Civil Procedure Section 2055. See Gates v. Pendleton, 71 Cal.App. 752, 236 Pac. 365 (1925); Goehring v. Rogers, 67 Cal.App. 260, 227 Pac. 689 (1924).

Subdivision (d). Subdivision (d) lists the classes of persons who are "identified with a party" as that phrase and variations of it are used in subdivisions (a) and (b) of Section 776. The persons named in paragraphs (1) and (2) are those described in the first sentence of Code of Civil Procedure Section 2055 as being subject to examination pursuant to the section because of a particular relationship to a party. See the definitions of "person," "public employee," and "public entity" in Evidence Code §§ 175, 195, and 200, respectively. In addition, paragraph (3) of this subdivision describes persons who were in any of the requisite relationships at the time of the act or omission giving rise to the cause of action. This states existing case law. Scott v. Del Monte Properties, Inc., 140 Cal.App.2d 756, 295 P.2d 947 (1956); Wells v. Lloyd, 35 Cal.App.2d 6, 94 P.2d 373 (1939). Similarly, paragraph (4) extends this principle to include any person who obtained relevant knowledge as a result of such a relationship but who does not fit the precise descriptions contained in paragraphs (1) through (3). For example, a person whose employment by a party began after the cause of action arose and terminated prior to the time of his examination at the trial would be included in the description contained in paragraph (4) if he obtained relevant knowledge of the incident as a result of his employment. It is not clear whether this states existing law, for no California decision has been found that decides this question. The paragraph is necessary, however, to preclude a party from preventing examination of his employee pursuant to this section by the simple expedient of discharging the employee prior to trial and reinstating him afterwards. *Cf.* Wells v. Lloyd, 35 Cal.App.2d 6, 12, 94 P.2d 373, 376–377 (1939). [7 Cal.L.Rev.Comm. Reports 1 (1965)].

Section 776 permits a party calling as a witness an employee of (or someone similarly identified in interest with) an adverse party to examine the witness as if under cross-examination, i.e., to use leading questions in his examination. Section 776 requires the party whose employee was thus called and examined to examine the witness as if under redirect examination, i.e., to refrain from the use of leading questions. If a party is able to persuade the court that the usual rule prescribed by Section 776 is not in the interest of justice in a particular case, the court may enlarge or restrict the right to use leading questions as provided in Section 767.

These rules are based on the premise that ordinarily such a witness will have a feeling of identification in the lawsuit with his employer rather than with the other party to the action.

Subdivision (b) has been amended, and subdivision (e) has been added, because the premise upon which Section 776 is based does not necessarily apply when the party calling the witness is also closely identified with the adverse party; hence, the adverse party should be entitled to the usual rights of a cross-examiner when he examines the witness. For example, when an employee sues his employer and calls a co-employee as a witness, there is no reason to assume that the witness will be adverse to the employee-party and in sympathy with the employer-party. The reverse may be the case. The amendment to Section 776 will permit an employer, as a general rule, to use leading questions in his cross-examination of an employee-witness who has been called to testify under Section 776 by a co-employee. However, if the party calling the witness can satisfy the court that the witness is in fact identified in interest with the employer or for some other reason is amenable to suggestive questioning by the employer, the court may limit the employer's use of leading questions during his examination of the witness pursuant to Section 767. See J. & B. Motors, Inc. v. Margolis, 75 Ariz. 392, 257 P.2d 588 (1953). [8 Cal.L.Rev.Comm. Reports 101 (1967)].

Research References

Rutter, Cal. Practice Guide: Civil Trials & Evidence Ch. 1-C, C. Marshalling the Evidence.
Rutter, Cal. Practice Guide: Civil Trials & Evidence Ch. 9-A, A. Preliminary Considerations.
Rutter, Cal. Practice Guide: Civil Trials & Evidence Ch. 9-B, B. Form of Questions.
Rutter, Cal. Practice Guide: Civil Trials & Evidence Ch. 9-C, C. Direct Examination of Adverse Witness (EV.C. § 776).
Rutter, Cal. Practice Guide: Civil Trials & Evidence Ch. 9-E, E. Conduct of Direct Examination.
Rutter, Cal. Practice Guide: Civil Trials & Evidence Ch. 10-C, C. Form of Questions.
Rutter, Cal. Practice Guide: Civil Trials & Evidence Ch. 10-D, D. Objectives of Cross-Examination.
Rutter, Cal. Practice Guide: Civil Trials & Evidence Ch. 11-E, E. Impeachment Evidence from Other Witnesses.
Rutter, Cal. Practice Guide: Civil Trials & Evidence Ch. 12-B, B. Motion for Nonsuit.
Rutter, Cal. Practice Guide: Civil Trials & Evidence Ch. 12-C, C. Motion for Directed Verdict.
Rutter, Cal. Practice Guide: Civil Trials & Evidence Ch. 16-C, C. Motion for Judgment (CCP § 631.8).
Rutter, Cal. Practice Guide: Civil Trials & Evidence Ch. 8C-A, A. Testimony.
Rutter, Cal. Practice Guide: Civil Trials & Evidence Ch. 8D-C, C. General Parameters Re Admissibility of Hearsay Evidence.
Rutter, Cal. Practice Guide: Civil Trials & Evidence Ch. 8E-A, A. Privileges.
Rutter, Cal. Practice Guide: Civil Trials & Evidence Ch. 9-C, Outline C.
Rutter, Cal. Practice Guide: Civil Trials & Evidence Ch. 10-C, Outline C.
Rutter, Cal. Practice Guide: Civil Trials & Evidence Ch. 16-C, Outline C.
Rutter, Cal. Practice Guide: Personal Injury Ch. 9-F, F. Examination of Witnesses.
Rutter, Cal. Practice Guide: Personal Injury Ch. 9-G, G. Expert Witnesses.
Rutter, Cal. Practice Guide: Prof. Responsibility Ch. 8-C, C. Restrictions on Advocacy in Court Proceedings.

8 Witkin Cal. Proc. 5th Enforcement of Judgment § 350, No Notice or Knowledge.
7 Witkin Cal. Proc. 5th Trial § 290, (S 290) Singling Out Witness.
7 Witkin Cal. Proc. 5th Trial § 432, (S 432) Evidence from Examination of Adverse Party.

§ 777. Exclusion of witness

(a) Subject to subdivisions (b) and (c), the court may exclude from the courtroom any witness not at the time under examination so that such witness cannot hear the testimony of other witnesses.

(b) A party to the action cannot be excluded under this section.

(c) If a person other than a natural person is a party to the action, an officer or employee designated by its attorney is entitled to be present. *(Stats.1965, c. 299, § 2, operative Jan. 1, 1967.)*

Law Revision Commission Comments

Section 777 is based on and supersedes Section 2043 of the Code of Civil Procedure. Under the existing law, the judge exercises broad discretion in regard to the exclusion of witnesses. People v. Lariscy, 14 Cal.2d 30, 92 P.2d 638 (1939); People v. Garbutt, 197 Cal. 200, 239 Pac. 1080 (1925). *Cf.* Penal Code § 867 (power of magistrate to exclude witnesses during preliminary examination). See also Code Civ.Proc. § 125 (general discretionary power of the court to exclude witnesses).

Under the existing law, the judge may not exclude a party to an action. If the party is a corporation, an officer designated by its attorney is entitled to be present. Section 777 permits the right of presence to be exercised by an employee as well as an officer. Also, because there is little practical distinction between corporations and other artificial entities and organizations, Section 777 extends the right of presence to all artificial parties. [7 Cal.L.Rev.Comm. Reports 1 (1965)].

Research References

Rutter, Cal. Practice Guide: Civil Trials & Evidence Ch. 4-I, I. Other Motions at Final Status Conference.
Rutter, Cal. Practice Guide: Civil Trials & Evidence Ch. 6-A, A. General Considerations.
2 Witkin Cal. Proc. 5th Courts § 33, General Requirement.
10 Witkin, California Summary 10th Parent and Child § 809, Victims and Support Persons.

§ 778. Recall of witness

After a witness has been excused from giving further testimony in the action, he cannot be recalled without leave of the court. Leave may be granted or withheld in the court's discretion. *(Stats.1965, c. 299, § 2, operative Jan. 1, 1967.)*

Law Revision Commission Comments

Section 778 restates the substance of and supersedes the second and third sentences of Section 2050 of the Code of Civil Procedure. [7 Cal.L.Rev.Comm. Reports 1 (1965)].

CHAPTER 6. CREDIBILITY OF WITNESSES

ARTICLE 1. CREDIBILITY GENERALLY

§ 780. Testimony; proof of truthfulness; considerations

Except as otherwise provided by statute, the court or jury may consider in determining the credibility of a witness any matter that has any tendency in reason to prove or disprove the truthfulness of his testimony at the hearing, including but not limited to any of the following:

(a) His demeanor while testifying and the manner in which he testifies.

(b) The character of his testimony.

(c) The extent of his capacity to perceive, to recollect, or to communicate any matter about which he testifies.

(d) The extent of his opportunity to perceive any matter about which he testifies.

(e) His character for honesty or veracity or their opposites.

(f) The existence or nonexistence of a bias, interest, or other motive.

(g) A statement previously made by him that is consistent with his testimony at the hearing.

(h) A statement made by him that is inconsistent with any part of his testimony at the hearing.

(i) The existence or nonexistence of any fact testified to by him.

(j) His attitude toward the action in which he testifies or toward the giving of testimony.

(k) His admission of untruthfulness. *(Stats.1965, c. 299, § 2, operative Jan. 1, 1967.)*

Law Revision Commission Comments

Section 780 is a restatement of the existing California law as declared in several sections of the Code of Civil Procedure, all of which are superseded by this section and other sections in Article 2 (commencing with Section 785) of this chapter. See, *e.g.*, Code Civ.Proc. §§ 1847, 2049, 2051, 2052, 2053.

Section 780 is a general catalog of those matters that have any tendency in reason to affect the credibility of a witness. So far as the admissibility of evidence relating to credibility is concerned, Section 780 is technically unnecessary because Section 351 declares that "all relevant evidence is admissible." However, this section makes it clear that matters that may not be "evidence" in a technical sense can affect the credibility of a witness, and it provides a useful list of the most common factors that bear on the question of credibility. See Davis v. Judson, 159 Cal. 121, 128, 113 Pac. 147, 150 (1910); La Jolla Casa de Manana v. Hopkins, 98 Cal.App.2d 339, 346, 219 P.2d 871, 876 (1950). See generally Witkin, California Evidence §§ 480–485 (1958). Limitations on the admissibility of evidence offered to attack or support the credibility of a witness are stated in Article 2 (commencing with Section 785).

There is no specific limitation in the Evidence Code on the use of impeaching evidence on the ground that it is "collateral". The so-called "collateral matter" limitation on attacking the credibility of a witness excludes evidence relevant to credibility unless such evidence is independently relevant to the issue being tried. It is based on the sensible notion that trials should be confined to settling those disputes between the parties upon which their rights in the litigation depend. Under existing law, this "collateral matter" doctrine has been treated as an inflexible rule excluding evidence relevant to the credibility of the witness. See, *e.g.*, People v. Wells, 33 Cal.2d 330, 340, 202 P.2d 53, 59 (1949), and cases cited therein.

The effect of Section 780 (together with Section 351) is to eliminate this inflexible rule of exclusion. This is not to say that all evidence of a collateral nature offered to attack the credibility of a witness would be admissible. Under Section 352, the court has substantial discretion to exclude collateral evidence. The effect of Section 780, therefore, is to change the present somewhat inflexible rule of exclusion to a rule of discretion to be exercised by the trial judge.

There is no limitation in the Evidence Code on the use of opinion evidence to prove the character of a witness for honesty, veracity, or the lack thereof. Hence, under Sections 780 and 1100, such evidence is admissible. This represents a change in the present law. See People v.

Methvin, 53 Cal. 68 (1878). However, the opinion evidence that may be offered by those persons intimately familiar with the witness is likely to be of more probative value than the generally admissible evidence of reputation. See 7 Wigmore, Evidence § 1986 (3d ed. 1940). [7 Cal.L.Rev.Comm. Reports 1 (1965)].

Research References

Rutter, Cal. Practice Guide: Civil Trials & Evidence Ch. 4-B, B. Preliminary Matters Discussed in Final Status Conference or In-Chambers Conference.

Rutter, Cal. Practice Guide: Civil Trials & Evidence Ch. 10-B, B. Scope of Permissible Cross-Examination.

Rutter, Cal. Practice Guide: Civil Trials & Evidence Ch. 10-C, C. Form of Questions.

Rutter, Cal. Practice Guide: Civil Trials & Evidence Ch. 10-D, D. Objectives of Cross-Examination.

Rutter, Cal. Practice Guide: Civil Trials & Evidence Ch. 11-D, D. Cross-Examination of Expert Witnesses.

Rutter, Cal. Practice Guide: Civil Trials & Evidence Ch. 13-D, D. Preparing for Closing Argument.

Rutter, Cal. Practice Guide: Civil Trials & Evidence Ch. 8B-A, A. General Considerations.

Rutter, Cal. Practice Guide: Civil Trials & Evidence Ch. 8E-E, E. Limitations on Character Evidence.

Rutter, Cal. Practice Guide: Civil Trials & Evidence Ch. 8E-F, F. Limitations on Impeachment and Rehabilitation.

Rutter, Cal. Practice Guide: Civil Trials & Evidence Gen. Matls., Highlights.

Rutter, Cal. Practice Guide: Landlord-Tenant Ch. 2E-1, Residential Units.

Rutter, Cal. Practice Guide: Personal Injury Ch. 9-F, F. Examination of Witnesses.

7 Witkin Cal. Proc. 5th Trial § 299, (S 299) Credibility and Impeachment.

1 Witkin Cal. Summ. 10th Contracts § 522, Statutory Regulation: in General.

§ 782. Sexual offenses; evidence of sexual conduct of complaining witness; procedure for admissibility; treatment of resealed affidavits

(a) In any of the circumstances described in subdivision (c), if evidence of sexual conduct of the complaining witness is offered to attack the credibility of the complaining witness under Section 780, the following procedure shall be followed:

(1) A written motion shall be made by the defendant to the court and prosecutor stating that the defense has an offer of proof of the relevancy of evidence of the sexual conduct of the complaining witness proposed to be presented and its relevancy in attacking the credibility of the complaining witness.

(2) The written motion shall be accompanied by an affidavit in which the offer of proof shall be stated. The affidavit shall be filed under seal and only unsealed by the court to determine if the offer of proof is sufficient to order a hearing pursuant to paragraph (3). After that determination, the affidavit shall be resealed by the court.

(3) If the court finds that the offer of proof is sufficient, the court shall order a hearing out of the presence of the jury, if any, and at the hearing allow the questioning of the complaining witness regarding the offer of proof made by the defendant.

(4) At the conclusion of the hearing, if the court finds that evidence proposed to be offered by the defendant regarding the sexual conduct of the complaining witness is relevant pursuant to Section 780, and is not inadmissible pursuant to Section 352, the court may make an order stating what evidence may be introduced by the defendant, and the nature of the questions to be permitted. The defendant may then offer evidence pursuant to the order of the court.

(5) An affidavit resealed by the court pursuant to paragraph (2) shall remain sealed, unless the defendant raises an issue on appeal or collateral review relating to the offer of proof contained in the sealed document. If the defendant raises that

issue on appeal, the court shall allow the Attorney General and appellate counsel for the defendant access to the sealed affidavit. If the issue is raised on collateral review, the court shall allow the district attorney and defendant's counsel access to the sealed affidavit. The use of the information contained in the affidavit shall be limited solely to the pending proceeding.

(b) As used in this section, "complaining witness" means:

(1) The alleged victim of the crime charged, the prosecution of which is subject to this section, pursuant to paragraph (1) of subdivision (c).

(2) An alleged victim offering testimony pursuant to paragraph (2) or (3) of subdivision (c).

(c) The procedure provided by subdivision (a) shall apply in any of the following circumstances:

(1) In a prosecution under Section 261, 262, 264.1, 286, 288, 288a, 288.5, or 289 of the Penal Code, or for assault with intent to commit, attempt to commit, or conspiracy to commit any crime defined in any of those sections, except if the crime is alleged to have occurred in a local detention facility, as defined in Section 6031.4 of the Penal Code, or in the state prison, as defined in Section 4504.

(2) When an alleged victim testifies pursuant to subdivision (b) of Section 1101 as a victim of a crime listed in Section 243.4, 261, 261.5, 269, 285, 286, 288, 288a, 288.5, 289, 314, or 647.6 of the Penal Code, except if the crime is alleged to have occurred in a local detention facility, as defined in Section 6031.4 of the Penal Code, or in the state prison, as defined in Section 4504 of the Penal Code.

(3) When an alleged victim of a sexual offense testifies pursuant to Section 1108, except if the crime is alleged to have occurred in a local detention facility, as defined in Section 6031.4 of the Penal Code, or in the state prison, as defined in Section 4504 of the Penal Code. *(Added by Stats.1974, c. 569, p. 1388, § 1. Amended by Stats.1981, c. 726, p. 2876, § 1; Stats.1987, c. 177, § 1; Stats.1989, c. 1402, § 2; Stats.1996, c. 1075 (S.B.1444), § 6; Stats.2004, c. 61 (A.B.2829), § 1; Stats.2006, c. 225 (A.B.1996), § 1; Stats.2007, c. 130 (A.B.299), § 83.)*

Research References

Rutter, Cal. Practice Guide: Civil Trials & Evidence Ch. 8E-E, E. Limitations on Character Evidence.

§ 783. Sexual harassment, sexual assault, or sexual battery cases; admissibility of evidence of plaintiff's sexual conduct; procedure

In any civil action alleging conduct which constitutes sexual harassment, sexual assault, or sexual battery, if evidence of sexual conduct of the plaintiff is offered to attack credibility of the plaintiff under Section 780, the following procedures shall be followed:

(a) A written motion shall be made by the defendant to the court and the plaintiff's attorney stating that the defense has an offer of proof of the relevancy of evidence of the sexual conduct of the plaintiff proposed to be presented.

(b) The written motion shall be accompanied by an affidavit in which the offer of proof shall be stated.

(c) If the court finds that the offer of proof is sufficient, the court shall order a hearing out of the presence of the jury, if any, and at the hearing allow the questioning of the plaintiff regarding the offer of proof made by the defendant.

(d) At the conclusion of the hearing, if the court finds that evidence proposed to be offered by the defendant regarding the sexual conduct of the plaintiff is relevant pursuant to Section 780, and is not inadmissible pursuant to Section 352, the court may make an order stating what evidence may be introduced by

the defendant, and the nature of the questions to be permitted. The defendant may then offer evidence pursuant to the order of the court. *(Added by Stats.1985, c. 1328, § 3.)*

Research References

Rutter, Cal. Practice Guide: Civil Trials & Evidence Ch. 8E-E, E. Limitations on Character Evidence.
Rutter, Cal. Practice Guide: Civil Trials & Evidence Ch. 8E-F, F. Limitations on Impeachment and Rehabilitation.
California Practice Guide: Employment Litigation Ch. 19-N, N. Evidence Issues.
2 Witkin Cal. Summ. 10th Workers' Compensation § 402, Evidence of Sexual Conduct.

ARTICLE 2. ATTACKING OR SUPPORTING CREDIBILITY

Section
785. Parties may attack or support credibility.
786. Character evidence generally.
787. Specific instances of conduct.
788. Prior felony conviction.
789. Religious belief.
790. Good character of witness.
791. Prior consistent statement of witness.

§ 785. Parties may attack or support credibility

The credibility of a witness may be attacked or supported by any party, including the party calling him. *(Stats.1965, c. 299, § 2, operative Jan. 1, 1967.)*

Law Revision Commission Comments

Section 785 eliminates the present restriction on attacking the credibility of one's own witness. Under the existing law, a party is precluded from attacking the credibility of his own witness unless he has been surprised and damaged by the witness' testimony. Code Civ.Proc. §§ 2049, 2052 (superseded by Evidence Code §§ 768, 769, 770, 785); People v. LeBeau, 39 Cal.2d 146, 148, 245 P.2d 302, 303 (1952). In large part, the present law rests upon the theory that a party producing a witness is bound by his testimony. See discussion in Smellie v. Southern Pac. Co., 212 Cal. 540, 555–556, 299 Pac. 529, 535 (1931). This theory has long been abandoned in several jurisdictions where the practical exigencies of litigation have been recognized. See McCormick, Evidence § 38 (1954). A party has no actual control over a person who witnesses an event and is required to testify to aid the trier of fact in its function of determining the truth. Hence, a party should not be "bound" by the testimony of a witness produced by him and should be permitted to attack the credibility of the witness without anachronistic limitations. Denial of the right to attack credibility may often work a hardship on a party where by necessity he must call a hostile witness. Expanded opportunity for testing credibility is in keeping with the interest of providing a forum for full and free disclosure. In regard to attacking the credibility of a "necessary" witness, see generally People v. McFarlane, 134 Cal. 618, 66 Pac. 865 (1901); Anthony v. Hobbie, 85 Cal.App.2d 798, 803–804, 193 P.2d 748, 751 (1948); First Nat'l Bank v. De Moulin, 56 Cal.App. 313, 321, 205 Pac. 92, 96 (1922). [7 Cal.L.Rev.Comm. Reports 1 (1965)].

Research References

Rutter, Cal. Practice Guide: Civil Trials & Evidence Ch. 4-B, B. Preliminary Matters Discussed in Final Status Conference or In-Chambers Conference.
Rutter, Cal. Practice Guide: Civil Trials & Evidence Ch. 9-F, F. Witnesses Needing Assistance in Testifying.
Rutter, Cal. Practice Guide: Civil Trials & Evidence Ch. 10-B, B. Scope of Permissible Cross-Examination.
Rutter, Cal. Practice Guide: Civil Trials & Evidence Ch. 11-D, D. Cross-Examination of Expert Witnesses.
Rutter, Cal. Practice Guide: Civil Trials & Evidence Ch. 8E-E, E. Limitations on Character Evidence.
Rutter, Cal. Practice Guide: Civil Trials & Evidence Ch. 8E-F, F. Limitations on Impeachment and Rehabilitation.
Rutter, Cal. Practice Guide: Personal Injury Ch. 9-F, F. Examination of Witnesses.

Rutter, Cal. Practice Guide: Personal Injury Ch. 9-H, H. Introduction of Discovered Evidence.

§ 786. Character evidence generally

Evidence of traits of his character other than honesty or veracity, or their opposites, is inadmissible to attack or support the credibility of a witness. *(Stats.1965, c. 299, § 2, operative Jan. 1, 1967.)*

Law Revision Commission Comments

Section 786 limits evidence relating to the character of a witness to the character traits necessarily involved in a proper determination of credibility. Other character traits are not sufficiently probative of a witness' honesty or veracity to warrant their consideration on the issue of credibility.

Section 786 is substantially in accord with the present California law. Code Civ.Proc. § 2051 (superseded by Evidence Code §§ 780, 785–788); People v. Yslas, 27 Cal. 630, 633 (1865). [7 Cal.L.Rev.Comm. Reports 1 (1965)].

Research References

Rutter, Cal. Practice Guide: Civil Trials & Evidence Ch. 10-D, D. Objectives of Cross-Examination.
Rutter, Cal. Practice Guide: Civil Trials & Evidence Ch. 8E-E, E. Limitations on Character Evidence.
Rutter, Cal. Practice Guide: Civil Trials & Evidence Ch. 8E-F, F. Limitations on Impeachment and Rehabilitation.
Rutter, Cal. Practice Guide: Personal Injury Ch. 9-F, F. Examination of Witnesses.

§ 787. Specific instances of conduct

Subject to Section 788, evidence of specific instances of his conduct relevant only as tending to prove a trait of his character is inadmissible to attack or support the credibility of a witness. *(Stats.1965, c. 299, § 2, operative Jan. 1, 1967.)*

Law Revision Commission Comments

Under Section 787, as under existing law, evidence of specific instances of a witness' conduct is inadmissible to prove a trait of his character for the purpose of attacking or supporting his credibility. See Sharon v. Sharon, 79 Cal. 633, 673–674, 22 Pac. 26, 38 (1889); Code Civ.Proc. § 2051 (superseded by Section 787 and several other sections in Chapter 6). Section 787 is subject, however, to Section 788, which permits certain kinds of criminal convictions to be used for the purpose of attacking a witness' credibility. [7 Cal.L.Rev.Comm. Reports 1 (1965)].

Research References

Rutter, Cal. Practice Guide: Civil Trials & Evidence Ch. 4-F, F. Motions in Limine.
Rutter, Cal. Practice Guide: Civil Trials & Evidence Ch. 10-D, D. Objectives of Cross-Examination.
Rutter, Cal. Practice Guide: Civil Trials & Evidence Ch. 8E-E, E. Limitations on Character Evidence.
Rutter, Cal. Practice Guide: Civil Trials & Evidence Ch. 8E-F, F. Limitations on Impeachment and Rehabilitation.
Rutter, Cal. Practice Guide: Personal Injury Ch. 9-F, F. Examination of Witnesses.
7 Witkin Cal. Proc. 5th Trial § 190, Conduct Constituting Contempt.

§ 788. Prior felony conviction

For the purpose of attacking the credibility of a witness, it may be shown by the examination of the witness or by the record of the judgment that he has been convicted of a felony unless:

(a) A pardon based on his innocence has been granted to the witness by the jurisdiction in which he was convicted.

(b) A certificate of rehabilitation and pardon has been granted to the witness under the provisions of Chapter 3.5 (commencing with Section 4852.01) of Title 6 of Part 3 of the Penal Code.

(c) The accusatory pleading against the witness has been dismissed under the provisions of Penal Code Section 1203.4, but this exception does not apply to any criminal trial where the witness is being prosecuted for a subsequent offense.

(d) The conviction was under the laws of another jurisdiction and the witness has been relieved of the penalties and disabilities arising from the conviction pursuant to a procedure substantially equivalent to that referred to in subdivision (b) or (c). *(Stats. 1965, c. 299, § 2, operative Jan. 1, 1967.)*

Research References

Rutter, Cal. Practice Guide: Civil Trials & Evidence Ch. 10-D, D. Objectives of Cross-Examination.
Rutter, Cal. Practice Guide: Civil Trials & Evidence Ch. 8E-E, E. Limitations on Character Evidence.
Rutter, Cal. Practice Guide: Civil Trials & Evidence Ch. 8E-F, F. Limitations on Impeachment and Rehabilitation.
Rutter, Cal. Practice Guide: Personal Injury Ch. 9-B, B. In-Chambers Conference Before Commencement of Trial.
Rutter, Cal. Practice Guide: Personal Injury Ch. 9-F, F. Examination of Witnesses.

§ 789. Religious belief

Evidence of his religious belief or lack thereof is inadmissible to attack or support the credibility of a witness. *(Stats.1965, c. 299, § 2, operative Jan. 1, 1967.)*

Law Revision Commission Comments

Section 789 codifies existing law as expressed in People v. Copsey, 71 Cal. 548, 12 Pac. 721 (1887), where the Supreme Court held that evidence relating to a witness' religious belief or lack thereof is incompetent on the issue of his credibility as a witness. See Cal.Const., Art. I, § 4. [7 Cal.L.Rev.Comm. Reports 1 (1965)].

Research References

Rutter, Cal. Practice Guide: Civil Trials & Evidence Ch. 10-D, D. Objectives of Cross-Examination.
Rutter, Cal. Practice Guide: Civil Trials & Evidence Ch. 8E-E, E. Limitations on Character Evidence.
Rutter, Cal. Practice Guide: Civil Trials & Evidence Ch. 8E-F, F. Limitations on Impeachment and Rehabilitation.

§ 790. Good character of witness

Evidence of the good character of a witness is inadmissible to support his credibility unless evidence of his bad character has been admitted for the purpose of attacking his credibility. *(Stats.1965, c. 299, § 2, operative Jan. 1, 1967.)*

Law Revision Commission Comments

Section 790 restates without substantive change a rule that is well recognized by statutory and case law in California. Code Civ.Proc. § 2053 (superseded by Evidence Code §§ 790, 1101); People v. Bush, 65 Cal. 129, 131, 3 Pac. 590, 591 (1884). Unless the credibility of a witness is put in issue by an attack impugning his character for honesty or veracity (see Section 786), evidence of the witness' good character admitted merely to support his credibility introduces collateral material that is unnecessary to a proper determination of any legitimate issue in the action. See People v. Sweeney, 55 Cal.2d 27, 38–39, 9 Cal.Rptr. 793, 799, 357 P.2d 1049, 1055 (1960). [7 Cal.L.Rev.Comm. Reports 1 (1965)].

Research References

Rutter, Cal. Practice Guide: Civil Trials & Evidence Ch. 8E-E, E. Limitations on Character Evidence.
Rutter, Cal. Practice Guide: Civil Trials & Evidence Ch. 8E-F, F. Limitations on Impeachment and Rehabilitation.

Rutter, Cal. Practice Guide: Personal Injury Ch. 9-F, F. Examination of Witnesses.

§ 791. Prior consistent statement of witness

Evidence of a statement previously made by a witness that is consistent with his testimony at the hearing is inadmissible to support his credibility unless it is offered after:

(a) Evidence of a statement made by him that is inconsistent with any part of his testimony at the hearing has been admitted for the purpose of attacking his credibility, and the statement was made before the alleged inconsistent statement; or

(b) An express or implied charge has been made that his testimony at the hearing is recently fabricated or is influenced by bias or other improper motive, and the statement was made before the bias, motive for fabrication, or other improper motive is alleged to have arisen. *(Stats.1965, c. 299, § 2, operative Jan. 1, 1967.)*

Law Revision Commission Comments

Section 791 sets forth the conditions for admitting a witness' prior consistent statements for the purpose of supporting his credibility as a witness. For a discussion of the effect to be given to the evidence admitted under this section, see Evidence Code § 1236 and the Comment thereto.

Subdivision (a). Subdivision (a) permits the introduction of a witness' prior consistent statement if evidence of an inconsistent statement of the witness has been admitted for the purpose of attacking his credibility and if the consistent statement was made *before* the alleged inconsistent statement.

Under existing California law, evidence of a prior consistent statement is admissible to rebut a charge of bias, interest, recent fabrication, or other improper motive. See the Comment to subdivision (b), *infra*. Existing law may preclude admission of a prior consistent statement to rehabilitate a witness where only a prior inconsistent statement has been admitted for the purpose of attacking his credibility. See People v. Doyell, 48 Cal. 85, 90–91 (1874). However, recent cases indicate that the offering of a prior inconsistent statement necessarily is an implied charge that the witness has fabricated his testimony since the time the inconsistent statement was made and justifies the admission of a consistent statement made prior to the alleged inconsistent statement. People v. Bias, 170 Cal.App.2d 502, 511–512, 339 P.2d 204, 210–211 (1959). Subdivision (a) makes it clear that evidence of a previous consistent statement is admissible under these circumstances to show that no such fabrication took place. Subdivision (a), thus, is no more than a logical extension of the general rule that evidence of a prior consistent statement is admissible to rehabilitate a witness following an express or implied charge of recent fabrication.

Subdivision (b). This subdivision codifies existing law. See People v. Kynette, 15 Cal.2d 731, 104 P.2d 794 (1940) (overruled on other grounds in People v. Snyder, 50 Cal.2d 190, 197, 324 P.2d 1, 6 (1958)). Of course, if the consistent statement was made *after* the time the improper motive is alleged to have arisen, the logical thrust of the evidence is lost and the statement is inadmissible. See People v. Doetschman, 69 Cal.App.2d 486, 159 P.2d 418 (1945). [7 Cal.L.Rev.Comm. Reports 1 (1965)].

Research References

Rutter, Cal. Practice Guide: Civ. Pro. Before Trial Ch. 8E-17, Use of Depositions at Trial.

Rutter, Cal. Practice Guide: Civil Trials & Evidence Ch. 9-G, G. Redirect Examination.

Rutter, Cal. Practice Guide: Civil Trials & Evidence Ch. 10-D, D. Objectives of Cross-Examination.

Rutter, Cal. Practice Guide: Civil Trials & Evidence Ch. 8C-I, I. Depositions and Discovery.

Rutter, Cal. Practice Guide: Civil Trials & Evidence Ch. 8D-D, D. Hearsay Exceptions.

Rutter, Cal. Practice Guide: Civil Trials & Evidence Ch. 8E-F, F. Limitations on Impeachment and Rehabilitation.

Rutter, Cal. Practice Guide: Personal Injury Ch. 9-F, F. Examination of Witnesses.

Rutter, Cal. Practice Guide: Personal Injury Ch. 9-H, H. Introduction of Discovered Evidence.

CHAPTER 7. HYPNOSIS OF WITNESSES

Section
795. Testimony of hypnosis subject; admissibility; conditions.

§ 795. Testimony of hypnosis subject; admissibility; conditions

(a) The testimony of a witness is not inadmissible in a criminal proceeding by reason of the fact that the witness has previously undergone hypnosis for the purpose of recalling events that are the subject of the witness's testimony, if all of the following conditions are met:

(1) The testimony is limited to those matters that the witness recalled and related prior to the hypnosis.

(2) The substance of the prehypnotic memory was preserved in a writing, audio recording, or video recording prior to the hypnosis.

(3) The hypnosis was conducted in accordance with all of the following procedures:

(A) A written record was made prior to hypnosis documenting the subject's description of the event, and information that was provided to the hypnotist concerning the subject matter of the hypnosis.

(B) The subject gave informed consent to the hypnosis.

(C) The hypnosis session, including the pre- and post-hypnosis interviews, was video recorded for subsequent review.

(D) The hypnosis was performed by a licensed physician and surgeon, psychologist, licensed clinical social worker, licensed marriage and family therapist, or licensed professional clinical counselor experienced in the use of hypnosis and independent of and not in the presence of law enforcement, the prosecution, or the defense.

(4) Prior to admission of the testimony, the court holds a hearing pursuant to Section 402 at which the proponent of the evidence proves by clear and convincing evidence that the hypnosis did not so affect the witness as to render the witness's prehypnosis recollection unreliable or to substantially impair the ability to cross-examine the witness concerning the witness's prehypnosis recollection. At the hearing, each side shall have the right to present expert testimony and to cross-examine witnesses.

(b) Nothing in this section shall be construed to limit the ability of a party to attack the credibility of a witness who has undergone hypnosis, or to limit other legal grounds to admit or exclude the testimony of that witness. *(Added by Stats.1984, c. 479, § 1. Amended by Stats.1987, c. 285, § 1; Stats.1996, c. 67 (A.B.2296), § 1; Stats.2002, c. 1013 (S.B.2026), § 77; Stats.2009, c. 88 (A.B.176), § 34; Stats.2011, c. 381 (S.B.146), § 20.)*

Law Revision Commission Comments

Section 795 is amended to reflect advances in recording technology and for consistency of terminology. For a similar reform, see 2002 Cal. Stat. ch. 1068 (replacing numerous references to "audiotape" in Civil Discovery Act with either "audio technology," "audio recording," or "audio record," as context required). [37 Cal. L. Revision Comm'n Reports 211 (2007)].

Research References

Rutter, Cal. Practice Guide: Civil Trials & Evidence Ch. 8C-G, G. Scientific Evidence.

Division 7

OPINION TESTIMONY AND SCIENTIFIC EVIDENCE

Law Revision Commission Comments

Two matters concerning the terminology used in this division should be noted: (1) The word "opinion" is used to include all opinions, inferences, conclusions, and other subjective statements made by a witness. (2) The word "matter" is used to encompass facts, data, and such matters as a witness' knowledge, experience, and other intangibles upon which an opinion may be based. Thus, every conceivable basis for an opinion is included within this term. [7 Cal.L.Rev.Comm. Reports 1 (1965)].

CHAPTER 1. EXPERT AND OTHER OPINION TESTIMONY

ARTICLE 1. EXPERT AND OTHER OPINION TESTIMONY GENERALLY

§ 800. Lay witnesses; opinion testimony

If a witness is not testifying as an expert, his testimony in the form of an opinion is limited to such an opinion as is permitted by law, including but not limited to an opinion that is:

(a) Rationally based on the perception of the witness; and

(b) Helpful to a clear understanding of his testimony. *(Stats. 1965, c. 299, § 2, operative Jan. 1, 1967.)*

Law Revision Commission Comments

This section codifies existing law. A witness who is not testifying as an expert may testify in the form of an opinion only if the opinion is based on his own perception. Stuart v. Dotts, 89 Cal.App.2d 683, 201 P.2d 820 (1949). See discussion in Manney v. Housing Authority, 79 Cal.App.2d 453, 459–460, 180 P.2d 69, 73 (1947). And, in addition, the opinion must be "helpful to a clear understanding of his testimony." See Tentative Recommendation and a Study Relating to the Uniform Rules of Evidence (Article VII. Expert and Other Opinion Testimony), 6 Cal.Law Revision Comm'n, Rep., Rec. & Studies 901, 931–935 (1964).

Section 800 does not make inadmissible an opinion that is admissible under existing law, even though the requirements of subdivisions (a) and (b) are not satisfied. Thus, the section does not affect the existing rule that a nonexpert witness may give his opinion as to the value of his property or the value of his own services. See Witkin, California Evidence § 179 (1958). The words "such an opinion as is permitted by law" in Section 800 make this clear. [7 Cal.L.Rev.Comm. Reports 1 (1965)].

Research References

Rutter, Cal. Practice Guide: Civil Appeals & Writs Ch. 8-C, C. Standards of Appellate Review.

Rutter, Cal. Practice Guide: Civil Trials & Evidence Ch. 4-B, B. Preliminary Matters Discussed in Final Status Conference or In-Chambers Conference.

Rutter, Cal. Practice Guide: Civil Trials & Evidence Ch. 8C-H, H. Opinion Evidence.

Rutter, Cal. Practice Guide: Civil Trials & Evidence Ch. 8D-D, D. Hearsay Exceptions.

California Practice Guide: Employment Litigation Ch. 19-N, N. Evidence Issues.

Rutter, Cal. Practice Guide: Personal Injury Ch. 3-C, C. Specific Items of Compensatory Damages.

Rutter, Cal. Practice Guide: Personal Injury Ch. 9-F, F. Examination of Witnesses.

Rutter, Cal. Practice Guide: Personal Injury Ch. 2(I)-B, B. General Investigation Tactics.

§ 801. Expert witnesses; opinion testimony

If a witness is testifying as an expert, his testimony in the form of an opinion is limited to such an opinion as is:

(a) Related to a subject that is sufficiently beyond common experience that the opinion of an expert would assist the trier of fact; and

(b) Based on matter (including his special knowledge, skill, experience, training, and education) perceived by or personally known to the witness or made known to him at or before the hearing, whether or not admissible, that is of a type that reasonably may be relied upon by an expert in forming an opinion upon the subject to which his testimony relates, unless an expert is precluded by law from using such matter as a basis for his opinion. *(Stats.1965, c. 299, § 2, operative Jan. 1, 1967.)*

Law Revision Commission Comments

Section 801 deals with opinion testimony of a witness testifying as an expert; it sets the standard for admissibility of such testimony.

Subdivision (a), which states *when* an expert may give his opinion upon a subject that is within the scope of his expertise, codifies the existing rule that expert opinion is limited to those subjects that are beyond the competence of persons of common experience, training, and education. People v. Cole, 47 Cal.2d 99, 103, 301 P.2d 854, 856 (1956). For examples of the variety of subjects upon which expert testimony is admitted, see Witkin, California Evidence §§ 190–195 (1958).

Subdivision (b) states a general rule in regard to the permissible bases upon which the opinion of an expert may be founded. The California courts have made it clear that the nature of the matter upon which an expert may base his opinion varies from case to case. In some fields of expert knowledge, an expert may rely on statements made by and information received from other persons; in some other fields of expert knowledge, an expert may not do so. For example, a physician may rely on statements made to him by the patient concerning the history of his condition. People v. Wilson, 25 Cal.2d 341, 153 P.2d 720 (1944). A physician may also rely on reports and opinions of other physicians. Kelley v. Bailey, 189 Cal.App.2d 728, 11 Cal.Rptr. 448 (1961); Hope v. Arrowhead & Puritas Waters, Inc., 174 Cal.App.2d 222, 344 P.2d 428 (1959). An expert on the valuation of real or personal property, too, may rely on inquiries made of others, commercial reports, market quotations, and relevant sales known to the witness. Betts v. Southern Cal. Fruit Exchange, 144 Cal. 402, 77 Pac. 993 (1904); Hammond Lumber Co. v. County of Los Angeles, 104 Cal.App. 235, 285 Pac. 896 (1930); Glantz v. Freedman, 100 Cal.App. 611, 280 Pac. 704 (1929). On the other hand, an expert on automobile accidents may not rely on extrajudicial statements of others as a partial basis for an opinion as to the point of impact, whether or not the statements would be admissible evidence. Hodges v. Severns, 201 Cal.App.2d 99, 20 Cal.Rptr. 129 (1962); Ribble v. Cook, 111 Cal.App.2d 903, 245 P.2d 593 (1952). See also Behr v. County of Santa Cruz, 172 Cal.App.2d 697, 342 P.2d 987 (1959) (report of fire ranger as to cause of fire held inadmissible because it was based primarily upon statements made to him by other persons).

Likewise, under existing law, irrelevant or speculative matters are not a proper basis for an expert's opinion. See Roscoe Moss Co. v. Jenkins, 55 Cal.App.2d 369, 130 P.2d 477 (1942) (expert may not base opinion upon a comparison if the matters compared are not reasonably comparable); People v. Luis, 158 Cal. 185, 110 Pac. 580 (1910) (physician may not base opinion as to person's feeblemindedness merely upon the person's exterior appearance); Long v. Cal.-Western States Life Ins. Co., 43 Cal.2d 871, 279 P.2d 43 (1955) (speculative or conjectural data); Eisenmayer v. Leonardt, 148 Cal. 596, 84 Pac. 43 (1906) (speculative or conjectural data). *Compare* People v. Wochnick, 98 Cal.App.2d 124, 219 P.2d 70 (1950) (expert may not give opinion as to the truth or falsity of certain statements on basis of lie detector test), with People v. Jones, 42 Cal.2d 219, 266 P.2d 38 (1954) (psychiatrist may consider an examination given under the influence of sodium pentothal—the so-called "truth serum"—in forming an opinion as to the mental state of the person examined).

The variation in the permissible bases of expert opinion is unavoidable in light of the wide variety of subjects upon which such opinion can be offered. In regard to some matters of expert opinion, an expert *must,* if he is going to give an opinion that will be helpful to the jury, rely on reports, statements, and other information that might not be admissible evidence. A physician in many instances cannot make a diagnosis without relying on the case history recited by the patient or on reports from various technicians or other physicians. Similarly, an appraiser must rely on reports of sales and other market data if he is to give an opinion that will be of value to the jury. In the usual case where a physician's or an appraiser's opinion is required, the adverse party also will have its expert who will be able to check the data relied upon by the adverse expert. On the other hand, a police officer can analyze skid marks, debris, and the condition of vehicles that have been involved in an accident without relying on the statements of bystanders; and it seems likely that the jury would be as able to evaluate the statements of others in the light of the physical facts, as interpreted by the officer, as would the officer himself. It is apparent that the extent to which an expert may base his opinion upon the statements of others is far from clear. It is at least clear, however, that it is permitted in a number of instances. See Young v. Bates Valve Bag Corp., 52 Cal.App.2d 86, 96–97, 125 P.2d 840, 846 (1942), and cases therein cited. *Cf.* People v. Alexander, 212 Cal.App.2d 84, 27 Cal.Rptr. 720 (1963).

It is not practical to formulate a detailed statutory rule that lists all of the matters upon which an expert may properly base his opinion, for it would be necessary to prescribe specific rules applicable to each field of expertise. This is clearly impossible; the subjects upon which expert opinion may be received are too numerous to make statutory prescription of applicable rules a feasible venture. It is possible, however, to formulate a general rule that specifies the minimum requisites that must be met in every case, leaving to the courts the task of determining particular detail within this general framework. This standard is expressed in subdivision (b) which states a general rule that is applicable whenever expert opinion is offered on a given subject.

Under subdivision (b), the matter upon which an expert's opinion is based must meet each of three separate but related tests. *First,* the matter must be perceived by or personally known to the witness or must be made known to him at or before the hearing at which the opinion is expressed. This requirement assures the expert's acquaintance with the facts of a particular case either by his personal perception or observation or by means of assuming facts not personally known to the witness. *Second,* and without regard to the means by which an expert familiarizes himself with the matter upon which his opinion is based, the matter relied upon by the expert in forming his opinion must be of a type that reasonably may be relied upon by experts in forming an opinion upon the subject to which his testimony relates. In large measure, this assures the reliability and trustworthiness of the information used by experts in forming their opinions. *Third,* an expert may not base his opinion upon any matter that is declared by the constitutional, statutory, or decisional law of this State to be an improper basis for an opinion. For example, the statements of bystanders as to the cause of a fire may be considered reliable for some purposes by an investigator of the fire, particularly when coupled with physical evidence found at the scene, but the courts have determined this to be an improper basis for an opinion since the trier of fact is as capable as the expert of evaluating such statements in light of the physical facts as interpreted by the expert. Behr v. County of Santa Cruz, 172 Cal.App.2d 697, 342 P.2d 987 (1959).

The rule stated in subdivision (b) thus permits an expert to base his opinion upon reliable matter, *whether or not admissible,* of a type that may reasonably be used in forming an opinion upon the subject to which his expert testimony relates. In addition, it provides assurance that the courts and the Legislature are free to continue to develop specific rules regarding

the proper bases for particular kinds of expert opinion in specific fields. See, *e.g.,* 3 Cal.Law Revision Comm'n, Rep., Rec. & Studies, Recommendation and Study Relating to Evidence in Eminent Domain Proceedings at A–1 (1961), Subdivision (b) thus provides a sensible standard of admissibility while, at the same time, it continues in effect the discretionary power of the courts to regulate abuses, thereby retaining in large measure the existing California law. [7 Cal.L.Rev.Comm. Reports 1 (1965)].

Research References

Rutter, Cal. Practice Guide: Civil Appeals & Writs Ch. 8-C, C. Standards of Appellate Review.

Rutter, Cal. Practice Guide: Civ. Pro. Before Trial Ch. 10-C, C. Procedural Requirements-Moving Party.

Rutter, Cal. Practice Guide: Civil Trials & Evidence Ch. 1-C, C. Marshalling the Evidence.

Rutter, Cal. Practice Guide: Civil Trials & Evidence Ch. 4-B, B. Preliminary Matters Discussed in Final Status Conference or In-Chambers Conference.

Rutter, Cal. Practice Guide: Civil Trials & Evidence Ch. 9-A, A. Preliminary Considerations.

Rutter, Cal. Practice Guide: Civil Trials & Evidence Ch. 11-A, A. Direct Examination of Expert Witnesses.

Rutter, Cal. Practice Guide: Civil Trials & Evidence Ch. 11-B, B. Procedures to Challenge Admissibility of Expert Witness Testimony.

Rutter, Cal. Practice Guide: Civil Trials & Evidence Ch. 11-D, D. Cross-Examination of Expert Witnesses.

Rutter, Cal. Practice Guide: Civil Trials & Evidence Ch. 8C-A, A. Testimony.

Rutter, Cal. Practice Guide: Civil Trials & Evidence Ch. 8C-G, G. Scientific Evidence.

Rutter, Cal. Practice Guide: Civil Trials & Evidence Ch. 8C-H, H. Opinion Evidence.

Rutter, Cal. Practice Guide: Civil Trials & Evidence Ch. 8D-D, D. Hearsay Exceptions.

Rutter, Cal. Practice Guide: Civil Trials & Evidence Ch. 8C-H, Outline H.

California Practice Guide: Employment Litigation Ch. 19-N, N. Evidence Issues.

Rutter, Cal. Practice Guide: Family Law Ch. 8-E, E. Division of Community Estate Upon Dissolution, Legal Separation or Nullity.

Rutter, Cal. Practice Guide: Family Law Ch. 13-B, B. Contested Family Law Trial.

Rutter, Cal. Practice Guide: Insurance Litigation Ch. 15-I, I. Trial.

Rutter, Cal. Practice Guide: Insurance Litigation Ch. 12C-E, E. Evidentiary Considerations.

Rutter, Cal. Practice Guide: Landlord-Tenant Ch. 2C-4, Establishing and Proving Unlawful Rental Discrimination.

Rutter, Cal. Practice Guide: Personal Injury Ch. 3-C, C. Specific Items of Compensatory Damages.

Rutter, Cal. Practice Guide: Personal Injury Ch. 9-F, F. Examination of Witnesses.

Rutter, Cal. Practice Guide: Personal Injury Ch. 9-G, G. Expert Witnesses.

Rutter, Cal. Practice Guide: Personal Injury Ch. 2(I)-D, D. Employment of Experts.

6 Witkin, California Summary 10th Torts § 1673, Loss of Enjoyment.

§ 802. Statement of basis of opinion

A witness testifying in the form of an opinion may state on direct examination the reasons for his opinion and the matter (including, in the case of an expert, his special knowledge, skill, experience, training, and education) upon which it is based, unless he is precluded by law from using such reasons or matter as a basis for his opinion. The court in its discretion may require that a witness before testifying in the form of an opinion be first examined concerning the matter upon which his opinion is based. *(Stats.1965, c. 299, § 2, operative Jan. 1, 1967.)*

Law Revision Commission Comments

Section 802 restates the substance of and supersedes a portion of Section 1872 of the Code of Civil Procedure. Section 802, however, relates to all witnesses who testify in the form of opinion, while Section 1872 relates only to experts.

Although Section 802 (like its predecessor, Code of Civil Procedure Section 1872) provides that a witness *may* state the basis for his opinion on direct examination, it is clear that, in some cases, a witness is *required* to

Evidence

do so in order to show that his opinion is applicable to the action before the court. Under existing law, where a witness testifies in the form of opinion not based upon his personal observation, the assumed facts upon which his opinion is based must be stated in order to show that the witness has some basis for forming an intelligent opinion and to permit the trier of fact to determine the applicability of the opinion in light of the existence or nonexistence of such facts. Eisenmayer v. Leonardt, 148 Cal. 596, 84 Pac. 43 (1906); Lemley v. Doak Gas Engine Co., 40 Cal.App. 146, 180 Pac. 671 (1919) (hearing denied). Evidence Code Section 802 will not affect the rule set forth in these cases, for it is based essentially on the requirement that all evidence must be shown to be applicable—or relevant—to the action. Evidence Code §§ 350, 403. But under Section 802, as under existing law, a witness testifying from his personal observation of the facts upon which his opinion is based need not be examined concerning such facts before testifying in the form of opinion; his personal observation is a sufficient basis upon which to found his opinion. Lumbermen's Mut. Cas. Co. v. Industrial Acc. Comm'n, 29 Cal.2d 492, 175 P.2d 823 (1946); Hart v. Olson, 68 Cal.App.2d 657, 157 P.2d 385 (1945); Lemley v. Doak Gas Engine Co., *supra*. However, the court may require a witness to state the facts observed before stating his opinion. In this respect Section 802 codifies the existing rule concerning lay witnesses and, although the existing law is unclear, probably states the existing rule as to expert witnesses. See Tentative Recommendation and a Study Relating to the Uniform Rules of Evidence (Article VII. Expert and Other Opinion Testimony), 6 Cal.Law Revision Comm'n, Rep., Rec. & Studies 901, 934 (lay witness), 939 (expert witness) (1964). [7 Cal.L.Rev.Comm. Reports 1 (1965)].

Research References

Rutter, Cal. Practice Guide: Civil Trials & Evidence Ch. 4-B, B. Preliminary Matters Discussed in Final Status Conference or In-Chambers Conference.
Rutter, Cal. Practice Guide: Civil Trials & Evidence Ch. 10-A, A. Preliminary Considerations.
Rutter, Cal. Practice Guide: Civil Trials & Evidence Ch. 11-A, A. Direct Examination of Expert Witnesses.
Rutter, Cal. Practice Guide: Civil Trials & Evidence Ch. 11-B, B. Procedures to Challenge Admissibility of Expert Witness Testimony.
Rutter, Cal. Practice Guide: Civil Trials & Evidence Ch. 11-D, D. Cross-Examination of Expert Witnesses.
Rutter, Cal. Practice Guide: Civil Trials & Evidence Ch. 8C-H, H. Opinion Evidence.
Rutter, Cal. Practice Guide: Personal Injury Ch. 9-F, F. Examination of Witnesses.
Rutter, Cal. Practice Guide: Personal Injury Ch. 9-G, G. Expert Witnesses.

§ 803.   Opinion based on improper matter

The court may, and upon objection shall, exclude testimony in the form of an opinion that is based in whole or in significant part on matter that is not a proper basis for such an opinion. In such case, the witness may, if there remains a proper basis for his opinion, then state his opinion after excluding from consideration the matter determined to be improper. *(Stats.1965, c. 299, § 2, operative Jan. 1, 1967.)*

Law Revision Commission Comments

Under Section 803, as under existing law, an opinion may be held inadmissible or may be stricken if it is based wholly or in substantial part upon improper considerations. Whether or not the opinion should be held inadmissible or stricken will depend in a particular case on the extent to which the improper considerations have influenced the opinion. "The question is addressed to the discretion of the trial court." People v. Lipari, 213 Cal.App.2d 485, 493, 28 Cal.Rptr. 808, 813–814 (1963). See discussion in City of Gilroy v. Filice, 221 Cal.App.2d 259, 271–272, 34 Cal.Rptr. 368, 375–376 (1963), and cases cited therein. If a witness' opinion is stricken because of reliance upon improper considerations, the second sentence of Section 803 assures the witness the opportunity to express his opinion after excluding from his consideration the matter determined to be improper. [7 Cal.L.Rev.Comm. Reports 1 (1965)].

Research References

Rutter, Cal. Practice Guide: Civil Trials & Evidence Ch. 4-B, B. Preliminary Matters Discussed in Final Status Conference or In-Chambers Conference.

Rutter, Cal. Practice Guide: Civil Trials & Evidence Ch. 4-F, F. Motions in Limine.
Rutter, Cal. Practice Guide: Civil Trials & Evidence Ch. 11-B, B. Procedures to Challenge Admissibility of Expert Witness Testimony.
Rutter, Cal. Practice Guide: Civil Trials & Evidence Ch. 11-D, D. Cross-Examination of Expert Witnesses.
Rutter, Cal. Practice Guide: Civil Trials & Evidence Ch. 8C-H, H. Opinion Evidence.
Rutter, Cal. Practice Guide: Insurance Litigation Ch. 15-I, I. Trial.
Rutter, Cal. Practice Guide: Personal Injury Ch. 9-F, F. Examination of Witnesses.
Rutter, Cal. Practice Guide: Personal Injury Ch. 9-G, G. Expert Witnesses.

§ 804.   Opinion based on opinion or statement of another

(a) If a witness testifying as an expert testifies that his opinion is based in whole or in part upon the opinion or statement of another person, such other person may be called and examined by any adverse party as if under cross-examination concerning the opinion or statement.

(b) This section is not applicable if the person upon whose opinion or statement the expert witness has relied is (1) a party, (2) a person identified with a party within the meaning of subdivision (d) of Section 776, or (3) a witness who has testified in the action concerning the subject matter of the opinion or statement upon which the expert witness has relied.

(c) Nothing in this section makes admissible an expert opinion that is inadmissible because it is based in whole or in part on the opinion or statement of another person.

(d) An expert opinion otherwise admissible is not made inadmissible by this section because it is based on the opinion or statement of a person who is unavailable for examination pursuant to this section. *(Stats.1965, c. 299, § 2, operative Jan. 1, 1967.)*

Law Revision Commission Comments

Section 804 is designed to provide protection to a party who is confronted with an expert witness who relies on the opinion or statement of some other person. (See the Comment to Section 801 for examples of opinions that may be based on the statements and opinions of others.) In such a situation, a party may find that cross-examination of the witness will not reveal the weakness in his opinion, for the crucial parts are based on the observations or opinions of someone else. Under existing law, if that other person is called as a witness, he is the witness of the party calling him and, therefore, that party may not subject him to cross-examination.

The existing law operates unfairly, for it unnecessarily restricts meaningful cross-examination. Hence, Section 804 permits a party to extend his cross-examination into the underlying bases of the opinion testimony introduced against him by calling the authors of opinions and statements relied on by adverse witnesses and examining them as if under cross-examination concerning the subject matter of their opinions and statements. See the Comment to Evidence Code § 1203. [7 Cal.L.Rev. Comm. Reports 1 (1965)].

Research References

Rutter, Cal. Practice Guide: Civil Trials & Evidence Ch. 4-B, B. Preliminary Matters Discussed in Final Status Conference or In-Chambers Conference.
Rutter, Cal. Practice Guide: Civil Trials & Evidence Ch. 9-C, C. Direct Examination of Adverse Witness (EV.C. § 776).
Rutter, Cal. Practice Guide: Civil Trials & Evidence Ch. 11-E, E. Impeachment Evidence from Other Witnesses.
Rutter, Cal. Practice Guide: Personal Injury Ch. 9-G, G. Expert Witnesses.

§ 805.   Opinion on ultimate issue

Testimony in the form of an opinion that is otherwise admissible is not objectionable because it embraces the ultimate issue to be decided by the trier of fact. *(Stats.1965, c. 299, § 2, operative Jan. 1, 1967.)*

Law Revision Commission Comments

Although several older cases indicated that an opinion could not be received on an ultimate issue, more recent cases have repudiated this rule. Hence, this section is declarative of existing law. People v. Wilson, 25 Cal.2d 341, 349–350, 153 P.2d 720, 725 (1944); Wells Truckways, Ltd. v. Cebrian, 122 Cal.App.2d 666, 265 P.2d 557 (1954); People v. King, 104 Cal.App.2d 298, 231 P.2d 156 (1951). [7 Cal.L.Rev.Comm. Reports 1 (1965)].

Research References

Rutter, Cal. Practice Guide: Civil Trials & Evidence Ch. 11-A, A. Direct Examination of Expert Witnesses.

Rutter, Cal. Practice Guide: Civil Trials & Evidence Ch. 8C-H, H. Opinion Evidence.

Rutter, Cal. Practice Guide: Personal Injury Ch. 3-C, C. Specific Items of Compensatory Damages.

Rutter, Cal. Practice Guide: Personal Injury Ch. 2(I)-D, D. Employment of Experts.

Rutter, Cal. Practice Guide: Prof. Responsibility Ch. 11-I, I. Trial Proceedings.

ARTICLE 2. EVIDENCE OF MARKET VALUE OF PROPERTY

Section

810. Application of article.
811. Value of property.
812. Market value; interpretation of meaning.
813. Value of property; authorized opinions; view of property; admissible evidence.
814. Matter upon which opinion must be based.
815. Sales of subject property.
816. Comparable sales.
817. Leases of subject property.
818. Comparable leases.
819. Capitalization of income.
820. Reproduction cost.
821. Conditions in general vicinity of subject property.
822. Matter upon which opinion may not be based.
823. Property with no relevant, comparable market.
824. Nonprofit, special use property.

§ 810. Application of article

(a) Except where another rule is provided by statute, this article provides special rules of evidence applicable to any action in which the value of property is to be ascertained.

(b) This article does not govern ad valorem property tax assessment or equalization proceedings. *(Added by Stats.1965, c. 1151, p. 2904, § 4, operative Jan. 1, 1967. Amended by Stats.1978, c. 294, p. 615, § 3; Stats.1980, c. 381, p. 757, § 1.)*

Research References

Rutter, Cal. Practice Guide: Landlord-Tenant Ch. 8-D, D. Answer to Unlawful Detainer Complaint.

Miller and Starr California Real Estate § 34:50, Determining "Value of the Property"; Comparison of the Terms of Sale.

Miller and Starr California Real Estate § 34:86, Compensatory Damages.

Miller and Starr California Real Estate § 30A:72, Valuation Testimony.

8 Witkin, California Summary 10th Constitutional Law § 1219, in General.

8 Witkin, California Summary 10th Constitutional Law § 1230, Determining Market Value.

§ 811. Value of property

As used in this article, "value of property" means market value of any of the following:

(a) Real property or any interest therein.

(b) Real property or any interest therein and tangible personal property valued as a unit. *(Added by Stats.1965, c. 1151, p.*

2904, § 4, operative Jan. 1, 1967. Amended by Stats.1975, c. 1240, p. 3202, § 15, operative July 1, 1976; Stats.1978, c. 294, p. 615, § 4; Stats.1980, c. 381, p. 757, § 2.)*

Law Revision Commission Comments

Section 811 is amended to conform to the numbering of the Eminent Domain Law.

Section 811 makes clear that this article as applied to eminent domain proceedings governs only evidence relating to the determination of property value and damages and benefits to the remainder. This article does not govern evidence relating to the determination of loss of goodwill (Code Civ.Proc. § 1263.510).

The evidence admissible to prove loss of goodwill is governed by the general provisions of the Evidence Code. Hence, nothing in this article should be deemed a limitation on the admissibility of evidence to prove loss of goodwill if such evidence is otherwise admissible. [12 Cal.L.Rev. Comm. Reports 1601 (1975)].

Research References

Rutter, Cal. Practice Guide: Family Law Ch. 8-E, E. Division of Community Estate Upon Dissolution, Legal Separation or Nullity.

Miller and Starr California Real Estate § 34:50, Determining "Value of the Property"; Comparison of the Terms of Sale.

Miller and Starr California Real Estate § 30A:72, Valuation Testimony.

§ 812. Market value; interpretation of meaning

This article is not intended to alter or change the existing substantive law, whether statutory or decisional, interpreting the meaning of "market value," whether denominated "fair market value" or otherwise. *(Added by Stats.1965, c. 1151, p. 2904, § 4, operative Jan. 1, 1967. Amended by Stats.1975, c. 1240, p. 3202, § 16, operative July 1, 1976; Stats.1978, c. 294, p. 615, § 5.)*

Law Revision Commission Comments

Section 812 is amended to conform to the numbering and terminology of the Eminent Domain Law. [12 Cal.L.Rev.Comm. Reports 1601 (1975)].

Research References

Miller and Starr California Real Estate § 34:50, Determining "Value of the Property"; Comparison of the Terms of Sale.

Miller and Starr California Real Estate § 30A:72, Valuation Testimony.

8 Witkin, California Summary 10th Constitutional Law § 1222, (S 1222) Valuation of Divided Interests.

§ 813. Value of property; authorized opinions; view of property; admissible evidence

(a) The value of property may be shown only by the opinions of any of the following:

(1) Witnesses qualified to express such opinions.

(2) The owner or the spouse of the owner of the property or property interest being valued.

(3) An officer, regular employee, or partner designated by a corporation, partnership, or unincorporated association that is the owner of the property or property interest being valued, if the designee is knowledgeable as to the value of the property or property interest.

(b) Nothing in this section prohibits a view of the property being valued or the admission of any other admissible evidence (including but not limited to evidence as to the nature and condition of the property and, in an eminent domain proceeding, the character of the improvement proposed to be constructed by the plaintiff) for the limited purpose of enabling the court, jury, or referee to understand and weigh the testimony given under subdivision (a); and such evidence, except evidence of the character of the improvement proposed to be constructed by the plaintiff in an eminent domain proceeding, is subject to impeachment and rebuttal.

(c) For the purposes of subdivision (a), "owner of the property or property interest being valued" includes, but is not limited to, the following persons:

(1) A person entitled to possession of the property.

(2) Either party in an action or proceeding to determine the ownership of the property between the parties if the court determines that it would not be in the interest of efficient administration of justice to determine the issue of ownership prior to the admission of the opinion of the party. *(Added by Stats.1965, c. 1151, p. 2904, § 4, operative Jan. 1, 1967. Amended by Stats.1978, c. 294, p. 615, § 6; Stats.1980, c. 381, p. 757, § 3.)*

Law Revision Commission Comments

Paragraph (3) is added to Section 813(a) to make clear that, where a corporation, partnership, or unincorporated association owns property being valued, a designated officer, regular employee, or partner who is knowledgeable as to the value of the property may testify to an opinion of its value as an owner, notwithstanding any contrary implications in City of Pleasant Hill v. First Baptist Church, 1 Cal.App.3d 384, 82 Cal.Rptr. 1 (1969). The designee may be knowledgeable as to the value of the property as a result of being instrumental in its acquisition or management or as a result of being knowledgeable as to its character and use; the designee need not qualify as a general valuation expert. Compare Section 720 (qualification as an expert witness). Nothing in Section 813 affects the authority of the court to limit the number of expert witnesses to be called by any party (see Section 723) or to limit cumulative evidence (see Section 352).

The phrase "value of property," as used in this section, is defined in Section 811. [14 Cal.L.Rev.Comm. Reports 105 (1978)].

Research References

Rutter, Cal. Practice Guide: Civil Trials & Evidence Ch. 8B-B, B. Particular Types of Evidence.
Rutter, Cal. Practice Guide: Civil Trials & Evidence Ch. 8C-H, H. Opinion Evidence.
Rutter, Cal. Practice Guide: Family Law Ch. 8-E, E. Division of Community Estate Upon Dissolution, Legal Separation or Nullity.
Rutter, Cal. Practice Guide: Landlord-Tenant Ch. 9-E, E. Trial of the Case-Selected Evidentiary Issues.
Miller and Starr California Real Estate § 12:47, Basic Rules for Determining Character of Property; Definitions--Property Acquired With Both Separate and Community Property--Property Acquired After 1984.
Miller and Starr California Real Estate § 34:50, Determining "Value of the Property"; Comparison of the Terms of Sale.
Miller and Starr California Real Estate § 34:86, Compensatory Damages.
Miller and Starr California Real Estate § 30A:26, Appraisal Methods of Determining Fair Market Value.
Miller and Starr California Real Estate § 30A:41, Valuation of Damage When Project Ongoing.
Miller and Starr California Real Estate § 30A:72, Valuation Testimony.

§ 814. Matter upon which opinion must be based

The opinion of a witness as to the value of property is limited to such an opinion as is based on matter perceived by or personally known to the witness or made known to the witness at or before the hearing, whether or not admissible, that is of a type that reasonably may be relied upon by an expert in forming an opinion as to the value of property, including but not limited to the matters listed in Sections 815 to 821, inclusive, unless a witness is precluded by law from using such matter as a basis for an opinion. *(Added by Stats.1965, c. 1151, p. 2904, § 4, operative Jan. 1, 1967. Amended by Stats.1975, c. 1240, p. 3202, § 17, operative July 1, 1976; Stats.1980, c. 381, p. 757, § 4.)*

Research References

Rutter, Cal. Practice Guide: Civil Trials & Evidence Ch. 8C-H, H. Opinion Evidence.
Rutter, Cal. Practice Guide: Family Law Ch. 8-E, E. Division of Community Estate Upon Dissolution, Legal Separation or Nullity.
Rutter, Cal. Practice Guide: Landlord-Tenant Ch. 9-E, E. Trial of the Case-Selected Evidentiary Issues.

Miller and Starr California Real Estate § 34:50, Determining "Value of the Property"; Comparison of the Terms of Sale.
Miller and Starr California Real Estate § 30A:72, Valuation Testimony.

§ 815. Sales of subject property

When relevant to the determination of the value of property, a witness may take into account as a basis for an opinion the price and other terms and circumstances of any sale or contract to sell and purchase which included the property or property interest being valued or any part thereof if the sale or contract was freely made in good faith within a reasonable time before or after the date of valuation, except that in an eminent domain proceeding where the sale or contract to sell and purchase includes only the property or property interest being taken or a part thereof, such sale or contract to sell and purchase may not be taken into account if it occurs after the filing of the lis pendens. *(Added by Stats.1965, c. 1151, p. 2904, § 4, operative Jan. 1, 1967. Amended by Stats.1978, c. 294, p. 615, § 7.)*

Research References

Rutter, Cal. Practice Guide: Civil Trials & Evidence Ch. 8B-B, B. Particular Types of Evidence.
Rutter, Cal. Practice Guide: Family Law Ch. 8-E, E. Division of Community Estate Upon Dissolution, Legal Separation or Nullity.
Miller and Starr California Real Estate § 30A:26, Appraisal Methods of Determining Fair Market Value.

§ 816. Comparable sales

When relevant to the determination of the value of property, a witness may take into account as a basis for his opinion the price and other terms and circumstances of any sale or contract to sell and purchase comparable property if the sale or contract was freely made in good faith within a reasonable time before or after the date of valuation. In order to be considered comparable, the sale or contract must have been made sufficiently near in time to the date of valuation, and the property sold must be located sufficiently near the property being valued, and must be sufficiently alike in respect to character, size, situation, usability, and improvements, to make it clear that the property sold and the property being valued are comparable in value and that the price realized for the property sold may fairly be considered as shedding light on the value of the property being valued. *(Added by Stats.1965, c. 1151, p. 2904, § 4, operative Jan. 1, 1967.)*

Research References

Rutter, Cal. Practice Guide: Civil Trials & Evidence Ch. 8B-B, B. Particular Types of Evidence.
Rutter, Cal. Practice Guide: Family Law Ch. 8-E, E. Division of Community Estate Upon Dissolution, Legal Separation or Nullity.
Rutter, Cal. Practice Guide: Landlord-Tenant Ch. 9-E, E. Trial of the Case-Selected Evidentiary Issues.
Miller and Starr California Real Estate § 34:50, Determining "Value of the Property"; Comparison of the Terms of Sale.
Miller and Starr California Real Estate § 30A:26, Appraisal Methods of Determining Fair Market Value.
9 Witkin, California Summary 10th Taxation § 216, Market Data or Comparable Sales Method.

§ 817. Leases of subject property

(a) Subject to subdivision (b), when relevant to the determination of the value of property, a witness may take into account as a basis for an opinion the rent reserved and other terms and circumstances of any lease which included the property or property interest being valued or any part thereof which was in effect within a reasonable time before or after the date of valuation, except that in an eminent domain proceeding where the lease includes only the property or property interest being taken or a part thereof, such lease may not be taken into account in the determination of the value of property if it is entered into after the filing of the lis pendens.

(b) A witness may take into account a lease providing for a rental fixed by a percentage or other measurable portion of gross sales or gross income from a business conducted on the leased property only for the purpose of arriving at an opinion as to the reasonable net rental value attributable to the property or property interest being valued as provided in Section 819 or determining the value of a leasehold interest. *(Added by Stats.1965, c. 1151, § 4, operative Jan. 1, 1967. Amended by Stats.1978, c. 294, p. 616, § 8.)*

Law Revision Commission Comments

Subdivision (a) of Section 817 is amended to add the limitation that a lease of the subject property is not a proper basis for an opinion of value of the property after the filing of the lis pendens in an eminent domain proceeding. This is comparable to a provision of Section 815 (sale of subject property). Nothing in subdivision (a) should be construed to limit the use of leases created after filing of the lis pendens to show damages to the property, such as those authorized by Klopping v. City of Whittier, 8 Cal.3d 39, 500 P.2d 1345, 104 Cal.Rptr. 1 (1972).

Subdivision (b) limits the extent to which a witness may take into account a lease based on gross sales or gross income of a business conducted on the property. This limitation applies only to valuation of the real property or an interest therein, or of tangible personal property, and does not apply to the determination of loss of goodwill. See Section 811 and Comment thereto; Code Civ.Proc. § 1263.510 and Comment thereto.

The phrase "value of property," as used in this section, is defined in Section 811. [14 Cal.L.Rev.Comm. Reports 105 (1978)].

Research References

Rutter, Cal. Practice Guide: Landlord-Tenant Ch. 9-E, E. Trial of the Case-Selected Evidentiary Issues.
Miller and Starr California Real Estate § 34:50, Determining "Value of the Property"; Comparison of the Terms of Sale.
8 Witkin, California Summary 10th Constitutional Law § 1222, (S 1222) Valuation of Divided Interests.

§ 818. Comparable leases

For the purpose of determining the capitalized value of the reasonable net rental value attributable to the property or property interest being valued as provided in Section 819 or determining the value of a leasehold interest, a witness may take into account as a basis for his opinion the rent reserved and other terms and circumstances of any lease of comparable property if the lease was freely made in good faith within a reasonable time before or after the date of valuation. *(Added by Stats.1965, c. 1151, p. 2904, § 4, operative Jan. 1, 1967.)*

Research References

Rutter, Cal. Practice Guide: Landlord-Tenant Ch. 9-E, E. Trial of the Case-Selected Evidentiary Issues.
Miller and Starr California Real Estate § 34:50, Determining "Value of the Property"; Comparison of the Terms of Sale.
Miller and Starr California Real Estate § 30A:26, Appraisal Methods of Determining Fair Market Value.

§ 819. Capitalization of income

When relevant to the determination of the value of property, a witness may take into account as a basis for his opinion the capitalized value of the reasonable net rental value attributable to the land and existing improvements thereon (as distinguished from the capitalized value of the income or profits attributable to the business conducted thereon). *(Added by Stats.1965, c. 1151, p. 2904, § 4, operative Jan. 1, 1967.)*

Research References

Miller and Starr California Real Estate § 34:50, Determining "Value of the Property"; Comparison of the Terms of Sale.

Miller and Starr California Real Estate § 30A:26, Appraisal Methods of Determining Fair Market Value.

§ 820. Reproduction cost

When relevant to the determination of the value of property, a witness may take into account as a basis for his opinion the value of the property or property interest being valued as indicated by the value of the land together with the cost of replacing or reproducing the existing improvements thereon, if the improvements enhance the value of the property or property interest for its highest and best use, less whatever depreciation or obsolescence the improvements have suffered. *(Added by Stats.1965, c. 1151, p. 2904, § 4, operative Jan. 1, 1967.)*

Research References

Miller and Starr California Real Estate § 34:50, Determining "Value of the Property"; Comparison of the Terms of Sale.
Miller and Starr California Real Estate § 30A:26, Appraisal Methods of Determining Fair Market Value.

§ 821. Conditions in general vicinity of subject property

When relevant to the determination of the value of property, a witness may take into account as a basis for his opinion the nature of the improvements on properties in the general vicinity of the property or property interest being valued and the character of the existing uses being made of such properties. *(Added by Stats.1965, c. 1151, p. 2904, § 4, operative Jan. 1, 1967.)*

Research References

Rutter, Cal. Practice Guide: Civil Trials & Evidence Ch. 8C-H, H. Opinion Evidence.
Miller and Starr California Real Estate § 34:50, Determining "Value of the Property"; Comparison of the Terms of Sale.
Miller and Starr California Real Estate § 30A:26, Appraisal Methods of Determining Fair Market Value.

§ 822. Matter upon which opinion may not be based

(a) In an eminent domain or inverse condemnation proceeding, notwithstanding the provisions of Sections 814 to 821, inclusive, the following matter is inadmissible as evidence and shall not be taken into account as a basis for an opinion as to the value of property:

(1) The price or other terms and circumstances of an acquisition of property or a property interest if the acquisition was for a public use for which the property could have been taken by eminent domain.

The price or other terms and circumstances shall not be excluded pursuant to this paragraph if the proceeding relates to the valuation of all or part of a water system as defined in Section 240 of the Public Utilities Code.

(2) The price at which an offer or option to purchase or lease the property or property interest being valued or any other property was made, or the price at which the property or interest was optioned, offered, or listed for sale or lease, except that an option, offer, or listing may be introduced by a party as an admission of another party to the proceeding; but nothing in this subdivision permits an admission to be used as direct evidence upon any matter that may be shown only by opinion evidence under Section 813.

(3) The value of any property or property interest as assessed for taxation purposes or the amount of taxes which may be due on the property, but nothing in this subdivision prohibits the consideration of actual or estimated taxes for the purpose of determining the reasonable net rental value attributable to the property or property interest being valued.

(4) An opinion as to the value of any property or property interest other than that being valued.

Evidence

(5) The influence upon the value of the property or property interest being valued of any noncompensable items of value, damage, or injury.

(6) The capitalized value of the income or rental from any property or property interest other than that being valued.

(b) In an action other than an eminent domain or inverse condemnation proceeding, the matters listed in subdivision (a) are not admissible as evidence, and may not be taken into account as a basis for an opinion as to the value of property, except to the extent permitted under the rules of law otherwise applicable. *(Added by Stats.1965, c. 1151, p. 2904, § 4, operative Jan. 1, 1967. Amended by Stats.1978, c. 294, p. 616, § 9; Stats.1980, c. 381, p. 758, § 5; Stats.1986, c. 1238, § 2; Stats. 1987, c. 1278, § 1; Stats.2000, c. 948 (A.B.321), § 1.)*

Law Revision Commission Comments

Subdivision (c) of Section 822 is amended to incorporate a provision formerly found in Revenue and Taxation Code Section 4986(b). Unlike the former provision, subdivision (c) does not provide for a mistrial for mention of the amount of taxes which may be due. Whether such mention is grounds for a mistrial is governed by the general principles of court discretion to declare a mistrial when evidence has been presented which is inadmissible, highly prejudicial, and cannot be corrected by an admonition to the jury.

Subdivision (d) does not prohibit a witness from testifying to adjustments made in sales of comparable property used as a basis for an opinion. Merced Irrigation Dist. v. Woolstenhulme, 4 Cal.3d 478, 501–03, 483 P.2d 1, 16–17, 93 Cal.Rptr. 833, 848–49 (1971).

Section 822 does not prohibit cross-examination of a witness on any matter precluded from admission as evidence if such cross-examination is for the limited purpose of determining whether a witness based an opinion in whole or in part on matter that is not a proper basis for an opinion; such cross-examination may not, however, serve as a means of placing improper matters before the trier of fact. See Evid. Code §§ 721, 802, 803.

The phrase "value of property," as used in this section, is defined in Section 811. [14 Cal.L.Rev.Comm. Reports 105 (1978)].

Subdivision (a)(1) of Section 822 is amended to delete the special exception relating to property appropriated to public use, in reliance on general evidentiary principles. See, e.g., Section 823 ("Notwithstanding any other provision of this article, the value of property for which there is no relevant, comparable market may be determined by any method of valuation that is just and equitable."); see also Code Civ. Proc. § 1263.320(b) (fair market value). Thus, evidence of an acquisition that is otherwise inadmissible under subdivision (a)(1) may, in an appropriate case, be admissible under Section 823 if a private market is lacking, e.g., the acquisition involves a special purpose property such as a school, church, cemetery, park, utility corridor, or similar property.

The new exception added to subdivision (a)(1) is intended to apply in an eminent domain or inverse condemnation proceeding that relates to a public agency's acquisition or taking of all or any part of a water system owned by a water company.

Subdivision (c) is deleted as obsolete. [30 Cal.L.Rev.Comm.Reports 723 (2000)].

Research References

Rutter, Cal. Practice Guide: Civil Trials & Evidence Ch. 8B-B, B. Particular Types of Evidence.

Rutter, Cal. Practice Guide: Civil Trials & Evidence Ch. 8C-H, H. Opinion Evidence.

Rutter, Cal. Practice Guide: Family Law Ch. 8-E, E. Division of Community Estate Upon Dissolution, Legal Separation or Nullity.

Rutter, Cal. Practice Guide: Landlord-Tenant Ch. 7-C, C. Bases for Terminating Tenancy.

Miller and Starr California Real Estate § 21:34, Who is Liable for Usury Penalties--Loans "Made or Arranged" by a Licensed Real Estate Broker.

Miller and Starr California Real Estate § 30A:26, Appraisal Methods of Determining Fair Market Value.

15 NO. 3 Miller & Starr, California Real Estate Newsalert 7, Eminent Domain.

23 NO. 2 Miller & Starr, California Real Estate Newsalert 10, Eminent Domain.

8 Witkin, California Summary 10th Constitutional Law § 1232, Inadmissible Matters.

§ 823. Property with no relevant, comparable market

Notwithstanding any other provision of this article, the value of property for which there is no relevant, comparable market may be determined by any method of valuation that is just and equitable. *(Added by Stats.1980, c. 381, p. 758, § 6. Amended by Stats.1992, c. 7 (S.B.821), § 4.)*

Research References

Miller and Starr California Real Estate § 17:27, Water Rights--Priority of Water Rights.

Miller and Starr California Real Estate § 34:50, Determining "Value of the Property"; Comparison of the Terms of Sale.

Miller and Starr California Real Estate § 34:86, Compensatory Damages.

Miller and Starr California Real Estate § 30A:26, Appraisal Methods of Determining Fair Market Value.

Miller and Starr California Real Estate § 30A:38, Valuing Severance Damage.

§ 824. Nonprofit, special use property

(a) Notwithstanding any other provision of this article, a just and equitable method of determining the value of nonprofit, special use property, as defined by Section 1235.155 of the Code of Civil Procedure, for which there is no relevant, comparable market, is the cost of purchasing land and the reasonable cost of making it suitable for the conduct of the same nonprofit, special use, together with the cost of constructing similar improvements. The method for determining compensation for improvements shall be as set forth in subdivision (b).

(b) Notwithstanding any other provision of this article, a witness providing opinion testimony on the value of nonprofit, special use property, as defined by Section 1235.155 of the Code of Civil Procedure, for which there is no relevant, comparable market, shall base his or her opinion on the value of reproducing the improvements without taking into consideration any depreciation or obsolescence of the improvements.

(c) This section does not apply to actions or proceedings commenced by a public entity or public utility to acquire real property or any interest in real property for the use of water, sewer, electricity, telephone, natural gas, or flood control facilities or rights-of-way where those acquisitions neither require removal or destruction of existing improvements, nor render the property unfit for the owner's present or proposed use. *(Added by Stats.1992, c. 7 (S.B.821), § 5.)*

Research References

Miller and Starr California Real Estate § 34:50, Determining "Value of the Property"; Comparison of the Terms of Sale.

Miller and Starr California Real Estate § 30A:22, Fair Market Value Defined.

Miller and Starr California Real Estate § 30A:26, Appraisal Methods of Determining Fair Market Value.

8 Witkin, California Summary 10th Constitutional Law § 1230, Determining Market Value.

ARTICLE 3. OPINION TESTIMONY ON PARTICULAR SUBJECTS

Section
870. Opinion as to sanity.

§ 870. Opinion as to sanity

A witness may state his opinion as to the sanity of a person when:

(a) The witness is an intimate acquaintance of the person whose sanity is in question;

(b) The witness was a subscribing witness to a writing, the validity of which is in dispute, signed by the person whose sanity is in question and the opinion relates to the sanity of such person at the time the writing was signed; or

(c) The witness is qualified under Section 800 or 801 to testify in the form of an opinion. *(Stats.1965, c. 299, § 2, operative Jan. 1, 1967.)*

Law Revision Commission Comments

Subdivisions (a) and (b) restate the substance of and supersede subdivision 10 of Section 1870 of the Code of Civil Procedure. Subdivision (c) merely makes it clear that a witness who meets the requirements of Section 800 or Section 801 is qualified to testify in the form of an opinion as to the sanity of a person. Section 870 does not disturb the present rule that permits a witness to testify to a person's rational or irrational appearance or conduct, even though the witness is not qualified under Section 870 to express an opinion on the person's sanity. See Pfingst v. Goetting, 96 Cal.App.2d 293, 215 P.2d 93 (1950). [7 Cal.L.Rev. Comm. Reports 1 (1965)].

Research References

Rutter, Cal. Practice Guide: Civil Trials & Evidence Ch. 8C-H, H. Opinion Evidence.
Miller and Starr California Real Estate § 8:23, Mental Incapacity to Convey.
14 Witkin, California Summary 10th Wills and Probate § 122, Showing Required.

Division 8

PRIVILEGES

CHAPTER 1. DEFINITIONS

§ 900. Application of definitions

Unless the provision or context otherwise requires, the definitions in this chapter govern the construction of this division. They do not govern the construction of any other division. *(Stats.1965, c. 299, § 2, operative Jan. 1, 1967.)*

Law Revision Commission Comments

Section 900 makes it clear that the definitions in Sections 901 through 905 apply only to Division 8 (Privileges) and that these definitions are not applicable where the context or language of a particular section in Division 8 requires that a word or phrase used in that section be given a different meaning. The definitions contained in Division 2 (commencing with Section 100) apply to the entire code, including Division 8. Definitions applicable only to a particular article are found in that article. [7 Cal.L.Rev.Comm. Reports 1 (1965)].

Research References

Rutter, Cal. Practice Guide: Civil Trials & Evidence Ch. 8E-A, A. Privileges.
Rutter, Cal. Practice Guide: Civil Trials & Evidence Ch. 8E-B, B. Attorney Work Product Doctrine.
Rutter, Cal. Practice Guide: Personal Injury Ch. 6-A, A. Scope of Discovery and Limitations.

§ 901. Proceeding

"Proceeding" means any action, hearing, investigation, inquest, or inquiry (whether conducted by a court, administrative agency, hearing officer, arbitrator, legislative body, or any other person authorized by law) in which, pursuant to law, testimony can be compelled to be given. *(Stats.1965, c. 299, § 2, operative Jan. 1, 1967.)*

Law Revision Commission Comments

"Proceeding" is defined to mean all proceedings of whatever kind in which testimony can be compelled by law to be given. It includes civil and criminal actions and proceedings, administrative proceedings, legislative hearings, grand jury proceedings, coroners' inquests, arbitration proceedings, and any other kind of proceeding in which a person can be compelled by law to appear and give evidence. This broad definition is necessary in order that Division 8 may be made applicable to all situations where a person can be compelled to testify. The reasons for giving this broad scope to Division 8 are stated in the Comment to Section 910. [7 Cal.L.Rev.Comm. Reports 1 (1965)].

Research References

Rutter, Cal. Practice Guide: Civil Trials & Evidence Ch. 8E-A, A. Privileges.
Rutter, Cal. Practice Guide: Prof. Responsibility Ch. 7-C, C. Attorney-Client Privilege.

§ 902. Civil proceeding

"Civil proceeding" means any proceeding except a criminal proceeding. *(Stats.1965, c. 299, § 2, operative Jan. 1, 1967.)*

Law Revision Commission Comments

"Civil proceeding" includes not only a civil action or proceeding, but also any nonjudicial proceeding in which, pursuant to law, testimony can be compelled to be given. See Evidence Code §§ 901 and 903. [7 Cal.L.Rev.Comm. Reports 1 (1965)].

§ 903. Criminal proceeding

"Criminal proceeding" means:

(a) A criminal action; and

(b) A proceeding pursuant to Article 3 (commencing with Section 3060) of Chapter 7 of Division 4 of Title 1 of the Government Code to determine whether a public officer should be removed from office for willful or corrupt misconduct in office. *(Stats.1965, c. 299, § 2, operative Jan. 1, 1967.)*

Law Revision Commission Comments

This division treats a proceeding by accusation for the removal of a public officer under Government Code Sections 3060–3073 the same as a criminal action. Proceedings by accusation and criminal actions are so nearly alike in their basic nature that, so far as privileges are concerned, this similar treatment is justified. [7 Cal.L.Rev.Comm. Reports 1 (1965)].

§ 905. Presiding officer

"Presiding officer" means the person authorized to rule on a claim of privilege in the proceeding in which the claim is made. *(Stats.1965, c. 299, § 2, operative Jan. 1, 1967.)*

"Presiding officer" is defined so that reference may be made in Division 8 to the person who makes rulings on questions of privilege in nonjudicial proceedings. The term includes arbitrators, hearing officers, referees, and any other person who is authorized to make rulings on claims of privilege. It, of course, includes the judge or other person presiding in a judicial proceeding. [7 Cal.L.Rev.Comm. Reports 1 (1965)].

CHAPTER 2. APPLICABILITY OF DIVISION

Section
910. Applicability of division.

§ 910. Applicability of division

Except as otherwise provided by statute, the provisions of this division apply in all proceedings. The provisions of any statute making rules of evidence inapplicable in particular proceedings, or limiting the applicability of rules of evidence in particular proceedings, do not make this division inapplicable to such proceedings. *(Stats.1965, c. 299, § 2, operative Jan. 1, 1967.)*

Law Revision Commission Comments

Most rules of evidence are designed for use in courts. Generally, their purpose is to keep unreliable or prejudicial evidence from being presented to the trier of fact. Privileges are granted, however, for reasons of policy unrelated to the reliability of the information involved. A privilege is granted because it is considered more important to keep certain information confidential than it is to require disclosure of all the information relevant to the issues in a pending proceeding. Thus, for example, to protect the attorney-client relationship, it is necessary to prevent disclosure of confidential communications made in the course of that relationship.

If confidentiality is to be protected effectively by a privilege, the privilege must be recognized in proceedings other than judicial proceedings. The protection afforded by a privilege would be insufficient if a court were the only place where the privilege could be invoked. Every officer with power to issue subpoenas for investigative purposes, every administrative agency, every local governing board, and many more persons could pry into the protected information if the privilege rules were applicable only in judicial proceedings.

Therefore, the policy underlying the privilege rules requires their recognition in all proceedings of any nature in which testimony can be compelled by law to be given. Section 910 makes the privilege rules applicable to all such proceedings. In this respect, it follows the precedent set in New Jersey when privilege rules, based in part on the Uniform Rules of Evidence, were enacted. See N.J.Laws 1960, Ch. 52, p. 452 (N.J.Rev.Stat. §§ 2A:84A–1 to 2A:84A–49).

Statutes that relax the rules of evidence in particular proceedings do not have the effect of making privileges inapplicable in such proceedings. For example, Labor Code Section 5708, which provides that the officer conducting an Industrial Accident Commission proceeding "shall not be bound by the common law or statutory rules of evidence," does not make privileges inapplicable in such proceedings. Thus, the lawyer-client privilege must be recognized in an Industrial Accident Commission proceeding. On the other hand, Division 8 and other statutes provide exceptions to particular privileges for particular types of proceedings. *E. g.,* Evidence Code § 998 (physician-patient privilege inapplicable in criminal proceeding); Labor Code §§ 4055, 6407, 6408 (testimony by physician and certain reports of physicians admissible as evidence in Industrial Accident Commission proceedings).

Whether Section 910 is declarative of existing law is uncertain. No California case has squarely decided whether the privileges which are recognized in judicial proceedings are also applicable in nonjudicial proceedings. By statute, however, they have been made applicable in all adjudicatory proceedings conducted under the terms of the Administrative Procedure Act. Govt. Code § 11513. The reported decisions indicate that, as a general rule, privileges are assumed to be applicable in nonjudicial proceedings. See, *e. g.,* McKnew v. Superior Court, 23 Cal.2d 58, 142 P.2d 1 (1943); Ex parte McDonough, 170 Cal. 230, 149 P. 566 (1915); Board of Educ. v. Wilkinson, 125 Cal.App.2d 100, 270 P.2d 82 (1954); In re Bruns, 15 Cal.App.2d 1, 58 P.2d 1318 (1936). Thus, Section 910 appears to be declarative of existing practice, but there is no authority as to whether it is declarative of existing law. Its enactment will remove the existing uncertainty concerning the right to claim a privilege in a nonjudicial proceeding. See generally Tentative Recommendation and a Study Relating to the Uniform Rules of Evidence (Article V. Privileges), 6 Cal.Law Revision Comm'n, Rep., Rec. & Studies 201, 309–327 (1964). [7 Cal.L.Rev.Comm. Reports 1 (1965)].

Research References

Rutter, Cal. Practice Guide: Civil Trials & Evidence Ch. 8E-A, A. Privileges.
Rutter, Cal. Practice Guide: Prof. Responsibility Ch. 7-C, C. Attorney-Client Privilege.

CHAPTER 3. GENERAL PROVISIONS RELATING TO PRIVILEGES

Section
911. Refusal to be or have another as witness, or disclose or produce any matter.
912. Waiver of privilege.
913. Comment on, and inferences from, exercise of privilege.
914. Determination of claim of privilege; limitation on punishment for contempt.
915. Disclosure of privileged information or attorney work product in ruling on claim of privilege.
916. Exclusion of privileged information where persons authorized to claim privilege are not present.
917. Presumption that certain communications are confidential; privileged character of electronic communications.
918. Error in overruling claim of privilege.
919. Admissibility where disclosure erroneously compelled; claim of privilege; coercion.
920. Implied repeal of other statutes related to privileges.

§ 911. Refusal to be or have another as witness, or disclose or produce any matter

Except as otherwise provided by statute:

(a) No person has a privilege to refuse to be a witness.

(b) No person has a privilege to refuse to disclose any matter or to refuse to produce any writing, object, or other thing.

(c) No person has a privilege that another shall not be a witness or shall not disclose any matter or shall not produce any writing, object, or other thing. *(Stats.1965, c. 299, § 2, operative Jan. 1, 1967.)*

Law Revision Commission Comments

This section codifies the existing law that privileges are not recognized in the absence of statute. See Chronicle Pub. Co. v. Superior Court, 54 Cal.2d 548, 565, 7 Cal.Rptr. 109, 117, 354 P.2d 637, 645 (1960); Tatkin v. Superior Court, 160 Cal.App.2d 745, 753, 326 P.2d 201, 205–206 (1958); Whitlow v. Superior Court, 87 Cal.App.2d 175, 196 P.2d 590 (1948). See also 8 Wigmore, Evidence § 2286 (McNaughton rev. 1961); Witkin, California Evidence § 396 at 446 (1958). This is one of the few instances where the Evidence Code precludes the courts from elaborating upon the statutory scheme. Even with respect to privileges, however, the courts to a limited extent are permitted to develop the details of declared principles. See, *e. g.,* Section 1060 (trade secret). [7 Cal.L.Rev.Comm. Reports 1 (1965)].

Research References

Rutter, Cal. Practice Guide: Civ. Pro. Before Trial Ch. 8C-3, "Not Privileged".
Rutter, Cal. Practice Guide: Civil Trials & Evidence Ch. 8C-D, D. Demonstrative Evidence.

Rutter, Cal. Practice Guide: Civil Trials & Evidence Ch. 8E-A, A. Privileges.

§ 912. Waiver of privilege

(a) Except as otherwise provided in this section, the right of any person to claim a privilege provided by Section 954 (lawyer-client privilege), 966 (lawyer referral service-client privilege), 980 (privilege for confidential marital communications), 994 (physician-patient privilege), 1014 (psychotherapist-patient privilege), 1033 (privilege of penitent), 1034 (privilege of * * * clergy member), 1035.8 (sexual assault counselor-victim privilege), or 1037.5 (domestic violence counselor- victim privilege) is waived with respect to a communication protected by the privilege if any holder of the privilege, without coercion, has disclosed a significant part of the communication or has consented to disclosure made by anyone. Consent to disclosure is manifested by any statement or other conduct of the holder of the privilege indicating consent to the disclosure, including failure to claim the privilege in any proceeding in which the holder has the legal standing and opportunity to claim the privilege.

(b) Where two or more persons are joint holders of a privilege provided by Section 954 (lawyer-client privilege), 966 (lawyer referral service-client privilege), 994 (physician-patient privilege), 1014 (psychotherapist-patient privilege), 1035.8 (sexual assault counselor-victim privilege), or 1037.5 (domestic violence counselor-victim privilege), a waiver of the right of a particular joint holder of the privilege to claim the privilege does not affect the right of another joint holder to claim the privilege. In the case of the privilege provided by Section 980 (privilege for confidential marital communications), a waiver of the right of one spouse to claim the privilege does not affect the right of the other spouse to claim the privilege.

(c) A disclosure that is itself privileged is not a waiver of any privilege.

(d) A disclosure in confidence of a communication that is protected by a privilege provided by Section 954 (lawyer-client privilege), 966 (lawyer referral service-client privilege), 994 (physician-patient privilege), 1014 (psychotherapist-patient privilege), 1035.8 (sexual assault counselor-victim privilege), or 1037.5 (domestic violence counselor-victim privilege), when disclosure is reasonably necessary for the accomplishment of the purpose for which the lawyer, lawyer referral service, physician, psychotherapist, sexual assault counselor, or domestic violence counselor was consulted, is not a waiver of the privilege. *(Stats.1965, c. 299, § 2, operative Jan. 1, 1967. Amended by Stats.1980, c. 917, p. 2915, § 1; Stats.2002, c. 72 (S.B.2061), § 1; Stats.2004, c. 405 (S.B.1796), § 1; Stats.2013, c. 123 (A.B.267), § 1.)*

Law Revision Commission Comments

Section 912 is amended to make clear that it applies to the privilege for confidential communications between a domestic violence victim and counselor, which did not exist when the statute was originally enacted in 1965. See Sections 1037–1037.7 (domestic violence victim). [31 Cal. L.Rev.Comm. Reports 255 (2002)].

Research References

Rutter, Cal. Practice Guide: Civ. Pro. Before Trial Ch. 6-C, C. Answer.
Rutter, Cal. Practice Guide: Civ. Pro. Before Trial Ch. 8C-3, "Not Privileged".
Rutter, Cal. Practice Guide: Civ. Pro. Before Trial Ch. 8E-12, Conduct of Deposition.
Rutter, Cal. Practice Guide: Civil Trials & Evidence Ch. 10-A, A. Preliminary Considerations.
Rutter, Cal. Practice Guide: Civil Trials & Evidence Ch. 8E-A, A. Privileges.
Rutter, Cal. Practice Guide: Civil Trials & Evidence Ch. 8E-C, C. Right of Privacy.

California Practice Guide: Employment Litigation Ch. 3-K, K. Right to Independent (Cumis) Counsel.
California Practice Guide: Employment Litigation Ch. 19-F, F. Discovery.
Rutter, Cal. Practice Guide: Family Law Ch. 1-B, B. General Objectives of First Interview.
Rutter, Cal. Practice Guide: Family Law Ch. 7-B, B. Contested Custody Proceedings, Generally.
Rutter, Cal. Practice Guide: Insurance Litigation Ch. 7B-K, K. Insurer's Duty to Provide Independent Counsel When Conflict of Interest Arises.
Rutter, Cal. Practice Guide: Insurance Litigation Ch. 12D-G, G. Insurer's Reliance on Advice of Counsel.
Rutter, Cal. Practice Guide: Personal Injury Ch. 1-D, D. General Concerns and Advice to Client Upon Accepting Employment; Execution of Necessary Authorizations.
Rutter, Cal. Practice Guide: Personal Injury Ch. 4-C, C. Effective Settlement Negotiations.
Rutter, Cal. Practice Guide: Personal Injury Ch. 6-A, A. Scope of Discovery and Limitations.
Rutter, Cal. Practice Guide: Prof. Responsibility Ch. 7-C, C. Attorney-Client Privilege.
Miller and Starr California Real Estate § 25A:23, Type of Action; Time to File; Preparation of Administrative Record.

§ 913. Comment on, and inferences from, exercise of privilege

(a) If in the instant proceeding or on a prior occasion a privilege is or was exercised not to testify with respect to any matter, or to refuse to disclose or to prevent another from disclosing any matter, neither the presiding officer nor counsel may comment thereon, no presumption shall arise because of the exercise of the privilege, and the trier of fact may not draw any inference therefrom as to the credibility of the witness or as to any matter at issue in the proceeding.

(b) The court, at the request of a party who may be adversely affected because an unfavorable inference may be drawn by the jury because a privilege has been exercised, shall instruct the jury that no presumption arises because of the exercise of the privilege and that the jury may not draw any inference therefrom as to the credibility of the witness or as to any matter at issue in the proceeding. *(Stats.1965, c. 299, § 2, operative Jan. 1, 1967.)*

Research References

Rutter, Cal. Practice Guide: Civil Trials & Evidence Ch. 13-B, B. Prop vs. Improper Closing Argument.
Rutter, Cal. Practice Guide: Civil Trials & Evidence Ch. 8E-A, Privileges.
Miller and Starr California Real Estate § 4:42, Disciplinary Proce Hearing Procedure.
3 Witkin Cal. Proc. 5th Actions § 937, Award of Expenses and Fee Prevailing Party.
2 Witkin Cal. Proc. 5th Courts § 86, Evidence.
7 Witkin Cal. Proc. 5th Trial § 225, (S 225) Other Acts.
7 Witkin Cal. Proc. 5th Trial § 253, (S 253) Comment on Evidence.
7 Witkin Cal. Proc. 5th Trial § 299, (S 299) Credibility and Impeach

§ 914. Determination of claim of privilege; limitati punishment for contempt

(a) The presiding officer shall determine a claim of pr in any proceeding in the same manner as a court determin a claim under Article 2 (commencing with Section Chapter 4 of Division 3.

(b) No person may be held in contempt for failure to information claimed to be privileged unless he has comply with an order of a court that he disclose such tion. This subdivision does not apply to any gove agency that has constitutional contempt power, nor do to hearings and investigations of the Industrial Accid mission, nor does it impliedly repeal Chapter 4 (co with Section 9400) of Part 1 of Division 2 of Titl Government Code. If no other statutory procedure ble, the procedure prescribed by Section 1991 of t

Civil Procedure shall be followed in seeking an order of a court that the person disclose the information claimed to be privileged. *(Stats.1965, c. 299, § 2, operative Jan. 1, 1967.)*

Research References

Rutter, Cal. Practice Guide: Civil Trials & Evidence Ch. 8E-A, A. Privileges.
Rutter, Cal. Practice Guide: Prof. Responsibility Ch. 7-C, C. Attorney-Client Privilege.

§ 915. Disclosure of privileged information or attorney work product in ruling on claim of privilege

(a) Subject to subdivision (b), the presiding officer may not require disclosure of information claimed to be privileged under this division or attorney work product under subdivision (a) of Section 2018.030 of the Code of Civil Procedure in order to rule on the claim of privilege; provided, however, that in any hearing conducted pursuant to subdivision (c) of Section 1524 of the Penal Code in which a claim of privilege is made and the court determines that there is no other feasible means to rule on the validity of the claim other than to require disclosure, the court shall proceed in accordance with subdivision (b).

(b) When a court is ruling on a claim of privilege under Article 9 (commencing with Section 1040) of Chapter 4 (official information and identity of informer) or under Section 1060 (trade secret) or under subdivision (b) of Section 2018.030 of the Code of Civil Procedure (attorney work product) and is unable to do so without requiring disclosure of the information claimed to be privileged, the court may require the person from whom disclosure is sought or the person authorized to claim the privilege, or both, to disclose the information in chambers out of the presence and hearing of all persons except the person authorized to claim the privilege and any other persons as the person authorized to claim the privilege is willing to have present.

If the judge determines that the information is privileged, neither the judge nor any other person may ever disclose, without the consent of a person authorized to permit disclosure, what was disclosed in the course of the proceedings in chambers. *(Stats.1965, c. 299, § 2, operative Jan. 1, 1967. Amended by Stats.1979, c. 1034, p. 3572, § 1; Stats.2001, c. 812 (S.B.205), § 13; Stats.2004, c. 182 (A.B.3081), § 29, operative July 1, 2005.)*

Law Revision Commission Comments

Subdivision (a) states the general rule that revelation of the information claimed to be privileged may not be compelled in order to determine whether it is privileged. This codifies existing law. See Collette v. Sarrasin, 184 Cal. 283, 288–289, 193 Pac. 571, 573 (1920); People v. Glen Arms Estate, Inc., 230 Cal.App.2d 841, 846 note 1, 41 Cal.Rptr. 303, 305

Subdivision (b) provides an exception to this general rule for information claimed to be privileged under Section 1040 (official information), 1041 (identity of an informer), or Section 1060 (trade secret). In these cases, generally if the interest in maintaining the secrecy of the information and the interest in seeing that justice is done in the particular case... In some cases, it will be necessary for the judge to examine the matter claimed to be privileged in order to balance these conflicting interests intelligently. See People v. Glen Arms Estate, Inc., supra, 841, 846 note 1, 41 Cal.Rptr. 303, 305 note 1... discussion thereof in 8 Wigmore, Evidence § 2379 at 812 note 6... and see United States v. Reynolds, 345 U.S. 1, ... discussion thereof in 8 Wigmore, Evidence ... (1961). Even in these cases, Section 915 affords some protection to the person claiming the privilege... information be disclosed in confidence to ... be kept in confidence if it is found to be ...

... applies only when a court is ruling on ... review of subdivision (a), disclosure of the ... for example, in an administrative ... Reports 1 (1965)].

Section 915 is amended to reflect nonsubstantive reorganization of the rules governing civil discovery. [33 Cal.L.Rev.Comm. Reports 1015 (2004)].

Research References

Rutter, Cal. Practice Guide: Civ. Pro. Before Trial Ch. 8C-3, "Not Privileged".
Rutter, Cal. Practice Guide: Civ. Pro. Before Trial Ch. 8C-4, Attorney Work Product Protection.
Rutter, Cal. Practice Guide: Civ. Pro. Before Trial Ch. 8H-5, Protective Orders.
Rutter, Cal. Practice Guide: Civil Trials & Evidence Ch. 8E-A, A. Privileges.
Rutter, Cal. Practice Guide: Civil Trials & Evidence Ch. 8E-B, B. Attorney Work Product Doctrine.
California Practice Guide: Employment Litigation Ch. 13-H, H. Contesting Citations and Related Orders and Notices.
Rutter, Cal. Practice Guide: Family Law Ch. 11-C, C. Optional "Formal" Discovery Procedures.
Rutter, Cal. Practice Guide: Insurance Litigation Ch. 15-G, G. Discovery.
Rutter, Cal. Practice Guide: Personal Injury Ch. 6-A, A. Scope of Discovery and Limitations.
Rutter, Cal. Practice Guide: Prof. Responsibility Ch. 7-C, C. Attorney-Client Privilege.

§ 916. Exclusion of privileged information where persons authorized to claim privilege are not present

(a) The presiding officer, on his own motion or on the motion of any party, shall exclude information that is subject to a claim of privilege under this division if:

(1) The person from whom the information is sought is not a person authorized to claim the privilege; and

(2) There is no party to the proceeding who is a person authorized to claim the privilege.

(b) The presiding officer may not exclude information under this section if:

(1) He is otherwise instructed by a person authorized to permit disclosure; or

(2) The proponent of the evidence establishes that there is no person authorized to claim the privilege in existence. *(Stats. 1965, c. 299, § 2, operative Jan. 1, 1967.)*

Research References

Rutter, Cal. Practice Guide: Civil Trials & Evidence Ch. 8E-A, A. Privileges.

§ 917. Presumption that certain communications are confidential; privileged character of electronic communications

(a) If a privilege is claimed on the ground that the matter sought to be disclosed is a communication made in confidence in the course of the lawyer-client, physician-patient, psychotherapist-patient, clergy-penitent, husband-wife, sexual assault counselor-victim, or domestic violence counselor-victim relationship, the communication is presumed to have been made in confidence and the opponent of the claim of privilege has the burden of proof to establish that the communication was not confidential.

(b) A communication between persons in a relationship listed in subdivision (a) does not lose its privileged character for the sole reason that it is communicated by electronic means or because persons involved in the delivery, facilitation, or storage of electronic communication may have access to the content of the communication.

(c) For purposes of this section, "electronic" has the same meaning provided in Section 1633.2 of the Civil Code. *(Stats. 1965, c. 299, § 2, operative Jan. 1, 1967. Amended by Stats.2002, c. 72 (S.B.2061), § 2; Stats.2003, c. 468 (S.B.851), § 2; Stats. 2004, c. 183 (A.B.3082), § 93; Stats.2006, c. 689 (S.B.1743), § 2.)*

Evidence

Law Revision Commission Comments

Subdivision (a) of Section 917 is amended to make clear that it also applies to confidential communication privileges created after its original enactment in 1965. See Sections 1035–1036.2 (sexual assault victim), 1037–1037.7 (domestic violence victim). The presumption set forth in subdivision (a) applies regardless of how a communication is transmitted. In each instance, the opponent of the claim of privilege has the burden of proof to establish that the communication was not confidential.

Subdivision (b) is drawn from New York law (N.Y. C.P.L.R. 4548 (McKinney 2001)) and from language formerly found in Section 952 relating to confidentiality of an electronic communication between a client and a lawyer. For waiver of privileges, see Section 912 & Comment.

Under subdivision (c), the definition of "electronic" is broad, including any "intangible media which are technologically capable of storing, transmitting and reproducing information in human perceivable form." Unif. Electronic Transactions Act, § 2 comment (1999) (enacted as Civ. Code § 1633.2).

For discussion of ethical considerations where a lawyer communicates with a client by electronic means, see Bus. & Prof. Code § 6068(e) (attorney has duty to "maintain inviolate the confidence, and at every peril to himself or herself to preserve the secrets, of his or her client"); ABA Standing Committee on Ethics & Professional Responsibility, Formal Op. 99–413 ("Protecting the Confidentiality of Unencrypted E–Mail"); ABA Standing Committee on Ethics & Professional Responsibility, Formal Op. 92–368 ("Inadvertent Disclosure of Confidential Materials").

For examples of provisions on the admissibility of electronic communications, see Evid. Code §§ 1521 & Comment (Secondary Evidence Rule), 1552 (printed representation of computer information or computer program), 1553 (printed representation of images stored on video or digital medium); Civ. Code § 1633.13 ("In a proceeding, evidence of a record or signature may not be excluded solely because it is in electronic form."). See also People v. Martinez, 22 Cal.4th 106, 990 P.2d 563, 91 Cal.Rptr.2d 687 (2000); People v. Hernandez, 55 Cal.App.4th 225, 63 Cal.Rptr.2d 769 (1997); Aguimatang v. California State Lottery, 234 Cal.App.3d 769, 286 Cal.Rptr. 57 (1991); People v. Lugashi, 205 Cal. App.3d 632, 252 Cal.Rptr. 434 (1988). [31 Cal.L.Rev.Comm. Reports 256 (2002)].

Research References

Rutter, Cal. Practice Guide: Civ. Pro. Before Trial Ch. 8C-3, "Not Privileged".

Rutter, Cal. Practice Guide: Civil Trials & Evidence Ch. 8E-A, A. Privileges.

California Practice Guide: Employment Litigation Ch. 5-K, K. Invasion of Privacy.

Rutter, Cal. Practice Guide: Personal Injury Ch. 6-A, A. Scope of Discovery and Limitations.

Rutter, Cal. Practice Guide: Prof. Responsibility Ch. 7-C, C. Attorney-Client Privilege.

§ 918. Error in overruling claim of privilege

A party may predicate error on a ruling disallowing a claim of privilege only if he is the holder of the privilege, except that a party may predicate error on a ruling disallowing a claim of privilege by his spouse under Section 970 or 971. *(Stats.1965, c. 299, § 2, operative Jan. 1, 1967.)*

Law Revision Commission Comments

This section is consistent with existing law. See People v. Gonzales, 56 Cal.App. 330, 204 Pac. 1088 (1922), and discussion of similar cases cited in Tentative Recommendation and a Study Relating to the Uniform Rules of Evidence (Article V. Privileges), 6 Cal.Law Revision Comm'n, Rep., Rec. & Studies 201, 525 note 5 (1964). [7 Cal.L.Rev.Comm. Reports 1 (1965)].

Research References

Rutter, Cal. Practice Guide: Civil Trials & Evidence Ch. 8E-A, A. Privileges.

§ 919. Admissibility where disclosure erroneously compelled; claim of privilege; coercion

(a) Evidence of a statement or other disclosure of privileged information is inadmissible against a holder of the privilege if:

(1) A person authorized to claim the privilege claimed it but nevertheless disclosure erroneously was required to be made; or

(2) The presiding officer did not exclude the privileged information as required by Section 916.

(b) If a person authorized to claim the privilege claimed it, whether in the same or a prior proceeding, but nevertheless disclosure erroneously was required by the presiding officer to be made, neither the failure to refuse to disclose nor the failure to seek review of the order of the presiding officer requiring disclosure indicates consent to the disclosure or constitutes a waiver and, under these circumstances, the disclosure is one made under coercion. *(Stats.1965, c. 299, § 2, operative Jan. 1, 1967. Amended by Stats.1974, c. 227, p. 426, § 1.)*

Law Revision Commission Comments

Section 919 protects a holder of a privilege from the detriment he would otherwise suffer in a later proceeding when, in a prior proceeding, the presiding officer erroneously overruled a claim of privilege and compelled revelation of the privileged information. Although Section 912 provides that such a coerced disclosure does not waive a privilege, it does not provide specifically that evidence of the prior disclosure is inadmissible; Section 919 assures the inadmissibility of such evidence in the subsequent proceeding.

Section 919 probably states existing law. See People v. Abair, 102 Cal.App.2d 765, 228 P.2d 336 (1951) (prior disclosure by an attorney held inadmissible in a later proceeding where the holder of the privilege had first opportunity to object to attorney's testifying). See also People v. Kor, 129 Cal.App.2d 436, 277 P.2d 94 (1954). However, there is little case authority upon the proposition. [7 Cal.L.Rev.Comm. Reports 1 (1965)].

Subdivision (b) has been added to Section 919 to make clear that, after disclosure of privileged information has been erroneously required to be made by order of a trial court or other presiding officer, neither the failure to refuse to disclose nor the failure to challenge the order (by, for example, a petition for a writ of habeas corpus or other special writ or by an appeal from a contempt order) amounts to a waiver and the disclosure is one made under coercion for the purposes of Sections 912(a) and 919(a) (1). See Section 905 (defining "presiding officer"). The addition of subdivision (b) will preclude any possibility of a contrary interpretation of Sections 912 and 919 based on the language found in Markwell v. Sykes, 173 Cal.App.2d 642, 649–650, 343 P.2d 769, 773–774 (1959). See Recommendation Relating to Erroneously Ordered Disclosure of Privileged Information, 11 Cal.L. Revision Comm'n Reports 1163 (1973).

The phrase "whether in the same or a prior proceeding" has been included in subdivision (b) to avoid any implication that might be drawn from the original Law Revision Commission Comment to Section 919 that subdivision (a) (1) applies only where the privilege was claimed in a prior proceeding. The protection afforded by Section 919, of course, also applies where a claim of privilege is made at an earlier stage in the same proceeding and the presiding officer erroneously overruled the claim and ordered disclosure of the privileged information to be made. [11 Cal.L.Rev.Comm. Reports 1163 (1974)].

Research References

Rutter, Cal. Practice Guide: Civil Trials & Evidence Ch. 8E-A, A. Privileges.

Rutter, Cal. Practice Guide: Prof. Responsibility Ch. 7-C, C. Attorney-Client Privilege.

§ 920. Implied repeal of other statutes related to privileges

Nothing in this division shall be construed to repeal by implication any other statute relating to privileges. *(Stats.1965, c. 299, § 2, operative Jan. 1, 1967.)*

Law Revision Commission Comments

Some of the statutes relating to privileges are found in other codes and are continued in force. See, *e.g.*, Penal Code §§ 266h and 266i (making the marital communications privilege inapplicable in prosecutions for pimping and pandering respectively). Section 920 assures that nothing in this division makes privileged any information declared by statute to be unprivileged or makes unprivileged any information declared by statute to be privileged. [7 Cal.L.Rev. Reports 1 (1965)].

CHAPTER 4. PARTICULAR PRIVILEGES

ARTICLE 1. PRIVILEGE OF DEFENDANT IN CRIMINAL CASE

Section
930. Privilege not to be called as a witness and not to testify.

§ 930. Privilege not to be called as a witness and not to testify

To the extent that such privilege exists under the Constitution of the United States or the State of California, a defendant in a criminal case has a privilege not to be called as a witness and not to testify. *(Stats.1965, c. 299, § 2, operative Jan. 1, 1967.)*

Law Revision Commission Comments

Section 930 recognizes that the defendant in a criminal case has a constitutional privilege not to be called as a witness and not to testify. Cal.Const., Art. I, § 13 [so in original; probably should read § 15]. See Killpatrick v. Superior Court, 153 Cal.App.2d 146, 314 P.2d 164 (1957); People v. Talle, 111 Cal.App.2d 650, 245 P.2d 633 (1952). Section 930 also recognizes that the defendant may have a similar privilege under the United States Constitution. See Malloy v. Hogan, 378 U.S. 1 (1964). [7 Cal.L.Rev.Comm. Reports 1 (1965)].

Research References

Rutter, Cal. Practice Guide: Civil Trials & Evidence Ch. 8E-A, A. Privileges.
2 Witkin Cal. Proc. 5th Courts § 301, (S 301) Admission and Exclusion of Evidence.

ARTICLE 2. PRIVILEGE AGAINST SELF–INCRIMINATION

Section
940. Privilege against self-incrimination.

§ 940. Privilege against self-incrimination

To the extent that such privilege exists under the Constitution of the United States or the State of California, a person has a privilege to refuse to disclose any matter that may tend to incriminate him. *(Stats.1965, c. 299, § 2, operative Jan. 1, 1967.)*

Law Revision Commission Comments

Section 940 recognizes the privilege (derived from the California and United States Constitutions) of a person to refuse, when testifying, to give information that might tend to incriminate him. See Fross v. Wotton, 3 Cal.2d 384, 44 P.2d 350 (1935); In re Leavitt, 174 Cal.App.2d 535, 345 P.2d 75 (1959). This privilege should be distinguished from the privilege

stated in Section 930 (privilege of defendant in a criminal case to refuse to testify at all).

Section 940 does not determine the scope of the privilege against self-incrimination; the scope of the privilege is determined by the pertinent provisions of the California and United States Constitutions as interpreted by the courts. See Cal.Const., Art. I, § 13 [so in original; probably should read § 15]. See also Malloy v. Hogan, 378 U.S. 1 (1964). Nor does Section 940 prescribe the exceptions to the privilege or indicate when it has been waived. This, too, is determined by the cases interpreting the pertinent provisions of the California and United States Constitutions. For a statement of the scope of the constitutional privilege and some of its exceptions, see Tentative Recommendation and a Study Relating to the Uniform Rules of Evidence (Article V. Privileges), 6 Cal.Law Revision Comm'n, Rep., Rec. & Studies 201, 215–218, 343–377 (1964). [7 Cal.L.Rev.Comm. Reports 1 (1965)].

Research References

Rutter, Cal. Practice Guide: Civ. Pro. Before Trial Ch. 8C-3, "Not Privileged".
Rutter, Cal. Practice Guide: Civil Trials & Evidence Ch. 4-B, B. Preliminary Matters Discussed in Final Status Conference or In-Chambers Conference.
Rutter, Cal. Practice Guide: Civil Trials & Evidence Ch. 8E-A, A. Privileges.
Rutter, Cal. Practice Guide: Civil Trials & Evidence Ch. 8G-B, B. Procedures on Objection.
Rutter, Cal. Practice Guide: Family Law Ch. 11-C, C. Optional "Formal" Discovery Procedures.
Rutter, Cal. Practice Guide: Personal Injury Ch. 6-A, A. Scope of Discovery and Limitations.
Rutter, Cal. Practice Guide: Personal Injury Ch. 9-E, E. Order of Trial and Proof and Related Matters.

ARTICLE 3. LAWYER–CLIENT PRIVILEGE

Section
950. Lawyer.
951. Client.
952. Confidential communication between client and lawyer.
953. Holder of the privilege.
954. Lawyer-client privilege.
955. When lawyer required to claim privilege.
956. Exception: Crime or fraud.
956.5. Exception: Prevention of criminal act likely to result in death or substantial bodily harm.
957. Exception: Parties claiming through deceased client.
958. Exception: Breach of duty arising out of lawyer-client relationship.
959. Exception: Lawyer as attesting witness.
960. Exception: Intention of deceased client concerning writing affecting property interest.
961. Exception: Validity of writing affecting property interest.
962. Exception: Joint clients.

§ 950. Lawyer

As used in this article, "lawyer" means a person authorized, or reasonably believed by the client to be authorized, to practice law in any state or nation. *(Stats.1965, c. 299, § 2, operative Jan. 1, 1967.)*

Law Revision Commission Comments

"Lawyer" is defined to include a person "reasonably believed by the client to be authorized" to practice law. Since the privilege is intended to encourage full disclosure, the client's reasonable belief that the person he is consulting is an attorney is sufficient to justify application of the privilege. See 8 Wigmore, Evidence § 2302 (McNaughton rev. 1961), and cases there cited in note 1. See also McCormick, Evidence § 92 (1954).

There is no requirement that the lawyer be licensed to practice in a jurisdiction that recognizes the lawyer-client privilege. Legal transactions frequently cross state and national boundaries and require consultation with attorneys from many different jurisdictions. When a California resident travels outside the State and has occasion to consult a lawyer during such travel, or when a lawyer from another state or nation participates in a transaction involving a California client, the client should be entitled to assume that his communications will be given as much protection as they would be if he consulted a California lawyer in California. A client should not be forced to inquire about the jurisdictions where the lawyer is authorized to practice and whether such jurisdictions recognize the lawyer-client privilege before he may safely communicate with the lawyer. [7 Cal.L.Rev.Comm. Reports 1 (1965)].

Research References

Rutter, Cal. Practice Guide: Civ. Pro. Before Trial Ch. 8C-3, "Not Privileged".

Rutter, Cal. Practice Guide: Civil Trials & Evidence Ch. 8E-A, A. Privileges.

Rutter, Cal. Practice Guide: Civil Trials & Evidence Ch. 8E-B, B. Attorney Work Product Doctrine.

Rutter, Cal. Practice Guide: Family Law Ch. 1-B, B. General Objectives of First Interview.

Rutter, Cal. Practice Guide: Family Law Ch. 11-C, C. Optional "Formal" Discovery Procedures.

Rutter, Cal. Practice Guide: Landlord-Tenant Ch. 1-B, B. Accepting a New Case.

Rutter, Cal. Practice Guide: Personal Injury Ch. 1-A, A. Initial Client Interview.

Rutter, Cal. Practice Guide: Personal Injury Ch. 4-C, C. Effective Settlement Negotiations.

Rutter, Cal. Practice Guide: Personal Injury Ch. 6-A, A. Scope of Discovery and Limitations.

Rutter, Cal. Practice Guide: Prof. Responsibility Ch. 7-C, C. Attorney-Client Privilege.

Rutter, Cal. Practice Guide: Prof. Responsibility Ch. 7-D, D. Attorney Work Product Doctrine.

Rutter, Cal. Practice Guide: Prof. Responsibility Ch. 7-E, E. Mediation Confidentiality.

14 Witkin, California Summary 10th Wills and Probate § 20, (S 20) Transfer of Documents.

§ 951. Client

As used in this article, "client" means a person who, directly or through an authorized representative, consults a lawyer for the purpose of retaining the lawyer or securing legal service or advice from him in his professional capacity, and includes an incompetent (a) who himself so consults the lawyer or (b) whose guardian or conservator so consults the lawyer in behalf of the incompetent. *(Stats.1965, c. 299, § 2, operative Jan. 1, 1967.)*

Law Revision Commission Comments

Under Section 951, public entities have a privilege insofar as communications made in the course of the lawyer-client relationship are concerned. This codifies existing law. See Holm v. Superior Court, 42 Cal.2d 500, 267 P.2d 1025 (1954). Likewise, such unincorporated organizations as labor unions, social clubs, and fraternal societies have a lawyer-client privilege when the organization (rather than its individual members) is the client. See Evidence Code § 175 (defining "person") and § 200 (defining "public entity"). [7 Cal.L.Rev.Comm. Reports 1 (1965)].

Research References

Rutter, Cal. Practice Guide: Civil Trials & Evidence Ch. 8E-A, A. Privileges.

Rutter, Cal. Practice Guide: Enforcing Judgments/Debts Ch. 1-B, B. Accepting the Collection Case.

Rutter, Cal. Practice Guide: Insurance Litigation Ch. 11-I, I. Conspiracy.

Rutter, Cal. Practice Guide: Personal Injury Ch. 1-B, B. Initial Evaluation of Case: Decision to Accept or Reject Employment or Undertake Further Evaluation of Claim.

Rutter, Cal. Practice Guide: Personal Injury Ch. 6-A, A. Scope of Discovery and Limitations.

Rutter, Cal. Practice Guide: Prof. Responsibility Ch. 3-A, A. Nature of Attorney-Client Relationship.

Rutter, Cal. Practice Guide: Prof. Responsibility Ch. 3-C, C. Identifying "Client".

Rutter, Cal. Practice Guide: Prof. Responsibility Ch. 7-C, C. Attorney-Client Privilege.

§ 952. Confidential communication between client and lawyer

As used in this article, "confidential communication between client and lawyer" means information transmitted between a client and his or her lawyer in the course of that relationship and in confidence by a means which, so far as the client is aware, discloses the information to no third persons other than those who are present to further the interest of the client in the consultation or those to whom disclosure is reasonably necessary for the transmission of the information or the accomplishment of the purpose for which the lawyer is consulted, and includes a legal opinion formed and the advice given by the lawyer in the course of that relationship. *(Stats.1965, c. 299, § 2, operative Jan. 1, 1967. Amended by Stats.1967, c. 650, p. 2006, § 3; Stats.1994, c. 186 (A.B.2662), § 1; Stats.1994, c. 587 (A.B.3600), § 9; Stats.2002, c. 72 (S.B.2061), § 3.)*

Law Revision Commission Comments

The requirement that the communication be made in the course of the lawyer-client relationship and be confidential is in accord with existing law. See City & County of San Francisco v. Superior Court, 37 Cal.2d 227, 234–235, 231 P.2d 26, 29–30 (1951).

Confidential communications also include those made to third parties—such as the lawyer's secretary, a physician, or similar expert—for the purpose of transmitting such information to the lawyer because they are "reasonably necessary for the transmission of the information." This codifies existing law. See, *e.g.,* City & County of San Francisco v. Superior Court, *supra* (communication to a physician); Loftin v. Glaser, Civil No. 789604 (L.A.Super.Ct., July 23, 1964) (communication to an accountant), as reported in Los Angeles Daily Journal Report Section, August 25, 1964 (memorandum opinion of Judge Philbrick McCoy).

A lawyer at times may desire to have a client reveal information to an expert consultant in order that the lawyer may adequately advise his client. The inclusion of the words "or the accomplishment of the purpose for which the lawyer is consulted" assures that these communications, too, are within the scope of the privilege. This part of the definition may change existing law. Himmelfarb v. United States, 175 F.2d 924, 938–939 (9th Cir.1949), applying California law, held that the presence of an accountant during a lawyer-client consultation destroyed the privilege, but no California case directly in point has been found. Of course, if the expert consultant is acting merely as a conduit for communications from the client to the attorney, the doctrine of City & County of San Francisco v. Superior Court, *supra,* applies and the communication would be privileged under existing law as well as under this section. See also Evidence Code § 912(d) and the Comment thereto.

The words "other than those who are present to further the interest of the client in the consultation" indicate that a communication to a lawyer is nonetheless confidential even though it is made in the presence of another person—such as a spouse, parent, business associate, or joint client—who is present to further the interest of the client in the consultation. These words refer, too, to another person and his attorney who may meet with the client and his attorney in regard to a matter of joint concern. This may change existing law, for the presence of a third person sometimes has been held to destroy the confidential character of the consultation, even where the third person was present because of his concern for the welfare of the client. See Attorney-Client Privilege in California, 10 Stan. L. Rev 297, 308 (1958), and authorities there cited in notes 67–71. See also Himmelfarb v. United States, *supra*. [7 Cal.L.Rev.Comm. Reports 1 (1965)].

The express inclusion of "a legal opinion" in the last clause will preclude a possible construction of this section that would leave the attorney's uncommunicated legal opinion—which includes his impressions and conclusions—unprotected by the privilege. Such a construction would virtually destroy the privilege. [8 Cal.L.Rev.Comm. Reports 101 (1967)].

Section 952 is amended to delete the last sentence concerning confidentiality of electronic communications, because this rule is generalized in Section 917(b)-(c) applicable to all confidential communication privileges. [31 Cal.L.Rev.Comm. Reports 258 (2002)].

Evidence

Research References

Rutter, Cal. Practice Guide: Civ. Pro. Before Trial Ch. 1-A, A. Accepting a New Case.

Rutter, Cal. Practice Guide: Civ. Pro. Before Trial Ch. 8C-3, "Not Privileged".

Rutter, Cal. Practice Guide: Civ. Pro. Before Trial Gen. Matls., Highlights.

Rutter, Cal. Practice Guide: Civil Trials & Evidence Ch. 17-E, E. Attorney Fees as Costs.

Rutter, Cal. Practice Guide: Civil Trials & Evidence Ch. 8E-A, A. Privileges.

California Practice Guide: Employment Litigation Ch. 2-J, J. Confidential and Privileged Information.

Rutter, Cal. Practice Guide: Family Law Ch. 1-E, E. Attorney Fees and Costs Arrangements.

Rutter, Cal. Practice Guide: Landlord-Tenant Ch. 1-B, B. Accepting a New Case.

Rutter, Cal. Practice Guide: Personal Injury Ch. 1-C, C. Formation of Attorney-Client Relationship: the Employment Agreement.

Rutter, Cal. Practice Guide: Personal Injury Ch. 6-A, A. Scope of Discovery and Limitations.

Rutter, Cal. Practice Guide: Real Prop. Transactions Ch. 1-B, B. Attorney Competence, Conflicts of Interest and Initial Client Communications.

Rutter, Cal. Practice Guide: Real Prop. Transactions Ch. 1-C, C. Attorney Fees and Costs Agreements.

Rutter, Cal. Practice Guide: Prof. Responsibility Ch. 7-A, A. Introduction.

Rutter, Cal. Practice Guide: Prof. Responsibility Ch. 7-B, B. Duty to Maintain Client Confidence and Secrets Under State Bar Act.

Rutter, Cal. Practice Guide: Prof. Responsibility Ch. 7-C, C. Attorney-Client Privilege.

Rutter, Cal. Practice Guide: Prof. Responsibility Ch. 7-B, Outline B.

1 Witkin Cal. Proc. 5th Attorneys § 156, When Written Agreement is Required.

§ 953. Holder of the privilege

As used in this article, "holder of the privilege" means:

(a) The client, if the client has no guardian or conservator.

(b) A guardian or conservator of the client, if the client has a guardian or conservator.

(c) The personal representative of the client if the client is dead, including a personal representative appointed pursuant to Section 12252 of the Probate Code.

(d) A successor, assign, trustee in dissolution, or any similar representative of a firm, association, organization, partnership, business trust, corporation, or public entity that is no longer in existence. *(Stats.1965, c. 299, § 2, operative Jan. 1, 1967. Amended by Stats.2009, c. 8 (A.B.1163), § 1.)*

Law Revision Commission Comments

Under subdivisions (a) and (b), the guardian of a client is the holder of the privilege if the client has a guardian, and the client becomes the holder of the privilege when he no longer has a guardian. For example, if an underage client or his guardian consults a lawyer, the guardian is the holder of the privilege under subdivision (b) until the guardianship is terminated; thereafter, the client himself is the holder of the privilege. The present California law is uncertain. The statutes do not deal with the problem, and no appellate decision has discussed it.

Under subdivision (c), the personal representative of a client is the holder of the privilege when the client is dead. He may either claim or waive the privilege on behalf of the deceased client. This may be a change in California law. Under existing law, it seems probable that the privilege survives the death of the client and that no one can waive it after the client's death. See Collette v. Sarrasin, 184 Cal. 283, 289, 193 Pac. 571, 573 (1920). Hence, the privilege apparently is recognized even when it would be clearly to the interest of the estate of the deceased client to waive it. Under Section 953, however, the personal representative of a deceased client may waive the privilege. The purpose underlying the privilege—to provide a client with the assurance of confidentiality—does not require the recognition of the privilege when to do so is detrimental to his interest or to the interests of his estate. [7 Cal.L.Rev.Comm. Reports 1 (1965)].

Subdivision (a) of Section 953 is amended to revise a gender reference.

Subdivision (c) is amended to make clear that a personal representative holds the decedent's lawyer-client privilege at any time while the personal representative has duties as a personal representative, including, without limitation, during any subsequent estate administration. See, e.g., Prob. Code § 12252 (appointment of personal representative for subsequent administration of estate); see also Prob. Code § 58 (personal representative). The personal representative holds the privilege during any action asserted, commenced, continued, or defended by a personal representative. See Code Civ. Proc. §§ 377.30 (commencement of surviving action by personal representative), 377.31 (continuation of surviving action by personal representative), 377.40 (defense by personal representative of surviving action), 377.60 (assertion by personal representative of wrongful death action); Prob. Code §§ 9000–9399 (creditor claims against estate). [38 Cal. L. Revision Comm'n Reports 163 (2008)].

Research References

Rutter, Cal. Practice Guide: Civil Trials & Evidence Ch. 8E-A, A. Privileges.

Rutter, Cal. Practice Guide: Civil Trials & Evidence Ch. 8E-B, B. Attorney Work Product Doctrine.

Rutter, Cal. Practice Guide: Personal Injury Ch. 6-A, A. Scope of Discovery and Limitations.

Rutter, Cal. Practice Guide: Prof. Responsibility Ch. 7-C, C. Attorney-Client Privilege.

Rutter, Cal. Practice Guide: Prof. Responsibility Ch. 7-D, D. Attorney Work Product Doctrine.

14 Witkin, California Summary 10th Wills and Probate § 744, Administration After Discharge.

§ 954. Lawyer-client privilege

Subject to Section 912 and except as otherwise provided in this article, the client, whether or not a party, has a privilege to refuse to disclose, and to prevent another from disclosing, a confidential communication between client and lawyer if the privilege is claimed by:

(a) The holder of the privilege;

(b) A person who is authorized to claim the privilege by the holder of the privilege; or

(c) The person who was the lawyer at the time of the confidential communication, but such person may not claim the privilege if there is no holder of the privilege in existence or if he is otherwise instructed by a person authorized to permit disclosure.

The relationship of attorney and client shall exist between a law corporation as defined in Article 10 (commencing with Section 6160) of Chapter 4 of Division 3 of the Business and Professions Code and the persons to whom it renders professional services, as well as between such persons and members of the State Bar employed by such corporation to render services to such persons. The word "persons" as used in this subdivision includes partnerships, corporations, limited liability companies, associations and other groups and entities. *(Stats.1965, c. 299, § 2, operative Jan. 1, 1967. Amended by Stats.1968, c. 1375, p. 2695, § 2; Stats.1994, c. 1010 (S.B.2053), § 104.)*

Law Revision Commission Comments

Section 954 is the basic statement of the lawyer-client privilege. Exceptions to this privilege are stated in Sections 956–962.

Persons entitled to claim the privilege. The persons entitled to claim the privilege are specified in subdivisions (a), (b), and (c). See Evidence Code § 953 for the definition of "holder of the privilege."

Eavesdroppers. Under Section 954, the lawyer-client privilege can be asserted to prevent *anyone* from testifying to a confidential communication. Thus, clients are protected against the risk of disclosure by eavesdroppers and other wrongful interceptors of confidential communications between lawyer and client. Probably no such protection was provided prior to the enactment of Penal Code Sections 653i and 653j. See People v. Castiel, 153 Cal.App.2d 653, 315 P.2d 79 (1957). See also Attorney-Client Privilege in California, 10 Stan. L. Rev 297, 310–312 (1958), and cases there cited in note 84.

Penal Code Section 653j makes evidence obtained by *electronic* eavesdropping or recording in violation of the section inadmissible in "any judicial, administrative, legislative, or other proceeding." The section also provides a criminal penalty and contains definitions and exceptions. Penal Code Section 653i makes it a felony to eavesdrop by an electronic or other device upon a conversation between a person in custody of a public officer or on public property and that person's lawyer, religious advisor, or physician.

Section 954 is consistent with Penal Code Sections 653i and 653j but provides broader protection, for it protects against disclosure of confidential communications by anyone who obtained knowledge of the communication without the client's consent. See also Evidence Code § 912 (when disclosure with client's consent constitutes a waiver of the privilege). The use of the privilege to prevent testimony by eavesdroppers and those to whom the communication was wrongfully disclosed does not, however, affect the rule that the making of the communication under circumstances where others could easily overhear it is evidence that the client did not intend the communication to be confidential. See Sharon v. Sharon, 79 Cal. 633, 677, 22 Pac. 26, 39 (1889).

Termination of privilege. The privilege may be claimed by a person listed in Section 954, or the privileged information excluded by the presiding officer under Section 916, only if there is a holder of the privilege in existence. Hence, the privilege ceases to exist when the client's estate is finally distributed and his personal representative is discharged. This is apparently a change in California law. Under the existing law, it seems likely that the privilege continues to exist indefinitely after the client's death and that no one has authority to waive the privilege. See Collette v. Sarrasin, 184 Cal. 283, 193 Pac. 571 (1920). See generally Paley v. Superior Court, 137 Cal.App.2d 450, 290 P.2d 617 (1955), and discussion of the analogous situation in connection with the physician-patient privilege in Tentative Recommendation and a Study Relating to the Uniform Rules of Evidence (Article V. Privileges), 6 Cal.Law Revision Comm'n, Rep., Rec. & Studies 201, 408–410 (1964). Although there is good reason for maintaining the privilege while the estate is being administered—particularly if the estate is involved in litigation—there is little reason to preserve secrecy at the expense of excluding relevant evidence after the estate is wound up and the representative is discharged. [7 Cal.L.Rev.Comm. Reports 1 (1965)].

Research References

Rutter, Cal. Practice Guide: Civ. Pro. Before Trial Ch. 1-A, A. Accepting a New Case.
Rutter, Cal. Practice Guide: Civil Trials & Evidence Ch. 4-B, B. Preliminary Matters Discussed in Final Status Conference or In-Chambers Conference.
Rutter, Cal. Practice Guide: Civil Trials & Evidence Ch. 17-E, E. Attorney Fees as Costs.
Rutter, Cal. Practice Guide: Civil Trials & Evidence Ch. 8E-A, A. Privileges.
California Practice Guide: Employment Litigation Ch. 2-J, J. Confidential and Privileged Information.
Rutter, Cal. Practice Guide: Personal Injury Ch. 6-A, A. Scope of Discovery and Limitations.
Rutter, Cal. Practice Guide: Prof. Responsibility Ch. 7-A, A. Introduction.
Rutter, Cal. Practice Guide: Prof. Responsibility Ch. 7-B, B. Duty to Maintain Client Confidence and Secrets Under State Bar Act.
Rutter, Cal. Practice Guide: Prof. Responsibility Ch. 7-C, C. Attorney-Client Privilege.

§ 955. When lawyer required to claim privilege

The lawyer who received or made a communication subject to the privilege under this article shall claim the privilege whenever he is present when the communication is sought to be disclosed and is authorized to claim the privilege under subdivision (c) of Section 954. *(Stats.1965, c. 299, § 2, operative Jan. 1, 1967.)*

Law Revision Commission Comments

The obligation of the lawyer to claim the privilege on behalf of the client, unless otherwise instructed by a person authorized to permit disclosure, is consistent with Section 6068(e) of the Business and Professions Code. [7 Cal.L.Rev.Comm. Reports 1 (1965)].

Research References

Rutter, Cal. Practice Guide: Civil Trials & Evidence Ch. 8E-A, A. Privileges.

Rutter, Cal. Practice Guide: Prof. Responsibility Ch. 7-C, C. Attorney-Client Privilege.

§ 956. Exception: Crime or fraud

There is no privilege under this article if the services of the lawyer were sought or obtained to enable or aid anyone to commit or plan to commit a crime or a fraud. *(Stats.1965, c. 299, § 2, operative Jan. 1, 1967.)*

Law Revision Commission Comments

California now recognizes this exception. Abbott v. Superior Court, 78 Cal.App.2d 19, 177 P.2d 317 (1947). *Cf.* Nowell v. Superior Court, 223 Cal.App.2d 652, 36 Cal.Rptr. 21 (1963). [7 Cal.L.Rev.Comm. Reports 1 (1965)].

Research References

Rutter, Cal. Practice Guide: Civ. Pro. Before Trial Ch. 8C-3, "Not Privileged".
Rutter, Cal. Practice Guide: Civ. Pro. Before Trial Ch. 8C-4, Attorney Work Product Protection.
Rutter, Cal. Practice Guide: Civil Trials & Evidence Ch. 8E-A, A. Privileges.
Rutter, Cal. Practice Guide: Civil Trials & Evidence Ch. 8E-B, B. Attorney Work Product Doctrine.
California Practice Guide: Employment Litigation Ch. 2-J, J. Confidential and Privileged Information.
Rutter, Cal. Practice Guide: Insurance Litigation Ch. 11-I, I. Conspiracy.
Rutter, Cal. Practice Guide: Prof. Responsibility Ch. 7-B, B. Duty to Maintain Client Confidence and Secrets Under State Bar Act.
Rutter, Cal. Practice Guide: Prof. Responsibility Ch. 7-C, C. Attorney-Client Privilege.
5 Witkin, California Summary 10th Torts § 661, (S 661) Wiretapping and Electronic Eavesdropping.

§ 956.5. Exception: Prevention of criminal act likely to result in death or substantial bodily harm

There is no privilege under this article if the lawyer reasonably believes that disclosure of any confidential communication relating to representation of a client is necessary to prevent a criminal act that the lawyer reasonably believes is likely to result in the death of, or substantial bodily harm to, an individual. *(Added by Stats.1993, c. 982 (S.B.645), § 8. Amended by Stats.2003, c. 765 (A.B.1101), § 2, operative July 1, 2004; Stats. 2004, c. 183 (A.B.3082), § 94.)*

Research References

Rutter, Cal. Practice Guide: Civ. Pro. Before Trial Ch. 1-A, A. Accepting a New Case.
Rutter, Cal. Practice Guide: Civ. Pro. Before Trial Ch. 8C-3, "Not Privileged".
Rutter, Cal. Practice Guide: Civil Trials & Evidence Ch. 8E-A, A. Privileges.
California Practice Guide: Employment Litigation Ch. 2-J, J. Confidential and Privileged Information.
Rutter, Cal. Practice Guide: Prof. Responsibility Ch. 7-B, B. Duty to Maintain Client Confidence and Secrets Under State Bar Act.
Rutter, Cal. Practice Guide: Prof. Responsibility Ch. 7-C, C. Attorney-Client Privilege.
Rutter, Cal. Practice Guide: Prof. Responsibility Ch. 1 App., California Rules of Professional Conduct.

§ 957. Exception: Parties claiming through deceased client

There is no privilege under this article as to a communication relevant to an issue between parties all of whom claim through a deceased client, regardless of whether the claims are by testate or intestate succession, nonprobate transfer, or inter vivos transaction. *(Stats.1965, c. 299, § 2, operative Jan. 1, 1967. Amended by Stats.2009, c. 8 (A.B.1163), § 2.)*

Law Revision Commission Comments

The lawyer-client privilege does not apply to a communication relevant to an issue between parties all of whom claim through a deceased client.

Evidence

Under existing law, all must claim through the client by testate or intestate succession in order for this exception to be applicable; a claim by inter vivos transaction apparently is not within the exception. Paley v. Superior Court, 137 Cal.App.2d 450, 457–460, 290 P.2d 617, 621–623 (1955). Section 957 extends this exception to include inter vivos transactions.

The traditional exception for litigation between claimants by testate or intestate succession is based on the theory that claimants in privity with the estate claim *through* the client, not adversely, and the deceased client presumably would want his communications disclosed in litigation between such claimants so that his desires in regard to the disposition of his estate might be correctly ascertained and carried out. This rationale is equally applicable where one or more of the parties is claiming by inter vivos transaction, as, for example, in an action between a party who claims under a deed (executed by a client in full possession of his faculties) and a party who claims under a will executed while the client's mental stability was dubious. See the discussion in Tentative Recommendation and a Study Relating to the Uniform Rules of Evidence (Article V. Privileges), 6 Cal.Law Revision Comm'n, Rep., Rec. & Studies 201, 392–396 (1964). [7 Cal.L.Rev.Comm. Reports 1 (1965)].

Section 957 is amended to clarify that the exception is applicable to parties who all claim through a deceased client, including a person who claims through a nonprobate transfer. [38 Cal. L. Revision Comm'n Reports 163 (2008)].

Research References

Rutter, Cal. Practice Guide: Civil Trials & Evidence Ch. 8E-A, A. Privileges.
Rutter, Cal. Practice Guide: Prof. Responsibility Ch. 7-B, B. Duty to Maintain Client Confidence and Secrets Under State Bar Act.
Rutter, Cal. Practice Guide: Prof. Responsibility Ch. 7-C, C. Attorney-Client Privilege.

§ 958. Exception: Breach of duty arising out of lawyer-client relationship

There is no privilege under this article as to a communication relevant to an issue of breach, by the lawyer or by the client, of a duty arising out of the lawyer-client relationship. *(Stats.1965, c. 299, § 2, operative Jan. 1, 1967.)*

Law Revision Commission Comments

This exception has not been recognized by a holding in any California case, although dicta in several opinions indicate that it would be recognized if the question were presented in a proper case. People v. Tucker, 61 Cal.2d 828, 40 Cal.Rptr. 609, 395 P.2d 449 (1964); Henshall v. Coburn, 177 Cal. 50, 169 Pac. 1014 (1917); Pacific Tel. & Tel. Co. v. Fink, 141 Cal.App.2d 332, 335, 296 P.2d 843, 845 (1956); Fleschler v. Strauss, 15 Cal.App.2d 735, 60 P.2d 193 (1936). See generally Witkin, California Evidence § 419 (1958).

It would be unjust to permit a client either to accuse his attorney of a breach of duty and to invoke the privilege to prevent the attorney from bringing forth evidence in defense of the charge or to refuse to pay his attorney's fee and invoke the privilege to defeat the attorney's claim. Thus, for example, if the defendant in a criminal action claims that his lawyer did not provide him with an adequate defense, communications between the lawyer and client relevant to that issue are not privileged. See People v. Tucker, 61 Cal.2d 828, 40 Cal.Rptr. 609, 395 P.2d 449 (1964). The duty involved must, of course, be one arising out of the lawyer-client relationship, *e.g.*, the duty of the lawyer to exercise reasonable diligence on behalf of his client, the duty of the lawyer to care faithfully and account for his client's property, or the client's duty to pay for the lawyer's services. [7 Cal.L.Rev.Comm. Reports 1 (1965)].

Research References

Rutter, Cal. Practice Guide: Civ. Pro. Before Trial Ch. 1-A, A. Accepting a New Case.
Rutter, Cal. Practice Guide: Civ. Pro. Before Trial Ch. 8C-3, "Not Privileged".
Rutter, Cal. Practice Guide: Civil Trials & Evidence Ch. 8E-A, A. Privileges.
California Practice Guide: Employment Litigation Ch. 2-J, J. Confidential and Privileged Information.
Rutter, Cal. Practice Guide: Fed.Civ.Pro. Before Trial Ch. 17-A, A. General Considerations.
Rutter, Cal. Practice Guide: Personal Injury Ch. 6-A, A. Scope of Discovery and Limitations.

Rutter, Cal. Practice Guide: Prof. Responsibility Ch. 5-K, K. Fee Recovery/Enforcing Fee Agreements.
Rutter, Cal. Practice Guide: Prof. Responsibility Ch. 7-B, B. Duty to Maintain Client Confidence and Secrets Under State Bar Act.
Rutter, Cal. Practice Guide: Prof. Responsibility Ch. 7-C, C. Attorney-Client Privilege.
Rutter, Cal. Practice Guide: Prof. Responsibility Ch. 10-B, B. Withdrawal (Termination) by Lawyer.
Rutter, Cal. Practice Guide: Prof. Responsibility Ch. 11-E, E. Receiving Complaints of Attorney Misconduct.
20 NO. 3 Miller & Starr, California Real Estate Newsalert 7, Alternative Dispute Resolution.

§ 959. Exception: Lawyer as attesting witness

There is no privilege under this article as to a communication relevant to an issue concerning the intention or competence of a client executing an attested document of which the lawyer is an attesting witness, or concerning the execution or attestation of such a document. *(Stats.1965, c. 299, § 2, operative Jan. 1, 1967.)*

Law Revision Commission Comments

This exception relates to the type of communication about which an attesting witness would testify. The mere fact that an attorney acts as an attesting witness should not destroy the lawyer-client privilege as to all statements made concerning the document attested; but the privilege should not prohibit the lawyer from performing the duties expected of an attesting witness. Under existing law, the attesting witness exception is broader, having been used as a device to obtain information which the lawyer who is an attesting witness received in his capacity as a lawyer rather than as an attesting witness. See In re Mullin, 110 Cal. 252, 42 Pac. 645 (1895). [7 Cal.L.Rev.Comm. Reports 1 (1965)].

Research References

Rutter, Cal. Practice Guide: Civil Trials & Evidence Ch. 8E-A, A. Privileges.
Rutter, Cal. Practice Guide: Prof. Responsibility Ch. 7-C, C. Attorney-Client Privilege.

§ 960. Exception: Intention of deceased client concerning writing affecting property interest

There is no privilege under this article as to a communication relevant to an issue concerning the intention of a client, now deceased, with respect to a deed of conveyance, will, or other writing, executed by the client, purporting to affect an interest in property. *(Stats.1965, c. 299, § 2, operative Jan. 1, 1967.)*

Law Revision Commission Comments

Although the attesting witness exception stated in Section 959 is limited to information of the kind to which one would expect an attesting witness to testify, there is merit to having an exception that applies to all dispositive instruments. A client ordinarily would desire his lawyer to communicate his true intention with regard to a dispositive instrument if the instrument itself leaves the matter in doubt and the client is deceased. Likewise, the client ordinarily would desire his attorney to testify to communications relevant to the validity of such instruments after the client dies. Accordingly, two additional exceptions—Sections 960 and 961—are provided for this purpose. These exceptions have been recognized by the California decisions only in cases where the lawyer is an attesting witness. See the Comment to Evidence Code § 959. [7 Cal.L.Rev.Comm. Reports 1 (1965)].

Research References

Rutter, Cal. Practice Guide: Civil Trials & Evidence Ch. 8E-A, A. Privileges.
Rutter, Cal. Practice Guide: Prof. Responsibility Ch. 7-C, C. Attorney-Client Privilege.

§ 961. Exception: Validity of writing affecting property interest

There is no privilege under this article as to a communication relevant to an issue concerning the validity of a deed of conveyance, will, or other writing, executed by a client, now deceased, purporting to affect an interest in property. *(Stats. 1965, c. 299, § 2, operative Jan. 1, 1967.)*

Law Revision Commission Comments

See the Comment to Section 960. [7 Cal.L.Rev.Comm. Reports 1 (1965)].

Research References

Rutter, Cal. Practice Guide: Civil Trials & Evidence Ch. 8E-A, A. Privileges.
Rutter, Cal. Practice Guide: Prof. Responsibility Ch. 7-C, C. Attorney-Client Privilege.

§ 962. Exception: Joint clients

Where two or more clients have retained or consulted a lawyer upon a matter of common interest, none of them, nor the successor in interest of any of them, may claim a privilege under this article as to a communication made in the course of that relationship when such communication is offered in a civil proceeding between one of such clients (or his successor in interest) and another of such clients (or his successor in interest). *(Stats.1965, c. 299, § 2, operative Jan. 1, 1967.)*

Law Revision Commission Comments

This section states existing law. Clyne v. Brock, 82 Cal.App.2d 958, 965, 188 P.2d 263, 267 (1947); Croce v. Superior Court, 21 Cal.App.2d 18, 68 P.2d 369 (1937). See also Harris v. Harris, 136 Cal. 379, 69 Pac. 23 (1902). [7 Cal.L.Rev.Comm. Reports 1 (1965)].

Research References

Rutter, Cal. Practice Guide: Civ. Pro. Before Trial Ch. 8C-3, "Not Privileged".
Rutter, Cal. Practice Guide: Civil Trials & Evidence Ch. 8E-A, A. Privileges.
California Practice Guide: Employment Litigation Ch. 2-D, D. Joint Representation of Codefendants.
California Practice Guide: Employment Litigation Ch. 2-J, J. Confidential and Privileged Information.
California Practice Guide: Employment Litigation Ch. 2-D, Outline D.
Rutter, Cal. Practice Guide: Family Law Ch. 1-D, D. Potential Ethical Problems in Accepting or Continuing Representation.
Rutter, Cal. Practice Guide: Family Law Ch. 11-C, C. Optional "Formal" Discovery Procedures.
Rutter, Cal. Practice Guide: Insurance Litigation Ch. 15-G, G. Discovery.
Rutter, Cal. Practice Guide: Insurance Litigation Ch. 7B-L, L. Defense Counsel's Obligations-Professional Responsibility Considerations.
Rutter, Cal. Practice Guide: Insurance Litigation Ch. 12B-B, B. Bad Faith Refusal to Settle.
Rutter, Cal. Practice Guide: Landlord-Tenant Ch. 1-B, B. Accepting a New Case.
Rutter, Cal. Practice Guide: Personal Injury Ch. 1-B, B. Initial Evaluation of Case: Decision to Accept or Reject Employment or Undertake Further Evaluation of Claim.
Rutter, Cal. Practice Guide: Personal Injury Ch. 4-C, C. Effective Settlement Negotiations.
Rutter, Cal. Practice Guide: Personal Injury Ch. 6-A, A. Scope of Discovery and Limitations.
Rutter, Cal. Practice Guide: Real Prop. Transactions Ch. 1-B, B. Attorney Competence, Conflicts of Interest and Initial Client Communications.
Rutter, Cal. Practice Guide: Prof. Responsibility Ch. 3-C, C. Identifying "Client".
Rutter, Cal. Practice Guide: Prof. Responsibility Ch. 4-B, B. Concurrent Representation of Clients With Conflicting Interests (Conflicts Between Present Clients).
Rutter, Cal. Practice Guide: Prof. Responsibility Ch. 4-C, C. Conflicts Between Present and Former Clients (Successive Representation).
Rutter, Cal. Practice Guide: Prof. Responsibility Ch. 7-C, C. Attorney-Client Privilege.
Rutter, Cal. Practice Guide: Prof. Responsibility Form 4:C, Disclosure Letter and Client Consent to Joint Representation.

Rutter, Cal. Practice Guide: Prof. Responsibility Ch. 1 App., California Rules of Professional Conduct.

ARTICLE 3.5. LAWYER REFERRAL SERVICE–CLIENT PRIVILEGE

Section

§ 965. Definitions

For purposes of this article, the following terms have the following meanings:

(a) "Client" means a person who, directly or through an authorized representative, consults a lawyer referral service for the purpose of retaining, or securing legal services or advice from, a lawyer in his or her professional capacity, and includes an incompetent who consults the lawyer referral service himself or herself or whose guardian or conservator consults the lawyer referral service on his or her behalf.

(b) "Confidential communication between client and lawyer referral service" means information transmitted between a client and a lawyer referral service in the course of that relationship and in confidence by a means that, so far as the client is aware, does not disclose the information to third persons other than those who are present to further the interests of the client in the consultation or those to whom disclosure is reasonably necessary for the transmission of the information or the accomplishment of the purpose for which the lawyer referral service is consulted.

(c) "Holder of the privilege" means any of the following:

(1) The client, if the client has no guardian or conservator.

(2) A guardian or conservator of the client, if the client has a guardian or conservator.

(3) The personal representative of the client if the client is dead, including a personal representative appointed pursuant to Section 12252 of the Probate Code.

(4) A successor, assign, trustee in dissolution, or any similar representative of a firm, association, organization, partnership, business trust, corporation, or public entity that is no longer in existence.

(d) "Lawyer referral service" means a lawyer referral service certified under, and operating in compliance with, Section 6155 of the Business and Professions Code or an enterprise reasonably believed by the client to be a lawyer referral service certified under, and operating in compliance with, Section 6155 of the Business and Professions Code. *(Added by Stats.2013, c. 123 (A.B.267), § 2.)*

§ 966. Lawyer referral service-client privilege

(a) Subject to Section 912 and except as otherwise provided in this article, the client, whether or not a party, has a privilege to refuse to disclose, and to prevent another from disclosing, a confidential communication between client and lawyer referral service if the privilege is claimed by any of the following:

(1) The holder of the privilege.

(2) A person who is authorized to claim the privilege by the holder of the privilege.

(3) The lawyer referral service or a staff person thereof, but the lawyer referral service or a staff person thereof may not claim the privilege if there is no holder of the privilege in existence or if the lawyer referral service or a staff person thereof

is otherwise instructed by a person authorized to permit disclosure.

(b) The relationship of lawyer referral service and client shall exist between a lawyer referral service, as defined in Section 965, and the persons to whom it renders services, as well as between such persons and anyone employed by the lawyer referral service to render services to such persons. The word "persons" as used in this subdivision includes partnerships, corporations, limited liability companies, associations, and other groups and entities. *(Added by Stats.2013, c. 123 (A.B.267), § 2.)*

§ 967. Claiming of privilege

A lawyer referral service that has received or made a communication subject to the privilege under this article shall claim the privilege if the communication is sought to be disclosed and the client has not consented to the disclosure. *(Added by Stats.2013, c. 123 (A.B.267), § 2.)*

§ 968. Exceptions to privilege

There is no privilege under this article if either of the following applies:

(a) The services of the lawyer referral service were sought or obtained to enable or aid anyone to commit or plan to commit a crime or a fraud.

(b) A staff person of the lawyer referral service who receives a confidential communication in processing a request for legal assistance reasonably believes that disclosure of the confidential communication is necessary to prevent a criminal act that the staff person of the lawyer referral service reasonably believes is likely to result in the death of, or substantial bodily harm to, an individual. *(Added by Stats.2013, c. 123 (A.B.267), § 2.)*

ARTICLE 4. PRIVILEGE NOT TO TESTIFY AGAINST SPOUSE

Section
970. Spouse's privilege not to testify against spouse; exceptions.
971. Privilege not to be called as a witness against spouse.
972. Exceptions to privilege.
973. Waiver of privilege.

§ 970. Spouse's privilege not to testify against spouse; exceptions

Except as otherwise provided by statute, a married person has a privilege not to testify against his spouse in any proceeding. *(Stats.1965, c. 299, § 2, operative Jan. 1, 1967.)*

Law Revision Commission Comments

Under this article, a married person has two privileges: (1) a privilege not to testify against his spouse in any proceeding (Section 970) and (2) a privilege not to be called as a witness in any proceeding to which his spouse is a party (Section 971).

The privileges under this article are not as broad as the privilege provided by existing law. Under existing law, a married person has a privilege to prevent his spouse from testifying against him, but only the witness spouse has a privilege under this article. Under the existing law, a married person may refuse to testify *for* the other spouse, but no such privilege exists under this article. For a discussion of the reasons for these changes in existing law, see the Law Revision Commission's Comment to Code of Civil Procedure Section 1881 (superseded by the Evidence Code).

The rationale of the privilege provided by Section 970 not to testify against one's spouse is that such testimony would seriously disturb or disrupt the marital relationship. Society stands to lose more from such disruption than it stands to gain from the testimony which would be available if the privilege did not exist. The privilege is based in part on a previous recommendation and study of the California Law Revision

Commission. See 1 Cal.Law Revision Comm'n, Rep., Rec. & Studies, Recommendation and Study Relating to the Marital "For and Against" Testimonial Privilege at F–1 (1957). [7 Cal.L.Rev.Comm. Reports 1 (1965)].

Research References

Rutter, Cal. Practice Guide: Civ. Pro. Before Trial Ch. 8C-3, "Not Privileged".

Rutter, Cal. Practice Guide: Civil Trials & Evidence Ch. 4-B, B. Preliminary Matters Discussed in Final Status Conference or In-Chambers Conference.

Rutter, Cal. Practice Guide: Civil Trials & Evidence Ch. 8E-A, A. Privileges.

California Practice Guide: Employment Litigation Ch. 10-F, F. Discovery Issues.

California Practice Guide: Employment Litigation Ch. 19-F, F. Discovery.

Rutter, Cal. Practice Guide: Enforcing Judgments/Debts Ch. 6G-1, Examination of Judgment Debtor and Third Parties.

Rutter, Cal. Practice Guide: Family Law Ch. 2-A, A. Status Remedies-Dissolution, Nullity, Legal Separation.

Rutter, Cal. Practice Guide: Family Law Ch. 17-G, G. Modification Procedure.

Rutter, Cal. Practice Guide: Family Law Ch. 11-C, C. Optional "Formal" Discovery Procedures.

Rutter, Cal. Practice Guide: Family Law Ch. 20-A, A. Nonmarital "Marvin" Cohabitation Relationships.

Rutter, Cal. Practice Guide: Family Law Ch. 20-B, B. Domestic Partnerships.

Rutter, Cal. Practice Guide: Personal Injury Ch. 6-A, A. Scope of Discovery and Limitations.

Miller and Starr California Real Estate § 11:46, Privileged Publication.

8 Witkin Cal. Proc. 5th Enforcement of Judgment § 285, Privileges.

§ 971. Privilege not to be called as a witness against spouse

Except as otherwise provided by statute, a married person whose spouse is a party to a proceeding has a privilege not to be called as a witness by an adverse party to that proceeding without the prior express consent of the spouse having the privilege under this section unless the party calling the spouse does so in good faith without knowledge of the marital relationship. *(Stats.1965, c. 299, § 2, operative Jan. 1, 1967.)*

Law Revision Commission Comments

The privilege of a married person not to be called as a witness against his spouse is somewhat similar to the privilege given the defendant in a criminal case not to be called as a witness (Section 930). This privilege is necessary to avoid the prejudicial effect. For example, of the prosecution's calling the defendant's wife as a witness, thus forcing her to object before the jury. The privilege not to be called as a witness does not apply, however, in a proceeding where the other spouse is not a party. Thus, a married person may be called as a witness in a grand jury proceeding because his spouse is not a party to that proceeding, but the witness in the grand jury proceeding may claim the privilege under Section 970 to refuse to answer a question that would compel him to testify *against* his spouse. [7 Cal.L.Rev.Comm. Reports 1 (1965)].

Research References

Rutter, Cal. Practice Guide: Civil Trials & Evidence Ch. 8E-A, A. Privileges.

California Practice Guide: Employment Litigation Ch. 10-F, F. Discovery Issues.

Rutter, Cal. Practice Guide: Family Law Ch. 17-G, G. Modification Procedure.

Rutter, Cal. Practice Guide: Family Law Ch. 11-C, C. Optional "Formal" Discovery Procedures.

§ 972. Exceptions to privilege

A married person does not have a privilege under this article in:

(a) A proceeding brought by or on behalf of one spouse against the other spouse.

(b) A proceeding to commit or otherwise place his or her spouse or his or her spouse's property, or both, under the control of another because of the spouse's alleged mental or physical condition.

(c) A proceeding brought by or on behalf of a spouse to establish his or her competence.

(d) A proceeding under the Juvenile Court Law, Chapter 2 (commencing with Section 200) of Part 1 of Division 2 of the Welfare and Institutions Code.

(e) A criminal proceeding in which one spouse is charged with:

(1) A crime against the person or property of the other spouse or of a child, parent, relative, or cohabitant of either, whether committed before or during marriage.

(2) A crime against the person or property of a third person committed in the course of committing a crime against the person or property of the other spouse, whether committed before or during marriage.

(3) Bigamy.

(4) A crime defined by Section 270 or 270a of the Penal Code.

(f) A proceeding resulting from a criminal act which occurred prior to legal marriage of the spouses to each other regarding knowledge acquired prior to that marriage if prior to the legal marriage the witness spouse was aware that his or her spouse had been arrested for or had been formally charged with the crime or crimes about which the spouse is called to testify.

(g) A proceeding brought against the spouse by a former spouse so long as the property and debts of the marriage have not been adjudicated, or in order to establish, modify, or enforce a child, family or spousal support obligation arising from the marriage to the former spouse; in a proceeding brought against a spouse by the other parent in order to establish, modify, or enforce a child support obligation for a child of a nonmarital relationship of the spouse; or in a proceeding brought against a spouse by the guardian of a child of that spouse in order to establish, modify, or enforce a child support obligation of the spouse. The married person does not have a privilege under this subdivision to refuse to provide information relating to the issues of income, expenses, assets, debts, and employment of either spouse, but may assert the privilege as otherwise provided in this article if other information is requested by the former spouse, guardian, or other parent of the child.

Any person demanding the otherwise privileged information made available by this subdivision, who also has an obligation to support the child for whom an order to establish[1], modify, or enforce child support is sought, waives his or her marital privilege to the same extent as the spouse as provided in this subdivision. *(Stats.1965, c. 299, § 2, operative Jan. 1, 1967. Amended by Stats.1975, c. 71, p. 132, § 2; Stats.1982, c. 256, p. 833, § 1; Stats.1983, c. 244, § 1; Stats.1986, c. 769, § 1, eff. Sept. 15, 1986; Stats.1989, c. 1359, § 9.7.)*

[1] So in enrolled bill.

Law Revision Commission Comments

The exceptions to the privileges under this article are similar to those contained in Code of Civil Procedure Section 1881(1) and Penal Code Section 1322, both of which are superseded by the Evidence Code. However, the exceptions in this section have been drafted so that they are consistent with those provided in Article 5 (commencing with Section 980) of this chapter (the privilege for confidential marital communications).

A discussion of comparable exceptions may be found in the Comments to the sections in Article 5 of this chapter. [7 Cal.L.Rev.Comm. Reports 1 (1965)].

Research References

Rutter, Cal. Practice Guide: Civil Trials & Evidence Ch. 8E-A, A. Privileges.

Rutter, Cal. Practice Guide: Family Law Ch. 17-G, G. Modification Procedure.

Rutter, Cal. Practice Guide: Family Law Ch. 11-C, C. Optional "Formal" Discovery Procedures.

10 Witkin, California Summary 10th Parent and Child § 620, (S 620) Privileges.

10 Witkin, California Summary 10th Parent and Child § 873, (S 873) Privileges.

§ 973. Waiver of privilege

(a) Unless erroneously compelled to do so, a married person who testifies in a proceeding to which his spouse is a party, or who testifies against his spouse in any proceeding, does not have a privilege under this article in the proceeding in which such testimony is given.

(b) There is no privilege under this article in a civil proceeding brought or defended by a married person for the immediate benefit of his spouse or of himself and his spouse. *(Stats.1965, c. 299, § 2, operative Jan. 1, 1967.)*

Research References

Rutter, Cal. Practice Guide: Civ. Pro. Before Trial Ch. 8C-3, "Not Privileged".

Rutter, Cal. Practice Guide: Civil Trials & Evidence Ch. 8E-A, A. Privileges.

California Practice Guide: Employment Litigation Ch. 10-F, F. Discovery Issues.

California Practice Guide: Employment Litigation Ch. 19-F, F. Discovery.

Rutter, Cal. Practice Guide: Family Law Ch. 2-A, A. Status Remedies-Dissolution, Nullity, Legal Separation.

Miller and Starr California Real Estate § 11:46, Privileged Publication.

ARTICLE 5. PRIVILEGE FOR CONFIDENTIAL MARITAL COMMUNICATIONS

Section

980. Confidential marital communication privilege.
981. Exception: Crime or fraud.
982. Commitment or similar proceedings.
983. Competency proceedings.
984. Proceeding between spouses.
985. Criminal proceedings.
986. Juvenile court proceedings.
987. Communication offered by spouse who is criminal defendant.

§ 980. Confidential marital communication privilege

Subject to Section 912 and except as otherwise provided in this article, a spouse (or his guardian or conservator when he has a guardian or conservator), whether or not a party, has a privilege during the marital relationship and afterwards to refuse to disclose, and to prevent another from disclosing, a communication if he claims the privilege and the communication was made in confidence between him and the other spouse while they were husband and wife. *(Stats.1965, c. 299, § 2, operative Jan. 1, 1967.)*

Law Revision Commission Comments

Section 980 is the basic statement of the privilege for confidential marital communications. Exceptions to this privilege are stated in Sections 981–987.

Who can claim the privilege. Under Section 980, both spouses are the holders of the privilege and either spouse may claim it. Under existing law, the privilege *may* belong only to the nontestifying spouse inasmuch as Code of Civil Procedure Section 1881(1), superseded by the Evidence Code, provides: "[N]or can either . . . be, *without the consent of the other,* examined as to any communication made by one to the other during the marriage." (Emphasis added.) It is likely, however, that Section 1881(1) would be construed to grant the privilege to both spouses. See In re De Neef, 42 Cal.App.2d 691, 109 P.2d 741 (1941). *But see* People v. Keller, 165 Cal.App.2d 419, 423–424, 332 P.2d 174, 176 (1958) (dictum).

A guardian of an incompetent spouse may claim the privilege on behalf of that spouse. However, when a spouse is dead, no one can claim the privilege for him; the privilege, if it is to be claimed at all, can be claimed only by or on behalf of the surviving spouse.

Termination of marriage. The privilege may be claimed as to confidential communications made during a marriage even though the marriage has been terminated at the time the privilege is claimed. This states existing law. Code Civ.Proc. § 1881(1) (superseded by the Evidence Code; People v. Mullings, 83 Cal. 138, 23 Pac. 229 (1890). Free and open communication between spouses would be unduly inhibited if one of the spouses could be compelled to testify as to the nature of such communications after the termination of the marriage.

Eavesdroppers. The privilege may be asserted to prevent testimony by anyone, including eavesdroppers. To a limited extent, this constitutes a change in California law. See the Comment to Evidence Code § 954. See generally People v. Peak, 66 Cal.App.2d 894, 153 P.2d 464 (1944); People v. Morhar, 78 Cal.App. 380, 248 Pac. 975 (1926); People v. Mitchell, 61 Cal.App. 569, 215 Pac. 117 (1923). Section 980 also changes the existing law which permits a third party, to whom one of the spouses had revealed a confidential communication, to testify concerning it. People v. Swaile, 12 Cal.App. 192, 195–196, 107 Pac. 134, 137 (1909); People v. Chadwick, 4 Cal.App. 63, 72, 87 Pac. 384, 387, 388 (1906). See also Wolfle v. United States, 291 U.S. 7 (1934). Under Section 912, such conduct would constitute a waiver of the privilege only as to the spouse who makes the disclosure. [7 Cal.L.Rev.Comm. Reports 1 (1965)].

Research References

Rutter, Cal. Practice Guide: Civ. Pro. Before Trial Ch. 8C-3, "Not Privileged".
Rutter, Cal. Practice Guide: Civil Trials & Evidence Ch. 4-B, B. Preliminary Matters Discussed in Final Status Conference or In-Chambers Conference.
Rutter, Cal. Practice Guide: Civil Trials & Evidence Ch. 8E-A, A. Privileges.
California Practice Guide: Employment Litigation Ch. 19-F, F. Discovery.
Rutter, Cal. Practice Guide: Enforcing Judgments/Debts Ch. 6G-1, Examination of Judgment Debtor and Third Parties.
Rutter, Cal. Practice Guide: Family Law Ch. 11-C, C. Optional "Formal" Discovery Procedures.
Rutter, Cal. Practice Guide: Family Law Ch. 20-A, A. Nonmarital "Marvin" Cohabitation Relationships.
11 Witkin, California Summary 10th Husband and Wife § 151, Relation Back Theory.

§ 981. Exception: Crime or fraud

There is no privilege under this article if the communication was made, in whole or in part, to enable or aid anyone to commit or plan to commit a crime or a fraud. *(Stats.1965, c. 299, § 2, operative Jan. 1, 1967.)*

Law Revision Commission Comments

California recognizes this as an exception to the lawyer-client privilege, but it does not appear to have been recognized in the California cases dealing with the confidential marital communications privilege. Nonetheless, the exception does not seem so broad that it would impair the values that the privilege is intended to preserve; in many cases, the evidence which would be admissible under this exception would be vital in order to do justice between the parties to a lawsuit. This exception would not, of course, infringe on the privileges accorded to a married person under Sections 970 and 971.

It is important to note that the exception provided by Section 981 is quite limited. It does not permit disclosure of communications that merely reveal a plan to commit a crime or fraud; it permits disclosure only of communications made to *enable* or *aid* anyone to commit or plan to commit a crime or a fraud. Thus, unless the communication is for the purpose of obtaining assistance in the commission of the crime or fraud or in furtherance thereof, it is not made admissible by the exception provided in this section. *Cf.* People v. Pierce, 61 Cal.2d 879, 40 Cal.Rptr. 845, 395 P.2d 893 (1964) (husband and wife who conspire only between themselves against others cannot claim immunity from prosecution for conspiracy on the basis of their marital status). [7 Cal.L.Rev.Comm. Reports 1 (1965)].

Research References

Rutter, Cal. Practice Guide: Civil Trials & Evidence Ch. 8E-A, A. Privileges.

§ 982. Commitment or similar proceedings

There is no privilege under this article in a proceeding to commit either spouse or otherwise place him or his property, or both, under the control of another because of his alleged mental or physical condition. *(Stats.1965, c. 299, § 2, operative Jan. 1, 1967.)*

Law Revision Commission Comments

Sections 982 and 983 express existing law. Code Civ.Proc. § 1881(1) (superseded by the Evidence Code). Commitment and competency proceedings are undertaken for the benefit of the subject person. Frequently, much or all of the evidence bearing on a spouse's competency or lack of competency will consist of communications to the other spouse. It would be undesirable to permit either spouse to invoke a privilege to prevent the presentation of this vital information inasmuch as these proceedings are of such vital importance both to society and to the spouse who is the subject of the proceedings. [7 Cal.L.Rev.Comm. Reports 1 (1965)].

Research References

Rutter, Cal. Practice Guide: Civil Trials & Evidence Ch. 8E-A, A. Privileges.

§ 983. Competency proceedings

There is no privilege under this article in a proceeding brought by or on behalf of either spouse to establish his competence. *(Stats.1965, c. 299, § 2, operative Jan. 1, 1967.)*

Law Revision Commission Comments

See the Comment to Section 982. [7 Cal.L.Rev.Comm. Reports 1 (1965)].

Research References

Rutter, Cal. Practice Guide: Civil Trials & Evidence Ch. 8E-A, A. Privileges.

§ 984. Proceeding between spouses

There is no privilege under this article in:

(a) A proceeding brought by or on behalf of one spouse against the other spouse.

(b) A proceeding between a surviving spouse and a person who claims through the deceased spouse, regardless of whether such claim is by testate or intestate succession or by inter vivos transaction. *(Stats.1965, c. 299, § 2, operative Jan. 1, 1967.)*

Law Revision Commission Comments

The exception to the marital communications privilege for litigation between the spouses states existing law. Code Civ.Proc. § 1881(1) (superseded by the Evidence Code). Section 984 extends the principle to cases where one of the spouses is dead and the litigation is between his successor and the surviving spouse. See generally Estate of Gillett, 73 Cal.App.2d 588, 166 P.2d 870 (1946). [7 Cal.L.Rev.Comm. Reports 1 (1965)].

Research References

Rutter, Cal. Practice Guide: Civil Trials & Evidence Ch. 8E-A, A. Privileges.
Rutter, Cal. Practice Guide: Family Law Ch. 11-C, C. Optional "Formal" Discovery Procedures.

§ 985. Criminal proceedings

There is no privilege under this article in a criminal proceeding in which one spouse is charged with:

(a) A crime committed at any time against the person or property of the other spouse or of a child of either.

(b) A crime committed at any time against the person or property of a third person committed in the course of committing a crime against the person or property of the other spouse.

(c) Bigamy.

(d) A crime defined by Section 270 or 270a of the Penal Code. *(Stats.1965, c. 299, § 2, operative Jan. 1, 1967. Amended by Stats.1975, c. 71, p. 133, § 3.)*

Law Revision Commission Comments

This exception restates with minor variations an exception that is recognized under existing law. Code Civ.Proc. § 1881(1) (superseded by the Evidence Code). Sections 985 and 986 together create an exception for all the proceedings mentioned in Section 1322 of the Penal Code (superseded by the Evidence Code). [7 Cal.L.Rev.Comm. Reports 1 (1965)].

Research References

Rutter, Cal. Practice Guide: Civil Trials & Evidence Ch. 8E-A, A. Privileges.

§ 986. Juvenile court proceedings

There is no privilege under this article in a proceeding under the Juvenile Court Law, Chapter 2 (commencing with Section 200) of Part 1 of Division 2 of the Welfare and Institutions Code. *(Stats.1965, c. 299, § 2, operative Jan. 1, 1967. Amended by Stats.1982, c. 256, p. 833, § 2.)*

Law Revision Commission Comments

See the Comment to Section 985. [7 Cal.L.Rev.Comm. Reports 1 (1965)].

Research References

Rutter, Cal. Practice Guide: Civil Trials & Evidence Ch. 8E-A, A. Privileges.

10 Witkin, California Summary 10th Parent and Child § 620, (S 620) Privileges.

10 Witkin, California Summary 10th Parent and Child § 873, (S 873) Privileges.

§ 987. Communication offered by spouse who is criminal defendant

There is no privilege under this article in a criminal proceeding in which the communication is offered in evidence by a defendant who is one of the spouses between whom the communication was made. *(Stats.1965, c. 299, § 2, operative Jan. 1, 1967.)*

Law Revision Commission Comments

This exception does not appear to have been recognized in any California case. Nonetheless, it is a desirable exception. When a married person is the defendant in a criminal proceeding and seeks to introduce evidence which is material to his defense, his spouse (or his former spouse) should not be privileged to withhold the information. [7 Cal.L.Rev.Comm. Reports 1 (1965)].

Research References

Rutter, Cal. Practice Guide: Civil Trials & Evidence Ch. 8E-A, A. Privileges.

Rutter, Cal. Practice Guide: Personal Injury Ch. 6-A, A. Scope of Discovery and Limitations.

ARTICLE 6. PHYSICIAN–PATIENT PRIVILEGE

§ 990. Physician

As used in this article, "physician" means a person authorized, or reasonably believed by the patient to be authorized, to practice medicine in any state or nation. *(Stats.1965, c. 299, § 2, operative Jan. 1, 1967.)*

Law Revision Commission Comments

Defining "physician" to include a person "reasonably believed by the patient to be authorized" to practice medicine changes the existing law which requires that the physician be licensed. See Code Civ.Proc. § 1881(4) (superseded by the Evidence Code). But, if this privilege is to be recognized, it should protect the patient from reasonable mistakes as to unlicensed practitioners. The privilege also should be applicable to communications made to a physician authorized to practice in any state or nation. When a California resident travels outside the State and has occasion to visit a physician during such travel, or when a physician from another state or nation participates in the treatment of a person in California, the patient should be entitled to assume that his communications will be given as much protection as they would be if he consulted a California physician in California. A patient should not be forced to inquire about the jurisdictions where the physician is authorized to practice medicine and whether such jurisdictions recognize the physician-patient privilege before he may safely communicate with the physician. [7 Cal.L.Rev.Comm. Reports 1 (1965)].

Research References

Rutter, Cal. Practice Guide: Civ. Pro. Before Trial Ch. 8C-3, "Not Privileged".

Rutter, Cal. Practice Guide: Civ. Pro. Before Trial Ch. 8C-5, Privacy Protection.

Rutter, Cal. Practice Guide: Civil Trials & Evidence Ch. 8E-A, A. Privileges.

Rutter, Cal. Practice Guide: Family Law Ch. 11-C, C. Optional "Formal" Discovery Procedures.

Rutter, Cal. Practice Guide: Personal Injury Ch. 6-A, A. Scope of Discovery and Limitations.

Rutter, Cal. Practice Guide: Personal Injury Gen. Matls., Highlights.

§ 991. Patient

As used in this article, "patient" means a person who consults a physician or submits to an examination by a physician for the purpose of securing a diagnosis or preventive, palliative, or curative treatment of his physical or mental or emotional condition. *(Stats.1965, c. 299, § 2, operative Jan. 1, 1967.)*

Research References

Rutter, Cal. Practice Guide: Civil Trials & Evidence Ch. 8E-A, A. Privileges.

Rutter, Cal. Practice Guide: Personal Injury Ch. 6-A, A. Scope of Discovery and Limitations.

§ 992. Confidential communication between patient and physician

As used in this article, "confidential communication between patient and physician" means information, including information obtained by an examination of the patient, transmitted between a patient and his physician in the course of that relationship and in confidence by a means which, so far as the patient is aware, discloses the information to no third persons other than those who are present to further the interest of the patient in the consultation or those to whom disclosure is reasonably necessary for the transmission of the information or the accomplishment of the purpose for which the physician is consulted, and includes a diagnosis made and the advice given by the physician in the course of that relationship. *(Stats.1965, c. 299, § 2, operative Jan. 1, 1967. Amended by Stats.1967, c. 650, p. 2006, § 4.)*

Law Revision Commission Comments

The express inclusion of "a diagnosis" in the last clause will preclude a possible construction of this section that would leave an uncommunicated diagnosis unprotected by the privilege. Such a construction would virtually destroy the privilege. [8 Cal.L.Rev.Comm. Reports 101 (1967)].

Research References

Rutter, Cal. Practice Guide: Civil Trials & Evidence Ch. 8E-A, A. Privileges.

Rutter, Cal. Practice Guide: Family Law Ch. 7-B, B. Contested Custody Proceedings, Generally.

Rutter, Cal. Practice Guide: Personal Injury Ch. 6-A, A. Scope of Discovery and Limitations.

§ 993. Holder of the privilege

As used in this article, "holder of the privilege" means:

(a) The patient when he has no guardian or conservator.

(b) A guardian or conservator of the patient when the patient has a guardian or conservator.

(c) The personal representative of the patient if the patient is dead. *(Stats.1965, c. 299, § 2, operative Jan. 1, 1967.)*

Law Revision Commission Comments

A guardian of the patient is the holder of the privilege if the patient has a guardian. If the patient has separate guardians of his estate and of his person, either guardian may claim the privilege. The provision making the personal representative of the patient the holder of the privilege when the patient is dead may change California law. The existing law may be that the privilege survives the death of the patient in some cases and that no one can waive it on behalf of the patient. See the discussion in Tentative Recommendation and a Study Relating to the Uniform Rules of Evidence (Article V. Privileges), 6 Cal.Law Revision Comm'n, Rep., Rec. & Studies 201, 408–410 (1964). Sections 993 and 994 enable the personal representative to protect the interest of the patient's estate in the confidentiality of these statements and to waive the privilege when the estate would benefit by waiver. When the patient's estate has no interest in preserving confidentiality, or when the estate has been distributed and the representative discharged, the importance of providing complete access to information relevant to a particular proceeding should prevail over whatever remaining interest the decedent may have had in secrecy. [7 Cal.L.Rev.Comm. Reports 1 (1965)].

Research References

Rutter, Cal. Practice Guide: Civil Trials & Evidence Ch. 8E-A, A. Privileges.

§ 994. Physician-patient privilege

Subject to Section 912 and except as otherwise provided in this article, the patient, whether or not a party, has a privilege to refuse to disclose, and to prevent another from disclosing, a confidential communication between patient and physician if the privilege is claimed by:

(a) The holder of the privilege;

(b) A person who is authorized to claim the privilege by the holder of the privilege; or

(c) The person who was the physician at the time of the confidential communication, but such person may not claim the privilege if there is no holder of the privilege in existence or if he or she is otherwise instructed by a person authorized to permit disclosure.

The relationship of a physician and patient shall exist between a medical or podiatry corporation as defined in the Medical Practice Act and the patient to whom it renders professional services, as well as between such patients and licensed physicians and surgeons employed by such corporation to render services to such patients. The word "persons" as used in this subdivision includes partnerships, corporations, limited liability companies, associations, and other groups and entities. *(Stats.1965, c. 299, § 2, operative Jan. 1, 1967. Amended by Stats.1968, c. 1375, p. 2696, § 3; Stats.1980, c. 1313, p. 4532, § 12; Stats.1994, c. 1010 (S.B.2053), § 105.)*

Law Revision Commission Comments

This section, like Section 954 (lawyer-client privilege), is based on the premise that the privilege must be claimed by a person who is authorized to claim the privilege. If there is no claim of privilege by a person with authority to make the claim, the evidence is admissible. See the Comments to Evidence Code §§ 993 and 954.

For the reasons indicated in the Comment to Section 954, an eavesdropper or other interceptor of a communication privileged under this section is not permitted to testify to the communication. [7 Cal.L.Rev.Comm. Reports 1 (1965)].

Research References

Rutter, Cal. Practice Guide: Civil Appeals & Writs Ch. 15-B, B. Common Law Writs.

Rutter, Cal. Practice Guide: Civil Appeals & Writs Gen. Matls., Highlights.

Rutter, Cal. Practice Guide: Civil Trials & Evidence Ch. 4-B, B. Preliminary Matters Discussed in Final Status Conference or In-Chambers Conference.

Rutter, Cal. Practice Guide: Civil Trials & Evidence Ch. 8E-A, A. Privileges.

Rutter, Cal. Practice Guide: Family Law Ch. 7-B, B. Contested Custody Proceedings, Generally.

§ 995. When physician required to claim privilege

The physician who received or made a communication subject to the privilege under this article shall claim the privilege whenever he is present when the communication is sought to be disclosed and is authorized to claim the privilege under subdivision (c) of Section 994. *(Stats.1965, c. 299, § 2, operative Jan. 1, 1967.)*

Law Revision Commission Comments

The obligation of the physician to claim the privilege on behalf of the patient, unless otherwise instructed by a person authorized to permit disclosure, is consistent with Section 2379 of the Business and Professions Code. [7 Cal.L.Rev.Comm. Reports 1 (1965)].

Research References

Rutter, Cal. Practice Guide: Civil Trials & Evidence Ch. 8E-A, A. Privileges.

§ 996. Patient-litigant exception

There is no privilege under this article as to a communication relevant to an issue concerning the condition of the patient if such issue has been tendered by:

(a) The patient;

(b) Any party claiming through or under the patient;

(c) Any party claiming as a beneficiary of the patient through a contract to which the patient is or was a party; or

(d) The plaintiff in an action brought under Section 376 or 377 of the Code of Civil Procedure for damages for the injury or death of the patient. *(Stats.1965, c. 299, § 2, operative Jan. 1, 1967.)*

Law Revision Commission Comments

Section 996 provides that the physician-patient privilege does not exist in any proceeding in which an issue concerning the condition of the patient has been tendered by the patient. If the patient himself tenders the issue of his condition, he should not be able to withhold relevant evidence from the opposing party by the exercise of the physician-patient privilege.

A limited form of this exception is recognized by Code of Civil Procedure Section 1881(4) (superseded by the Evidence Code) which makes the privilege inapplicable in personal injury actions. This exception is also recognized in various types of administrative proceedings where the patient tenders the issue of his condition. *E.g.,* Labor Code §§ 4055, 5701, 5703, 6407, 6408 (proceedings before the Industrial Accident Commission). The exception provided by Section 996 applies not only to proceedings before the Industrial Accident Commission but also to any other proceeding where the patient tenders the issue of his condition. The exception in Section 996 also states existing law in applying the exception to other situations where the patient himself has raised the issue of his condition. In re Cathey, 55 Cal.2d 679, 690–692, 12 Cal.Rptr. 762, 768, 361 P.2d 426, 432 (1961) (prisoner in state medical facility waived physician-patient privilege by putting his mental condition in issue by application for habeas corpus); see also City & County of San Francisco v. Superior Court, 37 Cal.2d 227, 232, 231 P.2d 26, 28 (1951) (personal injury case).

Section 996 also provides that there is no privilege in an action brought under Section 377 of the Code of Civil Procedure (wrongful death). Under Code of Civil Procedure Section 1881(4) (superseded by the Evidence Code), a person authorized to bring the wrongful death action may consent to the testimony by the physician. As far as testimony by the physician is concerned, there is no reason why the rules of evidence should be different in a case where the patient brings the action and a case where someone else sues for the patient's wrongful death.

Section 996 also provides that there is no privilege in an action brought under Section 376 of the Code of Civil Procedure (parent's action for injury to child). In this case, as in a case under the wrongful death statute, the same rule of evidence should apply when the parent brings the action as applies when the child is the plaintiff. [7 Cal.L.Rev.Comm. Reports 1 (1965)].

Research References

Rutter, Cal. Practice Guide: Civil Appeals & Writs Ch. 15-B, B. Common Law Writs.
Rutter, Cal. Practice Guide: Civil Appeals & Writs Gen. Matls., Highlights.
Rutter, Cal. Practice Guide: Civ. Pro. Before Trial Ch. 8C-3, "Not Privileged".
Rutter, Cal. Practice Guide: Civ. Pro. Before Trial Ch. 8C-5, Privacy Protection.
Rutter, Cal. Practice Guide: Civ. Pro. Before Trial Ch. 8I-5, Exchange of Medical Reports; Waiver of Privilege.
Rutter, Cal. Practice Guide: Civil Trials & Evidence Ch. 8E-A, A. Privileges.
Rutter, Cal. Practice Guide: Civil Trials & Evidence Ch. 8E-C, C. Right of Privacy.
Rutter, Cal. Practice Guide: Civil Trials & Evidence Gen. Matls., Highlights.
Rutter, Cal. Practice Guide: Family Law Ch. 6-B, B. Spousal Support.
Rutter, Cal. Practice Guide: Personal Injury Ch. 6-A, A. Scope of Discovery and Limitations.

§ 997. Exception: crime or tort

There is no privilege under this article if the services of the physician were sought or obtained to enable or aid anyone to commit or plan to commit a crime or a tort or to escape detection or apprehension after the commission of a crime or a tort. *(Stats.1965, c. 299, § 2, operative Jan. 1, 1967.)*

Law Revision Commission Comments

This section is considerably broader in scope than Section 956 which provides that the lawyer-client privilege does not apply when the communication was made to enable anyone to commit or plan to commit a crime or a *fraud*. Section 997 creates an exception to the physician-patient privilege where the services of the physician were sought or obtained to enable or aid anyone to commit or plan to commit a crime or a *tort*, or to escape detection or apprehension after commission of a crime or a *tort*. People seldom, if ever, consult their physicians in regard to matters which might subsequently be determined to be a tort, and there is no desirable end to be served by encouraging such communications. On the other hand, people often consult lawyers about matters which may later turn out to be torts and it is desirable to encourage discussion of such matters with lawyers. Whether the exception provided by Section 997 now exists in California has not been determined in any decided case, but it probably would be recognized in an appropriate case in view of the similar court-created exception to the lawyer-client privilege. See the Comment to Evidence Code § 956. [7 Cal.L.Rev.Comm. Reports 1 (1965)].

Research References

Rutter, Cal. Practice Guide: Civil Trials & Evidence Ch. 8E-A, A. Privileges.
Rutter, Cal. Practice Guide: Personal Injury Ch. 6-A, A. Scope of Discovery and Limitations.

§ 998. Criminal proceeding

There is no privilege under this article in a criminal proceeding. *(Stats.1965, c. 299, § 2, operative Jan. 1, 1967.)*

Research References

Rutter, Cal. Practice Guide: Civil Trials & Evidence Ch. 8E-A, A. Privileges.

§ 999. Communication relating to patient condition in proceeding to recover damages; good cause

There is no privilege under this article as to a communication relevant to an issue concerning the condition of the patient in a proceeding to recover damages on account of the conduct of the patient if good cause for disclosure of the communication is shown. *(Stats.1965, c. 299, § 2, operative Jan. 1, 1967. Amended by Stats.1975, c. 318, p. 764, § 1.)*

Research References

Rutter, Cal. Practice Guide: Civil Trials & Evidence Ch. 8E-A, A. Privileges.
Rutter, Cal. Practice Guide: Personal Injury Ch. 6-A, A. Scope of Discovery and Limitations.

§ 1000. Parties claiming through deceased patient

There is no privilege under this article as to a communication relevant to an issue between parties all of whom claim through a deceased patient, regardless of whether the claims are by testate or intestate succession or by inter vivos transaction. *(Stats.1965, c. 299, § 2, operative Jan. 1, 1967.)*

Law Revision Commission Comments

See the Comment to Section 957. [7 Cal.L.Rev.Comm. Reports 1 (1965)].

Research References

Rutter, Cal. Practice Guide: Civil Trials & Evidence Ch. 8E-A, A. Privileges.

§ 1001. Breach of duty arising out of physician-patient relationship

There is no privilege under this article as to a communication relevant to an issue of breach, by the physician or by the patient, of a duty arising out of the physician-patient relationship. *(Stats.1965, c. 299, § 2, operative Jan. 1, 1967.)*

Law Revision Commission Comments

See the Comment to Section 658. [7 Cal.L.Rev.Comm. Reports 1 (1965)].

Research References

Rutter, Cal. Practice Guide: Civil Trials & Evidence Ch. 8E-A, A. Privileges.
Rutter, Cal. Practice Guide: Personal Injury Ch. 6-A, A. Scope of Discovery and Limitations.

§ 1002. Intention of deceased patient concerning writing affecting property interest

There is no privilege under this article as to a communication relevant to an issue concerning the intention of a patient, now deceased, with respect to a deed of conveyance, will, or other writing, executed by the patient, purporting to affect an interest in property. *(Stats.1965, c. 299, § 2, operative Jan. 1, 1967.)*

Law Revision Commission Comments

Existing law provides exceptions virtually coextensive with those provided in Sections 1002 and 1003. Code Civ.Proc. § 1881(4) (superseded by the Evidence Code). See the Comment to Section 960. [7 Cal.L.Rev. Comm. Reports 1 (1965)].

Research References

Rutter, Cal. Practice Guide: Civil Trials & Evidence Ch. 8E-A, A. Privileges.

§ 1003. Validity of writing affecting property interest

There is no privilege under this article as to a communication relevant to an issue concerning the validity of a deed of conveyance, will, or other writing, executed by a patient, now deceased, purporting to affect an interest in property. *(Stats. 1965, c. 299, § 2, operative Jan. 1, 1967.)*

Law Revision Commission Comments

See the Comment to Section 1002. [7 Cal.L.Rev.Comm. Reports 1 (1965)].

Research References

Rutter, Cal. Practice Guide: Civil Trials & Evidence Ch. 8E-A, A. Privileges.

§ 1004. Commitment or similar proceeding

There is no privilege under this article in a proceeding to commit the patient or otherwise place him or his property, or both, under the control of another because of his alleged mental or physical condition. *(Stats.1965, c. 299, § 2, operative Jan. 1, 1967.)*

Law Revision Commission Comments

This exception covers not only commitments of mentally ill persons but also such cases as the appointment of a conservator under Probate Code Section 1751. In these cases, the proceedings are being conducted for the benefit of the patient and he should not have a privilege to withhold evidence that the court needs in order to act properly for his welfare. There is no similar exception in existing law. McClenahan v. Keyes, 188 Cal. 574, 584, 206 Pac. 454, 458 (1922) (dictum). *But see* 35 Ops.Cal.Atty. Gen. 226 (1960), regarding the unavailability of the present physician-patient privilege where the physician acts pursuant to court appointment for the explicit purpose of giving testimony. [7 Cal.L.Rev.Comm. Reports 1 (1965)].

Research References

Rutter, Cal. Practice Guide: Civil Trials & Evidence Ch. 8E-A, A. Privileges.

§ 1005. Proceeding to establish competence

There is no privilege under this article in a proceeding brought by or on behalf of the patient to establish his competence. *(Stats.1965, c. 299, § 2, operative Jan. 1, 1967.)*

Law Revision Commission Comments

This exception is new to California law. When a patient has placed his mental condition in issue by instituting a proceeding to establish his competence, he should not be permitted to withhold the most vital evidence relating thereto. [7 Cal.L.Rev.Comm. Reports 1 (1965)].

Research References

Rutter, Cal. Practice Guide: Civil Trials & Evidence Ch. 8E-A, A. Privileges.

§ 1006. Required report

There is no privilege under this article as to information that the physician or the patient is required to report to a public employee, or as to information required to be recorded in a public office, if such report or record is open to public inspection. *(Stats.1965, c. 299, § 2, operative Jan. 1, 1967.)*

Law Revision Commission Comments

This exception is not recognized by existing law. However, no valid purpose is served by preventing the use of relevant information when the law requiring the information to be reported to a public office does not restrict disclosure. [7 Cal.L.Rev.Comm. Reports 1 (1965)].

Research References

Rutter, Cal. Practice Guide: Civil Trials & Evidence Ch. 8E-A, A. Privileges.

§ 1007. Proceeding to terminate right, license or privilege

There is no privilege under this article in a proceeding brought by a public entity to determine whether a right, authority, license, or privilege (including the right or privilege to be employed by the public entity or to hold a public office) should be revoked, suspended, terminated, limited, or conditioned. *(Stats.1965, c. 299, § 2, operative Jan. 1, 1967.)*

Research References

Rutter, Cal. Practice Guide: Civil Trials & Evidence Ch. 8E-A, A. Privileges.
Rutter, Cal. Practice Guide: Family Law Ch. 11-C, C. Optional "Formal" Discovery Procedures.
Rutter, Cal. Practice Guide: Personal Injury Ch. 6-A, A. Scope of Discovery and Limitations.

ARTICLE 7. PSYCHOTHERAPIST–PATIENT PRIVILEGE

Section

1018. Exception: Crime or tort.
1019. Exception: Parties claiming through deceased patient.
1020. Exception: Breach of duty arising out of psychotherapist-patient relationship.
1021. Exception: Intention of deceased patient concerning writing affecting property interest.
1022. Exception: Validity of writing affecting property interest.
1023. Exception: Proceeding to determine sanity of criminal defendant.
1024. Exception: Patient dangerous to himself or others.
1025. Exception: Proceeding to establish competence.
1026. Exception: Required report.
1027. Exception: Child under 16 victim of crime.

§ 1010. Psychotherapist

As used in this article, "psychotherapist" means a person who is, or is reasonably believed by the patient to be:

(a) A person authorized to practice medicine in any state or nation who devotes, or is reasonably believed by the patient to devote, a substantial portion of his or her time to the practice of psychiatry.

(b) A person licensed as a psychologist under Chapter 6.6 (commencing with Section 2900) of Division 2 of the Business and Professions Code.

(c) A person licensed as a clinical social worker under Article 4 (commencing with Section 4996) of Chapter 14 of Division 2 of the Business and Professions Code, when he or she is engaged in applied psychotherapy of a nonmedical nature.

(d) A person who is serving as a school psychologist and holds a credential authorizing that service issued by the state.

(e) A person licensed as a marriage and family therapist under Chapter 13 (commencing with Section 4980) of Division 2 of the Business and Professions Code.

(f) A person registered as a psychological assistant who is under the supervision of a licensed psychologist or board certified psychiatrist as required by Section 2913 of the Business and Professions Code, or a person registered as a marriage and family therapist intern who is under the supervision of a licensed marriage and family therapist, a licensed clinical social worker, a licensed psychologist, or a licensed physician and surgeon certified in psychiatry, as specified in Section 4980.44 of the Business and Professions Code.

(g) A person registered as an associate clinical social worker who is under supervision as specified in Section 4996.23 of the Business and Professions Code.

(h) A person exempt from the Psychology Licensing Law pursuant to subdivision (d) of Section 2909 of the Business and Professions Code who is under the supervision of a licensed psychologist or board certified psychiatrist.

(i) A psychological intern as defined in Section 2911 of the Business and Professions Code who is under the supervision of a licensed psychologist or board certified psychiatrist.

(j) A trainee, as defined in subdivision (c) of Section 4980.03 of the Business and Professions Code, who is fulfilling his or her supervised practicum required by subparagraph (B) of paragraph (1) of subdivision (d) of Section 4980.36 of, or subdivision (c) of Section 4980.37 of, the Business and Professions Code and is supervised by a licensed psychologist, a board certified psychiatrist, a licensed clinical social worker, a licensed marriage and family therapist, or a licensed professional clinical counselor.

(k) A person licensed as a registered nurse pursuant to Chapter 6 (commencing with Section 2700) of Division 2 of the Business and Professions Code, who possesses a master's degree in psychiatric-mental health nursing and is listed as a psychiatric-mental health nurse by the Board of Registered Nursing.

(*l*) An advanced practice registered nurse who is certified as a clinical nurse specialist pursuant to Article 9 (commencing with Section 2838) of Chapter 6 of Division 2 of the Business and Professions Code and who participates in expert clinical practice in the specialty of psychiatric-mental health nursing.

(m) A person rendering mental health treatment or counseling services as authorized pursuant to Section 6924 of the Family Code.

(n) A person licensed as a professional clinical counselor under Chapter 16 (commencing with Section 4999.10) of Division 2 of the Business and Professions Code.

(*o*) A person registered as a clinical counselor intern who is under the supervision of a licensed professional clinical counselor, a licensed marriage and family therapist, a licensed clinical social worker, a licensed psychologist, or a licensed physician and surgeon certified in psychiatry, as specified in Sections 4999.42 to 4999.46, inclusive, of the Business and Professions Code.

(p) A clinical counselor trainee, as defined in subdivision (g) of Section 4999.12 of the Business and Professions Code, who is fulfilling his or her supervised practicum required by paragraph (3) of subdivision (c) of Section 4999.32 of, or paragraph (3) of subdivision (c) of Section 4999.33 of, the Business and Professions Code, and is supervised by a licensed psychologist, a board-certified psychiatrist, a licensed clinical social worker, a licensed marriage and family therapist, or a licensed professional clinical counselor. (*Stats.1965, c. 299, § 2, operative Jan. 1, 1967. Amended by Stats.1967, c. 1677, p. 4211, § 3; Stats.1970, c. 1396, p. 2624, § 1.5; Stats.1970, c. 1397, p. 2626, § 1.5; Stats.1972, c. 888, p. 1584, § 1; Stats.1974, c. 546, p. 1359, § 16; Stats.1983, c. 928, § 8; Stats.1987, c. 724, § 1; Stats.1988, c. 488, § 1; Stats.1989, c. 1104, § 37; Stats.1990, c. 662 (A.B.3613), § 1; Stats.1992, c. 308 (A.B.3035), § 2; Stats.1994, c. 1270 (A.B.2659), § 1; Stats.2001, c. 142 (S.B.716), § 1; Stats.2001, c. 420 (A.B. 1253), § 1, eff. Oct. 2, 2001; Stats.2001, c. 420 (A.B.1253), § 1.5, eff. Oct. 2, 2001, operative Jan. 1, 2002; Stats.2009, c. 26 (S.B.33), § 21; Stats.2011, c. 381 (S.B.146), § 21.)*

Law Revision Commission Comments

A "psychotherapist" is defined to include only a person who is or who is reasonably believed to be a psychiatrist or who is a California certified psychologist (see Bus. & Prof.Code § 2900 et seq.). See the Comment to Section 990. [7 Cal.L.Rev.Comm. Reports 1 (1965)].

Research References

Rutter, Cal. Practice Guide: Civ. Pro. Before Trial Ch. 8C-3, "Not Privileged".
Rutter, Cal. Practice Guide: Civ. Pro. Before Trial Ch. 8E-6, Subpoena to Nonparty Deponent or Business Records Custodian.
Rutter, Cal. Practice Guide: Civil Trials & Evidence Ch. 1-C, C. Marshalling the Evidence.
Rutter, Cal. Practice Guide: Civil Trials & Evidence Ch. 8E-A, A. Privileges.
Rutter, Cal. Practice Guide: Family Law Ch. 11-C, C. Optional "Formal" Discovery Procedures.
Rutter, Cal. Practice Guide: Personal Injury Ch. 6-A, A. Scope of Discovery and Limitations.
Rutter, Cal. Practice Guide: Personal Injury Ch. 2(II)-I, I. Negligence Liability Based on Omission to Act-Legal Duty Arising from "Special Relationship".
1 Witkin Cal. Summ. 10th Contracts § 45, Minor Needing Mental Health Treatment.

§ 1010.5. Privileged communication between patient and educational psychologist

A communication between a patient and an educational psychologist, licensed under Article 5 (commencing with Section

4986) of Chapter 13 of Division 2 of the Business and Professions Code, shall be privileged to the same extent, and subject to the same limitations, as a communication between a patient and a psychotherapist described in subdivisions (c), (d), and (e) of Section 1010. *(Added by Stats.1985, c. 545, § 1.)*

Research References

Rutter, Cal. Practice Guide: Civ. Pro. Before Trial Ch. 8C-3, "Not Privileged".

Rutter, Cal. Practice Guide: Civil Trials & Evidence Ch. 4-B, B. Preliminary Matters Discussed in Final Status Conference or In-Chambers Conference.

Rutter, Cal. Practice Guide: Civil Trials & Evidence Ch. 8E-A, A. Privileges.

Rutter, Cal. Practice Guide: Family Law Ch. 11-C, C. Optional "Formal" Discovery Procedures.

Rutter, Cal. Practice Guide: Personal Injury Ch. 6-A, A. Scope of Discovery and Limitations.

§ 1011. Patient

As used in this article, "patient" means a person who consults a psychotherapist or submits to an examination by a psychotherapist for the purpose of securing a diagnosis or preventive, palliative, or curative treatment of his mental or emotional condition or who submits to an examination of his mental or emotional condition for the purpose of scientific research on mental or emotional problems. *(Stats.1965, c. 299, § 2, operative Jan. 1, 1967.)*

Research References

Rutter, Cal. Practice Guide: Civil Trials & Evidence Ch. 8E-A, A. Privileges.

Rutter, Cal. Practice Guide: Personal Injury Ch. 6-A, A. Scope of Discovery and Limitations.

§ 1012. Confidential communication between patient and psychotherapist

As used in this article, "confidential communication between patient and psychotherapist" means information, including information obtained by an examination of the patient, transmitted between a patient and his psychotherapist in the course of that relationship and in confidence by a means which, so far as the patient is aware, discloses the information to no third persons other than those who are present to further the interest of the patient in the consultation, or those to whom disclosure is reasonably necessary for the transmission of the information or the accomplishment of the purpose for which the psychotherapist is consulted, and includes a diagnosis made and the advice given by the psychotherapist in the course of that relationship. *(Stats.1965, c. 299, § 2, operative Jan. 1, 1967. Amended by Stats.1967, c. 650, p. 2006, § 5; Stats.1970, c. 1396, p. 2625, § 2; Stats.1970, c. 1397, p. 2627, § 2.)*

Law Revision Commission Comments

See the Comment to Section 992. [7 Cal.L.Rev.Comm. Reports 1 (1965)].

The express inclusion of "a diagnosis" in the last clause will preclude a possible construction of this section that would leave an uncommunicated diagnosis unprotected by the privilege. Such a construction would virtually destroy the privilege. [8 Cal.L.Rev.Comm. Reports 101 (1967)].

Section 1012 is amended to add "including other patients present at joint therapy" in order to foreclose the possibility that the section would be construed not to embrace marriage counseling, family counseling, and other forms of group therapy. However, it should be noted that communications made in the course of joint therapy are within the privilege only if they are made "in confidence" and "by a means which . . . discloses the information to no third persons other than those . . . to whom disclosure is reasonably necessary for . . . the accomplishment of the purpose for which the psychotherapist is consulted." The making of a communication that meets these two requirements in the course of joint

therapy would not amount to a waiver of the privilege. See Evidence Code Section 912(c) and (d).

The other amendments are technical and conform the language of Section 1012 to that of Section 992, the comparable section relating to the physician-patient privilege. Deletion of the words "or examination" makes no substantive change since "consultation" is broad enough to cover an examination. See Section 992. Substitution of "for which the psychotherapist is consulted" for "of the consultation or examination" adopts the broader language used in subdivision (d) of Section 912 and in Section 992. [9 Cal.L.Rev.Comm. Reports 153 (1969)].

Research References

Rutter, Cal. Practice Guide: Civil Trials & Evidence Ch. 4-B, B. Preliminary Matters Discussed in Final Status Conference or In-Chambers Conference.

Rutter, Cal. Practice Guide: Civil Trials & Evidence Ch. 8E-A, A. Privileges.

Rutter, Cal. Practice Guide: Personal Injury Ch. 6-A, A. Scope of Discovery and Limitations.

10 Witkin, California Summary 10th Parent and Child § 620, (S 620) Privileges.

10 Witkin, California Summary 10th Parent and Child § 873, (S 873) Privileges.

§ 1013. Holder of the privilege

As used in this article, "holder of the privilege" means:

(a) The patient when he has no guardian or conservator.

(b) A guardian or conservator of the patient when the patient has a guardian or conservator.

(c) The personal representative of the patient if the patient is dead. *(Stats.1965, c. 299, § 2, operative Jan. 1, 1967.)*

Law Revision Commission Comments

See the Comment to Section 993. [7 Cal.L.Rev.Comm. Reports 1 (1965)].

Research References

Rutter, Cal. Practice Guide: Civil Trials & Evidence Ch. 8E-A, A. Privileges.

§ 1014. Psychotherapist-patient privilege; application to individuals and entities

Subject to Section 912 and except as otherwise provided in this article, the patient, whether or not a party, has a privilege to refuse to disclose, and to prevent another from disclosing, a confidential communication between patient and psychotherapist if the privilege is claimed by:

(a) The holder of the privilege.

(b) A person who is authorized to claim the privilege by the holder of the privilege.

(c) The person who was the psychotherapist at the time of the confidential communication, but the person may not claim the privilege if there is no holder of the privilege in existence or if he or she is otherwise instructed by a person authorized to permit disclosure.

The relationship of a psychotherapist and patient shall exist between a psychological corporation as defined in Article 9 (commencing with Section 2995) of Chapter 6.6 of Division 2 of the Business and Professions Code, a marriage and family therapist corporation as defined in Article 6 (commencing with Section 4987.5) of Chapter 13 of Division 2 of the Business and Professions Code, a licensed clinical social workers corporation as defined in Article 5 (commencing with Section 4998) of Chapter 14 of Division 2 of the Business and Professions Code, or a professional clinical counselor corporation as defined in Article 7 (commencing with Section 4999.123) of Chapter 16 of Division 2 of the Business and Professions Code, and the patient to whom it renders professional services, as well as between those patients and psychotherapists employed by those corporations to render services to those patients. The word "persons" as used in this subdivision includes partnerships, corporations, limited liability companies, associations, and other groups and entities. *(Stats.1965, c. 299, § 2, operative Jan. 1, 1967. Amended by Stats.1969, c. 1436, p. 2943, § 1; Stats.1972, c. 1286, p. 2569, § 6; Stats.1989, c. 1104, § 38; Stats.1990, c. 605 (S.B.2245), § 1; Stats.1994, c. 1010 (S.B.2053), § 106; Stats.2002, c. 1013 (S.B. 2026), § 78; Stats.2011, c. 381 (S.B.146), § 22.)*

Research References

Rutter, Cal. Practice Guide: Civ. Pro. Before Trial Ch. 8C-5, Privacy Protection.

Rutter, Cal. Practice Guide: Civil Trials & Evidence Ch. 8E-A, A. Privileges.

Rutter, Cal. Practice Guide: Civil Trials & Evidence Ch. 8E-C, C. Right of Privacy.

Rutter, Cal. Practice Guide: Family Law Ch. 7-B, B. Contested Custody Proceedings, Generally.

Rutter, Cal. Practice Guide: Family Law Ch. 11-C, C. Optional "Formal" Discovery Procedures.

8 Witkin Cal. Proc. 5th Extraordinary Writs § 159, in General.

10 Witkin, California Summary 10th Parent and Child § 284, Trial.

10 Witkin, California Summary 10th Parent and Child § 873, (S 873) Privileges.

§ 1015. When psychotherapist required to claim privilege

The psychotherapist who received or made a communication subject to the privilege under this article shall claim the privilege whenever he is present when the communication is sought to be disclosed and is authorized to claim the privilege under subdivision (c) of Section 1014. *(Stats.1965, c. 299, § 2, operative Jan. 1, 1967.)*

Law Revision Commission Comments

See the Comment to Section 995. [7 Cal.L.Rev.Comm. Reports 1 (1965)].

Research References

Rutter, Cal. Practice Guide: Civil Trials & Evidence Ch. 8E-A, A. Privileges.

§ 1016. Exception: Patient-litigant exception

There is no privilege under this article as to a communication relevant to an issue concerning the mental or emotional condition of the patient if such issue has been tendered by:

(a) The patient;

(b) Any party claiming through or under the patient;

(c) Any party claiming as a beneficiary of the patient through a contract to which the patient is or was a party; or

(d) The plaintiff in an action brought under Section 376 or 377 of the Code of Civil Procedure for damages for the injury or death of the patient. *(Stats.1965, c. 299, § 2, operative Jan. 1, 1967.)*

Law Revision Commission Comments

See the Comment to Section 996. [7 Cal.L.Rev.Comm. Reports 1 (1965)].

Research References

Rutter, Cal. Practice Guide: Civ. Pro. Before Trial Ch. 8I-5, Exchange of Medical Reports; Waiver of Privilege.

Rutter, Cal. Practice Guide: Civil Trials & Evidence Ch. 8E-A, A. Privileges.

Rutter, Cal. Practice Guide: Family Law Ch. 6-B, B. Spousal Support.

Rutter, Cal. Practice Guide: Family Law Ch. 7-B, B. Contested Custody Proceedings, Generally.

Rutter, Cal. Practice Guide: Personal Injury Ch. 6-A, A. Scope of Discovery and Limitations.

10 Witkin, California Summary 10th Parent and Child § 620, (S 620) Privileges.

§ 1017. Exception: Psychotherapist appointed by court or board of prison terms

(a) There is no privilege under this article if the psychotherapist is appointed by order of a court to examine the patient, but this exception does not apply where the psychotherapist is appointed by order of the court upon the request of the lawyer for the defendant in a criminal proceeding in order to provide the lawyer with information needed so that he or she may advise the defendant whether to enter or withdraw a plea based on insanity or to present a defense based on his or her mental or emotional condition.

(b) There is no privilege under this article if the psychotherapist is appointed by the Board of Prison Terms to examine a patient pursuant to the provisions of Article 4 (commencing with Section 2960) of Chapter 7 of Title 1 of Part 3 of the Penal Code. *(Stats.1965, c. 299, § 2, operative Jan. 1, 1967. Amended by Stats.1967, c. 650, p. 2007, § 6; Stats.1987, c. 687, § 1.)*

Law Revision Commission Comments

Section 1017 provides an exception to the psychotherapist-patient privilege if the psychotherapist is appointed by order of a court to examine the patient. Generally, where the relationship of psychotherapist and patient is created by court order, there is not a sufficiently confidential relationship to warrant extending the privilege to communications made in the course of that relationship. Moreover, when the psychotherapist is appointed by the court, it is most often for the purpose of having the psychotherapist testify concerning his conclusions as to the patient's condition. It would be inappropriate to have the privilege apply in this situation. See generally 35 Ops.Cal.Atty.Gen. 226 (1960), regarding the unavailability of the present physician-patient privilege under these circumstances.

On the other hand, it is essential that the privilege apply where the psychotherapist is appointed by order of the court to provide the defendant's lawyer with information needed so that he may advise the defendant whether to enter a plea based on insanity or to present a defense based on his mental or emotional condition. If the defendant determines not to tender the issue of his mental or emotional condition, the privilege will protect the confidentiality of the communication between him and his court-appointed psychotherapist. If, however, the defendant determines to tender this issue—by a plea of not guilty by reason of insanity, by presenting a defense based on his mental or emotional condition, or by raising the question of his sanity at the time of the trial—the exceptions provided in Sections 1016 and 1023 make the privilege unavailable to prevent disclosure of the communications between the defendant and the psychotherapist. [7 Cal.L.Rev.Comm. Reports 1 (1965)].

The words "or withdraw" are added to Section 1017 to make it clear that the psychotherapist-patient privilege applies in a case where the defendant in a criminal proceeding enters a plea based on insanity, submits to an examination by a court-appointed psychotherapist, and later withdraws the plea based on insanity prior to the trial on that issue. In such case, since the defendant does not tender an issue based on his mental or emotional condition at the trial, the privilege should remain applicable. Of course, if the defendant determines to go to trial on the plea based on insanity, the psychotherapist-patient privilege will not be applicable. See Section 1016.

It should be noted that violation of the constitutional right to counsel may require the exclusion of evidence that is not privileged under this article; and, even in cases where this constitutional right is not violated, the protection that this right affords may require certain procedural safeguards in the examination procedure and a limiting instruction if the psychotherapist's testimony is admitted. See In re Spencer, 63 Cal.2d 400, 46 Cal.Rptr. 753, 406 P.2d 33 (1965).

It is important to recognize that the attorney-client privilege may provide protection in some cases where an exception to the psychotherapist-patient privilege is applicable. See Section 952 and the *Comment* thereto. See also Sections 912(d) and 954 and the *Comments* thereto. [8 Cal.L.Rev.Comm. Reports 101 (1967)].

Evidence

Research References

Rutter, Cal. Practice Guide: Civil Trials & Evidence Ch. 8E-A, A. Privileges.

Rutter, Cal. Practice Guide: Personal Injury Ch. 6-A, A. Scope of Discovery and Limitations.

10 Witkin, California Summary 10th Parent and Child § 284, Trial.

10 Witkin, California Summary 10th Parent and Child § 620, (S 620) Privileges.

§ 1018. Exception: Crime or tort

There is no privilege under this article if the services of the psychotherapist were sought or obtained to enable or aid anyone to commit or plan to commit a crime or a tort or to escape detection or apprehension after the commission of a crime or a tort. *(Stats.1965, c. 299, § 2, operative Jan. 1, 1967.)*

Law Revision Commission Comments

See the Comment to Section 997. [7 Cal.L.Rev.Comm. Reports 1 (1965)].

Research References

Rutter, Cal. Practice Guide: Civil Trials & Evidence Ch. 8E-A, A. Privileges.

§ 1019. Exception: Parties claiming through deceased patient

There is no privilege under this article as to a communication relevant to an issue between parties all of whom claim through a deceased patient, regardless of whether the claims are by testate or intestate succession or by inter vivos transaction. *(Stats.1965, c. 299, § 2, operative Jan. 1, 1967.)*

Law Revision Commission Comments

See the Comment to Section 957. [7 Cal.L.Rev.Comm. Reports 1 (1965)].

Research References

Rutter, Cal. Practice Guide: Civil Trials & Evidence Ch. 8E-A, A. Privileges.

§ 1020. Exception: Breach of duty arising out of psychotherapist-patient relationship

There is no privilege under this article as to a communication relevant to an issue of breach, by the psychotherapist or by the patient, of a duty arising out of the psychotherapist-patient relationship. *(Stats.1965, c. 299, § 2, operative Jan. 1, 1967.)*

Law Revision Commission Comments

See the Comment to Section 958. [7 Cal.L.Rev.Comm. Reports 1 (1965)].

Research References

Rutter, Cal. Practice Guide: Civil Trials & Evidence Ch. 8E-A, A. Privileges.

Rutter, Cal. Practice Guide: Personal Injury Ch. 6-A, A. Scope of Discovery and Limitations.

§ 1021. Exception: Intention of deceased patient concerning writing affecting property interest

There is no privilege under this article as to a communication relevant to an issue concerning the intention of a patient, now deceased, with respect to a deed of conveyance, will, or other writing, executed by the patient, purporting to affect an interest in property. *(Stats.1965, c. 299, § 2, operative Jan. 1, 1967.)*

Law Revision Commission Comments

See the Comment to Section 1002. [7 Cal.L.Rev.Comm. Reports 1 (1965)].

Research References

Rutter, Cal. Practice Guide: Civil Trials & Evidence Ch. 8E-A, A. Privileges.

§ 1022. Exception: Validity of writing affecting property interest

There is no privilege under this article as to a communication relevant to an issue concerning the validity of a deed of conveyance, will, or other writing, executed by a patient, now deceased, purporting to affect an interest in property. *(Stats. 1965, c. 299, § 2, operative Jan. 1, 1967.)*

Law Revision Commission Comments

See the Comment to Section 1002. [7 Cal.L.Rev.Comm. Reports 1 (1965)].

Research References

Rutter, Cal. Practice Guide: Civil Trials & Evidence Ch. 8E-A, A. Privileges.

§ 1023. Exception: Proceeding to determine sanity of criminal defendant

There is no privilege under this article in a proceeding under Chapter 6 (commencing with Section 1367) of Title 10 of Part 2 of the Penal Code initiated at the request of the defendant in a criminal action to determine his sanity. *(Stats.1965, c. 299, § 2, operative Jan. 1, 1967.)*

Law Revision Commission Comments

Section 1023 is included to make it clear that the psychotherapist-patient privilege does not apply when the defendant raises the issue of his sanity at the time of trial. The section probably is unnecessary because the exception provided by Section 1016 is broad enough to cover this situation. [7 Cal.L.Rev.Comm. Reports 1 (1965)].

Research References

Rutter, Cal. Practice Guide: Civil Trials & Evidence Ch. 8E-A, A. Privileges.

§ 1024. Exception: Patient dangerous to himself or others

There is no privilege under this article if the psychotherapist has reasonable cause to believe that the patient is in such mental or emotional condition as to be dangerous to himself or to the person or property of another and that disclosure of the communication is necessary to prevent the threatened danger. *(Stats.1965, c. 299, § 2, operative Jan. 1, 1967.)*

Law Revision Commission Comments

This section provides a narrower exception to the psychotherapist-patient privilege than the comparable exceptions provided by Section 982 (privilege for confidential marital communications) and Section 1004 (physician-patient privilege). Although this exception might inhibit the relationship between the patient and his psychotherapist to a limited extent, it is essential that appropriate action be taken if the psychotherapist becomes convinced during the course of treatment that the patient is a menace to himself or others and the patient refuses to permit the psychotherapist to make the disclosure necessary to prevent the threatened danger. [7 Cal.L.Rev.Comm. Reports 1 (1965)].

Research References

Rutter, Cal. Practice Guide: Civil Trials & Evidence Ch. 8E-A, A. Privileges.

Rutter, Cal. Practice Guide: Personal Injury Ch. 6-A, A. Scope of Discovery and Limitations.

10 Witkin, California Summary 10th Parent and Child § 873, (S 873) Privileges.

6 Witkin, California Summary 10th Torts § 1050, in General.

§ 1025.   Exception: Proceeding to establish competence

There is no privilege under this article in a proceeding brought by or on behalf of the patient to establish his competence. *(Stats.1965, c. 299, § 2, operative Jan. 1, 1967.)*

Law Revision Commission Comments

See the Comment to Section 1005.   [7 Cal.L.Rev.Comm. Reports 1 (1965)].

Research References

Rutter, Cal. Practice Guide: Civil Trials & Evidence Ch. 8E-A, A. Privileges.

§ 1026.   Exception: Required report

There is no privilege under this article as to information that the psychotherapist or the patient is required to report to a public employee or as to information required to be recorded in a public office, if such report or record is open to public inspection.   *(Stats.1965, c. 299, § 2, operative Jan. 1, 1967.)*

Law Revision Commission Comments

See the Comment to Section 1006.   [7 Cal.L.Rev.Comm. Reports 1 (1965)].

Research References

Rutter, Cal. Practice Guide: Civil Trials & Evidence Ch. 8E-A, A. Privileges.

§ 1027.   Exception: Child under 16 victim of crime

There is no privilege under this article if all of the following circumstances exist:

(a) The patient is a child under the age of 16.

(b) The psychotherapist has reasonable cause to believe that the patient has been the victim of a crime and that disclosure of the communication is in the best interest of the child.   *(Added by Stats.1970, c. 1397, p. 2627, § 3.)*

Law Revision Commission Comments

Section 1027 provides an exception to the psychotherapist-patient privilege that is analogous to the exception provided by Section 1024 (patient dangerous to himself or others).   The exception provided by Section 1027 is necessary to permit court disclosure of communications to a psychotherapist by a child who has been the victim of a crime (such as child abuse) in a proceeding in which the commission of such crime is a subject of inquiry.   Although the exception provided by Section 1027 might inhibit the relationship between the patient and his psychotherapist to a limited extent, it is essential that appropriate action be taken if the psychotherapist becomes convinced during the course of treatment that the patient is the victim of a crime and that disclosure of the communication would be in the best interest of the child.

The text of both 1970 additions was identical.   [9 Cal.L.Rev.Comm. Reports 137 (1970)].

Research References

Rutter, Cal. Practice Guide: Civil Trials & Evidence Ch. 8E-A, A. Privileges.
Rutter, Cal. Practice Guide: Family Law Ch. 11-C, C. Optional "Formal" Discovery Procedures.
Rutter, Cal. Practice Guide: Personal Injury Ch. 6-A, A. Scope of Discovery and Limitations.

ARTICLE 8.   CLERGY PENITENT PRIVILEGES

§ 1030.   Member of the clergy

As used in this article, a "member of the clergy" means a priest, minister, religious practitioner, or similar functionary of a church or of a religious denomination or religious organization. *(Stats.1965, c. 299, § 2, operative Jan. 1, 1967.   Amended by Stats.2002, c. 806 (A.B.3027), § 19.)*

Law Revision Commission Comments

Clergyman is broadly defined in this section.   [7 Cal.L.Rev.Comm. Reports 1 (1965)].

Research References

Rutter, Cal. Practice Guide: Civ. Pro. Before Trial Ch. 8C-3, "Not Privileged".
Rutter, Cal. Practice Guide: Civil Trials & Evidence Ch. 8E-A, A. Privileges.
Rutter, Cal. Practice Guide: Family Law Ch. 11-C, C. Optional "Formal" Discovery Procedures.
Rutter, Cal. Practice Guide: Personal Injury Ch. 6-A, A. Scope of Discovery and Limitations.

§ 1031.   Penitent

As used in this article, "penitent" means a person who has made a penitential communication to a member of the clergy. *(Stats.1965, c. 299, § 2, operative Jan. 1, 1967.   Amended by Stats.2002, c. 806 (A.B.3027), § 20.)*

Law Revision Commission Comments

This section defines "penitent" by incorporating the definitions in Sections 1030 and 1032.   [7 Cal.L.Rev.Comm. Reports 1 (1965)].

Research References

Rutter, Cal. Practice Guide: Civil Trials & Evidence Ch. 8E-A, A. Privileges.

§ 1032.   Penitential communication

As used in this article, "penitential communication" means a communication made in confidence, in the presence of no third person so far as the penitent is aware, to a member of the clergy who, in the course of the discipline or practice of the clergy member's church, denomination, or organization, is authorized or accustomed to hear those communications and, under the discipline or tenets of his or her church, denomination, or organization, has a duty to keep those communications secret. *(Stats.1965, c. 299, § 2, operative Jan. 1, 1967.   Amended by Stats.2002, c. 806 (A.B.3027), § 21.)*

Law Revision Commission Comments

Under existing law, the communication must be a "confession."   Code Civ.Proc. § 1881(3) (superseded by the Evidence Code).   Section 1032 extends the protection that traditionally has been provided only to those persons whose religious practice involves "confessions."   [7 Cal.L.Rev. Comm. Reports 1 (1965)].

Research References

Rutter, Cal. Practice Guide: Civ. Pro. Before Trial Ch. 8C-3, "Not Privileged".
Rutter, Cal. Practice Guide: Civil Trials & Evidence Ch. 8E-A, A. Privileges.
Rutter, Cal. Practice Guide: Personal Injury Ch. 6-A, A. Scope of Discovery and Limitations.

§ 1033.   Privilege of penitent

Subject to Section 912, a penitent, whether or not a party, has a privilege to refuse to disclose, and to prevent another from disclosing, a penitential communication if he or she claims the privilege. *(Stats.1965, c. 299, § 2, operative Jan. 1, 1967. Amended by Stats.2002, c. 806 (A.B.3027), § 22.)*

Law Revision Commission Comments

This section provides the penitent with a privilege to refuse to disclose, and to prevent another from disclosing, a penitential communication. Because of the definition of "penitential communication," Section 1033 provides a broader privilege than the existing law.

Section 1033 differs from Code of Civil Procedure Section 1881(3) (superseded by the Evidence Code) in that Section 1881(3) gives a penitent a privilege only to prevent a clergyman from disclosing the communication. Literally, Section 1881(3) does not give the penitent himself the right to refuse disclosure. However, similar privilege statutes have been held to grant a privilege both to refuse to disclose and to prevent the other communicant from disclosing the privileged statement. See City & County of San Francisco v. Superior Court, 37 Cal.2d 227, 236, 231 P.2d 26, 31 (1951) (attorney-client privilege); Verdelli v. Gray's Harbor Commercial Co., 115 Cal. 517, 525–526, 47 Pac. 364, 366 (1897) ("a client cannot be compelled to disclose communications which his attorney cannot be permitted to disclose"). Hence, it is likely that Section 1881 (3) would be similarly construed.

Section 1033 also protects against disclosure by eavesdroppers. In this respect, the section provides the same scope of protection that is provided by the other confidential communication privileges. See the Comment to Section 954. [7 Cal.L.Rev.Comm. Reports 1 (1965)].

Research References

Rutter, Cal. Practice Guide: Civ. Pro. Before Trial Ch. 8C-3, "Not Privileged".

Rutter, Cal. Practice Guide: Civil Trials & Evidence Ch. 4-B, B. Preliminary Matters Discussed in Final Status Conference or In-Chambers Conference.

Rutter, Cal. Practice Guide: Civil Trials & Evidence Ch. 8E-A, A. Privileges.

Rutter, Cal. Practice Guide: Personal Injury Ch. 6-A, A. Scope of Discovery and Limitations.

§ 1034. Privilege of clergy

Subject to Section 912, a member of the clergy, whether or not a party, has a privilege to refuse to disclose a penitential communication if he or she claims the privilege. *(Stats.1965, c. 299, § 2, operative Jan. 1, 1967. Amended by Stats.2002, c. 806 (A.B.3027), § 23.)*

Law Revision Commission Comments

This section provides the clergyman with a privilege in his own right. Moreover, he may claim this privilege even if the penitent has waived the privilege granted him by Section 1033.

There may be several reasons for granting clergyman the traditional priest-penitent privilege. At least one underlying reason seems to be that the law will not compel a clergyman to violate—nor punish him for refusing to violate—the tenets of his church which require him to maintain secrecy as to confidential statements made to him in the course of his religious duties. See generally 8 Wigmore, Evidence §§ 2394–2396 (McNaughton rev. 1961).

The clergyman is under no legal compulsion to claim the privilege. Hence, a penitential communication will be admitted if the clergyman fails to claim the privilege and the penitent is deceased, incompetent, absent, or fails to claim the privilege. This probably changes existing law; but, if so, the change is desirable. For example, if a murderer had confessed the crime to a clergyman, the clergyman might under some circumstances (*e.g.,* if the murderer has died) decline to claim the privilege and instead, give the evidence on behalf of an innocent third party who had been indicted for the crime. The extent to which a clergyman should keep secret or reveal penitential communications is not an appropriate subject for legislation; the matter is better left to the discretion of the individual clergyman involved and the discipline of the religious body of which he is a member. [7 Cal.L.Rev.Comm. Reports 1 (1965)].

Research References

Rutter, Cal. Practice Guide: Civ. Pro. Before Trial Ch. 8C-3, "Not Privileged".

Rutter, Cal. Practice Guide: Civil Trials & Evidence Ch. 8E-A, A. Privileges.

Rutter, Cal. Practice Guide: Family Law Ch. 11-C, C. Optional "Formal" Discovery Procedures.

Rutter, Cal. Practice Guide: Personal Injury Ch. 6-A, A. Scope of Discovery and Limitations.

ARTICLE 8.5. SEXUAL ASSAULT COUNSELOR–VICTIM PRIVILEGE

§ 1035. Victim

As used in this article, "victim" means a person who consults a sexual assault counselor for the purpose of securing advice or assistance concerning a mental, physical, or emotional condition caused by a sexual assault. *(Added by Stats.1980, c. 917, p. 2916, § 2. Amended by Stats.2006, c. 689 (S.B.1743), § 4.)*

Research References

Rutter, Cal. Practice Guide: Civil Trials & Evidence Ch. 8E-A, A. Privileges.

Rutter, Cal. Practice Guide: Family Law Ch. 11-C, C. Optional "Formal" Discovery Procedures.

Rutter, Cal. Practice Guide: Personal Injury Ch. 6-A, A. Scope of Discovery and Limitations.

§ 1035.2. Sexual assault counselor

As used in this article, "sexual assault counselor" means any of the following:

(a) A person who is engaged in any office, hospital, institution, or center commonly known as a rape crisis center, whose primary purpose is the rendering of advice or assistance to victims of sexual assault and who has received a certificate evidencing completion of a training program in the counseling of sexual assault victims issued by a counseling center that meets the criteria for the award of a grant established pursuant to Section 13837 of the Penal Code and who meets one of the following requirements:

(1) Is a psychotherapist as defined in Section 1010; has a master's degree in counseling or a related field; or has one year of counseling experience, at least six months of which is in rape crisis counseling.

(2) Has 40 hours of training as described below and is supervised by an individual who qualifies as a counselor under paragraph (1). The training, supervised by a person qualified under paragraph (1), shall include, but not be limited to, the following areas:

(A) Law.

(B) Medicine.

(C) Societal attitudes.

(D) Crisis intervention and counseling techniques.

(E) Role playing.

(F) Referral services.

(G) Sexuality.

(b) A person who is employed by any organization providing the programs specified in Section 13835.2 of the Penal Code, whether financially compensated or not, for the purpose of counseling and assisting sexual assault victims, and who meets one of the following requirements:

(1) Is a psychotherapist as defined in Section 1010; has a master's degree in counseling or a related field; or has one year of counseling experience, at least six months of which is in rape assault counseling.

(2) Has the minimum training for sexual assault counseling required by guidelines established by the employing agency pursuant to subdivision (c) of Section 13835.10 of the Penal Code, and is supervised by an individual who qualifies as a counselor under paragraph (1). The training, supervised by a person qualified under paragraph (1), shall include, but not be limited to, the following areas:

(A) Law.

(B) Victimology.

(C) Counseling.

(D) Client and system advocacy.

(E) Referral services. *(Added by Stats.1980, c. 917, p. 2916, § 2. Amended by Stats.1983, c. 580, § 1; Stats.1983, c. 1072, § 1; Stats.1990, c. 1342 (S.B.2501), § 1; Stats.2006, c. 689 (S.B.1743), § 5.)*

Research References

Rutter, Cal. Practice Guide: Civil Trials & Evidence Ch. 8E-A, A. Privileges.

§ 1035.4. Confidential communication between the sexual assault counselor and the victim; disclosure

As used in this article, "confidential communication between the sexual assault counselor and the victim" means information transmitted between the victim and the sexual assault counselor in the course of their relationship and in confidence by a means which, so far as the victim is aware, discloses the information to no third persons other than those who are present to further the interests of the victim in the consultation or those to whom disclosures are reasonably necessary for the transmission of the information or an accomplishment of the purposes for which the sexual assault counselor is consulted. The term includes all information regarding the facts and circumstances involving the alleged sexual assault and also includes all information regarding the victim's prior or subsequent sexual conduct, and opinions regarding the victim's sexual conduct or reputation in sexual matters.

The court may compel disclosure of information received by the sexual assault counselor which constitutes relevant evidence of the facts and circumstances involving an alleged sexual assault about which the victim is complaining and which is the subject of a criminal proceeding if the court determines that the probative value outweighs the effect on the victim, the treatment relationship, and the treatment services if disclosure is compelled. The court may also compel disclosure in proceedings related to child abuse if the court determines the probative value outweighs the effect on the victim, the treatment relationship, and the treatment services if disclosure is compelled.

When a court is ruling on a claim of privilege under this article, the court may require the person from whom disclosure is sought or the person authorized to claim the privilege, or both, to disclose the information in chambers out of the presence and hearing of all persons except the person authorized to claim the privilege and such other persons as the person authorized to claim the privilege is willing to have present. If the judge determines that the information is privileged and must not be disclosed, neither he or she nor any other person may ever disclose, without the consent of a person authorized to permit disclosure, what was disclosed in the course of the proceedings in chambers.

If the court determines certain information shall be disclosed, the court shall so order and inform the defendant. If the court finds there is a reasonable likelihood that particular information is subject to disclosure pursuant to the balancing test provided in this section, the following procedure shall be followed:

(1) The court shall inform the defendant of the nature of the information which may be subject to disclosure.

(2) The court shall order a hearing out of the presence of the jury, if any, and at the hearing allow the questioning of the sexual assault counselor regarding the information which the court has determined may be subject to disclosure.

(3) At the conclusion of the hearing, the court shall rule which items of information, if any, shall be disclosed. The court may make an order stating what evidence may be introduced by the defendant and the nature of questions to be permitted. The defendant may then offer evidence pursuant to the order of the court. Admission of evidence concerning the sexual conduct of the complaining witness is subject to Sections 352, 782, and 1103. *(Added by Stats.1980, c. 917, p. 2916, § 2. Amended by Stats.1983, c. 1072, § 2.)*

Research References

Rutter, Cal. Practice Guide: Civil Trials & Evidence Ch. 4-B, B. Preliminary Matters Discussed in Final Status Conference or In-Chambers Conference.
Rutter, Cal. Practice Guide: Civil Trials & Evidence Ch. 8E-A, A. Privileges.

§ 1035.6. Holder of the privilege

As used in this article, "holder of the privilege" means:

(a) The victim when such person has no guardian or conservator.

(b) A guardian or conservator of the victim when the victim has a guardian or conservator.

(c) The personal representative of the victim if the victim is dead. *(Added by Stats.1980, c. 917, p. 2916, § 2.)*

Research References

Rutter, Cal. Practice Guide: Civil Trials & Evidence Ch. 8E-A, A. Privileges.

§ 1035.8. Sexual assault counselor privilege

A victim of a sexual assault, whether or not a party, has a privilege to refuse to disclose, and to prevent another from disclosing, a confidential communication between the victim and a sexual assault counselor if the privilege is claimed by any of the following:

(a) The holder of the privilege;

(b) A person who is authorized to claim the privilege by the holder of the privilege; or

(c) The person who was the sexual assault counselor at the time of the confidential communication, but that person may not claim the privilege if there is no holder of the privilege in existence or if he or she is otherwise instructed by a person authorized to permit disclosure. *(Added by Stats.1980, c. 917, p. 2916, § 2. Amended by Stats.2006, c. 689 (S.B.1743), § 6.)*

Research References

Rutter, Cal. Practice Guide: Civ. Pro. Before Trial Ch. 8C-3, "Not Privileged".
Rutter, Cal. Practice Guide: Civil Trials & Evidence Ch. 8E-A, A. Privileges.

§ 1036. Claim of privilege by sexual assault counselor

The sexual assault counselor who received or made a communication subject to the privilege under this article shall claim the privilege if he or she is present when the communication is sought to be disclosed and is authorized to claim the privilege under subdivision (c) of Section 1035.8. *(Added by Stats.1980, c. 917, p. 2916, § 2. Amended by Stats.2006, c. 689 (S.B.1743), § 7.)*

Research References

Rutter, Cal. Practice Guide: Civil Trials & Evidence Ch. 8E-A, A. Privileges.

§ 1036.2. Sexual assault

As used in this article, "sexual assault" includes all of the following:

(a) Rape, as defined in Section 261 of the Penal Code.

(b) Unlawful sexual intercourse, as defined in Section 261.5 of the Penal Code.

(c) Rape in concert with force and violence, as defined in Section 264.1 of the Penal Code.

(d) Rape of a spouse, as defined in Section 262 of the Penal Code.

(e) Sodomy, as defined in Section 286 of the Penal Code, except a violation of subdivision (e) of that section.

(f) A violation of Section 288 of the Penal Code.

(g) Oral copulation, as defined in Section 288a of the Penal Code, except a violation of subdivision (e) of that section.

(h) Sexual penetration, as defined in Section 289 of the Penal Code.

(i) Annoying or molesting a child under 18, as defined in Section 647a of the Penal Code.

(j) Any attempt to commit any of the above acts. *(Added by Stats.1980, c. 917, p. 2916, § 2. Amended by Stats.1988, c. 102, § 1; Stats.2001, c. 854 (S.B.205), § 4.)*

Research References

Rutter, Cal. Practice Guide: Civil Trials & Evidence Ch. 8E-A, A. Privileges.
Rutter, Cal. Practice Guide: Family Law Ch. 11-C, C. Optional "Formal" Discovery Procedures.
Rutter, Cal. Practice Guide: Personal Injury Ch. 6-A, A. Scope of Discovery and Limitations.

ARTICLE 8.7. DOMESTIC VIOLENCE COUNSELOR–VICTIM PRIVILEGE

Section

§ 1037. Victim

As used in this article, "victim" means any person who suffers domestic violence, as defined in Section 1037.7. *(Added by Stats.1986, c. 854, § 1.)*

Research References

Rutter, Cal. Practice Guide: Civil Trials & Evidence Ch. 8E-A, A. Privileges.
Rutter, Cal. Practice Guide: Family Law Ch. 11-C, C. Optional "Formal" Discovery Procedures.
11 Witkin, California Summary 10th Husband and Wife § 371, (S 371) Civil Remedies.

§ 1037.1. Domestic violence counselor; qualifications; domestic violence victim service organization

(a)(1) As used in this article, "domestic violence counselor" means a person who is employed by a domestic violence victim service organization, as defined in this article, whether financially compensated or not, for the purpose of rendering advice or assistance to victims of domestic violence and who has at least 40 hours of training as specified in paragraph (2).

(2) The 40 hours of training shall be supervised by an individual who qualifies as a counselor under paragraph (1), and who has at least one year of experience counseling domestic violence victims for the domestic violence victim service organization. The training shall include, but need not be limited to, the following areas: history of domestic violence, civil and criminal law as it relates to domestic violence, the domestic violence victim-counselor privilege and other laws that protect the confidentiality of victim records and information, societal attitudes towards domestic violence, peer counseling techniques, housing, public assistance and other financial resources available to meet the financial needs of domestic violence victims, and referral services available to domestic violence victims.

(3) A domestic violence counselor who has been employed by the domestic violence victim service organization for a period of less than six months shall be supervised by a domestic violence counselor who has at least one year of experience counseling domestic violence victims for the domestic violence victim service organization.

(b) As used in this article, "domestic violence victim service organization" means a nongovernmental organization or entity that provides shelter, programs, or services to victims of domestic violence and their children, including, but not limited to, either of the following:

(1) Domestic violence shelter-based programs, as described in Section 18294 of the Welfare and Institutions Code.

(2) Other programs with the primary mission to provide services to victims of domestic violence whether or not that program exists in an agency that provides additional services. *(Added by Stats.1986, c. 854, § 1. Amended by Stats.1990, c. 1342 (S.B.2501), § 2; Stats.2007, c. 206 (S.B.407), § 2.)*

Research References

Rutter, Cal. Practice Guide: Civil Trials & Evidence Ch. 8E-A, A. Privileges.
Rutter, Cal. Practice Guide: Family Law Ch. 11-C, C. Optional "Formal" Discovery Procedures.

§ 1037.2. Confidential communication; compulsion of disclosure by court; claim of privilege

(a) As used in this article, "confidential communication" means any information, including, but not limited to, written or oral communication, transmitted between the victim and the counselor in the course of their relationship and in confidence by a means which, so far as the victim is aware, discloses the information to no third persons other than those who are present to further the interests of the victim in the consultation or those to whom disclosures are reasonably necessary for the transmission of the information or an accomplishment of the purposes for which the domestic violence counselor is consulted. The term includes all information regarding the facts and circumstances involving all incidences of domestic violence, as well as all information about the children of the victim or abuser and the relationship of the victim with the abuser.

(b) The court may compel disclosure of information received by a domestic violence counselor which constitutes relevant evidence of the facts and circumstances involving a crime allegedly perpetrated against the victim or another household member and which is the subject of a criminal proceeding, if the court determines that the probative value of the information outweighs the effect of disclosure of the information on the victim, the counseling relationship, and the counseling services. The court may compel disclosure if the victim is either dead or not the complaining witness in a criminal action against the perpetrator. The court may also compel disclosure in proceedings related to child abuse if the court determines that the probative value of the evidence outweighs the effect of the disclosure on the victim, the counseling relationship, and the counseling services.

(c) When a court rules on a claim of privilege under this article, it may require the person from whom disclosure is sought or the person authorized to claim the privilege, or both, to disclose the information in chambers out of the presence and hearing of all persons except the person authorized to claim the privilege and such other persons as the person authorized to claim the privilege consents to have present. If the judge determines that the information is privileged and shall not be disclosed, neither he nor she nor any other person may disclose, without the consent of a person authorized to permit disclosure, any information disclosed in the course of the proceedings in chambers.

(d) If the court determines that information shall be disclosed, the court shall so order and inform the defendant in the criminal action. If the court finds there is a reasonable likelihood that any information is subject to disclosure pursuant to the balancing test provided in this section, the procedure specified in subdivisions (1), (2), and (3) of Section 1035.4 shall be followed. *(Added by Stats.1986, c. 854, § 1. Amended by Stats.2007, c. 206 (S.B.407), § 3.)*

Research References

Rutter, Cal. Practice Guide: Civil Trials & Evidence Ch. 8E-A, A. Privileges.
Rutter, Cal. Practice Guide: Family Law Ch. 11-C, C. Optional "Formal" Discovery Procedures.

§ 1037.3. Child abuse; reporting

Nothing in this article shall be construed to limit any obligation to report instances of child abuse as required by Section 11166 of the Penal Code. *(Added by Stats.1986, c. 854, § 1.)*

Research References

Rutter, Cal. Practice Guide: Civil Trials & Evidence Ch. 8E-A, A. Privileges.

§ 1037.4. Holder of the privilege

As used in this article, "holder of the privilege" means:

(a) The victim when he or she has no guardian or conservator.

(b) A guardian or conservator of the victim when the victim has a guardian or conservator, unless the guardian or conservator is accused of perpetrating domestic violence against the victim. *(Added by Stats.1986, c. 854, § 1. Amended by Stats. 2007, c. 206 (S.B.407), § 4.)*

Research References

Rutter, Cal. Practice Guide: Civil Trials & Evidence Ch. 8E-A, A. Privileges.

§ 1037.5. Privilege of refusal to disclose communication; claimants

A victim of domestic violence, whether or not a party to the action, has a privilege to refuse to disclose, and to prevent another from disclosing, a confidential communication between the victim and a domestic violence counselor in any proceeding specified in Section 901 if the privilege is claimed by any of the following persons:

(a) The holder of the privilege.

(b) A person who is authorized to claim the privilege by the holder of the privilege.

(c) The person who was the domestic violence counselor at the time of the confidential communication. However, that person may not claim the privilege if there is no holder of the privilege in existence or if he or she is otherwise instructed by a person authorized to permit disclosure. *(Added by Stats.1986, c. 854, § 1. Amended by Stats.2007, c. 206 (S.B.407), § 5.)*

Research References

Rutter, Cal. Practice Guide: Civ. Pro. Before Trial Ch. 8C-3, "Not Privileged".
Rutter, Cal. Practice Guide: Civil Trials & Evidence Ch. 8E-A, A. Privileges.

§ 1037.6. Claim of privilege by counselor

The domestic violence counselor who received or made a communication subject to the privilege granted by this article shall claim the privilege whenever he or she is present when the communication is sought to be disclosed and he or she is authorized to claim the privilege under subdivision (c) of Section 1037.5. *(Added by Stats.1986, c. 854, § 1.)*

Research References

Rutter, Cal. Practice Guide: Civ. Pro. Before Trial Ch. 8C-3, "Not Privileged".
Rutter, Cal. Practice Guide: Civil Trials & Evidence Ch. 8E-A, A. Privileges.

§ 1037.7. Domestic violence

As used in this article, "domestic violence" means "domestic violence" as defined in Section 6211 of the Family Code. *(Added by Stats.1993, c. 219 (A.B.1500), § 77.4.)*

Law Revision Commission Comments

Section 1037.7 substitutes a reference to the Family Code provision defining "domestic violence" for the definitions of "abuse," "domestic violence," and "family or household member" in the former section. This is not a substantive change, since the Family Code definition of "domestic violence" continues the substance of the omitted definitions. See Fam. Code § 6211 ("domestic violence" defined) & Comment. See also Fam. Code §§ 6203 ("abuse" defined), 6209 ("cohabitant" and "former cohabitant" defined). [23 Cal.L.Rev.Comm. Reports 1 (1993)].

Research References

Rutter, Cal. Practice Guide: Civil Trials & Evidence Ch. 8E-A, A. Privileges.

§ 1037.8. Notice; limitations on confidential communications

A domestic violence counselor shall inform a domestic violence victim of any applicable limitations on confidentiality of communications between the victim and the domestic violence counselor. This information may be given orally. *(Added by Stats.2002, c. 629 (S.B.1735), § 1.)*

Research References

Rutter, Cal. Practice Guide: Civil Trials & Evidence Ch. 8E-A, A. Privileges.

Rutter, Cal. Practice Guide: Family Law Ch. 11-C, C. Optional "Formal" Discovery Procedures.

ARTICLE 8.8. HUMAN TRAFFICKING CASEWORKER–VICTIM PRIVILEGE

Section
1038.　　　Privilege.
1038.1.　　Compulsion of disclosure by court.
1038.2.　　Definitions.

§ 1038. Privilege

(a) A trafficking victim, whether or not a party to the action, has a privilege to refuse to disclose, and to prevent another from disclosing, a confidential communication between the victim and a human trafficking caseworker if the privilege is claimed by any of the following persons:

(1) The holder of the privilege.

(2) A person who is authorized to claim the privilege by the holder of the privilege.

(3) The person who was the human trafficking caseworker at the time of the confidential communication. However, that person may not claim the privilege if there is no holder of the privilege in existence or if he or she is otherwise instructed by a person authorized to permit disclosure. The human trafficking caseworker who received or made a communication subject to the privilege granted by this article shall claim the privilege whenever he or she is present when the communication is sought to be disclosed and he or she is authorized to claim the privilege under this section.

(b) A human trafficking caseworker shall inform a trafficking victim of any applicable limitations on confidentiality of communications between the victim and the caseworker. This information may be given orally. *(Added by Stats.2005, c. 240 (A.B.22), § 4.)*

§ 1038.1. Compulsion of disclosure by court

(a) The court may compel disclosure of information received by a human trafficking caseworker that constitutes relevant evidence of the facts and circumstances involving a crime allegedly perpetrated against the victim and that is the subject of a criminal proceeding, if the court determines that the probative value of the information outweighs the effect of disclosure of the information on the victim, the counseling relationship, and the counseling services. The court may compel disclosure if the victim is either dead or not the complaining witness in a criminal action against the perpetrator.

(b) When a court rules on a claim of privilege under this article, it may require the person from whom disclosure is sought or the person authorized to claim the privilege, or both, to disclose the information in chambers out of the presence and hearing of all persons except the person authorized to claim the privilege and those other persons that the person authorized to claim the privilege consents to have present.

(c) If the judge determines that the information is privileged and shall not be disclosed, neither he nor she nor any other person may disclose, without the consent of a person authorized to permit disclosure, any information disclosed in the course of the proceedings in chambers. If the court determines that information shall be disclosed, the court shall so order and inform the defendant in the criminal action. If the court finds there is a reasonable likelihood that any information is subject to disclosure pursuant to the balancing test provided in this section, the procedure specified in paragraphs (1), (2), and (3) of Section 1035.4 shall be followed. *(Added by Stats.2005, c. 240 (A.B.22), § 4.)*

§ 1038.2. Definitions

(a) As used in this article, "victim" means any person who is a "trafficking victim" as defined in Section 236.1.[1]

(b) As used in this article, "human trafficking caseworker" means any of the following:

(1) A person who is employed by any organization providing the programs specified in Section 18294 of the Welfare and Institutions Code, whether financially compensated or not, for the purpose of rendering advice or assistance to victims of human trafficking, who has received specialized training in the counseling of human trafficking victims, and who meets one of the following requirements:

(A) Has a master's degree in counseling or a related field; or has one year of counseling experience, at least six months of which is in the counseling of human trafficking victims.

(B) Has at least 40 hours of training as specified in this paragraph and is supervised by an individual who qualifies as a counselor under subparagraph (A), or is a psychotherapist, as defined in Section 1010. The training, supervised by a person qualified under subparagraph (A), shall include, but need not be limited to, the following areas: history of human trafficking, civil and criminal law as it relates to human trafficking, societal attitudes towards human trafficking, peer counseling techniques, housing, public assistance and other financial resources available to meet the financial needs of human trafficking victims, and referral services available to human trafficking victims. A portion of this training must include an explanation of privileged communication.

(2) A person who is employed by any organization providing the programs specified in Section 13835.2 of the Penal Code, whether financially compensated or not, for the purpose of counseling and assisting human trafficking victims, and who meets one of the following requirements:

(A) Is a psychotherapist as defined in Section 1010, has a master's degree in counseling or a related field, or has one year of counseling experience, at least six months of which is in rape assault counseling.

(B) Has the minimum training for human trafficking counseling required by guidelines established by the employing agency pursuant to subdivision (c) of Section 13835.10 of the Penal Code, and is supervised by an individual who qualifies as a counselor under subparagraph (A). The training, supervised by a person qualified under subparagraph (A), shall include, but not be limited to, law, victimology, counseling techniques, client and system advocacy, and referral services. A portion of this training must include an explanation of privileged communication.

(c) As used in this article, "confidential communication" means information transmitted between the victim and the caseworker in the course of their relationship and in confidence by a means which, so far as the victim is aware, discloses the information to no third persons other than those who are present to further the interests of the victim in the consultation or those to whom disclosures are reasonably necessary for the transmission of the information or an accomplishment of the purposes for which the human trafficking counselor is consulted. It includes all information regarding the facts and circumstances involving all incidences of human trafficking.

(d) As used in this article, "holder of the privilege" means the victim when he or she has no guardian or conservator, or a guardian or conservator of the victim when the victim has a guardian or conservator. *(Added by Stats.2005, c. 240 (A.B.22), § 4.)*

¹ See Penal Code § 236.1.

ARTICLE 9. OFFICIAL INFORMATION AND IDENTITY OF INFORMER

Section
1040. Privilege for official information.
1041. Privilege for identity of informer.
1042. Adverse order or finding in certain cases.
1043. Peace or custodial officer personnel records; discovery or disclosure; procedure.
1044. Medical or psychological history records; right of access.
1045. Peace or custodial officers; access to records of complaints, investigations of complaints, or discipline imposed; relevancy; protective orders.
1046. Allegation of excessive force by peace or custodial officer; copy of police or crime report.
1047. Records of peace or custodial officers; exemption from disclosure.

§ 1040. Privilege for official information

(a) As used in this section, "official information" means information acquired in confidence by a public employee in the course of his or her duty and not open, or officially disclosed, to the public prior to the time the claim of privilege is made.

(b) A public entity has a privilege to refuse to disclose official information, and to prevent another from disclosing official information, if the privilege is claimed by a person authorized by the public entity to do so and:

(1) Disclosure is forbidden by an act of the Congress of the United States or a statute of this state; or

(2) Disclosure of the information is against the public interest because there is a necessity for preserving the confidentiality of the information that outweighs the necessity for disclosure in the interest of justice; but no privilege may be claimed under this paragraph if any person authorized to do so has consented that the information be disclosed in the proceeding. In determining whether disclosure of the information is against the public interest, the interest of the public entity as a party in the outcome of the proceeding may not be considered.

(c) Notwithstanding any other provision of law, the Employment Development Department shall disclose to law enforcement agencies, in accordance with the provisions of subdivision (k) of Section 1095 and subdivision (b) of Section 2714 of the Unemployment Insurance Code, information in its possession relating to any person if an arrest warrant has been issued for the person for commission of a felony. *(Stats.1965, c. 299, § 2, operative Jan. 1, 1967. Amended by Stats.1984, c. 1127, § 2.)*

Research References

Rutter, Cal. Practice Guide: Civ. Pro. Before Trial Ch. 8C-3, "Not Privileged".
Rutter, Cal. Practice Guide: Civil Trials & Evidence Ch. 4-B, B. Preliminary Matters Discussed in Final Status Conference or In-Chambers Conference.
Rutter, Cal. Practice Guide: Civil Trials & Evidence Ch. 8E-A, A. Privileges.
Rutter, Cal. Practice Guide: Family Law Ch. 1-F, F. Advising the Petitioner Client at the First Interview.
Rutter, Cal. Practice Guide: Family Law Ch. 7-B, B. Contested Custody Proceedings, Generally.
Rutter, Cal. Practice Guide: Personal Injury Ch. 6-A, A. Scope of Discovery and Limitations.
Rutter, Cal. Practice Guide: Prof. Responsibility Ch. 11-E, E. Receiving Complaints of Attorney Misconduct.

15 NO. 3 Miller & Starr, California Real Estate Newsalert 16, Regulation of the Real Estate Industry.
10 Witkin, California Summary 10th Parent and Child § 280, (S 280) Mediation Proceeding.
10 Witkin, California Summary 10th Parent and Child § 333, (S 333) Inspection of Records.
11 Witkin, California Summary 10th Husband and Wife § 91, Family Conciliation Courts.
7 Witkin, California Summary 10th Constitutional Law § 149, Court Cannot Inquire Into Legislative Motivation.

§ 1041. Privilege for identity of informer

(a) Except as provided in this section, a public entity has a privilege to refuse to disclose the identity of a person who has furnished information as provided in subdivision (b) purporting to disclose a violation of a law of the United States or of this state or of a public entity in this state, and to prevent another from disclosing * * * the person's identity, if the privilege is claimed by a person authorized by the public entity to do so and either of the following apply:

(1) Disclosure is forbidden by an act of the Congress of the United States or a statute of this state * * *.

(2) Disclosure of the identity of the informer is against the public interest because * * * the necessity for preserving the confidentiality of his or her identity * * * outweighs the necessity for disclosure in the interest of justice * * *. The privilege * * * shall not be claimed under this paragraph if a person authorized to do so has consented that the identity of the informer be disclosed in the proceeding. In determining whether disclosure of the identity of the informer is against the public interest, the interest of the public entity as a party in the outcome of the proceeding shall not be considered.

(b) The privilege described in this section applies only if the information is furnished in confidence by the informer to any of the following:

(1) A law enforcement officer.

(2) A representative of an administrative agency charged with the administration or enforcement of the law alleged to be violated * * *.

(3) Any person for the purpose of transmittal to a person listed in paragraph (1) or (2). As used in this paragraph, "person" includes a volunteer or employee of a crime stopper organization.

(c) * * * The privilege * * * described in this section shall not be construed to prevent the informer from disclosing his or her identity.

(d) As used in this section, "crime stopper organization" means a private, nonprofit organization that accepts and expends donations used to reward persons who report to the organization information concerning alleged criminal activity, and forwards the information to the appropriate law enforcement agency. *(Stats.1965, c. 299, § 2, operative Jan. 1, 1967. Amended by Stats.2013, c. 19 (A.B.1250), § 1.)*

Law Revision Commission Comments

Under existing law, the identity of an informer is protected by subdivision 5 of Code of Civil Procedure Section 1881 (which, like Section 1041, prohibits disclosure when the interest of the public would suffer thereby). Section 1881 is superseded by the Evidence Code.

This privilege may be claimed under the same conditions as the official information privilege may be claimed, except that it does not apply if a person is called as a witness and asked if he is the informer. [7 Cal.L.Rev.Comm. Reports 1 (1965)].

Evidence

Research References

Rutter, Cal. Practice Guide: Civil Trials & Evidence Ch. 8E-A, A. Privileges.

§ 1042. Adverse order or finding in certain cases

(a) Except where disclosure is forbidden by an act of the Congress of the United States, if a claim of privilege under this article by the state or a public entity in this state is sustained in a criminal proceeding, the presiding officer shall make such order or finding of fact adverse to the public entity bringing the proceeding as is required by law upon any issue in the proceeding to which the privileged information is material.

(b) Notwithstanding subdivision (a), where a search is made pursuant to a warrant valid on its face, the public entity bringing a criminal proceeding is not required to reveal to the defendant official information or the identity of an informer in order to establish the legality of the search or the admissibility of any evidence obtained as a result of it.

(c) Notwithstanding subdivision (a), in any preliminary hearing, criminal trial, or other criminal proceeding, any otherwise admissible evidence of information communicated to a peace officer by a confidential informant, who is not a material witness to the guilt or innocence of the accused of the offense charged, is admissible on the issue of reasonable cause to make an arrest or search without requiring that the name or identity of the informant be disclosed if the judge or magistrate is satisfied, based upon evidence produced in open court, out of the presence of the jury, that such information was received from a reliable informant and in his discretion does not require such disclosure.

(d) When, in any such criminal proceeding, a party demands disclosure of the identity of the informant on the ground the informant is a material witness on the issue of guilt, the court shall conduct a hearing at which all parties may present evidence on the issue of disclosure. Such hearing shall be conducted outside the presence of the jury, if any. During the hearing, if the privilege provided for in Section 1041 is claimed by a person authorized to do so or if a person who is authorized to claim such privilege refuses to answer any question on the ground that the answer would tend to disclose the identity of the informant, the prosecuting attorney may request that the court hold an in camera hearing. If such a request is made, the court shall hold such a hearing outside the presence of the defendant and his counsel. At the in camera hearing, the prosecution may offer evidence which would tend to disclose or which discloses the identity of the informant to aid the court in its determination whether there is a reasonable possibility that nondisclosure might deprive the defendant of a fair trial. A reporter shall be present at the in camera hearing. Any transcription of the proceedings at the in camera hearing, as well as any physical evidence presented at the hearing, shall be ordered sealed by the court, and only a court may have access to its contents. The court shall not order disclosure, nor strike the testimony of the witness who invokes the privilege, nor dismiss the criminal proceeding, if the party offering the witness refuses to disclose the identity of the informant, unless, based upon the evidence presented at the hearing held in the presence of the defendant and his counsel and the evidence presented at the in camera hearing, the court concludes that there is a reasonable possibility that nondisclosure might deprive the defendant of a fair trial. *(Stats.1965, c. 299, § 2, operative Jan. 1, 1967. Amended Stats.1965, c. 937, p. 2549, § 2, operative Jan. 1, 1967; Stats.1969, c. 1412, p. 2891, § 1.)*

§ 1043. Peace or custodial officer personnel records; discovery or disclosure; procedure

(a) In any case in which discovery or disclosure is sought of peace or custodial officer personnel records or records maintained pursuant to Section 832.5 of the Penal Code or information from those records, the party seeking the discovery or disclosure shall file a written motion with the appropriate court or administrative body upon written notice to the governmental agency which has custody and control of the records. The written notice shall be given at the times prescribed by subdivision (b) of Section 1005 of the Code of Civil Procedure. Upon receipt of the notice the governmental agency served shall immediately notify the individual whose records are sought.

(b) The motion shall include all of the following:

(1) Identification of the proceeding in which discovery or disclosure is sought, the party seeking discovery or disclosure, the peace or custodial officer whose records are sought, the governmental agency which has custody and control of the records, and the time and place at which the motion for discovery or disclosure shall be heard.

(2) A description of the type of records or information sought.

(3) Affidavits showing good cause for the discovery or disclosure sought, setting forth the materiality thereof to the subject matter involved in the pending litigation and stating upon reasonable belief that the governmental agency identified has the records or information from the records.

(c) No hearing upon a motion for discovery or disclosure shall be held without full compliance with the notice provisions of this section except upon a showing by the moving party of good cause for noncompliance, or upon a waiver of the hearing by the governmental agency identified as having the records. *(Added by Stats.1978, c. 630, p. 2082, § 1. Amended by Stats.1989, c. 693, § 7; Stats.2002, c. 391 (A.B.2040), § 1.)*

Research References

Rutter, Cal. Practice Guide: Civil Appeals & Writs Ch. 8-C, C. Standards of Appellate Review.
Rutter, Cal. Practice Guide: Civ. Pro. Before Trial Ch. 8C-3, "Not Privileged".
Rutter, Cal. Practice Guide: Civ. Pro. Before Trial Ch. 8H-6, Responding to Demand.
Rutter, Cal. Practice Guide: Civ. Pro. Before Trial Ch. 8K-6, Special Statutes and Court Rules.
Rutter, Cal. Practice Guide: Civ. Pro. Before Trial Ch. 9(I)-B, B. Preparing and Filing Motions.
Rutter, Cal. Practice Guide: Civil Trials & Evidence Ch. 8E-A, A. Privileges.
California Practice Guide: Employment Litigation Ch. 19-F, F. Discovery.
Rutter, Cal. Practice Guide: Family Law Ch. 11-C, C. Optional "Formal" Discovery Procedures.
Rutter, Cal. Practice Guide: Personal Injury Ch. 6-A, A. Scope of Discovery and Limitations.
Rutter, Cal. Practice Guide: Personal Injury Ch. 6-B, B. Overview of Selected Discovery Procedures.

§ 1044. Medical or psychological history records; right of access

Nothing in this article shall be construed to affect the right of access to records of medical or psychological history where such access would otherwise be available under Section 996 or 1016. *(Added by Stats.1978, c. 630, p. 2082, § 2.)*

Research References

Rutter, Cal. Practice Guide: Personal Injury Ch. 6-A, A. Scope of Discovery and Limitations.

§ 1045. Peace or custodial officers; access to records of complaints, investigations of complaints, or discipline imposed; relevancy; protective orders

(a) Nothing in this article shall be construed to affect the right of access to records of complaints, or investigations of complaints, or discipline imposed as a result of those investigations, concerning an event or transaction in which the peace officer or custodial officer, as defined in Section 831.5 of the Penal Code, participated, or which he or she perceived, and pertaining to the manner in which he or she performed his or her duties, provided that information is relevant to the subject matter involved in the pending litigation.

(b) In determining relevance, the court shall examine the information in chambers in conformity with Section 915, and shall exclude from disclosure:

(1) Information consisting of complaints concerning conduct occurring more than five years before the event or transaction that is the subject of the litigation in aid of which discovery or disclosure is sought.

(2) In any criminal proceeding the conclusions of any officer investigating a complaint filed pursuant to Section 832.5 of the Penal Code.

(3) Facts sought to be disclosed that are so remote as to make disclosure of little or no practical benefit.

(c) In determining relevance where the issue in litigation concerns the policies or pattern of conduct of the employing agency, the court shall consider whether the information sought may be obtained from other records maintained by the employing agency in the regular course of agency business which would not necessitate the disclosure of individual personnel records.

(d) Upon motion seasonably made by the governmental agency which has custody or control of the records to be examined or by the officer whose records are sought, and upon good cause showing the necessity thereof, the court may make any order which justice requires to protect the officer or agency from unnecessary annoyance, embarrassment or oppression.

(e) The court shall, in any case or proceeding permitting the disclosure or discovery of any peace or custodial officer records requested pursuant to Section 1043, order that the records disclosed or discovered may not be used for any purpose other than a court proceeding pursuant to applicable law. *(Added by Stats.1978, c. 630, p. 2082, § 3. Amended by Stats.1982, c. 946, p. 3432, § 1; Stats.2002, c. 391 (A.B.2040), § 2.)*

Research References

Rutter, Cal. Practice Guide: Civil Appeals & Writs Ch. 8-C, C. Standards of Appellate Review.
Rutter, Cal. Practice Guide: Civ. Pro. Before Trial Ch. 8C-3, "Not Privileged".
Rutter, Cal. Practice Guide: Family Law Ch. 11-C, C. Optional "Formal" Discovery Procedures.
Rutter, Cal. Practice Guide: Personal Injury Ch. 6-A, A. Scope of Discovery and Limitations.

§ 1046. Allegation of excessive force by peace or custodial officer; copy of police or crime report

In any case, otherwise authorized by law, in which the party seeking disclosure is alleging excessive force by a peace officer or custodial officer, as defined in Section 831.5 of the Penal Code, in connection with the arrest of that party, or for conduct alleged to have occurred within a jail facility, the motion shall include a copy of the police report setting forth the circumstances under which the party was stopped and arrested, or a copy of the crime report setting forth the circumstances under which the conduct is alleged to have occurred within a jail facility. *(Added by Stats.1985, c. 539, § 1. Amended by Stats.2002, c. 391 (A.B. 2040), § 3.)*

Research References

Rutter, Cal. Practice Guide: Civ. Pro. Before Trial Ch. 8C-3, "Not Privileged".

Rutter, Cal. Practice Guide: Civ. Pro. Before Trial Ch. 8H-6, Responding to Demand.
Rutter, Cal. Practice Guide: Civil Trials & Evidence Ch. 8E-A, A. Privileges.

§ 1047. Records of peace or custodial officers; exemption from disclosure

Records of peace officers or custodial officers, as defined in Section 831.5 of the Penal Code, including supervisorial officers, who either were not present during the arrest or had no contact with the party seeking disclosure from the time of the arrest until the time of booking, or who were not present at the time the conduct is alleged to have occurred within a jail facility, shall not be subject to disclosure. *(Added by Stats.1985, c. 539, § 2. Amended by Stats.2002, c. 391 (A.B.2040), § 4.)*

Research References

Rutter, Cal. Practice Guide: Civ. Pro. Before Trial Ch. 8C-3, "Not Privileged".
Rutter, Cal. Practice Guide: Personal Injury Ch. 6-A, A. Scope of Discovery and Limitations.

ARTICLE 10. POLITICAL VOTE

Section
1050. Privilege to protect secrecy of vote.

§ 1050. Privilege to protect secrecy of vote

If he claims the privilege, a person has a privilege to refuse to disclose the tenor of his vote at a public election where the voting is by secret ballot unless he voted illegally or he previously made an unprivileged disclosure of the tenor of his vote. *(Stats.1965, c. 299, § 2, operative Jan. 1, 1967.)*

Law Revision Commission Comments

Section 1050 declares existing law. The California cases declaring such a privilege have relied upon the provision of the Constitution that "secrecy in voting be preserved." Cal.Const., Art. II, § 5. See Bush v. Head, 154 Cal. 277, 97 Pac. 512 (1908); Smith v. Thomas, 121 Cal. 533, 54 Pac. 71 (1898). Since the policy of ballot secrecy extends only to legally cast ballots, the California cases—as well as Section 1050—recognize that there is no privilege as to the tenor of an illegal vote. Patterson v. Hanley, 136 Cal. 265, 68 Pac. 821 (1902). [7 Cal.L.Rev.Comm. Reports 1 (1965)].

Research References

Rutter, Cal. Practice Guide: Civ. Pro. Before Trial Ch. 8C-3, "Not Privileged".
Rutter, Cal. Practice Guide: Civil Trials & Evidence Ch. 8E-A, A. Privileges.

ARTICLE 11. TRADE SECRET

Section
1060. Privilege to protect trade secret.
1061. Procedure for assertion of trade secret privilege.
1062. Exclusion of public from criminal proceeding; motion; contents; hearing; determination.
1063. Sealing of articles protected by protective order; procedures.

§ 1060. Privilege to protect trade secret

If he or his agent or employee claims the privilege, the owner of a trade secret has a privilege to refuse to disclose the secret, and to prevent another from disclosing it, if the allowance of the privilege will not tend to conceal fraud or otherwise work injustice. *(Stats.1965, c. 299, § 2, operative Jan. 1, 1967.)*

Evidence

Law Revision Commission Comments

This privilege is granted so that secret information essential to the continued operation of a business or industry may be afforded some measure of protection against unnecessary disclosure. Thus, the privilege prevents the use of the witness' duty to testify as the means for injuring an otherwise profitable business where more important interests will not be jeopardized. See generally 8 Wigmore, Evidence § 2212(3) (McNaughton rev. 1961). Nevertheless, there are dangers in the recognition of such a privilege. Copyright and patent laws provide adequate protection for many of the matters that might otherwise be classified as trade secrets. Recognizing the privilege as to such information would serve only to hinder the courts in determining the truth without providing the owner of the secret any needed protection. Again, disclosure of the matters protected by the privilege may be essential to disclose unfair competition or fraud or to reveal the improper use of dangerous materials by the party asserting the privilege. Recognizing the privilege in such cases would amount to a legally sanctioned license to commit the wrongs complained of, for the wrongdoer would be privileged to withhold his wrongful conduct from legal scrutiny.

Therefore, the privilege exists under this section only if its application will not tend to conceal fraud or otherwise work injustice. The limits of the privilege are necessarily uncertain and will have to be worked out through judicial decisions.

Although no California case has been found holding evidence of a tradesecret to be privileged, at least one California case has recognized that such a privilege may exist unless its holder has injured another and the disclosure of the secret is indispensable to the ascertainment of the truth and the ultimate determination of the rights of the parties. Willson v. Superior Court, 66 Cal.App. 275, 225 Pac. 881 (1924) (trade secret held not subject to privilege because of plaintiff's need for information to establish case against the person asserting the privilege). Indirect recognition of such a privilege has also been given in Code of Civil Procedure Section 2019, which provides that in discovery proceedings the court may make protective orders prohibiting inquiry into "secret processes, developments or research." [7 Cal.L.Rev.Comm. Reports 1 (1965)].

Research References

Rutter, Cal. Practice Guide: Civ. Pro. Before Trial Ch. 8C-3, "Not Privileged".

Rutter, Cal. Practice Guide: Civ. Pro. Before Trial Ch. 8H-5, Protective Orders.

Rutter, Cal. Practice Guide: Civil Trials & Evidence Ch. 4-B, B. Preliminary Matters Discussed in Final Status Conference or In-Chambers Conference.

Rutter, Cal. Practice Guide: Civil Trials & Evidence Ch. 8E-A, A. Privileges.

Rutter, Cal. Practice Guide: Personal Injury Ch. 6-A, A. Scope of Discovery and Limitations.

§ 1061. Procedure for assertion of trade secret privilege

(a) For purposes of this section, and Sections 1062 and 1063:

(1) "Trade secret" means "trade secret," as defined in subdivision (d) of Section 3426.1 of the Civil Code, or paragraph (9) of subdivision (a) of Section 499c of the Penal Code.

(2) "Article" means "article," as defined in paragraph (2) of subdivision (a) of Section 499c of the Penal Code.

(b) In addition to Section 1062, the following procedure shall apply whenever the owner of a trade secret wishes to assert his or her trade secret privilege, as provided in Section 1060, during a criminal proceeding:

(1) The owner of the trade secret shall file a motion for a protective order, or the people may file the motion on the owner's behalf and with the owner's permission. The motion shall include an affidavit based upon personal knowledge listing the affiant's qualifications to give an opinion concerning the trade secret at issue, identifying, without revealing, the alleged trade secret and articles which disclose the secret, and presenting evidence that the secret qualifies as a trade secret under either subdivision (d) of Section 3426.1 of the Civil Code or paragraph (9) of subdivision (a) of Section 499c of the Penal Code. The

motion and affidavit shall be served on all parties in the proceeding.

(2) Any party in the proceeding may oppose the request for the protective order by submitting affidavits based upon the affiant's personal knowledge. The affidavits shall be filed under seal, but shall be provided to the owner of the trade secret and to all parties in the proceeding. Neither the owner of the trade secret nor any party in the proceeding may disclose the affidavit to persons other than to counsel of record without prior court approval.

(3) The movant shall, by a preponderance of the evidence, show that the issuance of a protective order is proper. The court may rule on the request without holding an evidentiary hearing. However, in its discretion, the court may choose to hold an in camera evidentiary hearing concerning disputed articles with only the owner of the trade secret, the people's representative, the defendant, and defendant's counsel present. If the court holds such a hearing, the parties' right to examine witnesses shall not be used to obtain discovery, but shall be directed solely toward the question of whether the alleged trade secret qualifies for protection.

(4) If the court finds that a trade secret may be disclosed during any criminal proceeding unless a protective order is issued and that the issuance of a protective order would not conceal a fraud or work an injustice, the court shall issue a protective order limiting the use and dissemination of the trade secret, including, but not limited to, articles disclosing that secret. The protective order may, in the court's discretion, include the following provisions:

(A) That the trade secret may be disseminated only to counsel for the parties, including their associate attorneys, paralegals, and investigators, and to law enforcement officials or clerical officials.

(B) That the defendant may view the secret only in the presence of his or her counsel, or if not in the presence of his or her counsel, at counsel's offices.

(C) That any party seeking to show the trade secret, or articles containing the trade secret, to any person not designated by the protective order shall first obtain court approval to do so:

(i) The court may require that the person receiving the trade secret do so only in the presence of counsel for the party requesting approval.

(ii) The court may require the person receiving the trade secret to sign a copy of the protective order and to agree to be bound by its terms. The order may include a provision recognizing the owner of the trade secret to be a third-party beneficiary of that agreement.

(iii) The court may require a party seeking disclosure to an expert to provide that expert's name, employment history, and any other relevant information to the court for examination. The court shall accept that information under seal, and the information shall not be disclosed by any court except upon termination of the action and upon a showing of good cause to believe the secret has been disseminated by a court-approved expert. The court shall evaluate the expert and determine whether the expert poses a discernible risk of disclosure. The court shall withhold approval if the expert's economic interests place the expert in a competitive position with the victim, unless no other experts are available. The court may interview the expert in camera in aid of its ruling. If the court rejects the expert, it shall state its reasons for doing so on the record and a transcript of those reasons shall be prepared and sealed.

(D) That no articles disclosing the trade secret shall be filed or otherwise made a part of the court record available to the public without approval of the court and prior notice to the owner of the secret. The owner of the secret may give either party permission to accept the notice on the owner's behalf.

(E) Other orders as the court deems necessary to protect the integrity of the trade secret.

(c) A ruling granting or denying a motion for a protective order filed pursuant to subdivision (b) shall not be construed as a determination that the alleged trade secret is or is not a trade secret as defined by subdivision (d) of Section 3426.1 of the Civil Code or paragraph (9) of subdivision (a) of Section 499c of the Penal Code. Such a ruling shall not have any effect on any civil litigation.

(d) This section shall have prospective effect only and shall not operate to invalidate previously entered protective orders. *(Added by Stats.1990, c. 149 (A.B.2986), § 1. Amended by Stats.1990, c. 714 (A.B.2553), § 1; Stats.2002, c. 784 (S.B.1316), § 103.)*

Law Revision Commission Comments

Former subdivision (d) of Section 1061 is deleted to reflect unification of the municipal and superior courts pursuant to Article VI, Section 5(e), of the California Constitution. On unification of the municipal and superior courts in a county, preexisting records of the municipal court automatically become records of the superior court. Cal. Const. art. VI, § 23(c)(3); Gov't Code § 70212[32 Cal.L.Rev.Comm. Reports 158 (2002)].(c).

Research References

Rutter, Cal. Practice Guide: Civ. Pro. Before Trial Ch. 8H-5, Protective Orders.
Rutter, Cal. Practice Guide: Civil Trials & Evidence Ch. 8E-A, A. Privileges.
Rutter, Cal. Practice Guide: Insurance Litigation Ch. 15-G, G. Discovery.
Rutter, Cal. Practice Guide: Personal Injury Ch. 6-A, A. Scope of Discovery and Limitations.

§ 1062. Exclusion of public from criminal proceeding; motion; contents; hearing; determination

(a) Notwithstanding any other provision of law, in a criminal case, the court, upon motion of the owner of a trade secret, or upon motion by the People with the consent of the owner, may exclude the public from any portion of a criminal proceeding where the proponent of closure has demonstrated a substantial probability that the trade secret would otherwise be disclosed to the public during that proceeding and a substantial probability that the disclosure would cause serious harm to the owner of the secret, and where the court finds that there is no overriding public interest in an open proceeding. No evidence, however, shall be excluded during a criminal proceeding pursuant to this section if it would conceal a fraud, work an injustice, or deprive the People or the defendant of a fair trial.

(b) The motion made pursuant to subdivision (a) shall identify, without revealing, the trade secrets which would otherwise be disclosed to the public. A showing made pursuant to subdivision (a) shall be made during an in camera hearing with only the owner of the trade secret, the People's representative, the defendant, and defendant's counsel present. A court reporter shall be present during the hearing. Any transcription of the proceedings at the in camera hearing, as well as any articles presented at that hearing, shall be ordered sealed by the court and only a court may allow access to its contents upon a showing of good cause. The court, in ruling upon the motion made pursuant to subdivision (a), may consider testimony presented or affidavits filed in any proceeding held in that action.

(c) If, after the in camera hearing described in subdivision (b), the court determines that exclusion of trade secret information from the public is appropriate, the court shall close only that portion of the criminal proceeding necessary to prevent disclosure of the trade secret. Before granting the motion, however, the court shall find and state for the record that the moving party has met its burden pursuant to subdivision (b), and that the closure of that portion of the proceeding will not deprive the People or the defendant of a fair trial.

(d) The owner of the trade secret, the People, or the defendant may seek relief from a ruling denying or granting closure by petitioning a higher court for extraordinary relief.

(e) Whenever the court closes a portion of a criminal proceeding pursuant to this section, a transcript of that closed proceeding shall be made available to the public as soon as practicable. The court shall redact any information qualifying as a trade secret before making that transcript available.

(f) The court, subject to Section 867 of the Penal Code, may allow witnesses who are bound by a protective order entered in the criminal proceeding protecting trade secrets, pursuant[1] to Section 1061, to remain within the courtroom during the closed portion of the proceeding. *(Added by Stats.1990, c. 149 (A.B. 2986), § 2. Amended by Stats.1990, c. 714 (A.B.2553), § 2.)*

[1]So in enrolled bill.

Research References

Rutter, Cal. Practice Guide: Civil Trials & Evidence Ch. 4-I, I. Other Motions at Final Status Conference.
Rutter, Cal. Practice Guide: Civil Trials & Evidence Ch. 8E-A, A. Privileges.

§ 1063. Sealing of articles protected by protective order; procedures

The following provisions shall govern requests to seal articles which are protected by a protective order entered pursuant to Evidence Code Section 1060 or 1061:

(a) The People shall request sealing of articles reasonably expected to be filed or admitted into evidence as follows:

(1) No less than 10 court days before trial, and no less than five court days before any other criminal proceeding, the People shall file with the court a list of all articles which the People reasonably expect to file with the court, or admit into evidence, under seal at that proceeding. That list shall be available to the public. The People may be relieved from providing timely notice upon showing that exigent circumstances prevent that notice.

(2) The court shall not allow the listed articles to be filed, admitted into evidence, or in any way made a part of the court record otherwise open to the public before holding a hearing to consider any objections to the People's request to seal the articles. The court at that hearing shall allow those objecting to the sealing to state their objections.

(3) After hearing any objections to sealing, the court shall conduct an in camera hearing with only the owner of the trade secret contained within those articles, the People's representative, defendant, and defendant's counsel present. The court shall review the articles sought to be sealed, evaluate objections to sealing, and determine whether the People have satisfied the constitutional standards governing public access to articles which are part of the judicial record. The court may consider testimony presented or affidavits filed in any proceeding held in that action. The People, defendant, and the owner of the trade secret may file affidavits based on the affiant's personal knowledge to be considered at that hearing. Those affidavits are to be sealed and not released to the public, but shall be made available to the parties. The court may rule on the request to seal without taking testimony. If the court takes testimony, examination of witnesses shall not be used to obtain discovery, but shall be directed solely toward whether sealing is appropriate.

(4) If the court finds that the movant has satisfied appropriate constitutional standards with respect to sealing particular arti-

cles, the court shall seal those articles if and when they are filed, admitted into evidence, or in any way made a part of the court record otherwise open to the public. The articles shall not be unsealed absent an order of a court upon a showing of good cause. Failure to examine the court file for notice of a request to seal shall not constitute good cause to consider objections to sealing.

(b) The following procedure shall apply to other articles made a part of the court record:

(1) Where any articles protected by a protective order entered pursuant to Section 1060 or 1061 are filed, admitted into evidence, or in any way made a part of the court record in such a way as to be otherwise open to the public, the People, a defendant, or the owner of a trade secret contained within those articles may request the court to seal those articles.

(2) The request to seal shall be made by noticed motion filed with the court. It may also be made orally in court at the time the articles are made a part of the court record. Where the request is made orally, the movant must file within 24 hours a written description of that request, including a list of the articles which are the subject of that request. These motions and lists shall be available to the public.

(3) The court shall promptly conduct hearings as provided in paragraphs (2), (3), and (4) of subdivision (a). The court shall, pending the hearings, seal those articles which are the subject of the request. Where a request to seal is made orally, the court may conduct hearings at the time the articles are made a part of the court record, but shall reconsider its ruling in light of additional objections made by objectors within two court days after the written record of the request to seal is made available to the public.

(4) Any articles sealed pursuant to these hearings shall not be unsealed absent an order of a court upon a showing of good cause. Failure to examine the court file for notice of a request to seal shall not constitute good cause to consider objections to sealing. *(Added by Stats.1990, c. 714 (A.B.2553), § 3.)*

Research References

Rutter, Cal. Practice Guide: Personal Injury Ch. 6-A, A. Scope of Discovery and Limitations.

CHAPTER 5. IMMUNITY OF NEWSMAN FROM CITATION FOR CONTEMPT

Section
1070. Refusal to disclose news source.

§ 1070. Refusal to disclose news source

(a) A publisher, editor, reporter, or other person connected with or employed upon a newspaper, magazine, or other periodical publication, or by a press association or wire service, or any person who has been so connected or employed, cannot be adjudged in contempt by a judicial, legislative, administrative body, or any other body having the power to issue subpoenas, for refusing to disclose, in any proceeding as defined in Section 901, the source of any information procured while so connected or employed for publication in a newspaper, magazine or other periodical publication, or for refusing to disclose any unpublished information obtained or prepared in gathering, receiving or processing of information for communication to the public.

(b) Nor can a radio or television news reporter or other person connected with or employed by a radio or television station, or any person who has been so connected or employed, be so adjudged in contempt for refusing to disclose the source of any information procured while so connected or employed for news or news commentary purposes on radio or television, or for refusing to disclose any unpublished information obtained or prepared in gathering, receiving or processing of information for communication to the public.

(c) As used in this section, "unpublished information" includes information not disseminated to the public by the person from whom disclosure is sought, whether or not related information has been disseminated and includes, but is not limited to, all notes, outtakes, photographs, tapes or other data of whatever sort not itself disseminated to the public through a medium of communication, whether or not published information based upon or related to such material has been disseminated. *(Stats.1965, c. 299, § 2, operative Jan. 1, 1967. Amended by Stats.1971, c. 1717, p. 3658, § 1; Stats.1972, c. 1431, p. 3126, § 1; Stats.1974, c. 1323, p. 2877, § 1; Stats.1974, c. 1456, p. 3184, § 2.)*

Research References

Rutter, Cal. Practice Guide: Civil Appeals & Writs Ch. 15-B, B. Common Law Writs.
Rutter, Cal. Practice Guide: Civ. Pro. Before Trial Ch. 8C-6, Protection for News Media.
Rutter, Cal. Practice Guide: Civ. Pro. Before Trial Ch. 7(II)-B, B. Exemptions (Actions Not Subject to SLAPP Statutes).
Rutter, Cal. Practice Guide: Civil Trials & Evidence Ch. 8E-A, A. Privileges.
Rutter, Cal. Practice Guide: Fed.Civ.Pro. Before Trial Ch. 11(III)-B, B. Scope of Discovery.
Rutter, Cal. Practice Guide: Landlord-Tenant Ch. 8-B, B. Unlawful Detainer Complaint.
Rutter, Cal. Practice Guide: Personal Injury Ch. 6-A, A. Scope of Discovery and Limitations.
5 Witkin Cal. Proc. 5th Pleading § 1026, in General.

Division 9

EVIDENCE AFFECTED OR EXCLUDED BY EXTRINSIC POLICIES

CHAPTER 1. EVIDENCE OF CHARACTER, HABIT, OR CUSTOM

Section
1100. Manner of proof of character.

Section

1106. Sexual harassment, sexual assault, or sexual battery cases; opinion or reputation evidence of plaintiff's sexual conduct; inadmissibility; exception; cross-examination.

1107. Intimate partner battering and its effects; expert testimony in criminal actions; sufficiency of foundation; abuse and domestic violence; applicability to Penal Code; impact on decisional law.

1108. Evidence of another sexual offense by defendant; disclosure; construction of section.

1109. Evidence of defendant's other acts of domestic violence.

§ 1100.　Manner of proof of character

Except as otherwise provided by statute, any otherwise admissible evidence (including evidence in the form of an opinion, evidence of reputation, and evidence of specific instances of such person's conduct) is admissible to prove a person's character or a trait of his character. *(Stats.1965, c. 299, § 2, operative Jan. 1, 1967.)*

Law Revision Commission Comments

Section 1100 states the *kinds* of evidence that may be used to prove a person's character or a trait of his character. The section makes it clear that reputation evidence, opinion evidence, and evidence of specific instances of conduct are admissible for this purpose.

Section 1100 is technically unnecessary because Section 351 declares that all relevant evidence is admissible. Hence, all of the evidence declared to be admissible by Section 1100 would be admissible anyway under the general provisions of Section 351. Section 1100 is included in the Evidence Code, however, to forestall the argument that Section 351 does not remove all judicially created restrictions on the kinds of evidence that may be used to prove character or a trait of character.

Subject to certain statutory restrictions, the character evidence described in Section 1100 is admissible under Section 351 whenever it is relevant. Evidence of a person's character or a trait of his character is relevant in three situations: (1) when offered on the issue of his credibility as a witness, (2) when offered as circumstantial evidence of his conduct in conformity with such character or trait of character, and (3) when his character or a trait of his character is an ultimate fact in dispute in the action.

Sections 786–790 establish restrictions that are applicable when character evidence is offered to attack or to support the *credibility of a witness*. See the Comments to Sections 787 and 788 for a discussion of the restrictions on the kinds of evidence admissible for this purpose.

Sections 1101–1104 substantially restrict the extent to which character evidence may be used as *circumstantial evidence of conduct*. See the Comments to those sections for a discussion of the restrictions on the kinds of evidence admissible for this purpose.

Section 1100 applies without restriction only when character or a trait of character is an *ultimate fact in dispute* in the action. As applied to this situation, Section 1100 is generally consistent with existing law, although the existing law is uncertain in some respects. Cases involving character as an ultimate issue have admitted opinion evidence (People v. Wade, 118 Cal. 672, 50 Pac. 841 (1897); People v. Samonset, 97 Cal. 448, 450, 32 Pac. 520, 521 (1893)), reputation evidence (Estate of Akers, 184 Cal. 514, 519–520, 194 Pac. 706, 708–709 (1920); People v. Samonset, *supra*), and evidence of specific acts (Guardianship of Wisdom, 146 Cal.App.2d 635, 304 P.2d 221 (1956); Currin v. Currin, 125 Cal.App.2d 644, 271 P.2d 61 (1954); Guardianship of Casad, 106 Cal.App.2d 134, 234 P.2d 647 (1951)). However, there are cases which exclude some kinds of evidence where particular traits are involved. For example, in cases involving the unfitness or incompetency of an employee, evidence of specific acts is admissible to prove such unfitness or incompetency, while evidence of reputation is not. *E.g.,* Gier v. Los Angeles Consol. Elec. Ry., 108 Cal. 129, 41 Pac. 22 (1895). Section 1100 eliminates the uncertainties in existing law and makes admissible any evidence that is relevant to prove the character in issue. [7 Cal.L.Rev.Comm. Reports 1 (1965)].

Research References

Rutter, Cal. Practice Guide: Civil Trials & Evidence Ch. 10-D, D. Objectives of Cross-Examination.

Rutter, Cal. Practice Guide: Civil Trials & Evidence Ch. 8E-E, E. Limitations on Character Evidence.

Rutter, Cal. Practice Guide: Personal Injury Ch. 9-F, F. Examination of Witnesses.

§ 1101.　Evidence of character to prove conduct

(a) Except as provided in this section and in Sections 1102, 1103, 1108, and 1109, evidence of a person's character or a trait of his or her character (whether in the form of an opinion, evidence of reputation, or evidence of specific instances of his or her conduct) is inadmissible when offered to prove his or her conduct on a specified occasion.

(b) Nothing in this section prohibits the admission of evidence that a person committed a crime, civil wrong, or other act when relevant to prove some fact (such as motive, opportunity, intent, preparation, plan, knowledge, identity, absence of mistake or accident, or whether a defendant in a prosecution for an unlawful sexual act or attempted unlawful sexual act did not reasonably and in good faith believe that the victim consented) other than his or her disposition to commit such an act.

(c) Nothing in this section affects the admissibility of evidence offered to support or attack the credibility of a witness. *(Stats.1965, c. 299, § 2, operative Jan. 1, 1967. Amended by Stats.1986, c. 1432, § 1; Stats.1995, c. 439 (A.B.882), § 1; Stats.1996, c. 261 (S.B.1876), § 1.)*

Law Revision Commission Comments

Section 1101 is concerned with evidence of a person's character (*i.e.,* his propensity or disposition to engage in a certain type of conduct) that is offered as a basis for an inference that he behaved in conformity with that character on a particular occasion. Section 1101 is not concerned with evidence offered to prove a person's character when that character is itself in issue; the admissibility of character evidence offered for this purpose is determined under Sections 351 and 1100. Nor is Section 1101 concerned with evidence of character offered on the issue of the credibility of a witness; the admissibility of such evidence is determined under Section 786–790. See Evidence Code § 1101(c).

Civil cases. Section 1101 excludes evidence of character to prove conduct in a civil case for the following reasons. *First,* character evidence is of slight probative value and may be very prejudicial. *Second,* character evidence tends to distract the trier of fact from the main question of what actually happened on the particular occasion and permits the trier of fact to reward the good man and to punish the bad man because of their respective characters. *Third,* introduction of character evidence may result in confusion of issues and require extended collateral inquiry.

Section 1101 states the general rule recognized under existing law. Code Civ.Proc. § 2053 ("Evidence of the good character of a party is not admissible in a civil action. . . .") (Section 2053 is superseded by various Evidence Code sections).); Deevy v. Tassi, 21 Cal.2d 109, 130 P.2d 389 (1942) (assault; evidence of defendant's bad character for peace and quiet held inadmissible); Vance v. Richardson, 110 Cal. 414, 42 Pac. 909 (1895) (assault; evidence of defendant's good character for peace and quiet held inadmissible); Van Horn v. Van Horn, 5 Cal.App. 719, 91 Pac. 260 (1907) (divorce for adultery; evidence of defendant's and the nonparty-corespondent's good character held inadmissible). Under existing law, however, there *may* be an exception to this general rule. Existing law may permit evidence to be introduced of the unchaste character of a plaintiff to show the likelihood of her consent to an alleged rape. Valencia v. Milliken, 31 Cal.App. 533, 160 Pac. 1086 (1916) (civil action for rape; error, but nonprejudicial, to limit evidence of unchaste character of plaintiff to issue of damages). The Evidence Code has no such exception for civil cases. *But see* Evidence Code § 1103 (criminal cases).

Criminal cases. Section 1101 states the general rule that evidence of character to prove conduct is inadmissible in a criminal case. Sections 1102 and 1103 state exceptions to this general principle. See the Comment to Section 1102.

Evidence of misconduct to show fact other than character. Section 1101 does not prohibit the admission of evidence of misconduct when it is offered as evidence of some other fact in issue, such as motive, common scheme or plan, preparation, intent, knowledge, identity, or absence of mistake or accident. Subdivision (b) of Section 1101 makes this clear. This codifies existing law. People v. Lisenba, 14 Cal.2d 403, 94 P.2d 569 (1939) (prior crime admissible to show general criminal plan and absence of accident); People v. David, 12 Cal.2d 639, 86 P.2d 811 (1939) (prior robbery admissible to show defendant's sanity and ability to devise and execute deliberate plan); People v. Morani, 196 Cal. 154, 236 Pac. 135 (1925) (prior abortion admissible to show that operation was not performed in ignorance of effect and, hence, to show necessary intent). See discussion in California Criminal Law Practice 491–498 (Cal. Cont.Ed.Bar 1964). [7 Cal.L.Rev.Comm. Reports 1 (1965)].

Research References

Rutter, Cal. Practice Guide: Civil Trials & Evidence Ch. 8B-B, B. Particular Types of Evidence.

Rutter, Cal. Practice Guide: Civil Trials & Evidence Ch. 8E-E, E. Limitations on Character Evidence.

Rutter, Cal. Practice Guide: Civil Trials & Evidence Ch. 8F-B, B. Particular Grounds.

Rutter, Cal. Practice Guide: Civil Trials & Evidence Gen. Matls., Highlights.

Rutter, Cal. Practice Guide: Civil Trials & Evidence Ch. 8B-B, Outline B.

California Practice Guide: Employment Litigation Ch. 7-A, A. Title VII and the California Fair Employment and Housing Act.

Rutter, Cal. Practice Guide: Insurance Litigation Ch. 15-I, I. Trial.

Rutter, Cal. Practice Guide: Personal Injury Ch. 9-F, F. Examination of Witnesses.

§ 1102. Opinion and reputation evidence of character of criminal defendant to prove conduct

In a criminal action, evidence of the defendant's character or a trait of his character in the form of an opinion or evidence of his reputation is not made inadmissible by Section 1101 if such evidence is:

(a) Offered by the defendant to prove his conduct in conformity with such character or trait of character.

(b) Offered by the prosecution to rebut evidence adduced by the defendant under subdivision (a). *(Stats.1965, c. 299, § 2, operative Jan. 1, 1967.)*

Law Revision Commission Comments

Section 1102 and 1103 state exceptions (applicable only in criminal cases) to the general rule of Section 1101 that character evidence is not admissible to prove conduct in conformity with that character.

Sections 1102 and 1103 generally. Under Section 1102, the accused in a criminal case may introduce evidence of his good character to show his innocence of the alleged crime—provided that the character or trait of character to be shown is relevant to the charge made against him. This codifies existing law. People v. Chrisman, 135 Cal. 282, 67 Pac. 136 (1901). Sections 1101 and 1102 make it clear that the prosecution may not, on its own initiative, use character evidence to prove that the defendant had the disposition to commit the crime charged; but, if the defendant first introduces evidence of his good character to show the likelihood of innocence, the prosecution may meet his evidence by introducing evidence of the defendant's bad character to show the likelihood of guilt. This also codifies existing law. People v. Jones, 42 Cal.2d 219, 266 P.2d 38 (1954) (prosecution for sexual molestation of child; error to exclude expert psychiatric opinion that defendant was not a sexual psychopath); People v. Stewart, 28 Cal. 395 (1865) (murder prosecution; error to exclude evidence of defendant's good character for peace and quiet); People v. Hughes, 123 Cal.App.2d 767, 267 P.2d 376 (1954) (assault prosecution; evidence of defendant's violent nature held admissible after introduction of evidence showing his good character for peace and quiet). See California Criminal Law Practice 489–490 (Cal.Cont.Ed.Bar 1964).

Likewise, under Section 1103, the defendant may introduce evidence of the character of the victim of the crime where the conduct of the victim in conformity with his character would tend to exculpate the defendant; and, if the defendant introduces evidence of the bad character of the victim, the prosecution may introduce evidence of the victim's good character. This codifies existing law. People v. Hoffman, 195 Cal. 295, 311–312, 232 Pac. 974, 980 (1925) (murder prosecution; evidence of victim's good reputation for peace and quiet held inadmissible when defendant had not attacked reputation of victim); People v. Lamar, 148 Cal. 564, 83 Pac. 993 (1906) (murder prosecution; error to exclude evidence of victim's bad character for violence offered to prove victim was aggressor and defendant acted in self-defense); People v. Shea, 125 Cal. 151, 57 Pac. 885 (1899) (rape prosecution; error to exclude evidence of the prosecutrix's

unchaste character offered to prove the likelihood of consent); People v. Fitch, 28 Cal.App.2d 31, 81 P.2d 1019 (1938) (murder prosecution; evidence of victim's good character for peace and quiet held admissible after defendant introduced evidence of victim's violent nature). See also Comment, 25 Cal.L.Rev. 459 (1937).

Thus, under Sections 1102 and 1103, the defendant in a criminal case is given the right to introduce character evidence that would be inadmissible in a civil case. However, evidence of the character of the defendant or the victim—though weak—may be enough to raise a reasonable doubt in the mind of the trier of fact concerning the defendant's guilt. And, since his life or liberty is at stake, the defendant should not be deprived of the right to introduce evidence even of such slight probative value.

Kinds of character evidence admissible to prove conduct under Sections 1102 and 1103. The three kinds of evidence that might be offered to prove character as circumstantial evidence of conduct are: (1) evidence as to reputation, (2) opinion evidence as to character, and (3) evidence of specific acts indicating character. The admissibility of each of these kinds of evidence when character is sought to be proved as circumstantial evidence of conduct under Sections 1102 and 1103 is discussed below.

Reputation evidence. Reputation evidence is the ordinary means sanctioned by the cases for proving character as circumstantial evidence of conduct. Witkin, California Evidence § 125 (1958). See People v. Fair, 43 Cal. 137 (1872). Both Sections 1102 and 1103 codify the existing law permitting character to be proved by reputation.

Opinion evidence. There is recent authority for the admission of opinion evidence to prove character as circumstantial evidence of conduct. People v. Jones, 42 Cal.2d 219, 266 P.2d 38 (1954) (error to exclude expert psychiatric opinion that the defendant was not a sexual psychopath and, hence, unlikely to have violated Penal Code Section 288). However, opinion evidence generally has been held inadmissible. See People v. Spigno, 156 Cal.App.2d 279, 319 P.2d 458 (1957) (full discussion of the Jones case); California Criminal Law Practice 489–490 (Cal.Cont.Ed.Bar 1964).

The general rule under existing law excludes the most reliable form of character evidence and admits the least reliable. The opinions of those whose personal intimacy with a person gives them firsthand knowledge of that person's character are a far more reliable indication of that character than is reputation, which is little more than accumulated hearsay. See 7 Wigmore, Evidence § 1986 (3d ed. 1940). The danger of collateral issues seems no greater than that inherent in reputation evidence. Accordingly, both Section 1102 and Section 1103 permit character to be proved by opinion evidence.

Evidence of specific acts. Under existing law, the admissibility of evidence of specific acts to prove character as circumstantial evidence of conduct depends upon the nature of the conduct sought to be proved. Evidence of specific acts of the accused is excluded as a general rule in order to avoid the possibility of prejudice, undue confusion of the issues with collateral matters, unfair surprise, and the like. Thus, it is usually held that evidence of specific acts by the defendant is inadmissible to prove his guilt even though the defendant has opened the question by introducing evidence of his good character. See discussion in People v. Gin Shue, 58 Cal.App.2d 625, 634, 137 P.2d 742, 747–748 (1943). On the other hand, it is well settled that in a rape case the defendant may show the unchaste character of the prosecutrix by evidence of prior voluntary intercourse in order to indicate the unlikelihood of resistance on the occasion in question. People v. Shea, 125 Cal. 151, 57 Pac. 885 (1899); People v. Benson, 6 Cal. 221 (1856); People v. Battilana, 52 Cal.App.2d 685, 126 P.2d 923 (1942). However, in a homicide or assault case where the defense is self-defense, evidence of specific acts of violence by the victim is inadmissible to prove his violent nature (and, hence, that the victim was the aggressor) unless the prior acts were directed against the defendant himself. People v. Yokum, 145 Cal.App.2d 245, 302 P.2d 406 (1956); People v. Soules, 41 Cal.App.2d 298, 106 P.2d 639 (1940). *But see* People v. Carmichael, 198 Cal. 534, 548, 246 Pac. 62, 68 (1926) (if defendant had knowledge of victim's statement evidencing violent nature, the "statement was material and might have had an important bearing upon his plea of self-defense"); People v. Swigart, 80 Cal.App. 31, 251 Pac. 343 (1926). See also Comment, 25 Cal.L.Rev. 459, 466–469 (1937).

Section 1102 codifies the general rule under existing law which precludes evidence of specific acts of the defendant to prove character as circumstantial evidence of his innocence or of his disposition to commit the crime with which he is charged.

Section 1103 permits both the defendant and the prosecution to use evidence of specific acts of the victim of the crime to prove the victim's character as circumstantial evidence of his conduct. In this respect, the section harmonizes conflicting rules found in existing law.   [7 Cal.L.Rev. Comm. Reports 1 (1965)].

Research References

Rutter, Cal. Practice Guide: Civil Trials & Evidence Ch. 8C-H, H. Opinion Evidence.
Rutter, Cal. Practice Guide: Civil Trials & Evidence Ch. 8E-E, E. Limitations on Character Evidence.
1 Witkin Cal. Proc. 5th Attorneys § 592, (S 592) in General.

§ 1103. Character evidence of crime victim to prove conduct; evidence of defendant's character or trait for violence; evidence of manner of dress of victim; evidence of complaining witness' sexual conduct

(a) In a criminal action, evidence of the character or a trait of character (in the form of an opinion, evidence of reputation, or evidence of specific instances of conduct) of the victim of the crime for which the defendant is being prosecuted is not made inadmissible by Section 1101 if the evidence is:

(1) Offered by the defendant to prove conduct of the victim in conformity with the character or trait of character.

(2) Offered by the prosecution to rebut evidence adduced by the defendant under paragraph (1).

(b) In a criminal action, evidence of the defendant's character for violence or trait of character for violence (in the form of an opinion, evidence of reputation, or evidence of specific instances of conduct) is not made inadmissible by Section 1101 if the evidence is offered by the prosecution to prove conduct of the defendant in conformity with the character or trait of character and is offered after evidence that the victim had a character for violence or a trait of character tending to show violence has been adduced by the defendant under paragraph (1) of subdivision (a).

(c)(1) Notwithstanding any other provision of this code to the contrary, and except as provided in this subdivision, in any prosecution under Section 261, 262, or 264.1 of the Penal Code, or under Section 286, 288a, or 289 of the Penal Code, or for assault with intent to commit, attempt to commit, or conspiracy to commit a crime defined in any of those sections, except where the crime is alleged to have occurred in a local detention facility, as defined in Section 6031.4, or in a state prison, as defined in Section 4504, opinion evidence, reputation evidence, and evidence of specific instances of the complaining witness' sexual conduct, or any of that evidence, is not admissible by the defendant in order to prove consent by the complaining witness.

(2) Notwithstanding paragraph (3), evidence of the manner in which the victim was dressed at the time of the commission of the offense shall not be admissible when offered by either party on the issue of consent in any prosecution for an offense specified in paragraph (1), unless the evidence is determined by the court to be relevant and admissible in the interests of justice. The proponent of the evidence shall make an offer of proof outside the hearing of the jury. The court shall then make its determination and at that time, state the reasons for its ruling on the record. For the purposes of this paragraph, "manner of dress" does not include the condition of the victim's clothing before, during, or after the commission of the offense.

(3) Paragraph (1) shall not be applicable to evidence of the complaining witness' sexual conduct with the defendant.

(4) If the prosecutor introduces evidence, including testimony of a witness, or the complaining witness as a witness gives testimony, and that evidence or testimony relates to the complaining witness' sexual conduct, the defendant may cross-examine the witness who gives the testimony and offer relevant evidence limited specifically to the rebuttal of the evidence introduced by the prosecutor or given by the complaining witness.

(5) Nothing in this subdivision shall be construed to make inadmissible any evidence offered to attack the credibility of the complaining witness as provided in Section 782.

(6) As used in this section, "complaining witness" means the alleged victim of the crime charged, the prosecution of which is subject to this subdivision. *(Stats.1965, c. 299, § 2, operative Jan. 1, 1967. Amended by Stats.1974, c. 569, p. 1388, § 2; Stats.1981, c. 726, p. 2876, § 2; Stats.1990, c. 268 (A.B.2615), § 1; Stats. 1991, c. 16 (A.B.263), § 1, eff. March 18, 1991; Stats.1996, c. 1075 (S.B.1444), § 7; Stats.1998, c. 127 (A.B.1926), § 1.)*

Law Revision Commission Comments

See the Comment to Section 1102.   [7 Cal.L.Rev.Comm. Reports 1 (1965)].

Research References

Rutter, Cal. Practice Guide: Civil Trials & Evidence Ch. 8E-E, E. Limitations on Character Evidence.

§ 1104. Character trait for care or skill

Except as provided in Sections 1102 and 1103, evidence of a trait of a person's character with respect to care or skill is inadmissible to prove the quality of his conduct on a specified occasion. *(Stats.1965, c. 299, § 2, operative Jan. 1, 1967.)*

Law Revision Commission Comments

Section 1104 places a further limitation on the use of character evidence. Under Section 1104, character evidence with respect to care or skill is inadmissible to prove that conduct on a specific occasion was either careless or careful, skilled or unskilled, except to the extent permitted by Sections 1102 and 1103.

Section 1104 codifies well-settled California law. Towle v. Pacific Improvement Co., 98 Cal. 342, 33 Pac. 207 (1893). The purpose of the rule is to prevent collateral issues from consuming too much time and distracting the attention of the trier of fact from what was actually done on the particular occasion. Here, the slight probative value of the evidence balanced against the danger of confusion of issues, collateral inquiry, prejudice, and the like, warrants a fixed exclusionary rule. [7 Cal.L.Rev. Comm. Reports 1 (1965)].

Research References

Rutter, Cal. Practice Guide: Civil Trials & Evidence Ch. 8E-E, E. Limitations on Character Evidence.
Rutter, Cal. Practice Guide: Personal Injury Ch. 9-F, F. Examination of Witnesses.
Rutter, Cal. Practice Guide: Personal Injury Ch. 2(II)-B, B. Liability Arising from Operation of Motor Vehicle.

§ 1105. Habit or custom to prove specific behavior

Any otherwise admissible evidence of habit or custom is admissible to prove conduct on a specified occasion in conformity with the habit or custom. *(Stats.1965, c. 299, § 2, operative Jan. 1, 1967.)*

Law Revision Commission Comments

Section 1105, like Section 1100, declares that certain evidence is admissible. Hence, Section 1105 is technically unnecessary because Section 351 declares that all relevant evidence is admissible. Nonetheless, Section 1105 is desirable to assure that evidence of custom or habit (a regular response to a repeated specific situation) is admissible even where evidence of a person's character (his general disposition or propensity to engage in a certain type of conduct) is inadmissible.

The admissibility of habit evidence to prove conduct in conformity with the habit has long been established in California. Wallis v. Southern Pac. Co., 184 Cal. 662, 195 Pac. 408 (1921) (distinguishing cases holding character evidence as to care or skill inadmissible); Craven v. Central Pac. R.R., 72 Cal. 345, 13 Pac. 878 (1887). The admissibility of evidence of the custom of a business or occupation is also well established. Hughes v. Pacific Wharf & Storage Co., 188 Cal. 210, 205 Pac. 105 (1922) (mailing letter). However, under existing law, evidence of habit is admissible only if there are no eyewitnesses. Boone v. Bank of America, 220 Cal. 93, 29

P.2d 409 (1934). In earlier cases, the Supreme Court criticized the "no eyewitness" limitation:

This limitation upon the introduction of such testimony seems rather illogical. If the fact of the existence of habits of caution in a given particular has any legitimate evidentiary weight, the party benefited ought to have the advantage of it for whatever it is worth, even against adverse eye-witnesses; and if the testimony of the eye-witnesses is in his favor, it would be at least a harmless cumulation of evidence to permit testimony of his custom or habit. [Wallis v. Southern Pac. Co., 184 Cal. 662, 665, 195 Pac. 408, 409 (1921)].

The "no eyewitness" limitation is undesirable. Eyewitnesses frequently are mistaken, and some are dishonest. The trier of fact should be entitled to weigh the habit evidence against the eyewitness testimony as well as all of the other evidence in the case. Hence, Section 1105 does not contain the "no eyewitness" limitation. [7 Cal.L.Rev.Comm. Reports 1 (1965)].

Research References

Rutter, Cal. Practice Guide: Civil Trials & Evidence Ch. 8E-E, E. Limitations on Character Evidence.
Rutter, Cal. Practice Guide: Insurance Litigation Ch. 5-A, A. Cancellation by Insurer.

§ 1106. Sexual harassment, sexual assault, or sexual battery cases; opinion or reputation evidence of plaintiff's sexual conduct; inadmissibility; exception; cross-examination

(a) In any civil action alleging conduct which constitutes sexual harassment, sexual assault, or sexual battery, opinion evidence, reputation evidence, and evidence of specific instances of plaintiff's sexual conduct, or any of such evidence, is not admissible by the defendant in order to prove consent by the plaintiff or the absence of injury to the plaintiff, unless the injury alleged by the plaintiff is in the nature of loss of consortium.

(b) Subdivision (a) shall not be applicable to evidence of the plaintiff's sexual conduct with the alleged perpetrator.

(c) If the plaintiff introduces evidence, including testimony of a witness, or the plaintiff as a witness gives testimony, and the evidence or testimony relates to the plaintiff's sexual conduct, the defendant may cross-examine the witness who gives the testimony and offer relevant evidence limited specifically to the rebuttal of the evidence introduced by the plaintiff or given by the plaintiff.

(d) Nothing in this section shall be construed to make inadmissible any evidence offered to attack the credibility of the plaintiff as provided in Section 783. *(Added by Stats.1985, c. 1328, § 4.)*

Research References

Rutter, Cal. Practice Guide: Civil Trials & Evidence Ch. 8E-E, E. Limitations on Character Evidence.
California Practice Guide: Employment Litigation Ch. 19-N, N. Evidence Issues.
Rutter, Cal. Practice Guide: Personal Injury Ch. 9-F, F. Examination of Witnesses.

§ 1107. Intimate partner battering and its effects; expert testimony in criminal actions; sufficiency of foundation; abuse and domestic violence; applicability to Penal Code; impact on decisional law

(a) In a criminal action, expert testimony is admissible by either the prosecution or the defense regarding intimate partner battering and its effects, including the nature and effect of physical, emotional, or mental abuse on the beliefs, perceptions, or behavior of victims of domestic violence, except when offered against a criminal defendant to prove the occurrence of the act or acts of abuse which form the basis of the criminal charge.

(b) The foundation shall be sufficient for admission of this expert testimony if the proponent of the evidence establishes its relevancy and the proper qualifications of the expert witness. Expert opinion testimony on intimate partner battering and its

effects shall not be considered a new scientific technique whose reliability is unproven.

(c) For purposes of this section, "abuse" is defined in Section 6203 of the Family Code, and "domestic violence" is defined in Section 6211 of the Family Code and may include acts defined in Section 242, subdivision (e) of Section 243, Section 262, 273.5, 273.6, 422, or 653m of the Penal Code.

(d) This section is intended as a rule of evidence only and no substantive change affecting the Penal Code is intended.

(e) This section shall be known, and may be cited, as the Expert Witness Testimony on Intimate Partner Battering and Its Effects Section of the Evidence Code.

(f) The changes in this section that become effective on January 1, 2005, are not intended to impact any existing decisional law regarding this section, and that decisional law should apply equally to this section as it refers to "intimate partner battering and its effects" in place of "battered women's syndrome." *(Added by Stats.1991, c. 812 (A.B.785), § 1. Amended by Stats.1992, c. 163 (A.B.2641), § 72, operative Jan. 1, 1994; Stats.1993, c. 589 (A.B.2211), § 60; Stats.1993, c. 219 (A.B.1500), § 77.5; Stats.2000, c. 1001 (S.B.1944), § 1; Stats. 2004, c. 609 (S.B.1385), § 1.)*

Law Revision Commission Comments

Subdivision (c) of Section 1107 is amended to substitute references to the provisions of the Family Code that replaced the relevant provisions of former Code of Civil Procedure Section 542. [23 Cal.L.Rev.Comm. Reports 1 (1993)].

Research References

Rutter, Cal. Practice Guide: Civil Trials & Evidence Ch. 8B-B, B. Particular Types of Evidence.
Rutter, Cal. Practice Guide: Civil Trials & Evidence Ch. 8C-G, G. Scientific Evidence.
Rutter, Cal. Practice Guide: Civil Trials & Evidence Ch. 8C-H, H. Opinion Evidence.
Rutter, Cal. Practice Guide: Family Law Ch. 7-C, C. Custody Awards, Generally.
11 Witkin, California Summary 10th Husband and Wife § 372, (S 372) Criminal Proceedings.

§ 1108. Evidence of another sexual offense by defendant; disclosure; construction of section

(a) In a criminal action in which the defendant is accused of a sexual offense, evidence of the defendant's commission of another sexual offense or offenses is not made inadmissible by Section 1101, if the evidence is not inadmissible pursuant to Section 352.

(b) In an action in which evidence is to be offered under this section, the people shall disclose the evidence to the defendant, including statements of witnesses or a summary of the substance of any testimony that is expected to be offered in compliance with the provisions of Section 1054.7 of the Penal Code.

(c) This section shall not be construed to limit the admission or consideration of evidence under any other section of this code.

(d) As used in this section, the following definitions shall apply:

(1) "Sexual offense" means a crime under the law of a state or of the United States that involved any of the following:

(A) Any conduct proscribed by Section 243.4, 261, 261.5, 262, 264.1, 266c, 269, 286, 288, 288a, 288.2, 288.5, or 289, or subdivision (b), (c), or (d) of Section 311.2 or Section 311.3, 311.4, 311.10, 311.11, 314, or 647.6, of the Penal Code.

(B) Any conduct proscribed by Section 220 of the Penal Code, except assault with intent to commit mayhem.

(C) Contact, without consent, between any part of the defendant's body or an object and the genitals or anus of another person.

(D) Contact, without consent, between the genitals or anus of the defendant and any part of another person's body.

(E) Deriving sexual pleasure or gratification from the infliction of death, bodily injury, or physical pain on another person.

(F) An attempt or conspiracy to engage in conduct described in this paragraph.

(2) "Consent" shall have the same meaning as provided in Section 261.6 of the Penal Code, except that it does not include consent which is legally ineffective because of the age, mental disorder, or developmental or physical disability of the victim. *(Added by Stats.1995, c. 439 (A.B.882), § 2. Amended by Stats.2001, c. 517 (A.B.380), § 1; Stats.2002, c. 194 (A.B.2252), § 1; Stats.2002, c. 828 (A.B.2499), § 1.)*

Research References

Rutter, Cal. Practice Guide: Civil Trials & Evidence Ch. 8E-E, E. Limitations on Character Evidence.

§ 1109. Evidence of defendant's other acts of domestic violence

(a)(1) Except as provided in subdivision (e) or (f), in a criminal action in which the defendant is accused of an offense involving domestic violence, evidence of the defendant's commission of other domestic violence is not made inadmissible by Section 1101 if the evidence is not inadmissible pursuant to Section 352.

(2) Except as provided in subdivision (e) or (f), in a criminal action in which the defendant is accused of an offense involving abuse of an elder or dependent person, evidence of the defendant's commission of other abuse of an elder or dependent person is not made inadmissible by Section 1101 if the evidence is not inadmissible pursuant to Section 352.

(3) Except as provided in subdivision (e) or (f) and subject to a hearing conducted pursuant to Section 352, which shall include consideration of any corroboration and remoteness in time, in a criminal action in which the defendant is accused of an offense involving child abuse, evidence of the defendant's commission of child abuse is not made inadmissible by Section 1101 if the evidence is not inadmissible pursuant to Section 352. Nothing in this paragraph prohibits or limits the admission of evidence pursuant to subdivision (b) of Section 1101.

(b) In an action in which evidence is to be offered under this section, the people shall disclose the evidence to the defendant, including statements of witnesses or a summary of the substance of any testimony that is expected to be offered, in compliance with the provisions of Section 1054. 7 of the Penal Code.

(c) This section shall not be construed to limit or preclude the admission or consideration of evidence under any other statute or case law.

(d) As used in this section:

(1) "Abuse of an elder or dependent person" means physical or sexual abuse, neglect, financial abuse, abandonment, isolation, abduction, or other treatment that results in physical harm, pain, or mental suffering, the deprivation of care by a caregiver, or other deprivation by a custodian or provider of goods or services that are necessary to avoid physical harm or mental suffering.

(2) "Child abuse" means an act proscribed by Section 273d of the Penal Code.

(3) "Domestic violence" has the meaning set forth in Section 13700 of the Penal Code. Subject to a hearing conducted pursuant to Section 352, which shall include consideration of any corroboration and remoteness in time, "domestic violence" has the further meaning as set forth in Section 6211 of the Family

Code, if the act occurred no more than five years before the charged offense.

(e) Evidence of acts occurring more than 10 years before the charged offense is inadmissible under this section, unless the court determines that the admission of this evidence is in the interest of justice.

(f) Evidence of the findings and determinations of administrative agencies regulating the conduct of health facilities licensed under Section 1250 of the Health and Safety Code is inadmissible under this section. *(Added by Stats.1996, c. 261 (S.B.1876), § 2. Amended by Stats.1998, c. 707 (S.B.1682), § 1; Stats.2000, c. 97 (A.B.2063), § 1; Stats.2004, c. 116 (A.B.141), § 1; Stats. 2004, c. 823 (A.B.20), § 6.5; Stats.2005, c. 464 (A.B.114), § 1.)*

Research References

Rutter, Cal. Practice Guide: Civil Trials & Evidence Ch. 8E-E, E. Limitations on Character Evidence.

CHAPTER 2. MEDIATION

§ 1115. Definitions

For purposes of this chapter:

(a) "Mediation" means a process in which a neutral person or persons facilitate communication between the disputants to assist them in reaching a mutually acceptable agreement.

(b) "Mediator" means a neutral person who conducts a mediation. "Mediator" includes any person designated by a mediator either to assist in the mediation or to communicate with the participants in preparation for a mediation.

(c) "Mediation consultation" means a communication between a person and a mediator for the purpose of initiating, considering, or reconvening a mediation or retaining the mediator. *(Added by Stats.1997, c. 772 (A.B.939), § 3.)*

Law Revision Commission Comments

Subdivision (a) of Section 1115 is drawn from Code of Civil Procedure Section 1775.1. To accommodate a wide range of mediation styles, the definition is broad, without specific limitations on format. For example, it would include a mediation conducted as a number of sessions, only some of which involve the mediator. The definition focuses on the nature of a proceeding, not its label. A proceeding may be a "mediation" for purposes of this chapter, even though it is denominated differently.

Under subdivision (b), a mediator must be neutral. The neutrality requirement is drawn from Code of Civil Procedure Section 1775.1. An attorney or other representative of a party is not neutral and so does not qualify as a "mediator" for purposes of this chapter.

A "mediator" may be an individual, group of individuals, or entity. See Section 175 ("person" defined). See also Section 10 (singular includes

Evidence

the plural). This definition of mediator encompasses not only the neutral person who takes the lead in conducting a mediation, but also any neutral who assists in the mediation, such as a case-developer, interpreter, or secretary. The definition focuses on a person's role, not the person's title. A person may be a "mediator" under this chapter even though the person has a different title, such as "ombudsperson." Any person who meets the definition of "mediator" must comply with Section 1121 (mediator reports and communications), which generally prohibits a mediator from reporting to a court or other tribunal concerning the mediated dispute.

Subdivision (c) is drawn from former Section 1152.5, which was amended in 1996 to explicitly protect mediation intake communications. See 1996 Cal. Stat. ch. 174, § 1. Subdivision (c) is not limited to communications to retain a mediator. It also encompasses contacts concerning whether to mediate, such as where a mediator contacts a disputant because another disputant desires to mediate, and contacts concerning initiation or recommencement of mediation, such as where a case-developer meets with a disputant before mediation.

For the scope of this chapter, see Section 1117. [1997–98 Annual Report, 27 Cal.L.Rev.Comm. Reports App. 5 (1997)].

Research References

Rutter, Cal. Practice Guide: A.D.R. Ch. 3-A, A. General Considerations.
Rutter, Cal. Practice Guide: A.D.R. Ch. 3-C, C. Confidentiality.
Rutter, Cal. Practice Guide: A.D.R. Ch. 3-F, F. Mini-Trial.
Rutter, Cal. Practice Guide: A.D.R. Ch. 4-C, C. Statutorily-Mandated Court Mediation Programs.
Rutter, Cal. Practice Guide: A.D.R. App. D Form 9, Mediation Agreement (Comprehensive Form).
Rutter, Cal. Practice Guide: A.D.R. App. D Form 10, Mini-Trial Agreement.
Rutter, Cal. Practice Guide: A.D.R. App. D Form 12, Confidentiality Provision.
Rutter, Cal. Practice Guide: Civ. Pro. Before Trial Ch. 1-E, E. Prelawsuit ADR Requirement.
Rutter, Cal. Practice Guide: Civ. Pro. Before Trial Ch. 13-A, A. Introduction.
Rutter, Cal. Practice Guide: Civil Trials & Evidence Ch. 8E-D, D. Other Public Policy Exclusions.
California Practice Guide: Employment Litigation Ch. 18-B, B. Nonbinding ADR Procedures.
California Practice Guide: Employment Litigation Ch. 18-E, E. Confidentiality of ADR Processes.
Rutter, Cal. Practice Guide: Family Law Ch. 9-E, E. Marital Settlement Agreements.
Rutter, Cal. Practice Guide: Insurance Litigation Ch. 15-I, I. Trial.
Rutter, Cal. Practice Guide: Personal Injury Ch. 7-A, A. Introduction-Nature and Purpose of "Judicial Arbitration" in General.
Rutter, Cal. Practice Guide: Prof. Responsibility Ch. 7-E, E. Mediation Confidentiality.
Miller and Starr California Real Estate § 35:6, --Confidentiality in Mediation.
Miller and Starr California Real Estate § 29:76, Systems for Resolving Defective Construction Disputes.
Miller and Starr California Real Estate § 35:16, Community Dispute Resolution Programs.
Miller and Starr California Real Estate § 35:22, Nature of Arbitration.
7 Witkin Cal. Proc. 5th Judgment § 180, Action Where No Contract was Formed.
6 Witkin Cal. Proc. 5th Proceedings Without Trial § 487, (S 487) Confidentiality.
6 Witkin Cal. Proc. 5th Proceedings Without Trial § 488, (S 488) Regulation of Mediation.
6 Witkin Cal. Proc. 5th Proceedings Without Trial § 491, Procedure.
12 Witkin, California Summary 10th Real Property § 125, (S 125) Alternative Dispute Resolution.

§ 1116. Effect of chapter

(a) Nothing in this chapter expands or limits a court's authority to order participation in a dispute resolution proceeding. Nothing in this chapter authorizes or affects the enforceability of a contract clause in which parties agree to the use of mediation.

(b) Nothing in this chapter makes admissible evidence that is inadmissible under Section 1152 or any other statute. (*Added by Stats.1997, c. 772 (A.B.939), § 3.*)

Law Revision Commission Comments

Subdivision (a) of Section 1116 establishes guiding principles for applying this chapter.

Subdivision (b) continues the first sentence of former Section 1152.5(c) without substantive change. [1997–98 Annual Report, 27 Cal.L.Rev. Comm. Reports App. 5 (1997)].

§ 1117. Application of chapter

(a) Except as provided in subdivision (b), this chapter applies to a mediation as defined in Section 1115.

(b) This chapter does not apply to either of the following:

(1) A proceeding under Part 1 (commencing with Section 1800) of Division 5 of the Family Code or Chapter 11 (commencing with Section 3160) of Part 2 of Division 8 of the Family Code.

(2) A settlement conference pursuant to Rule 3.1380 of the California Rules of Court. (*Added by Stats.1997, c. 772 (A.B. 939), § 3. Amended by Stats.2007, c. 130 (A.B.299), § 84.*)

Law Revision Commission Comments

Under subdivision (a) of Section 1117, mediation confidentiality and the other safeguards of this chapter apply to a broad range of mediations. See Section 1115 Comment.

Subdivision (b) sets forth two exceptions. Section 1117(b)(1) continues without substantive change former Section 1152.5(b). Special confidentiality rules apply to a proceeding in family conciliation court or a mediation of child custody or visitation issues. See Section 1040; Fam. Code §§ 1818, 3177.

Section 1117(b)(2) establishes that a court settlement conference is not a mediation within the scope of this chapter. A settlement conference is conducted under the aura of the court and is subject to special rules. [1997–98 Annual Report, 27 Cal.L.Rev.Comm. Reports App. 5 (1997)].

Research References

Rutter, Cal. Practice Guide: A.D.R. Ch. 3-C, C. Confidentiality.
Rutter, Cal. Practice Guide: A.D.R. Ch. 4-C, C. Statutorily-Mandated Court Mediation Programs.
Rutter, Cal. Practice Guide: Personal Injury Ch. 7-A, A. Introduction-Nature and Purpose of "Judicial Arbitration" in General.

§ 1118. Oral agreements

An oral agreement "in accordance with Section 1118" means an oral agreement that satisfies all of the following conditions:

(a) The oral agreement is recorded by a court reporter or reliable means of audio recording.

(b) The terms of the oral agreement are recited on the record in the presence of the parties and the mediator, and the parties express on the record that they agree to the terms recited.

(c) The parties to the oral agreement expressly state on the record that the agreement is enforceable or binding, or words to that effect.

(d) The recording is reduced to writing and the writing is signed by the parties within 72 hours after it is recorded. (*Added by Stats.1997, c. 772 (A.B.939), § 3. Amended by Stats.2009, c. 88 (A.B.176), § 35; Stats.2010, c. 328 (S.B.1330), § 64.*)

Law Revision Commission Comments

Section 1118 establishes a procedure for orally memorializing an agreement, in the interest of efficiency. Provisions permitting use of that procedure for certain purposes include Sections 1121 (mediator reports and communications), 1122 (disclosure by agreement), 1123 (written settlement agreements reached through mediation), and 1124 (oral agreements reached through mediation). See also Section 1125 (when mediation ends). For guidance on authority to bind a litigant, see Williams v. Saunders, 55 Cal.App.4th 1158, 64 Cal.Rptr.2d 571 (1997) ("The litigants' direct participation tends to ensure that the settlement is the result of their mature reflection and deliberate assent.") [1997–98 Annual Report, 27 Cal.L.Rev.Comm. Reports App. 5 (1997)].

Section 1118 is amended to reflect advances in recording technology and for consistency of terminology. For a similar reform, see 2002 Cal. Stat. ch. 1068 (replacing numerous references to "audiotape" in Civil Discovery Act with either "audio technology," "audio recording," or "audio record," as context required). [37 Cal. L. Revision Comm'n Reports 211 (2007)].

Research References

Rutter, Cal. Practice Guide: A.D.R. Ch. 1-E, E. Enforcing ADR Settlements.

Rutter, Cal. Practice Guide: A.D.R. Ch. 3-C, C. Confidentiality.

Rutter, Cal. Practice Guide: A.D.R. Ch. 3-D, D. "Classic" (Facilitative) Mediation.

Rutter, Cal. Practice Guide: A.D.R. Ch. 3-E, E. Voluntary Settlement Conference (Vsc) (Evaluative Mediation).

Rutter, Cal. Practice Guide: Civ. Pro. Before Trial Ch. 12(II)-F, F. Motion to Enforce Settlement (CCP §§ 664.6, 664.7).

Rutter, Cal. Practice Guide: Civil Trials & Evidence Ch. 8E-D, D. Other Public Policy Exclusions.

California Practice Guide: Employment Litigation Ch. 18-A, A. Settlement Considerations.

California Practice Guide: Employment Litigation Ch. 18-E, E. Confidentiality of ADR Processes.

Rutter, Cal. Practice Guide: Family Law Ch. 9-E, E. Marital Settlement Agreements.

Rutter, Cal. Practice Guide: Family Law Ch. 11-C, C. Optional "Formal" Discovery Procedures.

Rutter, Cal. Practice Guide: Personal Injury Ch. 4-G, G. Concluding and Enforcing Settlement.

Rutter, Cal. Practice Guide: Prof. Responsibility Ch. 7-E, E. Mediation Confidentiality.

Miller and Starr California Real Estate § 35:6, --Confidentiality in Mediation.

§ 1119. Written or oral communications during mediation process; admissibility

Except as otherwise provided in this chapter:

(a) No evidence of anything said or any admission made for the purpose of, in the course of, or pursuant to, a mediation or a mediation consultation is admissible or subject to discovery, and disclosure of the evidence shall not be compelled, in any arbitration, administrative adjudication, civil action, or other noncriminal proceeding in which, pursuant to law, testimony can be compelled to be given.

(b) No writing, as defined in Section 250, that is prepared for the purpose of, in the course of, or pursuant to, a mediation or a mediation consultation, is admissible or subject to discovery, and disclosure of the writing shall not be compelled, in any arbitration, administrative adjudication, civil action, or other noncriminal proceeding in which, pursuant to law, testimony can be compelled to be given.

(c) All communications, negotiations, or settlement discussions by and between participants in the course of a mediation or a mediation consultation shall remain confidential. *(Added by Stats.1997, c. 772 (A.B.939), § 3.)*

Law Revision Commission Comments

Subdivision (a) of Section 1119 continues without substantive change former Section 1152.5(a)(1), except that its protection explicitly applies in a subsequent arbitration or administrative adjudication, as well as in any civil action or proceeding. See Section 120 ("civil action" includes civil proceedings). In addition, the protection of Section 1119(a) extends to oral communications made for the purpose of or pursuant to a mediation, not just oral communications made in the course of the mediation.

Subdivision (b) continues without substantive change former Section 1152.5(a)(2), except that its protection explicitly applies in a subsequent arbitration or administrative adjudication, as well as in any civil action or proceeding. See Section 120 ("civil action" includes civil proceedings). In addition, subdivision (b) expressly encompasses any type of "writing" as defined in Section 250, regardless of whether the representations are on paper or on some other medium.

Subdivision (c) continues former Section 1152.5(a)(3) without substantive change. A mediation is confidential notwithstanding the presence of an observer, such as a person evaluating or training the mediator or studying the mediation process.

See Sections 1115(a) ("mediation" defined), 1115(c) ("mediation consultation" defined). See also Section 703.5 (testimony by a judge, arbitrator, or mediator).

For examples of specialized mediation confidentiality provisions, see Bus. & Prof. Code §§ 467.4–467.5 (community dispute resolution programs), 6200 (attorney-client fee disputes); Code Civ. Proc. §§ 1297.371 (international commercial disputes), 1775.10 (civil action mediation in participating courts); Fam. Code §§ 1818 (family conciliation court), 3177 (child custody); Food & Agric. Code § 54453 (agricultural cooperative bargaining associations); Gov't Code §§ 11420.20–11420.30 (administrative adjudication), 12984–12985 (housing discrimination), 66032–66033 (land use); Ins. Code § 10089.80 (earthquake insurance); Lab. Code § 65 (labor disputes); Welf. & Inst. Code § 350 (dependency mediation). See also Cal. Const. art. I, § 1 (right to privacy); Garstang v. Superior Court, 39 Cal.App.4th 526, 46 Cal.Rptr.2d 84, 88 (1995) (constitutional right of privacy protected communications made during mediation sessions before an ombudsperson). [1997–98 Annual Report, 27 Cal.L.Rev.Comm. Reports App. 5 (1997)].

Research References

Rutter, Cal. Practice Guide: A.D.R. Ch. 1-E, E. Enforcing ADR Settlements.

Rutter, Cal. Practice Guide: A.D.R. Ch. 2-E, E. Conducting Negotiations.

Rutter, Cal. Practice Guide: A.D.R. Ch. 3-A, A. General Considerations.

Rutter, Cal. Practice Guide: A.D.R. Ch. 3-C, C. Confidentiality.

Rutter, Cal. Practice Guide: A.D.R. Ch. 3-E, E. Voluntary Settlement Conference (Vsc) (Evaluative Mediation).

Rutter, Cal. Practice Guide: A.D.R. Ch. 3-F, F. Mini-Trial.

Rutter, Cal. Practice Guide: A.D.R. Ch. 4-C, C. Statutorily-Mandated Court Mediation Programs.

Rutter, Cal. Practice Guide: A.D.R. Ch. 7-A, A. Mediators.

Rutter, Cal. Practice Guide: A.D.R. Ch. 3B-B, B. ADR Options in Construction Disputes.

Rutter, Cal. Practice Guide: A.D.R. Gen. Matls., Highlights.

Rutter, Cal. Practice Guide: A.D.R. App. D Form 146, Stipulation for Appointment.

Rutter, Cal. Practice Guide: Civ. Pro. Before Trial Ch. 13-A, A. Introduction.

Rutter, Cal. Practice Guide: Civ. Pro. Before Trial Ch. 8C-3, "Not Privileged".

Rutter, Cal. Practice Guide: Civ. Pro. Before Trial Ch. 8C-5, Privacy Protection.

Rutter, Cal. Practice Guide: Civ. Pro. Before Trial Ch. 12(II)-F, F. Motion to Enforce Settlement (CCP §§ 664.6, 664.7).

Rutter, Cal. Practice Guide: Civil Trials & Evidence Ch. 4-F, F. Motions in Limine.

Rutter, Cal. Practice Guide: Civil Trials & Evidence Ch. 8E-D, D. Other Public Policy Exclusions.

California Practice Guide: Employment Litigation Ch. 18-B, B. Nonbinding ADR Procedures.

California Practice Guide: Employment Litigation Ch. 18-E, E. Confidentiality of ADR Processes.

Rutter, Cal. Practice Guide: Family Law Ch. 11-C, C. Optional "Formal" Discovery Procedures.

Rutter, Cal. Practice Guide: Insurance Litigation Ch. 15-I, I. Trial.

Rutter, Cal. Practice Guide: Personal Injury Ch. 4-G, G. Concluding and Enforcing Settlement.

Rutter, Cal. Practice Guide: Personal Injury Ch. 7-A, A. Introduction-Nature and Purpose of "Judicial Arbitration" in General.

Rutter, Cal. Practice Guide: Prof. Responsibility Ch. 3-D, D. Authority of Client vs. Authority of Attorney.

Rutter, Cal. Practice Guide: Prof. Responsibility Ch. 6-D, D. Professional Liability.

Rutter, Cal. Practice Guide: Prof. Responsibility Ch. 7-E, E. Mediation Confidentiality.

Miller and Starr California Real Estate § 35:6, --Confidentiality in Mediation.

Miller and Starr California Real Estate § 35:17, Efficacy of the Mediation Process; Enforceability.

Miller and Starr California Real Estate § 25B:105, Enforcement of the Restrictions--Requirement of Alternative Dispute Resolution.

15 NO. 3 Miller & Starr, California Real Estate Newsalert 2, Commercial Arbitration.

17 NO. 4 Miller & Starr, California Real Estate Newsalert 3, Commercial Arbitration.

20 NO. 3 Miller & Starr, California Real Estate Newsalert 7, Alternative Dispute Resolution.

21 NO. 4 Miller & Starr, California Real Estate Newsalert 19, Alternative Dispute Resolution.

6 Witkin Cal. Proc. 5th Proceedings Without Trial § 487, (S 487) Confidentiality.

6 Witkin Cal. Proc. 5th Proceedings Without Trial § 491, Procedure.

11 Witkin, California Summary 10th Husband and Wife § 10, (S 10) Imposition of Award as Sanction.

§ 1120. Evidence otherwise admissible

(a) Evidence otherwise admissible or subject to discovery outside of a mediation or a mediation consultation shall not be or become inadmissible or protected from disclosure solely by reason of its introduction or use in a mediation or a mediation consultation.

(b) This chapter does not limit any of the following:

(1) The admissibility of an agreement to mediate a dispute.

(2) The effect of an agreement not to take a default or an agreement to extend the time within which to act or refrain from acting in a pending civil action.

(3) Disclosure of the mere fact that a mediator has served, is serving, will serve, or was contacted about serving as a mediator in a dispute. *(Added by Stats.1997, c. 772 (A.B.939), § 3.)*

Law Revision Commission Comments

Subdivision (a) of Section 1120 continues former Section 1152.5(a)(6) without change. It limits the scope of Section 1119 (mediation confidentiality), preventing parties from using a mediation as a pretext to shield materials from disclosure.

Subdivision (b)(1) makes explicit that Section 1119 does not restrict admissibility of an agreement to mediate. Subdivision (b)(2) continues former Section 1152.5(e) without substantive change, but also includes an express exception for extensions of litigation deadlines. Subdivision (b)(3) makes clear that Section 1119 does not preclude a disputant from obtaining basic information about a mediator's track record, which may be significant in selecting an impartial mediator. Similarly, mediation participants may express their views on a mediator's performance, so long as they do not disclose anything said or done at the mediation.

See Sections 1115(a) ("mediation" defined), 1115(b) ("mediator" defined), 1115(c) ("mediation consultation" defined). [1997–98 Annual Report, 27 Cal.L.Rev.Comm. Reports App. 5 (1997)].

Research References

Rutter, Cal. Practice Guide: A.D.R. Ch. 3-C, C. Confidentiality.

Rutter, Cal. Practice Guide: A.D.R. Ch. 4-C, C. Statutorily-Mandated Court Mediation Programs.

Rutter, Cal. Practice Guide: Civ. Pro. Before Trial Ch. 13-A, A. Introduction.

Rutter, Cal. Practice Guide: Civil Trials & Evidence Ch. 8E-D, D. Other Public Policy Exclusions.

California Practice Guide: Employment Litigation Ch. 18-E, E. Confidentiality of ADR Processes.

Rutter, Cal. Practice Guide: Personal Injury Ch. 6-A, A. Scope of Discovery and Limitations.

Rutter, Cal. Practice Guide: Personal Injury Ch. 7-A, A. Introduction-Nature and Purpose of "Judicial Arbitration" in General.

Rutter, Cal. Practice Guide: Prof. Responsibility Ch. 6-D, D. Professional Liability.

6 Witkin Cal. Proc. 5th Proceedings Without Trial § 487, (S 487) Confidentiality.

§ 1121. Mediator's reports and findings

Neither a mediator nor anyone else may submit to a court or other adjudicative body, and a court or other adjudicative body may not consider, any report, assessment, evaluation, recommendation, or finding of any kind by the mediator concerning a mediation conducted by the mediator, other than a report that is

mandated by court rule or other law and that states only whether an agreement was reached, unless all parties to the mediation expressly agree otherwise in writing, or orally in accordance with Section 1118. *(Added by Stats.1997, c. 772 (A.B.939), § 3.)*

Law Revision Commission Comments

Section 1121 continues the first sentence of former Section 1152.6 without substantive change, except to make clear that (1) the section applies to all submissions, not just filings, (2) the section is not limited to court proceedings but rather applies to all types of adjudications, including arbitrations and administrative adjudications, (3) the section applies to any report or statement of opinion, however denominated, and (4) neither a mediator nor anyone else may submit the prohibited information. The section does not prohibit a mediator from providing a mediation participant with feedback on the dispute in the course of the mediation.

Rather, the focus is on preventing coercion. As Section 1121 recognizes, a mediator should not be able to influence the result of a mediation or adjudication by reporting or threatening to report to the decisionmaker on the merits of the dispute or reasons why mediation failed to resolve it. Similarly, a mediator should not have authority to resolve or decide the mediated dispute, and should not have any function for the adjudicating tribunal with regard to the dispute, except as a non-decisionmaking neutral. See Section 1117 (scope of chapter), which excludes settlement conferences from this chapter.

The exception to Section 1121 (permitting submission and consideration of a mediator's report where "all parties to the mediation expressly agree" in writing) is modified to allow use of the oral procedure in Section 1118 (recorded oral agreement) and to permit making of the agreement at any time, not just before the mediation. A mediator's report to a court may disclose mediation communications only if all parties to the mediation agree to the reporting and all persons who participate in the mediation agree to the disclosure. See Section 1122 (disclosure by agreement).

The second sentence of former Section 1152.6 is continued without substantive change in Section 1117 (scope of chapter), except that Section 1117 excludes proceedings under Part 1 (commencing with Section 1800) of Division 5 of the Family Code, as well as proceedings under Chapter 11 (commencing with Section 3160) of Part 2 of Division 8 of the Family Code.

See Sections 1115(a) ("mediation" defined), 1115(b) ("mediator" defined). See also Sections 703.5 (testimony by a judge, arbitrator, or mediator), 1127 (attorney's fees), 1128 (irregularity in proceedings). [1997–98 Annual Report, 27 Cal.L.Rev.Comm. Reports App. 5 (1997)].

Research References

Rutter, Cal. Practice Guide: A.D.R. Ch. 3-A, A. General Considerations.

Rutter, Cal. Practice Guide: A.D.R. Ch. 3-C, C. Confidentiality.

Rutter, Cal. Practice Guide: A.D.R. Ch. 4-C, C. Statutorily-Mandated Court Mediation Programs.

Rutter, Cal. Practice Guide: Civ. Pro. Before Trial Ch. 13-A, A. Introduction.

Rutter, Cal. Practice Guide: Civ. Pro. Before Trial Ch. 8C-3, "Not Privileged".

Rutter, Cal. Practice Guide: Civil Trials & Evidence Ch. 8E-D, D. Other Public Policy Exclusions.

California Practice Guide: Employment Litigation Ch. 18-B, B. Nonbinding ADR Procedures.

California Practice Guide: Employment Litigation Ch. 18-E, E. Confidentiality of ADR Processes.

Rutter, Cal. Practice Guide: Family Law Ch. 11-C, C. Optional "Formal" Discovery Procedures.

Rutter, Cal. Practice Guide: Personal Injury Ch. 4-G, G. Concluding and Enforcing Settlement.

Rutter, Cal. Practice Guide: Personal Injury Ch. 7-A, A. Introduction-Nature and Purpose of "Judicial Arbitration" in General.

§ 1122. Communications or writings; conditions to admissibility

(a) A communication or a writing, as defined in Section 250, that is made or prepared for the purpose of, or in the course of, or pursuant to, a mediation or a mediation consultation, is not made inadmissible, or protected from disclosure, by provisions of this chapter if either of the following conditions is satisfied:

(1) All persons who conduct or otherwise participate in the mediation expressly agree in writing, or orally in accordance with Section 1118, to disclosure of the communication, document, or writing.

(2) The communication, document, or writing was prepared by or on behalf of fewer than all the mediation participants, those participants expressly agree in writing, or orally in accordance with Section 1118, to its disclosure, and the communication, document, or writing does not disclose anything said or done or any admission made in the course of the mediation.

(b) For purposes of subdivision (a), if the neutral person who conducts a mediation expressly agrees to disclosure, that agreement also binds any other person described in subdivision (b) of Section 1115. *(Added by Stats.1997, c. 772 (A.B.939), § 3.)*

Law Revision Commission Comments

Section 1122 supersedes former Section 1152.5(a)(4) and part of former Section 1152.5(a)(2), which were unclear regarding precisely whose agreement was required for admissibility or disclosure of mediation communications and documents.

Subdivision (a)(1) states the general rule that mediation documents and communications may be admitted or disclosed only upon agreement of all participants, including not only parties but also the mediator and other nonparties attending the mediation (e.g., a disputant not involved in litigation, a spouse, an accountant, an insurance representative, or an employee of a corporate affiliate). Agreement must be express, not implied. For example, parties cannot be deemed to have agreed in advance to disclosure merely because they agreed to participate in a particular dispute resolution program.

Subdivision (a)(2) facilitates admissibility and disclosure of unilaterally prepared materials, but it only applies so long as those materials may be produced in a manner revealing nothing about the mediation discussion. Materials that necessarily disclose mediation communications may be admitted or disclosed only upon satisfying the general rule of subdivision (a)(1).

Mediation materials that satisfy the requirements of subdivisions (a)(1) or (a)(2) are not necessarily admissible or subject to disclosure. Although the provisions on mediation confidentiality do not bar admissibility or disclosure, there may be other bases for exclusion.

Subdivision (b) makes clear that if the person who takes the lead in conducting a mediation agrees to disclosure, it is unnecessary to seek out and obtain assent from each assistant to that person, such as a case developer, interpreter, or secretary.

For exceptions to Section 1122, see Sections 1123 (written settlement agreements reached through mediation) and 1124 (oral agreements reached through mediation) & Comments.

See Section 1115(a) ("mediation" defined), 1115(c) ("mediation consultation" defined). See also Sections 703.5 (testimony by a judge, arbitrator, or mediator), 1119 (mediation confidentiality), 1121 (mediator reports and communications). [1997–98 Annual Report, 27 Cal.L.Rev. Comm. Reports App. 5 (1997)].

Research References

Rutter, Cal. Practice Guide: A.D.R. Ch. 3-C, C. Confidentiality.
Rutter, Cal. Practice Guide: Civ. Pro. Before Trial Ch. 8C-3, "Not Privileged".
Rutter, Cal. Practice Guide: Civil Trials & Evidence Ch. 8E-D, D. Other Public Policy Exclusions.
California Practice Guide: Employment Litigation Ch. 18-E, E. Confidentiality of ADR Processes.
Rutter, Cal. Practice Guide: Family Law Ch. 11-C, C. Optional "Formal" Discovery Procedures.
Rutter, Cal. Practice Guide: Personal Injury Ch. 7-A, A. Introduction-Nature and Purpose of "Judicial Arbitration" in General.
Rutter, Cal. Practice Guide: Prof. Responsibility Ch. 7-E, E. Mediation Confidentiality.

6 Witkin Cal. Proc. 5th Proceedings Without Trial § 487, (S 487) Confidentiality.

§ 1123. Written settlement agreements; conditions to admissibility

A written settlement agreement prepared in the course of, or pursuant to, a mediation, is not made inadmissible, or protected from disclosure, by provisions of this chapter if the agreement is signed by the settling parties and any of the following conditions are satisfied:

(a) The agreement provides that it is admissible or subject to disclosure, or words to that effect.

(b) The agreement provides that it is enforceable or binding or words to that effect.

(c) All parties to the agreement expressly agree in writing, or orally in accordance with Section 1118, to its disclosure.

(d) The agreement is used to show fraud, duress, or illegality that is relevant to an issue in dispute. *(Added by Stats.1997, c. 772 (A.B.939), § 3.)*

Law Revision Commission Comments

Section 1123 consolidates and clarifies provisions governing written settlements reached through mediation. For guidance on binding a disputant to a written settlement agreement, see Williams v. Saunders, 55 Cal.App.4th 1158, 64 Cal.Rptr.2d 571 (1997) ("The litigants' direct participation tends to ensure that the settlement is the result of their mature reflection and deliberate assent.").

As to an executed written settlement agreement, subdivision (a) continues part of former Section 1152.5(a)(2). See also Ryan v. Garcia, 27 Cal.App.4th 1006, 1012, 33 Cal.Rptr.2d 158, 162 (1994) (Section 1152.5 "provides a simple means by which settlement agreements executed during mediation can be made admissible in later proceedings," i.e., the "parties may consent, as part of a writing, to subsequent admissibility of the agreement").

Subdivision (b) is new. It is added due to the likelihood that parties intending to be bound will use words to that effect, rather than saying their agreement is intended to be admissible or subject to disclosure.

As to fully executed written settlement agreements, subdivision (c) supersedes former Section 1152.5(a)(4). To facilitate enforceability of such agreements, disclosure pursuant to subdivision (c) requires only agreement of the parties. Agreement of the mediator and other mediation participants is not necessary. Subdivision (c) is thus an exception to the general rule governing disclosure of mediation communications by agreement. See Section 1122.

Subdivision (d) continues former Section 1152.5(a)(5) without substantive change.

A written settlement agreement that satisfies the requirements of subdivision (a), (b), (c), or (d) is not necessarily admissible or subject to disclosure. Although the provisions on mediation confidentiality do not bar admissibility or disclosure, there may be other bases for exclusion.

See Section 1115(a) ("mediation" defined). [1997–98 Annual Report, 27 Cal.L.Rev.Comm. Reports App. 5 (1997)].

Research References

Rutter, Cal. Practice Guide: A.D.R. Ch. 1-E, E. Enforcing ADR Settlements.
Rutter, Cal. Practice Guide: A.D.R. Ch. 3-C, C. Confidentiality.
Rutter, Cal. Practice Guide: A.D.R. Ch. 5-G, G. Procedures to Enforce Arbitration.
Rutter, Cal. Practice Guide: Civ. Pro. Before Trial Ch. 8C-3, "Not Privileged".
Rutter, Cal. Practice Guide: Civ. Pro. Before Trial Ch. 12(II)-F, F. Motion to Enforce Settlement (CCP §§ 664.6, 664.7).
Rutter, Cal. Practice Guide: Civil Trials & Evidence Ch. 8E-D, D. Other Public Policy Exclusions.
California Practice Guide: Employment Litigation Ch. 18-E, E. Confidentiality of ADR Processes.
Rutter, Cal. Practice Guide: Family Law Ch. 9-B, B. General Drafting and Analytical Considerations.
Rutter, Cal. Practice Guide: Family Law Ch. 9-E, E. Marital Settlement Agreements.

Evidence

Rutter, Cal. Practice Guide: Family Law Ch. 11-C, C. Optional "Formal" Discovery Procedures.

Rutter, Cal. Practice Guide: Personal Injury Ch. 4-G, G. Concluding and Enforcing Settlement.

Rutter, Cal. Practice Guide: Personal Injury Ch. 7-A, A. Introduction-Nature and Purpose of "Judicial Arbitration" in General.

Rutter, Cal. Practice Guide: Prof. Responsibility Ch. 7-E, E. Mediation Confidentiality.

Miller and Starr California Real Estate § 35:6, --Confidentiality in Mediation.

Miller and Starr California Real Estate § 35:17, Efficacy of the Mediation Process; Enforceability.

15 NO. 3 Miller & Starr, California Real Estate Newsalert 2, Commercial Arbitration.

17 NO. 4 Miller & Starr, California Real Estate Newsalert 3, Commercial Arbitration.

19 NO. 2 Miller & Starr, California Real Estate Newsalert 4, Alternative Dispute Resolution.

19 NO. 3 Miller & Starr, California Real Estate Newsalert 5, Alternative Dispute Resolution.

6 Witkin Cal. Proc. 5th Proceedings Without Trial § 487, (S 487) Confidentiality.

§ 1124. Oral agreements; conditions to admissibility

An oral agreement made in the course of, or pursuant to, a mediation is not made inadmissible, or protected from disclosure, by the provisions of this chapter if any of the following conditions are satisfied:

(a) The agreement is in accordance with Section 1118.

(b) The agreement is in accordance with subdivisions (a), (b), and (d) of Section 1118, and all parties to the agreement expressly agree, in writing or orally in accordance with Section 1118, to disclosure of the agreement.

(c) The agreement is in accordance with subdivisions (a), (b), and (d) of Section 1118, and the agreement is used to show fraud, duress, or illegality that is relevant to an issue in dispute. *(Added by Stats.1997, c. 772 (A.B.939), § 3.)*

Law Revision Commission Comments

Section 1124 sets forth specific circumstances under which mediation confidentiality is inapplicable to an oral agreement reached through mediation. Except in those circumstances, Sections 1119 (mediation confidentiality) and 1124 codify the rule of Ryan v. Garcia, 27 Cal.App.4th 1006, 33 Cal.Rptr.2d 158 (1994) (mediation confidentiality applies to oral statement of settlement terms), and reject the contrary approach of Regents of University of California v. Sumner, 42 Cal.App.4th 1209, 50 Cal.Rptr.2d 200 (1996) (mediation confidentiality does not protect oral statement of settlement terms).

Subdivision (a) of Section 1124 facilitates enforcement of an oral agreement that is recorded and memorialized in writing in accordance with Section 1118. For guidance in applying subdivision (a), see Section 1125 (when mediation ends) & Comment.

Subdivision (b) parallels Section 1123(c).

Subdivision (c) parallels Section 1123(d).

An oral agreement that satisfies the requirements of subdivision (a), (b), or (c) is not necessarily admissible or subject to disclosure. Although the provisions on mediation confidentiality do not bar admissibility or disclosure, there may be other bases for exclusion. For guidance on binding a disputant to a settlement agreement, see Williams v. Saunders, 55 Cal.App.4th 1158, 64 Cal.Rptr.2d 571 (1997) ("The litigants' direct participation tends to ensure that the settlement is the result of their mature reflection and deliberate assent.").

See Section 1115(a) ("mediation" defined). [1997–98 Annual Report, 27 Cal.L.Rev.Comm. Reports App. 5 (1997)].

Research References

Rutter, Cal. Practice Guide: A.D.R. Ch. 1-E, E. Enforcing ADR Settlements.

Rutter, Cal. Practice Guide: A.D.R. Ch. 3-C, C. Confidentiality.

Rutter, Cal. Practice Guide: A.D.R. Ch. 3-D, D. "Classic" (Facilitative) Mediation.

Rutter, Cal. Practice Guide: A.D.R. Ch. 3-E, E. Voluntary Settlement Conference (Vsc) (Evaluative Mediation).

Rutter, Cal. Practice Guide: Civil Trials & Evidence Ch. 8E-D, D. Other Public Policy Exclusions.

California Practice Guide: Employment Litigation Ch. 18-E, E. Confidentiality of ADR Processes.

Rutter, Cal. Practice Guide: Family Law Ch. 9-E, E. Marital Settlement Agreements.

Rutter, Cal. Practice Guide: Family Law Ch. 11-C, C. Optional "Formal" Discovery Procedures.

Rutter, Cal. Practice Guide: Prof. Responsibility Ch. 7-E, E. Mediation Confidentiality.

Miller and Starr California Real Estate § 35:6, --Confidentiality in Mediation.

6 Witkin Cal. Proc. 5th Proceedings Without Trial § 487, (S 487) Confidentiality.

§ 1125. End of mediation; satisfaction of conditions

(a) For purposes of confidentiality under this chapter, a mediation ends when any one of the following conditions is satisfied:

(1) The parties execute a written settlement agreement that fully resolves the dispute.

(2) An oral agreement that fully resolves the dispute is reached in accordance with Section 1118.

(3) The mediator provides the mediation participants with a writing signed by the mediator that states that the mediation is terminated, or words to that effect, which shall be consistent with Section 1121.

(4) A party provides the mediator and the other mediation participants with a writing stating that the mediation is terminated, or words to that effect, which shall be consistent with Section 1121. In a mediation involving more than two parties, the mediation may continue as to the remaining parties or be terminated in accordance with this section.

(5) For 10 calendar days, there is no communication between the mediator and any of the parties to the mediation relating to the dispute. The mediator and the parties may shorten or extend this time by agreement.

(b) For purposes of confidentiality under this chapter, if a mediation partially resolves a dispute, mediation ends when either of the following conditions is satisfied:

(1) The parties execute a written settlement agreement that partially resolves the dispute.

(2) An oral agreement that partially resolves the dispute is reached in accordance with Section 1118.

(c) This section does not preclude a party from ending a mediation without reaching an agreement. This section does not otherwise affect the extent to which a party may terminate a mediation. *(Added by Stats.1997, c. 772 (A.B.939), § 3.)*

Law Revision Commission Comments

By specifying when a mediation ends, Section 1125 provides guidance on which communications are protected by Section 1119 (mediation confidentiality).

Under subdivision (a)(1), if mediation participants reach an oral compromise and reduce it to a written settlement fully resolving their dispute, confidentiality extends until the agreement is signed by all the parties. For guidance on binding a disputant to a settlement agreement, see Williams v. Saunders, 55 Cal.App.4th 1158, 64 Cal.Rptr.2d 571 (1997) ("The litigants' direct participation tends to ensure that the settlement is the result of their mature reflection and deliberate assent.").

Subdivision (a)(2) applies where mediation participants fully resolve their dispute by an oral agreement that is recorded and memorialized in writing in accordance with Section 1118. The mediation is over upon completion of that procedure, and the confidentiality protections of this chapter do not apply to any later proceedings, such as attempts to further refine the content of the agreement. See Section 1124 (oral agreements reached through mediation). Subdivisions (a)(3) and (a)(4) are drawn from Rule 14 of the American Arbitration Association's Commercial Mediation Rules (as amended, Jan. 1, 1992). Subdivision (a)(5) applies where an affirmative act terminating a mediation for purposes of this chapter does not occur.

Subdivision (b) applies where mediation partially resolves a dispute, such as when the disputants resolve only some of the issues (e.g., contract, but not tort, liability) or when only some of the disputants settle.

Subdivision (c) limits the effect of Section 1125.

See Sections 1115(a) ("mediation" defined), 1115(b) ("mediator" defined). [1997–98 Annual Report, 27 Cal.L.Rev.Comm. Reports App. 5 (1997)].

Research References

Rutter, Cal. Practice Guide: A.D.R. Ch. 3-C, C. Confidentiality.
Rutter, Cal. Practice Guide: Civil Trials & Evidence Ch. 8E-D, D. Other Public Policy Exclusions.

§ 1126. Protections before and after mediation ends

Anything said, any admission made, or any writing that is inadmissible, protected from disclosure, and confidential under this chapter before a mediation ends, shall remain inadmissible, protected from disclosure, and confidential to the same extent after the mediation ends. *(Added by Stats.1997, c. 772 (A.B.939), § 3.)*

Law Revision Commission Comments

Section 1126 clarifies that mediation materials are confidential not only during a mediation, but also after the mediation ends pursuant to Section 1125 (when mediation ends).

See Section 1115(a) ("mediation" defined). [1997–98 Annual Report, 27 Cal.L.Rev.Comm. Reports App. 5 (1997)].

Research References

Rutter, Cal. Practice Guide: A.D.R. Ch. 3-C, C. Confidentiality.
Rutter, Cal. Practice Guide: Civil Trials & Evidence Ch. 8E-D, D. Other Public Policy Exclusions.
California Practice Guide: Employment Litigation Ch. 18-E, E. Confidentiality of ADR Processes.
Rutter, Cal. Practice Guide: Prof. Responsibility Ch. 7-E, E. Mediation Confidentiality.

§ 1127. Attorney's fees and costs

If a person subpoenas or otherwise seeks to compel a mediator to testify or produce a writing, as defined in Section 250, and the court or other adjudicative body determines that the testimony or writing is inadmissible under this chapter, or protected from disclosure under this chapter, the court or adjudicative body making the determination shall award reasonable attorney's fees and costs to the mediator against the person seeking the testimony or writing. *(Added by Stats.1997, c. 772 (A.B.939), § 3.)*

Law Revision Commission Comments

Section 1127 continues former Section 1152.5(d) without substantive change, except to clarify that either a court or another adjudicative body (e.g., an arbitrator or an administrative tribunal) may award the fees and costs. Because Section 1115 (definitions) defines "mediator" to include not only the neutral person who takes the lead in conducting a mediation, but also any neutral who assists in the mediation, fees are available regardless of the role played by the person subjected to discovery.

See Section 1115(b) ("mediator" defined). [1997–98 Annual Report, 27 Cal.L.Rev.Comm. Reports App. 5 (1997)].

Research References

Rutter, Cal. Practice Guide: A.D.R. Ch. 3-C, C. Confidentiality.
Miller and Starr California Real Estate § 35:6, --Confidentiality in Mediation.
6 Witkin Cal. Proc. 5th Proceedings Without Trial § 487, (S 487) Confidentiality.

§ 1128. Subsequent trials; references to mediation

Any reference to a mediation during any subsequent trial is an irregularity in the proceedings of the trial for the purposes of

Section 657 of the Code of Civil Procedure. Any reference to a mediation during any other subsequent noncriminal proceeding is grounds for vacating or modifying the decision in that proceeding, in whole or in part, and granting a new or further hearing on all or part of the issues, if the reference materially affected the substantial rights of the party requesting relief. *(Added by Stats.1997, c. 772 (A.B.939), § 3.)*

Law Revision Commission Comments

Section 1128 is drawn from Code of Civil Procedure Section 1775.12. The first sentence makes it an irregularity to refer to a mediation in a subsequent civil trial; the second sentence extends that rule to other noncriminal proceedings, such as an administrative adjudication. An appropriate situation for invoking this section is where a party urges the trier of fact to draw an adverse inference from an adversary's refusal to disclose mediation communications.

See Section 1115 ("mediation" defined). [1997–98 Annual Report, 27 Cal.L.Rev.Comm. Reports App. 5 (1997)].

Research References

Rutter, Cal. Practice Guide: A.D.R. Ch. 3-C, C. Confidentiality.
Rutter, Cal. Practice Guide: A.D.R. Ch. 3-F, F. Mini-Trial.
Rutter, Cal. Practice Guide: A.D.R. Ch. 4-C, C. Statutorily-Mandated Court Mediation Programs.
Rutter, Cal. Practice Guide: Civil Trials & Evidence Ch. 18-B, B. Motion for New Trial.
California Practice Guide: Employment Litigation Ch. 18-E, E. Confidentiality of ADR Processes.
Rutter, Cal. Practice Guide: Insurance Litigation Ch. 15-I, I. Trial.
Rutter, Cal. Practice Guide: Personal Injury Ch. 7-A, A. Introduction-Nature and Purpose of "Judicial Arbitration" in General.
Miller and Starr California Real Estate § 35:6, --Confidentiality in Mediation.
Miller and Starr California Real Estate § 29:76, Systems for Resolving Defective Construction Disputes.
Miller and Starr California Real Estate § 35:16, Community Dispute Resolution Programs.
6 Witkin Cal. Proc. 5th Proceedings Without Trial § 487, (S 487) Confidentiality.
6 Witkin Cal. Proc. 5th Proceedings Without Trial § 491, Procedure.

CHAPTER 3. OTHER EVIDENCE AFFECTED OR EXCLUDED BY EXTRINSIC POLICIES

Section

1160. Admissibility of expressions of sympathy or benevolence; definitions.

1161. Human trafficking; admissibility of evidence of engagement in commercial sexual act by victim or sexual history of victim.

Law Revision Commission Comments

The chapter heading is renumbered to reflect the addition of a new Chapter 2 (commencing with Section 1115) (Mediation). [1997–98 Annual Report, 27 Cal.L.Rev.Comm. Reports App. 5 (1997)].

§ 1150. Evidence to test a verdict

(a) Upon an inquiry as to the validity of a verdict, any otherwise admissible evidence may be received as to statements made, or conduct, conditions, or events occurring, either within or without the jury room, of such a character as is likely to have influenced the verdict improperly. No evidence is admissible to show the effect of such statement, conduct, condition, or event upon a juror either in influencing him to assent to or dissent from the verdict or concerning the mental processes by which it was determined.

(b) Nothing in this code affects the law relating to the competence of a juror to give evidence to impeach or support a verdict. *(Stats.1965, c. 299, § 2, operative Jan. 1, 1967.)*

Research References

Rutter, Cal. Practice Guide: Civ. Pro. Before Trial Ch. 8C-3, "Not Privileged".

Rutter, Cal. Practice Guide: Civil Trials & Evidence Ch. 5-I, I. Challenging Prospective Jurors.

Rutter, Cal. Practice Guide: Civil Trials & Evidence Ch. 7-F, F. Juror Misconduct During Trial.

Rutter, Cal. Practice Guide: Civil Trials & Evidence Ch. 15-D, D. Juror Requests for Additional Information During Deliberations.

Rutter, Cal. Practice Guide: Civil Trials & Evidence Ch. 15-F, F. Juror Misconduct During Deliberations.

Rutter, Cal. Practice Guide: Civil Trials & Evidence Ch. 18-B, B. Motion for New Trial.

Rutter, Cal. Practice Guide: Civil Trials & Evidence Ch. 15-F, Outline F.

Rutter, Cal. Practice Guide: Personal Injury Ch. 10-A, A. Motion for New Trial.

7 Witkin Cal. Proc. 5th Trial § 334, Inattentiveness at Trial.

7 Witkin Cal. Proc. 5th Trial § 383, Evidence of Overt Acts is Admissible.

7 Witkin Cal. Proc. 5th Trial § 384, Evidence of Jurors' Intentions is Not Admissible.

7 Witkin Cal. Proc. 5th Trial § 385, Distinction: Questioning Jurors Prior to Verdict.

§ 1151. Subsequent remedial conduct

When, after the occurrence of an event, remedial or precautionary measures are taken, which, if taken previously, would have tended to make the event less likely to occur, evidence of such subsequent measures is inadmissible to prove negligence or culpable conduct in connection with the event. *(Stats.1965, c. 299, § 2, operative Jan. 1, 1967.)*

Law Revision Commission Comments

Section 1151 codifies well-settled law. Helling v. Schindler, 145 Cal. 303, 78 Pac. 710 (1904); Sappenfield v. Main Street etc. R.R., 91 Cal. 48, 27 Pac. 590 (1891). The admission of evidence of subsequent repairs to prove negligence would substantially discourage persons from making repairs after the occurrence of an accident.

Section 1151 does not prevent the use of evidence of subsequent remedial conduct for the purpose of impeachment in appropriate cases. This is in accord with Pierce v. J. C. Penney Co., 167 Cal.App.2d 3, 334 P.2d 117 (1959). [7 Cal.L.Rev.Comm. Reports 1 (1965)].

Research References

Rutter, Cal. Practice Guide: Civ. Pro. Before Trial Ch. 8C-3, "Not Privileged".

Rutter, Cal. Practice Guide: Civ. Pro. Before Trial Ch. 8C-3, Outline 3.

Rutter, Cal. Practice Guide: Civil Trials & Evidence Ch. 4-F, F. Motions in Limine.

Rutter, Cal. Practice Guide: Civil Trials & Evidence Ch. 6-C, C. Improper Conduct During Opening Statement.

Rutter, Cal. Practice Guide: Civil Trials & Evidence Ch. 9-C, C. Direct Examination of Adverse Witness (EV.C. § 776).

Rutter, Cal. Practice Guide: Civil Trials & Evidence Ch. 10-B, B. Scope of Permissible Cross-Examination.

Rutter, Cal. Practice Guide: Civil Trials & Evidence Ch. 8E-D, D. Other Public Policy Exclusions.

Rutter, Cal. Practice Guide: Civil Trials & Evidence Ch. 8G-A, A. Objections and Motions Challenging Admissibility.

Rutter, Cal. Practice Guide: Civil Trials & Evidence Ch. 8E-D, Outline D.

Rutter, Cal. Practice Guide: Personal Injury Ch. 2(I)-C, C. Special Considerations Re Product Liability Investigations.

6 Witkin, California Summary 10th Torts § 1449, (S 1449) in General.

6 Witkin, California Summary 10th Torts § 1513, (S 1513) Physical Injury or Wrongful Death.

§ 1152. Offers to compromise

(a) Evidence that a person has, in compromise or from humanitarian motives, furnished or offered or promised to furnish money or any other thing, act, or service to another who has sustained or will sustain or claims that he or she has sustained or will sustain loss or damage, as well as any conduct or statements made in negotiation thereof, is inadmissible to prove his or her liability for the loss or damage or any part of it.

(b) In the event that evidence of an offer to compromise is admitted in an action for breach of the covenant of good faith and fair dealing or violation of subdivision (h) of Section 790.03 of the Insurance Code, then at the request of the party against whom the evidence is admitted, or at the request of the party who made the offer to compromise that was admitted, evidence relating to any other offer or counteroffer to compromise the same or substantially the same claimed loss or damage shall also be admissible for the same purpose as the initial evidence regarding settlement. Other than as may be admitted in an action for breach of the covenant of good faith and fair dealing or violation of subdivision (h) of Section 790.03 of the Insurance Code, evidence of settlement offers shall not be admitted in a motion for a new trial, in any proceeding involving an additur or remittitur, or on appeal.

(c) This section does not affect the admissibility of evidence of any of the following:

(1) Partial satisfaction of an asserted claim or demand without questioning its validity when such evidence is offered to prove the validity of the claim.

(2) A debtor's payment or promise to pay all or a part of his or her preexisting debt when such evidence is offered to prove the creation of a new duty on his or her part or a revival of his or her preexisting duty. *(Stats.1965, c. 299, § 2, operative Jan. 1, 1967. Amended by Stats.1967, c. 650, p. 2007, § 7; Stats.1987, c. 496, § 1.)*

Law Revision Commission Comments

Section 1152, like Section 2078 of the Code of Civil Procedure which it supersedes, declares that compromise offers are inadmissible to prove liability. Because of the particular wording of Section 2078, an offer of compromise probably may not be considered as an admission even though admitted without objection. See Tentative Recommendation and a Study Relating to the Uniform Rules of Evidence (Article VI. Extrinsic Policies Affecting Admissibility), 6 Cal.Law Revision Comm'n, Rep., Rec. & Studies 601, 675–676 (1964). See also Scott v. Wood, 81 Cal. 398, 405–406, 22 Pac. 871, 873 (1889). Under Section 1152, however, nothing prohibits the consideration of an offer of settlement on the issue of liability if the evidence is received without objection. This modest change in the law is desirable. An offer of compromise, like other incompetent evidence, should be considered to the extent that it is relevant when it is presented to the trier of fact without objection.

The words "as well as any conduct or statements made in negotiation thereof" make it clear that statements made by parties during negotiations for the settlement of a claim may not be used as admissions in later litigation. This language will change the existing law under which certain statements made during settlement negotiations may be used as admissions. People v. Forster, 58 Cal.2d 257, 23 Cal.Rptr. 582, 373 P.2d 630 (1962). The rule excluding offers is based upon the public policy in favor of the settlement of disputes without litigation. The same public policy requires that admissions made during settlement negotiations also be excluded. The rule of the Forster case that permits such statements to be admitted places a premium on the form of the statement. The statement "Assuming, for the purposes of these negotiations, that I was negligent . . . ." is inadmissible; but the statement "All right, I was negligent! Let's talk about damages . . . ." may be admissible. See the discussion in People v. Glen Arms Estate, Inc., 230 Cal.App.2d 841, 863, 864, 41 Cal.Rptr. 303, 316 (1964). The rule of the Forster case is changed by Section 1152 because that rule prevents the complete candor between the parties that is most conducive to settlement. [7 Cal.L.Rev.Comm. Reports 1 (1965)].

The amendment to Section 1152 is intended to clarify the meaning of the section without changing its substantive effect. The words "or will sustain" have been added to make it clear that the section applies to statements made in the course of negotiations concerning future loss or damage as well as past loss or damage. Such negotiations might occur as a result of an alleged anticipatory breach of contract or as an incident of an eminent domain proceeding. [8 Cal.L.Rev.Comm. Reports 101 (1967)].

Research References

Rutter, Cal. Practice Guide: A.D.R. Ch. 2-E, E. Conducting Negotiations.
Rutter, Cal. Practice Guide: A.D.R. Ch. 3-C, C. Confidentiality.
Rutter, Cal. Practice Guide: A.D.R. Ch. 4-C, C. Statutorily-Mandated Court Mediation Programs.
Rutter, Cal. Practice Guide: A.D.R. Ch. 4-D, D. Mandatory Settlement Conferences.
Rutter, Cal. Practice Guide: A.D.R. Ch. 3B-C, C. Statutorily-Mandated ADR.
Rutter, Cal. Practice Guide: A.D.R. App. D Form 2, Negotiation Clause (Two-Step Process: Correspondence Followed by Meeting).
Rutter, Cal. Practice Guide: Civil Appeals & Writs Ch. 8-C, C. Standards of Appellate Review.
Rutter, Cal. Practice Guide: Civ. Pro. Before Trial Ch. 13-A, A. Introduction.
Rutter, Cal. Practice Guide: Civ. Pro. Before Trial Ch. 8C-2, "Reasonably Calculated to Lead to Discovery of Admissible Evidence".
Rutter, Cal. Practice Guide: Civ. Pro. Before Trial Ch. 8C-3, "Not Privileged".
Rutter, Cal. Practice Guide: Civ. Pro. Before Trial Ch. 12(II)-A, A. Mandatory Settlement Conference ("Msc").
Rutter, Cal. Practice Guide: Civ. Pro. Before Trial Ch. 12(II)-C, C. Statutory Offer to Compromise (CCP § 998).
Rutter, Cal. Practice Guide: Civ. Pro. Before Trial Ch. 12(II)-H, H. Professional Responsibility Considerations Re Settlements.
Rutter, Cal. Practice Guide: Civil Trials & Evidence Ch. 4-F, F. Motions in Limine.
Rutter, Cal. Practice Guide: Civil Trials & Evidence Ch. 5-H, H. Challenging Improper Questions.
Rutter, Cal. Practice Guide: Civil Trials & Evidence Ch. 6-C, C. Improper Conduct During Opening Statement.
Rutter, Cal. Practice Guide: Civil Trials & Evidence Ch. 13-B, B. Proper vs. Improper Closing Argument.
Rutter, Cal. Practice Guide: Civil Trials & Evidence Ch. 8D-D, D. Hearsay Exceptions.
Rutter, Cal. Practice Guide: Civil Trials & Evidence Ch. 8E-D, D. Other Public Policy Exclusions.
California Practice Guide: Employment Litigation Ch. 18-B, B. Nonbinding ADR Procedures.
California Practice Guide: Employment Litigation Ch. 19-N, N. Evidence Issues.
California Practice Guide: Employment Litigation Ch. 19-N, Outline N.
Rutter, Cal. Practice Guide: Enforcing Judgments/Debts Ch. 6G-1, Examination of Judgment Debtor and Third Parties.
Rutter, Cal. Practice Guide: Insurance Litigation Ch. 15-I, I. Trial.
Rutter, Cal. Practice Guide: Insurance Litigation Ch. 12C-D, D. Application-Matters Held "Unreasonable".
Rutter, Cal. Practice Guide: Personal Injury Ch. 4-D, D. Techniques Where Settlement Not Forthcoming.

Rutter, Cal. Practice Guide: Personal Injury Ch. 4-F, F. Court-Conducted Settlement Proceedings.
Rutter, Cal. Practice Guide: Personal Injury Ch. 4-G, G. Concluding and Enforcing Settlement.
Rutter, Cal. Practice Guide: Personal Injury Ch. 6-A, A. Scope of Discovery and Limitations.
Rutter, Cal. Practice Guide: Personal Injury Ch. 7-A, A. Introduction-Nature and Purpose of "Judicial Arbitration" in General.
Miller and Starr California Real Estate § 35:22, Nature of Arbitration.
Miller and Starr California Real Estate § 7:188, Duty to Pay Claims; the Implied Covenant of Good Faith and Fair Dealing.
15 NO. 3 Miller & Starr, California Real Estate Newsalert 17, Remedies.
16 NO. 6 Miller & Starr, California Real Estate Newsalert 3, Adverse Possession.
9 Witkin Cal. Proc. 5th Administrative Proceedings § 63, in General.
8 Witkin Cal. Proc. 5th Enforcement of Judgment § 286, Testimony Concerning Settlement Negotiations.
7 Witkin Cal. Proc. 5th Judgment § 439, Judgment on Offer to Compromise.
6 Witkin Cal. Proc. 5th Proceedings Without Trial § 99, (S 99) Judgment on Compromise.
6 Witkin Cal. Proc. 5th Proceedings Without Trial § 491, Procedure.
2 Witkin, California Summary 10th Insurance § 246, (S 246) Conduct of Litigation.

§ 1153.   Offer to plead guilty or withdrawn plea of guilty by criminal defendant

Evidence of a plea of guilty, later withdrawn, or of an offer to plead guilty to the crime charged or to any other crime, made by the defendant in a criminal action is inadmissible in any action or in any proceeding of any nature, including proceedings before agencies, commissions, boards, and tribunals. *(Stats.1965, c. 299, § 2, operative Jan. 1, 1967.)*

Law Revision Commission Comments

Section 1153 is consistent with existing law. Under existing law, evidence of a rejected *offer* to plead guilty to the crime charged or to a lesser crime is inadmissible. Penal Code § 1192.4; People v. Wilson, 60 Cal.2d 139, 155–156, 32 Cal.Rptr. 44, 54–55, 383 P.2d 452, 462–463 (1963); People v. Hamilton, 60 Cal.2d 105, 113–114, 32 Cal.Rptr. 4, 8–9, 383 P.2d 412, 146–417 (1963). Likewise, a plea of guilty, later withdrawn, is inadmissible. People v. Quinn, 61 Cal.2d 551, 39 Cal.Rptr. 393, 393 P.2d 705 (1964). [7 Cal.L.Rev.Comm. Reports 1 (1965)].

Research References

Rutter, Cal. Practice Guide: Civil Trials & Evidence Ch. 8D-D, D. Hearsay Exceptions.
Rutter, Cal. Practice Guide: Civil Trials & Evidence Ch. 8E-D, D. Other Public Policy Exclusions.

§ 1153.5.   Offer for civil resolution of crimes against property

Evidence of an offer for civil resolution of a criminal matter pursuant to the provisions of Section 33 of the Code of Civil Procedure, or admissions made in the course of or negotiations for the offer shall not be admissible in any action. *(Added by Stats.1982, c. 1518, p. 5890, § 2.)*

Research References

Rutter, Cal. Practice Guide: Civil Trials & Evidence Ch. 8E-D, D. Other Public Policy Exclusions.

§ 1154.   Offer to discount a claim

Evidence that a person has accepted or offered or promised to accept a sum of money or any other thing, act, or service in satisfaction of a claim, as well as any conduct or statements made in negotiation thereof, is inadmissible to prove the invalidity of the claim or any part of it. *(Stats.1965, c. 299, § 2, operative Jan. 1, 1967.)*

Law Revision Commission Comments

Section 1154 stems from the same policy of encouraging settlement and compromise that is reflected in Section 1152. Except for the language "as well as any conduct or statements made in negotiation thereof," this section codifies existing law. Dennis v. Belt, 30 Cal. 247 (1866); Anderson v. Yousem, 177 Cal.App.2d 135, 1 Cal.Rptr. 889 (1960); Cramer v. Lee Wa Corp., 109 Cal.App.2d 691, 241 P.2d 550 (1952). The significance of the quoted language is indicated in the Comment to Section 1152. [7 Cal.L.Rev.Comm. Reports 1 (1965)].

Research References

Rutter, Cal. Practice Guide: Civil Appeals & Writs Ch. 8-C, C. Standards of Appellate Review.
Rutter, Cal. Practice Guide: Civil Trials & Evidence Ch. 8E-D, D. Other Public Policy Exclusions.
Rutter, Cal. Practice Guide: Enforcing Judgments/Debts Ch. 6G-1, Examination of Judgment Debtor and Third Parties.
Rutter, Cal. Practice Guide: Insurance Litigation Ch. 15-I, I. Trial.
Rutter, Cal. Practice Guide: Personal Injury Ch. 4-F, F. Court-Conducted Settlement Proceedings.
Rutter, Cal. Practice Guide: Personal Injury Ch. 4-G, G. Concluding and Enforcing Settlement.
Rutter, Cal. Practice Guide: Personal Injury Ch. 6-A, A. Scope of Discovery and Limitations.
8 Witkin Cal. Proc. 5th Enforcement of Judgment § 286, Testimony Concerning Settlement Negotiations.

§ 1155. Liability insurance

Evidence that a person was, at the time a harm was suffered by another, insured wholly or partially against loss arising from liability for that harm is inadmissible to prove negligence or other wrongdoing. *(Stats.1965, c. 299, § 2, operative Jan. 1, 1967.)*

Law Revision Commission Comments

Section 1155 codifies existing law. Roche v. Llewellyn Iron Works Co., 140 Cal. 563, 74 Pac. 147 (1903). Evidence of liability insurance might be inadmissible in the absence of Section 1155 because it is not relevant; Section 1155 assures its inadmissibility. [7 Cal.L.Rev.Comm. Reports 1 (1965)].

Research References

Rutter, Cal. Practice Guide: Civil Trials & Evidence Ch. 4-F, F. Motions in Limine.
Rutter, Cal. Practice Guide: Civil Trials & Evidence Ch. 5-G, G. Scope of Permissible Voir Dire-Proper vs. Improper Questions.
Rutter, Cal. Practice Guide: Civil Trials & Evidence Ch. 6-C, C. Improper Conduct During Opening Statement.
Rutter, Cal. Practice Guide: Civil Trials & Evidence Ch. 13-B, B. Proper vs. Improper Closing Argument.
Rutter, Cal. Practice Guide: Civil Trials & Evidence Ch. 8D-D, D. Hearsay Exceptions.
Rutter, Cal. Practice Guide: Civil Trials & Evidence Ch. 8E-D, D. Other Public Policy Exclusions.
Rutter, Cal. Practice Guide: Personal Injury Ch. 9-J, J. Final Arguments Upon Close of Evidence.
4 Witkin Cal. Proc. 5th Pleading § 377, (S 377) California Statute.
7 Witkin Cal. Proc. 5th Trial § 217, General Rule: Reference is Improper.
2 Witkin, California Summary 10th Insurance § 300, (S 300) Assignment of Cause of Action Against Insurer.

§ 1156. Records of medical or dental study of in–hospital staff committee

(a) In-hospital medical or medical-dental staff committees of a licensed hospital may engage in research and medical or dental study for the purpose of reducing morbidity or mortality, and may make findings and recommendations relating to such purpose. Except as provided in subdivision (b), the written records of interviews, reports, statements, or memoranda of such in-hospital medical or medical-dental staff committees relating to such medical or dental studies are subject to Title 4 (commencing with Section 2016.010) of Part 4 of the Code of Civil Procedure (relating to discovery proceedings) but, subject to subdivisions (c) and (d), shall not be admitted as evidence in any action or before any administrative body, agency, or person.

(b) The disclosure, with or without the consent of the patient, of information concerning him to such in-hospital medical or medical-dental staff committee does not make unprivileged any information that would otherwise be privileged under Section 994 or 1014; but, notwithstanding Sections 994 and 1014, such information is subject to discovery under subdivision (a) except that the identity of any patient may not be discovered under subdivision (a) unless the patient consents to such disclosure.

(c) This section does not affect the admissibility in evidence of the original medical or dental records of any patient.

(d) This section does not exclude evidence which is relevant evidence in a criminal action. *(Stats.1965, c. 299, § 2, operative Jan. 1, 1967. Amended by Stats.1975, c. 674, p. 1468, § 1; Stats.2004, c. 182 (A.B.3081), § 30, operative July 1, 2005.)*

Law Revision Commission Comments

Section 1156 supersedes Code of Civil Procedure Section 1936.1 (added by Cal.Stats.1963, Ch. 1558, § 1, p. 3142). Except as noted below, Section 1156 restates the substance of the superseded section.

The phrase "Sections 2016 to 2036, inclusive," has been inserted in Section 1156 in place of the phrase "Sections 2016 and 2036," which appears in Section 1936.1, to correct an apparent inadvertence. This substitution permits use of all kinds of discovery procedures, instead of depositions only, to discover material of the type described in Section 1156. *E.g.,* Code Civ.Proc. §§ 2030 (written interrogatories), 2031 (motion for order for production of documents.)

Section 1156 also makes it clear that the *names* of patients may not be disclosed without the consent of the patient. This limitation is necessary to preserve the physician-patient and psychotherapist-patient privileges.

Subdivision (a) of Section 1156 is amended to reflect nonsubstantive reorganization of the rules governing civil discovery. [33 Cal.L.Rev. Comm. Reports 1016 (2004)].

§ 1156.1. Records of medical or psychiatric studies of quality assurance committees

(a) A committee established in compliance with Sections 4070 and 5624 of the Welfare and Institutions Code may engage in research and medical or psychiatric study for the purpose of reducing morbidity or mortality, and may make findings and recommendations to the county and state relating to such purpose. Except as provided in subdivision (b), the written records of interviews, reports, statements, or memoranda of such committees relating to such medical or psychiatric studies are subject to Title 4 (commencing with Section 2016.010) of Part 4 of the Code of Civil Procedure but, subject to subdivisions (c) and (d), shall not be admitted as evidence in any action or before any administrative body, agency, or person.

(b) The disclosure, with or without the consent of the patient, of information concerning him or her to such committee does not make unprivileged any information that would otherwise be privileged under Section 994 or 1014. However, notwithstanding Sections 994 and 1014, such information is subject to discovery under subdivision (a) except that the identity of any patient may not be discovered under subdivision (a) unless the patient consents to such disclosure.

(c) This section does not affect the admissibility in evidence of the original medical or psychiatric records of any patient.

(d) This section does not exclude evidence which is relevant evidence in a criminal action. *(Added by Stats.1982, c. 234, p. 767, § 4, eff. June 2, 1982. Amended by Stats.2004, c. 182 (A.B.3081), § 31, operative July 1, 2005.)*

Law Revision Commission Comments

Subdivision (a) of Section 1156.1 is amended to reflect nonsubstantive reorganization of the rules governing civil discovery. [33 Cal.L.Rev. Comm. Reports 1017 (2004)].

§ 1157. Proceedings and records of organized committees having responsibility of evaluation and improvement of quality of care; exceptions

(a) Neither the proceedings nor the records of organized committees of medical, medical-dental, podiatric, registered dietitian, psychological, marriage and family therapist, licensed clinical social worker, professional clinical counselor, or veterinary staffs in hospitals, or of a peer review body, as defined in Section 805 of the Business and Professions Code, having the responsibility of evaluation and improvement of the quality of care rendered in the hospital, or for that peer review body, or medical or dental review or dental hygienist review or chiropractic review or podiatric review or registered dietitian review or veterinary review or acupuncturist review committees of local medical, dental, dental hygienist, podiatric, dietetic, veterinary, acupuncture, or chiropractic societies, marriage and family therapist, licensed clinical social worker, professional clinical counselor, or psychological review committees of state or local marriage and family therapist, state or local licensed clinical social worker, state or local licensed professional clinical counselor, or state or local psychological associations or societies having the responsibility of evaluation and improvement of the quality of care, shall be subject to discovery.

(b) Except as hereinafter provided, no person in attendance at a meeting of any of those committees shall be required to testify as to what transpired at that meeting.

(c) The prohibition relating to discovery or testimony does not apply to the statements made by any person in attendance at a meeting of any of those committees who is a party to an action or proceeding the subject matter of which was reviewed at that meeting, or to any person requesting hospital staff privileges, or in any action against an insurance carrier alleging bad faith by the carrier in refusing to accept a settlement offer within the policy limits.

(d) The prohibitions in this section do not apply to medical, dental, dental hygienist, podiatric, dietetic, psychological, marriage and family therapist, licensed clinical social worker, professional clinical counselor, veterinary, acupuncture, or chiropractic society committees that exceed 10 percent of the membership of the society, nor to any of those committees if any person serves upon the committee when his or her own conduct or practice is being reviewed.

(e) The amendments made to this section by Chapter 1081 of the Statutes of 1983, or at the 1985 portion of the 1985–86 Regular Session of the Legislature, at the 1990 portion of the 1989–90 Regular Session of the Legislature, at the 2000 portion of the 1999–2000 Regular Session of the Legislature, or at the 2011 portion of the 2011–12 Regular Session of the Legislature, do not exclude the discovery or use of relevant evidence in a criminal action. *(Added by Stats.1968, c. 1122, p. 2138, § 1. Amended by Stats.1975, c. 674, p. 1468, § 2; Stats.1978, c. 7, p. 62, § 1, eff. Feb. 10, 1978; Stats.1978, c. 503, p. 1648, § 2; Stats.1982, c. 705, p. 2864, § 3; Stats.1983, c. 289, § 3; Stats. 1983, c. 422, § 1; Stats.1983, c. 1081, § 2.5; Stats.1985, c. 725, § 1; Stats.1990, c. 196 (A.B.1565), § 2; Stats.1994, c. 815 (S.B.1279), § 3; Stats.2000, c. 136 (A.B.2374), § 1; Stats.2011, c. 381 (S.B.146), § 23.)*

Research References

Rutter, Cal. Practice Guide: Civ. Pro. Before Trial Ch. 8C-3, "Not Privileged".
Rutter, Cal. Practice Guide: Civil Trials & Evidence Ch. 8C-H, H. Opinion Evidence.
Rutter, Cal. Practice Guide: Civil Trials & Evidence Ch. 8E-D, D. Other Public Policy Exclusions.
Rutter, Cal. Practice Guide: Fed.Civ.Pro. Before Trial Ch. 11(III)-B, B. Scope of Discovery.
Rutter, Cal. Practice Guide: Personal Injury Ch. 6-A, A. Scope of Discovery and Limitations.
Rutter, Cal. Practice Guide: Personal Injury Ch. 2(II)-A, A. Vicarious Liability.
9 Witkin Cal. Proc. 5th Administrative Proceedings § 103, Subpenas in Aid of Investigation.
11 Witkin, California Summary 10th Husband and Wife § 16, (S 16) Licensing of Marriage and Family Therapists.
6 Witkin, California Summary 10th Torts § 1064, (S 1064) Distinction: Medical Proctor.

§ 1157.5. Organized committee of nonprofit medical care foundation or professional standards review organization; proceedings and records

Except in actions involving a claim of a provider of health care services for payment for such services, the prohibition relating to discovery or testimony provided by Section 1157 shall be applicable to the proceedings or records of an organized committee of any nonprofit medical care foundation or professional standards review organization which is organized in a manner which makes available professional competence to review health care services with respect to medical necessity, quality of care, or economic justification of charges or level of care. *(Added by Stats.1973, c. 848, p. 1515, § 1. Amended by Stats.1980, c. 524, p. 1461, § 1.)*

Research References

Rutter, Cal. Practice Guide: Civ. Pro. Before Trial Ch. 8C-3, "Not Privileged".

§ 1157.6. Proceedings and records of quality assurance committees for county health facilities

Neither the proceedings nor the records of a committee established in compliance with Sections 4070 and 5624 of the Welfare and Institutions Code having the responsibility of evaluation and improvement of the quality of mental health care rendered in county operated and contracted mental health facilities shall be subject to discovery. Except as provided in this section, no person in attendance at a meeting of any such committee shall be required to testify as to what transpired thereat. The prohibition relating to discovery or testimony shall not apply to the statements made by any person in attendance at such a meeting who is a party to an action or proceeding the subject matter of which was reviewed at such meeting, or to any person requesting facility staff privileges. *(Added by Stats.1982, c. 234, p. 767, § 5, eff. June 2, 1982.)*

Research References

Rutter, Cal. Practice Guide: Civ. Pro. Before Trial Ch. 8C-3, "Not Privileged".
Rutter, Cal. Practice Guide: Personal Injury Ch. 6-A, A. Scope of Discovery and Limitations.

§ 1157.7. Application of Section 1157 discovery or testimony prohibitions; application of public records and meetings provisions

The prohibition relating to discovery or testimony provided in Section 1157 shall be applicable to proceedings and records of any committee established by a local governmental agency to monitor, evaluate, and report on the necessity, quality, and level of specialty health services, including, but not limited to, trauma care services, provided by a general acute care hospital which has been designated or recognized by that governmental agency as qualified to render specialty health care services. The provisions of Chapter 3.5 (commencing with Section 6250) of Division 7 of Title 1 of the Government Code and Chapter 9 (commencing with Section 54950) of Division 2 of Title 5 of the Government Code shall not be applicable to the committee records and proceedings. *(Added by Stats.1983, c. 1237, § 1.)*

Evidence

Research References

Rutter, Cal. Practice Guide: Civ. Pro. Before Trial Ch. 8C-3, "Not Privileged".

§ 1158. Inspection and copying of patient's records; authorization; failure to comply; costs

Whenever, prior to the filing of any action or the appearance of a defendant in an action, an attorney at law or his or her representative presents a written authorization therefor signed by an adult patient, by the guardian or conservator of his or her person or estate, or, in the case of a minor, by a parent or guardian of the minor, or by the personal representative or an heir of a deceased patient, or a copy thereof, a physician and surgeon, dentist, registered nurse, dispensing optician, registered physical therapist, podiatrist, licensed psychologist, osteopathic physician and surgeon, chiropractor, clinical laboratory bioanalyst, clinical laboratory technologist, or pharmacist or pharmacy, duly licensed as such under the laws of the state, or a licensed hospital, shall make all of the patient's records under his, hers or its custody or control available for inspection and copying by the attorney at law or his, or her, representative, promptly upon the presentation of the written authorization.

No copying may be performed by any medical provider or employer enumerated above, or by an agent thereof, when the requesting attorney has employed a professional photocopier or anyone identified in Section 22451 of the Business and Professions Code as his or her representative to obtain or review the records on his or her behalf. The presentation of the authorization by the agent on behalf of the attorney shall be sufficient proof that the agent is the attorney's representative.

Failure to make the records available, during business hours, within five days after the presentation of the written authorization, may subject the person or entity having custody or control of the records to liability for all reasonable expenses, including attorney's fees, incurred in any proceeding to enforce this section.

All reasonable costs incurred by any person or entity enumerated above in making patient records available pursuant to this section may be charged against the person whose written authorization required the availability of the records.

"Reasonable cost," as used in this section, shall include, but not be limited to, the following specific costs: ten cents ($0.10) per page for standard reproduction of documents of a size 8½ by 14 inches or less; twenty cents ($0.20) per page for copying of documents from microfilm; actual costs for the reproduction of oversize documents or the reproduction of documents requiring special processing which are made in response to an authorization; reasonable clerical costs incurred in locating and making the records available to be billed at the maximum rate of sixteen dollars ($16) per hour per person, computed on the basis of four dollars ($4) per quarter hour or fraction thereof; actual postage charges; and actual costs, if any, charged to the witness by a third person for the retrieval and return of records held by that third person.

Where the records are delivered to the attorney or the attorney's representative for inspection or photocopying at the record custodian's place of business, the only fee for complying with the authorization shall not exceed fifteen dollars ($15), plus actual costs, if any, charged to the record custodian by a third person for retrieval and return of records held offsite by the third person. *(Added by Stats.1968, c. 1122, p. 2138, § 2. Amended by Stats.1970, c. 556, p. 1077, § 1; Stats.1974, c. 250, p. 461, § 1; Stats.1974, c. 667, p. 1530, § 1; Stats.1975, c. 563, p. 1144, § 1; Stats.1978, c. 493, p. 1625, § 1; Stats.1980, c. 697, p. 2099, § 1; Stats.1986, c. 603, § 5; Stats.1987, c. 19, § 1, eff. May 12, 1987; Stats.1993, c. 226 (A.B.1987), § 9; Stats.1997, c. 442 (A.B.758), § 15.)*

Research References

Rutter, Cal. Practice Guide: Civ. Pro. Before Trial Ch. 1-B, B. Prelawsuit Investigations, Research and Analysis.
Rutter, Cal. Practice Guide: Civ. Pro. Before Trial Ch. 1-C, C. Prelawsuit Notices, Claims and Demands.
Rutter, Cal. Practice Guide: Civ. Pro. Before Trial Ch. 8K-6, Special Statutes and Court Rules.
Rutter, Cal. Practice Guide: Personal Injury Ch. 1-D, D. General Concerns and Advice to Client Upon Accepting Employment; Execution of Necessary Authorizations.
3 Witkin, California Summary 10th Agency and Employment § 553, in General.

§ 1159. Animal experimentation in product liability actions

(a) No evidence pertaining to live animal experimentation, including, but not limited to, injury, impact, or crash experimentation, shall be admissible in any product liability action involving a motor vehicle or vehicles.

(b) This section shall apply to cases for which a trial has not actually commenced, as described in paragraph (6) of subdivision (a) of Section 581 of the Code of Civil Procedure, on January 1, 1993. *(Added by Stats.1992, c. 188 (A.B.3691), § 1.)*

Research References

Rutter, Cal. Practice Guide: Civ. Pro. Before Trial Ch. 8C-3, "Not Privileged".
Rutter, Cal. Practice Guide: Personal Injury Ch. 9-I, I. Use of Writings, Exhibits and Demonstrative Evidence.
6 Witkin, California Summary 10th Torts § 1443, (S 1443) Motor Vehicle Equipment.

§ 1160. Admissibility of expressions of sympathy or benevolence; definitions

(a) The portion of statements, writings, or benevolent gestures expressing sympathy or a general sense of benevolence relating to the pain, suffering, or death of a person involved in an accident and made to that person or to the family of that person shall be inadmissible as evidence of an admission of liability in a civil action. A statement of fault, however, which is part of, or in addition to, any of the above shall not be inadmissible pursuant to this section.

(b) For purposes of this section:

(1) "Accident" means an occurrence resulting in injury or death to one or more persons which is not the result of willful action by a party.

(2) "Benevolent gestures" means actions which convey a sense of compassion or commiseration emanating from humane impulses.

(3) "Family" means the spouse, parent, grandparent, stepmother, stepfather, child, grandchild, brother, sister, half brother, half sister, adopted children of parent, or spouse's parents of an injured party. *(Added by Stats.2000, c. 195 (A.B.2804), § 1.)*

Research References

Rutter, Cal. Practice Guide: Civil Trials & Evidence Ch. 8E-D, D. Other Public Policy Exclusions.

§ 1161. Human trafficking; admissibility of evidence of engagement in commercial sexual act by victim or sexual history of victim

(a) Evidence that a victim of human trafficking, as defined in Section 236.1 of the Penal Code, has engaged in any commercial sexual act as a result of being a victim of human trafficking is inadmissible to prove the victim's criminal liability for * * * the commercial sexual act.

(b) Evidence of sexual history or history of any commercial sexual act of a victim of human trafficking, as defined in Section 236.1 of the Penal Code, is inadmissible to attack the credibility or impeach the character of the victim in any civil or criminal proceeding. *(Added by Initiative Measure (Prop. 35, § 4, approved Nov. 6, 2012, eff. Nov. 7, 2012). Amended by Stats.2013, c. 126 (A.B.694), § 1.)*

Division 10

HEARSAY EVIDENCE

Law Revision Commission Comments

Division 10 contains the hearsay rule and the most commonly used exceptions to the rule. Other exceptions may be found in other statutes scattered throughout the codes. Under the Evidence Code, the hearsay objection is met if the evidence offered falls within any of the exceptions to the hearsay rule. But the fact that the hearsay objection is overcome does not necessarily make the evidence admissible. All other exclusionary rules apply and may require exclusion of the evidence. [7 Cal.L.Rev. Comm. Reports 1 (1965)].

CHAPTER 1. GENERAL PROVISIONS

§ 1200. The hearsay rule

(a) "Hearsay evidence" is evidence of a statement that was made other than by a witness while testifying at the hearing and that is offered to prove the truth of the matter stated.

(b) Except as provided by law, hearsay evidence is inadmissible.

(c) This section shall be known and may be cited as the hearsay rule. *(Stats.1965, c. 299, § 2, operative Jan. 1, 1967.)*

Research References

Rutter, Cal. Practice Guide: Civil Trials & Evidence Ch. 4-B, B. Preliminary Matters Discussed in Final Status Conference or In-Chambers Conference.
Rutter, Cal. Practice Guide: Civil Trials & Evidence Ch. 8D-A, A. the "Hearsay Rule"-An Overview.
Rutter, Cal. Practice Guide: Civil Trials & Evidence Ch. 8D-B, B. Hearsay vs. Nonhearsay.
Rutter, Cal. Practice Guide: Civil Trials & Evidence Ch. 8D-C, C. General Parameters Re Admissibility of Hearsay Evidence.
Rutter, Cal. Practice Guide: Civil Trials & Evidence Ch. 8D-D, D. Hearsay Exceptions.
Rutter, Cal. Practice Guide: Family Law Ch. 3-D, D. Family Rules and Mandatory Forms of Pleading-In General.
Rutter, Cal. Practice Guide: Family Law Ch. 13-B, B. Contested Family Law Trial.
Rutter, Cal. Practice Guide: Family Law Ch. 18-B, B. Enforcement Remedies and Procedures.
Rutter, Cal. Practice Guide: Personal Injury Ch. 9-N, N. Special Trial Rules in Limited Civil Cases (CCP § 90 et seq.).
Rutter, Cal. Practice Guide: Personal Injury Ch. 10-A, A. Motion for New Trial.
6 Witkin Cal. Proc. 5th Proceedings Without Trial § 231, (S 231) Documentary Evidence.

10 Witkin, California Summary 10th Parent and Child § 276, (S 276) Report.

§ 1201. Multiple hearsay

A statement within the scope of an exception to the hearsay rule is not inadmissible on the ground that the evidence of such statement is hearsay evidence if such hearsay evidence consists of one or more statements each of which meets the requirements of an exception to the hearsay rule. *(Stats.1965, c. 299, § 2, operative Jan. 1, 1967. Amended by Stats.1967, c. 650, p. 2007, § 8.)*

Law Revision Commission Comments

Section 1201 makes it possible to use admissible hearsay to prove another statement that is also admissible hearsay. For example, under Section 1201, an official reporter's transcript of the testimony at a previous trial may be used to prove the testimony previously given (Evidence Code § 1280); the former testimony may be used as evidence (Evidence Code § 1291) to prove that a party made a statement; and the party's statement is admissible against him as an admission (Evidence Code § 1220). Thus, under Section 1201, the evidence of the admission contained in the transcript is admissible because each of the hearsay statements involved is within an exception to the hearsay rule.

Although no California case has been found where the admissibility of "multiple hearsay" has been analyzed and discussed, the practice is apparently in accord with the rule stated in Section 1201. See, *e.g.,* People v. Collup, 27 Cal.2d 829, 167 P.2d 714 (1946) (transcript of former testimony used to prove admission). [7 Cal.L.Rev.Comm. Reports 1 (1965)].

This amendment is designed to clarify the meaning of Section 1201 without changing its substantive effect. [8 Cal.L.Rev.Comm. Reports 101 (1967)].

Research References

Rutter, Cal. Practice Guide: Civil Trials & Evidence Ch. 8D-B, B. Hearsay vs. Nonhearsay.
Rutter, Cal. Practice Guide: Civil Trials & Evidence Ch. 8D-C, C. General Parameters Re Admissibility of Hearsay Evidence.
Rutter, Cal. Practice Guide: Civil Trials & Evidence Ch. 8D-D, D. Hearsay Exceptions.

§ 1202. Credibility of hearsay declarant

Evidence of a statement or other conduct by a declarant that is inconsistent with a statement by such declarant received in evidence as hearsay evidence is not inadmissible for the purpose of attacking the credibility of the declarant though he is not given and has not had an opportunity to explain or to deny such inconsistent statement or other conduct. Any other evidence offered to attack or support the credibility of the declarant is admissible if it would have been admissible had the declarant been a witness at the hearing. For the purposes of this section, the deponent of a deposition taken in the action in which it is offered shall be deemed to be a hearsay declarant. *(Stats.1965, c. 299, § 2, operative Jan. 1, 1967.)*

Law Revision Commission Comments

Section 1202 deals with the impeachment of a declarant whose hearsay statement is in evidence as distinguished from the impeachment of a witness who has testified. It clarifies two points. *First,* evidence to impeach a hearsay declarant is not to be excluded on the ground that it is collateral. *Second,* the rule applying to the impeachment of a witness—that a witness may be impeached by an inconsistent statement only if he is provided with an opportunity to explain or deny it—does not apply to a hearsay declarant.

When hearsay evidence in the form of former testimony has been admitted, the California courts have permitted a party to impeach the hearsay declarant with evidence of an inconsistent statement made by the hearsay declarant *after* the former testimony was given, even though the declarant was never given an opportunity to explain or deny the inconsistency. People v. Collup, 27 Cal.2d 829, 167 P.2d 714 (1946). Apparently, however, former testimony may not be impeached by evidence of an inconsistent statement made *prior* to the former testimony unless the would-be impeacher either did not know of the inconsistent statement at the time the former testimony was given or unless he had provided the declarant with an opportunity to explain or deny the inconsistent statement. People v. Greenwell, 20 Cal.App.2d 266, 66 P.2d 674 (1937), as limited by People v. Collup, 27 Cal.2d 829, 167 P.2d 714 (1946). The courts permit dying declarations to be impeached by evidence of contradictory statements by the deceased despite the lack of any foundation, for only in very rare cases would it be possible to provide the declarant with an opportunity to explain or deny the inconsistency. People v. Lawrence, 21 Cal. 368 (1863).

Section 1202 substitutes for this case law a uniform rule permitting a hearsay declarant to be impeached by inconsistent statements in all cases, whether or not the declarant has been given an opportunity to explain or deny the inconsistency. If the hearsay declarant is unavailable as a witness, the party against whom the evidence is admitted should not be deprived of both his right to cross-examine and his right to impeach. *Cf.* People v. Lawrence, 21 Cal. 368, 372 (1863). If the hearsay declarant is available, the party electing to use the hearsay of such a declarant should have the burden of calling him to explain or deny any alleged inconsistencies.

Of course, the trial judge may curb efforts to impeach hearsay declarants if he determines that the inquiry is becoming too remote from the issues that are actually at stake in the litigation. Evidence Code § 352.

Section 1235 provides that evidence of inconsistent statements made by a trial witness may be admitted to prove the truth of the matter stated. No similar exception to the hearsay rule is applicable to a hearsay declarant's inconsistent statements that are admitted under Section 1202. Hence, the hearsay rule prohibits any such statement from being used to prove the truth of the matter stated. If the declarant is not a witness and is not subject to cross-examination upon the subject matter of his statements, there is no sufficient guarantee of the trustworthiness of the statements he has made out of court to warrant their reception as substantive evidence unless they fall within some recognized exception to the hearsay rule. [7 Cal.L.Rev.Comm. Reports 1 (1965)].

Research References

Rutter, Cal. Practice Guide: Civil Trials & Evidence Ch. 8D-B, B. Hearsay vs. Nonhearsay.

Rutter, Cal. Practice Guide: Civil Trials & Evidence Ch. 8D-C, C. General Parameters Re Admissibility of Hearsay Evidence.

Rutter, Cal. Practice Guide: Civil Trials & Evidence Ch. 8D-D, D. Hearsay Exceptions.

§ 1203. Cross-examination of hearsay declarant

(a) The declarant of a statement that is admitted as hearsay evidence may be called and examined by any adverse party as if under cross-examination concerning the statement.

(b) This section is not applicable if the declarant is (1) a party, (2) a person identified with a party within the meaning of subdivision (d) of Section 776, or (3) a witness who has testified in the action concerning the subject matter of the statement.

(c) This section is not applicable if the statement is one described in Article 1 (commencing with Section 1220), Article 3 (commencing with Section 1235), or Article 10 (commencing with Section 1300) of Chapter 2 of this division.

(d) A statement that is otherwise admissible as hearsay evidence is not made inadmissible by this section because the declarant who made the statement is unavailable for examination pursuant to this section. *(Stats.1965, c. 299, § 2, operative Jan. 1, 1967.)*

Research References

Rutter, Cal. Practice Guide: Civil Trials & Evidence Ch. 9-C, C. Direct Examination of Adverse Witness (EV.C. § 776).

Rutter, Cal. Practice Guide: Civil Trials & Evidence Ch. 8D-C, C. General Parameters Re Admissibility of Hearsay Evidence.

§ 1203.1. Hearsay offered at preliminary examination; application of § 1203

Section 1203 is not applicable if the hearsay statement is offered at a preliminary examination, as provided in Section 872 of the Penal Code. *(Added by Initiative Measure (Prop. 115), approved June 5, 1990, eff. June 6, 1990.)*

Research References

Rutter, Cal. Practice Guide: Civil Trials & Evidence Ch. 8D-C, C. General Parameters Re Admissibility of Hearsay Evidence.

§ 1204. Hearsay statement offered against criminal defendant

A statement that is otherwise admissible as hearsay evidence is inadmissible against the defendant in a criminal action if the statement was made, either by the defendant or by another, under such circumstances that it is inadmissible against the defendant under the Constitution of the United States or the State of California. *(Stats.1965, c. 299, § 2, operative Jan. 1, 1967.)*

§ 1205. No implied repeal

Nothing in this division shall be construed to repeal by implication any other statute relating to hearsay evidence. *(Stats.1965, c. 299, § 2, operative Jan. 1, 1967.)*

Law Revision Commission Comments

Although some of the statutes providing for the admission of hearsay evidence will be repealed when the Evidence Code is enacted, a number of statutes will remain in the various codes. For the most part, these statutes are narrowly drawn to make a particular type of hearsay evidence admissible under specifically limited circumstances. To assure the continued validity of these provisions, Section 1205 states that they will not be impliedly repealed by the enactment of the Evidence Code. [7 Cal.L.Rev.Comm. Reports 1 (1965)].

CHAPTER 2. EXCEPTIONS TO THE HEARSAY RULE

ARTICLE 1. CONFESSIONS AND ADMISSIONS

§ 1220. Admission of party

Evidence of a statement is not made inadmissible by the hearsay rule when offered against the declarant in an action to which he is a party in either his individual or representative capacity, regardless of whether the statement was made in his individual or representative capacity. *(Stats.1965, c. 299, § 2, operative Jan. 1, 1967.)*

Law Revision Commission Comments

Section 1220 states existing law as found in subdivision 2 of Section 1870 of the Code of Civil Procedure. The rationale underlying this exception is that the party cannot object to the lack of the right to cross-examine the declarant since the party himself made the statement. Moreover, the party can cross-examine the witness who testifies to the party's statement and can explain or deny the purported admission. The statement need not be one which would be admissible if made at the hearing. See Shields v. Oxnard Harbor Dist., 46 Cal.App.2d 477, 116 P.2d 121 (1941).

In a criminal action, a defendant's statement is not admissible under this section unless it was made voluntarily. Evidence Code § 1204. [7 Cal.L.Rev.Comm. Reports 1 (1965)].

Research References

Rutter, Cal. Practice Guide: Civ. Pro. Before Trial Ch. 8F-9, Use of Interrogatories at Trial.
Rutter, Cal. Practice Guide: Civil Trials & Evidence Ch. 4-B, B. Preliminary Matters Discussed in Final Status Conference or In-Chambers Conference.
Rutter, Cal. Practice Guide: Civil Trials & Evidence Ch. 8D-A, A. the "Hearsay Rule"-An Overview.
Rutter, Cal. Practice Guide: Civil Trials & Evidence Ch. 8D-D, D. Hearsay Exceptions.
California Practice Guide: Employment Litigation Ch. 19-N, N. Evidence Issues.
Rutter, Cal. Practice Guide: Family Law Ch. 4-E, E. Amended and Supplemental Pleadings.
Rutter, Cal. Practice Guide: Family Law Ch. 13-B, B. Contested Family Law Trial.
Rutter, Cal. Practice Guide: Family Law Ch. 19-A, A. Validity of Marriage.

6 Witkin Cal. Proc. 5th Proceedings Without Trial § 229, (S 229) Evidence Obtained by Discovery.

§ 1221. Adoptive admission

Evidence of a statement offered against a party is not made inadmissible by the hearsay rule if the statement is one of which the party, with knowledge of the content thereof, has by words or other conduct manifested his adoption or his belief in its truth. *(Stats.1965, c. 299, § 2, operative Jan. 1, 1967.)*

Law Revision Commission Comments

Section 1221 restates an exception found in subdivision 3 of Section 1870 of the Code of Civil Procedure. [7 Cal.L.Rev.Comm. Reports 1 (1965)].

Research References

Rutter, Cal. Practice Guide: Civil Trials & Evidence Ch. 8D-D, D. Hearsay Exceptions.
7 Witkin Cal. Proc. 5th Trial § 303, (S 303) Extrajudicial and Implied Admissions.

§ 1222. Authorized admission

Evidence of a statement offered against a party is not made inadmissible by the hearsay rule if:

(a) The statement was made by a person authorized by the party to make a statement or statements for him concerning the subject matter of the statement; and

(b) The evidence is offered either after admission of evidence sufficient to sustain a finding of such authority or, in the court's discretion as to the order of proof, subject to the admission of such evidence. *(Stats.1965, c. 299, § 2, operative Jan. 1, 1967.)*

Law Revision Commission Comments

Section 1222 provides a hearsay exception for authorized admissions. Under this exception, if a party authorized an agent to make statements on his behalf, such statements may be introduced against the party under the same conditions as if they had been made by the party himself. The authority of the declarant to make the statement need not be express; it may be implied. It is to be determined in each case under the substantive law of agency. Section 1222 restates an exception found in the first portion of subdivision 5 of Section 1870 of the Code of Civil Procedure. See Tentative Recommendation and a Study Relating to the Uniform Rules of Evidence (Article VIII. Hearsay Evidence), 6 Cal.Law Revision Comm'n, Rep., Rec. & Studies Appendix at 484–490 (1964). [7 Cal. L.Rev.Comm. Reports 1 (1965)].

Research References

Rutter, Cal. Practice Guide: Civil Trials & Evidence Ch. 8D-C, C. General Parameters Re Admissibility of Hearsay Evidence.
Rutter, Cal. Practice Guide: Civil Trials & Evidence Ch. 8D-D, D. Hearsay Exceptions.
Rutter, Cal. Practice Guide: Civil Trials & Evidence Ch. 8G-B, B. Procedures on Objection.

§ 1223. Admission of co-conspirator

Evidence of a statement offered against a party is not made inadmissible by the hearsay rule if:

(a) The statement was made by the declarant while participating in a conspiracy to commit a crime or civil wrong and in furtherance of the objective of that conspiracy;

(b) The statement was made prior to or during the time that the party was participating in that conspiracy; and

(c) The evidence is offered either after admission of evidence sufficient to sustain a finding of the facts specified in subdivisions (a) and (b) or, in the court's discretion as to the order of proof, subject to the admission of such evidence. *(Stats.1965, c. 299, § 2, operative Jan. 1, 1967.)*

Law Revision Commission Comments

Section 1223 is a specific example of a kind of authorized admission that is admissible under Section 1222. The statement is admitted because it is an act of the conspiracy for which the party, as a co-conspirator, is legally responsible. People v. Lorraine, 90 Cal.App. 317, 327, 265 Pac. 893, 897 (1928). See California Criminal Law Practice 471–472 (Cal.Cont.Ed.Bar 1964). Section 1223 restates an exception found in subdivision 6 of Section 1870 of the Code of Civil Procedure. [7 Cal.L.Rev.Comm. Reports 1 (1965)].

Research References

Rutter, Cal. Practice Guide: Civil Trials & Evidence Ch. 8D-D, D. Hearsay Exceptions.

§ 1224. Statement of declarant whose liability or breach of duty is in issue

When the liability, obligation, or duty of a party to a civil action is based in whole or in part upon the liability, obligation, or duty of the declarant, or when the claim or right asserted by a party to a civil action is barred or diminished by a breach of duty by the declarant, evidence of a statement made by the declarant is as admissible against the party as it would be if offered against the declarant in an action involving that liability, obligation, duty, or breach of duty. *(Stats.1965, c. 299, § 2, operative Jan. 1, 1967.)*

Law Revision Commission Comments

Section 1224 restates in substance a hearsay exception found in Code of Civil Procedure Section 1851 (superseded by Evidence Code Sections 1224 and 1302). See Butte County v. Morgan, 76 Cal. 1, 18 Pac. 115 (1888); Ingram v. Bob Jaffe Co., 139 Cal.App.2d 193, 293 P.2d 132 (1956); Standard Oil Co. v. Houser, 101 Cal.App.2d 480, 225 P.2d 539 (1950). Section 1224, however, limits this hearsay exception to civil actions. Much of the evidence within this exception is also covered by Section 1230, which makes declarations against interest admissible. However, to be admissible under Section 1230, the statement must have been against the declarant's interest when made; this requirement is not stated in Section 1224.

Code of Civil Procedure Section 1851 provides for the admission of a declarant's statements in an action where the liability of the party against whom the statements are offered is based on the declarant's breach of duty. Butte County v. Morgan, 76 Cal. 1, 18 Pac. 115 (1888); Nye & Nissen v. Central etc. Ins. Corp., 71 Cal.App.2d 570, 163 P.2d 100 (1945). Section 1224 of the Evidence Code refers specifically to "breach of duty" in order to admit statements of a declarant whose breach of duty is in issue without regard to whether that breach gives rise to a liability of the party against whom the statements are offered or merely defeats a right being asserted by that party. For example, in Ingram v. Bob Jaffe Co., 139 Cal.App.2d 193, 293 P.2d 132 (1956), a statement of a person permitted to operate a vehicle was admitted against the owner of the vehicle in an action seeking to hold the owner liable on the derivative liability of vehicle owners established by Vehicle Code Section 17150. Under Section 1224, the statement of the declarant would also be admissible against the owner in an action brought by the owner to recover for damage to his vehicle where the defense is based on the contributory negligence of the declarant.

Section 1302 supplements the rule stated in Section 1224. Section 1302 creates an exception for judgments against a third person when one of the issues between the parties is the liability, obligation, or duty of the third person and the judgment determines that liability, obligation, or duty. Together, Sections 1224 and 1302 codify the holdings of the cases applying Code of Civil Procedure Section 1851. See Tentative Recommendation and a Study Relating to the Uniform Rules of Evidence (Article VIII. Hearsay Evidence), 6 Cal.Law Revision Comm'n, Rep., Rec. & Studies Appendix at 491–496 (1964). [7 Cal.L.Rev.Comm. Reports 1 (1965)].

Research References

Rutter, Cal. Practice Guide: Civil Trials & Evidence Ch. 8D-D, D. Hearsay Exceptions.

California Practice Guide: Employment Litigation Ch. 2-G, G. Communicating With Adverse Party Represented by Counsel.

§ 1225. Statement of declarant whose right or title is in issue

When a right, title, or interest in any property or claim asserted by a party to a civil action requires a determination that a right, title, or interest exists or existed in the declarant, evidence of a statement made by the declarant during the time the party now claims the declarant was the holder of the right, title, or interest is as admissible against the party as it would be if offered against the declarant in an action involving that right, title, or interest. *(Stats.1965, c. 299, § 2, operative Jan. 1, 1967.)*

Law Revision Commission Comments

Section 1225 expresses a common law exception to the hearsay rule that is recognized in part in Section 1849 of the Code of Civil Procedure. Section 1849 (which is superseded by Section 1225) permits the statements of predecessors in interest of real property to be admitted against the successors; however, the California cases follow the general rule of permitting predecessors' statements to be admitted against successors of either real or personal property. Smith v. Goethe, 159 Cal. 628, 115 Pac. 223 (1911); 4 Wigmore, Evidence § 1082 *et seq.* (3d ed. 1940).

It should be noted that "statements made *before title accrued in the declarant* will not be receivable. On the other hand, the time of divestiture, *after* which no statements could be treated as admissions, is the time when the party against whom they are offered has by his own hypothesis acquired the title; thus, in a suit, for example, between A's heir and A's grantee, A's statements at any time before his death are receivable against the heir; but only his statements before the grant are receivable against the grantee." 4 Wigmore, Evidence § 1082 at 153 (3d ed. 1940).

Despite the limitations of Section 1225, some statements of a grantor made after divestiture of title will be admissible; but another theory of admissibility must be found. For example, later statement of his state of mind may be admissible on the issue of his intent. Evidence Code §§ 1950 and 1251. Where it is claimed that a conveyance was in fraud of creditors, the later statements of the grantor may be admissible not as hearsay but as evidence of the fraud itself (*cf.* Bush & Mallett Co. v. Helbing, 134 Cal. 676, 66 Pac. 967 (1901)) or as declarations of a co-conspirator in the fraud (*cf.* McGee v. Allen, 7 Cal.2d 468, 60 P.2d 1026 (1936)). See generally 4 Wigmore, Evidence § 1086 (3d ed. 1940).

Section 1225 supplements the rule provided in Section 1224. Under Section 1224, for example, a party suing an executor on an obligation incurred by the decedent prior to his death may introduce admissions of the decedent. Similarly, under Section 1225, a party sued by an executor on an obligation claimed to have been owed to the decedent may introduce admissions of the decedent. [7 Cal.L.Rev.Comm. Reports 1 (1965)].

Research References

Rutter, Cal. Practice Guide: Civil Trials & Evidence Ch. 8D-D, D. Hearsay Exceptions.

§ 1226. Statement of minor child in parent's action for child's injury

Evidence of a statement by a minor child is not made inadmissible by the hearsay rule if offered against the plaintiff in an action brought under Section 376 of the Code of Civil Procedure for injury to such minor child. *(Stats.1965, c. 299, § 2, operative Jan. 1, 1967.)*

Law Revision Commission Comments

See the Comment to Section 1227. [7 Cal.L.Rev.Comm. Reports 1 (1965)].

Research References

Rutter, Cal. Practice Guide: Civil Trials & Evidence Ch. 8D-D, D. Hearsay Exceptions.

§ 1227. Statement of declarant in action for his wrongful death

Evidence of a statement by the deceased is not made inadmissible by the hearsay rule if offered against the plaintiff in an action for wrongful death brought under Section 377 of the Code of Civil Procedure. *(Stats.1965, c. 299, § 2, operative Jan. 1, 1967.)*

Law Revision Commission Comments

Under existing law, an admission by a decedent is not admissible against his heirs or representatives in a wrongful death action brought by them. Marks v. Reissinger, 35 Cal.App. 44, 169 Pac. 243 (1917). *Cf.* Hedge v. Williams, 131 Cal. 455, 63 Pac. 721 (1901). The reason is that the action is a new action, but merely a survival of the decedent's action. This rule has been severely criticized and is contrary to the rule adopted by most American courts. Carr v. Duncan, 90 Cal.App.2d 282, 285, 202 P.2d 855, 856 (1949).

Under Section 1224, the admissions of a decedent are admissible to establish the liability of his executor. Similarly, when the executor brings an action for the decedent's death under Code of Civil Procedure Section 377, the defendant should be permitted to introduce the admissions of the decedent. Without Section 1227, in an action between two executors arising out of an accident which was fatal to both participants, the plaintiff executor would be able to introduce admissions of the defendant's decedent, but the defending executor would be unable to introduce admissions of the plaintiff's decedent.

Section 1227 changes the rule announced in the California cases and makes the admissions of the decedent admissible in wrongful death actions. Section 1226 provides a similar rule for the analogous cases arising under Code of Civil Procedure Section 376 (action by parent of injured child).

Section 1227 recognizes that, in an action brought under Code of Civil Procedure Section 377, the only reason for treating the admissions of a plaintiff's decedent differently from those of a defendant's decedent is a technical procedural rule. The plaintiff in a wrongful death action—and the parent of an injured child in an action under Code of Civil Procedure Section 376—stands in reality so completely on the right of the deceased or injured person that such person's admissions should be admitted against the plaintiff, even though (as a technical matter the plaintiff is asserting an independent right. [7 Cal.L.Rev.Comm. Reports 1 (1965)].

Research References

Rutter, Cal. Practice Guide: Civil Trials & Evidence Ch. 8D-D, D. Hearsay Exceptions.

§ 1228. Admissibility of certain out-of-court statements of minors under the age of 12; establishing elements of certain sexually oriented crimes; notice to defendant

Notwithstanding any other provision of law, for the purpose of establishing the elements of the crime in order to admit as evidence the confession of a person accused of violating Section 261, 264.1, 285, 286, 288, 288a, 289, or 647a of the Penal Code, a court, in its discretion, may determine that a statement of the complaining witness is not made inadmissible by the hearsay rule if it finds all of the following:

(a) The statement was made by a minor child under the age of 12, and the contents of the statement were included in a written report of a law enforcement official or an employee of a county welfare department.

(b) The statement describes the minor child as a victim of sexual abuse.

(c) The statement was made prior to the defendant's confession. The court shall view with caution the testimony of a person recounting hearsay where there is evidence of personal bias or prejudice.

(d) There are no circumstances, such as significant inconsistencies between the confession and the statement concerning material facts establishing any element of the crime or the identification of the defendant, that would render the statement unreliable.

(e) The minor child is found to be unavailable pursuant to paragraph (2) or (3) of subdivision (a) of Section 240 or refuses to testify.

(f) The confession was memorialized in a trustworthy fashion by a law enforcement official.

If the prosecution intends to offer a statement of the complaining witness pursuant to this section, the prosecution shall serve a written notice upon the defendant at least 10 days prior to the hearing or trial at which the prosecution intends to offer the statement.

If the statement is offered during trial, the court's determination shall be made out of the presence of the jury. If the statement is found to be admissible pursuant to this section, it shall be admitted out of the presence of the jury and solely for the purpose of determining the admissibility of the confession of the defendant. *(Added by Stats.1984, c. 1421, § 1. Amended by Stats.1985, c. 1572, § 1, eff. Oct. 2, 1985.)*

Research References

10 Witkin, California Summary 10th Parent and Child § 284, Trial.

§ 1228.1. Signature of parent or guardian on child welfare services case plan; acceptance of services; use in court of law; failure to cooperate

(a) Except as provided in subdivision (b), neither the signature of any parent or legal guardian on a child welfare services case plan nor the acceptance of any services prescribed in the child welfare services case plan by any parent or legal guardian shall constitute an admission of guilt or be used as evidence against the parent or legal guardian in a court of law.

(b) A parent's or guardian's failure to cooperate, except for good cause, in the provision of services specified in the child welfare services case plan may be used as evidence, if relevant, in any hearing held pursuant to Section 366.21, 366.22, or 388 of the Welfare and Institutions Code and at any jurisdictional or dispositional hearing held on a petition filed pursuant to Section 300, 342, or 387 of the Welfare and Institutions Code. *(Added by Stats.1995, c. 540 (A.B.1523), § 1. Amended by Stats.1997, c. 793 (A.B.1544), § 1.)*

ARTICLE 2. DECLARATIONS AGAINST INTEREST

Section
1230. Declarations against interest.

§ 1230. Declarations against interest

Evidence of a statement by a declarant having sufficient knowledge of the subject is not made inadmissible by the hearsay rule if the declarant is unavailable as a witness and the statement, when made, was so far contrary to the declarant's pecuniary or proprietary interest, or so far subjected him to the risk of civil or criminal liability, or so far tended to render invalid a claim by him against another, or created such a risk of making him an object of hatred, ridicule, or social disgrace in the community, that a reasonable man in his position would not have made the statement unless he believed it to be true. *(Stats.1965, c. 299, § 2, operative Jan. 1, 1967.)*

Research References

Rutter, Cal. Practice Guide: Civil Trials & Evidence Ch. 10-B, B. Scope of Permissible Cross-Examination.
Rutter, Cal. Practice Guide: Civil Trials & Evidence Ch. 8D-D, D. Hearsay Exceptions.
Rutter, Cal. Practice Guide: Civil Trials & Evidence Gen. Matls., Highlights.
Rutter, Cal. Practice Guide: Insurance Litigation Ch. 15-K, K. Judgment Creditor's Action to Enforce Judgment Debtor's Liability Insurance (INS.C. § 11580(B)(2)).

ARTICLE 2.5. SWORN STATEMENTS REGARDING GANG–RELATED CRIMES

Section

1231.   Prior statements of deceased declarant; hearsay exception.

1231.1.   Statements made by deceased declarant; admissibility; notice of statement to adverse party.

1231.2.   Administer and certify oaths.

1231.3.   Testimony of law enforcement officer; hearsay.

1231.4.   Cause of death; deceased declarant.

§ 1231. Prior statements of deceased declarant; hearsay exception

Evidence of a prior statement made by a declarant is not made inadmissible by the hearsay rule if the declarant is deceased and the proponent of introducing the statement establishes each of the following:

(a) The statement relates to acts or events relevant to a criminal prosecution under provisions of the California Street Terrorism Enforcement and Prevention Act (Chapter 11 (commencing with Section 186.20) of Title 7 of Part 1 of the Penal Code).

(b) A verbatim transcript, copy, or record of the statement exists. A record may include a statement preserved by means of an audio or video recording or equivalent technology.

(c) The statement relates to acts or events within the personal knowledge of the declarant.

(d) The statement was made under oath or affirmation in an affidavit; or was made at a deposition, preliminary hearing, grand jury hearing, or other proceeding in compliance with law, and was made under penalty of perjury.

(e) The declarant died from other than natural causes.

(f) The statement was made under circumstances that would indicate its trustworthiness and render the declarant's statement particularly worthy of belief. For purposes of this subdivision, circumstances relevant to the issue of trustworthiness include, but are not limited to, all of the following:

(1) Whether the statement was made in contemplation of a pending or anticipated criminal or civil matter, in which the declarant had an interest, other than as a witness.

(2) Whether the declarant had a bias or motive for fabricating the statement, and the extent of any bias or motive.

(3) Whether the statement is corroborated by evidence other than statements that are admissible only pursuant to this section.

(4) Whether the statement was a statement against the declarant's interest. *(Added by Stats.1997, c. 499 (S.B.941), § 1.)*

Research References

Rutter, Cal. Practice Guide: Civil Trials & Evidence Ch. 8D-D, D. Hearsay Exceptions.

§ 1231.1. Statements made by deceased declarant; admissibility; notice of statement to adverse party

A statement is admissible pursuant to Section 1231 only if the proponent of the statement makes known to the adverse party the intention to offer the statement and the particulars of the statement sufficiently in advance of the proceedings to provide the adverse party with a fair opportunity to prepare to meet the statement. *(Added by Stats.1997, c. 499 (S.B.941), § 1.)*

§ 1231.2. Administer and certify oaths

A peace officer may administer and certify oaths for purposes of this article. *(Added by Stats.1997, c. 499 (S.B.941), § 1. Amended by Stats.1998, c. 606 (S.B.1880), § 2.)*

§ 1231.3. Testimony of law enforcement officer; hearsay

Any law enforcement officer testifying as to any hearsay statement pursuant to this article shall either have five years of law enforcement experience or have completed a training course certified by the Commission on Peace Officer Standards and Training which includes training in the investigation and reporting of cases and testifying at preliminary hearings and trials. *(Added by Stats.1997, c. 499 (S.B.941), § 1.)*

§ 1231.4. Cause of death; deceased declarant

If evidence of a prior statement is introduced pursuant to this article, the jury may not be told that the declarant died from other than natural causes, but shall merely be told that the declarant is unavailable. *(Added by Stats.1997, c. 499 (S.B.941), § 1.)*

ARTICLE 3. PRIOR STATEMENTS OF WITNESSES

Section

1235.   Inconsistent statements.

1236.   Prior consistent statements.

1237.   Past recollection recorded.

1238.   Prior identification.

§ 1235. Inconsistent statements

Evidence of a statement made by a witness is not made inadmissible by the hearsay rule if the statement is inconsistent with his testimony at the hearing and is offered in compliance with Section 770. *(Stats.1965, c. 299, § 2, operative Jan. 1, 1967.)*

Law Revision Commission Comments

Under existing law, when a prior statement of a witness that is inconsistent with his testimony at the trial is admitted in evidence, it may not be used as evidence of the truth of the matters stated. Because of the hearsay rule, a witness' prior inconsistent statement may be used only to discredit his testimony given at the trial. Albert v. McKay & Co., 174 Cal. 451, 456, 163 Pac. 666, 668 (1917).

Because a witness' inconsistent statement is not substantive evidence, the courts do not permit a party—even when surprised by the testimony—to impeach his own witness with inconsistent statements if the witness' testimony at the trial has not damaged the party's case in any way. Evidence tending only to discredit the witness is irrelevant and immaterial when the witness has not given damaging testimony. People v. Crespi, 115 Cal. 50, 46 Pac. 863 (1896); People v. Mitchell, 94 Cal. 550, 29 Pac. 1106 (1892); People v. Brown, 81 Cal.App. 226, 253 Pac. 735 (1927).

Section 1235 permits an inconsistent statement of a witness to be used as substantive evidence if the statement is otherwise admissible under the conditions specified in Section 770—which do not include surprise on the part of the party calling the witness if he is the party offering the inconsistent statement. Because Section 1235 permits a witness' inconsistent statements to be considered as evidence of the matters stated and not merely as evidence casting discredit on the witness, it follows that a party may introduce evidence of inconsistent statements of his own witness whether or not the witness gave damaging testimony and whether or not the party was surprised by the testimony, for such evidence is no longer irrelevant (and, hence, inadmissible).

Section 1235 admits inconsistent statements of witnesses because the dangers against which the hearsay rule is designed to protect are largely nonexistent. The declarant is in court and may be examined and cross-examined in regard to his statements and their subject matter. In many cases, the inconsistent statement is more likely to be true than the testimony of the witness at the trial because it was made nearer in time to the matter to which it relates and is less likely to be influenced by the controversy that gave rise to the litigation. The trier of fact has the declarant before it and can observe his demeanor and the nature of his testimony as he denies or tries to explain away the inconsistency. Hence, it is in as good a position to determine the truth or falsity of the prior statement as it is to determine the truth or falsity of the inconsistent testimony given in court. Moreover, Section 1235 will provide a party with desirable protection against the "turn-coat" witness who changes his story on the stand and deprives the party calling him of evidence essential to his case. [7 Cal.L.Rev.Comm. Reports 1 (1965)].

Research References

Rutter, Cal. Practice Guide: Civ. Pro. Before Trial Ch. 3-E, E. Federal vs. State Courts.

Rutter, Cal. Practice Guide: Civ. Pro. Before Trial Ch. 8F-5, Responding to Interrogatories.

Rutter, Cal. Practice Guide: Civ. Pro. Before Trial Ch. 8F-9, Use of Interrogatories at Trial.

Rutter, Cal. Practice Guide: Civil Trials & Evidence Ch. 8D-D, D. Hearsay Exceptions.

Rutter, Cal. Practice Guide: Civil Trials & Evidence Ch. 8E-F, F. Limitations on Impeachment and Rehabilitation.

Rutter, Cal. Practice Guide: Fed.Civ.Pro. Before Trial Ch. 1-D, D. Choosing Between State and Federal Courts.

Rutter, Cal. Practice Guide: Personal Injury Ch. 9-F, F. Examination of Witnesses.

4 Witkin Cal. Proc. 5th Pleading § 458, Suppressed Allegation.

§ 1236. Prior consistent statements

Evidence of a statement previously made by a witness is not made inadmissible by the hearsay rule if the statement is consistent with his testimony at the hearing and is offered in compliance with Section 791. *(Stats.1965, c. 299, § 2, operative Jan. 1, 1967.)*

Law Revision Commission Comments

Under existing law, a prior statement of a witness that is consistent with his testimony at the trial is admissible under certain conditions when the credibility of the witness has been attacked. The statement is admitted, however, only to rehabilitate the witness—to support his credibility—and not as evidence of the truth of the matter stated. People v. Kynette, 15 Cal.2d 731, 753–754, 104 P.2d 794, 805–806 (1940) (overruled on other grounds in People v. Snyder, 50 Cal.2d 190, 197, 324 P.2d 1, 6 (1958)).

Section 1236, however, permits a prior consistent statement of a witness to be used as substantive evidence if the statement is otherwise admissible under the rules relating to the rehabilitation of impeached witnesses. See Evidence Code § 791.

There is no reason to perpetuate the subtle distinction made in the cases. It is not realistic to expect a jury to understand that it cannot believe that a witness was telling the truth on a former occasion even though it believes that the same story given at the hearing is true. [7 Cal.L.Rev.Comm. Reports 1 (1965)].

Research References

Rutter, Cal. Practice Guide: Civ. Pro. Before Trial Ch. 8F-5, Responding to Interrogatories.

Rutter, Cal. Practice Guide: Civil Trials & Evidence Ch. 9-G, G. Redirect Examination.

Rutter, Cal. Practice Guide: Civil Trials & Evidence Ch. 8D-D, D. Hearsay Exceptions.

Rutter, Cal. Practice Guide: Civil Trials & Evidence Ch. 8E-F, F. Limitations on Impeachment and Rehabilitation.

§ 1237. Past recollection recorded

(a) Evidence of a statement previously made by a witness is not made inadmissible by the hearsay rule if the statement would have been admissible if made by him while testifying, the statement concerns a matter as to which the witness has insufficient present recollection to enable him to testify fully and accurately, and the statement is contained in a writing which:

(1) Was made at a time when the fact recorded in the writing actually occurred or was fresh in the witness' memory;

(2) Was made (i) by the witness himself or under his direction or (ii) by some other person for the purpose of recording the witness' statement at the time it was made;

(3) Is offered after the witness testifies that the statement he made was a true statement of such fact; and

(4) Is offered after the writing is authenticated as an accurate record of the statement.

(b) The writing may be read into evidence, but the writing itself may not be received in evidence unless offered by an adverse party. *(Stats.1965, c. 299, § 2, operative Jan. 1, 1967.)*

Research References

Rutter, Cal. Practice Guide: Civil Trials & Evidence Ch. 9-F, F. Witnesses Needing Assistance in Testifying.

Rutter, Cal. Practice Guide: Civil Trials & Evidence Ch. 8C-B, B. Writings.

Rutter, Cal. Practice Guide: Civil Trials & Evidence Ch. 8D-D, D. Hearsay Exceptions.

Rutter, Cal. Practice Guide: Civil Trials & Evidence Ch. 8E-D, D. Other Public Policy Exclusions.

Rutter, Cal. Practice Guide: Personal Injury Ch. 3-C, C. Specific Items of Compensatory Damages.

Rutter, Cal. Practice Guide: Personal Injury Ch. 9-H, H. Introduction of Discovered Evidence.

Rutter, Cal. Practice Guide: Personal Injury Ch. 9-I, I. Use of Writings, Exhibits and Demonstrative Evidence.

§ 1238. Prior identification

Evidence of a statement previously made by a witness is not made inadmissible by the hearsay rule if the statement would have been admissible if made by him while testifying and:

(a) The statement is an identification of a party or another as a person who participated in a crime or other occurrence;

(b) The statement was made at a time when the crime or other occurrence was fresh in the witness' memory; and

(c) The evidence of the statement is offered after the witness testifies that he made the identification and that it was a true reflection of his opinion at that time. *(Stats.1965, c. 299, § 2, operative Jan. 1, 1967.)*

Law Revision Commission Comments

Under Section 1235, evidence of a prior identification is admissible if the witness denies having made the prior identification or in any other way testifies inconsistently with the prior statement. Under Section 1238, evidence of a prior identification is admissible if the witness admits the prior identification and vouches for its accuracy.

Sections 1235 and 1238 codify exceptions to the hearsay rule similar to that which was recognized in People v. Gould, 54 Cal.2d 621, 7 Cal.Rptr. 273, 354 P.2d 865 (1960). In the Gould case, evidence of a prior identification made by a witness who could not repeat the identification at the trial was held admissible "because the earlier identification has greater probative value than an identification made in the courtroom after the suggestions of others and the circumstances of the trial may have intervened to create a fancied recognition in the witness' mind. [Citations omitted.] The failure of the witness to repeat the extrajudicial identification in court does not destroy its probative value, for such failure may be explained by loss of memory or other circumstances. [Moreover,] the principal danger of admitting hearsay evidence is not present since the witness is available at the trial for cross-examination." 54 Cal.2d at 626, 7 Cal.Rptr. at 275, 354 P.2d at 867.

As there was no discussion in the Gould opinion of the preliminary showing necessary to warrant admission of evidence of a prior identification, it cannot be determined whether Sections 1235 and 1238 modify the law as declared in that case.

Sections 1235 and 1238 deal only with the admissibility of evidence; they do not determine what constitutes evidence sufficient to sustain a verdict or finding. Hence, these sections have no effect on the holding of the Gould case that evidence of an extrajudicial identification that cannot be confirmed by an identification at the trial is insufficient to sustain a criminal conviction in the absence of other evidence tending to connect the defendant with the crime. [7 Cal.L.Rev.Comm. Reports 1 (1965)].

Research References

Rutter, Cal. Practice Guide: Civil Trials & Evidence Ch. 8D-D, D. Hearsay Exceptions.

ARTICLE 4. SPONTANEOUS, CONTEMPORANEOUS, AND DYING DECLARATIONS

Section

1241. Contemporaneous statement.

1242. Dying declaration.

§ 1240. Spontaneous statement

Evidence of a statement is not made inadmissible by the hearsay rule if the statement:

(a) Purports to narrate, describe, or explain an act, condition, or event perceived by the declarant; and

(b) Was made spontaneously while the declarant was under the stress of excitement caused by such perception. *(Stats.1965, c. 299, § 2, operative Jan. 1, 1967.)*

Law Revision Commission Comments

Section 1240 is a codification of the existing exception to the hearsay rule for statements made spontaneously under the stress of excitement engendered by the event to which they relate. Showalter v. Western Pacific R.R., 16 Cal.2d 460, 106 P.2d 895 (1940). See Tentative Recommendation and a study relating to the Uniform Rules of Evidence, (Article, VIII. Hearsay Evidence), 6 Cal.Law Revision Comm'n, Rep., Rec. & Studies Appendix at 465–466 (1964). The rationale of this exception is that the spontaneity of such statements and the consequent lack of opportunity for reflection and deliberate fabrication provide an adequate guarantee of their trustworthiness. [7 Cal.L.Rev.Comm. Reports 1 (1965)].

Research References

Rutter, Cal. Practice Guide: Civil Trials & Evidence Ch. 8D-D, D. Hearsay Exceptions.

§ 1241. Contemporaneous statement

Evidence of a statement is not made inadmissible by the hearsay rule if the statement:

(a) Is offered to explain, qualify, or make understandable conduct of the declarant; and

(b) Was made while the declarant was engaged in such conduct. *(Stats.1965, c. 299, § 2, operative Jan. 1, 1967.)*

Research References

Rutter, Cal. Practice Guide: Civil Trials & Evidence Ch. 8D-D, D. Hearsay Exceptions.

§ 1242. Dying declaration

Evidence of a statement made by a dying person respecting the cause and circumstances of his death is not made inadmissible by the hearsay rule if the statement was made upon his personal knowledge and under a sense of immediately impending death. *(Stats.1965, c. 299, § 2, operative Jan. 1, 1967.)*

Law Revision Commission Comments

Section 1242 is a broadened form of the well-established exception to the hearsay rule for dying declarations relating to the cause and circumstances of the declarant's death. The existing law—Code of Civil Procedure Section 1870(4) as interpreted by the courts—makes such declarations admissible only in criminal homicide actions. People v. Hall, 94 Cal. 595, 30 Pac. 7 (1892); Thrasher v. Board of Medical Examiners, 44 Cal.App. 26, 185 Pac. 1006 (1919). For the purpose of the *admissibility* of dying declarations, there is no rational basis for differentiating between civil and criminal actions or among various types of criminal actions. Hence, Section 1242 makes the exception applicable in all actions.

Under Section 1242, as under existing law, the dying declaration is admissible only if the declarant made the statement on personal knowledge. People v. Wasson, 65 Cal. 538, 4 Pac. 555 (1884); People v. Taylor, 59 Cal. 640 (1881). [7 Cal.L.Rev.Comm. Reports 1 (1965)].

Research References

Rutter, Cal. Practice Guide: Civil Trials & Evidence Ch. 8D-D, D. Hearsay Exceptions.

ARTICLE 5. STATEMENTS OF MENTAL OR PHYSICAL STATE

Section

1250. Statement of declarant's then existing mental or physical state.

1251. Statement of declarant's previously existing mental or physical state.

1252. Restriction on admissibility of statement of mental or physical state.

1253. Statements for purposes of medical diagnosis or treatment; contents of statement; child abuse or neglect; age limitations.

§ 1250. Statement of declarant's then existing mental or physical state

(a) Subject to Section 1252, evidence of a statement of the declarant's then existing state of mind, emotion, or physical sensation (including a statement of intent, plan, motive, design, mental feeling, pain, or bodily health) is not made inadmissible by the hearsay rule when:

(1) The evidence is offered to prove the declarant's state of mind, emotion, or physical sensation at that time or at any other time when it is itself an issue in the action; or

(2) The evidence is offered to prove or explain acts or conduct of the declarant.

(b) This section does not make admissible evidence of a statement of memory or belief to prove the fact remembered or believed. *(Stats.1965, c. 299, § 2, operative Jan. 1, 1967.)*

Research References

Rutter, Cal. Practice Guide: Civil Trials & Evidence Ch. 8D-D, D. Hearsay Exceptions.

Rutter, Cal. Practice Guide: Civil Trials & Evidence Ch. 8D-D, Outline D.

Rutter, Cal. Practice Guide: Personal Injury Ch. 3-C, C. Specific Items of Compensatory Damages.

Miller and Starr California Real Estate § 8:55, Undue Influence.

§ 1251. Statement of declarant's previously existing mental or physical state

Subject to Section 1252, evidence of a statement of the declarant's state of mind, emotion, or physical sensation (including a statement of intent, plan, motive, design, mental feeling, pain, or bodily health) at a time prior to the statement is not made inadmissible by the hearsay rule if:

(a) The declarant is unavailable as a witness; and

(b) The evidence is offered to prove such prior state of mind, emotion, or physical sensation when it is itself an issue in the action and the evidence is not offered to prove any fact other than such state of mind, emotion, or physical sensation. *(Stats. 1965, c. 299, § 2, operative Jan. 1, 1967.)*

Law Revision Commission Comments

Section 1250 forbids the use of a statement of memory or belief to prove the fact remembered or believed. Section 1251, however, permits a statement of memory or belief of a past mental or physical state to be used to prove the previous mental or physical state when the previous mental or physical state is itself an issue in the case. If the past mental or physical state is to be used merely as circumstantial evidence of some other fact, the limitation in Section 1250 still applies and the statement of the past mental state is inadmissible hearsay.

The rule stated in Section 1251 is consistent with the California case law to the extent that it permits a statement of a prior mental state to be used as evidence of that mental state. See, *e.g.* People v. One 1948 Chevrolet

Conv. Coupe, 45 Cal.2d 613, 290 P.2d 538 (1955) (statement of prior knowledge admitted to prove such knowledge); Kelly v. Bank of America, 112 Cal.App.2d 388, 246 P.2d 92 (1952) (statement of previous intent to retain title admitted to prove such intent). However, the California cases have held that statements of previous bodily conditions and symptoms are inadmissible to prove the existence of such conditions or symptoms, although they may be admitted as a basis for an expert's opinion. People v. Brown, 49 Cal.2d 577, 320 P.2d 5 (1958); Willoughby v. Zylstra, 5 Cal.App.2d 297, 42 P.2d 685 (1935). Section 1251 eliminates the distinction between statements of previous mental conditions and statements of previous physical sensations; it permits both to be admitted as evidence of the matters stated. Both kinds of statements are equally subjective, and there is no reason to believe that one kind is more unreliable than the other.

Section 1251 requires that the declarant be unavailable as a witness. Some California cases seem to indicate that the unavailability of the declarant is a necessary condition for the admission of his statements to prove a previous state of mind. See, *e.g.*, Whitlow v. Durst, 20 Cal.2d 523, 524, 127 P.2d 530, 531 (1942) ("declarations of a *decedent*" admissible to show previous mental state); Kelly v. Bank of America, 112 Cal.App.2d 388, 246 P.2d 92 (1952). But other cases have admitted such statements without insisting on the declarant's unavailability. People v. One 1948 Chevrolet Conv. Coupe, 45 Cal.2d 613, 290 P.2d 538 (1955). Section 1251 requires a showing of the declarant's unavailability because the statements involved are narrations of past conditions. There is, therefore, a greater opportunity for the declarant to remember inaccurately or even to fabricate. Hence, Section 1251 permits such statements to be admitted only when the declarant's unavailability necessitates reliance upon his out-of-court statements.

A statement is not admissible under Section 1251 if the statement was made under circumstances indicating that the statement is not trustworthy. See Evidence Code 1252 and the Comment thereto. [7 Cal.L.Rev. Comm. Reports 1 (1965)].

Research References

Rutter, Cal. Practice Guide: Civil Trials & Evidence Ch. 8D-D, D. Hearsay Exceptions.

§ 1252. Restriction on admissibility of statement of mental or physical state

Evidence of a statement is inadmissible under this article if the statement was made under circumstances such as to indicate its lack of trustworthiness. *(Stats.1965, c. 299, § 2, operative Jan. 1, 1967.)*

Law Revision Commission Comments

Section 1252 limits the admissibility of hearsay statements that would otherwise be admissible under Sections 1250 and 1251. If a statement of mental or physical state was made with a motive to misrepresent or to manufacture evidence, the statement is not sufficiently reliable to warrant its reception in evidence. The limitation expressed in Section 1252 has been held to be a condition of admissibility in some of the California cases. See, *e.g.*, People v. Hamilton, 55 Cal.2d 881, 893, 895, 13 Cal.Rptr. 649, 656, 657, 362 P.2d 473, 480, 481 (1961); People v. Alcalde, 24 Cal.2d 177, 187, 148 P.2d 627, 632 (1944).

The Hamilton case mentions some additional limitations on the admissibility of statements offered in a criminal action to prove the declarant's mental statement. These additional limitations do not appear in the Evidence Code. In the Hamilton case, the court was concerned with a murder victim's statements that she was afraid of the accused, that the accused had threatened to kill her, and that the accused had beaten her. The statements were ostensibly offered to prove that the victim feared the accused and, therefore, to cast doubt on the accused's testimony that the victim had invited him to her house on the night of the murder. As the case was tried, however, the victim's declarations were used repeatedly in argument as a basis for the prosecution's claim that the beatings actually occurred, that the threats were actually made, and that the threats were carried out in the murder.

The court said that "testimony as to the 'state of mind' of the declarant . . . is admissible, but only when such testimony refers to threats as to future conduct on the part of the accused . . . and when [such declarations] show primarily the then state of mind of the declarant and not the state of mind of the accused. But . . . such testimony is not admissible if it refers solely to alleged past conduct on the part of the accused." 55 Cal.2d at 893–894, 13 Cal.Rptr. at 656, 362 P.2d at 480.

These additional limitations on the admissibility of state of mind evidence are not mentioned in the Evidence Code for two reasons. *First*, they are confusing and contradictory: The declarations are inadmissible if they refer to past conduct of the accused; nevertheless, they are admissible "only" when they refer to his past conduct, *i.e.*, his threats. The declarations, to be admissible, must show primarily the state of mind of the declarant and not the state of mind of the accused; nevertheless, such declarations are admissible "only" if they refer to the accused's statements of his state of mind, *i.e.*, his intent to do future harm to the victim.

Second, these additional limitations are unnecessary. Section 1200 makes it clear that statements of past events cannot be used to prove those events unless they fall within an exception to the hearsay rule; and Sections 1250 and 1251 make it clear that statements of a declarant's past state of mind may be used to prove only that state of mind and no other fact. The real problem in the Hamilton case was the fact that much of the evidence was offered ostensibly not as hearsay but as circumstantial evidence of the victim's fear (see Section 1200 and the Comment thereto); but the prosecution endeavored nevertheless to have the jury consider the evidence as hearsay evidence, *i.e.*, as evidence that the events related actually occurred. Evidence Code Section 352 provides the judge with ample power to exclude evidence of this sort where its prejudicial effect outweighs its probative value. But, under Section 352, the judge must weigh the need for the evidence against the danger of its misuse in each case. The Evidence Code does not freeze the courts to the arbitrary and contradictory standards mentioned in the Hamilton case for determining when prejudicial effect outweighs probative value. [7 Cal.L.Rev.Comm. Reports 1 (1965)].

Research References

Rutter, Cal. Practice Guide: Civil Trials & Evidence Ch. 8D-C, C. General Parameters Re Admissibility of Hearsay Evidence.
Rutter, Cal. Practice Guide: Civil Trials & Evidence Ch. 8D-D, D. Hearsay Exceptions.
Miller and Starr California Real Estate § 8:55, Undue Influence.

§ 1253. Statements for purposes of medical diagnosis or treatment; contents of statement; child abuse or neglect; age limitations

Subject to Section 1252, evidence of a statement is not made inadmissible by the hearsay rule if the statement was made for purposes of medical diagnosis or treatment and describes medical history, or past or present symptoms, pain, or sensations, or the inception or general character of the cause or external source thereof insofar as reasonably pertinent to diagnosis or treatment. This section applies only to a statement made by a victim who is a minor at the time of the proceedings, provided the statement was made when the victim was under the age of 12 describing any act, or attempted act, of child abuse or neglect. "Child abuse" and "child neglect," for purposes of this section, have the meanings provided in subdivision (c) of Section 1360. In addition, "child abuse" means any act proscribed by Chapter 5 (commencing with Section 281) of Title 9 of Part 1 of the Penal Code committed against a minor. *(Added by Stats.1995, c. 87 (A.B.355), § 2.)*

Research References

Rutter, Cal. Practice Guide: Civil Trials & Evidence Ch. 8D-D, D. Hearsay Exceptions.

ARTICLE 6. STATEMENTS RELATING TO WILLS AND TO CLAIMS AGAINST ESTATES

Evidence

§ 1260. Statements concerning declarant's will or revocable trust

(a) Except as provided in subdivision (b), evidence of any of the following statements made by a declarant who is unavailable as a witness is not made inadmissible by the hearsay rule:

(1) That the declarant has or has not made a will or established or amended a revocable trust.

(2) That the declarant has or has not revoked his or her will, revocable trust, or an amendment to a revocable trust.

(3) That identifies the declarant's will, revocable trust, or an amendment to a revocable trust.

(b) Evidence of a statement is inadmissible under this section if the statement was made under circumstances that indicate its lack of trustworthiness. *(Stats.1965, c. 299, § 2, operative Jan. 1, 1967. Amended by Stats.2010, c. 106 (S.B.1041), § 1.)*

Law Revision Commission Comments

Section 1260 codifies an exception recognized in California case law. Estate of Morrison, 198 Cal. 1, 242 Pac. 939 (1926); Estate of Thompson, 44 Cal.App.2d 774, 112 P.2d 937 (1941). The section is, of course, subject to the provisions of Probate Code Sections 350 and 351 which relate to the establishment of a lost or destroyed will.

The limitation in subdivision (b) is not mentioned in the few court decisions involving this exception. The limitation is desirable, however, to assure the reliability of the hearsay that is admissible under this section. [7 Cal.L.Rev.Comm. Reports 1 (1965)].

Research References

Rutter, Cal. Practice Guide: Civil Trials & Evidence Ch. 8D-D, D. Hearsay Exceptions.

§ 1261. Statement of decedent offered in action against his estate

(a) Evidence of a statement is not made inadmissible by the hearsay rule when offered in an action upon a claim or demand against the estate of the declarant if the statement was made upon the personal knowledge of the declarant at a time when the matter had been recently perceived by him and while his recollection was clear.

(b) Evidence of a statement is inadmissible under this section if the statement was made under circumstances such as to indicate its lack of trustworthiness. *(Stats.1965, c. 299, § 2, operative Jan. 1, 1967.)*

Law Revision Commission Comments

The dead man statute (subdivision 3 of Section 1880 of the Code of Civil Procedure) prohibits a party who sues on a claim against a decedent's estate from testifying to any fact occurring prior to the decedent's death. The theory apparently underlying the statute is that it would be unfair to permit the surviving claimant to testify to such facts when the decedent is precluded by his death from doing so. To balance the positions of the parties, the living may not speak because the dead cannot.

The dead man statute operates unsatisfactorily. It prohibits testimony concerning matters of which the decedent had no knowledge and, hence, to which he could not have testified even if he had survived. It operates unevenly since it does not prohibit testimony relating to claims *under,* as distinguished from claims *against,* the decedent's estate even though the effect of such a claim may be to frustrate the decedent's plan for the disposition of his property. See the Law Revision Commission's Comment to Code of Civil Procedure Section 1880 and 1 Cal.Law Revision Comm'n, Rep., Rec. & Studies, Recommendation and Study Relating to the Dead Man Statute at D-1 (1957). The dead man statute excludes otherwise relevant and competent evidence—even if it is the only available evidence—and frequently this forces the courts to decide cases with a minimum of information concerning the actual facts. See the Supreme Court's complaint in Light v. Stevens, 159 Cal. 288, 292, 113 Pac. 659, 660 (1911) ("Owing to the fact that the lips of one of the parties to the transaction are closed by death and those of the other party by the law, the

evidence on this question is somewhat unsatisfactory."). Hence, the dead man statute is not continued in the Evidence Code.

Under the Evidence Code, the positions of the parties are balanced by throwing more light, not less, on the actual facts. Repeal of the dead man statute permits the claimant to testify without restriction. To balance this advantage, Section 1261 permits hearsay evidence of the decedent's statements to be admitted. Certain safeguards—*i.e.,* personal knowledge, recent perception, and circumstantial evidence of trustworthiness—are included in the section to provide some protection for the party against whom the statements are offered, for he has no opportunity to test the hearsay by cross-examination. [7 Cal.L.Rev.Comm. Reports 1 (1965)].

Research References

Rutter, Cal. Practice Guide: Civil Trials & Evidence Ch. 8D-C, C. General Parameters Re Admissibility of Hearsay Evidence.
Rutter, Cal. Practice Guide: Civil Trials & Evidence Ch. 8D-D, D. Hearsay Exceptions.

ARTICLE 7.　BUSINESS RECORDS

Section
1270.　A business.
1271.　Admissible writings.
1272.　Absence of entry in business records.

§ 1270. A business

As used in this article, "a business" includes every kind of business, governmental activity, profession, occupation, calling, or operation of institutions, whether carried on for profit or not. *(Stats.1965, c. 299, § 2, operative Jan. 1, 1967.)*

Law Revision Commission Comments

This article restates and supersedes the Uniform Business Records as Evidence Act appearing in Sections 1953e through 1953h of the Code of Civil Procedure. The definition of "a business" in Section 1270 is substantially the same as that appearing in Code of Civil Procedure Section 1953e. A reference to "governmental activity" has been added to the Evidence Code definition to codify the decisions in cases holding the Uniform Act applicable to governmental records. See, *e.g.,* Nichols v. McCoy, 38 Cal.2d 447, 240 P.2d 569 (1952); Fox v. San Francisco Unified School Dist., 111 Cal.App.2d 885, 245 P.2d 603 (1952).

The definition is sufficiently broad to encompass institutions not customarily thought of as businesses. For example, the baptismal and wedding records of a church would be admissible under the section to prove the events recorded. 5 Wigmore, Evidence § 1523 (3d ed. 1940). *Cf.* Evidence Code § 1315. [7 Cal.L.Rev.Comm. Reports 1 (1965)].

Research References

Rutter, Cal. Practice Guide: Civ. Pro. Before Trial Ch. 8E-6, Subpoena to Nonparty Deponent or Business Records Custodian.
Rutter, Cal. Practice Guide: Civ. Pro. Before Trial Ch. 9(II)-D, D. Attachment.
Rutter, Cal. Practice Guide: Civil Trials & Evidence Ch. 8C-B, B. Writings.
Rutter, Cal. Practice Guide: Civil Trials & Evidence Ch. 8D-D, D. Hearsay Exceptions.
Rutter, Cal. Practice Guide: Personal Injury Ch. 3-C, C. Specific Items of Compensatory Damages.
Rutter, Cal. Practice Guide: Personal Injury Ch. 9-I, I. Use of Writings, Exhibits and Demonstrative Evidence.

§ 1271. Admissible writings

Evidence of a writing made as a record of an act, condition, or event is not made inadmissible by the hearsay rule when offered to prove the act, condition, or event if:

(a) The writing was made in the regular course of a business;

(b) The writing was made at or near the time of the act, condition, or event;

(c) The custodian or other qualified witness testifies to its identity and the mode of its preparation; and

(d) The sources of information and method and time of preparation were such as to indicate its trustworthiness. *(Stats. 1965, c. 299, § 2, operative Jan. 1, 1967.)*

Law Revision Commission Comments

Section 1271 is the business records exception to the hearsay rule. It is stated in language taken from the Uniform Business Records as Evidence Act (Sections 1953e–1953h of the Code of Civil Procedure) and from Rule 63(13) of the Uniform Rules of Evidence.

Section 1271 requires the judge to find that the sources of information and the method and time of preparation of the record "were such as to indicate its trustworthiness." Under the language of Code of Civil Procedure Section 1953f, the judge must determine that the sources of information and method and time of preparation "were such as to justify its admission." The language of Section 1271 is more accurate, for the cases hold that admission of a business record is not justified when there is no preliminary showing that the record is reliable or trustworthy. *E.g.,* People v. Grayson, 172 Cal.App.2d 372, 341 P.2d 820 (1959) (hotel register rejected because "not shown to be true and complete").

"The chief foundation of the special reliability of business records is the requirement that they must be based upon the first-hand observation of someone whose job it is to know the facts recorded. . . . But if the evidence in the particular case discloses that the record was not based upon the report of an informant having the business duty to observe and report, then the record is not admissible under this exception, to show the truth of the matter reported to the recorder." McCormick, Evidence § 286 at 602 (1954), as quoted in MacLean v. City & County of San Francisco, 151 Cal.App.2d 133, 143, 311 P.2d 158, 164 (1957).

Applying this standard, the cases have rejected a variety of business records on the ground that they were not based on the personal knowledge of the recorder or of someone with a business duty to report to the recorder. Police accident and arrest reports are usually held inadmissible because they are based on the narrations of persons who have no business duty to report to the police. MacLean v. City & County of San Francisco, 151 Cal.App.2d 133, 311 P.2d 158 (1957); Hoel v. City of Los Angeles, 136 Cal.App.2d 295, 288 P.2d 989 (1955). They are admissible, however, to prove the fact of the arrest. Harris v. Alcoholic Bev. Con. Appeals Bd., 212 Cal.App.2d 106, 23 Cal.Rptr. 74 (1963). Similar investigative reports on the origin of fires have been held inadmissible because they were not based on personal knowledge. Behr v. County of Santa Cruz, 172 Cal.App.2d 697, 342 P.2d 987 (1959); Harrigan v. Chaperon, 118 Cal.App.2d 167, 257 P.2d 716 (1953).

Section 1271 will continue the law developed in these cases that a business report is admissible only if the sources of information and the time and method of preparation are such as to indicate its trustworthiness. [7 Cal.L.Rev.Comm. Reports 1 (1965)].

Research References

Rutter, Cal. Practice Guide: Civ. Pro. Before Trial Ch. 8E-6, Subpoena to Nonparty Deponent or Business Records Custodian.
Rutter, Cal. Practice Guide: Civil Trials & Evidence Ch. 1-C, C. Marshalling the Evidence.
Rutter, Cal. Practice Guide: Civil Trials & Evidence Ch. 8D-C, C. General Parameters Re Admissibility of Hearsay Evidence.
Rutter, Cal. Practice Guide: Civil Trials & Evidence Ch. 8D-D, D. Hearsay Exceptions.
Rutter, Cal. Practice Guide: Civil Trials & Evidence Ch. 8G-A, A. Objections and Motions Challenging Admissibility.
Rutter, Cal. Practice Guide: Civil Trials & Evidence Ch. 8G-C, C. Presumptions.
Rutter, Cal. Practice Guide: Enforcing Judgments/Debts Ch. 3-C, C. Prelawsuit Considerations.
Rutter, Cal. Practice Guide: Enforcing Judgments/Debts Ch. 4-A, A. Attachment.
Rutter, Cal. Practice Guide: Landlord-Tenant Ch. 7-C, C. Bases for Terminating Tenancy.
Rutter, Cal. Practice Guide: Landlord-Tenant Ch. 9-C, C. Final Preparation for Trial.
Rutter, Cal. Practice Guide: Landlord-Tenant Ch. 9-E, E. Trial of the Case-Selected Evidentiary Issues.

6 Witkin Cal. Proc. 5th Proceedings Without Trial § 226, Admissibility of Evidence Recited.

§ 1272. Absence of entry in business records

Evidence of the absence from the records of a business of a record of an asserted act, condition, or event is not made inadmissible by the hearsay rule when offered to prove the nonoccurrence of the act or event, or the nonexistence of the condition, if:

(a) It was the regular course of that business to make records of all such acts, conditions, or events at or near the time of the act, condition, or event and to preserve them; and

(b) The sources of information and method and time of preparation of the records of that business were such that the absence of a record of an act, condition, or event is a trustworthy indication that the act or event did not occur or the condition did not exist. *(Stats.1965, c. 299, § 2, operative Jan. 1, 1967.)*

Law Revision Commission Comments

Technically, evidence of the absence of a record may not be hearsay. Section 1272 removes any doubt that might otherwise exist concerning the admissibility of such evidence under the hearsay rule. It codifies existing case law. People v. Torres, 201 Cal.App.2d 290, 20 Cal.Rptr. 315 (1962). [7 Cal.L.Rev.Comm. Reports 1 (1965)].

Research References

Rutter, Cal. Practice Guide: Civ. Pro. Before Trial Ch. 9(II)-D, D. Attachment.
Rutter, Cal. Practice Guide: Civil Trials & Evidence Ch. 8D-D, D. Hearsay Exceptions.
Rutter, Cal. Practice Guide: Personal Injury Ch. 3-C, C. Specific Items of Compensatory Damages.
Rutter, Cal. Practice Guide: Personal Injury Ch. 9-I, I. Use of Writings, Exhibits and Demonstrative Evidence.

ARTICLE 8. OFFICIAL RECORDS AND OTHER OFFICIAL WRITINGS

Section
1280. Record by public employee.
1281. Vital statistics records.
1282. Finding of presumed death by authorized federal employee.
1283. Record by federal employee that person is missing, captured, beleaguered, besieged, detained, or dead.
1284. Statement of absence of public record.

§ 1280. Record by public employee

Evidence of a writing made as a record of an act, condition, or event is not made inadmissible by the hearsay rule when offered in any civil or criminal proceeding to prove the act, condition, or event if all of the following applies:

(a) The writing was made by and within the scope of duty of a public employee.

(b) The writing was made at or near the time of the act, condition, or event.

(c) The sources of information and method and time of preparation were such as to indicate its trustworthiness. *(Stats. 1965, c. 299, § 2, operative Jan. 1, 1967. Amended by Stats.1996, c. 642 (A.B.1387), § 4.)*

Law Revision Commission Comments

Section 1280 restates the substance of and supersedes Sections 1920 and 1926 of the Code of Civil Procedure. Although Sections 1920 and 1926 declare unequivocally that entries in public records are prima facie evidence of the facts stated, "it has been held repeatedly that those sections cannot have universal literal application." Chandler v. Hibberd, 165 Cal.App.2d 39, 65, 332 P.2d 133, 149 (1958). In fact, the cases require the same showing of trustworthiness in regard to an official record as is required under the business records exception. Behr v. County of Santa Cruz, 172 Cal.App.2d 697, 342 P.2d 987 (1959); Hoel v. City of Los Angeles, 136 Cal.App.2d 295, 288 P.2d 989 (1955). Section 1280 continues the law declared in these cases by explicitly requiring the same showing of trustworthiness that is required in Section 1271. See the Comment to Section 1271.

The evidence that is admissible under this section is also admissible under Section 1271, the business records exception. However, Section 1271 requires a witness to testify as to the identity of the record and its mode of preparation in every instance. In contrast, Section 1280, as does existing law, permits the court to admit an official record or report without necessarily requiring a witness to testify as to its identity and mode of preparation if the court takes judicial notice or if sufficient independent evidence shows that the record or report was prepared in such a manner as to assure its trustworthiness. See, e.g., People v. Williams, 64 Cal. 87, 27 Pac. 939 (1883) (census report admitted, the court judicially noticing the statutes prescribing the method of preparing the report); Vallejo etc. R.R. v. Reed Orchard Co., 169 Cal. 545, 571, 147 Pac. 238, 250 (1915) (statistical report of state agency admitted, the court judicially noticing the statutory duty to prepare the report). [7 Cal.L.Rev.Comm. Reports 1 (1965)].

Research References

Rutter, Cal. Practice Guide: Civil Trials & Evidence Ch. 8D-C, C. General Parameters Re Admissibility of Hearsay Evidence.
Rutter, Cal. Practice Guide: Civil Trials & Evidence Ch. 8D-D, D. Hearsay Exceptions.
California Practice Guide: Employment Litigation Ch. 19-N, N. Evidence Issues.
Rutter, Cal. Practice Guide: Family Law Ch. 19-A, A. Validity of Marriage.
Rutter, Cal. Practice Guide: Landlord-Tenant Ch. 9-E, E. Trial of the Case-Selected Evidentiary Issues.
20 NO. 4 Miller & Starr, California Real Estate Newsalert 41, Regulation of the Real Estate Industry.

§ 1281. Vital statistics records

Evidence of a writing made as a record of a birth, fetal death, death, or marriage is not made inadmissible by the hearsay rule if the maker was required by law to file the writing in a designated public office and the writing was made and filed as required by law. (Stats.1965, c. 299, § 2, operative Jan. 1, 1967.)

Law Revision Commission Comments

Section 1281 provides a hearsay exception for official reports concerning birth, death, and marriage. Official reports of such events occurring within California are now admissible under the provisions of Section 10577 [103550] of the Health and Safety Code. Section 1281 provides a broader exception which includes similar reports from other jurisdictions. [7 Cal.L.Rev.Comm. Reports 1 (1965)].

Research References

Rutter, Cal. Practice Guide: Civil Trials & Evidence Ch. 8D-D, D. Hearsay Exceptions.
Rutter, Cal. Practice Guide: Family Law Ch. 19-A, A. Validity of Marriage.
Rutter, Cal. Practice Guide: Insurance Litigation Ch. 6C-B, B. Accidental Death Insurance.

§ 1282. Finding of presumed death by authorized federal employee

A written finding of presumed death made by an employee of the United States authorized to make such finding pursuant to the Federal Missing Persons Act (56 Stats. 143, 1092, and P.L. 408, Ch. 371, 2d Sess. 78th Cong.; 50 U.S.C. App. 1001–1016), as enacted or as heretofore or hereafter amended, shall be received in any court, office, or other place in this state as evidence of the death of the person therein found to be dead and of the date, circumstances, and place of his disappearance. (Stats.1965, c. 299, § 2, operative Jan. 1, 1967.)

Law Revision Commission Comments

Section 1282 restates and supersedes the provisions of Code of Civil Procedure Section 1928.1. The evidence made admissible under Section 1282 is limited to evidence of the fact of death and of the date, circumstances, and place of disappearance.

The determination by the federal employee of the date of the presumed death is a determination ordinarily made for the purpose of determining whether the pay of a missing person should be stopped and his name stricken from the payroll. The date so determined should not be given any consideration in the California courts since the issues involved in the California proceedings require determination of the date of death for a different purpose. Hence, Section 1282 does not make admissible the finding of the date of presumed death. On the other hand, the determination of the date, circumstances, and place of disappearance is reliable information that will assist the trier of fact in determining the date when the person died and is admissible under this section. Often the date of death may be inferred from the circumstances of the disappearance. See In re Thornburg's Estate, 186 Ore. 570, 208 P.2d 349 (1949); Lukens v. Camden Trust Co., 2 N.J.Super. 214, 62 A.2d 886 (Super.Ct.1948).

Section 1282 provides a convenient and reliable method of proof of death of persons covered by the Federal Missing Persons Act. See, e.g., In re Jacobsen's Estate, 208 Misc. 443, 143 N.Y.S.2d 432 (1955) (proof of death of 2-year-old dependent of serviceman where child was passenger on plane lost at sea). [7 Cal.L.Rev.Comm. Reports 1 (1965)].

Research References

Rutter, Cal. Practice Guide: Civil Trials & Evidence Ch. 8D-D, D. Hearsay Exceptions.

§ 1283. Record by federal employee that person is missing, captured, beleaguered, besieged, detained, or dead

An official written report or record that a person is missing, missing in action, interned in a foreign country, captured by a hostile force, beleaguered by a hostile force, besieged by a hostile force, or detained in a foreign country against his will, or is dead or is alive, made by an employee of the United States authorized by any law of the United States to make such report or record shall be received in any court, office, or other place in this state as evidence that such person is missing, missing in action, interned in a foreign country, captured by a hostile force, beleaguered by a hostile force, besieged by a hostile force, or detained in a foreign country against his will, or is dead or is alive. (Stats.1965, c. 299, § 2, operative Jan. 1, 1967.)

Law Revision Commission Comments

Section 1283 restates and supersedes the provisions of Code of Civil Procedure Section 1928.2. The language of Section 1928.2 has been revised to reflect the 1953 and 1964 amendments to the Federal Missing Persons Act. [7 Cal.L.Rev.Comm. Reports 1 (1965)].

Research References

Rutter, Cal. Practice Guide: Civil Trials & Evidence Ch. 8D-D, D. Hearsay Exceptions.
14 Witkin, California Summary 10th Wills and Probate § 948, Where Proposed Conservatee is Absentee.
14 Witkin, California Summary 10th Wills and Probate § 1074, Court Proceeding to Set Aside Property.

§ 1284. Statement of absence of public record

Evidence of a writing made by the public employee who is the official custodian of the records in a public office, reciting diligent search and failure to find a record, is not made inadmissible by the hearsay rule when offered to prove the absence of a record in that office. (Stats.1965, c. 299, § 2, operative Jan. 1, 1967.)

Research References

Rutter, Cal. Practice Guide: Civil Trials & Evidence Ch. 8D-D, D. Hearsay Exceptions.

ARTICLE 9. FORMER TESTIMONY

Section
1290. Former testimony.

§ 1290. Former testimony

As used in this article, "former testimony" means testimony given under oath in:

(a) Another action or in a former hearing or trial of the same action;

(b) A proceeding to determine a controversy conducted by or under the supervision of an agency that has the power to determine such a controversy and is an agency of the United States or a public entity in the United States;

(c) A deposition taken in compliance with law in another action; or

(d) An arbitration proceeding if the evidence of such former testimony is a verbatim transcript thereof. *(Stats.1965, c. 299, § 2, operative Jan. 1, 1967.)*

Law Revision Commission Comments

The purpose of Section 1290 is to provide a convenient term for use in the substantive provisions in the remainder of this article. It should be noted that depositions taken in *another* action are considered former testimony under Section 1290, and their admissibility is determined by Sections 1291 and 1292. The use of a deposition taken in the same action, however, is not covered by this article. Code of Civil Procedure Sections 2016–2036 deal comprehensively with the conditions and circumstances under which a deposition taken in a civil action may be used at the trial of the action in which the deposition was taken, and Penal Code Sections 1345 and 1362 prescribe the conditions for admitting the deposition of a witness that has been taken in the same criminal action. These sections will continue to govern the use of depositions in the action in which they are taken. [7 Cal.L.Rev.Comm. Reports 1 (1965)].

Research References

Rutter, Cal. Practice Guide: Civ. Pro. Before Trial Ch. 8E-17, Use of Depositions at Trial.

Rutter, Cal. Practice Guide: Civil Trials & Evidence Ch. 13-B, B. Proper vs. Improper Closing Argument.

Rutter, Cal. Practice Guide: Civil Trials & Evidence Ch. 8D-D, D. Hearsay Exceptions.

§ 1291. Former testimony offered against party to former proceeding

(a) Evidence of former testimony is not made inadmissible by the hearsay rule if the declarant is unavailable as a witness and:

(1) The former testimony is offered against a person who offered it in evidence in his own behalf on the former occasion or against the successor in interest of such person; or

(2) The party against whom the former testimony is offered was a party to the action or proceeding in which the testimony was given and had the right and opportunity to cross-examine the declarant with an interest and motive similar to that which he has at the hearing.

(b) The admissibility of former testimony under this section is subject to the same limitations and objections as though the declarant were testifying at the hearing, except that former testimony offered under this section is not subject to:

(1) Objections to the form of the question which were not made at the time the former testimony was given.

(2) Objections based on competency or privilege which did not exist at the time the former testimony was given. *(Stats. 1965, c. 299, § 2, operative Jan. 1, 1967.)*

Research References

Rutter, Cal. Practice Guide: Civ. Pro. Before Trial Ch. 8E-17, Use of Depositions at Trial.

Rutter, Cal. Practice Guide: Civil Trials & Evidence Ch. 4-B, B. Preliminary Matters Discussed in Final Status Conference or In-Chambers Conference.

Rutter, Cal. Practice Guide: Civil Trials & Evidence Ch. 8C-A, A. Testimony.

Rutter, Cal. Practice Guide: Civil Trials & Evidence Ch. 8C-I, I. Depositions and Discovery.

Rutter, Cal. Practice Guide: Civil Trials & Evidence Ch. 8D-C, C. General Parameters Re Admissibility of Hearsay Evidence.

Rutter, Cal. Practice Guide: Civil Trials & Evidence Ch. 8D-D, D. Hearsay Exceptions.

Rutter, Cal. Practice Guide: Family Law Ch. 13-B, B. Contested Family Law Trial.

Rutter, Cal. Practice Guide: Personal Injury Ch. 9-H, H. Introduction of Discovered Evidence.

§ 1292. Former testimony offered against person not a party to former proceeding

(a) Evidence of former testimony is not made inadmissible by the hearsay rule if:

(1) The declarant is unavailable as a witness;

(2) The former testimony is offered in a civil action; and

(3) The issue is such that the party to the action or proceeding in which the former testimony was given had the right and opportunity to cross-examine the declarant with an interest and motive similar to that which the party against whom the testimony is offered has at the hearing.

(b) The admissibility of former testimony under this section is subject to the same limitations and objections as though the declarant were testifying at the hearing, except that former testimony offered under this section is not subject to objections based on competency or privilege which did not exist at the time the former testimony was given. *(Stats.1965, c. 299, § 2, operative Jan. 1, 1967.)*

Research References

Rutter, Cal. Practice Guide: Civ. Pro. Before Trial Ch. 10-C, C. Procedural Requirements-Moving Party.

Rutter, Cal. Practice Guide: Civil Trials & Evidence Ch. 4-B, B. Preliminary Matters Discussed in Final Status Conference or In-Chambers Conference.

Rutter, Cal. Practice Guide: Civil Trials & Evidence Ch. 13-B, B. Proper vs. Improper Closing Argument.

Rutter, Cal. Practice Guide: Civil Trials & Evidence Ch. 8D-D, D. Hearsay Exceptions.

§ 1293. Former testimony by minor child complaining witness at preliminary examination

(a) Evidence of former testimony made at a preliminary examination by a minor child who was the complaining witness is not made inadmissible by the hearsay rule if:

(1) The former testimony is offered in a proceeding to declare the minor a dependent child of the court pursuant to Section 300 of the Welfare and Institutions Code.

(2) The issues are such that a defendant in the preliminary examination in which the former testimony was given had the right and opportunity to cross-examine the minor child with an interest and motive similar to that which the parent or guardian against whom the testimony is offered has at the proceeding to declare the minor a dependent child of the court.

(b) The admissibility of former testimony under this section is subject to the same limitations and objections as though the

Evidence

minor child were testifying at the proceeding to declare him or her a dependent child of the court.

(c) The attorney for the parent or guardian against whom the former testimony is offered or, if none, the parent or guardian may make a motion to challenge the admissibility of the former testimony upon a showing that new substantially different issues are present in the proceeding to declare the minor a dependent child than were present in the preliminary examination.

(d) As used in this section, "complaining witness" means the alleged victim of the crime for which a preliminary examination was held.

(e) This section shall apply only to testimony made at a preliminary examination on and after January 1, 1990. *(Added by Stats.1989, c. 322, § 1.)*

Research References

Rutter, Cal. Practice Guide: Civil Trials & Evidence Ch. 8D-D, D. Hearsay Exceptions.

§ 1294. Unavailable witnesses; prior inconsistent statements; preliminary hearing or prior proceeding

(a) The following evidence of prior inconsistent statements of a witness properly admitted in a preliminary hearing or trial of the same criminal matter pursuant to Section 1235 is not made inadmissible by the hearsay rule if the witness is unavailable and former testimony of the witness is admitted pursuant to Section 1291:

(1) A video recorded statement introduced at a preliminary hearing or prior proceeding concerning the same criminal matter.

(2) A transcript, containing the statements, of the preliminary hearing or prior proceeding concerning the same criminal matter.

(b) The party against whom the prior inconsistent statements are offered, at his or her option, may examine or cross-examine any person who testified at the preliminary hearing or prior proceeding as to the prior inconsistent statements of the witness. *(Added by Stats.1996, c. 560 (A.B.2483), § 1. Amended by Stats.2009, c. 88 (A.B.176), § 36.)*

Law Revision Commission Comments

Section 1294 is amended to reflect advances in recording technology and for consistency of terminology. For a similar reform, see 2002 Cal. Stat. ch. 1068 (replacing numerous references to "audiotape" in Civil Discovery Act with either "audio technology," "audio recording," or "audio record," as context required). [37 Cal. L. Revision Comm'n Reports 211 (2007)].

Research References

Rutter, Cal. Practice Guide: Civil Trials & Evidence Ch. 8D-D, D. Hearsay Exceptions.

ARTICLE 10. JUDGMENTS

Section
1300. Judgment of conviction of crime punishable as felony.
1301. Judgment against person entitled to indemnity.
1302. Judgment determining liability of third person.

§ 1300. Judgment of conviction of crime punishable as felony

Evidence of a final judgment adjudging a person guilty of a crime punishable as a felony is not made inadmissible by the hearsay rule when offered in a civil action to prove any fact essential to the judgment whether or not the judgment was based on a plea of nolo contendere. *(Stats.1965, c. 299, § 2, operative Jan. 1, 1967. Amended by Stats.1982, c. 390, p. 1724, § 2.)*

Law Revision Commission Comments

Analytically, a judgment that is offered to prove the matters determined by the judgment is hearsay evidence. Uniform Rules of Evidence, Rule 63(20) Comment (1953); Tentative Recommendation and a Study Relating to the Uniform Rules of Evidence (Article VIII. Hearsay Evidence), 6 Cal.Law Revision Comm'n, Rep., Rec. & Studies Appendix at 539–541 (1964). It is in substance a statement of the court that determined the previous action ("a statement that was made other than by a witness while testifying at the hearing") that is offered "to prove the truth of the matter stated." Evidence Code § 1200. Therefore, unless an exception to the hearsay rule is provided, a judgment would be inadmissible if offered in a subsequent action to prove the matters determined.

Of course, a judgment may, as a matter of substantive law, conclusively establish certain facts insofar as a party is concerned. Teitlebaum Furs, Inc. v. Dominion Ins. Co., 58 Cal.2d 601, 25 Cal.Rptr. 559, 375 P.2d 439 (1962); Bernhard v. Bank of America, 19 Cal.2d 807, 122 P.2d 892 (1942). The sections of this article do not purport to deal with the doctrines of res judicata and estoppel by judgment. These sections deal only with the evidentiary use of judgments in those cases where the substantive law does not require that the judgments be given conclusive effect.

Section 1300 provides an exception to the hearsay rule for a final judgment adjudging a person guilty of a crime punishable as a felony. Hence, if a plaintiff sues to recover a reward offered by the defendant for the arrest and conviction of a person who committed a particular crime, Section 1300 permits the plaintiff to use a judgment of conviction as evidence that the person convicted committed the crime. The exception does not, however, apply in criminal actions. Thus, Section 1300 does not permit the judgment to be used in a criminal action as evidence of the identity of the person who committed the crime or as evidence that the crime was committed.

Section 1300 will change the California law. Under existing law, a conviction of a crime is inadmissible as evidence in a subsequent action. Marceau v. Travelers' Ins. Co., 101 Cal. 338, 35 Pac. 856 (1894) (evidence of a murder conviction held inadmissible to prove the insured was intentionally killed); Burke v. Wells, Fargo & Co., 34 Cal. 60 (1867) (evidence of a robbery conviction held inadmissible to prove the identity of robber in an action to recover reward). The change, however, is desirable, for the evidence involved is peculiarly reliable. The seriousness of the charge assures that the facts will be thoroughly litigated, and the fact that the judgment must be based upon a determination that there was no reasonable doubt concerning the defendant's guilt assures that the question of guilt will be thoroughly considered.

Section 1300 applies to any crime punishable as a felony. The fact that a misdemeanor sentence is imposed does not affect the admissibility of the judgment of a conviction under this section. *Cf.* Penal Code § 17. The exclusion of judgments based on a plea of nolo contendere from the exception in Section 1300 is a reflection of the policy expressed in Penal Code Section 1016. [7 Cal.L.Rev.Comm. Reports 1 (1965)].

Research References

Rutter, Cal. Practice Guide: Civil Trials & Evidence Ch. 8D-D, D. Hearsay Exceptions.
California Practice Guide: Employment Litigation Ch. 13-H, H. Contesting Citations and Related Orders and Notices.
Rutter, Cal. Practice Guide: Insurance Litigation Ch. 15-K, K. Judgment Creditor's Action to Enforce Judgment Debtor's Liability Insurance (INS.C. § 11580(B)(2)).
Rutter, Cal. Practice Guide: Insurance Litigation Ch. 6C-A, A. Life Insurance.

§ 1301. Judgment against person entitled to indemnity

Evidence of a final judgment is not made inadmissible by the hearsay rule when offered by the judgment debtor to prove any fact which was essential to the judgment in an action in which he seeks to:

(a) Recover partial or total indemnity or exoneration for money paid or liability incurred because of the judgment;

(b) Enforce a warranty to protect the judgment debtor against the liability determined by the judgment; or

(c) Recover damages for breach of warranty substantially the same as the warranty determined by the judgment to have been breached. *(Stats.1965, c. 299, § 2, operative Jan. 1, 1967.)*

Law Revision Commission Comments

If a person entitled to indemnity, or if the obligee under a warranty contract, complies with certain conditions relating to notice and defense, the indemnitor or warrantor is conclusively bound by any judgment recovered. Civil Code § 2778 (5); Code Civ.Proc. § 1912; McCormick v. Marcy, 165 Cal. 386, 132 Pac. 449 (1913).

Where a judgment against an indemnitee or person protected by a warranty is not made conclusive on the indemnitor or warrantor, Section 1301 permits the judgment to be used as hearsay evidence in an action to recover on the indemnity or warranty. Section 1301 reflects the existing law relating to indemnity agreements. Civil Code § 2778(6). Section 1301 probably restates the law relating to warranties, too, but the law in that regard is not altogether clear. Erio City Iron Works v. Tatum, 1 Cal.App. 286, 82 Pac. 92 (1905). *But see* Peabody v. Phelps, 9 Cal. 213 (1858). [7 Cal.L.Rev.Comm. Reports 1 (1965)].

Research References

Rutter, Cal. Practice Guide: Civil Trials & Evidence Ch. 8D-D, D. Hearsay Exceptions.

§ 1302. Judgment determining liability of third person

When the liability, obligation, or duty of a third person is in issue in a civil action, evidence of a final judgment against that person is not made inadmissible by the hearsay rule when offered to prove such liability, obligation, or duty. *(Stats.1965, c. 299, § 2, operative Jan. 1, 1967.)*

Law Revision Commission Comments

Section 1302 expresses an exception contained in Code of Civil Procedure Section 1851. Ellsworth v. Bradford, 186 Cal. 316, 199 Pac. 335 (1921); Nordin v. Bank of America, 11 Cal.App.2d 98, 52 P.2d 1018 (1936). Evidence Code Sections 1302 and 1224 together restate and supersede the provisions of Code of Civil Procedure Section 1851. [7 Cal.L.Rev.Comm. Reports 1 (1965)].

Research References

Rutter, Cal. Practice Guide: Civil Trials & Evidence Ch. 8D-D, D. Hearsay Exceptions.

ARTICLE 11. FAMILY HISTORY

Section
1310. Statement concerning declarant's own family history.
1311. Statement concerning family history of another.
1312. Entries in family records and the like.
1313. Reputation in family concerning family history.
1314. Reputation in community concerning family history.
1315. Church records concerning family history.
1316. Marriage, baptismal and similar certificates.

§ 1310. Statement concerning declarant's own family history

(a) Subject to subdivision (b), evidence of a statement by a declarant who is unavailable as a witness concerning his own birth, marriage, divorce, a parent and child relationship, relationship by blood or marriage, race, ancestry, or other similar fact of his family history is not made inadmissible by the hearsay rule, even though the declarant had no means of acquiring personal knowledge of the matter declared.

(b) Evidence of a statement is inadmissible under this section if the statement was made under circumstances such as to indicate its lack of trustworthiness. *(Stats.1965, c. 299, § 2, operative Jan. 1, 1967. Amended by Stats.1975, c. 1244, p. 3202, § 15.)*

Law Revision Commission Comments

Section 1310 provides a hearsay exception for a statement concerning the declarant's own family history. It restates in substance and supersedes Section 1870(4) of the Code of Civil Procedure. Section 1870(4), however, requires that the declarant be dead whereas unavailability of the declarant for any of the reasons specified in Section 240 makes the statement admissible under Section 1310.

The statement is not admissible if it was made under circumstances such as to indicate its lack of trustworthiness. The requirement is similar to the requirement of existing case law that the statement be made at a time when no controversy existed as to the matters stated. See, *e.g.*, Estate of Walden, 166 Cal. 446, 137 Pac. 35 (1913); Estate of Nidever, 181 Cal.App.2d 367, 5 Cal.Rptr. 343 (1960). However, the language of Section 1310 permits the judge to consider the declarant's motives to tell the truth as well as his reasons to deviate therefrom in determining whether the statement is sufficiently trustworthy to be admitted as evidence. [7 Cal.L.Rev.Comm. Reports 1 (1965)].

Research References

Rutter, Cal. Practice Guide: Civil Trials & Evidence Ch. 8D-C, C. General Parameters Re Admissibility of Hearsay Evidence.
Rutter, Cal. Practice Guide: Civil Trials & Evidence Ch. 8D-D, D. Hearsay Exceptions.
Rutter, Cal. Practice Guide: Family Law Ch. 19-A, A. Validity of Marriage.

§ 1311. Statement concerning family history of another

(a) Subject to subdivision (b), evidence of a statement concerning the birth, marriage, divorce, death, parent and child relationship, race, ancestry, relationship by blood or marriage, or other similar fact of the family history of a person other than the declarant is not made inadmissible by the hearsay rule if the declarant is unavailable as a witness and:

(1) The declarant was related to the other by blood or marriage; or

(2) The declarant was otherwise so intimately associated with the other's family as to be likely to have had accurate information concerning the matter declared and made the statement (i) upon information received from the other or from a person related by blood or marriage to the other or (ii) upon repute in the other's family.

(b) Evidence of a statement is inadmissible under this section if the statement was made under circumstances such as to indicate its lack of trustworthiness. *(Stats.1965, c. 299, § 2, operative Jan. 1, 1967. Amended by Stats.1975, c. 1244, p. 3202, § 16.)*

Law Revision Commission Comments

Section 1311 provides a hearsay exception for a statement concerning the family history of another. Paragraph (1) of subdivision (a) restates in substance existing law as found in Section 1870(4) of the Code of Civil Procedure which it supersedes. Paragraph (2) is new to California law, but it is a sound extension of the present law to cover a situation where the declarant was a family housekeeper or doctor or so close a friend as to be included by the family in discussions of its family history.

There are two limitations on admissibility of a statement under Section 1311. *First*, a statement is admissible only if the declarant is unavailable as a witness within the meaning of Section 240. (Section 1870(4) requires that the declarant be deceased in order for his statement to be admissible.) *Second*, a statement is not admissible if it was made under circumstances such as to indicate its lack of trustworthiness. For a discussion of this requirement, see the Comment to Evidence Code § 1310. [7 Cal.L.Rev.Comm. Reports 1 (1965)].

Research References

Rutter, Cal. Practice Guide: Civil Trials & Evidence Ch. 8D-C, C. General Parameters Re Admissibility of Hearsay Evidence.
Rutter, Cal. Practice Guide: Civil Trials & Evidence Ch. 8D-D, D. Hearsay Exceptions.
Rutter, Cal. Practice Guide: Family Law Ch. 19-A, A. Validity of Marriage.

§ 1312. Entries in family records and the like

Evidence of entries in family Bibles or other family books or charts, engravings on rings, family portraits, engravings on urns, crypts, or tombstones, and the like, is not made inadmissible by the hearsay rule when offered to prove the birth, marriage, divorce, death, parent and child relationship, race, ancestry, relationship by blood or marriage, or other similar fact of the family history of a member of the family by blood or marriage. *(Stats.1965, c. 299, § 2, operative Jan. 1, 1967. Amended by Stats.1975, c. 1244, p. 3202, § 17.)*

Law Revision Commission Comments

Section 1312 restates the substance of and supersedes the provisions of Code of Civil Procedure Section 1870(13). [7 Cal.L.Rev.Comm. Reports 1 (1965)].

Research References

Rutter, Cal. Practice Guide: Civil Trials & Evidence Ch. 8D-D, D. Hearsay Exceptions.

Rutter, Cal. Practice Guide: Family Law Ch. 19-A, A. Validity of Marriage.

§ 1313. Reputation in family concerning family history

Evidence of reputation among members of a family is not made inadmissible by the hearsay rule if the reputation concerns the birth, marriage, divorce, death, parent and child relationship, race, ancestry, relationship by blood or marriage, or other similar fact of the family history of a member of the family by blood or marriage. *(Stats.1965, c. 299, § 2, operative Jan. 1, 1967. Amended by Stats.1975, c. 1244, p. 3202, § 18.)*

Law Revision Commission Comments

Section 1313 restates the substance of and supersedes the provisions of Code of Civil Procedure Sections 1852 and 1870(11). See Estate of Connors, 53 Cal.App.2d 484, 128 P.2d 200 (1942); Estate of Newman, 34 Cal.App.2d 706, 94 P.2d 356 (1939). However, Section 1870(11) requires the family reputation in question to have existed "previous to the controversy." This qualification is not included in Section 1313 because it is unlikely that a family reputation on a matter of pedigree would be influenced by the existence of a controversy even though the declaration of an individual member of the family, covered in Sections 1310 and 1311, might be.

The family reputation admitted under Section 1313 is necessarily multiple hearsay. If, however, such reputation were inadmissible because of the hearsay rule, and if direct statements of pedigree were inadmissible because they are based on such reputation (as most of them are), the courts would be virtually helpless in determining matters of pedigree. See Tentative Recommendation and a Study Relating to the Uniform Rules of Evidence (Article VIII. Hearsay Evidence), 6 Cal.Law Revision Comm'n, Rep., Rec. & Studies Appendix at 548 (1964). [7 Cal.L.Rev.Comm. Reports 1 (1965)].

Research References

Rutter, Cal. Practice Guide: Civil Trials & Evidence Ch. 8D-D, D. Hearsay Exceptions.

§ 1314. Reputation in community concerning family history

Evidence of reputation in a community concerning the date or fact of birth, marriage, divorce, or death of a person resident in the community at the time of the reputation is not made inadmissible by the hearsay rule. *(Stats.1965, c. 299, § 2, operative Jan. 1, 1967.)*

Law Revision Commission Comments

Section 1314 restates what has been held to be existing law under Code of Civil Procedure Section 1963(30) with respect to proof of the fact of marriage. See People v. Vogel, 46 Cal.2d 798, 299 P.2d 850 (1956); Estate of Baldwin, 162 Cal. 471, 123 Pac. 267 (1912). However, Section 1314 has no counterpart in California law insofar as proof of the date or fact of birth, divorce, or death is concerned, since proof of such facts by reputation is presently limited to reputation in the family. See Estate of Heaton, 135 Cal. 385, 67 Pac. 321 (1902). [7 Cal.L.Rev.Comm. Reports 1 (1965)].

Research References

Rutter, Cal. Practice Guide: Civil Trials & Evidence Ch. 8D-D, D. Hearsay Exceptions.

Rutter, Cal. Practice Guide: Family Law Ch. 19-A, A. Validity of Marriage.

11 Witkin, California Summary 10th Husband and Wife § 53, (S 53) in General.

§ 1315. Church records concerning family history

Evidence of a statement concerning a person's birth, marriage, divorce, death, parent and child relationship, race, ancestry, relationship by blood or marriage, or other similar fact of family history which is contained in a writing made as a record of a church, religious denomination, or religious society is not made inadmissible by the hearsay rule if:

(a) The statement is contained in a writing made as a record of an act, condition, or event that would be admissible as evidence of such act, condition, or event under Section 1271; and

(b) The statement is of a kind customarily recorded in connection with the act, condition, or event recorded in the writing. *(Stats.1965, c. 299, § 2, operative Jan. 1, 1967. Amended by Stats.1975, c. 1244, p. 3203, § 19.)*

Law Revision Commission Comments

Church records generally are admissible as business records under the provisions of Section 1271. Under Section 1271, such records would be admissible to prove the occurrence of the church activity—the baptism, confirmation, or marriage—recorded in the writing. However, it is unlikely that Section 1271 would permit such records to be used as evidence of the age or relationship of the participants, for the business records act has been held to authorize business records to be used to prove only facts known personally to the recorder of the information or to other employees of the business. Patek & Co. v. Vineberg, 210 Cal.App.2d 20, 23, 26 Cal.Rptr. 293, 294 (1962) (hearing denied); People v. Williams, 187 Cal.App.2d 355, 9 Cal.Rptr. 722 (1960); Gough v. Security Trust & Sav. Bank, 162 Cal.App.2d 90, 327 P.2d 555 (1958). Section 1315 permits church records to be used to prove certain additional information. Facts of family history, such as birth dates, relationships, marital histories, etc., that are ordinarily reported to church authorities and recorded in connection with the church's baptismal, confirmation, marriage, and funeral records may be proved by such records under Section 1315.

Section 1315 continues in effect and supersedes the provisions of Code of Civil Procedure Section 1919a without, however, the special and cumbersome authentication procedure specified in Code of Civil Procedure Section 1919b. Under Section 1315, church records may be authenticated in the same manner that other business records are authenticated. [7 Cal.L.Rev.Comm. Reports 1 (1965)].

Research References

Rutter, Cal. Practice Guide: Civil Trials & Evidence Ch. 8D-D, D. Hearsay Exceptions.

Rutter, Cal. Practice Guide: Family Law Ch. 19-A, A. Validity of Marriage.

§ 1316. Marriage, baptismal and similar certificates

Evidence of a statement concerning a person's birth, marriage, divorce, death, parent and child relationship, race, ancestry, relationship by blood or marriage, or other similar fact of family history is not made inadmissible by the hearsay rule if the statement is contained in a certificate that the maker thereof performed a marriage or other ceremony or administered a sacrament and:

(a) The maker was a clergyman, civil officer, or other person authorized to perform the acts reported in the certificate by law or by the rules, regulations, or requirements of a church, religious denomination, or religious society; and

(b) The certificate was issued by the maker at the time and place of the ceremony or sacrament or within a reasonable time thereafter. *(Stats.1965, c. 299, § 2, operative Jan. 1, 1967. Amended by Stats.1975, c. 1244, p. 3203, § 20.)*

Law Revision Commission Comments

Section 1316 provides a hearsay exception for marriage, baptismal, and similar certificates. This exception is somewhat broader than that found in Sections 1919a and 1919b of the Code of Civil Procedure (superseded by Evidence Code Sections 1315 and 1316). Sections 1919a and 1919b are limited to church records and, hence, with respect to marriages, to those performed by clergymen. Moreover, they establish an elaborate and detailed authentication procedure, whereas certificates made admissible by Section 1316 need meet only the general authentication requirement of Section 1401. [7 Cal.L.Rev.Comm. Reports 1 (1965)].

Research References

Rutter, Cal. Practice Guide: Civil Trials & Evidence Ch. 8D-D, D. Hearsay Exceptions.
Rutter, Cal. Practice Guide: Family Law Ch. 19-A, A. Validity of Marriage.

ARTICLE 12. REPUTATION AND STATEMENTS CONCERNING COMMUNITY HISTORY, PROPERTY INTERESTS, AND CHARACTER

Section
1320. Reputation concerning community history.
1321. Reputation concerning public interest in property.
1322. Reputation concerning boundary or custom affecting land.
1323. Statement concerning boundary.
1324. Reputation concerning character.

§ 1320. Reputation concerning community history

Evidence of reputation in a community is not made inadmissible by the hearsay rule if the reputation concerns an event of general history of the community or of the state or nation of which the community is a part and the event was of importance to the community. *(Stats.1965, c. 299, § 2, operative Jan. 1, 1967.)*

Law Revision Commission Comments

Section 1320 provides a wider rule of admissibility than does Code of Civil Procedure Section 1870(11) which it supersedes in part. Section 1870 provides in relevant part that proof may be made of "common reputation existing previous to the controversy, respecting facts of a public or general interest more than thirty years old." The 30-year limitation is essentially arbitrary. The important question would seem to be whether a community reputation on the matter involved exists; its age would appear to go more to its venerability than to its truth. Nor is it necessary to include in Section 1320 the requirement that the reputation existed previous to controversy. It is unlikely that a community reputation respecting an event of general history would be influenced by the existence of a controversy. [7 Cal.L.Rev.Comm. Reports 1 (1965)].

Research References

Rutter, Cal. Practice Guide: Civil Trials & Evidence Ch. 8D-D, D. Hearsay Exceptions.

§ 1321. Reputation concerning public interest in property

Evidence of reputation in a community is not made inadmissible by the hearsay rule if the reputation concerns the interest of the public in property in the community and the reputation arose before controversy. *(Stats.1965, c. 299, § 2, operative Jan. 1, 1967.)*

Law Revision Commission Comments

Section 1321 preserves the rule in Simons v. Inyo Cerro Gordo Co., 48 Cal.App. 524, 192 Pac. 144 (1920). It does not require, however, that the reputation be more than 30 years old; it requires merely that the reputation arose before there was a controversy concerning the matter.

See the Comment to Section 1320. [7 Cal.L.Rev.Comm. Reports 1 (1965)].

Research References

Rutter, Cal. Practice Guide: Civil Trials & Evidence Ch. 8D-D, D. Hearsay Exceptions.

§ 1322. Reputation concerning boundary or custom affecting land

Evidence of reputation in a community is not made inadmissible by the hearsay rule if the reputation concerns boundaries of, or customs affecting, land in the community and the reputation arose before controversy. *(Stats.1965, c. 299, § 2, operative Jan. 1, 1967.)*

Law Revision Commission Comments

Section 1322 restates the substance of existing law as found in Code of Civil Procedure Section 1870(11) which it supersedes in part. See Muller v. So. Pac. Branch Ry., 83 Cal. 240, 23 Pac. 265 (1890); Ferris v. Emmons, 214 Cal. 501, 6 P.2d 950 (1931). [7 Cal.L.Rev.Comm. Reports 1 (1965)].

Research References

Rutter, Cal. Practice Guide: Civil Trials & Evidence Ch. 8D-D, D. Hearsay Exceptions.

§ 1323. Statement concerning boundary

Evidence of a statement concerning the boundary of land is not made inadmissible by the hearsay rule if the declarant is unavailable as a witness and had sufficient knowledge of the subject, but evidence of a statement is not admissible under this section if the statement was made under circumstances such as to indicate its lack of trustworthiness. *(Stats.1965, c. 299, § 2, operative Jan. 1, 1967.)*

Law Revision Commission Comments

Section 1323 codifies existing law found in such cases as Morton v. Folger, 15 Cal. 275 (1860), and Morcom v. Baiersky, 16 Cal.App. 480, 117 Pac. 560 (1911). [7 Cal.L.Rev.Comm. Reports 1 (1965)].

Research References

Rutter, Cal. Practice Guide: Civil Trials & Evidence Ch. 8D-D, D. Hearsay Exceptions.

§ 1324. Reputation concerning character

Evidence of a person's general reputation with reference to his character or a trait of his character at a relevant time in the community in which he then resided or in a group with which he then habitually associated is not made inadmissible by the hearsay rule. *(Stats.1965, c. 299, § 2, operative Jan. 1, 1967.)*

Law Revision Commission Comments

Section 1324 codifies a well-settled exception to the hearsay rule. See, *e.g.,* People v. Cobb, 45 Cal.2d 158, 287 P.2d 752 (1955). Of course, character evidence is admissible only when the question of character is material to the matter being litigated. The only purpose of Section 1324 is to declare that reputation evidence as to character or a trait of character is not inadmissible under the hearsay rule. [7 Cal.L.Rev.Comm. Reports 1 (1965)].

Research References

Rutter, Cal. Practice Guide: Civil Trials & Evidence Ch. 8D-D, D. Hearsay Exceptions.
Rutter, Cal. Practice Guide: Civil Trials & Evidence Ch. 8E-E, E. Limitations on Character Evidence.

ARTICLE 13. DISPOSITIVE INSTRUMENTS AND ANCIENT WRITINGS

Section
1330. Recitals in writings affecting property.
1331. Recitals in ancient writings.

Evidence

§ 1330. Recitals in writings affecting property

Evidence of a statement contained in a deed of conveyance or a will or other writing purporting to affect an interest in real or personal property is not made inadmissible by the hearsay rule if:

(a) The matter stated was relevant to the purpose of the writing;

(b) The matter stated would be relevant to an issue as to an interest in the property; and

(c) The dealings with the property since the statement was made have not been inconsistent with the truth of the statement. *(Stats.1965, c. 299, § 2, operative Jan. 1, 1967.)*

Law Revision Commission Comments

Section 1330 restates the substance of existing California law relating to recitals in dispositive instruments. Although language in some cases appears to require that the dispositive instrument be ancient, cases may be found in which recitals in dispositive instruments have been admitted without regard to the age of the instrument. See Russell v. Langford, 135 Cal. 356, 67 Pac. 331 (1902) (recital in will); Pearson v. Pearson, 46 Cal. 609 (1873) (recital in will); Culver v. Newhart, 18 Cal.App. 614, 123 Pac. 975 (1912) (bill of sale). There is a sufficient likelihood that the statements made in a dispositive document, when related to the purpose of the document, will be true to warrant the admissibility of such documents without regard to their age. [7 Cal.L.Rev.Comm. Reports 1 (1965)].

Research References

Rutter, Cal. Practice Guide: Civil Trials & Evidence Ch. 8D-D, D. Hearsay Exceptions.

§ 1331. Recitals in ancient writings

Evidence of a statement is not made inadmissible by the hearsay rule if the statement is contained in a writing more than 30 years old and the statement has been since generally acted upon as true by persons having an interest in the matter. *(Stats.1965, c. 299, § 2, operative Jan. 1, 1967.)*

Law Revision Commission Comments

Section 1331 clarifies the existing law relating to the admissibility of recitals in ancient documents by providing that such recitals are admissible under an exception to the hearsay rule. Code of Civil Procedure Section 1963(34) (superseded by the Evidence Code) provides that a document more than 30 years old is presumed genuine if it has been generally acted upon as genuine by persons having an interest in the matter. The Supreme Court has held that a document meeting this section's requirements is presumed to be genuine—presumed to be what it purports to be—but that the genuineness of the document imports no verity to the recitals contained therein. Gwin v. Calegaris, 139 Cal. 384, 389, 73 Pac. 851, 853 (1903). Recent cases decided by district courts of appeal, however, have held that the recitals in such a document are admissible to prove the truth of the facts recited. Estate of Nidever, 181 Cal.App.2d 367, 5 Cal.Rptr. 343 (1960); Kirkpatrick v. Tapo Oil Co., 144 Cal.App.2d 404, 301 P.2d 274 (1956). In these latter cases, the courts have not insisted that the hearsay statement itself be acted upon as true by persons with an interest in the matter; the evidence has been admitted merely upon a showing that the document containing the statement is genuine. The age of a document alone is not a sufficient guarantee of the trustworthiness of a statement contained therein to warrant the admission of the statement into evidence. Accordingly, Section 1331 makes it clear that the statement itself must have been generally acted upon as true for at least 30 years by persons having an interest in the matter. [7 Cal.L.Rev.Comm. Reports 1 (1965)].

Research References

Rutter, Cal. Practice Guide: Civil Trials & Evidence Ch. 8D-D, D. Hearsay Exceptions.

Rutter, Cal. Practice Guide: Civil Trials & Evidence Ch. 8G-A, A. Objections and Motions Challenging Admissibility.

ARTICLE 14. COMMERCIAL, SCIENTIFIC, AND SIMILAR PUBLICATIONS

Section
1340. Publications relied upon as accurate in the course of business.
1341. Publications concerning facts of general notoriety and interests.

§ 1340. Publications relied upon as accurate in the course of business

Evidence of a statement, other than an opinion, contained in a tabulation, list, directory, register, or other published compilation is not made inadmissible by the hearsay rule if the compilation is generally used and relied upon as accurate in the course of a business as defined in Section 1270. *(Stats.1965, c. 299, § 2, operative Jan. 1, 1967.)*

Law Revision Commission Comments

Section 1340 codifies an exception that has been recognized by statute and by the courts in specific situations. See, *e.g.*, Com.Code § 2724; Emery v. So. Cal. Gas Co., 72 Cal.App.2d 821, 165 P.2d 695 (1946); Christiansen v. Hollings, 44 Cal.App.2d 332, 112 P.2d 723 (1941). [7 Cal.L.Rev.Comm. Reports 1 (1965)].

Research References

Rutter, Cal. Practice Guide: Civil Trials & Evidence Ch. 8D-D, D. Hearsay Exceptions.

§ 1341. Publications concerning facts of general notoriety and interests

Historical works, books of science or art, and published maps or charts, made by persons indifferent between the parties, are not made inadmissible by the hearsay rule when offered to prove facts of general notoriety and interest. *(Stats.1965, c. 299, § 2, operative Jan. 1, 1967.)*

Law Revision Commission Comments

Section 1341 recodifies without substantive change Section 1936 of the Code of Civil Procedure. [7 Cal.L.Rev.Comm. Reports 1 (1965)].

Research References

Rutter, Cal. Practice Guide: Civil Trials & Evidence Ch. 4-B, B. Preliminary Matters Discussed in Final Status Conference or In-Chambers Conference.

Rutter, Cal. Practice Guide: Civil Trials & Evidence Ch. 11-D, D. Cross-Examination of Expert Witnesses.

Rutter, Cal. Practice Guide: Civil Trials & Evidence Ch. 11-E, E. Impeachment Evidence from Other Witnesses.

Rutter, Cal. Practice Guide: Civil Trials & Evidence Ch. 8D-D, D. Hearsay Exceptions.

Rutter, Cal. Practice Guide: Family Law Ch. 13-B, B. Contested Family Law Trial.

ARTICLE 15. DECLARANT UNAVAILABLE AS WITNESS

Section
1350. Unavailable declarant; hearsay rule.

§ 1350. Unavailable declarant; hearsay rule

(a) In a criminal proceeding charging a serious felony, evidence of a statement made by a declarant is not made inadmissible by the hearsay rule if the declarant is unavailable as a witness, and all of the following are true:

(1) There is clear and convincing evidence that the declarant's unavailability was knowingly caused by, aided by, or solicited by the party against whom the statement is offered for the purpose of preventing the arrest or prosecution of the party and is the result of the death by homicide or the kidnapping of the declarant.

(2) There is no evidence that the unavailability of the declarant was caused by, aided by, solicited by, or procured on behalf of, the party who is offering the statement.

(3) The statement has been memorialized in a tape recording made by a law enforcement official, or in a written statement prepared by a law enforcement official and signed by the declarant and notarized in the presence of the law enforcement official, prior to the death or kidnapping of the declarant.

(4) The statement was made under circumstances which indicate its trustworthiness and was not the result of promise, inducement, threat, or coercion.

(5) The statement is relevant to the issues to be tried.

(6) The statement is corroborated by other evidence which tends to connect the party against whom the statement is offered with the commission of the serious felony with which the party is charged. The corroboration is not sufficient if it merely shows the commission of the offense or the circumstances thereof.

(b) If the prosecution intends to offer a statement pursuant to this section, the prosecution shall serve a written notice upon the defendant at least 10 days prior to the hearing or trial at which the prosecution intends to offer the statement, unless the prosecution shows good cause for the failure to provide that notice. In the event that good cause is shown, the defendant shall be entitled to a reasonable continuance of the hearing or trial.

(c) If the statement is offered during trial, the court's determination shall be made out of the presence of the jury. If the defendant elects to testify at the hearing on a motion brought pursuant to this section, the court shall exclude from the examination every person except the clerk, the court reporter, the bailiff, the prosecutor, the investigating officer, the defendant and his or her counsel, an investigator for the defendant, and the officer having custody of the defendant. Notwithstanding any other provision of law, the defendant's testimony at the hearing shall not be admissible in any other proceeding except the hearing brought on the motion pursuant to this section. If a transcript is made of the defendant's testimony, it shall be sealed and transmitted to the clerk of the court in which the action is pending.

(d) As used in this section, "serious felony" means any of the felonies listed in subdivision (c) of Section 1192.7 of the Penal Code or any violation of Section 11351, 11352, 11378, or 11379 of the Health and Safety Code.

(e) If a statement to be admitted pursuant to this section includes hearsay statements made by anyone other than the declarant who is unavailable pursuant to subdivision (a), those hearsay statements are inadmissible unless they meet the requirements of an exception to the hearsay rule. *(Added by Stats.1985, c. 783, § 1. Amended by Stats.2001, c. 854 (S.B.205), § 5.)*

ARTICLE 16. STATEMENTS BY CHILDREN UNDER THE AGE OF 12 IN CHILD NEGLECT AND ABUSE PROCEEDINGS

Section
1360. Statements describing an act or attempted act of child abuse or neglect; criminal prosecutions; requirements.

§ 1360. Statements describing an act or attempted act of child abuse or neglect; criminal prosecutions; requirements

(a) In a criminal prosecution where the victim is a minor, a statement made by the victim when under the age of 12 describing any act of child abuse or neglect performed with or on the child by another, or describing any attempted act of child abuse or neglect with or on the child by another, is not made inadmissible by the hearsay rule if all of the following apply:

(1) The statement is not otherwise admissible by statute or court rule.

(2) The court finds, in a hearing conducted outside the presence of the jury, that the time, content, and circumstances of the statement provide sufficient indicia of reliability.

(3) The child either:

(A) Testifies at the proceedings.

(B) Is unavailable as a witness, in which case the statement may be admitted only if there is evidence of the child abuse or neglect that corroborates the statement made by the child.

(b) A statement may not be admitted under this section unless the proponent of the statement makes known to the adverse party the intention to offer the statement and the particulars of the statement sufficiently in advance of the proceedings in order to provide the adverse party with a fair opportunity to prepare to meet the statement.

(c) For purposes of this section, "child abuse" means an act proscribed by Section 273a, 273d, or 288.5 of the Penal Code, or any of the acts described in Section 11165.1 of the Penal Code, and "child neglect" means any of the acts described in Section 11165.2 of the Penal Code. *(Added by Stats.1995, c. 87 (A.B.355), § 3.)*

Research References

Rutter, Cal. Practice Guide: Civil Trials & Evidence Ch. 8D-D, D. Hearsay Exceptions.
10 Witkin, California Summary 10th Parent and Child § 284, Trial.

ARTICLE 17. PHYSICAL ABUSE

Section
1370. Threat of infliction of injury.
1380. Elder and dependent adults; statements by victims of abuse.
1390. Statements against parties involved in causing unavailability of declarant as witness.

§ 1370. Threat of infliction of injury

(a) Evidence of a statement by a declarant is not made inadmissible by the hearsay rule if all of the following conditions are met:

(1) The statement purports to narrate, describe, or explain the infliction or threat of physical injury upon the declarant.

(2) The declarant is unavailable as a witness pursuant to Section 240.

(3) The statement was made at or near the time of the infliction or threat of physical injury. Evidence of statements made more than five years before the filing of the current action or proceeding shall be inadmissible under this section.

(4) The statement was made under circumstances that would indicate its trustworthiness.

(5) The statement was made in writing, was electronically recorded, or made to a physician, nurse, paramedic, or to a law enforcement official.

(b) For purposes of paragraph (4) of subdivision (a), circumstances relevant to the issue of trustworthiness include, but are not limited to, the following:

(1) Whether the statement was made in contemplation of pending or anticipated litigation in which the declarant was interested.

(2) Whether the declarant has a bias or motive for fabricating the statement, and the extent of any bias or motive.

(3) Whether the statement is corroborated by evidence other than statements that are admissible only pursuant to this section.

(c) A statement is admissible pursuant to this section only if the proponent of the statement makes known to the adverse party the intention to offer the statement and the particulars of the statement sufficiently in advance of the proceedings in order to provide the adverse party with a fair opportunity to prepare to meet the statement. *(Added by Stats.1996, c. 416 (A.B.2068), § 2, eff. Sept. 4, 1996. Amended by Stats.2000, c. 1001 (S.B. 1944), § 2.)*

Research References

Rutter, Cal. Practice Guide: Civil Trials & Evidence Ch. 8D-D, D. Hearsay Exceptions.

§ 1380. Elder and dependent adults; statements by victims of abuse

(a) In a criminal proceeding charging a violation, or attempted violation, of Section 368 of the Penal Code, evidence of a statement made by a declarant is not made inadmissible by the hearsay rule if the declarant is unavailable as a witness, as defined in subdivisions (a) and (b) of Section 240, and all of the following are true:

(1) The party offering the statement has made a showing of particularized guarantees of trustworthiness regarding the statement, the statement was made under circumstances which indicate its trustworthiness, and the statement was not the result of promise, inducement, threat, or coercion. In making its determination, the court may consider only the circumstances that surround the making of the statement and that render the declarant particularly worthy of belief.

(2) There is no evidence that the unavailability of the declarant was caused by, aided by, solicited by, or procured on behalf of, the party who is offering the statement.

(3) The entire statement has been memorialized in a videotape recording made by a law enforcement official, prior to the death or disabling of the declarant.

(4) The statement was made by the victim of the alleged violation.

(5) The statement is supported by corroborative evidence.

(6) The victim of the alleged violation is an individual who meets both of the following requirements:

(A) Was 65 years of age or older or was a dependent adult when the alleged violation or attempted violation occurred.

(B) At the time of any criminal proceeding, including, but not limited to, a preliminary hearing or trial, regarding the alleged violation or attempted violation, is either deceased or suffers from the infirmities of aging as manifested by advanced age or organic brain damage, or other physical, mental, or emotional dysfunction, to the extent that the ability of the person to provide adequately for the person's own care or protection is impaired.

(b) If the prosecution intends to offer a statement pursuant to this section, the prosecution shall serve a written notice upon the defendant at least 10 days prior to the hearing or trial at which the prosecution intends to offer the statement, unless the prosecution shows good cause for the failure to provide that

notice. In the event that good cause is shown, the defendant shall be entitled to a reasonable continuance of the hearing or trial.

(c) If the statement is offered during trial, the court's determination as to the availability of the victim as a witness shall be made out of the presence of the jury. If the defendant elects to testify at the hearing on a motion brought pursuant to this section, the court shall exclude from the examination every person except the clerk, the court reporter, the bailiff, the prosecutor, the investigating officer, the defendant and his or her counsel, an investigator for the defendant, and the officer having custody of the defendant. Notwithstanding any other provision of law, the defendant's testimony at the hearing shall not be admissible in any other proceeding except the hearing brought on the motion pursuant to this section. If a transcript is made of the defendant's testimony, it shall be sealed and transmitted to the clerk of the court in which the action is pending. *(Added by Stats.1999, c. 383 (A.B.526), § 1.)*

Validity

This section was held unconstitutional on its face as violating the Confrontation Clause in the decision of People v. Pirwani (App. 6 Dist. 2004) 14 Cal.Rptr.3d 673, 119 Cal.App.4th 770.

Research References

Rutter, Cal. Practice Guide: Civil Trials & Evidence Ch. 8D-D, D. Hearsay Exceptions.

§ 1390. Statements against parties involved in causing unavailability of declarant as witness

(a) Evidence of a statement is not made inadmissible by the hearsay rule if the statement is offered against a party that has engaged, or aided and abetted, in the wrongdoing that was intended to, and did, procure the unavailability of the declarant as a witness.

(b)(1) The party seeking to introduce a statement pursuant to subdivision (a) shall establish, by a preponderance of the evidence, that the elements of subdivision (a) have been met at a foundational hearing.

(2) The hearsay evidence that is the subject of the foundational hearing is admissible at the foundational hearing. However, a finding that the elements of subdivision (a) have been met shall not be based solely on the unconfronted hearsay statement of the unavailable declarant, and shall be supported by independent corroborative evidence.

(3) The foundational hearing shall be conducted outside the presence of the jury. However, if the hearing is conducted after a jury trial has begun, the judge presiding at the hearing may consider evidence already presented to the jury in deciding whether the elements of subdivision (a) have been met.

(4) In deciding whether or not to admit the statement, the judge may take into account whether it is trustworthy and reliable.

(c) This section shall apply to any civil, criminal, or juvenile case or proceeding initiated or pending as of January 1, 2011.

(d) This section shall remain in effect only until January 1, 2016, and as of that date is repealed, unless a later enacted statute, that is enacted before January 1, 2016, deletes or extends that date. If this section is repealed, the fact that it is repealed, should it occur, shall not be deemed to give rise to any ground for an appeal or a postverdict challenge based on its use in a criminal or juvenile case or proceeding before January 1, 2016. *(Added by Stats.2010, c. 537 (A.B.1723), § 2. Amended by Stats.2011, c. 296 (A.B.1023), § 90.)*

Repeal

For repeal of this section, see its terms.

Research References

Rutter, Cal. Practice Guide: Civil Trials & Evidence Ch. 8D-C, C. General Parameters Re Admissibility of Hearsay Evidence.

Division 11

WRITINGS

CHAPTER 1. AUTHENTICATION AND PROOF OF WRITINGS

ARTICLE 1. REQUIREMENT OF AUTHENTICATION

§ 1400. Authentication

Authentication of a writing means (a) the introduction of evidence sufficient to sustain a finding that it is the writing that the proponent of the evidence claims it is or (b) the establishment of such facts by any other means provided by law. *(Stats.1965, c. 299, § 2, operative Jan. 1, 1967.)*

Law Revision Commission Comments

Before any tangible object may be admitted into evidence, the party seeking to introduce the object must make a preliminary showing that the object is in some way relevant to the issues to be decided in the action. When the object sought to be introduced is a writing, this preliminary showing of relevancy usually entails some proof that the writing is authentic—*i.e.*, that the writing was made or signed by its purported maker. Hence, this showing is normally referred to as "authentication" of the writing. But authentication, correctly understood, may involve a preliminary showing that the writing is a forgery or is a writing found in particular files regardless of its authorship. *Cf.* People v. Adamson, 118 Cal.App.2d 714, 258 P.2d 1020 (1953). When the requisite preliminary showing has been made, the judge admits the writing into evidence for consideration by the trier of fact. However, the fact that the judge permits the writing to be admitted in evidence does not necessarily establish the authenticity of the writing; all that the judge has determined is that there has been a sufficient showing of the authenticity of the writing to permit the trier of fact to find that it is authentic. The trier of fact independently determines the question of authenticity, and, if the trier of fact does not believe the evidence of authenticity, it may find that the writing is not authentic despite the fact that the judge has determined that it was "authenticated." See 7 Wigmore, Evidence §§ 2129–2135 (3d ed. 1940).

This chapter sets forth the rules governing this process of authentication. Sections 1400–1402 (Article 1) define and state the general requirement of authentication—either by evidence sufficient to sustain a finding of authenticity or by other means sanctioned by law. Sections 1410–1454 (Articles 2 and 3) set forth some of the means that may be used to authenticate certain kinds of writings. The operation and effect of these sections is explained in separate Comments relating to them.

Under Section 1400, as under existing law, a writing may be authenticated by the presentation of evidence sufficient to sustain a finding of its authenticity. See Verzan v. McGregor, 23 Cal. 339, 342–343 (1863). Under Section 1400, as under existing law, the authenticity of a particular writing also may be established by some means other than the introduction of evidence of authenticity. Thus, the authenticity of a writing may be established by stipulation or by the pleadings. See *e.g.,* Code Civ.Proc. §§ 447 and 448. The requisite preliminary showing may also be supplied by a presumption. See, *e.g.,* Evidence Code §§ 1450–1454, 1530. In some instances, a presumption of authenticity may also attach to a writing authenticated in a particular manner. See, *e.g.,* Evidence Code § 643 (the ancient documents rule). Where a presumption applies, the trier of fact is required to find that the writing is authentic unless the requisite contrary showing is made. Evidence Code §§ 600, 604, 606. [7 Cal.L.Rev.Comm. Reports 1 (1965)].

Research References

Rutter, Cal. Practice Guide: Civ. Pro. Before Trial Ch. 10-C, C. Procedural Requirements-Moving Party.

Rutter, Cal. Practice Guide: Civ. Pro. Before Trial Ch. 9(II)-D, D. Attachment.

Rutter, Cal. Practice Guide: Civil Trials & Evidence Ch. 8C-B, B. Writings.

6 Witkin Cal. Proc. 5th Proceedings Without Trial § 231, (S 231) Documentary Evidence.

14 Witkin, California Summary 10th Wills and Probate § 547, Proof of Holographic Will.

§ 1401. Authentication required

(a) Authentication of a writing is required before it may be received in evidence.

(b) Authentication of a writing is required before secondary evidence of its content may be received in evidence. *(Stats.1965, c. 299, § 2, operative Jan. 1, 1967.)*

Research References

Rutter, Cal. Practice Guide: Civ. Pro. Before Trial Ch. 9(I)-B, B. Preparing and Filing Motions.

Rutter, Cal. Practice Guide: Civil Trials & Evidence Ch. 8C-B, B. Writings.

Rutter, Cal. Practice Guide: Landlord-Tenant Ch. 9-C, C. Final Preparation for Trial.

§ 1402. Authentication of altered writings

The party producing a writing as genuine which has been altered, or appears to have been altered, after its execution, in a part material to the question in dispute, must account for the alteration or appearance thereof. He may show that the alteration was made by another, without his concurrence, or was made with the consent of the parties affected by it, or otherwise properly or innocently made, or that the alteration did not change the meaning or language of the instrument. If he does that, he may give the writing in evidence, but not otherwise. *(Stats.1965, c. 299, § 2, operative Jan. 1, 1967.)*

Law Revision Commission Comments

Section 1402 restates and supersedes Code of Civil Procedure Section 1982. See Miller v. Luco, 80 Cal. 257, 265, 22 Pac. 195, 197 (1889); King v. Tarabino, 53 Cal.App. 157, 199 Pac. 890 (1921). [7 Cal.L.Rev.Comm. Reports 1 (1965)].

Research References

Rutter, Cal. Practice Guide: Civil Trials & Evidence Ch. 8C-B, B. Writings.

Rutter, Cal. Practice Guide: Civil Trials & Evidence Ch. 8C-E, E. Audio or Visual Recordings.

Miller and Starr California Real Estate § 1:97, Alteration of a Written Contract.

1 Witkin Cal. Summ. 10th Contracts § 970, Obligations Discharged.

ARTICLE 2. MEANS OF AUTHENTICATING AND PROVING WRITINGS

Section
1410.   Article not exclusive.
1410.5.   Graffiti constitutes a writing; admissibility.
1411.   Subscribing witness' testimony unnecessary.
1412.   Use of other evidence when subscribing witness' testimony required.
1413.   Witness to the execution of a writing.
1414.   Admission of authenticity; acting upon writing as authentic.
1415.   Authentication by handwriting evidence.
1416.   Proof of handwriting by person familiar therewith.
1417.   Comparison of handwriting by trier of fact.
1418.   Comparison of writing by expert witness.
1419.   Exemplars when writing is more than 30 years old.
1420.   Authentication by evidence of reply.
1421.   Authentication by content.

§ 1410. Article not exclusive

Nothing in this article shall be construed to limit the means by which a writing may be authenticated or proved. *(Stats.1965, c. 299, § 2, operative Jan. 1, 1967.)*

Law Revision Commission Comments

This article (Sections 1410–1421) lists many of the evidentiary means for authenticating writings and supersedes the existing statutory expressions of such means.

Section 1410 is included in this article in recognition of the fact that it would be impossible to specify all of the varieties of circumstantial evidence that may be sufficient in particular cases to sustain a finding of the authenticity of a writing. Hence, Section 1410 ensures that the means of authentication listed in this article or stated elsewhere in the codes will not be considered the exclusive means of authenticating writings. Although Section 1410 has no counterpart in previous legislation, the California courts have never considered the listing of certain means of authentication in the various California statutes as precluding reliance upon other means of authentication. See, *e.g.*, People v. Ramsey, 83 Cal.App.2d 707, 189 P.2d 802 (1948) (authentication by evidence of possession); Geary St. etc. R.R. v. Campbell, 39 Cal.App. 496, 179 Pac. 453 (1919) (corporate stock record book authenticated by age, appropriate custody, and unsuspicious appearance). See also the Comments to Sections 1420 and 1421. [7 Cal.L.Rev.Comm. Reports 1 (1965)].

Research References

Rutter, Cal. Practice Guide: Civ. Pro. Before Trial Ch. 10-C, C. Procedural Requirements-Moving Party.

Rutter, Cal. Practice Guide: Civil Trials & Evidence Ch. 8C-B, B. Writings.

Rutter, Cal. Practice Guide: Enforcing Judgments/Debts Ch. 4-A, A. Attachment.

§ 1410.5. Graffiti constitutes a writing; admissibility

(a) For purposes of this chapter, a writing shall include any graffiti consisting of written words, insignia, symbols, or any other markings which convey a particular meaning.

(b) Any writing described in subdivision (a), or any photograph thereof, may be admitted into evidence in an action for vandalism, for the purpose of proving that the writing was made by the defendant.

(c) The admissibility of any fact offered to prove that the writing was made by the defendant shall, upon motion of the defendant, be ruled upon outside the presence of the jury, and is subject to the requirements of Sections 1416, 1417, and 1418. *(Added by Stats.1989, c. 660, § 1.)*

Research References

Rutter, Cal. Practice Guide: Civil Trials & Evidence Ch. 8C-B, B. Writings.

§ 1411. Subscribing witness' testimony unnecessary

Except as provided by statute, the testimony of a subscribing witness is not required to authenticate a writing. *(Stats.1965, c. 299, § 2, operative Jan. 1, 1967.)*

Law Revision Commission Comments

When Section 1940 of the Code of Civil Procedure was enacted in 1872, it stated the common law rule that a subscribing witness to a witnessed writing must be produced to authenticate the writing or his absence must be satisfactorily accounted for. See Stevens v. Irwin, 12 Cal. 306 (1859). Section 1940 was amended by the Code Amendments of 1873–74 to remove the requirement that the subscribing witness be produced. Cal.Stats.1873–74, Ch. 383, § 231 (Code Amdts., p. 386). Instead, three alternative methods of authenticating a writing were listed.

Section 1411 states directly what the 1873–74 amendment to Code of Civil Procedure Section 1940 stated indirectly—that the common law rule requiring the production of a subscribing witness to a witnessed writing is not the law in California unless a statute specifically so requires. [7 Cal.L.Rev.Comm. Reports 1 (1965)].

Research References

Rutter, Cal. Practice Guide: Civil Trials & Evidence Ch. 8C-B, B. Writings.

§ 1412. Use of other evidence when subscribing witness' testimony required

If the testimony of a subscribing witness is required by statute to authenticate a writing and the subscribing witness denies or does not recollect the execution of the writing, the writing may be authenticated by other evidence. *(Stats.1965, c. 299, § 2, operative Jan. 1, 1967.)*

Law Revision Commission Comments

When enacted in 1872, Code of Civil Procedure Section 1941 stated a limitation on the common law rule requiring proof of witnessed writings by a subscribing witness. Section 1941 provided, in effect, that this rule did not prohibit the authentication of a witnessed writing by other evidence if the subscribing witness denied or did not remember the execution of the writing. Evidence Code Section 1412, which supersedes Code of Civil Procedure Section 1941, retains this limitation on the subscribing witness rule in those few cases, such as those involving wills, where a statute requires the testimony of a subscribing witness to authenticate a writing. [7 Cal.L.Rev.Comm. Reports 1 (1965)].

Research References

Rutter, Cal. Practice Guide: Civil Trials & Evidence Ch. 8C-B, B. Writings.

§ 1413. Witness to the execution of a writing

A writing may be authenticated by anyone who saw the writing made or executed, including a subscribing witness. *(Stats.1965, c. 299, § 2, operative Jan. 1, 1967.)*

Research References

Rutter, Cal. Practice Guide: Civil Trials & Evidence Ch. 8C-B, B. Writings.

§ 1414. Admission of authenticity; acting upon writing as authentic

A writing may be authenticated by evidence that:

(a) The party against whom it is offered has at any time admitted its authenticity; or

(b) The writing has been acted upon as authentic by the party against whom it is offered. *(Stats.1965, c. 299, § 2, operative Jan. 1, 1967.)*

Law Revision Commission Comments

Section 1414 restates and supersedes the provisions of Code of Civil Procedure Section 1942. Section 1942 is difficult to understand. It was amended in 1901 to make it more intelligible. Cal.Stats.1901, Ch. 102, § 480, p. 247. However, the code revision of which the 1901 amendment was a part was held unconstitutional because of technical defects in the title of the act and because the act embraced more than one subject. Lewis v. Dunne, 134 Cal. 291, 66 Pac. 478 (1901). Evidence Code Section 1414 is based on the 1901 amendment of Section 1942. [7 Cal.L.Rev. Comm. Reports 1 (1965)].

Research References

Rutter, Cal. Practice Guide: Civil Trials & Evidence Ch. 8C-B, B. Writings.

§ 1415. Authentication by handwriting evidence

A writing may be authenticated by evidence of the genuineness of the handwriting of the maker. *(Stats.1965, c. 299, § 2, operative Jan. 1, 1967.)*

Law Revision Commission Comments

Section 1415 restates and supersedes the provisions of subdivision 2 of Code of Civil Procedure Section 1940. [7 Cal.L.Rev.Comm. Reports 1 (1965)].

§ 1416. Proof of handwriting by person familiar therewith

A witness who is not otherwise qualified to testify as an expert may state his opinion whether a writing is in the handwriting of a supposed writer if the court finds that he has personal knowledge of the handwriting of the supposed writer. Such personal knowledge may be acquired from:

(a) Having seen the supposed writer write;

(b) Having seen a writing purporting to be in the handwriting of the supposed writer and upon which the supposed writer has acted or been charged;

(c) Having received letters in the due course of mail purporting to be from the supposed writer in response to letters duly addressed and mailed by him to the supposed writer; or

(d) Any other means of obtaining personal knowledge of the handwriting of the supposed writer. *(Stats.1965, c. 299, § 2, operative Jan. 1, 1967.)*

Law Revision Commission Comments

Section 1416 is based on Code of Civil Procedure Section 1943 as amended in the code revision of 1901. Cal.Stats.1901, Ch. 102, § 481, p. 247. See the Comment to Section 1414. [7 Cal.L.Rev.Comm. Reports 1 (1965)].

Research References

Rutter, Cal. Practice Guide: Civil Trials & Evidence Ch. 8C-B, B. Writings.
Rutter, Cal. Practice Guide: Civil Trials & Evidence Ch. 8C-H, H. Opinion Evidence.

§ 1417. Comparison of handwriting by trier of fact

The genuineness of handwriting, or the lack thereof, may be proved by a comparison made by the trier of fact with handwriting (a) which the court finds was admitted or treated as genuine by the party against whom the evidence is offered or (b) otherwise proved to be genuine to the satisfaction of the court. *(Stats.1965, c. 299, § 2, operative Jan. 1, 1967.)*

Law Revision Commission Comments

Section 1417 is based on that portion of Code of Civil Procedure Section 1944 that permits the trier of fact to compare questioned handwriting with handwriting the court has found to be genuine. [7 Cal.L.Rev.Comm. Reports 1 (1965)].

Research References

Rutter, Cal. Practice Guide: Civil Trials & Evidence Ch. 8C-B, B. Writings.

§ 1418. Comparison of writing by expert witness

The genuineness of writing, or the lack thereof, may be proved by a comparison made by an expert witness with writing (a) which the court finds was admitted or treated as genuine by the party against whom the evidence is offered or (b) otherwise proved to be genuine to the satisfaction of the court. *(Stats. 1965, c. 299, § 2, operative Jan. 1, 1967.)*

Law Revision Commission Comments

Section 1418 is based on that portion of Code of Civil Procedure Section 1944 that permits a witness to compare questioned handwriting with handwriting the court has found to be genuine. However, Section 1418 applies to any form of writing, not just handwriting. This is in recognition of the fact that experts can now compare typewriting specimens and other forms of writing as accurately as they could compare handwriting specimens in 1872.

Although Code of Civil Procedure Section 1944 does not expressly require that the witness making the comparison be an expert witness (as Evidence Code Section 1418 does), the cases have nonetheless imposed this requirement. *E.g.,* Spottiswood v. Weir, 80 Cal. 448, 22 Pac. 289 (1889). The witness' expertise may, of course, be derived from practical experience instead of from technical training. In re Newell's Estate, 75 Cal.App. 554, 243 Pac. 33 (1926) (experienced banker). [7 Cal.L.Rev. Comm. Reports 1 (1965)].

Research References

Rutter, Cal. Practice Guide: Civil Trials & Evidence Ch. 8C-B, B. Writings.

§ 1419. Exemplars when writing is more than 30 years old

Where a writing whose genuineness is sought to be proved is more than 30 years old, the comparison under Section 1417 or 1418 may be made with writing purporting to be genuine, and generally respected and acted upon as such, by persons having an interest in knowing whether it is genuine. *(Stats.1965, c. 299, § 2, operative Jan. 1, 1967.)*

Law Revision Commission Comments

Section 1419 restates and supersedes the provisions of Code of Civil Procedure Section 1945. The apparent purpose of Section 1945, continued without substantive change in Evidence Code Section 1419, is to permit the judge to be satisfied with a lesser degree of proof of the authenticity of an exemplar when the writing offered in evidence is more than 30 years old. [7 Cal.L.Rev.Comm. Reports 1 (1965)].

Research References

Rutter, Cal. Practice Guide: Civil Trials & Evidence Ch. 8C-B, B. Writings.

§ 1420. Authentication by evidence of reply

A writing may be authenticated by evidence that the writing was received in response to a communication sent to the person who is claimed by the proponent of the evidence to be the author of the writing. *(Stats.1965, c. 299, § 2, operative Jan. 1, 1967.)*

Law Revision Commission Comments

Section 1420 provides a method of authentication recognized in California case law but not previously reflected in California statutes. House Grain Co. v. Finerman & Sons, 116 Cal.App.2d 485, 253 P.2d 1034 (1953). [7 Cal.L.Rev.Comm. Reports 1 (1965)].

Research References

Rutter, Cal. Practice Guide: Civil Trials & Evidence Ch. 8C-B, B.
   Writings.

§ 1421. Authentication by content

A writing may be authenticated by evidence that the writing
refers to or states matters that are unlikely to be known to
anyone other than the person who is claimed by the proponent of
the evidence to be the author of the writing. *(Stats.1965, c. 299,
§ 2, operative Jan. 1, 1967.)*

Law Revision Commission Comments

Section 1421 provides a method of authentication recognized in
California case law but not previously reflected in California statutes.
Chaplin v. Sullivan, 67 Cal.App.2d 728, 734, 155 P.2d 368, 372 (1945). [7
Cal.L.Rev.Comm. Reports 1 (1965)].

Research References

Rutter, Cal. Practice Guide: Civil Trials & Evidence Ch. 8C-B, B.
   Writings.

ARTICLE 3. PRESUMPTIONS AFFECTING ACKNOWLEDGED WRITINGS AND OFFICIAL WRITINGS

§ 1450. Classification of presumptions in article

The presumptions established by this article are presumptions
affecting the burden of producing evidence. *(Stats.1965, c. 299,
§ 2, operative Jan. 1, 1967.)*

Law Revision Commission Comments

This article (Sections 1450–1454) lists several presumptions that may be
used to authenticate particular kinds of writings. Section 1450 prescribes
the effect of these presumptions. They require a finding of authenticity
unless the adverse party produces evidence sufficient to sustain a finding
that the writing in question is not authentic. See Evidence Code § 604
and the Comment thereto. [7 Cal.L.Rev.Comm. Reports 1 (1965)].

Research References

Rutter, Cal. Practice Guide: Civil Trials & Evidence Ch. 8C-B, B.
   Writings.
Miller and Starr California Real Estate § 11:8, Evidentiary Effect of
   Recording.

§ 1451. Acknowledged writings

A certificate of the acknowledgment of a writing other than a
will, or a certificate of the proof of such a writing, is prima facie
evidence of the facts recited in the certificate and the genuineness of the signature of each person by whom the writing
purports to have been signed if the certificate meets the
requirements of Article 3 (commencing with Section 1180) of
Chapter 4, Title 4, Part 4, Division 2 of the Civil Code.
(Stats.1965, c. 299, § 2, operative Jan. 1, 1967.)

Law Revision Commission Comments

Section 1451 continues in effect and restates a method of authenticating
private writings that is contained in Code of Civil Procedure Section 1948.
[7 Cal.L.Rev.Comm. Reports 1 (1965)].

Research References

Rutter, Cal. Practice Guide: Civil Trials & Evidence Ch. 8C-B, B.
   Writings.

Miller and Starr California Real Estate § 8:3, Requirements; Form and
   Content.
Miller and Starr California Real Estate § 11:8, Evidentiary Effect of
   Recording.
Miller and Starr California Real Estate § 8:40, Certificate of Acknowledg-
   ment.
Miller and Starr California Real Estate § 11:23, Purpose and Effect;
   Required for Recordation.
12 Witkin, California Summary 10th Real Property § 283, Nature of
   Requirement.

§ 1452. Official seals

A seal is presumed to be genuine and its use authorized if it
purports to be the seal of:

(a) The United States or a department, agency, or public
employee of the United States.

(b) A public entity in the United States or a department,
agency, or public employee of such public entity.

(c) A nation recognized by the executive power of the United
States or a department, agency, or officer of such nation.

(d) A public entity in a nation recognized by the executive
power of the United States or a department, agency, or officer of
such public entity.

(e) A court of admiralty or maritime jurisdiction.

(f) A notary public within any state of the United States.
(Stats.1965, c. 299, § 2, operative Jan. 1, 1967.)

Law Revision Commission Comments

Sections 1452 and 1453 eliminate the need for formal proof of the
genuineness of certain official seals and signatures when such proof would
otherwise be required by the general requirement of authentication.

Under existing law, formal proof of many of the signatures and seals
mentioned in Sections 1452 and 1453 is not required because such
signatures and seals are the subject of judicial notice. Code Civ.Proc.
§ 1875 (5), (6), (7), (8). (Section 1875 is superseded by Division 4
(Sections 450–460) of the Evidence Code.) The parties may not dispute a
matter that has been judicially noticed. Code Civ.Proc. § 2102 (superseded by Evidence Code § 457). Hence, judicial notice of facts should be
confined to matters concerning which there can be no reasonable dispute.
The authenticity of writings purporting to be official writings should not
be determined conclusively by the judge when there is serious dispute as
to such authenticity. Therefore, Sections 1452 and 1453 provide that the
official seals and signatures mentioned shall be presumed genuine and
authorized until evidence is introduced sufficient to sustain a finding that
they are not genuine or authorized. When there is such evidence
disputing the authenticity of an official seal or signature, the trier of fact is
required to determine the question of authenticity without regard to any
presumption created by this section. See Evidence Code § 604 and the
Comment thereto.

This procedure will dispense with the necessity for proof of authenticity
when there is no real dispute as to such authenticity, but it will assure the
parties the right to contest the authenticity of official writings when there
is a real dispute as to such authenticity. [7 Cal.L.Rev.Comm. Reports 1
(1965)].

Research References

Rutter, Cal. Practice Guide: Civil Trials & Evidence Ch. 8C-B, B.
   Writings.
Rutter, Cal. Practice Guide: Civil Trials & Evidence Ch. 8D-D, D.
   Hearsay Exceptions.
Rutter, Cal. Practice Guide: Enforcing Judgments/Debts Ch. 6J-2, Enforc-
   ing Sister State Judgments in California.
8 Witkin Cal. Proc. 5th Enforcement of Judgment § 455, (S 455) Form
   and Content.

§ 1453. Domestic official signatures

A signature is presumed to be genuine and authorized if it
purports to be the signature, affixed in his official capacity, of:

(a) A public employee of the United States.

(b) A public employee of any public entity in the United States.

(c) A notary public within any state of the United States. *(Stats.1965, c. 299, § 2, operative Jan. 1, 1967.)*

Law Revision Commission Comments

See the Comment to Section 1452. [7 Cal.L.Rev.Comm. Reports 1 (1965)].

Research References

Rutter, Cal. Practice Guide: Civil Trials & Evidence Ch. 8C-B, B. Writings.

Rutter, Cal. Practice Guide: Enforcing Judgments/Debts Ch. 6J-2, Enforcing Sister State Judgments in California.

8 Witkin Cal. Proc. 5th Enforcement of Judgment § 455, (S 455) Form and Content.

§ 1454. Foreign official signatures

A signature is presumed to be genuine and authorized if it purports to be the signature, affixed in his official capacity, of an officer, or deputy of an officer, of a nation or public entity in a nation recognized by the executive power of the United States and the writing to which the signature is affixed is accompanied by a final statement certifying the genuineness of the signature and the official position of (a) the person who executed the writing or (b) any foreign official who has certified either the genuineness of the signature and official position of the person executing the writing or the genuineness of the signature and official position of another foreign official who has executed a similar certificate in a chain of such certificates beginning with a certificate of the genuineness of the signature and official position of the person executing the writing. The final statement may be made only by a secretary of an embassy or legation, consul general, consul, vice consul, consular agent, or other officer in the foreign service of the United States stationed in the nation, authenticated by the seal of his office. *(Stats.1965, c. 299, § 2, operative Jan. 1, 1967.)*

Law Revision Commission Comments

Section 1454 supersedes the somewhat complex procedure for authenticating foreign official writings that is contained in subdivision 8 of Code of Civil Procedure Section 1918. Section 1454 is based on a proposed amendment to Rule 44 of the Federal Rules of Civil Procedure that has been prepared by the Advisory Committee on Civil Rules, the Commission and Advisory Committee on International Rules of Judicial Procedure, and the Columbia Law School Project on International Procedure. Proposed Amendments to Rules of Civil Procedure for the United States District Courts with Advisory Committee's Notes (mimeo., Feb. 25, 1964). Rule 44 and the proposed amendment, however, deal only with the question of authenticating *copies* of foreign official writings. Section 1454 relates to the authentication of *any* foreign official writing, whether it be an original or a copy.

The procedure set forth in Section 1454 is necessary for the reason that a United States foreign service officer may not be able to certify to the official position and signature of a particular foreign official. Accordingly, this section permits the original signature to be certified by a higher foreign official, whose signature can in turn be certified by a still higher official, and such certifications can be continued in a chain until a foreign official is reached as to whom the United States foreign service officer has adequate information upon which to base his final certification. See, *e.g.,* New York Life Ins. Co. v. Aronson, 38 F.Supp. 687 (W.D.Pa.1941).

See also the Comment to Section 1452. [7 Cal.L.Rev.Comm. Reports 1 (1965)].

Research References

Rutter, Cal. Practice Guide: Civ. Pro. Before Trial Ch. 9(II)-D, D. Attachment.

Rutter, Cal. Practice Guide: Civil Trials & Evidence Ch. 8C-B, B. Writings.

CHAPTER 2. SECONDARY EVIDENCE OF WRITINGS

ARTICLE 1. PROOF OF THE CONTENT OF A WRITING

§ 1520. Content of writing; proof

The content of a writing may be proved by an otherwise admissible original. *(Added by Stats.1998, c. 100 (S.B.177), § 2, operative Jan. 1, 1999.)*

Law Revision Commission Comments

Section 1520 continues former Section 1500 insofar as it permitted proof of the content of a writing by an original of the writing. See also Sections 1521 (Secondary Evidence Rule), 1522 (exclusion of secondary evidence in criminal action), 1523 (oral testimony of content of writing). [26 Cal.L.Rev.Comm. Reports 369 (1996)].

Research References

Rutter, Cal. Practice Guide: Civil Trials & Evidence Ch. 8C-B, B. Writings.

Rutter, Cal. Practice Guide: Civil Trials & Evidence Ch. 8E-G, G. Parol Evidence Rule.

Rutter, Cal. Practice Guide: Enforcing Judgments/Debts Ch. 4-A, A. Attachment.

Rutter, Cal. Practice Guide: Family Law Ch. 13-B, B. Contested Family Law Trial.

Rutter, Cal. Practice Guide: Insurance Litigation Ch. 15-I, I. Trial.

Rutter, Cal. Practice Guide: Landlord-Tenant Ch. 9-C, C. Final Preparation for Trial.

6 Witkin Cal. Proc. 5th Proceedings Without Trial § 231, (S 231) Documentary Evidence.

§ 1521. Secondary evidence rule

(a) The content of a writing may be proved by otherwise admissible secondary evidence. The court shall exclude secondary evidence of the content of writing if the court determines either of the following:

(1) A genuine dispute exists concerning material terms of the writing and justice requires the exclusion.

(2) Admission of the secondary evidence would be unfair.

(b) Nothing in this section makes admissible oral testimony to prove the content of a writing if the testimony is inadmissible under Section 1523 (oral testimony of the content of a writing).

(c) Nothing in this section excuses compliance with Section 1401 (authentication).

(d) This section shall be known as the "Secondary Evidence Rule." *(Added by Stats.1998, c. 100 (S.B.177), § 2, operative Jan. 1, 1999.)*

Law Revision Commission Comments

Sections 1520 (proof of content of writing by original), 1521 (Secondary Evidence Rule), 1522 (exclusion of secondary evidence in criminal action), and 1523 (oral testimony of content of writing) replace the Best Evidence Rule and its exceptions. For background, see *Best Evidence Rule*, 26 Cal. L. Revision Comm'n Reports 369 (1996). Because of the breadth of the exceptions to the Best Evidence Rule, this reform is not a major departure from former law, but primarily a matter of clarification and simplification. Discovery principles remain unchanged.

Subdivision (a) makes secondary evidence generally admissible to prove the content of a writing. The nature of the evidence offered affects its weight, not its admissibility. The normal motivation of parties to support their cases with convincing evidence is a deterrent to introduction of unreliable secondary evidence. See also Section 412 (if party offers weaker and less satisfactory evidence despite ability to produce stronger and more satisfactory evidence, the evidence offered should be viewed with distrust).

The mandatory exceptions set forth in subdivisions (a)(1) and (a)(2) provide further protection against unreliable secondary evidence. Those exceptions are modeled on the exceptions to former Section 1511 and to Rule 1003 of the Federal Rules of Evidence. Cases interpreting those statutes provide guidance in applying subdivisions (a)(1) and (a)(2). *See, e.g.,* United States v. Sinclair, 74 F.3d 753, 760–61 (7th Cir. 1996) (admitting copies of expense account reports was not unfair); Ruberto v. Commissioner of Internal Revenue, 774 F.2d 61, 64 (2d Cir. 1985) (tax court did not err in excluding photocopies of canceled checks, "since problems in matching the copies of the backs of the checks with copies of the fronts made them somewhat suspect"); Amoco Production Co. v. United States, 619 F.2d 1383, 1391 (10th Cir. 1980) (upholding trial court's determination that "admission of the file copy would be unfair because the most critical part of the original conformed copy.... is not completely reproduced in the 'duplicate'"); People v. Garcia, 201 Cal.App.3d 324, 330, 247 Cal.Rptr. 94 (1988) (claim of unfairness "must be based on substance, not mere speculation that the original might contain some relevant difference"). Courts may consider a broad range of factors, for example: (1) whether the proponent attempts to use the writing in a manner that could not reasonably have been anticipated, (2) whether the original was suppressed in discovery, (3) whether discovery conducted in a reasonably diligent (as opposed to exhaustive) manner failed to result in production of the original, (4) whether there are dramatic differences between the original and the secondary evidence (e.g., the original but not the secondary evidence is in color and the colors provide significant clues to interpretation), (5) whether the original is unavailable and, if so, why, and (6) whether the writing is central to the case or collateral. A classic circumstance for exclusion pursuant to subdivision (a)(2) is if the proponent destroyed the original with fraudulent intent or the doctrine of spoliation of evidence otherwise applies.

Subdivision (b) explicitly establishes that Section 1523 (oral testimony of the content of writing), not Section 1521, governs the admissibility of oral testimony to prove the content of a writing.

Subdivision (c) makes clear that like other evidence, secondary evidence is admissible only if it is properly authenticated. Under Section 1401, the proponent must not only authenticate the original writing, but must also establish that the proffered evidence is secondary evidence of the original. *See* B. Jefferson, Jefferson's Synopsis of California Evidence Law, 30.1, at 470–71 (1985). [26 Cal.L.Rev.Comm. Reports 369 (1996)].

Research References

Rutter, Cal. Practice Guide: Civil Appeals & Writs Ch. 8-C, C. Standards of Appellate Review.

Rutter, Cal. Practice Guide: Civ. Pro. Before Trial Ch. 5-D, D. Default Judgment by Court.

Rutter, Cal. Practice Guide: Civ. Pro. Before Trial Ch. 10-C, C. Procedural Requirements-Moving Party.

Rutter, Cal. Practice Guide: Civ. Pro. Before Trial Ch. 8G-5, Responses to Rfas.

Rutter, Cal. Practice Guide: Civ. Pro. Before Trial Ch. 9(I)-B, B. Preparing and Filing Motions.

Rutter, Cal. Practice Guide: Civ. Pro. Before Trial Ch. 9(II)-D, D. Attachment.

Rutter, Cal. Practice Guide: Civil Trials & Evidence Ch. 8C-B, B. Writings.

Rutter, Cal. Practice Guide: Enforcing Judgments/Debts Ch. 4-A, A. Attachment.

Rutter, Cal. Practice Guide: Family Law Ch. 13-B, B. Contested Family Law Trial.

Rutter, Cal. Practice Guide: Insurance Litigation Ch. 15-I, I. Trial.

Rutter, Cal. Practice Guide: Landlord-Tenant Ch. 9-C, C. Final Preparation for Trial.

18 NO. 3 Miller & Starr, California Real Estate Newsalert 6, Contracts.

§ 1522. Additional grounds for exclusion of secondary evidence

(a) In addition to the grounds for exclusion authorized by Section 1521, in a criminal action the court shall exclude secondary evidence of the content of a writing if the court determines that the original is in the proponent's possession, custody, or control, and the proponent has not made the original reasonably available for inspection at or before trial. This section does not apply to any of the following:

(1) A duplicate as defined in Section 260.

(2) A writing that is not closely related to the controlling issues in the action.

(3) A copy of a writing in the custody of a public entity.

(4) A copy of a writing that is recorded in the public records, if the record or a certified copy of it is made evidence of the writing by statute.

(b) In a criminal action, a request to exclude secondary evidence of the content of a writing, under this section or any other law, shall not be made in the presence of the jury. *(Added by Stats.1998, c. 100 (S.B.177), § 2, operative Jan. 1, 1999.)*

Law Revision Commission Comments

Subdivision (a) of Section 1522 sets forth a mandatory exception applicable only in criminal cases, which are governed by narrower discovery rules than civil cases. See Section 130 ("criminal action" includes criminal proceedings). See also Penal Code §§ 1054–1054.7 (discovery in criminal cases). Section 1522 does not expand discovery obligations, it simply conditions use of secondary evidence on making the original reasonably available for inspection if the proponent has it. In determining whether the proponent of secondary evidence has made the original "reasonably available," the court should examine specific circumstances, such as the time, place, and manner of allowing inspection. The concept is fluid, not rigid. For example, making the original available moments before using secondary evidence may in general suffice if a defendant is rebutting a surprise contention, but not if the prosecution is presenting its case in chief. Similarly, what constitutes reasonable access to computer evidence may vary from system to system.

The exceptions in subdivisions (a)(1)-(a)(4) are drawn from exceptions to the former Best Evidence Rule (former Section 1500). Subdivision (a)(1) is drawn from former Section 1511. Subdivision (a)(2) is drawn from former Section 1504. Subdivision (a)(3) is drawn from former Section 1506. Subdivision (a)(4) is drawn from former Section 1507.

Subdivision (b) continues the requirement of the second sentence of former Section 1503(a), but applies it to all requests for exclusion of secondary evidence in a criminal trial.

See also Sections 1520 (proof of content of writing by original), 1521 (Secondary Evidence Rule), and 1523 (oral testimony of content of writing). [26 Cal.L.Rev.Comm. Reports 369 (1996)].

Research References

Rutter, Cal. Practice Guide: Civil Trials & Evidence Ch. 8C-B, B. Writings.

§ 1523. Oral testimony of the content of a writing; admissibility

(a) Except as otherwise provided by statute, oral testimony is not admissible to prove the content of a writing.

(b) Oral testimony of the content of a writing is not made inadmissible by subdivision (a) if the proponent does not have possession or control of a copy of the writing and the original is lost or has been destroyed without fraudulent intent on the part of the proponent of the evidence.

(c) Oral testimony of the content of a writing is not made inadmissible by subdivision (a) if the proponent does not have possession or control of the original or a copy of the writing and either of the following conditions is satisfied:

(1) Neither the writing nor a copy of the writing was reasonably procurable by the proponent by use of the court's process or by other available means.

(2) The writing is not closely related to the controlling issues and it would be inexpedient to require its production.

(d) Oral testimony of the content of a writing is not made inadmissible by subdivision (a) if the writing consists of numerous accounts or other writings that cannot be examined in court without great loss of time, and the evidence sought from them is only the general result of the whole. *(Added by Stats.1998, c. 100 (S.B.177), § 2, operative Jan. 1, 1999.)*

Law Revision Commission Comments

Section 1523 preserves former law governing the admissibility of oral testimony to prove the content of a writing. See former Sections 1500, 1501–1509.

Subdivision (a) is based on an assumption that oral testimony as to the content of a writing is typically less reliable than other proof of the content of a writing. For background, see *Best Evidence Rule*, 26 Cal. L. Revision Comm'n Reports 369 (1996).

Subdivision (b) continues former Sections 1501 and 1505 without substantive change as to oral testimony of the content of a writing that is lost or has been destroyed.

Subdivision (c)(1) continues former Sections 1502 and 1505 without substantive change as to oral testimony of the content of a writing that was not reasonably procurable. In effect, subdivision (c)(1) also continues former Sections 1503 and 1505 without substantive change as to oral testimony of the content of a writing that the opponent has, but failed to produce at the hearing despite being expressly or impliedly notified that it would be needed. Under such circumstances, the writing was not reasonably procurable. Finally, subdivision (c)(1) continues former Sections 1506–1508 without substantive change as to oral testimony of the content of a writing where (1) the writing is in the custody of a public entity and the proponent could not have obtained it or a copy of it in the exercise of reasonable diligence, or (2) the writing has been recorded in the public records, the record or a certified copy of the writing is made evidence of the writing by statute, and the proponent could not have obtained it or a copy of it in the exercise of reasonable diligence. Subdivision (c)(2) continues former Sections 1504 and 1505 without substantive change as to oral testimony of the content of a collateral writing.

Subdivision (d) continues former Section 1509 without substantive change as to oral testimony of a voluminous writing.

See Sections 1520 (proof of content of writing by original), 1521 (Secondary Evidence Rule), and 1522 (exclusion of secondary evidence in criminal action). [26 Cal.L.Rev.Comm. Reports 369 (1996)].

Research References

Rutter, Cal. Practice Guide: Civil Trials & Evidence Ch. 8C-B, B. Writings.

Rutter, Cal. Practice Guide: Civil Trials & Evidence Ch. 8E-G, G. Parol Evidence Rule.

Rutter, Cal. Practice Guide: Enforcing Judgments/Debts Ch. 4-A, A. Attachment.

Rutter, Cal. Practice Guide: Family Law Ch. 13-B, B. Contested Family Law Trial.

Rutter, Cal. Practice Guide: Insurance Litigation Ch. 15-I, I. Trial.

Rutter, Cal. Practice Guide: Landlord-Tenant Ch. 9-C, C. Final Preparation for Trial.

ARTICLE 2. OFFICIAL WRITINGS AND RECORDED WRITINGS

Section

§ 1530. Copy of writing in official custody

(a) A purported copy of a writing in the custody of a public entity, or of an entry in such a writing, is prima facie evidence of the existence and content of such writing or entry if:

(1) The copy purports to be published by the authority of the nation or state, or public entity therein in which the writing is kept;

(2) The office in which the writing is kept is within the United States or within the Panama Canal Zone, the Trust Territory of the Pacific Islands, or the Ryukyu Islands, and the copy is attested or certified as a correct copy of the writing or entry by a public employee, or a deputy of a public employee, having the legal custody of the writing; or

(3) The office in which the writing is kept is not within the United States or any other place described in paragraph (2) and the copy is attested as a correct copy of the writing or entry by a person having authority to make attestation. The attestation must be accompanied by a final statement certifying the genuineness of the signature and the official position of (i) the person who attested the copy as a correct copy or (ii) any foreign official who has certified either the genuineness of the signature and official position of the person attesting the copy or the genuineness of the signature and official position of another foreign official who has executed a similar certificate in a chain of such certificates beginning with a certificate of the genuineness of the signature and official position of the person attesting the copy. Except as provided in the next sentence, the final statement may be made only by a secretary of an embassy or legation, consul general, consul, vice consul, or consular agent of the United States, or a diplomatic or consular official of the foreign country assigned or accredited to the United States. Prior to January 1, 1971, the final statement may also be made by a secretary of an embassy or legation, consul general, consul, vice consul, consular agent, or other officer in the foreign service of the United States stationed in the nation in which the writing is kept, authenticated by the seal of his office. If reasonable opportunity has been given to all parties to investigate the authenticity and accuracy of the documents, the court may, for good cause shown, (i) admit an attested copy without the final statement or (ii) permit the writing or entry in foreign custody to be evidenced by an attested summary with or without a final statement.

(b) The presumptions established by this section are presumptions affecting the burden of producing evidence. *(Stats.1965, c. 299, § 2, operative Jan. 1, 1967. Amended by Stats.1970, c. 41, p. 60, § 1, eff. April 3, 1970.)*

Law Revision Commission Comments

Section 1530 deals with three evidentiary problems. *First*, it is concerned with the problem of proving the content of an original writing by means of a copy, i.e., the best evidence rule. See Evidence Code § 1500. *Second*, it is concerned with authentication, for the copy must be authenticated as a copy of the original writing. Evidence Code § 1401. *Finally*, it is concerned with the hearsay rule, for a certification or attestation of authenticity is "a statement that was made other than by a witness while testifying at the hearing and that is offered to prove the truth of the matter stated." Evidence Code § 1200. Because this section is principally concerned with the use of a copy of a writing to prove the content of the original, it is located in the division relating to secondary evidence of writings.

Under existing California law, certain official records may be proved by copies purporting to have been published by official authority or by copies with attached certificates containing certain requisite seals and signatures. The rules are complex and detailed and appear for the most part in Article 2 (beginning with Section 1892) of Chapter 3, Title 2, Part IV of the Code of Civil Procedure.

Section 1530 substitutes for these rules a uniform rule that can be applied to all writings in official custody found within the United States and another rule applicable to all writings in official custody found outside the United States.

Subdivision (a)(1). Subdivision (a)(1) of Section 1530 provides that an official writing may be proved by a copy purporting to be published by official authority. Under Section 1918 of the Code of Civil Procedure, the acts and proceedings of the executive and legislature of any state, the United States, or a foreign government may be proved by documents and journals published by official authority. Subdivision (a)(1) in effect makes these provisions of Section 1918 applicable to all classes of official documents. This extension of the means of proving official documents will facilitate the proof of many official documents the authenticity of which is presumed (Evidence Code § 644) and is seldom subject to question.

Subdivision (a)(2) and (a)(3) generally. Paragraphs (2) and (3) of subdivision (a) of Section 1530 set forth the rules for proving the content of writings in official custody by attested or certified copies. A person who "attests" a writing merely affirms it to be true or genuine by his signature. Black, Law Dictionary (4th ed. 1951). Existing California statutes require certain writings to be "certified." Section 1923 of the Code of Civil Procedure (superseded by Evidence Code Section 1531) provides that the certificate affixed to a certified copy must state that the copy is a correct copy of the original, must be signed by the certifying officer, and must be under his seal of office, if he has one. Thus, the only difference between the words "attested" and "certified" is that the existing statutory definition of "certified" requires the use of a seal, if the authenticating officer has one, whereas the definition of "attested" does not. Section 1530 eliminates the requirement of the seal by the use of the word "attested." However, Section 1530 retains, in addition, the word "certified" because it is the more familiar term in California practice.

Subdivision (a)(2). Under existing law, copies of many records of the United States government and of the governments of sister states may be proved by a copy certified or attested by the custodian alone. See, *e.g.,* Code Civ.Proc. §§ 1901 and 1918(1), (2), (3), (9); Corp.Code § 6600. Yet, other official writings must be certified or attested not only by the custodian but also by a higher official certifying the authority and signature of the custodian. In order to provide a uniform rule for the proof of all domestic official writings, subdivision (a)(2) extends the simpler and more expeditious procedure to all official writings within the United States.

Subdivision (a)(3). Under existing law, some foreign official records may be proved by a copy certified or attested by the custodian alone. See Code Civ.Proc. §§ 1901 and 1918(4). Yet, other copies of foreign official writings must be accompanied by three certificates: one executed by the custodian, another by a higher official certifying the authority and signature of the custodian, and a third by still another official certifying the signature and official position of the second official. See Code Civ.Proc. §§ 1906 and 1918(8).

For these complex rules, subdivision (a)(3) of Section 1530 substitutes a relatively simple and uniform procedure that is applicable to all classes of foreign official writings. Subdivision (a)(3) is based on a proposed amendment to Rule 44 of the Federal Rules of Civil Procedure that has been prepared by the Advisory Committee on Civil Rules, the Commission and Advisory Committee on International Rules of Judicial Procedure, and the Columbia Law School Project on International Procedure, Proposed Amendments to Rules of Civil Procedure for the United States District Courts with Advisory Committee's Notes (mimeo., Feb. 25, 1964).

Subdivision (a)(3) requires that the copy be attested as a correct copy by "a person having authority to make the attestation." In some foreign countries, the person with authority to attest a copy of an official writing is not necessarily the person with legal custody of the writing. See 2B Barron & Holtzoff, Federal Practice Procedure § 992 (Wright ed. 1961). In such a case, subdivision (a)(3) requires that the attester's signature and official position be certified by another official. If this is a United States foreign service officer stationed in the country, no further certificates are required. If a United States foreign service officer is not able to certify to the signature and official position of the attester, subdivision (a)(3) permits the attester's signature and official position to be certified by a higher foreign official, whose signature can in turn be certified by a still higher official. Such certifications can be continued in a chain until a foreign official is reached as to whom the United States foreign service officer has adequate information upon which to base his final certification. See, *e.g.,* New York Life Ins. Co. v. Aronson, 38 F.Supp. 687 (W.D.Pa. 1941).

Subdivision (b). Where evidence is introduced that is sufficient to sustain a finding that the copy is not a correct copy, the trier of fact is required to determine whether the copy is a correct copy without regard to the presumptions created by this section. See Evidence Code § 604 and the Comment thereto. [7 Cal.L.Rev.Comm. Reports 1 (1965)].

Section 1530 of the Evidence Code is concerned with the use of a copy of a writing in official custody to prove the content of the original. Section 1530 was deficient insofar as it prescribed, in subdivision (a)(3), the procedure for proof of foreign official writings. Subdivision (a)(3) requires that the copy of the foreign official record be attested as a correct copy by "a person having authority to make the attestation." The subdivision further requires that the first attester's signature and his official position be certified by a higher foreign official, whose signature can in turn be certified by a still higher official. Under the section as it formerly read, such certifications could be continued in a chain until a foreign official was reached as to whom a United States foreign service officer "stationed in the nation in which the writing is kept" had adequate information upon which to base his final certification. In other words, to prove a copy of a foreign official record, it was necessary to have a certificate of a United States foreign service officer stationed in the nation in which the writing was kept.

In some situations, it was impossible to satisfy the basic requirement of subdivision (a)(3) of Section 1530 because there were no United States foreign service officials in the particular foreign country (such as East Germany) and, hence, there was no one who could make the certificate required by subdivision (a)(3). As a result, in some situations, it was extremely difficult and expensive or even impossible to establish such matters as birth, legitimacy, marriage, death, or a will.

The problem described above was particularly troublesome in the case of a foreign will because Probate Code Section 361 was amended at the 1969 session to provide that a copy of a foreign will (and the related documents concerning the establishment of proof of the will in the foreign country) can be admitted in California "if such copy or other evidence satisfies the requirements of Article 2 (commencing with Section 1530) of Chapter 2 of Division 11 of the Evidence Code."

When Section 1530 of the Evidence Code was drafted in 1964, the Commission had the benefit of a proposed amendment to Rule 44 of the Federal Rules of Civil Procedure and based subdivision (a)(3) on that proposed amendment. After the Evidence Code was enacted in 1965, Rule 44 was revised (in 1966) to provide for proof of foreign official records. In the revision of Rule 44 in 1966, the defect pointed out above was discovered and provision was made in Rule 44 to cover the problem.

Rule 44 (as revised in 1966) includes the following provision to deal with the East Germany type of case:

If reasonable opportunity has been given to all parties to investigate the authenticity and accuracy of the documents, the court may, for good cause shown, (i) admit an attested copy without final certification or (ii) permit the foreign official record to be evidenced by an attested summary with or without a final certification.

The Note of the Advisory Committee regarding revised Rule 44 states:

Although the amended rule will generally facilitate proof of foreign official records, it is recognized that in some situations it may be difficult or even impossible to satisfy the basic requirements of the rule. There may be no United States consul in a particular foreign country; the foreign officials may not cooperate; peculiarities may exist or arise hereafter in the law or practice of a foreign country. See United States v. Grabina, 119 F.2d 863 (2d Cir.1941); and, generally, Jones, International Judicial Assistance: Procedural Chaos and a Program for Reform, 62 Yale L.J. 515, 548–49 (1953). Therefore the final sentence of subdivision (a)(2) provides the court with discretion to admit an attested copy of a record without a final certification, or an attested summary of a record with or without a final certification. See Rep. of Comm. on Comparative Civ.Proc. & Prac., Proc. A.B.A., Sec. Int'l & Comp. L. 123, 130–31 (1952); Model Code of Evidence §§ 517, 519 (1942). This relaxation should be permitted only when it is shown that the party has been unable to satisfy the basic requirements of the amended rule despite his reasonable efforts. Moreover it is specially provided that the parties must be given a reasonable opportunity in these cases to examine into the authenticity and accuracy of the copy or summary.

Senate Bill No. 266 [Stats.1970, c. 41] adds the substance of the sentence of Rule 44 quoted above, making only those changes needed to conform the language of that sentence to the language used in Section 1530. The bill also adopts the language of Rule 44 which specifies the officers who can make the final certificate. The change made by adopting this language is to restrict the United States foreign service officers who can make the final certificate to certain specified responsible officers and to liberalize the provision by permitting "a diplomatic or consular official of the foreign country assigned or accredited to the United States" to make the final certificate. This latter conforming change achieves desirable conformity with Rule 44 and liberalizes the rule but at the same time assures that a responsible official will make the final certificate. [10 Cal.L.Rev.Comm. Reports 1022 (1970)].

Research References

Rutter, Cal. Practice Guide: Civil Trials & Evidence Ch. 8G-C, C. Presumptions.

Rutter, Cal. Practice Guide: Enforcing Judgments/Debts Ch. 6J-2, Enforcing Sister State Judgments in California.

8 Witkin Cal. Proc. 5th Enforcement of Judgment § 455, (S 455) Form and Content.

7 Witkin Cal. Proc. 5th Judgment § 349, Methods of Proof.

14 Witkin, California Summary 10th Wills and Probate § 67, Will Previously Admitted to Probate.

§ 1531. Certification of copy for evidence

For the purpose of evidence, whenever a copy of a writing is attested or certified, the attestation or certificate must state in substance that the copy is a correct copy of the original, or of a specified part thereof, as the case may be. *(Stats.1965, c. 299, § 2, operative Jan. 1, 1967.)*

Law Revision Commission Comments

Section 1531 is based on the provisions of Section 1923 of the Code of Civil Procedure. The language has been modified to define the process of attestation as well as the process of certification. Since Section 1530 permits a writing to be attested or certified for purposes of evidence without the attachment of an official seal, Section 1531 omits any requirement of a seal. [7 Cal.L.Rev.Comm. Reports 1 (1965)].

§ 1532. Official record of recorded writing

(a) The official record of a writing is prima facie evidence of the existence and content of the original recorded writing if:

(1) The record is in fact a record of an office of a public entity; and

(2) A statute authorized such a writing to be recorded in that office.

(b) The presumption established by this section is a presumption affecting the burden of producing evidence. *(Stats.1965, c. 299, § 2, operative Jan. 1, 1967.)*

Law Revision Commission Comments

Section 1530 authorizes the use of a copy of a writing in official custody to prove the content of that writing. When a writing has been recorded, Section 1530 merely permits a certified copy of the record to be used to prove the record, not the original recorded writing. Section 1532 permits the official record to be used to prove the content of the original recorded writing. However, under the provisions of Section 1401, the original recorded writing must be authenticated before the copy can be introduced. If the writing was executed by a public official, or if a certificate of acknowledgment or proof was attached to the writing, the original writing is presumed to be authentic and no further evidence of authenticity is required. Evidence Code §§ 1450, 1451, and 1453.

Where evidence is introduced that is sufficient to sustain a finding that the original writing is not authentic, the trier of fact is required to determine the authenticity of the original writing without regard to the presumption created by this section. See Evidence Code § 604 and the Comment thereto.

Code of Civil Procedure Section 1951 (superseded by Evidence Code Section 1600) is similar to Section 1532, but the Code of Civil Procedure section relates only to writings affecting property. Section 1532 extends the principle of the Code of Civil Procedure section to all recorded writings. There is no comparable provision in existing law. [7 Cal.L.Rev. Comm. Reports 1 (1965)].

Research References

Rutter, Cal. Practice Guide: Civil Trials & Evidence Ch. 8G-C, C. Presumptions.

Miller and Starr California Real Estate § 8:3, Requirements; Form and Content.

Miller and Starr California Real Estate § 11:8, Evidentiary Effect of Recording.

Miller and Starr California Real Estate § 8:42, Presumptions and Proof-- Generally.

ARTICLE 3. PHOTOGRAPHIC COPIES AND PRINTED REPRESENTATIONS OF WRITINGS

Section

Law Revision Commission Comments

The article heading is amended to reflect the repeal of the Best Evidence Rule and the addition of Sections 1552 (computer printouts) and 1553 (printouts of images stored on video or digital media) to this article. See Comments to Section 1521 and former Sections 1500.5 and 1500.6. [26 Cal.L.Rev.Comm. Reports 369 (1996)].

§ 1550. Photographic copies made as business records

Section prior to amendment by Stats.2002, c. 124 (A.B.2033), § 1. See, also, section as amended by Stats.2002, c. 124 (A.B.2033), § 1.

A nonerasable optical image reproduction provided that additions, deletions, or changes to the original document are not permitted by the technology, a photostatic, microfilm, microcard, miniature photographic, or other photographic copy or reproduction, or an enlargement thereof, of a writing is as admissible as the writing itself if the copy or reproduction was made and preserved as a part of the records of a business (as defined by Section 1270) in the regular course of that business. The introduction of the copy, reproduction, or enlargement does not preclude admission of the original writing if it is still in existence. A court may require the introduction of a hard copy printout of the document. *(Stats.1965, c. 299, § 2, operative Jan. 1, 1967. Amended by Stats.1992, c. 876 (A.B.3296), § 10.)*

Law Revision Commission Comments

Section 1550 continues in effect those provisions of the Uniform Photographic Copies of Business and Public Records as Evidence Act that are now found in Code of Civil Procedure Section 1953i.

Section 1550 omits the requirement, contained in Section 1953i of the Code of Civil Procedure, that the original writing be a business record. As long as the original writing is admissible under any exception to the hearsay rule, its trustworthiness is sufficiently assured; and the requirement that the photographic copy be made in the regular course of business sufficiently assures the trustworthiness of the copy. If the original is admissible not as an exception to the hearsay rule but as evidence of an ultimate fact in the case (*e.g.*, a will or a contract), a photographic copy, the trustworthiness of which is sufficiently assured by the fact that it was made in the regular course of business, should be as admissible as the original. [7 Cal.L.Rev.Comm. Reports 1 (1965)].

Research References

Rutter, Cal. Practice Guide: Civ. Pro. Before Trial Ch. 5-D, D. Default Judgment by Court.

Rutter, Cal. Practice Guide: Civ. Pro. Before Trial Ch. 10-C, C. Procedural Requirements-Moving Party.

Rutter, Cal. Practice Guide: Civil Trials & Evidence Ch. 8C-B, B. Writings.

Evidence

Rutter, Cal. Practice Guide: Civil Trials & Evidence Ch. 8G-C, C. Presumptions.

§ 1550. Types of evidence as writing admissible as the writing itself

Section as amended by Stats.2002, c. 124 (A.B.2033), § 1. See, also, section prior to amendment by Stats.2002, c. 124 (A.B.2033), § 1.

(a) If made and preserved as a part of the records of a business, as defined in Section 1270, in the regular course of that business, the following types of evidence of a writing are as admissible as the writing itself:

(1) A nonerasable optical image reproduction or any other reproduction of a public record by a trusted system, as defined in Section 12168.7 of the Government Code, if additions, deletions, or changes to the original document are not permitted by the technology.

(2) A photostatic copy or reproduction.

(3) A microfilm, microcard, or miniature photographic copy, reprint, or enlargement.

(4) Any other photographic copy or reproduction, or an enlargement thereof.

(b) The introduction of evidence of a writing pursuant to subdivision (a) does not preclude admission of the original writing if it is still in existence. A court may require the introduction of a hard copy printout of the document. *(Stats. 1965, c. 299, § 2, operative Jan. 1, 1967. Amended by Stats.1992, c. 876 (A.B.3296), § 10; Stats.2002, c. 124 (A.B.2033), § 1, operative contingent.)*

Operative Effect

Stats.2002, c. 124 (A.B.2033), § 2, provides that this act shall become operative on the date the Secretary of State adopts uniform standards for storing and recording permanent and nonpermanent documents in electronic media as required by Government Code § 12168.7.

Law Revision Commission Comments

Section 1550 continues in effect those provisions of the Uniform Photographic Copies of Business and Public Records as Evidence Act that are now found in Code of Civil Procedure Section 1953i.

Section 1550 omits the requirement, contained in Section 1953i of the Code of Civil Procedure, that the original writing be a business record. As long as the original writing is admissible under any exception to the hearsay rule, its trustworthiness is sufficiently assured; and the requirement that the photographic copy be made in the regular course of business sufficiently assures the trustworthiness of the copy. If the original is admissible not as an exception to the hearsay rule but as evidence of an ultimate fact in the case (*e.g.,* a will or a contract), a photographic copy, the trustworthiness of which is sufficiently assured by the fact that it was made in the regular course of business, should be as admissible as the original. [7 Cal.L.Rev.Comm. Reports 1 (1965)].

Research References

Rutter, Cal. Practice Guide: Civ. Pro. Before Trial Ch. 5-D, D. Default Judgment by Court.
Rutter, Cal. Practice Guide: Civ. Pro. Before Trial Ch. 10-C, C. Procedural Requirements-Moving Party.
Rutter, Cal. Practice Guide: Civil Trials & Evidence Ch. 8C-B, B. Writings.
Rutter, Cal. Practice Guide: Civil Trials & Evidence Ch. 8G-C, C. Presumptions.

§ 1550.1. Admissibility of reproductions of files, records, writings, photographs, and fingerprints

Reproductions of files, records, writings, photographs, fingerprints or other instruments in the official custody of a criminal justice agency that were microphotographed or otherwise reproduced in a manner that conforms with the provisions of Section 11106.1, 11106.2, or 11106.3 of the Penal Code shall be admissible to the same extent and under the same circumstances as the original file, record, writing or other instrument would be admissible. *(Added by Stats.2004, c. 65 (A.B.883), § 1.)*

Research References

Rutter, Cal. Practice Guide: Civil Trials & Evidence Ch. 8C-B, B. Writings.

§ 1551. Photographic copies where original destroyed or lost

A print, whether enlarged or not, from a photographic film (including a photographic plate, microphotographic film, photostatic negative, or similar reproduction) of an original writing destroyed or lost after such film was taken or a reproduction from an electronic recording of video images on magnetic surfaces is admissible as the original writing itself if, at the time of the taking of such film or electronic recording, the person under whose direction and control it was taken attached thereto, or to the sealed container in which it was placed and has been kept, or incorporated in the film or electronic recording, a certification complying with the provisions of Section 1531 and stating the date on which, and the fact that, it was so taken under his direction and control. *(Stats.1965, c. 299, § 2, operative Jan. 1, 1967. Amended by Stats.1969, c. 646, p. 1298, § 1.)*

Law Revision Commission Comments

Section 1551 restates without substantive change the provisions of Code of Civil Procedure Section 1920b. [7 Cal.L.Rev.Comm. Reports 1 (1965)].

§ 1552. Printed representation of computer-generated information

(a) A printed representation of computer information or a computer program is presumed to be an accurate representation of the computer information or computer program that it purports to represent. This presumption is a presumption affecting the burden of producing evidence. If a party to an action introduces evidence that a printed representation of computer information or computer program is inaccurate or unreliable, the party introducing the printed representation into evidence has the burden of proving, by a preponderance of evidence, that the printed representation is an accurate representation of the existence and content of the computer information or computer program that it purports to represent.

(b) Subdivision (a) applies to the printed representation of computer-generated information stored by an automated traffic enforcement system.

(c) Subdivision (a) shall not apply to computer-generated official records certified in accordance with Section 452.5 or 1530. *(Added by Stats.1998, c. 100 (S.B.177), § 4, operative Jan. 1, 1999. Amended by Stats.2012, c. 735 (S.B.1303), § 1.)*

Law Revision Commission Comments

Subdivision (a) of Section 1552 continues former Section 1500.5(c) without substantive change, except that the reference to "best available evidence" is changed to "an accurate representation," due to the replacement of the Best Evidence Rule with the Secondary Evidence Rule. See Section 1521 Comment. See also Section 255 (accurate printout of computer data is an "original").

Subdivision (b) continues former Section 1500.5(d) without substantive change. [26 Cal.L.Rev.Comm. Reports 369 (1996)].

Research References

Rutter, Cal. Practice Guide: Civil Trials & Evidence Ch. 8C-B, B. Writings.
Rutter, Cal. Practice Guide: Civil Trials & Evidence Ch. 8D-D, D. Hearsay Exceptions.
Rutter, Cal. Practice Guide: Civil Trials & Evidence Ch. 8G-C, C. Presumptions.

Rutter, Cal. Practice Guide: Insurance Litigation Ch. 15-I, I. Trial.

§ 1553. Printed representation of video or digital images

(a) A printed representation of images stored on a video or digital medium is presumed to be an accurate representation of the images it purports to represent. This presumption is a presumption affecting the burden of producing evidence. If a party to an action introduces evidence that a printed representation of images stored on a video or digital medium is inaccurate or unreliable, the party introducing the printed representation into evidence has the burden of proving, by a preponderance of evidence, that the printed representation is an accurate representation of the existence and content of the images that it purports to represent.

(b) Subdivision (a) applies to the printed representation of video or photographic images stored by an automated traffic enforcement system. *(Added by Stats.1998, c. 100 (S.B.177), § 5, operative Jan. 1, 1999. Amended by Stats.2012, c. 735 (S.B.1303), § 2.)*

Law Revision Commission Comments

Section 1553 continues the last three sentences of the second paragraph of former Section 1500.6 without substantive change, except that the reference to "best available evidence" is changed to "an accurate representation," due to the replacement of the Best Evidence Rule with the Secondary Evidence Rule. See Section 1521 Comment. [26 Cal. L.Rev.Comm. Reports 369 (1996)].

Research References

Rutter, Cal. Practice Guide: Civil Trials & Evidence Ch. 8C-B, B. Writings.
Rutter, Cal. Practice Guide: Civil Trials & Evidence Ch. 8G-C, C. Presumptions.

ARTICLE 4. PRODUCTION OF BUSINESS RECORDS

Section

§ 1560. Compliance with subpoena duces tecum for business records

(a) As used in this article:

(1) "Business" includes every kind of business described in Section 1270.

(2) "Record" includes every kind of record maintained by a business.

(b) Except as provided in Section 1564, when a subpoena duces tecum is served upon the custodian of records or other qualified witness of a business in an action in which the business is neither a party nor the place where any cause of action is alleged to have arisen, and the subpoena requires the production of all or any part of the records of the business, it is sufficient compliance therewith if the custodian or other qualified witness delivers by mail or otherwise a true, legible, and durable copy of all of the records described in the subpoena to the clerk of the court or to another person described in subdivision (d) of Section 2026.010 of the Code of Civil Procedure, together with

the affidavit described in Section 1561, within one of the following time periods:

(1) In any criminal action, five days after the receipt of the subpoena.

(2) In any civil action, within 15 days after the receipt of the subpoena.

(3) Within the time agreed upon by the party who served the subpoena and the custodian or other qualified witness.

(c) The copy of the records shall be separately enclosed in an inner envelope or wrapper, sealed, with the title and number of the action, name of witness, and date of subpoena clearly inscribed thereon; the sealed envelope or wrapper shall then be enclosed in an outer envelope or wrapper, sealed, and directed as follows:

(1) If the subpoena directs attendance in court, to the clerk of the court.

(2) If the subpoena directs attendance at a deposition, to the officer before whom the deposition is to be taken, at the place designated in the subpoena for the taking of the deposition or at the officer's place of business.

(3) In other cases, to the officer, body, or tribunal conducting the hearing, at a like address.

(d) Unless the parties to the proceeding otherwise agree, or unless the sealed envelope or wrapper is returned to a witness who is to appear personally, the copy of the records shall remain sealed and shall be opened only at the time of trial, deposition, or other hearing, upon the direction of the judge, officer, body, or tribunal conducting the proceeding, in the presence of all parties who have appeared in person or by counsel at the trial, deposition, or hearing. Records that are original documents and that are not introduced in evidence or required as part of the record shall be returned to the person or entity from whom received. Records that are copies may be destroyed.

(e) As an alternative to the procedures described in subdivisions (b), (c), and (d), the subpoenaing party in a civil action may direct the witness to make the records available for inspection or copying by the party's attorney, the attorney's representative, or deposition officer as described in Section 2020.420 of the Code of Civil Procedure, at the witness' business address under reasonable conditions during normal business hours. Normal business hours, as used in this subdivision, means those hours that the business of the witness is normally open for business to the public. When provided with at least five business days' advance notice by the party's attorney, attorney's representative, or deposition officer, the witness shall designate a time period of not less than six continuous hours on a date certain for copying of records subject to the subpoena by the party's attorney, attorney's representative, or deposition officer. It shall be the responsibility of the attorney's representative to deliver any copy of the records as directed in the subpoena. Disobedience to the deposition subpoena issued pursuant to this subdivision is punishable as provided in Section 2020.240 of the Code of Civil Procedure. *(Stats.1965, c. 299, § 2, operative Jan. 1, 1967. Amended by Stats.1969, c. 199, p. 484, § 2; Stats.1982, c. 452, p. 1824, § 2.5; Stats.1984, c. 481, § 2; Stats.1986, c. 603, § 6; Stats.1991, c. 1090 (A.B.1484), § 14; Stats.1997, c. 442 (A.B.758), § 16; Stats.1999, c. 444 (A.B.794), § 4; Stats.2000, c. 287 (S.B.1955), § 1; Stats.2004, c. 182 (A.B.3081), § 32, operative July 1, 2005; Stats.2004, c. 162 (A.B.1249), § 1; Stats.2005, c. 294 (A.B.333), § 18; Stats.2006, c. 538 (S.B.1852), § 155.)*

Law Revision Commission Comments

Section 1560 is the same in substance as Code of Civil Procedure Section 1998, except for the clarifying definition of "hospital" added in subdivision (a). [7 Cal.L.Rev.Comm. Reports 1 (1965)].

Section 1560 is amended to reflect nonsubstantive reorganization of the rules governing civil discovery. See 2004 Cal. Stat. ch. 182.

Section 1560 is also amended to delete language authorizing the judge to substitute for the clerk if there is no clerk. Every superior court has a clerk. See Gov't Code §§ 69840 (court clerk's powers, duties, and responsibilities), 71620 (court executive or administrative officer has authority of a court clerk). See also Code Civ. Proc. § 167 (judge may perform any act court clerk may perform).

Research References

Rutter, Cal. Practice Guide: Civ. Pro. Before Trial Ch. 8E-6, Subpoena to Nonparty Deponent or Business Records Custodian.
Rutter, Cal. Practice Guide: Civil Trials & Evidence Ch. 1-C, C. Marshalling the Evidence.
Rutter, Cal. Practice Guide: Civil Trials & Evidence Ch. 1-L, L. Assignment to Trial Department.
Rutter, Cal. Practice Guide: Civil Trials & Evidence Ch. 4-B, B. Preliminary Matters Discussed in Final Status Conference or In-Chambers Conference.
Rutter, Cal. Practice Guide: Civil Trials & Evidence Ch. 8C-B, B. Writings.
Rutter, Cal. Practice Guide: Civil Trials & Evidence Ch. 8D-D, D. Hearsay Exceptions.
California Practice Guide: Employment Litigation Ch. 13-H, H. Contesting Citations and Related Orders and Notices.
Rutter, Cal. Practice Guide: Family Law Ch. 11-E, E. Securing Witness Attendance and Document Production at Trial.
Rutter, Cal. Practice Guide: Landlord-Tenant Ch. 9-C, C. Final Preparation for Trial.
Rutter, Cal. Practice Guide: Personal Injury Ch. 6-B, B. Overview of Selected Discovery Procedures.
Rutter, Cal. Practice Guide: Personal Injury Ch. 8-C, C. Two Months Before Trial.

§ 1561.   Affidavit accompanying records

(a) The records shall be accompanied by the affidavit of the custodian or other qualified witness, stating in substance each of the following:

(1) The affiant is the duly authorized custodian of the records or other qualified witness and has authority to certify the records.

(2) The copy is a true copy of all the records described in the subpoena duces tecum, or pursuant to subdivision (e) of Section 1560 the records were delivered to the attorney, the attorney's representative, or deposition officer for copying at the custodian's or witness' place of business, as the case may be.

(3) The records were prepared by the personnel of the business in the ordinary course of business at or near the time of the act, condition, or event.

(4) The identity of the records.

(5) A description of the mode of preparation of the records.

(b) If the business has none of the records described, or only part thereof, the custodian or other qualified witness shall so state in the affidavit, and deliver the affidavit and those records that are available in one of the manners provided in Section 1560.

(c) Where the records described in the subpoena were delivered to the attorney or his or her representative or deposition officer for copying at the custodian's or witness' place of business, in addition to the affidavit required by subdivision (a), the records shall be accompanied by an affidavit by the attorney or his or her representative or deposition officer stating that the copy is a true copy of all the records delivered to the attorney or his or her representative or deposition officer for copying. (Stats.1965, c. 299, § 2, operative Jan. 1, 1967. Amended by Stats.1969, c. 199, p. 484, § 3; Stats.1986, c. 603, § 7; Stats.1987, c. 19, § 2, eff. May 12, 1987; Stats.1996, c. 146 (A.B.3001), § 1; Stats.1999, c. 444 (A.B.794), § 5.)

Law Revision Commission Comments

Section 1561 restates without substantive change the provisions of Code of Civil Procedure Section 1998.1.   [7 Cal.L.Rev.Comm. Reports 1 (1965)].

Research References

Rutter, Cal. Practice Guide: Civ. Pro. Before Trial Ch. 8E-6, Subpoena to Nonparty Deponent or Business Records Custodian.
Rutter, Cal. Practice Guide: Civ. Pro. Before Trial Ch. 8L-1, Limitations on Existing Discovery Procedures.
Rutter, Cal. Practice Guide: Civil Trials & Evidence Ch. 1-C, C. Marshalling the Evidence.
Rutter, Cal. Practice Guide: Civil Trials & Evidence Ch. 8D-D, D. Hearsay Exceptions.
Rutter, Cal. Practice Guide: Civil Trials & Evidence Ch. 8G-C, C. Presumptions.
Rutter, Cal. Practice Guide: Family Law Ch. 11-E, E. Securing Witness Attendance and Document Production at Trial.
Rutter, Cal. Practice Guide: Landlord-Tenant Ch. 9-C, C. Final Preparation for Trial.
Rutter, Cal. Practice Guide: Personal Injury Ch. 6-B, B. Overview of Selected Discovery Procedures.
Rutter, Cal. Practice Guide: Personal Injury Ch. 6-E, E. Special Discovery Rules and Procedures in Limited Civil Cases.
Rutter, Cal. Practice Guide: Personal Injury Ch. 8-C, C. Two Months Before Trial.
11 Witkin, California Summary 10th Husband and Wife § 291, (S 291) Discovery.

§ 1562.   Admissibility of affidavit and copy of records

If the original records would be admissible in evidence if the custodian or other qualified witness had been present and testified to the matters stated in the affidavit, and if the requirements of Section 1271 have been met, the copy of the records is admissible in evidence.   The affidavit is admissible as evidence of the matters stated therein pursuant to Section 1561 and the matters so stated are presumed true.   When more than one person has knowledge of the facts, more than one affidavit may be made.   The presumption established by this section is a presumption affecting the burden of producing evidence.   (Stats. 1965, c. 299, § 2, operative Jan. 1, 1967.   Amended by Stats.1989, c. 1416, § 31; Stats.1996, c. 146 (A.B.3001), § 2.)

Research References

Rutter, Cal. Practice Guide: Civ. Pro. Before Trial Ch. 8E-6, Subpoena to Nonparty Deponent or Business Records Custodian.
Rutter, Cal. Practice Guide: Civil Trials & Evidence Ch. 1-C, C. Marshalling the Evidence.
Rutter, Cal. Practice Guide: Civil Trials & Evidence Ch. 8C-B, B. Writings.
Rutter, Cal. Practice Guide: Civil Trials & Evidence Ch. 8D-D, D. Hearsay Exceptions.
Rutter, Cal. Practice Guide: Civil Trials & Evidence Ch. 8G-C, C. Presumptions.
Rutter, Cal. Practice Guide: Family Law Ch. 11-E, E. Securing Witness Attendance and Document Production at Trial.
Rutter, Cal. Practice Guide: Landlord-Tenant Ch. 9-C, C. Final Preparation for Trial.
Rutter, Cal. Practice Guide: Personal Injury Ch. 8-C, C. Two Months Before Trial.
11 Witkin, California Summary 10th Husband and Wife § 291, (S 291) Discovery.

§ 1563.   One witness and mileage fee

(a) This article shall not be interpreted to require tender or payment of more than one witness fee and one mileage fee or other charge, to a witness or witness' business, unless there is an agreement to the contrary between the witness and the requesting party.

(b) All reasonable costs incurred in a civil proceeding by any witness which is not a party with respect to the production of all or any part of business records the production of which is requested pursuant to a subpoena duces tecum may be charged against the party serving the subpoena duces tecum.

(1) "Reasonable cost," as used in this section, shall include, but not be limited to, the following specific costs: ten cents ($0.10) per page for standard reproduction of documents of a size 8½ by 14 inches or less; twenty cents ($0.20) per page for copying of documents from microfilm; actual costs for the reproduction of oversize documents or the reproduction of documents requiring special processing which are made in response to a subpoena; reasonable clerical costs incurred in locating and making the records available to be billed at the maximum rate of twenty-four dollars ($24) per hour per person, computed on the basis of six dollars ($6) per quarter hour or fraction thereof; actual postage charges; and the actual cost, if any, charged to the witness by a third person for the retrieval and return of records held offsite by that third person.

(2) The requesting party, or the requesting party's deposition officer, shall not be required to pay those costs or any estimate thereof prior to the time the records are available for delivery pursuant to the subpoena, but the witness may demand payment of costs pursuant to this section simultaneous with actual delivery of the subpoenaed records, and until payment is made, is under no obligation to deliver the records.

(3) The witness shall submit an itemized statement for the costs to the requesting party, or the requesting party's deposition officer, setting forth the reproduction and clerical costs incurred by the witness. Should the costs exceed those authorized in paragraph (1), or the witness refuses to produce an itemized statement of costs as required by paragraph (3), upon demand by the requesting party, or the requesting party's deposition officer, the witness shall furnish a statement setting forth the actions taken by the witness in justification of the costs.

(4) The requesting party may petition the court in which the action is pending to recover from the witness all or a part of the costs paid to the witness, or to reduce all or a part of the costs charged by the witness, pursuant to this subdivision, on the grounds that those costs were excessive. Upon the filing of the petition the court shall issue an order to show cause and from the time the order is served on the witness the court shall have jurisdiction over the witness. The court may hear testimony on the order to show cause and if it finds that the costs demanded and collected, or charged but not collected, exceed the amount authorized by this subdivision, it shall order the witness to remit to the requesting party, or reduce its charge to the requesting party by an amount equal to, the amount of the excess. In the event that the court finds the costs excessive and charged in bad faith by the witness, the court shall order the witness to remit the full amount of the costs demanded and collected, or excuse the requesting party from any payment of costs charged but not collected, and the court shall also order the witness to pay the requesting party the amount of the reasonable expenses incurred in obtaining the order including attorney's fees. If the court finds the costs were not excessive, the court shall order the requesting party to pay the witness the amount of the reasonable expenses incurred in defending the petition, including attorney's fees.

(5) If a subpoena is served to compel the production of business records and is subsequently withdrawn, or is quashed, modified or limited on a motion made other than by the witness, the witness shall be entitled to reimbursement pursuant to paragraph (1) for all costs incurred in compliance with the subpoena to the time that the requesting party has notified the witness that the subpoena has been withdrawn or quashed, modified or limited. In the event the subpoena is withdrawn or quashed, if those costs are not paid within 30 days after demand therefor, the witness may file a motion in the court in which the action is pending for an order requiring payment, and the court

shall award the payment of expenses and attorney's fees in the manner set forth in paragraph (4).

(6) Where the records are delivered to the attorney, the attorney's representative, or the deposition officer for inspection or photocopying at the witness' place of business, the only fee for complying with the subpoena shall not exceed fifteen dollars ($15), plus the actual cost, if any, charged to the witness by a third person for retrieval and return of records held offsite by that third person. If the records are retrieved from microfilm, the reasonable cost, as defined in paragraph (1), shall also apply.

(c) When the personal attendance of the custodian of a record or other qualified witness is required pursuant to Section 1564, in a civil proceeding, he or she shall be entitled to the same witness fees and mileage permitted in a case where the subpoena requires the witness to attend and testify before a court in which the action or proceeding is pending and to any additional costs incurred as provided by subdivision (b). *(Stats.1965, c. 299, § 2, operative Jan. 1, 1967. Amended by Stats.1972, c. 396, p. 719, § 1; Stats.1981, c. 1014, p. 3913, § 2; Stats.1982, c. 452, p. 1825, § 3; Stats.1986, c. 603, § 8; Stats.1987, c. 19, § 3, eff. May 12, 1987; Stats.1997, c. 442 (A.B.758), § 17; Stats.1999, c. 444 (A.B.794), § 6.)*

Fees and Charges

Commissioner's authority to increase or decrease fees, and schedule of fees and charges, see Insurance Code § 12978.

Law Revision Commission Comments

Section 1563 restates without substantive change the provisions of Code of Civil Procedure Section 1998.3. [7 Cal.L.Rev.Comm. Reports 1 (1965)].

Research References

Rutter, Cal. Practice Guide: Civ. Pro. Before Trial Ch. 8E-6, Subpoena to Nonparty Deponent or Business Records Custodian.
Rutter, Cal. Practice Guide: Civil Trials & Evidence Ch. 1-C, C. Marshalling the Evidence.
Rutter, Cal. Practice Guide: Family Law Ch. 11-C, C. Optional "Formal" Discovery Procedures.
Rutter, Cal. Practice Guide: Family Law Ch. 11-E, E. Securing Witness Attendance and Document Production at Trial.

§ 1564. Personal attendance of custodian and production of original records

The personal attendance of the custodian or other qualified witness and the production of the original records is not required unless, at the discretion of the requesting party, the subpoena duces tecum contains a clause which reads:

"The personal attendance of the custodian or other qualified witness and the production of the original records are required by this subpoena. The procedure authorized pursuant to subdivision (b) of Section 1560, and Sections 1561 and 1562, of the Evidence Code will not be deemed sufficient compliance with this subpoena." *(Stats.1965, c. 299, § 2, operative Jan. 1, 1967. Amended by Stats.1984, c. 603, § 2; Stats.1986, c. 603, § 9; Stats.1987, c. 19, § 4, eff. May 12, 1987.)*

Law Revision Commission Comments

Section 1564 restates without substantive change the provisions of Code of Civil Procedure Section 1998.4. [7 Cal.L.Rev.Comm. Reports 1 (1965)].

Research References

Rutter, Cal. Practice Guide: Civil Trials & Evidence Ch. 1-C, C. Marshalling the Evidence.
Rutter, Cal. Practice Guide: Family Law Ch. 11-E, E. Securing Witness Attendance and Document Production at Trial.

Rutter, Cal. Practice Guide: Landlord-Tenant Ch. 9-C, C. Final Preparation for Trial.

Rutter, Cal. Practice Guide: Personal Injury Ch. 8-C, C. Two Months Before Trial.

§ 1565. Service of more than one subpoena duces tecum

If more than one subpoena duces tecum is served upon the custodian of records or other qualified witness and the personal attendance of the custodian or other qualified witness is required pursuant to Section 1564, the witness shall be deemed to be the witness of the party serving the first such subpoena duces tecum. *(Stats.1965, c. 299, § 2, operative Jan. 1, 1967. Amended by Stats.1969, c. 199, p. 485, § 4.)*

Law Revision Commission Comments

Section 1565 restates without substantive change the provisions of Code of Civil Procedure Section 1998.5. [7 Cal.L.Rev.Comm. Reports 1 (1965)].

§ 1566. Applicability of article

This article applies in any proceeding in which testimony can be compelled. *(Stats.1965, c. 299, § 2, operative Jan. 1, 1967.)*

Law Revision Commission Comments

This section has no counterpart in the portion of the Code of Civil Procedure from which this article is taken. Section 1566 is intended to preserve the original effect of Code of Civil Procedure Sections 1998–1998.5 by removing Sections 1560–1565 from the limiting provisions of Section 300. [7 Cal.L.Rev.Comm. Reports 1 (1965)].

Research References

Rutter, Cal. Practice Guide: Civil Trials & Evidence Ch. 1-C, C. Marshalling the Evidence.

Rutter, Cal. Practice Guide: Landlord-Tenant Ch. 9-C, C. Final Preparation for Trial.

Rutter, Cal. Practice Guide: Personal Injury Ch. 8-C, C. Two Months Before Trial.

§ 1567. Employee income and benefit information; forms completed by employer; support modification or termination proceedings

A completed form described in Section 3664 of the Family Code for income and benefit information provided by the employer may be admissible in a proceeding for modification or termination of an order for child, family, or spousal support if both of the following requirements are met:

(a) The completed form complies with Sections 1561 and 1562.

(b) A copy of the completed form and notice was served on the employee named therein pursuant to Section 3664 of the Family Code. *(Added by Stats.1995, c. 506 (A.B.413), § 1.)*

Research References

Rutter, Cal. Practice Guide: Personal Injury Ch. 6-B, B. Overview of Selected Discovery Procedures.

11 Witkin, California Summary 10th Husband and Wife § 291, (S 291) Discovery.

CHAPTER 3. OFFICIAL WRITINGS AFFECTING PROPERTY

Section

§ 1600. Record of document affecting property interest

(a) The record of an instrument or other document purporting to establish or affect an interest in property is prima facie evidence of the existence and content of the original recorded document and its execution and delivery by each person by whom it purports to have been executed if:

(1) The record is in fact a record of an office of a public entity; and

(2) A statute authorized such a document to be recorded in that office.

(b) The presumption established by this section is a presumption affecting the burden of proof. *(Stats.1965, c. 299, § 2, operative Jan. 1, 1967. Amended by Stats.1967, c. 650, p. 2007, § 9.)*

Law Revision Commission Comments

The sections in this chapter all relate to official writings affecting property. The provisions of some sections provide hearsay exceptions; other sections provide exceptions to the best evidence rule; still others provide authentication procedures.

Section 1600 is based on Code of Civil Procedure Section 1951, which it supersedes. It is similar to Section 1532 of the Evidence Code, which applies to all recorded writings, but it gives an added effect to the writings covered by its provisions. Under Section 1600, as under existing law, if an instrument purporting to affect an interest in property is recorded, a presumption of execution and delivery of the instrument arises. Thomas v. Peterson, 213 Cal. 672, 3 P.2d 306 (1931). [7 Cal.L.Rev.Comm. Reports 1 (1965)].

One effect of making the official record "prima facie evidence" is to create a rebuttable presumption. See Evidence Code § 602 ("A statute providing that a fact or group of facts is prima facie evidence of another fact establishes a rebuttable presumption."). The classification of this presumption as one affecting the burden of proof is consistent with the prior case law. See Thomas v. Peterson, 213 Cal. 672, 3 P.2d 306 (1931); DuBois v. Larke, 175 Cal.App.2d 737, 346 P.2d 830 (1959); Osterberg v. Osterberg, 68 Cal.App.2d 254, 156 P.2d 46 (1945). Such a classification tends to support the record title to property by requiring that the record title be sustained unless the party attacking it can actually prove its invalidity. See Evidence Code § 606 and *Comment* thereto.

The word "official," which modified "record," has been deleted as unnecessary in light of the requirements of paragraphs (1) and (2) of subdivision (a).

Record of deed to regents of university as conclusive evidence, see Education Code § 23259. [8 Cal.L.Rev.Comm. Reports 1 (1965)].

Research References

Miller and Starr California Real Estate § 8:3, Requirements; Form and Content.

Miller and Starr California Real Estate § 11:8, Evidentiary Effect of Recording.

Miller and Starr California Real Estate § 8:42, Presumptions and Proof-- Generally.

12 Witkin, California Summary 10th Real Property § 295, (S 295) Presumptions and Inferences.

§ 1601. Proof of content of lost official record affecting property

(a) Subject to subdivisions (b) and (c), when in any action it is desired to prove the contents of the official record of any writing lost or destroyed by conflagration or other public calamity, after proof of such loss or destruction, the following may, without further proof, be admitted in evidence to prove the contents of such record:

(1) Any abstract of title made and issued and certified as correct prior to such loss or destruction, and purporting to have been prepared and made in the ordinary course of business by any person engaged in the business of preparing and making abstracts of title prior to such loss or destruction; or

(2) Any abstract of title, or of any instrument affecting title, made, issued, and certified as correct by any person engaged in

the business of insuring titles or issuing abstracts of title to real estate, whether the same was made, issued, or certified before or after such loss or destruction and whether the same was made from the original records or from abstract and notes, or either, taken from such records in the preparation and upkeeping of its plant in the ordinary course of its business.

(b) No proof of the loss of the original writing is required other than the fact that the original is not known to the party desiring to prove its contents to be in existence.

(c) Any party desiring to use evidence admissible under this section shall give reasonable notice in writing to all other parties to the action who have appeared therein, of his intention to use such evidence at the trial of the action, and shall give all such other parties a reasonable opportunity to inspect the evidence, and also the abstracts, memoranda, or notes from which it was compiled, and to take copies thereof. *(Stats.1965, c. 299, § 2, operative Jan. 1, 1967.)*

Law Revision Commission Comments

Section 1601 restates without substantive change the provisions of Section 1855a of the Code of Civil Procedure. [7 Cal.L.Rev.Comm. Reports 1 (1965)].

Research References

Miller and Starr California Real Estate § 11:9, Destruction of Public Records; Proof of Recorded Document.

§ 1603. Deed by officer in pursuance of court process

A deed of conveyance of real property, purporting to have been executed by a proper officer in pursuance of legal process of any of the courts of record of this state, acknowledged and recorded in the office of the recorder of the county wherein the real property therein described is situated, or the record of such deed, or a certified copy of such record, is prima facie evidence that the property or interest therein described was thereby conveyed to the grantee named in such deed. The presumption established by this section is a presumption affecting the burden of proof. *(Stats.1965, c. 299, § 2, operative Jan. 1, 1967. Amended by Stats.1967, c. 650, p. 2008, § 11.)*

Law Revision Commission Comments

Section 1603 restates without substantive change the provisions of Section 1928 of the Code of Civil Procedure. [7 Cal.L.Rev.Comm. Reports 1 (1965)].

One effect of Section 1603 is to create a rebuttable presumption. See Evidence Code § 602 ("A statute providing that a fact or group of facts is prima facie evidence of another fact establishes a rebuttable presumption.").

Prior to the enactment in 1911 of Code of Civil Procedure Section 1928 (upon which Section 1603 of the Evidence Code is based), the recitals in a sheriff's deed, made pursuant to legal process, could not be used as evidence of the judgment, the execution, and the sale upon which the deed was based. The existence of the prior proceedings were required to be proved with independent evidence. Heyman v. Babcock, 30 Cal. 367, 370 (1866); Hihn v. Peck, 30 Cal. 280, 287–288 (1966). The enactment of the predecessor of Evidence Code Section 1603 had two effects. First, it obviated the need for such independent proof. See, e.g., Oakes v. Fernandez, 108 Cal.App.2d 168, 238 P.2d 641 (1951); Wagnor v. Blume, 71 Cal.App.2d 94, 161 P.2d 1001 (1945). See also Basye, Clearing Land Titles § 41 (1953). Second, it obviated the need for proof of a chain of title prior to the execution of the need. Krug v. Warden, 57 Cal.App. 563, 207 Pac. 696 (1922).

The classification of the presumption in Section 1603 as a presumption affecting the burden of proof is consistent with the classification of the similar and overlapping presumptions contained in Evidence Code Sections 664 (official duty regularly performed) and 1600 (official record

of document affecting property). Like the presumption in Section 1600, the presumption in Section 1603 serves the purpose of supporting the record chain of title. [8 Cal.L.Rev.Comm. Reports 101 (1967)].

§ 1604. Certificate of purchase or of location of lands

A certificate of purchase, or of location, of any lands in this state, issued or made in pursuance of any law of the United States or of this state, is prima facie evidence that the holder or assignee of such certificate is the owner of the land described therein; but this evidence may be overcome by proof that, at the time of the location, or time of filing a preemption claim on which the certificate may have been issued, the land was in the adverse possession of the adverse party, or those under whom he claims, or that the adverse party is holding the land for mining purposes. *(Stats.1965, c. 299, § 2, operative Jan. 1, 1967.)*

Law Revision Commission Comments

Section 1604 restates without substantive change the provisions of Section 1925 of the Code of Civil Procedure. [7 Cal.L.Rev.Comm. Reports 1 (1965)].

Research References

Rutter, Cal. Practice Guide: Civil Trials & Evidence Ch. 8C-B, B. Writings.

Miller and Starr California Real Estate § 21:28, Mistake and Reformation.

Miller and Starr California Real Estate § 21:34, Who is Liable for Usury Penalties--Loans "Made or Arranged" by a Licensed Real Estate Broker.

18 NO. 2 Miller & Starr, California Real Estate Newsalert 25, Usury.

§ 1605. Authenticated Spanish title records

Duplicate copies and authenticated translations of original Spanish title papers relating to land claims in this state, derived from the Spanish or Mexican governments, prepared under the supervision of the Keeper of Archives by the Surveyor–General or his successor and by the Keeper of Archives, and filed with a county recorder, in accordance with Chapter 281 of the Statutes of 1865–66, are admissible as evidence with like force and effect as the originals and without proving the execution of such originals. *(Stats.1965, c. 299, § 2, operative Jan. 1, 1967. Amended by Stats.1967, c. 650, p. 2008, § 12.)*

Law Revision Commission Comments

Section 1605 restates without substantive change the provisions of Section 1927.5 of the Code of Civil Procedure. [7 Cal.L.Rev.Comm. Reports 1 (1965)].

Chapter 281 of the Statutes of 1865–66 required the California Secretary of State to cause copies to be made of all of the original Spanish title papers relating to land claims in this state derived from the Spanish and Mexican governments that were on file in the office of the United States Surveyor-General for California. These copies, authenticated by the Surveyor-General and the Keeper of Archives in his office, were then required to be recorded in the offices of the county recorders of the concerned counties.

Section 5 of the 1865–66 statute, which is now codified as Section 1605 of the Evidence Code, provided that the recorded copies would be admissible "as prima facie evidence" without proving the execution of the originals. It is apparent that the original purpose of the section was to provide an exception to the best evidence rule—which would have required production of the original or an excuse for its nonproduction before the recorded copy could be admitted—and an exception to the rule, now expressed in Evidence Code Section 1401(b), requiring the authentication of the original document as a condition of the admissibility of the copy. Section 1605, therefore, has been revised to reflect this original purpose. [8 Cal.L.Rev.Comm. Reports 101 (1967)].

Evidence

BUSINESS AND PROFESSIONS CODE

Division 3

PROFESSIONS AND VOCATIONS GENERALLY

CHAPTER 4. ATTORNEYS

ARTICLE 8.5. FEE AGREEMENTS

§ 6146. Limitations; periodic payments

(a) An attorney shall not contract for or collect a contingency fee for representing any person seeking damages in connection with an action for injury or damage against a health care provider based upon such person's alleged professional negligence in excess of the following limits:

(1) Forty percent of the first fifty thousand dollars ($50,000) recovered.

(2) Thirty-three and one-third percent of the next fifty thousand dollars ($50,000) recovered.

(3) Twenty-five percent of the next five hundred thousand dollars ($500,000) recovered.

(4) Fifteen percent of any amount on which the recovery exceeds six hundred thousand dollars ($600,000).

The limitations shall apply regardless of whether the recovery is by settlement, arbitration, or judgment, or whether the person for whom the recovery is made is a responsible adult, an infant, or a person of unsound mind.

(b) If periodic payments are awarded to the plaintiff pursuant to Section 667.7 of the Code of Civil Procedure, the court shall place a total value on these payments based upon the projected life expectancy of the plaintiff and include this amount in computing the total award from which attorney's fees are calculated under this section.

(c) For purposes of this section:

(1) "Recovered" means the net sum recovered after deducting any disbursements or costs incurred in connection with prosecution or settlement of the claim. Costs of medical care incurred by the plaintiff and the attorney's office-overhead costs or charges are not deductible disbursements or costs for such purpose.

(2) "Health care provider" means any person licensed or certified pursuant to Division 2 (commencing with Section 500), or licensed pursuant to the Osteopathic Initiative Act, or the Chiropractic Initiative Act, or licensed pursuant to Chapter 2.5 (commencing with Section 1440) of Division 2 of the Health and Safety Code; and any clinic, health dispensary, or health facility,

licensed pursuant to Division 2 (commencing with Section 1200) of the Health and Safety Code. "Health care provider" includes the legal representatives of a health care provider.

(3) "Professional negligence" is a negligent act or omission to act by a health care provider in the rendering of professional services, which act or omission is the proximate cause of a personal injury or wrongful death, provided that the services are within the scope of services for which the provider is licensed and which are not within any restriction imposed by the licensing agency or licensed hospital. *(Added by Stats.1975, 2nd Ex.Sess., c. 1, p. 3967, § 24.2. Amended by Stats.1975, 2nd Ex.Sess., c. 2, p. 3989, § 1.185, eff. Sept. 24, 1975, operative Dec. 12, 1975; Stats.1981, c. 714, p. 2580, § 23; Stats.1987, c. 1498, § 2.)*

Research References

Rutter, Cal. Practice Guide: Civil Appeals & Writs Ch. 1-G, G. Retaining an Appellate Specialist.
Rutter, Cal. Practice Guide: Civ. Pro. Before Trial Ch. 1-A, A. Accepting a New Case.
Rutter, Cal. Practice Guide: Civ. Pro. Before Trial Form 1:C, Contingency Fee Agreement.
Rutter, Cal. Practice Guide: Enforcing Judgments/Debts Ch. 1-B, B. Accepting the Collection Case.
Rutter, Cal. Practice Guide: Landlord-Tenant Ch. 2B-8, Successor Landlord Rights and Obligations Under Rental Agreements.
Rutter, Cal. Practice Guide: Personal Injury Ch. 1-C, C. Formation of Attorney-Client Relationship: the Employment Agreement.
Rutter, Cal. Practice Guide: Personal Injury Ch. 3-F, F. MICRA Provisions Affecting Damages.
Rutter, Cal. Practice Guide: Prof. Responsibility Ch. 5-A, A. Rules Governing Fee Negotiations With Client.
Rutter, Cal. Practice Guide: Prof. Responsibility Ch. 5-B, B. Types of Fees and Fee Arrangements.
Rutter, Cal. Practice Guide: Prof. Responsibility Ch. 5-C, C. Other Statutory Limits on Fees and Fee Agreements.
Rutter, Cal. Practice Guide: Prof. Responsibility Ch. 5-E, E. Costs Arrangements.
Rutter, Cal. Practice Guide: Prof. Responsibility Ch. 5-F, F. Formalizing Fee Agreements.
Rutter, Cal. Practice Guide: Prof. Responsibility Form 5:E, Fee Agreement Provision for "Graduated" Contingency Fee.
1 Witkin Cal. Proc. 5th Attorneys § 180, (S 180) Required Disclosures to Client.
1 Witkin Cal. Proc. 5th Attorneys § 182, Statutory Provisions.
1 Witkin Cal. Proc. 5th Attorneys § 183, Constitutionality.
1 Witkin Cal. Proc. 5th Attorneys § 184, Limits May Not be Waived.
1 Witkin Cal. Proc. 5th Attorneys § 185, Hybrid Proceeding.
1 Witkin Cal. Proc. 5th Attorneys § 186, Calculation of Fee.
1 Witkin Cal. Proc. 5th Attorneys § 188, Medical-Legal Consulting Fee.
1 Witkin Cal. Summ. 10th Contracts § 684, Miscellaneous Substantive Rights.
6 Witkin, California Summary 10th Torts § 942, Statutory Provisions.
6 Witkin, California Summary 10th Torts § 943, Constitutionality.
6 Witkin, California Summary 10th Torts § 944, Hybrid Action.
6 Witkin, California Summary 10th Torts § 945, Computation of Fee.
6 Witkin, California Summary 10th Torts § 970, Attorneys' Fees When Periodic Payments Are Awarded.
6 Witkin, California Summary 10th Torts § 1046, in General.
7 Witkin, California Summary 10th Constitutional Law § 633, General Rule.

14 Witkin, California Summary 10th Wills and Probate § 1070, (S 1070) in General.

§ 6147. Contingency fee contracts; duplicate copy; contents; effect of noncompliance; recovery of workers' compensation benefits

(a) An attorney who contracts to represent a client on a contingency fee basis shall, at the time the contract is entered into, provide a duplicate copy of the contract, signed by both the attorney and the client, or the client's guardian or representative, to the plaintiff, or to the client's guardian or representative. The contract shall be in writing and shall include, but is not limited to, all of the following:

(1) A statement of the contingency fee rate that the client and attorney have agreed upon.

(2) A statement as to how disbursements and costs incurred in connection with the prosecution or settlement of the claim will affect the contingency fee and the client's recovery.

(3) A statement as to what extent, if any, the client could be required to pay any compensation to the attorney for related matters that arise out of their relationship not covered by their contingency fee contract. This may include any amounts collected for the plaintiff by the attorney.

(4) Unless the claim is subject to the provisions of Section 6146, a statement that the fee is not set by law but is negotiable between attorney and client.

(5) If the claim is subject to the provisions of Section 6146, a statement that the rates set forth in that section are the maximum limits for the contingency fee agreement, and that the attorney and client may negotiate a lower rate.

(b) Failure to comply with any provision of this section renders the agreement voidable at the option of the plaintiff, and the attorney shall thereupon be entitled to collect a reasonable fee.

(c) This section shall not apply to contingency fee contracts for the recovery of workers' compensation benefits.

(d) This section shall become operative on January 1, 2000. *(Added by Stats.1993, c. 982 (S.B.645), § 5, operative Jan. 1, 1997. Amended by Stats.1994, c. 479 (A.B.3219), § 3, operative Jan. 1, 1997; Stats.1996, c. 1104 (A.B.2787), § 9, operative Jan. 1, 2000.)*

Research References

Rutter, Cal. Practice Guide: Civil Appeals & Writs Ch. 1-G, G. Retaining an Appellate Specialist.
Rutter, Cal. Practice Guide: Civil Appeals & Writs Ch. 8-D, D. Limits on Assertion of Issues on Appeal.
Rutter, Cal. Practice Guide: Civ. Pro. Before Trial Ch. 1-A, A. Accepting a New Case.
California Practice Guide: Employment Litigation Ch. 1-B, B. Plaintiffs' Evaluation of Claims.
California Practice Guide: Employment Litigation Ch. 2-B, B. Fee Arrangements.
California Practice Guide: Employment Litigation Form 2:A, State Bar of California Sample Contingency Fee Agreement.
Rutter, Cal. Practice Guide: Enforcing Judgments/Debts Ch. 1-B, B. Accepting the Collection Case.
Rutter, Cal. Practice Guide: Family Law Ch. 1-E, E. Attorney Fees and Costs Arrangements.
Rutter, Cal. Practice Guide: Landlord-Tenant Ch. 1-B, B. Accepting a New Case.
Rutter, Cal. Practice Guide: Personal Injury Ch. 1-C, C. Formation of Attorney-Client Relationship: the Employment Agreement.
Rutter, Cal. Practice Guide: Real Prop. Transactions Ch. 1-C, C. Attorney Fees and Costs Agreements.
Rutter, Cal. Practice Guide: Prof. Responsibility Ch. 1-I, I. Regulation of Sale of Law Practice.
Rutter, Cal. Practice Guide: Prof. Responsibility Ch. 2-D, D. In-Person Solicitation for Profit.

Rutter, Cal. Practice Guide: Prof. Responsibility Ch. 3-B, B. Formation of Relationship.
Rutter, Cal. Practice Guide: Prof. Responsibility Ch. 5-B, B. Types of Fees and Fee Arrangements.
Rutter, Cal. Practice Guide: Prof. Responsibility Ch. 5-C, C. Other Statutory Limits on Fees and Fee Agreements.
Rutter, Cal. Practice Guide: Prof. Responsibility Ch. 5-E, E. Costs Arrangements.
Rutter, Cal. Practice Guide: Prof. Responsibility Ch. 5-F, F. Formalizing Fee Agreements.
Rutter, Cal. Practice Guide: Prof. Responsibility Ch. 5-K, K. Fee Recovery/Enforcing Fee Agreements.
Rutter, Cal. Practice Guide: Prof. Responsibility Ch. 11-L, L. Determining Appropriate Discipline.
1 Witkin Cal. Proc. 5th Attorneys § 2, Statutory and Regulatory Framework.
1 Witkin Cal. Proc. 5th Attorneys § 180, (S 180) Required Disclosures to Client.
1 Witkin Cal. Proc. 5th Attorneys § 181, (S 181) Contracts Involving Claims Between Merchants.
1 Witkin Cal. Proc. 5th Attorneys § 425, Quantum Meruit Recovery.
6 Witkin, California Summary 10th Torts § 945, Computation of Fee.
14 Witkin, California Summary 10th Wills and Probate § 534, (S 534) Nature of Allowance.

§ 6147.5. Contingency fee contracts; recovery of claims between merchants

(a) Sections 6147 and 6148 shall not apply to contingency fee contracts for the recovery of claims between merchants as defined in Section 2104 of the Commercial Code, arising from the sale or lease of goods or services rendered, or money loaned for use, in the conduct of a business or profession if the merchant contracting for legal services employs 10 or more individuals.

(b) (1) In the instances in which no written contract for legal services exists as permitted by subdivision (a), an attorney shall not contract for or collect a contingency fee in excess of the following limits:

(A) Twenty percent of the first three hundred dollars ($300) collected.

(B) Eighteen percent of the next one thousand seven hundred dollars ($1,700) collected.

(C) Thirteen percent of sums collected in excess of two thousand dollars ($2,000).

(2) However, the following minimum charges may be charged and collected:

(A) Twenty-five dollars ($25) in collections of seventy-five dollars ($75) to one hundred twenty-five dollars ($125).

(B) Thirty-three and one-third percent of collections less than seventy-five dollars ($75). *(Added by Stats.1990, c. 713 (S.B. 2606), § 1.)*

Research References

Rutter, Cal. Practice Guide: Civ. Pro. Before Trial Ch. 1-A, A. Accepting a New Case.
Rutter, Cal. Practice Guide: Enforcing Judgments/Debts Ch. 1-B, B. Accepting the Collection Case.
Rutter, Cal. Practice Guide: Prof. Responsibility Ch. 5-C, C. Other Statutory Limits on Fees and Fee Agreements.
Rutter, Cal. Practice Guide: Prof. Responsibility Ch. 5-F, F. Formalizing Fee Agreements.
1 Witkin Cal. Proc. 5th Attorneys § 180, (S 180) Required Disclosures to Client.
1 Witkin Cal. Proc. 5th Attorneys § 181, (S 181) Contracts Involving Claims Between Merchants.

§ 6148. Contracts for services in cases not coming within § 6147; bills rendered by attorney; contents; failure to comply

(a) In any case not coming within Section 6147 in which it is reasonably foreseeable that total expense to a client, including attorney fees, will exceed one thousand dollars ($1,000), the contract for services in the case shall be in writing. At the time the contract is entered into, the attorney shall provide a duplicate copy of the contract signed by both the attorney and the client, or the client's guardian or representative, to the client or to the client's guardian or representative. The written contract shall contain all of the following:

(1) Any basis of compensation including, but not limited to, hourly rates, statutory fees or flat fees, and other standard rates, fees, and charges applicable to the case.

(2) The general nature of the legal services to be provided to the client.

(3) The respective responsibilities of the attorney and the client as to the performance of the contract.

(b) All bills rendered by an attorney to a client shall clearly state the basis thereof. Bills for the fee portion of the bill shall include the amount, rate, basis for calculation, or other method of determination of the attorney's fees and costs. Bills for the cost and expense portion of the bill shall clearly identify the costs and expenses incurred and the amount of the costs and expenses. Upon request by the client, the attorney shall provide a bill to the client no later than 10 days following the request unless the attorney has provided a bill to the client within 31 days prior to the request, in which case the attorney may provide a bill to the client no later than 31 days following the date the most recent bill was provided. The client is entitled to make similar requests at intervals of no less than 30 days following the initial request. In providing responses to client requests for billing information, the attorney may use billing data that is currently effective on the date of the request, or, if any fees or costs to that date cannot be accurately determined, they shall be described and estimated.

(c) Failure to comply with any provision of this section renders the agreement voidable at the option of the client, and the attorney shall, upon the agreement being voided, be entitled to collect a reasonable fee.

(d) This section shall not apply to any of the following:

(1) Services rendered in an emergency to avoid foreseeable prejudice to the rights or interests of the client or where a writing is otherwise impractical.

(2) An arrangement as to the fee implied by the fact that the attorney's services are of the same general kind as previously rendered to and paid for by the client.

(3) If the client knowingly states in writing, after full disclosure of this section, that a writing concerning fees is not required.

(4) If the client is a corporation.

(e) This section applies prospectively only to fee agreements following its operative date.

(f) This section shall become operative on January 1, 2000. *(Added by Stats.1993, c. 982 (S.B.645), § 6, operative Jan. 1, 1997. Amended by Stats.1994, c. 479 (A.B.3219), § 5, operative Jan. 1, 1997; Stats.1996, c. 1104 (A.B.2787), § 11, operative Jan. 1, 2000.)*

Research References

Rutter, Cal. Practice Guide: Civil Appeals & Writs Ch. 1-G, G. Retaining an Appellate Specialist.
Rutter, Cal. Practice Guide: Civ. Pro. Before Trial Ch. 1-A, A. Accepting a New Case.
California Practice Guide: Employment Litigation Ch. 1-B, B. Plaintiffs' Evaluation of Claims.
California Practice Guide: Employment Litigation Ch. 2-B, B. Fee Arrangements.
California Practice Guide: Employment Litigation Form 2:B, State Bar of California Sample Fee Agreement for Hourly Litigation.
Rutter, Cal. Practice Guide: Enforcing Judgments/Debts Ch. 1-B, B. Accepting the Collection Case.

Rutter, Cal. Practice Guide: Enforcing Judgments/Debts Ch. 3-C, C. Prelawsuit Considerations.
Rutter, Cal. Practice Guide: Family Law Ch. 1-E, E. Attorney Fees and Costs Arrangements.
Rutter, Cal. Practice Guide: Family Law Ch. 1-H, H. Special Concerns for Counsel Taking Over a Pending Dissolution Case.
Rutter, Cal. Practice Guide: Family Law Ch. 14-A, A. Fees and Costs Awards.
Rutter, Cal. Practice Guide: Family Law Ch. 14-B, B. Action Against Client for Payment of Fees.
Rutter, Cal. Practice Guide: Insurance Litigation Ch. 7B-K, K. Insurer's Duty to Provide Independent Counsel When Conflict of Interest Arises.
Rutter, Cal. Practice Guide: Landlord-Tenant Ch. 1-B, B. Accepting a New Case.
Rutter, Cal. Practice Guide: Landlord-Tenant Ch. 1-B, Outline B.
Rutter, Cal. Practice Guide: Personal Injury Ch. 1-C, C. Formation of Attorney-Client Relationship: the Employment Agreement.
Rutter, Cal. Practice Guide: Real Prop. Transactions Ch. 1-A, A. Scope of Work in Handling Real Estate Transactions.
Rutter, Cal. Practice Guide: Real Prop. Transactions Ch. 1-C, C. Attorney Fees and Costs Agreements.
Rutter, Cal. Practice Guide: Prof. Responsibility Ch. 1-I, I. Regulation of Sale of Law Practice.
Rutter, Cal. Practice Guide: Prof. Responsibility Ch. 3-B, B. Formation of Relationship.
Rutter, Cal. Practice Guide: Prof. Responsibility Ch. 5-B, B. Types of Fees and Fee Arrangements.
Rutter, Cal. Practice Guide: Prof. Responsibility Ch. 5-F, F. Formalizing Fee Agreements.
Rutter, Cal. Practice Guide: Prof. Responsibility Ch. 5-H, H. Billing Methods.
Rutter, Cal. Practice Guide: Prof. Responsibility Ch. 5-K, K. Fee Recovery/Enforcing Fee Agreements.
Rutter, Cal. Practice Guide: Prof. Responsibility Ch. 9-B, B. Establishing and Maintaining Client Trust Accounts.
Rutter, Cal. Practice Guide: Prof. Responsibility Ch. 11-L, L. Determining Appropriate Discipline.
Rutter, Cal. Practice Guide: Prof. Responsibility Form 5:M, Attorney-Client Fee Contract.
Rutter, Cal. Practice Guide: Prof. Responsibility Gen. Matls., Highlights.
3 Witkin Cal. Proc. 5th Actions § 514, Quasi-Contract Obligations.
1 Witkin Cal. Proc. 5th Attorneys § 102, Duty to Keep Client Informed.
1 Witkin Cal. Proc. 5th Attorneys § 155, Informal and Oral Agreements.
1 Witkin Cal. Proc. 5th Attorneys § 156, When Written Agreement is Required.
1 Witkin Cal. Proc. 5th Attorneys § 181, (S 181) Contracts Involving Claims Between Merchants.
1 Witkin Cal. Proc. 5th Attorneys § 425, Quantum Meruit Recovery.

§ 6149. Written fee contract as confidential communication

A written fee contract shall be deemed to be a confidential communication within the meaning of subdivision (e) of Section 6068 and of Section 952 of the Evidence Code. *(Added by Stats.1986, c. 475, § 8.)*

Research References

Rutter, Cal. Practice Guide: Civ. Pro. Before Trial Ch. 1-A, A. Accepting a New Case.
Rutter, Cal. Practice Guide: Civil Trials & Evidence Ch. 8E-A, A. Privileges.
Rutter, Cal. Practice Guide: Family Law Ch. 1-E, E. Attorney Fees and Costs Arrangements.
Rutter, Cal. Practice Guide: Landlord-Tenant Ch. 1-B, B. Accepting a New Case.
Rutter, Cal. Practice Guide: Personal Injury Ch. 1-C, C. Formation of Attorney-Client Relationship: the Employment Agreement.
Rutter, Cal. Practice Guide: Real Prop. Transactions Ch. 1-C, C. Attorney Fees and Costs Agreements.
Rutter, Cal. Practice Guide: Prof. Responsibility Ch. 5-H, H. Billing Methods.
Rutter, Cal. Practice Guide: Prof. Responsibility Ch. 5-K, K. Fee Recovery/Enforcing Fee Agreements.
Rutter, Cal. Practice Guide: Prof. Responsibility Ch. 7-B, B. Duty to Maintain Client Confidence and Secrets Under State Bar Act.

Rutter, Cal. Practice Guide: Prof. Responsibility Ch. 7-C, C. Attorney-Client Privilege.

1 Witkin Cal. Proc. 5th Attorneys § 156, When Written Agreement is Required.

§ 6149.5. Third-party liability claim; settlement by insurer; notice to claimant; effect on action or defense

(a) Upon the payment of one hundred dollars ($100) or more in settlement of any third-party liability claim the insurer shall provide written notice to the claimant if both of the following apply:

(1) The claimant is a natural person.

(2) The payment is delivered to the claimant's lawyer or other representative by draft, check, or otherwise.

(b) For purposes of this section, "written notice" includes providing to the claimant a copy of the cover letter sent to the claimant's attorney or other representative that accompanied the settlement payment.

(c) This section shall not create any cause of action for any person against the insurer based upon the insurer's failure to provide the notice to a claimant required by this section. This section shall not create a defense for any party to any cause of action based upon the insurer's failure to provide this notice. *(Added by Stats.1994, c. 479 (A.B.3219), § 6.)*

Research References

1 Witkin Cal. Proc. 5th Attorneys § 259, Receipt of Money in Settlement.

ARTICLE 13. ARBITRATION OF ATTORNEYS' FEES

Section

6200.   Establishment of system and procedure; arbitration and mediation; application of article; voluntary or mandatory nature; rules; immunity of arbitrator and mediator; powers of arbitrator; confidentiality of mediation.

6201.   Notice to client and State Bar; stay of action; right to arbitration; waiver by client.

6202.   Disclosure of attorney–client communication or attorney's work product; limitation.

6203.   Award; contents; damages and offset; fees and costs; finality of award; appellate fees and costs; attorney inactive status and penalties.

6204.   Agreement to be bound by award of arbitrator; trial after arbitration in absence of agreement; commencement of proceeding; prevailing party; effect of award and determination.

6204.5.   Disqualification of arbitrator or mediator; notice of right to judicial relief.

6206.   Limitation of actions tolled; judicial resolution of disputes subject to arbitration; effect of bar on civil actions requesting same relief.

§ 6200. Establishment of system and procedure; arbitration and mediation; application of article; voluntary or mandatory nature; rules; immunity of arbitrator and mediator; powers of arbitrator; confidentiality of mediation

(a) The board of trustees shall, by rule, establish, maintain, and administer a system and procedure for the arbitration, and may establish, maintain, and administer a system and procedure for mediation of disputes concerning fees, costs, or both, charged for professional services by members of the State Bar or by members of the bar of other jurisdictions. The rules may include provision for a filing fee in the amount as the board may, from time to time, determine.

(b) This article shall not apply to any of the following:

(1) Disputes where a member of the State Bar of California is also admitted to practice in another jurisdiction or where an attorney is only admitted to practice in another jurisdiction, and he or she maintains no office in the State of California, and no material portion of the services were rendered in the State of California.

(2) Claims for affirmative relief against the attorney for damages or otherwise based upon alleged malpractice or professional misconduct, except as provided in subdivision (a) of Section 6203.

(3) Disputes where the fee or cost to be paid by the client or on his or her behalf has been determined pursuant to statute or court order.

(c) Unless the client has agreed in writing to arbitration under this article of all disputes concerning fees, costs, or both, arbitration under this article shall be voluntary for a client and shall be mandatory for an attorney if commenced by a client. Mediation under this article shall be voluntary for an attorney and a client.

(d) The board of trustees shall adopt rules to allow arbitration and mediation of attorney fee and cost disputes under this article to proceed under arbitration and mediation systems sponsored by local bar associations in this state. Rules of procedure promulgated by local bar associations are subject to review by the board or a committee designated by the board to ensure that they provide for a fair, impartial, and speedy hearing and award.

(e) In adopting or reviewing rules of arbitration under this section, the board shall provide that the panel shall include one attorney member whose area of practice is either, at the option of the client, civil law, if the attorney's representation involved civil law, or criminal law, if the attorney's representation involved criminal law, as follows:

(1) If the panel is composed of three members the panel shall include one attorney member whose area of practice is either, at the option of the client, civil or criminal law, and shall include one lay member.

(2) If the panel is composed of one member, that member shall be an attorney whose area of practice is either, at the option of the client, civil or criminal law.

(f) In any arbitration or mediation conducted pursuant to this article by the State Bar or by a local bar association, pursuant to rules of procedure approved by the board of trustees, an arbitrator or mediator, as well as the arbitrating association and its directors, officers, and employees, shall have the same immunity which attaches in judicial proceedings.

(g) In the conduct of arbitrations under this article the arbitrator or arbitrators may do all of the following:

(1) Take and hear evidence pertaining to the proceeding.

(2) Administer oaths and affirmations.

(3) Issue subpoenas for the attendance of witnesses and the production of books, papers, and documents pertaining to the proceeding.

(h) Participation in mediation is a voluntary consensual process, based on direct negotiations between the attorney and his or her client, and is an extension of the negotiated settlement process. All discussions and offers of settlement are confidential and may not be disclosed in any subsequent arbitration or other proceedings. *(Added by Stats.1978, c. 719, p. 2249, § 1. Amended by Stats.1984, c. 825, § 1; Stats.1989, c. 1416, § 1; Stats.1990, c. 483 (S.B.2066), § 5; Stats.1990, c. 1020 (A.B.2682), § 2; Stats.1993, c. 1262 (A.B.1272), § 1; Stats.1994, c. 479 (A.B.3219), § 8; Stats.1996, c. 1104 (A.B.2787), § 12; Stats.2009, c. 54 (S.B.544), § 1; Stats.2011, c. 417 (S.B.163), § 55.)*

Research References

Rutter, Cal. Practice Guide: A.D.R. App. A, Selected Statutes Providing for ADR.

Rutter, Cal. Practice Guide: A.D.R. Ch. 5-A, A. General Considerations.

Rutter, Cal. Practice Guide: A.D.R. Ch. 5-D, D. Defenses to Enforcement.

Rutter, Cal. Practice Guide: A.D.R. Ch. 5-I, I. Arbitrator's Award.

Rutter, Cal. Practice Guide: A.D.R. Ch. 5-J, J. Challenging and Enforcing Arbitrator's Award in Court.

Rutter, Cal. Practice Guide: A.D.R. Ch. 7-B, B. Arbitrators.

Rutter, Cal. Practice Guide: A.D.R. App. D Form 78, Attorney Retainer or Contingent Fee Agreements.

Rutter, Cal. Practice Guide: Civ. Pro. Before Trial Ch. 1-A, A. Accepting a New Case.

Rutter, Cal. Practice Guide: Civ. Pro. Before Trial Ch. 1-E, E. Prelawsuit ADR Requirement.

Rutter, Cal. Practice Guide: Civ. Pro. Before Trial Ch. 3-A, A. Subject Matter Jurisdiction (Competency).

Rutter, Cal. Practice Guide: Civ. Pro. Before Trial Form 1:C, Contingency Fee Agreement.

Rutter, Cal. Practice Guide: Enforcing Judgments/Debts Ch. 3-A, A. Evaluating the Claim.

Rutter, Cal. Practice Guide: Family Law Ch. 1-E, E. Attorney Fees and Costs Arrangements.

Rutter, Cal. Practice Guide: Family Law Ch. 14-B, B. Action Against Client for Payment of Fees.

Rutter, Cal. Practice Guide: Personal Injury Ch. 1-C, C. Formation of Attorney-Client Relationship: the Employment Agreement.

Rutter, Cal. Practice Guide: Real Prop. Transactions Ch. 1-C, C. Attorney Fees and Costs Agreements.

Rutter, Cal. Practice Guide: Real Prop. Transactions Form 1:A, Sample Fee Letter.

Rutter, Cal. Practice Guide: Real Prop. Transactions Form 1:C, Notice of Client's Right to Arbitration.

Rutter, Cal. Practice Guide: Prof. Responsibility Ch. 1-J, J. Regulating Participation in Legal Service Programs and Referral Service Plans.

Rutter, Cal. Practice Guide: Prof. Responsibility Ch. 3-A, A. Nature of Attorney-Client Relationship.

Rutter, Cal. Practice Guide: Prof. Responsibility Ch. 5-D, D. Ethical Limitations on Attorney Fees.

Rutter, Cal. Practice Guide: Prof. Responsibility Ch. 5-F, F. Formalizing Fee Agreements.

Rutter, Cal. Practice Guide: Prof. Responsibility Ch. 5-K, K. Fee Recovery/Enforcing Fee Agreements.

Rutter, Cal. Practice Guide: Prof. Responsibility Ch. 9-B, B. Establishing and Maintaining Client Trust Accounts.

Miller and Starr California Real Estate § 35:22, Nature of Arbitration.

Miller and Starr California Real Estate § 35:25, Written Agreement Required.

Miller and Starr California Real Estate § 35:59, Loss of Right to Arbitrate by Waiver, Estoppel, or Forfeiture.

Miller and Starr California Real Estate § 35:66, Immunity of Arbitrators and Arbitration Associations.

Miller and Starr California Real Estate § 35:88, Limitations on Judicial Review of Arbitrators' Awards.

Miller and Starr California Real Estate § 35:97, Arbitrators Exceeded Their Powers.

Miller and Starr California Real Estate § 35:104, Award of Costs and Attorney's Fees in Order Confirming, Correcting, or Vacating an Arbitrator's Award.

14 NO. 3 Miller & Starr, California Real Estate Newsalert 4, Commercial Arbitration.

8 Witkin Cal. Proc. 5th Attack Judgment Trial Court § 147, (S 147) in General.

1 Witkin Cal. Proc. 5th Attorneys § 2, Statutory and Regulatory Framework.

1 Witkin Cal. Proc. 5th Attorneys § 208, (S 208) in General.

1 Witkin Cal. Proc. 5th Attorneys § 220, Methods Available.

1 Witkin Cal. Proc. 5th Attorneys § 221, Nature and Purpose of Arbitration Program.

1 Witkin Cal. Proc. 5th Attorneys § 222, Administration by State Bar.

1 Witkin Cal. Proc. 5th Attorneys § 223, Exceptions to Arbitration Requirement.

1 Witkin Cal. Proc. 5th Attorneys § 224, Scope of Jurisdiction.

1 Witkin Cal. Proc. 5th Attorneys § 225, Arbitrators.

1 Witkin Cal. Proc. 5th Attorneys § 232, in General.

2 Witkin Cal. Proc. 5th Courts § 243, (S 243) in General.

2 Witkin Cal. Proc. 5th Courts § 249, (S 249) Declaratory Relief.

2 Witkin Cal. Proc. 5th Courts § 282, (S 282) Particular Actions.

5 Witkin Cal. Proc. 5th Pleading § 850, (S 850) Nature of Action.

6 Witkin Cal. Proc. 5th Proceedings Without Trial § 482, (S 482) Programs and Legislation.

6 Witkin Cal. Proc. 5th Proceedings Without Trial § 571, (S 571) Arbitrator Exceeded Powers.

5 Witkin, California Summary 10th Torts § 174, Persons Engaged in Alternative Dispute Resolution.

§ 6201. Notice to client and State Bar; stay of action; right to arbitration; waiver by client

(a) The rules adopted by the board of trustees shall provide that an attorney shall forward a written notice to the client prior to or at the time of service of summons or claim in an action against the client, or prior to or at the commencement of any other proceeding against the client under a contract between attorney and client which provides for an alternative to arbitration under this article, for recovery of fees, costs, or both. The written notice shall be in the form that the board of trustees prescribes, and shall include a statement of the client's right to arbitration under this article. Failure to give this notice shall be a ground for the dismissal of the action or other proceeding. The notice shall not be required, however, prior to initiating mediation of the dispute.

The rules adopted by the board of trustees shall provide that the client's failure to request arbitration within 30 days after receipt of notice from the attorney shall be deemed a waiver of the client's right to arbitration under the provisions of this article.

(b) If an attorney, or the attorney's assignee, commences an action in any court or any other proceeding and the client is entitled to maintain arbitration under this article, and the dispute is not one to which subdivision (b) of Section 6200 applies, the client may stay the action or other proceeding by serving and filing a request for arbitration in accordance with the rules established by the board of trustees pursuant to subdivision (a) of Section 6200. The request for arbitration shall be served and filed prior to the filing of an answer in the action or equivalent response in the other proceeding; failure to so request arbitration prior to the filing of an answer or equivalent response shall be deemed a waiver of the client's right to arbitration under the provisions of this article if notice of the client's right to arbitration was given pursuant to subdivision (a).

(c) Upon filing and service of the request for arbitration, the action or other proceeding shall be automatically stayed until the award of the arbitrators is issued or the arbitration is otherwise terminated. The stay may be vacated in whole or in part, after a hearing duly noticed by any party or the court, if and to the extent the court finds that the matter is not appropriate for arbitration under the provisions of this article. The action or other proceeding may thereafter proceed subject to the provisions of Section 6204.

(d) A client's right to request or maintain arbitration under the provisions of this article is waived by the client commencing an action or filing any pleading seeking either of the following:

(1) Judicial resolution of a fee dispute to which this article applies.

(2) Affirmative relief against the attorney for damages or otherwise based upon alleged malpractice or professional misconduct.

(e) If the client waives the right to arbitration under this article, the parties may stipulate to set aside the waiver and to proceed with arbitration. *(Added by Stats.1978, c. 719, p. 2249, § 1. Amended by Stats.1979, c. 878, p. 3062, § 1; Stats.1982, c. 979, p. 3557, § 1; Stats.1984, c. 825, § 2; Stats.1989, c. 1416, § 2; Stats.1990, c. 483 (S.B.2066), § 6; Stats.1993, c. 1262 (A.B.1272),*

§ 2; Stats.1994, c. 479 (A.B.3219), § 9; Stats.1996, c. 1104 (A.B.2787), § 13; Stats.2011, c. 417 (S.B.163), § 56.)

Research References

Rutter, Cal. Practice Guide: A.D.R. Ch. 5-D, D. Defenses to Enforcement.
Rutter, Cal. Practice Guide: Civ. Pro. Before Trial Ch. 1-A, A. Accepting a New Case.
Rutter, Cal. Practice Guide: Civ. Pro. Before Trial Ch. 1-E, E. Prelawsuit ADR Requirement.
Rutter, Cal. Practice Guide: Civ. Pro. Before Trial Ch. 12(I)-G, G. Stays Caused by Other Proceedings.
Rutter, Cal. Practice Guide: Family Law Ch. 14-B, B. Action Against Client for Payment of Fees.
Rutter, Cal. Practice Guide: Personal Injury Ch. 1-C, C. Formation of Attorney-Client Relationship: the Employment Agreement.
Rutter, Cal. Practice Guide: Personal Injury Ch. 7-A, A. Introduction-Nature and Purpose of "Judicial Arbitration" in General.
Rutter, Cal. Practice Guide: Real Prop. Transactions Ch. 1-C, C. Attorney Fees and Costs Agreements.
Rutter, Cal. Practice Guide: Prof. Responsibility Ch. 5-F, F. Formalizing Fee Agreements.
Rutter, Cal. Practice Guide: Prof. Responsibility Ch. 5-K, K. Fee Recovery/Enforcing Fee Agreements.
Miller and Starr California Real Estate § 35:22, Nature of Arbitration.
1 Witkin Cal. Proc. 5th Attorneys § 208, (S 208) in General.
1 Witkin Cal. Proc. 5th Attorneys § 221, Nature and Purpose of Arbitration Program.
1 Witkin Cal. Proc. 5th Attorneys § 226, Notice, Request, and Stay.
1 Witkin Cal. Proc. 5th Attorneys § 227, Waiver of Right to Arbitration.
1 Witkin Cal. Proc. 5th Attorneys § 231, Trial After Arbitration.
7 Witkin Cal. Proc. 5th Trial § 41, Notice of Settlement or Stay.

§ 6202. Disclosure of attorney–client communication or attorney's work product; limitation

The provisions of Article 3 (commencing with Section 950) of Chapter 4 of Division 8 of the Evidence Code shall not prohibit the disclosure of any relevant communication, nor shall the provisions of Chapter 4 (commencing with Section 2018.010) of Title 4 of Part 4 of the Code of Civil Procedure be construed to prohibit the disclosure of any relevant work product of the attorney in connection with: (a) an arbitration hearing or mediation pursuant to this article; (b) a trial after arbitration; or (c) judicial confirmation, correction, or vacation of an arbitration award. In no event shall such disclosure be deemed a waiver of the confidential character of such matters for any other purpose. *(Added by Stats.1978, c. 719, p. 2249, § 1. Amended by Stats.1982, c. 979, p. 3558, § 2; Stats.1984, c. 825, § 3; Stats.1996, c. 1104 (A.B.2787), § 14; Stats.2004, c. 182 (A.B.3081), § 1, operative July 1, 2005.)*

Law Revision Commission Comments

Section 6202 is amended to reflect nonsubstantive reorganization of the rules governing civil discovery. [33 Cal.L.Rev.Comm. Reports 971 (2004)].

Research References

Rutter, Cal. Practice Guide: Prof. Responsibility Ch. 7-C, C. Attorney-Client Privilege.
Rutter, Cal. Practice Guide: Prof. Responsibility Ch. 7-D, D. Attorney Work Product Doctrine.
1 Witkin Cal. Proc. 5th Attorneys § 229, Evidence and Privilege.

§ 6203. Award; contents; damages and offset; fees and costs; finality of award; appellate fees and costs; attorney inactive status and penalties

(a) The award shall be in writing and signed by the arbitrators concurring therein. It shall include a determination of all the questions submitted to the arbitrators, the decision of which is necessary in order to determine the controversy. The award shall not include any award to either party for costs or attorney's fees incurred in preparation for or in the course of the fee arbitration proceeding, notwithstanding any contract between the parties providing for such an award or costs or attorney's fees. However, the filing fee paid may be allocated between the parties by the arbitrators. This section shall not preclude an award of costs or attorney's fees to either party by a court pursuant to subdivision (c) of this section or of subdivision (d) of Section 6204. The State Bar, or the local bar association delegated by the State Bar to conduct the arbitration, shall deliver to each of the parties with the award, an original declaration of service of the award.

Evidence relating to claims of malpractice and professional misconduct, shall be admissible only to the extent that those claims bear upon the fees, costs, or both, to which the attorney is entitled. The arbitrators shall not award affirmative relief, in the form of damages or offset or otherwise, for injuries underlying the claim. Nothing in this section shall be construed to prevent the arbitrators from awarding the client a refund of unearned fees, costs, or both previously paid to the attorney.

(b) Even if the parties to the arbitration have not agreed in writing to be bound, the arbitration award shall become binding upon the passage of 30 days after service of notice of the award, unless a party has, within the 30 days, sought a trial after arbitration pursuant to Section 6204. If an action has previously been filed in any court, any petition to confirm, correct, or vacate the award shall be to the court in which the action is pending, and may be served by mail on any party who has appeared, as provided in Chapter 4 (commencing with Section 1003) of Title 14 of Part 2 of the Code of Civil Procedure; otherwise it shall be in the same manner as provided in Chapter 4 (commencing with Section 1285) of Title 9 of Part 3 of the Code of Civil Procedure. If no action is pending in any court, the award may be confirmed, corrected, or vacated by petition to the court having jurisdiction over the amount of the arbitration award, but otherwise in the same manner as provided in Chapter 4 (commencing with Section 1285) of Title 9 of Part 3 of the Code of Civil Procedure.

(c) Neither party to the arbitration may recover costs or attorney's fees incurred in preparation for or in the course of the fee arbitration proceeding with the exception of the filing fee paid pursuant to subdivision (a) of this section. However, a court confirming, correcting, or vacating an award under this section may award to the prevailing party reasonable fees and costs incurred in obtaining confirmation, correction, or vacation of the award including, if applicable, fees and costs on appeal. The party obtaining judgment confirming, correcting, or vacating the award shall be the prevailing party except that, without regard to consideration of who the prevailing party may be, if a party did not appear at the arbitration hearing in the manner provided by the rules adopted by the board of trustees, that party shall not be entitled to attorney's fees or costs upon confirmation, correction, or vacation of the award.

(d)(1) In any matter arbitrated under this article in which the award is binding or has become binding by operation of law or has become a judgment either after confirmation under subdivision (c) or after a trial after arbitration under Section 6204, or in any matter mediated under this article, if: (A) the award, judgment, or agreement reached after mediation includes a refund of fees or costs, or both, to the client and (B) the attorney has not complied with that award, judgment, or agreement the State Bar shall enforce the award, judgment, or agreement by placing the attorney on involuntary inactive status until the refund has been paid.

(2) The State Bar shall provide for an administrative procedure to determine whether an award, judgment, or agreement should be enforced pursuant to this subdivision. An award, judgment, or agreement shall be so enforced if:

(A) The State Bar shows that the attorney has failed to comply with a binding fee arbitration award, judgment, or agreement rendered pursuant to this article.

(B) The attorney has not proposed a payment plan acceptable to the client or the State Bar.

However, the award, judgment, or agreement shall not be so enforced if the attorney has demonstrated that he or she (i) is not personally responsible for making or ensuring payment of the refund, or (ii) is unable to pay the refund.

(3) An attorney who has failed to comply with a binding award, judgment, or agreement shall pay administrative penalties or reasonable costs, or both, as directed by the State Bar. Penalties imposed shall not exceed 20 percent of the amount to be refunded to the client or one thousand dollars ($1,000), whichever is greater. Any penalties or costs, or both, that are not paid shall be added to the membership fee of the attorney for the next calendar year.

(4) The board shall terminate the inactive enrollment upon proof that the attorney has complied with the award, judgment, or agreement and upon payment of any costs or penalties, or both, assessed as a result of the attorney's failure to comply.

(5) A request for enforcement under this subdivision shall be made within four years from the date (A) the arbitration award was mailed, (B) the judgment was entered, or (C) the date the agreement was signed. In an arbitrated matter, however, in no event shall a request be made prior to 100 days from the date of the service of a signed copy of the award. In cases where the award is appealed, a request shall not be made prior to 100 days from the date the award has become final as set forth in this section. *(Added by Stats.1978, c. 719, p. 2249, § 1. Amended by Stats.1982, c. 979, p. 3559, § 3; Stats.1984, c. 825, § 4; Stats. 1989, c. 1416, § 3; Stats.1990, c. 483 (S.B.2066), § 7; Stats.1992, c. 1265 (S.B.1405), § 5; Stats.1993, c. 1262 (A.B.1272), § 3; Stats.1996, c. 1104 (A.B.2787), § 15; Stats.2009, c. 54 (S.B.544), § 2; Stats.2011, c. 417 (S.B.163), § 57.)*

Research References

Rutter, Cal. Practice Guide: A.D.R. App. A, Selected Statutes Providing for ADR.
Rutter, Cal. Practice Guide: A.D.R. Ch. 5-D, D. Defenses to Enforcement.
Rutter, Cal. Practice Guide: A.D.R. Ch. 5-J, J. Challenging and Enforcing Arbitrator's Award in Court.
Rutter, Cal. Practice Guide: Civil Appeals & Writs Ch. 14-B, B. Recovery of Appellate Costs and Attorney Fees.
Rutter, Cal. Practice Guide: Civ. Pro. Before Trial Ch. 3-A, A. Subject Matter Jurisdiction (Competency).
Rutter, Cal. Practice Guide: Civ. Pro. Before Trial Ch. 13-G, G. Trial De Novo.
Rutter, Cal. Practice Guide: Family Law Ch. 14-B, B. Action Against Client for Payment of Fees.
Rutter, Cal. Practice Guide: Real Prop. Transactions Ch. 1-C, C. Attorney Fees and Costs Agreements.
Rutter, Cal. Practice Guide: Prof. Responsibility Ch. 1-D, D. Unauthorized Practice of Law.
Rutter, Cal. Practice Guide: Prof. Responsibility Ch. 5-K, K. Fee Recovery/Enforcing Fee Agreements.
Rutter, Cal. Practice Guide: Prof. Responsibility Ch. 11-A, A. Grounds for Discipline.
Rutter, Cal. Practice Guide: Prof. Responsibility Ch. 11-B, B. Disciplinary Proceedings-In General.
Rutter, Cal. Practice Guide: Prof. Responsibility Ch. 1 App., California Rules of Professional Conduct.
1 Witkin Cal. Proc. 5th Attorneys § 223, Exceptions to Arbitration Requirement.
1 Witkin Cal. Proc. 5th Attorneys § 224, Scope of Jurisdiction.
1 Witkin Cal. Proc. 5th Attorneys § 229, Evidence and Privilege.
1 Witkin Cal. Proc. 5th Attorneys § 230, Arbitration Award.
1 Witkin Cal. Proc. 5th Attorneys § 232, in General.
1 Witkin Cal. Proc. 5th Attorneys § 233, Proceedings to Enforce Award.

1 Witkin Cal. Proc. 5th Attorneys § 234, Proceedings for Inactive Enrollment.
1 Witkin Cal. Proc. 5th Attorneys § 352, Noncompliance With Reporting or Disciplinary Requirements.

§ 6204. Agreement to be bound by award of arbitrator; trial after arbitration in absence of agreement; commencement of proceeding; prevailing party; effect of award and determination

(a) The parties may agree in writing to be bound by the award of arbitrators appointed pursuant to this article at any time after the dispute over fees, costs, or both, has arisen. In the absence of such an agreement, either party shall be entitled to a trial after arbitration if sought within 30 days, pursuant to subdivisions (b) and (c), except that if either party willfully fails to appear at the arbitration hearing in the manner provided by the rules adopted by the board of trustees, that party shall not be entitled to a trial after arbitration. The determination of willfulness shall be made by the court. The party who failed to appear at the arbitration shall have the burden of proving that the failure to appear was not willful. In making its determination, the court may consider any findings made by the arbitrators on the subject of a party's failure to appear.

(b) If there is an action pending, the trial after arbitration shall be initiated by filing a rejection of arbitration award and request for trial after arbitration in that action within 30 days after service of notice of the award. If the rejection of arbitration award has been filed by the plaintiff in the pending action, all defendants shall file a responsive pleading within 30 days following service upon the defendant of the rejection of arbitration award and request for trial after arbitration. If the rejection of arbitration award has been filed by the defendant in the pending action, all defendants shall file a responsive pleading within 30 days after the filing of the rejection of arbitration award and request for trial after arbitration. Service may be made by mail on any party who has appeared; otherwise service shall be made in the manner provided in Chapter 4 (commencing with Section 413.10) of Title 5 of Part 2 of the Code of Civil Procedure. Upon service and filing of the rejection of arbitration award, any stay entered pursuant to Section 6201 shall be vacated, without the necessity of a court order.

(c) If no action is pending, the trial after arbitration shall be initiated by the commencement of an action in the court having jurisdiction over the amount of money in controversy within 30 days after service of notice of the award. After the filing of such an action, the action shall proceed in accordance with the provisions of Part 2 (commencing with Section 307) of the Code of Civil Procedure, concerning civil actions generally.

(d) The party seeking a trial after arbitration shall be the prevailing party if that party obtains a judgment more favorable than that provided by the arbitration award, and in all other cases the other party shall be the prevailing party. The prevailing party may, in the discretion of the court, be entitled to an allowance for reasonable attorney's fees and costs incurred in the trial after arbitration, which allowance shall be fixed by the court. In fixing the attorney's fees, the court shall consider the award and determinations of the arbitrators, in addition to any other relevant evidence.

(e) Except as provided in this section, the award and determinations of the arbitrators shall not be admissible nor operate as collateral estoppel or res judicata in any action or proceeding. *(Added by Stats.1978, c. 719, p. 2249, § 1. Amended by Stats.1979, c. 878, p. 3063, § 2; Stats.1982, c. 979, p. 3559, § 4; Stats.1984, c. 825, § 5; Stats.1992, c. 1265 (S.B.1405), § 6; Stats.1996, c. 1104 (A.B.2787), § 16; Stats.1998, c. 798 (A.B. 1374), § 1; Stats.2009, c. 54 (S.B.544), § 3; Stats.2011, c. 417 (S.B.163), § 58.)*

Bus. & Prof.

Research References

Rutter, Cal. Practice Guide: A.D.R. Ch. 5-A, A. General Considerations.
Rutter, Cal. Practice Guide: A.D.R. Ch. 5-D, D. Defenses to Enforcement.
Rutter, Cal. Practice Guide: A.D.R. App. D Form 78, Attorney Retainer or Contingent Fee Agreements.
Rutter, Cal. Practice Guide: Civ. Pro. Before Trial Ch. 1-A, A. Accepting a New Case.
Rutter, Cal. Practice Guide: Civ. Pro. Before Trial Ch. 13-G, G. Trial De Novo.
Rutter, Cal. Practice Guide: Civ. Pro. Before Trial Form 1:C, Contingency Fee Agreement.
Rutter, Cal. Practice Guide: Family Law Ch. 1-E, E. Attorney Fees and Costs Arrangements.
Rutter, Cal. Practice Guide: Family Law Ch. 14-B, B. Action Against Client for Payment of Fees.
Rutter, Cal. Practice Guide: Personal Injury Ch. 1-C, C. Formation of Attorney-Client Relationship: the Employment Agreement.
Rutter, Cal. Practice Guide: Real Prop. Transactions Ch. 1-C, C. Attorney Fees and Costs Agreements.
Rutter, Cal. Practice Guide: Prof. Responsibility Ch. 5-F, F. Formalizing Fee Agreements.
Rutter, Cal. Practice Guide: Prof. Responsibility Ch. 5-K, K. Fee Recovery/Enforcing Fee Agreements.
Miller and Starr California Real Estate § 35:22, Nature of Arbitration.
Miller and Starr California Real Estate § 35:59, Loss of Right to Arbitrate by Waiver, Estoppel, or Forfeiture.
17 NO. 5 Miller & Starr, California Real Estate Newsalert 3, Commercial Arbitration.
1 Witkin Cal. Proc. 5th Attorneys § 221, Nature and Purpose of Arbitration Program.
1 Witkin Cal. Proc. 5th Attorneys § 230, Arbitration Award.
1 Witkin Cal. Proc. 5th Attorneys § 231, Trial After Arbitration.
1 Witkin Cal. Proc. 5th Attorneys § 232, in General.
2 Witkin Cal. Proc. 5th Courts § 282, (S 282) Particular Actions.
6 Witkin Cal. Proc. 5th Proceedings Without Trial § 32, Implied Limitations.

§ 6204.5. Disqualification of arbitrator or mediator; notice of right to judicial relief

(a) The State Bar shall provide by rule for an appropriate procedure to disqualify an arbitrator or mediator upon request of either party.

(b) The State Bar, or the local bar association delegated by the State Bar to conduct the arbitration, shall deliver a notice to the parties advising them of their rights to judicial relief subsequent to the arbitration proceeding. *(Added by Stats.1986, c. 475, § 9. Amended by Stats.1996, c. 1104 (A.B.2787), § 17.)*

Research References

Rutter, Cal. Practice Guide: Prof. Responsibility Ch. 5-K, K. Fee Recovery/Enforcing Fee Agreements.
1 Witkin Cal. Proc. 5th Attorneys § 225, Arbitrators.
1 Witkin Cal. Proc. 5th Attorneys § 231, Trial After Arbitration.

§ 6206. Limitation of actions tolled; judicial resolution of disputes subject to arbitration; effect of bar on civil actions requesting same relief

The time for filing a civil action seeking judicial resolution of a dispute subject to arbitration under this article shall be tolled from the time an arbitration is initiated in accordance with the rules adopted by the board of trustees until (a) 30 days after receipt of notice of the award of the arbitrators, or (b) receipt of notice that the arbitration is otherwise terminated, whichever comes first. Arbitration may not be commenced under this article if a civil action requesting the same relief would be barred by any provision of Title 2 (commencing with Section 312) of Part 2 of the Code of Civil Procedure; provided that this limitation shall not apply to a request for arbitration by a client, pursuant to the provisions of subdivision (b) of Section 6201, following the filing of a civil action by the attorney. *(Added by Stats.1978, c. 719, p. 2249, § 1. Amended by Stats.1984, c. 825, § 6; Stats.2011, c. 417 (S.B.163), § 59.)*

Research References

Rutter, Cal. Practice Guide: Real Prop. Transactions Form 1:C, Notice of Client's Right to Arbitration.
1 Witkin Cal. Proc. 5th Attorneys § 223, Exceptions to Arbitration Requirement.
1 Witkin Cal. Proc. 5th Attorneys § 226, Notice, Request, and Stay.

GOVERNMENT CODE

Title 1

GENERAL

Division 3.6

CLAIMS AND ACTIONS AGAINST PUBLIC ENTITIES AND PUBLIC EMPLOYEES

Part 1

DEFINITIONS

Section
810. Construction of division; short title.
810.2. Employee.
810.4. Employment.
810.6. Enactment.
810.8. Injury.
811. Law.
811.2. Public entity.
811.4. Public employee.
811.6. Regulation.
811.8. Statute.
811.9. Judges, subordinate judicial officers, and court executive officers in superior courts; state officer status.

§ 810. Construction of division; short title

(a) Unless the provision or context otherwise requires, the definitions contained in this part govern the construction of this division.

(b) This division may be referred to as the Government Claims Act. *(Added by Stats.1963, c. 1681, p. 3267, § 1. Amended by Stats.2012, c. 759 (A.B.2690), § 5.)*

Law Revision Commission Comments

Subdivision (a) [of § 45 of Stats.1963, c. 1681, p. 3288, set out in full under Historical and Statutory Notes to this section] provides that this act states the law governing the extent to which public entities may be liable for injury even in those cases where the injury occurred prior to the effective date of the act, prior to the moratorium legislation (Chapter 1404, Statutes of 1961), or prior to the decision in Muskopf v. Corning Hospital District, 55 Cal.2d 211, 11 Cal.Rptr. 89, 359 P.2d 457 (1961). Such retroactive application of this act may create new liabilities and may abolish recognized causes of action. The subdivision recognizes, however, that there may be a constitutional limitation on the extent to which it can be applied retroactively. But whether there is such a limitation, and if so what the extent of such limitation is, must be determined by the courts.

Subdivision (b) declares that this act does not revive any cause of action that has been barred because of a failure to comply with a claims presentation requirement or a statute of limitations. Subdivision (b), together with subdivision (c), also declares that a cause of action newly created by the retroactive application of this act is nonetheless barred if there has been no compliance with the claims procedure or statute of limitations that would have been applicable if the cause of action had accrued at the time of the injury. These provisions are to prevent stale claims and actions from being asserted on causes of action where the injury occurred long before the effective date of the act.

Subdivision (d) provides a limited period within which vested rights to causes of action that cannot be abolished by this act must be asserted. Of course, if the courts should hold that there is no constitutional impediment to the giving of full retroactive effect to this act, subdivision (d) would become unnecessary. [4 Cal.L.Rev.Comm. Reports 801 (1963)].

Section 810 is amended to adopt the short title "Government Claims Act." For background, see City of Stockton v. Superior Court, 42 Cal. 4th 730, 734, 741–42, 171 P.3d 20, 68 Cal. Rptr. 3d 295 (2007). [41 Cal.L.Rev.Comm. Reports 285 (2011)].

Research References

Rutter, Cal. Practice Guide: Civ. Pro. Before Trial Ch. 1-C, C. Prelawsuit Notices, Claims and Demands.
Rutter, Cal. Practice Guide: Civ. Pro. Before Trial Ch. 6-C, C. Answer.
Rutter, Cal. Practice Guide: Personal Injury Ch. 3-A, A. Introduction.
Rutter, Cal. Practice Guide: Personal Injury Ch. 5-A, A. Prelawsuit Filings.
Rutter, Cal. Practice Guide: Prof. Responsibility Ch. 10-A, A. Termination by Client.
Miller and Starr California Real Estate § 14:37, Liability of Governmental Entity for Land Use Decisions Affecting Views and Sunlight.
Miller and Starr California Real Estate § 22:18, Governmental Agencies.
Miller and Starr California Real Estate § 22:47, Liability to Persons Injured Due to Dangerous Conditions Off the Premises.
Miller and Starr California Real Estate § 22:76, Liability of a Government Entity.
Miller and Starr California Real Estate § 30:32, Remedies for a Regulatory Taking.
Miller and Starr California Real Estate § 30A:74, Judgment.
17 NO. 2 Miller & Starr, California Real Estate Newsalert 17, Inverse Condemnation.
3 Witkin Cal. Proc. 5th Actions § 233, (S 233) Revised Law.
1 Witkin Cal. Proc. 5th Attorneys § 318, Liability of Public Officers.
1 Witkin Cal. Proc. 5th Attorneys § 569, (S 569) Communications Are Privileged.
2 Witkin Cal. Proc. 5th Courts § 342, in General.
7 Witkin Cal. Proc. 5th Judgment § 235, (S 235) Statutory Authorization.
9 Witkin, California Summary 10th Taxation § 324, Other Taxes.
5 Witkin, California Summary 10th Torts § 216, (S 216) Adoption.
5 Witkin, California Summary 10th Torts § 217, (S 217) Statutory Framework.
5 Witkin, California Summary 10th Torts § 345, Statutory Framework.
8 Witkin, California Summary 10th Constitutional Law § 1254, Payment and Final Order.
14 Witkin, California Summary 10th Wills and Probate § 941, Investigation and Report.
2 Witkin Cal. Summ. 10th Workers' Compensation § 147, (S 147) Insurers.

§ 810.2. Employee

"Employee" includes an officer, judicial officer as defined in Section 327 of the Elections Code, employee, or servant, whether or not compensated, but does not include an independent contractor. *(Added by Stats.1963, c. 1681, p. 3267, § 1. Amended by Stats.1977, c. 745, p. 2333, § 1; Stats.1994, c. 923 (S.B.1546), § 30.)*

Research References

Rutter, Cal. Practice Guide: Personal Injury Ch. 5-A, A. Prelawsuit Filings.
3 Witkin Cal. Proc. 5th Actions § 251, in General.
5 Witkin, California Summary 10th Torts § 166, in General.
5 Witkin, California Summary 10th Torts § 219, (S 219) "Employee.".

§ 810.4. Employment

"Employment" includes office or employment. *(Added by Stats.1963, c. 1681, p. 3267, § 1.)*

2347

Law Revision Commission Comments

This definition obviates unnecessary repetition in later sections. [4 Cal.L.Rev.Comm. Reports 801 (1963)].

Research References

5 Witkin, California Summary 10th Torts § 220, (S 220) Other Definitions.

§ 810.6. Enactment

"Enactment" means a constitutional provision, statute, charter provision, ordinance or regulation. *(Added by Stats.1963, c. 1681, p. 3267, § 1.)*

Law Revision Commission Comments

This definition is intended to refer to all measures of a formal legislative or quasi-legislative nature. "Regulation" is defined in Section 811.6 to carry out this intent more fully. [4 Cal.L.Rev.Comm. Reports 801 (1963)].

Research References

5 Witkin, California Summary 10th Torts § 220, (S 220) Other Definitions.
5 Witkin, California Summary 10th Torts § 245, Statutory Rule of Liability.

§ 810.8. Injury

"Injury" means death, injury to a person, damage to or loss of property, or any other injury that a person may suffer to his person, reputation, character, feelings or estate, of such nature that it would be actionable if inflicted by a private person. *(Added by Stats.1963, c. 1681, p. 3267, § 1.)*

Law Revision Commission Comments

This definition merely defines "injury"; it does not impose liability for an injury. The standards and conditions of liability for an injury are found in other provisions of this division and in other statutes. The purpose of the definition is to make clear that public entities and public employees may be held liable only for injuries to the kind of interests that have been protected by the courts in actions between private persons. [4 Cal.L.Rev.Comm. Reports 801 (1963)].

Research References

15 NO. 5 Miller & Starr, California Real Estate Newsalert 15, Mechanics' Liens.
5 Witkin, California Summary 10th Torts § 220, (S 220) Other Definitions.
5 Witkin, California Summary 10th Torts § 245, Statutory Rule of Liability.
5 Witkin, California Summary 10th Torts § 262, Recovery for Emotional Distress.
5 Witkin, California Summary 10th Torts § 289, (S 289) Tax Collection or Administration.
3 Witkin, California Summary 10th Agency and Employment § 390, (S 390) No Action Against Agency Under Tort Claims Act.

§ 811. Law

"Law" includes not only enactments but also the decisional law applicable within this State as determined and declared from time to time by the courts of this State and of the United States. *(Added by Stats.1963, c. 1681, p. 3267, § 1.)*

Law Revision Commission Comments

Section 810.6 defines enactment to mean a measure of a formal legislative or quasi-legislative nature. The definition of "law" contained in this section includes enactments and also the common law applicable within the State as determined by the courts. [4 Cal.L.Rev.Comm. Reports 801 (1963)].

Research References

5 Witkin, California Summary 10th Torts § 220, (S 220) Other Definitions.

§ 811.2. Public entity

"Public entity" includes the state, the Regents of the University of California, the Trustees of the California State University and the California State University, a county, city, district, public authority, public agency, and any other political subdivision or public corporation in the State. *(Added by Stats.1963, c. 1681, p. 3267, § 1. Amended by Stats.2010, c. 636 (S.B.1046), § 1.)*

Law Revision Commission Comments

This definition is intended to include every kind of independent political or governmental entity in the State. [4 Cal.L.Rev.Comm. Reports 801 (1963)].

Research References

Rutter, Cal. Practice Guide: Personal Injury Ch. 3-E, E. Punitive Damages.
1 Witkin Cal. Summ. 10th Contracts § 464, Exemptions.
10 Witkin, California Summary 10th Parent and Child § 416, (S 416) Application and Order.
11 Witkin, California Summary 10th Husband and Wife § 250, (S 250) Definitions.
5 Witkin, California Summary 10th Torts § 220, (S 220) Other Definitions.
5 Witkin, California Summary 10th Torts § 222, (S 222) in General.
14 Witkin, California Summary 10th Wills and Probate § 621, (S 621) Filing Requirement.

§ 811.4. Public employee

"Public employee" means an employee of a public entity. *(Added by Stats.1963, c. 1681, p. 3267, § 1.)*

Law Revision Commission Comments

Liability and immunity provisions in Division 3.6 are often made applicable to "public employees." These provisions will not be applicable to independent contractors since the term "employee" is defined in Section 810.2 to exclude independent contractors. [4 Cal.L.Rev.Comm. Reports 801 (1963)].

Research References

5 Witkin, California Summary 10th Torts § 220, (S 220) Other Definitions.

§ 811.6. Regulation

"Regulation" means a rule, regulation, order or standard, having the force of law, adopted by an employee or agency of the United States pursuant to the federal Administrative Procedure Act (Chapter 5 (commencing with Section 500) of Title 5 of the United States Code) or as a regulation by an agency of the state pursuant to the Administrative Procedure Act (Chapter 3.5 (commencing with Section 11340) of Part 1 of Division 3 of Title 2). *(Added by Stats.1963, c. 1681, p. 3266, § 1. Amended by Stats.1987, c. 1201, § 14; Stats.1987, c. 1207, § 3; Stats.1988, c. 160, § 50.)*

Law Revision Commission Comments

See the comment under Section 810.6. [4 Cal.L.Rev.Comm. Reports 801 (1963)].

Research References

5 Witkin, California Summary 10th Torts § 220, (S 220) Other Definitions.

6 Witkin, California Summary 10th Torts § 877, (S 877) Agency Manual is Not Regulation.

§ 811.8. Statute

"Statute" means an act adopted by the Legislature of this State or by the Congress of the United States, or a statewide initiative act. *(Added by Stats.1963, c. 1681, p. 3267, § 1.)*

Law Revision Commission Comments

Section 810.6 defines enactment to mean a legislative or quasilegislative measure adopted by any employee or agency of government that has power to legislate. "Statute" is here defined to include only those enactments that are adopted by Congress, the Legislature of California, or the people of California (by initiative act). [4 Cal.L.Rev.Comm. Reports 801 (1963)].

Research References

5 Witkin, California Summary 10th Torts § 220, (S 220) Other Definitions.

§ 811.9. Judges, subordinate judicial officers, and court executive officers in superior courts; state officer status

(a) Notwithstanding any other provision of law, judges, subordinate judicial officers, and court executive officers of the superior courts are state officers for purposes of Part 1 (commencing with Section 810) to Part 7 (commencing with Section 995), inclusive, and trial court employees are employees of the trial court for purposes of Part 1 (commencing with Section 810) to Part 7 (commencing with Section 995), inclusive. The Judicial Council shall provide for representation, defense, and indemnification of those individuals and the court pursuant to Part 1 (commencing with Section 810) to Part 7 (commencing with Section 995), inclusive. The Judicial Council shall provide for that representation or defense through the county counsel, the Attorney General, or other counsel. The county counsel and the Attorney General may, but are not required to, provide representation or defense for the Judicial Council. The fact that a justice, judge, subordinate judicial officer, court executive officer, court employee, the court, the Judicial Council, or the Administrative Office of the Courts is or was represented or defended by the county counsel, the Attorney General, or other counsel shall not be the sole basis for a judicial determination of disqualification of a justice, judge, subordinate judicial officer, the county counsel, the Attorney General, or other counsel in unrelated actions.

(b) To promote the cost-effective, prompt, and fair resolution of actions, proceedings, and claims affecting the trial courts, the Judicial Council shall adopt rules of court requiring the Administrative Office of the Courts to manage actions, proceedings, and claims that affect the trial courts and involve superior courts, superior court judges, subordinate judicial officers, court executive officers, or trial court employees in consultation with the affected courts and individuals. The Administrative Office of the Courts' management of these actions, proceedings, and claims shall include, but not be limited to, case management and administrative responsibilities such as selection of counsel and making strategic and settlement decisions.

(c) Nothing in this section shall be construed to affect the employment status of subordinate judicial officers, court executive officers, and trial court employees related to any matters not covered by subdivision (a). *(Added by Stats.2000, c. 447 (S.B.1533), § 4.5. Amended by Stats.2005, c. 706 (A.B.1742), § 16.)*

Research References

3 Witkin Cal. Proc. 5th Actions § 1057, Officers.
2 Witkin Cal. Proc. 5th Courts § 342, in General.

5 Witkin, California Summary 10th Torts § 219, (S 219) "Employee.".

Part 2

LIABILITY OF PUBLIC ENTITIES AND PUBLIC EMPLOYEES

CHAPTER 1. GENERAL PROVISIONS RELATING TO LIABILITY

ARTICLE 1. SCOPE OF PART

Section
814.   Effect upon liability based on contract or right to relief other than money or damages.
814.2.   Workers' compensation provisions not repealed.

§ 814. Effect upon liability based on contract or right to relief other than money or damages

Nothing in this part affects liability based on contract or the right to obtain relief other than money or damages against a public entity or public employee. *(Added by Stats.1963, c. 1681, p. 3267, § 1.)*

Research References

Miller and Starr California Real Estate § 30:1, Basis for Inverse Condemnation.
Miller and Starr California Real Estate § 22:18, Governmental Agencies.
Miller and Starr California Real Estate § 26:21, Informal Acceptance by Public Authority.
18 NO. 4 Miller & Starr, California Real Estate Newsalert 28, Construction Contracts.
3 Witkin Cal. Proc. 5th Actions § 238, (S 238) Other Money Claims.
5 Witkin, California Summary 10th Torts § 217, (S 217) Statutory Framework.
5 Witkin, California Summary 10th Torts § 218, (S 218) Exclusions and Limitations.
5 Witkin, California Summary 10th Torts § 241, (S 241) Immunity Rule.
5 Witkin, California Summary 10th Torts § 289, (S 289) Tax Collection or Administration.
5 Witkin, California Summary 10th Torts § 294, (S 294) Exceptions.
5 Witkin, California Summary 10th Torts § 348, Nature of Immunities and Defenses.

§ 814.2. Workers' compensation provisions not repealed

Nothing in this part shall be construed to impliedly repeal any provision of Division 4 (commencing with Section 3201) or Division 4.5 (commencing with Section 6100) of the Labor Code. *(Added by Stats.1963, c. 1681, p. 3267, § 1.)*

Research References

5 Witkin, California Summary 10th Torts § 218, (S 218) Exclusions and Limitations.
5 Witkin, California Summary 10th Torts § 294, (S 294) Exceptions.

ARTICLE 2. LIABILITY OF PUBLIC ENTITIES

Section
815.   Liability for injuries generally; immunity of public entity; defenses.
815.2.   Injuries by employee within scope of employment; immunity of employee.
815.3.   Intentional torts.
815.4.   Injuries by independent contractors.
815.6.   Mandatory duty of public entity to protect against particular kinds of injuries.
816.   Injuries by members of National Guard; legislative intent.
818.   Exemplary damages.

Section

818.2.   Adoption or failure to adopt or enforce enactment.

818.4.   Issuance, denial, suspension or revocation of permit, license, or similar authorization.

818.5.   Injury caused by omission of lienholder's name from ownership certificate for motor vehicle.

818.6.   Failure to inspect, or negligent inspection of, property.

818.7.   Publication of records relating to controlled substance law violators; confidential information.

818.8.   Misrepresentations by employees.

818.9.   Advice to small claims court litigants.

§ 815. Liability for injuries generally; immunity of public entity; defenses

Except as otherwise provided by statute:

(a) A public entity is not liable for an injury, whether such injury arises out of an act or omission of the public entity or a public employee or any other person.

(b) The liability of a public entity established by this part (commencing with Section 814) is subject to any immunity of the public entity provided by statute, including this part, and is subject to any defenses that would be available to the public entity if it were a private person. *(Added by Stats.1963, c. 1681, p. 3268, § 1.)*

Research References

California Practice Guide: Employment Litigation Ch. 5-A, A. Wrongful Discharge in Violation of Public Policy (Tameny Claims).

Miller and Starr California Real Estate § 30:5, Physical Invasion by Water Discharge--Surface Water; Artificial Drainage Systems.

Miller and Starr California Real Estate § 17:28, Airspace.

Miller and Starr California Real Estate § 22:76, Liability of a Government Entity.

Miller and Starr California Real Estate § 29:45, Fraud of Building Inspector.

17 NO. 5 Miller & Starr, California Real Estate Newsalert 1, Flood Control System Failure, Property Damage, and Theories of Liability-Inverse Condemnation or Mere Negligence, If Any.

22 NO. 6 Miller & Starr, California Real Estate Newsalert 19, Landowners' Liability.

3 Witkin Cal. Proc. 5th Actions § 231, (S 231) Nature and Purpose of Requirement.

4 Witkin Cal. Proc. 5th Pleading § 617, (S 617) Government Claims Act.

5 Witkin, California Summary 10th Torts § 57, Between Tortfeasors Subject and Not Subject to Liability.

5 Witkin, California Summary 10th Torts § 216, (S 216) Adoption.

5 Witkin, California Summary 10th Torts § 222, (S 222) in General.

5 Witkin, California Summary 10th Torts § 223, (S 223) No Common Law Liability.

5 Witkin, California Summary 10th Torts § 226, (S 226) Statutory Immunities.

5 Witkin, California Summary 10th Torts § 227, (S 227) Defenses of Private Person Are Available.

5 Witkin, California Summary 10th Torts § 285, Protective Measures Against Earth Movement.

5 Witkin, California Summary 10th Torts § 310, in General.

5 Witkin, California Summary 10th Torts § 319, Confinement or Release of Mental Patient or Addict.

5 Witkin, California Summary 10th Torts § 339, (S 339) Nuisances.

5 Witkin, California Summary 10th Torts § 343, 911 Calls.

5 Witkin, California Summary 10th Torts § 369, (S 369) False Arrest or Imprisonment.

6 Witkin, California Summary 10th Torts § 930, (S 930) Occurrence or Allegation of Prior Assault.

3 Witkin, California Summary 10th Agency and Employment § 285, Disclosure to State Auditor.

§ 815.2. Injuries by employee within scope of employment; immunity of employee

(a) A public entity is liable for injury proximately caused by an act or omission of an employee of the public entity within the scope of his employment if the act or omission would, apart from

this section, have given rise to a cause of action against that employee or his personal representative.

(b) Except as otherwise provided by statute, a public entity is not liable for an injury resulting from an act or omission of an employee of the public entity where the employee is immune from liability. *(Added by Stats.1963, c. 1681, p. 3268, § 1.)*

Research References

California Practice Guide: Employment Litigation Ch. 5-H, H. Negligence.

Rutter, Cal. Practice Guide: Family Law Ch. 6-A, A. Child Support.

Miller and Starr California Real Estate § 30:5, Physical Invasion by Water Discharge--Surface Water; Artificial Drainage Systems.

Miller and Starr California Real Estate § 22:57, Negligence of an Independent Contractor; Injuries to a Contractor's Employees.

Miller and Starr California Real Estate § 29:45, Fraud of Building Inspector.

19 NO. 1 Miller & Starr, California Real Estate Newsalert 19, Landowners' Liability.

4 Witkin Cal. Proc. 5th Pleading § 617, (S 617) Government Claims Act.

5 Witkin, California Summary 10th Torts § 223, (S 223) No Common Law Liability.

5 Witkin, California Summary 10th Torts § 224, (S 224) Liability Under Statutes and Constitution.

5 Witkin, California Summary 10th Torts § 228, (S 228) Immunity Where Employee is Immune.

5 Witkin, California Summary 10th Torts § 237, Statutory Rule of Liability.

5 Witkin, California Summary 10th Torts § 238, Employment by Public Entity.

5 Witkin, California Summary 10th Torts § 240, (S 240) Sexual Misconduct by Employee.

5 Witkin, California Summary 10th Torts § 241, (S 241) Immunity Rule.

5 Witkin, California Summary 10th Torts § 248, Availability of Immunities.

5 Witkin, California Summary 10th Torts § 290, (S 290) in General.

5 Witkin, California Summary 10th Torts § 299, (S 299) Duty to Warn Where Special Relationship Exists.

5 Witkin, California Summary 10th Torts § 310, in General.

5 Witkin, California Summary 10th Torts § 316, Liabilities.

5 Witkin, California Summary 10th Torts § 321, in General.

5 Witkin, California Summary 10th Torts § 323, Activities Outside School Grounds.

5 Witkin, California Summary 10th Torts § 324, Extracurricular Activities.

5 Witkin, California Summary 10th Torts § 328, Injury to Nonstudent.

5 Witkin, California Summary 10th Torts § 331, in General.

5 Witkin, California Summary 10th Torts § 338, (S 338) Use of Pesticides.

5 Witkin, California Summary 10th Torts § 343, 911 Calls.

5 Witkin, California Summary 10th Torts § 344, (S 344) National Guard Operations.

5 Witkin, California Summary 10th Torts § 355, (S 355) Immunity Not Applicable.

5 Witkin, California Summary 10th Torts § 607, Governmental Defendants.

§ 815.3. Intentional torts

(a) Notwithstanding any other provision of this part, unless the elected official and the public entity are named as codefendants in the same action, a public entity is not liable to a plaintiff under this part for any act or omission of an elected official employed by or otherwise representing that public entity, which act or omission constitutes an intentional tort, including, but not limited to, harassment, sexual battery, and intentional infliction of emotional distress. For purposes of this section, harassment in violation of state or federal law constitutes an intentional tort, to the extent permitted by federal law. This section shall not apply to defamation.

(b) If the elected official is held liable for an intentional tort other than defamation in such an action, the trier of fact in reaching the verdict shall determine if the act or omission constituting the intentional tort arose from and was directly related to the elected official's performance of his or her official duties. If the trier of fact determines that the act or omission arose from and was directly related to the elected official's performance of his or her official duties, the public entity shall be liable for the judgment as provided by law. For the purpose of this subdivision, employee managerial functions shall be deemed to arise from, and to directly relate to, the elected official's official duties. However, acts or omissions constituting sexual harassment shall not be deemed to arise from, and to directly relate to, the elected official's official duties.

(c) If the trier of fact determines that the elected official's act or omission did not arise from and was not directly related to the elected official's performance of his or her official duties, upon a final judgment, including any appeal, the plaintiff shall first seek recovery of the judgment against the assets of the elected official. If the court determines that the elected official's assets are insufficient to satisfy the total judgment, including plaintiff's costs as provided by law, the court shall determine the amount of the deficiency and the plaintiff may seek to collect that remainder of the judgment from the public entity. The public entity may pay that deficiency if the public entity is otherwise authorized by law to pay that judgment.

(d) To the extent the public entity pays any portion of the judgment against the elected official pursuant to subdivision (c) or has expended defense costs in an action in which the trier of fact determines the elected official's action did not arise from and did not directly relate to his or her performance of official duties, the public entity shall pursue all available creditor's remedies against the elected official in indemnification, including garnishment, until the elected official has fully reimbursed the public entity.

(e) If the public entity elects to appeal the judgment in an action brought pursuant to this section, the entity shall continue to provide a defense for the official until the case is finally adjudicated, as provided by law.

(f) It is the intent of the Legislature that elected officials assume full fiscal responsibility for their conduct which constitutes an intentional tort not directly related to their official duties committed for which the public entity they represent may also be liable, while maintaining fair compensation for those persons injured by such conduct.

(g) This section shall not apply to a criminal or civil enforcement action brought on behalf of the state by an elected district attorney, city attorney, or Attorney General.

(h) If any provision of this section or the application thereof to any person or circumstances is held invalid, that invalidity shall not affect other provisions or applications of the section which can be given effect without the invalid provision or application, and to this end the provisions of this section are severable. *(Added by Stats.1994, c. 796 (A.B.2508), § 1.)*

Research References

Rutter, Cal. Practice Guide: Personal Injury Ch. 5-C, C. Selected Issues Affecting Parties.
5 Witkin, California Summary 10th Torts § 243, Intentional Torts of Elected Officials.

§ 815.4. Injuries by independent contractors

A public entity is liable for injury proximately caused by a tortious act or omission of an independent contractor of the public entity to the same extent that the public entity would be subject to such liability if it were a private person. Nothing in this section subjects a public entity to liability for the act or omission of an independent contractor if the public entity would not have been liable for the injury had the act or omission been that of an employee of the public entity. *(Added by Stats.1963, c. 1681, p. 3268, § 1.)*

Law Revision Commission Comments

The California courts have held that public entities—and private persons, too—may at times be liable for the acts of their independent contractors. Snyder v. Southern Cal. Edison Co., 44 Cal.2d 793, 285 P.2d 912 (1955) (discussing general rule); Los Angeles County Flood Control Dist. v. Southern Cal. Bldg. & Loan Assn., 188 Cal.App.2d 850, 10 Cal.Rptr. 811 (1961). This section retains that liability. Under the terms of this section, though, a public entity cannot be held liable for an independent contractor's act if the entity would have been immune had the act been that of a public employee. [4 Cal.L.Rev.Comm. Reports 801 (1963)].

Research References

Miller and Starr California Real Estate § 22:53, Liability for Condition Arising After the Tenant Takes Possession.
Miller and Starr California Real Estate § 22:57, Negligence of an Independent Contractor; Injuries to a Contractor's Employees.
13 NO. 6 Miller & Starr, California Real Estate Newsalert 8, Inverse Condemnation.
19 NO. 1 Miller & Starr, California Real Estate Newsalert 19, Landowners' Liability.
4 Witkin Cal. Proc. 5th Pleading § 617, (S 617) Government Claims Act.
5 Witkin, California Summary 10th Torts § 224, (S 224) Liability Under Statutes and Constitution.
5 Witkin, California Summary 10th Torts § 228, (S 228) Immunity Where Employee is Immune.
5 Witkin, California Summary 10th Torts § 244, (S 244) Liability for Torts of Independent Contractors.

§ 815.6. Mandatory duty of public entity to protect against particular kinds of injuries

Where a public entity is under a mandatory duty imposed by an enactment that is designed to protect against the risk of a particular kind of injury, the public entity is liable for an injury of that kind proximately caused by its failure to discharge the duty unless the public entity establishes that it exercised reasonable diligence to discharge the duty. *(Added by Stats.1963, c. 1681, p. 3268, § 1.)*

Law Revision Commission Comments

This section declares the familiar rule, applicable to both public entities and private persons, that failure to comply with applicable statutory or regulatory standards is negligence unless reasonable diligence has been exercised in an effort to comply with those standards. Alarid v. Vanier, 50 Cal.2d 617, 327 P.2d 897 (1958) (setting forth general rule); Lehmann v. Los Angeles City Bd. of Educ., 154 Cal.App.2d 256, 316 P.2d 55 (1957) (applying rule to public entity).

In the sections that follow in this division, there are stated some immunities from this general rule of liability. See, for example, Section 818.2. [4 Cal.L.Rev.Comm. Reports 801 (1963)].

Research References

Rutter, Cal. Practice Guide: Civ. Pro. Before Trial Ch. 6-B, B. Complaints.
Rutter, Cal. Practice Guide: Insurance Litigation Ch. 6I-B, B. Particular Surety Bond Coverages.
Miller and Starr California Real Estate § 7:8, Regulatory Provisions.
Miller and Starr California Real Estate § 14:19, Lateral Support--Common Law Rule.
Miller and Starr California Real Estate § 14:37, Liability of Governmental Entity for Land Use Decisions Affecting Views and Sunlight.
Miller and Starr California Real Estate § 22:29, Residential Buildings Which Do Not Comply With Code.
Miller and Starr California Real Estate § 27:20, Private Remedies.
Miller and Starr California Real Estate § 29:44, Exceptions.
17 NO. 5 Miller & Starr, California Real Estate Newsalert 1, Flood Control System Failure, Property Damage, and Theories of Liability-Inverse Condemnation or Mere Negligence, If Any.
17 NO. 2 Miller & Starr, California Real Estate Newsalert 17, Inverse Condemnation.
20 NO. 5 Miller & Starr, California Real Estate Newsalert 8, Covenants.
20 NO. 5 Miller & Starr, California Real Estate Newsalert 18, Landowners' Liability.
3 Witkin Cal. Proc. 5th Actions § 243, (S 243) Mechanics' Liens.

Government

1 Witkin Cal. Proc. 5th Attorneys § 366, (S 366) No Liability for Delay in Investigation.

10 Witkin, California Summary 10th Parent and Child § 9, (S 9) Rights and Responsibilities of Foster Parents.

9 Witkin, California Summary 10th Corporations § 403, (S 403) Commissioner, Rules, and Forms.

5 Witkin, California Summary 10th Torts § 224, (S 224) Liability Under Statutes and Constitution.

5 Witkin, California Summary 10th Torts § 237, Statutory Rule of Liability.

5 Witkin, California Summary 10th Torts § 245, Statutory Rule of Liability.

5 Witkin, California Summary 10th Torts § 246, Illustrations Finding Liability.

5 Witkin, California Summary 10th Torts § 247, Illustrations Finding No Liability.

5 Witkin, California Summary 10th Torts § 248, Availability of Immunities.

5 Witkin, California Summary 10th Torts § 287, (S 287) Action or Inaction on License.

5 Witkin, California Summary 10th Torts § 288, (S 288) Inspection of Private Property.

5 Witkin, California Summary 10th Torts § 307, (S 307) Failure to Prevent Driving.

5 Witkin, California Summary 10th Torts § 328, Injury to Nonstudent.

5 Witkin, California Summary 10th Torts § 343, 911 Calls.

3 Witkin, California Summary 10th Agency and Employment § 390, (S 390) No Action Against Agency Under Tort Claims Act.

§ 816. Injuries by members of National Guard; legislative intent

A public entity is not liable for injury arising out of any activity conducted by a member of the California National Guard pursuant to Section 316, 502, 503, 504, or 505 of Title 32 of the United States Code and compensated pursuant to the Federal Tort Claims Act.

It is the intent of the Legislature, in enacting this section, to conform state law regarding liability for activities of the National Guard to federal law as expressed in Public Law 97–124. *(Added by Stats.1982, c. 616, p. 2600, § 1.)*

Research References

5 Witkin, California Summary 10th Torts § 185, Privilege of Member of Military.

5 Witkin, California Summary 10th Torts § 344, (S 344) National Guard Operations.

§ 818. Exemplary damages

Notwithstanding any other provision of law, a public entity is not liable for damages awarded under Section 3294 of the Civil Code or other damages imposed primarily for the sake of example and by way of punishing the defendant. *(Added by Stats.1963, c. 1681, p. 3266, § 1.)*

Law Revision Commission Comments

This section exempts public entities from liability for punitive or exemplary damages. [4 Cal.L.Rev.Comm. Reports 801 (1963)].

Research References

Rutter, Cal. Practice Guide: Personal Injury Ch. 3-E, E. Punitive Damages.

Miller and Starr California Real Estate § 34:93, Punitive Damages--Basis of the Award; Burden of Proof.

5 Witkin, California Summary 10th Torts § 230, (S 230) No Punitive Damages.

5 Witkin, California Summary 10th Torts § 347, Punitive Damages May be Recoverable.

5 Witkin, California Summary 10th Torts § 378, (S 378) Payment of Punitive Damages.

6 Witkin, California Summary 10th Torts § 1579, Recovery by Public Entities.

6 Witkin, California Summary 10th Torts § 1580, in General.

8 Witkin, California Summary 10th Constitutional Law § 895, Hate Crimes, Intimidation, and Threats of Violence.

2 Witkin Cal. Summ. 10th Workers' Compensation § 316, (S 316) Nature of Increased Award.

§ 818.2. Adoption or failure to adopt or enforce enactment

A public entity is not liable for an injury caused by adopting or failing to adopt an enactment or by failing to enforce any law. *(Added by Stats.1963, c. 1681, p. 3268, § 1.)*

Law Revision Commission Comments

This section would be unnecessary except for a possible implication that might arise from Section 815.6, which imposes liability upon public entities for failure to exercise reasonable diligence to comply with a mandatory duty imposed by an enactment. This section recognizes that the wisdom of legislative or quasi-legislative action, and the discretion of law enforcement officers in carrying out their duties, should not be subject to review in tort suits for damages if political responsibility for these decisions is to be retained.

The New York courts recognize a similar immunity in the absence of statute. Under the Federal Tort Claims Act, this immunity falls within the general immunity for discretionary acts. [4 Cal.L.Rev.Comm. Reports 801 (1963)].

Research References

5 Witkin, California Summary 10th Torts § 248, Availability of Immunities.

5 Witkin, California Summary 10th Torts § 278, Exceptions.

5 Witkin, California Summary 10th Torts § 286, (S 286) Legislation or Law Enforcement.

§ 818.4. Issuance, denial, suspension or revocation of permit, license, or similar authorization

A public entity is not liable for an injury caused by the issuance, denial, suspension or revocation of, or by the failure or refusal to issue, deny, suspend or revoke, any permit, license, certificate, approval, order, or similar authorization where the public entity or an employee of the public entity is authorized by enactment to determine whether or not such authorization should be issued, denied, suspended or revoked. *(Added by Stats.1963, c. 1681, p. 3268, § 1.)*

Research References

Rutter, Cal. Practice Guide: Prof. Responsibility Ch. 8-A, A. Duties to Administration of Justice-In General.

Miller and Starr California Real Estate § 14:37, Liability of Governmental Entity for Land Use Decisions Affecting Views and Sunlight.

Miller and Starr California Real Estate § 29:44, Exceptions.

Miller and Starr California Real Estate § 29:45, Fraud of Building Inspector.

1 Witkin Cal. Proc. 5th Attorneys § 366, (S 366) No Liability for Delay in Investigation.

5 Witkin, California Summary 10th Torts § 229, (S 229) Tort Claims Act Immunities Extend to Liabilities Imposed by Other Statutes.

5 Witkin, California Summary 10th Torts § 248, Availability of Immunities.

5 Witkin, California Summary 10th Torts § 287, (S 287) Action or Inaction on License.

§ 818.5. Injury caused by omission of lienholder's name from ownership certificate for motor vehicle

The Department of Motor Vehicles is liable for any injury to a lienholder or good faith purchaser of a vehicle proximately caused by the department's negligent omission of the lienholder's name from an ownership certificate issued by the department. The liability of the department under this section shall not exceed the actual cash value of the vehicle. *(Added by Stats.1985, c. 437, § 2.)*

§ 818.6. Failure to inspect, or negligent inspection of, property

A public entity is not liable for injury caused by its failure to make an inspection, or by reason of making an inadequate or negligent inspection, of any property, other than its property (as defined in subdivision (c) of Section 830), for the purpose of determining whether the property complies with or violates any enactment or contains or constitutes a hazard to health or safety. *(Added by Stats.1963, c. 1681, p. 3269, § 1.)*

§ 818.7. Publication of records relating to controlled substance law violators; confidential information

No board, commission, or any public officer or employee of the state or of any district, county, city and county, or city is liable for any damage or injury to any person resulting from the publication of any reports, records, prints, or photographs of or concerning any person convicted of violation of any law relating to the use, sale, or possession of controlled substances, when such publication is to school authorities for use in instruction on the subject of controlled substances or to any person when used for the purpose of general education. However, the name of any person concerning whom any such reports, records, prints, or photographs are used shall be kept confidential and every reasonable effort shall be made to maintain as confidential any information which may tend to identify such person. *(Added by Stats.1968, c. 182, p. 469, § 36. Amended by Stats.1984, c. 1635, § 40.)*

§ 818.8. Misrepresentations by employees

A public entity is not liable for an injury caused by misrepresentation by an employee of the public entity, whether or not such misrepresentation be negligent or intentional. *(Added by Stats.1963, c. 1681, p. 3269, § 1.)*

§ 818.9. Advice to small claims court litigants

A court or county, its employees, independent contractors, and volunteers shall not be liable because of any advice provided to small claims court litigants or potential litigants as a public service on behalf of the court or county pursuant to the Small Claims Act (Chapter 5.5 (commencing with Section 116.110) of Title 1 of Part 1 of the Code of Civil Procedure). *(Added by Stats.1981, c. 958, p. 3643, § 10. Amended by Stats.1990, c. 1305 (S.B.2627), § 10; Stats.2002, c. 806 (A.B.3027), § 24.)*

ARTICLE 3. LIABILITY OF PUBLIC EMPLOYEES

§ 820. Liability for injuries generally; defenses

(a) Except as otherwise provided by statute (including Section 820.2), a public employee is liable for injury caused by his act or omission to the same extent as a private person.

(b) The liability of a public employee established by this part (commencing with Section 814) is subject to any defenses that would be available to the public employee if he were a private person. *(Added by Stats.1963, c. 1681, p. 3269, § 1.)*

§ 820.2. Discretionary acts

Except as otherwise provided by statute, a public employee is not liable for an injury resulting from his act or omission where the act or omission was the result of the exercise of the discretion vested in him, whether or not such discretion be abused. *(Added by Stats.1963, c. 1681, p. 3269, § 1.)*

Research References

Rutter, Cal. Practice Guide: Civ. Pro. Before Trial Ch. 6-B, B. Complaints.

Rutter, Cal. Practice Guide: Prof. Responsibility Ch. 6-D, D. Professional Liability.

4 Witkin Cal. Proc. 5th Pleading § 624, Tort Actions Against Public Employees.

5 Witkin, California Summary 10th Torts § 228, (S 228) Immunity Where Employee is Immune.

5 Witkin, California Summary 10th Torts § 229, (S 229) Tort Claims Act Immunities Extend to Liabilities Imposed by Other Statutes.

5 Witkin, California Summary 10th Torts § 292, (S 292) Immunity Rule.

5 Witkin, California Summary 10th Torts § 296, Injury Caused by Escaped Prisoner.

5 Witkin, California Summary 10th Torts § 298, (S 298) Immunity Rule.

5 Witkin, California Summary 10th Torts § 299, (S 299) Duty to Warn Where Special Relationship Exists.

5 Witkin, California Summary 10th Torts § 308, (S 308) Failure to Remove Parked Car.

5 Witkin, California Summary 10th Torts § 319, Confinement or Release of Mental Patient or Addict.

5 Witkin, California Summary 10th Torts § 338, (S 338) Use of Pesticides.

5 Witkin, California Summary 10th Torts § 347, Punitive Damages May be Recoverable.

5 Witkin, California Summary 10th Torts § 348, Nature of Immunities and Defenses.

5 Witkin, California Summary 10th Torts § 351, Immunity Rule.

5 Witkin, California Summary 10th Torts § 352, What Constitutes Discretionary Act.

5 Witkin, California Summary 10th Torts § 353, Causes of Action Subject to Immunity.

5 Witkin, California Summary 10th Torts § 354, (S 354) Immunity Applicable.

5 Witkin, California Summary 10th Torts § 355, (S 355) Immunity Not Applicable.

5 Witkin, California Summary 10th Torts § 356, (S 356) Police Officers.

5 Witkin, California Summary 10th Torts § 357, (S 357) Parole Officers.

5 Witkin, California Summary 10th Torts § 358, (S 358) Public Defenders.

6 Witkin, California Summary 10th Torts § 930, (S 930) Occurrence or Allegation of Prior Assault.

6 Witkin, California Summary 10th Torts § 983, Failure to Prevent Birth.

6 Witkin, California Summary 10th Torts § 1050, in General.

3 Witkin, California Summary 10th Agency and Employment § 288, False Claims Act.

8 Witkin, California Summary 10th Constitutional Law § 895, Hate Crimes, Intimidation, and Threats of Violence.

8 Witkin, California Summary 10th Constitutional Law § 915, Nature and Purpose of Act.

14 Witkin, California Summary 10th Wills and Probate § 416, Nature of Office.

§ 820.21.   Juvenile court and child protection workers; exceptions to immunity; malice

(a) Notwithstanding any other provision of the law, the civil immunity of juvenile court social workers, child protection workers, and other public employees authorized to initiate or conduct investigations or proceedings pursuant to Chapter 2 (commencing with Section 200) of Part 1 of Division 2 of the Welfare and Institutions Code shall not extend to any of the following, if committed with malice:

(1) Perjury.

(2) Fabrication of evidence.

(3) Failure to disclose known exculpatory evidence.

(4) Obtaining testimony by duress, as defined in Section 1569 of the Civil Code, fraud, as defined in either Section 1572 or Section 1573 of the Civil Code, or undue influence, as defined in Section 1575 of the Civil Code.

(b) As used in this section, "malice" means conduct that is intended by the person described in subdivision (a) to cause injury to the plaintiff or despicable conduct that is carried on by the person described in subdivision (a) with a willful and conscious disregard of the rights or safety of others. *(Added by Stats.1995, c. 977 (A.B.1355), § 1.)*

Research References

5 Witkin, California Summary 10th Torts § 349, Particular Employees.

5 Witkin, California Summary 10th Torts § 368, (S 368) Institution or Prosecution of Judicial or Administrative Proceeding.

§ 820.25.   Peace officers or law enforcement officials; decisions not to render assistance or to respond to an emergency

(a) For purposes of Section 820.2, the decision of a peace officer, as defined in Sections 830.1 and 830.2 of the Penal Code, or a state or local law enforcement official, to render assistance to a motorist who has not been involved in an accident or to leave the scene after rendering assistance, upon learning of a reasonably apparent emergency requiring his immediate attention elsewhere or upon instructions from a superior to assume duties elsewhere, shall be deemed an exercise of discretion.

(b) The provision in subdivision (a) shall not apply if the act or omission occurred pursuant to the performance of a ministerial duty. For purposes of this section, "ministerial duty" is defined as a plain and mandatory duty involving the execution of a set task and to be performed without the exercise of discretion. *(Added by Stats.1979, c. 806, § 1, eff. Sept. 19, 1979.)*

Research References

5 Witkin, California Summary 10th Torts § 309, (S 309) Inadequate Assistance to Stranded Motorist.

5 Witkin, California Summary 10th Torts § 356, (S 356) Police Officers.

§ 820.4.   Execution or enforcement of laws; exception

A public employee is not liable for his act or omission, exercising due care, in the execution or enforcement of any law. Nothing in this section exonerates a public employee from liability for false arrest or false imprisonment. *(Added by Stats.1963, c. 1681, p. 3269, § 1.)*

Law Revision Commission Comments

This immunity, by virtue of Section 815.2, will inure to the benefit of the public entity employing the particular public employee. A similar immunity in almost identical language appears in the Federal Tort Claims Act. [4 Cal.L.Rev.Comm. Reports 801 (1963)].

Research References

5 Witkin, California Summary 10th Torts § 346, Nature of Liability.

5 Witkin, California Summary 10th Torts § 348, Nature of Immunities and Defenses.

5 Witkin, California Summary 10th Torts § 369, (S 369) False Arrest or Imprisonment.

§ 820.6.   Acting under unconstitutional, invalid or inapplicable enactments

If a public employee acts in good faith, without malice, and under the apparent authority of an enactment that is unconstitutional, invalid or inapplicable, he is not liable for an injury caused thereby except to the extent that he would have been liable had the enactment been constitutional, valid and applicable. *(Added by Stats.1963, c. 1681, p. 3269, § 1.)*

Research References

5 Witkin, California Summary 10th Torts § 348, Nature of Immunities and Defenses.

6 Witkin, California Summary 10th Torts § 877, (S 877) Agency Manual is Not Regulation.

7 Witkin, California Summary 10th Constitutional Law § 105, (S 105) Effect of Determination of Unconstitutionality.

8 Witkin, California Summary 10th Constitutional Law § 895, Hate Crimes, Intimidation, and Threats of Violence.

§ 820.8.   Acts or omissions of others

Except as otherwise provided by statute, a public employee is not liable for an injury caused by the act or omission of another person. Nothing in this section exonerates a public employee from liability for injury proximately caused by his own negligent or wrongful act or omission. *(Added by Stats.1963, c. 1681, p. 3269, § 1.)*

Research References

5 Witkin, California Summary 10th Torts § 346, Nature of Liability.
5 Witkin, California Summary 10th Torts § 348, Nature of Immunities and Defenses.
8 Witkin, California Summary 10th Constitutional Law § 895, Hate Crimes, Intimidation, and Threats of Violence.

§ 820.9.   Mayors, members of local public entities, boards, commissions and advisory bodies; vicarious liability for injuries caused by public entity

Members of city councils, mayors, members of boards of supervisors, members of school boards, members of governing boards of other local public entities, members of locally appointed boards and commissions, and members of locally appointed or elected advisory bodies are not vicariously liable for injuries caused by the act or omission of the public entity or advisory body. Nothing in this section exonerates an official from liability for injury caused by that individual's own wrongful conduct. Nothing in this section affects the immunity of any other public official.

This section shall become operative January 1, 2000. *(Added by Stats.1997, c. 132 (S.B.1159), § 2, operative Jan. 1, 2000.)*

Research References

5 Witkin, California Summary 10th Torts § 349, Particular Employees.

§ 821.   Adoption or failure to adopt or enforce enactment

A public employee is not liable for an injury caused by his adoption of or failure to adopt an enactment or by his failure to enforce an enactment. *(Added by Stats.1963, c. 1681, p. 3269, § 1.)*

Law Revision Commission Comments

This section continues an existing immunity of public employees. Martelli v. Pollock, 162 Cal.App.2d 655, 328 P.2d 795 (1958) (city councilman immune for actions as councilman); Rubinow v. County of San Bernardino, 169 Cal.App.2d 67, 336 P.2d 968 (1959) (no liability for failure to arrest drunk driver). [4 Cal.L.Rev.Comm. Reports 801 (1963)].

Research References

5 Witkin, California Summary 10th Torts § 348, Nature of Immunities and Defenses.

§ 821.2.   Issuance, denial, suspension, or revocation of permit or license

A public employee is not liable for an injury caused by his issuance, denial, suspension or revocation of, or by his failure or refusal to issue, deny, suspend or revoke, any permit, license, certificate, approval, order, or similar authorization where he is authorized by enactment to determine whether or not such authorization should be issued, denied, suspended or revoked. *(Added by Stats.1963, c. 1681, p. 3269, § 1.)*

Law Revision Commission Comments

The immunity stated here has been long established in California. Downer v. Lent, 6 Cal. (94 (1856) (pilot commissioners immune from liability for maliciously revoking pilot's license). [4 Cal.L.Rev.Comm. Reports 801 (1963)].

Research References

Rutter, Cal. Practice Guide: Prof. Responsibility Ch. 8-A, A. Duties to Administration of Justice-In General.
Miller and Starr California Real Estate § 29:45, Fraud of Building Inspector.
1 Witkin Cal. Proc. 5th Attorneys § 366, (S 366) No Liability for Delay in Investigation.
5 Witkin, California Summary 10th Torts § 229, (S 229) Tort Claims Act Immunities Extend to Liabilities Imposed by Other Statutes.
5 Witkin, California Summary 10th Torts § 287, (S 287) Action or Inaction on License.
5 Witkin, California Summary 10th Torts § 348, Nature of Immunities and Defenses.

§ 821.4.   Failure to inspect, or negligent inspection of, property

A public employee is not liable for injury caused by his failure to make an inspection, or by reason of making an inadequate or negligent inspection, of any property, other than the property (as defined in subdivision (c) of Section 830) of the public entity employing the public employee, for the purpose of determining whether the property complies with or violates any enactment or contains or constitutes a hazard to health or safety. *(Added by Stats.1963, c. 1681, p. 3270, § 1.)*

Research References

5 Witkin, California Summary 10th Torts § 346, Nature of Liability.
5 Witkin, California Summary 10th Torts § 348, Nature of Immunities and Defenses.

§ 821.5.   Failure to restrict or prohibit tunnel traffic of vehicles carrying flammable liquids

A public entity or a public employee acting within the scope of his employment is not liable for failing to prohibit or restrict the time that cargo tank vehicles required to display flammable liquid placards may travel through a tunnel. *(Added by Stats. 1982, c. 1255, p. 4600, § 1.)*

Research References

5 Witkin, California Summary 10th Torts § 315, (S 315) Protection from Hazardous Substances.

§ 821.6.   Institution or prosecution of judicial or administrative proceeding

A public employee is not liable for injury caused by his instituting or prosecuting any judicial or administrative proceeding within the scope of his employment, even if he acts maliciously and without probable cause. *(Added by Stats.1963, c. 1681, p. 3270, § 1.)*

Research References

Rutter, Cal. Practice Guide: Family Law Ch. 6-A, A. Child Support.
Rutter, Cal. Practice Guide: Personal Injury Gen. Matls., Highlights.
Rutter, Cal. Practice Guide: Prof. Responsibility Ch. 8-A, A. Duties to Administration of Justice-In General.
5 Witkin, California Summary 10th Torts § 57, Between Tortfeasors Subject and Not Subject to Liability.
5 Witkin, California Summary 10th Torts § 180, in General.
5 Witkin, California Summary 10th Torts § 182, Administrative Agency Officers.
5 Witkin, California Summary 10th Torts § 228, (S 228) Immunity Where Employee is Immune.
5 Witkin, California Summary 10th Torts § 248, Availability of Immunities.
5 Witkin, California Summary 10th Torts § 348, Nature of Immunities and Defenses.
5 Witkin, California Summary 10th Torts § 368, (S 368) Institution or Prosecution of Judicial or Administrative Proceeding.
5 Witkin, California Summary 10th Torts § 369, (S 369) False Arrest or Imprisonment.
5 Witkin, California Summary 10th Torts § 442, Warrant Defective on Face.

Government

5 Witkin, California Summary 10th Torts § 663, (S 663) Capturing Impression of Personal or Familial Activity.

8 Witkin, California Summary 10th Constitutional Law § 895, Hate Crimes, Intimidation, and Threats of Violence.

§ 821.8. Entry upon property

A public employee is not liable for an injury arising out of his entry upon any property where such entry is expressly or impliedly authorized by law. Nothing in this section exonerates a public employee from liability for an injury proximately caused by his own negligent or wrongful act or omission. *(Added by Stats.1963, c. 1681, p. 3270, § 1.)*

Law Revision Commission Comments

This section expresses a principle contained in a large number of statutes scattered through the codes providing particular public employees with a similar immunity. The section nullifies the common law rule that a public employee who enters property under authority of law but then commits a negligent or wrongful act is a trespasser ab initio and liable for all damages resulting from his entry. [4 Cal.L.Rev.Comm. Reports 801 (1963)].

Research References

5 Witkin, California Summary 10th Torts § 340, (S 340) Condemnor's Entry to Survey Land.
5 Witkin, California Summary 10th Torts § 346, Nature of Liability.
5 Witkin, California Summary 10th Torts § 348, Nature of Immunities and Defenses.

§ 822. Money stolen from custody

A public employee is not liable for money stolen from his official custody. Nothing in this section exonerates a public employee from liability if the loss was sustained as a result of his own negligent or wrongful act or omission. *(Added by Stats. 1963, c. 1681, p. 3270, § 1.)*

Research References

5 Witkin, California Summary 10th Torts § 346, Nature of Liability.
5 Witkin, California Summary 10th Torts § 348, Nature of Immunities and Defenses.

§ 822.2. Misrepresentations

A public employee acting in the scope of his employment is not liable for an injury caused by his misrepresentation, whether or not such misrepresentation be negligent or intentional, unless he is guilty of actual fraud, corruption or actual malice. *(Added by Stats.1963, c. 1681, p. 3270, § 1.)*

Research References

Miller and Starr California Real Estate § 1:148, Reliance by Injured Party.
Miller and Starr California Real Estate § 29:45, Fraud of Building Inspector.
5 Witkin, California Summary 10th Torts § 166, in General.
5 Witkin, California Summary 10th Torts § 241, (S 241) Immunity Rule.
5 Witkin, California Summary 10th Torts § 242, (S 242) Requirement of Commercial Relationship or Transaction.
5 Witkin, California Summary 10th Torts § 346, Nature of Liability.
5 Witkin, California Summary 10th Torts § 348, Nature of Immunities and Defenses.
5 Witkin, California Summary 10th Torts § 368, (S 368) Institution or Prosecution of Judicial or Administrative Proceeding.
5 Witkin, California Summary 10th Torts § 821, in General.

§ 823. Liability of widow, widower or heirs for act or omission by peace officer

Neither the widow, widower, nor the heirs of a peace officer, as defined in Sections 830.1, 830.2, and 830.32 of the Penal Code, shall be liable individually for any injury or death that may result from an act or omission of a peace officer that occurs in his or her line of duty, including an act or omission not directly related to the officer's death, if the officer was slain while in the line of duty. Nothing in this section shall preclude any action from being brought against the estate of the peace officer. *(Added by Stats.1998, c. 559 (A.B.1865), § 2.)*

Research References

5 Witkin, California Summary 10th Torts § 349, Particular Employees.

ARTICLE 4. INDEMNIFICATION OF PUBLIC EMPLOYEES

Section

825. Defense by public entity; payments of judgments, compromises or settlements; punitive damages; memorandum of understanding; elected officials; tortious influencing of judicial actions.

825.2. Recovery of payment from public entity; memorandum of understanding.

825.4. Indemnification of public entity by employee generally.

825.6. Grounds for indemnification of public entity by employee; memorandum of understanding.

§ 825. Defense by public entity; payments of judgments, compromises or settlements; punitive damages; memorandum of understanding; elected officials; tortious influencing of judicial actions

(a) Except as otherwise provided in this section, if an employee or former employee of a public entity requests the public entity to defend him or her against any claim or action against him or her for an injury arising out of an act or omission occurring within the scope of his or her employment as an employee of the public entity and the request is made in writing not less than 10 days before the day of trial, and the employee or former employee reasonably cooperates in good faith in the defense of the claim or action, the public entity shall pay any judgment based thereon or any compromise or settlement of the claim or action to which the public entity has agreed.

If the public entity conducts the defense of an employee or former employee against any claim or action with his or her reasonable good-faith cooperation, the public entity shall pay any judgment based thereon or any compromise or settlement of the claim or action to which the public entity has agreed. However, where the public entity conducted the defense pursuant to an agreement with the employee or former employee reserving the rights of the public entity not to pay the judgment, compromise, or settlement until it is established that the injury arose out of an act or omission occurring within the scope of his or her employment as an employee of the public entity, the public entity is required to pay the judgment, compromise, or settlement only if it is established that the injury arose out of an act or omission occurring in the scope of his or her employment as an employee of the public entity.

Nothing in this section authorizes a public entity to pay that part of a claim or judgment that is for punitive or exemplary damages.

(b) Notwithstanding subdivision (a) or any other provision of law, a public entity is authorized to pay that part of a judgment that is for punitive or exemplary damages if the governing body of that public entity, acting in its sole discretion except in cases involving an entity of the state government, finds all of the following:

(1) The judgment is based on an act or omission of an employee or former employee acting within the course and scope of his or her employment as an employee of the public entity.

(2) At the time of the act giving rise to the liability, the employee or former employee acted, or failed to act, in good

faith, without actual malice and in the apparent best interests of the public entity.

(3) Payment of the claim or judgment would be in the best interests of the public entity.

As used in this subdivision with respect to an entity of state government, "a decision of the governing body" means the approval of the Legislature for payment of that part of a judgment that is for punitive damages or exemplary damages, upon recommendation of the appointing power of the employee or former employee, based upon the finding by the Legislature and the appointing authority of the existence of the three conditions for payment of a punitive or exemplary damages claim. The provisions of subdivision (a) of Section 965.6 shall apply to the payment of any claim pursuant to this subdivision.

The discovery of the assets of a public entity and the introduction of evidence of the assets of a public entity shall not be permitted in an action in which it is alleged that a public employee is liable for punitive or exemplary damages.

The possibility that a public entity may pay that part of a judgment that is for punitive damages shall not be disclosed in any trial in which it is alleged that a public employee is liable for punitive or exemplary damages, and that disclosure shall be grounds for a mistrial.

(c) Except as provided in subdivision (d), if the provisions of this section are in conflict with the provisions of a memorandum of understanding reached pursuant to Chapter 10 (commencing with Section 3500) of Division 4 of Title 1, the memorandum of understanding shall be controlling without further legislative action, except that if those provisions of a memorandum of understanding require the expenditure of funds, the provisions shall not become effective unless approved by the Legislature in the annual Budget Act.

(d) The subject of payment of punitive damages pursuant to this section or any other provision of law shall not be a subject of meet and confer under the provisions of Chapter 10 (commencing with Section 3500) of Division 4 of Title 1, or pursuant to any other law or authority.

(e) Nothing in this section shall affect the provisions of Section 818 prohibiting the award of punitive damages against a public entity. This section shall not be construed as a waiver of a public entity's immunity from liability for punitive damages under Section 1981, 1983, or 1985 of Title 42 of the United States Code.

(f)(1) Except as provided in paragraph (2), a public entity shall not pay a judgment, compromise, or settlement arising from a claim or action against an elected official, if the claim or action is based on conduct by the elected official by way of tortiously intervening or attempting to intervene in, or by way of tortiously influencing or attempting to influence the outcome of, any judicial action or proceeding for the benefit of a particular party by contacting the trial judge or any commissioner, court-appointed arbitrator, court-appointed mediator, or court-appointed special referee assigned to the matter, or the court clerk, bailiff, or marshal after an action has been filed, unless he or she was counsel of record acting lawfully within the scope of his or her employment on behalf of that party. Notwithstanding Section 825.6, if a public entity conducted the defense of an elected official against such a claim or action and the elected official is found liable by the trier of fact, the court shall order the elected official to pay to the public entity the cost of that defense.

(2) If an elected official is held liable for monetary damages in the action, the plaintiff shall first seek recovery of the judgment against the assets of the elected official. If the elected official's assets are insufficient to satisfy the total judgment, as determined

by the court, the public entity may pay the deficiency if the public entity is authorized by law to pay that judgment.

(3) To the extent the public entity pays any portion of the judgment or is entitled to reimbursement of defense costs pursuant to paragraph (1), the public entity shall pursue all available creditor's remedies against the elected official, including garnishment, until that party has fully reimbursed the public entity.

(4) This subdivision shall not apply to any criminal or civil enforcement action brought in the name of the people of the State of California by an elected district attorney, city attorney, or attorney general. *(Added by Stats.1963, c. 1681, p. 3270, § 1. Amended by Stats.1972, c. 1352, p. 2685, § 1; Stats.1979, c. 1072, § 47, eff. Sept. 28, 1979; Stats.1985, c. 1373, § 1; Stats.1994, c. 794 (A.B.2467), § 1; Stats.1995, c. 799 (A.B.1361), § 1.)*

Research References

Rutter, Cal. Practice Guide: Civ. Pro. Before Trial Ch. 1-C, C. Prelawsuit Notices, Claims and Demands.

Rutter, Cal. Practice Guide: Civ. Pro. Before Trial Ch. 12(II)-E, E. Motion to Determine "Good Faith" of "Piecemeal" Settlement (CCP § 877.6).

Rutter, Cal. Practice Guide: Fed.Civ.Pro. Before Trial Ch. 2E-10, Eleventh Amendment as Limitation on Actions Against States.

Rutter, Cal. Practice Guide: Personal Injury Ch. 1-A, A. Initial Client Interview.

Rutter, Cal. Practice Guide: Personal Injury Ch. 3-E, E. Punitive Damages.

Rutter, Cal. Practice Guide: Personal Injury Ch. 4-D, D. Techniques Where Settlement Not Forthcoming.

Rutter, Cal. Practice Guide: Personal Injury Ch. 5-A, A. Prelawsuit Filings.

Rutter, Cal. Practice Guide: Personal Injury Ch. 6-A, A. Scope of Discovery and Limitations.

Rutter, Cal. Practice Guide: Prof. Responsibility Ch. 4-B, B. Concurrent Representation of Clients With Conflicting Interests (Conflicts Between Present Clients).

Rutter, Cal. Practice Guide: Prof. Responsibility Ch. 6-D, D. Professional Liability.

3 Witkin Cal. Proc. 5th Actions § 214, Steps by Defendant.

3 Witkin Cal. Proc. 5th Actions § 252, Requirement of Claim Against Entity.

5 Witkin, California Summary 10th Torts § 91, Claims for Contractual or Statutory Indemnity.

5 Witkin, California Summary 10th Torts § 166, in General.

5 Witkin, California Summary 10th Torts § 331, in General.

5 Witkin, California Summary 10th Torts § 347, Punitive Damages May be Recoverable.

5 Witkin, California Summary 10th Torts § 352, What Constitutes Discretionary Act.

5 Witkin, California Summary 10th Torts § 375, (S 375) in General.

5 Witkin, California Summary 10th Torts § 376, (S 376) Employee Must Act Within Scope of Employment.

5 Witkin, California Summary 10th Torts § 377, (S 377) Where Entity Fails to Defend or Defends Under Reservation of Rights.

5 Witkin, California Summary 10th Torts § 378, (S 378) Payment of Punitive Damages.

5 Witkin, California Summary 10th Torts § 380, (S 380) Elected Officials.

6 Witkin, California Summary 10th Torts § 1580, in General.

§ 825.2. Recovery of payment from public entity; memorandum of understanding

(a) Subject to subdivision (b), if an employee or former employee of a public entity pays any claim or judgment against him, or any portion thereof, that the public entity is required to pay under Section 825, he is entitled to recover the amount of such payment from the public entity.

(b) If the public entity did not conduct his defense against the action or claim, or if the public entity conducted such defense pursuant to an agreement with him reserving the rights of the public entity against him, an employee or former employee of a public entity may recover from the public entity under subdivision (a) only if he establishes that the act or omission upon which the claim or judgment is based occurred within the scope of his employment as an employee of the public entity and the public entity fails to establish that he acted or failed to act because of actual fraud, corruption or actual malice or that he willfully failed or refused to conduct the defense of the claim or action in good faith or to reasonably cooperate in good faith in the defense conducted by the public entity.

(c) If the provisions of this section are in conflict with the provisions of a memorandum of understanding reached pursuant to Chapter 12 (commencing with Section 3560) of Division 4 of Title 1, the memorandum of understanding shall be controlling without further legislative action, except that if such provisions of a memorandum of understanding require the expenditure of funds, the provisions shall not become effective unless approved by the Legislature in the annual Budget Act. *(Added by Stats.1963, c. 1681, p. 3271, § 1. Amended by Stats.1972, c. 1352, p. 2685, § 2; Stats.1979, c. 1072, § 48, eff. Sept. 28, 1979.)*

Law Revision Commission Comments

This section permits a public employee to enforce his right of indemnity against the public entity where he has been required to pay a judgment that the entity is required to pay under Section 825. [4 Cal.L.Rev.Comm. Reports 801 (1963)].

Research References

5 Witkin, California Summary 10th Torts § 375, (S 375) in General.
5 Witkin, California Summary 10th Torts § 376, (S 376) Employee Must Act Within Scope of Employment.
5 Witkin, California Summary 10th Torts § 377, (S 377) Where Entity Fails to Defend or Defends Under Reservation of Rights.

§ 825.4. Indemnification of public entity by employee generally

Except as provided in Section 825.6, if a public entity pays any claim or judgment against itself or against an employee or former employee of the public entity, or any portion thereof, for an injury arising out of an act or omission of the employee or former employee of the public entity, he is not liable to indemnify the public entity. *(Added by Stats.1963, c. 1681, p. 3271, § 1.)*

Research References

5 Witkin, California Summary 10th Torts § 352, What Constitutes Discretionary Act.
5 Witkin, California Summary 10th Torts § 375, (S 375) in General.

§ 825.6. Grounds for indemnification of public entity by employee; memorandum of understanding

(a)(1) Except as provided in subdivision (b), if a public entity pays any claim or judgment, or any portion thereof, either against itself or against an employee or former employee of the public entity, for an injury arising out of an act or omission of the employee or former employee of the public entity, the public entity may recover from the employee or former employee the amount of that payment if he or she acted or failed to act because of actual fraud, corruption, or actual malice, or willfully failed or refused to conduct the defense of the claim or action in good faith. Except as provided in paragraph (2) or (3), a public entity may not recover any payments made upon a judgment or claim against an employee or former employee if the public entity conducted his or her defense against the action or claim.

(2) If a public entity pays any claim or judgment, or any portion thereof, against an employee or former employee of the public entity for an injury arising out of his or her act or omission, and if the public entity conducted his or her defense against the claim or action pursuant to an agreement with him or her reserving the rights of the public entity against him or her, the public entity may recover the amount of the payment from him or her unless he or she establishes that the act or omission

upon which the claim or judgment is based occurred within the scope of his or her employment as an employee of the public entity and the public entity fails to establish that he or she acted or failed to act because of actual fraud, corruption, or actual malice or that he or she willfully failed or refused to reasonably cooperate in good faith in the defense conducted by the public entity.

(3) If a public entity pays any claim or judgment, or any portion thereof, against an employee or former employee of the public entity for an injury arising out of his or her act or omission, and if the public entity conducted the defense against the claim or action in the absence of an agreement with him or her reserving the rights of the public entity against him or her, the public entity may recover the amount of that payment from him or her if he or she willfully failed or refused to reasonably cooperate in good faith in the defense conducted by the public entity.

(b)(1) Upon a felony conviction for a violation of Section 1195 of this code, or of Section 68, 86, 93, 165, 504, or 518 of the Penal Code, by an elected official or former elected official of a public entity for an act or omission of that person while in office, the elected official or former elected official shall forfeit any rights to defense or indemnification under Section 825 with respect to a claim for damages for an injury arising from that act or omission.

(2) If a public entity pays any claim or judgment, or any portion thereof, either against itself or against an elected official or former elected official of the public entity, for an injury arising out of an act or omission of the elected official or former elected official of the public entity, which act or omission constituted a felony violation of Section 1195 of this code, or of Section 68, 86, 93, 165, 504, or 518 of the Penal Code, the public entity shall recover from the elected official or former elected official the amount of that payment upon the felony conviction of the elected official or former elected official for that act or omission. Upon that conviction, the public entity shall also recover from the elected official the costs of any defense to a civil action filed against the elected official for that act or omission.

(c) If the provisions of this section are in conflict with the provisions of a memorandum of understanding reached pursuant to Chapter 12 (commencing with Section 3560) of Division 4 of Title 1, the memorandum of understanding shall be controlling without further legislative action, except that if the provisions of a memorandum of understanding require the expenditure of funds, the provisions shall not become effective unless approved by the Legislature in the annual Budget Act. *(Added by Stats.1963, c. 1681, p. 3271, § 1. Amended by Stats.1972, c. 1352, p. 2685, § 3; Stats.1979, c. 1072, § 49, eff. Sept. 28, 1979; Stats.1994, c. 797 (A.B.2522), § 1; Stats.1995, c. 91 (S.B.975), § 43.)*

Research References

Rutter, Cal. Practice Guide: Civ. Pro. Before Trial Ch. 1-C, C. Prelawsuit Notices, Claims and Demands.
5 Witkin, California Summary 10th Torts § 352, What Constitutes Discretionary Act.
5 Witkin, California Summary 10th Torts § 375, (S 375) in General.
5 Witkin, California Summary 10th Torts § 380, (S 380) Elected Officials.

ARTICLE 5. INDEMNIFICATION OF CERTAIN STATE AGENTS

Section
827. Health care providers; extent of indemnification.

§ 827. Health care providers; extent of indemnification

A provider of health care, as defined in Section 56.05 of the Civil Code, its officers, employees, agents, and subcontractors, who are defended by the Attorney General pursuant to Section 12511.5, or other legal counsel provided by the state, shall be indemnified in accordance with Section 825, subject to the same conditions and limitations applicable to state employees, except that no provider of health care shall be indemnified in a civil rights action unless the health care provider maintains insurance for professional negligence. To the extent that negligence constitutes the basis of liability of the health care provider, the provider's private insurance shall be the source of recovery. *(Added by Stats.1995, c. 749 (A.B.1177), § 3, eff. Oct. 10, 1995.)*

Research References

5 Witkin, California Summary 10th Torts § 375, (S 375) in General.

CHAPTER 2. DANGEROUS CONDITIONS OF PUBLIC PROPERTY

ARTICLE 1. GENERAL

§ 830. Definitions

As used in this chapter:

(a) "Dangerous condition" means a condition of property that creates a substantial (as distinguished from a minor, trivial or insignificant) risk of injury when such property or adjacent property is used with due care in a manner in which it is reasonably foreseeable that it will be used.

(b) "Protect against" includes repairing, remedying or correcting a dangerous condition, providing safeguards against a dangerous condition, or warning of a dangerous condition.

(c) "Property of a public entity" and "public property" mean real or personal property owned or controlled by the public entity, but do not include easements, encroachments and other property that are located on the property of the public entity but are not owned or controlled by the public entity. *(Added by Stats.1963, c. 1681, p. 3272, § 1.)*

Law Revision Commission Comments

This section defines the terms used in this chapter. The definition of "dangerous condition" defines the type of property conditions for which a public entity may be held liable but does not impose liability. A public entity may be held liable for a "dangerous condition" of public property only if it has acted unreasonably in creating or failing to remedy or warn against the condition under the circumstances described in subsequent sections.

A "dangerous condition" is defined in terms of "foreseeable use." This does not change the pre-existing law relating to cities, counties and school districts. These entities are liable under Government Code [former] Section 53051 for maintaining property in a condition that creates a hazard to foreseeable users even if those persons use the property for a purpose for which it is not designed to be used or for a purpose that is illegal. Acosta v. County of Los Angeles, 56 Cal.2d 208, 14 Cal.Rptr. 433, 363 P.2d 473 (1961); Torkelson v. City of Redlands, 198 Cal.App.2d 354, 17 Cal.Rptr. 899 (1961).

The definition of "dangerous condition" is quite broad because it incorporates the broad definition of "injury" contained in Section 810.8. Thus, the danger involved need not be a danger of physical injury; it may be a danger of injury to intangible interests so long as the injury is of a kind that the law would redress if it were inflicted by a private person. For example, liability for an offensive odor may be imposed if the requirements of this chapter are satisfied.

Under the previous law, public entities were liable for maintaining a nuisance; but under this statute liability for conditions that would constitute a nuisance will have to be based on the somewhat more rigorous standards set forth in this chapter. Liability for such conditions cannot be imposed upon a nuisance theory because Section 815 provides public entities with immunity from liability unless liability is imposed by an enactment, and there is no enactment imposing liability on a nuisance theory.

"Adjacent property" as used in the definition of "dangerous condition" refers to the area that is exposed to the risk created by a dangerous condition of the public property. For example, the hazard created by a condition of public property may not be a hazard to persons using the public property itself, but may be a hazard to other property or to those using other property. A tree located on public property may have a decayed limb overhanging private property and creating a hazard to that property and the persons on it. Explosives on public property may create a hazard to a wide area of private property adjacent to the public property.

Under the definition as it is used in subsequent sections, a public entity cannot be held liable for dangerous conditions of "adjacent property." A public entity may be liable only for dangerous conditions of its own property. But its own property may be considered dangerous if it creates a substantial risk of injury to adjacent property or to persons on adjacent property; and its own property may be considered dangerous if a condition on the adjacent property exposes those using the public property to a substantial risk of injury.

A condition is not dangerous within the meaning of this chapter unless it creates a hazard to those who foreseeably will use the property or adjacent property with due care. Thus, even though it is foreseeable that persons may use public property without due care, a public entity may not be held liable for failing to take precautions to protect such persons. The definition would, however, take into consideration the standard of care that would be applicable to foreseeable users of the property. Where it is reasonably foreseeable that persons to whom a lower standard of care is applicable—such as children—may be exposed to a substantial risk of injury from the property, the public entity should be required to take reasonable precautions to protect such persons from that risk. Thus, a public entity may be expected to fence a swimming pool or to fence or lock up a dangerous instrumentality if it is reasonably foreseeable that small children may be injured if such precautions are not taken.

Although the condition will not be considered dangerous within the meaning of this chapter unless it creates a hazard to those who foreseeably will use the property or adjacent property with due care, this does not require that the injured person prove that he was free from contributory negligence. Contributory negligence is a matter of defense under subdivision (b) of Section 815. The plaintiff is, however, required to establish that the condition was one that created a hazard to a person who foreseeably would use the property or adjacent property with due care.

A condition will not be considered dangerous unless it creates a substantial (as distinguished from a minor, trivial or insignificant) risk of injury.

The definition of "protect against" is self-explanatory.

"Property of a public entity" excludes easements, encroachments and similar property, not owned or controlled by the public entity, that may be located on the property of a public entity in order to make clear that it is not the duty of the owner of the servient estate to inspect such property for hazards; rather, it is the duty of the person or entity that owns the easement, encroachment, etc. Of course, if the condition of the easement or encroachment renders the public property dangerous—as, for example, where a privately owned power line falls or sags across a public highway— the public entity will have an obligation to take reasonable precautions after it receives notice of the condition. [4 Cal.L.Rev.Comm. Reports 1001 (1963)].

Research References

Miller and Starr California Real Estate § 22:44, Landowners' Liability for Dangerous Conditions.
Miller and Starr California Real Estate § 22:76, Liability of a Government Entity.
Miller and Starr California Real Estate § 26:34, in General; Duty to Maintain.
18 NO. 4 Miller & Starr, California Real Estate Newsalert 38, Landowners' Liability.
19 NO. 1 Miller & Starr, California Real Estate Newsalert 19, Landowners' Liability.
19 NO. 2 Miller & Starr, California Real Estate Newsalert 19, Landowners' Liability.
20 NO. 5 Miller & Starr, California Real Estate Newsalert 18, Landowners' Liability.
22 NO. 6 Miller & Starr, California Real Estate Newsalert 19, Landowners' Liability.
4 Witkin Cal. Proc. 5th Pleading § 617, (S 617) Government Claims Act.
4 Witkin Cal. Proc. 5th Pleading § 621, Elements of Cause of Action.
4 Witkin Cal. Proc. 5th Pleading § 622, Illustrations.
5 Witkin, California Summary 10th Torts § 224, (S 224) Liability Under Statutes and Constitution.
5 Witkin, California Summary 10th Torts § 228, (S 228) Immunity Where Employee is Immune.
5 Witkin, California Summary 10th Torts § 249, Governing Statute.
5 Witkin, California Summary 10th Torts § 250, (S 250) Property Covered.
5 Witkin, California Summary 10th Torts § 251, (S 251) Property Not Owned or Controlled.
5 Witkin, California Summary 10th Torts § 253, Illustrations.
5 Witkin, California Summary 10th Torts § 259, What Constitutes Dangerous Condition.
5 Witkin, California Summary 10th Torts § 267, in General.
5 Witkin, California Summary 10th Torts § 268, Criminal Assault.
5 Witkin, California Summary 10th Torts § 269, (S 269) Condition on Adjacent Property.
5 Witkin, California Summary 10th Torts § 271, (S 271) Notice of Condition.
5 Witkin, California Summary 10th Torts § 288, (S 288) Inspection of Private Property.
5 Witkin, California Summary 10th Torts § 290, (S 290) in General.
5 Witkin, California Summary 10th Torts § 316, Liabilities.

§ 830.1. Seismic safety or fire sprinkler improvements; private ownership

For purposes of this chapter, seismic safety improvements or fire sprinkler improvements which are owned, built, controlled, operated, and maintained by the private owner of the building in which they are installed are not public property or property of a public entity solely because the improvements were financed, in whole or in part, by means of the formation of a special assessment district. (*Added by Stats.1990, c. 1318 (S.B.2819), § 1.*)

§ 830.2.   Minor, trivial or insignificant nature of risk

A condition is not a dangerous condition within the meaning of this chapter if the trial or appellate court, viewing the evidence most favorably to the plaintiff, determines as a matter of law that the risk created by the condition was of such a minor, trivial or insignificant nature in view of the surrounding circumstances that no reasonable person would conclude that the condition created a substantial risk of injury when such property or adjacent property was used with due care in a manner in which it was reasonably foreseeable that it would be used. (*Added by Stats.1963, c. 1681, p. 3272, § 1.*)

Law Revision Commission Comments

This section declares a rule that has been applied by the courts in cases involving dangerous conditions of sidewalks. Technically it is unnecessary, for it merely declares the rule that would be applied in any event when a court rules upon the sufficiency of the evidence. It is included in the chapter to emphasize that the courts are required to determine that there is evidence from which a reasonable person could conclude that a substantial, as opposed to a possible, risk is involved before they may permit the jury to find that a condition is dangerous. [4 Cal.L.Rev. Comm. Reports 1001 (1963)].

Research References

Miller and Starr California Real Estate § 22:44, Landowners' Liability for Dangerous Conditions.
Miller and Starr California Real Estate § 22:76, Liability of a Government Entity.
19 NO. 1 Miller & Starr, California Real Estate Newsalert 19, Landowners' Liability.
23 NO. 1 Miller & Starr, California Real Estate Newsalert 16, Landowners' Liability.
5 Witkin, California Summary 10th Torts § 261, Minor or Trivial Defect.

§ 830.4.   Failure to provide traffic control signals or signs

A condition is not a dangerous condition within the meaning of this chapter merely because of the failure to provide regulatory traffic control signals, stop signs, yield right-of-way signs, or speed restriction signs, as described by the Vehicle Code, or distinctive roadway markings as described in Section 21460 of the Vehicle Code. (*Added by Stats.1963, c. 1681, p. 3272, § 1.*)

Law Revision Commission Comments

This section prevents the liability of a public entity for dangerous conditions of public property from being based upon the failure to provide regulatory traffic signs. The California courts have held public entities immune from liability for failure to provide stop signs. Perry v. City of Santa Monica, 130 Cal.App.2d 370, 279 P.2d 92 (1955). This section would not, however, prevent the imposition of liability where a dangerous condition exists and a warning signal or device of the kind mentioned in Section 830.8 would be required. [4 Cal.L.Rev.Comm. Reports 1001 (1963)].

Research References

23 NO. 1 Miller & Starr, California Real Estate Newsalert 16, Landowners' Liability.
5 Witkin, California Summary 10th Torts § 264, Lack of Signal.
5 Witkin, California Summary 10th Torts § 265, Defective Signal.

§ 830.5. Happening of accident or action taken to correct condition after accident not evidence of dangerous condition

(a) Except where the doctrine of res ipsa loquitur is applicable, the happening of the accident which results in the injury is not in and of itself evidence that public property was in a dangerous condition.

(b) The fact that action was taken after an injury occurred to protect against a condition of public property is not evidence that the public property was in a dangerous condition at the time of the injury. *(Added by Stats.1963, c. 1681, p. 3272, § 1.)*

Research References

Rutter, Cal. Practice Guide: Civil Trials & Evidence Ch. 8G-C, C. Presumptions.

5 Witkin, California Summary 10th Torts § 259, What Constitutes Dangerous Condition.

§ 830.6. Plan or design of, or improvement to, public property; remedial work; warnings

Neither a public entity nor a public employee is liable under this chapter for an injury caused by the plan or design of a construction of, or an improvement to, public property where such plan or design has been approved in advance of the construction or improvement by the legislative body of the public entity or by some other body or employee exercising discretionary authority to give such approval or where such plan or design is prepared in conformity with standards previously so approved, if the trial or appellate court determines that there is any substantial evidence upon the basis of which (a) a reasonable public employee could have adopted the plan or design or the standards therefor or (b) a reasonable legislative body or other body or employee could have approved the plan or design or the standards therefor. Notwithstanding notice that constructed or improved public property may no longer be in conformity with a plan or design or a standard which reasonably could be approved by the legislative body or other body or employee, the immunity provided by this section shall continue for a reasonable period of time sufficient to permit the public entity to obtain funds for and carry out remedial work necessary to allow such public property to be in conformity with a plan or design approved by the legislative body of the public entity or other body or employee, or with a plan or design in conformity with a standard previously approved by such legislative body or other body or employee. In the event that the public entity is unable to remedy such public property because of practical impossibility or lack of sufficient funds, the immunity provided by this section shall remain so long as such public entity shall reasonably attempt to provide adequate warnings of the existence of the condition not conforming to the approved plan or design or to the approved standard. However, where a person fails to heed such warning or occupies public property despite such warning, such failure or occupation shall not in itself constitute an assumption of the risk of the danger indicated by the warning. *(Added by Stats.1963, c. 1681, p. 3272, § 1. Amended by Stats.1979, c. 481, § 1.)*

Law Revision Commission Comments

Sections 830.6 to 831.6, inclusive, describe certain limitations on the liability of public entities for conditions of public property. Some of these limitations have been previously established by the courts of this State in determining the liability of entities under the Public Liability Act of 1923; some have been established by the courts of other states where public entities are liable generally for their torts. Still others reflect policies previously adopted by the Legislature or logical extensions of the legislatively and judicially established policies. The immunities are stated here in statutory form so that litigation will not be needed to determine whether or not there is liability in these situations under this statute.

Section 830.6 provides immunity where a governmental body exercises the discretion given to it under the laws of the State in the planning and designing of public construction and improvements. No similar immunity for liability is provided entities under the Public Liability Act of 1923. The immunity provided by Section 830.6 is an immunity from liability under this chapter (Sections 830 to 840.6) only; hence, a public entity in some cases may be held liable under some enactment not contained in this chapter. For example, a public entity might be held liable under Section 815.6 for an injury resulting from its failure to exercise reasonable diligence to discharge a mandatory duty imposed by an enactment.

The immunity provided by Section 830.6 is similar to an immunity that has been granted by judicial decision to public entities in New York. See Weiss v. Fote, 7 N.Y.2d 579, 200 N.Y.S.2d 409, 167 N.E.2d 63 (1960). [4 Cal.L.Rev.Comm. Reports (1963)].

Research References

Miller and Starr California Real Estate § 22:76, Liability of a Government Entity.

Miller and Starr California Real Estate § 26:34, in General; Duty to Maintain.

19 NO. 1 Miller & Starr, California Real Estate Newsalert 19, Landowners' Liability.

20 NO. 3 Miller & Starr, California Real Estate Newsalert 20, Landowners' Liability.

5 Witkin Cal. Proc. 5th Pleading § 1107, Public Entity and Officer Defenses.

5 Witkin, California Summary 10th Torts § 229, (S 229) Tort Claims Act Immunities Extend to Liabilities Imposed by Other Statutes.

5 Witkin, California Summary 10th Torts § 272, (S 272) Reasonable Act or Omission.

5 Witkin, California Summary 10th Torts § 280, Nature of Defense.

5 Witkin, California Summary 10th Torts § 281, Causation of Injury by Design.

5 Witkin, California Summary 10th Torts § 282, Advance Discretionary Approval.

5 Witkin, California Summary 10th Torts § 283, Reasonableness of Design.

5 Witkin, California Summary 10th Torts § 284, Effect of Changed Conditions.

5 Witkin, California Summary 10th Torts § 360, Immunities.

§ 830.8. Failure to provide traffic or warning signals; exception

Neither a public entity nor a public employee is liable under this chapter for an injury caused by the failure to provide traffic or warning signals, signs, markings or devices described in the Vehicle Code. Nothing in this section exonerates a public entity or public employee from liability for injury proximately caused by such failure if a signal, sign, marking or device (other than one described in Section 830.4) was necessary to warn of a dangerous condition which endangered the safe movement of traffic and which would not be reasonably apparent to, and would not have been anticipated by, a person exercising due care. *(Added by Stats.1963, c. 1681, p. 3273, § 1.)*

Law Revision Commission Comments

This section prevents the imposition of liability based on the failure to provide traffic regulatory or warning signals or devices of a type not listed in Section 830.4, but liability may exist for failure to provide such a signal or device where the condition constitutes a trap to a person using the street or highway with due care. [4 Cal.L.Rev.Comm. Reports 801 (1963)].

Research References

Miller and Starr California Real Estate § 22:76, Liability of a Government Entity.

19 NO. 2 Miller & Starr, California Real Estate Newsalert 19, Landowners' Liability.

5 Witkin, California Summary 10th Torts § 264, Lack of Signal.

5 Witkin, California Summary 10th Torts § 265, Defective Signal.

5 Witkin, California Summary 10th Torts § 360, Immunities.

§ 830.9. Traffic signals under control of emergency vehicle

Neither a public entity nor a public employee is liable for an injury caused by the operation or nonoperation of official traffic control signals when controlled by an emergency vehicle in accordance with the provisions of subdivision (a) of Section 25258 of the Vehicle Code. *(Added by Stats.1967, c. 1037, p. 2640, § 2.)*

Government

Research References

5 Witkin, California Summary 10th Torts § 265, Defective Signal.

§ 831. Weather conditions; effect on use of streets and highways

Neither a public entity nor a public employee is liable for an injury caused by the effect on the use of streets and highways of weather conditions as such. Nothing in this section exonerates a public entity or public employee from liability for injury proximately caused by such effect if it would not be reasonably apparent to, and would not be anticipated by, a person exercising due care. For the purpose of this section, the effect on the use of streets and highways of weather conditions includes the effect of fog, wind, rain, flood, ice or snow but does not include physical damage to or deterioration of streets and highways resulting from weather conditions. *(Added by Stats.1963, c. 1681, p. 3273, § 1.)*

Law Revision Commission Comments

This section may be unnecessary in view of the other provisions of this chapter setting forth the conditions of liability for dangerous conditions of public property. Nonetheless, it is included to forestall unmeritorious litigation that might be brought in an effort to hold public entitles responsible for injuries caused by weather. [4 Cal.L.Rev.Comm. Reports 801 (1963)].

Research References

Miller and Starr California Real Estate § 26:34, in General; Duty to Maintain.
5 Witkin, California Summary 10th Torts § 279, (S 279) Accident Caused by Weather Conditions.
5 Witkin, California Summary 10th Torts § 348, Nature of Immunities and Defenses.
5 Witkin, California Summary 10th Torts § 360, Immunities.

§ 831.2. Natural condition of unimproved public property

Neither a public entity nor a public employee is liable for an injury caused by a natural condition of any unimproved public property, including but not limited to any natural condition of any lake, stream, bay, river or beach. *(Added by Stats.1963, c. 1681, p. 3273, § 1.)*

Research References

Miller and Starr California Real Estate § 14:8, Ownership of Trees; Overhanging Branches and Roots.
Miller and Starr California Real Estate § 22:69, Persons Entitled to the Exemption.
Miller and Starr California Real Estate § 22:72, Recreational or Hazardous Activities on Certain Public Property.
Miller and Starr California Real Estate § 26:34, in General; Duty to Maintain.
5 Witkin, California Summary 10th Torts § 252, Property in Natural Condition: General Rule of Nonliability.
5 Witkin, California Summary 10th Torts § 253, Illustrations.
5 Witkin, California Summary 10th Torts § 254, Effect of Assuming Duty to Protect Public.
5 Witkin, California Summary 10th Torts § 255, Roads, Trails, and Paths.
5 Witkin, California Summary 10th Torts § 257, Injury or Damage on Adjacent Land.

§ 831.21. Public beaches; natural condition and unimproved notwithstanding public safety services; application of section

(a) Public beaches shall be deemed to be in a natural condition and unimproved notwithstanding the provision or absence of public safety services such as lifeguards, police or sheriff patrols, medical services, fire protection services, beach cleanup services, or signs. The provisions of this section shall apply only to natural conditions of public property and shall not limit any liability or immunity that may otherwise exist pursuant to this division.

(b) This section shall only be applicable to causes of action based upon acts or omissions occurring on or after January 1, 1988. *(Added by Stats.1987, c. 1209, § 1.)*

Research References

Miller and Starr California Real Estate § 22:72, Recreational or Hazardous Activities on Certain Public Property.
5 Witkin, California Summary 10th Torts § 254, Effect of Assuming Duty to Protect Public.

§ 831.25. Land failure caused by natural condition; failure to warn; duty of care

(a) Neither a public entity nor a public employee is liable for any damage or injury to property, or for emotional distress unless the plaintiff has suffered substantial physical injury, off the public entity's property caused by land failure of any unimproved public property if the land failure was caused by a natural condition of the unimproved public property.

(b) For the purposes of this section, a natural condition exists and property shall be deemed unimproved notwithstanding the intervention of minor improvements made for the preservation or prudent management of the property in its unimproved state that did not contribute to the land failure.

(c) As used in this section, "land failure" means any movement of land, including a landslide, mudslide, creep, subsidence, and any other gradual or rapid movement of land.

(d) This section shall not benefit any public entity or public employee who had actual notice of probable damage that is likely to occur outside the public property because of land failure and who fails to give a reasonable warning of the danger to the affected property owners. Neither a public entity nor a public employee is liable for any damage or injury arising from the giving of a warning under this section.

(e) Nothing in this section shall limit the immunity provided by Section 831.2.

(f) Nothing in this section creates a duty of care or basis of liability for damage or injury to property or of liability for emotional distress. *(Added by Stats.1984, c. 1071, § 1. Amended by Stats.1988, c. 1034, § 1.)*

Research References

Miller and Starr California Real Estate § 30:8, Interference With Land Stability.
Miller and Starr California Real Estate § 22:18, Governmental Agencies.
5 Witkin, California Summary 10th Torts § 257, Injury or Damage on Adjacent Land.

§ 831.3. Nondedicated roads

Neither a public entity nor a public employee is liable for any injury occurring on account of the grading or the performance of other maintenance or repair on or reconstruction or replacement of any road which has not officially been accepted as a part of the road system under the jurisdiction of the public entity if the grading, maintenance, repair, or reconstruction or replacement is performed with reasonable care and leaves the road in no more dangerous or unsafe condition than it was before the work commenced. No act of grading, maintenance, repair, or reconstruction or replacement within the meaning of this section shall be deemed to give rise to any duty of the public entity to continue any grading, maintenance, repair, or reconstruction or replacement on any road not a part of the road system under the public entity's jurisdiction. As used in this section "reconstruction or replacement" means reconstruction or replacement performed pursuant to Article 3 (commencing with Section 1160) of Chapter 4 of Division 2 of the Streets and Highways Code. *(Added by Stats.1981, c. 260, p. 1337, § 1. Amended by Stats.1986, c. 578, § 1, eff. Aug. 26, 1986.)*

5 Witkin, California Summary 10th Torts § 255, Roads, Trails, and Paths.

§ 831.4. Unpaved access roads to recreational or scenic areas; trails; paved paths on easements of way granted to public entities

A public entity, public employee, or a grantor of a public easement to a public entity for any of the following purposes, is not liable for an injury caused by a condition of:

(a) Any unpaved road which provides access to fishing, hunting, camping, hiking, riding, including animal and all types of vehicular riding, water sports, recreational or scenic areas and which is not a (1) city street or highway or (2) county, state or federal highway or (3) public street or highway of a joint highway district, boulevard district, bridge and highway district or similar district formed for the improvement or building of public streets or highways.

(b) Any trail used for the above purposes.

(c) Any paved trail, walkway, path, or sidewalk on an easement of way which has been granted to a public entity, which easement provides access to any unimproved property, so long as such public entity shall reasonably attempt to provide adequate warnings of the existence of any condition of the paved trail, walkway, path, or sidewalk which constitutes a hazard to health or safety. Warnings required by this subdivision shall only be required where pathways are paved, and such requirement shall not be construed to be a standard of care for any unpaved pathways or roads. *(Added by Stats.1963, c. 1681, p. 3273, § 1. Amended by Stats.1968, c. 714, p. 1416, § 1; Stats.1970, c. 807, p. 1530, § 2; Stats.1972, c. 1200, p. 2323, § 2; Stats.1979, c. 1010, § 1.)*

Miller and Starr California Real Estate § 22:69, Persons Entitled to the Exemption.
Miller and Starr California Real Estate § 22:72, Recreational or Hazardous Activities on Certain Public Property.
Miller and Starr California Real Estate § 26:34, in General; Duty to Maintain.
22 NO. 2 Miller & Starr, California Real Estate Newsalert 17, Landowners' Liability.
5 Witkin, California Summary 10th Torts § 255, Roads, Trails, and Paths.

§ 831.5. Legislative declaration; innovative public access programs

(a) The Legislature declares that innovative public access programs, such as agreements with public land trusts, can provide effective and responsible alternatives to costly public acquisition programs. The Legislature therefore declares that it is beneficial to the people of this state to encourage private nonprofit entities such as public land trusts to carry out programs that preserve open space or increase opportunities for the public to enjoy access to and use of natural resources if the programs are consistent (1) with public safety, (2) with the protection of the resources, and (3) with public and private rights.

(b) For the purposes of Sections 831.2, 831.25, 831.4, and 831.7, "public entity" includes a public land trust which meets all of the following conditions:

(1) It is a nonprofit organization existing under the provisions of Section 501(c) of the United States Internal Revenue Code.

(2) It has specifically set forth in its articles of incorporation, as among its principal charitable purposes, the conservation of land for public access, agricultural, scientific, historical, educational, recreational, scenic, or open-space opportunities.

(3) It has entered into an agreement with the State Coastal Conservancy for lands located within the coastal zone, as defined in Section 31006 of the Public Resources Code, with the California Tahoe Conservancy or its designee for lands located within the Lake Tahoe region, as defined in subdivision (c) of Section 66953 of the Government Code, or with the State Public Works Board or its designee for lands not located within the coastal zone or the Lake Tahoe region, on such terms and conditions as are mutually agreeable, requiring the public land trust to hold the lands or, where appropriate, to provide nondiscriminatory public access consistent with the protection and conservation of either coastal or other natural resources, or both. The conservancy or the board, as appropriate, shall periodically review the agreement and determine whether the public land trust is in compliance with the terms and conditions. In the event the conservancy or the board determines that the public land trust is not in substantial compliance with the agreement, the conservancy or the board shall cancel the agreement, and the provisions of Sections 831.2, 831.25, 831.4, and 831.7 shall no longer apply with regard to that public land trust.

(c) For the purposes of Sections 831.2, 831.25, 831.4, and 831.7, "public employee" includes an officer, authorized agent, or employee of any public land trust which is a public entity. *(Added by Stats.1980, c. 1123, p. 3621, § 1. Amended by Stats.1980, c. 1234, p. 4183, § 1, eff. Sept. 29, 1980, operative Jan. 1, 1981; Stats.1984, c. 1222, § 1, eff. Sept. 17, 1984; Stats.1984, c. 1239, § 1, eff. Sept. 17, 1984; Stats.1990, c. 934 (A.B.3570), § 2.)*

Miller and Starr California Real Estate § 22:69, Persons Entitled to the Exemption.
Miller and Starr California Real Estate § 22:72, Recreational or Hazardous Activities on Certain Public Property.

§ 831.6. Unimproved and unoccupied portions of tidelands, submerged lands and school lands

Neither the State nor an employee of the State is liable under this chapter for any injury caused by a condition of the unimproved and unoccupied portions of:

(a) The ungranted tidelands and submerged lands, and the beds of navigable rivers, streams, lakes, bays, estuaries, inlets and straits, owned by the State.

(b) The unsold portions of the 16th and 36th sections of school lands, the unsold portions of the 500,000 acres granted to the State for school purposes, and the unsold portions of the listed lands selected of the United States in lieu of the 16th and 36th sections and losses to the school grant. *(Added by Stats.1963, c. 1681, p. 3273, § 1.)*

Law Revision Commission Comments

This section exempts the State from liability under the dangerous conditions statute for conditions of the vast amounts of property, title to which has vested in the State because of its sovereignty, but which it has never occupied or improved. The descriptions of the property are taken from Public Resources Code Sections 6301 and 7301.

The immunity provided by this section, like that provided by Section 830.6, is an immunity from liability under this chapter (Sections 830 to 840.6) only. In a proper case, liability may be based on a provision in some other enactment. [4 Cal.L.Rev.Comm. Reports 801 (1963)].

5 Witkin, California Summary 10th Torts § 256, Tidelands, Submerged Lands, and School Lands.
5 Witkin, California Summary 10th Torts § 360, Immunities.

§ 831.7. Hazardous recreational activities; failure to guard or warn; negligence; duty of care

(a) Neither a public entity nor a public employee is liable to any person who participates in a hazardous recreational activity, including any person who assists the participant, or to any spectator who knew or reasonably should have known that the

Government

hazardous recreational activity created a substantial risk of injury to himself or herself and was voluntarily in the place of risk, or having the ability to do so failed to leave, for any damage or injury to property or persons arising out of that hazardous recreational activity.

(b) As used in this section, "hazardous recreational activity" means a recreational activity conducted on property of a public entity that creates a substantial, as distinguished from a minor, trivial, or insignificant, risk of injury to a participant or a spectator.

"Hazardous recreational activity" also means:

(1) Water contact activities, except diving, in places where, or at a time when, lifeguards are not provided and reasonable warning thereof has been given, or the injured party should reasonably have known that there was no lifeguard provided at the time.

(2) Any form of diving into water from other than a diving board or diving platform, or at any place or from any structure where diving is prohibited and reasonable warning thereof has been given.

(3) Animal riding, including equestrian competition, archery, bicycle racing or jumping, mountain bicycling, boating, cross-country and downhill skiing, hang gliding, kayaking, motorized vehicle racing, off-road motorcycling or four-wheel driving of any kind, orienteering, pistol and rifle shooting, rock climbing, rocketeering, rodeo, self-contained underwater breathing apparatus (SCUBA) diving, spelunking, skydiving, sport parachuting, paragliding, body contact sports, surfing, trampolining, tree climbing, tree rope swinging, waterskiing, white water rafting, and windsurfing. For the purposes of this subdivision, "mountain bicycling" does not include riding a bicycle on paved pathways, roadways, or sidewalks. For the purpose of this paragraph, "body contact sports" means sports in which it is reasonably foreseeable that there will be rough bodily contact with one or more participants.

(c)(1) Notwithstanding subdivision (a), this section does not limit liability that would otherwise exist for any of the following:

(A) Failure of the public entity or employee to guard or warn of a known dangerous condition or of another hazardous recreational activity known to the public entity or employee that is not reasonably assumed by the participant as inherently a part of the hazardous recreational activity out of which the damage or injury arose.

(B) Damage or injury suffered in any case where permission to participate in the hazardous recreational activity was granted for a specific fee. For the purpose of this subparagraph, "specific fee" does not include a fee or consideration charged for a general purpose such as a general park admission charge, a vehicle entry or parking fee, or an administrative or group use application or permit fee, as distinguished from a specific fee charged for participation in the specific hazardous recreational activity out of which the damage or injury arose.

(C) Injury suffered to the extent proximately caused by the negligent failure of the public entity or public employee to properly construct or maintain in good repair any structure, recreational equipment or machinery, or substantial work of improvement utilized in the hazardous recreational activity out of which the damage or injury arose.

(D) Damage or injury suffered in any case where the public entity or employee recklessly or with gross negligence promoted the participation in or observance of a hazardous recreational activity. For purposes of this subparagraph, promotional literature or a public announcement or advertisement that merely describes the available facilities and services on the property does not in itself constitute a reckless or grossly negligent promotion.

(E) An act of gross negligence by a public entity or a public employee that is the proximate cause of the injury.

(2) Nothing in this subdivision creates a duty of care or basis of liability for personal injury or damage to personal property.

(d) Nothing in this section limits the liability of an independent concessionaire, or any person or organization other than the public entity, whether or not the person or organization has a contractual relationship with the public entity to use the public property, for injuries or damages suffered in any case as a result of the operation of a hazardous recreational activity on public property by the concessionaire, person, or organization. *(Added by Stats.1983, c. 863, § 1. Amended by Stats.1995, c. 597 (A.B.700), § 1; Stats.2010, c. 73 (A.B.634), § 1; Stats.2011, c. 296 (A.B.1023), § 109.)*

Research References

Miller and Starr California Real Estate § 22:69, Persons Entitled to the Exemption.
Miller and Starr California Real Estate § 22:72, Recreational or Hazardous Activities on Certain Public Property.
5 Witkin, California Summary 10th Torts § 275, in General.
5 Witkin, California Summary 10th Torts § 276, Participants and Spectators.
5 Witkin, California Summary 10th Torts § 277, Nature of Activity.
5 Witkin, California Summary 10th Torts § 278, Exceptions.

§ 831.7.5. Liability of public entity owning or operating a dog park; actions of a dog in the dog park

(a) A public entity that owns or operates a dog park shall not be held liable for injury or death of a person or pet resulting solely from the actions of a dog in the dog park.

(b) This section shall not be construed to affect the liability of a public entity that exists under the law.

(c) "Public entity" has the same meaning as Section 811.2, and includes, but is not limited to, cities, counties, cities and counties, and special districts. *(Added by Stats.2013, c. 74 (A.B.265), § 1.)*

§ 831.8. Reservoirs, canals, conduits, or drains; exoneration of liability; exceptions

(a) Subject to subdivisions (d) and (e), neither a public entity nor a public employee is liable under this chapter for an injury caused by the condition of a reservoir if at the time of the injury the person injured was using the property for any purpose other than that for which the public entity intended or permitted the property to be used.

(b) Subject to subdivisions (d) and (e), neither an irrigation district nor an employee thereof nor the state nor a state employee is liable under this chapter for an injury caused by the condition of canals, conduits, or drains used for the distribution of water if at the time of the injury the person injured was using the property for any purpose other than that for which the district or state intended it to be used.

(c) Subject to subdivisions (d) and (e), neither a public agency operating flood control and water conservation facilities nor its employees are liable under this chapter for an injury caused by the condition or use of unlined flood control channels or adjacent groundwater recharge spreading grounds if, at the time of the injury, the person injured was using the property for any purpose other than that for which the public entity intended it to be used, and, if all of the following conditions are met:

(1) The public agency operates and maintains dams, pipes, channels, and appurtenant facilities to provide flood control protection and water conservation for a county whose population exceeds nine million residents.

(2) The public agency operates facilities to recharge a groundwater basin system which is the primary water supply for more than one million residents.

(3) The groundwater supply is dependent on imported water recharge which must be conducted in accordance with court-imposed basin management restrictions.

(4) The basin recharge activities allow the conservation and storage of both local and imported water supplies when these waters are available.

(5) The public agency posts conspicuous signs warning of any increase in waterflow levels of an unlined flood control channel or any spreading ground receiving water.

(d) Nothing in this section exonerates a public entity or a public employee from liability for injury proximately caused by a dangerous condition of property if all of the following occur:

(1) The injured person was not guilty of a criminal offense under Article 1 (commencing with Section 552) of Chapter 12 of Title 13 of Part 1 of the Penal Code in entering on or using the property.

(2) The condition created a substantial and unreasonable risk of death or serious bodily harm when the property or adjacent property was used with due care in a manner in which it was reasonably foreseeable that it would be used.

(3) The dangerous character of the condition was not reasonably apparent to, and would not have been anticipated by, a mature, reasonable person using the property with due care.

(4) The public entity or the public employee had actual knowledge of the condition and knew or should have known of its dangerous character a sufficient time prior to the injury to have taken measures to protect against the condition.

(e) Nothing in this section exonerates a public entity or a public employee from liability for injury proximately caused by a dangerous condition of property if all of the following occur:

(1) The person injured was less than 12 years of age.

(2) The dangerous condition created a substantial and unreasonable risk of death or serious bodily harm to children under 12 years of age using the property or adjacent property with due care in a manner in which it was reasonably foreseeable that it would be used.

(3) The person injured, because of his or her immaturity, did not discover the condition or did not appreciate its dangerous character.

(4) The public entity or the public employee had actual knowledge of the condition and knew or should have known of its dangerous character a sufficient time prior to the injury to have taken measures to protect against the condition.

(f) Nothing in subdivision (c) exonerates a public agency or public employee subject to that subdivision from liability for injury proximately caused by a dangerous condition of public property if all of the following occur:

(1) The person injured was 16 years of age or younger.

(2) The dangerous condition created a substantial and unreasonable risk of death or serious bodily harm to children 16 years of age or younger using the property or adjacent property with due care in a manner in which it was reasonably foreseeable that it would be used.

(3) The person injured did not discover the condition or did not appreciate its dangerous character because of his or her immaturity.

(4) The public entity or public employee had actual knowledge of the condition and knew or should have known of its dangerous character a sufficient time prior to the injury to have taken measures to protect against the condition. *(Added by*

Stats.1963, c. 1681, p. 3274, § 1. Amended by Stats.1998, c. 659 (A.B.2023), § 1; Stats.2001, c. 756 (A.B.92), § 1; Stats.2008, c. 633 (A.B.1903), § 1, eff. Sept. 30, 2008; Stats.2012, c. 110 (A.B.1558), § 1.)

Research References

Miller and Starr California Real Estate § 22:76, Liability of a Government Entity.

19 NO. 3 Miller & Starr, California Real Estate Newsalert 4, Landowners' Liability.

19 NO. 4 Miller & Starr, California Real Estate Newsalert 20, Landowners' Liability.

5 Witkin, California Summary 10th Torts § 273, Statutory Rule.

5 Witkin, California Summary 10th Torts § 274, Exceptions.

5 Witkin, California Summary 10th Torts § 360, Immunities.

ARTICLE 2.   LIABILITY OF PUBLIC ENTITIES

Section

835.   Conditions of liability.

835.2.   Actual notice; constructive notice; evidence of due care.

835.4.   Reasonableness of act or omission creating condition or of action to protect against risk of injury created by condition.

§ 835.   Conditions of liability

Except as provided by statute, a public entity is liable for injury caused by a dangerous condition of its property if the plaintiff establishes that the property was in a dangerous condition at the time of the injury, that the injury was proximately caused by the dangerous condition, that the dangerous condition created a reasonably foreseeable risk of the kind of injury which was incurred, and that either:

(a) A negligent or wrongful act or omission of an employee of the public entity within the scope of his employment created the dangerous condition; or

(b) The public entity had actual or constructive notice of the dangerous condition under Section 835.2 a sufficient time prior to the injury to have taken measures to protect against the dangerous condition. *(Added by Stats.1963, c. 1681, p. 3275, § 1.)*

Research References

Rutter, Cal. Practice Guide: Civil Trials & Evidence Ch. 8G-C, C. Presumptions.

Rutter, Cal. Practice Guide: Personal Injury Ch. 5-E, E. Selected Pleading Issues.

Rutter, Cal. Practice Guide: Personal Injury Gen. Matls., Highlights.

Miller and Starr California Real Estate § 22:18, Governmental Agencies.

Miller and Starr California Real Estate § 22:44, Landowners' Liability for Dangerous Conditions.

Miller and Starr California Real Estate § 22:57, Negligence of an Independent Contractor; Injuries to a Contractor's Employees.

Miller and Starr California Real Estate § 22:69, Persons Entitled to the Exemption.

Miller and Starr California Real Estate § 22:72, Recreational or Hazardous Activities on Certain Public Property.

Miller and Starr California Real Estate § 22:76, Liability of a Government Entity.

Miller and Starr California Real Estate § 26:34, in General; Duty to Maintain.

18 NO. 4 Miller & Starr, California Real Estate Newsalert 38, Landowners' Liability.

19 NO. 1 Miller & Starr, California Real Estate Newsalert 19, Landowners' Liability.

20 NO. 6 Miller & Starr, California Real Estate Newsalert 17, Landowners' Liability.

21 NO. 1 Miller & Starr, California Real Estate Newsalert 19, Landowners' Liability.

Government

22 NO. 2 Miller & Starr, California Real Estate Newsalert 17, Landowners' Liability.
23 NO. 1 Miller & Starr, California Real Estate Newsalert 16, Landowners' Liability.
4 Witkin Cal. Proc. 5th Pleading § 622, Illustrations.
7 Witkin Cal. Proc. 5th Trial § 268, (S 268) Language of Statute.
5 Witkin, California Summary 10th Torts § 258, Elements of Liability.
5 Witkin, California Summary 10th Torts § 260, Illustrations of Dangerous and Non-Dangerous Conditions.
5 Witkin, California Summary 10th Torts § 262, Recovery for Emotional Distress.
5 Witkin, California Summary 10th Torts § 263, Causation.
5 Witkin, California Summary 10th Torts § 265, Defective Signal.
5 Witkin, California Summary 10th Torts § 267, in General.
5 Witkin, California Summary 10th Torts § 268, Criminal Assault.
5 Witkin, California Summary 10th Torts § 270, (S 270) Act or Omission of Employee.
5 Witkin, California Summary 10th Torts § 271, (S 271) Notice of Condition.
5 Witkin, California Summary 10th Torts § 285, Protective Measures Against Earth Movement.
5 Witkin, California Summary 10th Torts § 296, Injury Caused by Escaped Prisoner.
5 Witkin, California Summary 10th Torts § 317, Immunities.
6 Witkin, California Summary 10th Torts § 1089, (S 1089) Natural Conditions.

§ 835.2. Actual notice; constructive notice; evidence of due care

(a) A public entity had actual notice of a dangerous condition within the meaning of subdivision (b) of Section 835 if it had actual knowledge of the existence of the condition and knew or should have known of its dangerous character.

(b) A public entity had constructive notice of a dangerous condition within the meaning of subdivision (b) of Section 835 only if the plaintiff establishes that the condition had existed for such a period of time and was of such an obvious nature that the public entity, in the exercise of due care, should have discovered the condition and its dangerous character. On the issue of due care, admissible evidence includes but is not limited to evidence as to:

(1) Whether the existence of the condition and its dangerous character would have been discovered by an inspection system that was reasonably adequate (considering the practicability and cost of inspection weighed against the likelihood and magnitude of the potential danger to which failure to inspect would give rise) to inform the public entity whether the property was safe for the use or uses for which the public entity used or intended others to use the public property and for uses that the public entity actually knew others were making of the public property or adjacent property.

(2) Whether the public entity maintained and operated such an inspection system with due care and did not discover the condition. (Added by Stats.1963, c. 1681, p. 3275, § 1.)

Research References

22 NO. 6 Miller & Starr, California Real Estate Newsalert 19, Landowners' Liability.
5 Witkin, California Summary 10th Torts § 271, (S 271) Notice of Condition.

§ 835.4. Reasonableness of act or omission creating condition or of action to protect against risk of injury created by condition

(a) A public entity is not liable under subdivision (a) of Section 835 for injury caused by a condition of its property if the public entity establishes that the act or omission that created the condition was reasonable. The reasonableness of the act or omission that created the condition shall be determined by weighing the probability and gravity of potential injury to persons and property foreseeably exposed to the risk of injury

against the practicability and cost of taking alternative action that would not create the risk of injury or of protecting against the risk of injury.

(b) A public entity is not liable under subdivision (b) of Section 835 for injury caused by a dangerous condition of its property if the public entity establishes that the action it took to protect against the risk of injury created by the condition or its failure to take such action was reasonable. The reasonableness of the action or inaction of the public entity shall be determined by taking into consideration the time and opportunity it had to take action and by weighing the probability and gravity of potential injury to persons and property foreseeably exposed to the risk of injury against the practicability and cost of protecting against the risk of such injury. (Added by Stats.1963, c. 1681, p. 3275, § 1.)

Law Revision Commission Comments

Under this section, a public entity may absolve itself from liability for creating or failing to remedy a dangerous condition by showing that it would have been too costly and impractical for the public entity to have done anything else.

This defense has been provided public entities in recognition that, despite limited manpower and budgets, there is much that they are required to do. Unlike private enterprise, a public entity often cannot weigh the advantage of engaging in an activity against the cost and decide not to engage in it. Government cannot "go out of the business" of governing. Therefore, a public entity should not be liable for injuries caused by a dangerous condition if it is able to show that under all the circumstances, including the alternative courses of action available to it and the practicability and cost of pursuing such alternatives, its action in creating or failing to remedy the condition was not unreasonable.

No similar defense is provided to public entities by the Public Liability Act of 1923.

In addition to the defense specified here, the defenses normally available to private litigants—contributory negligence and assumption of the risk—are available to the public entity under subdivision (b) of Section 815. [4 Cal.L.Rev.Comm. Reports 801 (1963)].

Research References

5 Witkin Cal. Proc. 5th Pleading § 1107, Public Entity and Officer Defenses.
5 Witkin, California Summary 10th Torts § 258, Elements of Liability.
5 Witkin, California Summary 10th Torts § 272, (S 272) Reasonable Act or Omission.
5 Witkin, California Summary 10th Torts § 274, Exceptions.
5 Witkin, California Summary 10th Torts § 284, Effect of Changed Conditions.
5 Witkin, California Summary 10th Torts § 285, Protective Measures Against Earth Movement.
5 Witkin, California Summary 10th Torts § 360, Immunities.
7 Witkin, California Summary 10th Constitutional Law § 625, (S 625) Rule and Test.

ARTICLE 3. LIABILITY OF PUBLIC EMPLOYEES

Section
840.   Liability for injuries generally; immunity; defenses.
840.2. Dangerous condition of public property; conditions of liability.
840.4. Notice; actual; constructive.
840.6. Standard of care; reasonableness of act or omission.

§ 840. Liability for injuries generally; immunity; defenses

Except as provided in this article, a public employee is not liable for injury caused by a condition of public property where such condition exists because of any act or omission of such employee within the scope of his employment. The liability established by this article is subject to any immunity of the public employee provided by statute and is subject to any defenses that would be available to the public employee if he were a private person. (Added by Stats.1963, c. 1681, p. 3276, § 1.)

Law Revision Commission Comments

Government Code [former] Section 1953 has provided the exclusive basis for the liability of public officers and employees for dangerous conditions of public property since its enactment in 1919. This article supersedes [former] Section 1953, and the provisions of that section that make it the exclusive basis of liability are carried forward, in substance, in this section. Hence, liability, if any, of a public employee for a condition of public property must be grounded upon this article and upon no other statute.

On the other hand, the general liability of public employees that is described here is subject to statutory immunities from liability that are found in other statutes, such as the immunities of Article 1 of this chapter and the immunities found in Article 3 of Chapter 1. It also is subject to the defenses normally available to private litigants. [4 Cal.L.Rev.Comm. Reports 801 (1963)].

Research References

5 Witkin, California Summary 10th Torts § 359, Liability.

§ 840.2. Dangerous condition of public property; conditions of liability

An employee of a public entity is liable for injury caused by a dangerous condition of public property if the plaintiff establishes that the property of the public entity was in a dangerous condition at the time of the injury, that the injury was proximately caused by the dangerous condition, that the dangerous condition created a reasonably foreseeable risk of the kind of injury which was incurred, and that either:

(a) The dangerous condition was directly attributable wholly or in substantial part to a negligent or wrongful act of the employee and the employee had the authority and the funds and other means immediately available to take alternative action which would not have created the dangerous condition; or

(b) The employee had the authority and it was his responsibility to take adequate measures to protect against the dangerous condition at the expense of the public entity and the funds and other means for doing so were immediately available to him, and he had actual or constructive notice of the dangerous condition under Section 840.4 a sufficient time prior to the injury to have taken measures to protect against the dangerous condition. (Added by Stats.1963, c. 1681, p. 3276, § 1.)

Law Revision Commission Comments

Subdivision (a) of this section subjects a public employee to liability for injuries caused by conditions which he has negligently created. The cases that have arisen under Government Code [former] Section 1953, are in conflict upon the question whether public employees are subject to such liability, although the more recent authority seems to indicate that they are not.

Under this section, a public employee who has negligently created a dangerous condition may not be held liable for injuries caused thereby if someone other than the employee has taken adequate measures to protect against the condition. For example, if an employee through negligence creates a dangerous condition in a street, the employee may not be held liable to an automobile passenger who is injured when the auto strikes the condition if the entity has placed lights, warnings or barriers sufficient to prevent injury to careful motorists, even though the defense of contributory negligence may not be available against the passenger.

Subdivision (b) is comparable to Government Code [former] Section 1953. However, unlike [former] Section 1953, this section does not leave the question of notice to judicial construction. The requisite conditions for notice are stated in Section 840.4.

Under this section, a public employee may not be held liable for injuries caused by a dangerous condition of public property if it was not reasonably foreseeable that the particular type of injury incurred would occur. There is no similar provision in [former] Section 1953. See the comment under Section 835. [4 Cal.L.Rev.Comm. Reports 801 (1963)].

Research References

5 Witkin, California Summary 10th Torts § 359, Liability.

§ 840.4. Notice; actual; constructive

(a) A public employee had actual notice of a dangerous condition within the meaning of subdivision (b) of Section 840.2 if he had actual personal knowledge of the existence of the condition and knew or should have known of its dangerous character.

(b) A public employee had constructive notice of a dangerous condition within the meaning of subdivision (b) of Section 840.2 only if the plaintiff establishes (1) that the public employee had the authority and it was his responsibility as a public employee to inspect the property of the public entity or to see that inspections were made to determine whether dangerous conditions existed in the public property, (2) that the funds and other means for making such inspections or for seeing that such inspections were made were immediately available to the public employee, and (3) that the dangerous condition had existed for such a period of time and was of such an obvious nature that the public employee, in the exercise of his authority and responsibility with due care, should have discovered the condition and its dangerous character. (Added by Stats.1963, c. 1681, p. 3276, § 1.)

Law Revision Commission Comments

This section prescribes the conditions under which a public employee may be charged with notice of a dangerous condition. See the discussion under Section 835.2. [4 Cal.L.Rev.Comm. Reports 801 (1963)].

Research References

5 Witkin, California Summary 10th Torts § 359, Liability.

§ 840.6. Standard of care; reasonableness of act or omission

(a) A public employee is not liable under subdivision (a) of Section 840.2 for injury caused by a dangerous condition of public property if he establishes that the act or omission that created the condition was reasonable. The reasonableness of the act or omission that created the condition shall be determined by weighing the probability and gravity of potential injury to persons and property foreseeably exposed to the risk of injury against the practicability and cost of taking alternative action that would not create the risk of injury or of protecting against the risk of injury.

(b) A public employee is not liable under subdivision (b) of Section 840.2 for injury caused by a dangerous condition of public property if he establishes that the action taken to protect against the risk of injury created by the condition or the failure to take such action was reasonable. The reasonableness of the inaction or action shall be determined by taking into consideration the time and opportunity the public employee had to take action and by weighing the probability and gravity of potential injury to persons and property foreseeably exposed to the risk of injury against the practicability and cost of protecting against the risk of such injury. (Added by Stats.1963, c. 1681, p. 3277, § 1.)

Law Revision Commission Comments

This section makes available to a public employee a defense similar to that given public entities by Section 835.4. See the comment to that section. [4 Cal.L.Rev.Comm. Reports 801 (1963)].

Research References

5 Witkin, California Summary 10th Torts § 360, Immunities.

CHAPTER 3. POLICE AND CORRECTIONAL ACTIVITIES

Section
844. Prisoner.

Government

Section

844.6.   Injuries by and to prisoners.

845.   Police protection services; failure to provide.

845.2.   Prison, jail or correctional facilities; failure to provide.

845.4.   Interference with right of prisoner to judicial determination or review of legality of confinement.

845.6.   Medical care for prisoners; failure to obtain.

845.8.   Parole or release of prisoner; escape of prisoners; persons resisting arrest.

846.   Failure to make arrest or to retain person arrested in custody.

§ 844. Prisoner

As used in this chapter, "prisoner" includes an inmate of a prison, jail, or penal or correctional facility. For the purposes of this chapter, a lawfully arrested person who is brought into a law enforcement facility for the purpose of being booked, as described in Section 7 of the Penal Code, becomes a prisoner, as a matter of law, upon his or her initial entry into a prison, jail, or penal or correctional facility, pursuant to penal processes. *(Added by Stats.1963, c. 1681, p. 3277, § 1. Amended by Stats.1996, c. 395 (S.B.1493), § 1.)*

Research References

4 Witkin Cal. Proc. 5th Pleading § 617, (S 617) Government Claims Act.

5 Witkin, California Summary 10th Torts § 224, (S 224) Liability Under Statutes and Constitution.

5 Witkin, California Summary 10th Torts § 290, (S 290) in General.

5 Witkin, California Summary 10th Torts § 293, (S 293) Who Are Prisoners.

§ 844.6. Injuries by and to prisoners

(a) Notwithstanding any other provision of this part, except as provided in this section and in Sections 814, 814.2, 845.4, and 845.6, or in Title 2.1 (commencing with Section 3500) of Part 3 of the Penal Code, a public entity is not liable for:

(1) An injury proximately caused by any prisoner.

(2) An injury to any prisoner.

(b) Nothing in this section affects the liability of a public entity under Article 1 (commencing with Section 17000) of Chapter 1 of Division 9 of the Vehicle Code.

(c) Except for an injury to a prisoner, nothing in this section prevents recovery from the public entity for an injury resulting from the dangerous condition of public property under Chapter 2 (commencing with Section 830) of this part.

(d) Nothing in this section exonerates a public employee from liability for injury proximately caused by his negligent or wrongful act or omission. The public entity may but is not required to pay any judgment, compromise or settlement, or may but is not required to indemnify any public employee, in any case where the public entity is immune from liability under this section; except that the public entity shall pay, as provided in Article 4 (commencing with Section 825) of Chapter 1 of this part, any judgment based on a claim against a public employee who is lawfully engaged in the practice of one of the healing arts under any law of this state for malpractice arising from an act or omission in the scope of his employment, and shall pay any compromise or settlement of a claim or action, based on such malpractice, to which the public entity has agreed. *(Added by Stats.1963, c. 1681, p. 3277, § 1. Amended by Stats.1970, c. 1099, p. 1957, § 5; Stats.1977, c. 1250, p. 4276, § 2.)*

Research References

5 Witkin, California Summary 10th Torts § 290, (S 290) in General.

5 Witkin, California Summary 10th Torts § 292, (S 292) Immunity Rule.

5 Witkin, California Summary 10th Torts § 293, (S 293) Who Are Prisoners.

5 Witkin, California Summary 10th Torts § 294, (S 294) Exceptions.

5 Witkin, California Summary 10th Torts § 295, (S 295) Failure to Furnish Medical Care to Prisoner.

5 Witkin, California Summary 10th Torts § 356, (S 356) Police Officers.

5 Witkin, California Summary 10th Torts § 361, Liabilities.

5 Witkin, California Summary 10th Torts § 375, (S 375) in General.

2 Witkin Cal. Summ. 10th Workers' Compensation § 26, (S 26) Pleading to Negate or Uphold Jurisdiction.

§ 845. Police protection services; failure to provide

Neither a public entity nor a public employee is liable for failure to establish a police department or otherwise to provide police protection service or, if police protection service is provided, for failure to provide sufficient police protection service.

A police department shall not fail to respond to a request for service via a burglar alarm system or an alarm company referral service solely on the basis that a permit from the city has not been obtained. *(Added by Stats.1963, c. 1681, p. 3278, § 1. Amended by Stats.1992, c. 547 (A.B.2611), § 1.)*

Law Revision Commission Comments

This section grants a general immunity for failure to provide police protection or for failure to provide enough police protection. Whether police protection should be provided at all, and the extent to which it should be provided, are political decisions which are committed to the policy-making officials of government. To permit review of these decisions by judges and juries would remove the ultimate decision-making authority from those politically responsible for making the decisions. [4 Cal.L.Rev.Comm. Reports 801 (1963)].

Research References

Miller and Starr California Real Estate § 22:59, Liability for Wrongful or Criminal Conduct of Third Persons.

21 NO. 1 Miller & Starr, California Real Estate Newsalert 19, Landowners' Liability.

5 Witkin, California Summary 10th Torts § 302, (S 302) Immunity Rule.

5 Witkin, California Summary 10th Torts § 303, (S 303) Discriminatory Allocation of Protective Services During Riot.

5 Witkin, California Summary 10th Torts § 309, (S 309) Inadequate Assistance to Stranded Motorist.

5 Witkin, California Summary 10th Torts § 356, (S 356) Police Officers.

5 Witkin, California Summary 10th Torts § 362, Immunities.

6 Witkin, California Summary 10th Torts § 930, (S 930) Occurrence or Allegation of Prior Assault.

8 Witkin, California Summary 10th Constitutional Law § 898, in General.

§ 845.2. Prison, jail or correctional facilities; failure to provide

Except as provided in Chapter 2 (commencing with Section 830), neither a public entity nor a public employee is liable for failure to provide a prison, jail or penal or correctional facility or, if such facility is provided, for failure to provide sufficient equipment, personnel or facilities therein. *(Added by Stats.1963, c. 1681, p. 3278, § 1.)*

Research References

5 Witkin, California Summary 10th Torts § 290, (S 290) in General.

5 Witkin, California Summary 10th Torts § 302, (S 302) Immunity Rule.

5 Witkin, California Summary 10th Torts § 361, Liabilities.

5 Witkin, California Summary 10th Torts § 362, Immunities.

§ 845.4. Interference with right of prisoner to judicial determination or review of legality of confinement

Neither a public entity nor a public employee acting within the scope of his employment is liable for interfering with the right of a prisoner to obtain a judicial determination or review of the legality of his confinement; but a public employee, and the public entity where the employee is acting within the scope of his employment, is liable for injury proximately caused by the employee's intentional and unjustifiable interference with such right, but no cause of action for such injury shall be deemed to accrue until it has first been determined that the confinement was illegal. *(Added by Stats.1963, c. 1681, p. 3278, § 1. Amended by Stats.1970, c. 1099, p. 1958, § 6.)*

Law Revision Commission Comments

Section 845.4 is amended to refer to the time of the accrual of the cause of action. This amendment clarifies the relationship of this section to the claims statute. As originally enacted, the statute of limitations might have expired before illegality of the imprisonment was determined—a determination that must be made before the action may be commenced. [9 Cal.L.Rev.Comm. Reports 801 (1969)].

Research References

5 Witkin, California Summary 10th Torts § 290, (S 290) in General.
5 Witkin, California Summary 10th Torts § 294, (S 294) Exceptions.
5 Witkin, California Summary 10th Torts § 306, Interference With Prisoner's Right to Judicial Review.
5 Witkin, California Summary 10th Torts § 361, Liabilities.
5 Witkin, California Summary 10th Torts § 362, Immunities.

§ 845.6. Medical care for prisoners; failure to obtain

Neither a public entity nor a public employee is liable for injury proximately caused by the failure of the employee to furnish or obtain medical care for a prisoner in his custody; but, except as otherwise provided by Sections 855.8 and 856, a public employee, and the public entity where the employee is acting within the scope of his employment, is liable if the employee knows or has reason to know that the prisoner is in need of immediate medical care and he fails to take reasonable action to summon such medical care. Nothing in this section exonerates a public employee who is lawfully engaged in the practice of one of the healing arts under any law of this state from liability for injury proximately caused by malpractice or exonerates the public entity from its obligation to pay any judgment, compromise, or settlement that it is required to pay under subdivision (d) of Section 844.6. *(Added by Stats.1963, c. 1681, p. 3278, § 1. Amended by Stats.1970, c. 1099, p. 1958, § 7.)*

Law Revision Commission Comments

This section limits the duty to provide medical care for prisoners to cases where there is actual or constructive knowledge that the prisoner is in need of immediate medical care. The standards of medical care to be provided to prisoners involve basic governmental policy that should not be subject to review in tort suits for damages. The immunity from liability for damages that is provided by this section exists even where some other statute might be construed to impose a mandatory duty to provide medical care to prisoners under other circumstances. In cases where another statute is so construed, the prisoner is left to the other remedies provided by law to compel public employees to perform their duties. [4 Cal.L.Rev. Comm. Reports 801 (1963)].

Section 845.6 is amended to expand the group of public employees who are referred to as potentially liable for medical malpractice to include all types of medical personnel, not merely those who are "licensed" under the Business and Professions Code. This conforms Section 845.6 to amended Section 844.6. The amendment also clarifies the relationship of Section 845.6 and subdivision (d) of Section 844.6. [9 Cal.L.Rev.Comm. Reports 801 (1969)].

Research References

Rutter, Cal. Practice Guide: Personal Injury Ch. 1-C, C. Formation of Attorney-Client Relationship: the Employment Agreement.
Rutter, Cal. Practice Guide: Personal Injury Ch. 3-F, F. MICRA Provisions Affecting Damages.
5 Witkin, California Summary 10th Torts § 290, (S 290) in General.
5 Witkin, California Summary 10th Torts § 293, (S 293) Who Are Prisoners.
5 Witkin, California Summary 10th Torts § 294, (S 294) Exceptions.
5 Witkin, California Summary 10th Torts § 295, (S 295) Failure to Furnish Medical Care to Prisoner.
5 Witkin, California Summary 10th Torts § 301, (S 301) Release of Suicidal Arrestee.
5 Witkin, California Summary 10th Torts § 361, Liabilities.

5 Witkin, California Summary 10th Torts § 362, Immunities.
6 Witkin, California Summary 10th Torts § 958, in General.

§ 845.8. Parole or release of prisoner; escape of prisoners; persons resisting arrest

Neither a public entity nor a public employee is liable for:

(a) Any injury resulting from determining whether to parole or release a prisoner or from determining the terms and conditions of his parole or release or from determining whether to revoke his parole or release.

(b) Any injury caused by:

(1) An escaping or escaped prisoner;

(2) An escaping or escaped arrested person; or

(3) A person resisting arrest. *(Added by Stats.1963, c. 1681, p. 3279, § 1. Amended by Stats.1970, c. 1099, p. 1958, § 8.)*

Law Revision Commission Comments

This section is a specific application of the discretionary immunity recognized in California cases and in Section 820.2. The extent of the freedom that must be accorded to prisoners for rehabilitative purposes and the nature of the precautions necessary to prevent escape of prisoners are matters that should be determined by the proper public officials unfettered by any fear that their decisions may result in liability. [4 Cal.L.Rev.Comm. Reports 801 (1963)].

Subdivision (b) of Section 845.8 has been amended to extend the immunity to include persons resisting or escaping from arrest. This probably codifies former law. See Ne Casek v. City of Los Angeles, 233 Cal.App.2d 131, 43 Cal.Rptr. 294 (1965) (city not liable to pedestrian injured by escaping arrestee). But see Johnson v. State, 69 Cal.2d 782, 447 P.2d 352, 73 Cal.Rptr. 240 (1968). [9 Cal.L.Rev.Comm. Reports 801 (1969)].

Research References

5 Witkin, California Summary 10th Torts § 296, Injury Caused by Escaped Prisoner.
5 Witkin, California Summary 10th Torts § 297, Injury Caused by Arrested Person.
5 Witkin, California Summary 10th Torts § 298, (S 298) Immunity Rule.
5 Witkin, California Summary 10th Torts § 299, (S 299) Duty to Warn Where Special Relationship Exists.
5 Witkin, California Summary 10th Torts § 331, in General.
5 Witkin, California Summary 10th Torts § 333, Operation of Vehicle.
5 Witkin, California Summary 10th Torts § 356, (S 356) Police Officers.
5 Witkin, California Summary 10th Torts § 357, (S 357) Parole Officers.
5 Witkin, California Summary 10th Torts § 362, Immunities.
6 Witkin, California Summary 10th Torts § 1048, (S 1048) Other Illustrations.

§ 846. Failure to make arrest or to retain person arrested in custody

Neither a public entity nor a public employee is liable for injury caused by the failure to make an arrest or by the failure to retain an arrested person in custody. *(Added by Stats.1963, c. 1681, p. 3279, § 1.)*

Law Revision Commission Comments

This section is a specific application of the principle stated in Section 818.2 and 821. [4 Cal.L.Rev.Comm. Reports 801 (1963)].

Research References

Rutter, Cal. Practice Guide: Civ. Pro. Before Trial Ch. 6-B, B. Complaints.
Miller and Starr California Real Estate § 22:69, Persons Entitled to the Exemption.
Miller and Starr California Real Estate § 22:72, Recreational or Hazardous Activities on Certain Public Property.
5 Witkin, California Summary 10th Torts § 304, (S 304) Duty to Protect Where Special Relationship Exists.
5 Witkin, California Summary 10th Torts § 305, Injury from Failure to Arrest or Retain in Custody.
5 Witkin, California Summary 10th Torts § 356, (S 356) Police Officers.

Government

5 Witkin, California Summary 10th Torts § 362, Immunities.

CHAPTER 4.　FIRE PROTECTION

Section
850.　Failure to provide fire protection service.
850.2.　Failure to provide or maintain sufficient personnel, equipment or facilities.
850.4.　Condition of equipment or facilities; injuries caused in fighting fires.
850.6.　Service provided outside regular area; indemnity; claims.
850.8.　Transportation of person injured by fire to physician and surgeon or hospital.

§ 850.　Failure to provide fire protection service

Neither a public entity nor a public employee is liable for failure to establish a fire department or otherwise to provide fire protection service. *(Added by Stats.1963, c. 1681, p. 3279, § 1.)*

Law Revision Commission Comments

Sections 850, 850.2 and 850.4 provide for a broad immunity from liability for injuries resulting in connection with fire protection service.

Sections 850 and 850.2 provide an absolute immunity from liability for injury resulting from failure to provide fire protection or from failure to provide enough personnel, equipment or other fire protection facilities. Whether fire protection should be provided at all, and the extent to which fire protection should be provided, are political decisions which are committed to the policy-making officials of government. To permit review of these decisions by judges and juries would remove the ultimate decision-making authority from those politically responsible for making the decisions.

Section 850.4 provides for absolute immunity from liability for injury caused in fighting fires (other than injuries resulting from operation of motor vehicles) or from failure to properly maintain fire protection equipment or facilities. There are adequate incentives to careful maintenance of fire equipment without imposing tort liability; and firemen should not be deterred from any action they may desire to take in combatting fires by a fear that liability might be imposed if a jury believes such action to be unreasonable. [4 Cal.L.Rev.Comm. Reports 801 (1963)].

Research References

4 Witkin Cal. Proc. 5th Pleading § 617, (S 617) Government Claims Act.
5 Witkin, California Summary 10th Torts § 224, (S 224) Liability Under Statutes and Constitution.
5 Witkin, California Summary 10th Torts § 310, in General.
5 Witkin, California Summary 10th Torts § 313, (S 313) Immunity Despite Wilful Misconduct.
5 Witkin, California Summary 10th Torts § 314, Fire on Public Property.
5 Witkin, California Summary 10th Torts § 363, (S 363) Fire Protection.

§ 850.2.　Failure to provide or maintain sufficient personnel, equipment or facilities

Neither a public entity that has undertaken to provide fire protection service, nor an employee of such a public entity, is liable for any injury resulting from the failure to provide or maintain sufficient personnel, equipment or other fire protection facilities. *(Added by Stats.1963, c. 1681, p. 3279, § 1.)*

Research References

5 Witkin, California Summary 10th Torts § 310, in General.
5 Witkin, California Summary 10th Torts § 314, Fire on Public Property.
5 Witkin, California Summary 10th Torts § 363, (S 363) Fire Protection.

§ 850.4.　Condition of equipment or facilities; injuries caused in fighting fires

Neither a public entity, nor a public employee acting in the scope of his employment, is liable for any injury resulting from the condition of fire protection or firefighting equipment or facilities or, except as provided in Article 1 (commencing with

Section 17000) of Chapter 1 of Division 9 of the Vehicle Code, for any injury caused in fighting fires. *(Added by Stats.1963, c. 1681, p. 3279, § 1.)*

Research References

5 Witkin, California Summary 10th Torts § 310, in General.
5 Witkin, California Summary 10th Torts § 311, (S 311) General Immunity Rule.
5 Witkin, California Summary 10th Torts § 312, (S 312) Exceptions and Distinctions.
5 Witkin, California Summary 10th Torts § 313, (S 313) Immunity Despite Wilful Misconduct.
5 Witkin, California Summary 10th Torts § 363, (S 363) Fire Protection.

§ 850.6.　Service provided outside regular area; indemnity; claims

(a) Whenever a public entity provides fire protection or firefighting service outside of the area regularly served and protected by the public entity providing that service, the public entity providing the service is liable for any injury for which liability is imposed by statute caused by its act or omission or the act or omission of its employee occurring in the performance of that fire protection or firefighting service. Notwithstanding any other law, the public entity receiving the fire protection or firefighting service is not liable for any act or omission of the public entity providing the service or for any act or omission of an employee of the public entity providing the service; but the public entity providing the service and the public entity receiving the service may by agreement determine the extent, if any, to which the public entity receiving the service will be required to indemnify the public entity providing the service.

(b) Notwithstanding any other provision of this section, any claims against the state shall be presented to the California Victim Compensation and Government Claims Board in accordance with Part 3 (commencing with Section 900) and Part 4 (commencing with Section 940) of Division 3.6 of Title 1. *(Added by Stats.1963, c. 1681, p. 3279, § 1. Amended by Stats.1965, c. 1203, p. 3024, § 1; Stats.2006, c. 538 (S.B.1852), § 217.)*

Law Revision Commission Comments

This section makes clear which public entity is liable when one entity calls for the assistance of another in fighting a fire. Unless the entities agree, each entity is financially responsible only for the torts of its own personnel. [4 Cal.L.Rev.Comm. Reports 801 (1963)].

Research References

5 Witkin, California Summary 10th Torts § 312, (S 312) Exceptions and Distinctions.

§ 850.8.　Transportation of person injured by fire to physician and surgeon or hospital

Any member of an organized fire department, fire protection district, or other firefighting unit of either the state or any political subdivision, any employee of the Department of Forestry and Fire Protection, or any other public employee when acting in the scope of his or her employment, may transport or arrange for the transportation of any person injured by a fire, or by a fire protection operation, to a physician and surgeon or hospital if the injured person does not object to the transportation.

Neither a public entity nor a public employee is liable for any injury sustained by the injured person as a result of or in connection with that transportation or for any medical, ambulance, or hospital bills incurred by or in behalf of the injured person or for any other damages, but a public employee is liable for injury proximately caused by his or her willful misconduct in transporting the injured person or arranging for the transportation. *(Added by Stats.1963, c. 1681, p. 3279, § 1. Amended by*

Stats.1981, c. 714, p. 2648, § 158; Stats.1992, c. 427 (A.B.3355), § 45.)

Law Revision Commission Comments

This section is based on [former] Section 1957 of the Government Code which provides a similar immunity to firefighting personnel for transporting persons injured by a fire or by a fire protection operation. [4 Cal.L.Rev.Comm. Reports 801 (1963)].

Research References

5 Witkin, California Summary 10th Torts § 310, in General.
5 Witkin, California Summary 10th Torts § 363, (S 363) Fire Protection.

CHAPTER 5. MEDICAL, HOSPITAL AND PUBLIC HEALTH ACTIVITIES

§ 854. "Medical facility" defined

As used in this chapter, unless the context otherwise requires, "medical facility" includes a hospital, infirmary, clinic, dispensary, mental institution, or similar facility. *(Added by Stats.1963, c. 1681, p. 3280, § 1.)*

Research References

4 Witkin Cal. Proc. 5th Pleading § 617, (S 617) Government Claims Act.
5 Witkin, California Summary 10th Torts § 224, (S 224) Liability Under Statutes and Constitution.
5 Witkin, California Summary 10th Torts § 316, Liabilities.
5 Witkin, California Summary 10th Torts § 317, Immunities.

§ 854.1. Continuity of care for clients of Agnews Developmental Center and Lanterman Developmental Center; legislative intent; definitions

(a) It is the intent of the Legislature to ensure continuity of care for clients of Agnews Developmental Center and Lanterman Developmental Center.

(b) In the effort to achieve these goals, it is the intent of the Legislature to seek and implement recommendations that in-clude all of the following services to retain Agnews and Lanterman staff as employees:

(1) Crisis management teams that provide behavioral, medical, and dental treatment, training, and technical assistance.

(2) Specialized services, including adaptive equipment design and fabrication, and medical, dental, psychological, and assessment services.

(3) Staff support in community homes to assist individuals with behavioral or psychiatric needs.

(c) As used in this chapter, the terms "mental institution" or "medical facility" also include a developmental services facility. For the purposes of this chapter "developmental services facility" means any facility or place where a public employee provides developmental services relating to the closure of Agnews Developmental Center or Lanterman Developmental Center. *(Added by Stats.2005, c. 538 (A.B.1378), § 1. Amended by Stats.2010, c. 717 (S.B.853), § 2, eff. Oct. 19, 2010.)*

§ 854.2. "Mental institution" defined

As used in this chapter, "mental institution" means a state hospital for the care and treatment of the mentally disordered or persons with intellectual disabilities, the California Rehabilitation Center referred to in Section 3300 of the Welfare and Institutions Code, or a county psychiatric hospital. *(Added by Stats.1963, c. 1681, p. 3280, § 1. Amended by Stats.1970, c. 1099, p. 1959, § 9; Stats.2012, c. 448 (A.B.2370), § 13; Stats.2012, c. 457 (S.B.1381), § 13.)*

Law Revision Commission Comments

Section 854.2 is amended to specify more precisely the institutions that are embraced within the definition. Formerly, the definition included only facilities "for the care or treatment of persons committed for mental illness or addiction." The amendment makes clear that the designated institutions are "mental institutions" even though they are used primarily for persons voluntarily admitted or involuntarily detained (but not "committed") for observation and diagnosis or for treatment. See, e.g., Welf. & Inst.Code §§ 703 (90-day court-ordered observation in state hospital of minors appearing to be mentally ill), 705 (temporary holding of minor in county psychiatric hospital pending hearing), 5206 (court-ordered evaluation for mentally disordered persons), 5304 (90-day court-ordered involuntary treatment of imminently dangerous persons), 6512 (detention of mentally retarded juvenile pending commitment hearings).

Section 7200 of the Welfare and Institutions Code lists the state hospitals for the care and treatment of the mentally disordered, and Section 7500 of the Welfare and Institutions Code lists the state hospitals for the care and treatment of the mentally retarded.

The principal purpose of the California Rehabilitation Center, established by Section 3300 of the Welfare and Institutions Code, is "the receiving, control, confinement, employment, education, treatment and rehabilitation of persons under the custody of the Department of Corrections or any agency thereof who are addicted to the use of narcotics or are in imminent danger of becoming so addicted." Welf. & Inst.Code § 3301.

"County psychiatric hospital" is defined in Section 854.3 of the Government Code. See also Goff v. County of Los Angeles, 254 Cal.App.2d 45, 61 Cal.Rptr. 840 (1967) (county psychiatric unit of county hospital as "mental institution").

Not included within the scope of this section 854.2 are certain units provided on the grounds of an institution under this jurisdiction of the Department of Corrections (see Welf. & Inst.Code § 6326) and farms, road camps, and rehabilitation centers under county jurisdiction (see Welf. & Inst.Code §§ 6404, 6406). These facilities, however, come within the ambit of Government Code Section 844, and the broad general immunity for liability for injuries to mental patients conferred by Section 854.8 is extended to cover liability to inmates of these facilities by Section 844.6. [9 Cal.L.Rev.Comm. Reports 801 (1969)].

Research References

5 Witkin, California Summary 10th Torts § 316, Liabilities.

Government

5 Witkin, California Summary 10th Torts § 317, Immunities.

§ 854.3. "County psychiatric hospital" defined

As used in this chapter, "county psychiatric hospital" means the hospital, ward, or facility provided by the county pursuant to the provisions of Section 7100 of the Welfare and Institutions Code. *(Added by Stats.1970, c. 1099, p. 1959, § 10.)*

Law Revision Commission Comments

The term "county psychiatric hospital" is defined to include the county facilities for the detention, care, and treatment of persons who are or are alleged to be mentally disordered or mentally retarded. See Welf. & Inst.Code § 7100. The definition takes the same form as in other statutes. See, e.g., Welf. & Inst.Code §§ 6003, 7101. [9 Cal.L.Rev. Comm. Reports 801 (1969)].

§ 854.4. "Mental illness or addiction" defined

As used in this chapter, "mental illness or addiction" means any condition for which a person may be detained, cared for, or treated in a mental institution, in a facility designated by a county pursuant to Chapter 2 (commencing with Section 5150) of Part 1 of Division 5 of the Welfare and Institutions Code, or in a similar facility. *(Added by Stats.1963, c. 1681, p. 3280, § 1. Amended by Stats.1970, c. 1099, p. 1959, § 11.)*

Law Revision Commission Comments

Section 854.4 is amended to eliminate the specific listing of mental or emotional conditions for which a person could, at the time the section was enacted by committed to a public medical facility and to substitute general language that includes all mental or emotional conditions, including addiction, for which a person may be voluntarily admitted or involuntarily detained in a mental institution (see Section 854.2, defining "mental institution") or in a "72-hour" evaluation facility (see Welf. & Inst.Code § 5150), or in any similar facility.

Since enactment of Section 854.4 in 1963, the Welfare and Institutions Code has been revised to make a number of changes in the categories of mental illness previously specified in this section. The amendment eliminates the inconsistency between Section 854.4 and the revised provisions of the Welfare and Institutions Code relating to mental illness and minimizes, if not eliminates, the possibility that future revisions of those provisions will create a similar inconsistency. [9 Cal.L.Rev.Comm. Reports 801 (1969)].

Research References

5 Witkin, California Summary 10th Torts § 317, Immunities.

§ 854.5. "Confine" defined

As used in this chapter, "confine" includes admit, commit, place, detain, or hold in custody. *(Added by Stats.1970, c. 1099, p. 1959, § 12.)*

Law Revision Commission Comments

Section 854.5 has been added to make clear that Sections 856 and 856.2 apply to all cases within the rationale of those sections. [9 Cal.L.Rev. Comm. Reports 801 (1969)].

§ 854.8. Liability of public entity generally

(a) Notwithstanding any other provision of this part, except as provided in this section and in Sections 814, 814.2, 855, and 855.2, a public entity is not liable for:

(1) An injury proximately caused by a patient of a mental institution.

(2) An injury to an inpatient of a mental institution.

(b) Nothing in this section affects the liability of a public [entit]y under Article 1 (commencing with Section 17000) of [Chap]ter 1 of Division 9 of the Vehicle Code.

(c) [E]xcept for an injury to an inpatient of a mental institution, [nothing] in this section prevents recovery from the public entity [for in]jury resulting from the dangerous condition of public property under Chapter 2 (commencing with Section 830) of this part.

(d) Nothing in this section exonerates a public employee from liability for injury proximately caused by his negligent or wrongful act or omission. The public entity may but is not required to pay any judgment, compromise or settlement, or may but is not required to indemnify any public employee, in any case where the public entity is immune from liability under this section; except that the public entity shall pay, as provided in Article 4 (commencing with Section 825) of Chapter 1 of this part, any judgment based on a claim against a public employee who is lawfully engaged in the practice of one of the healing arts under any law of this state for malpractice arising from an act or omission in the scope of his employment, and shall pay any compromise or settlement of a claim or action, based on such malpractice, to which the public entity has agreed. *(Added by Stats.1963, c. 1681, p. 3280, § 1. Amended by Stats.1970, c. 1099, p. 1959, § 13.)*

Law Revision Commission Comments

The changes in subdivisions (c) and (d) and in the introductory portion of subdivision (a) of Section 854.8 parallel the similar amendments to Section 844.6 and are explained in the Comment to that section. See also Moxon v. County of Kern, 233 Cal.App.2d 393, 43 Cal.Rptr. 481 (1965) (no liability for death of mental patient killed by fellow patient). Subdivision (a) is further amended to clarify the scope of the immunity. The terms "patient" and "inpatient" are used in place of "any person committed or admitted." The term "inpatient" refers only to inmates of mental institutions and not outpatients; the broader term "patient" refers to both inpatients and outpatients. [9 Cal.L.Rev.Comm. Reports 801 (1969)].

Research References

2 Witkin Cal. Proc. 5th Jurisdiction § 90, (S 90) Sovereign Immunity.
5 Witkin, California Summary 10th Torts § 298, (S 298) Immunity Rule.
5 Witkin, California Summary 10th Torts § 316, Liabilities.
5 Witkin, California Summary 10th Torts § 317, Immunities.
5 Witkin, California Summary 10th Torts § 364, Liabilities.
5 Witkin, California Summary 10th Torts § 375, (S 375) in General.
6 Witkin, California Summary 10th Torts § 983, Failure to Prevent Birth.

§ 855. Failure to provide adequate or sufficient equipment, personnel or facilities required by statute or regulation

(a) A public entity that operates or maintains any medical facility that is subject to regulation by the State Department of Health Services, Social Services, Developmental Services, or Mental Health is liable for injury proximately caused by the failure of the public entity to provide adequate or sufficient equipment, personnel or facilities required by any statute or any regulation of the State Department of Health Services, Social Services, Developmental Services, or Mental Health prescribing minimum standards for equipment, personnel or facilities, unless the public entity establishes that it exercised reasonable diligence to comply with the applicable statute or regulation.

(b) A public entity that operates or maintains any medical facility that is not subject to regulation by the State Department of Health Services, Social Services, Developmental Services, or Mental Health is liable for injury proximately caused by the failure of the public entity to provide adequate or sufficient equipment, personnel or facilities substantially equivalent to those required by any statute or any regulation of the State Department of Health Services, Social Services, Developmental Services, or Mental Health prescribing minimum standards for equipment, personnel or facilities applicable to a public medical facility of the same character and class, unless the public entity establishes that it exercised reasonable diligence to conform with such minimum standards.

(c) Nothing in this section confers authority upon, or augments the authority of, the State Department of Health Services,

Social Services, Developmental Services, or Mental Health to adopt, administer or enforce any regulation. Any regulation establishing minimum standards for equipment, personnel or facilities in any medical facility operated or maintained by a public entity, to be effective, must be within the scope of authority conferred by law. *(Added by Stats.1963, c. 1681, p. 3281, § 1. Amended by Stats.1978, c. 429, § 49.5, eff. July 17, 1978, operative July 1, 1978.)*

Law Revision Commission Comments

This section imposes liability upon a public entity operating or maintaining medical facilities where the public entity fails to comply with applicable minimum standards for equipment, personnel or facilities, unless the public entity establishes that it exercised reasonable diligence to comply. The minimum standards for equipment, personnel or facilities may be established by statute or by regulations promulgated by the State Department of Public Health or the State Department of Mental Hygiene.

Paragraph (c) makes clear that this section grants no authority to adopt or enforce regulations; such authority must be granted by some other statute. [4 Cal.L.Rev.Comm. Reports 801 (1963)].

Research References

5 Witkin, California Summary 10th Torts § 316, Liabilities.

§ 855.2. Interference with right of inmate to judicial determination or review of legality of confinement

Neither a public entity nor a public employee acting within the scope of his employment is liable for interfering with the right of an inmate of a medical facility operated or maintained by a public entity to obtain a judicial determination or review of the legality of his confinement; but a public employee, and the public entity where the employee is acting within the scope of his employment, is liable for injury proximately caused by the employee's intentional and unjustifiable interference with such right, but no cause of action for such injury shall be deemed to accrue until it has first been determined that the confinement was illegal. *(Added by Stats.1963, c. 1681, p. 3281, § 1. Amended by Stats.1970, c. 1099, p. 1960, § 14.)*

Law Revision Commission Comments

This section, like Section 845.4, makes clear that liability exists for the intentional and unjustifiable interference with a basic legal right—the right to obtain judicial review of the legality of confinement. [4 Cal.L.Rev.Comm. Reports 801 (1963)].

The amendment to Section 855.2 is similar to that made to Section 845.4. See the Comment to Section 845.4. [9 Cal.L.Rev.Comm. Reports 801 (1969)].

Research References

5 Witkin, California Summary 10th Torts § 316, Liabilities.
5 Witkin, California Summary 10th Torts § 317, Immunities.
5 Witkin, California Summary 10th Torts § 364, Liabilities.
5 Witkin, California Summary 10th Torts § 365, Immunities.

§ 855.4. Prevention of disease or controlling communication of disease; discretion

(a) Neither a public entity nor a public employee is liable for an injury resulting from the decision to perform or not to perform any act to promote the public health of the community by preventing disease or controlling the communication of disease within the community if the decision whether the act was or was not to be performed was the result of the exercise of discretion vested in the public entity or the public employee, whether or not such discretion be abused.

(b) Neither a public entity nor a public employee is liable for an injury caused by an act or omission in carrying out with due care a decision described in subdivision (a). *(Added by Stats. 1963, c. 1681, p. 3281, § 1.)*

Law Revision Commission Comments

This section declares a specific rule of discretionary immunity for acts or omissions relating to quarantines or other measures for the prevention or control of disease. [4 Cal.L.Rev.Comm. Reports 801 (1963)].

Research References

5 Witkin, California Summary 10th Torts § 317, Immunities.
5 Witkin, California Summary 10th Torts § 365, Immunities.

§ 855.6. Failure to make physical or mental examination or to make adequate examination

Except for an examination or diagnosis for the purpose of treatment, neither a public entity nor a public employee acting within the scope of his employment is liable for injury caused by the failure to make a physical or mental examination, or to make an adequate physical or mental examination, of any person for the purpose of determining whether such person has a disease or physical or mental condition that would constitute a hazard to the health or safety of himself or others. *(Added by Stats.1963, c. 1681, p. 3282, § 1.)*

Law Revision Commission Comments

This section declares an immunity that has been recognized by the New York courts in the absence of statute. It grants an immunity for failure to perform adequately public health examinations, such as public tuberculosis examinations, physical examinations to determine the qualifications of boxers and other athletes, and eye examinations for vehicle operator applicants. It does not apply to examinations for the purpose of treatment such as are made in doctors' offices and public hospitals. In those situations, the ordinary rules of liability would apply.

The immunity provided by this section relates only to failure to make any examination or, if an examination is made, to the "adequacy" of the examination; the section does not provide immunity, for example, where a public employee negligently injures a person while making an examination. [4 Cal.L.Rev.Comm. Reports 801 (1963)].

Research References

5 Witkin, California Summary 10th Torts § 316, Liabilities.
5 Witkin, California Summary 10th Torts § 317, Immunities.
5 Witkin, California Summary 10th Torts § 318, Failure to Conduct Physical or Mental Examination.
5 Witkin, California Summary 10th Torts § 358, (S 358) Public Defenders.
5 Witkin, California Summary 10th Torts § 364, Liabilities.
5 Witkin, California Summary 10th Torts § 365, Immunities.

§ 855.8. Diagnosing or failing to diagnose or prescribe for mental illness or addiction

(a) Neither a public entity nor a public employee acting within the scope of his employment is liable for injury resulting from diagnosing or failing to diagnose that a person is afflicted with mental illness or addiction or from failing to prescribe for mental illness or addiction.

(b) A public employee acting within the scope of his employment is not liable for administering with due care the treatment prescribed for mental illness or addiction.

(c) Nothing in this section exonerates a public employee who has undertaken to prescribe for mental illness or addiction from liability for injury proximately caused by his negligence or by his wrongful act in so prescribing.

(d) Nothing in this section exonerates a public employee from liability for injury proximately caused by his negligent or wrongful act or omission in administering any treatment prescribed for mental illness or addiction. *(Added by Stats.1963, c. 1681, p. 3282, § 1.)*

Research References

5 Witkin, California Summary 10th Torts § 295, (S 295) Failure Furnish Medical Care to Prisoner.
5 Witkin, California Summary 10th Torts § 301, (S 301) Release Suicidal Arrestee.

Government

5 Witkin, California Summary 10th Torts § 317, Immunities.
5 Witkin, California Summary 10th Torts § 364, Liabilities.
5 Witkin, California Summary 10th Torts § 365, Immunities.

§ 856. Confinement of persons for mental illness or addictions; determinations in accordance with applicable enactments

(a) Neither a public entity nor a public employee acting within the scope of his employment is liable for any injury resulting from determining in accordance with any applicable enactment:

(1) Whether to confine a person for mental illness or addiction.

(2) The terms and conditions of confinement for mental illness or addiction.

(3) Whether to parole, grant a leave of absence to, or release a person confined for mental illness or addiction.

(b) A public employee is not liable for carrying out with due care a determination described in subdivision (a).

(c) Nothing in this section exonerates a public employee from liability for injury proximately caused by his negligent or wrongful act or omission in carrying out or failing to carry out:

(1) A determination to confine or not to confine a person for mental illness or addiction.

(2) The terms or conditions of confinement of a person for mental illness or addiction.

(3) A determination to parole, grant a leave of absence to, or release a person confined for mental illness or addiction. *(Added by Stats.1963, c. 1681, p. 3282, § 1. Amended by Stats.1970, c. 1099, p. 1960, § 15.)*

Law Revision Commission Comments

This section declares an immunity from liability for determining whether to confine a person for "mental illness or addiction," for determining the terms and conditions of any such confinement and for determining whether to parole or release a person from confinement for such conditions. The phrase "mental illness or addiction" is used to describe certain mental or emotional conditions for which a person may be committed to a public hospital under the provisions of Welfare and Institutions Code Sections 5000 et seq. [repealed] and 5100 et seq. [repealed] (mental illness), 5075 et seq. [repealed] (mental disorder bordering on mental illness), 5250 et seq. [repealed] (mental deficiency), 5300 et seq. [repealed] (epilepsy), 5350 et seq. [repealed] (narcotic drug addiction), 5400 et seq. [repealed] (habit forming drug addiction or dipsomania or inebriety), 5500 et seq. [repealed] (sexual psychopathy), and 5600 et seq. [repealed] (such mental abnormality as to evidence utter lack of power to control sexual impulses). The determination whether to confine or release a person who may be suffering from such a condition and the determination of the terms and conditions of his confinement necessarily involve a high degree of discretion.

The section also declares an immunity from liability for carrying out with due care the discretionary determinations that are made. Liability may be imposed, however, for failure to use reasonable care in carrying out whatever determination has been made, for the act or omission causing injury in this case would be a departure from a defined standard of care. [4 Cal.L.Rev.Comm. Reports 801 (1963)].

Section 856 is amended to make reference to "leave of absence" since the Welfare and Institutions Code appears to consider such leaves equivalent to paroles. See Welf. & Inst.Code § 7351. The phrase "in a medical facility operated or maintained by a public entity", which appeared four times in the section, has been deleted because, to the extent that this phrase had any substantive effect, it resulted in an undesirable limitation on the immunity provided by Section 856. [9 Cal.L.Rev.Comm. Reports 801 (1969)].

Research References

Witkin, California Summary 10th Torts § 295, (S 295) Failure to ~~F~~urnish Medical Care to Prisoner.

~~Witk~~in, California Summary 10th Torts § 301, (S 301) Release of ~~Su~~idal Arrestee.

California Summary 10th Torts § 317, Immunities.

5 Witkin, California Summary 10th Torts § 319, Confinement or Release of Mental Patient or Addict.
5 Witkin, California Summary 10th Torts § 364, Liabilities.
5 Witkin, California Summary 10th Torts § 365, Immunities.
6 Witkin, California Summary 10th Torts § 1050, in General.

§ 856.2. Escape of persons confined

(a) Neither a public entity nor a public employee is liable for:

(1) An injury caused by an escaping or escaped person who has been confined for mental illness or addiction.

(2) An injury to, or the wrongful death of, an escaping or escaped person who has been confined for mental illness or addiction.

(b) Nothing in this section exonerates a public employee from liability:

(1) If he acted or failed to act because of actual fraud, corruption, or actual malice.

(2) For injuries inflicted as a result of his own negligent or wrongful act or omission on an escaping or escaped mental patient in recapturing him. *(Added by Stats.1963, c. 1681, p. 3283, § 1. Amended by Stats.1970, c. 1099, p. 1960, § 16.)*

Law Revision Commission Comments

The amendment of Section 856.2—by the addition of paragraph (2) to subdivision (a)—makes clear that the injury or death of an escaping or escaped mental patient is not a basis of liability. Other jurisdictions have determined that, when a mental patient escapes as a result of negligent or wrongful acts or omissions of custodial employees, injuries sustained by the escapee (as a result of his inability due to mental deficiency or illness to cope with ordinary risks encountered) may be a basis of state liability. See, e.g., Callahan v. State of New York, 179 Misc. 781, 40 N.Y.S.2d 109 (Ct.Cl.1943), aff'd, 266 App.Div. 1054, 46 N.Y.S.2d 104 (1943) (frostbite sustained by escaped mental patient); White v. United States, 317 F.2d 13 (4th Cir.1963) (escaped mental patient killed by train). The immunity provided by Section 856.2 makes certain that California will not follow these cases.

Formerly, Section 856.2 covered only persons who had been "committed" for mental illness or addiction. The substitution of "confined" for "committed" makes clear that the immunity covers all persons who are confined for mental illness or addiction, whether or not they are "committed."

Subdivision (b) has been added to limit the immunity under subdivision (a) for injuries to an escaping or escaped mental patient to cases where such immunity is appropriate. Paragraph (1) adopts language used in other provisions of the Governmental Liability Act. See, e.g., Section 995.2 (grounds for refusal to provide for defense of action against public employee). Paragraph (2) is consistent with the general rule that a public employee is liable for his negligent or wrongful act in caring for mental patients. [9 Cal.L.Rev.Comm. Reports 801 (1969)].

Research References

Rutter, Cal. Practice Guide: Civ. Pro. Before Trial Ch. 9(III)-D, D. Other Sanctions Statutes and Rules.
7 Witkin Cal. Proc. 5th Judgment § 238, (S 238) Award is Proper Where Plaintiffs Lacked Either Reasonable Cause or Good Faith.
5 Witkin, California Summary 10th Torts § 317, Immunities.
5 Witkin, California Summary 10th Torts § 319, Confinement or Release of Mental Patient or Addict.
5 Witkin, California Summary 10th Torts § 320, Escape of Mental Patient or Addict.
5 Witkin, California Summary 10th Torts § 365, Immunities.

§ 856.4. Failure to admit person to public medical facility

Except as provided in Section 815.6, neither a public entity nor a public employee acting in the scope of his employment is liable for an injury resulting from the failure to admit a person to a public medical facility. *(Added by Stats.1963, c. 1681, p. 3283, § 1.)*

Research References

5 Witkin, California Summary 10th Torts § 316, Liabilities.

5 Witkin, California Summary 10th Torts § 317, Immunities.
5 Witkin, California Summary 10th Torts § 364, Liabilities.
5 Witkin, California Summary 10th Torts § 365, Immunities.

§ 856.6. National Influenza Program of 1976; exemption of participants from liability; exception for willful misconduct; notice

(a) A public entity, public employee, or volunteer, participating in the National Influenza Program of 1976, shall not be liable for an injury caused by an act or omission in the promotion of a community program or the administration of vaccine in a community program, including the residual effects of the vaccine, unless the act or omission constitutes willful misconduct.

(b) All promotions of a community program and oral and written information provided for purposes of consent to a person requesting inoculation shall contain notice of the provisions of subdivision (a) of this section. In the event the person to be inoculated is a minor, the parents or legal guardian of said minor must be informed orally or in writing of the provisions of subdivision (a) of this section and said parents or legal guardian must consent in writing to the inoculation of said minor person. The State Department of Health shall prescribe a form to be used in community programs which notifies a person of the provisions of subdivision (a) and contains a provision by which the person acknowledges that he has been so notified and understands the legal effect of the subdivision.

(c) As used in the section:

(1) "Community program" means a public program conducted by a state, city, county, or district health agency under the National Influenza Program of 1976 or a public or private organization which has entered into a contract with a state, city, county, or district health agency, with the approval of the State Department of Health, to provide services pursuant to the National Influenza Program of 1976.

(2) "Volunteer" means a licensed health professional, licensed health facility, organization, or individual participating in a community program.

(d) Notwithstanding any other provision of law, an individual authorized by the State Department of Health may administer influenza vaccine under the supervision of a licensed health professional in a community program using a jet injection apparatus. *(Added by Stats.1976, c. 427, p. 1093, § 1, eff. July 10, 1976.)*

Research References

5 Witkin, California Summary 10th Torts § 365, Immunities.

CHAPTER 6. ADMINISTRATION OF TAX LAWS

Section
860. Tax.
860.2. Injuries caused by proceedings or application of laws.
860.4. Application of chapter.

§ 860. Tax

As used in this chapter, "tax" includes a tax, assessment, fee or charge. *(Added by Stats.1963, c. 1681, p. 3283, § 1.)*

Research References

3 Witkin Cal. Proc. 5th Actions § 988, (S 988) Validating Proceedings.
5 Witkin, California Summary 10th Torts § 289, (S 289) Tax Collection or Administration.

§ 860.2. Injuries caused by proceedings or application of laws

Neither a public entity nor a public employee is liable for an injury caused by:

(a) Instituting any judicial or administrative proceeding or action for or incidental to the assessment or collection of a tax.

(b) An act or omission in the interpretation or application of any law relating to a tax. *(Added by Stats.1963, c. 1681, p. 3283, § 1.)*

Research References

Miller and Starr California Real Estate § 30B:6, Tax Increment Financing.
5 Witkin, California Summary 10th Torts § 289, (S 289) Tax Collection or Administration.
5 Witkin, California Summary 10th Torts § 348, Nature of Immunities and Defenses.

§ 860.4. Application of chapter

Nothing in this chapter affects any law relating to refund, rebate, exemption, cancellation, amendment or adjustment of taxes. *(Added by Stats.1963, c. 1681, p. 3283, § 1.)*

CHAPTER 7. USE OF PESTICIDES

Section
862. Use of economic poison or injurious material; definitions; application of other laws.

§ 862. Use of economic poison or injurious material; definitions; application of other laws

(a) As used in this section, "pesticide" means:

(1) An "economic poison" as defined in Section 12753 of the Agricultural Code;

(2) An "injurious material" the use of which is regulated or prohibited under Chapter 3 (commencing with Section 14001) of Division 7 of the Agricultural Code; or

(3) Any material used for the same purpose as material referred to in paragraphs (1) and (2).

(b) A public entity is liable for injuries caused by its use of a pesticide to the same extent as a private person except that no presumption of negligence arises from the failure of a public entity or a public employee to comply with a provision of a statute or regulation relating to the use of a pesticide if the statute or regulation by its terms is made inapplicable to the public entity or the public employee.

(c) Sections 11761 to 11765 of the Agricultural Code, relating to reports of loss or damages from the use of pesticides, apply in an action against a public entity under this section. *(Added by Stats.1970, c. 1099, p. 1961, § 17.)*

Law Revision Commission Comments

Section 862 is added to clarify the law as to the liability of public entities for injuries resulting from the use of pesticides. The section probably codifies former law. See Recommendation Relating to Sovereign Immunity: Number 10—Revisions of the Governmental Liability Act, 9 Cal.L.Revision Comm'n Reports 801, 833–836 (1969). Enactment of the section has no effect on the rules that determine the liability of public entities for injuries arising from the use of a chemical that is not a "pesticide."

Subdivision (a). The term "pesticide" is broadly defined in subdivision (a) to include not only materials used to control, destroy, or mitigate "pests," but also materials used to eliminate or control weeds, brush, and the like. See Agri.Code §§ 12753, 14001, 14031, 14061, 14091.

Subdivision (b). Although it appears that the effect of the California statutes and regulations relating to the use of pesticides is to impose "strict" liability for injuries resulting from such use, this conclusion will remain uncertain until there has been a judicial determination of th question in California. See Recommendation Relating to Sovere' Immunity: Number 10—Revisions of the Governmental Liability Ac' Cal.L.Revision Comm'n Reports 801, 833–836 (1969). At any subdivision (b) makes clear that the standard of liability applica' private persons applies equally to the public entities. However, subdivision (b) also makes clear that the presumption of failure to exercise due care that arises upon violation of a statute, ordinance, or regulation designed to protect life or property does not apply to a public entity or public employee if the entity or employee is exempted from the particular statute or regulation. See Evidence Code § 669. For example, the requirement of Agricultural Code Section 11701 that a person obtain an agricultural pest control license if he is "to engage for hire in the business of pest control" would not be applicable to a public employee who is engaged in pest control in the course of his employment since he is not engaged "for hire in the business of pest control." See County of Contra Costa v. Cowell Portland Cement Co., 126 Cal.App. 267, 14 P.2d 606 (1932). On the other hand, statutes such as Agricultural Code Section 12972 (prevention of any substantial drift of chemicals to other crops) and Sections 14001–14011 (application of chemicals to be in accordance with regulations issued by Director of Agriculture) are applicable to public entities.

To a considerable extent, the regulations adopted by the Director of Agriculture governing the use of injurious agricultural chemicals are applicable to public entities. However, some regulations by their terms are made inapplicable to certain public entities or their employees. E.g., 3 Cal.Admin.Code §§ 2451(a)(6) (permit not required by state or state employees to engage in research on injurious herbicides), 2462(b), (d) (public agencies engaged in mosquito control under cooperative agreement with California Department of Public Health exempt from some, but not all, of the conditions prescribed by regulation governing time and conditions for use of pest control chemicals). Compare 3 Cal.Admin.Code § 3114 (departure from certain requirements, but no substantial drift, permitted when pesticide used for experimental purposes under direction and supervision of qualified federal, state, or county personnel).

Subdivision (c). Subdivision (c) makes clear that the provisions relating to a report of loss or damage apply in an action against a public entity. Failure to file the report within the time prescribed in the Agricultural Code is evidence that no loss or damage occurred. Agri.Code § 11765. The general statute that governs claims against public entities is, of course, also applicable. See Govt.Code § 911.2 (claim for "death or for injury to person or to personal property or growing crops" must be presented not later than the 100th day after the accrual of the cause of action). [9 Cal.L.Rev.Comm. Reports 801 (1969)].

Research References

5 Witkin, California Summary 10th Torts § 338, (S 338) Use of Pesticides.

CHAPTER 8. ACTIVITIES TO ABATE AN IMPENDING PERIL

Section
865. Legislative findings and declarations; legislative intent.
866. Gradual earth movement; liability of local public entity; immunity; defenses.
867. Injuries from impending peril or actions to abate peril.

§ 865. Legislative findings and declarations; legislative intent

The Legislature hereby finds and declares that:

(a) The gradual movement of land, such as in prehistoric slide areas, or as a result of subsidence due to the depletion of underground or subterranean supporting substances, such as minerals, petroleum sources, water, and similar substances, can result in danger to persons or property. Although the movement is gradual and expressed in terms of numbers of inches, feet or meters per day, week or year, at some point the forces that are exerted by the movement will sever underground utilities, such as water, sewer, gas, electricity or telephone ervices and can cause the destruction of aboveground structures ose foundations become undermined or where support is ied altogether. Unlike an earthquake or rapid rockslide or slide, these gradual earth movements permit possible inter- n to arrest the movement and avoid harm which is posed ons or property. If there is an adequate manifestation of blem before actual harm to persons or property, it is to make some determinations as to a method of

remedial action which can abate the hazard. However, any undertaking to arrest the earth movement may not be successful or may have within it the potential for hastening the movement and the damages resulting from such movement. Regardless of how slight that potential for aggravating the damages, local public entities are unwilling to undertake action to alleviate the hazard if such undertaking may invite potential liability.

(b) It is the intent of the Legislature in enacting this chapter to create an incentive for local public entities, upon learning of the particular earth movement which will result in possible damage to substantial areas of property and constitute a threat of injury to persons, to undertake remedial action to abate the earth movement or protect against the danger therefrom without fear of incurring liability as a result of undertaking such action. *(Added by Stats.1979, c. 1119, § 1, eff. Sept. 28, 1979.)*

Research References

5 Witkin, California Summary 10th Torts § 285, Protective Measures Against Earth Movement.

§ 866. Gradual earth movement; liability of local public entity; immunity; defenses

(a) Subject to the provisions of subdivisions (b) and (c), in the event of public necessity and to avoid impending peril to persons or property as a result of gradual earth movement, a local public entity is not liable for damages for injury to persons or property resulting from such impending peril or from any action taken to abate such peril providing the legislative body of the local public entity has, on the basis of expert opinion or other reasonable basis, done all of the following:

(1) On the basis of adequate evidence such as expert opinion or otherwise, found the existence of such impending peril.

(2) Determined appropriate remedial action to halt, stabilize, or abate such impending peril.

(3) Undertaken to implement such remedial action.

As used in this chapter, "gradual earth movements" includes, but is not limited to, perceptible changes in the earth either in a subterranean area or at the surface, or both, which if not arrested or contained will over a gradual period of time result in damage to or destruction of underground or aboveground property or harm to persons. However, "gradual earth movement" does not include movement which is caused by activity undertaken by a local public entity for purposes other than the abatement of peril caused by gradual earth movement.

As used in this chapter, "local public entity" has the meaning set forth in Section 900.4.

(b) If the local public entity is unable to complete the steps described in paragraphs (1) to (3), inclusive, of subdivision (a) because of the cessation of the hazard or because such actions cannot be completed before the occurrence of the hazard sought to be avoided, or because such legislative body of such entity shall reasonably determine that such remedial action will not abate such danger, the immunity provided herein shall nevertheless apply to such actions by such local public entity.

(c) The immunity provided herein is in addition to any other immunity of the local public entity provided by law or statute, including this part, and any claim of liability based upon the impending peril or any action of the local public entity is subject to such immunities and any defenses that would be available to the local public entity if it were a private person. *(Added by Stats.1979, c. 1119, § 1, eff. Sept. 28, 1979.)*

Research References

Miller and Starr California Real Estate § 30:2, Types of Activity and General Rules Applicable to Inverse Condemnation.

5 Witkin, California Summary 10th Torts § 285, Protective Measures Against Earth Movement.

§ 867.   Injuries from impending peril or actions to abate peril

An employee of a local public entity is not liable for damages for injury to persons or property resulting from an impending peril or from any action taken to abate such peril pursuant to Section 866. *(Added by Stats.1979, c. 1119, § 1, eff. Sept. 28, 1979.)*

Research References

5 Witkin, California Summary 10th Torts § 285, Protective Measures Against Earth Movement.

5 Witkin, California Summary 10th Torts § 348, Nature of Immunities and Defenses.

5 Witkin, California Summary 10th Torts § 360, Immunities.

CHAPTER 21.   TORT LIABILITY UNDER AGREEMENTS BETWEEN PUBLIC ENTITIES

Section
895.   Agreement.
895.2.   Joint and several liability; limitations.
895.4.   Contribution or indemnification provisions.
895.6.   Right of contribution in absence of agreement.
895.8.   Application of chapter.

§ 895.   Agreement

As used in this chapter "agreement" means a joint powers agreement entered into pursuant to Chapter 5 (commencing with Section 6500) of Division 7 of Title 1 of the Government Code, an agreement to transfer the functions of a public entity or an employee thereof to another public entity pursuant to Part 2 (commencing with Section 51300) of Division 1 of Title 5 of the Government Code, and any other agreement under which a public entity undertakes to perform any function, service or act with or for any other public entity or employee thereof with its consent, whether such agreement is expressed by resolution, contract, ordinance or in any other manner provided by law; but "agreement" does not include an agreement between public entities which is designed to implement the disbursement or subvention of public funds from one of the public entities to the other, whether or not it provides standards or controls governing the expenditure of such funds. *(Added by Stats.1963, c. 1681, p. 3283, § 1.)*

Law Revision Commission Comments

"Agreement" is used here to refer to any consensual arrangement between public entities under which some service, function or act is to be performed with or for any or all of the participating public entities. The broad definition is used so that the liability standards of this chapter will be applicable to all such arrangements regardless of whether the agreement is entered into under the authority of Government Code Section 6502 or under the authority of any other law. [4 Cal.L.Rev. Comm. Reports 801 (1963)].

Research References

5 Witkin, California Summary 10th Torts § 232, Liability Under Joint Powers Agreements.

§ 895.2.   Joint and several liability; limitations

Whenever any public entities enter into an agreement, they are jointly and severally liable upon any liability which is imposed by any law other than this chapter upon any one of the entities or upon any entity created by the agreement for injury caused by a negligent or wrongful act or omission occurring in the performance of such agreement.

Notwithstanding any other law, if a judgment is recovered against a public entity for injury caused in the performance of an agreement, the time within which a claim for such injury may be presented or an action commenced against any other public entity that is subject to the liability determined by the judgment under the provisions of this section begins to run when the judgment is rendered. *(Added by Stats.1963, c. 1681, p. 3283, § 1.)*

Law Revision Commission Comments

This section makes each of the public entities that are parties to an agreement jointly and severally liable to the injured party for any torts that may occur in the performance of the agreement for which any one of the entities, or an entity created by the agreement, is otherwise made liable by law.

The time for presenting claims or filing actions against other entities is extended by the second paragraph so that the rights granted by this section will not become unenforceable during the time the first judgment is being obtained. [4 Cal.L.Rev.Comm. Reports 801 (1963)].

Research References

5 Witkin, California Summary 10th Torts § 232, Liability Under Joint Powers Agreements.

§ 895.4.   Contribution or indemnification provisions

As part of any agreement, the public entities may provide for contribution or indemnification by any or all of the public entities that are parties to the agreement upon any liability arising out of the performance of the agreement. *(Added by Stats.1963, c. 1681, p. 3283, § 1.)*

Law Revision Commission Comments

This section permits public entities that are parties to an agreement to allocate the ultimate financial responsibility among themselves in whatever manner seems most desirable to them. The section does not affect the right of the injured person to recover the full amount of his damages from any one of the public entities under Section 895.2. [4 Cal.L.Rev.Comm. Reports 801 (1963)].

Research References

5 Witkin, California Summary 10th Torts § 232, Liability Under Joint Powers Agreements.

§ 895.6.   Right of contribution in absence of agreement

Unless the public entities that are parties to an agreement otherwise provide in the agreement, if a public entity is held liable upon any judgment for damages caused by a negligent or wrongful act or omission occurring in the performance of the agreement and pays in excess of its pro rata share in satisfaction of such judgment, such public entity is entitled to contribution from each of the other public entities that are parties to the agreement. The pro rata share of each public entity is determined by dividing the total amount of the judgment by the number of public entities that are parties to the agreement. The right of contribution is limited to the amount paid in satisfaction of the judgment in excess of the pro rata share of the public entity so paying. No public entity may be compelled to make contribution beyond its own pro rata share of the entire judgment. *(Added by Stats.1963, c. 1681, p. 3284, § 1.)*

Law Revision Commission Comments

Where an agreement between public entities fails to specify how the responsibility for tort liability is to be allocated, this section requires each entity to contribute a pro rata share of the amount of any judgment based on a tort that occurs in the performance of the agreement. Where it would not be appropriate to determine contributions according to the formula set out in this section, the public entities may by agreement provide another method of allocating responsibility for tort liability. Section 895.4. [4 Cal.L.Rev.Comm. Reports 801 (1963)].

Research References

5 Witkin, California Summary 10th Torts § 232, Liability Under Joint Powers Agreements.

§ 895.8. Application of chapter

Except for Section 895.6, this chapter applies to any agreement between public entities, whether entered into before or after the effective date of this chapter. Section 895.6 applies to any agreement between public entities entered into, or renewed, modified, or extended, after the effective date of this chapter. *(Added by Stats.1963, c. 1681, p. 3266, § 1.)*

Part 3

CLAIMS AGAINST PUBLIC ENTITIES

CHAPTER 1. GENERAL

ARTICLE 1. DEFINITIONS

Section
900.   Definitions governing construction of part.
900.2.   Board.
900.3.   Judicial branch entity.
900.4.   Local public entity.
900.6.   State.
901.   Date of accrual of cause of action.

§ 900. Definitions governing construction of part

Unless the provision or context otherwise requires, the definitions contained in this article govern the construction of this part. *(Added by Stats.1963, c. 1715, p. 3372, § 1.)*

Research References

Rutter, Cal. Practice Guide: Civ. Pro. Before Trial Ch. 1-C, C. Prelawsuit Notices, Claims and Demands.
Rutter, Cal. Practice Guide: Personal Injury Ch. 5-B, B. When to Sue-Statute of Limitations.
Miller and Starr California Real Estate § 27:49, Provisions for Arbitration and Mediation of Disputes--Public Works.
Miller and Starr California Real Estate § 30A:19, Resolution of Necessity.
3 Witkin Cal. Proc. 5th Actions § 233, (S 233) Revised Law.
3 Witkin Cal. Proc. 5th Actions § 235, in General.
3 Witkin Cal. Proc. 5th Actions § 284, Illustrations: Defects Waived.
7 Witkin Cal. Proc. 5th Judgment § 285, (S 285) Public Entity.
5 Witkin, California Summary 10th Torts § 217, (S 217) Statutory Framework.
5 Witkin, California Summary 10th Torts § 218, (S 218) Exclusions and Limitations.

§ 900.2. Board

"Board" means:

(a) In the case of a local public entity, the governing body of the local public entity.

(b) In the case of the state, except as provided by subdivisions (c) and (d), the Victim Compensation and Government Claims Board.

(c) In the case of a judicial branch entity or judge of one of those entities, the Judicial Council.

In the case of the California State University, the Trustees California State University. *(Added by Stats.1963, c. 1715, § 1. Amended by Stats.2002, c. 1007 (A.B.2321), § 1; ...0, c. 636 (S.B.1046), § 2.)*

Law Revision Commission Comments

"Board" has been defined to facilitate the drafting of provisions that apply both to the State and to local public entities. [4 Cal.L.Rev.Comm. Reports 1001 (1963)].

Research References

Rutter, Cal. Practice Guide: Personal Injury Ch. 5-A, A. Prelawsuit Filings.
3 Witkin Cal. Proc. 5th Actions § 233, (S 233) Revised Law.
3 Witkin Cal. Proc. 5th Actions § 273, (S 273) Judicial Branch Entity.
3 Witkin Cal. Proc. 5th Actions § 273A, (S 273A) (New)-California State University.

§ 900.3. Judicial branch entity

A "judicial branch entity" is a public entity and means any superior court, court of appeals, the Supreme Court, the Judicial Council, or the Administrative Office of the Courts. *(Added by Stats.2002, c. 1007 (A.B.2321), § 2.)*

Research References

Rutter, Cal. Practice Guide: Enforcing Judgments/Debts Ch. 6A-6, Payment of Final Judgments Against Public Entities.
Rutter, Cal. Practice Guide: Personal Injury Ch. 5-A, A. Prelawsuit Filings.
3 Witkin Cal. Proc. 5th Actions § 233, (S 233) Revised Law.
3 Witkin Cal. Proc. 5th Actions § 267, (S 267) Judicial Branch Entity.
8 Witkin Cal. Proc. 5th Enforcement of Judgment § 429, (S 429) Against State.

§ 900.4. Local public entity

"Local public entity" includes a county, city, district, public authority, public agency, and any other political subdivision or public corporation in the State, but does not include the State. *(Added by Stats.1963, c. 1715, p. 3372, § 1.)*

Law Revision Commission Comments

The definitions of "State" and "local public entity" are based on the definition of "local public entity" contained in Government Code [former] Section 700. [4 Cal.L.Rev.Comm. Reports 1001 (1963)].

Research References

3 Witkin Cal. Proc. 5th Actions § 233, (S 233) Revised Law.

§ 900.6. State

"State" means the State and any office, officer, department, division, bureau, board, commission or agency of the State claims against which are paid by warrants drawn by the Controller. *(Added by Stats.1963, c. 1715, p. 3372, § 1.)*

Law Revision Commission Comments

The definitions of "State" and "local public entity" are based on the definition of "local public entity" contained in Government Code [former] Section 700. [4 Cal.L.Rev.Comm. Reports 1001 (1963)].

Research References

3 Witkin Cal. Proc. 5th Actions § 233, (S 233) Revised Law.

§ 901. Date of accrual of cause of action

For the purpose of computing the time limits prescribed by Sections 911.2, 911.4, 945.6, and 946.6, the date of the accrual of a cause of action to which a claim relates is the date upon which the cause of action would be deemed to have accrued within the meaning of the statute of limitations which would be applicable thereto if there were no requirement that a claim be presented to and be acted upon by the public entity before an action could be commenced thereon. However, the date upon which a cause of action for equitable indemnity or partial equitable indemnity accrues shall be the date upon which a defendant is served with the complaint giving rise to the defendant's claim for equitable indemnity or partial equitable indemnity against the public entity. *(Added by Stats.1963, c. 1715, p. 3372, § 1. Amended by Stats.1968, c. 134, p. 349, § 1; Stats.1981, c. 856, p. 3286, § 1; Stats.2011, c. 296 (A.B.1023), § 110.)*

Law Revision Commission Comments

This section is based on the second paragraph of Government Code [former] Section 715, which applies to claims against local public entities. There is no existing comparable statutory provision that applies to claims against the State. [4 Cal.L.Rev.Comm. Reports 1001 (1963)].

Research References

Rutter, Cal. Practice Guide: Civ. Pro. Before Trial Ch. 1-C, C. Prelawsuit Notices, Claims and Demands.

Rutter, Cal. Practice Guide: Personal Injury Ch. 5-A, A. Prelawsuit Filings.

Rutter, Cal. Practice Guide: Personal Injury Ch. 5-B, B. When to Sue-Statute of Limitations.

3 Witkin Cal. Proc. 5th Actions § 256, Statute of Limitations Rule Governs.

3 Witkin Cal. Proc. 5th Actions § 260, (S 260) Former Rule of Postponed Accrual.

3 Witkin Cal. Proc. 5th Actions § 261, (S 261) Legislative Repudiation of Rule.

3 Witkin Cal. Proc. 5th Actions § 268, (S 268) Notice of Rejection of Late Claim.

3 Witkin Cal. Proc. 5th Actions § 691, (S 691) Two-Year Period.

ARTICLE 2. GENERAL PROVISIONS

Section

905. Claims for money or damages against local public entities; exceptions.

905.1. Inverse condemnation; claim unnecessary to maintain action; procedure if claim filed.

905.2. Claims for money or damages against state filed with California Victim Compensation and Government Claims Board; filing fee; reimbursement; surcharge to state entity; application.

905.3. Claims against state for additional reimbursement.

905.4. Chapters 1 and 2 not exclusive means for presenting claims.

905.5. School districts' civil liability for asbestos exposures.

905.6. Claims against Regents of the University of California.

905.7. Claims against judicial branch entity.

905.8. Necessity of existence of liability.

905.9. Claims against California State University; presentment.

906. Amount allowed on the claim by California Victim Compensation and Government Claims Board; interest.

907. Offset of delinquent amounts due for services rendered to other public entities; notice; disputes.

§ 905. Claims for money or damages against local public entities; exceptions

There shall be presented in accordance with Chapter 1 (commencing with Section 900) and Chapter 2 (commencing with Section 910) all claims for money or damages against local public entities except any of the following:

(a) Claims under the Revenue and Taxation Code or other statute prescribing procedures for the refund, rebate, exemption, cancellation, amendment, modification, or adjustment of any tax, assessment, fee, or charge or any portion thereof, or of any penalties, costs, or charges related thereto.

(b) Claims in connection with which the filing of a notice of lien, statement of claim, or stop notice is required under any law relating to liens of mechanics, laborers, or materialmen.

(c) Claims by public employees for fees, salaries, wages, mileage, or other expenses and allowances.

(d) Claims for which the workers' compensation authorized by Division 4 (commencing with Section 3200) of the Labor Code is the exclusive remedy.

(e) Applications or claims for any form of public assistance under the Welfare and Institutions Code or other provisions of law relating to public assistance programs, and claims for goods, services, provisions, or other assistance rendered for or on behalf of any recipient of any form of public assistance.

(f) Applications or claims for money or benefits under any public retirement or pension system.

(g) Claims for principal or interest upon any bonds, notes, warrants, or other evidences of indebtedness.

(h) Claims that relate to a special assessment constituting a specific lien against the property assessed and that are payable from the proceeds of the assessment, by offset of a claim for damages against it or by delivery of any warrant or bonds representing it.

(i) Claims by the state or by a state department or agency or by another local public entity or by a judicial branch entity.

(j) Claims arising under any provision of the Unemployment Insurance Code, including, but not limited to, claims for money or benefits, or for refunds or credits of employer or worker contributions, penalties, or interest, or for refunds to workers of deductions from wages in excess of the amount prescribed.

(k) Claims for the recovery of penalties or forfeitures made pursuant to Article 1 (commencing with Section 1720) of Chapter 1 of Part 7 of Division 2 of the Labor Code.

(*l*) Claims governed by the Pedestrian Mall Law of 1960 (Part 1 (commencing with Section 11000) of Division 13 of the Streets and Highways Code).

(m) Claims made pursuant to Section 340.1 of the Code of Civil Procedure for the recovery of damages suffered as a result of childhood sexual abuse. This subdivision shall apply only to claims arising out of conduct occurring on or after January 1, 2009.

(n) Claims made pursuant to Section 701.820 of the Code of Civil Procedure for the recovery of money pursuant to Section 26680.

(*o*) Claims made pursuant to Section 49013 of the Education Code for reimbursement of pupil fees for participation in educational activities. *(Added by Stats.1963, c. 1715, p. 3372, § 1. Amended by Stats.2005, c. 706 (A.B.1742), § 17; Stats.2007, c. 130 (A.B.299), § 105; Stats.2008, c. 383 (S.B.640), § 1; Stats.2010, c. 4 (A.B.680), § 4; Stats.2012, c. 776 (A.B.1575), § 2.)*

Law Revision Commission Comments

This section is the same in substance as Government Code [former] Section 703. See new Section 935 for procedure for claims excepted from Chapters 1 and 2. [4 Cal.L.Rev.Comm. Reports 1001 (1963)].

Research References

Rutter, Cal. Practice Guide: Civ. Pro. Before Trial Ch. 1-C, C. Prelawsuit Notices, Claims and Demands.

Rutter, Cal. Practice Guide: Enforcing Judgments/Debts Ch. 6D-2, Writ of Execution.

Rutter, Cal. Practice Guide: Personal Injury Ch. 5-A, A. Prelawsuit Filings.

Rutter, Cal. Practice Guide: Prof. Responsibility Ch. 8-D, D. Restrictions on Speech and Behavior Outside Courtroom.

Miller and Starr California Real Estate § 27:49, Provisions for Arbitration and Mediation of Disputes--Public Works.

18 NO. 4 Miller & Starr, California Real Estate Newsalert 28, Construction Contracts.

19 NO. 2 Miller & Starr, California Real Estate Newsalert 7, Construction Contracts.

calculated and included in claims paid after June 30, 2004, or the effective date of the statute adding this subdivision [2].

(h) This section shall not apply to claims made for a violation of the California Whistleblower Protection Act (Article 3 (commencing with Section 8547) of Chapter 6.5 of Division 1 of Title 2). *(Added by Stats.1963, c. 1715, p. 3372, § 1. Amended by Stats.1976, c. 96, p. 155, § 2; Stats.2004, c. 227 (S.B.1102), § 19, eff. Aug. 16, 2004; Stats.2005, c. 184 (A.B.346), § 1, eff. Sept. 6, 2005, operative July 11, 2005; Stats.2013, c. 781 (S.B.496), § 1.)*

[1] Acts of Congress, alternate or descriptive name of acts, enacting credit, and sections, if any, classified to U.S.C.A., see Popular Name Table for Acts of Congress.

[2] Stats.2004, c. 227 (S.B.1102), § 19, eff. Aug. 16, 2004.

Law Revision Commission Comments

This section—which restates the substance of portions of Government Code [former] Sections 620, 621 and 641—is patterned after Section 630 (Title 2 of the Cal.Admin.Code) of the Rules of the State Board of Control. [4 Cal.L.Rev.Comm. Report 1001 (1963)].

Research References

Rutter, Cal. Practice Guide: Civ. Pro. Before Trial Ch. 1-C, C. Prelawsuit Notices, Claims and Demands.
Rutter, Cal. Practice Guide: Personal Injury Ch. 5-A, A. Prelawsuit Filings.
Miller and Starr California Real Estate § 27:49, Provisions for Arbitration and Mediation of Disputes--Public Works.
3 Witkin Cal. Proc. 5th Actions § 231, (S 231) Nature and Purpose of Requirement.
3 Witkin Cal. Proc. 5th Actions § 235, in General.
3 Witkin Cal. Proc. 5th Actions § 238, (S 238) Other Money Claims.
3 Witkin Cal. Proc. 5th Actions § 253, (S 253) Statutory Requirements.
3 Witkin Cal. Proc. 5th Actions § 418, Trial Court Costs.

§ 905.3. Claims against state for additional reimbursement

Notwithstanding any other provision of law to the contrary, no claim shall be submitted by a local agency or school district, nor shall a claim be considered by the California Victim Compensation and Government Claims Board pursuant to Section 905.2, if that claim is eligible for consideration by the Commission on State Mandates pursuant to Article 1 (commencing with Section 17550) of Chapter 4 of Part 7 of Division 4 of Title 2. *(Added by Stats.1977, c. 1135, p. 3646, § 3.5. Amended by Stats.1994, c. 726 (A.B.3069), § 2, eff. Sept. 22, 1994; Stats.2006, c. 538 (S.B.1852), § 218.)*

§ 905.4. Chapters 1 and 2 not exclusive means for presenting claims

Chapter 1 (commencing with Section 900) and Chapter 2 (commencing with Section 910) of this part shall not be construed to be an exclusive means for presenting claims to the Legislature nor as preventing the Legislature from making such appropriations as it deems proper for the payment of claims against the State which have not been submitted to the board or recommended for payment by it pursuant to Chapters 1 and 2 of this part. *(Added by Stats.1963, c. 1715, p. 3372, § 1.)*

Law Revision Commission Comments

This section is the same in substance as Government Code [former] Section 625. [4 Cal.L.Rev.Comm. Reports 1001 (1963)].

Research References

3 Witkin Cal. Proc. 5th Actions § 235, in General.

§ 905.5. School districts' civil liability for asbestos exposures

A school district, its officers, directors, or employees shall have no civil liability in any civil action for injury, disease, death, or economic loss arising out of exposure on or after January 1, 1989, to asbestos contained in buildings owned, leased, or otherwise used by a school district, except upon proof that the injury, disease, death, or economic loss was caused by the negligence of the school district, its officers, directors, or employees. Notwithstanding the provisions of Section 815.6 of the Government Code and Section 669 of the Evidence Code, no presumption of negligence shall apply to any action under this section. This section applies only to actions against school districts, and shall not apply to any other action, including, but not limited to, actions against a manufacturer, contractor, or any person who makes, sells, distributes, furnishes, or installs asbestos-containing materials. This section shall not affect, alter, or otherwise modify the law pertaining to workers' compensation claims. This section shall not affect the right of a school district, its officers, directors, or employees to seek indemnification. *(Added by Stats.1988, c. 1022, § 1.)*

Research References

5 Witkin, California Summary 10th Torts § 330, Exposure to Asbestos.

§ 905.6. Claims against Regents of the University of California

This part does not apply to claims against the Regents of the University of California. *(Added by Stats.1963, c. 1715, p. 3372, § 1.)*

Law Revision Commission Comments

This section codifies existing law as declared by two trial court decisions which, the Commission is advised, held that neither the State nor the local public entity claims presentation procedures apply to claims against the University of California. [4 Cal.L.Rev.Comm. Reports 1001 (1963)].

Research References

Rutter, Cal. Practice Guide: Personal Injury Ch. 5-A, A. Prelawsuit Filings.
3 Witkin Cal. Proc. 5th Actions § 235, in General.

§ 905.7. Claims against judicial branch entity

All claims against a judicial branch entity for money or damages based upon an express contract or for an injury for which the judicial branch entity is liable shall be presented in accordance with Chapter 1 (commencing with Section 900) and Chapter 2 (commencing with Section 910) of this part. *(Added by Stats.2005, c. 706 (A.B.1742), § 18.)*

Research References

Rutter, Cal. Practice Guide: Personal Injury Ch. 5-A, A. Prelawsuit Filings.
3 Witkin Cal. Proc. 5th Actions § 235, in General.
3 Witkin Cal. Proc. 5th Actions § 238, (S 238) Other Money Claims.

§ 905.8. Necessity of existence of liability

Nothing in this part imposes liability upon a public entity unless such liability otherwise exists. *(Added by Stats.1963, c. 1715, p. 3372, § 1.)*

Law Revision Commission Comments

This section is new. It makes clear that the claims presentation provisions do not impose substantive liability; some other statute must be found that imposes liability. [4 Cal.L.Rev.Comm. Reports 1001 (1963)].

Research References

3 Witkin Cal. Proc. 5th Actions § 233, (S 233) Revised Law.

§ 905.9. Claims against California State University; presentment

All claims against the California State University for money or damages based upon an express contract or for an injury for which the Trustees of the California State University is liable shall be presented in accordance with Chapter 1 (commencing with Section 900) and Chapter 2 (commencing with Section 910) of this part. *(Added by Stats.2010, c. 636 (S.B.1046), § 3.)*

Research References

3 Witkin Cal. Proc. 5th Actions § 235, in General.
3 Witkin Cal. Proc. 5th Actions § 238, (S 238) Other Money Claims.

§ 906. Amount allowed on the claim by California Victim Compensation and Government Claims Board; interest

(a) As used in this section, "amount allowed on the claim" means the amount allowed by the California Victim Compensation and Government Claims Board on a claim allowed, in whole or in part, or the amount offered by the board to settle or compromise a claim.

(b) Except as otherwise provided in this subdivision, no interest is payable on the amount allowed on the claim if payment of the claim is subject to approval of an appropriation by the Legislature. If an appropriation is made for the payment of a claim described in this subdivision, interest on the amount appropriated for the payment of the claim commences to accrue 180 days after the effective date of the act by which the appropriation is enacted. *(Added by Stats.1980, c. 215, § 4. Amended by Stats.2012, c. 19 (S.B.1504), § 1, eff. June 15, 2012.)*

Research References

8 Witkin Cal. Proc. 5th Enforcement of Judgment § 61, (S 61) Governmental Property.

§ 907. Offset of delinquent amounts due for services rendered to other public entities; notice; disputes

A local public entity, as defined in Section 900.4, may offset any delinquent amount due it for services rendered to any other local public entity. The offset may be charged, against any amount reciprocally owing, upon the giving of 30 days advance written notice, if no written dispute is received from the debtor within the 30-day notice period. Notices from the creditor or the debtor shall be made through certified mail.

If the offset would result in the debtor's inability to meet encumbered bonded indebtedness repayments, the debtor shall so state in a written dispute within the time period stated above.

If a dispute notice is received and the dispute is subsequently resolved in favor of the entity to whom an amount is due, interest on the principal amount from the date that amount was originally owing shall be assessed at the legal rate per annum established pursuant to Section 685.010 of the Code of Civil Procedure.

For purposes of this section, an amount reciprocally owing includes any tax revenue collected by a local public entity for disbursement to another local public entity. *(Added by Stats. 1990, c. 697 (A.B.3463), § 1.)*

CHAPTER 2. PRESENTATION AND CONSIDERATION OF CLAIMS

ARTICLE 1. GENERAL

Section
910.　　Contents of claim.
910.2.　Signature.
910.4.　Forms.
910.6.　Amendment of claim; failure or refusal to amend.
910.8.　Notice of insufficiency of claim.
911.　　Failure to give notice of insufficiency; waiver of defenses based on defect or omission.
911.2.　Time of presentation of claims; limitation.
911.3.　Claim presented without application; notice of return without action; form.

Section
911.4.　Application to present late claim; one year limitation; computation of limitation period; tolling.
911.6.　Grant or denial of application by board.
911.8.　Notice of board's action.
912.2.　Claim deemed presented to board upon day leave to present claim granted.
912.4.　Time for action by board; extension of time by agreement; failure or refusal to act within time prescribed.
912.5.　Procedure; adoption of rules; claims mistakenly presented.
912.6.　Action by board on claim against local public entity.
912.7.　Action on claim against judicial branch entity or judge by Judicial Council.
912.8.　Action by board on claims against state; procedure; report to Legislature; recommendations.
913.　　Notice of rejection of claim.
913.2.　Re-examination of rejected claim.

§ 910. Contents of claim

A claim shall be presented by the claimant or by a person acting on his or her behalf and shall show all of the following:

(a) The name and post office address of the claimant.

(b) The post office address to which the person presenting the claim desires notices to be sent.

(c) The date, place and other circumstances of the occurrence or transaction which gave rise to the claim asserted.

(d) A general description of the indebtedness, obligation, injury, damage or loss incurred so far as it may be known at the time of presentation of the claim.

(e) The name or names of the public employee or employees causing the injury, damage, or loss, if known.

(f) The amount claimed if it totals less than ten thousand dollars ($10,000) as of the date of presentation of the claim, including the estimated amount of any prospective injury, damage, or loss, insofar as it may be known at the time of the presentation of the claim, together with the basis of computation of the amount claimed. If the amount claimed exceeds ten thousand dollars ($10,000), no dollar amount shall be included in the claim. However, it shall indicate whether the claim would be a limited civil case. *(Added by Stats.1963, c. 1715, p. 3374, § 1. Amended by Stats.1965, c. 653, p. 2010, § 1; Stats.1987, c. 1201, § 17; Stats.1987, c. 1208, § 2; Stats.1998, c. 931 (S.B.2139), § 174, eff. Sept. 28, 1998.)*

Law Revision Commission Comments

This section will substitute a more specific statement of the contents of a claim for the very general statement found in Government Code [former] Section 621, which applies to the State and requires that "any person having a claim against the State . . . shall present it to the board . . . , accompanied by a statement showing the facts constituting the claim." [4 Cal.L.Rev.Comm. Reports 1001 (1963)].

This amendment to Section 910 merely makes a technical correction in punctuation to clarify the relationship of subdivision (f) to the remaining subdivisions in this section. [7 Cal.L.Rev.Comm. Reports 401 (1965)].

Section 910 is amended to accommodate unification of the municipal and superior courts in a county. Cal. Const. art. VI, § 5(e). See also Code Civ. Proc. § 85 (limited civil cases) & Comment. [28 Cal.L.Rev.Comm. Reports App. 7 (1998)].

Research References

Rutter, Cal. Practice Guide: Civ. Pro. Before Trial Ch. 1-C, C. Prelawsuit Notices, Claims and Demands.
Rutter, Cal. Practice Guide: Civ. Pro. Before Trial Ch. 14-C, C. Procedural Issues.
Rutter, Cal. Practice Guide: Civ. Pro. Before Trial Gen. Matls., Highlights.

Rutter, Cal. Practice Guide: Personal Injury Ch. 5-A, A. Prelawsuit Filings.
Rutter, Cal. Practice Guide: Personal Injury Ch. 5-B, B. When to Sue-Statute of Limitations.
Miller and Starr California Real Estate § 27:49, Provisions for Arbitration and Mediation of Disputes--Public Works.
19 NO. 2 Miller & Starr, California Real Estate Newsalert 7, Construction Contracts.
3 Witkin Cal. Proc. 5th Actions § 235, in General.
3 Witkin Cal. Proc. 5th Actions § 239, (S 239) Claims in Class Actions.
3 Witkin Cal. Proc. 5th Actions § 243, (S 243) Mechanics' Liens.
3 Witkin Cal. Proc. 5th Actions § 253, (S 253) Statutory Requirements.
3 Witkin Cal. Proc. 5th Actions § 254, (S 254) Illustrations.
3 Witkin Cal. Proc. 5th Actions § 262, Manner of Presentation.
3 Witkin Cal. Proc. 5th Actions § 284, Illustrations: Defects Waived.
3 Witkin Cal. Proc. 5th Actions § 304, Filing and Service of Petition.
3 Witkin Cal. Proc. 5th Actions § 308, (S 308) Effect of New Facts Not in Original Claim.
4 Witkin Cal. Proc. 5th Pleading § 620, Conformance of Complaint to Claim.
9 Witkin, California Summary 10th Taxation § 292, in General.
9 Witkin, California Summary 10th Taxation § 297, (S 297) Constitutional Restriction.
9 Witkin, California Summary 10th Taxation § 322, Utility Users' Taxes.
6 Witkin, California Summary 10th Torts § 953, in General.

§ 910.2. Signature

The claim shall be signed by the claimant or by some person on his behalf. Claims against local public entities for supplies, materials, equipment or services need not be signed by the claimant or on his behalf if presented on a billhead or invoice regularly used in the conduct of the business of the claimant. *(Added by Stats.1963, c. 1715, p. 3374, § 1.)*

Law Revision Commission Comments

This section is the same as the second paragraph of Government Code [former] Section 711, which applies to local public entities. It will eliminate the requirement of Government Code Section 621 that claims against the State be "verified in the same manner as complaints in civil actions." Claims against local public entities are not required by existing law to be verified. [4 Cal.L.Rev.Comm. Reports 1001 (1963)].

Research References

Rutter, Cal. Practice Guide: Civ. Pro. Before Trial Ch. 1-C, C. Prelawsuit Notices, Claims and Demands.
Rutter, Cal. Practice Guide: Personal Injury Ch. 5-A, A. Prelawsuit Filings.
3 Witkin Cal. Proc. 5th Actions § 253, (S 253) Statutory Requirements.
3 Witkin Cal. Proc. 5th Actions § 284, Illustrations: Defects Waived.

§ 910.4. Forms

The board shall provide forms specifying the information to be contained in claims against the state or a judicial branch entity. The person presenting a claim shall use the form in order that his or her claim is deemed in conformity with Sections 910 and 910.2. A claim may be returned to the person if it was not presented using the form. Any claim returned to a person may be resubmitted using the appropriate form. *(Added by Stats. 1963, c. 1715, p. 3374, § 1. Amended by Stats.1965, c. 653, p. 2010, § 2; Stats.2002, c. 1124 (A.B.3000), § 6, eff. Sept. 30, 2002, operative March 30, 2003; Stats.2004, c. 227 (S.B.1102), § 20, eff. Aug. 16, 2004; Stats.2005, c. 706 (A.B.1742), § 19.)*

Law Revision Commission Comments

This section is new. It permits public entities to provide a form that a claimant may use in lieu of submitting a claim containing the information specified in new Section 910. However, a claimant is not required to use the form provided by the public entity; he may submit his claim in compliance with new Sections 910 and 910.2. [4 Cal.L.Rev.Comm. Reports 1001 (1963)].

The last sentence in this section as originally enacted has created uncertainty. In some cases, particular claim forms provided by a public entity impose requirements not required by Section 910; for example, the claim form prescribed by the State Board of Control (2 Cal.Admin.Code §§ 631, 632.5) requires that the claim be verified. Thus, this section might be construed to bar suit where a claimant failed to comply with the requirements of a particular form supplied by the public entity even though he fully complied with the requirements of Sections 910 and 910.2. The amendment makes it clear that a claim presented on an officially prescribed form (such as the State Board of Control form) is sufficient if the information given substantially satisfies the requirements either of Sections 910 and 910.2 or of the form. [7 Cal.L.Rev.Comm. Reports 401 (1965)].

Research References

Rutter, Cal. Practice Guide: Civ. Pro. Before Trial Ch. 1-C, C. Prelawsuit Notices, Claims and Demands.
Rutter, Cal. Practice Guide: Personal Injury Ch. 5-A, A. Prelawsuit Filings.
3 Witkin Cal. Proc. 5th Actions § 253, (S 253) Statutory Requirements.

§ 910.6. Amendment of claim; failure or refusal to amend

(a) A claim may be amended at any time before the expiration of the period designated in Section 911.2 or before final action thereon is taken by the board, whichever is later, if the claim as amended relates to the same transaction or occurrence which gave rise to the original claim. The amendment shall be considered a part of the original claim for all purposes.

(b) A failure or refusal to amend a claim, whether or not notice of insufficiency is given under Section 910.8, shall not constitute a defense to any action brought upon the cause of action for which the claim was presented if the court finds that the claim as presented complied substantially with Sections 910 and 910.2 or a form provided under Section 910.4. *(Added by Stats.1963, c. 1715, p. 3372, § 1.)*

Law Revision Commission Comments

Paragraph (a) governs the amendment of claims. Existing law applying to local public entities (Government Code [former] Section 711) provides that "a claim may be amended at any time, and the amendment shall be considered a part of the original claim for all purposes." There is no existing statutory provision relating to amendment of claims against the State.

Paragraph (b) is based on a portion of Government Code [former] Section 712 which applies to local public entities. [4 Cal.L.Rev.Comm. Reports 1001 (1963)].

Research References

Rutter, Cal. Practice Guide: Civ. Pro. Before Trial Ch. 1-C, C. Prelawsuit Notices, Claims and Demands.
Rutter, Cal. Practice Guide: Personal Injury Ch. 5-A, A. Prelawsuit Filings.
3 Witkin Cal. Proc. 5th Actions § 282, (S 282) Correction by Amendment.
3 Witkin Cal. Proc. 5th Actions § 283, Statutory Procedure.
3 Witkin Cal. Proc. 5th Actions § 308, (S 308) Effect of New Facts Not in Original Claim.

§ 910.8. Notice of insufficiency of claim

If, in the opinion of the board or the person designated by it, a claim as presented fails to comply substantially with the requirements of Sections 910 and 910.2, or with the requirements of a form provided under Section 910.4 if a claim is presented pursuant thereto, the board or the person may, at any time within 20 days after the claim is presented, give written notice of its insufficiency, stating with particularity the defects or omissions therein. The notice shall be given in the manner prescribed by Section 915.4. The board may not take action on the claim for a period of 15 days after the notice is given. *(Added by Stats.1963, c. 1715, p. 3372, § 1. Amended by Stats.1970, c. 104, p. 323, § 2, operative Jan. 1, 1971; Stats.2004, c. 227 (S.B.1102), § 21, eff. Aug. 16, 2004; Stats.2005, c. 184 (A.B.346), § 2, eff. Sept. 6, 2005.)*

Government

Law Revision Commission Comments

This section is the same as Government Code [former] Section 712, which applies to local public entities, except that (1) Section 712 provides for notice of insufficiency within 50 days instead of within 20 days, and (2) Section 712 prohibits board action on the claim for a period of 20 days instead of 15 days. The shorter time limits under new Section 910.8 are necessary because this legislation is designed to give the board an opportunity to consider the claim before court action may be commenced. Under existing law, there is no similar provision that provides for notice of insufficiency of claims against the State.

The board may delegate to an employee of the entity the function of ruling on the sufficiency of claims and giving notice of insufficiency if the board deems it more convenient to do so than to perform this function itself. See new Sections 912.8 and 935.4. [4 Cal.L.Rev.Comm. Reports 1001 (1963)].

See the Comment to Section 915.4. [9 Cal.L.Rev.Comm. Reports 175 (1969)].

Research References

Rutter, Cal. Practice Guide: Civ. Pro. Before Trial Ch. 1-C, C. Prelawsuit Notices, Claims and Demands.
Rutter, Cal. Practice Guide: Personal Injury Ch. 5-A, A. Prelawsuit Filings.
3 Witkin Cal. Proc. 5th Actions § 283, Statutory Procedure.
3 Witkin Cal. Proc. 5th Actions § 284, Illustrations: Defects Waived.

§ 911. Failure to give notice of insufficiency; waiver of defenses based on defect or omission

Any defense as to the sufficiency of the claim based upon a defect or omission in the claim as presented is waived by failure to give notice of insufficiency with respect to the defect or omission as provided in Section 910.8, except that no notice need be given and no waiver shall result when the claim as presented fails to state either an address to which the person presenting the claim desires notices to be sent or an address of the claimant. *(Added by Stats.1963, c. 1715, p. 3372, § 1. Amended by Stats.2004, c. 227 (S.B.1102), § 22, eff. Aug. 16, 2004; Stats.2005, c. 184 (A.B.346), § 3, eff. Sept. 6, 2005.)*

Law Revision Commission Comments

This section is the same as Government Code [former] Section 713, which applies to local public entities. No comparable statutory provision now exists with respect to claims against the State. [4 Cal.L.Rev.Comm. Reports 1001 (1963)].

Research References

Rutter, Cal. Practice Guide: Civ. Pro. Before Trial Ch. 1-C, C. Prelawsuit Notices, Claims and Demands.
Rutter, Cal. Practice Guide: Personal Injury Ch. 5-A, A. Prelawsuit Filings.
3 Witkin Cal. Proc. 5th Actions § 283, Statutory Procedure.
3 Witkin Cal. Proc. 5th Actions § 284, Illustrations: Defects Waived.

§ 911.2. Time of presentation of claims; limitation

(a) A claim relating to a cause of action for death or for injury to person or to personal property or growing crops shall be presented as provided in Article 2 (commencing with Section 915) not later than six months after the accrual of the cause of action. A claim relating to any other cause of action shall be presented as provided in Article 2 (commencing with Section 915) not later than one year after the accrual of the cause of action.

(b) For purposes of determining whether a claim was commenced within the period provided by law, the date the claim was presented to the California Victim Compensation and Government Claims Board is one of the following:

(1) The date the claim is submitted with a twenty-five dollar ($25) filing fee.

(2) If a fee waiver is granted, the date the claim was submitted with the affidavit requesting the fee waiver.

(3) If a fee waiver is denied, the date the claim was submitted with the affidavit requesting the fee waiver, provided the filing fee is paid to the board within 10 calendar days of the mailing of the notice of the denial of the fee waiver. *(Added by Stats.1963, c. 1715, p. 3372, § 1. Amended by Stats.1987, c. 1201, § 18; Stats.1987, c. 1208, § 3; Stats.2005, c. 184 (A.B.346), § 4, eff. Sept. 6, 2005.)*

Law Revision Commission Comments

This section is substantially the same as the first paragraph of Government Code [former] Section 715, which applies to local public entities. It will provide a shorter period of time for presenting a claim against the State than the existing law (Government Code [former] Sections 643 and 644), which provides that a claim arising under Sections 17000 to 17003, inclusive, of the Vehicle Code shall be presented to the board within one year after the claim first arose or accrued and that other claims shall be presented within two years after the claim first arose or accrued. [4 Cal.L.Rev.Comm. Reports 1001 (1963)].

Research References

Rutter, Cal. Practice Guide: Civ. Pro. Before Trial Ch. 1-C, C. Prelawsuit Notices, Claims and Demands.
Rutter, Cal. Practice Guide: Fed.Civ.Pro. Before Trial Ch. 1-B, B. Federal vs. State Law.
Rutter, Cal. Practice Guide: Insurance Litigation Ch. 9-D, D. Nature of Subrogation.
Rutter, Cal. Practice Guide: Personal Injury Ch. 1-A, A. Initial Client Interview.
Rutter, Cal. Practice Guide: Personal Injury Ch. 1-B, B. Initial Evaluation of Case: Decision to Accept or Reject Employment or Undertake Further Evaluation of Claim.
Rutter, Cal. Practice Guide: Personal Injury Ch. 5-A, A. Prelawsuit Filings.
Miller and Starr California Real Estate § 22:40, Limitations Period for Recovery of Damages; Permanent and Continuing Nuisance Distinguished.
Miller and Starr California Real Estate § 27:49, Provisions for Arbitration and Mediation of Disputes--Public Works.
Miller and Starr California Real Estate § 29:45, Fraud of Building Inspector.
3 Witkin Cal. Proc. 5th Actions § 178, Action Under Federal Civil Rights Act.
3 Witkin Cal. Proc. 5th Actions § 236, Failure to Furnish Information.
3 Witkin Cal. Proc. 5th Actions § 245, (S 245) Civil Rights Actions.
3 Witkin Cal. Proc. 5th Actions § 253, (S 253) Statutory Requirements.
3 Witkin Cal. Proc. 5th Actions § 255, (S 255) Statutory Requirements.
3 Witkin Cal. Proc. 5th Actions § 256, Statute of Limitations Rule Governs.
3 Witkin Cal. Proc. 5th Actions § 259, (S 259) Postponed Accrual for Subrogation Claim.
3 Witkin Cal. Proc. 5th Actions § 260, (S 260) Former Rule of Postponed Accrual.
3 Witkin Cal. Proc. 5th Actions § 268, (S 268) Notice of Rejection of Late Claim.
3 Witkin Cal. Proc. 5th Actions § 270, Excluded Claims Governed by Local Procedures.
3 Witkin Cal. Proc. 5th Actions § 286, (S 286) in General.
3 Witkin Cal. Proc. 5th Actions § 301, Claim by Minor.
3 Witkin Cal. Proc. 5th Actions § 462, in General.
3 Witkin Cal. Proc. 5th Actions § 689, Scope and Accrual.
3 Witkin Cal. Proc. 5th Actions § 690, Personal Injury Claim Not Involving Medical Malpractice.
8 Witkin Cal. Proc. 5th Attack Judgment Trial Court § 194, Relief for Inexcusable Neglect.

§ 911.3. Claim presented without application; notice of return without action; form

(a) When a claim that is required by Section 911.2 to be presented not later than six months after accrual of the cause of action is presented after such time without the application provided in Section 911.4, the board or other person designated by it may, at any time within 45 days after the claim is presented, give written notice to the person presenting the claim that the claim was not filed timely and that it is being returned without further action. The notice shall be in substantially the following form:

"The claim you presented to the (insert title of board or officer) on (indicate date) is being returned because it was not presented within six months after the event or occurrence as required by law. See Sections 901 and 911.2 of the Government Code. Because the claim was not presented within the time allowed by law, no action was taken on the claim.

Your only recourse at this time is to apply without delay to (name of public entity) for leave to present a late claim. See Sections 911.4 to 912.2, inclusive, and Section 946.6 of the Government Code. Under some circumstances, leave to present a late claim will be granted. See Section 911.6 of the Government Code.

You may seek the advice of an attorney of your choice in connection with this matter. If you desire to consult an attorney, you should do so immediately."

(b) Any defense as to the time limit for presenting a claim described in subdivision (a) is waived by failure to give the notice set forth in subdivision (a) within 45 days after the claim is presented, except that no notice need be given and no waiver shall result when the claim as presented fails to state either an address to which the person presenting the claim desires notices to be sent or an address of the claimant. (Added by Stats.1983, c. 107, § 1. Amended by Stats.1987, c. 1201, § 19; Stats.1987, c. 1208, § 4.)

Research References

Rutter, Cal. Practice Guide: Civ. Pro. Before Trial Ch. 1-C, C. Prelawsuit Notices, Claims and Demands.
Rutter, Cal. Practice Guide: Personal Injury Ch. 5-A, A. Prelawsuit Filings.
3 Witkin Cal. Proc. 5th Actions § 268, (S 268) Notice of Rejection of Late Claim.
3 Witkin Cal. Proc. 5th Actions § 284, Illustrations: Defects Waived.
3 Witkin Cal. Proc. 5th Actions § 305, Hearing and Determination.

§ 911.4. Application to present late claim; one year limitation; computation of limitation period; tolling

(a) When a claim that is required by Section 911.2 to be presented not later than six months after the accrual of the cause of action is not presented within that time, a written application may be made to the public entity for leave to present that claim.

(b) The application shall be presented to the public entity as provided in Article 2 (commencing with Section 915) within a reasonable time not to exceed one year after the accrual of the cause of action and shall state the reason for the delay in presenting the claim. The proposed claim shall be attached to the application.

(c) In computing the one-year period under subdivision (b), the following shall apply:

(1) The time during which the person who sustained the alleged injury, damage, or loss is a minor shall be counted, but the time during which he or she is mentally incapacitated and does not have a guardian or conservator of his or her person shall not be counted.

(2) The time shall not be counted during which the person is detained or adjudged to be a dependent child of the juvenile court under the Arnold–Kennick Juvenile Court Law (Chapter 2 (commencing with Section 200) of Part 1 of Division 2 of the Welfare and Institutions Code), if both of the following conditions exist:

(A) The person is in the custody and control of an agency of the public entity to which a claim is to be presented.

(B) The public entity or its agency having custody and control of the minor is required by statute or other law to make a report

of injury, abuse, or neglect to either the juvenile court or the minor's attorney, and that entity or its agency fails to make this report within the time required by the statute or other enactment, with this time period to commence on the date on which the public entity or its agency becomes aware of the injury, neglect, or abuse. In circumstances where the public entity or its agency makes a late report, the claim period shall be tolled for the period of the delay caused by the failure to make a timely report.

(3) The time shall not be counted during which a minor is adjudged to be a dependent child of the juvenile court under the Arnold–Kennick Juvenile Court Law (Chapter 2 (commencing with Section 200) of Part 1 of Division 2 of the Welfare and Institutions Code), if the minor is without a guardian ad litem or conservator for purposes of filing civil actions. (Added by Stats.1963, c. 1715, p. 3372, § 1. Amended by Stats.1965, c. 653, p. 2010, § 3; Stats.1970, c. 411, p. 822, § 1; Stats.1987, c. 1201, § 20; Stats.1987, c. 1208, § 5; Stats.1999, c. 620 (A.B.118), § 1; Stats.2003, c. 847 (A.B.1151), § 2.)

Law Revision Commission Comments

Sections 911.4 to 911.8 are new. These sections permit public entities to grant leave to present a late claim under certain circumstances. This will make a court proceeding to obtain leave to present a late claim necessary only in those cases where the public entity does not grant such leave. Under the existing law applicable to local public entities, late claims may be presented only in limited types of cases and a court proceeding is necessary in every case before a late claim may be presented. New Section 911.6 states the types of cases where late claims may be presented. [4 Cal.L.Rev.Comm. Reports 1001 (1963)].

The amendment merely divides this section into two subdivisions to facilitate the inclusion of cross-references to subdivision (b) in Section 930.4 (added) and in Section 935 (amended). [7 Cal.L.Rev.Comm. Reports 401 (1965)].

Research References

Rutter, Cal. Practice Guide: Civ. Pro. Before Trial Ch. 1-C, C. Prelawsuit Notices, Claims and Demands.
Rutter, Cal. Practice Guide: Personal Injury Ch. 5-A, A. Prelawsuit Filings.
Rutter, Cal. Practice Guide: Personal Injury Ch. 5-B, B. When to Sue-Statute of Limitations.
Miller and Starr California Real Estate § 27:49, Provisions for Arbitration and Mediation of Disputes--Public Works.
3 Witkin Cal. Proc. 5th Actions § 256, Statute of Limitations Rule Governs.
3 Witkin Cal. Proc. 5th Actions § 268, (S 268) Notice of Rejection of Late Claim.
3 Witkin Cal. Proc. 5th Actions § 287, (S 287) Minority.
3 Witkin Cal. Proc. 5th Actions § 289, Current Law: Mandatory Relief on Application.
3 Witkin Cal. Proc. 5th Actions § 295, (S 295) Failure to File Second Claim.
3 Witkin Cal. Proc. 5th Actions § 299, in General.
3 Witkin Cal. Proc. 5th Actions § 300, Claim by Mentally Incapacitated Person.
3 Witkin Cal. Proc. 5th Actions § 301, Claim by Minor.
3 Witkin Cal. Proc. 5th Actions § 305, Hearing and Determination.
3 Witkin Cal. Proc. 5th Actions § 308, (S 308) Effect of New Facts Not in Original Claim.
3 Witkin Cal. Proc. 5th Actions § 312, Current Law Applying Doctrine.
3 Witkin Cal. Proc. 5th Actions § 689, Scope and Accrual.

§ 911.6. Grant or denial of application by board

(a) The board shall grant or deny the application within 45 days after it is presented to the board. The claimant and the board may extend the period within which the board is required to act on the application by written agreement made before the expiration of the period.

(b) The board shall grant the application where one or more of the following is applicable:

(1) The failure to present the claim was through mistake, inadvertence, surprise or excusable neglect and the public entity was not prejudiced in its defense of the claim by the failure to present the claim within the time specified in Section 911.2.

(2) The person who sustained the alleged injury, damage or loss was a minor during all of the time specified in Section 911.2 for the presentation of the claim.

(3) The person who sustained the alleged injury, damage or loss was physically or mentally incapacitated during all of the time specified in Section 911.2 for the presentation of the claim and by reason of such disability failed to present a claim during such time.

(4) The person who sustained the alleged injury, damage or loss died before the expiration of the time specified in Section 911.2 for the presentation of the claim.

(c) If the board fails or refuses to act on an application within the time prescribed by this section, the application shall be deemed to have been denied on the 45th day or, if the period within which the board is required to act is extended by agreement pursuant to this section, the last day of the period specified in the agreement. *(Added by Stats.1963, c. 1715, p. 3372, § 1. Amended by Stats.1965, c. 653, p. 2010, § 4; Stats.1979, c. 769, § 1; Stats.1987, c. 1201, § 21; Stats.1987, c. 1208, § 6.)*

Law Revision Commission Comments

Government Code [former] Section 716 (which applies to local public entities) permits presentation of a late claim only if the public entity would not be unduly prejudiced thereby, and then only in cases where the claimant was a minor, was physically or mentally incapacitated, or has died. New Sections 911.6 and 912, on the other hand, permit presentation of late claims in these cases even though the public entity may be prejudiced thereby. In addition these sections permit the presentation of late claims in cases where the failure to present the claim was through mistake, inadvertence, surprise or excusable neglect if the public entity would not be unduly prejudiced thereby.

Government Code [former] Section 646 (which applies to claims against the State) permits late presentation of a claim of a minor, an insane person, a person imprisoned on a criminal charge or undergoing execution of sentence of a criminal court, a married woman if her husband is a necessary party with her in commencing the action thereon, or an incompetent person. No showing of lack of prejudice is required under [former] Section 646. [4 Cal.L.Rev.Comm. Reports 1001 (1963)].

By extending the time for board action an additional 10 days, the amendment to subdivision (a) makes the time within which the board may act on an application for leave to present a late claim the same as that within which it may act on a claim or an amended claim. See Section 912.4.

Subdivision (b) has been amended to identify more accurately the person to whom the section refers. By definition, he is not a "claimant" because he has filed no claim. [7 Cal.L.Rev.Comm. Reports 401 (1965)].

Research References

Rutter, Cal. Practice Guide: Civ. Pro. Before Trial Ch. 1-C, C. Prelawsuit Notices, Claims and Demands.
Rutter, Cal. Practice Guide: Personal Injury Ch. 5-A, A. Prelawsuit Filings.
3 Witkin Cal. Proc. 5th Actions § 268, (S 268) Notice of Rejection of Late Claim.
3 Witkin Cal. Proc. 5th Actions § 270, Excluded Claims Governed by Local Procedures.
3 Witkin Cal. Proc. 5th Actions § 271, Procedure Established by Agreement.
3 Witkin Cal. Proc. 5th Actions § 286, (S 286) in General.
3 Witkin Cal. Proc. 5th Actions § 287, (S 287) Minority.
3 Witkin Cal. Proc. 5th Actions § 289, Current Law: Mandatory Relief on Application.
3 Witkin Cal. Proc. 5th Actions § 290, Theory of Relief.
3 Witkin Cal. Proc. 5th Actions § 302, Action by Agency.
3 Witkin Cal. Proc. 5th Actions § 303, in General.

3 Witkin Cal. Proc. 5th Actions § 689, Scope and Accrual.

§ 911.8.　Notice of board's action

(a) Written notice of the board's action upon the application shall be given in the manner prescribed by Section 915.4.

(b) If the application is denied, the notice shall include a warning in substantially the following form:

"WARNING

"If you wish to file a court action on this matter, you must first petition the appropriate court for an order relieving you from the provisions of Government Code Section 945.4 (claims presentation requirement). See Government Code Section 946.6. Such petition must be filed with the court within six (6) months from the date your application for leave to present a late claim was denied.

"You may seek the advice of an attorney of your choice in connection with this matter. If you desire to consult an attorney, you should do so immediately." *(Added by Stats.1963, c. 1715, p. 3372, § 1. Amended by Stats.1970, c. 104, p. 323, § 3, operative Jan. 1, 1971; Stats.1974, c. 620, p. 1467, § 1.)*

Law Revision Commission Comments

Sections 911.4 to 911.8 are new. These sections permit public entities to grant leave to present a late claim under certain circumstances. This will make a court proceeding to obtain leave to present a late claim necessary only in those cases where the public entity does not grant such leave. Under the existing law applicable to local public entities, late claims may be presented only in limited types of cases and a court proceeding is necessary in every case before a late claim may be presented. New Section 911.6 states the types of cases where late claims may be presented. [4 Cal.L.Rev.Comm. 1001 (1963)].

See the Comment to Section 915.4. [9 Cal.L.Rev.Comm. Reports 175 (1969)].

Research References

Rutter, Cal. Practice Guide: Personal Injury Ch. 5-A, A. Prelawsuit Filings.
Miller and Starr California Real Estate § 27:49, Provisions for Arbitration and Mediation of Disputes--Public Works.
3 Witkin Cal. Proc. 5th Actions § 302, Action by Agency.

§ 912.2.　Claim deemed presented to board upon day leave to present claim granted

If an application for leave to present a claim is granted by the board pursuant to Section 911.6, the claim shall be deemed to have been presented to the board upon the day that leave to present the claim is granted. *(Added by Stats.1963, c. 1715, p. 3372, § 1. Amended by Stats.1965, c. 653, p. 2011, § 6.)*

Law Revision Commission Comments

Section 912.2 is new. It is necessary in order to fix the date from which to compute the time within which the board must act on the claim under new Section 912.4. [4 Cal.L.Rev.Comm. Reports 1001 (1963)].

This amendment merely strikes the reference to the procedure specified in Section 912 because that procedure is superseded by the more simplified procedure set out in Section 946.6 (added). [7 Cal.L.Rev. Comm. Reports 401 (1965)].

Research References

Rutter, Cal. Practice Guide: Personal Injury Ch. 5-A, A. Prelawsuit Filings.
3 Witkin Cal. Proc. 5th Actions § 268, (S 268) Notice of Rejection of Late Claim.
3 Witkin Cal. Proc. 5th Actions § 302, Action by Agency.

§ 912.4.　Time for action by board; extension of time by agreement; failure or refusal to act within time prescribed

(a) The board shall act on a claim in the manner provided in Section 912.6, 912.7, or 912.8 within 45 days after the claim has been presented. If a claim is amended, the board shall act on the amended claim within 45 days after the amended claim is presented.

(b) The claimant and the board may extend the period within which the board is required to act on the claim by written agreement made either:

(1) Before the expiration of the period.

(2) After the expiration of the period if an action based on the claim has not been commenced and is not yet barred by the period of limitations provided in Section 945.6.

(c) If the board fails or refuses to act on a claim within the time prescribed by this section, the claim shall be deemed to have been rejected by the board on the last day of the period within which the board was required to act upon the claim. If the period within which the board is required to act is extended by agreement pursuant to this section, the last day of the period within which the board is required to act shall be the last day of the period specified in the agreement. *(Added by Stats.1963, c. 1715, p. 3372, § 1. Amended by Stats.1965, c. 653, p. 2011, § 7; Stats.2002, c. 1007 (A.B.2321), § 3.)*

Law Revision Commission Comments

This section is new. Under Government Code [former] Sections 643 and 644, an action may not be brought against the State until the claim is rejected or disallowed in whole or in part, and no time is prescribed within which the State Board of Control must act on the claim. On the other hand, under existing law, an action may be brought against a local public entity as soon as the claim has been presented.

Although this section provides that a claim is deemed to be rejected if the board does not act within 45 days, it expressly authorizes the claimant and the board to extend the 45-day period by agreement. In addition, new Section 913.2 authorizes reconsideration and settlement of claims within the period allowed for commencing an action. Settlement or compromise of pending litigation is covered by new Sections 948 (State) and 949 (local public entities). [4 Cal.L.Rev.Comm. Reports 1001 (1963)].

This amendment makes it clear that an agreement extending the board's time to act on a claim must be entered into before an action is commenced or before the action is barred by the applicable statute of limitations (the six-month period allowed by Section 945.6 after rejection of the claim), thus conforming this section to Section 913.2 (which permits previously rejected claims to be reconsidered and settled before, but not after, they are barred by the applicable statute of limitations). [7 Cal.L.Rev.Comm. Reports 401 (1965)].

Research References

Rutter, Cal. Practice Guide: Civ. Pro. Before Trial Ch. 1-C, C. Prelawsuit Notices, Claims and Demands.
Rutter, Cal. Practice Guide: Civ. Pro. Before Trial Ch. 6-B, B. Complaints.
Rutter, Cal. Practice Guide: Personal Injury Ch. 5-A, A. Prelawsuit Filings.
Miller and Starr California Real Estate § 27:49, Provisions for Arbitration and Mediation of Disputes--Public Works.
3 Witkin Cal. Proc. 5th Actions § 264, Time to Act.
3 Witkin Cal. Proc. 5th Actions § 267, (S 267) Judicial Branch Entity.
3 Witkin Cal. Proc. 5th Actions § 270, Excluded Claims Governed by Local Procedures.
3 Witkin Cal. Proc. 5th Actions § 688, (S 688) in General.
3 Witkin Cal. Proc. 5th Actions § 689, Scope and Accrual.
3 Witkin Cal. Proc. 5th Actions § 767, (S 767) Other Representations.

§ 912.5. Procedure; adoption of rules; claims mistakenly presented

(a) The Trustees of the California State University shall act on a claim against the California State University in accordance with the procedure that the Trustees of the California State University provide by rule.

(b) Nothing in this section authorizes the Trustees of the California State University to adopt any rule that is inconsistent with this part.

(c) If a claim for money or damages against the California State University is mistakenly presented to the Victim Compensation and Government Claims Board, the Victim Compensation and Government Claims Board shall immediately notify the claimant of the error and shall include information on proper filing of the claim. *(Added by Stats.2010, c. 636 (S.B.1046), § 4. Amended by Stats.2011, c. 296 (A.B.1023), § 111.)*

Research References

3 Witkin Cal. Proc. 5th Actions § 267A, (S 267A) (New)-California State University.

§ 912.6. Action by board on claim against local public entity

(a) In the case of a claim against a local public entity, the board may act on a claim in one of the following ways:

(1) If the board finds the claim is not a proper charge against the public entity, it shall reject the claim.

(2) If the board finds the claim is a proper charge against the public entity and is for an amount justly due, it shall allow the claim.

(3) If the board finds the claim is a proper charge against the public entity but is for an amount greater than is justly due, it shall either reject the claim or allow it in the amount justly due and reject it as to the balance.

(4) If legal liability of the public entity or the amount justly due is disputed, the board may reject the claim or may compromise the claim.

(b) In the case of a claim against a local public entity, if the board allows the claim in whole or in part or compromises the claim, it may require the claimant, if the claimant accepts the amount allowed or offered to settle the claim, to accept it in settlement of the entire claim.

(c) Subject to subdivision (b), the local public entity shall pay the amount allowed on the claim or in compromise of the claim in the same manner as if the claimant had obtained a final judgment against the local public entity for that amount, but the claim may be paid in not exceeding 10 equal annual installments as provided in Section 970.6 only if the claimant agrees in writing to that method of payment and in such case no court order authorizing installment payments is required. If an agreement for payment of the claim in installments is made, the local public entity, in its discretion, may prepay any one or more installments or any part of an installment. *(Added by Stats.1963, c. 1715, p. 3372, § 1. Amended by Stats.1980, c. 215, § 5.)*

Law Revision Commission Comments

This section is based on Government Code [former] Section 717; but subdivision (a)(4), authorizing compromise of claims, is new. [4 Cal. L.Rev.Comm. Reports 1001 (1963)].

Section 912.6 is amended to add subdivision (c) which provides a means of enforcing the payment of the amount allowed on a claim or in compromise of a claim. See Section 942 (writ of mandate to compel payment). See also Sections 970–971.2 (payment of money judgments against local public entities). [15 Cal.L.Rev.Comm. Reports 1257 (1980)].

Research References

Rutter, Cal. Practice Guide: Personal Injury Ch. 5-A, A. Prelawsuit Filings.
Miller and Starr California Real Estate § 27:49, Provisions for Arbitration and Mediation of Disputes--Public Works.
3 Witkin Cal. Proc. 5th Actions § 263, Allowance, Rejection, Partial Rejection, or Compromise.
3 Witkin Cal. Proc. 5th Actions § 266, (S 266) State.
8 Witkin Cal. Proc. 5th Enforcement of Judgment § 61, (S 61) Governmental Property.

Government

8 Witkin Cal. Proc. 5th Enforcement of Judgment § 430, in General.
8 Witkin Cal. Proc. 5th Enforcement of Judgment § 431, Payment Obligation.

§ 912.7. Action on claim against judicial branch entity or judge by Judicial Council

The Judicial Council shall act on a claim against a judicial branch entity or judge of one of those entities in accordance with the procedure that the Judicial Council provides by rule of court. The Judicial Council may authorize any committee of the Judicial Council or employee of the Administrative Office of the Courts to perform the functions of the Judicial Council under this part. *(Added by Stats.2002, c. 1007 (A.B.2321), § 4.)*

Research References

3 Witkin Cal. Proc. 5th Actions § 267, (S 267) Judicial Branch Entity.
5 Witkin, California Summary 10th Torts § 233, Compromise and Settlement of Claims.

§ 912.8. Action by board on claims against state; procedure; report to Legislature; recommendations

Except as provided in Section 912.7, in the case of claims against the state, the board shall act on claims in accordance with that procedure as the board, by rule, may prescribe. It may hear evidence for and against the claims and, with the approval of the Governor, report to the Legislature those facts and recommendations concerning the claims as it deems proper. In making recommendations, the board may state and use any official or personal knowledge that any member may have regarding any claim. The board may authorize any employee of the state to perform the functions of the board under this part as are prescribed by the board. *(Added by Stats.1963, c. 1715, p. 3372, § 1. Amended by Stats.1998, c. 872 (A.B.2771), § 6; Stats.2002, c. 1007 (A.B.2321), § 5; Stats.2004, c. 183 (A.B.3082), § 131.)*

Law Revision Commission Comments

This section is based on Government Code [former] Sections 620 (second paragraph) and 622, which apply to the State. It authorizes the Board of Control to prescribe, by rule, the procedure for disposition of claims. Giving the board this broad authority permits the elimination of the provisions of Government Code [former] Section 621 relating to notice of time and place of hearing on the claim and allows the repeal of Government Code Section 624, which permits the automatic denial of any claim covered by insurance. See new Section 965, which provides for payment of allowed claims when a sufficient appropriation for payment exists. [4 Cal.L.Rev.Comm. Reports 1001 (1963)].

Research References

Rutter, Cal. Practice Guide: Personal Injury Ch. 5-A, A. Prelawsuit Filings.
3 Witkin Cal. Proc. 5th Actions § 266, (S 266) State.
8 Witkin Cal. Proc. 5th Enforcement of Judgment § 429, (S 429) Against State.

§ 913. Notice of rejection of claim

(a) Written notice of the action taken under Section 912.5, 912.6, 912.7, or 912.8 or the inaction that is deemed rejection under Section 912.4 shall be given in the manner prescribed by Section 915.4. The notice may be in substantially the following form:

"Notice is hereby given that the claim that you presented to the (insert title of board or officer) on (indicate date) was (indicate whether rejected, allowed, allowed in the amount of $___ and rejected as to the balance, rejected by operation of law, or other appropriate language, whichever is applicable) on (indicate date of action or rejection by operation of law)."

(b) If the claim is rejected, in whole or in part, the notice required by subdivision (a) shall include a warning in substantially the following form:

"WARNING

"Subject to certain exceptions, you have only six (6) months from the date this notice was personally delivered or deposited in the mail to file a court action on this claim. See Government Code Section 945.6.

"You may seek the advice of an attorney of your choice in connection with this matter. If you desire to consult an attorney, you should do so immediately." *(Added by Stats.1963, c. 1715, p. 3372, § 1. Amended by Stats.1970, c. 104, p. 323, § 4, operative Jan. 1, 1971; Stats.2002, c. 1007 (A.B.2321), § 6; Stats.2010, c. 636 (S.B.1046), § 5.)*

Law Revision Commission Comments

This section is based on the second paragraph of Government Code [former] Section 717, which applies to local public entities. There is no similar statutory provision relating to claims against the State. [4 Cal.L.Rev.Comm. Reports 1001 (1963)].

Subdivision (a) of Section 913 is amended to require that written notice of either acceptance or rejection be given by the public entity in every case in which a claim is required to be presented under Chapters 1 and 2 of Part 3 of Division 3.6. The notice serves to keep each claimant aware of the status of his claim and guards against an inadvertent failure to sue on a rejected claim within the applicable time limit. The notice must be given in compliance with the uniform procedure prescribed by Section 915.4. An optional form of notice is set forth in subdivision (a).

If the claim is rejected either in whole or in part, subdivision (b) requires the public entity to include with the notice a warning concerning the applicable statute of limitations and advice to secure the services of an attorney. The notice and warning will alert the claimant, at the time of rejection, of the time allowed to pursue his claim in the courts and will protect a minor or incompetent against an inadvertent reliance on the general tolling provisions of Code of Civil Procedure Section 352. See Code of Civil Procedure Section 352 and Government Code Section 945.6(a). The last two sentences of the notice are based on the language of the notice required by Code of Civil Procedure Section 407 to be included in a summons. [9 Cal.L.Rev.Comm. Reports 175 (1969)].

Research References

Rutter, Cal. Practice Guide: Civ. Pro. Before Trial Ch. 1-C, C. Prelawsuit Notices, Claims and Demands.
Rutter, Cal. Practice Guide: Personal Injury Ch. 5-A, A. Prelawsuit Filings.
3 Witkin Cal. Proc. 5th Actions § 265, Notice of Action Taken.
3 Witkin Cal. Proc. 5th Actions § 266, (S 266) State.
3 Witkin Cal. Proc. 5th Actions § 267, (S 267) Judicial Branch Entity.
3 Witkin Cal. Proc. 5th Actions § 272, Payment by Controller or Authorized State Agency.
3 Witkin Cal. Proc. 5th Actions § 303, in General.
3 Witkin Cal. Proc. 5th Actions § 689, Scope and Accrual.
3 Witkin Cal. Proc. 5th Actions § 691, (S 691) Two-Year Period.
3 Witkin Cal. Proc. 5th Actions § 741, General Rule.
3 Witkin Cal. Proc. 5th Actions § 267A, (S 267A) (New)-California State University.

§ 913.2. Re-examination of rejected claim

The board may, in its discretion, within the time prescribed by Section 945.6 for commencing an action on the claim, re-examine a previously rejected claim in order to consider a settlement of the claim. *(Added by Stats.1963, c. 1715, p. 3372, § 1.)*

Research References

Rutter, Cal. Practice Guide: Personal Injury Ch. 5-A, A. Prelawsuit Filings.
3 Witkin Cal. Proc. 5th Actions § 264, Time to Act.
3 Witkin Cal. Proc. 5th Actions § 266, (S 266) State.
3 Witkin Cal. Proc. 5th Actions § 267, (S 267) Judicial Branch Entity.

3 Witkin Cal. Proc. 5th Actions § 267A, (S 267A) (New)-California State University.

ARTICLE 2. MANNER OF PRESENTATION AND OF GIVING NOTICE

Section

915.   Presentation to local public entity or to state; means of presentation.

915.2.   Mailing manner; time of presentation and receipt; proof of mailing.

915.4.   Manner of giving notice of insufficiency of claim, board's action upon application, or rejection of claim.

§ 915. Presentation to local public entity or to state; means of presentation

(a) A claim, any amendment thereto, or an application to the public entity for leave to present a late claim shall be presented to a local public entity by either of the following means:

(1) Delivering it to the clerk, secretary or auditor thereof.

(2) Mailing it to the clerk, secretary, auditor, or to the governing body at its principal office.

(b) Except as provided in subdivisions (c) and (d), a claim, any amendment thereto, or an application for leave to file a late claim shall be presented to the state by either of the following means:

(1) Delivering it to an office of the Victim Compensation and Government Claims Board.

(2) Mailing it to the Victim Compensation and Government Claims Board at its principal office.

(c) A claim, any amendment thereto, or an application for leave to file a late claim shall be presented to a judicial branch entity in accordance with the following means:

(1) Delivering or mailing it to the court executive officer, if against a superior court or a judge, court executive officer, or trial court employee, as defined in Section 811.9, of that court.

(2) Delivering or mailing it to the clerk/administrator of the court of appeals, if against a court of appeals or a judge of that court.

(3) Delivering or mailing it to the Clerk of the Supreme Court, if against the Supreme Court or a judge of that court.

(4) Delivering or mailing it to the Secretariat of the Judicial Council, if against the Judicial Council or the Administrative Office of the Courts.

(d) A claim, any amendment thereto, or an application for leave to file a late claim shall be presented to the Trustees of the California State University by delivering or mailing it to the Office of Risk Management at the Office of the Chancellor of the California State University.

(e) A claim, amendment or application shall be deemed to have been presented in compliance with this section even though it is not delivered or mailed as provided in this section if, within the time prescribed for presentation thereof, any of the following apply:

(1) It is actually received by the clerk, secretary, auditor or board of the local public entity.

(2) It is actually received at an office of the Victim Compensation and Government Claims Board.

(3) If against the California State University, it is actually received by the Trustees of the California State University.

(4) If against a judicial branch entity or judge, it is actually received by the court executive officer, court clerk/administrator, court clerk, or secretariat of the judicial branch entity.

(f) A claim, amendment or application shall be deemed to have been presented in compliance with this section to a public agency as defined in Section 53050 if it is delivered or mailed within the time prescribed for presentation thereof in conformity with the information contained in the statement in the Roster of Public Agencies pertaining to that public agency which is on file at the time the claim, amendment or application is delivered or mailed. As used in this subdivision, "statement in the Roster of Public Agencies" means the statement or amended statement in the Roster of Public Agencies in the office of the Secretary of State or in the office of the county clerk of any county in which the statement or amended statement is on file. *(Added by Stats.1963, c. 1715, p. 3372, § 1. Amended by Stats.1965, c. 653, p. 2012, § 8; Stats.2002, c. 1007 (A.B.2321), § 7; Stats.2010, c. 636 (S.B.1046), § 6.)*

Law Revision Commission Comments

This section is based on Government Code [former] Section 714, which applies to local public entities. There is no similar statutory provision relating to claims against the State. [4 Cal.L.Rev.Comm. Reports 1001 (1963)].

Subdivision (d) of this section is necessary to fill in a gap in the 1963 legislation requiring certain public agencies to file and maintain in a Roster of Public Agencies certain information necessary to facilitate compliance with the claims filing procedure. Section 945.5 (repealed) dispensed with the necessity of presenting a claim to any public agency that had not complied with the Roster requirements. It was silent, however, as to the effect to be given a claim presented in accord with the information filed in the Roster if the information was incomplete, inaccurate or for any other reason deviated from the actual facts. This amendment makes it clear that the presentation of a claim, amendment or application in conformity with the information filed by the public entity in the Roster of Public Agencies constitutes sufficient presentation even if the information does not reflect the actual facts. [7 Cal.L.Rev.Comm. Reports 401 (1965)].

Research References

Rutter, Cal. Practice Guide: Civ. Pro. Before Trial Ch. 1-C, C. Prelawsuit Notices, Claims and Demands.

Rutter, Cal. Practice Guide: Personal Injury Ch. 5-A, A. Prelawsuit Filings.

3 Witkin Cal. Proc. 5th Actions § 254, (S 254) Illustrations.

3 Witkin Cal. Proc. 5th Actions § 262, Manner of Presentation.

3 Witkin Cal. Proc. 5th Actions § 276, Compliance Sufficient.

3 Witkin Cal. Proc. 5th Actions § 277, Compliance Insufficient.

5 Witkin, California Summary 10th Torts § 233, Compromise and Settlement of Claims.

§ 915.2. Mailing manner; time of presentation and receipt; proof of mailing

(a) If a claim, amendment to a claim, or application to a public entity for leave to present a late claim is presented or sent by mail under this chapter, or if any notice under this chapter is given by mail, the claim, amendment, application, or notice shall be mailed in the manner prescribed in this section. The claim, amendment, application, or notice shall be deposited in the United States post office, a mailbox, sub-post office, substation, mail chute, or other similar facility regularly maintained by the government of the United States, in a sealed envelope, properly addressed, with postage paid. The claim, amendment, application, or notice shall be deemed to have been presented and received at the time of the deposit.

(b) Any period of notice and any duty to respond after receipt of service of a claim, amendment, application, or notice is extended five days upon service by mail, if the place of address is within the State of California, 10 days if the place of address is within the United States, and 20 days if the place of address is outside the United States. This subdivision shall not apply to the written notice set forth in Section 945.6 or the filing of a complaint after denial of a claim.

(c) As applied to this section, proof of mailing may be made in the manner prescribed by Section 1013a of the Code of Civil Procedure. *(Added by Stats.1963, c. 1715, p. 3372, § 1. Amended by Stats.2002, c. 1124 (A.B.3000), § 7, eff. Sept. 30, 2002; Stats.2011, c. 308 (S.B.647), § 7.)*

Law Revision Commission Comments

This section is new. It makes clear that a claim, amendment to a claim, application to present a late claim, or any notice, is deemed to have been presented and received at the time of deposit in the mail. The section is based in part on Section 1013 of the Code of Civil Procedure relating to service by mail. [4 Cal.L.Rev.Comm. Reports 1001 (1963)].

Research References

Rutter, Cal. Practice Guide: Civ. Pro. Before Trial Ch. 1-C, C. Prelawsuit Notices, Claims and Demands.
Rutter, Cal. Practice Guide: Personal Injury Ch. 5-A, A. Prelawsuit Filings.
3 Witkin Cal. Proc. 5th Actions § 262, Manner of Presentation.

§ 915.4.　Manner of giving notice of insufficiency of claim, board's action upon application, or rejection of claim

(a) The notices provided for in Sections 910.8, 911.8, and 913 shall be given by either of the following methods:

(1) Personally delivering the notice to the person presenting the claim or making the application.

(2) Mailing the notice to the address, if any, stated in the claim or application as the address to which the person presenting the claim or making the application desires notices to be sent or, if no such address is stated in the claim or application, by mailing the notice to the address, if any, of the claimant as stated in the claim or application.

(b) No notice need be given where the claim or application fails to state either an address to which the person presenting the claim or making the application desires notices to be sent or an address of the claimant. *(Added by Stats.1970, c. 104, p. 324, § 5, operative Jan. 1, 1971.)*

Law Revision Commission Comments

Section 915.4 is new, but it incorporates the substance of former Sections 910.8(b), 911.8, and 913. It makes uniform the manner of giving all notices under this chapter. Where notice is given by mail, Section 915.2 is applicable. [9 Cal.L.Rev.Comm. Reports 175 (1969)].

Research References

Rutter, Cal. Practice Guide: Civ. Pro. Before Trial Ch. 1-C, C. Prelawsuit Notices, Claims and Demands.
3 Witkin Cal. Proc. 5th Actions § 265, Notice of Action Taken.
3 Witkin Cal. Proc. 5th Actions § 283, Statutory Procedure.
3 Witkin Cal. Proc. 5th Actions § 302, Action by Agency.

CHAPTER 3.　PROCEEDINGS TO DETERMINE CONSTITUTIONALITY OF CLAIMS AGAINST THE STATE

§ 920.　"Omnibus claim appropriation" defined

As used in this chapter, "omnibus claim appropriation" means an act of appropriation, or an item of appropriation in a budget act, by which the Legislature appropriates a lump sum to pay the claim of the California Victim Compensation and Government Claims Board or its secretary against the state in an amount that the Legislature has determined is properly chargeable to the state. *(Added by Stats.1963, c. 1715, p. 3372, § 1. Amended by Stats.2006, c. 538 (S.B.1852), § 219.)*

§ 920.2.　Submission to Controller of claim covering full amount of omnibus claim appropriation

Promptly following the effective date of an omnibus claim appropriation, the board or its secretary shall submit to the Controller a claim covering the full amount of the appropriation made in the omnibus claim appropriation. Any such claim is exempt from the provisions of Chapter 4 (commencing with Section 925) of this part, and the board shall have those powers necessary to administer and disburse the omnibus claim appropriation. *(Added by Stats.1963, c. 1715, p. 3372, § 1.)*

§ 920.4.　Withholding payment of questioned portion of omnibus claim appropriation; notice to Joint Legislative Budget Committee

If the Controller believes or has reason to believe that the payment of any portion of the omnibus claim appropriation may violate the provisions of the Constitution, he shall withhold payment of the questioned portion and shall issue his warrant for the remainder of the appropriation. The secretary, subject to the board's approval, shall promptly disburse the undisputed portion of the omnibus claim appropriation and shall promptly give notice to the Joint Legislative Budget Committee of the Controller's action concerning the withheld portion. *(Added by Stats.1963, c. 1715, p. 3372, § 1.)*

§ 920.6.　Advice of committee; proceedings to compel Controller to issue warrant for balance of appropriation

Unless the Joint Legislative Budget Committee within 60 days after receipt of such notice advises the board in writing that the Legislature desires to reconsider any part of the withheld portion, the board shall institute proceedings to compel the Controller to issue his warrant for the balance of the omnibus claim appropriation. The board shall prosecute any such proceeding to final determination and shall disburse the funds finally paid over to it. Funds subject to such proceedings shall continue to be available until the end of the fiscal year in which final determination of the proceeding occurs. *(Added by Stats. 1963, c. 1715, p. 3372, § 1.)*

§ 920.8.　Decision of committee to reconsider questioned portion of appropriation; action to compel payment of remainder

If the Joint Legislative Budget Committee advises the board that the Legislature desires to reconsider any part of the omnibus claim appropriation withheld by the Controller, no further action shall be taken with respect to that part and the money appropriated therefor shall revert to funds from which they were appropriated, pending further legislative action. The board, however, shall institute proceedings as provided in Section 920.6 to compel payment of the remainder of the omnibus claim appropriation withheld by the Controller. *(Added by Stats.1963, c. 1715, p. 3372, § 1.)*

CHAPTER 4. PRESENTATION OF CLAIMS TO STATE CONTROLLER

§ 925. "Board" defined

As used in this chapter, "board" means the California Victim Compensation and Government Claims Board. *(Added by Stats.1963, c. 1715, p. 3372, § 1. Amended by Stats.2006, c. 538 (S.B.1852), § 220.)*

Research References

3 Witkin Cal. Proc. 5th Actions § 272, Payment by Controller or Authorized State Agency.

§ 925.2. Claims exempt from chapter and Section 13920

Claims for expenses of either house of the Legislature or members or committees thereof are exempt from Section 13920 and this chapter, except Section 925.6, and claims for official salaries fixed by statute are exempt from this chapter and Section 13920. *(Added by Stats.1963, c. 1715, p. 3372, § 1. Amended by Stats.1989, c. 592, § 2.)*

§ 925.4. Form and manner of presentation

Any person having a claim against the State for which appropriations have been made, or for which state funds are available, may present it to the Controller in the form and manner prescribed by the general rules and regulations adopted by the board for the presentation and audit of claims. *(Added by Stats.1963, c. 1715, p. 3372, § 1.)*

§ 925.6. Audit

(a) The Controller shall not draw his or her warrant for any claim until it has been audited by him or her in conformity with law and the general rules and regulations adopted by the board, governing the presentation and audit of claims. Whenever the Controller is directed by law to draw his or her warrant for any purpose, the direction is subject to this section.

(b) Notwithstanding the provisions of subdivision (a), the Assembly Committee on Rules, the Senate Committee on Rules, and the Joint Rules Committee, in cooperation with the Controller, shall adopt rules and regulations to govern the presentation of claims of the committees to the Controller. The Controller, in cooperation with the committees, shall adopt rules and regulations governing the audit and recordkeeping of claims of the committees. All rules and regulations shall be adopted by January 31, 1990, shall be published in the Assembly and Senate Journals, and shall be made available to the public.

(c) Rules and regulations adopted pursuant to subdivision (b) shall not be subject to the review by or approval of the Office of Administrative Law.

(d) Records of claims kept by the Controller pursuant to subdivision (b) shall be open to public inspection as permitted by the California Public Records Act (Chapter 3.5 (commencing with Section 6250) of Division 7 of Title 1). *(Added by Stats.1963, c. 1715, p. 3372, § 1. Amended by Stats.1989, c. 592, § 3.)*

§ 925.8. Approval; drawing of warrant

If the Controller approves a claim he shall draw his warrant for the amount approved in favor of the claimant. *(Added by Stats.1963, c. 1715, p. 3372, § 1.)*

§ 926. Disapproval; filing with board

If he disapproves a claim, the Controller shall file it and a statement of his disapproval and his reasons with the board as prescribed in the rules and regulations of the board. *(Added by Stats.1963, c. 1715, p. 3372, § 1.)*

§ 926.2. Reconsideration of rejected claim

The Controller shall not entertain for a second time a claim against the State once rejected by him or by the Legislature unless such facts are subsequently presented to the board as in suits between individuals would furnish sufficient ground for granting a new trial. *(Added by Stats.1963, c. 1715, p. 3381, § 1.)*

§ 926.4. Appeal to board

Any person who is aggrieved by the disapproval of a claim by the Controller, may appeal to the board. If the board finds that facts are presented justifying such action, the Controller shall reconsider his rejection of the claim. *(Added by Stats.1963, c. 1715, p. 3381, § 1.)*

Research References

3 Witkin Cal. Proc. 5th Actions § 272, Payment by Controller or Authorized State Agency.

§ 926.6. Appeal to Legislature; filing of notice; transmission of papers

After final rejection of a claim by the Controller following reconsideration, any person interested may appeal to the Legislature by filing with the board a notice of appeal. Upon receipt of such notice the board shall transmit to the Legislature the rejected claim, all papers accompanying it, and a statement of the evidence taken before the board. *(Added by Stats.1963, c. 1715, p. 3381, § 1.)*

Research References

3 Witkin Cal. Proc. 5th Actions § 272, Payment by Controller or Authorized State Agency.

§ 926.8. Claim by federal agency against credits owing by state

Whenever a governmental agency of the United States, in the collection of taxes or amounts owing to it, is authorized by federal law to levy administratively on credits owing to a debtor, it may avail itself of the provisions of this section and claim credits owing by the State to such debtor, in manner as follows:

It shall file a certification of the facts with the state department, board, office or commission owing the credit to the debtor prior to the time the state agency presents the claims of the debtor therefor to the State Controller or to the State Personnel Board. The state agency in presenting the claim of the debtor shall note thereon the fact of the filing of the certificate and shall also note any amounts owed by the debtor to the State by reason of advances or for any other purpose.

Subject to the provisions of Sections 12419.4 and 12419.5, the State Controller shall issue his warrant payable to the United States Treasurer for the net amount due the debtor, after offsetting for any amounts advanced to the debtor or by him owing to the State, or as much thereof as will satisfy in full the amount owing by the debtor to the United States as so certified;

Government

any balance shall be paid to the debtor. *(Added by Stats.1963, c. 1715, p. 3372, § 1.)*

§ 926.10. Interest on liquidated claim against public entity

Any public entity as defined by Section 811.2 having a liquidated claim against any other public entity based on contract or statute of the State of California, or any person having such a claim against a public agency, shall be entitled to interest commencing the 61st day after such public entity or person files a liquidated claim known or agreed to be valid when filed pursuant to such statute or contract, and such claim is due and payable. Interest shall be 6 percent per annum. *(Added by Stats.1971, c. 1526, p. 3018, § 1.)*

Research References

Miller and Starr California Real Estate § 34:35, Rate of Interest; Compound Interest.

1 Witkin Cal. Summ. 10th Contracts § 889, (S 889) Liquidated Sum Due.

CHAPTER 4.5. PROMPT PAYMENT OF CLAIMS

§ 927. Short title; legislative intent; application

(a) This chapter shall be known and may be cited as the California Prompt Payment Act.

(b) It is the intent of the Legislature that state agencies pay properly submitted, undisputed invoices, refunds, or other undisputed payments due to individuals within 45 days of receipt or notification thereof, or automatically calculate and pay the appropriate late payment penalties as specified in this chapter.

(c) Notwithstanding any other provision of law, this chapter shall apply to all state agencies, including, but not limited to, the Public Employees' Retirement System, the State Teachers' Retirement System, the Treasurer, and the Department of General Services. *(Added by Stats.1998, c. 916 (A.B.2275), § 5. Amended by Stats.2010, c. 719 (S.B.856), § 13, eff. Oct. 19, 2010.)*

§ 927.1. Payment for property or services; payment for grant; late payment penalties

(a)(1) A state agency that acquires property or services pursuant to a contract with a business, including any approved change order or contract amendment, shall make payment to the person or business on the date required by the contract and as required by Section 927.4 or be subject to a late payment penalty.

(2) A state agency that awards a grant, as defined in subdivision (b) of Section 927.2, shall make payment to the person or business that is the recipient of the grant on the date required by the grant and as required by Section 927.4 or be subject to a late payment penalty.

(b) Except in the event of an emergency as provided in Section 927.11, effective January 1, 1999, the late payment penalties specified in this chapter may not be waived, altered, or limited by either of the following:

(1) A state agency acquiring property or services pursuant to a contract or that awards a grant.

(2) Any person or business contracting with a state agency to provide property or services or that is the recipient of a grant. *(Added by Stats.1998, c. 916 (A.B.2275), § 5. Amended by Stats.2000, c. 151 (A.B.1936), § 1; Stats.2006, c. 861 (A.B.2541), § 1.)*

§ 927.2. Definitions

The following definitions apply to this chapter:

(a) "Claim schedule" means a schedule of payment requests prepared and submitted by a state agency to the Controller for payment to the named claimant.

(b) "Grant" means a signed final agreement between any state agency and a local government agency or organization authorized to accept grant funding for victim services or prevention programs administered by any state agency. Any such grant is a contract and subject to this chapter.

(c) "Invoice" means a bill or claim that requests payment on a contract under which a state agency acquires property or services or pursuant to a signed final grant agreement.

(d) "Medi–Cal program" means the program established pursuant to Chapter 7 (commencing with Section 14000) of Part 3 of Division 9 of the Welfare and Institutions Code.

(e) "Nonprofit public benefit corporation" means a corporation, as defined by subdivision (b) of Section 5046 of the Corporations Code, that has registered with the Department of General Services as a small business.

(f) "Nonprofit service organization" means a nonprofit entity that is organized to provide services to the public.

(g) "Notice of refund or other payment due" means a state agency provides notice to the person that a refund or payment is owed to that person or the state agency receives notice from the person that a refund or undisputed payment is due.

(h) "Payment" means any form of the act of paying, including, but not limited to, the issuance of a warrant or a registered warrant by the Controller, or the issuance of a revolving fund check by a state agency, to a claimant in the amount of an undisputed invoice.

(i) "Reasonable cause" means a determination by a state agency that any of the following conditions are present:

(1) There is a discrepancy between the invoice or claimed amount and the provisions of the contract or grant.

(2) There is a discrepancy between the invoice or claimed amount and either the claimant's actual delivery of property or services to the state or the state's acceptance of those deliveries.

(3) Additional evidence supporting the validity of the invoice or claimed amount is required to be provided to the state agency by the claimant.

(4) The invoice has been improperly executed or needs to be corrected by the claimant.

(5) There is a discrepancy between the refund or other payment due as calculated by the person to whom the money is owed and by the state agency.

(j) "Received by a state agency" means the date an invoice is delivered to the state location or party specified in the contract or grant or, if a state location or party is not specified in the contract or grant, wherever otherwise specified by the state agency.

(k) "Required payment approval date" means the date on which payment is due as specified in a contract or grant or, if a specific date is not established by the contract or grant, 30 calendar days following the date upon which an undisputed invoice is received by a state agency.

(l) "Revolving fund" means a fund established pursuant to Article 5 (commencing with Section 16400) of Division 4 of Title 2.

(m) "Small business" means a business certified as a "small business" in accordance with subdivision (d) of Section 14837, including certified small businesses engaged in the development, design, and construction of California's high-speed rail system pursuant to the California High–Speed Rail Act (Division 19.5 (commencing with Section 185000) of the Public Utilities Code).

(n) "Small business" and "nonprofit organization" mean, in reference to providers under the Medi–Cal program, a business or organization that meets all of the following criteria:

(1) The principal office is located in California.

(2) The officers, if any, are domiciled in California.

(3) If a small business, it is independently owned and operated.

(4) The business or organization is not dominant in its field of operation.

(5) Together with any affiliates, the business or organization has gross receipts from business operations that do not exceed three million dollars ($3,000,000) per year, except that the Director of Health Services may increase this amount if the director deems that this action would be in furtherance of the intent of this chapter. *(Added by Stats.1998, c. 916 (A.B.2275), § 5. Amended by Stats.1999, c. 784 (A.B.724), § 8, eff. Oct. 10, 1999; Stats.2006, c. 861 (A.B.2541), § 2; Stats.2009–2010, 4th Ex.Sess., c. 23 (S.B.16), § 4, eff. July 28, 2009; Stats.2010, c. 719 (S.B.856), § 14, eff. Oct. 19, 2010; Stats.2012, c. 199 (A.B.2181), § 1.)*

§ 927.3. Undisputed invoice payment; dispute; notice of refund or other payment due

(a) Except where payment is made directly by a state agency pursuant to Section 927.6, an undisputed invoice received by a state agency shall be submitted to the Controller for payment by the required payment approval date. A state agency may dispute an invoice submitted by a claimant for reasonable cause if the state agency notifies the claimant within 15 working days from receipt of the invoice, or delivery of property or services, whichever is later. No state employee shall dispute an invoice, on the basis of minor or technical defects, in order to circumvent or avoid the general intent or any of the specific provisions of this chapter.

(b) Except where payment is made directly by a state agency pursuant to Section 927.13, a notice of refund or other payment due received by a state agency shall be submitted to the Controller within 30 calendar days of the agency's receipt of the notice. A state agency may dispute a refund request for reasonable cause if the state agency notifies the claimant within 15 working days after the state agency receives notice from the individual that the refund is due. *(Added by Stats.1998, c. 916 (A.B.2275), § 5. Amended by Stats.2006, c. 861 (A.B.2541), § 3; Stats.2010, c. 719 (S.B.856), § 15, eff. Oct. 19, 2010.)*

§ 927.4. Undisputed invoices; time for payment; late payment penalties

Except as otherwise provided in this chapter, to avoid late payment penalties, the maximum time from state agency receipt of an undisputed invoice to the date of payment is 45 calendar days. If payment is not issued within 45 calendar days from the state agency receipt of an undisputed invoice, late payment penalties shall be paid to the claimant in accordance with Sections 927.6 and 927.7. *(Added by Stats.1998, c. 916 (A.B. 2275), § 5. Amended by Stats.2009–2010, 4th Ex.Sess., c. 23 (S.B.16), § 5, eff. July 28, 2009.)*

Research References

Miller and Starr California Real Estate § 27:91, Prompt Payment of Progress Payments and Contract Retention.

§ 927.5. Medi–Cal program; reimbursement for health care services; time

This chapter shall not apply to claims for reimbursement for health care services provided under the Medi–Cal program, unless the Medi–Cal health care services provider is a small business or nonprofit organization. In applying this section to claims submitted to the state, or its fiscal intermediary, by providers of services or equipment under the Medi–Cal program, payment for claims shall be due 30 days after a claim is received by the state or its fiscal intermediary, unless reasonable cause for nonpayment exists. With regard to Medi–Cal claims, reasonable cause shall include review of claims to determine medical necessity, review of claims for providers subject to special prepayment fraud and abuse controls, and claims that require review by the fiscal intermediary or State Department of Health Care Services due to special circumstances. Claims requiring special review as specified above shall not be eligible for a late payment penalty. *(Added by Stats.1998, c. 916 (A.B.2275), § 5. Amended by Stats.1999, c. 784 (A.B.724), § 9, eff. Oct. 10, 1999; Stats.2010, c. 719 (S.B.856), § 16, eff. Oct. 19, 2010.)*

§ 927.6. Penalties

(a) State agencies shall pay applicable penalties, without requiring that the claimant submit an additional invoice for these amounts, whenever the state agency fails to submit a correct claim schedule to the Controller by the required payment approval date and payment is not issued within 45 calendar days from the state agency receipt of an undisputed invoice. The penalty shall cease to accrue on the date the state agency submits the claim schedule to the Controller for payment or pays the claimant directly, and shall be paid for out of the state agency's support appropriation. If the claimant is a certified small business, a nonprofit organization, a nonprofit public benefit corporation, or a small business or nonprofit organization that provides services or equipment under the Medi–Cal program, the state agency shall pay to the claimant a penalty at a rate of 10 percent above the United States Prime Rate on June 30 of the prior fiscal year. However, a nonprofit organization shall only be eligible to receive a penalty payment if it has been awarded a contract or grant in an amount less than five hundred thousand dollars ($500,000). If the amount of the penalty is ten dollars ($ 10) or less, the penalty shall be waived and not paid by the state agency.

(b) For all other businesses, the state agency shall pay a penalty at a rate of 1 percent above the Pooled Money Investment Account daily rate on June 30 of the prior fiscal year, not to exceed a rate of 15 percent. If the amount of the penalty is one hundred dollars ($100) or less, the penalty shall be waived and not paid by the state agency. On an exception basis, state agencies may avoid payment of penalties for failure to submit a correct claim schedule to the Controller by the required payment approval date by paying the claimant directly from the state agency's revolving fund within 45 calendar days following the date upon which an undisputed invoice is received by the state agency. *(Added by Stats.1998, c. 916 (A.B.2275), § 5. Amended by Stats.2006, c. 861 (A.B.2541), § 4; Stats.2009–2010, 4th Ex.Sess., c. 23 (S.B.16), § 6, eff. July 28, 2009; Stats.2010, c. 719 (S.B.856), § 17, eff. Oct. 19, 2010.)*

Research References

1 Witkin Cal. Summ. 10th Contracts § 911, (S 911) Works of Improvement Contracts.

§ 927.7. Controller payment to claimants; penalties

The Controller shall pay claimants within 15 calendar days of receipt of a correct claim schedule from the state agency. If the Controller fails to make payment within 15 calendar days of receipt of the claim schedule from a state agency, and payment is not issued within 45 calendar days from state agency receipt of an undisputed invoice, the Controller shall pay applicable penalties to the claimant without requiring that the claimant submit an invoice for these amounts. Penalties shall cease to accrue on the date full payment is made, and shall be paid for out of the Controller's funds. If the claimant is a certified small business, a nonprofit organization, a nonprofit public benefit corporation, or a small business or nonprofit organization that provides services or equipment under the Medi–Cal program, the Controller shall pay to the claimant a penalty at a rate of 10 percent above the United States Prime Rate on June 30 of the prior fiscal year, from the 16th calendar day following receipt of the claim schedule from the state agency. However, a nonprofit organization shall only be eligible to receive a penalty payment if it has been awarded a contract or grant in an amount less than five hundred thousand dollars ($500,000). If the amount of the penalty is ten dollars ($ 10) or less, the penalty shall be waived and not paid by the Controller. For all other businesses, the Controller shall pay penalties at a rate of 1 percent above the Pooled Money Investment Account daily rate on June 30 of the prior fiscal year, not to exceed a rate of 15 percent. If the amount of the penalty is one hundred dollars ($100) or less, the penalty shall be waived and not paid by the Controller. *(Added by Stats.1998, c. 916 (A.B.2275), § 5. Amended by Stats.2006, c. 861 (A.B.2541), § 5; Stats.2009–2010, 4th Ex.Sess., c. 23 (S.B.16), § 7, eff. July 28, 2009; Stats.2010, c. 719 (S.B.856), § 18, eff. Oct. 19, 2010.)*

§ 927.8. Appropriations to pay penalties

State agencies shall avoid seeking any additional appropriation to pay penalties that accrue as a result of the agency's failure to make timely payments as required by this chapter. Any state agency that requests that the Legislature make a deficiency appropriation for the agency shall identify what portion, if any, of the requested amount is required because of any penalties imposed by this chapter. *(Added by Stats.1998, c. 916 (A.B. 2275), § 5.)*

§ 927.9. Late payment penalties; report

(a) Except as provided in subdivision (c), on an annual basis, within 90 calendar days following the end of each fiscal year, state agencies shall provide the Director of General Services with a report on late payment penalties that were paid by the state agency in accordance with this chapter during the preceding fiscal year.

(b) The report shall separately identify the total number and dollar amount of late payment penalties paid to small businesses, other businesses, and refunds or other payments to individuals. State agencies may, at their own initiative, provide the director with other relevant performance measures. The director shall prepare a report separately listing the number and total dollar amount of all late payment penalties paid to small businesses,

other businesses, and refunds and other payments to individuals by each state agency during the preceding fiscal year, together with other relevant performance measures, and shall make the information available to the public.

(c) The reporting requirements of subdivisions (a) and (b) are not applicable to the Department of Forestry and Fire Protection. *(Added by Stats.1998, c. 916 (A.B.2275), § 5. Amended by Stats.2010, c. 719 (S.B.856), § 19, eff. Oct. 19, 2010; Stats.2013, c. 356 (S.B.96), § 4, eff. Sept. 26, 2013.)*

§ 927.10. Prime contractors payment to subcontractors and suppliers; state agency encouragement

State agencies shall encourage claimants to promptly pay their subcontractors and suppliers, especially those that are small businesses. In furtherance of this policy, state agencies shall utilize expedited payment processes to enable faster payment by prime contractors to their subcontractors and suppliers, and shall promptly respond to any subcontractor or supplier inquiries regarding the status of payments made to prime contractors. *(Added by Stats.1998, c. 916 (A.B.2275), § 5. Amended by Stats.2006, c. 861 (A.B.2541), § 6.)*

§ 927.11. Declared fire season; passage of Budget Act; major disaster; payments and penalties

(a) Except in the case of a contract with a certified small business, a nonprofit organization, or a nonprofit public benefit corporation, if an invoice from a business under a contract with the Department of Forestry and Fire Protection would become subject to late payment penalties during the annually declared fire season, as declared by the Director of Forestry and Fire Protection, then the required payment approval date shall be extended by 30 calendar days.

(b) No nonprofit public benefit corporation shall be eligible for a late payment penalty if a state agency fails to make timely payment because no Budget Act has been enacted.

(c) If the Director of Finance determines that a state agency or the Controller is unable to promptly pay an invoice as provided for by this chapter due to a major calamity, disaster, or criminal act, then otherwise applicable late payment penalty provisions contained in Sections 927.6 and 927.7 shall be suspended except as they apply to a claimant that is either a certified small business, a nonprofit organization, a nonprofit public benefit corporation, or a small business or nonprofit organization that provides services or equipment under the Medi–Cal program. The suspension shall remain in effect until the Director of Finance determines that the suspended late payment penalty provisions of this section should be reinstated.

(d) Except as provided in subdivision (b), in the event a state agency fails to make timely payment because no Budget Act has been enacted, penalties shall continue to accrue until the time that the invoice is paid. *(Added by Stats.1998, c. 916 (A.B.2275), § 5. Amended by Stats.2006, c. 861 (A.B.2541), § 7; Stats.2009– 2010, 4th Ex.Sess., c. 23 (S.B.16), § 8, eff. July 28, 2009.)*

§ 927.12. Application of § 926.10

Section 926.10 shall not apply to any contract covered by this chapter. *(Added by Stats.1998, c. 916 (A.B.2275), § 5.)*

§ 927.13. Failure of state agencies to submit claim schedule to Controller; penalties; payment of claimants; interest payments; exemptions

(a) Unless otherwise provided for by statute, any state agency that fails to submit a correct claim schedule to the Controller within 30 days of receipt of a notice of refund or other payment due, and fails to issue payment within 45 days from the notice of refund or other payment due, shall be liable for penalties on the undisputed amount pursuant to this section. The penalties shall be paid out of the agency's funds at a rate equal to the Pooled Money Investment Account daily rate on June 30 of the prior fiscal year minus 1 percent. The penalties shall cease to accrue on the date full payment or refund is made. If the amount of the penalty is ten dollars ($10) or less, the penalty shall be waived and not paid by the state agency. On an exception basis, state agencies may avoid payment of penalties for failure to submit a correct claim schedule to the Controller by paying the claimant directly from the state agency's revolving fund within 45 calendar days following the agency's receipt of the notice of refund or other payment due.

(b) The Controller shall pay claimants within 15 calendar days of receipt of a correct claim schedule from the state agency. If the Controller fails to make payment within 15 calendar days of receipt of the claim schedule from a state agency, and payment is not issued within 45 calendar days following the agency's receipt of a notice of refund or undisputed payment due, the Controller shall pay applicable penalties to the claimant. Penalties shall cease to accrue on the date full payment is made, and shall be paid out of the Controller's funds. If the amount of the penalty is ten dollars ($10) or less, the penalty shall be waived and not paid by the Controller.

(c) No person shall receive an interest payment pursuant to this section if it is determined that the person has intentionally overpaid on a liability solely for the purpose of receiving a penalty payment.

(d) No penalty shall accrue during any time period for which there is no Budget Act in effect, nor on any payment or refund that is the result of a federally mandated program or that is directly dependent upon the receipt of federal funds by a state agency.

(e) This section shall not apply to any of the following:

(1) Payments, refunds, or credits for income tax purposes.

(2) Payment of claims for reimbursement for health care services or mental health services provided under the Medi-Cal program, pursuant to Chapter 7 (commencing with Section 14000) of Part 3 of Division 9 of the Welfare and Institutions Code.

(3) Any payment made pursuant to a public social service or public health program to a recipient of benefits under that program.

(4) Payments made on claims by the California Victim Compensation and Government Claims Board.

(5) Payments made by the Commission on State Mandates.

(6) Payments made by the Department of Human Resources pursuant to Section 19823. *(Added by Stats.2010, c. 719 (S.B. 856), § 20, eff. Oct. 19, 2010. Amended by Gov.Reorg.Plan No. 1 of 2011, § 33, eff. Sept. 9, 2011, operative July 1, 2012; Stats.2012, c. 665 (S.B.1308), § 31.)*

CHAPTER 5. CLAIMS PROCEDURES ESTABLISHED BY AGREEMENT

§ 930. Agreement of state agency establishing claims procedure

(a) Any state agency may include in any written agreement to which the agency is a party, provisions governing the following:

(1) The presentation, by or on behalf of any party thereto, of any or all claims that are required to be presented to the board arising out of or related to the agreement.

(2) The consideration and payment of the claims described in paragraph (1).

(b) As used in this section, "state agency" means any office, officer, department, division, bureau, board, commission or agency of the state, claims against which are paid by warrants drawn by the Controller. *(Added by Stats.1963, c. 1715, p. 3372, § 1. Amended by Stats.1965, c. 653, p. 2012, § 9; Stats.1994, c. 726 (A.B.3069), § 3, eff. Sept. 22, 1994.)*

Law Revision Commission Comments

This section is new and is based on new Section 930.2, which relates to local public entities. See the comment to that section.

This section relates only to claims which are required to be presented to the State Board of Control. Thus, the section will have no effect on contract provisions, such as those contained in contracts entered into by the Department of Public Works, which require the contractor to give prompt notice of claims for extra services. These provisions will be valid without authorization of the State Board of Control, for these provisions do not relate to "claims which are required to be presented to the board." [4 Cal.L.Rev.Comm. Reports 1001 (1963)].

The amendments to Sections 930 and 930.2 are necessary because the deleted language is superseded by Section 930.4 (added), which states in detail how the late claim procedure of Sections 911.4 to 912.2 applies to claims governed by the contractual procedures here authorized. [7 Cal.L.Rev.Comm. Reports 401 (1965)].

Research References

3 Witkin Cal. Proc. 5th Actions § 271, Procedure Established by Agreement.
3 Witkin Cal. Proc. 5th Actions § 273, (S 273) Judicial Branch Entity.
3 Witkin Cal. Proc. 5th Actions § 273A, (S 273A) (New)-California State University.

§ 930.2. Agreement of governing body of local public entity establishing claims procedure

The governing body of a local public entity may include in any written agreement to which the entity, its governing body, or any board or employee thereof in an official capacity is a party, provisions governing the presentation, by or on behalf of any party thereto, of any or all claims arising out of or related to the agreement and the consideration and payment of such claims. The written agreement may incorporate by reference claim provisions set forth in a specifically identified ordinance or resolution theretofore adopted by the governing body. *(Added by Stats.1963, c. 1715, p. 3372, § 1. Amended by Stats.1965, c. 653, p. 2012, § 10.)*

Law Revision Commission Comments

This section is the same in substance as Government Code [former] Section 705, except that Section 705 provides that the agreement may not provide a shorter time for presentation of claims than the time specified for presentation of claims under the general claims statute applicable to local public entities. [4 Cal.L.Rev.Comm. Reports 1001 (1963)].

See the Comment to Section 930. [7 Cal.L.Rev.Comm. Reports 401 (1965)].

Research References

3 Witkin Cal. Proc. 5th Actions § 236, Failure to Furnish Information.

3 Witkin Cal. Proc. 5th Actions § 269, in General.

§ 930.4. Application for leave to present claim not presented within required time

A claims procedure established by agreement made pursuant to Section 930 or Section 930.2 exclusively governs the claims to which it relates, except that if the procedure so prescribed requires a claim to be presented within a period of less than one year after the accrual of the cause of action and such claim is not presented within the required time, an application may be made to the public entity for leave to present such claim. Subdivision (b) of Section 911.4, Sections 911.6 to 912.2, inclusive, and Section 946.6 are applicable to all such claims, and the time specified in the agreement shall be deemed the "time specified in Section 911.2" within the meaning of Sections 911.6 and 946.6. *(Added by Stats.1965, c. 653, p. 2013, § 11.)*

Law Revision Commission Comments

The purpose of this new section is to spell out the limitations on contractual claims procedures and to clarify the application of the late claim procedure to such claims.

In the interest of uniformity of policy and in order to prevent the setting of an excessively short presentation time by a "small print" clause in a contract form prepared by the public entity, the 100-day period specified in Section 911.2 is declared in this section to be a minimum period for contractual claims procedures. Thus, all claimants will know that they always have at least 100 days in which to present a claim whether the claim is governed by the statutory rule of Section 911.2, by the contractual procedures specified in an agreement with a public entity as authorized under Section 930 or 930.2 or by a local ordinance or charter provision adopted pursuant to Section 935. [7 Cal.L.Rev.Comm. Reports 401 (1965)].

Research References

Rutter, Cal. Practice Guide: Civ. Pro. Before Trial Ch. 1-C, C. Prelawsuit Notices, Claims and Demands.
Miller and Starr California Real Estate § 27:49, Provisions for Arbitration and Mediation of Disputes--Public Works.
3 Witkin Cal. Proc. 5th Actions § 269, in General.
3 Witkin Cal. Proc. 5th Actions § 271, Procedure Established by Agreement.
3 Witkin Cal. Proc. 5th Actions § 273, (S 273) Judicial Branch Entity.
3 Witkin Cal. Proc. 5th Actions § 273A, (S 273A) (New)-California State University.

§ 930.6. Presentation of claim as prerequisite to suit

A claims procedure established by agreement made pursuant to Section 930 or Section 930.2 may include a requirement that a claim be presented and acted upon as a prerequisite to suit thereon. If such requirement is included, any action brought against the public entity on the claim shall be subject to the provisions of Section 945.6 and Section 946. *(Added by Stats. 1965, c. 653, p. 2013, § 12.)*

Law Revision Commission Comments

This new section makes applicable to claims governed by contractual claims procedures the same six-month statute of limitations (Section 945.6) and the same general rules limiting suit on a claim to that portion of the claim rejected by the board and not waived by the claimant (Section 946) as apply to claims governed by other claims procedures. [7 Cal.L.Rev.Comm. Reports 401 (1965)].

Research References

3 Witkin Cal. Proc. 5th Actions § 269, in General.
3 Witkin Cal. Proc. 5th Actions § 271, Procedure Established by Agreement.
3 Witkin Cal. Proc. 5th Actions § 273, (S 273) Judicial Branch Entity.
3 Witkin Cal. Proc. 5th Actions § 692, Public Entity: Where Claim is Not Required.

3 Witkin Cal. Proc. 5th Actions § 273A, (S 273A) (New)-California State University.

CHAPTER 6. CLAIMS PROCEDURES ESTABLISHED BY PUBLIC ENTITIES

Section
935.   Procedure established by charter, ordinance or regulation of local public entity; requirements.
935.2.   Claims board or commission; establishment; membership; duties; warrants.
935.4.   Delegation of authority to employee of local public entity; allowance, compromise or settlement of claims; warrants.
935.6.   Delegation of authority to state agencies to settle and pay specified claims; reports.
935.7.   Department of Transportation; denial or adjustment and payment of claims without prior approval; notice; claims procedure.
935.8.   Adjustment and payment of claims arising out of activities of judicial branch entity or judge; adoption of rules by Judicial Council.
935.9.   Adjustment and payment of claims arising out of activities of California State University; adoption of rules by Trustees.

§ 935. Procedure established by charter, ordinance or regulation of local public entity; requirements

(a) Claims against a local public entity for money or damages which are excepted by Section 905 from Chapter 1 (commencing with Section 900) and Chapter 2 (commencing with Section 910) of this part, and which are not governed by any other statutes or regulations expressly relating thereto, shall be governed by the procedure prescribed in any charter, ordinance or regulation adopted by the local public entity.

(b) The procedure so prescribed may include a requirement that a claim be presented and acted upon as a prerequisite to suit thereon. If such requirement is included, any action brought against the public entity on the claim shall be subject to the provisions of Section 945.6 and Section 946.

(c) The procedure so prescribed may not require a shorter time for presentation of any claim than the time provided in Section 911.2.

(d) The procedure so prescribed may not provide a longer time for the board to take action upon any claim than the time provided in Section 912.4.

(e) When a claim required by the procedure to be presented within a period of less than one year after the accrual of the cause of action is not presented within the required time, an application may be made to the public entity for leave to present such claim. Subdivision (b) of Section 911.4, Sections 911.6 to 912.2, inclusive, and Sections 946.4 and 946.6 are applicable to all such claims, and the time specified in the charter, ordinance or regulation shall be deemed the "time specified in Section 911.2" within the meaning of Sections 911.6 and 946.6. *(Added by Stats.1963, c. 1715, p. 3372, § 1. Amended by Stats.1965, c. 653, p. 2013, § 13.)*

Law Revision Commission Comments

Section 935 is the same as Government Code [former] Section 730, except Section 935 provides that the procedure prescribed pursuant to Section 935 may include a requirement that the claim be acted upon as a prerequisite to suit thereon. This change conforms to new Section 945.4, which bars suit until claim is rejected or deemed to be rejected.

It should be noted that where claims provisions impose a requirement of presentation or presentation and rejection prior to commencement of suit on the cause of action represented by the claim, the action cannot be commenced and the statute of limitations does not begin to run until the prescribed conditions have been satisfied. Spencer v. City of Los Angeles, 180 Cal. 103, 179 P. 163 (1919); Southern Pac. Co. v. City of Santa Cruz, 26 Cal.App. 26, 145 P. 736 (1914). See also Hochfelder v. County of Los Angeles, 126 Cal.App.2d 370, 272 P.2d 844 (1954); Walton v. County of Kern, 39 Cal.App.2d 32, 102 P.2d 531 (1940). [4 Cal.L.Rev.Comm. Reports 1001 (1963)].

The amendment to this section makes applicable to claims procedures prescribed by local charter or ordinance provisions the same basic policies recommended in regard to claims governed by contractual claims procedures. See Sections 930 and 930.02 (amended) and Sections 930.4 and 930.6 (added) and the Comments thereto. Taken together, these several sections provide with respect to all claims—whether governed by statute, by contract procedures or by local charter or ordinance provisions—that:

(1) At least 100 days must be allowed in which to present claim.

(2) The board may not be given more than 45 days after presentation to act on a claim (unless the period for consideration is extended by agreement).

(3) Where prior presentation and rejection of a claim is required as a prerequisite to commencing a suit, a uniform six-month period of limitations is applicable.

(4) Where the time for presentation of a claim is less than one year, the late claim procedures are applicable. [7 Cal.L.Rev.Comm. Reports 401 (1965)].

Research References

Rutter, Cal. Practice Guide: Civ. Pro. Before Trial Ch. 1-C, C. Prelawsuit Notices, Claims and Demands.

3 Witkin Cal. Proc. 5th Actions § 270, Excluded Claims Governed by Local Procedures.

3 Witkin Cal. Proc. 5th Actions § 689, Scope and Accrual.

3 Witkin Cal. Proc. 5th Actions § 692, Public Entity: Where Claim is Not Required.

§ 935.2. Claims board or commission; establishment; membership; duties; warrants

A charter provision, or a local public entity by ordinance or resolution, may establish a claims board or commission of not less than three members to perform such functions of the governing body of the public entity under this part as are prescribed by the local public entity. A charter provision, ordinance or resolution may provide that, upon the written order of the claims board or commission, the auditor or other fiscal officer of the local public entity shall cause a warrant to be drawn upon the treasury of the local public entity in the amount for which a claim has been allowed or compromised or settled. *(Added by Stats.1963, c. 1715, p. 3383, § 1. Amended by Stats.1965, c. 653, p. 2014, § 14.)*

Law Revision Commission Comments

Sections 935.2 and 935.4 are new. They authorize a local public entity to delegate to a claims board or to an employee such functions relating to claims as the local public entity designates. However, an employee may not be delegated authority to settle finally a claim where the amount to be paid exceeds $5,000. These sections will permit the public entity, for example, to delegate such functions as ruling on the sufficiency of claims or automatically rejecting certain classes of claims. [4 Cal.L.Rev.Comm. Reports 1001 (1963)].

As originally drafted, Section 935.2 authorized local public entities to establish claims boards to perform the functions of the governing body in passing on claims and late claims applications, and Section 935.4 authorized local public entities to delegate these functions to claims officers. In the course of consideration by the Legislature, Section 935.4 was amended to refer to "commissions," thus causing the two sections to overlap substantially.

This overlap creates an ambiguity because Section 935.4 contains an express limitation of $5,000 on the authority to delegate settlement of claims except where a higher figure is authorized by a city or county charter approved by the voters, whereas no such dollar limit is contained in Section 935.2. The amendments to Sections 935.2 and 935.4 eliminate this ambiguity. [7 Cal.L.Rev.Comm. Reports 401 (1965)].

Research References

3 Witkin Cal. Proc. 5th Actions § 269, in General.

§ 935.4. Delegation of authority to employee of local public entity; allowance, compromise or settlement of claims; warrants

A charter provision, or a local public entity by ordinance or resolution, may authorize an employee of the local public entity to perform those functions of the governing body of the public entity under this part that are prescribed by the local public entity, but only a charter provision may authorize that employee to allow, compromise, or settle a claim against the local public entity if the amount to be paid pursuant to the allowance, compromise or settlement exceeds fifty thousand dollars ($50,-000). A charter provision, ordinance, or resolution may provide that, upon the written order of that employee, the auditor or other fiscal officer of the local public entity shall cause a warrant to be issued upon the treasury of the local public entity in the amount for which a claim has been allowed, compromised, or settled. *(Added by Stats.1963, c. 1715, p. 3383, § 1. Amended by Stats.1965, c. 653, p. 2014, § 15; Stats.1981, c. 317, p. 1457, § 1; Stats.1989, c. 159, § 1.)*

Law Revision Commission Comments

Sections 935.2 and 935.4 are new. The authorize a local public entity to delegate to a claims board or to an employee such functions relating to claims as the local public entity designates. However, an employee may not be delegated authority to settle finally a claim where the amount to be paid exceeds $5,000. These sections will permit the public entity, for example, to delegate such functions as ruling on the sufficiency of claims or automatically rejecting certain classes of claims. [4 Cal.L.Rev.Comm. Reports 1001 (1963)].

See the Comment to Section 935.2 regarding the deletion of the reference to "commission" in this section. The remaining changes simply clarify the section. [7 Cal.L.Rev.Comm. Reports 401 (1965)].

Research References

3 Witkin Cal. Proc. 5th Actions § 269, in General.

§ 935.6. Delegation of authority to state agencies to settle and pay specified claims; reports

(a) The Victim Compensation and Government Claims Board may authorize any state agency to settle and pay claims filed pursuant to Section 905.2 if the settlement does not exceed one thousand dollars ($1,000) or a lesser amount as the board may determine, or to reject the claim and provide the notice required by Section 913. The board may require state agencies that it so authorizes to report annually to the board concerning the claims resolved pursuant to this section.

(b) As used in this section, "state agency" means any office, officer, department, division, bureau, board, commission, or agency of the state, claims against which are paid by warrants drawn by the Controller, but does not mean any judicial branch entity, as defined in Section 900.3, or any judge thereof. *(Added by Stats.1963, c. 1715, p. 3383, § 1. Amended by Stats.1965, c. 1004, p. 2634, § 2; Stats.1980, c. 215, § 6; Stats.1983, c. 591, § 1; Stats.1994, c. 726 (A.B.3069), § 4, eff. Sept. 22, 1994; Stats.2002, c. 1007 (A.B.2321), § 8; Stats.2007, c. 509 (A.B.1273), § 1, eff. Oct. 11, 2007.)*

Law Revision Commission Comments

This section is new. It permits the Board of Control to delegate the authority to settle certain small claims to the state agencies immediately concerned. [4 Cal.L.Rev.Comm. Reports 1001 (1963)].

Section 935.6 is amended to eliminate the exclusion for claims arising from activities of the "Department of Public Works," now the Department of Transportation. [15 Cal.L.Rev.Comm. Reports 1257 (1980)].

Government

Research References

3 Witkin Cal. Proc. 5th Actions § 272, Payment by Controller or
  Authorized State Agency.

§ 935.7. Department of Transportation; denial or adjustment and payment of claims without prior approval; notice; claims procedure

(a) Notwithstanding Section 935.6, the Department of Transportation may deny or adjust and pay any claim arising out of the activities of the department without the prior approval of the California Victim Compensation and Government Claims Board if both of the following conditions exist:

(1) The amount claimed is equal to or less than the amount specified as the small claims court jurisdictional amount in Section 116.221 of the Code of Civil Procedure.

(2) The Director of Finance or the Director of Transportation certifies that a sufficient appropriation for the payment of the claim exists.

(b) If the department elects not to pay any claim, the department shall provide the notice required by Section 913.

(c) Any person who submits any claim arising out of any activity of the Department of Transportation shall comply with every other applicable provision of this part relating to claims against state agencies. *(Added by Stats.1987, c. 350, § 1. Amended by Stats.2002, c. 1124 (A.B.3000), § 8, eff. Sept. 30, 2002; Stats.2003, c. 228 (A.B.1756), § 11, eff. Aug. 11, 2003; Stats.2012, c. 769 (A.B.2679), § 1.)*

§ 935.8. Adjustment and payment of claims arising out of activities of judicial branch entity or judge; adoption of rules by Judicial Council

The Judicial Council may adjust and pay any claim arising out of the activities of a judicial branch entity or judge thereof. The Judicial Council may adopt rules of court authorizing any committee of the Judicial Council or employee of the Administrative Office of the Courts to perform the functions of the Judicial Council under this section. *(Added by Stats.2002, c. 1007 (A.B.2321), § 9.)*

Research References

3 Witkin Cal. Proc. 5th Actions § 273, (S 273) Judicial Branch Entity.

§ 935.9. Adjustment and payment of claims arising out of activities of California State University; adoption of rules by Trustees

The Trustees of the California State University may adjust and pay any claim arising out of the activities of the California State University. The Trustees of the California State University may, by rule, authorize the Office of Risk Management at the Office of the Chancellor of the California State University to perform the functions of the Trustees of the California State University under this section. *(Added by Stats.2010, c. 636 (S.B.1046), § 7. Amended by Stats.2011, c. 296 (A.B.1023), § 112.)*

Research References

3 Witkin Cal. Proc. 5th Actions § 273A, (S 273A) (New)-California State
  University.

Part 4

ACTIONS AGAINST PUBLIC ENTITIES AND PUBLIC EMPLOYEES

CHAPTER 1. GENERAL

ARTICLE 1. DEFINITIONS

§ 940. Definitions governing construction of part

Unless the provision or context otherwise requires, the definitions contained in this article govern the construction of this part. *(Added by Stats.1963, c. 1715, c. 3384, § 2.)*

Research References

5 Witkin, California Summary 10th Torts § 217, (S 217) Statutory
  Framework.

§ 940.2. Board

"Board" means:

(a) In the case of a local public entity, the governing body of the local public entity.

(b) In the case of the state, except as provided by subdivisions (c) and (d), the Victim Compensation and Government Claims Board.

(c) In the case of a judicial branch entity or a judge thereof, the Judicial Council.

(d) In the case of the California State University, the Trustees of the California State University. *(Added by Stats.1963, c. 1715, p. 3384, § 2. Amended by Stats.2002, c. 1007 (A.B.2321), § 10; Stats.2010, c. 636 (S.B.1046), § 8.)*

Law Revision Commission Comments

"Board" has been defined to facilitate the drafting of provisions that apply both to the State and to local public entities. [4 Cal.L.Rev.Comm. Reports 1001 (1963)].

§ 940.3. Judicial branch entity

A "judicial branch entity" is a public entity and means any superior court, court of appeals, the Supreme Court, the Judicial Council, or the Administrative Office of the Courts. *(Added by Stats.2002, c. 1007 (A.B.2321), § 11.)*

Research References

Rutter, Cal. Practice Guide: Enforcing Judgments/Debts Ch. 6A-6,
  Payment of Final Judgments Against Public Entities.
8 Witkin Cal. Proc. 5th Enforcement of Judgment § 429, (S 429) Against
  State.

§ 940.4. Local public entity

"Local public entity" includes a county, city, district, public authority, public agency, and any other political subdivision or public corporation in the State, but does not include the State. *(Added by Stats.1963, c. 1715, p. 3384, § 2.)*

Law Revision Commission Comments

The definitions of "State" and "local public entity" are based on the definition of "local public entity" contained in Government Code [former] Section 700. [4 Cal.L.Rev.Comm. Reports 1001 (1963)].

§ 940.6. State

"State" means the State and any office, officer, department, division, bureau, board, commission or agency of the State claims against which are paid by warrants drawn by the Controller. *(Added by Stats.1963, c. 1715, p. 3384, § 2.)*

Law Revision Commission Comments

The definitions of "State" and "local public entity" are based on the definition of "local public entity" contained in Government Code [former] Section 700. [4 Cal.L.Rev.Comm. Reports 1001 (1963)].

ARTICLE 2. CONSTRUCTION

Section
942. Other remedies.
943. Application of part to claims or actions against regents of University of California or employees.
944. Necessity of existence of liability.

§ 942. Other remedies

Nothing in this division shall be construed to deprive a claimant of the right to resort to writ of mandate or other proceeding against the public entity or the board or any employee of the public entity to compel payment of a claim when and to the extent that it has been allowed and is required by this division to be paid. *(Added by Stats.1963, c. 1715, p. 3383, § 2. Amended by Stats.1980, c. 215, § 7.)*

Law Revision Commission Comments

This section is the same in substance as the second paragraph of Government Code [former] Section 718, which applies to claims against local public entities. In some circumstances, a claimant might be able to compel payment of a claim allowed by the State Board of Control. [4 Cal.L.Rev.Comm. Reports 1001 (1963)].

Section 942 is amended to limit the application of the section to cases where a claim is required by this division to be paid. In the case of the state, a claim is required to be paid only where the Director of Finance certifies that there is a sufficient appropriation for the payment of the claim. See, e.g., Sections 935.6, 965, 965.6. See also Section 965.8 (writ of mandate to compel Director of Finance to certify that sufficient appropriation exists). A writ of mandate is not available where no such sufficient appropriation exists. See Veterans of Foreign Wars v. State, 36 Cal.App.3d 688, 697, 111 Cal.Rptr. 750, 756 (1974) ("judgment against the State, even when authorized by law, may be paid only out of appropriated funds"). Instead, the claim is reported to the Legislature. See Sections 912.8, 965, and 965.4. A writ of mandate is an appropriate remedy to compel a local public entity to pay an allowed claim. See Sections 912.6(c) and 970.2. [15 Cal.L.Rev.Comm. Reports 1257 (1980)].

Research References

Rutter, Cal. Practice Guide: Enforcing Judgments/Debts Ch. 6A-6, Payment of Final Judgments Against Public Entities.
Rutter, Cal. Practice Guide: Enforcing Judgments/Debts Ch. 6D-2, Writ of Execution.
8 Witkin Cal. Proc. 5th Enforcement of Judgment § 429, (S 429) Against State.
8 Witkin Cal. Proc. 5th Enforcement of Judgment § 432, Enforcement Mechanisms.

§ 943. Application of part to claims or actions against regents of University of California or employees

This part does not apply to claims or actions against the Regents of the University of California nor to claims or actions against an employee or former employee of the Regents of the University of California arising out of such employment. *(Added by Stats.1963, c. 1715, p. 3383, § 2. Amended by Stats.1965, c. 653, p. 2014, § 16.)*

Law Revision Commission Comments

This part, like the previous part, does not apply to the University of California. See new Section 905.6 and the comment thereto. [4 Cal.L.Rev.Comm. Reports 1001 (1963)].

The reference to "this part" includes the procedural provisions governing actions against public employees as well as actions against public entities. As enacted, this section only declared the provisions in question inapplicable to claims or actions against the university itself, thereby leaving in doubt the applicability (or inapplicability) of the provisions to claims and actions against university employees. The amendment eliminates this ambiguity. [7 Cal.L.Rev.Comm. Reports 401 (1965)].

Research References

Rutter, Cal. Practice Guide: Personal Injury Ch. 5-A, A. Prelawsuit Filings.

§ 944. Necessity of existence of liability

Nothing in this part imposes liability upon a public entity unless such liability otherwise exists. *(Added by Stats.1963, c. 1715, p. 3383, § 2.)*

Law Revision Commission Comments

This section makes clear that this part is procedural only; some other statute must be found to impose liability. [4 Cal.L.Rev.Comm. Reports 1001 (1963)].

CHAPTER 2. ACTIONS AGAINST PUBLIC ENTITIES

Section
945. Power to sue and be sued.
945.2. Rules of practice.
945.3. Person charged with criminal offense; prohibition from bringing civil action for money or damages while charges pending; tolling of statute of limitations.
945.4. Necessity of written claim acted upon by board or deemed to have been rejected.
945.6. Limitation practices on claims required to be presented in accordance with chapters 1 and 2 of part 3; persons imprisoned in state prisons.
945.8. Limitation of actions on claims not required to be presented in accordance with chapters 1 and 2 of part 3.
946. Maintenance of suit barred after allowance of claim in full or in part and acceptance by claimant of amount allowed.
946.4. Statement of public agency not on file or inaccurate; failure to present claim not bar or defense.
946.6. Denial of application for leave to present claim; relief from provisions of section 945.4; place of filing petition.
948. Settlement, adjustment or compromise of action by head of state agency.
948.1. Adjustment or compromise of any pending action; rules of Judicial Council.
949. Compromise, or delegation of authority to compromise, action against local public entity.

§ 945. Power to sue and be sued

A public entity may sue and be sued. *(Added by Stats.1963, c. 1715, p. 3383, § 2.)*

Law Revision Commission Comments

Section 945 is new. This section will eliminate any doubt that might otherwise exist as to whether a tort action might be defeated on the technical ground that a particular local public entity is not subject to suit. The section does not, however, impose substantive liability; some other statute must be found that imposes such liability. See new Section 944. [4 Cal.L.Rev.Comm. Reports 1001 (1963)].

Research References

4 Witkin Cal. Proc. 5th Pleading § 105, as Plaintiffs.
4 Witkin Cal. Proc. 5th Pleading § 108, (S 108) Statutory Consent in California.
5 Witkin Cal. Proc. 5th Pleading § 905, (S 905) Public Entity.

§ 945.2. Rules of practice

Except as otherwise provided by law, the rules of practice in civil actions apply to actions brought against public entities. *(Added by Stats.1963, c. 1715, p. 3383, § 2.)*

Government

Law Revision Commission Comments

This section is based on Government Code [former] Section 642, which applies to actions against the State based on express contract, negligence or inverse condemnation. [4 Cal.L.Rev.Comm. Reports 1001 (1963)].

Research References

4 Witkin Cal. Proc. 5th Pleading § 108, (S 108) Statutory Consent in California.

§ 945.3. Person charged with criminal offense; prohibition from bringing civil action for money or damages while charges pending; tolling of statute of limitations

No person charged by indictment, information, complaint, or other accusatory pleading charging a criminal offense may bring a civil action for money or damages against a peace officer or the public entity employing a peace officer based upon conduct of the peace officer relating to the offense for which the accused is charged, including an act or omission in investigating or reporting the offense or arresting or detaining the accused, while the charges against the accused are pending before a superior court.

Any applicable statute of limitations for filing and prosecuting these actions shall be tolled during the period that the charges are pending before a superior court.

For the purposes of this section, charges pending before a superior court do not include appeals or criminal proceedings diverted pursuant to Chapter 2.5 (commencing with Section 1000), Chapter 2.6 (commencing with Section 1000.6), Chapter 2.7 (commencing with Section 1001), Chapter 2.8 (commencing with Section 1001.20), or Chapter 2.9 (commencing with Section 1001.50) of Title 6 of Part 2 of the Penal Code.

Nothing in this section shall prohibit the filing of a claim with the board of a public entity, and this section shall not extend the time within which a claim is required to be presented pursuant to Section 911.2. *(Added by Stats.1981, c. 285, p. 1403, § 1. Amended by Stats.1983, c. 272, § 1; Stats.1998, c. 931 (S.B.2139), § 175, eff. Sept. 28, 1998; Stats.2002, c. 784 (S.B.1316), § 121.)*

Law Revision Commission Comments

Section 945.3 is amended to reflect elimination of the justice court. Cal. Const. art. VI, §§ 1, 5(b). [28 Cal.L.Rev.Comm. Reports 51 (1998)].

Section 945.3 is amended to reflect unification of the municipal and superior courts pursuant to Article VI, Section 5(e), of the California Constitution. [32 Cal.L.Rev.Comm. Reports 177 (2002)].

Research References

Rutter, Cal. Practice Guide: Civ. Pro. Before Trial Ch. 1-C, C. Prelawsuit Notices, Claims and Demands.
Rutter, Cal. Practice Guide: Personal Injury Ch. 5-A, A. Prelawsuit Filings.
Rutter, Cal. Practice Guide: Personal Injury Ch. 5-B, B. When to Sue-Statute of Limitations.
Rutter, Cal. Practice Guide: Personal Injury Ch. 5-B, Outline B.
3 Witkin Cal. Proc. 5th Actions § 59, Federal Statute With Express Limitation.
3 Witkin Cal. Proc. 5th Actions § 257, (S 257) in General.
3 Witkin Cal. Proc. 5th Actions § 721, in General.

§ 945.4. Necessity of written claim acted upon by board or deemed to have been rejected

Except as provided in Sections 946.4 and 946.6, no suit for money or damages may be brought against a public entity on a cause of action for which a claim is required to be presented in accordance with Chapter 1 (commencing with Section 900) and Chapter 2 (commencing with Section 910) of Part 3 of this division until a written claim therefor has been presented to the public entity and has been acted upon by the board, or has been deemed to have been rejected by the board, in accordance with Chapters 1 and 2 of Part 3 of this division. *(Added by Stats.1963,*

c. 1715, p. 3383, § 2. Amended by Stats.1965, c. 653, p. 2014, § 17.)

Law Revision Commission Comments

This section prevents a claimant from bringing an action against a public entity until his claim has been acted upon or is deemed to have been rejected. The section is designed to provide the public entity with a short period of time (45 days) to consider the claim. See new Section 912.4.

Under Government Code [former] Section 641, an action may not be brought against the State until the claim is rejected or disallowed, and no time is prescribed within which the State Board of Control must act on the claim. On the other hand, under Government Code [former] Section 710, an action may be brought against a local public entity as soon as the claim is presented.

Section 945.4 applies only to claims that are required to be presented in accordance with Chapters 1 and 2 of Part 3. [4 Cal.L.Rev.Comm. Reports 1001 (1963)].

The amendment to this section directs attention to the exceptions to Section 945.4 that are stated in Sections 946.4 and 946.6 (added). See the Comments to the cited sections. [7 Cal.L.Rev.Comm. Reports 401 (1965)].

Research References

Rutter, Cal. Practice Guide: Civ. Pro. Before Trial Ch. 1-C, C. Prelawsuit Notices, Claims and Demands.
Rutter, Cal. Practice Guide: Civ. Pro. Before Trial Ch. 6-B, B. Complaints.
Rutter, Cal. Practice Guide: Civ. Pro. Before Trial Ch. 6-E, E. Amended and Supplemental Pleadings.
Rutter, Cal. Practice Guide: Enforcing Judgments/Debts Ch. 6D-2, Writ of Execution.
Rutter, Cal. Practice Guide: Personal Injury Ch. 5-A, A. Prelawsuit Filings.
Miller and Starr California Real Estate § 27:49, Provisions for Arbitration and Mediation of Disputes--Public Works.
3 Witkin Cal. Proc. 5th Actions § 238, (S 238) Other Money Claims.
3 Witkin Cal. Proc. 5th Actions § 246, (S 246) Actions Under Fair Employment and Housing Act.
3 Witkin Cal. Proc. 5th Actions § 248, (S 248) Actions on Judgment.
3 Witkin Cal. Proc. 5th Actions § 254, (S 254) Illustrations.
3 Witkin Cal. Proc. 5th Actions § 307, (S 307) Where Original Complaint is on File.
4 Witkin Cal. Proc. 5th Pleading § 620, Conformance of Complaint to Claim.
5 Witkin Cal. Proc. 5th Pleading § 1107, Public Entity and Officer Defenses.

§ 945.6. Limitation practices on claims required to be presented in accordance with chapters 1 and 2 of part 3; persons imprisoned in state prisons

(a) Except as provided in Sections 946.4 and 946.6 and subject to subdivision (b), any suit brought against a public entity on a cause of action for which a claim is required to be presented in accordance with Chapter 1 (commencing with Section 900) and Chapter 2 (commencing with Section 910) of Part 3 of this division must be commenced:

(1) If written notice is given in accordance with Section 913, not later than six months after the date such notice is personally delivered or deposited in the mail.

(2) If written notice is not given in accordance with Section 913, within two years from the accrual of the cause of action. If the period within which the public entity is required to act is extended pursuant to subdivision (b) of Section 912.4, the period of such extension is not part of the time limited for the commencement of the action under this paragraph.

(b) When a person is unable to commence a suit on a cause of action described in subdivision (a) within the time prescribed in that subdivision because he has been sentenced to imprisonment in a state prison, the time limit for the commencement of such suit is extended to six months after the date that the civil right to commence such action is restored to such person, except that the time shall not be extended if the public entity establishes that the plaintiff failed to make a reasonable effort to commence the suit, or to obtain a restoration of his civil right to do so, before the expiration of the time prescribed in subdivision (a).

(c) A person sentenced to imprisonment in a state prison may not commence a suit on a cause of action described in subdivision (a) unless he presented a claim in accordance with Chapter 1 (commencing with Section 900) and Chapter 2 (commencing with Section 910) of Part 3 of this division. *(Added by Stats.1963, c. 1715, p. 3383, § 2. Amended by Stats.1965, c. 653, p. 2015, § 19; Stats.1968, c. 134, p. 349, § 2; Stats.1970, c. 346, p. 739, § 1; Stats.1970, c. 104, p. 324, § 6, operative Jan. 1, 1971; Stats.1971, c. 438, p. 882, § 92.)*

Law Revision Commission Comments

This section requires that an action must be commenced within six months after the claim is acted upon or is deemed to be rejected. The normal statute of limitations will not apply. The section applies only to claims that are required to be presented in accordance with Chapters 1 and 2 of Part 3. See new Sections 905 to 905.6.

This section is based upon Government Code [former] Sections 643 and 644, which apply to claims against the State. Government Code [former] Section 719, which applies to actions on claims against local public entities, requires that an actions on claims within the period of time prescribed by the applicable statute of limitations. The recommended legislation prevents the commencing of an action until the claim is acted upon or is deemed to be rejected. This is designed to provide the public entity with an opportunity to consider the claim and makes it desirable to provide for a special statute of limitations that commences to run when the entity has acted on the claim. [4 Cal.L.Rev.Comm. Reports 1001 (1963)].

Although the imposition of a sentence to imprisonment in a state prison constitutes the operative fact making effective a loss of civil rights (see Penal Code § 2600), this section as enacted provided no standards for determining when failure to sue within a six-month period could be said to be "because" of the imposition of the sentence. The amendment clarifies this causal relationship by defining it in terms of whether the claimant had made a reasonable effort to commence the action (e.g., prior to sentence) or to obtain a restoration of his civil right to do so. (Penal Code Sections 2600, 2601 and 3054 authorize a prisoner to apply for a limited restoration of civil rights.)

The amendment to subdivision (a) directs attention to the exceptions to Section 945.6 that are stated in Sections 946.4 and 946.6 (added). See the Comments to the cited sections.

The last sentence has been recast as a new subdivision with appropriate rewording in the interest of clarity. Elimination of the last five words in the original sentence precludes a contention that the late claim procedures do not apply to prisoners' claims. [7 Cal.L.Rev.Comm. Reports 401 (1965)].

Subdivision (a) of Section 945.6 is amended to require that an action be commenced within six months after notice of rejection (by action or nonaction) is given pursuant to Section 913. If such notice is not given, the claimant has two years from the accrual of his cause of action in which to file suit. If the period within which the public entity is required to act is extended pursuant to subdivision (b) of Section 912.4, the period of such extension is added to the two years allowed.

The triggering date generally will be the date the notice is deposited in the mail or personally delivered to the claimant, at which time the claimant will receive a warning that he has a limited time within which to sue and a suggestion that he consult an attorney of his choice. See Government Code Section 913. No time limit is prescribed within which the public entity must give the notice, but the claimant is permitted six months from the date that the notice is given to file suit.

If notice is not given, the two-year period allows ample time within which the claimant may file a court action.

Section 945.6 does not, of course, preclude the claimant from filing an action at an earlier date after his claim is deemed to have been rejected pursuant to Sections 912.4 and 945.4.

Section 352 of the Code of Civil Procedure does not apply to actions described in Section 945.6. See Code of Civil Procedure Section 352(b). However, the other general provisions of the Code of Civil Procedure relating to the time within which actions must be commenced—Sections

350, 351, 353 to 363—are applicable. See Williams v. Los Angeles Metropolitan Transit Authority, 68 Cal.2d 599, 68 Cal.Rptr. 297, 440 P.2d 497 (1968). [9 Cal.L.Rev.Comm. Reports 175 (1969)].

Research References

Rutter, Cal. Practice Guide: Civ. Pro. Before Trial Ch. 1-C, C. Prelawsuit Notices, Claims and Demands.

Rutter, Cal. Practice Guide: Civ. Pro. Before Trial Ch. 6-E, E. Amended and Supplemental Pleadings.

Rutter, Cal. Practice Guide: Civ. Pro. Before Trial Ch. 11-A, A. Voluntary Dismissals.

Rutter, Cal. Practice Guide: Insurance Litigation Ch. 9-H, H. Defenses to Subrogation Action by Insurer.

Rutter, Cal. Practice Guide: Personal Injury Ch. 5-A, A. Prelawsuit Filings.

Rutter, Cal. Practice Guide: Personal Injury Ch. 5-B, B. When to Sue-Statute of Limitations.

Rutter, Cal. Practice Guide: Personal Injury Ch. 5-B, Outline B.

Miller and Starr California Real Estate § 27:49, Provisions for Arbitration and Mediation of Disputes--Public Works.

Miller and Starr California Real Estate § 29:45, Fraud of Building Inspector.

3 Witkin Cal. Proc. 5th Actions § 262, Manner of Presentation.

3 Witkin Cal. Proc. 5th Actions § 264, Time to Act.

3 Witkin Cal. Proc. 5th Actions § 265, Notice of Action Taken.

3 Witkin Cal. Proc. 5th Actions § 270, Excluded Claims Governed by Local Procedures.

3 Witkin Cal. Proc. 5th Actions § 271, Procedure Established by Agreement.

3 Witkin Cal. Proc. 5th Actions § 480, (S 480) One Hundred Eighty Days or Six Months.

3 Witkin Cal. Proc. 5th Actions § 482, (S 482) Two Years.

3 Witkin Cal. Proc. 5th Actions § 506, (S 506) Alternative Remedy With Longer Period.

3 Witkin Cal. Proc. 5th Actions § 586, Limitations Periods.

3 Witkin Cal. Proc. 5th Actions § 688, (S 688) In General.

3 Witkin Cal. Proc. 5th Actions § 689, Scope and Accrual.

3 Witkin Cal. Proc. 5th Actions § 690, Personal Injury Claim Not Involving Medical Malpractice.

3 Witkin Cal. Proc. 5th Actions § 703, Exceptions and Distinctions.

3 Witkin Cal. Proc. 5th Actions § 741, General Rule.

3 Witkin Cal. Proc. 5th Actions § 743, Effect of Federal Tolling Statute.

2 Witkin Cal. Proc. 5th Courts § 50, (S 50) Where Last Day is Holiday.

4 Witkin Cal. Proc. 5th Pleading § 486, (S 486) Exception: Public Entity Defendant.

6 Witkin, California Summary 10th Torts § 954, Extension of Applicable Statute of Limitations.

6 Witkin, California Summary 10th Torts § 955, Government Tort Claim is Not Notice of Intent to Sue.

§ 945.8. Limitation of actions on claims not required to be presented in accordance with chapters 1 and 2 of part 3

Except where a different statute of limitations is specifically applicable to the public entity, and except as provided in Sections 930.6 and 935, any action against a public entity upon a cause of action for which a claim is not required to be presented in accordance with Chapter 1 (commencing with Section 900) and Chapter 2 (commencing with Section 910) of Part 3 of this division must be commenced within the time prescribed by the statute of limitations that would be applicable if the action were brought against a defendant other than a public entity. *(Added by Stats.1963, c. 1715, p. 3383, § 2. Amended by Stats.1965, c. 653, p. 2015, § 20.)*

Law Revision Commission Comments

This section is based on Government Code [former] Section 719, which applies to claims against local public entities. [4 Cal.L.Rev.Comm. Reports 1001 (1963)].

This amendment conforms Section 945.8 to the proposal, incorporated in the language of new Section 930.6 (applicable to claims procedures established by agreement) and amended Section 935 (applicable to claims procedures established by local charter or ordinance), that the maximum period of limitations for commencement of an action on a rejected claim should be uniformly set at six months (except for plaintiffs without civil rights). [7 Cal.L.Rev.Comm. Reports 401 (1965)].

Research References

3 Witkin Cal. Proc. 5th Actions § 692, Public Entity: Where Claim is Not Required.

§ 946. Maintenance of suit barred after allowance of claim in full or in part and acceptance by claimant of amount allowed

Where a claim that is required to be presented to a public entity in accordance with Chapter 1 (commencing with Section 900) and Chapter 2 (commencing with Section 910) of Part 3 of this division is so presented and action thereon is taken by the board:

(a) If the claim is allowed in full and the claimant accepts the amount allowed, no suit may be maintained on any part of the cause of action to which the claim relates.

(b) If the claim is allowed in part and the claimant accepts the amount allowed, no suit may be maintained on that part of the cause of action which is represented by the allowed portion of the claim.

(c) If the claim is allowed in part, no suit may be maintained on any portion of the cause of action where, pursuant to a requirement of the board to such effect, the claimant has accepted the amount allowed in settlement of the entire claim. *(Added by Stats.1963, c. 1715, p. 3383, § 2.)*

Law Revision Commission Comments

This section is the same in substance as the first paragraph of Government Code [former] Section 718, which applies to claims against local public entities. Government Code [former] Section 645, which applies to claims against the State, contains somewhat comparable provisions. [4 Cal.L.Rev.Comm. Reports 1001 (1963)].

Research References

3 Witkin Cal. Proc. 5th Actions § 270, Excluded Claims Governed by Local Procedures.
3 Witkin Cal. Proc. 5th Actions § 271, Procedure Established by Agreement.

§ 946.4. Statement of public agency not on file or inaccurate; failure to present claim not bar or defense

(a) Where provision is made by or pursuant to law that no suit may be brought against a public agency as defined in Section 53050 unless and until a claim is presented to the agency, the failure to present a claim does not constitute a bar or defense to the maintenance of a suit against such public agency if, during the 70 days immediately following the accrual of the cause of action:

(1) No statement pertaining to the public agency is on file, or is placed on file, in the Roster of Public Agencies in the office of the Secretary of State and of the county clerk of each county in which the public agency then maintains an office, as required by Section 53051; or

(2) A statement or amended statement pertaining to the public agency is on file, or is placed on file, in the Roster of Public Agencies in the office of the Secretary of State and of the county clerk of each county in which the public agency then maintains an office, but the information contained therein is so inaccurate or incomplete that it does not substantially conform to the requirements of Section 53051.

(b) On any question of fact arising within the scope of paragraphs (1) and (2) of subdivision (a), the burden of proof is upon the public agency.

(c) This section is inapplicable where the presentation of a claim is required by a claims procedure established by agreement made pursuant to Section 930.2 unless the procedure so prescribed requires that the claim be presented to the governing body of the public agency or to a person listed in Section 53051. *(Added by Stats.1965, c. 653, p. 2015, § 21.)*

Law Revision Commission Comments

This section replaces present Section 945.5, enacted in 1963 as a part of a State Bar legislative program. Section 945.5 is unclear as to when the public agency's failure to have its statement on file in the Roster of Public Agencies is critical: when the cause of action accrued, when an effort to present a claim was undertaken, when the action was commenced or at some other time? The amendment makes it clear that the Roster requirement is satisfied if the agency is in compliance not later than 70 days after the cause of action accrues. By checking the Roster at the end of 70 days, a person can determine whether he must present a claim within the remaining 30-day or 295-day period (depending on the kind of claim asserted) available for that purpose. If the agency is not then listed, he need not file a claim. The public agency cannot thereafter file the required statement—perhaps on the last day for presentation of the claim or of an application for leave to present a late claim—and then contend that nonpresentation bars suit. Seventy days gives the public agency a reasonable time within which to comply with the Roster procedure. On the other hand, compliance within 70 days would not unduly prejudice the claimant and should be permitted to cure any earlier default on the part of the agency. The same considerations that govern the failure of a public agency to have a statement on file in the Roster of Public Agencies apply with equal force in a case where the information supplied by the agency is not in substantial compliance with the Roster requirements.

Because an agency required to comply with the Roster procedure is in a better position than a claimant to know the facts concerning its duty under the Roster procedure, subdivision (b) places the burden of proof on questions arising under subdivision (a) on the agency.

Subdivision (c) makes this section inapplicable to local claims procedures established by agreement unless the procedure requires a claim to be presented to the same persons required to be listed in the Roster. Moreover, the very purpose of the contract procedure may be to require the filing of claims with persons other than those named in the Roster of Public Agencies legislation. In these cases, a claimant normally will have prior notice as to the applicable claims procedure by reason of the agreement. [7 Cal.L.Rev.Comm. Reports 401 (1965)].

Research References

Rutter, Cal. Practice Guide: Civ. Pro. Before Trial Ch. 1-C, C. Prelawsuit Notices, Claims and Demands.
Rutter, Cal. Practice Guide: Personal Injury Ch. 5-A, A. Prelawsuit Filings.
3 Witkin Cal. Proc. 5th Actions § 236, Failure to Furnish Information.

§ 946.6. Denial of application for leave to present claim; relief from provisions of section 945.4; place of filing petition

(a) If an application for leave to present a claim is denied or deemed to be denied pursuant to Section 911.6, a petition may be made to the court for an order relieving the petitioner from Section 945.4. The proper court for filing the petition is a superior court that would be a proper court for the trial of an action on the cause of action to which the claim relates. If the petition is filed in a court which is not a proper court for the determination of the matter, the court, on motion of any party, shall transfer the proceeding to a proper court. If an action on the cause of action to which the claim relates would be a limited civil case, a proceeding pursuant to this section is a limited civil case.

(b) The petition shall show each of the following:

(1) That application was made to the board under Section 911.4 and was denied or deemed denied.

(2) The reason for failure to present the claim within the time limit specified in Section 911.2.

(3) The information required by Section 910.

The petition shall be filed within six months after the application to the board is denied or deemed to be denied pursuant to Section 911.6.

(c) The court shall relieve the petitioner from the requirements of Section 945.4 if the court finds that the application to the board under Section 911.4 was made within a reasonable time not to exceed that specified in subdivision (b) of Section 911.4 and was denied or deemed denied pursuant to Section 911.6 and that one or more of the following is applicable:

(1) The failure to present the claim was through mistake, inadvertence, surprise, or excusable neglect unless the public entity establishes that it would be prejudiced in the defense of the claim if the court relieves the petitioner from the requirements of Section 945.4.

(2) The person who sustained the alleged injury, damage or loss was a minor during all of the time specified in Section 911.2 for the presentation of the claim.

(3) The person who sustained the alleged injury, damage or loss was physically or mentally incapacitated during all of the time specified in Section 911.2 for the presentation of the claim and by reason of that disability failed to present a claim during that time.

(4) The person who sustained the alleged injury, damage or loss died before the expiration of the time specified in Section 911.2 for the presentation of the claim.

(d) A copy of the petition and a written notice of the time and place of hearing shall be served before the hearing as prescribed by subdivision (b) of Section 1005 of the Code of Civil Procedure on (1) the clerk or secretary or board of the local public entity, if the respondent is a local public entity, or (2) the Attorney General, if the respondent is the state. If the petition involves a claim arising out of alleged actions or inactions of the Department of Transportation, service of the petition and notice of the hearing shall be made on the Attorney General or the Director of Transportation. Service on the Attorney General may be accomplished at any of the Attorney General's offices in Los Angeles, Sacramento, San Diego, or San Francisco. Service on the Director of Transportation may be accomplished only at the Department of Transportation's headquarters office in Sacramento. If the petition involves a claim arising out of alleged actions or inactions of a judicial branch entity, service of the petition and notice of the hearing shall be made in accordance with the following:

(1) If the petition involves a claim arising out of alleged actions or inactions of a superior court or a judge, court executive officer, or trial court employee, as defined in Section 811.9, of the court, service shall be made on the court executive officer.

(2) If the petition involves a claim arising out of alleged actions or inactions of a court of appeals or a judge thereof, service shall be made on the Clerk/Administrator of the court of appeals.

(3) If the petition involves a claim arising out of alleged actions or inactions of the Supreme Court or a judge thereof, service shall be made on the Clerk of the Supreme Court.

(4) If the petition involves a claim arising out of alleged actions or inactions of the Judicial Council or the Administrative Office of the Courts, service shall be made on the secretariat of the Judicial Council.

(e) The court shall make an independent determination upon the petition. The determination shall be made upon the basis of the petition, any affidavits in support of or in opposition to the petition, and any additional evidence received at the hearing on the petition.

(f) If the court makes an order relieving the petitioner from Section 945.4, suit on the cause of action to which the claim relates shall be filed with the court within 30 days thereafter. *(Added by Stats.1965, c. 653, p. 2016, § 22. Amended by* *Stats.1970, c. 411, p. 822, § 2; Stats.1987, c. 1201, § 22; Stats.1987, c. 1208, § 7; Stats.1989, c. 148, § 1; Stats.1989, c. 693, § 8; Stats.2001, c. 44 (S.B.562), § 9; Stats.2002, c. 1007 (A.B.2321), § 12.)*

Law Revision Commission Comments

Section 946.6 establishes a new procedure for obtaining a judicial determination of the issue following a public entity's rejection of an application for leave to present a late claim. Under the original procedure enacted in 1963, a claimant was required to file (within 20 days after the application for leave to present a late claim was denied or deemed denied pursuant to Section 911.6) a petition in court for leave to present a late claim to the public entity. See Section 912 (repealed). As to claims against the State, venue for such a petition lay only in those counties in which the Attorney General maintains an office (Sacramento, San Francisco and Los Angeles). This time for filing was to short and the State venue provisions were inconvenient both for claimants and the State.

Another defect in the original procedure is that it required a successful petitioner to present his late claim to the entity, to be acted upon in the ordinary way. Any benefit to be gained from so proceeding appears to be outweighed by the delay involved.

Accordingly, the Commission recommends that the petition to a court, following the presentation and rejection of an application to the public entity to present a late claim, be a petition for relief from having to present any claim at all instead of one for leave to present a late claim. The State venue problem is eliminated by providing that the proper court for hearing the petition is a court of competent jurisdiction in which a suit on the cause of action to which the claim relates could be brought. The petition may be filed within six months after the application for leave to present a late claim is denied or deemed to be denied, the same period of time specified in Section 945.6 for commencing legal action on a claim that has been denied or deemed denied on the merits.

The notice required to be given, the matters required to be shown in the petition, the basis of the determination and the grounds upon which relief may be granted remain the same as under existing law.

Subdivision (f) provides a special period of limitations on actions that can be commenced only after relief from the claims presentation requirements is granted pursuant to the provisions of this section. [7 Cal.L.Rev.Comm. Reports 401 (1965)].

Section 946.6 is amended to reflect elimination of the municipal courts as a result of unification with the superior courts pursuant to Article VI, Section 5(e), of the California Constitution, and the consequent elimination of associated judicial districts. See Section 38 (judicial districts).

Section 946.6 is also amended to clarify the jurisdictional classification of a proceeding for relief from the requirements of Section 945.4 following rejection of an application for leave to present a late claim. This is declaratory of existing law. See Code Civ. Proc. 85 (limited civil cases) & Comment. See also Code Civ. Proc. 88 (unlimited civil case). [40 Cal.L.Rev.Comm. Reports 479 (2000)].

Research References

Rutter, Cal. Practice Guide: Civil Appeals & Writs Ch. 2-B, B. Appealable Judgments and Orders.

Rutter, Cal. Practice Guide: Civil Appeals & Writs Ch. 8-C, C. Standards of Appellate Review.

Rutter, Cal. Practice Guide: Civil Appeals & Writs Ch. 15-B, B. Common Law Writs.

Rutter, Cal. Practice Guide: Civ. Pro. Before Trial Ch. 1-C, C. Prelawsuit Notices, Claims and Demands.

Rutter, Cal. Practice Guide: Personal Injury Ch. 5-A, A. Prelawsuit Filings.

Rutter, Cal. Practice Guide: Prof. Responsibility Ch. 6-A, A. Sources of Duty of Competence.

3 Witkin Cal. Proc. 5th Actions § 268, (S 268) Notice of Rejection of Late Claim.

3 Witkin Cal. Proc. 5th Actions § 270, Excluded Claims Governed by Local Procedures.

3 Witkin Cal. Proc. 5th Actions § 271, Procedure Established by Agreement.

3 Witkin Cal. Proc. 5th Actions § 286, (S 286) in General.

3 Witkin Cal. Proc. 5th Actions § 289, Current Law: Mandatory Relief on Application.

3 Witkin Cal. Proc. 5th Actions § 290, Theory of Relief.

3 Witkin Cal. Proc. 5th Actions § 301, Claim by Minor.

3 Witkin Cal. Proc. 5th Actions § 303, in General.

3 Witkin Cal. Proc. 5th Actions § 304, Filing and Service of Petition.

3 Witkin Cal. Proc. 5th Actions § 305, Hearing and Determination.

3 Witkin Cal. Proc. 5th Actions § 306, (S 306) Time and Statute of Limitations.

3 Witkin Cal. Proc. 5th Actions § 307, (S 307) Where Original Complaint is on File.

3 Witkin Cal. Proc. 5th Actions § 308, (S 308) Effect of New Facts Not in Original Claim.

3 Witkin Cal. Proc. 5th Actions § 475, (S 475) Thirty Days.

3 Witkin Cal. Proc. 5th Actions § 723, Medical Malpractice.

8 Witkin Cal. Proc. 5th Extraordinary Writs § 52, Lack or Excess of Jurisdiction.

5 Witkin Cal. Proc. 5th Pleading § 1228, Substitution for Fictitious Defendants.

6 Witkin Cal. Proc. 5th Proceedings Without Trial § 391, When Statute is Not Tolled.

7 Witkin Cal. Proc. 5th Trial § 94, Special Proceedings.

§ 948. Settlement, adjustment or compromise of action by head of state agency

(a) The head of the state agency concerned, upon recommendation of the Attorney General or other attorney authorized to represent the state, may settle, adjust, or compromise any pending action where the Director of Finance certifies that a sufficient appropriation for the payment of claims exists. Claims arising out of the activities of the State Department of Transportation may be paid if either the Director of Transportation or the Director of Finance certifies that a sufficient appropriation for the payment of the claim exists.

(b) If no funds or insufficient funds for the payment exist, the head of the state agency concerned, upon recommendation of the Attorney General or other attorney authorized to represent the state, may settle, adjust or compromise any pending action with the approval of the Department of Finance.

(c) As used in this section, "state agency" means any office, officer, department, division, bureau, board, commission or agency of the state claims against which are paid by warrants drawn by the Controller, but does not mean any "judicial branch entity" as defined in Section 940.3 or any judge thereof. *(Added by Stats.1963, c. 1715, p. 3383, § 2. Amended by Stats.1965, c. 1004, p. 2634, § 3; Stats.1980, c. 215, § 8; Stats.1985, c. 778, § 1; Stats.2002, c. 1007 (A.B.2321), § 13.)*

Law Revision Commission Comments

This section specifies the conditions under which a pending action against the State may be settled or compromised. There is no comparable provision in the existing statutes. [4 Cal.L.Rev.Comm. Reports 1001 (1963)].

Section 948 is amended to delete the former exclusion for the "Department of Public Works" (now the Department of Transportation) and to add a provision in subdivision (b) for reporting the settlement, adjustment, or compromise to the Legislature so that provision for payment may be made. See also Sections 965–965.4. [15 Cal.L.Rev. Comm. Reports 1257 (1980)].

Research References

5 Witkin, California Summary 10th Torts § 233, Compromise and Settlement of Claims.

§ 948.1. Adjustment or compromise of any pending action; rules of Judicial Council

The Judicial Council may settle, adjust, or compromise any pending action arising out of the activities of a judicial branch entity or judge thereof. The Judicial Council may adopt rules of court authorizing any committee of the Judicial Council or employee of the Administrative Office of the Courts to perform the functions of the Judicial Council under this section. *(Added by Stats.2002, c. 1007 (A.B.2321), § 14.)*

§ 949. Compromise, or delegation of authority to compromise, action against local public entity

The governing body of a local public entity may compromise, or may delegate the authority to its attorney or an employee to compromise, any pending action. *(Added by Stats.1963, c. 1715, p. 3383, § 2.)*

Law Revision Commission Comments

This section is based of Government Code [former] Section 720. Section 720, however, confers the authority to compromise only by implication and does not expressly authorize such authority to be delegated. Section 949 should be compared with new Section 935.4. Under these two sections, claims settlement authority can be delegated only within prescribed limits until suit is filed. Thereafter, there is no limit on the authority to delegate claims settlement authority. [4 Cal.L.Rev.Comm. Reports 1001 (1963)].

Research References

5 Witkin, California Summary 10th Torts § 233, Compromise and Settlement of Claims.

CHAPTER 3. ACTIONS AGAINST PUBLIC EMPLOYEES

§ 950. Necessity for presentation of claim against public employee

Except as otherwise provided in this chapter, a claim need not be presented as a prerequisite to the maintenance of an action against a public employee or former public employee for injury resulting from an act or omission in the scope of his employment as a public employee. *(Added by Stats.1963, c. 1715, p. 3383, § 2.)*

Law Revision Commission Comments

Sections 950 to 950.8 cover *all* employees (officers, agents and employees) and both negligent and intentional torts.

The provisions of these sections make it unnecessary to present a claim against a public employee. The proposed sections will, however, bar an action against an employee if the action against the employing public entity is barred.

Sections 950 to 950.8 are based on [former] Section 803 of the Government Code. In 1951, the Legislature enacted Section 2003 (now Section 803 [repealed]) of the Government Code in an attempt to accomplish the result achieved under Sections 950 to 950.8. The attempt was not completely successful, however, for Section 803 [repealed] does not apply to State personnel, nor to officers (as distinguished from "employees") of other entities. Moreover, since Section 803 [repealed] applies only to actions based on "negligence," it appears that a plaintiff at times would be able to evade the public policy expressed in Section 803 [repealed] by framing his complaint on a theory other than negligence. Somewhat overlapping provisions of the Government Code (Sections 801 and 802 [repealed]) require that a claim be presented to the employee as a condition to bringing an action against him. [4 Cal.L.Rev.Comm. Reports 1001 (1963)].

Government

Research References

Rutter, Cal. Practice Guide: Personal Injury Ch. 5-B, B. When to Sue-Statute of Limitations.

3 Witkin Cal. Proc. 5th Actions § 308, (S 308) Effect of New Facts Not in Original Claim.

5 Witkin, California Summary 10th Torts § 217, (S 217) Statutory Framework.

5 Witkin, California Summary 10th Torts § 370, in General.

§ 950.2. Grounds for barring cause of action

Except as provided in Section 950.4, a cause of action against a public employee or former public employee for injury resulting from an act or omission in the scope of his employment as a public employee is barred if an action against the employing public entity for such injury is barred under Part 3 (commencing with Section 900) of this division or under Chapter 2 (commencing with Section 945) of Part 4 of this division. This section is applicable even though the public entity is immune from liability for the injury. *(Added by Stats.1963, c. 1715, p. 3383, § 2. Amended by Stats.1965, c. 653, p. 2017, § 23.)*

Law Revision Commission Comments

See the comment to Section 950. [4 Cal.L.Rev.Comm. Reports 1001 (1963)].

This amendment makes it clear that suit against a public employee or former employee is barred when a suit against the entity is barred (1) by failure to present any claim at all or (2) by presenting a claim that is insufficient, too late or for any other reason inadequate to support an action against the employing public entity. (The blanket reference to Part 3 makes the rule stated in this section applicable as well to contractual claims procedures (see Section 930 et seq.) and local ordinance or charter claims procedures (see Section 935).) Likewise, if suit against a public entity is barred by the applicable statute of limitations or by any other provision in Chapter 2 of Part 4 dealing with actions against public entities, suit against the public employee or former employee is also barred.

The addition of the last sentence to this section eliminates an existing ambiguity by providing that the presentation of a claim to the employing public entity is a prerequisite to suit against an employee notwithstanding the fact that the applicable substantive law may declare the entity to be immune from liability for the injury. Because the employing public entity is financially responsible for judgments against its employees (see Section 825), the presentation of a claim is required in all cases. [7 Cal.L.Rev. Comm. Reports 401 (1965)].

Research References

Rutter, Cal. Practice Guide: Civ. Pro. Before Trial Ch. 1-C, C. Prelawsuit Notices, Claims and Demands.

Rutter, Cal. Practice Guide: Personal Injury Ch. 5-A, A. Prelawsuit Filings.

3 Witkin Cal. Proc. 5th Actions § 251, in General.

3 Witkin Cal. Proc. 5th Actions § 251, in General.

3 Witkin Cal. Proc. 5th Actions § 251, in General.

3 Witkin Cal. Proc. 5th Actions § 252, Requirement of Claim Against Entity.

5 Witkin, California Summary 10th Torts § 240, (S 240) Sexual Misconduct by Employee.

§ 950.4. Exception to bar of cause of action

A cause of action against a public employee or former public employee is not barred by Section 950.2 if the plaintiff pleads and proves that he did no.t know or have reason to know, within the period for the presentation of a claim to the employing public entity as a condition to maintaining an action for such injury against the employing public entity, as that period is prescribed by Section 911.2 or by such other claims procedure as may be applicable, that the injury was caused by an act or omission of the public entity or by an act or omission of an employee of the public entity in the scope of his employment as a public employee. *(Added by Stats.1963, c. 1715, p. 3383, § 2. Amended by Stats.1965, c. 653, p. 2017, § 24.)*

Law Revision Commission Comments

This section makes it unnecessary to present a claim where the plaintiff does not know the injury was caused by the public entity or a public employee. There is no similar provision in existing law. [4 Cal.L.Rev. Comm. Reports 1001 (1963)].

This amendment makes it clear that "the period for the presentation of a claim" refers to the original claim presentation period only and does not include the period within which a late claim application could be submitted. [7 Cal.L.Rev.Comm. Reports 401 (1965)].

Research References

Rutter, Cal. Practice Guide: Personal Injury Ch. 5-A, A. Prelawsuit Filings.

3 Witkin Cal. Proc. 5th Actions § 252, Requirement of Claim Against Entity.

3 Witkin Cal. Proc. 5th Actions § 308, (S 308) Effect of New Facts Not in Original Claim.

§ 950.6. Necessity of written claim rejected, or deemed to have been rejected, by public entity; limitations

When a written claim for money or damages for injury has been presented to the employing public entity:

(a) A cause of action for such injury may not be maintained against the public employee or former public employee whose act or omission caused such injury until the claim has been rejected, or has been deemed to have been rejected, in whole or in part by the public entity.

(b) A suit against the public employee or former public employee for such injury must be commenced within the time prescribed by Section 945.6 for bringing an action against the public entity.

(c) When a person is unable to commence the suit within the time prescribed in subdivision (b) because he has been sentenced to imprisonment in a state prison, the time limited for the commencement of such suit is extended to six months after the date that the civil right to commence such action is restored to such person, except that the time shall not be extended if the public employee or former public employee establishes that the plaintiff failed to make a reasonable effort to commence the suit, or to obtain a restoration of his civil right to do so, before the expiration of the time prescribed in subdivision (b). *(Added by Stats.1963, c. 1715, p. 3383, § 2. Amended by Stats.1965, c. 653, p. 2017, § 25; Stats.1970, c. 104, p. 325, § 7, operative Jan. 1, 1971.)*

Law Revision Commission Comments

See the comments to Sections 945.6 and 950. See new Sections 945.4 and 945.6 for similar provisions applicable to actions against public entities. [4 Cal.L.Rev.Comm. Reports 1001 (1963)].

This amendment to Section 950.6 conforms the present section to the amended version of Section 945.6. [7 Cal.L.Rev.Comm. Reports 401 (1965)].

The amendment of subdivision (b) of Section 950.6 conforms that subdivision to subdivision (a) of Section 945.6. The effect of this amendment is indicated in the Comment to Section 945.6. [9 Cal.L.Rev. Comm. Reports 175 (1969)].

Research References

3 Witkin Cal. Proc. 5th Actions § 252, Requirement of Claim Against Entity.

3 Witkin Cal. Proc. 5th Actions § 693, Public Employee.

5 Witkin, California Summary 10th Torts § 217, (S 217) Statutory Framework.

5 Witkin, California Summary 10th Torts § 370, in General.

§ 950.8. Invalidity of provision of charter, ordinance or regulation requiring presentation of claim as prerequisite to suit against public employee

Any provision of a charter, ordinance or regulation heretofore or hereafter adopted by a local public entity which requires the presentation of a claim as a prerequisite to the maintenance of an action against a public employee to enforce his personal liability is invalid. *(Added by Stats.1963, c. 1715, p. 3383, § 2.)*

Law Revision Commission Comments

This section is new. It makes clear that local provisions cannot replace the provisions of Sections 950 to 950.6. [4 Cal.L.Rev.Comm. Reports 1001 (1963)].

Research References

3 Witkin Cal. Proc. 5th Actions § 251, in General.

§ 951. Civil actions against public officers; sufficiency of complaint

Notwithstanding Section 425.10 of the Code of Civil Procedure, any complaint for damages in any civil action brought against a publicly elected or appointed state or local officer, in his or her individual capacity, where the alleged injury is proximately caused by the officer acting under color of law, shall allege with particularity sufficient material facts to establish the individual liability of the publicly elected or appointed state or local officer and the plaintiff's right to recover therefrom. *(Added by Stats.1996, c. 562 (S.B.1368), § 1. Amended by Stats.1997, c. 17 (S.B.947), § 46.)*

Research References

Rutter, Cal. Practice Guide: Civ. Pro. Before Trial Ch. 6-B, B. Complaints.
Rutter, Cal. Practice Guide: Personal Injury Ch. 5-E, E. Selected Pleading Issues.
3 Witkin Cal. Proc. 5th Actions § 350, (S 350) in General.
3 Witkin Cal. Proc. 5th Actions § 352, (S 352) Statutory Revision.
4 Witkin Cal. Proc. 5th Pleading § 624, Tort Actions Against Public Employees.
5 Witkin, California Summary 10th Torts § 370, in General.

CHAPTER 4. SPECIAL PROVISIONS RELATING TO ACTIONS AGAINST THE STATE

§ 955. Venue; actions for taking or damaging private property for public use; other actions

The proper court for trial of actions against the State for the taking or damaging of private property for public use is a court of competent jurisdiction in the county in which the property is situate.

Except as provided in Sections 955.2 and 955.3, upon written demand of the Attorney General made on or before answering, the place of trial in other actions shall be changed to Sacramento County. *(Added by Stats.1963, c. 1715, p. 3383, § 2. Amended by Stats.1980, c. 387, § 1.)*

Law Revision Commission Comments

This section is the same in substance as Government Code [former] Section 651, except that [former] Section 651 is not qualified by a provision similar to new Section 955.2. [4 Cal.L.Rev.Comm. Reports 1001 (1963)].

Research References

Rutter, Cal. Practice Guide: Civ. Pro. Before Trial Ch. 3-D, D. Venue.
3 Witkin Cal. Proc. 5th Actions § 803, Inverse Condemnation.
3 Witkin Cal. Proc. 5th Actions § 816, Miscellaneous Local Proceedings.
3 Witkin Cal. Proc. 5th Actions § 862, Nature of Problem.
3 Witkin Cal. Proc. 5th Actions § 863, Where Attorney General Has Office.
3 Witkin Cal. Proc. 5th Actions § 865, Local Actions.
3 Witkin Cal. Proc. 5th Actions § 866, Transitory Actions.
3 Witkin Cal. Proc. 5th Actions § 867, Actions by Cities, Counties, and Local Agencies.
3 Witkin Cal. Proc. 5th Actions § 868, (S 868) Actions Against State Agency.
5 Witkin, California Summary 10th Torts § 217, (S 217) Statutory Framework.

§ 955.1. Earthquake predictions; public warning and governmental action; liability for injuries; legislative intent; basis for declaration of state of emergency or local emergency

(a) The science of earthquake prediction is developing rapidly and, although still largely in a research stage, these predictions are now being initiated and are certain to continue into the future. Administrative procedures exist within the Office of Emergency Services to advise the Governor on the validity of earthquake predictions. Numerous important actions can be taken by state and local governments and special districts to protect life and property in response to earthquake predictions and associated warnings. It is the intent of this legislation to ensure that those actions are taken in the public interest by government agencies acting in a responsible manner without fear of consequent financial liabilities.

(b) The Governor may, at his or her discretion, issue a warning as to the existence of an earthquake or volcanic prediction determined to have scientific validity. The state and its agencies and employees shall not be liable for any injury resulting from the issuance or nonissuance of a warning pursuant to this subdivision or for any acts or omissions in fact gathering, evaluation, or other activities leading up to the issuance or nonissuance of a warning.

(c) Public entities and public employees may, on the basis of a warning issued pursuant to subdivision (b), take, or fail or refuse to take, any action or execute or fail or refuse to execute any earthquake or volcanic prediction response plan with relation to the warning which is otherwise authorized by law. In taking, or failing or refusing to take, such action, neither public entities nor public employees shall be liable for any injuries caused thereby or for any injuries resulting from the preparation of, or failure or refusal to prepare, any earthquake hazard or damage prediction maps, plans for evacuation of endangered areas, and other plan elements.

(d) An earthquake or volcanic warning issued by the Governor pursuant to subdivision (b) is a sufficient basis for a declaration of a state of emergency or local emergency as defined by Section 8558. Public entities and public employees shall be immune from liability in accordance with all immunity provisions applicable during such state of emergency or local emergency. *(Added by Stats.1976, c. 1267, p. 5614, § 1, eff. Sept. 28, 1976. Amended by Stats.1979, c. 1131, § 1; Stats.1984, c. 1284, § 1; Stats.2010, c. 618 (A.B.2791), § 18; Gov.Reorg.Plan No. 2 of 2011–2012, § 82, eff. July 3, 2012, operative July 1, 2013; Stats.2013, c. 352 (A.B.1317), § 103, eff. Sept. 26, 2013, operative July 1, 2013.)*

Research References

5 Witkin, California Summary 10th Torts § 342, Earthquake and Volcanic Warnings.

§ 955.2. Venue in actions for death or injury to persons or personal property

Notwithstanding any other provision of law, where the State is named as a defendant in any action or proceeding for death or injury to person or personal property and the injury or the injury causing death occurred within this State, the proper court for the trial of the action is a court of competent jurisdiction in the county where the injury occurred or where the injury causing death occurred. The court may, on motion, change the place of the trial in the same manner and under the same circumstances as the place of trial may be changed where an action is between private parties. *(Added by Stats.1963, c. 1715, p. 3383, § 2.)*

Law Revision Commission Comments

This section is new. It requires that certain tort actions against the State be tried in the county where the injury occurred. [4 Cal.L.Rev. Comm. Reports 1001 (1963)].

Research References

Rutter, Cal. Practice Guide: Civ. Pro. Before Trial Ch. 3-D, D. Venue.
3 Witkin Cal. Proc. 5th Actions § 816, Miscellaneous Local Proceedings.
3 Witkin Cal. Proc. 5th Actions § 863, Where Attorney General Has Office.
3 Witkin Cal. Proc. 5th Actions § 866, Transitory Actions.
3 Witkin Cal. Proc. 5th Actions § 904, (S 904) Joinder of Private and Governmental Defendants.

§ 955.3. Venue; action or proceeding by local entity against state; change to Sacramento County

Notwithstanding any provision of law, when a city, county, or city and county, or local agency is a plaintiff in an action or proceeding against the State of California, the action may be tried in any city or county, or city and county, where the city, county, or city and county, or local agency is situated.

The Attorney General may, on behalf of the State of California, before answering, move to change the place of trial to Sacramento County in accordance with the provisions of Section 397 of the Code of Civil Procedure.

For the purposes of this section, "local agency" means any governmental district, board, or agency, or any other local governmental body or corporation, or elected local public official, but shall not include the State of California or any of its agencies, departments, commissions, or boards, or elected public officials in the executive branch of the state government. *(Added by Stats.1980, c. 387, § 2. Amended by Stats.1994, c. 155 (A.B.860), § 2, eff. July 11, 1994; Stats.1994, c. 156 (S.B.2127), § 2, eff. July 11, 1994.)*

Research References

Rutter, Cal. Practice Guide: Civ. Pro. Before Trial Ch. 3-D, D. Venue.
3 Witkin Cal. Proc. 5th Actions § 867, Actions by Cities, Counties, and Local Agencies.

3 Witkin Cal. Proc. 5th Actions § 904, (S 904) Joinder of Private and Governmental Defendants.

§ 955.4. Service of summons generally; defense by attorney general

Except as provided in Sections 811.9, 955.6, 955.8, and 955.9:

(a) Service of summons in all actions on claims against the state shall be made on the Attorney General.

(b) The Attorney General shall defend all actions on claims against the state. *(Added by Stats.1963, c. 1715, p. 3383, § 2. Amended by Stats.2002, c. 1007 (A.B.2321), § 15.)*

Law Revision Commission Comments

This section is the same in substance as Government Code [former] Section 649, except that [former] Section 649 requires service on both the Governor and the Attorney General. [4 Cal.L.Rev.Comm. Reports 1001 (1963)].

Research References

Rutter, Cal. Practice Guide: Civ. Pro. Before Trial Ch. 4-D, D. Service of Summons.
3 Witkin Cal. Proc. 5th Actions § 1057, Officers.

§ 955.6. Actions for taking or damaging private property; work done by department of transportation; service of summons; defense

In actions for the taking or damaging of private property for public use within the meaning of Section 19 of Article I of the Constitution on claims arising out of work done by the Department of Transportation:

(a) Service of summons shall be made on the Attorney General or the Director of Transportation.

(b) The defense shall be conducted by the attorney for the Department of Transportation. *(Added by Stats.1963, c. 1715, p. 3383, § 2. Amended by Stats.1980, c. 215, § 10.)*

Law Revision Commission Comments

This section is the same as Government Code [former] Section 648, except that [former] Section 648 permits service only on the Director of Public Works. [4 Cal.L.Rev.Comm. Reports 1001 (1963)].

Section 955.6 is amended to substitute references to the Director of Transportation and Department of Transportation. This reflects the fact that the Department of Transportation has replaced the Department of Public Works. See Sts. & Hy. Code § 20. [15 Cal.L.Rev.Comm. Reports 1257 (1980)].

Research References

Rutter, Cal. Practice Guide: Civ. Pro. Before Trial Ch. 4-D, D. Service of Summons.
3 Witkin Cal. Proc. 5th Actions § 1057, Officers.
5 Witkin, California Summary 10th Torts § 217, (S 217) Statutory Framework.

§ 955.8. Actions for taking or damaging private property; work done by department of water resources; service of summons; defense

In actions for the taking or damaging of private property for public use within the meaning of Section 14 of Article I of the Constitution on claims arising out of work done by the Department of Water Resources:

(a) Service of summons shall be made on the Attorney General or the Director of Water Resources.

(b) The defense shall be conducted by the legal counsel of the department, if authorized by the Attorney General pursuant to Section 127 of the Water Code; otherwise the defense shall be conducted by the Attorney General. *(Added by Stats.1963, c. 1715, p. 3383, § 2.)*

Law Revision Commission Comments

This section is the same in substance as Government Code [former] Section 650, except, that [former] Section 650 requires service on both the Attorney General and the Directors of Water Resources. [4 Cal.L.Rev. Comm. Reports 1001 (1963)].

Research References

Rutter, Cal. Practice Guide: Civ. Pro. Before Trial Ch. 4-D, D. Service of Summons.

3 Witkin Cal. Proc. 5th Actions § 1057, Officers.

§ 955.9. Service of summons in actions on claims against judicial branch entity

In actions on claims against a judicial branch entity, service of summons shall be made on:

(a) The court executive officer, in actions on claims against a superior court or a judge thereof.

(b) The Clerk/Administrator of the Court of Appeal, in actions on claims against a court of appeals or a judge thereof.

(c) The Clerk of the Supreme Court, in actions on claims against the Supreme Court or a judge thereof.

(d) The Secretariat of the Judicial Council, in actions on claims against the Judicial Council or the Administrative Office of the Courts. *(Added by Stats.2002, c. 1007 (A.B.2321), § 16.)*

Research References

3 Witkin Cal. Proc. 5th Actions § 1057, Officers.

§ 956. Joinder of state in certain actions involving real property in which state has remainder or undivided fractional interest; complaint; process; powers of attorney general

Whenever the State has acquired by gift, under the will of a decedent or through a decree of distribution in the estate of a decedent, or otherwise than by purchase or the exercise of the power of eminent domain, a remainder interest, whether contingent or vested, in real property, or an undivided fractional interest in real property, the holder or holders of the precedent estate or of other undivided fractional interests, as the case may be, may join the State as a party defendant in any action to partition said property, brought pursuant to the Code of Civil Procedure or in any action in declaratory relief brought pursuant to the Code of Civil Procedure. In the complaint in any such action the nature of the interest of the State shall be set forth and the manner in which the same was acquired and process in any such action shall be served upon the Attorney General and the Director of Finance. In any such action the Attorney General shall represent the State and may on behalf of the State execute such stipulations, disclaimers or consents as may be appropriate. *(Added by Stats.1963, c. 1450, p. 3005, § 2.)*

CHAPTER 5. SPECIAL PROVISIONS RELATING TO ACTIONS AGAINST LOCAL PUBLIC ENTITIES

§ 960. Public agency

As used in this chapter, "public agency" has the meaning given that term by Section 53050. *(Added by Stats.1963, c. 1805, p. 3650, § 3.)*

§ 960.2. Statement of public agency not on file or inaccurate; service of process

Notwithstanding any provision of law to the contrary, service of process in an action or proceeding against a public agency may be made in the manner provided in Section 960.3 if, during the 10 days immediately following the commencement of the action or proceeding:

(a) No statement pertaining to the public agency is on file, or is placed on file, in the Roster of Public Agencies in the office of the Secretary of State and of the county clerk of each county in which the public agency then maintains an office, as required by Section 53051; or

(b) A statement or amended statement pertaining to the public agency is on file, or is placed on file, in the Roster of Public Agencies in the office of the Secretary of State and of the county clerk of each county in which the public agency then maintains an office, but the information contained therein is so inaccurate or incomplete that it does not substantially conform to the requirements of Section 53051; or

(c) A statement or amended statement pertaining to the public agency is on file, or is placed on file, in the Roster of Public Agencies in the office of the Secretary of State and of the county clerk of each county in which the public agency then maintains an office, but neither the governing body nor any officer or agent of the public agency upon whom personal service of process constitutes service upon the public agency can thereafter, with due diligence, be personally served at the address or addresses set forth in the statement. *(Added by Stats.1965, c. 653, p. 2018, § 27.)*

Law Revision Commission Comments

This new section defines the circumstances in which substituted service on the Secretary of State is permitted and clarifies several matters dealt with in former Section 960.2.

Failure to comply with Section 53051 is defined in the new section as either the absence of a statement in the Roster of Public Agencies or the presence in the Roster of a statement that is not in substantial compliance with the requirements of Section 53051.

As enacted, Section 960.2 (repealed) authorized substituted service if the governing board could not be found at the last known "official mailing address" of the entity and if service could not be effected with due diligence. Except as reflected in subdivision (c), this basis for substituted service has been omitted in the new section. Under both the repealed and the new section, no showing of diligence was or is required if no statement is in the Roster; on the other hand, if a statement is on file, all that would appear to be necessary to establish diligence is a good faith effort to accomplish service at the addresses set forth in the statement. In any event, a court order must be obtained under new Section 960.3 as under former Section 960.2. [7 Cal.L.Rev.Comm. Reports 401 (1965)].

Research References

3 Witkin Cal. Proc. 5th Actions § 1059, (S 1059) Effect of Agency's Failure to Comply.

§ 960.3. Manner of service

(a) If it is shown by affidavit to the satisfaction of the court or judge that the circumstances required by Section 960.2 exist, the court or judge may make an order that service of process be made upon the public agency as provided in this section.

(b) Service of process shall be made by:

(1) Leaving two copies of the process for each public agency defendant to be served, together with two copies of the order

authorizing the service, in the hands of the Secretary of State or in his or her office at Sacramento; or

(2) Mailing two copies of the process for each public agency defendant to be served, together with two copies of the order authorizing the service, to the office of the Secretary of State in Sacramento by certified or registered mail, addressee only, return receipt requested. Service shall be effective as of the day the return receipt is received from the office of the Secretary of State.

(c) Service in this manner constitutes personal service upon the public agency.

(d) A fee of fifty dollars ($50) shall be paid by the plaintiff to the Secretary of State for each public agency on which service is made in this manner. *(Added by Stats.1965, c. 653, p. 2018, § 28. Amended by Stats.1990, c. 479 (S.B.2633), § 1.)*

Law Revision Commission Comments

This section is new. It is an adaptation of part of former Section 960.2 which has been recast as two separate sections in the present proposal. See new Section 960.2 and the Comment thereto. The means by which service may be made by delivery to the Secretary of State are similar to the means for substituted service provided in Vehicle Code Section 17454. [7 Cal.L.Rev.Comm. Reports 401 (1965)].

Research References

3 Witkin Cal. Proc. 5th Actions § 1058, (S 1058) Nature and Purpose.
3 Witkin Cal. Proc. 5th Actions § 1059, (S 1059) Effect of Agency's Failure to Comply.

§ 960.4. Notice to public agency; copies to attorney general

Upon receipt of the copies of process pursuant to Section 960.3, the Secretary of State shall give notice of the service of the process to the governing body of the public agency at its principal office in this state, by forwarding to such office, by registered mail with request for return receipt, a copy of the process. If the only address disclosed by the records of the Secretary of State of the principal office of the governing body of the public agency is the county in which it is situated, then the process shall be mailed to the county seat, addressed to the public agency in care of the county clerk, or it may be mailed to any address for the public agency specified in the court order. If the process is mailed in care of the county clerk, the county clerk shall promptly send it to the public agency at its address within the county, if known to him, and if unknown shall cause the process to be posted at the courthouse of the county for 30 days. If the records of the Secretary of State disclose no address for the public agency, then the Secretary of State shall mail a copy of the process to the county clerk of either (a) the county in which the transaction or occurrence took place, or (b) the county where real property of the agency is situated, and the county clerk shall promptly send the process to the public agency at its address within the county, if known to him, or if unknown shall cause the process to be posted at the courthouse of the county for 30 days.

Upon receipt of such copies of process, the Secretary of State shall immediately forward to the Attorney General a copy of all papers served upon him. The Attorney General, upon receipt of any such process, may locate the responsible officers of the public agency involved, and the governing body of such public agency may relieve the Attorney General of any further responsibility hereunder, and may designate any other attorneys to defend said action or take such other action as they may determine. *(Added by Stats.1963, c. 1805, p. 3650, § 3. Amended by Stats.1965, c. 653, p. 2019, § 29.)*

Law Revision Commission Comments

The change of reference in this section is required because of the division of former Section 960.2 into two new sections, Sections 960.2 and

960.3; only the latter need be referred to in this section. [7 Cal.L.Rev. Comm. Reports 401 (1965)].

Research References

3 Witkin Cal. Proc. 5th Actions § 1059, (S 1059) Effect of Agency's Failure to Comply.

§ 960.5. Duties of attorney general; delegation of responsibility; costs and expenses

The Attorney General, until he is relieved of further responsibility in the manner provided in Section 960.4, or until the matter has been reduced to final judgment, shall have the duty to defend such public agency by taking whatever steps he considers appropriate or necessary. The Attorney General, until he is so relieved of further responsibility, shall have full authority to bind the public agency by stipulation or admission.

The Attorney General may delegate his responsibility hereunder in any particular case, to any county counsel or district attorney willing to accept such delegation. When such responsibility has been delegated, the district attorney or county counsel, as the case may be, shall have the same power and authority with reference to the matter as is hereinabove provided for the Attorney General.

All costs and expenses, without limitation, of the Attorney General or district attorney or county counsel, pursuant to this chapter shall be a charge against the public agency in whose behalf he appears. *(Added by Stats.1963, c. 1805, p. 3650, § 3.)*

Research References

3 Witkin Cal. Proc. 5th Actions § 1059, (S 1059) Effect of Agency's Failure to Comply.

§ 960.8. Service of process in conformity with information contained in statement in roster of public agencies

Service of process in an action or proceeding against a public agency may be made in conformity with the information contained in the statement in the Roster of Public Agencies pertaining to that public agency which is on file at the time of such service. Service in this manner, if otherwise made in compliance with law, constitutes personal service upon the public agency.

As used in this section, "statement in the Roster of Public Agencies" means the statement or amended statement in the Roster of Public Agencies in the office of the Secretary of State or in the office of the county clerk of any county in which such statement or amended statement is on file. *(Added by Stats. 1965, c. 653, p. 2019, § 30.)*

Law Revision Commission Comments

The addition of Section 960.8 completes the disposition of matters covered in former Section 960.2 by providing that service of process in accord with the information contained in the Roster of Public Agencies constitutes sufficient service on the public entity. As enacted, Section 960.2 (repealed) was silent as to the effect to be given service of process in accord with the information filed in the Roster. [7 Cal.L.Rev.Comm. Reports 401 (1965)].

Research References

3 Witkin Cal. Proc. 5th Actions § 1058, (S 1058) Nature and Purpose.

CHAPTER 6. POSTJUDGMENT SETTLEMENT CONFERENCE

Section

962. Entry of verdict over $100,000 in action for personal injury or wrongful death; request in writing; review and consideration of structured payment plans; time; rules.

Government

§ 962. Entry of verdict over $100,000 in action for personal injury or wrongful death; request in writing; review and consideration of structured payment plans; time; rules

Upon entry of a verdict against a public entity in excess of one hundred thousand dollars ($100,000) in an action for personal injury or wrongful death, the public entity may, within the time set in Section 659 of the Code of Civil Procedure, request in writing a mandatory settlement conference for the purpose of discussing available methods by which the judgment shall be satisfied. The court shall then set a date for the conference. The request may be noticed with any motions pursuant to Sections 984 and 985 of the Government Code or Section 659 of the Code of Civil Procedure. At the conference the parties shall negotiate in good faith and shall review and consider structured payment plans presented by either party. The conference shall not occur until after determination of any motion for a new trial, motion for judgment notwithstanding the verdict, motion for remittitur and motion for additur, but shall occur before hearing on any motions pursuant to Sections 984 and 985.

The Judicial Council shall adopt rules providing for a reasonable extension of the time for filing the notice of appeal from a judgment on the verdict to permit a request for the mandatory settlement conference and the mandatory settlement conference itself. *(Added by Stats.1987, c. 1204, § 2.)*

Research References

Rutter, Cal. Practice Guide: Civil Appeals & Writs Ch. 3-C, C. Extensions of Filing Deadline.
Rutter, Cal. Practice Guide: Personal Injury Ch. 3-A, A. Introduction.
Rutter, Cal. Practice Guide: Personal Injury Ch. 4-E, E. Special Considerations Re "Structured Settlements".
Rutter, Cal. Practice Guide: Personal Injury Ch. 4-F, F. Court-Conducted Settlement Proceedings.
Rutter, Cal. Practice Guide: Personal Injury Ch. 9-M, M. Verdicts and Judgment.
Rutter, Cal. Practice Guide: Personal Injury Ch. 10-D, D. Government Entity Defendant Post-Trial Elections, Requests, Motions and Hearings.
Rutter, Cal. Practice Guide: Personal Injury Ch. 4-F, Outline F.
Rutter, Cal. Practice Guide: Personal Injury Ch. 10-D, Outline D.
9 Witkin Cal. Proc. 5th Appeal § 606, (S 606) Judgment Against Public Entity.
8 Witkin Cal. Proc. 5th Enforcement of Judgment § 433, (S 433) Postjudgment Settlement Conference.
8 Witkin Cal. Proc. 5th Enforcement of Judgment § 435, (S 435) Reduction of Judgment for Collateral Source Payments.
5 Witkin, California Summary 10th Torts § 234, Conference on Satisfaction of Judgment.
6 Witkin, California Summary 10th Torts § 1638, Motion, Discovery, and Settlement Conference.

Part 5

PAYMENT OF CLAIMS AND JUDGMENTS

CHAPTER 1. PAYMENT OF CLAIMS AND JUDGMENTS AGAINST THE STATE

§ 965. Designation of fund; payment of claim; report to Legislature in event of insufficient appropriation; authorization of payment by Judicial Council

(a) Upon the allowance by the California Victim Compensation and Government Claims Board of all or part of a claim for which the Director of Finance certifies that a sufficient appropriation for the payment of the claim exists, and the execution and presentation of documents the board may require that discharge the state of all liability under the claim, the board shall designate the fund from which the claim is to be paid, and the state agency concerned shall pay the claim from that fund. If there is no sufficient appropriation for the payment available, the board shall report to the Legislature in accordance with Section 912.8. Claims arising out of the activities of the State Department of Transportation may be paid if either the Director of Transportation or the Director of Finance certifies that a sufficient appropriation for the payment of the claim exists.

(b) Notwithstanding subdivision (a), if there is no sufficient appropriation for the payment of claims, settlements, or judgments against the state arising from an action in which the state is represented by the Attorney General, the Attorney General shall report the claims, settlements, and judgments to the chairperson of either the Senate Committee on Appropriations or the Assembly Committee on Appropriations, who shall cause to be introduced legislation appropriating funds for the payment of the claims, settlements, or judgments.

(c) Notwithstanding subdivision (a) or (b), claims, settlements, or judgments arising out of the activities of a judicial branch entity, as defined by Sections 900.3 and 940.3, or a judge thereof may be paid if the Judicial Council authorizes payment and the Administrative Director of the Courts certifies that sufficient funds for that payment exist from funds allocated to settlement, adjustment, and compromise of actions and claims. If sufficient funds for payment of settlements or judgments do not exist, the Administrative Director of the Courts shall report the settlements and judgments to the chairperson of either the Senate Committee on Appropriations or the Assembly Committee on Appropriations, who shall cause to be introduced legislation appropriating funds for the payment of the settlements or judgments. If sufficient funds for payment of claims do not exist, the Administrative Director of the Courts shall report the claims to the California Victim Compensation and Government Claims Board, which shall have 90 days to object to payment. The Administrative Director of the Courts shall confer with the Chairperson of the California Victim Compensation and Government Claims Board regarding any objection received during the 90-day period. If the California Victim Compensation and Government Claims Board withdraws the objection, or if no objection was received, the Administrative Director of the Courts shall report the claims to the chairperson of either the Senate Committee on Appropriations or the Assembly Committee on Appropriations, who shall cause to be introduced legislation appropriating funds for the payment of the claims. The Judicial Council may authorize any committee of the Judicial Council or any employee of the Administrative Office of the Courts to perform the functions of the Judicial Council under this section. The Administrative Director of the Courts may designate an executive staff member of the Administrative Office of the Courts to perform the functions of the Administrative Director of the Courts under this section. *(Added by Stats.1963, c. 1715, p. 3388, § 3. Amended by Stats.1965, c. 1004, p. 2634, § 4; Stats.1980, c. 212, § 1; Stats.1980, c. 215, § 11; Stats.1985, c. 778, § 2; Stats.1989, c. 1126, § 1, eff. Sept. 30, 1989; Stats.2002, c. 1007 (A.B.2321), § 17; Stats.2011, c. 11 (S.B.80), § 4, eff. March 24, 2011; Stats.2011, c. 31 (A.B.119), § 1, eff. June 29, 2011; Stats.2012, c. 19 (S.B.1504), § 2, eff. June 15, 2012.)*

Law Revision Commission Comments

This section is based on Government Code [former] Section 623 which applies to the State. Government Code [former] Section 623 is limited to payment of claims arising under Section 17000 to 17003, inclusive, of the Vehicle Code. [4 Cal.L.Rev.Comm. Reports 1001 (1963)].

Section 965 is amended to make clear that the Department of Transportation (formerly the Department of Public Works) has the duty to pay a claim allowed by the Board of Control when the requirements of the section are satisfied. See Sections 965.7 and 965.8 (compelling performance by writ of mandate). [15 Cal.L.Rev.Comm. Reports 1257 (1980)].

Research References

Rutter, Cal. Practice Guide: Enforcing Judgments/Debts Ch. 6A-7, Period During Which Judgment Enforceable; Renewal Procedures.
8 Witkin Cal. Proc. 5th Enforcement of Judgment § 41, Exceptions to Application of Provisions.
8 Witkin Cal. Proc. 5th Enforcement of Judgment § 61, (S 61) Governmental Property.
8 Witkin Cal. Proc. 5th Enforcement of Judgment § 429, (S 429) Against State.
5 Witkin, California Summary 10th Torts § 217, (S 217) Statutory Framework.
5 Witkin, California Summary 10th Torts § 370, in General.

§ 965.1. Authority delegated to executive officer to allow or reject claims

Pursuant to Section 13909, the California Victim Compensation and Government Claims Board may delegate to the executive officer the authority to allow a claim filed pursuant to subdivision (c) of Section 905.2 if the settlement amount of that claim does not exceed fifty thousand dollars ($50,000), or to reject any claim as so described. *(Added by Stats.1994, c. 726 (A.B.3069), § 5, eff. Sept. 22, 1994. Amended by Stats.2006, c. 538 (S.B.1852), § 222.)*

§ 965.2. Drawing a warrant for payment of final judgment or settlement; certification of sufficient funds

(a) The Controller shall draw a warrant for the payment of any final judgment or settlement against the state whenever the Director of Finance certifies that a sufficient appropriation for the payment of the judgment or settlement exists. Claims upon those judgments and settlements are exempt from Section 925.6. Claims arising out of the activities of the State Department of Transportation may be paid if either the Director of Transportation or the Director of Finance certifies that a sufficient appropriation for the payment of the claim exists.

(b) Notwithstanding subdivision (a), the Controller shall draw a warrant for the payment of any final judgment or settlement based on claims arising out of the activities of a judicial branch entity, as defined by Sections 900.3 and 940.3, or a judge thereof, whenever the Administrative Director of the Courts certifies that sufficient funds for that payment exist from funds allocated to settlement, adjustment, and compromise of actions and claims.

Claims upon those judgments and settlements are exempt from Section 925.6. Claims arising out of the activities of a judicial branch entity, as defined by Sections 900.3 and 940.3, or a judge thereof, may be paid if the Administrative Director of the Courts certifies that sufficient funds for the payment exist from funds allocated to settlement, adjustment, and compromise of actions and claims. The Administrative Director of the Courts may designate an executive staff member of the Administrative Office of the Courts to perform the certification of funds pursuant to this section. *(Added by Stats.1963, c. 1715, p. 3388, § 3. Amended by Stats.1965, c. 1004, p. 2634, § 5; Stats.1980, c. 676, § 100; Stats.1980, c. 212, § 2; Stats.1980, c. 215, § 12; Stats. 1985, c. 778, § 3; Stats.2002, c. 1007 (A.B.2321), § 18.)*

Law Revision Commission Comments

This section is based on Government Code [former] Sections 653 and 654. The existing statutes, however, apply only to judgments and do not include settlements. [4 Cal.L.Rev.Comm. Reports 1001 (1963)].

Section 965.2 is amended to eliminate the exclusion of the Department of Transportation (formerly the Department of Public Works) from the application of the section. A writ of mandate is an appropriate remedy to compel the Director of Finance to certify that a sufficient appropriation exists for the payment if such appropriation does in fact exist. See Sections 965.7 and 965.8. [15 Cal.L.Rev.Comm. Reports 1257 (1980)].

Research References

Rutter, Cal. Practice Guide: Enforcing Judgments/Debts Ch. 6A-6, Payment of Final Judgments Against Public Entities.
8 Witkin Cal. Proc. 5th Enforcement of Judgment § 429, (S 429) Against State.

§ 965.3. Notice of payment; reversion of funds

(a) The Attorney General shall notify the Controller in writing when all claims for which an appropriation is made to the the Department of Justice or the Attorney General pursuant to subdivision (b) of Section 965 have been paid. The Controller shall, at the close of the fiscal year in which notice of payment is received from the Attorney General, cause any undisbursed balance to revert to the fund from which the appropriation was made.

(b) Whenever an appropriation exceeds the actual amount necessary to satisfy a settlement in accordance with the settlement agreement or a judgment, the excess shall revert to the fund from which the appropriation was made. *(Added by Stats.1990, c. 1244, (S.B.1768), § 1, eff. Sept. 24, 1990.)*

§ 965.4. Report of judgments or settlements to Legislature

The Governor shall report to the Legislature, at each session, all judgments or settlements against the State not theretofore reported. *(Added by Stats.1963, c. 1715, p. 3389, § 3.)*

Law Revision Commission Comments

This section is based on Government Code [former] Section 655, which, does not, however, require that judgments based on injuries arising out of operation of motor vehicles by state employees be reported nor does the section require that settlements be reported. [4 Cal.L.Rev.Comm. Reports 1001 (1963)].

§ 965.5. Enforcement of money judgment against state or state agency; time; law governing; accrual of interest; interest rate; exclusions

(a) A judgment for the payment of money against the state or a state agency is enforceable until 10 years after the time the judgment becomes final or, if the judgment is payable in installments, until 10 years after the final installment becomes due.

(b) A judgment for the payment of money against the state or a state agency is not enforceable under Title 9 (commencing with

Government

Section 680.010) of Part 2 of the Code of Civil Procedure, but is enforceable under this chapter.

(c) Interest on the amount of a judgment or settlement for the payment of <u>moneys</u> against the state shall commence to accrue 180 days from the date of the final judgment or settlement. * * *

(d) Unless another statute provides a different interest rate, interest on a tax or fee judgment for the payment of moneys against the state shall accrue at a rate equal to the weekly average one year constant maturity United States Treasury yield at the time of the judgment plus 2 percent, but shall not exceed 7 percent per annum.

(e) Subdivisions (c) and (d) shall not apply to any claim approved by the California Victim Compensation and Government Claims Board. *(Added by Stats.1980, c. 215, § 13. Amended by Stats.1982, c. 497, p. 2192, § 94, operative July 1, 1983; Stats.2012, c. 19 (S.B.1504), § 3, eff. June 15, 2012; Stats.2013, c. 424 (A.B.748), § 2.)*

Law Revision Commission Comments

Section 965.5 is amended to correct the cross-reference. [15 Cal.L.Rev. Comm. Reports 2001 (1980)].

Research References

Rutter, Cal. Practice Guide: Enforcing Judgments/Debts Ch. 6A-2, Enforcement of Judgments Law ("Ejl")-Background.
Rutter, Cal. Practice Guide: Enforcing Judgments/Debts Ch. 6A-7, Period During Which Judgment Enforceable; Renewal Procedures.
Rutter, Cal. Practice Guide: Enforcing Judgments/Debts Ch. 6D-2, Writ of Execution.
Rutter, Cal. Practice Guide: Enforcing Judgments/Debts Ch. 6I-1, Writ of Possession or Sale.
Rutter, Cal. Practice Guide: Personal Injury Ch. 9-M, M. Verdicts and Judgment.
Miller and Starr California Real Estate § 34:35, Rate of Interest; Compound Interest.
Miller and Starr California Real Estate § 19:208, Termination of the Lease; Landlord's Recovery of Rent or Damages--Recovery in an Unlawful Detainer Proceeding.
20 NO. 3 Miller & Starr, California Real Estate Newsalert 18, Judicial Remedies.
3 Witkin Cal. Proc. 5th Actions § 675, Action on Judgment: Ten Years.
8 Witkin Cal. Proc. 5th Enforcement of Judgment § 41, Exceptions to Application of Provisions.
8 Witkin Cal. Proc. 5th Enforcement of Judgment § 61, (S 61) Governmental Property.
8 Witkin Cal. Proc. 5th Enforcement of Judgment § 429, (S 429) Against State.
8 Witkin Cal. Proc. 5th Extraordinary Writs § 114, Enforcing or Vacating Judgment.

§ 965.6. No payment or offset of claim, settlement of judgment against state, judicial branch entity, or officers or employees; exception; conditions

Notwithstanding any other provision of law, neither the state nor a judicial branch entity, nor any officers or employees thereof, may be required by any court in any proceeding to pay or offset a tort liability claim, settlement, or judgment for which the state or judicial branch entity is liable, unless one of the following conditions exists:

(a) The Legislature has authorized the payment or offset of the specific tort liability claim, settlement, or judgment.

(b) The Director of Finance, or the Director of Transportation for claims arising out of the activities of the Department of Transportation, has certified that a sufficient appropriation for the payment of the claim, settlement, or judgment or to provide for that offset exists. This subdivision does not apply to claims arising out of the activities of a judicial branch entity or a judge thereof.

(c) In the case of claims arising out of the activities of a judicial branch entity, as defined in Sections 900.3 and 940.3, or a judge thereof, the Administrative Director of the Courts has certified that sufficient funds for payment of the claim, settlement, or judgment, or to provide for that offset, exist from funds allocated to settlement, adjustment, and compromise of pending actions and claims. The Administrative Director of the Courts may designate an executive staff member of the Administrative Office of the Courts to perform the certification of funds pursuant to this section. *(Added by Stats.1980, c. 215, § 14. Amended by Stats.1985, c. 778, § 4; Stats.2002, c. 1007 (A.B. 2321), § 19.)*

Law Revision Commission Comments

Section 965.6 continues the substance of the first sentence of former Section 955.5. [15 Cal.L.Rev.Comm. Reports 1257 (1980)].

Research References

Rutter, Cal. Practice Guide: Enforcing Judgments/Debts Ch. 6A-6, Payment of Final Judgments Against Public Entities.
8 Witkin Cal. Proc. 5th Enforcement of Judgment § 429, (S 429) Against State.
8 Witkin Cal. Proc. 5th Extraordinary Writs § 114, Enforcing or Vacating Judgment.
5 Witkin, California Summary 10th Torts § 378, (S 378) Payment of Punitive Damages.

§ 965.65. Prevention of future claims; application of section; reports

(a) If a request is made for certification of availability of funds, approval of a settlement, or inclusion of a claim in a claims bill pursuant to Section 948, 965, or 965.2 for a claim in excess of thirty-five thousand dollars ($35,000) against the state which arose from the activities of any state agency or employee, the agency shall report to the Director of Finance concerning any action it has taken or proposes to take to prevent the future occurrence of circumstances similar to those upon which the claim was based, including any imposition of disciplinary action.

(b) This section does not apply to a judicial branch entity, as defined in Sections 900.3 and 940.3, or claims arising out of the activities of a judicial branch entity or a judge or employee thereof. However, in the case of the categories of claims and settlements described in subdivision (a) arising out of activities of a judicial branch entity or a judge, court executive officer, or employee thereof, the Administrative Director of the Courts shall report to the Judicial Council concerning any action the Administrative Office of the Courts has taken or proposes to take to prevent the future occurrence of circumstances similar to those upon which the claim was based, including any imposition of disciplinary action. *(Added by Stats.1990, c. 1244 (S.B.1768), § 3, eff. Sept. 24, 1990. Amended by Stats.1992, c. 1296 (S.B.986), § 10, eff. Sept. 30, 1992; Stats.2002, c. 1007 (A.B. 2321), § 20.)*

§ 965.7. Compelling state, officer or employee to act; writ of mandate; legislative discretion

(a) A writ of mandate is an appropriate remedy to compel the state, or an officer or employee of the state, to perform any act required by this chapter.

(b) Nothing in this division affects the discretion of the Legislature in determining whether or not to:

(1) Make an appropriation for the payment of a claim, compromise, settlement, or judgment or to provide an offset for a claim, compromise, settlement, or judgment.

(2) Authorize such a payment or offset. *(Added by Stats.1980, c. 215, § 15.)*

Law Revision Commission Comments

Section 965.7 is a new provision that makes clear that the state, or an officer or employee, can be compelled to pay an approved claim, settlement, compromise, or judgment when required by this chapter or to perform other duties under this chapter. Payment can be compelled only where there is a sufficient appropriation for the payment of the claim, settlement, compromise, or judgment. See Section 965.8. The traditional forms of enforcement of a money judgment (execution and other remedies under the Code of Civil Procedure) are not available to enforce a judgment against the state or a state agency. See Section 965.5(b). See also Sections 942 (writ of mandate to compel payment of allowed claim when payment is required to be made), 965.6 (necessity of authorization of payment of tort claims), 965.8 (writ of mandate to compel Director of Finance to certify that sufficient appropriate exists for payment). But see Section 965.9 (Regents of the University of California).

Subdivision (b) is included to make clear that a writ of mandate may not be used to compel the Legislature to make an appropriation or to authorize a payment or offset. This codifies existing law. See Myers v. English, 9 Cal. 341 (1858); Veterans of Foreign Wars v. State, 36 Cal.App.3d 688, 111 Cal.Rptr. 750 (1974); California State Employees' Ass'n v. State, 32 Cal.App.3d 103, 108 Cal.Rptr. 60 (1973). [15 Cal.L.Rev.Comm. Reports 1257 (1980)].

Research References

Rutter, Cal. Practice Guide: Enforcing Judgments/Debts Ch. 6A-6, Payment of Final Judgments Against Public Entities.
Rutter, Cal. Practice Guide: Enforcing Judgments/Debts Ch. 6D-2, Writ of Execution.
8 Witkin Cal. Proc. 5th Enforcement of Judgment § 429, (S 429) Against State.
8 Witkin Cal. Proc. 5th Extraordinary Writs § 114, Enforcing or Vacating Judgment.

§ 965.8. Certification of existence of sufficient appropriation for payment or offset; writ of mandate

Where any provision of this division requires a certificate of the Director of Finance or the Director of Transportation that a sufficient appropriation exists for the payment of a claim, settlement, compromise, or judgment or requires a certificate of the Director of Finance or the Director of Transportation that a sufficient appropriation exists to provide for an offset, a writ of mandate is an appropriate remedy to compel the Director of Finance or the Director of Transportation to so certify if a sufficient appropriation in fact exists for that purpose. *(Added by Stats.1980, c. 215, § 16. Amended by Stats.1985, c. 778, § 5.)*

Law Revision Commission Comments

Section 965.8 is a new provision that makes clear that a writ of mandate is an appropriate remedy if the Director of Finance wrongfully fails or refuses to certify that a sufficient appropriation exists when one does in fact exist. [15 Cal.L.Rev.Comm. Reports 1257 (1980)].

Research References

Rutter, Cal. Practice Guide: Enforcing Judgments/Debts Ch. 6A-6, Payment of Final Judgments Against Public Entities.
Rutter, Cal. Practice Guide: Enforcing Judgments/Debts Ch. 6D-2, Writ of Execution.
8 Witkin Cal. Proc. 5th Enforcement of Judgment § 429, (S 429) Against State.

§ 965.9. Regents of University of California; inapplicability of chapter to claims, settlements and judgments

This chapter does not apply to claims, settlements, and judgments against the Regents of the University of California. *(Added by Stats.1980, c. 215, § 17.)*

Law Revision Commission Comments

Section 965.9 makes clear that this chapter does not apply to claims, settlements, and judgments against the University of California. The section is consistent with Sections 905.6 and 943. [15 Cal.L.Rev.Comm. Reports 1257 (1980)].

Research References

Rutter, Cal. Practice Guide: Enforcing Judgments/Debts Ch. 6A-2, Enforcement of Judgments Law ("Ejl")-Background.
Rutter, Cal. Practice Guide: Enforcing Judgments/Debts Ch. 6A-6, Payment of Final Judgments Against Public Entities.
Rutter, Cal. Practice Guide: Enforcing Judgments/Debts Ch. 6A-7, Period During Which Judgment Enforceable; Renewal Procedures.
Rutter, Cal. Practice Guide: Enforcing Judgments/Debts Ch. 6I-1, Writ of Possession or Sale.
8 Witkin Cal. Proc. 5th Enforcement of Judgment § 429, (S 429) Against State.

CHAPTER 2. PAYMENT OF JUDGMENTS AGAINST LOCAL PUBLIC ENTITIES

Law Revision Commission Comments

The heading for Chapter 2 is amended to delete "Tort" in recognition of the fact that Article 2 of the chapter applies to any judgment and Article 1 has been amended to include inverse condemnation judgments. [12 Cal.L.Rev.Comm. Reports 575 (1974)].

ARTICLE 1. GENERAL

Section
970. Definitions.
970.1. Enforcement of judgments; time; law governing; interest rate.
970.2. Manner of payment; compelling performance of acts by writ of mandate.
970.4. Funds available for payment of judgments with interest.
970.5. Payment of judgment with interest in year of judgment's finality or ensuing year.
970.6. Installment payments; conditions.
970.8. Budget provision for funds to pay judgments; appropriation of funds.
971. Application of limitations on taxes, assessments, or rates; court mandated costs.
971.2. Legal investments.

§ 970. Definitions

As used in this article:

(a) "Fiscal year" means a year beginning on July 1 and ending on June 30 unless the local public entity has adopted a different fiscal year as authorized by law, in which case "fiscal year" means the fiscal year adopted by such local public entity.

(b) "Judgment" means a final judgment for the payment of money rendered against a local public entity.

(c) "Local public entity" includes a county, city, district, public authority, public agency, and any other political subdivision or public corporation in the state, but does not include the Regents of the University of California and does not include the state or any office, officer, department, division, bureau, board, commission or agency of the state claims against which are paid by warrants drawn by the Controller. *(Added by Stats.1963, c. 1715, p. 3388, § 3. Amended by Stats.1975, c. 285, p. 705, § 2; Stats.1980, c. 215, § 18.)*

Law Revision Commission Comments

Section 970 is amended to substitute a definition of "judgment" for the former definition of "tort judgment." The effect of this substitution is to make clear that Article 1 (commencing with Section 970) applies to inverse condemnation judgments. See Recommendation Relating to Payment of Judgments Against Local Public Entities, 12 Cal.L.Revision Comm'n Reports 575 (1974). Cf. Govt.Code §§ 990, 11007.4 (authorizing public entities to obtain insurance against "any tort or inverse condemnation liability").

The definition of "judgment" provided by subdivision (b) applies only to this article. The term "judgment" used in Article 2 (commencing with Section 975) refers to judgments generally without limitation. [12 Cal.L.Rev.Comm. Reports 575 (1974)].

Section 970 is amended to expand the definition of "judgment" to include all money judgments. This change makes this article a comprehensive statute that applies to money judgments generally without limitation. See *Recommendation Relating to Enforcement of Claims and Judgments Against Public Entities,* 15 Cal.L. Revision Comm'n Reports 1257 (1980).

The expansion of the scope of this article permits the repeal of a number of special statutes applying to particular types of local public entities: Educ. Code §§ 35201 (duty of school district to pay "any judgment for debts, liabilities, or damages"), 72501 (duty of community college district to pay "any judgment for debts, liabilities, or damages"); Gov't Code §§ 50170–50175 (duty of city or county to pay any "final judgment"); Water Code §§ 31091–31096 (duty of county water district to pay any "final judgment"). [15 Cal.L.Rev.Comm. Reports 1257 (1980)].

Research References

Rutter, Cal. Practice Guide: Enforcing Judgments/Debts Ch. 6A-2, Enforcement of Judgments Law ("Ejl")-Background.
Rutter, Cal. Practice Guide: Enforcing Judgments/Debts Ch. 6A-6, Payment of Final Judgments Against Public Entities.
Rutter, Cal. Practice Guide: Enforcing Judgments/Debts Ch. 6A-7, Period During Which Judgment Enforceable; Renewal Procedures.
Rutter, Cal. Practice Guide: Enforcing Judgments/Debts Ch. 6I-1, Writ of Possession or Sale.
8 Witkin Cal. Proc. 5th Enforcement of Judgment § 41, Exceptions to Application of Provisions.
8 Witkin Cal. Proc. 5th Enforcement of Judgment § 61, (S 61) Governmental Property.
8 Witkin Cal. Proc. 5th Enforcement of Judgment § 430, in General.
8 Witkin Cal. Proc. 5th Enforcement of Judgment § 431, Payment Obligation.
8 Witkin Cal. Proc. 5th Enforcement of Judgment § 432, Enforcement Mechanisms.
3 Witkin, California Summary 10th Agency and Employment § 263, (S 263) Other Terminations.
8 Witkin, California Summary 10th Constitutional Law § 1168, Costs and Attorneys' Fees.

§ 970.1. Enforcement of judgments; time; law governing; interest rate

(a) A judgment is enforceable until 10 years after the time the judgment becomes final or, if the judgment is payable in installments, until 10 years after the final installment becomes due.

(b) A judgment, whether or not final, is not enforceable under Title 9 (commencing with Section 680.010) of Part 2 of the Code of Civil Procedure but is enforceable under this article after it becomes final.

(c) Unless another statute provides a different interest rate, interest on a tax or fee judgment against a local public entity shall accrue at a rate equal to the weekly average one year constant maturity United States Treasury yield at the time of the judgment plus 2 percent, but shall not exceed 7 percent per annum. *(Added by Stats.1980, c. 215, § 19. Amended by Stats.1982, c. 497, p. 2192, § 95, operative July 1, 1983; Stats.2013, c. 424 (A.B.748), § 3.)*

Law Revision Commission Comments

Section 970.1 is a new provision that prescribes the time within which a money judgment against a local public entity is enforceable and the method of enforcement. See also Section 970(b) (defining "judgment").

Subdivision (a) is drawn from former Government Code Section 50175 and former Water Code Section 31096 and from Code of Civil Procedure Section 681. The 10-year period is drawn from Code of Civil Procedure Section 681. Subdivision (a)—not Code of Civil Procedure Sections 681 and 685—prescribes the period of enforceability of a money judgment against a local public entity. Where the judgment is payable in installments, the 10-year period does not run until the last installment

becomes due. Thus, if a court order is obtained under Section 970.6 permitting the payment of the judgment in installments, the 10-year period commences to run when the last installment payment becomes due.

Subdivision (b) changes prior law to provide that execution and other remedies under the Code of Civil Procedure for enforcement of money judgments do not apply to enforcement of a money judgment against a local public entity. Such a judgment is payable under this article, and a writ of mandate is an appropriate remedy to compel payment. See Section 970.2. Under prior law, property of a local public entity was not subject to execution under the Code of Civil Procedure if the property was used or held for use for a public purpose. On the other hand, property held by a local public entity merely as a proprietor, devoted to no use of a public character, such as land acquired or held for other than public purposes and not held in trust for public use, was subject to execution unless some statutory or constitutional provision forbade it. See Marin Water & Power Co. v. Town of Sausalito, 49 Cal.App. 78, 83, 193 P. 294, 296 (1920) (opinion of Supreme Court denying hearing and stating the governing rules). See also C.J. Kubach Co. v. City of Long Beach, 8 Cal.App.2d 567, 48 P.2d 181 (1935) (no execution against property of city held for public purposes; United Taxpayers Co. v. City & County of San Francisco, 202 Cal. 264, 259 P. 1101 (1927) (property of local public entity retains its public character notwithstanding temporary disuse). [15 Cal.L.Rev.Comm. Reports 1257 (1980)].

Section 970.1 is amended to correct the cross-reference and to make technical revisions. [15 Cal.L.Rev.Comm. Reports 2001 (1980)].

Research References

Rutter, Cal. Practice Guide: Civil Trials & Evidence Ch. 17-F, F. Prejudgment Interest.
Rutter, Cal. Practice Guide: Enforcing Judgments/Debts Ch. 6A-2, Enforcement of Judgments Law ("Ejl")-Background.
Rutter, Cal. Practice Guide: Enforcing Judgments/Debts Ch. 6A-7, Period During Which Judgment Enforceable; Renewal Procedures.
Rutter, Cal. Practice Guide: Enforcing Judgments/Debts Ch. 6D-2, Writ of Execution.
Rutter, Cal. Practice Guide: Enforcing Judgments/Debts Ch. 6I-1, Writ of Possession or Sale.
3 Witkin Cal. Proc. 5th Actions § 675, Action on Judgment: Ten Years.
8 Witkin Cal. Proc. 5th Enforcement of Judgment § 41, Exceptions to Application of Provisions.
8 Witkin Cal. Proc. 5th Enforcement of Judgment § 42, in General.
8 Witkin Cal. Proc. 5th Enforcement of Judgment § 61, (S 61) Governmental Property.
8 Witkin Cal. Proc. 5th Enforcement of Judgment § 430, in General.
8 Witkin Cal. Proc. 5th Enforcement of Judgment § 432, Enforcement Mechanisms.
8 Witkin Cal. Proc. 5th Extraordinary Writs § 114, Enforcing or Vacating Judgment.
7 Witkin Cal. Proc. 5th Judgment § 328, Rate Applicable to Local Public Entities.

§ 970.2. Manner of payment; compelling performance of acts by writ of mandate

A local public entity shall pay any judgment in the manner provided in this article. A writ of mandate is an appropriate remedy to compel a local public entity to perform any act required by this article. *(Added by Stats.1963, c. 1715, p. 3388, § 3. Amended by Stats.1975, c. 285, p. 705, § 3.)*

Law Revision Commission Comments

This section imposes a duty upon local public entities to pay tort judgments in the manner provided in this article and gives the judgment creditor the right to obtain a writ of mandate to enforce this duty. Depending upon the financial condition of the public entity, it can comply with the duty to pay a tort judgment by: (1) paying the judgment in the fiscal year in which it becomes final; (2) paying the judgment in the next fiscal year; (3) paying the judgment in not more than 10 annual instalments; or (4) paying the judgment with the proceeds of a bond issue as authorized by Article 2 (commencing with Section 975) of this chapter. [4 Cal.L.Rev.Comm. Reports 1001 (1963)].

See Comment to Section 970. [12 Cal.L.Rev.Comm. Reports 575 (1974)].

Research References

Rutter, Cal. Practice Guide: Enforcing Judgments/Debts Ch. 6A-5, Amount Recoverable Under Judgment.

Rutter, Cal. Practice Guide: Enforcing Judgments/Debts Ch. 6A-6, Payment of Final Judgments Against Public Entities.

Rutter, Cal. Practice Guide: Enforcing Judgments/Debts Ch. 6D-2, Writ of Execution.

8 Witkin Cal. Proc. 5th Enforcement of Judgment § 431, Payment Obligation.

8 Witkin Cal. Proc. 5th Enforcement of Judgment § 432, Enforcement Mechanisms.

8 Witkin Cal. Proc. 5th Extraordinary Writs § 114, Enforcing or Vacating Judgment.

§ 970.4. Funds available for payment of judgments with interest

Except as provided in Section 970.6, the governing body of a local public entity shall pay, to the extent funds are available in the fiscal year in which it becomes final, any judgment, with interest thereon, out of any funds to the credit of the local public entity that are:

(a) Unappropriated for any other purpose unless the use of such funds is restricted by law or contract to other purposes; or

(b) Appropriated for the current fiscal year for the payment of judgments and not previously encumbered. *(Added by Stats.1963, c. 1715, p. 3388, § 3. Amended by Stats.1975, c. 285, p. 705, § 4; Stats.1980, c. 215, § 20.)*

Law Revision Commission Comments

Sections 970.4 and 970.6 provide the procedure by which local public entities must pay tort judgments. The judgment must be paid to the extent funds are available in the fiscal year in which it becomes final. If the judgment cannot be paid in full in such fiscal year, the public entity must pay the balance of the judgment in the ensuing fiscal year unless this would result in undue hardship to the entity. In case of undue hardship, the public entity is authorized to spread the payment of the balance of the judgment over a period not to exceed 10 years. The procedure provided by Sections 970.4 and 970.6 is based on Government Code Sections 50170–50175 (cities and counties), Water Code Sections 31091–31096 (county water districts), and Education Code Section 904 [repealed] (school districts). [4 Cal.L.Rev.Comm. Reports 1001 (1963)].

See Comment to Section 970. [12 Cal.L.Rev.Comm. Reports 575 (1974)].

Section 970.4 is amended to add a reference to Section 970.6 (payment of judgment in installments). This addition makes clear that installment payments may be authorized under Section 970.6 as an alternative to paying the entire judgment in the fiscal year in which the judgment becomes final. A writ of mandate is an appropriate remedy to enforce the duty imposed by this section. See Section 970.2. [15 Cal.L.Rev. Comm. Reports 1257 (1980)].

Research References

Rutter, Cal. Practice Guide: Enforcing Judgments/Debts Ch. 6A-6, Payment of Final Judgments Against Public Entities.

8 Witkin Cal. Proc. 5th Enforcement of Judgment § 431, Payment Obligation.

§ 970.5. Payment of judgment with interest in year of judgment's finality or ensuing year

Except as provided in Section 970.6, if a local public entity does not pay a judgment, with interest thereon, during the fiscal year in which it becomes final, the governing body shall pay the judgment, with interest thereon, during the ensuing fiscal year immediately upon the obtaining of sufficient funds for that purpose. *(Added by Stats.1980, c. 215, § 21.)*

Law Revision Commission Comments

Section 970.5 continues a provision formerly found in Section 970.6. A writ of mandate is an appropriate remedy to enforce the duty imposed by this section. See Section 970.2. See also Section 970.8 (duty to include in budget a provision for payment). [15 Cal.L.Rev.Comm. Reports 1257 (1980)].

Research References

Rutter, Cal. Practice Guide: Enforcing Judgments/Debts Ch. 6A-6, Payment of Final Judgments Against Public Entities.

8 Witkin Cal. Proc. 5th Enforcement of Judgment § 61, (S 61) Governmental Property.

8 Witkin Cal. Proc. 5th Enforcement of Judgment § 431, Payment Obligation.

§ 970.6. Installment payments; conditions

(a) The court which enters the judgment shall order that the governing body pay the judgment, with interest thereon, in not exceeding 10 equal annual installments if both of the following conditions are satisfied:

(1) The governing body of the local public entity has adopted an ordinance or resolution finding that an unreasonable hardship will result unless the judgment is paid in installments.

(2) The court, after hearing, has found that payment of the judgment in installments as ordered by the court is necessary to avoid an unreasonable hardship.

(b) Each installment payment shall be of an equal amount, consisting of a portion of the principal of the judgment and the unpaid interest on the judgment to the date of the payment. The local public entity, in its discretion, may prepay any one or more installments or any part of an installment. *(Added by Stats.1963, c. 1715, p. 3388, § 3. Amended by Stats.1975, c. 285, p. 705, § 5; Stats.1980, c. 215, § 22.)*

Law Revision Commission Comments

Sections 970.4 and 970.6 provide the procedure by which local public entities must pay tort judgments. The judgment must be paid to the extent funds are available in the fiscal year in which it becomes final. the judgment cannot be paid in full in such fiscal year, the public ent must pay the balance of the judgment in the ensuing fiscal year unless would result in undue hardship to the entity. In case of undue hardsh the public entity is authorized to spread the payment of the balance of judgment over a period not to exceed 10 years. The procedure provi by Sections 970.4 and 970.6 is based on Government Code Sect 50170–50175 (cities and counties), Water Code Sections 31091–3 (county water districts) and Education Code Section 904 [repealed. now, § 1013] (school districts). [4 Cal.L.Rev.Comm. Reports (1963)].

See Comment to Section 970. [12 Cal.L.Rev.Comm. Report (1974)].

Subdivision (b) of Section 970.6 is amended to require th installment payments be equal in amount. Accordingly, the amo the principal paid in each installment will increase with each p since the amount of accrued interest required to be included payment will decrease as the amount of the unpaid principal judgment decreases. Formerly this section required payment of amount of the principal of the judgment each year, together accrued interest. This requirement tended to defeat the purpo section since the installment payments required during the first of the 10-year period were substantially greater in amount payments required in the last few years. A writ of mand appropriate remedy to enforce the duty imposed by an order section. See Section 970.2. Former subdivision (a) is co Section 970.5. Former subdivision (d) has been omitted as unr view of the repeal of the other provisions of former law which local public entities to pay judgments in installments. See C Section 970.

In determining whether to order installment payments section, the court should consider all potential sources from are available. For example, insurance may cover some or all entity liability or the payment of the judgment in whole or ir passed on to the United States or some other entity ur contract, or other arrangement. Section 970.6 is not inter an insurance company or other source to minimize its oblig payment by permitting payment in installments. [15 Cal. Reports 1257 (1980)].

Research References

Rutter, Cal. Practice Guide: Enforcing Judgments/Debts Ch. 6A-6, Payment of Final Judgments Against Public Entities.

Rutter, Cal. Practice Guide: Personal Injury Ch. 10-D, D. Government Entity Defendant Post-Trial Elections, Requests, Motions and Hearings.

8 Witkin Cal. Proc. 5th Enforcement of Judgment § 430, in General.

8 Witkin Cal. Proc. 5th Enforcement of Judgment § 431, Payment Obligation.

8 Witkin Cal. Proc. 5th Enforcement of Judgment § 434, (S 434) Periodic Payments.

5 Witkin, California Summary 10th Torts § 235, Periodic Payment of Judgment.

8 Witkin, California Summary 10th Constitutional Law § 1254, Payment and Final Order.

§ 970.8. Budget provision for funds to pay judgments; appropriation of funds

(a) Each local public entity shall in each fiscal year include in its budget a provision to provide funds in an amount sufficient to pay all judgments in accordance with this article.

(b) If all or any portion of the revenue used for the maintenance and operation of a local public entity (other than an entity created by an agreement described in Section 895) liable for a judgment is derived from appropriations of another local public entity, such other local public entity shall in each fiscal year appropriate funds equal to its pro rata share of an amount sufficient to permit the local public entity liable for the judgment to pay the judgment in accordance with this article. Such amount shall be paid to the local public entity liable for the judgment and shall be used by such entity to satisfy the judgment. The pro rata share of such other local public entity [for] each judgment is an amount bearing the same proportion to [the t]otal amount of the judgment as the revenue derived from [such] other local public entity for maintenance and operation [during] the fiscal year in which the cause of action on such [judgme]nt accrued bears to the total revenues used for mainte-[nance a]nd operation during such fiscal year of the local public [entity lia]ble for the judgment. For this purpose, such other local [public en]tity shall include in its budget a provision to provide [funds suf]ficient in amount to make the appropriation and [payment re]quired by this section. (Added by Stats.1963, c. 1715, [§] 3. Amended by Stats.1975, c. 285, p. 706, § 6; [c.] 215, § 23.)

Law Revision Commission Comments

[...] of this section is necessary to ensure that local public [entity takes] appropriate action to raise funds to pay tort judgments. [... is] needed to ensure payment of a tort judgment against a [local public entity] other than an entity created by an agreement described [... tha]t is financially dependent upon some other public [... en]tity is created by an agreement described in Section [... financi]al ability to pay is provided by imposing liability [... parti]es to the agreement. [4 Cal.L.Rev.Comm. Reports

[... Se]ction 970. [12 Cal.L.Rev.Comm. Reports 575

[...] to substitute a requirement that the budget [... prov]ide funds for the payment of all judgments in [... e] for the former requirement that the local [... oth]erwise provide funds for such payment. This [... b]udget make provision for the payment of [... Hig]her Education Code Sections 35201 (school [...] college district). A writ of mandate is an [...] the duty imposed by this section that the [...] [an]d pay all judgments in accordance with [...] [15 Cal.L.Rev.Comm. Reports 1257

References

[... Enf]orcing Judgments/Debts Ch. 6A-6, [... Aga]inst Public Entities.

8 Witkin Cal. Proc. 5th Enforcement of Judgment § 431, Payment Obligation.

9 Witkin, California Summary 10th Taxation § 126, General Rule.

§ 971. Application of limitations on taxes, assessments, or rates; court mandated costs

(a) As used in this section:.

(1) "Judgment resulting from a discretionary act" means a judgment arising from a liability which the local public entity has discretion to incur or not to incur and includes a judgment rendered in an eminent domain proceeding and a judgment requiring specific performance of a contractual obligation or awarding damages for failure to perform a contractual obligation.

(2) "Judgment resulting from a nondiscretionary act" means a judgment other than one described in paragraph (1) and includes a judgment founded upon tort or inverse condemnation liability.

(b) Any limitation on the amount of taxes, assessments or rates and charges that may be levied or collected by a local public entity, and any limitation on the amount of appropriations and payments that may be made by a local public entity, and any limitation on the amount of liability or indebtedness that may be incurred by a local public entity, contained in any other statute or in any charter or ordinance:

(1) Applies to the taxes, assessments, rates and charges or appropriations levied, collected or made to pay pursuant to this article a judgment resulting from a discretionary act.

(2) Does not apply to the taxes, assessments, rates and charges or appropriations levied, collected or made to pay pursuant to this article a judgment resulting from a nondiscretionary act.

(c) For the purposes of Section 2271 of the Revenue and Taxation Code, taxes levied to pay pursuant to this article a judgment resulting from a nondiscretionary act are levied to pay costs mandated by the courts. (Added by Stats.1963, c. 1715, § 3. Amended by Stats.1975, c. 285, p. 706, § 7; Stats.1980, c. 215, § 24.)

Law Revision Commission Comments

This section makes clear that the statutory restrictions upon incurring debts or liabilities and the statutory limitations upon the maximum permissible rate of property taxation by local public entities do not apply to tort judgments. The section is necessary to ensure that these restrictions and limitations do not operate to confer for practical purposes an immunity from tort liability. [4 Cal.L.Rev.Comm.Reports 1001 (1963)].

Section 971 is amended to make clear that Revenue and Taxation Code Sections 2201 to 2326 do not limit the levy of a tax pursuant to this article to pay a tort or inverse condemnation judgment. This clarifying amendment makes no substantive change in existing law and is consistent with both the purposes of this article and the Revenue and Taxation Code sections. See Rev. & Tax.Code § 2205, defining "costs mandated by the courts" to mean: any increased costs incurred by a local agency in order to comply with a final court order issued after January 1, 1973 or with a final court order issued prior to July 1, 1972, if the costs incurred by a local agency as a result thereof are not incurred until after June 30, 1973. "Costs mandated by the courts" do not include (i) costs incurred as a result of a judgment in an eminent domain or condemnation proceeding, or (ii) costs incurred in order to comply with a final court order mandating the specific performance, or awarding damages as a result of nonperformance, of any contract or agreement entered into after January 1, 1973.

The procedure provided by Sections 970 to 971.2 does not include judgments in an eminent domain or condemnation proceeding or judgments arising out of failure to perform a contract. [12 Cal.L.Rev. Comm. Reports 575 (1974)].

Section 971 is revised to reflect the expansion of Sections 970–971.2 to cover all money judgments. Revision of Section 971 is necessary because this article formerly covered only tort and inverse condemnation judgments. Formerly, Section 971 made tax and similar limitations inapplicable with respect to the payment of tort and inverse condemnation judgments; the revised section continues this rule for tort and inverse condemnation judgments and expands the rule to include other money judgments that result from a nondiscretionary act.

The standard used in subdivision (a)—which distinguishes between judgments that result from a discretionary act and those that do not—is drawn from cases interpreting constitutional limits on liabilities or indebtedness (see, e.g., Martin v. Fisher, 108 Cal.App, 34, 40–41, 291 P. 276, 278 (1930) and from Section 2205 of the Revenue and Taxation Code. Section 971, however, merely makes inapplicable limitations contained in a statute, charter, or ordinance; the section does not affect the applicability of any constitutional limits. [15 Cal.L.Rev.Comm. Reports 1257 (1980)].

Research References

Rutter, Cal. Practice Guide: Enforcing Judgments/Debts Ch. 6A-6, Payment of Final Judgments Against Public Entities.
8 Witkin Cal. Proc. 5th Enforcement of Judgment § 431, Payment Obligation.
9 Witkin, California Summary 10th Taxation § 126, General Rule.

§ 971.2. Legal investments

(a) All judgments for which a local public entity is liable are legal investments for all trust funds, and for the funds of all insurance companies, banks (both commercial and savings) and trust companies, and for every other local public entity within this state, to the same extent as bonds of the local public entity liable for the judgment.

(b) Whenever any money or funds may by law be invested in or loaned upon the security of bonds of a local public entity, such money or funds may be invested in or loaned upon the security of a judgment for which such local public entity is liable; and whenever bonds of a local public entity may be used as security for the faithful performance or execution of any court or private trust or of any other act, a judgment for which such local public entity is liable may be so used.

(c) All judgments for which a local public entity is liable, to the same extent as bonds of such local public entity, are legal for use by any state or national bank or banks in the state as security for the deposit of funds of any local public entity within this state. *(Added by Stats.1963, c. 1715, p. 3388, § 3. Amended by Stats.1975, c. 285, p. 707, § 8.)*

Law Revision Commission Comments

This section makes a tort judgment against a local public entity an authorized legal investment for trust funds, banks and insurance companies, to the same extent as the bonds of such local public entity. It also provides that a tort judgment against a local public entity may be used as security in certain circumstances to the same extent as bonds of such entity. The section is necessary to provide assurance that tort judgments against local public entities will be marketable. [4 Cal.L.Rev.Comm. Reports 1001 (1963)].

See Comment to Section 970. [12 Cal.L.Rev.Comm. Reports 575 (1974)].

Research References

8 Witkin Cal. Proc. 5th Enforcement of Judgment § 431, Payment Obligation.
13 Witkin, California Summary 10th Trusts § 80, (S 80) Standard of Care.

ARTICLE 2. FUNDING JUDGMENTS WITH BONDS

Law Revision Commission Comments

This article authorizes all local public entities that levy taxes or assessments—and thus have the power to raise the revenues to discharge a bonded indebtedness—to issue bonds to obtain funds to pay judgments. This authority will permit these public entities to fund their tort liabilities with bonds so that they may meet such obligations without seriously impairing their financial resources. Not all of these public entities have such authority under existing law. Inasmuch as the exercise of this power may result in the imposition of taxes to discharge the bonded indebtedness, the power may be exercised only when two-thirds of the voters, voting at an election called for that purpose, authorize the public entity to issue the bonds.

This article is based for the most part on the bond authorization provisions of the Community Services District Law—Government Code Sections 61650 to 61673. [4 Cal.L.Rev.Comm. Reports 1001 (1963)].

§ 975. Definitions

As used in this article:

(a) "Board" means the governing body of a local taxing entity.

(b) "Local taxing entity" means a local public entity that has the power to levy ad valorem taxes, or ad valorem assessments, upon property within the territory of the entity. *(Added by Stats.1963, c. 1715, p. 3388, § 3.)*

Law Revision Commission Comments

This section defines certain terms used in this article. The definition of "local taxing entity" is based in part on Government Code Section 5401, which defines "bonds" as "bonds or other evidences of indebtedness the principal and interest of which are payable or may be paid from ad valorem taxes or assessments levied by or on behalf of a public body." [4 Cal.L.Rev.Comm. Reports 1001 (1963)].

Research References

8 Witkin Cal. Proc. 5th Enforcement of Judgment § 431, Payment Obligation.

§ 975.2. Resolution of necessity to incur bonded indebtedness; contents

Whenever the board deems it necessary for the local taxing entity to incur a bonded indebtedness to fund all or any portion of an outstanding judgment against the entity, it shall by resolution state:

(a) The necessity for the indebtedness.

(b) The purpose for which the proposed debt is to be incurred.

Government (margin tab)

(c) The amount of the proposed debt.

(d) The time and place for a hearing by the board on the question whether the local taxing entity should incur a bonded indebtedness to fund all or any portion of an outstanding judgment against the entity. *(Added by Stats.1963, c. 1715, p. 3388, § 3.)*

Law Revision Commission Comments

This section is based primarily on Government Code Section 61650. [4 Cal.L.Rev.Comm. Reports 1001 (1963)].

§ 975.4. Notice of hearing; publication; posting

Notice of the hearing shall be given by publication of a copy of the resolution pursuant to Section 6066 in a newspaper of general circulation circulated within the local taxing entity. If there is no such newspaper, the resolution shall be posted in three public places in the local taxing entity for two succeeding weeks. No other notice of the hearing need be given. *(Added by Stats.1963, c. 1715, p. 3388, § 3.)*

Law Revision Commission Comments

This section is based in part on Government Code Section 43611 and in part on Government Code Section 61651. [4 Cal.L.Rev.Comm. Reports 1001 (1963)].

§ 975.6. Notice accompanying copy of resolution published or posted; contents

The copy of the resolution published or posted shall be accompanied by a notice subscribed by the clerk or secretary of the local taxing entity that:

(a) The hearing referred to in the resolution will be had at the time and place specified in the resolution.

(b) At that time and place, any person interested, including persons owning property within the local taxing entity, will be heard upon the question stated in the resolution. *(Added by Stats.1963, c. 1715, p. 3388, § 3.)*

Law Revision Commission Comments

This section is based on Government Code Section 61652. [4 Cal.L.Rev.Comm. Reports 1001 (1963)].

§ 975.8. Hearing; determination of board

At the time and place fixed for the hearing on the resolution or at any time and place to which the hearing is adjourned, the board shall proceed with the hearing. Any person interested, including persons owning property within the local taxing entity, may appear and present any matters material to the question set forth in the resolution. Thereafter, the board shall determine whether it is necessary to incur the bonded indebtedness. The board's determination on the question of necessity is conclusive. *(Added by Stats.1963, c. 1715, p. 3388, § 3.)*

Law Revision Commission Comments

This section is based on Government Code Sections 61653 to 61658. [4 Cal.L.Rev.Comm. Reports 1001 (1963)].

§ 976. Resolution of determination to incur bonded indebtedness

After the board has made its determination pursuant to Section 975.8, if it deems it necessary to incur the bonded indebtedness, it shall by resolution state:

(a) That it deems it necessary to incur the bonded indebtedness.

(b) The purpose for which the bonded indebtedness will be incurred.

(c) The amount of the debt to be incurred, which amount may include legal and other fees and costs incidental to or connected with the authorization, issuance and sale of the bonds, including but not limited to the costs of printing the bonds.

(d) The maximum term the bonds to be issued shall run before maturity, which term shall not exceed 40 years.

(e) The annual rate of interest to be paid, which rate shall not exceed 7 percent, payable annually or semiannually, or in part annually and in part semiannually.

(f) The proposition to be submitted to the voters.

(g) The date of the special election of the local taxing entity (which may be consolidated with any other election of the local taxing entity) at which such proposition shall be submitted to the voters; the manner of holding the election and the procedure for voting for or against the proposition. *(Added by Stats.1963, c. 1715, p. 3388, § 3.)*

Law Revision Commission Comments

This section is based on Government Code Sections 29901, 43610.1, 43653, 61659 and 61659.1. [4 Cal.L.Rev.Comm. Reports 1001 (1963)].

§ 976.2. Resolution as notice of election; publication; posting

The resolution made pursuant to Section 976 shall constitute the notice of such election and such resolution shall be published pursuant to Section 6066 in a newspaper of general circulation circulated within the local taxing entity. If there is no such newspaper, the resolution shall be posted in three public places in the local taxing entity for two succeeding weeks. No other notice of the election need be given. *(Added by Stats.1963, c. 1715, p. 3388, § 3.)*

Law Revision Commission Comments

This section is based on Government Code Sections 29906, 43611 and 61660. [4 Cal.L.Rev.Comm. Reports 1001 (1963)].

§ 976.4. Manner of holding election

The board shall provide for holding the election in the same manner as provided by law in respect to general elections of the local taxing entity so far as applicable, except as otherwise provided in this article. *(Added by Stats.1963, c. 1715, p. 3388, § 3.)*

Law Revision Commission Comments

This section is based on Government Code Section 61661. [4 Cal.L.Rev.Comm. Reports 1001 (1963)].

§ 976.6. Persons entitled to vote

Every elector authorized to vote in general elections of the local taxing entity may vote on the proposition to authorize the bonds. *(Added by Stats.1963, c. 1715, p. 3388, § 3.)*

Law Revision Commission Comments

This section is based in part on Government Code Section 61663. [4 Cal.L.Rev.Comm. Reports 1001 (1963)].

§ 976.8. Favorable vote; authority to issue bonds

If two-thirds or more of the votes cast upon the proposition at the election are in favor of incurring the bonded indebtedness, the board may issue the bonds at the time or times it deems proper. *(Added by Stats.1963, c. 1715, p. 3388, § 3.)*

Law Revision Commission Comments

This section is based on Government Code Sections 43614 and 29908. [4 Cal.L.Rev.Comm. Reports 1001 (1963)].

§ 977. Form of bonds; denominations; time and place for payment

The board shall prescribe the form of the bonds. The bonds may be issued in denominations not to exceed one thousand dollars ($1,000) and not less than one hundred dollars ($100). The board shall fix, and designate in the bonds, a time and place for payment of the bonds. *(Added by Stats.1963, c. 1715, p. 3388, § 3.)*

§ 977.2. Redemption prior to maturity; publication of notice of redemption

The board may provide for the redemption of bonds issued under this article before maturity at prices determined by it. A bond shall not be subject to call or redemption prior to maturity unless it contains a recital to that effect. Notice of redemption shall be published at such time and in such manner as the board may provide in the resolution providing for the issuance of the bonds. *(Added by Stats.1963, c. 1715, p. 3388, § 3.)*

§ 977.4. Signatures; countersignatures

The bonds shall be signed by the presiding officer of the board and countersigned by the clerk or secretary of the local taxing entity, and the coupons shall be signed by the clerk or secretary. All signatures except that of the clerk or secretary on the bonds may be printed, lithographed or engraved. If any officer whose signature appears on the bonds or coupons ceases to be such officer before the delivery of the bonds, his signature is as effective as if he had remained in office. *(Added by Stats.1963, c. 1715, p. 3388, § 3.)*

§ 977.6. Sale of bonds

The local taxing entity may sell the bonds at the times or in the manner the board deems to be to the public interest. The bonds shall be sold on sealed proposals to the highest bidder after advertising for bids by publication of notice of sale pursuant to Section 6061, not less than 10 days prior to the date of sale, in a newspaper of general circulation circulating in the local taxing entity. If there is no such newspaper, the notice of sale shall be posted in three places in the local public entity for two succeeding weeks ending not less than 10 days prior to the date of sale. If satisfactory bids are received, the bonds offered for sale shall be awarded to the highest responsible bidder. If no bids are received or if the board determines that the bids received are not satisfactory as to price or responsibility of the bidders, the board may reject all bids received, if any, and either readvertise or sell the bonds at private sale. *(Added by Stats.1963, c. 1715, p. 3388, § 3.)*

§ 977.8. Action to determine validity of bonds

An action to determine the validity of bonds may be brought pursuant to Chapter 9 (commencing with Section 860) of Title 10 of Part 2 of the Code of Civil Procedure. *(Added by Stats.1963, c. 1715, p. 3388, § 3.)*

§ 978. Force, value and use of bonds; exemption from taxation; legal investments

Any bonds issued by any local taxing entity under the provisions of this article have the same force, value and use as bonds issued by any municipality and are exempt from all taxation within the State.

Such bonds are legal investments for all trust funds, for the funds of all insurance companies, banks (both commercial and savings) and trust companies, for the state school funds, and for any funds which may be invested in bonds of cities, counties, school districts, or municipalities in the State. *(Added by Stats.1963, c. 1715, p. 3388, § 3.)*

§ 978.2. Bonds as general obligations of local taxing entity; taxes and assessments

Bonds issued under this article constitute general obligations of the local taxing entity for the payment of both principal and interest of which all property in the local taxing entity subject to ad valorem taxation by the local taxing entity or subject to ad valorem assessment by the local taxing entity shall be taxed or assessed without limitation of rate or amount.

The board shall, at the time and in the manner provided by law for levying taxes or assessments, fix an ad valorem rate of tax or assessment sufficient to pay the principal of and interest on all bonds issued under this article as they become due. Such ad valorem taxes or assessments shall be in addition to all other taxes or assessments levied by the local taxing entity, and when collected shall be used for no purpose other than the payment of such bonds and the interest thereon.

Nothing in this section shall be construed to prohibit the use of other revenues of the local taxing entity for the payment of principal and interest on bonds issued under this article. *(Added by Stats.1963, c. 1715, p. 3393, § 3.)*

§ 978.4. Use of proceeds only for purpose stated in bond resolution

The proceeds from the sale of bonds issued pursuant to this article shall not be used for any purpose other than the purpose stated in the resolution authorizing the issuance of the bonds. *(Added by Stats.1963, c. 1715, p. 3388, § 3.)*

§ 978.6. Voiding of unsold portion of bond issue

The board may by resolution adopted by two-thirds vote of all its members declare that no part of a described bond issue authorized under this article which remains unsold shall be issued or sold. When the resolution takes effect, the bonds described in the resolution which remain unsold are voided. *(Added by Stats.1963, c. 1715, p. 3388, § 3.)*

§ 978.8. Authority to issue bonds additional and supplementary

The authority provided in this article is in addition and supplementary to any other law authorizing public entities to issue bonds to fund an outstanding indebtedness. *(Added by Stats.1963, c. 1715, p. 3388, § 3.)*

Law Revision Commission Comments

This section is included merely to make clear that this article is not intended to supersede any other law that permits a public entity to fund judgments against it with bonds. [4 Cal.L.Rev.Comm. Reports 1001 (1963)].

CHAPTER 3.7. PROCEDURES APPLICABLE TO STATE AND LOCAL PUBLIC ENTITIES

Section
984. Order for periodic payments; conditions; applicable provisions.

§ 984. Order for periodic payments; conditions; applicable provisions

(a) As used in this section, "not insured" includes a public entity that has no liability insurance or is self-insured by itself, or through an insurance pooling arrangement, a joint powers agreement, the Local Agency Self Insurance Authority, or any other similar arrangement.

(b) If a public entity has commercial insurance as to a portion of the judgment, this section shall only apply to that portion of the judgment which is "not insured" as defined in this section.

(c) A judgment against a public entity may be ordered to be paid by periodic payments only if ordered under Section 667.7 of the Code of Civil Procedure or Section 970.6, or if the public entity has made an election under subdivision (d), or if the parties have agreed to it.

(d) If, after making any deductions pursuant to Section 985 of the Government Code, the judgment on a tort claims action against a public entity that is not insured is greater than five hundred thousand dollars ($500,000), the public entity may elect to pay the judgment in periodic payments as provided in this subdivision.

Effective January 1, 1990, the five hundred thousand dollar ($500,000) threshold amount shall be five hundred fifty thousand dollars ($550,000). Effective January 1, 1992, that amount shall be six hundred thousand dollars ($600,000). Effective January 1, 1994, that amount shall be six hundred fifty thousand dollars ($650,000). Effective January 1, 1996, that amount shall be seven hundred twenty-five thousand dollars ($725,000), and thereafter, the seven hundred twenty-five thousand dollar ($725,-000) amount shall be increased 5 percent on January 1 of each year.

After any amounts reimbursed pursuant to Section 985, the judgment-debtor shall pay 50 percent of the remainder immediately, and the other 50 percent of the remainder shall be paid over a period of time to be determined by the court, not to exceed 10 years or the length of the judgment-creditor's remaining life expectancy at the time the judgment is entered, whichever is less.

(e) The following provisions apply to all judgments for periodic payment under this section against a public entity:

(1) Payments shall not terminate upon the death of the judgment-creditor.

(2) Interest at the same rate as one-year United States Treasury bills as of January 1, each year shall accrue to the unpaid balance of the judgment, and on each January 1 thereafter throughout the duration of the installment payments the interest shall be adjusted until the judgment is fully satisfied.

(3) Throughout the term of the installment payments until the judgment is fully satisfied, the public entity shall remain liable for all payments due on the judgment and the interest.

(4) The court shall retain jurisdiction in order to enforce, amend, modify, or approve settlement of the installment payments as may be just. Upon a motion by the judgment-creditor, the court shall accelerate the installment payments if it finds any unreasonable delay in, or failure to make payments.

(5) The court, upon motion, may modify the installment payments consistent with Sections 1431 to 1431.5, inclusive, of the Civil Code to account for the insolvency or uncollectability of amounts of the judgment owed by joint tortfeasors. The defendant shall bring a motion for that adjustment under Section 1010 of the Code of Civil Procedure.

(f) Nothing in this section shall prevent the parties from agreeing to settle an action on any other terms.

(g) The Judicial Council shall adopt rules providing for a reasonable extension of the time for filing the notice of appeal from a judgment on the verdict to permit an election pursuant to this section and any hearing pursuant to subdivision (d).

(h) This section does not apply to contribution and indemnity between joint tortfeasors. *(Added by Stats.1987, c. 1204, § 3.)*

Research References

Rutter, Cal. Practice Guide: Civil Appeals & Writs Ch. 3-C, C. Extensions of Filing Deadline.
Rutter, Cal. Practice Guide: Enforcing Judgments/Debts Ch. 6A-5, Amount Recoverable Under Judgment.
Rutter, Cal. Practice Guide: Enforcing Judgments/Debts Ch. 6A-6, Payment of Final Judgments Against Public Entities.
Rutter, Cal. Practice Guide: Personal Injury Ch. 3-A, A. Introduction.
Rutter, Cal. Practice Guide: Personal Injury Ch. 9-M, M. Verdicts and Judgment.
Rutter, Cal. Practice Guide: Personal Injury Ch. 10-D, D. Government Entity Defendant Post-Trial Elections, Requests, Motions and Hearings.
Rutter, Cal. Practice Guide: Personal Injury Ch. 10-D, Outline D.
9 Witkin Cal. Proc. 5th Appeal § 606, (S 606) Judgment Against Public Entity.
8 Witkin Cal. Proc. 5th Enforcement of Judgment § 433, (S 433) Postjudgment Settlement Conference.
8 Witkin Cal. Proc. 5th Enforcement of Judgment § 434, (S 434) Periodic Payments.
8 Witkin Cal. Proc. 5th Enforcement of Judgment § 435, (S 435) Reduction of Judgment for Collateral Source Payments.
5 Witkin, California Summary 10th Torts § 234, Conference on Satisfaction of Judgment.
5 Witkin, California Summary 10th Torts § 235, Periodic Payment of Judgment.
6 Witkin, California Summary 10th Torts § 1638, Motion, Discovery, and Settlement Conference.
6 Witkin, California Summary 10th Torts § 1639, Hearing and Determination.

CHAPTER 4. PROCEDURES APPLICABLE TO STATE AND LOCAL PUBLIC ENTITIES

Section
985. Collateral source payments.

Explanatory Note

For another Chapter 4, "Procedures Applicable to State and Local Public Entities", added by Stats.1987, c. 1208, § 8, see Government Code § 985.

§ 985. Collateral source payments

Section added by Stats.1987, c. 1201, § 25. See, also, another section of the same number added by Stats.1987, c. 1208, § 8.

(a) As used in this section:

(1) "Collateral source payment" includes either of the following:

(A) The direct provision of services prior to the commencement of trial to the plaintiff for the same injury or death by prepaid health maintenance organizations providing services to their members or by nonfederal publicly funded health service providers.

(B) Monetary payments paid or obligated to be paid for services or benefits that were provided prior to the commencement of trial to or on behalf of the plaintiff for the same injury or death from a provider of collateral source payments described in paragraphs (1) and (2) of subdivision (f).

(2) "Plaintiff" includes, but is not limited to, a person or entity who is entitled to make a claim under Part 2 (commencing with Section 6400) of Division 6 of the Probate Code for the collateral source benefits against the tortfeasor or alleged tortfeasor, and in the case of a minor, the minor and the minor's parent, legal guardian or guardian ad litem.

(3) "Commencement of trial" occurs as defined in paragraph (6) of subdivision (a) of Section 581 of the Code of Civil Procedure.

(b) Any collateral source payment paid or owed to or on behalf of a plaintiff shall be inadmissible in any action for personal injuries or wrongful death where a public entity is a defendant. However, after a verdict has been returned against a public entity that includes damages for which payment from a collateral source listed below has already been paid or is obligated to be paid for services or benefits that were provided prior to the commencement of trial, and the total of the collateral source payments is greater than five thousand dollars ($5,000), that amount to be increased 5 percent compounded on January 1, 1989, and each January 1 thereafter, the defendant public entity may, by a motion noticed within the time set in Section 659 of the Code of Civil Procedure, request a posttrial hearing for a reduction of the judgment against the defendant public entity for collateral source payments paid or obligated to be paid for services or benefits that were provided prior to the commencement of trial. The hearing may be noticed with any motions pursuant to Sections 962 and 984 of the Government Code or Section 659 of the Code of Civil Procedure; however, the hearing shall not occur until after the determination of any motions for a new trial, for judgment notwithstanding the verdict, for remittitur, for additur, and after any mandatory settlement conference pursuant to Section 962 of the Government Code.

(c) A defendant public entity may, by interrogatory or in writing at the trial-setting conference, request from the plaintiff a list of the names and addresses of any provider of a collateral source payment affected by this section that has provided collateral source payments directly to or on behalf of the plaintiff and the amount provided to the plaintiff from each collateral source. The plaintiff shall produce the requested list within 30 days of such request. The plaintiff shall have a continuing duty to disclose to the public entity defendant the name and address of any provider of a collateral source payment affected by this section but not disclosed in plaintiff's response if that provider pays or owes collateral source payments to or on behalf of plaintiff between the time of plaintiff's response and the commencement of trial.

The public entity shall provide written notice to each provider of a collateral source payment listed by the plaintiff or identified by defendant of the date set for any pretrial settlement conference.

The provider of a collateral source shall not be required to attend a settlement conference unless requested to do so by the court. The court may request a provider of a collateral source to attend a settlement conference or to provide written information, to be available by telephone, or to otherwise participate in the conference, and a provider of a collateral source shall waive its rights to reimbursement unless it attends or otherwise complies with the request.

(d) If the plaintiff fails or refuses to supply to the defendant public entity information as to the identity of a provider of a collateral source payment, as required by this section, the defendant public entity may, upon discovery of the identity of the provider of a collateral source payment, within five years of the date of entry of judgment, request a reduction of the judgment for payment made or for services provided prior to the commencement of trial by that source. Failure of plaintiff to provide the names of collateral source providers affected by this section and known to plaintiff, shall subject plaintiff or plaintiff's attorney to sanctions pursuant to Section 128.5 of the Code of Civil Procedure.

(e) The public entity shall also give 20 days notice to the provider of a collateral source payment of any posttrial settlement conference or hearing regarding collateral source payments under this section.

Proof of service of any notice sent pursuant to this section shall be filed with the court and a copy served on all parties to the action.

(f) At the hearing the trial court shall, in its discretion and on terms as may be just, make a final determination as to any pending lien and subrogation rights, and, subject to paragraphs (1) to (3), inclusive, determine what portion of collateral source payments should be reimbursed from the judgment to the provider of a collateral source payment, deducted to the verdict, or accrue to the benefit of the plaintiff. No provider of collateral source payments pursuant to this section shall recover any amount against the plaintiff nor shall it be subrogated to the rights of the plaintiff against a public entity defendant other than in the amount so determined by the court. The following provisions shall apply to the court's adjustments:

(1) If the court has determined that the verdict included money damages for which the plaintiff has already received payment from or had his or her expenses paid by the following collateral sources: Medi–Cal, county health care, Aid to Families with Dependent Children, Victims of Crime, or other nonfederal publicly funded sources of benefit with statutory lien rights, the court shall order reimbursement from the judgment of those amounts to the provider of a collateral source payment pursuant to this section and on terms as may be just.

(2) If the court has determined that the verdict includes money damages for which the plaintiff has already received payment from or had his or her expenses paid by the following collateral sources: private medical programs, health maintenance organizations, state disability, unemployment insurance, private disability insurance, or other sources of compensation similar to those listed in this paragraph, the court may, after considering the totality of all circumstances and on terms as may be just, determine what portion of the collateral source benefits will be reimbursed from the judgment to the provider of the collateral source payment, used to reduce the verdict, or accrue to the benefit of the plaintiff. However, nothing in this section shall create subrogation or lien rights that do not already exist.

Government

(3) In determining the amount to be reimbursed from the judgment to a provider of a collateral source payment, or the amount by which the judgment will be reduced to account for collateral source payments, the court shall make the following adjustments:

(A) Where plaintiff has been found partially at fault, the reimbursement or reduction shall be decreased by the same percentage as the entire judgment is reduced to take into account the plaintiff's comparative fault.

(B) The court shall deduct from the reimbursement or reduction the amount of premiums the court determines were paid by or on behalf of the plaintiff to the provider of a collateral source payment.

(C) After making the adjustments described in subparagraphs (A) and (B) above, the court shall reduce that amount by a percentage equal to the percentage of the entire judgment that the plaintiff paid or owes for his or her attorney fees and costs and reasonable expenses incurred.

(g) In no event shall the total dollar amount deducted from the verdict, paid to lienholders or reimbursed to all collateral source providers, exceed one-half of the plaintiff's net recovery for all damages after deducting for attorney's fees, medical services paid by the plaintiff, and litigation costs; however, the court may order no reimbursement or verdict reduction if the reimbursement or reduction would result in undue financial hardship upon the person who suffered the injury.

(h) Unless otherwise ordered by the court, 50 percent of any amount reimbursed pursuant to this section shall be due immediately. The court may order the remaining 50 percent to be paid in installments over a period of time to be determined by the court pursuant to Section 984, not to exceed 10 years.

(i) In any case involving multiple defendants, a reduction pursuant to this section shall be proportional to the percentage of the judgment actually paid by the public entity and shall satisfy the judgment as to the portion reduced so that no other judgment debtor shall be jointly liable for the portion of the judgment reduced pursuant to this section. If, after a hearing and determination pursuant to this section, the public entity judgment debtor is required to satisfy a portion of a joint and several judgment beyond that public entity judgment debtor's several portion due to the uncollectability of a joint tortfeasor's portion, the public entity may make a motion to reduce the additional portion in an amount proportional to the determination of the court pursuant to this section.

(j) In all actions affected by this section, the court shall instruct the jury with the following language:

"You shall award damages in an amount that fully compensates plaintiff for damages in accordance with instructions from the court. You shall not speculate or consider any other possible sources of benefit the plaintiff may have received. After you have returned your verdict the court will make whatever adjustments are necessary in this regard."

(k) The Judicial Council shall adopt rules providing for a reasonable extension of the time for filing the notice of appeal from a judgment on the verdict to permit a motion for the hearing and the hearing itself.

(*l*) If the defendant public entity or defendant public employee is also a health care provider as defined in Section 3333.1 of the Civil Code, that section controls as to that defendant.

(m) This chapter does not apply to lien or subrogation rights provided in Chapter 5 (commencing with Section 385¹) of Part 1 of Division 4 of the Labor Code. *(Added by Stats.1987, c. 1201, § 25.)*

¹ So in enrolled bill, should be section 3850.

Research References

Rutter, Cal. Practice Guide: A.D.R. Ch. 4-D, D. Mandatory Settlement Conferences.

Rutter, Cal. Practice Guide: Civil Appeals & Writs Ch. 3-C, C. Extensions of Filing Deadline.

Rutter, Cal. Practice Guide: Civ. Pro. Before Trial Ch. 8F-3, Propounding Interrogatories.

Rutter, Cal. Practice Guide: Civ. Pro. Before Trial Ch. 8K-6, Special Statutes and Court Rules.

Rutter, Cal. Practice Guide: Civ. Pro. Before Trial Ch. 12(II)-A, A. Mandatory Settlement Conference ("Msc").

Rutter, Cal. Practice Guide: Civil Trials & Evidence Ch. 8E-D, D. Other Public Policy Exclusions.

Rutter, Cal. Practice Guide: Enforcing Judgments/Debts Ch. 6A-6, Payment of Final Judgments Against Public Entities.

Rutter, Cal. Practice Guide: Personal Injury Ch. 1-A, A. Initial Client Interview.

Rutter, Cal. Practice Guide: Personal Injury Ch. 3-A, A. Introduction.

Rutter, Cal. Practice Guide: Personal Injury Ch. 3-C, C. Specific Items of Compensatory Damages.

Rutter, Cal. Practice Guide: Personal Injury Ch. 4-F, F. Court-Conducted Settlement Proceedings.

Rutter, Cal. Practice Guide: Personal Injury Ch. 6-B, B. Overview of Selected Discovery Procedures.

Rutter, Cal. Practice Guide: Personal Injury Ch. 8-A, A. Case Management.

Rutter, Cal. Practice Guide: Personal Injury Ch. 9-M, M. Verdicts and Judgment.

Rutter, Cal. Practice Guide: Personal Injury Ch. 10-D, D. Government Entity Defendant Post-Trial Elections, Requests, Motions and Hearings.

Rutter, Cal. Practice Guide: Personal Injury Ch. 3-C, Outline C.

Rutter, Cal. Practice Guide: Personal Injury Ch. 4-F, Outline F.

Rutter, Cal. Practice Guide: Personal Injury Ch. 10-D, Outline D.

9 Witkin Cal. Proc. 5th Appeal § 606, (S 606) Judgment Against Public Entity.

8 Witkin Cal. Proc. 5th Enforcement of Judgment § 433, (S 433) Postjudgment Settlement Conference.

8 Witkin Cal. Proc. 5th Enforcement of Judgment § 434, (S 434) Periodic Payments.

8 Witkin Cal. Proc. 5th Enforcement of Judgment § 435, (S 435) Reduction of Judgment for Collateral Source Payments.

5 Witkin, California Summary 10th Torts § 234, Conference on Satisfaction of Judgment.

5 Witkin, California Summary 10th Torts § 235, Periodic Payment of Judgment.

6 Witkin, California Summary 10th Torts § 1631, Nature of Rule.

6 Witkin, California Summary 10th Torts § 1637, Nature of Statute.

6 Witkin, California Summary 10th Torts § 1638, Motion, Discovery, and Settlement Conference.

6 Witkin, California Summary 10th Torts § 1639, Hearing and Determination.

CHAPTER 4. PROCEDURES APPLICABLE TO STATE AND LOCAL PUBLIC ENTITIES

Section
985. Collateral source payments.

Explanatory Note

For another Chapter 4, added as "Procedures Applicable to State and Local Public Entities", by Stats.1987, c. 1201, § 25, see Government Code § 985.

§ 985. Collateral source payments

Section added by Stats.1987, c. 1208, § 8. See, also, another section of the same number added by Stats.1987, c. 1201, § 25.

(a) As used in this section:

(1) "Collateral source payment" includes either of the following:

(A) The direct provision of services prior to the commencement of trial to the plaintiff for the same injury or death by prepaid health maintenance organizations providing services to their members or by nonfederal publicly funded health service providers.

(B) Monetary payments paid or obligated to be paid for services or benefits that were provided prior to the commencement of trial to or on behalf of the plaintiff for the same injury or death from a provider of collateral source payments described in paragraphs (1) and (2) of subdivision (f).

(2) "Plaintiff" includes, but is not limited to, a person or entity who is entitled to make a claim under Part 2 (commencing with Section 6400) of Division 6 of the Probate Code for the collateral source benefits against the tortfeasor or alleged tortfeasor, and in the case of a minor, the minor and the minor's parent, legal guardian or guardian ad litem.

(3) "Commencement of trial" occurs as defined in paragraph (6) of subdivision (a) of Section 581 of the Code of Civil Procedure.

(b) Any collateral source payment paid or owed to or on behalf of a plaintiff shall be inadmissible in any action for personal injuries or wrongful death where a public entity is a defendant. However, after a verdict has been returned against a public entity that includes damages for which payment from a collateral source listed below has already been paid or is obligated to be paid for services or benefits that were provided prior to the commencement of trial, and the total of the collateral source payments is greater than five thousand dollars ($5,000), that amount to be increased 5 percent compounded on January 1, 1989, and each January 1 thereafter, the defendant public entity may, by a motion noticed within the time set in Section 659 of the Code of Civil Procedure, request a posttrial hearing for a reduction of the judgment against the defendant public entity for collateral source payments paid or obligated to be paid for services or benefits that were provided prior to the commencement of trial. The hearing may be noticed with any motions pursuant to Sections 962 and 984 of the Government Code or Section 659 of the Code of Civil Procedure; however, the hearing shall not occur until after the determination of any motions for a new trial, for judgment notwithstanding the verdict, for remittitur, for additur, and after any mandatory settlement conference pursuant to Section 962 of the Government Code.

(c) A defendant public entity may, by interrogatory or in writing at the trial-setting conference, request from the plaintiff a list of the names and addresses of any provider of a collateral source payment affected by this section that has provided collateral source payments directly to or on behalf of the plaintiff and the amount provided to the plaintiff from each collateral source. The plaintiff shall produce the requested list within 30 days of such request. The plaintiff shall have a continuing duty to disclose to the public entity defendant the name and address of any provider of a collateral source payment affected by this section but not disclosed in plaintiff's response if that provider pays or owes collateral source payments to or on behalf of plaintiff between the time of plaintiff's response and the commencement of trial.

The public entity shall provide written notice to each provider of a collateral source payment listed by the plaintiff or identified by defendant of the date set for any pretrial settlement conference.

The provider of a collateral source shall not be required to attend a settlement conference unless requested to do so by the court. The court may request a provider of a collateral source to attend a settlement conference or to provide written information, to be available by telephone, or to otherwise participate in the conference, and a provider of a collateral source shall waive its rights to reimbursement unless it attends or otherwise complies with the request.

(d) If the plaintiff fails or refuses to supply to the defendant public entity information as to the identity of a provider of a collateral source payment, as required by this section, the defendant public entity may, upon discovery of the identity of the provider of a collateral source payment, within five years of the date of entry of judgment, request a reduction of the judgment for payment made or for services provided prior to the commencement of trial by that source. Failure of plaintiff to provide the names of collateral source providers affected by this section and known to plaintiff, shall subject plaintiff or plaintiff's attorney to sanctions pursuant to Section 128.5 of the Code of Civil Procedure.

(e) The public entity shall also give 20 days notice to the provider of a collateral source payment of any posttrial settlement conference or hearing regarding collateral source payments under this section.

Proof of service of any notice sent pursuant to this section shall be filed with the court and a copy served on all parties to the action.

(f) At the hearing the trial court shall, in its discretion and on terms as may be just, make a final determination as to any pending lien and subrogation rights, and, subject to subdivisions [1] (1) to (3), inclusive, determine what portion of collateral source payments should be reimbursed from the judgment to the provider of a collateral source payment, deducted from the verdict, or accrue to the benefit of the plaintiff. No provider of collateral source payments pursuant to this section shall recover any amount against the plaintiff nor shall it be subrogated to the rights of the plaintiff against a public entity defendant other than in the amount so determined by the court. The following provisions shall apply to the court's adjustments:

(1) If the court has determined that the verdict included money damages for which the plaintiff has already received payment from or had his or her expenses paid by the following collateral sources: Medi–Cal, county health care, Aid to Families with Dependent Children, Victims of Crime, or other nonfederal publicly funded sources of benefit with statutory lien rights, the court shall order reimbursement from the judgment of those amounts to the provider of a collateral source payment pursuant to this section and on terms as may be just.

(2) If the court has determined that the verdict includes money damages for which the plaintiff has already received payment from or had his or her expenses paid by the following collateral sources: private medical programs, health maintenance organizations, state disability, unemployment insurance, private disability insurance, or other sources of compensation similar to those listed in this paragraph, the court may, after considering the totality of all circumstances and on terms as may be just, determine what portion of the collateral source benefits will be reimbursed from the judgment to the provider of the collateral source payment, used to reduce the verdict, or accrue to the benefit of the plaintiff. However, nothing in this section shall create subrogation or lien rights that do not already exist.

(3) In determining the amount to be reimbursed from the judgment to a provider of a collateral source payment, or the amount by which the judgment will be reduced to account for collateral source payments, the court shall make the following adjustments:

(A) Where plaintiff has been found partially at fault, the reimbursement or reduction shall be decreased by the same percentage as the entire judgment is reduced to take into account the plaintiff's comparative fault.

(B) The court shall deduct from the reimbursement or reduction the amount of premiums the court determines were paid by or on behalf of the plaintiff to the provider of a collateral source payment.

(C) After making the adjustments described in subparagraphs (A) and (B) above, the court shall reduce that amount by a percentage equal to the percentage of the entire judgment that the plaintiff paid or owes for his or her attorney fees and costs and reasonable expenses incurred.

(g) In no event shall the total dollar amount deducted from the verdict, paid to lienholders or reimbursed to all collateral source providers, exceed one-half of the plaintiff's net recovery for all damages after deducting for attorney's fees, medical services paid by the plaintiff, and litigation costs; however, the court may order no reimbursement or verdict reduction if the reimbursement or reduction would result in undue financial hardship upon the person who suffered the injury.

(h) Unless otherwise ordered by the court, 50 percent of any amount reimbursed pursuant to this section shall be due immediately. The court may order the remaining 50 percent to be paid in installments over a period of time to be determined by the court pursuant to Section 984, not to exceed 10 years.

(i) In any case involving multiple defendants, a reduction pursuant to this section shall be proportional to the percentage of the judgment actually paid by the public entity and shall satisfy the judgment as to the portion reduced so that no other judgment debtor shall be jointly liable for the portion of the judgment reduced pursuant to this section. If, after a hearing and determination pursuant to this section, the public entity judgment debtor is required to satisfy a portion of a joint and several judgment beyond that public entity judgment debtor's several portion due to the uncollectability of a joint tortfeasor's portion, the public entity may make a motion to reduce the additional portion in an amount proportional to the determination of the court pursuant to this section.

(j) In all actions affected by this section, the court shall instruct the jury with the following language:

"You shall award damages in an amount that fully compensates plaintiff for damages in accordance with instructions from the court. You shall not speculate or consider any other possible sources of benefit the plaintiff may have received. After you have returned your verdict the court will make whatever adjustments are necessary in this regard."

(k) The Judicial Council shall adopt rules providing for a reasonable extension of the time for filing the notice of appeal from a judgment on the verdict to permit a motion for the hearing and the hearing itself.

(*l*) If the defendant public entity or defendant public employee is also a health care provider as defined in Section 3333.1 of the Civil Code, that section controls as to that defendant.

(m) This chapter does not apply to lien or subrogation rights provided in Chapter 5 (commencing with Section 3850) of Part 1 of Division 4 of the Labor Code. *(Added by Stats.1987, c. 1208, § 8.)*

¹ So in enrolled bill.

Research References

Rutter, Cal. Practice Guide: A.D.R. Ch. 4-D, D. Mandatory Settlement Conferences.
Rutter, Cal. Practice Guide: Civil Appeals & Writs Ch. 3-C, C. Extensions of Filing Deadline.
Rutter, Cal. Practice Guide: Civ. Pro. Before Trial Ch. 8F-3, Propounding Interrogatories.
Rutter, Cal. Practice Guide: Civ. Pro. Before Trial Ch. 8K-6, Special Statutes and Court Rules.

Rutter, Cal. Practice Guide: Civ. Pro. Before Trial Ch. 12(II)-A, A. Mandatory Settlement Conference ("Msc").
Rutter, Cal. Practice Guide: Civil Trials & Evidence Ch. 8E-D, D. Other Public Policy Exclusions.
Rutter, Cal. Practice Guide: Enforcing Judgments/Debts Ch. 6A-6, Payment of Final Judgments Against Public Entities.
Rutter, Cal. Practice Guide: Personal Injury Ch. 1-A, A. Initial Client Interview.
Rutter, Cal. Practice Guide: Personal Injury Ch. 3-A, A. Introduction.
Rutter, Cal. Practice Guide: Personal Injury Ch. 3-C, C. Specific Items of Compensatory Damages.
Rutter, Cal. Practice Guide: Personal Injury Ch. 4-F, F. Court-Conducted Settlement Proceedings.
Rutter, Cal. Practice Guide: Personal Injury Ch. 6-B, B. Overview of Selected Discovery Procedures.
Rutter, Cal. Practice Guide: Personal Injury Ch. 8-A, A. Case Management.
Rutter, Cal. Practice Guide: Personal Injury Ch. 9-M, M. Verdicts and Judgment.
Rutter, Cal. Practice Guide: Personal Injury Ch. 10-D, D. Government Entity Defendant Post-Trial Elections, Requests, Motions and Hearings.
Rutter, Cal. Practice Guide: Personal Injury Ch. 3-C, Outline C.
Rutter, Cal. Practice Guide: Personal Injury Ch. 4-F, Outline F.
Rutter, Cal. Practice Guide: Personal Injury Ch. 10-D, Outline D.
9 Witkin Cal. Proc. 5th Appeal § 606, (S 606) Judgment Against Public Entity.
8 Witkin Cal. Proc. 5th Enforcement of Judgment § 433, (S 433) Postjudgment Settlement Conference.
8 Witkin Cal. Proc. 5th Enforcement of Judgment § 434, (S 434) Periodic Payments.
8 Witkin Cal. Proc. 5th Enforcement of Judgment § 435, (S 435) Reduction of Judgment for Collateral Source Payments.
5 Witkin, California Summary 10th Torts § 234, Conference on Satisfaction of Judgment.
5 Witkin, California Summary 10th Torts § 235, Periodic Payment of Judgment.
6 Witkin, California Summary 10th Torts § 1631, Nature of Rule.
6 Witkin, California Summary 10th Torts § 1637, Nature of Statute.
6 Witkin, California Summary 10th Torts § 1638, Motion, Discovery, and Settlement Conference.
6 Witkin, California Summary 10th Torts § 1639, Hearing and Determination.

Part 6

INSURANCE

Section

§ 989. Local public entity

As used in this part, "local public entity" means any public entity except a state agency covered by Section 11007.4 of the Government Code. *(Added by Stats.1963, c. 1682, p. 3294, § 12.)*

Research References

8 Witkin Cal. Proc. 5th Enforcement of Judgment § 431, Payment Obligation.
5 Witkin, California Summary 10th Torts § 217, (S 217) Statutory Framework.

5 Witkin, California Summary 10th Torts § 231, Insurance Coverage.

§ 990. Authority to insure

Except for a liability which may be insured against pursuant to Division 4 (commencing with Section 3200) of the Labor Code, a local public entity may:

(a) Insure itself against all or any part of any tort or inverse condemnation liability.

(b) Insure any employee of the local public entity against all or any part of his liability for injury resulting from an act or omission in the scope of his employment.

(c) Insure, contract or provide against the expense of defending a claim against the local public entity or its employee, whether or not liability exists on such claim, including a claim for damages under Section 3294 of the Civil Code or otherwise for the sake of example or by way of punishment, where such liability arose from an act or omission in the scope of his employment, and an insurance contract for such purpose is valid and binding notwithstanding Section 1668 of the Civil Code, Section 533 of the Insurance Code, or any other provision of law.

(d) A hospital district may participate in a reciprocal or interinsurance exchange with the members of its medical staff as provided in Section 1284 of the Insurance Code.

Nothing in this section shall be construed to authorize a local public entity to pay for, or to insure, contract, or provide for payment for, such part of a claim or judgment against an employee of the local entity as is for punitive or exemplary damages. *(Added by Stats.1963, c. 1682, p. 3294, § 12. Amended by Stats.1967, c. 298, p. 1480, § 1; Stats.1971, c. 140, p. 187, § 1; Stats.1976, c. 1465, p. 6575, § 2; Stats.1977, c. 904, p. 2761, § 1.)*

Law Revision Commission Comments

Section 990 is amended to make clear that a local public entity has authority to insure against all inverse condemnation liabilities. See Recommendation Relating to Inverse Condemnation: Insurance Coverage, 10 Cal.L.Revision Comm'n Reports 1051 (1971). This effectuates the original intent of Section 990 that "a public entity's authority to insure is as broad as its potential liability." See Recommendation Relating to Sovereign Immunity: Number 3—Insurance Coverage for Public Entities and Public Employees. [4 Cal.L.Rev.Comm. Reports 1201, 1206 (1963)].

Research References

5 Witkin, California Summary 10th Torts § 231, Insurance Coverage.
5 Witkin, California Summary 10th Torts § 350, Insurance Coverage.
8 Witkin, California Summary 10th Constitutional Law § 1143, Nature of Action.

§ 990.2. Court officers and attachés; authority to insure

A county may insure any officer or attaché of its superior and municipal courts against all or any part of the officer or attaché's liability for injury resulting from any act or omission in the scope of the officer or attaché's employment, and also may insure against the expense of defending any claim against such officer or attaché, whether or not liability exists on such claim. *(Added by Stats.1963, c. 1682, p. 3294, § 12. Amended by Stats.1998, c. 931 (S.B.2139), § 176, eff. Sept. 28, 1998.)*

Law Revision Commission Comments

Section 990.2 is amended to reflect elimination of the justice court. Cal. Const. art. VI, §§ 1, 5(b). [28 Cal.L.Rev.Comm. Reports 51 (1998)].

Research References

5 Witkin, California Summary 10th Torts § 350, Insurance Coverage.

§ 990.4. Manner of providing insurance

The insurance authorized by this part may be provided by:

(a) Self-insurance, which may be, but is not required to be, funded by appropriations to establish or maintain reserves for self-insurance purposes.

(b) Insurance in any insurer authorized to transact such insurance in this state.

(c) Insurance secured in accordance with Chapter 6 (commencing with Section 1760) of Part 2 of Division 1 of the Insurance Code.

(d) Participation by a hospital district and its medical staff in a reciprocal or interinsurance exchange as provided in Section 1284 of the Insurance Code.

(e) Any combination of insurance authorized by subdivisions (a), (b), (c), and (d). *(Added by Stats.1963, c. 1682, p. 3294, § 12. Amended by Stats.1976, c. 1465, p. 6576, § 3; Stats.1977, c. 904, p. 2761, § 2.)*

Research References

5 Witkin, California Summary 10th Torts § 231, Insurance Coverage.

§ 990.6. Cost of insurance

The cost of the insurance authorized by this part is a proper charge against the local public entity. *(Added by Stats.1963, c. 1682, p. 3294, § 12.)*

§ 990.8. Insurance by two or more local public entities; pooling

(a) Two or more local public entities, by a joint powers agreement made pursuant to Article 1 (commencing with Section 6500) of Chapter 5 of Division 7, may provide insurance authorized by this part or for any other purpose by any one or more of the methods specified in Section 990.4. Where two or more hospital districts have joined together to pool their self-insurance claims or losses, any nonprofit corporation created pursuant to subdivision (p) of Section 32121 of the Health and Safety Code, and affiliated with a hospital district which is a party to the pool may participate in the pool.

(b) Two or more local public entities having the same governing board may be coinsured under a master policy and the total premium may be prorated among those entities.

(c) The pooling of self-insured claims or losses among entities as authorized in subdivision (a) of Section 990.4 shall not be considered insurance nor be subject to regulation under the Insurance Code.

(d) Any liability or loss under a joint powers agreement for the pooling of self-insured claims or losses authorized by this part and provided pursuant to this section may, notwithstanding Section 620 of the Insurance Code or any other provision of law, be reinsured to the same extent and the same manner as insurance provided by an insurer.

(e) Where a joint powers agreement authorized by this part or authorized pursuant to Section 6516 provides for the pooling of self-insured claims or losses among entities, if any peril insured or covered under contract has existed, and the joint powers authority or other parties to the pool have been liable for any period, however short, the agreement may provide that the party insured or covered under contract is not entitled to the return of premiums, contributions, payments, or advances so far as that particular risk is concerned. *(Added by Stats.1963, c. 1682, p. 3294, § 12. Amended by Stats.1976, c. 1459, p. 6536, § 1; Stats.1982, c. 454, p. 1839, § 34; Stats.1986, c. 1355, § 1; Stats.1996, c. 181 (S.B.2047), § 1; Stats.1997, c. 131 (S.B.1153), § 1.)*

Research References

2 Witkin, California Summary 10th Insurance § 1, (S 1) in General.

5 Witkin, California Summary 10th Torts § 231, Insurance Coverage.

§ 990.9. Health care providers; voluntary care of low-income patients

Any city, county, city and county, or any other local public entity with authority to provide health care services may provide insurance or provide indemnity through self-insurance for medical or other health-care tort claims against any person who, in good faith and without compensation, renders voluntary care to low-income patients within the scope of his or her practice at a community clinic or free clinic, as those terms are defined in subdivision (a) of Section 1204 of the Health and Safety Code, serving residents within the jurisdiction of the local public entity, and who is licensed under Division 2 (commencing with Section 500) of the Business and Professions Code or under an initiative act referred to in those provisions. However, the insurance or indemnity provided pursuant to this section shall not cover liability for which there is other insurance coverage in effect. *(Added by Stats.1993, c. 154 (A.B.2058), § 1.)*

§ 991. Other enactments requiring local public entity to insure

Where an enactment, other than this part, authorizes or requires a local public entity to insure against its liability or the liability of its employees:

(a) The authority provided by this part to insure does not affect such other enactment.

(b) Such other enactment does not limit or restrict the authority to insure under this part; but, except to the extent authorized by Section 1251 of the Education Code, nothing in this part permits a school district to self-insure in any case where the school district is required to insure. *(Added by Stats.1963, c. 1682, p. 3294, § 12.)*

Research References

5 Witkin, California Summary 10th Torts § 231, Insurance Coverage.

§ 991.2. Application of part

Neither the authority provided by this part to insure, nor the exercise of such authority, shall:

(a) Impose any liability upon the local public entity or its employee unless such liability otherwise exists.

(b) Impair any defense the local public entity or its employee otherwise may have. *(Added by Stats.1963, c. 1682, p. 3294, § 12.)*

Research References

5 Witkin, California Summary 10th Torts § 231, Insurance Coverage.

Part 7

DEFENSE OF PUBLIC EMPLOYEES

§ 995. Authority to provide for defense of civil action or proceeding

Except as otherwise provided in Sections 995.2 and 995.4, upon request of an employee or former employee, a public entity shall provide for the defense of any civil action or proceeding brought against him, in his official or individual capacity or both, on account of an act or omission in the scope of his employment as an employee of the public entity.

For the purposes of this part, a cross-action, counterclaim or cross-complaint against an employee or former employee shall be deemed to be a civil action or proceeding brought against him. *(Added by Stats.1963, c. 1683, p. 3302, § 16.)*

Research References

Rutter, Cal. Practice Guide: Personal Injury Ch. 1-A, A. Initial Client Interview.
Miller and Starr California Real Estate § 22:72, Recreational or Hazardous Activities on Certain Public Property.
5 Witkin, California Summary 10th Torts § 166, in General.
5 Witkin, California Summary 10th Torts § 217, (S 217) Statutory Framework.
5 Witkin, California Summary 10th Torts § 219, (S 219) "Employee.".
5 Witkin, California Summary 10th Torts § 371, (S 371) Employee's Right to Defense.
5 Witkin, California Summary 10th Torts § 376, (S 376) Employee Must Act Within Scope of Employment.

§ 995.2. Grounds for refusal to provide defense; request of defense; refusal because of conflict of interest

(a) A public entity may refuse to provide for the defense of a civil action or proceeding brought against an employee or former employee if the public entity determines any of the following:

(1) The act or omission was not within the scope of his or her employment.

(2) He or she acted or failed to act because of actual fraud, corruption, or actual malice.

(3) The defense of the action or proceeding by the public entity would create a specific conflict of interest between the public entity and the employee or former employee. For the purposes of this section, "specific conflict of interest" means a conflict of interest or an adverse or pecuniary interest, as specified by statute or by a rule or regulation of the public entity.

(b) If an employee or former employee requests in writing that the public entity, through its designated legal counsel, provide for a defense, the public entity shall, within 20 days, inform the employee or former employee whether it will or will not provide a defense, and the reason for the refusal to provide a defense.

(c) If an actual and specific conflict of interest becomes apparent subsequent to the 20-day period following the employee's written request for defense, nothing herein shall prevent the public entity from refusing to provide further defense to the employee. The public entity shall inform the employee of the reason for the refusal to provide further defense. *(Added by Stats.1963, c. 1683, p. 3300, § 16. Amended by Stats.1982, c. 1046, p. 3806, § 1.)*

Research References

Rutter, Cal. Practice Guide: Personal Injury Ch. 1-A, A. Initial Client Interview.
1 Witkin Cal. Proc. 5th Attorneys § 144, (S 144) General Principles.
5 Witkin, California Summary 10th Torts § 372, (S 372) When Defense May be Refused.

5 Witkin, California Summary 10th Torts § 377, (S 377) Where Entity Fails to Defend or Defends Under Reservation of Rights.

§ 995.3. Defense against allegations of use of official authority or influence to interfere with disclosure of information

(a) If a state employee provides his or her own defense against an action brought for an alleged violation of Section 8547.3, and if it is established that no violation of Section 8547.3 occurred, the public entity shall reimburse the employee for any costs incurred in the defense.

(b) A public entity which does provide for the defense of a state employee charged with a violation of Section 8547.3 shall reserve all rights to be reimbursed for any costs incurred in that defense. If a state employee is found to have violated Section 8547.3, he or she is liable for all defense costs and shall reimburse the public entity for those costs. *(Added by Stats. 1984, c. 1212, § 1. Amended by Stats.1986, c. 353, § 2; Stats.1995, c. 277 (A.B.1097), § 1.)*

§ 995.4. Actions or proceedings brought by public entity

A public entity may, but is not required to, provide for the defense of:

(a) An action or proceeding brought by the public entity to remove, suspend or otherwise penalize its own employee or former employee, or an appeal to a court from an administrative proceeding by the public entity to remove, suspend or otherwise penalize its own employee or former employee.

(b) An action or proceeding brought by the public entity against its own employee or former employee as an individual and not in his official capacity, or an appeal therefrom. *(Added by Stats.1963, c. 1683, p. 3300, § 16.)*

Research References

5 Witkin, California Summary 10th Torts § 373, (S 373) When Defense is Optional.

§ 995.6. Administrative proceedings

A public entity is not required to provide for the defense of an administrative proceeding brought against an employee or former employee, but a public entity may provide for the defense of an administrative proceeding brought against an employee or former employee if:

(a) The administrative proceeding is brought on account of an act or omission in the scope of his employment as an employee of the public entity; and

(b) The public entity determines that such defense would be in the best interests of the public entity and that the employee or former employee acted, or failed to act, in good faith, without actual malice and in the apparent interests of the public entity. *(Added by Stats.1963, c. 1683, p. 3300, § 16.)*

Research References

5 Witkin, California Summary 10th Torts § 373, (S 373) When Defense is Optional.

§ 995.8. Criminal actions and proceedings

A public entity is not required to provide for the defense of a criminal action or proceeding (including a proceeding to remove an officer under Sections 3060 to 3073, inclusive, of the Government Code) brought against an employee or former employee, but a public entity may provide for the defense of a criminal action or proceeding (including a proceeding to remove an officer under Sections 3060 to 3073, inclusive, of the Government Code) brought against an employee or former employee if:

(a) The criminal action or proceeding is brought on account of an act or omission in the scope of his employment as an employee of the public entity; and

(b) The public entity determines that such defense would be in the best interests of the public entity and that the employee or former employee acted, or failed to act, in good faith, without actual malice and in the apparent interests of the public entity. *(Added by Stats.1963, c. 1683, p. 3300, § 16.)*

Research References

5 Witkin, California Summary 10th Torts § 373, (S 373) When Defense is Optional.
3 Witkin, California Summary 10th Agency and Employment § 124, Illustrations: Indemnification Denied.

§ 995.9. Defense or indemnification of witness by public entity

Notwithstanding any other provision of law, upon a request made in writing to a public entity, the public entity may defend or indemnify or defend and indemnify any witness who has testified on behalf of the public entity in any criminal, civil, or administrative action. The decision of the public entity to defend or indemnify or defend and indemnify such a witness shall rest within the sound discretion of the public entity and may be based on any relevant factors, including, but not limited to, whether the provision of defense or indemnity would serve the public interest. The public entity may defend or indemnify or defend and indemnify the witness only if it is determined by the public entity that the action being brought against the witness is based directly upon the conduct which the public entity requested of the witness related to the witness' testimony or provision of evidence. The public entity has the discretion to provide a defense alone apart from indemnity, and the public entity may offer to defend or indemnify or defend and indemnify while reserving all rights to subsequently withdraw these offers upon reasonable notice.

Neither defense nor indemnification shall be provided if the testimony giving rise to the action against the witness was false in any material respect, or was otherwise not given by the witness with a good faith belief in its truth; nor shall representation or indemnification under this section be offered or promised unless the action has been commenced and the witness has requested the public entity to act for the witness' benefit under this section. The public entity shall not be liable for indemnification of a defendant witness for punitive damages awarded to the plaintiff in such an action. If the plaintiff prevails in a claim for punitive damages in an action defended at the expense of the public entity, the defendant shall be liable to the public entity for the full costs incurred by the public entity in providing representation to the defendant witness. *(Added by Stats.1995, c. 799 (A.B.1361), § 2.)*

Research References

3 Witkin Cal. Proc. 5th Actions § 214, Steps by Defendant.
5 Witkin, California Summary 10th Torts § 236, Defense or Indemnification of Witness.

§ 996. Counsel; insurance; expenses

A public entity may provide for a defense pursuant to this part by its own attorney or by employing other counsel for this purpose or by purchasing insurance which requires that the insurer provide the defense. All of the expenses of providing a defense pursuant to this part are proper charges against a public entity. A public entity has no right to recover such expenses from the employee or former employee defended. *(Added by Stats.1963, c. 1683, p. 3300, § 16.)*

Research References

5 Witkin, California Summary 10th Torts § 374, (S 374) Methods of Providing Defense.

§ 996.4.   Failure or refusal to provide defense

If after request a public entity fails or refuses to provide an employee or former employee with a defense against a civil action or proceeding brought against him and the employee retains his own counsel to defend the action or proceeding, he is entitled to recover from the public entity such reasonable attorney's fees, costs and expenses as are necessarily incurred by him in defending the action or proceeding if the action or proceeding arose out of an act or omission in the scope of his employment as an employee of the public entity, but he is not entitled to such reimbursement if the public entity establishes (a) that he acted or failed to act because of actual fraud, corruption or actual malice, or (b) that the action or proceeding is one described in Section 995.4.

Nothing in this section shall be construed to deprive an employee or former employee of the right to petition for a writ of mandate to compel the public entity or the governing body or an employee thereof to perform the duties imposed by this part. *(Added by Stats.1963, c. 1683, p. 3300, § 16.)*

Research References

5 Witkin, California Summary 10th Torts § 371, (S 371) Employee's Right to Defense.
5 Witkin, California Summary 10th Torts § 375, (S 375) in General.

§ 996.6.   Rights of employee under contract or other enactments

The rights of an employee or former employee under this part are in addition to and not in lieu of any rights he may have under any contract or under any other enactment providing for his defense. *(Added by Stats.1963, c. 1683, p. 3300, § 16.)*

Research References

Rutter, Cal. Practice Guide: Civ. Pro. Before Trial Ch. 6-C, C. Answer.
Miller and Starr California Real Estate § 30:32, Remedies for a Regulatory Taking.
5 Witkin, California Summary 10th Torts § 371, (S 371) Employee's Right to Defense.
3 Witkin, California Summary 10th Agency and Employment § 124, Illustrations: Indemnification Denied.

Title 2

GOVERNMENT OF THE STATE OF CALIFORNIA

Division 3

EXECUTIVE DEPARTMENT

Part 1

STATE DEPARTMENTS AND AGENCIES

CHAPTER 3.5.   ADMINISTRATIVE REGULATIONS AND RULEMAKING

ARTICLE 1.   GENERAL

§ 11340.   Legislative findings and declarations

The Legislature finds and declares as follows:

(a) There has been an unprecedented growth in the number of administrative regulations in recent years.

(b) The language of many regulations is frequently unclear and unnecessarily complex, even when the complicated and technical nature of the subject matter is taken into account. The language is often confusing to the persons who must comply with the regulations.

(c) Substantial time and public funds have been spent in adopting regulations, the necessity for which has not been established.

(d) The imposition of prescriptive standards upon private persons and entities through regulations where the establishment of performance standards could reasonably be expected to produce the same result has placed an unnecessary burden on California citizens and discouraged innovation, research, and development of improved means of achieving desirable social goals.

(e) There exists no central office in state government with the power and duty to review regulations to ensure that they are written in a comprehensible manner, are authorized by statute, and are consistent with other law.

(f) Correcting the problems that have been caused by the unprecedented growth of regulations in California requires the direct involvement of the Legislature as well as that of the executive branch of state government.

(g) The complexity and lack of clarity in many regulations put small businesses, which do not have the resources to hire experts to assist them, at a distinct disadvantage. *(Added by Stats.1979, c. 567, § 1, operative July 1, 1980. Amended by Stats.1981, c. 865, p. 3305, § 2; Stats.1983, c. 874, § 1; Stats.1993, c. 870 (S.B.726), § 1.)*

Research References

California Practice Guide: Employment Litigation Ch. 1-A, A. Background.

California Practice Guide: Employment Litigation Ch. 11-B, B. Coverage and Exemptions-In General.

Rutter, Cal. Practice Guide: Insurance Litigation Ch. 14-A, A. The California Regulator (*).

Rutter, Cal. Practice Guide: Prof. Responsibility Ch. 4-B, B. Concurrent Representation of Clients With Conflicting Interests (Conflicts Between Present Clients).

Rutter, Cal. Practice Guide: Prof. Responsibility Ch. 8-D, D. Restrictions on Speech and Behavior Outside Courtroom.

Miller and Starr California Real Estate § 4:3, The Real Estate Commissioner.

Miller and Starr California Real Estate § 4:22, Regulations; Generally.

21 NO. 5 Miller & Starr, California Real Estate Newsalert 9, Deeds.

9 Witkin Cal. Proc. 5th Administrative Proceedings § 34, (S 34) in General.

9 Witkin Cal. Proc. 5th Administrative Proceedings § 37, (S 37) Legislative Authority.

9 Witkin Cal. Proc. 5th Administrative Proceedings § 38, History, Legislative Intent, and Revision.

9 Witkin Cal. Proc. 5th Administrative Proceedings § 41, Interpretive Policies.

9 Witkin Cal. Proc. 5th Administrative Proceedings § 43, (S 43) Drafting Requirements.

9 Witkin Cal. Proc. 5th Administrative Proceedings § 51, (S 51) in General.

9 Witkin Cal. Proc. 5th Administrative Proceedings § 73, (S 73) Reliance on Appropriate Authority.

9 Witkin Cal. Proc. 5th Administrative Proceedings § 144, Grounds for Declaration of Invalidity.

9 Witkin Cal. Proc. 5th Administrative Proceedings § 203, (S 203) Office of Administrative Law.

8 Witkin Cal. Proc. 5th Extraordinary Writs § 264, Public Administrative Agencies.

8 Witkin Cal. Proc. 5th Extraordinary Writs § 307, Period and Extensions.

§ 11340.1. Legislative intent

(a) The Legislature therefore declares that it is in the public interest to establish an Office of Administrative Law which shall be charged with the orderly review of adopted regulations. It is the intent of the Legislature that the purpose of such review shall be to reduce the number of administrative regulations and to improve the quality of those regulations which are adopted. It is the intent of the Legislature that agencies shall actively seek to reduce the unnecessary regulatory burden on private individuals and entities by substituting performance standards for prescriptive standards wherever performance standards can be reasonably expected to be as effective and less burdensome, and that this substitution shall be considered during the course of the agency rulemaking process. It is the intent of the Legislature that neither the Office of Administrative Law nor the court should substitute its judgment for that of the rulemaking agency as expressed in the substantive content of adopted regulations. It is the intent of the Legislature that while the Office of Administrative Law will be part of the executive branch of state government, that the office work closely with, and upon request report directly to, the Legislature in order to accomplish regulatory reform in California.

(b) It is the intent of the Legislature that the California Code of Regulations made available on the Internet by the office pursuant to Section 11344 include complete authority and reference citations and history notes. *(Added by Stats.1979, c. 567, § 1, operative July 1, 1980. Amended by Stats.1981, c. 865, p. 3306, § 3; Stats.1983, c. 874, § 2; Stats.1996, c. 501 (S.B.1910), § 1.)*

Research References

9 Witkin Cal. Proc. 5th Administrative Proceedings § 38, History, Legislative Intent, and Revision.

9 Witkin Cal. Proc. 5th Administrative Proceedings § 43, (S 43) Drafting Requirements.

9 Witkin Cal. Proc. 5th Administrative Proceedings § 51, (S 51) in General.

9 Witkin Cal. Proc. 5th Administrative Proceedings § 55, (S 55) in General.

§ 11340.2. Establishment of office; director and deputy director

(a) The Office of Administrative Law is hereby established in state government in the Government Operations Agency. The office shall be under the direction and control of an executive officer who shall be known as the director. There shall also be a deputy director. The director's term and the deputy director's term of office shall be coterminous with that of the appointing power, except that they shall be subject to reappointment.

(b) The director and deputy director shall have the same qualifications as a hearing officer and shall be appointed by the Governor subject to the confirmation of the Senate. *(Added by Stats.1979, c. 567, § 1, operative July 1, 1980. Amended by Stats.1980, c. 992, p. 3138, § 1.5; Gov.Reorg.Plan No. 2 of 2011–2012, § 175, eff. July 3, 2012, operative July 1, 2013; Stats.2013, c. 352 (A.B.1317), § 235, eff. Sept. 26, 2013, operative July 1, 2013.)*

Research References

9 Witkin Cal. Proc. 5th Administrative Proceedings § 38, History, Legislative Intent, and Revision.

§ 11340.3. Personnel

The director may employ and fix the compensation, in accordance with law, of such professional assistants and clerical and other employees as is deemed necessary for the effective conduct of the work of the office. *(Added by Stats.1979, c. 567, § 1, operative July 1, 1980.)*

§ 11340.4. Authorized actions; access to records and information

(a) The office is authorized and directed to do the following:

(1) Study the subject of administrative rulemaking in all its aspects.

(2) In the interest of fairness, uniformity, and the expedition of business, submit its suggestions to the various agencies.

(3) Report its recommendations to the Governor and Legislature at the commencement of each general session.

(b) All agencies of the state shall give the office ready access to their records and full information and reasonable assistance in any matter of research requiring recourse to them or to data within their knowledge or control. Nothing in this subdivision authorizes an agency to provide access to records required by statute to be kept confidential. *(Added by Stats.1995, c. 938 (S.B.523), § 14, operative July 1, 1997.)*

Law Revision Commission Comments

Section 11340.4 transfers to the Office of Administrative Law authority formerly found in Section 11370.5 relating to the study of "administrative law" by the Office of Administrative Hearings, to the extent that authority related to administrative rulemaking. [25 Cal.L.Rev.Comm. Reports 55 (1995)].

§ 11340.5. Agency guidelines, criteria, bulletins, manuals, instructions, orders, standards of general application or other rules: adoption as regulation; filing; determination of status as regulation

(a) No state agency shall issue, utilize, enforce, or attempt to enforce any guideline, criterion, bulletin, manual, instruction, order, standard of general application, or other rule, which is a regulation as defined in Section 11342.600, unless the guideline, criterion, bulletin, manual, instruction, order, standard of general application, or other rule has been adopted as a regulation and filed with the Secretary of State pursuant to this chapter.

(b) If the office is notified of, or on its own, learns of the issuance, enforcement of, or use of, an agency guideline, criterion, bulletin, manual, instruction, order, standard of general application, or other rule that has not been adopted as a regulation and filed with the Secretary of State pursuant to this chapter, the office may issue a determination as to whether the guideline, criterion, bulletin, manual, instruction, order, standard of general application, or other rule, is a regulation as defined in Section 11342.600.

(c) The office shall do all of the following:

(1) File its determination upon issuance with the Secretary of State.

(2) Make its determination known to the agency, the Governor, and the Legislature.

(3) Publish its determination in the California Regulatory Notice Register within 15 days of the date of issuance.

(4) Make its determination available to the public and the courts.

(d) Any interested person may obtain judicial review of a given determination by filing a written petition requesting that the determination of the office be modified or set aside. A petition shall be filed with the court within 30 days of the date the determination is published.

(e) A determination issued by the office pursuant to this section shall not be considered by a court, or by an administrative agency in an adjudicatory proceeding if all of the following occurs:

(1) The court or administrative agency proceeding involves the party that sought the determination from the office.

(2) The proceeding began prior to the party's request for the office's determination.

(3) At issue in the proceeding is the question of whether the guideline, criterion, bulletin, manual, instruction, order, standard of general application, or other rule that is the legal basis for the adjudicatory action is a regulation as defined in Section 11342.600. *(Added by Stats.1994, c. 1039 (A.B.2531), § 4. Amended by Stats.1995, c. 938 (S.B.523), § 15, operative Jan. 1, 1996; Stats.2000, c. 1060 (A.B.1822), § 3.)*

Law Revision Commission Comments

Section 11340.5 is amended to correct references to the definition of "regulation" in former Section 11342(g), which is continued in Section 11342.600. Amendment of this section is not intended to ratify or abrogate the opinion in Tidewater Marine Western, Inc. v. Bradshaw, 14 Cal.4th 557, 927 P.2d 296, 59 Cal.Rptr.2d 186 (1996). [29 Cal.L.Rev.Comm.Reports 459 (2000)].

Research References

9 Witkin Cal. Proc. 5th Administrative Proceedings § 40, What Constitutes Regulation.
9 Witkin Cal. Proc. 5th Administrative Proceedings § 41, Interpretive Policies.
9 Witkin Cal. Proc. 5th Administrative Proceedings § 53, (S 53) Determination Whether Uncodified Agency Action Constitutes Regulation.
9 Witkin Cal. Proc. 5th Administrative Proceedings § 73, (S 73) Reliance on Appropriate Authority.

§ 11340.6. Petition for adoption or repeal; contents

Except where the right to petition for adoption of a regulation is restricted by statute to a designated group or where the form of procedure for such a petition is otherwise prescribed by statute, any interested person may petition a state agency requesting the adoption, amendment, or repeal of a regulation as provided in Article 5 (commencing with Section 11346). This petition shall state the following clearly and concisely:

(a) The substance or nature of the regulation, amendment, or repeal requested.

(b) The reason for the request.

(c) Reference to the authority of the state agency to take the action requested. *(Added by Stats.1994, c. 1039 (A.B.2531), § 5.)*

Research References

Rutter, Cal. Practice Guide: Insurance Litigation Ch. 14-A, A. The California Regulator (*).
9 Witkin Cal. Proc. 5th Administrative Proceedings § 45, (S 45) Petition by Interested Person.

§ 11340.7. Petition for adoption, amendment or repeal; relief; reconsideration; decision

(a) Upon receipt of a petition requesting the adoption, amendment, or repeal of a regulation pursuant to Article 5 (commencing with Section 11346), a state agency shall notify the petitioner in writing of the receipt and shall within 30 days deny the petition indicating why the agency has reached its decision on the merits of the petition in writing or schedule the matter for public hearing in accordance with the notice and hearing requirements of that article.

(b) A state agency may grant or deny the petition in part, and may grant any other relief or take any other action as it may determine to be warranted by the petition and shall notify the petitioner in writing of this action.

(c) Any interested person may request a reconsideration of any part or all of a decision of any agency on any petition submitted. The request shall be submitted in accordance with Section 11340.6 and include the reason or reasons why an agency should reconsider its previous decision no later than 60 days after the date of the decision involved. The agency's reconsideration of any matter relating to a petition shall be subject to subdivision (a).

(d) Any decision of a state agency denying in whole or in part or granting in whole or in part a petition requesting the adoption, amendment, or repeal of a regulation pursuant to Article 5 (commencing with Section 11346) shall be in writing and shall be transmitted to the Office of Administrative Law for publication in the California Regulatory Notice Register at the earliest practicable date. The decision shall identify the agency, the party submitting the petition, the provisions of the California Code of Regulations requested to be affected, reference to authority to take the action requested, the reasons supporting the agency determination, an agency contact person, and the right of interested persons to obtain a copy of the petition from the agency. *(Added by Stats.1994, c. 1039 (A.B.2531), § 6.)*

Research References

Rutter, Cal. Practice Guide: Insurance Litigation Ch. 14-A, A. The California Regulator (*).
9 Witkin Cal. Proc. 5th Administrative Proceedings § 45, (S 45) Petition by Interested Person.
9 Witkin Cal. Proc. 5th Administrative Proceedings § 55, (S 55) in General.

§ 11340.85. Electronic communications

(a) As used in this section, "electronic communication" includes electronic transmission of written or graphical material by electronic mail, facsimile, or other means, but does not include voice communication.

(b) Notwithstanding any other provision of this chapter that refers to mailing or sending, or to oral or written communication:

(1) An agency may permit and encourage use of electronic communication, but may not require use of electronic communication.

(2) An agency may publish or distribute a document required by this chapter or by a regulation implementing this chapter by means of electronic communication, but shall not make that the exclusive means by which the document is published or distributed.

(3) A notice required or authorized by this chapter or by a regulation implementing this chapter may be delivered to a person by means of electronic communication if the person has expressly indicated a willingness to receive the notice by means of electronic communication.

(4) A comment regarding a regulation may be delivered to an agency by means of electronic communication.

(5) A petition regarding a regulation may be delivered to an agency by means of electronic communication if the agency has expressly indicated a willingness to receive a petition by means of electronic communication.

(c) An agency that maintains an Internet Web site or other similar forum for the electronic publication or distribution of written material shall publish on that Web site or other forum information regarding a proposed regulation or regulatory repeal or amendment, that includes, but is not limited to, the following:

(1) Any public notice required by this chapter or by a regulation implementing this chapter.

(2) The initial statement of reasons prepared pursuant to subdivision (b) of Section 11346.2.

(3) The final statement of reasons prepared pursuant to subdivision (a) of Section 11346.9.

(4) Notice of a decision not to proceed prepared pursuant to Section 11347.

(5) The text of a proposed action or instructions on how to obtain a copy of the text.

(6) A statement of any decision made by the office regarding a proposed action.

(7) The date a rulemaking action is filed with the Secretary of State.

(8) The effective date of a rulemaking action.

(9) A statement to the effect that a business or person submitting a comment regarding a proposed action has the right to request a copy of the final statement of reasons.

(10) The text of a proposed emergency adoption, amendment, or repeal of a regulation pursuant to Section 11346.1 and the date it was submitted to the office for review and filing.

(d) A document that is required to be posted pursuant to subdivision (c) shall be posted within a reasonable time after issuance of the document, and shall remain posted until at least 15 days after (1) the rulemaking action is filed with the Secretary of State, or (2) notice of a decision not to proceed is published pursuant to Section 11347. Publication under subdivision (c) supplements any other required form of publication or distribution. Failure to comply with this section is not grounds for disapproval of a proposed regulation. Subdivision (c) does not require an agency to establish or maintain a Web site or other forum for the electronic publication or distribution of written material.

(e) Nothing in this section precludes the office from requiring that the material submitted to the office for publication in the California Code of Regulations or the California Regulatory Notice Register be submitted in electronic form.

(f) This section is intended to make the regulatory process more user-friendly and to improve communication between interested parties and the regulatory agencies. *(Added by Stats.2000, c. 1060 (A.B.1822), § 4. Amended by Stats.2001, c. 59 (S.B.561), § 2; Stats.2002, c. 389 (A.B.1857), § 2; Stats.2006, c. 713 (A.B.1302), § 1.)*

Law Revision Commission Comments

Section 11340.85 is new. Subdivision (b) authorizes the use of electronic communications in adopting a regulation under this chapter.

Subdivision (c) requires electronic publication of certain rulemaking documents by an agency that maintains a website or similar electronic communication forum. Provisions requiring a "public notice" as defined in paragraph (1) include Sections 11346.4 (notice of proposed action), 11346.8(a) (notice of hearing), and 11346.8(b) (notice of continuance or postponement of hearing), and Section 44 of Title 1 of the California Code of Regulations (notice of changes to proposed regulation).

Use of electronic communications pursuant to this section supplements other required forms of publication or distribution. See subdivisions (b)(2) & (d). See also Section 11342(b) ("office" means Office of Administrative Law). [30 Cal.L.Rev.Comm.Reports 725 (2000)].

Section 11340.85 is amended to harmonize its requirements with those of former Section 11340.8.

Subdivision (b)(4) is amended to provide that agencies are required to accept comments by facsimile or electronic mail. The mandatory aspect of this rule is drawn from former Section 11340.8(a). Subdivision (b)(5) makes clear that an agency is not required to accept rulemaking petitions by facsimile or electronic mail.

Subdivision (c)(1) is amended to improve its clarity. This is a nonsubstantive change. Provisions requiring a "public notice" as defined in paragraph (1) include Sections 11346.4 (notice of proposed action), 11346.8(a) (notice of hearing), 11346.8(b) (notice of continuance or postponement of hearing), and Section 44 of Title 1 of the California Code of Regulations (notice of changes to proposed regulation).

Subdivision (c)(6)-(9) continues former Section 11340.8(b)(6)-(9) without substantive change.

Subdivision (f) continues the introductory statement of intent in former Section 11340.8 without substantive change. [31 Cal.L.Rev.Comm. Reports 71 (2001)].

Subdivision (c) of Section 11340.85 is amended to extend the existing Internet publication requirement to include the text of a proposed emergency rulemaking action. See Section 11349.6 (review of emergency regulation), 1 Cal. Code Regs. § 55 (public comments regarding emergency regulation).

Subdivision (d) is amended to specify when and for how long a document must be posted under subdivision (c). 31 Cal.L.Rev.Comm. Reports 267 (2001)].

Research References

9 Witkin Cal. Proc. 5th Administrative Proceedings § 38, History, Legislative Intent, and Revision.

9 Witkin Cal. Proc. 5th Administrative Proceedings § 39, Nature and Scope.

9 Witkin Cal. Proc. 5th Administrative Proceedings § 44, (S 44) Notice Requirements.

§ 11340.9. Application of chapter

This chapter does not apply to any of the following:

(a) An agency in the judicial or legislative branch of the state government.

(b) A legal ruling of counsel issued by the Franchise Tax Board or State Board of Equalization.

(c) A form prescribed by a state agency or any instructions relating to the use of the form, but this provision is not a limitation on any requirement that a regulation be adopted pursuant to this chapter when one is needed to implement the law under which the form is issued.

(d) A regulation that relates only to the internal management of the state agency.

(e) A regulation that establishes criteria or guidelines to be used by the staff of an agency in performing an audit, investiga-

Government

tion, examination, or inspection, settling a commercial dispute, negotiating a commercial arrangement, or in the defense, prosecution, or settlement of a case, if disclosure of the criteria or guidelines would do any of the following:

(1) Enable a law violator to avoid detection.

(2) Facilitate disregard of requirements imposed by law.

(3) Give clearly improper advantage to a person who is in an adverse position to the state.

(f) A regulation that embodies the only legally tenable interpretation of a provision of law.

(g) A regulation that establishes or fixes rates, prices, or tariffs.

(h) A regulation that relates to the use of public works, including streets and highways, when the effect of the regulation is indicated to the public by means of signs or signals or when the regulation determines uniform standards and specifications for official traffic control devices pursuant to Section 21400 of the Vehicle Code.

(i) A regulation that is directed to a specifically named person or to a group of persons and does not apply generally throughout the state. *(Added by Stats.2000, c. 1060 (A.B.1822), § 5.)*

Law Revision Commission Comments

Section 11340.9 is new. It collects various exemptions from the requirements of this chapter.

Subdivision (a) continues former Section 11342(a) without substantive change.

Subdivisions (b)-(d) continue provisions of former Section 11342(g) without substantive change.

Subdivision (e) establishes a new exception for agency rules that should not be disclosed to the public. It is drawn from 1981 Model State APA §3–116(2). Note that "examination" includes both an inspection and a test administered to determine a person's knowledge or ability. See, e.g., Corp. Code §25217 (passage of examination administered by Department of Corporations may be required for licensing of securities agent); Fin. Code §17405 (Department of Corporations may examine business, accounts, and records of escrow agent). Subdivision (e) is intended to create an exception for data that relates to an examination only where disclosure of that data would give a clearly improper advantage to a person taking the examination.

Subdivision (f) establishes a new exception for an agency rule embodying the only legally tenable interpretation of a provision of law. This principle has been recognized by the courts. *See, e.g.,* Engelmann v. State Bd. of Educ., 2 Cal.App.4th 47, 62, 3 Cal.Rptr.2d 264, 274–75 (1991) (statement of policy or procedure that simply reiterates statutory law, without departing from or embellishing it, need not be adopted as regulation). *Cf.* Grier v. Kizer, 219 Cal.App.3d 422, 438–39, 268 Cal.Rptr. 244, 255 (1990) (agency policy was not "only legally tenable interpretation" of law and should have been adopted as regulation). The rule is also consistent with the current practice of the Office of Administrative Law. *See, e.g.,* 1988 OAL Determination No. 10, Cal. Regulatory Notice Reg. 88, No. 28–Z, July 8, 1988, p. 2313 (agency rule reflecting only legally tenable interpretation of statute was not regulation). *Cf.* 1989 OAL Determination No. 15, Cal. Regulatory Notice Reg. 89, No. 44–Z, Nov. 3 1989, p. 3122 (law interpreted by agency regulation was subject to more than one legally tenable interpretation). The addition of this exception does not expand the definition of "regulation." See Section 11342.600 ("regulation" defined). For a similar exception, see Section 18212(a).

Subdivisions (g)-(i) continue without substantive change former Section 11343(a)(1)-(3) and part of the former first sentence of Section 11346.1(a) ("This article does not apply to any regulation not required to be filed with the Secretary of State under this chapter."). Enactment of subdivision (i) is not intended to ratify or abrogate the opinion in Tidewater Marine Western, Inc. v. Bradshaw, 14 Cal.4th 557, 927 P.2d 296, 59 Cal.Rptr.2d 186 (1996). [29 Cal.L.Rev.Comm.Reports 459 (2000)].

Research References

Rutter, Cal. Practice Guide: Insurance Litigation Ch. 14-A, A. The California Regulator (*).

Miller and Starr California Real Estate § 27:18, Department of Industrial Relations--Administrative Powers and Proceedings.
21 NO. 5 Miller & Starr, California Real Estate Newsalert 9, Deeds.
9 Witkin Cal. Proc. 5th Administrative Proceedings § 38, History, Legislative Intent, and Revision.
9 Witkin Cal. Proc. 5th Administrative Proceedings § 39, Nature and Scope.
9 Witkin Cal. Proc. 5th Administrative Proceedings § 40, What Constitutes Regulation.
9 Witkin Cal. Proc. 5th Administrative Proceedings § 41, Interpretive Policies.

§ 11341. Unique identification numbers for regulatory actions; use and application of identification numbers

(a) The office shall establish a system to give a unique identification number to each regulatory action.

(b) The office and the state agency taking the regulatory action shall use the identification number given by the office pursuant to subdivision (a) to refer to the regulatory action for which a notice has already been published in the California Regulatory Notice Register.

(c) The identification number shall be sufficient information for a member of the public to identify and track a regulatory action both with the office and the state agency taking the regulatory action. No other information pertaining to the regulatory action shall be required of a member of the public if the identification number of the regulatory action has been provided. *(Added by Stats.2000, c. 1059 (A.B.505), § 5.)*

§ 11342.1. Scope of authority

Except as provided in Section 11342.4, nothing in this chapter confers authority upon or augments the authority of any state agency to adopt, administer, or enforce any regulation. Each regulation adopted, to be effective, shall be within the scope of authority conferred and in accordance with standards prescribed by other provisions of law. *(Added by Stats.1979, c. 567, § 1, operative July 1, 1980. Amended by Stats.1987, c. 1375, § 2.)*

Research References

9 Witkin Cal. Proc. 5th Administrative Proceedings § 37, (S 37) Legislative Authority.

§ 11342.2. Validity of regulations

Whenever by the express or implied terms of any statute a state agency has authority to adopt regulations to implement, interpret, make specific or otherwise carry out the provisions of the statute, no regulation adopted is valid or effective unless consistent and not in conflict with the statute and reasonably necessary to effectuate the purpose of the statute. *(Added by Stats.1979, c. 567, § 1, operative July 1, 1980.)*

Research References

Rutter, Cal. Practice Guide: Insurance Litigation Ch. 14-B, B. Courts and Regulation.
22 NO. 4 Miller & Starr, California Real Estate Newsalert 44, Hazardous Materials Charge on Businesses With 50 or More Employees Upheld as Valid Regulation and Constitutional Tax.
9 Witkin Cal. Proc. 5th Administrative Proceedings § 37, (S 37) Legislative Authority.

§ 11342.4. Regulations to carry out provisions of chapter

The office shall adopt, amend, or repeal regulations for the purpose of carrying out the provisions of this chapter. *(Formerly § 11344.6, added by Stats.1981, c. 865, p. 3310, § 19. Amended by Stats.1982, c. 1573, p. 6201, § 1. Renumbered § 11342.4 and amended by Stats.1983, c. 797, § 12.)*

Research References

9 Witkin Cal. Proc. 5th Administrative Proceedings § 42, Incorporation by Reference.

ARTICLE 2. DEFINITIONS

§ 11342.510. Definitions; construction of chapter

Unless the provision or context otherwise requires, the definitions in this article govern the construction of this chapter. *(Added by Stats.2000, c. 1060 (A.B.1822), § 8.)*

Law Revision Commission Comments

Section 11342.510 continues the introductory paragraph of former Section 11342 without substantive change. [29 Cal.L.Rev.Comm.Reports 459 (2000)].

Research References

9 Witkin Cal. Proc. 5th Administrative Proceedings § 38, History, Legislative Intent, and Revision.

§ 11342.520. Agency

"Agency" means state agency. *(Added by Stats.2000, c. 1060 (A.B.1822), § 8.)*

Law Revision Commission Comments

Section 11342.520 is new. It clarifies part of the substance of former Section 11342(a). See also Section 11000 ("state agency" defined for purposes of this title). [29 Cal.L.Rev.Comm.Reports 459 (2000)].

§ 11342.530. Building standard

"Building standard" has the same meaning provided in Section 18909 of the Health and Safety Code. *(Added by Stats.2000, c. 1060 (A.B.1822), § 8.)*

Law Revision Commission Comments

Section 11342.530 is new. It is added for drafting convenience. [29 Cal.L.Rev.Comm.Reports 459 (2000)].

§ 11342.535. Cost impact

"Cost impact" means the amount of reasonable range of direct costs, or a description of the type and extent of direct costs, that a representative private person or business necessarily incurs in reasonable compliance with the proposed action. *(Added by Stats.2000, c. 1059 (A.B.505), § 6.5.)*

§ 11342.540. Director

"Director" means the director of the office. *(Added by Stats.2000, c. 1060 (A.B.1822), § 8.)*

Law Revision Commission Comments

Section 11342.540 is new. It is added for drafting convenience. [29 Cal.L.Rev.Comm.Reports 459 (2000)].

§ 11342.545. Emergency

"Emergency" means a situation that calls for immediate action to avoid serious harm to the public peace, health, safety, or general welfare. *(Added by Stats.2006, c. 713 (A.B.1302), § 2.)*

Research References

Rutter, Cal. Practice Guide: Insurance Litigation Ch. 14-A, A. The California Regulator (*).

§ 11342.548. Major regulation

"Major regulation" means any proposed adoption, amendment, or repeal of a regulation subject to review by the Office of Administrative Law pursuant to Article 6 (commencing with Section 11349) that will have an economic impact on California business enterprises and individuals in an amount exceeding fifty million dollars ($50,000,000), as estimated by the agency. *(Added by Stats.2011, c. 496 (S.B.617), § 1.)*

§ 11342.550. Office

"Office" means the Office of Administrative Law. *(Added by Stats.2000, c. 1060 (A.B.1822), § 8.)*

Law Revision Commission Comments

Section 11342.550 continues former Section 11342(b) without change. [29 Cal.L.Rev.Comm.Reports 459 (2000)].

§ 11342.560. Order of repeal

"Order of repeal" means any resolution, order, or other official act of a state agency that expressly repeals a regulation in whole or in part. *(Added by Stats.2000, c. 1060 (A.B.1822), § 8.)*

Law Revision Commission Comments

Section 11342.560 continues former Section 11342(c) without change. [29 Cal.L.Rev.Comm.Reports 459 (2000)].

§ 11342.570. Performance standard

"Performance standard" means a regulation that describes an objective with the criteria stated for achieving the objective. *(Added by Stats.2000, c. 1060 (A.B.1822), § 8.)*

Law Revision Commission Comments

Section 11342.570 continues former Section 11342(d) without change. [29 Cal.L.Rev.Comm.Reports 459 (2000)].

Research References

9 Witkin Cal. Proc. 5th Administrative Proceedings § 38, History, Legislative Intent, and Revision.

§ 11342.580. Plain English

"Plain English" means language that satisfies the standard of clarity provided in Section 11349. *(Added by Stats.2000, c. 1060 (A.B.1822), § 8.)*

Law Revision Commission Comments

Section 11342.580 is drawn from former Section 11342(e). This section differs from former Section 11342(e) in that it refers to the "clarity" standard provided in Section 11349(c) (regulations must be written or displayed so that their meaning will be easily understood by persons directly affected by them). Plain English requirements may be found in Sections 11346.2 and 11346.5. [29 Cal.L.Rev.Comm.Reports 459 (2000)].

Research References

9 Witkin Cal. Proc. 5th Administrative Proceedings § 38, History, Legislative Intent, and Revision.

9 Witkin Cal. Proc. 5th Administrative Proceedings § 43, (S 43) Drafting Requirements.

§ 11342.590. Prescriptive standard

"Prescriptive standard" means a regulation that specifies the sole means of compliance with a performance standard by specific actions, measurements, or other quantifiable means. *(Added by Stats.2000, c. 1060 (A.B.1822), § 8.)*

Law Revision Commission Comments

Section 11342.590 continues former Section 11342(f) without change. [29 Cal.L.Rev.Comm.Reports 459 (2000).

Research References

9 Witkin Cal. Proc. 5th Administrative Proceedings § 38, History, Legislative Intent, and Revision.

§ 11342.595. Proposed action

"Proposed action" means the regulatory action, notice of which is submitted to the office for publication in the California Regulatory Notice Register. *(Added by Stats.2000, c. 1059 (A.B.505), § 6.7. Amended by Stats.2001, c. 59 (S.B.561), § 3.)*

Law Revision Commission Comments

Section 11342.595 is amended to correct a technical defect. It is the notice of proposed action, not the proposed action itself, that is published in the California Regulatory Notice Register. See Section 11344.1(a) (contents of California Regulatory Notice Register). [30 Cal.L.Rev. Comm. Reports 533 (2000)].

§ 11342.600. Regulation

"Regulation" means every rule, regulation, order, or standard of general application or the amendment, supplement, or revision of any rule, regulation, order, or standard adopted by any state agency to implement, interpret, or make specific the law enforced or administered by it, or to govern its procedure. *(Added by Stats.2000, c. 1060 (A.B.1822), § 8.)*

Law Revision Commission Comments

Section 11342.600 continues part of former Section 11342(g) without substantive change. The parts of former Section 11342(g) that are not continued in this section are continued without substantive change in Section 11340.9(b)-(d). [29 Cal.L.Rev.Comm.Reports 459 (2000)].

Research References

Rutter, Cal. Practice Guide: Insurance Litigation Ch. 14-A, A. The California Regulator (*).
9 Witkin Cal. Proc. 5th Administrative Proceedings § 40, What Constitutes Regulation.
9 Witkin Cal. Proc. 5th Administrative Proceedings § 41, Interpretive Policies.
9 Witkin Cal. Proc. 5th Administrative Proceedings § 64, When Provisions Apply.

§ 11342.610. Small business

(a) "Small business" means a business activity in agriculture, general construction, special trade construction, retail trade, wholesale trade, services, transportation and warehousing, manufacturing, generation and transmission of electric power, or a health care facility, unless excluded in subdivision (b), that is both of the following:

(1) Independently owned and operated.

(2) Not dominant in its field of operation.

(b) "Small business" does not include the following professional and business activities:

(1) A financial institution including a bank, a trust, a savings and loan association, a thrift institution, a consumer finance company, a commercial finance company, an industrial finance company, a credit union, a mortgage and investment banker, a securities broker-dealer, or an investment adviser.

(2) An insurance company, either stock or mutual.

(3) A mineral, oil, or gas broker.

(4) A subdivider or developer.

(5) A landscape architect, an architect, or a building designer.

(6) An entity organized as a nonprofit institution.

(7) An entertainment activity or production, including a motion picture, a stage performance, a television or radio station, or a production company.

(8) A utility, a water company, or a power transmission company generating and transmitting more than 4.5 million kilowatt hours annually.

(9) A petroleum producer, a natural gas producer, a refiner, or a pipeline.

(10) A manufacturing enterprise exceeding 250 employees.

(11) A health care facility exceeding 150 beds or one million five hundred thousand dollars ($1,500,000) in annual gross receipts.

(c) "Small business" does not include the following business activities:

(1) Agriculture, where the annual gross receipts exceed one million dollars ($1,000,000).

(2) General construction, where the annual gross receipts exceed nine million five hundred thousand dollars ($9,500,000).

(3) Special trade construction, where the annual gross receipts exceed five million dollars ($5,000,000).

(4) Retail trade, where the annual gross receipts exceed two million dollars ($2,000,000).

(5) Wholesale trade, where the annual gross receipts exceed nine million five hundred thousand dollars ($9,500,000).

(6) Services, where the annual gross receipts exceed two million dollars ($2,000,000).

(7) Transportation and warehousing, where the annual gross receipts exceed one million five hundred thousand dollars ($1,500,000). *(Added by Stats.2000, c. 1060 (A.B.1822), § 8.)*

Law Revision Commission Comments

Section 11342.610 continues former Section 11342(h) without substantive change. [29 Cal.L.Rev.Comm.Reports 459 (2000)].

ARTICLE 3. FILING AND PUBLICATION

§ 11343. Transmittal of certified copies of regulations; orders of repeal; posting on Internet Web site; exceptions; duplicate copies and citation of authority; notice of proposed action; certification and delegation

Every state agency shall:

(a) Transmit to the office for filing with the Secretary of State a certified copy of every regulation adopted or amended by it except one that is a building standard.

(b) Transmit to the office for filing with the Secretary of State a certified copy of every order of repeal of a regulation required to be filed under subdivision (a).

(c)(1) Within 15 days of the office filing a state agency's regulation with the Secretary of State, post the regulation on its Internet Web site in an easily marked and identifiable location. The state agency shall keep the regulation on its Internet Web site for at least six months from the date the regulation is filed with the Secretary of State.

(2) Within five days of posting, the state agency shall send to the office the Internet Web site link of each regulation that the agency posts on its Internet Web site pursuant to paragraph (1).

(3) This subdivision shall not apply to a state agency that does not maintain an Internet Web site.

(d) Deliver to the office, at the time of transmittal for filing a regulation or order of repeal, six duplicate copies of the regulation or order of repeal, together with a citation of the authority pursuant to which it or any part thereof was adopted.

(e) Deliver to the office a copy of the notice of proposed action required by Section 11346.4.

(f) Transmit to the California Building Standards Commission for approval a certified copy of every regulation, or order of repeal of a regulation, that is a building standard, together with a citation of authority pursuant to which it or any part thereof was adopted, a copy of the notice of proposed action required by Section 11346.4, and any other records prescribed by the State Building Standards Law (Part 2.5 (commencing with Section 18901) of Division 13 of the Health and Safety Code).

(g) Whenever a certification is required by this section, it shall be made by the head of the state agency that is adopting, amending, or repealing the regulation, or by a designee of the agency head, and the certification and delegation shall be in writing. *(Added by Stats.1979, c. 567, § 1. Amended by Stats.1979, c. 1152, § 12.2, operative July 1, 1980; Stats.1980, c. 204, § 1, eff. June 20, 1980; Stats.1981, c. 865, p. 3307, § 5; Stats.1982, c. 749, p. 2965, § 1, eff. Sept. 8, 1982; Stats.1983, c. 291, § 1; Stats.1987, c. 1375, § 3; Stats.1988, c. 1194, § 1.2, operative Jan. 1, 1989; Stats.2000, c. 1060 (A.B.1822), § 9; Stats.2002, c. 389 (A.B.1857), § 3; Stats.2012, c. 295 (S.B.1099), § 1.)*

Law Revision Commission Comments

Section 11343 is amended to make technical improvements. Former subdivision (a)(1)-(3) is continued without substantive change in Section 11340.9(g)-(i).

Subdivision (e) is amended to reflect the change in the name of the California Building Standards Commission. See also Section 11342.530 ("building standard" defined). [29 Cal.L.Rev.Comm.Reports 459 (2000)].

Subdivision (f) of Section 11343 is amended to reflect the fact that the head of an agency may be its governing body, rather than an individual officer. This is a technical, nonsubstantive change. [31 Cal.L.Rev.Comm. Reports 270 (2002)].

Research References

9 Witkin Cal. Proc. 5th Administrative Proceedings § 39, Nature and Scope.

9 Witkin Cal. Proc. 5th Administrative Proceedings § 51, (S 51) in General.

9 Witkin Cal. Proc. 5th Administrative Proceedings § 54, Filing.

§ 11343.1. Style; endorsement

(a) All regulations transmitted to the Office of Administrative Law for filing with the Secretary of State shall conform to the style prescribed by the office.

(b) Regulations approved by the office shall bear an endorsement by the office affixed to the certified copy which is filed with the Secretary of State. *(Added by Stats.1983, c. 797, § 2. Amended by Stats.1994, c. 1039 (A.B.2531), § 12.)*

Research References

9 Witkin Cal. Proc. 5th Administrative Proceedings § 43, (S 43) Drafting Requirements.

9 Witkin Cal. Proc. 5th Administrative Proceedings § 54, Filing.

§ 11343.2. Endorsement of time and date of filing; public inspection; fees; prohibition

The Secretary of State shall endorse on the certified copy of each regulation or order of repeal filed with or delivered to him or her, the time and date of filing and shall maintain a permanent file of the certified copies of regulations and orders of repeal for public inspection.

No fee shall be charged by any state officer or public official for the performance of any official act in connection with the certification or filing of regulations pursuant to this article. *(Added by Stats.1994, c. 1039 (A.B.2531), § 14.)*

§ 11343.3. Agencies required to promulgate regulations; required considerations regarding vehicle weight

Notwithstanding any other law, a state agency that is required to promulgate administrative regulations, including, but not limited to, the State Air Resources Board, the California Environmental Protection Agency, the State Energy Resources Conservation and Development Commission, and the Department of Motor Vehicles, shall take into account vehicle weight impacts and the ability of vehicle manufacturers or vehicle operators to comply with laws limiting the weight of vehicles. *(Added by Stats.2012, c. 771 (A.B.1706), § 2.)*

§ 11343.4. Regulation or order of repeal; effective date; exceptions

(a) Except as otherwise provided in subdivision (b), a regulation or an order of repeal required to be filed with the Secretary of State shall become effective on a quarterly basis as follows:

(1) January 1 if the regulation or order of repeal is filed on September 1 to November 30, inclusive.

(2) April 1 if the regulation or order of repeal is filed on December 1 to February 29, inclusive.

(3) July 1 if the regulation or order of repeal is filed on March 1 to May 31, inclusive.

(4) October 1 if the regulation or order of repeal is filed on June 1 to August 31, inclusive.

(b) The effective dates in subdivision (a) shall not apply in all of the following:

(1) The effective date is specifically provided by the statute pursuant to which the regulation or order of repeal was adopted, in which event it becomes effective on the day prescribed by the statute.

(2) A later date is prescribed by the state agency in a written instrument filed with, or as part of, the regulation or order of repeal.

(3) The agency makes a written request to the office demonstrating good cause for an earlier effective date, in which case the office may prescribe an earlier date.

(4)(A) A regulation adopted by the Fish and Game Commission pursuant to Article 1 (commencing with Section 200) of Chapter 2 of Division 1 of the Fish and Game Code.

(B) A regulation adopted by the Fish and Game Commission that requires a different effective date in order to conform to a federal regulation. *(Added by Stats.1994, c. 1039 (A.B.2531), § 16. Amended by Stats.2000, c. 1060 (A.B.1822), § 10; Stats. 2012, c. 295 (S.B.1099), § 2.)*

Law Revision Commission Comments

Subdivision (a) of Section 11343.4 is amended to eliminate an ambiguity. Former subdivision (b) is deleted as redundant. See Fin. Code 3373(b)(3) (effective date of regulation adopted pursuant to that section), 8054(c) (regulation adopted pursuant to that section subject to Gov't Code §11346.1); Gov't Code §11346.1(d) (effective date of regulation adopted pursuant to that section). [29 Cal.L.Rev.Comm.Reports 459 (2000)].

Research References

Rutter, Cal. Practice Guide: Insurance Litigation Ch. 14-A, A. The California Regulator (*).

9 Witkin Cal. Proc. 5th Administrative Proceedings § 47, (S 47) Determination by Agency.

9 Witkin Cal. Proc. 5th Administrative Proceedings § 54, Filing.

§ 11343.5. Filing of regulatory code or supplement in office of county clerk or delegated person

Within 10 days from the receipt of printed copies of the California Code of Regulations or of the California Code of Regulations Supplement from the State Printing Office, the office shall file one copy of the particular issue of the code or supplement in the office of the county clerk of each county in this state, or if the authority to accept filings on his or her behalf has been delegated by the county clerk of any county pursuant to Section 26803.5, in the office of the person to whom that authority has been delegated. *(Formerly § 11343.6, added by Stats.1979, c. 567, p. 1780, § 1, operative July 1, 1980. Renumbered § 11343.5 and amended by Stats.1981, c. 865, p. 3308, § 9. Amended by Stats.1987, c. 1375, § 3.2; Stats.2000, c. 1060 (A.B.1822), § 11.)*

Law Revision Commission Comments

Section 11343.5 is amended to conform to the change in the name of the former California Regulatory Code Supplement. See Section 11344. [29 Cal.L.Rev.Comm.Reports 459 (2000)].

Research References

9 Witkin Cal. Proc. 5th Administrative Proceedings § 38, History, Legislative Intent, and Revision.

9 Witkin Cal. Proc. 5th Administrative Proceedings § 55, (S 55) in General.

§ 11343.6. Rebuttable presumptions; judicial notice

The filing of a certified copy of a regulation or an order of repeal with the Secretary of State raises the rebuttable presumptions that:

(a) It was duly adopted.

(b) It was duly filed and made available for public inspection at the day and hour endorsed on it.

(c) All requirements of this chapter and the regulations of the office relative to such regulation have been complied with.

(d) The text of the certified copy of a regulation or order of repeal is the text of the regulation or order of repeal as adopted.

The courts shall take judicial notice of the contents of the certified copy of each regulation and of each order of repeal duly

filed. *(Formerly § 11343.7, added by Stats.1979, c. 567, p. 1780, § 1, operative July 1, 1980. Renumbered § 11343.6 and amended by Stats.1981, c. 865, p. 3308, § 10.)*

Research References

9 Witkin Cal. Proc. 5th Administrative Proceedings § 54, Filing.

§ 11343.8. Filing and publication other than required by article

Upon the request of a state agency, the office may file with the Secretary of State and the office may publish in such manner as it believes proper, any regulation or order of repeal of a regulation not required by this article to be filed with the Secretary of State. *(Formerly § 11343.9, added by Stats.1979, c. 567, p. 1781, § 1, operative July 1, 1980. Renumbered § 11343.8 and amended by Stats.1981, c. 865, p. 3308, § 12.)*

ARTICLE 4. THE CALIFORNIA CODE OF REGULATIONS, THE CALIFORNIA CODE OF REGULATIONS SUPPLEMENT, AND THE CALIFORNIA REGULATORY NOTICE REGISTER

Section

§ 11344. Code of regulations; publication; internet; updating

The office shall do all of the following:

(a) Provide for the official compilation, printing, and publication of adoption, amendment, or repeal of regulations, which shall be known as the California Code of Regulations. On and after July 1, 1998, the office shall make available on the Internet, free of charge, the full text of the California Code of Regulations, and may contract with another state agency or a private entity in order to provide this service.

(b) Make available on its Internet Web site a list of, and a link to the full text of, each regulation filed with the Secretary of State that is pending effectiveness pursuant to Section 11343.4.

(c) Provide for the compilation, printing, and publication of weekly updates of the California Code of Regulations. This publication shall be known as the California Code of Regulations Supplement and shall contain amendments to the code.

(d) Provide for the publication dates and manner and form in which regulations shall be printed and distributed and ensure that regulations are available in printed form at the earliest practicable date after filing with the Secretary of State.

(e) Ensure that each regulation is printed together with a reference to the statutory authority pursuant to which it was enacted and the specific statute or other provision of law which the regulation is implementing, interpreting, or making specific. *(Added by Stats.1983, c. 797, § 7. Amended by Stats.1987, c. 1375, § 3.5; Stats.1994, c. 1039 (A.B.2531), § 17; Stats.1996, c.*

501 (S.B.1910), § 2; Stats.2000, c. 1060 (A.B.1822), § 13; Stats.2012, c. 295 (S.B.1099), § 3.)

Law Revision Commission Comments

Section 11344 is amended to change the name of the California Regulatory Code Supplement to conform to the name of the California Code of Regulations, which it supplements. [29 Cal.L.Rev.Comm.Reports 459 (2000)].

Research References

9 Witkin Cal. Proc. 5th Administrative Proceedings § 38, History, Legislative Intent, and Revision.
9 Witkin Cal. Proc. 5th Administrative Proceedings § 55, (S 55) in General.

§ 11344.1. Regulatory notice register; publication

The office shall do all of the following:

(a) Provide for the publication of the California Regulatory Notice Register, which shall be an official publication of the State of California and which shall contain the following:

(1) Notices of proposed action prepared by regulatory agencies, subject to the notice requirements of this chapter, and which have been approved by the office.

(2) A summary of all regulations filed with the Secretary of State in the previous week.

(3) Summaries of all regulation decisions issued in the previous week detailing the reasons for disapproval of a regulation, the reasons for not filing an emergency regulation, and the reasons for repealing an emergency regulation. The California Regulatory Notice Register shall also include a quarterly index of regulation decisions.

(4) Material that is required to be published under Sections 11349.5, 11349.7, and 11349.9.

(5) Determinations issued pursuant to Section 11340.5.

(b) Establish the publication dates and manner and form in which the California Regulatory Notice Register shall be prepared and published and ensure that it is published and distributed in a timely manner to the presiding officer and rules committee of each house of the Legislature and to all subscribers.

(c) Post on its website, on a weekly basis:

(1) The California Regulatory Notice Register. Each issue of the California Regulatory Notice Register on the office's website shall remain posted for a minimum of 18 months.

(2) One or more Internet links to assist the public to gain access to the text of regulations proposed by state agencies. (Added by Stats.1983, c. 797, § 9. Amended by Stats.1987, c. 1375, § 4; Stats.1994, c. 1039 (A.B.2531), § 18; Stats.2000, c. 1059 (A.B.505), § 7; Stats.2000, c. 1060 (A.B.1822), § 14.5.)

Law Revision Commission Comments

Subdivision (a)(3) of Section 11344.1 is amended to ratify the existing practice of publishing detailed summaries of regulation decisions, rather than the decisions themselves. The complete decisions are public documents and can be obtained from the Office of Administrative Law.

Subdivision (a)(4) is amended to improve its clarity. This change is technical and is not intended to affect the meaning of the section.

This section also contains language from 2000 Cal. Stat. ch. 1059, §7, which was chaptered out by the bill amending this section. See 2000 Cal. Stat. ch. 1060, §§14.5 & 44. 30 Cal.L.Rev.Comm.Reports 725 (2000)].

Research References

9 Witkin Cal. Proc. 5th Administrative Proceedings § 55, (S 55) in General.

§ 11344.2. Supplying sets to county clerks or delegated persons

The office shall supply a complete set of the California Code of Regulations, and of the California Code of Regulations Supplement to the county clerk of any county or to the delegatee of the county clerk pursuant to Section 26803.5, provided the director makes the following two determinations:

(a) The county clerk or the delegatee of the county clerk pursuant to Section 26803.5 is maintaining the code and supplement in complete and current condition in a place and at times convenient to the public.

(b) The California Code of Regulations and California Code of Regulations Supplement are not otherwise reasonably available to the public in the community where the county clerk or the delegatee of the county clerk pursuant to Section 26803.5 would normally maintain the code and supplements by distribution to libraries pursuant to Article 6 (commencing with Section 14900) of Chapter 7 of Part 5.5. (Added by Stats.1979, c. 567, § 1, operative July 1, 1980. Amended by Stats.1979, c. 1203, § 2; Stats.1981, c. 865, p. 3309, § 14; Stats.1987, c. 1375, § 4.5; Stats.2000, c. 1060 (A.B.1822), § 15.)

Law Revision Commission Comments

Section 11344.2 is amended to reflect existing practice and to conform to the change in the name of the former California Regulatory Code Supplement. See Section 11344. [29 Cal.L.Rev.Comm.Reports 459 (2000)].

§ 11344.3. Publication in notice register

Every document, other than a notice of proposed rulemaking action, required to be published in the California Regulatory Notice Register by this chapter, shall be published in the first edition of the California Regulatory Notice Register following the date of the document. (Formerly § 11349.9, added by Stats.1985, c. 1044, § 9. Renumbered § 11344.3 and amended by Stats.1987, c. 1375, § 23.)

§ 11344.4. Sale; prices; disposition of proceeds

(a) The California Code of Regulations, the California Code of Regulations Supplement, and the California Regulatory Notice Register shall be sold at prices which will reimburse the state for all costs incurred for printing, publication, and distribution.

(b) All money received by the state from the sale of the publications listed in subdivision (a) shall be deposited in the treasury and credited to the General Fund, except that, where applicable, an amount necessary to cover the printing, publication, and distribution costs shall be credited to the fund from which the costs have been paid. (Added by Stats.1979, c. 567, § 1, operative July 1, 1980. Amended by Stats.1979, c. 1203, § 4; Stats.1981, c. 865, p. 3310, § 16; Stats.1987, c. 1375, § 5; Stats.1988, c. 1194, § 1.3, operative Jan. 1, 1989; Stats.2000, c. 1060 (A.B.1822), § 16.)

Law Revision Commission Comments

Section 11344.4 is amended to conform to the change in the name of the former California Regulatory Code Supplement. See Section 11344. [29 Cal.L.Rev.Comm.Reports 459 (2000)].

§ 11344.6. Presumption from publication in code or supplement; judicial notice of contents of regulation or repeal

The publication of a regulation in the California Code of Regulations or California Code of Regulations Supplement raises a rebuttable presumption that the text of the regulation as so published is the text of the regulation adopted.

The courts shall take judicial notice of the contents of each regulation which is printed or which is incorporated by appropriate reference into the California Code of Regulations as compiled by the office.

The courts shall also take judicial notice of the repeal of a regulation as published in the California Code of Regulations Supplement compiled by the office. *(Formerly § 11343.8, added by Stats.1979, c. 567, p. 1781, § 1, operative July 1, 1980. Renumbered § 11343.7 and amended by Stats.1981, c. 865, p. 3308, § 11. Renumbered § 11344.6 and amended by Stats.1983, c. 797, § 5. Amended by Stats.1987, c. 1375, § 6; Stats.2000, c. 1060 (A.B.1822), § 17.)*

Law Revision Commission Comments

Section 11344.6 is amended to conform to the change in the name of the former California Regulatory Code Supplement. See Section 11344. [29 Cal.L.Rev.Comm.Reports 459 (2000)].

Research References

9 Witkin Cal. Proc. 5th Administrative Proceedings § 38, History, Legislative Intent, and Revision.
9 Witkin Cal. Proc. 5th Administrative Proceedings § 42, Incorporation by Reference.
9 Witkin Cal. Proc. 5th Administrative Proceedings § 55, (S 55) in General.

§ 11344.7. Purchase by person; state agencies; special editions

Nothing in this chapter precludes any person or state agency from purchasing copies of the California Code of Regulations, the California Code of Regulations Supplement, or the California Regulatory Notice Register or of any unit of either, nor from printing special editions of any such units and distributing the same. However, where the purchase and printing is by a state agency, the state agency shall do so at the cost or at less than the cost to the agency if it is authorized to do so by other provisions of law. *(Added by Stats.1979, c. 567, § 1, operative July 1, 1980. Amended by Stats.1981, c. 865, p. 3310, § 20; Stats.1987, c. 1375, § 6.5; Stats.2000, c. 1060 (A.B.1822), § 18.)*

Law Revision Commission Comments

Section 11344.7 is amended to conform to the change in the name of the former California Regulatory Code Supplement. See Section 11344. [29 Cal.L.Rev.Comm.Reports 459 (2000)].

§ 11344.9. California administrative code; California administrative notice register; California administrative code supplement

(a) Whenever the term "California Administrative Code" appears in law, official legal paper, or legal publication, it means the "California Code of Regulations."

(b) Whenever the term "California Administrative Notice Register" appears in any law, official legal paper, or legal publication, it means the "California Regulatory Notice Register."

(c) Whenever the term "California Administrative Code Supplement" or "California Regulatory Code Supplement" appears in any law, official legal paper, or legal publication, it means the "California Code of Regulations Supplement." *(Formerly § 11342.02, added by Stats.1988, c. 1194, § 1, operative Jan. 1, 1989. Renumbered § 11344.9 and amended by Stats.1994, c. 1039 (A.B.2531), § 9. Amended by Stats.2000, c. 1060 (A.B.1822), § 19.)*

Law Revision Commission Comments

Section 11344.9 is amended to conform to the change in the name of the former California Regulatory Code Supplement. See Section 11344. [29 Cal.L.Rev.Comm.Reports 459 (2000)].

§ 11345. Effective date of unique identification number system for regulatory actions

The office is not required to develop a unique identification number system for each regulatory action pursuant to Section 11341 or to make the California Regulatory Notice Register available on its website pursuant to subdivision (c) of Section 11344.1 until January 1, 2002. *(Added by Stats.2000, c. 1059 (A.B.505), § 8.)*

ARTICLE 5. PUBLIC PARTICIPATION: PROCEDURE FOR ADOPTION OF REGULATIONS

Section
11346.   Purpose; application; construction.
11346.1.   Adoption, amendment, and repeal of emergency regulations; notice of proposed emergency action; building standards; effective date and filing requirements.
11346.2.   Notification of proposed agency action; public information.
11346.3.   Action with potential or significant adverse economic impact on California business enterprises and individuals; potential cost impact; exemption from reporting; standard regulatory impact analysis.
11346.36.   Standardized regulatory impact analysis regulations.
11346.4.   Notice of proposed action; methods; effective period; notice of changes after completion and approval; refusal to publish; regulatory notice register.
11346.45.   Public discussions of proposed regulations.
11346.5.   Notice of proposed adoption, amendment or repeal; contents; availability to public.
11346.6.   Notice of certain proposed regulations; submission of description of changes in California Code of Regulations in response to requests by persons with visual disability or other disability for which effective communication is required under state or federal law; right of requester to submit public comment on proposed regulation; agency reports to Governor and Legislature.
11346.7.   Website link to Small Business Advocate website.
11346.8.   Hearing; actions affecting regulations; public notification; conditions.
11346.9.   Final statement of reasons; updated informative digest; adoption or amendment of federal regulations.
11347.   Failure to proceed with proposed action; notice for publication.
11347.   Failure to proceed with proposed action; notice for publication.
11347.1.   Rulemaking; documents made available.
11347.3.   File of rulemaking proceeding.
11348.   Rulemaking records; currency and location.

§ 11346. Purpose; application; construction

(a) It is the purpose of this chapter to establish basic minimum procedural requirements for the adoption, amendment, or repeal of administrative regulations. Except as provided in Section 11346.1, the provisions of this chapter are applicable to the exercise of any quasi-legislative power conferred by any statute heretofore or hereafter enacted, but nothing in this chapter repeals or diminishes additional requirements imposed by any statute. This chapter shall not be superseded or modified by any subsequent legislation except to the extent that the legislation shall do so expressly.

(b) An agency that is considering adopting, amending, or repealing a regulation may consult with interested persons before initiating regulatory action pursuant to this article. *(Added by Stats.1979, c. 567, § 1, operative July 1, 1980. Amended by Stats.1994, c. 1039 (A.B.2531), § 20; Stats.2000, c. 1060 (A.B.1822), § 20.)*

Law Revision Commission Comments

Subdivision (b) of Section 11346 is added to clarify the legality of an existing agency practice C consultation with interested persons in developing a proposed regulation. For example, an agency that is considering the adoption of a regulation may hold a workshop in which interested persons can share their views on the proposal. Informal communication of this type provides useful information to the agency and may reduce opposition to the proposed regulation from persons who participated in its development. [29 Cal.L.Rev.Comm.Reports 459 (2000)].

Research References

9 Witkin Cal. Proc. 5th Administrative Proceedings § 39, Nature and Scope.
9 Witkin Cal. Proc. 5th Administrative Proceedings § 41, Interpretive Policies.
9 Witkin Cal. Proc. 5th Administrative Proceedings § 48, in General.
7 Witkin, California Summary 10th Constitutional Law § 675, (S 675) Statutory Requirement.

§ 11346.1. Adoption, amendment, and repeal of emergency regulations; notice of proposed emergency action; building standards; effective date and filing requirements

(a)(1) The adoption, amendment, or repeal of an emergency regulation is not subject to any provision of this article or Article 6 (commencing with Section 11349), except this section and Sections 11349.5 and 11349.6.

(2) At least five working days before submitting an emergency regulation to the office, the adopting agency shall, except as provided in paragraph (3), send a notice of the proposed emergency action to every person who has filed a request for notice of regulatory action with the agency. The notice shall include both of the following:

(A) The specific language proposed to be adopted.

(B) The finding of emergency required by subdivision (b).

(3) An agency is not required to provide notice pursuant to paragraph (2) if the emergency situation clearly poses such an immediate, serious harm that delaying action to allow public comment would be inconsistent with the public interest.

(b)(1) Except as provided in subdivision (c), if a state agency makes a finding that the adoption of a regulation or order of repeal is necessary to address an emergency, the regulation or order of repeal may be adopted as an emergency regulation or order of repeal.

(2) Any finding of an emergency shall include a written statement that contains the information required by paragraphs (2) to (6), inclusive, of subdivision (a) of Section 11346.5 and a description of the specific facts demonstrating the existence of an emergency and the need for immediate action, and demonstrating, by substantial evidence, the need for the proposed regulation to effectuate the statute being implemented, interpreted, or made specific and to address only the demonstrated emergency. The finding of emergency shall also identify each technical, theoretical, and empirical study, report, or similar document, if any, upon which the agency relies. The enactment of an urgency statute shall not, in and of itself, constitute a need for immediate action.

A finding of emergency based only upon expediency, convenience, best interest, general public need, or speculation, shall not be adequate to demonstrate the existence of an emergency. If the situation identified in the finding of emergency existed and was known by the agency adopting the emergency regulation in sufficient time to have been addressed through nonemergency regulations adopted in accordance with the provisions of Article 5 (commencing with Section 11346), the finding of emergency shall include facts explaining the failure to address the situation through nonemergency regulations.

(3) The statement and the regulation or order of repeal shall be filed immediately with the office.

(c) Notwithstanding any other provision of law, no emergency regulation that is a building standard shall be filed, nor shall the building standard be effective, unless the building standard is submitted to the California Building Standards Commission, and is approved and filed pursuant to Sections 18937 and 18938 of the Health and Safety Code.

(d) The emergency regulation or order of repeal shall become effective upon filing or upon any later date specified by the state agency in a written instrument filed with, or as a part of, the regulation or order of repeal.

(e) No regulation, amendment, or order of repeal initially adopted as an emergency regulatory action shall remain in effect more than 180 days unless the adopting agency has complied with Sections 11346.2 to 11347.3, inclusive, either before adopting an emergency regulation or within the 180–day period. The adopting agency, prior to the expiration of the 180–day period, shall transmit to the office for filing with the Secretary of State the adopted regulation, amendment, or order of repeal, the rulemaking file, and a certification that Sections 11346.2 to 11347.3, inclusive, were complied with either before the emergency regulation was adopted or within the 180–day period.

(f) If an emergency amendment or order of repeal is filed and the adopting agency fails to comply with subdivision (e), the regulation as it existed prior to the emergency amendment or order of repeal shall thereupon become effective and after notice to the adopting agency by the office shall be reprinted in the California Code of Regulations.

(g) If a regulation is originally adopted and filed as an emergency and the adopting agency fails to comply with subdivision (e), this failure shall constitute a repeal of the regulation and after notice to the adopting agency by the office, shall be deleted.

(h) The office may approve not more than two readoptions, each for a period not to exceed 90 days, of an emergency regulation that is the same as or substantially equivalent to an emergency regulation previously adopted by that agency. Readoption shall be permitted only if the agency has made substantial progress and proceeded with diligence to comply with subdivision (e). *(Added by Stats.1979, c. 567, § 1, operative July 1, 1980. Amended by Stats.1979, c. 1152, § 12.4, operative July 1, 1980; Stats.1980, c. 204, § 2, eff. June 20, 1980; Stats.1980, c. 1238, p. 4202, § 1, eff. Sept. 29, 1980; Stats.1981, c. 274, p. 1376, § 7, eff. Aug. 26, 1981; Stats.1981, c. 865, p. 3310, § 22; Stats.1982, c. 86, p. 251, § 3, eff. March 1, 1982; Stats.1982, c. 1573, p. 6201, § 2; Stats.1983, c. 797, § 13; Stats.1984, c. 287, § 45, eff. July 6, 1984; Stats.1985, c. 956, § 10, eff. Sept. 26, 1985; Stats.1987, c. 1375, § 7; Stats.1994, c. 1039 (A.B.2531), § 21; Stats.2000, c. 1060 (A.B.1822), § 21; Stats.2006, c. 713 (A.B. 1302), § 3.)*

Law Revision Commission Comments

Subdivision (a) of Section 11346.1 is amended to make three technical changes:

(1) The provision establishing an exception to the requirements of this article for "any regulation not required to be filed with the Secretary of State under this chapter" is deleted. The substance of this exception is continued in Section 11340.9(g)-(i). This change also resolves an inconsistency between Section 11356(b), which expressly requires building standards to be adopted under this article, and the deleted language, which exempted building standards from the requirements of this article.

(2) An inconsistency between this section and Financial Code Section 3373 is eliminated.

(3) A redundant reference to Financial Code Section 8054 is eliminated.

Subdivision (c) is amended to use the defined term "building standard," to correct a grammatical error, and to reflect the change in the name of the California Building Standards Commission. See Section 11342.530 ("building standard" defined).

Subdivision (e) is amended to correct an underinclusive reference.

Subdivision (h) is amended to improve its clarity, without affecting its substance. [30 Cal.L.Rev.Comm. Reports 725 (2000)].

Subdivision (a) of Section 11346.1 is amended to make clear that the exemption of emergency rulemaking from the requirements of this chapter only applies to the procedures provided in this article and in Article 6 (commencing with Section 11349). Former subdivision (a) could be read to preclude application of a number of sections that should apply to an emergency regulation. See, e.g., Sections 11340.85(c)(10) (Internet publication of emergency regulation), 11343 (filing regulation with Secretary of State), 11344.1(a)(3) (publication of emergency regulation decisions in California Regulatory Notice Register), 11350 (judicial review of emergency regulation), 11350.3 (judicial review of emergency regulation decisions). [34 Cal.L.Rev.Comm. Reports 227 (2004)].

Research References

Rutter, Cal. Practice Guide: Insurance Litigation Ch. 14-A, A. The California Regulator (*).
9 Witkin Cal. Proc. 5th Administrative Proceedings § 48, in General.
9 Witkin Cal. Proc. 5th Administrative Proceedings § 49, Interim Regulations to Comply With Federal Legislation.
9 Witkin Cal. Proc. 5th Administrative Proceedings § 143, Matters Considered and Excluded.
9 Witkin Cal. Proc. 5th Administrative Proceedings § 144, Grounds for Declaration of Invalidity.
9 Witkin Cal. Proc. 5th Appeal § 760, Illustrations.

§ 11346.2. Notification of proposed agency action; public information

Every agency subject to this chapter shall prepare, submit to the office with the notice of the proposed action as described in Section 11346.5, and make available to the public upon request, all of the following:

(a) A copy of the express terms of the proposed regulation.

(1) The agency shall draft the regulation in plain, straightforward language, avoiding technical terms as much as possible, and using a coherent and easily readable style. The agency shall draft the regulation in plain English.

(2) The agency shall include a notation following the express terms of each California Code of Regulations section, listing the specific statutes or other provisions of law authorizing the adoption of the regulation and listing the specific statutes or other provisions of law being implemented, interpreted, or made specific by that section in the California Code of Regulations.

(3) The agency shall use underline or italics to indicate additions to, and strikeout to indicate deletions from, the California Code of Regulations.

(b) An initial statement of reasons for proposing the adoption, amendment, or repeal of a regulation. This statement of reasons shall include, but not be limited to, all of the following:

(1) A statement of the specific purpose of each adoption, amendment, or repeal, the problem the agency intends to address, and the rationale for the determination by the agency that each adoption, amendment, or repeal is reasonably necessary to carry out the purpose and address the problem for which it is proposed. The statement shall enumerate the benefits anticipated from the regulatory action, including the benefits or goals provided in the authorizing statute. These benefits may include, to the extent applicable, nonmonetary benefits such as the protection of public health and safety, worker safety, or the environment, the prevention of discrimination, the promotion of fairness or social equity, and the increase in openness and transparency in business and government, among other things. Where the adoption or amendment of a regulation would mandate the use of specific technologies or equipment, a statement of the reasons why the agency believes these mandates or prescriptive standards are required.

(2) For a major regulation proposed on or after November 1, 2013, the standardized regulatory impact analysis required by Section 11346.3.

(3) An identification of each technical, theoretical, and empirical study, report, or similar document, if any, upon which the agency relies in proposing the adoption, amendment, or repeal of a regulation.

(4)(A) A description of reasonable alternatives to the regulation and the agency's reasons for rejecting those alternatives. Reasonable alternatives to be considered include, but are not limited to, alternatives that are proposed as less burdensome and equally effective in achieving the purposes of the regulation in a manner that ensures full compliance with the authorizing statute or other law being implemented or made specific by the proposed regulation. In the case of a regulation that would mandate the use of specific technologies or equipment or prescribe specific actions or procedures, the imposition of performance standards shall be considered as an alternative.

(B) A description of reasonable alternatives to the regulation that would lessen any adverse impact on small business and the agency's reasons for rejecting those alternatives.

(C) Notwithstanding subparagraph (A) or (B), an agency is not required to artificially construct alternatives or describe unreasonable alternatives.

(5)(A) Facts, evidence, documents, testimony, or other evidence on which the agency relies to support an initial determination that the action will not have a significant adverse economic impact on business.

(B)(i) If a proposed regulation * * * is a building standard * * *, the initial statement of reasons shall include the estimated cost of compliance, the estimated potential benefits, and the related assumptions used to determine the estimates.

(ii) The model codes adopted pursuant to Section 18928 of the Health and Safety Code shall be exempt from the requirements of this subparagraph. However, if an interested party has made a request in writing to the agency, at least 30 days before the submittal of the initial statement of reasons, to examine a specific section for purposes of estimating the cost of compliance and the potential benefits for that section, and including the related assumptions used to determine the estimates, then the agency shall comply with the requirements of this subparagraph with regard to that requested section.

(6) A department, board, or commission within the Environmental Protection Agency, the Natural Resources Agency, or the Office of the State Fire Marshal shall describe its efforts, in connection with a proposed rulemaking action, to avoid unnecessary duplication or conflicts with federal regulations contained in the Code of Federal Regulations addressing the same issues. These agencies may adopt regulations different from federal regulations contained in the Code of Federal Regulations addressing the same issues upon a finding of one or more of the following justifications:

(A) The differing state regulations are authorized by law.

(B) The cost of differing state regulations is justified by the benefit to human health, public safety, public welfare, or the environment.

(c) A state agency that adopts or amends a regulation mandated by federal law or regulations, the provisions of which are identical to a previously adopted or amended federal regulation, shall be deemed to have complied with subdivision (b) if a statement to the effect that a federally mandated regulation or amendment to a regulation is being proposed, together with a citation to where an explanation of the provisions of the regulation can be found, is included in the notice of proposed adoption or amendment prepared pursuant to Section 11346.5. However, the agency shall comply fully with this chapter with respect to any provisions in the regulation that the agency proposes to adopt or amend that are different from the corresponding provisions of the federal regulation.

(d) This section shall be inoperative from January 1, 2012, until January 1, 2014. *(Added by Stats.1994, c. 1039 (A.B.2531), § 23. Amended by Stats.1995, c. 938 (S.B.523), § 15.3, operative Jan. 1, 1996; Stats.2000, c. 1059 (A.B.505), § 9; Stats.2000, c. 1060 (A.B.1822), § 22.5; Stats.2002, c. 389 (A.B.1857), § 4; Stats.2010, c. 398 (A.B.2738), § 1, eff. Sept. 27, 2010; Stats.2011, c. 496 (S.B.617), § 3; Stats.2012, c. 471 (A.B.1612), § 2; Stats.2013, c. 212 (S.B.401), § 2.)*

Operative Effect

For period of time during which this section was inoperative, see its terms.

Law Revision Commission Comments

Subdivision (a)(1) of Section 11346.2 is a specific application of Section 6215(a) (state agency "shall write each document which it produces in plain, straightforward language, avoiding technical terms as much as possible, and using a coherent and easily readable style"). The requirement that a regulation be written in plain English has been expanded to include all regulations and not just those that affect small business. Plain English means language that satisfies the clarity standard expressed in Section 11349. See Section 11342.580 ("plain English" defined). Note that the former provision requiring the preparation of a plain English summary of a proposed regulation affecting small businesses, where the regulation cannot be drafted in plain English, has been broadened to apply to all regulations and continued in Section 11346.5(a)(3)(B). See Sections 11342.580 ("plain English" defined), 11349(c) (clarity standard).

Former subdivision (b)(1) (description of problem addressed) is deleted as unnecessary; the same information is required by former subdivision (b)(2) (statement of purpose for proposed action).

Former subdivision (b)(5) is revised to eliminate the implication that a final finding is required before the agency has received comment on a proposed action.

This section also contains language from 2000 Cal. Stat. ch. 1059, §9, which was chaptered out by the bill amending this section. See 2000 Cal. Stat. ch. 1060, §§22.5 & 44. [30 Cal.L.Rev.Comm.Reports 725 (2000)].

Subdivision (b)(3) of Section 11346.2 is amended to make clear that the former second sentence of subdivision (b)(3)(B) applies to subdivision (b)(3)(A) and (B). This is a technical, nonsubstantive change. Subdivision (b)(3)(B) is amended to more closely conform to subdivision (b)(3)(A). This is a nonsubstantive change except that an agency is now required to give reasons for rejecting reasonable alternatives that would lessen any adverse impact on small business. [31 Cal.L.Rev.Comm. Reports 271 (2002)].

Research References

Rutter, Cal. Practice Guide: Insurance Litigation Ch. 14-A, A. The California Regulator (*).

9 Witkin Cal. Proc. 5th Administrative Proceedings § 44, (S 44) Notice Requirements.

§ 11346.3. Action with potential or significant adverse economic impact on California business enterprises and individuals; potential cost impact; exemption from reporting; standard regulatory impact analysis

(a) State agencies proposing to adopt, amend, or repeal any administrative regulation shall assess the potential for adverse economic impact on California business enterprises and individuals, avoiding the imposition of unnecessary or unreasonable regulations or reporting, recordkeeping, or compliance requirements. For purposes of this subdivision, assessing the potential for adverse economic impact shall require agencies, when proposing to adopt, amend, or repeal a regulation, to adhere to the following requirements, to the extent that these requirements do not conflict with other state or federal laws:

(1) The proposed adoption, amendment, or repeal of a regulation shall be based on adequate information concerning the need for, and consequences of, proposed governmental action.

(2) The state agency, prior to submitting a proposal to adopt, amend, or repeal a regulation to the office, shall consider the proposal's impact on business, with consideration of industries affected including the ability of California businesses to compete with businesses in other states. For purposes of evaluating the impact on the ability of California businesses to compete with businesses in other states, an agency shall consider, but not be limited to, information supplied by interested parties.

(3) An economic assessment prepared pursuant to this subdivision for a proposed regulation that is not a major regulation or that is a major regulation proposed prior to November 1, 2013, shall be prepared in accordance with subdivision (b). An economic assessment prepared pursuant to this subdivision for a major regulation proposed on or after November 1, 2013, shall be prepared in accordance with subdivision (c), and shall be included in the initial statement of reasons as required by Section 11346.2.

(b)(1) All state agencies proposing to adopt, amend, or repeal a regulation that is not a major regulation or that is a major regulation proposed prior to November 1, 2013, shall prepare an economic impact assessment that assesses whether and to what extent it will affect the following:

(A) The creation or elimination of jobs within the state.

(B) The creation of new businesses or the elimination of existing businesses within the state.

(C) The expansion of businesses currently doing business within the state.

(D) The benefits of the regulation to the health and welfare of California residents, worker safety, and the state's environment.

(2) This subdivision does not apply to the University of California, the Hastings College of the Law, or the Fair Political Practices Commission.

(3) Information required from state agencies for the purpose of completing the assessment may come from existing state publications.

(c)(1) Each state agency proposing to adopt, amend, or repeal a major regulation on or after November 1, 2013, shall prepare a standardized regulatory impact analysis in the manner prescribed by the Department of Finance pursuant to Section 11346.36. The standardized regulatory impact analysis shall address all of the following:

(A) The creation or elimination of jobs within the state.

(B) The creation of new businesses or the elimination of existing businesses within the state.

(C) The competitive advantages or disadvantages for businesses currently doing business within the state.

(D) The increase or decrease of investment in the state.

(E) The incentives for innovation in products, materials, or processes.

(F) The benefits of the regulations, including, but not limited to, benefits to the health, safety, and welfare of California residents, worker safety, and the state's environment and quality of life, among any other benefits identified by the agency.

(2) This subdivision shall not apply to the University of California, the Hastings College of the Law, or the Fair Political Practices Commission.

(3) Information required from state agencies for the purpose of completing the analysis may be derived from existing state, federal, or academic publications.

(d) Any administrative regulation adopted on or after January 1, 1993, that requires a report shall not apply to businesses, unless the state agency adopting the regulation makes a finding that it is necessary for the health, safety, or welfare of the people of the state that the regulation apply to businesses.

(e) Analyses conducted pursuant to this section are intended to provide agencies and the public with tools to determine whether the regulatory proposal is an efficient and effective means of implementing the policy decisions enacted in statute or by other provisions of law in the least burdensome manner. Regulatory impact analyses shall inform the agencies and the public of the economic consequences of regulatory choices, not reassess statutory policy. The baseline for the regulatory analysis shall be the most cost-effective set of regulatory measures that are equally effective in achieving the purpose of the regulation in a manner that ensures full compliance with the authorizing statute or other law being implemented or made specific by the proposed regulation.

(f) Each state agency proposing to adopt, amend, or repeal a major regulation on or after November 1, 2013, and that has prepared a standardized regulatory impact analysis pursuant to subdivision (c), shall submit that analysis to the Department of Finance upon completion. The department shall comment, within 30 days of receiving that analysis, on the extent to which the analysis adheres to the regulations adopted pursuant to Section 11346.36. Upon receiving the comments from the department, the agency may update its analysis to reflect any comments received from the department and shall summarize the comments and the response of the agency along with a statement of the results of the updated analysis for the statement required by paragraph (10) of subdivision (a) of Section 11346.5. *(Added by Stats.1994, c. 1039 (A.B.2531), § 24. Amended by Stats.2000, c. 1059 (A.B.505), § 10; Stats.2000, c. 1060 (A.B. 1822), § 23; Stats.2011, c. 496 (S.B.617), § 4; Stats.2012, c. 766 (S.B.1520), § 2, eff. Sept. 29, 2012.)*

Law Revision Commission Comments

Subdivision (a) of Section 11346.3 is amended to provide that it applies to the repeal of a regulation as well as the adoption or amendment of a regulation.

Subdivision (b)(2) is amended to recast the definition provision as a substantive limitation. This change is technical and does not affect the meaning of the section. See Sections 11000 ("state agency" defined), 11340.9(a) (requirements of chapter do not apply to agency in judicial or legislative branch). [29 Cal.L.Rev.Comm.Reports 459 (2000)].

Research References

22 NO. 5 Miller & Starr, California Real Estate Newsalert 21, Property Tax Developments.
9 Witkin Cal. Proc. 5th Administrative Proceedings § 44, (S 44) Notice Requirements.

§ 11346.36. Standardized regulatory impact analysis regulations

(a) Prior to November 1, 2013, the Department of Finance, in consultation with the office and other state agencies, shall adopt regulations for conducting the standardized regulatory impact analyses required by subdivision (c) of Section 11346.3.

(b) The regulations, at a minimum, shall assist the agencies in specifying the methodologies for:

(1) Assessing and determining the benefits and costs of the proposed regulation, expressed in monetary terms to the extent feasible and appropriate. Assessing the value of nonmonetary benefits such as the protection of public health and safety, worker safety, or the environment, the prevention of discrimination, the promotion of fairness or social equity, the increase in the openness and transparency of business and government and other nonmonetary benefits consistent with the statutory policy or other provisions of law.

(2) Comparing proposed regulatory alternatives with an established baseline so agencies can make analytical decisions for the adoption, amendment, or repeal of regulations necessary to determine that the proposed action is the most effective, or equally effective and less burdensome, alternative in carrying out the purpose for which the action is proposed, or the most cost-effective alternative to the economy and to affected private persons that would be equally effective in implementing the statutory policy or other provision of law.

(3) Determining the impact of a regulatory proposal on the state economy, businesses, and the public welfare, as described in subdivision (c) of Section 11346.3.

(4) Assessing the effects of a regulatory proposal on the General Fund and special funds of the state and affected local government agencies attributable to the proposed regulation.

(5) Determining the cost of enforcement and compliance to the agency and to affected business enterprises and individuals.

(6) Making the estimation described in Section 11342.548.

(c) To the extent required by this chapter, the department shall convene a public hearing or hearings and take public comment on any draft regulation. Representatives from state agencies and the public at large shall be afforded the opportunity to review and comment on the draft regulation before the regulation is adopted in final form.

(d) State agencies shall provide the Director of Finance and the office ready access to their records and full information and reasonable assistance in any matter requested for purposes of developing the regulations required by this section. This subdivision shall not be construed to authorize an agency to provide access to records required by statute to be kept confidential.

(e) The standardized regulatory impact analysis prepared by the proposing agency shall be included in the initial statement of reasons for the regulation as provided in subdivision (b) of Section 11346.2.

(f) On or before November 1, 2013, the department shall submit the adopted regulations to the Senate and Assembly Committees on Governmental Organization and shall publish the adopted regulations in the State Administrative Manual. *(Added by Stats.2011, c. 496 (S.B.617), § 5.)*

Research References

9 Witkin Cal. Proc. 5th Administrative Proceedings § 44, (S 44) Notice Requirements.

§ 11346.4. Notice of proposed action; methods; effective period; notice of changes after completion and approval; refusal to publish; regulatory notice register

(a) At least 45 days prior to the hearing and close of the public comment period on the adoption, amendment, or repeal of a regulation, notice of the proposed action shall be:

(1) Mailed to every person who has filed a request for notice of regulatory actions with the state agency. Each state agency shall give a person filing a request for notice of regulatory

actions the option of being notified of all proposed regulatory actions or being notified of regulatory actions concerning one or more particular programs of the state agency.

(2) In cases in which the state agency is within a state department, mailed or delivered to the director of the department.

(3) Mailed to a representative number of small business enterprises or their representatives that are likely to be affected by the proposed action. "Representative" for the purposes of this paragraph includes, but is not limited to, a trade association, industry association, professional association, or any other business group or association of any kind that represents a business enterprise or employees of a business enterprise.

(4) When appropriate in the judgment of the state agency, mailed to any person or group of persons whom the agency believes to be interested in the proposed action and published in the form and manner as the state agency shall prescribe.

(5) Published in the California Regulatory Notice Register as prepared by the office for each state agency's notice of regulatory action.

(6) Posted on the state agency's website if the agency has a website.

(b) The effective period of a notice issued pursuant to this section shall not exceed one year from the date thereof. If the adoption, amendment, or repeal of a regulation proposed in the notice is not completed and transmitted to the office within the period of one year, a notice of the proposed action shall again be issued pursuant to this article.

(c) Once the adoption, amendment, or repeal is completed and approved by the office, no further adoption, amendment, or repeal to the noticed regulation shall be made without subsequent notice being given.

(d) The office may refuse to publish a notice submitted to it if the agency has failed to comply with this article.

(e) The office shall make the California Regulatory Notice Register available to the public and state agencies at a nominal cost that is consistent with a policy of encouraging the widest possible notice distribution to interested persons.

(f) Where the form or manner of notice is prescribed by statute in any particular case, in addition to filing and mailing notice as required by this section, the notice shall be published, posted, mailed, filed, or otherwise publicized as prescribed by that statute. The failure to mail notice to any person as provided in this section shall not invalidate any action taken by a state agency pursuant to this article. *(Added by Stats.1979, c. 567, § 1, operative July 1, 1980. Amended by Stats.1979, c. 1203, § 5; Stats.1981, c. 865, p. 3312, § 24; Stats.1982, c. 1083, p. 3950, § 3; Stats.1985, c. 1044, § 1; Stats.1987, c. 1375, § 9; Stats.1994, c. 1039 (A.B.2531), § 25; Stats.2000, c. 1059 (A.B.505), § 11.)*

Research References

Rutter, Cal. Practice Guide: Insurance Litigation Ch. 14-A, A. The California Regulator (*).
9 Witkin Cal. Proc. 5th Administrative Proceedings § 44, (S 44) Notice Requirements.
9 Witkin Cal. Proc. 5th Administrative Proceedings § 50, (S 50) No Amendment of Regulation by Interpretation.

§ 11346.45. Public discussions of proposed regulations

(a) In order to increase public participation and improve the quality of regulations, state agencies proposing to adopt regulations shall, prior to publication of the notice required by Section 11346.5, involve parties who would be subject to the proposed regulations in public discussions regarding those proposed regulations, when the proposed regulations involve complex proposals or a large number of proposals that cannot easily be reviewed during the comment period.

(b) This section does not apply to a state agency in any instance where that state agency is required to implement federal law and regulations for which there is little or no discretion on the part of the state to vary.

(c) If the agency does not or cannot comply with the provisions of subdivision (a), it shall state the reasons for noncompliance with reasonable specificity in the rulemaking record.

(d) The provisions of this section shall not be subject to judicial review or to the provisions of Section 11349.1. *(Added by Stats.2000, c. 1059 (A.B.505), § 12.)*

Research References

Rutter, Cal. Practice Guide: Insurance Litigation Ch. 14-A, A. The California Regulator (*).

§ 11346.5. Notice of proposed adoption, amendment or repeal; contents; availability to public

(a) The notice of proposed adoption, amendment, or repeal of a regulation shall include the following:

(1) A statement of the time, place, and nature of proceedings for adoption, amendment, or repeal of the regulation.

(2) Reference to the authority under which the regulation is proposed and a reference to the particular code sections or other provisions of law that are being implemented, interpreted, or made specific.

(3) An informative digest drafted in plain English in a format similar to the Legislative Counsel's digest on legislative bills. The informative digest shall include the following:

(A) A concise and clear summary of existing laws and regulations, if any, related directly to the proposed action and of the effect of the proposed action.

(B) If the proposed action differs substantially from an existing comparable federal regulation or statute, a brief description of the significant differences and the full citation of the federal regulations or statutes.

(C) A policy statement overview explaining the broad objectives of the regulation and the specific benefits anticipated by the proposed adoption, amendment, or repeal of a regulation, including, to the extent applicable, nonmonetary benefits such as the protection of public health and safety, worker safety, or the environment, the prevention of discrimination, the promotion of fairness or social equity, and the increase in openness and transparency in business and government, among other things.

(D) An evaluation of whether the proposed regulation is inconsistent or incompatible with existing state regulations.

(4) Any other matters as are prescribed by statute applicable to the specific state agency or to any specific regulation or class of regulations.

(5) A determination as to whether the regulation imposes a mandate on local agencies or school districts and, if so, whether the mandate requires state reimbursement pursuant to Part 7 (commencing with Section 17500) of Division 4.

(6) An estimate, prepared in accordance with instructions adopted by the Department of Finance, of the cost or savings to any state agency, the cost to any local agency or school district that is required to be reimbursed under Part 7 (commencing with Section 17500) of Division 4, other nondiscretionary cost or savings imposed on local agencies, and the cost or savings in federal funding to the state.

For purposes of this paragraph, "cost or savings" means additional costs or savings, both direct and indirect, that a public agency necessarily incurs in reasonable compliance with regulations.

(7) If a state agency, in proposing to adopt, amend, or repeal any administrative regulation, makes an initial determination that the action may have a significant, statewide adverse economic impact directly affecting business, including the ability of California businesses to compete with businesses in other states, it shall include the following information in the notice of proposed action:

(A) Identification of the types of businesses that would be affected.

(B) A description of the projected reporting, recordkeeping, and other compliance requirements that would result from the proposed action.

(C) The following statement: "The (name of agency) has made an initial determination that the (adoption/amendment/repeal) of this regulation may have a significant, statewide adverse economic impact directly affecting business, including the ability of California businesses to compete with businesses in other states. The (name of agency) (has/has not) considered proposed alternatives that would lessen any adverse economic impact on business and invites you to submit proposals. Submissions may include the following considerations:

(i) The establishment of differing compliance or reporting requirements or timetables that take into account the resources available to businesses.

(ii) Consolidation or simplification of compliance and reporting requirements for businesses.

(iii) The use of performance standards rather than prescriptive standards.

(iv) Exemption or partial exemption from the regulatory requirements for businesses."

(8) If a state agency, in adopting, amending, or repealing any administrative regulation, makes an initial determination that the action will not have a significant, statewide adverse economic impact directly affecting business, including the ability of California businesses to compete with businesses in other states, it shall make a declaration to that effect in the notice of proposed action. In making this declaration, the agency shall provide in the record facts, evidence, documents, testimony, or other evidence upon which the agency relies to support its initial determination.

An agency's initial determination and declaration that a proposed adoption, amendment, or repeal of a regulation may have or will not have a significant, adverse impact on businesses, including the ability of California businesses to compete with businesses in other states, shall not be grounds for the office to refuse to publish the notice of proposed action.

(9) A description of all cost impacts, known to the agency at the time the notice of proposed action is submitted to the office, that a representative private person or business would necessarily incur in reasonable compliance with the proposed action.

If no cost impacts are known to the agency, it shall state the following:

"The agency is not aware of any cost impacts that a representative private person or business would necessarily incur in reasonable compliance with the proposed action."

(10) A statement of the results of the economic impact assessment required by subdivision (b) of Section 11346.3 or the standardized regulatory impact analysis if required by subdivision (c) of Section 11346.3, a summary of any comments submitted to the agency pursuant to subdivision (f) of Section 11346.3 and the agency's response to those comments.

(11) The finding prescribed by subdivision (d) of Section 11346.3, if required.

(12)(A) A statement that the action would have a significant effect on housing costs, if a state agency, in adopting, amending, or repealing any administrative regulation, makes an initial determination that the action would have that effect.

(B) The agency officer designated in paragraph (14) shall make available to the public, upon request, the agency's evaluation, if any, of the effect of the proposed regulatory action on housing costs.

(C) The statement described in subparagraph (A) shall also include the estimated costs of compliance and potential benefits of a building standard, if any, that were included in the initial statement of reasons.

(D) For purposes of model codes adopted pursuant to Section 18928 of the Health and Safety Code, the agency shall comply with the requirements of this paragraph only if an interested party has made a request to the agency to examine a specific section for purposes of estimating the costs of compliance and potential benefits for that section, as described in Section 11346.2.

(13) A statement that the adopting agency must determine that no reasonable alternative considered by the agency or that has otherwise been identified and brought to the attention of the agency would be more effective in carrying out the purpose for which the action is proposed, would be as effective and less burdensome to affected private persons than the proposed action, or would be more cost effective to affected private persons and equally effective in implementing the statutory policy or other provision of law. For a major regulation, as defined by Section 11342.548, proposed on or after November 1, 2013, the statement shall be based, in part, upon the standardized regulatory impact analysis of the proposed regulation, as required by Section 11346.3, as well as upon the benefits of the proposed regulation identified pursuant to subparagraph (C) of paragraph (3).

(14) The name and telephone number of the agency representative and designated backup contact person to whom inquiries concerning the proposed administrative action may be directed.

(15) The date by which comments submitted in writing must be received to present statements, arguments, or contentions in writing relating to the proposed action in order for them to be considered by the state agency before it adopts, amends, or repeals a regulation.

(16) Reference to the fact that the agency proposing the action has prepared a statement of the reasons for the proposed action, has available all the information upon which its proposal is based, and has available the express terms of the proposed action, pursuant to subdivision (b).

(17) A statement that if a public hearing is not scheduled, any interested person or his or her duly authorized representative may request, no later than 15 days prior to the close of the written comment period, a public hearing pursuant to Section 11346.8.

(18) A statement indicating that the full text of a regulation changed pursuant to Section 11346.8 will be available for at least 15 days prior to the date on which the agency adopts, amends, or repeals the resulting regulation.

(19) A statement explaining how to obtain a copy of the final statement of reasons once it has been prepared pursuant to subdivision (a) of Section 11346.9.

(20) If the agency maintains an Internet Web site or other similar forum for the electronic publication or distribution of written material, a statement explaining how materials published or distributed through that forum can be accessed.

(21) If the proposed regulation is subject to Section 11346.6, a statement that the agency shall provide, upon request, a description of the proposed changes included in the proposed action, in the manner provided by Section 11346.6, to accommodate a person with a visual or other disability for which effective communication is required under state or federal law and that providing the description of proposed changes may require extending the period of public comment for the proposed action.

(b) The agency representative designated in paragraph (14) of subdivision (a) shall make available to the public upon request the express terms of the proposed action. The representative shall also make available to the public upon request the location of public records, including reports, documentation, and other materials, related to the proposed action. If the representative receives an inquiry regarding the proposed action that the representative cannot answer, the representative shall refer the inquiry to another person in the agency for a prompt response.

(c) This section shall not be construed in any manner that results in the invalidation of a regulation because of the alleged inadequacy of the notice content or the summary or cost estimates, or the alleged inadequacy or inaccuracy of the housing cost estimates, if there has been substantial compliance with those requirements. *(Added by Stats.1979, c. 567, § 1, operative July 1, 1980. Amended by Stats.1979, c. 1203, § 6; Stats.1981, c. 865, p. 3313, § 25; Stats.1982, c. 327, p. 1434, § 30, eff. June 30, 1982; Stats.1983, c. 797, § 15; Stats.1986, c. 879, § 1; Stats.1987, c. 1375, § 10; Stats.1993, c. 1046 (A.B.1144), § 1; Stats.1994, c. 1039 (A.B.2531), § 26; Stats.2000, c. 1059 (A.B.505), § 13; Stats.2000, c. 1060 (A.B.1822), § 24.5; Stats.2002, c. 389 (A.B. 1857), § 5; Stats.2011, c. 495 (A.B.410), § 2; Stats.2011, c. 496 (S.B.617), § 6; Stats.2012, c. 471 (A.B.1612), § 3; Stats.2012, c. 723 (A.B.2041), § 1.5.)*

Law Revision Commission Comments

Subdivision (a)(3)(B) of Section 11346.5 is amended to broaden the plain English policy statement requirement to apply to all proposed actions, and not just those affecting small business. The informative digest is also expanded to include a plain English summary of the regulation. See Sections 11342.580 ("plain English" defined), 11349(c) (clarity standard).

Paragraphs (7)-(8) and former paragraph (11) of subdivision (a) are amended to make clear that final findings are not required before the agency has received comment on a proposed action. Paragraphs (7)-(8) are also amended to provide that those provisions apply to the repeal of a regulation, as well as the adoption, or amendment of a regulation.

Paragraph (11) is added to subdivision (a) to include a finding that it is necessary for the health, safety, or welfare of the people of the state that a regulation requiring a report apply to businesses. This implements Section 11346.3(c).

Paragraphs (18)-(19) are added to subdivision (a) to provide that the notice of proposed action must include statements explaining how to obtain the final statement of reasons and any electronically published documents. See also Sections 11340.85(c) (electronic publication of rulemaking materials),

This section also contains language from 2000 Cal. Stat. ch. 1059, §13, which was chaptered out by the bill amending this section. See 2000 Cal. Stat. ch. 1060, §§24.5 & 44. [30 Cal.L.Rev.Comm.Reports 725 (2000)].

Subdivision (a)(7)(C) of Section 11346.5 is amended to conform to the language used in the introductory paragraph of subdivision (a)(7). This is a technical, nonsubstantive change.

Subdivisions (a)(14) and (b) are amended to require that inquiries received by an agency representative be answered promptly, either by the agency representative or by another person in the agency. [31 Cal.L.Rev. Comm. Reports 273 (2002)].

Research References

9 Witkin Cal. Proc. 5th Administrative Proceedings § 38, History, Legislative Intent, and Revision.

9 Witkin Cal. Proc. 5th Administrative Proceedings § 43, (S 43) Drafting Requirements.

9 Witkin Cal. Proc. 5th Administrative Proceedings § 44, (S 44) Notice Requirements.

9 Witkin Cal. Proc. 5th Administrative Proceedings § 50, (S 50) No Amendment of Regulation by Interpretation.

9 Witkin Cal. Proc. 5th Administrative Proceedings § 144, Grounds for Declaration of Invalidity.

§ 11346.6. Notice of certain proposed regulations; submission of description of changes in California Code of Regulations in response to requests by persons with visual disability or other disability for which effective communication is required under state or federal law; right of requester to submit public comment on proposed regulation; agency reports to Governor and Legislature

(a) This section shall only apply to the following proposed regulations:

(1) Regulations proposed by the Department of Rehabilitation.

(2) Regulations that must be submitted to the California Building Standards Commission that pertain to disability access compliance, including, but not limited to, regulations proposed by the State Fire Marshal, the Department of Housing and Community Development, the Division of the State Architect, and the California Commission on Disability Access.

(3) Regulations proposed by the State Department of Education that pertain to special education.

(4) Regulations proposed by the State Department of Health Care Services that pertain to the Medi–Cal program.

(b) Upon request from a person with a visual disability or other disability for which effective communication is required under state or federal law, the agency shall provide that person a narrative description of the additions to, and deletions from, the California Code of Regulations or other publication. The description shall identify each addition to or deletion from the California Code of Regulations by reference to the subdivision, paragraph, subparagraph, clause, or subclause within the proposed regulation containing the addition or deletion. The description shall provide the express language proposed to be added to or deleted from the California Code of Regulations or other publication and any portion of the surrounding language necessary to understand the change in a manner that allows for accurate translation by reading software used by the visually impaired.

(c) The agency shall provide the information described in subdivision (b) within 10 business days, unless the agency determines that compliance with this requirement would be impractical and notifies the requester of the date on which the information will be provided.

(d) Notwithstanding any other law, if information is provided to a requester pursuant to this section, the agency shall provide that requester at least 45 days from the date upon which the information was provided to the requester to submit a public comment regarding the proposed regulation. The agency shall not take final action to adopt the regulation until the requester has submitted a public comment or the extended 45–day comment period expires, whichever occurs first.

(e) The requirements imposed pursuant to subdivisions (b) to (d), inclusive, for a proposed regulation described in subdivision (a) shall apply to an agency only for purposes of that proposed regulation until the proposed regulation is filed with the Secretary of State or until the agency otherwise concludes the regulatory adoption process.

(f)(1) Not later than February 1, 2014, an agency that adopted a proposed regulation subject to the requirements of this section shall submit a report, for both the 2012 and 2013 calendar years, to the Governor, the fiscal committee in each house of the Legislature, and the appropriate policy committee in each house of the Legislature, that specifies the number of requests submit-

Government

ted for a narrative description of a proposed regulation, and the number of narrative descriptions actually provided pursuant to this section.

(2) The report shall be submitted to the Legislature in the manner required pursuant to Section 9795.

(3) The reporting requirement imposed by this subdivision shall become inoperative on February 1, 2018, as required pursuant to Section 10231.5.

(4) It is the intent of the Legislature to evaluate the reports submitted pursuant to this subdivision to determine whether the requirements of this section should be applied to all regulations adopted by all agencies. *(Added by Stats.2011, c. 495 (A.B.410), § 3.)*

Research References

9 Witkin Cal. Proc. 5th Administrative Proceedings § 44, (S 44) Notice Requirements.

§ 11346.7. Website link to Small Business Advocate website

The office shall maintain a link on its website to the website maintained by the Small Business Advocate that also includes the telephone number of the Small Business Advocate. *(Added by Stats.2000, c. 1059 (A.B.505), § 15.)*

§ 11346.8. Hearing; actions affecting regulations; public notification; conditions

(a) If a public hearing is held, both oral and written statements, arguments, or contentions, shall be permitted. The agency may impose reasonable limitations on oral presentations. If a public hearing is not scheduled, the state agency shall, consistent with Section 11346.4, afford any interested person or his or her duly authorized representative, the opportunity to present statements, arguments or contentions in writing. In addition, a public hearing shall be held if, no later than 15 days prior to the close of the written comment period, an interested person or his or her duly authorized representative submits in writing to the state agency, a request to hold a public hearing. The state agency shall, to the extent practicable, provide notice of the time, date, and place of the hearing by mailing the notice to every person who has filed a request for notice thereby with the state agency. The state agency shall consider all relevant matter presented to it before adopting, amending, or repealing any regulation.

(b) In any hearing under this section, the state agency or its duly authorized representative shall have authority to administer oaths or affirmations. An agency may continue or postpone a hearing from time to time to the time and at the place as it determines. If a hearing is continued or postponed, the state agency shall provide notice to the public as to when it will be resumed or rescheduled.

(c) No state agency may adopt, amend, or repeal a regulation which has been changed from that which was originally made available to the public pursuant to Section 11346.5, unless the change is (1) nonsubstantial or solely grammatical in nature, or (2) sufficiently related to the original text that the public was adequately placed on notice that the change could result from the originally proposed regulatory action. If a sufficiently related change is made, the full text of the resulting adoption, amendment, or repeal, with the change clearly indicated, shall be made available to the public for at least 15 days before the agency adopts, amends, or repeals the resulting regulation. Any written comments received regarding the change must be responded to in the final statement of reasons required by Section 11346.9.

(d) No state agency shall add any material to the record of the rulemaking proceeding after the close of the public hearing or comment period, unless the agency complies with Section 11347.1. This subdivision does not apply to material prepared pursuant to Section 11346.9.

(e) If a comment made at a public hearing raises a new issue concerning a proposed regulation and a member of the public requests additional time to respond to the new issue before the state agency takes final action, it is the intent of the Legislature that rulemaking agencies consider granting the request for additional time if, under the circumstances, granting the request is practical and does not unduly delay action on the regulation. *(Added by Stats.1981, c. 865, p. 3315, § 29. Amended by Stats.1981, c. 1091, p. 4194, § 2; Stats.1982, c. 86, p. 252, § 4, eff. March 1, 1982; Stats.1983, c. 797, § 19; Stats.1987, c. 1375, § 15; Stats.1994, c. 1039 (A.B.2531), § 32; Stats.2000, c. 1059 (A.B. 505), § 16; Stats.2000, c. 1060 (A.B.1822), § 26.5.)*

Law Revision Commission Comments

Subdivision (a) of Section 11346.8 is amended to make clear that oral testimony must be allowed at a public hearing, subject to reasonable time, repetition, or other limitations by the agency.

Subdivision (d) is amended to refer to Section 11347.1, which codifies the existing procedure for providing an additional opportunity for public comment in response to material added to the rulemaking file. See 1 Cal. Code Regs. §45. Section 11347.1 requires additional public comment on certain material that is added to the rulemaking file after publication of the notice of proposed action. This is a broader requirement than that provided in subdivision (d), which only requires an opportunity for additional comment regarding material that is added to the rulemaking file after the close of the public hearing or comment period. The broader requirement is consistent with existing practice. Subdivision (d) is also amended to exempt material that is required to be added to the rulemaking file after the close of the public hearing or comment period. See Section 11346.9 (final statement of reasons and updated informative digest). However, if the final statement of reasons refers to documents not previously included in the rulemaking file, an opportunity for additional public comment regarding those documents must be provided. See Section 11346.9(a)(1).

This section also contains language from 2000 Cal. Stat. ch. 1059, §16, which was chaptered out by the bill amending this section. See 2000 Cal. Stat. ch. 1060, §§26.5 & 44. [30 Cal.L.Rev.Comm.Reports 725 (2000)].

Research References

Rutter, Cal. Practice Guide: Insurance Litigation Ch. 14-A, A. The California Regulator (*).
9 Witkin Cal. Proc. 5th Administrative Proceedings § 38, History, Legislative Intent, and Revision.
9 Witkin Cal. Proc. 5th Administrative Proceedings § 46, (S 46) Hearing.
9 Witkin Cal. Proc. 5th Administrative Proceedings § 47, (S 47) Determination by Agency.
9 Witkin Cal. Proc. 5th Administrative Proceedings § 50, (S 50) No Amendment of Regulation by Interpretation.
7 Witkin, California Summary 10th Constitutional Law § 675, (S 675) Statutory Requirement.

§ 11346.9. Final statement of reasons; updated informative digest; adoption or amendment of federal regulations

Every agency subject to this chapter shall do the following:

(a) Prepare and submit to the office with the adopted regulation a final statement of reasons that shall include all of the following:

(1) An update of the information contained in the initial statement of reasons. If the update identifies any data or any technical, theoretical or empirical study, report, or similar document on which the agency is relying in proposing the adoption, amendment, or repeal of a regulation that was not identified in the initial statement of reasons, or which was otherwise not identified or made available for public review prior to the close of the public comment period, the agency shall comply with Section 11347.1.

(2) A determination as to whether adoption, amendment, or repeal of the regulation imposes a mandate on local agencies or school districts. If the determination is that adoption, amendment, or repeal of the regulation would impose a local mandate, the agency shall state whether the mandate is reimbursable pursuant to Part 7 (commencing with Section 17500) of Division 4. If the agency finds that the mandate is not reimbursable, it shall state the reasons for that finding.

(3) A summary of each objection or recommendation made regarding the specific adoption, amendment, or repeal proposed, together with an explanation of how the proposed action has been changed to accommodate each objection or recommendation, or the reasons for making no change. This requirement applies only to objections or recommendations specifically directed at the agency's proposed action or to the procedures followed by the agency in proposing or adopting the action. The agency may aggregate and summarize repetitive or irrelevant comments as a group, and may respond to repetitive comments or summarily dismiss irrelevant comments as a group. For the purposes of this paragraph, a comment is " irrelevant" if it is not specifically directed at the agency' s proposed action or to the procedures followed by the agency in proposing or adopting the action.

(4) A determination with supporting information that no alternative considered by the agency would be more effective in carrying out the purpose for which the regulation is proposed, would be as effective and less burdensome to affected private persons than the adopted regulation, or would be more cost effective to affected private persons and equally effective in implementing the statutory policy or other provision of law. For a major regulation, as defined by Section 11342.548 proposed on or after November 1, 2013, the determination shall be based, in part, upon the standardized regulatory impact analysis of the proposed regulation and, in part, upon the statement of benefits identified in subparagraph (C) of paragraph (3) of subdivision (a) of Section 11346.5.

(5) An explanation setting forth the reasons for rejecting any proposed alternatives that would lessen the adverse economic impact on small businesses. The agency shall include, as supporting information, the standardized regulatory impact analysis for a major regulation, if required by subdivision (c) of Section 11346.3, as well as the benefits of the proposed regulation identified pursuant to paragraph (3) of subdivision (a) of Section 11346.5.

(b) Prepare and submit to the office with the adopted regulation an updated informative digest containing a clear and concise summary of the immediately preceding laws and regulations, if any, relating directly to the adopted, amended, or repealed regulation and the effect of the adopted, amended, or repealed regulation. The informative digest shall be drafted in a format similar to the Legislative Counsel's Digest on legislative bills.

(c) A state agency that adopts or amends a regulation mandated by federal law or regulations, the provisions of which are identical to a previously adopted or amended federal regulation, shall be deemed to have complied with this section if a statement to the effect that a federally mandated regulation or amendment to a regulation is being proposed, together with a citation to where an explanation of the provisions of the regulation can be found, is included in the notice of proposed adoption or amendment prepared pursuant to Section 11346.5. However, the agency shall comply fully with this chapter with respect to any provisions in the regulation which the agency proposes to adopt or amend that are different from the corresponding provisions of the federal regulation.

(d) If an agency determines that a requirement of this section can be satisfied by reference to an agency statement made pursuant to Sections 11346.2 to 11346.5, inclusive, the agency may satisfy the requirement by incorporating the relevant statement by reference. *(Added by Stats.1994, c. 1039 (A.B. 2531), § 33. Amended by Stats.2000, c. 1060 (A.B.1822), § 27; Stats.2011, c. 496 (S.B.617), § 7.)*

Law Revision Commission Comments

Subdivision (a)(1) of Section 11346.9 is amended to refer to Section 11347.1, which codifies the existing procedure for providing an additional opportunity for public comment in response to material added to the rulemaking file. See 1 Cal. Code Regs. §45. Subdivision (a) requires additional public comment on certain material that is added to the rulemaking file after publication of the notice of proposed action. This is a broader requirement than that provided in Section 11346.8(d), which only requires an opportunity for additional comment regarding material that is added to the rulemaking file after the close of the public hearing or comment period. The broader requirement is consistent with existing practice.

Subdivision (a)(1)-(2) is also amended to make clear that those provisions apply to the repeal of a regulation as well as the adoption or amendment of a regulation.

Subdivision (a)(3) is amended to codify the existing practice of grouping repetitive comments and summarily dismissing irrelevant comments for purposes of this section. The Office of Administrative Law may disapprove a proposed regulation if an agency improperly aggregates dissimilar comments or summarily dismisses a relevant comment. See Section 11349.3 (office may disapprove regulation for failure to comply with this chapter).

Subdivision (d) is added to authorize incorporation of a prior statement by reference. This reflects the fact that no purpose is served by requiring an agency to reiterate a statement that was made earlier in the rulemaking process. For example, where an agency determines pursuant to Section 11346.5(a)(6) that a proposed rule would not impose a cost on a local agency or school district and, at the time of preparing the final statement of reasons, determines that its prior determination is correct and complete, the agency may incorporate the statement made pursuant to Section 11346.5(a)(6) in complying with Section 11346.9(a)(2). [30 Cal. L.Rev.Comm. Reports 725 (2000)].

Research References

Rutter, Cal. Practice Guide: Insurance Litigation Ch. 14-A, A. The California Regulator (*).

9 Witkin Cal. Proc. 5th Administrative Proceedings § 44, (S 44) Notice Requirements.

§ 11347. Failure to proceed with proposed action; notice for publication

Section added by Stats.2000, c. 1059 (A.B.505), § 17. See, also, another section of the same number added by Stats.2000, c. 1060 (A.B.1822), § 28.

(a) If, after publication of a notice of proposed action pursuant to Section 11346.4, but before the notice of proposed action becomes ineffective pursuant to subdivision (b) of that section, an agency decides not to proceed with the proposed action, it shall deliver notice of its decision to the office for publication in the California Regulatory Notice Register.

(b) Publication of a notice under this section terminates the effect of the notice of proposed action referred to in the notice. Nothing in this section precludes an agency from proposing a new regulatory action that is similar or identical to a regulatory action that was previously the subject of a notice published under this section. *(Added by Stats.2000, c. 1059 (A.B.505), § 17.)*

Law Revision Commission Comments

Section 11347 is new. The purpose of this section is to require notice where an agency decides to completely abandon a proposed regulatory action. A decision not to proceed with part of a proposed regulatory action, while proceeding with the remainder, would not require notice under this section. See also Section 11342(b) ("office" means Office of Administrative Law). [30 Cal.L.Rev.Comm.Reports 524 (2000)].

Research References

9 Witkin Cal. Proc. 5th Administrative Proceedings § 44, (S 44) Notice Requirements.

§ 11347. Failure to proceed with proposed action; notice for publication

Section added by Stats.2000, c. 1060 (A.B.1822), § 28. See, also, another section of the same number added by Stats.2000, c. 1059 (A.B.505), § 17.

(a) If, after publication of a notice of proposed action pursuant to Section 11346.4, but before the notice of proposed action becomes ineffective pursuant to subdivision (b) of that section, an agency decides not to proceed with the proposed action, it shall deliver notice of its decision to the office for publication in the California Regulatory Notice Register.

(b) Publication of a notice under this section terminates the effect of the notice of proposed action referred to in the notice. Nothing in this section precludes an agency from proposing a new regulatory action that is similar or identical to a regulatory action that was previously the subject of a notice published under this section. *(Added by Stats.2000, c. 1060 (A.B.1822), § 28.)*

Law Revision Commission Comments

Section 11347 is new. The purpose of this section is to require notice where an agency decides to completely abandon a proposed regulatory action. A decision not to proceed with part of a proposed regulatory action, while proceeding with the remainder, would not require notice under this section. See also Section 11342(b) ("office" means Office of Administrative Law). [30 Cal.L.Rev.Comm.Reports 524 (2000)].

Research References

9 Witkin Cal. Proc. 5th Administrative Proceedings § 44, (S 44) Notice Requirements.

§ 11347.1. Rulemaking; documents made available

(a) An agency that adds any technical, theoretical, or empirical study, report, or similar document to the rulemaking file after publication of the notice of proposed action and relies on the document in proposing the action shall make the document available as required by this section.

(b) At least 15 calendar days before the proposed action is adopted by the agency, the agency shall mail to all of the following persons a notice identifying the added document and stating the place and business hours that the document is available for public inspection:

(1) Persons who testified at the public hearing.

(2) Persons who submitted written comments at the public hearing.

(3) Persons whose comments were received by the agency during the public comment period.

(4) Persons who requested notification from the agency of the availability of changes to the text of the proposed regulation.

(c) The document shall be available for public inspection at the location described in the notice for at least 15 calendar days before the proposed action is adopted by the agency.

(d) Written comments on the document or information received by the agency during the availability period shall be summarized and responded to in the final statement of reasons as provided in Section 11346.9.

(e) The rulemaking file shall contain a statement confirming that the agency complied with the requirements of this section and stating the date on which the notice was mailed.

(f) If there are no persons in categories listed in subdivision (b), then the rulemaking file shall contain a confirming statement to that effect. *(Added by Stats.2000, c. 1060 (A.B.1822), § 29.)*

Law Revision Commission Comments

Section 11347.1 is drawn from 1 Cal. Code Regs. §45. It codifies the existing procedure for providing an additional opportunity for public comment in response to material added to the rulemaking file pursuant to Sections 11346.8(d) and 11346.9(a)(1). Section 11347.1 requires additional public comment on certain material that is added to the rulemaking file after publication of the notice of proposed action. This is a broader requirement than that provided in Section 11346.8(d), which only requires an opportunity for additional comment regarding material that is added to the rulemaking file after the close of the public hearing or comment period. The broader requirement is consistent with existing practice. This section does not require an additional opportunity for comment in response to a written public comment that is added to the rulemaking file, unless the public comment includes a technical, theoretical, or empirical study, report, or similar document on which the agency chooses to rely in proposing the rulemaking action. [29 Cal.L.Rev.Comm.Reports 459 (2000)].

§ 11347.3. File of rulemaking proceeding

(a) Every agency shall maintain a file of each rulemaking that shall be deemed to be the record for that rulemaking proceeding. Commencing no later than the date that the notice of the proposed action is published in the California Regulatory Notice Register, and during all subsequent periods of time that the file is in the agency's possession, the agency shall make the file available to the public for inspection and copying during regular business hours.

(b) The rulemaking file shall include:

(1) Copies of any petitions received from interested persons proposing the adoption, amendment, or repeal of the regulation, and a copy of any decision provided for by subdivision (d) of Section 11340.7, which grants a petition in whole or in part.

(2) All published notices of proposed adoption, amendment, or repeal of the regulation, and an updated informative digest, the initial statement of reasons, and the final statement of reasons.

(3) The determination, together with the supporting data required by paragraph (5) of subdivision (a) of Section 11346.5.

(4) The determination, together with the supporting data required by paragraph (8) of subdivision (a) of Section 11346.5.

(5) The estimate, together with the supporting data and calculations, required by paragraph (6) of subdivision (a) of Section 11346.5.

(6) All data and other factual information, any studies or reports, and written comments submitted to the agency in connection with the adoption, amendment, or repeal of the regulation.

(7) All data and other factual information, technical, theoretical, and empirical studies or reports, if any, on which the agency is relying in the adoption, amendment, or repeal of a regulation, including any economic impact assessment or standardized regulatory impact analysis as required by Section 11346.3.

(8) A transcript, recording, or minutes of any public hearing connected with the adoption, amendment, or repeal of the regulation.

(9) The date on which the agency made the full text of the proposed regulation available to the public for 15 days prior to the adoption, amendment, or repeal of the regulation, if required to do so by subdivision (c) of Section 11346.8.

(10) The text of regulations as originally proposed and the modified text of regulations, if any, that were made available to the public prior to adoption.

(11) Any other information, statement, report, or data that the agency is required by law to consider or prepare in connection with the adoption, amendment, or repeal of a regulation.

(12) An index or table of contents that identifies each item contained in the rulemaking file. The index or table of contents shall include an affidavit or a declaration under penalty of perjury in the form specified by Section 2015.5 of the Code of Civil Procedure by the agency official who has compiled the rulemaking file, specifying the date upon which the record was closed, and that the file or the copy, if submitted, is complete.

(c) Every agency shall submit to the office with the adopted regulation, the rulemaking file or a complete copy of the rulemaking file.

(d) The rulemaking file shall be made available by the agency to the public, and to the courts in connection with the review of the regulation.

(e) Upon filing a regulation with the Secretary of State pursuant to Section 11349.3, the office shall return the related rulemaking file to the agency, after which no item contained in the file shall be removed, altered, or destroyed or otherwise disposed of. The agency shall maintain the file unless it elects to transmit the file to the State Archives pursuant to subdivision (f).

(f) The agency may transmit the rulemaking file to the State Archives. The file shall include instructions that the Secretary of State shall not remove, alter, or destroy or otherwise dispose of any item contained in the file. Pursuant to Section 12223.5, the Secretary of State may designate a time for the delivery of the rulemaking file to the State Archives in consideration of document processing or storage limitations. *(Added by Stats. 1979, c. 567, § 1, operative July 1, 1980. Amended by Stats.1979, c. 1203, § 8; Stats.1981, c. 865, p. 3316, § 31; Stats.1982, c. 327, p. 1437, § 35, eff. June 30, 1982; Stats.1983, c. 797, § 21; Stats.1984, c. 1444, § 5, eff. Sept. 26, 1984; Stats.1987, c. 1375, § 16; Stats.1991, c. 899 (S.B.327), § 3, eff. Oct. 14, 1991; Stats.1994, c. 1039 (A.B.2531), § 36; Stats.1996, c. 928 (S.B. 1507), § 3; Stats.2000, c. 1060 (A.B.1822), § 30; Stats.2011, c. 496 (S.B.617), § 8.)*

Law Revision Commission Comments

Subdivision (a) of Section 11347.3 is amended to make clear that the rulemaking file is available to the public throughout the rulemaking process. The amendment is not intended to affect agency practice regarding where the agency makes the record available to the public. If an agency properly limits the locations at which the rulemaking file may be inspected, it may continue to do so.

Subdivision (b)(9) is amended to improve its clarity, without affecting its substance. [30 Cal.L.Rev.Comm.Reports 725 (2000)].

Research References

Rutter, Cal. Practice Guide: Insurance Litigation Ch. 14-A, A. The California Regulator (*).
9 Witkin Cal. Proc. 5th Administrative Proceedings § 51, (S 51) in General.
9 Witkin Cal. Proc. 5th Administrative Proceedings § 143, Matters Considered and Excluded.

§ 11348. Rulemaking records; currency and location

Each agency subject to this chapter shall keep its rulemaking records on all of that agency's pending rulemaking actions, in which the notice has been published in the California Regulatory Notice Register, current and in one central location. *(Added by Stats.2000, c. 1059 (A.B.505), § 19.)*

Research References

9 Witkin Cal. Proc. 5th Administrative Proceedings § 55, (S 55) in General.

ARTICLE 6. REVIEW OF PROPOSED REGULATIONS

§ 11349. Definitions

The following definitions govern the interpretation of this chapter:

(a) "Necessity" means the record of the rulemaking proceeding demonstrates by substantial evidence the need for a regulation to effectuate the purpose of the statute, court decision, or other provision of law that the regulation implements, interprets, or makes specific, taking into account the totality of the record. For purposes of this standard, evidence includes, but is not limited to, facts, studies, and expert opinion.

(b) "Authority" means the provision of law which permits or obligates the agency to adopt, amend, or repeal a regulation.

(c) "Clarity" means written or displayed so that the meaning of regulations will be easily understood by those persons directly affected by them.

(d) "Consistency" means being in harmony with, and not in conflict with or contradictory to, existing statutes, court decisions, or other provisions of law.

(e) "Reference" means the statute, court decision, or other provision of law which the agency implements, interprets, or makes specific by adopting, amending, or repealing a regulation.

(f) "Nonduplication" means that a regulation does not serve the same purpose as a state or federal statute or another regulation. This standard requires that an agency proposing to amend or adopt a regulation must identify any state or federal statute or regulation which is overlapped or duplicated by the proposed regulation and justify any overlap or duplication. This standard is not intended to prohibit state agencies from printing relevant portions of enabling legislation in regulations when the duplication is necessary to satisfy the clarity standard in paragraph (3) of subdivision (a) of Section 11349.1. This standard is intended to prevent the indiscriminate incorporation of statutory language in a regulation. *(Added by Stats.1979, c. 567, § 1, operative July 1, 1980. Amended by Stats.1981, c. 983, p. 3814, § 4; Stats.1982, c. 1573, p. 6205, § 4; Stats.1983, c. 797, § 22; Stats.1985, c. 1044, § 3; Stats.1994, c. 1039 (A.B.2531), § 39; Stats.2000, c. 1060 (A.B.1822), § 31.)*

Law Revision Commission Comments

Subdivision (a) of Section 11349 is amended to clarify the meaning of "necessity," by placing it in the context of the purpose of the regulation. This is consistent with other provisions that relate to the necessity of a regulation. See Gov't Code §§11342.2 (regulation not valid unless "reasonably necessary to effectuate the purpose of statute" authorizing the regulation), 11350 (court may find regulation invalid if agency determination that the regulation "is reasonably necessary to effectuate the purpose of the statute, court decision, or other provision of law that is being implemented, interpreted, or made specific by the regulation" is not supported by substantial evidence). This is a nonsubstantive change. [30 Cal.L.Rev.Comm.Reports 725 (2000)].

Research References

9 Witkin Cal. Proc. 5th Administrative Proceedings § 48, in General.
9 Witkin Cal. Proc. 5th Administrative Proceedings § 51, (S 51) in General.

§ 11349.1. Review of regulations

(a) The office shall review all regulations adopted, amended, or repealed pursuant to the procedure specified in Article 5 (commencing with Section 11346) and submitted to it for publication in the California Code of Regulations Supplement and for transmittal to the Secretary of State and make determinations using all of the following standards:

(1) Necessity.

(2) Authority.

(3) Clarity.

(4) Consistency.

(5) Reference.

(6) Nonduplication.

In reviewing regulations pursuant to this section, the office shall restrict its review to the regulation and the record of the rulemaking proceeding. The office shall approve the regulation or order of repeal if it complies with the standards set forth in this section and with this chapter.

(b) In reviewing proposed regulations for the criteria in subdivision (a), the office may consider the clarity of the proposed regulation in the context of related regulations already in existence.

(c) The office shall adopt regulations governing the procedures it uses in reviewing regulations submitted to it. The regulations shall provide for an orderly review and shall specify the methods, standards, presumptions, and principles the office uses, and the limitations it observes, in reviewing regulations to establish compliance with the standards specified in subdivision (a). The regulations adopted by the office shall ensure that it does not substitute its judgment for that of the rulemaking agency as expressed in the substantive content of adopted regulations.

(d) The office shall return any regulation subject to this chapter to the adopting agency if any of the following occur:

(1) The adopting agency has not prepared the estimate required by paragraph (6) of subdivision (a) of Section 11346.5 and has not included the data used and calculations made and the summary report of the estimate in the file of the rulemaking.

(2) The agency has not complied with Section 11346.3. "Noncompliance" means that the agency failed to complete the economic impact assessment or standardized regulatory impact analysis required by Section 11346.3 or failed to include the assessment or analysis in the file of the rulemaking proceeding as required by Section 11347.3.

(3) The adopting agency has prepared the estimate required by paragraph (6) of subdivision (a) of Section 11346.5, the estimate indicates that the regulation will result in a cost to local agencies or school districts that is required to be reimbursed under Part 7 (commencing with Section 17500) of Division 4, and the adopting agency fails to do any of the following:

(A) Cite an item in the Budget Act for the fiscal year in which the regulation will go into effect as the source from which the Controller may pay the claims of local agencies or school districts.

(B) Cite an accompanying bill appropriating funds as the source from which the Controller may pay the claims of local agencies or school districts.

(C) Attach a letter or other documentation from the Department of Finance which states that the Department of Finance has approved a request by the agency that funds be included in the Budget Bill for the next following fiscal year to reimburse local agencies or school districts for the costs mandated by the regulation.

(D) Attach a letter or other documentation from the Department of Finance which states that the Department of Finance has authorized the augmentation of the amount available for expenditure under the agency's appropriation in the Budget Act which is for reimbursement pursuant to Part 7 (commencing with Section 17500) of Division 4 to local agencies or school districts from the unencumbered balances of other appropriations in the Budget Act and that this augmentation is sufficient to reimburse local agencies or school districts for their costs mandated by the regulation.

(4) The proposed regulation conflicts with an existing state regulation and the agency has not identified the manner in which the conflict may be resolved.

(5) The agency did not make the alternatives determination as required by paragraph (4) of subdivision (a) of Section 11346.9.

(e) The office shall notify the Department of Finance of all regulations returned pursuant to subdivision (d).

(f) The office shall return a rulemaking file to the submitting agency if the file does not comply with subdivisions (a) and (b) of Section 11347.3. Within three state working days of the receipt of a rulemaking file, the office shall notify the submitting agency of any deficiency identified. If no notice of deficiency is mailed to the adopting agency within that time, a rulemaking file shall be deemed submitted as of the date of its original receipt by the office. A rulemaking file shall not be deemed submitted until each deficiency identified under this subdivision has been corrected.

(g) Notwithstanding any other law, return of the regulation to the adopting agency by the office pursuant to this section is the exclusive remedy for a failure to comply with subdivision (c) of Section 11346.3 or paragraph (10) of subdivision (a) of Section 11346.5. *(Added by Stats.1979, c. 567, § 1, operative July 1, 1980. Amended by Stats.1979, c. 1152, § 12.8, operative July 1, 1980; Stats.1981, c. 865, p. 3317, § 32; Stats.1982, c. 86, p. 253, § 5, eff. March 1, 1982; Stats.1982, c. 327, p. 1438, § 36, eff. June 30, 1982; Stats.1982, c. 1544, p. 6014, § 1; Stats.1982, c. 1573, p. 6206, § 5; Stats.1985, c. 1044, § 4; Stats.1987, c. 1375, § 17.5; Stats.1991, c. 794 (A.B.2061), § 4; Stats.1994, c. 1039 (A.B.2351), § 40; Stats.2000, c. 1060 (A.B.1822), § 32; Stats.2011, c. 496 (S.B.617), § 9.)*

Law Revision Commission Comments

Section 11349.1 is amended (1) to make clear that it requires review of the repeal of a regulation, as well as the adoption or amendment of a regulation, and (2) to conform to the change in the name of the former California Regulatory Code Supplement. See Section 11344. [29 Cal.L.Rev.Comm.Reports 459 (2000)].

Research References

Rutter, Cal. Practice Guide: Insurance Litigation Ch. 14-A, A. The California Regulator (*).
9 Witkin Cal. Proc. 5th Administrative Proceedings § 51, (S 51) in General.

9 Witkin Cal. Proc. 5th Administrative Proceedings § 145, Declaration of Validity of Disapproved Regulation.

§ 11349.1.5. Review of standardized regulatory impact analyses; report; notification of noncompliance

(a) The Department of Finance and the office shall, from time to time, review the standardized regulatory impact analyses required by subdivision (c) of Section 11346.3 and submitted to the office pursuant to Section 11347.3, for adherence to the regulations adopted by the department pursuant to Section 11346.36.

(b) On or before November 1, 2015, the office shall submit to the Senate and Assembly Committees on Governmental Organization a report describing the extent to which submitted standardized regulatory impact analyses for proposed major regulations adhere to the regulations adopted pursuant to Section 11346.36. The report shall include a discussion of agency adherence to the regulations as well as a comparison between various state agencies on the question of adherence. The report may also include any recommendations from the office for actions the Legislature might consider for improving state agency performance.

(c) In addition to the report required by subdivision (b), the office may notify the Legislature of noncompliance by a state agency with the regulations adopted pursuant to Section 11346.36, in any manner or form determined by the office. *(Added by Stats.2011, c. 496 (S.B.617), § 10.)*

Research References

9 Witkin Cal. Proc. 5th Administrative Proceedings § 44, (S 44) Notice Requirements.

§ 11349.2. Rulemaking file; material added

An agency may add material to a rulemaking file that has been submitted to the office for review pursuant to this article if addition of the material does not violate other requirements of this chapter. *(Added by Stats.2000, c. 1060 (A.B.1822), § 33.)*

Law Revision Commission Comments

Section 11349.2 is new. It allows an agency to add inadvertently omitted material to a rulemaking file that has been submitted for review by the Office of Administrative Law. See Sections 11346.8(d) (limitation on addition of material to rulemaking file after close of public comment), 11346.9(a)(1) (limitation on use of new data in final statement of reasons), 11347.1 (procedure for additional public comment on material added to rulemaking file). [29 Cal.L.Rev.Comm.Reports 459 (2000)].

§ 11349.3. Approval or disapproval; return upon request of agency

(a) The office shall either approve a regulation submitted to it for review and transmit it to the Secretary of State for filing or disapprove it within 30 working days after the regulation has been submitted to the office for review. If the office fails to act within 30 days, the regulation shall be deemed to have been approved and the office shall transmit it to the Secretary of State for filing.

(b) If the office disapproves a regulation, it shall return it to the adopting agency within the 30-day period specified in subdivision (a) accompanied by a notice specifying the reasons for disapproval. Within seven calendar days of the issuance of the notice, the office shall provide the adopting agency with a written decision detailing the reasons for disapproval. No regulation shall be disapproved except for failure to comply with the standards set forth in Section 11349.1 or for failure to comply with this chapter.

(c) If an agency determines, on its own initiative, that a regulation submitted pursuant to subdivision (a) should be returned by the office prior to completion of the office's review,

it may request the return of the regulation. All requests for the return of a regulation shall be memorialized in writing by the submitting agency no later than one week following the request. Any regulation returned pursuant to this subdivision shall be resubmitted to the office for review within the one-year period specified in subdivision (b) of Section 11346.4 or shall comply with Article 5 (commencing with Section 11346) prior to resubmission.

(d) The office shall not initiate the return of a regulation pursuant to subdivision (c) as an alternative to disapproval pursuant to subdivision (b). *(Added by Stats.1979, c. 567, § 1, operative July 1, 1980. Amended by Stats.1981, c. 865, p. 3317, § 33; Stats.1982, c. 1236, p. 4557, § 1; Stats.1985, c. 1044, § 5; Stats.1987, c. 1375, § 19; Stats.1991, c. 794 (A.B.2061), § 5; Stats.1992, c. 1306 (A.B.3511), § 2.)*

Research References

Rutter, Cal. Practice Guide: Insurance Litigation Ch. 14-A, A. The California Regulator (*).
9 Witkin Cal. Proc. 5th Administrative Proceedings § 51, (S 51) in General.

§ 11349.4. Returned regulations; readoption; limited review

(a) A regulation returned to an agency because of failure to meet the standards of Section 11349.1, because of an agency's failure to comply with this chapter may be rewritten and resubmitted within 120 days of the agency's receipt of the written opinion required by subdivision (b) of Section 11349.3 without complying with the notice and public hearing requirements of Sections 11346.4, 11346.5, and 11346.8 unless the substantive provisions of the regulation have been significantly changed. If the regulation has been significantly changed or was not submitted within 120 days of receipt of the written opinion, the agency shall comply with Article 5 (commencing with Section 11346) and readopt the regulation. The director of the office may, upon a showing of good cause, grant an extension to the 120-day time period specified in this subdivision.

(b) Upon resubmission of a disapproved regulation to the office pursuant to subdivision (a), the office shall only review the resubmitted regulation for those reasons expressly identified in the written opinion required by subdivision (b) of Section 11349.3, or for those issues arising as a result of a substantial change to a provision of the resubmitted regulation or as a result of intervening statutory changes or intervening court orders or decisions.

(c) When an agency resubmits a withdrawn or disapproved regulation to the office it shall identify the prior withdrawn or disapproved regulation by date of submission to the office, shall specify the portion of the prior rulemaking record that should be included in the resubmission, and shall submit to the office a copy of the prior rulemaking record if that record has been returned to the agency by the office.

(d) The office shall expedite the review of a regulation submitted without significant substantive change. *(Added by Stats.1979, c. 567, § 1, operative July 1, 1980. Amended by Stats.1981, c. 865, p. 3317, § 34; Stats.1982, c. 1573, p. 6207, § 7; Stats.1983, c. 142, § 37; Stats.1985, c. 1044, § 6; Stats.1987, c. 1375, § 20.)*

Research References

Rutter, Cal. Practice Guide: Insurance Litigation Ch. 14-A, A. The California Regulator (*).

Government

9 Witkin Cal. Proc. 5th Administrative Proceedings § 52, (S 52) Review of Rewritten Regulations.

§ 11349.5. Review by Governor of decision by office of administrative law; written request for review; contents; delivery; response; written decision; publication; overruling decision of office

(a) To initiate a review of a decision by the office, the agency shall file a written Request for Review with the Governor's Legal Affairs Secretary within 10 days of receipt of the written opinion provided by the office pursuant to subdivision (b) of Section 11349.3. The Request for Review shall include a complete statement as to why the agency believes the decision is incorrect and should be overruled. Along with the Request for Review, the agency shall submit all of the following:

(1) The office's written decision detailing the reasons for disapproval required by subdivision (b) of Section 11349.3.

(2) Copies of all regulations, notices, statements, and other documents which were submitted to the office.

(b) A copy of the agency's Request for Review shall be delivered to the office on the same day it is delivered to the Governor's office. The office shall file its written response to the agency's request with the Governor's Legal Affairs Secretary within 10 days and deliver a copy of its response to the agency on the same day it is delivered to the Governor's office.

(c) The Governor's office shall provide the requesting agency and the office with a written decision within 15 days of receipt of the response by the office to the agency's Request for Review. Upon receipt of the decision, the office shall publish in the California Regulatory Notice Register the agency's Request for Review, the office's response thereto, and the decision of the Governor's office.

(d) The time requirements set by subdivisions (a) and (b) may be shortened by the Governor's office for good cause.

(e) The Governor may overrule the decision of the office disapproving a proposed regulation, an order repealing an emergency regulation adopted pursuant to subdivision (b) of Section 11346.1, or a decision refusing to allow the readoption of an emergency regulation pursuant to Section 11346.1. In that event, the office shall immediately transmit the regulation to the Secretary of State for filing.

(f) Upon overruling the decision of the office, the Governor shall immediately transmit to the Committees on Rules of both houses of the Legislature a statement of his or her reasons for overruling the decision of the office, along with copies of the adopting agency's initial statement of reasons issued pursuant to Section 11346.2 and the office's statement regarding the disapproval of a regulation issued pursuant to subdivision (b) of Section 11349.3. The Governor's action and the reasons therefor shall be published in the California Regulatory Notice Register. *(Added by Stats.1979, c. 567, § 1, operative July 1, 1980. Amended by Stats.1980, c. 1238, p. 4205, § 5, eff. Sept. 29, 1980; Stats.1981, c. 865, p. 3318, § 34.5; Stats.1982, c. 86, p. 253, § 6, eff. March 1, 1982; Stats.1982, c. 1236, p. 4557, § 2; Stats.1983, c. 724, § 1; Stats.1985, c. 1044, § 7; Stats.1987, c. 1375, § 20.2; Stats.1994, c. 1039 (A.B.2351), § 41; Stats.1995, c. 938 (S.B.523), § 15.6, operative Jan. 1, 1996.)*

Research References

Rutter, Cal. Practice Guide: Insurance Litigation Ch. 14-A, A. The California Regulator (*).
9 Witkin Cal. Proc. 5th Administrative Proceedings § 48, in General.
9 Witkin Cal. Proc. 5th Administrative Proceedings § 51, (S 51) in General.

9 Witkin Cal. Proc. 5th Administrative Proceedings § 55, (S 55) in General.

§ 11349.6. Emergency regulations

(a) If the adopting agency has complied with Sections 11346.2 to 11347.3, inclusive, prior to the adoption of the regulation as an emergency, the office shall approve or disapprove the regulation in accordance with this article.

(b) Emergency regulations adopted pursuant to subdivision (b) of Section 11346.1 shall be reviewed by the office within 10 calendar days after their submittal to the office. After posting a notice of the filing of a proposed emergency regulation on its Internet Web site, the office shall allow interested persons five calendar days to submit comments on the proposed emergency regulations unless the emergency situation clearly poses such an immediate serious harm that delaying action to allow public comment would be inconsistent with the public interest. The office shall disapprove the emergency regulations if it determines that the situation addressed by the regulations is not an emergency, or if it determines that the regulation fails to meet the standards set forth in Section 11349.1, or if it determines the agency failed to comply with Section 11346.1.

(c) If the office considers any information not submitted to it by the rulemaking agency when determining whether to file emergency regulations, the office shall provide the rulemaking agency with an opportunity to rebut or comment upon that information.

(d) Within 30 working days of the filing of a certificate of compliance, the office shall review the regulation and hearing record and approve or order the repeal of an emergency regulation if it determines that the regulation fails to meet the standards set forth in Section 11349.1, or if it determines that the agency failed to comply with this chapter. *(Added by Stats.1979, c. 567, § 1, operative July 1, 1980. Amended by Stats.1979, c. 1203, § 9; Stats.1980, c. 1238, p. 4206, § 6, eff. Sept. 29, 1980; Stats.1981, c. 865, p. 3318, § 35; Stats.1982, c. 1236, p. 4558, § 3; Stats.1982, c. 1573, p. 6208, § 8; Stats.1983, c. 797, § 23; Stats.1985, c. 1044, § 8; Stats.1987, c. 1375, § 20.5; Stats.1994, c. 1039 (A.B.2351), § 42; Stats.2000, c. 1060 (A.B.1822), § 34; Stats.2006, c. 713 (A.B.1302), § 4.)*

Law Revision Commission Comments

Subdivision (a) of Section 11349.6 is amended to correct an underinclusive reference.

Subdivision (d) is amended to conform the period for review of an emergency regulation under that subdivision to the period for review of nonemergency regulations under Section 11343.3. [29 Cal.L.Rev.Comm.Reports 459 (2000)].

Research References

9 Witkin Cal. Proc. 5th Administrative Proceedings § 48, in General.

ARTICLE 7. REVIEW OF EXISTING REGULATIONS

§ 11349.7. Priority review of regulations; notice; repeal procedures

The office, at the request of any standing, select, or joint committee of the Legislature, shall initiate a priority review of any regulation, group of regulations, or series of regulations that the committee believes does not meet the standards set forth in Section 11349.1.

The office shall notify interested persons and shall publish notice in the California Regulatory Notice Register that a priority review has been requested, shall consider the written comments submitted by interested persons, the information contained in the rulemaking record, if any, and shall complete each priority review made pursuant to this section within 90 calendar days of the receipt of the committee's written request. During the period of any priority review made pursuant to this section, all information available to the office relating to the priority review shall be made available to the public. In the event that the office determines that a regulation does not meet the standards set forth in Section 11349.1, it shall order the adopting agency to show cause why the regulation should not be repealed and shall proceed to seek repeal of the regulation as provided by this section in accordance with the following:

(a) In the event it determines that any of the regulations subject to the review do not meet the standards set forth in Section 11349.1, the office shall within 15 days of the determination order the adopting agency to show cause why the regulation should not be repealed. In issuing the order, the office shall specify in writing the reasons for its determination that the regulation does not meet the standards set forth in Section 11349.1. The reasons for its determination shall be made available to the public. The office shall also publish its order and the reasons therefor in the California Regulatory Notice Register. In the case of a regulation for which no, or inadequate, information relating to its necessity can be furnished by the adopting agency, the order shall specify the information which the office requires to make its determination.

(b) No later than 60 days following receipt of an order to show cause why a regulation should not be repealed, the agency shall respond in writing to the office. Upon written application by the agency, the office may extend the time for an additional 30 days.

(c) The office shall review and consider all information submitted by the agency in a timely response to the order to show cause why the regulation should not be repealed, and determine whether the regulation meets the standards set forth in Section 11349.1. The office shall make this determination within 60 days of receipt of an agency's response to the order to show cause. If the office does not make a determination within 60 days of receipt of an agency's response to the order to show cause, the regulation shall be deemed to meet the standards set forth in subdivision (a) of Section 11349.1. In making this determination, the office shall also review any written comments submitted to it by the public within 30 days of the publication of the order to show cause in the California Regulatory Notice Register. During the period of review and consideration, the information available to the office relating to each regulation for which the office has issued an order to show cause shall be made available to the public. The office shall notify the adopting agency within two working days of the receipt of information submitted by the public regarding a regulation for which an order to show cause has been issued. If the office determines that a regulation fails to meet the standards, it shall prepare a statement specifying the reasons for its determination. The statement shall be delivered to the adopting agency, the Legislature, and the Governor and shall be made available to the public and the courts. Thirty days after delivery of the statement required by this subdivision the office shall prepare an order of repeal of the regulation and shall transmit it to the Secretary of State for filing.

(d) The Governor, within 30 days after the office has delivered the statement specifying the reasons for its decision to repeal, as required by subdivision (c), may overrule the decision of the office ordering the repeal of a regulation. The regulation shall then remain in full force and effect. Notice of the

Governor's action and the reasons therefor shall be published in the California Regulatory Notice Register.

The Governor shall transmit to the rules committee of each house of the Legislature a statement of reasons for overruling the decision of the office, plus any other information that may be requested by either of the rules committees.

(e) In the event that the office orders the repeal of a regulation, it shall publish the order and the reasons therefor in the California Regulatory Notice Register. *(Added by Stats. 1994, c. 1039 (A.B.2531), § 43.)*

Research References

9 Witkin Cal. Proc. 5th Administrative Proceedings § 51, (S 51) in General.
9 Witkin Cal. Proc. 5th Administrative Proceedings § 55, (S 55) in General.

§ 11349.8. Repeal for lack of statutory authority; procedure

(a) If the office is notified of, or on its own becomes aware of, an existing regulation in the California Code of Regulations for which the statutory authority has been repealed or becomes ineffective or inoperative by its own terms, the office shall order the adopting agency to show cause why the regulation should not be repealed for lack of statutory authority and shall notify the Legislature in writing of this order. In issuing the order, the office shall specify in writing the reasons for issuance of the order. "Agency," for purposes of this section and Section 11349.9, refers to the agency that adopted the regulation and, if applicable, the agency that is responsible for administering the regulation in issue.

(b) The agency may, within 30 days after receipt of the written notification, submit in writing to the office any citations, legal arguments, or other information opposing the repeal, including public comments during this period. This section shall not apply where the agency demonstrates in its response that any of the following conditions exists:

(1) The statute or section thereof is simultaneously repealed and substantially reenacted through a single piece of legislation, or where subsequent legislation evinces a specific legislative intent to reenact the substance of the statute or section. When a regulation cites more than one specific statute or section as reference or authority for the adoption of a regulation, and one or more of the statutes or sections are repealed or become ineffective or inoperative, then the only provisions of the regulation which remain in effect shall be those for which the remaining statutes or sections provide specific or general authority.

(2) The statute is temporarily repealed, or rendered ineffective or inoperative by a provision of law which is effective only for a limited period, in which case any regulation described in subdivision (a) is thereby also temporarily repealed, rendered ineffective, or inoperative during that limited period. Any regulation so affected shall have the same force and effect upon the expiration of the limited period during which the provision of law was effective as if that temporary provision had not been enacted.

(3) The statute or section of a statute being repealed, or becoming ineffective or inoperative by its own terms, is to remain in full force and effect as regards events occurring prior to the date of repeal or ineffectiveness, in which case any regulation adopted to implement or interpret that statute shall likewise be deemed to remain in full force and effect in regards to those same events.

(c) This section shall not be construed to deprive any person or public agency of any substantial right which would have existed prior to, or hereafter exists subsequent to, the effective date of this section.

(d) Thirty days after receipt of the agency's opposition material, or the close of the 30-day agency and public response period if no response is submitted, the office shall do one of the following:

(1) Inform the agency and the Legislature in writing that the office has withdrawn its order to show cause.

(2) Issue a written notice to the agency specifying the reasons for the repeal and its intent to file a Notice of Repeal of the invalid regulation with the Secretary of State. Within seven calendar days of the filing of the Notice of Repeal, the office shall provide the agency, the Governor, and the Legislature with a written decision detailing the reasons for the repeal and a copy of the Notice of Repeal, and publish the office's written decision in the California Regulatory Notice Register.

(e) The office shall order the removal of the repealed regulation from the California Code of Regulations within 30 days after filing the Notice of Repeal, if the agency has not appealed the office's decision, or upon receipt of notification of the Governor's decision upholding the office's decision, if an appeal has been filed pursuant to Section 11349.9. *(Formerly § 11349.10, added by Stats.1989, c. 1170, § 1. Renumbered § 11349.8 and amended by Stats.1994, c. 1039 (A.B.2531), § 44.)*

Research References

9 Witkin Cal. Proc. 5th Administrative Proceedings § 51, (S 51) in General.

§ 11349.9. Notice of repeal pursuant to § 11349.8; request for review; written decision; overrule

(a) To initiate a review of the office's Notice of Repeal pursuant to Section 11349.8, the agency shall appeal the office's decision by filing a written Request for Review with the Governor's Legal Affairs Secretary within 10 days of receipt of the Notice of Repeal and written decision provided for by paragraph (2) of subdivision (d) of Section 11349.8. The Request for Review shall include a complete statement as to why the agency believes the decision is incorrect and should be overruled. Along with the Request for Review, the agency shall submit all of the following:

(1) The office's written opinion detailing the reasons for repeal required by paragraph (2) of subdivision (d) of Section 11349.8.

(2) Copies of all statements and other documents that were submitted to the office.

(b) A copy of the agency's Request for Review shall be delivered to the office on the same day it is delivered to the Governor's office. The office shall file its written response to the agency's request with the Governor's Legal Affairs Secretary within 10 days, and deliver a copy of its response to the agency on the same day it is delivered to the Governor's office.

(c) The Governor's office shall provide the requesting agency and the office with a written decision within 15 days of receipt of the response by the office to the agency's Request for Review. Upon receipt of the decision, the office shall publish in the California Regulatory Notice Register the agency's Request for Review, the office's response thereto, and the decision of the Governor's office.

(d) The time requirements set by subdivisions (a) and (b) may be shortened by the Governor's office for good cause.

(e) In the event the Governor overrules the decision of the office, the office shall immediately transmit the regulation to the Secretary of State for filing.

(f) Upon overruling the decision of the office, the Governor shall transmit to the rules committees of both houses of the Legislature a statement of the reasons for overruling the decision of the office. *(Formerly § 11349.11, added by Stats.1989, c. 1170, § 2. Renumbered § 11349.9 and amended by Stats.1994, c. 1039 (A.B.2531), § 45. Amended by Stats.1995, c. 938 (S.B.523), § 15.7, operative Jan. 1, 1996.)*

Research References

9 Witkin Cal. Proc. 5th Administrative Proceedings § 51, (S 51) in General.
9 Witkin Cal. Proc. 5th Administrative Proceedings § 55, (S 55) in General.

ARTICLE 8. JUDICIAL REVIEW

Section
11350.   Declaratory relief; grounds for declaration of invalidity; evidence allowed.
11350.3.   Judicial declaration as to validity of regulation disapproved or ordered repealed; action for declaratory relief.

§ 11350. Declaratory relief; grounds for declaration of invalidity; evidence allowed

(a) Any interested person may obtain a judicial declaration as to the validity of any regulation or order of repeal by bringing an action for declaratory relief in the superior court in accordance with the Code of Civil Procedure. The right to judicial determination shall not be affected by the failure either to petition or to seek reconsideration of a petition filed pursuant to Section 11340.7 before the agency promulgating the regulation or order of repeal. The regulation or order of repeal may be declared to be invalid for a substantial failure to comply with this chapter, or, in the case of an emergency regulation or order of repeal, upon the ground that the facts recited in the finding of emergency prepared pursuant to subdivision (b) of Section 11346.1 do not constitute an emergency within the provisions of Section 11346.1.

(b) In addition to any other ground that may exist, a regulation or order of repeal may be declared invalid if either of the following exists:

(1) The agency's determination that the regulation is reasonably necessary to effectuate the purpose of the statute, court decision, or other provision of law that is being implemented, interpreted, or made specific by the regulation is not supported by substantial evidence.

(2) The agency declaration pursuant to paragraph (8) of subdivision (a) of Section 11346.5 is in conflict with substantial evidence in the record.

(c) The approval of a regulation or order of repeal by the office or the Governor's overruling of a decision of the office disapproving a regulation or order of repeal shall not be considered by a court in any action for declaratory relief brought with respect to a regulation or order of repeal.

(d) In a proceeding under this section, a court may only consider the following evidence:

(1) The rulemaking file prepared under Section 11347.3.

(2) The finding of emergency prepared pursuant to subdivision (b) of Section 11346.1.

(3) An item that is required to be included in the rulemaking file but is not included in the rulemaking file, for the sole purpose of proving its omission.

(4) Any evidence relevant to whether a regulation used by an agency is required to be adopted under this chapter. *(Added by*

Stats.1979, c. 567, § 1, operative July 1, 1980. Amended by Stats.1981, c. 592, p. 2305, § 1; Stats.1981, c. 865, p. 3321, § 37; Stats.1982, c. 86, p. 256, § 9, eff. March 1, 1982; Stats.1982, c. 1573, p. 6211, § 10; Stats.1991, c. 794 (A.B.2061), § 6; Stats. 1994, c. 1039 (A.B.2531), § 47; Stats.1995, c. 938 (S.B.523), § 15.8, operative Jan. 1, 1996; Stats.2000, c. 1060 (A.B.1822), § 35; Stats.2006, c. 713 (A.B.1302), § 5.)

Law Revision Commission Comments

Section 11350 is amended to provide for judicial review of an order of repeal, as well as a regulation. This is consistent with the provision authorizing review of an emergency order of repeal.

Subdivision (a) is also amended to eliminate an ambiguity regarding the statement an agency prepares on proposing an emergency regulation. This change is technical and is not intended to affect the meaning of the section.

Subdivision (d) is added to correct inadequacies in the former provision limiting the record of review to the rulemaking file. Subdivision (d)(1) restates part of the substance of the former second paragraph of Section 11350(b)(2), limiting the record of review to the rulemaking file prepared under Section 11347.3. Subdivision (d)(2) permits consideration of an agency statement prepared under Section 11346.1(b) (justifying emergency regulation). Such a statement is not part of a rulemaking file prepared under Section 11347.3. See Section 11346.1(a). Subdivision (d)(3) permits consideration of a document that should have been included in the rulemaking file but was not, in order to prove its omission. Such evidence may be necessary to prove a substantial failure to follow required procedures. For example, an agency's failure to include a public comment in the rulemaking file may constitute a substantial failure to follow required procedures. See Section 11347.3(b)(6) (written public comments must be included in rulemaking file). Proof of such an omission requires consideration of the omitted item. Subdivision (d)(4) permits consideration of any relevant evidence for the purpose of determining whether a regulation used by an agency is required to be adopted under this chapter C i.e., whether it is an invalid "underground regulation." See Section 11340.5 (issuance or use of regulation that has not been adopted is prohibited). Note that evidence offered to prove that an agency has used a regulation that is required to be adopted under the rulemaking procedure will typically be documentary evidence, but a court may consider oral testimony in appropriate circumstances (e.g., to judge the credibility of an affiant or declarant). [30 Cal.L.Rev.Comm. Reports 725 (2000)].

Subdivision (a) of Section 11350 is amended to correct a typographical error. Subdivisions (a) and (d)(2) are amended to make clear that it is the entire finding of emergency that is subject to review, and not just the "written statement" that is required as part of the finding of emergency. See Section 11346.1(b). These are nonsubstantive changes. [34 Cal. L.Rev.Comm. Reports 229 (2004)].

Research References

Rutter, Cal. Practice Guide: Insurance Litigation Ch. 14-B, B. Courts and Regulation.

Miller and Starr California Real Estate § 4:3, The Real Estate Commissioner.

3 Witkin Cal. Proc. 5th Actions § 336, (S 336) in General.

9 Witkin Cal. Proc. 5th Administrative Proceedings § 38, History, Legislative Intent, and Revision.

9 Witkin Cal. Proc. 5th Administrative Proceedings § 121, (S 121) Forms of Relief.

9 Witkin Cal. Proc. 5th Administrative Proceedings § 122, (S 122) Standing to Obtain Review.

9 Witkin Cal. Proc. 5th Administrative Proceedings § 138, (S 138) in General.

9 Witkin Cal. Proc. 5th Administrative Proceedings § 141, in General.

9 Witkin Cal. Proc. 5th Administrative Proceedings § 142, Standing.

9 Witkin Cal. Proc. 5th Administrative Proceedings § 143, Matters Considered and Excluded.

9 Witkin Cal. Proc. 5th Administrative Proceedings § 144, Grounds for Declaration of Invalidity.

8 Witkin Cal. Proc. 5th Extraordinary Writs § 270, in General.

8 Witkin Cal. Proc. 5th Extraordinary Writs § 275, (S 275) Purpose of Study.

5 Witkin Cal. Proc. 5th Pleading § 859, (S 859) Statute, Ordinance, or Regulation.

5 Witkin Cal. Proc. 5th Pleading § 865, Probable Future Controversy.

5 Witkin Cal. Proc. 5th Pleading § 873, (S 873) Express Prohibition by Statute.

3 Witkin, California Summary 10th Agency and Employment § 460, Decision as Precedent.

7 Witkin, California Summary 10th Constitutional Law § 78, (S 78) Standing Shown.

7 Witkin, California Summary 10th Constitutional Law § 675, (S 675) Statutory Requirement.

§ 11350.3. Judicial declaration as to validity of regulation disapproved or ordered repealed; action for declaratory relief

Any interested person may obtain a judicial declaration as to the validity of a regulation or order of repeal which the office has disapproved pursuant to Section 11349.3, or 11349.6, or of a regulation that has been ordered repealed pursuant to Section 11349.7 by bringing an action for declaratory relief in the superior court in accordance with the Code of Civil Procedure. The court may declare the regulation valid if it determines that the regulation meets the standards set forth in Section 11349.1 and that the agency has complied with this chapter. If the court so determines, it may order the office to immediately file the regulation with the Secretary of State. *(Added by Stats.1982, c. 1544, p. 6016, § 2; Stats.1982, c. 1573, p. 6212, § 11. Amended by Stats.1987, c. 1375, § 23.5; Stats.1994, c. 1039 (A.B.2531), § 48; Stats.2000, c. 1060 (A.B.1822), § 36.)*

Law Revision Commission Comments

Section 11350.3 is amended to provide for judicial review of an order of repeal that is disapproved by the Office of Administrative Law. [29 Cal.L.Rev.Comm.Reports 459 (2000)].

Research References

9 Witkin Cal. Proc. 5th Administrative Proceedings § 138, (S 138) in General.

9 Witkin Cal. Proc. 5th Administrative Proceedings § 145, Declaration of Validity of Disapproved Regulation.

ARTICLE 9.   SPECIAL PROCEDURES

§ 11351.　Application of articles to public utilities commission and worker's compensation appeals board

(a) Except as provided in subdivision (b), Article 5 (commencing with Section 11346), Article 6 (commencing with Section 11349), Article 7 (commencing with Section 11349.7), and Article 8 (commencing with Section 11350) shall not apply to the Public Utilities Commission or the Workers' Compensation

Appeals Board, and Article 3 (commencing with Section 11343) and Article 4 (commencing with Section 11344) shall apply only to the rules of procedure of these state agencies.

(b) The Public Utilities Commission and the Workers' Compensation Appeals Board shall comply with paragraph (5) of subdivision (a) of Section 11346.4 with respect to regulations that are required to be filed with the Secretary of State pursuant to Section 11343.

(c) Article 8 (commencing with Section 11350) shall not apply to the Division of Workers' Compensation. *(Formerly § 11445, added by Stats.1979, c. 567, § 1, operative July 1, 1980. Renumbered § 11351 and amended by Stats.1980, c. 204, § 6, eff. June 20, 1980. Amended by Stats.1982, c. 86, p. 257, § 10, eff. March 1, 1982; Stats.1983, c. 797, § 26; Stats.1987, c. 1375, § 24; Stats.1994, c. 1039 (A.B.2531), § 50; Stats.1996, c. 14 (A.B.1859), § 1.)*

Research References

9 Witkin Cal. Proc. 5th Administrative Proceedings § 39, Nature and Scope.

§ 11352. Water quality certification; waste discharge requirements, permits, and waivers; guidance document; application of chapter to certain actions

The following actions are not subject to this chapter:

(a) The issuance, denial, or waiver of any water quality certification as authorized under Section 13160 of the Water Code.

(b) The issuance, denial, or revocation of waste discharge requirements and permits pursuant to Sections 13263 and 13377 of the Water Code and waivers issued pursuant to Section 13269 of the Water Code.

(c) The development, issuance, and use of the guidance document pursuant to Section 13383.7 of the Water Code. *(Added by Stats.1992, c. 1112 (A.B.3359), § 1. Amended by Stats.2007, c. 610 (A.B.739), § 1.5.)*

Research References

12 Witkin, California Summary 10th Real Property § 895, Other California Statutes.

§ 11353. State water quality control policies, plans, and guidelines; adoption or revision; application of chapter; review; procedures; requirements

(a) Except as provided in subdivision (b), this chapter does not apply to the adoption or revision of state policy for water quality control and the adoption or revision of water quality control plans and guidelines pursuant to Division 7 (commencing with Section 13000) of the Water Code.

(b)(1) Any policy, plan, or guideline, or any revision thereof, that the State Water Resources Control Board has adopted or that a court determines is subject to this part, after June 1, 1992, shall be submitted to the office.

(2) The State Water Resources Control Board shall include in its submittal to the office all of the following:

(A) A clear and concise summary of any regulatory provisions adopted or approved as part of that action, for publication in the California Code of Regulations.

(B) The administrative record for the proceeding. Proposed additions to a policy, plan, or guideline shall be indicated by underlined text and proposed deletions shall be indicated by strike-through text in documents submitted as part of the administrative record for the proceeding.

(C) A summary of the necessity for the regulatory provision.

(D) A certification by the chief legal officer of the State Water Resources Control Board that the action was taken in compliance with all applicable procedural requirements of Division 7 (commencing with Section 13000) of the Water Code.

(3) Paragraph (2) does not limit the authority of the office to review any regulatory provision which is part of the policy, plan, or guideline submitted by the State Water Resources Control Board.

(4) The office shall review the regulatory provisions to determine compliance with the standards of necessity, authority, clarity, consistency, reference, and nonduplication set forth in subdivision (a) of Section 11349.1. The office shall also review the responses to public comments prepared by the State Water Resources Control Board or the appropriate regional water quality control board to determine compliance with the public participation requirements of the Federal Water Pollution Control Act (33 U.S.C. Sec. 1251 et seq.). The office shall restrict its review to the regulatory provisions and the administrative record of the proceeding. Sections 11349.3, 11349.4, 11349.5, and 11350.3 shall apply to the review by the office to the extent that those sections are consistent with this section.

(5) The policy, plan, guideline, or revision shall not become effective unless and until the regulatory provisions are approved by the office in accordance with subdivision (a) of Section 11349.3.

(6) Upon approval of the regulatory provisions, the office shall transmit to the Secretary of State for filing the clear and concise summary of the regulatory provisions submitted by the State Water Resources Control Board.

(7) Any proceedings before the State Water Resources Control Board or a California regional water quality control board to take any action subject to this subdivision shall be conducted in accordance with the procedural requirements of Division 7 (commencing with Section 13000) of the Water Code, together with any applicable requirements of the Federal Water Pollution Control Act (33 U.S.C. Sec. 1251 et seq.), and the requirements of this chapter, other than the requirement for review by the office in accordance with this subdivision, shall not apply.

(8) This subdivision shall not provide a basis for review by the office under this subdivision or Article 6 (commencing with Section 11349) of any such policy, plan, or guideline adopted or revised prior to June 1, 1992.

(c) Subdivision (a) does not apply to a provision of any policy, plan, guideline, or revision, as applied to any person who, as of June 1, 1992, was a party to a civil action challenging that provision on the grounds that it has not been adopted as a regulation pursuant to this chapter.

(d) Copies of the policies, plans, and guidelines to which subdivision (a) applies shall be maintained at central locations for inspection by the public. The State Water Resources Control Board shall maintain, at its headquarters in Sacramento, a current copy of each policy, plan, or guideline in effect. Each regional water quality control board shall maintain at its headquarters a current copy of each policy, plan, or guideline in effect in its respective region. Any revision of a policy, plan, or guideline shall be made available for inspection by the public within 30 days of its effective date. *(Added by Stats.1992, c. 1112 (A.B.3359), § 2. Amended by Stats.2000, c. 1060 (A.B.1822), § 37.)*

Law Revision Commission Comments

Subdivision (b)(2)(B) of Section 11353 is amended to require that amendments and deletions be clearly indicated in material submitted to the Office of Administrative Law for review. For a similar provision, see Section 11354.1(d)(2)(B) (underscore and strike-through required to indicate changes in plans of San Francisco Bay Conservation and Development Commission). [29 Cal.L.Rev.Comm.Reports 459 (2000)].

§ 11354. Application of §§ 11352 and 11353 in civil actions pending on June 1, 1992

Sections 11352 and 11353 do not affect any court's determination, relating to the applicability of this chapter to any provision of a policy, plan, or guideline, in a civil action which was pending on June 1, 1992, and on that date included a challenge to a provision of a policy, plan, or guideline on the grounds that it has not been adopted in accordance with this chapter. *(Added by Stats.1992, c. 1112 (A.B.3359), § 2.)*

§ 11354.1. Application of chapter; amendments or changes to plans; submission to office; documents; review; approval

(a) For purposes of this section, "commission" means the San Francisco Bay Conservation and Development Commission.

(b) This chapter does not apply to any policy, plan, or guideline adopted by the commission prior to January 1, 1996, pursuant to Chapter 5 (commencing with Section 66650) of Title 7.2 of this code or Division 19 (commencing with Section 29000) of the Public Resources Code.

(c) The issuance or denial by the commission of any permit pursuant to subdivision (a) of Section 66632, and the issuance or denial by, or appeal to, the commission of any permit pursuant to Chapter 6 (commencing with Section 29500) of Division 19 of the Public Resources Code, are not subject to this chapter.

(d)(1) Any amendments or other changes to the San Francisco Bay Plan or to a special area plan pursuant to Chapter 5 (commencing with Section 66650) of Title 7.2, adopted by the commission on or after January 1, 1996, and any amendments or other changes to the Suisun Marsh Protection Plan, as defined in Section 29113 of the Public Resources Code, or in the Suisun Marsh local protection program, as defined in Section 29111 of the Public Resources Code, adopted by the commission on and after January 1, 1996, shall be submitted to the office but are not subject to this chapter except as provided in this subdivision.

(2) The commission shall include in its submittal to the office pursuant to paragraph (1) both of the following documents:

(A) A clear and concise summary of any regulatory provision adopted or approved by the commission as part of the proposed change for publication in the California Code of Regulations.

(B) The administrative record for the proceeding, and a list of the documents relied upon in making the change. Proposed additions to the plans shall be indicated by underlined text, and proposed deletions shall be indicated by strike-through text in documents submitted as part of the administrative record for the proceeding.

(3) The office shall review the regulatory provisions to determine compliance with the standards of necessity, authority, clarity, consistency, reference, and nonduplication set forth in subdivision (a) of Section 11349.1. The office shall also review the responses to public comments prepared by the commission to determine compliance with the public participation requirements of Sections 11000 to 11007, inclusive, of Title 14 of the California Code of Regulations, and to ensure that the commission considers all relevant matters presented to it before adopting, amending, or repealing any regulatory provision, and that the commission explains the reasons for not modifying a proposed plan change to accommodate an objection or recommendation. The office shall restrict its review to the regulatory provisions and the administrative record of the proceeding. Sections 11349.3, 11349.4, 11349.5, and 11350.3 shall apply to the review by the office to the extent that those sections are consistent with this section.

(4) In reviewing proposed changes to the commission's plans for the criteria specified in subdivision (a) of Section 11349.1, the office shall consider the clarity of the proposed plan change in the context of the commission's existing plans.

(5) The proposed plan or program change subject to this subdivision shall not become effective unless and until the regulatory provisions are approved by the office in accordance with subdivision (a) of Section 11349.3.

(6) Upon approval of the regulatory provisions, the office shall transmit to the Secretary of State for filing the clear and concise summary of the regulatory provisions submitted by the commission.

(e) Except as provided in subdivisions (b), (c), and (d), the adoption of any regulation by the commission shall be subject to this chapter in all respects. *(Added by Stats.1995, c. 951 (A.B.1102), § 1. Amended by Stats.1996, c. 124 (A.B.3470), § 35; Stats.2002, c. 389 (A.B.1857), § 7.)*

§ 11356. Building standards; application of articles 5 and 6

(a) Article 6 (commencing with Section 11349) is not applicable to a building standard.

(b) Article 5 (commencing with Section 11346) is applicable to those building standards, except that the office shall not disapprove those building standards nor refuse to publish any notice of proposed building standards if either has been approved by, and submitted to, the office by the California Building Standards Commission pursuant to Section 18935 of the Health and Safety Code. *(Formerly § 11446, added by Stats.1979, c. 1152, p. 4232, § 13.5, operative July 1, 1980. Renumbered § 11356 and amended by Stats.1980, c. 676, p. 1918, § 106. Amended by Stats.1984, c. 677, § 1; Stats.1987, c. 1375, § 25; Stats.1988, c. 1194, § 1.5, operative Jan. 1, 1989; Stats.2000, c. 1060 (A.B.1822), § 38.)*

Law Revision Commission Comments

Subdivision (a) of Section 11356 is amended to eliminate the implication that the exemption of building standards from review by the Office of Administrative Law is conditioned on approval of the California Building Standards Commission. Note, however, that building standards are subject to review by the California Building Standards Commission under Health and Safety Code Section 18930. Subdivision (a) is also amended to use the defined term "building standard." See Section 11342.530 ("building standard" defined).

Subdivision (b) is amended to reflect the change in the name of the California Building Standards Commission. [29 Cal.L.Rev.Comm.Reports 459 (2000)].

§ 11357. Financial instructions for inclusion in the state administrative manual; exemptions; review of estimates

(a) The Department of Finance shall adopt and update, as necessary, instructions for inclusion in the State Administrative Manual prescribing the methods that any agency subject to this chapter shall use in making the determination required by paragraph (5) and the estimate required by paragraph (6) of subdivision (a) of Section 11346.5. The instructions shall include, but need not be limited to, the following:

(1) Guidelines governing the types of data or assumptions, or both, that may be used, and the methods that shall be used, to calculate the estimate of the cost or savings to public agencies mandated by the regulation for which the estimate is being prepared.

(2) The types of direct or indirect costs and savings that should be taken into account in preparing the estimate.

(3) The criteria that shall be used in determining whether the cost of a regulation must be funded by the state pursuant to Section 6 of Article XIII B of the California Constitution and Part 7 (commencing with Section 17500) of Division 4.

(4) The format the agency preparing the estimate shall follow in summarizing and reporting its estimate of the cost or savings to state and local agencies, school districts, and in federal funding of state programs that will result from the regulation.

(b) Any action by the Department of Finance to adopt and update, as necessary, instructions to any state or local agency for the preparation, development, or administration of the state budget, including any instructions included in the State Administrative Manual, shall be exempt from this chapter.

(c) The Department of Finance may review any estimate prepared pursuant to this section for content including, but not limited to, the data and assumptions used in its preparation. *(Added by Stats.1994, c. 1039 (A.B.2531), § 51.)*

§ 11359. Fire and panic safety regulations; approval requirement; exemption

(a) Except as provided in subdivision (b), on and after January 1, 1982, no new regulation, or the amendment or repeal of any regulation, which regulation is intended to promote fire and panic safety or provide fire protection and prevention, including fire suppression systems, equipment, or alarm regulation, is valid or effective unless it is submitted by, or approved in writing by, the State Fire Marshal before transmittal to the Secretary of State or the Office of Administrative Law.

(b) Approval of the State Fire Marshal is not required if the regulation is expressly required to be at least as effective as federal standards published in the Federal Register pursuant to Section 6 of the Occupational Safety and Health Act of 1970 (P.L. 91-596) within the time period specified by federal law and as provided in subdivision (b) of Section 142.4 of the Labor Code, and as approved by the Occupational Safety and Health Administration of the United States Department of Labor as meeting the requirements of subdivision (a) of Section 142.3 of the Labor Code, unless the regulation is determined by the State Fire Marshal to be less effective in promoting fire and panic safety than regulations adopted by the State Fire Marshal. *(Formerly § 11342.3, added by Stats.1981, c. 1177, p. 4740, § 1. Renumbered § 11359 and amended by Stats.1994, c. 1039 (A.B. 2531), § 10.)*

§ 11361. Application of chapter to specified acts

This chapter does not apply to the adoption or revision of regulations, guidelines, or criteria to implement the Safe Neighborhood Parks, Clean Water, Clean Air, and Coastal Protection Bond Act of 2000 (the Villaraigosa–Keeley Act) (Chapter 1.692 (commencing with Section 5096.300) of Division 5 of the Public Resources Code), the California Clean Water, Clean Air, Safe Neighborhood Parks, and Coastal Protection Act of 2002 (Chapter 1.696 (commencing with Section 5096.600) of Division 5 of the Public Resources Code), or the Water Security, Clean Drinking Water, Coastal and Beach Protection Act of 2002 (Division 26.5 (commencing with Section 79500) of the Water Code). The adoption or revision of regulations, guidelines, or criteria, if necessary to implement those respective acts, shall instead be accomplished by means of a public process reasonably calculated to give those persons interested in their adoption or revision an opportunity to be heard. *(Added by Stats.2000, c. 87 (S.B.1679), § 5, eff. July 5, 2000. Amended by Stats.2003, c. 240 (A.B.1747), § 2, eff. Aug. 13, 2003.)*

CHAPTER 4.   OFFICE OF ADMINISTRATIVE HEARINGS

ARTICLE 1.   GENERAL PROVISIONS

Section
11370.   Citation.

Section
11370.1.   "Director" defined.
11370.2.   Office of administrative hearings; existence; director.
11370.3.   Administrative law judges and other personnel; appointment; assignment.
11370.4.   Costs; determination and collection.
11370.5.   Administrative adjudication; study; recommendations.

Law Revision Commission Comments

Chapter 4 (commencing with Section 11370) is divided into articles for organizational purposes. [25 Cal.L.Rev.Comm. Reports 55 (1995)].

§ 11370.   Citation

Chapter 3.5 (commencing with Section 11340), Chapter 4 (commencing with Section 11370), Chapter 4.5 (commencing with Section 11400), and Chapter 5 (commencing with Section 11500) constitute, and may be cited as, the Administrative Procedure Act. *(Added by Stats.1947, c. 1425, p. 2985, § 1. Amended by Stats.1961, c. 2048, p. 4267, § 2; Stats.1981, c. 714, p. 2659, § 176; Stats.1995, c. 938 (S.B.523), § 16.5, operative July 1, 1997.)*

Law Revision Commission Comments

Section 11370 is amended to recognize the addition of Sections 11400–11470.50. The administrative adjudication provisions of the Administrative Procedure Act are found in Chapters 4.5 (administrative adjudication: general provisions) and 5 (administrative adjudication: formal hearing). Section 11400 (administrative adjudication provisions of Administrative Procedure Act). [25 Cal.L.Rev.Comm. Reports 55 (1995)].

Research References

9 Witkin Cal. Proc. 5th Administrative Proceedings § 34, (S 34) in General.
9 Witkin Cal. Proc. 5th Administrative Proceedings § 202, (S 202) Office of Administrative Hearings.

§ 11370.1.   "Director" defined

As used in the Administrative Procedure Act "director" means the executive officer of the Office of Administrative Hearings. *(Added by Stats.1961, c. 2048, p. 4267, § 3. Amended by Stats.1971, c. 1303, p. 2554, § 2.)*

Research References

9 Witkin Cal. Proc. 5th Administrative Proceedings § 58, (S 58) Office of Administrative Hearings.

§ 11370.2.   Office of administrative hearings; existence; director

(a) There is in the Department of General Services the Office of Administrative Hearings which is under the direction and control of an executive officer who shall be known as the director.

(b) The director shall have the same qualifications as administrative law judges, and shall be appointed by the Governor subject to the confirmation of the Senate.

(c) Any and all references in any law to the Office of Administrative Procedure shall be deemed to be the Office of Administrative Hearings. *(Added by Stats.1961, c. 2048, p. 4268, § 4. Amended by Stats.1963, c. 1786, p. 3580, § 13, operative Oct. 1, 1963; Stats.1971, c. 1303, p. 2554, § 3; Stats.1985, c. 324, § 13.)*

Research References

9 Witkin Cal. Proc. 5th Administrative Proceedings § 58, (S 58) Office of Administrative Hearings.

§ 11370.3. Administrative law judges and other personnel; appointment; assignment

The director shall appoint and maintain a staff of full-time, and may appoint pro tempore part-time, administrative law judges qualified under Section 11502 which is sufficient to fill the needs of the various state agencies. The director shall also appoint any other technical and clerical personnel as may be required to perform the duties of the office. The director shall assign an administrative law judge for any proceeding arising under Chapter 5 (commencing with Section 11500) and, upon request from any agency, may assign an administrative law judge to conduct other administrative proceedings not arising under that chapter and shall assign hearing reporters as required. Any administrative law judge or other employee so assigned shall be deemed an employee of the office and not of the agency to which he or she is assigned. When not engaged in hearing cases, administrative law judges may be assigned by the director to perform other duties vested in or required of the office, including those provided for in Section 11370.5. *(Added by Stats.1961, c. 2048, p. 4268, § 5. Amended by Stats.1971, c. 1303, p. 2554, § 3.5; Stats.1979, c. 199, § 2; Stats.1984, c. 1005, § 2; Stats.1985, c. 324, § 14; Stats.1995, c. 938 (S.B.523), § 17, operative July 1, 1997.)*

Law Revision Commission Comments

The references in Section 11370.3 to hearing officers and shorthand reporters are deleted to reflect current practice. The fourth sentence is deleted as unnecessary. See Bus. & Prof.Code § 22460.5. [25 Cal.L.Rev. Comm. Reports 55 (1995)].

Research References

California Practice Guide: Employment Litigation Ch. 7-A, A. Title VII and the California Fair Employment and Housing Act.

9 Witkin Cal. Proc. 5th Administrative Proceedings § 58, (S 58) Office of Administrative Hearings.

§ 11370.4. Costs; determination and collection

The total cost to the state of maintaining and operating the Office of Administrative Hearings shall be determined by, and collected by the Department of General Services in advance or upon such other basis as it may determine from the state or other public agencies for which services are provided by the office. *(Added by Stats.1961, c. 2048, p. 4268, § 6. Amended by Stats.1963, c. 1553, p. 3139, § 1; Stats.1965, c. 462, p. 1769, § 1; Stats.1971, c. 1303, p. 2555, § 4.)*

§ 11370.5. Administrative adjudication; study; recommendations

(a) The office is authorized and directed to study the subject of administrative adjudication in all its aspects; to submit its suggestions to the various agencies in the interests of fairness, uniformity and the expedition of business; and to report its recommendations to the Governor and Legislature. All departments, agencies, officers, and employees of the state shall give the office ready access to their records and full information and reasonable assistance in any matter of research requiring recourse to them or to data within their knowledge or control. Nothing in this section authorizes an agency to provide access to records required by statute to be kept confidential.

(b) The office may adopt rules and regulations to carry out the functions and duties of the office under the Administrative Procedure Act. The regulations are subject to Chapter 3.5 (commencing with Section 11340). *(Added by Stats.1961, c. 2048, p. 4268, § 7. Amended by Stats.1995, c. 938 (S.B.523), § 18, operative July 1, 1997; Stats.2002, c. 370 (A.B.2283), § 3.)*

Law Revision Commission Comments

Subdivision (a) of Section 11370.5 is amended to limit the authority of the Office of Administrative Hearings to administrative adjudication. For authority of the Office of Administrative Law to study administrative rulemaking, see Section 11340.4. Subdivision (a) is also amended to add language protecting confidentiality of records.

Subdivision (b) is added to make clear the general authority of the Office of Administrative Hearings to adopt implementing regulations concerning the office and proceedings under the Administrative Procedure Act. For specific regulation authority of the office, see, e.g., Sections 11420.20 (regulations governing ADR), 11465.70 (regulations governing declaratory decision). [25 Cal.L.Rev.Comm. Reports 711 (1995)].

Research References

9 Witkin Cal. Proc. 5th Administrative Proceedings § 58, (S 58) Office of Administrative Hearings.

ARTICLE 2. MEDICAL QUALITY HEARING PANEL

Law Revision Commission Comments

Chapter 4 (commencing with Section 11370) is divided into articles for organizational purposes. [25 Cal.L.Rev.Comm. Reports 55 (1995)].

§ 11371. Medical Quality Hearing Panel

(a) There is within the Office of Administrative Hearings a Medical Quality Hearing Panel, consisting of no fewer than five full-time administrative law judges. The administrative law judges shall have medical training as recommended by the Division of Medical Quality of the Medical Board of California and approved by the Director of the Office of Administrative Hearings.

(b) The director shall determine the qualifications of panel members, supervise their training, and coordinate the publication of a reporter of decisions pursuant to this section. The panel shall include only those persons specifically qualified and shall at no time constitute more than 25 percent of the total number of administrative law judges within the Office of Administrative Hearings. If the members of the panel do not have a full workload, they may be assigned work by the Director of the Office of Administrative Hearings. When the medically related case workload exceeds the capacity of the members of the panel, additional judges shall be requested to be added to the panels as appropriate. When this workload overflow occurs on a temporary basis, the Director of the Office of Administrative Hearings shall supply judges from the Office of Administrative Hearings to adjudicate the cases.

(c) The administrative law judges of the panel shall have panels of experts available. The panels of experts shall be appointed by the Director of the Office of Administrative Hearings, with the advice of the Medical Board of California. These panels of experts may be called as witnesses by the administrative law judges of the panel to testify on the record about any matter relevant to a proceeding and subject to cross-examination by all parties, and Section 11430.30 does not apply in a proceeding under this section. The administrative law judge may award reasonable expert witness fees to any person or persons serving on a panel of experts, which shall be paid from the Contingent Fund of the Medical Board of California upon appropriation by the Legislature. *(Added by Stats.1993, c. 1267*

(S.B.916), § 51. Amended by Stats.1994, c. 1206 (S.B.1775), § 27; Stats.1995, c. 938 (S.B.523), § 19.5, operative July 1, 1997; Stats.1998, c. 878 (S.B.2239), § 56; Stats.2002, c. 1085 (S.B. 1950), § 31; Stats.2005, c. 674 (S.B.231), § 21.)

Law Revision Commission Comments

Subdivision (d) of Section 11371 is amended to make certain ex parte communications exceptions inapplicable in proceedings under this section. [25 Cal.L.Rev.Comm. Reports 711 (1995)].

§ 11372. Adjudicative hearings and proceedings relating to discipline or reinstatement of licensees of medical board; presiding judge; interim orders

(a) Except as provided in subdivision (b), all adjudicative hearings and proceedings relating to the discipline or reinstatement of licensees of the Medical Board of California, including licensees of affiliated health agencies within the jurisdiction of the Medical Board of California, that are heard pursuant to the Administrative Procedure Act, shall be conducted by an administrative law judge as designated in Section 11371, sitting alone if the case is so assigned by the agency filing the charging pleading.

(b) Proceedings relating to interim orders shall be heard in accordance with Section 11529. *(Added by Stats.1990, c. 1597 (S.B.2375), § 32. Amended by Stats.1993, c. 1267 (S.B.916), § 52; Stats.2007, c. 588 (S.B.1048), § 89.)*

§ 11373. Conduct of adjudicative hearings and proceedings by administrative law judge

All adjudicative hearings and proceedings conducted by an administrative law judge as designated in Section 11371 shall be conducted under the terms and conditions set forth in the Administrative Procedure Act, except as provided in the Medical Practice Act (Chapter 5 (commencing with Section 2000) of Division 2 of the Business and Professions Code). *(Added by Stats.1990, c. 1597 (S.B.2375), § 33. Amended by Stats.1993, c. 1267 (S.B.916), § 53.)*

§ 11373.3. Provision of facilities and support personnel; assessment

The Office of Administrative Hearings shall provide facilities and support personnel for the review committee panel and shall assess the Medical Board of California for facilities and personnel, where used to adjudicate cases involving the Medical Board of California. *(Added by Stats.1990, c. 1597 (S.B.2375), § 34. Amended by Stats.1991, c. 1091 (A.B.1487), § 44.)*

ARTICLE 3. STATE AGENCY REPORTS AND FORMS APPEALS

Section
11380. Decisions; procedures.

§ 11380. Decisions; procedures

(a)(1) The office shall hear and render a decision on any appeal filed by a business, pursuant to subdivision (c) of Section 14775, in the event the business contests the certification by a state agency head that reporting requirements meet established criteria and shall not be eliminated.

(2) Before a business may file an appeal with the office pursuant to subdivision (c) of Section 14775, the business shall file a challenge to a form or report required by a state agency with that state agency. Within 60 days of filing the challenge with a state agency, the state agency shall either eliminate the form or report or provide written justification for its continued use.

(3) A business may appeal a state agency's written justification for the continued use of a form or report with the office.

(4) If a state agency fails to respond within 60 days of the filing of a challenge pursuant to paragraph (2), the business shall have an immediate right to file an appeal with the office.

(b) No later than January 1, 1996, the office shall adopt procedures governing the filing, hearing, and disposition of appeals. The procedures shall include, but shall not be limited to, provisions that assure that appeals are heard and decisions rendered by the office in a fair, impartial, and timely fashion.

(c) The office may charge appellants a reasonable fee to pay for costs it incurs in complying with this section. *(Added by Stats.1995, c. 938 (S.B.523), § 20, operative July 1, 1997.)*

Law Revision Commission Comments

Section 11380 continues former Section 11530 without change. [25 Cal.L.Rev.Comm. Reports 55 (1995)].

CHAPTER 4.5. ADMINISTRATIVE ADJUDICATION: GENERAL PROVISIONS

ARTICLE 1. PRELIMINARY PROVISIONS

Section
11400.   Administrative adjudication provisions; references to prior law.
11400.10.   Operative date and application of chapter.
11400.20.   Regulations.

§ 11400. Administrative adjudication provisions; references to prior law

(a) This chapter and Chapter 5 (commencing with Section 11500) constitute the administrative adjudication provisions of the Administrative Procedure Act.

(b) A reference in any other statute or in a rule of court, executive order, or regulation, to a provision formerly found in Chapter 5 (commencing with Section 11500) that is superseded by a provision of this chapter, means the applicable provision of this chapter. *(Added by Stats.1995, c. 938 (S.B.523), § 21, operative July 1, 1997.)*

Law Revision Commission Comments

Section 11400 makes clear that references to the administrative adjudication provisions of the Administrative Procedure Act include both this chapter (general provisions) and Chapter 5 (formal hearing). The formal hearing provisions of Chapter 5 apply to an adjudicative proceeding as determined by the statutes relating to the proceeding. Section 11501. The general provisions of this chapter apply to all statutorily and constitutionally required state agency adjudicative proceedings, including proceedings under Chapter 5. See Section 11410.10 and sections following.

Various statutes and regulations incorporate provisions of the existing Administrative Procedure Act by referring to specific section numbers. See, e.g., Ins. Code § 1861.08 (Proposition 103). This chapter is not intended to change those incorporated provisions. See Section 11415.10 & Comment (governing procedure determined by applicable statutes; this chapter supplements and does not replace governing procedure). Where a specific provision that is incorporated by reference has been moved to a differently numbered section of this chapter, it is intended that the obligation will continue to apply as provided in this chapter. Subdivision (b).

References in section Comments in this chapter and Chapter 5 to the "1981 Model State APA" mean the Model State Administrative Procedure Act (1981) promulgated by the National Conference of Commissioners on Uniform State Laws. See 15 U.L.A. 1 (1990). References to the "Federal APA" mean the Federal Administrative Procedure Act, 5 U.S.C. §§ 551–583, 701–706, 1305, 3105, 3344, 5372, 7521 (1988 & Supp. V 1993), and related sections (originally enacted as Act of June 11, 1946, ch. 324, 60 Stat. 237). A number of the administrative adjudication provisions of the Administrative Procedure Act are drawn from the Federal APA. [25 Cal.L.Rev.Comm. Reports 711 (1995)].

Research References

Miller and Starr California Real Estate § 4:43, Disciplinary Process--Penalties and Other Remedies.

9 Witkin Cal. Proc. 5th Administrative Proceedings § 34, (S 34) in General.

9 Witkin Cal. Proc. 5th Administrative Proceedings § 57, (S 57) Nature and Scope of A.P.A. Adjudication Provisions.

9 Witkin Cal. Proc. 5th Administrative Proceedings § 60, (S 60) Administrative Adjudication Code of Ethics.

9 Witkin Cal. Proc. 5th Administrative Proceedings § 63, in General.

9 Witkin Cal. Proc. 5th Administrative Proceedings § 64, When Provisions Apply.

9 Witkin Cal. Proc. 5th Administrative Proceedings § 65, Specific Statute Prevails.

9 Witkin Cal. Proc. 5th Administrative Proceedings § 66, Optional and Mandatory Provisions.

9 Witkin Cal. Proc. 5th Administrative Proceedings § 68, in General.

9 Witkin Cal. Proc. 5th Administrative Proceedings § 84, (S 84) in General.

9 Witkin Cal. Proc. 5th Administrative Proceedings § 88, (S 88) Service and Notice.

9 Witkin Cal. Proc. 5th Administrative Proceedings § 96, (S 96) Nature and Scope of A.P.A. Formal Hearing Provisions.

10 Witkin, California Summary 10th Parent and Child § 971, (S 971) Notice and Hearing.

3 Witkin, California Summary 10th Agency and Employment § 657, (S 657) Agricultural Labor Relations Board.

3 Witkin, California Summary 10th Agency and Employment § 670, (S 670) Procedure.

8 Witkin, California Summary 10th Constitutional Law § 1107, (S 1107) Hearing and Determination.

§ 11400.10. Operative date and application of chapter

(a) This chapter is operative on July 1, 1997.

(b) This chapter is applicable to an adjudicative proceeding commenced on or after July 1, 1997.

(c) This chapter is not applicable to an adjudicative proceeding commenced before July 1, 1997, except an adjudicative proceeding conducted on a remand from a court or another agency on or after July 1, 1997. *(Added by Stats.1995, c. 938 (S.B.523), § 21, operative July 1, 1997.)*

Law Revision Commission Comments

Section 11400.10 provides a deferred operative date to enable state agencies to make any necessary preparations for operation under this chapter. [25 Cal.L.Rev.Comm. Reports 55 (1995)].

§ 11400.20. Regulations

(a) Before, on, or after July 1, 1997, an agency may adopt interim or permanent regulations to govern an adjudicative proceeding under this chapter or Chapter 5 (commencing with Section 11500). Nothing in this section authorizes an agency to adopt regulations to govern an adjudicative proceeding required to be conducted by an administrative law judge employed by the Office of Administrative Hearings, except to the extent the regulations are otherwise authorized by statute.

(b) Except as provided in Section 11351:

(1) Interim regulations need not comply with Article 5 (commencing with Section 11346) or Article 6 (commencing with Section 11349) of Chapter 3.5, but are governed by Chapter 3.5 (commencing with Section 11340) in all other respects.

(2) Interim regulations expire on December 31, 1998, unless earlier terminated or replaced by or readopted as permanent regulations under paragraph (3). If on December 31, 1998, an agency has completed proceedings to replace or readopt interim regulations and has submitted permanent regulations for review by the Office of Administrative Law, but permanent regulations have not yet been filed with the Secretary of State, the interim regulations are extended until the date permanent regulations are filed with the Secretary of State or March 31, 1999, whichever is earlier.

(3) Permanent regulations are subject to all the provisions of Chapter 3.5 (commencing with Section 11340), except that if by December 31, 1998, an agency has submitted the regulations for review by the Office of Administrative Law, the regulations are not subject to review for necessity under Section 11349.1 or 11350. *(Added by Stats.1995, c. 938 (S.B.523), § 21, operative July 1. 1997. Amended by Stats.1996, c. 390 (S.B.794), § 5, eff. Aug. 19, 1996, operative July 1, 1997.)*

Law Revision Commission Comments

Subdivision (a) of Section 11400.20 makes clear that an agency may act to adopt regulations under this division after enactment but before the division becomes operative. This will enable the agency to have any necessary regulations in place on the operative date. It should be noted that revisions of regulations that merely conform to the new law may be adopted by simplified procedures under the rulemaking provisions of the Administrative Procedure Act pursuant to 1 California Code of Regulations Section 100.

Under subdivision (b), an agency may adopt interim procedural regulations without the normal notice and hearing and Office of Administrative Law review processes of the Administrative Procedure Act. However, this does not excuse compliance with the other provisions of the Administrative Procedure Act, including but not limited to the requirements that (1) regulations be consistent and not in conflict with statute and reasonably necessary to effectuate the purpose of the statute (Section 11342.2), (2) regulations be filed and published (Sections 11343–11344.9), and (3) regulations are subject to judicial review (Section 11350). Compliance with these provisions is not required for agencies exempted by statute. See Section 11351.

Interim regulations are only valid through December 31, 1998. They may be replaced by or readopted as permanent regulations before then, through the standard administrative rulemaking process. In case permanent regulations are pending on December 31, 1998, interim regulations may be extended up to three months.

Subdivision (b)(3) makes clear that permanent regulations governing administrative adjudication are subject to normal rulemaking procedures, other than review for necessity under Section 11349.1 (Office of Administrative Law) or 11350 (declaratory relief) in the case of permanent regulations promulgated during the transitional period. [25 Cal.L.Rev. Comm. Reports 55 (1995)].

Subdivision (a) of Section 11400.20 is amended to permit use of the procedure provided in this section for adoption of interim or permanent regulations under the formal hearing procedure, Chapter 5 (commencing with Section 11500).

Subdivision (a) makes clear that the authority of an agency to adopt regulations governing its hearings does not apply to hearings required to be conducted for it by the Office of Administrative Hearings, unless there is express statutory authority for the regulations. Examples of express statutory authority include:

Section 11420.10 (alternative dispute resolution)

Section 11425.50 (penalty guidelines)

Section 11440.10 (administrative review)

Section 11440.50 (intervention)

Sections 11445.20 and 11445.50 (informal hearing procedure)

Section 11460.20 (emergency decision)

Section 11518.5 (correction of mistakes and clerical errors in decision)

It should be noted that the provision of Section 11425.40(d) allowing an agency that conducts an adjudicative proceeding to provide by regulation for peremptory challenge of the presiding officer applies to the Office of Administrative Hearings and not the agency for which the Office of Administrative Hearings is conducting the proceeding. See Comment to Section 11425.40(d).

Nothing in subdivision (a) precludes regulations governing matters peripheral to administrative adjudication proceedings, such as a requirement that a person maintain an address with the agency for the purpose of notice. [26 Cal.L.Rev.Comm. Reports 107 (1996) (App. 4)].

Government

Research References

9 Witkin Cal. Proc. 5th Administrative Proceedings § 57, (S 57) Nature
and Scope of A.P.A. Adjudication Provisions.

ARTICLE 2. DEFINITIONS

Section

11405.10. Construction of chapter.
11405.20. Adjudicative proceeding.
11405.30. Agency.
11405.40. Agency head.
11405.50. Decision.
11405.60. Party.
11405.70. Person.
11405.80. Presiding officer.

§ 11405.10. Construction of chapter

Unless the provision or context requires otherwise, the definitions in this article govern the construction of this chapter.
*(Added by Stats.1995, c. 938 (S.B.523), § 21, operative July 1,
1997.)*

Law Revision Commission Comments

Section 11405.10 limits these definitions to the general provisions on
administrative adjudication. For definitions governing the formal hearing
procedure under Chapter 5, see Section 11500. [25 Cal.L.Rev.Comm.
Reports 55 (1995)].

Research References

9 Witkin Cal. Proc. 5th Administrative Proceedings § 63, in General.

§ 11405.20. Adjudicative proceeding

"Adjudicative proceeding" means an evidentiary hearing for
determination of facts pursuant to which an agency formulates
and issues a decision. *(Added by Stats.1995, c. 938 (S.B.523),
§ 21, operative July 1, 1997.)*

Law Revision Commission Comments

Section 11405.20 is intended for drafting convenience. [25 Cal.L.Rev.
Comm. Reports 55 (1995)].

Research References

9 Witkin Cal. Proc. 5th Administrative Proceedings § 63, in General.
9 Witkin Cal. Proc. 5th Administrative Proceedings § 64, When Provisions Apply.
9 Witkin Cal. Proc. 5th Administrative Proceedings § 74, (S 74) General
Prohibition.

§ 11405.30. Agency

"Agency" means a board, bureau, commission, department,
division, office, officer, or other administrative unit, including
the agency head, and one or more members of the agency head
or agency employees or other persons directly or indirectly
purporting to act on behalf of or under the authority of the
agency head. To the extent it purports to exercise authority
pursuant to this chapter, an administrative unit otherwise
qualifying as an agency shall be treated as a separate agency even
if the unit is located within or subordinate to another agency.
*(Added by Stats.1995, c. 938 (S.B.523), § 21, operative July 1,
1997.)*

Law Revision Commission Comments

Section 11405.30 is drawn from 1981 Model State APA § 1–102(1). It
supplements Section 11000. See also Section 11500(a). The intent of the
definition is to subject as many governmental units as possible to this
chapter. The definition explicitly includes the agency head and those
others who act for an agency, so as to effect the broadest possible
coverage. The definition also would include a committee or council.

The last sentence of the section is in part derived from Federal APA
§ 551(1) (1988), treating as an agency "each authority of the Government
of the United States, whether or not it is within or subject to review by
another agency." A similar provision is desirable here to avoid difficulty
in ascertaining which is *the* agency in a situation where an administrative
unit is within or subject to the jurisdiction of another administrative unit.

An administrative unit of an agency that has no authority to issue
decisions or take other action on behalf of the agency is not an "agency"
within the meaning of this section. [25 Cal.L.Rev.Comm. Reports 55
(1995)].

Research References

9 Witkin Cal. Proc. 5th Administrative Proceedings § 63, in General.
9 Witkin Cal. Proc. 5th Administrative Proceedings § 64, When Provisions Apply.

§ 11405.40. Agency head

"Agency head" means a person or body in which the ultimate
legal authority of an agency is vested, and includes a person or
body to which the power to act is delegated pursuant to authority
to delegate the agency's power to hear and decide. *(Added by
Stats.1995, c. 938 (S.B.523), § 21, operative July 1, 1997.)*

Law Revision Commission Comments

The first portion of Section 11405.40 is drawn from 1981 Model State
APA § 1–102(3). The definition of agency head is included to differentiate for some purposes between the agency as an organic entity that
includes all of its employees, and those particular persons in which the
final legal authority over its operations is vested.

The last portion is drawn from Section 11500(a), relating to use of the
term "agency itself" to refer to a nondelegable power to act. An agency
may delegate review authority. Section 11440.10. [25 Cal.L.Rev.Comm.
Reports 55 (1995)].

Research References

9 Witkin Cal. Proc. 5th Administrative Proceedings § 63, in General.

§ 11405.50. Decision

(a) "Decision" means an agency action of specific application
that determines a legal right, duty, privilege, immunity, or other
legal interest of a particular person.

(b) Nothing in this section limits any of the following:

(1) The precedential effect of a decision under Section
11425.60.

(2) The authority of an agency to make a declaratory decision
pursuant to Article 14 (commencing with Section 11465.10).
*(Added by Stats.1995, c. 938 (S.B.523), § 21, operative July 1,
1997.)*

Law Revision Commission Comments

Section 11405.50 is drawn from 1981 Model State APA § 1–102(5).
The definition of "decision" makes clear that it includes only legal
determinations made by an agency that are of specific applicability
because they are addressed to particular or named persons. More than
one identified person may be the subject of a decision. See Section 13
(singular includes plural). "Person" includes legal entity and governmental subdivision. Section 11405.70 ("person" defined); see also Section 17
("person" defined).

A decision includes every agency action that determines any of the legal
rights, duties, privileges, or immunities of a specific, identified individual
or individuals. This is to be compared to a regulation, which is an agency
action of general application, applicable to all members of a described
class. See Section 11342 ("regulation" defined). This section is not
intended to expand the types of cases in which an adjudicative proceeding
is required; an adjudicative proceeding under this chapter is required only
where another statute or the constitution requires one. Section 11410.10
(application to constitutionally and statutorily required hearings).

Consistent with the definition in this section, rate making and licensing
determinations of specific application, addressed to named or particular
parties such as a certain power company or a certain licensee, are
decisions subject to this chapter. Cf. Federal APA § 551(4) (1988)

(defining all rate making as rulemaking). On the other hand, rate making and licensing actions of general application, addressed to all members of a described class of providers or licensees, are regulations under the Administrative Procedure Act. Section 11342 ("regulation" defined). However, some decisions may have precedential effect pursuant to Section 11425.60 (precedent decisions). [25 Cal.L.Rev.Comm. Reports 55 (1995)].

Research References

9 Witkin Cal. Proc. 5th Administrative Proceedings § 63, in General.
9 Witkin Cal. Proc. 5th Administrative Proceedings § 64, When Provisions Apply.

§ 11405.60. Party

"Party" includes the agency that is taking action, the person to which the agency action is directed, and any other person named as a party or allowed to appear or intervene in the proceeding. If the agency that is taking action and the agency that is conducting the adjudicative proceeding are separate agencies, the agency that is taking action is a party and the agency that is conducting the adjudicative proceeding is not a party. *(Added by Stats.1995, c. 938 (S.B.523), § 21, operative July 1, 1997.)*

Law Revision Commission Comments

The first sentence of Section 11405.60 is drawn from subdivision (b) of Section 11500; see also 1981 Model State APA § 1–102(6). The second sentence is new.

"Person" includes legal entity and governmental subdivision. Section 11405.70 ("person" defined); see also Section 17 ("person" defined).

Under this definition, if an officer or employee of an agency appears in an official capacity, the agency and not the person is a party. A staff division authorized to act on behalf of the agency may be a party under this chapter. See Section 11405.30 & Comment ("agency" defined).

This section is not intended to address the question of whether a person is entitled to judicial review. Standing to seek judicial review is dealt with in other law. [25 Cal.L.Rev.Comm. Reports 55 (1995)].

Research References

9 Witkin Cal. Proc. 5th Administrative Proceedings § 63, in General.

§ 11405.70. Person

"Person" includes an individual, partnership, corporation, governmental subdivision or unit of a governmental subdivision, or public or private organization or entity of any character. *(Added by Stats.1995, c. 938 (S.B.523), § 21, operative July 1, 1997.)*

Law Revision Commission Comments

Section 11405.70 supplements the definition of "person" in Section 17 ("person" defined). It is drawn from 1981 Model State APA § 1–102(8). It would include the trustee of a trust or other fiduciary.

The definition is broader than Section 17 in its application to a governmental subdivision or unit; this would include an agency other than the agency against which rights under this chapter are asserted by the person. Inclusion of such agencies and units of government insures, therefore, that other agencies or other governmental bodies can, for example, apply to an agency for a decision, and will be accorded all the other rights that a person has under this chapter. [25 Cal.L.Rev.Comm. Reports 55 (1995)].

Research References

9 Witkin Cal. Proc. 5th Administrative Proceedings § 63, in General.
9 Witkin Cal. Proc. 5th Administrative Proceedings § 81, (S 81) Procedure.

§ 11405.80. Presiding officer

"Presiding officer" means the agency head, member of the agency head, administrative law judge, hearing officer, or other person who presides in an adjudicative proceeding. *(Added by Stats.1995, c. 938 (S.B.523), § 21, operative July 1, 1997.)*

Law Revision Commission Comments

Section 11405.80 is intended for drafting convenience. [25 Cal.L.Rev. Comm. Reports 55 (1995)].

Research References

9 Witkin Cal. Proc. 5th Administrative Proceedings § 63, in General.
9 Witkin Cal. Proc. 5th Administrative Proceedings § 70, Separation of Adjudicative Function from Other Functions.
9 Witkin Cal. Proc. 5th Administrative Proceedings § 74, (S 74) General Prohibition.

ARTICLE 3. APPLICATION OF CHAPTER

§ 11410.10. Evidentiary hearing required

This chapter applies to a decision by an agency if, under the federal or state Constitution or a federal or state statute, an evidentiary hearing for determination of facts is required for formulation and issuance of the decision. *(Added by Stats.1995, c. 938 (S.B.523), § 21, operative July 1, 1997.)*

Law Revision Commission Comments

Section 11410.10 limits application of this chapter to constitutionally and statutorily required hearings of state agencies. See Section 11410.20 (application to state). The provisions do not govern local agency hearings except to the extent expressly made applicable by another statute. Section 11410.30 (application to local agencies).

Section 11410.10 states the general principle that an agency must conduct an appropriate adjudicative proceeding before issuing a decision where a statute or the due process clause of the federal or state constitutions necessitates an evidentiary hearing for determination of facts. Such a hearing is a process in which a neutral decision maker makes a decision based exclusively on evidence contained in a record made at the hearing or on matters officially noticed. The hearing must at least permit a party to introduce evidence, make an argument to the presiding officer, and rebut opposing evidence.

The coverage of this chapter is the same as coverage by the existing provision for administrative mandamus under Code of Civil Procedure Section 1094.5(a). That section applies only where an agency has issued a final decision "as the result of a proceeding in which by law a hearing is required to be given, evidence is required to be taken, and discretion in the determination of facts is vested in the [agency]." Numerous cases have applied Code of Civil Procedure Section 1094.5(a) broadly to administrative proceedings in which a statute requires an "administrative appeal" or some other functional equivalent of an evidentiary hearing for determination of facts—an on-the-record or trial-type hearing. See, e.g., Eureka Teachers Ass'n v. Board of Educ., 199 Cal.App.3d 353, 244 Cal.Rptr. 240 (1988) (teacher's right to appeal grade change was right to hearing—Code Civ. Proc. § 1094.5 applies); Chavez v. Civil Serv. Comm'n, 86 Cal. App.3d 324, 150 Cal.Rptr. 197 (1978) (right of "appeal" means hearing required—Code Civ. Proc. § 1094.5 available).

In many cases, statutes or the constitution call for administrative proceedings that do not rise to the level of an evidentiary hearing as defined in this section. For example, the constitution or a statute might require only a consultation or a decision that is not based on an exclusive record or a purely written procedure or an opportunity for the general public to make statements. In some cases, the agency has discretion to provide or not provide the procedure. In other cases, the hearing called for by the statute is informal and investigative in nature, and any decision that results is not final but is subject to a full administrative hearing at a higher agency level. See, e.g., Rev. & Tax. Code §§ 19044, 19084 (statutory oral hearing available, with opportunity for full administrative hearing before State Board of Equalization). This chapter does not apply in such cases. Examples of cases in which the required procedure does not meet the standard of an evidentiary hearing for determination of facts are:

Government

Goss v. Lopez, 419 U.S. 565 (1975) (informal consultation between student and disciplinarian before brief suspension from school); Hewitt v. Helms, 459 U.S. 460 (1983) (informal nonadversary review of decision to place prisoner in administrative segregation—prisoner has right to file written statement); Skelly v. State Personnel Bd., 15 Cal.3d 194, 539 P.2d 774, 124 Cal.Rptr. 14 (1975) (informal opportunity for employee to respond orally or in writing to charges of misconduct prior to removal from government job); Wasko v. Department of Corrections, 211 Cal.App.3d 996, 1001–02, 259 Cal.Rptr. 764 (1989) (prisoner's right to appeal decision does not require a hearing—Code Civ. Proc. § 1094.5 inapplicable); Marina County Water Dist. v. State Water Resources Control Bd., 163 Cal.App.3d 132, 209 Cal.Rptr. 212 (1984) (hearing discretionary, not mandatory—Code Civ. Proc. § 1094.5 inapplicable).

Agency action pursuant to statutes that do not require evidentiary hearings are not subject to this chapter. Such statutes include the California Environmental Quality Act (Pub. Res. Code §§ 21000–21178.1), the Bagley–Keene Open Meeting Act (Gov't Code §§ 11120–11132), and the California Public Records Act (Gov't Code §§ 6250–6268).

This chapter applies only to proceedings for issuing a "decision." A decision is an agency action of specific application that determines a legal right, duty, privilege, immunity, or other legal interest of a particular person. Section 11405.50(a) ("decision" defined). Therefore this chapter does not apply to agency actions that do not determine a person's legal interests and does not apply to rulemaking, which is agency action of general applicability.

This chapter does not apply where agency regulations or practice, rather than a statute or the constitution, call for a hearing. For example, an agency may provide an informal "hearing" as part of its process for deciding whether to issue a license or for deciding whether a particular educational program meets requirements established by regulation for continuing education credits; if a statute does not require a hearing in such a case, this chapter does not apply. Agencies are encouraged to provide procedural protections by regulation even though not required to do so by statute or the constitution. An agency may provide any appropriate procedure for a decision for which an adjudicative proceeding is not required. Section 11415.50 (when adjudicative proceeding not required).

This section does not specify what type of adjudicative proceeding should be conducted. If an adjudicative proceeding is required by this section, the proceeding may be a formal hearing procedure under Chapter 5 (commencing with Section 11500), or may be a special hearing procedure provided by a statute applicable to the particular proceeding. This chapter also makes available the alternatives of an informal hearing, an emergency decision, or a declaratory decision, where appropriate under the circumstances. See Articles 10 (commencing with Section 11445.10), 13 (commencing with Section 11460.10), and 14 (commencing with Section 11465.10).

This section does not preclude the waiver of any procedure, or the settlement of any case without use of all available proceedings, under the general waiver and settlement provisions of Sections 11415.40 (waiver of provisions) and 11415.60 (settlement). [25 Cal.L.Rev.Comm. Reports 711 (1995)].

Research References

9 Witkin Cal. Proc. 5th Administrative Proceedings § 64, When Provisions Apply.

3 Witkin, California Summary 10th Agency and Employment § 318, (S 318) Investigation, Hearing, and Decision.

§ 11410.20. Agencies; legislative, judicial and executive branches

Except as otherwise expressly provided by statute:

(a) This chapter applies to all agencies of the state.

(b) This chapter does not apply to the Legislature, the courts or judicial branch, or the Governor or office of the Governor. *(Added by Stats.1995, c. 938 (S.B.523), § 21, operative July 1, 1997.)*

Law Revision Commission Comments

Section 11410.20 applies this chapter to all state agencies unless specifically excepted. The intent of this statute is to apply the provisions to as many state governmental units as possible.

Subdivision (a) is drawn from 1981 Model State APA § 1–103(a).

Subdivision (b) is drawn from 1981 Model State APA § 1–102(1). Exemptions from this chapter are to be construed narrowly.

Subdivision (b) exempts the entire judicial branch, and is not limited to the courts. Judicial branch agencies include the Judicial Council, the Commission on Judicial Appointments, the Commission on Judicial Performance, and the Judicial Criminal Justice Planning Committee.

Subdivision (b) exempts the Governor's office, and is not limited to the Governor. For an express statutory exception to the Governor's exemption from this chapter, see Bus. & Prof.Code § 106.5 ("The proceedings for removal [by the Governor of a board member in the Department of Consumer Affairs] shall be conducted in accordance with the provisions of Chapter 5 of Part 1 of Division 3 of Title 2 of the Government Code, and the Governor shall have all the powers granted therein.")

This chapter is not applicable to specified proceedings of the following state agencies:

Alcoholic Beverage Control Appeals Board (Bus. & Prof.Code § 23083)

University of California (Educ.Code § 92001)

Public Employment Relations Board (Gov't Code §§ 3541.3, 3563)

Commission on State Mandates (Gov't Code § 17533)

Agricultural Labor Relations Board (Lab.Code § 1144.5)

Military Department (Mil. & Vet.Code § 105)

Department of Corrections, Board of Prison Terms, Youth Authority, Youthful Offender Parole Board, and Narcotic Evaluation Authority (Pen.Code § 3066; Welf. & Inst.Code §§ 1788, 3158)

Public Utilities Commission (Pub.Util.Code § 1701)

This chapter is not applicable to the State Bar of California. Bus. & Prof.Code § 6001.

Nothing in this chapter precludes an agency from electing to have an exempt proceeding governed by this division. Section 11410.40. [25 Cal.L.Rev.Comm. Reports 55 (1995)].

Research References

9 Witkin Cal. Proc. 5th Administrative Proceedings § 64, When Provisions Apply.

§ 11410.30. Local agencies

(a) As used in this section, "local agency" means a county, city, district, public authority, public agency, or other political subdivision or public corporation in the state other than the state.

(b) This chapter does not apply to a local agency except to the extent the provisions are made applicable by statute.

(c) This chapter applies to an agency created or appointed by joint or concerted action of the state and one or more local agencies. *(Added by Stats.1995, c. 938 (S.B.523), § 21, operative July 1, 1997.)*

Law Revision Commission Comments

Section 11410.30 is drawn from 1981 Model State APA § 1–102(1). Local agencies are excluded because of the very different circumstances of local government units when compared to state agencies. The section explicitly includes joint state and local bodies, so as to effect the broadest possible coverage.

The administrative adjudication provisions of the Administrative Procedure Act are made applicable by statute to local agencies in a number of instances, including:

Suspension or dismissal of permanent employee by school district. Educ.Code § 44944.

Nonreemployment of probationary employee by school district. Educ.Code § 44948.5.

Evaluation, dismissal, and imposition of penalties on certificated personnel by community college district. Educ.Code § 87679.

See also Sections 11410.50 (application where formal hearing procedure required), 11501 (application of chapter). [25 Cal.L.Rev.Comm. Reports 55 (1995)]

§ 11410.40. Adoption by exempt agency

Notwithstanding any other provision of this article, by regulation, ordinance, or other appropriate action, an agency may adopt this chapter or any of its provisions for the formulation and issuance of a decision, even though the agency or decision is exempt from application of this chapter. *(Added by Stats.1995, c. 938 (S.B.523), § 21, operative July 1, 1997.)*

Law Revision Commission Comments

Section 11410.40 is new. An agency may elect to apply this chapter even though the agency would otherwise be exempt or the particular action taken by the agency would otherwise be exempt. See Sections 11410.20 & Comment (application to state) and 11410.30 (application to local agencies); Section 11410.10 (application to constitutionally and statutorily required hearings). [25 Cal.L.Rev.Comm. Reports 55 (1995)].

§ 11410.50. Adjudicative proceeding under Chapter 5

This chapter applies to an adjudicative proceeding required to be conducted under Chapter 5 (commencing with Section 11500) unless the statutes relating to the proceeding provide otherwise. *(Added by Stats.1995, c. 938 (S.B.523), § 21, operative July 1, 1997.)*

Law Revision Commission Comments

Section 11410.50 makes clear that the provisions of this chapter supplement the formal hearing provisions of Chapter 5. See also Section 11501(c) (application of chapter). Thus if an agency is required by statute to conduct a hearing under Chapter 5, the agency may, unless a statute provides otherwise, elect to use alternative dispute resolution or the informal hearing procedure or other appropriate provisions of this chapter. Likewise, the general provisions of this chapter restricting ex parte communications, regulating precedent decisions, and the like, apply to a hearing under Chapter 5. [25 Cal.L.Rev.Comm. Reports 55 (1995)].

§ 11410.60. Quasi-public entities

(a) As used in this section, "quasi-public entity" means an entity, other than a governmental agency, whether characterized by statute as a public corporation, public instrumentality, or otherwise, that is expressly created by statute for the purpose of administration of a state function.

(b) This chapter applies to an adjudicative proceeding conducted by a quasi-public entity if all of the following conditions are satisfied:

(1) A statute vests the power of decision in the quasi-public entity.

(2) A statute, the United States Constitution, or the California Constitution, requires an evidentiary hearing for determination of facts for formulation and issuance of the decision. Nothing in this section is intended to create an evidentiary hearing requirement that is not otherwise statutorily or constitutionally imposed.

(3) The decision is not otherwise subject to administrative review in an adjudicative proceeding to which this chapter applies.

(c) For the purpose of application of this chapter to a decision by a quasi-public entity:

(1) "Agency," as defined in Section 11405.30, also includes the quasi-public entity.

(2) "Regulation" includes a rule promulgated by the quasi-public entity.

(3) Article 8 (commencing with Section 11435.05), requiring language assistance in an adjudicative proceeding, applies to a quasi-public entity to the same extent as a state agency under Section 11018.

(d) This section shall be strictly construed to effectuate the intent of the Legislature to apply this chapter only to a decision by a quasi-public entity that is expressly created by statute for the purpose of administration of a state function.

(e) This section shall not apply to a decision made on authority of an approved plan of operations of a quasi-public entity that is subject to the regulation or supervision of the Insurance Commissioner. *(Added by Stats.1997, c. 220 (S.B.68), § 9, eff. Aug. 4, 1997.)*

Law Revision Commission Comments

Section 11410.60 applies this chapter to adjudicative decisions of quasi-public entities for which an evidentiary hearing by the quasi-public entity is statutorily or constitutionally required. A typical decision of this type might involve resolution of a membership assessment protest or a hearing on a claim that has been denied (provided the statute or Constitution requires a hearing for a decision of that type). *Cf.* Section 11405.50 ("decision" is action of specific application that determines legal right or other legal interest of particular person). This chapter does not apply to legislative actions such as an election or negotiation and adoption of a health and welfare benefits plan, pension trust, or collective bargaining agreement by an industry or labor organization.

This section does not apply to an entity unless the entity was expressly created by statute for the purpose of administering a state function. Thus this chapter governs hearings required to be held by a statutory entity such as the Winegrowers of California Commission (Food & Agric. Code § 74061) or the Escrow Agents' Fidelity Corporation (Fin. Code § 17311). But the statute does not govern hearings of a private entity such as a licensed health care provider (Health and Safety Code § 1200 *et seq.*), a labor organization, or a board of trustees established pursuant to statute under an interindemnity, reciprocal, or interinsurance contract between members of a cooperative corporation (Insurance Code § 1280.7).

This section does not apply to the State Bar, including proceedings of the State Bar Court. See Business and Professions Code § 6001.

The intent of this section is to provide fair hearing rules where a statute or the Constitution requires a hearing. This section is not intended to create any new hearing requirements. Thus, for example, this section does not apply to a decision of the Travel Consumer Restitution Corporation where the statute requires that the claim be decided on the written record, "with no hearing to be held." Bus. & Prof. Code § 17550.47.

Although subdivision (b) makes this chapter inapplicable to a quasi-public entity decision if the decision is otherwise reviewable in a proceeding governed by this chapter, the quasi-public entity may voluntarily adopt the procedural protections provided in this chapter. *Cf.* Section 11410.40 (election to apply administrative adjudication provisions). [1997–1998 Annual Report, 27 Cal.L.Rev.Comm. Reports 531 (1997)].

ARTICLE 4. GOVERNING PROCEDURE

§ 11415.10.   Statutes and regulations; Administrative Procedure Act

(a) The governing procedure by which an agency conducts an adjudicative proceeding is determined by the statutes and regulations applicable to that proceeding. If no other governing procedure is provided by statute or regulation, an agency may conduct an adjudicative proceeding under the administrative adjudication provisions of the Administrative Procedure Act.

(b) This chapter supplements the governing procedure by which an agency conducts an adjudicative proceeding. *(Added by Stats.1995, c. 938 (S.B.523), § 21, operative July 1, 1997.)*

Law Revision Commission Comments

The first sentence of subdivision (a) of Section 11415.10 is drawn from Section 11501(a) (formal hearing procedure applies to agency as determined by statutes relating to agency). The second sentence enables an agency to use the procedures provided in this chapter and Chapter 5 without further action in a case where there is no other applicable governing procedure. See Section 11400 (administrative adjudication provisions of Administrative Procedure Act).

Subdivision (b) makes clear that the provisions of this chapter supplement the applicable hearing procedure. Some provisions of this chapter are optional, e.g., the informal hearing procedure (Article 10 (commencing with Section 11445.10)), the emergency decision procedure (Article 13 (commencing with Section 11460.10)), and the declaratory decision procedure (Article 14 (commencing with Section 11465.10)). The agency determines whether to use any of the optional provisions. The optional provisions do not replace any other agency procedures that serve the same purpose. For example, the informal hearing procedure provided in this chapter does not replace an agency's own informal hearing procedure, but offers a supplemental alternative. Likewise, the emergency decision procedure does not replace an agency's own procedures for interim suspension or other immediate action, but provides an alternative means of proceeding that an agency may wish to use.

Other provisions of this chapter are mandatory. See, e.g., Section 11425.10 (administrative adjudication bill of rights). The mandatory provisions govern any adjudicative proceeding to which this chapter is applicable, and supplement the governing procedure by which an agency conducts an adjudicative proceeding, subject to a contrary statute applicable to the particular agency or proceeding. Section 11415.20 (conflicting or inconsistent statute controls). [25 Cal.L.Rev.Comm. Reports 55 (1995)].

Research References

9 Witkin Cal. Proc. 5th Administrative Proceedings § 65, Specific Statute Prevails.

9 Witkin Cal. Proc. 5th Administrative Proceedings § 66, Optional and Mandatory Provisions.

§ 11415.20.   Controlling law

A state statute or a federal statute or regulation applicable to a particular agency or decision prevails over a conflicting or inconsistent provision of this chapter. *(Added by Stats.1995, c. 938 (S.B.523), § 21, operative July 1, 1997.)*

Law Revision Commission Comments

Section 11415.20 makes clear that the provisions of this chapter are not intended to override a conflicting or inconsistent statute or applicable federal law that governs a particular matter. It should also be noted that if application of a provision of this chapter would cause loss or delay of federal funds, the Governor may suspend the provision. Section 11415.30. [25 Cal.L.Rev.Comm. Reports 55 (1995)].

Research References

9 Witkin Cal. Proc. 5th Administrative Proceedings § 65, Specific Statute Prevails.

9 Witkin Cal. Proc. 5th Administrative Proceedings § 67, Procedure Where Adjudicative Proceeding is Not Required.

§ 11415.30.   Executive orders; authorized actions

(a) To the extent necessary to avoid a loss or delay of funds or services from the federal government that would otherwise be available to the state, the Governor may do any of the following by executive order:

(1) Suspend, in whole or in part, any administrative adjudication provision of the Administrative Procedure Act.

(2) Adopt a rule of procedure that will avoid the loss or delay.

(b) The Governor shall rescind an executive order issued under this section as soon as it is no longer necessary to prevent the loss or delay of funds or services from the federal government.

(c) If an administrative adjudication provision is suspended or rule of procedure is adopted pursuant to this section, the Governor shall promptly report the suspension or adoption to the Legislature. The report shall include recommendations concerning any legislation that may be necessary to conform the provision to federal law. *(Added by Stats.1995, c. 938 (S.B.523), § 21, operative July 1, 1997.)*

Law Revision Commission Comments

Section 11415.30 is drawn from 1981 Model State APA § 1–104. *Cf.* Section 8571 (power of Governor to suspend statute in emergency). It is extended to include a delay in receipt as well as a loss of federal funds, and actions that may be taken include provision of an alternate procedure as well as suspension of an existing procedure. The administrative adjudication provisions of the Administrative Procedure Act are found in this chapter and in Chapter 5. See Section 11400 (administrative adjudication provisions of Administrative Procedure Act).

This section permits specific functions of agencies to be exempted from applicable administrative adjudication provisions of the Administrative Procedure Act only to the extent necessary to prevent the loss or delay of federal funds or services. The test to be met is simply whether, as a matter of fact, there will actually be a loss or delay of federal funds or services if there is no suspension or adoption of an alternate procedure. The suspension or adoption is effective only so long as and to the extent necessary to avoid the contemplated loss or delay.

The Governor cannot issue an executive order merely on the receipt of a federal agency certification that a suspension or adoption of an alternate procedure is necessary. That is, the Governor must first decide that the federal agency is correct in its assertion that federal funds may *lawfully* be delayed or withheld from the state agency if that agency complies with certain administrative adjudication provisions of the Administrative Procedure Act, and that the federal agency intends to exercise its authority to withhold or delay those funds if certain administrative adjudication provisions of the Administrative Procedure Act are followed. However, if these two requirements are met, the Governor may suspend the provision or adopt an alternate procedure. [25 Cal.L.Rev.Comm. Reports 55 (1995)].

§ 11415.40.   Waiver of rights

Except to the extent prohibited by another statute or regulation, a person may waive a right conferred on the person by the administrative adjudication provisions of the Administrative Procedure Act. *(Added by Stats.1995, c. 938 (S.B.523), § 21, operative July 1, 1997.)*

Law Revision Commission Comments

Section 11415.40 is drawn from 1981 Model State APA § 1–105. It embodies the standard notion of waiver, which requires an intentional relinquishment of a known right. This section applies to all affected persons, whether or not parties.

A right under the administrative adjudication provisions of the Administrative Procedure Act is subject to waiver in the same way that a right under any other civil statute is normally subject to waiver. Although a right may be waived by inaction, a written waiver is ordinarily preferable. A waiver by inaction may be the procedural result of a failure to act. See, e.g., Section 11506 (failure to file notice of defense is waiver of right to hearing).

The administrative adjudication provisions of the Administrative Procedure Act are found in this chapter and in Chapter 5. See Section 11400 (administrative adjudication provisions of Administrative Procedure Act). [25 Cal.L.Rev.Comm. Reports 55 (1995)].

Research References

9 Witkin Cal. Proc. 5th Administrative Proceedings § 63, in General.

§ 11415.50. Procedure where adjudicative proceeding not required; informal investigations

(a) An agency may provide any appropriate procedure for a decision for which an adjudicative proceeding is not required.

(b) An adjudicative proceeding is not required for informal factfinding or an informal investigatory hearing, or a decision to initiate or not to initiate an investigation, prosecution, or other proceeding before the agency, another agency, or a court, whether in response to an application for an agency decision or otherwise. *(Added by Stats.1995, c. 938 (S.B.523), § 21, operative July 1, 1997.)*

Law Revision Commission Comments

Subdivision (a) of Section 11415.50 is subject to statutory specification of the applicable procedure for decisions not governed by this chapter. See Section 11415.20 (conflicting or inconsistent statute controls).

Subdivision (b) is drawn in part from 1981 Model State APA § 4–101(a). The provision lists situations in which an agency may issue a decision without first conducting an adjudicative proceeding. For example, a law enforcement officer may, without first conducting an adjudicative proceeding, issue a "ticket" that will lead to a proceeding before an agency or court. Likewise, an agency may commence an adjudicative proceeding without first conducting a proceeding to decide whether to issue the pleading. Nothing in this subdivision implies that this chapter applies in a proceeding in which a hearing is not statutorily or constitutionally required. Section 11410.10 (application to constitutionally and statutorily required hearings).

Nothing in this section excuses compliance with this chapter in an agency decision for which an evidentiary hearing may be statutorily or constitutionally required. See Section 11410.10 (application to constitutionally and statutorily required hearings). A hearing may be statutorily or constitutionally required for a decision that an occupational license should be granted, revoked, suspended, limited, or conditioned. See, e.g., Bus. & Prof. Code §§ 485 (denial of license), 2555 (suspension, revocation, or probation of medical license); Suckow v. Alderson, 182 Cal. 247, 187 P. 965 (1920) (occupational license a vested property right that cannot be impaired without affording licensee an opportunity for a hearing). [25 Cal.L.Rev.Comm. Reports 711 (1995)].

Research References

9 Witkin Cal. Proc. 5th Administrative Proceedings § 67, Procedure Where Adjudicative Proceeding is Not Required.

§ 11415.60. Decision by settlement

(a) An agency may formulate and issue a decision by settlement, pursuant to an agreement of the parties, without conducting an adjudicative proceeding. Subject to subdivision (c), the settlement may be on any terms the parties determine are appropriate. Notwithstanding any other provision of law, no evidence of an offer of compromise or settlement made in settlement negotiations is admissible in an adjudicative proceeding or civil action, whether as affirmative evidence, by way of impeachment, or for any other purpose, and no evidence of conduct or statements made in settlement negotiations is admissible to prove liability for any loss or damage except to the extent provided in Section 1152 of the Evidence Code. Nothing in this subdivision makes inadmissible any public document created by a public agency.

(b) A settlement may be made before or after issuance of an agency pleading, except that in an adjudicative proceeding to determine whether an occupational license should be revoked, suspended, limited, or conditioned, a settlement may not be made before issuance of the agency pleading. A settlement may be made before, during, or after the hearing.

(c) A settlement is subject to any necessary agency approval. An agency head may delegate the power to approve a settlement. The terms of a settlement may not be contrary to statute or regulation, except that the settlement may include sanctions the agency would otherwise lack power to impose. *(Added by Stats.1995, c. 938 (S.B.523), § 21, operative July 1, 1997. Amended by Stats.1996, c. 390 (S.B.794), § 7, eff. Aug. 19, 1996, operative July 1, 1997.)*

Law Revision Commission Comments

Subdivision (a) of Section 11415.60 codifies the rule in Rich Vision Centers, Inc. v. Board of Medical Examiners, 144 Cal.App.3d 110, 192 Cal.Rptr. 455 (1983).

Subdivision (a) is analogous to Section 11420.30 (confidentiality of communications in alternative dispute resolution). The parties are, of course, free to make a stipulation concerning confidentiality of offers of compromise or settlement that goes beyond or otherwise varies the protection of this section.

Section 11415.60 is subject to a specific statute to the contrary governing the matter. Section 11415.20 (conflicting or inconsistent statute controls). Subdivision (c) recognizes that some other statutes provide for agency approval of a settlement. See, e.g., Gov't Code § 18681 (authority of State Personnel Board to approve settlements), Lab.Code §§ 98.2(d) (approval in labor standards enforcement), 5001 (approval of workers' compensation settlement), Pub.Res.Code § 6107 (approval by Governor of settlement by State Lands Commission), Rev. & Tax.Code §§ 7093.5, 9271, 19442, 30459.1, 32471, 40211, 41171, 43522, 45867, 50156.11, 55332 (approval of tax settlements). [25 Cal.L.Rev. Comm. Reports 55 (1995)].

Section 11415.60 is amended to protect conduct and statements made in settlement negotiations from admissibility, parallel to the protection provided in Section 1152 of the Evidence Code. This provision supplements the existing protection from admissibility of evidence of an offer of compromise or settlement (as opposed to evidence of conduct or statements made in settlement negotiations). [26 Cal.L.Rev.Comm. Reports 107 (1996) (App. 4)].

Research References

9 Witkin Cal. Proc. 5th Administrative Proceedings § 63, in General.

ARTICLE 5. ALTERNATIVE DISPUTE RESOLUTION

Section

§ 11420.10. Referral of proceedings

(a) An agency, with the consent of all the parties, may refer a dispute that is the subject of an adjudicative proceeding for resolution by any of the following means:

(1) Mediation by a neutral mediator.

(2) Binding arbitration by a neutral arbitrator. An award in a binding arbitration is subject to judicial review in the manner provided in Chapter 4 (commencing with Section 1285) of Title 9 of Part 3 of the Code of Civil Procedure.

(3) Nonbinding arbitration by a neutral arbitrator. The arbitrator's decision in a nonbinding arbitration is final unless within 30 days after the arbitrator delivers the award to the agency head a party requests that the agency conduct a de novo adjudicative proceeding. If the decision in the de novo proceed-

ing is not more favorable to the party electing the de novo proceeding, the party shall pay the costs and fees specified in Section 1141.21 of the Code of Civil Procedure insofar as applicable in the adjudicative proceeding.

(b) If another statute requires mediation or arbitration in an adjudicative proceeding, that statute prevails over this section.

(c) This section does not apply in an adjudicative proceeding to the extent an agency by regulation provides that this section is not applicable in a proceeding of the agency. *(Added by Stats.1995, c. 938 (S.B.523), § 21, operative July 1, 1997.)*

Law Revision Commission Comments

The introductory portion of subdivision (a) of Section 11420.10 makes clear that alternative dispute resolution is not mandatory, but may only be used if all parties consent. The relative cost of alternative dispute resolution is a factor an agency should consider in determining whether to refer a dispute for alternative resolution proceedings.

Under subdivision (a)(1), the mediator may use any mediation technique.

Subdivision (a)(2) authorizes delegation of the agency's authority to decide, with the consent of all parties.

Subdivision (a)(3) parallels the procedure applicable in judicial arbitration. See Code Civ. Proc. §§ 1141.20–1141.21. The costs and fees specified in Section 1141.21 for a civil proceeding may not all be applicable in an adjudicative proceeding, but subdivision (a)(3) requires such costs and fees to be assessed to the extent they are applicable.

Subdivision (b) recognizes that some statutes require alternative dispute resolution techniques.

If there is no statute requiring the agency to use mediation or arbitration, this section applies unless the agency makes it inapplicable by regulation under subdivision (c). [25 Cal.L.Rev.Comm. Reports 711 (1995)].

Research References

Rutter, Cal. Practice Guide: A.D.R. Ch. 1-B, B. Why ADR?
9 Witkin Cal. Proc. 5th Administrative Proceedings § 66, Optional and Mandatory Provisions.
9 Witkin Cal. Proc. 5th Administrative Proceedings § 84, (S 84) in General.
9 Witkin Cal. Proc. 5th Administrative Proceedings § 85, (S 85) Judicial Review of Award.
9 Witkin Cal. Proc. 5th Administrative Proceedings § 104, (S 104) Prehearing Conference.

§ 11420.20. Model regulations; contents

(a) The Office of Administrative Hearings shall adopt and promulgate model regulations for alternative dispute resolution under this article. The model regulations govern alternative dispute resolution by an agency under this article, except to the extent the agency by regulation provides inconsistent rules or provides that the model regulations are not applicable in a proceeding of the agency.

(b) The model regulations shall include provisions for selection and compensation of a mediator or arbitrator, qualifications of a mediator or arbitrator, and confidentiality of the mediation or arbitration proceeding. *(Added by Stats.1995, c. 938 (S.B. 523), § 21, operative July 1, 1997.)*

Law Revision Commission Comments

Section 11420.20 provides for regulations to govern the detail of alternative dispute resolution proceedings. In addition to the matters listed in subdivision (b), the regulations may address other issues such as cost allocation, discovery, and enforcement and review of alternative dispute resolutions.

This section does not require each agency to adopt regulations. The model regulations developed by the Office of Administrative Hearings will automatically govern mediation or arbitration for an agency, unless the agency provides otherwise. The agency may choose to preclude mediation or arbitration altogether. Section 11420.10 (ADR authorized). The Office of Administrative Hearings could maintain a roster of neutral mediators and arbitrators who are available for alternative dispute

settlement in all administrative agencies. [25 Cal.L.Rev.Comm. Reports 55 (1995)].

Research References

Rutter, Cal. Practice Guide: A.D.R. Ch. 1-B, B. Why ADR?
9 Witkin Cal. Proc. 5th Administrative Proceedings § 84, (S 84) in General.

§ 11420.30. Confidentiality of communications

Notwithstanding any other provision of law, a communication made in alternative dispute resolution under this article is protected to the following extent:

(a) Anything said, any admission made, and any document prepared in the course of, or pursuant to, mediation under this article is a confidential communication, and a party to the mediation has a privilege to refuse to disclose and to prevent another from disclosing the communication, whether in an adjudicative proceeding, civil action, or other proceeding. This subdivision does not limit the admissibility of evidence if all parties to the proceedings consent.

(b) No reference to nonbinding arbitration proceedings, a decision of the arbitrator that is rejected by a party's request for a de novo adjudicative proceeding, the evidence produced, or any other aspect of the arbitration may be made in an adjudicative proceeding or civil action, whether as affirmative evidence, by way of impeachment, or for any other purpose.

(c) No mediator or arbitrator is competent to testify in a subsequent administrative or civil proceeding as to any statement, conduct, decision, or order occurring at, or in conjunction with, the alternative dispute resolution.

(d) Evidence otherwise admissible outside of alternative dispute resolution under this article is not inadmissible or protected from disclosure solely by reason of its introduction or use in alternative dispute resolution under this article. *(Added by Stats.1995, c. 938 (S.B.523), § 21, operative July 1, 1997.)*

Law Revision Commission Comments

The policy of Section 11420.30 is not to restrict access to information but to encourage dispute resolution.

Subdivision (a) is analogous to Evidence Code Section 1152.5(a) (mediation).

Subdivision (b) is drawn from Code of Civil Procedure Section 1141.25 (arbitration) and California Rules of Court 1616(c) (arbitration). Subdivision (b) protects confidentiality of a proposed decision in nonbinding arbitration that is rejected by a party; it does not protect a decision accepted by the parties in a nonbinding arbitration, nor does it protect an award in a binding arbitration. See also Section 11425.20 (open hearings).

Subdivision (c) is drawn from Evidence Code Section 703.5.

Subdivision (d) is drawn from Evidence Code Section 1152.5(a)(6). [25 Cal.L.Rev.Comm. Reports 55 (1955)].

Research References

9 Witkin Cal. Proc. 5th Administrative Proceedings § 86, (S 86) Protection of Communications.

ARTICLE 6.   ADMINISTRATIVE ADJUDICATION BILL OF RIGHTS

§ 11425.10. Governing procedures; requirements

(a) The governing procedure by which an agency conducts an adjudicative proceeding is subject to all of the following requirements:

(1) The agency shall give the person to which the agency action is directed notice and an opportunity to be heard, including the opportunity to present and rebut evidence.

(2) The agency shall make available to the person to which the agency action is directed a copy of the governing procedure, including a statement whether Chapter 5 (commencing with Section 11500) is applicable to the proceeding.

(3) The hearing shall be open to public observation as provided in Section 11425.20.

(4) The adjudicative function shall be separated from the investigative, prosecutorial, and advocacy functions within the agency as provided in Section 11425.30.

(5) The presiding officer is subject to disqualification for bias, prejudice, or interest as provided in Section 11425.40.

(6) The decision shall be in writing, be based on the record, and include a statement of the factual and legal basis of the decision as provided in Section 11425.50.

(7) A decision may not be relied on as precedent unless the agency designates and indexes the decision as precedent as provided in Section 11425.60.

(8) Ex parte communications shall be restricted as provided in Article 7 (commencing with Section 11430.10).

(9) Language assistance shall be made available as provided in Article 8 (commencing with Section 11435.05) by an agency described in Section 11018 or 11435.15.

(b) The requirements of this section apply to the governing procedure by which an agency conducts an adjudicative proceeding without further action by the agency, and prevail over a conflicting or inconsistent provision of the governing procedure, subject to Section 11415.20. The governing procedure by which an agency conducts an adjudicative proceeding may include provisions equivalent to, or more protective of the rights of the person to which the agency action is directed than, the requirements of this section. *(Added by Stats.1995, c. 938 (S.B.523), § 21, operative July 1, 1997.)*

Law Revision Commission Comments

Section 11425.10 specifies the minimum due process and public interest requirements that must be satisfied in a hearing that is subject to this chapter, including a hearing under Chapter 5 (formal hearing). See Sections 11410.50 (application where formal hearing procedure required) and 11501 (application of chapter).

Under subdivision (b), this section is self-executing—it is part of the governing procedure by which an agency conducts an adjudicative proceeding whether or not regulations address the matter. The section does not, however, override conflicting or inconsistent state statutes, or federal statutes or regulations. Section 11415.20 (conflicting or inconsistent statute controls). If the governing procedure includes regulations that are at variance with the requirements of this section, it is desirable, but not necessary, that the agency revise the regulations; the requirements of this section apply regardless of the regulations. Conforming regulations may be adopted by a simplified procedure under the rulemaking provisions of the Administrative Procedure Act pursuant to 1 California Code of Regulations Section 100. Nothing in this section precludes the agency from adopting additional or more extensive requirements than those prescribed by this section.

Subdivision (a)(1), providing a person the opportunity to present and rebut evidence, is subject to reasonable control and limitation by the agency conducting the hearing, including the manner of presentation of evidence, whether oral, written, or electronic, limitation on lengthy or repetitious testimony or other evidence, and other controls or limitations appropriate to the character of the hearing.

Subdivision (a)(2) requires only that the agency "make available" a copy of the applicable hearing procedure. This requirement is subject to a rule of reasonableness in the circumstances and does not necessarily require the agency routinely to provide a copy to a person each time agency action is directed to the person. The requirement may be satisfied, for example, by the agency's offer to provide a copy on request.

Subdivision (a)(9), relating to language assistance, is limited to agencies listed in Sections 11018 (state agency not subject to Chapter 5) and 11435.15 (application of language assistance provisions). [25 Cal.L.Rev. Comm. Reports 711 (1995)].

Research References

9 Witkin Cal. Proc. 5th Administrative Proceedings § 66, Optional and Mandatory Provisions.
9 Witkin Cal. Proc. 5th Administrative Proceedings § 68, in General.
9 Witkin Cal. Proc. 5th Administrative Proceedings § 70, Separation of Adjudicative Function from Other Functions.
9 Witkin Cal. Proc. 5th Administrative Proceedings § 71, (S 71) in General.
9 Witkin Cal. Proc. 5th Administrative Proceedings § 77, Language Assistance.

§ 11425.20. Open hearings; exceptions

(a) A hearing shall be open to public observation. Nothing in this subdivision limits the authority of the presiding officer to order closure of a hearing or make other protective orders to the extent necessary or proper for any of the following purposes:

(1) To satisfy the United States Constitution, the California Constitution, federal or state statute, or other law, including but not limited to laws protecting privileged, confidential, or other protected information.

(2) To ensure a fair hearing in the circumstances of the particular case.

(3) To conduct the hearing, including the manner of examining witnesses, in a way that is appropriate to protect a minor witness or a witness with a developmental disability, as defined in Section 4512 of the Welfare and Institutions Code, from intimidation or other harm, taking into account the rights of all persons.

(b) To the extent a hearing is conducted by telephone, television, or other electronic means, subdivision (a) is satisfied if members of the public have an opportunity to do both of the following:

(1) At reasonable times, hear or inspect the agency's record, and inspect any transcript obtained by the agency.

(2) Be physically present at the place where the presiding officer is conducting the hearing.

(c) This section does not apply to a prehearing conference, settlement conference, or proceedings for alternative dispute resolution other than binding arbitration. *(Added by Stats.1995, c. 938 (S.B.523), § 21, operative July 1, 1997.)*

Law Revision Commission Comments

Section 11425.20 supplements the Bagley–Keene Open Meeting Act, Government Code §§ 11120–11132. Closure of a hearing should be done only to the extent necessary under this section, taking into account the substantial public interest in open proceedings. It should be noted that under the open meeting law deliberations on a decision to be reached based on evidence introduced in an adjudicative proceeding may be made in closed session. Section 11126(d). And under the open meeting law, a settlement proposal may be considered by the agency in closed session if it sustains its substantial burden of showing the prejudice to be suffered from conducting an open meeting. Section 11126(d), (q).

Subdivision (a) codifies existing practice. See 1 G. Ogden, California Public Agency Practice § 37.03 (1994).

Statutory protection of trade secrets and other confidential or privileged information is covered by subdivision (a)(1). See, e.g., Evid.Code §§ 1060–1063; Fin.Code §§ 1939, 16120, 18496.

Government

Subdivision (a)(3) codifies and broadens an aspect of Seering v. Department of Social Serv., 194 Cal.App.3d 298, 239 Cal.Rptr. 422 (1987). It should be noted that the rights of persons to be taken into account includes the right of the parties to observe the proceedings in an appropriate manner.

Subdivision (b) is drawn in part from 1981 Model State APA § 4–211(6). The right of the public to be present where a hearing is being conducted telephonically does not include the right to participate, and the right of the public to inspect the record does not impose a duty on the agency to provide a copy independent of the California Public Records Act. [25 Cal.L.Rev.Comm. Reports 55 (1955)].

Research References

9 Witkin Cal. Proc. 5th Administrative Proceedings § 7, Statutes and Ordinances.
9 Witkin Cal. Proc. 5th Administrative Proceedings § 68, in General.
9 Witkin Cal. Proc. 5th Administrative Proceedings § 69, Open Hearing.

§ 11425.30. Presiding officer; disqualification

(a) A person may not serve as presiding officer in an adjudicative proceeding in any of the following circumstances:

(1) The person has served as investigator, prosecutor, or advocate in the proceeding or its preadjudicative stage.

(2) The person is subject to the authority, direction, or discretion of a person who has served as investigator, prosecutor, or advocate in the proceeding or its preadjudicative stage.

(b) Notwithstanding subdivision (a):

(1) A person may serve as presiding officer at successive stages of an adjudicative proceeding.

(2) A person who has participated only as a decisionmaker or as an advisor to a decisionmaker in a determination of probable cause or other equivalent preliminary determination in an adjudicative proceeding or its preadjudicative stage may serve as presiding officer in the proceeding.

(c) The provisions of this section governing separation of functions as to the presiding officer also govern separation of functions as to the agency head or other person or body to which the power to hear or decide in the proceeding is delegated. *(Added by Stats.1995, c. 938 (S.B.523), § 21, operative July 1, 1997.)*

Law Revision Commission Comments

Subdivision (a) of Section 11425.30 is drawn from 1981 Model State APA § 4–214(a)–(b). See also Veh.Code § 14112 (exemption for drivers' licensing proceedings).

Under this provision, a person has "served" in any of the capacities mentioned if the person has personally carried out the function, and not merely supervised or been organizationally connected with a person who has personally carried out the function. The separation of functions requirements are intended to apply to substantial involvement in a case by a person, and not merely marginal or trivial participation. The sort of participation intended to be disqualifying is meaningful participation that is likely to affect an individual with a commitment to a particular result in the case.

Subdivision (b) is drawn from 1981 Model State APA § 4–214(c)–(d). It allows a person to be involved as a decisionmaker in both a probable cause determination and in the subsequent hearing; it does not allow a person to serve as a presiding officer at the hearing if the person was involved in a probable cause determination as an investigator, prosecutor, or advocate.

This provision, dealing with the extent to which a person may serve as presiding officer at different stages of the same proceeding, should be distinguished from Section 11430.10, which prohibits certain ex parte communications. The policy issues in Section 11430.10 regarding ex parte communication between two persons differ from the policy issues in subdivision (b) regarding the participation by one individual in two stages of the same proceeding. There may be other grounds for disqualification, however, in the event of improper ex parte communications. See Sections 11430.60 (disqualification of presiding officer), 11425.40 (disqualification of presiding officer for bias, prejudice, or interest). [25 Cal.L.Rev.Comm. Reports 55 (1995)].

Research References

9 Witkin Cal. Proc. 5th Administrative Proceedings § 68, in General.
9 Witkin Cal. Proc. 5th Administrative Proceedings § 70, Separation of Adjudicative Function from Other Functions.

§ 11425.40. Bias, prejudice or interest

(a) The presiding officer is subject to disqualification for bias, prejudice, or interest in the proceeding.

(b) It is not alone or in itself grounds for disqualification, without further evidence of bias, prejudice, or interest, that the presiding officer:

(1) Is or is not a member of a racial, ethnic, religious, sexual, or similar group and the proceeding involves the rights of that group.

(2) Has experience, technical competence, or specialized knowledge of, or has in any capacity expressed a view on, a legal, factual, or policy issue presented in the proceeding.

(3) Has as a lawyer or public official participated in the drafting of laws or regulations or in the effort to pass or defeat laws or regulations, the meaning, effect, or application of which is in issue in the proceeding.

(c) The provisions of this section governing disqualification of the presiding officer also govern disqualification of the agency head or other person or body to which the power to hear or decide in the proceeding is delegated.

(d) An agency that conducts an adjudicative proceeding may provide by regulation for peremptory challenge of the presiding officer. *(Added by Stats.1995, c. 938 (S.B.523), § 21, operative July 1, 1997.)*

Law Revision Commission Comments

Section 11425.40 applies in all administrative adjudications subject to this chapter, including a hearing under Chapter 5 (formal hearing). See Sections 11410.50 (application where formal hearing procedure required) and 11501 (application of chapter). It supersedes a provision formerly found in Section 11512(c) (disqualification of presiding officer in formal hearing). Section 11425.40 applies whether the presiding officer serves alone or with others. For separation of functions requirements, see Section 11425.30.

Subdivision (a) is drawn from 1981 Model State APA § 4–202(b).

Subdivision (b) is drawn from Code of Civil Procedure Section 170.2 (disqualification of judges). Although subdivision (b)(2) provides that, as a general principle, expression of a view on a legal, factual, or policy issue in the proceeding is not in itself bias, prejudice, or interest under Section 11425.40, expression of a view could be a basis for disqualification in conjunction with other acts of the presiding officer. Moreover, expression of a view concerning the particular proceeding before the presiding officer could be grounds for disqualification, and disqualification in such a situation might also occur under Section 11425.30 (neutrality of presiding officer).

Subdivision (d) adds authority for an agency to allow for peremptory challenge of the presiding officer. This is consistent with existing practice in some agencies. See, e.g., 8 Cal. Code Reg. § 10453 (Workers' Compensation Appeals Board). In the case of a proceeding conducted under Chapter 5 (formal hearing procedure) by an administrative law judge employed by the Office of Administrative Hearings, this provision authorizes the Office of Administrative Hearings, and not the agency for which the Office of Administrative Hearings is conducting the proceeding, to provide for peremptory challenge of the administrative law judge. [25 Cal.L.Rev.Comm. Reports 711 (1995)].

Research References

California Practice Guide: Employment Litigation Ch. 13-H, H. Contesting Citations and Related Orders and Notices.
9 Witkin Cal. Proc. 5th Administrative Proceedings § 68, in General.
9 Witkin Cal. Proc. 5th Administrative Proceedings § 70, Separation of Adjudicative Function from Other Functions.

9 Witkin Cal. Proc. 5th Administrative Proceedings § 110, Disqualification of Judge or Agency Member.

§ 11425.50. Written decision; contents

(a) The decision shall be in writing and shall include a statement of the factual and legal basis for the decision.

(b) The statement of the factual basis for the decision may be in the language of, or by reference to, the pleadings. If the statement is no more than mere repetition or paraphrase of the relevant statute or regulation, the statement shall be accompanied by a concise and explicit statement of the underlying facts of record that support the decision. If the factual basis for the decision includes a determination based substantially on the credibility of a witness, the statement shall identify any specific evidence of the observed demeanor, manner, or attitude of the witness that supports the determination, and on judicial review the court shall give great weight to the determination to the extent the determination identifies the observed demeanor, manner, or attitude of the witness that supports it.

(c) The statement of the factual basis for the decision shall be based exclusively on the evidence of record in the proceeding and on matters officially noticed in the proceeding. The presiding officer's experience, technical competence, and specialized knowledge may be used in evaluating evidence.

(d) Nothing in this section limits the information that may be contained in the decision, including a summary of evidence relied on.

(e) A penalty may not be based on a guideline, criterion, bulletin, manual, instruction, order, standard of general application or other rule subject to Chapter 3.5 (commencing with Section 11340) unless it has been adopted as a regulation pursuant to Chapter 3.5 (commencing with Section 11340). (Added by Stats.1995, c. 938 (S.B.523), § 21, operative July 1, 1997.)

Law Revision Commission Comments

Section 11425.50 supersedes the first two sentences of Section 11518. See also former subdivision (f)(4) of Section 11500.

Subdivision (a) is drawn from the first sentence of 1981 Model State APA § 4–215(c). The decision must be supported by findings that link the evidence in the proceeding to the ultimate decision. Topanga Ass'n for a Scenic Community v. County of Los Angeles, 11 Cal.3d 506, 522 P. 2d 12, 113 Cal.Rptr. 836 (1974). The requirement that the decision must include a statement of the basis for the decision is particularly significant when an agency develops new policy through the adjudication of specific cases rather than through rulemaking. Articulation of the basis for the agency's decision facilitates administrative and judicial review, helps clarify the effect of any precedential decision (see Section 11425.60), and focuses attention on questions that the agency should address in subsequent rulemaking to supersede the policy that has been developed through adjudicative proceedings. The decision must only explain its actual basis. It need not eliminate other possible bases that could have been, but were not, relied upon as the basis for the decision. Thus, for example, if the decision imposes terms and conditions, it need not explain why other terms and conditions were not imposed.

Subdivision (a) requires the decision to contain a statement of the "factual . . . basis for the decision," while former Section 11518 required the decision to contain "findings of fact." The new language more accurately reflects case law, and is not a substantive change. See Topanga Ass'n for a Scenic Community v. County of Los Angeles, supra; Swars v. Council of the City of Vallejo, 33 Cal.2d 867, 872–73, 206 P.2d 355 (1949).

The requirement in subdivision (b) that a mere repetition or paraphrase of the relevant statute or regulation be accompanied by a statement of the underlying facts is drawn from the second sentence of 1981 Model APA § 4–215(c).

Subdivision (b) adopts the rule of Universal Camera Corp. v. NLRB, 340 U.S. 474 (1951), requiring that the reviewing court weigh more heavily findings by the trier of fact (the presiding officer in an administrative adjudication) based on observation of witnesses than findings based on other evidence. This generalizes the standard of review used by a number of California agencies. See, e.g., Garza v. Workmen's Compensation

Appeals Bd., 3 Cal.3d 312, 318–19, 475 P. 2d 451, 90 Cal.Rptr. 355 (1970) (Workers' Compensation Appeals Board); Millen v. Swoap, 58 Cal. App.3d 943, 947–48, 130 Cal.Rptr. 387 (1976) (Department of Social Services); Apte v. Regents of Univ. of Cal., 198 Cal.App.3d 1084, 1092, 244 Cal.Rptr. 312 (1988) (University of California); Unemp. Ins. App. Bd., Precedent Decisions P–B–10, P–T–13, P–B–57; Lab. Code § 1148 (Agricultural Labor Relations Board). It reverses the existing practice under the administrative procedure act and other California administrative procedures that gives no weight to the findings of the presiding officer at the hearing. See Asimow, *Toward a New California Administrative Procedure Act: Adjudication Fundamentals*, 39 UCLA L.Rev. 1067, 1114 (1992), *reprinted in* 25 Cal. L. Revision Comm'n Reports 321, 368 (1995).

Findings based substantially on credibility of a witness must be identified by the presiding officer in the decision made in the adjudicative proceeding. This requirement is derived from Washington law. See Wash. Rev. Code Ann. §§ 34.05.461(3), 34.05.464(4) (West 1990). However, the presiding officer's identification of such findings in not binding on the agency or the courts, which may make their own determinations whether a particular finding is based substantially on credibility of a witness. Even though the presiding officer's determination is based substantially on credibility of a witness, the determination is entitled to great weight only to the extent the determination derives from the presiding officer's observation of the demeanor, manner, or attitude of the witness. Nothing in subdivision (b) precludes the agency head or court from overturning a credibility determination of the presiding officer, after giving the observational elements of the credibility determination great weight, whether on the basis of nonobservational elements of credibility or otherwise. See Evid. Code § 780. Nor does if preclude the agency head from overturning a factual finding based on the presiding officer's assessment of expert witness testimony.

The first sentence of subdivision (c) codifies existing California case law. See, e.g., Vollstedt v. City of Stockton, 220 Cal.App.3d 265, 269 Cal.Rptr. 404 (1990). It is drawn from the first sentence of 1981 Model State APA § 4–215(d). Official notice of some matters may be taken by the presiding officer. See Section 11515 (official notice). The second sentence is drawn from 1981 Model State APA § 4–215(d).

Subdivision (e) is consistent with the rulemaking provisions of the Administrative Procedure Act. See Section 11340.5 ("underground regulations"). A penalty based on a precedent decision does not violate subdivision (e). See Section 11425.60 (precedent decision). If a penalty is based on an "underground rule" — one not adopted as a regulation as required by the rulemaking provisions of the Administrative Procedure Act — a reviewing court should exercise discretion in deciding the appropriate remedy. Generally the court should remand to the agency to set a new penalty without reliance on the underground rule but without setting aside the balance of the decision. Remand would not be appropriate in the event that the penalty is, in light of the evidence, the *only* reasonable application of duly adopted law. Or a court might decide the appropriate penalty itself without giving the normal deference to agency discretionary judgments. See Armistead v. State Personnel Bd., 22 Cal.3d 198, 583 P.2d 744, 149 Cal.Rptr. 1 (1978). [25 Cal.L.Rev. Comm. Reports 55 (1995)].

Research References

9 Witkin Cal. Proc. 5th Administrative Proceedings § 68, in General.

9 Witkin Cal. Proc. 5th Administrative Proceedings § 71, (S 71) in General.

9 Witkin Cal. Proc. 5th Administrative Proceedings § 72, (S 72) Statement of Factual Basis.

9 Witkin Cal. Proc. 5th Administrative Proceedings § 73, (S 73) Reliance on Appropriate Authority.

9 Witkin Cal. Proc. 5th Administrative Proceedings § 115, Filing and Service.

§ 11425.60. Precedent; designation; index

(a) A decision may not be expressly relied on as precedent unless it is designated as a precedent decision by the agency.

(b) An agency may designate as a precedent decision a decision or part of a decision that contains a significant legal or policy determination of general application that is likely to recur. Designation of a decision or part of a decision as a precedent decision is not rulemaking and need not be done under Chapter 3.5 (commencing with Section 11340). An agency's designation of a decision or part of a decision, or failure to designate a

Government

decision or part of a decision, as a precedent decision is not subject to judicial review.

(c) An agency shall maintain an index of significant legal and policy determinations made in precedent decisions. The index shall be updated not less frequently than annually, unless no precedent decision has been designated since the last preceding update. The index shall be made available to the public by subscription, and its availability shall be publicized annually in the California Regulatory Notice Register.

(d) This section applies to decisions issued on or after July 1, 1997. Nothing in this section precludes an agency from designating and indexing as a precedent decision a decision issued before July 1, 1997. *(Added by Stats.1995, c. 938 (S.B.523), § 21, operative July 1, 1997. Amended by Stats.1996, c. 390 (S.B.794), § 8, eff. Aug. 19, 1996, operative July 1, 1997.)*

Law Revision Commission Comments

Section 11425.60 limits the authority of an agency to rely on previous decisions unless the decisions have been publicly announced as precedential.

The first sentence of subdivision (b) recognizes the need of agencies to be able to make law and policy through adjudication as well as through rulemaking. It codifies the practice of a number of agencies to designate important decisions as precedential. See Sections 12935(h) (Fair Employment and Housing Commission), 19582.5 (State Personnel Board); Unemp.Ins.Code § 409 (Unemployment Insurance Appeals Board). Section 11425.60 is intended to encourage agencies to articulate what they are doing when they make new law or policy in an adjudicative decision. An agency may not by precedent decision revise or amend an existing regulation or adopt a rule that has no adequate legislative basis.

Under the second sentence of subdivision (b), this section applies notwithstanding Section 11340.5 ("underground regulations"). See 1993 OAL Det. No. 1 (determination by Office of Administrative Law that agency designation of decision as precedential violates former Government Code Section 11347.5 [now 11340.5] unless made pursuant to rulemaking procedures). The provision is drawn from Government Code Section 19582.5 (expressly exempting the State Personnel Board's precedent decision designations from rulemaking procedures). See also Unemp.Ins.Code § 409 (Unemployment Insurance Appeals Board). Nonetheless, agencies are encouraged to express precedent decisions in the form of regulations, to the extent practicable.

The index required by subdivision (c) is a public record, available for public inspection and copying.

Subdivision (d) minimizes the potential burden on agencies by making the precedent decision requirements prospective only. [25 Cal.L.Rev. Comm. Reports 55 (1995)].

Subdivision (d) of Section 11425.60 is amended to make clear that if an agency designates as precedential a decision issued before July 1, 1997, the decision must be indexed pursuant to subdivision (c). [26 Cal.L.Rev. Comm. Reports 107 (1996) (App. 4)].

Research References

9 Witkin Cal. Proc. 5th Administrative Proceedings § 53, (S 53) Determination Whether Uncodified Agency Action Constitutes Regulation.
9 Witkin Cal. Proc. 5th Administrative Proceedings § 68, in General.
9 Witkin Cal. Proc. 5th Administrative Proceedings § 73, (S 73) Reliance on Appropriate Authority.
3 Witkin, California Summary 10th Agency and Employment § 460, Decision as Precedent.

ARTICLE 7.   EX PARTE COMMUNICATIONS

§ 11430.10.   Pending proceedings

(a) While the proceeding is pending there shall be no communication, direct or indirect, regarding any issue in the proceeding, to the presiding officer from an employee or representative of an agency that is a party or from an interested person outside the agency, without notice and opportunity for all parties to participate in the communication.

(b) Nothing in this section precludes a communication, including a communication from an employee or representative of an agency that is a party, made on the record at the hearing.

(c) For the purpose of this section, a proceeding is pending from the issuance of the agency's pleading, or from an application for an agency decision, whichever is earlier. *(Added by Stats.1995, c. 938 (S.B.523), § 21, operative July 1, 1997.)*

Law Revision Commission Comments

Section 11430.10 is drawn from former Section 11513.5(a) and (b). See also 1981 Model State APA § 4–213(a), (c). This provision also applies to the agency head, or other person or body to which the power to hear or decide is delegated. See Section 11430.70 (application of provisions to agency head or other person). For exceptions to this section, see Sections 11430.20 (permissible ex parte communications generally) and 11430.30 (permissible ex parte communications from agency personnel).

The reference to an "interested person outside the agency" replaces the former reference to a "person who has a direct or indirect interest in the outcome of the proceeding," and is drawn from federal law. See Federal APA § 557(d)(1)(A) (1988); see also Professional Air Traffic Controllers Org. v. Federal Labor Relations Auth., 685 F.2d 547, 562 (D.C.Cir.1982) (construing the federal standard to include person with an interest beyond that of a member of the general public).

Where the agency conducting the hearing is not a party to the proceeding, the presiding officer may consult with other agency personnel. The ex parte communications prohibition only applies as between the presiding officer and parties and other interested persons, not as between the presiding officer and disinterested personnel of a non-party agency conducting the hearing. However, the presiding officer may not consult with the agency head. Section 11430.80 (communications between presiding officer and agency head).

While this section precludes an adversary from communicating with the presiding officer, it does not preclude the presiding officer from communicating with an adversary. This reverses a provision of former Section 11513.5(a). Thus it would not prohibit an agency head from communicating to an adversary that a particular case should be settled or dismissed. However, a presiding officer should give assistance or advice with caution, since there may be an appearance of unfairness if assistance or advice is given to some parties but not others.

Nothing in this section limits the authority of the presiding officer to conduct an in camera examination of proffered evidence. *Cf.* Section 11507.7(d)-(e).

Subdivision (c) defines the pendency of a proceeding to include any period between the time an application for a hearing is made and the time the agency's pleading is issued. Treatment of communications made to a person during pendency of the proceeding but before the person becomes presiding officer is dealt with in Section 11430.40 (prior ex parte communication). [25 Cal.L.Rev.Comm. Reports 711 (1995)].

Research References

Rutter, Cal. Practice Guide: Prof. Responsibility Ch. 4-B, B. Concurrent Representation of Clients With Conflicting Interests (Conflicts Between Present Clients).
Rutter, Cal. Practice Guide: Prof. Responsibility Ch. 8-D, D. Restrictions on Speech and Behavior Outside Courtroom.
9 Witkin Cal. Proc. 5th Administrative Proceedings § 60, (S 60) Administrative Adjudication Code of Ethics.
9 Witkin Cal. Proc. 5th Administrative Proceedings § 68, in General.

9 Witkin Cal. Proc. 5th Administrative Proceedings § 74, (S 74) General Prohibition.

9 Witkin Cal. Proc. 5th Administrative Proceedings § 94, (S 94) Sanctions.

§ 11430.20. Permissible communications

A communication otherwise prohibited by Section 11430.10 is permissible in any of the following circumstances:

(a) The communication is required for disposition of an ex parte matter specifically authorized by statute.

(b) The communication concerns a matter of procedure or practice, including a request for a continuance, that is not in controversy. *(Added by Stats.1995, c. 938 (S.B.523), § 21, operative July 1, 1997.)*

Law Revision Commission Comments

Subdivision (a) of Section 11430.20 is drawn from former Section 11513.5(a) and (b). This provision also applies to the agency head, or other person or body to which the power to hear or decide is delegated. See Section 11430.70 (application of provisions to agency head or other person).

This article is not intended to preclude communications made to a presiding officer or staff assistant regarding noncontroversial matters of procedure and practice, such as the format of pleadings, number of copies required, manner of service, and calendaring and status discussions. Subdivision (b). Such topics are not part of the merits of the matter, provided they appear to be noncontroversial in context of the specific case. [25 Cal.L.Rev.Comm. Reports 55 (1995)].

Research References

Rutter, Cal. Practice Guide: Prof. Responsibility Ch. 8-D, D. Restrictions on Speech and Behavior Outside Courtroom.

9 Witkin Cal. Proc. 5th Administrative Proceedings § 75, (S 75) Permissible Communications.

§ 11430.30. Permissible communications from employees or representatives of agencies

A communication otherwise prohibited by Section 11430.10 from an employee or representative of an agency that is a party to the presiding officer is permissible in any of the following circumstances:

(a) The communication is for the purpose of assistance and advice to the presiding officer from a person who has not served as investigator, prosecutor, or advocate in the proceeding or its preadjudicative stage. An assistant or advisor may evaluate the evidence in the record but shall not furnish, augment, diminish, or modify the evidence in the record.

(b) The communication is for the purpose of advising the presiding officer concerning a settlement proposal advocated by the advisor.

(c) The communication is for the purpose of advising the presiding officer concerning any of the following matters in an adjudicative proceeding that is nonprosecutorial in character:

(1) The advice involves a technical issue in the proceeding and the advice is necessary for, and is not otherwise reasonably available to, the presiding officer, provided the content of the advice is disclosed on the record and all parties are given an opportunity to address it in the manner provided in Section 11430.50.

(2) The advice involves an issue in a proceeding of the San Francisco Bay Conservation and Development Commission, California Tahoe Regional Planning Agency, Delta Protection Commission, Water Resources Control Board, or a regional water quality control board. *(Added by Stats.1995, c. 938 (S.B.523), § 21, operative July 1, 1997.)*

Law Revision Commission Comments

The exceptions to the prohibition on ex parte communications provided in Section 11430.30 are most likely to be useful in hearings where the presiding officer is employed by an agency that is a party. This provision also applies to the agency head, or other person or body to which the power to hear or decide is delegated. See Section 11430.70 (application of provisions to agency head or other person).

This article does not limit on-the-record communications between agency personnel and the presiding officer. Section 11430.10(b) (ex parte communications prohibited). Only advice or assistance given outside the hearing is prohibited.

The first sentence of subdivision (a) is drawn from 1981 Model State APA § 4–214(a)-(b). The second sentence is drawn from 1981 Model State APA § 4–213(b). Under this provision, a person has "served" in any of the capacities mentioned if the person has personally carried out the function, and not merely supervised or been organizationally connected with a person who has personally carried out the function. The limitation is intended to apply to substantial involvement in a case by a person, and not merely marginal or trivial participation. The sort of participation intended to be disqualifying is meaningful participation that is likely to affect an individual with a commitment to a particular result in the case. Thus a person who merely participated in a preliminary determination in an adjudicative proceeding or its pre-adjudicative stage would ordinarily be able to assist or advise the presiding officer in the proceeding. *Cf.* Section 11425.30 (neutrality of presiding officer). For this reason also, a staff member who plays a meaningful but neutral role without becoming an adversary would not be barred by this section.

This provision is not limited to agency personnel, but includes participants in the proceeding not employed by the agency. A deputy attorney general who prosecuted the case at the administrative trial level, for example, would be precluded from advising the agency head or other person delegated the power to hear or decide at the final decision level, except with respect to settlement matters. Subdivision (b).

Subdivision (b), permitting an investigator, prosecutor, or advocate to advise the presiding officer regarding a settlement proposal, is limited to advice in support of the proposed settlement; the insider may not use the opportunity to argue against a previously agreed-to settlement. *Cf.* Alhambra Teachers Ass'n CTA/NEA v. Alhambra City and High Sch. Dists. (1986), PERB Decision No. 560. Insider access is permitted here in furtherance of public policy favoring settlement, and because of the consonance of interest of the parties in this situation.

Subdivision (c) applies to nonprosecutorial types of administrative adjudications, such as power plant siting, land use decisions, and proceedings allocating water or setting water quality protection or instream flow requirements. The provision recognizes that the length and complexity of many cases of this type may as a practical matter make it impossible for an agency to adhere to the restrictions of this article, given limited staffing and personnel. Subdivision (c)(1) recognizes that such an adjudication may require advice from a person with special technical knowledge whose advice would not otherwise be available to the presiding officer under standard doctrine. Subdivision (c)(2) recognizes the need for policy advice from planning staff in proceedings such as land use and environmental matters. [25 Cal.L.Rev.Comm. Reports 711 (1995)].

Research References

Rutter, Cal. Practice Guide: Prof. Responsibility Ch. 8-D, D. Restrictions on Speech and Behavior Outside Courtroom.

9 Witkin Cal. Proc. 5th Administrative Proceedings § 75, (S 75) Permissible Communications.

§ 11430.40. Communications received prior to serving as presiding officer; disclosure

If, while the proceeding is pending but before serving as presiding officer, a person receives a communication of a type that would be in violation of this article if received while serving as presiding officer, the person, promptly after starting to serve, shall disclose the content of the communication on the record and give all parties an opportunity to address it in the manner provided in Section 11430.50. *(Added by Stats.1995, c. 938 (S.B.523), § 21, operative July 1, 1997.)*

Law Revision Commission Comments

Section 11430.40 is drawn from former Section 11513.5(c), but is limited to communications received during pendency of the proceeding. See also 1981 Model State APA § 4–213(d). This provision also applies to the agency head, or other person or body to which the power to hear or decide is delegated. See Section 11430.70 (application of provisions to agency head or other person). For the purpose of this section, a proceeding is pending on the earlier of issuance of an agency pleading or submission of an application for an agency decision. Section 11430.10(c) (ex parte communications prohibited). [25 Cal.L.Rev.Comm. Reports 55 (1995)].

Research References

9 Witkin Cal. Proc. 5th Administrative Proceedings § 76, (S 76) Disclosure of Communications.

§ 11430.50. Violations; duty of presiding officer

(a) If a presiding officer receives a communication in violation of this article, the presiding officer shall make all of the following a part of the record in the proceeding:

(1) If the communication is written, the writing and any written response of the presiding officer to the communication.

(2) If the communication is oral, a memorandum stating the substance of the communication, any response made by the presiding officer, and the identity of each person from whom the presiding officer received the communication.

(b) The presiding officer shall notify all parties that a communication described in this section has been made a part of the record.

(c) If a party requests an opportunity to address the communication within 10 days after receipt of notice of the communication:

(1) The party shall be allowed to comment on the communication.

(2) The presiding officer has discretion to allow the party to present evidence concerning the subject of the communication, including discretion to reopen a hearing that has been concluded. *(Added by Stats.1995, c. 938 (S.B.523), § 21, operative July 1, 1997.)*

Law Revision Commission Comments

Section 11430.50 is drawn from former Section 11513.5(d). This provision also applies to the agency head, or other person or body to which the power to hear or decide is delegated. See Section 11430.70 (application of provisions to agency head or other person). See also Section 11440.20 (notice). [25 Cal.L.Rev.Comm. Reports 55 (1995)].

Research References

9 Witkin Cal. Proc. 5th Administrative Proceedings § 75, (S 75) Permissible Communications.
9 Witkin Cal. Proc. 5th Administrative Proceedings § 76, (S 76) Disclosure of Communications.

§ 11430.60. Disqualification of presiding officer

Receipt by the presiding officer of a communication in violation of this article may be grounds for disqualification of the presiding officer. If the presiding officer is disqualified, the portion of the record pertaining to the ex parte communication may be sealed by protective order of the disqualified presiding officer. *(Added by Stats.1995, c. 938 (S.B.523), § 21, operative July 1, 1997.)*

Law Revision Commission Comments

Section 11430.60 is drawn from former Section 11513.5(e). This provision also applies to the agency head, or other person or body to which the power to hear or decide is delegated. See Section 11430.70 (application of provisions to agency head or other person).

Section 11430.60 permits the disqualification of a presiding officer if necessary to eliminate the effect of an ex parte communication.

In addition, this section permits the pertinent portions of the record to be sealed by protective order. The intent of this provision is to remove the improper communication from the view of the successor presiding officer, while preserving it as a sealed part of the record, for purposes of subsequent administrative or judicial review. Issuance of a protective order under this section is permissive, not mandatory, and is therefore

within the discretion of a presiding officer who has knowledge of the improper communication. [25 Cal.L.Rev.Comm. Reports 55 (1995)].

Research References

9 Witkin Cal. Proc. 5th Administrative Proceedings § 74, (S 74) General Prohibition.
9 Witkin Cal. Proc. 5th Administrative Proceedings § 110, Disqualification of Judge or Agency Member.

§ 11430.70. Agency heads or other persons with power to hear or decide

(a) Subject to subdivisions (b) and (c), the provisions of this article governing ex parte communications to the presiding officer also govern ex parte communications in an adjudicative proceeding to the agency head or other person or body to which the power to hear or decide in the proceeding is delegated.

(b) An ex parte communication to the agency head or other person or body to which the power to hear or decide in the proceeding is delegated is permissible in an individualized ratemaking proceeding if the content of the communication is disclosed on the record and all parties are given an opportunity to address it in the manner provided in Section 11430.50.

(c) An ex parte communication to the agency head or other person or body to which the power to hear or decide in the proceeding is delegated is permissible in an individualized determination of an application for site certification pursuant to Chapter 6 (commencing with Section 25500) of Division 15 of the Public Resources Code, that is before the State Energy Resources Conservation and Development Commission, if the communication is made by an employee of another state agency and is made for the purpose of enabling the presiding officer to effectively manage the proceeding. *(Added by Stats.1995, c. 938 (S.B.523), § 21, operative July 1, 1997. Amended by Stats.2009–2010, 8th Ex.Sess., c. 9 (S.B.34), § 4, eff. March 22, 2010.)*

Law Revision Commission Comments

Under Section 11430.70, this article is applicable to the agency head or other person or body to which the power to act is delegated. For an additional limitation on communications between the presiding officer and agency head, see Section 11430.80.

Section 11430.70 applies only in administrative adjudication proceedings; it does not apply in rulemaking proceedings. Cf. Sections 11405.20 ("adjudicative proceeding" defined); 11405.50 ("decision" defined). See also Sections 11400 (administrative adjudication provisions); 11410.10 (application of chapter). While subdivision (b) permits ex parte communications to the agency head in an individualized ratemaking proceeding, it does not require an agency head to accept ex parte communications. Moreover, an agency may provide greater limitations on acceptance of ex parte communications than would be permitted by this provision. See Section 11425.10(b) & Comment (administrative adjudication bill of rights). [25 Cal.L.Rev.Comm. Reports 711 (1995)].

Research References

Rutter, Cal. Practice Guide: Prof. Responsibility Ch. 8-D, D. Restrictions on Speech and Behavior Outside Courtroom.
9 Witkin Cal. Proc. 5th Administrative Proceedings § 74, (S 74) General Prohibition.
9 Witkin Cal. Proc. 5th Administrative Proceedings § 75, (S 75) Permissible Communications.

§ 11430.80. Communications between presiding officer and agency head regarding the merits of any issue

(a) There shall be no communication, direct or indirect, while a proceeding is pending regarding the merits of any issue in the proceeding, between the presiding officer and the agency head or other person or body to which the power to hear or decide in the proceeding is delegated.

(b) This section does not apply where the agency head or other person or body to which the power to hear or decide in the proceeding is delegated serves as both presiding officer and agency head, or where the presiding officer does not issue a decision in the proceeding. *(Added by Stats.1995, c. 938 (S.B.523), § 21, operative July 1, 1997.)*

Law Revision Commission Comments

Section 11430.80 is a special application of a provision of former Section 11513.5(a), which precluded a presiding officer from communicating with a person who presided in an earlier phase of the proceeding. Section 11430.80 extends the ex parte communications limitation of Section 11430.70 (application of provisions to agency head or other person) to include communications with an agency or non-agency presiding officer as well. This limitation does not apply where the presiding officer does not issue a decision to the parties, but merely prepares a recommended decision for the agency head or other person or body to which the power to decide is delegated.

This section enforces the general principle that the presiding officer should not be an advocate for the proposed decision to the agency head, including a person or body to which the power to act is delegated. See Section 11405.40 ("agency head" defined). The decision of the agency head should be based on the record and not on off-the-record discussions from which the parties are excluded. Nothing in this section restricts on-the-record communications between the presiding officer and the agency head. Section 11430.10(b).

This section precludes only communications concerning the merits of an issue in the proceeding while the proceeding is pending. It does not preclude, for example, the agency head from directing the presiding officer to elaborate portions of the proposed decision in the proceeding, from asking the presiding officer for tapes of settlement discussions in the proceeding, or from informing the presiding officer of an investigation concerning disciplinary action involving the presiding officer arising out of the proceeding.

References in this section to a "person or body to which the power to hear or decide in the proceeding is delegated" mean a referral by the agency head pursuant to legal authority vested in the agency head. Cf. Section 11405.40 & Comment ("agency head" defined). [25 Cal.L.Rev. Comm. Reports 711 (1995)].

Research References

Rutter, Cal. Practice Guide: Prof. Responsibility Ch. 4-B, B. Concurrent Representation of Clients With Conflicting Interests (Conflicts Between Present Clients).
9 Witkin Cal. Proc. 5th Administrative Proceedings § 74, (S 74) General Prohibition.
9 Witkin Cal. Proc. 5th Administrative Proceedings § 75, (S 75) Permissible Communications.

ARTICLE 8. LANGUAGE ASSISTANCE

§ 11435.05. Language assistance

As used in this article, "language assistance" means oral interpretation or written translation into English of a language other than English or of English into another language for a party or witness who cannot speak or understand English or who can do so only with difficulty. *(Added by Stats.1995, c. 938 (S.B.523), § 21, operative July 1, 1997.)*

Law Revision Commission Comments

Section 11435.05 supersedes former subdivision (g) of Section 11500. It extends this article to language translation for witnesses. [25 Cal. L.Rev.Comm. Reports 55 (1995)].

Research References

9 Witkin Cal. Proc. 5th Administrative Proceedings § 68, in General.
9 Witkin Cal. Proc. 5th Administrative Proceedings § 77, Language Assistance.
2 Witkin Cal. Summ. 10th Workers' Compensation § 264, Reimbursement for Examination Expenses.
2 Witkin Cal. Summ. 10th Workers' Compensation § 396, Procedure.

§ 11435.10. Application of Evidence Code § 754

Nothing in this article limits the application or effect of Section 754 of the Evidence Code to interpretation for a deaf or hard-of-hearing party or witness in an adjudicative proceeding. *(Added by Stats.1995, c. 938 (S.B.523), § 21, operative July 1, 1997.)*

Law Revision Commission Comments

Section 11435.10 makes clear that the language assistance provisions of this article are not intended to limit the application of Evidence Code Section 754 in adjudicative proceedings. [25 Cal.L.Rev.Comm. Reports 55 (1995)].

Research References

9 Witkin Cal. Proc. 5th Administrative Proceedings § 77, Language Assistance.

§ 11435.15. State agencies providing language assistance

(a) The following state agencies shall provide language assistance in adjudicative proceedings to the extent provided in this article:

(1) Agricultural Labor Relations Board.

(2) State Department of Alcohol and Drug * * * Programs.

(3) State Athletic Commission.

(4) California Unemployment Insurance Appeals Board.

(5) Board of * * * Parole Hearings.

(6) State Board of Barbering and Cosmetology.

(7) State Department of Developmental Services.

(8) Public Employment Relations Board.

(9) Franchise Tax Board.

(10) State Department of Health Care Services.

(11) Department of Housing and Community Development.

(12) Department of Industrial Relations.

(13) State Department of State Hospitals.

(14) Department of Motor Vehicles.

(15) Notary Public Section, Office of the Secretary of State.

(16) Public Utilities Commission.

(17) Office of Statewide Health Planning and Development.

(18) State Department of Social Services.

(19) Workers' Compensation Appeals Board.

* * *

Government

(20) Division of Juvenile Justice.

(21) Division of Juvenile Parole Operations.

(22) Department of Insurance.

(23) State Personnel Board.

(24) California Board of Podiatric Medicine.

(25) Board of Psychology.

(b) Nothing in this section prevents an agency other than an agency listed in subdivision (a) from electing to adopt any of the procedures in this article, provided that any selection of an interpreter is subject to Section 11435.30.

(c) Nothing in this section prohibits an agency from providing an interpreter during a proceeding to which this chapter does not apply, including an informal factfinding or informal investigatory hearing.

(d) This article applies to an agency listed in subdivision (a) notwithstanding a general provision that this chapter does not apply to some or all of an agency's adjudicative proceedings. *(Added by Stats.1995, c. 938 (S.B.523), § 21, operative July 1, 1997. Amended by Stats.1996, c. 390 (S.B.794), § 9, eff. Aug. 19, 1996, operative July 1, 1997; Stats.2012, c. 440 (A.B.1488), § 11, eff. Sept. 22, 2012; Stats.2013, c. 76 (A.B.383), § 82.)*

Law Revision Commission Comments

Subdivisions (a) and (b) of Section 11435.15 restate former Section 11501.5. Subdivision (c) restates a portion of former subdivision (f) of Section 11500. Subdivision (d) is added to make clear that even though this chapter does not otherwise apply to a hearing, the hearing is not exempt from the requirements of this article if the agency is listed in this section.

The application of this article is limited to adjudicative proceedings in which, under the federal or state constitution or a federal or state statute, an evidentiary hearing for determination of facts is required for formulation and issuance of a decision. Section 11410.10. This continues the general effect of the first paragraph of former subdivision (f) of Section 11500 ("adjudicatory hearing" defined).

In addition to the proceedings listed in this section, language assistance is also required of state agencies whose hearings are not governed by Chapter 5. Section 11018. [25 Cal.L.Rev.Comm. Reports 55 (1995)].

Section 11435.15 is amended to correct a printing error. [26 Cal.L.Rev. Comm. Reports 107 (1996) (App. 4)].

Research References

9 Witkin Cal. Proc. 5th Administrative Proceedings § 77, Language Assistance.

§ 11435.20. Hearings or medical examinations; English language required

(a) The hearing, or any medical examination conducted for the purpose of determining compensation or monetary award, shall be conducted in English.

(b) If a party or the party's witness does not proficiently speak or understand English and before commencement of the hearing or medical examination requests language assistance, an agency subject to the language assistance requirement of this article shall provide the party or witness an interpreter. *(Added by Stats.1995, c. 938 (S.B.523), § 21, operative July 1, 1997.)*

Law Revision Commission Comments

Section 11435.20 continues the first sentence of former subdivision (d) of Section 11513 and extends it to witnesses as well as parties. See Section 11435.05 ("language assistance" defined). [25 Cal.L.Rev.Comm. Reports 55 (1995)].

Research References

9 Witkin Cal. Proc. 5th Administrative Proceedings § 77, Language Assistance.

§ 11435.25. Cost of interpreters; payment; workers' compensation proceedings

(a) The cost of providing an interpreter under this article shall be paid by the agency having jurisdiction over the matter if the presiding officer so directs, otherwise by the party at whose request the interpreter is provided.

(b) The presiding officer's decision to direct payment shall be based upon an equitable consideration of all the circumstances in each case, such as the ability of the party in need of the interpreter to pay.

(c) Notwithstanding any other provision of this section, in a hearing before the Workers' Compensation Appeals Board or the Division of Workers' Compensation relating to workers' compensation claims, the payment of the costs of providing an interpreter shall be governed by the rules and regulations promulgated by the Workers' Compensation Appeals Board or the Administrative Director of the Division of Workers' Compensation, as appropriate. *(Added by Stats.1995, c. 938 (S.B. 523), § 21, operative July 1, 1997.)*

Law Revision Commission Comments

Section 11435.25 continues the fourth sentence and the second paragraph of former subdivision (d) of Section 11513 without substantive change. [25 Cal.L.Rev.Comm. Reports 55 (1995)].

Research References

9 Witkin Cal. Proc. 5th Administrative Proceedings § 77, Language Assistance.

§ 11435.30. Certified administrative hearing interpreters; annual list; court interpreters

(a) The State Personnel Board shall establish, maintain, administer, and publish annually an updated list of certified administrative hearing interpreters it has determined meet the minimum standards in interpreting skills and linguistic abilities in languages designated pursuant to Section 11435.40. Any interpreter so listed may be examined by each employing agency to determine the interpreter's knowledge of the employing agency's technical program terminology and procedures.

(b) Court interpreters certified pursuant to Section 68562, and interpreters listed on the State Personnel Board's recommended lists of court and administrative hearing interpreters prior to July 1, 1993, shall be deemed certified for purposes of this section.

(c)(1) In addition to the certification procedure provided pursuant to subdivision (a), the Administrative Director of the Division of Workers' Compensation may establish, maintain, administer, and publish annually an updated list of certified administrative hearing interpreters who, based on testing by an independent organization designated by the administrative director, have been determined to meet the minimum standards in interpreting skills and linguistic abilities in languages designated pursuant to Section 11435.40, for purposes of administrative hearings conducted pursuant to proceedings of the Workers' Compensation Appeals Board. The independent testing organization shall have no financial interest in the training of interpreters or in the employment of interpreters for administrative hearings.

(2)(A) A fee, as determined by the administrative director, shall be collected from each interpreter seeking certification. The fee shall not exceed the reasonable regulatory costs of administering the testing and certification program and of publishing the list of certified administrative hearing interpreters on the Division of Workers' Compensation' Internet Web site.

(B) The Legislature finds and declares that the services described in this section are of such a special and unique nature that they may be contracted out pursuant to paragraph (3) of subdivision (b) of Section 19130. The Legislature further finds and declares that the services described in this section are a new state function pursuant to paragraph (2) of subdivision (b) of Section 19130. *(Added by Stats.1995, c. 938 (S.B.523), § 21, operative July 1, 1997. Amended by Stats.2012, c. 363 (S.B.863), § 2.)*

Research References

9 Witkin Cal. Proc. 5th Administrative Proceedings § 77, Language Assistance.

§ 11435.35. Certified medical examination interpreters; annual list; court interpreters

(a) The State Personnel Board shall establish, maintain, administer, and publish annually, an updated list of certified medical examination interpreters it has determined meet the minimum standards in interpreting skills and linguistic abilities in languages designated pursuant to Section 11435.40.

(b) Court interpreters certified pursuant to Section 68562 and administrative hearing interpreters certified pursuant to Section 11435.30 shall be deemed certified for purposes of this section.

(c)(1) In addition to the certification procedure provided pursuant to subdivision (a), the Administrative Director of the Division of Workers' Compensation may establish, maintain, administer, and publish annually an updated list of certified medical examination interpreters who, based on testing by an independent organization designated by the administrative director, have been determined to meet the minimum standards in interpreting skills and linguistic abilities in languages designated pursuant to Section 11435.40, for purposes of medical examinations conducted pursuant to proceedings of the Workers' Compensation Appeals Board, and medical examinations conducted pursuant to Division 4 (commencing with Section 3200) of the Labor Code. The independent testing organization shall have no financial interest in the training of interpreters or in the employment of interpreters for * * * <u>medical examinations.</u>

(2)(A) A fee, as determined by the administrative director, shall be collected from each interpreter seeking certification. The fee shall not exceed the reasonable regulatory costs of administering the testing and certification program and of publishing the list of certified medical examination interpreters on the Division of Workers' Compensation's Internet Web site.

(B) The Legislature finds and declares that the services described in this section are of such a special and unique nature that they may be contracted out pursuant to paragraph (3) of subdivision (b) of Section 19130. The Legislature further finds and declares that the services described in this section are a new state function pursuant to paragraph (2) of subdivision (b) of Section 19130. *(Added by Stats.1995, c. 938 (S.B.523), § 21, operative July 1, 1997. Amended by Stats.2012, c. 363 (S.B.863), § 3; Stats.2013, c. 287 (S.B.375), § 1.)*

Research References

9 Witkin Cal. Proc. 5th Administrative Proceedings § 77, Language Assistance.

§ 11435.40. Certification; languages

(a) The Department of Human Resources shall designate the languages for which certification shall be established under Sections 11435.30 and 11435.35. The languages designated shall include, but not be limited to, Spanish, Tagalog, Arabic, Cantonese, Japanese, Korean, Portuguese, and Vietnamese until the Department of Human Resources finds that there is an insufficient need for interpreting assistance in these languages.

(b) The language designations shall be based on the following:

(1) The language needs of non–English-speaking persons appearing before the administrative agencies, as determined by consultation with the agencies.

(2) The cost of developing a language examination.

(3) The availability of experts needed to develop a language examination.

(4) Other information the department deems relevant. *(Added by Stats.1995, c. 938 (S.B.523), § 21, operative July 1, 1997. Amended by Stats.2012, c. 360 (S.B.1309), § 6.)*

Research References

9 Witkin Cal. Proc. 5th Administrative Proceedings § 77, Language Assistance.

§ 11435.45. Fees; interpreter examinations; certificate renewal

(a) The Department of Human Resources shall establish and charge fees for applications to take interpreter examinations and for renewal of certifications. The purpose of these fees is to cover the annual projected costs of carrying out this article. The fees may be adjusted each fiscal year by a percent that is equal to or less than the percent change in the California Necessities Index prepared by the Commission on State Finance.

(b) Each certified administrative hearing interpreter and each certified medical examination interpreter shall pay a fee, due on July 1 of each year, for the renewal of the certification. Court interpreters certified under Section 68562 shall not pay any fees required by this section.

(c) If the amount of money collected in fees is not sufficient to cover the costs of carrying out this article, the department shall charge and be reimbursed a pro rata share of the additional costs by the state agencies that conduct administrative hearings. *(Added by Stats.1995, c. 938 (S.B.523), § 21, operative July 1, 1997. Amended by Stats.2012, c. 360 (S.B.1309), § 7.)*

Research References

9 Witkin Cal. Proc. 5th Administrative Proceedings § 77, Language Assistance.

§ 11435.50. Removal of name from list of certified interpreters; grounds

The Department of Human Resources may remove the name of a person from the list of certified interpreters if any of the following conditions occurs:

Government

(a) The person is deceased.

(b) The person notifies the department that the person is unavailable for work.

(c) The person does not submit a renewal fee as required by Section 11435. 45. *(Added by Stats.1995, c. 938 (S.B.523), § 21, operative July 1, 1997. Amended by Stats.2012, c. 360 (S.B.1309), § 8.)*

Law Revision Commission Comments

Section 11435.50 continues former subdivision (j) of Section 11513 without substantive change. [25 Cal.L.Rev.Comm. Reports 55 (1995)].

Research References

9 Witkin Cal. Proc. 5th Administrative Proceedings § 77, Language Assistance.

§ 11435.55. Certification requirement; use of noncertified interpreters

(a) An interpreter used in a hearing shall be certified pursuant to Section 11435.30. However, if an interpreter certified pursuant to Section 11435.30 cannot be present at the hearing, the hearing agency shall have discretionary authority to provisionally qualify and use another interpreter.

(b) An interpreter used in a medical examination shall be certified pursuant to Section 11435.35. However, if an interpreter certified pursuant to Section 11435.35 cannot be present at the medical examination, the physician provisionally may use another interpreter if that fact is noted in the record of the medical evaluation. *(Added by Stats.1995, c. 938 (S.B.523), § 21, operative July 1, 1997.)*

Law Revision Commission Comments

Section 11435.55 continues the second and third sentences of former subdivision (d) and former subdivision (k) of Section 11513 without substantive change. [25 Cal.L.Rev.Comm. Reports 55 (1995)].

Research References

9 Witkin Cal. Proc. 5th Administrative Proceedings § 77, Language Assistance.

§ 11435.60. Notice of right to interpreter

Every agency subject to the language assistance requirement of this article shall advise each party of the right to an interpreter at the same time that each party is advised of the hearing date or medical examination. Each party in need of an interpreter shall also be encouraged to give timely notice to the agency conducting the hearing or medical examination so that appropriate arrangements can be made. *(Added by Stats.1995, c. 938 (S.B.523), § 21, operative July 1, 1997.)*

Law Revision Commission Comments

Section 11435.60 continues former subdivision (*l*) of Section 11513 without substantive change. [25 Cal.L.Rev.Comm. Reports 55 (1995)].

Research References

9 Witkin Cal. Proc. 5th Administrative Proceedings § 77, Language Assistance.

§ 11435.65. Confidentiality; interest of interpreter

(a) The rules of confidentiality of the agency, if any, that apply in an adjudicative proceeding shall apply to any interpreter in the hearing or medical examination, whether or not the rules so state.

(b) The interpreter shall not have had any involvement in the issues of the case prior to the hearing. *(Added by Stats.1995, c. 938 (S.B.523), § 21, operative July 1, 1997.)*

Law Revision Commission Comments

Section 11435.65 continues former subdivisions (m) and (n) of Section 11513 without substantive change. [25 Cal.L.Rev.Comm. Reports 55 (1995)].

Research References

9 Witkin Cal. Proc. 5th Administrative Proceedings § 77, Language Assistance.

ARTICLE 9. GENERAL PROCEDURAL PROVISIONS

Section

§ 11440.10. Authority of agency head following decision

(a) The agency head may do any of the following with respect to a decision of the presiding officer or the agency:

(1) Determine to review some but not all issues, or not to exercise any review.

(2) Delegate its review authority to one or more persons.

(3) Authorize review by one or more persons, subject to further review by the agency head.

(b) By regulation an agency may mandate review, or may preclude or limit review, of a decision of the presiding officer or the agency. *(Added by Stats.1995, c. 938 (S.B.523), § 21, operative July 1, 1997.)*

Law Revision Commission Comments

Section 11440.10 is drawn from Section 11500(a) (power to act may be delegated by agency) and 1981 Model State APA § 4–216(a)(1)–(2). This section is subject to a contrary statute that may, for example, require the agency head itself to hear and decide a specific issue. Section 11415.20 (conflicting or inconsistent statute controls). See, e.g., Greer v. Board of Educ., 47 Cal.App.3d 98, 121 Cal.Rptr. 542 (1975) (school board, rather than hearing officer, formerly required to determine issues under Educ.Code § 13443). See also Section 11500(a) (power to act may not be delegated where action required by "agency itself" under formal hearing procedure). [25 Cal.L.Rev.Comm. Reports 55 (1995)].

Research References

9 Witkin Cal. Proc. 5th Administrative Proceedings § 66, Optional and Mandatory Provisions.
9 Witkin Cal. Proc. 5th Administrative Proceedings § 95, (S 95) Administrative Review.

§ 11440.20. Service; notice

Service of a writing on, or giving of a notice to, a person in a procedure provided in this chapter is subject to the following provisions:

(a) The writing or notice shall be delivered personally or sent by mail or other means to the person at the person's last known address or, if the person is a party with an attorney or other authorized representative of record in the proceeding, to the party's attorney or other authorized representative. If a party is required by statute or regulation to maintain an address with an agency, the party's last known address is the address maintained with the agency.

(b) Unless a provision specifies the form of mail, service or notice by mail may be by first-class mail, registered mail, or certified mail, by mail delivery service, by facsimile transmission if complete and without error, or by other electronic means as provided by regulation, in the discretion of the sender. *(Added by Stats.1995, c. 938 (S.B.523), § 21, operative July 1, 1997.)*

Law Revision Commission Comments

The application of Section 11440.20 is limited to the procedures in this chapter. It does not apply to Chapter 5 (formal hearing), which includes its own notice and service provisions. See Section 11505.

Subdivision (b) authorizes delivery by a commercial delivery service as well as by the United States Postal Service. Proof of service under subdivision (b) may be made by any appropriate method, including proof in the manner provided for civil actions and proceedings. See Code Civ.Proc. § 1013a; Cal.R.Ct. 2008(e) (proof of service by facsimile transmission). [25 Cal.L.Rev.Comm. Reports 55 (1995)].

Research References

9 Witkin Cal. Proc. 5th Administrative Proceedings § 66, Optional and Mandatory Provisions.
9 Witkin Cal. Proc. 5th Administrative Proceedings § 88, (S 88) Service and Notice.

§ 11440.30. Conduct of hearing by electronic means

(a) The presiding officer may conduct all or part of a hearing by telephone, television, or other electronic means if each participant in the hearing has an opportunity to participate in and to hear the entire proceeding while it is taking place and to observe exhibits.

(b) The presiding officer may not conduct all or part of a hearing by telephone, television, or other electronic means if a party objects. *(Added by Stats.1995, c. 938 (S.B.523), § 21, operative July 1, 1997.)*

Law Revision Commission Comments

Subdivision (a) of Section 11440.30 is drawn from 1981 Model State APA § 4–211(4), allowing the presiding officer to conduct all or part of the hearing by telephone, television, or other electronic means, such as a conference telephone call. The opportunity to observe exhibits includes a reasonable opportunity to examine and object to exhibits before or at the hearing. While subdivision (a) permits the conduct of proceedings by telephone, television, or other electronic means, the presiding officer may of course conduct the proceeding in the physical presence of all participants. [25 Cal.L.Rev.Comm. Reports 55 (1995)].

Research References

California Practice Guide: Employment Litigation Ch. 13-H, H. Contesting Citations and Related Orders and Notices.
9 Witkin Cal. Proc. 5th Administrative Proceedings § 66, Optional and Mandatory Provisions.
9 Witkin Cal. Proc. 5th Administrative Proceedings § 92, (S 92) Hearing by Electronic Means.

§ 11440.40. Sexual harassment, sexual assault or sexual battery; evidence

(a) In any proceeding under subdivision (h) or (i) of Section 12940, or Section 19572 or 19702, alleging conduct that constitutes sexual harassment, sexual assault, or sexual battery, evidence of specific instances of a complainant's sexual conduct with individuals other than the alleged perpetrator is subject to all of the following limitations:

(1) The evidence is not discoverable unless it is to be offered at a hearing to attack the credibility of the complainant as provided for under subdivision (b). This paragraph is intended only to limit the scope of discovery; it is not intended to affect the methods of discovery allowed by statute.

(2) The evidence is not admissible at the hearing unless offered to attack the credibility of the complainant as provided for under subdivision (b). Reputation or opinion evidence regarding the sexual behavior of the complainant is not admissible for any purpose.

(b) Evidence of specific instances of a complainant's sexual conduct with individuals other than the alleged perpetrator is presumed inadmissible absent an offer of proof establishing its relevance and reliability and that its probative value is not substantially outweighed by the probability that its admission will create substantial danger of undue prejudice or confuse the issue.

(c) As used in this section "complainant" means a person claiming to have been subjected to conduct that constitutes sexual harassment, sexual assault, or sexual battery. *(Added by Stats.1995, c. 938 (S.B.523), § 21, operative July 1, 1997.)*

Law Revision Commission Comments

Section 11440.40 expands the application of provisions formerly limited to proceedings under Chapter 5 (commencing with Section 11500) to apply in all cases covered by this chapter. Subdivision (a) restates former subdivision (g) of Section 11507.6 and the unnumbered paragraph formerly located between subdivisions (c) and (d) of Section 11513, correcting the reference to Section 12940(h) and (i). Subdivision (b) restates former subdivision (o) of Section 11513. Subdivision (c) restates former subdivision (p) of Section 11513. [25 Cal.L.Rev.Comm. Reports 55 (1995)].

Research References

9 Witkin Cal. Proc. 5th Administrative Proceedings § 66, Optional and Mandatory Provisions.
9 Witkin Cal. Proc. 5th Administrative Proceedings § 93, (S 93) Specific Evidentiary Rules.

§ 11440.45. Admissibility of expressions of sympathy or benevolence; definitions

(a) In any proceedings pursuant to this chapter or Chapter 5 (commencing with Section 11500), the portion of statements, writings, or benevolent gestures expressing sympathy or a general sense of benevolence relating to the pain, suffering, or death of a person involved in an accident and made to that person or to the family of that person shall be inadmissible as evidence of an admission of liability. A statement of fault, however, which is part of, or in addition to, any of the above shall not be inadmissible pursuant to this section.

(b) For purposes of this section:

(1) "Accident" means an occurrence resulting in injury or death to one or more persons which is not the result of willful action by a party.

(2) "Benevolent gestures" means actions which convey a sense of compassion or commiseration emanating from humane impulses.

(3) "Family" means the spouse, parent, grandparent, stepmother, stepfather, child, grandchild, brother, sister, half brother, half sister, adopted children of parent, or spouse's parents of an injured party. *(Added by Stats.2002, c. 92 (A.B.2723), § 1.)*

Research References

9 Witkin Cal. Proc. 5th Administrative Proceedings § 93, (S 93) Specific Evidentiary Rules.

§ 11440.50. Intervention

(a) This section applies in adjudicative proceedings of an agency if the agency by regulation provides that this section is applicable in the proceedings.

(b) The presiding officer shall grant a motion for intervention if all of the following conditions are satisfied:

(1) The motion is submitted in writing, with copies served on all parties named in the agency's pleading.

(2) The motion is made as early as practicable in advance of the hearing. If there is a prehearing conference, the motion shall be made in advance of the prehearing conference and shall be resolved at the prehearing conference.

(3) The motion states facts demonstrating that the applicant's legal rights, duties, privileges, or immunities will be substantially affected by the proceeding or that the applicant qualifies as an intervenor under a statute or regulation.

(4) The presiding officer determines that the interests of justice and the orderly and prompt conduct of the proceeding will not be impaired by allowing the intervention.

(c) If an applicant qualifies for intervention, the presiding officer may impose conditions on the intervenor's participation in the proceeding, either at the time that intervention is granted or at a subsequent time. Conditions may include the following:

(1) Limiting the intervenor's participation to designated issues in which the intervenor has a particular interest demonstrated by the motion.

(2) Limiting or excluding the use of discovery, cross-examination, and other procedures involving the intervenor so as to promote the orderly and prompt conduct of the proceeding.

(3) Requiring two or more intervenors to combine their presentations of evidence and argument, cross-examination, discovery, and other participation in the proceeding.

(4) Limiting or excluding the intervenor's participation in settlement negotiations.

(d) As early as practicable in advance of the hearing the presiding officer shall issue an order granting or denying the motion for intervention, specifying any conditions, and briefly stating the reasons for the order. The presiding officer may modify the order at any time, stating the reasons for the modification. The presiding officer shall promptly give notice of an order granting, denying, or modifying intervention to the applicant and to all parties.

(e) Whether the interests of justice and the orderly and prompt conduct of the proceedings will be impaired by allowing intervention is a determination to be made in the sole discretion, and based on the knowledge and judgment at that time, of the presiding officer. The determination is not subject to administrative or judicial review.

(f) Nothing in this section precludes an agency from adopting a regulation that permits participation by a person short of intervention as a party, subject to Article 7 (commencing with Section 11430.10) of Chapter 4.5. *(Added by Stats.1995, c. 938 (S.B.523), § 21, operative July 1, 1997.)*

Law Revision Commission Comments

Subdivision (a) of Section 11440.50 makes clear that this section does not apply to a proceeding unless an agency has acted to make it applicable. This section provides an optional means by which an agency can provide for intervention. This section does not provide an exclusive intervention procedure, and an agency may adopt other intervention rules or may preclude intervention entirely, subject to due process limitations.

Subdivision (b)(1) is drawn from 1981 Model State APA § 4–209(a). It provides that the presiding officer must grant the motion to intervene if a party satisfies the standards of the section. Subdivision (b)(3) confers standing on an applicant to intervene on demonstrating that the applicant's "legal rights, duties, privileges, or immunities will be substantially affected by the proceeding." This provision is not intended to permit intervention by a person such as a victim or interest group whose legal rights are not affected by the proceeding, but to permit intervention only by a person who has a legal right entitled to protection by due process of law that will be substantially impaired by the proceeding. *Cf.* Horn v. County of Ventura, 24 Cal.3d 605, 596 P.2d 1134, 156 Cal.Rptr. 718 (1979) (right to notice and hearing if agency action will constitute substantial deprivation of property rights). However, subdivision (b)(4) imposes the further limitation that the presiding officer may grant the

motion for intervention only on determining that "the interests of justice and the orderly and prompt conduct of the proceeding will not be impaired by allowing the intervention." The presiding officer is thus required to weigh the impact that the proceeding will have on the legal rights of the applicant for intervention (subdivision (b)(3)) against the interests of justice and the need for orderly and prompt proceedings (subdivision (b)(4)).

Subdivision (c) is drawn from 1981 Model State APA § 4–209(c). This provision, authorizing the presiding officer to impose conditions on the intervenor's participation in the proceeding, is intended to permit the presiding officer to facilitate reasonable involvement of intervenors without subjecting the proceeding to unreasonably burdensome or repetitious presentations.

Subdivision (d) is drawn from 1981 Model State APA § 4–209(d). By requiring advance notice of the presiding officer's order granting, denying, or modifying intervention, this provision is intended to give the parties and the applicants for intervention an opportunity to prepare for the adjudicative proceeding.

Subdivision (f) recognizes that there are ways whereby an interested person can have an impact on an ongoing adjudication without assuming the substantial litigation costs of becoming a party and without unnecessarily complicating the proceeding through the addition of more parties. Agency regulations may provide, for example, for filing of amicus briefs, testifying as a witness, or contributing to the fees of a party. [25 Cal.L.Rev.Comm. Reports 711 (1995)].

Research References

9 Witkin Cal. Proc. 5th Administrative Proceedings § 66, Optional and Mandatory Provisions.
9 Witkin Cal. Proc. 5th Administrative Proceedings § 91, (S 91) Intervention.

§ 11440.60. Written communications in quasi–judicial proceedings; indication of person who paid to produce document or client on whose behalf communication is submitted

(a) For purposes of this section, the following terms have the following meaning:

(1) "Quasi–judicial proceeding" means any of the following:

(A) A proceeding to determine the rights or duties of a person under existing laws, regulations, or policies.

(B) A proceeding involving the issuance, amendment, or revocation of a permit or license.

(C) A proceeding to enforce compliance with existing law or to impose sanctions for violations of existing law.

(D) A proceeding at which action is taken involving the purchase or sale of property, goods, or services by an agency.

(E) A proceeding at which an action is taken awarding a grant or a contract.

(2) "Written communication" means any report, study, survey, analysis, letter, or any other written document.

(b) Any person submitting a written communication, which is specifically generated for the purpose of being presented at the agency hearing to which it is being communicated, to a state agency in a quasi-judicial proceeding that is directly paid for by anyone other than the person who submitted the written communication shall clearly indicate any person who paid to produce the written communication.

(c) A state agency may refuse or ignore a written communication submitted by an attorney or any other authorized representative on behalf of a client in a quasi-judicial proceeding, unless the written communication clearly indicates the client on whose behalf the communication is submitted to the state agency. *(Added by Stats.1997, c. 192 (S.B.504), § 1.)*

Research References

9 Witkin Cal. Proc. 5th Administrative Proceedings § 90, (S 90) Client Identification.

ARTICLE 10. INFORMAL HEARING

Section

11445.10.   Informal hearing procedure; legislative findings and declarations.

11445.20.   Proceedings.

11445.30.   Notice of hearing; objection.

11445.40.   Hearing procedures applicable; authority of presiding officer.

11445.50.   Denial of use of informal hearing procedure; cross examination; judicial review.

11445.60.   Material facts in dispute; presentation of proof.

§ 11445.10. Informal hearing procedure; legislative findings and declarations

(a) Subject to the limitations in this article, an agency may conduct an adjudicative proceeding under the informal hearing procedure provided in this article.

(b) The Legislature finds and declares the following:

(1) The informal hearing procedure is intended to satisfy due process and public policy requirements in a manner that is simpler and more expeditious than hearing procedures otherwise required by statute, for use in appropriate circumstances.

(2) The informal hearing procedure provides a forum in the nature of a conference in which a party has an opportunity to be heard by the presiding officer.

(3) The informal hearing procedure provides a forum that may accommodate a hearing where by regulation or statute a member of the public may participate without appearing or intervening as a party. *(Added by Stats.1995, c. 938 (S.B.523), § 21, operative July 1, 1997.)*

Law Revision Commission Comments

Section 11445.10 states the policy that underlies the informal hearing procedure. The circumstances where the simplified procedure is appropriate are provided in Section 11445.20 (when informal hearing may be used). The simplified procedures are outlined in Section 11445.40 (procedure for informal hearing).

Basic due process and public policy protections of the administrative adjudication bill of rights are preserved in the informal hearing. Sections 11445.40(a) (procedure for informal hearing), 11425.10 (administrative adjudication bill of rights). Thus, for example, the presiding officer must be free of bias, prejudice, and interest; the presiding officer must be neutral, the adjudicative function being separated from the investigative, prosecutorial, and advocacy functions within the agency; the hearing must be open to public observation; the agency must make available language assistance; ex parte communications are restricted; the decision must be in writing, be based on the record, and include a statement of the factual and legal basis of the decision; and the agency must designate and index significant decisions as precedent.

Reference in this article to the "presiding officer" is not intended to imply unnecessary formality in the proceeding. The presiding officer may be the agency head, an agency member, an administrative law judge, or another person who presides over the hearing. Section 11405.80 ("presiding officer" defined).

It should be noted that a decision made pursuant to the informal hearing procedure is subject to judicial review to the same extent and in the same manner as a decision made pursuant to a formal hearing procedure. See, e.g., Code Civ. Proc. § 1094.5(a) (administrative mandamus for decisions "made as the result of a proceeding in which by law a hearing is required to be given, evidence is required to be taken, and discretion in the determination of facts is vested in the [agency]"; see also Sections 11445.40 (procedure for informal hearing) and 11410.10 ("This chapter applies to a decision by an agency if, under the federal or state Constitution or a federal or state statute, an evidentiary hearing for

determination of facts is required for formulation and issuance of the decision.") [25 Cal.L.Rev.Comm. Reports 711 (1995)].

Research References

9 Witkin Cal. Proc. 5th Administrative Proceedings § 66, Optional and Mandatory Provisions.

9 Witkin Cal. Proc. 5th Administrative Proceedings § 78, (S 78) in General.

9 Witkin Cal. Proc. 5th Administrative Proceedings § 79, (S 79) Procedure.

9 Witkin Cal. Proc. 5th Administrative Proceedings § 104, (S 104) Prehearing Conference.

§ 11445.20. Proceedings

Subject to Section 11445.30, an agency may use an informal hearing procedure in any of the following proceedings, if in the circumstances its use does not violate another statute or the federal or state Constitution:

(a) A proceeding where there is no disputed issue of material fact.

(b) A proceeding where there is a disputed issue of material fact, if the matter is limited to any of the following:

(1) A monetary amount of not more than one thousand dollars ($1,000).

(2) A disciplinary sanction against a student that does not involve expulsion from an academic institution or suspension for more than 10 days.

(3) A disciplinary sanction against an employee that does not involve discharge from employment, demotion, or suspension for more than 5 days.

(4) A disciplinary sanction against a licensee that does not involve an actual revocation of a license or an actual suspension of a license for more than five days. Nothing in this section precludes an agency from imposing a stayed revocation or a stayed suspension of a license in an informal hearing.

(c) A proceeding where, by regulation, the agency has authorized use of an informal hearing.

(d) A proceeding where an evidentiary hearing for determination of facts is not required by statute but where the agency determines the federal or state Constitution may require a hearing. *(Added by Stats.1995, c. 938 (S.B.523), § 21, operative July 1, 1997.)*

Law Revision Commission Comments

Subdivision (a) of Section 11445.20 permits the informal hearing to be used, regardless of the type or amount at issue, if no disputed issue of material fact has appeared, e.g., a power plant siting proceeding in which the power company and the Energy Commission have agreed on all material facts. However, if consumers intervene and dispute material facts, the proceeding may be subject to conversion from an informal hearing procedure to a formal or other type of hearing procedure in accordance with Sections 11470.10–11470.50.

Subdivision (b) permits the informal hearing to be used, even if a disputed issue of material fact has appeared, where the amount or other stake involved is relatively minor. The reference to a "licensee" in subdivision (b)(4) includes a certificate holder. Under subdivision (b), an informal hearing procedure may be used if the sanction imposed in the decision falls within the limitations of the subdivision, even though a greater penalty may result if a party fails to comply with the sanction imposed in the decision.

Subdivision (c) imposes no limits on the authority of the agency to adopt the informal hearing by regulation, other than the general limitation that use of the informal hearing procedure is subject to statutory and constitutional due process requirements. Thus, an agency by regulation may authorize use of the informal hearing procedure in a case where the amount in issue or sanction exceeds the amount provided in subdivision (b), so long as use of the informal hearing procedure would not contravene other statutes or due process of law.

Each subdivision in this section provides an independent basis for conducting an informal hearing. For example, if there is no issue of material fact, an agency may conduct an informal hearing under subdivision (a) whether or not a disciplinary sanction that exceeds the limits of subdivision (b) may result from the hearing.

Nothing in this section implies that this procedure is required in a proceeding in which a hearing is not statutorily or constitutionally required, including an agency's authority in minor disciplinary matters to make an investigation with or without a hearing as it deems necessary. Sections 11410.10 (application to constitutionally and statutorily required hearings), 11415.50 (when adjudicative proceeding not required). [25 Cal.L.Rev.Comm. Reports 711 (1995)].

Research References

9 Witkin Cal. Proc. 5th Administrative Proceedings § 78, (S 78) in General.

§ 11445.30.   Notice of hearing; objection

(a) The notice of hearing shall state the agency's selection of the informal hearing procedure.

(b) Any objection of a party to use of the informal hearing procedure shall be made in the party's pleading.

(c) An objection to use of the informal hearing procedure shall be resolved by the presiding officer before the hearing on the basis of the pleadings and any written submissions in support of the pleadings. An objection to use of the informal hearing procedure in a disciplinary proceeding involving an occupational license shall be resolved in favor of the licensee. *(Added by Stats.1995, c. 938 (S.B.523), § 21, operative July 1, 1997.)*

Law Revision Commission Comments

Section 11445.30 provides a procedure for resolving objections to use of the informal hearing procedure in advance of the hearing. See also Section 11511.5 (prehearing conference). However, conversion to a formal hearing or other type of hearing may be appropriate if during the course of the hearing circumstances indicate the need for it. See Sections 11445.50 (cross-examination), 11445.60 (proposed proof). [25 Cal.L.Rev. Comm. Reports 55 (1995)].

Research References

9 Witkin Cal. Proc. 5th Administrative Proceedings § 79, (S 79) Procedure.

§ 11445.40.   Hearing procedures applicable; authority of presiding officer

(a) Except as provided in this article, the hearing procedures otherwise required by statute for an adjudicative proceeding apply to an informal hearing.

(b) In an informal hearing the presiding officer shall regulate the course of the proceeding. The presiding officer shall permit the parties and may permit others to offer written or oral comments on the issues. The presiding officer may limit the use of witnesses, testimony, evidence, and argument, and may limit or eliminate the use of pleadings, intervention, discovery, prehearing conferences, and rebuttal. *(Added by Stats.1995, c. 938 (S.B.523), § 21, operative July 1, 1997.)*

Law Revision Commission Comments

Section 11445.40 is drawn from 1981 Model State APA § 4-402. The section indicates that the informal hearing is a simplified version of a formal hearing. The informal hearing need not have a prehearing conference, discovery, or testimony of anyone other than the parties. However, it is intended to permit agencies to allow public participation where appropriate. Section 11445.10 (purpose of informal hearing procedure). [25 Cal.L.Rev.Comm. Reports 55 (1995)].

Research References

9 Witkin Cal. Proc. 5th Administrative Proceedings § 79, (S 79) Procedure.

§ 11445.50.   Denial of use of informal hearing procedure; cross examination; judicial review

(a) The presiding officer may deny use of the informal hearing procedure, or may convert an informal hearing to a formal hearing after an informal hearing is commenced, if it appears to the presiding officer that cross-examination is necessary for proper determination of the matter and that the delay, burden, or complication due to allowing cross-examination in the informal hearing will be more than minimal.

(b) An agency, by regulation, may specify categories of cases in which cross-examination is deemed not necessary for proper determination of the matter under the informal hearing procedure. The presiding officer may allow cross-examination of witnesses in an informal hearing notwithstanding an agency regulation if it appears to the presiding officer that in the circumstances cross-examination is necessary for proper determination of the matter.

(c) The actions of the presiding officer under this section are not subject to judicial review. *(Added by Stats.1995, c. 938 (S.B.523), § 21, operative July 1, 1997.)*

Law Revision Commission Comments

Subdivision (a) of Section 11445.50 gives the presiding officer discretion to limit availability of the informal hearing in situations where it appears that substantial cross-examination will be necessary. For provisions on conversion, see Sections 11470.10–11470.50.

Subdivision (b) permits an agency to specify types of informal hearings in which cross-examination will be precluded. In recognition of the possibility that on occasion a case may demand cross-examination for proper determination of a matter, the presiding officer has limited authority to depart from the general procedure for cases of that type. [25 Cal.L.Rev.Comm. Reports 55 (1995)].

Research References

9 Witkin Cal. Proc. 5th Administrative Proceedings § 79, (S 79) Procedure.

§ 11445.60.   Material facts in dispute; presentation of proof

(a) If the presiding officer has reason to believe that material facts are in dispute, the presiding officer may require a party to state the identity of the witnesses or other sources through which the party would propose to present proof if the proceeding were converted to a formal or other applicable hearing procedure. If disclosure of a fact, allegation, or source is privileged or expressly prohibited by a regulation, statute, or the federal or state Constitution, the presiding officer may require the party to indicate that confidential facts, allegations, or sources are involved, but not to disclose the confidential facts, allegations, or sources.

(b) If a party has reason to believe that essential facts must be obtained in order to permit an adequate presentation of the case, the party may inform the presiding officer regarding the general nature of the facts and the sources from which the party would propose to obtain the facts if the proceeding were converted to a formal or other applicable hearing procedure. *(Added by Stats.1995, c. 938 (S.B.523), § 21, operative July 1, 1997.)*

Law Revision Commission Comments

Section 11445.60 is drawn from 1981 Model State APA § 4-403. For conversion of proceedings, see Sections 11470.10–11470.50. [25 Cal. L.Rev.Comm. Reports 55 (1995)].

Research References

9 Witkin Cal. Proc. 5th Administrative Proceedings § 79, (S 79) Procedure.

ARTICLE 11. SUBPOENAS

Section

11450.05.   Application of article.
11450.10.   Issuance.
11450.20.   Issuer; service.
11450.30.   Objections; protective orders.
11450.40.   Witnesses; mileage and fees.
11450.50.   Written notice.

§ 11450.05. Application of article

(a) This article applies in an adjudicative proceeding required to be conducted under Chapter 5 (commencing with Section 11500).

(b) An agency may use the subpoena procedure provided in this article in an adjudicative proceeding not required to be conducted under Chapter 5 (commencing with Section 11500), in which case all the provisions of this article apply including, but not limited to, issuance of a subpoena at the request of a party or by the attorney of record for a party under Section 11450.20. *(Added by Stats.1995, c. 938 (S.B.523), § 21, operative July 1, 1997.)*

Law Revision Commission Comments

Subdivision (a) of Section 11450.05 makes clear that the subpoena provisions of this article apply automatically in hearings required to be conducted under Chapter 5. Under subdivision (b), application of the subpoena provisions in other hearings is discretionary with the agency. But if the agency uses the subpoena procedure in other hearings, all provisions of this article apply, including the service and protective provisions, as well as the requirement for issuance of a subpoena on request of a party or by the attorney of record for a party. See Section 11450.20(a) (issuance of subpoena). [25 Cal.L.Rev.Comm. Reports 711 (1995)].

Research References

Miller and Starr California Real Estate § 4:42, Disciplinary Process-- Hearing Procedure.
9 Witkin Cal. Proc. 5th Administrative Proceedings § 66, Optional and Mandatory Provisions.
9 Witkin Cal. Proc. 5th Administrative Proceedings § 89, (S 89) Subpenas.

§ 11450.10. Issuance

(a) Subpoenas and subpoenas duces tecum may be issued for attendance at a hearing and for production of documents at any reasonable time and place or at a hearing.

(b) The custodian of documents that are the subject of a subpoena duces tecum may satisfy the subpoena by delivery of the documents or a copy of the documents, or by making the documents available for inspection or copying, together with an affidavit in compliance with Section 1561 of the Evidence Code. *(Added by Stats.1995, c. 938 (S.B.523), § 21, operative July 1, 1997.)*

Law Revision Commission Comments

Subdivision (a) of Section 11450.10 supersedes a portion of former Section 11510(a). This article gives subpoena power to all adjudicating agencies, presiding officers, and attorneys for parties. See Section 11450.20 (issuance of subpoena). The Coastal Commission previously lacked statutory subpoena power. This section also makes clear that a subpoena duces tecum may be issued to provide documents at any reasonable time and place as well as at the hearing.

Subdivision (b) provides an alternative means of satisfying a subpoena duces tecum without the custodian's appearance. This is analogous to the procedure available in court proceedings. See Code Civ.Proc. § 2020. A custodian of subpoenaed documents who fails to comply with the

subpoena may be compelled to appear and produce the documents. See Section 11455.10 (misconduct in proceeding).

This article incorporates privacy protections from civil practice Section 11450.20(a). [25 Cal.L.Rev.Comm. Reports 55 (1995)].

Research References

9 Witkin Cal. Proc. 5th Administrative Proceedings § 89, (S 89) Subpenas.
7 Witkin Cal. Proc. 5th Trial § 169, Any Judicial Tribunal.

§ 11450.20. Issuer; service

(a) Subpoenas and subpoenas duces tecum shall be issued by the agency or presiding officer at the request of a party, or by the attorney of record for a party, in accordance with Sections 1985 to 1985.4, inclusive, of the Code of Civil Procedure.

(b) The process extends to all parts of the state and shall be served in accordance with Sections 1987 and 1988 of the Code of Civil Procedure. A subpoena or subpoena duces tecum may also be delivered by certified mail return receipt requested or by messenger. Service by messenger shall be effected when the witness acknowledges receipt of the subpoena to the sender, by telephone, by mail, or in person, and identifies himself or herself either by reference to date of birth and driver's license number or Department of Motor Vehicles identification number, or the sender may verify receipt of the subpoena by obtaining other identifying information from the recipient. The sender shall make a written notation of the acknowledgment. A subpoena issued and acknowledged pursuant to this section has the same force and effect as a subpoena personally served. Failure to comply with a subpoena issued and acknowledged pursuant to this section may be punished as a contempt and the subpoena may so state. A party requesting a continuance based upon the failure of a witness to appear at the time and place required for the appearance or testimony pursuant to a subpoena, shall prove that the party has complied with this section. The continuance shall only be granted for a period of time that would allow personal service of the subpoena and in no event longer than that allowed by law.

(c) No witness is obliged to attend unless the witness is a resident of the state at the time of service. *(Added by Stats.1995, c. 938 (S.B.523), § 21, operative July 1, 1997.)*

Law Revision Commission Comments

Section 11450.20 restates a portion of former Section 11510(a)–(b), and expands it to include issuance by an attorney and to incorporate civil practice privacy protections. See Code Civ.Proc. §§ 1985–1985.4. See also Sehlmeyer v. Department of Gen. Serv., 17 Cal.App.4th 1072, 21 Cal.Rptr.2d 840 (1993). For enforcement of a subpoena, see Sections 11455.10–11455.20.

Subdivision (a) requires a subpoena or subpoena duces tecum to be issued in accordance with Sections 1985–1985.4 of the Code of Civil Procedure. For a subpoena duces tecum, this includes the requirement of an affidavit showing good cause for production of the matters and things described in the subpoena. Code Civ.Proc. § 1985. [25 Cal.L.Rev. Comm. Reports 55 (1995)].

Research References

9 Witkin Cal. Proc. 5th Administrative Proceedings § 89, (S 89) Subpenas.

§ 11450.30. Objections; protective orders

(a) A person served with a subpoena or a subpoena duces tecum may object to its terms by a motion for a protective order, including a motion to quash.

(b) The objection shall be resolved by the presiding officer on terms and conditions that the presiding officer declares. The presiding officer may make another order that is appropriate to protect the parties or the witness from unreasonable or oppressive demands, including violations of the right to privacy.

(c) A subpoena or a subpoena duces tecum issued by the agency on its own motion may be quashed by the agency.

(Added by Stats.1995, c. 938 (S.B.523), § 21, operative July 1, 1997.)

Research References

9 Witkin Cal. Proc. 5th Administrative Proceedings § 89, (S 89) Subpenas.

§ 11450.40. Witnesses; mileage and fees

A witness appearing pursuant to a subpoena or a subpoena duces tecum, other than a party, shall receive for the appearance the following mileage and fees, to be paid by the party at whose request the witness is subpoenaed:

(a) The same mileage allowed by law to a witness in a civil case.

(b) The same fees allowed by law to a witness in a civil case. This subdivision does not apply to an officer or employee of the state or a political subdivision of the state. *(Added by Stats.1995, c. 938 (S.B.523), § 21, operative July 1, 1997.)*

Research References

9 Witkin Cal. Proc. 5th Administrative Proceedings § 89, (S 89) Subpenas.

§ 11450.50. Written notice

(a) In the case of the production of a party to the record of a proceeding or of a person for whose benefit a proceeding is prosecuted or defended, the service of a subpoena on the witness is not required if written notice requesting the witness to attend, with the time and place of the hearing, is served on the attorney of the party or person.

(b) Service of written notice to attend under this section shall be made in the manner and is subject to the conditions provided in Section 1987 of the Code of Civil Procedure for service of written notice to attend in a civil action or proceeding. *(Added by Stats.1995, c. 938 (S.B.523), § 21, operative July 1, 1997.)*

Research References

Miller and Starr California Real Estate § 4:42, Disciplinary Process-- Hearing Procedure.
9 Witkin Cal. Proc. 5th Administrative Proceedings § 89, (S 89) Subpenas.

ARTICLE 12. ENFORCEMENT OF ORDERS AND SANCTIONS

Section
11455.10.   Contempt sanction; grounds.
11455.20.   Order to show cause; purge of contempt.
11455.30.   Expenses; attorney fees; review.

§ 11455.10. Contempt sanction; grounds

A person is subject to the contempt sanction for any of the following in an adjudicative proceeding before an agency:

(a) Disobedience of or resistance to a lawful order.

(b) Refusal to take the oath or affirmation as a witness or thereafter refusal to be examined.

(c) Obstruction or interruption of the due course of the proceeding during a hearing or near the place of the hearing by any of the following:

(1) Disorderly, contemptuous, or insolent behavior toward the presiding officer while conducting the proceeding.

(2) Breach of the peace, boisterous conduct, or violent disturbance.

(3) Other unlawful interference with the process or proceedings of the agency.

(d) Violation of the prohibition of ex parte communications under Article 7 (commencing with Section 11430.10).

(e) Failure or refusal, without substantial justification, to comply with a deposition order, discovery request, subpoena, or other order of the presiding officer, or moving, without substantial justification, to compel discovery. *(Added by Stats.1995, c. 938 (S.B.523), § 21, operative July 1, 1997.)*

Research References

9 Witkin Cal. Proc. 5th Administrative Proceedings § 66, Optional and Mandatory Provisions.
9 Witkin Cal. Proc. 5th Administrative Proceedings § 94, (S 94) Sanctions.

§ 11455.20. Order to show cause; purge of contempt

(a) The presiding officer or agency head may certify the facts that justify the contempt sanction against a person to the superior court in and for the county where the proceeding is conducted. The court shall thereupon issue an order directing the person to appear before the court at a specified time and place, and then and there to show cause why the person should not be punished for contempt. The order and a copy of the certified statement shall be served on the person. Upon service of the order and a copy of the certified statement, the court has jurisdiction of the matter.

(b) The same proceedings shall be had, the same penalties may be imposed, and the person charged may purge the contempt in the same way, as in the case of a person who has committed a contempt in the trial of a civil action before a superior court. *(Added by Stats.1995, c. 938 (S.B.523), § 21, operative July 1, 1997.)*

Research References

9 Witkin Cal. Proc. 5th Administrative Proceedings § 94, (S 94) Sanctions.

§ 11455.30. Expenses; attorney fees; review

(a) The presiding officer may order a party, the party's attorney or other authorized representative, or both, to pay reasonable expenses, including attorney's fees, incurred by another party as a result of bad faith actions or tactics that are frivolous or solely intended to cause unnecessary delay as defined in Section 128.5 of the Code of Civil Procedure.

(b) The order, or denial of an order, is subject to judicial review in the same manner as a decision in the proceeding. The order is enforceable in the same manner as a money judgment or by the contempt sanction. *(Added by Stats.1995, c. 938 (S.B. 523), § 21, operative July 1, 1997.)*

Law Revision Commission Comments

Section 11455.30 permits monetary sanctions against a party (including the agency) for bad faith actions or tactics. Bad faith actions or tactics could include failure or refusal to comply with a deposition order, discovery request, subpoena, or other order of the presiding officer in discovery, or moving to compel discovery, frivolously or solely intended to cause delay. A person who requests a hearing without legal grounds would not be subject to sanctions under this section unless the request was made in bad faith and frivolous or solely intended to cause unnecessary delay. An order imposing sanctions (or denial of such an order) is reviewable in the same manner as administrative decisions generally.

For authority to seek the contempt sanction, see Section 11455.20. [25 Cal.L.Rev.Comm. Reports 55 (1995)].

Research References

9 Witkin Cal. Proc. 5th Administrative Proceedings § 94, (S 94) Sanctions.

ARTICLE 13. EMERGENCY DECISION

Section
11460.10. Authority.
11460.20. Emergency decision for temporary, interim relief; regulation.
11460.30. Immediate danger to public health, safety or welfare.
11460.40. Notice and hearing.
11460.50. Emergency decision; contents.
11460.60. Adjudicative proceeding.
11460.70. Agency record.
11460.80. Judicial review.

§ 11460.10. Authority

Subject to the limitations in this article, an agency may conduct an adjudicative proceeding under the emergency decision procedure provided in this article. *(Added by Stats.1995, c. 938 (S.B.523), § 21, operative July 1, 1997.)*

Law Revision Commission Comments

Section 11460.10 makes available an emergency decision procedure for decisions in which an adjudicative proceeding is required. See Section 11410.10 (application to constitutionally and statutorily required hearings). The emergency decision procedure does not apply to an agency decision to seek injunctive relief. See Section 11415.50 (when adjudicative proceeding not required). The decision whether to use the emergency procedure, if available, is in the discretion of the agency.

This article supplements and does not replace other statutes that provide for interim suspension orders or other emergency orders. See Section 11415.10 & Comment (applicable procedure). For other statutes on interim suspension orders and other emergency orders, see Bus. & Prof.Code §§ 494 (order for interim suspension of licensee), 6007(c) (attorney), 10086(a) (real estate licensee); Educ.Code §§ 66017 (immediate suspension of disruptive student, teacher, staff member, or administrator), 94319.12 (emergency suspension of approval of private postsecondary institution to operate); Fin.Code § 8201(f) (immediate removal of officer or employee of savings association); Food & Agric.Code §§ 56535–56537 (farm products licenses); Health and Safety Code §§ 1550.5 (community care facilities), 1569.50 (residential care facilities for the elderly), 1596.886 (child daycare facilities); Pub.Util.Code § 1070.5 (trucking license); Veh.Code § 11706 (DMV licenses of manufacturers, transporters, and dealers). [25 Cal.L.Rev.Comm. Reports 55 (1995)].

Research References

9 Witkin Cal. Proc. 5th Administrative Proceedings § 66, Optional and Mandatory Provisions.
9 Witkin Cal. Proc. 5th Administrative Proceedings § 80, (S 80) in General.
9 Witkin Cal. Proc. 5th Administrative Proceedings § 117, Effect, Enforcement, and Stay.

§ 11460.20. Emergency decision for temporary, interim relief; regulation

(a) An agency may issue an emergency decision for temporary, interim relief under this article if the agency has adopted a regulation that provides that the agency may use the procedure provided in this article.

(b) The regulation shall elaborate the application of the provisions of this article to an emergency decision by the agency, including all of the following:

(1) Define the specific circumstances in which an emergency decision may be issued under this article.

(2) State the nature of the temporary, interim relief that the agency may order.

(3) Prescribe the procedures that will be available before and after issuance of an emergency decision under this article. The procedures may be more protective of the person to which the agency action is directed than those provided in this article.

(c) This article does not apply to an emergency decision, including a cease and desist order or an interim or temporary suspension order, issued pursuant to other express statutory authority. *(Added by Stats.1995, c. 938 (S.B.523), § 21, operative July 1, 1997.)*

Law Revision Commission Comments

Section 11460.20 requires specificity in agency regulations that adopt an emergency decision procedure. Notwithstanding this article, a statute on emergency decisions, including cease and desist orders and interim and temporary suspension orders, applicable to a particular agency or proceeding prevails over the provisions of this article. Section 11415.20 (conflicting or inconsistent statute controls). [25 Cal.L.Rev.Comm. Reports 711 (1995)].

Research References

9 Witkin Cal. Proc. 5th Administrative Proceedings § 80, (S 80) in General.

§ 11460.30. Immediate danger to public health, safety or welfare

(a) An agency may only issue an emergency decision under this article in a situation involving an immediate danger to the public health, safety, or welfare that requires immediate agency action.

(b) An agency may only take action under this article that is necessary to prevent or avoid the immediate danger to the public health, safety, or welfare that justifies issuance of an emergency decision.

(c) An emergency decision issued under this article is limited to temporary, interim relief. The temporary, interim relief is subject to judicial review under Section 11460.80, and the underlying issue giving rise to the temporary, interim relief is subject to an adjudicative proceeding pursuant to Section 11460.60. *(Added by Stats.1995, c. 938 (S.B.523), § 21, operative July 1, 1997.)*

Law Revision Commission Comments

Section 11460.30 is drawn from 1981 Model State APA § 4–501(a)–(b). The emergency decision procedure is available only if the agency has adopted an authorizing regulation. Section 11460.20.

The authority for an emergency decision to avoid immediate danger to the public health, safety, or welfare includes avoiding adverse effects on the environment, such as to fish and wildlife. [25 Cal.L.Rev.Comm. Reports 55 (1995)].

Research References

9 Witkin Cal. Proc. 5th Administrative Proceedings § 80, (S 80) in General.

9 Witkin Cal. Proc. 5th Administrative Proceedings § 81, (S 81) Procedure.

§ 11460.40. Notice and hearing

(a) Before issuing an emergency decision under this article, the agency shall, if practicable, give the person to which the agency action is directed notice and an opportunity to be heard.

(b) Notice and hearing under this section may be oral or written, including notice and hearing by telephone, facsimile transmission, or other electronic means, as the circumstances permit. The hearing may be conducted in the same manner as an informal hearing. *(Added by Stats.1995, c. 938 (S.B.523), § 21, operative July 1, 1997.)*

Law Revision Commission Comments

Section 11460.40 applies to the extent practicable in the circumstances of the particular emergency situation. The agency must use its discretion to determine the extent of the practicability, and give appropriate notice and opportunity to be heard accordingly. For the conduct of a hearing in the manner of an informal hearing, see Section 11445.40 (procedure for informal hearing).

By regulation the agency may prescribe the emergency notice and hearing procedure. *Cf.* Transitional Rules of Procedure of the State Bar, Rules 789–798 (proceedings re involuntary transfer to inactive status upon a finding that the attorney's conduct poses a substantial threat of harm to the public or the attorney's clients). The regulation may be more protective of the person to which the agency action is directed than the provisions of this article. Section 11460.20 (agency regulation required). [25 Cal.L.Rev.Comm. Reports 55 (1995)].

Research References

9 Witkin Cal. Proc. 5th Administrative Proceedings § 81, (S 81) Procedure.

§ 11460.50. Emergency decision; contents

(a) The agency shall issue an emergency decision, including a brief explanation of the factual and legal basis and reasons for the emergency decision, to justify the determination of an immediate danger and the agency's emergency decision to take the specific action.

(b) The agency shall give notice to the extent practicable to the person to which the agency action is directed. The emergency decision is effective when issued or as provided in the decision. *(Added by Stats.1995, c. 938 (S.B.523), § 21, operative July 1, 1997.)*

Law Revision Commission Comments

Section 11460.50 is drawn from 1981 Model State APA § 4–501(c)–(d). Under this section the agency has flexibility to issue its emergency decision orally, if necessary to cope with the emergency. [25 Cal.L.Rev.Comm. Reports 55 (1995)].

Research References

9 Witkin Cal. Proc. 5th Administrative Proceedings § 81, (S 81) Procedure.

§ 11460.60. Adjudicative proceeding

(a) After issuing an emergency decision under this article for temporary, interim relief, the agency shall conduct an adjudicative proceeding under a formal, informal, or other applicable hearing procedure to resolve the underlying issues giving rise to the temporary, interim relief.

(b) The agency shall commence an adjudicative proceeding under another procedure within 10 days after issuing an emergency decision under this article, notwithstanding the pendency of proceedings for judicial review of the emergency decision. *(Added by Stats.1995, c. 938 (S.B.523), § 21, operative July 1, 1997.)*

Law Revision Commission Comments

Section 11460.60 is drawn from 1981 Model State APA § 4–501(e). If the emergency proceedings have rendered the matter completely moot, this section does not direct the agency to conduct useless follow-up proceedings, since these would not be required in the circumstances. [25 Cal.L.Rev.Comm. Reports 55 (1995)].

Research References

9 Witkin Cal. Proc. 5th Administrative Proceedings § 81, (S 81) Procedure.

§ 11460.70. Agency record

The agency record consists of any documents concerning the matter that were considered or prepared by the agency. The agency shall maintain these documents as its official record. *(Added by Stats.1995, c. 938 (S.B.523), § 21, operative July 1, 1997.)*

Law Revision Commission Comments

Section 11460.70 is drawn from 1981 Model State APA § 4–501(f). [25 Cal.L.Rev.Comm. Reports 55 (1995)].

Research References

9 Witkin Cal. Proc. 5th Administrative Proceedings § 81, (S 81) Procedure.

§ 11460.80. Judicial review

(a) On issuance of an emergency decision under this article, the person to which the agency action is directed may obtain judicial review of the decision in the manner provided in this section without exhaustion of administrative remedies.

(b) Judicial review under this section shall be pursuant to Section 1094.5 of the Code of Civil Procedure, subject to the following provisions:

(1) The hearing shall be on the earliest day that the business of the court will admit of, but not later than 15 days after service of the petition on the agency.

(2) Where it is claimed that the findings are not supported by the evidence, abuse of discretion is established if the court determines that the findings are not supported by substantial evidence in the light of the whole record.

(3) A party, on written request to another party, before the proceedings for review and within 10 days after issuance of the emergency decision, is entitled to appropriate discovery.

(4) The relief that may be ordered on judicial review is limited to a stay of the emergency decision. *(Added by Stats.1995, c. 938 (S.B.523), § 21, operative July 1, 1997.)*

Law Revision Commission Comments

Section 11460.80 is drawn from Section 11529(h) (interim suspension of medical care professional). [25 Cal.L.Rev.Comm. Reports 55 (1995)].

Research References

9 Witkin Cal. Proc. 5th Administrative Proceedings § 81, (S 81) Procedure.

ARTICLE 14.   DECLARATORY DECISION

Section

11465.10.   Authority.

§ 11465.10. Authority

Subject to the limitations in this article, an agency may conduct an adjudicative proceeding under the declaratory decision procedure provided in this article. *(Added by Stats.1995, c. 938 (S.B.523), § 21, operative July 1, 1997.)*

Law Revision Commission Comments

Article 14 (commencing with Section 11465.10) creates, and establishes all of the requirements for, a special proceeding to be known as a "declaratory decision" proceeding. The purpose of the proceeding is to provide an inexpensive and generally available means by which a person may obtain fully reliable information as to the applicability of agency administered law to the person's particular circumstances.

The declaratory decision procedure is thus quasi-adjudicative in nature, enabling an agency to issue in effect an advisory opinion concerning assumed facts submitted by a person. The procedure does not authorize an agency "declaration" of a guideline, criterion, bulletin, manual, instruction, order, standard of general application, or other rule that is an "underground regulation." See Section 11340.5.

The declaratory decision procedure provided in this article applies only to decisions subject to this chapter, including a hearing under Chapter 5 (formal hearing). See Sections 11410.50 (application where formal hearing procedure required), 11501 (application of chapter). See also Section 11410.10 (application to constitutionally and statutorily required hearings).

It should be noted that an agency not governed by this chapter nonetheless has general power to issue a declaratory decision. This power is derived from the power to adjudicate. See, e.g., M. Asimow, Advice to the Public from Federal Administrative Agencies 121–22 (1973). [25 Cal.L.Rev.Comm. Reports 711 (1995)].

Research References

9 Witkin Cal. Proc. 5th Administrative Proceedings § 66, Optional and Mandatory Provisions.
9 Witkin Cal. Proc. 5th Administrative Proceedings § 82, (S 82) in General.
9 Witkin Cal. Proc. 5th Administrative Proceedings § 83, (S 83) Procedure.

§ 11465.20. Application; issuance

(a) A person may apply to an agency for a declaratory decision as to the applicability to specified circumstances of a statute, regulation, or decision within the primary jurisdiction of the agency.

(b) The agency in its discretion may issue a declaratory decision in response to the application. The agency shall not issue a declaratory decision if any of the following applies:

(1) Issuance of the decision would be contrary to a regulation adopted under this article.

(2) The decision would substantially prejudice the rights of a person who would be a necessary party and who does not consent in writing to the determination of the matter by a declaratory decision proceeding.

(3) The decision involves a matter that is the subject of pending administrative or judicial proceedings.

(c) An application for a declaratory decision is not required for exhaustion of the applicant's administrative remedies for purposes of judicial review. *(Added by Stats.1995, c. 938 (S.B.523), § 21, operative July 1, 1997.)*

Law Revision Commission Comments

Subdivisions (a) and (b) of Section 11465.20 are drawn from 1981 Model State APA § 2–103(a). For the procedure by which an interested person may petition requesting adoption, amendment, or repeal of a regulation, see Sections 11347–11347.1. Unlike the model act, issuance of a declaratory decision under Section 11465.20 is discretionary with the agency, rather than mandatory.

Under subdivision (a), a declaratory decision may determine whether the subject of the proceeding is or is not within the agency's primary jurisdiction. See Abelleira v. District Court of Appeal, 17 Cal.2d 280, 302–03, 109 P.2d 942 (1941); United Ins. Co. of Chicago v. Maloney, 127 Cal.App.2d 155, 157–58, 273 P.2d 579 (1954).

Subdivision (b)(2) prohibits an agency from issuing a declaratory decision that would substantially prejudice the rights of a person who would be a necessary party, and who does not consent to the determination of the matter by a declaratory decision proceeding. A necessary party is one that is constitutionally entitled to notice and an opportunity to be heard—a flexible concept depending on the nature of the competing interests involved. Horn v. County of Ventura, 24 Cal.3d 605, 612, 617, 596 P.2d 1134, 156 Cal.Rptr. 718 (1979). Such a person may refuse to give consent because in a declaratory decision proceeding the person might not have all of the same procedural rights the person would have in another type of adjudicative proceeding to which the person would be entitled.

Subdivision (c) makes clear that application for a declaratory decision is not a necessary part of the administrative process. A person may seek judicial review of an agency action after other administrative remedies have been exhausted; the person is not required to seek declaratory relief as well. Nothing in this subdivision authorizes judicial review without exhaustion of other applicable administrative remedies. [25 Cal.L.Rev. Comm. Reports 55 (1995)].

Research References

9 Witkin Cal. Proc. 5th Administrative Proceedings § 83, (S 83) Procedure.

§ 11465.30. Notice

Within 30 days after receipt of an application for a declaratory decision, an agency shall give notice of the application to all persons to which notice of an adjudicative proceeding is otherwise required, and may give notice to any other person. *(Added by Stats.1995, c. 938 (S.B.523), § 21, operative July 1, 1997.)*

Law Revision Commission Comments

Section 11465.30 is drawn from 1981 Model State APA § 2–103(c). See also Section 11440.20 (notice). [25 Cal.L.Rev.Comm. Reports 55 (1995)].

Research References

9 Witkin Cal. Proc. 5th Administrative Proceedings § 83, (S 83) Procedure.

§ 11465.40. Applicable law

The provisions of a formal, informal, or other applicable hearing procedure do not apply to an agency proceeding for a declaratory decision except to the extent provided in this article or to the extent the agency so provides by regulation or order. *(Added by Stats.1995, c. 938 (S.B.523), § 21, operative July 1, 1997.)*

Law Revision Commission Comments

Section 11465.40 is drawn from 1981 Model State APA § 2–103(d). It makes clear that the specific procedural requirements for adjudications imposed by the formal hearing procedure or other applicable hearing procedure on an agency when it conducts an adjudicative proceeding are inapplicable to a proceeding for a declaratory decision unless the agency elects to make some or all of them applicable.

Regulations specifying precise procedures available in a declaratory proceeding may be adopted under Section 11465.70. The reason for exempting a declaratory decision from usual procedural requirements for adjudications is to encourage an agency to issue a decision by eliminating requirements it might deem onerous. Moreover, many adjudicative provisions have no applicability. For example, cross-examination is unnecessary since the application establishes the facts on which the agency should rule. Oral argument could also be dispensed with.

Note that there are no contested issues of fact in a declaratory decision proceeding because its function is to declare the applicability of the law in question to facts furnished by the applicant. The actual existence of the facts on which the decision is based will usually become an issue only in a later proceeding in which a party to the declaratory decision proceeding seeks to use the decision as a justification of the party's conduct.

Note also that the party requesting a declaratory decision has the choice of refraining from filing such an application and awaiting the ordinary agency adjudicative process.

A declaratory decision is, of course, subject to provisions governing judicial review of agency decisions and for public inspection and indexing of agency decisions. See, e.g., Sections 6250–6268 (California Public Records Act). A declaratory decision may be given precedential effect, subject to the provisions governing precedent decisions. See Section 11425.60 (precedent decisions). [25 Cal.L.Rev.Comm. Reports 55 (1995)].

Research References

9 Witkin Cal. Proc. 5th Administrative Proceedings § 83, (S 83) Procedure.

§ 11465.50.   Agency action

(a) Within 60 days after receipt of an application for a declaratory decision, an agency shall do one of the following, in writing:

(1) Issue a decision declaring the applicability of the statute, regulation, or decision in question to the specified circumstances.

(2) Set the matter for specified proceedings.

(3) Agree to issue a declaratory decision by a specified time.

(4) Decline to issue a declaratory decision, stating in writing the reasons for its action. Agency action under this paragraph is not subject to judicial review.

(b) A copy of the agency's action under subdivision (a) shall be served promptly on the applicant and any other party.

(c) If an agency has not taken action under subdivision (a) within 60 days after receipt of an application for a declaratory decision, the agency is considered to have declined to issue a declaratory decision on the matter. *(Added by Stats.1995, c. 938 (S.B.523), § 21, operative July 1, 1997.)*

Law Revision Commission Comments

Subdivision (a) of Section 11465.50 is drawn from 1981 Model State APA § 2–103(e). The requirement that an agency dispose of an application within 60 days ensures a timely agency response to a declaratory decision application, thereby facilitating planning by affected parties.

Subdivision (b) is drawn from 1981 Model State APA § 2–103(f). It requires that the agency communicate to the applicant and to any other parties any action it takes in response to an application for a declaratory decision. This includes each of the types of actions listed in paragraphs (1)–(4) of subdivision (a). Service is made by personal delivery or mail or other means to the last known address of the person to which the agency action is directed. Section 11440.20 (notice).

The decision by an agency not to issue a declaratory decision is within the absolute discretion of the agency and is therefore not reviewable. Subdivision (a)(4). See also Section 11465.20 & Comment (declaratory decision permissive). [25 Cal.L.Rev.Comm. Reports 55 (1995)].

Research References

9 Witkin Cal. Proc. 5th Administrative Proceedings § 83, (S 83) Procedure.

§ 11465.60.   Contents of decision; status

(a) A declaratory decision shall contain the names of all parties to the proceeding, the particular facts on which it is based, and the reasons for its conclusion.

(b) A declaratory decision has the same status and binding effect as any other decision issued by the agency in an adjudicative proceeding. *(Added by Stats.1995, c. 938 (S.B.523), § 21, operative July 1, 1997.)*

Law Revision Commission Comments

Section 11465.60 is drawn from 1981 Model State APA § 2–103(g). A declaratory decision issued by an agency is judicially reviewable; is binding on the applicant, other parties to that declaratory proceeding, and the agency, unless reversed or modified on judicial review; and has the same precedential effect as other agency adjudications.

A declaratory decision, like other decisions, only determines the legal rights of the particular parties to the proceeding in which it was issued.

The requirement in subdivision (a) that each declaratory decision issued contain the facts on which it is based and the reasons for its conclusion will facilitate any subsequent judicial review of the decision's legality. It also ensures a clear record of what occurred for the parties and for persons interested in the decision because of its possible precedential effect. [25 Cal.L.Rev.Comm. Reports 55 (1995)].

Research References

9 Witkin Cal. Proc. 5th Administrative Proceedings § 83, (S 83) Procedure.

§ 11465.70.   Model regulations

(a) The Office of Administrative Hearings shall adopt and promulgate model regulations under this article that are consistent with the public interest and with the general policy of this article to facilitate and encourage agency issuance of reliable advice. The model regulations shall provide for all of the following:

(1) A description of the classes of circumstances in which an agency will not issue a declaratory decision.

(2) The form, contents, and filing of an application for a declaratory decision.

(3) The procedural rights of a person in relation to an application.

(4) The disposition of an application.

(b) The regulations adopted by the Office of Administrative Hearings under this article apply in an adjudicative proceeding unless an agency adopts its own regulations to govern declaratory decisions of the agency.

(c) This article does not apply in an adjudicative proceeding to the extent an agency by regulation provides inconsistent rules or provides that this article is not applicable in a proceeding of the agency. *(Added by Stats.1995, c. 938 (S.B.523), § 21, operative July 1, 1997.)*

Law Revision Commission Comments

Section 11465.70 is drawn from 1981 Model State APA § 2–103(b). An agency may choose to preclude declaratory decisions altogether.

Regulations should specify all of the details surrounding the declaratory decision process including a specification of the precise form and contents of the application; when, how, and where an application is to be filed; whether an applicant has the right to an oral argument; the circumstances in which the agency will not issue a decision; and the like.

Regulations also should require a clear and precise presentation of facts, so that an agency will not be required to rule on the application of law to unclear or excessively general facts. The regulations should make clear that, if the facts are not sufficiently precise, the agency can require additional facts or a narrowing of the application.

Agency regulations on this subject will be valid so long as the requirements they impose are reasonable and are within the scope of agency discretion. To be valid these rules must also be consistent with the public interest—which includes the efficient and effective accomplishment of the agency's mission—and the express general policy of this article to facilitate and encourage the issuance of reliable agency advice. Within these general limits, therefore, an agency may include in its rules reasonable standing, ripeness, and other requirements for obtaining a declaratory decision. [25 Cal.L.Rev.Comm. Reports 55 (1995)].

Research References

9 Witkin Cal. Proc. 5th Administrative Proceedings § 82, (S 82) in General.

ARTICLE 15. CONVERSION OF PROCEEDING

Section

11470.10.   Authority of presiding officer or other agency official; notice.
11470.20.   Appointment of successor.
11470.30.   Record of original proceeding.
11470.40.   Duties of presiding officer or other agency official responsible for new proceeding.
11470.50.   Regulations.

§ 11470.10. Authority of presiding officer or other agency official; notice

(a) Subject to any applicable regulation adopted under Section 11470.50, at any point in an agency proceeding the presiding officer or other agency official responsible for the proceeding:

(1) May convert the proceeding to another type of agency proceeding provided for by statute if the conversion is appropriate, is in the public interest, and does not substantially prejudice the rights of a party.

(2) Shall convert the proceeding to another type of agency proceeding provided for by statute, if required by regulation or statute.

(b) A proceeding of one type may be converted to a proceeding of another type only on notice to all parties to the original proceeding. *(Added by Stats.1995, c. 938 (S.B.523), § 21, operative July 1, 1997.)*

Law Revision Commission Comments

Section 11470.10 is drawn from 1981 Model State APA § 1–107(a)–(b). A reference in this section to a "party," in the case of an adjudicative proceeding means "party" as defined in Section 11405.60, and in the case of a rulemaking proceeding means an active participant in the proceeding or one primarily interested in its outcome. Agency proceedings covered by this article include a rulemaking proceeding as well as an adjudicative proceeding. The conversion provisions may be irrelevant to some types of proceedings by some agencies, and in that case this article would be inapplicable.

Under subdivision (a)(1), a proceeding may not be converted to another type that would be inappropriate for the action being taken. For example, if an agency elects to conduct a formal hearing in a case where it could have elected an informal hearing initially, a subsequent decision to convert to an informal hearing would be appropriate under subdivision (a)(1).

The further limitation in subdivision (a)(1)—that the conversion may not substantially prejudice the rights of a party—must also be satisfied. The courts will have to decide on a case-by-case basis what constitutes substantial prejudice. The concept includes both the right to an appropriate procedure that enables a party to protect its interests, and freedom of the party from great inconvenience caused by the conversion in terms of time, cost, availability of witnesses, necessity of continuances and other delays, and other practical consequences of the conversion. Of course, even if the rights of a party are substantially prejudiced by a conversion, the party may voluntarily waive them. Section 11415.40.

It should be noted that the substantial-prejudice-to-the-rights-of-a-party limitation on discretionary conversion of an agency proceeding from one type to another is not intended to disturb an existing body of law. In certain situations an agency may lawfully deny an individual an adjudicative proceeding to which the individual otherwise would be entitled by conducting a rulemaking proceeding that determines for an entire class an issue that otherwise would be the subject of a necessary adjudicative proceeding. See Note, *The Use of Agency Rulemaking To Deny Adjudications Apparently Required by Statute*, 54 Iowa L.Rev. 1086 (1969). Similarly, the substantial prejudice limitation is not intended to disturb the

existing body of law allowing an agency, in certain situations, to make a determination through an adjudicative proceeding that has the effect of denying a person an opportunity the person might otherwise be afforded if a rulemaking proceeding were used instead.

Subdivision (a)(2) makes clear that an agency must convert a proceeding of one type to a proceeding of another type when required by regulation or statute, even if a nonconsenting party is prejudiced thereby. Under subdivision (b), however, both a discretionary and a mandatory conversion must be accompanied by notice to all parties to the original proceeding so that they will have a fully adequate opportunity to protect their interests.

Within the limits of this section, an agency should be authorized to use procedures in a proceeding that are most likely to be effective and efficient under the particular circumstances. Subdivision (a) allows an agency this flexibility. For example, an agency that wants to convert a formal hearing into an informal hearing, or an informal hearing into a formal hearing, may do so under this provision if the conversion is appropriate and in the public interest, if adequate notice is given, and if the rights of the parties are not substantially prejudiced.

Similarly, an agency called on to explore a new area of law in a declaratory decision proceeding may prefer to do so by rulemaking. That is, the agency may decide to have full public participation in developing its policy in the area and to declare law of general applicability instead of issuing a determination of only particular applicability at the request of a specific party in a more limited proceeding. So long as all of the standards in this section are met, this section would authorize such a conversion from one type of agency proceeding to another.

While it is unlikely that a conversion consistent with all of the statutory standards could occur more than once in the course of a proceeding, the possibility of multiple conversions in the course of a particular proceeding is left open by the statutory language. In an adjudication, the prehearing conference could be used to choose the most appropriate form of proceeding at the outset, thereby diminishing the likelihood of a later conversion. [25 Cal.L.Rev.Comm. Reports 55 (1995)].

Research References

9 Witkin Cal. Proc. 5th Administrative Proceedings § 66, Optional and Mandatory Provisions.
9 Witkin Cal. Proc. 5th Administrative Proceedings § 87, Conversion of Proceeding from One Type to Another.

§ 11470.20. Appointment of successor

If the presiding officer or other agency official responsible for the original proceeding would not have authority over the new proceeding to which it is to be converted, the agency head shall appoint a successor to preside over or be responsible for the new proceeding. *(Added by Stats.1995, c. 938 (S.B.523), § 21, operative July 1, 1997.)*

Law Revision Commission Comments

Section 11470.20 is drawn from 1981 Model State APA § 1–107(c). It deals with the mechanics of transition from one type of proceeding to another. [25 Cal.L.Rev.Comm. Reports 55 (1995)].

Research References

9 Witkin Cal. Proc. 5th Administrative Proceedings § 87, Conversion of Proceeding from One Type to Another.

§ 11470.30. Record of original proceeding

To the extent practicable and consistent with the rights of parties and the requirements of this article relating to the new proceeding, the record of the original agency proceeding shall be used in the new agency proceeding. *(Added by Stats.1995, c. 938 (S.B.523), § 21, operative July 1, 1997.)*

Law Revision Commission Comments

Section 11470.30 is drawn from 1981 Model State APA § 1–107(d). It seeks to avoid unnecessary duplication of proceedings by requiring the use of as much of the agency record in the first proceeding as is possible in the second proceeding, consistent with the rights of the parties and the requirements of the applicable statute governing the hearing procedure. [25 Cal.L.Rev.Comm. Reports 55 (1995)].

Government

Research References

9 Witkin Cal. Proc. 5th Administrative Proceedings § 87, Conversion of Proceeding from One Type to Another.

§ 11470.40. Duties of presiding officer or other agency official responsible for new proceeding

After a proceeding is converted from one type to another, the presiding officer or other agency official responsible for the new proceeding shall do all of the following:

(a) Give additional notice to parties or other persons necessary to satisfy the statutory requirements relating to the new proceeding.

(b) Dispose of the matters involved without further proceedings if sufficient proceedings have already been held to satisfy the statutory requirements relating to the new proceeding.

(c) Conduct or cause to be conducted any additional proceedings necessary to satisfy the statutory requirements relating to the new proceeding, and allow the parties a reasonable time to prepare for the new proceeding. *(Added by Stats.1995, c. 938 (S.B.523), § 21, operative July 1, 1997.)*

Law Revision Commission Comments

Section 11470.40 is drawn from 1981 Model State APA § 1–107(e). [25 Cal.L.Rev.Comm. Reports 55 (1995)].

Research References

9 Witkin Cal. Proc. 5th Administrative Proceedings § 87, Conversion of Proceeding from One Type to Another.

§ 11470.50. Regulations

An agency may adopt regulations to govern the conversion of one type of proceeding to another. The regulations may include an enumeration of the factors to be considered in determining whether and under what circumstances one type of proceeding will be converted to another. *(Added by Stats.1995, c. 938 (S.B.523), § 21, operative July 1, 1997.)*

Law Revision Commission Comments

Section 11470.50 is drawn from 1981 Model State APA § 1–107(f). Adoption of regulations is permissive, rather than mandatory. [25 Cal.L.Rev.Comm. Reports 55 (1995)].

Research References

9 Witkin Cal. Proc. 5th Administrative Proceedings § 87, Conversion of Proceeding from One Type to Another.

ARTICLE 16.   ADMINISTRATIVE ADJUDICATION CODE OF ETHICS

§ 11475.   Administrative Adjudication Code of Ethics

The rules imposed by this article may be referred to as the Administrative Adjudication Code of Ethics. *(Added by Stats. 1998, c. 95 (A.B.2164), § 1.)*

Research References

9 Witkin Cal. Proc. 5th Administrative Proceedings § 60, (S 60) Administrative Adjudication Code of Ethics.
2 Witkin Cal. Proc. 5th Courts § 52, (S 52) Development and Adoption.
2 Witkin Cal. Proc. 5th Courts § 60, (S 60) Compliance With Code (Canon 6).

§ 11475.10. Application of article; administrative law judge; defined

(a) This article applies to the following persons:

(1) An administrative law judge. As used in this subdivision, "administrative law judge" means an incumbent of that position, as defined by the State Personnel Board, for each class specification for Administrative Law Judge.

(2) A presiding officer to which this article is made applicable by statute or regulation.

(b) This article shall apply notwithstanding any general statutory provision that this chapter does not apply to some or all of a state agency's adjudicative proceedings. *(Added by Stats.1998, c. 95 (A.B.2164), § 1.)*

Law Revision Commission Comments

Section 11475.10 limits application of the Administrative Adjudication Code of Ethics to specified classes of hearing officers. See Section 11475.20 (application of Code of Judicial Ethics).

Subdivision (a)(1) includes not only an administrative law judge who presides at a hearing but also a supervisory or management level administrative law judge or chief administrative law judge, whose function may relate directly or indirectly to the adjudicative process.

This article does not apply to an agency head or hearing officer who presides in an administrative adjudication but who is not an administrative law judge, absent a special statute or regulation. See subdivision (a)(2). However, other ethical considerations apply to the hearing and nonhearing conduct of state agency presiding officers. See, e.g., Section 19572 (cause for discipline).

An agency may make the Administrative Adjudication Code of Ethics applicable to its non-administrative law judge presiding officers by regulation where this article would not otherwise apply. See Section 11410.40 (election to apply administrative adjudication provisions); see also Section 11405.80 ("presiding officer" defined).

Under subdivision (b), the Administrative Adjudication Code of Ethics applies to an administrative law judge even though the proceedings in which the administrative law judge presides might otherwise be statutorily exempt from this chapter. See, e.g., Section 15609.5 (State Board of Equalization); Pub. Util. Code § 1701 (Public Utilities Commission). [28 Cal.L.Rev.Comm. Reports App. 5 (1998)].

Research References

9 Witkin Cal. Proc. 5th Administrative Proceedings § 60, (S 60) Administrative Adjudication Code of Ethics.

§ 11475.20. Governing code for hearing and nonhearing conduct of judge or other presiding officer

Except as otherwise provided in this article, the Code of Judicial Ethics adopted by the Supreme Court pursuant to subdivision (m) of Section 18 of Article VI of the California Constitution for the conduct of judges governs the hearing and nonhearing conduct of an administrative law judge or other presiding officer to which this article applies. *(Added by Stats.1998, c. 95 (A.B.2164), § 1.)*

Law Revision Commission Comments

Section 11475.20 applies the Code of Judicial Ethics in administrative adjudication. For the persons to which this article applies, see Section 11475.10 (application of article).

The Code of Judicial Ethics adopted by the Supreme Court is effective January 15, 1996. The incorporation by reference includes subsequent amendments and additions to the Code. Section 9.

It is intended that interpretations of the Code of Judicial Ethics in its application to the judicial system, whether made by court rule or decision, should also be applied in administrative adjudication, to the extent relevant to the circumstances of administrative adjudication. *Cf.* Section 11475.40 (provisions of Code excepted from application).

The Code of Judicial Ethics supplements other standards applicable to conduct of an administrative law judge, including disqualification for bias (Section 11425.40) and disciplinary action for failure of good behavior (Section 19572). See also Section 11475.50 & Comment (enforcement). These requirements are also in addition to the requirements pursuant to Chapter 9.5 (commencing with Section 89500) of Title 9, applicable to designated employees of state agencies, including administrative law judges and other presiding officers. [28 Cal.L.Rev.Comm. Reports App. 5 (1998)].

Research References

9 Witkin Cal. Proc. 5th Administrative Proceedings § 60, (S 60) Administrative Adjudication Code of Ethics.

§ 11475.30. Definitions

For the purpose of this article, the following terms used in the Code of Judicial Ethics have the meanings provided in this section:

(a) "Appeal" means administrative review.

(b) "Court" means the agency conducting an adjudicative proceeding.

(c) "Judge" means administrative law judge or other presiding officer to which this article applies. Related terms, including "judicial," "judiciary," and "justice," mean comparable concepts in administrative adjudication.

(d) "Law" includes regulation and precedent decision. *(Added by Stats.1998, c. 95 (A.B.2164), § 1.)*

Law Revision Commission Comments

Section 11475.30 provides a general guide to conversion of terminology in the Code of Judicial Ethics for application to administrative adjudication. It is intended to be applied in a manner to effectuate that general purpose without requiring strict or grammatically precise rigidity in the conversion. Likewise, terms not specified in this section should be converted in an appropriate manner to effectuate the general intent of this statute to apply the Code of Judicial Ethics to the circumstances of administrative adjudication. [26 Cal.L.Rev.Comm. Reports 335 (1996)].

Research References

9 Witkin Cal. Proc. 5th Administrative Proceedings § 60, (S 60) Administrative Adjudication Code of Ethics.

§ 11475.40. Code of Judicial Ethics; application of article

The following provisions of the Code of Judicial Ethics do not apply under this article:

(a) Canon 3B(7), to the extent it relates to ex parte communications.

(b) Canon 3B(10).

(c) Canon 3D(3).

(d) Canon 4C.

(e) Canons 4E(1), 4F, and 4G.

(f) Canons 5A–5D. However, the introductory paragraph of Canon 5 applies to persons subject to this article notwithstanding Chapter 9.5 (commencing with Section 3201) of Division 4 of Title 1, relating to political activities of public employees.

(g) Canon 6. *(Added by Stats.1998, c. 95 (A.B.2164), § 1.)*

Law Revision Commission Comments

Section 11475.40 adapts the Code of Judicial Ethics for application to administrative law judges. Some provisions of the Code of Judicial Ethics, although not excepted by this section, may be minimally relevant to an administrative law judge. See, e.g., Canon 3C(4) (administrative responsibilities).

Subdivision (a) of Section 11475.40 excepts the portion of Canon 3B(7) relating to ex parte communications. It reflects the fact that special provisions, and not the Code of Judicial Ethics, govern ex parte communications in administrative adjudication. See, e.g., Article 7 (commencing with Section 11430.10).

Subdivision (b) excepts Canon 3B(10), relating to juries. It reflects the fact that juries are not used in administrative adjudication.

Subdivision (c) excepts Canon 3D(3), which requires a judge who is criminally charged to report that fact to the Commission on Judicial Performance. This duty is not relevant to administrative law judges, who are not under the jurisdiction of the Commission on Judicial Performance.

Subdivision (d) excepts Canon 4C, relating to governmental, civic, or charitable activities. An administrative law judge is not precluded from engaging in activities of this type, except to the extent the activities may conflict with general limitations on the administrative law judge's conduct. See, e.g., Canon 4A (extrajudicial activities in general).

Subdivision (e) excepts Canons 4E(1), 4F, and 4G, relating to fiduciary activities, private employment in alternative dispute resolution, and the practice of law. These matters are the subject of the employing agency's incompatible activity statement pursuant to Section 19990.

Subdivision (f) applies the introductory portion of Canon 5 to an administrative law judge or other presiding officer, but not Canons 5A–5D. Under this provision an administrative law judge or other presiding officer must avoid political activity that may create the appearance of political bias or impropriety. This would preclude participation in political activity related to an issue that may come before the administrative law judge or other presiding officer.

Subdivision (f) limits the political activities of administrative law judges even though other public employees might be able to participate in those activities under the *Hatch Act* (Sections 3201–3209). This subdivision is not intended to preclude an administrative law judge or other presiding officer to which this article applies from appearing at a public hearing or officially consulting with an executive or legislative body or public official in matters concerning the judge's private economic or personal interests, or to otherwise engage in political activities relating to salary, benefits, and working conditions. *Cf.* Section 11475.70 (collective bargaining rights not affected).

Subdivision (g) excepts Canon 6, which is superseded by Sections 11475.50 (enforcement) and 11475.60 (compliance). [28 Cal.L.Rev.Comm. Reports App. 5 (1998)].

Research References

9 Witkin Cal. Proc. 5th Administrative Proceedings § 60, (S 60) Administrative Adjudication Code of Ethics.

§ 11475.50. Acceptance of honoraria, gifts, or travel; violation of code; discipline

A violation of an applicable provision of the Code of Judicial Ethics, or a violation of the restrictions and prohibitions on accepting honoraria, gifts, or travel that otherwise apply to elected state officers pursuant to Chapter 9.5 (commencing with Section 89500) of Title 9, by an administrative law judge or other presiding officer to which this article applies is cause for discipline by the employing agency pursuant to Section 19572. *(Added by Stats.1998, c. 95 (A.B.2164), § 1.)*

Law Revision Commission Comments

Section 11475.50 supersedes Canon 6A of the Code of Judicial Ethics. The compliance requirement is not precatory in administrative adjudication, but is mandatory.

Appropriate discipline under this section is the responsibility of the agency that employs the administrative law judge. Thus if an administrative law judge employed by the Office of Administrative Hearings violates the code of ethics in a hearing conducted for another agency, the Office of Administrative Hearings is the disciplining entity, and not the other agency. An agency may apply appropriate disciplinary procedures. It should be noted that a person may also institute disciplinary proceedings directly before the State Personnel Board with the consent of the board. Gov't Code § 19583.5; 2 Cal. Code Regs. 51.9 (1996).

A violation of the code of ethics by the administrative law judge is not per se grounds for disqualification, or reversal of a decision, of the administrative law judge. But the violation may be indicative of the administrative law judge's violation of other procedural requirements.

See, e.g., Section 11425.40 (disqualification of presiding officer for bias, prejudice, or interest). [28 Cal.L.Rev.Comm. Reports App. 5 (1998)].

Research References

9 Witkin Cal. Proc. 5th Administrative Proceedings § 60, (S 60) Administrative Adjudication Code of Ethics.

§ 11475.60. Application of article; compliance with provisions

(a) Except as provided in subdivision (b), a person to whom this article applies shall comply immediately with all applicable provisions of the Code of Judicial Ethics.

(b) A person to whom this article applies shall comply with Canon 4D(2) of the Code of Judicial Ethics as soon as reasonably possible and shall do so in any event within a period of one year after the article becomes applicable. *(Added by Stats.1998, c. 95 (A.B.2164), § 1.)*

Law Revision Commission Comments

Section 11475.60 supersedes Canon 6F of the Code of Judicial Ethics. [26 Cal.L.Rev.Comm. Reports 335 (1996)].

Research References

9 Witkin Cal. Proc. 5th Administrative Proceedings § 60, (S 60) Administrative Adjudication Code of Ethics.

§ 11475.70. Construction of article

Nothing in this article shall be construed or is intended to limit or affect the rights of an administrative law judge or other presiding officer under Chapter 10.3 (commencing with Section 3512) of Division 4 of Title 1. *(Added by Stats.1998, c. 95 (A.B.2164), § 1.)*

Law Revision Commission Comments

Section 11475.70 makes clear that the Administrative Adjudication Code of Ethics is not intended to interfere with collective bargaining rights guaranteed state employees under the Ralph C. Dills Act. These include the right to form, join, and participate in activities of employee organizations of their own choosing for the purpose of representation on all matters of employer-employee relations, to refuse to join or participate in the activities of employee organizations, or to represent themselves individually in their employment relations with the state. See Section 3515. [26 Cal.L.Rev.Comm. Reports 335 (1996)].

Research References

9 Witkin Cal. Proc. 5th Administrative Proceedings § 60, (S 60) Administrative Adjudication Code of Ethics.

CHAPTER 5. ADMINISTRATIVE ADJUDICATION: FORMAL HEARING

§ 11500. Definitions

In this chapter unless the context or subject matter otherwise requires:

(a) "Agency" includes the state boards, commissions, and officers to which this chapter is made applicable by law, except that wherever the word "agency" alone is used the power to act may be delegated by the agency, and wherever the words "agency itself" are used the power to act shall not be delegated unless the statutes relating to the particular agency authorize the delegation of the agency's power to hear and decide.

(b) "Party" includes the agency, the respondent, and any person, other than an officer or an employee of the agency in his or her official capacity, who has been allowed to appear or participate in the proceeding.

(c) "Respondent" means any person against whom an accusation or District Statement of Reduction in Force is filed pursuant to Section 11503 or against whom a statement of issues is filed pursuant to Section 11504.

(d) "Administrative law judge" means an individual qualified under Section 11502.

(e) "Agency member" means any person who is a member of any agency to which this chapter is applicable and includes any person who himself or herself constitutes an agency. *(Added by Stats.1945, c. 867, p. 1626, § 1. Amended by Stats.1947, c. 491, p.*

1469, § 1; Stats.1977, c. 1057, p. 3195, § 1, operative July 1, 1978; Stats.1985, c. 324, § 15; Stats.1995, c. 938 (S.B.523), § 23, operative July 1, 1997; Stats.2013, c. 90 (S.B.546), § 2.)

Law Revision Commission Comments

Subdivision (a) of Section 11500 is amended to reflect the deletion of the enumeration of agencies formerly found in Section 11501. The application of this chapter to the hearings of an agency is determined by the statutes relating to the agency. Section 11501.

Former subdivision (f) is superseded by Sections 11410.10 (application to constitutionally and statutorily required hearings), 11410.20 (application to state), 11405.50 ("decision" defined), 11425.50 (decision), and 11435.15 (language assistance).

Former subdivision (g) is superseded by Section 11435.05 ("language assistance" defined). [25 Cal.L.Rev.Comm. Reports 55 (1995)].

Research References

Rutter, Cal. Practice Guide: Insurance Litigation Ch. 14-A, A. The California Regulator (*).

Rutter, Cal. Practice Guide: Real Prop. Transactions Ch. 2-B, B. Licensing and Regulatory Requirements.

Miller and Starr California Real Estate § 4:42, Disciplinary Process-- Hearing Procedure.

Miller and Starr California Real Estate § 4:86, Licensing and Registration of Mortgage Loan Originators by Department of Corporations.

Miller and Starr California Real Estate § 25C:45, Violation of the Subdivided Lands Act; Enforcement by the Commissioner.

14 NO. 5 Miller & Starr, California Real Estate Newsalert 9, Discrimination.

9 Witkin Cal. Proc. 5th Administrative Proceedings § 11, Scope of Act.

9 Witkin Cal. Proc. 5th Administrative Proceedings § 12, Exceptions.

9 Witkin Cal. Proc. 5th Administrative Proceedings § 34, (S 34) in General.

9 Witkin Cal. Proc. 5th Administrative Proceedings § 57, (S 57) Nature and Scope of A.P.A. Adjudication Provisions.

9 Witkin Cal. Proc. 5th Administrative Proceedings § 58, (S 58) Office of Administrative Hearings.

9 Witkin Cal. Proc. 5th Administrative Proceedings § 64, When Provisions Apply.

9 Witkin Cal. Proc. 5th Administrative Proceedings § 68, in General.

9 Witkin Cal. Proc. 5th Administrative Proceedings § 96, (S 96) Nature and Scope of A.P.A. Formal Hearing Provisions.

9 Witkin Cal. Proc. 5th Administrative Proceedings § 97, Filing.

9 Witkin Cal. Proc. 5th Administrative Proceedings § 114, Time for Decision.

9 Witkin Cal. Proc. 5th Administrative Proceedings § 116, Correction.

2 Witkin, California Summary 10th Insurance § 10, Ratemaking Process.

12 Witkin, California Summary 10th Real Property § 501, (S 501) Sanctions for Violations.

9 Witkin, California Summary 10th Corporations § 440, (S 440) Discontinuance of Activities and Administrative Penalties.

§ 11501. Application of chapter; application of other law

(a) This chapter applies to any agency as determined by the statutes relating to that agency.

(b) This chapter applies to an adjudicative proceeding of an agency created on or after July 1, 1997, unless the statutes relating to the proceeding provide otherwise.

(c) Chapter 4.5 (commencing with Section 11400) applies to an adjudicative proceeding required to be conducted under this chapter, unless the statutes relating to the proceeding provide otherwise. *(Added by Stats.1995, c. 938 (S.B.523), § 24.5, operative July 1, 1997.)*

Law Revision Commission Comments

Section 11501 is revised to make this chapter the default procedure, absent a contrary statute, for agencies created after the operative date of the revision.

This chapter is supplemented by the general provisions on administrative adjudication found in Chapter 4.5 (commencing with Section 11400), which apply to proceedings under this chapter. See subdivision (c). See also Section 11410.50 (application where formal hearing procedure required). Thus if an agency is required by statute to conduct a hearing

under this chapter, the agency may, unless a statute provides otherwise, elect to use alternative dispute resolution or the informal hearing procedure or other appropriate provisions of Chapter 4.5. Likewise, the general provisions of Chapter 4.5 restricting ex parte communications, regulating precedent decisions, and the like, apply to a hearing under this chapter. See also Section 11502 (use of administrative law judges under Chapter 4.5).

The enumeration of agencies formerly found in subdivision (b) is deleted as obsolete. The application of this chapter to the hearings of an agency is determined by the statutes relating to the agency. See also Section 11500(a) ("agency" defined). [25 Cal.L.Rev.Comm. Reports 711 (1995)].

Research References

9 Witkin Cal. Proc. 5th Administrative Proceedings § 64, When Provisions Apply.

9 Witkin Cal. Proc. 5th Administrative Proceedings § 96, (S 96) Nature and Scope of A.P.A. Formal Hearing Provisions.

9 Witkin Cal. Proc. 5th Administrative Proceedings § 109, Conduct of Hearing.

§ 11502. Administrative law judges; duties; appointment; qualifications

(a) All hearings of state agencies required to be conducted under this chapter shall be conducted by administrative law judges on the staff of the Office of Administrative Hearings. This subdivision applies to a hearing required to be conducted under this chapter that is conducted under the informal hearing or emergency decision procedure provided in Chapter 4.5 (commencing with Section 11400).

(b) The Director of the Office of Administrative Hearings has power to appoint a staff of administrative law judges for the office as provided in Section 11370.3. Each administrative law judge shall have been admitted to practice law in this state for at least five years immediately preceding his or her appointment and shall possess any additional qualifications established by the State Personnel Board for the particular class of position involved. *(Added by Stats.1945, c. 867, p. 1627, § 1. Amended by Stats.1961, c. 2048, p. 4269, § 10; Stats.1971, c. 1303, p. 2555, § 7; Stats.1985, c. 324, § 16; Stats.1995, c. 938 (S.B.523), § 26, operative July 1, 1997.)*

Law Revision Commission Comments

Section 11502 is amended to make clear that where use of an administrative law judge employed by the Office of Administrative Hearings is required for an adjudicative proceeding under this chapter, such use is also required in informal and emergency proceedings under Chapter 4.5 (administrative adjudication: general provisions). An administrative law judge employed by the Office of Administrative Hearings is not required for a declaratory decision or for alternative dispute resolution under Chapter 4.5. [25 Cal.L.Rev.Comm. Reports 55 (1995)].

Research References

California Practice Guide: Employment Litigation Ch. 7-A, A. Title VII and the California Fair Employment and Housing Act.

Miller and Starr California Real Estate § 27:19, Civil Wage and Penalty Assessments.

9 Witkin Cal. Proc. 5th Administrative Proceedings § 58, (S 58) Office of Administrative Hearings.

9 Witkin Cal. Proc. 5th Administrative Proceedings § 79, (S 79) Procedure.

9 Witkin Cal. Proc. 5th Administrative Proceedings § 81, (S 81) Procedure.

9 Witkin Cal. Proc. 5th Administrative Proceedings § 109, Conduct of Hearing.

§ 11503. Revocation, suspension, limitation, or condition of a right, authority, license or privilege; accusation or District Statement of Reduction in Force; contents; verification; hearing

(a) A hearing to determine whether a right, authority, license, or privilege should be revoked, suspended, limited, or conditioned shall be initiated by filing an accusation or District Statement of Reduction in Force. The accusation or District Statement of Reduction in Force shall be a written statement of charges that shall set forth in ordinary and concise language the acts or omissions with which the respondent is charged, to the end that the respondent will be able to prepare his or her defense. It shall specify the statutes and rules that the respondent is alleged to have violated, but shall not consist merely of charges phrased in the language of those statutes and rules. The accusation or District Statement of Reduction in Force shall be verified unless made by a public officer acting in his or her official capacity or by an employee of the agency before which the proceeding is to be held. The verification may be on information and belief.

(b) In a hearing involving a reduction in force that is conducted pursuant to Section 44949 of the Education Code, the hearing shall be initiated by filing a "District Statement of Reduction in Force." For purposes of this chapter, a "District Statement of Reduction in Force" shall have the same meaning as an "accusation." Respondent's responsive pleading shall be entitled "Notice of Participation in Reduction in Force Hearing." *(Added by Stats.1945, c. 867, p. 1628, § 1. Amended by Stats.1947, c. 491, p. 1470, § 3; Stats.2013, c. 90 (S.B.546), § 3.)*

Research References

Rutter, Cal. Practice Guide: Real Prop. Transactions Ch. 2-B, B. Licensing and Regulatory Requirements.
Miller and Starr California Real Estate § 4:41, Disciplinary Process--Complaint, Investigation and Accusation.
Miller and Starr California Real Estate § 4:42, Disciplinary Process--Hearing Procedure.
9 Witkin Cal. Proc. 5th Administrative Proceedings § 97, Filing.

§ 11504. Grant, issuance, or renewal of right, authority, license, or privilege; statement of issues; contents; verification; service

A hearing to determine whether a right, authority, license, or privilege should be granted, issued, or renewed shall be initiated by filing a statement of issues. The statement of issues shall be a written statement specifying the statutes and rules with which the respondent must show compliance by producing proof at the hearing and, in addition, any particular matters that have come to the attention of the initiating party and that would authorize a denial of the agency action sought. The statement of issues shall be verified unless made by a public officer acting in his or her official capacity or by an employee of the agency before which the proceeding is to be held. The verification may be on information and belief. The statement of issues shall be served in the same manner as an accusation, except that, if the hearing is held at the request of the respondent, Sections 11505 and 11506 shall not apply and the statement of issues together with the notice of hearing shall be delivered or mailed to the parties as provided in Section 11509. Unless a statement to respondent is served pursuant to Section 11505, a copy of Sections 11507.5, 11507.6, and 11507.7, and the name and address of the person to whom requests permitted by Section 11505 may be made, shall be served with the statement of issues. *(Added by Stats.1945, c. 867, p. 1628, § 1. Amended by Stats.1947, c. 491, p. 1471, § 4; Stats.1968, c. 808, p. 1559, § 1; Stats.1996, c. 124 (A.B.3470), § 36; Stats.1997, c. 17 (S.B.947), § 50.)*

Research References

Miller and Starr California Real Estate § 4:42, Disciplinary Process--Hearing Procedure.
9 Witkin Cal. Proc. 5th Administrative Proceedings § 97, Filing.
9 Witkin Cal. Proc. 5th Administrative Proceedings § 98, Service.

9 Witkin Cal. Proc. 5th Administrative Proceedings § 100, (S 100) Notice of Defense.

§ 11504.5. Statements of issues; law applicable

In the following sections of this chapter, all references to accusations shall be deemed to be applicable to statements of issues except in those cases mentioned in subdivision (a) of Section 11505 and Section 11506 where compliance is not required. *(Added by Stats.1963, c. 856, p. 2081, § 1.)*

Research References

9 Witkin Cal. Proc. 5th Administrative Proceedings § 100, (S 100) Notice of Defense.

§ 11505. Service of accusation or District Statement of Reduction in Force; notice of defense or participation; request for hearing; discovery; postponement

(a) Upon the filing of the accusation or District Statement of Reduction in Force the agency shall serve a copy thereof on the respondent as provided in subdivision (c). The agency may include with the accusation or District Statement of Reduction in Force any information that it deems appropriate, but it shall include a postcard or other form entitled Notice of Defense * * *, or, as applicable, Notice of Participation, that, when signed by or on behalf of the respondent and returned to the agency, will acknowledge service of the accusation or District Statement of Reduction in Force and constitute a notice of defense, or, as applicable, notice of participation, under Section 11506. The copy of the accusation or District Statement of Reduction in Force shall include or be accompanied by (1) a statement that respondent may request a hearing by filing a notice of defense, or, as applicable, notice of participation, as provided in Section 11506 within 15 days after service upon the respondent of the accusation or District Statement of Reduction in Force, and that failure to do so will constitute a waiver of the respondent's right to a hearing, and (2) copies of Sections 11507.5, 11507.6, and 11507.7.

(b) The statement to respondent shall be substantially in the following form:

Unless a written request for a hearing signed by or on behalf of the person named as respondent in the accompanying accusation or District Statement of Reduction in Force is delivered or mailed to the agency within 15 days after the accusation or District Statement of Reduction in Force was personally served on you or mailed to you, (here insert name of agency) may proceed upon the accusation or District Statement of Reduction in Force without a hearing. The request for a hearing may be made by delivering or mailing the enclosed form entitled Notice of Defense, or, as applicable, Notice of Participation, or by delivering or mailing a notice of defense, or, as applicable, notice of participation, as provided by Section 11506 of the Government Code to: (here insert name and address of agency). You may, but need not, be represented by counsel at any or all stages of these proceedings.

If you desire the names and addresses of witnesses or an opportunity to inspect and copy the items mentioned in Section 11507.6 of the Government Code in the possession, custody, or control of the agency, you may contact: (here insert name and address of appropriate person).

The hearing may be postponed for good cause. If you have good cause, you are obliged to notify the agency or, if an administrative law judge has been assigned to the hearing, the Office of Administrative Hearings, within 10 working days after you discover the good cause. Failure to give notice within 10 days will deprive you of a postponement.

(c) The accusation or District Statement of Reduction in Force and all accompanying information may be sent to the respondent by any means selected by the agency. But no order adversely affecting the rights of the respondent shall be made by the agency in any case unless the respondent shall have been served personally or by registered mail as provided herein, or shall have filed a notice of defense, or, as applicable, notice of participation, or otherwise appeared. Service may be proved in the manner authorized in civil actions. Service by registered mail shall be effective if a statute or agency rule requires the respondent to file the respondent's address with the agency and to notify the agency of any change, and if a registered letter containing the accusation or District Statement of Reduction in Force and accompanying material is mailed, addressed to the respondent at the latest address on file with the agency.

(d) For purposes of this chapter, for hearings involving a reduction in force that are conducted pursuant to Section 44949 of the Education Code, a "Notice of Participation" shall have the same meaning as a "Notice of Defense." *(Added by Stats.1945, c. 867, p. 1628, § 1. Amended by Stats.1968, c. 808, p. 1560, § 2; Stats.1970, c. 828, p. 1562, § 1; Stats.1979, c. 199, § 3; Stats. 1995, c. 938 (S.B.523), § 28, operative July 1, 1997; Stats.2013, c. 90 (S.B.546), § 4.)*

Law Revision Commission Comments

Section 11505 is amended to correct the portion of the statement to the respondent relating to postponement of the hearing. See Section 11524 (continuances). [25 Cal.L.Rev.Comm. Reports 55 (1995)].

Research References

Miller and Starr California Real Estate § 4:42, Disciplinary Process-- Hearing Procedure.

9 Witkin Cal. Proc. 5th Administrative Proceedings § 88, (S 88) Service and Notice.

9 Witkin Cal. Proc. 5th Administrative Proceedings § 98, Service.

9 Witkin Cal. Proc. 5th Administrative Proceedings § 117, Effect, Enforcement, and Stay.

§ 11506. Notice of defense or participation; grounds; right to hearing

(a) Within 15 days after service of the accusation or District Statement of Reduction in Force the respondent may file with the agency a notice of defense, or, as applicable, notice of participation, in which the respondent may:

(1) Request a hearing.

(2) Object to the accusation or District Statement of Reduction in Force upon the ground that it does not state acts or omissions upon which the agency may proceed.

(3) Object to the form of the accusation or District Statement of Reduction in Force on the ground that it is so indefinite or uncertain that the respondent cannot identify the transaction or prepare a defense.

(4) Admit the accusation or District Statement of Reduction in Force in whole or in part.

(5) Present new matter by way of defense.

(6) Object to the accusation or District Statement of Reduction in Force upon the ground that, under the circumstances, compliance with the requirements of a regulation would result in a material violation of another regulation enacted by another department affecting substantive rights.

(b) Within the time specified the respondent may file one or more notices of defense, or, as applicable, notices of participation, upon any or all of these grounds but all of these notices shall be filed within that period unless the agency in its discretion authorizes the filing of a later notice.

(c) The respondent shall be entitled to a hearing on the merits if the respondent files a notice of defense or notice of participation, and the notice shall be deemed a specific denial of all parts of the accusation or District Statement of Reduction in Force not expressly admitted. Failure to file a notice of defense or notice of participation shall constitute a waiver of respondent's right to a hearing, but the agency in its discretion may nevertheless grant a hearing. Unless objection is taken as provided in paragraph (3) of subdivision (a), all objections to the form of the accusation or District Statement of Reduction in Force shall be deemed waived.

(d) The notice of defense or notice of participation shall be in writing signed by or on behalf of the respondent and shall state the respondent's mailing address. It need not be verified or follow any particular form.

(e) As used in this section, "file," "files," "filed," or " filing" means "delivered or mailed" to the agency as provided in Section 11505. *(Added by Stats.1945, c. 867, p. 1629, § 1. Amended by Stats.1963, c. 931, p. 2184, § 1; Stats.1982, c. 606, p. 2588, § 1; Stats.1986, c. 951, § 20; Stats.1995, c. 938 (S.B.523), § 29, operative July 1, 1997; Stats.2013, c. 90 (S.B.546), § 5.)*

Law Revision Commission Comments

Section 11506 is amended to delete the statement by way of mitigation. A default may be cured pursuant to Section 11520, and evidence in favor of mitigation may be made as a defense. [25 Cal.L.Rev.Comm. Report 55 (1995)].

Research References

Miller and Starr California Real Estate § 4:42, Disciplinary Process-- Hearing Procedure.

9 Witkin Cal. Proc. 5th Administrative Proceedings § 100, (S 100) Notice of Defense.

§ 11507. Amended or supplemental accusation or District Statement of Reduction in Force before submission of case

At any time before the matter is submitted for decision, the agency may file or permit the filing of an amended or supplemental accusation or District Statement of Reduction in Force. All parties shall be notified * * * of the filing. If the amended or supplemental accusation or District Statement of Reduction in Force presents new charges the agency shall afford the respondent a reasonable opportunity to prepare his or her defense thereto, but he or she shall not be entitled to file a further pleading unless the agency in its discretion so orders. Any new charges shall be deemed controverted, and any objections to the amended or supplemental accusation or District Statement of Reduction in Force may be made orally and shall be noted in the record. *(Added by Stats.1945, c. 867, p. 1629, § 1. Amended by Stats.2013, c. 90 (S.B.546), § 6.)*

Research References

Miller and Starr California Real Estate § 4:42, Disciplinary Process-- Hearing Procedure.

9 Witkin Cal. Proc. 5th Administrative Proceedings § 99, Amendment and Supplementation.

§ 11507.3. Consolidation of proceedings

(a) When proceedings that involve a common question of law or fact are pending, the administrative law judge on the judge's own motion or on motion of a party may order a joint hearing of any or all the matters at issue in the proceedings. The administrative law judge may order all the proceedings consolidated and may make orders concerning the procedure that may tend to avoid unnecessary costs or delay.

(b) The administrative law judge on the judge's own motion or on motion of a party, in furtherance of convenience or to avoid prejudice or when separate hearings will be conducive to expedition and economy, may order a separate hearing of any issue, including an issue raised in the notice of defense or notice of participation, or of any number of issues. *(Added by*

Stats.1995, c. 938 (S.B.523), § 30, operative July 1, 1997. Amended by Stats.2013, c. 90 (S.B.546), § 7.)

Law Revision Commission Comments

Section 11507.3 is drawn from Code of Civil Procedure Section 1048. Subdivision (a) is sufficiently broad to enable related cases brought before several agencies to be consolidated in a single proceeding. See also Section 13 (singular includes plural). [25 Cal.L.Rev.Comm. Reports 55 (1995)].

Research References

9 Witkin Cal. Proc. 5th Administrative Proceedings § 101, (S 101) Consolidation and Severance.

§ 11507.5. Discovery; exclusive provisions

The provisions of Section 11507.6 provide the exclusive right to and method of discovery as to any proceeding governed by this chapter. *(Added by Stats.1968, c. 808, p. 1561, § 3.)*

Research References

Rutter, Cal. Practice Guide: Civ. Pro. Before Trial Ch. 8A-8, Discovery in Nonjudicial Proceedings.
Miller and Starr California Real Estate § 4:42, Disciplinary Process-- Hearing Procedure.
9 Witkin Cal. Proc. 5th Administrative Proceedings § 102, Limited Discovery.

§ 11507.6. Request for discovery; statements; writings; investigative reports

After initiation of a proceeding in which a respondent or other party is entitled to a hearing on the merits, a party, upon written request made to another party, prior to the hearing and within 30 days after service by the agency of the initial pleading or within 15 days after the service of an additional pleading, is entitled to (1) obtain the names and addresses of witnesses to the extent known to the other party, including, but not limited to, those intended to be called to testify at the hearing, and (2) inspect and make a copy of any of the following in the possession or custody or under the control of the other party:

(a) A statement of a person, other than the respondent, named in the initial administrative pleading, or in any additional pleading, when it is claimed that the act or omission of the respondent as to this person is the basis for the administrative proceeding;

(b) A statement pertaining to the subject matter of the proceeding made by any party to another party or person;

(c) Statements of witnesses then proposed to be called by the party and of other persons having personal knowledge of the acts, omissions or events which are the basis for the proceeding, not included in (a) or (b) above;

(d) All writings, including, but not limited to, reports of mental, physical and blood examinations and things which the party then proposes to offer in evidence;

(e) Any other writing or thing which is relevant and which would be admissible in evidence;

(f) Investigative reports made by or on behalf of the agency or other party pertaining to the subject matter of the proceeding, to the extent that these reports (1) contain the names and addresses of witnesses or of persons having personal knowledge of the acts, omissions or events which are the basis for the proceeding, or (2) reflect matters perceived by the investigator in the course of his or her investigation, or (3) contain or include by attachment any statement or writing described in (a) to (e), inclusive, or summary thereof.

For the purpose of this section, "statements" include written statements by the person signed or otherwise authenticated by him or her, stenographic, mechanical, electrical or other recordings, or transcripts thereof, of oral statements by the person, and written reports or summaries of these oral statements.

Nothing in this section shall authorize the inspection or copying of any writing or thing which is privileged from disclosure by law or otherwise made confidential or protected as the attorney's work product. *(Added by Stats.1968, c. 808, p. 1561, § 4. Amended by Stats.1985, c. 1328, § 5; Stats.1995, c. 938 (S.B.523), § 31, operative July 1, 1997.)*

Law Revision Commission Comments

Former subdivision (g) of Section 11507.6 is restated in Section 11440.40 (evidence of sexual conduct). [25 Cal.L.Rev.Comm. Reports 55 (1995)].

Research References

Rutter, Cal. Practice Guide: Insurance Litigation Ch. 14-A, A. The California Regulator (*).
Miller and Starr California Real Estate § 4:42, Disciplinary Process-- Hearing Procedure.
9 Witkin Cal. Proc. 5th Administrative Proceedings § 102, Limited Discovery.
9 Witkin Cal. Proc. 5th Administrative Proceedings § 104, (S 104) Prehearing Conference.

§ 11507.7. Motion to compel discovery

(a) Any party claiming the party's request for discovery pursuant to Section 11507.6 has not been complied with may serve and file with the administrative law judge a motion to compel discovery, naming as respondent the party refusing or failing to comply with Section 11507.6. The motion shall state facts showing the respondent party failed or refused to comply with Section 11507.6, a description of the matters sought to be discovered, the reason or reasons why the matter is discoverable under that section, that a reasonable and good faith attempt to contact the respondent for an informal resolution of the issue has been made, and the ground or grounds of respondent's refusal so far as known to the moving party.

(b) The motion shall be served upon respondent party and filed within 15 days after the respondent party first evidenced failure or refusal to comply with Section 11507.6 or within 30 days after request was made and the party has failed to reply to the request, or within another time provided by stipulation, whichever period is longer.

(c) The hearing on the motion to compel discovery shall be held within 15 days after the motion is made, or a later time that the administrative law judge may on the judge's own motion for good cause determine. The respondent party shall have the right to serve and file a written answer or other response to the motion before or at the time of the hearing.

(d) Where the matter sought to be discovered is under the custody or control of the respondent party and the respondent party asserts that the matter is not a discoverable matter under the provisions of Section 11507.6, or is privileged against disclosure under those provisions, the administrative law judge may order lodged with it [1] matters provided in subdivision (b) of Section 915 of the Evidence Code and examine the matters in accordance with its provisions.

(e) The administrative law judge shall decide the case on the matters examined in camera, the papers filed by the parties, and such oral argument and additional evidence as the administrative law judge may allow.

(f) Unless otherwise stipulated by the parties, the administrative law judge shall no later than 15 days after the hearing make its order denying or granting the motion. The order shall be in writing setting forth the matters the moving party is entitled to discover under Section 11507.6. A copy of the order shall forthwith be served by mail by the administrative law judge upon the parties. Where the order grants the motion in whole or in part, the order shall not become effective until 10 days after the date the order is served. Where the order denies relief to the moving party, the order shall be effective on the date it is served. *(Added by Stats.1968, c. 808, p. 1562, § 5. Amended by Stats.1971, c. 1303, p. 2556, § 8; Stats.1980, c. 548, § 2; Stats.1995, c. 938 (S.B.523), § 32, operative July 1, 1997.)*

1 So in chaptered copy.

Law Revision Commission Comments

Section 11507.7 is amended to provide for proceedings to compel discovery before the administrative law judge rather than the superior court. The administrative law judge may continue the proceeding if necessary to allow adequate briefing of the motion. Cf. Section 11524(a) (continuances granted for good cause).

An order of the administrative law judge compelling discovery is enforceable by certification to the superior court of facts to justify the contempt sanction. Sections 11455.10–11455.20. A court judgment of contempt is not appealable. Code Civ. Proc. §§ 1222, 904.1(a). The administrative law judge may also impose monetary sanctions for bad faith tactics, which are reviewable in the same manner as the decision in the proceeding. Section 11455.30. [25 Cal.L.Rev.Comm. Reports 711 (1995)].

Research References

California Practice Guide: Employment Litigation Ch. 13-H, H. Contesting Citations and Related Orders and Notices.
Miller and Starr California Real Estate § 4:42, Disciplinary Process-- Hearing Procedure.
9 Witkin Cal. Proc. 5th Administrative Proceedings § 102, Limited Discovery.

§ 11508. Time and place of hearing

(a) The agency shall consult the office, and subject to the availability of its staff, shall determine the time and place of the hearing. The hearing shall be held at a hearing facility maintained by the office in Sacramento, Oakland, Los Angeles, or San Diego and shall be held at the facility that is closest to the location where the transaction occurred or the respondent resides.

(b) Notwithstanding subdivision (a), the hearing may be held at either of the following places:

(1) A place selected by the agency that is closer to the location where the transaction occurred or the respondent resides.

(2) A place within the state selected by agreement of the parties.

(c) The respondent may move for, and the administrative law judge has discretion to grant or deny, a change in the place of the hearing. A motion for a change in the place of the hearing shall be made within 10 days after service of the notice of hearing on the respondent.

Unless good cause is identified in writing by the administrative law judge, hearings shall be held in a facility maintained by the office. *(Added by Stats.1945, c. 867, p. 1629, § 1. Amended by Stats.1963, c. 710, p. 1715, § 1; Stats.1967, c. 17, p. 837, § 39; Stats.1987, c. 50, § 1; Stats.1995, c. 938 (S.B.523), § 33, operative July 1, 1997; Stats.2005, c. 674 (S.B.231), § 22.)*

Law Revision Commission Comments

Subdivision (a) of Section 11508 is amended to reflect relocation of the San Francisco branch of the Office of Administrative Hearings to Oakland and to recognize creation of a branch of the Office of Administrative Hearings in San Diego.

Subdivision (c) codifies practice authorizing a motion for change of venue. See 1 G. Ogden, California Public Agency Practice § 33.02[4][d] (1994). Grounds for change of venue include selection of an improper county and promotion of the convenience of witnesses and ends of justice. Cf. Code Civ. Proc. § 397. In making a change of venue determination the administrative law judge may weigh the detriment to the moving party of the initial location against the cost to the agency and other parties of

relocating the site. Failure to move for a change in the place of the hearing within the 10 day period waives the right to object to the place of the hearing. [25 Cal.L.Rev.Comm. Reports 711 (1995)].

Research References

Miller and Starr California Real Estate § 25C:45, Violation of the Subdivided Lands Act; Enforcement by the Commissioner.
9 Witkin Cal. Proc. 5th Administrative Proceedings § 106, Time and Place.

§ 11509. Notice of hearing

The agency shall deliver or mail a notice of hearing to all parties at least 10 days prior to the hearing. The hearing shall not be prior to the expiration of the time within which the respondent is entitled to file a notice of defense, or, as applicable, notice of participation.

The notice to respondent shall be substantially in the following form but may include other information:

You are hereby notified that a hearing will be held before [here insert name of agency] at [here insert place of hearing] on the ___ day of ___, 20__, at the hour of ___, upon the charges made in the accusation or District Statement of Reduction in Force served upon you. If you object to the place of hearing, you must notify the presiding officer within 10 days after this notice is served on you. Failure to notify the presiding officer within 10 days will deprive you of a change in the place of the hearing. You may be present at the hearing. You have the right to be represented by an attorney at your own expense. You are not entitled to the appointment of an attorney to represent you at public expense. You are entitled to represent yourself without legal counsel. You may present any relevant evidence, and will be given full opportunity to cross-examine all witnesses testifying against you. You are entitled to the issuance of subpoenas to compel the attendance of witnesses and the production of books, documents or other things by applying to [here insert appropriate office of agency]. *(Added by Stats.1945, c. 867, p. 1630, § 1. Amended by Stats.1988, c. 362, § 2; Stats.1995, c. 938 (S.B.523), § 34, operative July 1, 1997; Stats. 2013, c. 90 (S.B.546), § 8.)*

Law Revision Commission Comments

Section 11509 is amended to include notification of the right to seek change of venue. See Section 11508 (time and place of hearing). [25 Cal.L.Rev.Comm. Reports 55 (1995)].

Research References

Miller and Starr California Real Estate § 4:42, Disciplinary Process-- Hearing Procedure.
9 Witkin Cal. Proc. 5th Administrative Proceedings § 98, Service.
9 Witkin Cal. Proc. 5th Administrative Proceedings § 106, Time and Place.
9 Witkin Cal. Proc. 5th Administrative Proceedings § 107, Notice of Hearing.
7 Witkin, California Summary 10th Constitutional Law § 665, Counsel.

§ 11511. Depositions

On verified petition of any party, an administrative law judge or, if an administrative law judge has not been appointed, an agency may order that the testimony of any material witness residing within or without the state be taken by deposition in the manner prescribed by law for depositions in civil actions under Title 4 (commencing with Section 2016.010) of Part 4 of the Code of Civil Procedure. The petition shall set forth the nature of the pending proceeding; the name and address of the witness whose testimony is desired; a showing of the materiality of the testimony; a showing that the witness will be unable or cannot be compelled to attend; and shall request an order requiring the witness to appear and testify before an officer named in the petition for that purpose. The petitioner shall serve notice of

Government

hearing and a copy of the petition on the other parties at least 10 days before the hearing. Where the witness resides outside the state and where the administrative law judge or agency has ordered the taking of the testimony by deposition, the agency shall obtain an order of court to that effect by filing a petition therefor in the superior court in Sacramento County. The proceedings thereon shall be in accordance with the provisions of Section 11189. *(Added by Stats.1945, c. 867, p. 1631, § 1. Amended by Stats.1995, c. 938 (S.B.523), § 36, operative July 1, 1997; Stats.1998, c. 931 (S.B.2139), § 182, eff. Sept. 28, 1998; Stats.2004, c. 182 (A.B.3081), § 42, operative July 1, 2005.)*

Law Revision Commission Comments

Section 11511 is amended to extend to the administrative law judge the authority to order a deposition, and to provide for notice of the petition. [25 Cal.L.Rev.Comm. Reports 55 (1995)].

Section 11511 is amended to accommodate unification of the municipal and superior courts in a county. Cal. Const. art. VI, § 5(e). [28 Cal.L.Rev.Comm. Reports 51 (1998)].

Section 11511 is amended to reflect nonsubstantive reorganization of the rules governing civil discovery. [33 Cal.L.Rev.Comm. Reports 1034 (2004)].

Research References

Miller and Starr California Real Estate § 4:42, Disciplinary Process--Hearing Procedure.
9 Witkin Cal. Proc. 5th Administrative Proceedings § 102, Limited Discovery.
7 Witkin, California Summary 10th Constitutional Law § 666, (S 666) General Rule.

§ 11511.5. Prehearing conference; subject matter; prehearing order

(a) On motion of a party or by order of an administrative law judge, the administrative law judge may conduct a prehearing conference. The administrative law judge shall set the time and place for the prehearing conference, and shall give reasonable written notice to all parties.

(b) The prehearing conference may deal with one or more of the following matters:

(1) Exploration of settlement possibilities.

(2) Preparation of stipulations.

(3) Clarification of issues.

(4) Rulings on identity and limitation of the number of witnesses.

(5) Objections to proffers of evidence.

(6) Order of presentation of evidence and cross-examination.

(7) Rulings regarding issuance of subpoenas and protective orders.

(8) Schedules for the submission of written briefs and schedules for the commencement and conduct of the hearing.

(9) Exchange of witness lists and of exhibits or documents to be offered in evidence at the hearing.

(10) Motions for intervention.

(11) Exploration of the possibility of using alternative dispute resolution provided in Article 5 (commencing with Section 11420.10) of, or the informal hearing procedure provided in Article 10 (commencing with Section 11445.10) of, Chapter 4.5, and objections to use of the informal hearing procedure. Use of alternative dispute resolution or of the informal hearing procedure is subject to subdivision (d).

(12) Any other matters as shall promote the orderly and prompt conduct of the hearing.

(c) The administrative law judge may conduct all or part of the prehearing conference by telephone, television, or other electronic means if each participant in the conference has an opportunity to participate in and to hear the entire proceeding while it is taking place.

(d) With the consent of the parties, the prehearing conference may be converted immediately into alternative dispute resolution or an informal hearing. With the consent of the parties, the proceeding may be converted into alternative dispute resolution to be conducted at another time. With the consent of the agency, the proceeding may be converted into an informal hearing to be conducted at another time subject to the right of a party to object to use of the informal hearing procedure as provided in Section 11445.30.

(e) The administrative law judge shall issue a prehearing order incorporating the matters determined at the prehearing conference. The administrative law judge may direct one or more of the parties to prepare a prehearing order. *(Added by Stats.1986, c. 899, § 1. Amended by Stats.1995, c. 938 (S.B.523), § 37, operative July 1, 1997.)*

Law Revision Commission Comments

Subdivision (a) of Section 11511.5 is amended to reflect the practice of the administrative law judge, rather than the agency, giving the required notice.

Subdivision (b)(9) is not intended to provide a new discovery procedure. If a party has not availed itself of discovery within the time periods provided by Section 11507.6, it should not be permitted to use the prehearing conference as a substitute for statutory discovery. The prehearing conference is limited to an exchange of witness lists and of exhibits or documents to be offered in evidence at the hearing.

Subdivision (b)(10) implements Section 11440.50 (intervention) for those proceedings in which an agency has by regulation provided for intervention.

Subdivision (c) is a procedural innovation drawn from 1981 Model State APA § 4–205(a) that allows the presiding officer to conduct all or part of the prehearing conference by telephone, television, or other electronic means, such as a conference telephone call. While subdivision (c) permits the conduct of proceedings by telephone, television, or other electronic means, the administrative law judge may of course conduct the proceedings in the physical presence of all participants.

Subdivision (d) is drawn from 1981 Model State APA § 4–204(3)(vii), expanded to include alternative dispute resolution. [25 Cal.L.Rev.Comm. Reports 711 (1995)].

Research References

Miller and Starr California Real Estate § 4:42, Disciplinary Process--Hearing Procedure.
9 Witkin Cal. Proc. 5th Administrative Proceedings § 104, (S 104) Prehearing Conference.

§ 11511.7. Settlement conferences

(a) The administrative law judge may order the parties to attend and participate in a settlement conference. The administrative law judge shall set the time and place for the settlement conference, and shall give reasonable written notice to all parties.

(b) The administrative law judge at the settlement conference shall not preside as administrative law judge at the hearing unless otherwise stipulated by the parties. The administrative law judge may conduct all or part of the settlement conference by telephone, television, or other electronic means if each participant in the conference has an opportunity to participate in and to hear the entire proceeding while it is taking place. *(Added by Stats.1995, c. 938 (S.B.523), § 38, operative July 1, 1997.)*

Law Revision Commission Comments

Under Section 11511.7 a settlement conference may, but need not, be separate from the prehearing conference (at which exploration of settlement issues may occur).

Attendance and participation in the settlement conference is mandatory. Communications made in settlement negotiations are protected. Section 11415.60 (settlement). [25 Cal.L.Rev.Comm. Reports 55 (1995)].

Research References

Miller and Starr California Real Estate § 4:42, Disciplinary Process--Hearing Procedure.
9 Witkin Cal. Proc. 5th Administrative Proceedings § 105, (S 105) Settlement Conference.

§ 11512. Presiding officer; participation of agency in hearing; conduct of hearing; disqualification of administrative law judge or agency member; reporter; proposed decision

(a) Every hearing in a contested case shall be presided over by an administrative law judge. The agency itself shall determine whether the administrative law judge is to hear the case alone or whether the agency itself is to hear the case with the administrative law judge.

(b) When the agency itself hears the case, the administrative law judge shall preside at the hearing, rule on the admission and exclusion of evidence, and advise the agency on matters of law; the agency itself shall exercise all other powers relating to the conduct of the hearing but may delegate any or all of them to the administrative law judge. When the administrative law judge alone hears a case, he or she shall exercise all powers relating to the conduct of the hearing. A ruling of the administrative law judge admitting or excluding evidence is subject to review in the same manner and to the same extent as the administrative law judge's proposed decision in the proceeding.

(c) An administrative law judge or agency member shall voluntarily disqualify himself or herself and withdraw from any case in which there are grounds for disqualification, including disqualification under Section 11425.40. The parties may waive the disqualification by a writing that recites the grounds for disqualification. A waiver is effective only when signed by all parties, accepted by the administrative law judge or agency member, and included in the record. Any party may request the disqualification of any administrative law judge or agency member by filing an affidavit, prior to the taking of evidence at a hearing, stating with particularity the grounds upon which it is claimed that the administrative law judge or agency member is disqualified. Where the request concerns an agency member, the issue shall be determined by the other members of the agency. Where the request concerns the administrative law judge, the issue shall be determined by the agency itself if the agency itself hears the case with the administrative law judge, otherwise the issue shall be determined by the administrative law judge. No agency member shall withdraw voluntarily or be subject to disqualification if his or her disqualification would prevent the existence of a quorum qualified to act in the particular case, except that a substitute qualified to act may be appointed by the appointing authority.

(d) The proceedings at the hearing shall be reported by a stenographic reporter. However, upon the consent of all the parties, the proceedings may be reported electronically.

(e) Whenever, after the agency itself has commenced to hear the case with an administrative law judge presiding, a quorum no longer exists, the administrative law judge who is presiding shall complete the hearing as if sitting alone and shall render a proposed decision in accordance with subdivision (b) of Section 11517. *(Added by Stats.1945, c. 867, p. 1631, § 1. Amended by Stats.1973, c. 231, p. 616, § 1; Stats.1983, c. 635, § 1; Stats.1985, c. 324, § 19; Stats.1995, c. 938 (S.B.523), § 39, operative July 1, 1997.)*

Law Revision Commission Comments

Subdivision (b) of Section 11512 is amended to overrule any contrary implication that might otherwise be drawn from the language of subdivision (b).

Grounds for disqualification under subdivision (c) include bias, prejudice, or interest of presiding officer (Section 11425.40) and receipt of ex parte communications (Section 11430.60). A waiver of disqualification is a voluntary relinquishment of rights by the parties. The administrative law judge need not accept a waiver; the waiver is effective only if accepted by the administrative law judge. The provision for appointment of a substitute for an agency member is drawn from 1981 Model State APA § 4–202(e). In cases where there is no appointing authority, e.g., the agency member is an elected official, the "rule of necessity" still applies and the agency member shall not withdraw or be disqualified. See 1 G. Ogden, California Public Agency Practice § 36.14 (1994). [25 Cal.L.Rev. Comm. Reports 711 (1995)].

Research References

Miller and Starr California Real Estate § 4:42, Disciplinary Process--Hearing Procedure.
Miller and Starr California Real Estate § 25C:45, Violation of the Subdivided Lands Act; Enforcement by the Commissioner.
9 Witkin Cal. Proc. 5th Administrative Proceedings § 109, Conduct of Hearing.
9 Witkin Cal. Proc. 5th Administrative Proceedings § 110, Disqualification of Judge or Agency Member.

§ 11513. Evidence; examination of witnesses

(a) Oral evidence shall be taken only on oath or affirmation.

(b) Each party shall have these rights: to call and examine witnesses,[1] to introduce exhibits; to cross-examine opposing witnesses on any matter relevant to the issues even though that matter was not covered in the direct examination; to impeach any witness regardless of which party first called him or her to testify; and to rebut the evidence against him or her. If respondent does not testify in his or her own behalf he or she may be called and examined as if under cross-examination.

(c) The hearing need not be conducted according to technical rules relating to evidence and witnesses, except as hereinafter provided. Any relevant evidence shall be admitted if it is the sort of evidence on which responsible persons are accustomed to rely in the conduct of serious affairs, regardless of the existence of any common law or statutory rule which might make improper the admission of the evidence over objection in civil actions.

(d) Hearsay evidence may be used for the purpose of supplementing or explaining other evidence but over timely objection shall not be sufficient in itself to support a finding unless it would be admissible over objection in civil actions. An objection is timely if made before submission of the case or on reconsideration.

(e) The rules of privilege shall be effective to the extent that they are otherwise required by statute to be recognized at the hearing.

(f) The presiding officer has discretion to exclude evidence if its probative value is substantially outweighed by the probability that its admission will necessitate undue consumption of time. *(Added by Stats.1992, c. 1302 (A.B.3107), § 9, eff. Sept. 30, 1992, operative July 1, 1995. Amended by Stats.1995, c. 938 (S.B.523), § 40, operative July 1, 1997.)*

[1] Punctuation so in chaptered copy.

Law Revision Commission Comments

Subdivision (d) of Section 11513 is intended to avoid or eliminate routine objections to administrative hearsay. If a proposed finding is supported only by hearsay evidence, a single objection at the conclusion of testimony, or on petition for reconsideration by the agency, is sufficient and timely.

The "irrelevant and unduly repetitious" standard formerly found in Section 11513 is replaced in subdivision (f) by the general standard of

Government

Evidence Code Section 352. The basic standard of admissibility of relevant evidence is stated in subdivision (c); nothing in subdivision (f) authorizes admission of irrelevant evidence.

The unnumbered paragraph formerly located between subdivisions (c) and (d) is restated in Section 11440.40(a).

Former subdivisions (d)-(n) are restated in Sections 11435.20–11435.65.

Former subdivision (*o*) is restated in Section 11440.40(b).

Former subdivision (p) is restated in Section 11440.40(c).

Former subdivision (q) is deleted as obsolete. [25 Cal.L.Rev.Comm. Reports 711 (1995)].

Research References

Rutter, Cal. Practice Guide: Civil Trials & Evidence Ch. 8D-C, C. General Parameters Re Admissibility of Hearsay Evidence.

Miller and Starr California Real Estate § 4:42, Disciplinary Process-- Hearing Procedure.

16 NO. 1 Miller & Starr, California Real Estate Newsalert 22, Regulation of the Real Estate Industry.

20 NO. 4 Miller & Starr, California Real Estate Newsalert 41, Regulation of the Real Estate Industry.

9 Witkin Cal. Proc. 5th Administrative Proceedings § 74, (S 74) General Prohibition.

9 Witkin Cal. Proc. 5th Administrative Proceedings § 111, Evidence.

§ 11514. Affidavits

(a) At any time 10 or more days prior to a hearing or a continued hearing, any party may mail or deliver to the opposing party a copy of any affidavit which he proposes to introduce in evidence, together with a notice as provided in subdivision (b). Unless the opposing party, within seven days after such mailing or delivery, mails or delivers to the proponent a request to cross-examine an affiant, his right to cross-examine such affiant is waived and the affidavit, if introduced in evidence, shall be given the same effect as if the affiant had testified orally. If an opportunity to cross-examine an affiant is not afforded after request therefor is made as herein provided, the affidavit may be introduced in evidence, but shall be given only the same effect as other hearsay evidence.

(b) The notice referred to in subdivision (a) shall be substantially in the following form:

The accompanying affidavit of (here insert name of affiant) will be introduced as evidence at the hearing in (here insert title of proceeding). (Here insert name of affiant) will not be called to testify orally and you will not be entitled to question him unless you notify (here insert name of proponent or his attorney) at (here insert address) that you wish to cross-examine him. To be effective your request must be mailed or delivered to (here insert name of proponent or his attorney) on or before (here insert a date seven days after the date of mailing or delivering the affidavit to the opposing party). *(Added by Stats.1947, c. 491, p. 1471, § 6.)*

Research References

Miller and Starr California Real Estate § 4:42, Disciplinary Process-- Hearing Procedure.

9 Witkin Cal. Proc. 5th Administrative Proceedings § 111, Evidence.

§ 11515. Official notice

In reaching a decision official notice may be taken, either before or after submission of the case for decision, of any generally accepted technical or scientific matter within the agency's special field, and of any fact which may be judicially noticed by the courts of this State. Parties present at the hearing shall be informed of the matters to be noticed, and those matters shall be noted in the record, referred to therein, or appended thereto. Any such party shall be given a reasonable opportunity on request to refute the officially noticed matters by evidence or by written or oral presentation of authority, the manner of such refutation to be determined by the agency. *(Added by Stats. 1945, c. 867, p. 1633, § 1.)*

Research References

Miller and Starr California Real Estate § 4:42, Disciplinary Process-- Hearing Procedure.

9 Witkin Cal. Proc. 5th Administrative Proceedings § 72, (S 72) Statement of Factual Basis.

9 Witkin Cal. Proc. 5th Administrative Proceedings § 111, Evidence.

§ 11516. Amendment of accusation or District Statement of Reduction in Force after submission of case

The agency may order amendment of the accusation or District Statement of Reduction in Force after submission of the case for decision. Each party shall be given notice of the intended amendment and opportunity to show that he or she will be prejudiced thereby unless the case is reopened to permit the introduction of additional evidence on his or her behalf. If such prejudice is shown, the agency shall reopen the case to permit the introduction of additional evidence. *(Added by Stats.1945, c. 867, p. 1633, § 1. Amended by Stats.2013, c. 90 (S.B.546), § 9.)*

Research References

9 Witkin Cal. Proc. 5th Administrative Proceedings § 99, Amendment and Supplementation.

§ 11517. Contested case; original hearing; agency or administrative law judge

(a) A contested case may be originally heard by the agency itself and subdivision (b) shall apply. Alternatively, at the discretion of the agency, an administrative law judge may originally hear the case alone and subdivision (c) shall apply.

(b) If a contested case is originally heard before an agency itself, all of the following provisions apply:

(1) An administrative law judge shall be present during the consideration of the case and, if requested, shall assist and advise the agency in the conduct of the hearing.

(2) No member of the agency who did not hear the evidence shall vote on the decision.

(3) The agency shall issue its decision within 100 days of submission of the case.

(c)(1) If a contested case is originally heard by an administrative law judge alone, he or she shall prepare within 30 days after the case is submitted to him or her a proposed decision in a form that may be adopted by the agency as the final decision in the case. Failure of the administrative law judge to deliver a proposed decision within the time required does not prejudice the rights of the agency in the case. Thirty days after the receipt by the agency of the proposed decision, a copy of the proposed decision shall be filed by the agency as a public record and a copy shall be served by the agency on each party and his or her attorney. The filing and service is not an adoption of a proposed decision by the agency.

(2) Within 100 days of receipt by the agency of the administrative law judge's proposed decision, the agency may act as prescribed in subparagraphs (A) to (E), inclusive. If the agency fails to act as prescribed in subparagraphs (A) to (E), inclusive, within 100 days of receipt of the proposed decision, the proposed decision shall be deemed adopted by the agency. The agency may do any of the following:

(A) Adopt the proposed decision in its entirety.

(B) Reduce or otherwise mitigate the proposed penalty and adopt the balance of the proposed decision.

(C) Make technical or other minor changes in the proposed decision and adopt it as the decision. Action by the agency under this paragraph is limited to a clarifying change or a change of a similar nature that does not affect the factual or legal basis of the proposed decision.

(D) Reject the proposed decision and refer the case to the same administrative law judge if reasonably available, otherwise to another administrative law judge, to take additional evidence. If the case is referred to an administrative law judge pursuant to this subparagraph, he or she shall prepare a revised proposed decision, as provided in paragraph (1), based upon the additional evidence and the transcript and other papers that are part of the record of the prior hearing. A copy of the revised proposed decision shall be furnished to each party and his or her attorney as prescribed in this subdivision.

(E) Reject the proposed decision, and decide the case upon the record, including the transcript, or upon an agreed statement of the parties, with or without taking additional evidence. By stipulation of the parties, the agency may decide the case upon the record without including the transcript. If the agency acts pursuant to this subparagraph, all of the following provisions apply:

(i) A copy of the record shall be made available to the parties. The agency may require payment of fees covering direct costs of making the copy.

(ii) The agency itself shall not decide any case provided for in this subdivision without affording the parties the opportunity to present either oral or written argument before the agency itself. If additional oral evidence is introduced before the agency itself, no agency member may vote unless the member heard the additional oral evidence.

(iii) The authority of the agency itself to decide the case under this subdivision includes authority to decide some but not all issues in the case.

(iv) If the agency elects to proceed under this subparagraph, the agency shall issue its final decision not later than 100 days after rejection of the proposed decision. If the agency elects to proceed under this subparagraph, and has ordered a transcript of the proceedings before the administrative law judge, the agency shall issue its final decision not later than 100 days after receipt of the transcript. If the agency finds that a further delay is required by special circumstance, it shall issue an order delaying the decision for no more than 30 days and specifying the reasons therefor. The order shall be subject to judicial review pursuant to Section 11523.

(d) The decision of the agency shall be filed immediately by the agency as a public record and a copy shall be served by the agency on each party and his or her attorney. *(Added by Stats.1999, c. 339 (A.B.1692), § 2.)*

Research References

Rutter, Cal. Practice Guide: Insurance Litigation Ch. 14-A, A. The California Regulator (*).
Miller and Starr California Real Estate § 4:42, Disciplinary Process--Hearing Procedure.
Miller and Starr California Real Estate § 25C:45, Violation of the Subdivided Lands Act; Enforcement by the Commissioner.
9 Witkin Cal. Proc. 5th Administrative Proceedings § 74, (S 74) General Prohibition.
9 Witkin Cal. Proc. 5th Administrative Proceedings § 109, Conduct of Hearing.
9 Witkin Cal. Proc. 5th Administrative Proceedings § 113, Rendition.
9 Witkin Cal. Proc. 5th Administrative Proceedings § 114, Time for Decision.
9 Witkin Cal. Proc. 5th Administrative Proceedings § 115, Filing and Service.
9 Witkin Cal. Proc. 5th Administrative Proceedings § 118, (S 118) Reconsideration.
8 Witkin Cal. Proc. 5th Extraordinary Writs § 316, (S 316) in General.

§ 11518. Delivery of copies to parties

Copies of the decision shall be delivered to the parties personally or sent to them by registered mail. *(Added by*

Stats.1945, c. 867, p. 1634, § 1. Amended by Stats.1947, c. 491, p. 1472, § 7; Stats.1995, c. 938 (S.B.523), § 43, operative July 1, 1997.)

Law Revision Commission Comments

The first two sentences of Section 11518 are superseded by Section 11425.50 (contents of decision).

The California Public Records Act governs the accessibility of a decision to the public, including exclusions from coverage, confidentiality, and agency regulations affecting access. Gov't Code §§ 6250–6268. [25 Cal.L.Rev.Comm. Reports 55 (1995)].

Research References

9 Witkin Cal. Proc. 5th Administrative Proceedings § 71, (S 71) in General.
9 Witkin Cal. Proc. 5th Administrative Proceedings § 115, Filing and Service.

§ 11518.5. Appeals for correction of mistake or clerical error

(a) Within 15 days after service of a copy of the decision on a party, but not later than the effective date of the decision, the party may apply to the agency for correction of a mistake or clerical error in the decision, stating the specific ground on which the application is made. Notice of the application shall be given to the other parties to the proceeding. The application is not a prerequisite for seeking judicial review.

(b) The agency may refer the application to the administrative law judge who formulated the proposed decision or may delegate its authority under this section to one or more persons.

(c) The agency may deny the application, grant the application and modify the decision, or grant the application and set the matter for further proceedings. The application is considered denied if the agency does not dispose of it within 15 days after it is made or a longer time that the agency provides by regulation.

(d) Nothing in this section precludes the agency, on its own motion or on motion of the administrative law judge, from modifying the decision to correct a mistake or clerical error. A modification under this subdivision shall be made within 15 days after issuance of the decision.

(e) The agency shall, within 15 days after correction of a mistake or clerical error in the decision, serve a copy of the correction on each party on which a copy of the decision was previously served. *(Added by Stats.1995, c. 938 (S.B.523), § 44, operative July 1, 1997.)*

Law Revision Commission Comments

Section 11518.5 is drawn from 1981 Model State APA § 4–218. "Party" includes the agency that is a party to the proceedings. Section 11500(b) ("party" defined).

The section is intended to provide parties a limited right to remedy mistakes in the decision without the need for judicial review. Instances where this procedure is intended to apply include correction of factual or legal errors in the decision. This supplements the authority in 11517 of the agency head to adopt a proposed decision with technical or other minor changes. [25 Cal.L.Rev.Comm. Reports 55 (1995)].

Research References

9 Witkin Cal. Proc. 5th Administrative Proceedings § 116, Correction.

§ 11519. Effective date of decision; stay of execution; notification; restitution

(a) The decision shall become effective 30 days after it is delivered or mailed to respondent unless: a reconsideration is ordered within that time, or the agency itself orders that the decision shall become effective sooner, or a stay of execution is granted.

(b) A stay of execution may be included in the decision or if not included therein may be granted by the agency at any time

Government

before the decision becomes effective. The stay of execution provided herein may be accompanied by an express condition that respondent comply with specified terms of probation; provided, however, that the terms of probation shall be just and reasonable in the light of the findings and decision.

(c) If respondent was required to register with any public officer, a notification of any suspension or revocation shall be sent to the officer after the decision has become effective.

(d) As used in subdivision (b), specified terms of probation may include an order of restitution. Where restitution is ordered and paid pursuant to the provisions of this subdivision, the amount paid shall be credited to any subsequent judgment in a civil action.

(e) The person to which the agency action is directed may not be required to comply with a decision unless the person has been served with the decision in the manner provided in Section 11505 or has actual knowledge of the decision.

(f) A nonparty may not be required to comply with a decision unless the agency has made the decision available for public inspection and copying or the nonparty has actual knowledge of the decision.

(g) This section does not preclude an agency from taking immediate action to protect the public interest in accordance with Article 13 (commencing with Section 11460.10) of Chapter 4.5. *(Added by Stats.1945, c. 867, p. 1634, § 1. Amended by Stats.1949, c. 314, p. 604, § 2; Stats.1976, c. 476, p. 1221, § 1; Stats.1977, c. 680, p. 2206, § 1; Stats.1995, c. 938 (S.B.523), § 45, operative July 1, 1997.)*

Law Revision Commission Comments

Subdivision (d) of Section 11519 is amended to simplify and broaden the application of the restitution provisions.

Subdivisions (e)-(g) are drawn from 1981 Model State APA § 4–220(c)-(d). They distinguish between the effective date of a decision and the time when it can be enforced.

The requirement of "actual knowledge" in subdivisions (e) and (f) is intended to include not only knowledge that a decision has been issued, but also knowledge of the general contents of the decision insofar as it pertains to the person who is required to comply with it. If a question arises whether a particular person had actual knowledge of a decision, this must be resolved in the same manner as other fact questions.

The binding effect of a decision on nonparties who have actual knowledge may be illustrated by a state law that prohibits wholesalers from delivering alcoholic beverages to liquor dealers unless the dealers hold valid licenses from the state beverage agency. If the agency issues a decision revoking the license of a particular dealer, this decision is binding on any wholesaler who has actual knowledge of it, even before the decision is made available for public inspection and copying; the decision binds all wholesalers, including those without actual knowledge, after it has been made available for public inspection and copying. [25 Cal. L.Rev.Comm. Reports 55 (1995)].

Research References

Miller and Starr California Real Estate § 4:42, Disciplinary Process--Hearing Procedure.

Miller and Starr California Real Estate § 4:43, Disciplinary Process--Penalties and Other Remedies.

9 Witkin Cal. Proc. 5th Administrative Proceedings § 117, Effect, Enforcement, and Stay.

9 Witkin Cal. Proc. 5th Administrative Proceedings § 150, (S 150) Stay Pending Review.

§ 11519.1. Restitution; vehicle manufacturers, transporters, and dealers

(a) A decision rendered against a licensee under Article 1 (commencing with Section 11700) of Chapter 4 of Division 5 of the Vehicle Code may include an order of restitution for any financial loss or damage found to have been suffered by a person in the case.

(b) The failure to make the restitution in accordance with the terms of the decision is separate grounds for the Department of Motor Vehicles to refuse to issue a license under Article 1 (commencing with Section 11700) of Chapter 4 of Division 5 of the Vehicle Code, and constitutes a violation of the terms of any applicable probationary order in the decision.

(c) Nothing in this section is intended to limit or restrict actions, remedies, or procedures otherwise available to an aggrieved party pursuant to any other provision of law. *(Added by Stats.2007, c. 93 (S.B.525), § 1.)*

Research References

Miller and Starr California Real Estate § 4:42, Disciplinary Process--Hearing Procedure.

§ 11520. Defaults and uncontested cases

(a) If the respondent either fails to file a notice of defense, or, as applicable, notice of participation, or to appear at the hearing, the agency may take action based upon the respondent's express admissions or upon other evidence and affidavits may be used as evidence without any notice to respondent; and where the burden of proof is on the respondent to establish that the respondent is entitled to the agency action sought, the agency may act without taking evidence.

(b) Notwithstanding the default of the respondent, the agency or the administrative law judge, before a proposed decision is issued, has discretion to grant a hearing on reasonable notice to the parties. If the agency and administrative law judge make conflicting orders under this subdivision, the agency's order takes precedence. The administrative law judge may order the respondent, or the respondent's attorney or other authorized representative, or both, to pay reasonable expenses, including attorney's fees, incurred by another party as a result of the respondent's failure to appear at the hearing.

(c) Within seven days after service on the respondent of a decision based on the respondent's default, the respondent may serve a written motion requesting that the decision be vacated and stating the grounds relied on. The agency in its discretion may vacate the decision and grant a hearing on a showing of good cause. As used in this subdivision, good cause includes, but is not limited to, any of the following:

(1) Failure of the person to receive notice served pursuant to Section 11505.

(2) Mistake, inadvertence, surprise, or excusable neglect. *(Added by Stats.1945, c. 867, p. 1634, § 1. Amended by Stats.1947, c. 491, p. 1472, § 8; Stats.1963, c. 931, p. 2184, § 2; Stats.1995, c. 938 (S.B.523), § 46, operative July 1, 1997; Stats. 2013, c. 90 (S.B.546), § 10.)*

Law Revision Commission Comments

Subdivision (a) of Section 11520 is amended to make clear that either failure to respond or to appear is a default.

Former subdivision (b), relating to the right of a defaulting respondent to make a showing by way of mitigation, is superseded by the procedures to cure a default in subdivisions (b) and (c). The respondent may make a showing by way of mitigation as a defense in the hearing.

Subdivision (b) parallels Section 11506(c), with the addition of the provision enabling the administrative law judge to waive a default and impose costs, and requiring reasonable notice.

Subdivision (c) is drawn in part from procedures used by the Unemployment Insurance Appeals Board. [25 Cal.L.Rev.Comm. Reports 55 (1995)].

Research References

Miller and Starr California Real Estate § 4:42, Disciplinary Process--Hearing Procedure.

9 Witkin Cal. Proc. 5th Administrative Proceedings § 100, (S 100) Notice of Defense.

9 Witkin Cal. Proc. 5th Administrative Proceedings § 112, (S 112) Default.

§ 11521. Reconsideration

(a) The agency itself may order a reconsideration of all or part of the case on its own motion or on petition of any party. The agency shall notify a petitioner of the time limits for petitioning for reconsideration. The power to order a reconsideration shall expire 30 days after the delivery or mailing of a decision to a respondent, or on the date set by the agency itself as the effective date of the decision if that date occurs prior to the expiration of the 30–day period or at the termination of a stay of not to exceed 30 days which the agency may grant for the purpose of filing an application for reconsideration. If additional time is needed to evaluate a petition for reconsideration filed prior to the expiration of any of the applicable periods, an agency may grant a stay of that expiration for no more than 10 days, solely for the purpose of considering the petition. If no action is taken on a petition within the time allowed for ordering reconsideration, the petition shall be deemed denied.

(b) The case may be reconsidered by the agency itself on all the pertinent parts of the record and such additional evidence and argument as may be permitted, or may be assigned to an administrative law judge. A reconsideration assigned to an administrative law judge shall be subject to the procedure provided in Section 11517. If oral evidence is introduced before the agency itself, no agency member may vote unless he or she heard the evidence. *(Added by Stats.1945, c. 867, p. 1634, § 1. Amended by Stats.1953, c. 964, p. 2340, § 1; Stats.1985, c. 324, § 22; Stats.1987, c. 305, § 1; Stats.2004, c. 865 (S.B.1914), § 34.)*

Research References

Miller and Starr California Real Estate § 4:14, Requirements to Obtain a License.
Miller and Starr California Real Estate § 4:42, Disciplinary Process--Hearing Procedure.
15 NO. 4 Miller & Starr, California Real Estate Newsalert 4, Construction Contracts.
9 Witkin Cal. Proc. 5th Administrative Proceedings § 118, (S 118) Reconsideration.
8 Witkin Cal. Proc. 5th Extraordinary Writs § 308, What Does Not Extend Period.

§ 11522. Reinstatement of license or reduction of penalty

A person whose license has been revoked or suspended may petition the agency for reinstatement or reduction of penalty after a period of not less than one year has elapsed from the effective date of the decision or from the date of the denial of a similar petition. The agency shall give notice to the Attorney General of the filing of the petition and the Attorney General and the petitioner shall be afforded an opportunity to present either oral or written argument before the agency itself. The agency itself shall decide the petition, and the decision shall include the reasons therefor, and any terms and conditions that the agency reasonably deems appropriate to impose as a condition of reinstatement. This section shall not apply if the statutes dealing with the particular agency contain different provisions for reinstatement or reduction of penalty. *(Added by Stats.1945, c. 867, p. 1634, § 1. Amended by Stats.1985, c. 587, § 4.)*

Research References

Rutter, Cal. Practice Guide: Real Prop. Transactions Ch. 2-B, B. Licensing and Regulatory Requirements.
Miller and Starr California Real Estate § 4:43, Disciplinary Process--Penalties and Other Remedies.

9 Witkin Cal. Proc. 5th Administrative Proceedings § 119, (S 119) Reinstatement of License or Reduction of Penalty.

§ 11523. Judicial review

Judicial review may be had by filing a petition for a writ of mandate in accordance with the provisions of the Code of Civil Procedure, subject, however, to the statutes relating to the particular agency. Except as otherwise provided in this section, the petition shall be filed within 30 days after the last day on which reconsideration can be ordered. The right to petition shall not be affected by the failure to seek reconsideration before the agency. On request of the petitioner for a record of the proceedings, the complete record of the proceedings, or the parts thereof as are designated by the petitioner in the request, shall be prepared by the Office of Administrative Hearings or the agency and shall be delivered to the petitioner, within 30 days after the request, which time shall be extended for good cause shown, upon the payment of the cost for the preparation of the transcript, the cost for preparation of other portions of the record and for certification thereof. The complete record includes the pleadings, all notices and orders issued by the agency, any proposed decision by an administrative law judge, the final decision, a transcript of all proceedings, the exhibits admitted or rejected, the written evidence and any other papers in the case. If the petitioner, within 10 days after the last day on which reconsideration can be ordered, requests the agency to prepare all or any part of the record, the time within which a petition may be filed shall be extended until 30 days after its delivery to him or her. The agency may file with the court the original of any document in the record in lieu of a copy thereof. If the petitioner prevails in overturning the administrative decision following judicial review, the agency shall reimburse the petitioner for all costs of transcript preparation, compilation of the record, and certification. *(Added by Stats.1945, c. 867, p. 1635, § 1. Amended by Stats.1947, c. 491, p. 1472, § 9; Stats.1953, c. 962, p. 2339, § 1; Stats.1955, c. 246, p. 709, § 1; Stats.1965, c. 1458, p. 3416, § 10; Stats.1971, c. 984, p. 1896, § 1; Stats.1985, c. 324, § 23; Stats.1985, c. 973, § 1; Stats.1986, c. 597, § 3; Stats.1994, c. 1206 (S.B.1775), § 29; Stats.1995, c. 938 (S.B.523), § 47, operative July 1, 1997; Stats.2005, c. 674 (S.B. 231), § 23.)*

Fees and Charges

Commissioner's authority to increase or decrease fees, and schedule of fees and charges, see Insurance Code § 12978.

Law Revision Commission Comments

Section 11523 is amended to clarify how long the agency must wait for the petitioner to designate a part of the record before it may proceed on the assumption that the complete record is required. This revision is intended to reduce confusion and delay encountered in the appeal process. [25 Cal.L.Rev.Comm. Reports 55 (1995)].

Research References

Miller and Starr California Real Estate § 4:14, Requirements to Obtain a License.
Miller and Starr California Real Estate § 4:42, Disciplinary Process--Hearing Procedure.
Miller and Starr California Real Estate § 4:44, Disciplinary Process--Judicial Review.
Miller and Starr California Real Estate § 20:22, California Fair Employment and Housing Act--Administrative Proceedings.
Miller and Starr California Real Estate § 23:54, Remedies.
Miller and Starr California Real Estate § 25C:45, Violation of the Subdivided Lands Act; Enforcement by the Commissioner.
14 NO. 5 Miller & Starr, California Real Estate Newsalert 9, Discrimination.
3 Witkin Cal. Proc. 5th Actions § 329, Application for Rehearing by Administrative Body.
3 Witkin Cal. Proc. 5th Actions § 419, Costs of Appeal.

Government

3 Witkin Cal. Proc. 5th Actions § 684, (S 684) Mandamus.
9 Witkin Cal. Proc. 5th Administrative Proceedings § 114, Time for Decision.
9 Witkin Cal. Proc. 5th Administrative Proceedings § 121, (S 121) Forms of Relief.
9 Witkin Cal. Proc. 5th Administrative Proceedings § 124, (S 124) Finality and Ripeness.
9 Witkin Cal. Proc. 5th Administrative Proceedings § 129, (S 129) Statutes of Limitations.
9 Witkin Cal. Proc. 5th Administrative Proceedings § 148, (S 148) Administrative Mandamus as Remedy.
9 Witkin Cal. Proc. 5th Administrative Proceedings § 149, (S 149) Petition.
9 Witkin Cal. Proc. 5th Administrative Proceedings § 151, (S 151) Record on Review.
8 Witkin Cal. Proc. 5th Extraordinary Writs § 303, (S 303) in General.
8 Witkin Cal. Proc. 5th Extraordinary Writs § 307, Period and Extensions.
8 Witkin Cal. Proc. 5th Extraordinary Writs § 309, (S 309) Content.
8 Witkin Cal. Proc. 5th Extraordinary Writs § 311, (S 311) Obtaining and Filing Record.
8 Witkin Cal. Proc. 5th Extraordinary Writs § 313, Legislative Abrogation of Rule.
8 Witkin Cal. Proc. 5th Extraordinary Writs § 314, in General.
8 Witkin Cal. Proc. 5th Extraordinary Writs § 315, Record Prepared for Administrative Proceeding.
2 Witkin, California Summary 10th Insurance § 10, Ratemaking Process.
12 Witkin, California Summary 10th Real Property § 884, Forests.
8 Witkin, California Summary 10th Constitutional Law § 953, in General.

§ 11524. Continuances; good cause; judicial review

(a) The agency may grant continuances. When an administrative law judge of the Office of Administrative Hearings has been assigned to the hearing, no continuance may be granted except by him or her or by the presiding judge of the appropriate regional office of the Office of Administrative Hearings, for good cause shown.

(b) When seeking a continuance, a party shall apply for the continuance within 10 working days following the time the party discovered or reasonably should have discovered the event or occurrence which establishes the good cause for the continuance. A continuance may be granted for good cause after the 10 working days have lapsed if the party seeking the continuance is not responsible for and has made a good faith effort to prevent the condition or event establishing the good cause.

(c) In the event that an application for a continuance by a party is denied by an administrative law judge of the Office of Administrative Hearings, and the party seeks judicial review thereof, the party shall, within 10 working days of the denial, make application for appropriate judicial relief in the superior court or be barred from judicial review thereof as a matter of jurisdiction. A party applying for judicial relief from the denial shall give notice to the agency and other parties. Notwithstanding Section 1010 of the Code of Civil Procedure, the notice may be either oral at the time of the denial of application for a continuance or written at the same time application is made in court for judicial relief. This subdivision does not apply to the Department of Alcoholic Beverage Control. (Added by Stats. 1945, c. 867, p. 1635, § 1. Amended by Stats.1953, c. 962, p. 2339, § 2; Stats.1963, c. 842, p. 2069, § 1; Stats.1971, c. 1303, p. 2557, § 9; Stats.1979, c. 199, § 5; Stats.1985, c. 324, § 24; Stats.1995, c. 938 (S.B.523), § 48, operative July 1, 1997.)

Law Revision Commission Comments
Section 11524 is amended to reflect current practice. [25 Cal.L.Rev. Comm. Reports 55 (1995)].

Research References
9 Witkin Cal. Proc. 5th Administrative Proceedings § 108, Continuance.

§ 11526. Voting by mail or other method

The members of an agency qualified to vote on any question may vote by mail or another appropriate method. (Added by Stats.1945, c. 867, p. 1635, § 1. Amended by Stats.1995, c. 938 (S.B.523), § 50, operative July 1, 1997.)

Law Revision Commission Comments
Section 11526 is broadened to allow telephonic or other appropriate means of voting. An agency member is not qualified to vote when a contested case is heard before the agency itself if the agency member did not hear the evidence. Section 11517(a).

Under the open meeting law, deliberations on a decision to be reached based on evidence introduced in an adjudicative proceeding may be made in closed session. Section 11126(d). [25 Cal.L.Rev.Comm. Reports 55 (1995)].

Research References
9 Witkin Cal. Proc. 5th Administrative Proceedings § 113, Rendition.

§ 11527. Charge against funds of agency

Any sums authorized to be expended under this chapter by any agency shall be a legal charge against the funds of the agency. (Added by Stats.1945, c. 867, p. 1635, § 1.)

§ 11528. Oaths

In any proceedings under this chapter any agency, agency member, secretary of an agency, hearing reporter, or administrative law judge has power to administer oaths and affirmations and to certify to official acts. (Added by Stats.1945, c. 867, p. 1635, § 1. Amended by Stats.1969, c. 191, p. 469, § 1; Stats. 1985, c. 324, § 25.)

Research References
Miller and Starr California Real Estate § 25C:45, Violation of the Subdivided Lands Act; Enforcement by the Commissioner.
9 Witkin Cal. Proc. 5th Administrative Proceedings § 109, Conduct of Hearing.

§ 11529. Interim orders suspending or imposing restrictions on license of medical care professional

(a) The administrative law judge of the Medical Quality Hearing Panel established pursuant to Section 11371 may issue an interim order suspending a license, * * * imposing drug testing, continuing education, supervision of procedures, limitations on the authority to prescribe, furnish, administer, or dispense controlled substances, or other license restrictions. Interim orders may be issued only if the affidavits in support of the petition show that the licensee has engaged in, or is about to engage in, acts or omissions constituting a violation of the Medical Practice Act or the appropriate practice act governing each allied health profession, or is unable to practice safely due to a mental or physical condition, and that permitting the licensee to continue to engage in the profession for which the license was issued will endanger the public health, safety, or welfare. The failure to comply with an order issued pursuant to Section 820 of the Business and Professions Code may constitute grounds to issue an interim suspension order under this section.

(b) All orders authorized by this section shall be issued only after a hearing conducted pursuant to subdivision (d), unless it appears from the facts shown by affidavit that serious injury would result to the public before the matter can be heard on notice. Except as provided in subdivision (c), the licensee shall receive at least 15 days' prior notice of the hearing, which notice shall include affidavits and all other information in support of the order.

(c) If an interim order is issued without notice, the administrative law judge who issued the order without notice shall cause the licensee to be notified of the order, including affidavits and all other information in support of the order by a 24–hour delivery service. That notice shall also include the date of the hearing on the order, which shall be conducted in accordance with the requirement of subdivision (d), not later than 20 days from the date of issuance. The order shall be dissolved unless the requirements of subdivision (a) are satisfied.

(d) For the purposes of the hearing conducted pursuant to this section, the licentiate shall, at a minimum, have the following rights:

(1) To be represented by counsel.

(2) To have a record made of the proceedings, copies of which may be obtained by the licentiate upon payment of any reasonable charges associated with the record.

(3) To present written evidence in the form of relevant declarations, affidavits, and documents.

The discretion of the administrative law judge to permit testimony at the hearing conducted pursuant to this section shall be identical to the discretion of a superior court judge to permit testimony at a hearing conducted pursuant to Section 527 of the Code of Civil Procedure.

(4) To present oral argument.

(e) Consistent with the burden and standards of proof applicable to a preliminary injunction entered under Section 527 of the Code of Civil Procedure, the administrative law judge shall grant the interim order if, in the exercise of discretion, the administrative law judge concludes that:

(1) There is a reasonable probability that the petitioner will prevail in the underlying action.

(2) The likelihood of injury to the public in not issuing the order outweighs the likelihood of injury to the licensee in issuing the order.

(f) In all cases * * * in which an interim order is issued, and an accusation is not filed and served pursuant to Sections 11503 and 11505 within 30 days of the date on which the parties to the hearing on the interim order have submitted the matter, the order shall be dissolved.

Upon service of the accusation the licensee shall have, in addition to the rights granted by this section, all of the rights and privileges available as specified in this chapter. If the licensee requests a hearing on the accusation, the board shall provide the licensee with a hearing within 30 days of the request, unless the licensee stipulates to a later hearing, and a decision within 15 days of the date the decision is received from the administrative law judge, or the board shall nullify the interim order previously issued, unless good cause can be shown by the Division of Medical Quality for a delay.

(g) If an interim order is issued, a written decision shall be prepared within 15 days of the hearing, by the administrative law judge, including findings of fact and a conclusion articulating the connection between the evidence produced at the hearing and the decision reached.

(h) Notwithstanding the fact that interim orders issued pursuant to this section are not issued after a hearing as otherwise required by this chapter, interim orders so issued shall be subject to judicial review pursuant to Section 1094.5 of the Code of Civil Procedure. The relief that may be ordered shall be limited to a stay of the interim order. Interim orders issued pursuant to this section are final interim orders and, if not dissolved pursuant to subdivision (c) or (f), may only be challenged administratively at the hearing on the accusation.

(i) The interim order provided for by this section shall be:

(1) In addition to, and not a limitation on, the authority to seek injunctive relief provided for in the Business and Professions Code.

(2) A limitation on the emergency decision procedure provided in Article 13 (commencing with Section 11460.10) of Chapter 4.5. *(Added by Stats.1990, c. 1597 (S.B.2375), § 35. Amended*

by Stats.1993, c. 1267 (S.B.916), § 54; Stats.1995, c. 938 (S.B. 523), § 51, operative July 1, 1997; Stats.1998, c. 878 (S.B.2239), § 57; Stats.2013, c. 399 (S.B.670), § 3; Stats.2013, c. 515 (S.B.304), § 29.5.)

Law Revision Commission Comments

Section 11529 is amended to substitute the administrative law judge for the court in subdivision (e).

Subdivision (i) is amended to make clear that, notwithstanding Section 11415.10, the emergency decision procedure of the Administrative Procedure Act may not be used as an alternative to the interim order procedure provided in this section for interim suspension of a license, or imposition of drug testing, continuing education, supervision of procedures, or other license restrictions. [25 Cal.L.Rev.Comm. Reports 711 (1995)].

Research References

14 NO. 5 Miller & Starr, California Real Estate Newsalert 9, Discrimination.

Part 4.5

BUSINESS, TRANSPORTATION AND HOUSING AGENCY

CHAPTER 2. INTELLECTUAL PROPERTY

Section
13988.   Findings and declarations.
13988.1. Definitions.
13988.2. Functions of department; application of section.
13988.3. Sharing of records and information; public disclosure prohibited.
13988.4. Application of chapter.

§ 13988. Findings and declarations

The Legislature finds and declares all of the following:

(a) The state is home to many of the world's top research universities, national laboratories, and leading-edge high-technology companies that generate significant intellectual property.

(b) It is in the interest of the state to ensure that the results of state-funded research are promptly developed and protected and to make the research available in the public domain, where appropriate.

(c) The commercialization of technology developed with the investment of taxpayer dollars in the form of contracts, grants, and agreements could generate public benefit, including, but not limited to, state revenues, favorable pricing, revenue sharing, reinvestment into research, development of new technologies, the commercialization of the product of state-funded research, and the jobs created from these types of research.

(d) It is in the interest of the state to facilitate, promote, and enhance technology transfer programs that will facilitate the transfer of technology into the marketplace for the public benefit.

(e) The Legislature supports the use of efficient models to develop and streamline infrastructures, policies, and processes for the management of intellectual property developed under state funding in order to stimulate economic development in the state while, at the same time, minimizing costs of administering policies in this area.

(f) It is the intent of the Legislature that the rights of state agencies and departments to track and manage intellectual property created with any state funds shall be interpreted so as to promote the benefit to the public.

(g) It is the intent of the Legislature that the Department of General Services have access to information about intellectual property created by state employees and by state-funded research, consistent with state and federal laws and regulations governing access to this information.

(h) The Legislature recognizes that the licensing of or limitations on the use of intellectual property should accommodate free expression and, therefore, state agencies and departments should not develop policies or procedures to license or otherwise limit the use of the state's intellectual property in expressive works created by nonstate employees or without state funding. *(Added by Stats.2012, c. 463 (A.B.744), § 1.)*

§ 13988.1. Definitions

Unless the context otherwise requires, the definitions in this section govern the construction of this chapter:

(a) "Department" means the Department of General Services.

(b) "Databases" means compilations of data, typically generated from research, sometimes from one source, but often combined from many sources.

(c) "Expressive works" means a play, book, magazine, newspaper, musical composition, audiovisual work, radio or television program, work of art, work of political or newsworthy value, or an advertisement or commercial announcement for any of these works, if it is fictional or nonfictional entertainment, or a dramatic, literary, or musical work.

(d) "Intellectual property" means intangible assets that are subject to statutory protection under applicable patent, copyright, and trademark law. Intellectual property includes, but is not limited to, inventions, industrial designs, identifying marks and symbols, electronic publications, trade secrets, and literary, musical, artistic, photographic, and film works.

(e) "State funding" shall not include either of the following:

(1) Funding from the California Film and Television Tax Credit Program established pursuant to Sections 17053.85 and 23685 of the Revenue and Taxation Code and Chapter 7.75 (commencing with Section 5500) of Title 10 of the California Code of Regulations.

(2) Any fee, tax, fine, or penalty assessed, collected, or received by an air pollution control district or an air quality management district, including any fee, tax, fine, or penalty that is authorized by the state but is not remitted to a state agency. However, state funding shall include a fee, tax, fine, or penalty that is collected by an air pollution control district or an air quality management district that is remitted to a state agency, such as the State Air Resources Board. *(Added by Stats.2012, c. 463 (A.B.744), § 1.)*

§ 13988.2. Functions of department; application of section

(a) The department shall perform all of the following functions:

(1) Commencing January 1, 2015, and every three years thereafter, track intellectual property generated by state employees or with state funding.

(2) Develop a database that includes, but is not limited to, tracking intellectual property by category of protection, date of creation, owner of intellectual property, grantee, state agency or granting entity, sources of funding, and status of licensing, including invention utilization updates. Failure to include an

item in the database does not create any presumption regarding ownership. Prior to January 1, 2018, the database shall include the summary of state-owned intellectual property found in the California State Auditor's Report 2011–106 on intellectual property. After January 1, 2018, and every three years thereafter, the database shall be updated using information collected by the department pursuant to this section.

(3) Develop a sample maintenance plan of an inventory of intellectual property.

(4) Develop factors that state agencies should consider when deciding whether to sell their intellectual property or license it to others.

(5) Develop an outreach campaign informing state agencies of their rights and abilities concerning intellectual property created by their employees.

(6) Develop sample invention assignment agreements that state agencies can consider if they believe it is necessary to secure the rights to potentially patentable items created by their employees on worktime using state resources.

(7) Develop sample language for licenses or terms-of-use agreements that state agencies can use to limit the use of their intellectual property by others to only appropriate purposes.

(b) This section shall not apply to the use of expressive works created by nonstate employees or without state funding. *(Added by Stats.2012, c. 463 (A.B.744), § 1.)*

§ 13988.3. Sharing of records and information; public disclosure prohibited

(a) Notwithstanding any other law, state agencies and departments may, upon request, share records and information related to intellectual property generated by state employees or with state funding with the department.

(b) Any employee or former employee of the department who has access to or knowledge of the records and information described in subdivision (a), shall not divulge or make known to any person not employed by the department in any manner not expressly permitted by law any particulars of these records or information that is restricted by law from public disclosure, or represents a first publication of research results, or information pertaining to patent rights that would not otherwise be publicly available. *(Added by Stats.2012, c. 463 (A.B.744), § 1.)*

§ 13988.4. Application of chapter

(a) This chapter shall not apply to intellectual property or intellectual property related agreements administered by the Regents of the University of California, the subcontractors of the Regents of the University of California, and the Trustees of the California State University. This chapter shall apply to a funding agreement from a state agency for the performance of research, and these funding agreements shall be subject to the model contract provisions developed pursuant to Chapter 14. 27 (commencing with Section 67325) of Part 40 of Division 5 of Title 3 of the Education Code.

(b) This chapter shall not apply to intellectual property agreements governed by the California Stem Cell Research and Cures Bond Act (Chapter 3 (commencing with Section 125290.10) of Part 5 of Division 106 of the Health and Safety Code). *(Added by Stats.2012, c. 463 (A.B.744), § 1.)*

Title 3

GOVERNMENT OF COUNTIES

Division 2

OFFICERS

Part 3

OTHER OFFICERS

CHAPTER 2. SHERIFF

ARTICLE 7. FEES

§ 26720. Collection of fees

For services performed by them sheriffs shall charge and collect the fees fixed in this article. *(Added by Stats.1947, c. 424, p. 1144, § 1.)*

Research References

3 Witkin Cal. Proc. 5th Actions § 418, Trial Court Costs.
3 Witkin Cal. Proc. 5th Actions § 429C, (New)-Costs Excused.
2 Witkin Cal. Proc. 5th Courts § 388, (S 388) In General.
8 Witkin Cal. Proc. 5th Enforcement of Judgment § 30, Deposit to Cover Expenses.
6 Witkin Cal. Proc. 5th Provisional Remedies § 4, (S 4) Fees.

§ 26720.5. Proceeding in forma pauperis; waiver or refund of fees

Notwithstanding Section 26720, fees otherwise payable by a litigant pursuant to this article shall be waived or, if paid, refunded, in any case in which the litigant is permitted by the court to proceed in forma pauperis under rules adopted by the Judicial Council pursuant to Section 68511.3.

This section is declaratory of existing law, and the enumeration in this section of fees to be waived shall not be construed to limit the power of the court to waive fees in other instances, as permitted or required under rules adopted by the Judicial Council pursuant to Section 68511.3. *(Added by Stats.1980, c. 1372, p. 4985, § 4.5.)*

§ 26720.9. Fee amounts for specified sections

Notwithstanding any other provision of law, the amounts set forth in Sections 26721, 26721.1, 26725, 26728, 26734, 26742, and 26743 shall be thirty-five dollars ($35).

This section shall become operative on January 1, 2011. *(Added by Stats.2010, c. 4 (A.B.680), § 7, operative Jan. 1, 2011.)*

Research References

Rutter, Cal. Practice Guide: Enforcing Judgments/Debts Ch. 4-A, A. Attachment.
Rutter, Cal. Practice Guide: Enforcing Judgments/Debts Ch. 6D-3, Levy of Writ of Execution-In General.
6 Witkin Cal. Proc. 5th Provisional Remedies § 4, (S 4) Fees.

§ 26721. Service of process or notice

Except as provided in this article, the fee for serving or executing any process or notice required by law or the litigants to be served shall be the amount described in Section 26720.9, and there shall be no additional fee for substitute service when substitute service is authorized.

However, no fee shall be charged for serving an emergency protective order, protective order, or restraining order issued pursuant to Division 10 of the Family Code (the Domestic Violence Prevention Act) on a respondent who is in custody.

In any case where property has been levied upon and, pursuant to the levy, a copy of the writ of execution and a notice of levy are required by statute to be served either personally or by mail upon the judgment debtor or other person, no fee shall be charged for that service. *(Added by Stats.1947, c. 424, p. 1144, § 1. Amended by Stats.1951, c. 956, p. 2564, § 1; Stats.1961, c. 310, p. 1354, § 1; Stats.1966, 1st Ex.Sess., c. 120, p. 600, § 7; Stats.1975, c. 368, p. 816, § 1; Stats.1980, c. 1372, p. 4985, § 5; Stats.1981, c. 1034, p. 3971, § 2; Stats.1985, c. 1296, § 1; Stats.1987, c. 328, § 1; Stats.1991, c. 810 (A.B.709), § 1; Stats.1992, c. 687 (S.B.1732), § 2, operative July 1, 1993; Stats. 1994, c. 689 (A.B.3033), § 1; Stats.2000, c. 629 (A.B.1768), § 2.)*

Research References

Rutter, Cal. Practice Guide: Civ. Pro. Before Trial Ch. 4-D, D. Service of Summons.
8 Witkin Cal. Proc. 5th Enforcement of Judgment § 103, (S 103) Levy by Registered Process Server.
8 Witkin Cal. Proc. 5th Enforcement of Judgment § 117, (S 117) in General.
6 Witkin Cal. Proc. 5th Provisional Remedies § 4, (S 4) Fees.
6 Witkin Cal. Proc. 5th Provisional Remedies § 152, Levy by Registered Process Server.

§ 26721.1. Unlawful detainer actions; service of summons, complaint, and prejudgment claim of right to possession

In an action for unlawful detainer, the fee for service of a summons, complaint, and prejudgment claim of right to possession pursuant to Section 415.46 of the Code of Civil Procedure shall be the amount described in Section 26720.9 for all occupants not named in the summons. The fee is not refundable. *(Added by Stats.1990, c. 1535 (S.B.2508), § 4. Amended by Stats.2000, c. 629 (A.B.1768), § 3.)*

§ 26721.2. Superior court; service of summons

(a) For any action commenced in the superior court, the fee for the service of the summons, the complaint for which the summons is issued, and all other documents or notices required to be served with the summons and complaint, is thirty-five dollars ($35).

(b) This section shall become operative on January 1, 2008. *(Added by Stats.2006, c. 365 (S.B.432), § 2, operative Jan. 1, 2008.)*

§ 26722. Serving, executing or processing any writ or order to take possession of property

The fee for serving, executing, or processing any writ or order where the levying officer is required to take immediate possession of the property levied upon is eighty-five dollars ($85). *(Added by Stats.1991, c. 810 (A.B.709), § 2. Amended by Stats.2000, c. 629 (A.B.1768), § 4.)*

§ 26723. Fee to open safe-deposit box

The fee for opening a safe-deposit box pursuant to Sections 488.460 and 700.150 of the Code of Civil Procedure is one hundred twenty-five dollars ($125). *(Added by Stats.2003, c. 888 (A.B.394), § 4.)*

Research References

Rutter, Cal. Practice Guide: Enforcing Judgments/Debts Ch. 6D-4, Levy on Specific Property.
8 Witkin Cal. Proc. 5th Enforcement of Judgment § 133, (S 133) Safe Deposit Boxes.
6 Witkin Cal. Proc. 5th Provisional Remedies § 177, Safe Deposit Boxes.

§ 26725. Service, execution or processing writs of attachment, execution or sale or order on realty

The fee for serving, executing, or processing a writ of attachment, writ of execution, writ of sale, or order on real estate, as to the initial service or posting of a continuous unbroken parcel or tract, and the fee for serving a record owner

other than the defendant shall be the amount described in Section 26720.9. *(Added by Stats.1947, c. 424, p. 1144, § 1. Amended by Stats.1951, c. 956, p. 2565, § 3; Stats.1953, c. 1797, p. 3581, § 1; Stats.1966, 1st Ex.Sess., c. 120, p. 601, § 11; Stats.1975, c. 368, p. 816, § 5; Stats.1978, c. 1419, p. 4688, § 5; Stats.1980, c. 1372, p. 4985, § 6; Stats.1981, c. 1034, p. 3971, § 4; Stats.1982, c. 497, p. 2195, § 105, operative July 1, 1983; Stats.1985, c. 1296, § 2; Stats.1987, c. 328, § 2; Stats.1991, c. 810 (A.B.709), § 3; Stats.2000, c. 629 (A.B.1768), § 5.)*

Law Revision Commission Comments

Section 26725 is amended to add a reference to a writ of sale. See Code Civ.Proc. §§ 716.010–716.030 [16 Cal.L.Rev.Comm. Reports 1839 (1982)].

Research References

6 Witkin Cal. Proc. 5th Provisional Remedies § 4, (S 4) Fees.

§ 26725.1. Serving or posting additional notices or orders

The fee for the serving or posting of any additionally required notices or orders on other parcels is ten dollars ($10) each. *(Added by Stats.1975, c. 368, p. 817, § 6. Amended by Stats.1987, c. 328, § 3; Stats.1991, c. 810 (A.B.709), § 4.)*

§ 26726. Keeping and caring for property under writ of attachment, execution, possession, or sale

(a) The fee for keeping and caring for property under a writ of attachment, execution, possession, or sale shall be one hundred forty dollars ($140) when necessarily employed for any eight-hour period or any part thereof. If an additional keeper or keepers are required during these periods, the fee for the additional keeper or keepers shall be the same as fixed, but, in no event shall any one keeper receive more than two hundred eighty dollars ($280) during any 24-hour period when so employed.

(b) In addition to the fees provided by Section 26721, the fee for maintaining custody of property under levy by the use of a keeper is thirty-five dollars ($35) for each day custody is maintained after the first day.

(c) Notwithstanding any other fee charged, a keeper shall receive fifty dollars ($50) when, pursuant to Section 26738, a levying officer prepares a not-found return.

(d) This section shall become operative on January 1, 2011. *(Added by Stats.2010, c. 4 (A.B.680), § 9, operative Jan. 1, 2011.)*

Research References

Rutter, Cal. Practice Guide: Enforcing Judgments/Debts Ch. 6D-4, Levy on Specific Property.
8 Witkin Cal. Proc. 5th Enforcement of Judgment § 126, Property of Going Business.
6 Witkin Cal. Proc. 5th Provisional Remedies § 4, (S 4) Fees.

§ 26727. Copies

The fee for a copy of any writ, process, paper, order, or notice actually made by him or her when required or demanded is fifty cents ($0.50) a page, except that when correct copies are furnished to him or her for use no charge shall be made for those copies. *(Added by Stats.1947, c. 424, p. 1144, § 1. Amended by Stats.1966, 1st Ex.Sess., c. 120, p. 601, § 13; Stats.1975, c. 368, p. 817, § 8; Stats.1987, c. 328, § 5; Stats.1991, c. 810 (A.B.709), § 6.)*

§ 26728. Posting notices of personal property sale

The fee for preparing and posting the initial notice of personal property sale under a writ of attachment, execution, or sale or order of court shall be the amount described in Section 26720.9. *(Added by Stats.1947, c. 424, p. 1145, § 1. Amended by Stats.1951, c. 956, p. 2565, § 4; Stats.1966, 1st Ex.Sess., c. 120, p.*

601, § 14; Stats.1975, c. 368, p. 817, § 9; Stats.1980, c. 1372, p. 4986, § 7; Stats.1981, c. 1034, p. 3971, § 7; Stats.1982, c. 497, p. 2196, § 107, operative July 1, 1983; Stats.1985, c. 1296, § 4; Stats.1987, c. 328, § 6; Stats.1991, c. 810 (A.B.709), § 7; Stats.2000, c. 629 (A.B.1768), § 7.)

Law Revision Commission Comments

Section 26728 is amended to add a reference to a writ of sale. See Code Civ.Proc. §§ 716.010–716.030. [16 Cal.L.Rev.Comm. Reports 1839 (1982)].

§ 26728.1. Preparing and posting additional notices

The fee for preparing and posting additionally required notices of personal property sales is ten dollars ($10) each. (Added by Stats.1975, c. 368, p. 817, § 10. Amended by Stats.1987, c. 328, § 7; Stats.1991, c. 810 (A.B.709), § 8.)

§ 26729. Furnishing notice for publication

The fee for furnishing a notice for publication is ten dollars ($10). (Added by Stats.1947, c. 424, p. 1145, § 1. Amended by Stats.1951, c. 956, p. 2565, § 5; Stats.1966, 1st Ex.Sess., c. 120, p. 601, § 15; Stats.1975, c. 368, p. 817, § 11; Stats.1987, c. 328, § 8; Stats.1991, c. 810 (A.B.709), § 9.)

§ 26730. Conducting sale of property

The fee for conducting or postponing the sale of real or personal property as required by law or the litigant is eighty-five dollars ($85). (Added by Stats.1947, c. 424, p. 1145, § 1. Amended by Stats.1951, c. 1114, p. 2869, § 2; Stats.1966, 1st Ex.Sess., c. 120, p. 601, § 16; Stats.1975, c. 368, p. 817, § 12; Stats.1980, c. 1372, p. 4986, § 8; Stats.1981, c. 1034, p. 3971, § 9; Stats.1985, c. 1296, § 5; Stats.1987, c. 328, § 9; Stats.1991, c. 810 (A.B.709), § 10; Stats.2000, c. 629 (A.B.1768), § 8.)

§ 26731. Special fund; deposit of certain fees collected by sheriff's civil division or marshal; expenditures restricted

Fifteen dollars ($15) of any fee collected by the sheriff's civil division or marshal under Sections 26721, 26722, 26725, 26726, 26728, 26730, 26733.5, 26734, 26736, 26738, 26742, 26743, 26744, and 26750 of the Government Code shall be deposited in a special fund in the county treasury. A separate accounting of funds deposited shall be maintained for each depositor, and funds deposited shall be for the exclusive use of the sheriff's civil division or marshal.

Ninety-five percent of the moneys in the special fund shall be expended to supplement the costs of the depositor for the implementation, maintenance, and purchase of auxiliary equipment and furnishings for automated systems or other nonautomated operational equipment and furnishings deemed necessary by the sheriff's civil division or marshal. Five percent of the moneys in the special fund shall be used to supplement the expenses of the sheriff's civil division or marshal in administering the funds.

This section shall become operative on January 1, 2011. (Added by Stats.2010, c. 4 (A.B.680), § 11, operative Jan. 1, 2011.)

§ 26732. Publication of newspaper notice

The fee for publication of a notice in a newspaper is the reasonable cost of the publication. (Added by Stats.1947, c. 424, p. 1145, § 1. Amended by Stats.1951, c. 1114, p. 2869, § 3.)

§ 26733.5. Service of writ of possession; removing occupants from premises and putting person in possession; reposting notice to vacate

The fee for serving a writ of possession of real property on an occupant or the occupants or for posting and serving a copy on the judgment debtor is seventy-five dollars ($75). The addition-al fee for removing an occupant or occupants from the premises and putting a person in possession of the premises is fifty dollars ($50). The fee for reposting of a notice to vacate shall be pursuant to Section 26721. (Added by Stats.1985, c. 1296, § 7. Amended by Stats.1987, c. 328, § 10; Stats.1991, c. 810 (A.B.709), § 12; Stats.2004, c. 327 (A.B.2137), § 3.)

Research References

8 Witkin Cal. Proc. 5th Enforcement of Judgment § 333, (S 333) Execution of Writ of Possession.

§ 26734. Levy on personalty in possession of officer

The fee for making a levy on personal property already in possession of the officer who is holding it under attachment in the same action shall be the amount described in Section 26720.9. (Added by Stats.1947, c. 424, p. 1145, § 1. Amended by Stats.1951, c. 956, p. 2565, § 8; Stats.1953, c. 1797, p. 3581, § 2; Stats.1966, 1st Ex.Sess., c. 120, p. 601, § 19; Stats.1969, c. 514, p. 1124, § 2; Stats.1975, c. 368, p. 818, § 15; Stats.1980, c. 1372, p. 4986, § 10; Stats.1981, c. 1034, p. 3971, § 13; Stats.1985, c. 1296, § 8; Stats.1987, c. 328, § 11; Stats.1991, c. 810 (A.B.709), § 13; Stats.2000, c. 629 (A.B.1768), § 10.)

§ 26736. Cancellation of service or execution of process or notice prior to completion

The fee for cancellation of the service or execution of any process or notice prior to its completion shall be thirty-five dollars ($35). The fee provided by this section shall not be charged where a charge is made pursuant to any other section of this article in attempting to serve or execute the process or notice.

This section shall become operative on January 1, 2011. (Added by Stats.2010, c. 4 (A.B.680), § 13, operative Jan. 1, 2011.)

§ 26738. Not-found return

The fee for making a not-found return on a summons, affidavit and order, order for appearance, subpoena, writ of attachment, writ of execution, writ of possession, order for delivery of personal property, or other process or notice required to be served, certifying that the person or property cannot be found at the address specified is thirty-five dollars ($35).

This section shall become operative on January 1, 2011. (Added by Stats.2010, c. 4 (A.B.680), § 15, operative Jan. 1, 2011.)

Research References

6 Witkin Cal. Proc. 5th Provisional Remedies § 4, (S 4) Fees.

§ 26740. Execution and delivery of deed

The fee for the execution and delivery of a deed or certificate of redemption is ten dollars ($10). (Added by Stats.1947, c. 424, p. 1145, § 1. Amended by Stats.1951, c. 956, p. 2565, § 12; Stats.1953, c. 1797, p. 3581, § 5; Stats.1966, 1st Ex.Sess., c. 120, p. 602, § 24; Stats.1987, c. 328, § 14; Stats.1991, c. 810 (A.B.709), § 17.)

§ 26741. Execution and delivery of certificate or deed of sale

The fee for executing and delivering a certificate or deed of sale is ten dollars ($10). (Added by Stats.1947, c. 424, p. 1145, § 1. Amended by Stats.1951, c. 956, p. 2565, § 13; Stats.1951, c. 1114, p. 2869, § 7; Stats.1966, 1st Ex.Sess., c. 120, p. 602, § 25; Stats.1982, c. 497, p. 2196, § 110, operative July 1, 1983; Stats.1987, c. 328, § 15; Stats.1991, c. 810 (A.B.709), § 18.)

Law Revision Commission Comments

Section 26741 is amended to add a reference to the deed of sale. See Code Civ.Proc. § 701.660. [16 Cal.L.Rev.Comm. Reports 1840 (1982)].

§ 26742. Execution and delivery of other instruments

The fee for executing and delivering any other instrument shall be the amount described in Section 26720.9. *(Added by Stats.1947, c. 424, p. 1145, § 1. Amended by Stats.1953, c. 1797, p. 3581, § 6; Stats.1966, 1st Ex.Sess., c. 120, p. 602, § 26; Stats.1975, c. 368, p. 818, § 21; Stats.1980, c. 1372, p. 4988, § 14; Stats.1981, c. 1034, p. 3972, § 21; Stats.1985, c. 1296, § 12; Stats.1987, c. 328, § 16; Stats.1991, c. 810 (A.B.709), § 19; Stats.1992, c. 687 (S.B.1732), § 5, operative July 1, 1993; Stats. 2000, c. 629 (A.B.1768), § 13.)*

§ 26743. Subpoenaing witnesses

The fee for subpoenaing a witness, including a copy of the subpoena and any affidavit required to be served therewith, shall be the amount described in Section 26720.9. *(Added by Stats.1947, c. 424, p. 1145, § 1. Amended by Stats.1949, c. 597, p. 1092, § 1; Stats.1951, c. 956, p. 2565, § 14; Stats.1966, 1st Ex.Sess., c. 120, p. 602, § 27; Stats.1969, c. 514, p. 1125, § 4; Stats.1975, c. 368, p. 818, § 22; Stats.1980, c. 1372, p. 4988, § 15; Stats.1981, c. 1034, p. 3972, § 23; Stats.1985, c. 1296, § 13; Stats.1987, c. 328, § 17; Stats.1991, c. 810 (A.B.709), § 20; Stats.2000, c. 629 (A.B.1768), § 14.)*

§ 26744. Serving or executing bench warrant arising out of order of appearance

The fee for serving or executing a bench warrant arising from an order of appearance issued under subparagraph (A) of paragraph (1) of subdivision (a) of Section 491.160 or subparagraph (A) of paragraph (1) of subdivision (a) of Section 708.170 of the Code of Civil Procedure is fifty dollars ($50). *(Added by Stats.1947, c. 424, p. 1145, § 1. Amended by Stats.1961, c. 310, p. 1354, § 2; Stats.1966, 1st Ex.Sess., c. 120, p. 602, § 28; Stats. 1975, c. 368, p. 818, § 23; Stats.1980, c. 1372, p. 4988, § 16; Stats.1981, c. 1034, p. 3972, § 25; Stats.1982, c. 497, p. 2196, § 111, operative July 1, 1983; Stats.1982, c. 1198, p. 4326, § 66, operative July 1, 1983; Stats.1985, c. 1296, § 14; Stats.1987, c. 328, § 18; Stats.1991, c. 810 (A.B.709), § 21; Stats.2006, c. 277 (A.B.2369), § 4.)*

Law Revision Commission Comments

Section 26744 is amended to correct cross-references. [16 Cal.L.Rev. Comm. Reports 1840 (1982)].

§ 26744.5. Processing warrant for absent witness; waiver

(a) The fees for processing a warrant issued pursuant to Section 1993 of the Code of Civil Procedure shall be paid by the moving party, as follows:

(1) Thirty-five dollars ($35) to receive and process the warrant, which shall include the issuance and mailing of a notice advising the person to be arrested of the issuance of the warrant and demanding that the person appear in court.

(2) Thirty-five dollars ($35) to cancel the service of the warrant.

(3) Seventy-five dollars ($75) if unable to find the person at the address specified using due diligence.

(4) Eighty-five dollars ($85) to arrest the person, which shall include the arrest and release of the person on a promise to appear pursuant to Section 1993.2 of the Code of Civil Procedure.

(b) The in forma pauperis fee waiver provisions under Rules 3.50 to 3.63, inclusive, of the California Rules of Court shall apply to the collection of fees under this section.

(c) This section shall become operative on January 1, 2011. *(Added by Stats.2010, c. 4 (A.B.680), § 17, operative Jan. 1, 2011.)*

§ 26745. Summoning trial jury

The fee for summoning a trial jury of 12 or less is two dollars ($2), and for each additional juror, ten cents ($0.10). *(Added by Stats.1947, c. 424, p. 1145, § 1.)*

§ 26746. Processing fee for disbursement of money collected under writs of attachment; child support exclusion; special fund; expenditures

In addition to any other fees required by law, a processing fee of twelve dollars ($12) shall be assessed for each disbursement of money collected under a writ of attachment, execution, possession, or sale, but excluding any action by the local child support agency for the establishment or enforcement of a child support obligation. The fee shall be collected from the judgment debtor in addition to, and in the same manner as, the moneys collected under the writ. All proceeds of this fee shall be deposited in a special fund in the county treasury. A separate accounting of funds deposited shall be maintained for each depositor, and funds deposited shall be for the exclusive use of the depositor.

The special fund shall be expended to supplement the county's cost for vehicle fleet replacement and equipment, maintenance, and civil process operations.

A fee may not be charged if the only disbursement is the return of the judgment creditor's deposit for costs. *(Added by Stats.1987, c. 1330, § 1. Amended by Stats.2000, c. 629 (A.B. 1768), § 15; Stats.2000, c. 808 (A.B.1358), § 100.1, eff. Sept. 28, 2000; Stats.2003, c. 888 (A.B.394), § 6; Stats.2010, c. 4 (A.B. 680), § 18.)*

Research References

8 Witkin Cal. Proc. 5th Enforcement of Judgment § 254, in General.

§ 26746.1. Certification of correction on citation requiring proof of correction of violation pursuant to Vehicle Code § 40616; disposition of proceeds of fee

A seventeen-dollar ($17) fee shall be assessed by the sheriff or marshal for certification of correction on each citation that requires inspection for proof of correction of any violation pursuant to Section 40616 of the Vehicle Code.

All proceeds of the fee shall be deposited in a special fund in the county treasury. A separate accounting of funds deposited shall be maintained for each depositor, and funds deposited shall be for the exclusive use of the sheriff's civil division or marshal.

Ninety-five percent of the moneys in the special fund shall be expended to supplement the costs of the depositor for the implementation, maintenance, and purchase of auxiliary equipment and furnishings for automated systems or other nonautomated operational equipment and furnishings deemed necessary by the sheriff's civil division or marshal. Five percent of the moneys in the special fund shall be used to supplement the expenses of the sheriff's civil division or marshal in administering the funds.

This section shall become operative on January 1, 2011. *(Added by Stats.2010, c. 4 (A.B.680), § 20, operative Jan. 1, 2011.)*

§ 26747. Transporting prisoners

For transporting prisoners to the county jail, the sheriff shall charge the actual cost of such transportation. *(Added by Stats.1947, c. 424, p. 1146, § 1.)*

§ 26748. Other charges

In addition to the fees provided by this article, the sheriff may collect from the litigant or person requiring his services, his actual expenses for inspection, checking, releasing, or any other handling of property under his custody, charge, or keeping pursuant to any process, writ, order, paper, or notice, and actual postal charges paid for mailing by registered mail or certified mail any notice or demand required or authorized by law to be sent by registered mail or certified mail. *(Added by Stats.1947, c. 424, p. 1146, § 1. Amended by Stats.1953, c. 1797, p. 3581, § 7; Stats.1957, c. 1737, p. 3120, § 1; Stats.1975, c. 368, p. 819, § 25.)*

§ 26749. Transportation expenses for conveying insane persons or prisoners or deportees

The sheriff shall receive expenses necessarily incurred in conveying insane persons to and from the state hospitals and in conveying persons to and from the state prisons or other state institutions, or to other destinations for the purpose of deportation to other states, or in advancing actual traveling expenses to any person committed to a state institution who is permitted to report to an institution without escort, which expenses shall be allowed as provided by Chapter 6 (commencing with Section 4750) of Title 5 of Part 3 of the Penal Code for cases subject to that chapter, and, otherwise, by the California Victim Compensation and Government Claims Board and paid by the state. *(Added by Stats.1947, c. 424, p. 1146, § 1. Amended by Stats.1951, c. 181, p. 433, § 1; Stats.1986, c. 1310, § 1; Stats. 2006, c. 538 (S.B.1852), § 301.)*

§ 26750. Service of earnings withholding order; prohibition of other fees for performance of duties under Wage Garnishment Law

(a) The fee for serving an earnings withholding order under the Wage Garnishment Law (Chapter 5 (commencing with Section 706.010) of Division 2 of Title 9 of Part 2 of the Code of Civil Procedure), including, but not limited to, the costs of postage or traveling, and for performing all other duties of the levying officer under that law with respect to the levy shall be thirty dollars ($30).

(b) Except as provided in Section 26746, no additional fees, costs, or expenses may be charged by the levying officer for performing the duties under the Wage Garnishment Law (Chapter 5 (commencing with Section 706.010) of Division 2 of Title 9 of Part 2 of the Code of Civil Procedure).

(c) This section shall become operative on January 1, 2008. *(Added by Stats.2006, c. 365 (S.B.432), § 4, operative Jan. 1, 2008.)*

Research References

Rutter, Cal. Practice Guide: Enforcing Judgments/Debts Ch. 6F-3, Issuance and Service of Earnings Withholding Orders.
8 Witkin Cal. Proc. 5th Enforcement of Judgment § 254, in General.
8 Witkin Cal. Proc. 5th Enforcement of Judgment § 256, Service by Registered Process Server.

§ 26751. Report of repossession; receipt and filing fee; release of vehicle

After possession is taken of any vehicle by or on behalf of any legal owner thereof under the terms of a security agreement or lease agreement, the debtor shall pay the sheriff a fee of fifteen dollars ($15) for the receipt and filing of the report of repossession pursuant to Section 28 of the Vehicle Code before the vehicle may be redeemed by the debtor. Except as provided herein, any person in possession of the vehicle shall not release it to the debtor without first obtaining proof of payment of the fee to the sheriff. At the request of the debtor, a person in possession of the vehicle, or the legal owner, may also release the vehicle to the debtor provided the debtor pays the fifteen dollar ($15) fee, plus an administrative fee not to exceed five dollars ($5), to the person in possession or the legal owner, who shall transmit the fifteen dollar ($15) fee to the sheriff within three business days. The failure to transmit the fee within three business days shall subject the person in possession or legal owner receiving the fee from the debtor to a fine of fifty dollars

($50). The proof of payment, or a copy thereof, shall be retained by the party releasing possession to the debtor for the period required by law, and the party releasing possession shall provide a copy of the proof of payment to the debtor upon request of the debtor. *(Added by Stats.1993, c. 1269 (A.B.1972), § 10. Amended by Stats.1994, c. 1114 (A.B.2781), § 7.)*

CHAPTER 3. COUNTY CLERK

ARTICLE 2. FEES

§ 26820. Collection of fees

The county clerk shall charge and collect the fees fixed in this article for service performed by the clerk, when not otherwise provided by law. *(Added by Stats.1947, c. 424, p. 1146, § 1. Amended by Stats.1955, c. 862, p. 1477, § 1; Stats.1998, c. 931 (S.B.2139), § 200, eff. Sept. 28, 1998; Stats.2005, c. 75 (A.B.145), § 49, eff. July 19, 2005, operative Jan. 1, 2006.)*

Law Revision Commission Comments

Section 26820 is amended to accommodate unification of the municipal and superior courts in a county. Cal. Const. art. VI, § 5(e). [28 Cal.L.Rev.Comm. Reports 51 (1998)].

Research References

4 Witkin, California Summary 10th Security Transactions in Real Property § 163, (S 163) Conflicting Claims.

§ 26831. Fee for copies

The county clerk may charge a reasonable fee to cover the cost of preparing copies of any record, proceeding, or paper on file in his or her office. *(Added by Stats.1947, c. 424, p. 1147, § 1. Amended by Stats.1949, c. 739, p. 1359, § 10; Stats.1955, c. 1880, p. 3477, § 1; Stats.1976, c. 822, p. 1890, § 2; Stats.2005, c. 75 (A.B.145), § 72, eff. July 19, 2005, operative Jan. 1, 2006.)*

§ 26833. Certifying copy

The fee for certifying to a copy of any paper, record, or proceeding on file in the office of the county clerk is one dollar and seventy-five cents ($1.75). *(Added by Stats.1947, c. 424, p. 1148, § 1. Amended by Stats.1949, c. 739, p. 1359, § 12; Stats.1966, 1st Ex.Sess., c. 120, p. 603, § 35; Stats.1977, c. 1257, p. 4771, § 45, eff. Oct. 3, 1977; Stats.1980, c. 1372, p. 4991, § 36; Stats.1982, c. 327, § 74.)*

§ 26836. Other certificates

For every certificate the fee for which is not otherwise fixed, the fee is one dollar and seventy-five cents ($1.75). *(Added by Stats.1947, c. 424, p. 1148, § 1. Amended by Stats.1980, c. 1372, p. 4991, § 38; Stats.1982, c. 327, p. 1456, § 76, eff. June 30, 1982.)*

§ 26837. Fee for comparison of papers

For comparing with the original on file in the office of the county clerk, the copy of any paper, record, or proceeding prepared by another and presented for his or her certificate, the fee is fifty cents ($0.50) a page, in addition to the fee for the certificate. *(Added by Stats.1947, c. 424, p. 1148, § 1. Amended by Stats.1949, c. 739, p. 1359, § 13; Stats.1955, c. 1880, p. 3478, § 3; Stats.1966, 1st Ex.Sess., c. 120, p. 604, § 37; Stats.1969, c. 178, p. 428, § 1; Stats.1977, c. 1257, p. 4771, § 46, eff. Oct. 3, 1977; Stats.1980, c. 1372, p. 4991, § 39; Stats.2005, c. 75 (A.B.145), § 80, eff. July 19, 2005, operative Jan. 1, 2006.)*

§ 26839. Exemplification of record

For an exemplification of a record or other paper on file, the fee is twenty dollars ($20) and the charges allowed for copying or comparing. *(Added by Stats.1947, c. 424, p. 1148, § 1. Amended by Stats.1949, c. 739, p. 1359, § 15; Stats.1966, 1st Ex.Sess., c. 120, p. 604, § 38; Stats.1980, c. 1372, p. 4992, § 41; Stats.1982, c. 327, p. 1457, § 78, eff. June 30, 1982; Stats.1993, c. 158 (A.B.392), § 9, eff. July 21, 1993.)*

§ 26840. Marriage license; disposition of fees

The fee for issuing a marriage license is ten dollars ($10), to be collected at the time it is issued. One dollar ($1) of this fee shall be paid to the county recorder, one dollar ($1) of this fee shall be paid to the county clerk, and one dollar ($1) of this fee shall be paid to the State Registrar of Vital Statistics and seven dollars ($7) of this fee shall be disposed of pursuant to the provisions of Section 54 of Chapter 120, Statutes of 1966, First Extraordinary Session. In counties where the salary of the county recorder is the sole compensation allowed by law, this fee shall be paid to the county treasurer who shall credit one dollar ($1) to the county recorder and shall pay one dollar ($1) to the State Registrar of Vital Statistics. The fee provided by this section is in full for all services of the clerk and recorder in connection with the issuance of a marriage license and the filing of a certificate of registry of marriage. *(Added by Stats.1947, c. 424, p. 1148, § 1. Amended by Stats.1947, c. 1303, p. 2840, § 1; Stats.1966, 1st Ex.Sess., c. 120, p. 604, § 39; Stats.1967, c. 1500, p. 3509, § 6, operative Jan. 1, 1968; Stats.1979, c. 139, p. 327, § 3.)*

Research References

11 Witkin, California Summary 10th Husband and Wife § 45, (S 45) License.

§ 26840.1. Marriage certificate

(a) The fee for filing a marriage certificate pursuant to Part 4 (commencing with Section 500) of Division 3 of the Family Code is fourteen dollars ($14), to be collected at the time an authorization for the performance of the marriage is issued or a blank authorization form is obtained from the county clerk pursuant to Part 4 (commencing with Section 500) of Division 3 of the Family Code. Four dollars ($4) of the fee shall be paid to the State Registrar of Vital Statistics. One dollar ($1) of the fee shall be paid to the county treasurer and shall be used to defray any local costs incurred pursuant to Part 4 (commencing with Section 500) of Division 3 of the Family Code.

(b) Notwithstanding subdivision (a), in addition to the amount authorized by subdivision (a) the county clerk may impose an additional amount, not to exceed three dollars ($3), if he or she determines that the additional amount is necessary to defray local costs. *(Added by Stats.1971, c. 1244, p. 2444, § 2. Amended by Stats.1979, c. 139, p. 327, § 4; Stats.1981, c. 872, p. 3336, § 3; Stats.1992, c. 163 (A.B.2641), § 81, operative Jan. 1, 1994.)*

Law Revision Commission Comments

Subdivisions (a) of Section 26840.1 is amended to substitute references to the Family Code provisions that replaced the former Civil Code provisions. [22 Cal.L.Rev.Comm.Reports 1 (1992)].

Research References

11 Witkin, California Summary 10th Husband and Wife § 48, (S 48) Confidential Marriage.

§ 26840.2. Marriage license; issuance outside of normal business hours; additional fee

Whenever the board of supervisors of a county makes provision by ordinance for the issuance of marriage licenses outside of the normal business hours, the board may establish a fee, in addition to that provided in Section 26840, not to exceed five dollars ($5), which shall be paid to the county treasury. *(Added by Stats.1971, c. 1527, p. 3019, § 1. Amended by Stats.1981, c. 199, p. 1123, § 1.)*

Research References

11 Witkin, California Summary 10th Husband and Wife § 45, (S 45) License.

§ 26840.3. Increase of fees for support of family conciliation court and mediation services

(a) For the support of the family conciliation court or for conciliation and mediation services provided pursuant to Chapter 11 (commencing with Section 3160) of Part 2 of Division 8 of the Family Code, to provide all space costs and indirect overhead costs from other sources, the board of supervisors in any county may increase:

(1) The fee for issuing a marriage license, by an amount not to exceed five dollars ($5).

(2) The fee for issuing a marriage certificate pursuant to Part 4 (commencing with Section 500) of Division 3 of the Family Code, by an amount not to exceed five dollars ($5).

(b) The county shall distribute the moneys received under subdivision (a) to the court to be used exclusively to pay the costs of maintaining the family conciliation court or conciliation and mediation services provided pursuant to Chapter 11 (commencing with Section 3160) of Part 2 of Division 8 of the Family Code. *(Added by Stats.1976, c. 1356, p. 6180, § 1. Amended by Stats.1977, c. 786, p. 2430, § 1; Stats.1980, c. 48, p. 134, § 6, eff. March 27, 1980; Stats.1982, c. 1071, p. 3855, § 2; Stats.1983, c. 1277, § 2; Stats.1992, c. 163 (A.B.2641), § 82; Stats.1992, c. 696 (A.B.1344), § 19, eff. Sept. 15, 1992; Stats.1993, c. 219 (A.B. 1500), § 214; Stats.2005, c. 75 (A.B.145), § 83, eff. July 19, 2005, operative Jan. 1, 2006.)*

Law Revision Commission Comments

Section 26840.3 is amended to substitute references to the Family Code provisions that replaced the former Civil Code provisions. [23 Cal.L.Rev. Comm. Reports 1 (1993)].

Research References

4 Witkin Cal. Proc. 5th Pleading § 26, Additional Fees.
11 Witkin, California Summary 10th Husband and Wife § 45, (S 45) License.
11 Witkin, California Summary 10th Husband and Wife § 48, (S 48) Confidential Marriage.
11 Witkin, California Summary 10th Husband and Wife § 90, in General.

§ 26840.7. Marriage license; additional fee upon issuance; use of fee

In addition to the fee prescribed by Section 26840 and as authorized by Section 26840.3, the county clerk shall collect a fee of twenty-three dollars ($23) at the time of issuance of the license. The fee shall be disposed of by the clerk pursuant to Chapter 5 (commencing with Section 18290) of Part 6 of Division 9 of the Welfare and Institutions Code. Of this amount, four dollars ($4) shall be used, to the extent feasible, to develop or expand domestic violence shelter-based programs to target underserved areas and populations. *(Added by Stats.1980, c. 146, p. 339, § 1, eff. June 4, 1980. Amended by Stats.1982, c. 522, p. 2450, § 1; Stats.1984, c. 112, § 1; Stats.1992, c. 916 (S.B.5), § 1; Stats.1993, c. 420 (S.B.5), § 1; Stats.2006, c. 857 (A.B.2084), § 1.)*

Research References

11 Witkin, California Summary 10th Husband and Wife § 45, (S 45) License.
11 Witkin, California Summary 10th Husband and Wife § 371, (S 371) Civil Remedies.

§ 26840.8. Marriage authorization; additional fee upon filing; use of fee

In addition to the fee prescribed by Section 26840.1 and as authorized by Section 26840.3, the person issuing an authorization for the performance of a marriage pursuant to Part 4 (commencing with Section 500) of Division 3 of the Family Code or the county clerk, upon providing a blank authorization form pursuant to Part 4 (commencing with Section 500) of Division 3 of the Family Code, shall collect a fee of twenty-three dollars ($23) at the time of providing the authorization. The fee shall be disposed of pursuant to Chapter 5 (commencing with Section 18290) of Part 6 of Division 9 of the Welfare and Institutions Code. Of this amount, four dollars ($4) shall be used, to the extent feasible, to develop or expand domestic violence shelter-based programs to target underserved areas and populations. *(Added by Stats.1980, c. 146, p. 339, § 1.5, eff. June 4, 1980. Amended by Stats.1981, c. 872, p. 3337, § 4; Stats.1982, c. 449, p. 1819, § 2; Stats.1982, c. 522, p. 2450, § 2.5; Stats.1984, c. 112, § 2; Stats.1992, c. 163 (A.B.2641), § 83, operative Jan. 1, 1994; Stats.1992, c. 916 (S.B.5), § 2; Stats.1993, c. 420 (S.B.5), § 2; Stats.2006, c. 857 (A.B.2084), § 2.)*

Research References

11 Witkin, California Summary 10th Husband and Wife § 48, (S 48) Confidential Marriage.
11 Witkin, California Summary 10th Husband and Wife § 371, (S 371) Civil Remedies.

§ 26840.10. Alameda County Board of Supervisors; domestic violence; fee increase for marriage and confidential marriage licenses; collection; report

Section operative until Jan. 1, 2015. See, also, section operative Jan. 1, 2015.

(a) The Alameda County Board of Supervisors, upon making findings and declarations on the need for governmental oversight and coordination of the multiple agencies dealing with domestic violence, may authorize an increase in the fees for marriage licenses and confidential marriage licenses, up to a maximum increase of two dollars ($2).

(b) Effective July 1 of each year, the Alameda County Board of Supervisors may authorize an increase in these fees by an amount equal to the increase in the Consumer Price Index for the San Francisco metropolitan area for the preceding calendar year, rounded to the nearest half-dollar ($0.50). The fees shall be allocated pursuant to Section 18309 of the Welfare and Institutions Code.

(c) In addition to the fee prescribed by Section 26840.1, in Alameda County, the person issuing authorization for the performance of a marriage or confidential marriage, or the county clerk upon providing a blank authorization form pursuant to Part 4 (commencing with Section 500) of Division 3 of the Family Code, shall collect the fees specified in subdivisions (a) and (b), at the time of providing the authorization.

(d) If it elects to increase fees pursuant to this section, the Alameda County Board of Supervisors shall submit to the Assembly and Senate Committees on Judiciary a preliminary report no later than July 1, 2009, and a final report no later than July 1, 2014. Both reports shall contain the following information:

(1) The annual amounts of funds received and expended from fee increases for the purpose of governmental oversight and coordination of domestic violence prevention, intervention, and prosecution efforts in the county.

(2) Outcomes achieved as a result of the activities associated with the implementation of this section.

(e) This section shall remain in effect only until January 1, 2015, and as of that date is repealed, unless a later enacted statute, that is enacted before January 1, 2015, deletes or extends that date. *(Added by Stats.2004, c. 830 (A.B.2010), § 2. Amended by Stats.2009, c. 215 (A.B.73), § 2.)*

Repeal

For repeal of this section, see its terms.

§ 26840.10. Alameda County Board of Supervisors; domestic violence; fee increase for marriage and confidential marriage licenses; collection

Section operative Jan. 1, 2015. See, also, section operative until Jan. 1, 2015.

(a) The Alameda County Board of Supervisors, upon making findings and declarations for the need for governmental oversight and coordination of the multiple agencies dealing with domestic violence, may authorize an increase in the fees for marriage licenses and confidential marriage licenses, up to a maximum increase of two dollars ($2).

(b) Effective July 1 of each year, the Alameda County Board of Supervisors may authorize an increase in these fees by an amount equal to the increase in the Consumer Price Index for the San Francisco metropolitan area for the preceding calendar year, rounded to the nearest half-dollar ($0.50). The fees shall be allocated pursuant to Section 18309 of the Welfare and Institutions Code.

(c) In addition to the fee prescribed by Section 26840.1, in Alameda County, the person issuing authorization for the performance of a marriage or confidential marriage, or the county clerk upon providing a blank authorization form pursuant to Part 4 (commencing with Section 500) of Division 3 of the Family Code, shall collect the fees specified in subdivisions (a) and (b), at the time of providing the authorization.

(d) This section shall become operative on January 1, 2015. *(Added by Stats.2009, c. 215 (A.B.73), § 3, operative Jan. 1, 2015.)*

§ 26840.11. Solano County Board of Supervisors; domestic violence; fee increase for marriage and confidential marriage licenses; collection; preliminary and followup reports

(a) The Solano County Board of Supervisors, upon making findings and declarations for the need for governmental oversight and coordination of the multiple agencies dealing with domestic violence, may authorize an increase in the fees for marriage licenses and confidential marriage licenses, up to a maximum increase of two dollars ($2).

(b) Effective July 1 of each year, the Solano County Board of Supervisors may authorize an increase in these fees by an amount equal to the increase in the Consumer Price Index for the San Francisco metropolitan area for the preceding calendar year, rounded to the nearest one-half dollar ($0.50). The fees shall be allocated pursuant to Section 18309.5 of the Welfare and Institutions Code.

(c) In addition to the fee prescribed by Section 26840.1, in Solano County, the person issuing authorization for the performance of a marriage or confidential marriage, or the county clerk upon providing a blank authorization form pursuant to Part 4 (commencing with Section 500) of Division 3 of the Family Code, shall collect the fees specified in subdivisions (a) and (b), at the time of providing the authorization.

(d) The Solano County Board of Supervisors shall submit to the Assembly and Senate Committees on Judiciary, no later than July 1, 2009, a preliminary report and a followup report no later than July 1, 2014, containing the following information:

(1) The annual amounts of funds received and expended from fee increases for the purpose of governmental oversight and coordination of domestic violence prevention, intervention, and prosecution efforts in the county.

(2) Outcomes achieved as a result of the activities associated with the implementation of this section. *(Added by Stats.2004, c. 830 (A.B.2010), § 3. Amended by Stats.2009, c. 356 (S.B.635), § 1; Stats.2010, c. 520 (S.B.1222), § 1; Stats.2011, c. 120 (S.B.154), § 1.)*

§ 26840.12. Sonoma County Board of Supervisors; domestic violence; fee increase for marriage and confidential marriage licenses; collection; report

(a) The Sonoma County Board of Supervisors, upon making findings and declarations on the need for governmental oversight and coordination of the multiple agencies dealing with domestic violence, may authorize an increase in the fees for marriage licenses and confidential marriage licenses, up to a maximum increase of two dollars ($2).

(b) Effective July 1 of each year, the Sonoma County Board of Supervisors may authorize an increase in these fees by an amount equal to the increase in the Consumer Price Index for the San Francisco metropolitan area for the preceding calendar year, rounded to the nearest one-half dollar ($0.50). The fees

shall be allocated pursuant to Section 18309.6 of the Welfare and Institutions Code.

(c) In addition to the fee prescribed by Section 26840.1, in Sonoma County, the person issuing authorization for the performance of a marriage or confidential marriage, or the county clerk upon providing a blank authorization form pursuant to Part 4 (commencing with Section 500) of Division 3 of the Family Code, shall collect the fees specified in subdivisions (a) and (b), at the time of providing the authorization.

(d) The Sonoma County Board of Supervisors shall submit to the Assembly and Senate Committees on Judiciary a preliminary report no later than July 1, 2013, and a final report no later than July 1, 2014. Both reports shall contain the following information:

(1) The annual amounts of funds received and expended from fee increases for the purpose of governmental oversight and coordination of domestic violence prevention, intervention, and prosecution efforts in the county.

(2) Outcomes achieved as a result of the activities associated with the implementation of this section.

(e) This section shall remain in effect only until January 1, 2015, and as of that date is repealed, unless a later enacted statute, that is enacted before January 1, 2015, deletes or extends that date. *(Added by Stats.2009, c. 356 (S.B.635), § 2.)*

Repeal

For repeal of this section, see its terms.

§ 26847. Certificate of revivor

The fee for making a record of a certificate of revivor is two dollars ($2). *(Added by Stats.1947, c. 424, p. 1148, § 1. Amended by Stats.1949, c. 739, p. 1360, § 23.)*

§ 26849.1. Filing, cancelling, revoking, or withdrawing bond of notary; recording fee

The fee for filing, canceling, revoking, or withdrawing the bond of a notary public is seven dollars ($7).

The recording fee for the notice of cancellation, revocation, or withdrawal and any related document by the surety shall be paid to the county clerk, who shall transmit it to the county recorder. *(Added by Stats.1949, c. 272, p. 491, § 11. Amended by Stats.1979, c. 139, p. 327, § 5; Stats.1991, c. 1090 (A.B.1484), § 15.)*

§ 26850. Filing and indexing of other papers

For filing and indexing all papers for which a charge is not elsewhere provided, other than papers filed in actions or special proceedings, official bonds, or certificates of appointment, the fee is two dollars and twenty-five cents ($2.25). *(Added by Stats.1947, c. 424, p. 1149, § 1. Amended by Stats.1949, c. 739, p. 1360, § 26; Stats.1982, c. 327, p. 1457, § 79, eff. June 30, 1982.)*

§ 26851. Recording other licenses or certificates

For either recording or registering any license or certificate or issuing any certificate, or both, in connection with a license, required by law for which a charge is not otherwise prescribed, the fee is two dollars and twenty-five cents ($2.25). *(Added by Stats.1947, c. 424, p. 1149, § 1. Amended by Stats.1949, c. 739, p. 1360, § 27; Stats.1982, c. 327, p. 1457, § 80, eff. June 30, 1982.)*

§ 26852. Certificate to official capacity of public official

The fee for each certificate to the official capacity of any public official is two dollars and twenty-five cents ($2.25). *(Added by Stats.1947, c. 424, p. 1149, § 1. Amended by Stats.1949, c. 272, p. 491, § 12; Stats.1949, c. 739, p. 1360, § 28;*

Stats.1966, 1st Ex.Sess., c. 120, p. 604, § 41; Stats.1979, c. 139, p. 327, § 6; Stats.1982, c. 327, p. 1457, § 81, eff. June 30, 1982.)

§ 26853. Affidavits; exception

The fee for taking an affidavit, except in criminal cases or adoption proceedings, is two dollars and twenty-five cents ($2.25). *(Added by Stats.1947, c. 424, p. 1149, § 1. Amended by Stats.1966, 1st Ex.Sess., c. 120, p. 604, § 42; Stats.1980, c. 1372, p. 4992, § 42; Stats.1982, c. 327, p. 1457, § 82, eff. June 30, 1982.)*

§ 26854. Searching records or files

The fee for searching records or files is five dollars ($5) for each file. *(Formerly § 16854, added by Stats.1947, c. 424, p. 1149, § 1. Renumbered § 26854 and amended by Stats.1947, c. 1353, p. 2907, § 3. Amended by Stats.1980, c. 1372, p. 4992, § 43; Stats.1982, c. 327, p. 1457, § 83, eff. June 30, 1982; Stats.1991, c. 651 (S.B.757), § 1.)*

§ 26855. Acknowledgments

The fee for taking acknowledgment of any deed or other instrument, including the certificate, is two dollars and twenty-five cents ($2.25) for each signature. *(Added by Stats.1947, c. 424, p. 1149, § 1. Amended by Stats.1966, 1st Ex.Sess., c. 120, p. 604, § 43; Stats.1979, c. 139, p. 327, § 7; Stats.1982, c. 327, p. 1457, § 84, eff. June 30, 1982.)*

§ 26855.1. Power of attorney, or notice of cancellation, revocation or withdrawal of power of attorney; admitted surety insurer

The fee for filing a power of attorney for an admitted surety insurer, or a notice of cancellation, revocation, or withdrawal of a power of attorney for an admitted surety insurer, is three dollars and fifty cents ($3.50), or, if more than one name is designated, two dollars and twenty-five cents ($2.25) for each name. *(Added by Stats.1955, c. 800, p. 1421, § 1. Amended by Stats.1979, c. 139, p. 327, § 8; Stats.1982, c. 327, p. 1457, § 85, eff. June 30, 1982; Stats.1992, c. 876 (A.B.3296), § 11.)*

§ 26855.2. Financial statement of admitted surety insurer

The fee for filing a financial statement of an admitted surety insurer is three dollars and fifty cents ($3.50), but nothing in this section shall be construed to require an admitted surety insurer to file such a statement. *(Added by Stats.1955, c. 800, p. 1421, § 2. Amended by Stats.1957, c. 1050, p. 2285, § 1; Stats.1979, c. 139, p. 328, § 9; Stats.1982, c. 327, p. 1457, § 86, eff. June 30, 1982.)*

§ 26855.3. Certificate stating whether admitted surety insurer's certificate of authority has been surrendered, revoked, etc.

The fee for issuing a certificate pursuant to Section 995.640 of the Code of Civil Procedure is three dollars and fifty cents ($3.50). *(Added by Stats.1955, c. 800, p. 1421, § 3. Amended by Stats.1957, c. 1050, p. 2285, § 2; Stats.1979, c. 139, p. 328, § 10; Stats.1982, c. 517, p. 2391, § 254; Stats.1982, c. 327, p. 1458, § 87, eff. June 30, 1982; Stats.1983, c. 18, § 23, eff. April 21, 1983.)*

Law Revision Commission Comments

Section 26855.3 is amended to correct a section reference. [16 Cal.L.Rev.Comm.Reports 2247 (1982)].

§ 26857. Services not subject to fees

No fee shall be charged by the clerk for service rendered to any municipality or county in the state, or to the state or national government, nor for any service relating thereto. *(Added by Stats.1947, c. 424, p. 1149, § 1. Amended by Stats.1965, c. 456, p. 1766, § 1; Stats.1978, c. 809, p. 2592, § 1; Stats.1986, c. 823,*

§ 1.1; Stats.1996, c. 1023 (S.B.1497), § 94, eff. Sept. 29, 1996; Stats.1997, c. 850 (A.B.233), § 23; Stats.1998, c. 146 (A.B.1301), § 2, eff. July 13, 1998; Stats.2005, c. 75 (A.B.145), § 92, eff. July 19, 2005, operative Jan. 1, 2006.)

Research References

3 Witkin Cal. Proc. 5th Actions § 76, (S 76) Mandamus.

§ 26858. Fees not to be charged in pension matters

No fees or other compensation shall be charged by any county clerk for taking and certifying affidavits for pension claimants, the payment of a pension voucher, or any matters relating thereto under the laws of the United States. *(Added by Stats.1947, c. 424, p. 1149, § 1.)*

§ 26861. Performance of marriage

A fee of fifteen dollars ($15) may be charged for performing a marriage ceremony pursuant to Section 401 of the Family Code, which shall be paid into the county treasury. *(Added by Stats.1973, c. 979, p. 1885, § 3. Amended by Stats.1974, c. 974, p. 2023, § 1; Stats.1979, c. 139, p. 328, § 11; Stats.1992, c. 163 (A.B.2641), § 85, operative Jan. 1, 1994.)*

Law Revision Commission Comments

Section 26861 is amended to substitute a reference to the Family Code provision that replaced former Civil Code Section 4205.1. [22 Cal.L.Rev.Comm.Reports 1 (1992)].

Research References

11 Witkin, California Summary 10th Husband and Wife § 47, (S 47) Solemnization.

CHAPTER 6. RECORDER

ARTICLE 5. FEES

Government

Section

27383.   No fees for services to state or political subdivisions; exception.

27387.   Abstract of judgment or other document creating an involuntary lien on real property; recordation.

27387.1.   Additional recording fees; deeds filed with Los Angeles County Recorder; amount not to exceed cost of mailing notice and actual cost to provide information, counseling, or assistance; administrative costs.

27387.1.   Additional recording fees; deeds filed with Los Angeles County Recorder; amount not to exceed cost of mailing notice.

27388.   Recording fees; real estate instrument, paper, or notice; Real Estate Fraud Prosecution Trust Fund; distribution; district attorney review; purpose.

§ 27360.   Required fees

For services performed by him, the county recorder shall charge and collect the fees fixed in this article. (*Added by Stats.1947, c. 424, p. 1165, § 1.*)

Research References

12 Witkin, California Summary 10th Real Property § 320, Fees.

§ 27360.5.   "Folio" defined

As used in this code, the word "folio" means 100 words. Each figure, character, symbol, and initial, excluding punctuation marks, shall be regarded as a word for the purpose of computing fees by a recorder. (*Added by Stats.1963, c. 22, p. 630, § 1.*)

Research References

12 Witkin, California Summary 10th Real Property § 320, Fees.

§ 27361.   Recording and indexing fees

(a) The fee for recording and indexing every instrument, paper, or notice required or permitted by law to be recorded shall not exceed ten dollars ($10) for recording the first page and three dollars ($3) for each additional page, to reimburse the county for the costs of services rendered pursuant to this subdivision, except the recorder may charge additional fees as follows:

(1) If the printing on printed forms is spaced more than nine lines per vertical inch or more than 22 characters and spaces per inch measured horizontally for not less than three inches in one sentence, the recorder shall charge one dollar ($1) extra for each page or sheet on which printing appears, except, however, the extra charge shall not apply to printed words which are directive or explanatory in nature for completion of the form or on vital statistics forms. Fees collected under this paragraph are not subject to subdivision (b) or (c).

(2) If a page or sheet does not conform with the dimensions described in subdivision (a) of Section 27361.5, the recorder shall charge three dollars ($3) extra per page or sheet of the document. The funds generated by the extra charge authorized under this paragraph shall be available solely to support, maintain, improve, and provide for the full operation for modernized creation, retention, and retrieval of information in each county's system of recorded documents. Fees collected under this paragraph are not subject to subdivision (b) or (c).

(b) One dollar ($1) of each three dollar ($3) fee for each additional page shall be deposited in the county general fund.

(c) Notwithstanding Section 68085, one dollar ($1) for recording the first page and one dollar ($1) for each additional page shall be available solely to support, maintain, improve, and provide for the full operation for modernized creation, retention,

and retrieval of information in each county's system of recorded documents.

(d)(1) In addition to all other fees authorized by this section, a county recorder may charge a fee of one dollar ($1) for recording the first page of every instrument, paper, or notice required or permitted by law to be recorded, as authorized by each county's board of supervisors. The funds generated by this fee shall be used only by the county recorder collecting the fee for the purpose of implementing a social security number truncation program pursuant to Article 3.5 (commencing with Section 27300).

(2) A county recorder shall not charge the fee described in paragraph (1) after December 31, 2017, unless the county recorder has received reauthorization by the county's board of supervisors. A county recorder shall not seek reauthorization of the fee by the board before June 1, 2017, or after December 31, 2017. In determining the additional period of authorization, the board shall consider the review described in paragraph (4).

(3) Notwithstanding paragraph (2), a county recorder who, pursuant to subdivision (c) of Section 27304, secures a revenue anticipation loan, or other outside source of funding, for the implementation of a social security number truncation program, may be authorized to charge the fee described in paragraph (1) for a period not to exceed the term of repayment of the loan or other outside source of funding.

(4) A county board of supervisors that authorizes the fee described in this subdivision shall require the county auditor to conduct two reviews to verify that the funds generated by this fee are used only for the purpose of the program, as described in Article 3.5 (commencing with Section 27300) and for conducting these reviews. The reviews shall state the progress of the county recorder in truncating recorded documents pursuant to subdivision (a) of Section 27301, and shall estimate any ongoing costs to the county recorder of complying with subdivisions (a) and (b) of Section 27301. The board shall require that the first review be completed not before June 1, 2012, or after December 31, 2013, and that the second review be completed not before June 1, 2017, or after December 31, 2017. The reviews shall adhere to generally accepted accounting standards, and the review results shall be made available to the public. (*Added by Stats.1947, c. 424, p. 1165, § 1. Amended by Stats.1955, c. 542, p. 1011, § 1; Stats.1957, c. 954, p. 2197, § 2, eff. June 8, 1957; Stats.1971, c. 59, p. 77, § 1; Stats.1984, c. 1156, § 1; Stats.1988, c. 344, § 1; Stats.1991, c. 331 (S.B.21), § 2, eff. Aug. 5, 1991; Stats.1991, c. 1168 (A.B.2142), § 2.5, eff. Oct. 14, 1991; Stats.1992, c. 87 (A.B.689), § 4, operative July 1, 1994; Stats.1997, c. 850 (A.B. 233), § 26; Stats.1998, c. 146 (A.B.1301), § 3; Stats.2007, c. 627 (A.B.1168), § 9; Stats.2008, c. 179 (S.B.1498), § 102; Stats.2009, c. 606 (S.B.676), § 2.*)

Research References

Miller and Starr California Real Estate § 11:15, Transfer Taxes and Other Fees Charged on Recordation.

12 Witkin, California Summary 10th Real Property § 320, Fees.

§ 27361.1.   Two or more instruments, papers or notices serially incorporated on one form or sheet

Whenever two or more instruments, papers, or notices are serially incorporated on one form or sheet, or are attached to one another, except as an exhibit marked as such, each instrument, paper, or notice shall be considered to be a separate instrument, paper, or notice for the purpose of computing the fee established by Section 27361 of this code. (*Added by Stats.1967, c. 56, p. 957, § 4.*)

Research References

Miller and Starr California Real Estate § 11:19, Indexing Systems; Indexing by Title of Documents Submitted.

§ 27361.2. Document requiring additional indexing; additional fee

Whenever any instrument, paper, or notice is recorded which contains references to more than one previously recorded document and which requires additional indexing by the county recorder to give notice required by law, an additional fee of one dollar ($1) shall be charged for each reference to a previously recorded document, other than the first such reference, requiring additional indexing. References to group mining claims listed on a proof of labor shall be considered as only one reference when they are consecutively numbered or lettered alphabetically, and each break in consecutive numbers or letters shall be considered as an additional mine for fee purposes under this section and shall be so indexed in the index. *(Added by Stats.1969, c. 36, p. 143, § 1. Amended by Stats.1971, c. 889, p. 1742, § 1.)*

Research References

Miller and Starr California Real Estate § 11:19, Indexing Systems; Indexing by Title of Documents Submitted.

§ 27361.3. Release of lien, encumbrance or notice executed by state or local government

Notwithstanding any contrary provision of the law, the fee for recording every release of lien, encumbrance, or notice executed by the state, or any municipality, county, city, district or other political subdivision shall be eight dollars ($8) if the original lien, encumbrance, or notice was recorded without fee as provided by Section 27383 of the Government Code.

No fee shall be charged for recording a release of lien, encumbrance, or notice which was recorded in error by the state, or any municipality, county, city, district or other political subdivision if there is noted on the face of the release of lien, encumbrance, or notice a statement to that effect.

Two dollars ($2) for recording each release of lien pursuant to this section shall be available solely to support, maintain, improve, and provide for the full operation for modernized creation, retention, and retrieval of information in each county's system of recorded documents. *(Added by Stats.1974, c. 220, p. 419, § 1. Amended by Stats.1975, c. 473, p. 978, § 1; Stats.1984, c. 1156, § 2; Stats.1988, c. 344, § 2.)*

Research References

12 Witkin, California Summary 10th Real Property § 320, Fees.

§ 27361.4. Defraying cost of converting document storage system to micrographics; additional fee

(a) The board of supervisors of any county may provide for an additional fee of one dollar ($1) for filing every instrument, paper, or notice for record, in order to defray the cost of converting the county recorder's document storage system to micrographics. Upon completion of the conversion and payment of the costs therefor, this additional fee shall no longer be imposed.

(b) The board of supervisors of any county may provide for an additional fee, other than the fees authorized in subdivisions (a) and (c), of one dollar ($1) for filing every instrument, paper, or notice for record provided that the resolution providing for the additional fee establishes the days of operation of the county recorder's offices as every business day except for legal holidays and those holidays designated as judicial holidays pursuant to Section 135 of the Code of Civil Procedure.

(c) The board of supervisors of any county may provide for an additional fee, other than the fees authorized in subdivisions (a) and (b), of one dollar ($1) for filing every instrument, paper, or notice for record provided that the resolution providing for the additional fee requires that the instrument, paper, or notice be indexed within two business days after the date of recordation. *(Added by Stats.1980, c. 1002, p. 3194, § 1, eff. Sept. 21, 1980. Amended by Stats.1993, c. 710 (A.B.130), § 1.)*

Research References

12 Witkin, California Summary 10th Real Property § 320, Fees.

§ 27361.5. Page and sheet defined

(a) As used in Section 27361, a page shall be one printed side of a single piece of paper being 8½ inches by 11 inches.

(b) A sheet shall be one printed side of a single piece of paper which is not exactly 8½ inches by 11 inches but not greater than 8½ inches by 14 inches. *(Added by Stats.1992, c. 87 (A.B.689), § 6, operative July 1, 1994.)*

Research References

Miller and Starr California Real Estate § 11:10, Required Form and Contents--In General.

§ 27361.6. Margins and blank spaces; quality of paper; instruments modifying, releasing, or cancelling previously recorded documents

Except as otherwise provided by law or regulation, all documents submitted for recording shall have at least a ½-inch margin on the two vertical sides except in the space reserved for recording information. At least the top 2½ inches of the first page or sheet shall be reserved for recording information. The left-hand 3½ inches of the space shall be used by the public to show the name of the person requesting recording and the name and address to which the document is to be returned following recording. In the event the first page or sheet of a document does not comply with these requirements, a separate page shall be attached by the party requesting recording to the front of the document which meets these criteria and which reflects the title or titles of the document as required by Section 27324. Any printed form accepted for recordation that does not comply with the foregoing shall not affect the notice otherwise imparted by recording.

All instruments, papers, or notices presented for recordation shall be on a quality of paper and contain print of a size and color which will reproduce legibly by microphotographic or imaging processes as set forth in Sections 26205.5 and 27322.2.

Any instrument, paper, or notice presented for recordation which in any way modifies, releases, or cancels the provisions of a previously recorded document shall state the recorder identification number or book and page of the document number being modified, released, or canceled. *(Added by Stats.1992, c. 87 (A.B.689), § 8, operative July 1, 1994.)*

Research References

California Real Estate Forms (Miller & Starr) § 3:8, Deed of Trust, Security Agreement, and Fixture Filing With Assignment of Rents and Agreements.

California Real Estate Forms (Miller & Starr) § 3:9, Assignment of Lessor's Interest in Leases and Seller's Interest in Contracts for Sale.

California Real Estate Forms (Miller & Starr) § 3:14, Construction Deed of Trust, Security Agreement, and Fixture Filing With Assignment of Rents and Agreements.

California Real Estate Forms (Miller & Starr) § 3:21, Deed of Trust, Assignment of Rents, Security Agreement and Fixture Filing–Conduit Loan.

California Real Estate Forms (Miller & Starr) § 3:22, Assignment of Leases and Rents–Conduit Loans.

California Real Estate Forms (Miller & Starr) § 3:34, Short Form Deed of Trust and Assignment of Rents.

California Real Estate Forms (Miller & Starr) § 3:35, Long Form Deed of Trust and Assignment of Rents.

California Real Estate Forms (Miller & Starr) § 3:56, Subordination Agreement (Deed of Trust to Deed of Trust).

California Real Estate Forms (Miller & Starr) § 3:68, Deed in Lieu of Foreclosure–Amendment of Note and Deed of Trust (Exhibit C to Transfer Agreement).

Miller and Starr California Real Estate § 11:10, Required Form and Contents--In General.

12 Witkin, California Summary 10th Real Property § 319, General Requirements.

§ 27361.7. Illegible documents; substitution of legible original or preparation of true copy; certification

Whenever the text of a document presented for record may be made out but is not sufficiently legible to reproduce a readable photographic record, the recorder may require the person presenting it for record to substitute a legible original document or to prepare a legible copy of the first document by handwriting or typewriting and attach the same to the original as a part of the document for making the permanent photographic record. The handwritten or typewritten legible copy shall be certified by the party creating the copy under penalty of perjury as being a true copy of the original. As used in this section, the word "text" includes the notary seal, certificates, and other appendages thereto. *(Added by Stats.1963, c. 22, p. 631, § 2. Amended by Stats.1975, c. 252, p. 653, § 1; Stats.1981, c. 187, p. 1112, § 1.)*

Research References

Miller and Starr California Real Estate § 11:10, Required Form and Contents--In General.

Miller and Starr California Real Estate § 11:18, Reproduction of Documents.

12 Witkin, California Summary 10th Real Property § 319, General Requirements.

§ 27361.8. Document requiring indexing of more than 10 names; additional fee

Whenever any instrument, paper, or notice is recorded which requires additional indexing by the county recorder to give notice required by law and does not refer to a previously recorded document by reference, as covered in Section 27361.2, an additional fee of one dollar ($1) shall be charged for each group of 10 names or fractional portion thereof after the initial group of 10 names. *(Added by Stats.1980, c. 299, p. 627, § 1.)*

Research References

12 Witkin, California Summary 10th Real Property § 320, Fees.

§ 27361.9. Additional fee; filing preliminary notice by mechanics lien claimant

The board of supervisors of any county may provide for an additional fee for filing every preliminary notice pursuant to subdivision (a) of Section 8214 of the Civil Code for the exclusive purpose of defraying the cost of implementing and maintaining a system to facilitate compliance with subdivision (b) of Section 8214 of the Civil Code. *(Added by Stats.1987, c. 716, § 2. Amended by Stats.2010, c. 697 (S.B.189), § 34, operative July 1, 2012.)*

Law Revision Commission Comments

Section 27361.9 is amended to correct cross references and obsolete terminology. [40 Cal.L.Rev.Comm. Reports 49 (2010)].

§ 27364. Certificates under seal

The fee for each certificate under seal shall be set by the board of supervisors in an amount necessary to recover the direct and indirect costs of providing the product or service or the cost of enforcing any regulation for which the fee or charge is levied. *(Added by Stats.1947, c. 424, p. 1165 § 1. Amended by Stats. 1957, c. 869, p. 2083, § 4; Stats.1967, c. 57, p. 958, § 1; Stats.1993, c. 710 (A.B.130), § 2.)*

Research References

12 Witkin, California Summary 10th Real Property § 320, Fees.

§ 27365. Copies of vital statistics certificates

The fee for any copy of a birth, death, or marriage certificate, when the copy is made by the recorder, is the same as is payable to a state or local registrar of vital statistics. *(Added by Stats.1947, c. 424, p. 1165, § 1.)*

§ 27366. Copies of records on file

The fee for any copy of any other record or paper on file in the office of the recorder, when the copy is made by the recorder, shall be set by the board of supervisors in an amount necessary to recover the direct and indirect costs of providing the product or service or the cost of enforcing any regulation for which the fee or charge is levied. *(Added by Stats.1947, c. 424, p. 1165, § 1. Amended by Stats.1951, c. 1364, p. 3279, § 1; Stats.1957, c. 1865, p. 3267, § 4; Stats.1984, c. 1397, § 6; Stats.1993, c. 710 (A.B.130), § 3.)*

Research References

12 Witkin, California Summary 10th Real Property § 320, Fees.

§ 27369. Searching vital statistics records

The fee for searching the records of his office for a birth, death, or marriage certificate is the same as is payable to a state or local registrar of vital statistics; in all other cases, for each year, fifty cents ($0.50). *(Added by Stats.1947, c. 424, p. 1166, § 1.)*

§ 27371. Maps or plats; photographic method

The fee for recording each map or plat where it is copied in a book of record is ten cents ($0.10) for each course, plus ten cents ($0.10) a folio for letters and figures on the map or plat.

When recording is by a photographic method the fee for recording each map or plat shall be the same as provided for under Sections 27361 and 27361.5 of this code. *(Added by Stats.1947, c. 424, p. 1166, § 1. Amended by Stats.1951, c. 1308, p. 3199, § 1; Stats.1957, c. 1865, p. 3267, § 5.)*

§ 27372. Subdivision maps

The fee for recording or filing and indexing each map wherein land is subdivided in lots, tracts, or parcels is five dollars ($5) for the first page and two dollars ($2) for each additional page. *(Added by Stats.1947, c. 424, p. 1166, § 1. Amended by Stats.1957, c. 1865, p. 3268, § 6.)*

Research References

Miller and Starr California Real Estate § 11:15, Transfer Taxes and Other Fees Charged on Recordation.

§ 27375. Acknowledgments

The fee for taking an acknowledgment of any instrument is seventy-five cents ($0.75). *(Added by Stats.1947, c. 424, p. 1166, § 1. Amended by Stats.1957, c. 869, p. 2083, § 6.)*

§ 27379. Administering oaths

The fee for administering and certifying each oath or affirmation is fifty cents ($0.50). *(Added by Stats.1947, c. 424, p. 1166, § 1.)*

§ 27380. Papers not required to be recorded

The fee for filing, indexing, and keeping each paper not required by law to be recorded is three dollars ($3). *(Added by Stats.1947, c. 424, p. 1166, § 1. Amended by Stats.1949, c. 62, p. 81, § 1; Stats.1957, c. 954, p. 2197, § 3, eff. June 8, 1957; Stats.1971, c. 59, p. 77, § 2.)*

§ 27381. Exemptions

No charge or fee shall be made for recording, indexing, or issuing certified copies of any discharge, certificate of service, certificate of satisfactory service, report of separation, or notice of separation of any officer, commissioned warrant officer, warrant officer, flight officer, cadet, midshipman, noncommissioned officer, petty officer, soldier, sailor, or marine separated, released, or discharged from the Army, Navy, Marine Corps, Coast Guard of the United States, Women's Army Corps, Women's Army Auxiliary Corps, Women's Reserve of Navy, Marine Corps, or Coast Guard, or from the Army and Navy Nurse Corps. *(Added by Stats.1947, c. 424, p. 1166, § 1.)*

§ 27383. No fees for services to state or political subdivisions; exception

No fee shall be charged by the recorder for services rendered to the State, to any municipality, county in the State or other political subdivision thereof, except for making a copy of a paper or record. *(Added by Stats.1955, c. 488, p. 963, § 1.)*

Research References

12 Witkin, California Summary 10th Real Property § 320, Fees.

§ 27387. Abstract of judgment or other document creating an involuntary lien on real property; recordation

In addition to any other fee, the county recorder shall collect a fee from any lienor, other than a governmental entity, for the recordation of an abstract of judgment or other document creating an involuntary lien within the meaning of Section 27297.5 affecting title to real property. The fee shall not exceed the actual cost to the recorder of providing the notice required by Section 27297.5. *(Added by Stats.1980, c. 1281, p. 4328, § 4. Amended by Stats.1984, c. 144, § 146.)*

Research References

Rutter, Cal. Practice Guide: Enforcing Judgments/Debts Ch. 6B-4, Notice of Lien.

Miller and Starr California Real Estate § 32:47, Contents of the Abstract of Judgment.

12 Witkin, California Summary 10th Real Property § 320, Fees.

§ 27387.1. Additional recording fees; deeds filed with Los Angeles County Recorder; amount not to exceed cost of mailing notice and actual cost to provide information, counseling, or assistance; administrative costs

Section operative until Jan. 1, 2015. See, also, section operative Jan. 1, 2015.

(a) In addition to any other recording fee, the recorder, pursuant to Section 27297.6, may collect a fee from the party filing a deed, quitclaim deed, deed of trust, notice of default, or notice of sale, unless that party is a government entity. The fee shall not exceed the mailing cost of the notice specified in Section 27297.6 and the actual cost to provide information, counseling, or assistance to a person who receives the notice, not to exceed seven dollars ($7).

(b) The actual costs comprising the fee described in subdivision (a) may include administrative costs incurred by the recorder in performing the actions described in that subdivision. However, the administrative costs shall not exceed 10 percent of the total fee collected pursuant to subdivision (a).

(c) This section shall remain in effect only until January 1, 2015, and as of that date is repealed, unless a later enacted statute, that is enacted before January 1, 2015, deletes or extends that date. *(Added by Stats.1996, c. 177 (S.B.1631), § 2. Amended by Stats.2011, c. 141 (S.B.62), § 3.)*

Repeal

For repeal of this section, see its terms.

Research References

Miller and Starr California Real Estate § 11:10, Required Form and Contents--In General.

§ 27387.1. Additional recording fees; deeds filed with Los Angeles County Recorder; amount not to exceed cost of mailing notice

Section operative Jan. 1, 2015. See, also, section operative until Jan. 1, 2015.

(a) In addition to any other recording fee, the recorder may collect a fee from the party filing a deed, quitclaim deed, or deed of trust, other than a government entity, pursuant to Section 27297.6. The fee shall not exceed the mailing cost of the notice specified in Section 27297.6, not to exceed seven dollars ($7).

(b) This section shall become operative on January 1, 2015. *(Added by Stats.2011, c. 141 (S.B.62), § 4, operative Jan. 1, 2015.)*

Research References

Miller and Starr California Real Estate § 11:10, Required Form and Contents--In General.

§ 27388. Recording fees; real estate instrument, paper, or notice; Real Estate Fraud Prosecution Trust Fund; distribution; district attorney review; purpose

(a) In addition to any other recording fees specified in this code, upon the adoption of a resolution by the county board of supervisors, a fee of up to ten dollars ($10) shall be paid at the time of recording of every real estate instrument, paper, or notice required or permitted by law to be recorded within that county, except those expressly exempted from payment of recording fees. For purposes of this section, " real estate instrument" means a deed of trust, an assignment of deed of trust, an amended deed of trust, an abstract of judgment, an affidavit, an assignment of rents, an assignment of a lease, a construction trust deed, covenants, conditions, and restrictions (CC&Rs), a declaration of homestead, an easement, a lease, a lien, a lot line adjustment, a mechanics lien, a modification for deed of trust, a notice of completion, a quitclaim deed, a subordination agreement, a release, a reconveyance, a request for notice, a notice of default, a substitution of trustee, a notice of trustee sale, a trustee's deed upon sale, or a notice of rescission of declaration of default, or any Uniform Commercial Code amendment, assignment, continuation, statement, or termination. "Real estate instrument" does not include any deed, instrument, or writing recorded in connection with a transfer subject to the imposition of a documentary transfer tax as defined in Section 11911 of the Revenue and Taxation Code. The fees, after deduction of any actual and necessary administrative costs incurred by the county recorder in carrying out this section, shall be paid quarterly to the county auditor or director of finance, to be placed in the Real Estate Fraud Prosecution Trust Fund. The amount deducted for administrative costs shall not exceed 10 percent of the fees paid pursuant to this section.

(b) Money placed in the Real Estate Fraud Prosecution Trust Fund shall be expended to fund programs to enhance the capacity of local police and prosecutors to deter, investigate, and prosecute real estate fraud crimes. After deduction of the actual and necessary administrative costs referred to in subdivision (a), 60 percent of the funds shall be distributed to district attorneys subject to review pursuant to subdivision (d), and 40 percent of the funds shall be distributed to local law enforcement agencies within the county in accordance with subdivision (c). In those counties where the investigation of real estate fraud is done exclusively by the district attorney, after deduction of the actual and necessary administrative costs referred to in subdivision (a), 100 percent of the funds shall be distributed to the district attorney, subject to review pursuant to subdivision (d). A portion of the funds may be directly allocated to the county recorder to support county recorder fraud prevention programs, including, but not limited to, the fraud prevention program provided for in Section 27297.7. Prior to establishing or increasing fees pursuant to this section, the board of supervisors may consider support for county recorder fraud prevention programs. The funds so distributed shall be expended for the exclusive purpose of deterring, investigating, and prosecuting real estate fraud crimes.

(c) The county auditor or director of finance shall distribute funds in the Real Estate Fraud Prosecution Trust Fund to eligible law enforcement agencies within the county pursuant to subdivision (b), as determined by a Real Estate Fraud Prosecution Trust Fund Committee composed of the district attorney, the county chief administrative officer, the chief officer responsible for consumer protection within the county, and the chief law enforcement officer of one law enforcement agency receiving funding from the Real Estate Fraud Prosecution Trust Fund, the latter being selected by a majority of the other three members of the committee. The chief law enforcement officer shall be a nonvoting member of the committee and shall serve a one-year term, which may be renewed. Members may appoint representatives of their offices to serve on the committee. If a county lacks a chief officer responsible for consumer protection, the county board of supervisors may appoint an appropriate representative to serve on the committee. The committee shall establish and publish deadlines and written procedures for local law enforcement agencies within the county to apply for the use of funds and shall review applications and make determinations by majority vote as to the award of funds using the following criteria:

(1) Each law enforcement agency that seeks funds shall submit a written application to the committee setting forth in detail the agency's proposed use of the funds.

(2) In order to qualify for receipt of funds, each law enforcement agency submitting an application shall provide written evidence that the agency either:

(A) Has a unit, division, or section devoted to the investigation or prosecution of real estate fraud, or both, and the unit, division, or section has been in existence for at least one year prior to the application date.

(B) Has on a regular basis, during the three years immediately preceding the application date, accepted for investigation or prosecution, or both, and assigned to specific persons employed by the agency, cases of suspected real estate fraud, and actively investigated and prosecuted those cases.

(3) The committee's determination to award funds to a law enforcement agency shall be based on, but not be limited to, (A) the number of real estate fraud cases filed in the prior year; (B) the number of real estate fraud cases investigated in the prior year; (C) the number of victims involved in the cases filed; and (D) the total aggregated monetary loss suffered by victims, including individuals, associations, institutions, or corporations, as a result of the real estate fraud cases filed, and those under active investigation by that law enforcement agency.

(4) Each law enforcement agency that, pursuant to this section, has been awarded funds in the previous year, upon reapplication for funds to the committee in each successive year, in addition to any information the committee may require in paragraph (3), shall be required to submit a detailed accounting of funds received and expended in the prior year. The accounting shall include (A) the amount of funds received and expended; (B) the uses to which those funds were put, including payment of salaries and expenses, purchase of equipment and supplies, and other expenditures by type; (C) the number of filed complaints, investigations, arrests, and convictions that resulted from the expenditure of the funds; and (D) other relevant information the committee may reasonably require.

(d) The county board of supervisors shall annually review the effectiveness of the district attorney in deterring, investigating, and prosecuting real estate fraud crimes based upon information provided by the district attorney in an annual report. The district attorney shall submit the annual report to the board on or before September 1 of each year.

(e) A county shall not expend funds held in that county's Real Estate Fraud Prosecution Trust Fund until the county's auditor-controller verifies that the county's district attorney has submitted an annual report for the county's most recent full fiscal year pursuant to the requirements of subdivision (d).

(f) The intent of the Legislature in enacting this section is to have an impact on real estate fraud involving the largest number of victims. To the extent possible, an emphasis should be placed on fraud against individuals whose residences are in danger of, or are in, foreclosure as defined in subdivision (b) of Section 1695.1 of the Civil Code. Case filing decisions continue to be at the discretion of the prosecutor.

(g) A district attorney's office or a local enforcement agency that has undertaken investigations and prosecutions that will continue into a subsequent program year may receive nonexpended funds from the previous fiscal year subsequent to the annual submission of information detailing the accounting of funds received and expended in the prior year.

(h) No money collected pursuant to this section shall be expended to offset a reduction in any other source of funds. Funds from the Real Estate Fraud Prosecution Trust Fund shall be used only in connection with criminal investigations or prosecutions involving recorded real estate documents. *(Added by Stats.1995, c. 942 (S.B.537), § 1. Amended by Stats.2000, c. 765 (S.B.762), § 1; Stats.2003, c. 46 (A.B.241), § 1; Stats.2005, c. 531 (A.B.901), § 2; Stats.2008, c. 405 (S.B.1396), § 1; Stats. 2009, c. 35 (S.B.174), § 4; Stats.2012, c. 104 (S.B.1342), § 2.)*

Research References

Miller and Starr California Real Estate § 11:15, Transfer Taxes and Other Fees Charged on Recordation.
16 NO. 4 Miller & Starr, California Real Estate Newsalert 18, Regulation of the Real Estate Industry.
16 NO. 5 Miller & Starr, California Real Estate Newsalert 26, State Board of Equalization Issues Comprehensive Summary and Qs and As for Transfers of Base Year Values of Principal Residences.
19 NO. 4 Miller & Starr, California Real Estate Newsalert 23, Recording and Priorities.

ARTICLE 6. ELECTRONIC RECORDING DELIVERY ACT OF 2004

Section

Section

27393.   Development and adoption of regulations for review, approval, and oversight of electronic recording delivery systems; local inspection and review by Attorney General.

27394.   Eligibility for establishment of electronic recording delivery system; contract with computer security auditor approved by Attorney General; criteria for approval; audit of electronic recording delivery systems; considerations; transmittal and disclosure of audit reports; scope of access of computer security auditor; notification and action in event of reasonable belief that system is vulnerable to fraud or intrusion.

27395.   Computer security auditors; prohibited persons; criminal records checks and subsequent arrest notification; notification of ineligibility for access to electronic recording delivery service; fees; "secure access".

27396.   Attorney General; monitoring of security of electronic recording delivery systems; authority to suspend electronic recording delivery systems; authority of Attorney General, district attorney, or city prosecutor to bring action for relief.

27397.   Regulation and oversight costs; authorized fees; deposit of fees paid to Attorney General.

27397.5.   Authority of county recorder to include in electronic recording delivery system a secure method for accepting for recording a digital or digitized electronic record that is an instrument of reconveyance, substitution of trustee, or assignment of deed of trust; authority to contract; application of security audit and criminal records check requirements; certification requirements; withdrawal of certification.

27398.   Attorney General; evaluation of electronic recording delivery systems and report to legislature; content of evaluation.

27399.   Scope of article.

§ 27390. Citation of article; definitions

(a) This article shall be known and may be cited as the Electronic Recording Delivery Act of 2004.

(b) For the purposes of this article, the following definitions shall apply:

(1) "Authorized submitter" means a party that has entered into a contract with a county recorder pursuant to subdivision (b) of Section 27391 and is not disqualified pursuant to Section 27395.

(2) "Computer security auditor" means computer security personnel hired to perform an independent audit of the electronic recording delivery system. The computer security auditor shall be independent of the county recorder and the authorized submitter and shall not be the same contractor hired to establish or participate in a county's electronic recording delivery system or in the authorized submitter's portion of that system.

(3) "Digital electronic record" means a record containing information that is created, generated, sent, communicated, received, or stored by electronic means, but not created in original paper form.

(4) "Digitized electronic record" means a scanned image of the original paper document.

(5) "Electronic recording delivery system" means a system to deliver for recording, and to return to the party requesting recording, digitized or digital electronic records.

(6) "Security testing" means an independent security audit by a computer security auditor, including, but not limited to, attempts to penetrate an electronic recording delivery system for the purpose of testing the security of that system.

(7) "Source code" means a program or set of programs, readable and maintainable by humans, translated or interpreted into a form that the electronic recording delivery system can execute.

(8) "System certification" means the issuance of a confirmation letter regarding a county's electronic recording delivery system by the Attorney General. *(Added by Stats.2004, c. 621 (A.B.578), § 2, eff. Sept. 21, 2004.)*

Research References

Rutter, Cal. Practice Guide: Real Prop. Transactions Ch. 4-F, F. Use of an Escrow.

Miller and Starr California Real Estate § 11:11, Required Form and Contents--Digital Recording Systems.

15 NO. 4 Miller & Starr, California Real Estate Newsalert 15, Recording and Priorities.

12 Witkin, California Summary 10th Real Property § 319, General Requirements.

§ 27391. Establishment of electronic recording delivery system; contracting; termination or suspension of access; mailing copy of recorded electronic document; electronic signatures

(a) Upon approval by resolution of the board of supervisors and system certification by the Attorney General, a county recorder may establish an electronic recording delivery system.

(b) Upon system certification, a county recorder may enter into a contract with a title insurer, as defined in Section 12340.4 of the Insurance Code, underwritten title company, as defined in Section 12340.5 of the Insurance Code, institutional lender, as defined in paragraph (1), (2), or (4) of subdivision (j) of Section 50003 of the Financial Code, or an entity of local, state, or federal government for the delivery for recording, and return to the party requesting recording, of a digitized electronic record that is an instrument affecting a right, title, or interest in real property. The contract may provide for the delivery of documents by an agent. However, the agent shall not be a vendor of electronic recording delivery systems.

(c) A county recorder may refuse to enter into a contract with any party or may terminate or suspend access to a system for any good faith reason, including, but not limited to, a determination by the county recorder that termination or suspension is necessary to protect the public interest, to protect the integrity of public records, or to protect homeowners from financial harm, or if the volume or quality of instruments submitted by the requester is not sufficient to warrant electronic recordation. A county recorder may also terminate or suspend access to a system if a party commits a substantive breach of the contract, the requirements of this article, or the regulations adopted pursuant to this article.

(d) Notwithstanding Section 27321, a county recorder may require a party electronically submitting records to mail a copy of the recorded electronic document to the address specified in the instructions for mailing upon completion of recording.

(e) When a signature is required to be accompanied by a notary's seal or stamp, that requirement is satisfied if the electronic signature of the notary contains all of the following:

(1) The name of the notary.

(2) The words "Notary Public."

(3) The name of the county where the bond and oath of office of the notary are filed.

Government

(4) The sequential identification number assigned to the notary, if any.

(5) The sequential identification number assigned to the manufacturer or vendor of the notary's physical or electronic seal, if any. *(Added by Stats.2004, c. 621 (A.B.578), § 2, eff. Sept. 21, 2004.)*

Research References

Miller and Starr California Real Estate § 11:11, Required Form and Contents--Digital Recording Systems.
15 NO. 4 Miller & Starr, California Real Estate Newsalert 15, Recording and Priorities.

§ 27392. System certification by Attorney General

(a) No electronic recording delivery system may become operational without system certification by the Attorney General. The certification shall affirm that the proposed county system conforms to this article and any regulations adopted pursuant to this article, that security testing has confirmed that the system is secure and that the proposed operating procedures are sufficient to assure the continuing security and lawful operation of that system. The certification may include any agreements between the county recorder and the Attorney General as to the operation of the system, including, but not limited to, the nature and frequency of computer security audits. Certification may be withdrawn for good cause.

(b) The Attorney General shall approve software and other services for electronic recording delivery systems pursuant to regulations adopted as described in paragraph (7) of subdivision (b) of Section 27393. *(Added by Stats.2004, c. 621 (A.B.578), § 2, eff. Sept. 21, 2004.)*

Research References

Miller and Starr California Real Estate § 11:11, Required Form and Contents--Digital Recording Systems.
15 NO. 4 Miller & Starr, California Real Estate Newsalert 15, Recording and Priorities.

§ 27393. Development and adoption of regulations for review, approval, and oversight of electronic recording delivery systems; local inspection and review by Attorney General

(a) The Attorney General shall, in consultation with interested parties, adopt regulations for the review, approval, and oversight of electronic recording delivery systems. Regulations shall be adopted pursuant to the Administrative Procedure Act (Chapter 3.5 (commencing with Section 11340) of Part 1 of Division 3). The regulations shall comply with Section 12168.7.

(b) The regulations adopted pursuant to subdivision (a) may include, but need not be limited to, all of the following:

(1) Establishment of baseline technological and procedural specifications for electronic recording delivery systems.

(2) Requirements for security, capacity, reliability, and uniformity.

(3) Requirements as to the nature and frequency of computer security audits.

(4) A statement of a detailed and uniform definition of the term "source code" consistent with paragraph (7) of subdivision (b) of Section 27390, and as used in this article, and applicable to each county's electronic recording delivery system.

(5) Requirements for placement of a copy of the operating system, source code, compilers, and all related software associated with each county's electronic recording delivery system in an approved escrow facility prior to that system's first use.

(6) Requirements to ensure that substantive modifications to an operating system, compilers, related software, or source code are approved by the Attorney General.

(7) Procedures for initial certification of vendors offering software and other services to counties for electronic recording delivery systems.

(8) Requirements for system certification and for oversight of approved systems.

(9) Requirements for fingerprinting and criminal records checks required by Section 27395, including a list of employment positions or classifications subject to criminal records checks under subdivision (f) of that section.

(10) Requirements for uniform index information that shall be included in every digitized or digital electronic record.

(11) Requirements for protecting proprietary information accessed pursuant to subdivision (e) of Section 27394 from public disclosure.

(12) Requirements for certification under Section 27397.5.

(c) The Attorney General may promulgate any other regulations necessary to fulfill his or her obligations under this article.

(d) An electronic recording delivery system shall be subject to local inspection and review by the Attorney General. The Attorney General shall furnish a statement of any relevant findings associated with a local inspection of an electronic recording delivery system, to the county recorder and the district attorney of the affected county, and to all technology vendors associated with that system. *(Added by Stats.2004, c. 621 (A.B.578), § 2, eff. Sept. 21, 2004. Amended by Stats.2005, c. 22 (S.B.1108), § 87.)*

Research References

Miller and Starr California Real Estate § 11:11, Required Form and Contents--Digital Recording Systems.
15 NO. 4 Miller & Starr, California Real Estate Newsalert 15, Recording and Priorities.

§ 27394. Eligibility for establishment of electronic recording delivery system; contract with computer security auditor approved by Attorney General; criteria for approval; audit of electronic recording delivery systems; considerations; transmittal and disclosure of audit reports; scope of access of computer security auditor; notification and action in event of reasonable belief that system is vulnerable to fraud or intrusion

(a) To be eligible to establish an electronic recording delivery system, a county recorder shall contract with, and obtain a report from, a computer security auditor selected from a list of computer security auditors approved by the Attorney General.

(b) The Attorney General shall approve computer security auditors on the basis of significant experience in the evaluation and analysis of Internet security design, the conduct of security testing procedures, and specific experience performing Internet penetration studies. The Attorney General shall complete the approval of security auditors within 90 days of a request from a county recorder. The list shall be a public record.

(c) An electronic recording delivery system shall be audited, at least once during the first year of operation and periodically thereafter, as set forth in regulation and in the system certification, by a computer security auditor. The computer security auditor shall conduct security testing of the electronic recording delivery system. The reports of the computer security auditor shall include, but not be limited to, all of the following considerations:

(1) Safety and security of the system, including the vulnerability of the electronic recording delivery system to fraud or penetration.

(2) Results of testing of the system's protections against fraud or intrusion, including security testing and penetration studies.

(3) Recommendations for any additional precautions needed to ensure that the system is secure.

(d) Upon completion, the reports and any response to any recommendations shall be transmitted to the board of supervisors, the county recorder, the county district attorney, and the Attorney General. These reports shall be exempt from disclosure under the California Public Records Act (Chapter 3.5 (commencing with Section 6250) of Division 7 of Title 1).

(e) A computer security auditor shall have access to any aspect of an electronic recording delivery system, in any form requested. Computer security auditor access shall include, but not be limited to, permission for a thorough examination of source code and the associated approved escrow facility, and necessary authorization and assistance for a penetration study of that system.

(f) If the county recorder, a computer security auditor, a district attorney for a county participating in the electronic recording delivery system, or the Attorney General reasonably believes that an electronic recording delivery system is vulnerable to fraud or intrusion, the county recorder, the board of supervisors, the district attorney, and the Attorney General shall be immediately notified. The county recorder shall immediately take the necessary steps to guard against any compromise of the electronic recording delivery system, including, if necessary, the suspension of an authorized submitter or of the electronic recording delivery system. *(Added by Stats.2004, c. 621 (A.B. 578), § 2, eff. Sept. 21, 2004.)*

Research References

Miller and Starr California Real Estate § 11:11, Required Form and Contents--Digital Recording Systems.
15 NO. 4 Miller & Starr, California Real Estate Newsalert 15, Recording and Priorities.

§ 27395. Computer security auditors; prohibited persons; criminal records checks and subsequent arrest notification; notification of ineligibility for access to electronic recording delivery service; fees; "secure access"

(a) No person shall be a computer security auditor or be granted secure access to an electronic recording delivery system if he or she has been convicted of a felony, has been convicted of a misdemeanor related to theft, fraud, or a crime of moral turpitude, or if he or she has pending criminal charges for any of these crimes. A plea of guilty or no contest, a verdict resulting in conviction, or the forfeiture of bail, shall be a conviction within the meaning of this section, irrespective of a subsequent order under Section 1203.4 of the Penal Code.

(b) All persons entrusted with secure access to an electronic recording delivery system shall submit fingerprints to the Attorney General for a criminal records check according to regulations adopted pursuant to Section 27393.

(c)(1) The Attorney General shall submit to the Department of Justice the fingerprint images and related information of persons with secure access to the electronic recording delivery system and computer security auditors for the purpose of obtaining information as to the existence and nature of a record of state or federal convictions and arrests for which the Department of Justice establishes that the applicant was released on bail or on his or her own recognizance pending trial.

(2) The Department of Justice shall respond to the Attorney General for criminal offender record information requests submitted pursuant to this section, with information as delineated in subdivision (*l*) of Section 11105 of the Penal Code.

(3) The Department of Justice shall forward requests from the Attorney General to the Federal Bureau of Investigation for federal summary criminal history information pursuant to this section.

(4) The Attorney General shall review and compile the information from the Department of Justice and the Federal Bureau of Investigation to determine whether a person is eligible to access an electronic recording delivery system pursuant to this article.

(5) The Attorney General shall request subsequent arrest notification service, pursuant to Section 11105.2 of the Penal Code, for all persons with secure access to the electronic recording delivery system and all computer security auditors.

(d) The Attorney General shall deliver written notification of an individual's ineligibility for access to an electronic recording delivery system to the individual, his or her known employer, the computer security auditor, and the county recorder.

(e) The Department of Justice shall charge a fee sufficient to cover the cost of processing a state or federal criminal offender record information request and any other costs incurred pursuant to this section.

(f) The Attorney General shall define "secure access" by regulation and by agreement with the county recorder in the system certification. *(Added by Stats.2004, c. 621 (A.B.578), § 2, eff. Sept. 21, 2004. Amended by Stats.2005, c. 520 (A.B.1738), § 1.)*

Research References

Miller and Starr California Real Estate § 11:11, Required Form and Contents--Digital Recording Systems.
15 NO. 4 Miller & Starr, California Real Estate Newsalert 15, Recording and Priorities.
16 NO. 4 Miller & Starr, California Real Estate Newsalert 17, Recording and Priorities.
16 NO. 5 Miller & Starr, California Real Estate Newsalert 26, State Board of Equalization Issues Comprehensive Summary and Qs and As for Transfers of Base Year Values of Principal Residences.

§ 27396. Attorney General; monitoring of security of electronic recording delivery systems; authority to suspend electronic recording delivery systems; authority of Attorney General, district attorney, or city prosecutor to bring action for relief

(a) The Attorney General shall monitor the security of electronic recording delivery systems statewide, in close cooperation with county recorders and public prosecutors. In the event of an emergency involving multiple fraudulent transactions linked to one county's use of an electronic recording delivery system, the Attorney General may order the suspension of electronic recording delivery systems in any county or in multiple counties, if necessary to protect the security of the system, for a period of up to seven court days. The Attorney General may seek an order from the superior court if it is necessary to extend this order.

(b)(1) The Attorney General, a district attorney, or a city prosecutor may bring an action in the name of the people of the state seeking declaratory or injunctive relief, restitution for damages or economic loss, rescission, or other equitable relief pertaining to any alleged violation of this article or regulations adopted pursuant to this article. Injunctive relief may include, but is not limited to, an order suspending a party from participation in the electronic recording delivery system, on a temporary or permanent basis.

(2) Nothing in this subdivision shall be construed to prevent the Attorney General, a district attorney, or a city prosecutor from seeking legal or equitable relief under any other provision of law. *(Added by Stats.2004, c. 621 (A.B.578), § 2, eff. Sept. 21, 2004.)*

Research References

15 NO. 4 Miller & Starr, California Real Estate Newsalert 15, Recording and Priorities.

§ 27397. Regulation and oversight costs; authorized fees; deposit of fees paid to Attorney General

(a) A county establishing an electronic recording delivery system under this article shall pay for the direct cost of regulation and oversight by the Attorney General.

(b) The Attorney General may charge a fee directly to a vendor seeking approval of software and other services as part of an electronic recording delivery system. The fee shall not exceed the reasonable costs of approving software or other services for vendors.

(c) In order to pay costs under this section, a county may do any of the following:

(1) Impose a fee in an amount up to and including one dollar ($1) for each instrument that is recorded by the county. This fee may, at the county's discretion, be limited to instruments that are recorded pursuant to the electronic recording delivery system.

(2) Impose a fee upon any vendor seeking approval of software and other services as part of an electronic recording delivery system.

(3) Impose a fee upon any person seeking to contract as an authorized submitter.

(d) The total fees assessed by a county recorder pursuant to this section may not exceed the reasonable total costs of the electronic recording delivery system, the review and approval of vendors and potential authorized submitters, security testing as required by this article and the regulations of the Attorney General, and reimbursement to the Attorney General for regulation and oversight of the electronic recording delivery system.

(e) Fees paid to the Attorney General pursuant to subdivisions (a) and (b) shall be deposited in the Electronic Recording Authorization Account, which is hereby created in the Special Deposit Fund, and, notwithstanding Section 13340, is continuously appropriated, without regard to fiscal years, to the Attorney General for the costs described in those subdivisions. *(Added by Stats.2004, c. 621 (A.B.578), § 2, eff. Sept. 21, 2004.)*

Research References

15 NO. 4 Miller & Starr, California Real Estate Newsalert 15, Recording and Priorities.

§ 27397.5. Authority of county recorder to include in electronic recording delivery system a secure method for accepting for recording a digital or digitized electronic record that is an instrument of reconveyance, substitution of trustee, or assignment of deed of trust; authority to contract; application of security audit and criminal records check requirements; certification requirements; withdrawal of certification

(a) A county recorder may include in the county's electronic recording delivery system a secure method for accepting for recording a digital or digitized electronic record that is an instrument of reconveyance, substitution of trustee, or assignment of deed of trust.

(b) A county recorder may contract with a title insurer, as defined in Section 12340.4 of the Insurance Code, underwritten title company, as defined in Section 12340.5 of the Insurance Code, an entity of state, local, or federal government, or an institutional lender, as defined in Section 50003 of the Financial Code, or their authorized agents, to be an authorized submitter of the documents specified in subdivision (a).

(c) With respect to the electronic submission of the records described in subdivision (a), the requirements that an authorized submitter be subject to a security audit under Section 27394 and a criminal records check under Section 27395 shall not apply where the certification requirements of subdivision (d) have been met.

(d)(1) In order for subdivision (c) to apply, the county recorder and the Attorney General shall certify that the method of submission allowed under the system will not permit an authorized submitter or its employees and agents, or any third party, to modify, manipulate, insert, or delete information in the public record, maintained by the county recorder, or information in electronic records submitted pursuant to subdivision (b) of Section 27391.

(2) Certification under this section may be withdrawn by either the county recorder or the Attorney General at any time either determines that the requirements of this subdivision are not met.

(e) For purposes of this section, an agent of an authorized submitter shall not include a vendor of electronic recording delivery systems. *(Added by Stats.2004, c. 621 (A.B.578), § 2, eff. Sept. 21, 2004.)*

Research References

Miller and Starr California Real Estate § 11:11, Required Form and Contents--Digital Recording Systems.
15 NO. 4 Miller & Starr, California Real Estate Newsalert 15, Recording and Priorities.

§ 27398. Attorney General; evaluation of electronic recording delivery systems and report to legislature; content of evaluation

(a) The Attorney General shall conduct an evaluation of electronic recording delivery systems authorized by this article, and report to both houses of the Legislature on or before June 30, 2009.

(b) It is the intent of the Legislature that the evaluation include an analysis of costs, cost savings, security and real estate fraud prevention, and recommendations as to improvements and possible expansion of the provisions of this article.

(c) The evaluation shall also include a study of the feasibility of expanding the provisions of this article to cover the delivery, recording, and return of other electronic records. *(Added by Stats.2004, c. 621 (A.B.578), § 2, eff. Sept. 21, 2004.)*

Research References

15 NO. 4 Miller & Starr, California Real Estate Newsalert 15, Recording and Priorities.

§ 27399. Scope of article

(a) Nothing in this article shall be construed to authorize any state agency to administer any of the processes or procedures relating to the business of the county recorders of the state in any manner not otherwise specifically set forth in this article.

(b) The authority granted in this article is in addition to any other authority or obligation under state or federal law.

(c) Nothing in this article shall be construed to repeal or affect Section 27279, 27279.1, 27279.2, 27297.6, 27387.1, or 27399.7, or the authority of the Counties of Orange and San Bernardino to act under those provisions. *(Added by Stats.2004, c. 621 (A.B.578), § 2, eff. Sept. 21, 2004.)*

Title 8

THE ORGANIZATION AND GOVERNMENT OF COURTS

CHAPTER 1. GENERAL PROVISIONS

§ 68070. Rules of court; authority to make; restrictions; uniformity

(a) Every court may make rules for its own government and the government of its officers not inconsistent with law or with the rules adopted and prescribed by the Judicial Council. These rules shall not:

(1) Impose any tax, charge, or penalty upon any legal proceeding, or for filing any pleading allowed by law.

(2) Give any allowance to any officer for services.

(b) The Judicial Council is encouraged to adopt rules to provide for uniformity in rules and procedures throughout all courts in a county and statewide. The subjects on which uniformity should be sought shall include, but are not limited to, (1) the form of papers, (2) limitations on the filing of papers, (3) rules relating to law and motion, and (4) requirements concerning documents to be filed at or prior to trial. *(Added by Stats.1953, c. 206, p. 1238, § 1. Amended by Stats.1977, c. 1257, § 48, eff. Oct. 3, 1977; Stats.1993, c. 925 (S.B.425), § 3; Stats.1998, c. 1004 (A.B.1935), § 1.5.)*

Research References

Rutter, Cal. Practice Guide: Civ. Pro. Before Trial Ch. 13-A, A. Introduction.

Rutter, Cal. Practice Guide: Civ. Pro. Before Trial Ch. 9(I)-A, A. Introduction.

Rutter, Cal. Practice Guide: Civ. Pro. Before Trial Ch. 12(I)-A, A. Rules Governing Trial Setting Process.

Government

Rutter, Cal. Practice Guide: Civil Trials & Evidence Ch. 1-A, A. Importance of Statewide and Local Rules of Court.

Rutter, Cal. Practice Guide: Civil Trials & Evidence Ch. 4-A, A. General Considerations.

Rutter, Cal. Practice Guide: Personal Injury Ch. 8-A, A. Case Management.

2 Witkin Cal. Proc. 5th Courts § 181, Rules Must be Consistent With Statute.

2 Witkin Cal. Proc. 5th Courts § 187, (S 187) in General.

2 Witkin Cal. Proc. 5th Courts § 199, (S 199) in General.

2 Witkin Cal. Proc. 5th Courts § 201, (S 201) Local Policy.

2 Witkin Cal. Proc. 5th Courts § 203, Invalid Rules.

§ 68070.5. Communications between judges or judicial officers; cases on appeal; petitions for an original writ naming a court as party

(a) When a case is appealed, there shall be no communication direct or indirect between the judge or judicial officer who heard the case and any judge of the reviewing court concerning the facts or merits of the case.

(b) When a petition for an original writ names a court as a party, there shall be no communication direct or indirect between any judge hearing the writ and the judge or judicial officer of the court named as a party.

(c) The prohibitions of subdivisions (a) and (b) shall not apply to a written communication if at the time the communication is transmitted all the parties are sent a copy. *(Added by Stats.1978, c. 596, p. 2035, § 1.)*

Research References

2 Witkin Cal. Proc. 5th Courts § 66, (S 66) Communications Between Judges.

§ 68071. Rules of superior courts; effective dates; exceptions

No rule adopted by a superior court shall take effect until January 1 or July 1, whichever comes first, following the 45th day after it has been filed with the Judicial Council and the clerk of the court, and made immediately available for public examination. The Judicial Council may establish, by rule, a procedure for exceptions to these effective dates. *(Added by Stats.1953, c. 206, p. 1238, § 1. Amended by Stats.1977, c. 1257, p. 4771, § 49, eff. Oct. 3, 1977; Stats.1984, c. 1249, § 3; Stats.1985, c. 1311, § 1; Stats.1988, c. 1133, § 1; Stats.1992, c. 305 (A.B.2948), § 1; Stats.1998, c. 931 (S.B.2139), § 220, eff. Sept. 28, 1998; Stats. 2002, c. 784 (S.B.1316), § 199; Stats.2008, c. 218 (A.B.1949), § 3.)*

Law Revision Commission Comments

Section 68071 is amended to reflect elimination of the justice court. Cal. Const. art. VI, §§ 1, 5(b). [28 Cal.L.Rev.Comm. Reports 51 (1998)].

Section 68071 is amended to reflect unification of the municipal and superior courts pursuant to Article VI, Section 5(e), of the California Constitution. [32 Cal.L.Rev.Comm. Reports 226 (2002)].

Research References

Rutter, Cal. Practice Guide: Civ. Pro. Before Trial Ch. 9(I)-A, A. Introduction.

Rutter, Cal. Practice Guide: Civil Trials & Evidence Ch. 4-A, A. General Considerations.

2 Witkin Cal. Proc. 5th Courts § 188, (S 188) Filing, Publication, and Effective Date.

2 Witkin Cal. Proc. 5th Courts § 200, (S 200) Adoption and Publication.

2 Witkin Cal. Proc. 5th Courts § 259, (S 259) Local Standards and Procedure.

§ 68072. Rules of judicial council, supreme court, or court of appeal; effective date

Rules adopted by the Judicial Council, the Supreme Court, or a court of appeal shall take effect on a date to be fixed in the order of adoption. If no effective date is fixed, those rules shall take effect 60 days after their adoption. Rules adopted by a superior court shall take effect as provided in Section 68071. *(Added by Stats.1953, c. 206, p. 1238, § 1. Amended by Stats.1967, c. 17, p. 838, § 42; Stats.1977, c. 1257, p. 4771, § 50, eff. Oct. 3, 1977; Stats.1989, c. 1416, § 34; Stats.1992, c. 305 (A.B.2948), § 2; Stats.1998, c. 931 (S.B.2139), § 221, eff. Sept. 28, 1998; Stats.2002, c. 784 (S.B.1316), § 200.)*

Law Revision Commission Comments

Section 68072 is amended to reflect elimination of the justice court. Cal. Const. art. VI, §§ 1, 5(b). [28 Cal.L.Rev.Comm. Reports 51 (1998)].

Research References

2 Witkin Cal. Proc. 5th Courts § 188, (S 188) Filing, Publication, and Effective Date.

§ 68081. Appellate review; supplemental briefing; rehearing

Before the Supreme Court, a court of appeal, or the appellate division of a superior court renders a decision in a proceeding other than a summary denial of a petition for an extraordinary writ, based upon an issue which was not proposed or briefed by any party to the proceeding, the court shall afford the parties an opportunity to present their views on the matter through supplemental briefing. If the court fails to afford that opportunity, a rehearing shall be ordered upon timely petition of any party. *(Added by Stats.1986, c. 1098, § 1. Amended by Stats. 1987, c. 56, § 92; Stats.1989, c. 262, § 1; Stats.1998, c. 931 (S.B.2139), § 224, eff. Sept. 28, 1998.)*

Law Revision Commission Comments

Section 68081 is amended to reflect the creation of an appellate division in the superior court. Cal. Const. art. VI, § 4. [28 Cal.L.Rev.Comm. Reports 51 (1998)].

Research References

Rutter, Cal. Practice Guide: Civil Appeals & Writs Ch. 9-D, D. Procedural Rules.

Rutter, Cal. Practice Guide: Civil Appeals & Writs Ch. 11-A, A. the Decisionmaking Process.

Rutter, Cal. Practice Guide: Civil Appeals & Writs Ch. 11-C, C. Rendition of Opinion and Judgment.

Rutter, Cal. Practice Guide: Civil Appeals & Writs Ch. 12-B, B. Grounds for Rehearing.

Rutter, Cal. Practice Guide: Civil Appeals & Writs Ch. 13-F, F. Petition for Rehearing.

9 Witkin Cal. Proc. 5th Appeal § 693, Supplementary Briefs.

9 Witkin Cal. Proc. 5th Appeal § 905, Grounds.

9 Witkin Cal. Proc. 5th Appeal § 1019, (S 1019) Rehearing.

§ 68084.1. Disposition of unclaimed money deposited with a superior court or that court is holding in trust; notice; claims; disposition of funds

(a) Except as otherwise provided by law, any money, excluding restitution to victims, that has been deposited with a superior court, or that a superior court is holding in trust for the lawful owner, in a court bank account or in a court trust account in a county treasury, that remains unclaimed for three years shall become the property of the superior court if, after published notice pursuant to this section, the money is not claimed or no verified complaint is filed and served. After published notice pursuant to this section, if the money is not claimed or no verified complaint is filed and served, money representing restitution collected on behalf of victims that remains unclaimed for three years shall be deposited either into the State Restitution Fund exclusively for the purposes of providing victim services or into the general fund of a county that administers a victim services program exclusively for the provision of victim services.

(b) At any time after the expiration of the three-year period specified in subdivision (a), the executive officer of the superior court may cause a notice to be published once a week for two successive weeks in a newspaper of general circulation published in the county in which the court is located. The notice shall state the amount of money, the fund in which it is held, and that it is proposed that the money will become the property of the court on a designated date not less than 45 days nor more than 60 days after the first publication of the notice.

(c) Before or after publication, a party of interest may file a claim with the court executive officer that shall include the claimant's name, address, amount of claim, the grounds on which the claim is founded, and any other information that may be required by the court executive officer. The claim shall be filed before the designated date on which unclaimed money becomes the property of the court as provided under subdivision (b), and the executive officer shall accept or reject that claim.

(d) If the superior court executive officer rejects the claim, or takes no action on the claim within 30 days after it is filed, the party that submitted the claim may file a verified complaint seeking to recover all, or a specified part, of the money in the court in the county in which the notice is published. The copy of the complaint and summons shall be served on the court executive officer. The court executive officer shall withhold the release of the portion of unclaimed money for which a court action has been filed as provided in this section until the court renders a decision or the claim is settled. Any portion of the unclaimed money not covered by the verified complaint shall become the property of the court if no other claim or verified complaint has been filed regarding it within the time specified in this section. If the party that submitted the claim does not file a verified complaint within 30 days after the date that the court mailed notice that the claim was rejected or within 60 days after the claim was filed, the money shall become the property of the court.

(e) Notwithstanding subdivisions (c) and (d), the court executive officer may release the unclaimed money to the depositor of the unclaimed money, or the depositor's heir, beneficiary, or duly appointed representative, if the depositor or the depositor's heir, beneficiary, or duly appointed representative claims the money before the date that the money becomes the property of the superior court, upon submitting proof satisfactory to the court executive officer.

(f) If no claim is filed under subdivision (c) and the time for filing claims has expired, the money shall become the property of the court. If a claim or claims are filed with respect to a portion of the money, but not the remainder of the money, and the time for filing claims under subdivision (c) has expired, the remainder of the money shall become the property of the court.

(g) Notwithstanding any other provision of this section, the presiding judge may direct the transfer of any individual deposit of twenty dollars ($20) or less, or any amount if the name of the original depositor is unknown, that remains unclaimed for one year to the Trial Court Operations Fund without the need for publication of notice.

(h) The court executive officer may delegate the responsibilities provided in this section to appropriate superior court staff.

(i) When any money deposited and held under this section becomes the property of a superior court, the presiding judge shall transfer it to the Trial Court Operations Fund. *(Added by Stats.2005, c. 75 (A.B.145), § 100, eff. July 19, 2005, operative Jan. 1, 2006. Amended by Stats.2007, c. 738 (A.B.1248), § 16; Stats.2010, c. 212 (A.B.2767), § 9.)*

Research References

Miller and Starr California Real Estate § 18:8, The Unclaimed Property Law--Property Exempt.

2 Witkin Cal. Proc. 5th Courts § 306, Payment to Court.

13 Witkin, California Summary 10th Personal Property § 41, Exemptions.

§ 68085.1. Fees and fines collected on or after Jan. 1, 2006; deposit into bank account; distribution; remittance

Section operative until July 1, 2017. See, also, section operative July 1, 2017.

(a) This section applies to all fees and fines that are collected on or after January 1, 2006, under all of the following:

(1) Sections 177.5, 209, 403.060, 491.150, 631.3, 683.150, 704.750, 708.160, 724.100, 1134, 1161.2, 1218, and 1993.2 of, subdivision (g) of Section 411.20 and subdivisions (c) and (g) of Section 411.21 of, subdivision (b) of Section 631 of, and Chapter 5.5 (commencing with Section 116.110) of Title 1 of Part 1 of, the Code of Civil Procedure.

(2) Section 3112 of the Family Code.

(3) Section 31622 of the Food and Agricultural Code.

(4) Subdivision (d) of Section 6103.5, Sections 68086 and 68086.1, subdivision (d) of Section 68511.3, Sections 68926.1 and 69953.5, and Chapter 5.8 (commencing with Section 70600).

(5) Section 103470 of the Health and Safety Code.

(6) Subdivisions (b) and (c) of Section 166 and Section 1214.1 of the Penal Code.

(7) Sections 1835, 1851.5, 2343, 7660, and 13201 of the Probate Code.

(8) Sections 14607.6 and 16373 of the Vehicle Code.

(9) Section 71386 of this code, Sections 304, 7851.5, and 9002 of the Family Code, and Section 1513.1 of the Probate Code, if the reimbursement is for expenses incurred by the court.

(10) Section 3153 of the Family Code, if the amount is paid to the court for the cost of counsel appointed by the court to represent a child.

(b) On and after January 1, 2006, each superior court shall deposit all fees and fines listed in subdivision (a), as soon as practicable after collection and on a regular basis, into a bank account established for this purpose by the Administrative Office of the Courts. Upon direction of the Administrative Office of the Courts, the county shall deposit civil assessments under Section 1214.1 of the Penal Code and any other money it collects under the sections listed in subdivision (a) as soon as practicable after collection and on a regular basis into the bank account established for this purpose and specified by the Administrative Office of the Courts. The deposits shall be made as required by rules adopted by, and financial policies and procedures authorized by, the Judicial Council under subdivision (a) of Section 77206. Within 15 days after the end of the month in which the fees and fines are collected, each court, and each county that collects any fines or fees under subdivision (a), shall provide the Administrative Office of the Courts with a report of the fees by categories as specified by the Administrative Office of the Courts. The Administrative Office of the Courts and any court may agree upon a time period greater than 15 days, but in no case more than 30 days after the end of the month in which the fees and fines are collected. The fees and fines listed in subdivision (a) shall be distributed as provided in this section.

(c)(1) Within 45 calendar days after the end of the month in which the fees and fines listed in subdivision (a) are collected, the Administrative Office of the Courts shall make the following distributions:

(A) To the small claims advisory services, as described in subdivision (f) of Section 116.230 of the Code of Civil Procedure.

(B) To dispute resolution programs, as described in subdivision (b) of Section 68085.3 and subdivision (b) of Section 68085.4.

(C) To the county law library funds, as described in Sections 116.230 and 116.760 of the Code of Civil Procedure, subdivision (b) of Section 68085.3, subdivision (b) of Section 68085.4, and Section 70621 of this code, and Section 14607.6 of the Vehicle Code.

(D) To the courthouse construction funds in the Counties of Riverside, San Bernardino, and San Francisco, as described in Sections 70622, 70624, and 70625.

(E) Commencing July 1, 2011, to the Trial Court Trust Fund, as described in subdivision (d) of Section 70626, to be used by the Judicial Council to implement and administer the civil representation pilot program under Section 68651.

(2) If any distribution under this subdivision is delinquent, the Administrative Office of the Courts shall add a penalty to the distribution as specified in subdivision (i).

(d) Within 45 calendar days after the end of the month in which the fees and fines listed in subdivision (a) are collected, the amounts remaining after the distributions in subdivision (c) shall be transmitted to the State Treasury for deposit in the Trial Court Trust Fund and other funds as required by law. This remittance shall be accompanied by a remittance advice identifying the collection month and the appropriate account in the Trial Court Trust Fund or other fund to which it is to be deposited. Upon the receipt of any delinquent payment required under this subdivision, the Controller shall calculate a penalty as provided under subdivision (i).

(e) From the money transmitted to the State Treasury under subdivision (d), the Controller shall make deposits as follows:

(1) Into the State Court Facilities Construction Fund, the Judges' Retirement Fund, and the Equal Access Fund, as described in subdivision (c) of Section 68085.3 and subdivision (c) of Section 68085.4.

(2) Into the Health Statistics Special Fund, as described in subdivision (b) of Section 70670 of this code and Section 103730 of the Health and Safety Code.

(3) Into the Family Law Trust Fund, as described in Section 70674.

(4) Into the Immediate and Critical Needs Account of the State Court Facilities Construction Fund, established in Section 70371.5, as described in Sections 68085.3, 68085.4, and 70657.5, and subdivision (e) of Section 70617.

(5) The remainder of the money shall be deposited into the Trial Court Trust Fund.

(f) The amounts collected by each superior court under Section 116.232, subdivision (g) of Section 411.20, and subdivision (g) of Section 411.21 of the Code of Civil Procedure, Sections 304, 3112, 3153, 7851.5, and 9002 of the Family Code, subdivision (d) of Section 6103.5, subdivision (d) of Section 68511.3 and Sections 68926.1, 69953.5, 70627, 70631, 70640, 70661, 70678, and 71386 of this code, and Sections 1513.1, 1835, 1851.5, and 2343 of the Probate Code shall be added to the monthly apportionment for that court under subdivision (a) of Section 68085.

(g) If any of the fees provided in subdivision (a) are partially waived by court order or otherwise reduced, and the fee is to be divided between the Trial Court Trust Fund and any other fund or account, the amount of the reduction shall be deducted from the amount to be distributed to each fund in the same proportion as the amount of each distribution bears to the total amount of the fee. If the fee is paid by installment payments, the amount distributed to each fund or account from each installment shall bear the same proportion to the installment payment as the full distribution to that fund or account does to the full fee. If a court collects a fee that was incurred before January 1, 2006, under a provision that was the predecessor to one of the

paragraphs contained in subdivision (a), the fee may be deposited as if it were collected under the paragraph of subdivision (a) that corresponds to the predecessor of that paragraph and distributed in prorated amounts to each fund or account to which the fee in subdivision (a) must be distributed.

(h) Except as provided in Sections 470.5 and 6322.1 of the Business and Professions Code, and Sections 70622, 70624, and 70625 of this code, no agency may take action to change the amounts allocated to any of the funds described in subdivision (c), (d), or (e).

(i) The amount of the penalty on any delinquent payment under subdivision (c) or (d) shall be calculated by multiplying the amount of the delinquent payment at a daily rate equivalent to 1 ½ percent per month for the number of days the payment is delinquent. The penalty shall be paid from the Trial Court Trust Fund. Penalties on delinquent payments under subdivision (d) shall be calculated only on the amounts to be distributed to the Trial Court Trust Fund and the State Court Facilities Construction Fund, and each penalty shall be distributed proportionately to the funds to which the delinquent payment was to be distributed.

(j) If a delinquent payment under subdivision (c) or (d) results from a delinquency by a superior court under subdivision (b), the court shall reimburse the Trial Court Trust Fund for the amount of the penalty. Notwithstanding Section 77009, any penalty on a delinquent payment that a court is required to reimburse pursuant to this section shall be paid from the court operations fund for that court. The penalty shall be paid by the court to the Trial Court Trust Fund no later than 45 days after the end of the month in which the penalty was calculated. If the penalty is not paid within the specified time, the Administrative Office of the Courts may reduce the amount of a subsequent monthly allocation to the court by the amount of the penalty on the delinquent payment.

(k) If a delinquent payment under subdivision (c) or (d) results from a delinquency by a county in transmitting fees and fines listed in subdivision (a) to the bank account established for this purpose, as described in subdivision (b), the county shall reimburse the Trial Court Trust Fund for the amount of the penalty. The penalty shall be paid by the county to the Trial Court Trust Fund no later than 45 days after the end of the month in which the penalty was calculated.

(*l*) This section shall become inoperative on July 1, 2017, and, as of January 1, 2018, is repealed, unless a later enacted statute, that becomes operative on or before January 1, 2018, deletes or extends the dates on which it becomes inoperative and is repealed. *(Added by Stats.2005, c. 75 (A.B.145), § 102, eff. July 19, 2005, operative Jan. 1, 2006. Amended by Stats.2005, c. 706 (A.B.1742), § 23; Stats.2007, c. 738 (A.B.1248), § 17; Stats.2008, c. 311 (S.B.1407), § 1.5; Stats.2009, c. 457 (A.B.590), § 4; Stats.2012, c. 41 (S.B.1021), § 18, eff. June 27, 2012.)*

Inoperative Date and Repeal

For inoperative date and repeal of this section, see its terms.

Research References

4 Witkin Cal. Proc. 5th Pleading § 28, Distribution of Fees.

§ 68085.1. Fees and fines collected on or after Jan. 1, 2006; deposit into bank account; distribution; remittance

Section operative July 1, 2017. See, also, section operative until July 1, 2017.

(a) This section applies to all fees and fines that are collected on or after January 1, 2006, under all of the following:

(1) Sections 177.5, 209, 403.060, 491.150, 631.3, 683.150, 704.750, 708.160, 724.100, 1134, 1161.2, 1218, and 1993.2 of,

subdivision (g) of Section 411.20 and subdivisions (c) and (g) of Section 411.21 of, subdivision (b) of Section 631 of, and Chapter 5.5 (commencing with Section 116.110) of Title 1 of Part 1 of, the Code of Civil Procedure.

(2) Section 3112 of the Family Code.

(3) Section 31622 of the Food and Agricultural Code.

(4) Subdivision (d) of Section 6103.5, Sections 68086 and 68086.1, subdivision (d) of Section 68511.3, Sections 68926.1 and 69953.5, and Chapter 5.8 (commencing with Section 70600).

(5) Section 103470 of the Health and Safety Code.

(6) Subdivisions (b) and (c) of Section 166 and Section 1214.1 of the Penal Code.

(7) Sections 1835, 1851.5, 2343, 7660, and 13201 of the Probate Code.

(8) Sections 14607.6 and 16373 of the Vehicle Code.

(9) Section 71386 of this code, Sections 304, 7851.5, and 9002 of the Family Code, and Section 1513.1 of the Probate Code, if the reimbursement is for expenses incurred by the court.

(10) Section 3153 of the Family Code, if the amount is paid to the court for the cost of counsel appointed by the court to represent a child.

(b) On and after January 1, 2006, each superior court shall deposit all fees and fines listed in subdivision (a), as soon as practicable after collection and on a regular basis, into a bank account established for this purpose by the Administrative Office of the Courts. Upon direction of the Administrative Office of the Courts, the county shall deposit civil assessments under Section 1214.1 of the Penal Code and any other money it collects under the sections listed in subdivision (a) as soon as practicable after collection and on a regular basis into the bank account established for this purpose and specified by the Administrative Office of the Courts. The deposits shall be made as required by rules adopted by, and financial policies and procedures authorized by, the Judicial Council under subdivision (a) of Section 77206. Within 15 days after the end of the month in which the fees and fines are collected, each court, and each county that collects any fines or fees under subdivision (a), shall provide the Administrative Office of the Courts with a report of the fees by categories as specified by the Administrative Office of the Courts. The Administrative Office of the Courts and any court may agree upon a time period greater than 15 days, but in no case more than 30 days after the end of the month in which the fees and fines are collected. The fees and fines listed in subdivision (a) shall be distributed as provided in this section.

(c)(1) Within 45 calendar days after the end of the month in which the fees and fines listed in subdivision (a) are collected, the Administrative Office of the Courts shall make the following distributions:

(A) To the small claims advisory services, as described in subdivision (f) of Section 116.230 of the Code of Civil Procedure.

(B) To dispute resolution programs, as described in subdivision (b) of Section 68085.3 and subdivision (b) of Section 68085.4.

(C) To the county law library funds, as described in Sections 116.230 and 116.760 of the Code of Civil Procedure, subdivision (b) of Section 68085.3, subdivision (b) of Section 68085.4, and Section 70621 of this code, and Section 14607.6 of the Vehicle Code.

(D) To the courthouse construction funds in the Counties of Riverside, San Bernardino, and San Francisco, as described in Sections 70622, 70624, and 70625.

(2) If any distribution under this subdivision is delinquent, the Administrative Office of the Courts shall add a penalty to the distribution as specified in subdivision (i).

(d) Within 45 calendar days after the end of the month in which the fees and fines listed in subdivision (a) are collected, the amounts remaining after the distributions in subdivision (c) shall be transmitted to the State Treasury for deposit in the Trial Court Trust Fund and other funds as required by law. This remittance shall be accompanied by a remittance advice identifying the collection month and the appropriate account in the Trial Court Trust Fund or other fund to which it is to be deposited. Upon the receipt of any delinquent payment required under this subdivision, the Controller shall calculate a penalty as provided under subdivision (i).

(e) From the money transmitted to the State Treasury under subdivision (d), the Controller shall make deposits as follows:

(1) Into the State Court Facilities Construction Fund, the Judges' Retirement Fund, and the Equal Access Fund, as described in subdivision (c) of Section 68085.3 and subdivision (c) of Section 68085.4.

(2) Into the Health Statistics Special Fund, as described in subdivision (b) of Section 70670 of this code and Section 103730 of the Health and Safety Code.

(3) Into the Family Law Trust Fund, as described in Section 70674.

(4) Into the Immediate and Critical Needs Account of the State Court Facilities Construction Fund, established in Section 70371.5, as described in Sections 68085.3, 68085.4, and 70657.5, and subdivision (e) of Section 70617.

(5) The remainder of the money shall be deposited into the Trial Court Trust Fund.

(f) The amounts collected by each superior court under Section 116.232, subdivision (g) of Section 411.20, and subdivision (g) of Section 411.21 of the Code of Civil Procedure, Sections 304, 3112, 3153, 7851.5, and 9002 of the Family Code, subdivision (d) of Section 6103.5, subdivision (d) of Section 68511.3 and Sections 68926.1, 69953.5, 70627, 70631, 70640, 70661, 70678, and 71386 of this code, and Sections 1513.1, 1835, 1851.5, and 2343 of the Probate Code shall be added to the monthly apportionment for that court under subdivision (a) of Section 68085.

(g) If any of the fees provided in subdivision (a) are partially waived by court order or otherwise reduced, and the fee is to be divided between the Trial Court Trust Fund and any other fund or account, the amount of the reduction shall be deducted from the amount to be distributed to each fund in the same proportion as the amount of each distribution bears to the total amount of the fee. If the fee is paid by installment payments, the amount distributed to each fund or account from each installment shall bear the same proportion to the installment payment as the full distribution to that fund or account does to the full fee. If a court collects a fee that was incurred before January 1, 2006, under a provision that was the predecessor to one of the paragraphs contained in subdivision (a), the fee may be deposited as if it were collected under the paragraph of subdivision (a) that corresponds to the predecessor of that paragraph and distributed in prorated amounts to each fund or account to which the fee in subdivision (a) must be distributed.

(h) Except as provided in Sections 470.5 and 6322.1 of the Business and Professions Code, and Sections 70622, 70624, and 70625 of this code, no agency may take action to change the amounts allocated to any of the funds described in subdivision (c), (d), or (e).

(i) The amount of the penalty on any delinquent payment under subdivision (c) or (d) shall be calculated by multiplying the

Government

amount of the delinquent payment at a daily rate equivalent to 1 ½ percent per month for the number of days the payment is delinquent. The penalty shall be paid from the Trial Court Trust Fund. Penalties on delinquent payments under subdivision (d) shall be calculated only on the amounts to be distributed to the Trial Court Trust Fund and the State Court Facilities Construction Fund, and each penalty shall be distributed proportionately to the funds to which the delinquent payment was to be distributed.

(j) If a delinquent payment under subdivision (c) or (d) results from a delinquency by a superior court under subdivision (b), the court shall reimburse the Trial Court Trust Fund for the amount of the penalty. Notwithstanding Section 77009, any penalty on a delinquent payment that a court is required to reimburse pursuant to this section shall be paid from the court operations fund for that court. The penalty shall be paid by the court to the Trial Court Trust Fund no later than 45 days after the end of the month in which the penalty was calculated. If the penalty is not paid within the specified time, the Administrative Office of the Courts may reduce the amount of a subsequent monthly allocation to the court by the amount of the penalty on the delinquent payment.

(k) If a delinquent payment under subdivision (c) or (d) results from a delinquency by a county in transmitting fees and fines listed in subdivision (a) to the bank account established for this purpose, as described in subdivision (b), the county shall reimburse the Trial Court Trust Fund for the amount of the penalty. The penalty shall be paid by the county to the Trial Court Trust Fund no later than 45 days after the end of the month in which the penalty was calculated.

(*l*) This section shall become operative on July 1, 2017. (Added by Stats.2009, c. 457 (A.B.590), § 5, operative July 1, 2017. Amended by Stats.2012, c. 41 (S.B.1021), § 19, eff. June 27, 2012, operative July 1, 2017.)

Research References

4 Witkin Cal. Proc. 5th Pleading § 28, Distribution of Fees.

§ 68085.2. Reduction of amount of each county's annual remittance to Trial Court Trust Fund

(a) Notwithstanding Section 77201.1, commencing with the 2005–06 fiscal year, the amount of each county's annual remittance to the Trial Court Trust Fund under paragraph (2) of subdivision (b) of Section 77201.1 shall be reduced by the amount determined under this section. In the 2005–06 fiscal year, the remittance shall be reduced by one-half the amount determined in subdivision (b). In the 2006–07 fiscal year and thereafter, the remittance shall be reduced in each fiscal year by the full amount determined in subdivision (b).

(b) The amount of the reduction under this section for each county shall be the actual receipts into the county general fund for retention by the county for civil fees under Sections 26823, 26827.4, 26830, 26832, 26832.1, 26833.1, 26835.1, 26836.1, 26837.1, 26838, 26850.1, 26851.1, 26852.1, 26853.1, 26855.4, and 72060 of this code and Section 116.230 of the Code of Civil Procedure for the fiscal year ending June 30, 2004. This reduction is intended to compensate the counties for the loss of the revenue, as measured by receipts for the 2003–04 fiscal year, that was allocated to them from these fees by statute before January 1, 2006.

(c) In each county, the superior court and the county shall exchange relevant information to determine the amount of reduction they believe is correct under subdivision (b) and jointly report it to the California State Association of Counties (CSAC) and the Administrative Office of the Courts (AOC) on or before January 1, 2006. If the superior court and the county do not agree on the amount, the superior court and the county shall

each report the amount it believes is correct to the CSAC and the AOC on or before January 1, 2006.

(d) The AOC and the CSAC shall agree on the amount of the reduction for each county on or before January 1, 2006. If a court or county disagrees with the amount agreed to by the AOC and the CSAC for that county, the court or county may appeal to the AOC and the CSAC for an adjustment. The CSAC and the AOC shall determine whether to make any requested adjustment.

(e) If the CSAC and the AOC do not agree on the amount of the reduction for a county, they may request a mutually agreed-upon third party to arbitrate and determine the amount. The amount shall be determined by March 1, 2006. (Added by Stats.2005, c. 75 (A.B.145), § 103, eff. July 19, 2005, operative Jan. 1, 2006.)

§ 68085.3. Fees collected under enumerated sections to be deposited in bank account established by Administrative Office of the Courts; distributions; transmittal of remaining fees

(a) Fees collected under Sections 70611, 70612, 70650, 70651, 70652, 70653, 70655, 70658, and 70670 shall be deposited in a bank account established by the Administrative Office of the Courts for deposit of fees collected by the courts.

(b) For each three-hundred-fifty-five-dollar ($355) fee listed in subdivision (a), the Administrative Office of the Courts shall distribute specified amounts in each county as follows:

(1) To the county law library fund, the amount described in Sections 6321 and 6322.1 of the Business and Professions Code.

(2) To the account to support dispute resolution programs, the amount described in Section 470.5 of the Business and Professions Code.

(c) The remainder of the fees in subdivision (a) shall be transmitted monthly to the Treasurer for deposit. For each three-hundred-fifty-five-dollar ($355) fee listed in subdivision (a), the Controller shall make deposits as follows:

(1) To the State Court Facilities Construction Fund, as provided in Article 6 (commencing with Section 70371) of Chapter 5.7, thirty-five dollars ($35).

(2) To the Immediate and Critical Needs Account of the State Court Facilities Construction Fund, established in Section 70371.5, thirty dollars ($30), unless the fee is collected under Section 70658, in which case the amount distributed to that fund shall be one hundred seventy dollars ($170).

(3) To the Judges' Retirement Fund, as established in Section 75100, two dollars and fifty cents ($2.50).

(4) To the Trial Court Trust Fund for use as part of the Equal Access Fund program administered by the Judicial Council, four dollars and eighty cents ($4.80).

(5) To the Trial Court Trust Fund, as provided in Section 68085.1, the remainder of the fee.

(d) If any of the fees listed in subdivision (a) are reduced or partially waived, the amount of the reduction or partial waiver shall be deducted from the amount to be distributed to each fund or account in the same proportion as the amount of each distribution bears to the total amount of the fee.

(e) As used in this section, "law library fund" includes a law library account described in Section 6320 of the Business and Professions Code. (Added by Stats.2005, c. 75 (A.B.145), § 104, eff. July 19, 2005, operative Jan. 1, 2006. Amended by Stats.2008, c. 311 (S.B.1407), § 2; Stats.2009, c. 342 (S.B.75), § 2.)

Research References

4 Witkin Cal. Proc. 5th Pleading § 28, Distribution of Fees.

§ 68085.4. Certain fees to be deposited into bank account; distribution; transmittal

(a) Fees collected under Sections 70613, 70614, 70621, 70654, and 70656 of this code, Section 103470 of the Health and Safety Code, and Section 7660 of the Probate Code shall be deposited in a bank account established by the Administrative Office of the Courts for deposit of fees collected by the courts.

(b) For each three-hundred-thirty-dollar ($330) fee and each two-hundred-five-dollar ($205) fee listed in subdivision (a), the Administrative Office of the Courts shall distribute specified amounts in each county as follows:

(1) To the county law library fund, the amount described in Sections 6321 and 6322.1 of the Business and Professions Code.

(2) To the account to support dispute resolution programs, the amount described in Section 470.5 of the Business and Professions Code.

(c) The remainder of the fees in subdivision (a) shall be transmitted monthly to the Treasurer for deposit. For each three-hundred-thirty-dollar ($330) fee and each two-hundred-five-dollar ($205) fee listed in subdivision (a), the Controller shall make deposits as follows:

(1) To the State Court Facilities Construction Fund, as provided in Article 6 (commencing with Section 70371) of Chapter 5.7, twenty-five dollars ($25) if the fee is three hundred thirty dollars ($330), and twenty dollars ($20) if the fee is two hundred five dollars ($205).

(2) To the Immediate and Critical Needs Account of the State Court Facilities Construction Fund, established in Section 70371.5, twenty-five dollars ($25) if the fee is three hundred thirty dollars ($330), and twenty dollars ($20) if the fee is two hundred five dollars ($205), except as otherwise provided in Section 6322.1 of the Business and Professions Code.

(3) To the Judges' Retirement Fund, as established in Section 75100, two dollars and fifty cents ($2.50).

(4) To the Trial Court Trust Fund for use as part of the Equal Access Fund program administered by the Judicial Council, four dollars and eighty cents ($4.80).

(5) To the Trial Court Trust Fund, as provided in Section 68085.1, the remainder of the fee.

(d) If any of the fees listed in subdivision (a) are reduced or partially waived, the amount of the reduction or partial waiver shall be deducted from the amount to be distributed to each fund or account in the same proportion as the amount of each distribution bears to the total amount of the fee.

(e) As used in this section, "law library fund" includes a law library account described in Section 6320 of the Business and Professions Code. *(Added by Stats.2005, c. 75 (A.B.145), § 105, eff. July 19, 2005, operative Jan. 1, 2006. Amended by Stats.2005, c. 706 (A.B.1742), § 24; Stats.2007, c. 738 (A.B.1248), § 18; Stats.2008, c. 311 (S.B.1407), § 3; Stats.2009, c. 342 (S.B.75), § 3.)*

Research References

4 Witkin Cal. Proc. 5th Pleading § 28, Distribution of Fees.

§ 68085.45. State Trial Court Operations Trust Fund

(a) There is hereby established the State Trial Court Operations Trust Fund. Upon the retirement of all bonded indebtedness that may be incurred in connection with immediate and critical trial court projects, any moneys remaining in, or that would otherwise be payable into, the Immediate and Critical Needs Account of the State Court Facilities Construction Fund, shall be transferred to the Controller for deposit into the State Trial Court Operations Trust Fund.

(b) The proceeds of the State Trial Court Operations Trust Fund shall be available, upon appropriation by the Legislature in the annual Budget Act, only for trial court operations as defined in Section 77003. *(Added by Stats.2008, c. 311 (S.B.1407), § 3.7. Amended by Stats.2009–2010, 2nd Ex.Sess., c. 10 (S.B.12), § 1, eff. May 21, 2009.)*

§ 68085.5. Deposit of specified fees and fines in the Trial Court Trust Fund; distribution of revenue pursuant to prior agreements or practices; reports of revenue; effective date of transfers of certain fees and fines; application to certain fees and fines

(a) Notwithstanding any other provision of law, except subdivision (h) and Section 68085.6, the fees and fines collected pursuant to Sections 116.390, 116.570, 116.760, 116.860, 491.150, 704.750, 708.160, 724.100, 1134, and 1161.2 of the Code of Civil Procedure, Sections 26824, 26828, 26829, 26834, and 72059 of the Government Code, and Section 1835 of the Probate Code, that are not part of a local revenue sharing agreement or practice shall be deposited in a special account in the county treasury and transmitted therefrom monthly to the Controller for deposit in the Trial Court Trust Fund.

(b) Notwithstanding any other provision of law, except subdivision (h) and Section 68085.6, the fees and fines collected pursuant to Sections 26827. 6, 26827.7, 26840.1, 26847, 26854, 26855.1, 26855.2, 26859, 27293, 71386, and 72061 of the Government Code, Section 103470 of the Health and Safety Code, Sections 1203.4 and 1203.45 of the Penal Code, Sections 2343, 7660, and 13201 of the Probate Code, and Section 14607.6 of the Vehicle Code, that are not subject to a local revenue sharing agreement or practice, shall be deposited in a special account in the county treasury.

(c) However, if a superior court incurs the cost or provides the services specified in subdivision (b), the fees and fines collected shall be transmitted from the special account in the county treasury monthly to the Controller for deposit in the Trial Court Trust Fund.

(d)(1) Until July 1, 2005, each superior court and each county shall maintain the distribution of revenue from the fees specified in subdivisions (a) and (b) that is in effect pursuant to an agreement or practice that is in place at the time this section takes effect.

(2) In order to ensure that expenditures from revenue sharing agreements are consistent with Judicial Council fiscal and budgetary policy, the Administrative Director of the Courts shall review and approve all distribution of revenue agreements that are negotiated after the effective date of this section. If approval of an agreement negotiated after the effective date of this section is not granted, the director shall advise the court and county of the reasons for not granting approval and suggest modifications that will make the agreement consistent with the Judicial Council fiscal and budgetary policies.

(e) The Administrative Office of the Courts and the California State Association of Counties shall jointly determine and administer on or after January 1, 2004, and on or after January 1, 2005, all of the following:

(1) The amount of revenue that was deposited in the Trial Court Trust Fund pursuant to subdivisions (a) and (b) during the calendar year that just ended.

(2) The difference between the amount specified in subdivision (c) and thirty-one million dollars ($31,000,000).

Government

(3) A county-by-county transfer of the amount specified in paragraph (2) to the Trial Court Trust Fund in two equal installments, on February 15 and May 15, in each fiscal year.

(4) Any payment to correct for an overpayment or underpayment made for the 2003–04 fiscal year, shall be paid to the appropriate party on or before September 15, 2004. Any payment to correct for an overpayment or underpayment made for the 2004–05 fiscal year, shall be paid to the appropriate party on or before November 15, 2005.

(5) The sum of the amounts specified in paragraphs (1) and (2) may not exceed thirty-one million dollars ($31,000,000), and shall be deposited in the Trial Court Trust Fund.

(6) Counties that have not paid amounts billed under this section for the 2003–04 or 2004–05 fiscal year shall pay the amounts still owing to the Trial Court Trust Fund on or before September 1, 2005. If payment is not received on or before September 1, 2005, it shall be considered delinquent and subject to the penalties set forth in Section 68085.

(7) Penalty amounts calculated under paragraph (6) shall be paid by the county or the city and county to the Trial Court Trust Fund no later than 45 days after the end of the month in which the penalty was calculated.

(f) Each superior court and each county shall provide detailed quarterly reports of the revenues generated by the fees and fines specified in subdivisions (a) and (b), Sections 177.5 and 1218 of the Code of Civil Procedure, and Sections 166 and 1214.1 of the Penal Code. The reports shall include the total amount collected and retained by the court or county and the existing distribution of those fees.

(g) No other transfers of the fees and fines specified in subdivisions (a) and (b), Sections 177.5 and 1218 of the Code of Civil Procedure, and Sections 166 and 1214.1 of the Penal Code shall take effect prior to July 1, 2005.

(h) This section does not apply to fees and fines specified in subdivisions (a), (b), and (f) that are collected on or after July 1, 2005.

(i) Nothing in this section shall be deemed to alter or make void the shift of responsibility for court funding from the counties to the state. *(Added by Stats.2003, c. 159 (A.B.1759), § 13, eff. Aug. 2, 2003. Amended by Stats.2004, c. 183 (A.B. 3082), § 178; Stats.2005, c. 74 (A.B.139), § 43, eff. July 19, 2005.)*

§ 68085.6. Counties' obligations to remit funds to Trial Court Trust Fund; corrective payments; delinquencies and penalty amounts; determination of amount; methodology to determine revenue growth exceeding projected levels and effect thereof

(a) Commencing July 1, 2005, the counties' obligation to remit to the Trial Court Trust Fund each fiscal year the difference between thirty-one million dollars ($31,000,000) and the amount remitted to the Trial Court Trust Fund under Section 68085.5 shall expire. The counties thereafter shall be obligated to remit to the Trial Court Trust Fund the following amounts:

(1) In the 2005–06 fiscal year, twenty million dollars ($20,000,-000).

(2) In the 2006–07 fiscal year, fifteen million dollars ($15,000,-000).

(3) In the 2007–08 fiscal year, ten million dollars ($10,000,-000).

(4) In the 2008–09 fiscal year, five million dollars ($5,000,-000).

(5) In the 2009–10 fiscal year and thereafter, the obligation shall expire.

(b) If the amounts remitted annually to the Trial Court Trust Fund, pursuant to subdivision (a) of this section, and the amendments made to Section 68085.5 of the Government Code and Section 1214.1 of the Penal Code by the act that added this section, are less than the differences between thirty-one million dollars ($31,000,000) and the amounts specified in paragraphs (1) to (5), inclusive, of subdivision (a), no additional state funds shall be appropriated to the courts to mitigate these revenue shortfalls.

(c) In the 2005–06 fiscal year, the amount described in paragraph (1) of subdivision (a) shall be remitted to the Trial Court Trust Fund in two equal installments on February 15, 2006, and May 15, 2006. In each subsequent fiscal year, the amount described in subdivision (a) shall be remitted to the Trial Court Trust Fund in four equal installments, due on October 1, January 1, April 1, and May 1. Each county shall pay the installments from all available resources, including the county's general fund.

(d) Any payment to correct for an overpayment or underpayment made in any fiscal year shall be paid to the appropriate party on or before November 15 of the subsequent fiscal year.

(e) All moneys required to be paid to the Trial Court Trust Fund under this section shall be considered delinquent if not paid by the dates specified in this section, and shall be subject to the penalties set forth in Section 68085.

(f) Penalty amounts calculated under subdivision (e) shall be paid by the county or the city and county to the Trial Court Trust Fund no later than 45 days after the end of the month in which the penalty was calculated.

(g) The portion of the amount in subdivision (a) to be paid by each county shall be determined by the Administrative Office of the Courts (AOC) and the California State Association of Counties (CSAC) with the following conditions:

(1) Any county that did not receive a reduction of county remittances for support of trial courts to compensate for loss of civil assessment revenue under Section 68085.7 shall not be required to make any payments under this section.

(2) No county's payment in any year, commencing in the 2005–06 fiscal year, shall be greater than 90 percent of the annual payment that county was required to pay toward the thirty-one million dollars ($31,000,000) in subdivision (e) of Section 68085.5 as it read on January 1, 2004.

(3) The AOC and the CSAC shall determine the portion of the amounts in subdivision (a) to be paid by each county on or before October 31, 2005. If the AOC and the CSAC do not agree on the portions, they may request a mutually agreed-upon third party to arbitrate and determine the portion for each county. The portions shall be determined on or before December 31, 2005.

(h) On or before June 30, 2006, the AOC and the CSAC shall agree upon a methodology to determine whether the growth in revenue to the Trial Court Trust Fund created by the transfer of revenues under this section and Section 68085.7 has significantly exceeded projected levels so that a reduction in the counties' obligation under paragraph (4) of subdivision (a) should be recommended to the Legislature.

(i) Nothing in this section shall be deemed to alter or make void the shift of responsibility for court funding from the counties to the state. *(Added by Stats.2005, c. 74 (A.B.139), § 44, eff. July 19, 2005.)*

§ 68085.7. Application of Trial Court Trust Fund depositary provision to specified fees and fines; reduction of counties' remittance; determination of reduction amount

(a)(1) Notwithstanding any other provision of law, Section 68085.5 does not apply to the following fees and fines collected on or after July 1, 2005: any fees and fines specified in subdivision (a) or (b) of Section 68085.5, Section 177.5 or 1218 of the Code of Civil Procedure, or Section 166 or 1214.1 of the Penal Code. Commencing July 1, 2005, these fees and fines shall be distributed as provided by Section 68085, except that the fees listed in subdivision (b) of Section 68085.5 and the fee in Section 1835 of the Probate Code shall be distributed to the court or the county, whichever provided the services for which the fee is charged or incurred the costs reimbursed by the fee.

(2) Notwithstanding any other provision of law, until January 1, 2006, upon direction of the Administrative Office of the Courts, the court and the county shall deposit the money each collects under the sections listed in paragraph (2) of subdivision (c) of Section 68085 as soon as practicable after collection and on a regular basis into a bank account established for this purpose and specified by the Administrative Office of the Courts. The deposits shall be made as required by rules adopted by and financial policies and procedures authorized by the Judicial Council under subdivision (a) of Section 77206 of the Government Code. Within 15 days after the end of the month in which the money is collected, the court and the county each shall provide the Administrative Office of the Courts with a report of the money it collects, as specified by the Administrative Office of the Courts. The money shall be transmitted to the State Controller for deposit in the Trial Court Trust Fund by the Administrative Office of the Courts.

(3) Commencing January 1, 2006, the fees and fines listed in Section 68085.5 shall be distributed as provided by Section 68085.1, or if no provision is made in Section 68085.1, as specified in the section that provides for the fee or fine. The fees in Sections 26840.1, 26847, 26854, 26855.1, 26855.2, and 27293 shall be distributed to the county.

(b) Commencing July 1, 2005, in each fiscal year, the amount of each county's annual remittance to the state Trial Court Trust Fund under paragraph (2) of subdivision (b) of Section 77201.1 shall be reduced by the amount that the county received from civil assessments under Section 1214.1 of the Penal Code, after deducting the cost of collecting those civil assessments as defined in subdivision (f), in the 2003–04 fiscal year. The reduction provided by this subdivision for the 2005–06 fiscal year shall apply only to a county that transmits to the Trial Court Trust Fund any money received by the county between July 1, 2005, and the effective date of this section that would have been transmitted to the Trial Court Trust Fund pursuant to subdivision (a), and the amendments to Section 68085 of this code and Section 1214.1 of the Penal Code, if this section had been effective on July 1, 2005.

(c) The amount of the reduction under this section for each county shall be determined by agreement between the Administrative Office of the Courts (AOC) and the California State Association of Counties (CSAC). Each county and each superior court shall exchange relevant factual information to determine and jointly report to the AOC and the CSAC the total amount the county received from civil assessments for the 2003–04 fiscal year, both gross and net after costs, on or before August 31, 2005. If the court and the county do not agree on the amount, the court and the county shall each report the amount each believes is correct to the AOC and the CSAC on or before August 31, 2005.

(d) The AOC and the CSAC shall agree on the amount of the reduction for each county under this section on or before October 31, 2005. If a court or county disagrees with the

amount agreed to by the AOC and the CSAC for that county, the court or county may appeal to the AOC and the CSAC for an adjustment. The AOC and the CSAC shall determine whether to make any requested adjustment.

(e) If the AOC and the CSAC do not agree on the amount of the reduction for a county, they may request a mutually agreed-upon third party to arbitrate and determine the amount. The amount shall be determined on or before December 31, 2005.

(f) Guidelines of the Controller shall apply to the determination of revenues from civil assessments under Section 1214.1 of the Penal Code. The costs of collecting civil assessments applied in determining net civil assessments are only those costs used to collect those civil assessments. *(Added by Stats.2005, c. 74 (A.B.139), § 45, eff. July 19, 2005. Amended by Stats.2005, c. 705 (S.B.67), § 2, eff. Oct. 7, 2005.)*

§ 68085.8. Initial review of impact on counties and courts of revenue distribution and payment obligation changes; correction of inequities

(a) On or before December 31, 2005, the Administrative Office of the Courts (AOC) and the California State Association of Counties (CSAC) shall complete an initial review of the impact upon individual counties and courts of the changes in revenue distributions and payment obligations under Sections 68085.6, and 68085.7 for the purpose of correcting inequities that may result from these changes. The AOC and CSAC shall work with counties and courts to develop and implement procedures to correct inequities resulting from either the implementation of these changes or any changes in the provision of services or benefits under any of the following circumstances:

(1) Institution of new civil assessment programs after the 2003–04 fiscal year.

(2) Substantial impacts on memoranda of understanding or other agreements that are existing or pending as of June 10, 2005, or practices in effect at that time, which agreements and practices contemplate the use of revenues transferred under the act that added this section.

(3) The demonstration by clear evidence that the information used as the basis for determining a reduction under Section 68085.7, or for determining a county's obligation under Section 68085.6, results in an inequity, and that the inequity imposes an undue hardship on the court or county.

(b) Inequities may be corrected by one or more of the following mechanisms:

(1) Adjustment of the reduction under subdivision (b) of Section 68085.7.

(2) Adjustment of the amount of a county's obligation under subdivision (a) of Section 68085.6.

(3) Adjustment of allocations to a trial court from the Trial Court Trust Fund under subdivision (a) of Section 68085.

(4) If necessary, with agreement of the court and county, adjustments of the rights and duties of the parties under memoranda of understanding or other agreements or practices.

The adjustments under paragraphs (1) to (4), inclusive, may be temporary or permanent. Adjustments under this section shall be made only with the mutual agreement of the AOC and CSAC. *(Added by Stats.2005, c. 74 (A.B.139), § 46, eff. July 19, 2005. Amended by Stats.2005, c. 705 (S.B.67), § 3, eff. Oct. 7, 2005.)*

§ 68085.9. Deposit of all moneys into bank account; consent

Section as added by Stats.2005, c. 705 (S.B.67), § 4, eff. Oct. 7, 2005. See, also, section as added by Stats.2005, c. 706, (A.B.1742), § 25.

Notwithstanding any other provision of law requiring a trial court or officer of a trial court to deposit money received by the court or officer into the county treasury or with the county treasurer, including but not limited to Sections 24353, 68085, 68085.5, and 68101 of this code and Section 1463.001 of the Penal Code, the court or officer, with the consent of the county and the Administrative Director of the Courts, may deposit all money required to be deposited into the county treasury or with the county treasurer into a bank account established by the Administrative Office of the Courts separate from the county treasury. Money collected pursuant to Section 68085.1 of this code shall be deposited as provided in that section. The Judicial Council, with the consent of the county, may require the court and officer to deposit money into a bank account established by the Administrative Office of the Courts separate from the county treasury. *(Added by Stats.2005, c. 705 (S.B.67), § 4, eff. Oct. 7, 2005.)*

§ 68085.9. Deposit of all moneys into bank account; consent

Section as added by Stats.2005, c. 706 (A.B.1742), § 25.
See, also, section as added by Stats.2005, c. 705
(S.B.67), § 4, eff. Oct. 7, 2005.

Notwithstanding any other provision of law requiring a trial court or officer of a trial court to deposit money received by the court or officer into the county treasury or with the county treasurer, including, but not limited to, Sections 24353, 68085, 68085.5, and 68101 of this code and Section 1463.001 of the Penal Code, the court or officer, with the consent of the county and the Administrative Director of the Courts, may deposit all money required to be deposited into the county treasury or with the county treasurer into a bank account established by the Administrative Office of the Courts separate from the county treasury. Money collected pursuant to Section 68085.1 shall be deposited as provided in that section. The Judicial Council, with the consent of the county, may require the court and officer to deposit money into a bank account established by the Administrative Office of the Courts separate from the county treasury. *(Added by Stats.2005, c. 706 (A.B.1742), § 25.)*

§ 68086. Official court reporting services; fees; waiver; recovery of costs; adoption of rules; use of fees; report to Joint Legislative Budget Committee

* * * The following provisions apply in superior court:

(a) In addition to any other fee required in civil actions or cases:

(1) For each proceeding * * * anticipated to last one hour or less, a fee of thirty dollars ($30) shall be charged for the reasonable cost of the * * * court reporting services provided at the expense of the court by an official court reporter pursuant to Section 269 of the Code of Civil Procedure. * * *

(A) The fee shall be charged to the party, or parties if filing jointly, that filed the paper that resulted in the proceeding being scheduled. If no fee has been charged, and a party subsequently requests a court reporter, that party shall be charged the fee if a reporter is to be provided by the court.

(B) All parties paying the fee shall deposit the fee with the clerk of the court as specified by the court, but not later than the conclusion of each day's court session.

(C) The fee shall be charged once per case for all proceedings conducted within the same hour if the total time taken by those proceedings is one hour or less. If the total time taken exceeds one hour, the fee shall be charged and collected pursuant to paragraph (2).

(D) The fee shall be deposited into the Trial Court Trust Fund and distributed back to the court from which the fee was collected on a dollar-for-dollar basis.

(E) The fee shall be refunded as soon as practicable to the remitting party or parties if no court reporting services were provided.

(2) For each proceeding lasting more than one hour, a fee equal to the actual cost of providing that service shall be charged per one-half day of services to the parties, on a pro rata basis, for the services of an official court reporter on the first and each succeeding judicial day those services are provided pursuant to Section 269 of the Code of Civil Procedure.

(A) All parties shall deposit their pro rata shares of these fees with the clerk of the court as specified by the court, but not later than the conclusion of each day's court session.

(B) For purposes of this paragraph, "one-half day" means any period of judicial time, in excess of one hour, but not more than four hours, during either the morning or afternoon court session.

(b) The fee shall be waived for a person who has been granted a fee waiver under Section 68631.

(c) The costs for the services of the official court reporter shall be recoverable as taxable costs by the prevailing party as otherwise provided by law.

(d) The Judicial Council shall adopt rules to ensure all of the following:

(1) That parties are given adequate and timely notice of the availability of an official court reporter.

(2) That if an official court reporter is not available, a party may arrange for the presence of a certified shorthand reporter to serve as an official pro tempore reporter, the costs therefor recoverable as provided in * * * subdivision (c).

(3) That if the services of an official pro tempore reporter are utilized pursuant to * * * paragraph (2), no other charge shall be made to the parties.

(e) The fees collected pursuant to this section shall be used only to pay the cost for services of an official court reporter in civil proceedings.

(f) The Judicial Council shall report on or before February 1 of each year to the Joint Legislative Budget Committee on the fees collected by courts pursuant to this section and Section 68086.1 and on the total amount spent for services of official court reporters in civil proceedings statewide in the prior fiscal year. *(Added by Stats.1992, c. 696 (A.B.1344), § 21, eff. Sept. 15, 1992. Amended by Stats.1993, c. 70 (S.B.86), § 2, eff. June 30, 1993; Stats.1998, c. 931 (S.B.2139), § 226, eff. Sept. 28, 1998; Stats.2001, c. 115 (S.B.153), § 15; Stats.2003, c. 159 (A.B.1759), § 14, eff. Aug. 2, 2003; Stats.2003, c. 757 (A.B.296), § 5; Stats.2004, c. 183 (A.B.3082), § 179; Stats.2005, c. 75 (A.B.145), § 106, eff. July 19, 2005, operative Jan. 1, 2006; Stats.2005, c. 706 (A.B.1742), § 26; Stats.2012, c. 41 (S.B.1021), § 20, eff. June 27, 2012; Stats.2013, c. 31 (S.B.75), § 3, eff. June 27, 2013; Stats. 2013, c. 454 (A.B.648), § 1.)*

Law Revision Commission Comments

Section 68086 is amended to reflect elimination of the justice court. Cal. Const. art. VI, §§ 1, 5(b). [28 Cal.L.Rev.Comm. Reports 51 (1998)].

Section 68086 is amended to delete obsolete references to former Code of Civil Procedure Section 270. [30 Cal.L.Rev.Comm. Reports 327 (2000)].

Research References

2 Witkin Cal. Proc. 5th Courts § 379, (S 379) Appointment and Qualifications.
2 Witkin Cal. Proc. 5th Courts § 385, Advance Payment in Civil Cases.
7 Witkin Cal. Proc. 5th Judgment § 135, (S 135) Reporter's Fees.

4 Witkin Cal. Proc. 5th Pleading § 26, Additional Fees.

§ 68086.1. Use of fees collected for court reporter services in civil proceedings

(a) For each three-hundred-fifty-five-dollar ($355) fee collected under Section 70611, 70612, or 70670, thirty dollars ($30) of the amount distributed to the Trial Court Trust Fund shall be used for services of an official court reporter in civil proceedings.

(b) For each three-hundred-thirty-dollar ($330) fee collected under subdivision (a) of Section 70613 or subdivision (a) of Section 70614, thirty dollars ($30) of the amount distributed to the Trial Court Trust Fund shall be used for services of an official court reporter in civil proceedings.

(c) It is the intent of the Legislature, in approving the thirty-dollar ($30) distribution out of each filing fee listed in subdivisions (a) and (b), to continue an incentive to courts to use the services of an official court reporter in civil proceedings. However, nothing in this section shall affect the Judicial Council's authority to allocate these revenues to replace reductions in the General Fund appropriation to the Trial Court Trust Fund.

(d) The portion of the distribution to the Trial Court Trust Fund to be used for services of an official court reporter in civil proceedings pursuant to subdivisions (a) and (b) shall be used only in trial courts that utilize the services of an official court reporter in civil proceedings. *(Added by Stats.2005, c. 75 (A.B.145), § 107, eff. July 19, 2005, operative Jan. 1, 2006. Amended by Stats.2005, c. 706 (A.B.1742), § 27; Stats.2008, c. 311 (S.B.1407), § 4; Stats.2009–2010, 4th Ex.Sess., c. 22 (S.B.13), § 2, eff. July 28, 2009.)*

§ 68088. Racial, ethnic, and gender bias and sexual harassment training

The Judicial Council may provide by rule of court for racial, ethnic, and gender bias, and sexual harassment training and training for any other bias based on any characteristic listed or defined in Section 11135 for judges, commissioners, and referees. *(Added by Stats.1997, c. 850 (A.B.233), § 31. Amended by Stats.2007, c. 568 (A.B.14), § 36.)*

Research References

2 Witkin Cal. Proc. 5th Courts § 396, (S 396) Specialized Programs.

§ 68089. Vouchers; return or destruction

Two years after judgment in any civil action or proceeding has become final the court may order any vouchers on file for the action or proceeding delivered to the person who filed them or to his attorney. If such person or his attorney cannot be located or fails after reasonable notice to obtain such vouchers, the court may order them destroyed by the clerk of the court. *(Added by Stats.1953, c. 206, p. 1240, § 1.)*

§ 68092. Interpreters' and translators' fees; payment

Court interpreters' and translators' fees or other compensation shall be paid:

(a) In criminal cases, by the court.

(b) In civil cases, by the litigants, in proportions as the court may direct, to be taxed and collected as other costs. *(Added by Stats.1953, c. 206, p. 1241, § 1. Amended by Stats.2010, c. 212 (A.B.2767), § 10.)*

Law Revision Commission Comments

Section 68092 is amended to reflect enactment of the Lockyer–Isenberg Trial Court Funding Act, 1997 Cal. Stat. ch. 850 (see generally Sections 77000–77655). Under that act, the state, not the county, funds the cost of "court operations." See, e.g., Sections 77003 ("court operations" defined), 77200 (state funding of "court operations"). Interpretation by a court interpreter for a court proceeding is a court operation and therefore payable by the court and ultimately by the state. See Cal. R. Ct. 810, Function 4 (court interpreters). In contrast, interpretation beyond the court context (e.g., during a client interview), or for a coroner's case, is not a court operation and thus remains payable by the county. See Cal. R. Ct. 810 (listing matters classified as court operations).

The material relevant to coroner's cases in subdivision (a) is relocated to Section 27473 of the Government Code.

Section 68092 is also amended to refer to compensation, not just fees. Under the Trial Court Interpreter Employment and Labor Relations Act (Sections 71801–71829), interpreters may be paid a salary (e.g., as court employees) or may be paid on a daily basis (e.g., as independent contractors). See Section 71802.

Section 68092 is further amended to make stylistic revisions.

For provisions governing the cost of translation of a writing offered in evidence, see Evidence Code Section 753. For provisions governing compensation of an interpreter for a witness, see Evidence Code Section 752.

The purpose of the revisions in the act that amended this section is to remove material made obsolete by trial court restructuring. See Gov't Code § 71674. The revisions should not be construed as a re-evaluation of the extent to which interpretation or translation should be provided in court proceedings, or who should bear the expense of interpretation or translation. [39 Cal.L.Rev.Comm. Reports 109 (2009)].

Research References

Rutter, Cal. Practice Guide: Civil Trials & Evidence Ch. 9-F, F. Witnesses Needing Assistance in Testifying.

§ 68092.5. Expert witnesses; compensation; service; notice of continuance or cancellation; deposition

(a) A party requiring testimony before any court, tribunal, or arbiter in any civil action or proceeding from any expert witness, other than a party or employee of a party, who is either, (1) an expert described in subdivision (b) of Section 2034.210 of the Code of Civil Procedure, (2) a treating physician and surgeon or other treating health care practitioner who is to be asked to express an opinion during the action or proceeding, or (3) an architect, professional engineer, or licensed land surveyor who was involved with the original project design or survey for which he or she is asked to express an opinion within his or her expertise and relevant to the action or proceeding, shall pay the reasonable and customary hourly or daily fee for the actual time consumed in the examination of that witness by any party attending the action or proceeding. The hourly or daily fee shall not exceed the fee charged the party who retained the expert except where the expert donated his or her services to a charitable or other nonprofit organization. A daily fee shall only be charged for a full day of attendance at a deposition or where the expert was required by the deposing party to be available for a full day and the expert necessarily had to forego all business he or she would have otherwise conducted that day but for the request that he or she be available all day for the scheduled deposition.

The party requiring the attendance shall either accompany the service of the subpoena or notice with a tender of the expert's fee based on the anticipated length of time the expert is required to remain at such place pursuant to the notice or subpoena or tender that fee at the required time of appearance. The expert's fee shall be delivered to the attorney for the party designating the expert. If the appearance of the expert takes longer than anticipated, the party serving the subpoena or notice shall pay the balance of the expert's fee within five days of receipt of an itemized statement from the expert. The party designating the expert is responsible for any fee charged by the expert for preparing for the testimony and for traveling to the place of the civil action or proceeding, as well as for any travel expenses of the expert, unless otherwise determined by the court.

(b) The service of a proper subpoena or notice accompanied by the tender of the expert witness fee described in subdivision

(a) is effective to require the party employing or retaining the expert to produce the expert for testimony. If the party serving the notice or subpoena fails to tender the expert's fee under subdivision (a), the expert shall not be required to appear at that time unless the parties stipulate otherwise.

(c) If a party requiring the appearance by subpoena or notice of another party's expert witness under this subdivision deems that the hourly or daily fee of that expert for providing testimony is unreasonable, that party may move for an order setting the compensation of that expert. This motion shall be accompanied by a declaration stating facts showing a reasonable and good faith attempt at an informal resolution of each issue presented by the motion. Notice of this motion shall also be given to the expert.

In any such attempt at an informal resolution, either the party or the expert shall provide the other with (A) proof of the ordinary and customary fee actually charged and received by that expert for similar services provided outside the subject litigation, (B) the total number of times the presently demanded fee has ever been charged and received by that expert, and (C) the frequency and regularity with which the presently demanded fee has been charged and received by that expert within the two-year period preceding the hearing on the motion. Provisions (B) and (C) shall apply to actions filed after January 1, 1994.

In addition to any other facts or evidence, the expert or the party designating the expert shall provide, and the court's determination as to the reasonableness of the fee shall be based upon, (1) proof of the ordinary and customary fee actually charged and received by that expert for similar services provided outside the subject litigation, (2) the total number of times the presently demanded fee has ever been charged and received by that expert, and (3) the frequency and regularity with which the presently demanded and any other fee has been charged and received by that expert within the two-year period preceding the hearing on the motion. The court may also consider (4) the ordinary and customary fees charged by similar experts for similar services within the relevant community, and (5) any other factors the court deems necessary or appropriate to make its determination.

Upon a determination that the fee demanded by that expert is unreasonable, and based upon the evidence and factors considered, the court shall set the fee of the expert providing testimony.

(d) In the event the proceeding at which the expert witness has been notified his or her attendance is required is continued or canceled in advance of the time for which it is scheduled, such witness shall be notified of the continuance or cancellation by the party requiring his or her attendance by the quickest and most reliable means of giving notice under the circumstances. In the event such party fails to give notice as required by this subdivision, then the expert witness shall be entitled to receive the compensation specified in subdivision (a) of this section, notwithstanding his or her failure to give any testimony.

(e) An express contract entered into between a person and the party requesting or requiring the person to testify, relating to compensation, shall be enforceable and shall prevail over the provisions of this section.

(f) The deposition of an expert witness is governed by Chapter 18 (commencing with Section 2034.010) of Title 4 of Part 4 of the Code of Civil Procedure. *(Added by Stats.1979, c. 746, p. 2593, § 7, operative Jan. 1, 1983. Amended by Stats.1986, c. 560, § 2; Stats.1988, c. 275, § 1; Stats.1990, c. 771 (S.B.247), § 3; Stats.1990, c. 1392 (A.B.3136), § 4; Stats.1993, c. 678 (A.B.907), § 2; Stats.2004, c. 182 (A.B.3081), § 45, operative July 1, 2005.)*

Law Revision Commission Comments

Subdivisions (a) and (f) of Section 68092.5 are amended to reflect nonsubstantive reorganization of the rules governing civil discovery. [33 Cal.L.Rev.Comm. Reports 1036 (2004)].

Research References

Rutter, Cal. Practice Guide: Civ. Pro. Before Trial Ch. 8J-6, Exchange Required.
Rutter, Cal. Practice Guide: Civ. Pro. Before Trial Ch. 8J-7, Deposing Opposing Experts.
Rutter, Cal. Practice Guide: Civ. Pro. Before Trial Ch. 12(II)-C, C. Statutory Offer to Compromise (CCP § 998).
Rutter, Cal. Practice Guide: Civil Trials & Evidence Ch. 1-C, C. Marshalling the Evidence.
Rutter, Cal. Practice Guide: Civil Trials & Evidence Ch. 4-I, I. Other Motions at Final Status Conference.
Rutter, Cal. Practice Guide: Civil Trials & Evidence Ch. 17-D, D. Costs.
Rutter, Cal. Practice Guide: Personal Injury Ch. 4-D, D. Techniques Where Settlement Not Forthcoming.
Rutter, Cal. Practice Guide: Personal Injury Ch. 6-B, B. Overview of Selected Discovery Procedures.
7 Witkin Cal. Proc. 5th Judgment § 133, (S 133) Fees of Expert Witness.
6 Witkin Cal. Proc. 5th Proceedings Without Trial § 112, Expert Witness Fees Allowable.

§ 68093. Witness fees and mileage; civil actions; superior courts

Except as otherwise provided by law, witness' fees for each day's actual attendance, when legally required to attend a civil action or proceeding in the superior courts, are thirty-five dollars ($35) a day and mileage actually traveled, both ways, twenty cents ($0.20) a mile. *(Added by Stats.1953, c. 206, p. 1241, § 1. Amended by Stats.1957, c. 1908, p. 3339, § 2; Stats.1970, c. 1061, p. 1892, § 2; Stats.1977, c. 1257, p. 4772, § 54, eff. Oct. 3, 1977; Stats.1981, c. 184, p. 1106, § 4; Stats.1998, c. 931 (S.B.2139), § 228, eff. Sept. 28, 1998; Stats.2002, c. 784 (S.B.1316), § 207.)*

Law Revision Commission Comments

Section 68093 is amended to reflect elimination of the justice court. Cal. Const. art. VI, §§ 1, 5(b). [28 Cal.L.Rev.Comm. Reports 51 (1998)].
Section 68093 is amended to reflect unification of the municipal and superior courts pursuant to Article VI, Section 5(e), of the California Constitution. [32 Cal.L.Rev.Comm. Reports 231 (2002)].

Research References

Rutter, Cal. Practice Guide: Civ. Pro. Before Trial Ch. 8E-6, Subpoena to Nonparty Deponent or Business Records Custodian.
Rutter, Cal. Practice Guide: Civil Trials & Evidence Ch. 1-C, C. Marshalling the Evidence.
Rutter, Cal. Practice Guide: Enforcing Judgments/Debts Ch. 6G-1, Examination of Judgment Debtor and Third Parties.
Rutter, Cal. Practice Guide: Personal Injury Ch. 6-B, B. Overview of Selected Discovery Procedures.
Rutter, Cal. Practice Guide: Personal Injury Ch. 8-C, C. Two Months Before Trial.
Rutter, Cal. Practice Guide: Personal Injury Ch. 9-M, M. Verdicts and Judgment.
Rutter, Cal. Practice Guide: Prof. Responsibility Ch. 11-I, I. Trial Proceedings.
8 Witkin Cal. Proc. 5th Enforcement of Judgment § 279, Issuance and Service of Order.
7 Witkin Cal. Proc. 5th Judgment § 132, (S 132) Fees of Ordinary Witness.
7 Witkin Cal. Proc. 5th Judgment § 134, (S 134) Mileage.
10 Witkin, California Summary 10th Parent and Child § 566, (S 566) Notices, Citations, Warrants, and Subpenas.
10 Witkin, California Summary 10th Parent and Child § 781, Subpenas to Witnesses.

§ 68094. Witness fees and mileage; grand jury

Except as otherwise provided by law, witness' fees for each day's actual attendance, when legally required to attend before a grand jury, are twelve dollars ($12) a day and mileage for each mile actually traveled in attendance as such witness, one way only twenty cents ($0.20). Such per diem and mileage are discretionary and shall only be allowed upon a showing that the allowances are necessary for the expenses of the witness in attending. The court may disallow any fees to a witness unnecessarily subpoenaed. *(Added by Stats.1953, c. 206, p. 1241, § 1. Amended by Stats.1957, c. 1908, p. 3339, § 3; Stats.1970, c. 1061, p. 1892, § 3.)*

§ 68095. Witness fees and mileage; coroner's jury; county charge

Except as otherwise provided by law, witness' fees for each day's actual attendance, when legally required to attend, or if the witness attends voluntarily and is called to testify, before a coroner's jury, are twelve dollars ($12) a day and mileage for each mile actually traveled in attendance as a witness, one way only, twenty cents ($0.20). That per diem and mileage shall be a county charge. *(Added by Stats.1953, c. 206, p. 1241, § 1. Amended by Stats.1957, c. 1908, p. 3339, § 4; Stats.1970, c. 1061, p. 1893, § 4; Stats.2003, c. 62 (S.B.600), § 161.)*

§ 68096.1. Local agency employees subpoenaed as witnesses; compensation and expenses; reimbursement to agency

(a) Any employee of a local agency who is obliged by a subpoena to attend a civil action or proceeding as a witness in litigation in a matter regarding an event or transaction which he or she perceived or investigated in the course of his or her duties, to which that local agency is not a party, shall receive the salary or other compensation to which he or she is normally entitled from that local agency during the time that he or she prepares for his or her response and appearance, during the time that he or she travels to and from the place where the court or other tribunal is located and while he or she is required to remain at that place pursuant to the subpoena. He or she shall also receive from that local agency the actual necessary and reasonable traveling expenses he or she incurred in complying with the subpoena.

(b) The party at whose request the subpoena is issued shall reimburse the local agency for the full cost incurred by the local agency in paying the employee his or her salary or other compensation and traveling expenses as provided for in this section, for each day that the employee is required to remain in attendance pursuant to the subpoena. The amount of one hundred fifty dollars ($150), together with the subpoena, shall be tendered to that local agency for each day that the employee is required to remain in attendance pursuant to the subpoena.

(c) If the actual expenses should later prove to be less than the amount tendered, the excess of the amount tendered shall be refunded.

(d) If the actual expenses should later prove to be more than the amount tendered, the difference shall be paid to the local agency by the party at whose request the subpoena was issued.

(e) If a court continues a proceeding on its own motion, no additional witness fee shall be required prior to the issuance of a subpoena or the making of any order directing the employee to appear on the date to which the proceeding is continued.

(f) As used in this section, "local agency" means a city, county, city and county, special district, redevelopment agency, or any other political subdivision of the state. *(Added by Stats.1991, c. 230 (S.B.109), § 2. Amended by Stats.1993, c. 1195 (S.B.405), § 17.)*

Research References

Rutter, Cal. Practice Guide: Civil Trials & Evidence Ch. 1-C, C. Marshalling the Evidence.
Rutter, Cal. Practice Guide: Personal Injury Ch. 6-B, B. Overview of Selected Discovery Procedures.

Rutter, Cal. Practice Guide: Personal Injury Ch. 8-C, C. Two Months Before Trial.

§ 68097. Witness fees and mileage; civil cases; demand for advance payment; exceptions

Witnesses in civil cases may demand the payment of their mileage and fees for one day, in advance, and when so demanded may not be compelled to attend until the allowances are paid except as hereinafter provided for employees of the Department of Justice who are peace officers or analysts in technical fields, peace officers of the Department of the California Highway Patrol, peace officer members of the State Fire Marshal's Office, other state employees, trial court employees, sheriffs, deputy sheriffs, marshals, deputy marshals, district attorney inspectors, probation officers, building inspectors, firefighters, and city police officers. For the purposes of this section and Sections 68097.1 to 68097.10, inclusive, only, the term "peace officer of the California Highway Patrol" shall include those persons employed as vehicle inspection specialists by the Department of the California Highway Patrol, the term "firefighter" has the definition provided in Section 50925, and a volunteer firefighter shall be deemed to be employed by the public entity for which he or she volunteers as a firefighter. *(Added by Stats.1953, c. 206, p. 1241, § 1. Amended by Stats.1963, c. 1485, p. 3050, § 4; Stats.1970, c. 58, p. 74, § 1; Stats.1972, c. 256, p. 507, § 1; Stats.1974, c. 986, p. 2054, § 1; Stats.1974, c. 1290, p. 2801, § 1; Stats.1977, c. 471, c. 1534, § 1; Stats.1977, c. 593, p. 1964, § 1.5; Stats.1992, c. 381 (S.B.1546), § 1, eff. July 30, 1992; Stats.1992, c. 887 (A.B.3816), § 1.5; Stats.1993, c. 158 (A.B.392), § 11, eff. July 21, 1993; Stats.1993, c. 727 (A.B.1522), § 1; Gov.Reorg.Plan No. 1 of 1995, § 33, eff. July 12, 1995; Stats.1996, c. 305 (A.B.3103), § 34; Stats.2003, c. 449 (A.B.1712), § 19.)*

Research References

Rutter, Cal. Practice Guide: Civil Trials & Evidence Ch. 1-C, C. Marshalling the Evidence.

§ 68097.1. State employees; civil witnesses; matters pertaining to duties; subpoenas; attendance

(a) Whenever an employee of the Department of Justice who is a peace officer or an analyst in a technical field, peace officer of the Department of the California Highway Patrol, peace officer member of the State Fire Marshal's Office, sheriff, deputy sheriff, marshal, deputy marshal, district attorney inspector, probation officer, building inspector, firefighter, or city police officer is required as a witness before any court or other tribunal in any civil action or proceeding in connection with a matter regarding an event or transaction which he or she has perceived or investigated in the course of his or her duties, a subpoena requiring his or her attendance may be served by delivering a copy either to the person personally, or by delivering two copies to his or her immediate superior at the public entity by which he or she is employed or an agent designated by that immediate superior to receive that service.

(b) Whenever any other state employee or any employee of the trial courts is required as a witness before any court or other tribunal in any civil action or proceeding in connection with a matter, event, or transaction concerning which he or she has expertise gained in the course of his or her duties, a subpoena requiring his or her attendance may be served by delivering a copy either to the person personally or by delivering two copies to his or her immediate superior or agent designated by that immediate superior to receive that service.

(c) The attendance of any person described in subdivisions (a) and (b) may be required pursuant to this section only in accordance with Section 1989 of the Code of Civil Procedure.

(d) As used in this section and in Sections 68097.2 and 68097.5, "tribunal" means any person or body before whom or which attendance of witnesses may be required by subpoena, including an arbitrator in arbitration proceedings. *(Added by Stats.1963, c. 1485, p. 3050, § 5. Amended by Stats.1965, c. 561, p. 1885, § 1; Stats.1969, c. 172, p. 423, § 1; Stats.1974, c. 986, p. 2054, § 2; Stats.1974, c. 1290, p. 2802, § 2; Stats.1977, c. 471, p. 1534, § 2; Stats.1977, c. 593, p. 1964, § 2.5; Stats.1990, c. 1695 (S.B.2140), § 2.5; Stats.1992, c. 381 (S.B.1546), § 2, eff. July 30, 1992; Stats.1992, c. 887 (A.B.3816), § 2.5; Stats.1993, c. 158 (A.B.392), § 12, eff. July 21, 1993; Stats.1993, c. 727 (A.B.1522), § 2; Gov.Reorg.Plan No. 1 of 1995, § 34, eff. July 12, 1995; Stats.1996, c. 305 (A.B.3103), § 35; Stats.2003, c. 449 (A.B.1712), § 20.)*

Research References

Rutter, Cal. Practice Guide: Civ. Pro. Before Trial Ch. 8E-6, Subpoena to Nonparty Deponent or Business Records Custodian.

Rutter, Cal. Practice Guide: Civil Trials & Evidence Ch. 1-C, C. Marshalling the Evidence.

§ 68097.2. Witnesses employed by public entity; compensation; expenses; reimbursement of public entity

(a) Any peace officer, as that term is defined in Chapter 4.5 (commencing with Section 830) of Title 3 of Part 2 of the Penal Code, any firefighter, any state employee, any trial court employee, or any county employee, who is obliged by a subpoena issued pursuant to Section 68097.1 to attend as a witness, shall receive the salary or other compensation to which he or she is normally entitled from the public entity by which he or she is employed during the time that he or she travels to and from the place where the court or other tribunal is located and while he or she is required to remain at that place pursuant to the subpoena. He or she shall also receive from the public entity by which he or she is employed the actual necessary and reasonable traveling expenses incurred by him or her in complying with the subpoena.

(b) The party at whose request the subpoena is issued shall reimburse the public entity for the full cost to the public entity incurred in paying the peace officer, firefighter, state employee, trial court employee, or specified county employee his or her salary or other compensation and traveling expenses as provided for in this section, for each day that the peace officer, firefighter, state employee, trial court employee, or specified county employee is required to remain in attendance pursuant to the subpoena. The amount of two hundred seventy-five dollars ($275), together with the subpoena, shall be tendered to the person accepting the subpoena for each day that the peace officer, firefighter, state employee, trial court employee, or specified county employee is required to remain in attendance pursuant to the subpoena.

(c) If the actual expenses should later prove to be less than the amount tendered, the excess of the amount tendered shall be refunded.

(d) If the actual expenses should later prove to be more than the amount deposited, the difference shall be paid to the public entity by the party at whose request the subpoena is issued.

(e) If a court continues a proceeding on its own motion, no additional witness fee shall be required prior to the issuance of a subpoena or the making of an order directing the peace officer, firefighter, state employee, or trial court employee to appear on the date to which the proceeding is continued.

(f) For the purposes of the payment of the salary or other compensation of a volunteer firefighter pursuant to subdivision (a), a volunteer firefighter who is subpoenaed to appear as a witness in connection with a matter regarding an event or transaction that he or she has perceived or investigated in the course of his or her duties as a volunteer firefighter, shall be deemed to be entitled to reasonable compensation evidenced by the compensation paid to firefighters in jurisdictions with similar geographic and economic characteristics. However, the require-

ments of subdivision (a) and of this subdivision are not applicable if a volunteer firefighter will receive his or her regular salary or other compensation pursuant to the policy of his or her regular employer, for the periods during which compensation is required under subdivision (a). *(Added by Stats.1963, c. 1485, p. 3050, § 6. Amended by Stats.1965, c. 561, p. 1885, § 2; Stats.1969, c. 172, p. 423, § 2; Stats.1969, c. 342, p. 717, § 2; Stats.1969, c. 1187, p. 2317, § 2; Stats.1974, c. 986, p. 2054, § 3; Stats.1974, c. 1290, p. 2802, § 3; Stats.1977, c. 471, p. 1534, § 3; Stats.1977, c. 593, p. 1965, § 3.5; Stats.1980, c. 472, p. 984, § 1; Stats.1986, c. 747, § 1; Stats.1988, c. 588, § 1; Stats.1989, c. 1416, § 35; Stats.1990, c. 511 (S.B.163), § 2, eff. Aug. 13, 1990; Stats.1992, c. 427 (A.B.3355), § 73; Stats.1992, c. 381 (S.B.1546), § 3, eff. July 30, 1992; Stats.1992, c. 876 (A.B.3296), § 13; Stats.1993, c. 158 (A.B.392), § 13, eff. July 21, 1993; Stats.1993, c. 727 (A.B.1522), § 3; Stats.2003, c. 449 (A.B.1712), § 21; Stats. 2012, c. 377 (A.B.2612), § 1.)*

Fees and Charges

Commissioner's authority to increase or decrease fees, and schedule of fees and charges, see Insurance Code § 12978.

Research References

Rutter, Cal. Practice Guide: Civ. Pro. Before Trial Ch. 8E-6, Subpoena to Nonparty Deponent or Business Records Custodian.

Rutter, Cal. Practice Guide: Civil Trials & Evidence Ch. 1-C, C. Marshalling the Evidence.

Rutter, Cal. Practice Guide: Personal Injury Ch. 6-B, B. Overview of Selected Discovery Procedures.

Rutter, Cal. Practice Guide: Personal Injury Ch. 8-C, C. Two Months Before Trial.

§ 68097.3. Appearance of highway patrol members; service of subpoenas

Whenever a member of the California Highway Patrol is not subject to a subpoena pursuant to Section 1989 of the Code of Civil Procedure, he may nevertheless be required to appear as a witness before any court located in this state, in any civil action or proceeding in connection with a matter regarding an event or transaction which he has perceived or investigated in the course of his duties, by a subpoena requiring his attendance. The subpoena may be served by delivering a copy (1) to the member personally or to his immediate superior or (2) during usual office hours, at least five days prior to the date of the member's required attendance, to the person in charge of the office of the California Highway Patrol where the member filed his report of the event or transaction. *(Added by Stats.1963, c. 1485, p. 3050, § 7. Amended by Stats.1976, c. 10, § 1.)*

§ 68097.4. Highway patrol members; compensation; expenses; reimbursement of state; refund of excess

Any member of the California Highway Patrol who is obliged to appear pursuant to a subpoena issued under the provisions of Section 68097.3 as a witness, shall receive from the State the salary or other compensation to which he is normally entitled as a member of the patrol during the time that he travels to and from the place where the court is located and while he is required to remain at such place pursuant to such subpoena. He shall also receive from the State the actual necessary and reasonable traveling expenses incurred by him in complying with such subpoena.

The party at whose request a subpoena is issued pursuant to Section 68097.3 shall reimburse the State for the amount of the salary or other compensation to which the member of the California Highway Patrol involved is normally entitled from the State during the time that he travels to and from the place where the court is located and while he is required to remain at such place pursuant to such subpoena; and in addition, such party shall reimburse the State for the actual, necessary and reasonable traveling expenses incurred by the member of the California Highway Patrol in complying with such subpoena. An amount equal to the estimated amount of such salary or other compensation and expenses shall be deposited with the clerk of the court prior to the issuance of such subpoena. If the actual amount of such salary or other compensation and expenses should later prove to be more than the amount deposited, the party shall also deposit the difference with the clerk. If the actual amount should later prove to be less than the amount deposited, the excess of the amount deposited shall be refunded. All amounts received by the clerk to which the State is entitled shall be remitted to the Department of the California Highway Patrol for deposit in the State Treasury. *(Added by Stats.1963, c. 1485, p. 3051, § 8.)*

§ 68097.5. Return for subsequent proceedings; tender of funds

No employee of the Department of Justice who is a peace officer or an analyst in a technical field, peace officer of the Department of the California Highway Patrol, peace officer member of the State Fire Marshal's office, sheriff, deputy sheriff, marshal, deputy marshal, firefighter, or city police officer shall be ordered to return by the court for subsequent proceedings beyond the day stated in the subpoena referred to in Sections 68097.1, 68097.2, 68097.3 and 68097.4, or the day upon which the witness appeared pursuant to the provisions of Section 68097.9, unless the party at whose request the subpoena was issued or the party at whose request the witness is ordered to return, shall first tender to the public entity by which the witness is employed the same sum required to be tendered for the issuance of a subpoena in the first instance. *(Added by Stats.1963, c. 1485, p. 3051, § 9. Amended by Stats.1965, c. 561, p. 1886, § 3; Stats.1967, c. 115, p. 1032, § 1; Stats.1970, c. 58, p. 74, § 2; Stats.1974, c. 986, p. 2055, § 4; Stats.1974, c. 1290, p. 2803, § 4; Stats.1977, c. 471, p. 1535, § 4; Stats.1977, c. 593, p. 1966, § 4.5; Stats.1990, c. 511 (S.B.163), § 3, eff. Aug. 13, 1990; Stats.1992, c. 887 (A.B.3816), § 3; Gov.Reorg.Plan No. 1 of 1995, § 35, eff. July 12, 1995; Stats.1996, c. 305 (A.B.3103), § 36.)*

§ 68097.55. Relief from duty to make deposit

Notwithstanding the provisions of Section 68097.5, the court, upon good cause shown, including the fact that the party is proceeding in forma pauperis pursuant to Section 68511.3, may relieve a party of the duty to make any deposit or payment, or portion thereof, required by Sections 68096.1, 68097.1, 68097.2, 68097.3, 68097.4, and 68097.5. *(Added by Stats.1967, c. 115, p. 1032, § 2. Amended by Stats.1980, c. 472, p. 985, § 2; Stats. 1993, c. 93 (A.B.1348), § 1.)*

Research References

Rutter, Cal. Practice Guide: Civ. Pro. Before Trial Ch. 8E-6, Subpoena to Nonparty Deponent or Business Records Custodian.
Rutter, Cal. Practice Guide: Civil Trials & Evidence Ch. 1-C, C. Marshalling the Evidence.
Rutter, Cal. Practice Guide: Personal Injury Ch. 6-B, B. Overview of Selected Discovery Procedures.

§ 68097.6. Subpoenas for taking depositions of peace officers and others; sections which apply

Sections 68097.1, 68097.2, 68097.3, 68097.4, and 68097.5 apply to subpoenas issued for the taking of depositions of employees of the Department of Justice who are peace officers or analysts in technical fields, peace officers of the Department of the California Highway Patrol, peace officer members of the State Fire Marshal's office, sheriffs, deputy sheriffs, marshals, deputy marshals, firefighters, or city police officers pursuant to Chapter 9 (commencing with Section 2025.010) of Title 4 of Part 4 of the Code of Civil Procedure. *(Added by Stats.1963, c. 1485, p. 3051,*

§ 10. Amended by Stats.1970, c. 58, p. 74, § 3; Stats.1974, c. 986, p. 2055, § 5; Stats.1974, c. 1290, p. 2803, § 5; Stats.1977, c. 471, p. 1535, § 5; Stats.1977, c. 593, p. 1967, § 5.5; Stats.1992, c. 887 (A.B.3816), § 4; Gov.Reorg.Plan No. 1 of 1995, § 36, eff. July 12, 1995; Stats.1996, c. 305 (A.B.3103), § 37; Stats.2005, c. 294 (A.B.333), § 21.)

Law Revision Commission Comments

Section 68097.6 is amended to reflect revision and relocation of the civil discovery provision referenced in it (former Code Civ. Proc. § 2019), which set forth guidelines for taking an oral deposition in the state. Former Code of Civil Procedure Section 2019 was repealed in 1986 and its substance relocated to Code of Civil Procedure Section 2025. 1986 Cal. Stat. ch. 1334, §§ 1, 2; see also 1963 Cal. Stat. ch. 519, § 1 (former Code Civ. Proc. § 2019); 1963 Cal. Stat. ch. 1485, § 10 (earlier version of Section 68097.6). Section 68097.6 was not revised at that time to reflect the repeal of former Code of Civil Procedure Section 2019 and the relocation of its substance. It is now amended to reflect that change, as well as a subsequent nonsubstantive reorganization of the provisions governing civil discovery. See 2004 Cal. Stat. ch. 182, §§ 22, 23, 23.5, 61, 62; *Civil Discovery: Nonsubstantive Reform*, 33 Cal. L. Revision Comm'n Reports 789 (2003).

Section 68097.6 is also amended to delete unnecessary language.

§ 68097.7. Offer or payment of other consideration; asking or receiving other payment; offense

Any person who pays or offers to pay any money or other form of consideration for the services of any employee of the Department of Justice who is a peace officer or an analyst in a technical field, peace officer of the Department of the California Highway Patrol, peace officer member of the State Fire Marshal's office, sheriff, deputy sheriff, marshal, deputy marshal, firefighter, or city police officer as a witness in any action or proceeding in connection with a matter regarding an event or transaction which he or she has perceived or investigated in the course of his or her duties in any manner other than as provided in Sections 68097.1, 68097.2, 68097.3, 68097.4, 68097.5, and 68097.6 is guilty of a misdemeanor, and any employee of the Department of Justice who is a peace officer or an analyst in a technical field, peace officer of the Department of the California Highway Patrol, peace officer member of the State Fire Marshal's office, sheriff, deputy sheriff, marshal, deputy marshal, firefighter, or city police officer who asks or receives a payment except as provided in Sections 68097.2 and 68097.4 is likewise guilty of a misdemeanor. *(Added by Stats.1963, c. 1485, p. 3052, § 11. Amended by Stats.1970, c. 58, p. 75, § 4; Stats.1974, c. 986, p. 2055, § 6; Stats.1974, c. 1290, p. 2803, § 6; Stats.1977, c. 471, p. 1535, § 6; Stats.1977, c. 593, p. 1967, § 6.5; Stats.1992, c. 887 (A.B.3816), § 5; Gov.Reorg.Plan No. 1 of 1995, § 37, eff. July 12, 1995; Stats.1996, c. 305 (A.B.3103), § 38.)*

§ 68097.8. Deposits taxable as costs

All deposits made pursuant to Sections 68097.2 or 68097.4 of this code, except such deposits as the party may be entitled to have refunded, shall be taxable as costs by the prevailing party. *(Added by Stats.1963, c. 1485, p. 3052, § 12.)*

§ 68097.9. Agreement to appear at time other than specified in subpoena

An employee of the Department of Justice who is a peace officer or an analyst in a technical field, peace officer of the Department of the California Highway Patrol, peace officer member of the State Fire Marshal's office, sheriff, deputy sheriff, marshal, deputy marshal, firefighter, or city police officer who has been subpoenaed pursuant to Section 68097.1, 68097.3, or 68097.6, may, in lieu of attendance at the time specified in the subpoena, agree with the party at whose request the subpoena was issued to appear at another time or pursuant to notice as may be agreed upon. *(Added by Stats.1967, c. 115, p. 1032, § 3. Amended by Stats.1970, c. 58, p. 75, § 5; Stats.1974, c. 986, p.*

Government

2056, § 7; Stats.1974, c. 1290, p. 2803, § 7; Stats.1977, c. 471, p. 1536, § 7; Stats.1977, c. 593, p. 1968, § 7.5; Stats.1992, c. 887 (A.B.3816), § 6; Gov.Reorg.Plan No. 1 of 1995, § 38, eff. July 12, 1995; Stats.1996, c. 305 (A.B.3103), § 39.)

§ 68097.10.　Action to recover compensation for expenses

Whenever an employee of the Department of Justice who is a peace officer or an analyst in a technical field, peace officer of the Department of the California Highway Patrol, peace officer member of the State Fire Marshal's office, sheriff, deputy sheriff, marshal, deputy marshal, firefighter, or city police officer appears as a witness pursuant to Section 68097.1 and reimbursement is not made as provided for in Section 68097.2, then the Department of Justice, the Department of the California Highway Patrol, the State Fire Marshal's office, or the public entity employing the employee, sheriff, deputy sheriff, marshal, deputy marshal, firefighter, or city police officer shall have standing to bring an action in order to recover the funds. (Added by Stats.1967, c. 1240, p. 3011, § 1.　Amended by Stats.1970, c. 58, p. 75, § 6; Stats.1974, c. 986, p. 2056, § 8; Stats.1974, c. 1290, p. 2804, § 8; Stats.1977, c. 471, p. 1536, § 8; Stats.1977, c. 593, p. 1968, § 8.5; Stats.1992, c. 887 (A.B.3816), § 7; Gov.Reorg.Plan No. 1 of 1995, § 39, eff. July 12, 1995; Stats.1996, c. 305 (A.B.3103), § 40.)

§ 68098.　Witness fees; criminal cases; superior courts; charges against funds; exception

Witness' fees in criminal cases in superior courts, other than fees for expert witnesses appointed by the court for the court's needs pursuant to Section 730 of the Evidence Code, are charges against the same funds as grand jurors' fees in criminal cases. (Added by Stats.1953, c. 206, p. 1242, § 1.　Amended by Stats.1977, c. 1257, p. 4772, § 56, eff. Oct. 3, 1977; Stats.1998, c. 931 (S.B.2139), § 229, eff. Sept. 28, 1998; Stats.2012, c. 470 (A.B.1529), § 48.)

Law Revision Commission Comments

Section 68098 is amended to reflect elimination of the justice court. Cal. Const. art. VI, §§ 1, 5(b).　[28 Cal.L.Rev.Comm. Reports 51 (1998)].

Section 68098 is amended to reflect enactment of the Lockyer–Isenberg Trial Court Funding Act, 1997 Cal. Stat. ch. 850 (see generally Sections 77000–77655). See Sections 77003 ("court operations" defined), 77200 (state funding of "court operations"); see also Cal. R. Ct. 10.810(b)(6) & (d), Functions 2 (jury services) & 10 ("court-appointed expert witness fees (for the court's needs)").

The section is also amended to reflect unification of the municipal and superior courts pursuant to former Section 5(e) of Article VI of the California Constitution.

Section 68098 is further amended to make a stylistic revision.　[39 Cal.L.Rev.Comm. Reports 157 (2009)].

CHAPTER 2.　THE JUDICIAL COUNCIL

ARTICLE 4.　COURT INTERPRETER SERVICES

Section
68560.　Legislative findings and declarations.
68560.5.　Definitions.
68561.　Certified court interpreters; qualifications; appointment of noncertified interpreters.
68566.　"Certified court interpreter" defined.

§ 68560.　Legislative findings and declarations

The Legislature finds and declares that:

(a)　Resolution Chapter 179 of the Statutes of 1973 requested the Judicial Council of California to undertake a comprehensive survey of the language needs of California citizens and residents in relation to the judicial process.

(b)　The Judicial Council performed this undertaking with the aid and assistance of a special advisory committee appointed by the Chief Justice of California and significant work was done by a private consultant under contract to the Judicial Council.

(c)　During 1976 and 1977, the Judicial Council submitted to the Legislature a series of detailed reports identifying specific language needs of California citizens and residents, describing language services that had been provided by California's justice system, indicating special problem areas in need of solution, and setting forth specific objectives to be achieved by providing adequate interpreter services to non-English-speaking citizens and residents in California.　These reports resulted in adoption of this article by Chapter 158 of the Statutes of 1978.

(d)　In 1990 the Chief Justice of California appointed the Judicial Council Advisory Committee on Court Interpreters to propose actions to the Judicial Council to (1) improve the quality of interpreter services provided to courts, (2) increase the number of available, qualified court interpreters, and (3) provide non-English-speaking persons with increased access to the court system.　At the request of the advisory committee, the Judicial Council proposed to the Legislature changes in this article to clarify the law, to create a program to certify court interpreters, and to coordinate programs for interpreter recruiting, training, testing, certification, and continuing education and evaluation.

(e)　The Legislature recognizes that the number of non-English-speaking persons in California is increasing, and recognizes the need to provide equal justice under the law to all California citizens and residents and to provide for their special needs in their relations with the judicial and administrative law system.

(f)　Competent interpreter services in the courts and judicial and administrative agencies should be provided through programs to recruit, train, test, certify, and evaluate interpreters. Continuing education and evaluation would also help ensure adequate interpreter services to the courts.

(g)　To plan, monitor, and coordinate interpreter services, reliable and uniform data are needed on the continuing use of and need for interpreters in the courts. (Added by Stats.1978, c. 158, p. 388, § 1, eff. May 24, 1978.　Amended by Stats.1992, c. 770 (S.B.1304), § 2.)

Research References

2 Witkin Cal. Proc. 5th Courts § 387, Interpreters and Translators.

§ 68560.5.　Definitions

As used in this article:

(a)　"Court proceeding" means a civil, criminal, or juvenile proceeding, or a deposition in a civil case filed in a court of record.　However, "court proceeding" does not include a small claims proceeding.

(b)　"Interpreter" does not include (1) an interpreter qualified under Section 754 of the Evidence Code to interpret for deaf or hearing impaired persons, or (2) an interpreter qualified for administrative hearings or noncourt settings under Article 8 (commencing with Section 11435.05) of Chapter 4.5 of Part 1 of Division 3 of Title 2. (Added by Stats.1995, c. 938 (S.B.523), § 58.5, operative July 1, 1997.)

Law Revision Commission Comments

Section 68560.5 is revised to correct the reference to the Administrative Procedure Act. [25 Cal.L.Rev.Comm. Reports 711 (1995)].

Research References

2 Witkin Cal. Proc. 5th Courts § 387, Interpreters and Translators.

§ 68561. Certified court interpreters; qualifications; appointment of noncertified interpreters

(a) Except for good cause as provided in subdivision (c), any person who interprets in a court proceeding using a language designated by the Judicial Council under subdivision (a) of Section 68562 shall be a certified court interpreter as defined in Section 68566 for the language used.

(b) Interpreters named and maintained on the list of recommended court interpreters (1) previously established by the State Personnel Board, or (2) established by an entity provisionally approved under subdivision (b) of Section 68562, shall be deemed certified under this article until January 1, 1996. After that date, those interpreters shall not be deemed certified unless they have complied with the procedures for certification adopted under subdivision (c) of Section 68562. Interpreters approved by the State Personnel Board or any other agency or entity for use in administrative hearings or nonjudicial settings shall not be deemed certified as court interpreters. These interpreters also shall not be used in court proceedings unless they are qualified by the court under subdivision (c) or (d).

(c) A court may for good cause appoint an interpreter for a language designated by the Judicial Council who does not hold a court interpreter certificate. The court shall follow the good cause and qualification procedures and guidelines adopted by the Judicial Council.

(d) Any person who interprets in a court proceeding using a language not designated by the Judicial Council shall be qualified by the court under the qualification procedures and guidelines adopted by the Judicial Council. If this qualified interpreter also passes an English fluency examination offered by a testing entity approved by the Judicial Council, this person shall be designated a "registered interpreter."

(e) Interpreters shall establish to the court that they meet the requirements of this section under procedures adopted by the Judicial Council. The court record shall show that the interpreter (1) is a certified court interpreter as defined by Section 68566 for the language used, or (2) was qualified by the court under subdivision (c), after a finding of good cause, or under subdivision (d), if the language is not designated by the Judicial Council. *(Added by Stats.1992, c. 770 (S.B.1304), § 5. Amended by Stats.1997, c. 376 (A.B.1445), § 2.)*

Research References

2 Witkin Cal. Proc. 5th Courts § 387, Interpreters and Translators.

§ 68566. "Certified court interpreter" defined

A natural person who either (1) holds a valid certificate as a certified court interpreter issued by a certification entity approved by the Judicial Council, or (2) until January 1, 1996, is named and maintained on the list of recommended court interpreters previously established by the State Personnel Board or established by an entity provisionally approved under subdivision (b) of Section 68562, shall be designated a "certified court interpreter." No other person or entity shall use the title "certified court interpreter" or represent that he or she or it is certified to interpret in or for the courts. *(Added by Stats.1992, c. 770 (S.B.1304), § 14.)*

Research References

2 Witkin Cal. Proc. 5th Courts § 387, Interpreters and Translators.
2 Witkin Cal. Summ. 10th Workers' Compensation § 264, Reimbursement for Examination Expenses.

2 Witkin Cal. Summ. 10th Workers' Compensation § 396, Procedure.

ARTICLE 5. THE TRIAL COURT DELAY REDUCTION ACT

§ 68600. Short title

This article shall be known and may be cited as the Trial Court Delay Reduction Act. *(Added by Stats.1990, c. 1232 (A.B.3820), § 3.)*

Research References

Rutter, Cal. Practice Guide: A.D.R. Ch. 4-C, C. Statutorily-Mandated Court Mediation Programs.
Rutter, Cal. Practice Guide: A.D.R. Ch. 4-D, D. Mandatory Settlement Conferences.
Rutter, Cal. Practice Guide: A.D.R. Ch. 6-B, B. Temporary Judges.
Rutter, Cal. Practice Guide: A.D.R. Ch. 6-C, C. Referees.
Rutter, Cal. Practice Guide: Civ. Pro. Before Trial Ch. 11-B, B. Involuntary Dismissals.
Rutter, Cal. Practice Guide: Civ. Pro. Before Trial Ch. 13-A, A. Introduction.
Rutter, Cal. Practice Guide: Civ. Pro. Before Trial Ch. 8A-4, Use of Technology in Discovery.
Rutter, Cal. Practice Guide: Civ. Pro. Before Trial Ch. 12(I)-B, B. Case Management ("Fast Track") System.
Rutter, Cal. Practice Guide: Civil Trials & Evidence Ch. 1-L, L. Assignment to Trial Department.
Rutter, Cal. Practice Guide: Civil Trials & Evidence Ch. 4-A, A. General Considerations.
Rutter, Cal. Practice Guide: Personal Injury Ch. 7-A, A. Introduction- Nature and Purpose of "Judicial Arbitration" in General.

Government

Rutter, Cal. Practice Guide: Personal Injury Ch. 7-B, B. Tactical Considerations-Pros and Cons of Judicial Arbitration.

Rutter, Cal. Practice Guide: Personal Injury Ch. 8-A, A. Case Management.

2 Witkin Cal. Proc. 5th Courts § 145, Exception: Local Delay Reduction Rule.

2 Witkin Cal. Proc. 5th Courts § 257, (S 257) Nature and Scope.

2 Witkin Cal. Proc. 5th Courts § 266, Sanctions Improper.

5 Witkin Cal. Proc. 5th Pleading § 1186, (S 1186) Right to Amend Pleadings.

6 Witkin Cal. Proc. 5th Proceedings Without Trial § 281, Local Rules.

6 Witkin Cal. Proc. 5th Proceedings Without Trial § 319, Authority.

6 Witkin Cal. Proc. 5th Proceedings Without Trial § 442, in General.

6 Witkin Cal. Proc. 5th Proceedings Without Trial § 451, in General.

6 Witkin Cal. Proc. 5th Proceedings Without Trial § 490, Time for Mediation.

7 Witkin Cal. Proc. 5th Trial § 37, (S 37) Procedural Framework.

7 Witkin Cal. Proc. 5th Trial § 38, (S 38) Trial Court Delay Reduction Act.

6 Witkin, California Summary 10th Torts § 1603, (S 1603) Time Limits.

§ 68603. Standards of timely disposition of civil and criminal actions; adoption

(a) The Judicial Council shall adopt standards of timely disposition for the processing and disposition of civil and criminal actions. The standards shall be guidelines by which the progress of litigation in the superior court of every county may be measured. In establishing these standards, the Judicial Council shall be guided by the principles that litigation, from commencement to resolution, should require only that time reasonably necessary for pleadings, discovery, preparation, and court events, and that any additional elapsed time is delay and should be eliminated.

(b) The Judicial Council may adopt the standards of timely disposition adopted by the National Conference of State Trial Judges and the American Bar Association or may adopt different standards, but in the latter event shall specify reasons for approval of any standard which permits greater elapsed time for the resolution of litigation than that provided in the standards of the National Conference of State Trial Judges.

(c) The Judicial Council shall adopt rules effective July 1, 1991, to be used by all delay reduction courts, establishing a case differentiation classification system based on the relative complexity of cases. The rules shall provide longer periods for the timely disposition of more complex cases. The rules may provide a presumption that all cases, when filed, shall be classified in the least complex category. *(Added by Stats.1990, c. 1232 (A.B.3820), § 3.)*

Research References

Rutter, Cal. Practice Guide: Civ. Pro. Before Trial Ch. 12(I)-B, B. Case Management ("Fast Track") System.

Rutter, Cal. Practice Guide: Personal Injury Ch. 8-A, A. Case Management.

2 Witkin Cal. Proc. 5th Courts § 145, Exception: Local Delay Reduction Rule.

2 Witkin Cal. Proc. 5th Courts § 259, (S 259) Local Standards and Procedure.

2 Witkin Cal. Proc. 5th Courts § 260, in General.

2 Witkin Cal. Proc. 5th Courts § 263, (S 263) Differential Case Management.

7 Witkin Cal. Proc. 5th Trial § 38, (S 38) Trial Court Delay Reduction Act.

12 Witkin, California Summary 10th Real Property § 125, (S 125) Alternative Dispute Resolution.

§ 68604. Statistics regarding compliance with standards of timely disposition; collection and maintenance; method

The Judicial Council shall collect and maintain statistics, and shall publish them at least on a yearly basis, regarding the compliance of the superior court of each county and of each branch court with the standards of timely disposition adopted pursuant to Section 68603. In collecting and publishing these statistics, the Judicial Council shall measure the time required for the resolution of civil cases from the filing of the first document invoking court jurisdiction, and for the resolution of criminal cases from the date of arrest, including a separate measurement in felony cases from the first appearance in superior court. The Judicial Council shall report its findings and recommendations to the Legislature in a biennial Report on the State of California's Civil and Criminal Justice Systems.

The Judicial Council shall conduct a two-year study on the stipulated continuance authorized by subdivision (c) of Section 68616. *(Added by Stats.1990, c. 1232 (A.B.3820), § 3. Amended by Stats.2001, c. 745 (S.B.1191), § 112, eff. Oct. 12, 2001.)*

Research References

2 Witkin Cal. Proc. 5th Courts § 259, (S 259) Local Standards and Procedure.

2 Witkin Cal. Proc. 5th Courts § 260, in General.

§ 68605. Exemplary delay reduction program

The Judicial Council shall designate the four superior courts with 18 or more judicial positions which, as of June 30, 1986, had the highest ratio per judicial position of at-issue civil cases pending more than one year, and the five superior courts with more than eight judicial positions, not otherwise designated, with the highest such ratio. In each such court, an exemplary delay reduction program shall be established. The superior court of any other county, at the option of the presiding judge, may elect to establish an exemplary delay reduction program, and the Judicial Council may designate additional superior courts for participation in an exemplary delay reduction program.

This section shall cease to be operative on July 1, 1992. *(Added by Stats.1990, c. 1232 (A.B.3820), § 3.)*

Inoperative Date

This section became inoperative July 1, 1992, by its own terms.

§ 68605.5. Application of article

On and after July 1, 1992, this article shall apply to all actions and proceedings in the superior court in each county, except actions and proceedings subject to subdivision (a) of Section 68608 or subdivision (b) of Section 68609. *(Added by Stats.1990, c. 1232 (A.B.3820), § 3.)*

Research References

Rutter, Cal. Practice Guide: Civ. Pro. Before Trial Ch. 12(I)-B, B. Case Management ("Fast Track") System.

2 Witkin Cal. Proc. 5th Courts § 257, (S 257) Nature and Scope.

7 Witkin Cal. Proc. 5th Trial § 38, (S 38) Trial Court Delay Reduction Act.

§ 68606. Exemplary delay reduction program; selection of judges to provide basis for determining effective methods; identification of judges who will participate in program

In each of the counties in which an exemplary delay reduction program is established, the presiding judge shall, (a) select a sufficient number of judges for the program that will provide, consistent with the size of the court, an adequate basis for determining the effectiveness of the methods for reducing delay specified in this article; and (b) identify the particular judges who will participate in the program. However, a minimum of four judges shall be included in the program. Each presiding judge may select, and is encouraged to select, all the judges of the superior court or the branch of a superior court as the judges of an exemplary delay reduction program.

This section shall cease to be operative on July 1, 1992. *(Added by Stats.1990, c. 1232 (A.B.3820), § 3.)*

Inoperative Date

This section became inoperative July 1, 1992, by its own terms.

§ 68607. Judges; responsibilities

In accordance with this article and consistent with statute, judges shall have the responsibility to eliminate delay in the progress and ultimate resolution of litigation, to assume and maintain control over the pace of litigation, to actively manage the processing of litigation from commencement to disposition, and to compel attorneys and litigants to prepare and resolve all litigation without delay, from the filing of the first document invoking court jurisdiction to final disposition of the action.

The judges of the program shall, consistent with the policies of this article:

(a) Actively monitor, supervise and control the movement of all cases assigned to the program from the time of filing of the first document invoking court jurisdiction through final disposition.

(b) Seek to meet the standards for timely disposition adopted pursuant to Section 68603.

(c) Establish procedures for early identification of cases within the program which may be protracted and for giving those cases special administrative and judicial attention as appropriate, including special assignment.

(d) Establish procedures for early identification and timely and appropriate handling of cases within the program which may be amenable to settlement or other alternative disposition techniques.

(e) Adopt a trial setting policy which, to the maximum extent possible, schedules a trial date within the time standards adopted pursuant to Section 68603 and which schedules a sufficient number of cases to ensure efficient use of judicial time while minimizing resetting caused by overscheduling.

(f) Commence trials on the date scheduled.

(g) Adopt and utilize a firm, consistent policy against continuances, to the maximum extent possible and reasonable, in all stages of the litigation. *(Added by Stats.1990, c. 1232 (A.B.3820), § 3.)*

Research References

Rutter, Cal. Practice Guide: Civ. Pro. Before Trial Ch. 12(I)-B, B. Case Management ("Fast Track") System.
Rutter, Cal. Practice Guide: Civ. Pro. Before Trial Ch. 12(I)-F, F. Motions to Continue Trial.
Rutter, Cal. Practice Guide: Civil Trials & Evidence Ch. 1-K, K. Continuance Motions.
Rutter, Cal. Practice Guide: Fed.Civ.Pro. Before Trial Ch. 1-D, D. Choosing Between State and Federal Courts.
Rutter, Cal. Practice Guide: Personal Injury Ch. 8-A, A. Case Management.
Rutter, Cal. Practice Guide: Personal Injury Ch. 9-A, A. Assignment to Trial.
2 Witkin Cal. Proc. 5th Courts § 258, (S 258) Duties and Powers of Judge.
2 Witkin Cal. Proc. 5th Courts § 259, (S 259) Local Standards and Procedure.
2 Witkin Cal. Proc. 5th Courts § 263, (S 263) Differential Case Management.
2 Witkin Cal. Proc. 5th Courts § 266, Sanctions Improper.

§ 68607.5. Challenge; removal of action or proceeding from delay reduction program

No action or proceeding may be removed from a delay reduction program because of a challenge filed under Section 170.6 of the Code of Civil Procedure. *(Added by Stats.1990, c. 1232 (A.B.3820), § 3.)*

Research References

Rutter, Cal. Practice Guide: Civ. Pro. Before Trial Ch. 12(I)-B, B. Case Management ("Fast Track") System.
Rutter, Cal. Practice Guide: Personal Injury Ch. 9-A, A. Assignment to Trial.
2 Witkin Cal. Proc. 5th Courts § 257, (S 257) Nature and Scope.

§ 68608. Cases not to be assigned; sanctions for noncompliance

(a) Juvenile, probate, and domestic relations cases shall not be assigned to a delay reduction program, and cases which have been assigned to a judge or judges for all purposes based on subject matter need not be assigned to the program.

(b) Judges shall have all the powers to impose sanctions authorized by law, including the power to dismiss actions or strike pleadings, if it appears that less severe sanctions would not be effective after taking into account the effect of previous sanctions or previous lack of compliance in the case. Judges are encouraged to impose sanctions to achieve the purposes of this article.

(c) This section shall become operative July 1, 1992. *(Added by Stats.1990, c. 1232 (A.B.3820), § 3, operative July 1, 1992.)*

Research References

Rutter, Cal. Practice Guide: Civ. Pro. Before Trial Ch. 4-A, A. Requirements-In General.
Rutter, Cal. Practice Guide: Civ. Pro. Before Trial Ch. 9(I)-D, D. Hearing.
Rutter, Cal. Practice Guide: Civ. Pro. Before Trial Ch. 12(I)-B, B. Case Management ("Fast Track") System.
Rutter, Cal. Practice Guide: Civ. Pro. Before Trial Ch. 9(III)-A, A. Sources of Sanctions Power.
Rutter, Cal. Practice Guide: Personal Injury Ch. 8-A, A. Case Management.
2 Witkin Cal. Proc. 5th Courts § 177, (S 177) Imposition of Money Sanctions.
2 Witkin Cal. Proc. 5th Courts § 257, (S 257) Nature and Scope.
2 Witkin Cal. Proc. 5th Courts § 264, in General.
2 Witkin Cal. Proc. 5th Courts § 266, Sanctions Improper.
6 Witkin Cal. Proc. 5th Proceedings Without Trial § 281, Local Rules.
7 Witkin Cal. Proc. 5th Trial § 38, (S 38) Trial Court Delay Reduction Act.
7 Witkin Cal. Proc. 5th Trial § 58, (S 58) in General.
7 Witkin Cal. Proc. 5th Trial § 63, (S 63) Imposition of Ultimate Sanction in First Instance.

§ 68609. Assignment of new and existing cases; cases not to be assigned; challenge; removal of case from program; judges; power to impose sanctions

(a) The presiding judge of each superior court with an exemplary delay reduction program shall assign a pro rata share of new cases, and an appropriate number of existing cases, to the program, and these cases shall thereafter be handled by the judges of the program for all purposes.

(b) Juvenile, probate, and domestic relations cases shall not be assigned to an exemplary delay reduction program, and cases which have been assigned to a judge or judges for all purposes based on subject matter need not be assigned to the program.

(c) No case shall be removed from an exemplary delay reduction program because of a challenge filed under Section 170.6 of the Code of Civil Procedure.

(d) In order to enforce the requirements of an exemplary delay reduction program and orders issued in cases assigned to it, the judges of the program shall have all the powers to impose sanctions authorized by law, including the power to dismiss actions or strike pleadings, if it appears that less severe sanctions would not be effective after taking into account the effect of previous sanctions or previous lack of compliance in the case. Judges are encouraged to impose sanctions to achieve the purposes of this article.

(e) This section shall cease to be operative on July 1, 1992. *(Added by Stats.1990, c. 1232 (A.B.3820), § 3.)*

Inoperative Date

This section became inoperative July 1, 1992, by its own terms.

Research References

Rutter, Cal. Practice Guide: Civ. Pro. Before Trial Ch. 12(I)-B, B. Case Management ("Fast Track") System.
Rutter, Cal. Practice Guide: Personal Injury Ch. 9-A, A. Assignment to Trial.
2 Witkin Cal. Proc. 5th Courts § 264, in General.
2 Witkin Cal. Proc. 5th Courts § 265, Sanctions Proper.
7 Witkin Cal. Proc. 5th Trial § 63, (S 63) Imposition of Ultimate Sanction in First Instance.

§ 68609.5. Uninsured motorist

Each court and the Judicial Council, under subdivision (b) of Section 68619, shall adopt rules to allow for the arbitration of cases designated by the court as "Uninsured Motorist" in which an action is filed against a defendant who is an uninsured motorist and the plaintiff's claim is subject to an arbitration provision. *(Added by Stats.1990, c. 1232 (A.B.3820), § 3.)*

Research References

Rutter, Cal. Practice Guide: Civ. Pro. Before Trial Ch. 12(I)-B, B. Case Management ("Fast Track") System.
Rutter, Cal. Practice Guide: Personal Injury Ch. 7-J, J. Arbitration of Uninsured Motorist Claims.
2 Witkin Cal. Proc. 5th Courts § 259, (S 259) Local Standards and Procedure.

§ 68610. Training judges; program

The Judicial Council, in conjunction with other interested groups as it determines appropriate, may prepare and administer a program, consistent with the policies and requirements of this article, for the training of judges in administering the delay reduction program. *(Added by Stats.1990, c. 1232 (A.B.3820), § 3.)*

§ 68612. Procedures, standards, and policies; development and publication; Rules of Court requirements

Judges shall, in consultation with the bar of the county to the maximum extent feasible develop and publish the procedures, standards, and policies which will be used in the program, including time standards for the conclusion of all critical steps in the litigation process, including discovery, and shall meet on a regular basis with the bar of the county in order to explain and publicize the program and the procedures, standards, and policies which shall govern cases assigned to the program. The procedures, standards, and policies to be used in the program shall be filed, distributed, and maintained pursuant to Section 68071 and the California Rules of Court, and shall also be published for general distribution. In its discretion, the Judicial Council may assist in the development of, or may develop and adopt, any or all of such procedures, standards, or policies on a statewide basis. *(Added by Stats.1990, c. 1232 (A.B.3820), § 3.)*

Research References

Rutter, Cal. Practice Guide: Civ. Pro. Before Trial Ch. 12(I)-B, B. Case Management ("Fast Track") System.
Rutter, Cal. Practice Guide: Civil Trials & Evidence Ch. 1-L, L. Assignment to Trial Department.
Rutter, Cal. Practice Guide: Civil Trials & Evidence Ch. 4-A, A. General Considerations.

Rutter, Cal. Practice Guide: Personal Injury Ch. 8-A, A. Case Management.
2 Witkin Cal. Proc. 5th Courts § 145, Exception: Local Delay Reduction Rule.
2 Witkin Cal. Proc. 5th Courts § 259, (S 259) Local Standards and Procedure.
2 Witkin Cal. Proc. 5th Courts § 264, in General.
7 Witkin Cal. Proc. 5th Trial § 38, (S 38) Trial Court Delay Reduction Act.
7 Witkin Cal. Proc. 5th Trial § 69, (S 69) Party Over Age 70.

§ 68613. Funds; receipt and expenditure

The Judicial Council may receive and expend on the programs established by this article any funds available from county, state, or federal government or other sources which may be available for such purposes. *(Added by Stats.1990, c. 1232 (A.B.3820), § 3.)*

§ 68614. Scope of article; judges not part of exemplary delay reduction program

Nothing in this article is intended to prevent a presiding judge from directing the use of the methods of delay reduction specified in Section 68607 by judges who are not part of an exemplary delay reduction program.

This section shall cease to be operative on July 1, 1992. *(Added by Stats.1990, c. 1232 (A.B.3820), § 3.)*

Inoperative Date

This section became inoperative July 1, 1992, by its own terms.

§ 68615. Judicial council; contracting out for performance of duties

In its discretion, the Judicial Council may contract out for performance of any of the duties imposed by this article. *(Added by Stats.1990, c. 1232 (A.B.3820), § 3.)*

§ 68616. Minimum time periods for certain actions

Delay reduction rules shall not require shorter time periods than as follows:

(a) Service of the complaint within 60 days after filing. Exceptions, for longer periods of time, (1) may be granted as authorized by local rule, and (2) shall be granted on a showing that service could not reasonably be achieved within the time required with the exercise of due diligence, consistent with the amount in controversy.

(b) Service of responsive pleadings within 30 days after service of the complaint. The parties may stipulate to an additional 15 days. Exceptions, for longer periods of time, may be granted as authorized by local rule.

(c) Time for service of notice or other paper under Sections 1005 and 1013 of the Code of Civil Procedure, and time to plead after service of summons under Section 412.20 of the Code of Civil Procedure, shall not be shortened, except as provided in those sections.

(d) Within 30 days of service of the responsive pleadings, the parties may, by stipulation filed with the court, agree to a single continuance not to exceed 30 days.

It is the intent of the Legislature that these stipulations not detract from the efforts of the courts to comply with standards of timely disposition. To this extent, the Judicial Council shall develop statistics that distinguish between cases involving, and not involving, these stipulations.

(e) A status conference, or similar event, other than a challenge to the jurisdiction of the court, shall not be required to be conducted sooner than 30 days after service of the first responsive pleadings, or 30 days after expiration of a stipulated continuance, if any, pursuant to subdivision (d).

(f) Title 4 (commencing with Section 2016.010) of Part 4 of the Code of Civil Procedure shall govern discovery, except in arbitration proceedings.

(g) A case shall not be referred to arbitration prior to 210 days after the filing of the complaint, exclusive of the stipulated period provided for in subdivision (d). Any rule adopted pursuant to this article shall not contravene Sections 638 and 639 of the Code of Civil Procedure.

(h) Unnamed (DOE) defendants shall not be dismissed or severed prior to the conclusion of the introduction of evidence at trial, except upon stipulation or motion of the parties. *(Added by Stats.1999, c. 67 (A.B.1105), § 10, eff. July 6, 1999, operative Jan. 1, 2004. Amended by Stats.2004, c. 182 (A.B.3081), § 46, operative July 1, 2005; Stats.2007, c. 146 (A.B.1264), § 1; Stats.2010, c. 131 (A.B.1894), § 2.)*

Law Revision Commission Comments

Subdivision (f) of Section 68616 is amended to reflect nonsubstantive reorganization of the rules governing civil discovery. [33 Cal.L.Rev. Comm. Reports 1039 (2004)].

Research References

Rutter, Cal. Practice Guide: A.D.R. Ch. 4-C, C. Statutorily-Mandated Court Mediation Programs.
Rutter, Cal. Practice Guide: Civ. Pro. Before Trial Ch. 4-D, D. Service of Summons.
Rutter, Cal. Practice Guide: Civ. Pro. Before Trial Ch. 5-B, B. Entry of Default.
Rutter, Cal. Practice Guide: Civ. Pro. Before Trial Ch. 13-A, A. Introduction.
Rutter, Cal. Practice Guide: Civ. Pro. Before Trial Ch. 8E-2, When Depositions May be Taken.
Rutter, Cal. Practice Guide: Civ. Pro. Before Trial Ch. 12(I)-B, B. Case Management ("Fast Track") System.
Rutter, Cal. Practice Guide: Civil Trials & Evidence Ch. 1-K, K. Continuance Motions.
Rutter, Cal. Practice Guide: Civil Trials & Evidence Ch. 4-A, A. General Considerations.
Rutter, Cal. Practice Guide: Civil Trials & Evidence Ch. 4-B, B. Preliminary Matters Discussed in Final Status Conference or In-Chambers Conference.
Rutter, Cal. Practice Guide: Personal Injury Ch. 1-B, B. Initial Evaluation of Case: Decision to Accept or Reject Employment or Undertake Further Evaluation of Claim.
Rutter, Cal. Practice Guide: Personal Injury Ch. 7-A, A. Introduction-Nature and Purpose of "Judicial Arbitration" in General.
Rutter, Cal. Practice Guide: Personal Injury Ch. 7-B, B. Tactical Considerations-Pros and Cons of Judicial Arbitration.
Rutter, Cal. Practice Guide: Personal Injury Ch. 7-G, G. Arbitration Hearing.
Rutter, Cal. Practice Guide: Personal Injury Ch. 8-A, A. Case Management.
2 Witkin Cal. Proc. 5th Courts § 142, 10-Day/5-Day Rule.
2 Witkin Cal. Proc. 5th Courts § 146, Codification.
2 Witkin Cal. Proc. 5th Courts § 262, Minimum Time Standards.
6 Witkin Cal. Proc. 5th Proceedings Without Trial § 586, on Order of Court.
7 Witkin Cal. Proc. 5th Trial § 36, (S 36) Stipulation.
7 Witkin Cal. Proc. 5th Trial § 38, (S 38) Trial Court Delay Reduction Act.
7 Witkin Cal. Proc. 5th Trial § 45, Current Procedure.

§ 68617.   Centers for complex litigation report; contents

On or before October 30, 2002, the Judicial Council shall submit a report to the Legislature and the Governor regarding the effectiveness of the Centers for Complex Litigation established pursuant to the Budget Act of 1999. The report shall examine, among other things, the number of complex cases filed, the impact of the centers on case and calendar management, and the impact on the trial courts, the attorneys, and the parties, and

shall make recommendations to the Legislature and the Governor. *(Added by Stats.1999, c. 67 (A.B.1105), § 11, eff. July 6, 1999.)*

§ 68619.   Judicial council; local rules; review and recommendations; uniform delay reduction rules; adoption

(a) The Judicial Council shall review all local delay reduction rules adopted by courts and any revisions or new rules adopted by them and make recommendations to the courts of revisions so that these rules are consistent, to the extent desirable, with other court rules.

(b) The Judicial Council shall adopt uniform delay reduction rules which shall apply to any court that adopts a delay reduction program pursuant to Section 68618.

This subdivision shall cease to be operative on July 1, 1992. *(Added by Stats.1990, c. 1232 (A.B.3820), § 3.)*

§ 68620.   Delay reduction program for limited civil cases; establishment; actions and proceedings; discovery

(a) Each superior court shall establish a delay reduction program for limited civil cases in consultation with the local bar that is consistent with the provisions of this article. In its discretion, the Judicial Council may assist in the development of, or may develop and adopt, any or all procedures, standards, or policies for a delay reduction program for limited civil cases in superior courts on a statewide basis which are consistent with the provisions of the Trial Court Delay Reduction Act.

(b) Actions and proceedings subject to the provisions of Chapter 5.5 (commencing with Section 116.110) of Title 1 of Part 1 of the Code of Civil Procedure or provisions of Chapter 4 (commencing with Section 1159) of Title 3 of Part 3 of the Code of Civil Procedure may not be assigned to or governed by the provisions of any delay reduction program established pursuant to this section.

(c) It is the intent of the Legislature that the civil discovery in actions and proceedings subject to a program established pursuant to Article 2 (commencing with Section 90) of Chapter 5.1 of Title 1 of Part 1 of the Code of Civil Procedure shall be governed by the times and procedures specified in that article. Civil discovery in these actions and proceedings is not affected by the provisions of any delay reduction program adopted pursuant to this section. *(Added by Stats.1991, c. 90 (A.B.1297), § 12, eff. June 30, 1991. Amended by Stats.1991, c. 189 (A.B.544), § 8.5, eff. July 29, 1991; Stats.1994, c. 587 (A.B.3600), § 11; Stats.1998, c. 931 (S.B.2139), § 247, eff. Sept. 28, 1998; Stats.2002, c. 784 (S.B.1316), § 223; Stats.2003, c. 62 (S.B.600), § 163; Stats.2003, c. 149 (S.B.79), § 28.)*

Law Revision Commission Comments

Section 68620 is amended to reflect elimination of the justice court. Cal. Const. art. VI, §§ 1, 5(b). [28 Cal.L.Rev.Comm. Reports 51 (1998)].

Subdivision (a) of Section 68620 is amended to reflect unification of the municipal and superior courts pursuant to Article VI, Section 5(e), of the California Constitution. See Code Civ. Proc. § 85 (limited civil cases) & Comment. [32 Cal.L.Rev.Comm. Reports 246 (2002)].

Subdivision (c) of Section 68620 is amended to correct the reference to former Chapter 5. [33 Cal.L.Rev.Comm. Reports 208 (2003)].

Research References

Rutter, Cal. Practice Guide: Civ. Pro. Before Trial Ch. 12(I)-B, B. Case Management ("Fast Track") System.
2 Witkin Cal. Proc. 5th Courts § 257, (S 257) Nature and Scope.

Government

7 Witkin Cal. Proc. 5th Trial § 38, (S 38) Trial Court Delay Reduction
Act.

CHAPTER 3.   THE SUPREME COURT

ARTICLE 2.   THE CHIEF CLERK

Section
68847.   Fees; collection.

§ 68847.   Fees; collection

The Clerk of the Supreme Court shall collect in advance the
fees specified in Article 4 (commencing with Section 68926) of
this chapter.   *(Added by Stats.1953, c. 206, p. 1246, § 1.
Amended by Stats.1963, c. 873, p. 2121, § 1.)*

ARTICLE 3.5.   TRANSFER OF CASES APPEALED TO THE SUPREME COURT AND COURTS OF APPEAL

Section
68915.   Appeals not taken to proper court.

§ 68915.   Appeals not taken to proper court

No appeal taken to the Supreme Court or to a court of appeal
shall be dismissed for the reason only that the same was not
taken to the proper court, but the cause shall be transferred to
the proper court upon such terms as to costs or otherwise as may
be just, and shall be proceeded with therein, as if regularly
appealed thereto.   *(Added by Stats.1966, 1st Ex.Sess., c. 161, p.
716, § 18, operative Nov. 8, 1966.)*

ARTICLE 4.   FEES IN THE SUPREME COURT AND COURTS OF APPEAL

Section
68926.   Notice of appeal, petition for writ, or first document;
            rules governing time and method of payment.
68926.1.   Notice of appeal; deposit by applicant; forfeitures;
            additional fees.
68926.3.   Deposit of fees collected in court of appeal civil
            cases to California State Law Library Special
            Account; use of moneys deposited.
68927.   Petition for review in a civil case after decision in a
            court of appeal; first document.
68928.   Copies of records or documents; waiver.
68929.   Comparing documents.
68930.   Certificate under seal.
68931.   Administering oaths for verification of claims
            against state.
68932.   Other services.
68933.   Appellate Court Trust Fund; establishment; appor-
            tionment; deposits; investment.

§ 68926.   Notice of appeal, petition for writ, or first document; rules governing time and method of payment

(a)(1) The fee for filing a notice of appeal in a civil case
appealed to a court of appeal is six hundred five dollars ($605).

(2) The fee for filing a petition for a writ within the original
civil jurisdiction of the Supreme Court is five hundred forty
dollars ($540).

(3) The fee for filing a petition for a writ within the original
civil jurisdiction of a court of appeal is six hundred five dollars
($605).

(b)(1) The fee for a party other than appellant filing its first
document in a civil case appealed to a court of appeal is three
hundred ninety dollars ($390).

(2) The fee for a party other than petitioner filing its first
document in a writ proceeding within the original jurisdiction of
the Supreme Court is three hundred ninety dollars ($390).

(3) The fee for a party other than petitioner filing its first
document in a writ proceeding within the original jurisdiction of
a court of appeal is three hundred ninety dollars ($390).

(c) These fees are in full, for all services, through the
rendering of the judgment or the issuing of the remittitur or
peremptory writ, except the fees imposed by subdivision (b) of
Section 68926.1 and Section 68927.   The Judicial Council may
make rules governing the time and method of payment of these
fees, and providing for excuse therefrom in appropriate cases.
A fee may not be charged in appeals from, nor petitions for writs
involving, juvenile cases or proceedings to declare a minor free
from parental custody or control, or proceedings under the
Lanterman–Petris–Short Act (Part 1 (commencing with Section
5000) of Division 5 of the Welfare and Institutions Code).
*(Added by Stats.1963, c. 873, p. 2121, § 3.   Amended by
Stats.1967, c. 17, p. 842, § 68; Stats.1975, c. 986, § 1; Stats.1982,
c. 327, p. 1459, § 91, eff. June 30, 1982; Stats.1986, c. 823, § 1.2;
Stats.1992, c. 1149 (A.B.3692), § 2, eff. Sept. 30, 1992; Stats.1999,
c. 78 (A.B.1115), § 55, eff. July 7, 1999; Stats.2003, c. 159
(A.B.1759), § 15, eff. Aug. 2, 2003, operative Aug. 17, 2003;
Stats.2004, c. 811 (A.B.3079), § 8; Stats.2011, c. 193 (A.B.110),
§ 2, eff. Aug. 30, 2011; Stats.2012, c. 41 (S.B.1021), § 24, eff.
June 27, 2012.)*

Research References

Rutter, Cal. Practice Guide: Civil Appeals & Writs Ch. 3-E, E. Filing
    Steps.
Rutter, Cal. Practice Guide: Civil Appeals & Writs Ch. 5-C, C. Motion,
    Application and Request Procedures.
Rutter, Cal. Practice Guide: Civil Appeals & Writs Ch. 9-D, D.
    Procedural Rules.
Rutter, Cal. Practice Guide: Civil Appeals & Writs Ch. 15-E, E.
    Procedures on Writ Review.
Rutter, Cal. Practice Guide: Civil Appeals & Writs Gen. Matls., High-
    lights.
Rutter, Cal. Practice Guide: Family Law Gen. Matls, Highlights.
3 Witkin Cal. Proc. 5th Actions § 429C, (New)-Costs Excused.
9 Witkin Cal. Proc. 5th Appeal § 12, Serve and File.
9 Witkin Cal. Proc. 5th Appeal § 16A, (New)-Waiver of Fees and Costs.
9 Witkin Cal. Proc. 5th Appeal § 556, (S 556) Payment of Fees.
2 Witkin Cal. Proc. 5th Courts § 180, Court Fees.
10 Witkin, California Summary 10th Parent and Child § 709, in General.
10 Witkin, California Summary 10th Parent and Child § 716, (S 716) in
    General.
10 Witkin, California Summary 10th Parent and Child § 918, in General.
10 Witkin, California Summary 10th Parent and Child § 920, (S 920)
    Review by Extraordinary Writ.
11 Witkin, California Summary 10th Husband and Wife § 123, Certifica-
    tion Procedure for Bifurcated Issues.

§ 68926.1.   Notice of appeal; deposit by applicant; forfeitures; additional fees

(a)(1) Upon filing a notice of appeal for which a fee is paid
pursuant to Section 68926, the appellant shall deposit the sum of
one hundred dollars ($100) with the clerk of the originating
court.   The deposit shall be credited against the amount
chargeable for the preparation of the clerk's transcript or any
other appeal processing or notification.

(2) The deposit shall be forfeited in the event of abandonment or dismissal of appeal prior to filing of the record in the
reviewing court.

(3) The amount charged for preparation of the transcript or any deposit that is forfeited shall be distributed to the court in which it was collected.

(b) Upon filing a notice of appeal, a petition for a writ, or a petition for a hearing for which a fee is paid pursuant to subdivision (a) of Section 68926 or subdivision (a) of Section 68927, the appellant shall pay an additional fee in the amount of one hundred seventy dollars ($170). Upon filing its first document for which a fee is paid pursuant to subdivision (b) of Section 68926 or subdivision (b) of Section 68927, a party other than the appellant or petitioner is not required to pay this additional fee. The fees collected pursuant to this subdivision shall be transmitted to the State Treasury for deposit in the Appellate Court Trust Fund. *(Added by Stats.1983, c. 493, § 1. Amended by Stats.1993, c. 158 (A.B.392), § 15, eff. July 21, 1993; Stats.2003, c. 159 (A.B.1759), § 16, eff. Aug. 2, 2003, operative Aug. 17, 2003; Stats.2005, c. 75 (A.B.145), § 114, eff. July 19, 2005, operative Jan. 1, 2006; Stats.2011, c. 193 (A.B.110), § 3, eff. Aug. 30, 2011.)*

Research References

Rutter, Cal. Practice Guide: Civil Appeals & Writs Ch. 3-E, E. Filing Steps.

Rutter, Cal. Practice Guide: Civil Appeals & Writs Ch. 4-C, C. Record Preparation Procedure.

Rutter, Cal. Practice Guide: Civil Appeals & Writs Ch. 5-B, B. Types of Motions, Applications and Requests.

Rutter, Cal. Practice Guide: Civil Appeals & Writs Ch. 13-B, B. Petition for Review Procedures.

Rutter, Cal. Practice Guide: Civil Appeals & Writs Ch. 15-E, E. Procedures on Writ Review.

Rutter, Cal. Practice Guide: Civil Appeals & Writs Gen. Matls., Highlights.

3 Witkin Cal. Proc. 5th Actions § 429C, (New)-Costs Excused.

9 Witkin Cal. Proc. 5th Appeal § 556, (S 556) Payment of Fees.

9 Witkin Cal. Proc. 5th Appeal § 557, (S 557) Effect of Nonpayment.

9 Witkin Cal. Proc. 5th Appeal § 649, (S 649) Cost and Preparation.

11 Witkin, California Summary 10th Husband and Wife § 123, Certification Procedure for Bifurcated Issues.

§ 68926.3. Deposit of fees collected in court of appeal civil cases to California State Law Library Special Account; use of moneys deposited

(a) Notwithstanding any other provision of law, sixty-five dollars ($65) of each fee collected in a civil case by the clerk of each court of appeal pursuant to subdivision (a) of Section 68926 shall be paid into the State Treasury for deposit in a special account in the General Fund to be known as the California State Law Library Special Account, which account is hereby established.

(b) Moneys deposited in the California State Law Library Special Account shall be available for the support of the California State Law Library upon appropriation thereto by the Legislature in the annual Budget Act.

(c) This section shall remain in effect only until January 1, 2015, and as of that date, is repealed, unless a later statute that is enacted before that date extends or repeals that date. *(Added by Stats.1992, c. 1149 (A.B.3692), § 3, eff. Sept. 30, 1992. Amended by Stats.1994, c. 234 (S.B.1865), § 1; Stats.1999, c. 78 (A.B.1115), § 56, eff. July 7, 1999; Stats.2004, c. 216 (S.B.1108), § 27, eff. Aug. 11, 2004; Stats.2009, c. 187 (S.B.511), § 10; Stats.2011, c. 193 (A.B.110), § 4, eff. Aug. 30, 2011.)*

Repeal

For repeal of this section, see its terms.

§ 68927. Petition for review in a civil case after decision in a court of appeal; first document

(a) The fee for filing a petition for review in a civil case in the Supreme Court after a decision in a court of appeal is five hundred forty dollars ($540).

(b) The fee for a party other than petitioner filing its first document in a civil case in the Supreme Court after a decision in a court of appeal is three hundred ninety dollars ($390).

(c) A fee may not be charged for petitions for review from decisions in juvenile cases or proceedings to declare a minor free from parental custody or control or proceedings under the Lanterman–Petris–Short Act (Part 1 (commencing with Section 5000) of Division 5 of the Welfare and Institutions Code). *(Added by Stats.1963, c. 873, p. 2121, § 3. Amended by Stats.1967, c. 17, p. 842, § 69; Stats.1982, c. 327, p. 1459, § 92, eff. June 30, 1982; Stats.2003, c. 159 (A.B.1759), § 17, eff. Aug. 2, 2003, operative Aug. 17, 2003; Stats.2004, c. 811 (A.B.3079), § 9; Stats.2005, c. 22 (S.B.1108), § 107; Stats.2011, c. 193 (A.B.110), § 5, eff. Aug. 30, 2011; Stats.2012, c. 41 (S.B.1021), § 25, eff. June 27, 2012.)*

Research References

Rutter, Cal. Practice Guide: Civil Appeals & Writs Ch. 13-B, B. Petition for Review Procedures.

Rutter, Cal. Practice Guide: Civil Appeals & Writs Ch. 13-C, C. Briefs on the Merits After Grant of Review.

3 Witkin Cal. Proc. 5th Actions § 429C, (New)-Costs Excused.

9 Witkin Cal. Proc. 5th Appeal § 12, Serve and File.

9 Witkin Cal. Proc. 5th Appeal § 16A, (New)-Waiver of Fees and Costs.

§ 68928. Copies of records or documents; waiver

The fee for copies of any record or document in the office of the Clerk of the Supreme Court or the clerk of a court of appeal is the prevailing commercial rate as determined by the clerk. The Supreme Court and each court of appeal may waive the charge for copies of opinions furnished to parties to the litigation and other interested persons. *(Added by Stats.1963, c. 873, p. 2121, § 3. Amended by Stats.1967, c. 17, p. 842, § 70.)*

§ 68929. Comparing documents

The fee for comparing any document requiring a certificate is five cents ($0.05) a folio, except that when the document to be compared was printed or typewritten from the same type or at the same time as the original on file and has been corrected in all respects to conform with it, such charge shall be one cent ($0.01) a folio. Such fee is in addition to the fee for the certificate. *(Added by Stats.1963, c. 873, p. 2121, § 3.)*

§ 68930. Certificate under seal

The fee for each certificate under seal is one dollar ($1). *(Added by Stats.1963, c. 873, p. 2121, § 3.)*

§ 68931. Administering oaths for verification of claims against state

There shall be no fee for administering oaths for verification of claims against the State. *(Added by Stats.1963, c. 873, p. 2121, § 3.)*

§ 68932. Other services

For all other services not specified in this article the fee shall be the same as that prescribed by law for similar services by notaries public. *(Added by Stats.1963, c. 873, p. 2121, § 3.)*

§ 68933. Appellate Court Trust Fund; establishment; apportionment; deposits; investment

(a) There is hereby established the Appellate Court Trust Fund, the proceeds of which shall be used for the purpose of funding the courts of appeal and the Supreme Court.

(b) The fund, upon appropriation by the Legislature, shall be apportioned by the Judicial Council to the courts of appeal and the Supreme Court as determined by the Judicial Council, taking into consideration all other funds available to each court and the needs of each court, in a manner that promotes equal access to the courts, ensures the ability of the courts to carry out their functions, and promotes implementation of statewide policies.

(c) Notwithstanding any other provision of law, the fees listed in subdivision (d) shall all be transmitted for deposit in the Appellate Court Trust Fund within the State Treasury.

(d) This section applies to all fees collected pursuant to Section 68926, excluding that portion subject to Section 68926.3; subdivision (b) of Section 68926.1; and Sections 68927, 68928, 68929, 68930, and 68932.

(e) The Appellate Court Trust Fund shall be invested in the Surplus Money Investment Fund and all interest earned shall be allocated to the Appellate Court Trust Fund semiannually and used as specified in this section. *(Added by Stats.2003, c. 159 (A.B.1759), § 18, eff. Aug. 2, 2003, operative Aug. 17, 2003. Amended by Stats.2003, c. 757 (A.B.296), § 6.)*

Research References

Rutter, Cal. Practice Guide: Civil Appeals & Writs Ch. 3-E, E. Filing Steps.
Rutter, Cal. Practice Guide: Civil Appeals & Writs Ch. 13-B, B. Petition for Review Procedures.
Rutter, Cal. Practice Guide: Civil Appeals & Writs Ch. 15-E, E. Procedures on Writ Review.

CHAPTER 5. THE SUPERIOR COURTS

ARTICLE 9. OFFICIAL REPORTERS GENERALLY

§ 69947. Fees

Except in counties where a statute provides otherwise, the official reporter shall receive for his services the fees prescribed in this article. *(Added by Stats.1953, c. 206, p. 1265, § 1.)*

Research References

2 Witkin Cal. Proc. 5th Courts § 180, Court Fees.
2 Witkin Cal. Proc. 5th Courts § 384, Fees in Civil Cases.

§ 69948. Fees

(a) The fee for reporting testimony and proceedings in contested cases is fifty-five dollars ($55) a day, or any fractional part thereof.

(b) In San Joaquin County, the compensation for superior court reporters shall be that prescribed by Section 69993.

(c) In Madera County, the board of supervisors may, by ordinance or resolution, prescribe a higher rate of compensation for superior court reporters.

(d) In Kings County, the fee for reporting testimony and proceedings in contested cases is one hundred forty dollars ($140) a day, or any fractional part thereof.

(e) In Mariposa County, the board of supervisors may, by ordinance or resolution, prescribe the rate of compensation for superior court reporters.

(f) In Siskiyou County, the board of supervisors may, by ordinance, prescribe a higher rate of compensation for superior court reporters.

(g) In Yuba County, the board of supervisors may, by ordinance or resolution, prescribe a higher rate of compensation for superior court reporters.

(h) In Butte County, pro tempore reporters shall receive a fee of seventy-five dollars ($75) a day, or any fractional part thereof, for reporting testimony and proceedings in contested cases.

(i) In Sutter County, except as may otherwise be provided in Sections 70045.11 and 74839, the fee for reporting testimony and proceedings in contested cases is one hundred ten dollars ($110) per day, or any fractional part thereof. However, the board of supervisors may, by ordinance, prescribe a higher rate of compensation for superior court reporters.

(j) In Napa County, the board of supervisors may, by ordinance, prescribe a higher rate of compensation for superior court reporters.

(k) In Tehama County, the board of supervisors may, by ordinance, prescribe a higher rate of compensation for superior court reporters.

(*l*) In Monterey County, the fee for reporting testimony and proceedings in contested cases in any court is seventy-five dollars ($75) a day or any fractional part thereof.

(m) In Nevada County, the board of supervisors may, by ordinance, prescribe a higher rate of compensation for superior court reporters.

(n) In Calaveras County, the fee for reporting testimony and proceedings in contested cases is seventy-five dollars ($75) per day, or any fractional part thereof. However, the board of supervisors may, by ordinance, prescribe a higher rate of compensation for superior court reporters.

(o) In Placer County, the board of supervisors may, by ordinance, prescribe a higher rate of compensation for superior court reporters.

(p) In Sierra County, the board of supervisors may, by ordinance, prescribe a higher rate of compensation for superior court reporters.

(q) In Trinity County, the board of supervisors may, by ordinance, prescribe a higher rate of compensation for superior court reporters.

(r) In Humboldt County, the fee for reporting testimony and proceedings in contested cases is seventy-five dollars ($75) per day, or any fractional part thereof.

(s) In Del Norte County, the fee for reporting testimony and proceedings in contested cases is seventy-five dollars ($75) per day, or any fractional part thereof.

(t) In Alpine County, the board of supervisors may, by ordinance, prescribe a higher rate of compensation for superior court reporters.

(u) In Glenn County, the board of supervisors may, by ordinance, prescribe a higher rate of compensation for superior court reporters.

(v) In Colusa County, the fee for reporting testimony and proceedings in contested cases is one hundred twenty-five dollars ($125) per day, or any fractional part thereof.

(w) In Shasta County, the board of supervisors may prescribe a higher rate of compensation for superior court reporters.

(x) In Solano County, the fee for reporting testimony and proceedings in contested cases is ninety dollars ($90) per day, or fifty-five dollars ($55) per half day or fractional part thereof. However, the board of supervisors may, by ordinance, prescribe a higher rate of compensation for superior court reporters.

(y) In Inyo County, the board of supervisors may, by ordinance, prescribe a higher rate of compensation for superior court reporters.

(z) In Mono County, the board of supervisors may, by ordinance, prescribe a higher rate of compensation for superior court reporters. *(Added by Stats.1953, c. 206, p. 1265, § 1. Amended by Stats.1955, c. 1303, p. 2371, § 1; Stats.1961, c. 2061, p. 4288, § 1; Stats.1967, c. 653, p. 2010, § 1; Stats.1970, c. 614, p. 1200, § 1; Stats.1975, c. 330, § 1; Stats.1976, c. 1460, § 2; Stats.1977, c. 224, p. 1021, § 2, eff. July 5, 1977; Stats.1977, c. 905, p. 2766, § 2; Stats.1978, c. 179, p. 410, § 2, eff. June 1, 1978; Stats.1980, c. 79, p. 199, § 2; Stats.1980, c. 1361, p. 4942, § 4; Stats.1981, c. 499, p. 1851, § 1; Stats.1982, c. 307, p. 972, § 1, eff. June 28, 1982; Stats.1982, c. 1033, p. 3766, § 2; Stats.1983, c. 363, § 1, eff. July 25, 1983; Stats.1983, c. 1253, § 3; Stats.1985, c. 370, § 1; Stats.1985, c. 1374, § 1, eff. Oct. 1, 1985; Stats.1986, c. 15, § 1, eff. March 11, 1986; Stats.1986, c. 1418, § 5; Stats.1987, c. 641, § 1, eff. Sept. 15, 1987; Stats.1987, c. 749, § 1; Stats.1988, c. 3, § 1, eff. Jan. 26, 1988; Stats.1989, c. 670, § 1, eff. Sept. 22, 1989; Stats.1989, c. 703, § 2; Stats.1990, c. 1447 (S.B.1818), § 1.)*

Research References

2 Witkin Cal. Proc. 5th Courts § 384, Fees in Civil Cases.

§ 69948.5. Superior court in Modoc County; fees for reporter

Notwithstanding Section 69948, in Modoc County, the board of supervisors may, by ordinance, prescribe a higher rate of compensation for superior court reporters. *(Added by Stats. 1983, c. 230, § 1.)*

§ 69949. Defaults; fee

The fee for reporting each default or uncontested action or proceeding is ten dollars ($10). If more than four defaults or uncontested matters are reported in any one day, or two or more defaults are reported in conjunction with any contested case, the fee is forty-five dollars ($45) a day, or any fractional part thereof. *(Added by Stats.1953, c. 206, p. 1265, § 1. Amended by Stats.1961, c. 2061, p. 4288, § 2; Stats.1967, c. 653, p. 2010, § 1.3.)*

Research References

2 Witkin Cal. Proc. 5th Courts § 384, Fees in Civil Cases.

§ 69950. Transcription fees

(a) The fee for transcription for original ribbon or printed copy is eighty-five cents ($0.85) for each 100 words, and for each copy purchased at the same time by the court, party, or other person purchasing the original, fifteen cents ($0.15) for each 100 words.

(b) The fee for a first copy to any court, party, or other person who does not simultaneously purchase the original shall be twenty cents ($0.20) for each 100 words, and for each additional copy, purchased at the same time, fifteen cents ($0.15) for each 100 words.

(c) Notwithstanding subdivisions (a) and (b), if a trial court had established transcription fees that were in effect on January 1, 2012 based on an estimate or assumption as to the number of words or folios on a typical transcript page, those transcription fees shall be the transcription fees for proceedings in those trial courts, and the policy or practice for determining transcription fees in those trial courts shall not be unilaterally changed. *(Added by Stats.1953, c. 206, p. 1266, § 1. Amended by Stats.1961, c. 2220, p. 4576, § 1; Stats.1967, c. 1668, p. 4188, § 1; Stats.1972, c. 537, p. 928, § 1; Stats.1980, c. 1350, p. 4784, § 16; Stats.1986, c. 373, § 2; Stats.1986, c. 529, § 13, eff. July 28, 1986; Stats.1987, c. 56, § 95; Stats.1990, c. 505 (S.B.2376), § 11; Stats.2002, c. 71 (S.B.1371), § 4; Stats.2012, c. 41 (S.B.1021), § 37, eff. June 27, 2012.)*

Law Revision Commission Comments

Section 69950 is amended to conform to the rule that a nonparty is generally entitled to obtain a transcript. See Code Civ. Proc. § 269 & Comment.

The section is also amended to reflect changes in technology. When the provision was first enacted, carbon paper was still in use and it was routine to create a copy at the same time as the original. Now the original typically is made first, then copied.

The section is further amended to specify the fee where the person who purchases the original subsequently (as opposed to simultaneously) purchases a copy. [31 Cal.L.Rev.Comm. Reports 240 (2002)].

Research References

2 Witkin Cal. Proc. 5th Courts § 384, Fees in Civil Cases.
8 Witkin Cal. Proc. 5th Extraordinary Writs § 314, in General.

§ 69951. Transcription; daily copy service; fee

For transcription, in civil cases, the reporter may charge an additional 50 percent for special daily copy service. *(Added by Stats.1953, c. 206, p. 1266, § 1.)*

Research References

2 Witkin Cal. Proc. 5th Courts § 384, Fees in Civil Cases.

§ 69952. Verbatim record; payment from county treasury; fees

(a) The court may specifically direct the making of a verbatim record and payment therefor shall be from the county treasury on order of the court in the following cases:

(1) Criminal matters.

(2) Juvenile proceedings.

(3) Proceedings to declare a minor free from custody.

(4) Proceedings under the Lanterman–Petris–Short Act, (Part 1 (commencing with Section 5000) of Division 5 of the Welfare and Institutions Code).

(5) As otherwise provided by law.

(b) Except as otherwise authorized by law, the court shall not order to be transcribed and paid for out of the county treasury any matter or material except that reported by the reporter pursuant to Section 269 of the Code of Civil Procedure. When there is no official reporter in attendance and a reporter pro tempore is appointed, his or her reasonable expenses for traveling and detention shall be fixed and allowed by the court and paid in like manner. When the court orders a daily transcript, necessitating the services of two phonographic reporters, the reporting fee for each of the reporters and the transcript fee shall be proper charges against the county treasury, and the daily transcript shall be pursuant to Section 269 of the Code of Civil Procedure. When the daily transcript is prepared by a single reporter, an additional fee for technological services, as set by the court with the agreement of the reporter, may be imposed. However, the total of the fee for a single reporter and the fee for technological services shall be less than the total fee for two reporters. *(Added by Stats.1953, c. 206, p. 1266, § 1. Amended by Stats.1965, c. 2053, p. 4791, § 2; Stats.1985, c. 1391, § 1; Stats.1986, c. 823, § 2.)*

Research References

2 Witkin Cal. Proc. 5th Courts § 386, Free Transcript in Criminal and Specified Civil Proceedings.

7 Witkin Cal. Proc. 5th Judgment § 135, (S 135) Reporter's Fees.

§ 69953. Verbatim record not made at public expense; payment by parties

In any case where a verbatim record is not made at public expense pursuant to Section 69952 or other provisions of law, the cost of making any verbatim record shall be paid by the parties in equal proportion; and either party at his option may pay the whole. In either case, all amounts so paid by the party to whom costs are awarded shall be taxed as costs in the case. The fees for transcripts and copies ordered by the parties shall be paid by the party ordering them. Except as provided in Section 69952, no reporter shall perform any service in a civil action other than transcriptions until his fee for it has been deposited with the clerk of the court or with the reporter. *(Added by Stats.1953, c. 206, p. 1266, § 1. Amended by Stats.1961, c. 2062, p. 4289, § 3; Stats.1986, c. 823, § 3.)*

Research References

Rutter, Cal. Practice Guide: Personal Injury Ch. 9-M, M. Verdicts and Judgment.

2 Witkin Cal. Proc. 5th Courts § 385, Advance Payment in Civil Cases.

7 Witkin Cal. Proc. 5th Judgment § 135, (S 135) Reporter's Fees.

§ 69953.5. Request for daily transcript requiring services of reporter; fee per day; distribution of fee

Notwithstanding any other provision of law, whenever a daily transcript is ordered in a civil case requiring the services of more than one phonographic reporter, the party requesting the daily transcript, in addition to any other required fee, shall pay a fee per day, or portion thereof, equal to the per diem rate for pro tempore reporters established by statute, local rule, or ordinance for the services of each additional reporter for the first day and each subsequent day the additional reporters are required. This fee shall be distributed to the court in which it was collected to offset the cost of the additional reporter. *(Added by Stats.1986, c. 675, § 1. Amended by Stats.2005, c. 75 (A.B.145), § 116, eff. July 19, 2005, operative Jan. 1, 2006.)*

Research References

2 Witkin Cal. Proc. 5th Courts § 384, Fees in Civil Cases.

§ 69954. Transcripts prepared with computer assistance; fees

(a) Transcripts prepared by a reporter using computer assistance and delivered on a medium other than paper shall be compensated at the same rate set for paper transcripts, except the reporter may also charge an additional fee not to exceed the cost of the medium or any copies thereof.

(b) The fee for a second copy of a transcript on appeal in computer-readable format ordered by or on behalf of a requesting party within 120 days of the filing or delivery of the original transcript shall be compensated at one-third the rate set forth for a second copy of a transcript as provided in Section 69950. A reporter may also charge an additional fee not to exceed the cost of the medium or any copies thereof.

(c) The fee for a computer-readable transcript shall be paid by the requesting court, party, or person, unless the computer-readable transcript is requested by a party in lieu of a paper transcript required to be delivered to that party by the rules of court. In that event, the fee shall be chargeable as statute or rule provides for the paper transcript.

(d) Any court, party, or person who has purchased a transcript may, without paying a further fee to the reporter, reproduce a copy or portion thereof as an exhibit pursuant to court order or rule, or for internal use, but shall not otherwise provide or sell a copy or copies to any other party or person. *(Added by Stats.1985, c. 1391, § 2. Amended by Stats.1993, c. 1016 (A.B. 1929), § 2.)*

Research References

Rutter, Cal. Practice Guide: Civil Appeals & Writs Ch. 4-C, C. Record Preparation Procedure.

Rutter, Cal. Practice Guide: Civil Appeals & Writs Ch. 4-E, E. Filing and Correction of Record.

2 Witkin Cal. Proc. 5th Courts § 384, Fees in Civil Cases.

CHAPTER 5.8. SUPERIOR COURT FEES

ARTICLE 1. CIVIL FEES GENERALLY

Section

70633.   Fees for adoption proceedings, proceedings to declare a minor free from parental custody or control, criminal actions, and service to public entities.

70640.   Filing fee surcharge for children's waiting rooms.

§ 70600. Legislative intent; citation to chapter

It is the intent of the Legislature to establish a uniform schedule of filing fees and other civil fees for the superior courts throughout the state. This chapter shall be known, and may be cited, as the Uniform Civil Fees and Standard Fee Schedule Act of 2005. *(Added by Stats.2005, c. 75 (A.B.145), § 121, eff. July 19, 2005, operative Jan. 1, 2006.)*

Research References

2 Witkin Cal. Proc. 5th Courts § 180, Court Fees.
4 Witkin Cal. Proc. 5th Pleading § 25, Basic Fees.
4 Witkin Cal. Proc. 5th Pleading § 26, Additional Fees.
6 Witkin Cal. Proc. 5th Proceedings Without Trial § 33, (S 33) General Requirements.

§ 70601. Legislative intent; moratorium on increases in filing fees; task force

(a) It is the intent of the Legislature to establish a moratorium on increases in filing fees until January 1, 2008. No fee provided for in this chapter may be changed before January 1, 2008, except as may be required by the following:

(1) Legislative implementation of recommendations of the Task Force on County Law Libraries.

(2) Legislative implementation of recommendations for changes to the graduated filing fee for petitions in probate proceedings under subdivision (a) of Section 70650.

(b) The Judicial Council shall establish a Task Force on Civil Fees, including, but not limited to, representatives from the trial courts, the counties, the county law libraries, and the State Bar. On or before February 1, 2007, the task force shall make recommendations to the Judicial Council and the Legislature on the following:

(1) The effectiveness of the uniform fee structure, any operational or revenue problems, and how to address these issues.

(2) Whether a fee differential should be implemented based on the number of cases a party files in a year.

(3) A process to adjust fees in the future to accommodate inflation and other factors affecting operating costs for trial courts, county law libraries, and county programs that rely on court fees. *(Added by Stats.2005, c. 75 (A.B.145), § 121, eff. July 19, 2005, operative Jan. 1, 2006. Amended by Stats.2005, c. 706 (A.B.1742), § 30.)*

§ 70602.5. Legislative intent to supplement certain first paper filing fees; decrease

Notwithstanding any other law, it is the intent of the Legislature to supplement certain first paper filing fees as provided below:

(a) A supplemental fee of forty dollars ($40) shall be collected for filing any first paper subject to the uniform fee that is set at three hundred fifty-five dollars ($355) under Sections 70611, 70612, 70650, 70651, 70652, 70653, 70655, 70658, and 70670. The total fee collected under these sections, which includes the supplemental fee, shall be deposited and distributed as provided in Sections 68085.3 and 68086.1, as applicable.

(b) A supplemental fee of forty dollars ($40) shall be collected for filing any first paper subject to the uniform fee that is set at three hundred thirty dollars ($330) under Sections 70613, 70614, and 70621. The total fee collected under these sections, which includes the supplemental fee, shall be deposited and distributed as provided in Sections 68085.4 and 68086.1, as applicable.

(c) A supplemental fee of twenty dollars ($20) shall be collected for filing any first paper subject to the uniform fee that is set at two hundred five dollars ($205) under Sections 70613, 70614, 70621, 70654, and 70656 of this code, and Section 103470 of the Health and Safety Code. The total fee collected under these sections, which includes the supplemental fee, shall be deposited and distributed as provided in Section 68085.4. *(Added by Stats.2010, c. 720 (S.B.857), § 18, eff. Oct. 19, 2010. Amended by Stats.2011, c. 193 (A.B.110), § 6, eff. Aug. 30, 2011; Stats.2012, c. 41 (S.B.1021), § 39, eff. June 27, 2012.)*

Research References

2 Witkin Cal. Proc. 5th Courts § 180, Court Fees.
13 Witkin, California Summary 10th Trusts § 226, (S 226) in General.
13 Witkin, California Summary 10th Trusts § 279, (S 279) Petition.
14 Witkin, California Summary 10th Wills and Probate § 356, Petition.
14 Witkin, California Summary 10th Wills and Probate § 384, Petition or Report.
14 Witkin, California Summary 10th Wills and Probate § 540, in General.
14 Witkin, California Summary 10th Wills and Probate § 577, (S 577) Objection, Summons, and Response.
14 Witkin, California Summary 10th Wills and Probate § 585, Filing Fee.
14 Witkin, California Summary 10th Wills and Probate § 782, (S 782) Petition to Set Aside.
14 Witkin, California Summary 10th Wills and Probate § 874, (S 874) Petition.
14 Witkin, California Summary 10th Wills and Probate § 898, (S 898) Petition.
14 Witkin, California Summary 10th Wills and Probate § 1008, (S 1008) in General.
14 Witkin, California Summary 10th Wills and Probate § 1044, Procedure.
14 Witkin, California Summary 10th Wills and Probate § 1064, Petition, Notice, and Hearing.
14 Witkin, California Summary 10th Wills and Probate § 1070, (S 1070) in General.
14 Witkin, California Summary 10th Wills and Probate § 380A, (S 380A) (New)-In General.
14 Witkin, California Summary 10th Wills and Probate § 380B, (S 380B) (New)-Decedents' Estates.
14 Witkin, California Summary 10th Wills and Probate § 380C, (S 380C) (New)-Trusts.
14 Witkin, California Summary 10th Wills and Probate § 380D, (S 380D) (New)-Guardianships and Conservatorships.
14 Witkin, California Summary 10th Wills and Probate § 380E, (S 380E) (New)-Specified Proceedings.

§ 70602.6. Supplemental fee for filing first paper under specified sections

(a) Notwithstanding any other law, a supplemental fee of forty dollars ($40) shall be collected for filing any first paper subject to the uniform fee that is set at three hundred fifty-five dollars ($355) under Sections 70611, 70612, 70650, 70651, 70652, 70653, 70655, 70658, and 70670. The total fee collected under these sections, which includes the supplemental fee, shall be deposited and distributed as provided in Sections 68085.3 and 68086.1, as applicable.

(b) The fee imposed under this section is in addition to any other fees authorized by law, including, but not limited to, the fees authorized in Section 70602.5.

(c) After the 2013–14 fiscal year, if the amount of the General Fund transfer to the Trial Court Trust Fund is decreased more than 10 percent from the amount appropriated in the 2013–14 fiscal year and is not offset by another source of revenue other than court fees so as to result in a net reduction in funding greater than 10 percent, then the amount of the supplemental fees provided in subdivision (a) shall be decreased proportionally. The Judicial Council shall adopt and publish a schedule setting the fees resulting from the decrease.

(d) This section shall become inoperative on July 1, 2015, and, as of January 1, 2016, is repealed, unless a later enacted statute, that becomes operative on or before January 1, 2016, deletes or extends the dates on which it becomes inoperative and is repealed. *(Added by Stats.2012, c. 41 (S.B.1021), § 40, eff. June 27, 2012.)*

Inoperative Date and Repeal

For inoperative date and repeal of this section, see its terms.

§ 70603. Statewide uniformity of fees; exceptions; courthouse construction surcharge

(a) Except as provided in this section, the fees charged for filings and services under this chapter are intended to be uniform statewide and to be the only allowable fees for those services and filings. The only charges that may be added to the fees in this chapter are the following:

(1) In a complex case, the fee provided for in Section 70616 may be added to the first paper and first responsive paper filing fees in Sections 70611, 70612, 70613, and 70614.

(2) In an unlawful detainer action subject to Section 1161.2 of the Code of Civil Procedure, a charge of fifteen dollars ($15) as provided under that section may be added to the fee in Section 70613 for filing a first appearance by a plaintiff.

(3) In Riverside County, a surcharge as provided in Section 70622 may be added to the first paper and first responsive paper filing fees in Sections 70611, 70612, 70613, 70614, 70650, 70651, 70652, 70653, 70655, and 70670.

(4) In San Bernardino County, a surcharge as provided in Section 70624 may be added to the first paper and first responsive paper filing fees in Sections 70611, 70612, 70613, 70614, 70650, 70651, 70652, 70653, 70655, and 70670. This paragraph applies to fees collected under Sections 70611, 70612, 70613, 70614, 70650, 70651, 70652, 70653, 70655, and 70670, beginning January 1, 2006.

(5) In the City and County of San Francisco, a surcharge as provided in Section 70625 may be added to the first paper and first responsive paper filing fees in Sections 70611, 70612, 70613, 70614, 70650, 70651, 70652, 70653, 70655, and 70670.

(b) Notwithstanding paragraph (1) of subdivision (c) of Section 68085.3 and paragraph (1) of subdivision (c) of Section 68085.4, when a charge for courthouse construction in the City and County of San Francisco or in the Counties of Riverside or San Bernardino is added to the uniform filing fee as provided under paragraph (3), (4), or (5) of subdivision (a), the amount distributed to the State Court Facilities Construction Fund under Section 68085.3 or 68085.4 shall be reduced by an amount equal to the charge added under paragraph (3), (4), or (5) of subdivision (a), up to the amount that would otherwise be distributed to the State Court Facilities Construction Fund. If the amount added under paragraph (3), (4), or (5) of subdivision (a) is greater than the amount that would be distributed to the State Court Facilities Construction Fund under Section 68085.3 or 68085.4, no distribution shall be made to the State Court Facilities Construction Fund, but the amount charged to the party may be greater than the amount of the uniform fee otherwise allowed, in order to collect the surcharge under paragraph (3), (4), or (5) of subdivision (a).

(c) If a filing fee is reduced by twenty-four dollars ($24) under subdivision (c) of Section 6322.1 of the Business and Professions Code, and a courthouse construction surcharge is added to the filing fee as provided under paragraph (3), (4), or (5) of subdivision (a), the amount distributed to the State Court Facilities Construction Fund under Section 68085.4 shall be reduced as provided in subdivision (b). If the amount added under paragraph (3), (4), or (5) of subdivision (a) is greater than

the amount that would be distributed to the State Court Facilities Construction Fund under Section 68085.4, no distribution shall be made to the State Court Facilities Construction Fund, but the amount charged to the party may be greater than one hundred eighty-one dollars ($181), in order to collect the surcharge under paragraph (3), (4), or (5) of subdivision (a).

(d) This section shall become operative on July 1, 2013. *(Added by Stats.2010, c. 720 (S.B.857), § 20, operative July 1, 2013.)*

Research References

2 Witkin Cal. Proc. 5th Courts § 180, Court Fees.
4 Witkin Cal. Proc. 5th Pleading § 26, Additional Fees.

§ 70611. Filing fee for first paper in civil action; documents included

The uniform fee for filing the first paper in a civil action or proceeding in the superior court, other than in a limited civil case, an adoption proceeding, a proceeding under the Probate Code, or a proceeding under the Family Code, is three hundred fifty-five dollars ($355). The fee shall be distributed as provided in Section 68085.3.

This section applies to the initial complaint, petition, or application, and the papers transmitted from another court on the transfer of a civil action or proceeding, but does not include documents filed pursuant to Section 491.150, 704.750, or 708.160 of the Code of Civil Procedure. *(Formerly § 26820.4, added by Stats.1980, c. 1372, p. 4988, § 17. Amended by Stats.1982, c. 454, p. 1825, § 73; Stats.1982, c. 327, p. 1453, § 63, eff. June 30, 1982; Stats.1982, c. 1198, p. 4326, § 67, operative July 1, 1983; Stats.1982, c. 1364, p. 5235, § 2.4, eff. July 1, 1983; Stats.1983, c. 155, § 27, eff. June 30, 1983, operative July 1, 1983; Stats.1983, c. 938, § 6, eff. Sept. 20, 1983; Stats.1992, c. 696 (A.B.1344), § 12, eff. Sept. 15, 1992; Stats.1997, c. 850 (A.B.233), § 6; Stats.1998, c. 931 (S.B.2139), § 201, eff. Sept. 28, 1998. Renumbered § 70611 and amended by Stats.2005, c. 75 (A.B.145), § 50, eff. July 19, 2005, operative Jan. 1, 2006. Amended by Stats.2008, c. 311 (S.B.1407), § 10; Stats.2009–2010, 4th Ex.Sess., c. 22 (S.B.13), § 12, eff. July 28, 2009.)*

Law Revision Commission Comments

Section 26820.4 is amended to insert a reference to the provision that replaced former Section 722 and to add a reference to Section 704.750. [16 Cal.L.Rev.Comm. Reports 1840 (1982)].

[Former] Section 26820.4 is amended to correct a cross-reference. [16 Cal.L. Rev. Comm. Reports 2203 (1982)].

[Former] Section 26820.4 is amended to accommodate unification of the municipal and superior courts in a county. Cal. Const. art. VI, § 5(e). See also Code Civ. Proc. §§ 85, 85.1 (limited civil cases) & Comments. [28 Cal.L.Rev.Comm. Reports 51 (1998)].

Research References

Rutter, Cal. Practice Guide: Civ. Pro. Before Trial Ch. 1-H, H. Filing Fee Considerations.
Rutter, Cal. Practice Guide: Civ. Pro. Before Trial Ch. 9(I)-B, B. Preparing and Filing Motions.
2 Witkin Cal. Proc. 5th Courts § 367, (S 367) Fees.
4 Witkin Cal. Proc. 5th Pleading § 25, Basic Fees.
3 Witkin, California Summary 10th Agency and Employment § 319, (S 319) Notice of Appeal.

§ 70612. Fee for filing first paper on behalf of defendant and others

(a) The uniform fee for filing the first paper in the action or proceeding described in Section 70611 on behalf of any defendant, intervenor, respondent, or adverse party, whether separately or jointly, except for the purpose of making disclaimer, is three hundred fifty-five dollars ($355). The fee shall be distributed as provided in Section 68085.3.

(b) As used in this section, the term "paper" does not include a stipulation for the appointment of a temporary judge or of a court investigator, or the report made by the court investigator. *(Formerly § 26826, added by Stats.1947, c. 424, p. 1147, § 1. Amended by Stats.1949, c. 55, p. 73, § 1; Stats.1949, c. 272, p. 490, § 2; Stats.1949, c. 739, p. 1358, § 5; Stats.1953, c. 806, p. 2111, § 1; Stats.1957, c. 1891, p. 3297, § 1; Stats.1963, c. 356, p. 1146, § 1; Stats.1966, 1st Ex.Sess., c. 120, p. 603, § 31; Stats. 1974, c. 1285, p. 2790, § 9; Stats.1975, c. 766, p. 1784, § 9; Stats.1980, c. 1372, p. 4990, § 28; Stats.1981, c. 109, p. 841, § 1; Stats.1982, c. 327, p. 1454, § 66, eff. June 30, 1982; Stats.1983, c. 1159, § 13, operative July 1, 1984; Stats.1985, c. 96, § 2; Stats.1985, c. 1239, § 4; Stats.1992, c. 696 (A.B.1344), § 16, eff. Sept. 15, 1992; Stats.1993, c. 2 (A.B.32), § 1, eff. March 2, 1993; Stats.1998, c. 931 (S.B.2139), § 203, eff. Sept. 28, 1998. Renumbered § 70612 and amended by Stats.2005, c. 75 (A.B.145), § 56, eff. July 19, 2005, operative Jan. 1, 2006. Amended by Stats.2007, c. 738 (A.B.1248), § 23; Stats.2008, c. 311 (S.B.1407), § 11; Stats.2009–2010, 4th Ex.Sess., c. 22 (S.B.13), § 13, eff. July 28, 2009.)*

Law Revision Commission Comments

[Former] Section 26826 is amended to accommodate unification of the municipal and superior courts in a county. Cal. Const. art. VI, § 5(e). [28 Cal.L.Rev.Comm. Reports 51 (1998)].

Research References

4 Witkin Cal. Proc. 5th Pleading § 25, Basic Fees.
4 Witkin Cal. Proc. 5th Pleading § 27, Exemptions.
9 Witkin, California Summary 10th Taxation § 136, (S 136) Definition of Special Taxes After Proposition 218.

§ 70613. Uniform fee for filing first papers in specified cases; application; waiver

(a) The uniform fee for filing the first paper in a limited civil case is three hundred thirty dollars ($330), except as provided in subdivision (b).

(b) In a case where the amount demanded, excluding attorney's fees and costs, is ten thousand dollars ($10,000) or less, the uniform fee for filing the first paper is two hundred five dollars ($205). The first page of the first paper shall state whether the amount demanded exceeds or does not exceed ten thousand dollars ($10,000).

(c) This section applies to the initial complaint, petition, or application, and any papers transmitted from another court on the transfer of a civil action or proceeding, but does not include documents filed pursuant to Section 491.150, 704.750, or 708.160 of the Code of Civil Procedure.

(d) The fee for a paper filed under this section shall be distributed as provided in Section 68085.4.

(e) The fee shall be waived in any action for damages against a defendant, based upon the defendant's commission of a felony offense, upon presentation to the clerk of the court of a certified copy of the abstract of judgment of conviction of the defendant of the felony giving rise to the claim for damages. If the plaintiff would have been entitled to recover those fees from the defendant had they been paid, the court may assess the amount of the waived fees against the defendant and order the defendant to pay that sum to the court. *(Formerly § 72055, added by Stats.1983, c. 969, § 10, operative Jan. 1, 1988. Amended by Stats.1990, c. 56 (S.B.1609), § 4, eff. April 20, 1990; Stats.1992, c. 696 (A.B.1344), § 73, eff. Sept. 15, 1992; Stats.1996, c. 942 (A.B.2953), § 2; Stats.1997, c. 850 (A.B.233), § 37; Stats.1998, c. 931 (S.B.2139), § 315, eff. Sept. 28, 1998; Stats.2000, c. 447 (S.B.1533), § 7; Stats.2001, c. 812 (A.B.223), § 18; Stats.2003, c. 159 (A.B.1759), § 21, eff. Aug. 2, 2003, operative Aug. 17, 2003. Renumbered § 70613 and amended by Stats.2005, c. 75 (A.B.145), § 126, eff. July 19, 2005, operative Jan. 1, 2006. Amended by*

Stats.2008, c. 311 (S.B.1407), § 12; Stats.2009–2010, 4th Ex.Sess., c. 22 (S.B.13), § 14, eff. July 28, 2009.)

Law Revision Commission Comments

[Former] Section 72055 is amended to accommodate unification of the municipal and superior courts in a county. Cal. Const. art. VI, § 5(e). See also Code Civ. Proc. §§ 85, 85.1 (limited civil cases) & Comments. [28 Cal.L.Rev.Comm. Reports 51 (1998)].

Subdivision (a) of [former] Section 72055 is amended to delete the requirement that the amount of the demand in a limited civil case be stated on the first page of the first paper immediately below the caption. It is sufficient to state whether the amount demanded exceeds $10,000, so as to permit determination of the proper filing fee. For formatting requirements, see Cal. R. Ct. 201(f)(8). See also Code Civ. Proc. 422.30 (caption of complaint in limited civil case shall identify case as a limited civil case). Technical changes are also made for conformity with preferred drafting style. [31 Cal.L.Rev.Comm. Reports 85 (2001)].

Research References

Rutter, Cal. Practice Guide: Civ. Pro. Before Trial Ch. 6-B, B. Complaints.
Rutter, Cal. Practice Guide: Personal Injury Ch. 5-E, E. Selected Pleading Issues.
4 Witkin Cal. Proc. 5th Pleading § 17, Format of First Page.
4 Witkin Cal. Proc. 5th Pleading § 25, Basic Fees.
4 Witkin Cal. Proc. 5th Pleading § 26, Additional Fees.
4 Witkin Cal. Proc. 5th Pleading § 27, Exemptions.
4 Witkin Cal. Proc. 5th Pleading § 496, Form.
4 Witkin Cal. Proc. 5th Pleading § 500, Other Procedures Distinguished.
4 Witkin Cal. Proc. 5th Pleading § 511, (S 511) in General.

§ 70613.5. Amending complaint or cross-complaint to increase amount demanded into higher fee range; fee charge equal to difference between original filing fee and filing fee for new amount demanded; reimbursement for amendment to lower amount to lower fee range

(a) Notwithstanding Section 472 of the Code of Civil Procedure, if a plaintiff or petitioner who previously was charged the filing fee under subdivision (b) of Section 70613 files an amended complaint or other initial pleading that increases the amount demanded to an amount that exceeds ten thousand dollars ($10,000) but does not exceed twenty-five thousand dollars ($25,000), so that the higher filing fee under subdivision (a) of Section 70613 would have been required if such a demand had been made in the original pleading, a fee equal to the difference between the fee for the original filing fee and the filing fee for the new amount demanded shall be charged to make up the difference between the filing fees. This fee shall be distributed to the Trial Court Trust Fund.

(b) Notwithstanding Section 472 of the Code of Civil Procedure, if a party who previously was charged the filing fee under subdivision (b) of Section 70614 files a cross-complaint, amended cross-complaint, or amendment to a cross-complaint demanding an amount that exceeds ten thousand dollars ($10,000) but does not exceed twenty-five thousand dollars ($25,000), a fee equal to the difference between the fee for the original filing fee and the filing fee under subdivision (a) of Section 70614 shall be charged to make up the difference between the filing fees. This fee shall be distributed to the Trial Court Trust Fund.

(c) The court shall not reimburse a party if the party's complaint or cross-complaint is amended to demand a lower amount that falls within the range for a filing fee lower than that originally paid. *(Added by Stats.2007, c. 738 (A.B.1248), § 24.)*

Research References

4 Witkin Cal. Proc. 5th Pleading § 25, Basic Fees.

§ 70614. Uniform fee for filing first papers in specified cases on behalf of party other than plaintiff; application; waiver

(a) The uniform fee for filing the first paper in a limited civil case on behalf of any party other than a plaintiff is three hundred thirty dollars ($330), except as provided in subdivision (b).

(b) In a case where the amount demanded, excluding attorney's fees and costs, is ten thousand dollars ($10,000) or less, the uniform fee for filing the first paper is two hundred five dollars ($205).

(c) The fees in this section do not apply to papers filed for the purpose of making disclaimer.

(d) The fee for a paper filed under this section shall be distributed as provided in Section 68085.4. *(Formerly § 72056, added by Stats.1953, c. 206, p. 1289, § 1. Amended by Stats.1955, c. 604, p. 1098, § 3; Stats.1955, c. 955, p. 1850, § 39; Stats.1980, c. 1372, p. 4933, § 56; Stats.1982, c. 327, p. 1460, § 95, eff. June 30, 1982; Stats.1992, c. 696 (A.B.1344), § 75, eff. Sept. 15, 1992; Stats.1998, c. 931 (S.B.2139), § 316, eff. Sept. 28, 1998; Stats. 2003, c. 159 (A.B.1759), § 23, eff. Aug. 2, 2003, operative Aug. 17, 2003. Renumbered § 70614 and amended by Stats.2005, c. 75 (A.B.145), § 128, eff. July 19, 2005, operative Jan. 1, 2006. Amended by Stats.2008, c. 311 (S.B.1407), § 13; Stats.2009–2010, 4th Ex.Sess., c. 22 (S.B.13), § 15, eff. July 28, 2009.)*

Law Revision Commission Comments

[Former] Section 72056 is amended to accommodate unification of the municipal and superior courts in a county. Cal. Const. art. VI, § 5(e). See also Code Civ. Proc. §§ 85, 85.1 (limited civil cases) & Comments. [28 Cal.L.Rev.Comm. Reports 51 (1998)].

Research References

8 Witkin Cal. Proc. 5th Enforcement of Judgment § 334, in General.
4 Witkin Cal. Proc. 5th Pleading § 25, Basic Fees.
4 Witkin Cal. Proc. 5th Pleading § 27, Exemptions.

§ 70615. Fee for specified appeals to superior court

The fee for filing any of the following appeals to the superior court is twenty-five dollars ($25):

(a) An appeal of a local agency's decision regarding an administrative fine or penalty under Section 53069.4.

(b) An appeal under Section 40230 of the Vehicle Code of an administrative agency's decision regarding a parking violation.

(c) An appeal under Section 99582 of the Public Utilities Code of a hearing officer's determination regarding an administrative penalty for fare evasion or a passenger conduct violation. *(Added by Stats.2007, c. 738 (A.B.1248), § 25.)*

Research References

2 Witkin Cal. Proc. 5th Courts § 180, Court Fees.
4 Witkin Cal. Proc. 5th Pleading § 26, Additional Fees.

§ 70616. Complex case fees

Section operative until July 1, 2015. See, also, section operative July 1, 2015.

(a) In addition to the first paper filing fee required by Section 70611 or 70613, a single complex case fee shall be paid to the clerk on behalf of all plaintiffs, whether filing separately or jointly, either at the time of the filing of the first paper if the case is designated as complex pursuant to the California Rules of Court, or, if no such designation was made, in each case in which a court determines that the case is a complex case pursuant to the California Rules of Court, within 10 calendar days of the filing of the court's order.

(b) In addition to the first appearance fee required under Section 70612 or 70614, a complex case fee shall be paid on behalf of each defendant, intervenor, respondent, or adverse party, whether filing separately or jointly, either at the time that party files its first paper in a case if the case is designated or counterdesignated as complex pursuant to the California Rules of Court, or, if no such designation was made, in each case in which a court determines that the case is a complex case pursuant to the California Rules of Court, within 10 calendar

days of the filing of the court's order. This additional complex fee shall be charged to each defendant, intervenor, respondent, or adverse party appearing in the case, but the total complex fees collected from all the defendants, intervenors, respondents, or other adverse parties appearing in a complex case shall not exceed eighteen thousand dollars ($18,000).

(c) In each case in which the court determines that a case that has been designated or counterdesignated as complex is not a complex case, the court shall order reimbursement to the parties of the amount of any complex case fees that the parties have previously paid pursuant to subdivision (a) or (b).

(d) In each case determined to be complex in which the total fees actually collected exceed, or if collected would exceed, the limit in subdivision (b), the court shall make any order as is necessary to ensure that the total complex fees paid by the defendants, intervenors, respondents, or other adverse parties appearing in the case do not exceed the limit and that the complex fees paid by those parties are apportioned fairly among those parties.

(e) The complex case fee established by this section shall be one thousand dollars ($1,000), unless the fee is reduced pursuant to this section. The fee shall be transmitted to the Trial Court Trust Fund as provided in Section 68085.1.

(f) The fees provided by this section are in addition to the filing fee authorized by Section 70611, 70612, 70613, or 70614.

(g) Failure to pay the fees required by this section shall have the same effect as the failure to pay a filing fee, and shall be subject to the same enforcement and penalties.

(h) The amendments made to this section during the 2011–12 Regular Session of the Legislature do not constitute a change in, but are declaratory of, existing law [1].

(i) This section shall become inoperative on July 1, 2015, and, as of January 1, 2016, is repealed, unless a later enacted statute, that becomes operative on or before January 1, 2016, deletes or extends the dates on which it becomes inoperative and is repealed. *(Formerly § 26826.4, added by Stats.2003, c. 159 (A.B.1759), § 8, eff. Aug. 2, 2003, operative Aug. 17, 2003. Amended by Stats.2003, c. 757 (A.B.296), § 3.5. Renumbered § 70616 and amended by Stats.2005, c. 75 (A.B.145), § 60, eff. July 19, 2005, operative Jan. 1, 2006. Amended by Stats.2011, c. 419 (S.B.384), § 5; Stats.2012, c. 41 (S.B.1021), § 41, eff. June 27, 2012.)*

[1]   Subd. (h) was added by Stats.2011, c. 419 (S.B.384).

Inoperative Date and Repeal

For inoperative date and repeal of this section, see its terms.

Research References

Rutter, Cal. Practice Guide: Civ. Pro. Before Trial Ch. 9(I)-B, B. Preparing and Filing Motions.
Rutter, Cal. Practice Guide: Civ. Pro. Before Trial Ch. 12(I)-B, B. Case Management ("Fast Track") System.
4 Witkin Cal. Proc. 5th Pleading § 26, Additional Fees.

§ 70616. Complex case fees

Section operative July 1, 2015. See, also, section operative until July 1, 2015.

(a) In addition to the first paper filing fee required by Section 70611 or 70613, a single complex case fee shall be paid to the clerk on behalf of all plaintiffs, whether filing separately or jointly, either at the time of the filing of the first paper if the case is designated as complex pursuant to the California Rules of Court, or, if no such designation was made, in each case in which a court determines that the case is a complex case pursuant to the California Rules of Court, within 10 calendar days of the filing of the court's order.

(b) In addition to the first appearance fee required under Section 70612 or 70614, a complex case fee shall be paid on behalf of each defendant, intervenor, respondent, or adverse party, whether filing separately or jointly, either at the time that party files its first paper in a case if the case is designated or counterdesignated as complex pursuant to the California Rules of Court, or, if no such designation was made, in each case in which a court determines that the case is a complex case pursuant to the California Rules of Court, within 10 calendar days of the filing of the court's order. This additional complex fee shall be charged to each defendant, intervenor, respondent, or adverse party appearing in the case, but the total complex fees collected from all the defendants, intervenors, respondents, or other adverse parties appearing in a complex case shall not exceed ten thousand dollars ($10,000).

(c) In each case in which the court determines that a case that has been designated or counterdesignated as complex is not a complex case, the court shall order reimbursement to the parties of the amount of any complex case fees that the parties have previously paid pursuant to subdivision (a) or (b).

(d) In each case determined to be complex in which the total fees actually collected exceed, or if collected would exceed, the limit in subdivision (b), the court shall make any order as is necessary to ensure that the total complex fees paid by the defendants, intervenors, respondents, or other adverse parties appearing in the case do not exceed the limit and that the complex fees paid by those parties are apportioned fairly among those parties.

(e) The complex case fee established by this section shall be five hundred fifty dollars ($550), unless the fee is reduced pursuant to this section. The fee shall be transmitted to the Trial Court Trust Fund as provided in Section 68085.1.

(f) The fees provided by this section are in addition to the filing fee authorized by Section 70611, 70612, 70613, or 70614.

(g) Failure to pay the fees required by this section shall have the same effect as the failure to pay a filing fee, and shall be subject to the same enforcement and penalties.

(h) The amendments made to the predecessor to this section during the 2011–12 Regular Session of the Legislature do not constitute a change in, but are declaratory of, existing law [1].

(i) This section shall become operative on July 1, 2015. *(Added by Stats.2012, c. 41 (S.B.1021), § 42, eff. June 27, 2012, operative July 1, 2015.)*

[1] Subd. (h) was added to the predecessor to this section by Stats.2011, c. 419 (S.B.384).

Research References

Rutter, Cal. Practice Guide: Civ. Pro. Before Trial Ch. 9(I)-B, B. Preparing and Filing Motions.
Rutter, Cal. Practice Guide: Civ. Pro. Before Trial Ch. 12(I)-B, B. Case Management ("Fast Track") System.
4 Witkin Cal. Proc. 5th Pleading § 26, Additional Fees.

§ 70617. Filing fees, generally

Section operative until July 1, 2015. See, also, section operative July 1, 2015.

(a) Except as provided in subdivisions (d) and (e), the uniform fee for filing a motion, application, or any other paper requiring a hearing subsequent to the first paper, is sixty dollars ($60). Papers for which this fee shall be charged include the following:

(1) A motion listed in paragraphs (1) to (12), inclusive, of subdivision (a) of Section 1005 of the Code of Civil Procedure.

(2) A motion or application to continue a trial date.

(3) An application for examination of a third person controlling defendant's property under Section 491.110 or 491.150 of the Code of Civil Procedure.

(4) Discovery motions under Title 4 (commencing with Section 2016.010) of Part 4 of the Code of Civil Procedure.

(5) A motion for a new trial of any civil action or special proceeding.

(6) An application for an order for a judgment debtor examination under Section 708.110 or 708.160 of the Code of Civil Procedure.

(7) An application for an order of sale of a dwelling under Section 704.750 of the Code of Civil Procedure.

(8) An ex parte application that requires a party to give notice of the ex parte appearance to other parties.

(b) There shall be no fee under subdivision (a) or (c) for filing any of the following:

(1) A motion, application, demurrer, request, notice, or stipulation and order that is the first paper filed in an action and on which a first paper filing fee is paid.

(2) An amended notice of motion.

(3) A civil case management statement.

(4) A request for trial de novo after judicial arbitration.

(5) A stipulation that does not require an order.

(6) A request for an order to prevent civil harassment.

(7) A request for an order to prevent domestic violence.

(8) A request for entry of default or default judgment.

(9) A paper requiring a hearing on a petition for emancipation of a minor.

(10) A paper requiring a hearing on a petition for an order to prevent abuse of an elder or dependent adult.

(11) A paper requiring a hearing on a petition for a writ of review, mandate, or prohibition.

(12) A paper requiring a hearing on a petition for a decree of change of name or gender.

(13) A paper requiring a hearing on a petition to approve the compromise of a claim of a minor.

(c) The fee for filing the following papers not requiring a hearing is twenty dollars ($20):

(1) A request, application, or motion for, or a notice of, the continuance of a hearing or case management conference. The fee shall be charged no more than once for each continuance. The fee shall not be charged if the continuance is required by the court.

(2) A stipulation and order.

(3) A request for an order authorizing service of summons by posting or by publication under Section 415.45 or 415.50 of the Code of Civil Procedure.

(d) The fee for filing a motion for summary judgment or summary adjudication of issues is five hundred dollars ($500).

(e)(1) The fee for filing in the superior court an application to appear as counsel pro hac vice is five hundred dollars ($500). This fee is in addition to any other fee required of the applicant. Two hundred fifty dollars ($250) of the fee collected under this paragraph shall be transmitted to the state for deposit into the Immediate and Critical Needs Account of the State Court Facilities Construction Fund, established in Section 70371.5. The remaining two hundred fifty dollars ($250) of the fee shall be transmitted to the state for deposit into the Trial Court Trust Fund, established in Section 68085.

(2) An attorney whose application to appear as counsel pro hac vice has been granted shall pay to the superior court, on or before the anniversary of the date the application was granted, an annual renewal fee of five hundred dollars ($500) for each year that the attorney maintains pro hac vice status in the case in which the application was granted. The entire fee collected under this paragraph shall be transmitted to the state for deposit into the Trial Court Trust Fund, established in Section 68085.

(f) Regardless of whether each motion or matter is heard at a single hearing or at separate hearings, the filing fees required by subdivisions (a), (c), (d), and (e) apply separately to each motion or other paper filed. The Judicial Council may publish rules to give uniform guidance to courts in applying fees under this section.

(g) This section shall become inoperative on July 1, 2015, and, as of January 1, 2016, is repealed, unless a later enacted statute, that becomes operative on or before January 1, 2016, deletes or extends the dates on which it becomes inoperative and is repealed. *(Added by Stats.2005, c. 75 (A.B.145), § 121, eff. July 19, 2005, operative Jan. 1, 2006. Amended by Stats.2007, c. 738 (A.B.1248), § 26; Stats.2008, c. 311 (S.B.1407), § 13.5; Stats. 2010, c. 720 (S.B.857), § 21, eff. Oct. 19, 2010; Stats.2012, c. 41 (S.B.1021), § 43, eff. June 27, 2012.)*

Inoperative Date and Repeal

For inoperative date and repeal of this section, see its terms.

Research References

Rutter, Cal. Practice Guide: Civ. Pro. Before Trial Ch. 10-C, C. Procedural Requirements-Moving Party.
Rutter, Cal. Practice Guide: Civ. Pro. Before Trial Ch. 9(I)-B, B. Preparing and Filing Motions.
Rutter, Cal. Practice Guide: Civil Trials & Evidence Ch. 1-K, K. Continuance Motions.
Rutter, Cal. Practice Guide: Enforcing Judgments/Debts Ch. 4-A, A. Attachment.
Rutter, Cal. Practice Guide: Enforcing Judgments/Debts Ch. 6D-8, Special Requirements for Sale of Real Property Dwellings.
Rutter, Cal. Practice Guide: Enforcing Judgments/Debts Ch. 6G-1, Examination of Judgment Debtor and Third Parties.
8 Witkin Cal. Proc. 5th Attack Judgment Trial Court § 52, Filing Fee.
1 Witkin Cal. Proc. 5th Attorneys § 389, (S 389) Counsel Pro Hac Vice.
2 Witkin Cal. Proc. 5th Courts § 290, (S 290) Uniform Fees.
2 Witkin Cal. Proc. 5th Courts § 302, (S 302) in General.
8 Witkin Cal. Proc. 5th Enforcement of Judgment § 220, (S 220) Application.
8 Witkin Cal. Proc. 5th Enforcement of Judgment § 287, (S 287) Proper Court for Examination.
4 Witkin Cal. Proc. 5th Pleading § 25, Basic Fees.
6 Witkin Cal. Proc. 5th Proceedings Without Trial § 33, (S 33) General Requirements.
6 Witkin Cal. Proc. 5th Provisional Remedies § 196, (S 196) Application.
11 Witkin, California Summary 10th Husband and Wife § 12A, (S 12A) (New)-Filing Fees.
14 Witkin, California Summary 10th Wills and Probate § 380E, (S 380E) (New)-Specified Proceedings.

§ 70617. Filing fees, generally

Section operative July 1, 2015. See, also, section operative until July 1, 2015.

(a) Except as provided in subdivisions (d) and (e), the uniform fee for filing a motion, application, or any other paper requiring a hearing subsequent to the first paper, is forty dollars ($40). Papers for which this fee shall be charged include the following:

(1) A motion listed in paragraphs (1) to (12), inclusive, of subdivision (a) of Section 1005 of the Code of Civil Procedure.

(2) A motion or application to continue a trial date.

(3) An application for examination of a third person controlling defendant's property under Section 491.110 or 491.150 of the Code of Civil Procedure.

(4) Discovery motions under Title 4 (commencing with Section 2016.010) of Part 4 of the Code of Civil Procedure.

(5) A motion for a new trial of any civil action or special proceeding.

(6) An application for an order for a judgment debtor examination under Section 708.110 or 708.160 of the Code of Civil Procedure.

(7) An application for an order of sale of a dwelling under Section 704.750 of the Code of Civil Procedure.

(8) An ex parte application that requires a party to give notice of the ex parte appearance to other parties.

(b) There shall be no fee under subdivision (a) or (c) for filing any of the following:

(1) A motion, application, demurrer, request, notice, or stipulation and order that is the first paper filed in an action and on which a first paper filing fee is paid.

(2) An amended notice of motion.

(3) A civil case management statement.

(4) A request for trial de novo after judicial arbitration.

(5) A stipulation that does not require an order.

(6) A request for an order to prevent civil harassment.

(7) A request for an order to prevent domestic violence.

(8) A request for entry of default or default judgment.

(9) A paper requiring a hearing on a petition for emancipation of a minor.

(10) A paper requiring a hearing on a petition for an order to prevent abuse of an elder or dependent adult.

(11) A paper requiring a hearing on a petition for a writ of review, mandate, or prohibition.

(12) A paper requiring a hearing on a petition for a decree of change of name or gender.

(13) A paper requiring a hearing on a petition to approve the compromise of a claim of a minor.

(c) The fee for filing the following papers not requiring a hearing is twenty dollars ($20):

(1) A request, application, or motion for, or a notice of, the continuance of a hearing or case management conference. The fee shall be charged no more than once for each continuance. The fee shall not be charged if the continuance is required by the court.

(2) A stipulation and order.

(3) A request for an order authorizing service of summons by posting or by publication under Section 415.45 or 415.50 of the Code of Civil Procedure.

(d) The fee for filing a motion for summary judgment or summary adjudication of issues is five hundred dollars ($500).

(e)(1) The fee for filing in the superior court an application to appear as counsel pro hac vice is five hundred dollars ($500). This fee is in addition to any other fee required of the applicant. Two hundred fifty dollars ($250) of the fee collected under this paragraph shall be transmitted to the state for deposit into the Immediate and Critical Needs Account of the State Court Facilities Construction Fund, established in Section 70371.5. The remaining two hundred fifty dollars ($250) of the fee shall be transmitted to the state for deposit into the Trial Court Trust Fund, established in Section 68085.

(2) An attorney whose application to appear as counsel pro hac vice has been granted shall pay to the superior court, on or before the anniversary of the date the application was granted, an annual renewal fee of five hundred dollars ($500) for each year that the attorney maintains pro hac vice status in the case in which the application was granted. The entire fee collected under this paragraph shall be transmitted to the state for deposit into the Trial Court Trust Fund, established in Section 68085.

(f) Regardless of whether each motion or matter is heard at a single hearing or at separate hearings, the filing fees required by subdivisions (a), (c), (d), and (e) apply separately to each motion or other paper filed. The Judicial Council may publish rules to give uniform guidance to courts in applying fees under this section.

(g) This section shall become operative on July 1, 2015. *(Added by Stats.2010, c. 720 (S.B.857), § 22, operative July 1, 2013. Amended by Stats.2012, c. 41 (S.B.1021), § 44, eff. June 27, 2012, operative July 1, 2015.)*

Research References

Rutter, Cal. Practice Guide: Civ. Pro. Before Trial Ch. 10-C, C. Procedural Requirements-Moving Party.
Rutter, Cal. Practice Guide: Civ. Pro. Before Trial Ch. 9(I)-B, B. Preparing and Filing Motions.
Rutter, Cal. Practice Guide: Civil Trials & Evidence Ch. 1-K, K. Continuance Motions.
Rutter, Cal. Practice Guide: Enforcing Judgments/Debts Ch. 4-A, A. Attachment.
Rutter, Cal. Practice Guide: Enforcing Judgments/Debts Ch. 6D-8, Special Requirements for Sale of Real Property Dwellings.
Rutter, Cal. Practice Guide: Enforcing Judgments/Debts Ch. 6G-1, Examination of Judgment Debtor and Third Parties.
8 Witkin Cal. Proc. 5th Attack Judgment Trial Court § 52, Filing Fee.
1 Witkin Cal. Proc. 5th Attorneys § 389, (S 389) Counsel Pro Hac Vice.
2 Witkin Cal. Proc. 5th Courts § 290, (S 290) Uniform Fees.
2 Witkin Cal. Proc. 5th Courts § 302, (S 302) in General.
8 Witkin Cal. Proc. 5th Enforcement of Judgment § 220, (S 220) Application.
8 Witkin Cal. Proc. 5th Enforcement of Judgment § 287, (S 287) Proper Court for Examination.
4 Witkin Cal. Proc. 5th Pleading § 25, Basic Fees.
6 Witkin Cal. Proc. 5th Proceedings Without Trial § 33, (S 33) General Requirements.
6 Witkin Cal. Proc. 5th Provisional Remedies § 196, (S 196) Application.
11 Witkin, California Summary 10th Husband and Wife § 12A, (S 12A) (New)-Filing Fees.
14 Witkin, California Summary 10th Wills and Probate § 380E, (S 380E) (New)-Specified Proceedings.

§ 70618. Change of venue; transmission of transcript and papers; filing feed

When the venue in a case is changed, the fee for making up and transmitting the transcript and papers is fifty dollars ($ 50) and a further sum equal to the uniform fee for filing in the court to which the case is transferred. The clerk shall transmit the uniform filing fee with the papers in the case to the clerk or judge of the court to which the case is transferred. *(Formerly § 26823, added by Stats.1947, c. 424, p. 1147, § 1. Amended by Stats.1949, c. 739, p. 1358, § 3; Stats.1951, c. 1553, p. 3542, § 45, operative in part Jan. 1, 1952, and in part Jan. 5, 1953; Stats.1957, c. 1579, p. 2932, § 3; Stats.1974, c. 1285, p. 2789, § 6; Stats.1975, c. 766, p. 1784, § 6; Stats.1980, c. 1372, p. 4990, § 26; Stats.1982, c. 327, p. 1454, § 65, eff. June 30, 1982; Stats.1997, c. 850 (A.B.233), § 7. Renumbered § 70618 and amended by Stats. 2005, c. 75 (A.B.145), § 54, eff. July 19, 2005, operative Jan. 1, 2006.)*

Research References

4 Witkin Cal. Proc. 5th Pleading § 26, Additional Fees.

§ 70619. Fee for reclassification of case

The fee for reclassification of a case from a limited civil case to an unlimited civil case under Section 403.060 of the Code of Civil Procedure is one hundred forty dollars ($140). *(Added by Stats.2005, c. 75 (A.B.145), § 121, eff. July 19, 2005, operative Jan. 1, 2006.)*

Research References

Rutter, Cal. Practice Guide: Civ. Pro. Before Trial Ch. 3-A, A. Subject Matter Jurisdiction (Competency).
2 Witkin Cal. Proc. 5th Jurisdiction § 412, (S 412) Reclassification Fees.
4 Witkin Cal. Proc. 5th Pleading § 26, Additional Fees.

§ 70620. Fee for certificate on appeal

The fee for a certificate required by courts of appeal or the Supreme Court on filing a notice of motion prior to the filing of the record on appeal in the reviewing court is twenty dollars ($20). *(Formerly § 26838, added by Stats.1947, c. 424, p. 1148, § 1. Amended by Stats.1949, c. 272, p. 491, § 8; Stats.1949, c. 739, p. 1359, § 14; Stats.1963, c. 459, p. 1308, § 1; Stats.1971, c. 806, p. 1563, § 1; Stats.1980, c. 1372, p. 4992, § 40; Stats.1982, c. 327, p. 1457, § 77, eff. June 30, 1982; Stats.1997, c. 850 (A.B.233), § 17. Renumbered § 70620 and amended by Stats.2005, c. 75 (A.B.145), § 82, eff. July 19, 2005, operative Jan. 1, 2006.)*

§ 70621. Fee for filing notice of appeal in limited civil case

(a)(1) The fee for filing a notice of appeal to the appellate division of the superior court in a limited civil case is three hundred thirty dollars ($330), except as provided in subdivision (b).

(2) The fee for filing a petition for a writ within the original jurisdiction of the appellate division of the superior court is three hundred thirty dollars ($330), except as provided in subdivision (b).

(b) If the amount demanded in the limited civil case, excluding attorney's fees and costs, is ten thousand dollars ($10,000) or less, the fee for filing a petition for a writ or a notice of appeal to the appellate division of the superior court is two hundred five dollars ($205).

(c) The fees provided for in this section shall be distributed as provided in Section 68085.4.

(d) The Judicial Council may make rules governing the time and method of payment of the fees in this section and providing for excuse. *(Formerly § 26824, added by Stats.1947, c. 424, p. 1147, § 1. Amended by Stats.1949, c. 739, p. 1358, § 4; Stats.1951, c. 1553, p. 3543, § 46, operative in part Jan. 1, 1952, and in part Jan. 5, 1953; Stats.1957, c. 1579, p. 2932, § 4; Stats.1974, c. 1285, p. 2789, § 7; Stats.1975, c. 766, p. 1784, § 7; Stats.1977, c. 1257, p. 4771, § 43, eff. Oct. 3, 1977; Stats.1979, c. 212, p. 458, § 5; Stats.1980, c. 1372, p. 4990, § 27; Stats.1993, c. 158 (A.B.392), § 4, eff. July 21, 1993; Stats.1998, c. 931 (S.B. 2139), § 202, eff. Sept. 28, 1998. Renumbered § 70621 and amended by Stats.2005, c. 75 (A.B.145), § 55, eff. July 19, 2005, operative Jan. 1, 2006. Amended by Stats.2007, c. 738 (A.B.1248), § 27; Stats.2008, c. 311 (S.B.1407), § 14; Stats.2009–2010, 4th Ex.Sess., c. 22 (S.B.13), § 16, eff. July 28, 2009.)*

Law Revision Commission Comments

[Former] Section 26824 is amended to accommodate unification of the municipal and superior courts in a county. Cal. Const. art. VI, § 5(e). See also Code Civ. Proc. 85, 85.1 (limited civil cases) & Comments. [28 Cal.L.Rev.Comm. Reports 51 (1998)].

Government

Research References

Rutter, Cal. Practice Guide: Civil Appeals & Writs Ch. 16-C, C. Notice of Appeal.

Rutter, Cal. Practice Guide: Civil Appeals & Writs Ch. 16-L, L. Writs. 9 Witkin Cal. Proc. 5th Appeal § 1006, Form and Filing.

§ 70622. Riverside County; surcharge for filings in superior court for court facilities construction fund

(a) In addition to the uniform filing fee authorized pursuant to Section 70611, 70612, 70613, 70614, 70650, 70651, 70652, 70653, 70655, or 70670, after giving notice and holding a public hearing on the proposal, the Board of Supervisors of Riverside County may impose a surcharge not to exceed fifty dollars ($50) for the filing in superior court of any of the following:

(1) A complaint, petition, or other first paper in a civil or probate action or special proceeding.

(2) A first paper on behalf of any defendant, respondent, intervenor, or adverse party.

(3) A petition for dissolution of marriage, dissolution of domestic partnership, legal separation, or nullity of marriage.

(4) A response to such a petition.

(5) A first paper on behalf of any party in a proceeding under Section 98.2 of the Labor Code.

(b) The county shall notify in writing the Superior Court of Riverside County and the Administrative Office of the Courts of any change in a surcharge under this section.

(c) When a surcharge under this section is imposed on a filing fee, the distribution that would otherwise be made to the State Court Facilities Construction Fund under subdivision (c) of Section 68085.3 or subdivision (c) of Section 68085.4 shall be reduced as provided in Section 70603.

(d) The surcharge shall be in an amount determined to be necessary by the board of supervisors to cover the costs of the seismic stabilization, construction, and rehabilitation of the Riverside County Courthouse, the Indio Branch Courthouse, and the family law courthouse, and collection thereof shall terminate upon repayment of the amortized costs incurred. When the amortized costs have been repaid, the county shall notify in writing the Superior Court of Riverside County and the Administrative Office of the Courts. *(Formerly § 26826.1, added by Stats.1992, c. 1285 (S.B.1478), § 1. Amended by Stats.1993, c. 2 (A.B.32), § 1.5, eff. March 2, 1993. Renumbered § 70622 and amended by Stats.2005, c. 75 (A.B.145), § 57, eff. July 19, 2005, operative Jan. 1, 2006. Amended by Stats.2006, c. 538 (S.B.1852), § 331.)*

Research References

4 Witkin Cal. Proc. 5th Pleading § 26, Additional Fees.

§ 70624. San Bernardino County Board of Supervisors; surcharge for listed filings; deposit and use of funds; termination of surcharge

(a) In addition to the uniform filing fee authorized pursuant to Section 70611, 70612, 70613, 70614, 70650, 70651, 70652, 70653, 70655, or 70670, after giving notice and holding a public hearing on the proposal, the Board of Supervisors of San Bernardino County may impose a surcharge not to exceed thirty-five dollars ($35) for the filing in superior court of (1) a complaint, petition, or other first paper in a civil, family, or probate action or special proceeding, and (2) a first paper on behalf of any defendant, respondent, intervenor, or adverse party. The county shall notify in writing the superior court and the Administrative Office of the Courts of any change in a surcharge under this section. If a surcharge under this section is imposed on a filing fee, the distribution that would otherwise be made to the State Court Facilities Construction Fund under

subdivision (c) of Section 68085.3 or subdivision (c) of Section 68085.4 shall be reduced as provided in Section 70603. This section shall apply to fees collected under Sections 70611, 70612, 70613, 70614, 70650, 70651, 70652, 70653, 70655, and 70670, beginning January 1, 2006.

(b) The surcharge shall be in an amount determined to be necessary by the board of supervisors to supplement the Courthouse Construction Fund, to be deposited in that fund and used solely for the purposes authorized for expenditures from that fund, including, but not limited to, earthquake retrofitting, renovation, and remodeling of all portions of the Central San Bernardino Courthouse in need of retrofitting, renovation, or remodeling, whether or not necessitated by the retrofitting work, including the original courthouse built in 1926 and all subsequent additions thereto. Expenditures made from the Courthouse Construction Fund that are funded from the surcharge shall be made in order of priority to ensure that all necessary earthquake retrofitting of the Central San Bernardino Courthouse will be completed. Collection of the surcharge authorized by this section shall terminate upon repayment of the amortized costs incurred, or 30 years from the sale of the bond, whichever occurs first. However, the surcharge shall not apply in instances in which no filing fee is charged or the filing fee is waived. If the amortized costs have been repaid, or 30 years have passed since the sale of the bond, the county shall notify in writing the superior court and the Administrative Office of the Courts. *(Formerly § 76236, added by Stats.2002, c. 367 (A.B.2022), § 2. Renumbered § 70624 and amended by Stats.2005, c. 75 (A.B.145), § 136, eff. July 19, 2005, operative Jan. 1, 2006. Amended by Stats.2007, c. 738 (A.B.1248), § 28.)*

Research References

4 Witkin Cal. Proc. 5th Pleading § 26, Additional Fees.

§ 70625. San Francisco City and County; deposit of funds; use of funds; rental of excess space; surcharge for filing fees

(a) Notwithstanding any other law, for the purpose of assisting the City and County of San Francisco in the acquisition, rehabilitation, construction, and financing of courtrooms or of a courtroom building or buildings containing facilities necessary or incidental to the operation of the justice system, the Board of Supervisors of the City and County of San Francisco may require the amounts collected pursuant to subdivision (d) to be deposited in the Courthouse Construction Fund established pursuant to Section 76100. In the City and County of San Francisco, the moneys of the Courthouse Construction Fund together with any interest earned thereon shall be payable only for the foregoing purposes and at the time necessary therefor, and for the purposes set forth in subdivision (b) and at the time necessary therefor.

(b) In conjunction with the acquisition, rehabilitation, construction, or financing of courtrooms or of a courtroom building or buildings referred to in subdivision (a), the City and County of San Francisco may use the moneys of the Courthouse Construction Fund (1) to rehabilitate existing courtrooms or an existing courtroom building or buildings for other uses if new courtrooms or a courtroom building or buildings are acquired, constructed, or financed or (2) to acquire, rehabilitate, construct, or finance excess courtrooms or an excess courtroom building or buildings if that excess is anticipated to be needed at a later time.

(c) Any excess courtrooms or excess courtroom building or buildings that are acquired, rehabilitated, constructed, or financed pursuant to subdivision (b) may be leased or rented for uses other than the operation of the justice system until such time as the excess courtrooms or excess courtroom building or buildings are needed for the operation of the justice system.

Any amounts received as lease or rental payments pursuant to this subdivision shall be deposited in the Courthouse Construction Fund.

(d) In the City and County of San Francisco, a surcharge for the purpose and for the time set forth in this section may be added to the filing fees under Sections 70611, 70612, 70613, 70614, 70650, 70651, 70652, 70653, 70655, and 70670 in any civil, family, or probate action in the superior court. The surcharge shall be in an amount, not to exceed fifty dollars ($50), as set forth in a resolution adopted by the Board of Supervisors of the City and County of San Francisco. If a surcharge under this section is imposed on a filing fee, the distribution that would otherwise be made to the State Court Facilities Construction Fund under subdivision (c) of Section 68085.3 or subdivision (c) of Section 68085.4 shall be reduced as provided in Section 70603. The county shall notify in writing the superior court and the Administrative Office of the Courts of any change in a surcharge under this section. When the amortized costs that are to be repaid from this fund have been repaid, the county shall notify in writing the superior court and the Administrative Office of Courts, and the surcharge under this section shall terminate, as provided in subdivision (b) of Section 70375. *(Formerly § 76238, added by Stats.1991, c. 189 (A.B.544), § 11, eff. July 29, 1991. Amended by Stats.1992, c. 427 (A.B.3355), § 77; Stats. 2002, c. 784 (S.B.1316), § 503. Renumbered § 70625 and amended by Stats.2005, c. 75 (A.B.145), § 137, eff. July 16, 2005, operative Jan. 1, 2006. Amended by Stats.2010, c. 709 (S.B.1062), § 6.)*

Law Revision Commission Comments

[Former] Subdivision (d) of Section 76238 is amended to reflect unification of the municipal and superior courts in the City and County of San Francisco pursuant to Article VI, Section 5(e), of the California Constitution, effective December 31, 1998. [32 Cal.L.Rev.Comm. Reports 423 (2002)].

Research References

4 Witkin Cal. Proc. 5th Pleading § 26, Additional Fees.

§ 70626. Fees for miscellaneous services

Section operative until July 1, 2017. See, also, section operative July 1, 2017.

(a) The fee for each of the following services is twenty-five dollars ($25). Subject to subdivision (e), amounts collected shall be distributed to the Trial Court Trust Fund under Section 68085.1.

(1) Issuing a writ of attachment, a writ of mandate, a writ of execution, a writ of sale, a writ of possession, a writ of prohibition, or any other writ for the enforcement of any order or judgment.

(2) Issuing an abstract of judgment.

(3) Issuing a certificate of satisfaction of judgment under Section 724.100 of the Code of Civil Procedure.

(4) Certifying a copy of any paper, record, or proceeding on file in the office of the clerk of any court.

(5) Taking an affidavit, except in criminal cases or adoption proceedings.

(6) Acknowledgment of any deed or other instrument, including the certificate.

(7) Recording or registering any license or certificate, or issuing any certificate in connection with a license, required by law, for which a charge is not otherwise prescribed.

(8) Issuing any certificate for which the fee is not otherwise fixed.

(b) The fee for each of the following services is thirty dollars ($30). Subject to subdivision (e), amounts collected shall be distributed to the Trial Court Trust Fund under Section 68085.1.

(1) Issuing an order of sale.

(2) Receiving and filing an abstract of judgment rendered by a judge of another court and subsequent services based on it, unless the abstract of judgment is filed under Section 704.750 or 708.160 of the Code of Civil Procedure.

(3) Filing a confession of judgment under Section 1134 of the Code of Civil Procedure.

(4) Filing an application for renewal of judgment under Section 683.150 of the Code of Civil Procedure.

(5) Issuing a commission to take a deposition in another state or place under Section 2026.010 of the Code of Civil Procedure, or issuing a subpoena under Section 2029.300 to take a deposition in this state for purposes of a proceeding pending in another jurisdiction.

(6) Filing and entering an award under the Workers' Compensation Law (Division 4 (commencing with Section 3200) of the Labor Code).

(7) Filing an affidavit of publication of notice of dissolution of partnership.

(8) Filing an appeal of a determination whether a dog is potentially dangerous or vicious under Section 31622 of the Food and Agricultural Code.

(9) Filing an affidavit under Section 13200 of the Probate Code, together with the issuance of one certified copy of the affidavit under Section 13202 of the Probate Code.

(10) Filing and indexing all papers for which a charge is not elsewhere provided, other than papers filed in actions or special proceedings, official bonds, or certificates of appointment.

(c) The fee for filing a first petition under Section 2029.600 or 2029.620 of the Code of Civil Procedure, if the petitioner is not a party to the out-of-state case, is eighty dollars ($80). Amounts collected shall be distributed to the Trial Court Trust Fund pursuant to Section 68085.1.

(d) The fee for delivering a will to the clerk of the superior court in which the estate of a decedent may be administered, as required by Section 8200 of the Probate Code, is fifty dollars ($50).

(e) From July 1, 2011, to June 30, 2017, inclusive, ten dollars ($10) of each fee collected pursuant to subdivisions (a) and (b) shall be used by the Judicial Council for the expenses of the Judicial Council in implementing and administering the civil representation pilot program under Section 68651.

(f) This section shall become inoperative on July 1, 2017, and, as of January 1, 2018, is repealed, unless a later enacted statute, that becomes operative on or before January 1, 2018, deletes or extends the dates on which it becomes inoperative and is repealed. *(Added by Stats.2005, c. 75 (A.B.145), § 121, eff. July 19, 2005, operative Jan. 1, 2006. Amended by Stats.2005, c. 706 (A.B.1742), § 31; Stats.2008, c. 231 (A.B.2193), § 4; Stats.2009–2010, 4th Ex.Sess., c. 22 (S.B.13), § 17, eff. July 28, 2009; Stats.2009, c. 457 (A.B.590), § 7; Stats.2012, c. 41 (S.B.1021), § 45, eff. June 27, 2012.)*

Inoperative Date and Repeal

For inoperative date and repeal of this section, see its terms.

Law Revision Commission Comments

Subdivision (b) of Section 70626 is amended to specify the fee for obtaining a subpoena from a California court to take a deposition in this state for purposes of a proceeding pending in another jurisdiction. If a person seeks multiple subpoenas, a separate fee is payable under this subdivision for each subpoena sought.

Subdivision (c) is added to specify the fee applicable when discovery is taken in this state for an out-of-state case, and a person who is not a party to the out-of-state case petitions for relief in this state. This fee applies only to the first petition that a non-party files in a particular superior court. If that person files another petition in the same court relating to the same out-of-state case, a motion fee is payable under Section 70617(a). See Code Civ. Proc. § 2029.620(c)(2). [38 Cal.L.Rev.Comm. Reports Apx.4 (2008)].

Research References

Rutter, Cal. Practice Guide: Civ. Pro. Before Trial Ch. 8E-7, Foreign Subpoenas.
Rutter, Cal. Practice Guide: Enforcing Judgments/Debts Ch. 4-A, A. Attachment.
Rutter, Cal. Practice Guide: Enforcing Judgments/Debts Ch. 4-B, B. Claim and Delivery.
Rutter, Cal. Practice Guide: Enforcing Judgments/Debts Ch. 6A-7, Period During Which Judgment Enforceable; Renewal Procedures.
Rutter, Cal. Practice Guide: Enforcing Judgments/Debts Ch. 6B-3, Creation of Judgment Lien.
Rutter, Cal. Practice Guide: Enforcing Judgments/Debts Ch. 6D-2, Writ of Execution.
Rutter, Cal. Practice Guide: Enforcing Judgments/Debts Ch. 6D-8, Special Requirements for Sale of Real Property Dwellings.
Rutter, Cal. Practice Guide: Enforcing Judgments/Debts Ch. 6I-1, Writ of Possession or Sale.
Rutter, Cal. Practice Guide: Enforcing Judgments/Debts Ch. 6K-1, Acknowledgment of Full Satisfaction of Judgment.
Rutter, Cal. Practice Guide: Prof. Responsibility Ch. 8-B, B. Accepting or Rejecting Employment.
2 Witkin Cal. Proc. 5th Courts § 290, (S 290) Uniform Fees.
2 Witkin Cal. Proc. 5th Courts § 303, (S 303) Enforcement and Stay.
8 Witkin Cal. Proc. 5th Enforcement of Judgment § 36, (S 36) Application.
8 Witkin Cal. Proc. 5th Enforcement of Judgment § 107, Application to Clerk.
8 Witkin Cal. Proc. 5th Enforcement of Judgment § 222, (S 222) Determination and Order.
8 Witkin Cal. Proc. 5th Enforcement of Judgment § 326, (S 326) Issuance of Writ of Possession or Sale.
8 Witkin Cal. Proc. 5th Enforcement of Judgment § 338, (S 338) Writ of Sale.
8 Witkin Cal. Proc. 5th Enforcement of Judgment § 391, (S 391) Certificate of Satisfaction.
4 Witkin Cal. Proc. 5th Pleading § 26, Additional Fees.
12 Witkin, California Summary 10th Real Property § 288, (S 288) in General.
11 Witkin, California Summary 10th Husband and Wife § 12A, (S 12A) (New)-Filing Fees.
14 Witkin, California Summary 10th Wills and Probate § 807, Nature of Proceeding.

§ 70626. Fees for miscellaneous services

Section operative July 1, 2017. See, also, section operative until July 1, 2017.

(a) The fee for each of the following services is fifteen dollars ($15). Amounts collected shall be distributed to the Trial Court Trust Fund under Section 68085.1.

(1) Issuing a writ of attachment, a writ of mandate, a writ of execution, a writ of sale, a writ of possession, a writ of prohibition, or any other writ for the enforcement of any order or judgment.

(2) Issuing an abstract of judgment.

(3) Issuing a certificate of satisfaction of judgment under Section 724.100 of the Code of Civil Procedure.

(4) Certifying a copy of any paper, record, or proceeding on file in the office of the clerk of any court.

(5) Taking an affidavit, except in criminal cases or adoption proceedings.

(6) Acknowledgment of any deed or other instrument, including the certificate.

(7) Recording or registering any license or certificate, or issuing any certificate in connection with a license, required by law, for which a charge is not otherwise prescribed.

(8) Issuing any certificate for which the fee is not otherwise fixed.

(b) The fee for each of the following services is twenty dollars ($20). Amounts collected shall be distributed to the Trial Court Trust Fund under Section 68085.1.

(1) Issuing an order of sale.

(2) Receiving and filing an abstract of judgment rendered by a judge of another court and subsequent services based on it, unless the abstract of judgment is filed under Section 704.750 or 708.160 of the Code of Civil Procedure.

(3) Filing a confession of judgment under Section 1134 of the Code of Civil Procedure.

(4) Filing an application for renewal of judgment under Section 683.150 of the Code of Civil Procedure.

(5) Issuing a commission to take a deposition in another state or place under Section 2026.010 of the Code of Civil Procedure, or issuing a subpoena under Section 2029.300 to take a deposition in this state for purposes of a proceeding pending in another jurisdiction.

(6) Filing and entering an award under the Workers' Compensation Law (Division 4 (commencing with Section 3200) of the Labor Code).

(7) Filing an affidavit of publication of notice of dissolution of partnership.

(8) Filing an appeal of a determination whether a dog is potentially dangerous or vicious under Section 31622 of the Food and Agricultural Code.

(9) Filing an affidavit under Section 13200 of the Probate Code, together with the issuance of one certified copy of the affidavit under Section 13202 of the Probate Code.

(10) Filing and indexing all papers for which a charge is not elsewhere provided, other than papers filed in actions or special proceedings, official bonds, or certificates of appointment.

(c) The fee for filing a first petition under Section 2029.600 or 2029.620 of the Code of Civil Procedure, if the petitioner is not a party to the out-of-state case, is eighty dollars ($80). Amounts collected shall be distributed to the Trial Court Trust Fund pursuant to Section 68085.1.

(d) The fee for delivering a will to the clerk of the superior court in which the estate of a decedent may be administered, as required by Section 8200 of the Probate Code, is fifty dollars ($50).

(e) This section shall become operative on July 1, 2017. *(Added by Stats.2009, c. 457 (A.B.590), § 8, operative July 1, 2017. Amended by Stats.2012, c. 41 (S.B.1021), § 46, eff. June 27, 2012, operative July 1, 2017.)*

Research References

Rutter, Cal. Practice Guide: Civ. Pro. Before Trial Ch. 8E-7, Foreign Subpoenas.
Rutter, Cal. Practice Guide: Enforcing Judgments/Debts Ch. 4-A, A. Attachment.
Rutter, Cal. Practice Guide: Enforcing Judgments/Debts Ch. 4-B, B. Claim and Delivery.
Rutter, Cal. Practice Guide: Enforcing Judgments/Debts Ch. 6A-7, Period During Which Judgment Enforceable; Renewal Procedures.
Rutter, Cal. Practice Guide: Enforcing Judgments/Debts Ch. 6B-3, Creation of Judgment Lien.

Rutter, Cal. Practice Guide: Enforcing Judgments/Debts Ch. 6D-2, Writ of Execution.

Rutter, Cal. Practice Guide: Enforcing Judgments/Debts Ch. 6D-8, Special Requirements for Sale of Real Property Dwellings.

Rutter, Cal. Practice Guide: Enforcing Judgments/Debts Ch. 6I-1, Writ of Possession or Sale.

Rutter, Cal. Practice Guide: Enforcing Judgments/Debts Ch. 6K-1, Acknowledgment of Full Satisfaction of Judgment.

Rutter, Cal. Practice Guide: Prof. Responsibility Ch. 8-B, B. Accepting or Rejecting Employment.

2 Witkin Cal. Proc. 5th Courts § 290, (S 290) Uniform Fees.

2 Witkin Cal. Proc. 5th Courts § 303, (S 303) Enforcement and Stay.

8 Witkin Cal. Proc. 5th Enforcement of Judgment § 36, (S 36) Application.

8 Witkin Cal. Proc. 5th Enforcement of Judgment § 107, Application to Clerk.

8 Witkin Cal. Proc. 5th Enforcement of Judgment § 222, (S 222) Determination and Order.

8 Witkin Cal. Proc. 5th Enforcement of Judgment § 326, (S 326) Issuance of Writ of Possession or Sale.

8 Witkin Cal. Proc. 5th Enforcement of Judgment § 338, (S 338) Writ of Sale.

8 Witkin Cal. Proc. 5th Enforcement of Judgment § 391, (S 391) Certificate of Satisfaction.

4 Witkin Cal. Proc. 5th Pleading § 26, Additional Fees.

12 Witkin, California Summary 10th Real Property § 288, (S 288) in General.

11 Witkin, California Summary 10th Husband and Wife § 12A, (S 12A) (New)-Filing Fees.

14 Witkin, California Summary 10th Wills and Probate § 807, Nature of Proceeding.

§ 70627. Fees for copying, comparing, and search of records or files

The fees collected under this section shall be distributed to the court in which they were collected.

(a) The clerk of the court shall charge fifty cents ($0.50) per page to cover the cost of preparing copies of any record, proceeding, or paper on file in the clerk's office.

(b) For comparing with the original on file in the office of the clerk of any court, the copy of any paper, record, or proceeding prepared by another and presented for the clerk's certificate, the fee is one dollar ($1) per page, in addition to the fee for the certificate.

(c) The fee for a search of records or files conducted by a court employee that requires more than 10 minutes is fifteen dollars ($15) for each search. *(Added by Stats.2005, c. 75 (A.B.145), § 121, eff. July 19, 2005, operative Jan. 1, 2006.)*

§ 70628. Fee for exemplification of paper on file

For an exemplification of a record or other paper on file, the fee is fifty dollars * * * ($50), in addition to the charges allowed for copying or comparing each page of the record or other paper. *(Added by Stats.2005, c. 75 (A.B.145), § 121, eff. July 19, 2005, operative Jan. 1, 2006. Amended by Stats.2013, c. 31 (S.B.75), § 7, eff. June 27, 2013.)*

§ 70629. Fee for authentication of documents by clerk of court

(a) The clerk of the court shall collect a fee of fifteen dollars ($15) per signature for any document that is required to be authenticated pursuant to court order.

(b) Each document authenticated by the clerk of the court shall contain the following statement:

"___, Clerk of the Superior Court, County of ___, State of California. Signed pursuant to court order dated ___ in the matter of ___ petitioner v. ___, respondent, Case No. ___." *(Formerly § 26835.1, added by Stats.1997, c. 850 (A.B.233), § 14. Amended by Stats.2002, c. 784 (S.B.1316), § 182. Renumbered § 70629 and amended by Stats.2005, c. 75 (A.B.145), § 78, eff. July 19, 2005, operative Jan. 1, 2006.)*

Law Revision Commission Comments

Subdivision (b) of [former] Section 26835.1 is amended to reflect elimination of the county clerk's role as ex officio clerk of the superior court. See former Section 26800 (county clerk acting as clerk of superior court). The powers, duties, and responsibilities formerly exercised by the county clerk as ex officio clerk of the court are delegated to the court administrative or executive officer, and the county clerk is relieved of those powers, duties, and responsibilities. See Sections 69840 (powers, duties, and responsibilities of clerk of court and deputy clerk of court), 71620 (trial court personnel). [32 Cal.L.Rev.Comm. Reports 214 (2002)].

§ 70630. Fee for appearance by videoconferencing

If the court has made videoconferencing services available, the clerk of the court shall charge a reasonable fee to cover the costs of permitting parties to appear by videoconferencing. This fee shall be deposited into the Trial Court Trust Fund. *(Added by Stats.2005, c. 75 (A.B.145), § 121, eff. July 19, 2005, operative Jan. 1, 2006.)*

§ 70631. Fees for services or products not otherwise legislated or regulated

In the absence of a statute or rule authorizing or prohibiting a fee by the superior court for a particular service or product, the court may charge a reasonable fee not to exceed the costs of providing the service or product, if the Judicial Council approves the fee. The fee shall be distributed to the court in which it was collected. *(Added by Stats.2005, c. 75 (A.B.145), § 121, eff. July 19, 2005, operative Jan. 1, 2006.)*

Research References

2 Witkin Cal. Proc. 5th Courts § 180, Court Fees.

§ 70632. Fees for handling funds held in trust

The clerk of the court shall charge a reasonable fee for handling funds held in trust for non-court parties or entities. The amount of the fee for handling the funds shall be based on rules adopted by, or guidelines and policies authorized by, the Judicial Council under subdivision (a) of Section 77206. This fee shall be deposited into the Trial Court Trust Fund. *(Added by Stats.2005, c. 75 (A.B.145), § 121, eff. July 19, 2005, operative Jan. 1, 2006.)*

§ 70633. Fees for adoption proceedings, proceedings to declare a minor free from parental custody or control, criminal actions, and service to public entities

(a) No fee shall be charged by the clerk for service rendered to the petitioner in any adoption proceeding except as provided in Section 103730 of the Health and Safety Code, nor shall any fees be charged for any service to the state or for any proceeding brought pursuant to Section 7841 of the Family Code to declare a minor free from parental custody or control. No fee shall be charged by the clerk for services rendered in an action to compel registration of a voter under Section 2142 of the Elections Code or to compel counting of provisional ballots under Section 14310 of the Elections Code.

(b) No fee shall be charged by the clerk for services rendered in any criminal action unless otherwise specifically authorized by law, except that the clerk may charge the fee specified in Section 70627 for making or certifying to a copy of any filed paper, record, or proceeding in a criminal action. If a criminal defendant has been granted a fee waiver or the court finds that the defendant does not have the ability to pay the fee, the court may reduce or waive the fee.

(c) Except as permitted in subdivision (b), no fee shall be charged by the clerk for service to any municipality or county in the state, to the state government, nor to the United States of America or any of its officers acting in his or her official capacity. *(Added by Stats.2005, c. 75 (A.B.145), § 121, eff. July 19, 2005, operative Jan. 1, 2006. Amended by Stats.2007, c. 738 (A.B.1248), § 29.)*

Research References

2 Witkin Cal. Proc. 5th Courts § 180, Court Fees.

4 Witkin Cal. Proc. 5th Pleading § 27, Exemptions.

§ 70640. Filing fee surcharge for children's waiting rooms

(a) It is the policy of the state that each court shall endeavor to provide a children's waiting room in each courthouse for children whose parents or guardians are attending a court hearing as a litigant, witness, or for other court purposes as determined by the court. To defray that expense, monthly allocations for children's waiting rooms shall be added to the monthly apportionment under subdivision (a) of Section 68085 for each court where a children's waiting room has been established or where the court has elected to establish that service.

(b) The amount allocated to each court under this section shall be equal to the following: for each first paper filing fee as provided under Section 70611, 70612, 70613, 70614, or 70670, and each first paper or petition filing fee in a probate matter as provided under Section 70650, 70651, 70652, 70653, 70654, 70655, 70656, or 70658, the same amount as was required to be collected as of December 31, 2005, to the Children's Waiting Room Fund under former Section 26826.3 in the county in which the court is located when a fee was collected for the filing of a first paper in a civil action under former Section 26820.4.

(c) Notwithstanding any other provision of law, the court may make expenditures from these allocations in payment of any cost, excluding capital outlay, related to the establishment and maintenance of the children's waiting room, including personnel, heat, light, telephone, security, rental of space, furnishings, toys, books, or any other item in connection with the operation of a children's waiting room.

(d) If, as of January 1, 2006, there is a Children's Waiting Room Fund in the county treasury established under former Section 26826.3, the county immediately shall transfer the moneys in that fund to the court's operations fund as a restricted fund. By February 15, 2006, the county shall provide an accounting of the fund to the Administrative Office of the Courts.

(e) After January 1, 2006, the court may apply to the Judicial Council for an adjustment of the amount distributed to the fund for each uniform filing fee. A court that wishes to establish a children's waiting room, and does not yet have a distribution under this section, may apply to the Judicial Council for a distribution. Applications under this subdivision shall be made according to trial court financial policies and procedures authorized by the Judicial Council under subdivision (a) of Section 77206. Adjustments and new distributions shall be effective January 1 or July 1 of any year beginning January 1, 2006.

(f) The distribution to a court under this section per each filing fee shall be not less than two dollars ($2) and not more than five dollars ($5). *(Formerly § 26826.3, added by Stats.1999, c. 115 (A.B.177), § 1. Renumbered § 70640 and amended by Stats.2005, c. 75 (A.B.145), § 59, eff. July 19, 2005, operative Jan. 1, 2006. Amended by Stats.2005, c. 706 (A.B.1742), § 32; Stats.2007, c. 130 (A.B.299), § 135.)*

Research References

4 Witkin Cal. Proc. 5th Pleading § 28, Distribution of Fees.

ARTICLE 2. FEES IN PROBATE PROCEEDINGS

Section

70650.　Fees for filing papers in probate proceedings.

§ 70650. Fees for filing papers in probate proceedings

(a) The uniform filing fee for the first petition for letters of administration or letters testamentary, or the first petition for special letters of administration with the powers of a general personal representative pursuant to Section 8545 of the Probate Code, is three hundred fifty-five dollars ($355).

(b) The uniform filing fee for the first objections to the probate of any will or codicil under Section 8250 of the Probate Code, or the first petition for revocation of probate of any will or codicil under Section 8270 of the Probate Code, is three hundred fifty-five dollars ($355). The uniform filing fee for the first petition for special letters of administration without the powers of a general personal representative is the fee provided in Section 70657.5. Where objections to the probate of a will or codicil or a petition for revocation of probate of a will or codicil are filed together with a petition for appointment of a personal representative described in subdivision (c) filed by the same person, only the fee provided in subdivision (c) shall be charged to that person.

(c) A fee of three hundred fifty-five dollars ($355) shall also be charged for filing each subsequent petition or objections of a type described in subdivision (a) in the same proceeding by a person other than the original petitioner or contestant. The same fee as provided in subdivision (b) shall be charged for filing each subsequent petition or objections of a type described in that subdivision in the same proceeding by a person other than the original petitioner or contestant.

(d) Notwithstanding Section 70658.5, if a petition for special letters of administration is filed together with a petition for letters of administration or letters testamentary under subdivision (a) or (c) by the same person, the person filing the petitions shall be charged the applicable filing fees for both petitions.

(e) The uniform filing fee charged under this section shall be distributed as provided in Section 68085.3. *(Formerly § 26827, added by Stats.1974, c. 1285, p. 2791, § 11.5. Amended by Stats.1975, c. 766, p. 1785, § 11; Stats.1980, c. 1372, p. 4990, § 30; Stats.1982, c. 327, p. 1455, § 68, eff. June 30, 1982; Stats.1988, c. 113, § 8, eff. May 25, 1988, operative July 1, 1988; Stats.1992, c. 696 (A.B.1344), § 17, eff. Sept. 15, 1992; Stats.1997, c. 850 (A.B.233), § 9; Stats.2003, c. 159 (A.B.1759), § 9, eff. Aug. 2, 2003, operative Aug. 17, 2003; Stats.2003, c. 757, (A.B.296), § 4. Renumbered § 70650 and amended by Stats.2005, c. 75 (A.B.145), § 61, eff. July 19, 2005, operative Jan. 1, 2006. Amended by Stats.2007, c. 738 (A.B.1248), § 30; Stats.2008, c. 310 (A.B.171), § 1; Stats.2008, c. 311 (S.B.1407), § 15; Stats. 2009–2010, 4th Ex.Sess., c. 22 (S.B.13), § 18, eff. July 28, 2009.)*

Validity

A prior version of this section was held unconstitutional as an amendment of an initiative prohibiting estate taxes in the decision of In re Estate of Claeyssens (App. 2 Dist. 2008) 74 Cal.Rptr.3d 304, 161 Cal.App.4th 465.

Law Revision Commission Comments

Subdivision (a) of [former] Section 26827 is revised to clarify the testamentary trust accountings that are subject to this provision. Subdivision (a) is also revised to include petitions under Probate Code Sections 13151 (order determining succession to real property) and 13650 (order determining or confirming property passing or belonging to surviving spouse). Subdivision (a) also recognizes the exception provided in Probate Code Section 13652, which excuses the fee otherwise applicable to a petition under Section 13650 if probate proceedings are already pending.

Subdivision (b) is revised to eliminate language repeated from subdivision (a). The provision relating to fees payable by a public administrator or the Department of Mental Health, formerly in subdivision (b), is generalized in Section 26827.5. [See Section 70659.] [19 Cal.L.Rev.Comm.Reports 1037 (1988)].

Research References

2 Witkin Cal. Proc. 5th Courts § 180, Court Fees.
4 Witkin Cal. Proc. 5th Pleading § 25, Basic Fees.
13 Witkin, California Summary 10th Trusts § 237, (S 237) Nature and Scope of Continuing Jurisdiction.
14 Witkin, California Summary 10th Wills and Probate § 577, (S 577) Objection, Summons, and Response.
14 Witkin, California Summary 10th Wills and Probate § 581, (S 581) Petition, Summons, and Response.
14 Witkin, California Summary 10th Wills and Probate § 585, Filing Fee.
14 Witkin, California Summary 10th Wills and Probate § 380A, (S 380A) (New)-In General.
14 Witkin, California Summary 10th Wills and Probate § 380B, (S 380B) (New)-Decedents' Estates.
14 Witkin, California Summary 10th Wills and Probate § 380C, (S 380C) (New)-Trusts.
14 Witkin, California Summary 10th Wills and Probate § 380E, (S 380E) (New)-Specified Proceedings.

§ 70651. Fee for filing opposition to petition described in § 70650(a)

(a) The uniform filing fee for objections or any other paper in opposition to a petition described in subdivision (a) of Section 70650, other than a petition described in subdivision (c) of Section 70650, is three hundred fifty-five dollars ($355). If objections or any other paper in opposition are filed together with a petition described in subdivision (c) of Section 70650 by the same person, only the fee provided in subdivision (c) of Section 70650 shall be charged to that person.

(b) The uniform filing fee charged under this section shall be distributed as provided in Section 68085.3. *(Added by Stats. 2005, c. 75 (A.B.145), § 121, eff. July 19, 2005, operative Jan. 1,*

2006. Amended by Stats.2007, c. 738 (A.B.1248), § 31; Stats. 2008, c. 310 (A.B.171), § 2; Stats.2008, c. 311 (S.B.1407), § 16; Stats.2009–2010, 4th Ex.Sess., c. 22 (S.B.13), § 19, eff. July 28, 2009.)

Research References

14 Witkin, California Summary 10th Wills and Probate § 585, Filing Fee.
14 Witkin, California Summary 10th Wills and Probate § 380A, (S 380A) (New)-In General.
14 Witkin, California Summary 10th Wills and Probate § 380B, (S 380B) (New)-Decedents' Estates.
14 Witkin, California Summary 10th Wills and Probate § 380C, (S 380C) (New)-Trusts.
14 Witkin, California Summary 10th Wills and Probate § 380E, (S 380E) (New)-Specified Proceedings.

§ 70652. Fee for filing petition and opposition papers concerning internal affairs of certain trusts or first accounts of trustees of certain testamentary trusts

(a) The uniform filing fee for each petition concerning the internal affairs of a trust under Chapter 3 (commencing with Section 17200) of Part 5 of Division 9 of the Probate Code, or a first account of a trustee of a testamentary trust that is subject to the continuing jurisdiction of the court pursuant to Chapter 4 (commencing with Section 17300) of Part 5 of Division 9 of the Probate Code, is three hundred fifty-five dollars ($355).

(b) The uniform filing fee for each paper filed in opposition to a petition or first account of a trustee of a testamentary trust under subdivision (a) is three hundred fifty-five dollars ($355).

(c) To avoid hardship, or for other good cause, the court may direct the clerk of the court to refund all or any part of a filing fee paid under this section.

(d) This section does not apply to petitions or opposition filed concerning trusts created by court order under Article 10 (commencing with Section 2580) of Chapter 6 of Part 3 of Division 4 of the Probate Code, Article 1 (commencing with Section 3100) of Chapter 3 of Part 6 of Division 4 of the Probate Code, Article 1 (commencing with Section 3600) of Chapter 4 of Part 8 of Division 4 of the Probate Code.

(e) The uniform filing fee charged under this section shall be distributed as provided in Section 68085.3. *(Added by Stats. 2005, c. 75 (A.B.145), § 121, eff. July 19, 2005, operative Jan. 1, 2006. Amended by Stats.2008, c. 310 (A.B.171), § 3; Stats.2008, c. 311 (S.B.1407), § 17; Stats.2009–2010, 4th Ex.Sess., c. 22 (S.B.13), § 20, eff. July 28, 2009.)*

Research References

13 Witkin, California Summary 10th Trusts § 226, (S 226) in General.
13 Witkin, California Summary 10th Trusts § 237, (S 237) Nature and Scope of Continuing Jurisdiction.
14 Witkin, California Summary 10th Wills and Probate § 380A, (S 380A) (New)-In General.
14 Witkin, California Summary 10th Wills and Probate § 380C, (S 380C) (New)-Trusts.
14 Witkin, California Summary 10th Wills and Probate § 380E, (S 380E) (New)-Specified Proceedings.

§ 70653. Fee for filing petition and opposition papers concerning appointment of conservator, guardian of estate, or guardian of person and estate

(a) The uniform filing fee for a petition for appointment of a conservator, a guardian of the estate, or a guardian of the person and estate, pursuant to Division 4 (commencing with Section 1400) of the Probate Code, is three hundred fifty-five dollars ($355).

(b) Except as provided in subdivision (f), the uniform filing fee for objections or any other paper in opposition to a petition

Government

under subdivision (a) or (d) is three hundred fifty-five dollars ($355).

(c) If a competing petition for appointment of a guardian or conservator subject to the fee under subdivision (a) is filed together with opposition to the petition of another by the same person, the person filing the competing petition and opposition shall be charged a filing fee only for the competing petition.

(d) Notwithstanding Section 70658.5, if a petition for appointment of a temporary guardian or conservator is filed together with a petition for appointment of a guardian or conservator under subdivision (a), or a competing petition under subdivision (c) by the same person, the person filing the petitions shall be charged the applicable filing fees for both petitions.

(e) The uniform filing fee charged under this section shall be distributed as provided in Section 68085.3.

(f) No fee under this section shall be charged for objections or any other paper in opposition filed by or on behalf of the proposed conservatee, or the minor or a parent of the minor who is the subject of a guardianship proceeding. *(Added by Stats. 2005, c. 75 (A.B.145), § 121, eff. July 19, 2005, operative Jan. 1, 2006. Amended by Stats.2007, c. 738 (A.B.1248), § 32; Stats. 2008, c. 311 (S.B.1407), § 18; Stats.2009–2010, 4th Ex.Sess., c. 22 (S.B.13), § 21, eff. July 28, 2009.)*

Research References

14 Witkin, California Summary 10th Wills and Probate § 918, (S 918) Who May File.
14 Witkin, California Summary 10th Wills and Probate § 938, (S 938) Content and Form.
14 Witkin, California Summary 10th Wills and Probate § 380A, (S 380A) (New)-In General.
14 Witkin, California Summary 10th Wills and Probate § 380D, (S 380D) (New)-Guardianships and Conservatorships.

§ 70654. Fee for filing petition and opposition papers concerning appointment of guardian of person

(a) The uniform filing fee for a petition for appointment of a guardian of the person only, is two hundred five dollars ($205).

(b) Except as provided in subdivision (e), the uniform filing fee for objections or any other paper in opposition to a petition under subdivision (a) is two hundred five dollars ($205).

(c) If a competing petition for appointment of a guardian subject to the fee under subdivision (a) is filed together with opposition to the petition of another by the same person, the person filing the competing petition and opposition shall be charged a filing fee only for the competing petition.

(d) Notwithstanding Section 70658.5, if a petition for appointment of a temporary guardian is filed together with a petition for appointment of a guardian under subdivision (a), or a competing petition under subdivision (c) by the same person, the person filing the petitions shall be charged the applicable filing fees for both petitions.

(e) No fee under this section shall be charged for objections or any other paper in opposition filed by or on behalf of the minor or a parent of the minor who is the subject of the proceeding.

(f) The uniform filing fee charged under this section shall be distributed as provided in Section 68085.4.

(g) No other fees shall be charged for filing a paper under this section in addition to the uniform filing fee provided for in this section. *(Added by Stats.2005, c. 75 (A.B.145), § 121, eff. July 19, 2005, operative Jan. 1, 2006. Amended by Stats.2007, c. 738 (A.B.1248), § 33; Stats.2008, c. 311 (S.B.1407), § 19; Stats. 2009–2010, 4th Ex.Sess., c. 22 (S.B.13), § 22, eff. July 28, 2009.)*

Research References

14 Witkin, California Summary 10th Wills and Probate § 918, (S 918) Who May File.
14 Witkin, California Summary 10th Wills and Probate § 380A, (S 380A) (New)-In General.
14 Witkin, California Summary 10th Wills and Probate § 380D, (S 380D) (New)-Guardianships and Conservatorships.
14 Witkin, California Summary 10th Wills and Probate § 380E, (S 380E) (New)-Specified Proceedings.

§ 70655. Fee for filing petition commencing or opposition papers concerning certain probate proceedings

(a) The uniform filing fee for a petition that commences any of the proceedings under the Probate Code listed in subdivision (c) is three hundred fifty-five dollars ($355).

(b) The uniform filing fee for objections or any other paper filed in opposition to a petition under subdivision (a) is three hundred fifty-five dollars ($355).

(c) This section applies to petitions or opposition concerning the following proceedings:

(1) A petition for compromise of a minor's claim pursuant to Section 3600 of the Probate Code.

(2) A petition to determine succession to real property pursuant to Section 13151 of the Probate Code.

(3) A spousal or domestic partnership property petition pursuant to Section 13650 of the Probate Code, except as provided in Section 13652 of the Probate Code.

(4) A petition to establish the fact of death to determine title to real property under Section 200 of the Probate Code.

(5) A petition for an order concerning a particular transaction pursuant to Section 3100 of the Probate Code.

(6) A petition concerning capacity determination and health care decision for an adult without conservator pursuant to Section 3200 of the Probate Code.

(7) A petition concerning an advance health care directive pursuant to Section 4766 of the Probate Code.

(8) A petition concerning a power of attorney pursuant to Section 4541 of the Probate Code.

(9) A petition for approval, compromise, or settlement of claims against a deceased settlor, or for allocation of amounts due between trusts, pursuant to Section 19020 of the Probate Code.

(10) Any other petition that commences a proceeding under the Probate Code not otherwise provided for in this article.

(d) The uniform filing fee charged under this section shall be distributed as provided in Section 68085.3. *(Added by Stats. 2005, c. 75 (A.B.145), § 121, eff. July 19, 2005, operative Jan. 1, 2006. Amended by Stats.2007, c. 738 (A.B.1248), § 34; Stats. 2008, c. 311 (S.B.1407), § 20; Stats.2009–2010, 4th Ex.Sess., c. 22 (S.B.13), § 23, eff. July 28, 2009.)*

Research References

11 Witkin, California Summary 10th Community Property § 163, Petition.
13 Witkin, California Summary 10th Trusts § 279, (S 279) Petition.
14 Witkin, California Summary 10th Wills and Probate § 14, (S 14) Statutory Proceeding to Establish Death.
14 Witkin, California Summary 10th Wills and Probate § 814, Petition.
14 Witkin, California Summary 10th Wills and Probate § 830, Petition.
14 Witkin, California Summary 10th Wills and Probate § 874, (S 874) Petition.
14 Witkin, California Summary 10th Wills and Probate § 898, (S 898) Petition.
14 Witkin, California Summary 10th Wills and Probate § 1014, (S 1014) Procedure for Court Approval.
14 Witkin, California Summary 10th Wills and Probate § 1064, Petition, Notice, and Hearing.

14 Witkin, California Summary 10th Wills and Probate § 1070, (S 1070) in General.

14 Witkin, California Summary 10th Wills and Probate § 380A, (S 380A) (New)-In General.

14 Witkin, California Summary 10th Wills and Probate § 380E, (S 380E) (New)-Specified Proceedings.

§ 70656. Fee for filing petition commencing or opposition papers concerning setting aside decedent's estate of small value

(a) The uniform filing fee for a petition requesting an order setting aside a decedent's estate of small value pursuant to Section 6602 of the Probate Code, if no estate proceeding is pending for the decedent, is two hundred five dollars ($205).

(b) The uniform filing fee for objections or any other paper filed in opposition to a petition under subdivision (a) is two hundred five dollars ($205).

(c) If a petition or objections or any other paper in opposition under this section is filed concurrently with a petition for appointment of a personal representative described in Section 70650, the petitioner or objector shall be charged only for the filing fee provided in Section 70650.

(d) The uniform filing fee charged under this section shall be distributed as provided in Section 68085.4.

(e) Except as provided in subdivision (c), no other fee shall be charged for filing a paper under this section in addition to the uniform filing fee provided for in this section. *(Added by Stats.2005, c. 75 (A.B.145), § 121, eff. July 19, 2005, operative Jan. 1, 2006. Amended by Stats.2008, c. 311 (S.B.1407), § 21; Stats.2009–2010, 4th Ex.Sess., c. 22 (S.B.13), § 24, eff. July 28, 2009.)*

Research References

14 Witkin, California Summary 10th Wills and Probate § 782, (S 782) Petition to Set Aside.

14 Witkin, California Summary 10th Wills and Probate § 380A, (S 380A) (New)-In General.

14 Witkin, California Summary 10th Wills and Probate § 380B, (S 380B) (New)-Decedents' Estates.

§ 70657. Fee for filing motion or other paper requiring a hearing

Section operative until July 1, 2015. See, also, section operative July 1, 2015.

(a) Except as provided in subdivision (c), the uniform fee for filing a motion or other paper requiring a hearing subsequent to the first paper in a proceeding under the Probate Code, other than a petition or application or opposition described in Sections 70657.5 and 70658, is sixty dollars ($60). This fee shall be charged for the following papers:

(1) Papers listed in subdivision (a) of Section 70617.

(2) Applications for ex parte relief, whether or not notice of the application to any person is required, except an ex parte petition for discharge of a personal representative, conservator, or guardian upon completion of a court-ordered distribution or transfer, for which no fee shall be charged.

(3) Petitions or applications, or objections, filed subsequent to issuance of temporary letters of conservatorship or guardianship or letters of conservatorship or guardianship that are not subject to the filing fee provided in subdivision (a) of Section 70658.

(4) The first or subsequent petition for temporary letters of conservatorship or guardianship.

(b) There shall be no fee under subdivision (a) for filing any of the papers listed under subdivision (b) of Section 70617.

(c) The summary judgment fee provided in subdivision (d) of Section 70617 shall apply to summary judgment motions in proceedings under the Probate Code.

(d) Regardless of whether each motion or matter is heard at a single hearing or at separate hearings, the filing fees required by subdivisions (a) and (c) apply separately to each motion or other paper filed. The Judicial Council may publish rules to give uniform guidance to courts in applying fees under this section.

(e) No fee is payable under this section for a petition or opposition filed subsequent to issuance of letters of temporary guardianship or letters of guardianship in a guardianship described in Section 70654.

(f) This section shall become inoperative on July 1, 2015, and, as of January 1, 2016, is repealed, unless a later enacted statute, that becomes operative on or before January 1, 2016, deletes or extends the dates on which it becomes inoperative and is repealed. *(Added by Stats.2005, c. 75 (A.B.145), § 121, eff. July 19, 2005, operative Jan. 1, 2006. Amended by Stats.2007, c. 738 (A.B.1248), § 35; Stats.2008, c. 311 (S.B.1407), § 22; Stats.2012, c. 41 (S.B.1021), § 47, eff. June 27, 2012.)*

Inoperative Date and Repeal

For inoperative date and repeal of this section, see its terms.

Research References

14 Witkin, California Summary 10th Wills and Probate § 975, Appointment.

14 Witkin, California Summary 10th Wills and Probate § 380A, (S 380A) (New)-In General.

14 Witkin, California Summary 10th Wills and Probate § 380D, (S 380D) (New)-Guardianships and Conservatorships.

14 Witkin, California Summary 10th Wills and Probate § 380E, (S 380E) (New)-Specified Proceedings.

§ 70657. Fee for filing motion or other paper requiring a hearing

Section operative July 1, 2015. See, also, section operative until July 1, 2015.

(a) Except as provided in subdivision (c), the uniform fee for filing a motion or other paper requiring a hearing subsequent to the first paper in a proceeding under the Probate Code, other than a petition or application or opposition described in Sections 70657.5 and 70658, is forty dollars ($40). This fee shall be charged for the following papers:

(1) Papers listed in subdivision (a) of Section 70617.

(2) Applications for ex parte relief, whether or not notice of the application to any person is required, except an ex parte petition for discharge of a personal representative, conservator, or guardian upon completion of a court-ordered distribution or transfer, for which no fee shall be charged.

(3) Petitions or applications, or objections, filed subsequent to issuance of temporary letters of conservatorship or guardianship or letters of conservatorship or guardianship that are not subject to the filing fee provided in subdivision (a) of Section 70658.

(4) The first or subsequent petition for temporary letters of conservatorship or guardianship.

(b) There shall be no fee under subdivision (a) for filing any of the papers listed under subdivision (b) of Section 70617.

(c) The summary judgment fee provided in subdivision (d) of Section 70617 shall apply to summary judgment motions in proceedings under the Probate Code.

(d) Regardless of whether each motion or matter is heard at a single hearing or at separate hearings, the filing fees required by subdivisions (a) and (c) apply separately to each motion or other

Government

paper filed. The Judicial Council may publish rules to give uniform guidance to courts in applying fees under this section.

(e) No fee is payable under this section for a petition or opposition filed subsequent to issuance of letters of temporary guardianship or letters of guardianship in a guardianship described in Section 70654.

(f) This section shall become operative on July 1, 2015. *(Added by Stats.2012, c. 41 (S.B.1021), § 48, eff. June 27, 2012, operative July 1, 2015.)*

Research References

14 Witkin, California Summary 10th Wills and Probate § 975, Appointment.

14 Witkin, California Summary 10th Wills and Probate § 380A, (S 380A) (New)-In General.

14 Witkin, California Summary 10th Wills and Probate § 380D, (S 380D) (New)-Guardianships and Conservatorships.

14 Witkin, California Summary 10th Wills and Probate § 380E, (S 380E) (New)-Specified Proceedings.

§ 70657.5. Uniform fee for filing specified petitions, applications, objections or other opposition; exceptions

(a) The uniform fee for filing the following petitions or applications, and objections or other opposition, is two hundred dollars ($200):

(1) Petitions or applications, or opposition, concerning the internal affairs of a trust that are not subject to the filing fees provided in Section 70650, 70651, or 70652.

(2) Petitions or applications, or objections, filed subsequent to issuance of special letters of administration or letters testamentary or of administration in decedent's estate proceedings that are not subject to the filing fee provided in subdivision (a) of Section 70658.

(3) The first or subsequent petition for special letters of administration without the powers of a general personal representative.

(b) One hundred sixty dollars ($160) of each two-hundred-dollar ($200) fee collected under subdivision (a) shall be transmitted to the state for deposit into the Immediate and Critical Needs Account of the State Court Facilities Construction Fund, established in Section 70371.5.

(c) No fee is payable under this section for a disclaimer of an interest in a decedent's estate. *(Added by Stats.2007, c. 738 (A.B.1248), § 36. Amended by Stats.2008, c. 310 (A.B.171), § 4; Stats.2008, c. 311 (S.B.1407), § 23.)*

Research References

14 Witkin, California Summary 10th Wills and Probate § 334, in General.

14 Witkin, California Summary 10th Wills and Probate § 426, Procedure for Appointment.

14 Witkin, California Summary 10th Wills and Probate § 585, Filing Fee.

14 Witkin, California Summary 10th Wills and Probate § 380A, (S 380A) (New)-In General.

14 Witkin, California Summary 10th Wills and Probate § 380B, (S 380B) (New)-Decedents' Estates.

14 Witkin, California Summary 10th Wills and Probate § 380C, (S 380C) (New)-Trusts.

14 Witkin, California Summary 10th Wills and Probate § 380E, (S 380E) (New)-Specified Proceedings.

§ 70658. Uniform fee for filing petition or opposition paper concerning appealable order filed after issuance of letters; application; exceptions

(a) Except as provided in subdivision (c), the uniform fee for filing a petition or application, or objections or any other paper in opposition to a petition or application listed in this subdivision, filed after issuance of letters testamentary, letters of administration, letters of special administration to a personal representative of a decedent's estate, or letters of guardianship or conservatorship, or letters of temporary guardianship or conservatorship to a guardian or conservator, is three hundred fifty-five dollars ($355). This section shall apply to the following petitions or applications, or opposition:

(1) Petition or application for or opposition to an order directing, authorizing, approving, or confirming the sale, lease, encumbrance, grant of an option, purchase, conveyance, or exchange of property.

(2) Petition or application for or opposition to an order settling an account of a fiduciary.

(3) Petition or application for or opposition to an order authorizing, instructing, or directing a fiduciary, or approving or confirming the acts of a fiduciary.

(4) Petition or application for or opposition to an order fixing, authorizing, allowing, or directing payment of compensation or expenses of an attorney.

(5) Petition or application for or opposition to an order fixing, authorizing, allowing, or directing payment of compensation or expenses of a fiduciary.

(6) Petition or application for or opposition to an order surcharging or removing a fiduciary.

(7) Petition or application for or opposition to an order transferring or authorizing the transfer of the property of an estate to a fiduciary in another jurisdiction.

(8) Petition or application for or opposition to an order allowing a fiduciary's request to resign.

(9) Petition or application for or opposition to an order adjudicating the merits of a claim made under Part 19 (commencing with Section 850) of Division 2 of the Probate Code.

(10) Petition or application for or opposition to an order granting permission to fix the residence of a ward or conservatee at a place not within this state.

(11) Petition or application for or opposition to an order directing, authorizing, approving, or modifying payments for support, maintenance, or education of a ward or conservatee or for a person entitled to support, maintenance, or education from a ward or conservatee.

(12) Petition or application for or opposition to an order granting or denying a request under Section 2423, concerning payment of surplus income to the relatives of a conservatee, or Section 2580, concerning substituted judgment, of the Probate Code.

(13) Petition or application for or opposition to an order affecting the legal capacity of a conservatee pursuant to Chapter 4 (commencing with Section 1870) of Part 3 of Division 4 of the Probate Code.

(14) Petition or application for or opposition to an order adjudicating the merits of a claim under Article 5 (commencing with Section 2500) of Chapter 6 of Part 4 of Division 4 of the Probate Code.

(b) The uniform fee in subdivision (a) shall be distributed as provided in Section 68085.3. No other fee shall be charged for filing a paper under this section in addition to the uniform filing fee provided for in this section.

(c) The fee provided in this section shall not be charged for filing any of the following papers:

(1) A petition or application, or opposition, in a guardianship proceeding under Section 70654.

(2) A disclaimer of an interest in a decedent's estate.

(d) One hundred seventy dollars ($170) of each three hundred fifty-five dollar ($355) fee collected under this section shall be transmitted to the Controller for deposit into the Immediate and Critical Needs Account of the State Court Facilities Construction Fund, established in Section 70371.5. *(Added by Stats.2005, c. 75 (A.B.145), § 121, eff. July 19, 2005, operative Jan. 1, 2006. Amended by Stats.2007, c. 738 (A.B.1248), § 37; Stats.2008, c. 310 (A.B.171), § 5; Stats.2008, c. 311 (S.B.1407), § 24; Stats.2009–2010, 4th Ex.Sess., c. 22 (S.B.13), § 25, eff. July 28, 2009.)*

Research References

14 Witkin, California Summary 10th Wills and Probate § 334, in General.

14 Witkin, California Summary 10th Wills and Probate § 356, Petition.

14 Witkin, California Summary 10th Wills and Probate § 384, Petition or Report.

14 Witkin, California Summary 10th Wills and Probate § 459, Petition, Citation, Hearing, and Determination.

14 Witkin, California Summary 10th Wills and Probate § 460, (S 460) Death, Resignation, Removal, or Other Termination.

14 Witkin, California Summary 10th Wills and Probate § 540, in General.

14 Witkin, California Summary 10th Wills and Probate § 751, in General.

14 Witkin, California Summary 10th Wills and Probate § 955, (S 955) Court Order Broadening Capacity.

14 Witkin, California Summary 10th Wills and Probate § 990, Fixing Residence.

14 Witkin, California Summary 10th Wills and Probate § 1001, (S 1001) Duty to Manage Estate.

14 Witkin, California Summary 10th Wills and Probate § 1008, (S 1008) in General.

14 Witkin, California Summary 10th Wills and Probate § 1009, (S 1009) Distribution of Surplus Income.

14 Witkin, California Summary 10th Wills and Probate § 1014, (S 1014) Procedure for Court Approval.

14 Witkin, California Summary 10th Wills and Probate § 1026, (S 1026) Petition, Notice, and Hearing.

14 Witkin, California Summary 10th Wills and Probate § 1044, Procedure.

14 Witkin, California Summary 10th Wills and Probate § 1049, Procedure for Removal.

14 Witkin, California Summary 10th Wills and Probate § 1050, Resignation.

14 Witkin, California Summary 10th Wills and Probate § 1053, (S 1053) Transfer of Property Out of State.

14 Witkin, California Summary 10th Wills and Probate § 380A, (S 380A) (New)-In General.

14 Witkin, California Summary 10th Wills and Probate § 380B, (S 380B) (New)-Decedents' Estates.

14 Witkin, California Summary 10th Wills and Probate § 380E, (S 380E) (New)-Specified Proceedings.

§ 70658.5. Filing combining requests for relief or opposition to relief that could have been stated in separate petitions; one filing fee; amount

If a petition or application, or opposition to a petition or application, described in Sections 70650 to 70656, inclusive, or Sections 70657.5 to 70658, inclusive, is filed combining requests for relief or opposition to relief that could have been stated in separate petitions or applications, or objections or other opposition, only one filing fee shall be charged under this article. If a filing combines petitions, applications, or objections, or other opposition to a petition or application, that would be subject to different filing fees under this article, the higher of the applicable filing fees shall be charged. *(Added by Stats.2007, c. 738 (A.B.1248), § 38.)*

Research References

14 Witkin, California Summary 10th Wills and Probate § 380A, (S 380A) (New)-In General.

§ 70659. Probate proceedings where petitioner is specified public official; fee payable from estate

Where the public administrator, public guardian, or public conservator, or an employee of the State Department of State Hospitals or the State Department of Developmental Services is

the petitioner in an official capacity in a proceeding described in Section 70650, 70653, 70657, or 70658, the fee is payable only out of the assets of the estate coming into the official's possession or control. *(Formerly § 26827.5, added by Stats.1988, c. 113, § 10, eff. May 25, 1988, operative July 1, 1988. Renumbered § 70659 and amended by Stats.2005, c. 75 (A.B.145), § 65, eff. July 19, 2005, operative Jan. 1, 2006. Amended by Stats.2012, c. 440 (A.B.1488), § 33, eff. Sept. 22, 2012.)*

Law Revision Commission Comments

[Former] Section 26827.5 is a new provision that generalizes a provision formerly set out in Section 26827(b). This section applies to all filing fees described in Sections 26827 and 26827.4, whereas the former provision appeared to apply only to part of Section 26827. In addition, this section refers to assets under the control of the official. [19 Cal.L.Rev.Comm.Reports 1038 (1988)].

§ 70660. Estate planning documents; storage; reduction or waiver of fees

(a) The fee for receiving and storing each document transferred to the clerk of the superior court under Section 732 of the Probate Code is twenty dollars ($20).

(b) The superior court may reduce or waive the fee established pursuant to this section under either of the following circumstances:

(1) The court has assumed jurisdiction under Article 11 (commencing with Section 6180) of Chapter 4 of Division 3 of the Business and Professions Code over the law practice of the attorney with whom the document is deposited.

(2) On a showing of hardship. *(Formerly § 26827.6, added by Stats.1993, c. 519 (A.B.209), § 2. Amended by Stats.2001, c. 824 (A.B.1700), § 14. Renumbered § 70660 and amended by Stats. 2005, c. 75 (A.B.145), § 66, eff. July 19, 2005, operative Jan. 1, 2006.)*

Law Revision Commission Comments

[Former] Section 26827.6 is new. [23 Cal.L.Rev.Comm. Reports 989 (1993)].

§ 70661. Estate planning documents; fee for searching

The fee for searching a document transferred to the clerk of the superior court under Section 732 of the Probate Code is the same as the fee under subdivision (c) of Section 70627 for searching records or files. *(Formerly § 26827.7, added by Stats.1993, c. 519 (A.B.209), § 3. Renumbered § 70661 and amended by Stats.2005, c. 75 (A.B.145), § 67, eff. July 19, 2005, operative Jan. 1, 2006.)*

Law Revision Commission Comments

[Former] Section 26827.7 is new. [23 Cal.L.Rev.Comm. Reports 901 (1993) (Annual Report, App. 8)].

§ 70662. Request for special notice pursuant to Probate Code §§ 1250, 2700, and 17204; filing fees

(a) The filing fee for a request for special notice pursuant to Sections 1250, 2700, and 17204 of the Probate Code is forty dollars ($40). This fee shall be in addition to any other fee charged for a paper filed concurrently with a request for special notice.

(b) This section shall remain in effect only until January 1, 2019, and as of that date is repealed, unless a later enacted statute, that is enacted before January 1, 2019, deletes or extends that date. *(Added by Stats.2013, c. 382 (A.B.1293), § 1.)*

Repeal

For repeal of this section, see its terms.

ARTICLE 3.　FEES IN FAMILY LAW MATTERS

Section
70670.　Fee for filing first paper in Family Code proceeding.
70671.　"Paper" defined.
70672.　Filing fees for issues relating to cases involving child support agency services.
70673.　Member of armed forces; respondent or defendant in dissolution, separation or paternity action; exemption.
70674.　Fee for marriage or domestic partnership dissolution record.
70676.　Exemption from fee for certain certified copies of order for indigent petitioner.
70677.　Filing fee for motion or other paper requiring a hearing.
70677.　Filing fee for motion or other paper requiring a hearing.
70678.　Filing fee for filing motion, order or other proceeding to modify or enforce order or judgment regarding custody or visitation of children.

§ 70670.　Fee for filing first paper in Family Code proceeding

(a) The uniform fee for filing the first paper in a proceeding under the Family Code, other than a proceeding for dissolution of marriage or domestic partnership, legal separation, or nullity, is three hundred fifty-five dollars ($355). The fee shall be distributed as provided in Section 68085.3.

(b) The uniform fee for filing the first paper in a proceeding for dissolution of marriage or domestic partnership, legal separation, or nullity, is three hundred fifty-five dollars ($355). The fee shall be distributed as provided in Section 68085.3, except that two dollars ($2) of the funds that would otherwise be distributed to the Trial Court Trust Fund shall be transmitted to the Treasurer for deposit in the Health Statistics Special Fund.

(c) The uniform fee for filing the first paper in a proceeding under subdivision (a) on behalf of any respondent, defendant, intervenor, or adverse party, whether separately or jointly, is three hundred fifty-five dollars ($355). The fee shall be distributed as provided in Section 68085.3.

(d) The uniform fee for filing the first paper in a proceeding under subdivision (b) on behalf of any respondent, defendant, intervenor, or adverse party, whether separately or jointly, is three hundred fifty-five dollars ($355). The fee shall be distributed as provided in Section 68085.3.

(e) The fees in this section do not apply to papers filed for the purpose of making a disclaimer. *(Added by Stats.2005, c. 75 (A.B.145), § 121, eff. July 19, 2005, operative Jan. 1, 2006. Amended by Stats.2008, c. 311 (S.B.1407), § 25; Stats.2009–2010, 4th Ex.Sess., c. 22 (S.B.13), § 26, eff. July 28, 2009.)*

Research References
2 Witkin Cal. Proc. 5th Courts § 180, Court Fees.
4 Witkin Cal. Proc. 5th Pleading § 25, Basic Fees.
11 Witkin, California Summary 10th Husband and Wife § 12A, (S 12A) (New)-Filing Fees.

§ 70671.　"Paper" defined

As used in subdivision (c) or (d) of Section 70670, the term "paper" does not include any of the following:

(a) The declaration of a spouse or domestic partner filed in an order to show cause proceeding.

(b) A settlement agreement or a stipulation for judgment that is signed by a defaulted respondent and intended for incorporation in a proposed decree of dissolution of marriage or domestic partnership.

(c) A stipulation regarding the date of termination of the marital or domestic partnership status if the court has retained jurisdiction over that date.

(d) A document relating to a stipulated postjudgment modification of child support.

(e) A stipulation to modify a settlement agreement that was signed by a defaulted respondent and incorporated in a decree of dissolution if the stipulation is presented by the petitioner.

(f) A request for an order to prevent domestic violence or a responsive declaration to that request. *(Added by Stats.2005, c. 75 (A.B.145), § 121, eff. July 19, 2005, operative Jan. 1, 2006.)*

Research References
11 Witkin, California Summary 10th Husband and Wife § 12A, (S 12A) (New)-Filing Fees.

§ 70672.　Filing fees for issues relating to cases involving child support agency services

Notwithstanding any other provision of law, no fee shall be charged to file a first paper or any subsequent pleading or document on issues relating to parentage or support in a case in which a Title IV–D child support agency is providing services under Section 17400 of the Family Code. *(Added by Stats.2005, c. 75 (A.B.145), § 121, eff. July 19, 2005, operative Jan. 1, 2006.)*

§ 70673.　Member of armed forces; respondent or defendant in dissolution, separation or paternity action; exemption

Notwithstanding any other provision of law, no fee shall be charged to file a respondent's appearance, stipulation if any, and waiver of rights in the action under the Service members Civil Relief Act (50 U.S.C. App. Secs. 501 to 596, inclusive) in an action for dissolution of marriage or domestic partnership, legal separation, or nullity, or to establish parentage, in any case wherein the respondent is a member of the armed forces of the United States and does not contest the action for dissolution of marriage or domestic partnership, legal separation, or nullity, or to establish parentage. *(Formerly § 26857.5, added by Stats. 1974, c. 39, p. 52, § 1. Amended by Stats.1996, c. 348 (A.B.3148), § 1. Renumbered § 70673 and amended by Stats.2005, c. 75 (A.B.145), § 93, eff. July 19, 2005, operative Jan. 1, 2006.)*

Research References
4 Witkin Cal. Proc. 5th Pleading § 27, Exemptions.
11 Witkin, California Summary 10th Husband and Wife § 12A, (S 12A) (New)-Filing Fees.

§ 70674.　Fee for marriage or domestic partnership dissolution record

(a) Except as provided by Section 6103.9, and notwithstanding the fee authorized by paragraph (4) of subdivision (a) of Section 70626, a fee of ten dollars ($10) shall be paid by a public agency applicant for a certified copy of a marriage or domestic partnership dissolution record that the agency is required to obtain in the ordinary course of business. A fee of fifteen dollars ($15) shall be paid by any other applicant for a certified copy of a marriage or domestic partnership dissolution record. Five dollars ($5) of any fifteen dollar ($15) fee shall be transmitted monthly to the state for deposit into the Family Law Trust Fund as provided by Section 1852 of the Family Code. The remainder of the fees collected under this section shall be deposited into the Trial Court Trust Fund.

(b) As used in this section, "marriage or domestic partnership dissolution record" means the judgment. *(Formerly § 26832.1, added by Stats.1997, c. 850 (A.B.233), § 12. Renumbered § 70674 and amended by Stats.2005, c. 75 (A.B.145), § 74, eff. July 19, 2005, operative Jan. 1, 2006.)*

Research References

11 Witkin, California Summary 10th Husband and Wife § 17, (S 17) Vital Statistics.

11 Witkin, California Summary 10th Husband and Wife § 12A, (S 12A) (New)-Filing Fees.

§ 70676. Exemption from fee for certain certified copies of order for indigent petitioner

No fee shall be charged to an indigent petitioner for certified copies of any order issued pursuant to any of the following:

(a) Article 2 (commencing with Section 2045), Article 3 (commencing with Section 2047), or Article 4 (commencing with Section 2049) of Chapter 4 of Part 1 of Division 6 of the Family Code.

(b) Division 10 (commencing with Section 6200) of the Family Code.

(c) Article 2 (commencing with Section 7710), Article 3 (commencing with Section 7720), or Article 4 (commencing with Section 7730) of Chapter 6 of Part 3 of Division 12 of the Family Code. *(Formerly § 26833.5, added by Stats.1979, c. 795, p. 2713, § 11, operative July 1, 1980. Amended by Stats.1992, c. 163 (A.B.2641), § 80, operative Jan. 1, 1994; Stats.1993, c. 219 (A.B.1500), § 213.5. Renumbered § 70676 and amended by Stats.2005, c. 75 (A.B.145), § 76, eff. July 19, 2005, operative Jan. 1, 2006.)*

Law Revision Commission Comments

[Former] Section 26833.5 is amended to substitute references to the Family Code provisions that replaced the former provisions in the Civil Code and Code of Civil Procedure. The references to restraining orders included in a judgment have been added. [23 Cal.L.Rev.Comm. Reports 1 (1993)].

Research References

11 Witkin, California Summary 10th Husband and Wife § 12A, (S 12A) (New)-Filing Fees.

§ 70677. Filing fee for motion or other paper requiring a hearing

Section operative until July 1, 2015. See,
also, section operative July 1, 2015.

(a) The uniform fee for filing any motion, application, order to show cause, or any other paper requiring a hearing subsequent to the first paper is sixty dollars ($60). Papers for which this fee shall be charged include the following:

(1) Papers listed in subdivision (a) of Section 70617.

(2) An order to show cause or notice of motion seeking temporary prejudgment or postjudgment orders, including, but not limited to, orders to establish, modify, or enforce child, spousal, or partner support, custody and visitation of children, division and control of property, attorney's fees, and bifurcation of issues.

(b) There shall be no fee under subdivision (a) of this section for filing any of the following:

(1) A motion, motion to quash proceeding, application, or demurrer that is the first paper filed in an action and on which a first paper filing fee is paid.

(2) An amended notice of motion or amended order to show cause.

(3) A statement to register foreign support under Section 4951 of the Family Code.

(4) An application to determine the judgment after entry of default.

(5) A request for an order to prevent domestic violence.

(6) A paper requiring a hearing on a petition for writ of review, mandate, or prohibition that is the first paper filed in an action and on which a first paper filing fee has been paid.

(7) A stipulation that does not require an order.

(c) The uniform fee for filing the following papers not requiring a hearing is twenty dollars ($20):

(1) A request, application, or motion for the continuance of a hearing or case management conference.

(2) A stipulation and order.

(d) Regardless of whether each motion or matter is heard at a single hearing or at separate hearings, the filing fees required under paragraph (1) of subdivision (a) and under subdivision (c) apply separately to each motion or other paper filed. If an order to show cause or notice of motion is filed as specified in paragraph (2) of subdivision (a) combining requests for relief or opposition to relief on more than one issue, only one filing fee shall be charged under this section. The Judicial Council may publish rules to give uniform guidance to courts in applying fees under this section.

(e) This section shall become inoperative on July 1, 2015, and, as of January 1, 2016, is repealed, unless a later enacted statute, that becomes operative on or before January 1, 2016, deletes or extends the dates on which it becomes inoperative and is repealed. *(Added by Stats.2005, c. 75 (A.B.145), § 121, eff. July 19, 2005, operative Jan. 1, 2006. Amended by Stats.2007, c. 738 (A.B.1248), § 39; Stats.2012, c. 41 (S.B.1021), § 49, eff. June 27, 2012.)*

Inoperative Date and Repeal

For inoperative date and repeal of this section, see its terms.

Research References

4 Witkin Cal. Proc. 5th Pleading § 25, Basic Fees.

11 Witkin, California Summary 10th Husband and Wife § 12A, (S 12A) (New)-Filing Fees.

§ 70677. Filing fee for motion or other paper requiring a hearing

Section operative July 1, 2015. See, also,
section operative until July 1, 2015.

(a) The uniform fee for filing any motion, application, order to show cause, or any other paper requiring a hearing subsequent to the first paper is forty dollars ($40). Papers for which this fee shall be charged include the following:

(1) Papers listed in subdivision (a) of Section 70617.

(2) An order to show cause or notice of motion seeking temporary prejudgment or postjudgment orders, including, but not limited to, orders to establish, modify, or enforce child, spousal, or partner support, custody and visitation of children, division and control of property, attorney's fees, and bifurcation of issues.

(b) There shall be no fee under subdivision (a) of this section for filing any of the following:

(1) A motion, motion to quash proceeding, application, or demurrer that is the first paper filed in an action and on which a first paper filing fee is paid.

(2) An amended notice of motion or amended order to show cause.

(3) A statement to register foreign support under Section 4951 of the Family Code.

(4) An application to determine the judgment after entry of default.

(5) A request for an order to prevent domestic violence.

(6) A paper requiring a hearing on a petition for writ of review, mandate, or prohibition that is the first paper filed in an action and on which a first paper filing fee has been paid.

(7) A stipulation that does not require an order.

(c) The uniform fee for filing the following papers not requiring a hearing is twenty dollars ($20):

(1) A request, application, or motion for the continuance of a hearing or case management conference.

(2) A stipulation and order.

(d) Regardless of whether each motion or matter is heard at a single hearing or at separate hearings, the filing fees required under paragraph (1) of subdivision (a) and under subdivision (c) apply separately to each motion or other paper filed. If an order to show cause or notice of motion is filed as specified in paragraph (2) of subdivision (a) combining requests for relief or opposition to relief on more than one issue, only one filing fee shall be charged under this section. The Judicial Council may publish rules to give uniform guidance to courts in applying fees under this section.

(e) This section shall become operative on July 1, 2015. *(Added by Stats.2012, c. 41 (S.B.1021), § 50, eff. June 27, 2012, operative July 1, 2015.)*

Research References

4 Witkin Cal. Proc. 5th Pleading § 25, Basic Fees.

11 Witkin, California Summary 10th Husband and Wife § 12A, (S 12A) (New)-Filing Fees.

§ 70678. Filing fee for filing motion, order or other proceeding to modify or enforce order or judgment regarding custody or visitation of children

In addition to the fee set forth in Section 70677, a fee of twenty-five dollars ($25) shall be paid to the clerk of the court at the time of filing a motion, order to show cause, or other proceeding seeking to modify or enforce that portion of any judgment or order entered in this state or any other state which orders or awards the custody of a minor child or children or which specifies the rights of any party to the proceeding to visitation of a minor child or children. Fifteen dollars ($15) of the fee authorized in this section shall be used exclusively to pay the costs of maintaining mediation services provided under Chapter 11 (commencing with Section 3160) of Part 2 of Division 8 of the Family Code, and ten dollars ($10) of the fee shall be used exclusively to pay the costs of services provided by the family law facilitator under Section 10005 of the Family Code. *(Formerly § 26862, added by Stats.1980, c. 48, p. 134, § 7, eff. March 27, 1980. Amended by Stats.1997, c. 850 (A.B.233), § 24. Renumbered § 70678 and amended by Stats.2005, c. 75 (A.B.145), § 95, eff. July 19, 2005, operative Jan. 1, 2006.)*

Research References

11 Witkin, California Summary 10th Husband and Wife § 12A, (S 12A) (New)-Filing Fees.

RULES OF THE STATE BAR OF CALIFORNIA
CALIFORNIA RULES OF PROFESSIONAL CONDUCT

Chapter 1

PROFESSIONAL INTEGRITY IN GENERAL

Rule

Rule 1–100.   Rules of Professional Conduct, in General

(A) Purpose and Function.

The following rules are intended to regulate professional conduct of members of the State Bar through discipline. They have been adopted by the Board of Governors of the State Bar of California and approved by the Supreme Court of California pursuant to Business and Professions Code sections 6076 and 6077 to protect the public and to promote respect and confidence in the legal profession. These rules together with any standards adopted by the Board of Governors pursuant to these rules shall be binding upon all members of the State Bar.

For a willful breach of any of these rules, the Board of Governors has the power to discipline members as provided by law.

The prohibition of certain conduct in these rules is not exclusive. Members are also bound by applicable law including the State Bar Act (Bus. & Prof.Code, § 6000 et seq.) and opinions of California courts. Although not binding, opinions of ethics committees in California should be consulted by members for guidance on proper professional conduct. Ethics opinions and rules and standards promulgated by other jurisdictions and bar associations may also be considered.

These rules are not intended to create new civil causes of action. Nothing in these rules shall be deemed to create, augment, diminish, or eliminate any substantive legal duty of lawyers or the non-disciplinary consequences of violating such a duty.

(B) Definitions.

(1) "Law Firm" means:

(a) two or more lawyers whose activities constitute the practice of law, and who share its profits, expenses, and liabilities; or

(b) a law corporation which employs more than one lawyer; or

(c) a division, department, office, or group within a business entity, which includes more than one lawyer who performs legal services for the business entity; or

(d) a publicly funded entity which employs more than one lawyer to perform legal services.

(2) "Member" means a member of the State Bar of California.

(3) "Lawyer" means a member of the State Bar of California or a person who is admitted in good standing of and eligible to practice before the bar of any United States court or the highest court of the District of Columbia or any state, territory, or insular possession of the United States, or is licensed to practice law in, or is admitted in good standing and eligible to practice before the bar of the highest court of, a foreign country or any political subdivision thereof.

(4) "Associate" means an employee or fellow employee who is employed as a lawyer.

(5) "Shareholder" means a shareholder in a professional corporation pursuant to Business and Professions Code section 6160 et seq.

(C) Purpose of Discussions.

Because it is a practical impossibility to convey in black letter form all of the nuances of these disciplinary rules, the comments contained in the Discussions of the rules, while they do not add independent basis for imposing discipline, are intended to provide guidance for interpreting the rules and practicing in compliance with them.

(D) Geographic Scope of Rules.

(1) As to members:

These rules shall govern the activities of members in and outside this state, except as members lawfully practicing outside this state may be specifically required by a jurisdiction in which they are practicing to follow rules of professional conduct different from these rules.

(2) As to lawyers from other jurisdictions who are not members:

These rules shall also govern the activities of lawyers while engaged in the performance of lawyer functions in this state; but nothing contained in these rules shall be deemed to authorize the performance of such functions by such persons in this state except as otherwise permitted by law.

(E) These rules may be cited and referred to as "Rules of Professional Conduct of the State Bar of California."

DISCUSSION

The Rules of Professional Conduct are intended to establish the standards for members for purposes of discipline. (See *Ames v. State Bar* (1973) 8 Cal.3d 910 [106 Cal.Rptr. 489].) The fact that a member has engaged in conduct that may be contrary to these rules does not automatically give rise to a civil cause of action. (See *Noble v. Sears, Roebuck & Co.* (1973) 33 Cal. App.3d 654 [109 Cal.Rptr. 269]; *Wilhelm v. Pray, Price, Williams & Russell* (1986) 186 Cal.App.3d 1324 [231 Cal.Rptr. 355].)

These rules are not intended to supercede existing law relating to members in non-disciplinary contexts. (See, e.g., *Klemm v. Superior Court* (1977) 75 Cal.App.3d 893 [142 Cal.Rptr. 509] (motion for disqualification of counsel due to a conflict of interest); *Academy of California Optometrists, Inc. v. Superior Court* (1975) 51 Cal.App.3d 999 [124 Cal.Rptr. 668] (duty to return client files); *Chronometrics, Inc. v. Sysgen, Inc.* (1980) 110 Cal.App.3d 597 [168 Cal.Rptr. 196] (disqualification of member appropriate remedy for improper communication with adverse party).)

Law firm, as defined by subparagraph (B)(1), is not intended to include an association of lawyers who do not share profits, expenses, and liabilities. The subparagraph is not intended to imply that a law firm may include a person who is not a member in violation of the law governing the unauthorized practice of law.

(Adopted Nov. 28, 1988, eff. May 27, 1989. As amended, eff. Sept. 14, 1992.)

Research References

Rutter, Cal. Practice Guide: Civ. Pro. Before Trial Ch. 1-A, A. Accepting a New Case.

Rutter, Cal. Practice Guide: Civ. Pro. Before Trial Ch. 1-B, B. Prelawsuit Investigations, Research and Analysis.

California Practice Guide: Employment Litigation Ch. 2-A, A. Sources of Rules Governing Attorney Conduct.

California Practice Guide: Employment Litigation Ch. 2-G, G. Communicating With Adverse Party Represented by Counsel.

Rutter, Cal. Practice Guide: Personal Injury Ch. 1-B, B. Initial Evaluation of Case: Decision to Accept or Reject Employment or Undertake Further Evaluation of Claim.

Rutter, Cal. Practice Guide: Real Prop. Transactions Ch. 1-B, B. Attorney Competence, Conflicts of Interest and Initial Client Communications.

Rutter, Cal. Practice Guide: Prof. Responsibility Ch. 1-A, A. Sources of Regulation of Practice of Law in California-Overview.

Rutter, Cal. Practice Guide: Prof. Responsibility Ch. 1-E, E. Regulation of Form of Practice.

Rutter, Cal. Practice Guide: Prof. Responsibility Ch. 2-A, A. Regulations Generally.

Rutter, Cal. Practice Guide: Prof. Responsibility Ch. 2-D, D. In-Person Solicitation for Profit.

Rutter, Cal. Practice Guide: Prof. Responsibility Ch. 2-E, E. Targeted or Mass Mailings.

Rutter, Cal. Practice Guide: Prof. Responsibility Ch. 2-F, F. Print Media Advertising.

Rutter, Cal. Practice Guide: Prof. Responsibility Ch. 2-G, G. Electronic Media Advertising.

Rutter, Cal. Practice Guide: Prof. Responsibility Ch. 5-D, D. Ethical Limitations on Attorney Fees.

Rutter, Cal. Practice Guide: Prof. Responsibility Ch. 6-A, A. Sources of Duty of Competence.

Rutter, Cal. Practice Guide: Prof. Responsibility Ch. 6-B, B. Elements of Attorney Competence.

Rutter, Cal. Practice Guide: Prof. Responsibility Ch. 6-D, D. Professional Liability.

Rutter, Cal. Practice Guide: Prof. Responsibility Ch. 8-A, A. Duties to Administration of Justice-In General.

1 Witkin Cal. Proc. 5th Attorneys § 19, Partnership Practice.

1 Witkin Cal. Proc. 5th Attorneys § 409, Adoption.

1 Witkin Cal. Proc. 5th Attorneys § 411, in General (Rules 1-100 to 1-120).

1 Witkin Cal. Proc. 5th Attorneys § 558, (S 558) in General.

Rule 1–110. Disciplinary Authority of the State Bar

A member shall comply with conditions attached to public or private reprovals or other discipline administered by the State Bar pursuant to Business and Professions Code sections 6077 and 6078 and rule 9.19, California Rules of Court. *(Adopted Nov. 28, 1988, eff. May 27, 1989. As amended, eff. July 11, 2008.)*

Research References

Rutter, Cal. Practice Guide: Prof. Responsibility Ch. 11-L, L. Determining Appropriate Discipline.

1 Witkin Cal. Proc. 5th Attorneys § 411, in General (Rules 1-100 to 1-120).

Rule 1–120. Assisting, Soliciting, or Inducing Violations

A member shall not knowingly assist in, solicit, or induce any violation of these rules or the State Bar Act. *(Adopted Nov. 28, 1988, eff. May 27, 1989.)*

Research References

Rutter, Cal. Practice Guide: Prof. Responsibility Ch. 2-D, D. In-Person Solicitation for Profit.

Rutter, Cal. Practice Guide: Prof. Responsibility Ch. 10-B, B. Withdrawal (Termination) by Lawyer.

1 Witkin Cal. Proc. 5th Attorneys § 411, in General (Rules 1-100 to 1-120).

Rule 1–200. False Statement Regarding Admission to the State Bar

(A) A member shall not knowingly make a false statement regarding a material fact or knowingly fail to disclose a material fact in connection with an application for admission to the State Bar.

(B) A member shall not further an application for admission to the State Bar of a person whom the member knows to be unqualified in respect to character, education, or other relevant attributes.

(C) This rule shall not prevent a member from serving as counsel of record for an applicant for admission to practice in proceedings related to such admission.

DISCUSSION

For purposes of rule 1–200 "admission" includes readmission.

(Adopted Nov. 28, 1988, eff. May 27, 1989.)

Research References

Rutter, Cal. Practice Guide: Prof. Responsibility Ch. 1-B, B. Regulation of Admission to Practice Law.

1 Witkin Cal. Proc. 5th Attorneys § 365, (S 365) Duties of Applicant and Attorneys.

1 Witkin Cal. Proc. 5th Attorneys § 412, False Statements Regarding Admission (Rule 1-200).

Rule 1–300. Unauthorized Practice of Law

(A) A member shall not aid any person or entity in the unauthorized practice of law.

(B) A member shall not practice law in a jurisdiction where to do so would be in violation of regulations of the profession in that jurisdiction. *(Adopted Nov. 28, 1988, eff. May 27, 1989.)*

Research References

Rutter, Cal. Practice Guide: A.D.R. Ch. 3-D, D. "Classic" (Facilitative) Mediation.

Rutter, Cal. Practice Guide: Real Prop. Transactions Ch. 2-A, A. Preliminary Considerations.

Rutter, Cal. Practice Guide: Real Prop. Transactions Ch. 6-I, I. Real Property Foreclosures and Antideficiency Laws.

Rutter, Cal. Practice Guide: Prof. Responsibility Ch. 1-D, D. Unauthorized Practice of Law.

Rutter, Cal. Practice Guide: Prof. Responsibility Ch. 1-E, E. Regulation of Form of Practice.

Rutter, Cal. Practice Guide: Prof. Responsibility Ch. 2-B, B. Regulation of Firm Name.

1 Witkin Cal. Proc. 5th Attorneys § 379, (S 379) General Prohibitions.

1 Witkin Cal. Proc. 5th Attorneys § 413, Unauthorized Practice of Law (Rule 1-300).

1 Witkin Cal. Proc. 5th Attorneys § 530, (S 530) Statutory Prohibition and Rules.

Rule 1–310. Forming a Partnership With a Non–Lawyer

A member shall not form a partnership with a person who is not a lawyer if any of the activities of that partnership consist of the practice of law.

DISCUSSION

Rule 1–310 is not intended to govern members' activities which cannot be considered to constitute the practice of law. It is intended solely to preclude a member from being involved in the practice of law with a person who is not a lawyer.

(Adopted Nov. 28, 1988, eff. May 27, 1989. As amended, eff. Sept. 14, 1992.)

Research References

Rutter, Cal. Practice Guide: Prof. Responsibility Ch. 1-E, E. Regulation of Form of Practice.

Rutter, Cal. Practice Guide: Prof. Responsibility Ch. 5-D, D. Ethical Limitations on Attorney Fees.

1 Witkin Cal. Proc. 5th Attorneys § 19, Partnership Practice.

1 Witkin Cal. Proc. 5th Attorneys § 414, Dealings With Nonlawyer (Rules 1-310, 1-320).

1 Witkin Cal. Proc. 5th Attorneys § 530, (S 530) Statutory Prohibition and Rules.

Rule 1–311. Employment of Disbarred, Suspended, Resigned, or Involuntarily Inactive Member

(A) For purposes of this rule:

(1) "Employ" means to engage the services of another, including employees, agents, independent contractors and consultants, regardless of whether any compensation is paid;

(2) "Involuntarily inactive member" means a member who is ineligible to practice law as a result of action taken pursuant to Business and Professions Code sections 6007, 6203(c), or California Rule of Court 9.31; and

(3) "Resigned member" means a member who has resigned from the State Bar while disciplinary charges are pending.

(B) A member shall not employ, associate professionally with, or aid a person the member knows or reasonably should know is a disbarred, suspended, resigned, or involuntarily inactive member to perform the following on behalf of the member's client:

(1) Render legal consultation or advice to the client;

(2) Appear on behalf of a client in any hearing or proceeding or before any judicial officer, arbitrator, mediator, court, public agency, referee, magistrate, commissioner, or hearing officer;

(3) Appear as a representative of the client at a deposition or other discovery matter;

(4) Negotiate or transact any matter for or on behalf of the client with third parties;

(5) Receive, disburse or otherwise handle the client's funds; or

(6) Engage in activities which constitute the practice of law.

(C) A member may employ, associate professionally with, or aid a disbarred, suspended, resigned, or involuntarily inactive member to perform research, drafting or clerical activities, including but not limited to:

(1) Legal work of a preparatory nature, such as legal research, the assemblage of data and other necessary information, drafting of pleadings, briefs, and other similar documents;

(2) Direct communication with the client or third parties regarding matters such as scheduling, billing, updates, confirmation of receipt or sending of correspondence and messages; or

(3) Accompanying an active member in attending a deposition or other discovery matter for the limited purpose of providing clerical assistance to the active member who will appear as the representative of the client.

(D) Prior to or at the time of employing a person the member knows or reasonably should know is a disbarred, suspended, resigned, or involuntarily inactive member, the member shall serve upon the State Bar written notice of the employment, including a full description of such person's current bar status. The written notice shall also list the activities prohibited in paragraph (B) and state that the disbarred, suspended, resigned, or involuntarily inactive member will not perform such activities. The member shall serve similar written notice upon each client on whose specific matter such person will work, prior to or at the time of employing such person to work on the client's specific matter. The member shall obtain proof of service of the client's written notice and shall retain such proof and a true and correct copy of the client's written notice for two years following termination of the member's employment with the client.

(E) A member may, without client or State Bar notification, employ a disbarred, suspended, resigned, or involuntarily inactive member whose sole function is to perform office physical plant or equipment maintenance, courier or delivery services, catering, reception, typing or transcription, or other similar support activities.

(F) Upon termination of the disbarred, suspended, resigned, or involuntarily inactive member, the member shall promptly serve upon the State Bar written notice of the termination.

DISCUSSION

For discussion of the activities that constitute the practice of law, see *Farnham v. State Bar* (1976) 17 Cal.3d 605 [131 Cal.Rptr. 611]; *Bluestein v. State Bar* (1974) 13 Cal.3d 162 [118 Cal.Rptr. 175]; *Baron v. City of Los Angeles* (1970) 2 Cal.3d 535 [86 Cal.Rptr. 673]; *Crawford v. State Bar* (1960) 54 Cal.2d 659 [7 Cal.Rptr. 746]; *People v. Merchants Protective Corporation* (1922) 189 Cal. 531, 535 [209 P. 363]; *People v. Landlords Professional Services* (1989) 215 Cal.App.3d 1599 [264 Cal.Rptr. 548]; and *People v. Sipper* (1943) 61 Cal.App.2d Supp. 844 [142 P.2d 960].) [1]

Paragraph (D) is not intended to prevent or discourage a member from fully discussing with the client the activities that will be performed by the disbarred, suspended, resigned, or involuntarily inactive member on the client's matter. If a member's client is an organization, then the written notice required by paragraph (D) shall be served upon the highest authorized officer, employee, or constituent overseeing the particular engagement. (See rule 3–600.)

Nothing in rule 1–311 shall be deemed to limit or preclude any activity engaged in pursuant to rules 9.40, 9.41, 9.42, and 9.44 of the California Rules of Court, or any local rule of a federal district court concerning admission pro hac vice.

(Adopted July 11, 1996, eff. Aug. 1, 1996. As amended, eff. July 11, 2008.)

[1] Supplied copy contains no opening parenthesis.

Research References

Rutter, Cal. Practice Guide: Enforcing Judgments/Debts Ch. 1-C, C. Efficient Debt Collection Office Procedures.

Rutter, Cal. Practice Guide: Prof. Responsibility Ch. 1-D, D. Unauthorized Practice of Law.

Rutter, Cal. Practice Guide: Prof. Responsibility Form 1:A, Notice of Employment of Disbarred, Resigned, Suspended or Involuntarily Inactive State Bar Member.

Rutter, Cal. Practice Guide: Prof. Responsibility Form 1:B, Notice to Client of Employment of a Disbarred, Resigned, Suspended or Involuntarily Inactive Member of the State Bar of California.

Rutter, Cal. Practice Guide: Prof. Responsibility Form 1:C, Notice of Termination of Employment of Disbarred, Resigned, Suspended or Involuntarily Inactive State Bar Member.

1 Witkin Cal. Proc. 5th Attorneys § 415, Employment of Disbarred or Suspended Lawyer (Rule 1-311).

Prof. Conduct

Rule 1–320.   Financial Arrangements With Non–Lawyers

(A) Neither a member nor a law firm shall directly or indirectly share legal fees with a person who is not a lawyer, except that:

(1) An agreement between a member and a law firm, partner, or associate may provide for the payment of money after the member's death to the member's estate or to one or more specified persons over a reasonable period of time; or

(2) A member or law firm undertaking to complete unfinished legal business of a deceased member may pay to the estate of the deceased member or other person legally entitled thereto that proportion of the total compensation which fairly represents the services rendered by the deceased member; or

(3) A member or law firm may include non-member employees in a compensation, profit-sharing, or retirement plan even though the plan is based in whole or in part on a profit-sharing arrangement, if such plan does not circumvent these rules or Business and Professions Code section 6000 et seq.; or

(4) A member may pay a prescribed registration, referral, or participation fee to a lawyer referral service established, sponsored, and operated in accordance with the State Bar of California's Minimum Standards for a Lawyer Referral Service in California.

(B) A member shall not compensate, give, or promise anything of value to any person or entity for the purpose of recommending or securing employment of the member or the member's law firm by a client, or as a reward for having made a recommendation resulting in employment of the member or the member's law firm by a client. A member's offering of or giving a gift or gratuity to any person or entity having made a recommendation resulting in the employment of the member or the member's law firm shall not of itself violate this rule, provided that the gift or gratuity was not offered or given in consideration of any promise, agreement, or understanding that such a gift or gratuity would be forthcoming or that referrals would be made or encouraged in the future.

(C) A member shall not compensate, give, or promise anything of value to any representative of the press, radio, television, or other communication medium in anticipation of or in return for publicity of the member, the law firm, or any other member as such in a news item, but the incidental provision of food or beverage shall not of itself violate this rule.

DISCUSSION

Rule 1–320(C) is not intended to preclude compensation to the communications media in exchange for advertising the member's or law firm's availability for professional employment.

(Adopted Nov. 28, 1988, eff. May 27, 1989. As amended, eff. Sept. 14, 1992.)

Research References

Rutter, Cal. Practice Guide: Civ. Pro. Before Trial Ch. 1-A, A. Accepting a New Case.

California Practice Guide: Employment Litigation Ch. 2-B, B. Fee Arrangements.

Rutter, Cal. Practice Guide: Personal Injury Ch. 1-C, C. Formation of Attorney-Client Relationship: the Employment Agreement.

Rutter, Cal. Practice Guide: Real Prop. Transactions Ch. 6-I, I. Real Property Foreclosures and Antideficiency Laws.

Rutter, Cal. Practice Guide: Prof. Responsibility Ch. 1-E, E. Regulation of Form of Practice.

Rutter, Cal. Practice Guide: Prof. Responsibility Ch. 1-I, I. Regulation of Sale of Law Practice.

Rutter, Cal. Practice Guide: Prof. Responsibility Ch. 1-J, J. Regulating Participation in Legal Service Programs and Referral Service Plans.

Rutter, Cal. Practice Guide: Prof. Responsibility Ch. 2-D, D. In-Person Solicitation for Profit.

Rutter, Cal. Practice Guide: Prof. Responsibility Ch. 2-F, F. Print Media Advertising.

Rutter, Cal. Practice Guide: Prof. Responsibility Ch. 2-G, G. Electronic Media Advertising.

Rutter, Cal. Practice Guide: Prof. Responsibility Ch. 2-H, H. Lawyer Referral Services.

Rutter, Cal. Practice Guide: Prof. Responsibility Ch. 5-B, B. Types of Fees and Fee Arrangements.

Rutter, Cal. Practice Guide: Prof. Responsibility Ch. 5-D, D. Ethical Limitations on Attorney Fees.

Rutter, Cal. Practice Guide: Prof. Responsibility Ch. 5-G, G. Accepting Property or Services in Exchange for Legal Services (Barter).

1 Witkin Cal. Proc. 5th Attorneys § 414, Dealings With Nonlawyer (Rules 1-310, 1-320).

1 Witkin Cal. Proc. 5th Attorneys § 519, in General.

1 Witkin Cal. Proc. 5th Attorneys § 527, in General.

1 Witkin Cal. Proc. 5th Attorneys § 530, (S 530) Statutory Prohibition and Rules.

Rule 1–400.   Advertising and Solicitation

(A) For purposes of this rule, "communication" means any message or offer made by or on behalf of a member concerning the availability for professional employment of a member or a law firm directed to any former, present, or prospective client, including but not limited to the following:

(1) Any use of firm name, trade name, fictitious name, or other professional designation of such member or law firm; or

(2) Any stationery, letterhead, business card, sign, brochure, or other comparable written material describing such member, law firm, or lawyers; or

(3) Any advertisement (regardless of medium) of such member or law firm directed to the general public or any substantial portion thereof; or

(4) Any unsolicited correspondence from a member or law firm directed to any person or entity.

(B) For purposes of this rule, a "solicitation" means any communication:

(1) Concerning the availability for professional employment of a member or a law firm in which a significant motive is pecuniary gain; and

(2) Which is:

(a) delivered in person or by telephone, or

(b) directed by any means to a person known to the sender to be represented by counsel in a matter which is a subject of the communication.

(C) A solicitation shall not be made by or on behalf of a member or law firm to a prospective client with whom the member or law firm has no family or prior professional relationship, unless the solicitation is protected from abridgment by the Constitution of the United States or by the Constitution of the State of California. A solicitation to a former or present client in the discharge of a member's or law firm's professional duties is not prohibited.

(D) A communication or a solicitation (as defined herein) shall not:

(1) Contain any untrue statement; or

(2) Contain any matter, or present or arrange any matter in a manner or format which is false, deceptive, or which tends to confuse, deceive, or mislead the public; or

(3) Omit to state any fact necessary to make the statements made, in the light of circumstances under which they are made, not misleading to the public; or

(4) Fail to indicate clearly, expressly, or by context, that it is a communication or solicitation, as the case may be; or

(5) Be transmitted in any manner which involves intrusion, coercion, duress, compulsion, intimidation, threats, or vexatious or harassing conduct.

(6) State that a member is a "certified specialist" unless the member holds a current certificate as a specialist issued by the Board of Legal Specialization, or any other entity accredited by the State Bar to designate specialists pursuant to standards adopted by the Board of Governors, and states the complete name of the entity which granted certification.

(E) The Board of Governors of the State Bar shall formulate and adopt standards as to communications which will be presumed to violate this rule 1–400. The standards shall only be used as presumptions affecting the burden of proof in disciplinary proceedings involving alleged violations of these rules. "Presumption affecting the burden of proof" means that presumption defined in Evidence Code sections 605 and 606. Such standards formulated and adopted by the Board, as from time to time amended, shall be effective and binding on all members.

(F) A member shall retain for two years a true and correct copy or recording of any communication made by written or electronic media. Upon written request, the member shall make any such copy or recording available to the State Bar, and, if requested, shall provide to the State Bar evidence to support any factual or objective claim contained in the communication.

[Publisher's Note: Former rule 1–400 (D)(6) repealed by order of the Supreme Court effective November 30, 1992. New rule 1–400 (D)(6) added by order of the Supreme Court effective June 1, 1997.]

STANDARDS

Pursuant to rule 1–400(E) the Board of Governors of the State Bar has adopted the following standards, effective May 27, 1989, unless noted otherwise, as forms of "communication" defined in rule 1–400(A) which are presumed to be in violation of rule 1–400:

(1) A "communication" which contains guarantees, warranties, or predictions regarding the result of the representation.

(2) A "communication" which contains testimonials about or endorsements of a member unless such communication also contains an express disclaimer such as "this testimonial or endorsement does not constitute a guarantee, warranty, or prediction regarding the outcome of your legal matter."

(3) A "communication" which is delivered to a potential client whom the member knows or should reasonably know is in such a physical, emotional, or mental state that he or she would not be expected to exercise reasonable judgment as to the retention of counsel.

(4) A "communication" which is transmitted at the scene of an accident or at or en route to a hospital, emergency care center, or other health care facility.

(5) A "communication," except professional announcements, seeking professional employment for pecuniary gain, which is transmitted by mail or equivalent means which does not bear the word "Advertisement," "Newsletter" or words of similar import in 12 point print on the first page. If such communication, including firm brochures, newsletters, recent legal development advisories, and similar materials, is transmitted in an envelope, the envelope shall bear the word "Advertisement," "Newsletter" or words of similar import on the outside thereof.

(6) A "communication" in the form of a firm name, trade name, fictitious name, or other professional designation which states or implies a relationship between any member in private practice and a government agency or instrumentality or a public or non-profit legal services organization.

(7) A "communication" in the form of a firm name, trade name, fictitious name, or other professional designation which states or implies that a member has a relationship to any other lawyer or a law firm as a partner or associate, or officer or shareholder pursuant to Business and Professions Code sections 6160–6172 unless such relationship in fact exists.

(8) A "communication" which states or implies that a member or law firm is "of counsel" to another lawyer or a law firm unless the former has a relationship with the latter (other than as a partner or associate, or officer or shareholder pursuant to Business and Professions Code sections 6160–6172) which is close, personal, continuous, and regular.

(9) A "communication" in the form of a firm name, trade name, fictitious name, or other professional designation used by a member or law firm in private practice which differs materially from any other such designation used by such member or law firm at the same time in the same community.

(10) A "communication" which implies that the member or law firm is participating in a lawyer referral service which has been certified by the State Bar of California or as having satisfied the Minimum Standards for Lawyer Referral Services in California, when that is not the case.

(11) [Repealed eff. June 1, 1997]

(Publisher's Note: Repealed. See rule 1–400(D)(6) for the operative language on this subject.)

(12) A "communication," except professional announcements, in the form of an advertisement primarily directed to seeking professional employment primarily for pecuniary gain transmitted to the general public or any substantial portion thereof by mail or equivalent means or by means of television, radio, newspaper, magazine or other form of commercial mass media which does not state the name of the member responsible for the communication. When the communication is made on behalf of a law firm, the communication shall state the name of at least one member responsible for it.

(13) A "communication" which contains a dramatization unless such communication contains a disclaimer which states "this is a dramatization" or words of similar import.

(14) A "communication" which states or implies "no fee without recovery" unless such communication also expressly discloses whether or not the client will be liable for costs.

(15) A "communication" which states or implies that a member is able to provide legal services in a language other than English unless the member can actually provide legal services in such language or the communication also states in the language of the communication (a) the employment title of the person who speaks such language and (b) that the person is not a member of the State Bar of California, if that is the case.

(16) An unsolicited "communication" transmitted to the general public or any substantial portion thereof primarily directed to seeking professional employment primarily for pecuniary gain which sets

forth a specific fee or range of fees for a particular service where, in fact, the member charges a greater fee than advertised in such communication within a period of 90 days following dissemination of such communication, unless such communication expressly specifies a shorter period of time regarding the advertised fee. Where the communication is published in the classified or "yellow pages" section of telephone, business or legal directories or in other media not published more frequently than once a year, the member shall conform to the advertised fee for a period of one year from initial publication, unless such communication expressly specifies a shorter period of time regarding the advertised fee.

(Adopted Nov. 28, 1988, eff. May 27, 1989. As amended, eff. Aug. 13, 1992; Oct. 29, 1992; April 9, 1994; June 1, 1997.)

Research References

Rutter, Cal. Practice Guide: Civ. Pro. Before Trial Ch. 14-C, C. Procedural Issues.
California Practice Guide: Employment Litigation Ch. 2-G, G. Communicating With Adverse Party Represented by Counsel.
Rutter, Cal. Practice Guide: Enforcing Judgments/Debts Ch. 1-B, B. Accepting the Collection Case.
Rutter, Cal. Practice Guide: Real Prop. Transactions Ch. 6-I, I. Real Property Foreclosures and Antideficiency Laws.
Rutter, Cal. Practice Guide: Prof. Responsibility Ch. 1-E, E. Regulation of Form of Practice.
Rutter, Cal. Practice Guide: Prof. Responsibility Ch. 1-I, I. Regulation of Sale of Law Practice.
Rutter, Cal. Practice Guide: Prof. Responsibility Ch. 1-J, J. Regulating Participation in Legal Service Programs and Referral Service Plans.
Rutter, Cal. Practice Guide: Prof. Responsibility Ch. 2-A, A. Regulations Generally.
Rutter, Cal. Practice Guide: Prof. Responsibility Ch. 2-B, B. Regulation of Firm Name.
Rutter, Cal. Practice Guide: Prof. Responsibility Ch. 2-C, C. Description of Lawyer or Practice in Letterheads, Signs, Brochures, etc.
Rutter, Cal. Practice Guide: Prof. Responsibility Ch. 2-D, D. In-Person Solicitation for Profit.
Rutter, Cal. Practice Guide: Prof. Responsibility Ch. 2-E, E. Targeted or Mass Mailings.
Rutter, Cal. Practice Guide: Prof. Responsibility Ch. 2-F, F. Print Media Advertising.
Rutter, Cal. Practice Guide: Prof. Responsibility Ch. 2-G, G. Electronic Media Advertising.
Rutter, Cal. Practice Guide: Prof. Responsibility Ch. 2-H, H. Lawyer Referral Services.
Rutter, Cal. Practice Guide: Prof. Responsibility Ch. 2-I, I. Legal Services Programs.
Rutter, Cal. Practice Guide: Prof. Responsibility Ch. 2-J, J. Other Statutes Regulating Lawyer Advertising and Solicitation.
Rutter, Cal. Practice Guide: Prof. Responsibility Ch. 5-F, F. Formalizing Fee Agreements.
Rutter, Cal. Practice Guide: Prof. Responsibility Ch. 5-H, H. Billing Methods.
Rutter, Cal. Practice Guide: Prof. Responsibility Ch. 8-D, D. Restrictions on Speech and Behavior Outside Courtroom.
Rutter, Cal. Practice Guide: Prof. Responsibility Ch. 10-E, E. Law Firm Break-Ups.
Rutter, Cal. Practice Guide: Prof. Responsibility Ch. 2-A , Outline a.
Rutter, Cal. Practice Guide: Prof. Responsibility Ch. 8-D , Outline D.
Rutter, Cal. Practice Guide: Prof. Responsibility Ch. 10-E , Outline E.
1 Witkin Cal. Proc. 5th Attorneys § 6, (S 6) Preventive Law.
1 Witkin Cal. Proc. 5th Attorneys § 19, Partnership Practice.
1 Witkin Cal. Proc. 5th Attorneys § 37, in General.
1 Witkin Cal. Proc. 5th Attorneys § 416, (S 416) Definitions.
1 Witkin Cal. Proc. 5th Attorneys § 417, (S 417) Prohibited Solicitation.
1 Witkin Cal. Proc. 5th Attorneys § 418, (S 418) State Bar Standards.
1 Witkin Cal. Proc. 5th Attorneys § 423, (S 423) Nature and Scope of Rule.
1 Witkin Cal. Proc. 5th Attorneys § 516, (S 516) First Amendment Right to Advertise.

1 Witkin Cal. Proc. 5th Attorneys § 518, (S 518) False and Misleading Communications.
1 Witkin Cal. Proc. 5th Attorneys § 519, in General.
1 Witkin Cal. Proc. 5th Attorneys § 520, Using Media for Self-Laudatory Statements.
1 Witkin Cal. Proc. 5th Attorneys § 522, (S 522) Permissible Listings and Announcements.
1 Witkin Cal. Proc. 5th Attorneys § 523, in General.
1 Witkin Cal. Proc. 5th Attorneys § 525, Distinction: Free Services in Civil Liberties Case.

Rule 1–500. Agreements Restricting a Member's Practice

(A) A member shall not be a party to or participate in offering or making an agreement, whether in connection with the settlement of a lawsuit or otherwise, if the agreement restricts the right of a member to practice law, except that this rule shall not prohibit such an agreement which:

(1) Is a part of an employment, shareholders', or partnership agreement among members provided the restrictive agreement does not survive the termination of the employment, shareholder, or partnership relationship; or

(2) Requires payments to a member upon the member's retirement from the practice of law; or

(3) Is authorized by Business and Professions Code sections 6092.5 subdivision (i), or 6093.

(B) A member shall not be a party to or participate in offering or making an agreement which precludes the reporting of a violation of these rules.

DISCUSSION

Paragraph (A) makes it clear that the practice, in connection with settlement agreements, of proposing that a member refrain from representing other clients in similar litigation, is prohibited. Neither counsel may demand or suggest such provisions nor may opposing counsel accede or agree to such provisions.

Paragraph (A) permits a restrictive covenant in a law corporation, partnership, or employment agreement. The law corporation shareholder, partner, or associate may agree not to have a separate practice during the existence of the relationship; however, upon termination of the relationship (whether voluntary or involuntary), the member is free to practice law without any contractual restriction except in the case of retirement from the active practice of law.

(Adopted Nov. 28, 1988, eff. May 27, 1989. As amended, eff. Sept. 14, 1992.)

Research References

Rutter, Cal. Practice Guide: Civ. Pro. Before Trial Ch. 12(II)-H, H. Professional Responsibility Considerations Re Settlements.
California Practice Guide: Employment Litigation Ch. 2-L, L. Settlements.
California Practice Guide: Employment Litigation Ch. 18-A, A. Settlement Considerations.
Rutter, Cal. Practice Guide: Personal Injury Ch. 4-G, G. Concluding and Enforcing Settlement.
Rutter, Cal. Practice Guide: Prof. Responsibility Ch. 1-F, F. Prohibition Against Agreements Restricting Right to Practice.
Rutter, Cal. Practice Guide: Prof. Responsibility Ch. 1-I, I. Regulation of Sale of Law Practice.
Rutter, Cal. Practice Guide: Prof. Responsibility Ch. 1-L, L. Reporting Claims, Judgments and Sanctions Against Attorney to State Bar.
Rutter, Cal. Practice Guide: Prof. Responsibility Ch. 5-F, F. Formalizing Fee Agreements.
Rutter, Cal. Practice Guide: Prof. Responsibility Ch. 6-F, F. Waiver/Settlement of Malpractice Claim.
Rutter, Cal. Practice Guide: Prof. Responsibility Ch. 7-B, B. Duty to Maintain Client Confidence and Secrets Under State Bar Act.
Rutter, Cal. Practice Guide: Prof. Responsibility Ch. 10-E, E. Law Firm Break-Ups.
Rutter, Cal. Practice Guide: Prof. Responsibility Ch. 1-F , Outline F.
1 Witkin Cal. Proc. 5th Attorneys § 33, General Rule and Exceptions.

1 Witkin Cal. Proc. 5th Attorneys § 34, (S 34) Agreements Are Not Prohibited.

1 Witkin Cal. Proc. 5th Attorneys § 35, (S 35) Rule of Reason Applies.

1 Witkin Cal. Proc. 5th Attorneys § 419, Agreements Restricting Practice (Rule 1-500).

Rule 1–600. Legal Service Programs

(A) A member shall not participate in a nongovernmental program, activity, or organization furnishing, recommending, or paying for legal services, which allows any third person or organization to interfere with the member's independence of professional judgment, or with the client-lawyer relationship, or allows unlicensed persons to practice law, or allows any third person or organization to receive directly or indirectly any part of the consideration paid to the member except as permitted by these rules, or otherwise violates the State Bar Act or these rules.

(B) The Board of Governors of the State Bar shall formulate and adopt Minimum Standards for Lawyer Referral Services, which, as from time to time amended, shall be binding on members.

DISCUSSION

The participation of a member in a lawyer referral service established, sponsored, supervised, and operated in conformity with the Minimum Standards for a Lawyer Referral Service in California is encouraged and is not, of itself, a violation of these rules.

Rule 1–600 is not intended to override any contractual agreement or relationship between insurers and insureds regarding the provision of legal services.

Rule 1–600 is not intended to apply to the activities of a public agency responsible for providing legal services to a government or to the public.

For purposes of paragraph (A), "a nongovernmental program, activity, or organization" includes, but is not limited to group, prepaid, and voluntary legal service programs, activities, or organizations.

(Adopted Nov. 28, 1988, eff. May 27, 1989.)

Research References

Rutter, Cal. Practice Guide: Prof. Responsibility Ch. 1-J, J. Regulating Participation in Legal Service Programs and Referral Service Plans.
Rutter, Cal. Practice Guide: Prof. Responsibility Ch. 2-C, C. Description of Lawyer or Practice in Letterheads, Signs, Brochures, etc.
Rutter, Cal. Practice Guide: Prof. Responsibility Ch. 2-I, I. Legal Services Programs.
Rutter, Cal. Practice Guide: Prof. Responsibility Ch. 5-D, D. Ethical Limitations on Attorney Fees.
Rutter, Cal. Practice Guide: Prof. Responsibility Ch. 7-B, B. Duty to Maintain Client Confidence and Secrets Under State Bar Act.
1 Witkin Cal. Proc. 5th Attorneys § 11, in General.
1 Witkin Cal. Proc. 5th Attorneys § 14, in General.
1 Witkin Cal. Proc. 5th Attorneys § 420, Legal Service Programs (Rule 1-600).
1 Witkin Cal. Proc. 5th Attorneys § 529, Distinction: Attorney Referral Service.
1 Witkin Cal. Proc. 5th Attorneys § 535, (S 535) Authorized Legal Service Programs.

Rule 1–650. Limited Legal Services Programs

(A) A member who, under the auspices of a program sponsored by a court, government agency, bar association, law school, or nonprofit organization, provides short-term limited legal services to a client without expectation by either the member or the client that the member will provide continuing representation in the matter:

(1) is subject to rule 3–310 only if the member knows that the representation of the client involves a conflict of interest; and

(2) has an imputed conflict of interest only if the member knows that another lawyer associated with the member in a law firm would have a conflict of interest under rule 3–310 with respect to the matter.

(B) Except as provided in paragraph (A)(2), a conflict of interest that arises from a member's participation in a program under paragraph (A) will not be imputed to the member's law firm.

(C) The personal disqualification of a lawyer participating in the program will not be imputed to other lawyers participating in the program.

DISCUSSION

[1] Courts, government agencies, bar associations, law schools and various nonprofit organizations have established programs through which lawyers provide short-term limited legal services—such as advice or the completion of legal forms—that will assist persons in addressing their legal problems without further representation by a lawyer. In these programs, such as legal-advice hotlines, advice-only clinics or pro se counseling programs, whenever a lawyer-client relationship is established, there is no expectation that the lawyer's representation of the client will continue beyond that limited consultation. Such programs are normally operated under circumstances in which it is not feasible for a lawyer to systematically screen for conflicts of interest as is generally required before undertaking a representation.

[2] A member who provides short-term limited legal services pursuant to rule 1–650 must secure the client's informed consent to the limited scope of the representation. If a short-term limited representation would not be reasonable under the circumstances, the member may offer advice to the client but must also advise the client of the need for further assistance of counsel. See rule 3–110. Except as provided in this rule 1–650, the Rules of Professional Conduct and the State Bar Act, including the member's duty of confidentiality under Business and Professions Code § 6068(e)(1), are applicable to the limited representation.

[3] A member who is representing a client in the circumstances addressed by rule 1–650 ordinarily is not able to check systematically for conflicts of interest. Therefore, paragraph (A)(1) requires compliance with rule 3–310 only if the member knows that the representation presents a conflict of interest for the member. In addition, paragraph (A)(2) imputes conflicts of interest to the member only if the member knows that another lawyer in the member's law firm would be disqualified under rule 3–310.

[4] Because the limited nature of the services significantly reduces the risk of conflicts of interest with other matters being handled by the member's law firm, paragraph (B) provides that imputed conflicts of interest are inapplicable to a representation governed by this rule except as provided by paragraph (A)(2). Paragraph (A)(2) imputes conflicts of interest to the participating member when the member knows that any lawyer in the member's firm would be disqualified under rule 3–310. By virtue of paragraph (B), moreover, a member's participation in a short-term limited legal services program will not be imputed to the member's law firm or preclude the member's law firm from undertaking or continuing the representation of a client with interests adverse to a client being represented under the program's auspices. Nor will the personal disqualification of a lawyer participating in the program be imputed to other lawyers participating in the program.

[5] If, after commencing a short-term limited representation in accordance with rule 1–650, a member undertakes to represent the client in the matter on an ongoing basis, rule 3–310 and all other rules become applicable.

(Adopted, eff. Aug. 28, 2009.)

Research References

Rutter, Cal. Practice Guide: Prof. Responsibility Ch. 1-J, J. Regulating Participation in Legal Service Programs and Referral Service Plans.
Rutter, Cal. Practice Guide: Prof. Responsibility Ch. 3-A, A. Nature of Attorney-Client Relationship.

Rutter, Cal. Practice Guide: Prof. Responsibility Ch. 3-B, B. Formation of Relationship.

Rutter, Cal. Practice Guide: Prof. Responsibility Ch. 4-A, A. General Considerations.

Rutter, Cal. Practice Guide: Prof. Responsibility Ch. 4-B, B. Concurrent Representation of Clients With Conflicting Interests (Conflicts Between Present Clients).

Rutter, Cal. Practice Guide: Prof. Responsibility Ch. 4-C, C. Conflicts Between Present and Former Clients (Successive Representation).

1 Witkin Cal. Proc. 5th Attorneys § 420A, (S 420A) (New)-Limited Legal Services Programs (Rule 1-650).

Rule 1–700. Member as Candidate for Judicial Office

(A) A member who is a candidate for judicial office in California shall comply with Canon 5 of the Code of Judicial Ethics.

(B) For purposes of this rule, "candidate for judicial office" means a member seeking judicial office by election. The determination of when a member is a candidate for judicial office is defined in the terminology section of the California Code of Judicial Ethics. A member's duty to comply with paragraph (A) shall end when the member announces withdrawal of the member's candidacy or when the results of the election are final, whichever occurs first.

DISCUSSION

Nothing in rule 1-700 shall be deemed to limit the applicability of any other rule or law.

(Adopted, eff. Nov. 21, 1997.)

Research References

Rutter, Cal. Practice Guide: Prof. Responsibility Ch. 1-D, D. Unauthorized Practice of Law.

Rutter, Cal. Practice Guide: Prof. Responsibility Ch. 8-D, D. Restrictions on Speech and Behavior Outside Courtroom.

1 Witkin Cal. Proc. 5th Attorneys § 421, Attorney as Judicial Candidate or Acting in Judicial Capacity (Rules 1-700, 1-710).

Rule 1–710. Member as Temporary Judge, Referee, or Court-Appointed Arbitrator

A member who is serving as a temporary judge, referee, or court-appointed arbitrator, and is subject under the Code of Judicial Ethics to Canon 6D, shall comply with the terms of that canon.

DISCUSSION

This rule is intended to permit the State Bar to discipline members who violate applicable portions of the Code of Judicial Ethics while acting in a judicial capacity pursuant to an order or appointment by a court.

Nothing in rule 1–710 shall be deemed to limit the applicability of any other rule or law.

[*Publisher's Note: The California Code of Judicial Ethics is available on-line at the official website of the California Courts located at www.courtinfo.ca.gov. Select "Code of Judicial Ethics" in the "Rules" area of the website.*]

(Adopted, eff. March 18, 1999.)

Research References

Rutter, Cal. Practice Guide: A.D.R. Ch. 7-B, B. Arbitrators.

Rutter, Cal. Practice Guide: A.D.R. Ch. 7-C, C. Private Judges.

Rutter, Cal. Practice Guide: A.D.R. Ch. 7-D, D. Referees.

Rutter, Cal. Practice Guide: Civil Trials & Evidence Ch. 16-G, G. Trial by Reference.

Rutter, Cal. Practice Guide: Prof. Responsibility Ch. 8-D, D. Restrictions on Speech and Behavior Outside Courtroom.

1 Witkin Cal. Proc. 5th Attorneys § 421, Attorney as Judicial Candidate or Acting in Judicial Capacity (Rules 1-700, 1-710).

2 Witkin Cal. Proc. 5th Courts § 348, (S 348) Nature of Position.

Chapter 2

RELATIONSHIP AMONG MEMBERS

Rule

2–100. Communication With a Represented Party.

2–200. Financial Arrangements Among Lawyers.

2–300. Sale or Purchase of a Law Practice of a Member, Living or Deceased.

2–400. Prohibited Discriminatory Conduct in a Law Practice.

Rule 2–100. Communication With a Represented Party

(A) While representing a client, a member shall not communicate directly or indirectly about the subject of the representation with a party the member knows to be represented by another lawyer in the matter, unless the member has the consent of the other lawyer.

(B) For purposes of this rule, a "party" includes:

(1) An officer, director, or managing agent of a corporation or association, and a partner or managing agent of a partnership; or

(2) An association member or an employee of an association, corporation, or partnership, if the subject of the communication is any act or omission of such person in connection with the matter which may be binding upon or imputed to the organization for purposes of civil or criminal liability or whose statement may constitute an admission on the part of the organization.

(C) This rule shall not prohibit:

(1) Communications with a public officer, board, committee, or body; or

(2) Communications initiated by a party seeking advice or representation from an independent lawyer of the party's choice; or

(3) Communications otherwise authorized by law.

DISCUSSION

Rule 2–100 is intended to control communications between a member and persons the member knows to be represented by counsel unless a statutory scheme or case law will override the rule. There are a number of express statutory schemes which authorize communications between a member and person who would otherwise be subject to this rule. These statutes protect a variety of other rights such as the right of employees to organize and to engage in collective bargaining, employee health and safety, or equal employment opportunity. Other applicable law also includes the authority of government prosecutors and investigators to conduct criminal investigations, as limited by the relevant decisional law.

Rule 2–100 is not intended to prevent the parties themselves from communicating with respect to the subject matter of the representation, and nothing in the rule prevents a member from advising the client that such communication can be made. Moreover, the rule does not prohibit a member who is also a party to a legal matter from directly or indirectly communicating on his or her own behalf with a represented party. Such a member has independent rights as a party which should not be abrogated because of his or her professional status. To prevent any possible abuse in such situations, the counsel for the opposing party may advise that party (1) about the risks and benefits of communications with a lawyer-party, and (2) not to accept or engage in communications with the lawyer-party.

Rule 2–100 also addresses the situation in which member A is contacted by an opposing party who is represented and, because of dissatisfaction with that party's counsel, seeks A's independent advice. Since A is employed by the opposition, the member cannot give independent advice.

As used in paragraph (A), "the subject of the representation," "matter," and "party" are not limited to a litigation context.

Paragraph (B) is intended to apply only to persons employed at the time of the communication. (See Triple A Machine Shop, Inc. v. State of California (1989) 213 Cal.App.3d 131 [261 Cal.Rptr. 493].)

Subparagraph (C)(2) is intended to permit a member to communicate with a party seeking to hire new counsel or to obtain a second opinion. A member contacted by such a party continues to be bound by other Rules of Professional Conduct. (See, e.g., rules 1–400 and 3–310.)

(Adopted Nov. 28, 1988, eff. May 27, 1989. As amended, eff. Sept. 14, 1992.)

Research References

Rutter, Cal. Practice Guide: A.D.R. Ch. 3-B, B. Commencing Mediation Process.

Rutter, Cal. Practice Guide: Civ. Pro. Before Trial Ch. 1-B, B. Prelawsuit Investigations, Research and Analysis.

Rutter, Cal. Practice Guide: Civ. Pro. Before Trial Ch. 1-C, C. Prelawsuit Notices, Claims and Demands.

Rutter, Cal. Practice Guide: Civ. Pro. Before Trial Ch. 14-C, C. Procedural Issues.

Rutter, Cal. Practice Guide: Civ. Pro. Before Trial Ch. 8D-3, Obtaining Proof.

Rutter, Cal. Practice Guide: Civ. Pro. Before Trial Ch. 12(II)-H, H. Professional Responsibility Considerations Re Settlements.

Rutter, Cal. Practice Guide: Civil Trials & Evidence Ch. 4-I, I. Other Motions at Final Status Conference.

California Practice Guide: Employment Litigation Ch. 2-G, G. Communicating With Adverse Party Represented by Counsel.

Rutter, Cal. Practice Guide: Enforcing Judgments/Debts Ch. 4-A, A. Attachment.

Rutter, Cal. Practice Guide: Fed.Civ.Pro. Before Trial Ch. 10-C, C. Class Actions.

Rutter, Cal. Practice Guide: Fed.Civ.Pro. Before Trial Ch. 11(I)-B, B. Informal Methods of Obtaining Information.

Rutter, Cal. Practice Guide: Insurance Litigation Ch. 12B-B, B. Bad Faith Refusal to Settle.

Rutter, Cal. Practice Guide: Personal Injury Ch. 1-D, D. General Concerns and Advice to Client Upon Accepting Employment; Execution of Necessary Authorizations.

Rutter, Cal. Practice Guide: Personal Injury Ch. 4-A, A. General Considerations.

Rutter, Cal. Practice Guide: Personal Injury Ch. 4-G, G. Concluding and Enforcing Settlement.

Rutter, Cal. Practice Guide: Prof. Responsibility Ch. 2-D, D. In-Person Solicitation for Profit.

Rutter, Cal. Practice Guide: Prof. Responsibility Ch. 2-E, E. Targeted or Mass Mailings.

Rutter, Cal. Practice Guide: Prof. Responsibility Ch. 4-A, A. General Considerations.

Rutter, Cal. Practice Guide: Prof. Responsibility Ch. 5-J, J. Fee Disputes With Existing Clients.

Rutter, Cal. Practice Guide: Prof. Responsibility Ch. 7-B, B. Duty to Maintain Client Confidence and Secrets Under State Bar Act.

Rutter, Cal. Practice Guide: Prof. Responsibility Ch. 8-B, B. Accepting or Rejecting Employment.

Rutter, Cal. Practice Guide: Prof. Responsibility Ch. 8-D, D. Restrictions on Speech and Behavior Outside Courtroom.

Rutter, Cal. Practice Guide: Prof. Responsibility Ch. 8-D , Outline D.

1 Witkin Cal. Proc. 5th Attorneys § 109, (S 109) in General.

1 Witkin Cal. Proc. 5th Attorneys § 236, (S 236) Distinctions.

1 Witkin Cal. Proc. 5th Attorneys § 240, (S 240) Adverse Party Must Deal With Attorney.

1 Witkin Cal. Proc. 5th Attorneys § 422, (S 422) Prohibited and Authorized Activity.

1 Witkin Cal. Proc. 5th Attorneys § 423, (S 423) Nature and Scope of Rule.

1 Witkin Cal. Proc. 5th Attorneys § 536, (S 536) Rules of Professional Conduct.

1 Witkin Cal. Proc. 5th Attorneys § 537, (S 537) Violation of Rule.

1 Witkin Cal. Proc. 5th Attorneys § 538, (S 538) Distinction: Communication With Former Employees of Corporation.

Rule 2–200.   Financial Arrangements Among Lawyers

(A) A member shall not divide a fee for legal services with a lawyer who is not a partner of, associate of, or shareholder with the member unless:

(1) The client has consented in writing thereto after a full disclosure has been made in writing that a division of fees will be made and the terms of such division; and

(2) The total fee charged by all lawyers is not increased solely by reason of the provision for division of fees and is not unconscionable as that term is defined in rule 4–200.

(B) Except as permitted in paragraph (A) of this rule or rule 2–300, a member shall not compensate, give, or promise anything of value to any lawyer for the purpose of recommending or securing employment of the member or the member's law firm by a client, or as a reward for having made a recommendation resulting in employment of the member or the member's law firm by a client. A member's offering of or giving a gift or gratuity to any lawyer who has made a recommendation resulting in the employment of the member or the member's law firm shall not of itself violate this rule, provided that the gift or gratuity was not offered in consideration of any promise, agreement, or understanding that such a gift or gratuity would be forthcoming or that referrals would be made or encouraged in the future. *(Adopted Nov. 28, 1988, eff. May 27, 1989.)*

Research References

Rutter, Cal. Practice Guide: Civil Appeals & Writs Ch. 1-E, E. Preappeal Evaluation and "Housekeeping" Steps.

Rutter, Cal. Practice Guide: Civ. Pro. Before Trial Ch. 1-A, A. Accepting a New Case.

Rutter, Cal. Practice Guide: Civil Trials & Evidence Ch. 1-N, N. Associating Trial Counsel.

California Practice Guide: Employment Litigation Ch. 2-B, B. Fee Arrangements.

Rutter, Cal. Practice Guide: Enforcing Judgments/Debts Ch. 1-B, B. Accepting the Collection Case.

Rutter, Cal. Practice Guide: Personal Injury Ch. 1-B, B. Initial Evaluation of Case: Decision to Accept or Reject Employment or Undertake Further Evaluation of Claim.

Rutter, Cal. Practice Guide: Real Prop. Transactions Ch. 1-B, B. Attorney Competence, Conflicts of Interest and Initial Client Communications.

Rutter, Cal. Practice Guide: Real Prop. Transactions Ch. 1-C, C. Attorney Fees and Costs Agreements.

Rutter, Cal. Practice Guide: Prof. Responsibility Ch. 1-E, E. Regulation of Form of Practice.

Rutter, Cal. Practice Guide: Prof. Responsibility Ch. 1-F, F. Prohibition Against Agreements Restricting Right to Practice.

Rutter, Cal. Practice Guide: Prof. Responsibility Ch. 1-I, I. Regulation of Sale of Law Practice.

Rutter, Cal. Practice Guide: Prof. Responsibility Ch. 2-D, D. In-Person Solicitation for Profit.

Rutter, Cal. Practice Guide: Prof. Responsibility Ch. 5-D, D. Ethical Limitations on Attorney Fees.

Rutter, Cal. Practice Guide: Prof. Responsibility Ch. 5-E, E. Costs Arrangements.

Rutter, Cal. Practice Guide: Prof. Responsibility Ch. 5-K, K. Fee Recovery/Enforcing Fee Agreements.

Rutter, Cal. Practice Guide: Prof. Responsibility Ch. 10-E, E. Law Firm Break-Ups.

Rutter, Cal. Practice Guide: Prof. Responsibility Ch. 5-D , Outline D.

Rutter, Cal. Practice Guide: Prof. Responsibility Ch. 5-E , Outline E.

Rutter, Cal. Practice Guide: Prof. Responsibility Ch. 5-K , Outline K.

1 Witkin Cal. Proc. 5th Attorneys § 161, Ethical Considerations.

1 Witkin Cal. Proc. 5th Attorneys § 162, Referral Fee is Valid.

1 Witkin Cal. Proc. 5th Attorneys § 424, in General.

1 Witkin Cal. Proc. 5th Attorneys § 425, Quantum Meruit Recovery.

1 Witkin Cal. Proc. 5th Attorneys § 426, Outside Attorney as Associate.

1 Witkin Cal. Proc. 5th Attorneys § 427, (S 427) Inducements to Recommend Employment.

Prof. Conduct

Rule 2–300. Sale or Purchase of a Law Practice of a Member, Living or Deceased

All or substantially all of the law practice of a member, living or deceased, including goodwill, may be sold to another member or law firm subject to all the following conditions:

(A) Fees charged to clients shall not be increased solely by reason of such sale.

(B) If the sale contemplates the transfer of responsibility for work not yet completed or responsibility for client files or information protected by Business and Professions Code section 6068, subdivision (e), then;

(1) if the seller is deceased, or has a conservator or other person acting in a representative capacity, and no member has been appointed to act for the seller pursuant to Business and Professions Code section 6180.5, then prior to the transfer;

(a) the purchaser shall cause a written notice to be given to the client stating that the interest in the law practice is being transferred to the purchaser; that the client has the right to retain other counsel; that the client may take possession of any client papers and property, as required by rule 3–700(D); and that if no response is received to the notification within 90 days of the sending of such notice, or in the event the client's rights would be prejudiced by a failure to act during that time, the purchaser may act on behalf of the client until otherwise notified by the client. Such notice shall comply with the requirements as set forth in rule 1–400(D) and any provisions relating to attorney-client fee arrangements, and

(b) the purchaser shall obtain the written consent of the client provided that such consent shall be presumed until otherwise notified by the client if no response is received to the notification specified in subparagraph (a) within 90 days of the date of the sending of such notification to the client's last address as shown on the records of the seller, or the client's rights would be prejudiced by a failure to act during such 90-day period.

(2) in all other circumstances, not less than 90 days prior to the transfer;

(a) the seller, or the member appointed to act for the seller pursuant to Business and Professions Code section 6180.5, shall cause a written notice to be given to the client stating that the interest in the law practice is being transferred to the purchaser; that the client has the right to retain other counsel; that the client may take possession of any client papers and property, as required by rule 3–700(D); and that if no response is received to the notification within 90 days of the sending of such notice, the purchaser may act on behalf of the client until otherwise notified by the client. Such notice shall comply with the requirements as set forth in rule 1–400(D) and any provisions relating to attorney-client fee arrangements, and

(b) the seller, or the member appointed to act for the seller pursuant to Business and Professions Code section 6180.5, shall obtain the written consent of the client prior to the transfer provided that such consent shall be presumed until otherwise notified by the client if no response is received to the notification specified in subparagraph (a) within 90 days of the date of the sending of such notification to the client's last address as shown on the records of the seller.

(C) If substitution is required by the rules of a tribunal in which a matter is pending, all steps necessary to substitute a member shall be taken.

(D) All activity of a purchaser or potential purchaser under this rule shall be subject to compliance with rules 3–300 and 3–310 where applicable.

(E) Confidential information shall not be disclosed to a non-member in connection with a sale under this rule.

(F) Admission to or retirement from a law partnership or law corporation, retirement plans and similar arrangements, or sale of tangible assets of a law practice shall not be deemed a sale or purchase under this rule.

DISCUSSION

Paragraph (A) is intended to prohibit the purchaser from charging the former clients of the seller a higher fee than the purchaser is charging his or her existing clients.

"All or substantially all of the law practice of a member" means, for purposes of rule 2–300, that, for example, a member may retain one or two clients who have such a longstanding personal and professional relationship with the member that transfer of those clients' files is not feasible. Conversely, rule 2–300 is not intended to authorize the sale of a law practice in a piecemeal fashion except as may be required by subparagraph (B)(1)(a) or paragraph (D).

Transfer of individual client matters, where permitted, is governed by rule 2–200. Payment of a fee to a non-lawyer broker for arranging the sale or purchase of a law practice is governed by rule 1–320.

(Adopted Nov. 28, 1988, eff. May 27, 1989. As amended, eff. Sept. 14, 1992.)

Research References

Rutter, Cal. Practice Guide: Prof. Responsibility Ch. 1-I, I. Regulation of Sale of Law Practice.
Rutter, Cal. Practice Guide: Prof. Responsibility Ch. 2-A, A. Regulations Generally.
Rutter, Cal. Practice Guide: Prof. Responsibility Ch. 5-D, D. Ethical Limitations on Attorney Fees.
1 Witkin Cal. Proc. 5th Attorneys § 36, (S 36) Sale of Law Practice.
1 Witkin Cal. Proc. 5th Attorneys § 427, (S 427) Inducements to Recommend Employment.
1 Witkin Cal. Proc. 5th Attorneys § 428, (S 428) Sale to Attorney or Law Firm.
1 Witkin Cal. Proc. 5th Attorneys § 429, (S 429) Transfer of Responsibility for Work or Files.

Rule 2–400. Prohibited Discriminatory Conduct in a Law Practice

(A) For purposes of this rule:

(1) "law practice" includes sole practices, law partnerships, law corporations, corporate and governmental legal departments, and other entities which employ members to practice law;

(2) "knowingly permit" means a failure to advocate corrective action where the member knows of a discriminatory policy or practice which results in the unlawful discrimination prohibited in paragraph (B); and

(3) "unlawfully" and "unlawful" shall be determined by reference to applicable state or federal statutes or decisions making unlawful discrimination in employment and in offering goods and services to the public.

(B) In the management or operation of a law practice, a member shall not unlawfully discriminate or knowingly permit unlawful discrimination on the basis of race, national origin, sex, sexual orientation, religion, age or disability in:

(1) hiring, promoting, discharging, or otherwise determining the conditions of employment of any person; or

(2) accepting or terminating representation of any client.

(C) No disciplinary investigation or proceeding may be initiated by the State Bar against a member under this rule unless and until a tribunal of competent jurisdiction, other than a disciplinary tribunal, shall have first adjudicated a complaint of alleged discrimination and found that unlawful conduct occurred. Upon such adjudication, the tribunal finding or verdict shall then be admissible evidence of the occurrence or non-occurrence of the alleged discrimination in any disciplinary proceeding initiated under this rule. In order for discipline to be imposed under this rule, however, the finding of unlawfulness must be upheld and final after appeal, the time for filing an appeal must have expired, or the appeal must have been dismissed.

DISCUSSION

In order for discriminatory conduct to be actionable under this rule, it must first be found to be unlawful by an appropriate civil administrative or judicial tribunal under applicable state or federal law. Until there is a finding of civil unlawfulness, there is no basis for disciplinary action under this rule.

A complaint of misconduct based on this rule may be filed with the State Bar following a finding of unlawfulness in the first instance even though that finding is thereafter appealed.

A disciplinary investigation or proceeding for conduct coming within this rule may be initiated and maintained, however, if such conduct warrants discipline under California Business and Professions Code sections 6106 and 6068, the California Supreme Court's inherent authority to impose discipline, or other disciplinary standard.

(Adopted March 6, 1993, eff. March 1, 1994.)

Research References

Rutter, Cal. Practice Guide: Prof. Responsibility Ch. 1-G, G. Prohibition Against Discriminatory Practices.
Rutter, Cal. Practice Guide: Prof. Responsibility Ch. 6-B, B. Elements of Attorney Competence.
Rutter, Cal. Practice Guide: Prof. Responsibility Ch. 6-C, C. Sexual Relations With Client Affecting Competence.
Rutter, Cal. Practice Guide: Prof. Responsibility Ch. 6-E, E. Malpractice Insurance.
Rutter, Cal. Practice Guide: Prof. Responsibility Ch. 10-B, B. Withdrawal (Termination) by Lawyer.
1 Witkin Cal. Proc. 5th Attorneys § 430, Discriminatory Conduct in Law Practice (Rule 2-400).

Chapter 3

PROFESSIONAL RELATIONSHIP WITH CLIENTS

Rule 3–100. Confidential Information of a Client

(A) A member shall not reveal information protected from disclosure by Business and Professions Code section 6068, subdivision (e)(1) without the informed consent of the client, or as provided in paragraph (B) of this rule.

(B) A member may, but is not required to, reveal confidential information relating to the representation of a client to the extent that the member reasonably believes the disclosure is necessary to prevent a criminal act that the member reasonably believes is likely to result in death of, or substantial bodily harm to, an individual.

(C) Before revealing confidential information to prevent a criminal act as provided in paragraph (B), a member shall, if reasonable under the circumstances:

(1) make a good faith effort to persuade the client: (i) not to commit or to continue the criminal act or (ii) to pursue a course of conduct that will prevent the threatened death or substantial bodily harm; or do both (i) and (ii); and

(2) inform the client, at an appropriate time, of the member's ability or decision to reveal information as provided in paragraph (B).

(D) In revealing confidential information as provided in paragraph (B), the member's disclosure must be no more than is necessary to prevent the criminal act, given the information known to the member at the time of the disclosure.

(E) A member who does not reveal information permitted by paragraph (B) does not violate this rule.

DISCUSSION

[1] Duty of confidentiality. Paragraph (A) relates to a member's obligations under Business and Professions Code section 6068, subdivision (e)(1), which provides it is a duty of a member: "To maintain inviolate the confidence, and at every peril to himself or herself to preserve the secrets, of his or her client." A member's duty to preserve the confidentiality of client information involves public policies of paramount importance. (*In Re Jordan* (1974) 12 Cal.3d 575, 580 [116 Cal.Rptr. 371].) Preserving the confidentiality of client information contributes to the trust that is the hallmark of the client-lawyer relationship. The client is thereby encouraged to seek legal assistance and to communicate fully and frankly with the lawyer even as to embarrassing or legally damaging subject matter. The lawyer needs this information to represent the client effectively and, if necessary, to advise the client to refrain from wrongful conduct. Almost without exception, clients come to lawyers in order to determine their rights and what is, in the complex of laws and regulations, deemed to be legal and correct. Based upon experience, lawyers know that almost all clients follow the advice given, and the law is upheld. Paragraph (A) thus recognizes a fundamental principle in the client-lawyer relationship that, in the absence of the client's informed consent, a member must not reveal information relating to the representation. (See, e.g., *Commercial Standard Title Co. v. Superior Court* (1979) 92 Cal.App.3d 934, 945 [155 Cal.Rptr.393].)

[2] Client-lawyer confidentiality encompasses the attorney-client privilege, the work-product doctrine and ethical standards of confidentiality. The principle of client-lawyer confidentiality applies to information relating to the representation, whatever its source, and encompasses matters communicated in confidence by the client, and therefore protected by the attorney-client privilege, matters protected by the work product doctrine, and matters protected under ethical standards of confidentiality, all as established in law, rule and policy. (See *In the Matter of Johnson* (Rev. Dept. 2000) 4 Cal. State Bar Ct. Rptr. 179; *Goldstein v. Lees* (1975) 46 Cal.App.3d 614 [120 Cal.Rptr. 253].) The attorney-client privilege and work-product doctrine apply in judicial and other proceedings in which a member may be called as a witness or be otherwise compelled to produce evidence concerning a client. A member's ethical duty of confidentiality is not so limited in its scope of protection for the client-lawyer relationship of trust and prevents a member from revealing the client's confidential information even when not confronted with such compulsion. Thus, a member may not reveal such information except with the consent of the client or as authorized or required by the State Bar Act, these rules, or other law.

[3] Narrow exception to duty of confidentiality under this Rule. Notwithstanding the important public policies promoted by lawyers adhering to the core duty of confidentiality, the overriding value of life permits disclosures otherwise prohibited under Business & Professions Code section 6068(e), subdivision (1). Paragraph (B), which restates Business and Professions

Prof. Conduct

Code section 6068, subdivision (e)(2), identifies a narrow confidentiality exception, absent the client's informed consent, when a member reasonably believes that disclosure is necessary to prevent a criminal act that the member reasonably believes is likely to result in the death of, or substantial bodily harm to an individual. Evidence Code section 956.5, which relates to the evidentiary attorney-client privilege, sets forth a similar express exception. Although a member is not permitted to reveal confidential information concerning a client's past, completed criminal acts, the policy favoring the preservation of human life that underlies this exception to the duty of confidentiality and the evidentiary privilege permits disclosure to prevent a future or ongoing criminal act.

[4] Member not subject to discipline for revealing confidential information as permitted under this Rule. Rule 3–100, which restates Business and Professions Code section 6068, subdivision (e)(2), reflects a balancing between the interests of preserving client confidentiality and of preventing a criminal act that a member reasonably believes is likely to result in death or substantial bodily harm to an individual. A member who reveals information as permitted under this rule is not subject to discipline.

[5] No duty to reveal confidential information. Neither Business and Professions Code section 6068, subdivision (e)(2) nor this rule imposes an affirmative obligation on a member to reveal information in order to prevent harm. (See rule 1–100(A).) A member may decide not to reveal confidential information. Whether a member chooses to reveal confidential information as permitted under this rule is a matter for the individual member to decide, based on all the facts and circumstances, such as those discussed in paragraph [6] of this discussion.

[6] Deciding to reveal confidential information as permitted under paragraph (B). Disclosure permitted under paragraph (B) is ordinarily a last resort, when no other available action is reasonably likely to prevent the criminal act. Prior to revealing information as permitted under paragraph (B), the member must, if reasonable under the circumstances, make a good faith effort to persuade the client to take steps to avoid the criminal act or threatened harm. Among the factors to be considered in determining whether to disclose confidential information are the following:

(1) the amount of time that the member has to make a decision about disclosure;

(2) whether the client or a third party has made similar threats before and whether they have ever acted or attempted to act upon them;

(3) whether the member believes the member's efforts to persuade the client or a third person not to engage in the criminal conduct have or have not been successful;

(4) the extent of adverse effect to the client's rights under the Fifth, Sixth and Fourteenth Amendments of the United States Constitution and analogous rights and privacy rights under Article 1 of the Constitution of the State of California that may result from disclosure contemplated by the member;

(5) the extent of other adverse effects to the client that may result from disclosure contemplated by the member; and

(6) the nature and extent of information that must be disclosed to prevent the criminal act or threatened harm.

A member may also consider whether the prospective harm to the victim or victims is imminent in deciding whether to disclose the confidential information. However, the imminence of the harm is not a prerequisite to disclosure and a member may disclose the information without waiting until immediately before the harm is likely to occur.

[7] Counseling client or third person not to commit a criminal act reasonably likely to result in death of substantial bodily harm. Subparagraph (C)(1) provides that before a member may reveal confidential information, the member must, if reasonable under the circumstances, make a good faith effort to persuade the client not to commit or to continue the criminal act, or to persuade the client to otherwise pursue a course of conduct that will prevent the threatened death or substantial bodily harm, or if necessary, do both. The interests protected by

such counseling is the client's interest in limiting disclosure of confidential information and in taking responsible action to deal with situations attributable to the client. If a client, whether in response to the member's counseling or otherwise, takes corrective action—such as by ceasing the criminal act before harm is caused—the option for permissive disclosure by the member would cease as the threat posed by the criminal act would no longer be present. When the actor is a nonclient or when the act is deliberate or malicious, the member who contemplates making adverse disclosure of confidential information may reasonably conclude that the compelling interests of the member or others in their own personal safety preclude personal contact with the actor. Before counseling an actor who is a nonclient, the member should, if reasonable under the circumstances, first advise the client of the member's intended course of action. If a client or another person has already acted but the intended harm has not yet occurred, the member should consider, if reasonable under the circumstances, efforts to persuade the client or third person to warn the victim or consider other appropriate action to prevent the harm. Even when the member has concluded that paragraph (B) does not permit the member to reveal confidential information, the member nevertheless is permitted to counsel the client as to why it may be in the client's best interest to consent to the attorney's disclosure of that information.

[8] Disclosure of confidential information must be no more than is reasonably necessary to prevent the criminal act. Under paragraph (D), disclosure of confidential information, when made, must be no more extensive than the member reasonably believes necessary to prevent the criminal act. Disclosure should allow access to the confidential information to only those persons who the member reasonably believes can act to prevent the harm. Under some circumstances, a member may determine that the best course to pursue is to make an anonymous disclosure to the potential victim or relevant law-enforcement authorities. What particular measures are reasonable depends on the circumstances known to the member. Relevant circumstances include the time available, whether the victim might be unaware of the threat, the member's prior course of dealings with the client, and the extent of the adverse effect on the client that may result from the disclosure contemplated by the member.

[9] Informing client of member's ability or decision to reveal confidential information under subparagraph (C)(2). A member is required to keep a client reasonably informed about significant developments regarding the employment or representation. Rule 3–500; Business and Professions Code, section 6068, subdivision (m). Paragraph (C)(2), however, recognizes that under certain circumstances, informing a client of the member's ability or decision to reveal confidential information under paragraph (B) would likely increase the risk of death or substantial bodily harm, not only to the originally-intended victims of the criminal act, but also to the client or members of the client's family, or to the member or the member's family or associates. Therefore, paragraph (C)(2) requires a member to inform the client of the member's ability or decision to reveal confidential information as provided in paragraph (B) only if it is reasonable to do so under the circumstances. Paragraph (C)(2) further recognizes that the appropriate time for the member to inform the client may vary depending upon the circumstances. (See paragraph [10] of this discussion.) Among the factors to be considered in determining an appropriate time, if any, to inform a client are:

(1) whether the client is an experienced user of legal services;

(2) the frequency of the member's contact with the client;

(3) the nature and length of the professional relationship with the client;

(4) whether the member and client have discussed the member's duty of confidentiality or any exceptions to that duty;

(5) the likelihood that the client's matter will involve information within paragraph (B);

(6) the member's belief, if applicable, that so informing the client is likely to increase the likelihood that a criminal act likely to result in the death of, or substantial bodily harm to, an individual; and

(7) the member's belief, if applicable, that good faith efforts to persuade a client not to act on a threat have failed.

[10] Avoiding a chilling effect on the lawyer-client relationship. The foregoing flexible approach to the member's informing a client of his or her ability or decision to reveal confidential information recognizes the concern that informing a client about limits on confidentiality may have a chilling effect on client communication. (See Discussion paragraph [1].) To avoid that chilling effect, one member may choose to inform the client of the member's ability to reveal information as early as the outset of the representation, while another member may choose to inform a client only at a point when that client has imparted information that may fall under paragraph (B), or even choose not to inform a client until such time as the member attempts to counsel the client as contemplated in Discussion paragraph [7]. In each situation, the member will have discharged properly the requirement under subparagraph (C)(2), and will not be subject to discipline.

[11] Informing client that disclosure has been made; termination of the lawyer-client relationship. When a member has revealed confidential information under paragraph (B), in all but extraordinary cases the relationship between member and client will have deteriorated so as to make the member's representation of the client impossible. Therefore, the member is required to seek to withdraw from the representation (see rule 3-700(B)), unless the member is able to obtain the client's informed consent to the member's continued representation. The member must inform the client of the fact of the member's disclosure unless the member has a compelling interest in not informing the client, such as to protect the member, the member's family or a third person from the risk of death or substantial bodily harm.

[12] Other consequences of the member's disclosure. Depending upon the circumstances of a member's disclosure of confidential information, there may be other important issues that a member must address. For example, if a member will be called as a witness in the client's matter, then rule 5-210 should be considered. Similarly, the member should consider his or her duties of loyalty and competency (rule 3-110).

[13] Other exceptions to confidentiality under California law. Rule 3-100 is not intended to augment, diminish, or preclude reliance upon, any other exceptions to the duty to preserve the confidentiality of client information recognized under California law.

(Adopted, eff. July 1, 2004.)

Research References

Rutter, Cal. Practice Guide: Personal Injury Ch. 1-D, D. General Concerns and Advice to Client Upon Accepting Employment; Execution of Necessary Authorizations.

Rutter, Cal. Practice Guide: Prof. Responsibility Ch. 7-A, A. Introduction.

Rutter, Cal. Practice Guide: Prof. Responsibility Ch. 7-B, B. Duty to Maintain Client Confidence and Secrets Under State Bar Act.

Rutter, Cal. Practice Guide: Prof. Responsibility Ch. 7-C, C. Attorney-Client Privilege.

1 Witkin Cal. Proc. 5th Attorneys § 90, in General.

1 Witkin Cal. Proc. 5th Attorneys § 110, (S 110) Representation on Unrelated Matter.

1 Witkin Cal. Proc. 5th Attorneys § 431, Confidential Information of Client (Rule 3-100).

Rule 3-110. Failing to Act Competently

(A) A member shall not intentionally, recklessly, or repeatedly fail to perform legal services with competence.

(B) For purposes of this rule, "competence" in any legal service shall mean to apply the 1) diligence, 2) learning and skill, and 3) mental, emotional, and physical ability reasonably necessary for the performance of such service.

(C) If a member does not have sufficient learning and skill when the legal service is undertaken, the member may nonetheless perform such services competently by 1) associating with or, where appropriate, professionally consulting another lawyer reasonably believed to be competent, or 2) by acquiring sufficient learning and skill before performance is required.

DISCUSSION

The duties set forth in rule 3-110 include the duty to supervise the work of subordinate attorney and non-attorney employees or agents. (See, e.g., *Waysman v. State Bar* (1986) 41 Cal.3d 452; *Trousil v. State Bar* (1985) 38 Cal.3d 337, 342 [211 Cal.Rptr. 525]; *Palomo v. State Bar* (1984) 36 Cal.3d 785 [205 Cal.Rptr. 834]; *Crane v. State Bar* (1981) 30 Cal.3d 117, 122; *Black v. State Bar* (1972) 7 Cal.3d 676, 692 [103 Cal.Rptr. 288; 499 P.2d 968]; *Vaughn v. State Bar* (1972) 6 Cal.3d 847, 857-858 [100 Cal.Rptr. 713; 494 P.2d 1257]; *Moore v. State Bar* (1964) 62 Cal.2d 74, 81 [41 Cal.Rptr. 161; 396 P.2d 577].)

In an emergency a lawyer may give advice or assistance in a matter in which the lawyer does not have the skill ordinarily required where referral to or consultation with another lawyer would be impractical. Even in an emergency, however, assistance should be limited to that reasonably necessary in the circumstances.

(Adopted Nov. 28, 1988, eff. May 27, 1989. As amended, eff. Sept. 14, 1992.)

Research References

Rutter, Cal. Practice Guide: A.D.R. Ch. 1-C, C. Attorneys' Obligation Re ADR.

Rutter, Cal. Practice Guide: A.D.R. Ch. 2-C, C. Preparing for Negotiations.

Rutter, Cal. Practice Guide: Civil Appeals & Writs Ch. 1-E, E. Preappeal Evaluation and "Housekeeping" Steps.

Rutter, Cal. Practice Guide: Civ. Pro. Before Trial Ch. 1-A, A. Accepting a New Case.

Rutter, Cal. Practice Guide: Civ. Pro. Before Trial Ch. 1-B, B. Prelawsuit Investigations, Research and Analysis.

Rutter, Cal. Practice Guide: Civil Trials & Evidence Ch. 1-N, N. Associating Trial Counsel.

California Practice Guide: Employment Litigation Ch. 18-B, B. Non-binding ADR Procedures.

Rutter, Cal. Practice Guide: Enforcing Judgments/Debts Ch. 1-B, B. Accepting the Collection Case.

Rutter, Cal. Practice Guide: Personal Injury Ch. 1-B, B. Initial Evaluation of Case: Decision to Accept or Reject Employment or Undertake Further Evaluation of Claim.

Rutter, Cal. Practice Guide: Personal Injury Ch. 4-G, G. Concluding and Enforcing Settlement.

Rutter, Cal. Practice Guide: Real Prop. Transactions Ch. 1-B, B. Attorney Competence, Conflicts of Interest and Initial Client Communications.

Rutter, Cal. Practice Guide: Real Prop. Transactions Ch. 6-I, I. Real Property Foreclosures and Antideficiency Laws.

Rutter, Cal. Practice Guide: Real Prop. Transactions Ch. 9-D, D. Prenegotiation/Predrafting Considerations.

Rutter, Cal. Practice Guide: Real Prop. Transactions Ch. 12-B, B. Agreements Regarding Co-Ownership Rights and Obligations.

Rutter, Cal. Practice Guide: Prof. Responsibility Ch. 3-E, E. Duties Owed to Client.

Rutter, Cal. Practice Guide: Prof. Responsibility Ch. 5-F, F. Formalizing Fee Agreements.

Rutter, Cal. Practice Guide: Prof. Responsibility Ch. 5-K, K. Fee Recovery/Enforcing Fee Agreements.

Rutter, Cal. Practice Guide: Prof. Responsibility Ch. 6-A, A. Sources of Duty of Competence.

Rutter, Cal. Practice Guide: Prof. Responsibility Ch. 6-B, B. Elements of Attorney Competence.

Rutter, Cal. Practice Guide: Prof. Responsibility Ch. 6-C, C. Sexual Relations With Client Affecting Competence.

Rutter, Cal. Practice Guide: Prof. Responsibility Ch. 6-D, D. Professional Liability.

Rutter, Cal. Practice Guide: Prof. Responsibility Ch. 7-B, B. Duty to Maintain Client Confidence and Secrets Under State Bar Act.

Rutter, Cal. Practice Guide: Prof. Responsibility Ch. 8-B, B. Accepting or Rejecting Employment.

Rutter, Cal. Practice Guide: Prof. Responsibility Ch. 9-A, A. Introduction.

Prof. Conduct

Rutter, Cal. Practice Guide: Prof. Responsibility Ch. 9-F, F. Duties Re Nonclient Funds.

Rutter, Cal. Practice Guide: Prof. Responsibility Ch. 9-G, G. Misappropriation of Entrusted Funds or Property.

Rutter, Cal. Practice Guide: Prof. Responsibility Ch. 11-G, G. Commencement of Disciplinary Proceedings.

1 Witkin Cal. Proc. 5th Attorneys § 294, Duty to Refer to Specialist.

1 Witkin Cal. Proc. 5th Attorneys § 432, Failing to Act Competently (Rule 3-110).

1 Witkin Cal. Proc. 5th Attorneys § 433, Sexual Relations With Client (Rule 3-120).

1 Witkin Cal. Proc. 5th Attorneys § 492, (S 492) Earlier Cases.

1 Witkin Cal. Proc. 5th Attorneys § 494, Sexual Relations With Client.

Rule 3–120. Sexual Relations With Client

(A) For purposes of this rule, "sexual relations" means sexual intercourse or the touching of an intimate part of another person for the purpose of sexual arousal, gratification, or abuse.

(B) A member shall not:

(1) Require or demand sexual relations with a client incident to or as a condition of any professional representation; or

(2) Employ coercion, intimidation, or undue influence in entering into sexual relations with a client; or

(3) Continue representation of a client with whom the member has sexual relations if such sexual relations cause the member to perform legal services incompetently in violation of rule 3–110.

(C) Paragraph (B) shall not apply to sexual relations between members and their spouses or to ongoing consensual sexual relationships which predate the initiation of the lawyer-client relationship.

(D) Where a lawyer in a firm has sexual relations with a client but does not participate in the representation of that client, the lawyers in the firm shall not be subject to discipline under this rule solely because of the occurrence of such sexual relations.

DISCUSSION

Rule 3–120 is intended to prohibit sexual exploitation by a lawyer in the course of a professional representation. Often, based upon the nature of the underlying representation, a client exhibits great emotional vulnerability and dependence upon the advice and guidance of counsel. Attorneys owe the utmost duty of good faith and fidelity to clients. (See, e.g., *Greenbaum v. State Bar* (1976) 15 Cal.3d 893, 903 [126 Cal.Rptr. 785]; *Alkow v. State Bar* (1971) 3 Cal.3d 924, 935 [92 Cal.Rptr. 278]; *Cutler v. State Bar* (1969) 71 Cal.2d 241, 251 [78 Cal.Rptr. 172]; *Clancy v. State Bar* (1969) 71 Cal.2d 140, 146 [77 Cal.Rptr. 657].) The relationship between an attorney and client is a fiduciary relationship of the very highest character and all dealings between an attorney and client that are beneficial to the attorney will be closely scrutinized with the utmost strictness for unfairness. (See, e.g., *Giovanazzi v. State Bar* (1980) 28 Cal.3d 465, 472 [169 Cal.Rptr. 581]; *Benson v. State Bar* (1975) 13 Cal.3d 581, 586 [119 Cal.Rptr. 297]; *Lee v. State Bar* (1970) 2 Cal.3d 927, 939 [88 Cal.Rptr. 361]; *Clancy v. State Bar* (1969) 71 Cal.2d 140, 146 [77 Cal.Rptr. 657].) Where attorneys exercise undue influence over clients or take unfair advantage of clients, discipline is appropriate. (See, e.g., *Magee v. State Bar* (1962) 58 Cal.2d 423 [24 Cal.Rptr. 839]; *Lantz v. State Bar* (1931) 212 Cal. 213 [298 P. 497].) In all client matters, a member is advised to keep clients' interests paramount in the course of the member's representation.

For purposes of this rule, if the client is an organization, any individual overseeing the representation shall be deemed to be the client. (See rule 3–600.)

Although paragraph (C) excludes representation of certain clients from the scope of rule 3–120, such exclusion is not intended to preclude the applicability of other Rules of Professional Conduct, including rule 3–110.

(Adopted, eff. Sept. 14, 1992.)

Research References

Rutter, Cal. Practice Guide: Prof. Responsibility Ch. 6-C, C. Sexual Relations With Client Affecting Competence.

1 Witkin Cal. Proc. 5th Attorneys § 101, Personal Relationship With Client.

1 Witkin Cal. Proc. 5th Attorneys § 433, Sexual Relations With Client (Rule 3-120).

1 Witkin Cal. Proc. 5th Attorneys § 494, Sexual Relations With Client.

Rule 3–200. Prohibited Objectives of Employment

A member shall not seek, accept, or continue employment if the member knows or should know that the objective of such employment is:

(A) To bring an action, conduct a defense, assert a position in litigation, or take an appeal, without probable cause and for the purpose of harassing or maliciously injuring any person; or

(B) To present a claim or defense in litigation that is not warranted under existing law, unless it can be supported by a good faith argument for an extension, modification, or reversal of such existing law. *(Adopted Nov. 28, 1988, eff. May 27, 1989.)*

Research References

Rutter, Cal. Practice Guide: Civil Appeals & Writs Ch. 1-E, E. Preappeal Evaluation and "Housekeeping" Steps.

Rutter, Cal. Practice Guide: Civil Appeals & Writs Ch. 13-B, B. Petition for Review Procedures.

Rutter, Cal. Practice Guide: Civ. Pro. Before Trial Ch. 1-A, A. Accepting a New Case.

Rutter, Cal. Practice Guide: Civ. Pro. Before Trial Ch. 1-B, B. Prelawsuit Investigations, Research and Analysis.

Rutter, Cal. Practice Guide: Enforcing Judgments/Debts Ch. 1-B, B. Accepting the Collection Case.

Rutter, Cal. Practice Guide: Personal Injury Ch. 1-B, B. Initial Evaluation of Case: Decision to Accept or Reject Employment or Undertake Further Evaluation of Claim.

Rutter, Cal. Practice Guide: Real Prop. Transactions Ch. 6-I, I. Real Property Foreclosures and Antideficiency Laws.

Rutter, Cal. Practice Guide: Prof. Responsibility Ch. 3-A, A. Nature of Attorney-Client Relationship.

Rutter, Cal. Practice Guide: Prof. Responsibility Ch. 5-K, K. Fee Recovery/Enforcing Fee Agreements.

Rutter, Cal. Practice Guide: Prof. Responsibility Ch. 6-D, D. Professional Liability.

Rutter, Cal. Practice Guide: Prof. Responsibility Ch. 8-A, A. Duties to Administration of Justice-In General.

Rutter, Cal. Practice Guide: Prof. Responsibility Ch. 8-B, B. Accepting or Rejecting Employment.

Rutter, Cal. Practice Guide: Prof. Responsibility Ch. 10-B, B. Withdrawal (Termination) by Lawyer.

1 Witkin Cal. Proc. 5th Attorneys § 330, (S 330) Conflicting Public Obligation.

1 Witkin Cal. Proc. 5th Attorneys § 434, Prohibited Objectives of Employment (Rule 3-200).

1 Witkin Cal. Proc. 5th Attorneys § 505, in General.

1 Witkin Cal. Proc. 5th Attorneys § 541, (S 541) Improper Support of Client's Cause.

Rule 3–210. Advising the Violation of Law

A member shall not advise the violation of any law, rule, or ruling of a tribunal unless the member believes in good faith that such law, rule, or ruling is invalid. A member may take appropriate steps in good faith to test the validity of any law, rule, or ruling of a tribunal.

DISCUSSION

Rule 3–210 is intended to apply not only to the prospective conduct of a client but also to the interaction between the member and client and to the specific legal service sought by the client from the member. An example of the former is the handling of physical evidence of a crime in the possession of the client and offered to the member. (See *People v. Meredith* (1981) 29 Cal.3d 682 [175 Cal.Rptr. 612].) An example of the latter is a request that the member negotiate the return of stolen property in exchange for the owner's agreement not to report the theft to the police or prosecutorial authorities. (See *People v. Pic'l* (1982) 31 Cal.3d 731 [183 Cal.Rptr. 685].)

(Adopted Nov. 28, 1988, eff. May 27, 1989.)

Research References

Rutter, Cal. Practice Guide: Prof. Responsibility Ch. 3-A, A. Nature of Attorney-Client Relationship.

Rutter, Cal. Practice Guide: Prof. Responsibility Ch. 7-B, B. Duty to Maintain Client Confidence and Secrets Under State Bar Act.

Rutter, Cal. Practice Guide: Prof. Responsibility Ch. 8-C, C. Restrictions on Advocacy in Court Proceedings.

Rutter, Cal. Practice Guide: Prof. Responsibility Ch. 8-D, D. Restrictions on Speech and Behavior Outside Courtroom.

1 Witkin Cal. Proc. 5th Attorneys § 105, Motion in Trial Court.

1 Witkin Cal. Proc. 5th Attorneys § 435, Advising Violation of Law (Rule 3-210).

1 Witkin Cal. Proc. 5th Attorneys § 541, (S 541) Improper Support of Client's Cause.

Rule 3–300. Avoiding Interests Adverse to a Client

A member shall not enter into a business transaction with a client; or knowingly acquire an ownership, possessory, security, or other pecuniary interest adverse to a client, unless each of the following requirements has been satisfied:

(A) The transaction or acquisition and its terms are fair and reasonable to the client and are fully disclosed and transmitted in writing to the client in a manner which should reasonably have been understood by the client; and

(B) The client is advised in writing that the client may seek the advice of an independent lawyer of the client's choice and is given a reasonable opportunity to seek that advice; and

(C) The client thereafter consents in writing to the terms of the transaction or the terms of the acquisition.

DISCUSSION

Rule 3–300 is not intended to apply to the agreement by which the member is retained by the client, unless the agreement confers on the member an ownership, possessory, security, or other pecuniary interest adverse to the client. Such an agreement is governed, in part, by rule 4–200.

Rule 3–300 is not intended to apply where the member and client each make an investment on terms offered to the general public or a significant portion thereof. For example, rule 3–300 is not intended to apply where A, a member, invests in a limited partnership syndicated by a third party. B, A's client, makes the same investment. Although A and B are each investing in the same business, A did not enter into the transaction "with" B for the purposes of the rule.

Rule 3–300 is intended to apply where the member wishes to obtain an interest in client's property in order to secure the amount of the member's past due or future fees.

(Adopted Nov. 28, 1988, eff. May 27, 1989. As amended, eff. Sept. 14, 1992.)

Research References

Rutter, Cal. Practice Guide: Civ. Pro. Before Trial Ch. 1-A, A. Accepting a New Case.

California Practice Guide: Employment Litigation Ch. 2-B, B. Fee Arrangements.

Rutter, Cal. Practice Guide: Fed.Civ.Pro. Before Trial Ch. 17-B, Rule 11.

Rutter, Cal. Practice Guide: Personal Injury Ch. 1-B, B. Initial Evaluation of Case: Decision to Accept or Reject Employment or Undertake Further Evaluation of Claim.

Rutter, Cal. Practice Guide: Personal Injury Ch. 1-C, C. Formation of Attorney-Client Relationship: the Employment Agreement.

Rutter, Cal. Practice Guide: Personal Injury Ch. 4-G, G. Concluding and Enforcing Settlement.

Rutter, Cal. Practice Guide: Personal Injury Ch. 1-C , Outline C.

Rutter, Cal. Practice Guide: Real Prop. Transactions Ch. 1-B, B. Attorney Competence, Conflicts of Interest and Initial Client Communications.

Rutter, Cal. Practice Guide: Real Prop. Transactions Ch. 1-C, C. Attorney Fees and Costs Agreements.

Rutter, Cal. Practice Guide: Real Prop. Transactions Ch. 1-C Outline, Outline C.

Rutter, Cal. Practice Guide: Prof. Responsibility Ch. 1-I, I. Regulation of Sale of Law Practice.

Rutter, Cal. Practice Guide: Prof. Responsibility Ch. 2-D, D. In-Person Solicitation for Profit.

Rutter, Cal. Practice Guide: Prof. Responsibility Ch. 3-A, A. Nature of Attorney-Client Relationship.

Rutter, Cal. Practice Guide: Prof. Responsibility Ch. 3-D, D. Authority of Client vs. Authority of Attorney.

Rutter, Cal. Practice Guide: Prof. Responsibility Ch. 4-E, E. Conflicts Based on Lawyer's Personal Interests or Relationships.

Rutter, Cal. Practice Guide: Prof. Responsibility Ch. 4-F, F. Rules Limiting Business or Financial Dealings With Client.

Rutter, Cal. Practice Guide: Prof. Responsibility Ch. 5-A, A. Rules Governing Fee Negotiations With Client.

Rutter, Cal. Practice Guide: Prof. Responsibility Ch. 5-B, B. Types of Fees and Fee Arrangements.

Rutter, Cal. Practice Guide: Prof. Responsibility Ch. 5-D, D. Ethical Limitations on Attorney Fees.

Rutter, Cal. Practice Guide: Prof. Responsibility Ch. 5-E, E. Costs Arrangements.

Rutter, Cal. Practice Guide: Prof. Responsibility Ch. 5-F, F. Formalizing Fee Agreements.

Rutter, Cal. Practice Guide: Prof. Responsibility Ch. 5-G, G. Accepting Property or Services in Exchange for Legal Services (Barter).

Rutter, Cal. Practice Guide: Prof. Responsibility Ch. 5-H, H. Billing Methods.

Rutter, Cal. Practice Guide: Prof. Responsibility Ch. 5-I, I. Paying Client's Personal or Financial Expenses.

Rutter, Cal. Practice Guide: Prof. Responsibility Ch. 5-J, J. Fee Disputes With Existing Clients.

Rutter, Cal. Practice Guide: Prof. Responsibility Ch. 5-K, K. Fee Recovery/Enforcing Fee Agreements.

Rutter, Cal. Practice Guide: Prof. Responsibility Ch. 6-D, D. Professional Liability.

Rutter, Cal. Practice Guide: Prof. Responsibility Ch. 9-B, B. Establishing and Maintaining Client Trust Accounts.

Rutter, Cal. Practice Guide: Prof. Responsibility Ch. 9-G, G. Misappropriation of Entrusted Funds or Property.

Rutter, Cal. Practice Guide: Prof. Responsibility Ch. 11-L, L. Determining Appropriate Discipline.

Rutter, Cal. Practice Guide: Prof. Responsibility Form 4:E, Disclosure Letter and Client Consent and Waiver Re Lawyer-Client Business Transaction.

Rutter, Cal. Practice Guide: Prof. Responsibility Form 5:C, Contingency Fee Agreement.

Rutter, Cal. Practice Guide: Prof. Responsibility Ch. 4-F , Outline F.

Rutter, Cal. Practice Guide: Prof. Responsibility Ch. 5-A , Outline a.

Rutter, Cal. Practice Guide: Prof. Responsibility Ch. 5-F , Outline F.

Rutter, Cal. Practice Guide: Prof. Responsibility Ch. 5-I , Outline I.

Rutter, Cal. Practice Guide: Prof. Responsibility Ch. 5-J , Outline J.

1 Witkin Cal. Proc. 5th Attorneys § 90, in General.

1 Witkin Cal. Proc. 5th Attorneys § 92, Scope of Rule.

1 Witkin Cal. Proc. 5th Attorneys § 95, Showing to Overcome Presumption.

1 Witkin Cal. Proc. 5th Attorneys § 147, (S 147) Enforcement of Collective Bargaining Rights.

1 Witkin Cal. Proc. 5th Attorneys § 168, Express Contract.

1 Witkin Cal. Proc. 5th Attorneys § 436, (S 436) Nature and Scope of Rule.

1 Witkin Cal. Proc. 5th Attorneys § 437, (S 437) Illustrations.

1 Witkin Cal. Proc. 5th Attorneys § 455, Expenses Incurred (Rule 4-210).

1 Witkin Cal. Proc. 5th Attorneys § 514, (S 514) Acquiring Adverse Interests.

1 Witkin Cal. Proc. 5th Attorneys § 625, (S 625) Increase in Punishment.

11 Witkin, California Summary 10th Community Property § 149, Distinction: Family Law Attorney's Lien.

3 Witkin, California Summary 10th Agency and Employment § 579, Attorneys Employed by County Counsel.

Prof. Conduct

Rule 3–310. Avoiding the Representation of Adverse Interests

(A) For purposes of this rule:

(1) "Disclosure" means informing the client or former client of the relevant circumstances and of the actual and reasonably foreseeable adverse consequences to the client or former client;

(2) "Informed written consent" means the client's or former client's written agreement to the representation following written disclosure;

(3) "Written" means any writing as defined in Evidence Code section 250.

(B) A member shall not accept or continue representation of a client without providing written disclosure to the client where:

(1) The member has a legal, business, financial, professional, or personal relationship with a party or witness in the same matter; or

(2) The member knows or reasonably should know that:

(a) the member previously had a legal, business, financial, professional, or personal relationship with a party or witness in the same matter; and

(b) the previous relationship would substantially affect the member's representation; or

(3) The member has or had a legal, business, financial, professional, or personal relationship with another person or entity the member knows or reasonably should know would be affected substantially by resolution of the matter; or

(4) The member has or had a legal, business, financial, or professional interest in the subject matter of the representation.

(C) A member shall not, without the informed written consent of each client:

(1) Accept representation of more than one client in a matter in which the interests of the clients potentially conflict; or

(2) Accept or continue representation of more than one client in a matter in which the interests of the clients actually conflict; or

(3) Represent a client in a matter and at the same time in a separate matter accept as a client a person or entity whose interest in the first matter is adverse to the client in the first matter.

(D) A member who represents two or more clients shall not enter into an aggregate settlement of the claims of or against the clients without the informed written consent of each client.

(E) A member shall not, without the informed written consent of the client or former client, accept employment adverse to the client or former client where, by reason of the representation of the client or former client, the member has obtained confidential information material to the employment.

(F) A member shall not accept compensation for representing a client from one other than the client unless:

(1) There is no interference with the member's independence of professional judgment or with the client-lawyer relationship; and

(2) Information relating to representation of the client is protected as required by Business and Professions Code section 6068, subdivision (e); and

(3) The member obtains the client's informed written consent, provided that no disclosure or consent is required if:

(a) such nondisclosure is otherwise authorized by law; or

(b) the member is rendering legal services on behalf of any public agency which provides legal services to other public agencies or the public.

DISCUSSION

Rule 3–310 is not intended to prohibit a member from representing parties having antagonistic positions on the same legal question that has arisen in different cases, unless representation of either client would be adversely affected.

Other rules and laws may preclude making adequate disclosure under this rule. If such disclosure is precluded, informed written consent is likewise precluded. (See, e.g., Business and Professions Code section 6068, subdivision (e).)

Paragraph (B) is not intended to apply to the relationship of a member to another party's lawyer. Such relationships are governed by rule 3–320.

Paragraph (B) is not intended to require either the disclosure of the new engagement to a former client or the consent of the former client to the new engagement. However, both disclosure and consent are required if paragraph (E) applies.

While paragraph (B) deals with the issues of adequate disclosure to the present client or clients of the member's present or past relationships to other parties or witnesses or present interest in the subject matter of the representation, paragraph (E) is intended to protect the confidences of another present or former client. These two paragraphs are to apply as complementary provisions.

Paragraph (B) is intended to apply only to a member's own relationships or interests, unless the member knows that a partner or associate in the same firm as the member has or had a relationship with another party or witness or has or had an interest in the subject matter of the representation.

Subparagraphs (C)(1) and (C)(2) are intended to apply to all types of legal employment, including the concurrent representation of multiple parties in litigation or in a single transaction or in some other common enterprise or legal relationship. Examples of the latter include the formation of a partnership for several partners or a corporation for several shareholders, the preparation of an ante-nuptial agreement, or joint or reciprocal wills for a husband and wife, or the resolution of an "uncontested" marital dissolution. In such situations, for the sake of convenience or economy, the parties may well prefer to employ a single counsel, but a member must disclose the potential adverse aspects of such multiple representation (e.g., Evid. Code, § 962) and must obtain the informed written consent of the clients thereto pursuant to subparagraph (C)(1). Moreover, if the potential adversity should become actual, the member must obtain the further informed written consent of the clients pursuant to subparagraph (C)(2).

Subparagraph (C)(3) is intended to apply to representations of clients in both litigation and transactional matters.

In *State Farm Mutual Automobile Insurance Company v. Federal Insurance Company* (1999) 72 Cal.App.4th 1422 [86 Cal.Rptr.2d 20], the court held that subparagraph (C)(3) was violated when a member, retained by an insurer to defend one suit, and while that suit was still pending, filed a direct action against the same insurer in an unrelated action without securing the insurer's consent. Notwithstanding *State Farm*, subparagraph (C)(3) is not intended to apply with respect to the relationship between an insurer and a member when, in each matter, the insurer's interest is only as an indemnity provider and not as a direct party to the action.

There are some matters in which the conflicts are such that written consent may not suffice for non-disciplinary purposes. (See *Woods v. Superior Court* (1983) 149 Cal.App.3d 931 [197 Cal.Rptr. 185]; *Klemm v. Superior Court* (1977) 75 Cal.App.3d 893 [142 Cal.Rptr. 509]; *Ishmael v. Millington* (1966) 241 Cal.App.2d 520 [50 Cal.Rptr. 592].)

Paragraph (D) is not intended to apply to class action settlements subject to court approval.

Paragraph (F) is not intended to abrogate existing relationships between insurers and insureds whereby the insurer has the contractual right to unilaterally select counsel for the insured, where there is no conflict of interest. (See *San Diego Navy*

Federal Credit Union v. Cumis Insurance Society (1984) 162 Cal.App.3d 358 [208 Cal.Rptr. 494].)

(Adopted Nov. 28, 1988, eff. May 27, 1989. As amended, eff. Sept. 14, 1992; March 3, 2003.)

Research References

Rutter, Cal. Practice Guide: A.D.R. Ch. 3-D, D. "Classic" (Facilitative) Mediation.

Rutter, Cal. Practice Guide: A.D.R. Ch. 7-A, A. Mediators.

Rutter, Cal. Practice Guide: A.D.R. Ch. 3A-C, C. "Classic" Mediation in Domestic Relations Cases.

Rutter, Cal. Practice Guide: Civil Appeals & Writs Ch. 15-B, B. Common Law Writs.

Rutter, Cal. Practice Guide: Civ. Pro. Before Trial Ch. 1-A, A. Accepting a New Case.

Rutter, Cal. Practice Guide: Civ. Pro. Before Trial Ch. 12(II)-H, H. Professional Responsibility Considerations Re Settlements.

Rutter, Cal. Practice Guide: Civ. Pro. Before Trial Ch. 9(III)-B, B. Sanctions Under CCP § 128.5 (Pre-1995 and SLAPP Cases).

Rutter, Cal. Practice Guide: Civil Trials & Evidence Ch. 4-I, I. Other Motions at Final Status Conference.

Rutter, Cal. Practice Guide: Civil Trials & Evidence Ch. 12-A, A. Motion for Mistrial.

Rutter, Cal. Practice Guide: Civil Trials & Evidence Ch. 13-B, B. Proper vs. Improper Closing Argument.

Rutter, Cal. Practice Guide: Civil Trials & Evidence Ch. 8E-A, A. Privileges.

California Practice Guide: Employment Litigation Ch. 2-C, C. Disclosure of Adverse Interests-In General.

California Practice Guide: Employment Litigation Ch. 2-D, D. Joint Representation of Codefendants.

California Practice Guide: Employment Litigation Ch. 2-E, E. Employment of Separate Counsel to Represent Employee.

California Practice Guide: Employment Litigation Ch. 2-F, F. Conflicts Between Present and Former Clients.

California Practice Guide: Employment Litigation Ch. 2-J, J. Confidential and Privileged Information.

California Practice Guide: Employment Litigation Ch. 2-L, L. Settlements.

California Practice Guide: Employment Litigation Ch. 19-H, H. Other Pretrial Procedures.

Rutter, Cal. Practice Guide: Enforcing Judgments/Debts Ch. 1-B, B. Accepting the Collection Case.

Rutter, Cal. Practice Guide: Family Law Gen. Matls, Highlights.

Rutter, Cal. Practice Guide: Fed.Civ.Pro. Before Trial Ch. 10-C, C. Class Actions.

Rutter, Cal. Practice Guide: Insurance Litigation Ch. 7B-K, K. Insurer's Duty to Provide Independent Counsel When Conflict of Interest Arises.

Rutter, Cal. Practice Guide: Insurance Litigation Ch. 7B-L, L. Defense Counsel's Obligations-Professional Responsibility Considerations.

Rutter, Cal. Practice Guide: Insurance Litigation Form 7:A, Joint Consent to Continued Representation.

Rutter, Cal. Practice Guide: Insurance Litigation Form 12:B, Sample Excess Liability Letter.

Rutter, Cal. Practice Guide: Personal Injury Ch. 1-B, B. Initial Evaluation of Case: Decision to Accept or Reject Employment or Undertake Further Evaluation of Claim.

Rutter, Cal. Practice Guide: Personal Injury Ch. 4-G, G. Concluding and Enforcing Settlement.

Rutter, Cal. Practice Guide: Real Prop. Transactions Ch. 1-B, B. Attorney Competence, Conflicts of Interest and Initial Client Communications.

Rutter, Cal. Practice Guide: Real Prop. Transactions Ch. 8-B, B. Options to Purchase.

Rutter, Cal. Practice Guide: Real Prop. Transactions Ch. 9-D, D. Prenegotiation/Predrafting Considerations.

Rutter, Cal. Practice Guide: Real Prop. Transactions Ch. 12-B, B. Agreements Regarding Co-Ownership Rights and Obligations.

Rutter, Cal. Practice Guide: Real Prop. Transactions Form 1:D, Client Waiver of Conflict of Interest.

Rutter, Cal. Practice Guide: Prof. Responsibility Ch. 1-I, I. Regulation of Sale of Law Practice.

Rutter, Cal. Practice Guide: Prof. Responsibility Ch. 1-J, J. Regulating Participation in Legal Service Programs and Referral Service Plans.

Rutter, Cal. Practice Guide: Prof. Responsibility Ch. 2-D, D. In-Person Solicitation for Profit.

Rutter, Cal. Practice Guide: Prof. Responsibility Ch. 3-B, B. Formation of Relationship.

Rutter, Cal. Practice Guide: Prof. Responsibility Ch. 3-C, C. Identifying "Client".

Rutter, Cal. Practice Guide: Prof. Responsibility Ch. 3-E, E. Duties Owed to Client.

Rutter, Cal. Practice Guide: Prof. Responsibility Ch. 4-A, A. General Considerations.

Rutter, Cal. Practice Guide: Prof. Responsibility Ch. 4-B, B. Concurrent Representation of Clients With Conflicting Interests (Conflicts Between Present Clients).

Rutter, Cal. Practice Guide: Prof. Responsibility Ch. 4-C, C. Conflicts Between Present and Former Clients (Successive Representation).

Rutter, Cal. Practice Guide: Prof. Responsibility Ch. 4-E, E. Conflicts Based on Lawyer's Personal Interests or Relationships.

Rutter, Cal. Practice Guide: Prof. Responsibility Ch. 4-F, F. Rules Limiting Business or Financial Dealings With Client.

Rutter, Cal. Practice Guide: Prof. Responsibility Ch. 4-G, G. Procedural Considerations for Disqualification Based on Conflict of Interest.

Rutter, Cal. Practice Guide: Prof. Responsibility Ch. 5-B, B. Types of Fees and Fee Arrangements.

Rutter, Cal. Practice Guide: Prof. Responsibility Ch. 5-D, D. Ethical Limitations on Attorney Fees.

Rutter, Cal. Practice Guide: Prof. Responsibility Ch. 5-E, E. Costs Arrangements.

Rutter, Cal. Practice Guide: Prof. Responsibility Ch. 5-F, F. Formalizing Fee Agreements.

Rutter, Cal. Practice Guide: Prof. Responsibility Ch. 5-J, J. Fee Disputes With Existing Clients.

Rutter, Cal. Practice Guide: Prof. Responsibility Ch. 5-K, K. Fee Recovery/Enforcing Fee Agreements.

Rutter, Cal. Practice Guide: Prof. Responsibility Ch. 6-D, D. Professional Liability.

Rutter, Cal. Practice Guide: Prof. Responsibility Ch. 6-G, G. Professional Competence in Criminal Cases.

Rutter, Cal. Practice Guide: Prof. Responsibility Ch. 7-B, B. Duty to Maintain Client Confidence and Secrets Under State Bar Act.

Rutter, Cal. Practice Guide: Prof. Responsibility Ch. 7-C, C. Attorney-Client Privilege.

Rutter, Cal. Practice Guide: Prof. Responsibility Form 4:A, Disclosure Letter and Client Consent Re Law Firm Merger.

Rutter, Cal. Practice Guide: Prof. Responsibility Form 4:B, Disclosure Letter and Client Consent Re Payment of Fees by Nonclient.

Rutter, Cal. Practice Guide: Prof. Responsibility Form 4:C, Disclosure Letter and Client Consent to Joint Representation.

Rutter, Cal. Practice Guide: Prof. Responsibility Ch. 4-E , Outline E.

Rutter, Cal. Practice Guide: Prof. Responsibility Ch. 5-J , Outline J.

1 Witkin Cal. Proc. 5th Attorneys § 103, (S 103) in General.

1 Witkin Cal. Proc. 5th Attorneys § 105, Motion in Trial Court.

1 Witkin Cal. Proc. 5th Attorneys § 109, (S 109) in General.

1 Witkin Cal. Proc. 5th Attorneys § 111, (S 111) Representing Parent and Subsidiary Corporations.

1 Witkin Cal. Proc. 5th Attorneys § 112, (S 112) Withdrawal from Representation Does Not Avoid Conflict.

1 Witkin Cal. Proc. 5th Attorneys § 113, (S 113) No Duty to Advise Potential Client Where Conflict Exists.

1 Witkin Cal. Proc. 5th Attorneys § 114, (S 114) Vicarious Disqualification of Law Firm.

1 Witkin Cal. Proc. 5th Attorneys § 117, (S 117) Representing Insured and Insurer.

1 Witkin Cal. Proc. 5th Attorneys § 128, Adverse Interests Involving Multiple Parties.

1 Witkin Cal. Proc. 5th Attorneys § 129, (S 129) Joint Representation in Nonlitigation Matters.

1 Witkin Cal. Proc. 5th Attorneys § 130, (S 130) Knowing and Informed Waiver.

1 Witkin Cal. Proc. 5th Attorneys § 135, Vicarious Disqualification of Law Firm.

1 Witkin Cal. Proc. 5th Attorneys § 136, Vicarious Disqualification of Individual Attorney.

1 Witkin Cal. Proc. 5th Attorneys § 137, Former Corporate Attorney.

1 Witkin Cal. Proc. 5th Attorneys § 138, (S 138) Relationship was Never Created.

1 Witkin Cal. Proc. 5th Attorneys § 140, (S 140) Client's Consent or Waiver.

Prof. Conduct

Rule 3–320.   Relationship With Other Party's Lawyer

A member shall not represent a client in a matter in which another party's lawyer is a spouse, parent, child, or sibling of the member, lives with the member, is a client of the member, or has an intimate personal relationship with the member, unless the member informs the client in writing of the relationship.

DISCUSSION

Rule 3–320 is not intended to apply to circumstances in which a member fails to advise the client of a relationship with another lawyer who is merely a partner or associate in the same law firm as the adverse party's counsel, and who has no direct involvement in the matter.

(Adopted Nov. 28, 1988, eff. May 27, 1989. As amended, eff. Sept. 14, 1992.)

Research References

Rutter, Cal. Practice Guide: Civ. Pro. Before Trial Ch. 1-A, A. Accepting a New Case.

Rutter, Cal. Practice Guide: Civil Trials & Evidence Ch. 3-A, A. Challenges for Cause.

California Practice Guide: Employment Litigation Ch. 2-C, C. Disclosure of Adverse Interests-In General.

Rutter, Cal. Practice Guide: Prof. Responsibility Ch. 4-E, E. Conflicts Based on Lawyer's Personal Interests or Relationships.

Rutter, Cal. Practice Guide: Prof. Responsibility Ch. 6-C, C. Sexual Relations With Client Affecting Competence.

Rutter, Cal. Practice Guide: Prof. Responsibility Ch. 4-E , Outline E.

1 Witkin Cal. Proc. 5th Attorneys § 439, (S 439) Relationship With Party or Witness or Interest in Subject Matter.

1 Witkin Cal. Proc. 5th Attorneys § 443, Relationship With Other Party's Lawyer (Rule 3-320).

Rule 3–400.   Limiting Liability to Client

A member shall not:

(A) Contract with a client prospectively limiting the member's liability to the client for the member's professional malpractice; or

(B) Settle a claim or potential claim for the member's liability to the client for the member's professional malpractice, unless the client is informed in writing that the client may seek the advice of an independent lawyer of the client's choice regarding the settlement and is given a reasonable opportunity to seek that advice.

DISCUSSION

Rule 3–400 is not intended to apply to customary qualifications and limitations in legal opinions and memoranda, nor is it intended to prevent a member from reasonably limiting the scope of the member's employment or representation.

(Adopted Nov. 28, 1988, eff. May 27, 1989. As amended, eff. Sept. 14, 1992.)

Research References

Rutter, Cal. Practice Guide: Real Prop. Transactions Ch. 1-B, B. Attorney Competence, Conflicts of Interest and Initial Client Communications.

Rutter, Cal. Practice Guide: Prof. Responsibility Ch. 3-A, A. Nature of Attorney-Client Relationship.

Rutter, Cal. Practice Guide: Prof. Responsibility Ch. 3-B, B. Formation of Relationship.

Rutter, Cal. Practice Guide: Prof. Responsibility Ch. 4-E, E. Conflicts Based on Lawyer's Personal Interests or Relationships.

Rutter, Cal. Practice Guide: Prof. Responsibility Ch. 5-F, F. Formalizing Fee Agreements.

Rutter, Cal. Practice Guide: Prof. Responsibility Ch. 5-J, J. Fee Disputes With Existing Clients.

Rutter, Cal. Practice Guide: Prof. Responsibility Ch. 6-A, A. Sources of Duty of Competence.

Rutter, Cal. Practice Guide: Prof. Responsibility Ch. 6-B, B. Elements of Attorney Competence.

Rutter, Cal. Practice Guide: Prof. Responsibility Ch. 6-D, D. Professional Liability.

Rutter, Cal. Practice Guide: Prof. Responsibility Ch. 6-F, F. Waiver/Settlement of Malpractice Claim.

Rutter, Cal. Practice Guide: Prof. Responsibility Ch. 5-J , Outline J.

1 Witkin Cal. Proc. 5th Attorneys § 444, Limiting Malpractice Liability to Client (Rule 3-400).

Rule 3–410.   Disclosure of Professional Liability Insurance

(A) A member who knows or should know that he or she does not have professional liability insurance shall inform a client in writing, at the time of the client's engagement of the member, that the member does not have professional liability insurance whenever it is reasonably foreseeable that the total amount of the member's legal representation of the client in the matter will exceed four hours.

(B) If a member does not provide the notice required under paragraph (A) at the time of a client's engagement of the member, and the member subsequently knows or should know that he or she no longer has professional liability insurance during the representation of the client, the member shall inform the client in writing within thirty days of the date that the member knows or should know that he or she no longer has professional liability insurance.

(C) This rule does not apply to a member who is employed as a government lawyer or in-house counsel when that member is representing or providing legal advice to a client in that capacity.

(D) This rule does not apply to legal services rendered in an emergency to avoid foreseeable prejudice to the rights or interests of the client.

(E) This rule does not apply where the member has previously advised the client under Paragraph (A) or (B) that the member does not have professional liability insurance.

DISCUSSION

[1] The disclosure obligation imposed by Paragraph (A) of this rule applies with respect to new clients and new engagements with returning clients.

[2] A member may use the following language in making the disclosure required by Rule 3–410(A), and may include that language in a written fee agreement with the client or in a separate writing:

"Pursuant to California Rule of Professional Conduct 3–410, I am informing you in writing that I do not have professional liability insurance."

[3] A member may use the following language in making the disclosure required by Rule 3–410(B):

"Pursuant to California Rule of Professional Conduct 3–410, I am informing you in writing that I no longer have professional liability insurance."

[4] Rule 3–410(C) provides an exemption for a "government lawyer or in-house counsel when that member is representing or providing legal advice to a client in that capacity." The basis of both exemptions is essentially the same. The purpose of this rule is to provide information directly to a client if a member is not covered by professional liability insurance. If a member is employed directly by and provides legal services directly for a private entity or a federal, state or local governmental entity, that entity presumably knows whether the member is or is not covered by professional liability insurance. The exemptions under this rule are limited to situations involving direct employment and representation, and do not, for example, apply to outside counsel for a private or governmental entity, or to counsel retained by an insurer to represent an insured.

(Adopted, eff. Jan. 1, 2010.)

Research References

Rutter, Cal. Practice Guide: Civ. Pro. Before Trial Ch. 1-A, A. Accepting a New Case.
Rutter, Cal. Practice Guide: Civ. Pro. Before Trial Form 1:C, Contingency Fee Agreement.
Rutter, Cal. Practice Guide: Landlord-Tenant Form 1:B, Sample Attorney Fee Agreement (Hourly Rate).
Rutter, Cal. Practice Guide: Personal Injury Ch. 1-C, C. Formation of Attorney-Client Relationship: the Employment Agreement.
Rutter, Cal. Practice Guide: Real Prop. Transactions Ch. 1-B, B. Attorney Competence, Conflicts of Interest and Initial Client Communications.
Rutter, Cal. Practice Guide: Real Prop. Transactions Form 1:A, Sample Fee Letter.
Rutter, Cal. Practice Guide: Prof. Responsibility Ch. 1-K, K. Additional Regulations Affecting Lawyer Conduct.
Rutter, Cal. Practice Guide: Prof. Responsibility Ch. 3-B, B. Formation of Relationship.
Rutter, Cal. Practice Guide: Prof. Responsibility Ch. 5-F, F. Formalizing Fee Agreements.
Rutter, Cal. Practice Guide: Prof. Responsibility Ch. 6-E, E. Malpractice Insurance.
Rutter, Cal. Practice Guide: Prof. Responsibility Form 5:C, Contingency Fee Agreement.
Rutter, Cal. Practice Guide: Prof. Responsibility Form 5:FF, Fee Agreement Provision Disclosing Lack of Professional Liability Insurance.
1 Witkin Cal. Proc. 5th Attorneys § 444A, (S 444A) (New)-Disclosure of Lack of Professional Liability Insurance (Rule 3-410).

Rule 3–500. Communication

A member shall keep a client reasonably informed about significant developments relating to the employment or representation, including promptly complying with reasonable requests for information and copies of significant documents when necessary to keep the client so informed.

DISCUSSION

Rule 3–500 is not intended to change a member's duties to his or her clients. It is intended to make clear that, while a client must be informed of significant developments in the matter, a member will not be disciplined for failing to communicate insignificant or irrelevant information. (See Bus. & Prof. Code, § 6068, subd. (m).)

A member may contract with the client in their employment agreement that the client assumes responsibility for the cost of copying significant documents. This rule is not intended to prohibit a claim for the recovery of the member's expense in any subsequent legal proceeding.

Rule 3–500 is not intended to create, augment, diminish, or eliminate any application of the work product rule. The obligation of the member to provide work product to the client shall be governed by relevant statutory and decisional law. Additionally, this rule is not intended to apply to any document or correspondence that is subject to a protective order or non-disclosure agreement, or to override applicable statutory or decisional law requiring that certain information not be provided to criminal defendants who are clients of the member.

(Adopted Nov. 28, 1988, eff. May 27, 1989. As amended, eff. June 5, 1997.)

Research References

Rutter, Cal. Practice Guide: Civil Appeals & Writs Ch. 1-F, F. Postjudgment Settlement Considerations.
Rutter, Cal. Practice Guide: Civil Trials & Evidence Ch. 1-N, N. Associating Trial Counsel.
California Practice Guide: Employment Litigation Ch. 2-L, L. Settlements.
Rutter, Cal. Practice Guide: Personal Injury Ch. 1-D, D. General Concerns and Advice to Client Upon Accepting Employment; Execution of Necessary Authorizations.
Rutter, Cal. Practice Guide: Personal Injury Ch. 4-C, C. Effective Settlement Negotiations.
Rutter, Cal. Practice Guide: Real Prop. Transactions Ch. 1-B, B. Attorney Competence, Conflicts of Interest and Initial Client Communications.
Rutter, Cal. Practice Guide: Prof. Responsibility Ch. 3-E, E. Duties Owed to Client.
Rutter, Cal. Practice Guide: Prof. Responsibility Ch. 5-D, D. Ethical Limitations on Attorney Fees.
Rutter, Cal. Practice Guide: Prof. Responsibility Ch. 5-J, J. Fee Disputes With Existing Clients.
Rutter, Cal. Practice Guide: Prof. Responsibility Ch. 6-A, A. Sources of Duty of Competence.
Rutter, Cal. Practice Guide: Prof. Responsibility Ch. 6-B, B. Elements of Attorney Competence.
Rutter, Cal. Practice Guide: Prof. Responsibility Ch. 6-D, D. Professional Liability.
Rutter, Cal. Practice Guide: Prof. Responsibility Ch. 7-B, B. Duty to Maintain Client Confidence and Secrets Under State Bar Act.
Rutter, Cal. Practice Guide: Prof. Responsibility Ch. 9-C, C. Duty to Notify Clients on Receipt of Funds or Property.
Rutter, Cal. Practice Guide: Prof. Responsibility Ch. 10-E, E. Law Firm Break-Ups.
1 Witkin Cal. Proc. 5th Attorneys § 102, Duty to Keep Client Informed.
1 Witkin Cal. Proc. 5th Attorneys § 445, Communications With Client (Rules 3-500, 3-510).

Rule 3–510. Communication of Settlement Offer

(A) A member shall promptly communicate to the member's client:

(1) All terms and conditions of any offer made to the client in a criminal matter; and

(2) All amounts, terms, and conditions of any written offer of settlement made to the client in all other matters.

(B) As used in this rule, "client" includes a person who possesses the authority to accept an offer of settlement or plea, or, in a class action, all the named representatives of the class.

DISCUSSION

Rule 3–510 is intended to require that counsel in a criminal matter convey all offers, whether written or oral, to the client, as give and take negotiations are less common in criminal matters, and, even were they to occur, such negotiations should require the participation of the accused.

Any oral offers of settlement made to the client in a civil matter should also be communicated if they are "significant" for the purposes of rule 3–500.

(Adopted Nov. 28, 1988, eff. May 27, 1989.)

Research References

Rutter, Cal. Practice Guide: A.D.R. Ch. 2-E, E. Conducting Negotiations.
Rutter, Cal. Practice Guide: Civ. Pro. Before Trial Ch. 12(II)-H, H. Professional Responsibility Considerations Re Settlements.
California Practice Guide: Employment Litigation Ch. 2-L, L. Settlements.

Rutter, Cal. Practice Guide: Personal Injury Ch. 4-C, C. Effective Settlement Negotiations.

Rutter, Cal. Practice Guide: Prof. Responsibility Ch. 3-C, C. Identifying "Client".

Rutter, Cal. Practice Guide: Prof. Responsibility Ch. 3-E, E. Duties Owed to Client.

Rutter, Cal. Practice Guide: Prof. Responsibility Ch. 5-B, B. Types of Fees and Fee Arrangements.

Rutter, Cal. Practice Guide: Prof. Responsibility Ch. 6-G, G. Professional Competence in Criminal Cases.

1 Witkin Cal. Proc. 5th Attorneys § 238, (S 238) Duty to Inform Client of Settlement Offer.

1 Witkin Cal. Proc. 5th Attorneys § 445, Communications With Client (Rules 3-500, 3-510).

Rule 3–600. Organization as Client

(A) In representing an organization, a member shall conform his or her representation to the concept that the client is the organization itself, acting through its highest authorized officer, employee, body, or constituent overseeing the particular engagement.

(B) If a member acting on behalf of an organization knows that an actual or apparent agent of the organization acts or intends or refuses to act in a manner that is or may be a violation of law reasonably imputable to the organization, or in a manner which is likely to result in substantial injury to the organization, the member shall not violate his or her duty of protecting all confidential information as provided in Business and Professions Code section 6068, subdivision (e). Subject to Business and Professions Code section 6068, subdivision (e), the member may take such actions as appear to the member to be in the best lawful interest of the organization. Such actions may include among others:

(1) Urging reconsideration of the matter while explaining its likely consequences to the organization; or

(2) Referring the matter to the next higher authority in the organization, including, if warranted by the seriousness of the matter, referral to the highest internal authority that can act on behalf of the organization.

(C) If, despite the member's actions in accordance with paragraph (B), the highest authority that can act on behalf of the organization insists upon action or a refusal to act that is a violation of law and is likely to result in substantial injury to the organization, the member's response is limited to the member's right, and, where appropriate, duty to resign in accordance with rule 3–700.

(D) In dealing with an organization's directors, officers, employees, members, shareholders, or other constituents, a member shall explain the identity of the client for whom the member acts, whenever it is or becomes apparent that the organization's interests are or may become adverse to those of the constituent(s) with whom the member is dealing. The member shall not mislead such a constituent into believing that the constituent may communicate confidential information to the member in a way that will not be used in the organization's interest if that is or becomes adverse to the constituent.

(E) A member representing an organization may also represent any of its directors, officers, employees, members, shareholders, or other constituents, subject to the provisions of rule 3–310. If the organization's consent to the dual representation is required by rule 3–310, the consent shall be given by an appropriate constituent of the organization other than the individual or constituent who is to be represented, or by the shareholder(s) or organization members.

DISCUSSION

Rule 3–600 is not intended to enmesh members in the intricacies of the entity and aggregate theories of partnership.

Rule 3–600 is not intended to prohibit members from representing both an organization and other parties connected with it, as for instance (as simply one example) in establishing employee benefit packages for closely held corporations or professional partnerships.

Rule 3–600 is not intended to create or to validate artificial distinctions between entities and their officers, employees, or members, nor is it the purpose of the rule to deny the existence or importance of such formal distinctions. In dealing with a close corporation or small association, members commonly perform professional engagements for both the organization and its major constituents. When a change in control occurs or is threatened, members are faced with complex decisions involving personal and institutional relationships and loyalties and have frequently had difficulty in perceiving their correct duty. (See *People ex rel Deukmejian v. Brown* (1981) 29 Cal.3d 150 [172 Cal.Rptr. 478]; *Goldstein v. Lees* (1975) 46 Cal.App.3d 614 [120 Cal.Rptr. 253]; *Woods v. Superior Court* (1983) 149 Cal.App.3d 931 [197 Cal.Rptr. 185]; *In re Banks* (1978) 283 Ore. 459 [584 P.2d 284]; 1 A.L.R.4th 1105.) In resolving such multiple relationships, members must rely on case law.

(Adopted Nov. 28, 1988, eff. May 27, 1989.)

Research References

California Practice Guide: Employment Litigation Ch. 2-D, D. Joint Representation of Codefendants.

California Practice Guide: Employment Litigation Ch. 2-J, J. Confidential and Privileged Information.

Rutter, Cal. Practice Guide: Real Prop. Transactions Ch. 1-B, B. Attorney Competence, Conflicts of Interest and Initial Client Communications.

Rutter, Cal. Practice Guide: Prof. Responsibility Ch. 3-C, C. Identifying "Client".

Rutter, Cal. Practice Guide: Prof. Responsibility Ch. 4-B, B. Concurrent Representation of Clients With Conflicting Interests (Conflicts Between Present Clients).

Rutter, Cal. Practice Guide: Prof. Responsibility Ch. 5-F, F. Formalizing Fee Agreements.

Rutter, Cal. Practice Guide: Prof. Responsibility Ch. 6-C, C. Sexual Relations With Client Affecting Competence.

Rutter, Cal. Practice Guide: Prof. Responsibility Ch. 7-A, A. Introduction.

Rutter, Cal. Practice Guide: Prof. Responsibility Ch. 7-B, B. Duty to Maintain Client Confidence and Secrets Under State Bar Act.

Rutter, Cal. Practice Guide: Prof. Responsibility Ch. 8-D, D. Restrictions on Speech and Behavior Outside Courtroom.

1 Witkin Cal. Proc. 5th Attorneys § 111, (S 111) Representing Parent and Subsidiary Corporations.

1 Witkin Cal. Proc. 5th Attorneys § 115, (S 115) in General.

1 Witkin Cal. Proc. 5th Attorneys § 116, (S 116) No Automatic Representation of Officers or Partners.

1 Witkin Cal. Proc. 5th Attorneys § 446, (S 446) General Principle.

1 Witkin Cal. Proc. 5th Attorneys § 447, (S 447) Response to Acts of Agents of Organization.

1 Witkin Cal. Proc. 5th Attorneys § 448, (S 448) Dealing With Constituents of Organization.

1 Witkin Cal. Proc. 5th Attorneys § 449, (S 449) Representation of Constituents.

Rule 3–700. Termination of Employment

(A) In General.

(1) If permission for termination of employment is required by the rules of a tribunal, a member shall not withdraw from employment in a proceeding before that tribunal without its permission.

(2) A member shall not withdraw from employment until the member has taken reasonable steps to avoid reasonably foreseeable prejudice to the rights of the client, including giving due notice to the client, allowing time for employment of other counsel, complying with rule 3–700(D), and complying with applicable laws and rules.

(B) Mandatory Withdrawal.

A member representing a client before a tribunal shall withdraw from employment with the permission of the tribunal, if required by its rules, and a member representing a client in other matters shall withdraw from employment, if:

(1) The member knows or should know that the client is bringing an action, conducting a defense, asserting a position in litigation, or taking an appeal, without probable cause and for the purpose of harassing or maliciously injuring any person; or

(2) The member knows or should know that continued employment will result in violation of these rules or of the State Bar Act; or

(3) The member's mental or physical condition renders it unreasonably difficult to carry out the employment effectively.

(C) Permissive Withdrawal.

If rule 3–700(B) is not applicable, a member may not request permission to withdraw in matters pending before a tribunal, and may not withdraw in other matters, unless such request or such withdrawal is because:

(1) The client

  (a) insists upon presenting a claim or defense that is not warranted under existing law and cannot be supported by good faith argument for an extension, modification, or reversal of existing law, or

  (b) seeks to pursue an illegal course of conduct, or

  (c) insists that the member pursue a course of conduct that is illegal or that is prohibited under these rules or the State Bar Act, or

  (d) by other conduct renders it unreasonably difficult for the member to carry out the employment effectively, or

  (e) insists, in a matter not pending before a tribunal, that the member engage in conduct that is contrary to the judgment and advice of the member but not prohibited under these rules or the State Bar Act, or

  (f) breaches an agreement or obligation to the member as to expenses or fees.

(2) The continued employment is likely to result in a violation of these rules or of the State Bar Act; or

(3) The inability to work with co-counsel indicates that the best interests of the client likely will be served by withdrawal; or

(4) The member's mental or physical condition renders it difficult for the member to carry out the employment effectively; or

(5) The client knowingly and freely assents to termination of the employment; or

(6) The member believes in good faith, in a proceeding pending before a tribunal, that the tribunal will find the existence of other good cause for withdrawal.

(D) Papers, Property, and Fees.

A member whose employment has terminated shall:

(1) Subject to any protective order or non-disclosure agreement, promptly release to the client, at the request of the client, all the client papers and property. "Client papers and property" includes correspondence, pleadings, deposition transcripts, exhibits, physical evidence, expert's reports, and other items reasonably necessary to the client's representation, whether the client has paid for them or not; and

(2) Promptly refund any part of a fee paid in advance that has not been earned. This provision is not applicable to a true retainer fee which is paid solely for the purpose of ensuring the availability of the member for the matter.

DISCUSSION

Subparagraph (A)(2) provides that "a member shall not withdraw from employment until the member has taken reasonable steps to avoid reasonably foreseeable prejudice to the rights of the clients." What such steps would include, of course, will vary according to the circumstances. Absent special circumstances, "reasonable steps" do not include providing additional services to the client once the successor counsel has been employed and rule 3–700(D) has been satisfied.

Paragraph (D) makes clear the member's duties in the recurring situation in which new counsel seeks to obtain client files from a member discharged by the client. It codifies existing case law. (See *Academy of California Optometrists v. Superior Court* (1975) 51 Cal.App.3d 999 [124 Cal.Rptr. 668]; *Weiss v. Marcus* (1975) 51 Cal.App.3d 590 [124 Cal.Rptr. 297].) Paragraph (D) also requires that the member "promptly" return unearned fees paid in advance. If a client disputes the amount to be returned, the member shall comply with rule 4–100(A)(2).

Paragraph (D) is not intended to prohibit a member from making, at the member's own expense, and retaining copies of papers released to the client, nor to prohibit a claim for the recovery of the member's expense in any subsequent legal proceeding.

(Adopted Nov. 28, 1988, eff. May 27, 1989.)

Research References

Rutter, Cal. Practice Guide: Civil Appeals & Writs Ch. 1-E, E. Preappeal Evaluation and "Housekeeping" Steps.

Rutter, Cal. Practice Guide: Civil Appeals & Writs Ch. 11-E, E. Appellate Costs and Sanctions.

Rutter, Cal. Practice Guide: Civil Appeals & Writs Ch. 13-B, B. Petition for Review Procedures.

Rutter, Cal. Practice Guide: Civ. Pro. Before Trial Ch. 1-A, A. Accepting a New Case.

Rutter, Cal. Practice Guide: Civ. Pro. Before Trial Ch. 9(I)-G, G. Motions Regulating Counsel.

Rutter, Cal. Practice Guide: Civ. Pro. Before Trial Ch. 9(III)-B, B. Sanctions Under CCP § 128.5 (Pre-1995 and SLAPP Cases).

Rutter, Cal. Practice Guide: Enforcing Judgments/Debts Ch. 1-B, B. Accepting the Collection Case.

Rutter, Cal. Practice Guide: Personal Injury Ch. 1-B, B. Initial Evaluation of Case: Decision to Accept or Reject Employment or Undertake Further Evaluation of Claim.

Rutter, Cal. Practice Guide: Personal Injury Ch. 1-C, C. Formation of Attorney-Client Relationship: the Employment Agreement.

Rutter, Cal. Practice Guide: Real Prop. Transactions Ch. 1-C, C. Attorney Fees and Costs Agreements.

Rutter, Cal. Practice Guide: Real Prop. Transactions Ch. 1-D, D. Termination of Employment/Withdrawal as Counsel.

Rutter, Cal. Practice Guide: Prof. Responsibility Ch. 1-I, I. Regulation of Sale of Law Practice.

Rutter, Cal. Practice Guide: Prof. Responsibility Ch. 3-E, E. Duties Owed to Client.

Rutter, Cal. Practice Guide: Prof. Responsibility Ch. 4-B, B. Concurrent Representation of Clients With Conflicting Interests (Conflicts Between Present Clients).

Rutter, Cal. Practice Guide: Prof. Responsibility Ch. 4-C, C. Conflicts Between Present and Former Clients (Successive Representation).

Rutter, Cal. Practice Guide: Prof. Responsibility Ch. 5-B, B. Types of Fees and Fee Arrangements.

Rutter, Cal. Practice Guide: Prof. Responsibility Ch. 5-D, D. Ethical Limitations on Attorney Fees.

Rutter, Cal. Practice Guide: Prof. Responsibility Ch. 5-F, F. Formalizing Fee Agreements.

Rutter, Cal. Practice Guide: Prof. Responsibility Ch. 5-H, H. Billing Methods.

Rutter, Cal. Practice Guide: Prof. Responsibility Ch. 5-J, J. Fee Disputes With Existing Clients.

Rutter, Cal. Practice Guide: Prof. Responsibility Ch. 5-K, K. Fee Recovery/Enforcing Fee Agreements.

Rutter, Cal. Practice Guide: Prof. Responsibility Ch. 6-A, A. Sources of Duty of Competence.

Rutter, Cal. Practice Guide: Prof. Responsibility Ch. 6-B, B. Elements of Attorney Competence.

Prof. Conduct

Rutter, Cal. Practice Guide: Prof. Responsibility Ch. 7-B, B. Duty to Maintain Client Confidence and Secrets Under State Bar Act.

Rutter, Cal. Practice Guide: Prof. Responsibility Ch. 8-A, A. Duties to Administration of Justice-In General.

Rutter, Cal. Practice Guide: Prof. Responsibility Ch. 8-B, B. Accepting or Rejecting Employment.

Rutter, Cal. Practice Guide: Prof. Responsibility Ch. 8-C, C. Restrictions on Advocacy in Court Proceedings.

Rutter, Cal. Practice Guide: Prof. Responsibility Ch. 9-E, E. Duty to Deliver Funds or Property Upon Demand.

Rutter, Cal. Practice Guide: Prof. Responsibility Ch. 10-B, B. Withdrawal (Termination) by Lawyer.

Rutter, Cal. Practice Guide: Prof. Responsibility Ch. 10-E, E. Law Firm Break-Ups.

Rutter, Cal. Practice Guide: Prof. Responsibility Ch. 10-F, F. Attorney Obligations Upon Termination of Representation.

Rutter, Cal. Practice Guide: Prof. Responsibility Ch. 11-A, A. Grounds for Discipline.

Rutter, Cal. Practice Guide: Prof. Responsibility Ch. 10-F , Outline F.

1 Witkin Cal. Proc. 5th Attorneys § 98, Where Fee Agreement Creates Conflict of Interest.

1 Witkin Cal. Proc. 5th Attorneys § 113, (S 113) No Duty to Advise Potential Client Where Conflict Exists.

1 Witkin Cal. Proc. 5th Attorneys § 175, Invalid Possessory Lien.

1 Witkin Cal. Proc. 5th Attorneys § 434, Prohibited Objectives of Employment (Rule 3-200).

1 Witkin Cal. Proc. 5th Attorneys § 447, (S 447) Response to Acts of Agents of Organization.

1 Witkin Cal. Proc. 5th Attorneys § 450, (S 450) in General.

1 Witkin Cal. Proc. 5th Attorneys § 451, (S 451) Mandatory Withdrawal.

1 Witkin Cal. Proc. 5th Attorneys § 452, (S 452) Permissive Withdrawal.

Chapter 4

FINANCIAL RELATIONSHIP WITH CLIENTS

Rule

4–100.   Preserving Identity of Funds and Property of a Client.

4–200.   Fees for Legal Services.

4–210.   Payment of Personal or Business Expenses Incurred by or for a Client.

4–300.   Purchasing Property at a Foreclosure or a Sale Subject to Judicial Review.

4–400.   Gifts From Client.

Rule 4–100. Preserving Identity of Funds and Property of a Client

(A) All funds received or held for the benefit of clients by a member or law firm, including advances for costs and expenses, shall be deposited in one or more identifiable bank accounts labeled "Trust Account," "Client's Funds Account" or words of similar import, maintained in the State of California, or, with written consent of the client, in any other jurisdiction where there is a substantial relationship between the client or the client's business and the other jurisdiction. No funds belonging to the member or the law firm shall be deposited therein or otherwise commingled therewith except as follows:

(1) Funds reasonably sufficient to pay bank charges.

(2) In the case of funds belonging in part to a client and in part presently or potentially to the member or the law firm, the portion belonging to the member or law firm must be withdrawn at the earliest reasonable time after the member's interest in that portion becomes fixed. However, when the right of the member or law firm to receive a portion of trust funds is disputed by the client, the disputed portion shall not be withdrawn until the dispute is finally resolved.

(B) A member shall:

(1) Promptly notify a client of the receipt of the client's funds, securities, or other properties.

(2) Identify and label securities and properties of a client promptly upon receipt and place them in a safe deposit box or other place of safekeeping as soon as practicable.

(3) Maintain complete records of all funds, securities, and other properties of a client coming into the possession of the member or law firm and render appropriate accounts to the client regarding them; preserve such records for a period of no less than five years after final appropriate distribution of such funds or properties; and comply with any order for an audit of such records issued pursuant to the Rules of Procedure of the State Bar.

(4) Promptly pay or deliver, as requested by the client, any funds, securities, or other properties in the possession of the member which the client is entitled to receive.

(C) The Board of Governors of the State Bar shall have the authority to formulate and adopt standards as to what "records" shall be maintained by members and law firms in accordance with subparagraph (B)(3). The standards formulated and adopted by the Board, as from time to time amended, shall be effective and binding on all members.

STANDARDS

Pursuant to rule 4–100(C) the Board of Governors of the State Bar adopted the following standards, effective January 1, 1993, as to what "records" shall be maintained by members and law firms in accordance with subparagraph (B)(3).

(1) A member shall, from the date of receipt of client funds through the period ending five years from the date of appropriate disbursement of such funds, maintain:

(a) a written ledger for each client on whose behalf funds are held that sets forth:

(i) the name of such client,

(ii) the date, amount and source of all funds received on behalf of such client,

(iii) the date, amount, payee and purpose of each disbursement made on behalf of such client, and

(iv) the current balance for such client;

(b) a written journal for each bank account that sets forth:

(i) the name of such account,

(ii) the date, amount and client affected by each debit and credit, and

(iii) the current balance in such account;

(c) all bank statements and canceled checks for each bank account; and

(d) each monthly reconciliation (balancing) of (a), (b), and (c).

(2) A member shall, from the date of receipt of all securities and other properties held for the benefit of client through the period ending five years from the date of appropriate disbursement of such securities and other properties, maintain a written journal that specifies:

(a) each item of security and property held;

(b) the person on whose behalf the security or property is held;

(c) the date of receipt of the security or property;

(d) the date of distribution of the security or property; and

(e) person to whom the security or property was distributed.

(PUBLISHER'S NOTE: Trust Account Record Keeping Standards as adopted by the Board of Governors on July 11, 1992, effective January 1, 1993.)

(Adopted Nov. 28, 1988, eff. May 27, 1989. As amended, eff. Jan. 1, 1993.)

Research References

Rutter, Cal. Practice Guide: Civ. Pro. Before Trial Ch. 1-A, A. Accepting a New Case.

Rutter, Cal. Practice Guide: Enforcing Judgments/Debts Ch. 1-B, B. Accepting the Collection Case.

Rutter, Cal. Practice Guide: Personal Injury Ch. 1-C, C. Formation of Attorney-Client Relationship: the Employment Agreement.

Rutter, Cal. Practice Guide: Personal Injury Ch. 4-G, G. Concluding and Enforcing Settlement.

Rutter, Cal. Practice Guide: Real Prop. Transactions Ch. 1-C, C. Attorney Fees and Costs Agreements.

Rutter, Cal. Practice Guide: Real Prop. Transactions Ch. 1-D, D. Termination of Employment/Withdrawal as Counsel.

Rutter, Cal. Practice Guide: Prof. Responsibility Ch. 1-I, I. Regulation of Sale of Law Practice.

Rutter, Cal. Practice Guide: Prof. Responsibility Ch. 3-E, E. Duties Owed to Client.

Rutter, Cal. Practice Guide: Prof. Responsibility Ch. 5-B, B. Types of Fees and Fee Arrangements.

Rutter, Cal. Practice Guide: Prof. Responsibility Ch. 5-F, F. Formalizing Fee Agreements.

Rutter, Cal. Practice Guide: Prof. Responsibility Ch. 5-H, H. Billing Methods.

Rutter, Cal. Practice Guide: Prof. Responsibility Ch. 5-K, K. Fee Recovery/Enforcing Fee Agreements.

Rutter, Cal. Practice Guide: Prof. Responsibility Ch. 9-A, A. Introduction.

Rutter, Cal. Practice Guide: Prof. Responsibility Ch. 9-B, B. Establishing and Maintaining Client Trust Accounts.

Rutter, Cal. Practice Guide: Prof. Responsibility Ch. 9-C, C. Duty to Notify Clients on Receipt of Funds or Property.

Rutter, Cal. Practice Guide: Prof. Responsibility Ch. 9-D, D. Recordkeeping and Accounting Duties Re Client Funds and Property.

Rutter, Cal. Practice Guide: Prof. Responsibility Ch. 9-E, E. Duty to Deliver Funds or Property Upon Demand.

Rutter, Cal. Practice Guide: Prof. Responsibility Ch. 9-F, F. Duties Re Nonclient Funds.

Rutter, Cal. Practice Guide: Prof. Responsibility Ch. 9-G, G. Misappropriation of Entrusted Funds or Property.

Rutter, Cal. Practice Guide: Prof. Responsibility Ch. 10-F, F. Attorney Obligations Upon Termination of Representation.

Rutter, Cal. Practice Guide: Prof. Responsibility Ch. 11-L, L. Determining Appropriate Discipline.

Rutter, Cal. Practice Guide: Prof. Responsibility Ch. 9-F , Outline F.

1 Witkin Cal. Proc. 5th Attorneys § 285, (S 285) Nature and Scope of Liability.

1 Witkin Cal. Proc. 5th Attorneys § 450, (S 450) in General.

1 Witkin Cal. Proc. 5th Attorneys § 453, Preserving Funds and Property (Rule 4-100).

1 Witkin Cal. Proc. 5th Attorneys § 483, Misappropriating Funds or Property.

1 Witkin Cal. Proc. 5th Attorneys § 509, (S 509) in General.

1 Witkin Cal. Proc. 5th Attorneys § 511, (S 511) Technical Violation.

1 Witkin Cal. Proc. 5th Attorneys § 512, (S 512) Misuse of Trust Account.

1 Witkin Cal. Proc. 5th Attorneys § 577, Examination of Books and Records.

Rule 4–200. Fees for Legal Services

(A) A member shall not enter into an agreement for, charge, or collect an illegal or unconscionable fee.

(B) Unconscionability of a fee shall be determined on the basis of all the facts and circumstances existing at the time the agreement is entered into except where the parties contemplate that the fee will be affected by later events. Among the factors to be considered, where appropriate, in determining the consciability of a fee are the following:

(1) The amount of the fee in proportion to the value of the services performed.

(2) The relative sophistication of the member and the client.

(3) The novelty and difficulty of the questions involved and the skill requisite to perform the legal service properly.

(4) The likelihood, if apparent to the client, that the acceptance of the particular employment will preclude other employment by the member.

(5) The amount involved and the results obtained.

(6) The time limitations imposed by the client or by the circumstances.

(7) The nature and length of the professional relationship with the client.

(8) The experience, reputation, and ability of the member or members performing the services.

(9) Whether the fee is fixed or contingent.

(10) The time and labor required.

(11) The informed consent of the client to the fee. *(Adopted Nov. 28, 1988, eff. May 27, 1989. As amended, eff. Sept. 14, 1992; May 12, 2009.)*

Research References

Rutter, Cal. Practice Guide: A.D.R. Ch. 5-J, J. Challenging and Enforcing Arbitrator's Award in Court.

Rutter, Cal. Practice Guide: Civil Appeals & Writs Ch. 1-G, G. Retaining an Appellate Specialist.

Rutter, Cal. Practice Guide: Civ. Pro. Before Trial Ch. 1-A, A. Accepting a New Case.

Rutter, Cal. Practice Guide: Civ. Pro. Before Trial Ch. 8C-2, "Reasonably Calculated to Lead to Discovery of Admissible Evidence".

Rutter, Cal. Practice Guide: Civ. Pro. Before Trial Ch. 8C-4, Attorney Work Product Protection.

Rutter, Cal. Practice Guide: Civil Trials & Evidence Ch. 1-N, N. Associating Trial Counsel.

California Practice Guide: Employment Litigation Ch. 2-B, B. Fee Arrangements.

Rutter, Cal. Practice Guide: Enforcing Judgments/Debts Ch. 1-B, B. Accepting the Collection Case.

Rutter, Cal. Practice Guide: Personal Injury Ch. 1-B, B. Initial Evaluation of Case: Decision to Accept or Reject Employment or Undertake Further Evaluation of Claim.

Rutter, Cal. Practice Guide: Personal Injury Ch. 1-C, C. Formation of Attorney-Client Relationship: the Employment Agreement.

Rutter, Cal. Practice Guide: Personal Injury Ch. 4-E, E. Special Considerations Re "Structured Settlements".

Rutter, Cal. Practice Guide: Real Prop. Transactions Ch. 1-C, C. Attorney Fees and Costs Agreements.

Rutter, Cal. Practice Guide: Real Prop. Transactions Ch. 6-I, I. Real Property Foreclosures and Antideficiency Laws.

Rutter, Cal. Practice Guide: Real Prop. Transactions Form 1:A, Sample Fee Letter.

Rutter, Cal. Practice Guide: Prof. Responsibility Ch. 1-D, D. Unauthorized Practice of Law.

Rutter, Cal. Practice Guide: Prof. Responsibility Ch. 1-F, F. Prohibition Against Agreements Restricting Right to Practice.

Rutter, Cal. Practice Guide: Prof. Responsibility Ch. 5-A, A. Rules Governing Fee Negotiations With Client.

Rutter, Cal. Practice Guide: Prof. Responsibility Ch. 5-B, B. Types of Fees and Fee Arrangements.

Rutter, Cal. Practice Guide: Prof. Responsibility Ch. 5-D, D. Ethical Limitations on Attorney Fees.

Rutter, Cal. Practice Guide: Prof. Responsibility Ch. 5-F, F. Formalizing Fee Agreements.

Rutter, Cal. Practice Guide: Prof. Responsibility Ch. 5-G, G. Accepting Property or Services in Exchange for Legal Services (Barter).

Rutter, Cal. Practice Guide: Prof. Responsibility Ch. 5-H, H. Billing Methods.

Rutter, Cal. Practice Guide: Prof. Responsibility Ch. 5-K, K. Fee Recovery/Enforcing Fee Agreements.

Rutter, Cal. Practice Guide: Prof. Responsibility Ch. 8-D, D. Restrictions on Speech and Behavior Outside Courtroom.

Rutter, Cal. Practice Guide: Prof. Responsibility Ch. 10-F, F. Attorney Obligations Upon Termination of Representation.

Rutter, Cal. Practice Guide: Prof. Responsibility Ch. 11-L, L. Determining Appropriate Discipline.

1 Witkin Cal. Proc. 5th Attorneys § 153, (S 153) General Principle and Distinctions.

1 Witkin Cal. Proc. 5th Attorneys § 165, (S 165) Attorney's Agreement to Bear Expenses.

1 Witkin Cal. Proc. 5th Attorneys § 200, Rules of Professional Conduct.

1 Witkin Cal. Proc. 5th Attorneys § 201, Contingency of Success.

1 Witkin Cal. Proc. 5th Attorneys § 205, Illustrations of Large Awards Upheld.

1 Witkin Cal. Proc. 5th Attorneys § 454, Fees for Legal Services (Rule 4-200).

1 Witkin Cal. Proc. 5th Attorneys § 490, (S 490) Exorbitant Fees.

Rule 4–210. Payment of Personal or Business Expenses Incurred by or for a Client

(A) A member shall not directly or indirectly pay or agree to pay, guarantee, represent, or sanction a representation that the member or member's law firm will pay the personal or business expenses of a prospective or existing client, except that this rule shall not prohibit a member:

(1) With the consent of the client, from paying or agreeing to pay such expenses to third persons from funds collected or to be collected for the client as a result of the representation; or

(2) After employment, from lending money to the client upon the client's promise in writing to repay such loan; or

(3) From advancing the costs of prosecuting or defending a claim or action or otherwise protecting or promoting the client's interests, the repayment of which may be contingent on the outcome of the matter. Such costs within the meaning of this subparagraph (3) shall be limited to all reasonable expenses of litigation or reasonable expenses in preparation for litigation or in providing any legal services to the client.

(B) Nothing in rule 4–210 shall be deemed to limit rules 3–300, 3–310, and 4–300. *(Adopted Nov. 28, 1988, eff. May 27, 1989.)*

Research References

Rutter, Cal. Practice Guide: Civ. Pro. Before Trial Ch. 1-A, A. Accepting a New Case.

California Practice Guide: Employment Litigation Ch. 1-B, B. Plaintiffs' Evaluation of Claims.

Rutter, Cal. Practice Guide: Fed.Civ.Pro. Before Trial Ch. 10-C, C. Class Actions.

Rutter, Cal. Practice Guide: Personal Injury Ch. 1-C, C. Formation of Attorney-Client Relationship: the Employment Agreement.

Rutter, Cal. Practice Guide: Real Prop. Transactions Ch. 1-C, C. Attorney Fees and Costs Agreements.

Rutter, Cal. Practice Guide: Prof. Responsibility Ch. 2-D, D. In-Person Solicitation for Profit.

Rutter, Cal. Practice Guide: Prof. Responsibility Ch. 4-E, E. Conflicts Based on Lawyer's Personal Interests or Relationships.

Rutter, Cal. Practice Guide: Prof. Responsibility Ch. 5-E, E. Costs Arrangements.

Rutter, Cal. Practice Guide: Prof. Responsibility Ch. 5-H, H. Billing Methods.

Rutter, Cal. Practice Guide: Prof. Responsibility Ch. 5-I, I. Paying Client's Personal or Financial Expenses.

Rutter, Cal. Practice Guide: Prof. Responsibility Ch. 9-B, B. Establishing and Maintaining Client Trust Accounts.

1 Witkin Cal. Proc. 5th Attorneys § 165, (S 165) Attorney's Agreement to Bear Expenses.

1 Witkin Cal. Proc. 5th Attorneys § 455, Expenses Incurred (Rule 4-210).

Rule 4–300. Purchasing Property at a Foreclosure or a Sale Subject to Judicial Review

(A) A member shall not directly or indirectly purchase property at a probate, foreclosure, receiver's, trustee's, or judicial sale in an action or proceeding in which such member or any lawyer affiliated by reason of personal, business, or professional relationship with that member or with that member's law firm is acting as a lawyer for a party or as executor, receiver, trustee, administrator, guardian, or conservator.

(B) A member shall not represent the seller at a probate, foreclosure, receiver, trustee, or judicial sale in an action or proceeding in which the purchaser is a spouse or relative of the member or of another lawyer in the member's law firm or is an employee of the member or the member's law firm. *(Adopted Nov. 28, 1988, eff. May 27, 1989. As amended, eff. Sept. 14, 1992.)*

Research References

Rutter, Cal. Practice Guide: Real Prop. Transactions Ch. 1-C, C. Attorney Fees and Costs Agreements.

Rutter, Cal. Practice Guide: Real Prop. Transactions Ch. 1-C Outline, Outline C.

Rutter, Cal. Practice Guide: Prof. Responsibility Ch. 4-F, F. Rules Limiting Business or Financial Dealings With Client.

Rutter, Cal. Practice Guide: Prof. Responsibility Ch. 5-E, E. Costs Arrangements.

Rutter, Cal. Practice Guide: Prof. Responsibility Ch. 5-F, F. Formalizing Fee Agreements.

1 Witkin Cal. Proc. 5th Attorneys § 456, Purchasing Property (Rule 4-300).

1 Witkin Cal. Proc. 5th Attorneys § 485, (S 485) Concealing Personal Interest.

Rule 4–400. Gifts From Client

A member shall not induce a client to make a substantial gift, including a testamentary gift, to the member or to the member's parent, child, sibling, or spouse, except where the client is related to the member.

DISCUSSION

A member may accept a gift from a member's client, subject to general standards of fairness and absence of undue influence. The member who participates in the preparation of an instrument memorializing a gift which is otherwise permissible ought not to be subject to professional discipline. On the other hand, where impermissible influence occurred, discipline is appropriate. (See *Magee v. State Bar* (1962) 58 Cal.2d 423 [24 Cal.Rptr. 839].)

(Adopted Nov. 28, 1988, eff. May 27, 1989.)

Research References

Rutter, Cal. Practice Guide: Real Prop. Transactions Ch. 1-B, B. Attorney Competence, Conflicts of Interest and Initial Client Communications.

Rutter, Cal. Practice Guide: Real Prop. Transactions Gen. Matls., Highlights.

Rutter, Cal. Practice Guide: Prof. Responsibility Ch. 4-F, F. Rules Limiting Business or Financial Dealings With Client.

Rutter, Cal. Practice Guide: Prof. Responsibility Ch. 5-G, G. Accepting Property or Services in Exchange for Legal Services (Barter).

1 Witkin Cal. Proc. 5th Attorneys § 457, Gifts from Client (Rule 4-400).

1 Witkin Cal. Proc. 5th Attorneys § 487, (S 487) Miscellaneous Frauds.

Chapter 5

ADVOCACY AND REPRESENTATION

Rule

5–100. Threatening Criminal, Administrative, or Disciplinary Charges.

Rule

Rule 5–100. Threatening Criminal, Administrative, or Disciplinary Charges

(A) A member shall not threaten to present criminal, administrative, or disciplinary charges to obtain an advantage in a civil dispute.

(B) As used in paragraph (A) of this rule, the term "administrative charges" means the filing or lodging of a complaint with a federal, state, or local governmental entity which may order or recommend the loss or suspension of a license, or may impose or recommend the imposition of a fine, pecuniary sanction, or other sanction of a quasi-criminal nature but does not include filing charges with an administrative entity required by law as a condition precedent to maintaining a civil action.

(C) As used in paragraph (A) of this rule, the term "civil dispute" means a controversy or potential controversy over the rights and duties of two or more parties under civil law, whether or not an action has been commenced, and includes an administrative proceeding of a quasi-civil nature pending before a federal, state, or local governmental entity.

DISCUSSION

Rule 5–100 is not intended to apply to a member's threatening to initiate contempt proceedings against a party for a failure to comply with a court order.

Paragraph (B) is intended to exempt the threat of filing an administrative charge which is a prerequisite to filing a civil complaint on the same transaction or occurrence.

For purposes of paragraph (C), the definition of "civil dispute" makes clear that the rule is applicable prior to the formal filing of a civil action.

(Adopted Nov. 28, 1988, eff. May 27, 1989.)

Research References

Rutter, Cal. Practice Guide: Civ. Pro. Before Trial Ch. 1-C, C. Prelawsuit Notices, Claims and Demands.

Rutter, Cal. Practice Guide: Civ. Pro. Before Trial Ch. 12(II)-H, H. Professional Responsibility Considerations Re Settlements.

California Practice Guide: Employment Litigation Ch. 2-L, L. Settlements.

Rutter, Cal. Practice Guide: Enforcing Judgments/Debts Ch. 2-D, D. Criminal Liability.

Rutter, Cal. Practice Guide: Enforcing Judgments/Debts Ch. 3-B, B. Collection Without Suit.

Rutter, Cal. Practice Guide: Insurance Litigation Ch. 6F-D, D. ERISA Preemption and Remedies.

Rutter, Cal. Practice Guide: Prof. Responsibility Ch. 5-K, K. Fee Recovery/Enforcing Fee Agreements.

Rutter, Cal. Practice Guide: Prof. Responsibility Ch. 8-A, A. Duties to Administration of Justice-In General.

Rutter, Cal. Practice Guide: Prof. Responsibility Ch. 8-D, D. Restrictions on Speech and Behavior Outside Courtroom.

Rutter, Cal. Practice Guide: Prof. Responsibility Ch. 8-D , Outline D.

1 Witkin Cal. Proc. 5th Attorneys § 458, Threatening Charges (Rule 5-100).

1 Witkin Cal. Proc. 5th Attorneys § 541, (S 541) Improper Support of Client's Cause.

Rule 5–110. Performing the Duty of Member in Government Service

A member in government service shall not institute or cause to be instituted criminal charges when the member knows or should know that the charges are not supported by probable cause. If, after the institution of criminal charges, the member in government service having responsibility for prosecuting the charges becomes aware that those charges are not supported by probable cause, the member shall promptly so advise the court in which the criminal matter is pending. *(Adopted Nov. 28, 1988, eff. May 27, 1989.)*

Research References

Rutter, Cal. Practice Guide: Prof. Responsibility Ch. 8-A, A. Duties to Administration of Justice-In General.

1 Witkin Cal. Proc. 5th Attorneys § 459, Government Attorney Instituting Charges (Rule 5-110).

1 Witkin Cal. Proc. 5th Attorneys § 541, (S 541) Improper Support of Client's Cause.

Rule 5–120. Trial Publicity

(A) A member who is participating or has participated in the investigation or litigation of a matter shall not make an extrajudicial statement that a reasonable person would expect to be disseminated by means of public communication if the member knows or reasonably should know that it will have a substantial likelihood of materially prejudicing an adjudicative proceeding in the matter.

(B) Notwithstanding paragraph (A), a member may state:

(1) the claim, offense or defense involved and, except when prohibited by law, the identity of the persons involved;

(2) the information contained in a public record;

(3) that an investigation of the matter is in progress;

(4) the scheduling or result of any step in litigation;

(5) a request for assistance in obtaining evidence and information necessary thereto;

(6) a warning of danger concerning the behavior of a person involved, when there is reason to believe that there exists the likelihood of substantial harm to an individual or the public interest; and

(7) in a criminal case, in addition to subparagraphs (1) through (6):

(a) the identity, residence, occupation, and family status of the accused;

(b) if the accused has not been apprehended, the information necessary to aid in apprehension of that person;

(c) the fact, time, and place of arrest; and

(d) the identity of investigating and arresting officers or agencies and the length of the investigation.

(C) Notwithstanding paragraph (A), a member may make a statement that a reasonable member would believe is required to protect a client from the substantial undue prejudicial effect of recent publicity not initiated by the member or the member's client. A statement made pursuant to this paragraph shall be limited to such information as is necessary to mitigate the recent adverse publicity.

DISCUSSION

Rule 5–120 is intended to apply equally to prosecutors and criminal defense counsel.

Whether an extrajudicial statement violates rule 5–120 depends on many factors, including: (1) whether the extrajudicial statement presents information clearly inadmissible as evidence in the matter for the purpose of proving or disproving a material fact in issue; (2) whether the extrajudicial statement presents information the member knows is false, deceptive, or the use of which would violate Business and Professions Code section 6068(d); (3) whether the extrajudicial statement violates a lawful "gag" order, or protective order, statute, rule of court, or special rule of confidentiality (for example, in juvenile, domestic, mental disability, and certain criminal proceedings); and (4) the timing of the statement.

Paragraph (A) is intended to apply to statements made by or on behalf of the member.

Subparagraph (B)(6) is not intended to create, augment, diminish, or eliminate any application of the lawyer-client privilege or of Business and Professions Code section 6068(e) regarding the member's duty to maintain client confidence and secrets.

(Adopted Sept. 14, 1995, eff. Oct. 1, 1995.)

Research References

Rutter, Cal. Practice Guide: Civil Trials & Evidence Ch. 1-O, O. Addressing the Media.
California Practice Guide: Employment Litigation Ch. 2-K, K. Statements to News Media.
Rutter, Cal. Practice Guide: Prof. Responsibility Ch. 8-D, D. Restrictions on Speech and Behavior Outside Courtroom.
Rutter, Cal. Practice Guide: Prof. Responsibility Ch. 8-D , Outline D.
1 Witkin Cal. Proc. 5th Attorneys § 460, Publicizing Litigation (Rule 5-120).
1 Witkin Cal. Proc. 5th Attorneys § 521, Publicizing Litigation.
5 Witkin, California Summary 10th Torts § 588, Limitations on Communications to Public Journals.

Rule 5-200.   Trial Conduct

In presenting a matter to a tribunal, a member:

(A) Shall employ, for the purpose of maintaining the causes confided to the member such means only as are consistent with truth;

(B) Shall not seek to mislead the judge, judicial officer, or jury by an artifice or false statement of fact or law;

(C) Shall not intentionally misquote to a tribunal the language of a book, statute, or decision;

(D) Shall not, knowing its invalidity, cite as authority a decision that has been overruled or a statute that has been repealed or declared unconstitutional; and

(E) Shall not assert personal knowledge of the facts at issue, except when testifying as a witness. *(Adopted Nov. 28, 1988, eff. May 27, 1989.)*

Research References

Rutter, Cal. Practice Guide: Civ. Pro. Before Trial Ch. 9(I)-B, B. Preparing and Filing Motions.
Rutter, Cal. Practice Guide: Civil Trials & Evidence Ch. 1-E, E. Preparing Witnesses to Testify.
Rutter, Cal. Practice Guide: Civil Trials & Evidence Ch. 6-C, C. Improper Conduct During Opening Statement.
Rutter, Cal. Practice Guide: Civil Trials & Evidence Ch. 9-A, A. Preliminary Considerations.
Rutter, Cal. Practice Guide: Civil Trials & Evidence Ch. 12-A, A. Motion for Mistrial.
Rutter, Cal. Practice Guide: Civil Trials & Evidence Ch. 13-B, B. Proper vs. Improper Closing Argument.
Rutter, Cal. Practice Guide: Fed.Civ.Pro. Before Trial Ch. 11(III)-A, A. Limitations on Right to Discovery.
Rutter, Cal. Practice Guide: Prof. Responsibility Ch. 3-A, A. Nature of Attorney-Client Relationship.
Rutter, Cal. Practice Guide: Prof. Responsibility Ch. 7-B, B. Duty to Maintain Client Confidence and Secrets Under State Bar Act.
Rutter, Cal. Practice Guide: Prof. Responsibility Ch. 8-C, C. Restrictions on Advocacy in Court Proceedings.
Rutter, Cal. Practice Guide: Prof. Responsibility Ch. 11-A, A. Grounds for Discipline.
9 Witkin Cal. Proc. 5th Appeal § 708, Honesty and Fairness.
9 Witkin Cal. Proc. 5th Appeal § 772, (S 772) Practice.

1 Witkin Cal. Proc. 5th Attorneys § 461, Trial Conduct (Rules 5-200, 5-220).
1 Witkin Cal. Proc. 5th Attorneys § 480, Statutory Framework.
1 Witkin Cal. Proc. 5th Attorneys § 497, (S 497) Misleading Court.

Rule 5-210.   Member as Witness

A member shall not act as an advocate before a jury which will hear testimony from the member unless:

(A) The testimony relates to an uncontested matter; or

(B) The testimony relates to the nature and value of legal services rendered in the case; or

(C) The member has the informed, written consent of the client. If the member represents the People or a governmental entity, the consent shall be obtained from the head of the office or a designee of the head of the office by which the member is employed and shall be consistent with principles of recusal.

DISCUSSION

Rule 5-210 is intended to apply to situations in which the member knows or should know that he or she ought to be called as a witness in litigation in which there is a jury. This rule is not intended to encompass situations in which the member is representing the client in an adversarial proceeding and is testifying before a judge. In non-adversarial proceedings, as where the member testifies on behalf of the client in a hearing before a legislative body, rule 5-210 is not applicable.

Rule 5-210 is not intended to apply to circumstances in which a lawyer in an advocate's firm will be a witness.

(Adopted Nov. 28, 1988, eff. May 27, 1989. As amended, eff. Sept. 14, 1992.)

Research References

Rutter, Cal. Practice Guide: Civ. Pro. Before Trial Ch. 6-B, B. Complaints.
Rutter, Cal. Practice Guide: Civ. Pro. Before Trial Ch. 8F-5, Responding to Interrogatories.
Rutter, Cal. Practice Guide: Civil Trials & Evidence Ch. 1-E, E. Preparing Witnesses to Testify.
Rutter, Cal. Practice Guide: Civil Trials & Evidence Ch. 4-I, I. Other Motions at Final Status Conference.
Rutter, Cal. Practice Guide: Civil Trials & Evidence Ch. 9-A, A. Preliminary Considerations.
Rutter, Cal. Practice Guide: Civil Trials & Evidence Ch. 8C-A, A. Testimony.
California Practice Guide: Employment Litigation Ch. 2-I, I. Investigations.
Rutter, Cal. Practice Guide: Fed.Civ.Pro. Before Trial Ch. 11(I)-B, B. Informal Methods of Obtaining Information.
Rutter, Cal. Practice Guide: Insurance Litigation Ch. 13-B, B. Extracontractual Compensatory Damages.
Rutter, Cal. Practice Guide: Insurance Litigation Ch. 15-G, G. Discovery.
Rutter, Cal. Practice Guide: Personal Injury Ch. 1-B, B. Initial Evaluation of Case: Decision to Accept or Reject Employment or Undertake Further Evaluation of Claim.
Rutter, Cal. Practice Guide: Personal Injury Gen. Matls., Highlights.
Rutter, Cal. Practice Guide: Real Prop. Transactions Ch. 9-D, D. Prenegotiation/Predrafting Considerations.
Rutter, Cal. Practice Guide: Prof. Responsibility Ch. 4-E, E. Conflicts Based on Lawyer's Personal Interests or Relationships.
Rutter, Cal. Practice Guide: Prof. Responsibility Ch. 6-D, D. Professional Liability.
Rutter, Cal. Practice Guide: Prof. Responsibility Ch. 8-C, C. Restrictions on Advocacy in Court Proceedings.
1 Witkin Cal. Proc. 5th Attorneys § 462, Attorney as Witness (Rule 5-210).

Rule 5-220.   Suppression of Evidence

A member shall not suppress any evidence that the member or the member's client has a legal obligation to reveal or to produce. *(Adopted Nov. 28, 1988, eff. May 27, 1989.)*

Research References

Rutter, Cal. Practice Guide: Civil Trials & Evidence Ch. 12-A, A. Motion for Mistrial.

California Practice Guide: Employment Litigation Ch. 2-I, I. Investigations.

Rutter, Cal. Practice Guide: Insurance Litigation Ch. 11-J, J. Other Torts Not Necessarily Related to Insurer "Bad Faith".

Rutter, Cal. Practice Guide: Prof. Responsibility Ch. 7-B, B. Duty to Maintain Client Confidence and Secrets Under State Bar Act.

Rutter, Cal. Practice Guide: Prof. Responsibility Ch. 8-C, C. Restrictions on Advocacy in Court Proceedings.

1 Witkin Cal. Proc. 5th Attorneys § 461, Trial Conduct (Rules 5-200, 5-220).

1 Witkin Cal. Proc. 5th Attorneys § 541, (S 541) Improper Support of Client's Cause.

Rule 5–300. Contact With Officials

(A) A member shall not directly or indirectly give or lend anything of value to a judge, official, or employee of a tribunal unless the personal or family relationship between the member and the judge, official, or employee is such that gifts are customarily given and exchanged. Nothing contained in this rule shall prohibit a member from contributing to the campaign fund of a judge running for election or confirmation pursuant to applicable law pertaining to such contributions.

(B) A member shall not directly or indirectly communicate with or argue to a judge or judicial officer upon the merits of a contested matter pending before such judge or judicial officer, except:

(1) In open court; or

(2) With the consent of all other counsel in such matter; or

(3) In the presence of all other counsel in such matter; or

(4) In writing with a copy thereof furnished to such other counsel; or

(5) In ex parte matters.

(C) As used in this rule, "judge" and "judicial officer" shall include law clerks, research attorneys, or other court personnel who participate in the decision-making process. *(Adopted Nov. 28, 1988, eff. May 27, 1989. As amended, eff. Sept. 14, 1992.)*

Research References

California Practice Guide: Employment Litigation Ch. 2-H, H. Ex Parte Communication With Court.

Rutter, Cal. Practice Guide: Prof. Responsibility Ch. 8-D, D. Restrictions on Speech and Behavior Outside Courtroom.

1 Witkin Cal. Proc. 5th Attorneys § 463, Contact With Officials (Rule 5-300).

Rule 5–310. Prohibited Contact With Witnesses

A member shall not:

(A) Advise or directly or indirectly cause a person to secrete himself or herself or to leave the jurisdiction of a tribunal for the purpose of making that person unavailable as a witness therein.

(B) Directly or indirectly pay, offer to pay, or acquiesce in the payment of compensation to a witness contingent upon the content of the witness's testimony or the outcome of the case.

Except where prohibited by law, a member may advance, guarantee, or acquiesce in the payment of:

(1) Expenses reasonably incurred by a witness in attending or testifying.

(2) Reasonable compensation to a witness for loss of time in attending or testifying.

(3) A reasonable fee for the professional services of an expert witness. *(Adopted Nov. 28, 1988, eff. May 27, 1989. As amended, eff. May 12, 2009.)*

Research References

Rutter, Cal. Practice Guide: Civil Trials & Evidence Ch. 1-C, C. Marshalling the Evidence.

California Practice Guide: Employment Litigation Ch. 2-I, I. Investigations.

Rutter, Cal. Practice Guide: Fed.Civ.Pro. Before Trial Ch. 11(I)-B, B. Informal Methods of Obtaining Information.

Rutter, Cal. Practice Guide: Prof. Responsibility Ch. 5-E, E. Costs Arrangements.

Rutter, Cal. Practice Guide: Prof. Responsibility Ch. 8-D, D. Restrictions on Speech and Behavior Outside Courtroom.

1 Witkin Cal. Proc. 5th Attorneys § 464, Contact With Witnesses (Rule 5-310).

1 Witkin Cal. Proc. 5th Attorneys § 541, (S 541) Improper Support of Client's Cause.

Rule 5–320. Contact With Jurors

(A) A member connected with a case shall not communicate directly or indirectly with anyone the member knows to be a member of the venire from which the jury will be selected for trial of that case.

(B) During trial a member connected with the case shall not communicate directly or indirectly with any juror.

(C) During trial a member who is not connected with the case shall not communicate directly or indirectly concerning the case with anyone the member knows is a juror in the case.

(D) After discharge of the jury from further consideration of a case a member shall not ask questions of or make comments to a member of that jury that are intended to harass or embarrass the juror or to influence the juror's actions in future jury service.

(E) A member shall not directly or indirectly conduct an out of court investigation of a person who is either a member of the venire or a juror in a manner likely to influence the state of mind of such person in connection with present or future jury service.

(F) All restrictions imposed by this rule also apply to communications with, or investigations of, members of the family of a person who is either a member of the venire or a juror.

(G) A member shall reveal promptly to the court improper conduct by a person who is either a member of a venire or a juror, or by another toward a person who is either a member of a venire or a juror or a member of his or her family, of which the member has knowledge.

(H) This rule does not prohibit a member from communicating with persons who are members of a venire or jurors as a part of the official proceedings.

(I) For purposes of this rule, "juror" means any empanelled, discharged, or excused juror. *(Adopted Nov. 28, 1988, eff. May 27, 1989. As amended, eff. Sept. 14, 1992.)*

Research References

Rutter, Cal. Practice Guide: Civil Trials & Evidence Ch. 5-E, E. Preparation for Attorney Voir Dire.

Rutter, Cal. Practice Guide: Civil Trials & Evidence Ch. 7-F, F. Juror Misconduct During Trial.

Rutter, Cal. Practice Guide: Civil Trials & Evidence Ch. 12-A, A. Motion for Mistrial.

Rutter, Cal. Practice Guide: Civil Trials & Evidence Ch. 15-F, F. Juror Misconduct During Deliberations.

Rutter, Cal. Practice Guide: Personal Injury Ch. 9-M, M. Verdicts and Judgment.

Rutter, Cal. Practice Guide: Personal Injury Ch. 10-A, A. Motion for New Trial.

Rutter, Cal. Practice Guide: Prof. Responsibility Ch. 8-D, D. Restrictions on Speech and Behavior Outside Courtroom.

1 Witkin Cal. Proc. 5th Attorneys § 465, Contact With Jurors (Rule 5-320).

7 Witkin Cal. Proc. 5th Trial § 136, (S 136) in General.

7 Witkin Cal. Proc. 5th Trial § 225, (S 225) Other Acts.

7 Witkin Cal. Proc. 5th Trial § 320, (S 320) Secrecy of Deliberations.

Prof. Conduct

7 Witkin Cal. Proc. 5th Trial § 331, (S 331) With Party, Attorney, or Witness.

CALIFORNIA RULES OF COURT

Selected Provisions

Title 1

RULES APPLICABLE TO ALL COURTS

Chapter 1

PRELIMINARY RULES

Rule
1.1. The California Rules of Court.
1.2. Title.
1.3. Authority.
1.4. Contents of the rules.
1.5. Construction of rules and standards.
1.6. Definitions and use of terms.

Rule 1.1. The California Rules of Court

These rules are entitled the California Rules of Court. *(Adopted, eff. Jan. 1, 2007.)*

Research References

2 Witkin Cal. Proc. 5th Courts § 189, (S 189) Rules Applicable to All Courts.

Rule 1.2. Title

The rules in this title of the California Rules of Court may be referred to as the Rules Applicable to All Courts. *(Adopted, eff. Jan. 1, 2007.)*

Rule 1.3. Authority

The rules in the California Rules of Court are adopted by the Judicial Council of California under the authority of article VI, section 6, of the Constitution of the State of California, unless otherwise indicated. The rules in division 5 of title 8 and in title 9 were adopted by the Supreme Court. *(Adopted, eff. Jan. 1, 2007. As amended, eff. Jan. 1, 2008.)*

Rule 1.4. Contents of the rules

(a) The titles

The California Rules of Court includes the following titles:

(1) *Title 1.* Rules Applicable to All Courts;

(2) *Title 2.* Trial Court Rules;

(3) *Title 3.* Civil Rules;

(4) *Title 4.* Criminal Rules;

(5) *Title 5.* Family and Juvenile Rules;

(6) *Title 6.* [Reserved];

(7) *Title 7.* Probate Rules;

(8) *Title 8.* Appellate Rules;

(9) *Title 9.* Rules on Law Practice, Attorneys, and Judges; and

(10) *Title 10.* Judicial Administration Rules.

(b) Standards of Judicial Administration

The California Rules of Court includes the Standards of Judicial Administration adopted by the Judicial Council.

(c) Ethics Standards for Neutral Arbitrators in Contractual Arbitrations

The California Rules of Court includes Ethics Standards for Neutral Arbitrators in Contractual Arbitrations adopted by the Judicial Council under the authority of Code of Civil Procedure section 1281.85.

(d) The appendixes

The California Rules of Court includes the following appendixes:

(1) *Appendix A.* Judicial Council Legal Forms List;

(2) *Appendix B.* Liability Limits of a Parent or Guardian Having Custody and Control of a Minor for the Torts of a Minor;

(3) *Appendix C.* Guidelines for the Operation of Family Law Information Centers and Family Law Facilitator Offices;

(4) *Appendix D.* Judicial Council Governance Policies;

(5) *Appendix E.* Guidelines for Determining Financial Eligibility for County Payment of the Cost of Counsel Appointed by the Court in Proceedings Under the Guardianship–Conservatorship Law; and

(6) *Appendix F.* Guidelines for the Juvenile Dependency Counsel Collections Program.; and

(7) *Appendix G.* Parliamentary Procedures for the Judicial Council of California. *(Adopted, eff. Jan. 1, 2007. As amended, eff. Jan. 1, 2008; Aug. 14, 2009; Jan. 1, 2013; Feb. 26, 2013.)*

Research References

2 Witkin Cal. Proc. 5th Courts § 187, (S 187) in General.

Rule 1.5. Construction of rules and standards

(a) Construction

The rules and standards of the California Rules of Court must be liberally construed to ensure the just and speedy determination of the proceedings that they govern.

(b) Terminology

As used in the rules and standards:

(1) "Must" is mandatory;

(2) "May" is permissive;

(3) "May not" means not permitted to;

(4) "Will" expresses a future contingency or predicts action by a court or person in the ordinary course of events, but does not signify a mandatory duty; and

(5) "Should" expresses a preference or a nonbinding recommendation.

(c) Standards

Standards are guidelines or goals recommended by the Judicial Council. The nonbinding nature of standards is indicat-

Ct. Rules

ed by the use of "should" in the standards instead of the mandatory "must" used in the rules.

(d) Construction of additional terms

In the rules:

(1) Each tense (past, present, or future) includes the others;

(2) Each gender (masculine, feminine, or neuter) includes the others; and

(3) Each number (singular or plural) includes the other. *(Adopted, eff. Jan. 1, 2007.)*

Research References

9 Witkin Cal. Proc. 5th Appeal § 11, in General.
2 Witkin Cal. Proc. 5th Courts § 187, (S 187) in General.
2 Witkin Cal. Proc. 5th Courts § 198, (S 198) Additional Elements.

Rule 1.6.   Definitions and use of terms

As used in the California Rules of Court, unless the context or subject matter otherwise requires:

(1) "Action" includes special proceeding.

(2) "Case" includes action or proceeding.

(3) "Civil case" means a case prosecuted by one party against another for the declaration, enforcement, or protection of a right or the redress or prevention of a wrong. Civil cases include all cases except criminal cases and petitions for habeas corpus.

(4) "General civil case" means all civil cases except probate, guardianship, conservatorship, juvenile, and family law proceedings (including proceedings under divisions 6–9 of the Family Code, Uniform Parentage Act, Domestic Violence Prevention Act, and Uniform Interstate Family Support Act; freedom from parental custody and control proceedings; and adoption proceedings), small claims proceedings, unlawful detainer proceedings, and "other civil petitions" described in (5).

(5) "Civil petitions" that are not general civil cases include petitions to prevent civil harassment, elder abuse, and workplace violence; petitions for name change; election contest petitions; and petitions for relief from late claims.

(6) "Unlimited civil cases" and "limited civil cases" are defined in Code of Civil Procedure section 85 et seq.

(7) "Criminal case" means a proceeding by which a party charged with a public offense is accused and prosecuted for the offense.

(8) "Rule" means a rule of the California Rules of Court.

(9) "Local rule" means every rule, regulation, order, policy, form, or standard of general application adopted by a court to govern practice and procedure in that court or by a judge of the court to govern practice or procedure in that judge's courtroom.

(10) "Chief Justice" and "presiding justice" include the Acting Chief Justice and the acting presiding justice, respectively.

(11) "Presiding judge" includes the acting presiding judge or the judicial officer designated by the presiding judge.

(12) "Judge" includes, as applicable, a judge of the superior court, a commissioner, or a temporary judge.

(13) "Temporary judge" means an active or inactive member of the State Bar of California who, under article VI, section 21 of the California Constitution and these rules, serves or expects to serve as a judge once, sporadically, or regularly on a part-time basis under a separate court appointment for each period of service or each case heard.

(14) "Person" includes a corporation or other legal entity as well as a natural person.

(15) "Party" is a person appearing in an action. Parties include both self-represented persons and persons represented by an attorney of record. "Party," "plaintiff," "People of the State of California," "applicant," "petitioner," "defendant," "respondent," "other parent," or any other designation of a party includes the party's attorney of record.

(16) "Attorney" means a member of the State Bar of California.

(17) "Counsel" means an attorney.

(18) "Sheriff" includes marshal.

(19) "Service" means service in the manner prescribed by a statute or rule.

(20) "Memorandum" means a written document containing: a statement of facts; a concise statement of the law, evidence, and arguments relied on; and a discussion of the statutes, cases, rules, and other legal sources relied on in support of the position advanced.

(21) "Declaration" includes "affidavit."

(22) "Recycled" as applied to paper means "recycled printing and writing paper" as defined by section 12209 of the Public Contract Code.

(23) "California Courts Web Site" means the Web site established by the Judicial Council that includes news and information, reference materials, rules and forms, and a self-help center. The address is: *www.courtinfos.ca.gov*. *(Formerly Rule 200.1, adopted, eff. Jan. 1, 2003. Renumbered Rule 1.6 and amended, eff. Jan. 1, 2007. As amended, eff. July 1, 2007; July 1, 2008; July 1, 2013.)*

Research References

Rutter, Cal. Practice Guide: Civ. Pro. Before Trial Ch. 9(I)-D, D. Hearing.
Rutter, Cal. Practice Guide: Civ. Pro. Before Trial Ch. 12(I)-B, B. Case Management ("Fast Track") System.
9 Witkin Cal. Proc. 5th Appeal § 11, in General.
9 Witkin Cal. Proc. 5th Appeal § 631, (S 631) Form of Record.
2 Witkin Cal. Proc. 5th Courts § 30, (S 30) Use of Recycled Paper.
2 Witkin Cal. Proc. 5th Courts § 189, (S 189) Rules Applicable to All Courts.
2 Witkin Cal. Proc. 5th Courts § 261, Maximum Time Standards.
2 Witkin Cal. Proc. 5th Courts § 263, (S 263) Differential Case Management.
2 Witkin Cal. Proc. 5th Courts § 348, (S 348) Nature of Position.
4 Witkin Cal. Proc. 5th Pleading § 14, Paper.
4 Witkin Cal. Proc. 5th Pleading § 29, (S 29) Service.
4 Witkin Cal. Proc. 5th Pleading § 67, (S 67) Designation of Parties.

Chapter 2

TIMING AND HOLIDAYS

Rule
1.10.   Time for actions.
1.11.   Holiday falling on a Saturday or Sunday.

Rule 1.10.   Time for actions

(a) Computation of time

The time in which any act provided by these rules is to be performed is computed by excluding the first day and including the last, unless the last day is a Saturday, Sunday, or other legal holiday, and then it is also excluded.

(b) Holidays

Unless otherwise provided by law, if the last day for the performance of any act that is required by these rules to be performed within a specific period of time falls on a Saturday,

Sunday, or other legal holiday, the period is extended to and includes the next day that is not a holiday.

(c) Extending or shortening time

Unless otherwise provided by law, the court may extend or shorten the time within which a party must perform any act under the rules. *(Formerly Rule 200.3, adopted, eff. Jan. 1, 2003. Renumbered Rule 1.10 and amended, eff. Jan. 1, 2007.)*

Research References

Rutter, Cal. Practice Guide: Civ. Pro. Before Trial Ch. 9(I)-B, B. Preparing and Filing Motions.
2 Witkin Cal. Proc. 5th Courts § 50, (S 50) Where Last Day is Holiday.
2 Witkin Cal. Proc. 5th Courts § 189, (S 189) Rules Applicable to All Courts.
4 Witkin Cal. Proc. 5th Pleading § 8, (S 8) Time Prescribed by Court.
4 Witkin Cal. Proc. 5th Pleading § 9, (S 9) Computation of Time.
4 Witkin Cal. Proc. 5th Pleading § 10, Extension to Ordinary Party.
6 Witkin Cal. Proc. 5th Proceedings Without Trial § 18, Extension by Stipulation or Court Order.

Rule 1.11. Holiday falling on a Saturday or Sunday

When a judicial holiday specified by Code of Civil Procedure section 135 falls on a Saturday, the courts must observe the holiday on the preceding Friday. When a judicial holiday specified by Code of Civil Procedure section 135 falls on a Sunday, the courts must observe the holiday on the following Monday. *(Formerly Rule 987, adopted, eff. Jan. 1, 1986, operative Jan. 1, 1989. Renumbered Rule 1.11 and amended, eff. Jan. 1, 2007.)*

Research References

2 Witkin Cal. Proc. 5th Courts § 189, (S 189) Rules Applicable to All Courts.

Chapter 3

SERVICE AND FILING

Rule
1.20. Filing.
1.21. Service.
1.22. Recycled paper.

Rule 1.20. Filing

(a) Effective date of filing

Unless otherwise provided, a document is deemed filed on the date it is received by the court clerk.

(b) Protection of privacy

(1) *Scope*

The requirements of this subdivision that parties or their attorneys must not include, or must redact, certain identifiers from documents or records filed with the court do not apply to documents or records that by court order or operation of law are filed in their entirety either confidentially or under seal.

(2) *Exclusion or redaction of identifiers*

To protect personal privacy and other legitimate interests, parties and their attorneys must not include, or must redact where inclusion is necessary, the following identifiers from all pleadings and other papers filed in the court's public file, whether filed in paper or electronic form, unless otherwise provided by law or ordered by the court:

(A) Social security numbers. If an individual's social security number is required in a pleading or other paper filed in the public file, only the last four digits of that number may be used.

(B) Financial account numbers. If financial account numbers are required in a pleading or other paper filed in the public file, only the last four digits of these numbers may be used.

(3) *Responsibility of the filer*

The responsibility for excluding or redacting identifiers identified in (b)(2) from all documents filed with the court rests solely with the parties and their attorneys. The court clerk will not review each pleading or other paper for compliance with this provision.

(4) *Confidential reference list*

If the court orders on a showing of good cause, a party filing a document containing identifiers listed in (b)(2) may file, along with the redacted document that will be placed in the public file, a reference list. The reference list is confidential. A party filing a confidential reference list must use *Confidential Reference List of Identifiers* (form MC–120) for that purpose. The confidential list must identify each item of redacted information and specify an appropriate reference that uniquely corresponds to each item of redacted information listed. All references in the case to the redacted identifiers included in the confidential reference list will be understood to refer to the corresponding complete identifier. A party may amend its reference list as of right. *(Adopted, eff. Jan. 1, 2007. As amended, eff. Jan. 1, 2008.)*

Research References

Rutter, Cal. Practice Guide: Civ. Pro. Before Trial Ch. 6-A, A. Introduction.
Rutter, Cal. Practice Guide: Civ. Pro. Before Trial Ch. 8C-5, Privacy Protection.
Rutter, Cal. Practice Guide: Prof. Responsibility Ch. 6-D, D. Professional Liability.
2 Witkin Cal. Proc. 5th Courts § 189, (S 189) Rules Applicable to All Courts.
5 Witkin Cal. Proc. 5th Pleading § 1030, (S 1030) Illegal Speech.
5 Witkin Cal. Proc. 5th Pleading § 1037, (S 1037) Plaintiff's Inability to Meet Burden as Matter of Law.
5 Witkin, California Summary 10th Torts § 567, in General.

Rule 1.21. Service

(a) Service on a party or attorney

Whenever a document is required to be served on a party, the service must be made on the party's attorney if the party is represented.

(b) "Serve and file"

As used in these rules, unless a statute or rule provides for a different method for filing or service, a requirement to "serve and file" a document means that a copy of the document must be served on the attorney for each party separately represented, on each self-represented party, and on any other person or entity when required by statute, rule, or court order, and that the document and a proof of service of the document must be filed with the court.

(c) "Proof of service"

As used in these rules, "proof of service" means a declaration stating that service has been made as provided in (a) and (b). If the proof of service names attorneys for separately represented parties, it must also state which party or parties each of the attorneys served is representing. *(Adopted, eff. Jan. 1, 2007. As amended, eff. Jan. 1, 2007.)*

Research References

6 Witkin Cal. Proc. 5th Proceedings Without Trial § 12, (S 12) in General.
6 Witkin Cal. Proc. 5th Proceedings Without Trial § 13, General Rule.
6 Witkin Cal. Proc. 5th Proceedings Without Trial § 20, Proof of Service.

Ct. Rules

6 Witkin Cal. Proc. 5th Proceedings Without Trial § 23, Proof of Service.

Rule 1.22. Recycled paper

(a) Use of recycled paper required

Recycled paper, as defined in rule 1.6, must be used for all original papers filed with the trial and appellate courts and for all copies of papers, documents, and exhibits, whether filed with the courts or served on other parties.

(b) Certification

Whenever the use of recycled paper is required by these rules, the attorney, party, or other person filing or serving a document certifies, by the act of filing or service, that the document was produced on paper purchased as recycled. *(Adopted, eff. Jan. 1, 2007.)*

Research References

2 Witkin Cal. Proc. 5th Courts § 30, (S 30) Use of Recycled Paper.
2 Witkin Cal. Proc. 5th Courts § 189, (S 189) Rules Applicable to All Courts.

Chapter 4

JUDICIAL COUNCIL FORMS

Rule
1.30. Judicial Council forms.
1.31. Mandatory forms.
1.35. Optional forms.
1.37. Use of forms.
1.40. Statutory references on forms.
1.41. Proofs of service on forms.
1.42. Forms not to be rejected.
1.43. Legibility.
1.44. Electronically produced forms.
1.45. Judicial Council pleading forms.
1.51. California Law Enforcement Telecommunications System (CLETS) information form.

Rule 1.30. Judicial Council forms

(a) Application

The rules in this chapter apply to Judicial Council forms.

(b) Mandatory or optional forms

Judicial Council forms are either mandatory or optional. *(Formerly Rule 982 adopted eff. Jan. 1, 1970. As amended, eff. July 1, 1971; Jan. 2, 1972; March 4, 1972; July 1, 1972; March 7, 1973; Jan. 1, 1975; July 1, 1975; July 1, 1976; Jan. 1, 1977; July 1, 1977; July 28, 1977; Jan. 1, 1978; Oct. 1, 1978; Jan. 1, 1979; Jan. 15, 1979; July 1, 1980; Jan. 1, 1981; April 30, 1981; July 1, 1981; Jan. 1, 1982; Jan. 1, 1983; July 1, 1983; Jan. 1, 1984; Jan. 1, 1985; July 1, 1986; Jan. 1, 1987; July 1, 1987; July 1, 1988; Jan. 1, 1990; Jan. 1, 1991; Sept. 30, 1991; Jan. 1, 1993; July 1, 1999. Renumbered Rule 201.1 and amended, eff. Jan. 1, 2003. As amended, eff. Jan. 1, 2006. Renumbered Rule 1.30 and amended, eff. Jan. 1, 2007.)*

Research References

2 Witkin Cal. Proc. 5th Courts § 189, (S 189) Rules Applicable to All Courts.
2 Witkin Cal. Proc. 5th Courts § 398, (S 398) in General.
4 Witkin Cal. Proc. 5th Pleading § 13, in General.
10 Witkin, California Summary 10th Parent and Child § 445, (S 445) Judicial Council Forms.
10 Witkin, California Summary 10th Parent and Child § 712, Notice of Appeal.

Rule 1.31. Mandatory forms

(a) Use of mandatory forms and acceptance for filing

Forms adopted by the Judicial Council for mandatory use are forms prescribed under Government Code section 68511. Wherever applicable, they must be used by all parties and must be accepted for filing by all courts. In some areas, alternative mandatory forms have been adopted.

(b) List of mandatory forms

Each mandatory Judicial Council form is identified as mandatory by an asterisk (*) on the list of Judicial Council forms in Appendix A to the California Rules of Court. The list is available on the California Courts Web site at *www.courtinfo.ca. gov/forms*.

(c) Identification of mandatory forms

Forms adopted by the Judicial Council for mandatory use bear the words "Form Adopted for Mandatory Use," "Mandatory Form," or "Form Adopted for Alternative Mandatory Use" in the lower left corner of the first page.

(d) Words on forms

Publishers and courts reprinting a mandatory Judicial Council form in effect before July 1, 1999, must add the words "Mandatory Form" to the bottom of the first page.

(e) No alteration of forms

Except as provided in rule 3.52(6), concerning court fee waiver orders, rule 5.504, concerning court orders in juvenile court proceedings, and rule 7.101.5, concerning court orders in proceedings under the Probate Code, courts may not require the use of an altered mandatory Judicial Council form in place of the Judicial Council form. However, a judicial officer may modify a Judicial Council form order as necessary or appropriate to adjudicate a particular case.

(f) No colored forms

Courts may not require that any mandatory Judicial Council form be submitted on any color of paper other than white.

(g) Orders not on mandatory forms

An otherwise legally sufficient court order for which there is a mandatory Judicial Council form is not invalid or unenforceable because the order is not prepared on a Judicial Council form or the correct Judicial Council form. *(Adopted, eff. Jan. 1, 2007. As amended, eff. Jan. 1, 2007; Jan. 1, 2009; July 1, 2009.)*

Research References

Rutter, Cal. Practice Guide: Civil Appeals & Writs Ch. 3-B, B. Filing Deadlines.
Rutter, Cal. Practice Guide: Civ. Pro. Before Trial Ch. 8E-6, Subpoena to Nonparty Deponent or Business Records Custodian.
Rutter, Cal. Practice Guide: Civ. Pro. Before Trial Ch. 9(I)-E, E. Posthearing Procedures.
2 Witkin Cal. Proc. 5th Courts § 398, (S 398) in General.
10 Witkin, California Summary 10th Parent and Child § 445, (S 445) Judicial Council Forms.
10 Witkin, California Summary 10th Parent and Child § 564, in General.

Rule 1.35. Optional forms

(a) Use of optional forms and acceptance for filing

Forms approved by the Judicial Council for optional use, wherever applicable, may be used by parties and must be accepted for filing by all courts.

(b) List of optional forms

Each optional Judicial Council form appears without an asterisk (*) on the list of Judicial Council forms in Appendix A to the California Rules of Court. The list is available on the California Courts Web site at *www.courtinfo.ca.gov/forms*.

(c) Identification of optional forms

Forms approved by the Judicial Council for optional use bear the words "Form Approved for Optional Use" or "Optional Form" in the lower left corner of the first page.

(d) Words on forms

Publishers and courts reprinting an optional Judicial Council form in effect before July 1, 1999, must add the words "Optional Form" to the bottom of the first page.

(e) No alteration of forms

Courts may not require the use of an altered optional Judicial Council form in place of the Judicial Council form. However, a judicial officer may modify a Judicial Council form order as necessary or appropriate to adjudicate a particular case.

(f) No colored forms

Courts may not require that any optional Judicial Council form be submitted on any color of paper other than white. *(Adopted, eff. Jan. 1, 2007. As amended, eff. Jan. 1, 2009.)*

Research References

2 Witkin Cal. Proc. 5th Courts § 398, (S 398) in General.
10 Witkin, California Summary 10th Parent and Child § 564, in General.

Rule 1.37. Use of forms

A person serving and filing a Judicial Council form must use the current version of the form adopted or approved by the council, unless a rule in the California Rules of Court allows the use of a different form. *(Adopted, eff. Jan. 1, 2007.)*

Research References

2 Witkin Cal. Proc. 5th Courts § 398, (S 398) in General.
10 Witkin, California Summary 10th Parent and Child § 445, (S 445) Judicial Council Forms.

Rule 1.40. Statutory references on forms

The references to statutes and rules at the bottom of Judicial Council forms are advisory only. The presence or absence of a particular reference is not a ground for rejecting a form otherwise applicable in the action or proceeding for the purpose presented. *(Adopted, eff. Jan. 1, 2007.)*

Research References

2 Witkin Cal. Proc. 5th Courts § 398, (S 398) in General.

Rule 1.41. Proofs of service on forms

Proofs of service are included on some Judicial Council forms solely for the convenience of the parties. A party may use an included proof of service or any other proper proof of service. *(Adopted, eff. Jan. 1, 2007.)*

Research References

2 Witkin Cal. Proc. 5th Courts § 398, (S 398) in General.

Rule 1.42. Forms not to be rejected

A court must not reject for filing a Judicial Council form for any of the following reasons:

(1) The form lacks the preprinted title and address of the court;

(2) The form lacks the name of the clerk;

(3) The preprinted title and address of another court or its clerk's name is legibly modified;

(4) The form lacks the court's local form number;

(5) The form lacks any other material added by a court, unless the material is required by the Judicial Council;

(6) The form is printed by a publisher or another court;

(7) The form is imprinted with the name or symbol of the publisher, unless the name or symbol replaces or obscures any material on the printed form;

(8) The form is legibly and obviously modified to correct a code section number or to comply with the law under which the form is filed; or

(9) The form is not the latest version of the form adopted or approved by the Judicial Council. *(Adopted, eff. Jan. 1, 2007. As amended, eff. Jan. 1, 2007.)*

Research References

2 Witkin Cal. Proc. 5th Courts § 398, (S 398) in General.
4 Witkin Cal. Proc. 5th Pleading § 13, in General.

Rule 1.43. Legibility

A Judicial Council form filed must be a true copy of the original form and must be as legible as a printed form. *(Adopted, eff. Jan. 1, 2007.)*

Research References

2 Witkin Cal. Proc. 5th Courts § 399, (S 399) Format Requirements.

Rule 1.44. Electronically produced forms

A party or attorney may file a duplicate of a Judicial Council form produced by a computer and a printer or similar device with a resolution of at least 300 dots per inch. *(Adopted, eff. Jan. 1, 2007.)*

Research References

2 Witkin Cal. Proc. 5th Courts § 399, (S 399) Format Requirements.

Rule 1.45. Judicial Council pleading forms

(a) Pleading forms

The forms listed under the "Pleading" heading on the list of Judicial Council forms in Appendix A to the California Rules of Court are approved by the Judicial Council.

(b) Cause of action forms

Any approved cause of action form may be attached to any approved form of complaint or cross-complaint.

(c) Other causes of action

A cause of action for which no form has been approved may be prepared in the format prescribed by the rules in chapter 1 of division 2 of title 2 and attached to any approved form of complaint or cross-complaint. Each paragraph within a cause of action must be numbered consecutively beginning with one. Each paragraph number must be preceded with one or more identifying letters derived from the title of the cause of action. *(Formerly Rule 982.1 adopted eff. Jan. 1, 1982. As amended, eff. July 1, 1999. Renumbered Rule 201.2 and amended, eff. Jan. 1, 2003. As amended, eff. Jan. 1, 2005. Renumbered Rule 1.45 and amended, eff. Jan. 1, 2007. As amended, eff. July 1, 2008.)*

Research References

2 Witkin Cal. Proc. 5th Courts § 189, (S 189) Rules Applicable to All Courts.
2 Witkin Cal. Proc. 5th Courts § 398, (S 398) in General.
4 Witkin Cal. Proc. 5th Pleading § 382, (S 382) Judicial Council Forms.

Rule 1.51. California Law Enforcement Telecommunications System (CLETS) information form

(a) *Confidential CLETS Information* form to be submitted to the court

A person requesting protective orders under Code of Civil Procedure section 527.6, 527.8, or 527.85; Family Code section

6320; or Welfare and Institutions Code section 213.5 or 15657.03 must submit to the court with the request a completed *Confidential CLETS Information* form.

(b) Confidentiality of the form

The *Confidential CLETS Information* form is confidential, and access to the information on the form is limited to the persons listed in (c).

(c) Access to information on the form

The *Confidential CLETS Information* form must not be included in the court file. After the form is submitted to the court, only the following persons may have access to the information on the form:

(1) Authorized court personnel; and

(2) Law enforcement and other personnel authorized by the California Department of Justice to transmit or receive CLETS information.

(d) Amendment of the form

A person requesting protective orders or the person's attorney may submit an amended *Confidential CLETS Information* form as a matter of right to provide updated or more complete and accurate information.

(e) Retention and destruction of the form

(1) When a *Confidential CLETS Information* form is submitted to the court, the court, if a temporary restraining order or order after hearing is entered, may:

(A) Transmit the form to a law enforcement agency for entry into CLETS and not retain any copy; or

(B) Enter the information on the form into CLETS itself and promptly destroy the form or delete it from its records.

(2) If no temporary restraining order or order after hearing is entered, the court may promptly destroy the form or delete it from its records.

(3) Until the court has completed (1) or (2), the form must be retained in a secure manner that prevents access to the information on the form except to those persons identified in (c). *(Adopted, eff. Jan. 1, 2011.)*

Research References

6 Witkin Cal. Proc. 5th Provisional Remedies § 315A, (S 315A) (New)-Abuse of Elder or Dependent Adult.
6 Witkin Cal. Proc. 5th Provisional Remedies § 330D, (S 330D) (New)-Petition, Service, and Response.
11 Witkin, California Summary 10th Husband and Wife § 382, in General.
6 Witkin, California Summary 10th Torts § 1686, Statutory Remedies.

Chapter 5

ACCOMMODATIONS

Rule
1.100. Requests for accommodations by persons with disabilities.

Rule 1.100. Requests for accommodations by persons with disabilities

(a) Definitions

As used in this rule:

(1) "Persons with disabilities" means individuals covered by California Civil Code section 51 et seq.; the Americans With Disabilities Act of 1990 (42 U.S.C. § 12101 et seq.); or other applicable state and federal laws. This definition includes persons who have a physical or mental impairment that limits one or more of the major life activities, have a record of such an impairment, or are regarded as having such an impairment.

(2) "Applicant" means any lawyer, party, witness, juror, or other person with an interest in attending any proceeding before any court of this state.

(3) "Accommodations" means actions that result in court services, programs, or activities being readily accessible to and usable by persons with disabilities. Accommodations may include making reasonable modifications in policies, practices, and procedures; furnishing, at no charge, to persons with disabilities, auxiliary aids and services, equipment, devices, materials in alternative formats, readers, or certified interpreters for persons with hearing impairments; relocating services or programs to accessible facilities; or providing services at alternative sites. Although not required where other actions are effective in providing access to court services, programs, or activities, alteration of existing facilities by the responsible entity may be an accommodation.

(b) Policy

It is the policy of the courts of this state to ensure that persons with disabilities have equal and full access to the judicial system. To ensure access to the courts for persons with disabilities, each superior and appellate court must delegate at least one person to be the ADA coordinator, also known as the access coordinator, or designee to address requests for accommodations. This rule is not intended to impose limitations or to invalidate the remedies, rights, and procedures accorded to persons with disabilities under state or federal law.

(c) Process for requesting accommodations

The process for requesting accommodations is as follows:

(1) Requests for accommodations under this rule may be presented ex parte on a form approved by the Judicial Council, in another written format, or orally. Requests must be forwarded to the ADA coordinator, also known as the access coordinator, or designee, within the time frame provided in (c)(3).

(2) Requests for accommodations must include a description of the accommodation sought, along with a statement of the impairment that necessitates the accommodation. The court, in its discretion, may require the applicant to provide additional information about the impairment.

(3) Requests for accommodations must be made as far in advance as possible, and in any event must be made no fewer than 5 court days before the requested implementation date. The court may, in its discretion, waive this requirement.

(4) The court must keep confidential all information of the applicant concerning the request for accommodation, unless confidentiality is waived in writing by the applicant or disclosure is required by law. The applicant's identity and confidential information may not be disclosed to the public or to persons other than those involved in the accommodation process. Confidential information includes all medical information pertaining to the applicant, and all oral or written communication from the applicant concerning the request for accommodation.

(d) Permitted communication

Communications under this rule must address only the accommodation requested by the applicant and must not address, in any manner, the subject matter or merits of the proceedings before the court.

(e) Response to accommodation request

The court must respond to a request for accommodation as follows:

(1) In determining whether to grant an accommodation request or provide an appropriate alternative accommodation, the court must consider, but is not limited by, California Civil

Code section 51 et seq., the provisions of the Americans With Disabilities Act of 1990 (42 U.S.C. § 12101, et seq.), and other applicable state and federal laws.

(2) The court must promptly inform the applicant of the determination to grant or deny an accommodation request. If the accommodation request is denied in whole or in part, the response must be in writing. On request of the applicant, the court may also provide an additional response in an alternative format. The response to the applicant must indicate:

(A) Whether the request for accommodation is granted or denied, in whole or in part, or an alternative accommodation is granted;

(B) If the request for accommodation is denied, in whole or in part, the reason therefor;

(C) The nature of any accommodation to be provided;

(D) The duration of any accommodation to be provided; and

(E) If the response is in writing, the date the response was delivered in person or sent to the applicant.

(f) Denial of accommodation request

A request for accommodation may be denied only when the court determines that:

(1) The applicant has failed to satisfy the requirements of this rule;

(2) The requested accommodation would create an undue financial or administrative burden on the court; or

(3) The requested accommodation would fundamentally alter the nature of the service, program, or activity.

(g) Review procedure

(1) If the determination to grant or deny a request for accommodation is made by nonjudicial court personnel, an applicant or any participant in the proceeding may submit a written request for review of that determination to the presiding judge or designated judicial officer. The request for review must be submitted within 10 days of the date the response under (e)(2) was delivered in person or sent.

(2) If the determination to grant or deny a request for accommodation is made by a presiding judge or another judicial officer, an applicant or any participant in the proceeding may file a petition for a writ of mandate under rules 8.485–8.493 or 8.930–8.936 in the appropriate reviewing court. The petition must be filed within 10 days of the date the response under (e)(2) was delivered in person or sent to the petitioner. For purposes of this rule, only those participants in the proceeding who were notified by the court of the determination to grant or deny the request for accommodation are considered real parties in interest in a writ proceeding. The petition for the writ must be served on the respondent court and any real party in interest as defined in this rule.

(3) The confidentiality of all information of the applicant concerning the request for accommodation and review under (g)(1) or (2) must be maintained as required under (c)(4).

(h) Duration of accommodations

The accommodation by the court must be provided for the duration indicated in the response to the request for accommodation and must remain in effect for the period specified. The court may provide an accommodation for an indefinite period of time, for a limited period of time, or for a particular matter or appearance. *(Formerly Rule 989.3, adopted, eff. Jan. 1, 1996. As amended, eff. Jan. 1, 2006. Renumbered Rule 1.100 and amended, eff. Jan. 1, 2007. As amended, eff. Jan. 1, 2010.)*

Advisory Committee Comment

Subdivision (g)(2). Which court is the "appropriate reviewing court" under this rule depends on the court in which the accommodation decision is made and the nature of the underlying case. If the accommodation decision is made by a superior court judicial officer and the underlying case is a limited civil, misdemeanor, or infraction case, the appropriate reviewing court is the appellate division of the superior court. If the accommodation decision is made by a superior court judicial officer and the case is anything other than a limited civil, misdemeanor, or infraction case, such as a family law, unlimited civil, or felony case, the appropriate reviewing court is the Court of Appeal. If the accommodation decision is made by a judicial officer of the Court of Appeal, the appropriate reviewing court is the California Supreme Court.

Research References

Rutter, Cal. Practice Guide: Civil Appeals & Writs Ch. 8-C, C. Standards of Appellate Review.

Rutter, Cal. Practice Guide: Civil Appeals & Writs Ch. 8-E, E. Limits on Reversal or Modification-"Prejudicial Error" Rule.

Rutter, Cal. Practice Guide: Civil Appeals & Writs Ch. 15-C, C. Statutory Writs.

Rutter, Cal. Practice Guide: Civ. Pro. Before Trial Ch. 9(I)-D, D. Hearing.

Rutter, Cal. Practice Guide: Civil Trials & Evidence Ch. 1-K, K. Continuance Motions.

Rutter, Cal. Practice Guide: Civil Trials & Evidence Ch. 12-D, D. Other Motions During Trial.

Rutter, Cal. Practice Guide: Personal Injury Ch. 9-A, A. Assignment to Trial.

2 Witkin Cal. Proc. 5th Courts § 32, (S 32) Accommodation of Persons With Disabilities.

2 Witkin Cal. Proc. 5th Courts § 189, (S 189) Rules Applicable to All Courts.

Chapter 6

PUBLIC ACCESS TO COURT PROCEEDINGS

Rule

1.150. Photographing, recording, and broadcasting in court.

Rule 1.150. Photographing, recording, and broadcasting in court

(a) Introduction

The judiciary is responsible for ensuring the fair and equal administration of justice. The judiciary adjudicates controversies, both civil and criminal, in accordance with established legal procedures in the calmness and solemnity of the courtroom. Photographing, recording, and broadcasting of courtroom proceedings may be permitted as circumscribed in this rule if executed in a manner that ensures that the fairness and dignity of the proceedings are not adversely affected. This rule does not create a presumption for or against granting permission to photograph, record, or broadcast court proceedings.

(b) Definitions

As used in this rule:

(1) "Media coverage" means any photographing, recording, or broadcasting of court proceedings by the media using television, radio, photographic, or recording equipment.

(2) "Media" or "media agency" means any person or organization engaging in news gathering or reporting and includes any newspaper, radio or television station or network, news service, magazine, trade paper, in-house publication, professional journal, or other news-reporting or news-gathering agency.

(3) "Court" means the courtroom at issue, the courthouse, and its entrances and exits.

Ct. Rules

(4) "Judge" means the judicial officer or officers assigned to or presiding at the proceeding, except as provided in (e)(1) if no judge has been assigned.

(5) "Photographing" means recording a likeness, regardless of the method used, including by digital or photographic methods. As used in this rule, photographing does not include drawings or sketchings of the court proceedings.

(6) "Recording" means the use of any analog or digital device to aurally or visually preserve court proceedings. As used in this rule, recording does not include handwritten notes on the court record, whether by court reporter or by digital or analog preservation.

(7) "Broadcasting" means a visual or aural transmission or signal, by any method, of the court proceedings, including any electronic transmission or transmission by sound waves.

(c) Photographing, recording, and broadcasting prohibited

Except as provided in this rule, court proceedings may not be photographed, recorded, or broadcast. This rule does not prohibit courts from photographing or videotaping sessions for judicial education or publications and is not intended to apply to closed-circuit television broadcasts solely within the courthouse or between court facilities if the broadcasts are controlled by the court and court personnel.

(d) Personal recording devices

The judge may permit inconspicuous personal recording devices to be used by persons in a courtroom to make sound recordings as personal notes of the proceedings. A person proposing to use a recording device must obtain advance permission from the judge. The recordings must not be used for any purpose other than as personal notes.

(e) Media coverage

Media coverage may be permitted only on written order of the judge as provided in this subdivision. The judge in his or her discretion may permit, refuse, limit, or terminate media coverage. This rule does not otherwise limit or restrict the right of the media to cover and report court proceedings.

(1) *Request for order*

The media may request an order on *Media Request to Photograph, Record, or Broadcast* (form MC–500). The form must be filed at least five court days before the portion of the proceeding to be covered unless good cause is shown. A completed, proposed order on *Order on Media Request to Permit Coverage* (form MC–510) must be filed with the request. The judge assigned to the proceeding must rule on the request. If no judge has been assigned, the request will be submitted to the judge supervising the calendar department, and thereafter be ruled on by the judge assigned to the proceeding. The clerk must promptly notify the parties that a request has been filed.

(2) *Hearing on request*

The judge may hold a hearing on the request or may rule on the request without a hearing.

(3) *Factors to be considered by the judge*

In ruling on the request, the judge is to consider the following factors:

(A) The importance of maintaining public trust and confidence in the judicial system;

(B) The importance of promoting public access to the judicial system;

(C) The parties' support of or opposition to the request;

(D) The nature of the case;

(E) The privacy rights of all participants in the proceeding, including witnesses, jurors, and victims;

(F) The effect on any minor who is a party, prospective witness, victim, or other participant in the proceeding;

(G) The effect on the parties' ability to select a fair and unbiased jury;

(H) The effect on any ongoing law enforcement activity in the case;

(I) The effect on any unresolved identification issues;

(J) The effect on any subsequent proceedings in the case;

(K) The effect of coverage on the willingness of witnesses to cooperate, including the risk that coverage will engender threats to the health or safety of any witness;

(L) The effect on excluded witnesses who would have access to the televised testimony of prior witnesses;

(M) The scope of the coverage and whether partial coverage might unfairly influence or distract the jury;

(N) The difficulty of jury selection if a mistrial is declared;

(O) The security and dignity of the court;

(P) Undue administrative or financial burden to the court or participants;

(Q) The interference with neighboring courtrooms;

(R) The maintenance of the orderly conduct of the proceeding; and

(S) Any other factor the judge deems relevant.

(4) *Order permitting media coverage*

The judge ruling on the request to permit media coverage is not required to make findings or a statement of decision. The order may incorporate any local rule or order of the presiding or supervising judge regulating media activity outside of the courtroom. The judge may condition the order permitting media coverage on the media agency's agreement to pay any increased court-incurred costs resulting from the permitted media coverage (for example, for additional court security or utility service). Each media agency is responsible for ensuring that all its media personnel who cover the court proceeding know and follow the provisions of the court order and this rule.

(5) *Modified order*

The order permitting media coverage may be modified or terminated on the judge's own motion or on application to the judge without the necessity of a prior hearing or written findings. Notice of the application and any modification or termination ordered under the application must be given to the parties and each media agency permitted by the previous order to cover the proceeding.

(6) *Prohibited coverage*

The judge may not permit media coverage of the following:

(A) Proceedings held in chambers;

(B) Proceedings closed to the public;

(C) Jury selection;

(D) Jurors or spectators; or

(E) Conferences between an attorney and a client, witness, or aide; between attorneys; or between counsel and the judge at the bench.

(7) *Equipment and personnel*

The judge may require media agencies to demonstrate that proposed personnel and equipment comply with this rule. The judge may specify the placement of media personnel and equipment to permit reasonable media coverage without disruption of the proceedings.

(8) *Normal requirements for media coverage of proceedings*

Unless the judge in his or her discretion orders otherwise, the following requirements apply to media coverage of court proceedings:

(A) One television camera and one still photographer will be permitted.

(B) The equipment used may not produce distracting sound or light. Signal lights or devices to show when equipment is operating may not be visible.

(C) An order permitting or requiring modification of existing sound or lighting systems is deemed to require that the modifications be installed, maintained, and removed without public expense or disruption of proceedings.

(D) Microphones and wiring must be unobtrusively located in places approved by the judge and must be operated by one person.

(E) Operators may not move equipment or enter or leave the courtroom while the court is in session, or otherwise cause a distraction.

(F) Equipment or clothing must not bear the insignia or marking of a media agency.

(9) *Media pooling*

If two or more media agencies of the same type request media coverage of a proceeding, they must file a joint statement of agreed arrangements. If they are unable to agree, the judge may deny media coverage by that type of media agency.

(f) Sanctions

Any violation of this rule or an order made under this rule is an unlawful interference with the proceedings of the court and may be the basis for an order terminating media coverage, a citation for contempt of court, or an order imposing monetary or other sanctions as provided by law. *(Formerly Rule 980, adopted, eff. July 1, 1984. As amended, eff. Jan. 1, 1997; Jan. 1, 2006. Renumbered Rule 1.150 and amended, eff. Jan. 1, 2007.)*

Research References

Rutter, Cal. Practice Guide: Civil Appeals & Writs Ch. 5-B, B. Types of Motions, Applications and Requests.

Rutter, Cal. Practice Guide: Civ. Pro. Before Trial Ch. 12(II)-A, A. Mandatory Settlement Conference ("MSC").

Rutter, Cal. Practice Guide: Civil Trials & Evidence Ch. 4-I, I. Other Motions at Final Status Conference.

Rutter, Cal. Practice Guide: Civil Trials & Evidence Ch. 10-E, E. Preparing for Cross-Examination-A Checklist.

Rutter, Cal. Practice Guide: Prof. Responsibility Ch. 11-I, I. Trial Proceedings.

2 Witkin Cal. Proc. 5th Courts § 37, (S 37) Scope of Current Restrictions.

2 Witkin Cal. Proc. 5th Courts § 38, (S 38) Order Limiting Coverage.

2 Witkin Cal. Proc. 5th Courts § 189, (S 189) Rules Applicable to All Courts.

Chapter 7

FORM AND FORMAT OF PAPERS

Rule
1.200.   Format of citations.

Rule 1.200.   Format of citations

Citations to cases and other authorities in all documents filed in the courts must be in the style established by either the *California Style Manual* or *The Bluebook: A Uniform System of Citation*, at the option of the party filing the document. The same style must be used consistently throughout the document. *(Adopted, eff. Jan. 1, 2008.)*

Research References

Rutter, Cal. Practice Guide: Civil Appeals & Writs Ch. 9-B, B. Approaches to Briefwriting.

Rutter, Cal. Practice Guide: Civ. Pro. Before Trial Ch. 9(I)-B, B. Preparing and Filing Motions.

2 Witkin Cal. Proc. 5th Courts § 189, (S 189) Rules Applicable to All Courts.

5 Witkin Cal. Proc. 5th Pleading § 980, (S 980) Supporting Memorandum.

Title 2

TRIAL COURT RULES

Division 1

GENERAL PROVISIONS

Chapter 1

TITLE AND APPLICATION

Rule
2.1.   Title.
2.2.   Application.

Rule 2.1.   Title

The rules in this title may be referred to as the Trial Court Rules. *(Adopted, eff. Jan. 1, 2007.)*

Research References

2 Witkin Cal. Proc. 5th Courts § 166, Consolidation of Municipal and Superior Court.

2 Witkin Cal. Proc. 5th Courts § 190, (S 190) Trial Court Rules.

Rule 2.2.   Application

The Trial Court Rules apply to all cases in the superior courts unless otherwise specified by a rule or statute. *(Formerly Rule 200, adopted, eff. Jan. 1, 2001. As amended, eff. Jan. 1, 2002; Jan. 1, 2003. Renumbered Rule 2.2 and amended, eff. Jan. 1, 2007.)*

Research References

2 Witkin Cal. Proc. 5th Courts § 166, Consolidation of Municipal and Superior Court.

2 Witkin Cal. Proc. 5th Courts § 190, (S 190) Trial Court Rules.

Chapter 2

DEFINITIONS AND SCOPE OF RULES

Rule
2.3.   Definitions.

Ct. Rules

Rule 2.3. Definitions

As used in the Trial Court Rules, unless the context or subject matter otherwise requires:

(1) "Court" means the superior court;

(2) "Papers" includes all documents, except exhibits and copies of exhibits, that are offered for filing in any case, but does not include Judicial Council and local court forms, records on appeal in limited civil cases, or briefs filed in appellate divisions; and

(3) "Written," "writing," "typewritten," and "typewriting" include other methods equivalent in legibility to typewriting. *(Adopted, eff. Jan. 1, 2007.)*

Research References

2 Witkin Cal. Proc. 5th Courts § 190, (S 190) Trial Court Rules.
4 Witkin Cal. Proc. 5th Pleading § 13, in General.

Chapter 3

TIMING

Rule
2.20.   Application for an order extending time.

Rule 2.20. Application for an order extending time

(a) Application—to whom made

An application for an order extending the time within which any act is required by law to be done must be heard and determined by the judge before whom the matter is pending; provided, however, that in case of the inability, death, or absence of such judge, the application may be heard and determined by another judge of the same court.

(b) Disclosure of previous extensions

An application for an order extending time must disclose in writing the nature of the case and what extensions, if any, have previously been granted by order of court or stipulation of counsel.

(c) Filing and service

An order extending time must be filed immediately and copies served within 24 hours after the making of the order or within such other time as may be fixed by the court. *(Formerly Rule 235, adopted, eff. Jan. 1, 1949. Renumbered Rule 2.20 and amended, eff. Jan. 1, 2007.)*

Research References

Rutter, Cal. Practice Guide: Civ. Pro. Before Trial Ch. 9(I)-F, F. Ex Parte Motions.
2 Witkin Cal. Proc. 5th Courts § 190, (S 190) Trial Court Rules.
4 Witkin Cal. Proc. 5th Pleading § 12, Procedure.
6 Witkin Cal. Proc. 5th Proceedings Without Trial § 18, Extension by Stipulation or Court Order.
7 Witkin Cal. Proc. 5th Trial § 393, (S 393) in General.

Chapter 4

SANCTIONS

Rule
2.30.   Sanctions for rules violations in civil cases.

Rule 2.30. Sanctions for rules violations in civil cases

(a) Application

This sanctions rule applies to the rules in the California Rules of Court relating to general civil cases, unlawful detainer cases, probate proceedings, civil proceedings in the appellate division of the superior court, and small claims cases.

(b) Sanctions

In addition to any other sanctions permitted by law, the court may order a person, after written notice and an opportunity to be heard, to pay reasonable monetary sanctions to the court or an aggrieved person, or both, for failure without good cause to comply with the applicable rules. For the purposes of this rule, "person" means a party, a party's attorney, a witness, and an insurer or any other individual or entity whose consent is necessary for the disposition of the case. If a failure to comply with an applicable rule is the responsibility of counsel and not of the party, any penalty must be imposed on counsel and must not adversely affect the party's cause of action or defense thereto.

(c) Notice and procedure

Sanctions must not be imposed under this rule except on noticed motion by the party seeking sanctions or on the court's own motion after the court has provided notice and an opportunity to be heard. A party's motion for sanctions must (1) state the applicable rule that has been violated, (2) describe the specific conduct that is alleged to have violated the rule, and (3) identify the attorney, law firm, party, witness, or other person against whom sanctions are sought. The court on its own motion may issue an order to show cause that must (1) state the applicable rule that has been violated, (2) describe the specific conduct that appears to have violated the rule, and (3) direct the attorney, law firm, party, witness, or other person to show cause why sanctions should not be imposed against them for violation of the rule.

(d) Award of expenses

In addition to the sanctions awardable under (b), the court may order the person who has violated an applicable rule to pay to the party aggrieved by the violation that party's reasonable expenses, including reasonable attorney's fees and costs, incurred in connection with the motion for sanctions or the order to show cause.

(e) Order

An order imposing sanctions must be in writing and must recite in detail the conduct or circumstances justifying the order. *(Formerly Rule 227, adopted, eff. Jan. 1, 1985. As amended, eff. Jan. 1, 1994; July 1, 2001; Jan. 1, 2004. Renumbered Rule 2.30 and amended, eff. Jan. 1, 2007.)*

Research References

Rutter, Cal. Practice Guide: A.D.R. Ch. 4-D, D. Mandatory Settlement Conferences.
Rutter, Cal. Practice Guide: A.D.R. Ch. 6-B, B. Temporary Judges.
Rutter, Cal. Practice Guide: A.D.R. Ch. 6-C, C. Referees.
Rutter, Cal. Practice Guide: Civil Appeals & Writs Ch. 16-A, A. Introduction.
Rutter, Cal. Practice Guide: Civ. Pro. Before Trial Ch. 6-B, B. Complaints.
Rutter, Cal. Practice Guide: Civ. Pro. Before Trial Ch. 11-B, B. Involuntary Dismissals.
Rutter, Cal. Practice Guide: Civ. Pro. Before Trial Ch. 12(II)-A, A. Mandatory Settlement Conference ("MSC").
Rutter, Cal. Practice Guide: Civ. Pro. Before Trial Ch. 12(II)-D, D. Plaintiff's Duties Upon Settlement.
Rutter, Cal. Practice Guide: Civ. Pro. Before Trial Ch. 9(III)-A, A. Sources of Sanctions Power.
Rutter, Cal. Practice Guide: Civ. Pro. Before Trial Ch. 9(III)-D, D. Other Sanctions Statutes and Rules.
Rutter, Cal. Practice Guide: Civil Trials & Evidence Ch. 2-D, D. Securing Trial by Jury.
Rutter, Cal. Practice Guide: Enforcing Judgments/Debts Ch. 3-C, C. Prelawsuit Considerations.
Rutter, Cal. Practice Guide: Personal Injury Ch. 3-A, A. Introduction.

Rutter, Cal. Practice Guide: Personal Injury Ch. 4-F, F. Court-Conducted Settlement Proceedings.

Rutter, Cal. Practice Guide: Personal Injury Ch. 4-G, G. Concluding and Enforcing Settlement.

Rutter, Cal. Practice Guide: Personal Injury Ch. 8-A, A. Case Management.

Rutter, Cal. Practice Guide: Personal Injury Ch. 3-A , Outline a.

Rutter, Cal. Practice Guide: Prof. Responsibility Ch. 1-A, A. Sources of Regulation of Practice of Law in California-Overview.

Rutter, Cal. Practice Guide: Prof. Responsibility Ch. 3-D, D. Authority of Client vs. Authority of Attorney.

Rutter, Cal. Practice Guide: Prof. Responsibility Ch. 8-E, E. Consequences of Improper Advocacy.

2 Witkin Cal. Proc. 5th Courts § 177, (S 177) Imposition of Money Sanctions.

2 Witkin Cal. Proc. 5th Courts § 187, (S 187) in General.

2 Witkin Cal. Proc. 5th Courts § 190, (S 190) Trial Court Rules.

2 Witkin Cal. Proc. 5th Courts § 264, in General.

4 Witkin Cal. Proc. 5th Pleading § 18, Other Requirements.

6 Witkin Cal. Proc. 5th Proceedings Without Trial § 55, (S 55) Statutory Authorization.

6 Witkin Cal. Proc. 5th Proceedings Without Trial § 127, Plaintiff's Duties After Settlement.

7 Witkin Cal. Proc. 5th Trial § 37, (S 37) Procedural Framework.

7 Witkin Cal. Proc. 5th Trial § 38, (S 38) Trial Court Delay Reduction Act.

7 Witkin Cal. Proc. 5th Trial § 58, (S 58) in General.

7 Witkin Cal. Proc. 5th Trial § 59, (S 59) Judicial Council Rules.

7 Witkin Cal. Proc. 5th Trial § 63, (S 63) Imposition of Ultimate Sanction in First Instance.

7 Witkin Cal. Proc. 5th Trial § 226, (S 226) in General.

Division 2

PAPERS AND FORMS TO BE FILED

Chapter 1

PAPERS

Rule

2.100.   Form and format of papers presented for filing in the trial courts.

2.101.   Use of recycled paper; certification by attorney or party.

2.102.   One–sided paper.

2.103.   Quality, color, and size of paper.

2.104.   Printing; type size.

2.105.   Type style.

2.106.   Color of print.

2.107.   Margins.

2.108.   Spacing and numbering of lines.

2.109.   Page numbering.

2.110.   Footer.

2.111.   Format of first page.

2.112.   Separate causes of action, counts, and defenses.

2.113.   Binding.

2.114.   Exhibits.

2.115.   Hole punching.

2.116.   Changes on face of paper.

2.117.   Conformed copies of papers.

2.118.   Acceptance of papers for filing.

2.119.   Exceptions for forms.

Research References

Rutter, Cal. Practice Guide: Civ. Pro. Before Trial Ch. 6-B, B. Complaints.

Rutter, Cal. Practice Guide: Civ. Pro. Before Trial Ch. 6-C, C. Answer.

Rutter, Cal. Practice Guide: Civ. Pro. Before Trial Ch. 6-D, D. Cross-Complaint.

Rutter, Cal. Practice Guide: Civ. Pro. Before Trial Ch. 9(I)-F, F. Ex Parte Motions.

Rutter, Cal. Practice Guide: Civil Trials & Evidence Ch. 1-G, G. Preparing Trial Notebook.

Rutter, Cal. Practice Guide: Civil Trials & Evidence Ch. 4-F, F. Motions in Limine.

Rutter, Cal. Practice Guide: Civil Trials & Evidence Ch. 14-C, C. Procedural Requirements.

Rutter, Cal. Practice Guide: Civil Trials & Evidence Ch. 14-D, D. Preparing Jury Instructions.

Rutter, Cal. Practice Guide: Personal Injury Ch. 5-B, B. When to Sue-Statute of Limitations.

Rutter, Cal. Practice Guide: Personal Injury Ch. 8-D, D. Final Preparation (One Month Before Trial).

Rutter, Cal. Practice Guide: Real Prop. Transactions Ch. 11-I, I. Lis Pendens.

2 Witkin Cal. Proc. 5th Courts § 190, (S 190) Trial Court Rules.

2 Witkin Cal. Proc. 5th Courts § 398, (S 398) in General.

4 Witkin Cal. Proc. 5th Pleading § 13, in General.

4 Witkin Cal. Proc. 5th Pleading § 20, Fax Filing.

4 Witkin Cal. Proc. 5th Pleading § 382, (S 382) Judicial Council Forms.

4 Witkin Cal. Proc. 5th Pleading § 470, Nature of Pleading.

6 Witkin Cal. Proc. 5th Proceedings Without Trial § 9, Formal Requisites.

7 Witkin Cal. Proc. 5th Trial § 263, Formal Requisites.

Rule 2.100.   Form and format of papers presented for filing in the trial courts

(a) Preemption of local rules

The Judicial Council has preempted local rules relating to the form and format of papers to be filed in the trial courts. No trial court, or any division or branch of a trial court, may enact or enforce any local rule concerning the form or format of papers.

(b) Rules prescribe form and format

The rules in this chapter prescribe the form and format of papers to be filed in the trial courts. *(Formerly Rule 201, as amended, eff. April 1, 1962; May 1, 1962; July 1, 1964; Jan. 1, 1966; July 1, 1969; July 1, 1971; Jan. 1, 1973; July 1, 1974; Jan. 1, 1976; Jan. 1, 1978; May 6, 1978; Jan. 1, 1984; April 1, 1990; July 1, 1990; Jan. 1, 1992; July 1, 1992; Jan. 1, 1993; July 1, 1993; Jan. 1, 1994; Jan. 1, 1998; Jan. 1, 1999; July 1, 1999; July 1, 2000; Jan. 1, 2001; Jan. 1, 2002; Jan. 1, 2003; Jan. 1, 2006. Renumbered Rule 2.100 and amended, eff. Jan. 1, 2007.)*

Rule 2.101.   Use of recycled paper; certification by attorney or party

(a) Use of recycled paper

Recycled paper must be used for the following:

(1) All original papers filed with the court and all copies of papers, documents, and exhibits, whether filed with the court or served on other parties; and

(2) The original record on appeal from a limited civil case, any brief filed with the court in a matter to be heard in the appellate division, and all copies of such documents, whether filed with the court or served on other parties.

(b) Certification

Whenever recycled paper must be used under the rules in this chapter, the attorney, party, or other person filing or serving a document certifies, by the act of filing or service, that the document was produced on paper purchased as recycled. *(Adopted, eff. Jan. 1, 2007.)*

Ct. Rules

Research References

Rutter, Cal. Practice Guide: Civ. Pro. Before Trial Ch. 6-B, B. Complaints.

Rutter, Cal. Practice Guide: Civ. Pro. Before Trial Ch. 9(I)-B, B. Preparing and Filing Motions.

Rutter, Cal. Practice Guide: Civil Trials & Evidence Ch. 14-D, D. Preparing Jury Instructions.

Rutter, Cal. Practice Guide: Insurance Litigation Ch. 14-A, A. The California Regulator (*).

2 Witkin Cal. Proc. 5th Courts § 30, (S 30) Use of Recycled Paper.

4 Witkin Cal. Proc. 5th Pleading § 14, Paper.

Rule 2.102.   One–sided paper

On papers, only one side of each page may be used. *(Adopted, eff. Jan. 1, 2007.)*

Research References

4 Witkin Cal. Proc. 5th Pleading § 15, Printing.

Rule 2.103.   Quality, color, and size of paper

All papers must be on opaque, unglazed paper, white or unbleached, of standard quality not less than 20–pound weight, 8½ by 11 inches. *(Adopted, eff. Jan. 1, 2007.)*

Research References

Rutter, Cal. Practice Guide: Civ. Pro. Before Trial Ch. 6-B, B. Complaints.

Rutter, Cal. Practice Guide: Civ. Pro. Before Trial Ch. 9(I)-B, B. Preparing and Filing Motions.

Rutter, Cal. Practice Guide: Civil Trials & Evidence Ch. 14-D, D. Preparing Jury Instructions.

4 Witkin Cal. Proc. 5th Pleading § 14, Paper.

Rule 2.104.   Printing; type size

All papers must be printed or typewritten or be prepared by a photocopying or other duplication process that will produce clear and permanent copies equally as legible as printing in type not smaller than 12 points. *(Adopted, eff. Jan. 1, 2007.)*

Research References

Rutter, Cal. Practice Guide: Civ. Pro. Before Trial Ch. 6-C, C. Answer.

4 Witkin Cal. Proc. 5th Pleading § 15, Printing.

Rule 2.105.   Type style

The typeface must be essentially equivalent to Courier, Times New Roman, or Arial. *(Adopted, eff. Jan. 1, 2007.)*

Research References

4 Witkin Cal. Proc. 5th Pleading § 15, Printing.

Rule 2.106.   Color of print

The color of print must be black or blue-black. *(Adopted, eff. Jan. 1, 2007.)*

Research References

Rutter, Cal. Practice Guide: Civ. Pro. Before Trial Ch. 6-B, B. Complaints.

Rutter, Cal. Practice Guide: Civil Trials & Evidence Ch. 14-D, D. Preparing Jury Instructions.

4 Witkin Cal. Proc. 5th Pleading § 15, Printing.

Rule 2.107.   Margins

The left margin of each page must be at least one inch from the left edge of the paper and the right margin at least 1/2 inch from the right edge of the paper. *(Adopted, eff. Jan. 1, 2007.)*

Research References

4 Witkin Cal. Proc. 5th Pleading § 15, Printing.

Rule 2.108.   Spacing and numbering of lines

The spacing and numbering of lines on a page must be as follows:

(1) The lines on each page must be one and one-half spaced or double-spaced and numbered consecutively.

(2) Descriptions of real property may be single-spaced.

(3) Footnotes, quotations, and printed forms of corporate surety bonds and undertakings may be single-spaced and have unnumbered lines if they comply generally with the space requirements of rule 2.111.

(4) Line numbers must be placed at the left margin and separated from the text of the paper by a vertical column of space at least 1/5 inch wide or a single or double vertical line. Each line number must be aligned with a line of type, or the line numbers must be evenly spaced vertically on the page. Line numbers must be consecutively numbered, beginning with the number 1 on each page. There must be at least three line numbers for every vertical inch on the page. *(Adopted, eff. Jan. 1, 2007.)*

Research References

Rutter, Cal. Practice Guide: Civ. Pro. Before Trial Ch. 6-B, B. Complaints.

Rutter, Cal. Practice Guide: Civ. Pro. Before Trial Ch. 9(I)-B, B. Preparing and Filing Motions.

Rutter, Cal. Practice Guide: Insurance Litigation Ch. 14-A, A. The California Regulator (*).

4 Witkin Cal. Proc. 5th Pleading § 15, Printing.

4 Witkin Cal. Proc. 5th Pleading § 16, Numbering.

Rule 2.109.   Page numbering

Each page must be numbered consecutively at the bottom unless a rule provides otherwise for a particular type of document. *(Adopted, eff. Jan. 1, 2007.)*

Research References

Rutter, Cal. Practice Guide: Civ. Pro. Before Trial Ch. 6-B, B. Complaints.

Rutter, Cal. Practice Guide: Civ. Pro. Before Trial Ch. 6-C, C. Answer.

Rutter, Cal. Practice Guide: Civ. Pro. Before Trial Ch. 9(I)-B, B. Preparing and Filing Motions.

4 Witkin Cal. Proc. 5th Pleading § 16, Numbering.

Rule 2.110.   Footer

(a) Location

Except for exhibits, each paper filed with the court must bear a footer in the bottom margin of each page, placed below the page number and divided from the rest of the document page by a printed line.

(b) Contents

The footer must contain the title of the paper (examples: "Complaint," "XYZ Corp.'s Motion for Summary Judgment") or some clear and concise abbreviation.

(c) Type size

The title of the paper in the footer must be in at least 10–point type. *(Adopted, eff. Jan. 1, 2007.)*

Research References

Rutter, Cal. Practice Guide: Civ. Pro. Before Trial Ch. 6-B, B. Complaints.

Rutter, Cal. Practice Guide: Civ. Pro. Before Trial Ch. 6-C, C. Answer.

Rutter, Cal. Practice Guide: Civ. Pro. Before Trial Ch. 7(I)-A, A. Demurrers.

Rutter, Cal. Practice Guide: Civ. Pro. Before Trial Ch. 9(I)-B, B. Preparing and Filing Motions.

4 Witkin Cal. Proc. 5th Pleading § 15, Printing.

Rule 2.111. Format of first page

The first page of each paper must be in the following form:

(1) In the space commencing 1 inch from the top of the page with line 1, to the left of the center of the page, the name, office address or, if none, residence address or mailing address (if different), telephone number, fax number and e-mail address (if available), and State Bar membership number of the attorney for the party in whose behalf the paper is presented, or of the party if he or she is appearing in person. The inclusion of a fax number or e-mail address on any document does not constitute consent to service by fax or e-mail unless otherwise provided by law.

(2) In the first 2 inches of space between lines 1 and 7 to the right of the center of the page, a blank space for the use of the clerk.

(3) On line 8, at or below 3 1/3 inches from the top of the paper, the title of the court.

(4) Below the title of the court, in the space to the left of the center of the page, the title of the case. In the title of the case on each initial complaint or cross-complaint, the name of each party must commence on a separate line beginning at the left margin of the page. On any subsequent pleading or paper, it is sufficient to provide a short title of the case (1) stating the name of the first party on each side, with appropriate indication of other parties, and (2) stating that a cross-action or cross-actions are involved (e.g., "and Related Cross–action"), if applicable.

(5) To the right of and opposite the title, the number of the case.

(6) Below the number of the case, the nature of the paper and, on all complaints and petitions, the character of the action or proceeding. In a case having multiple parties, any answer, response, or opposition must specifically identify the complaining, propounding, or moving party and the complaint, motion, or other matter being answered or opposed.

(7) Below the nature of the paper or the character of the action or proceeding, the name of the judge and department, if any, to which the case is assigned.

(8) Below the nature of the paper or the character of the action or proceeding, the word "Referee:" followed by the name of the referee, on any paper filed in a case pending before a referee appointed under Code of Civil Procedure section 638 or 639.

(9) On the complaint, petition, or application filed in a limited civil case, below the character of the action or proceeding, the amount demanded in the complaint, petition, or application, stated as follows: "Amount demanded exceeds $10,000" or "Amount demanded does not exceed $10,000," as required by Government Code section 70613.

(10) In the caption of every pleading and every other paper filed in a limited civil case, the words "Limited Civil Case," as required by Code of Civil Procedure section 422.30(b).

(11) If a case is reclassified by an amended complaint, cross-complaint, amended cross-complaint, or other pleading under Code of Civil Procedure section 403.020 or 403.030, the caption must indicate that the action or proceeding is reclassified by this pleading. If a case is reclassified by stipulation under Code of Civil Procedure section 403.050, the title of the stipulation must state that the action or proceeding is reclassified by this stipulation. The caption or title must state that the case is a limited civil case reclassified as an unlimited civil case, or an unlimited civil case reclassified as a limited civil case, or other words to that effect. (*Adopted, eff. Jan. 1, 2007. As amended, eff. Jan. 1, 2008.*)

Research References

Rutter, Cal. Practice Guide: A.D.R. Ch. 6-C, C. Referees.
Rutter, Cal. Practice Guide: Civ. Pro. Before Trial Ch. 3-A, A. Subject Matter Jurisdiction (Competency).
Rutter, Cal. Practice Guide: Civ. Pro. Before Trial Ch. 6-B, B. Complaints.
Rutter, Cal. Practice Guide: Civ. Pro. Before Trial Ch. 6-D, D. Cross-Complaint.
Rutter, Cal. Practice Guide: Civ. Pro. Before Trial Ch. 9(I)-B, B. Preparing and Filing Motions.
Rutter, Cal. Practice Guide: Personal Injury Ch. 5-D, D. Classification as Limited or Unlimited Civil Case.
Rutter, Cal. Practice Guide: Personal Injury Ch. 5-E, E. Selected Pleading Issues.
4 Witkin Cal. Proc. 5th Pleading § 15, Printing.
4 Witkin Cal. Proc. 5th Pleading § 17, Format of First Page.
4 Witkin Cal. Proc. 5th Pleading § 471, Superior Court.

Rule 2.112. Separate causes of action, counts, and defenses

Each separately stated cause of action, count, or defense must specifically state:

(1) Its number (e.g., "first cause of action");

(2) Its nature (e.g., "for fraud");

(3) The party asserting it if more than one party is represented on the pleading (e.g., "by plaintiff Jones"); and

(4) The party or parties to whom it is directed (e.g., "against defendant Smith"). (*Adopted, eff. Jan. 1, 2007.*)

Research References

Rutter, Cal. Practice Guide: Civ. Pro. Before Trial Ch. 6-B, B. Complaints.
Rutter, Cal. Practice Guide: Civ. Pro. Before Trial Ch. 6-C, C. Answer.
Rutter, Cal. Practice Guide: Civ. Pro. Before Trial Ch. 6-D, D. Cross-Complaint.
Rutter, Cal. Practice Guide: Personal Injury Ch. 5-E, E. Selected Pleading Issues.
4 Witkin Cal. Proc. 5th Pleading § 18, Other Requirements.
4 Witkin Cal. Proc. 5th Pleading § 471, Superior Court.
5 Witkin Cal. Proc. 5th Pleading § 1084, in General.

Rule 2.113. Binding

Each paper must consist entirely of original pages without riders and must be firmly bound together at the top. (*Adopted, eff. Jan. 1, 2007.*)

Research References

Rutter, Cal. Practice Guide: Civil Trials & Evidence Ch. 14-D, D. Preparing Jury Instructions.
4 Witkin Cal. Proc. 5th Pleading § 14, Paper.

Rule 2.114. Exhibits

Exhibits may be fastened to pages of the specified size and, when prepared by a machine copying process, must be equal to typewritten material in legibility and permanency of image. (*Adopted, eff. Jan. 1, 2007.*)

Rule 2.115. Hole punching

Each paper presented for filing must contain two prepunched normal-sized holes, centered 2½ inches apart and 5/8 inch from the top of the paper. (*Adopted, eff. Jan. 1, 2007.*)

Research References

Rutter, Cal. Practice Guide: Civ. Pro. Before Trial Ch. 6-B, B. Complaints.
4 Witkin Cal. Proc. 5th Pleading § 14, Paper.

Ct. Rules

Rule 2.116. Changes on face of paper

Any addition, deletion, or interlineation to a paper must be initialed by the clerk or judge at the time of filing. *(Adopted, eff. Jan. 1, 2007.)*

Research References

Rutter, Cal. Practice Guide: Civ. Pro. Before Trial Ch. 6-B, B. Complaints.
4 Witkin Cal. Proc. 5th Pleading § 18, Other Requirements.

Rule 2.117. Conformed copies of papers

All copies of papers served must conform to the original papers filed, including the numbering of lines, pagination, additions, deletions, and interlineations except that, with the agreement of the other party, a party may serve that other party with papers printed on both sides of the page. *(Adopted, eff. Jan. 1, 2007. As amended, eff. July 1, 2012.)*

Research References

4 Witkin Cal. Proc. 5th Pleading § 18, Other Requirements.

Rule 2.118. Acceptance of papers for filing

(a) Papers not in compliance

The clerk of the court must not accept for filing or file any papers that do not comply with the rules in this chapter, except the clerk must not reject a paper for filing solely on the ground that:

(1) It is handwritten or hand-printed; or

(2) The handwriting or hand printing on the paper is in a color other than black or blue-black.

(b) Absence of fax number or e-mail address

The clerk must not reject a paper for filing solely on the ground that it does not contain an attorney's or a party's fax number or e-mail address on the first page.

(c) Filing of papers for good cause

For good cause shown, the court may permit the filing of papers that do not comply with the rules in this chapter. *(Adopted, eff. Jan. 1, 2007.)*

Research References

Rutter, Cal. Practice Guide: Civ. Pro. Before Trial Ch. 6-B, B. Complaints.
2 Witkin Cal. Proc. 5th Courts § 202, (S 202) Duty of Clerk to Accept Filing Inconsistent With Local Rule.
4 Witkin Cal. Proc. 5th Pleading § 13, in General.

Rule 2.119. Exceptions for forms

Except as provided elsewhere in the California Rules of Court, the rules in this chapter do not apply to Judicial Council forms, local court forms, or forms for juvenile dependency proceedings produced by the California State Department of Social Services Child Welfare Systems Case Management System. *(Adopted, eff. Jan. 1, 2007.)*

Advisory Committee Comment

The California Department of Social Services (CDSS) has begun to distribute a new, comprehensive, computerized case management system to county welfare agencies. This system is not able to exactly conform to Judicial Council format in all instances. However, item numbering on the forms will remain the same. The changes allow CDSS computer-generated Judicial Council forms to be used in juvenile court proceedings.

Research References

Rutter, Cal. Practice Guide: Civ. Pro. Before Trial Ch. 6-B, B. Complaints.

Rutter, Cal. Practice Guide: Civ. Pro. Before Trial Ch. 6-C, C. Answer.
Rutter, Cal. Practice Guide: Civ. Pro. Before Trial Ch. 6-D, D. Cross-Complaint.
Rutter, Cal. Practice Guide: Civ. Pro. Before Trial Ch. 9(I)-B, B. Preparing and Filing Motions.
Rutter, Cal. Practice Guide: Civil Trials & Evidence Ch. 1-G, G. Preparing Trial Notebook.
Rutter, Cal. Practice Guide: Civil Trials & Evidence Ch. 4-F, F. Motions in Limine.
Rutter, Cal. Practice Guide: Civil Trials & Evidence Ch. 14-C, C. Procedural Requirements.
Rutter, Cal. Practice Guide: Civil Trials & Evidence Ch. 14-D, D. Preparing Jury Instructions.
Rutter, Cal. Practice Guide: Personal Injury Ch. 5-B, B. When to Sue-Statute of Limitations.
Rutter, Cal. Practice Guide: Personal Injury Ch. 8-D, D. Final Preparation (One Month Before Trial).
2 Witkin Cal. Proc. 5th Courts § 190, (S 190) Trial Court Rules.

Chapter 2

GENERAL RULES ON FORMS

Rule
2.130.   Application.
2.132.   True copy certified.
2.133.   Hole punching.
2.134.   Forms longer than one page.
2.135.   Filing of handwritten or hand-printed forms.
2.140.   Judicial Council forms.
2.141.   Local court forms.

Rule 2.130. Application

The rules in this chapter apply to Judicial Council forms, local court forms, and all other official forms to be filed in the trial courts. *(Adopted, eff. Jan. 1, 2007.)*

Research References

2 Witkin Cal. Proc. 5th Courts § 190, (S 190) Trial Court Rules.
2 Witkin Cal. Proc. 5th Courts § 399, (S 399) Format Requirements.
4 Witkin Cal. Proc. 5th Pleading § 13, in General.

Rule 2.132. True copy certified

A party or attorney who files a form certifies by filing the form that it is a true copy of the form. *(Adopted, eff. Jan. 1, 2007.)*

Research References

2 Witkin Cal. Proc. 5th Courts § 399, (S 399) Format Requirements.

Rule 2.133. Hole punching

All forms must contain two prepunched normal-sized holes, centered 2½ inches apart and ⅝ inch from the top of the form. *(Adopted, eff. Jan. 1, 2007.)*

Research References

Rutter, Cal. Practice Guide: Civ. Pro. Before Trial Ch. 6-B, B. Complaints.
2 Witkin Cal. Proc. 5th Courts § 399, (S 399) Format Requirements.

Rule 2.134. Forms longer than one page

(a) Single side may be used

If a form is longer than one page, the form may be printed on sheets printed only on one side even if the original has two sides to a sheet.

(b) Two–sided forms must be tumbled

If a form is filed on a sheet printed on two sides, the reverse side must be rotated 180 degrees (printed head to foot).

(c) Multiple–page forms must be bound

If a form is longer than one page, it must be firmly bound at the top. *(Adopted, eff. Jan. 1, 2007.)*

Research References

Rutter, Cal. Practice Guide: Civ. Pro. Before Trial Ch. 6-B, B. Complaints.

Rutter, Cal. Practice Guide: Civ. Pro. Before Trial Ch. 9(I)-B, B. Preparing and Filing Motions.

2 Witkin Cal. Proc. 5th Courts § 399, (S 399) Format Requirements.

4 Witkin Cal. Proc. 5th Pleading § 15, Printing.

10 Witkin, California Summary 10th Parent and Child § 445, (S 445) Judicial Council Forms.

Rule 2.135. Filing of handwritten or hand-printed forms

The clerk must not reject for filing or refuse to file any Judicial Council or local court form solely on the ground that:

(1) It is completed in handwritten or hand-printed characters; or

(2) The handwriting or hand-printing is a color other than blue-black or black. *(Formerly Rule 201.4, adopted, eff. Jan. 1, 2003. Renumbered Rule 2.135 and amended, eff. Jan. 1, 2007.)*

Research References

2 Witkin Cal. Proc. 5th Courts § 399, (S 399) Format Requirements.

4 Witkin Cal. Proc. 5th Pleading § 13, in General.

Rule 2.140. Judicial Council forms

Judicial Council forms are governed by the rules in this chapter and chapter 4 of title 1. *(Adopted, eff. Jan. 1, 2007.)*

Research References

4 Witkin Cal. Proc. 5th Pleading § 13, in General.

Rule 2.141. Local court forms

Local court forms are governed by the rules in this chapter and rules 10.613 and 10.614. *(Adopted, eff. Jan. 1, 2007.)*

Research References

2 Witkin Cal. Proc. 5th Courts § 190, (S 190) Trial Court Rules.

2 Witkin Cal. Proc. 5th Courts § 399, (S 399) Format Requirements.

Chapter 3

OTHER FORMS

Rule

2.150. Authorization for computer-generated or typewritten forms for proof of service of summons and complaint.

Rule 2.150. Authorization for computer-generated or typewritten forms for proof of service of summons and complaint

(a) Computer–generated or typewritten forms; conditions

Notwithstanding the adoption of mandatory form *Proof of Service of Summons* (form POS–010), a form for proof of service of a summons and complaint prepared entirely by word processor, typewriter, or similar process may be used for proof of service in any applicable action or proceeding if the following conditions are met:

(1) The form complies with the rules in chapter 1 of this division except as otherwise provided in this rule, but numbered lines are not required.

(2) The left, right, and bottom margins of the proof of service must be at least ½ inch. The top margin must be at least ¾ of an inch. The typeface must be Times New Roman, Courier, Arial, or an equivalent typeface not smaller than 9 points. Text must be single-spaced and a blank line must precede each main numbered item.

(3) The title and all the text of form POS–010 that is not accompanied by a check box must be copied word for word except for any instructions, which need not be copied. In addition, the optional text describing the particular method of service used must be copied word for word, except that the check boxes must not be copied. Any optional text not describing such service need not be included.

(4) The Judicial Council number of the *Proof of Service of Summons* must be typed as follows either in the left margin of the first page opposite the last line of text or at the bottom of each page: "Judicial Council form POS–010."

(5) The text of form POS–010 must be copied in the same order as it appears on the printed form using the same item numbers. A declaration of diligence may be attached to the proof of service or inserted as item 5b(5).

(6) Areas marked "For Court Use" must be copied in the same general locations and occupy approximately the same amount of space as on the printed form.

(7) The telephone number of the attorney or party must appear flush with the left margin and below the attorney's or party's address.

(8) The name of the court must be flush with the left margin. The address of the court is not required.

(9) Material that would have been typed onto the printed form must be typed with each line indented 3 inches from the left margin.

(b) Compliance with rule

The act of filing a computer-generated or typewritten form under this rule constitutes a certification by the party or attorney filing the form that it complies with this rule and is a true and correct copy of the form to the extent required by this rule. *(Formerly Rule 1280, adopted, eff. Jan. 1, 1985. As amended, eff. July 1, 1985; Jan. 1, 1986; Jan. 1, 1987. Renumbered Rule 982.9 and amended, eff. July 1, 1987. As amended, eff. Jan. 1, 1988; Jan. 1, 1989; July 1, 1999; Jan. 1, 2004; July 1, 2004. Renumbered Rule 2.150 and amended, eff. Jan. 1, 2007.)*

Advisory Committee Comment

This rule is intended to permit process servers and others to prepare their own shortened versions of *Proof of Service of Summons* (form POS–010) containing only the information that is relevant to show the method of service used.

Research References

Rutter, Cal. Practice Guide: Civ. Pro. Before Trial Ch. 4-E, E. Proof of Service of Summons.

2 Witkin Cal. Proc. 5th Courts § 190, (S 190) Trial Court Rules.

2 Witkin Cal. Proc. 5th Courts § 398, (S 398) in General.

Division 3

FILING AND SERVICE

Chapter 1

GENERAL PROVISIONS

Rule

2.200. Service and filing of notice of change of address or other contact information.

2.210. Drop box for filing documents.

Rule 2.200. Service and filing of notice of change of address or other contact information

An ~~party or~~ attorney or self-represented party whose mailing address, telephone number, fax number, or e-mail address (if it was provided under rule 2.111(1)) changes while an action is pending must serve on all parties and file a written notice of the change ~~of address~~. *(Formerly Rule 385, adopted, eff. Jan. 1, 1984. Renumbered Rule 2.200 and amended, eff. Jan. 1, 2007. As amended, eff. Jan. 1, 2013.)*

Research References

Rutter, Cal. Practice Guide: Civ. Pro. Before Trial Ch. 9(I)-B, B. Preparing and Filing Motions.

2 Witkin Cal. Proc. 5th Courts § 190, (S 190) Trial Court Rules.

7 Witkin Cal. Proc. 5th Trial § 76, (S 76) Mandatory Requirement.

Rule 2.210. Drop box for filing documents

(a) Use of drop box

Whenever a clerk's office filing counter is closed at any time between 8:30 a.m. and 4:00 p.m. on a court day, the court must provide a drop box for depositing documents to be filed with the clerk. A court may provide a drop box during other times.

(b) Documents deemed filed on day of deposit

Any document deposited in a court's drop box up to and including 4:00 p.m. on a court day is deemed to have been deposited for filing on that day. A court may provide for same-day filing of a document deposited in its drop box after 4:00 p.m. on a court day. If so, the court must give notice of the deadline for same-day filing of a document deposited in its drop box.

(c) Documents deemed filed on next court day

Any document deposited in a court's drop box is deemed to have been deposited for filing on the next court day if:

(1) It is deposited on a court day after 4:00 p.m. or after the deadline for same-day filing if a court provides for a later time; or

(2) It is deposited on a judicial holiday.

(d) Date and time documents deposited

A court must have a means of determining whether a document was deposited in the drop box by 4:00 p.m., or after the deadline for same-day filing if a court provides for a later time, on a court day. *(Formerly Rule 201.6, adopted, eff. Jan. 1, 2005. Renumbered Rule 2.210 and amended, eff. Jan. 1, 2007.)*

Advisory Committee Comment

The notice required by (b) may be provided by the same means a court provides notice of its clerk's office hours. The means of providing notice may include the following: information on the court's Web site, a local rule provision, a notice in a legal newspaper, a sign in the clerk's office, or a sign near the drop box.

Research References

Rutter, Cal. Practice Guide: Civil Appeals & Writs Ch. 3-E, E. Filing Steps.

2 Witkin Cal. Proc. 5th Courts § 190, (S 190) Trial Court Rules.

4 Witkin Cal. Proc. 5th Pleading § 19, in General.

Chapter 2

FILING AND SERVICE BY ELECTRONIC MEANS

Rule

2.250. Construction and definitions.

2.251. Electronic service.

2.252. General rules on electronic filing of documents.

2.253. Permissive electronic filing, mandatory electronic filing, and electronic filing by court order .

2.254. Responsibilities of court.

2.255. Contracts with electronic filing service providers.

2.256. Responsibilities of electronic filer.

2.257. Requirements for signatures on documents.

2.258. Payment of filing fees.

2.259. Actions by court on receipt of electronic filing.

2.261. Authorization for courts to continue modifying forms for the purpose of electronic filing and forms generation.

Rule 2.250. Construction and definitions

(a) Construction of rules

The rules in this chapter must be construed to authorize and permit filing and service by electronic means to the extent feasible.

(b) Definitions

As used in this chapter, unless the context otherwise requires:

(1) A "document" is a pleading, a paper, a declaration, an exhibit, or another filing submitted by a party or by an agent of a party on the party's behalf. A document may be in paper or electronic form.

(2) "Electronic service" is service of a document on a party or other person by either electronic transmission or electronic notification. Electronic service may be performed directly by a party, by an agent of a party including the party's attorney, through an electronic filing service provider, or by a court.

(3) "Electronic transmission" means the transmission of a document by electronic means to the electronic service address at or through which a party or other person has authorized electronic service.

(4) "Electronic notification" means the notification of a party or other person that a document is served by sending an electronic message to the electronic service address at or through which the party or other person has authorized electronic service, specifying the exact name of the document served and providing a hyperlink at which the served document can be viewed and downloaded.

(5) "Electronic service address" of a party means the electronic address at or through which the party has authorized electronic service.

(6) An "electronic filer" is a party filing a document in electronic form directly with the court, by an agent, or through an electronic filing service provider.

(7) "Electronic filing" is the electronic transmission to a court of a document in electronic form. For the purposes of this chapter, this definition concerns the activity of filing and does not include the processing and review of the document, and its entry into the court records, which are necessary for the document to be officially filed.

(8) An "electronic filing service provider" is a person or entity that receives an electronic filing from a party for retransmission to the court or for electronic service on other parties, or both. In submission of filings, the electronic filing service provider does so on behalf of the electronic filer and not as an agent of the court.

(9) "Regular filing hours" are the hours during which a court accepts documents for filing at its filing counter.

(10) "Close of business" is 5 p.m. or any other time on a court day at which the court stops accepting documents for filing at its filing counter, whichever is earlier. The court must provide notice of its close-of-business time electronically. The court may give this notice in any additional manner it deems appropriate. *(Formerly Rule 2050, adopted, eff. Jan. 1, 2003. As amended, eff. Jan. 1, 2006. Renumbered Rule 2.250 and amended, eff. Jan. 1, 2007. As amended, eff. Jan. 1, 2008; Jan. 1, 2011; July 1, 2013.)*

Advisory Committee Comment

The definition of "electronic service" has been amended to provide that a party may effectuate service not only by the electronic transmission of a document, but also by providing electronic notification of where a document served electronically may be located and downloaded. This amendment is intended to modify the rules on electronic service to expressly authorize electronic notification as a legally effective alternative means of service to electronic transmission. This rules amendment is consistent with the amendment of Code of Civil Procedure section 1010.6, effective January 1, 2011, to authorize service by electronic notification. (See Stats. 2010, ch. 156 (Sen. Bill 1274).) The amendments change the law on electronic service as understood by the appellate court in *Insyst, Ltd. v. Applied Materials, Inc.* (2009) 170 Cal.App.4th 1129, which interpreted the rules as authorizing electronic transmission as the only effective means of electronic service.

Research References

Rutter, Cal. Practice Guide: Civil Appeals & Writs Ch. 3-B, B. Filing Deadlines.
Rutter, Cal. Practice Guide: Civil Appeals & Writs Ch. 3-C, C. Extensions of Filing Deadline.
Rutter, Cal. Practice Guide: Civil Appeals & Writs Ch. 16-C, C. Notice of Appeal.
Rutter, Cal. Practice Guide: Civ. Pro. Before Trial Ch. 8E-4, Notice of Deposition.
Rutter, Cal. Practice Guide: Civ. Pro. Before Trial Ch. 8E-6, Subpoena to Nonparty Deponent or Business Records Custodian.
Rutter, Cal. Practice Guide: Civ. Pro. Before Trial Ch. 7(I)-A, A. Demurrers.
Rutter, Cal. Practice Guide: Civ. Pro. Before Trial Ch. 7(I)-B, B. Motions to Strike.
Rutter, Cal. Practice Guide: Civ. Pro. Before Trial Ch. 9(I)-B, B. Preparing and Filing Motions.
Rutter, Cal. Practice Guide: Civ. Pro. Before Trial Ch. 7(II)-F, F. Procedure.
Rutter, Cal. Practice Guide: Civil Trials & Evidence Ch. 18-A, A. Motion for Judgment Notwithstanding the Verdict ("JNOV").
Rutter, Cal. Practice Guide: Civil Trials & Evidence Ch. 18-B, B. Motion for New Trial.
9 Witkin Cal. Proc. 5th Appeal § 698, Filing and Service of Original and Copies.
2 Witkin Cal. Proc. 5th Courts § 190, (S 190) Trial Court Rules.
4 Witkin Cal. Proc. 5th Pleading § 21, (S 21) Nature of Filing Process.

6 Witkin Cal. Proc. 5th Proceedings Without Trial § 27, When Permitted.
6 Witkin Cal. Proc. 5th Proceedings Without Trial § 28, Mechanics of Service.
6 Witkin Cal. Proc. 5th Proceedings Without Trial § 35, (S 35) Electronic Filing.

Rule 2.251.   Electronic service

(a) ~~Consent to~~Authorization for electronic service

~~(1)~~ When a document may be served by mail, express mail, overnight delivery, or fax transmission, ~~electronic service of~~ the document may be served electronically under ~~is permitted when authorized by~~ Code of Civil Procedure section 1010.6 and ~~these~~ rules in this chapter.

(b) Electronic service by consent of the parties

~~(2)~~(1) Electronic service may be established by consent of the parties in an action. A party indicates that the party agrees to accept electronic service by:

(A) Serving a notice on all parties that the party accepts electronic service and filing the notice with the court. The notice must include the electronic service address at which the party agrees to accept service; or

(B) Electronically filing any document with the court. The act of electronic filing is evidence that the party agrees to accept service at the electronic service address the party has furnished to the court under rule 2. 256(a)(4). This subparagraph (B) does not apply to self-represented parties; they must affirmatively consent to electronic service under subparagraph (A).

~~(3)~~(2) A party that has consented to electronic service under ~~(2)~~(1) and has used an electronic filing service provider to serve and file documents in a case consents to service on that electronic filing service provider as the designated agent for service for the party in the case, until such time as the party designates a different agent for service.

(c) Electronic service required by local rule or court order

(1) A court may require parties to serve documents electronically in specified actions by local rule or court order, as provided in Code of Civil Procedure section 1010.6 and the rules in this chapter.

(2) Except when personal service is otherwise required by statute or rule, a party that is required to file documents electronically in an action must also serve documents and accept service of documents electronically from all other parties, unless:

(A) The court orders otherwise, or

(B) The action includes parties that are not required to file or serve documents electronically, including self-represented parties; those parties are to be served by non-electronic methods unless they affirmatively consent to electronic service.

(3) Each party that is required to serve and accept service of documents electronically must provide all other parties in the action with its electronic service address and must promptly notify all other parties and the court of any changes under (f).

~~(b)~~(d) Maintenance of electronic service lists

A court that ~~orders or~~ permits or requires electronic filing in a case must maintain and make available electronically to the parties an electronic service list that contains the parties' current electronic service addresses, as provided by the parties that have filed electronically in the case.

~~(c)~~(e) Service by the parties

(1) Notwithstanding ~~(b)~~(d), parties are responsible for electronic service on all other parties in the case. A party may serve documents electronically directly, by an agent, or through a designated electronic filing service provider.

Ct. Rules

(2) A document may not be electronically served on a nonparty unless the nonparty consents to electronic service or electronic service is otherwise provided for by law or court order.

~~(d)~~(f) **Change of electronic service address**

(1) A party whose electronic service address changes while the action or proceeding is pending must promptly file a notice of change of address electronically with the court and must serve this notice electronically on all other parties.

(2) A party's election to contract with an electronic filing service provider to electronically file and serve documents or to receive electronic service of documents on the party's behalf does not relieve the party of its duties under (1).

(3) An electronic service address is presumed valid for a party if the party files electronic documents with the court from that address and has not filed and served notice that the address is no longer valid.

~~(e)~~(g) **Reliability and integrity of documents served by electronic notification**

A party that serves a document by means of electronic notification must:

(1) Ensure that the documents served can be viewed and downloaded using the hyperlink provided;

(2) Preserve the document served without any change, alteration, or modification from the time the document is posted until the time the hyperlink is terminated; and

(3) Maintain the hyperlink until either:

(A) All parties in the case have settled or the case has ended and the time for appeals has expired; or

(B) If the party is no longer in the case, the party has provided notice to all other parties that it is no longer in the case and that they have 60 days to download any documents, and 60 days have passed after the notice was given.

~~(f)~~(h) **When service is complete**

(1) Electronic service of a document is complete at the time of the electronic transmission of the document or at the time that the electronic notification of service of the document is sent. If an electronic filing service provider is used for service, the service is complete at the time that the electronic filing service provider electronically transmits the document or sends electronic notification of service.

(2) If a document is served electronically, any period of notice, or any right or duty to act or respond within a specified period or on a date certain after service of the document, is extended by two court days, unless otherwise provided by a statute or a rule.

(3) The extension under (2) does not extend the time for filing:

(A) A notice of intent to move for a new trial;

(B) A notice of intent to move to vacate the judgment under Code of Civil Procedure section 663a; or

(C) A notice of appeal.

(4) Service that occurs after the close of business is deemed to have occurred on the next court day.

~~(g)~~(i) **Proof of service**

(1) Proof of electronic service may be by any of the methods provided in Code of Civil Procedure section 1013a, except that the proof of service must state:

(A) The electronic service address of the person making the service, in addition to that person's residence or business address;

(B) The date and time of the electronic service, instead of the date and place of deposit in the mail;

(C) The name and electronic service address of the person served, in place of that person's name and address as shown on the envelope; and

(D) That the document was served electronically in place of the statement that the envelope was sealed and deposited in the mail with postage fully prepaid.

(2) Proof of electronic service may be in electronic form and may be filed electronically with the court.

(3) Under rule 3.1300(c), proof of service of the moving papers must be filed at least five court days before the hearing.

(4) The party filing the proof of electronic service must maintain the printed form of the document bearing the declarant's original signature and must make the document available for inspection and copying on the request of the court or any party to the action or proceeding in which it is filed, in the manner provided in rule 2.257(a).

~~(h)~~(j) **Electronic service by court**

The court may electronically serve any notice, order, judgment, or other document issued by the court in the same manner that parties may serve documents by electronic service. *(Formerly Rule 2060, adopted, eff. Jan. 1, 2003.   Renumbered Rule 2.260 and amended, eff. Jan. 1, 2007.   As amended, eff. Jan. 1, 2008; Jan. 1, 2009; July 1, 2009; Jan. 1, 2010.   Renumbered Rule 2.251 and amended, eff. Jan. 1, 2011.   As amended, eff. July 1, 2013.)*

Research References

Rutter, Cal. Practice Guide: Civ. Pro. Before Trial Ch. 9(I)-B, B. Preparing and Filing Motions.
Rutter, Cal. Practice Guide: Civ. Pro. Before Trial Ch. 9(II)-A, A. Injunctions.
Rutter, Cal. Practice Guide: Civil Trials & Evidence Ch. 18-B, B. Motion for New Trial.
4 Witkin Cal. Proc. 5th Pleading § 24, (S 24) Electronic Service.
6 Witkin Cal. Proc. 5th Proceedings Without Trial § 27, When Permitted.
6 Witkin Cal. Proc. 5th Proceedings Without Trial § 28, Mechanics of Service.
6 Witkin Cal. Proc. 5th Proceedings Without Trial § 29, Proof of Service.
7 Witkin Cal. Proc. 5th Trial § 6B, (S 6B) (New)-Pretrial Proceedings.

Rule 2.252.   ~~Documents that may be filed electronically~~General rules on electronic filing of documents

(a) In general

A court may ~~permit~~ provide for electronic filing of ~~a~~ documents in ~~any~~ actions ~~or~~ and proceedings as provided under Code of Civil Procedure section 1010.6 and the rules in this chapter ~~unless the rules in this chapter or other legal authority expressly prohibit electronic filing~~.

(b) Direct and indirect electronic filing

Except as otherwise provided by law, a court may provide for the electronic filing of documents directly with the court, indirectly through one or more approved electronic filing service providers, or through a combination of direct and indirect means.

(c) Effect of document filed electronically

(1) A document that the court or a party files electronically under the rules in this chapter has the same legal effect as a document in paper form.

(2) Filing a document electronically does not alter any filing deadline.

(d) Filing in paper form

When it is not feasible for a party to convert a document to electronic form by scanning, imaging, or another means, a court may allow that party to file the document in paper form.

(b)(e) Original documents

In a proceeding that requires the filing of an original document, an electronic filer may file an electronic copy of a document if the original document is then filed with the court within 10 calendar days.

(c)(f) Application for waiver of court fees and costs

The court may permit electronic filing of an application for waiver of court fees and costs in any proceeding in which the court accepts electronic filings.

(d)(g) Orders and judgments

The court may electronically file any notice, order, minute order, judgment, or other document prepared by the court.

(e)(h) Proposed orders

Proposed orders may be filed and submitted electronically as provided in rule 3.1312.

(f) Effect of document filed electronically

(1) A document that the court or a party files electronically under the rules in this chapter has the same legal effect as a document in paper form.

(2) Filing a document electronically does not alter any filing deadline. *(Formerly Rule 2052, adopted, eff. Jan. 1, 2003. Renumbered Rule 2.252 and amended, eff. Jan. 1, 2007. As amended, eff. Jan. 1, 2011; July 1, 2013.)*

Research References

Rutter, Cal. Practice Guide: Civ. Pro. Before Trial Ch. 9(I)-B, B. Preparing and Filing Motions.
4 Witkin Cal. Proc. 5th Pleading § 21, (S 21) Nature of Filing Process.
6 Witkin Cal. Proc. 5th Proceedings Without Trial § 35, (S 35) Electronic Filing.

Rule 2.253. Permissive electronic filing, mandatory electronic filing, and electronic filing by court order ~~requiring electronic service or filing~~

(a) Permissive electronic filing

A court may permit parties by local rule to file documents electronically in any types of cases, directly or through approved electronic service providers, subject to the conditions in Code of Civil Procedure section 1010.6 and the rules in this chapter.

(b) Mandatory electronic filing

A court may require parties by local rule to electronically file documents in civil actions directly with the court, or directly with the court and through one or more approved electronic filing service providers, or through more than one approved electronic filing service provider, subject to the conditions in Code of Civil Procedure section 1010.6, the rules in this chapter, and the following conditions:

(1) The court must specify the types or categories of civil actions in which parties are required to file and serve documents electronically. The court may designate any of the following as eligible for mandatory electronic filing and service:

(A) All civil cases;

(B) All civil cases of a specific category, such as unlimited or limited civil cases;

(C) All civil cases of a specific case type, including but not limited to, contract, collections, personal injury, or employment;

(D) All civil cases assigned to a judge for all purposes;

(E) All civil cases assigned to a specific department, courtroom or courthouse;

(F) Any class actions, consolidated actions, or group of actions, coordinated actions, or actions that are complex under rule 3.403; or

(G) Any combination of the cases described in subparagraphs (A) to (F), inclusive.

(2) Self–represented parties are exempt from any mandatory electronic filing and service requirements adopted by courts under this rule and Code of Civil Procedure section 1010.6.

(3) In civil cases involving both represented and self-represented parties, represented parties may be required to file and serve documents electronically; however, in these cases, each self-represented party is to file, serve, and be served with documents by non-electronic means unless the self-represented party affirmatively agrees otherwise.

(4) A party that is required to file and serve documents electronically must be excused from the requirements if the party shows undue hardship or significant prejudice. A court requiring the electronic filing and service of documents must have a process for parties, including represented parties, to apply for relief and a procedure for parties excused from filing documents electronically to file them by conventional means.

(5) Any fees charged by the court shall be for no more than the cost actually incurred by the court in providing for the electronic filing and service of the documents. Any fees charged by an electronic filing service provider shall be reasonable.

(6) Any fees for electronic filing charged by the court or by an electronic filing service provider must be waived when deemed appropriate by the court, including providing a waiver of the fees for any party that has received a fee waiver.

(7) Any document required to be electronically filed with the court under this subdivision that is received electronically after the close of business on any day is deemed to have been filed on the next court day, unless by local rule the court provides that any document required to be electronically filed with the court under this subdivision that is received electronically before midnight on a court day is deemed to have been filed on that court day, and any document received electronically after midnight is deemed filed on the next court day. This paragraph concerns only the effective date of filing. Any document that is received electronically must be processed and satisfy all other legal filing requirements to be filed as an official court record.

(8) A court that adopts a mandatory electronic filing program under this subdivision must report semiannually to the Judicial Council on the operation and effectiveness of the court's program.

(a)(c) Electronic filing and service required by court order

(1) The court may, on the motion of any party or on its own motion, provided that the order would not cause undue hardship or significant prejudice to any party, order all parties in any class action, a consolidated action, a group of actions, a coordinated action, or an action that is complex under rule 3.403 to:

(A) Serve all documents electronically, except when personal service is required by statute or rule;

(B) File all documents electronically; or

(C) Serve and file all documents electronically, except when personal service is required by statute or rule.

(2) If the court proposes to make any order under (1) on its own motion, the court must mail notice to the parties. Any party may serve and file an opposition within 10 days after notice is mailed or such later time as the court may specify.

(3) If the court has previously ordered parties in a case to electronically serve or file documents and a new party is added

that the court determines should also be ordered to do so under (1), the court may follow the notice procedures under (2) or may order the party to electronically serve or file documents and in its order state that the new party may object within 10 days after service of the order or by such later time as the court may specify.

(b) Additional provisions of order

(4) The court's order may also provide that:

(1)(A) Documents previously filed in paper form may be resubmitted in electronic form; and

(2)(B) When the court sends confirmation of filing to all parties, receipt of the confirmation constitutes service of the filing if the filed document is available electronically.

(c) Filing in paper form

When it is not feasible for a party to convert a document to electronic form by scanning, imaging, or another means, a court may allow that party to serve, file, or serve and file the document in paper form. *(Formerly Rule 2053, adopted, eff. Jan. 1, 2003. Renumbered Rule 2.253 and amended, eff. Jan. 1, 2007. As amended, eff. Jan. 1, 2008; Jan. 1, 2011; July 1, 2013.)*

Advisory Committee Comment

Subdivision (b)(1). This subdivision allows courts to institute mandatory electronic filing and service in any type of civil case for which the court determines that mandatory electronic filing is appropriate. The scope of this authorization is meant to be broad. It will enable courts to implement mandatory electronic filing in a flexible yet expansive manner. However, in initiating mandatory electronic filing, courts should take into account the fact that some civil case types may be easier and more cost-effective to implement at the outset while other types may require special procedures or other considerations (such as the need to preserve the confidentiality of filed records) that may make them less appropriate for inclusion in initial mandatory e-filing efforts.

Subdivision (b)(2). Although this rule exempts self-represented parties from any mandatory electronic filing and service requirements, these parties are encouraged to participate voluntarily in electronic filing and service. To the extent feasible, courts and other entities should assist self-represented parties to electronically file and serve documents.

Subdivision (c). Court–ordered electronic filing and service under this subdivision are not subject to the provisions in (b) and Code of Civil Procedure section 1010.6 requiring that, where mandatory electronic filing and service are established by local rule, the court and the parties must have access to more than one electronic filing service provider.

Research References

Rutter, Cal. Practice Guide: Civ. Pro. Before Trial Ch. 9(I)-B, B. Preparing and Filing Motions.
4 Witkin Cal. Proc. 5th Pleading § 21, (S 21) Nature of Filing Process.

Rule 2.254. Responsibilities of court

(a) Publication of electronic filing requirements

Each court that permits or mandates electronic filing must publish, in both electronic and print formats, the court's electronic filing requirements.

(b) Problems with electronic filing

If the court is aware of a problem that impedes or precludes electronic filing during the court's regular filing hours, it must promptly take reasonable steps to provide notice of the problem.

(c) Public access to electronically filed documents

Except as provided in rules 2.250–2.259 and 2.500–2.506, an electronically filed document is a public document at the time it is filed unless it is sealed under rule 2.551(b) or made confidential by law. *(Formerly Rule 2054, adopted, eff. Jan. 1, 2003.*

Renumbered Rule 2.254 and amended, eff. Jan. 1, 2007. As amended, eff. Jan. 1, 2011; July 1, 2013.)

Research References

Rutter, Cal. Practice Guide: Civ. Pro. Before Trial Ch. 9(I)-B, B. Preparing and Filing Motions.
4 Witkin Cal. Proc. 5th Pleading § 22, (S 22) Duties of Courts and Filers.

Rule 2.255. Contracts with electronic filing service providers

(a) Right to contract

(1) A court may contract with one or more electronic filing service providers to furnish and maintain an electronic filing system for the court.

(2) If the court contracts with an electronic filing service provider, it may require electronic filers to transmit the documents to the provider.

(3) If the court contracts with an electronic service provider or the court has an in-house system, the provider or system must accept filing from other electronic filing service providers to the extent the provider or system is compatible with them.

(b) Provisions of contract

The court's contract with an electronic filing service provider may allow the provider to charge electronic filers a reasonable fee in addition to the court's filing fee. The contract may also allow the electronic filing service provider to make other reasonable requirements for use of the electronic filing system.

(c) Transmission of filing to court

An electronic filing service provider must promptly transmit any electronic filing, and any applicable filing fee to the court.

(d) Confirmation of receipt and filing of document

(1) An electronic filing service provider must promptly send to an electronic filer its confirmation of the receipt of any document that the filer has transmitted to the provider for filing with the court.

(2) The electronic filing service provider must send its confirmation to the filer's electronic service address and must indicate the date and time of receipt, in accordance with rule 2.259(a).

(3) After reviewing the documents, the court must promptly transmit to the electronic filing service provider and the electronic filer the court's confirmation of filing or notice of rejection of filing, in accordance with rule 2.259.

(e) Ownership of information

All contracts between the court and electronic filing service providers must acknowledge that the court is the owner of the contents of the filing system and has the exclusive right to control the system's use. *(Formerly Rule 2055, adopted, eff. Jan. 1, 2003. Renumbered Rule 2.255 and amended, eff. Jan. 1, 2007. As amended, eff. Jan. 1, 2011.)*

Research References

4 Witkin Cal. Proc. 5th Pleading § 22, (S 22) Duties of Courts and Filers.
6 Witkin Cal. Proc. 5th Proceedings Without Trial § 35, (S 35) Electronic Filing.

Rule 2.256. Responsibilities of electronic filer

(a) Conditions of filing

Each electronic filer must:

(1) Comply with any court requirements designed to ensure the integrity of electronic filing and to protect sensitive personal information;

(2) Furnish information the court requires for case processing;

(3) Take all reasonable steps to ensure that the filing does not contain computer code, including viruses, that might be harmful to the court's electronic filing system and to other users of that system;

(4) Furnish one or more electronic service addresses, in the manner specified by the court, at which the electronic filer agrees to accept service; and

(5) Immediately provide the court and all parties with any change to the electronic filer's electronic service address.; and

(6) If the electronic filer uses an electronic filing service provider, provide the electronic filing service provider with the electronic address at which the filer is to be sent all documents and immediately notify the electronic filing service provider of any change in that address.

(b) Format of documents to be filed electronically

A document that is filed electronically with the court must be in a format specified by the court unless it cannot be created in that format. The format adopted by a court must meet the following requirements:

(1) The software for creating and reading documents must be in the public domain or generally available at a reasonable cost.

(2) The printing of documents must not result in the loss of document text, format, or appearance.

If a document is filed electronically under the rules in this chapter and cannot be formatted to be consistent with a formatting rule elsewhere in the California Rules of Court, the rules in this chapter prevail. *(Formerly Rule 2056, adopted, eff. Jan. 1, 2003. As amended, eff. Jan. 1, 2006. Renumbered Rule 2.256 and amended, eff. Jan. 1, 2007. As amended, eff. Jan. 1, 2008; Jan. 1, 2010; Jan. 1, 2011; July 1, 2013.)*

Research References

Rutter, Cal. Practice Guide: Civ. Pro. Before Trial Ch. 9(I)-B, B. Preparing and Filing Motions.
4 Witkin Cal. Proc. 5th Pleading § 22, (S 22) Duties of Courts and Filers.
4 Witkin Cal. Proc. 5th Pleading § 23, (S 23) Court Action on Receipt of Filing.
6 Witkin Cal. Proc. 5th Proceedings Without Trial § 35, (S 35) Electronic Filing.

Rule 2.257. Requirements for signatures on documents

(a) Documents signed under penalty of perjury

When a document to be filed electronically provides for a signature under penalty of perjury, the following applies:

(1) The document is deemed signed by the declarant if, before filing, the declarant has signed a printed form of the document.

(2) By electronically filing the document, the electronic filer certifies that (1) has been complied with and that the original, signed document is available for inspection and copying at the request of the court or any other party.

(3) At any time after the document is filed, any other party may serve a demand for production of the original signed document. The demand must be served on all other parties but need not be filed with the court.

(4) Within five days of service of the demand under (3), the party on whom the demand is made must make the original signed document available for inspection and copying by all other parties.

(5) At any time after the document is filed, the court may order the filing party to produce the original signed document in court for inspection and copying by the court. The order must specify the date, time, and place for the production and must be served on all parties.

(b) Documents not signed under penalty of perjury

If a document does not require a signature under penalty of perjury, the document is deemed signed by the party if the document is filed electronically.

(c) Documents requiring signatures of opposing parties

When a document to be filed electronically, such as a stipulation, requires the signatures of opposing parties, the following procedure applies:

(1) The party filing the document must obtain the signatures of all parties on a printed form of the document.

(2) The party filing the document must maintain the original, signed document and must make it available for inspection and copying as provided in (a)(2). The court and any other party may demand production of the original signed document in the manner provided in (a)(3)–(5).

(3) By electronically filing the document, the electronic filer indicates that all parties have signed the document and that the filer has the signed original in his or her possession.

(d) Digital signature

A party is not required to use a digital signature on an electronically filed document.

(e) Judicial signatures

If a document requires a signature by a court or a judicial officer, the document may be electronically signed in any manner permitted by law. *(Formerly Rule 2057, adopted, eff. Jan. 1, 2003. Renumbered Rule 2.257 and amended, eff. Jan. 1, 2007. As amended, eff. Jan. 1, 2008.)*

Research References

Rutter, Cal. Practice Guide: Civ. Pro. Before Trial Ch. 9(I)-B, B. Preparing and Filing Motions.
4 Witkin Cal. Proc. 5th Pleading § 22, (S 22) Duties of Courts and Filers.
6 Witkin Cal. Proc. 5th Proceedings Without Trial § 28, Mechanics of Service.
6 Witkin Cal. Proc. 5th Proceedings Without Trial § 35, (S 35) Electronic Filing.

Rule 2.258. Payment of filing fees

(a) Use of credit cards and other methods

A court may permit the use of credit cards, debit cards, electronic fund transfers, or debit accounts for the payment of filing fees associated with electronic filing, as provided in Government Code section 6159, rule 10.820, and other applicable law. A court may also authorize other methods of payment.

(b) Fee waivers

Eligible persons may seek a waiver of court fees and costs, as provided in Government Code sections 68630–68641, rule 2.252(e)(f), and division 2 of title 3 of these rules. *(Formerly Rule 2058, adopted, eff. Jan. 1, 2003. Renumbered Rule 2.258 and amended, eff. Jan. 1, 2007. As amended, eff. Jan. 1, 2010; July 1, 2013.)*

Research References

Rutter, Cal. Practice Guide: Civ. Pro. Before Trial Ch. 9(I)-B, B. Preparing and Filing Motions.
4 Witkin Cal. Proc. 5th Pleading § 22, (S 22) Duties of Courts and Filers.

Rule 2.259.   Actions by court on receipt of electronic filing

(a) Confirmation of receipt and filing of document

(1) Confirmation of receipt

When a court receives an electronically submitted document, the court must promptly send the electronic filer confirmation of the court's receipt of the document, indicating the date and time of receipt. A document is considered received at the date and time the confirmation of receipt is created.

(2) Confirmation of filing

If the document received by the court under (1) complies with filing requirements and all required filing fees have been paid, the court must promptly send the electronic filer confirmation that the document has been filed. The filing confirmation must indicate the date and time of filing and is proof that the document was filed on the date and at the time specified. The filing confirmation must also specify:

(A) Any transaction number associated with the filing;

(B) The titles of the documents as filed by the court; and

(C) The fees assessed for the filing.

(3) Transmission of confirmations

The court must send receipt and filing confirmation to the electronic filer at the electronic service address the filer furnished to the court under rule 2.256(a)(4). The court must maintain a record of all receipt and filing confirmations.

(4) Filer responsible for verification

In the absence of the court's confirmation of receipt and filing, there is no presumption that the court received and filed the document. The electronic filer is responsible for verifying that the court received and filed any document that the electronic filer submitted to the court electronically.

(b) Notice of rejection of document for filing

If the clerk does not file a document because it does not comply with applicable filing requirements or because the required filing fee has not been paid, the court must promptly send notice of the rejection of the document for filing to the electronic filer. The notice must state the reasons that the document was rejected for filing.

(c) Document received after close of business

A document that is received electronically by the court after the close of business is deemed to have been received on the next court day, unless the court has provided by local rule, with respect to documents filed under the mandatory electronic filing provisions in rule 2.253(b)(7), that documents received electronically before midnight on a court day are deemed to have been filed on that court day, and documents received electronically after midnight are deemed filed on the next court day. This provision concerns only the effective date of filing. Any document that is electronically filed must be processed and satisfy all other legal filing requirements to be filed as an official court record.

(d) Delayed delivery

If a technical problem with a court's electronic filing system prevents the court from accepting an electronic filing during its regular filing hours on a particular court day, and the electronic filer demonstrates that he or she attempted to electronically file the document on that day, the court must deem the document as filed on that day. This subdivision does not apply to the filing of a complaint or any other initial pleading in an action or proceeding.

(e) Endorsement

(1) The court's endorsement of a document electronically filed must contain the following: "Electronically filed by Superi-

or Court of California, County of _____, on _____ (date)," followed by the name of the court clerk.

(2) The endorsement required under (1) has the same force and effect as a manually affixed endorsement stamp with the signature and initials of the court clerk.

(3) A complaint or another initial pleading in an action or proceeding that is filed and endorsed electronically may be printed and served on the defendant or respondent in the same manner as if it had been filed in paper form.

(f) Issuance of electronic summons

(1) On the electronic filing of a complaint, a petition, or another document that must be served with a summons, the court may transmit a summons electronically to the electronic filer.

(2) The electronically transmitted summons must contain an image of the court's seal and the assigned case number.

(3) Personal service of the printed form of a summons transmitted electronically to the electronic filer has the same legal effect as personal service of a copy of an original summons. *(Formerly Rule 2059, adopted, eff. Jan. 1, 2003. Renumbered Rule 2.259 and amended, eff. Jan. 1, 2007. As amended, eff. Jan. 1, 2008; Jan. 1, 2011; July 1, 2013.)*

Research References

Rutter, Cal. Practice Guide: Civ. Pro. Before Trial Ch. 4-B, B. Issuance of Summons.
Rutter, Cal. Practice Guide: Civ. Pro. Before Trial Ch. 8E-4, Notice of Deposition.
Rutter, Cal. Practice Guide: Civ. Pro. Before Trial Ch. 8E-6, Subpoena to Nonparty Deponent or Business Records Custodian.
Rutter, Cal. Practice Guide: Civ. Pro. Before Trial Ch. 7(I)-A, A. Demurrers.
Rutter, Cal. Practice Guide: Civ. Pro. Before Trial Ch. 7(I)-B, B. Motions to Strike.
Rutter, Cal. Practice Guide: Civ. Pro. Before Trial Ch. 9(I)-B, B. Preparing and Filing Motions.
Rutter, Cal. Practice Guide: Civ. Pro. Before Trial Ch. 7(II)-F, F. Procedure.
4 Witkin Cal. Proc. 5th Pleading § 22, (S 22) Duties of Courts and Filers.
4 Witkin Cal. Proc. 5th Pleading § 23, (S 23) Court Action on Receipt of Filing.

Rule 2.261.   Authorization for courts to continue modifying forms for the purpose of electronic filing and forms generation

Courts that participated in pilot projects for electronic filing and forms generation under former rule 981.5 are authorized to continue to modify Judicial Council forms for the purpose of accepting electronic filing or providing electronic generation of court documents provided that the modification of the forms is consistent with the rules in this chapter. *(Formerly Rule 2061, adopted, eff. July 1, 2004. Renumbered Rule 2.261 and amended, eff. Jan. 1, 2007.)*

Research References

Rutter, Cal. Practice Guide: Civil Appeals & Writs Ch. 3-B, B. Filing Deadlines.
Rutter, Cal. Practice Guide: Civil Appeals & Writs Ch. 3-C, C. Extensions of Filing Deadline.
Rutter, Cal. Practice Guide: Civil Appeals & Writs Ch. 16-C, C. Notice of Appeal.
Rutter, Cal. Practice Guide: Civil Trials & Evidence Ch. 18-A, A. Motion for Judgment Notwithstanding the Verdict ("JNOV").
Rutter, Cal. Practice Guide: Civil Trials & Evidence Ch. 18-B, B. Motion for New Trial.
2 Witkin Cal. Proc. 5th Courts § 190, (S 190) Trial Court Rules.

Chapter 3

FILING AND SERVICE BY FAX

Rule
2.300. Application.
2.301. Definitions.
2.302. Compliance with the rules on the form and format of papers.
2.303. Filing through fax filing agency.
2.304. Direct filing.
2.305. Requirements for signatures on documents.
2.306. Service of papers by fax transmission.

Rule 2.300. Application

(a) Proceedings to which rules apply

The rules in this chapter apply to civil, probate, and family law proceedings in all trial courts. Rule 5.386 applies to fax filing of a protective order issued by a tribal court. Rule 5.522 applies to fax filing in juvenile law proceedings.

(b) Documents that may not be issued by fax

Notwithstanding any provision in the rules in this chapter, no will, codicil, bond, or undertaking may be filed by fax nor may a court issue by fax any document intended to carry the original seal of the court. *(Formerly Rule 2002, adopted, eff. March 1, 1992. As amended, eff. Jan. 1, 1999. Renumbered Rule 2.300 and amended, eff. Jan. 1, 2007. As amended, eff. July 1, 2012.)*

Research References

Rutter, Cal. Practice Guide: Civ. Pro. Before Trial Ch. 9(I)-B, B. Preparing and Filing Motions.
Rutter, Cal. Practice Guide: Personal Injury Ch. 5-B, B. When to Sue-Statute of Limitations.
2 Witkin Cal. Proc. 5th Courts § 190, (S 190) Trial Court Rules.
4 Witkin Cal. Proc. 5th Pleading § 20, Fax Filing.
6 Witkin Cal. Proc. 5th Proceedings Without Trial § 24, When Permitted.
6 Witkin Cal. Proc. 5th Proceedings Without Trial § 34, (S 34) Filing by Fax.

Rule 2.301. Definitions

As used in this chapter, unless the context otherwise requires:

(1) "Fax" is an abbreviation for "facsimile" and refers, as indicated by the context, to facsimile transmission or to a document so transmitted.

(2) "Fax transmission" means the transmission of a document by a system that encodes a document into electrical signals, transmits these electrical signals over a telephone line, and reconstructs the signals to print a duplicate of the original document at the receiving end.

(3) "Fax machine" means a machine that can send a facsimile transmission using the international standard for scanning, coding, and transmission established for Group 3 machines by the Consultative Committee of International Telegraphy and Telephone of the International Telecommunications Union (CCITT),[1] in regular resolution. Any fax machine used to send documents to a court under rule 2.305 must send at an initial transmission speed of no less than 4800 baud and be able to generate a transmission record. "Fax machine" includes a fax modem that is connected to a personal computer.

(4) "Fax filing" means the fax transmission of a document to a court that accepts such documents.

(5) "Service by fax" means the transmission of a document to a party or the attorney for a party under the rules in this chapter.

(6) "Transmission record" means the document printed by the sending fax machine, stating the telephone number of the receiving fax machine, the number of pages sent, the transmission time and date, and an indication of any errors in transmission.

(7) "Fax filing agency" means an entity that receives documents by fax for processing and filing with the court. *(Formerly Rule 2003, adopted, eff. March 1, 1992. Renumbered Rule 2.301 and amended, eff. Jan. 1, 2007.)*

[1] Recommendations T.4 and T.30, Volume VII—Facsimile VII.3, CCITT Red Book, Malaga–Torremolinos, 1984, U.N. Bookstore Code ITU 6731. [Footnote is supplied in copy]

Research References

4 Witkin Cal. Proc. 5th Pleading § 20, Fax Filing.
6 Witkin Cal. Proc. 5th Proceedings Without Trial § 24, When Permitted.
6 Witkin Cal. Proc. 5th Proceedings Without Trial § 34, (S 34) Filing by Fax.

Rule 2.302. Compliance with the rules on the form and format of papers

The document used for transmitting a fax must comply with the rules in division 2, chapter 1 of this title regarding form or format of papers. Any exhibit that exceeds 8–1/2 by 11 inches must be reduced in size to not more than 8–1/2 by 11 inches before it is transmitted. The court may require the filing party to file the original of an exhibit that the party has filed by fax. *(Formerly Rule 2004, adopted, eff. March 1, 1992. Renumbered Rule 2.302 and amended, eff. Jan. 1, 2007.)*

Research References

Rutter, Cal. Practice Guide: Civ. Pro. Before Trial Ch. 9(I)-B, B. Preparing and Filing Motions.
4 Witkin Cal. Proc. 5th Pleading § 20, Fax Filing.
6 Witkin Cal. Proc. 5th Proceedings Without Trial § 34, (S 34) Filing by Fax.

Rule 2.303. Filing through fax filing agency

(a) Transmission of document for filing

A party may transmit a document by fax to a fax filing agency for filing with any trial court. The agency acts as the agent of the filing party and not as an agent of the court.

(b) Duties of fax filing agency

The fax filing agency that receives a document for filing must:

(1) Prepare the document so that it complies with the rules in division 2, chapter 1 of this title and any other requirements for filing with the court;

(2) Physically transport the document to the court; and

(3) File the document with the court, paying any applicable filing fee.

(c) Requirement of advance arrangements

A fax filing agency is not required to accept papers for filing from any party unless appropriate arrangements for payment of filing fees and service charges have been made in advance of any transmission to the agency. If an agency receives a document from a party with whom it does not have prior arrangements, the agency may discard the document without notice to the sender.

(d) Confidentiality

A fax filing agency must keep all documents transmitted to it confidential except as provided in the rules in this chapter.

(e) Certification

A fax filing agency, by filing a document with the court, certifies that it has complied with the rules in this chapter and that the document filed is the full and unaltered fax–produced document received by it. The agency is not required to give any additional certification.

(f) Notation of fax filing

Each document filed by a fax filing agency must contain the phrase "By fax" immediately below the title of the document. *(Formerly Rule 2005, adopted, eff. March 1, 1992. Renumbered Rule 2.303 and amended, eff. Jan. 1, 2007.)*

Research References

Rutter, Cal. Practice Guide: Civil Appeals & Writs Ch. 3-E, E. Filing Steps.

Rutter, Cal. Practice Guide: Civ. Pro. Before Trial Ch. 9(I)-B, B. Preparing and Filing Motions.

4 Witkin Cal. Proc. 5th Pleading § 20, Fax Filing.

6 Witkin Cal. Proc. 5th Proceedings Without Trial § 34, (S 34) Filing by Fax.

Rule 2.304. Direct filing

(a) Courts in which applicable

A party may file by fax directly to any court that, by local rule, has provided for direct fax filing. The local rule must state that direct fax filing may be made under the rules in this chapter and must provide the fax telephone number for filings and specific telephone numbers for any departments to which fax filings should be made directly. The court must also accept agency filings under rule 2.303.

(b) Mandatory cover sheet

A party filing a document directly by fax must use the *Facsimile Transmission Cover Sheet (Fax Filing)* (form MC–005). The cover sheet must be the first page transmitted, to be followed by any special handling instructions needed to ensure that the document will comply with local rules. Neither the cover sheet nor the special handling instructions are to be filed in the case. The court must ensure that any credit card information on the cover sheet is not publicly disclosed. The court is not required to keep a copy of the cover sheet.

(c) Notation of fax filing

Each document transmitted for direct filing with the court must contain the phrase "By fax" immediately below the title of the document.

(d) Presumption of filing

A party filing by fax must cause the transmitting fax machine to print a transmission record of each filing by fax. If the document transmitted to the court by fax machine is not filed with the court because of (1) an error in the transmission of the document to the court that was unknown to the sending party or (2) a failure to process the document after it has been received by the court, the sending party may move the court for an order filing the document nunc pro tunc. The motion must be accompanied by the transmission record and a proof of transmission in the following form:

"~~At the time of transmission I was at least 18 years of age and not a party to this legal proceeding.~~ On (date) _____ at (time) _____, I transmitted to the (court name) _____ the following documents (name) _____ by fax machine, under California Rules of Court, rule 2.304. The court's fax telephone number that I used was (fax telephone number) ___. The fax machine I used complied with rule 2.301 and no error was reported by the machine. Under rule 2.304, I caused the machine to print a transmission record of the transmission, a copy of which is attached to this declaration.

"I declare under penalty of perjury under the laws of the State of California that the foregoing is true and correct."

(e) Payment of fees by credit card

(1) *Credit or debit card payments*

The court may permit credit cards, debit cards, electronic funds transfers, or debit accounts to be used to pay filing fees for fax filings made directly with the court, as provided in Government Code section 6159, rule 10.820, and other applicable laws. The cover sheet for these filings must include (1) the credit or debit card account number to which the fees may be charged, (2) the signature of the cardholder authorizing the charging of the fees, and (3) the expiration date of the credit or debit card.

(2) *Rejection of charge*

If the charge is rejected by the credit or debit card issuing company, the court must proceed in the same manner as under Code of Civil Procedure section 411.20 relating to returned checks. This provision does not prevent a court from seeking authorization for the charge before the filing and rejecting the filing if the charge is not approved by the issuing company.

(3) *Amount of charge*

The amount charged is the applicable filing fee plus any fee or discount imposed by the card issuer or draft purchaser.

(f) Filing fee accounts

If a court so provides in its local rule establishing a direct fax filing program, an account may be used to pay for documents filed by fax by an attorney or party who has established an account with the court before filing a paper by fax. The court may require the deposit in advance of an amount not to exceed $1,000, or the court may agree to bill the attorney or party not more often than monthly. *(Formerly Rule 2006, adopted, eff. March 1, 1992. As amended, eff. July 1, 2006. Renumbered Rule 2.304 and amended, eff. Jan. 1, 2007. As amended, eff. July 1, 2013.)*

Research References

Rutter, Cal. Practice Guide: Civil Appeals & Writs Ch. 3-E, E. Filing Steps.

Rutter, Cal. Practice Guide: Civ. Pro. Before Trial Ch. 9(I)-B, B. Preparing and Filing Motions.

4 Witkin Cal. Proc. 5th Pleading § 20, Fax Filing.

6 Witkin Cal. Proc. 5th Proceedings Without Trial § 34, (S 34) Filing by Fax.

Rule 2.305. Requirements for signatures on documents

(a) Possession of original document

A party who files or serves a signed document by fax under the rules in this chapter represents that the original signed document is in the party's possession or control.

(b) Demand for original; waiver

At any time after filing or service of a signed fax document, any other party may serve a demand for production of the original physically signed document. The demand must be served on all other parties but not filed with the court.

(c) Examination of original

If a demand for production of the original signed document is made, the parties must arrange a meeting at which the original signed document can be examined.

(d) Fax signature as original

Notwithstanding any provision of law to the contrary, including Evidence Code sections 255 and 260, a signature produced by fax transmission is deemed to be an original. *(Formerly Rule 2007, adopted, eff. March 1, 1992. Renumbered Rule 2.305 and amended, eff. Jan. 1, 2007.)*

Research References

Rutter, Cal. Practice Guide: Civ. Pro. Before Trial Ch. 9(I)-B, B. Preparing and Filing Motions.

4 Witkin Cal. Proc. 5th Pleading § 20, Fax Filing.

6 Witkin Cal. Proc. 5th Proceedings Without Trial § 25, Mechanics of Service.

6 Witkin Cal. Proc. 5th Proceedings Without Trial § 34, (S 34) Filing by Fax.

Rule 2.306.   Service of papers by fax transmission

(a) Service by fax

(1) *Agreement of parties required*

Service by fax transmission is permitted only if the parties agree and a written confirmation of that agreement is made.

(2) *Service on last-given fax number*

Any notice or other document to be served must be transmitted to a fax machine maintained by the person on whom it is served at the fax machine telephone number as last given by that person on any document that the party has filed in the case and served on the party making service.

(b) Service lists

(1) *Duties of first-named plaintiff or petitioner*

In a case in which the parties have agreed to service by fax, the plaintiff or petitioner named first in the complaint or petition, in addition to its responsibilities under rule 3.254, must:

(A) Maintain a current list of the parties that includes their fax numbers for service of notice on each party; and

(B) Furnish a copy of the list on request to any party or the court.

(2) *Duties of each party*

In a case in which the parties have agreed to service by fax, each party, in addition to its responsibilities under rule 3.254, must:

(A) Furnish the first-named plaintiff or petitioner with the party's current fax number for service of notice when it first appears in the action; and

(B) If the party serves an order, notice, or pleading on a party that has not yet appeared in the action, serve a copy of the service list under (1) at the same time that the order, notice, or pleading is served.

(c) Transmission of papers by court

A court may serve any notice by fax in the same manner that parties may serve papers by fax.

(d) Notice period extended

Except as provided in (e), any prescribed period of notice and any right or duty to do any act or make any response within any prescribed period or on a date certain after the service of a document served by fax transmission is extended by two court days.

(e) Extension inapplicable to certain motions

The extension provided in (d) does not apply to extend the time for the filing of:

(1) A notice of intent to move for new trial;

(2) A notice of intent to move to vacate a judgment under Code of Civil Procedure section 663; or

(3) A notice of appeal.

(f) Availability of fax

A party or attorney agreeing to accept service by fax must make his or her fax machine generally available for receipt of served documents between the hours of 9 a.m. and 5 p.m. on days that are not court holidays under Code of Civil Procedure section 136.   This provision does not prevent the party or attorney from sending other documents by means of the fax machine or providing for normal repair and maintenance of the fax machine during these hours.

(g) When service complete

Service by fax is complete on transmission of the entire document to the receiving party's fax machine.   Service that is completed after 5 p.m. is deemed to have occurred on the next court day.   Time is extended as provided by this rule.

(h) Proof of service by fax

Proof of service by fax may be made by any of the methods provided in Code of Civil Procedure section 1013(a), except that:

(1) The time, date, and sending fax machine telephone number must be used instead of the date and place of deposit in the mail;

(2) The name and fax machine telephone number of the person served must be used instead of the name and address of the person served as shown on the envelope;

(3) A statement that the document was sent by fax transmission and that the transmission was reported as complete and without error must be used instead of the statement that the envelope was sealed and deposited in the mail with the postage thereon fully prepaid;

(4) A copy of the transmission report must be attached to the proof of service and the proof of service must declare that the transmission report was properly issued by the sending fax machine; and

(5) Service of papers by fax is ineffective if the transmission does not fully conform to these provisions.   *(Formerly Rule 2008, adopted, eff. March 1, 1992.   As amended, eff. July 1, 1997; May 1, 1998.   Renumbered Rule 2.306 and amended, eff. Jan. 1, 2007. As amended, eff. Jan. 1, 2008; July 1, 2008.)*

Research References

Rutter, Cal. Practice Guide: Civ. Pro. Before Trial Ch. 9(I)-B, B. Preparing and Filing Motions.

Rutter, Cal. Practice Guide: Civ. Pro. Before Trial Ch. 9(II)-A, A. Injunctions.

Rutter, Cal. Practice Guide: Personal Injury Ch. 4-D, D. Techniques Where Settlement Not Forthcoming.

Rutter, Cal. Practice Guide: Personal Injury Ch. 5-B, B. When to Sue-Statute of Limitations.

2 Witkin Cal. Proc. 5th Courts § 190, (S 190) Trial Court Rules.

6 Witkin Cal. Proc. 5th Proceedings Without Trial § 24, When Permitted.

6 Witkin Cal. Proc. 5th Proceedings Without Trial § 25, Mechanics of Service.

6 Witkin Cal. Proc. 5th Proceedings Without Trial § 26, Proof of Service.

Ct. Rules

Division 4

COURT RECORDS

Chapter 1

GENERAL PROVISIONS

Rule

2.400.   Court records.

Rule 2.400.   Court records

(a) Removal of records

Only the clerk may remove and replace records in the court's files. Unless otherwise provided by these rules or ordered by the court, court records may only be inspected by the public in the office of the clerk and released to authorized court personnel or an attorney of record for use in a court facility. No original court records may be used in any location other than a court facility, unless so ordered by the presiding judge or his or her designee.

(b) Original documents filed with the clerk; duplicate documents for temporary judge or referee

(1) All original documents in a case pending before a temporary judge or referee must be filed with the clerk in the same manner as would be required if the case were being heard by a judge, including filing within any time limits specified by law and paying any required fees. The filing party must provide a filed-stamped copy to the temporary judge or referee of each document relevant to the issues before the temporary judge or referee.

(2) If a document must be filed with the court before it is considered by a judge, the temporary judge or referee must not accept or consider any copy of that document unless the document has the clerk's file stamp or is accompanied by a declaration stating that the original document has been submitted to the court for filing.

(3) If a document would ordinarily be filed with the court after it is submitted to a judge or if a party submits an ex parte application, the party that submits the document or application to a temporary judge or referee must file the original with the court no later than the next court day after the document or application was submitted to the temporary judge or referee and must promptly provide a filed-stamped copy of the document or application to the temporary judge or referee.

(4) A party that has submitted a document to a temporary judge or referee must immediately notify the temporary judge or referee if the document is not accepted for filing by the court or if the filing is subsequently canceled.

(c) Return of exhibits

(1) The clerk must not release any exhibit except on order of the court. The clerk must require a signed receipt for a released exhibit.

(2) If proceedings are conducted by a temporary judge or a referee outside of court facilities, the temporary judge or referee must keep all exhibits and deliver them, properly marked, to the clerk at the conclusion of the proceedings, unless the parties file, and the court approves, a written stipulation providing for a different disposition of the exhibits. On request of the temporary judge or referee, the clerk must deliver exhibits filed or lodged with the court to the possession of the temporary judge or referee, who must not release them to any person other than the clerk, unless the court orders otherwise.

(d) Access to documents and exhibits in matters before temporary judges and referees

(1) Documents and exhibits in the possession of a temporary judge or referee that would be open to the public if filed or lodged with the court must be made available during business hours for inspection by any person within a reasonable time after request and under reasonable conditions.

(2) Temporary judges and referees must file a statement in each case in which they are appointed that provides the name, telephone number, and mailing address of a person who may be contacted to obtain access to any documents or exhibits submitted to the temporary judge or referee that would be open to the public if filed or lodged with the court. The statement must be filed at the same time as the temporary judge's or referee's certification under rule 2.831(b), 3.904(a), or 3.924(a). If there is any change in this contact information, the temporary judge or referee must promptly file a revised statement with the court.

(e) Definition

For purposes of this rule, "court facility" consists of those areas within a building required or used for court functions. *(Formerly Rule 243, adopted, eff. Jan. 1, 1949. As amended, eff. July 1, 1993. Renumbered Rule 2.400 and amended, eff. Jan. 1, 2007. As amended, eff. Jan. 1, 2008; Jan. 1, 2009; Jan. 1, 2010.)*

Advisory Committee Comment

Subdivision (b)(1). Rules 2.810 and 2.830 provide definitions of temporary judges appointed by the court and temporary judges requested by the parties, respectively.

Subdivision (d)(1). Public access to documents and exhibits in the possession of a temporary judge or referee should be the same as if the case were being heard by a judge. Documents and exhibits are not normally available to the public during a hearing or when needed by the judge for hearing or decision preparation. A temporary judge or referee may direct that access to documents and exhibits be available by scheduled appointment.

Research References

Rutter, Cal. Practice Guide: A.D.R. Ch. 6-B, B. Temporary Judges.
Rutter, Cal. Practice Guide: A.D.R. Ch. 6-C, C. Referees.
Rutter, Cal. Practice Guide: A.D.R. App. D Form 147, Statement of Temporary Judge Re Contact/Web Site Information.
Rutter, Cal. Practice Guide: A.D.R. App. D Form 129.3, Statement of Referee Re Contact/Web Site Information.
2 Witkin Cal. Proc. 5th Courts § 190, (S 190) Trial Court Rules.
2 Witkin Cal. Proc. 5th Courts § 350, (S 350) Temporary Judge Requested by Parties.
2 Witkin Cal. Proc. 5th Courts § 370, (S 370) in General.
2 Witkin Cal. Proc. 5th Courts § 372, Custody.
6 Witkin Cal. Proc. 5th Proceedings Without Trial § 498, (S 498) Procedure.

Chapter 2

PUBLIC ACCESS TO ELECTRONIC TRIAL COURT RECORDS

Rule

2.500.   Statement of purpose.
2.501.   Application and scope.
2.502.   Definitions.
2.503.   Public access.
2.504.   Limitations and conditions.

Rule
2.505.   Contracts with vendors.
2.506.   Fees for electronic access.
2.507.   Electronic access to court calendars, indexes, and registers of actions.

Rule 2.500.   Statement of purpose

(a) Intent

The rules in this chapter are intended to provide the public with reasonable access to trial court records that are maintained in electronic form, while protecting privacy interests.

(b) Benefits of electronic access

Improved technologies provide courts with many alternatives to the historical paper-based record receipt and retention process, including the creation and use of court records maintained in electronic form. Providing public access to trial court records that are maintained in electronic form may save the courts and the public time, money, and effort and encourage courts to be more efficient in their operations. Improved access to trial court records may also foster in the public a more comprehensive understanding of the trial court system.

(c) No creation of rights

The rules in this chapter are not intended to give the public a right of access to any record that they are not otherwise entitled to access. The rules do not create any right of access to records that are sealed by court order or confidential as a matter of law. *(Formerly Rule 2070, adopted, eff. July 1, 2002. Renumbered Rule 2.500 and amended, eff. Jan. 1, 2007.)*

Advisory Committee Comment

The rules in this chapter acknowledge the benefits that electronic court records provide but attempt to limit the potential for unjustified intrusions into the privacy of individuals involved in litigation that can occur as a result of remote access to electronic court records. The proposed rules take into account the limited resources currently available in the trial courts. It is contemplated that the rules may be modified to provide greater electronic access as the courts' technical capabilities improve and with the knowledge gained from the experience of the courts in providing electronic access under these rules.

Research References

2 Witkin Cal. Proc. 5th Courts § 40, Public Access to Electronic Trial Court Records.
2 Witkin Cal. Proc. 5th Courts § 190, (S 190) Trial Court Rules.
2 Witkin Cal. Proc. 5th Courts § 374, in General.

Rule 2.501.   Application and scope

(a) Application

The rules in this chapter apply only to trial court records.

(b) Access by parties and attorneys

The rules in this chapter apply only to access to court records by the public. They do not limit access to court records by a party to an action or proceeding, by the attorney of a party, or by other persons or entities that are entitled to access by statute or rule. *(Formerly Rule 2071, adopted, eff. July 1, 2002. Renumbered Rule 2.501 and amended, eff. Jan. 1, 2007.)*

Research References

2 Witkin Cal. Proc. 5th Courts § 40, Public Access to Electronic Trial Court Records.

Rule 2.502.   Definitions

As used in this chapter, the following definitions apply:

(1) "Court record" is any document, paper, or exhibit filed by the parties to an action or proceeding; any order or judgment of the court; and any item listed in Government Code section 68151(a), excluding any reporter's transcript for which the reporter is entitled to receive a fee for any copy. The term does not include the personal notes or preliminary memoranda of judges or other judicial branch personnel.

(2) "Electronic record" is a computerized court record, regardless of the manner in which it has been computerized. The term includes both a document that has been filed electronically and an electronic copy or version of a record that was filed in paper form. The term does not include a court record that is maintained only on microfiche, paper, or any other medium that can be read without the use of an electronic device.

(3) "The public" means an individual, a group, or an entity, including print or electronic media, or the representative of an individual, a group, or an entity.

(4) "Electronic access" means computer access to court records available to the public through both public terminals at the courthouse and remotely, unless otherwise specified in the rules in this chapter. *(Formerly Rule 2072, adopted, eff. July 1, 2002. Renumbered Rule 2.502 and amended, eff. Jan. 1, 2007.)*

Research References

2 Witkin Cal. Proc. 5th Courts § 40, Public Access to Electronic Trial Court Records.

Rule 2.503.   Public access

(a) General right of access

All electronic records must be made reasonably available to the public in some form, whether in electronic or in paper form, except those that are sealed by court order or made confidential by law.

(b) Electronic access required to extent feasible

A court that maintains the following records in electronic form must provide electronic access to them, both remotely and at the courthouse, to the extent it is feasible to do so:

(1) Registers of actions (as defined in Gov. Code, § 69845), calendars, and indexes in all cases; and

(2) All records in civil cases, except those listed in (c)(1)–(9).

(c) Courthouse electronic access only

A court that maintains the following records in electronic form must provide electronic access to them at the courthouse, to the extent it is feasible to do so, but may provide remote electronic access only to the records governed by (b):

(1) Records in a proceeding under the Family Code, including proceedings for dissolution, legal separation, and nullity of marriage; child and spousal support proceedings; child custody proceedings; and domestic violence prevention proceedings;

(2) Records in a juvenile court proceeding;

(3) Records in a guardianship or conservatorship proceeding;

(4) Records in a mental health proceeding;

(5) Records in a criminal proceeding;

(6) Records in a civil harassment proceeding under Code of Civil Procedure section 527.6;

(7) Records in a workplace violence prevention proceeding under Code of Civil Procedure section 527.8;

(8) Records in a private postsecondary school violence prevention proceeding under Code of Civil Procedure section 527.85;

(9) Records in an elder or dependent adult abuse prevention proceeding under Welfare and Institutions Code section 15657.03; and

(10) Records in proceedings to compromise the claims of a minor or a person with a disability.

(d) "Feasible" defined

As used in this rule, the requirement that a court provide electronic access to its electronic records "to the extent it is feasible to do so" means that a court is required to provide electronic access to the extent it determines it has the resources and technical capacity to do so.

(e) Remote electronic access allowed in extraordinary criminal cases

Notwithstanding (c)(5), the presiding judge of the court, or a judge assigned by the presiding judge, may exercise discretion, subject to (e)(1), to permit electronic access by the public to all or a portion of the public court records in an individual criminal case if (1) the number of requests for access to documents in the case is extraordinarily high and (2) responding to those requests would significantly burden the operations of the court. An individualized determination must be made in each case in which such remote electronic access is provided.

(1) In exercising discretion under (e), the judge should consider the relevant factors, such as:

(A) The privacy interests of parties, victims, witnesses, and court personnel, and the ability of the court to redact sensitive personal information;

(B) The benefits to and burdens on the parties in allowing remote electronic access, including possible impacts on jury selection; and

(C) The burdens on the court in responding to an extraordinarily high number of requests for access to documents.

(2) The court should, to the extent feasible, redact the following information from records to which it allows remote access under (e): driver license numbers; dates of birth; social security numbers; Criminal Identification and Information and National Crime Information numbers; addresses and phone numbers of parties, victims, witnesses, and court personnel; medical or psychiatric information; financial information; account numbers; and other personal identifying information. The court may order any party who files a document containing such information to provide the court with both an original unredacted version of the document for filing in the court file and a redacted version of the document for remote electronic access. No juror names or other juror identifying information may be provided by remote electronic access. This subdivision does not apply to any document in the original court file; it applies only to documents that are available by remote electronic access.

(3) Five days' notice must be provided to the parties and the public before the court makes a determination to provide remote electronic access under this rule. Notice to the public may be accomplished by posting notice on the court's Web site. Any person may file comments with the court for consideration, but no hearing is required.

(4) The court's order permitting remote electronic access must specify which court records will be available by remote electronic access and what categories of information are to be redacted. The court is not required to make findings of fact. The court's order must be posted on the court's Web site and a copy sent to the Judicial Council.

(f) Access only on a case-by-case basis

The court may only grant electronic access to an electronic record when the record is identified by the number of the case, the caption of the case, or the name of a party, and only on a case-by-case basis. This case-by-case limitation does not apply to the court's electronic records of a calendar, register of actions, or index.

(g) Bulk distribution

The court may provide bulk distribution of only its electronic records of a calendar, register of actions, and index. "Bulk distribution" means distribution of all, or a significant subset, of the court's electronic records.

(h) Records that become inaccessible

If an electronic record to which the court has provided electronic access is made inaccessible to the public by court order or by operation of law, the court is not required to take action with respect to any copy of the record that was made by the public before the record became inaccessible.

(i) Off-site access

Courts should encourage availability of electronic access to court records at public off-site locations. *(Formerly Rule 2073, adopted, eff. July 1, 2002. As amended, eff. July 1, 2004; Jan. 1, 2005. Renumbered Rule 2.503 and amended, eff. Jan. 1, 2007. As amended, eff. Jan. 1, 2008; Jan. 1, 2010; Jan. 1, 2012.)*

Advisory Committee Comment

The rule allows a level of access by the public to all electronic records that is at least equivalent to the access that is available for paper records and, for some types of records, is much greater. At the same time, it seeks to protect legitimate privacy concerns.

Subdivision (c). This subdivision excludes certain records (those other than the register, calendar, and indexes) in specified types of cases (notably criminal, juvenile, and family court matters) from remote electronic access. The committee recognized that while these case records are public records and should remain available at the courthouse, either in paper or electronic form, they often contain sensitive personal information. The court should not publish that information over the Internet. However, the committee also recognized that the use of the Internet may be appropriate in certain criminal cases of extraordinary public interest where information regarding a case will be widely disseminated through the media. In such cases, posting of selected nonconfidential court records, redacted where necessary to protect the privacy of the participants, may provide more timely and accurate information regarding the court proceedings, and may relieve substantial burdens on court staff in responding to individual requests for documents and information. Thus, under subdivision (e), if the presiding judge makes individualized determinations in a specific case, certain records in criminal cases may be made available over the Internet.

Subdivisions (f) (g). These subdivisions limit electronic access to records (other than the register, calendars, or indexes) to a case-by-case basis and prohibit bulk distribution of those records. These limitations are based on the qualitative difference between obtaining information from a specific case file and obtaining bulk information that may be manipulated to compile personal information culled from any document, paper, or exhibit filed in a lawsuit. This type of aggregate information may be exploited for commercial or other purposes unrelated to the operations of the courts, at the expense of privacy rights of individuals.

Courts must send a copy of the order permitting remote electronic access in extraordinary criminal cases to: Secretariat, Executive Office Programs Division, Administrative Office of the Courts, 455 Golden Gate Avenue, San Francisco, CA 94102–3688 or secretariat@jud.ca.gov.

Research References

Rutter, Cal. Practice Guide: Civ. Pro. Before Trial Ch. 9(I)-B, B. Preparing and Filing Motions.

2 Witkin Cal. Proc. 5th Courts § 40, Public Access to Electronic Trial Court Records.

Rule 2.504. Limitations and conditions

(a) Means of access

A court that maintains records in electronic form must provide electronic access to those records by means of a network or software that is based on industry standards or is in the public domain.

(b) Official record

Unless electronically certified by the court, a trial court record available by electronic access is not the official record of the court.

(c) Conditions of use by persons accessing records

A court may condition electronic access to its records on:

(1) The user's consent to access the records only as instructed by the court; and

(2) The user's consent to the court's monitoring of access to its records.

The court must give notice of these conditions, in any manner it deems appropriate. The court may deny access to a member of the public for failure to comply with either of these conditions of use.

(d) Notices to persons accessing records

The court must give notice of the following information to members of the public accessing its records electronically, in any manner it deems appropriate:

(1) The identity of the court staff member to be contacted about the requirements for accessing the court's records electronically.

(2) That copyright and other proprietary rights may apply to information in a case file, absent an express grant of additional rights by the holder of the copyright or other proprietary right. This notice must advise the public that:

    (A) Use of such information in a case file is permissible only to the extent permitted by law or court order; and

    (B) Any use inconsistent with proprietary rights is prohibited.

(3) Whether electronic records are the official records of the court. The notice must describe the procedure and any fee required for obtaining a certified copy of an official record of the court.

(4) That any person who willfully destroys or alters any court record maintained in electronic form is subject to the penalties imposed by Government Code section 6201.

(e) Access policy

The court must post a privacy policy on its public-access Web site to inform members of the public accessing its electronic records of the information it collects regarding access transactions and the uses that the court may make of the collected information. *(Formerly Rule 2074, adopted, eff. July 1, 2002. Renumbered Rule 2.504 and amended, eff. Jan. 1, 2007.)*

Research References

2 Witkin Cal. Proc. 5th Courts § 40, Public Access to Electronic Trial Court Records.

Rule 2.505. Contracts with vendors

(a) Contract must provide access consistent with rules

The court's contract with a vendor to provide public access to its electronic records must be consistent with the rules in this chapter and must require the vendor to provide public access to court records and to protect the confidentiality of court records as required by law or by court order.

(b) Contract must provide that court owns the records

Any contract between the court and a vendor to provide public access to the court's electronic records must provide that the court is the owner of these records and has the exclusive right to control their use. *(Formerly Rule 2075, adopted, eff. July 1, 2002. Renumbered Rule 2.505 and amended, eff. Jan. 1, 2007.)*

Rule 2.506. Fees for electronic access

(a) Court may impose fees

The court may impose fees for the costs of providing public access to its electronic records, under Government Code section 68150(h*l*). On request, the court must provide the public with a statement of the costs on which these fees are based.

(b) Fees of vendor must be reasonable

To the extent that public access to a court's electronic records is provided exclusively through a vendor, the court must ensure that any fees the vendor imposes for the costs of providing access are reasonable. *(Formerly Rule 2076, adopted, eff. July 1, 2002. Renumbered Rule 2.506 and amended, eff. Jan. 1, 2007. As amended, eff. July 1, 2013.)*

Research References

2 Witkin Cal. Proc. 5th Courts § 40, Public Access to Electronic Trial Court Records.

Rule 2.507. Electronic access to court calendars, indexes, and registers of actions

(a) Intent

This rule specifies information to be included in and excluded from the court calendars, indexes, and registers of actions to which public access is available by electronic means under rule 2.503(b). To the extent it is feasible to do so, the court must maintain court calendars, indexes, and registers of actions available to the public by electronic means in accordance with this rule.

(b) Minimum contents for electronically accessible court calendars, indexes, and registers of actions

(1) The electronic court calendar must include:

    (A) Date of court calendar;

    (B) Time of calendared event;

    (C) Court department number;

    (D) Case number; and

    (E) Case title (unless made confidential by law).

(2) The electronic index must include:

    (A) Case title (unless made confidential by law);

    (B) Party names (unless made confidential by law);

    (C) Party type;

    (D) Date on which the case was filed; and

    (E) Case number.

(3) The register of actions must be a summary of every proceeding in a case, in compliance with Government Code section 69845, and must include:

    (A) Date case commenced;

    (B) Case number;

    (C) Case type;

    (D) Case title (unless made confidential by law);

    (E) Party names (unless made confidential by law);

    (F) Party type;

    (G) Date of each activity; and

    (H) Description of each activity.

Ct. Rules

(c) Information that must be excluded from court calendars, indexes, and registers of actions

The following information must be excluded from a court's electronic calendar, index, and register of actions:

(1) Social security number;

(2) Any financial information;

(3) Arrest warrant information;

(4) Search warrant information;

(5) Victim information;

(6) Witness information;

(7) Ethnicity;

(8) Age;

(9) Gender;

(10) Government–issued identification card numbers (i.e., military);

(11) Driver's license number; and

(12) Date of birth. *(Formerly Rule 2077, adopted, eff. July 1, 2003. Renumbered Rule 2.507 and amended, eff. Jan. 1, 2007.)*

Research References

2 Witkin Cal. Proc. 5th Courts § 40, Public Access to Electronic Trial Court Records.
2 Witkin Cal. Proc. 5th Courts § 190, (S 190) Trial Court Rules.

Chapter 3

SEALED RECORDS

Rule
2.550. Sealed records.
2.551. Procedures for filing records under seal.

Rule 2.550. Sealed records

(a) Application

(1) Rules 2.550–2.551 apply to records sealed or proposed to be sealed by court order.

(2) These rules do not apply to records that are required to be kept confidential by law.

(3) These rules do not apply to discovery motions and records filed or lodged in connection with discovery motions or proceedings. However, the rules do apply to discovery materials that are used at trial or submitted as a basis for adjudication of matters other than discovery motions or proceedings.

(b) Definitions

As used in this chapter:

(1) "Record." Unless the context indicates otherwise, "record" means all or a portion of any document, paper, exhibit, transcript, or other thing filed or lodged with the court.

(2) "Sealed." A "sealed" record is a record that by court order is not open to inspection by the public.

(3) "Lodged." A "lodged" record is a record that is temporarily placed or deposited with the court, but not filed.

(c) Court records presumed to be open

Unless confidentiality is required by law, court records are presumed to be open.

(d) Express factual findings required to seal records

The court may order that a record be filed under seal only if it expressly finds facts that establish:

(1) There exists an overriding interest that overcomes the right of public access to the record;

(2) The overriding interest supports sealing the record;

(3) A substantial probability exists that the overriding interest will be prejudiced if the record is not sealed;

(4) The proposed sealing is narrowly tailored; and

(5) No less restrictive means exist to achieve the overriding interest.

(e) Content and scope of the order

(1) An order sealing the record must:

(A) Specifically state the facts that support the findings; and

(B) Direct the sealing of only those documents and pages, or, if reasonably practicable, portions of those documents and pages, that contain the material that needs to be placed under seal. All other portions of each document or page must be included in the public file.

(2) Consistent with Code of Civil Procedure sections 639 and 645.1, if the records that a party is requesting be placed under seal are voluminous, the court may appoint a referee and fix and allocate the referee's fees among the parties. *(Formerly Rule 243.1, adopted, eff. Jan. 1, 2001. As amended, eff. Jan. 1, 2004. Renumbered Rule 2.550 and amended, eff. Jan. 1, 2007.)*

Advisory Committee Comment

This rule and rule 2.551 provide a standard and procedures for courts to use when a request is made to seal a record. The standard is based on *NBC Subsidiary (KNBC–TV), Inc. v. Superior Court* (1999) 20 Cal.4th 1178. These rules apply to civil and criminal cases. They recognize the First Amendment right of access to documents used at trial or as a basis of adjudication. The rules do not apply to records that courts must keep confidential by law. Examples of confidential records to which public access is restricted by law are records of the family conciliation court (Family Code, § 1818(b)), in forma pauperis applications (Cal. Rules of Court, rules 3.54 and 8.26), and search warrant affidavits sealed under *People v. Hobbs* (1994) 7 Cal.4th 948. The sealed records rules also do not apply to discovery proceedings, motions, and materials that are not used at trial or submitted to the court as a basis for adjudication. (See *NBC Subsidiary, supra,* 20 Cal.4th at pp. 1208–1209, fn. 25.)

Rule 2.550(d)–(e) is derived from *NBC Subsidiary*. That decision contains the requirements that the court, before closing a hearing or sealing a transcript, must find an "overriding interest" that supports the closure or sealing, and must make certain express findings. (*Id.* at pp. 1217–1218.) The decision notes that the First Amendment right of access applies to records filed in both civil and criminal cases as a basis for adjudication. (*Id.* at pp. 1208–1209, fn. 25.) Thus, the *NBC Subsidiary* test applies to the sealing of records.

NBC Subsidiary provides examples of various interests that courts have acknowledged may constitute "overriding interests." (See *id.* at p. 1222, fn. 46.) Courts have found that, under appropriate circumstances, various statutory privileges, trade secrets, and privacy interests, when properly asserted and not waived, may constitute "overriding interests." The rules do not attempt to define what may constitute an "overriding interest," but leave this to case law.

Research References

Rutter, Cal. Practice Guide: Civil Appeals & Writs Ch. 5-B, B. Types of Motions, Applications and Requests.
Rutter, Cal. Practice Guide: Civil Appeals & Writs Ch. 8-C, C. Standards of Appellate Review.
Rutter, Cal. Practice Guide: Civil Appeals & Writs Ch. 16-E, E. Motions, Applications and Requests.
Rutter, Cal. Practice Guide: Civ. Pro. Before Trial Ch. 2-B, B. Capacity to Sue or Defend.

Rutter, Cal. Practice Guide: Civ. Pro. Before Trial Ch. 8C-5, Privacy Protection.

Rutter, Cal. Practice Guide: Civ. Pro. Before Trial Ch. 9(I)-I, I. Motion to Seal Court Records.

Rutter, Cal. Practice Guide: Civ. Pro. Before Trial Ch. 9(II)-D, D. Attachment.

Rutter, Cal. Practice Guide: Civ. Pro. Before Trial Ch. 12(II)-E, E. Motion to Determine "Good Faith" of "Piecemeal" Settlement (CCP § 877.6).

Rutter, Cal. Practice Guide: Civ. Pro. Before Trial Ch. 12(II)-H, H. Professional Responsibility Considerations Re Settlements.

Rutter, Cal. Practice Guide: Civil Trials & Evidence Ch. 4-B, B. Preliminary Matters Discussed in Final Status Conference or In-Chambers Conference.

2 Witkin Cal. Proc. 5th Courts § 41, in General.

2 Witkin Cal. Proc. 5th Courts § 42, (S 42) in General.

2 Witkin Cal. Proc. 5th Courts § 43, (S 43) Review of Sealing Orders.

2 Witkin Cal. Proc. 5th Courts § 44, Sealed Records in Reviewing Courts.

2 Witkin Cal. Proc. 5th Courts § 190, (S 190) Trial Court Rules.

7 Witkin, California Summary 10th Constitutional Law § 423, (S 423) Civil Trial.

Rule 2.551.   Procedures for filing records under seal

(a) Court approval required

A record must not be filed under seal without a court order. The court must not permit a record to be filed under seal based solely on the agreement or stipulation of the parties.

(b) Motion or application to seal a record

(1) *Motion or application required*

A party requesting that a record be filed under seal must file a motion or an application for an order sealing the record. The motion or application must be accompanied by a memorandum and a declaration containing facts sufficient to justify the sealing.

(2) *Service of motion or application*

A copy of the motion or application must be served on all parties that have appeared in the case. Unless the court orders otherwise, any party that already possesses copies of the records to be placed under seal must be served with a complete, unredacted version of all papers as well as a redacted version.

(3) *Procedure for party not intending to file motion or application*

(A) A party that files or intends to file with the court, for the purposes of adjudication or to use at trial, records produced in discovery that are subject to a confidentiality agreement or protective order, and does not intend to request to have the records sealed, must:

(i) Lodge the unredacted records subject to the confidentiality agreement or protective order and any pleadings, memorandums, declarations, and other documents that disclose the contents of the records, in the manner stated in (d);

(ii) File copies of the documents in (i) that are redacted so that they do not disclose the contents of the records that are subject to the confidentiality agreement or protective order; and

(iii) Give written notice to the party that produced the records that the records and the other documents lodged under (i) will be placed in the public court file unless that party files a timely motion or application to seal the records under this rule.

(B) If the party that produced the documents and was served with the notice under (A)(iii) fails to file a motion or an application to seal the records within 10 days or to obtain a court order extending the time to file such a motion or an application, the clerk must promptly remove all the documents in (A)(i) from the envelope or container where they are located and place them in the public file. If the party files a motion or an application to seal within 10 days or such later time as the court has ordered, these documents are to remain conditionally under seal until the court rules on the motion or application and thereafter are to be filed as ordered by the court.

(4) *Lodging of record pending determination of motion or application*

The party requesting that a record be filed under seal must lodge it with the court under (d) when the motion or application is made, unless good cause exists for not lodging it or the record has previously been lodged under (3)(A)(i). Pending the determination of the motion or application, the lodged record will be conditionally under seal.

(5) *Redacted and unredacted versions*

If necessary to prevent disclosure, any motion or application, any opposition, and any supporting documents must be filed in a public redacted version and lodged in a complete version conditionally under seal.

(6) *Return of lodged record*

If the court denies the motion or application to seal, the clerk must return the lodged record to the submitting party and must not place it in the case file unless that party notifies the clerk in writing within 10 days after the order denying the motion or application that the record is to be filed.

(c) References to nonpublic material in public records

A record filed publicly in the court must not disclose material contained in a record that is sealed, conditionally under seal, or subject to a pending motion or an application to seal.

(d) Procedure for lodging of records

(1) A record that may be filed under seal must be put in an envelope or other appropriate container, sealed in the envelope or container, and lodged with the court.

(2) The envelope or container lodged with the court must be labeled "CONDITIONALLY UNDER SEAL."

(3) The party submitting the lodged record must affix to the envelope or container a cover sheet that:

(A) Contains all the information required on a caption page under rule 2.111; and

(B) States that the enclosed record is subject to a motion or an application to file the record under seal.

(4) On receipt of a record lodged under this rule, the clerk must endorse the affixed cover sheet with the date of its receipt and must retain but not file the record unless the court orders it filed.

(e) Order

(1) If the court grants an order sealing a record, the clerk must substitute on the envelope or container for the label required by (d)(2) a label prominently stating "SEALED BY ORDER OF THE COURT ON *(DATE)*," and must replace the cover sheet required by (d)(3) with a filed-endorsed copy of the court's order.

(2) The order must state whether—in addition to records in the envelope or container—the order itself, the register of actions, any other court records, or any other records relating to the case are to be sealed.

(3) The order must state whether any person other than the court is authorized to inspect the sealed record.

(4) Unless the sealing order provides otherwise, it prohibits the parties from disclosing the contents of any materials that have been sealed in any subsequently filed records or papers.

(f) Custody of sealed records

Ct. Rules

Sealed records must be securely filed and kept separate from the public file in the case.

(g) Custody of voluminous records

If the records to be placed under seal are voluminous and are in the possession of a public agency, the court may by written order direct the agency instead of the clerk to maintain custody of the original records in a secure fashion. If the records are requested by a reviewing court, the trial court must order the public agency to deliver the records to the clerk for transmission to the reviewing court under these rules.

(h) Motion, application, or petition to unseal records

(1) A sealed record must not be unsealed except on order of the court.

(2) A party or member of the public may move, apply, or petition, or the court on its own motion may move, to unseal a record. Notice of any motion, application, or petition to unseal must be filed and served on all parties in the case. The motion, application, or petition and any opposition, reply, and supporting documents must be filed in a public redacted version and a sealed complete version if necessary to comply with (c).

(3) If the court proposes to order a record unsealed on its own motion, the court must mail notice to the parties stating the reason therefor. Any party may serve and file an opposition within 10 days after the notice is mailed or within such time as the court specifies. Any other party may file a response within 5 days after the filing of an opposition.

(4) In determining whether to unseal a record, the court must consider the matters addressed in rule 2.550(c)–(e).

(5) The order unsealing a record must state whether the record is unsealed entirely or in part. If the court's order unseals only part of the record or unseals the record only as to certain persons, the order must specify the particular records that are unsealed, the particular persons who may have access to the record, or both. If, in addition to the records in the envelope or container, the court has previously ordered the sealing order, the register of actions, or any other court records relating to the case to be sealed, the unsealing order must state whether these additional records are unsealed. *(Formerly Rule 243.2, adopted, eff. Jan. 1, 2001. As amended, eff. Jan. 1, 2004. Renumbered Rule 2.551 and amended, eff. Jan. 1, 2007.)*

Research References

Rutter, Cal. Practice Guide: Civil Appeals & Writs Ch. 16-E, E. Motions, Applications and Requests.
Rutter, Cal. Practice Guide: Civ. Pro. Before Trial Ch. 8H-5, Protective Orders.
Rutter, Cal. Practice Guide: Civ. Pro. Before Trial Ch. 9(I)-I, I. Motion to Seal Court Records.
Rutter, Cal. Practice Guide: Civ. Pro. Before Trial Ch. 12(II)-H, H. Professional Responsibility Considerations Re Settlements.
Rutter, Cal. Practice Guide: Civil Trials & Evidence Ch. 4-B, B. Preliminary Matters Discussed in Final Status Conference or In-Chambers Conference.
Rutter, Cal. Practice Guide: Civil Trials & Evidence Ch. 17-E, E. Attorney Fees as Costs.
2 Witkin Cal. Proc. 5th Courts § 41, in General.
2 Witkin Cal. Proc. 5th Courts § 42, (S 42) in General.
2 Witkin Cal. Proc. 5th Courts § 43, (S 43) Review of Sealing Orders.
2 Witkin Cal. Proc. 5th Courts § 44, Sealed Records in Reviewing Courts.
2 Witkin Cal. Proc. 5th Courts § 190, (S 190) Trial Court Rules.
7 Witkin, California Summary 10th Constitutional Law § 423, (S 423) Civil Trial.

Chapter 4

RECORDS IN FALSE CLAIMS ACT CASES

Rule
2.570. Filing False Claims Act records under seal.
2.571. Procedures for filing records under seal in a False Claims Act case.
2.572. Ex parte application for an extension of time.
2.573. Unsealing of records and management of False Claims Act cases.

Rule 2.570. Filing False Claims Act records under seal

(a) Application

Rules 2.570–2.573 apply to records initially filed under seal pursuant to the False Claims Act, Government Code section 12650 et seq. As to these records, rules 2.550–2.551 on sealed records do not apply.

(b) Definitions

As used in this chapter, unless the context or subject matter otherwise requires:

(1) "Attorney General" means the Attorney General of the State of California.

(2) "Prosecuting authority" means the county counsel, city attorney, or other local government official charged with investigating, filing, and conducting civil legal proceedings on behalf of or in the name of a particular political subdivision.

(3) *"Qui tam* plaintiff" means a person who files a complaint under the False Claims Act.

(4) The definitions in Government Code section 12650 apply to the rules in this chapter.

(c) Confidentiality of records filed under the False Claims Act

Records of actions filed by a *qui tam* plaintiff must initially be filed as confidential and under seal as required by Government Code section 12652(c). Until the seal is lifted, the records in the action must remain under seal, except to the extent otherwise provided in this rule.

(d) Persons permitted access to sealed records in a False Claims Act case

(1) *Public access prohibited*

As long as the records in a False Claims Act case are under seal, public access to the records in the case is prohibited. The prohibition on public access applies not only to filed documents but also to electronic records that would disclose information about the case, including the identity of any plaintiff or defendant.

(2) *Information on register of actions*

As long as the records in a False Claims Act case are under seal, only the information concerning filed records contained on the confidential cover sheet prescribed under rule 2.571(c) may be entered into the register of actions that is accessible to the public.

(3) *Parties permitted access to the sealed court file*

As long as the records in a False Claims Act case are under seal, the only parties permitted access to the court file are:

(A) The Attorney General;

(B) A prosecuting authority for the political subdivision on whose behalf the action is brought, unless the political subdivision is named as a defendant; and

(C) A prosecuting authority for any other political subdivision interested in the matter whose identity has been provided to the court by the Attorney General.

(4) *Parties not permitted access to the sealed court file*

As long as records in a False Claims Act case are under seal, no defendant is permitted to have access to the court records or other information concerning the case. Defendants not permitted access include any political subdivision that has been named as a defendant in a False Claims Act action.

(5) Qui tam *plaintiff's limited access to sealed court file*

The *qui tam* plaintiff in a False Claims Act case may have access to all documents filed by the *qui tam* plaintiff and to such other documents as the court may order. *(Formerly Rule 243.5, adopted, eff. July 1, 2002. Renumbered Rule 2.570 and amended, eff. Jan. 1, 2007.)*

Research References

2 Witkin Cal. Proc. 5th Courts § 42, (S 42) in General.
2 Witkin Cal. Proc. 5th Courts § 190, (S 190) Trial Court Rules.

Rule 2.571. Procedures for filing records under seal in a False Claims Act case

(a) No sealing order required

On the filing of an action under the False Claims Act,[1] the complaint, motions for extensions of time, and other papers filed with the court must be kept under seal. Under Government Code section 12652, no order sealing these records is necessary.

(b) Filing a False Claims Act case in a county where filings are accepted in multiple locations

In a county where complaints in civil cases may be filed in more than one location, the presiding judge must designate one particular location where all filings in False Claims Act cases must be made.

(c) Special cover sheet omitting names of the parties

In a False Claims Act case, the complaint and every other paper filed while the case is under seal must have a completed *Confidential Cover Sheet—False Claims Action* (form MC–060) affixed to the first page.

(d) Filing of papers under seal

When the complaint or other paper in a False Claims Act case is filed under seal, the clerk must stamp both the cover sheet and the caption page of the paper.

(e) Custody of sealed records

Records in a False Claims Act case that are confidential and under seal must be securely filed and kept separate from the public file in the case. *(Formerly Rule 243.6, adopted, eff. July 1, 2002. Renumbered Rule 2.571 and amended, eff. Jan. 1, 2007.)*

[1] See Government Code § 12650 et seq.

Rule 2.572. Ex parte application for an extension of time

A party in a False Claims Act case may apply under the ex parte rules in title 3 for an extension of time under Government Code section 12. *(Formerly Rule 243.7, adopted, eff. July 1, 2002. Renumbered Rule 2.572 and amended, eff. Jan. 1, 2007.)*

Rule 2.573. Unsealing of records and management of False Claims Act cases

(a) Expiration or lifting of seal

(1) Records in a False Claims Act case to which public access has been prohibited under Government Code section 12652(c) must remain under seal until the Attorney General and all local prosecuting authorities involved in the action have notified the court of their decision to intervene or not intervene.

(2) The Attorney General and all local prosecuting authorities involved in the action must give the notice required under (1) within 60 days of the filing of the complaint or before an order extending the time to intervene has expired, unless a new motion to extend time to intervene is pending, in which case the seal remains in effect until a ruling is made on the motion.

(b) Coordination of state and local authorities

The Attorney General and all local prosecuting authorities must coordinate their activities to provide timely and effective notice to the court that:

(1) A political subdivision or subdivisions remain interested in the action and have not yet determined whether to intervene; or

(2) The seal has been extended by the filing or grant of a motion to extend time to intervene, and therefore the seal has not expired.

(c) Designation of lead local prosecuting authority

In a False Claims Act [1] case in which the Attorney General is not involved or has declined to intervene and local prosecuting authorities remain interested in the action, the court may designate a lead prosecuting authority to keep the court apprised of whether all the prosecuting authorities have either intervened or declined to intervene, and whether the seal is to be lifted.

(d) Order unsealing record

The Attorney General or other prosecuting authority filing a notice of intervention or nonintervention must submit a proposed order indicating the documents that are to be unsealed or to remain sealed.

(e) Case management

(1) *Case management conferences*

The court, at the request of the parties or on its own motion, may hold a conference at any time in a False Claims Act case to determine what case management is appropriate for the case, including the lifting or partial lifting of the seal, the scheduling of trial and other events, and any other matters that may assist in managing the case.

(2) *Exemption from case management rules*

Cases under the False Claims Act are exempt from rule 3.110 and the case management rules in title 3, division 7, but are subject to such case management orders as the court may issue. *(Formerly Rule 243.8, adopted, eff. July 1, 2002. Renumbered Rule 2.573 and amended, eff. Jan. 1, 2007.)*

[1] See Government Code § 12650 et seq.

Research References

Rutter, Cal. Practice Guide: Civ. Pro. Before Trial Ch. 12(I)-B, B. Case Management ("Fast Track") System.
2 Witkin Cal. Proc. 5th Courts § 190, (S 190) Trial Court Rules.

Chapter 5

NAME CHANGE PROCEEDINGS UNDER ADDRESS CONFIDENTIALITY PROGRAM

Rule 2.575. Confidential information in name change proceedings under address confidentiality program

(a) Definitions

As used in this chapter, unless the context or subject matter otherwise requires:

(1) "Confidential name change petitioner" means a petitioner who is a participant in the address confidentiality program created by the Secretary of State under chapter 3.1 (commencing with section 6205) of division 7 of title 1 of the Government Code.

(2) "Record" means all or a portion of any document, paper, exhibit, transcript, or other thing that is filed or lodged with the court.

(3) "Lodged" means temporarily placed or deposited with the court but not filed.

(b) Application of chapter

The rules in this chapter apply to records filed in a change of name proceeding under Code of Civil Procedure section 1277(b) by a confidential name change petitioner who alleges any of the following reasons or circumstances as a reason for the name change:

(1) The petitioner is seeking to avoid domestic violence, as defined in Family Code section 6211.

(2) The petitioner is seeking to avoid stalking, as defined in Penal Code section 646.9.

(3) The petitioner is, or is filing on behalf of, a victim of sexual assault, as defined in Evidence Code section 1036.2.

(c) Confidentiality of current name of the petitioner

The current legal name of a confidential name change petitioner must be kept confidential by the court as required by Code of Civil Procedure section 1277(b)(3) and not be published or posted in the court's calendars, indexes, or register of actions, or by any means or in any public forum. Only the information concerning filed records contained on the confidential cover sheet prescribed under (d) may be entered into the register of actions or any other forum that is accessible to the public.

(d) Special cover sheet omitting names of the petitioner

To maintain the confidentiality provided under Code of Civil Procedure section 1277(b) for the petitioner's current name, the petitioner must attach a completed *Confidential Cover Sheet—Name Change Proceeding Under Address Confidentiality Program (Safe at Home)* (form NC–400) to the front of the petition for name change and every other document filed in the proceedings. The name of the petitioner must not appear on that cover sheet.

(e) Confidentiality of proposed name of the petitioner

To maintain the confidentiality provided under Code of Civil Procedure section 1277(b) for the petitioner's proposed name, the petitioner must not include the proposed name on the petition for name change or any other record in the proceedings. In any form that requests the petitioner's proposed name, the petitioner and the court must indicate that the proposed name is confidential and on file with the Secretary of State under the provisions of the Safe at Home address confidentiality program. *(Adopted, eff. Jan. 1, 2010.)*

Research References

2 Witkin Cal. Proc. 5th Courts § 190, (S 190) Trial Court Rules.
13 Witkin, California Summary 10th Personal Property § 24, Right to Change Name.

Rule 2.576. Access to name of the petitioner

(a) Termination of confidentiality

The current name of a confidential name change petitioner must remain confidential until a determination is made that:

(1) Petitioner's participation in the address confidentiality program has ended under Government Code section 6206.7; or

(2) The court finds by clear and convincing evidence that the allegations of domestic violence or stalking in the petition are false.

(b) Procedure to obtain access

A determination under (a) must be made by noticed motion, with service by mail on the confidential name change petitioner in care of the Secretary of State's address confidentiality program as stated in Government Code section 6206(a)(5)(A). *(Adopted, eff. Jan. 1, 2010.)*

Research References

13 Witkin, California Summary 10th Personal Property § 24, Right to Change Name.

Rule 2.577. Procedures for filing confidential name change records under seal

(a) Court approval required

Records in a name change proceeding may not be filed under seal without a court order. A request by a confidential name change petitioner to file records under seal may be made under the procedures in this chapter. A request by any other petitioner to file records under seal must be made under rules 2.550–2.573.

(b) Application to file records in confidential name change proceedings under seal

An application by a confidential name change petitioner to file records under seal must be filed at the time the petition for name change is submitted to the court. The application must be made on the *Application to File Documents Under Seal in Name Change Proceeding Under Address Confidentiality Program (Safe at Home)* (NC–410) and be accompanied by a *Declaration in Support of Application to File Documents Under Seal in Name Change Proceeding Under Address Confidentiality Program (Safe at Home)* (form NC–420), containing facts sufficient to justify the sealing.

(c) Confidentiality

The application to file under seal must be kept confidential by the court until the court rules on it.

(d) Procedure for lodging of petition for name change

(1) The records that may be filed under seal must be lodged with the court in a sealed envelope.

(2) The petitioner must complete and affix to the envelope a completed *Confidential Cover Sheet—Name Change Proceeding Under Address Confidentiality Program (Safe at Home)* (form NC–400) and in the space under the title and case number mark it "CONDITIONALLY UNDER SEAL."

(3) On receipt of a petition lodged under this rule, the clerk must endorse the affixed cover sheet with the date of its receipt and must retain but not file the record unless the court orders it filed.

(4) If the court denies the application to seal, the clerk must return the lodged record to the petitioner and must not place it in the case file unless the petitioner notifies the clerk in writing within 10 days after the order denying the application that the unsealed petition and related papers are to be filed.

(e) Consideration of application to file under seal

The court may order that the record be filed under seal if it finds that all of the following factors apply:

(1) There exists an overriding interest that overcomes the right of public access to the record;

(2) The overriding interest supports sealing the record;

(3) A substantial probability exists that the overriding interest will be prejudiced if the record is not sealed;

(4) The proposed order to seal the record is narrowly tailored; and

(5) No less restrictive means exist to achieve the overriding interest.

(f) Order

(1) The order may be issued on *Order on Application to File Documents Under Seal in Name Change Proceeding Under Address Confidentiality Program (Safe at Home)* (form NC–425).

(2) Any order granting the application to seal must state whether the declaration in support of the application, the order itself, and any other record in the proceeding are to be sealed as well as the petition for name change.

(3) If the court grants an order sealing a record, the clerk must strike out the notation required by (d)(2) on the *Confidential Cover Sheet* that the matter is filed "CONDITIONALLY UNDER SEAL" and add a notation to that sheet prominently stating "SEALED BY ORDER OF THE COURT ON (DATE)."

(4) If the court grants the application to file under seal and issues an order under (e), the petition and any associated records may be filed under seal and ruled on by the court immediately.

(5) The order must identify any person other than the court who is authorized to inspect the sealed records.

(g) Custody of sealed records

Sealed records must be securely filed and kept separate from the public file in the case.

(h) Motion, application, or petition to unseal record

(1) A sealed record may not be unsealed except by order of the court.

(2) Any member of the public seeking to unseal a record or a court proposing to do so on its own motion must follow the procedures described in rule 2.551(h). *(Adopted, eff. Jan. 1, 2010.)*

Research References

2 Witkin Cal. Proc. 5th Courts § 190, (S 190) Trial Court Rules.
13 Witkin, California Summary 10th Personal Property § 24, Right to Change Name.

Chapter 6

OTHER SEALED OR CLOSED RECORDS

Rule 2.580.　Request for delayed public disclosure

In an action in which the prejudgment attachment remedy under Code of Civil Procedure section 483.010 et seq. is sought, if the plaintiff requests at the time a complaint is filed that the records in the action or the fact of the filing of the action be made temporarily unavailable to the public under Code of Civil Procedure section 482.050, the plaintiff must file a declaration stating one of the following:

(1) "This action is on a claim for money based on contract against a defendant who is not a natural person. The claim is not secured within the meaning of Code of Civil Procedure section 483.010(b)."—or—

(2) "This action is on a claim for money based on contract against a defendant who is a natural person. The claim arises out of the defendant's conduct of a trade, business, or profession, and the money, property, or services were not used by the defendant primarily for personal, family, or household purposes. The claim is not secured within the meaning of Code of Civil Procedure section 483.010(b)." *(Formerly Rule 243.3, adopted, eff. Jan. 1, 2001. Renumbered Rule 2.580, eff. Jan. 1, 2007.)*

Research References

Rutter, Cal. Practice Guide: Civ. Pro. Before Trial Ch. 9(II)-D, D. Attachment.
Rutter, Cal. Practice Guide: Enforcing Judgments/Debts Ch. 4-A, A. Attachment.
2 Witkin Cal. Proc. 5th Courts § 190, (S 190) Trial Court Rules.
6 Witkin Cal. Proc. 5th Provisional Remedies § 94, (S 94) Request for Secrecy.

Rule 2.585.　Confidential in-camera proceedings

(a) Minutes of proceedings

If a confidential in-camera proceeding is held in which a party is excluded from being represented, the clerk must include in the minutes the nature of the hearing and only such references to writings or witnesses as will not disclose privileged information.

(b) Disposition of examined records

Records examined by the court in confidence under (a), or copies of them, must be filed with the clerk under seal and must not be disclosed without court order. *(Formerly Rule 243.4, adopted, eff. Jan. 1, 2001. Renumbered Rule 2.585, eff. Jan. 1, 2007.)*

Research References

2 Witkin Cal. Proc. 5th Courts § 190, (S 190) Trial Court Rules.
2 Witkin Cal. Proc. 5th Courts § 364, in General.

Division 6

APPOINTMENTS BY THE COURT OR AGREEMENT OF THE PARTIES

Chapter 1

COURT–APPOINTED TEMPORARY JUDGES

Rule 2.810.　Temporary judges appointed by the trial courts

(a) Scope of rule

Rules 2.810–2.819 apply to attorneys who serve as court-appointed temporary judges in the trial courts. The rules do not apply to subordinate judicial officers or to attorneys designated by the courts to serve as temporary judges at the parties' request.

(b) Definition of "court-appointed temporary judge"

A "court-appointed temporary judge" means an attorney who has satisfied the requirements for appointment under rule 2.812 and has been appointed by the court to serve as a temporary judge in that court.

(c) Appointment of attorneys as temporary judges

Trial courts may appoint an attorney as a temporary judge only if the attorney has satisfied the requirements of rule 2.812.

(d) Exception for extraordinary circumstances

A presiding judge may appoint an attorney who is qualified under 2.812(a), but who has not satisfied the other requirements of that rule, only in case of extraordinary circumstances. Any appointment under this subdivision based on extraordinary circumstances must be made before the attorney serves as a temporary judge, must be recorded for reporting purposes under rule 10.742(c)(3), and must not last more than 10 court days in a three-year period. *(Formerly Rule 243.11, adopted, eff. July 1, 2006, operative Jan. 1, 2007. Renumbered Rule 2.810 and amended, eff. Jan. 1, 2007. As amended, eff. Jan. 1, 2009.)*

Research References

Rutter, Cal. Practice Guide: A.D.R. Ch. 6-B, B. Temporary Judges.
Rutter, Cal. Practice Guide: A.D.R. Ch. 7-C, C. Private Judges.
Rutter, Cal. Practice Guide: Prof. Responsibility Ch. 8-D, D. Restrictions on Speech and Behavior Outside Courtroom.
2 Witkin Cal. Proc. 5th Courts § 190, (S 190) Trial Court Rules.
2 Witkin Cal. Proc. 5th Courts § 348, (S 348) Nature of Position.
2 Witkin Cal. Proc. 5th Courts § 349, (S 349) Temporary Judge Appointed by Court.

Rule 2.811.   Court appointment of temporary judges

(a) Purpose of court appointment

The purpose of court appointment of attorneys as temporary judges is to assist the public by providing the court with a panel of trained, qualified, and experienced attorneys who may serve as temporary judges at the discretion of the court if the court needs judicial assistance that it cannot provide using its full-time judicial officers.

(b) Appointment and service discretionary

Court-appointed attorneys are appointed and serve as temporary judges solely at the discretion of the presiding judge.

(c) No employment relationship

Court appointment and service of an attorney as a temporary judge do not establish an employment relationship between the court and the attorney.

(d) Responsibility of the presiding judge for appointments

The appointment of attorneys to serve as temporary judges is the responsibility of the presiding judge, who may designate another judge or committee of judges to perform this responsibility. In carrying out this responsibility, the presiding judge is assisted by a Temporary Judge Administrator as prescribed by rule 10.743. *(Formerly Rule 243.12, adopted, eff. July 1, 2006, operative Jan. 1, 2007. Renumbered Rule 2.811 and amended, eff. Jan. 1, 2007.)*

Research References

2 Witkin Cal. Proc. 5th Courts § 349, (S 349) Temporary Judge Appointed by Court.

Rule 2.812.   Requirements for court appointment of an attorney to serve as a temporary judge

(a) Experience required for appointment and service

The presiding judge may not appoint an attorney to serve as a temporary judge unless the attorney has been admitted to practice as a member of the State Bar of California for at least 10 years before the appointment. However, for good cause, the presiding judge may permit an attorney who has been admitted to practice for at least 5 years to serve as a temporary judge.

(b) Conditions for appointment by the court

The presiding judge may appoint an attorney to serve as a temporary judge only if the attorney:

(1) Is a member in good standing of the State Bar and has no disciplinary action pending;

(2) Has not pled guilty or no contest to a felony, or has not been convicted of a felony that has not been reversed;

(3) Has satisfied the education and training requirements in (c);

(4) Has satisfied all other general conditions that the court may establish for appointment of an attorney as a temporary judge in that court; and

(5) Has satisfied any additional conditions that the court may require for an attorney to be appointed as a temporary judge for a particular assignment or type of case in that court.

(c) Education and training requirements

The presiding judge may appoint an attorney to serve as a temporary judge only if the following minimum training requirements are satisfied:

(1) *Mandatory training on bench conduct and demeanor*

Before appointment, the attorney must have attended and successfully completed, within the previous three years, a course of at least 3 hours' duration on the subjects identified in rule 2.813(a) approved by the court in which the attorney will serve. This course must be taken in person and be taught by a qualified judicial officer.

(2) *Mandatory training in ethics*

Before appointment, the attorney must have attended and successfully completed, within the previous three years, a course of at least 3 hours' duration on the subjects identified in rule 2.813(b) approved by the court in which the attorney will serve. This course may be taken by any means approved by the court, including in-person, by broadcast with participation, or online.

(3) *Substantive training*

Before appointment, the attorney must have attended and successfully completed, within the previous three years, a course on the substantive law in each subject area in which the attorney will serve as a temporary judge. These courses may be taken by any means approved by the court, including in-person, by broadcast with participation, or online. The substantive courses have the following minimum requirements:

(A) Small claims

An attorney serving as a temporary judge in small claims cases must have attended and successfully completed, within the previous three years, a course of at least 3 hours' duration on the subjects identified in rule 2.813(c) approved by the court in which the attorney will serve.

(B) Traffic

An attorney serving as a temporary judge in traffic cases must have attended and completed, within the previous three years, a course of at least 3 hours' duration on the subjects identified in rule 2.813(d) approved by the court in which the attorney will serve.

(C) Other subject areas

If the court assigns attorneys to serve as temporary judges in other substantive areas such as civil law, family law, juvenile law, unlawful detainers, or case management, the court must determine what additional training is required and what additional courses are required before an attorney may serve as a temporary judge in each of those subject areas. The training required in each area must be of at least 3 hours' duration. The court may also require that an attorney possess additional years of practical experience in each substantive area before being assigned to serve as a temporary judge in that subject area.

(D) Settlement

An attorney need not be a temporary judge to assist the court in settlement conferences. However, an attorney assisting the court with settlement conferences who performs any judicial function, such as entering a settlement on the record under Code of Civil Procedure section 664.6, must be a qualified temporary judge who has satisfied the training requirements under (c)(1) and (c)(2) of this rule.

(E) The substantive training requirements in (3)(A)–(C) do not apply to courts in which temporary judges are used fewer than 10 times altogether in a calendar year.

(d) Requirements for retired judicial officers

Commencing five years after the retired judicial officer last served in a judicial position either as a full-time judicial officer or as an assigned judge, a retired judicial officer serving as a temporary judge must satisfy all the education and training requirements of this rule. However, a retired judicial officer serving as a temporary judge in a small claims case must satisfy all the requirements of Code of Civil Procedure section 116.240(b) and the rules in this chapter before serving in the case.

(e) Additional requirements

The presiding judge in each court should establish additional experience and training requirements for temporary judges beyond the minimum requirements provided in this rule if it is feasible for the court to do so.

(f) Records of attendance

A court that uses temporary judges must maintain records verifying that each attorney who serves as a temporary judge in that court has attended and successfully completed the courses required under this rule.

(g) Application and appointment

To serve as a temporary judge, an attorney must complete the application required under rule 10.744, must satisfy the requirements prescribed in this rule, and must satisfy such other requirements as the court appointing the attorney in its discretion may determine are appropriate. *(Formerly Rule 243.13, adopted, eff. July 1, 2006, operative Jan. 1, 2007. Renumbered Rule 2.812 and amended, eff. Jan. 1, 2007. As amended, eff. Jan. 1, 2009.)*

Advisory Committee Comment

The goal of this rule is to ensure that attorneys who serve as court-appointed temporary judges are qualified and properly trained.

Subdivision (a). If a court determines that there is good cause under (a) to appoint an attorney with less than 10 years of practice as a temporary judge, the attorney must still satisfy the other requirements of the rule before being appointed.

Subdivision (b). "Good standing" means that the attorney is currently eligible to practice law in the State of California. An attorney in good standing may be either an active or a voluntarily inactive member of the State Bar. The rule does not require that an attorney be an active member of the State Bar to serve as

a court-appointed temporary judge. Voluntarily inactive members may be appointed as temporary judges if the court decides to appoint them.

Subdivision (c). A court may use attorneys who are not temporary judges to assist in the settlement of cases. For example, attorneys may work under the presiding judge or individual judges and may assist them in settling cases. However, these attorneys may not perform any judicial functions such as entering a settlement on the record under Code of Civil Procedure section 664.6. Settlement attorneys who are not temporary judges are not required to satisfy the requirements of these rules, but must satisfy any requirements established by the court for attorneys who assist in the settlement of cases.

Research References

2 Witkin Cal. Proc. 5th Courts § 349, (S 349) Temporary Judge Appointed by Court.

Rule 2.813.　Contents of training programs

(a) Bench conduct

Before the court may appoint an attorney to serve as a temporary judge in any type of case, the attorney must have received training under rule 2.812(c)(1) in the following subjects:

(1) Bench conduct, demeanor, and decorum;

(2) Access, fairness, and elimination of bias; and

(3) Adjudicating cases involving self-represented parties.

(b) Ethics

Before the court may appoint an attorney to serve as a temporary judge in any type of case, the attorney must have received ethics training under rule 2.812(c)(2) in the following subjects:

(1) Judicial ethics generally;

(2) Conflicts;

(3) Disclosures, disqualifications, and limitations on appearances; and

(4) Ex parte communications.

(c) Small claims

Before the court may appoint an attorney to serve as a temporary judge in small claims cases, the attorney must have received training under rule 2.812(c)(3)(A) in the following subjects:

(1) Small claims procedures and practices;

(2) Consumer sales;

(3) Vehicular sales, leasing, and repairs;

(4) Credit and financing transactions;

(5) Professional and occupational licensing;

(6) Tenant rent deposit law;

(7) Contract, warranty, tort, and negotiable instruments law; and

(8) Other subjects deemed appropriate by the presiding judge based on local needs and conditions.

In addition, an attorney serving as a temporary judge in small claims cases must be familiar with the publications identified in Code of Civil Procedure section 116.930.

(d) Traffic

Before the court may appoint an attorney to serve as a temporary judge in traffic cases, the attorney must have received training under rule 2.812(c)(3)(B) in the following subjects:

(1) Traffic court procedures and practices;

(2) Correctable violations;

(3) Discovery;

Ct. Rules

(4) Driver licensing;

(5) Failure to appear;

(6) Mandatory insurance;

(7) Notice to appear citation forms;

(8) Red–light enforcement;

(9) Sentencing and court-ordered traffic school;

(10) Speed enforcement;

(11) Settlement of the record;

(12) Uniform bail and penalty schedules;

(13) Vehicle registration and licensing; and

(14) Other subjects deemed appropriate by the presiding judge based on local needs and conditions. *(Formerly Rule 243.14, adopted, eff. July 1, 2006, operative Jan. 1, 2007. Renumbered Rule 2.813 and amended, eff. Jan. 1, 2007.)*

Advisory Committee Comment

The purpose of this rule is to ensure that all court-appointed temporary judges have proper training in bench conduct and demeanor, ethics, and each substantive area in which they adjudicate cases. Each court is responsible for approving the training and instructional materials for the temporary judges appointed by that court. The training in bench conduct and demeanor must be in person, but in other areas each court may determine the approved method or methods by which the training is provided. The methods may include in-person courses, broadcasts with participation, and online courses. Courts may offer MCLE credit for courses that they provide and may approve MCLE courses provided by others as satisfying the substantive training requirements under this rule. Courts may work together with other courts, or may cooperate on a regional basis, to develop and provide training programs for court-appointed temporary judges under this rule.

Research References

2 Witkin Cal. Proc. 5th Courts § 349, (S 349) Temporary Judge Appointed by Court.

Rule 2.814.   Appointment of temporary judge

An attorney may serve as a temporary judge for the court only after the court has issued an order appointing him or her to serve. Before serving, the attorney must subscribe the oath of office and must certify that he or she is aware of and will comply with applicable provisions of canon 6 of the Code of Judicial Ethics and the California Rules of Court. *(Formerly Rule 243.15, adopted, eff. July 1, 2006. Renumbered Rule 2.814, eff. Jan. 1, 2007.)*

Research References

2 Witkin Cal. Proc. 5th Courts § 349, (S 349) Temporary Judge Appointed by Court.

Rule 2.815.   Continuing education

(a) Continuing education required

Each attorney appointed as a temporary judge must attend and successfully complete every three years a course on bench conduct and demeanor, an ethics course, and a course in each substantive area in which the attorney will serve as a temporary judge. The courses must cover the same subjects and be of the same duration as the courses prescribed in rule 2.812(c). These courses must be approved by the court that appoints the attorney.

(b) Records of attendance

A court that uses temporary judges must maintain records verifying that each attorney who serves as a temporary judge in that court has attended and successfully completed the courses

required under this rule. *(Formerly Rule 243.17, adopted, eff. July 1, 2006. Renumbered Rule 2.815 and amended, eff. Jan. 1, 2007.)*

Research References

2 Witkin Cal. Proc. 5th Courts § 349, (S 349) Temporary Judge Appointed by Court.

Rule 2.816.   Stipulation to court-appointed temporary judge

(a) Application

This rule governs a stipulation for a matter to be heard by a temporary judge when the court has appointed and assigned an attorney to serve as a temporary judge in that court.

(b) Contents of notice

Before the swearing in of the first witness at a small claims hearing, before the entry of a plea by the defendant at a traffic arraignment, or before the commencement of any other proceeding, the court must give notice to each party that:

(1) A temporary judge will be hearing the matters for that calendar;

(2) The temporary judge is a qualified member of the State Bar and the name of the temporary judge is provided; and

(3) The party has a right to have the matter heard before a judge, commissioner, or referee of the court.

(c) Form of notice

The court may give the notice in (b) by either of the following methods:

(1) A conspicuous sign posted inside or just outside the courtroom, accompanied by oral notification or notification by videotape or audiotape by a court officer on the day of the hearing; or

(2) A written notice provided to each party.

(d) Methods of stipulation

After notice has been given under (a) and (b), a party stipulates to a court-appointed temporary judge by either of the following:

(1) The party is deemed to have stipulated to the attorney serving as a temporary judge if the party fails to object to the matter being heard by the temporary judge before the temporary judge begins the proceeding; or

(2) The party signs a written stipulation agreeing that the matter may be heard by the temporary judge.

(e) Application or motion to withdraw stipulation

An application or motion to withdraw a stipulation for the appointment of a temporary judge must be supported by a declaration of facts establishing good cause for permitting the party to withdraw the stipulation. In addition:

(1) The application or motion must be heard by the presiding judge or a judge designated by the presiding judge.

(2) A declaration that a ruling by a temporary judge is based on an error of fact or law does not establish good cause for withdrawing a stipulation.

(3) The application or motion must be served and filed, and the moving party must mail or deliver a copy to the presiding judge.

(4) If the application or motion for withdrawing the stipulation is based on grounds for the disqualification of, or limitation of the appearance by, the temporary judge first learned or arising after the temporary judge has made one or more rulings, but before the temporary judge has completed judicial action in the proceeding, the temporary judge, unless the disqualification or termination is waived, must disqualify himself or herself. But in

the absence of good cause, the rulings the temporary judge has made up to that time must not be set aside by the judicial officer or temporary judge who replaces the temporary judge. *(Formerly Rule 1727, adopted, eff. Jan. 1, 2001. Renumbered Rule 243.18 and amended, eff. July 1, 2006. Renumbered Rule 2.816 and amended, eff. Jan. 1, 2007.)*

Research References

2 Witkin Cal. Proc. 5th Courts § 349, (S 349) Temporary Judge Appointed by Court.

Rule 2.817. Disclosures to the parties

A temporary judge must make all disclosures required under the Code of Judicial Ethics. *(Formerly Rule 243.19, adopted, eff. July 1, 2006. Renumbered Rule 2.817, eff. Jan. 1, 2007.)*

Research References

Rutter, Cal. Practice Guide: Prof. Responsibility Ch. 8-D, D. Restrictions on Speech and Behavior Outside Courtroom.

2 Witkin Cal. Proc. 5th Courts § 349, (S 349) Temporary Judge Appointed by Court.

Rule 2.818. Disqualifications and limitations

(a) Code of Judicial Ethics

A temporary judge must disqualify himself or herself as a temporary judge in proceedings as provided under the Code of Judicial Ethics.

(b) Limitations on service

In addition to being disqualified as provided in (a), an attorney may not serve as a court-appointed temporary judge:

(1) If the attorney, in any type of case, is appearing on the same day in the same courthouse as an attorney or as a party;

(2) If the attorney, in the same type of case, is presently a party to any action or proceeding in the court; or

(3) If, in a family law or unlawful detainer case, one party is self-represented and the other party is represented by an attorney or is an attorney.

For good cause, the presiding judge may waive the limitations established in this subdivision.

(c) Waiver of disqualifications or limitations

(1) After a temporary judge who has determined himself or herself to be disqualified under the Code of Judicial Ethics or prohibited from serving under (b) has disclosed the basis for his or her disqualification or limitation on the record, the parties and their attorneys may agree to waive the disqualification or limitation and the temporary judge may accept the waiver. The temporary judge must not seek to induce a waiver and must avoid any effort to discover which attorneys or parties favored or opposed a waiver. The waiver must be in writing, must recite the basis for the disqualification or limitation, and must state that it was knowingly made. The waiver is effective only when signed by all parties and their attorneys and filed in the record.

(2) No waiver is permitted where the basis for the disqualification is any of the following:

(A) The temporary judge has a personal bias or prejudice concerning a party;

(B) The temporary judge has served as an attorney in the matter in controversy; or

(C) The temporary judge has been a material witness in the controversy.

(d) Late discovery of grounds for disqualification or limitation

In the event that grounds for disqualification or limitation are first learned of or arise after the temporary judge has made one or more rulings in a proceeding, but before the temporary judge has completed judicial action in the proceeding, the temporary judge, unless the disqualification or limitation is waived, must disqualify himself or herself. But in the absence of good cause, the rulings the temporary judge has made up to that time must not be set aside by the judicial officer or temporary judge who replaces the temporary judge.

(e) Notification of the court

Whenever a temporary judge determines himself or herself to be disqualified or limited from serving, the temporary judge must notify the presiding judge or the judge designated by the presiding judge of his or her withdrawal and must not further participate in the proceeding, unless his or her disqualification or limitation is waived by the parties as provided in (c).

(f) Requests for disqualifications

A party may request that a temporary judge withdraw on the ground that he or she is disqualified or limited from serving. If a temporary judge who should disqualify himself or herself or who is limited from serving in a case fails to withdraw, a party may apply to the presiding judge under rule 2.816(e) of the California Rules of Court for a withdrawal of the stipulation. The presiding judge or the judge designated by the presiding judge must determine whether good cause exists for granting withdrawal of the stipulation. *(Formerly Rule 243.20, adopted, eff. July 1, 2006. As amended, eff. July 1, 2006. Renumbered Rule 2.818 and amended, eff. Jan. 1, 2007.)*

Advisory Committee Comment

Subdivision (a) indicates that the rules concerning the disqualification of temporary judges are provided in the Code of Judicial Ethics. Subdivision (b) establishes additional limitations that prohibit attorneys from serving as court-appointed temporary judges under certain specified circumstances. Under subdivisions (c)–(e), the provisions of Code of Civil Procedure section 170.3 on waiver of disqualifications, the effect of late discovery of the grounds of disqualification, and notification of disqualification of judicial officers are made applicable to temporary judges. Under subdivision (f), requests for disqualification are handled as withdrawals of the stipulation to a temporary judge and are ruled on by the presiding judge. This procedure is different from that for seeking the disqualification of a judge under Code of Civil Procedure section 170.3.

Research References

Rutter, Cal. Practice Guide: Prof. Responsibility Ch. 8-D, D. Restrictions on Speech and Behavior Outside Courtroom.

2 Witkin Cal. Proc. 5th Courts § 349, (S 349) Temporary Judge Appointed by Court.

Rule 2.819. Continuing duty to disclose and disqualify

A temporary judge has a continuing duty to make disclosures, to disqualify himself or herself, and to limit his or her service as provided under the Code of Judicial Ethics. *(Formerly Rule 243.21, adopted, eff. July 1, 2006. Renumbered Rule 2.819, eff. Jan. 1, 2007.)*

Research References

Rutter, Cal. Practice Guide: A.D.R. Ch. 6-B, B. Temporary Judges.

Rutter, Cal. Practice Guide: Prof. Responsibility Ch. 8-D, D. Restrictions on Speech and Behavior Outside Courtroom.

2 Witkin Cal. Proc. 5th Courts § 190, (S 190) Trial Court Rules.

2 Witkin Cal. Proc. 5th Courts § 349, (S 349) Temporary Judge Appointed by Court.

Chapter 2

TEMPORARY JUDGES REQUESTED BY THE PARTIES

Rule

2.830. Temporary judges requested by the parties.

Rule

2.831.   Temporary judge—stipulation, order, oath, assignment, disclosure, and disqualification.
2.832.   Compensation.
2.833.   Documents and exhibits.
2.834.   Open proceedings; notices of proceedings, use of court facilities, and order for hearing site.
2.835.   Motions or applications to be heard by the court.

Rule 2.830.   Temporary judges requested by the parties

(a) Application

Rules 2.830–2.834 apply to attorneys designated as temporary judges under article VI, section 21 of the California Constitution at the request of the parties rather than by prior appointment of the court, including privately compensated temporary judges and attorneys who serve as temporary judges pro bono at the request of the parties.

(b) Definition

"Privately compensated" means that the temporary judge is paid by the parties.

(c) Limitation

These rules do not apply to subordinate judicial officers or to attorneys who are appointed by the court to serve as temporary judges for the court. *(Formerly Rule 243.30, adopted, eff. July 1, 2006. Renumbered Rule 2.830 and amended, eff. Jan. 1, 2007.)*

Research References

Rutter, Cal. Practice Guide: A.D.R. Ch. 6-B, B. Temporary Judges.
Rutter, Cal. Practice Guide: A.D.R. Ch. 7-C, C. Private Judges.
Rutter, Cal. Practice Guide: Civ. Pro. Before Trial Ch. 1-B, B. Prelawsuit Investigations, Research and Analysis.
2 Witkin Cal. Proc. 5th Courts § 190, (S 190) Trial Court Rules.
2 Witkin Cal. Proc. 5th Courts § 348, (S 348) Nature of Position.
2 Witkin Cal. Proc. 5th Courts § 350, (S 350) Temporary Judge Requested by Parties.

Rule 2.831.   Temporary judge—stipulation, order, oath, assignment, disclosure, and disqualification

(a) Stipulation

When the parties request that an attorney be designated by the court to serve as a temporary judge on a case, the stipulation of the parties that a case may be tried by a temporary judge must be in writing and must state the name and office address of the member of the State Bar agreed on. The stipulation must be submitted for approval to the presiding judge or the judge designated by the presiding judge.

(b) Order, oath, and certification

The order designating the temporary judge must be signed by the presiding judge or the presiding judge's designee and refer to the stipulation. The stipulation and order must then be filed. The temporary judge must take and subscribe the oath of office and certify that he or she is aware of and will comply with applicable provisions of canon 6 of the Code of Judicial Ethics and the California Rules of Court.

(c) When the temporary judge may proceed

The temporary judge may proceed with the hearing, trial, and determination of the cause after the stipulation, order, oath, and certification have been filed.

(d) Disclosure to the parties

In addition to any other disclosure required by law, no later than five days after designation as a temporary judge or, if the temporary judge is not aware of his or her designation or of a matter subject to disclosure at that time, as soon as practicable thereafter, a temporary judge must disclose to the parties any matter subject to disclosure under the Code of Judicial Ethics.

(e) Disqualification

In addition to any other disqualification required by law, a temporary judge requested by the parties and designated by the court under this rule must disqualify himself or herself as provided under the Code of Judicial Ethics.

(f) Motion to withdraw stipulation

A motion to withdraw a stipulation for the appointment of a temporary judge must be supported by a declaration of facts establishing good cause for permitting the party to withdraw the stipulation, and must be heard by the presiding judge or a judge designated by the presiding judge. A declaration that a ruling is based on error of fact or law does not establish good cause for withdrawing a stipulation. Notice of the motion must be served and filed, and the moving party must mail or deliver a copy to the temporary judge. If the motion to withdraw the stipulation is based on grounds for the disqualification of the temporary judge first learned or arising after the temporary judge has made one or more rulings, but before the temporary judge has completed judicial action in the proceeding, the provisions of rule 2.816(e)(4) apply. If a motion to withdraw a stipulation is granted, the presiding judge must assign the case for hearing or trial as promptly as possible. *(Formerly Rule 244, adopted, eff. Jan. 1, 1949. As amended, eff. April 1, 1962; July 1, 1981; July 1, 1987; July 1, 1993; July 1, 1995; Jan. 1, 2001; July 1, 2001. Renumbered Rule 243.31 and amended, eff. July 1, 2006. As amended, eff. July 1, 2006. Renumbered Rule 2.831 and amended, eff. Jan. 1, 2007.)*

Research References

Rutter, Cal. Practice Guide: A.D.R. Ch. 3-B, B. Commencing Mediation Process.
Rutter, Cal. Practice Guide: A.D.R. Ch. 6-B, B. Temporary Judges.
Rutter, Cal. Practice Guide: A.D.R. Ch. 7-C, C. Private Judges.
Rutter, Cal. Practice Guide: A.D.R. Ch. 7-D, D. Referees.
Rutter, Cal. Practice Guide: A.D.R. App. D Form 146, Stipulation for Appointment.
Rutter, Cal. Practice Guide: A.D.R. App. D Form 147, Statement of Temporary Judge Re Contact/Web Site Information.
Rutter, Cal. Practice Guide: A.D.R. App. D Form 149, Motion to Withdraw Stipulation for Appointment.
Rutter, Cal. Practice Guide: A.D.R. Ch. 6-B , Outline B.
Rutter, Cal. Practice Guide: A.D.R. App. D Form Intro. 6, Practice and Procedure Forms for Trial by Temporary (Pro Tem) Judge.
California Practice Guide: Employment Litigation Ch. 18-F, F. Selecting the Neutral.
Rutter, Cal. Practice Guide: Prof. Responsibility Ch. 8-D, D. Restrictions on Speech and Behavior Outside Courtroom.
1 Witkin Cal. Proc. 5th Attorneys § 254, Stipulation for Temporary Judge.
2 Witkin Cal. Proc. 5th Courts § 350, (S 350) Temporary Judge Requested by Parties.
6 Witkin Cal. Proc. 5th Proceedings Without Trial § 497, (S 497) Temporary Judge.
10 Witkin, California Summary 10th Parent and Child § 466, (S 466) Referee as Temporary Judge.

Rule 2.832.   Compensation

A temporary judge selected by the parties may not be compensated by the parties unless the parties agree in writing on a rate of compensation that they will pay. *(Formerly Rule 243.32, adopted, eff. July 1, 2006. Renumbered Rule 2.832, eff. Jan. 1, 2007.)*

Research References

Rutter, Cal. Practice Guide: A.D.R. Ch. 6-B, B. Temporary Judges.
2 Witkin Cal. Proc. 5th Courts § 350, (S 350) Temporary Judge Requested by Parties.
6 Witkin Cal. Proc. 5th Proceedings Without Trial § 497, (S 497) Temporary Judge.

Rule 2.833. Documents and exhibits

All temporary judges requested by the parties and parties in proceedings before these temporary judges must comply with the applicable requirements of rule 2.400 concerning the filing and handling of documents and exhibits. *(Adopted, eff. Jan. 1, 2010.)*

Research References

2 Witkin Cal. Proc. 5th Courts § 350, (S 350) Temporary Judge Requested by Parties.

6 Witkin Cal. Proc. 5th Proceedings Without Trial § 498, (S 498) Procedure.

Rule 2.834. Open proceedings; notices of proceedings, use of court facilities, and order for hearing site

(a) Open proceedings

All proceedings before a temporary judge requested by the parties that would be open to the public if held before a judge must be open to the public, regardless of whether they are held in or outside a court facility.

(b) Notice regarding proceedings before temporary judge requested by the parties

(1) In each case in which he or she is appointed, a temporary judge requested by the parties must file a statement that provides the name, telephone number, and mailing address of a person who may be contacted to obtain information about the date, time, location, and general nature of all hearings and other proceedings scheduled in the matter that would be open to the public if held before a judge. This statement must be filed at the same time as the temporary judge's certification under rule 2.831(b). If there is any change in this contact information, the temporary judge must promptly file a revised statement with the court.

(2) In addition to providing the information required under (1), the statement filed by a temporary judge may also provide the address of a publicly accessible Web site at which the temporary judge will maintain a current calendar setting forth the date, time, location, and general nature of any hearings scheduled in the matter that would be open to the public if held before a judge.

(3) The clerk must post the information from the statement filed by the temporary judge in the court facility.

(c) Use of court facilities, court personnel, and summoned jurors

A party who has elected to use the services of a temporary judge requested by the parties is deemed to have elected to proceed outside court facilities. Court facilities, court personnel, and summoned jurors may not be used in proceedings pending before a temporary judge requested by the parties except on a finding by the presiding judge or his or her designee that their use would further the interests of justice.

(d) Appropriate hearing site

(1) The presiding judge or his or her designee, on application of any person or on the judge's own motion, may order that a case before a temporary judge requested by the parties must be heard at a site easily accessible to the public and appropriate for seating those who have made known their plan to attend hearings. The application must state facts showing good cause for granting the application, and must be served on all parties and the temporary judge and filed with the court. The proceedings are not stayed while the application is pending unless the presiding judge or his or her designee orders that they be stayed. The issuance of an order for an accessible and appropriate hearing site is not a ground for withdrawal of a stipulation that a case may be heard by a temporary judge.

(2) If a court staff mediator or evaluator is required to attend a hearing before a temporary judge requested by the parties, unless otherwise ordered by the presiding judge or his or her designee, that hearing must take place at a location requiring no more than 15 minutes' travel time from the mediator's or evaluator's work site. *(Formerly Rule 243.33, adopted, eff. July 1, 2006. Renumbered Rule 2.833, eff. Jan. 1, 2007. Renumbered Rule 2.834 and amended, eff. Jan. 1, 2010.)*

Research References

Rutter, Cal. Practice Guide: A.D.R. Ch. 6-B, B. Temporary Judges.

Rutter, Cal. Practice Guide: A.D.R. App. D Form 146, Stipulation for Appointment.

Rutter, Cal. Practice Guide: A.D.R. App. D Form 147, Statement of Temporary Judge Re Contact/Web Site Information.

Rutter, Cal. Practice Guide: A.D.R. App. D Form 148, Motion to Seal Records.

Rutter, Cal. Practice Guide: Civ. Pro. Before Trial Ch. 9(I)-D, D. Hearing.

2 Witkin Cal. Proc. 5th Courts § 190, (S 190) Trial Court Rules.

2 Witkin Cal. Proc. 5th Courts § 350, (S 350) Temporary Judge Requested by Parties.

4 Witkin Cal. Proc. 5th Pleading § 220, (S 220) Application and Ex Parte Order.

6 Witkin Cal. Proc. 5th Proceedings Without Trial § 498, (S 498) Procedure.

Rule 2.835. Motions or applications to be heard by the court

(a) Motion or application to seal records

A motion or application to seal records in a case pending before a temporary judge requested by the parties must be filed with the court and must be served on all parties that have appeared in the case and the temporary judge. The motion or application must be heard by the trial court judge to whom the case is assigned or, if the case has not been assigned, by the presiding judge or his or her designee. Rules 2.550–2.551 on sealed records apply to motions or applications filed under this rule.

(b) Motion for leave to file complaint for intervention

A motion for leave to file a complaint for intervention in a case pending before a temporary judge requested by the parties must be filed with the court and served on all parties and the temporary judge. The motion must be heard by the trial court judge to whom the case is assigned or, if the case has not been assigned, by the presiding judge or his or her designee. If intervention is allowed, the case must be returned to the trial court docket unless all parties stipulate in the manner prescribed in rule 2.831(a) to proceed before the temporary judge. *(Formerly Rule 243.34, adopted, eff. July 1, 2006. Renumbered Rule 2.834 and amended, eff. Jan. 1, 2007. Renumbered Rule 2.835 and amended, eff. Jan. 1, 2010.)*

Research References

Rutter, Cal. Practice Guide: A.D.R. Ch. 6-B, B. Temporary Judges.

Rutter, Cal. Practice Guide: Civ. Pro. Before Trial Ch. 9(I)-I, I. Motion to Seal Court Records.

2 Witkin Cal. Proc. 5th Courts § 190, (S 190) Trial Court Rules.

2 Witkin Cal. Proc. 5th Courts § 350, (S 350) Temporary Judge Requested by Parties.

4 Witkin Cal. Proc. 5th Pleading § 220, (S 220) Application and Ex Parte Order.

6 Witkin Cal. Proc. 5th Proceedings Without Trial § 498, (S 498) Procedure.

Chapter 4

COURT INTERPRETERS

Rule

2.890. Professional conduct for interpreters.

Ct. Rules

Rule

2.891. Periodic review of court interpreter skills and professional conduct.

2.892. Guidelines for approval of certification programs for interpreters for deaf and hard-of-hearing persons.

2.893. Appointment of noncertified interpreters in criminal cases and juvenile delinquency proceedings.

2.894. Reports on appointments of certified and registered interpreters and noncertified and nonregistered interpreters.

Rule 2.890. Professional conduct for interpreters

(a) Representation of qualifications

An interpreter must accurately and completely represent his or her certifications, training, and relevant experience.

(b) Complete and accurate interpretation

An interpreter must use his or her best skills and judgment to interpret accurately without embellishing, omitting, or editing. When interpreting for a party, the interpreter must interpret everything that is said during the entire proceedings. When interpreting for a witness, the interpreter must interpret everything that is said during the witness's testimony.

(c) Impartiality and avoidance of conflicts of interest

(1) *Impartiality*

An interpreter must be impartial and unbiased and must refrain from conduct that may give an appearance of bias.

(2) *Disclosure of conflicts*

An interpreter must disclose to the judge and to all parties any actual or apparent conflict of interest. Any condition that interferes with the objectivity of an interpreter is a conflict of interest. A conflict may exist if the interpreter is acquainted with or related to any witness or party to the action or if the interpreter has an interest in the outcome of the case.

(3) *Conduct*

An interpreter must not engage in conduct creating the appearance of bias, prejudice, or partiality.

(4) *Statements*

An interpreter must not make statements to any person about the merits of the case until the litigation has concluded.

(d) Confidentiality of privileged communications

An interpreter must not disclose privileged communications between counsel and client to any person.

(e) Giving legal advice

An interpreter must not give legal advice to parties and witnesses, nor recommend specific attorneys or law firms.

(f) Impartial professional relationships

An interpreter must maintain an impartial, professional relationship with all court officers, attorneys, jurors, parties, and witnesses.

(g) Continuing education and duty to the profession

An interpreter must, through continuing education, maintain and improve his or her interpreting skills and knowledge of procedures used by the courts. An interpreter should seek to elevate the standards of performance of the interpreting profession.

(h) Assessing and reporting impediments to performance

An interpreter must assess at all times his or her ability to perform interpreting services. If an interpreter has any reservation about his or her ability to satisfy an assignment competently, the interpreter must immediately disclose that reservation to the court or other appropriate authority.

(i) Duty to report ethical violations

An interpreter must report to the court or other appropriate authority any effort to impede the interpreter's compliance with the law, this rule, or any other official policy governing court interpreting and legal translating. *(Formerly Rule 984.4, adopted, eff. Jan. 1, 1999. Renumbered Rule 2.890 and amended, eff. Jan. 1, 2007.)*

Research References

2 Witkin Cal. Proc. 5th Courts § 190, (S 190) Trial Court Rules.
2 Witkin Cal. Proc. 5th Courts § 387, Interpreters and Translators.

Rule 2.891. Periodic review of court interpreter skills and professional conduct

Each trial court must establish a procedure for biennial, or more frequent, review of the performance and skills of each court interpreter certified under Government Code section 68560 et seq. The court may designate a review panel, which must include at least one person qualified in the interpreter's language. The review procedure may include interviews, observations of courtroom performance, rating forms, and other evaluation techniques. *(Formerly Rule 984, adopted, eff. July 1, 1979. As amended, eff. Jan. 1, 1996. Renumbered Rule 2.891 and amended, eff. Jan. 1, 2007.)*

Rule 2.892. Guidelines for approval of certification programs for interpreters for deaf and hard-of-hearing persons

Each organization, agency, or educational institution that administers tests for certification of court interpreters for deaf and hard-of-hearing persons under Evidence Code section 754 must comply with the guidelines adopted by the Judicial Council effective February 21, 1992, and any subsequent revisions, and must hold a valid, current approval by the Judicial Council to administer the tests as a certifying organization. The guidelines are stated in the *Judicial Council Guidelines for Approval of Certification Programs for Interpreters for Deaf and Hard-of-Hearing Persons*, published by the Administrative Office of the Courts. *(Formerly Rule 984.1, adopted, eff. Jan. 1, 1994. Renumbered Rule 2.892 and amended, eff. Jan. 1, 2007.)*

Rule 2.893. Appointment of noncertified interpreters in criminal cases and juvenile delinquency proceedings

(a) Application

This rule applies to trial court proceedings in criminal cases and juvenile delinquency proceedings under Welfare and Institutions Code section 602 et seq. in which the court determines that an interpreter is required.

(b) Appointment of noncertified interpreters

An interpreter who is not certified by the Judicial Council to interpret a language designated by the Judicial Council under Government Code section 68560 et seq. may be appointed under Government Code section 68561(c) in a proceeding if:

(1) *Noncertified interpreter provisionally qualified*

(A) The presiding judge of the court, or other judicial officer designated by the presiding judge:

(i) Finds the noncertified interpreter to be provisionally qualified following the *Procedures and Guidelines to Appoint a Noncertified Interpreter in Criminal and Juvenile Delinquency Proceedings (Designated Languages)* (form IN–100); and

(ii) Signs an order allowing the interpreter to be considered for appointment on *Qualifications of a Noncertified Interpreter* (form IN–110); and

(B) The judge in the proceeding finds on the record that:

(i) Good cause exists to appoint the noncertified interpreter; and

(ii) The interpreter is qualified to interpret the proceeding, following procedures adopted by the Judicial Council (see forms IN–100, IN–110, and IN–120).

(C) Each order of the presiding judge under (b)(1) finding a noncertified interpreter to be provisionally qualified and allowing the interpreter to be considered for appointment in a proceeding is for a six-month period.

(2) *Noncertified interpreter not provisionally qualified*

(A) To prevent burdensome delay or in other unusual circumstances, at the request of the defendant, or of the minor in a juvenile delinquency proceeding, the judge in the proceeding may appoint a noncertified interpreter who is not provisionally qualified under (b)(1) to interpret a brief, routine matter provided the judge, on the record:

(i) Indicates that the defendant or minor has waived the appointment of a certified interpreter and the appointment of an interpreter found provisionally qualified by the presiding judge;

(ii) Finds that good cause exists to appoint an interpreter who is neither certified nor provisionally qualified; and

(iii) Finds that the interpreter is qualified to interpret that proceeding.

(B) The findings and appointment under (b)(2)(A) made by the judge in the proceeding are effective only in that proceeding. The appointment must not be extended to subsequent proceedings without an additional waiver, findings, and appointment.

(c) Limit on appointment of noncertified interpreters

(1) A noncertified interpreter allowed to be appointed under (b) may not interpret in the trial courts for more than any four 6–month periods, except that:

(A) In counties with a population greater than 80,000, a noncertified interpreter of Spanish may be allowed to interpret for no more than any two 6–month periods.

(B) A noncertified interpreter may be allowed to interpret beyond four 6–month periods, or two 6–month periods for an interpreter of Spanish under (A), if the judge in the proceeding makes a specific finding on the record in each case in which the interpreter is sworn that good cause exists to appoint the interpreter notwithstanding that he or she has failed to achieve Judicial Council certification.

(2) Except as provided in (3), each six-month period under (1) begins on the date a presiding judge signs an order under (b)(1)(A)(ii) allowing the noncertified interpreter to be considered for appointment.

(3) If an interpreter is provisionally qualified under (b)(1) in more than one court at the same time, each six-month period runs concurrently for purposes of determining the maximum periods allowed in this subdivision.

(d) Waiver of certified interpreter or objection to noncertified interpreter

(1) If after a diligent search a certified interpreter is not available in a criminal case or in a juvenile delinquency proceeding, the judge in the proceeding must inform the defendant or the minor that:

(A) The proposed interpreter is not certified;

(B) The court has found good cause to appoint a noncertified interpreter; and

(C) The court has found the proposed interpreter to be qualified to interpret in the proceeding.

(2) If the defendant or minor objects to the appointment of the proposed interpreter or waives the appointment of a certified interpreter, the objection or waiver must be on the record.

(e) Court record

The minute order or docket must record the information in (1) or (2) below for each proceeding requiring the appointment of an interpreter:

(1) *Certified interpreters*

For each certified interpreter, the following information must be recorded:

(A) The name of the interpreter;

(B) The language to be interpreted;

(C) The fact that the interpreter is certified to interpret in the language to be interpreted; and

(D) Whether the interpreter was administered the interpreter's oath or has an oath on file with the court (only certified interpreters may have an oath on file).

(2) *Noncertified interpreters*

For each noncertified interpreter, the following information must be recorded:

(A) The name of the interpreter;

(B) The language to be interpreted;

(C) The fact that the interpreter was administered the interpreter's oath;

(D) The fact that the interpreter is not certified to interpret in the language to be interpreted;

(E) Whether a *Certification of Unavailability of Certified Interpreters* (form IN–120) for the language to be interpreted is on file for this date with the court administrator;

(F) The court's finding that good cause exists for the court to appoint a noncertified interpreter;

(G) The court's finding that the interpreter is qualified to interpret in the proceeding;

(H) If applicable, the court's finding under (c)(1)(B) that good cause exists for the court to appoint a noncertified interpreter beyond the time allowed in (c); and

(I) If applicable, the objection or waiver of the defendant or minor under (d).

(Formerly Rule 984.2, adopted, eff. Jan. 1, 1996. Renumbered Rule 2.893 and amended, eff. Jan. 1, 2007.)

Research References

2 Witkin Cal. Proc. 5th Courts § 387, Interpreters and Translators.

Rule 2.894. Reports on appointments of certified and registered interpreters and noncertified and nonregistered interpreters

Each superior court must report to the Judicial Council on:

(1) The appointment of certified and registered interpreters under Government Code section 71802, as required by the Administrative Office of the Courts; and

(2) The appointment of noncertified interpreters of languages designated under Government Code section 68562(a), and registered and nonregistered interpreters of nondesignated languages. *(Formerly Rule 984.3, adopted, eff. Jan. 1, 1996. As amended, eff. March 1, 2003. Renumbered Rule 2.894 and amended, eff. Jan. 1, 2007.)*

Research References

2 Witkin Cal. Proc. 5th Courts § 190, (S 190) Trial Court Rules.

Ct. Rules

Division 7

PROCEEDINGS

Chapter 1

GENERAL PROVISIONS

Rule

2.900. Submission of a cause in a trial court.

Rule 2.900.   Submission of a cause in a trial court

(a) Submission

A cause is deemed submitted in a trial court when either of the following first occurs:

(1) The date the court orders the matter submitted; or

(2) The date the final paper is required to be filed or the date argument is heard, whichever is later.

(b) Vacating submission

The court may vacate submission only by issuing an order served on the parties stating reasons constituting good cause and providing for resubmission.

(c) Pendency of a submitted cause

A submitted cause is pending and undetermined unless the court has announced its tentative decision or the cause is terminated. The time required to finalize a tentative decision is not time in which the cause is pending and undetermined. For purposes of this rule only, a motion that has the effect of vacating, reconsidering, or rehearing the cause will be considered a separate and new cause and will be deemed submitted as provided in (a). *(Formerly Rule 825, adopted, eff. Jan. 1, 1989. Renumbered Rule 2.900 and amended, eff. Jan. 1, 2007.)*

Research References

Rutter, Cal. Practice Guide: Civil Trials & Evidence Ch. 16-E, E. Statement of Decision.

2 Witkin Cal. Proc. 5th Courts § 190, (S 190) Trial Court Rules.

2 Witkin Cal. Proc. 5th Courts § 236, (S 236) Duty to Monitor Pending Cases.

Chapter 2

RECORDS OF PROCEEDINGS

Rule

2.950. Sequential list of reporters.

2.952. Electronic recording as official record of proceedings.

2.954. Specifications for electronic recording equipment.

2.956. Court reporting services in civil cases.

2.958. Assessing fee for official reporter.

Rule 2.950.   Sequential list of reporters

During any reported court proceeding, the clerk must keep a sequential list of all reporters working on the case, indicating the date the reporter worked and the reporter's name, business address, and Certified Shorthand Reporter license number. If more than one reporter reports a case during one day, the information pertaining to each reporter must be listed with the first reporter designated "A," the second designated "B," etc. If reporter "A" returns during the same day, that reporter will be designated as both reporter "A" and reporter "C" on the list. The list of reporters may be kept in an electronic database maintained by the clerk; however, a hard copy must be available to members of the public within one working day of a request for

the list of reporters. *(Formerly Rule 980.4, adopted, eff. July 1, 1991.   Renumbered Rule 2.950 and amended, eff. Jan. 1, 2007.)*

Research References

2 Witkin Cal. Proc. 5th Courts § 190, (S 190) Trial Court Rules.

2 Witkin Cal. Proc. 5th Courts § 379, (S 379) Appointment and Qualifications.

10 Witkin, California Summary 10th Parent and Child § 712, Notice of Appeal.

Rule 2.952.   Electronic recording as official record of proceedings

(a) Application

This rule applies when a court has ordered proceedings to be electronically recorded on a device of a type approved by the Judicial Council or conforming to specifications adopted by the Judicial Council.

(b) Definitions

As used in this rule, the following definitions apply:

(1) "Reel" means an individual reel or cassette of magnetic recording tape or a comparable unit of the medium on which an electronic recording is made.

(2) "Monitor" means any person designated by the court to operate electronic recording equipment and to make appropriate notations to identify the proceedings recorded on each reel, including the date and time of the recording. The trial judge, a courtroom clerk, or a bailiff may be the monitor, but when recording is of sound only, a separate monitor without other substantial duties is recommended.

(c) Reel numbers

Each reel must be distinctively marked with the date recorded, the department number of the court, if any, and, if possible, a serial number.

(d) Certificate of monitor

As soon as practicable after the close of each day's court proceedings, the monitor must execute a certificate for each reel recorded during the day, stating:

(1) That the person executing the certificate was designated by the court as monitor;

(2) The number or other identification assigned to the reel;

(3) The date of the proceedings recorded on that reel;

(4) The titles and numbers of actions and proceedings, or portions thereof, recorded on the reel, and the general nature of the proceedings; and

(5) That the recording equipment was functioning normally, and that all of the proceedings in open court between designated times of day were recorded, except for such matters as were expressly directed to be "off the record" or as otherwise specified.

(e) Two or more monitors

If two or more persons acted as monitors during the recording of a single reel, each monitor must execute a certificate as to the portion of the reel that he or she monitored. The certificate of a person other than a judge, clerk, or deputy clerk of the court must be in the form of an affidavit or declaration under penalty of perjury.

(f) Storage

The monitor's certificate, the recorded reel, and the monitor's notes must be retained and safely stored by the clerk in a manner that will permit their convenient retrieval and use.

(g) Transcripts

(1) Written transcripts of electronic recordings may be made by or under the direction of the clerk or a person designated by the court. The person making the transcript must execute a declaration under penalty of perjury that:

(A) Identifies the reel or reels transcribed, or the portions thereof, by reference to the numbers assigned thereto and, where only portions of a reel are transcribed, by reference to index numbers or other means of identifying the portion transcribed; and

(B) States that the transcript is a full, true, and correct transcript of the identified reel or reels or the designated portions thereof.

(2) The transcript must conform, as nearly as possible, to the requirements for a reporter's transcript as provided for in these rules.

(h) Use of transcripts

A transcript prepared and certified under (g), and accompanied by a certified copy of the monitor's certificate pertaining to each reel transcribed, is prima facie a true and complete record of the oral proceedings it purports to cover, and satisfies any requirement in the California Rules of Court or in any statute for a reporter's transcript of oral proceedings.

(i) Original reels

A reviewing court may order the transmittal to it of the original reels containing electronic recordings of proceedings being reviewed by it, or electronic copies of them.

(j) Record on appeal

(1) *Stipulation and approval of record without transcription*

On stipulation of the parties approved by the reviewing court, the original reels or electronic copies of them may be transmitted as the record of oral proceedings without being transcribed, in which case the reels or copies satisfy the requirements in the California Rules of Court or in any statute for a reporter's transcript.

(2) *Request for preparation of transcript*

In the absence of a stipulation and approval under (1), the appellant must, within 10 days after filing a notice of appeal in a civil case, serve and file with the clerk directions indicating the portions of the oral proceedings to be transcribed and must, at the same time, deposit with the clerk the approximate cost computed as specified in rule 8.130. Other steps necessary to complete preparation of the record on appeal must be taken following, as nearly as possible, the procedures in rules 8.120 and 8.130.

(3) *Preparation of transcript*

On receiving directions to have a transcript prepared, the clerk may have the material transcribed by a court employee, but should ordinarily send the reels in question to a professional recording service that has been certified by the federal court system or the Administrative Office of the Courts or verified by the clerk to be skilled in producing transcripts. *(Formerly Rule 980.5, adopted, eff. Jan. 1, 1976. As amended, eff. Jan. 1, 1990; Jan. 1, 1993. Renumbered Rule 2.952 and amended, eff. Jan. 1, 2007.)*

Research References

Rutter, Cal. Practice Guide: Civil Appeals & Writs Ch. 4-C, C. Record Preparation Procedure.

Rutter, Cal. Practice Guide: Civil Appeals & Writs Ch. 16-D, D. Designation of the Record.

9 Witkin Cal. Proc. 5th Appeal § 645, (S 645) Electronic Recording of Proceeding.

9 Witkin Cal. Proc. 5th Appeal § 1014A, (New)-Record Where Trial Proceedings Are Electronically Recorded.

2 Witkin Cal. Proc. 5th Courts § 375, Preservation.

2 Witkin Cal. Proc. 5th Courts § 383, Electronic Recording.

Rule 2.954. Specifications for electronic recording equipment

(a) Specifications mandated

Electronic recording equipment used in making the official verbatim record of oral courtroom proceedings must conform to the specifications in this rule.

(b) Sound recording only

The following specifications for electronic recording devices and appurtenant equipment apply when only sound is to be recorded:

(1) *Mandatory specifications*

(A) The device must be capable of simultaneously recording at least four separate channels or "tracks," each of which has a separate playback control so that any one channel separately or any combination of channels may be played back.

(B) The device must not have an operative erase head.

(C) The device must have a digital counter or comparable means of logging and locating the place on a reel where specific proceedings were recorded.

(D) Earphones must be provided for monitoring the recorded signal.

(E) The signal going to the earphones must come from a separate playback head, so that the monitor will hear what has actually been recorded on the tape.

(F) The device must be capable of recording at least two hours without interruption. This requirement may be satisfied by a device that automatically switches from one recording deck to another at the completion of a reel of tape of less than two hours in duration.

(G) A separate visual indicator of signal level must be provided for each recording channel.

(H) The appurtenant equipment must include at least four microphones, which should include one at the witness stand, one at the bench, and one at each counsel table. In the absence of unusual circumstances, all microphones must be directional (cardioid).

(I) A loudspeaker must be provided for courtroom playback.

(2) *Recommended features*

The following features are recommended, but not required:

(A) The recording level control should be automatic rather than manual.

(B) The device should be equipped to prevent recording over a previously recorded segment of tape.

(C) The device should give a warning signal at the end of a reel of tape.

(c) Audio–and–video recording

The following specifications for electronic audio-video recording devices and appurtenant equipment apply when audio and video are to be recorded simultaneously.

(1) *Mandatory specifications*

The system must include:

(A) At least five charge-coupled-device color video cameras in fixed mounts, equipped with lenses appropriate to the courtroom. Cameras must conform to EIA standard, accept

C–mount lenses, have 2000 lux sensitivity at f4.0 at 3200 degrees Kelvin so as to produce an adequate picture with 30 lux minimum illumination and an f1.4 lens, and be approximately 2.6″ × 2.4″ × 8.0.″

(B) At least eight phase-coherent cardioid (directional) microphones, Crown PCC–160 or equivalent, appropriately placed.

(C) At least two VHS videotape recorders with hi-fi sound on video, specially modified to record 4 channels of audio (2 linear channels with Dolby noise reduction and 2 hi-fi sound on video channels), capable of recording up to 6 hours on T–120 cassettes, modified to prevent automatic rewind at end of tape, and wired for remote control. The two recorders must simultaneously record the same audio and video signals, as selected by the audio-video mixer.

(D) A computer-controlled audio-video mixer and switching system that:

(i) Automatically selects for the VCRs the signal from the video camera that is associated with the active microphone; and

(ii) Compares microphone active signal to ambient noise signal so that microphones are recorded only when a person is speaking, and so that only the microphone nearest a speaker is active, thus minimizing recording of ambient noise.

(E) A sound system that serves both as a sound reinforcement system while recording is in progress, and as a playback amplification system, integrated with other components to minimize feedback.

(F) A time-date generator that is active and records at all times the system is recording.

(G) A color monitor.

(H) Appropriate cables, distribution amplifiers, switches, and the like.

(I) The system must produce:

(i) A signal visible to the judge, the in-court clerk, and counsel indicating that the system is recording;

(ii) An audible signal at end-of-tape or if the tape jams while the controls are set to record; and

(iii) Blanking of the judge's bench monitor when the system is not actually recording.

(2) *Recommended features*

The system should normally include:

(A) A chambers camera and microphone or microphones that, when in use, will override any signals originating in the courtroom, and that will be inactivated when not in use.

(B) Two additional videocassette recorders that will produce tapes with the same video and audio as the main two, but may have fewer channels of sound, for the use of parties in cases recorded.

(d) Substantial compliance

A sound or video and sound system that substantially conforms to these specifications is approved if the deviation does not significantly impair a major function of the system. Subdivision (c)(1)(D)(ii) of this rule describes a specification from which deviation is permissible, if the system produces adequate sound quality.

(e) Previous equipment

The Administrative Director of the Courts is authorized to approve any electronic recording devices and equipment acquired before the adoption or amendment of this rule that has been found by the court to produce satisfactory recordings of proceedings. *(Formerly Rule 980.6, adopted, eff. Jan. 1, 1990. Renumbered Rule 2.954 and amended, eff. Jan. 1, 2007.)*

Research References

2 Witkin Cal. Proc. 5th Courts § 375, Preservation.
2 Witkin Cal. Proc. 5th Courts § 383, Electronic Recording.

Rule 2.956.   Court reporting services in civil cases

(a) Statutory reference; application

This rule is adopted solely to effectuate the statutory mandate of Government Code sections 68086(a)–(b) and must be applied so as to give effect to these sections.   It applies to trial courts.

(b) Notice of availability; parties' request

(1) *Local policy to be adopted and posted*

Each trial court must adopt and post in the clerk's office a local policy enumerating the departments in which the services of official court reporters are normally available, and the departments in which the services of official court reporters are not normally available during regular court hours.   If the services of official court reporters are normally available in a department only for certain types of matters, those matters must be identified in the policy.

(2) *Publication of policy*

The court must publish its policy in a newspaper if one is published in the county.   Instead of publishing the policy, the court may:

(A) Send each party a copy of the policy at least 10 days before any hearing is held in a case; or

(B) Adopt the policy as a local rule.

(3) *Requests for official court reporter for civil trials and notices to parties*

Unless the court's policy states that all courtrooms normally have the services of official court reporters available for civil trials, the court must require that each party file a statement before the trial date indicating whether the party requests the presence of an official court reporter.   If a party requests the presence of an official court reporter and it appears that none will be available, the clerk must notify the party of that fact as soon as possible before the trial.   If the services of official court reporters are normally available in all courtrooms, the clerk must notify the parties to a civil trial as soon as possible if it appears that those services will not be available.

(4) *Notice of nonavailability of court reporter for nontrial matters*

If the services of an official court reporter will not be available during a hearing on law and motion or other nontrial matters in civil cases, that fact must be noted on the court's official calendar.

(c) Party may procure reporter

If the services of an official court reporter are not available for a hearing or trial in a civil case, a party may arrange for the presence of a certified shorthand reporter to serve as an official pro tempore reporter.   It is that party's responsibility to pay the reporter's fee for attendance at the proceedings, but the expense may be recoverable as part of the costs, as provided by law.

(d) No additional charge if party arranges for reporter

If a party arranges and pays for the attendance of a certified shorthand reporter at a hearing in a civil case because of the unavailability of the services of an official court reporter, none of the parties may be charged the reporter's attendance fee provided for in Government Code sections 68086(a)(1) or (b)(1).

(e) Definitions

As used in this rule and in Government Code section 68086:

(1) "Civil case" includes all matters other than criminal and juvenile matters.

(2) "Official reporter" and "official reporting services" both include an official court reporter or official reporter as those phrases are used in statutes, including Code of Civil Procedure sections 269 and 274c and Government Code section 69941; and include an official reporter pro tempore as the phrase is used in Government Code section 69945 and other statutes, whose fee for attending and reporting proceedings is paid for by the court or the county, and who attends court sessions as directed by the court, and who was not employed to report specific causes at the request of a party or parties. "Official reporter" and "official reporting services" do not include official reporters pro tempore employed by the court expressly to report only criminal, or criminal and juvenile, matters. "Official reporting services" include electronic recording equipment operated by the court to make the official verbatim record of proceedings where it is permitted. *(Formerly Rule 891, adopted, eff. Jan. 1, 1994. As amended, eff. Jan. 31, 1997. Renumbered Rule 2.956 and amended, eff. Jan. 1, 2007.)*

Research References

Rutter, Cal. Practice Guide: Civ. Pro. Before Trial Ch. 9(I)-D, D. Hearing.
7 Witkin Cal. Proc. 5th Judgment § 135, (S 135) Reporter's Fees.

Rule 2.958. Assessing fee for official reporter

The half-day fee to be charged under Government Code section 68086 for the services of an official reporter must be established by the trial court as follows: for a proceeding or portion of a proceeding in which a certified shorthand reporter is used, the fee is equal to the average salary and benefit costs of the reporter, plus indirect costs of up to 18 percent of salary and benefits. For purposes of this rule, the daily salary is determined by dividing the average annual salary of temporary and full-time reporters by 225 workdays. *(Formerly Rule 892, adopted, eff. Jan. 1, 1994. As amended, eff. Jan. 31, 1997; Aug. 17, 2003; Jan. 1, 2004; July 1, 2004. Renumbered Rule 2.958 and amended, eff. Jan. 1, 2007.)*

Research References

2 Witkin Cal. Proc. 5th Courts § 190, (S 190) Trial Court Rules.
2 Witkin Cal. Proc. 5th Courts § 385, Advance Payment in Civil Cases.
4 Witkin Cal. Proc. 5th Pleading § 26, Additional Fees.

Division 8

TRIALS

Chapter 1

JURY SERVICE

Rule
2.1002. Length of juror service.
2.1004. Scheduling accommodations for jurors.
2.1006. Deferral of jury service.
2.1008. Excuses from jury service.
2.1010. Juror motion to set aside sanctions imposed by default.

Rule 2.1002. Length of juror service

(a) Purpose

This rule implements Government Code section 68550, which is intended to make jury service more convenient and alleviate the problem of potential jurors refusing to appear for jury duty by shortening the time a person would be required to serve to one day or one trial. The exemptions authorized by the rule are intended to be of limited scope and duration, and they must be applied with the goal of achieving full compliance throughout the state as soon as possible.

(b) Definitions

As used in this rule:

(1) "Trial court system" means all the courts of a county.

(2) "One trial" means jury service provided by a citizen after being sworn as a trial juror.

(3) "One day" means the hours of one normal court working day (the hours a court is open to the public for business).

(4) "On call" means all same-day notice procedures used to inform prospective jurors of the time they are to report for jury service.

(5) "Telephone standby" means all previous-day notice procedures used to inform prospective jurors of their date to report for service.

(c) One–day/one–trial

Each trial court system must implement a juror management program under which a person has fulfilled his or her jury service obligation when the person has:

(1) Served on one trial until discharged;

(2) Been assigned on one day to one or more trial departments for jury selection and served through the completion of jury selection or until excused by the jury commissioner;

(3) Attended court but was not assigned to a trial department for selection of a jury before the end of that day;

(4) Served one day on call; or

(5) Served no more than five court days on telephone standby.

(d) Exemption

(1) *Good cause*

The Judicial Council may grant an exemption from the requirements of this rule for a specified period of time if the trial court system demonstrates good cause by establishing that:

(A) The cost of implementing a one–day/one–trial system is so high that the trial court system would be unable to provide essential services to the public if required to implement such a system; or

(B) The requirements of this rule cannot be met because of the size of the population in the county compared to the number of jury trials.

(2) *Application*

Any application for exemption from the requirements of this rule must be submitted to the Judicial Council no later than September 1, 1999. The application must demonstrate good cause for the exemption sought and must include either:

(A) A plan to fully comply with this rule by a specified date; or

(B) An alternative plan that would advance the purposes of this rule to the extent possible, given the conditions in the county.

(3) *Decision*

If the council finds good cause, it may grant an exemption for a limited period of time and on such conditions as it deems appropriate to further the purposes of this rule. *(Formerly Rule 861, adopted, eff. July 1, 1999. Renumbered Rule 2.1002 and amended, eff. Jan. 1, 2007.)*

Research References

Rutter, Cal. Practice Guide: Civil Trials & Evidence Ch. 5-A, A. Obtaining Prospective Jurors.
7 Witkin Cal. Proc. 5th Trial § 114, (S 114) Length of Jury Service.

Rule 2.1004.   Scheduling accommodations for jurors

(a) Accommodations for all jurors

The jury commissioner should accommodate a prospective juror's schedule by granting a prospective juror's request for a one-time deferral of jury service. If the request for a deferral is made under penalty of perjury in writing or through the court's established electronic means, and in accordance with the court's local procedure, the jury commissioner should not require the prospective juror to appear at court to make the request in person.

(b) Scheduling accommodations for peace officers

If a prospective juror is a peace officer, as defined by Penal Code section 830.5, the jury commissioner must make scheduling accommodations on application of the peace officer stating the reason a scheduling accommodation is necessary. The jury commissioner must establish procedures for the form and timing of the application. If the request for special accommodations is made under penalty of perjury in writing or through the court's established electronic means, and in accordance with the court's local procedure, the jury commissioner must not require the prospective juror to appear at court to make the request in person. *(Formerly Rule 858, adopted, eff. Jan. 1, 2005. Renumbered Rule 2.1004 and amended, eff. Jan. 1, 2007.)*

Research References

Rutter, Cal. Practice Guide: Civil Trials & Evidence Ch. 5-A, A. Obtaining Prospective Jurors.
7 Witkin Cal. Proc. 5th Trial § 112, in General.

Rule 2.1006.   Deferral of jury service

A mother who is breastfeeding a child may request that jury service be deferred for up to one year, and may renew that request as long as she is breastfeeding. If the request is made in writing, under penalty of perjury, the jury commissioner must grant it without requiring the prospective juror to appear at court. *(Formerly Rule 859, adopted, eff. July 1, 2001. Renumbered Rule 2.1006, eff. Jan. 1, 2007.)*

Research References

Rutter, Cal. Practice Guide: Civil Trials & Evidence Ch. 5-A, A. Obtaining Prospective Jurors.

Rule 2.1008.   Excuses from jury service

(a) Duty of citizenship

Jury service, unless excused by law, is a responsibility of citizenship. The court and its staff must employ all necessary and appropriate means to ensure that citizens fulfill this important civic responsibility.

(b) Principles

The following principles govern the granting of excuses from jury service by the jury commissioner on grounds of undue hardship under Code of Civil Procedure section 204:

(1) No class or category of persons may be automatically excluded from jury duty except as provided by law.

(2) A statutory exemption from jury service must be granted only when the eligible person claims it.

(3) Deferring jury service is preferred to excusing a prospective juror for a temporary or marginal hardship.

(4) Inconvenience to a prospective juror or an employer is not an adequate reason to be excused from jury duty, although it may be considered a ground for deferral.

(c) Requests to be excused from jury service

All requests to be excused from jury service that are granted for undue hardship must be put in writing by the prospective juror, reduced to writing, or placed on the court's record. The prospective juror must support the request with facts specifying the hardship and a statement why the circumstances constituting the undue hardship cannot be avoided by deferring the prospective juror's service.

(d) Reasons for excusing a juror because of undue hardship

An excuse on the ground of undue hardship may be granted for any of the following reasons:

(1) The prospective juror has no reasonably available means of public or private transportation to the court.

(2) The prospective juror must travel an excessive distance. Unless otherwise established by statute or local rule, an excessive distance is reasonable travel time that exceeds one-and-one-half hours from the prospective juror's home to the court.

(3) The prospective juror will bear an extreme financial burden. In determining whether to excuse the prospective juror for this reason, consideration must be given to:

(A) The sources of the prospective juror's household income;

(B) The availability and extent of income reimbursement;

(C) The expected length of service; and

(D) Whether service can reasonably be expected to compromise the prospective juror's ability to support himself or herself or his or her dependents, or so disrupt the economic stability of any individual as to be against the interests of justice.

(4) The prospective juror will bear an undue risk of material injury to or destruction of the prospective juror's property or property entrusted to the prospective juror, and it is not feasible to make alternative arrangements to alleviate the risk. In determining whether to excuse the prospective juror for this reason, consideration must be given to:

(A) The nature of the property;

(B) The source and duration of the risk;

(C) The probability that the risk will be realized;

(D) The reason alternative arrangements to protect the property cannot be made; and

(E) Whether material injury to or destruction of the property will so disrupt the economic stability of any individual as to be against the interests of justice.

(5) The prospective juror has a physical or mental disability or impairment, not affecting that person's competence to act as a juror, that would expose the potential juror to undue risk of mental or physical harm. In any individual case, unless the person is aged 70 years or older, the prospective juror may be required to furnish verification or a method of verification of the disability or impairment, its probable duration, and the particular reasons for the person's inability to serve as a juror.

(6) The prospective juror's services are immediately needed for the protection of the public health and safety, and it is not feasible to make alternative arrangements to relieve the person

of those responsibilities during the period of service as a juror without substantially reducing essential public services.

(7) The prospective juror has a personal obligation to provide actual and necessary care to another, including sick, aged, or infirm dependents, or a child who requires the prospective juror's personal care and attention, and no comparable substitute care is either available or practical without imposing an undue economic hardship on the prospective juror or person cared for. If the request to be excused is based on care provided to a sick, disabled, or infirm person, the prospective juror may be required to furnish verification or a method of verification that the person being cared for is in need of regular and personal care.

(e) Excuse based on previous jury service

A prospective juror who has served on a grand or trial jury or was summoned and appeared for jury service in any state or federal court during the previous 12 months must be excused from service on request. The jury commissioner, in his or her discretion, may establish a longer period of repose. *(Formerly Rule 860, adopted, eff. July 1, 1997. Renumbered Rule 2.1008 and amended, eff. Jan. 1, 2007.)*

Research References

Rutter, Cal. Practice Guide: Civil Trials & Evidence Ch. 5-A, A. Obtaining Prospective Jurors.
Rutter, Cal. Practice Guide: Civil Trials & Evidence Ch. 5-D, D. Examination by Trial Judge.
7 Witkin Cal. Proc. 5th Trial § 113, Rule of Court.

Rule 2.1010. Juror motion to set aside sanctions imposed by default

(a) Motion

A prospective juror against whom sanctions have been imposed by default under Code of Civil Procedure section 209 may move to set aside the default. The motion must be brought no later than 60 days after sanctions have been imposed.

(b) Contents of motion

A motion to set aside sanctions imposed by default must contain a short and concise statement of the reasons the prospective juror was not able to attend when summoned for jury duty and any supporting documentation.

(c) Judicial Council form may be used

A motion to set aside sanctions imposed by default may be made by completing and filing *Juror's Motion to Set Aside Sanctions and Order* (form MC–070).

(d) Hearing

The court may decide the motion with or without a hearing.

(e) Good cause required

If the motion demonstrates good cause, a court must set aside sanctions imposed against a prospective juror.

(f) Continuing obligation to serve

Nothing in this rule relieves a prospective juror of the obligation of jury service.

(g) Notice to juror

The court must provide a copy of this rule to the prospective juror against whom sanctions have been imposed. *(Formerly Rule 862, adopted, eff. Jan. 1, 2005. Renumbered Rule 2.1010 and amended, eff. Jan. 1, 2007. As amended, eff. Jan. 1, 2010.)*

Research References

Rutter, Cal. Practice Guide: Civil Trials & Evidence Ch. 5-A, A. Obtaining Prospective Jurors.

2 Witkin Cal. Proc. 5th Courts § 190, (S 190) Trial Court Rules.
7 Witkin Cal. Proc. 5th Trial § 120, Ordinary Panel.

Chapter 2

CONDUCT OF TRIAL

Rule 2.1030. Communications from or with jury

(a) Preservation of written jury communications

The trial judge must preserve and deliver to the clerk for inclusion in the record all written communications, formal or informal, received from the jury or from individual jurors or sent by the judge to the jury or individual jurors, from the time the jury is sworn until it is discharged.

(b) Recording of oral jury communications

The trial judge must ensure that the reporter, or any electronic recording system used instead of a reporter, records all oral communications, formal or informal, received from the jury or from individual jurors or communicated by the judge to the jury or individual jurors, from the time the jury is sworn until it is discharged. *(Formerly Rule 231, adopted eff. Jan. 1, 1990. Renumbered Rule 2.1030 and amended, eff. Jan. 1, 2007.)*

Research References

Rutter, Cal. Practice Guide: Civil Appeals & Writs Ch. 4-C, C. Record Preparation Procedure.
2 Witkin Cal. Proc. 5th Courts § 190, (S 190) Trial Court Rules.
7 Witkin Cal. Proc. 5th Trial § 330, (S 330) in General.

Rule 2.1031. Juror note–taking

Jurors must be permitted to take written notes in all civil and criminal trials. At the beginning of a trial, a trial judge must inform jurors that they may take written notes during the trial. The court must provide materials suitable for this purpose. *(Adopted, eff. Jan. 1, 2007.)*

Research References

Rutter, Cal. Practice Guide: Civil Trials & Evidence Ch. 7-B, B. Explanations, Admonitions and Preinstructions.
Rutter, Cal. Practice Guide: Personal Injury Ch. 9-C, C. Impanelment of Jury.
7 Witkin Cal. Proc. 5th Trial § 281, Functions of Court and Jury.
7 Witkin Cal. Proc. 5th Trial § 323, (S 323) Papers and Exhibits in Jury Room.

Rule 2.1032. Juror notebooks in complex civil cases

A trial judge should encourage counsel in complex civil cases to include key documents, exhibits, and other appropriate materials in notebooks for use by jurors during trial to assist them in performing their duties. *(Adopted, eff. Jan. 1, 2007.)*

Research References

Rutter, Cal. Practice Guide: Civil Trials & Evidence Ch. 7-B, B. Explanations, Admonitions and Preinstructions.
Rutter, Cal. Practice Guide: Civil Trials & Evidence Ch. 7-D, D. Jurors' Notes.
Rutter, Cal. Practice Guide: Civil Trials & Evidence Ch. 14-F, F. Instructing the Jury.
7 Witkin Cal. Proc. 5th Trial § 323, (S 323) Papers and Exhibits in Jury Room.

Ct. Rules

Rule 2.1033. Juror questions

A trial judge should allow jurors to submit written questions directed to witnesses. An opportunity must be given to counsel to object to such questions out of the presence of the jury. (Adopted, eff. Jan. 1, 2007.)

Research References

Rutter, Cal. Practice Guide: Civil Trials & Evidence Ch. 7-E, E. Juror Questioning of Witnesses.
Rutter, Cal. Practice Guide: Personal Injury Ch. 9-F, F. Examination of Witnesses.

Rule 2.1035. Preinstruction

Immediately after the jury is sworn, the trial judge may, in his or her discretion, preinstruct the jury concerning the elements of the charges or claims, its duties, its conduct, the order of proceedings, the procedure for submitting written questions for witnesses as set forth in rule 2.1033 if questions are allowed, and the legal principles that will govern the proceeding. (Adopted, eff. Jan. 1, 2007.)

Research References

Rutter, Cal. Practice Guide: Civil Trials & Evidence Ch. 5-D, D. Examination by Trial Judge.
Rutter, Cal. Practice Guide: Civil Trials & Evidence Ch. 14-A, A. General Considerations.
Rutter, Cal. Practice Guide: Civil Trials & Evidence Ch. 14-F, F. Instructing the Jury.
Rutter, Cal. Practice Guide: Personal Injury Ch. 9-C, C. Impanelment of Jury.
7 Witkin Cal. Proc. 5th Trial § 281, Functions of Court and Jury.

Rule 2.1036. Assisting the jury at impasse

(a) Determination

After a jury reports that it has reached an impasse in its deliberations, the trial judge may, in the presence of counsel, advise the jury of its duty to decide the case based on the evidence while keeping an open mind and talking about the evidence with each other. The judge should ask the jury if it has specific concerns which, if resolved, might assist the jury in reaching a verdict.

(b) Possible further action

If the trial judge determines that further action might assist the jury in reaching a verdict, the judge may:

(1) Give additional instructions;

(2) Clarify previous instructions;

(3) Permit attorneys to make additional closing arguments; or

(4) Employ any combination of these measures. (Adopted, eff. Jan. 1, 2007.)

Research References

Rutter, Cal. Practice Guide: Civil Trials & Evidence Ch. 13-A, A. Procedural Considerations Re Closing Argument.
Rutter, Cal. Practice Guide: Civil Trials & Evidence Ch. 15-D, D. Juror Requests for Additional Information During Deliberations.
7 Witkin Cal. Proc. 5th Trial § 326, (S 326) Assisting Jury at Impasse.

Chapter 3

TESTIMONY AND EVIDENCE

Rule
2.1040. Electronic recordings presented or offered into evidence.

Rule 2.1040. Electronic recordings presented or offered into evidence

(a) Electronic recordings of deposition or other prior testimony

(1) Before a party may present or offer into evidence an electronic sound or sound-and-video recording of deposition or other prior testimony, the party must lodge a transcript of the deposition or prior testimony with the court. At the time the recording is played, the party must identify on the record the page and line numbers where the testimony presented or offered appears in the transcript.

(2) Except as provided in (3), at the time the presentation of evidence closes or within five days after the recording in (1) is presented or offered into evidence, whichever is later, the party presenting or offering the recording into evidence must serve and file a copy of the transcript cover showing the witness name and a copy of the pages of the transcript where the testimony presented or offered appears. The transcript pages must be marked to identify the testimony that was presented or offered into evidence.

(3) If the court reporter takes down the content of all portions of the recording in (1) that were presented or offered into evidence, the party offering or presenting the recording is not required to provide a transcript of that recording under (2).

(b) Other electronic recordings

(1) Except as provided in (2) and (3), before a party may present or offer into evidence any electronic sound or sound-and-video recording not covered under (a), the party must provide to the court and to opposing parties a transcript of the electronic recording and provide opposing parties with a duplicate of the electronic recording, as defined in Evidence Code section 260. The transcript may be prepared by the party presenting or offering the recording into evidence; a certified transcript is not required.

(2) For good cause, the trial judge may permit the party to provide the transcript or the duplicate recording at the time the presentation of evidence closes or within five days after the recording is presented or offered into evidence, whichever is later.

(3) No transcript is required to be provided under (1):

(A) In proceedings that are uncontested or in which the responding party does not appear, unless otherwise ordered by the trial judge;

(B) If the parties stipulate in writing or on the record that the sound portion of a sound-and-video recording does not contain any words that are relevant to the issues in the case; or

(C) If, for good cause, the trial judge orders that a transcript is not required.

(c) Clerk's duties

An electronic recording provided to the court under this rule must be marked for identification. A transcript provided under (a)(2) or (b)(1) must be filed by the clerk.

(d) Reporting by court reporter

Unless otherwise ordered by the trial judge, the court reporter need not take down the content of an electronic recording that is presented or offered into evidence. (Formerly Rule 203.5, adopted, eff. July 1, 1988. As amended, eff. Jan. 1, 1997. Renumbered Rule 243.9, and amended, eff. Jan. 1, 2003. Renumbered Rule 2.1040 and amended, eff. Jan. 1, 2007. As amended, eff. July 1, 2011.)

Advisory Committee Comment

This rule is designed to ensure that, in the event of an appeal, there is an appropriate record of any electronic sound or sound-and-video recording that was presented or offered into evidence in the trial court. The rules on felony, misdemeanor, and infraction appeals require that any transcript provided by a party under this rule be included in the clerk's transcript on appeal (see rules 8.320, 8.861, and 8.912). In civil appeals, the parties may designate such a transcript for inclusion in the clerk's transcript (see rules 8.122(b) and 8.832(a)). The transcripts required under this rule may also assist the court or jurors during the trial court proceedings. For this purpose, it may be helpful for the trial court to request that the party offering an electronic recording provide additional copies of such transcripts for jurors to follow while the recording is played.

Subdivision (a). Note that, under Code of Civil Procedure section 2025.510(g), if the testimony at a deposition is recorded both stenographically and by audio or video technology, the stenographic transcript is the official record of that testimony for the purpose of the trial and any subsequent hearing or appeal.

Subdivision (a)(2). The party offering or presenting the electronic recording may serve and file a copy of the cover and of the relevant pages of the deposition or other transcript; a new transcript need not be prepared.

Subdivision (b). Note that, with the exception of recordings covered by Code of Civil Procedure section 2025.510(g), the recording itself, not the transcript, is the evidence that was offered or presented (see *People v. Sims* (1993) 5 Cal.4th 405, 448). Sometimes, a party may present or offer into evidence only a portion of a longer electronic recording. In such circumstances, the transcript provided to the court and opposing parties should contain only a transcription of those portions of the electronic recording that are actually presented or offered into evidence. If a party believes that a transcript provided under this subdivision is inaccurate, the party can raise an objection in the trial court.

Subdivision (b)(3)(C). Good cause to waive the requirement for a transcript may include such factors as (1) the party presenting or offering the electronic recording into evidence lacks the capacity to prepare a transcript or (2) the electronic recording is of such poor quality that preparing a useful transcript is not feasible.

Subdivision (c). The requirement to file a transcript provided to the court under (a)(2) or (b)(1) is intended to ensure that the transcript is available for inclusion in a clerk's transcript in the event of an appeal.

Subdivision (d). In some circumstances it may be helpful to have the court reporter take down the content of an electronic recording. For example, when short portions of a sound or sound-and-video recording of deposition or other testimony are played to impeach statements made by a witness on the stand, the best way to create a useful record of the proceedings may be for the court reporter to take down the portions of recorded testimony that are interspersed with the live testimony.

Research References

Rutter, Cal. Practice Guide: Civil Appeals & Writs Ch. 4-C, C. Record Preparation Procedure.

Rutter, Cal. Practice Guide: Civil Appeals & Writs Ch. 4-I, I. Special Rules for Record on Certain Appeals.

Rutter, Cal. Practice Guide: Civ. Pro. Before Trial Ch. 8E-14, Deposition Transcript.

Rutter, Cal. Practice Guide: Civil Trials & Evidence Ch. 8C-E, E. Audio or Visual Recordings.

Rutter, Cal. Practice Guide: Personal Injury Ch. 9-B, B. In-Chambers Conference Before Commencement of Trial.

Rutter, Cal. Practice Guide: Personal Injury Ch. 9-H, H. Introduction of Discovered Evidence.

Rutter, Cal. Practice Guide: Personal Injury Ch. 9-I, I. Use of Writings, Exhibits and Demonstrative Evidence.

9 Witkin Cal. Proc. 5th Appeal § 646, (S 646) Matters Automatically Included.

9 Witkin Cal. Proc. 5th Appeal § 647, (S 647) Matters Designated.

2 Witkin Cal. Proc. 5th Courts § 190, (S 190) Trial Court Rules.

2 Witkin Cal. Proc. 5th Courts § 381, Transcription.

10 Witkin, California Summary 10th Parent and Child § 713, in General.

Chapter 4

JURY INSTRUCTIONS

Rule

2.1050. Judicial Council jury instructions.

2.1055. Proposed jury instructions.

2.1058. Use of gender–neutral language in jury instructions.

Rule 2.1050. Judicial Council jury instructions

(a) Purpose

The California jury instructions approved by the Judicial Council are the official instructions for use in the state of California. The goal of these instructions is to improve the quality of jury decision making by providing standardized instructions that accurately state the law in a way that is understandable to the average juror.

(b) Accuracy

The Judicial Council endorses these instructions for use and makes every effort to ensure that they accurately state existing law. The articulation and interpretation of California law, however, remains within the purview of the Legislature and the courts of review.

(c) Public access

The Administrative Office of the Courts must provide copies and updates of the approved jury instructions to the public on the California Courts Web site. The Administrative Office of the Courts may contract with an official publisher to publish the instructions in both paper and electronic formats. The Judicial Council intends that the instructions be freely available for use and reproduction by parties, attorneys, and the public, except as limited by this subdivision. The Administrative Office of the Courts may take steps necessary to ensure that publication of the instructions by commercial publishers does not occur without its permission, including, without limitation, ensuring that commercial publishers accurately publish the Judicial Council's instructions, accurately credit the Judicial Council as the source of the instructions, and do not claim copyright of the instructions. The Administrative Office of the Courts may require commercial publishers to pay fees or royalties in exchange for permission to publish the instructions. As used in this rule, "commercial publishers" means entities that publish works for sale, whether for profit or otherwise.

(d) Updating and amendments

The Judicial Council instructions will be regularly updated and maintained through its advisory committees on jury instructions. Amendments to these instructions will be circulated for public comment before publication. Trial judges and attorneys may submit for the advisory committees' consideration suggestions for improving or modifying these instructions or creating new instructions, with an explanation of why the change is proposed. Suggestions should be sent to the Administrative Office of the Courts, Office of the General Counsel.

(e) Use of instructions

Use of the Judicial Council instructions is strongly encouraged. If the latest edition of the jury instructions approved by the Judicial Council contains an instruction applicable to a case and the trial judge determines that the jury should be instructed on the subject, it is recommended that the judge use the Judicial Council instruction unless he or she finds that a different instruction would more accurately state the law and be understood by jurors. Whenever the latest edition of the Judicial

Ct. Rules

Council jury instructions does not contain an instruction on a subject on which the trial judge determines that the jury should be instructed, or when a Judicial Council instruction cannot be modified to submit the issue properly, the instruction given on that subject should be accurate, brief, understandable, impartial, and free from argument. *(Formerly Rule 855, adopted, eff. Sept. 1, 2003. As amended, eff. Aug. 26, 2005. Renumbered Rule 2.1050 and amended, eff. Jan. 1, 2007.)*

Research References

Rutter, Cal. Practice Guide: Civil Trials & Evidence Ch. 4-C, C. Jury Matters.
Rutter, Cal. Practice Guide: Civil Trials & Evidence Ch. 14-B, B. Proper vs. Improper Jury Instructions.
Rutter, Cal. Practice Guide: Civil Trials & Evidence Ch. 14-D, D. Preparing Jury Instructions.
California Practice Guide: Employment Litigation Ch. 19-R, R. Jury Instructions.
California Practice Guide: Employment Litigation Form 19:D, List of Judicial Council Jury Instructions.
Rutter, Cal. Practice Guide: Personal Injury Ch. 9-K, K. Submission of Case to Jury.
2 Witkin Cal. Proc. 5th Courts § 190, (S 190) Trial Court Rules.
7 Witkin Cal. Proc. 5th Trial § 266, (S 266) General Principles.
7 Witkin Cal. Proc. 5th Trial § 270, (S 270) Approved Forms.
7 Witkin Cal. Proc. 5th Trial § 271, in General.

Rule 2.1055.   Proposed jury instructions

(a) Application

(1) This rule applies to proposed jury instructions that a party submits to the court, including:

(A) "Approved jury instructions," meaning jury instructions approved by the Judicial Council of California; and

(B) "Special jury instructions," meaning instructions from other sources, those specially prepared by the party, or approved instructions that have been substantially modified by the party.

(2) This rule does not apply to the form or format of the instructions presented to the jury, which is a matter left to the discretion of the court.

(b) Form and format of proposed instructions

(1) All proposed instructions must be submitted to the court in the form and format prescribed for papers in the rules in division 2 of this title.

(2) Each set of proposed jury instructions must have a cover page, containing the caption of the case and stating the name of the party proposing the instructions, and an index listing all the proposed instructions.

(3) In the index, approved jury instructions must be identified by their reference numbers and special jury instructions must be numbered consecutively. The index must contain a checklist that the court may use to indicate whether the instruction was:

(A) Given as proposed;

(B) Given as modified;

(C) Refused; or

(D) Withdrawn.

(4) Each set of proposed jury instructions must be bound loosely.

(c) Format of each proposed instruction

Each proposed instruction must:

(1) Be on a separate page or pages;

(2) Include the instruction number and title of the instruction at the top of the first page of the instruction; and

(3) Be prepared without any blank lines or unused bracketed portions, so that it can be read directly to the jury.

(d) Citation of authorities

For each special instruction, a citation of authorities that support the instruction must be included at the bottom of the page. No citation is required for approved instructions.

(e) Form and format are exclusive

No local court form or rule for the filing or submission of proposed jury instructions may require that the instructions be submitted in any manner other than as prescribed by this rule. *(Formerly Rule 229, adopted, eff. Jan. 1, 1949. As amended, eff. April 1, 1962; July 1, 1988; Jan. 1, 2003; Jan. 1, 2004; Aug. 26, 2005. Renumbered Rule 2.1055 and amended, eff. Jan. 1, 2007.)*

Advisory Committee Comment

This rule does not preclude a judge from requiring the parties in an individual case to transmit the jury instructions to the court electronically.

Research References

Rutter, Cal. Practice Guide: Civil Trials & Evidence Ch. 1-G, G. Preparing Trial Notebook.
Rutter, Cal. Practice Guide: Civil Trials & Evidence Ch. 4-C, C. Jury Matters.
Rutter, Cal. Practice Guide: Civil Trials & Evidence Ch. 14-C, C. Procedural Requirements.
Rutter, Cal. Practice Guide: Civil Trials & Evidence Ch. 14-D, D. Preparing Jury Instructions.
Rutter, Cal. Practice Guide: Civil Trials & Evidence Ch. 14-E, E. Argument and Settlement Re Proposed Instructions.
Rutter, Cal. Practice Guide: Personal Injury Ch. 8-D, D. Final Preparation (One Month Before Trial).
7 Witkin Cal. Proc. 5th Trial § 263, Formal Requisites.
7 Witkin Cal. Proc. 5th Trial § 264, (S 264) in General.

Rule 2.1058.   Use of gender–neutral language in jury instructions

All instructions submitted to the jury must be written in gender-neutral language. If standard jury instructions (*CALCRIM and CACI*) are to be submitted to the jury, the court or, at the court's request, counsel must recast the instructions as necessary to ensure that gender-neutral language is used in each instruction. *(Formerly Rule 989, adopted, eff. Jan. 1, 1991. Renumbered Rule 2.1058 and amended, eff. Jan. 1, 2007.)*

Research References

Rutter, Cal. Practice Guide: Civil Trials & Evidence Ch. 14-D, D. Preparing Jury Instructions.
2 Witkin Cal. Proc. 5th Courts § 31, (S 31) Avoidance of Gender or Other Bias.
2 Witkin Cal. Proc. 5th Courts § 190, (S 190) Trial Court Rules.
7 Witkin Cal. Proc. 5th Trial § 267, (S 267) Gender Neutrality.

Division 9

JUDGMENTS

Rule

2.1100.   Notice when statute or regulation declared unconstitutional.

Rule 2.1100.   Notice when statute or regulation declared unconstitutional

Within 10 days after a court has entered judgment in a contested action or special proceeding in which the court has declared unconstitutional a state statute or regulation, the prevailing party, or as otherwise ordered by the court, must mail a copy of the judgment and a notice of entry of judgment to the Attorney General and file a proof of service with the court. *(Formerly Rule 826, adopted, eff. Jan. 1, 1999.   Renumbered Rule 2.1100 and amended, eff. Jan. 1, 2007.)*

Research References

Rutter, Cal. Practice Guide: Civil Trials & Evidence Ch. 17-C, C. Entry of Judgment.

2 Witkin Cal. Proc. 5th Courts § 190, (S 190) Trial Court Rules.

7 Witkin Cal. Proc. 5th Judgment § 57, Purpose and Entry.

Title 3

CIVIL RULES

Division 1

GENERAL PROVISIONS

Chapter 1

PRELIMINARY RULES

Rule

3.1.   Title.

Rule 3.1.   Title

The rules in this title may be referred to as the Civil Rules. *(Adopted, eff. Jan. 1, 2007.)*

Research References

2 Witkin Cal. Proc. 5th Courts § 191, (S 191) Civil Rules.

Chapter 2

SCOPE OF THE CIVIL RULES

Rule

3.10.   Application.

3.20.   Preemption of local rules.

Rule 3.10.   Application

The Civil Rules apply to all civil cases in the superior courts, including general civil, family, juvenile, and probate cases, unless otherwise provided by a statute or rule in the California Rules of Court.   *(Adopted, eff. Jan. 1, 2007.)*

Research References

2 Witkin Cal. Proc. 5th Courts § 191, (S 191) Civil Rules.

Rule 3.20.   Preemption of local rules

(a)   Fields occupied

The Judicial Council has preempted all local rules relating to pleadings, demurrers, ex parte applications, motions, discovery, provisional remedies, and the form and format of papers.   No trial court, or any division or branch of a trial court, may enact or enforce any local rule concerning these fields.   All local rules concerning these fields are null and void unless otherwise permitted or required by a statute or a rule in the California Rules of Court.

(b)   Application

This rule applies to all matters identified in (a) except:

(1)   Trial and post-trial proceedings including but not limited to motions in limine (see rule 3.112(f) [1]);

(2)   Proceedings under Code of Civil Procedure sections 527.6, 527.7, and 527.8;   the Family Code;   the Probate Code;   the Welfare and Institutions Code;   and the Penal Code and all other criminal proceedings;

(3)   Eminent domain proceedings;   and

(4)   Local court rules adopted under the Trial Court Delay Reduction Act [2].   *(Formerly Rule 302, adopted, eff. July 1, 1997. Renumbered Rule 981.1 and amended, eff. July 1, 2000.   As amended, eff. July 1, 2000; Jan. 1, 2002.   Renumbered Rule 3.20 and amended, eff. Jan. 1, 2007.)*

[1] So in copy.   See California Rules of Court, Rule 3.1112(f).

[2] See Government Code § 68600 et seq.

Research References

Rutter, Cal. Practice Guide: Civ. Pro. Before Trial Ch. 5-C, C. Default Judgment by Clerk.

Rutter, Cal. Practice Guide: Civ. Pro. Before Trial Ch. 5-D, D. Default Judgment by Court.

Rutter, Cal. Practice Guide: Civ. Pro. Before Trial Ch. 6-B, B. Complaints.

Rutter, Cal. Practice Guide: Civ. Pro. Before Trial Ch. 10-C, C. Procedural Requirements-Moving Party.

Rutter, Cal. Practice Guide: Civ. Pro. Before Trial Ch. 10-D, D. Procedural Requirements-Opposing Party.

Rutter, Cal. Practice Guide: Civ. Pro. Before Trial Ch. 14-B, B. Class Action Requirements-In General.

Rutter, Cal. Practice Guide: Civ. Pro. Before Trial Ch. 8E-3, Whose Deposition May be Taken.

Rutter, Cal. Practice Guide: Civ. Pro. Before Trial Ch. 8E-4, Notice of Deposition.

Rutter, Cal. Practice Guide: Civ. Pro. Before Trial Ch. 8F-3, Propounding Interrogatories.

Rutter, Cal. Practice Guide: Civ. Pro. Before Trial Ch. 8F-7, Motion to Compel Answers.

Ct. Rules

Rutter, Cal. Practice Guide: Civ. Pro. Before Trial Ch. 8H-6, Responding to Demand.

Rutter, Cal. Practice Guide: Civ. Pro. Before Trial Ch. 8J-6, Exchange Required.

Rutter, Cal. Practice Guide: Civ. Pro. Before Trial Ch. 8K-1, Request for Statement of Damages (Personal Injury or Death Cases).

Rutter, Cal. Practice Guide: Civ. Pro. Before Trial Ch. 9(I)-A, A. Introduction.

Rutter, Cal. Practice Guide: Civ. Pro. Before Trial Ch. 9(I)-B, B. Preparing and Filing Motions.

Rutter, Cal. Practice Guide: Civ. Pro. Before Trial Ch. 9(I)-C, C. Opposing the Motion-And Rebutting the Opposition.

Rutter, Cal. Practice Guide: Civ. Pro. Before Trial Ch. 9(I)-E, E. Posthearing Procedures.

Rutter, Cal. Practice Guide: Civ. Pro. Before Trial Ch. 9(I)-F, F. Ex Parte Motions.

Rutter, Cal. Practice Guide: Civ. Pro. Before Trial Ch. 12(I)-A, A. Rules Governing Trial Setting Process.

Rutter, Cal. Practice Guide: Civ. Pro. Before Trial Ch. 12(I)-B, B. Case Management ("Fast Track") System.

Rutter, Cal. Practice Guide: Civ. Pro. Before Trial Ch. 9(II)-A, A. Injunctions.

Rutter, Cal. Practice Guide: Civ. Pro. Before Trial Ch. 9(III)-D, D. Other Sanctions Statutes and Rules.

Rutter, Cal. Practice Guide: Civ. Pro. Before Trial Ch. 9(I)-A , Outline a.

Rutter, Cal. Practice Guide: Civil Trials & Evidence Ch. 4-F, F. Motions in Limine.

Rutter, Cal. Practice Guide: Enforcing Judgments/Debts Ch. 4-A, A. Attachment.

Rutter, Cal. Practice Guide: Enforcing Judgments/Debts Ch. 4-B, B. Claim and Delivery.

Rutter, Cal. Practice Guide: Enforcing Judgments/Debts Ch. 4-C, C. Receiverships.

Rutter, Cal. Practice Guide: Enforcing Judgments/Debts Ch. 6D-2, Writ of Execution.

Rutter, Cal. Practice Guide: Enforcing Judgments/Debts Ch. 6G-1, Examination of Judgment Debtor and Third Parties.

Rutter, Cal. Practice Guide: Personal Injury Ch. 8-A, A. Case Management.

2 Witkin Cal. Proc. 5th Courts § 191, (S 191) Civil Rules.

2 Witkin Cal. Proc. 5th Courts § 199, (S 199) in General.

4 Witkin Cal. Proc. 5th Pleading § 4, (S 4) in General.

4 Witkin Cal. Proc. 5th Pleading § 13, in General.

7 Witkin Cal. Proc. 5th Trial § 38, (S 38) Trial Court Delay Reduction Act.

Chapter 3

ATTORNEYS

Rule

3.35. Definition of limited scope representation; application of rules.

3.36. Notice of limited scope representation and application to be relieved as attorney.

3.37. Nondisclosure of attorney assistance in preparation of court documents.

Rule 3.35. Definition of limited scope representation; application of rules

(a) Definition

"Limited scope representation" is a relationship between an attorney and a person seeking legal services in which they have agreed that the scope of the legal services will be limited to specific tasks that the attorney will perform for the person.

(b) Application

Rules 3.35 through 3.37 apply to limited scope representation in civil cases, except in family law cases. Rules 5.70 and 5.71 apply to limited scope representation in family law cases.

(c) Types of limited scope representation

These rules recognize two types of limited scope representation:

(1) *Noticed representation*

Rule 3.36 provides procedures for cases in which an attorney and a party notify the court and other parties of the limited scope representation.

(2) *Undisclosed representation*

Rule 3.37 applies to cases in which the limited scope representation is not disclosed. *(Adopted, eff. Jan. 1, 2007.)*

Research References

Rutter, Cal. Practice Guide: Enforcing Judgments/Debts Ch. 1-B, B. Accepting the Collection Case.

Rutter, Cal. Practice Guide: Personal Injury Ch. 1-C, C. Formation of Attorney-Client Relationship: the Employment Agreement.

Rutter, Cal. Practice Guide: Prof. Responsibility Ch. 3-A, A. Nature of Attorney-Client Relationship.

Rutter, Cal. Practice Guide: Prof. Responsibility Ch. 3-B, B. Formation of Relationship.

Rutter, Cal. Practice Guide: Prof. Responsibility Ch. 10-B, B. Withdrawal (Termination) by Lawyer.

1 Witkin Cal. Proc. 5th Attorneys § 5, (S 5) Classification of Professional Activities.

2 Witkin Cal. Proc. 5th Courts § 191, (S 191) Civil Rules.

11 Witkin, California Summary 10th Husband and Wife § 74, (S 74) Limited Scope Legal Representation.

Rule 3.36. Notice of limited scope representation and application to be relieved as attorney

(a) Notice of limited scope representation

A party and an attorney may provide notice of their agreement to limited scope representation by serving and filing a *Notice of Limited Scope Representation* (form MC–950).

(b) Notice and service of papers

After the notice in (a) is received and until either a substitution of attorney or an order to be relieved as attorney is filed and served, papers in the case must be served on both the attorney providing the limited scope representation and the client.

(c) Procedures to be relieved as counsel on completion of representation

Notwithstanding rule 3.1362, an attorney who has completed the tasks specified in the *Notice of Limited Scope Representation* (form MC–950) may use the procedures in this rule to request that he or she be relieved as attorney in cases in which the attorney has appeared before the court as an attorney of record and the client has not signed a *Substitution of Attorney—Civil* (form MC–050).

(d) Application

An application to be relieved as attorney on completion of limited scope representation under Code of Civil Procedure section 284(2) must be directed to the client and made on the *Application to Be Relieved as Attorney on Completion of Limited Scope Representation* (form MC–955).

(e) Filing and service of application

The application to be relieved as attorney must be filed with the court and served on the client and on all other parties or attorneys for parties in the case. The client must also be served with a blank *Objection to Application to Be Relieved as Attorney on Completion of Limited Scope Representation* (form MC–956).

(f) No objection

If no objection is served and filed with the court within 15 days from the date that the *Application to Be Relieved as Attorney on Completion of Limited Scope Representation* (form MC–955) is served on the client, the attorney making the application must file an updated form MC–955 indicating the lack of objection, along with a proposed *Order on Application to Be Relieved as Attorney on Completion of Limited Scope Representation* (form MC–958). The clerk must then forward the order for judicial signature.

(g) Objection

If an objection to the application is served and filed within 15 days, the clerk must set a hearing date on the *Objection to Application to Be Relieved as Attorney on Completion of Limited Scope Representation* (form MC–956). The hearing must be scheduled no later than 25 days from the date the objection is filed. The clerk must send the notice of the hearing to the parties and the attorney.

(h) Service of the order

If no objection is served and filed and the proposed order is signed under (f), the attorney who filed the *Application to Be Relieved as Attorney on Completion of Limited Scope Representation* (form MC–955) must serve a copy of the signed order on the client and on all parties or the attorneys for all parties who have appeared in the case. The court may delay the effective date of the order relieving the attorney until proof of service of a copy of the signed order on the client has been filed with the court. *(Adopted, eff. Jan. 1, 2007.)*

Research References

Rutter, Cal. Practice Guide: Civ. Pro. Before Trial Ch. 1-A, A. Accepting a New Case.
Rutter, Cal. Practice Guide: Civ. Pro. Before Trial Ch. 9(I)-G, G. Motions Regulating Counsel.
Rutter, Cal. Practice Guide: Enforcing Judgments/Debts Ch. 1-B, B. Accepting the Collection Case.
Rutter, Cal. Practice Guide: Personal Injury Ch. 1-C, C. Formation of Attorney-Client Relationship: the Employment Agreement.
Rutter, Cal. Practice Guide: Prof. Responsibility Ch. 3-B, B. Formation of Relationship.
Rutter, Cal. Practice Guide: Prof. Responsibility Ch. 10-B, B. Withdrawal (Termination) by Lawyer.
1 Witkin Cal. Proc. 5th Attorneys § 5, (S 5) Classification of Professional Activities.

Rule 3.37. Nondisclosure of attorney assistance in preparation of court documents

(a) Nondisclosure

In a civil proceeding, an attorney who contracts with a client to draft or assist in drafting legal documents, but not to make an appearance in the case, is not required to disclose within the text of the documents that he or she was involved in preparing the documents.

(b) Attorney's fees

If a litigant seeks a court order for attorney's fees incurred as a result of document preparation, the litigant must disclose to the court information required for a proper determination of the attorney's fees, including:

(1) The name of the attorney who assisted in the preparation of the documents;

(2) The time involved or other basis for billing;

(3) The tasks performed; and

(4) The amount billed.

(c) Application of rule

This rule does not apply to an attorney who has made a general appearance in a case. *(Adopted, eff. Jan. 1, 2007.)*

Research References

Rutter, Cal. Practice Guide: Civ. Pro. Before Trial Ch. 1-A, A. Accepting a New Case.
Rutter, Cal. Practice Guide: Enforcing Judgments/Debts Ch. 1-B, B. Accepting the Collection Case.
Rutter, Cal. Practice Guide: Personal Injury Ch. 1-C, C. Formation of Attorney-Client Relationship: the Employment Agreement.
Rutter, Cal. Practice Guide: Prof. Responsibility Ch. 3-A, A. Nature of Attorney-Client Relationship.
Rutter, Cal. Practice Guide: Prof. Responsibility Ch. 3-B, B. Formation of Relationship.
1 Witkin Cal. Proc. 5th Attorneys § 5, (S 5) Classification of Professional Activities.
2 Witkin Cal. Proc. 5th Courts § 191, (S 191) Civil Rules.

Division 2

WAIVER OF FEES AND COSTS

Rule
3.50. Application of rules.
3.51. Method of application.
3.52. Procedure for determining application.
3.53. Application granted unless acted on by the court.
3.54. Confidentiality.
3.55. Court fees and costs included in all initial fee waivers .
3.56. Additional court fees and costs that may be included in initial fee waiver .
3.57. Amount of lien for waived fees and costs.
3.58. Posting notice.

Rule 3.50. Application of rules

(a) Application

The rules in this division govern applications in the trial court for an initial waiver of court fees and costs because of the applicant's financial condition. As provided in Government Code sections 68631 and following, any waiver may later be ended, modified, or retroactively withdrawn if the court determines that the applicant is not eligible for the waiver. As provided in Government Code sections 68636 and 68637, the court may, at a later time, determine that the previously waived fees and costs be paid.

(b) Definitions

For purpose of the rules in this division, "initial fee waiver" means the initial waiver of court fees and costs that may be granted at any stage of the proceedings and includes both the fees and costs specified in rule 3.55 and any additional fees and costs specified in rule 3.56. *(Adopted, eff. Jan. 1, 2007. As amended, eff. July 1, 2009.)*

Research References

Rutter, Cal. Practice Guide: A.D.R. Ch. 6-C, C. Referees.
Rutter, Cal. Practice Guide: Civil Appeals & Writs Ch. 3-E, E. Filing Steps.
Rutter, Cal. Practice Guide: Civil Trials & Evidence Ch. 2-D, D. Securing Trial by Jury.
3 Witkin Cal. Proc. 5th Actions § 416, (S 416) in General.
3 Witkin Cal. Proc. 5th Actions § 418, Trial Court Costs.
3 Witkin Cal. Proc. 5th Actions § 419, Costs of Appeal.
3 Witkin Cal. Proc. 5th Actions § 423, (S 423) No Right to Reporter's Transcript.
3 Witkin Cal. Proc. 5th Actions § 425, (S 425) Legislative Directive to Judicial Council.
3 Witkin Cal. Proc. 5th Actions § 426, (S 426) Application and Forms.
3 Witkin Cal. Proc. 5th Actions § 428, (S 428) in General.
3 Witkin Cal. Proc. 5th Actions § 429A, (S 429A) (New)-In General.
3 Witkin Cal. Proc. 5th Actions § 429B, (New)-In General.

3 Witkin Cal. Proc. 5th Actions § 429E, (New)-Judicial Council Rules and Forms.
9 Witkin Cal. Proc. 5th Appeal § 556, (S 556) Payment of Fees.
9 Witkin Cal. Proc. 5th Appeal § 557, (S 557) Effect of Nonpayment.
9 Witkin Cal. Proc. 5th Appeal § 558, (S 558) Waiver of Fees in Indigent Appeal.
9 Witkin Cal. Proc. 5th Appeal § 649, (S 649) Cost and Preparation.
2 Witkin Cal. Proc. 5th Courts § 191, (S 191) Civil Rules.

Rule 3.51. Method of application

An application for initial fee waiver under rule 3.55 must be made on *Request to Waive Court Fees* (form FW–001). An application for initial fee waiver under rule 3.56 must be made on *Request to Waive Additional Court Fees (Superior Court)* (form FW–002). The clerk must provide the forms and the *Information Sheet on Waiver of Superior Court Fees and Costs* (form FW–001-INFO) without charge to any person who requests any fee waiver application or indicates that he or she is unable to pay any court fee or cost. *(Adopted, eff. Jan. 1, 2007. As amended, eff. Jan. 1, 2007; July 1, 2009.)*

Research References

Rutter, Cal. Practice Guide: Civ. Pro. Before Trial Ch. 1-A, A. Accepting a New Case.
3 Witkin Cal. Proc. 5th Actions § 426, (S 426) Application and Forms.
3 Witkin Cal. Proc. 5th Actions § 429G, (S 429G) (New)-Requirements for Specific Proceedings.

Rule 3.52. Procedure for determining application

The procedure for determining an application is as follows:

(1) The trial court must consider and determine the application as required by Government Code sections 68634 and 68635.

(2) An order determining an application for an initial fee waiver must be made on *Order on Court Fee Waiver (Superior Court)* (form FW–003), except as provided in (6) below.

(3) An order determining an application for an initial fee waiver after a hearing in the trial court must be made on *Order on Court Fee Waiver After Hearing (Superior Court)* (form FW–008).

(4) Any order granting a fee waiver must be accompanied by a blank *Notice of Improved Financial Situation or Settlement* (form FW–010).

(5) Any order denying an application without a hearing on the ground that the information on the application conclusively establishes that the applicant is not eligible for a waiver must be accompanied by a blank *Request for Hearing About Fee Waiver Order (Superior Court)* (form FW–006).

(6) Until January 1, 2013, a court with a computerized case management system may produce electronically generated court fee waiver orders as long as:

(A) The document is substantively identical to the mandatory Judicial Council form it is replacing;

(B) Any electronically generated form is identical in both language and legally mandated elements, including all notices and advisements, to the mandatory Judicial Council form it is replacing; and

(C) The order is an otherwise legally sufficient court order, as provided in rule 1.31(g), concerning orders not on Judicial Council mandatory forms.

(Formerly Rule 3.56, adopted, eff. Jan. 1, 2007. As amended, eff. Jan. 1, 2007. Renumbered Rule 3.52 and amended, eff. July 1, 2009.)

Research References

3 Witkin Cal. Proc. 5th Actions § 427, (S 427) Determination of Application.

3 Witkin Cal. Proc. 5th Actions § 428, (S 428) in General.
3 Witkin Cal. Proc. 5th Actions § 429H, (New)-Determination of Trial Court Applications.
3 Witkin Cal. Proc. 5th Actions § 429J, (New)-Fee Waiver Requests by Prisoners.

Rule 3.53. Application granted unless acted on by the court

The application for initial fee waiver is deemed granted unless the court gives notice of action on the application within five court days after it is filed. If the application is deemed granted under this provision, the clerk must prepare and serve a *Notice: Waiver of Court Fees (Superior Court)* (form FW–005) five court days after the application is filed. *(Formerly Rule 3.57, adopted, eff. Jan. 1, 2007. As amended, eff. Jan. 1, 2007. Renumbered Rule 3.53 and amended, eff. July 1, 2009.)*

Research References

3 Witkin Cal. Proc. 5th Actions § 426, (S 426) Application and Forms.
3 Witkin Cal. Proc. 5th Actions § 428, (S 428) in General.
3 Witkin Cal. Proc. 5th Actions § 429H, (New)-Determination of Trial Court Applications.

Rule 3.54. Confidentiality

(a) Confidential records

No person may have access to an application for an initial fee waiver except the court and authorized court personnel, any persons authorized by the applicant, and any persons authorized by order of the court. No person may reveal any information contained in the application except as authorized by law or order of the court.

(b) Request for access to confidential records

Any person seeking access to an application or financial information provided to the court by an applicant must make the request by noticed motion, supported by a declaration showing good cause regarding why the confidential information should be released.

(c) Order

An order granting access to an application or financial information may include limitations on who may access the information and on the use of the information after it has been released. *(Formerly Rule 3.60, adopted, eff. Jan. 1, 2007. As amended, eff. Jan. 1, 2008. Renumbered Rule 3.54 and amended, eff. July 1, 2009.)*

Research References

Rutter, Cal. Practice Guide: Civ. Pro. Before Trial Ch. 1-A, A. Accepting a New Case.
3 Witkin Cal. Proc. 5th Actions § 427, (S 427) Determination of Application.
3 Witkin Cal. Proc. 5th Actions § 429F, (S 429F) (New)-General Requirements.

Rule 3.55. Court fees and costs included in all initial fee waivers

Court fees and costs that must be waived upon granting an application for an initial fee waiver include:

(1) Clerk's fees for filing papers;

(2) Clerk's fees for reasonably necessary certification and copying;

(3) Clerk's fees for issuance of process and certificates;

(4) Clerk's fees for transmittal of papers;

(5) Court-appointed interpreter's fees for parties in small claims actions;

(6) Sheriff's and marshal's fees under article 7 of chapter 2 of part 3 of division 2 of title 3 of the Government Code (commencing with section 26720);

(7) Reporter's daily fees for attendance at hearings and trials held within 60 days of the date of the order granting the application;

(8) The court fee for a telephone appearance under Code of Civil Procedure section 367.5; and

(9) Clerk's fees for preparing, copying, certifying, and transmitting the clerk's transcript on appeal to the reviewing court and the party. A party proceeding under an initial fee waiver must specify with particularity the documents to be included in the clerk's transcript on appeal. *(Formerly Rule 3.61, adopted, eff. Jan. 1, 2007. As amended, eff. Jan. 1, 2009. Renumbered Rule 3.55 and amended, eff. July 1, 2009.)*

Research References

3 Witkin Cal. Proc. 5th Actions § 418, Trial Court Costs.
3 Witkin Cal. Proc. 5th Actions § 427, (S 427) Determination of Application.
3 Witkin Cal. Proc. 5th Actions § 429C, (New)-Costs Excused.
3 Witkin Cal. Proc. 5th Actions § 429E, (New)-Judicial Council Rules and Forms.
3 Witkin Cal. Proc. 5th Actions § 429G, (S 429G) (New)-Requirements for Specific Proceedings.

Rule 3.56. Additional court fees and costs that may be included in initial fee waiver

Necessary court fees and costs that may be waived upon granting an application for an initial fee waiver, either at the outset or upon later application, include:

(1) Jury fees and expenses;

(2) Court-appointed interpreter's fees for witnesses;

(3) Witness fees of peace officers whose attendance is reasonably necessary for prosecution or defense of the case;

(4) Reporter's fees for attendance at hearings and trials held more than 60 days after the date of the order granting the application;

(5) Witness fees of court-appointed experts; and

(6) Other fees or expenses as itemized in the application. *(Formerly Rule 3.62, adopted, eff. Jan. 1, 2007. Renumbered Rule 3.56 and amended, eff. July 1, 2009.)*

Research References

3 Witkin Cal. Proc. 5th Actions § 418, Trial Court Costs.
3 Witkin Cal. Proc. 5th Actions § 427, (S 427) Determination of Application.
3 Witkin Cal. Proc. 5th Actions § 429C, (New)-Costs Excused.
3 Witkin Cal. Proc. 5th Actions § 429E, (New)-Judicial Council Rules and Forms.
3 Witkin Cal. Proc. 5th Actions § 429G, (S 429G) (New)-Requirements for Specific Proceedings.

Rule 3.57. Amount of lien for waived fees and costs

To determine the amount of the court lien for waived fees and costs, any party to a civil action in which an initial fee waiver has been granted may ask the clerk to calculate the total amount of court fees and costs that have been waived as of the date of the request. *(Adopted, eff. July 1, 2009.)*

Research References

3 Witkin Cal. Proc. 5th Actions § 427, (S 427) Determination of Application.
3 Witkin Cal. Proc. 5th Actions § 429L, (New)-In General.

Rule 3.58. Posting notice

Each trial court must post in a conspicuous place near the filing window or counter a notice, 8½ by 11 inches or larger, advising litigants in English and Spanish that they may ask the court to waive court fees and costs. The notice must be substantially as follows:

"NOTICE: If you are unable to pay fees and costs, you may ask the court to permit you to proceed without paying them. Ask the clerk for the *Information Sheet on Waiver of Superior Court Fees and Costs* or *Information Sheet on Waiver of Court Fees and Costs for Appeal or Writ Proceedings* and the *Request to Waive Court Fees*." *(Formerly Rule 3.63, adopted, eff. Jan. 1, 2007. Renumbered Rule 3.58 and amended, eff. July 1, 2009.)*

Research References

Rutter, Cal. Practice Guide: A.D.R. Ch. 6-C, C. Referees.
Rutter, Cal. Practice Guide: Civil Trials & Evidence Ch. 2-D, D. Securing Trial by Jury.
3 Witkin Cal. Proc. 5th Actions § 427, (S 427) Determination of Application.
3 Witkin Cal. Proc. 5th Actions § 429G, (S 429G) (New)-Requirements for Specific Proceedings.
2 Witkin Cal. Proc. 5th Courts § 191, (S 191) Civil Rules.

Division 3

FILING AND SERVICE

Chapter 1

FILING

Rule
3.100. Payment of filing fees by credit or debit card.

Rule 3.100. Payment of filing fees by credit or debit card

A party may pay a filing fee by credit or debit card provided the court is authorized to accept payment by this method under Government Code section 6159, rule 10.820, and other applicable law. *(Adopted, eff. Jan. 1, 2007.)*

Research References

2 Witkin Cal. Proc. 5th Courts § 191, (S 191) Civil Rules.
2 Witkin Cal. Proc. 5th Courts § 367, (S 367) Fees.

Chapter 2

TIME FOR SERVICE

Rule
3.110. Time for service of complaint, cross-complaint, and response.

Rule 3.110. Time for service of complaint, cross-complaint, and response

(a) Application

This rule applies to the service of pleadings in civil cases except for collections cases under rule 3.740(a), unlawful detainer actions, proceedings under the Family Code, and other proceedings for which different service requirements are prescribed by law.

(b) Service of complaint

The complaint must be served on all named defendants and proofs of service on those defendants must be filed with the court within 60 days after the filing of the complaint. When the complaint is amended to add a defendant, the added defendant must be served and proof of service must be filed within 30 days after the filing of the amended complaint.

(c) Service of cross–complaint

A cross-complaint against a party who has appeared in the action must be accompanied by proof of service of the cross-complaint at the time it is filed. If the cross-complaint adds new parties, the cross-complaint must be served on all parties and proofs of service on the new parties must be filed within 30 days of the filing of the cross-complaint.

(d) Timing of responsive pleadings

The parties may stipulate without leave of court to one 15–day extension beyond the 30–day time period prescribed for the response after service of the initial complaint.

(e) Modification of timing; application for order extending time

The court, on its own motion or on the application of a party, may extend or otherwise modify the times provided in (b)–(d). An application for a court order extending the time to serve a pleading must be filed before the time for service has elapsed. The application must be accompanied by a declaration showing why service has not been completed, documenting the efforts that have been made to complete service, and specifying the date by which service is proposed to be completed.

(f) Failure to serve

If a party fails to serve and file pleadings as required under this rule, and has not obtained an order extending time to serve its pleadings, the court may issue an order to show cause why sanctions shall not be imposed.

(g) Request for entry of default

If a responsive pleading is not served within the time limits specified in this rule and no extension of time has been granted, the plaintiff must file a request for entry of default within 10 days after the time for service has elapsed. The court may issue an order to show cause why sanctions should not be imposed if the plaintiff fails to timely file the request for the entry of default.

(h) Default judgment

When a default is entered, the party who requested the entry of default must obtain a default judgment against the defaulting party within 45 days after the default was entered, unless the court has granted an extension of time. The court may issue an order to show cause why sanctions should not be imposed if that party fails to obtain entry of judgment against a defaulting party or to request an extension of time to apply for a default judgment within that time.

(i) Order to show cause

Responsive papers to an order to show cause issued under this rule must be filed and served at least 5 calendar days before the hearing. *(Formerly Rule 201.7, adopted, eff. July 1, 2002. Renumbered Rule 3.110 and amended, eff. Jan. 1, 2007. As amended, eff. July 1, 2007.)*

Research References

Rutter, Cal. Practice Guide: Civ. Pro. Before Trial Ch. 4-D, D. Service of Summons.
Rutter, Cal. Practice Guide: Civ. Pro. Before Trial Ch. 5-A, A. General.
Rutter, Cal. Practice Guide: Civ. Pro. Before Trial Ch. 5-B, B. Entry of Default.
Rutter, Cal. Practice Guide: Civ. Pro. Before Trial Ch. 6-C, C. Answer.

Rutter, Cal. Practice Guide: Civ. Pro. Before Trial Ch. 6-D, D. Cross-Complaint.
Rutter, Cal. Practice Guide: Civ. Pro. Before Trial Ch. 11-B, B. Involuntary Dismissals.
Rutter, Cal. Practice Guide: Civ. Pro. Before Trial Ch. 9(III)-D, D. Other Sanctions Statutes and Rules.
Rutter, Cal. Practice Guide: Enforcing Judgments/Debts Ch. 3-C, C. Prelawsuit Considerations.
Rutter, Cal. Practice Guide: Personal Injury Ch. 5-B, B. When to Sue-Statute of Limitations.
Rutter, Cal. Practice Guide: Personal Injury Ch. 5-E, E. Selected Pleading Issues.
6 Witkin Cal. Proc. 5th Proceedings Without Trial § 10, Statement of Grounds.

Chapter 3

PAPERS TO BE SERVED

Rule
3.220.   Case cover sheet.
3.221.   Information about alternative dispute resolution.
3.222.   Papers to be served on cross-defendants.

Rule 3.220.   Case cover sheet

(a) Cover sheet required

The first paper filed in an action or proceeding must be accompanied by a case cover sheet as required in (b). The cover sheet must be on a form prescribed by the Judicial Council and must be filed in addition to any cover sheet required by local court rule. If the plaintiff indicates on the cover sheet that the case is complex under rule 3.400 et seq., or a collections case under rule 3.740, the plaintiff must serve a copy of the cover sheet with the complaint. In all other cases, the plaintiff is not required to serve the cover sheet. The cover sheet is used for statistical purposes and may affect the assignment of a complex case.

(b) List of cover sheets

(1) *Civil Case Cover Sheet* (form CM–010) must be filed in each civil action or proceeding, except those filed in small claims court or filed under the Probate Code, Family Code, or Welfare and Institutions Code.

(2) [**Note:** Case cover sheets will be added for use in additional areas of the law as the data collection program expands.]

(c) Failure to provide cover sheet

If a party that is required to provide a cover sheet under this rule or a similar local rule fails to do so or provides a defective or incomplete cover sheet at the time the party's first paper is submitted for filing, the clerk of the court must file the paper. Failure of a party or a party's counsel to file a cover sheet as required by this rule may subject that party, its counsel, or both, to sanctions under rule 2.30. *(Formerly Rule 982.2, adopted, eff. July 1, 1996. As amended, eff. Jan. 1, 2000; Jan. 1, 2002. Renumbered Rule 201.8 and amended, eff. July 1, 2002. As amended, eff. July 1, 2003. Renumbered Rule 3.220 and amended, eff. Jan. 1, 2007. As amended, eff. Jan. 1, 2009.)*

Research References

Rutter, Cal. Practice Guide: Civ. Pro. Before Trial Ch. 3-D, D. Venue.
Rutter, Cal. Practice Guide: Civ. Pro. Before Trial Ch. 4-A, A. Requirements-In General.
Rutter, Cal. Practice Guide: Civ. Pro. Before Trial Ch. 6-B, B. Complaints.
Rutter, Cal. Practice Guide: Civ. Pro. Before Trial Ch. 9(I)-B, B. Preparing and Filing Motions.

Rutter, Cal. Practice Guide: Enforcing Judgments/Debts Ch. 3-C, C. Prelawsuit Considerations.
4 Witkin Cal. Proc. 5th Pleading § 18, Other Requirements.
4 Witkin Cal. Proc. 5th Pleading § 364, What Constitutes Complex Case.

Rule 3.221. Information about alternative dispute resolution

(a) Court to provide information package

Each court must make available to the plaintiff, at the time the complaint is filed in all general civil cases, an alternative dispute resolution (ADR) information package that includes, at a minimum, all of the following:

(1) General information about the potential advantages and disadvantages of ADR and descriptions of the principal ADR processes. The Administrative Office of the Courts has prepared model language that the courts may use to provide this information.

(2) Information about the ADR programs available in that court, including citations to any applicable local court rules and directions for contacting any court staff responsible for providing parties with assistance regarding ADR.

(3) In counties that are participating in the Dispute Resolution Programs Act (DRPA), information about the availability of local dispute resolution programs funded under the DRPA. This information may take the form of a list of the applicable programs or directions for contacting the county's DRPA coordinator.

(4) An ADR stipulation form that parties may use to stipulate to the use of an ADR process.

(b) Court may make package available on Web site

A court may make the ADR information package available on its Web site as long as paper copies are also made available in the clerk's office.

(c) Plaintiff to serve information package

In all general civil cases, the plaintiff must serve a copy of the ADR information package on each defendant together with the complaint. Cross–complainants must serve a copy of the ADR information package on any new parties to the action together with the cross-complaint. *(Formerly Rule 1590.1, adopted, eff. Jan. 1, 2001. Renumbered Rule 201.9 and amended, eff. July 1, 2002. Renumbered Rule 3.221 and amended, eff. Jan. 1, 2007.)*

Research References

Rutter, Cal. Practice Guide: A.D.R. Ch. 1-B, B. Why ADR?
Rutter, Cal. Practice Guide: A.D.R. Ch. 4-A, A. General Considerations.
Rutter, Cal. Practice Guide: Civ. Pro. Before Trial Ch. 1-B, B. Prelawsuit Investigations, Research and Analysis.
Rutter, Cal. Practice Guide: Civ. Pro. Before Trial Ch. 4-A, A. Requirements-In General.
6 Witkin Cal. Proc. 5th Proceedings Without Trial § 483, (S 483) Judicial Standards and Rules.

Rule 3.222. Papers to be served on cross-defendants

A cross-complainant must serve a copy of the complaint or, if it has been amended, the most recently amended complaint and any answers thereto on cross-defendants who have not previously appeared. *(Formerly Rule 202, adopted, eff. Jan. 1, 1985. As amended, eff. Jan. 1, 2003. Renumbered Rule 3.222 and amended, eff. Jan. 1, 2007.)*

Research References

Rutter, Cal. Practice Guide: Civ. Pro. Before Trial Ch. 6-D, D. Cross-Complaint.
5 Witkin Cal. Proc. 5th Pleading § 1172, Joinder of Cross-Defendants.

Chapter 4

MISCELLANEOUS

Rule
3.250. Limitations on the filing of papers.
3.252. Service of papers on the clerk when a party's address is unknown.
3.254. List of parties.

Rule 3.250. Limitations on the filing of papers

(a) Papers not to be filed

The following papers, whether offered separately or as attachments to other documents, may not be filed unless they are offered as relevant to the determination of an issue in a law and motion proceeding or other hearing or are ordered filed for good cause:

(1) Subpoena;

(2) Subpoena duces tecum;

(3) Deposition notice, and response;

(4) Notice to consumer or employee, and objection;

(5) Notice of intention to record testimony by audio or video tape;

(6) Notice of intention to take an oral deposition by telephone, videoconference, or other remote electronic means;

(7) Agreement to set or extend time for deposition, agreement to extend time for response to discovery requests, and notice of these agreements;

(8) Interrogatories, and responses or objections to interrogatories;

(9) Demand for production or inspection of documents, things, and places, and responses or objections to demand;

(10) Request for admissions, and responses or objections to request;

(11) Agreement for physical and mental examinations;

(12) Demand for delivery of medical reports, and response;

(13) Demand for exchange of expert witnesses;

(14) Demand for production of discoverable reports and writings of expert witnesses;

(15) List of expert witnesses whose opinion a party intends to offer in evidence at trial and declaration;

(16) Statement that a party does not presently intend to offer the testimony of any expert witness;

(17) Declaration for additional discovery;

(18) Stipulation to enlarge the scope of number of discovery requests from that specified by statute, and notice of the stipulation;

(19) Demand for bill of particulars or an accounting, and response;

(20) Request for statement of damages, and response, unless it is accompanied by a request to enter default and is the notice of special and general damages;

Ct. Rules

(21) Notice of deposit of jury fees;

(22) Notice to produce party, agent, or tangible things before a court, and response; and

(23) Offer to compromise, unless accompanied by an original proof of acceptance and a written judgment for the court's signature and entry of judgment.

(b) Retaining originals of papers not filed

Unless the paper served is a response, the party who serves a paper listed in (a) must retain the original with the original proof of service affixed. The original of a response must be served, and it must be retained by the person upon whom it is served. All original papers must be retained until six months after final disposition of the case, unless the court on motion of any party and for good cause shown orders the original papers preserved for a longer period.

(c) Papers defined

As used in this rule, papers include printed forms furnished by the clerk, but do not include notices filed and served by the clerk. *(Formerly Rule 201.5, adopted, eff. July 1, 1987. As amended, eff. Jan. 1, 2001; Jan. 1, 2003. Renumbered Rule 3.250 and amended, eff. Jan. 1, 2007.)*

Research References

Rutter, Cal. Practice Guide: Civ. Pro. Before Trial Ch. 6-B, B. Complaints.
Rutter, Cal. Practice Guide: Civ. Pro. Before Trial Ch. 8E-2, When Depositions May be Taken.
Rutter, Cal. Practice Guide: Civ. Pro. Before Trial Ch. 8E-4, Notice of Deposition.
Rutter, Cal. Practice Guide: Civ. Pro. Before Trial Ch. 8E-6, Subpoena to Nonparty Deponent or Business Records Custodian.
Rutter, Cal. Practice Guide: Civ. Pro. Before Trial Ch. 8F-3, Propounding Interrogatories.
Rutter, Cal. Practice Guide: Civ. Pro. Before Trial Ch. 8F-6, Custody of Interrogatories and Responses.
Rutter, Cal. Practice Guide: Civ. Pro. Before Trial Ch. 8J-4, Demand Procedure.
Rutter, Cal. Practice Guide: Civ. Pro. Before Trial Ch. 8K-1, Request for Statement of Damages (Personal Injury or Death Cases).
Rutter, Cal. Practice Guide: Civ. Pro. Before Trial Ch. 8K-2, Demand for Bill of Particulars.
Rutter, Cal. Practice Guide: Civ. Pro. Before Trial Ch. 12(II)-C, C. Statutory Offer to Compromise (CCP § 998).
Rutter, Cal. Practice Guide: Civil Trials & Evidence Ch. 1-C, C. Marshalling the Evidence.
Rutter, Cal. Practice Guide: Personal Injury Ch. 4-D, D. Techniques Where Settlement Not Forthcoming.
Rutter, Cal. Practice Guide: Personal Injury Ch. 5-E, E. Selected Pleading Issues.
Rutter, Cal. Practice Guide: Personal Injury Ch. 8-A, A. Case Management.
Rutter, Cal. Practice Guide: Personal Injury Ch. 8-C, C. Two Months Before Trial.
2 Witkin Cal. Proc. 5th Courts § 191, (S 191) Civil Rules.
4 Witkin Cal. Proc. 5th Pleading § 503, (S 503) Defendant's Demand.
4 Witkin Cal. Proc. 5th Pleading § 512, (S 512) Service and Filing of Statement.
6 Witkin Cal. Proc. 5th Proceedings Without Trial § 85, Formal Requirements.
6 Witkin Cal. Proc. 5th Proceedings Without Trial § 99, (S 99) Judgment on Compromise.
7 Witkin Cal. Proc. 5th Trial § 99, Advance and Subsequent Deposits.

Rule 3.252. Service of papers on the clerk when a party's address is unknown

(a) Service of papers

When service is made under Code of Civil Procedure section 1011(b) and a party's residence address is unknown, the notice or papers delivered to the clerk, or to the judge if there is no clerk, must be enclosed in an envelope addressed to the party in care of the clerk or the judge.

(b) Information on the envelope

The back of the envelope delivered under (a) must bear the following information:

"Service is being made under Code of Civil Procedure section 1011(b) on a party whose residence address is unknown."

[Name of party whose residence address is unknown]

[Case name and number] *(Formerly Rule 202.5, adopted, eff. July 1, 1997. As amended, eff. Jan. 1, 2003. Renumbered Rule 3.252, eff. Jan. 1, 2007.)*

Research References

Rutter, Cal. Practice Guide: Civ. Pro. Before Trial Ch. 9(I)-G, G. Motions Regulating Counsel.
Rutter, Cal. Practice Guide: Prof. Responsibility Ch. 10-B, B. Withdrawal (Termination) by Lawyer.
6 Witkin Cal. Proc. 5th Proceedings Without Trial § 19, on Attorney or Party.

Rule 3.254. List of parties

(a) Duties of first-named plaintiff or petitioner

If more than two parties have appeared in a case and are represented by different counsel, the plaintiff or petitioner named first in the complaint or petition must:

(1) Maintain a current list of the parties and their addresses for service of notice on each party; and

(2) Furnish a copy of the list on request to any party or the court.

(b) Duties of each party

Each party must:

(1) Furnish the first-named plaintiff or petitioner with its current address for service of notice when it first appears in the action;

(2) Furnish the first-named plaintiff or petitioner with any changes in its address for service of notice; and

(3) If it serves an order, notice, or pleading on a party who has not yet appeared in the action, serve a copy of the list required under (a) at the same time as the order, notice, or pleading is served. *(Formerly Rule 387, adopted, eff. July 1, 1984. Renumbered Rule 202.7, and amended, eff. Jan. 1, 2003. Renumbered Rule 3.254 and amended, eff. Jan. 1, 2007.)*

Research References

Rutter, Cal. Practice Guide: Civ. Pro. Before Trial Ch. 6-B, B. Complaints.
Rutter, Cal. Practice Guide: Civ. Pro. Before Trial Ch. 9(I)-B, B. Preparing and Filing Motions.
2 Witkin Cal. Proc. 5th Courts § 191, (S 191) Civil Rules.
6 Witkin Cal. Proc. 5th Proceedings Without Trial § 12, (S 12) in General.

Division 4

PARTIES AND ACTIONS

Chapter 3

RELATED CASES

Rule
3.300.   Related cases.

Rule 3.300.   Related cases

(a) Definition of "related case"

A pending civil case is related to another pending civil case, or to a civil case that was dismissed with or without prejudice, or to a civil case that was disposed of by judgment, if the cases:

(1) Involve the same parties and are based on the same or similar claims;

(2) Arise from the same or substantially identical transactions, incidents, or events requiring the determination of the same or substantially identical questions of law or fact;

(3) Involve claims against, title to, possession of, or damages to the same property; or

(4) Are likely for other reasons to require substantial duplication of judicial resources if heard by different judges.

(b) Duty to provide notice

Whenever a party in a civil action knows or learns that the action or proceeding is related to another action or proceeding pending, dismissed, or disposed of by judgment in any state or federal court in California, the party must serve and file a Notice of Related Case.

(c) Contents of the notice

The Notice of Related Case must:

(1) List all civil cases that are related by court, case name, case number, and filing date;

(2) Identify the case that has the earliest filing date and the court and department in which that case is pending; and

(3) Describe the manner in which the cases are related.

(d) Service and filing of notice

The Notice of Related Case must be filed in all pending cases listed in the notice and must be served on all parties in those cases.

(e) Time for service

The Notice of Related Case must be served and filed as soon as possible, but no later than 15 days after the facts concerning the existence of related cases become known.

(f) Continuing duty to provide notice

The duty under (b)–(e) is a continuing duty that applies when a party files a case with knowledge of a related action or proceeding, and that applies thereafter whenever a party learns of a related action or proceeding.

(g) Response

Within 5 days after service on a party of a Notice of Related Case, the party may serve and file a response supporting or opposing the notice. The response must state why one or more of the cases listed in the notice are not related or why other good cause exists for the court not to transfer the cases to or from a particular court or department. The response must be filed in all pending cases listed in the notice and must be served on all parties in those cases.

(h) Judicial action

(1) *Related cases pending in one superior court*

If all the related cases have been filed in one superior court, the court, on notice to all parties, may order that the cases, including probate and family law cases, be related and may assign them to a single judge or department. In a superior court where there is a master calendar, the presiding judge may order the cases related. In a court in which cases are assigned to a single judge or department, cases may be ordered related as follows:

(A) Where all the cases listed in the notice are unlimited civil cases, or where all the cases listed in the notice are limited civil cases, the judge who has the earliest filed case must determine whether the cases must be ordered related and assigned to his or her department;

(B) Where the cases listed in the notice include both unlimited and limited civil cases, the judge who has the earliest filed unlimited civil case must determine whether the cases should be ordered related and assigned to his or her department;

(C) Where the cases listed in the notice contain a probate or family law case, the presiding judge or a judge designated by the presiding judge must determine whether the cases should be ordered related and, if so, to which judge or department they should be assigned;

(D) In the event that any of the cases listed in the notice are not ordered related under (A), (B), or (C), any party in any of the cases listed in the notice may file a motion to have the cases related. The motion must be filed with the presiding judge or the judge designated by the presiding judge; and

(E) If the procedures for relating pending cases under this rule do not apply, the procedures under Code of Civil Procedure section 1048 and rule 3.350 must be followed to consolidate cases pending in the same superior court.

(2) *Related cases pending in different superior courts*

(A) If the related cases are pending in more than one superior court on notice to all parties, the judge to whom the earliest filed case is assigned may confer informally with the parties and with the judges to whom each related case is assigned, to determine the feasibility and desirability of joint discovery orders and other informal or formal means of coordinating proceedings in the cases.

(B) If it is determined that related cases pending in different superior courts should be formally coordinated, the procedures in Code of Civil Procedure section 403 and rule 3.500 must be followed for noncomplex cases, and the procedures in Code of Civil Procedure section 404 et seq. and rules 3.501 et seq. must be followed for complex cases.

(3) *Complex cases*

The provisions in (1) of this subdivision do not apply to cases that have been designated as complex by the parties or determined to be complex by the court.

(i) Ruling on related cases

The court, department, or judge issuing an order relating cases under this rule must either:

(1) File a notice of the order in all pending cases and serve a copy of the notice on all parties listed in the Notice of Related Case; or

(2) Direct counsel for a party to file the notice in all pending cases and serve a copy on all parties.

(j) Cases not ordered related

If for any reason a case is not ordered related under this rule, that case will remain assigned to the court, judge, or department where it was pending at the time of the filing and service of the Notice of Related Case.

(k) Exception

A party is not required to serve and file Notice of Related Case under this rule if another party has already filed a notice and served all parties under this rule on the same case. *(Formerly Rule 804, adopted, eff. Jan. 1, 1996. Renumbered Rule 3.300 and amended, eff. Jan. 1, 2007. As amended, eff. Jan. 1, 2008.)*

Research References

Rutter, Cal. Practice Guide: Civ. Pro. Before Trial Ch. 6-B, B. Complaints.
Rutter, Cal. Practice Guide: Civ. Pro. Before Trial Ch. 7(I)-A, A. Demurrers.
Rutter, Cal. Practice Guide: Civ. Pro. Before Trial Ch. 12(I)-B, B. Case Management ("Fast Track") System.
Rutter, Cal. Practice Guide: Personal Injury Ch. 9-A, A. Assignment to Trial.
1 Witkin Cal. Proc. 5th Attorneys § 105, Motion in Trial Court.
2 Witkin Cal. Proc. 5th Courts § 191, (S 191) Civil Rules.
4 Witkin Cal. Proc. 5th Pleading § 352, (S 352) in General.
4 Witkin Cal. Proc. 5th Pleading § 375, (S 375) Coordination of Related Cases.

Chapter 4

CONSOLIDATED CASES

Rule
3.350. Consolidation of cases.

Rule 3.350. Consolidation of cases

(a) Requirements of motion

(1) A notice of motion to consolidate must:

(A) List all named parties in each case, the names of those who have appeared, and the names of their respective attorneys of record;

(B) Contain the captions of all the cases sought to be consolidated, with the lowest numbered case shown first; and

(C) Be filed in each case sought to be consolidated.

(2) The motion to consolidate:

(A) Is deemed a single motion for the purpose of determining the appropriate filing fee, but memorandums, declarations, and other supporting papers must be filed only in the lowest numbered case;

(B) Must be served on all attorneys of record and all nonrepresented parties in all of the cases sought to be consolidated; and

(C) Must have a proof of service filed as part of the motion.

(b) Lead case

Unless otherwise provided in the order granting the motion to consolidate, the lowest numbered case in the consolidated case is the lead case.

(c) Order

An order granting or denying all or part of a motion to consolidate must be filed in each case sought to be consolidated. If the motion is granted for all purposes including trial, any subsequent document must be filed only in the lead case.

(d) Caption and case number

All documents filed in the consolidated case must include the caption and case number of the lead case, followed by the case numbers of all of the other consolidated cases. *(Formerly Rule 367, adopted, eff. Jan. 1, 1984. As amended, eff. July 1, 1999. Renumbered Rule 3.350 and amended, eff. Jan. 1, 2007.)*

Research References

Rutter, Cal. Practice Guide: Civ. Pro. Before Trial Ch. 12(I)-E, E. Consolidation, Coordination and Bifurcation.
4 Witkin Cal. Proc. 5th Pleading § 344, (S 344) Procedure.

Chapter 5

COMPLEX CASES

Rule
3.400. Definition.
3.401. Complex case designation.
3.402. Complex case counterdesignations.
3.403. Action by court.

Rule 3.400. Definition

(a) Definition

A "complex case" is an action that requires exceptional judicial management to avoid placing unnecessary burdens on the court or the litigants and to expedite the case, keep costs reasonable, and promote effective decision making by the court, the parties, and counsel.

(b) Factors

In deciding whether an action is a complex case under (a), the court must consider, among other things, whether the action is likely to involve:

(1) Numerous pretrial motions raising difficult or novel legal issues that will be time-consuming to resolve;

(2) Management of a large number of witnesses or a substantial amount of documentary evidence;

(3) Management of a large number of separately represented parties;

(4) Coordination with related actions pending in one or more courts in other counties, states, or countries, or in a federal court; or

(5) Substantial postjudgment judicial supervision.

(c) Provisional designation

Except as provided in (d), an action is provisionally a complex case if it involves one or more of the following types of claims:

(1) Antitrust or trade regulation claims;

(2) Construction defect claims involving many parties or structures;

(3) Securities claims or investment losses involving many parties;

(4) Environmental or toxic tort claims involving many parties;

(5) Claims involving mass torts;

(6) Claims involving class actions; or

(7) Insurance coverage claims arising out of any of the claims listed in (c)(1) through (c)(6).

(d) Court's discretion

Notwithstanding (c), an action is not provisionally complex if the court has significant experience in resolving like claims involving similar facts and the management of those claims has become routine. A court may declare by local rule that certain types of cases are or are not provisionally complex under this subdivision. *(Formerly Rule 1800, adopted, eff. Jan. 1, 2000. Renumbered Rule 3.400 and amended, eff. Jan. 1, 2007.)*

Research References

Rutter, Cal. Practice Guide: Civ. Pro. Before Trial Ch. 4-A, A. Requirements-In General.

Rutter, Cal. Practice Guide: Civ. Pro. Before Trial Ch. 6-B, B. Complaints.

Rutter, Cal. Practice Guide: Civ. Pro. Before Trial Ch. 14-C, C. Procedural Issues.

Rutter, Cal. Practice Guide: Civ. Pro. Before Trial Ch. 9(I)-A, A. Introduction.

Rutter, Cal. Practice Guide: Civ. Pro. Before Trial Ch. 12(I)-B, B. Case Management ("Fast Track") System.

Rutter, Cal. Practice Guide: Civil Trials & Evidence Ch. 4-H, H. Motions to Consolidate or Coordinate Separate Cases.

Rutter, Cal. Practice Guide: Enforcing Judgments/Debts Ch. 3-C, C. Prelawsuit Considerations.

Rutter, Cal. Practice Guide: Personal Injury Ch. 8-A, A. Case Management.

2 Witkin Cal. Proc. 5th Courts § 239, in General.

4 Witkin Cal. Proc. 5th Pleading § 18, Other Requirements.

4 Witkin Cal. Proc. 5th Pleading § 357, in General.

4 Witkin Cal. Proc. 5th Pleading § 359, (S 359) Motion in Court.

4 Witkin Cal. Proc. 5th Pleading § 364, What Constitutes Complex Case.

4 Witkin Cal. Proc. 5th Pleading § 366, (S 366) Transfer of Noncomplex Actions.

7 Witkin Cal. Proc. 5th Trial § 6, Complex Litigation.

7 Witkin Cal. Proc. 5th Trial § 46, Complex Cases.

Rule 3.401. Complex case designation

A plaintiff may designate an action as a complex case by filing and serving with the initial complaint the *Civil Case Cover Sheet* (form CM–010) marked to indicate that the action is a complex case. *(Formerly Rule 1810, adopted, eff. Jan. 1, 2000. As amended, eff. July 1, 2002; July 1, 2004. Renumbered Rule 3.401, eff. Jan. 1, 2007.)*

Research References

Rutter, Cal. Practice Guide: Civ. Pro. Before Trial Ch. 12(I)-B, B. Case Management ("Fast Track") System.

2 Witkin Cal. Proc. 5th Courts § 239, in General.

4 Witkin Cal. Proc. 5th Pleading § 364, What Constitutes Complex Case.

Rule 3.402. Complex case counterdesignations

(a) Noncomplex counterdesignation

If a *Civil Case Cover Sheet* (form CM–010) designating an action as a complex case has been filed and served and the court has not previously declared the action to be a complex case, a defendant may file and serve no later than its first appearance a counter *Civil Case Cover Sheet* (form CM–010) designating the action as not a complex case. The court must decide, with or without a hearing, whether the action is a complex case within 30 days after the filing of the counterdesignation.

(b) Complex counterdesignation

A defendant may file and serve no later than its first appearance a counter *Civil Case Cover Sheet* (form CM–010) designating the action as a complex case. The court must decide, with or without a hearing, whether the action is a complex case within 30 days after the filing of the counterdesignation.

(c) Joint complex designation

A defendant may join the plaintiff in designating an action as a complex case. *(Formerly Rule 1811, adopted, eff. Jan. 1, 2000. As amended, eff. July 1, 2004. Renumbered Rule 3.402 and amended, eff. Jan. 1, 2007.)*

Research References

Rutter, Cal. Practice Guide: Civ. Pro. Before Trial Ch. 12(I)-B, B. Case Management ("Fast Track") System.

2 Witkin Cal. Proc. 5th Courts § 239, in General.

4 Witkin Cal. Proc. 5th Pleading § 364, What Constitutes Complex Case.

Rule 3.403. Action by court

(a) Decision on complex designation

Except as provided in rule 3.402, if a *Civil Case Cover Sheet* (form CM–010) that has been filed and served designates an action as a complex case or checks a case type described as provisionally complex civil litigation, the court must decide as soon as reasonably practicable, with or without a hearing, whether the action is a complex case.

(b) Court's continuing power

With or without a hearing, the court may decide on its own motion, or on a noticed motion by any party, that a civil action is a complex case or that an action previously declared to be a complex case is not a complex case. *(Formerly Rule 1812, adopted, eff. Jan. 1, 2000. As amended, eff. July 1, 2004. Renumbered Rule 3.403 and amended, eff. Jan. 1, 2007.)*

Research References

Rutter, Cal. Practice Guide: Civ. Pro. Before Trial Ch. 12(I)-B, B. Case Management ("Fast Track") System.

2 Witkin Cal. Proc. 5th Courts § 239, in General.

4 Witkin Cal. Proc. 5th Pleading § 21, (S 21) Nature of Filing Process.

4 Witkin Cal. Proc. 5th Pleading § 364, What Constitutes Complex Case.

Chapter 6

COORDINATION OF NONCOMPLEX ACTIONS

Rule

3.500. Transfer and consolidation of noncomplex common-issue actions filed in different courts.

Rule 3.500. Transfer and consolidation of noncomplex common-issue actions filed in different courts

(a) Application

This rule applies when a motion under Code of Civil Procedure section 403 is filed requesting transfer and consolidation of noncomplex cases involving a common issue of fact or law filed in different courts.

(b) Preliminary step

A party that intends to file a motion under Code of Civil Procedure section 403 must first make a good-faith effort to obtain agreement of all parties to each case to the proposed transfer and consolidation.

(c) Motion and hearing

A motion to transfer an action under Code of Civil Procedure section 403 must conform to the requirements generally applicable to motions, and must be supported by a declaration stating facts showing that:

(1) The actions are not complex;

(2) The moving party has made a good-faith effort to obtain agreement to the transfer and consolidation from all parties to the actions; and

(3) The moving party has notified all parties of their obligation to disclose to the court any information they may have concerning any other motions requesting transfer of any case

that would be affected by the granting of the motion before the court.

(d) Findings and order

If the court orders that the case or cases be transferred from another court, the order must specify the reasons supporting a finding that the transfer will promote the ends of justice, with reference to the following standards:

(1) The actions are not complex;

(2) Whether the common question of fact or law is predominating and significant to the litigation;

(3) The convenience of the parties, witnesses, and counsel;

(4) The relative development of the actions and the work product of counsel;

(5) The efficient utilization of judicial facilities and staff resources;

(6) The calendar of the courts;

(7) The disadvantages of duplicative and inconsistent rulings, orders, or judgments; and

(8) The likelihood of settlement of the actions without further litigation should coordination be denied.

(e) Moving party to provide copies of order

If the court orders that the case or cases be transferred from another court, the moving party must promptly serve the order on all parties to each case and send it to the Judicial Council and to the presiding judge of the court from which each case is to be transferred.

(f) Moving party to take necessary action to complete transfer and consolidation

If the court orders a case or cases transferred, the moving party must promptly take all appropriate action necessary to assure that the transfer takes place and that proceedings are initiated in the other court or courts to complete consolidation with the case pending in that court.

(g) Conflicting orders

The coordination staff in the Administrative Office of the Courts must review all transfer orders submitted under (e) and must promptly confer with the presiding judges of any courts that have issued conflicting orders under Code of Civil Procedure section 403. The presiding judges of those courts must confer with each other and with the judges who have issued the orders to the extent necessary to resolve the conflict. If it is determined that any party to a case has failed to disclose information concerning pending motions, the court may, after a duly noticed hearing, find that the party's failure to disclose is an unlawful interference with the processes of the court.

(h) Alternative disposition of motion

If after considering the motion the judge determines that the action or actions pending in another court should not be transferred to the judge's court but instead all the actions that are subject to the motion to transfer should be transferred and consolidated in another court, the judge may order the parties to prepare, serve, and file a motion to have the actions transferred to the appropriate court. *(Formerly Rule 1500, adopted, eff. Sept. 21, 1996. Renumbered Rule 3.500 and amended, eff. Jan. 1, 2007.)*

Research References

Rutter, Cal. Practice Guide: Civ. Pro. Before Trial Ch. 12(I)-E, E. Consolidation, Coordination and Bifurcation.

Rutter, Cal. Practice Guide: Civil Trials & Evidence Ch. 4-H, H. Motions to Consolidate or Coordinate Separate Cases.

4 Witkin Cal. Proc. 5th Pleading § 352, (S 352) in General.

4 Witkin Cal. Proc. 5th Pleading § 366, (S 366) Transfer of Noncomplex Actions.

4 Witkin Cal. Proc. 5th Pleading § 375, (S 375) Coordination of Related Cases.

Chapter 7

COORDINATION OF COMPLEX ACTIONS

Article 1

GENERAL PROVISIONS

Rule
3.501.   Definitions.
3.502.   Complex case—determination.
3.503.   Requests for extensions of time or to shorten time.
3.504.   General law applicable.
3.505.   Appellate review.
3.506.   Liaison counsel.

Rule 3.501. Definitions

As used in this chapter, unless the context or subject matter otherwise requires:

(1) "Action" means any civil action or proceeding that is subject to coordination or that affects an action subject to coordination.

(2) "Add–on case" means an action that is proposed for coordination, under Code of Civil Procedure section 404.4, with actions previously ordered coordinated.

(3) "Assigned judge" means any judge assigned by the Chair of the Judicial Council or by a presiding judge authorized by the Chair of the Judicial Council to assign a judge under Code of Civil Procedure section 404 or 404.3, including a "coordination motion judge" and a "coordination trial judge."

(4) "Clerk," unless otherwise indicated, means any person designated by an assigned judge to perform any clerical duties required by the rules in this chapter.

(5) "Coordinated action" means any action that has been ordered coordinated with one or more other actions under chapter 3 (commencing with section 404) of title 4 of part 2 of the Code of Civil Procedure and the rules in this chapter.

(6) "Coordination attorney" means an attorney in the Administrative Office of the Courts appointed by the Chair of the Judicial Council to perform such administrative functions as may be appropriate under the rules in this chapter, including but not limited to the functions described in rules 3.524 and 3.550.

(7) "Coordination motion judge" means an assigned judge designated under Code of Civil Procedure section 404 to determine whether coordination is appropriate.

(8) "Coordination proceeding" means any procedure authorized by chapter 3 (commencing with section 404) of title 4 of part 2 of the Code of Civil Procedure and by the rules in this chapter.

(9) "Coordination trial judge" means an assigned judge designated under Code of Civil Procedure section 404.3 to hear and determine coordinated actions.

(10) "Expenses" means all necessary costs that are reimbursable under Code of Civil Procedure section 404.8, including the compensation of the assigned judge and other necessary judicial officers and employees, the costs of any necessary travel and subsistence determined under rules of the State Board of Control, and all necessarily incurred costs of facilities, supplies, materials, and telephone and mailing expenses.

(11) "Included action" means any action or proceeding included in a petition for coordination.

(12) "Liaison counsel" means an attorney of record for a party to an included action or a coordinated action who has been appointed by an assigned judge to serve as representative of all parties on a side with the following powers and duties, as appropriate:

(A) To receive on behalf of and promptly distribute to the parties for whom he or she acts all notices and other documents from the court;

(B) To act as spokesperson for the side that he or she represents at all proceedings set on notice before trial, subject to the right of each party to present individual or divergent positions; and

(C) To call meetings of counsel for the purpose of proposing joint action.

(13) "Party" includes all parties to all included actions or coordinated actions, and the word "party," "petitioner," or any other designation of a party includes that party's attorney of record. When a notice or other paper is required to be given or served on a party, the notice or paper must be given to or served on the party's attorney of record, if any.

(14) "Petition for coordination" means any petition, motion, application, or request for coordination of actions submitted to the Chair of the Judicial Council or to a coordination trial judge under rule 3.544.

(15) "Remand" means to return a coordinated action or a severable claim or issue in a coordinated action from a coordination proceeding to the court in which the action was pending at the time the coordination of that action was ordered. If a remanded action or claim had been transferred by the coordination trial judge under rule 3.543 from the court in which the remanded action or claim was pending, the remand must include the retransfer of that action or claim to that court.

(16) "Serve and file" means that a paper filed in a court must be accompanied by proof of prior service of a copy of the paper on each party required to be served under the rules in this chapter.

(17) "Serve and submit" means that a paper to be submitted to an assigned judge under the rules in this chapter must be submitted to that judge at a designated court address. Every paper so submitted must be accompanied by proof of prior service on each party required to be served under the rules in this chapter. If there is no assigned judge or if the paper is of a type included in rule 3.511(a), the paper must be submitted to the Chair of the Judicial Council.

(18) "Side" means all parties to an included or a coordinated action who have a common or substantially similar interest in the issues, as determined by the assigned judge for the purpose of appointing liaison counsel or of allotting peremptory challenges in jury selection, or for any other appropriate purpose. Except as defined in rule 3.515, a side may include less than all plaintiffs or all defendants.

(19) "Transfer" means to remove a coordinated action or severable claim in that action from the court in which it is pending to any other court under rule 3.543, without removing the action or claim from the coordination proceeding. "Transfer" includes "retransfer." *(Formerly Rule 1501, adopted, eff. Jan. 1, 1974. As amended, eff. July 1, 1974; Jan. 1, 2005. Renumbered Rule 3.501 and amended, eff. Jan. 1, 2007.)*

Research References

Rutter, Cal. Practice Guide: Civ. Pro. Before Trial Ch. 12(I)-B, B. Case Management ("Fast Track") System.

Rutter, Cal. Practice Guide: Civ. Pro. Before Trial Ch. 12(I)-E, E. Consolidation, Coordination and Bifurcation.

Rutter, Cal. Practice Guide: Civil Trials & Evidence Ch. 3-B, B. Peremptory Challenge of Judge (CCP § 170.6).

Rutter, Cal. Practice Guide: Personal Injury Ch. 5-E, E. Selected Pleading Issues.

Rutter, Cal. Practice Guide: Personal Injury Ch. 9-A, A. Assignment to Trial.

2 Witkin Cal. Proc. 5th Courts § 191, (S 191) Civil Rules.

4 Witkin Cal. Proc. 5th Pleading § 352, (S 352) in General.

4 Witkin Cal. Proc. 5th Pleading § 354, (S 354) Applicable Procedure.

4 Witkin Cal. Proc. 5th Pleading § 356, (S 356) Service, Filing, and Submission of Papers.

4 Witkin Cal. Proc. 5th Pleading § 361, Assignment of Coordination Motion Judge.

4 Witkin Cal. Proc. 5th Pleading § 365, Determination and Order.

4 Witkin Cal. Proc. 5th Pleading § 369, Liaison Counsel.

4 Witkin Cal. Proc. 5th Pleading § 370, Remand of Action or Claim.

4 Witkin Cal. Proc. 5th Pleading § 371, Transfer of Action or Claim.

4 Witkin Cal. Proc. 5th Pleading § 372, Add-On Cases.

4 Witkin Cal. Proc. 5th Pleading § 375, (S 375) Coordination of Related Cases.

Rule 3.502. Complex case—determination

The court must consider rule 3.400 et seq. in determining whether a case is or is not a complex case within the meaning of Code of Civil Procedure sections 403 and 404. *(Formerly Rule 1501.1, adopted, eff. Sept. 21, 1996. As amended, eff. Jan. 1, 2000. Renumbered Rule 1502 and amended, eff. Jan. 1, 2005. Renumbered Rule 3.502 and amended, eff. Jan. 1, 2007.)*

Research References

4 Witkin Cal. Proc. 5th Pleading § 364, What Constitutes Complex Case.

4 Witkin Cal. Proc. 5th Pleading § 366, (S 366) Transfer of Noncomplex Actions.

Rule 3.503. Requests for extensions of time or to shorten time

(a) Assigned judge may grant request

The assigned judge, on terms that are just, may shorten or extend the time within which any act is permitted or required to be done by a party. Unless otherwise ordered, any motion or application for an extension of time to perform an act required by these rules must be served and submitted in accordance with rule 3.501(17).

(b) Stipulation requires consent of assigned judge

A stipulation for an extension of time for the filing and service of documents required by the rules in this chapter requires approval of the assigned judge.

(c) Extension does not extend time for bringing action to trial

Nothing in this rule extends the time within which a party must bring an action to trial under Code of Civil Procedure section 583.310. *(Formerly Rule 1503, adopted, eff. Jan. 1, 1974. As amended, eff. Jan. 1, 2005. Renumbered Rule 3.503 and amended, eff. Jan. 1, 2007.)*

Research References

4 Witkin Cal. Proc. 5th Pleading § 354, (S 354) Applicable Procedure.

6 Witkin Cal. Proc. 5th Proceedings Without Trial § 362, (S 362) Coordinated Actions.

Rule 3.504. General law applicable

(a) General law applicable

Except as otherwise provided in the rules in this chapter, all provisions of law applicable to civil actions generally apply to an action included in a coordination proceeding.

(b) Rules prevail over conflicting general provisions of law

To the extent that the rules in this chapter conflict with provisions of law applicable to civil actions generally, the rules in this chapter prevail, as provided by Code of Civil Procedure section 404.7.

(c) Manner of proceeding may be prescribed by assigned judge

If the manner of proceeding is not prescribed by chapter 3 (commencing with section 404) of title 4 of part 2 of the Code of Civil Procedure or by the rules in this chapter, or if the prescribed manner of proceeding cannot, with reasonable diligence, be followed in a particular coordination proceeding, the assigned judge may prescribe any suitable manner of proceeding that appears most consistent with those statutes and rules.

(d) Specification of applicable local rules

At the beginning of a coordination proceeding, the assigned judge must specify, subject to rule 3.20, any local court rules to be followed in that proceeding, and thereafter all parties must comply with those rules. Except as otherwise provided in the rules in this chapter or as directed by the assigned judge, the local rules of the court designated in the order appointing the assigned judge apply in all respects if they would otherwise apply without reference to the rules in this chapter. *(Formerly Rule 1504, adopted, eff. Jan. 1, 1974. As amended, eff. Jan. 1, 2005. Renumbered Rule 3.504 and amended, eff. Jan. 1, 2007.)*

Research References

Rutter, Cal. Practice Guide: Civ. Pro. Before Trial Ch. 12(I)-E, E. Consolidation, Coordination and Bifurcation.
Rutter, Cal. Practice Guide: Civil Trials & Evidence Ch. 4-H, H. Motions to Consolidate or Coordinate Separate Cases.
4 Witkin Cal. Proc. 5th Pleading § 354, (S 354) Applicable Procedure.
6 Witkin Cal. Proc. 5th Proceedings Without Trial § 362, (S 362) Coordinated Actions.

Rule 3.505. Appellate review

(a) Coordination order to specify reviewing court

If the actions to be coordinated are within the jurisdiction of more than one reviewing court, the coordination motion judge must select and the order granting a petition for coordination must specify, in accordance with Code of Civil Procedure section 404.2, the court having appellate jurisdiction of the coordinated actions.

(b) Court for review of order granting or denying coordination

A petition for a writ relating to an order granting or denying coordination may be filed, subject to the provisions of rule 10.1000, in any reviewing court having jurisdiction under the rules applicable to civil actions generally. *(Formerly Rule 1505, adopted, eff. Jan. 1, 1974. As amended, eff. Jan. 1, 2005. Renumbered Rule 3.505 and amended, eff. Jan. 1, 2007.)*

Research References

Rutter, Cal. Practice Guide: Civil Appeals & Writs Ch. 15-C, C. Statutory Writs.
California Practice Guide: Employment Litigation Ch. 19-T, T. Appeals.
4 Witkin Cal. Proc. 5th Pleading § 374, (S 374) Review.

Rule 3.506. Liaison counsel

(a) Selection and appointment

An assigned judge may at any time request that the parties on each side of the included or coordinated actions select one or more of the attorneys of record on that side for appointment as liaison counsel, and may appoint liaison counsel if the parties are unable to agree.

(b) Duration of appointment by coordination motion judge

Unless otherwise stipulated to or directed by an assigned judge, the appointment of a liaison counsel by a coordination motion judge terminates on the final determination of the issue whether coordination is appropriate. For good cause shown, the coordination motion judge, on the court's own motion or on the motion of any party, may remove previously appointed counsel as liaison counsel.

(c) Service on party that has requested special notice

Except as otherwise directed by the assigned judge, any party that has made a written request for special notice must be served with a copy of any document thereafter served on the party's liaison counsel. *(Formerly Rule 1506, adopted, eff. Jan. 1, 1974. As amended, eff. Jan. 1, 2005. Renumbered Rule 3.506 and amended, eff. Jan. 1, 2007.)*

Research References

2 Witkin Cal. Proc. 5th Courts § 191, (S 191) Civil Rules.
4 Witkin Cal. Proc. 5th Pleading § 356, (S 356) Service, Filing, and Submission of Papers.
4 Witkin Cal. Proc. 5th Pleading § 368, Case Management Conference.
4 Witkin Cal. Proc. 5th Pleading § 369, Liaison Counsel.

Article 2

PROCEDURAL RULES APPLICABLE TO ALL COMPLEX COORDINATION PROCEEDINGS

Rule
3.510. Service of papers.
3.511. Papers to be submitted to the Chair of the Judicial Council.
3.512. Electronic submission of documents to the Chair of the Judicial Council.
3.513. Service of memorandums and declarations.
3.514. Evidence presented at court hearings.
3.515. Motions and orders for a stay.
3.516. Motions under Code of Civil Procedure section 170.6.

Rule 3.510. Service of papers

(a) Proof of service

Except as otherwise provided in the rules in this chapter, all papers filed or submitted must be accompanied by proof of prior service on all other parties to the coordination proceeding, including all parties appearing in all included actions and coordinated actions. Service and proof of such service must be made as provided for in civil actions generally.

(b) Service on liaison counsel

Except as provided in rule 3.506(c), any party for whom liaison counsel has been designated may be served by serving the liaison counsel.

(c) Effect of failure to serve

Failure to serve any defendant with a copy of the summons and of the complaint, or failure to serve any party with any other paper or order as required by the rules in this chapter, will not preclude the coordination of the actions, but the unserved defendant or party may assert the failure to serve as a basis for appropriate relief. *(Formerly Rule 1510, adopted, eff. Jan. 1, 1974. As amended, eff. Jan. 1, 2005. Renumbered Rule 3.510 and amended, eff. Jan. 1, 2007.)*

Research References

Rutter, Cal. Practice Guide: Civ. Pro. Before Trial Ch. 11-B, B. Involuntary Dismissals.
2 Witkin Cal. Proc. 5th Courts § 191, (S 191) Civil Rules.

4 Witkin Cal. Proc. 5th Pleading § 356, (S 356) Service, Filing, and Submission of Papers.
4 Witkin Cal. Proc. 5th Pleading § 369, Liaison Counsel.
4 Witkin Cal. Proc. 5th Pleading § 372, Add-On Cases.

Rule 3.511. Papers to be submitted to the Chair of the Judicial Council

(a) Types of papers

A copy of the following papers must be submitted to the Chair of the Judicial Council at the Judicial Council's San Francisco office:

(1) Petition for coordination, including a petition for coordination of add-on cases;

(2) Notice of submission of petition for coordination, along with the caption page of the original action;

(3) Order assigning coordination motion judge, if made by a presiding judge;

(4) Order assigning coordination trial judge, if made by a presiding judge;

(5) Notice of opposition;

(6) Response in opposition to or in support of a petition for coordination;

(7) Motion for a stay order;

(8) Notice of hearing on petition;

(9) Order granting or denying coordination, including coordination of add-on cases;

(10) Order of remand;

(11) Order of transfer;

(12) Order terminating a coordination proceeding in whole or in part;

(13) Order dismissing an included or coordinated action;

(14) Notice of appeal; and

(15) Notice of disposition of appeal.

(b) Obligation of party

The papers listed in (a) are to be submitted by the party that filed or submitted and served the papers or that was directed to give notice of entry of the order. Notice of submission must be filed with the court as part of the proof of service. *(Formerly Rule 1511, adopted, eff. Jan. 1, 1974. As amended, eff. Jan. 1, 2005. Renumbered Rule 3.511 and amended, eff. Jan. 1, 2007.)*

Research References

4 Witkin Cal. Proc. 5th Pleading § 356, (S 356) Service, Filing, and Submission of Papers.

Rule 3.512. Electronic submission of documents to the Chair of the Judicial Council

(a) Documents that may be submitted electronically

Any paper listed in rule 3.511(a) may be submitted electronically to coordination@jud.ca.gov.

(b) Responsibilities of party submitting documents electronically

A party submitting a document electronically must:

(1) Take all reasonable steps to ensure that the submission does not contain computer code, including viruses, that might be harmful to the Judicial Council's electronic system and to other users of that system; and

(2) Furnish one or more electronic notification addresses and immediately provide any change to his or her electronic notification addresses.

(c) Format of documents to be submitted electronically

A document that is submitted electronically must meet the following requirements:

(1) The software for creating and reading the document must be in the public domain or generally available at a reasonable cost; and

(2) The printing of documents must not result in the loss of document text, format, or appearance.

(d) Signature on documents under penalty of perjury

(1) When a document to be submitted electronically requires a signature under penalty of perjury, the document is deemed signed by the declarant if, before submission, the declarant has signed a printed form of the document.

(2) By electronically submitting the document, the party submitting it indicates that he or she has complied with subdivision (d)(1) of this rule and that the original, signed document is available for review and copying at the request of the court or any party.

(3) At any time after the document is submitted, any other party may serve a demand for production of the original signed document. The demand must be served on all other parties but need not be filed with the court.

(4) Within five days of service of the demand, the party on whom the demand is made must make the original signed document available for review and copying by all other parties.

(e) Signature on documents not under penalty of perjury

If a document does not require a signature under penalty of perjury, the document is deemed signed by the party if the document is submitted electronically.

(f) Digital signature

A party is not required to use a digital signature on an electronically submitted document. *(Formerly Rule 1511.5, adopted, eff. July 1, 2005. Renumbered Rule 3.512 and amended, eff. Jan. 1, 2007. As amended, eff. Jan. 1, 2008.)*

Research References

4 Witkin Cal. Proc. 5th Pleading § 356, (S 356) Service, Filing, and Submission of Papers.

Rule 3.513. Service of memorandums and declarations

Unless otherwise provided in the rules in this chapter or directed by the assigned judge, all memorandums and declarations in support of or opposition to any petition, motion, or application must be served and submitted at least nine court days before any hearing on the matter at issue. *(Formerly Rule 1512, adopted, eff. Jan. 1, 1974. As amended, eff. Jan. 1, 2005. Renumbered Rule 3.513 and amended, eff. Jan. 1, 2007.)*

Research References

4 Witkin Cal. Proc. 5th Pleading § 356, (S 356) Service, Filing, and Submission of Papers.

Rule 3.514. Evidence presented at court hearings

All factual matters to be heard on any petition for coordination, or on any other petition, motion, or application under the rules in this chapter, must be initially presented and heard on declarations, answers to interrogatories or requests for admissions, depositions, or matters judicially noticed. Oral testimony will not be permitted at a hearing except as the assigned judge may permit to resolve factual issues shown by the declarations, responses to discovery, or matters judicially noticed to be in dispute. Only parties that have submitted a petition or motion, or a written response or opposition to a petition or motion, will be permitted to appear at the hearing, except the assigned judge may permit other parties to appear, on a showing of good cause.

(Formerly Rule 1513, adopted, eff. Jan. 1, 1974. As amended, eff. Jan. 1, 2005. Renumbered Rule 3.514, eff. Jan. 1, 2007.)

Research References

4 Witkin Cal. Proc. 5th Pleading § 354, (S 354) Applicable Procedure.
4 Witkin Cal. Proc. 5th Pleading § 363, Hearing.

Rule 3.515. Motions and orders for a stay

(a) Motion for stay

Any party may file a motion for an order under Code of Civil Procedure section 404.5 staying the proceedings in any action being considered for, or affecting an action being considered for, coordination, or the court may stay the proceedings on its own motion. The motion for a stay may be included with a petition for coordination or may be served and submitted to the Chair of the Judicial Council and the coordination motion judge by any party at any time prior to the determination of the petition.

(b) Contents of motion

A motion for a stay order must:

(1) List all known pending related cases;

(2) State whether the stay order should extend to any such related case; and

(3) Be supported by a memorandum and by declarations establishing the facts relied on to show that a stay order is necessary and appropriate to effectuate the purposes of coordination.

(c) Service requirements for certain motions for stay orders

If the action to be stayed is not included in the petition for coordination or any response to that petition, the motion for a stay order and all supporting documents must be served on each party to the action to be stayed and any such party may serve and submit opposition to the motion for a stay order.

(d) Opposition to motion for stay order

Any memorandums and declarations in opposition to a motion for a stay order must be served and submitted within 10 days after service of the motion.

(e) Hearing on motion for stay order

A stay order may be issued with or without a hearing. A party filing a motion for a stay order or opposition thereto may request a hearing to determine whether the stay order should be granted. A request for hearing should be made at the time the requesting party files the motion or opposition. If the coordination motion judge grants the request for a hearing, the requesting party must provide notice.

(f) Determination of motion for stay order

In ruling on a motion for a stay order, the assigned judge must determine whether the stay will promote the ends of justice, considering the imminence of any trial or other proceeding that might materially affect the status of the action to be stayed, and whether a final judgment in that action would have a res judicata or collateral estoppel effect with regard to any common issue of the included actions.

(g) Issuance of stay order and termination of stay

If a stay order is issued, the party that requested the stay must serve and file a copy of the order in each included action that is stayed. Thirty or more days following issuance of the stay order, any party that is subject to the stay order may move to terminate the stay.

(h) Effect of stay order

Unless otherwise specified in the order, a stay order suspends all proceedings in the action to which it applies. A stay order may be limited by its terms to specified proceedings, orders, motions, or other phases of the action to which the order applies.

(i) Effect of absence of stay order

In the absence of a stay order, a court receiving an order assigning a coordination motion judge may continue to exercise jurisdiction over the included action for purposes of all pretrial and discovery proceedings, but no trial may be commenced and no judgment may be entered in that action unless trial of the action had commenced before the assignment of the coordination motion judge.

(j) Effect of stay order on dismissal for lack of prosecution

The time during which any stay of proceedings is in effect under the rules in this chapter must not be included in determining whether the action stayed should be dismissed for lack of prosecution under chapter 1.5 (§ 583.110 et seq.) of title 8 of part 2 of the Code of Civil Procedure. *(Formerly Rule 1514, adopted, eff. Jan. 1, 1974. As amended, eff. July 1, 1974; Jan. 1, 1986; Jan. 1, 2005. Renumbered Rule 3.515, eff. Jan. 1, 2007.)*

Research References

Rutter, Cal. Practice Guide: Civ. Pro. Before Trial Ch. 11-B, B. Involuntary Dismissals.
4 Witkin Cal. Proc. 5th Pleading § 357, in General.
4 Witkin Cal. Proc. 5th Pleading § 362, Stay Pending Determination.
4 Witkin Cal. Proc. 5th Pleading § 372, Add-On Cases.
6 Witkin Cal. Proc. 5th Proceedings Without Trial § 362, (S 362) Coordinated Actions.

Rule 3.516. Motions under Code of Civil Procedure section 170.6

A party making a peremptory challenge by motion or affidavit of prejudice regarding an assigned judge must submit it in writing to the assigned judge within 20 days after service of the order assigning the judge to the coordination proceeding. All plaintiffs or similar parties in the included or coordinated actions constitute a side and all defendants or similar parties in such actions constitute a side for purposes of applying Code of Civil Procedure section 170.6. *(Formerly Rule 1515, adopted, eff. Jan. 1, 1974. As amended, eff. June 19, 1982; Jan. 1, 2005. Renumbered Rule 3.516, eff. Jan. 1, 2007.)*

Research References

Rutter, Cal. Practice Guide: Civil Appeals & Writs Ch. 14-C, C. Trial Court Proceedings After Reversal.
Rutter, Cal. Practice Guide: Civ. Pro. Before Trial Ch. 9(I)-D, D. Hearing.
Rutter, Cal. Practice Guide: Civ. Pro. Before Trial Ch. 12(I)-E, E. Consolidation, Coordination and Bifurcation.
Rutter, Cal. Practice Guide: Civil Trials & Evidence Ch. 3-B, B. Peremptory Challenge of Judge (CCP § 170.6).
Rutter, Cal. Practice Guide: Personal Injury Ch. 9-A, A. Assignment to Trial.
2 Witkin Cal. Proc. 5th Courts § 140, (S 140) General Rule and Limitations.
2 Witkin Cal. Proc. 5th Courts § 150, (S 150) Coordination Judge.
2 Witkin Cal. Proc. 5th Courts § 191, (S 191) Civil Rules.
4 Witkin Cal. Proc. 5th Pleading § 355, (S 355) Peremptory Challenge of Assigned Judge.

Article 3

PETITIONS AND PROCEEDINGS FOR COORDINATION OF COMPLEX ACTIONS

Rule
3.520. Motions filed in the trial court.
3.521. Petition for coordination.

Rule

Rule 3.520. Motions filed in the trial court

(a) General requirements

A motion filed in the trial court under this rule must specify the matters required by rule 3.521(a) and must be made in the manner provided by law for motions in civil actions generally.

(b) Permission to submit a petition for coordination

(1) *Request for permission to submit coordination petition*

If a direct petition is not authorized by Code of Civil Procedure section 404, a party may request permission from the presiding judge of the court in which one of the included actions is pending to submit a petition for coordination to the Chair of the Judicial Council. The request must be made by noticed motion accompanied by a proposed order. The proposed order must state that the moving party has permission to submit a petition for coordination to the Chair of the Judicial Council under rules 3.521–3.523.

(2) *Order to be prepared*

If permission to submit a petition is granted, the moving party must serve and file the signed order and submit it to the Chair of the Judicial Council.

(3) *Stay permitted pending preparation of petition*

To provide sufficient time for a party to submit a petition, the presiding judge may stay all related actions pending in that court for a reasonable time not to exceed 30 calendar days. *(Formerly Rule 1520, adopted, eff. Jan. 1, 1974. As amended, eff. Jan. 1, 1983; Jan. 1, 2005; July 1, 2006. Renumbered Rule 3.520 and amended, eff. Jan. 1, 2007.)*

Research References

2 Witkin Cal. Proc. 5th Courts § 191, (S 191) Civil Rules.
4 Witkin Cal. Proc. 5th Pleading § 357, in General.
4 Witkin Cal. Proc. 5th Pleading § 359, (S 359) Motion in Court.
4 Witkin Cal. Proc. 5th Pleading § 372, Add-On Cases.
6 Witkin Cal. Proc. 5th Proceedings Without Trial § 362, (S 362) Coordinated Actions.

Rule 3.521. Petition for coordination

(a) Contents of petition

A request submitted to the Chair of the Judicial Council for the assignment of a judge to determine whether the coordination of certain actions is appropriate, or a request that a coordination trial judge make such a determination concerning an add-on case, must be designated a "Petition for Coordination" and may be made at any time after filing of the complaint. The petition must state whether a hearing is requested and must be supported by a memorandum and declarations showing:

(1) The name of each petitioner or, when the petition is submitted by a presiding or sole judge, the name of each real party in interest, and the name and address of each party's attorney of record, if any;

(2) The names of the parties to all included actions, and the name and address of each party's attorney of record, if any;

(3) If the party seeking to submit a petition for coordination is a plaintiff, whether the party's attorney has served the summons and complaint on all parties in all included actions in which the attorney has appeared;

(4) For each included action, the complete title and case number, the date the complaint was filed, and the title of the court in which the action is pending;

(5) The complete title and case number of any other action known to the petitioner to be pending in a court of this state that shares a common question of fact or law with the included actions, and a statement of the reasons for not including the other action in the petition for coordination or a statement that the petitioner knows of no other actions sharing a common question of fact or law;

(6) The status of each included action, including the status of any pretrial or discovery motions or orders in that action, if known to petitioner;

(7) The facts relied on to show that each included action meets the coordination standards specified in Code of Civil Procedure section 404.1; and

(8) The facts relied on in support of a request that a particular site or sites be selected for a hearing on the petition for coordination.

(b) Submit proof of filing and service

Within five court days of submitting the petition for coordination, the petitioner must submit to the Chair of the Judicial Council proof of filing of the notice of submission of petition required by rule 3.522, and proof of service of the notice of submission of petition and of the petition required by rule 3.523.

(c) Copies of pleadings in lieu of proof by declaration

In lieu of proof by declaration of any fact required by (a)(2), (4), (7), and (8), a certified or endorsed copy of the respective pleadings may be attached to the petition for coordination, provided that the petitioner specifies with particularity the portions of the pleadings that are relied on to show the fact.

(d) Effect of imminent trial date

The imminence of a trial in any action otherwise appropriate for coordination may be a ground for summary denial of a petition for coordination, in whole or in part. *(Formerly Rule 1521, adopted, eff. Jan. 1, 1974. As amended, eff. Jan. 1, 2005. Renumbered Rule 3.521 and amended, eff. Jan. 1, 2007.)*

Research References

Rutter, Cal. Practice Guide: Civ. Pro. Before Trial Ch. 12(I)-E, E. Consolidation, Coordination and Bifurcation.
Rutter, Cal. Practice Guide: Civil Trials & Evidence Ch. 4-H, H. Motions to Consolidate or Coordinate Separate Cases.
4 Witkin Cal. Proc. 5th Pleading § 353, (S 353) Test: Common Question in Different Courts.
4 Witkin Cal. Proc. 5th Pleading § 357, in General.
4 Witkin Cal. Proc. 5th Pleading § 358, Notice and Opposition.
4 Witkin Cal. Proc. 5th Pleading § 359, (S 359) Motion in Court.
4 Witkin Cal. Proc. 5th Pleading § 372, Add-On Cases.

Rule 3.522. Notice of submission of petition for coordination

(a) Contents of notice of submission

In each included action, the petitioner must file a "Notice of Submission of Petition for Coordination" and the petition for coordination. Each notice must bear the title of the court in which the notice is to be filed and the title and case number of each included action that is pending in that court. Each notice must include:

(1) The date that the petition for coordination was submitted to the Chair of the Judicial Council;

(2) The name and address of the petitioner's attorney of record;

(3) The title and case number of each included action to which the petitioner is a party and the title of the court in which each action is pending; and

(4) The statement that any written opposition to the petition must be submitted and served at least nine court days before the hearing date.

(b) Copies of notice

The petitioner must submit the notice and proof of filing in each included action to the Chair of the Judicial Council within five court days of submitting the petition for coordination. *(Formerly Rule 1522, adopted, eff. Jan. 1, 1974. As amended, eff. Jan. 1, 2005; Jan. 1, 2006. Renumbered Rule 3.522 and amended, eff. Jan. 1, 2007.)*

Research References

Rutter, Cal. Practice Guide: Civ. Pro. Before Trial Ch. 12(I)-E, E. Consolidation, Coordination and Bifurcation.
Rutter, Cal. Practice Guide: Civil Trials & Evidence Ch. 4-H, H. Motions to Consolidate or Coordinate Separate Cases.
4 Witkin Cal. Proc. 5th Pleading § 358, Notice and Opposition.

Rule 3.523. Service of notice of submission on party

The petitioner must serve the notice of submission of petition for coordination that was filed in each included action, the petition for coordination, and supporting documents on each party appearing in each included action and submit the notice to the Chair of the Judicial Council within five court days of submitting the petition for coordination. *(Formerly Rule 1523, adopted, eff. Jan. 1, 1974. As amended, eff. Jan. 1, 2005. Renumbered Rule 3.523 and amended, eff. Jan. 1, 2007.)*

Research References

Rutter, Cal. Practice Guide: Civ. Pro. Before Trial Ch. 12(I)-E, E. Consolidation, Coordination and Bifurcation.
Rutter, Cal. Practice Guide: Civil Trials & Evidence Ch. 4-H, H. Motions to Consolidate or Coordinate Separate Cases.
4 Witkin Cal. Proc. 5th Pleading § 358, Notice and Opposition.

Rule 3.524. Order assigning coordination motion judge

(a) Contents of order

An order by the Chair of the Judicial Council assigning a coordination motion judge to determine whether coordination is appropriate, or authorizing the presiding judge of a court to assign the matter to judicial officers of the court to make the determination in the same manner as assignments are made in other civil cases, must include the following:

(1) The special title and number assigned to the coordination proceeding; and

(2) The court address for submitting all subsequent documents to be considered by the coordination motion judge.

(b) Service of order

The petitioner must serve the order described in (a) on each party appearing in an included action and send it to each court in which an included action is pending with directions to the clerk to file the order in the included action. *(Formerly Rule 1524, adopted, eff. Jan. 1, 1974. As amended, eff. Jan. 1, 2005. Renumbered Rule 3.524, eff. Jan. 1, 2007.)*

Research References

Rutter, Cal. Practice Guide: Civil Trials & Evidence Ch. 4-H, H. Motions to Consolidate or Coordinate Separate Cases.

4 Witkin Cal. Proc. 5th Pleading § 361, Assignment of Coordination Motion Judge.

Rule 3.525. Response in opposition to petition for coordination

Any party to an included action that opposes coordination may serve and submit a memorandum and declarations in opposition to the petition. Any response in opposition must be served and filed at least nine court days before the date set for hearing. *(Formerly Rule 1525, adopted, eff. Jan. 1, 1974. As amended, eff. Jan. 1, 2005. Renumbered Rule 3.525 and amended, eff. Jan. 1, 2007.)*

Research References

Rutter, Cal. Practice Guide: Civ. Pro. Before Trial Ch. 12(I)-E, E. Consolidation, Coordination and Bifurcation.
Rutter, Cal. Practice Guide: Civil Trials & Evidence Ch. 4-H, H. Motions to Consolidate or Coordinate Separate Cases.
4 Witkin Cal. Proc. 5th Pleading § 358, Notice and Opposition.

Rule 3.526. Response in support of petition for coordination

Any party to an included action that supports coordination may serve and submit a written statement in support of the petition. Any response in support must be served and filed at least nine court days before the date set for hearing. If a party that supports coordination does not support the particular site or sites requested by the petitioner for the hearing on the petition for coordination, that party may request that a different site or sites be selected and include in his or her response the facts relied on in support thereof. *(Formerly Rule 1526, adopted, eff. Jan. 1, 1974. As amended, eff. Jan. 1, 2005. Renumbered Rule 3.526 and amended, eff. Jan. 1, 2007.)*

Research References

Rutter, Cal. Practice Guide: Civ. Pro. Before Trial Ch. 12(I)-E, E. Consolidation, Coordination and Bifurcation.
4 Witkin Cal. Proc. 5th Pleading § 358, Notice and Opposition.

Rule 3.527. Notice of hearing on petition for coordination

(a) Timing and notice of hearing

The coordination motion judge must set a hearing date on a petition for coordination within 30 days of the date of the order assigning the coordination motion judge. When a coordination motion judge is assigned to decide a petition for coordination that lists additional included actions sharing a common question of law or fact with included actions in a petition for coordination already pending before the judge, the judge may continue the hearing date on the first petition no more than 30 calendar days in order to hear both petitions at the same time. The petitioner must provide notice of the hearing to each party appearing in an included action. If the coordination motion judge determines that a party that should be served with notice of the petition for coordination has not been served with notice, the coordination motion judge must order the petitioner to promptly serve that party. If the coordination motion judge determines that a hearing is not required under (b), the hearing date must be vacated and notice provided to the parties.

(b) Circumstances in which hearing required

A hearing must be held to decide a petition for coordination if a party opposes coordination. A petition for coordination may not be denied unless a hearing has been held.

(c) Report to the Chair of the Judicial Council

If the petition for coordination has not been decided within 30 calendar days after the hearing, the coordination motion judge must promptly submit to the Chair of the Judicial Council a written report describing:

(1) The present status of the petition for coordination proceeding;

(2) Any factors or circumstances that may have caused undue or unanticipated delay in the decision on the petition for coordination; and

(3) Any stay orders that are in effect. *(Formerly Rule 1527, adopted, eff. Jan. 1, 1974. As amended, eff. Jan. 1, 2005. Renumbered Rule 3.527, eff. Jan. 1, 2007.)*

Research References

Rutter, Cal. Practice Guide: Civ. Pro. Before Trial Ch. 12(I)-E, E. Consolidation, Coordination and Bifurcation.
Rutter, Cal. Practice Guide: Civil Trials & Evidence Ch. 4-H, H. Motions to Consolidate or Coordinate Separate Cases.
4 Witkin Cal. Proc. 5th Pleading § 363, Hearing.
4 Witkin Cal. Proc. 5th Pleading § 365, Determination and Order.
4 Witkin Cal. Proc. 5th Pleading § 372, Add-On Cases.

Rule 3.528. Separate hearing on certain coordination issues

When a petition for coordination may be disposed of on the determination of a specified issue or issues, without a hearing on all issues raised by the petition and any opposition, the assigned judge may order that the specified issue or issues be heard and determined before a hearing on the remaining issues. *(Formerly Rule 1528, adopted, eff. Jan. 1, 1974. As amended, eff. Jan. 1, 2005. Renumbered Rule 3.528, eff. Jan. 1, 2007.)*

Research References

Rutter, Cal. Practice Guide: Civil Trials & Evidence Ch. 4-H, H. Motions to Consolidate or Coordinate Separate Cases.
4 Witkin Cal. Proc. 5th Pleading § 363, Hearing.
4 Witkin Cal. Proc. 5th Pleading § 372, Add-On Cases.

Rule 3.529. Order granting or denying coordination

(a) Filing, service, and submittal

When a petition for coordination is granted or denied, the petitioner must promptly file the order in each included action, serve it on each party appearing in an included action, and submit it to the Chair of the Judicial Council.

(b) Stay of further proceedings

When an order granting coordination is filed in an included action, all further proceedings in that action are automatically stayed, except as directed by the coordination trial judge or by the coordination motion judge under (c). The stay does not preclude the court in which the included action is pending from accepting and filing papers with proof of submission of a copy to the assigned judge or from exercising jurisdiction over any severable claim that has not been ordered coordinated.

(c) Authority of coordination motion judge pending assignment of coordination trial judge

After a petition for coordination has been granted and before a coordination trial judge has been assigned, the coordination motion judge may for good cause make any appropriate order as the ends of justice may require but may not commence a trial or enter judgment in any included action. Good cause includes a showing of an urgent need for judicial action to preserve the rights of a party pending assignment of a coordination trial judge.

(d) Order denying coordination

The authority of a coordination motion judge over an included action terminates when an order denying a petition for coordination is filed in the included action and served on the parties to the action. A stay ordered by the coordination motion judge terminates 10 days after the order denying coordination is filed. *(Formerly Rule 1529, adopted, eff. Jan. 1, 1974. As amended, eff. June 19, 1982; Jan. 1, 2005. Renumbered Rule 3.529 and amended, eff. Jan. 1, 2007.)*

Research References

Rutter, Cal. Practice Guide: Civil Trials & Evidence Ch. 4-H, H. Motions to Consolidate or Coordinate Separate Cases.
4 Witkin Cal. Proc. 5th Pleading § 362, Stay Pending Determination.
4 Witkin Cal. Proc. 5th Pleading § 365, Determination and Order.
4 Witkin Cal. Proc. 5th Pleading § 367, in General.
4 Witkin Cal. Proc. 5th Pleading § 372, Add-On Cases.
6 Witkin Cal. Proc. 5th Proceedings Without Trial § 362, (S 362) Coordinated Actions.

Rule 3.530. Site of coordination proceedings

(a) Recommendation by coordination motion judge

If a petition for coordination is granted, the coordination motion judge must, in the order granting coordination, recommend to the Chair of the Judicial Council a particular superior court for the site of the coordination proceedings.

(b) Factors to consider

The coordination motion judge may consider any relevant factors in making a recommendation for the site of the coordination proceedings, including the following:

(1) The number of included actions in particular locations;

(2) Whether the litigation is at an advanced stage in a particular court;

(3) The efficient use of court facilities and judicial resources;

(4) The locations of witnesses and evidence;

(5) The convenience of the parties and witnesses;

(6) The parties' principal places of business;

(7) The office locations of counsel for the parties; and

(8) The ease of travel to and availability of accommodations in particular locations. *(Formerly Rule 1530, adopted, eff. Jan. 1, 2005. Renumbered Rule 3.530, eff. Jan. 1, 2007.)*

Research References

4 Witkin Cal. Proc. 5th Pleading § 367, in General.

Rule 3.531. Potential add-on case

(a) Notice

Any party to an included action in a pending petition for coordination must promptly provide notice of any potential add-on cases in which that party is also named or in which that party's attorney has appeared. The party must submit notice to the coordination motion judge and the Chair of the Judicial Council and serve it on each party appearing in the included actions in the pending petition and each party appearing in the potential add-on cases.

(b) Stipulation or order

By stipulation of all parties or order of the coordination motion judge, each potential add-on case will be deemed an included action for purposes of the hearing on the petition for coordination. *(Formerly Rule 1531, adopted, eff. Jan. 1, 2005. Renumbered Rule 3.531, eff. Jan. 1, 2007.)*

Research References

4 Witkin Cal. Proc. 5th Pleading § 360, (S 360) Potential Add-On Cases.

Rule 3.532. Petition for coordination when cases already ordered coordinated

(a) Assignment of coordination trial judge

If it appears that included actions in a petition for coordination share a common question of law or fact with cases already ordered coordinated, the Chair of the Judicial Council may assign the petition to the coordination trial judge for the existing

Ct. Rules

coordinated cases to decide the petition as a request to coordinate an add-on case under rule 3.544.

(b) Order

The coordination trial judge's order must specify that the request to coordinate an add-on case is either granted or denied.

(c) Filing and service

The petitioner must promptly file the order in each included action, serve it on each party appearing in an included action, and submit a copy to the Chair of the Judicial Council.

(d) Cases added on and right to peremptory challenge

If the coordination trial judge grants the petition, the included actions will be coordinated as add-on cases and the right to file a peremptory challenge under Code of Civil Procedure section 170.6 will be limited by rule 3.516.

(e) Assignment of coordination motion judge if cases not added on

If the coordination trial judge denies the petition as a request to coordinate an add-on case under rule 3.544, the Chair of the Judicial Council must assign a coordination motion judge to determine whether coordination is appropriate under rule 3.524. *(Formerly Rule 1532, adopted, eff. Jan. 1, 2005. Renumbered Rule 3.532 and amended, eff. Jan. 1, 2007.)*

Research References

Rutter, Cal. Practice Guide: Civ. Pro. Before Trial Ch. 9(I)-D, D. Hearing.
Rutter, Cal. Practice Guide: Civ. Pro. Before Trial Ch. 12(I)-E, E. Consolidation, Coordination and Bifurcation.
2 Witkin Cal. Proc. 5th Courts § 191, (S 191) Civil Rules.
4 Witkin Cal. Proc. 5th Pleading § 372, Add-On Cases.

Article 4

PRETRIAL AND TRIAL RULES FOR COMPLEX COORDINATED ACTIONS

Rule
3.540.   Order assigning coordination trial judge.
3.541.   Duties of the coordination trial judge.
3.542.   Remand of action or claim.
3.543.   Transfer of action or claim.
3.544.   Add-on cases.
3.545.   Termination of coordinated action.

Rule 3.540.   Order assigning coordination trial judge

(a) Assignment by the Chair of the Judicial Council

When a petition for coordination is granted, the Chair of the Judicial Council must either assign a coordination trial judge to hear and determine the coordinated actions or authorize the presiding judge of a court to assign the matter to judicial officers of the court in the same manner as assignments are made in other civil cases, under Code of Civil Procedure section 404.3. The order assigning a coordination trial judge must designate an address for submission of papers to that judge.

(b) Powers of coordination trial judge

Immediately on assignment, the coordination trial judge may exercise all the powers over each coordinated action that are available to a judge of the court in which that action is pending.

(c) Filing and service of copies of assignment order

The petitioner must file the assignment order in each coordinated action and serve it on each party appearing in each action, and, if the assignment was made by the presiding judge, submit it to the Chair of the Judicial Council. Every paper filed in a coordinated action must be accompanied by proof of submission

of a copy of the paper to the coordination trial judge at the designated address. A copy of the assignment order must be included in any subsequent service of process on any defendant in the action. *(Formerly Rule 1540, adopted, eff. Jan. 1, 1974. As amended, eff. Jan. 1, 2005. Renumbered Rule 3.540 and amended, eff. Jan. 1, 2007. As amended, eff. Jan. 1, 2011.)*

Research References

Rutter, Cal. Practice Guide: Civil Trials & Evidence Ch. 4-H, H. Motions to Consolidate or Coordinate Separate Cases.
2 Witkin Cal. Proc. 5th Courts § 191, (S 191) Civil Rules.
4 Witkin Cal. Proc. 5th Pleading § 365, Determination and Order.
4 Witkin Cal. Proc. 5th Pleading § 367, in General.
6 Witkin Cal. Proc. 5th Proceedings Without Trial § 362, (S 362) Coordinated Actions.
7 Witkin Cal. Proc. 5th Trial § 42, (S 42) in General.

Rule 3.541.   Duties of the coordination trial judge

(a) Initial case management conference

The coordination trial judge must hold a case management conference within 45 days after issuance of the assignment order. Counsel and all self-represented persons must attend the conference and be prepared to discuss all matters specified in the order setting the conference. At any time following the assignment of the coordination trial judge, a party may serve and submit a proposed agenda for the conference and a proposed form of order covering such matters of procedure and discovery as may be appropriate. At the conference, the judge may:

(1) Appoint liaison counsel under rule 3.506;

(2) Establish a timetable for filing motions other than discovery motions;

(3) Establish a schedule for discovery;

(4) Provide a method and schedule for the submission of preliminary legal questions that might serve to expedite the disposition of the coordinated actions;

(5) In class actions, establish a schedule, if practicable, for the prompt determination of matters pertinent to the class action issue;

(6) Establish a central depository or depositories to receive and maintain for inspection by the parties evidentiary material and specified documents that are not required by the rules in this chapter to be served on all parties; and

(7) Schedule further conferences if appropriate.

(b) Management of proceedings by coordination trial judge

The coordination trial judge must assume an active role in managing all steps of the pretrial, discovery, and trial proceedings to expedite the just determination of the coordinated actions without delay. The judge may, for the purpose of coordination and to serve the ends of justice:

(1) Order any coordinated action transferred to another court under rule 3.543;

(2) Schedule and conduct hearings, conferences, and a trial or trials at any site within this state that the judge deems appropriate with due consideration to the convenience of parties, witnesses, and counsel; to the relative development of the actions and the work product of counsel; to the efficient use of judicial facilities and resources; and to the calendar of the courts; and

(3) Order any issue or defense to be tried separately and before trial of the remaining issues when it appears that the disposition of any of the coordinated actions might thereby be expedited. *(Formerly Rule 1541, adopted, eff. Jan. 1, 1974. As amended, eff. Jan. 1, 2005. Renumbered Rule 3.541 and amended, eff. Jan. 1, 2007.)*

Research References

Rutter, Cal. Practice Guide: Civ. Pro. Before Trial Ch. 12(I)-E, E. Consolidation, Coordination and Bifurcation.
Rutter, Cal. Practice Guide: Civil Trials & Evidence Ch. 2-B, B. What Constitutes Jury Trial.
Rutter, Cal. Practice Guide: Civil Trials & Evidence Ch. 4-H, H. Motions to Consolidate or Coordinate Separate Cases.
4 Witkin Cal. Proc. 5th Pleading § 367, in General.
4 Witkin Cal. Proc. 5th Pleading § 368, Case Management Conference.
4 Witkin Cal. Proc. 5th Pleading § 371, Transfer of Action or Claim.
6 Witkin Cal. Proc. 5th Proceedings Without Trial § 362, (S 362) Coordinated Actions.

Rule 3.542. Remand of action or claim

The coordination trial judge may at any time remand a coordinated action or any severable claim or issue in that action to the court in which the action was pending at the time the coordination of that action was ordered. Remand may be made on the stipulation of all parties or on the basis of evidence received at a hearing on the court's own motion or on the motion of any party to any coordinated action. No action or severable claim or issue in that action may be remanded over the objection of any party unless the evidence demonstrates a material change in the circumstances that are relevant to the criteria for coordination under Code of Civil Procedure section 404.1. If the order of remand requires that the action be transferred, the provisions of rule 3.543(c)–(e) are applicable to the transfer. A remanded action is no longer part of the coordination proceedings for purposes of the rules in this chapter. *(Formerly Rule 1542, adopted, eff. Jan. 1, 1974. As amended, eff. Jan. 1, 2005; July 1, 2006. Renumbered Rule 3.542 and amended, eff. Jan. 1, 2007.)*

Research References

Rutter, Cal. Practice Guide: Civ. Pro. Before Trial Ch. 12(I)-E, E. Consolidation, Coordination and Bifurcation.
4 Witkin Cal. Proc. 5th Pleading § 367, in General.
4 Witkin Cal. Proc. 5th Pleading § 370, Remand of Action or Claim.

Rule 3.543. Transfer of action or claim

(a) Court may transfer coordinated action

The coordination trial judge may order any coordinated action or severable claim in that action transferred from the court in which it is pending to another court for a specified purpose or for all purposes. Transfer may be made by the court on its own motion or on the motion of any party to any coordinated action.

(b) Hearing on motion to transfer

If a party objects to the transfer, the court must hold a hearing on at least 10 days' written notice served on all parties to that action. At any hearing to determine whether an action or claim should be transferred, the court must consider the convenience of parties, witnesses, and counsel; the relative development of the actions and the work product of counsel; the efficient use of judicial facilities and resources; the calendar of the courts; and any other relevant matter.

(c) Order transferring action

The order transferring the action or claim must designate the court to which the action is transferred and must direct that a copy of the order of transfer be filed in each coordinated action. The order must indicate whether the action remains part of the coordination proceedings for purposes of the rules in this chapter.

(d) Duties of transferor and transferee courts

(1) *Duty of transferor court*

The clerk of the court in which the action was pending must immediately prepare and transmit to the court to which the action is transferred a certified copy of the order of transfer and of the pleadings and proceedings in the transferred action and must serve a copy of the order of transfer on each party appearing in that action.

(2) *Duty of transferee court*

The court to which the action is transferred must file the action as if the action had been commenced in that court. No fees may be required for such transfer by either court.

(3) *Transmission of papers*

If it is necessary to have any of the original pleadings or other papers in the transferred action before the coordination trial judge, the clerk of the court from which the action was transferred must, on written request of a party to that action or of the coordination trial judge, transmit such papers or pleadings to the court to which the action is transferred and must retain a certified copy.

(e) Transferee court to exercise jurisdiction

On receipt of a transfer order, the court to which the action is transferred may exercise jurisdiction over the action in accordance with the orders and directions of the coordination trial judge, and no other court may exercise jurisdiction over that action except as provided in this rule. *(Formerly Rule 1543, adopted, eff. Jan. 1, 1974. As amended, eff. Jan. 1, 2005. Renumbered Rule 3.543 and amended, eff. Jan. 1, 2007.)*

Research References

Rutter, Cal. Practice Guide: Civil Trials & Evidence Ch. 4-H, H. Motions to Consolidate or Coordinate Separate Cases.
4 Witkin Cal. Proc. 5th Pleading § 367, in General.
4 Witkin Cal. Proc. 5th Pleading § 370, Remand of Action or Claim.
4 Witkin Cal. Proc. 5th Pleading § 371, Transfer of Action or Claim.

Rule 3.544. Add-on cases

(a) Request to coordinate add-on case

A request to coordinate an add-on case must comply with the requirements of rules 3.520 through 3.523, except that the request must be submitted to the coordination trial judge under Code of Civil Procedure section 404.4, with proof of mailing of one copy to the Chair of the Judicial Council and proof of service as required by rule 3.510.

(b) Opposition to request to coordinate an add-on case

Within 10 days after the service of a request, any party may serve and submit a notice of opposition to the request. Thereafter, within 15 days after submitting a notice of opposition, the party must serve and submit a memorandum and declarations in opposition to the request. Failure to serve and submit a memorandum and declarations in opposition may be a ground for granting the request to coordinate an add-on case.

(c) Hearing on request to coordinate an add-on case

The coordination trial judge may order a hearing on a request to coordinate an add-on case under rules 3.527 and 3.528 and may allow the parties to serve and submit additional written materials in support of or opposition to the request. In deciding the request to coordinate, the court must consider the relative development of the actions and the work product of counsel, in addition to any other relevant matter. An application for an order staying the add-on case must be made to the coordination trial judge under rule 3.515.

(d) Order on request to coordinate an add-on case

If no party has filed a notice of opposition within the time required under (b), the coordination trial judge may enter an order granting or denying the request without a hearing. An order granting or denying a request to coordinate an add-on case must be prepared and served under rule 3.529, and an order granting such request automatically stays all further proceedings in the add-on case under rule 3.529. *(Formerly Rule 1544, adopted, eff. Jan. 1, 1974. As amended, eff. Jan. 1, 2005. Renumbered Rule 3.544 and amended, eff. Jan. 1, 2007.)*

Research References

Rutter, Cal. Practice Guide: Civ. Pro. Before Trial Ch. 9(I)-D, D. Hearing.
Rutter, Cal. Practice Guide: Civil Trials & Evidence Ch. 3-B, B. Peremptory Challenge of Judge (CCP § 170.6).
4 Witkin Cal. Proc. 5th Pleading § 355, (S 355) Peremptory Challenge of Assigned Judge.
4 Witkin Cal. Proc. 5th Pleading § 367, in General.
4 Witkin Cal. Proc. 5th Pleading § 372, Add-On Cases.

Rule 3.545. Termination of coordinated action

(a) Coordination trial judge may terminate action

The coordination trial judge may terminate any coordinated action by settlement or final dismissal, summary judgment, or judgment, or may transfer the action so that it may be dismissed or otherwise terminated in the court where it was pending when coordination was ordered.

(b) Copies of order dismissing or terminating action and judgment

A certified copy of the order dismissing or terminating the action and of any judgment must be transmitted to:

(1) The clerk of the court in which the action was pending when coordination was ordered, who shall promptly enter any judgment and serve notice of entry of the judgment on all parties to the action and on the Chair of the Judicial Council; and

(2) The appropriate clerks for filing in each pending coordinated action.

(c) Judgment in coordinated action

The judgment entered in each coordinated action must bear the title and case number assigned to the action at the time it was filed.

(d) Proceedings in trial court after judgment

Until the judgment in a coordinated action becomes final or until a coordinated action is remanded, all further proceedings in that action to be determined by the trial court must be determined by the coordination trial judge. Thereafter, unless otherwise ordered by the coordination trial judge, all such proceedings must be conducted in the court where the action was pending when coordination was ordered. The coordination trial judge must also specify the court in which any ancillary proceedings will be heard and determined. For purposes of this rule, a judgment is final when it is no longer subject to appeal. *(Formerly Rule 1545, adopted, eff. Jan. 1, 1974. As amended, eff. Jan. 1, 2005. Renumbered Rule 3.545, eff. Jan. 1, 2007.)*

Research References

Rutter, Cal. Practice Guide: Civ. Pro. Before Trial Ch. 12(I)-E, E. Consolidation, Coordination and Bifurcation.
2 Witkin Cal. Proc. 5th Courts § 191, (S 191) Civil Rules.
4 Witkin Cal. Proc. 5th Pleading § 367, in General.
4 Witkin Cal. Proc. 5th Pleading § 373, Termination of Action.

Article 5

ADMINISTRATION OF COORDINATED COMPLEX ACTIONS

Rule
3.550. General administration by the Administrative Office of the Courts.

Rule 3.550. General administration by the Administrative Office of the Courts

(a) Coordination attorney

Except as otherwise provided in the rules in this chapter, all necessary administrative functions under this chapter will be performed at the direction of the Chair of the Judicial Council by a coordination attorney in the Administrative Office of the Courts.

(b) Duties of coordination attorney

The coordination attorney must at all times maintain:

(1) A list of active and retired judges who are qualified and currently available to conduct coordination proceedings; and

(2) A register of all coordination proceedings and a file for each proceeding, for public inspection during regular business hours at the San Francisco office of the Judicial Council.

(c) Coordination proceeding title and case number

The coordination attorney must assign each coordination proceeding a special title and coordination proceeding number. Thereafter all papers in that proceeding must bear that title and number. *(Formerly Rule 1550, adopted, eff. Jan. 1, 1974. As amended, eff. Jan. 1, 2005. Renumbered Rule 3.550 and amended, eff. Jan. 1, 2007.)*

Research References

Rutter, Cal. Practice Guide: Civ. Pro. Before Trial Ch. 12(I)-E, E. Consolidation, Coordination and Bifurcation.
Rutter, Cal. Practice Guide: Civil Trials & Evidence Ch. 4-H, H. Motions to Consolidate or Coordinate Separate Cases.
Rutter, Cal. Practice Guide: Personal Injury Ch. 5-E, E. Selected Pleading Issues.
2 Witkin Cal. Proc. 5th Courts § 191, (S 191) Civil Rules.
4 Witkin Cal. Proc. 5th Pleading § 352, (S 352) in General.
4 Witkin Cal. Proc. 5th Pleading § 356, (S 356) Service, Filing, and Submission of Papers.
4 Witkin Cal. Proc. 5th Pleading § 361, Assignment of Coordination Motion Judge.

Division 6

PROCEEDINGS

Chapter 2

STAY OF PROCEEDINGS

Rule
3.650. Duty to notify court and others of stay.

Rule 3.650. Duty to notify court and others of stay

(a) Notice of stay

The party who requested or caused a stay of a proceeding must immediately serve and file a notice of the stay and attach a copy of the order or other document showing that the proceeding is stayed. If the person who requested or caused the stay has not appeared, or is not subject to the jurisdiction of the court, the plaintiff must immediately file a notice of the stay and attach a copy of the order or other document showing that the proceeding is stayed. The notice of stay must be served on all parties who have appeared in the case.

(b) When notice must be provided

The party responsible for giving notice under (a) must provide notice if the case is stayed for any of the following reasons:

(1) An order of a federal court or a higher state court;

(2) Contractual arbitration under Code of Civil Procedure section 1281.4;

(3) Arbitration of attorney fees and costs under Business and Professions Code section 6201; or

(4) Automatic stay caused by a filing in another court, including a federal bankruptcy court.

(c) Contents of notice

The notice must state whether the case is stayed with regard to all parties or only certain parties. If it is stayed with regard to only certain parties, the notice must specifically identify those parties. The notice must also state the reason that the case is stayed.

(d) Notice that stay is terminated or modified

When a stay is vacated, is no longer in effect, or is modified, the party who filed the notice of the stay must immediately serve and file a notice of termination or modification of stay. If that party fails to do so, any other party in the action who has knowledge of the termination or modification of the stay must serve and file a notice of termination or modification of stay. Once one party in the action has served and filed a notice of termination or modification of stay, other parties in the action are not required to do so. *(Formerly Rule 224, adopted, eff. Jan. 1, 2004. As amended, eff. Jan. 1, 2006. Renumbered Rule 3.650 and amended, eff. Jan. 1, 2007.)*

Research References

Rutter, Cal. Practice Guide: A.D.R. Ch. 5-G, G. Procedures to Enforce Arbitration.
Rutter, Cal. Practice Guide: Civil Appeals & Writs Ch. 7-A, A. Overview.
Rutter, Cal. Practice Guide: Civil Appeals & Writs Ch. 7-A , Outline a.
Rutter, Cal. Practice Guide: Civ. Pro. Before Trial Ch. 9(I)-H, H. Motions Relating to Contractual Arbitration.
Rutter, Cal. Practice Guide: Civ. Pro. Before Trial Ch. 12(I)-G, G. Stays Caused by Other Proceedings.
Rutter, Cal. Practice Guide: Prof. Responsibility Ch. 5-K, K. Fee Recovery/Enforcing Fee Agreements.
1 Witkin Cal. Proc. 5th Attorneys § 226, Notice, Request, and Stay.
2 Witkin Cal. Proc. 5th Courts § 191, (S 191) Civil Rules.
7 Witkin Cal. Proc. 5th Trial § 41, Notice of Settlement or Stay.

Chapter 3

HEARINGS, CONFERENCES, AND PROCEEDINGS

Rule
3.670. Telephone appearance.

Rule 3.670. Telephone appearance

(a) Policy favoring telephone appearances

The intent of this rule is to promote uniformity in the practices and procedures relating to telephone appearances in civil cases. To improve access to the courts and reduce litigation costs, courts should permit parties, to the extent feasible, to appear by telephone at appropriate conferences, hearings, and proceedings in civil cases.

(b) Application

This rule applies to all general civil cases as defined in rule 1.6 and to unlawful detainer and probate proceedings.

(c) General provision authorizing parties to appear by telephone

Except as provided in (e)(2), a party may appear by telephone at the following conferences, hearings, and proceedings:

(1) Case management conferences, provided the party has made a good faith effort to meet and confer and has timely served and filed a case management statement before the conference date;

(2) Trial setting conferences;

(3) Hearings on law and motion, except motions in limine;

(4) Hearings on discovery motions;

(5) Status conferences, including conferences to review the status of an arbitration or a mediation; and

(6) Hearings to review the dismissal of an action.

(d) Required personal appearances

Except as provided in (e)(3), a personal appearance is required for hearings, conferences, and proceedings not listed in (c), including the following:

(1) Trials and hearings at which witnesses are expected to testify;

(2) Hearings on temporary restraining orders;

(3) Settlement conferences;

(4) Trial management conferences;

(5) Hearings on motions in limine; and

(6) Hearings on petitions to confirm the sale of property under the Probate Code.

In addition, except as provided in (e)(3), a personal appearance is required for the following persons:

(7) Applicants seeking an ex parte order, except when the applicant is seeking an order:

(A) For permission to file a memorandum in excess of the applicable page limits;

(B) For an extension of time to serve pleadings;

(C) To set hearing dates on alternative writs and orders to show cause; or

(D) By stipulation of the parties;

(8) Persons ordered to appear to show cause why sanctions should not be imposed for violation of a court order or a rule; or

(9) Persons ordered to appear in an order or citation issued under the Probate Code.

At the proceedings under (7), (8), and (9), parties who are not required to appear in person under this rule may appear by telephone.

(e) Court discretion to modify rule

(1) *Policy favoring telephone appearances in civil cases*

In exercising its discretion under this provision, the court should consider the general policy favoring telephone appearances in civil cases.

(2) *Court may require personal appearances*

The court may require a party to appear in person at a hearing, conference, or proceeding listed in (c) if the court determines on a hearing-by-hearing basis that a personal appearance would materially assist in the determination of the proceedings or in the effective management or resolution of the particular case.

(3) *Court may permit appearances by telephone*

The court may permit a party to appear by telephone at a hearing, conference, or proceeding under (d) if the court determines that a telephone appearance is appropriate.

Ct. Rules

(f) Need for personal appearance

If, at any time during a hearing, conference, or proceeding conducted by telephone, the court determines that a personal appearance is necessary, the court may continue the matter and require a personal appearance.

(g) Notice by party

(1) A party choosing to appear by telephone at a hearing, conference, or proceeding under this rule must either:

(A) Place the phrase "Telephone Appearance" below the title of the moving, opposing, or reply papers; or

(B) At least three court days before the appearance, notify the court and all other parties of the party's intent to appear by telephone. If the notice is oral, it must be given either in person or by telephone. If the notice is in writing, it must be given by filing a "Notice of Intent to Appear by Telephone" with the court at least three court days before the appearance and by serving the notice at the same time on all other parties by personal delivery, fax transmission, express mail, or other means reasonably calculated to ensure delivery to the parties no later than the close of the next business day.

(2) If after receiving notice from another party as provided under (1) a party that has not given notice also decides to appear by telephone, the party may do so by notifying the court and all other parties that have appeared in the action, no later than noon on the court day before the appearance, of its intent to appear by telephone.

(3) If a party that has given notice that it intends to appear by telephone under (1) subsequently chooses to appear in person, the party must so notify the court and all other parties that have appeared in the action, by telephone, at least two court days before the appearance.

(4) The court, on a showing of good cause, may permit a party to appear by telephone at a conference, hearing, or proceeding even if the party has not given the notice required under (1) or (2) and may permit a party to appear in person even if the party has not given the notice required in (3).

(h) Notice by court

After a party has requested a telephone appearance under (g), if the court requires the personal appearance of the party, the court must give reasonable notice to all parties before the hearing and may continue the hearing if necessary to accommodate the personal appearance. The court may direct the court clerk, a court-appointed vendor, a party, or an attorney to provide the notification. In courts using a telephonic tentative ruling system for law and motion matters, court notification that parties must appear in person may be given as part of the court's tentative ruling on a specific law and motion matter if that notification is given one court day before the hearing.

(i) Provision of telephone appearance services

A court may provide for telephone appearances only through one or more of the following methods:

(1) An agreement with one or more vendors under a state-wide master agreement or agreements.

(2) An agreement between a court and a vendor that was entered into before July 1, 2011, and that has not expired. If a contract is subject to cancellation by a court after July 1, 2011, that court must exercise its option to cancel the contract as soon after July 1, 2011 as is legally possible to do so.

(3)(2) The direct provision by the court of telephone appearance services. If a court directly provides telephone services, it must collect the telephone appearance fees specified in (j), except as provided in (k) and (*l*). A judge may, at his or her discretion, waive telephone appearance fees for parties appearing directly by telephone in that judge's courtroom.

(j) Telephone appearance fee amounts; time for making requests

The telephone appearance fees specified in this subdivision are the statewide, uniform fees to be paid by parties to a vendor or court for providing telephone appearance services. These fees supersede any fees paid by parties to vendors or courts under agreements or procedures existing before July 1, 2011. Except as provided under (k) and (*l*), the fees to be paid to appear by telephone are as follows:

(1) The fee to appear by telephone, made by a timely request to a vendor or court providing telephone appearance services, is $78 86 for each appearance.

(2) An additional late request fee of $30 is to be charged for an appearance by telephone if the request to the vendor or the court providing telephone services is not made at least three days before the scheduled appearance, except when:

(A) There is When an ex parte or other hearing or conference is set on shortened time for which three days' notice would not be feasible or practical, only the applying party—and not any responding party—is to be charged the late fee;

(B) When the court, on its own motion, sets a hearing or conference on shortened time, no late fee is to be charged to any party;

(C) When the matter has a tentative ruling posted within the three-day period, no late fee is to be charged to any party; or and

(D) When the request to appear by telephone is made by a party that received notice of another party's intent to appear and afterward decides also to appear by telephone under (g)(2), no late fee is to be charged to that party. The request of a party seeking to appear under (g)(2) is timely if the its request is made to the vendor or the court providing the service by noon on the court day before the hearing or conference.

(3) A fee of $5 is to be charged instead of the fees under (1) and (2) if a party cancels a telephone appearance request and no telephone appearance is made. A hearing or appearance that is taken off calendar or continued by the court is not a cancelation under this rule. If the hearing or appearance is taken off calendar by the court, there is no charge for the telephone appearance. If the hearing or appearance is continued by the court, the appearance fee must be refunded to the requesting party or, if the party agrees, be applied to the new hearing or appearance date.

(k) Fee waivers

(1) *Effect of fee waiver.*

A party that has received a fee waiver must not be charged the fees for telephone appearances provided under (j), subject to the provisions of Code of Civil Procedure section 367.6(b).

(2) *Responsibility of requesting party.*

To obtain telephone services without payment of a telephone appearance fee from a vendor or a court that provides telephone appearance services, a party must advise the vendor or the court that he or she has received a fee waiver from the court. If a vendor requests, the party must transmit a copy of the order granting the fee waiver to the vendor.

(3) *Lien on judgment.*

If a party based on a fee waiver receives telephone appearance services under this rule without payment of a fee, the vendor or court that provides the telephone appearance services has a lien on any judgment, including a judgment for costs, that the party may receive, in the amount of the fee that the party would have paid for the telephone appearance. There is no charge for filing the lien.

(*l*) Title IV-D proceedings

(1) *Court-provided telephone appearance services.*

If a court provides telephone appearance services in a proceeding for child or family support under Title IV-D of the Social Security Act brought by or otherwise involving a local child support agency, the court must not charge a fee for those services.

(2) *Vendor-provided telephone appearance services*

If a vendor provides for telephone appearance services in a proceeding for child or family support under Title IV–D, the amount of the fee for a telephone appearance under (j)(1) is $~~58~~ 66 instead of $~~78~~ 86. No portion of the fee received by the vendor for a telephone appearance under this subdivision is to be transmitted to the State Treasury under Government Code section 72011.

(3) *Responsibility of requesting party.*

When a party in a Title IV-D proceeding requests telephone appearance services from a court or a vendor, the party requesting the services must advise the court or the vendor that the requester is a party in a proceeding for child or family support under Title IV-D brought by or otherwise involving a local child support agency.

(4) *Fee waivers applicable.*

The fee waiver provisions in (k) apply to a request by a party in a Title IV-D proceeding for telephone appearance services from a vendor.

(m) Audibility and procedure

The court must ensure that the statements of participants are audible to all other participants and the court staff and that the statements made by a participant are identified as being made by that participant.

(n) Reporting

All proceedings involving telephone appearances must be reported to the same extent and in the same manner as if the participants had appeared in person.

(*o*) Conference call vendor or vendors

A court, by local rule, may designate the conference call vendor or vendors that must be used for telephone appearances.

(p) Information on telephone appearances

The court must publish notice providing parties with the particular information necessary for them to appear by telephone at conferences, hearings, and proceedings in that court under this rule. *(Formerly Rule 298, adopted, eff. March 1, 1988. As amended, eff. Jan. 1, 1989; July 1, 1998; Jan. 1, 1999; July 1, 1999; Jan. 1, 2001; July 1, 2002; Jan. 1, 2003. Renumbered Rule 3.670 and amended, eff. Jan. 1, 2007. As amended, eff. Jan. 1, 2008; July 1, 2011; July 1, 2013.)*

Advisory Committee Comment

This rule does not apply to criminal or juvenile matters, and it also does not apply to family law matters, except in certain respects as provided in rule 5.324 relating to telephone appearances in proceedings for child or family support under Title IV-D of the Social Security Act. (See Cal. Rules of Court, rule 3.670(b) [rule applies to general civil cases and unlawful detainer and probate proceedings]; rule 5.324(j) [subdivisions (i)–(p) of

rule 3.670 apply to telephone appearances in Title IV-D proceedings].)

Under subdivision (i)(3) of this rule and Government Code section 72010(c), even for proceedings in which fees are authorized, the fees may be waived by a judicial officer, in his or her discretion, for parties appearing directly by telephone in that judicial officer's courtroom.

Research References

Rutter, Cal. Practice Guide: Civ. Pro. Before Trial Ch. 9(I)-D, D. Hearing.

Rutter, Cal. Practice Guide: Civ. Pro. Before Trial Ch. 12(I)-B, B. Case Management ("Fast Track") System.

Rutter, Cal. Practice Guide: Personal Injury Ch. 8-A, A. Case Management.

2 Witkin Cal. Proc. 5th Courts § 191, (S 191) Civil Rules.

6 Witkin Cal. Proc. 5th Proceedings Without Trial § 39, Appearance by Telephone.

7 Witkin Cal. Proc. 5th Trial § 45, Current Procedure.

7 Witkin Cal. Proc. 5th Trial § 57, Appearance at Conferences by Telephone.

10 Witkin, California Summary 10th Parent and Child § 303, in General.

Chapter 4

SPECIAL PROCEEDINGS ON CONSTRUCTION–RELATED ACCESSIBILITY CLAIMS

Rule 3.680. Service of Notice of Stay and Early Evaluation Conference

(a) Service of Application and Notice

The defendant who requested a stay and early evaluation conference on a construction-related claim under Civil Code section 55.54 must, within 10 days of issuance of the notice, serve on all other parties the application for stay and any *Notice of Stay of Proceedings and Early Evaluation Conference* (form DAL–010) issued by the court.

(b) Filing Proof of Service

A proof of service must be filed with the court 15 days before the date set for the early evaluation conference. *Proof of Service–Disability Access Litigation* (form DAL–012) may be used to show service of the documents. *(Adopted, eff. July 1, 2013.)*

Rule 3.682. Notice of Mandatory Evaluation Conferences

(a) Service of Application and Notice

The party who requested a mandatory evaluation conference on a construction-related accessibility claim under Civil Code section 55.545 must, within 10 days of issuance of the notice, serve on all other parties the application and any *Notice of Mandatory Evaluation Conference* (form DAL–020) issued by the court.

(b) Filing Proof of Service

A proof of service must be filed with the court 15 days before the date set for the early evaluation conference. *Proof of Service–Disability Access Litigation* (form DAL–012) may be used to show service of the documents. *(Adopted, eff. July 1, 2013.)*

Ct. Rules

Division 7

CIVIL CASE MANAGEMENT

Chapter 1

GENERAL PROVISIONS

Rule
3.700.   Scope and purpose of the case management rules.

Rule 3.700.   Scope and purpose of the case management rules

The rules in this division are to be construed and administered to secure the fair, timely, and efficient disposition of every civil case. The rules are to be applied in a fair, practical, and flexible manner so as to achieve the ends of justice. *(Formerly Rule 204, adopted, eff. Jan. 1, 2004.   Renumbered Rule 3.700 and amended, eff. Jan. 1, 2007.)*

Research References

2 Witkin Cal. Proc. 5th Courts § 191, (S 191) Civil Rules.
2 Witkin Cal. Proc. 5th Courts § 263, (S 263) Differential Case Management.
6 Witkin Cal. Proc. 5th Proceedings Without Trial § 590, (S 590) Manner of Selection.
7 Witkin Cal. Proc. 5th Trial § 37, (S 37) Procedural Framework.
7 Witkin Cal. Proc. 5th Trial § 42, (S 42) in General.

Chapter 2

DIFFERENTIAL CASE MANAGEMENT

Rule
3.710.   Authority.
3.711.   Local court rules.
3.712.   Application and exceptions.
3.713.   Delay reduction goals.
3.714.   Differentiation of cases to achieve goals.
3.715.   Case evaluation factors.

Rule 3.710.   Authority

The rules in this chapter implement Government Code section 68603(c) under the Trial Court Delay Reduction Act of 1990. *(Formerly Rule 2101, adopted, eff. July 1, 1991.   Renumbered Rule 205, and amended, eff. July 1, 2002.   Renumbered Rule 3.710 and amended, eff. Jan. 1, 2007.)*

Research References

Rutter, Cal. Practice Guide: Civ. Pro. Before Trial Ch. 12(I)-B, B. Management ("Fast Track") System.
Rutter, Cal. Practice Guide: Personal Injury Ch. 7-J, J. Arbitration of Uninsured Motorist Claims.
Rutter, Cal. Practice Guide: Personal Injury Ch. 8-A, A. Case Management.
2 Witkin Cal. Proc. 5th Courts § 191, (S 191) Civil Rules.
7 Witkin Cal. Proc. 5th Trial § 38, (S 38) Trial Court Delay Reduction Act.
7 Witkin Cal. Proc. 5th Trial § 42, (S 42) in General.

Rule 3.711.   Local court rules

Each court must adopt local rules on differential case management as provided in this chapter consistent with the rules on case management in chapter 3 of this division and standard 2.1 of the California Standards of Judicial Administration.   *(Formerly Rule 2102, adopted, eff. July 1, 1991.   As amended, eff. Jan. 1, 1994; eff. Jan. 1, 2000.   Renumbered Rule 206 and amended, eff. July 1, 2002.   Renumbered Rule 3.711 and amended, eff. Jan. 1, 2007.)*

Research References

Rutter, Cal. Practice Guide: Civ. Pro. Before Trial Ch. 12(I)-A, A. Rules Governing Trial Setting Process.
Rutter, Cal. Practice Guide: Civ. Pro. Before Trial Ch. 12(I)-B, B. Case Management ("Fast Track") System.
Rutter, Cal. Practice Guide: Personal Injury Ch. 8-A, A. Case Management.
2 Witkin Cal. Proc. 5th Courts § 199, (S 199) in General.
2 Witkin Cal. Proc. 5th Courts § 263, (S 263) Differential Case Management.

Rule 3.712.   Application and exceptions

(a)   General application

The rules in this chapter apply to all general civil cases filed in the trial courts except those specified in (b), (c), and (d) and except those specified types or categories of general civil cases that have been exempted from the case management rules under rule 3.720(b).

(b)   Uninsured motorist cases

To allow for arbitration of the plaintiff's claim, the rules in this chapter do not apply to a case designated by the court as "uninsured motorist" until 180 days after the designation.

(c)   Coordinated cases

The rules in this chapter do not apply to any case included in a petition for coordination.   If the petition is granted, the coordination trial judge may establish a case progression plan for the cases, which may be assigned for review under the case management rules in chapter 3 of this division or, after appropriate findings, for treatment as an exceptional case.

(d)   Collections cases

The rules in this chapter do not apply to a collections case, as defined in rule 3.740(a), unless a defendant files a responsive pleading.   *(Formerly Rule 2103, adopted, eff. July 1, 1991.   As amended, eff. Jan. 1, 1994.   Renumbered Rule 207 and amended, eff. July 1, 2002.   Renumbered Rule 3.712 and amended, eff. Jan. 1, 2007.   As amended, eff. July 1, 2007; Feb. 26, 2013.)*

Research References

Rutter, Cal. Practice Guide: Civ. Pro. Before Trial Ch. 12(I)-B, B. Case Management ("Fast Track") System.
Rutter, Cal. Practice Guide: Enforcing Judgments/Debts Ch. 3-C, C. Prelawsuit Considerations.
Rutter, Cal. Practice Guide: Personal Injury Ch. 7-J, J. Arbitration of Uninsured Motorist Claims.
Rutter, Cal. Practice Guide: Personal Injury Ch. 8-A, A. Case Management.
2 Witkin Cal. Proc. 5th Courts § 263, (S 263) Differential Case Management.

Rule 3.713.   Delay reduction goals

(a)   Case management goals

The rules in this chapter are adopted to advance the goals of Government Code section 68607 and standard 2.1 of the California Standards of Judicial Administration.

(b)   Case disposition time goals

The goal of the court is to manage general civil cases from filing to disposition as provided under standard 2.2 of the California Standards of Judicial Administration.

(c)   Judges' responsibility

It is the responsibility of judges to achieve a just and effective resolution of each general civil case through active management and supervision of the pace of litigation from the date of filing to disposition. *(Formerly Rule 2104, adopted, eff. July 1, 1991. As amended, eff. Jan. 1, 1994. Renumbered Rule 208 and amended, eff. July 1, 2002. As amended, eff. Jan. 1, 2004. Renumbered Rule 3.713 and amended, eff. Jan. 1, 2007.)*

Research References

Rutter, Cal. Practice Guide: Civ. Pro. Before Trial Ch. 12(I)-B, B. Case Management ("Fast Track") System.
2 Witkin Cal. Proc. 5th Courts § 263, (S 263) Differential Case Management.

Rule 3.714.   Differentiation of cases to achieve goals

(a) Evaluation and assignment

The court must evaluate each case on its own merits as provided in rule 3.715, under procedures adopted by local court rules. After evaluation, the court must:

(1) Assign the case to the case management program for review under the case management rules in chapter 3 of this division for disposition under the case disposition time goals in (b) of this rule;

(2) Exempt the case as an exceptional case under (c) of this rule from the case disposition time goals specified in rule 3.713(b) and monitor it with the goal of disposing of it within three years; or

(3) Assign the case under (d) of this rule to a local case management plan for disposition within six to nine months after filing.

(b) Civil case disposition time goals

Civil cases assigned for review under the case management rules in chapter 3 of this division should be managed so as to achieve the following goals:

(1) *Unlimited civil cases*

The goal of each trial court should be to manage unlimited civil cases from filing so that:

(A) 75 percent are disposed of within 12 months;

(B) 85 percent are disposed of within 18 months; and

(C) 100 percent are disposed of within 24 months.

(2) *Limited civil cases*

The goal of each trial court should be to manage limited civil cases from filing so that:

(A) 90 percent are disposed of within 12 months;

(B) 98 percent are disposed of within 18 months; and

(C) 100 percent are disposed of within 24 months.

(3) *Individualized case management*

The goals in (1) and (2) are guidelines for the court's disposition of all unlimited and limited civil cases filed in that court. In managing individual civil cases, the court must consider each case on its merits. To enable the fair and efficient resolution of civil cases, each case should be set for trial as soon as appropriate for that individual case consistent with rule 3.729.

(c) Exemption of exceptional cases

(1) The court may in the interest of justice exempt a general civil case from the case disposition time goals under rule 3.713(b) if it finds the case involves exceptional circumstances that will prevent the court and the parties from meeting the goals and deadlines imposed by the program. In making the determination, the court is guided by rules 3.715 and 3.400.

(2) If the court exempts the case from the case disposition time goals, the court must establish a case progression plan and monitor the case to ensure timely disposition consistent with the exceptional circumstances, with the goal of disposing of the case within three years.

(d) Local case management plan for expedited case disposition

(1) For expedited case disposition, the court may by local rule adopt a case management plan that establishes a goal for disposing of appropriate cases within six to nine months after filing. The plan must establish a procedure to identify the cases to be assigned to the plan.

(2) The plan must be used only for uncomplicated cases amenable to early disposition that do not need a case management conference or review or similar event to guide the case to early resolution. *(Formerly Rule 2105, adopted, eff. July 1, 1991. As amended, eff. Jan. 1, 1994; eff. Jan. 1, 2000. Renumbered Rule 209 and amended, eff. July 1, 2002. As amended, eff. Jan. 1, 2004. Renumbered Rule 3.714 and amended, eff. Jan. 1, 2007.)*

Research References

Rutter, Cal. Practice Guide: A.D.R. Ch. 6-B, B. Temporary Judges.
Rutter, Cal. Practice Guide: A.D.R. Ch. 6-C, C. Referees.
Rutter, Cal. Practice Guide: Civ. Pro. Before Trial Ch. 12(I)-B, B. Case Management ("Fast Track") System.
Rutter, Cal. Practice Guide: Personal Injury Ch. 8-A, A. Case Management.
2 Witkin Cal. Proc. 5th Courts § 263, (S 263) Differential Case Management.

Rule 3.715.   Case evaluation factors

(a) Time estimate

In applying rule 3.714, the court must estimate the maximum time that will reasonably be required to dispose of each case in a just and effective manner. The court must consider the following factors and any other information the court deems relevant, understanding that no one factor or set of factors will be controlling and that cases may have unique characteristics incapable of precise definition:

(1) Type and subject matter of the action;

(2) Number of causes of action or affirmative defenses alleged;

(3) Number of parties with separate interests;

(4) Number of cross-complaints and the subject matter;

(5) Complexity of issues, including issues of first impression;

(6) Difficulty in identifying, locating, and serving parties;

(7) Nature and extent of discovery anticipated;

(8) Number and location of percipient and expert witnesses;

(9) Estimated length of trial;

(10) Whether some or all issues can be arbitrated or resolved through other alternative dispute resolution processes;

(11) Statutory priority for the issues;

(12) Likelihood of review by writ or appeal;

(13) Amount in controversy and the type of remedy sought, including measures of damages;

(14) Pendency of other actions or proceedings that may affect the case;

(15) Nature and extent of law and motion proceedings anticipated;

(16) Nature and extent of the injuries and damages;

(17) Pendency of underinsured claims; and

(18) Any other factor that would affect the time for disposition of the case. *(Formerly Rule 2106, adopted, eff. July 1, 1991.*

Ct. Rules

Renumbered Rule 210 and amended, eff. July 1, 2002. Renumbered Rule 3.715 and amended, eff. Jan. 1, 2007.)

Research References

Rutter, Cal. Practice Guide: Civ. Pro. Before Trial Ch. 12(I)-B, B. Case Management ("Fast Track") System.

Rutter, Cal. Practice Guide: Enforcing Judgments/Debts Ch. 3-C, C. Prelawsuit Considerations.

Rutter, Cal. Practice Guide: Personal Injury Ch. 8-A, A. Case Management.

2 Witkin Cal. Proc. 5th Courts § 191, (S 191) Civil Rules.

2 Witkin Cal. Proc. 5th Courts § 263, (S 263) Differential Case Management.

Chapter 3

CASE MANAGEMENT

Rule
3.720.   Application.
3.721.   Case management review.
3.722.   Case management conference.
3.723.   Additional case management conferences.
3.724.   Duty to meet and confer.
3.725.   Case Management Statement.
3.726.   Stipulation to alternative dispute resolution.
3.727.   Subjects to be considered at the case management conference.
3.728.   Case management order.
3.729.   Setting the trial date.
3.730.   Case management order controls.
3.734.   Assignment to one judge for all or limited purposes.
3.735.   Management of short cause cases.

Rule 3.720.   Application

(a)   General application

The rules in this chapter prescribe the procedures for the management of all applicable court cases. These rules may be referred to as "the case management rules."

(b)   Emergency suspension of rules

A court by local rule may exempt specified types or categories of general civil cases filed before January 1, 2016, from the case management rules in this chapter, provided that the court has in place alternative procedures for case processing and trial setting for such actions, including, without limitation, compliance with Code of Civil Procedure sections 1141.10 et seq. and 1775 et seq. The court must post the alternative procedures on its website.

(c)   Rules when case management conference set

In any case in which a court sets an initial case management conference, the rules in this chapter apply. *(Adopted, eff. Jan. 1, 2007. As amended, eff. Feb. 26, 2013.)*

Advisory Committee Comment

Subdivision (b) of this rule is an emergency measure in response to the limited fiscal resources available to the courts as a result of the current fiscal crisis and is not intended as a permanent change in the case.

Research References

Rutter, Cal. Practice Guide: Civ. Pro. Before Trial Ch. 7(I)-C, C. Motion for Judgment on the Pleadings.

Rutter, Cal. Practice Guide: Civil Trials & Evidence Ch. 4-I, I. Other Motions at Final Status Conference.

Rutter, Cal. Practice Guide: Personal Injury Ch. 8-A, A. Case Management.

Rutter, Cal. Practice Guide: Personal Injury Ch. 9-B, B. In-Chambers Conference Before Commencement of Trial.

2 Witkin Cal. Proc. 5th Courts § 191, (S 191) Civil Rules.

2 Witkin Cal. Proc. 5th Courts § 263, (S 263) Differential Case Management.

Rule 3.721.   Case management review

In every general civil case except complex cases and cases exempted under rules 3.712(b)–(d), 3.714(c)–(d), 3.735(b), 2.573(e), and 3.740(c), the court must review the case no later than 180 days after the filing of the initial complaint *(Adopted, eff. Jan. 1, 2007. As amended, eff. July 1, 2007.)*

Research References

Rutter, Cal. Practice Guide: A.D.R. Ch. 1-B, B. Why ADR?

Rutter, Cal. Practice Guide: A.D.R. Ch. 4-A, A. General Considerations.

Rutter, Cal. Practice Guide: Civ. Pro. Before Trial Ch. 12(I)-B, B. Case Management ("Fast Track") System.

Rutter, Cal. Practice Guide: Enforcing Judgments/Debts Ch. 3-C, C. Prelawsuit Considerations.

Rutter, Cal. Practice Guide: Personal Injury Ch. 8-A, A. Case Management.

7 Witkin Cal. Proc. 5th Trial § 45, Current Procedure.

Rule 3.722.   Case management conference

(a)   The initial conference

In each case, the court must set an initial case management conference to review the case. At the conference, the court must review the case comprehensively and decide whether to assign the case to an alternative dispute resolution process, whether to set the case for trial, and whether to take action regarding any of the other matters identified in rules 3.727 and 3.728. The initial case management conference should generally be the first case management event conducted by court order in each case, except for orders to show cause.

(b)   Notice of the initial conference

Notice of the date of the initial case management conference must be given to all parties no later than 45 days before the conference, unless otherwise ordered by the court. The court may provide by local rule for the time and manner of giving notice to the parties.

(c)   Preparation for the conference

At the conference, counsel for each party and each self-represented party must appear by telephone or personally as provided in rule 3.670; must be familiar with the case; and must be prepared to discuss and commit to the party's position on the issues listed in rules 3.724 and 3.727.

(d)   Case management order without appearance

If, based on its review of the written submissions of the parties and such other information as is available, the court determines that appearances at the conference are not necessary, the court may issue a case management order and notify the parties that no appearance is required.

(e)   Option to excuse attendance at initial conferences in limited civil cases

By local rule the court may provide that counsel and self-represented parties are not to attend an initial case management conference in limited civil cases unless ordered to do so by the court. *(Adopted, eff. Jan. 1, 2007. As amended, eff. Jan. 1, 2008.)*

Research References

Rutter, Cal. Practice Guide: A.D.R. Ch. 1-B, B. Why ADR?

Rutter, Cal. Practice Guide: Civ. Pro. Before Trial Ch. 12(I)-B, B. Case Management ("Fast Track") System.

Rutter, Cal. Practice Guide: Personal Injury Ch. 8-A, A. Case Management.

7 Witkin Cal. Proc. 5th Trial § 45, Current Procedure.

Rule 3.723.   Additional case management conferences

The court on its own motion may order, or a party or parties may request, that an additional case management conference be held at any time.   A party should be required to appear at an additional conference only if an appearance is necessary for the effective management of the case.   In determining whether to hold an additional conference, the court must consider each case individually on its own merits.   *(Adopted, eff. Jan. 1, 2007.)*

Advisory Committee Comment

Regarding additional case management conferences, in many civil cases one initial conference and one other conference before trial will be sufficient.   But in other cases, including complicated or difficult cases, the court may order an additional case management conference or conferences if that would promote the fair and efficient administration of the case.

Research References

Rutter, Cal. Practice Guide: Civ. Pro. Before Trial Ch. 12(I)-B, B. Case Management ("Fast Track") System.
Rutter, Cal. Practice Guide: Personal Injury Ch. 8-A, A. Case Management.
7 Witkin Cal. Proc. 5th Trial § 45, Current Procedure.

Rule 3.724.   Duty to meet and confer

Unless the court orders another time period, no later than 30 calendar days before the date set for the initial case management conference, the parties must meet and confer, in person or by telephone, to consider each of the issues identified in rule 3.727 and, in addition, to consider the following:

(1) Resolving any discovery disputes and setting a discovery schedule;

(2) Identifying and, if possible, informally resolving any anticipated motions;

(3) Identifying the facts and issues in the case that are uncontested and may be the subject of stipulation;

(4) Identifying the facts and issues in the case that are in dispute;

(5) Determining whether the issues in the case can be narrowed by eliminating any claims or defenses by means of a motion or otherwise;

(6) Determining whether settlement is possible;

(7) Identifying the dates on which all parties and their attorneys are available or not available for trial, including the reasons for unavailability;

(8) Any issues relating to the discovery of electronically stored information, including:

(A) Issues relating to the preservation of discoverable electronically stored information;

(B) The form or forms in which information will be produced;

(C) The time within which the information will be produced;

(D) The scope of discovery of the information;

(E) The method for asserting or preserving claims of privilege or attorney work product, including whether such claims may be asserted after production;

(F) The method for asserting or preserving the confidentiality, privacy, trade secrets, or proprietary status of information relating to a party or person not a party to the civil proceedings;

(G) How the cost of production of electronically stored information is to be allocated among the parties;

(H) Any other issues relating to the discovery of electronically stored information, including developing a proposed plan relating to the discovery of the information; and

(9) Other relevant matters.   *(Adopted, eff. Jan. 1, 2007.   As amended, eff. Aug. 14, 2009.)*

Research References

Rutter, Cal. Practice Guide: A.D.R. Ch. 1-B, B. Why ADR?
Rutter, Cal. Practice Guide: A.D.R. Ch. 4-A, A. General Considerations.
Rutter, Cal. Practice Guide: Civ. Pro. Before Trial Ch. 8H-2, What May be Inspected.
Rutter, Cal. Practice Guide: Civ. Pro. Before Trial Ch. 12(I)-B, B. Case Management ("Fast Track") System.
Rutter, Cal. Practice Guide: Personal Injury Ch. 8-A, A. Case Management.
7 Witkin Cal. Proc. 5th Trial § 45, Current Procedure.

Rule 3.725.   Case Management Statement

(a) Timing of statement

No later than 15 calendar days before the date set for the case management conference or review, each party must file a case management statement and serve it on all other parties in the case.

(b) Joint statement

In lieu of each party's filing a separate case management statement, any two or more parties may file a joint statement.

(c) Contents of statement

Parties must use the mandatory *Case Management Statement* (form CM–110).   All applicable items on the form must be completed.   *(Adopted, eff. Jan. 1, 2007.)*

Research References

Rutter, Cal. Practice Guide: A.D.R. Ch. 1-B, B. Why ADR?
Rutter, Cal. Practice Guide: A.D.R. Ch. 4-A, A. General Considerations.
Rutter, Cal. Practice Guide: A.D.R. Ch. 4-B, B. Judicial Arbitration.
Rutter, Cal. Practice Guide: Civ. Pro. Before Trial Ch. 12(I)-B, B. Case Management ("Fast Track") System.
Rutter, Cal. Practice Guide: Civil Trials & Evidence Ch. 1-A, A. Importance of Statewide and Local Rules of Court.
Rutter, Cal. Practice Guide: Civil Trials & Evidence Ch. 2-D, D. Securing Trial by Jury.
Rutter, Cal. Practice Guide: Personal Injury Ch. 8-A, A. Case Management.
7 Witkin Cal. Proc. 5th Trial § 45, Current Procedure.

Rule 3.726.   Stipulation to alternative dispute resolution

If all parties agree to use an alternative dispute resolution (ADR) process, they must jointly complete the ADR stipulation form provided for under rule 3.221 and file it with the court. *(Adopted, eff. Jan. 1, 2007.)*

Research References

Rutter, Cal. Practice Guide: A.D.R. Ch. 1-B, B. Why ADR?
Rutter, Cal. Practice Guide: A.D.R. Ch. 4-A, A. General Considerations.
Rutter, Cal. Practice Guide: A.D.R. Ch. 4-B, B. Judicial Arbitration.
Rutter, Cal. Practice Guide: Civ. Pro. Before Trial Ch. 12(I)-B, B. Case Management ("Fast Track") System.

Rule 3.727.   Subjects to be considered at the case management conference

In any case management conference or review conducted under this chapter, the parties must address, if applicable, and the court may take appropriate action with respect to, the following:

(1) Whether there are any related cases;

(2) Whether all parties named in the complaint or cross-complaint have been served, have appeared, or have been dismissed;

(3) Whether any additional parties may be added or the pleadings may be amended;

(4) Whether, if the case is a limited civil case, the economic litigation procedures under Code of Civil Procedure section 90 et seq. will apply to it or the party intends to bring a motion to exempt the case from these procedures;

(5) Whether any other matters (e.g., the bankruptcy of a party) may affect the court's jurisdiction or processing of the case;

(6) Whether the parties have stipulated to, or the case should be referred to, judicial arbitration in courts having a judicial arbitration program or to any other form of alternative dispute resolution (ADR) process and, if so, the date by which the judicial arbitration or other ADR process must be completed;

(7) Whether an early settlement conference should be scheduled and, if so, on what date;

(8) Whether discovery has been completed and, if not, the date by which it will be completed;

(9) What discovery issues are anticipated;

(10) Whether the case should be bifurcated or a hearing should be set for a motion to bifurcate under Code of Civil Procedure section 598;

(11) Whether there are any cross-complaints that are not ready to be set for trial and, if so, whether they should be severed;

(12) Whether the case is entitled to any statutory preference and, if so, the statute granting the preference;

(13) Whether a jury trial is demanded, and, if so, the identity of each party requesting a jury trial;

(14) If the trial date has not been previously set, the date by which the case will be ready for trial and the available trial dates;

(15) The estimated length of trial;

(16) The nature of the injuries;

(17) The amount of damages, including any special or punitive damages;

(18) Any additional relief sought;

(19) Whether there are any insurance coverage issues that may affect the resolution of the case; and

(20) Any other matters that should be considered by the court or addressed in its case management order. *(Adopted, eff. Jan. 1, 2007.)*

Research References

Rutter, Cal. Practice Guide: A.D.R. Ch. 1-B, B. Why ADR?
Rutter, Cal. Practice Guide: A.D.R. Ch. 4-A, A. General Considerations.
Rutter, Cal. Practice Guide: A.D.R. Ch. 4-B, B. Judicial Arbitration.
Rutter, Cal. Practice Guide: Civ. Pro. Before Trial Ch. 13-C, C. Civil Proceedings Subject to Judicial Arbitration.
Rutter, Cal. Practice Guide: Civ. Pro. Before Trial Ch. 12(I)-B, B. Case Management ("Fast Track") System.
Rutter, Cal. Practice Guide: Civ. Pro. Before Trial Ch. 12(I)-C, C. Claims for Trial Setting Preference.
Rutter, Cal. Practice Guide: Civ. Pro. Before Trial Ch. 12(I)-E, E. Consolidation, Coordination and Bifurcation.
Rutter, Cal. Practice Guide: Civil Trials & Evidence Ch. 1-A, A. Importance of Statewide and Local Rules of Court.
Rutter, Cal. Practice Guide: Civil Trials & Evidence Ch. 2-D, D. Securing Trial by Jury.
Rutter, Cal. Practice Guide: Personal Injury Ch. 4-C, C. Effective Settlement Negotiations.

Rutter, Cal. Practice Guide: Personal Injury Ch. 7-D, D. Screening Cases for Judicial Arbitration.
Rutter, Cal. Practice Guide: Personal Injury Ch. 8-A, A. Case Management.
7 Witkin Cal. Proc. 5th Trial § 45, Current Procedure.
7 Witkin Cal. Proc. 5th Trial § 66, (S 66) in General.
7 Witkin Cal. Proc. 5th Trial § 73, (S 73) Motion to Advance or Reset.

Rule 3.728. Case management order

The case management conference must be conducted in the manner provided by local rule. The court must enter a case management order setting a schedule for subsequent proceedings and otherwise providing for the management of the case. The order may include appropriate provisions, such as:

(1) Referral of the case to judicial arbitration or other alternative dispute resolution process;

(2) A date for completion of the judicial arbitration process or other alternative dispute resolution process if the case has been referred to such a process;

(3) In the event that a trial date has not previously been set, a date certain for trial if the case is ready to be set for trial;

(4) Whether the trial will be a jury trial or a nonjury trial;

(5) The identity of each party demanding a jury trial;

(6) The estimated length of trial;

(7) Whether all parties necessary to the disposition of the case have been served or have appeared;

(8) The dismissal or severance of unserved or not-appearing defendants from the action;

(9) The names and addresses of the attorneys who will try the case;

(10) The date, time, and place for a mandatory settlement conference as provided in rule 3.1380;

(11) The date, time, and place for the final case management conference before trial if such a conference is required by the court or the judge assigned to the case;

(12) The date, time, and place of any further case management conferences or review; and

(13) Any additional orders that may be appropriate, including orders on matters listed in rules 3.724 and 3.727. *(Adopted, eff. Jan. 1, 2007.)*

Research References

Rutter, Cal. Practice Guide: A.D.R. Ch. 1-B, B. Why ADR?
Rutter, Cal. Practice Guide: A.D.R. Ch. 4-B, B. Judicial Arbitration.
Rutter, Cal. Practice Guide: Civ. Pro. Before Trial Ch. 1-A, A. Accepting a New Case.
Rutter, Cal. Practice Guide: Civ. Pro. Before Trial Ch. 1-B, B. Prelawsuit Investigations, Research and Analysis.
Rutter, Cal. Practice Guide: Civ. Pro. Before Trial Ch. 13-C, C. Civil Proceedings Subject to Judicial Arbitration.
Rutter, Cal. Practice Guide: Civ. Pro. Before Trial Ch. 12(I)-B, B. Case Management ("Fast Track") System.
Rutter, Cal. Practice Guide: Civil Trials & Evidence Ch. 1-A, A. Importance of Statewide and Local Rules of Court.
Rutter, Cal. Practice Guide: Civil Trials & Evidence Ch. 2-D, D. Securing Trial by Jury.
Rutter, Cal. Practice Guide: Civil Trials & Evidence Ch. 4-A, A. General Considerations.
Rutter, Cal. Practice Guide: Personal Injury Ch. 7-D, D. Screening Cases for Judicial Arbitration.
Rutter, Cal. Practice Guide: Personal Injury Ch. 8-A, A. Case Management.
Rutter, Cal. Practice Guide: Personal Injury Ch. 9-L, L. Motions to Terminate Trial Before Verdict.
7 Witkin Cal. Proc. 5th Trial § 45, Current Procedure.
7 Witkin Cal. Proc. 5th Trial § 47, Preparation of Conference Order.
7 Witkin Cal. Proc. 5th Trial § 54, (S 54) in General.

Rule 3.729. Setting the trial date

In setting a case for trial, the court, at the initial case management conference or at any other proceeding at which the case is set for trial, must consider all the facts and circumstances that are relevant. These may include:

(1) The type and subject matter of the action to be tried;

(2) Whether the case has statutory priority;

(3) The number of causes of action, cross-actions, and affirmative defenses that will be tried;

(4) Whether any significant amendments to the pleadings have been made recently or are likely to be made before trial;

(5) Whether the plaintiff intends to bring a motion to amend the complaint to seek punitive damages under Code of Civil Procedure section 425.13;

(6) The number of parties with separate interests who will be involved in the trial;

(7) The complexity of the issues to be tried, including issues of first impression;

(8) Any difficulties in identifying, locating, or serving parties;

(9) Whether all parties have been served and, if so, the date by which they were served;

(10) Whether all parties have appeared in the action and, if so, the date by which they appeared;

(11) How long the attorneys who will try the case have been involved in the action;

(12) The trial date or dates proposed by the parties and their attorneys;

(13) The professional and personal schedules of the parties and their attorneys, including any conflicts with previously assigned trial dates or other significant events;

(14) The amount of discovery, if any, that remains to be conducted in the case;

(15) The nature and extent of law and motion proceedings anticipated, including whether any motions for summary judgment will be filed;

(16) Whether any other actions or proceedings that are pending may affect the case;

(17) The amount in controversy and the type of remedy sought;

(18) The nature and extent of the injuries or damages, including whether these are ready for determination;

(19) The court's trial calendar, including the pendency of other trial dates;

(20) Whether the trial will be a jury or a nonjury trial;

(21) The anticipated length of trial;

(22) The number, availability, and locations of witnesses, including witnesses who reside outside the county, state, or country;

(23) Whether there have been any previous continuances of the trial or delays in setting the case for trial;

(24) The achievement of a fair, timely, and efficient disposition of the case; and

(25) Any other factor that would significantly affect the determination of the appropriate date of trial. *(Adopted, eff. Jan. 1, 2007.)*

Research References

Rutter, Cal. Practice Guide: Civ. Pro. Before Trial Ch. 12(I)-B, B. Case Management ("Fast Track") System.

Rutter, Cal. Practice Guide: Civ. Pro. Before Trial Ch. 12(I)-C, C. Claims for Trial Setting Preference.

Rutter, Cal. Practice Guide: Civil Trials & Evidence Ch. 1-A, A. Importance of Statewide and Local Rules of Court.

Rutter, Cal. Practice Guide: Personal Injury Ch. 8-A, A. Case Management.

7 Witkin Cal. Proc. 5th Trial § 54, (S 54) in General.

Rule 3.730. Case management order controls

The order issued after the case management conference or review controls the subsequent course of the action or proceeding unless it is modified by a subsequent order. *(Adopted, eff. Jan. 1, 2007.)*

Research References

Rutter, Cal. Practice Guide: Civ. Pro. Before Trial Ch. 7(I)-C, C. Motion for Judgment on the Pleadings.

Rutter, Cal. Practice Guide: Civ. Pro. Before Trial Ch. 12(I)-B, B. Case Management ("Fast Track") System.

Rutter, Cal. Practice Guide: Civil Trials & Evidence Ch. 4-I, I. Other Motions at Final Status Conference.

Rutter, Cal. Practice Guide: Enforcing Judgments/Debts Ch. 3-C, C. Prelawsuit Considerations.

Rutter, Cal. Practice Guide: Personal Injury Ch. 8-A, A. Case Management.

Rutter, Cal. Practice Guide: Personal Injury Ch. 9-B, B. In-Chambers Conference Before Commencement of Trial.

7 Witkin Cal. Proc. 5th Trial § 48, (S 48) in General.

Rule 3.734. Assignment to one judge for all or limited purposes

The presiding judge may, on the noticed motion of a party or on the court's own motion, order the assignment of any case to one judge for all or such limited purposes as will promote the efficient administration of justice. *(Formerly Rule 213, adopted, eff. Jan. 1, 1985. As amended, eff. July 1, 2002. Renumbered Rule 3.734 and amended, eff. Jan. 1, 2007.)*

Research References

Rutter, Cal. Practice Guide: Civ. Pro. Before Trial Ch. 12(I)-B, B. Case Management ("Fast Track") System.

Rutter, Cal. Practice Guide: Civil Trials & Evidence Ch. 3-B, B. Peremptory Challenge of Judge (CCP § 170.6).

7 Witkin Cal. Proc. 5th Trial § 39, (S 39) Management and Distribution of Court Business.

Rule 3.735. Management of short cause cases

(a) Short cause case defined

A short cause case is a civil case in which the time estimated for trial by all parties or the court is five hours or less. All other civil cases are long cause cases.

(b) Exemption for short cause case and setting of case for trial

The court may order, upon the stipulation of all parties or the court's own motion, that a case is a short cause case exempted from the requirements of case management review and set the case for trial.

(c) Mistrial

If a short cause case is not completely tried within five hours, the judge may declare a mistrial or, in the judge's discretion, may complete the trial. In the event of a mistrial, the case will be treated as a long cause case and must promptly be set either for a new trial or for a case management conference. *(Formerly Rule 214, adopted, eff. July 1, 2002. Renumbered Rule 3.735 and amended, eff. Jan. 1, 2007.)*

Research References

Rutter, Cal. Practice Guide: Civ. Pro. Before Trial Ch. 12(I)-B, B. Case Management ("Fast Track") System.

Ct. Rules

Rutter, Cal. Practice Guide: Personal Injury Ch. 8-A, A. Case Management.

2 Witkin Cal. Proc. 5th Courts § 191, (S 191) Civil Rules.

7 Witkin Cal. Proc. 5th Trial § 55, (S 55) Short and Long Causes.

Chapter 4

MANAGEMENT OF COLLECTIONS CASES

Rule

3.740. Collections cases.

3.741. Settlement of collections case.

Rule 3.740. Collections cases

(a) Definition

"Collections case" means an action for recovery of money owed in a sum stated to be certain that is not more than $25,000, exclusive of interest and attorney fees, arising from a transaction in which property, services, or money was acquired on credit. A collections case does not include an action seeking any of the following:

(1) Tort damages;

(2) Punitive damages;

(3) Recovery of real property;

(4) Recovery of personal property; or

(5) A prejudgment writ of attachment.

(b) *Civil Case Cover Sheet*

If a case meets the definition in (a), a plaintiff must check the case type box on the *Civil Case Cover Sheet* (form CM–010) to indicate that the case is a collections case under rule 3.740 and serve the *Civil Case Cover Sheet* (form CM–010) with the initial complaint.

(c) Exemption from general time-for-service requirement and case management rules

A collections case is exempt from:

(1) The time-for-service requirement of rule 3.110(b); and

(2) The case management rules that apply to all general civil cases under rules 3.712–3.715 and 3.721–3.730, unless a defendant files a responsive pleading.

(d) Time for service

The complaint in a collections case must be served on all named defendants, and proofs of service on those defendants must be filed, or the plaintiff must obtain an order for publication of the summons, within 180 days after the filing of the complaint.

(e) Effect of failure to serve within required time

If proofs of service on all defendants are not filed or the plaintiff has not obtained an order for publication of the summons within 180 days after the filing of the complaint, the court may issue an order to show cause why reasonable monetary sanctions should not be imposed. If proofs of service on all defendants are filed or an order for publication of the summons is filed at least 10 court days before the order to show cause hearing, the court must continue the hearing to 360 days after the filing of the complaint.

(f) Effect of failure to obtain default judgment within required time

If proofs of service of the complaint are filed or service by publication is made and defendants do not file responsive pleadings, the plaintiff must obtain a default judgment within 360 days after the filing of the complaint. If the plaintiff has not obtained a default judgment by that time, the court must issue an order to show cause why reasonable monetary sanctions should not be imposed. The order to show cause must be vacated if the plaintiff obtains a default judgment at least 10 court days before the order to show cause hearing. *(Adopted, eff. July 1, 2007. As amended, eff. Jan. 1, 2009.)*

Research References

Rutter, Cal. Practice Guide: Civ. Pro. Before Trial Ch. 4-A, A. Requirements-In General.

Rutter, Cal. Practice Guide: Civ. Pro. Before Trial Ch. 4-D, D. Service of Summons.

Rutter, Cal. Practice Guide: Civ. Pro. Before Trial Ch. 5-A, A. General.

Rutter, Cal. Practice Guide: Civ. Pro. Before Trial Ch. 6-B, B. Complaints.

Rutter, Cal. Practice Guide: Civ. Pro. Before Trial Ch. 11-B, B. Involuntary Dismissals.

Rutter, Cal. Practice Guide: Civ. Pro. Before Trial Ch. 12(I)-B, B. Case Management ("Fast Track") System.

Rutter, Cal. Practice Guide: Enforcing Judgments/Debts Ch. 3-C, C. Prelawsuit Considerations.

2 Witkin Cal. Proc. 5th Courts § 191, (S 191) Civil Rules.

2 Witkin Cal. Proc. 5th Courts § 263, (S 263) Differential Case Management.

4 Witkin Cal. Proc. 5th Pleading § 18, Other Requirements.

7 Witkin Cal. Proc. 5th Trial § 42, (S 42) in General.

Rule 3.741. Settlement of collections case

If the plaintiff or other party seeking affirmative relief in a case meeting the definition of "collections case" in rule 3.740(a) files a notice of settlement under rule 3.1385, including a conditional settlement, the court must vacate all hearing, case management conference, and trial dates. *(Adopted, eff. July 1, 2007.)*

Research References

Rutter, Cal. Practice Guide: Civ. Pro. Before Trial Ch. 12(II)-D, D. Plaintiff's Duties Upon Settlement.

Rutter, Cal. Practice Guide: Enforcing Judgments/Debts Ch. 3-C, C. Prelawsuit Considerations.

2 Witkin Cal. Proc. 5th Courts § 191, (S 191) Civil Rules.

7 Witkin Cal. Proc. 5th Trial § 41, Notice of Settlement or Stay.

Chapter 5

MANAGEMENT OF COMPLEX CASES

Rule

3.750. Initial case management conference.

3.751. Electronic service.

Rule 3.750. Initial case management conference

(a) Timing of conference

The court in a complex case should hold an initial case management conference with all parties represented at the earliest practical date.

(b) Subjects for consideration

At the conference, the court should consider the following subjects:

(1) Whether all parties named in the complaint or cross-complaint have been served, have appeared, or have been dismissed;

(2) Whether any additional parties may be added or the pleadings may be amended;

(3) The deadline for the filing of any remaining pleadings and service of any additional parties;

(4) Whether severance, consolidation, or coordination with other actions is desirable;

(5) The schedule for discovery proceedings to avoid duplication and whether discovery should be stayed until all parties have been brought into the case;

(6) The schedule for settlement conferences or alternative dispute resolution;

(7) Whether to appoint liaison or lead counsel;

(8) The date for the filing of any dispositive motions;

(9) The creation of preliminary and updated lists of the persons to be deposed and the subjects to be addressed in each deposition;

(10) The exchange of documents and whether to establish an electronic document depository;

(11) Whether a special master should be appointed and the purposes for such appointment;

(12) Whether to establish a case-based Web site and other means to provide a current master list of addresses and telephone numbers of counsel; and

(13) The schedule for further conferences.

(c) Objects of conference

Principal objects of the initial case management conference are to expose at an early date the essential issues in the litigation and to avoid unnecessary and burdensome discovery procedures in the course of preparing for trial of those issues.

(d) Meet and confer requirement

The court may order counsel to meet privately before the initial case management conference to discuss the items specified in (a) and to prepare a joint statement of matters agreed upon, matters on which the court must rule at the conference, and a description of the major legal and factual issues involved in the litigation. *(Adopted, eff. Jan. 1, 2007.)*

Research References

Rutter, Cal. Practice Guide: Civ. Pro. Before Trial Ch. 12(I)-B, B. Case Management ("Fast Track") System.
2 Witkin Cal. Proc. 5th Courts § 191, (S 191) Civil Rules.
7 Witkin Cal. Proc. 5th Trial § 6, Complex Litigation.
7 Witkin Cal. Proc. 5th Trial § 46, Complex Cases.

Rule 3.751.   Electronic service

The court may provide in a case management order that documents filed electronically in a central electronic depository available to all parties are deemed served on all parties. *(Formerly Rule 1830, adopted, eff. Jan. 1, 2000. Renumbered Rule 3.751, eff. Jan. 1, 2007.)*

Research References

Rutter, Cal. Practice Guide: Civ. Pro. Before Trial Ch. 12(I)-B, B. Case Management ("Fast Track") System.
2 Witkin Cal. Proc. 5th Courts § 191, (S 191) Civil Rules.
4 Witkin Cal. Proc. 5th Pleading § 364, What Constitutes Complex Case.
7 Witkin Cal. Proc. 5th Trial § 46, Complex Cases.

Chapter 6

MANAGEMENT OF CLASS ACTIONS

Rule
3.760.   Application.
3.761.   Form of complaint.
3.762.   Case conference.
3.763.   Conference order.
3.764.   Motion to certify or decertify a class or amend or modify an order certifying a class.

Rule
3.765.   Class action order.
3.766.   Notice to class members.
3.767.   Orders in the conduct of class actions.
3.768.   Discovery from unnamed class members.
3.769.   Settlement of class actions.
3.770.   Dismissal of class actions.
3.771.   Judgment.

Rule 3.760.   Application

(a) Class actions

The rules in this chapter apply to each class action brought under Civil Code section 1750 et seq. or Code of Civil Procedure section 382 until the court finds the action is not maintainable as a class action or revokes a prior class certification.

(b) Relief from compliance with rules

The court, on its own motion or on motion of any named party, may grant relief from compliance with the rules in this chapter in an appropriate case. *(Formerly Rule 1850, adopted, eff. Jan. 1, 2002. Renumbered Rule 3.760 and amended, eff. Jan. 1, 2007.)*

Research References

Rutter, Cal. Practice Guide: Civ. Pro. Before Trial Ch. 14-B, B. Class Action Requirements-In General.
2 Witkin Cal. Proc. 5th Courts § 191, (S 191) Civil Rules.
4 Witkin Cal. Proc. 5th Pleading § 268, (S 268) California Law and Uniform Act.
4 Witkin Cal. Proc. 5th Pleading § 278, (S 278) in General.
7 Witkin Cal. Proc. 5th Trial § 42, (S 42) in General.

Rule 3.761.   Form of complaint

(a) Caption of pleadings

A complaint for or against a class party must include in the caption the designation "CLASS ACTION." This designation must be in capital letters on the first page of the complaint, immediately below the case number but above the description of the nature of the complaint.

(b) Heading and class action allegations

The complaint in a class action must contain a separate heading entitled "CLASS ACTION ALLEGATIONS," under which the plaintiff describes how the requirements for class certification are met. *(Formerly Rule 1851, adopted, eff. Jan. 1, 2002. Renumbered Rule 3.761, eff. Jan. 1, 2007.)*

Research References

Rutter, Cal. Practice Guide: Civ. Pro. Before Trial Ch. 14-C, C. Procedural Issues.
California Practice Guide: Employment Litigation Ch. 19-H, H. Other Pretrial Procedures.
4 Witkin Cal. Proc. 5th Pleading § 278, (S 278) in General.

Rule 3.762.   Case conference

(a) Purpose

One or more conferences between the court and counsel for the parties may be held to discuss class issues, conduct and scheduling of discovery, scheduling of hearings, and other matters. No evidence may be presented at the conference, but counsel must be fully prepared to discuss class issues and must possess authority to enter into stipulations.

(b) Notice by the parties

Notice of the conference may be given by any party. If notice is given by a named plaintiff, notice must be served on all named parties to the action. If notice is given by a defendant, notice must be served only on the parties who have appeared.

Ct. Rules

Within 10 calendar days after receipt of the notice, the plaintiff must serve a copy on each named party who has not appeared in the action and must file a declaration of service. If the plaintiff is unable to serve any party, the plaintiff must file a declaration stating the reasons for failure of service.

(c) Notice by the court

The court may give notice of the conference to the plaintiff. Within 10 calendar days after receipt of the notice given by the court, the plaintiff must serve a copy of the notice on all parties who have been served in the action, whether they have appeared or not, and must file a declaration of service. If the plaintiff is unable to serve any party, the plaintiff must file a declaration stating the reasons for failure of service.

(d) Timing of notice

The notice must be filed and served on the parties at least 20 calendar days before the scheduled date of the conference.

(e) Timing of conference

A conference may be held at any time after the first defendant has appeared. Before selecting a conference date, the party noticing the conference must:

(1) Obtain prior approval from the clerk of the department assigned to hear the class action; and

(2) Make reasonable efforts to accommodate the schedules of all parties entitled to receive notice under (b). *(Formerly Rule 1852, adopted, eff. Jan. 1, 2002. Renumbered Rule 3.762 and amended, eff. Jan. 1, 2007.)*

Research References

Rutter, Cal. Practice Guide: Civ. Pro. Before Trial Ch. 14-C, C. Procedural Issues.
4 Witkin Cal. Proc. 5th Pleading § 279, (S 279) Case Conference.

Rule 3.763. Conference order

At the conclusion of the conference, the court may make an order:

(1) Approving any stipulations of the parties;

(2) Establishing a schedule for discovery;

(3) Setting the date for the hearing on class certification;

(4) Setting the dates for any subsequent conferences; and

(5) Addressing any other matters related to management of the case. *(Formerly Rule 1853, adopted, eff. Jan. 1, 2002. Renumbered Rule 3.763, eff. Jan. 1, 2007.)*

Research References

Rutter, Cal. Practice Guide: Civ. Pro. Before Trial Ch. 14-C, C. Procedural Issues.
4 Witkin Cal. Proc. 5th Pleading § 279, (S 279) Case Conference.

Rule 3.764. Motion to certify or decertify a class or amend or modify an order certifying a class

(a) Purpose

Any party may file a motion to:

(1) Certify a class;

(2) Determine the existence of and certify subclasses;

(3) Amend or modify an order certifying a class; or

(4) Decertify a class.

(b) Timing of motion, hearing, extension, deferral

A motion for class certification should be filed when practicable. In its discretion, the court may establish a deadline for the filing of the motion, as part of the case conference or as part of other case management proceedings. Any such deadline must take into account discovery proceedings that may be necessary to the filing of the motion.

(c) Format and filing of motion

(1) *Time for service of papers*

Notice of a motion to certify or decertify a class or to amend or modify a certification order must be filed and served on all parties to the action at least 28 calendar days before the date appointed for hearing. Any opposition to the motion must be served and filed at least 14 calendar days before the noticed or continued hearing, unless the court for good cause orders otherwise. Any reply to the opposition must be served and filed at least 5 calendar days before the noticed or continued date of the hearing, unless the court for good cause orders otherwise. The provisions of Code of Civil Procedure section 1005 otherwise apply.

(2) *Length of papers*

An opening or responding memorandum filed in support of or in opposition to a motion for class certification must not exceed 20 pages. A reply memorandum must not exceed 15 pages. The provisions of rule 3.1113 otherwise apply.

(3) *Documents in support*

The documents in support of a motion for class certification consist of the notice of motion; a memorandum; evidence in support of the motion in the form of declarations of counsel, class representatives, or other appropriate declarants; and any requests for judicial notice.

(4) *Documents in opposition*

The documents in opposition to the motion consist of the opposing party's memorandum; the opposing party's evidence in opposition to the motion, including any declarations of counsel or other appropriate declarants; and any requests for judicial notice.

(d) Presentation of evidence

Evidence to be considered at the hearing must be presented in accordance with rule 3.1306.

(e) Stipulations

The parties should endeavor to resolve any uncontroverted issues by written stipulation before the hearing. If all class issues are resolved by stipulation of the named parties and approved by the court before the hearing, no hearing on class certification is necessary. *(Formerly Rule 1854, adopted, eff. Jan. 1, 2002. Renumbered Rule 3.764 and amended, eff. Jan. 1, 2007.)*

Research References

Rutter, Cal. Practice Guide: Civ. Pro. Before Trial Ch. 14-C, C. Procedural Issues.
Rutter, Cal. Practice Guide: Civ. Pro. Before Trial Ch. 9(I)-B, B. Preparing and Filing Motions.
4 Witkin Cal. Proc. 5th Pleading § 307, (S 307) Authority for Motion.
4 Witkin Cal. Proc. 5th Pleading § 313, Motion to Decertify.

Rule 3.765. Class action order

(a) Class described

An order certifying, amending, or modifying a class must contain a description of the class and any subclasses.

(b) Limited issues and subclasses

When appropriate, an action may be maintained as a class action limited to particular issues. A class may be divided into subclasses. *(Formerly Rule 1855, adopted, eff. Jan. 1, 2002. Renumbered Rule 3.765, eff. Jan. 1, 2007.)*

Research References

Rutter, Cal. Practice Guide: Civ. Pro. Before Trial Ch. 14-C, C. Procedural Issues.
4 Witkin Cal. Proc. 5th Pleading § 314, Order and Review of Order.

Rule 3.766.   Notice to class members

(a) Party to provide notice

If the class is certified, the court may require either party to notify the class of the action in the manner specified by the court.

(b) Statement regarding class notice

The class proponent must submit a statement regarding class notice and a proposed notice to class members. The statement must include the following items:

(1) Whether notice is necessary;

(2) Whether class members may exclude themselves from the action;

(3) The time and manner in which notice should be given;

(4) A proposal for which parties should bear the costs of notice; and,

(5) If cost shifting or sharing is proposed under subdivision (4), an estimate of the cost involved in giving notice.

(c) Order

Upon certification of a class, or as soon thereafter as practicable, the court must make an order determining:

(1) Whether notice to class members is necessary;

(2) Whether class members may exclude themselves from the action;

(3) The time and manner of notice;

(4) The content of the notice; and

(5) The parties responsible for the cost of notice.

(d) Content of class notice

The content of the class notice is subject to court approval. If class members are to be given the right to request exclusion from the class, the notice must include the following:

(1) A brief explanation of the case, including the basic contentions or denials of the parties;

(2) A statement that the court will exclude the member from the class if the member so requests by a specified date;

(3) A procedure for the member to follow in requesting exclusion from the class;

(4) A statement that the judgment, whether favorable or not, will bind all members who do not request exclusion; and

(5) A statement that any member who does not request exclusion may, if the member so desires, enter an appearance through counsel.

(e) Manner of giving notice

In determining the manner of the notice, the court must consider:

(1) The interests of the class;

(2) The type of relief requested;

(3) The stake of the individual class members;

(4) The cost of notifying class members;

(5) The resources of the parties;

(6) The possible prejudice to class members who do not receive notice; and

(7) The res judicata effect on class members.

(f) Court may order means of notice

If personal notification is unreasonably expensive or the stake of individual class members is insubstantial, or if it appears that all members of the class cannot be notified personally, the court may order a means of notice reasonably calculated to apprise the class members of the pendency of the action—for example, publication in a newspaper or magazine; broadcasting on television, radio, or the Internet; or posting or distribution through a trade or professional association, union, or public interest group. *(Formerly Rule 1856, adopted, eff. Jan. 1, 2002. Renumbered Rule 3.766 and amended, eff. Jan. 1, 2007.)*

Research References

Rutter, Cal. Practice Guide: Civ. Pro. Before Trial Ch. 14-C, C. Procedural Issues.
4 Witkin Cal. Proc. 5th Pleading § 315, in General.
4 Witkin Cal. Proc. 5th Pleading § 317, Manner of Notice.
4 Witkin Cal. Proc. 5th Pleading § 320, (S 320) Election to be Excluded.
4 Witkin Cal. Proc. 5th Pleading § 321, (S 321) Election to be Included.

Rule 3.767.   Orders in the conduct of class actions

(a) Court orders

In the conduct of a class action, the court may make orders that:

(1) Require that some or all of the members of the class be given notice in such manner as the court may direct of any action in the proceeding, or of their opportunity to seek to appear and indicate whether they consider the representation fair and adequate, or of the proposed extent of the judgment;

(2) Impose conditions on the representative parties or on intervenors;

(3) Require that the pleadings be amended to eliminate allegations as to representation of absent persons, and that the action proceed accordingly;

(4) Facilitate the management of class actions through consolidation, severance, coordination, bifurcation, intervention, or joinder; and

(5) Address similar procedural matters.

(b) Altered or amended orders

The orders may be altered or amended as necessary. *(Formerly Rule 1857, adopted, eff. Jan. 1, 2002. Renumbered Rule 3.767 and amended, eff. Jan. 1, 2007.)*

Research References

Rutter, Cal. Practice Guide: Civ. Pro. Before Trial Ch. 14-C, C. Procedural Issues.
4 Witkin Cal. Proc. 5th Pleading § 278, (S 278) in General.

Rule 3.768.   Discovery from unnamed class members

(a) Types of discovery permitted

The following types of discovery may be sought, through service of a subpoena and without a court order, from a member of a class who is not a party representative or who has not appeared:

(1) An oral deposition;

(2) A written deposition; and

(3) A deposition for production of business records and things.

(b) Motion for protective order

A party representative, deponent, or other affected person may move for a protective order to preclude or limit the discovery.

(c) Interrogatories require court order

A party may not serve interrogatories on a member of a class who is not a party representative or who has not appeared, without a court order.

(d) Determination by court

In deciding whether to allow the discovery requested under (a) or (c), the court must consider, among other relevant factors:

(1) The timing of the request;

(2) The subject matter to be covered;

(3) The materiality of the information being sought;

(4) The likelihood that class members have such information;

(5) The possibility of reaching factual stipulations that eliminate the need for such discovery;

(6) Whether class representatives are seeking discovery on the subject to be covered; and

(7) Whether discovery will result in annoyance, oppression, or undue burden or expense for the members of the class. *(Formerly Rule 1858, adopted, eff. Jan. 1, 2002. Renumbered Rule 3.768 and amended, eff. Jan. 1, 2007.)*

Research References

Rutter, Cal. Practice Guide: Civ. Pro. Before Trial Ch. 14-C, C. Procedural Issues.

Rutter, Cal. Practice Guide: Civ. Pro. Before Trial Ch. 8E-3, Whose Deposition May be Taken.

Rutter, Cal. Practice Guide: Civ. Pro. Before Trial Ch. 8F-2, to Whom Interrogatories May be Sent.

4 Witkin Cal. Proc. 5th Pleading § 280, (S 280) Discovery from Unnamed Members.

4 Witkin Cal. Proc. 5th Pleading § 322, (S 322) Interrogatories to Unnamed Members.

Rule 3.769.   Settlement of class actions

(a) Court approval after hearing

A settlement or compromise of an entire class action, or of a cause of action in a class action, or as to a party, requires the approval of the court after hearing.

(b) Attorney's fees

Any agreement, express or implied, that has been entered into with respect to the payment of attorney's fees or the submission of an application for the approval of attorney's fees must be set forth in full in any application for approval of the dismissal or settlement of an action that has been certified as a class action.

(c) Preliminary approval of settlement

Any party to a settlement agreement may serve and file a written notice of motion for preliminary approval of the settlement. The settlement agreement and proposed notice to class members must be filed with the motion, and the proposed order must be lodged with the motion.

(d) Order certifying provisional settlement class

The court may make an order approving or denying certification of a provisional settlement class after the preliminary settlement hearing.

(e) Order for final approval hearing

If the court grants preliminary approval, its order must include the time, date, and place of the final approval hearing; the notice to be given to the class; and any other matters deemed necessary for the proper conduct of a settlement hearing.

(f) Notice to class of final approval hearing

If the court has certified the action as a class action, notice of the final approval hearing must be given to the class members in the manner specified by the court. The notice must contain an explanation of the proposed settlement and procedures for class members to follow in filing written objections to it and in arranging to appear at the settlement hearing and state any objections to the proposed settlement.

(g) Conduct of final approval hearing

Before final approval, the court must conduct an inquiry into the fairness of the proposed settlement.

(h) Judgment and retention of jurisdiction to enforce

If the court approves the settlement agreement after the final approval hearing, the court must make and enter judgment. The judgment must include a provision for the retention of the court's jurisdiction over the parties to enforce the terms of the judgment. The court may not enter an order dismissing the action at the same time as, or after, entry of judgment. *(Formerly Rule 1859, adopted, eff. Jan. 1, 2002. Renumbered Rule 3.769 and amended, eff. Jan. 1, 2007. As amended, eff. Jan. 1, 2009.)*

Research References

Rutter, Cal. Practice Guide: Civ. Pro. Before Trial Ch. 14-C, C. Procedural Issues.

Rutter, Cal. Practice Guide: Personal Injury Ch. 1-B, B. Initial Evaluation of Case: Decision to Accept or Reject Employment or Undertake Further Evaluation of Claim.

Rutter, Cal. Practice Guide: Prof. Responsibility Ch. 5-D, D. Ethical Limitations on Attorney Fees.

4 Witkin Cal. Proc. 5th Pleading § 330, California Rules of Court.

Rule 3.770.   Dismissal of class actions

(a) Court approval of dismissal

A dismissal of an entire class action, or of any party or cause of action in a class action, requires court approval. The court may not grant a request to dismiss a class action if the court has entered judgment following final approval of a settlement. Requests for dismissal must be accompanied by a declaration setting forth the facts on which the party relies. The declaration must clearly state whether consideration, direct or indirect, is being given for the dismissal and must describe the consideration in detail.

(b) Hearing on request for dismissal

The court may grant the request without a hearing. If the request is disapproved, notice of tentative disapproval must be sent to the attorneys of record. Any party may seek, within 15 calendar days of the service of the notice of tentative disapproval, a hearing on the request. If no hearing is sought within that period, the request for dismissal will be deemed denied.

(c) Notice to class of dismissal

If the court has certified the class, and notice of the pendency of the action has been provided to class members, notice of the dismissal must be given to the class in the manner specified by the court. If the court has not ruled on class certification, or if notice of the pendency of the action has not been provided to class members in a case in which such notice was required, notice of the proposed dismissal may be given in the manner and to those class members specified by the court, or the action may be dismissed without notice to the class members if the court finds that the dismissal will not prejudice them. *(Formerly Rule 365, adopted, eff. Jan. 1, 1984. Renumbered Rule 1860 and amended, eff. Jan. 1, 2002. Renumbered Rule 3.770 and amended, eff. Jan. 1, 2007. As amended, eff. Jan. 1, 2009.)*

Research References

Rutter, Cal. Practice Guide: Civ. Pro. Before Trial Ch. 11-A, A. Voluntary Dismissals.

Rutter, Cal. Practice Guide: Civ. Pro. Before Trial Ch. 14-C, C. Procedural Issues.

California Practice Guide: Employment Litigation Ch. 19-F, F. Discovery.

4 Witkin Cal. Proc. 5th Pleading § 330, California Rules of Court.
6 Witkin Cal. Proc. 5th Proceedings Without Trial § 292, Plaintiff Not
   Sole Party in Interest.

Rule 3.771. Judgment

(a) Class members to be included in judgment

The judgment in an action maintained as a class action must include and describe those whom the court finds to be members of the class.

(b) Notice of judgment to class

Notice of the judgment must be given to the class in the manner specified by the court. *(Formerly Rule 1861, adopted, eff. Jan. 1, 2002. Renumbered Rule 3.771 and amended, eff. Jan. 1, 2007.)*

Research References

Rutter, Cal. Practice Guide: Civ. Pro. Before Trial Ch. 14-B, B. Class
   Action Requirements-In General.
Rutter, Cal. Practice Guide: Civ. Pro. Before Trial Ch. 14-C, C.
   Procedural Issues.
2 Witkin Cal. Proc. 5th Courts § 191, (S 191) Civil Rules.
4 Witkin Cal. Proc. 5th Pleading § 332, (S 332) Judgment.

Division 8

ALTERNATIVE DISPUTE RESOLUTION

Chapter 1

GENERAL PROVISIONS

Rule
3.800.   Definitions.

Rule 3.800. Definitions

As used in this division:

(1) "Alternative dispute resolution process" or "ADR process" means a process, other than formal litigation, in which a neutral person or persons resolve a dispute or assist parties in resolving their dispute.

(2) "Mediation" means a process in which a neutral person or persons facilitate communication between disputants to assist them in reaching a mutually acceptable agreement. As used in this division, mediation does not include a settlement conference under rule 3.1380. *(Formerly Rule 1580, adopted, eff. Jan. 1, 2001. As amended, eff. July 1, 2002. Renumbered Rule 3.800 and amended, eff. Jan. 1, 2007.)*

Research References

Rutter, Cal. Practice Guide: Civ. Pro. Before Trial Ch. 1-B, B.
   Prelawsuit Investigations, Research and Analysis.
2 Witkin Cal. Proc. 5th Courts § 191, (S 191) Civil Rules.

Chapter 2

JUDICIAL ARBITRATION

Rule
3.810.   Application.
3.811.   Cases subject to and exempt from arbitration.
3.812.   Assignment to arbitration.
3.813.   Arbitration program administration.
3.814.   Panels of arbitrators.
3.815.   Selection of the arbitrator.
3.816.   Disqualification for conflict of interest.
3.817.   Arbitration hearings; notice; when and where held.
3.818.   Continuances.
3.819.   Arbitrator's fees.
3.820.   Communication with the arbitrator.
3.821.   Representation by counsel; proceedings when party
         absent.
3.822.   Discovery.
3.823.   Rules of evidence at arbitration hearing.
3.824.   Conduct of the hearing.
3.825.   The award.
3.826.   Trial after arbitration.

Rule
3.827.   Entry of award as judgment.
3.828.   Vacating judgment on award.
3.829.   Settlement of case.
3.830.   Arbitration not pursuant to rules.

Rule 3.810. Application

The rules in this chapter (commencing with this rule) apply if Code of Civil Procedure, part 3, title 3, chapter 2.5 (commencing with section 1141.10) is in effect. *(Formerly Rule 1600.1, adopted, eff. Jan. 1, 1988. As amended, eff. July 1, 1999; Jan. 1, 2000. Renumbered Rule 1600 and amended, eff. Jan. 1, 2004. Renumbered Rule 3.810 and amended, eff. Jan. 1, 2007.)*

Research References

Rutter, Cal. Practice Guide: A.D.R. Ch. 4-B, B. Judicial Arbitration.
Rutter, Cal. Practice Guide: Civ. Pro. Before Trial Ch. 13-A, A.
   Introduction.
Rutter, Cal. Practice Guide: Personal Injury Ch. 7-A, A. Introduction-
   Nature and Purpose of "Judicial Arbitration" in General.
2 Witkin Cal. Proc. 5th Courts § 191, (S 191) Civil Rules.
6 Witkin Cal. Proc. 5th Proceedings Without Trial § 413, in General.
6 Witkin Cal. Proc. 5th Proceedings Without Trial § 483, (S 483)
   Judicial Standards and Rules.
6 Witkin Cal. Proc. 5th Proceedings Without Trial § 579, in General.

Rule 3.811. Cases subject to and exempt from arbitration

(a) Cases subject to arbitration

Except as provided in (b), the following cases must be arbitrated:

(1) In each superior court with 18 or more authorized judges, all unlimited civil cases where the amount in controversy does not exceed $50,000 as to any plaintiff;

(2) In each superior court with fewer than 18 authorized judges that so provides by local rule, all unlimited civil cases where the amount in controversy does not exceed $50,000 as to any plaintiff;

(3) All limited civil cases in courts that so provide by local rule;

(4) Upon stipulation, any limited or unlimited civil case in any court, regardless of the amount in controversy; and

(5) Upon filing of an election by all plaintiffs, any limited or unlimited civil case in any court in which each plaintiff agrees that the arbitration award will not exceed $50,000 as to that plaintiff.

(b) Cases exempt from arbitration

The following cases are exempt from arbitration:

(1) Cases that include a prayer for equitable relief that is not frivolous or insubstantial;

(2) Class actions;

(3) Small claims cases or trials de novo on appeal from the small claims court;

(4) Unlawful detainer proceedings;

(5) Family Law Act proceedings except as provided in Family Code section 2554;

(6) Any case otherwise subject to arbitration that is found by the court not to be amenable to arbitration on the ground that arbitration would not reduce the probable time and expense necessary to resolve the litigation;

(7) Any category of cases otherwise subject to arbitration but excluded by local rule as not amenable to arbitration on the ground that, under the circumstances relating to the particular court, arbitration of such cases would not reduce the probable time and expense necessary to resolve the litigation; and

(8) Cases involving multiple causes of action or a cross-complaint if the court determines that the amount in controversy as to any given cause of action or cross-complaint exceeds $50,000. *(Formerly Rule 1600, adopted, eff. July 1, 1979. As amended, eff. Jan. 1, 1982; Jan. 1, 1986; Jan. 1, 1988; July 1, 1999. Renumbered Rule 1601 and amended, eff. Jan. 1, 2004. Renumbered Rule 3.811, eff. Jan. 1, 2007.)*

Research References

Rutter, Cal. Practice Guide: A.D.R. App. A, Selected Statutes Providing for ADR.

Rutter, Cal. Practice Guide: A.D.R. Ch. 4-A, A. General Considerations.

Rutter, Cal. Practice Guide: A.D.R. Ch. 4-B, B. Judicial Arbitration.

Rutter, Cal. Practice Guide: Civ. Pro. Before Trial Ch. 13-C, C. Civil Proceedings Subject to Judicial Arbitration.

Rutter, Cal. Practice Guide: Civ. Pro. Before Trial Ch. 13-F, F. Arbitration Award.

Rutter, Cal. Practice Guide: Civ. Pro. Before Trial Ch. 13-G, G. Trial De Novo.

Rutter, Cal. Practice Guide: Personal Injury Ch. 7-C, C. Actions Subject to Judicial Arbitration.

Rutter, Cal. Practice Guide: Personal Injury Ch. 7-D, D. Screening Cases for Judicial Arbitration.

Rutter, Cal. Practice Guide: Personal Injury Ch. 7-H, H. Arbitration Award and Judgment.

Rutter, Cal. Practice Guide: Personal Injury Ch. 7-C , Outline C.

6 Witkin Cal. Proc. 5th Proceedings Without Trial § 457, Effect of Judicial Arbitration.

6 Witkin Cal. Proc. 5th Proceedings Without Trial § 582, (S 582) Cases that Must be Arbitrated.

6 Witkin Cal. Proc. 5th Proceedings Without Trial § 583, (S 583) Cases Excluded from Arbitration.

6 Witkin Cal. Proc. 5th Proceedings Without Trial § 606, (S 606) Amount of Damages.

6 Witkin Cal. Proc. 5th Proceedings Without Trial § 615, (S 615) Waiver by Plaintiff Electing Arbitration and Receiving Maximum Award.

Rule 3.812.   Assignment to arbitration

(a)   Stipulations to arbitration

When the parties stipulate to arbitration, the case must be set for arbitration forthwith. The stipulation must be filed no later than the time the initial case management statement is filed, unless the court orders otherwise.

(b)   Plaintiff election for arbitration

Upon written election of all plaintiffs to submit a case to arbitration, the case must be set for arbitration forthwith, subject to a motion by defendant for good cause to delay the arbitration hearing. The election must be filed no later than the time the

initial case management statement is filed, unless the court orders otherwise.

(c)   Cross–actions

A case involving a cross-complaint where all plaintiffs have elected to arbitrate must be removed from the list of cases assigned to arbitration if, upon motion of the cross-complainant made within 15 days after notice of the election to arbitrate, the court determines that the amount in controversy relating to the cross-complaint exceeds $50,000.

(d)   Case management conference

Absent a stipulation or an election by all plaintiffs to submit to arbitration, cases must be set for arbitration when the court determines that the amount in controversy does not exceed $50,000. The amount in controversy must be determined at the first case management conference or review under the rules on case management in division 7 of this title that takes place after all named parties have appeared or defaulted. *(Formerly Rule 1601, adopted, eff. July 1, 1976. As amended, eff. July 1, 1979; Jan. 1, 1982; Jan. 1, 1985; Jan. 1, 1986; Jan. 1, 1988; Jan. 1, 1991; Jan. 1, 2003. Renumbered Rule 1602 and amended, eff. Jan. 1, 2004. Renumbered Rule 3.812 and amended, eff. Jan. 1, 2007.)*

Research References

Rutter, Cal. Practice Guide: A.D.R. Ch. 4-B, B. Judicial Arbitration.

Rutter, Cal. Practice Guide: Civ. Pro. Before Trial Ch. 13-C, C. Civil Proceedings Subject to Judicial Arbitration.

Rutter, Cal. Practice Guide: Civ. Pro. Before Trial Ch. 13-D, D. the Arbitrator.

Rutter, Cal. Practice Guide: Personal Injury Ch. 7-C, C. Actions Subject to Judicial Arbitration.

Rutter, Cal. Practice Guide: Personal Injury Ch. 7-D, D. Screening Cases for Judicial Arbitration.

6 Witkin Cal. Proc. 5th Proceedings Without Trial § 584, on Stipulation.

6 Witkin Cal. Proc. 5th Proceedings Without Trial § 585, on Plaintiff's Election to Limit Award.

6 Witkin Cal. Proc. 5th Proceedings Without Trial § 586, on Order of Court.

6 Witkin Cal. Proc. 5th Proceedings Without Trial § 587, Effect of Submission.

6 Witkin Cal. Proc. 5th Proceedings Without Trial § 588, (S 588) in General.

Rule 3.813.   Arbitration program administration

(a)   Arbitration administrator

The presiding judge must designate the ADR administrator selected under rule 10.783 to serve as arbitration administrator. The arbitration administrator must supervise the selection of arbitrators for the cases on the arbitration hearing list, generally supervise the operation of the arbitration program, and perform any additional duties delegated by the presiding judge.

(b)   Responsibilities of ADR committee

The ADR committee established under rule 10.783 is responsible for:

(1) Appointing the panels of arbitrators provided for in rule 3.814;

(2) Removing a person from a panel of arbitrators;

(3) Establishing procedures for selecting an arbitrator not inconsistent with these rules or local court rules; and

(4) Reviewing the administration and operation of the arbitration program periodically and making recommendations to the Judicial Council as the committee deems appropriate to improve the program, promote the ends of justice, and serve the needs of the community. *(Formerly Rule 1603, adopted, eff. July 1, 1976. As amended, eff. July 1, 1979; July 1, 1999; Jan. 1, 2004. Renumbered Rule 3.813 and amended, eff. Jan. 1, 2007.)*

Research References

Rutter, Cal. Practice Guide: Civ. Pro. Before Trial Ch. 13-D, D. the Arbitrator.
Rutter, Cal. Practice Guide: Personal Injury Ch. 7-E, E. the Arbitrator.
6 Witkin Cal. Proc. 5th Proceedings Without Trial § 581, Administration.

Rule 3.814. Panels of arbitrators

(a) Creation of panels

Every court must have a panel of arbitrators for personal injury cases, and such additional panels as the presiding judge may, from time to time, determine are needed.

(b) Composition of panels

The panels of arbitrators must be composed of active or inactive members of the State Bar, retired court commissioners who were licensed to practice law before their appointment as commissioners, and retired judges. A former California judicial officer is not eligible for the panel of arbitrators unless he or she is an active or inactive member of the State Bar.

(c) Responsibilities of ADR committee

The ADR committee is responsible for determining the size and composition of each panel of arbitrators. The personal injury panel, to the extent feasible, must contain an equal number of those who usually represent plaintiffs and those who usually represent defendants.

(d) Service on panel

Each person appointed serves as a member of a panel of arbitrators at the pleasure of the ADR committee. A person may be on arbitration panels in more than one county. An appointment to a panel is effective when the person appointed:

(1) Agrees to serve;

(2) Certifies that he or she is aware of and will comply with applicable provisions of canon 6 of the Code of Judicial Ethics and these rules; and

(3) Files an oath or affirmation to justly try all matters submitted to him or her.

(e) Panel lists

Lists showing the names of panel arbitrators available to hear cases must be available for public inspection in the ADR administrator's office. *(Formerly Rule 1604, adopted, eff. July 1, 1976. As amended, eff. July 1, 1979; Jan. 1, 1996; July 1, 2001; Jan. 1, 2004. Renumbered Rule 3.814 and amended, eff. Jan. 1, 2007.)*

Research References

Rutter, Cal. Practice Guide: A.D.R. Ch. 4-B, B. Judicial Arbitration.
Rutter, Cal. Practice Guide: Civ. Pro. Before Trial Ch. 13-B, B. Judicial Arbitration Distinguished from Contract Arbitration.
Rutter, Cal. Practice Guide: Civ. Pro. Before Trial Ch. 13-D, D. the Arbitrator.
Rutter, Cal. Practice Guide: Personal Injury Ch. 7-E, E. the Arbitrator.
6 Witkin Cal. Proc. 5th Proceedings Without Trial § 579, in General.
6 Witkin Cal. Proc. 5th Proceedings Without Trial § 589, (S 589) Arbitration Panels.

Rule 3.815. Selection of the arbitrator

(a) Selection by stipulation

By stipulation, the parties may select any person to serve as arbitrator. If the parties select a person who is not on the court's arbitration panel to serve as the arbitrator, the stipulation will be effective only if:

(1) The selected person completes a written consent to serve and the oath required of panel arbitrators under these rules; and

(2) Both the consent and the oath are attached to the stipulation.

A stipulation may specify the maximum amount of the arbitrator's award. The stipulation to an arbitrator must be served and filed no later than 10 days after the case has been set for arbitration under rule 3.812.

(b) Selection absent stipulation or local procedures

If the arbitrator has not been selected by stipulation and the court has not adopted local rules or procedures for the selection of the arbitrator as permitted under (c), the arbitrator will be selected as follows:

(1) Within 15 days after a case is set for arbitration under rule 3.812, the administrator must determine the number of clearly adverse sides in the case; in the absence of a cross-complaint bringing in a new party, the administrator may assume there are two sides. A dispute as to the number or identity of sides must be decided by the presiding judge in the same manner as disputes in determining sides entitled to peremptory challenges of jurors.

(2) The administrator must select at random a number of names equal to the number of sides, plus one, and mail the list of randomly selected names to counsel for the parties.

(3) Each side has 10 days from the date of mailing to file a rejection, in writing, of no more than one name on the list; if there are two or more parties on a side, they must join in the rejection of a single name.

(4) Promptly on the expiration of the 10–day period, the administrator must appoint, at random, one of the persons on the list whose name was not rejected, if more than one name remains.

(5) The administrator must assign the case to the arbitrator appointed and must give notice of the appointment to the arbitrator and to all parties.

(c) Local selection procedures

Instead of the procedure in (b), a court that has an arbitration program may, by local rule or by procedures adopted by its ADR committee, establish any fair method of selecting an arbitrator that:

(1) Affords each side an opportunity to challenge at least one listed arbitrator peremptorily; and

(2) Ensures that an arbitrator is appointed within 30 days from the submission of a case to arbitration.

The local rule or procedure may require that all steps leading to the selection of the arbitrator take place during or immediately following the case management conference or review under the rules on case management in division 7 of this title at which the court determines the amount in controversy and the suitability of the case for arbitration.

(d) Procedure if first arbitrator declines to serve

If the first arbitrator selected declines to serve, the administrator must vacate the appointment of the arbitrator and may either:

(1) Return the case to the top of the arbitration hearing list, restore the arbitrator's name to the list of those available for selection to hear cases, and appoint a new arbitrator; or

(2) Certify the case to the court.

(e) Procedure if second arbitrator declines to serve or hearing is not timely held

If the second arbitrator selected declines to serve or if the arbitrator does not complete the hearing within 90 days after the date of the assignment of the case to him or her, including any time due to continuances granted under rule 3.818, the administrator must certify the case to the court.

(f) Cases certified to court

If a case is certified to the court under either (d) or (e), the court must hold a case management conference. If the inability to hold an arbitration hearing is due to the neglect or lack of cooperation of a party who elected or stipulated to arbitration, the court may set the case for trial and may make any other appropriate orders. In all other circumstances, the court may reassign the case to arbitration or make any other appropriate orders to expedite disposition of the case. *(Formerly Rule 1605, adopted, eff. July 1, 1976. As amended, eff. July 1, 1979; Jan. 1, 1982; Jan. 1, 1984; Jan. 1, 1991; Jan. 1, 1994; Jan. 1, 2004. Renumbered Rule 3.815 and amended, eff. Jan. 1, 2007.)*

Research References

Rutter, Cal. Practice Guide: A.D.R. Ch. 4-B, B. Judicial Arbitration.
Rutter, Cal. Practice Guide: Civ. Pro. Before Trial Ch. 13-A, A. Introduction.
Rutter, Cal. Practice Guide: Civ. Pro. Before Trial Ch. 13-D, D. the Arbitrator.
Rutter, Cal. Practice Guide: Civ. Pro. Before Trial Ch. 13-E, E. the Arbitration Hearing.
Rutter, Cal. Practice Guide: Personal Injury Ch. 7-A, A. Introduction-Nature and Purpose of "Judicial Arbitration" in General.
Rutter, Cal. Practice Guide: Personal Injury Ch. 7-D, D. Screening Cases for Judicial Arbitration.
Rutter, Cal. Practice Guide: Personal Injury Ch. 7-E, E. the Arbitrator.
6 Witkin Cal. Proc. 5th Proceedings Without Trial § 579, in General.
6 Witkin Cal. Proc. 5th Proceedings Without Trial § 587, Effect of Submission.
6 Witkin Cal. Proc. 5th Proceedings Without Trial § 588, (S 588) in General.
6 Witkin Cal. Proc. 5th Proceedings Without Trial § 590, (S 590) Manner of Selection.
6 Witkin Cal. Proc. 5th Proceedings Without Trial § 606, (S 606) Amount of Damages.

Rule 3.816. Disqualification for conflict of interest

(a) Arbitrator's duty to disqualify himself or herself

The arbitrator must determine whether any cause exists for disqualification upon any of the grounds set forth in Code of Civil Procedure section 170.1 governing the disqualification of judges. If any member of the arbitrator's law firm would be disqualified under subdivision (a)(2) of section 170.1, the arbitrator is disqualified. Unless the ground for disqualification is disclosed to the parties in writing and is expressly waived by all parties in writing, the arbitrator must promptly notify the administrator of any known ground for disqualification and another arbitrator must be selected as provided in rule 3.815.

(b) Disclosures by arbitrator

In addition to any other disclosure required by law, no later than five days before the deadline for parties to file a motion for disqualification of the arbitrator under Code of Civil Procedure section 170.6 or, if the arbitrator is not aware of his or her appointment or of a matter subject to disclosure at that time, as soon as practicable thereafter, an arbitrator must disclose to the parties:

(1) Any matter subject to disclosure under subdivisions (D)(5)(a) and (D)(5)(b) of canon 6 of the Code of Judicial Ethics; and

(2) Any significant personal or professional relationship the arbitrator has or has had with a party, attorney, or law firm in the instant case, including the number and nature of any other proceedings in the past 24 months in which the arbitrator has been privately compensated by a party, attorney, law firm, or insurance company in the instant case for any services, including service as an attorney, expert witness, or consultant or as a judge,

referee, arbitrator, mediator, settlement facilitator, or other alternative dispute resolution neutral.

(c) Request for disqualification

A copy of any request by a party for the disqualification of an arbitrator under Code of Civil Procedure section 170.1 or 170.6 must be sent to the ADR administrator.

(d) Arbitrator's failure to disqualify himself or herself

On motion of any party, made as promptly as possible under Code of Civil Procedure sections 170.1 and 1141.18(d) and before the conclusion of arbitration proceedings, the appointment of an arbitrator to a case must be vacated if the court finds that:

(1) The party has demanded that the arbitrator disqualify himself or herself;

(2) The arbitrator has failed to do so; and

(3) Any of the grounds specified in section 170.1 exists.

The ADR administrator must return the case to the top of the arbitration hearing list and appoint a new arbitrator. The disqualified arbitrator's name must be returned to the list of those available for selection to hear cases, unless the court orders that the circumstances of the disqualification be reviewed by the ADR administrator, the ADR committee, or the presiding judge for appropriate action. *(Formerly Rule 1606, adopted, eff. July 1, 1976. As amended, eff. July 1, 1979; July 1, 1990; Jan. 1, 1994; July 1, 2001; Jan. 1, 2004; July 1, 2004. Renumbered Rule 3.816 and amended, eff. Jan. 1, 2007. As amended, eff. Jan. 1, 2008.)*

Research References

Rutter, Cal. Practice Guide: A.D.R. Ch. 4-B, B. Judicial Arbitration.
Rutter, Cal. Practice Guide: Civ. Pro. Before Trial Ch. 13-A, A. Introduction.
Rutter, Cal. Practice Guide: Civ. Pro. Before Trial Ch. 13-D, D. the Arbitrator.
Rutter, Cal. Practice Guide: Civ. Pro. Before Trial Ch. 13-F, F. Arbitration Award.
Rutter, Cal. Practice Guide: Personal Injury Ch. 7-E, E. the Arbitrator.
6 Witkin Cal. Proc. 5th Proceedings Without Trial § 591, Disqualification.

Rule 3.817. Arbitration hearings; notice; when and where held

(a) Setting hearing; notice

Within 15 days after the appointment of the arbitrator, the arbitrator must set the time, date, and place of the arbitration hearing and notify each party and the administrator in writing of the time, date, and place set.

(b) Date of hearing; limitations

Except upon the agreement of all parties and the arbitrator, the arbitration hearing date must not be set:

(1) Earlier than 30 days after the date the arbitrator sends the notice of the hearing under (a); or

(2) On Saturdays, Sundays, or legal holidays.

(c) Hearing completion deadline

The hearing must be scheduled so as to be completed no later than 90 days from the date of the assignment of the case to the arbitrator, including any time due to continuances granted under rule 3.818.

(d) Hearing location

The hearing must take place in appropriate facilities provided by the court or selected by the arbitrator. *(Formerly Rule 1611, as amended, eff. July 1, 1979; Jan. 1, 1992. Renumbered Rule 1607 and amended, eff. Jan. 1, 2004. Renumbered Rule 3.817 and amended, eff. Jan. 1, 2007.)*

Research References

Rutter, Cal. Practice Guide: A.D.R. Ch. 4-B, B. Judicial Arbitration.
Rutter, Cal. Practice Guide: Civ. Pro. Before Trial Ch. 13-E, E. the Arbitration Hearing.
Rutter, Cal. Practice Guide: Personal Injury Ch. 7-G, G. Arbitration Hearing.
6 Witkin Cal. Proc. 5th Proceedings Without Trial § 597, Time and Place of Hearing.
6 Witkin Cal. Proc. 5th Proceedings Without Trial § 598, Notice of Hearing.

Rule 3.818. Continuances

(a) Stipulation to continuance; consent of arbitrator

Except as provided in (c), the parties may stipulate to a continuance in the case, with the consent of the assigned arbitrator. An arbitrator must consent to a request for a continuance if it appears that good cause exists. Notice of the continuance must be sent to the ADR administrator.

(b) Court grant of continuance

If the arbitrator declines to give consent to a continuance, upon the motion of a party and for good cause shown, the court may grant a continuance of the arbitration hearing. In the event the court grants the motion, the party who requested the continuance must notify the arbitrator and the arbitrator must reschedule the hearing, giving notice to all parties to the arbitration proceeding.

(c) Limitation on length of continuance

An arbitration hearing must not be continued to a date later than 90 days after the assignment of the case to the arbitrator, including any time due to continuances granted under this rule, except by order of the court upon the motion of a party as provided in (b). *(Formerly Rule 1607, as amended, eff. July 1, 1979; Jan. 1, 1984; Jan. 1, 1991; Jan. 1, 1992; Jan. 1, 1994. Renumbered Rule 1608 and amended, eff. Jan. 1, 2004. Renumbered Rule 3.818 and amended, eff. Jan. 1, 2007.)*

Research References

Rutter, Cal. Practice Guide: A.D.R. Ch. 4-B, B. Judicial Arbitration.
Rutter, Cal. Practice Guide: Civ. Pro. Before Trial Ch. 13-E, E. the Arbitration Hearing.
Rutter, Cal. Practice Guide: Personal Injury Ch. 7-G, G. Arbitration Hearing.
6 Witkin Cal. Proc. 5th Proceedings Without Trial § 597, Time and Place of Hearing.

Rule 3.819. Arbitrator's fees

(a) Filing of award ~~or notice of settlement~~ required

Except as provided in (b), the arbitrator's award must be timely filed with the clerk of the court under rule 3.825(b) ~~or a notice of settlement must have been filed~~ before a fee may be paid to the arbitrator.

(b) Exceptions for good cause

On the arbitrator's verified ex parte application, the court may for good cause authorize payment of a fee:

(1) If the arbitrator devoted a substantial amount of time to a case that was settled without a hearing <u>or without an award being filed. For this purpose, a case is considered settled when one of the following is filed:</u>

<u>(A) A notice of settlement of the entire case, under rule 3.1385; or</u>

<u>(B) A *Request for Dismissal* (form CIV–110) of the entire case or as to all parties to the arbitration is filed; or</u>

(2) If the award was not timely filed.

(c) Arbitrator's fee statement

The arbitrator's fee statement must be submitted to the administrator promptly upon the completion of the arbitrator's duties and must set forth the title and number of the cause arbitrated, the date of ~~the~~ <u>any</u> arbitration hearing, and the date the award ~~or~~<u>, notice of settlement, or request for dismissal</u> was filed. *(Formerly Rule 1608, as amended, eff. July 1, 1979; Jan. 1, 1987. Renumbered Rule 1609 and amended, eff. Jan. 1, 2004. Renumbered Rule 3.819 and amended, eff. Jan. 1, 2007. As amended, eff. Jan. 1, 2013.)*

Research References

Rutter, Cal. Practice Guide: Personal Injury Ch. 7-E, E. the Arbitrator.
6 Witkin Cal. Proc. 5th Proceedings Without Trial § 592, (S 592) in General.
6 Witkin Cal. Proc. 5th Proceedings Without Trial § 608, Filing.

Rule 3.820. Communication with the arbitrator

(a) Disclosure of settlement offers prohibited

No disclosure of any offers of settlement made by any party may be made to the arbitrator prior to the filing of the award.

(b) Ex parte communication prohibited

An arbitrator must not initiate, permit, or consider any ex parte communications or consider other communications made to the arbitrator outside the presence of all of the parties concerning a pending arbitration, except as follows:

(1) An arbitrator may communicate with a party in the absence of other parties about administrative matters, such as setting the time and place of hearings or making other arrangements for the conduct of the proceedings, as long as the arbitrator reasonably believes that the communication will not result in a procedural or tactical advantage for any party. When such a discussion occurs, the arbitrator must promptly inform the other parties of the communication and must give the other parties an opportunity to respond before making any final determination concerning the matter discussed.

(2) An arbitrator may initiate or consider any ex parte communication when expressly authorized by law to do so. *(Formerly Rule 1609. Renumbered Rule 1610 and amended, eff. Jan. 1, 2004. Renumbered Rule 3.820 and amended, eff. Jan. 1, 2007.)*

Research References

Rutter, Cal. Practice Guide: A.D.R. Ch. 4-B, B. Judicial Arbitration.
Rutter, Cal. Practice Guide: Personal Injury Ch. 7-E, E. the Arbitrator.
6 Witkin Cal. Proc. 5th Proceedings Without Trial § 595, in General.
6 Witkin Cal. Proc. 5th Proceedings Without Trial § 598, Notice of Hearing.

Rule 3.821. Representation by counsel; proceedings when party absent

(a) Representation by counsel

A party to the arbitration has a right to be represented by an attorney at any proceeding or hearing in arbitration, but this right may be waived. A waiver of this right may be revoked, but if revoked, the other party is entitled to a reasonable continuance for the purpose of obtaining counsel.

(b) Proceedings when party absent

The arbitration may proceed in the absence of any party who, after due notice, fails to be present and to obtain a continuance. An award must not be based solely on the absence of a party. In the event of a default by defendant, the arbitrator must require the plaintiff to submit such evidence as may be appropriate for the making of an award. *(Formerly Rule 1610. Renumbered Rule 1611 and amended, eff. Jan. 1, 2004. Renumbered Rule 3.821 and amended, eff. Jan. 1, 2007.)*

Research References

Rutter, Cal. Practice Guide: A.D.R. Ch. 4-B, B. Judicial Arbitration.
Rutter, Cal. Practice Guide: Civ. Pro. Before Trial Ch. 13-E, E. the Arbitration Hearing.
Rutter, Cal. Practice Guide: Personal Injury Ch. 7-G, G. Arbitration Hearing.
6 Witkin Cal. Proc. 5th Proceedings Without Trial § 595, in General.
6 Witkin Cal. Proc. 5th Proceedings Without Trial § 599, Persons Present.

Rule 3.822.   Discovery

(a) Right to discovery

The parties to the arbitration have the right to take depositions and to obtain discovery, and to that end may exercise all of the same rights, remedies, and procedures, and are subject to all of the same duties, liabilities, and obligations as provided in part 4, title 3, chapter 3 of the Code of Civil Procedure, except as provided in (b).

(b) Completion of discovery

All discovery must be completed not later than 15 days before the date set for the arbitration hearing unless the court, upon a showing of good cause, makes an order granting an extension of the time within which discovery must be completed. *(Formerly Rule 1612, adopted, eff. July 1, 1976. As amended, eff. July 1, 1979; Jan. 1, 2004. Renumbered Rule 3.822 and amended, eff. Jan. 1, 2007.)*

Research References

Rutter, Cal. Practice Guide: A.D.R. Ch. 4-B, B. Judicial Arbitration.
Rutter, Cal. Practice Guide: Civ. Pro. Before Trial Ch. 13-B, B. Judicial Arbitration Distinguished from Contract Arbitration.
Rutter, Cal. Practice Guide: Civ. Pro. Before Trial Ch. 13-E, E. the Arbitration Hearing.
Rutter, Cal. Practice Guide: Civ. Pro. Before Trial Ch. 13-G, G. Trial De Novo.
Rutter, Cal. Practice Guide: Civ. Pro. Before Trial Ch. 8E-2, When Depositions May be Taken.
Rutter, Cal. Practice Guide: Personal Injury Ch. 6-B, B. Overview of Selected Discovery Procedures.
Rutter, Cal. Practice Guide: Personal Injury Ch. 7-F, F. Preparing for Arbitration.
Rutter, Cal. Practice Guide: Personal Injury Ch. 7-G, G. Arbitration Hearing.
6 Witkin Cal. Proc. 5th Proceedings Without Trial § 580, Contractual Arbitration Distinguished.
6 Witkin Cal. Proc. 5th Proceedings Without Trial § 594, (S 594) Discovery.
6 Witkin Cal. Proc. 5th Proceedings Without Trial § 603, (S 603) Depositions.
7 Witkin Cal. Proc. 5th Trial § 74, Completion of Discovery.

Rule 3.823.   Rules of evidence at arbitration hearing

(a) Presence of arbitrator and parties

All evidence must be taken in the presence of the arbitrator and all parties, except where any of the parties has waived the right to be present or is absent after due notice of the hearing.

(b) Application of civil rules of evidence

The rules of evidence governing civil cases apply to the conduct of the arbitration hearing, except:

(1) *Written reports and other documents*

Any party may offer written reports of any expert witness, medical records and bills (including physiotherapy, nursing, and prescription bills), documentary evidence of loss of income, property damage repair bills or estimates, police reports concerning an accident that gave rise to the case, other bills and invoices, purchase orders, checks, written contracts, and similar documents prepared and maintained in the ordinary course of business.

(A) The arbitrator must receive them in evidence if copies have been delivered to all opposing parties at least 20 days before the hearing.

(B) Any other party may subpoena the author or custodian of the document as a witness and examine the witness as if under cross-examination.

(C) Any repair estimate offered as an exhibit, and the copies delivered to opposing parties, must be accompanied by:

(i) A statement indicating whether or not the property was repaired, and, if it was, whether the estimated repairs were made in full or in part; and

(ii) A copy of the receipted bill showing the items of repair made and the amount paid.

(D) The arbitrator must not consider any opinion as to ultimate fault expressed in a police report.

(2) *Witness statements*

The written statements of any other witness may be offered and must be received in evidence if:

(A) They are made by declaration under penalty of perjury;

(B) Copies have been delivered to all opposing parties at least 20 days before the hearing; and

(C) No opposing party has, at least 10 days before the hearing, delivered to the proponent of the evidence a written demand that the witness be produced in person to testify at the hearing. The arbitrator must disregard any portion of a statement received under this rule that would be inadmissible if the witness were testifying in person, but the inclusion of inadmissible matter does not render the entire statement inadmissible.

(3) *Depositions*

(A) The deposition of any witness may be offered by any party and must be received in evidence, subject to objections available under Code of Civil Procedure section 2025.410, notwithstanding that the deponent is not "unavailable as a witness" within the meaning of Evidence Code section 240 and no exceptional circumstances exist, if:

(i) The deposition was taken in the manner provided for by law or by stipulation of the parties and within the time provided for in these rules; and

(ii) Not less than 20 days before the hearing the proponent of the deposition delivered to all opposing parties notice of intention to offer the deposition in evidence.

(B) The opposing party, upon receiving the notice, may subpoena the deponent and, at the discretion of the arbitrator, either the deposition may be excluded from evidence or the deposition may be admitted and the deponent may be further cross-examined by the subpoenaing party. These limitations are not applicable to a deposition admissible under the terms of Code of Civil Procedure section 2025.620.

(c) Subpoenas

(1) *Compelling witnesses to appear*

The attendance of witnesses at arbitration hearings may be compelled through the issuance of subpoenas as provided in the Code of Civil Procedure, in section 1985 and elsewhere in part 4, title 3, chapters 2 and 3. It is the duty of the party requesting the subpoena to modify the form of subpoena so as to show that the appearance is before an arbitrator and to give the time and place set for the arbitration hearing.

(2) *Adjournment or continuances*

At the discretion of the arbitrator, nonappearance of a properly subpoenaed witness may be a ground for an adjournment or continuance of the hearing.

(3) *Contempt*

If any witness properly served with a subpoena fails to appear at the arbitration hearing or, having appeared, refuses to be sworn or to answer, proceedings to compel compliance with the subpoena on penalty of contempt may be had before the superior court as provided in Code of Civil Procedure section 1991 for other instances of refusal to appear and answer before an officer or commissioner out of court.

(d) Delivery of documents

For purposes of this rule, "delivery" of a document or notice may be accomplished manually or by mail in the manner provided by Code of Civil Procedure section 1013. If service is by mail, the times prescribed in this rule for delivery of documents, notices, and demands are increased by five days. *(Formerly Rule 1613, adopted, eff. July 1, 1976. As amended, eff. July 1, 1979; Jan. 1, 1984; Jan. 1, 1988; July 1, 1990; Jan. 1, 2004. Renumbered Rule 3.823 and amended, eff. Jan. 1, 2007. As amended, eff. Jan. 1, 2008.)*

Research References

Rutter, Cal. Practice Guide: A.D.R. Ch. 4-B, B. Judicial Arbitration.
Rutter, Cal. Practice Guide: Civ. Pro. Before Trial Ch. 13-B, B. Judicial Arbitration Distinguished from Contract Arbitration.
Rutter, Cal. Practice Guide: Civ. Pro. Before Trial Ch. 13-E, E. the Arbitration Hearing.
Rutter, Cal. Practice Guide: Civ. Pro. Before Trial Ch. 8E-18, Use of Depositions in Judicial Arbitration Hearings.
Rutter, Cal. Practice Guide: Civ. Pro. Before Trial Ch. 13-E , Outline E.
Rutter, Cal. Practice Guide: Personal Injury Ch. 3-C, C. Specific Items of Compensatory Damages.
Rutter, Cal. Practice Guide: Personal Injury Ch. 7-F, F. Preparing for Arbitration.
Rutter, Cal. Practice Guide: Personal Injury Ch. 7-G, G. Arbitration Hearing.
Rutter, Cal. Practice Guide: Personal Injury Ch. 7-G , Outline G.
6 Witkin Cal. Proc. 5th Proceedings Without Trial § 579, in General.
6 Witkin Cal. Proc. 5th Proceedings Without Trial § 580, Contractual Arbitration Distinguished.
6 Witkin Cal. Proc. 5th Proceedings Without Trial § 596, Subpenas.
6 Witkin Cal. Proc. 5th Proceedings Without Trial § 597, Time and Place of Hearing.
6 Witkin Cal. Proc. 5th Proceedings Without Trial § 599, Persons Present.
6 Witkin Cal. Proc. 5th Proceedings Without Trial § 600, (S 600) in General.
6 Witkin Cal. Proc. 5th Proceedings Without Trial § 601, (S 601) Reports and Records.
6 Witkin Cal. Proc. 5th Proceedings Without Trial § 602, (S 602) Written Statements.
6 Witkin Cal. Proc. 5th Proceedings Without Trial § 603, (S 603) Depositions.

Rule 3.824. Conduct of the hearing

(a) Arbitrator's powers

The arbitrator has the following powers; all other questions arising out of the case are reserved to the court:

(1) To administer oaths or affirmations to witnesses;

(2) To take adjournments upon the request of a party or upon his or her own initiative when deemed necessary;

(3) To permit testimony to be offered by deposition;

(4) To permit evidence to be offered and introduced as provided in these rules;

(5) To rule upon the admissibility and relevancy of evidence offered;

(6) To invite the parties, on reasonable notice, to submit arbitration briefs;

(7) To decide the law and facts of the case and make an award accordingly;

(8) To award costs, not to exceed the statutory costs of the suit; and

(9) To examine any site or object relevant to the case.

(b) Record of proceedings

(1) *Arbitrator's record*

The arbitrator may, but is not required to, make a record of the proceedings.

(2) *Record not subject to discovery*

Any records of the proceedings made by or at the direction of the arbitrator are deemed the arbitrator's personal notes and are not subject to discovery, and the arbitrator must not deliver them to any party to the case or to any other person, except to an employee using the records under the arbitrator's supervision or pursuant to a subpoena issued in a criminal investigation or prosecution for perjury.

(3) *No other record*

No other record may be made, and the arbitrator must not permit the presence of a stenographer or court reporter or the use of any recording device at the hearing, except as expressly permitted by (1). *(Formerly Rule 1614, adopted, eff. July 1, 1976. As amended, eff. Jan. 1, 2004. Renumbered Rule 3.824 and amended, eff. Jan. 1, 2007.)*

Research References

Rutter, Cal. Practice Guide: A.D.R. Ch. 4-B, B. Judicial Arbitration.
Rutter, Cal. Practice Guide: Civ. Pro. Before Trial Ch. 13-B, B. Judicial Arbitration Distinguished from Contract Arbitration.
Rutter, Cal. Practice Guide: Civ. Pro. Before Trial Ch. 13-E, E. the Arbitration Hearing.
Rutter, Cal. Practice Guide: Civ. Pro. Before Trial Ch. 13-F, F. Arbitration Award.
Rutter, Cal. Practice Guide: Personal Injury Ch. 7-G, G. Arbitration Hearing.
Rutter, Cal. Practice Guide: Personal Injury Ch. 7-H, H. Arbitration Award and Judgment.
6 Witkin Cal. Proc. 5th Proceedings Without Trial § 575, (S 575) Illustrations of Finality Rule.
6 Witkin Cal. Proc. 5th Proceedings Without Trial § 595, in General.
6 Witkin Cal. Proc. 5th Proceedings Without Trial § 607, (S 607) Award of Costs.
6 Witkin Cal. Proc. 5th Proceedings Without Trial § 624, (S 624) No Reference to Arbitration.

Rule 3.825. The award

(a) Form and content of the award

(1) *Award in writing*

The award must be in writing and signed by the arbitrator. It must determine all issues properly raised by the pleadings, including a determination of any damages and an award of costs if appropriate.

(2) *No findings or conclusions required*

The arbitrator is not required to make findings of fact or conclusions of law.

(b) Filing the award or amended award

(1) *Time for filing the award*

Within 10 days after the conclusion of the arbitration hearing, the arbitrator must file the award with the clerk, with proof of service on each party to the arbitration. On the arbitrator's application in cases of unusual length or complexity, the court may allow up to 20 additional days for the filing and service of the award.

(2) *Amended award*

Within the time for filing the award, the arbitrator may file and serve an amended award. *(Formerly Rule 1615, adopted, eff.*

Ct. Rules

July 1, 1976. As amended, eff. Jan. 1, 1983; Jan. 1, 1995; Jan. 1, 2003; Jan. 1, 2004. Renumbered Rule 3.825 and amended, eff. Jan. 1, 2007.)

Research References

Rutter, Cal. Practice Guide: A.D.R. Ch. 4-B, B. Judicial Arbitration.

Rutter, Cal. Practice Guide: Civ. Pro. Before Trial Ch. 13-F, F. Arbitration Award.

Rutter, Cal. Practice Guide: Civ. Pro. Before Trial Ch. 13-G, G. Trial De Novo.

Rutter, Cal. Practice Guide: Personal Injury Ch. 7-H, H. Arbitration Award and Judgment.

Rutter, Cal. Practice Guide: Personal Injury Ch. 7-I, I. Trial De Novo After Arbitration Award.

2 Witkin Cal. Proc. 5th Jurisdiction § 103, (S 103) Statute of Limitations and Other Time Provisions.

2 Witkin Cal. Proc. 5th Jurisdiction § 301, (S 301) Noncompliance With Condition Precedent.

6 Witkin Cal. Proc. 5th Proceedings Without Trial § 605, (S 605) in General.

6 Witkin Cal. Proc. 5th Proceedings Without Trial § 606, (S 606) Amount of Damages.

6 Witkin Cal. Proc. 5th Proceedings Without Trial § 607, (S 607) Award of Costs.

6 Witkin Cal. Proc. 5th Proceedings Without Trial § 608, Filing.

6 Witkin Cal. Proc. 5th Proceedings Without Trial § 609, Service.

6 Witkin Cal. Proc. 5th Proceedings Without Trial § 616, (S 616) Time for Request.

Rule 3.826. Trial after arbitration

(a) Request for trial; deadline

Within 60 days after the arbitration award is filed with the clerk of the court, a party may request a trial by filing with the clerk a request for trial, with proof of service of a copy upon all other parties appearing in the case. A request for trial filed after the parties have been served with a copy of the award by the arbitrator, but before the award has been filed with the clerk, is valid and timely filed. The 60–day period within which to request trial may not be extended.

(b) Prosecution of the case

If a party makes a timely request for a trial, the case must proceed as provided under an applicable case management order. If no pending order provides for the prosecution of the case after a request for a trial after arbitration, the court must promptly schedule a case management conference.

(c) References to arbitration during trial prohibited

The case must be tried as though no arbitration proceedings had occurred. No reference may be made during the trial to the arbitration award, to the fact that there had been arbitration proceedings, to the evidence adduced at the arbitration hearing, or to any other aspect of the arbitration proceedings, and none of the foregoing may be used as affirmative evidence, or by way of impeachment, or for any other purpose at the trial.

(d) Costs after trial

In assessing costs after the trial, the court must apply the standards specified in Code of Civil Procedure section 1141.21. *(Formerly Rule 1616, adopted, eff. July 1, 1976. As amended, eff. July 1, 1979; Jan. 1, 1985; July 1, 1990; Jan. 1, 2004. Renumbered Rule 3.826 and amended, eff. Jan. 1, 2007. As amended, eff. Jan. 1, 2012.)*

Research References

Rutter, Cal. Practice Guide: A.D.R. Ch. 4-B, B. Judicial Arbitration.

Rutter, Cal. Practice Guide: Civ. Pro. Before Trial Ch. 13-A, A. Introduction.

Rutter, Cal. Practice Guide: Civ. Pro. Before Trial Ch. 13-D, D. the Arbitrator.

Rutter, Cal. Practice Guide: Civ. Pro. Before Trial Ch. 13-G, G. Trial De Novo.

Rutter, Cal. Practice Guide: Civil Trials & Evidence Ch. 10-D, D. Objectives of Cross-Examination.

Rutter, Cal. Practice Guide: Civil Trials & Evidence Ch. 8D-D, D. Hearsay Exceptions.

Rutter, Cal. Practice Guide: Civil Trials & Evidence Ch. 8E-D, D. Other Public Policy Exclusions.

Rutter, Cal. Practice Guide: Civil Trials & Evidence Ch. 8E-F, F. Limitations on Impeachment and Rehabilitation.

Rutter, Cal. Practice Guide: Personal Injury Ch. 7-E, E. the Arbitrator.

Rutter, Cal. Practice Guide: Personal Injury Ch. 7-I, I. Trial De Novo After Arbitration Award.

2 Witkin Cal. Proc. 5th Courts § 203, Invalid Rules.

6 Witkin Cal. Proc. 5th Proceedings Without Trial § 415, Tolling Until New Trial Date.

6 Witkin Cal. Proc. 5th Proceedings Without Trial § 579, in General.

6 Witkin Cal. Proc. 5th Proceedings Without Trial § 580, Contractual Arbitration Distinguished.

6 Witkin Cal. Proc. 5th Proceedings Without Trial § 595, in General.

6 Witkin Cal. Proc. 5th Proceedings Without Trial § 609, Service.

6 Witkin Cal. Proc. 5th Proceedings Without Trial § 616, (S 616) Time for Request.

6 Witkin Cal. Proc. 5th Proceedings Without Trial § 617, (S 617) Form of Request.

6 Witkin Cal. Proc. 5th Proceedings Without Trial § 618, (S 618) Filing and Service.

6 Witkin Cal. Proc. 5th Proceedings Without Trial § 619, (S 619) Request by One of Several Coparties.

6 Witkin Cal. Proc. 5th Proceedings Without Trial § 621, (S 621) Subsequent Withdrawal of Request.

6 Witkin Cal. Proc. 5th Proceedings Without Trial § 622, (S 622) Calendaring.

6 Witkin Cal. Proc. 5th Proceedings Without Trial § 624, (S 624) No Reference to Arbitration.

6 Witkin Cal. Proc. 5th Proceedings Without Trial § 625, (S 625) Adoption of Arbitrator's Findings is Improper.

6 Witkin Cal. Proc. 5th Proceedings Without Trial § 626, (S 626) in General.

Rule 3.827. Entry of award as judgment

(a) Entry of award as judgment by clerk

The clerk must enter the award as a judgment immediately upon the expiration of 60 days after the award is filed if no party has, during that period, served and filed either:

(1) A request for trial as provided in these rules; or

(2) A *Request for Dismissal* (form CIV–110) of the entire case or as to all parties to the arbitration. The *Request for Dismissal* must be fully completed ~~and~~. If the request is for dismissal of the entire case, it must include the signatures of all parties ~~those whose consent is required for dismissal~~. If the request is for dismissal as to all parties to the arbitration, it must include the signatures of all those parties.

(b) Notice of entry of judgment

Promptly upon entry of the award as a judgment, the clerk must mail notice of entry of judgment to all parties who have appeared in the case and must execute a certificate of mailing and place it in the court's file in the case.

(c) Effect of judgment

The judgment so entered has the same force and effect in all respects as, and is subject to all provisions of law relating to, a judgment in a civil case or proceeding, except that it is not subject to appeal and it may not be attacked or set aside except as provided in rule 3.828. The judgment so entered may be enforced as if it had been rendered by the court in which it is entered. *(Adopted, eff. Jan. 1, 2007. As amended, eff. Jan. 1, 2012; Jan. 1, 2013.)*

Research References

Rutter, Cal. Practice Guide: A.D.R. Ch. 4-B, B. Judicial Arbitration.

Rutter, Cal. Practice Guide: Civ. Pro. Before Trial Ch. 11-A, A. Voluntary Dismissals.

Rutter, Cal. Practice Guide: Civ. Pro. Before Trial Ch. 13-B, B. Judicial Arbitration Distinguished from Contract Arbitration.

Rutter, Cal. Practice Guide: Civ. Pro. Before Trial Ch. 13-F, F. Arbitration Award.

Rutter, Cal. Practice Guide: Civ. Pro. Before Trial Ch. 13-G, G. Trial De Novo.

Rutter, Cal. Practice Guide: Civ. Pro. Before Trial Gen. Matls., Highlights.

Rutter, Cal. Practice Guide: Personal Injury Ch. 7-H, H. Arbitration Award and Judgment.

Rutter, Cal. Practice Guide: Personal Injury Ch. 7-I, I. Trial De Novo After Arbitration Award.

6 Witkin Cal. Proc. 5th Proceedings Without Trial § 579, in General.

6 Witkin Cal. Proc. 5th Proceedings Without Trial § 610, Effect.

6 Witkin Cal. Proc. 5th Proceedings Without Trial § 611, Appealability.

6 Witkin Cal. Proc. 5th Proceedings Without Trial § 619, (S 619) Request by One of Several Coparties.

Rule 3.828. Vacating judgment on award

(a) Motion to vacate

A party against whom a judgment is entered under an arbitration award may, within six months after its entry, move to vacate the judgment on the ground that the arbitrator was subject to a disqualification not disclosed before the hearing and of which the arbitrator was then aware, or upon one of the grounds set forth in Code of Civil Procedure sections 473 or 1286.2(a)(1), (2), and (3), and on no other grounds.

(b) Notice and grounds for granting motion

The motion must be heard upon notice to the adverse parties and to the arbitrator, and may be granted only upon clear and convincing evidence that the grounds alleged are true, and that the motion was made as soon as practicable after the moving party learned of the existence of those grounds. *(Adopted, eff. Jan. 1, 2007.)*

Research References

Rutter, Cal. Practice Guide: A.D.R. Ch. 4-B, B. Judicial Arbitration.

Rutter, Cal. Practice Guide: A.D.R. Ch. 5-A, A. General Considerations.

Rutter, Cal. Practice Guide: Civ. Pro. Before Trial Ch. 13-C, C. Civil Proceedings Subject to Judicial Arbitration.

Rutter, Cal. Practice Guide: Civ. Pro. Before Trial Ch. 13-F, F. Arbitration Award.

Rutter, Cal. Practice Guide: Personal Injury Ch. 7-H, H. Arbitration Award and Judgment.

Rutter, Cal. Practice Guide: Personal Injury Ch. 7-I, I. Trial De Novo After Arbitration Award.

6 Witkin Cal. Proc. 5th Proceedings Without Trial § 612, Vacation.

Rule 3.829. Settlement of case

If a case is settled, each plaintiff or other party seeking affirmative relief must notify the arbitrator and the court as required in rule 3.1385. *(Formerly Rule 1618, adopted, eff. Jan. 1, 1992. As amended, eff. Jan. 1, 2004. Renumbered Rule 3.829 and amended, eff. Jan. 1, 2007.)*

Research References

Rutter, Cal. Practice Guide: A.D.R. Ch. 4-B, B. Judicial Arbitration.

Rutter, Cal. Practice Guide: Civ. Pro. Before Trial Ch. 13-A, A. Introduction.

Rutter, Cal. Practice Guide: Civ. Pro. Before Trial Ch. 13-E, E. the Arbitration Hearing.

Rutter, Cal. Practice Guide: Personal Injury Ch. 7-G, G. Arbitration Hearing.

6 Witkin Cal. Proc. 5th Proceedings Without Trial § 593, (S 593) Source of Payment.

Rule 3.830. Arbitration not pursuant to rules

These rules do not prohibit the parties to any civil case or proceeding from entering into arbitration agreements under part 3, title 9 of the Code of Civil Procedure. Neither the ADR committee nor the ADR administrator may take any part in the conduct of an arbitration under an agreement not in conformity with these rules except that the administrator may, upon joint request of the parties, furnish the parties to the agreement with a randomly selected list of at least three names of members of the appropriate panel of arbitrators. *(Formerly Rule 1617, adopted, eff. July 1, 1976. As amended, eff. Jan. 1, 2004. Renumbered Rule 3.830 and amended, eff. Jan. 1, 2007.)*

Research References

Rutter, Cal. Practice Guide: A.D.R. Ch. 4-B, B. Judicial Arbitration.

Rutter, Cal. Practice Guide: Personal Injury Ch. 7-A, A. Introduction-Nature and Purpose of "Judicial Arbitration" in General.

2 Witkin Cal. Proc. 5th Courts § 191, (S 191) Civil Rules.

6 Witkin Cal. Proc. 5th Proceedings Without Trial § 580, Contractual Arbitration Distinguished.

Chapter 3

GENERAL RULES RELATING TO MEDIATION OF CIVIL CASES

Article 1

PROCEDURES FOR ALL COURT MEDIATION PROGRAMS

Rule
3.835. Application.
3.845. Form of mediator statements and reports.

Rule 3.835. Application

The rules in this article apply to all court mediation programs for general civil cases, as defined in rule 1.6, unless otherwise specified. *(Adopted, eff. July 1, 2012.)*

Research References

2 Witkin Cal. Proc. 5th Courts § 191, (S 191) Civil Rules.

Rule 3.845. Form of mediator statements and reports

If a mediator is required to submit a statement or report to the court concerning the status or result of the mediation, the statement or report must be submitted on the Judicial Council *Statement of Agreement or Nonagreement* (form ADR–100). The mediator's completed form ADR–100 must not disclose the terms of any agreement or any other communications or conduct that occurred in the course of the mediation, except as allowed in Evidence Code sections 1115–1128. *(Adopted, eff. July 1, 2012.)*

Advisory Committee Comment

This rule does not preclude courts from asking mediators to provide other information about court-program mediations on separate forms or surveys that do not request any information that will allow identification of a specific case or mediation participant and that will not become part of the court's case file.

Research References

Rutter, Cal. Practice Guide: A.D.R. Ch. 4-C, C. Statutorily-Mandated Court Mediation Programs.

Rutter, Cal. Practice Guide: Civ. Pro. Before Trial Ch. 13-A, A. Introduction.

2 Witkin Cal. Proc. 5th Courts § 191, (S 191) Civil Rules.

6 Witkin Cal. Proc. 5th Proceedings Without Trial § 491, Procedure.

Article 2

RULES OF CONDUCT FOR MEDIATORS IN COURT-CONNECTED MEDIATION PROGRAMS FOR CIVIL CASES

Rule
3.850. Purpose and function.
3.851. Application.
3.852. Definitions.
3.853. Voluntary participation and self–determination.
3.854. Confidentiality.
3.855. Impartiality, conflicts of interest, disclosure, and withdrawal.
3.856. Competence.
3.857. Quality of mediation process.
3.858. Marketing.
3.859. Compensation and gifts.
3.860. Attendance sheet and agreement to disclosure.

Rule 3.850. Purpose and function

(a) Standards of conduct

The rules in this article establish the minimum standards of conduct for mediators in court-connected mediation programs for general civil cases. These rules are intended to guide the conduct of mediators in these programs, to inform and protect participants in these mediation programs, and to promote public confidence in the mediation process and the courts. For mediation to be effective, there must be broad public confidence in the integrity and fairness of the process. Mediators in court-connected programs are responsible to the parties, the public, and the courts for conducting themselves in a manner that merits that confidence.

(b) Scope and limitations

These rules are not intended to:

(1) Establish a ceiling on what is considered good practice in mediation or discourage efforts by courts, mediators, or others to educate mediators about best practices;

(2) Create a basis for challenging a settlement agreement reached in connection with mediation; or

(3) Create a basis for a civil cause of action against a mediator. *(Formerly Rule 1620, adopted, eff. Jan. 1, 2003. Renumbered Rule 3.850 and amended, eff. Jan. 1, 2007.)*

Research References

Rutter, Cal. Practice Guide: A.D.R. Ch. 3-A, A. General Considerations.
Rutter, Cal. Practice Guide: A.D.R. Ch. 3-B, B. Commencing Mediation Process.
Rutter, Cal. Practice Guide: A.D.R. Ch. 4-C, C. Statutorily-Mandated Court Mediation Programs.
Rutter, Cal. Practice Guide: A.D.R. Ch. 7-A, A. Mediators.
Rutter, Cal. Practice Guide: Civ. Pro. Before Trial Ch. 13-A, A. Introduction.
Rutter, Cal. Practice Guide: Prof. Responsibility Ch. 1-K, K. Additional Regulations Affecting Lawyer Conduct.
2 Witkin Cal. Proc. 5th Courts § 191, (S 191) Civil Rules.
6 Witkin Cal. Proc. 5th Proceedings Without Trial § 488, (S 488) Regulation of Mediation.

Rule 3.851. Application

(a) Circumstances applicable

The rules in this article apply to mediations in which a mediator:

(1) Has agreed to be included on a superior court's list or panel of mediators for general civil cases and is notified by the court or the parties that he or she has been selected to mediate a case within that court's mediation program; or

(2) Has agreed to mediate a general civil case pending in a superior court after being notified by the court or the parties that he or she was recommended, selected, or appointed by that court or will be compensated by that court to mediate a case within that court's mediation program. A mediator who is not on a superior court list or panel and who is selected by the parties is not "recommended, selected, or appointed" by the court within the meaning of this subdivision simply because the court approves the parties' agreement to use this mediator or memorializes the parties' selection in a court order.

(b) Application to listed firms

If a court's panel or list includes firms that provide mediation services, all mediators affiliated with a listed firm are required to comply with the rules in this article when they are notified by the court or the parties that the firm was selected from the court list to mediate a general civil case within that court's mediation program.

(c) Time of applicability

Except as otherwise provided in these rules, the rules in this article apply from the time the mediator agrees to mediate a case until the end of the mediation in that case.

(d) Inapplicability to judges

The rules in this article do not apply to judges or other judicial officers while they are serving in a capacity in which they are governed by the Code of Judicial Ethics.

(e) Inapplicability to settlement conferences

The rules in this article do not apply to settlement conferences conducted under rule 3.1380. *(Formerly Rule 1620.1, adopted, eff. Jan. 1, 2003. Renumbered Rule 3.851 and amended, eff. Jan. 1, 2007. As amended, eff. July 1, 2007; Jan. 1, 2009; Jan. 1, 2010.)*

Advisory Committee Comment

Subdivision (d). Although these rules do not apply to them, judicial officers who serve as mediators in their courts' mediation programs are nevertheless encouraged to be familiar with and observe these rules when mediating, particularly the rules concerning subjects not covered in the Code of Judicial Ethics such as voluntary participation and self-determination.

Research References

Rutter, Cal. Practice Guide: A.D.R. Ch. 4-C, C. Statutorily-Mandated Court Mediation Programs.
Rutter, Cal. Practice Guide: Civ. Pro. Before Trial Ch. 13-A, A. Introduction.
6 Witkin Cal. Proc. 5th Proceedings Without Trial § 488, (S 488) Regulation of Mediation.

Rule 3.852. Definitions

As used in this article, unless the context or subject matter requires otherwise:

(1) "Mediation" means a process in which a neutral person or persons facilitate communication between the disputants to assist them in reaching a mutually acceptable agreement.

(2) "Mediator" means a neutral person who conducts a mediation.

(3) "Participant" means any individual, entity, or group, other than the mediator taking part in a mediation, including but not limited to attorneys for the parties.

(4) "Party" means any individual, entity, or group taking part in a mediation that is a plaintiff, a defendant, a cross-complainant, a cross-defendant, a petitioner, a respondent, or an interve-

nor in the case. *(Formerly Rule 1620.2, adopted, eff. Jan. 1, 2003. Renumbered Rule 3.852 and amended, eff. Jan. 1, 2007.)*

Advisory Committee Comment

The definition of "mediator" in this rule departs from the definition in Evidence Code section 1115(b) in that it does not include persons designated by the mediator to assist in the mediation or to communicate with a participant in preparation for the mediation. However, these definitions are applicable only to these rules of conduct and do not limit or expand mediation confidentiality under the Evidence Code or other law.

The definition of "participant" includes insurance adjusters, experts, and consultants as well as the parties and their attorneys.

Research References

Rutter, Cal. Practice Guide: A.D.R. Ch. 4-C, C. Statutorily-Mandated Court Mediation Programs.

Rutter, Cal. Practice Guide: Personal Injury Ch. 7-A, A. Introduction-Nature and Purpose of "Judicial Arbitration" in General.

6 Witkin Cal. Proc. 5th Proceedings Without Trial § 488, (S 488) Regulation of Mediation.

Rule 3.853. Voluntary participation and self–determination

A mediator must conduct the mediation in a manner that supports the principles of voluntary participation and self-determination by the parties. For this purpose a mediator must:

(1) Inform the parties, at or before the outset of the first mediation session, that any resolution of the dispute in mediation requires a voluntary agreement of the parties;

(2) Respect the right of each participant to decide the extent of his or her participation in the mediation, including the right to withdraw from the mediation at any time; and

(3) Refrain from coercing any party to make a decision or to continue to participate in the mediation. *(Formerly Rule 1620.3, adopted, eff. Jan. 1, 2003. Renumbered Rule 3.853 and amended, eff. Jan. 1, 2007.)*

Advisory Committee Comment

Voluntary participation and self-determination are fundamental principles of mediation that apply both to mediations in which the parties voluntarily elect to mediate and to those in which the parties are required to go to mediation in a mandatory court mediation program or by court order. Although the court may order participants to attend mediation, a mediator may not mandate the extent of their participation in the mediation process or coerce any party to settle the case.

After informing the parties of their choices and the consequences of those choices, a mediator can invoke a broad range of approaches to assist the parties in reaching an agreement without offending the principles of voluntary participation and self-determination, including (1) encouraging the parties to continue participating in the mediation when it reasonably appears to the mediator that the possibility of reaching an uncoerced, consensual agreement has not been exhausted and (2) suggesting that a party consider obtaining professional advice (for example, informing an unrepresented party that he or she may consider obtaining legal advice). Conversely, examples of conduct that violate the principles of voluntary participation and self-determination include coercing a party to continue participating in the mediation after the party has told the mediator that he or she wishes to terminate the mediation, providing an opinion or evaluation of the dispute in a coercive manner or over the objection of the parties, using abusive language, and threatening to make a report to the court about a party's conduct at the mediation.

Research References

Rutter, Cal. Practice Guide: A.D.R. Ch. 3-C, C. Confidentiality.

Rutter, Cal. Practice Guide: A.D.R. Ch. 4-C, C. Statutorily-Mandated Court Mediation Programs.

Rutter, Cal. Practice Guide: Civ. Pro. Before Trial Ch. 13-A, A. Introduction.

Rutter, Cal. Practice Guide: Personal Injury Ch. 7-A, A. Introduction-Nature and Purpose of "Judicial Arbitration" in General.

6 Witkin Cal. Proc. 5th Proceedings Without Trial § 488, (S 488) Regulation of Mediation.

Rule 3.854. Confidentiality

(a) Compliance with confidentiality law

A mediator must, at all times, comply with the applicable law concerning confidentiality.

(b) Informing participants of confidentiality

At or before the outset of the first mediation session, a mediator must provide the participants with a general explanation of the confidentiality of mediation proceedings.

(c) Confidentiality of separate communications; caucuses

If, after all the parties have agreed to participate in the mediation process and the mediator has agreed to mediate the case, a mediator speaks separately with one or more participants out of the presence of the other participants, the mediator must first discuss with all participants the mediator's practice regarding confidentiality for separate communications with the participants. Except as required by law, a mediator must not disclose information revealed in confidence during such separate communications unless authorized to do so by the participant or participants who revealed the information.

(d) Use of confidential information

A mediator must not use information that is acquired in confidence in the course of a mediation outside the mediation or for personal gain. *(Formerly Rule 1620.4, adopted, eff. Jan. 1, 2003. Renumbered Rule 3.854, eff. Jan. 1, 2007.)*

Advisory Committee Comment

Subdivision (a). The general law concerning mediation confidentiality is found in Evidence Code sections 703.5 and 1115–1128 and in cases interpreting those sections. (See, e.g., *Foxgate Homeowners' Association, Inc. v. Bramalea California, Inc.* (2001) 26 Cal.4th 1; *Rinaker v. Superior Court* (1998) 62 Cal.App.4th 155; and *Gilbert v. National Corp. for Housing Partnerships* (1999) 71 Cal.App.4th 1240.)

Research References

Rutter, Cal. Practice Guide: A.D.R. Ch. 4-C, C. Statutorily-Mandated Court Mediation Programs.

Rutter, Cal. Practice Guide: Civ. Pro. Before Trial Ch. 13-A, A. Introduction.

Rutter, Cal. Practice Guide: Personal Injury Ch. 7-A, A. Introduction-Nature and Purpose of "Judicial Arbitration" in General.

6 Witkin Cal. Proc. 5th Proceedings Without Trial § 488, (S 488) Regulation of Mediation.

Rule 3.855. Impartiality, conflicts of interest, disclosure, and withdrawal

(a) Impartiality

A mediator must maintain impartiality toward all participants in the mediation process at all times.

(b) Disclosure of matters potentially affecting impartiality

(1) A mediator must make reasonable efforts to keep informed about matters that reasonably could raise a question about his or her ability to conduct the proceedings impartially, and must disclose these matters to the parties. These matters include:

(A) Past, present, and currently expected interests, relationships, and affiliations of a personal, professional, or financial nature; and

Ct. Rules

(B) The existence of any grounds for disqualification of a judge specified in Code of Civil Procedure section 170.1.

(2) A mediator's duty to disclose is a continuing obligation, from the inception of the mediation process through its completion. Disclosures required by this rule must be made as soon as practicable after a mediator becomes aware of a matter that must be disclosed. To the extent possible, such disclosures should be made before the first mediation session, but in any event they must be made within the time required by applicable court rules or statutes.

(c) Proceeding if there are no objections or questions concerning impartiality

Except as provided in (f), if, after a mediator makes disclosures, no party objects to the mediator and no participant raises any question or concern about the mediator's ability to conduct the mediation impartially, the mediator may proceed.

(d) Responding to questions or concerns concerning impartiality

If, after a mediator makes disclosures or at any other point in the mediation process, a participant raises a question or concern about the mediator's ability to conduct the mediation impartially, the mediator must address the question or concern with the participants. Except as provided in (f), if, after the question or concern is addressed, no party objects to the mediator, the mediator may proceed.

(e) Withdrawal or continuation upon party objection concerning impartiality

In a two-party mediation, if any party objects to the mediator after the mediator makes disclosures or discusses a participant's question or concern regarding the mediator's ability to conduct the mediation impartially, the mediator must withdraw. In a mediation in which there are more than two parties, the mediator may continue the mediation with the nonobjecting parties, provided that doing so would not violate any other provision of these rules, any law, or any local court rule or program guideline.

(f) Circumstances requiring mediator recusal despite party consent

Regardless of the consent of the parties, a mediator either must decline to serve as mediator or, if already serving, must withdraw from the mediation if:

(1) The mediator cannot maintain impartiality toward all participants in the mediation process; or

(2) Proceeding with the mediation would jeopardize the integrity of the court or of the mediation process. *(Formerly Rule 1620.5, adopted, eff. Jan. 1, 2003. Renumbered Rule 3.855 and amended, eff. Jan. 1, 2007.)*

Advisory Committee Comment

Subdivision (b). This subdivision is intended to provide parties with information they need to help them determine whether a mediator can conduct the mediation impartially. A mediator's overarching duty under this subdivision is to make a "reasonable effort" to identify matters that, in the eyes of a reasonable person, could raise a question about the mediator's ability to conduct the mediation impartially, and to inform the parties about those matters. What constitutes a "reasonable effort" to identify such matters varies depending on the circumstances, including whether the case is scheduled in advance or received on the spot, and the information about the participants and the subject matter that is provided to the mediator by the court and the parties.

The interests, relationships, and affiliations that a mediator may need to disclose under (b)(1)(A) include: (1) prior, current, or currently expected service as a mediator in another mediation involving any of the participants in the present mediation; (2)

prior, current, or currently expected business relationships or transactions between the mediator and any of the participants; and (3) the mediator's ownership of stock or any other significant financial interest involving any participant in the mediation. Currently expected interests, relationships, and affiliations may include, for example, an intention to form a partnership or to enter into a future business relationship with one of the participants in the mediation.

Although (b)(1) specifies interests, relationships, affiliations, and matters that are grounds for disqualification of a judge under Code of Civil Procedure section 170.1, these are only examples of common matters that reasonably could raise a question about a mediator's ability to conduct the mediation impartially and, thus, must be disclosed. The absence of particular interests, relationships, affiliations, and section 170.1 matters does not necessarily mean that there is no matter that could reasonably raise a question about the mediator's ability to conduct the mediation impartially. A mediator must make determinations concerning disclosure on a case-by-case basis, applying the general criteria for disclosure under (b)(1).

Attorney mediators should be aware that under the section 170.1 standard, they may need to make disclosures when an attorney in their firm is serving or has served as a lawyer for any of the parties in the mediation. Section 170.1 does not specifically address whether a mediator must disclose when another member of the mediator's dispute resolution services firm is providing or has provided services to any of the parties in the mediation. Therefore, a mediator must evaluate such circumstances under the general criteria for disclosure under (b)(1)—that is, is it a matter that, in the eyes of a reasonable person, could raise a question about the mediator's ability to conduct the mediation impartially?

If there is a conflict between the mediator's obligation to maintain confidentiality and the mediator's obligation to make a disclosure, the mediator must determine whether he or she can make a general disclosure of the circumstance without revealing any confidential information, or must decline to serve.

Research References

Rutter, Cal. Practice Guide: A.D.R. Ch. 3-B, B. Commencing Mediation Process.

Rutter, Cal. Practice Guide: A.D.R. Ch. 4-C, C. Statutorily-Mandated Court Mediation Programs.

Rutter, Cal. Practice Guide: A.D.R. Ch. 7-A, A. Mediators.

Rutter, Cal. Practice Guide: Civ. Pro. Before Trial Ch. 13-A, A. Introduction.

Rutter, Cal. Practice Guide: Personal Injury Ch. 7-A, A. Introduction-Nature and Purpose of "Judicial Arbitration" in General.

6 Witkin Cal. Proc. 5th Proceedings Without Trial § 488, (S 488) Regulation of Mediation.

Rule 3.856.　Competence

(a) Compliance with court qualifications

A mediator must comply with experience, training, educational, and other requirements established by the court for appointment and retention.

(b) Truthful representation of background

A mediator has a continuing obligation to truthfully represent his or her background to the court and participants. Upon a request by any party, a mediator must provide truthful information regarding his or her experience, training, and education.

(c) Informing court of public discipline and other matters

A mediator must also inform the court if:

(1) Public discipline has been imposed on the mediator by any public disciplinary or professional licensing agency;

(2) The mediator has resigned his or her membership in the State Bar or another professional licensing agency while disciplinary or criminal charges were pending;

(3) A felony charge is pending against the mediator;

(4) The mediator has been convicted of a felony or of a misdemeanor involving moral turpitude; or

(5) There has been an entry of judgment against the mediator in any civil action for actual fraud or punitive damages.

(d) Assessment of skills; withdrawal

A mediator has a continuing obligation to assess whether or not his or her level of skill, knowledge, and ability is sufficient to conduct the mediation effectively. A mediator must decline to serve or withdraw from the mediation if the mediator determines that he or she does not have the level of skill, knowledge, or ability necessary to conduct the mediation effectively. *(Formerly Rule 1620.6, adopted, eff. Jan. 1, 2003. Renumbered Rule 3.856, eff. Jan. 1, 2007.)*

Advisory Committee Comment

Subdivision (d). No particular advanced academic degree or technical or professional experience is a prerequisite for competence as a mediator. Core mediation skills include communicating clearly, listening effectively, facilitating communication among all participants, promoting exploration of mutually acceptable settlement options, and conducting oneself in a neutral manner.

A mediator must consider and weigh a variety of issues in order to assess whether his or her level of skill, knowledge, and ability is sufficient to make him or her effective in a particular mediation. Issues include whether the parties (1) were involved or had input in the selection of the mediator; (2) had access to information about the mediator's background or level of skill, knowledge, and ability; (3) have a specific expectation or perception regarding the mediator's level of skill, knowledge, and ability; (4) have expressed a preference regarding the style of mediation they would like or expect; or (5) have expressed a desire to discuss legal or other professional information, to hear a personal evaluation of or opinion on a set of facts as presented, or to be made aware of the interests of persons who are not represented in mediation.

Research References

Rutter, Cal. Practice Guide: A.D.R. Ch. 4-C, C. Statutorily-Mandated Court Mediation Programs.

Rutter, Cal. Practice Guide: Civ. Pro. Before Trial Ch. 13-A, A. Introduction.

Rutter, Cal. Practice Guide: Personal Injury Ch. 7-A, A. Introduction-Nature and Purpose of "Judicial Arbitration" in General.

6 Witkin Cal. Proc. 5th Proceedings Without Trial § 488, (S 488) Regulation of Mediation.

Rule 3.857. Quality of mediation process

(a) Diligence

A mediator must make reasonable efforts to advance the mediation in a timely manner. If a mediator schedules a mediation for a specific time period, he or she must keep that time period free of other commitments.

(b) Procedural fairness

A mediator must conduct the mediation proceedings in a procedurally fair manner. "Procedural fairness" means a balanced process in which each party is given an opportunity to participate and make uncoerced decisions. A mediator is not obligated to ensure the substantive fairness of an agreement reached by the parties.

(c) Explanation of process

In addition to the requirements of rule 3.853 (voluntary participation and self–determination), rule 3.854(a) (confidentiality), and (d) of this rule (representation and other professional services), at or before the outset of the mediation the mediator must provide all participants with a general explanation of:

(1) The nature of the mediation process;

(2) The procedures to be used; and

(3) The roles of the mediator, the parties, and the other participants.

(d) Representation and other professional services

A mediator must inform all participants, at or before the outset of the first mediation session, that during the mediation he or she will not represent any participant as a lawyer or perform professional services in any capacity other than as an impartial mediator. Subject to the principles of impartiality and self-determination, a mediator may provide information or opinions that he or she is qualified by training or experience to provide.

(e) Recommending other services

A mediator may recommend the use of other services in connection with a mediation and may recommend particular providers of other services. However, a mediator must disclose any related personal or financial interests if recommending the services of specific individuals or organizations.

(f) Nonparticipants' interests

A mediator may bring to the attention of the parties the interests of others who are not participating in the mediation but who may be affected by agreements reached as a result of the mediation.

(g) Combining mediation with other ADR processes

A mediator must exercise caution in combining mediation with other alternative dispute resolution (ADR) processes and may do so only with the informed consent of the parties and in a manner consistent with any applicable law or court order. The mediator must inform the parties of the general natures of the different processes and the consequences of revealing information during any one process that might be used for decision making in another process, and must give the parties the opportunity to select another neutral for the subsequent process. If the parties consent to a combination of processes, the mediator must clearly inform the participants when the transition from one process to another is occurring.

(h) Settlement agreements

Consistent with (d), a mediator may present possible settlement options and terms for discussion. A mediator may also assist the parties in preparing a written settlement agreement, provided that in doing so the mediator confines the assistance to stating the settlement as determined by the parties.

(i) Discretionary termination and withdrawal

A mediator may suspend or terminate the mediation or withdraw as mediator when he or she reasonably believes the circumstances require it, including when he or she suspects that:

(1) The mediation is being used to further illegal conduct;

(2) A participant is unable to participate meaningfully in negotiations; or

(3) Continuation of the process would cause significant harm to any participant or a third party.

(j) Manner of withdrawal

When a mediator determines that it is necessary to suspend or terminate a mediation or to withdraw, the mediator must do so without violating the obligation of confidentiality and in a manner that will cause the least possible harm to the participants. *(Formerly Rule 1620.7, adopted, eff. Jan. 1, 2003. Renumbered Rule 3.857 and amended, eff. Jan. 1, 2007.)*

Advisory Committee Comment

Subdivision (c). The explanation of the mediation process should include a description of the mediator's style of mediation.

Subdivision (d). Subject to the principles of impartiality and self-determination, and if qualified to do so, a mediator may (1) discuss a party's options, including a range of possible outcomes in an adjudicative process; (2) offer a personal evaluation of or opinion on a set of facts as presented, which should be clearly identified as a personal evaluation or opinion; or (3) communicate the mediator's opinion or view of what the law is or how it applies to the subject of the mediation, provided that the mediator does not also advise any participant about how to adhere to the law or on what position the participant should take in light of that opinion.

One question that frequently arises is whether a mediator's assessment of claims, defenses, or possible litigation outcomes constitutes legal advice or the practice of law. Similar questions may arise when accounting, architecture, construction, counseling, medicine, real estate, or other licensed professions are relevant to a mediation. This rule does not determine what constitutes the practice of law or any other licensed profession. A mediator should be cautious when providing any information or opinion related to any field for which a professional license is required, in order to avoid doing so in a manner that may constitute the practice of a profession for which the mediator is not licensed, or in a manner that may violate the regulations of a profession that the mediator is licensed to practice. A mediator should exercise particular caution when discussing the law with unrepresented parties and should inform such parties that they may seek independent advice from a lawyer.

Subdivision (i). Subdivision (i)(2) is not intended to establish any new responsibility or diminish any existing responsibilities that a mediator may have, under the Americans With Disabilities Act or other similar law, to attempt to accommodate physical or mental disabilities of a participant in mediation.

Research References

Rutter, Cal. Practice Guide: A.D.R. Ch. 1-D, D. Planning for Private ADR.
Rutter, Cal. Practice Guide: A.D.R. Ch. 4-C, C. Statutorily-Mandated Court Mediation Programs.
Rutter, Cal. Practice Guide: Civ. Pro. Before Trial Ch. 13-A, A. Introduction.
6 Witkin Cal. Proc. 5th Proceedings Without Trial § 488, (S 488) Regulation of Mediation.

Rule 3.858. Marketing

(a) Truthfulness

A mediator must be truthful and accurate in marketing his or her mediation services. A mediator is responsible for ensuring that both his or her own marketing activities and any marketing activities carried out on his or her behalf by others comply with this rule.

(b) Representations concerning court approval

A mediator may indicate in his or her marketing materials that he or she is a member of a particular court's panel or list but, unless specifically permitted by the court, must not indicate that he or she is approved, endorsed, certified, or licensed by the court.

(c) Promises, guarantees, and implications of favoritism

In marketing his or her mediation services, a mediator must not:

(1) Promise or guarantee results; or

(2) Make any statement that directly or indirectly implies bias in favor of one party or participant over another.

(d) Solicitation of business

A mediator must not solicit business from a participant in a mediation proceeding while that mediation is pending. (Formerly Rule 1620.8, adopted, eff. Jan. 1, 2003. Renumbered Rule 3.858, eff. Jan. 1, 2007.)

Advisory Committee Comment

Subdivision (d). This rule is not intended to prohibit a mediator from accepting other employment from a participant

while a mediation is pending, provided that there was no express solicitation of this business by the mediator and that accepting that employment does not contravene any other provision of these rules, including the obligations to maintain impartiality, confidentiality, and the integrity of the process. If other employment is accepted from a participant while a mediation is pending, however, the mediator may be required to disclose this to the parties under rule 3.855.

This rule also is not intended to prohibit a mediator from engaging in general marketing activities. General marketing activities include, but are not limited to, running an advertisement in a newspaper and sending out a general mailing (either of which may be directed to a particular industry or market).

Research References

Rutter, Cal. Practice Guide: A.D.R. Ch. 4-C, C. Statutorily-Mandated Court Mediation Programs.
Rutter, Cal. Practice Guide: Civ. Pro. Before Trial Ch. 13-A, A. Introduction.
6 Witkin Cal. Proc. 5th Proceedings Without Trial § 488, (S 488) Regulation of Mediation.

Rule 3.859. Compensation and gifts

(a) Compliance with law

A mediator must comply with any applicable requirements concerning compensation established by statute or the court.

(b) Disclosure of and compliance with compensation terms

Before commencing the mediation, the mediator must disclose to the parties in writing any fees, costs, or charges to be paid to the mediator by the parties. A mediator must abide by any agreement that is reached concerning compensation.

(c) Contingent fees

The amount or nature of a mediator's fee must not be made contingent on the outcome of the mediation.

(d) Gifts and favors

A mediator must not at any time solicit or accept from or give to any participant or affiliate of a participant any gift, bequest, or favor that might reasonably raise a question concerning the mediator's impartiality. (Formerly Rule 1620.9, adopted, eff. Jan. 1, 2003. Renumbered Rule 3.859 and amended, eff. Jan. 1, 2007.)

Advisory Committee Comment

Subdivision (b). It is good practice to put mediation fee agreements in writing, and mediators are strongly encouraged to do so; however, nothing in this rule is intended to preclude enforcement of a compensation agreement for mediation services that is not in writing.

Subdivision (d). Whether a gift, bequest, or favor "might reasonably raise a question concerning the mediator's impartiality" must be determined on a case-by-case basis. This subdivision is not intended to prohibit a mediator from accepting other employment from any of the participants, consistent with rule 3.858(d).

Research References

Rutter, Cal. Practice Guide: A.D.R. Ch. 4-C, C. Statutorily-Mandated Court Mediation Programs.
Rutter, Cal. Practice Guide: Civ. Pro. Before Trial Ch. 13-A, A. Introduction.
6 Witkin Cal. Proc. 5th Proceedings Without Trial § 488, (S 488) Regulation of Mediation.

Rule 3.860. Attendance sheet and agreement to disclosure

(a) Attendance sheet

In each mediation to which these rules apply under rule 3.851(a), the mediator must request that all participants in the mediation complete an attendance sheet stating their names, mailing addresses, and telephone numbers; retain the attendance sheet for at least two years; and submit it to the court on request.

(b) Agreement to disclosure

The mediator must agree, in each mediation to which these rules apply under rule 3.851(a), that if an inquiry or a complaint is made about the conduct of the mediator, mediation communications may be disclosed solely for purposes of a complaint procedure conducted pursuant to rule 3.865 to address that complaint or inquiry. *(Formerly Rule 1621, adopted, eff. Jan. 1, 2006. Renumbered Rule 3.860 and amended, eff. Jan. 1, 2007. As amended, eff. Jan. 1, 2011.)*

Research References

Rutter, Cal. Practice Guide: A.D.R. Ch. 4-C, C. Statutorily-Mandated Court Mediation Programs.
Rutter, Cal. Practice Guide: Personal Injury Ch. 7-A, A. Introduction-Nature and Purpose of "Judicial Arbitration" in General.
2 Witkin Cal. Proc. 5th Courts § 191, (S 191) Civil Rules.
6 Witkin Cal. Proc. 5th Proceedings Without Trial § 488, (S 488) Regulation of Mediation.

Article 3

REQUIREMENTS FOR ADDRESSING COMPLAINTS ABOUT COURT–PROGRAM MEDIATORS

Rule
3.865.   Application and purpose.
3.866.   Definitions.
3.867.   Complaint coordinator.
3.868.   Complaint procedure required.
3.869.   General requirements for complaint procedures and complaint proceedings.
3.870.   Permissible court actions on complaints.
3.871.   Confidentiality of complaint proceedings, information, and records.
3.872.   Disqualification from subsequently serving as an adjudicator.

Rule 3.865.   Application and purpose

(a) Application

The rules in this article apply to each superior court that makes a list of mediators available to litigants in general civil cases or that recommends, selects, appoints, or compensates a mediator to mediate any general civil case pending in that court. A court that approves the parties' agreement to use a mediator who is selected by the parties and who is not on the court's list of mediators or that memorializes the parties' agreement in a court order has not thereby recommended, selected, or appointed that mediator within the meaning of this rule.

(b) Purpose

These rules are intended to promote the resolution of complaints that mediators in court-connected mediation programs for civil cases may have violated a provision of the rules of conduct for such mediators in article 2. They are intended to help courts promptly resolve any such complaints in a manner that is respectful and fair to the complainant and the mediator and consistent with the California mediation confidentiality statutes. *(Adopted, eff. Jan. 1, 2010. As amended, eff. Jan. 1, 2010.)*

Advisory Committee Comment

As used in this article, complaint means a written communication presented to a court's complaint coordinator indicating that

a mediator may have violated a provision of the rules of conduct for mediators in article 2.

Complaints about mediators are relatively rare. To ensure the quality of court mediation panels and public confidence in the mediation process and the courts, it is, nevertheless, important to ensure that any complaints that do arise are resolved through procedures that are consistent with California mediation confidentiality statutes (Evid. Code, §§ 703.5 and 1115 et seq.), as well as fair and respectful to the interested parties.

The requirements and procedures in this article do not abrogate or limit a court's inherent or other authority, in its sole and absolute discretion, to determine who may be included on or removed from a court list of mediators; to approve or revoke a mediator's eligibility to be recommended, selected, appointed, or compensated by the court; or to follow other procedures or take other actions to ensure the quality of mediators who serve in the court's mediation program in contexts other than when addressing a complaint. The failure to follow a requirement or procedure in this article will not invalidate any action taken by the court in addressing a complaint.

Research References

Rutter, Cal. Practice Guide: A.D.R. Ch. 4-C, C. Statutorily-Mandated Court Mediation Programs.
Rutter, Cal. Practice Guide: Civ. Pro. Before Trial Ch. 13-A, A. Introduction.
Rutter, Cal. Practice Guide: Personal Injury Ch. 7-A, A. Introduction-Nature and Purpose of "Judicial Arbitration" in General.
2 Witkin Cal. Proc. 5th Courts § 191, (S 191) Civil Rules.
6 Witkin Cal. Proc. 5th Proceedings Without Trial § 488, (S 488) Regulation of Mediation.

Rule 3.866.   Definitions

As used in this article, unless the context or subject matter requires otherwise:

(1) "The rules of conduct" means rules 3.850–3.860 of the California Rules of Court in article 2.

(2) "Court-program mediator" means a person subject to the rules of conduct under rule 3.851.

(3) "Inquiry" means an unwritten communication presented to the court's complaint coordinator indicating that a mediator may have violated a provision of the rules of conduct.

(4) "Complaint" means a written communication presented to the court's complaint coordinator indicating that a mediator may have violated a provision of the rules of conduct.

(5) "Complainant" means the person who makes or presents a complaint.

(6) "Complaint coordinator" means the person designated by the presiding judge under rule 3.867(a) to receive complaints and inquiries about the conduct of mediators.

(7) "Complaint committee" means a committee designated or appointed to investigate and make recommendations concerning complaints under rule 3.869(d)(2).

(8) "Complaint procedure" means a procedure for presenting, receiving, reviewing, responding to, investigating, and acting on any inquiry or complaint.

(9) "Complaint proceeding" means all of the proceedings that take place as part of a complaint procedure concerning a specific inquiry or complaint.

(10) "Mediation communication" means any statement that is made or any writing that is prepared for the purpose of, in the course of, or pursuant to a mediation or a mediation consultation, as defined in Evidence Code section 1115, and includes any communications, negotiations, and settlement discussions between participants in the course of a mediation or a mediation consultation. *(Adopted, eff. Jan. 1, 2010.)*

Advisory Committee Comment

Paragraph (2). Under rule 3.851, the rules of conduct apply when a mediator, or a firm with which a mediator is affiliated, has agreed to be included on a superior court's list or panel of mediators for general civil cases and is notified by the court or the parties that he or she has been selected to mediate a case within that court's mediation program or when a mediator has agreed to mediate a general civil case after being notified that he or she was recommended, selected, or appointed by a court, or will be compensated by a court, to mediate a case within a court's mediation program.

Paragraphs (3) and (4). The distinction between "inquiries" and "complaints" is significant because some provisions of this article apply only to complaints (i.e., written communications presented to the court's complaint coordinator indicating that a mediator may have violated a provision of the rules of conduct) and not to inquiries.

Research References

6 Witkin Cal. Proc. 5th Proceedings Without Trial § 488, (S 488) Regulation of Mediation.

Rule 3.867. Complaint coordinator

(a) Designation of the complaint coordinator

The presiding judge must designate a person who is knowledgeable about mediation to serve as the complaint coordinator.

(b) Identification of the complaint coordinator

The court must make the complaint coordinator's identity and contact information readily accessible to litigants and the public. *(Formerly Rule 1622.1, adopted, eff. Jan. 1, 2006. Renumbered Rule 3.866 and amended, eff. Jan. 1, 2007. Renumbered Rule 3.867 and amended, eff. Jan. 1, 2010.)*

Advisory Committee Comment

The alternative dispute resolution program administrator appointed under rule 10.783(a) may also be appointed as the complaint coordinator if that person is knowledgeable about mediation.

Research References

6 Witkin Cal. Proc. 5th Proceedings Without Trial § 488, (S 488) Regulation of Mediation.

Rule 3.868. Complaint procedure required

Each court to which this article applies under rule 3.865 must establish a complaint procedure by local rule of court that is consistent with this article. *(Formerly Rule 1622, adopted, eff. Jan. 1, 2003. As amended, eff. Jan. 1, 2006. Renumbered Rule 3.865 and amended, eff. Jan. 1, 2007. Renumbered Rule 3.868 and amended, eff. Jan. 1, 2010.)*

Research References

Rutter, Cal. Practice Guide: A.D.R. Ch. 4-C, C. Statutorily-Mandated Court Mediation Programs.
2 Witkin Cal. Proc. 5th Courts § 191, (S 191) Civil Rules.
6 Witkin Cal. Proc. 5th Proceedings Without Trial § 488, (S 488) Regulation of Mediation.

Rule 3.869. General requirements for complaint procedures and complaint proceedings

(a) Submission and referral of inquiries and complaints to the complaint coordinator

All inquiries and complaints should be submitted or referred to the complaint coordinator.

(b) Acknowledgment of complaint

The complaint coordinator must send the complainant a written acknowledgment that the court has received the complaint.

(c) Preliminary review and disposition of complaints

The complaint coordinator must conduct a preliminary review of all complaints to determine whether the complaint can be informally resolved or closed, or whether the complaint warrants investigation.

(d) Procedure for complaints not resolved through the preliminary review

The following procedures are required only if a complaint is not resolved or closed through the preliminary review.

(1) *Mediator's notice and opportunity to respond*

The mediator must be given notice of the complaint and an opportunity to respond.

(2) *Investigation and recommendation*

(A) Except as provided in (B), the complaint must be investigated and a recommendation concerning court action on the complaint must be made by either an individual who has experience as a mediator and who is familiar with the rules of conduct stated in article 2 or a complaint committee that has at least one such individual as a member.

(B) A court with eight or fewer authorized judges may waive the requirement in (A) for participation by an individual who has experience as a mediator in conducting the investigation and making the recommendation if the court cannot find a suitable qualified individual to perform the functions described in (A) or for other grounds of hardship.

(3) *Final decision*

The final decision on the complaint must be made by the presiding judge or his or her designee, who must not be the complaint coordinator or an individual who investigated the complaint before its submission for final decision.

(e) Notice of final action

(1) The court must send the complainant notice of the final action taken by the court on the complaint.

(2) If the complaint was not closed during the preliminary review, the court must send notice of the final action to the mediator.

(f) Promptness

The court must process complaints promptly at all stages.

(g) Records of complaints

The court should maintain sufficient information about each complaint and its disposition to identify any history or patterns of complaints submitted under these rules. *(Adopted, eff. Jan. 1, 2010.)*

Advisory Committee Comment

The Administrative Office of the Courts has developed model local rules that satisfy the requirements of this rule. These model local rules were developed with input from judicial officers, court administrators, alternative dispute resolution (ADR) program administrators, court-program mediators, and public commentators and are designed so that they can be readily adapted to the circumstances of individual courts and specific complaints. Courts are encouraged to adopt rules that follow the model rules, to the extent feasible. Courts can obtain copies of these model rules from civil ADR program staff at the Administrative Office of the Courts.

Subdivision (a). Coordination of inquiries and complaints by a person knowledgeable about mediation is important to help ensure that the requirements of this article are followed and that mediation confidentiality is preserved.

Subdivision (c). Courts are encouraged to resolve inquiries and complaints about mediators using the simplest, least formal procedures that are appropriate under the circumstances, provided that they meet the requirements stated in this article.

Most complaints can be appropriately resolved during the preliminary review stage of the complaint process, through informal discussions between or among the complaint coordinator, the complainant, and the mediator. Although complaint coordinators are not required to communicate with the mediator during the preliminary review, they are encouraged to consider doing so. For example, some complaints may arise from a misunderstanding of the mediator's role or from behavior that would not violate the standards of conduct. These types of complaints might appropriately be addressed by providing the complainant with additional information or by informing the mediator that certain behavior was upsetting to a mediation participant.

The circumstances under which a complaint coordinator might informally resolve or close a complaint include, for example, when (1) the complaint is withdrawn; (2) no violation of the rules of conduct appears to have occurred; (3) the alleged violation of the rules of conduct is very minor and the mediator has provided an acceptable explanation or response; and (4) the complainant, the mediator, and the complaint coordinator have agreed on a resolution. In determining whether to close a complaint, the complaint coordinator might also consider whether there are or have been other complaints about the mediator.

Subdivision (d). At the investigation and recommendation stage, all courts are encouraged to consider using a complaint committee comprised of members with a variety of backgrounds, including at least one person with experience as a mediator, to investigate and make recommendations concerning those rare complaints that are not resolved during the preliminary review.

Courts are also encouraged to have a judicial officer who is knowledgeable about mediation, or a committee that includes another person who is knowledgeable about mediation, make the final decision on complaints that are not resolved through the preliminary review.

Research References

Rutter, Cal. Practice Guide: A.D.R. Ch. 4-C, C. Statutorily-Mandated Court Mediation Programs.
Rutter, Cal. Practice Guide: Civ. Pro. Before Trial Ch. 13-A, A. Introduction.
6 Witkin Cal. Proc. 5th Proceedings Without Trial § 488, (S 488) Regulation of Mediation.

Rule 3.870. Permissible court actions on complaints

After an investigation has been conducted, the presiding judge or his or her designee may do one or more of the following:

(1) Direct that no action be taken on the complaint;

(2) Counsel, admonish, or reprimand the mediator;

(3) Impose additional training requirements as a condition of the mediator remaining on the court's panel or list;

(4) Suspend the mediator from the court's panel or list or otherwise temporarily prohibit the mediator from receiving future mediation referrals from the court; or

(5) Remove the mediator from the court's panel or list or otherwise prohibit the mediator from receiving future mediation referrals from the court. *(Adopted, eff. Jan. 1, 2010.)*

Advisory Committee Comment

This rule does not abrogate or limit any existing legal right or duty of the court to take other actions, including interim suspension of a mediator pending final action by the court on a complaint.

Research References

Rutter, Cal. Practice Guide: A.D.R. Ch. 4-C, C. Statutorily-Mandated Court Mediation Programs.
2 Witkin Cal. Proc. 5th Courts § 191, (S 191) Civil Rules.
6 Witkin Cal. Proc. 5th Proceedings Without Trial § 488, (S 488) Regulation of Mediation.
6 Witkin Cal. Proc. 5th Proceedings Without Trial § 489, Scope of Pilot Project.

Rule 3.871. Confidentiality of complaint proceedings, information, and records

(a) Intent

This rule is intended to:

(1) Preserve the confidentiality of mediation communications as required by Evidence Code sections 1115–1128;

(2) Promote cooperation in the reporting, investigation, and resolution of complaints about court-program mediators; and

(3) Protect mediators against damage to their reputations that might result from the disclosure of unfounded complaints against them.

(b) Preserving the confidentiality of mediation communications

All complaint procedures and complaint proceedings must be designed and conducted in a manner that preserves the confidentiality of mediation communications, including but not limited to the confidentiality of any communications between the mediator and individual mediation participants or subgroups of mediation participants.

(c) Confidentiality of complaint proceedings

All complaint proceedings must occur in private and must be kept confidential. No information or records concerning the receipt, investigation, or resolution of an inquiry or a complaint may be open to the public or disclosed outside the course of the complaint proceeding except as provided in (d) or as otherwise required by law.

(d) Authorized disclosures

After the decision on a complaint, the presiding judge, or a person whom the presiding judge designates to do so, may authorize the public disclosure of information or records concerning the complaint proceeding that do not reveal any mediation communications. The disclosures that may be authorized under this subdivision include the name of a mediator against whom action has been taken under rule 3.870, the action taken, and the general basis on which the action was taken. In determining whether to authorize the disclosure of information or records under this subdivision, the presiding judge or the designee should consider the purposes of the confidentiality of complaint proceedings stated in (a)(2) and (a)(3).

(e) Disclosures required by law

In determining whether the disclosure of information or records concerning a complaint proceeding is required by law, courts should consider the purposes of the confidentiality of complaint proceedings stated in (a). If it appears that the disclosure of information or records concerning a complaint proceeding that would reveal mediation communications is required by law, before the information or records are disclosed, notice should be given to any person whose mediation communications may thereby be revealed. *(Formerly Rule 1622.2, adopted, eff. Jan. 1, 2006. Renumbered Rule 3.867 and amended, eff. Jan. 1, 2007. Renumbered Rule 3.871 and amended, eff. Jan. 1, 2010.)*

Advisory Committee Comment

Under rule 3.866(9), the complaint proceedings covered by this rule include proceedings to address inquiries as well as complaints (i.e., to unwritten as well as written communications indicating that a mediator may have violated a provision of the rules of conduct).

Subdivision (a). See Evidence Code sections 1115 and 1119 concerning the scope and types of mediation communications protected by mediation confidentiality. Rule 3.871 is intended to supplement the confidentiality of mediation communications established by the Evidence Code by ensuring that disclosure of information or records about a complaint proceeding does not reveal confidential mediation communications. Rule 3.871 is not intended to supersede or abrogate the confidentiality of mediation communications established by the Evidence Code.

Subdivision (b). Private meetings, or "caucuses," between a mediator and subgroups of participants are common in court-connected mediations, and it is frequently understood that these communications will not be disclosed to other participants in the mediation. (See Cal. Rules of Court, rule 3.854(c).) It is important to protect the confidentiality of these communications in complaint proceedings so that one participant in the mediation does not learn what another participant discussed in confidence with the mediator without the consent of the participants in the caucus communication.

Subdivisions (c)–(e). The provisions of (c)–(e) that authorize the disclosure of information and records related to complaint proceedings do not create any new exceptions to mediation confidentiality. Although public disclosure of information and records about complaint proceedings that do not reveal mediation communications may be authorized under (d), information and records that *would* reveal mediation communications may be publicly disclosed only as required by law (e.g., in response to a subpoena or court order) and consistent with the statutes and case law governing mediation confidentiality. A person who is knowledgeable about California's mediation confidentiality laws should determine whether the disclosure of mediation communications is required by law.

Evidence Code sections 915 and 1040 establish procedures and criteria for deciding whether information acquired in confidence by a public employee in the course of his or her duty is subject to disclosure. These sections may be applicable or helpful in determining whether the disclosure of information or records acquired by judicial officers, court staff, and other persons in the course of a complaint proceeding is required by law or should be authorized in the discretion of the presiding judge.

Research References

Rutter, Cal. Practice Guide: A.D.R. Ch. 4-C, C. Statutorily-Mandated Court Mediation Programs.
Rutter, Cal. Practice Guide: Civ. Pro. Before Trial Ch. 13-A, A. Introduction.
Rutter, Cal. Practice Guide: Personal Injury Ch. 7-A, A. Introduction-Nature and Purpose of "Judicial Arbitration" in General.
6 Witkin Cal. Proc. 5th Proceedings Without Trial § 488, (S 488) Regulation of Mediation.
6 Witkin Cal. Proc. 5th Proceedings Without Trial § 489, Scope of Pilot Project.
6 Witkin Cal. Proc. 5th Proceedings Without Trial § 490, Time for Mediation.

Rule 3.872. Disqualification from subsequently serving as an adjudicator

A person who has participated in a complaint proceeding or otherwise received information about the substance of a complaint, other than information that is publicly disclosed under rule 3.871(d), must not subsequently hear or determine any contested issue of law, fact, or procedure concerning the dispute that was the subject of the underlying mediation or any other dispute that arises from the mediation as a judge, an arbitrator, a referee, or a juror, or in any other adjudicative capacity, in any court action or proceeding. *(Formerly Rule 1622.3, adopted, eff. Jan. 1, 2006. Renumbered Rule 3.868 and amended, eff. Jan. 1, 2007. Renumbered Rule 3.872 and amended, eff. Jan. 1, 2010.)*

Advisory Committee Comment

Persons who participated in a complaint proceeding are prohibited from subsequently adjudicating the dispute that was the subject of the underlying mediation or any other dispute that arises from the mediation because they may have learned of confidential mediation communications that were disclosed in the complaint proceeding or may have been influenced by what transpired in that proceeding. Because the information that can be disclosed publicly under rule 3.871(d) is limited and excludes

mediation communications, it is unnecessary to disqualify persons who received only publicly disclosed information from subsequently adjudicating the dispute.

Research References

Rutter, Cal. Practice Guide: A.D.R. Ch. 3-B, B. Commencing Mediation Process.
Rutter, Cal. Practice Guide: A.D.R. Ch. 4-C, C. Statutorily-Mandated Court Mediation Programs.
Rutter, Cal. Practice Guide: Civ. Pro. Before Trial Ch. 13-A, A. Introduction.
2 Witkin Cal. Proc. 5th Courts § 191, (S 191) Civil Rules.
6 Witkin Cal. Proc. 5th Proceedings Without Trial § 488, (S 488) Regulation of Mediation.
6 Witkin Cal. Proc. 5th Proceedings Without Trial § 491, Procedure.

Chapter 4

CIVIL ACTION MEDIATION PROGRAM RULES

Rule
3.890. Application.
3.891. Actions subject to mediation.
3.892. Panels of mediators.
3.893. Selection of mediators.
3.894. Attendance, participant lists, and mediation statements.
3.895. Filing of Statement of Agreement or Nonagreement by mediator.
3.896. Coordination with Trial Court Delay Reduction Act.
3.898. Educational material.

Rule 3.890. Application

The rules in this chapter implement the Civil Action Mediation Act, Code of Civil Procedure section 1775 et seq. Under section 1775.2, they apply in the Superior Court of California, County of Los Angeles and in other courts that elect to apply the act. *(Formerly Rule 1630, adopted, eff. March 1, 1994. Renumbered Rule 3.870 and amended, eff. Jan. 1, 2007. Renumbered Rule 3.890, eff. July 1, 2009.)*

Research References

Rutter, Cal. Practice Guide: A.D.R. Ch. 4-C, C. Statutorily-Mandated Court Mediation Programs.
Rutter, Cal. Practice Guide: Civ. Pro. Before Trial Ch. 13-A, A. Introduction.
Rutter, Cal. Practice Guide: Personal Injury Ch. 7-A, A. Introduction-Nature and Purpose of "Judicial Arbitration" in General.
2 Witkin Cal. Proc. 5th Courts § 191, (S 191) Civil Rules.
6 Witkin Cal. Proc. 5th Proceedings Without Trial § 489, Scope of Pilot Project.

Rule 3.891. Actions subject to mediation

(a) Actions that may be submitted to mediation

The following actions may be submitted to mediation under these provisions:

(1) By court order

Any action in which the amount in controversy, independent of the merits of liability, defenses, or comparative negligence, does not exceed $50,000 for each plaintiff. The court must determine the amount in controversy under Code of Civil Procedure section 1775.5. Determinations to send a case to mediation must be made by the court after consideration of the expressed views of the parties on the amenability of the case to mediation. The court must not require the parties or their counsel to personally appear in court for a conference held solely to determine whether to send their case to mediation.

(2) *By stipulation*

Any other action, regardless of the amount of controversy, in which all parties stipulate to such mediation. The stipulation must be filed not later than 90 days before trial unless the court permits a later time.

(b) Case–by–case determination

Amenability of a particular action for mediation must be determined on a case-by-case basis, rather than categorically. *(Formerly Rule 1631, adopted, eff. March 1, 1994. Renumbered Rule 3.871 and amended, eff. Jan. 1, 2007. Renumbered Rule 3.891, eff. July 1, 2009.)*

Research References

Rutter, Cal. Practice Guide: A.D.R. Ch. 4-C, C. Statutorily-Mandated Court Mediation Programs.
Rutter, Cal. Practice Guide: Civ. Pro. Before Trial Ch. 13-A, A. Introduction.
Rutter, Cal. Practice Guide: Personal Injury Ch. 7-A, A. Introduction-Nature and Purpose of "Judicial Arbitration" in General.
6 Witkin Cal. Proc. 5th Proceedings Without Trial § 489, Scope of Pilot Project.
6 Witkin Cal. Proc. 5th Proceedings Without Trial § 490, Time for Mediation.

Rule 3.892. Panels of mediators

Each court, in consultation with local bar associations, ADR providers, and associations of providers, must identify persons who may be appointed as mediators. The court must consider the criteria in standard 10.72 of the Standards of Judicial Administration and California Code of Regulations, title 16, section 3622, relating to the Dispute Resolution Program Act. *(Formerly Rule 1632, adopted, eff. March 1, 1994. Renumbered Rule 3.872 and amended, eff. Jan. 1, 2007. Renumbered Rule 3.892, eff. July 1, 2009.)*

Research References

Rutter, Cal. Practice Guide: A.D.R. Ch. 4-C, C. Statutorily-Mandated Court Mediation Programs.
Rutter, Cal. Practice Guide: Civ. Pro. Before Trial Ch. 13-A, A. Introduction.
Rutter, Cal. Practice Guide: Personal Injury Ch. 7-A, A. Introduction-Nature and Purpose of "Judicial Arbitration" in General.
6 Witkin Cal. Proc. 5th Proceedings Without Trial § 491, Procedure.

Rule 3.893. Selection of mediators

The parties may stipulate to any mediator, whether or not the person selected is among those identified under rule 3.892, within 15 days of the date an action is submitted to mediation. If the parties do not stipulate to a mediator, the court must promptly assign a mediator to the action from those identified under rule 3.892. *(Formerly Rule 1633, adopted, eff. March 1, 1994. Renumbered Rule 3.873 and amended, eff. Jan. 1, 2007. Renumbered Rule 3.893, eff. July 1, 2009. As amended, eff. Jan. 1, 2011.)*

Research References

Rutter, Cal. Practice Guide: A.D.R. Ch. 4-C, C. Statutorily-Mandated Court Mediation Programs.
Rutter, Cal. Practice Guide: Civ. Pro. Before Trial Ch. 13-A, A. Introduction.
Rutter, Cal. Practice Guide: Personal Injury Ch. 7-A, A. Introduction-Nature and Purpose of "Judicial Arbitration" in General.
6 Witkin Cal. Proc. 5th Proceedings Without Trial § 491, Procedure.

Rule 3.894. Attendance, participant lists, and mediation statements

(a) Attendance

(1) All parties and attorneys of record must attend all mediation sessions in person unless excused or permitted to attend by telephone as provided in (3). If a party is not a natural person, a representative of that party with authority to resolve the dispute or, in the case of a governmental entity that requires an agreement to be approved by an elected official or a legislative body, a representative with authority to recommend such agreement, must attend all mediation sessions in person, unless excused or permitted to attend by telephone as provided in (3).

(2) If any party is insured under a policy of insurance that provides or may provide coverage for a claim that is a subject of the action, a representative of the insurer with authority to settle or recommend settlement of the claim must attend all mediation sessions in person, unless excused or permitted to attend by telephone as provided in (3).

(3) The mediator may excuse a party, attorney, or representative from the requirement to attend a mediation session under (1) or (2) or permit attendance by telephone. The party, attorney, or representative who is excused or permitted to attend by telephone must promptly send a letter or an electronic communication to the mediator and to all parties confirming the excuse or permission.

(4) Each party may have counsel present at all mediation sessions that concern the party.

(b) Participant lists and mediation statements

(1) At least five court days before the first mediation session, each party must serve a list of its mediation participants on the mediator and all other parties. The list must include the names of all parties, attorneys, representatives of a party that is not a natural person, insurance representatives, and other persons who will attend the mediation with or on behalf of that party. A party must promptly serve a supplemental list if the party subsequently determines that other persons will attend the mediation with or on behalf of the party.

(2) The mediator may request that each party submit a short mediation statement providing information about the issues in dispute and possible resolutions of those issues and other information or documents that may appear helpful to resolve the dispute. *(Formerly Rule 1634, adopted, eff. March 1, 1994. Renumbered Rule 3.874 and amended, eff. Jan. 1, 2007. Renumbered Rule 3.894, eff. July 1, 2009.)*

Research References

Rutter, Cal. Practice Guide: A.D.R. Ch. 4-C, C. Statutorily-Mandated Court Mediation Programs.
Rutter, Cal. Practice Guide: Civ. Pro. Before Trial Ch. 13-A, A. Introduction.
Rutter, Cal. Practice Guide: Civ. Pro. Before Trial Ch. 9(III)-D, D. Other Sanctions Statutes and Rules.
Rutter, Cal. Practice Guide: Personal Injury Ch. 7-A, A. Introduction-Nature and Purpose of "Judicial Arbitration" in General.
6 Witkin Cal. Proc. 5th Proceedings Without Trial § 491, Procedure.

Rule 3.895. Filing of Statement of Agreement or Nonagreement by mediator

Within 10 days after conclusion of the mediation, or by another date set by the court, the mediator must complete, serve on all parties, and file a *Statement of Agreement or Nonagreement* (form ADR–100). If the mediation has not ended when the report is filed, the mediator must file a supplemental form ADR–100 within 10 days after the mediation is concluded or by another date set by the court. The completed form ADR–100 must not disclose the terms of any agreement or any other communications or conduct that occurred in the course of the mediation, except as allowed in Evidence Code sections 1115–1128. *(Formerly Rule 1635, adopted, eff. March 1, 1994. Renumbered Rule 3.875 and amended, eff. Jan. 1, 2007. Renumbered Rule 3.895, eff. July 1, 2009. As amended, eff. July 1, 2012.)*

Research References

Rutter, Cal. Practice Guide: A.D.R. Ch. 4-C, C. Statutorily-Mandated Court Mediation Programs.

Rutter, Cal. Practice Guide: Civ. Pro. Before Trial Ch. 13-A, A. Introduction.

Rutter, Cal. Practice Guide: Personal Injury Ch. 7-A, A. Introduction-Nature and Purpose of "Judicial Arbitration" in General.

6 Witkin Cal. Proc. 5th Proceedings Without Trial § 491, Procedure.

Rule 3.896. Coordination with Trial Court Delay Reduction Act

(a) Effect of mediation on time standards

Submission of an action to mediation under the rules in this chapter does not affect time periods specified in the Trial Court Delay Reduction Act (Gov. Code, § 68600 et seq.), except as provided in this rule.

(b) Exception to delay reduction time standards

On written stipulation of the parties filed with the court, the court may order an exception of up to 90 days to the delay reduction time standards to permit mediation of an action. The court must coordinate the timing of the exception period with its delay reduction calendar.

(c) Time for completion of mediation

Mediation must be completed within 60 days of a reference to a mediator, but that period may be extended by the court for up to 30 days on a showing of good cause.

(d) Restraint in discovery

The parties should exercise restraint in discovery while a case is in mediation. In appropriate cases to accommodate that objective, the court may issue a protective order under Code of Civil Procedure section 2017(c) and related provisions. *(Formerly Rule 1637, adopted, eff. March 1, 1994. Renumbered Rule 3.876 and amended, eff. Jan. 1, 2007. Renumbered Rule 3.896, eff. July 1, 2009.)*

Research References

Rutter, Cal. Practice Guide: A.D.R. Ch. 4-C, C. Statutorily-Mandated Court Mediation Programs.

Rutter, Cal. Practice Guide: Civ. Pro. Before Trial Ch. 13-A, A. Introduction.

Rutter, Cal. Practice Guide: Personal Injury Ch. 7-A, A. Introduction-Nature and Purpose of "Judicial Arbitration" in General.

6 Witkin Cal. Proc. 5th Proceedings Without Trial § 490, Time for Mediation.

6 Witkin Cal. Proc. 5th Proceedings Without Trial § 491, Procedure.

Rule 3.898. Educational material

Each court must make available educational material, adopted by the Judicial Council, or from other sources, describing available ADR processes in the community. *(Formerly Rule 1639, adopted, eff. March 1, 1994. Renumbered Rule 3.878 and amended, eff. Jan. 1, 2007. Renumbered Rule 3.898, eff. July 1, 2009.)*

Research References

2 Witkin Cal. Proc. 5th Courts § 191, (S 191) Civil Rules.

Division 9

REFERENCES

Chapter 1

REFERENCE BY AGREEMENT OF THE PARTIES UNDER CODE OF CIVIL PROCEDURE SECTION 638

Rule 3.900. Purposes of reference

A court must not use the reference procedure under Code of Civil Procedure section 638 to appoint a person to conduct a mediation. *(Adopted, eff. Jan. 1, 2007.)*

Advisory Committee Comment

Rule 3.900 is not intended to prohibit a court from appointing a referee to conduct a mandatory settlement conference or, following the conclusion of a reference, from appointing a person who previously served as a referee to conduct a mediation.

Research References

Rutter, Cal. Practice Guide: A.D.R. Ch. 6-A, A. General Considerations.

Rutter, Cal. Practice Guide: A.D.R. Ch. 7-A, A. Mediators.

California Practice Guide: Employment Litigation Ch. 18-D, D. Private Trials.

2 Witkin Cal. Proc. 5th Courts § 191, (S 191) Civil Rules.

2 Witkin Cal. Proc. 5th Courts § 346, (S 346) in General.

6 Witkin Cal. Proc. 5th Proceedings Without Trial § 63, (S 63) Nature and Purpose.

6 Witkin Cal. Proc. 5th Proceedings Without Trial § 64, (S 64) Voluntary Reference.

Rule 3.901. Application for order appointing referee

(a) Stipulation or motion for appointment

A written stipulation or motion for an order appointing a referee under Code of Civil Procedure section 638 must be presented to the judge to whom the case is assigned, or to the presiding judge or law and motion department if the case has not been assigned.

(b) Contents of application

The stipulation or motion for the appointment of a referee under section 638 must:

(1) Clearly state whether the scope of the requested reference includes all issues or is limited to specified issues;

(2) State whether the referee will be privately compensated;

(3) If authorization to use court facilities or court personnel is requested, describe the use requested and state the reasons that this would further the interests of justice;

(4) If the applicant is requesting or the parties have stipulated to the appointment of a particular referee, be accompanied by the proposed referee's certification as required by rule 3.904(a); and

(5) Be accompanied by a proposed order that includes the matters specified in rule 3.902. *(Adopted, eff. Jan. 1, 2007.)*

Research References

Rutter, Cal. Practice Guide: A.D.R. Ch. 6-C, C. Referees.

Rutter, Cal. Practice Guide: A.D.R. App. D Form 126, ADR Clause (Submission of Disputes to Referee).

Rutter, Cal. Practice Guide: A.D.R. App. D Form 128, ADR Clause (Trial by Reference of Discovery Issues).

Rutter, Cal. Practice Guide: A.D.R. App. D Form 129, ADR Clause (Referee for Purposes of Case Management in Event of Litigation).

Rutter, Cal. Practice Guide: A.D.R. App. D Form 130, Motion for Order of Reference (CCP §§ 638.

Rutter, Cal. Practice Guide: A.D.R. App. D Form 138, Stipulation and Order for General Reference.

Rutter, Cal. Practice Guide: Civ. Pro. Before Trial Ch. 8K-5, Appointment of Referee in Aid of Discovery.

6 Witkin Cal. Proc. 5th Proceedings Without Trial § 68, (S 68) Motion.

Rule 3.902. Order appointing referee

An order appointing a referee under Code of Civil Procedure section 638 must be filed with the clerk or entered in the minutes and must specify:

(1) The name, business address, and telephone number of the referee and, if he or she is a member of the State Bar, the referee's State Bar number;

(2) Whether the scope of the reference covers all issues or is limited to specified issues;

(3) Whether the referee will be privately compensated; and

(4) Whether the use of court facilities and court personnel is authorized. *(Adopted, eff. Jan. 1, 2007. As amended, eff. Jan. 1, 2010.)*

Research References

Rutter, Cal. Practice Guide: A.D.R. Ch. 6-C, C. Referees.

Rutter, Cal. Practice Guide: Civil Trials & Evidence Ch. 16-G, G. Trial by Reference.

6 Witkin Cal. Proc. 5th Proceedings Without Trial § 68, (S 68) Motion.

Rule 3.903. Selection and qualifications of referee

The court must appoint the referee or referees as provided in the Code of Civil Procedure section 640. If the proposed referee is a former judicial officer, he or she must be an active or an inactive member of the State Bar. *(Adopted, eff. Jan. 1, 2007.)*

Research References

Rutter, Cal. Practice Guide: A.D.R. Ch. 6-C, C. Referees.

Rule 3.904. Certification and disclosure by referee

(a) Certification by referee

Before a referee begins to serve:

(1) The referee must certify in writing that he or she consents to serve as provided in the order of appointment and is aware of and will comply with applicable provisions of canon 6 of the Code of Judicial Ethics and with the California Rules of Court; and

(2) The referee's certification must be filed with the court.

(b) Disclosure by referee

In addition to any other disclosure required by law, no later than five days before the deadline for parties to file a motion for disqualification of the referee under Code of Civil Procedure section 170.6 or, if the referee is not aware of his or her appointment or of a matter subject to disclosure at that time, as soon as practicable thereafter, a referee must disclose to the parties:

(1) Any matter subject to disclosure under either canon 6D(5)(a) or 6D(5)(b) of the Code of Judicial Ethics; and

(2) Any significant personal or professional relationship the referee has or has had with a party, attorney, or law firm in the current case, including the number and nature of any other proceedings in the past 24 months in which the referee has been privately compensated by a party, attorney, law firm, or insurance company in the current case for any services. The disclosure must include privately compensated service as an attorney, expert witness, or consultant or as a judge, referee, arbitrator, mediator, settlement facilitator, or other alternative dispute resolution neutral. *(Adopted, eff. Jan. 1, 2007.)*

Research References

Rutter, Cal. Practice Guide: A.D.R. Ch. 3-B, B. Commencing Mediation Process.

Rutter, Cal. Practice Guide: A.D.R. Ch. 6-C, C. Referees.

Rutter, Cal. Practice Guide: A.D.R. Ch. 7-D, D. Referees.

Rutter, Cal. Practice Guide: A.D.R. App. D Form 126, ADR Clause (Submission of Disputes to Referee).

Rutter, Cal. Practice Guide: A.D.R. App. D Form 128, ADR Clause (Trial by Reference of Discovery Issues).

Rutter, Cal. Practice Guide: A.D.R. App. D Form 129, ADR Clause (Referee for Purposes of Case Management in Event of Litigation).

Rutter, Cal. Practice Guide: A.D.R. App. D Form 130, Motion for Order of Reference (CCP §§ 638.

Rutter, Cal. Practice Guide: A.D.R. App. D Form 129.3, Statement of Referee Re Contact/Web Site Information.

Rutter, Cal. Practice Guide: Civ. Pro. Before Trial Ch. 8K-5, Appointment of Referee in Aid of Discovery.

Rutter, Cal. Practice Guide: Civil Trials & Evidence Ch. 16-G, G. Trial by Reference.

California Practice Guide: Employment Litigation Ch. 18-F, F. Selecting the Neutral.

6 Witkin Cal. Proc. 5th Proceedings Without Trial § 68, (S 68) Motion.

6 Witkin Cal. Proc. 5th Proceedings Without Trial § 70, (S 70) Objection to Referee.

Rule 3.905. Objections to the appointment

A stipulation or an agreement for an order appointing a referee does not constitute a waiver of grounds for objection to the appointment of a particular person as referee under Code of Civil Procedure section 641. Any objection to the appointment of a person as a referee must be made with reasonable diligence and in writing. The objection must be served on all parties and the referee and filed with the court. The objection must be heard by the judge to whom the case is assigned or by the presiding judge or law and motion judge if the case has not been assigned. *(Adopted, eff. Jan. 1, 2007.)*

Research References

Rutter, Cal. Practice Guide: A.D.R. Ch. 6-C, C. Referees.

Rutter, Cal. Practice Guide: A.D.R. Ch. 7-D, D. Referees.

Rutter, Cal. Practice Guide: Civil Trials & Evidence Ch. 16-G, G. Trial by Reference.

6 Witkin Cal. Proc. 5th Proceedings Without Trial § 70, (S 70) Objection to Referee.

Rule 3.906. Motion to withdraw stipulation

(a) Good cause requirement

A motion to withdraw a stipulation for the appointment of a referee must be supported by a declaration of facts establishing good cause for permitting the party to withdraw the stipulation. The following do not constitute good cause for withdrawing a stipulation:

(1) A declaration that a ruling is based on an error of fact or law.

(2) The issuance of an order for an appropriate hearing site under rule 3.910.

(b) Service, filing and hearing of motion

Notice of the motion must be served on all parties and the referee and filed with the court. The motion must be heard by the judge to whom the case is assigned or by the presiding judge or law and motion judge. If the motion is granted, the case must be transferred to the trial court docket. *(Adopted, eff. Jan. 1, 2007.)*

Research References

Rutter, Cal. Practice Guide: A.D.R. Ch. 6-C, C. Referees.

6 Witkin Cal. Proc. 5th Proceedings Without Trial § 71, (S 71) Withdrawal of Stipulation for Reference.

Rule 3.907. Use of court facilities and court personnel

A party who has elected to use the services of a referee appointed under Code of Civil Procedure section 638 is deemed to have elected to proceed outside court facilities. Court facilities, court personnel, and summoned jurors may not be used in proceedings pending before a such a referee except on a finding by the presiding judge or his or her designee that their use would further the interests of justice. *(Formerly Rule 3.909, adopted, eff. Jan. 1, 2007. Renumbered Rule 3.907 and amended, eff. Jan. 1, 2010.)*

Research References

Rutter, Cal. Practice Guide: A.D.R. Ch. 6-C, C. Referees.

Rutter, Cal. Practice Guide: A.D.R. App. D Form 138, Stipulation and Order for General Reference.

Rutter, Cal. Practice Guide: Civil Trials & Evidence Ch. 16-G, G. Trial by Reference.

2 Witkin Cal. Proc. 5th Courts § 191, (S 191) Civil Rules.

6 Witkin Cal. Proc. 5th Proceedings Without Trial § 73, (S 73) Hearing.

Chapter 2

COURT–ORDERED REFERENCE UNDER CODE OF CIVIL PROCEDURE SECTION 639

Rule

3.920. Purposes and conditions for appointment of referee.

3.921. Motion for appointment of a referee.

3.922. Form and contents of order appointing referee.

3.923. Selection and qualification of referee.

3.924. Certification and disclosure by referee.

3.925. Objection to reference.

3.926. Use of court facilities.

Rule 3.920. Purposes and conditions for appointment of referee

(a) Purposes prescribed by statute

A court may order the appointment of a referee under Code of Civil Procedure section 639 only for the purposes specified in that section.

(b) No references for mediation

A court must not use the reference procedure under Code of Civil Procedure section 639 to appoint a person to conduct a mediation.

(c) Conditions for appointment of discovery referee

A discovery referee must not be appointed under Code of Civil Procedure section 639(a)(5) unless the exceptional circumstances of the particular case require the appointment. *(Adopted, eff. Jan. 1, 2007.)*

Advisory Committee Comment

Rule 3.920(b) is not intended to prohibit a court from appointing a referee to conduct a mandatory settlement confer-

ence in a complex case or, following the conclusion of a reference, from appointing a person who previously served as a referee to conduct a mediation.

Research References

Rutter, Cal. Practice Guide: A.D.R. Ch. 3-C, C. Confidentiality.

Rutter, Cal. Practice Guide: A.D.R. Ch. 6-C, C. Referees.

Rutter, Cal. Practice Guide: A.D.R. Ch. 7-A, A. Mediators.

Rutter, Cal. Practice Guide: A.D.R. Ch. 3B-B, B. ADR Options in Construction Disputes.

Rutter, Cal. Practice Guide: A.D.R. App. D Form 143, Order Appointing Referee for the Purpose of Discovery.

Rutter, Cal. Practice Guide: A.D.R. App. D Form 145, Order of Reference for Case Management.

Rutter, Cal. Practice Guide: Civ. Pro. Before Trial Ch. 13-A, A. Introduction.

Rutter, Cal. Practice Guide: Civ. Pro. Before Trial Ch. 8K-5, Appointment of Referee in Aid of Discovery.

Rutter, Cal. Practice Guide: Civ. Pro. Before Trial Ch. 12(II)-A, A. Mandatory Settlement Conference ("MSC").

2 Witkin Cal. Proc. 5th Courts § 191, (S 191) Civil Rules.

2 Witkin Cal. Proc. 5th Courts § 346, (S 346) in General.

6 Witkin Cal. Proc. 5th Proceedings Without Trial § 65, in General.

Rule 3.921. Motion for appointment of a referee

(a) Filing and contents

A motion by a party for the appointment of a referee under Code of Civil Procedure section 639 must be served and filed. The motion must specify the matter or matters to be included in the requested reference. If the applicant is requesting the appointment of a particular referee, the motion must be accompanied by the proposed referee's certification as required by rule 3.924(a).

(b) Hearing

The motion must be heard by the judge to whom the case is assigned, or by the presiding judge or law and motion judge if the case has not been assigned. *(Adopted, eff. Jan. 1, 2007.)*

Research References

Rutter, Cal. Practice Guide: A.D.R. Ch. 6-C, C. Referees.

Rutter, Cal. Practice Guide: Civ. Pro. Before Trial Ch. 1-B, B. Prelawsuit Investigations, Research and Analysis.

Rutter, Cal. Practice Guide: Civ. Pro. Before Trial Ch. 8E-12, Conduct of Deposition.

Rutter, Cal. Practice Guide: Civil Trials & Evidence Ch. 16-G, G. Trial by Reference.

6 Witkin Cal. Proc. 5th Proceedings Without Trial § 68, (S 68) Motion.

Rule 3.922. Form and contents of order appointing referee

(a) Written order required

An order appointing a referee under Code of Civil Procedure section 639, on the motion of a party or on the court's own motion, must be in writing and must address the matters set forth in (b) through (g).

(b) Referee information

The order must state the name, business address, and telephone number of the referee and, if he or she is a member of the State Bar, the referee's State Bar number.

(c) Basis for reference

The order must specify whether the referee is appointed under paragraph (1), (2), (3), (4), or (5) of subdivision (a) of section 639 and:

(1) If the referee is appointed under section 639(a)(1)–(a)(4), the order must state the reason the referee is being appointed.

(2) If the referee is appointed under section 639(a)(5) to hear and determine discovery motions and disputes relevant to discovery, the order must state the exceptional circumstances of the particular case that require the reference.

(d) Subject matter and scope of reference

(1) The order must specify the subject matter or matters included in the reference.

(2) If the referee is appointed under section 639(a)(5) to hear and determine discovery motions and disputes relevant to discovery, the order must state whether the discovery referee is appointed for all purposes or only for limited purposes.

(e) Authority of discovery referee

If the referee is appointed under section 639(a)(5) to hear and determine discovery motions and disputes relevant to discovery, the order must state that the referee is authorized to set the date, time, and place for all hearings determined by the referee to be necessary; direct the issuance of subpoenas; preside over hearings; take evidence; and rule on objections, motions, and other requests made during the course of the hearing.

(f) Referee fees; apportionment

If the referee will be appointed at a cost to the parties, the order must:

(1) Specify the maximum hourly rate the referee may charge and, if any party so requests, the maximum number of hours for which the referee may charge;

(2) Include a finding that either:

(A) No party has established an economic inability to pay a pro rata share of the referee's fee; or

(B) One or more parties has established an economic inability to pay a pro rata share of the referee's fees and another party has agreed voluntarily to pay that additional share of the referee's fees.

(3) When the issue of economic hardship is raised before the referee begins performing services, the court must determine a fair and reasonable apportionment of reference costs. The court may modify its apportionment order and may consider a recommendation by the referee as a factor in determining any modification.

(g) Use of court facilities and court personnel

The order must specify the extent, if any, to which court facilities and court personnel may be used in connection with the reference. *(Adopted, eff. Jan. 1, 2007. As amended, eff. Jan. 1, 2010.)*

Research References

Rutter, Cal. Practice Guide: A.D.R. Ch. 6-C, C. Referees.
Rutter, Cal. Practice Guide: Civ. Pro. Before Trial Ch. 8K-5, Appointment of Referee in Aid of Discovery.
Rutter, Cal. Practice Guide: Civil Trials & Evidence Ch. 16-G, G. Trial by Reference.
6 Witkin Cal. Proc. 5th Proceedings Without Trial § 68, (S 68) Motion.
6 Witkin Cal. Proc. 5th Proceedings Without Trial § 69, (S 69) Appointment of Referee.
6 Witkin Cal. Proc. 5th Proceedings Without Trial § 77, in General.
6 Witkin Cal. Proc. 5th Proceedings Without Trial § 78, Consideration of Economic Hardship.

Rule 3.923. Selection and qualification of referee

The court must appoint the referee or referees as provided in Code of Civil Procedure section 640. If the referee is a former California judicial officer, he or she must be an active or inactive member of the State Bar. *(Adopted, eff. Jan. 1, 2007.)*

Research References

Rutter, Cal. Practice Guide: A.D.R. Ch. 6-C, C. Referees.
6 Witkin Cal. Proc. 5th Proceedings Without Trial § 69, (S 69) Appointment of Referee.

Rule 3.924. Certification and disclosure by referee

(a) Certification by referee

Before a referee begins to serve:

(1) The referee must certify in writing that he or she consents to serve as provided in the order of appointment and is aware of and will comply with applicable provisions of canon 6 of the Code of Judicial Ethics and with the California Rules of Court; and

(2) The referee's certification must be filed with the court.

(b) Disclosure by referee

In addition to any other disclosure required by law, no later than five days before the deadline for parties to file a motion for disqualification of the referee under Code of Civil Procedure section 170.6 or, if the referee is not aware of his or her appointment or of a matter subject to disclosure at that time, as soon as practicable thereafter, a referee must disclose to the parties:

(1) Any matter subject to disclosure under subdivisions (D)(5)(a) and (D)(5)(b) of canon 6 of the Code of Judicial Ethics; and

(2) Any significant personal or professional relationship the referee has or has had with a party, attorney, or law firm in the current case, including the number and nature of any other proceedings in the past 24 months in which the referee has been privately compensated by a party, attorney, law firm, or insurance company in the current case for any services. The disclosure must include privately compensated service as an attorney, expert witness, or consultant or as a judge, referee, arbitrator, mediator, settlement facilitator, or other alternative dispute resolution neutral. *(Adopted, eff. Jan. 1, 2007. As amended, eff. Jan. 1, 2008.)*

Research References

Rutter, Cal. Practice Guide: A.D.R. Ch. 6-C, C. Referees.
Rutter, Cal. Practice Guide: A.D.R. Ch. 7-D, D. Referees.
Rutter, Cal. Practice Guide: A.D.R. App. D Form 143, Order Appointing Referee for the Purpose of Discovery.
Rutter, Cal. Practice Guide: A.D.R. App. D Form 145, Order of Reference for Case Management.
Rutter, Cal. Practice Guide: A.D.R. App. D Form 129.3, Statement of Referee Re Contact/Web Site Information.
Rutter, Cal. Practice Guide: Civ. Pro. Before Trial Ch. 8K-5, Appointment of Referee in Aid of Discovery.
Rutter, Cal. Practice Guide: Civil Trials & Evidence Ch. 16-G, G. Trial by Reference.
6 Witkin Cal. Proc. 5th Proceedings Without Trial § 69, (S 69) Appointment of Referee.

Rule 3.925. Objection to reference

The filing of a motion for an order appointing a referee does not constitute a waiver of grounds for objection to the appointment of a particular person as referee under Code of Civil Procedure section 641, or objection to the rate or apportionment of compensation of the referee. Any objection to the appointment of a particular person as a referee must be made with reasonable diligence and in writing. The objection must be heard by the judge to whom the case is assigned, or by the presiding judge or the law and motion judge. *(Adopted, eff. Jan. 1, 2007.)*

Research References

Rutter, Cal. Practice Guide: A.D.R. Ch. 6-C, C. Referees.
Rutter, Cal. Practice Guide: A.D.R. Ch. 7-D, D. Referees.
Rutter, Cal. Practice Guide: Civ. Pro. Before Trial Ch. 8K-5, Appointment of Referee in Aid of Discovery.
Rutter, Cal. Practice Guide: Civil Trials & Evidence Ch. 16-G, G. Trial by Reference.

Ct. Rules

Rule 3.926. Use of court facilities

A reference ordered under Code of Civil Procedure section 639 entitles the parties to the use of court facilities and court personnel to the extent provided in the order of reference. The proceedings may be held in a private facility, but, if so, the private facility must be open to the public as provided in rule 3.931. *(Adopted, eff. Jan. 1, 2007. As amended, eff. Jan. 1, 2010.)*

Research References

Rutter, Cal. Practice Guide: A.D.R. Ch. 6-C, C. Referees.
Rutter, Cal. Practice Guide: A.D.R. App. D Form 143, Order Appointing Referee for the Purpose of Discovery.
Rutter, Cal. Practice Guide: A.D.R. App. D Form 145, Order of Reference for Case Management.
Rutter, Cal. Practice Guide: Civil Trials & Evidence Ch. 16-G, G. Trial by Reference.
2 Witkin Cal. Proc. 5th Courts § 191, (S 191) Civil Rules.
6 Witkin Cal. Proc. 5th Proceedings Without Trial § 73, (S 73) Hearing.

Chapter 3

RULES APPLICABLE TO REFERENCES UNDER CODE OF CIVIL PROCEDURE SECTION 638 OR 639

Rule
3.930.   Documents and exhibits.
3.931.   Open proceedings, notice of proceedings, and order for hearing site.
3.932.   Motions or applications to be heard by the court.

Rule 3.930. Documents and exhibits

All referees and parties in proceedings before a referee appointed under Code of Civil Procedure section 638 or 639 must comply with the applicable requirements of rule 2.400 concerning the filing and handling of documents and exhibits. *(Adopted, eff. Jan. 1, 2010.)*

Research References

2 Witkin Cal. Proc. 5th Courts § 191, (S 191) Civil Rules.

Rule 3.931. Open proceedings, notice of proceedings, and order for hearing site

(a) Open proceedings

All proceedings before a referee that would be open to the public if held before a judge must be open to the public, regardless of whether they are held in a court facility or in another location.

(b) Notice regarding proceedings before referee

(1) In each case in which he or she is appointed, a referee must file a statement that provides the name, telephone number, and mailing address of a person who may be contacted to obtain information about the date, time, location, and general nature of all hearings scheduled in matters pending before the referee that would be open to the public if held before a judge. This statement must be filed at the same time as the referee's certification under rule 3.904(a) or 3.924(a). If there is any change in this contact information, the referee must promptly file a revised statement with the court.

(2) In addition to providing the information required under (1), the statement filed by a referee may also provide the address of a publicly accessible Web site at which the referee will maintain a current calendar setting forth the date, time, location, and general nature of any hearings scheduled in the matter that would be open to the public if held before a judge.

(3) The clerk must post the information from the statement filed by the referee in the court facility.

(c) Appropriate hearing site

(1) The presiding judge or his or her designee, on application of any person or on the judge's own motion, may order that a case before a referee must be heard at a site easily accessible to the public and appropriate for seating those who have made known their plan to attend hearings. The application must state facts showing good cause for granting the application, must be served on all parties and the referee, and filed with the court. The proceedings are not stayed while the application is pending unless the presiding judge or his or her designee orders that they be stayed. The issuance of an order for an accessible and appropriate hearing site is not grounds for withdrawal of a stipulation for the appointment of a referee.

(2) If a court staff mediator or evaluator is required to attend a hearing before a referee, unless otherwise ordered by the presiding judge or his or her designee, that hearing must take place at a location requiring no more than 15 minutes' travel time from the mediator's or evaluator's work site. *(Adopted, eff. Jan. 1, 2010.)*

Research References

Rutter, Cal. Practice Guide: A.D.R. Ch. 6-C, C. Referees.
Rutter, Cal. Practice Guide: A.D.R. App. D Form 129.3, Statement of Referee Re Contact/Web Site Information.
Rutter, Cal. Practice Guide: Civ. Pro. Before Trial Ch. 8K-5, Appointment of Referee in Aid of Discovery.
Rutter, Cal. Practice Guide: Civ. Pro. Before Trial Ch. 9(I)-D, D. Hearing.
6 Witkin Cal. Proc. 5th Proceedings Without Trial § 73, (S 73) Hearing.

Rule 3.932. Motions or applications to be heard by the court

(a) Motion or application to seal records

A motion or application to seal records in a case pending before a referee must be filed with the court and served on all parties that have appeared in the case and the referee. The motion or application must be heard by the trial court judge to whom the case is assigned or, if the case has not been assigned, by the presiding judge or his or her designee. Rules 2.550 and 2.551 apply to the motion or application to seal the records.

(b) Motion for leave to file complaint for intervention

A motion for leave to file a complaint for intervention in a case pending before a referee must be filed with the court and served on all parties and the referee. The motion must be heard by the trial court judge to whom the case is assigned or, if the case has not been assigned, by the presiding judge or his or her designee. If intervention is allowed, the case must be returned to the trial court docket unless all parties stipulate in the manner prescribed in rule 3.901 to proceed before the referee. *(Adopted, eff. Jan. 1, 2010.)*

Research References

Rutter, Cal. Practice Guide: A.D.R. Ch. 6-C, C. Referees.
Rutter, Cal. Practice Guide: Civ. Pro. Before Trial Ch. 8K-5, Appointment of Referee in Aid of Discovery.
Rutter, Cal. Practice Guide: Civ. Pro. Before Trial Ch. 9(I)-I, I. Motion to Seal Court Records.
2 Witkin Cal. Proc. 5th Courts § 191, (S 191) Civil Rules.
6 Witkin Cal. Proc. 5th Proceedings Without Trial § 72, (S 72) Intervention.
6 Witkin Cal. Proc. 5th Proceedings Without Trial § 73, (S 73) Hearing.

Division 10

DISCOVERY

Chapter 1

FORMAT OF DISCOVERY

Rule
3.1000.   Format of supplemental and further discovery.

Rule 3.1000.   Format of supplemental and further discovery

(a) Supplemental interrogatories and responses, etc.

In each set of supplemental interrogatories, supplemental responses to interrogatories, amended answers to interrogatories, and further responses to interrogatories, inspection demands, and admission requests, the following must appear in the first paragraph immediately below the title of the case:

(1) The identity of the propounding, demanding, or requesting party;

(2) The identity of the responding party;

(3) The set number being propounded or responded to; and

(4) The nature of the paper.

(b) Identification of responses

Each supplemental or further response and each amended answer must be identified by the same number or letter and be in the same sequence as the corresponding interrogatory, inspection demand, or admission request, but the text of the interrogatory, demand, or request need not be repeated. *(Formerly Rule 331, adopted, eff. Jan. 1, 1984. As amended, eff. Jan. 1, 1986; July 1, 1987. Renumbered Rule 3.1000 and amended, eff. Jan. 1, 2007.)*

Research References

Rutter, Cal. Practice Guide: Civ. Pro. Before Trial Ch. 8F-3, Propounding Interrogatories.
Rutter, Cal. Practice Guide: Civ. Pro. Before Trial Ch. 8F-5, Responding to Interrogatories.
Rutter, Cal. Practice Guide: Civ. Pro. Before Trial Ch. 8G-5, Responses to Rfas.
2 Witkin Cal. Proc. 5th Courts § 191, (S 191) Civil Rules.

Chapter 2

CONDUCT OF DISCOVERY

Rule
3.1010.   Oral depositions by telephone, videoconference, or other remote electronic means.

Division 11

LAW AND MOTION

Chapter 1

GENERAL PROVISIONS

Rule
3.1100.   Application.
3.1103.   Definitions and construction.
3.1109.   Notice of determination of submitted matters.

Rule 3.1010.   Oral depositions by telephone, videoconference, or other remote electronic means

(a) Taking depositions

Any party may take an oral deposition by telephone, videoconference, or other remote electronic means, provided:

(1) Notice is served with the notice of deposition or the subpoena;

(2) That party makes all arrangements for any other party to participate in the deposition in an equivalent manner. However, each party so appearing must pay all expenses incurred by it or properly allocated to it;

(3) Any party may be personally present at the deposition without giving prior notice.

(b) Appearing and participating in depositions

Any party may appear and participate in an oral deposition by telephone, videoconference, or other remote electronic means, provided:

(1) Written notice of such appearance is served by personal delivery or fax at least three court days before the deposition;

(2) The party so appearing makes all arrangements and pays all expenses incurred for the appearance.

(c) Party deponent's appearance

A party deponent must appear at his or her deposition in person and be in the presence of the deposition officer.

(d) Nonparty deponent's appearance

A nonparty deponent may appear at his or her deposition by telephone, videoconference, or other remote electronic means with court approval upon a finding of good cause and no prejudice to any party. The deponent must be sworn in the presence of the deposition officer or by any other means stipulated to by the parties or ordered by the court. Any party may be personally present at the deposition.

(e) Court orders

On motion by any person, the court in a specific action may make such other orders as it deems appropriate. *(Formerly Rule 333, adopted, eff. Jan. 1, 2003. Renumbered Rule 3.1010 and amended, eff. Jan. 1, 2007.)*

Research References

Rutter, Cal. Practice Guide: Civ. Pro. Before Trial Ch. 8E-8, Place of Deposition.
2 Witkin Cal. Proc. 5th Courts § 191, (S 191) Civil Rules.

Rule 3.1100.   Application

The rules in this division apply to proceedings in civil law and motion, as defined in rule 3.1103, and to discovery proceedings in family law and probate. *(Formerly Rule 301, adopted, eff. Jan. 1, 1984. As amended, eff. July 1, 1984; July 1, 1997; Jan. 1, 2002. Renumbered Rule 3.1100 and amended, eff. Jan. 1, 2007.)*

Ct. Rules

Research References

Rutter, Cal. Practice Guide: Civ. Pro. Before Trial Ch. 7(I)-A, A. Demurrers.

2 Witkin Cal. Proc. 5th Courts § 191, (S 191) Civil Rules.

6 Witkin Cal. Proc. 5th Proceedings Without Trial § 2, (S 2) Types of Motions.

Rule 3.1103.   Definitions and construction

(a)   Law and motion defined

"Law and motion" includes any proceedings:

(1) On application before trial for an order, except for causes arising under the Welfare and Institutions Code, the Probate Code, the Family Code, or Code of Civil Procedure sections 527.6, 527.7, 527.8, and 527.85; or

(2) On application for an order regarding the enforcement of judgment, attachment of property, appointment of a receiver, obtaining or setting aside a judgment by default, writs of review, mandate and prohibition, a petition to compel arbitration, and enforcement of an award by arbitration.

(b)   Application of rules on extending or shortening time

Rules 1.10(c) and 2.20 on extending or shortening time apply to proceedings under this division.

(c)   Application to demurrers

Unless the context or subject matter otherwise requires, the rules in this division apply to demurrers. *(Formerly Rule 303, adopted, eff. Jan. 1, 1984. As amended, eff. July 1, 1984; July 1, 1997. Renumbered Rule 3.1103 and amended, eff. Jan. 1, 2007. As amended, eff. Jan. 1, 2011.)*

Research References

Rutter, Cal. Practice Guide: A.D.R. Ch. 5-G, G. Procedures to Enforce Arbitration.

Rutter, Cal. Practice Guide: Civ. Pro. Before Trial Ch. 7(I)-A, A. Demurrers.

6 Witkin Cal. Proc. 5th Proceedings Without Trial § 18, Extension by Stipulation or Court Order.

6 Witkin Cal. Proc. 5th Proceedings Without Trial § 525, (S 525) Hearing.

Rule 3.1109.   Notice of determination of submitted matters

(a)   Notice by clerk

When the court rules on a motion or makes an order or renders a judgment in a matter it has taken under submission, the clerk must immediately notify the parties of the ruling, order, or judgment. The notification, which must specifically identify the matter ruled on, may be given by mailing the parties a copy of the ruling, order, or judgment, and it constitutes service of notice only if the clerk is required to give notice under Code of Civil Procedure section 664.5.

(b)   Notice in a case involving more than two parties

In a case involving more than two parties, a clerk's notification made under this rule, or any notice of a ruling or order served by a party, must name the moving party, and the party against whom relief was requested, and specifically identify the particular motion or other matter ruled upon.

(c)   Time not extended by failure of clerk to give notice

The failure of the clerk to give the notice required by this rule does not extend the time provided by law for performing any act except as provided in rules 8.104(a) or 8.824(a). *(Formerly Rule 309, adopted, eff. Jan. 1, 1984. Renumbered Rule 3.1109 and amended, eff. Jan. 1, 2007.)*

Research References

Rutter, Cal. Practice Guide: Civil Appeals & Writs Ch. 3-B, B. Filing Deadlines.

Rutter, Cal. Practice Guide: Civ. Pro. Before Trial Ch. 7(I)-A, A. Demurrers.

9 Witkin Cal. Proc. 5th Appeal § 579, as Equivalent to Notice of Entry.

2 Witkin Cal. Proc. 5th Courts § 191, (S 191) Civil Rules.

5 Witkin Cal. Proc. 5th Pleading § 983, Notification and Service of Notice.

6 Witkin Cal. Proc. 5th Proceedings Without Trial § 45, (S 45) Notification and Notice.

6 Witkin Cal. Proc. 5th Proceedings Without Trial § 261, (S 261) Mandamus.

Chapter 2

FORMAT OF MOTION PAPERS

Rule

3.1110.   General format.

3.1112.   Motions—and other pleadings.

3.1113.   Memorandum.

3.1114.   Applications, motions, and petitions not requiring a memorandum.

3.1115.   Declarations.

3.1116.   Deposition testimony as an exhibit.

Rule 3.1110.   General format

(a)   Notice of motion

A notice of motion must state in the opening paragraph the nature of the order being sought and the grounds for issuance of the order.

(b)   Date of hearing and other information

The first page of each paper must specify immediately below the number of the case:

(1) The date, time, and location, if ascertainable, of any scheduled hearing and the name of the hearing judge, if ascertainable;

(2) The nature or title of any attached document other than an exhibit;

(3) The date of filing of the action; and

(4) The trial date, if set.

(c)   Pagination of documents

Documents bound together must be consecutively paginated.

(d)   Reference to previously filed papers

Any paper previously filed must be referred to by date of execution and title.

(e)   Binding

All pages of each document and exhibit must be attached together at the top by a method that permits pages to be easily turned and the entire content of each page to be read.

(f)   Format of exhibits

Each exhibit must be separated by a hard $8\frac{1}{2} \times 11$ sheet with hard paper or plastic tabs extending below the bottom of the page, bearing the exhibit designation. An index to exhibits must be provided. Pages from a single deposition and associated exhibits must be designated as a single exhibit.

(g)   Translation of exhibits

Exhibits written in a foreign language must be accompanied by an English translation, certified under oath by a qualified interpreter. *(Formerly Rule 311, adopted, eff. Jan. 1, 1984. As amended, eff. July 1, 1997. Renumbered Rule 3.1110 and amended, eff. Jan. 1, 2007.)*

Research References

Rutter, Cal. Practice Guide: Civ. Pro. Before Trial Ch. 6-E, E. Amended and Supplemental Pleadings.

Rutter, Cal. Practice Guide: Civ. Pro. Before Trial Ch. 10-C, C. Procedural Requirements-Moving Party.

Rutter, Cal. Practice Guide: Civ. Pro. Before Trial Ch. 9(I)-B, B. Preparing and Filing Motions.

Rutter, Cal. Practice Guide: Civil Trials & Evidence Ch. 4-F, F. Motions in Limine.

6 Witkin Cal. Proc. 5th Proceedings Without Trial § 9, Formal Requisites.

Rule 3.1112. Motions—and other pleadings

(a) Motions required papers

Unless otherwise provided by the rules in this division, the papers filed in support of a motion must consist of at least the following:

(1) A notice of hearing on the motion;

(2) The motion itself; and

(3) A memorandum in support of the motion or demurrer.

(b) Other papers

Other papers may be filed in support of a motion, including declarations, exhibits, appendices, and other documents or pleadings.

(c) Form of motion papers

The papers filed under (a) and (b) may either be filed as separate documents or combined in one or more documents if the party filing a combined pleading specifies these items separately in the caption of the combined pleading.

(d) Motion—required elements

A motion must:

(1) Identify the party or parties bringing the motion;

(2) Name the parties to whom it is addressed;

(3) Briefly state the basis for the motion and the relief sought; and

(4) If a pleading is challenged, state the specific portion challenged.

(e) Additional requirements for motions

In addition to the requirements of this rule, a motion relating to the subjects specified in chapter 6 of this division must comply with any additional requirements in that chapter.

(f) Motion in limine

Notwithstanding (a), a motion in limine filed before or during trial need not be accompanied by a notice of hearing. The timing and place of the filing and service of the motion are at the discretion of the trial judge. *(Formerly Rule 312, adopted, eff. July 1, 1997. Renumbered Rule 3.1112 and amended, eff. Jan. 1, 2007. As amended, eff. July 1, 2008.)*

Research References

Rutter, Cal. Practice Guide: Civ. Pro. Before Trial Ch. 6-E, E. Amended and Supplemental Pleadings.

Rutter, Cal. Practice Guide: Civ. Pro. Before Trial Ch. 7(I)-A, A. Demurrers.

Rutter, Cal. Practice Guide: Civ. Pro. Before Trial Ch. 7(I)-B, B. Motions to Strike.

Rutter, Cal. Practice Guide: Civ. Pro. Before Trial Ch. 9(I)-B, B. Preparing and Filing Motions.

Rutter, Cal. Practice Guide: Civ. Pro. Before Trial Ch. 12(I)-B, B. Case Management ("Fast Track") System.

Rutter, Cal. Practice Guide: Civil Trials & Evidence Ch. 4-F, F. Motions in Limine.

5 Witkin Cal. Proc. 5th Pleading § 979, (S 979) Service and Filing.

6 Witkin Cal. Proc. 5th Proceedings Without Trial § 6, (S 6) Required Papers and Elements.

6 Witkin Cal. Proc. 5th Proceedings Without Trial § 7, General Requirement of Notice.

Rule 3.1113. Memorandum

(a) Memorandum in support of motion

A party filing a motion, except for a motion listed in rule 3.1114, must serve and file a supporting memorandum. The court may construe the absence of a memorandum as an admission that the motion or special demurrer is not meritorious and cause for its denial and, in the case of a demurrer, as a waiver of all grounds not supported.

(b) Contents of memorandum

The memorandum must contain a statement of facts, a concise statement of the law, evidence and arguments relied on, and a discussion of the statutes, cases, and textbooks cited in support of the position advanced.

(c) Case citation format

A case citation must include the official report volume and page number and year of decision. The court must not require any other form of citation.

(d) Length of memorandum

Except in a summary judgment or summary adjudication motion, no opening or responding memorandum may exceed 15 pages. In a summary judgment or summary adjudication motion, no opening or responding memorandum may exceed 20 pages. No reply or closing memorandum may exceed 10 pages. The page limit does not include exhibits, declarations, attachments, the table of contents, the table of authorities, or the proof of service.

(e) Application to file longer memorandum

A party may apply to the court ex parte but with written notice of the application to the other parties, at least 24 hours before the memorandum is due, for permission to file a longer memorandum. The application must state reasons why the argument cannot be made within the stated limit.

(f) Format of longer memorandum

A memorandum that exceeds 10 pages must include a table of contents and a table of authorities. A memorandum that exceeds 15 pages must also include an opening summary of argument.

(g) Effect of filing an oversized memorandum

A memorandum that exceeds the page limits of these rules must be filed and considered in the same manner as a late-filed paper.

(h) Pagination of memorandum

Notwithstanding any other rule, a memorandum that includes a table of contents and a table of authorities must be paginated as follows:

(1) The caption page or pages must not be numbered;

(2) The pages of the tables must be numbered consecutively using lower-case roman numerals starting on the first page of the tables; and

(3) The pages of the text must be numbered consecutively using Arabic numerals starting on the first page of the text.

(i) Copies of authorities

(1) A judge may require that if any authority other than California cases, statutes, constitutional provisions, or state or local rules is cited, a copy of the authority must be lodged with the papers that cite the authority and tabbed as required by 3.1110(f).

(2) If a California case is cited before the time it is published in the advance sheets of the Official Reports, the party must include the title, case number, date of decision, and, if from the Court of Appeal, district of the Court of Appeal in which the case was decided. A judge may require that a copy of that case must be lodged and tabbed as required by rule 3.1110(f).

(3) Upon the request of a party to the action, any party citing any authority other than California cases, statutes, constitutional provisions, or state or local rules must promptly provide a copy of such authority to the requesting party.

(j) Attachments

To the extent practicable, all supporting memorandums and declarations must be attached to the notice of motion.

(k) Exhibit references

All references to exhibits or declarations in supporting or opposing papers must reference the number or letter of the exhibit, the specific page, and, if applicable, the paragraph or line number.

(l) Requests for judicial notice

Any request for judicial notice must be made in a separate document listing the specific items for which notice is requested and must comply with rule 3.1306(c).

(m) Proposed orders or judgments

If a proposed order or judgment is submitted, it must be lodged and served with the moving papers but must not be attached to them. *(Formerly Rule 313, adopted, eff. Jan. 1984. As amended, eff. July 1, 1984; Jan. 1, 1992; July 1, 1997; July 1, 2000; Jan. 1, 2003; Jan. 1, 2004. Renumbered Rule 3.1113 and amended, eff. Jan. 1, 2007. As amended, eff. Jan. 1, 2008; July 1, 2011.)*

Advisory Committee Comment

See also rule 1.200 concerning the format of citations.

Research References

Rutter, Cal. Practice Guide: A.D.R. App. D Form 87, Petition for Order Compelling Arbitration.
Rutter, Cal. Practice Guide: A.D.R. App. D Form 88, Motion for Order Compelling Arbitration and for Stay (Pending Lawsuit).
Rutter, Cal. Practice Guide: A.D.R. App. D Form 130, Motion for Order of Reference (CCP §§ 638).
Rutter, Cal. Practice Guide: Civil Appeals & Writs Ch. 8-C, C. Standards of Appellate Review.
Rutter, Cal. Practice Guide: Civ. Pro. Before Trial Ch. 6-E, E. Amended and Supplemental Pleadings.
Rutter, Cal. Practice Guide: Civ. Pro. Before Trial Ch. 10-C, C. Procedural Requirements-Moving Party.
Rutter, Cal. Practice Guide: Civ. Pro. Before Trial Ch. 10-D, D. Procedural Requirements-Opposing Party.
Rutter, Cal. Practice Guide: Civ. Pro. Before Trial Ch. 10-E, E. Procedural Requirements-Reply Papers.
Rutter, Cal. Practice Guide: Civ. Pro. Before Trial Ch. 14-A, A. General Considerations.
Rutter, Cal. Practice Guide: Civ. Pro. Before Trial Ch. 14-C, C. Procedural Issues.
Rutter, Cal. Practice Guide: Civ. Pro. Before Trial Ch. 7(I)-A, A. Demurrers.
Rutter, Cal. Practice Guide: Civ. Pro. Before Trial Ch. 7(I)-B, B. Motions to Strike.
Rutter, Cal. Practice Guide: Civ. Pro. Before Trial Ch. 9(I)-B, B. Preparing and Filing Motions.
Rutter, Cal. Practice Guide: Civil Trials & Evidence Ch. 4-F, F. Motions in Limine.
Rutter, Cal. Practice Guide: Civil Trials & Evidence Ch. 18-C, C. Other Post-Trial Motions.
Rutter, Cal. Practice Guide: Personal Injury Ch. 9-B, B. In-Chambers Conference Before Commencement of Trial.
Rutter, Cal. Practice Guide: Personal Injury Ch. 10-A, A. Motion for New Trial.

Rutter, Cal. Practice Guide: Personal Injury Ch. 10-B, B. Motion for Judgment Notwithstanding the Verdict.
Rutter, Cal. Practice Guide: Personal Injury Ch. 10-C, C. Motion to Vacate and Enter Different Judgment.
3 Witkin Cal. Proc. 5th Actions § 933, (S 933) Points and Authorities.
8 Witkin Cal. Proc. 5th Attack Judgment Trial Court § 66, (S 66) Supporting Memorandum.
8 Witkin Cal. Proc. 5th Attack Judgment Trial Court § 141, Notice of Motion.
8 Witkin Cal. Proc. 5th Attack Judgment Trial Court § 174, Form and Content.
4 Witkin Cal. Proc. 5th Pleading § 307, (S 307) Authority for Motion.
5 Witkin Cal. Proc. 5th Pleading § 980, (S 980) Supporting Memorandum.
6 Witkin Cal. Proc. 5th Proceedings Without Trial § 9, Formal Requisites.
6 Witkin Cal. Proc. 5th Proceedings Without Trial § 11, Supporting Memorandum.

Rule 3.1114. Applications, motions, and petitions not requiring a memorandum

(a) Memorandum not required

Civil motions, applications, and petitions filed on Judicial Council forms that do not require a memorandum include the following:

(1) Application for appointment of guardian ad litem in a civil case;

(2) Application for an order extending time to serve pleading;

(3) Motion to be relieved as counsel;

(4) Motion filed in small claims case;

(5) Petition for change of name or gender;

(6) Petition for declaration of emancipation of minor;

(7) Petition for injunction prohibiting harassment;

(8) Petition for protective order to prevent elder or dependent adult abuse;

(9) Petition for order to prevent postsecondary school violence;

(10) Petition of employer for injunction prohibiting workplace violence;

(11) Petition for order prohibiting abuse (transitional housing);

(12) Petition to approve compromise of claim of a minor or a person with a disability; and

(13) Petition for withdrawal of funds from blocked account.

(b) Submission of a memorandum

Notwithstanding (a), if it would further the interests of justice, a party may submit, or the court may order the submission of, a memorandum in support of any motion, application, or petition. The memorandum must comply with rule 3.1113. *(Formerly Rule 314, adopted, eff. Jan. 1, 2004. Renumbered Rule 3.1114 and amended, eff. Jan. 1, 2007. As amended, eff. Jan. 1, 2011.)*

Research References

Rutter, Cal. Practice Guide: Civ. Pro. Before Trial Ch. 9(I)-B, B. Preparing and Filing Motions.
6 Witkin Cal. Proc. 5th Proceedings Without Trial § 11, Supporting Memorandum.

Rule 3.1115. Declarations

The caption of a declaration must state the name of the declarant and must specifically identify the motion or other proceeding that it supports or opposes. *(Formerly Rule 315, adopted, eff. Jan. 1, 1984. Renumbered Rule 3.1115 and amended, eff. Jan. 1, 2007.)*

Rutter, Cal. Practice Guide: Civ. Pro. Before Trial Ch. 9(I)-B, B. Preparing and Filing Motions.

Rutter, Cal. Practice Guide: Civil Trials & Evidence Ch. 4-F, F. Motions in Limine.

Rule 3.1116. Deposition testimony as an exhibit

(a) Title page

The first page of any deposition used as an exhibit must state the name of the deponent and the date of the deposition.

(b) Deposition pages

Other than the title page, the exhibit must contain only the relevant pages of the transcript. The original page number of any deposition page must be clearly visible.

(c) Highlighting of testimony

The relevant portion of any testimony in the deposition must be marked in a manner that calls attention to the testimony. *(Formerly Rule 316, adopted, eff. Jan. 1, 1992. Renumbered Rule 3.1116 and amended, eff. Jan. 1, 2007.)*

Rutter, Cal. Practice Guide: Civ. Pro. Before Trial Ch. 10-C, C. Procedural Requirements-Moving Party.

Rutter, Cal. Practice Guide: Civ. Pro. Before Trial Ch. 8E-15, Motion to Compel Answers.

Rutter, Cal. Practice Guide: Civ. Pro. Before Trial Ch. 9(I)-B, B. Preparing and Filing Motions.

Rutter, Cal. Practice Guide: Civil Trials & Evidence Ch. 4-F, F. Motions in Limine.

Chapter 3

PROVISIONAL AND INJUNCTIVE RELIEF

Article 1

GENERAL PROVISIONS

Rule
3.1130. Bonds and undertakings.

Rule 3.1130. Bonds and undertakings

(a) Prerequisites to acceptance of corporate sureties

A corporation must not be accepted or approved as surety on a bond or undertaking unless the following conditions are met:

(1) The Insurance Commissioner has certified the corporation as being admitted to do business in the state as a surety insurer;

(2) There is filed in the office of the clerk a copy, duly certified by the proper authority, of the transcript or record of appointment entitling or authorizing the person or persons purporting to execute the bond or undertaking for and in behalf of the corporation to act in the premises; and

(3) The bond or undertaking has been executed under penalty of perjury as provided in Code of Civil Procedure section 995.630, or the fact of execution of the bond or undertaking by the officer or agent of the corporation purporting to become surety has been duly acknowledged before an officer of this state authorized to take and certify acknowledgements.

(b) Certain persons not eligible to act as sureties

An officer of the court or member of the State Bar may not act as a surety.

(c) Withdrawal of bonds and undertakings

An original bond or undertaking may be withdrawn from the files and delivered to the party by whom it was filed on order of the court only if all parties interested in the obligation so stipulate, or upon a showing that the purpose for which it was filed has been abandoned without any liability having been incurred. *(Formerly Rule 381, adopted, eff. Jan. 1, 1984. Renumbered Rule 3.1130 and amended, eff. Jan. 1, 2007.)*

Rutter, Cal. Practice Guide: Enforcing Judgments/Debts Ch. 4-A, A. Attachment.

6 Witkin Cal. Proc. 5th Provisional Remedies § 18, Filing and Service.

6 Witkin Cal. Proc. 5th Provisional Remedies § 20, (S 20) Qualification.

6 Witkin Cal. Proc. 5th Provisional Remedies § 23, (S 23) Authentication of Bond.

Article 2

WRITS

Rule
3.1140. Lodging of record in administrative mandate cases.
3.1142. Stay of driving license suspension.

Rule 3.1140. Lodging of record in administrative mandate cases

The party intending to use a part of the administrative record in a case brought under Code of Civil Procedure section 1094.5 must lodge that part of the record at least five days before the hearing. *(Formerly Rule 347, adopted, eff. Jan. 1, 1984. Renumbered Rule 3.1140 and amended, eff. Jan. 1, 2007.)*

Rule 3.1142. Stay of driving license suspension

A request for a stay of a suspension of a driving license must be accompanied by a copy of the petitioner's driving record from the Department of Motor Vehicles. *(Formerly Rule 355, adopted, eff. Jan. 1, 1984. Renumbered Rule 3.1142 and amended, eff. Jan. 1, 2007.)*

Article 3

INJUNCTIONS

Rule
3.1150. Preliminary injunctions and bonds.
3.1151. Requirements for injunction in certain cases.
3.1152. Requests for protective orders to prevent civil harassment, workplace violence, private postsecondary school violence, and elder or dependent adult abuse.

Rule 3.1150. Preliminary injunctions and bonds

(a) Manner of application and service

A party requesting a preliminary injunction may give notice of the request to the opposing or responding party either by serving a noticed motion under Code of Civil Procedure section 1005 or by obtaining and serving an order to show cause (OSC). An OSC must be used when a temporary restraining order (TRO) is sought, or if the party against whom the preliminary injunction is sought has not appeared in the action. If the responding party has not appeared, the OSC must be served in the same manner as a summons and complaint.

(b) Filing of complaint or obtaining of court file

If the action is initiated the same day a TRO or an OSC is sought, the complaint must be filed first. The moving party must provide a file-stamped copy of the complaint to the judge who will hear the application. If an application for a TRO or OSC is made in an existing case, the moving party must that the court file be made available to the judge hearing the application.

(c) Form of OSC and TRO

The OSC and TRO must be stated separately, with the OSC stated first. The restraining language sought in an OSC and a TRO must be separately stated in the OSC and the TRO and may not be incorporated by reference. The OSC must describe the injunction to be sought at the hearing. The TRO must describe the activities to be enjoined pending the hearing. A proposed OSC must contain blank spaces for the time and manner of service on responding parties, the date on which the proof of service must be delivered to the court hearing the OSC, a briefing schedule, and, if applicable, the expiration date of the TRO.

(d) Personal attendance

The moving party or counsel for the moving party must be personally present when the request for a TRO is made.

(e) Previous applications

An application for a TRO or an OSC must state whether there has been any previous application for similar relief and, if so, the result of the application.

(f) Undertaking

Notwithstanding rule 3.1312, whenever an application for a preliminary injunction is granted, a proposed order must be presented to the judge for signature, with an undertaking in the amount ordered, within one court day after the granting of the application or within the time ordered. Unless otherwise ordered, any restraining order previously granted remains in effect during the time allowed for presentation for signature of the order of injunction and undertaking. If the proposed order and the undertaking required are not presented within the time allowed, the TRO may be vacated without notice. All bonds and undertakings must comply with rule 3.1130.

(g) Ex parte temporary restraining orders

Applications for ex parte temporary restraining orders are governed by the ex parte rules in chapter 4 of this division. *(Formerly Rule 359, adopted, eff. Jan. 1, 1984. As amended, eff. July 1, 1997; July 1, 1999. Renumbered Rule 3.1150 and amended, eff. Jan. 1, 2007.)*

Research References

Rutter, Cal. Practice Guide: Civ. Pro. Before Trial Ch. 9(II)-A, A. Injunctions.
Rutter, Cal. Practice Guide: Enforcing Judgments/Debts Ch. 4-B, B. Claim and Delivery.
6 Witkin Cal. Proc. 5th Provisional Remedies § 364, Order to Show Cause and Restraining Order.
6 Witkin Cal. Proc. 5th Provisional Remedies § 368, (S 368) in General.
6 Witkin Cal. Proc. 5th Provisional Remedies § 384, (S 384) Amount and Form.
6 Witkin Cal. Proc. 5th Provisional Remedies § 385, (S 385) Time of Filing.

Rule 3.1151.   Requirements for injunction in certain cases

A petition for an injunction to limit picketing, restrain real property encroachments, or protect easements must depict by drawings, plot plans, photographs, or other appropriate means, or must describe in detail the premises involved, including, if applicable, the length and width of the frontage on a street or alley, the width of sidewalks, and the number, size, and location of entrances. *(Formerly Rule 361, adopted, eff. Jan. 1, 1984. Renumbered Rule 3.1151 and amended, eff. Jan. 1, 2007.)*

Research References

Rutter, Cal. Practice Guide: Civ. Pro. Before Trial Ch. 9(II)-A, A. Injunctions.

Rule 3.1152.   Requests for protective orders to prevent civil harassment, workplace violence, private postsecondary school violence, and elder or dependent adult abuse

(a) Application

This rule applies to requests for protective orders under Code of Civil Procedure sections 527.6, 527.8, and 527.85, and Welfare and Institutions Code section 15657.03.

(b) No memorandum required

Unless ordered by the court, no memorandum is required in support of or in opposition to a request for a protective order.

(c) Service of requests, notices, and orders

The request for a protective order, notice of hearing, and any temporary restraining order, must be personally served on the respondent at least five days before the hearing, unless the court for good cause orders a shorter time. Service must be made in the manner provided by law for personal service of summons in civil actions.

(d) Response

The response to a request for a protective order may be written or oral, or both. If a written is served on the petitioner or, if the petitioner is represented, on the petitioner's attorney at least two days before the hearing, the petitioner is not entitled to a continuance on account of the response.

(e) Continuance

A respondent may request continuance of the hearing upon a showing of good cause. If the court in its discretion grants the continuance, any temporary restraining order that has been granted remains in effect until the end of the continued hearing unless otherwise ordered by the court. *(Formerly Rule 363, adopted, eff. Jan. 1, 1984. As amended, eff. Jan. 1, 1993; July 1, 1995; Jan. 1, 2000; Jan. 1, 2002. Renumbered Rule 3.1152 and amended, eff. Jan. 1, 2007. As amended, eff. Jan. 1, 2012.)*

Research References

Rutter, Cal. Practice Guide: Civ. Pro. Before Trial Ch. 9(II)-A, A. Injunctions.
6 Witkin Cal. Proc. 5th Provisional Remedies § 321, (S 321) Petition, Service, and Response.
6 Witkin Cal. Proc. 5th Provisional Remedies § 322, (S 322) Hearing, Determination, and Enforcement Response.
6 Witkin Cal. Proc. 5th Provisional Remedies § 329, (S 329) Petition, Service, and Response.
6 Witkin Cal. Proc. 5th Provisional Remedies § 330, (S 330) Hearing, Determination, and Enforcement.
6 Witkin Cal. Proc. 5th Provisional Remedies § 315A, (S 315A) (New)-Abuse of Elder or Dependent Adult.
6 Witkin Cal. Proc. 5th Provisional Remedies § 330D, (S 330D) (New)-Petition, Service, and Response.
6 Witkin Cal. Proc. 5th Provisional Remedies § 330E, (S 330E) (New)-Hearing, Determination, and Enforcement.

Article 4

RECEIVERSHIPS

Rule 3.1175. Ex parte application for appointment of receiver

(a) Application

In addition to any other matters supporting an application for the ex parte appointment of a receiver, the applicant must show in detail by verified complaint or declaration:

(1) The nature of the emergency and the reasons irreparable injury would be suffered by the applicant during the time necessary for a hearing on notice;

(2) The names, addresses, and telephone numbers of the persons in actual possession of the property for which a receiver is requested, or of the president, manager, or principal agent of any corporation in possession of the property;

(3) The use being made of the property by the persons in possession; and

(4) If the property is a part of the plant, equipment, or stock in trade of any business, the nature and approximate size or extent of the business and facts sufficient to show whether the taking of the property by a receiver would stop or seriously interfere with the operation of the business.

If any of the matters listed above are unknown to the applicant and cannot be ascertained by the exercise of due diligence, the applicant's declaration or verified complaint must fully state the matters unknown and the efforts made to acquire the information. *(Formerly Rule 349, adopted, eff. Jan. 1, 1984. Renumbered Rule 1900 and amended, eff. Jan. 1, 2002. Renumbered Rule 3.1175 and amended, eff. Jan. 1, 2007.)*

Research References

Rutter, Cal. Practice Guide: Civ. Pro. Before Trial Ch. 9(II)-B, B. Receiverships.
Rutter, Cal. Practice Guide: Enforcing Judgments/Debts Ch. 4-C, C. Receiverships.
6 Witkin Cal. Proc. 5th Provisional Remedies § 446, Showing Required.

Rule 3.1176. Confirmation of ex parte appointment of receiver

(a) Order to show cause

Whenever a receiver is appointed without notice, the matter must be made returnable upon an order to show cause why the appointment should not be confirmed. The order to show cause must be made returnable on the earliest date that the business of the court will admit, but not later than 15 days or, if good cause appears to the court, 22 days from the date the order is issued.

(b) Service of complaint, order to show cause, declarations, and memorandum

The applicant must serve on each of the adverse parties:

(1) A copy of the complaint if not previously served;

(2) The order to show cause stating the date, time, and place of the hearing;

(3) Any declarations supporting the application; and

(4) A memorandum supporting the application.

Service must be made as soon as reasonably practical, but no later than 5 days after the date on which the order to show cause is issued, unless the court orders another time for service.

(c) Failure to proceed or serve adverse party

When the matter first comes on for hearing, the party that obtained the appointment must be ready to proceed. If that party is not ready to proceed or has failed to exercise diligence to effect service upon the adverse parties as provided in (b), the court may discharge the receiver.

(d) Continuance

The adverse parties are entitled to one continuance to enable them to oppose the confirmation. If a continuance is granted under this subdivision, the order to show cause remains in effect until the date of the continued hearing. *(Formerly Rule 351, adopted, eff. Jan. 1, 1984. Renumbered Rule 1901 and amended, eff. Jan. 1, 2002. Renumbered Rule 3.1176 and amended, eff. Jan. 1, 2007.)*

Research References

Rutter, Cal. Practice Guide: Civ. Pro. Before Trial Ch. 9(II)-B, B. Receiverships.
Rutter, Cal. Practice Guide: Enforcing Judgments/Debts Ch. 4-C, C. Receiverships.
6 Witkin Cal. Proc. 5th Provisional Remedies § 448, Confirmation of Appointment.

Rule 3.1177. Nomination of receivers

At the hearing of an application for appointment of a receiver on notice or at the hearing for confirmation of an ex parte appointment, each party appearing may, at the time of the hearing, suggest in writing one or more persons for appointment or substitution as receiver, stating the reasons. A party's suggestion is without prejudice to its objection to the appointment or confirmation of a receiver. *(Formerly Rule 353, adopted, eff. Jan. 1, 1984. Renumbered Rule 1902 and amended, eff. Jan. 1, 2002. Renumbered Rule 3.1177, eff. Jan. 1, 2007.)*

Research References

Rutter, Cal. Practice Guide: Civ. Pro. Before Trial Ch. 9(II)-B, B. Receiverships.
Rutter, Cal. Practice Guide: Enforcing Judgments/Debts Ch. 4-C, C. Receiverships.
6 Witkin Cal. Proc. 5th Provisional Remedies § 443, Appointment.

Rule 3.1178. Amount of undertakings

At the hearing of an application for appointment of a receiver on notice or ex parte, the applicant must, and other parties may, propose and state the reasons for the specific amounts of the undertakings required from (1) the applicant by Code of Civil Procedure section 529, (2) the applicant by Code of Civil Procedure section 566(b), and (3) the receiver by Code of Civil Procedure section 567(b), for any injunction that is ordered in or with the order appointing a receiver. *(Formerly Rule 1902.5, adopted eff. Jan. 1, 2004. Renumbered Rule 3.1178 and amended, eff. Jan. 1, 2007.)*

Research References

Rutter, Cal. Practice Guide: Civ. Pro. Before Trial Ch. 9(II)-B, B. Receiverships.
Rutter, Cal. Practice Guide: Enforcing Judgments/Debts Ch. 4-C, C. Receiverships.
6 Witkin Cal. Proc. 5th Provisional Remedies § 384, (S 384) Amount and Form.
6 Witkin Cal. Proc. 5th Provisional Remedies § 444, Qualification and Undertaking.
6 Witkin Cal. Proc. 5th Provisional Remedies § 447, Undertaking.

Rule 3.1179. The receiver

(a) Agent of the court

The receiver is the agent of the court and not of any party, and as such:

(1) Is neutral;

(2) Acts for the benefit of all who may have an interest in the receivership property; and

(3) Holds assets for the court and not for the plaintiff or the defendant.

(b) Prohibited contracts, agreements, arrangements, and understandings

The party seeking the appointment of the receiver may not, directly or indirectly, require any contract, agreement, arrangement, or understanding with any receiver whom it intends to nominate or recommend to the court, and the receiver may not enter into any such contract, arrangement, agreement, or understanding concerning:

(1) The role of the receiver with respect to the property following a trustee's sale or termination of a receivership, without specific court permission;

(2) How the receiver will administer the receivership or how much the receiver will charge for services or pay for services to appropriate or approved third parties hired to provide services;

(3) Who the receiver will hire, or seek approval to hire, to perform necessary services; or

(4) What capital expenditures will be made on the property. *(Formerly Rule 1903, adopted, eff. Jan. 1, 2002. Renumbered Rule 3.1179, eff. Jan. 1, 2007.)*

Research References

Rutter, Cal. Practice Guide: Civ. Pro. Before Trial Ch. 9(II)-B, B. Receiverships.
Rutter, Cal. Practice Guide: Enforcing Judgments/Debts Ch. 4-C, C. Receiverships.
6 Witkin Cal. Proc. 5th Provisional Remedies § 419, (S 419) Nature of Receivership.

Rule 3.1180. Employment of attorney

A receiver must not employ an attorney without the approval of the court. The application for approval to employ an attorney must be in writing and must state:

(1) The necessity for the employment;

(2) The name of the attorney whom the receiver proposes to employ; and

(3) That the attorney is not the attorney for, associated with, nor employed by an attorney for any party. *(Formerly Rule 1904, adopted, eff. Jan. 1, 2002. Renumbered Rule 3.1180 and amended, eff. Jan. 1, 2007.)*

Research References

Rutter, Cal. Practice Guide: Civ. Pro. Before Trial Ch. 9(II)-B, B. Receiverships.
Rutter, Cal. Practice Guide: Enforcing Judgments/Debts Ch. 4-C, C. Receiverships.
6 Witkin Cal. Proc. 5th Provisional Remedies § 457, Contracts.

Rule 3.1181. Receiver's inventory

(a) Filing of inventory

A receiver must, within 30 days after appointment, or within such other time as the court may order, file an inventory containing a complete and detailed list of all property of which the receiver has taken possession by virtue of the appointment.

(b) Supplemental inventory

The receiver must promptly file a supplementary inventory of all subsequently obtained property. *(Formerly Rule 1905, adopted, eff. Jan. 1, 2002. Renumbered Rule 3.1181 and amended, eff. Jan. 1, 2007.)*

Research References

Rutter, Cal. Practice Guide: Civ. Pro. Before Trial Ch. 9(II)-B, B. Receiverships.
Rutter, Cal. Practice Guide: Enforcing Judgments/Debts Ch. 4-C, C. Receiverships.
Witkin Cal. Proc. 5th Provisional Remedies § 454, Possession and Control of Property.

Rule 3.1182. Monthly reports

(a) Content of reports

The receiver must provide monthly reports to the parties and, if requested, to nonparty client lien holders. These reports must include:

(1) A narrative report of events;

(2) A financial report; and

(3) A statement of all fees paid to the receiver, employees, and professionals showing:

(A) Itemized services;

(B) A breakdown of the services by 1/10 hour increments;

(C) If the fees are hourly, the hourly fees; and

(D) If the fees are on another basis, that basis.

(b) Reports not to be filed

The monthly reports are not to be filed with the court unless the court so orders. *(Formerly Rule 1906, adopted, eff. Jan. 1, 2002. Renumbered Rule 3.1182 and amended, eff. Jan. 1, 2007.)*

Research References

Rutter, Cal. Practice Guide: Civ. Pro. Before Trial Ch. 9(II)-B, B. Receiverships.
Rutter, Cal. Practice Guide: Enforcing Judgments/Debts Ch. 4-C, C. Receiverships.
6 Witkin Cal. Proc. 5th Provisional Remedies § 458, (S 458) Accounts.

Rule 3.1183. Interim fees and objections

(a) Interim fees

Interim fees are subject to final review and approval by the court. The court retains jurisdiction to award a greater or lesser amount as the full, fair, and final value of the services received.

(b) Objections to interim accounts and reports

Unless good cause is shown, objections to a receiver's interim report and accounting must be made within 10 days of notice of the report and accounting, must be specific, and must be delivered to the receiver and all parties entitled to service of the interim report and accounting. *(Formerly Rule 1907, adopted, eff. Jan. 1, 2002. Renumbered Rule 3.1183, eff. Jan. 1, 2007.)*

Research References

Rutter, Cal. Practice Guide: Civ. Pro. Before Trial Ch. 9(II)-B, B. Receiverships.
Rutter, Cal. Practice Guide: Enforcing Judgments/Debts Ch. 4-C, C. Receiverships.
6 Witkin Cal. Proc. 5th Provisional Remedies § 458, (S 458) Accounts.

Rule 3.1184. Receiver's final account and report

(a) Motion or stipulation

A receiver must present by noticed motion or stipulation of all parties:

(1) A final account and report;

(2) A request for the discharge; and

(3) A request for exoneration of the receiver's surety.

(b) No memorandum required

No memorandum needs to be submitted in support of the motion or stipulation served and filed under (a) unless the court so orders.

(c) Notice

Notice of the motion or of the stipulation must be given to every person or entity known to the receiver to have a substantial, unsatisfied claim that will be affected by the order or stipulation, whether or not the person or entity is a party to the action or has appeared in it.

(d) Claim for compensation for receiver or attorney

If any allowance of compensation for the receiver or for an attorney employed by the receiver is claimed in an account, it must state in detail what services have been performed by the receiver or the attorney and whether previous allowances have been made to the receiver or attorney and the amounts. *(Formerly Rule 1908, adopted, eff. Jan. 1, 2002. As amended, eff. Jan. 1, 2004. Renumbered Rule 3.1184 and amended, eff. Jan. 1, 2007.)*

Research References

Rutter, Cal. Practice Guide: Civ. Pro. Before Trial Ch. 9(II)-B, B. Receiverships.
Rutter, Cal. Practice Guide: Enforcing Judgments/Debts Ch. 4-C, C. Receiverships.
6 Witkin Cal. Proc. 5th Provisional Remedies § 458, (S 458) Accounts.
6 Witkin Cal. Proc. 5th Provisional Remedies § 459, (S 459) Compensation.
6 Witkin Cal. Proc. 5th Provisional Remedies § 460, (S 460) Discharge.

Chapter 4

EX PARTE APPLICATIONS

Rule
3.1200. Application.
3.1201. Required documents.
3.1202. Contents of application.
3.1203. Time of notice to other parties.
3.1204. Contents of notice and declaration regarding notice.
3.1205. Filing and presentation of the ex parte application.
3.1206. Service of papers.
3.1207. Personal appearance requirements.

Rule 3.1200. Application

The rules in this chapter govern ex parte applications and orders in civil cases, unless otherwise provided by a statute or a rule. These rules may be referred to as "the ex parte rules." *(Adopted, eff. Jan. 1, 2007.)*

Research References

Rutter, Cal. Practice Guide: Civ. Pro. Before Trial Ch. 9(I)-F, F. Ex Parte Motions.
Rutter, Cal. Practice Guide: Civ. Pro. Before Trial Ch. 12(I)-C, C. Claims for Trial Setting Preference.
Rutter, Cal. Practice Guide: Civ. Pro. Before Trial Ch. 9(II)-A, A. Injunctions.
Rutter, Cal. Practice Guide: Civ. Pro. Before Trial Ch. 9(III)-C, C. Sanctions Under CCP § 128.7.
Rutter, Cal. Practice Guide: Enforcing Judgments/Debts Ch. 6D-2, Writ of Execution.
Rutter, Cal. Practice Guide: Personal Injury Ch. 8-A, A. Case Management.
6 Witkin Cal. Proc. 5th Proceedings Without Trial § 59, (S 59) Formal Requisites.
7 Witkin Cal. Proc. 5th Trial § 32, (S 32) Motion.
7 Witkin Cal. Proc. 5th Trial § 73, (S 73) Motion to Advance or Reset.

Rule 3.1201. Required documents

A request for ex parte relief must be in writing and must include all of the following:

(1) An application containing the case caption and stating the relief requested;

(2) A declaration in support of the application making the factual showing required under rule 3.1202(c);

(3) A declaration based on personal knowledge of the notice given under rule 3.1204;

(4) A memorandum; and

(5) A proposed order. *(Adopted, eff. Jan. 1, 2007.)*

Research References

Rutter, Cal. Practice Guide: Civ. Pro. Before Trial Ch. 9(I)-F, F. Ex Parte Motions.
Rutter, Cal. Practice Guide: Enforcing Judgments/Debts Ch. 4-A, A. Attachment.
Rutter, Cal. Practice Guide: Enforcing Judgments/Debts Ch. 4-B, B. Claim and Delivery.
6 Witkin Cal. Proc. 5th Proceedings Without Trial § 59, (S 59) Formal Requisites.

Rule 3.1202. Contents of application

(a) Identification of attorney or party

An ex parte application must state the name, address, and telephone number of any attorney known to the applicant to be an attorney for any party or, if no such attorney is known, the name, address, and telephone number of the party if known to the applicant.

(b) Disclosure of previous applications

If an ex parte application has been refused in whole or in part, any subsequent application of the same character or for the same relief, although made upon an alleged different state of facts, must include a full disclosure of all previous applications and of the court's actions.

(c) Affirmative factual showing required

An applicant must make an affirmative factual showing in a declaration containing competent testimony based on personal knowledge of irreparable harm, immediate danger, or any other statutory basis for granting relief ex parte. *(Adopted, eff. Jan. 1, 2007. As amended, eff. Jan. 1, 2007.)*

Research References

Rutter, Cal. Practice Guide: Civ. Pro. Before Trial Ch. 9(I)-F, F. Ex Parte Motions.
Rutter, Cal. Practice Guide: Enforcing Judgments/Debts Ch. 4-A, A. Attachment.
Rutter, Cal. Practice Guide: Enforcing Judgments/Debts Ch. 4-B, B. Claim and Delivery.
6 Witkin Cal. Proc. 5th Proceedings Without Trial § 59, (S 59) Formal Requisites.

Rule 3.1203. Time of notice to other parties

(a) Time of notice

A party seeking an ex parte order must notify all parties no later than 10:00 a.m. the court day before the ex parte appearance, absent a showing of exceptional circumstances that justify a shorter time for notice.

(b) Time of notice in unlawful detainer proceedings

A party seeking an ex parte order in an unlawful detainer proceeding may provide shorter notice than required under (a) provided that the notice given is reasonable. *(Adopted, eff. Jan. 1, 2007. As amended, eff. Jan. 1, 2008.)*

Research References

Rutter, Cal. Practice Guide: Civil Appeals & Writs Ch. 7-C, C. Stay by Posting Security (Bond or Undertaking).
Rutter, Cal. Practice Guide: Civ. Pro. Before Trial Ch. 2-E, E. Intervention.
Rutter, Cal. Practice Guide: Civ. Pro. Before Trial Ch. 6-E, E. Amended and Supplemental Pleadings.
Rutter, Cal. Practice Guide: Civ. Pro. Before Trial Ch. 7(I)-A, A. Demurrers.
Rutter, Cal. Practice Guide: Civ. Pro. Before Trial Ch. 9(I)-B, B. Preparing and Filing Motions.

Rutter, Cal. Practice Guide: Civ. Pro. Before Trial Ch. 9(I)-F, F. Ex Parte Motions.

Rutter, Cal. Practice Guide: Civ. Pro. Before Trial Ch. 9(II)-A, A. Injunctions.

California Practice Guide: Employment Litigation Ch. 2-H, H. Ex Parte Communication With Court.

Rutter, Cal. Practice Guide: Enforcing Judgments/Debts Ch. 4-A, A. Attachment.

Rutter, Cal. Practice Guide: Enforcing Judgments/Debts Ch. 4-B, B. Claim and Delivery.

6 Witkin Cal. Proc. 5th Proceedings Without Trial § 59, (S 59) Formal Requisites.

Rule 3.1204. Contents of notice and declaration regarding notice

(a) Contents of notice

When notice of an ex parte application is given, the person giving notice must:

(1) State with specificity the nature of the relief to be requested and the date, time, and place for the presentation of the application; and

(2) Attempt to determine whether the opposing party will appear to oppose the application.

(b) Declaration regarding notice

An ex parte application must be accompanied by a declaration regarding notice stating:

(1) The notice given, including the date, time, manner, and name of the party informed, the relief sought, any response, and whether opposition is expected and that, within the applicable time under rule 3.1203, the applicant informed the opposing party where and when the application would be made;

(2) That the applicant in good faith attempted to inform the opposing party but was unable to do so, specifying the efforts made to inform the opposing party; or

(3) That, for reasons specified, the applicant should not be required to inform the opposing party.

(c) Explanation for shorter notice

If notice was provided later than 10:00 a.m. the court day before the ex parte appearance, the declaration regarding notice must explain:

(1) The exceptional circumstances that justify the shorter notice; or

(2) In unlawful detainer proceedings, why the notice given is reasonable. *(Adopted, eff. Jan. 1, 2007.)*

Research References

Rutter, Cal. Practice Guide: Civ. Pro. Before Trial Ch. 9(I)-F, F. Ex Parte Motions.

Rutter, Cal. Practice Guide: Civ. Pro. Before Trial Ch. 9(II)-A, A. Injunctions.

Rutter, Cal. Practice Guide: Civ. Pro. Before Trial Ch. 9(II)-D, D. Attachment.

California Practice Guide: Employment Litigation Ch. 2-H, H. Ex Parte Communication With Court.

Rutter, Cal. Practice Guide: Enforcing Judgments/Debts Ch. 4-A, A. Attachment.

Rutter, Cal. Practice Guide: Enforcing Judgments/Debts Ch. 4-B, B. Claim and Delivery.

6 Witkin Cal. Proc. 5th Proceedings Without Trial § 59, (S 59) Formal Requisites.

14 Witkin, California Summary 10th Wills and Probate § 975A, (S 975A) (New)-Good Cause Exception to Notice Requirements.

Rule 3.1205. Filing and presentation of the ex parte application

Notwithstanding the failure of an applicant to comply with the requirements of rule 3.1203, the clerk must not reject an ex parte application for filing and must promptly present the application to the appropriate judicial officer for consideration. *(Adopted, eff. Jan. 1, 2007.)*

Research References

Rutter, Cal. Practice Guide: Civ. Pro. Before Trial Ch. 9(I)-F, F. Ex Parte Motions.

6 Witkin Cal. Proc. 5th Proceedings Without Trial § 59, (S 59) Formal Requisites.

Rule 3.1206. Service of papers

Parties appearing at the ex parte hearing must serve the ex parte application or any written opposition on all other appearing parties at the first reasonable opportunity. Absent exceptional circumstances, no hearing may be conducted unless such service has been made. *(Adopted, eff. Jan. 1, 2007.)*

Research References

Rutter, Cal. Practice Guide: Civ. Pro. Before Trial Ch. 9(I)-F, F. Ex Parte Motions.

Rutter, Cal. Practice Guide: Civ. Pro. Before Trial Ch. 9(II)-A, A. Injunctions.

Rutter, Cal. Practice Guide: Enforcing Judgments/Debts Ch. 4-A, A. Attachment.

Rutter, Cal. Practice Guide: Enforcing Judgments/Debts Ch. 4-B, B. Claim and Delivery.

6 Witkin Cal. Proc. 5th Proceedings Without Trial § 59, (S 59) Formal Requisites.

Rule 3.1207. Personal appearance requirements

An ex parte application will be considered without a personal appearance of the applicant in the following cases only:

(1) Applications to file a memorandum in excess of the applicable page limit;

(2) Applications for extensions of time to serve pleadings;

(3) Setting of hearing dates on alternative writs and orders to show cause; and

(4) Stipulations by the parties for an order. *(Adopted, eff. Jan. 1, 2007. As amended, eff. Jan. 1, 2008.)*

Research References

Rutter, Cal. Practice Guide: Civ. Pro. Before Trial Ch. 9(I)-F, F. Ex Parte Motions.

Rutter, Cal. Practice Guide: Civ. Pro. Before Trial Ch. 12(I)-C, C. Claims for Trial Setting Preference.

Rutter, Cal. Practice Guide: Civ. Pro. Before Trial Ch. 9(II)-A, A. Injunctions.

Rutter, Cal. Practice Guide: Civ. Pro. Before Trial Ch. 9(III)-C, C. Sanctions Under CCP § 128.7.

Rutter, Cal. Practice Guide: Enforcing Judgments/Debts Ch. 6D-2, Writ of Execution.

Rutter, Cal. Practice Guide: Personal Injury Ch. 8-A, A. Case Management.

6 Witkin Cal. Proc. 5th Proceedings Without Trial § 59, (S 59) Formal Requisites.

Chapter 5

NOTICED MOTIONS

Rule 3.1300.   Time for filing and service of motion papers

(a) In general

Unless otherwise ordered or specifically provided by law, all moving and supporting papers must be served and filed in accordance with Code of Civil Procedure section 1005.

(b) Order shortening time

The court, on its own motion or on application for an order shortening time supported by a declaration showing good cause, may prescribe shorter times for the filing and service of papers than the times specified in Code of Civil Procedure section 1005.

(c) Time for filing proof of service

Proof of service of the moving papers must be filed no later than five court days before the time appointed for the hearing.

(d) Filing of late papers

No paper may be rejected for filing on the ground that it was untimely submitted for filing. If the court, in its discretion, refuses to consider a late filed paper, the minutes or order must so indicate.

(e) Computation of time

A paper submitted before the close of the clerk's office to the public on the day the paper is due is deemed timely filed. *(Formerly Rule 317, adopted, eff. Jan. 1984. As amended, eff. Jan. 1, 1992; Jan. 1, 2000. Renumbered Rule 3.1300 and amended, eff. Jan. 1, 2007.)*

Research References

Rutter, Cal. Practice Guide: Civ. Pro. Before Trial Ch. 10-C, C. Procedural Requirements-Moving Party.
Rutter, Cal. Practice Guide: Civ. Pro. Before Trial Ch. 7(I)-A, A. Demurrers.
Rutter, Cal. Practice Guide: Civ. Pro. Before Trial Ch. 9(I)-B, B. Preparing and Filing Motions.
Rutter, Cal. Practice Guide: Civ. Pro. Before Trial Ch. 9(I)-C, C. Opposing the Motion-And Rebutting the Opposition.
Rutter, Cal. Practice Guide: Civ. Pro. Before Trial Ch. 9(II)-D, D. Attachment.
Rutter, Cal. Practice Guide: Civil Trials & Evidence Ch. 18-A, A. Motion for Judgment Notwithstanding the Verdict ("JNOV").
Rutter, Cal. Practice Guide: Enforcing Judgments/Debts Ch. 4-A, A. Attachment.
Rutter, Cal. Practice Guide: Enforcing Judgments/Debts Ch. 4-B, B. Claim and Delivery.
6 Witkin Cal. Proc. 5th Proceedings Without Trial § 12, (S 12) in General.
6 Witkin Cal. Proc. 5th Proceedings Without Trial § 16, (S 16) Shortening Time.
6 Witkin Cal. Proc. 5th Proceedings Without Trial § 20, Proof of Service.
6 Witkin Cal. Proc. 5th Proceedings Without Trial § 23, Proof of Service.
6 Witkin Cal. Proc. 5th Proceedings Without Trial § 26, Proof of Service.
6 Witkin Cal. Proc. 5th Proceedings Without Trial § 33, (S 33) General Requirements.
6 Witkin Cal. Proc. 5th Proceedings Without Trial § 41, Affidavits and Declarations.

Rule 3.1302.   Place and manner of filing

(a) Papers filed in clerk's office

Unless otherwise provided by local rule, all papers relating to a law and motion proceeding must be filed in the clerk's office.

(b) Requirements for lodged material

Material lodged with the clerk must be accompanied by an addressed envelope with sufficient postage for mailing the material. After determination of the matter, the clerk may mail the material to the party lodging it. *(Formerly Rule 319, adopted,*

eff. Jan. 1, 1984. Renumbered Rule 3.1302 and amended, eff. Jan. 1, 2007.)

Research References

Rutter, Cal. Practice Guide: Civ. Pro. Before Trial Ch. 9(I)-B, B. Preparing and Filing Motions.
Rutter, Cal. Practice Guide: Civ. Pro. Before Trial Ch. 9(I)-C, C. Opposing the Motion-And Rebutting the Opposition.
2 Witkin Cal. Proc. 5th Courts § 360, (S 360) Nature of Office.
6 Witkin Cal. Proc. 5th Proceedings Without Trial § 33, (S 33) General Requirements.
6 Witkin Cal. Proc. 5th Proceedings Without Trial § 42, Other Documentary Evidence.

Rule 3.1304.   Time of hearing

(a) General schedule

The clerk must post a general schedule showing the days and departments for holding each type of law and motion hearing.

(b) Duty to notify if matter not to be heard

The moving party must immediately notify the court if a matter will not be heard on the scheduled date.

(c) Notice of nonappearance

A party may give notice that he or she will not appear at a law and motion hearing and submit the matter without an appearance unless the court orders otherwise. The court must rule on the motion as if the party had appeared.

(d) Action if no party appears

If a party fails to appear at a law and motion hearing without having given notice under (c), the court may take the matter off calendar, to be reset only upon motion, or may rule on the matter. *(Formerly Rule 321, adopted, eff. Jan. 1, 1984. As amended, eff. Jan. 1, 1992; Jan. 1, 2003. Renumbered Rule 3.1304, eff. Jan. 1, 2007.)*

Research References

Rutter, Cal. Practice Guide: Civ. Pro. Before Trial Ch. 9(I)-D, D. Hearing.
6 Witkin Cal. Proc. 5th Proceedings Without Trial § 36, (S 36) Nature of Hearing.
6 Witkin Cal. Proc. 5th Proceedings Without Trial § 38, Making of Motion.

Rule 3.1306.   Evidence at hearing

(a) Restrictions on oral testimony

Evidence received at a law and motion hearing must be by declaration or request for judicial notice without testimony or cross-examination, unless the court orders otherwise for good cause shown.

(b) Request to present oral testimony

A party seeking permission to introduce oral evidence, except for oral evidence in rebuttal to oral evidence presented by the other party, must file, no later than three court days before the hearing, a written statement stating the nature and extent of the evidence proposed to be introduced and a reasonable time estimate for the hearing. When the statement is filed less than five court days before the hearing, the filing party must serve a copy on the other parties in a manner to assure delivery to the other parties no later than two days before the hearing.

(c) Judicial notice

A party requesting judicial notice of material under Evidence Code sections 452 or 453 must provide the court and each party with a copy of the material. If the material is part of a file in the court in which the matter is being heard, the party must:

(1) Specify in writing the part of the court file sought to be judicially noticed; and

Ct. Rules

(2) Make arrangements with the clerk to have the file in the courtroom at the time of the hearing. *(Formerly Rule 323, adopted, eff. Jan. 1, 1984. As amended, eff. Jan. 1, 2003. Renumbered Rule 3.1306 and amended, eff. Jan. 1, 2007.)*

Research References

Rutter, Cal. Practice Guide: Civ. Pro. Before Trial Ch. 14-C, C. Procedural Issues.

Rutter, Cal. Practice Guide: Civ. Pro. Before Trial Ch. 7(I)-A, A. Demurrers.

Rutter, Cal. Practice Guide: Civ. Pro. Before Trial Ch. 9(I)-B, B. Preparing and Filing Motions.

Rutter, Cal. Practice Guide: Civ. Pro. Before Trial Ch. 9(I)-D, D. Hearing.

Rutter, Cal. Practice Guide: Civ. Pro. Before Trial Ch. 9(II)-A, A. Injunctions.

Rutter, Cal. Practice Guide: Civil Trials & Evidence Ch. 8C-J, J. Judicial Notice.

8 Witkin Cal. Proc. 5th Attack Judgment Trial Court § 221, Effect of Denial of Motion.

4 Witkin Cal. Proc. 5th Pleading § 307, (S 307) Authority for Motion.

5 Witkin Cal. Proc. 5th Pleading § 980, (S 980) Supporting Memorandum.

6 Witkin Cal. Proc. 5th Proceedings Without Trial § 11, Supporting Memorandum.

6 Witkin Cal. Proc. 5th Proceedings Without Trial § 40, Restrictions on Oral Testimony.

6 Witkin Cal. Proc. 5th Proceedings Without Trial § 41, Affidavits and Declarations.

6 Witkin Cal. Proc. 5th Proceedings Without Trial § 43, Judicial Notice.

Rule 3.1308.   Tentative rulings

(a) Tentative ruling procedures

A trial court that offers a tentative ruling procedure in civil law and motion matters must follow one of the following procedures:

(1) *Notice of intent to appear required*

The court must make its tentative ruling available by telephone and also, at the option of the court, by any other method designated by the court, by no later than 3:00 p.m. the court day before the scheduled hearing. If the court desires oral argument, the tentative ruling must so direct. The tentative ruling may also note any issues on which the court wishes the parties to provide further argument. If the court has not directed argument, oral argument must be permitted only if a party notifies all other parties and the court by 4:00 p.m. on the court day before the hearing of the party's intention to appear. A party must notify all other parties by telephone or in person. The court must accept notice by telephone and, at its discretion, may also designate alternative methods by which a party may notify the court of the party's intention to appear. The tentative ruling will become the ruling of the court if the court has not directed oral argument by its tentative ruling and notice of intent to appear has not been given.

(2) *No notice of intent to appear required*

The court must make its tentative ruling available by telephone and also, at the option of the court, by any other method designated by the court, by a specified time before the hearing. The tentative ruling may note any issues on which the court wishes the parties to provide further argument at the hearing. This procedure must not require the parties to give notice of intent to appear, and the tentative ruling will not automatically become the ruling of the court if such notice is not given. The tentative ruling, or such other ruling as the court may render, will not become the final ruling of the court until the hearing.

(b) No other procedures permitted

Other than following one of the tentative ruling procedures authorized in (a), courts must not issue tentative rulings except:

(1) By posting a calendar note containing tentative rulings on the day of the hearing; or

(2) By announcing the tentative ruling at the time of oral argument.

(c) Notice of procedure

A court that follows one of the procedures described in (a) must so state in its local rules. The local rule must specify the telephone number for obtaining the tentative rulings and the time by which the rulings will be available.

(d) Uniform procedure within court or branch

If a court or a branch of a court adopts a tentative ruling procedure, that procedure must be used by all judges in the court or branch who issue tentative rulings.

(e) Tentative rulings not required

This rule does not require any judge to issue tentative rulings. *(Formerly Rule 324, adopted, eff. July 1, 1992. As amended, eff. July 1, 2000. Renumbered Rule 3.1308 and amended, eff. Jan. 1, 2007.)*

Research References

Rutter, Cal. Practice Guide: Civ. Pro. Before Trial Ch. 11-A, A. Voluntary Dismissals.

Rutter, Cal. Practice Guide: Civ. Pro. Before Trial Ch. 9(I)-A, A. Introduction.

Rutter, Cal. Practice Guide: Civ. Pro. Before Trial Ch. 9(I)-D, D. Hearing.

6 Witkin Cal. Proc. 5th Proceedings Without Trial § 37, (S 37) Tentative Ruling.

Rule 3.1310.   Reporting of proceedings on motions

A court that does not regularly provide for reporting or electronic recording of hearings on motions must so state in its local rules. The rules must also provide a procedure by which a party may obtain a reporter or a recording of the proceedings in order to provide an official verbatim transcript. *(Formerly Rule 324.5, adopted, eff. Jan. 1, 1992. Renumbered Rule 3.1310 and amended, eff. Jan. 1, 2007.)*

Research References

Rutter, Cal. Practice Guide: Civ. Pro. Before Trial Ch. 9(I)-D, D. Hearing.

6 Witkin Cal. Proc. 5th Proceedings Without Trial § 36, (S 36) Nature of Hearing.

Rule 3.1312.   Preparation and submission of proposed order

(a) Prevailing party to prepare

Unless the parties waive notice or the court orders otherwise, the party prevailing on any motion must, within five days of the ruling, serve by any means authorized by law and reasonably calculated to ensure delivery to the other party or parties no later than the close of the next business day a proposed order for approval as conforming to the court's order. Within five days after service, the other party or parties must notify the prevailing party as to whether or not the proposed order is so approved. The opposing party or parties must state any reasons for disapproval. Failure to notify the prevailing party within the time required shall be deemed an approval. The extensions of time based on a method of service provided under any statute or rule do not apply to this rule.

(b) Submission of proposed order to court

The prevailing party must, upon expiration of the five-day period provided for approval, promptly transmit the proposed order to the court together with a summary of any responses of the other parties or a statement that no responses were received.

(c) Submission of proposed order by electronic means

If a proposed order is submitted to the court electronically in a case in which the parties are electronically filing documents under rules 2.250–2. 261 two versions of the proposed order must be submitted:

(1) A version of the proposed order must be attached to a completed *Proposed Order (Cover Sheet)* (form EFS–020), and the combined document in Portable Document Format (PDF) must be filed electronically; and

(2) A version of the proposed order in an editable word-processing format must also be sent electronically to the court, with a copy of the e-mail and proposed order also being sent to all parties in the action.

Each court that provides for electronic filing must provide an electronic address or addresses to which the editable versions of proposed orders are to be sent and must specify any particular requirements regarding the editable word-processing format for proposed orders.

(d) Failure of prevailing party to prepare proposed order

If the prevailing party fails to prepare and submit a proposed order as required by (a) and (b) above, any other party may do so.

(e) Motion unopposed

This rule does not apply if the motion was unopposed and a proposed order was submitted with the moving papers, unless otherwise ordered by the court. *(Formerly Rule 391, adopted, eff. July 1, 1992. As amended, eff. July 1, 2000. Renumbered Rule 3.1312 and amended, eff. Jan. 1, 2007. As amended, eff. Jan. 1, 2011.)*

Research References

Rutter, Cal. Practice Guide: Civil Appeals & Writs Ch. 3-B, B. Filing Deadlines.
Rutter, Cal. Practice Guide: Civil Appeals & Writs Ch. 16-C, C. Notice of Appeal.
Rutter, Cal. Practice Guide: Civil Appeals & Writs Ch. 3-B , Outline B.
Rutter, Cal. Practice Guide: Civ. Pro. Before Trial Ch. 1-C, C. Prelawsuit Notices, Claims and Demands.
Rutter, Cal. Practice Guide: Civ. Pro. Before Trial Ch. 5-G, G. Relief from Default.
Rutter, Cal. Practice Guide: Civ. Pro. Before Trial Ch. 6-E, E. Amended and Supplemental Pleadings.
Rutter, Cal. Practice Guide: Civ. Pro. Before Trial Ch. 10-C, C. Procedural Requirements-Moving Party.
Rutter, Cal. Practice Guide: Civ. Pro. Before Trial Ch. 10-D, D. Procedural Requirements-Opposing Party.
Rutter, Cal. Practice Guide: Civ. Pro. Before Trial Ch. 10-E, E. Procedural Requirements-Reply Papers.
Rutter, Cal. Practice Guide: Civ. Pro. Before Trial Ch. 10-H, H. Entry of Judgment or Order.
Rutter, Cal. Practice Guide: Civ. Pro. Before Trial Ch. 7(I)-A, A. Demurrers.
Rutter, Cal. Practice Guide: Civ. Pro. Before Trial Ch. 9(I)-B, B. Preparing and Filing Motions.
Rutter, Cal. Practice Guide: Civ. Pro. Before Trial Ch. 9(I)-C, C. Opposing the Motion-And Rebutting the Opposition.
Rutter, Cal. Practice Guide: Civ. Pro. Before Trial Ch. 9(I)-E, E. Posthearing Procedures.
Rutter, Cal. Practice Guide: Civil Trials & Evidence Ch. 18-A, A. Motion for Judgment Notwithstanding the Verdict ("JNOV").
Rutter, Cal. Practice Guide: Personal Injury Ch. 5-A, A: Prelawsuit Filings.
9 Witkin Cal. Proc. 5th Appeal § 591, (S 591) Entry of Order in Minutes.
9 Witkin Cal. Proc. 5th Appeal § 607, (S 607) Nature of Rules.
9 Witkin Cal. Proc. 5th Appeal § 610, (S 610) by Direction in Minute Order.
7 Witkin Cal. Proc. 5th Judgment § 46, Minute Order on Motion.
7 Witkin Cal. Proc. 5th Judgment § 54, Other Orders.
7 Witkin Cal. Proc. 5th Judgment § 56, Minute Orders.
4 Witkin Cal. Proc. 5th Pleading § 21, (S 21) Nature of Filing Process.

6 Witkin Cal. Proc. 5th Proceedings Without Trial § 31, Express Limitations.
6 Witkin Cal. Proc. 5th Proceedings Without Trial § 35, (S 35) Electronic Filing.
6 Witkin Cal. Proc. 5th Proceedings Without Trial § 44, (S 44) How Order is Made.
6 Witkin Cal. Proc. 5th Provisional Remedies § 385, (S 385) Time of Filing.

Chapter 6

PARTICULAR MOTIONS

Article 1

PLEADING AND VENUE MOTIONS

Rule
3.1320. Demurrers.
3.1322. Motions to strike.
3.1324. Amended pleadings and amendments to pleadings.
3.1326. Motions for change of venue.
3.1327. Motions to quash or to stay action in summary proceeding involving possession of real property.

Rule 3.1320. Demurrers

(a) Grounds separately stated

Each ground of demurrer must be in a separate paragraph and must state whether it applies to the entire complaint, cross-complaint, or answer, or to specified causes of action or defenses.

(b) Demurrer not directed to all causes of action

A demurrer to a cause of action may be filed without answering other causes of action.

(c) Notice of hearing

A party filing a demurrer must serve and file therewith a notice of hearing that must specify a hearing date in accordance with the provisions of Code of Civil Procedure section 1005.

(d) Date of hearing

Demurrers must be set for hearing not more than 35 days following the filing of the demurrer or on the first date available to the court thereafter. For good cause shown, the court may order the hearing held on an earlier or later day on notice prescribed by the court.

(e) Caption

A demurrer must state, on the first page immediately below the number of the case, the name of the party filing the demurrer and the name of the party whose pleading is the subject of the demurrer.

(f) Failure to appear at hearing

When a demurrer is regularly called for hearing and one of the parties does not appear, the demurrer must be disposed of on the merits at the request of the party appearing unless for good cause the hearing is continued. Failure to appear in support of a special demurrer may be construed by the court as an admission that the demurrer is not meritorious and as a waiver of all grounds thereof. If neither party appears, the demurrer may be disposed of on its merits or dropped from the calendar, to be restored on notice or on terms as the court may deem proper, or the hearing may be continued to such time as the court orders.

(g) Leave to answer or amend

Following a ruling on a demurrer, unless otherwise ordered, leave to answer or amend within 10 days is deemed granted, except for actions in forcible entry, forcible detainer, or unlawful detainer in which case 5 calendar days is deemed granted.

(h) Ex parte application to dismiss following failure to amend

A motion to dismiss the entire action and for entry of judgment after expiration of the time to amend following the sustaining of a demurrer may be made by ex parte application to the court under Code of Civil Procedure section 581(f)(2).

(i) Motion to strike late-filed amended pleading

If an amended pleading is filed after the time allowed, an order striking the amended pleading must be obtained by noticed motion under Code of Civil Procedure section 1010.

(j) Time to respond after demurrer

Unless otherwise ordered, defendant has 10 days to answer or otherwise plead to the complaint or the remaining causes of action following:

(1) The overruling of the demurrer;

(2) The expiration of the time to amend if the demurrer was sustained with leave to amend; or

(3) The sustaining of the demurrer if the demurrer was sustained without leave to amend. *(Formerly Rule 325, adopted, eff. Jan. 1, 1984. As amended, eff. July 1, 1984; July 1, 1995; July 1, 2000. Renumbered Rule 3.1320 and amended, eff. Jan. 1, 2007. As amended, eff. Jan. 1, 2009; Jan. 1, 2011.)*

Research References

Rutter, Cal. Practice Guide: Civ. Pro. Before Trial Ch. 5-B, B. Entry of Default.
Rutter, Cal. Practice Guide: Civ. Pro. Before Trial Ch. 6-E, E. Amended and Supplemental Pleadings.
Rutter, Cal. Practice Guide: Civ. Pro. Before Trial Ch. 11-B, B. Involuntary Dismissals.
Rutter, Cal. Practice Guide: Civ. Pro. Before Trial Ch. 7(I)-A, A. Demurrers.
Rutter, Cal. Practice Guide: Civ. Pro. Before Trial Ch. 7(I)-B, B. Motions to Strike.
Rutter, Cal. Practice Guide: Civ. Pro. Before Trial Ch. 9(I)-B, B. Preparing and Filing Motions.
Rutter, Cal. Practice Guide: Civ. Pro. Before Trial Ch. 9(I)-E, E. Posthearing Procedures.
2 Witkin Cal. Proc. 5th Courts § 191, (S 191) Civil Rules.
5 Witkin Cal. Proc. 5th Pleading § 954, Demurrer to Entire Complaint.
5 Witkin Cal. Proc. 5th Pleading § 956, (S 956) Separate Causes of Action.
5 Witkin Cal. Proc. 5th Pleading § 961, (S 961) Form.
5 Witkin Cal. Proc. 5th Pleading § 968, (S 968) Form.
5 Witkin Cal. Proc. 5th Pleading § 981, (S 981) Hearing.
5 Witkin Cal. Proc. 5th Pleading § 982, Overruling or Sustaining.
5 Witkin Cal. Proc. 5th Pleading § 990, (S 990) Dismissal on Failure to Amend.
5 Witkin Cal. Proc. 5th Pleading § 1001, (S 1001) Time to Plead After Ruling on Partial Demurrer.
6 Witkin Cal. Proc. 5th Proceedings Without Trial § 2, (S 2) Types of Motions.
6 Witkin Cal. Proc. 5th Proceedings Without Trial § 144, Failure to Answer After Demurrer is Overruled.
6 Witkin Cal. Proc. 5th Proceedings Without Trial § 477, Demurrer Sustained.
6 Witkin Cal. Proc. 5th Proceedings Without Trial § 480, Improper Grounds for Dismissal.

Rule 3.1322. Motions to strike

(a) Contents of notice

A notice of motion to strike a portion of a pleading must quote in full the portions sought to be stricken except where the motion is to strike an entire paragraph, cause of action, count, or defense. Specifications in a notice must be numbered consecutively.

(b) Timing

A notice of motion to strike must be given within the time allowed to plead, and if a demurrer is interposed, concurrently therewith, and must be noticed for hearing and heard at the same time as the demurrer. *(Formerly Rule 329, adopted, eff. Jan. 1, 1984. Renumbered Rule 3.1322 and amended, eff. Jan. 1, 2007.)*

Research References

Rutter, Cal. Practice Guide: Civ. Pro. Before Trial Ch. 7(I)-B, B. Motions to Strike.
5 Witkin Cal. Proc. 5th Pleading § 981, (S 981) Hearing.
5 Witkin Cal. Proc. 5th Pleading § 1014, (S 1014) in General.
5 Witkin Cal. Proc. 5th Pleading § 1015, (S 1015) Motion With or Without Demurrer.

Rule 3.1324. Amended pleadings and amendments to pleadings

(a) Contents of motion

A motion to amend a pleading before trial must:

(1) Include a copy of the proposed amendment or amended pleading, which must be serially numbered to differentiate it from previous pleadings or amendments;

(2) State what allegations in the previous pleading are proposed to be deleted, if any, and where, by page, paragraph, and line number, the deleted allegations are located; and

(3) State what allegations are proposed to be added to the previous pleading, if any, and where, by page, paragraph, and line number, the additional allegations are located.

(b) Supporting declaration

A separate declaration must accompany the motion and must specify:

(1) The effect of the amendment;

(2) Why the amendment is necessary and proper;

(3) When the facts giving rise to the amended allegations were discovered; and

(4) The reasons why the request for amendment was not made earlier.

(c) Form of amendment

The court may deem a motion to file an amendment to a pleading to be a motion to file an amended pleading and require the filing of the entire previous pleading with the approved amendments incorporated into it.

(d) Requirements for amendment to a pleading

An amendment to a pleading must not be made by alterations on the face of a pleading except by permission of the court. All alterations must be initialed by the court or the clerk. *(Formerly Rule 327, adopted, eff. Jan. 1, 1984. As amended, eff. Jan. 1, 2002. Renumbered Rule 3.1324, eff. Jan. 1, 2007.)*

Research References

Rutter, Cal. Practice Guide: Civ. Pro. Before Trial Ch. 6-E, E. Amended and Supplemental Pleadings.
5 Witkin Cal. Proc. 5th Pleading § 1240, (S 1240) Application and Notice.
5 Witkin Cal. Proc. 5th Pleading § 1241, (S 1241) Amendment or Amended Pleading.

Rule 3.1326. Motions for change of venue

Following denial of a motion to transfer under Code of Civil Procedure section 396b, unless otherwise ordered, 30 calendar days are deemed granted defendant to move to strike, demur, or otherwise plead if the defendant has not previously filed a response. If a motion to transfer is granted, 30 calendar days are deemed granted from the date the receiving court mails notice of receipt of the case and its new case number. *(Formerly Rule 326, adopted, eff. Jan. 1, 1984. As amended, eff. July 1, 1984. Renumbered Rule 3.1326 and amended, eff. Jan. 1, 2007.)*

Research References

Rutter, Cal. Practice Guide: Civ. Pro. Before Trial Ch. 3-D, D. Venue.
3 Witkin Cal. Proc. 5th Actions § 936, Transmission of Papers.
3 Witkin Cal. Proc. 5th Actions § 939, (S 939) Pleading After Denial of Motion.

Rule 3.1327. Motions to quash or to stay action in summary proceeding involving possession of real property

(a) Notice

In an unlawful detainer action or other action brought under chapter 4 of title 3 of part 3 of the Code of Civil Procedure (commencing with section 1159), notice of a motion to quash service of summons on the ground of lack of jurisdiction or to stay or dismiss the action on the ground of inconvenient forum must be given in compliance with Code of Civil Procedure sections 1013 and 1167.4.

(b) Opposition and reply at hearing

Any opposition to the motion and any reply to an opposition may be made orally at the time of hearing or in writing as set forth in (c).

(c) Written opposition in advance of hearing

If a party seeks to have a written opposition considered in advance of the hearing, the written opposition must be filed and served on or before the court day before the hearing. Service must be by personal delivery, facsimile transmission, express mail, or other means consistent with Code of Civil Procedure sections 1010, 1011, 1012, and 1013, and reasonably calculated to ensure delivery to the other party or parties no later than the close of business on the court day before the hearing. The court, in its discretion, may consider written opposition filed later. *(Adopted, eff. Jan. 1, 2009.)*

Research References

2 Witkin Cal. Proc. 5th Courts § 191, (S 191) Civil Rules.

Article 2

PROCEDURAL MOTIONS

Rule
3.1330. Motion concerning arbitration.
3.1332. Motion or application for continuance of trial.
3.1335. Motion or application to advance, specially set, or reset trial date.

Rule 3.1330. Motion concerning arbitration

A petition to compel arbitration or to stay proceedings pursuant to Code of Civil Procedure sections 1281.2 and 1281.4 must state, in addition to other required allegations, the provisions of the written agreement and the paragraph that provides for arbitration. The provisions must be stated verbatim or a copy must be attached to the petition and incorporated by reference. *(Formerly Rule 371, adopted, eff. Jan. 1, 1984. Renumbered Rule 3.1330 and amended, eff. Jan. 1, 2007.)*

Research References

Rutter, Cal. Practice Guide: A.D.R. Ch. 5-G, G. Procedures to Enforce Arbitration.
6 Witkin Cal. Proc. 5th Proceedings Without Trial § 524, (S 524) in General.

Rule 3.1332. Motion or application for continuance of trial

(a) Trial dates are firm

To ensure the prompt disposition of civil cases, the dates assigned for a trial are firm. All parties and their counsel must regard the date set for trial as certain.

(b) Motion or application

A party seeking a continuance of the date set for trial, whether contested or uncontested or stipulated to by the parties, must make the request for a continuance by a noticed motion or an ex parte application under the rules in chapter 4 of this division, with supporting declarations. The party must make the motion or application as soon as reasonably practical once the necessity for the continuance is discovered.

(c) Grounds for continuance

Although continuances of trials are disfavored, each request for a continuance must be considered on its own merits. The court may grant a continuance only on an affirmative showing of good cause requiring the continuance. Circumstances that may indicate good cause include:

(1) The unavailability of an essential lay or expert witness because of death, illness, or other excusable circumstances;

(2) The unavailability of a party because of death, illness, or other excusable circumstances;

(3) The unavailability of trial counsel because of death, illness, or other excusable circumstances;

(4) The substitution of trial counsel, but only where there is an affirmative showing that the substitution is required in the interests of justice;

(5) The addition of a new party if:

    (A) The new party has not had a reasonable opportunity to conduct discovery and prepare for trial; or

    (B) The other parties have not had a reasonable opportunity to conduct discovery and prepare for trial in regard to the new party's involvement in the case;

(6) A party's excused inability to obtain essential testimony, documents, or other material evidence despite diligent efforts; or

(7) A significant, unanticipated change in the status of the case as a result of which the case is not ready for trial.

(d) Other factors to be considered

In ruling on a motion or application for continuance, the court must consider all the facts and circumstances that are relevant to the determination. These may include:

(1) The proximity of the trial date;

(2) Whether there was any previous continuance, extension of time, or delay of trial due to any party;

(3) The length of the continuance requested;

(4) The availability of alternative means to address the problem that gave rise to the motion or application for a continuance;

(5) The prejudice that parties or witnesses will suffer as a result of the continuance;

(6) If the case is entitled to a preferential trial setting, the reasons for that status and whether the need for a continuance outweighs the need to avoid delay;

(7) The court's calendar and the impact of granting a continuance on other pending trials;

(8) Whether trial counsel is engaged in another trial;

(9) Whether all parties have stipulated to a continuance;

(10) Whether the interests of justice are best served by a continuance, by the trial of the matter, or by imposing conditions on the continuance; and

(11) Any other fact or circumstance relevant to the fair determination of the motion or application. *(Formerly Rule 375, adopted, eff. Jan. 1, 1984. As amended, eff. Jan. 1, 1985; Jan. 1, 1995; Jan. 1, 2004. Renumbered Rule 3.1332 and amended, eff. Jan. 1, 2007.)*

Research References

Rutter, Cal. Practice Guide: Civ. Pro. Before Trial Ch. 11-A, A. Voluntary Dismissals.

Rutter, Cal. Practice Guide: Civ. Pro. Before Trial Ch. 12(I)-F, F. Motions to Continue Trial.

Rutter, Cal. Practice Guide: Civil Trials & Evidence Ch. 1-K, K. Continuance Motions.

Rutter, Cal. Practice Guide: Civil Trials & Evidence Ch. 1-L, L. Assignment to Trial Department.

Rutter, Cal. Practice Guide: Civil Trials & Evidence Ch. 12-D, D. Other Motions During Trial.

Rutter, Cal. Practice Guide: Civil Trials & Evidence Ch. 17-E, E. Attorney Fees as Costs.

Rutter, Cal. Practice Guide: Personal Injury Ch. 8-A, A. Case Management.

Rutter, Cal. Practice Guide: Personal Injury Ch. 9-A, A. Assignment to Trial.

7 Witkin Cal. Proc. 5th Trial § 8, (S 8) Limitations.

7 Witkin Cal. Proc. 5th Trial § 9, (S 9) Judicial Council Rules.

7 Witkin Cal. Proc. 5th Trial § 13, (S 13) Unavailability of Attorney.

7 Witkin Cal. Proc. 5th Trial § 14, (S 14) Substitution of Attorney.

7 Witkin Cal. Proc. 5th Trial § 16, When Continuance Will be Granted.

7 Witkin Cal. Proc. 5th Trial § 18, (S 18) Absence of Evidence.

7 Witkin Cal. Proc. 5th Trial § 19, Death, Illness, or Unavailability.

7 Witkin Cal. Proc. 5th Trial § 24, (S 24) Surprise at Trial.

7 Witkin Cal. Proc. 5th Trial § 25, (S 25) Changes in Parties or Pleadings.

7 Witkin Cal. Proc. 5th Trial § 32, (S 32) Motion.

7 Witkin Cal. Proc. 5th Trial § 33, (S 33) Affidavits and Deposition.

Rule 3.1335. Motion or application to advance, specially set, or reset trial date

(a) Noticed motion or application required

A party seeking to advance, specially set, or reset a case for trial must make this request by noticed motion or ex parte application under the rules in chapter 4 of this division.

(b) Grounds for motion or application

The request may be granted only upon an affirmative showing by the moving party of good cause based on a declaration served and filed with the motion or application. *(Formerly Rule 375.1, adopted, eff. Jan. 1, 2004. Renumbered Rule 3.1335 and amended, eff. Jan. 1, 2007.)*

Research References

Rutter, Cal. Practice Guide: Civ. Pro. Before Trial Ch. 12(I)-C, C. Claims for Trial Setting Preference.

Rutter, Cal. Practice Guide: Personal Injury Ch. 8-A, A. Case Management.

7 Witkin Cal. Proc. 5th Trial § 73, (S 73) Motion to Advance or Reset.

8 Witkin, California Summary 10th Constitutional Law § 1220, Contesting Right to Take.

Article 3

MOTIONS TO DISMISS

Rule

Rule 3.1340. Motion for discretionary dismissal after two years for delay in prosecution

(a) Discretionary dismissal two years after filing

The court on its own motion or on motion of the defendant may dismiss an action under Code of Civil Procedure sections 583.410–583.430 for delay in prosecution if the action has not been brought to trial or conditionally settled within two years after the action was commenced against the defendant.

(b) Notice of court's intention to dismiss

If the court intends to dismiss an action on its own motion, the clerk must set a hearing on the dismissal and mail notice to all parties at least 20 days before the hearing date.

(c) Definition of "conditionally settled"

"Conditionally settled" means:

(1) A settlement agreement conditions dismissal on the satisfactory completion of specified terms that are not to be fully performed within two years after the filing of the case; and

(2) Notice of the settlement is filed with the court as provided in rule 3.1385. *(Formerly Rule 372, adopted, eff. Jan. 1, 1990. Renumbered Rule 3.1340 and amended, eff. Jan. 1, 2007.)*

Research References

Rutter, Cal. Practice Guide: A.D.R. Ch. 4-B, B. Judicial Arbitration.

Rutter, Cal. Practice Guide: Civil Appeals & Writs Ch. 14-C, C. Trial Court Proceedings After Reversal.

Rutter, Cal. Practice Guide: Civ. Pro. Before Trial Ch. 11-B, B. Involuntary Dismissals.

Rutter, Cal. Practice Guide: Civ. Pro. Before Trial Ch. 13-C, C. Civil Proceedings Subject to Judicial Arbitration.

Rutter, Cal. Practice Guide: Civ. Pro. Before Trial Ch. 9(I)-B, B. Preparing and Filing Motions.

6 Witkin Cal. Proc. 5th Proceedings Without Trial § 440, Premature Dismissal is Improper.

6 Witkin Cal. Proc. 5th Proceedings Without Trial § 451, in General.

6 Witkin Cal. Proc. 5th Proceedings Without Trial § 468, (S 468) Absent or Incorrect Statement of Grounds.

6 Witkin Cal. Proc. 5th Proceedings Without Trial § 469, (S 469) in General.

7 Witkin Cal. Proc. 5th Trial § 38, (S 38) Trial Court Delay Reduction Act.

Rule 3.1342. Motion to dismiss for delay in prosecution

(a) Notice of motion

A party seeking dismissal of a case under Code of Civil Procedure sections 583.410–583.430 must serve and file a notice of motion at least 45 days before the date set for hearing of the motion. The party may, with the memorandum, serve and file a declaration stating facts in support of the motion. The filing of the notice of motion must not preclude the opposing party from further prosecution of the case to bring it to trial.

(b) Written opposition

Within 15 days after service of the notice of motion, the opposing party may serve and file a written opposition. The failure of the opposing party to serve and file a written opposition may be construed by the court as an admission that the motion is meritorious, and the court may grant the motion without a hearing on the merits.

(c) Response to opposition

Within 15 days after service of the written opposition, if any, the moving party may serve and file a response.

(d) Reply

Within five days after service of the response, if any, the opposing party may serve and file a reply.

(e) Relevant matters

In ruling on the motion, the court must consider all matters relevant to a proper determination of the motion, including:

(1) The court's file in the case and the declarations and supporting data submitted by the parties and, where applicable, the availability of the moving party and other essential parties for service of process;

(2) The diligence in seeking to effect service of process;

(3) The extent to which the parties engaged in any settlement negotiations or discussions;

(4) The diligence of the parties in pursuing discovery or other pretrial proceedings, including any extraordinary relief sought by either party;

(5) The nature and complexity of the case;

(6) The law applicable to the case, including the pendency of other litigation under a common set of facts or determinative of the legal or factual issues in the case;

(7) The nature of any extensions of time or other delay attributable to either party;

(8) The condition of the court's calendar and the availability of an earlier trial date if the matter was ready for trial;

(9) Whether the interests of justice are best served by dismissal or trial of the case; and

(10) Any other fact or circumstance relevant to a fair determination of the issue.

The court must be guided by the policies set forth in Code of Civil Procedure section 583.130.

(f) Court action

The court may grant or deny the motion or, where the facts warrant, the court may continue or defer its ruling on the matter pending performance by either party of any conditions relating to trial or dismissal of the case that may be required by the court to effectuate substantial justice. *(Formerly Rule 373, adopted, eff. Jan. 1, 1984. As amended, eff. Jan. 1, 1986. Renumbered Rule 3.1342 and amended, eff. Jan. 1, 2007. As amended, eff. Jan. 1, 2009.)*

Research References

Rutter, Cal. Practice Guide: A.D.R. Ch. 4-B, B. Judicial Arbitration.
Rutter, Cal. Practice Guide: Civ. Pro. Before Trial Ch. 11-B, B. Involuntary Dismissals.
Rutter, Cal. Practice Guide: Civ. Pro. Before Trial Ch. 9(I)-B, B. Preparing and Filing Motions.
Rutter, Cal. Practice Guide: Civ. Pro. Before Trial Ch. 11-B , Outline B.
6 Witkin Cal. Proc. 5th Proceedings Without Trial § 427, (S 427) Preferential Setting Required.
6 Witkin Cal. Proc. 5th Proceedings Without Trial § 439, Criteria Governing Exercise of Discretion.
6 Witkin Cal. Proc. 5th Proceedings Without Trial § 442, in General.
6 Witkin Cal. Proc. 5th Proceedings Without Trial § 444, (S 444) Doe Defendant.
6 Witkin Cal. Proc. 5th Proceedings Without Trial § 446, (S 446) Necessity for Showing.
6 Witkin Cal. Proc. 5th Proceedings Without Trial § 447, (S 447) Sufficiency of Showing.
6 Witkin Cal. Proc. 5th Proceedings Without Trial § 449, (S 449) Dismissal Upheld.
6 Witkin Cal. Proc. 5th Proceedings Without Trial § 451, in General.
6 Witkin Cal. Proc. 5th Proceedings Without Trial § 463, Later Decisions.
6 Witkin Cal. Proc. 5th Proceedings Without Trial § 464, (S 464) Delay in New Trial.
6 Witkin Cal. Proc. 5th Proceedings Without Trial § 465, Notice of Motion.
6 Witkin Cal. Proc. 5th Proceedings Without Trial § 466, Opposition, Response, and Reply.
6 Witkin Cal. Proc. 5th Proceedings Without Trial § 467, (S 467) Ruling May be Conditioned.

6 Witkin Cal. Proc. 5th Proceedings Without Trial § 469, (S 469) in General.
6 Witkin Cal. Proc. 5th Proceedings Without Trial § 470, (S 470) After Motion to Specially Set.

Article 4

DISCOVERY MOTIONS

Rule
3.1345.   Format of discovery motions.
3.1346.   Service of motion papers on nonparty deponent.
3.1347.   Discovery motions in summary proceeding involving possession of real property.
3.1348.   Sanctions for failure to provide discovery.

Rule 3.1345.   Format of discovery motions

(a) Separate statement required

Any motion involving the content of a discovery request or the responses to such a request must be accompanied by a separate statement. The motions that require a separate statement include a motion:

(1) To compel further responses to requests for admission;

(2) To compel further responses to interrogatories;

(3) To compel further responses to a demand for inspection of documents or tangible things;

(4) To compel answers at a deposition;

(5) To compel or to quash the production of documents or tangible things at a deposition;

(6) For medical examination over objection; and

(7) For issue or evidentiary sanctions.

(b) Separate statement not required

A separate statement is not required when no response has been provided to the request for discovery.

(c) Contents of separate statement

A separate statement is a separate document filed and served with the discovery motion that provides all the information necessary to understand each discovery request and all the responses to it that are at issue. The separate statement must be full and complete so that no person is required to review any other document in order to determine the full request and the full response. Material must not be incorporated into the separate statement by reference. The separate statement must include—for each discovery request (e.g., each interrogatory, request for admission, deposition question, or inspection demand) to which a further response, answer, or production is requested—the following:

(1) The text of the request, interrogatory, question, or inspection demand;

(2) The text of each response, answer, or objection, and any further responses or answers;

(3) A statement of the factual and legal reasons for compelling further responses, answers, or production as to each matter in dispute;

(4) If necessary, the text of all definitions, instructions, and other matters required to understand each discovery request and the responses to it;

(5) If the response to a particular discovery request is dependent on the response given to another discovery request, or if the reasons a further response to a particular discovery request is deemed necessary are based on the response to some other discovery request, the other request and the response to it must be set forth; and

(6) If the pleadings, other documents in the file, or other items of discovery are relevant to the motion, the party relying on them must summarize each relevant document.

(d) Identification of interrogatories, demands, or requests

A motion concerning interrogatories, inspection demands, or admission requests must identify the interrogatories, demands, or requests by set and number. *(Formerly Rule 335, adopted, eff. Jan. 1, 1984. As amended, eff. July 1, 1987; Jan. 1, 1992; Jan. 1, 1997; July 1, 2001. Renumbered Rule 3.1020 and amended, eff. Jan. 1, 2007. Renumbered Rule 3.1345, eff. Jan. 1, 2009.)*

Research References

Rutter, Cal. Practice Guide: Civ. Pro. Before Trial Ch. 8E-5, Subpoena Not Necessary for Party or "Party-Affiliated" Witnesses.
Rutter, Cal. Practice Guide: Civ. Pro. Before Trial Ch. 8E-6, Subpoena to Nonparty Deponent or Business Records Custodian.
Rutter, Cal. Practice Guide: Civ. Pro. Before Trial Ch. 8F-7, Motion to Compel Answers.
Rutter, Cal. Practice Guide: Civ. Pro. Before Trial Ch. 8F-8, Sanctions in Enforcing Discovery.
Rutter, Cal. Practice Guide: Civ. Pro. Before Trial Ch. 8H-8, Enforcing Demand.
Rutter, Cal. Practice Guide: Civ. Pro. Before Trial Ch. 8I-3, Examination Upon Court Order.
Rutter, Cal. Practice Guide: Civ. Pro. Before Trial Ch. 8E-15, Motion to Compel Answers.
2 Witkin Cal. Proc. 5th Courts § 191, (S 191) Civil Rules.

Rule 3.1346. Service of motion papers on nonparty deponent

A written notice and all moving papers supporting a motion to compel an answer to a deposition question or to compel production of a document or tangible thing from a nonparty deponent must be personally served on the nonparty deponent unless the nonparty deponent agrees to accept service by mail at an address specified on the deposition record. *(Formerly Rule 337, adopted, eff. Jan. 1, 1984. As amended, eff. July 1, 1987. Renumbered Rule 3.1025 and amended, eff. Jan. 1, 2007. Renumbered Rule 3.1346, eff. Jan. 1, 2009.)*

Research References

Rutter, Cal. Practice Guide: Civ. Pro. Before Trial Ch. 8E-15, Motion to Compel Answers.

Rule 3.1347. Discovery motions in summary proceeding involving possession of real property

(a) Notice

In an unlawful detainer action or other action brought under chapter 4 of title 3 of part 3 of the Code of Civil Procedure (commencing with section 1159), notice of a discovery motion must be given in compliance with Code of Civil Procedure sections 1013 and 1170.8.

(b) Opposition and reply at hearing

Any opposition to the motion and any reply to an opposition may be made orally at the time of hearing or in writing as set forth in (c).

(c) Written opposition in advance of hearing

If a party seeks to have a written opposition considered in advance of the hearing, the written opposition must be served and filed on or before the court day before the hearing. Service must be by personal delivery, facsimile transmission, express mail, or other means consistent with Code of Civil Procedure sections 1010, 1011, 1012, and 1013, and reasonably calculated to ensure delivery to the other party or parties no later than the close of business on the court day before the hearing. The court, in its discretion, may consider written opposition filed later. *(Adopted, eff. Jan. 1, 2009.)*

Research References

Rutter, Cal. Practice Guide: Civ. Pro. Before Trial Ch. 9(I)-C, C. Opposing the Motion-And Rebutting the Opposition.

Rule 3.1348. Sanctions for failure to provide discovery

(a) Sanctions despite no opposition

The court may award sanctions under the Discovery Act in favor of a party who files a motion to compel discovery, even though no opposition to the motion was filed, or opposition to the motion was withdrawn, or the requested discovery was provided to the moving party after the motion was filed.

(b) Failure to oppose not an admission

The failure to file a written opposition or to appear at a hearing or the voluntary provision of discovery shall not be deemed an admission that the motion was proper or that sanctions should be awarded. *(Formerly Rule 341, adopted, eff. July 1, 2001. Renumbered Rule 3.1030, eff. Jan. 1, 2007. Renumbered Rule 3.1348, eff. Jan. 1, 2009.)*

Research References

Rutter, Cal. Practice Guide: Civ. Pro. Before Trial Ch. 8F-8, Sanctions in Enforcing Discovery.
Rutter, Cal. Practice Guide: Civ. Pro. Before Trial Ch. 8I-4, Sanctions.
Rutter, Cal. Practice Guide: Civ. Pro. Before Trial Ch. 8E-16, Sanctions Re Depositions.
2 Witkin Cal. Proc. 5th Courts § 191, (S 191) Civil Rules.

Article 5

SUMMARY JUDGMENT MOTIONS

Rule
3.1350.   Motion for summary judgment or summary adjudication.
3.1351.   Motions for summary judgment in summary proceeding involving possession of real property.
3.1352.   Objections to evidence.
3.1354.   Written objections to evidence.

Rule 3.1350. Motion for summary judgment or summary adjudication

(a) Motion

As used in this rule, "motion" refers to either a motion for summary judgment or a motion for summary adjudication.

(b) Motion for summary adjudication

If made in the alternative, a motion for summary adjudication may make reference to and depend on the same evidence submitted in support of the summary judgment motion. If summary adjudication is sought, whether separately or as an alternative to the motion for summary judgment, the specific cause of action, affirmative defense, claims for damages, or issues of duty must be stated specifically in the notice of motion and be repeated, verbatim, in the separate statement of undisputed material facts.

(c) Documents in support of motion

Except as provided in Code of Civil Procedure section 437c(r) and rule 3.1351, the motion must contain and be supported by the following documents:

(1) Notice of motion by *[moving party]* for summary judgment or summary adjudication or both;

(2) Separate statement of undisputed material facts in support of *[moving party's]* motion for summary judgment or summary adjudication or both;

(3) Memorandum in support of [*moving party's*] motion for summary judgment or summary adjudication or both;

(4) Evidence in support of [*moving party's*] motion for summary judgment or summary adjudication or both; and

(5) Request for judicial notice in support of [*moving party's*] motion for summary judgment or summary adjudication or both (if appropriate).

(d) Separate statement in support of motion

The Separate Statement of Undisputed Material Facts in support of a motion must separately identify each cause of action, claim, issue of duty, or affirmative defense, and each supporting material fact claimed to be without dispute with respect to the cause of action, claim, issue of duty, or affirmative defense. In a two-column format, the statement must state in numerical sequence the undisputed material facts in the first column followed by the evidence that establishes those undisputed facts in that same column. Citation to the evidence in support of each material fact must include reference to the exhibit, title, page, and line numbers.

(e) Documents in opposition to motion

Except as provided in Code of Civil Procedure section 437c(r) and rule 3.1351, the opposition to a motion must consist of the following documents, separately stapled and titled as shown:

(1) [*Opposing party's*] memorandum in opposition to [*moving party's*] motion for summary judgment or summary adjudication or both;

(2) [*Opposing party's*] separate statement of undisputed material facts in opposition to [*moving party's*] motion for summary judgment or summary adjudication or both;

(3) [*Opposing party's*] evidence in opposition to [*moving party's*] motion for summary judgment or summary adjudication or both (if appropriate); and

(4) [*Opposing party's*] request for judicial notice in opposition to [*moving party's*] motion for summary judgment or summary adjudication or both (if appropriate).

(f) Opposition to motion; content of separate statement

Each material fact claimed by the moving party to be undisputed must be set out verbatim on the left side of the page, below which must be set out the evidence said by the moving party to establish that fact, complete with the moving party's references to exhibits. On the right side of the page, directly opposite the recitation of the moving party's statement of material facts and supporting evidence, the response must unequivocally state whether that fact is "disputed" or "undisputed." An opposing party who contends that a fact is disputed must state, on the right side of the page directly opposite the fact in dispute, the nature of the dispute and describe the evidence that supports the position that the fact is controverted. That evidence must be supported by citation to exhibit, title, page, and line numbers in the evidence submitted.

(g) Documentary evidence

If evidence in support of or in opposition to a motion exceeds 25 pages, the evidence must be separately bound and must include a table of contents.

(h) Format for separate statements

Supporting and opposing separate statements in a motion for summary judgment must follow this format:

Supporting Statement:

Moving Party's Undisputed Material Facts and Supporting Evidence:	Opposing Party's Response and Supporting Evidence:
1. Plaintiff and defendant entered into a written contract for the sale of widgets. Jackson declaration, 2:17–21; contract, Ex. A to Jackson declaration.	
2. No widgets were ever received. Jackson declaration, 3:7–21.	

Opposing statement:

Moving Party's Undisputed Material Facts and Alleged Supporting Evidence:	Opposing Party's Response and Evidence:
1. Plaintiff and defendant entered into a written contract for the sale of widgets. Jackson declaration, 2:17–21; contract, Ex. A to Jackson declaration.	Undisputed.
2. No widgets were ever received. Jackson declaration, 3:7–21.	Disputed. The widgets were received in New Zealand on August 31, 2001. Baygi declaration, 7:2–5.

Supporting and opposing separate statements in a motion for summary adjudication must follow this format:

Supporting statement:

ISSUE 1—THE FIRST CAUSE OF ACTION FOR NEGLIGENCE IS BARRED BECAUSE PLAINTIFF EXPRESSLY ASSUMED THE RISK OF INJURY

Moving Party's Undisputed Material Facts and Supporting Evidence:	Opposing Party's Response and Supporting Evidence:
1. Plaintiff was injured while mountain climbing on a trip with Any Company USA. Plaintiff's deposition, 12:3–4.	
2. Before leaving on the mountain climbing trip, plaintiff signed a waiver of liability for acts of negligence. Smith declaration, 5:4–5; waiver of liability, Ex. A to Smith declaration.	

Opposing statement:

ISSUE 1—THE FIRST CAUSE OF ACTION FOR NEGLIGENCE IS BARRED BECAUSE PLAINTIFF EXPRESSLY ASSUMED THE RISK OF INJURY

Moving Party's Undisputed Material Facts and Alleged Supporting Evidence:	Opposing Party's Response and Evidence:
1. Plaintiff was injured while mountain climbing on a trip with Any Company	Undisputed.

USA. Plaintiff's deposition, 12:3–4.

| 2. Before leaving on the mountain climbing trip, plaintiff signed a waiver of liability for acts of negligence. Smith declaration, 5:4–5; waiver of liability, Ex. A to Smith declaration. | Disputed. Plaintiff did not sign the waiver of liability; the signature on the waiver is forged. Jones declaration, 3:6–7. |

(i) Request for electronic version of separate statement

On request, a party must within three days provide to any other party or the court an electronic version of its separate statement. The electronic version may be provided in any form on which the parties agree. If the parties are unable to agree on the form, the responding party must provide to the requesting party the electronic version of the separate statement that it used to prepare the document filed with the court. Under this subdivision, a party is not required to create an electronic version or any new version of any document for the purpose of transmission to the requesting party. *(Formerly Rule 342, adopted, eff. July 1, 1997. As amended, eff. Jan. 1, 1999; Jan. 1, 2002. Renumbered Rule 3.1350 and amended, eff. Jan. 1, 2007. As amended, eff. Jan. 1, 2008; July 1, 2008; Jan. 1, 2009.)*

Research References

Rutter, Cal. Practice Guide: Civ. Pro. Before Trial Ch. 10-A, A. Introduction.
Rutter, Cal. Practice Guide: Civ. Pro. Before Trial Ch. 10-C, C. Procedural Requirements-Moving Party.
Rutter, Cal. Practice Guide: Civ. Pro. Before Trial Ch. 10-D, D. Procedural Requirements-Opposing Party.
6 Witkin Cal. Proc. 5th Proceedings Without Trial § 213, (S 213) in General.
6 Witkin Cal. Proc. 5th Proceedings Without Trial § 215, (S 215) Notice of Motion.
6 Witkin Cal. Proc. 5th Proceedings Without Trial § 216, (S 216) Statement of Material Facts.
6 Witkin Cal. Proc. 5th Proceedings Without Trial § 217, (S 217) in General.
6 Witkin Cal. Proc. 5th Proceedings Without Trial § 218, (S 218) Statement of Material Facts.
6 Witkin Cal. Proc. 5th Proceedings Without Trial § 275, Motion by Itself or in Alternative.
6 Witkin Cal. Proc. 5th Proceedings Without Trial § 216A, (S 216A) (New)-Stipulation to Circumvent Motion Requirements.

Rule 3.1351. Motions for summary judgment in summary proceeding involving possession of real property

(a) Notice

In an unlawful detainer action or other action brought under chapter 4 of title 3 of part 3 of the Code of Civil Procedure (commencing with section 1159), notice of a motion for summary judgment must be given in compliance with Code of Civil Procedure sections 1013 and 1170.7.

(b) Opposition and reply at hearing

Any opposition to the motion and any reply to an opposition may be made orally at the time of hearing or in writing as set forth in (c).

(c) Written opposition in advance of hearing

If a party seeks to have a written opposition considered in advance of the hearing, the written opposition must be filed and served on or before the court day before the hearing. Service must be by personal delivery, facsimile transmission, express mail, or other means consistent with Code of Civil Procedure sections 1010, 1011, 1012, and 1013, and reasonably calculated to ensure delivery to the other party or parties no later than the close of business on the court day before the hearing. The court, in its discretion, may consider written opposition filed later. *(Adopted, eff. Jan. 1, 2009.)*

Research References

Rutter, Cal. Practice Guide: Civ. Pro. Before Trial Ch. 10-C, C. Procedural Requirements-Moving Party.

Rule 3.1352. Objections to evidence

A party desiring to make objections to evidence in the papers on a motion for summary judgment must either:

(1) Submit objections in writing under rule 3.1354; or

(2) Make arrangements for a court reporter to be present at the hearing. *(Formerly Rule 343, adopted, eff. Jan. 1, 1984. As amended, eff. Jan. 1, 2002. Renumbered Rule 3.1352 and amended, eff. Jan. 1, 2007.)*

Research References

Rutter, Cal. Practice Guide: Civ. Pro. Before Trial Ch. 10-D, D. Procedural Requirements-Opposing Party.
Rutter, Cal. Practice Guide: Civ. Pro. Before Trial Ch. 10-G, G. Ruling on Motion.
6 Witkin Cal. Proc. 5th Proceedings Without Trial § 233, (S 233) Objections to Evidence.

Rule 3.1354. Written objections to evidence

(a) Time for filing and service of objections

Unless otherwise excused by the court on a showing of good cause, all written objections to evidence in support of or in opposition to a motion for summary judgment or summary adjudication must be served and filed at the same time as the objecting party's opposition or reply papers are served and filed.

(b) Format of objections

All written objections to evidence must be served and filed separately from the other papers in support of or in opposition to the motion. Objections on specific evidence may be referenced by the objection number in the right column of a separate statement in opposition or reply to a motion, but the objections must not be restated or reargued in the separate statement. Each written objection must be numbered consecutively and must:

(1) Identify the name of the document in which the specific material objected to is located;

(2) State the exhibit, title, page, and line number of the material objected to;

(3) Quote or set forth the objectionable statement or material; and

(4) State the grounds for each objection to that statement or material.

Written objections to evidence must follow one of the following two formats:

(First Format):

Objections to Jackson Declaration

Objection Number 1

"Johnson told me that no widgets were ever received." (Jackson declaration, page 3, lines 7–8.)

Grounds for Objection 1: Hearsay (Evid. Code, § 1200); lack of personal knowledge (Evid. Code, § 702(a)).

Objection Number 2

"A lot of people find widgets to be very useful." (Jackson declaration, page 17, line 5.)

Grounds for Objection 2: Irrelevant (Evid. Code, §§ 210, 350–351).

(Second Format):

Objections to Jackson Declaration

Material Objected to:	Grounds for Objection:
1. Jackson declaration, page 3, lines 7–8: "Johnson told me that no widgets were ever received."	Hearsay (Evid. Code, § 1200); lack of personal knowledge (Evid. Code, § 702(a)).
2. Jackson declaration, page 17, line 5: "A lot of people find widgets to be very useful."	Irrelevant (Evid. Code, §§ 210, 350–351).

(c) Proposed order

A party submitting written objections to evidence must submit with the objections a proposed order. The proposed order must include places for the court to indicate whether it has sustained or overruled each objection. It must also include a place for the signature of the judge. The proposed order must be in one of the following two formats:

(First Format):

Objections to Jackson Declaration

Objection Number 1

"Johnson told me that no widgets were ever received." (Jackson declaration, page 3, lines 7–8.)

Grounds for Objection 1: Hearsay (Evid. Code, § 1200); lack of personal knowledge (Evid. Code, § 702(a)).

Court's Ruling on Objection 1:   Sustained: _____

                                            Overruled: _____

Objection Number 2

"A lot of people find widgets to be very useful." (Jackson declaration, page 17, line 5.)

Grounds for Objection 2: Irrelevant (Evid. Code, §§ 210, 350–351).

Court's Ruling on Objection 2:   Sustained: _____

                                            Overruled: _____

(Second Format):

Objections to Jackson Declaration

Material Objected to:	Grounds for Objection:	Ruling on the Objection
1. Jackson declaration, page 3, lines 7–8: "Johnson told me	Hearsay (Evid. Code, § 1200); lack of personal knowledge	Sustained: _____ Overruled: _____

that no widgets were ever received."

(Evid. Code, § 702(a)).

2. Jackson declaration, page 17, line 5: "A lot of people find widgets to be very useful."

Irrelevant (Evid. Code, §§ 210, 350–351).

Sustained: _____
Overruled: _____

Date: _____ _____
Judge

(Formerly Rule 345, adopted, eff. Jan. 1, 1984. As amended, eff. Jan. 1, 2002. Renumbered Rule 3.1354 and amended, eff. Jan. 1, 2007.)

Research References

Rutter, Cal. Practice Guide: Civ. Pro. Before Trial Ch. 10-D, D. Procedural Requirements-Opposing Party.

Rutter, Cal. Practice Guide: Civ. Pro. Before Trial Ch. 9(I)-C, C. Opposing the Motion-And Rebutting the Opposition.

Rutter, Cal. Practice Guide: Civ. Pro. Before Trial Ch. 9(II)-A, A. Injunctions.

Rutter, Cal. Practice Guide: Civ. Pro. Before Trial Ch. 9(II)-B, B. Receiverships.

6 Witkin Cal. Proc. 5th Proceedings Without Trial § 233, (S 233) Objections to Evidence.

Article 6

MISCELLANEOUS MOTIONS

Rule

3.1360. Motion to grant lien on cause of action.

3.1362. Motion to be relieved as counsel.

Rule 3.1360. Motion to grant lien on cause of action

A motion that a lien be granted on a cause of action, right to relief, or judgment must be accompanied by an authenticated record of the judgment on which the judgment creditor relies and a declaration as to the identity of the party involved and the amount due. *(Formerly Rule 369, adopted, eff. Jan. 1, 1984. Renumbered Rule 3.1360 and amended, eff. Jan. 1, 2007.)*

Research References

Rutter, Cal. Practice Guide: Enforcing Judgments/Debts Ch. 6G-8, Lien in Pending Action.

Rule 3.1362. Motion to be relieved as counsel

(a) Notice

A notice of motion and motion to be relieved as counsel under Code of Civil Procedure section 284(2) must be directed to the client and must be made on the *Notice of Motion and Motion to Be Relieved as Counsel—Civil* (form MC–051).

(b) Memorandum

Notwithstanding any other rule of court, no memorandum is required to be filed or served with a motion to be relieved as counsel.

(c) Declaration

The motion to be relieved as counsel must be accompanied by a declaration on the *Declaration in Support of Attorney's Motion to Be Relieved as Counsel—Civil* (form MC–052). The declaration must state in general terms and without compromising the confidentiality of the attorney-client relationship why a motion under Code of Civil Procedure section 284(2) is brought instead of filing a consent under Code of Civil Procedure section 284(1).

(d) Service

The notice of motion and motion, the declaration, and the proposed order must be served on the client and on all other parties who have appeared in the case. The notice may be by personal service or mail. If the notice is served on the client by mail under Code of Civil Procedure section 1013, it must be accompanied by a declaration stating facts showing that either:

(1) The service address is the current residence or business address of the client; or

(2) The service address is the last known residence or business address of the client and the attorney has been unable to locate a more current address after making reasonable efforts to do so within 30 days before the filing of the motion to be relieved.

As used in this rule, "current" means that the address was confirmed within 30 days before the filing of the motion to be relieved. Merely demonstrating that the notice was sent to the client's last known address and was not returned is not, by itself, sufficient to demonstrate that the address is current. If the service is by mail, Code of Civil Procedure section 1011(b) applies.

(e) Order

The proposed order relieving counsel must be prepared on the *Order Granting Attorney's Motion to Be Relieved as Counsel—Civil* (form MC–053) and must be lodged with the court with the moving papers. The order must specify all hearing dates scheduled in the action or proceeding, including the date of trial, if known. If no hearing date is presently scheduled, the court may set one and specify the date in the order. After the order is signed, a copy of the signed order must be served on the client and on all parties that have appeared in the case. The court may delay the effective date of the order relieving counsel until proof of service of a copy of the signed order on the client has been filed with the court. *(Formerly Rule 376, adopted, eff. July 1, 1984. As amended, eff. July 1, 1991; Jan. 1, 1996; July 1, 2000. Renumbered Rule 3.1362 and amended, eff. Jan. 1, 2007. As amended, eff. Jan. 1, 2009.)*

Research References

Rutter, Cal. Practice Guide: Civil Appeals & Writs Ch. 1-E, E. Preappeal Evaluation and "Housekeeping" Steps.

Rutter, Cal. Practice Guide: Civ. Pro. Before Trial Ch. 9(I)-G, G. Motions Regulating Counsel.

Rutter, Cal. Practice Guide: Prof. Responsibility Ch. 5-K, K. Fee Recovery/Enforcing Fee Agreements.

Rutter, Cal. Practice Guide: Prof. Responsibility Ch. 7-B, B. Duty to Maintain Client Confidence and Secrets Under State Bar Act.

Rutter, Cal. Practice Guide: Prof. Responsibility Ch. 10-B, B. Withdrawal (Termination) by Lawyer.

1 Witkin Cal. Proc. 5th Attorneys § 69, (S 69) Motion to Withdraw.

11 Witkin, California Summary 10th Husband and Wife § 74, (S 74) Limited Scope Legal Representation.

Chapter 7

PETITIONS UNDER THE CALIFORNIA ENVIRONMENTAL QUALITY ACT

Rule

3.1365. Form and format of administrative record lodged in a CEQA proceeding.

Rule

3.1366.   Lodging and service.
3.1367.   Electronic format.
3.1368.   Paper format.

Rule 3.1365.   Form and format of administrative record lodged in a CEQA proceeding

(a) Organization

(1) *Order of documents*

Except as permitted in (a)(3), the administrative record must be organized in the following order, as applicable:

(A) The Notice of Determination;

(B) The resolutions or ordinances adopted by the lead agency approving the project;

(C) The findings required by Public Resources Code section 21081, including any statement of overriding considerations;

(D) The final environmental impact report, including the draft environmental impact report or a revision of the draft, all other matters included in the final environmental impact report, and other types of environmental impact documents prepared under the California Environmental Quality Act, such as a negative declaration, mitigated negative declaration, or addenda;

(E) The initial study;

(F) Staff reports prepared for the administrative bodies providing subordinate approvals or recommendations to the lead agency, in chronological order;

(G) Transcripts and minutes of hearings, in chronological order; and

(H) The remainder of the administrative record, in chronological order.

(2) *List not limiting*

The list of documents in (1) is not intended to limit the content of the administrative record, which is prescribed in Public Resources Code section 21167.6(e).

(3) *Different order permissible*

The documents may be organized in a different order from that set out in (1) if the court so orders on;

(A) A party's motion;

(B) The parties' stipulation; or

(C) The court's own motion.

(4) *Oversized documents*

Oversized documents included in the record must be presented in a manner that allows them to be easily unfolded and viewed.

(5) *Use of tabs or electronic bookmarks*

The administrative record must be separated by tabs or marked with electronic bookmarks that identify each part of the record listed above.

(b) Index

A detailed index must be placed at the beginning of the administrative record. The index must list each document in the administrative record in the order presented, or in chronological order if ordered by the court, including title, date of the document, brief description, and the volume and page where it begins. The index must list any included exhibits or appendixes and must list each document contained in the exhibit or appendix (including environmental impact report appendixes) and the volume and page where each document begins. A copy of the index must be filed in the court at the time the administrative record is lodged with the court.

(c) Appendix of excerpts

A court may require each party filing a brief to prepare and lodge an appendix of excerpts that contains the documents or pages of the record cited in that party's brief. *(Adopted, eff. Jan. 1, 2010.)*

Research References

2 Witkin Cal. Proc. 5th Courts § 191, (S 191) Civil Rules.
12 Witkin, California Summary 10th Real Property § 857, (S 857) Preparation of Record.

Rule 3.1366.   Lodging and service

The party preparing the administrative record must lodge it with the court and serve it on each party. A record in electronic format must comply with rule 3.1367. A record in paper format must comply with rule 3.1368. If the party preparing the administrative record elects or is ordered to prepare an electronic version of the record, (1) a court may require the party to lodge one copy of the record in paper format and (2) a party may request the record in paper format and pay the reasonable cost or show good cause for a court order requiring the party preparing the administrative record to serve the requesting party with one copy of the record in paper format. *(Adopted, eff. Jan. 1, 2010.)*

Research References

12 Witkin, California Summary 10th Real Property § 857, (S 857) Preparation of Record.

Rule 3.1367.   Electronic format

(a) Requirements

The electronic version of the administrative record lodged in the court in a proceeding brought under the California Environmental Quality Act must be:

(1) In compliance with rule 3.1365;

(2) Created in portable document format (PDF) or other format for which the software for creating and reading documents is in the public domain or generally available at a reasonable cost;

(3) Divided into a series of electronic files and include electronic bookmarks that identify each part of the record and clearly state the volume and page numbers contained in each part of the record;

(4) Contained on a CD–ROM, DVD, or other medium in a manner that cannot be altered; and

(5) Capable of full text searching.

The electronic version of the index required under rule 3.1365(b) may include hyperlinks to the indexed documents.

(b) Documents not included

Any document that is part of the administrative record and for which it is not feasible to create an electronic version may be provided in paper format only. Not feasible means that it would be reduced in size or otherwise altered to such an extent that it would not be easily readable. *(Adopted, eff. Jan. 1, 2010.)*

Research References

12 Witkin, California Summary 10th Real Property § 857, (S 857) Preparation of Record.

Rule 3.1368.   Paper format

(a) Requirements

In the paper format of the administrative record lodged in the court in a proceeding brought under the California Environmental Quality Act:

(1) The paper must be recycled;

(2) Both sides of each page must be used;

(3) The paper must be opaque, unglazed, white or un-bleached, 8 ½ by 11 inches, and of standard quality no less than 20–pound weight, except that maps, charts, and other demonstrative materials may be larger; and

(4) Each page must be numbered consecutively at the bottom.

(b) Binding and cover

The paper format of the administrative record must be bound on the left margin or contained in three-ring binders. Bound volumes must contain no more than 300 pages, and binders must contain no more than 400 pages. If bound, each page must have an adequate margin to allow unimpaired readability. The cover of each volume must contain the information required in rule 2.111, be prominently entitled "ADMINISTRATIVE RECORD," and state the volume number and the page numbers included in the volume. *(Adopted, eff. Jan. 1, 2010.)*

Research References

2 Witkin Cal. Proc. 5th Courts § 191, (S 191) Civil Rules.
12 Witkin, California Summary 10th Real Property § 857, (S 857) Preparation of Record.

Chapter 8

OTHER CIVIL PETITIONS

Rule
3.1370. Emancipation of minors.
3.1372. Petitions for relief from financial obligations during military service.

Division 12

SETTLEMENT

Rule
3.1380. Mandatory settlement conferences.
3.1382. Good faith settlement and dismissal.
3.1384. Petition for approval of the compromise of a claim of a minor or a person with a disability; order for deposit of funds; and petition for withdrawal.
3.1385. Duty to notify court and others of settlement of entire case.

Rule 3.1380. Mandatory settlement conferences

(a) Setting conferences

On the court's own motion or at the request of any party, the court may set one or more mandatory settlement conferences.

(b) Persons attending

Trial counsel, parties, and persons with full authority to settle the case must personally attend the conference, unless excused by the court for good cause. If any consent to settle is required for any reason, the party with that consensual authority must be personally present at the conference.

(c) Settlement conference statement

No later than five court days before the initial date set for the settlement conference, each party must submit to the court and serve on each party a mandatory settlement conference statement containing:

(1) A good faith settlement demand;

Rule 3.1370. Emancipation of minors

A petition for declaration of the emancipation of a minor must comply with rule 5.605. *(Formerly Rule 270, adopted, eff. July 1, 1994. Renumbered Rule 3.1370 and amended, eff. Jan. 1, 2007.)*

Research References

Rutter, Cal. Practice Guide: Civ. Pro. Before Trial Ch. 7(I)-A, A. Demurrers.
2 Witkin Cal. Proc. 5th Courts § 191, (S 191) Civil Rules.
10 Witkin, California Summary 10th Parent and Child § 303, in General.
10 Witkin, California Summary 10th Parent and Child § 304, Notice of Hearing.

Rule 3.1372. Petitions for relief from financial obligations during military service

(a) Application

This rule applies to petitions for relief from financial obligations made by a servicemember under Military and Veterans Code section 409.3.

(b) Service of petition

Service of the petition for relief and all supporting papers must be made in the manner provided by law for service of summons in civil actions.

(c) No memorandum required

Unless ordered by the court, no memorandum is required in support of or opposition to a petition for relief. *(Adopted, eff. Jan. 1, 2012.)*

Research References

2 Witkin Cal. Proc. 5th Courts § 191, (S 191) Civil Rules.

(2) An itemization of economic and noneconomic damages by each plaintiff;

(3) A good faith offer of settlement by each defendant; and

(4) A statement identifying and discussing in detail all facts and law pertinent to the issues of liability and damages involved in the case as to that party.

The settlement conference statement must comply with any additional requirement imposed by local rule.

(d) Restrictions on appointments

A court must not:

(1) Appoint a person to conduct a settlement conference under this rule at the same time as that person is serving as a mediator in the same action; or

(2) Appoint a person to conduct a mediation under this rule. *(Formerly Rule 222, adopted, eff. Jan. 1, 1985. As amended, eff. Jan. 1, 1995; July 1, 2001; July 1, 2002. Renumbered Rule 3.1380 and amended, eff. Jan. 1, 2007. As amended, eff. Jan. 1, 2008.)*

Advisory Committee Comment

Subdivision (d) This provision is not intended to discourage settlement conferences or mediations. However, problems have arisen in several cases, such as *Jeld–Wen v. Superior Court of San Diego County* (2007) 146 Cal.App.4th 536, when distinctions between different ADR processes have been blurred. To prevent confusion about the confidentiality of the proceedings, it is important to clearly distinguish between settlement conferences held under this rule and mediations. The special confidentiality requirements for mediations established by Evidence Code sections 1115–1128 expressly do not apply to settlement conferences under this rule. This provision is not intended to prohibit a court from appointing a person who has previously served as a mediator in a case to conduct a settlement conference in that case following the conclusion of the mediation.

Research References

Rutter, Cal. Practice Guide: A.D.R. Ch. 1-D, D. Planning for Private ADR.

Rutter, Cal. Practice Guide: A.D.R. Ch. 3-C, C. Confidentiality.

Rutter, Cal. Practice Guide: A.D.R. Ch. 3-E, E. Voluntary Settlement Conference (VSC) (Evaluative Mediation).

Rutter, Cal. Practice Guide: A.D.R. Ch. 4-D, D. Mandatory Settlement Conferences.

Rutter, Cal. Practice Guide: Civ. Pro. Before Trial Ch. 12(I)-B, B. Case Management ("Fast Track") System.

Rutter, Cal. Practice Guide: Civ. Pro. Before Trial Ch. 12(II)-A, A. Mandatory Settlement Conference ("MSC").

Rutter, Cal. Practice Guide: Civil Trials & Evidence Ch. 1-A, A. Importance of Statewide and Local Rules of Court.

Rutter, Cal. Practice Guide: Personal Injury Ch. 4-C, C. Effective Settlement Negotiations.

Rutter, Cal. Practice Guide: Personal Injury Ch. 4-F, F. Court-Conducted Settlement Proceedings.

1 Witkin Cal. Proc. 5th Attorneys § 7, (S 7) Settlement.

2 Witkin Cal. Proc. 5th Courts § 191, (S 191) Civil Rules.

6 Witkin Cal. Proc. 5th Proceedings Without Trial § 492, Settlement Conference.

6 Witkin Cal. Proc. 5th Proceedings Without Trial § 594, (S 594) Discovery.

7 Witkin Cal. Proc. 5th Trial § 47, Preparation of Conference Order.

7 Witkin Cal. Proc. 5th Trial § 53, Settlement Conference.

7 Witkin Cal. Proc. 5th Trial § 63, (S 63) Imposition of Ultimate Sanction in First Instance.

5 Witkin, California Summary 10th Torts § 168, Nonjudicial Acts.

Rule 3.1382. Good faith settlement and dismissal

A motion or application for determination of good faith settlement may include a request to dismiss a pleading or a portion of a pleading. The notice of motion or application for determination of good faith settlement must list each party and pleading or portion of pleading affected by the settlement and the date on which the affected pleading was filed. *(Formerly Rule 330, adopted, eff. July 1, 1999. Renumbered Rule 3.1382 and amended, eff. Jan. 1, 2007.)*

Research References

Rutter, Cal. Practice Guide: Civ. Pro. Before Trial Ch. 12(II)-E, E. Motion to Determine "Good Faith" of "Piecemeal" Settlement (CCP § 877.6).

Rutter, Cal. Practice Guide: Personal Injury Ch. 4-D, D. Techniques Where Settlement Not Forthcoming.

6 Witkin Cal. Proc. 5th Proceedings Without Trial § 82, (S 82) in General.

Rule 3.1384. Petition for approval of the compromise of a claim of a minor or a person with a disability; order for deposit of funds; and petition for withdrawal

(a) Petition for approval of the compromise of a claim

A petition for court approval of a compromise or covenant not to sue under Code of Civil Procedure section 372 must comply with rules 7.950, 7.951, and 7.952.

(b) Order for the deposit of funds and petition for withdrawal

An order for the deposit of funds of a minor or a person with a disability, and a petition for the withdrawal of such funds, must comply with rules 7.953 and 7.954. *(Formerly Rule 378, adopted, eff. Jan. 1, 2002. Renumbered Rule 3.1384 and amended, eff. Jan. 1, 2007.)*

Research References

Rutter, Cal. Practice Guide: Civ. Pro. Before Trial Ch. 12(II)-B, B. Settlements on Behalf of Minors or Incompetents.

Rutter, Cal. Practice Guide: Personal Injury Ch. 4-G, G. Concluding and Enforcing Settlement.

4 Witkin Cal. Proc. 5th Pleading § 81, Petition.

4 Witkin Cal. Proc. 5th Pleading § 82, Hearing and Order.

Rule 3.1385. Duty to notify court and others of settlement of entire case

(a) Notice of settlement

(1) Court and other persons to be notified

If an entire case is settled or otherwise disposed of, each plaintiff or other party seeking affirmative relief must immediately file written notice of the settlement or other disposition with the court and serve the notice on all parties and any arbitrator or other court-connected alternative dispute resolution (ADR) neutral involved in the case. Each plaintiff or other party seeking affirmative relief must also immediately give oral notice to all of the above if a hearing, conference, or trial is scheduled to take place within 10 days.

(2) Compensation for failure to provide notice

If the plaintiff or other party seeking affirmative relief does not notify an arbitrator or other court-connected ADR neutral involved in the case of a settlement at least 2 days before the scheduled hearing or session with that arbitrator or neutral, the court may order the party to compensate the arbitrator or other neutral for the scheduled hearing time. The amount of compensation ordered by the court must not exceed the maximum amount of compensation the arbitrator would be entitled to receive for service as an arbitrator under Code of Civil Procedure section 1141.18(b) or that the neutral would have been entitled to receive for service as a neutral at the scheduled hearing or session.

(b) Dismissal of case

Except as provided in (c) or (d), each plaintiff or other party seeking affirmative relief must serve and file a request for dismissal of the entire case within 45 days after the date of settlement of the case. If the plaintiff or other party required to serve and file the request for dismissal does not do so, the court must dismiss the entire case 45 days after it receives notice of settlement unless good cause is shown why the case should not be dismissed.

(c) Conditional settlement

(1) Notice

If the settlement agreement conditions dismissal of the entire case on the satisfactory completion of specified terms that are not to be performed within 45 days of the settlement, including payment in installment payments, the notice of conditional settlement served and filed by each plaintiff or other party seeking affirmative relief must specify the date by which the dismissal is to be filed. ~~If the plaintiff or other party required to serve and file a request for dismissal within 45 days after the dismissal date specified in the notice does not do so, the court must dismiss the entire case unless good cause is shown why the case should not be dismissed.~~

(2) Dismissal

If the plaintiff or other party required to serve and file a request for dismissal within 45 days after the dismissal date specified in the notice does not do so, the court must dismiss the entire case unless good cause is shown why the case should not be dismissed.

(3) Hearings vacated

(A) Except as provided in (B), on the filing of the notice of conditional settlement, the court must vacate all hearings and other proceedings requiring the appearance of a party and may not set any hearing or other proceeding requiring the appearance of a party earlier than 45 days after the dismissal date specified in the notice, unless requested by a party.

(B) The court need not vacate a hearing on an order to show cause or other proceeding relating to sanctions, or for determination of good faith settlement at the request of a party under Code of Civil Procedure section 877.6.

(4) *Case disposition time*

Under standard 2.2(n)(1)(A), the filing of a notice of conditional settlement removes the case from the computation of time used to determine case disposition time.

(d) Compromise of claims of a minor or disabled person

If the settlement of the case involves the compromise of the claim of a minor or person with a disability, the court must not hold an order to show cause hearing under (b) before the court has held a hearing to approve the settlement, provided the parties have filed appropriate papers to seek court approval of the settlement.

(e) Request for additional time to complete settlement

If a party who has served and filed a notice of settlement under (a) determines that the case cannot be dismissed within the prescribed 45 days, that party must serve and file a notice and a supporting declaration advising the court of that party's inability to dismiss the case within the prescribed time, showing good cause for its inability to do so, and proposing an alternative date for dismissal. The notice and a supporting declaration must be served and filed at least 5 court days before the time for requesting dismissal has elapsed. If good cause is shown, the court must continue the matter to allow additional time to

complete the settlement. The court may take such other actions as may be appropriate for the proper management and disposition of the case. *(Formerly Rule 225, adopted, eff. Jan. 1, 1985. As amended, eff. Jan. 1, 1989; Jan. 1, 1992; July 1, 2001; July 1, 2002; Jan. 1, 2004; Jan. 1, 2006. Renumbered Rule 3.1385 and amended, eff. Jan. 1, 2007. As amended, eff. Jan. 1, 2009; July 1, 2013.)*

Research References

Rutter, Cal. Practice Guide: A.D.R. Ch. 1-E, E. Enforcing ADR Settlements.

Rutter, Cal. Practice Guide: A.D.R. Ch. 4-B, B. Judicial Arbitration.

Rutter, Cal. Practice Guide: A.D.R. Ch. 1-E , Outline E.

Rutter, Cal. Practice Guide: Civ. Pro. Before Trial Ch. 11-B, B. Involuntary Dismissals.

Rutter, Cal. Practice Guide: Civ. Pro. Before Trial Ch. 13-E, E. the Arbitration Hearing.

Rutter, Cal. Practice Guide: Civ. Pro. Before Trial Ch. 12(II)-D, D. Plaintiff's Duties Upon Settlement.

Rutter, Cal. Practice Guide: Civil Trials & Evidence Ch. 8C-K, K. Stipulations.

Rutter, Cal. Practice Guide: Enforcing Judgments/Debts Ch. 3-C, C. Prelawsuit Considerations.

Rutter, Cal. Practice Guide: Personal Injury Ch. 4-G, G. Concluding and Enforcing Settlement.

Rutter, Cal. Practice Guide: Personal Injury Ch. 7-G, G. Arbitration Hearing.

Rutter, Cal. Practice Guide: Personal Injury Ch. 4-G , Outline G.

2 Witkin Cal. Proc. 5th Courts § 191, (S 191) Civil Rules.

6 Witkin Cal. Proc. 5th Proceedings Without Trial § 127, Plaintiff's Duties After Settlement.

6 Witkin Cal. Proc. 5th Proceedings Without Trial § 451, in General.

6 Witkin Cal. Proc. 5th Proceedings Without Trial § 593, (S 593) Source of Payment.

7 Witkin Cal. Proc. 5th Trial § 41, Notice of Settlement or Stay.

Division 13

DISMISSAL OF ACTIONS

Rule
3.1390. Service and filing of notice of entry of dismissal.

Rule 3.1390. Service and filing of notice of entry of dismissal

A party that requests dismissal of an action must serve on all parties and file notice of entry of the dismissal. *(Formerly Rule 383, adopted, eff. Jan. 1, 1984. Renumbered Rule 3.1390 and amended, eff. Jan. 1, 2007.)*

Research References

Rutter, Cal. Practice Guide: Civ. Pro. Before Trial Ch. 11-A, A. Voluntary Dismissals.

2 Witkin Cal. Proc. 5th Courts § 191, (S 191) Civil Rules.

6 Witkin Cal. Proc. 5th Proceedings Without Trial § 305, Request and Clerk's Entry.

Division 15

TRIAL

Chapter 4

JURY TRIALS

Rule
3.1540. Examination of prospective jurors in civil cases.

Rule 3.1540. Examination of prospective jurors in civil cases

(a) Application

This rule applies to all civil jury trials.

(b) Examination of jurors by the trial judge

To select a fair and impartial jury, the trial judge must examine the prospective jurors orally, or by written question-

naire, or by both methods. In examining prospective jurors in civil cases, the judge should consider the policies and recommendations in standard 3.25 of the Standards of Judicial Administration. The judge may use the *Juror Questionnaire for Civil Cases* (form MC-001).

(c) Additional questions and examination by counsel

On completion of the initial examination, the trial judge must permit counsel for each party that so requests to submit additional questions that the judge will put to the jurors. On request of counsel, the trial judge must permit counsel to supplement the judge's examination by oral and direct questioning of any of the prospective jurors. The scope of the additional questions or supplemental examination must be within reason-

~~able limits prescribed by the trial judge in the judge's sound discretion.~~

~~(d) Examination of juror outside the judge's presence~~

~~The court may, upon stipulation by counsel for all parties appearing in the action, permit counsel to examine the prospective jurors outside a judge's presence.~~ *(Formerly Rule 228, adopted, eff. Jan. 1, 1949. As amended, eff. Jan. 1, 1972; Jan. 1, 1974; Jan. 1, 1975; Jan. 1, 1988; Jan. 1, 1990; June 6, 1990; July 1, 1993. Renumbered Rule 3.1540 and amended, eff. Jan. 1, 2007. As amended, eff. Jan. 1, 2013.)*

Research References

Rutter, Cal. Practice Guide: Civ. Pro. Before Trial Ch. 3-E, E. Federal vs. State Courts.
Rutter, Cal. Practice Guide: Civil Trials & Evidence Ch. 5-C, C. Voir Dire-General Considerations.
Rutter, Cal. Practice Guide: Civil Trials & Evidence Ch. 5-D, D. Examination by Trial Judge.
Rutter, Cal. Practice Guide: Civil Trials & Evidence Ch. 5-G, G. Scope of Permissible Voir Dire-Proper vs. Improper Questions.
Rutter, Cal. Practice Guide: Fed.Civ.Pro. Before Trial Ch. 1-D, D. Choosing Between State and Federal Courts.
2 Witkin Cal. Proc. 5th Courts § 191, (S 191) Civil Rules.
7 Witkin Cal. Proc. 5th Trial § 137, (S 137) Voir Dire Procedure.

Chapter 4.5

EXPEDITED JURY TRIALS

Rule
3.1545.   Expedited jury trials.
3.1546.   Assignment of judicial officers.
3.1547.   Consent order.
3.1548.   Pretrial submissions.
3.1549.   Voir dire.
3.1550.   Time limits.
3.1551.   Case presentation.
3.1552.   Presentation of evidence.

Rule 3.1545.   Expedited jury trials

(a) Application

The rules in this chapter apply to civil actions in which the parties agree to an expedited jury trial under chapter 4.5 (commencing with section 630.01) of title 8 of part 2 of the Code of Civil Procedure.

(b) Definitions

As used in this chapter, unless the context or subject matter otherwise requires:

(1) "Consent order" means the consent order granting an expedited jury trial described in Code of Civil Procedure section 630.03.

(2) "Expedited jury trial," "high/low agreement," and "post-trial motions" have the same meanings as stated in Code of Civil Procedure section 630.01.

(c) Other programs

This chapter does not limit the adoption or use of other expedited trial or alternative dispute resolution programs or procedures. *(Adopted, eff. Jan. 1, 2011.)*

Research References

Rutter, Cal. Practice Guide: Civ. Pro. Before Trial Ch. 12(I)-H, H. Expedited Jury Trials.
Rutter, Cal. Practice Guide: Civil Trials & Evidence Ch. 2-A, A. Sources of Right to Jury Trial.
Rutter, Cal. Practice Guide: Personal Injury Ch. 8-A, A. Case Management.

2 Witkin Cal. Proc. 5th Courts § 191, (S 191) Civil Rules.
7 Witkin Cal. Proc. 5th Trial § 6A, (S 6A) (New)-In General.

Rule 3.1546.   Assignment of judicial officers

The presiding judge is responsible for the assignment of a judicial officer to conduct an expedited jury trial. The presiding judge may assign a temporary judge appointed by the court under rules 2.810—2.819 to conduct an expedited jury trial. A temporary judge requested by the parties under rules 2.830—2.835, whether or not privately compensated, may not be appointed to conduct an expedited jury trial. *(Adopted, eff. Jan. 1, 2011.)*

Research References

Rutter, Cal. Practice Guide: A.D.R. Ch. 6-B, B. Temporary Judges.
Rutter, Cal. Practice Guide: Civ. Pro. Before Trial Ch. 12(I)-H, H. Expedited Jury Trials.
7 Witkin Cal. Proc. 5th Trial § 6B, (S 6B) (New)-Pretrial Proceedings.

Rule 3.1547.   Consent order

(a) Submitting proposed consent order to the court

(1) Unless the court otherwise allows, to be eligible to participate in an expedited jury trial, the parties must submit to the court, no later than 30 days before any assigned trial date, a proposed consent order granting an expedited jury trial.

(2) The parties may enter into written stipulations regarding any high/low agreements or other matters. Only in the following circumstances may a high/low agreement be submitted to the court with the proposed consent order or disclosed later in the action:

(A) Upon agreement of the parties;

(B) In any case involving either

(i) A self-represented litigant, or

(ii) A minor, an incompetent person, or a person for whom a conservator has been appointed; or

(C) If necessary for entry or enforcement of the judgment.

(b) Optional content of proposed consent order

In addition to complying with the provisions of Code of Civil Procedure section 630.03(e), the proposed consent order may include other agreements of the parties, including the following:

(1) Modifications of the timelines for pretrial submissions required by rule 3.1548;

(2) Limitations on the number of witnesses per party, including expert witnesses;

(3) Modification of statutory or rule provisions regarding exchange of expert witness information and presentation of testimony by such witnesses;

(4) Allocation of the time periods stated in rule 3.1550, including how arguments and cross-examination may be used by each party in the three-hour time frame;

(5) Any evidentiary matters agreed to by the parties, including any stipulations or admissions regarding factual matters;

(6) Any agreements about what constitutes necessary or relevant evidence for a particular factual determination;

(7) Agreements about admissibility of particular exhibits or demonstrative evidence that are presented without the legally required authentication or foundation;

(8) Agreements about admissibility of video or written depositions and declarations;

(9) Agreements about any other evidentiary issues or the application of any of the rules of evidence;

(10) Agreements to use photographs, diagrams, slides, electronic presentations, overhead projections, notebooks of exhibits, or other methods for presenting information to the jury;

(11) Agreements concerning the time frame for filing and serving motions in limine; and

(12) Agreements concerning numbers of jurors required for jury verdicts in cases with fewer than eight jurors. *(Adopted, eff. Jan. 1, 2011.)*

Research References

Rutter, Cal. Practice Guide: Civ. Pro. Before Trial Ch. 12(I)-H, H. Expedited Jury Trials.

Rutter, Cal. Practice Guide: Civil Trials & Evidence Ch. 1-A, A. Importance of Statewide and Local Rules of Court.

Rutter, Cal. Practice Guide: Civil Trials & Evidence Ch. 4-B, B. Preliminary Matters Discussed in Final Status Conference or In-Chambers Conference.

Rutter, Cal. Practice Guide: Personal Injury Ch. 8-A, A. Case Management.

7 Witkin Cal. Proc. 5th Trial § 6A, (S 6A) (New)-In General.

Rule 3.1548. Pretrial submissions

(a) Service

Service under this rule must be by a means consistent with Code of Civil Procedure sections 1010.6, 1011, 1012, and 1013 or rule 2.251 and be reasonably calculated to assure delivery to the other party or parties no later than the close of business on the last allowable day for service as specified below.

(b) Pretrial exchange

No later than 25 days before trial, each party must serve on all other parties the following:

(1) Copies of any documentary evidence that the party intends to introduce at trial (except for documentary evidence to be used solely for impeachment or rebuttal), including, but not limited to, medical bills, medical records, and lost income records;

(2) A list of all witnesses whom the party intends to call at trial, except for witnesses to be used solely for impeachment or rebuttal, and designation of whether the testimony will be in person, by video, or by deposition transcript;

(3) A list of depositions that the party intends to use at trial, except for depositions to be used solely for impeachment or rebuttal;

(4) A copy of any audiotapes, videotapes, digital video discs (DVDs), compact discs (CDs), or other similar recorded materials that the party intends to use at trial for evidentiary purposes, except recorded materials to be used solely for impeachment or rebuttal and recorded material intended to be used solely in closing argument;

(5) A copy of any proposed jury questionnaires (parties are encouraged to agree in advance on a questionnaire);

(6) A list of proposed approved introductory instructions, preinstructions, and instructions to be read by the judge to the jury;

(7) A copy of any proposed special jury instructions in the form and format described in rule 2.1055;

(8) Any proposed verdict forms;

(9) A special glossary, if the case involves technical or unusual vocabulary; and

(10) Motions in limine.

(c) Supplemental exchange

No later than 20 days before trial, a party may serve on any other party any additional documentary evidence and a list of any additional witnesses whom the party intends to use at trial in light of the exchange of information under subdivision (b).

(d) Submissions to court

No later than 20 days before trial, each party must file all motions in limine and must lodge with the court any items served under (b)(2)–(9) and (c).

(e) Preclusionary effect

Unless good cause is shown for any omission, failure to serve documentary evidence as required under this rule will be grounds for preclusion of the evidence at the time of trial.

(f) Pretrial conference

No later than 15 days before trial, unless that period is modified by the consent order, the judicial officer assigned to the case must conduct a pretrial conference, at which time objections to any documentary evidence previously submitted will be ruled on. If there are no objections at that time, counsel must stipulate in writing to the admissibility of the evidence. Matters to be addressed at the pretrial conference, in addition to the evidentiary objections, include the following:

(1) Any evidentiary matters agreed to by the parties, including any stipulations or admissions regarding factual matters;

(2) Any agreement of the parties regarding limitations on necessary or relevant evidence, including any limitations on expert witness testimony;

(3) Any agreements of the parties to use photographs, diagrams, slides, electronic presentations, overhead projections, notebooks of exhibits, or other methods of presenting information to the jury;

(4) Admissibility of any exhibits or demonstrative evidence without legally required authentication or foundation;

(5) Admissibility of video or written depositions and declarations and objections to any portions of them;

(6) Objections to and admissibility of any recorded materials that a party has designated for use at trial;

(7) Jury questionnaires;

(8) Jury instructions;

(9) Special verdict forms;

(10) Allocation of time for each party's case; and

(11) Motions in limine filed before the pretrial conference.

(g) Expert witness documents

Any documents produced at the deposition of an expert witness are deemed to have been timely exchanged for the purpose of (c) above. *(Adopted, eff. Jan. 1, 2011.)*

Research References

Rutter, Cal. Practice Guide: Civ. Pro. Before Trial Ch. 12(I)-H, H. Expedited Jury Trials.

Rutter, Cal. Practice Guide: Civil Trials & Evidence Ch. 4-A, A. General Considerations.

Rutter, Cal. Practice Guide: Civil Trials & Evidence Ch. 4-B, B. Preliminary Matters Discussed in Final Status Conference or In-Chambers Conference.

Rutter, Cal. Practice Guide: Civil Trials & Evidence Ch. 4-C, C. Jury Matters.

Rutter, Cal. Practice Guide: Civil Trials & Evidence Ch. 4-F, F. Motions in Limine.

Rutter, Cal. Practice Guide: Civil Trials & Evidence Ch. 8B-C, C. Procedural Considerations.

Rutter, Cal. Practice Guide: Personal Injury Ch. 8-A, A. Case Management.

7 Witkin Cal. Proc. 5th Trial § 6B, (S 6B) (New)-Pretrial Proceedings.

Rule 3.1549. Voir dire

Approximately one hour will be devoted to voir dire, with 15 minutes allotted to the judicial officer and 15 minutes to each side. Parties are encouraged to submit a joint form questionnaire to be used with prospective jurors to help expedite the voir dire process. *(Adopted, eff. Jan. 1, 2011.)*

Research References

Rutter, Cal. Practice Guide: Civ. Pro. Before Trial Ch. 12(I)-H, H. Expedited Jury Trials.

Rutter, Cal. Practice Guide: Civil Trials & Evidence Ch. 5-C, C. Voir Dire-General Considerations.

Rutter, Cal. Practice Guide: Personal Injury Ch. 8-A, A. Case Management.

7 Witkin Cal. Proc. 5th Trial § 6C, (S 6C) (New)-Conduct of Trial.

Rule 3.1550. Time limits

Excluding jury selection, each side will be allowed three hours to present its case, including opening statements and closing arguments, unless the court, upon a finding of good cause, allows additional time. The amount of time allotted for each side includes the time that the side spends on cross-examination. The parties are encouraged to streamline the trial process by limiting the number of live witnesses. The goal is to complete an expedited jury trial within one full trial day. *(Adopted, eff. Jan. 1, 2011.)*

Research References

Rutter, Cal. Practice Guide: Civ. Pro. Before Trial Ch. 12(I)-H, H. Expedited Jury Trials.

Rutter, Cal. Practice Guide: Civil Trials & Evidence Ch. 4-B, B. Preliminary Matters Discussed in Final Status Conference or In-Chambers Conference.

Rutter, Cal. Practice Guide: Civil Trials & Evidence Ch. 4-C, C. Jury Matters.

Rutter, Cal. Practice Guide: Civil Trials & Evidence Ch. 6-A, A. General Considerations.

Rutter, Cal. Practice Guide: Civil Trials & Evidence Ch. 10-A, A. Preliminary Considerations.

Rutter, Cal. Practice Guide: Civil Trials & Evidence Ch. 13-A, A. Procedural Considerations Re Closing Argument.

Rutter, Cal. Practice Guide: Personal Injury Ch. 8-A, A. Case Management.

7 Witkin Cal. Proc. 5th Trial § 6C, (S 6C) (New)-Conduct of Trial.

Rule 3.1551. Case presentation

(a) Methods of presentation

Upon agreement of the parties and with the approval of the judicial officer, the parties may present summaries and may use photographs, diagrams, slides, electronic presentations, overhead projections, individual notebooks of exhibits for submission to the jurors, or other innovative methods of presentation approved at the pretrial conference.

(b) Exchange of items

Anything to be submitted to the jury as part of the evidentiary presentation of the case in chief must be exchanged 20 days in advance of the trial, unless that period is modified by the consent order. This rule does not apply to items to be used solely for closing argument.

(c) Stipulations regarding facts

The parties should stipulate to factual and evidentiary matters to the greatest extent possible. *(Adopted, eff. Jan. 1, 2011.)*

Research References

Rutter, Cal. Practice Guide: Civ. Pro. Before Trial Ch. 12(I)-H, H. Expedited Jury Trials.

Rutter, Cal. Practice Guide: Civil Trials & Evidence Ch. 4-B, B. Preliminary Matters Discussed in Final Status Conference or In-Chambers Conference.

Rutter, Cal. Practice Guide: Personal Injury Ch. 8-A, A. Case Management.

7 Witkin Cal. Proc. 5th Trial § 6C, (S 6C) (New)-Conduct of Trial.

Rule 3.1552. Presentation of evidence

(a) Stipulations regarding rules of evidence

The parties may offer such evidence as is relevant and material to the dispute. An agreement to modify the rules of evidence for the trial made pursuant to the expedited jury trial statutes commencing with Code of Civil Procedure section 630.01 may be included in the consent order. To the extent feasible, the parties should stipulate to modes and methods of presentation that will expedite the process, either in the consent order or at the pretrial conference.

(b) Objections

Objections to evidence and motions to exclude evidence must be submitted in a timely manner. Except as provided in rule 3.1548(f), failure to raise an objection before trial does not preclude making an objection or motion to exclude at trial. *(Adopted, eff. Jan. 1, 2011.)*

Research References

Rutter, Cal. Practice Guide: Civ. Pro. Before Trial Ch. 12(I)-H, H. Expedited Jury Trials.

Rutter, Cal. Practice Guide: Civil Trials & Evidence Ch. 4-B, B. Preliminary Matters Discussed in Final Status Conference or In-Chambers Conference.

Rutter, Cal. Practice Guide: Civil Trials & Evidence Ch. 8A-A, A. Types of Evidence.

Rutter, Cal. Practice Guide: Civil Trials & Evidence Ch. 8B-C, C. Procedural Considerations.

2 Witkin Cal. Proc. 5th Courts § 191, (S 191) Civil Rules.

7 Witkin Cal. Proc. 5th Trial § 6C, (S 6C) (New)-Conduct of Trial.

Chapter 7

JURY INSTRUCTIONS

Rule
3.1560. Application.

Rule 3.1560. Application

The rules on jury instructions in chapter 4 of division 8 of title 2 of these rules apply to civil cases. *(Adopted, eff. Jan. 1, 2007.)*

Chapter 8

SPECIAL VERDICTS

Rule
3.1580. Request for special findings by jury.

Rule 3.1580. Request for special findings by jury

Whenever a party desires special findings by a jury, the party must, before argument, unless otherwise ordered, present to the judge in writing the issues or questions of fact on which the findings are requested, in proper form for submission to the jury, and serve copies on all other parties. *(Formerly Rule 230, adopted, eff. Jan. 1, 1949. Renumbered Rule 3.1580 and amended, eff. Jan. 1, 2007.)*

Research References

Rutter, Cal. Practice Guide: Civil Trials & Evidence Ch. 4-C, C. Jury Matters.

Rutter, Cal. Practice Guide: Civil Trials & Evidence Ch. 17-A, A. Verdicts.

Rutter, Cal. Practice Guide: Personal Injury Ch. 3-F, F. MICRA Provisions Affecting Damages.

Rutter, Cal. Practice Guide: Personal Injury Ch. 9-M, M. Verdicts and Judgment.

7 Witkin Cal. Proc. 5th Trial § 348, Procedure and Judge's Discretion.

Chapter 9

STATEMENT OF DECISION

Rule

3.1590. Announcement of tentative decision, statement of decision, and judgment.

3.1591. Statement of decision, judgment, and motion for new trial following bifurcated trial.

Rule 3.1590. Announcement of tentative decision, statement of decision, and judgment

(a) Announcement and service of tentative decision

On the trial of a question of fact by the court, the court must announce its tentative decision by an oral statement, entered in the minutes, or by a written statement filed with the clerk. Unless the announcement is made in open court in the presence of all parties that appeared at the trial, the clerk must immediately serve on all parties that appeared at the trial a copy of the minute entry or written tentative decision.

(b) Tentative decision not binding

The tentative decision does not constitute a judgment and is not binding on the court. If the court subsequently modifies or changes its announced tentative decision, the clerk must serve a copy of the modification or change on all parties that appeared at the trial.

(c) Provisions in tentative decision

The court in its tentative decision may:

(1) State that it is the court's proposed statement of decision, subject to a party's objection under (g);

(2) Indicate that the court will prepare a statement of decision;

(3) Order a party to prepare a statement of decision; or

(4) Direct that the tentative decision will become the statement of decision unless, within 10 days after announcement or service of the tentative decision, a party specifies those principal controverted issues as to which the party is requesting a statement of decision or makes proposals not included in the tentative decision.

(d) Request for statement of decision

Within 10 days after announcement or service of the tentative decision, whichever is later, any party that appeared at trial may request a statement of decision to address the principal controverted issues. The principal controverted issues must be specified in the request.

(e) Other party's response to request for statement of decision

If a party requests a statement of decision under (d), any other party may make proposals as to the content of the statement of decision within 10 days after the date of request for a statement of decision.

(f) Preparation and service of proposed statement of decision and judgment

If a party requests a statement of decision under (d), the court must, within 30 days of announcement or service of the tentative decision, prepare and serve a proposed statement of decision and a proposed judgment on all parties that appeared at the trial, unless the court has ordered a party to prepare the statement. A party that has been ordered to prepare the statement must within 30 days after the announcement or service of the tentative decision, serve and submit to the court a proposed statement of decision and a proposed judgment. If the proposed statement of decision and judgment are not served and submitted within that time, any other party that appeared at the trial may within 10 days thereafter: (1) prepare, serve, and submit to the court a proposed statement of decision and judgment or (2) serve on all other parties and file a notice of motion for an order that a statement of decision be deemed waived.

(g) Objections to proposed statement of decision

Any party may, within 15 days after the proposed statement of decision and judgment have been served, serve and file objections to the proposed statement of decision or judgment.

(h) Preparation and filing of written judgment when statement of decision not prepared

If no party requests or is ordered to prepare a statement of decision and a written judgment is required, the court must prepare and serve a proposed judgment on all parties that appeared at the trial within 20 days after the announcement or service of the tentative decision or the court may order a party to prepare, serve, and submit the proposed judgment to the court within 10 days after the date of the order.

(i) Preparation and filing of written judgment when statement of decision deemed waived

If the court orders that the statement of decision is deemed waived and a written judgment is required, the court must, within 10 days of the order deeming the statement of decision waived, either prepare and serve a proposed judgment on all parties that appeared at the trial or order a party to prepare, serve, and submit the proposed judgment to the court within 10 days.

(j) Objection to proposed judgment

Any party may, within 10 days after service of the proposed judgment, serve and file objections thereto.

(k) Hearing

The court may order a hearing on proposals or objections to a proposed statement of decision or the proposed judgment.

(l) Signature and filing of judgment

If a written judgment is required, the court must sign and file the judgment within 50 days after the announcement or service of the tentative decision, whichever is later, or, if a hearing was held under (k), within 10 days after the hearing. The judgment constitutes the decision on which judgment is to be entered under Code of Civil Procedure section 664.

(m) Extension of time; relief from noncompliance

The court may, by written order, extend any of the times prescribed by this rule and at any time before the entry of judgment may, for good cause shown and on such terms as may be just, excuse a noncompliance with the time limits prescribed for doing any act required by this rule.

(n) Trial within one day

When a trial is completed within one day or in less than eight hours over more than one day, a request for statement of decision must be made before the matter is submitted for decision and the statement of decision may be made orally on the record in the presence of the parties. *(Formerly Rule 232, adopted, eff. Jan. 1, 1949. As amended, eff. Jan. 1, 1969; July 1, 1973; Jan. 1, 1982; Jan. 1, 1983. Renumbered Rule 3.1590 and amended, eff. Jan. 1, 2007. As amended, eff. Jan. 1, 2010.)*

Research References

Rutter, Cal. Practice Guide: Civil Appeals & Writs Ch. 8-B, B. Presumption of Correctness.

Rutter, Cal. Practice Guide: Civil Appeals & Writs Ch. 8-D, D. Limits on Assertion of Issues on Appeal.

Rutter, Cal. Practice Guide: Civil Trials & Evidence Ch. 16-E, E. Statement of Decision.

Rutter, Cal. Practice Guide: Civil Trials & Evidence Ch. 17-B, B. Decision in Nonjury Trials.

Rutter, Cal. Practice Guide: Civil Trials & Evidence Ch. 17-C, C. Entry of Judgment.

Rutter, Cal. Practice Guide: Civil Trials & Evidence Ch. 18-B, B. Motion for New Trial.

Rutter, Cal. Practice Guide: Personal Injury Ch. 9-M, M. Verdicts and Judgment.

9 Witkin Cal. Proc. 5th Appeal § 161, (S 161) Order for Judgment.

2 Witkin Cal. Proc. 5th Courts § 191, (S 191) Civil Rules.

7 Witkin Cal. Proc. 5th Judgment § 9, (S 9) Announcement of Decision and Proposed Judgment.

7 Witkin Cal. Proc. 5th Judgment § 47, Judgment After Trial or Hearing.

7 Witkin Cal. Proc. 5th Judgment § 55, Judgments.

7 Witkin Cal. Proc. 5th Judgment § 139, (S 139) in General.

7 Witkin Cal. Proc. 5th Trial § 393, (S 393) in General.

7 Witkin Cal. Proc. 5th Trial § 394, (S 394) Announcement of Tentative Decision.

7 Witkin Cal. Proc. 5th Trial § 395, (S 395) Request by Party.

7 Witkin Cal. Proc. 5th Trial § 396, (S 396) Preparation of Statement.

7 Witkin Cal. Proc. 5th Trial § 397, (S 397) Proposed Judgment Where Statement is Not Required.

7 Witkin Cal. Proc. 5th Trial § 398, (S 398) Objections.

7 Witkin Cal. Proc. 5th Trial § 400, (S 400) Procedure in Bifurcated Trial.

7 Witkin Cal. Proc. 5th Trial § 402, (S 402) Insufficient Statement.

7 Witkin Cal. Proc. 5th Trial § 404, (S 404) Waiver by Failure to Object.

11 Witkin, California Summary 10th Community Property § 241, Statutory Requirement of Division.

11 Witkin, California Summary 10th Husband and Wife § 107, (S 107) Statement of Decision.

Rule 3.1591. Statement of decision, judgment, and motion for new trial following bifurcated trial

(a) Separate trial of an issue

When a factual issue raised by the pleadings is tried by the court separately and before the trial of other issues, the judge conducting the separate trial must announce the tentative decision on the issue so tried and must, when requested under Code of Civil Procedure section 632, issue a statement of decision as prescribed in rule 3.1590; but the court must not prepare any proposed judgment until the other issues are tried, except when an interlocutory judgment or a separate judgment may otherwise be properly entered at that time.

(b) Trial of issues by a different judge

If the other issues are tried by a different judge or judges, each judge must perform all acts required by rule 3.1590 as to the issues tried by that judge and the judge trying the final issue must prepare the proposed judgment.

(c) Trial of subsequent issues before issuance of statement of decision

A judge may proceed with the trial of subsequent issues before the issuance of a statement of decision on previously tried issues. Any motion for a new trial following a bifurcated trial must be made after all the issues are tried and, if the issues were tried by different judges, each judge must hear and determine the motion as to the issues tried by that judge. *(Formerly Rule 232.5, adopted, eff. Jan. 1, 1975. As amended, eff. Jan. 1, 1982; Jan. 1, 1985. Renumbered Rule 3.1591 and amended, eff. Jan. 1, 2007.)*

Research References

Rutter, Cal. Practice Guide: Civil Trials & Evidence Ch. 4-G, G. Motion to Sever or Bifurcate.

Rutter, Cal. Practice Guide: Civil Trials & Evidence Ch. 16-E, E. Statement of Decision.

Rutter, Cal. Practice Guide: Civil Trials & Evidence Ch. 18-A, A. Motion for Judgment Notwithstanding the Verdict ("JNOV").

Rutter, Cal. Practice Guide: Civil Trials & Evidence Ch. 18-B, B. Motion for New Trial.

Rutter, Cal. Practice Guide: Personal Injury Ch. 9-M, M. Verdicts and Judgment.

Rutter, Cal. Practice Guide: Personal Injury Ch. 10-A, A. Motion for New Trial.

8 Witkin Cal. Proc. 5th Attack Judgment Trial Court § 56, What Constitutes Decision.

8 Witkin Cal. Proc. 5th Attack Judgment Trial Court § 70, (S 70) Trial Judge.

2 Witkin Cal. Proc. 5th Courts § 191, (S 191) Civil Rules.

7 Witkin Cal. Proc. 5th Judgment § 47, Judgment After Trial or Hearing.

7 Witkin Cal. Proc. 5th Trial § 393, (S 393) in General.

7 Witkin Cal. Proc. 5th Trial § 400, (S 400) Procedure in Bifurcated Trial.

11 Witkin, California Summary 10th Husband and Wife § 106, (S 106) Court Rule.

11 Witkin, California Summary 10th Husband and Wife § 107, (S 107) Statement of Decision.

Division 16

POST-TRIAL

Rule
3.1600. Notice of intention to move for new trial.
3.1602. Hearing of motion to vacate judgment.

Rule 3.1600. Notice of intention to move for new trial

(a) Time for service of memorandum

Within 10 days after filing notice of intention to move for a new trial in a civil case, the moving party must serve and file a memorandum in support of the motion, and within 10 days thereafter any adverse party may serve and file a memorandum in reply.

(b) Effect of failure to serve memorandum

If the moving party fails to serve and file a memorandum within the time prescribed in (a), the court may deny the motion for a new trial without a hearing on the merits. *(Formerly Rule 203, as amended, eff. April 1, 1962; Jan. 1, 1984; Jan. 1, 1987. Renumbered Rule 236.5, and amended, eff. Jan. 1, 2003. Renumbered Rule 3.1600 and amended, eff. Jan. 1, 2007.)*

Research References

Rutter, Cal. Practice Guide: Civ. Pro. Before Trial Ch. 5-G, G. Relief from Default.

Rutter, Cal. Practice Guide: Civ. Pro. Before Trial Ch. 10-I, I. Challenging Judgment or Order in Trial Court.

Rutter, Cal. Practice Guide: Civil Trials & Evidence Ch. 18-A, A. Motion for Judgment Notwithstanding the Verdict ("JNOV").

Rutter, Cal. Practice Guide: Civil Trials & Evidence Ch. 18-B, B. Motion for New Trial.

Rutter, Cal. Practice Guide: Personal Injury Ch. 10-A, A. Motion for New Trial.

8 Witkin Cal. Proc. 5th Attack Judgment Trial Court § 66, (S 66) Supporting Memorandum.

2 Witkin Cal. Proc. 5th Courts § 191, (S 191) Civil Rules.

Rule 3.1602. Hearing of motion to vacate judgment

A motion to vacate judgment under Code of Civil Procedure section 663 must be heard and determined by the judge who presided at the trial; provided, however, that in case of the inability or death of such judge or if at the time noticed for the hearing thereon he is absent from the county where the trial was had, the motion may be heard and determined by another judge of the same court. *(Formerly Rule 236, adopted, eff. Jan. 1, 1949. Renumbered Rule 3.1602 and amended, eff. Jan. 1, 2007.)*

Research References

Rutter, Cal. Practice Guide: Personal Injury Ch. 10-C, C. Motion to Vacate and Enter Different Judgment.

8 Witkin Cal. Proc. 5th Attack Judgment Trial Court § 142, Hearing and Determination.

2 Witkin Cal. Proc. 5th Courts § 19, What Successor Can Do.

2 Witkin Cal. Proc. 5th Courts § 191, (S 191) Civil Rules.

Division 17

ATTORNEY'S FEES AND COSTS

Rule

3.1700.   Prejudgment costs.

3.1702.   Claiming attorney's fees.

Rule 3.1700.   Prejudgment costs

(a) Claiming costs

(1) *Trial costs*

A prevailing party who claims costs must serve and file a memorandum of costs within 15 days after the date of mailing of the notice of entry of judgment or dismissal by the clerk under Code of Civil Procedure section 664.5 or the date of service of written notice of entry of judgment or dismissal, or within 180 days after entry of judgment, whichever is first. The memorandum of costs must be verified by a statement of the party, attorney, or agent that to the best of his or her knowledge the items of cost are correct and were necessarily incurred in the case.

(2) *Costs on default*

A party seeking a default judgment who claims costs must request costs on the *Request for Entry of Default (Application to Enter Default)* (form CIV–100) at the time of applying for the judgment.

(b) Contesting costs

(1) *Striking and taxing costs*

Any notice of motion to strike or to tax costs must be served and filed 15 days after service of the cost memorandum. If the cost memorandum was served by mail, the period is extended as provided in Code of Civil Procedure section 1013.

(2) *Form of motion*

Unless objection is made to the entire cost memorandum, the motion to strike or tax costs must refer to each item objected to by the same number and appear in the same order as the corresponding cost item claimed on the memorandum of costs and must state why the item is objectionable.

(3) *Extensions of time*

The party claiming costs and the party contesting costs may agree to extend the time for serving and filing the cost memorandum and a motion to strike or tax costs. This agreement must be confirmed in writing, specify the extended date for service, and be filed with the clerk. In the absence of an agreement, the court may extend the times for serving and filing the cost memorandum or the notice of motion to strike or tax costs for a period not to exceed 30 days.

(4) *Entry of costs*

After the time has passed for a motion to strike or tax costs or for determination of that motion, the clerk must immediately enter the costs on the judgment. *(Formerly Rule 870, adopted,*

eff. Jan. 1, 1987. Renumbered Rule 3.1700 and amended, eff. Jan. 1, 2007. As amended, eff. July 1, 2007.)

Research References

Rutter, Cal. Practice Guide: A.D.R. Ch. 6-B, B. Temporary Judges.

Rutter, Cal. Practice Guide: Civil Appeals & Writs Ch. 14-B, B. Recovery of Appellate Costs and Attorney Fees.

Rutter, Cal. Practice Guide: Civil Appeals & Writs Ch. 15-E, E. Procedures on Writ Review.

Rutter, Cal. Practice Guide: Civ. Pro. Before Trial Ch. 11-A, A. Voluntary Dismissals.

Rutter, Cal. Practice Guide: Civ. Pro. Before Trial Ch. 8G-10, Sanctions in Enforcing Rfas.

Rutter, Cal. Practice Guide: Civil Trials & Evidence Ch. 17-D, D. Costs.

Rutter, Cal. Practice Guide: Civil Trials & Evidence Ch. 17-E, E. Attorney Fees as Costs.

Rutter, Cal. Practice Guide: Enforcing Judgments/Debts Ch. 6A-5, Amount Recoverable Under Judgment.

Rutter, Cal. Practice Guide: Personal Injury Ch. 7-H, H. Arbitration Award and Judgment.

Rutter, Cal. Practice Guide: Personal Injury Ch. 9-M, M. Verdicts and Judgment.

9 Witkin Cal. Proc. 5th Appeal § 977, Motion to Tax.

2 Witkin Cal. Proc. 5th Courts § 191, (S 191) Civil Rules.

7 Witkin Cal. Proc. 5th Judgment § 139, (S 139) in General.

7 Witkin Cal. Proc. 5th Judgment § 140, Time Limits.

7 Witkin Cal. Proc. 5th Judgment § 141, Late Filing.

7 Witkin Cal. Proc. 5th Judgment § 142, Premature Service or Filing.

7 Witkin Cal. Proc. 5th Judgment § 144, (S 144) Motion to Strike or Tax Costs.

7 Witkin Cal. Proc. 5th Judgment § 145, (S 145) Service and Filing.

7 Witkin Cal. Proc. 5th Judgment § 146, (S 146) Burden of Proof.

7 Witkin Cal. Proc. 5th Judgment § 147, (S 147) Inclusion of Cost Award.

7 Witkin Cal. Proc. 5th Judgment § 148, (S 148) Failure to Include Costs.

7 Witkin Cal. Proc. 5th Judgment § 297, (S 297) Fees Based on Statute.

6 Witkin Cal. Proc. 5th Proceedings Without Trial § 164, (S 164) Application and Accompanying Documents.

6 Witkin Cal. Proc. 5th Proceedings Without Trial § 166, Contents of Judgment.

6 Witkin Cal. Proc. 5th Proceedings Without Trial § 305, Request and Clerk's Entry.

Rule 3.1702.   Claiming attorney's fees

(a) Application

Except as otherwise provided by statute, this rule applies in civil cases to claims for statutory attorney's fees and claims for attorney's fees provided for in a contract. Subdivisions (b) and (c) apply when the court determines entitlement to the fees, the amount of the fees, or both, whether the court makes that determination because the statute or contract refers to "reasonable" fees, because it requires a determination of the prevailing party, or for other reasons.

(b) Attorney's fees before trial court judgment

(1) *Time for motion*

A notice of motion to claim attorney's fees for services up to and including the rendition of judgment in the trial court—including attorney's fees on an appeal before the rendition of judgment in the trial court—must be served and filed within the time for filing a notice of appeal under rules 8.104 and 8.108 in an unlimited civil case or under rules 8.822 and 8.823 in a limited civil case.

(2) *Stipulation for extension of time*

The parties may, by stipulation filed before the expiration of the time allowed under (b)(1), extend the time for filing a motion for attorney's fees:

(A) Until 60 days after the expiration of the time for filing a notice of appeal in an unlimited civil case or 30 days after the expiration of the time in a limited civil case; or

(B) If a notice of appeal is filed, until the time within which a memorandum of costs must be served and filed under rule 8.278(c) in an unlimited civil case or under rule 8.891(b)(2) 8.891(c)(1) in a limited civil case.

(c) Attorney's fees on appeal

(1) *Time for motion*

A notice of motion to claim attorney's fees on appeal—other than the attorney's fees on appeal claimed under (b)—under a statute or contract requiring the court to determine entitlement to the fees, the amount of the fees, or both, must be served and filed within the time for serving and filing the memorandum of costs under rule 8.278(c)(1) in an unlimited civil case or under rule 8.891(c)(1) in a limited civil case.

(2) *Stipulation for extension of time*

The parties may by stipulation filed before the expiration of the time allowed under (c)(1) extend the time for filing the motion up to an additional 60 days in an unlimited civil case or 30 days in a limited civil case.

(d) Extensions

For good cause, the trial judge may extend the time for filing a motion for attorney's fees in the absence of a stipulation or for a longer period than allowed by stipulation.

(e) Attorney's fees fixed by formula

If a party is entitled to statutory or contractual attorney's fees that are fixed without the necessity of a court determination, the fees must be claimed in the memorandum of costs. *(Formerly Rule 870.2, adopted, eff. Jan. 1, 1994. As amended, eff. Jan. 1, 1999; Jan. 1, 2006. Renumbered Rule 3.1702 and amended, eff.*

Jan. 1, 2007. As amended, eff. July 1, 2008; Jan. 1, 2009; Jan. 1, 2011; July 1, 2013.)

Research References

Rutter, Cal. Practice Guide: Civil Appeals & Writs Ch. 14-B, B. Recovery of Appellate Costs and Attorney Fees.

Rutter, Cal. Practice Guide: Civil Appeals & Writs Ch. 14-B , Outline B.

Rutter, Cal. Practice Guide: Civ. Pro. Before Trial Ch. 1-A, A. Accepting a New Case.

Rutter, Cal. Practice Guide: Civ. Pro. Before Trial Ch. 11-A, A. Voluntary Dismissals.

Rutter, Cal. Practice Guide: Civ. Pro. Before Trial Ch. 8G-10, Sanctions in Enforcing RFAs.

Rutter, Cal. Practice Guide: Civ. Pro. Before Trial Ch. 7(II)-F, F. Procedure.

Rutter, Cal. Practice Guide: Civ. Pro. Before Trial Ch. 12(II)-C, C. Statutory Offer to Compromise (CCP § 998).

Rutter, Cal. Practice Guide: Civil Trials & Evidence Ch. 17-D, D. Costs.

Rutter, Cal. Practice Guide: Civil Trials & Evidence Ch. 17-E, E. Attorney Fees as Costs.

Rutter, Cal. Practice Guide: Enforcing Judgments/Debts Ch. 3-C, C. Prelawsuit Considerations.

Rutter, Cal. Practice Guide: Enforcing Judgments/Debts Ch. 4-A, A. Attachment.

Rutter, Cal. Practice Guide: Family Law Ch. 7-C, C. Custody Awards, Generally.

Rutter, Cal. Practice Guide: Personal Injury Ch. 3-A, A. Introduction.

Rutter, Cal. Practice Guide: Personal Injury Ch. 9-M, M. Verdicts and Judgment.

Rutter, Cal. Practice Guide: Real Prop. Transactions Ch. 11-C, C. Seller's Remedies Upon Buyer's Breach-Damages and Specific Performance.

9 Witkin Cal. Proc. 5th Appeal § 968, in General.

9 Witkin Cal. Proc. 5th Appeal § 982, (S 982) Procedure for Request.

8 Witkin Cal. Proc. 5th Attack Judgment Trial Court § 176, (S 176) When Time Begins to Run.

2 Witkin Cal. Proc. 5th Courts § 191, (S 191) Civil Rules.

7 Witkin Cal. Proc. 5th Judgment § 295, (S 295) in General.

7 Witkin Cal. Proc. 5th Judgment § 296, (S 296) Fees Based on Contract.

7 Witkin Cal. Proc. 5th Judgment § 297, (S 297) Fees Based on Statute.

7 Witkin Cal. Proc. 5th Judgment § 300, in General.

7 Witkin Cal. Proc. 5th Judgment § 301, Fees Determined by Trial Court.

7 Witkin Cal. Proc. 5th Judgment § 302, Fees Determined by Appellate Court.

7 Witkin Cal. Proc. 5th Judgment § 303, Fees Awarded Under.

10 Witkin, California Summary 10th Parent and Child § 283, Sexual Abuse Allegation.

11 Witkin, California Summary 10th Husband and Wife § 10, (S 10) Imposition of Award as Sanction.

13 Witkin, California Summary 10th Trusts § 60, Attorneys' Fees and Costs.

Division 18

JUDGMENTS

Rule 3.1800.   Default judgments

(a) Documents to be submitted

A party seeking a default judgment on declarations must use mandatory *Request for Entry of Default (Application to Enter Default)* (form CIV–100). In an unlawful detainer case, a party may, in addition, use optional *Declaration for Default Judgment by*

Court (form UD–116) when seeking a court judgment based on declarations. The following must be included in the documents filed with the clerk:

(1) Except in unlawful detainer cases, a brief summary of the case identifying the parties and the nature of plaintiff's claim;

(2) Declarations or other admissible evidence in support of the judgment requested;

(3) Interest computations as necessary;

(4) A memorandum of costs and disbursements;

(5) A declaration of nonmilitary status for each defendant against whom judgment is sought;

(6) A proposed form of judgment;

(7) A dismissal of all parties against whom judgment is not sought or an application for separate judgment against specified parties under Code of Civil Procedure section 579, supported by a showing of grounds for each judgment;

(8) Exhibits as necessary; and

(9) A request for attorney fees if allowed by statute or by the agreement of the parties.

(b) Fee schedule

A court may by local rule establish a schedule of attorney's fees to be used by that court in determining the reasonable amount of attorney's fees to be allowed in the case of a default judgment. *(Formerly Rule 388, adopted, eff. July, 1, 2000. As amended, eff. Jan. 1, 2005. Renumbered Rule 3.1800 and amended, eff. Jan. 1, 2007. As amended, eff. July 1, 2007.)*

Research References

Rutter, Cal. Practice Guide: Civ. Pro. Before Trial Ch. 5-B, B. Entry of Default.
Rutter, Cal. Practice Guide: Civ. Pro. Before Trial Ch. 5-C, C. Default Judgment by Clerk.
Rutter, Cal. Practice Guide: Civ. Pro. Before Trial Ch. 5-D, D. Default Judgment by Court.
Rutter, Cal. Practice Guide: Enforcing Judgments/Debts Ch. 3-C, C. Prelawsuit Considerations.
2 Witkin Cal. Proc. 5th Courts § 191, (S 191) Civil Rules.
2 Witkin Cal. Proc. 5th Courts § 199, (S 199) in General.
6 Witkin Cal. Proc. 5th Proceedings Without Trial § 166, Contents of Judgment.

Rule 3.1802. Inclusion of interest in judgment

The clerk must include in the judgment any interest awarded by the court and the interest accrued since the entry of the verdict. *(Formerly Rule 875, adopted, eff. Jan. 1, 1987. Renumbered Rule 3.1802 and amended, eff. Jan. 1, 2007.)*

Research References

Rutter, Cal. Practice Guide: Civil Trials & Evidence Ch. 17-D, D. Costs.
Rutter, Cal. Practice Guide: Civil Trials & Evidence Ch. 17-F, F. Prejudgment Interest.
Rutter, Cal. Practice Guide: Enforcing Judgments/Debts Ch. 3-C, C. Prelawsuit Considerations.
Rutter, Cal. Practice Guide: Insurance Litigation Ch. 13-C, C. Punitive Damages.
Rutter, Cal. Practice Guide: Personal Injury Ch. 3-A, A. Introduction.
Rutter, Cal. Practice Guide: Personal Injury Ch. 4-D, D. Techniques Where Settlement Not Forthcoming.
Rutter, Cal. Practice Guide: Personal Injury Ch. 9-M, M. Verdicts and Judgment.
8 Witkin Cal. Proc. 5th Enforcement of Judgment § 43, When Accrual Commences.
7 Witkin Cal. Proc. 5th Judgment § 325, Interest on Verdict or Decision.

Rule 3.1804. Periodic payment of judgments against public entities

(a) Notice of election or hearing

A public entity electing to pay a judgment against it by periodic payments under Government Code section 984 must serve and file a notice of election stipulating to the terms of such payments, or a notice of hearing on such terms, by the earlier of:

(1) 30 days after the clerk sends, or a party serves, notice of entry of judgment; or

(2) 60 days after entry of judgment.

(b) Time for hearing

Notwithstanding any contrary local rule or practice, a hearing under (a) must be held within 30 days after service of the notice. The court must make an order for periodic payments at the hearing. *(Formerly Rule 389, adopted, eff. Jan. 1, 2002. Renumbered Rule 3.1804 and amended, eff. Jan. 1, 2007.)*

Research References

Rutter, Cal. Practice Guide: Civil Appeals & Writs Ch. 3-C, C. Extensions of Filing Deadline.
Rutter, Cal. Practice Guide: Personal Injury Ch. 3-A, A. Introduction.
Rutter, Cal. Practice Guide: Personal Injury Ch. 10-D, D. Government Entity Defendant Post-Trial Elections, Requests, Motions and Hearings.
9 Witkin Cal. Proc. 5th Appeal § 606, (S 606) Judgment Against Public Entity.
8 Witkin Cal. Proc. 5th Enforcement of Judgment § 434, (S 434) Periodic Payments.

Rule 3.1806. Notation on written instrument of rendition of judgment

In all cases in which judgment is rendered upon a written obligation to pay money, the clerk must, at the time of entry of judgment, unless otherwise ordered, note over the clerk's official signature and across the face of the writing the fact of rendition of judgment with the date of the judgment and the title of the court and the case. *(Formerly Rule 234, adopted, eff. Jan. 1, 1949. Renumbered Rule 3.1806 and amended, eff. Jan. 1, 2007.)*

Research References

Rutter, Cal. Practice Guide: Civ. Pro. Before Trial Ch. 5-C, C. Default Judgment by Clerk.
Rutter, Cal. Practice Guide: Civ. Pro. Before Trial Ch. 5-D, D. Default Judgment by Court.
Rutter, Cal. Practice Guide: Civ. Pro. Before Trial Ch. 10-C, C. Procedural Requirements-Moving Party.
Rutter, Cal. Practice Guide: Civ. Pro. Before Trial Ch. 9(I)-B, B. Preparing and Filing Motions.
2 Witkin Cal. Proc. 5th Courts § 191, (S 191) Civil Rules.
7 Witkin Cal. Proc. 5th Judgment § 49, (S 49) in General.
6 Witkin Cal. Proc. 5th Proceedings Without Trial § 164, (S 164) Application and Accompanying Documents.

Division 19

POSTJUDGMENT AND ENFORCEMENT OF JUDGMENTS

Rule
3.1900. Notice of renewal of judgment.

Rule 3.1900. Notice of renewal of judgment

A copy of the application for renewal of judgment must be attached to the notice of renewal of judgment required by Code of Civil Procedure section 683.160. *(Formerly Rule 986, adopted,* *eff. July 1, 1983. Renumbered Rule 3.1900 and amended, eff. Jan. 1, 2007.)*

Research References

Rutter, Cal. Practice Guide: Enforcing Judgments/Debts Ch. 6A-7, Period During Which Judgment Enforceable; Renewal Procedures.
2 Witkin Cal. Proc. 5th Courts § 191, (S 191) Civil Rules.

Division 20

UNLAWFUL DETAINERS

Rule
3.2000.   Unlawful detainer—supplemental costs.

Rule 3.2000.   Unlawful detainer—supplemental costs

(a) Time for filing supplemental cost memorandum

In unlawful detainer proceedings, the plaintiff who has complied with Code of Civil Procedure section 1034.5 may, no later than 10 days after being advised by the sheriff or marshal of the exact amount necessarily used and expended to effect the eviction, file a supplemental cost memorandum claiming the additional costs and specifying the items paid and the amount.

(b) Motion to tax costs

The defendant may move to tax those costs within 10 days after service of the supplemental cost memorandum.

(c) Entry of judgment for costs and enforcement

After costs have been fixed by the court, or on failure of the defendant to file a timely notice of motion to tax costs, the clerk must immediately enter judgment for the costs. The judgment may be enforced in the same manner as a money judgment. *(Formerly Rule 870.4, adopted, eff. Jan. 1, 1987. Renumbered Rule 3.2000 and amended, eff. Jan. 1, 2007.)*

Research References

Rutter, Cal. Practice Guide: Civil Trials & Evidence Ch. 17-D, D. Costs.
Rutter, Cal. Practice Guide: Enforcing Judgments/Debts Ch. 6A-5, Amount Recoverable Under Judgment.
2 Witkin Cal. Proc. 5th Courts § 191, (S 191) Civil Rules.
8 Witkin Cal. Proc. 5th Enforcement of Judgment § 47, Memorandum of Costs.
7 Witkin Cal. Proc. 5th Judgment § 139, (S 139) in General.

Division 21

RULES FOR SMALL CLAIMS ACTIONS

Chapter 1

TRIAL RULES

Rule
3.2100.   Compliance with fictitious business name laws.
3.2102.   Substituted service.
3.2104.   Defendant's claim.
3.2106.   Venue challenge.
3.2107.   Request for court order.
3.2108.   Form of judgment.
3.2110.   Role of clerk in assisting small claims litigants.

Rule 3.2100.   Compliance with fictitious business name laws

(a) Filing of declaration of compliance

A claimant who is required to file a declaration of compliance with the fictitious business name laws under Code of Civil Procedure section 116.430 must file the declaration in each case filed.

(b) Available methods

The clerk must make the declaration of compliance available to the claimant in any one of the following ways:

(1) The declaration of compliance may be placed on a separate form approved by the Judicial Council;

(2) The approved Judicial Council form may be placed on the reverse of the Plaintiff's Statement to the Clerk or on the back of any Judicial Council small claims form with only one side; or

(3) The precise language of the declaration of compliance that appears on the approved Judicial Council form may be incorporated into the Plaintiff's Statement to the Clerk. *(Formerly Rule 1701, adopted, eff. Jan. 1, 1986. As amended, eff. July 1, 1991. Renumbered Rule 3.2100 and amended, eff. Jan. 1, 2007.)*

Research References

2 Witkin Cal. Proc. 5th Courts § 191, (S 191) Civil Rules.
2 Witkin Cal. Proc. 5th Courts § 269, (S 269) Judicial Council Rules and Forms.
2 Witkin Cal. Proc. 5th Courts § 293, Use of Fictitious Business Name.

Rule 3.2102.   Substituted service

If substituted service is authorized by Code of Civil Procedure section 116.340 or other provisions of law, no due diligence is required in a small claims court action. *(Formerly Rule 1702, adopted, eff. July 1, 1991. Renumbered Rule 3.2102, eff. Jan. 1, 2007.)*

Research References

2 Witkin Cal. Proc. 5th Courts § 294, (S 294) Notice to Appear.

Rule 3.2104.   Defendant's claim

A defendant may file a claim against the plaintiff even if the claim does not relate to the same subject or event as the plaintiff's claim, so long as the claim is within the jurisdictional limit of the small claims court. *(Formerly Rule 1703, adopted, eff. July 1, 1991. Renumbered Rule 3.2104, eff. Jan. 1, 2007.)*

Research References

2 Witkin Cal. Proc. 5th Courts § 295, Claim in Same Action.

Rule 3.2106.   Venue challenge

A defendant may challenge venue by writing to the court. The defendant is not required to personally appear at the hearing on the venue challenge. If the court denies the challenge and the defendant is not present, the hearing must be continued to another appropriate date. The parties must be given notice of the venue determination and hearing date. *(Formerly Rule 1704, adopted, eff. July 1, 1991. Renumbered Rule 3.2106 and amended, eff. Jan. 1, 2007.)*

Research References

2 Witkin Cal. Proc. 5th Courts § 291, (S 291) Venue, Location, and Sessions.

Rule 3.2107.   Request for court order

(a) Request before trial

If a party files a written request for a court order before the hearing on the claim, the requesting party must mail or personally deliver a copy to all other parties in the case. The other parties must be given an opportunity to answer or respond to the request before or at the hearing. This subdivision does not apply to a request to postpone the hearing date if the plaintiff's claim has not been served.

(b) Request after trial

If a party files a written request for a court order after notice of entry of judgment, the clerk must mail a copy of the request to all other parties in the action. A party has 10 calendar days from the date on which the clerk mailed the request to file a response before the court makes an order. The court may schedule a hearing on the request, except that if the request is to vacate the judgment for lack of appearance by the plaintiff, the court must hold a hearing. The court may give notice of any scheduled hearing with notice of the request, but the hearing must be scheduled at least 11 calendar days after the clerk has mailed the request. *(Adopted, eff. Jan. 1, 2007.)*

Rule 3.2108. Form of judgment

The court may give judgment for damages, equitable relief, or both, and may make other orders as the court deems just and equitable for the resolution of the dispute. If specific property is referred to in the judgment, whether it be personal or real, tangible or intangible, the property must be identified with sufficient detail to permit efficient implementation or enforcement of the judgment. *(Formerly Rule 1705, adopted, eff. July 1, 1991. Renumbered Rule 3.2108 and amended, eff. Jan. 1, 2007.)*

Research References

2 Witkin Cal. Proc. 5th Courts § 302, (S 302) in General.

Rule 3.2110. Role of clerk in assisting small claims litigants

(a) Provision of forms and pamphlets

The clerk must provide forms and pamphlets from the Judicial Council.

(b) Provision of Department of Consumer Affairs materials

The clerk must provide materials from the Department of Consumer Affairs when available.

(c) Information about small claims advisory service

The clerk must inform litigants of the small claims advisory service.

(d) Answering questions

The clerk may answer questions relative to filing and service of the claim, designation of the parties, scheduling of hearings, and similar matters. *(Formerly Rule 1706, adopted, eff. July 1, 1991. Renumbered Rule 3.2110 and amended, eff. Jan. 1, 2007.)*

Research References

2 Witkin Cal. Proc. 5th Courts § 191, (S 191) Civil Rules.

Chapter 2

SMALL CLAIMS ADVISORS

Rule
3.2120. Advisor assistance.

Rule 3.2120. Advisor assistance

(a) Notice to parties

The clerk must inform the parties, orally or in writing, about:

(1) The availability of advisors to assist small claims litigants at no additional charge as provided in Code of Civil Procedure sections 116.260 and 116.940; and

(2) The provisions of Government Code section 818.9.

(b) Training

All small claims advisors must receive training sufficient to ensure competence in the areas of:

(1) Small claims court practice and procedure;

(2) Alternative dispute resolution programs;

(3) Consumer sales;

(4) Vehicular sales, leasing, and repairs;

(5) Credit and financing transactions;

(6) Professional and occupational licensing;

(7) Landlord–tenant law; and

(8) Contract, warranty, tort, and negotiable instruments law.

It is the intent of this rule that the county must provide this training.

(c) Qualifications

In addition to the training required in subdivision (b), each county may establish additional qualifications for small claims advisors.

(d) Conflict of interest

A small claims advisor must disclose any known direct or indirect relationship the advisor may have with any party or witness in the action. An advisor must not disclose information obtained in the course of the advisor's duties or use the information for financial or other advantage. *(Formerly Rule 1725, adopted, eff. Jan. 1, 1986. As amended, eff. July 1, 1991. Renumbered Rule 3.2120 and amended, eff. Jan. 1, 2007.)*

Research References

2 Witkin Cal. Proc. 5th Courts § 191, (S 191) Civil Rules.
2 Witkin Cal. Proc. 5th Courts § 271, (S 271) Small Claims Legal Advisers.

Title 4

CRIMINAL RULES

[**Editor's Note:** For Title Four Rules, consult *California Rules of Court* pamphlet.]

Division 2

PRETRIAL

Chapter 1

PRETRIAL PROCEEDINGS

Rule

4.104.   Procedures and eligibility criteria for attending traffic violator school.

Rule 4.104.   Procedures and eligibility criteria for attending traffic violator school

(a) Purpose

The purpose of this rule is to establish uniform statewide procedures and criteria for eligibility to attend traffic violator school.

(b) Authority of a court clerk to grant a request to attend traffic violator school

(1) *Eligible offenses*

Except as provided in (2), a court clerk is authorized to grant a request to attend traffic violator school when a defendant with a valid driver's license requests to attend an 8–hour traffic violator school under Vehicle Code sections 41501(a) and 42005 for any infraction under divisions 11 and 12 (rules of the road and equipment violations) of the Vehicle Code if the violation is reportable to the Department of Motor Vehicles.

(2) *Ineligible offenses*

A court clerk is not authorized to grant a request to attend traffic violator school for a misdemeanor or any of the following infractions:

(A) A violation that carries a negligent operator point count of more than one point under Vehicle Code section 12810 or one and one-half points or more under Vehicle Code section 12810.5(b)(2);

(B) A violation that occurs within 18 months after the date of a previous violation and the defendant either attended or elected to attend a traffic violator school for the previous violation (Veh. Code, §§ 1808.7 and 1808.10);

(C) A violation of Vehicle Code section 22406.5 (tank vehicles);

(D) A violation related to alcohol use or possession or drug use or possession;

(E) A violation on which the defendant failed to appear under Vehicle Code section 40508(a) unless the failure-to-appear charge has been adjudicated and any fine imposed has been paid;

(F) A violation on which the defendant has failed to appear under Penal Code section 1214.1 unless the civil monetary assessment has been paid;

(G) A speeding violation in which the speed alleged is more than 25 miles over a speed limit as stated in Chapter 7 (commencing with section 22348) of Division 11 of the Vehicle Code; and

(H) A violation that occurs in a commercial vehicle as defined in Vehicle Code section 15210(b).

(c) Judicial discretion

(1) A judicial officer may in his or her discretion order attendance at a traffic violator school in an individual case as permitted under Vehicle Code section 41501(a) or 42005 or for any other purpose permitted by law. A defendant having a class A, class B, or commercial class C driver's license ~~or~~ may request to attend traffic violator school if the defendant was operating a vehicle requiring only a noncommercial class C or class M license. The record of conviction after completion of traffic violator school by a driver who holds a class A, class B, or commercial class C license must not be reported as confidential. A defendant charged with a violation that occurs in a commercial vehicle, as defined in Vehicle Code section 15210(b), is not eligible to attend traffic violator school under Vehicle Code sections 41501 or 42005 in lieu of adjudicating an offense, to receive a confidential conviction, or to avoid violator point counts.

(2) A defendant who is otherwise eligible for traffic violator school is not made ineligible by entering a plea other than guilty or by exercising his or her right to trial. A traffic violator school request must be considered based on the individual circumstances of the specific case. The court is not required to state on the record a reason for granting or denying a traffic violator school request. *(Formerly Rule 851, adopted, eff. Jan. 1, 1997. As amended, eff. Jan. 1, 1998; July 1, 2001; Jan. 1, 2003; Sept. 20, 2005. Renumbered Rule 4.104 and amended, eff. Jan. 1, 2007. As amended, eff. July 1, 2011; Jan. 1, 2013.)*

Advisory Committee Comment

Subdivision (c)(1). Rule 4.104(c)(1) reflects that under Vehicle Code sections 1808.10, 41501, and 42005, the record of a driver with a class A, class B, or commercial class C license who completes a traffic violator school program is not confidential and must be reported to and disclosed by the Department of Motor Vehicles for purposes of Title 49 of the Federal Code of Regulations and to insurers for underwriting and rating purposes.

Subdivision (c)(2). Rule 4.104(c)(2) reflects court rulings in cases where defendants wished to plead not guilty and have the court order attendance of traffic violator school if found guilty after trial. A court has discretion to grant or not grant traffic violator school. (*People v. Schindler* (1993) 20 Cal.App.4th 431, 433; *People v. Levinson* (1984) 155 Cal.App.3d Supp. 13, 21.) However, the court may not arbitrarily refuse to consider a request for traffic violator school because a defendant pleads not guilty. (*Schindler*, supra, at p. 433; *People v. Wozniak* (1987) 197 Cal.App.3d Supp. 43, 44; *People v. Enochs* (1976) 62 Cal.App.3d Supp. 42, 44.) If a judicial officer believes that a defendant's circumstances indicate that a defendant would benefit from attending school, such attendance should be authorized and should not be affected by the order in which the plea, explanation, and request for traffic violator school are presented. (*Enochs*, supra, at p. 44.) A court is not required to state its reasons for granting or denying traffic violator school following a defendant's conviction for a traffic violation. (*Schindler*, supra, at p. 433.)

Division 3

TRIALS

Rule 4.210.   Traffic court—trial by written declaration

(a) Applicability

This rule establishes the minimum procedural requirements for trials by written declaration under Vehicle Code section 40902. The procedures established by this rule must be followed in all trials by written declaration under that section.

(b) Procedure

(1) *Definition of due date*

As used in this subdivision, "due date" means the last date on which the defendant's appearance is timely.

(2) *Extending due date*

If the clerk receives the defendant's written request for a trial by written declaration by the appearance date indicated on the *Notice to Appear*, the clerk must, within 15 calendar days after receiving the defendant's written request, extend the appearance date 25 calendar days and must give or mail notice to the defendant of the extended due date on the *Request for Trial by Written Declaration* (form TR–205) with a copy of the *Instructions to Defendant* (form TR–200) and any other required forms.

(3) *Election*

The defendant must file a *Request for Trial by Written Declaration* (form TR–205) with the clerk by the appearance date indicated on the *Notice to Appear* or the extended due date as provided in (2). The *Request for Trial by Written Declaration* (form TR–205) must be filed in addition to the defendant's written request for a trial by written declaration, unless the defendant's request was made on the election form.

(4) *Bail*

The defendant must deposit bail with the clerk by the appearance date indicated on the *Notice to Appear* or the extended due date as provided in (2).

(5) *Instructions to arresting officer*

If the clerk receives the defendant's *Request for Trial by Written Declaration* (form TR–205) and bail by the due date, the clerk must deliver or mail to the arresting officer's agency *Notice and Instructions to Arresting Officer* (form TR–210) and *Officer's Declaration* (form TR–235) with a copy of the *Notice to Appear* and a specified return date for receiving the officer's declaration. After receipt of the officer's declaration, or at the close of the officer's return date if no officer's declaration is filed, the clerk must submit the case file with all declarations and other evidence received to the court for decision.

(6) *Court decision*

After the court decides the case and returns the file and decision, the clerk must immediately deliver or mail the *Decision and Notice of Decision* (form TR–215) to the defendant and the arresting agency.

(7) *Trial de novo*

If the defendant files a *Request for New Trial (Trial de Novo)* (form TR–220) within 20 calendar days after the date of delivery or mailing of the *Decision and Notice of Decision* (form TR–215), the clerk must set a trial date within 45 calendar days of receipt of the defendant's written request for a new trial. The clerk must deliver or mail to the defendant and to the arresting officer's agency the *Order and Notice to Defendant of New Trial (Trial de Novo)* (form TR–225). If the defendant's request is not timely received, no new trial may be held and the case must be closed.

(8) *Case and time standard*

The clerk must deliver or mail the *Decision and Notice of Decision* (form TR–215) within 90 calendar days after the due date. Acts for which no specific time is stated in this rule must be performed promptly so that the *Decision and Notice of Decision* can be timely delivered or mailed by the clerk. Failure of the clerk or the court to comply with any time limit does not void or invalidate the decision of the court, unless prejudice to the defendant is shown.

(c) Due dates and time limits

Due dates and time limits must be as stated in this rule, unless changed or extended by the court. The court may extend any date, but the court need not state the reasons for granting or denying an extension on the record or in the minutes.

(d) Ineligible defendants

If the defendant requests a trial by written declaration and the clerk or the court determines that the defendant is not eligible for a trial by written declaration, the clerk must extend the due date 25 calendar days and notify the defendant by mail of the determination and due date.

(e) Noncompliance

If the defendant does not comply with this rule (including submitting the required bail amount, signing and filing all required forms, and complying with all time limits and due dates), the court may deny a trial by written declaration and may proceed as otherwise provided by statute and court rules.

(f) Evidence

Testimony and other relevant evidence may be introduced in the form of a *Notice to Appear* issued under Vehicle Code section 40500; a business record or receipt; a sworn declaration of the arresting officer; and, on behalf of the defendant, a sworn declaration of the defendant.

(g) Fines, assessments, or penalties

The statute and the rules do not prevent or preclude the court from imposing on a defendant who is found guilty any lawful fine, assessment, or other penalty, and the court is not limited to imposing money penalties in the bail amount, unless the bail amount is the maximum and the only lawful penalty.

(h) Additional forms and procedures

The clerk may approve and prescribe forms, time limits, and procedures that are not in conflict with or not inconsistent with the statute or this rule.

(i) Forms

The following forms are to be used to implement the procedures under this rule:

(1) *Instructions to Defendant* (form TR–200)

(2) *Request for Trial by Written Declaration* (form TR–205)

(3) *Notice and Instructions to Arresting Officer* (form TR–210)

(4) *Officer's Declaration* (form TR–235)

(5) *Decision and Notice of Decision* (form TR–215)

(6) *Request for New Trial (Trial de Novo)* (form TR–220)

(7) *Order and Notice to Defendant of New Trial (Trial de Novo)* (form TR–225)

(j) Local forms

A court may adopt additional forms as may be required to implement this rule and the court's local procedures not inconsistent with this rule. *(Formerly Rule 828, adopted, eff. Jan. 1, 1999. As amended, eff. Jan. 1, 2000; July 1, 2000. Renumbered Rule 4.210 and amended, eff. Jan. 1. 2007.)*

Research References

2 Witkin Cal. Proc. 5th Courts § 192, (S 192) Criminal Rules.

Rule 4.220. Remote Video Proceedings in Traffic Infraction Cases

(a) Authorization for pilot project

(1) With the approval of the Judicial Council, a superior court may establish by local rule a pilot project through December 31, 2015, to permit arraignments, trials, and related proceedings concerning the traffic infractions specified in (b) to be conducted by two-way remote video communication methods under the conditions stated below.

(2) To obtain approval of the Judicial Council to conduct a pilot project for remote video proceedings under this rule, a court must submit an application to the council that includes details on what procedures and forms the court intends to institute for processing cases in the pilot project.

(b) Definitions

For the purposes of this rule:

(1) "Infraction" means any alleged infraction involving a violation of the Vehicle Code or any local ordinance adopted under the Vehicle Code, other than an infraction cited under article 2 (commencing with section 23152) of chapter 12 of division 11 of the Vehicle Code, except that the procedures for remote video trials authorized by this rule do not apply to any case in which an informal juvenile and traffic court exercises jurisdiction over a violation under sections 255 and 256 of the Welfare and Institutions Code.

(2) "Remote video proceeding" means an arraignment, trial, or related proceeding conducted by two-way electronic audiovisual communication between the defendant, any witnesses, and the court in lieu of the physical presence of both the defendant and any witnesses in the courtroom.

(3) "Due date" means the last date on which the defendant's appearance is timely under this rule.

(c) Application

This rule establishes the minimum procedural requirements and options for courts that conduct a pilot project for remote video proceedings for cases in which a defendant is charged with an infraction as defined in (b) and the defendant's request to proceed according to this rule is for a trial or related proceeding that is set for a date after January 31, 2013.

(d) Designation of locations and presence of court clerk

(1) The court must designate the location or locations at which defendants may appear with any witnesses for a remote video proceeding in traffic infraction cases.

(2) The locations must be in a public place, and the remote video proceedings must be viewable by the public at the remote location as well as at the courthouse.

(3) A court clerk must be present at the remote location for all remote video proceedings.

(e) Scope of court pilot project and request by defendant

The following procedures and required forms in this section must be included in the court's pilot project for remote video proceedings. In addition to following the standard provisions for processing traffic infraction cases, the defendant may request to proceed by remote video proceeding as provided below.

(1) *Arraignment and trial on the same date*

The following procedures apply to a remote video proceeding when the court grants a defendant's request to have an arraignment and trial on the same date:

(A) The defendant must review a copy of the *Instructions to Defendant for Remote Video Proceeding* (form TR–500–INFO).

(B) To proceed by remote video arraignment and trial, the defendant must sign and file a *Notice and Waiver of Rights and Request for Remote Video Arraignment and Trial* (form TR–505) with the clerk by the appearance date indicated on the *Notice to Appear* or a continuation of that date granted by the court and must deposit bail when filing the form.

(C) A defendant who is dissatisfied with the judgment in a remote video trial may appeal the judgment under rules 8.901–8.902.

(2) *Arraignment on a date that is separate from a trial date*

The following procedures apply to a remote video proceeding when the court grants a defendant's request to have an arraignment that is set for a date that is separate from the trial date:

(A) The defendant must review a copy of the *Instructions to Defendant for Remote Video Proceeding* (form TR–500–INFO).

(B) To proceed by remote video arraignment on a date that is separate from a trial date, the defendant must sign and file a *Notice and Waiver of Rights and Request for Remote Video Proceeding* (form TR–510) with the clerk by the appearance date indicated on the *Notice to Appear* or a continuation of that date granted by the court.

(3) *Trial on a date that is separate from the date of arraignment*

The following procedures apply to a remote video proceeding when the court grants a defendant's request at arraignment to have a trial set for a date that is separate from the date of the arraignment:

(A) The defendant must review a copy of the *Instructions to Defendant for Remote Video Proceeding* (form TR–500–INFO).

(B) To proceed by remote video trial, the defendant must sign and file a *Notice and Waiver of Rights and Request for Remote Video Proceeding* (form TR–510) with the clerk by the appearance date indicated on the *Notice to Appear* or a continuation of that date granted by the court and deposit bail with the form as required by the court.

(C) A defendant who is dissatisfied with the judgment in a remote video trial may appeal the judgment under rules 8.901–8.902.

(4) *Judicial Council forms for remote video proceedings*

The following forms must be made available by the court and used by the defendant to implement the procedures that are required by a court's pilot project under this rule:

(A) *Instructions to Defendant for Remote Video Proceeding* (form TR–500–INFO);

(B) *Notice and Waiver of Rights and Request for Remote Video Arraignment and Trial* (form TR–505); and

(C) *Notice and Waiver of Rights and Request for Remote Video Proceeding* (form TR–510).

(f) Deposit of bail

(1) If a defendant requests to proceed by remote video arraignment and trial as provided in section (e)(1), the defendant must deposit bail, at the same time the request is filed, in

Ct. Rules

the amount established in the uniform traffic penalty schedule under Vehicle Code section 40310.

(2) If a defendant requests to proceed by remote video proceeding for a trial as provided in section (e)(3), the judicial officer may require deposit of bail, at the same time the request for remote video proceeding is filed, in the amount established in the uniform traffic penalty schedule under Vehicle Code section 40310.

(g) Appearance of witnesses

On receipt of the defendant's waiver of rights and request to appear for trial as specified in section (e)(1) or (e)(3), the court may permit law enforcement officers and other witnesses to testify at the remote location or in court and be cross-examined by the defendant from the remote location.

(h) Authority of court to require physical presence of defendant and witnesses

Nothing in this rule is intended to limit the authority of the court to issue an order requiring the defendant or any witnesses to be physically present in the courtroom in any proceeding or portion of a proceeding if the court finds that circumstances require the physical presence of the defendant or witness in the courtroom.

(i) Extending due date for remote video trial

If the clerk receives the defendant's written request for a remote video arraignment and trial on form TR–505 or remote video trial on form TR–510 by the appearance date indicated on the *Notice to Appear* and the request is granted, the clerk must, within 10 court days after receiving the defendant's request, extend the appearance date by 25 calendar days and must provide notice to the defendant of the extended due date on the *Notice and Waiver of Rights and Request for Remote Video Arraignment and Trial* (form TR–505) or *Notice and Waiver of Rights and Request for Remote Video Proceeding* (form TR–510) with a copy of any required local forms.

(j) Notice to arresting officer

If a court grants the defendant's request for a remote video proceeding after receipt of the defendant's *Notice and Waiver of Rights and Request for Remote Video Arraignment and Trial* (form TR–505) or *Notice and Waiver of Rights and Request for Remote Video Proceeding* (form TR–510) and bail deposit, if required, the clerk must deliver, mail, or e-mail a notice of the remote video proceedings to the arresting or citing law enforcement officer. The notice to the officer must specify the location and date for the remote video proceeding and provide an option for the officer to request at least five calendar days before the appearance date to appear in court instead of at the remote location.

(k) Due dates and time limits

Due dates and time limits must be as stated in this rule, unless extended by the court. The court may extend any date, and the court need not state the reasons for granting or denying an extension on the record or in the minutes.

(*l*) Ineligible defendants

If the defendant requests a remote video proceeding and the court determines that the defendant is ineligible, the clerk must extend the due date by 25 calendar days and notify the defendant of the determination and the new due date.

(m) Noncompliance

If the defendant fails to comply with this rule (including depositing the bail amount, signing and filing all required forms, and complying with all time limits and due dates), the court may deny a request for a remote video proceeding and may proceed as otherwise provided by statute.

(n) Fines, assessments, or penalties

This rule does not prevent or preclude the court from imposing on a defendant who is found guilty any lawful fine, assessment, or other penalty, and the court is not limited to imposing money penalties in the bail amount, unless the bail amount is the maximum and the only lawful penalty.

(*o*) Local rules and forms

A court establishing a remote video trial project under this rule may adopt such local rules and additional forms as may be necessary or appropriate to implement the rule and the court's local procedures not inconsistent with this rule.

(p) Collection of information and reports on pilot project

Each court that establishes a pilot project under this rule must institute procedures as required by the Judicial Council for collecting and evaluating information about that court's pilot project and must prepare semiannual reports to the Judicial Council that include an assessment of the costs and benefits of the project.

(q) Effective dates

This rule is adopted effective February 1, 2013, and remains in effect only until January 1, 2016, and as of that date is repealed, unless a rule adopted before January 1, 2016, repeals or extends that date. *(Adopted, eff. Feb. 1, 2013.)*

Repeal

For repeal of this rule, see its terms.

Title 7

PROBATE RULES

Chapter 1

GENERAL PROVISIONS

Rule 7.1. Probate Rules

The rules in this title may be referred to as the Probate Rules. *(Adopted, eff. Jan. 1, 2007.)*

Research References

2 Witkin Cal. Proc. 5th Courts § 194, (S 194) Probate Rules.
13 Witkin, California Summary 10th Trusts § 226, (S 226) in General.
14 Witkin, California Summary 10th Wills and Probate § 4, Probate Rules.
14 Witkin, California Summary 10th Wills and Probate § 372, Probate Rules.
14 Witkin, California Summary 10th Wills and Probate § 960, Governing Law.

Rule 7.2.   Preliminary provisions

(a)   Application of rules

The rules in this title apply to every action and proceeding to which the Probate Code applies and, unless they are elsewhere explicitly made applicable, do not apply to any other action or proceeding.

(b)   Purpose of rules

The rules in this title are designed to implement the purposes of the probate law by promoting uniformity in practice and procedure.

(c)   Rules of construction

Unless the context otherwise requires, these preliminary provisions and the following rules of construction govern the construction of the rules in this title:

(1) To the extent that the rules in this title are substantially the same as existing statutory provisions relating to the same subject matter, they must be construed as a restatement and a continuation of those statutes; and

(2) To the extent that the rules in this title may add to existing statutory provisions relating to the same subject matter, they must be construed so as to implement the purposes of the probate law.

(d)   Jurisdiction

The rules in this title are not intended to expand, limit, or restrict the jurisdiction of the court in proceedings under the Probate Code. *(Formerly Rule 7.1, adopted, eff. Jan. 1, 2000. As amended, eff. Jan. 1, 2003. Renumbered Rule 7.2 and amended, eff. Jan. 1, 2007.)*

Research References

14 Witkin, California Summary 10th Wills and Probate § 372, Probate Rules.

14 Witkin, California Summary 10th Wills and Probate § 377, Amended and Supplemental Pleadings.

14 Witkin, California Summary 10th Wills and Probate § 385, in General.

Rule 7.3.   Definitions and use of terms

As used in the rules in this title, unless the context or subject matter otherwise requires:

(1) The definitions in division 1, part 2 of the Probate Code [1] apply.

(2) "Pleading" means a contest, answer, petition, application, objection, response, statement of interest, report, or account filed in proceedings under the Probate Code.

(3) "Amended pleading" means a pleading that completely restates and supersedes the pleading it amends for all purposes.

(4) "Amendment to a pleading" means a pleading that modifies another pleading and alleges facts or requests relief materially different from the facts alleged or the relief requested in the modified pleading. An amendment to a pleading does not restate or supersede the modified pleading but must be read together with that pleading.

(5) "Supplement to a pleading" and "supplement" mean a pleading that modifies another pleading but does not allege facts or request relief materially different from the facts alleged or the relief requested in the supplemented pleading. A supplement to a pleading may add information to or may correct omissions in the modified pleading. *(Formerly Rule 7.2, adopted, eff. Jan. 1, 2000. As amended, eff. Jan. 1, 2002; Jan. 1, 2003. Renumbered Rule 7.3 and amended, eff. Jan. 1, 2007.)*

[1] See Probate Code § 20 et seq.

Research References

14 Witkin, California Summary 10th Wills and Probate § 4, Probate Rules.

14 Witkin, California Summary 10th Wills and Probate § 372, Probate Rules.

14 Witkin, California Summary 10th Wills and Probate § 377, Amended and Supplemental Pleadings.

14 Witkin, California Summary 10th Wills and Probate § 385, in General.

Rule 7.4.   Waiver of rules in probate proceedings

The court for good cause may waive the application of the rules in this title in an individual case. *(Formerly Rule 7.3, adopted, eff. Jan. 1, 2000. As amended, eff. Jan. 1, 2003. Renumbered Rule 7.4, eff. Jan. 1, 2007.)*

Research References

14 Witkin, California Summary 10th Wills and Probate § 4, Probate Rules.

14 Witkin, California Summary 10th Wills and Probate § 372, Probate Rules.

Rule 7.10.   Ex parte communications in proceedings under the Probate Code and certain other proceedings

(a)   Definitions

As used in this rule, the following terms have the meanings stated below:

(1) "Fiduciary" has the meaning specified in Probate Code section 39, and includes LPS conservators.

(2) "Person" has the meaning specified in Probate Code section 56.

(3) "Pleading" has the meaning specified in rule 7.3, but also includes petitions and objections or other opposition filed in LPS conservatorships. The term does not include creditors' claims and requests for special notice.

(4) A "party" is a fiduciary appointed in a proceeding under the Probate Code or an LPS conservatorship proceeding, and any other person who has filed a pleading in the proceeding concerning a matter then pending in the court.

(5) A "ward" is a minor subject to a guardianship under Division 4 of the Probate Code, including a proposed ward concerning whom a petition for appointment of a guardian has been filed.

(6) "Ex parte communication" is a communication between any party, attorney, or person in a proceeding under the Probate Code or an LPS conservatorship proceeding and the court outside the presence of all parties and attorneys, including written communications sent to the court without copies having been provided to other interested persons.

(7) "LPS Act" is the Lanterman–Petris–Short Act, part 1 of division 5 of the Welfare and Institutions Code, commencing with section 5000.

(8) "LPS Conservatorship" is a conservatorship proceeding under chapter 3 of the LPS Act, commencing with section 5350 of the Welfare and Institutions Code, for persons gravely disabled as the result of a mental disorder or impairment by chronic alcoholism.

(9) A "conservatee" is a person subject to a conservatorship under division 4 of the Probate Code or chapter 3 of the LPS Act, including a proposed conservatee concerning whom a petition for appointment of a conservator has been filed.

(10) A "matter then pending in the court" in proceedings under the Probate Code or in an LPS conservatorship proceeding refers to a request for relief or opposition in pleadings filed

in the proceeding that has not yet been resolved by a decision of the court or an agreement of the parties.

(11) Concerning a proceeding under the Probate Code or an LPS conservatorship proceeding, the term "open proceeding" refers to a proceeding that has been commenced and has not been concluded by the final discharge of all fiduciaries or otherwise terminated as provided by law, whether or not there is a matter then pending in the court in the proceeding at any point in time.

(b) Ex parte communications by parties and attorneys prohibited

(1) Except under a stipulation of all parties to the contrary, no ex parte communications may be made by a party or an attorney for a party and the court concerning a matter then pending in the court in proceedings under the Probate Code or in an LPS conservatorship proceeding.

(2) Except as provided in (c)(1), the court must treat an ex parte communication to the court described in (1) in the same way that an ex parte communication from a party or attorney for a party must be treated in other civil actions or proceedings or in criminal actions.

(c) Ex parte communications received and considered

(1) Notwithstanding (b)(2), a judicial officer or court staff may receive an ex parte communication concerning an open proceeding under the Probate Code or an open LPS conservatorship proceeding for the limited purpose of ascertaining whether it is a communication described in (b) or a communication described in (c)(2).

(2) Subject to the requirements of (c)(3), a judicial officer may consider an ex parte communication from a person about a fiduciary's performance of his or her duties and responsibilities or regarding a conservatee or ward in an open proceeding under the Probate Code or an open LPS conservatorship proceeding. The court may decline to take further action on the communication, with or without replying to the person or returning any written communication received from the person. The court may also take appropriate action, consistent with due process and California law, including one or any combination of the following:

(A) Review the court file and take any action that is supported by the record, including ordering a status report or accounting if it appears that a status report or accounting should have been filed by a fiduciary but is delinquent.

(B) Refer the communication to a court investigator for further action, and receive, consider, and respond to any report from the investigator concerning it;

(C) If the communication discloses possible criminal activity, refer the matter to the appropriate law enforcement agency or prosecutor's office;

(D) If the communication discloses conduct that might subject a person or organization to disciplinary action on a license, refer the matter to the appropriate licensing agency;

(E) If the communication discloses possible elder or dependent adult abuse, or child abuse, refer the matter to appropriate state or local governmental agencies, including adult protective or child protective service departments; and

(F) Set a hearing regarding the communication, compel the fiduciary's attendance, and require a response from the fiduciary concerning the issues raised by the communication.

(3) The court must fully disclose communications described in (c)(2) and any response made by the court to the fiduciary and all other parties to any matter then pending in the court, and their attorneys, unless the court finds good cause to dispense with the disclosure if necessary to protect a conservatee or ward from harm. If the court dispenses with disclosure to any party or attorney, it must make written findings in support of its determination of good cause, and preserve the communication received and any response made by the court. The court may place its findings and the preserved communication under seal or otherwise secure their confidentiality. *(Adopted, eff. Jan. 1, 2008.)*

Research References

2 Witkin Cal. Proc. 5th Courts § 194, (S 194) Probate Rules.
14 Witkin, California Summary 10th Wills and Probate § 378, Hearings.

Chapter 2

NOTICES, PUBLICATION, AND SERVICE

Rule
7.50. Description of pleading in notice of hearing.
7.51. Service of notice of hearing.
7.52. Service of notice when recipient's address unknown.
7.53. Notice of hearing of amended or supplemented pleadings.
7.54. Publication of Notice of Petition to Administer Estate.
7.55. Ex parte application for order.

Rule 7.50. Description of pleading in notice of hearing

The notice of hearing on a pleading filed in a proceeding under the Probate Code must state the complete title of the pleading to which the notice relates. *(Adopted, eff. Jan. 1, 2003.)*

Research References

2 Witkin Cal. Proc. 5th Courts § 194, (S 194) Probate Rules.
14 Witkin, California Summary 10th Wills and Probate § 4, Probate Rules.
14 Witkin, California Summary 10th Wills and Probate § 386, General Form of Notice.

Rule 7.51. Service of notice of hearing

(a) Direct notice required

(1) Except as otherwise permitted in the Probate Code, a notice sent by mail under Probate Code section 1220 must be mailed individually and directly to the person entitled to notice.

(2) A notice mailed to a person in care of another person is insufficient unless the person entitled to notice is an adult and has directed the party giving notice in writing to send the notice in care of the second person.

(3) Notices mailed to more than one person in the same household must be sent separately to each person.

(b) Notice to attorney

If a notice is required or permitted to be given to a person who is represented by an attorney of record in the proceeding, the notice must be sent as required in Probate Code section 1214.

(c) Notice to guardian or conservator

(1) When a guardian or conservator has been appointed for a person entitled to notice, the notice must be sent to the guardian or conservator.

(2) A copy of the notice must also be sent to the ward or conservatee unless:

(A) The court dispenses with such notice; or

(B) Under Probate Code section 1210 in a decedent's estate proceeding, the notice is personally served on a California-resident guardian or conservator of the estate of the ward or conservatee.

(d) Notice to minor

Except as permitted in Probate Code section 1460.1 for guardianships, conservatorships, and certain protective proceedings under division 4 of the Probate Code, notice to a minor must be sent directly to the minor. A separate copy of the notice must be sent to the person or persons having legal custody of the minor, with whom the minor resides.

(e) Notice required in a decedent's estate when a beneficiary has died

(1) *Notice when a beneficiary dies after the decedent*

Notice must be sent to the personal representative of a beneficiary who died after the decedent and survived for a period required by the decedent's will. If no personal representative has been appointed for the postdeceased beneficiary, notice must be sent to his or her beneficiaries or other persons entitled to succeed to his or her interest in the decedent's estate.

(2) *Notice when a beneficiary of the decedent's will dies before the decedent*

When a beneficiary under the will of the decedent died before the decedent or fails to survive the decedent for a period required by the decedent's will, notice must be sent to the persons named in the decedent's will as substitute beneficiaries of the gift to the predeceased beneficiary. If the decedent's will does not make a substitute disposition of that gift, notice must be sent as follows:

(A) If the predeceased beneficiary is a "transferee" under Probate Code section 21110(c), to the issue of the predeceased beneficiary determined under Probate Code section 240 and to the residuary beneficiaries of the decedent or to the decedent's heirs if decedent's will does not provide for distribution of the residue of the estate.

(B) If the predeceased beneficiary is not a "transferee" under Probate Code section 21110(c), to the residuary beneficiaries of the decedent or to the decedent's heirs if decedent's will does not provide for distribution of the residue of the estate.

(Adopted, eff. Jan. 1, 2003. As amended, eff. Jan. 1, 2004.)

Research References

14 Witkin, California Summary 10th Wills and Probate § 388, (S 388) Heirs and Devisees.
14 Witkin, California Summary 10th Wills and Probate § 390, (S 390) Other Persons.
14 Witkin, California Summary 10th Wills and Probate § 392, (S 392) Manner of Mailing.
14 Witkin, California Summary 10th Wills and Probate § 910, General Notice Requirement.

Rule 7.52. Service of notice when recipient's address unknown

(a) Declaration of diligent search

Petitioner must file a declaration describing efforts made to locate a person entitled to notice in a proceeding under the Probate Code, but whose address is unknown, before the court will prescribe an alternate form of notice or dispense with notice under (c). The declaration must state the name of the person whose address is unknown, the last known address of the person, the approximate date when the person was last known to reside there, the efforts made to locate the person, and any facts that explain why the person's address cannot be obtained. The declaration must include a description of the attempts to learn of the person's business and residence addresses by:

(1) Inquiry of the relatives, friends, acquaintances, and employers of the person entitled to notice and of the person who is the subject of the proceeding;

(2) Review of appropriate city telephone directories and directory assistance; and

(3) Search of the real and personal property indexes in the recorder's and assessor's offices for the county where the person was last known or believed to reside.

(b) Mailed notice to county seat

Mailing notice to a person at a county seat is not a manner of giving notice reasonably calculated to give actual notice.

(c) The court may prescribe or dispense with notice

If a person entitled to notice cannot be located after diligent search, the court may prescribe the manner of giving notice to that person or may dispense with notice to that person. *(Adopted, eff. Jan. 1, 2003.)*

Research References

14 Witkin, California Summary 10th Wills and Probate § 391, (S 391) in General.

Rule 7.53. Notice of hearing of amended or supplemented pleadings

(a) Amended pleading and amendment to a pleading

An amended pleading or an amendment to a pleading requires the same notice of hearing (including publication) as the pleading it amends.

(b) Supplement to a pleading

A supplement to a pleading does not require additional notice of hearing, but a copy of a supplement to a pleading must be served if service of a copy of the pleading was required, unless waived by the court. *(Adopted, eff. Jan. 1, 2003.)*

Research References

14 Witkin, California Summary 10th Wills and Probate § 377, Amended and Supplemental Pleadings.
14 Witkin, California Summary 10th Wills and Probate § 385, in General.

Rule 7.54. Publication of *Notice of Petition to Administer Estate*

Publication and service of a *Notice of Petition to Administer Estate* (form DE–121) under Probate Code sections 8110–8125 is sufficient notice of any instrument offered for probate that is filed with, and specifically referred to in, the petition for which notice is given. Any other instrument must be presented in an amended petition, and a new notice must be published and served. *(Adopted, eff. Jan. 1, 2003. As amended, eff. Jan. 1, 2007.)*

Research References

14 Witkin, California Summary 10th Wills and Probate § 589, Publication of Notice.

Rule 7.55. Ex parte application for order

(a) Special notice allegation

An ex parte application for an order must allege whether special notice has been requested.

(b) Allegation if special notice requested

If special notice has been requested, the application must identify each person who has requested special notice and must allege that special notice has been given to or waived by each person who has requested it.

(c) Proof of service or waiver of special notice

Proofs of service of special notice or written waivers of special notice must be filed with the application. *(Adopted, eff. Jan. 1, 2003. As amended, eff. Jan. 1, 2007.)*

Research References

2 Witkin Cal. Proc. 5th Courts § 194, (S 194) Probate Rules.

14 Witkin, California Summary 10th Wills and Probate § 4, Probate Rules.

14 Witkin, California Summary 10th Wills and Probate § 395, (S 395) in General.

Chapter 3

PLEADINGS

Rule

7.101.   Use of Judicial Council forms.
7.102.   Titles of pleadings and orders.
7.103.   Signature and verification of pleadings.
7.104.   Execution and verification of amended pleadings, amendments to pleadings, and supplements to pleadings; use of Judicial Council forms.

Rule 7.101.   Use of Judicial Council forms

(a) Use of mandatory forms

If a petition, an order, or another document to be submitted to the court is one for which the Judicial Council has adopted a mandatory form, that form must be used. Except as provided in this rule, if the Judicial Council has adopted a mandatory form in more than one alternative version, one of the alternative versions must be used. If that form is inadequate in a particular situation, an addendum may be attached to it.

(b) Alternative mandatory forms

The following forms have been adopted by the Judicial Council as alternative mandatory forms for use in probate proceedings or other proceedings governed by provisions of the Probate Code:

(1) Petition for Appointment of Guardian of Minor (form GC–210) and Petition for Appointment of Guardian of the Person (form GC–210(P));

(2) *Petition for Appointment of Temporary Guardian* (form GC–110) and *Petition for Appointment of Temporary Guardian of the Person* (form GC–110(P));

(3) *Petition to Approve Compromise of Disputed Claim or Pending Action or Disposition of Proceeds of Judgment for Minor or Person With a Disability* (form MC–350) and *Expedited Petition to Approve Compromise of Disputed Claim or Pending Action or Disposition of Proceeds of Judgment for Minor or Person With a Disability* (form MC–350EX).

(c) Use of guardianship petitions

Notwithstanding any other provision of this rule, a party petitioning for appointment of a temporary guardian of the person of a minor may file either form GC–110 or form GC–110(P). A party petitioning for appointment of a general guardian of the person of a minor may file either form GC–210 or form GC–210(P). A party petitioning for appointment of a temporary guardian of the estate or the person and estate of a minor must file form GC–110. A party petitioning for appointment of a general guardian of the estate or the person and estate of a minor must file form GC–210. *(Adopted, eff. Jan. 1, 2001. As amended, eff. Jan. 1, 2002; Jan. 1, 2007; Jan. 1, 2010.)*

Research References

2 Witkin Cal. Proc. 5th Courts § 194, (S 194) Probate Rules.
13 Witkin, California Summary 10th Trusts § 226, (S 226) in General.
14 Witkin, California Summary 10th Wills and Probate § 4, Probate Rules.
14 Witkin, California Summary 10th Wills and Probate § 373, Judicial Council Forms.
14 Witkin, California Summary 10th Wills and Probate § 915, (S 915) Judicial Council Forms.

14 Witkin, California Summary 10th Wills and Probate § 919, (S 919) Content and Form.
14 Witkin, California Summary 10th Wills and Probate § 975, Appointment.

Rule 7.102.   Titles of pleadings and orders

The title of each pleading and of each proposed order must clearly and completely identify the nature of the relief sought or granted. *(Adopted, eff. Jan. 1, 2001. As amended, eff. Jan. 1, 2002; Jan. 1, 2003.)*

Research References

13 Witkin, California Summary 10th Trusts § 226, (S 226) in General.
14 Witkin, California Summary 10th Wills and Probate § 376, Petitions and Other Papers.

Rule 7.103.   Signature and verification of pleadings

(a) Signature of parties

A pleading must be in writing and must be signed by all persons joining in it.

(b) Verification by parties

All pleadings filed in proceedings under the Probate Code must be verified. If two or more persons join in a pleading, it may be verified by any of them.

(c) Signature and verification by attorney

If a person is absent from the county where his or her attorney's office is located, or for some other cause is unable to sign or verify a pleading, the attorney may sign or verify it, unless the person is, or is seeking to become, a fiduciary appointed in the proceeding. *(Adopted, eff. Jan. 1, 2003.)*

Research References

14 Witkin, California Summary 10th Wills and Probate § 376, Petitions and Other Papers.

Rule 7.104.   Execution and verification of amended pleadings, amendments to pleadings, and supplements to pleadings; use of Judicial Council forms

(a) Amended pleading and amendment to a pleading

(1) All persons required to sign a pleading must sign an amended pleading. One of the persons required to verify a pleading must verify an amended pleading.

(2) All persons required to sign a pleading must sign an amendment to that pleading. One of the persons required to verify a pleading must verify an amendment to that pleading.

(3) A Judicial Council form must be used for an amended pleading, with the word "Amended" added to its caption, if the form was used for the pleading that is amended. A Judicial Council form must not be used for an amendment to a pleading.

(b) Supplement to a pleading

(1) A supplement to a pleading must be signed and verified by one of the persons who were required to sign and verify the pleading that is supplemented. However, the court may, in the exercise of its discretion, accept for filing and consider a supplement to a pleading signed under penalty of perjury by an attorney for the party offering it, where the information contained in the supplement is particularly within the knowledge of the attorney.

(2) A Judicial Council form must not be used for a supplement to a pleading. *(Adopted, eff. Jan. 1, 2003.)*

Research References

2 Witkin Cal. Proc. 5th Courts § 194, (S 194) Probate Rules.
14 Witkin, California Summary 10th Wills and Probate § 4, Probate Rules.

14 Witkin, California Summary 10th Wills and Probate § 376, Petitions and Other Papers.

14 Witkin, California Summary 10th Wills and Probate § 377, Amended and Supplemental Pleadings.

Chapter 4

APPOINTMENT OF EXECUTORS AND ADMINISTRATORS

Rule

7.150.   Acknowledgment of receipt of statement of duties and liabilities of personal representative.

7.151.   Reimbursement of graduated filing fee by successful subsequent petitioner.

Rule 7.150.   Acknowledgment of receipt of statement of duties and liabilities of personal representative

Before the court issues letters, each personal representative of a decedent's estate (other than a company authorized to conduct a trust business in California) must execute and file an acknowledgment of receipt of *Duties and Liabilities of Personal Representative* (form DE–147).   (*Adopted, eff. Jan. 1, 2000.   As amended, eff. Jan. 1, 2002; Jan. 1, 2007.*)

Research References

2 Witkin Cal. Proc. 5th Courts § 194, (S 194) Probate Rules.

14 Witkin, California Summary 10th Wills and Probate § 4, Probate Rules.

14 Witkin, California Summary 10th Wills and Probate § 447, (S 447) Statement of Duties and Liabilities.

Rule 7.151.   Reimbursement of graduated filing fee by successful subsequent petitioner

(a)   Duty to reimburse

In decedents' estates commenced on or after August 18, 2003, and before January 1, 2008, a general personal representative appointed on a *Petition for Probate* (form DE–111) that was not the first-filed petition for appointment of a general personal representative in the proceeding must reimburse the unsuccessful petitioner on the first-filed petition for a portion of the filing fee paid by the unsuccessful petitioner.

(b)   Amount of reimbursement

The reimbursement required under this rule is in the amount of:

(1)   The filing fee paid by the unsuccessful petitioner in excess of the filing fee that would have been payable on that date for a *Petition for Probate* filed to commence administration of an estate valued at less than $250,000, less

(2)   The unpaid amount of any costs or sanctions awarded against the unsuccessful petitioner in favor of the party that sought the personal representative's appointment in the proceeding.

(c)   When reimbursement payable

The personal representative must make the reimbursement payment required under this rule in cash and in full no later than the date the *Inventory and Appraisal* (form DE–160/GC–040) is due under Probate Code section 8800(b), including additional time allowed by the court under that provision.

(d)   Payment from estate funds

The reimbursement payment under this rule is an authorized expense of administration and may be made from estate funds without a prior court order.

(e)   Receipt from unsuccessful petitioner

The unsuccessful petitioner must give a signed receipt for the reimbursement payment made under this rule.

(f)   Personal representative's right to claim refund

A personal representative that is required to but fails to make the reimbursement payment under this rule may not claim a refund of the difference between the estimated filing fee and the corrected filing fee under rule 7.552(c).

(g)   Petitioner on dismissed *Petition for Probate*

A petitioner that is eligible to receive a refund of filing fee for a dismissed *Petition for Probate* under rule 7.552(d) is not an unsuccessful petitioner within the meaning of this rule.   (*Adopted, eff. Jan. 1, 2004.   As amended, eff. Jan. 1, 2007; March 1, 2008.*)

Research References

2 Witkin Cal. Proc. 5th Courts § 194, (S 194) Probate Rules.

14 Witkin, California Summary 10th Wills and Probate § 4, Probate Rules.

14 Witkin, California Summary 10th Wills and Probate § 585, Filing Fee.

Chapter 5

BONDING OF PERSONAL REPRESENTATIVES, GUARDIANS, CONSERVATORS, AND TRUSTEES

Rule

7.201.   Waiver of bond in will.

7.202.   Two or more personal representatives.

7.203.   Separate bonds for individuals.

7.204.   Duty to apply for order increasing bond.

7.205.   Independent power to sell real property.

7.206.   Bond upon sale of real property.

7.207.   Bonds of conservators and guardians.

Rule 7.201.   Waiver of bond in will

(a)   Statement of waiver in petition

If the will waives bond, the Petition for Probate must so state.

(b)   Court's discretion to require bond

The court may require bond if the proposed personal representative resides outside California or for other good cause, even if the will waives bond.   (*Adopted, eff. Jan. 1, 2000.   As amended, eff. Jan. 1, 2001; Jan. 1, 2002; Jan. 1, 2007.*)

Research References

2 Witkin Cal. Proc. 5th Courts § 194, (S 194) Probate Rules.

13 Witkin, California Summary 10th Trusts § 226, (S 226) in General.

14 Witkin, California Summary 10th Wills and Probate § 4, Probate Rules.

14 Witkin, California Summary 10th Wills and Probate § 450, Waiver.

14 Witkin, California Summary 10th Wills and Probate § 960, Governing Law.

Rule 7.202.   Two or more personal representatives

If a will admitted to probate names two or more persons to serve as executors but not all serve and the will does not expressly waive bond if fewer than all of the named persons serve, the court must require each executor to give a bond unless the court waives this requirement under Probate Code section 8481(a)(2).   (*Adopted, eff. Jan. 1, 2000.   As amended, eff. Jan. 1, 2002.*)

Research References

14 Witkin, California Summary 10th Wills and Probate § 448, in General.

Rule 7.203. Separate bonds for individuals

Because a corporate fiduciary (whether personal representative, guardian, conservator, or trustee) cannot assume responsibility for the acts of an individual cofiduciary, an individual cofiduciary who is required to give a bond must provide a separate bond, except to the extent that the court orders the assets to be held solely by the corporate cofiduciary. *(Adopted, eff. Jan. 1, 2000. As amended, eff. Jan. 1, 2002.)*

Research References

13 Witkin, California Summary 10th Trusts § 48, (S 48) Bond.

14 Witkin, California Summary 10th Wills and Probate § 448, in General.

14 Witkin, California Summary 10th Wills and Probate § 983, Requirement.

Rule 7.204. Duty to apply for order increasing bond

(a) Ex parte application for order

Immediately upon the occurrence of facts making it necessary or appropriate to increase the amount of the bond, the personal representative, or the guardian or conservator of the estate, must make an ex parte application for an order increasing the bond.

(b) Attorney's duty

If the personal representative, or the guardian or conservator of the estate, has not already made application under (a), the attorney for the personal representative, or the attorney for the guardian or conservator of the estate, must make the ex parte application immediately upon becoming aware of the need to increase bond.

(c) Amount

(1) The application by a personal representative under (a) or by the attorney for a personal representative under (b) must show the value of the estate's personal property and the probable annual gross income of the estate.

(2) The application by a guardian or conservator of the estate under (a) or by the attorney for a guardian or conservator of the estate under (b) must show the value of the estate's personal property, the probable annual gross income of all of the property of the estate, and the sum of the probable annual gross payments of the public benefits of the ward or conservatee identified in Probate Code section 2320(c)(3).

(3) If the personal representative has full Independent Administration of Estates Act (IAEA) [1] authority or the guardian or conservator of the estate has authority to sell estate real property without court confirmation, the application must also show the amount of the equity in estate real property. *(Adopted, eff. Jan. 1, 2000. As amended, eff. Jan. 1, 2002; Jan. 1, 2003.)*

[1] See Probate Code § 10400 et seq.

Research References

14 Witkin, California Summary 10th Wills and Probate § 449, Amount.

14 Witkin, California Summary 10th Wills and Probate § 592, Requirement of Inventory and Appraisal.

14 Witkin, California Summary 10th Wills and Probate § 985, Amount of Bond.

14 Witkin, California Summary 10th Wills and Probate § 1033, (S 1033) in General.

Rule 7.205. Independent power to sell real property

If the personal representative requests or has been granted an independent power to sell or hypothecate real estate or to lease it for a term of more than one year, the personal representative

must state in the request to fix the amount of the bond the value of the real property less encumbrances. *(Adopted, eff. Jan. 1, 2000. As amended, eff. Jan. 1, 2002.)*

Research References

14 Witkin, California Summary 10th Wills and Probate § 449, Amount.

Rule 7.206. Bond upon sale of real property

If a bond or additional bond is required in an order confirming sale of real estate, the court must not file the order until the additional bond is filed. *(Adopted, eff. Jan. 1, 2000. As amended, eff. Jan. 1, 2002.)*

Research References

14 Witkin, California Summary 10th Wills and Probate § 4, Probate Rules.

14 Witkin, California Summary 10th Wills and Probate § 449, Amount.

Rule 7.207. Bonds of conservators and guardians

(a) Bond includes reasonable amount for recovery on the bond

Except as otherwise provided by statute, every conservator or guardian of the estate must furnish a bond that includes an amount determined under (b) as a reasonable amount for the cost of recovery to collect on the bond under Probate Code section 2320(c)(4).

(b) Amount of bond for the cost of recovery on the bond

The reasonable amount of bond for the cost of recovery to collect on the bond, including attorney's fees and costs, under Probate Code section 2320(c)(4) is:

(1) Ten percent (10%) of the value up to and including $500,000 of the following:

(A) The value of personal property of the estate;

(B) The value, less encumbrances, of real property of the estate that the guardian or conservator has the independent power to sell without approval or confirmation of the court under Probate Code sections 2590 and 2591(d);

(C) The probable annual income from all assets of the estate; and

(D) The probable annual gross payments described in Probate Code section 2320(c)(3); and

(2) Twelve percent (12%) of the value above $500,000 up to and including $1,000,000 of the property, income, and payments described in (1); and

(3) Two percent (2%) of the value above $1,000,000 of the property, income, and payments described in (1). *(Adopted, eff. Jan. 1, 2008. As amended, eff. Jan. 1, 2010.)*

Research References

2 Witkin Cal. Proc. 5th Courts § 194, (S 194) Probate Rules.

14 Witkin, California Summary 10th Wills and Probate § 985, Amount of Bond.

Chapter 6

INDEPENDENT ADMINISTRATION
OF ESTATES

Rule

7.250. Report of actions taken under the Independent Administration of Estates Act.

Rule 7.250. Report of actions taken under the Independent Administration of Estates Act [1]

(a) Report required

In any accounting, report, petition for preliminary distribution, or petition for final distribution, the petitioner must list and describe all actions taken without prior court approval under the Independent Administration of Estates Act (IAEA) if notice of the proposed action was required. The description of the action must include the following:

(1) The nature of the action;

(2) When the action was taken;

(3) A statement of when and to whom notice was given;

(4) Whether notice was waived, and if so, by whom; and

(5) Whether any objections were received.

(b) Actions reported in previous reports

An action taken under the IAEA that was (1) properly listed and described in a prior accounting, report, or petition for distribution, and (2) approved by the court, need not be listed and described in a subsequent account, report, or petition for distribution. *(Adopted, eff. Jan. 1, 2000. As amended, eff. Jan. 1, 2002; Jan. 1, 2007.)*

[1] See Probate Code § 10400 et seq.

Research References

2 Witkin Cal. Proc. 5th Courts § 194, (S 194) Probate Rules.
14 Witkin, California Summary 10th Wills and Probate § 4, Probate Rules.
14 Witkin, California Summary 10th Wills and Probate § 384, Petition or Report.
14 Witkin, California Summary 10th Wills and Probate § 730, Distribution Under Independent Administration of Estates Act.
14 Witkin, California Summary 10th Wills and Probate § 731, in General.

Chapter 7

SPOUSAL OR DOMESTIC PARTNER PROPERTY PETITIONS

Rule
7.301. Spousal or domestic partner property petition filed with petition for probate.

Rule 7.301. Spousal or domestic partner property petition filed with petition for probate

A petition for spousal or domestic partner property determination or confirmation must be filed separately from a petition for probate of will or for letters of administration, even if both petitions are filed at the same time. The two petitions must be filed under the same case number. *(Adopted, eff. Jan. 1, 2000. As amended, eff. Jan. 1, 2002; Jan. 1, 2007.)*

Research References

2 Witkin Cal. Proc. 5th Courts § 194, (S 194) Probate Rules.
14 Witkin, California Summary 10th Wills and Probate § 4, Probate Rules.
14 Witkin, California Summary 10th Wills and Probate § 829, Nature of Proceeding.

Chapter 9

CREDITORS' CLAIMS

Rule
7.401. Personal representative's action on the claim.

Rule
7.402. Court's action on the claim.
7.403. Listing all claims in the final report.

Rule 7.401. Personal representative's action on the claim

For each creditor's claim filed with the court, the personal representative (whether or not acting under the Independent Administration of Estates Act (IAEA)) [1] must:

(1) Allow or reject in whole or in part the claim in writing;

(2) Serve a copy of the allowance or rejection on the creditor and the creditor's attorney; and

(3) File a copy of the allowance or rejection with proof of service with the court. *(Adopted, eff. Jan. 1, 2000. As amended, eff. Jan. 1, 2002.)*

[1] See Probate Code § 10400 et seq.

Research References

2 Witkin Cal. Proc. 5th Courts § 194, (S 194) Probate Rules.
14 Witkin, California Summary 10th Wills and Probate § 4, Probate Rules.
14 Witkin, California Summary 10th Wills and Probate § 640, Allowance or Rejection by Personal Representative.

Rule 7.402. Court's action on the claim

Except as to claims of the personal representative or the attorney, if the personal representative has authority to act under the Independent Administration of Estates Act (IAEA), [1] the court must not act on the personal representative's allowance or rejection of a creditor's claim unless good cause is shown. *(Adopted, eff. Jan. 1, 2000. As amended, eff. Jan. 1, 2002.)*

[1] See Probate Code § 10400 et seq.

Research References

14 Witkin, California Summary 10th Wills and Probate § 641, Approval or Rejection by Court.

Rule 7.403. Listing all claims in the final report

For each claim presented, the personal representative must state in the final report or petition for final distribution:

(1) The claimant's name;

(2) The date of filing of the claim;

(3) The nature of the claim;

(4) The amount claimed;

(5) The disposition of the claim; and

(6) If the claim was rejected, the date of service of the rejection and whether or not a lawsuit was filed. *(Adopted, eff. Jan. 1, 2000. As amended, eff. Jan. 1, 2002.)*

Research References

2 Witkin Cal. Proc. 5th Courts § 194, (S 194) Probate Rules.
14 Witkin, California Summary 10th Wills and Probate § 4, Probate Rules.
14 Witkin, California Summary 10th Wills and Probate § 640, Allowance or Rejection by Personal Representative.
14 Witkin, California Summary 10th Wills and Probate § 731, in General.

Chapter 10

SALES OF REAL AND PERSONAL PROPERTY

Rule
7.451. Refusal to show property to prospective buyers.
7.452. Petitioner or attorney required at hearing.
7.453. Petition for exclusive listing.

Rule

7.454. Ex parte application for order authorizing sale of securities or other personal property.

Rule 7.451. Refusal to show property to prospective buyers

Upon a showing that the fiduciary has denied any bona fide prospective buyer or his or her broker a reasonable opportunity to inspect the property, the court must not confirm the sale but must continue the sale to allow inspection unless good cause is shown for the court to confirm the sale. *(Adopted, eff. Jan. 1, 2000. As amended, eff. Jan. 1, 2002.)*

Research References

2 Witkin Cal. Proc. 5th Courts § 194, (S 194) Probate Rules.
14 Witkin, California Summary 10th Wills and Probate § 4, Probate Rules.
14 Witkin, California Summary 10th Wills and Probate § 689, (S 689) Report and Hearing.
14 Witkin, California Summary 10th Wills and Probate § 695, (S 695) Report and Hearing.
14 Witkin, California Summary 10th Wills and Probate § 1017, (S 1017) Procedure.

Rule 7.452. Petitioner or attorney required at hearing

The court must not proceed with the hearing on a petition to confirm a sale of property unless the petitioner's attorney or petitioner, if unrepresented, is present. *(Adopted, eff. Jan. 1, 2000. As amended, eff. Jan. 1, 2002.)*

Research References

14 Witkin, California Summary 10th Wills and Probate § 689, (S 689) Report and Hearing.
14 Witkin, California Summary 10th Wills and Probate § 695, (S 695) Report and Hearing.
14 Witkin, California Summary 10th Wills and Probate § 1017, (S 1017) Procedure.

Rule 7.453. Petition for exclusive listing

A petition for approval of an exclusive listing under Probate Code section 10150(c) must state the following:

(1) A description of the property to be sold;

(2) The name of the broker to be employed;

(3) A summary of the terms of the exclusive listing agreement or include a copy of the listing agreement; and

(4) A detailed statement of the facts supporting the "necessity and the advantage" to the estate of having the exclusive listing. *(Adopted, eff. Jan. 1, 2000. As amended, eff. Jan. 1, 2002.)*

Research References

14 Witkin, California Summary 10th Wills and Probate § 678, (S 678) Agent or Broker.

Rule 7.454. Ex parte application for order authorizing sale of securities or other personal property

An ex parte application for authority to sell or to surrender tangible or intangible personal property must state whether or not the property is specifically devised. If it is specifically devised, the written consent of the specific devisee to the sale or surrender must be filed. *(Adopted, eff. Jan. 1, 2003.)*

Research References

2 Witkin Cal. Proc. 5th Courts § 194, (S 194) Probate Rules.
14 Witkin, California Summary 10th Wills and Probate § 4, Probate Rules.
14 Witkin, California Summary 10th Wills and Probate § 684, (S 684) Notice of Sale.
14 Witkin, California Summary 10th Wills and Probate § 700, (S 700) Securities.

Chapter 11

INVENTORY AND APPRAISAL

Rule

7.501. Inventory and Appraisal to show sufficiency of bond.

Rule 7.501. Inventory and Appraisal to show sufficiency of bond

(a) Statement required

Every Inventory and Appraisal must contain one of the following statements:

(1) "Bond is waived";

(2) "Bond has been filed in the amount of $ *(specify amount)* and is insufficient"; or

(3) "Bond has been filed in the amount of $ *(specify amount)* and is sufficient."

(b) Insufficient bond

If the bond is insufficient, the fiduciary (the personal representative, or the guardian or conservator of the estate), or the attorney for the fiduciary, must immediately make ex parte application as provided in rule 7.204 for an order increasing the amount of the bond.

(c) Statement signed by attorney

The statement required by (a) must be signed by the attorney of record for each fiduciary who has an attorney of record and by each fiduciary who does not. *(Adopted, eff. Jan. 1, 2000. As amended, eff. Jan. 1, 2002; Jan. 1, 2003; Jan. 1, 2007.)*

Research References

2 Witkin Cal. Proc. 5th Courts § 194, (S 194) Probate Rules.
14 Witkin, California Summary 10th Wills and Probate § 4, Probate Rules.
14 Witkin, California Summary 10th Wills and Probate § 592, Requirement of Inventory and Appraisal.
14 Witkin, California Summary 10th Wills and Probate § 1033, (S 1033) in General.

Chapter 12

ACCOUNTS AND REPORTS OF EXECUTORS, ADMINISTRATORS, CONSERVATORS, AND GUARDIANS

Rule

7.550. Effect of waiver of account.
7.551. Final accounts or reports in estates with nonresident beneficiaries.
7.552. Graduated filing fee adjustments for estates commenced on or after August 18, 2003, and before January 1, 2008.
7.553. Graduated filing fee statements for decedents' estates commenced on or after January 1, 2008.
7.575. Accounts of conservators and guardians.

Rule 7.550. Effect of waiver of account

(a) Waiver of account

Except as provided in (b), if an accounting is waived under Probate Code section 10954, the details of receipts and disbursements need not be listed in the report required under section 10954(c)(1).

(b) Information required in report on waiver of account

The report required when an account has been waived must list the information required by law, including information as to:

(1) Creditors' claims;

(2) Sales, purchases, or exchanges of assets;

(3) Changes in the form of assets;

(4) Assets on hand;

(5) Whether the estate is solvent;

(6) Detailed schedules of receipts and gains or losses on sale (where an amount other than the amount of the Inventory and Appraisal is used as a basis for calculating fees or commissions);

(7) Costs of administration (if reimbursement of these costs is requested);

(8) The amount of any fees or commissions paid or to be paid;

(9) The calculation of such fees or commissions as described in rule 7.705; and

(10) For decedent's estate proceedings commenced on or after August 18, 2003, the information required by rule 7.552(a) and (b). *(Adopted, eff. Jan. 1, 2003. As amended, eff. Jan. 1, 2004; Jan. 1, 2007.)*

Research References

2 Witkin Cal. Proc. 5th Courts § 194, (S 194) Probate Rules.
14 Witkin, California Summary 10th Wills and Probate § 4, Probate Rules.
14 Witkin, California Summary 10th Wills and Probate § 529, Statutory Schedule.
14 Witkin, California Summary 10th Wills and Probate § 712, When Account is Not Required.

Rule 7.551. Final accounts or reports in estates with nonresident beneficiaries

(a) Final account

Under Revenue and Taxation Code section 19513 and the regulations of the Franchise Tax Board, the court must not approve a final account in an estate that has a total appraised value greater than $1,000,000 and from which more than $250,000 in the aggregate has been distributed or is distributable to beneficiaries who are not residents of California, until the executor or administrator has filed the Franchise Tax Board's state income tax certificate showing that all state personal income taxes, additions to tax, penalties, and interest imposed on the estate or the decedent have been paid or that payment has been secured.

(b) Final report

If a final account is waived under Probate Code section 10954 in an estate described in (a), the court must not approve the final report required by section 10954(c)(1) until the executor or administrator has filed the Franchise Tax Board's state income tax certificate showing that all state personal income taxes, additions to tax, penalties, and interest imposed on the estate or the decedent have been paid or that payment has been secured.

(c) Expiration date of certificate

If the certificate described in (a) or (b) is issued on the condition that the final account or report must be approved before a date specified in the certificate, the court must not approve the final account or report after that date unless the executor or administrator first files a new or revised certificate. *(Adopted, eff. Jan. 1, 2004.)*

Research References

14 Witkin, California Summary 10th Wills and Probate § 717, Hearing and Determination.

Rule 7.552. Graduated filing fee adjustments for estates commenced on or after August 18, 2003, and before January 1, 2008

This rule applies to decedents' estate proceedings commenced on or after August 18, 2003, and before January 1, 2008. Rule 7.553 applies to decedents' estate proceedings commenced on or after January 1, 2008.

(a) Separate schedule for graduated fee information

The final account or report filed in every decedent's estate proceeding commenced on or after August 18, 2003, and before January 1, 2008, must include a separate schedule showing the following information:

(1) The name of each petitioner on the first-filed *Petition for Probate* (form DE–111) in the proceeding;

(2) The date the first-filed *Petition for Probate* was filed in the proceeding;

(3) The estimated value of the estate shown in item 3, "estimated value of the estate for filing fee purposes," of the first-filed *Petition for Probate* in the proceeding;

(4) The filing fee paid by or for the petitioner on the first-filed *Petition for Probate* in the proceeding; and

(5) The following information from the inventories filed in the proceeding:

  (A) The date each partial, supplemental, final, or corrected *Inventory and Appraisal* (form DE–160/GC–040) was filed;

  (B) The total appraised value of the assets of the estate shown in each filed partial, supplemental, or final *Inventory and Appraisal;*

  (C) Changes in the appraised value of the assets of the estate shown in each filed corrected *Inventory and Appraisal;* and

  (D) The combined total appraised value of the estate shown in all filed partial, supplemental, final, and corrected inventories.

(6) A statement of the amount of filing fee that would have been payable under Government Code section 70650, as amended effective on the date the first-filed *Petition for Probate* was filed in the proceeding, if the total actual appraised value of the estate had been used as the estimated value for filing fee purposes (the "corrected filing fee");

(7) Calculation of the difference between the estimated filing fee paid under Government Code section 70650 on filing the first *Petition for Probate* in the proceeding (the "estimated filing fee") and the "corrected filing fee," as determined under (6) and subdivision (e) of this rule; and

(8) The following information concerning filing fee reimbursement payments made by a personal representative in the proceeding under rule 7.151:

  (A) The amount of each payment;

  (B) The date each payment was made; and

  (C) The name, address, and telephone number of the payee and of any attorney of record for the payee in the proceeding.

(b) If estimated filing fee less than corrected filing fee

If the estimated filing fee is less than the corrected filing fee, as determined under (a) and (e), the petition filed with the final account or report must allege that the difference between them has been paid to the clerk of the court. A copy of the clerk's receipt for the payment, and, if applicable, a receipt or other evidence satisfactory to the court of payment of the reimbursement required under rule 7.151, must be attached as an exhibit to the account or report.

(c) If estimated filing fee more than corrected filing fee

(1) Subject to the provisions of rule 7.151, if the estimated filing fee is more than the corrected filing fee, as determined under (a) and (e), the personal representative of the decedent's estate is eligible under this subdivision to receive a refund of the difference between them, without interest.

(2) The personal representative must apply to the court for the refund, in accordance with the court's local rules and practices for such payments.

(3) Unless authorized to retain a reserve against closing expenses that expressly is to include the court's refund payment after the personal representative's discharge, the personal representative must not apply for a discharge while an application for refund of filing fee under this subdivision is pending and before the court's refund payment is received.

(d) Refund on voluntarily dismissed *Petition for Probate*

(1) A petitioner that files a *Petition for Probate* on or after August 18, 2003, and voluntarily dismisses the petition at any time within 90 days after it is filed and before an order granting or denying the petition is filed, is eligible under this subdivision to receive a refund, without interest, of all filing fees paid in excess of the filing fees that would have been payable on the original filing date for a *Petition for Probate* of an estate valued at less than $250,000.

(2) The petitioner on a dismissed *Petition for Probate* under (1) must apply to the court for the refund, in accordance with the court's local rules and practices for such payments.

(e) Additional adjustment in corrected filing fee in insolvent estates

If the property of the estate is insufficient to pay the expenses of administration in full, the court may approve a determination of the corrected filing fee that reflects the proportionate reduction of those expenses under Probate Code section 11420. The corrected filing fee may not be reduced below the minimum fee required by Government Code section 70650 on the date the estimated fee was paid.

(f) Sample schedule of graduated fee information

The schedule of graduated fee information required under (a) may be substantially as follows:

SCHEDULE ____

Graduated Filing Fee Information

1. The first-filed *Petition for Probate* in this proceeding was filed on [Date] by [name of each petitioner].

2. The estimated value of the estate for filing fee purposes shown on the first-filed *Petition for Probate* in this proceeding is $_____.

3. The filing fee paid by or for the petitioners on the first-filed *Petition for Probate* in this proceeding was $_____.

4. The following inventories have been filed in this proceeding:

Type	Date Filed	Appraised Value
[Partial no. ___]	[09/30/09]	$
[Partial no. ___]		$
Final		$
[Supplemental]		$
[Correcting]		$ (or $)_____
Total appraised value of estate:		$ _____

5. Corrected Filing Fee:

Total appraised value of estate: $

Filing fee as of the date in 1 above, based on total appraised value of estate: $

Adjustment to reflect proportional reduction of expenses of administration for insolvent estate under Cal. Rules of Court, rule 7.552(e):   ($ _____)

Corrected Filing Fee: $ _____

6. Difference between estimated and corrected filing fee:

Estimated filing fee from 3 above: $

Corrected filing fee from 5 above: ($ _____)

Difference: $ (or $) _____

7. Filing fee reimbursements under rule 7.151:

Payee(s) [Name, address, and telephone number of each payee and attorney of record in the proceeding]	Date Paid [10/25/09]	Amount $

(Adopted, eff. Jan. 1, 2004. As amended, eff. Jan. 1, 2007; March 1, 2008.)

Validity

This rule was held unconstitutional for containing a graduated fee which amends an initiative prohibiting estate taxes in the decision of In re Estate of Claeyssens (App. 2 Dist. 2008) 74 Cal.Rptr.3d 304, 161 Cal.App.4th 465.

Research References

14 Witkin, California Summary 10th Wills and Probate § 383, Schedules.

14 Witkin, California Summary 10th Wills and Probate § 585, Filing Fee.

Rule 7.553. Graduated filing fee statements for decedents' estates commenced on or after January 1, 2008

This rule applies to decedents' estates commenced on or after January 1, 2008.

(a) Separate schedule for graduated fee information

The final account or report or petition for final distribution filed in every decedent's estate proceeding commenced on or after January 1, 2008, must include a separate schedule showing the following information:

(1) The date the first-filed *Petition for Probate* (form DE–111) was filed in the proceeding; and

(2) The following information from the inventories filed in the proceeding:

(A) The date each partial, supplemental, final, or corrected *Inventory and Appraisal* (form DE–160/GC–040) was filed;

(B) The total appraised value of the assets of the estate shown in each filed partial, supplemental, or final *Inventory and Appraisal;*

(C) Changes in the appraised value of the assets of the estate shown in each filed corrected *Inventory and Appraisal;* and

(D) The combined total appraised value of the estate shown in all filed partial, supplemental, final, and corrected inventories.

(b) Adjustment in corrected filing fee in insolvent estates

If the property of the estate is insufficient to pay expenses of administration in full, the court may approve a determination of the corrected filing fee under this rule that reflects the proportionate reduction of those expenses under Probate Code section 11420. The corrected filing fee may not be reduced below the minimum fee required by Government Code section 70650 on the date the estate was commenced.

(c) Sample schedule of filing fee information

The schedule of graduated fee information required under (a) may be substantially as follows:

SCHEDULE ___

Graduated Filing Fee Information

1. The first-filed *Petition for Probate* in this proceeding was filed on [Date] by [name of each petitioner].

2. The following inventories have been filed in this proceeding:

Type	Date Filed	Appraised Value
[Partial no.___]	[09/30/09]	$
[Partial no.___]		$
Final		$
[Supplemental]		$
[Correcting]		$ (or $) _____
Total appraised value of estate:		$ _____

3. Graduated Filing Fee:

Total appraised value of estate: $

Filing fee as of the date in 1 above, based on total appraised value of estate: $

Adjustment to reflect proportional reduction of expenses of administration for insolvent estate under Cal. Rules of Court, rule 7.553(b):   ($ _____)

Corrected Filing Fee: $ _____

(Adopted, eff. March 1, 2008.)

Research References

14 Witkin, California Summary 10th Wills and Probate § 4, Probate Rules.

14 Witkin, California Summary 10th Wills and Probate § 585, Filing Fee.

Rule 7.575. Accounts of conservators and guardians

This rule defines standard and simplified accountings filed by conservators and guardians under Probate Code section 2620(a), provides when each type of accounting must or may be filed, and prescribes the use of Judicial Council accounting forms in both types of accountings.

(a) Standard and simplified accountings

A standard accounting lists receipts and disbursements in subject-matter categories, with each receipt and disbursement category subtotaled. A simplified accounting lists receipts and disbursements chronologically, by receipt or payment date, without subject-matter categories.

(b) Standard accounting authorized or required

A conservator or guardian may file any accounting required or authorized by Probate Code section 2620 as a standard accounting under this rule and must file a standard accounting if:

(1) The estate contains income real property;

(2) The estate contains a whole or partial interest in a trade or business;

(3) The appraised value of the estate is $500,000 or more, exclusive of the conservatee's or ward's personal residence;

(4) Except as provided in (c), Schedule A (receipts) or Schedule C (disbursements) prepared in a simplified accounting format exceeds five pages in length; or

(5) The court directs that a standard accounting be filed.

(c) Simplified accounting authorized

A conservator or guardian may file a simplified accounting in all cases not listed in (b). If required by this rule to file a standard accounting only because a receipts or disbursements schedule is longer than five pages under (b)(4), a conservator or guardian may file a simplified accounting, except for that schedule, which must be prepared in a standard accounting format.

(d) Standard and simplified accounting forms

Judicial Council forms designated as GC–400 are standard accounting forms. Forms designated as GC–405 are simplified accounting forms. Forms designated as GC–400/GC–405 are forms for both standard and simplified accountings. Each form is also designated by a suffix following its accounting designator that identifies the form's intended use, based either on the form's schedule letter as shown in the *Summary of Account* (form GC–400(SUM)/GC–405(SUM)) or the form's subject matter.

(e) Mandatory and optional forms

(1) Judicial Council accounting forms adopted as mandatory forms must be used by standard and simplified accounting filers. Judicial Council accounting forms approved as optional forms may be used by all accounting filers. Judicial Council accounting forms designated as GC–400/GC–405 that are approved as optional forms may be used by standard accounting filers but must be used by simplified accounting filers.

(2) Standard accounting filers electing not to use optional Judicial Council accounting forms must:

(A) State receipts and disbursements in the subject-matter categories specified in the optional Judicial Council forms for receipts and disbursements schedules;

(B) Provide the same information about any asset, property, transaction, receipt, disbursement, or other matter that is required by the applicable Judicial Council accounting form; and

(C) Provide the information in the same general layout as the applicable Judicial Council accounting form, but instructional material contained in the form and material contained or requested in the form's header and footer need not be provided.

(f) Required information in all accounts

Notwithstanding any other provision of this rule and the Judicial Council accounting forms, all standard and simplified accounting filers must provide all information in their accounting schedules or their *Summary of Account* that is required by Probate Code sections 1060–1063 and must provide all information required by Probate Code section 1064 in the petition for approval of their account or the report accompanying their account. *(Adopted, eff. Jan. 1, 2008.)*

Research References

2 Witkin Cal. Proc. 5th Courts § 194, (S 194) Probate Rules.

14 Witkin, California Summary 10th Wills and Probate § 1036A, (S 1036A) (New)-Simplified and Standard Accountings.

Ct. Rules

Chapter 14

PRELIMINARY AND FINAL DISTRIBUTIONS

Rule

7.650.　Decree of distribution establishing testamentary trusts.

7.651.　Description of property in petition for distribution.

7.652.　Allegations in petition for distribution concerning character of property.

Rule 7.650.　Decree of distribution establishing testamentary trusts

(a)　Determining the trust

Upon distribution, the court must:

(1)　Determine whether or not a valid trust has been created by the will;

(2)　Determine the terms of the trust;　and

(3)　Order distribution of the trust property to the trustee.

(b)　Terms of the trust

The order for distribution must incorporate the terms of the trust so as to give effect to the conditions existing at the time distribution is ordered.　The pertinent provisions must be stated in the present tense and in the third person instead of quoting the will verbatim.　*(Adopted, eff. Jan. 1, 2000.　As amended, eff. Jan. 1, 2002.)*

Research References

2 Witkin Cal. Proc. 5th Courts § 194, (S 194) Probate Rules.
14 Witkin, California Summary 10th Wills and Probate § 4, Probate Rules.
14 Witkin, California Summary 10th Wills and Probate § 731, in General.

Rule 7.651.　Description of property in petition for distribution

(a)　Property description

A petition for distribution must list and describe in detail the property to be distributed, in the body of the petition or in an attachment that is incorporated in the petition by reference.　If an account is filed with the petition, the description must be included in a schedule in the account.

(b)　Specific description requirements

The description under (a) must:

(1)　Include the amount of cash on hand;

(2)　Indicate whether promissory notes are secured or unsecured, and describe in detail the security interest of any secured notes;

(3)　Include the complete legal description, street address (if any), and assessor's parcel number (if any) of real property;　and

(4)　Include the complete description of each individual security held in "street name" in security brokers' accounts.　*(Adopted, eff. Jan. 1, 2004.)*

Research References

14 Witkin, California Summary 10th Wills and Probate § 731, in General.

Rule 7.652.　Allegations in petition for distribution concerning character of property

(a)　Required allegations

If the character of property to be distributed may affect the distribution, a petition for distribution must allege:

(1)　The character of the property to be distributed, whether separate, community, or quasi-community;　and

(2)　That the community or quasi-community property to be distributed is either the decedent's one-half interest only, or the entire interest of the decedent and the decedent's spouse.

(b)　Compliance with Probate Code section 13502

If any property is to be distributed outright to the surviving spouse, a written election by the surviving spouse that complies with Probate Code section 13502 must have been filed, and the petition must show the filing date of the election.　*(Adopted, eff. Jan. 1, 2004.)*

Research References

2 Witkin Cal. Proc. 5th Courts § 194, (S 194) Probate Rules.
14 Witkin, California Summary 10th Wills and Probate § 4, Probate Rules.
14 Witkin, California Summary 10th Wills and Probate § 731, in General.

Chapter 15

COMPENSATION OF PERSONAL REPRESENTATIVES AND ATTORNEYS

Rule

7.700.　Compensation paid in advance.

7.701.　Allowance on account of statutory compensation.

7.702.　Petition for extraordinary compensation.

7.703.　Extraordinary compensation.

7.704.　Apportionment of statutory compensation.

7.705.　Calculation of statutory compensation.

7.706.　Compensation when personal representative is an attorney.

7.707.　Application of compensation provisions.

Rule 7.700.　Compensation paid in advance

(a)　No compensation in advance of court order

The personal representative must neither pay nor receive, and the attorney for the personal representative must not receive, statutory commissions or fees or fees for extraordinary services in advance of an order of the court authorizing their payment.

(b)　Surcharge for payment or receipt of advance compensation

In addition to removing the personal representative and imposing any other sanctions authorized by law against the personal representative or the attorney for the personal representative, the court may surcharge the personal representative for payment or receipt of statutory commissions or fees or fees for extraordinary services in advance of an order of the court authorizing their payment.　The surcharge may include interest at the legal rate from the date of payment.　*(Adopted, eff. Jan. 1, 2003.)*

Research References

2 Witkin Cal. Proc. 5th Courts § 194, (S 194) Probate Rules.
14 Witkin, California Summary 10th Wills and Probate § 4, Probate Rules.
14 Witkin, California Summary 10th Wills and Probate § 451, in General.
14 Witkin, California Summary 10th Wills and Probate § 541, Advance Payment.
14 Witkin, California Summary 10th Wills and Probate § 1044, Procedure.

Rule 7.701.　Allowance on account of statutory compensation

The court may authorize an allowance of statutory fees or commissions on account before approval of the final account and the decree of final distribution. Any allowance made before settlement of the final account must be low enough to avoid the possibility of overpayment. The allowance:

(1) Must be based on the estimated amount of statutory compensation payable on the estate determined as of the date of the petition for allowance;

(2) Must be in proportion to the work actually performed; and

(3) Must be based upon a detailed description of the ordinary services performed and remaining to be performed. *(Adopted, eff. Jan. 1, 2003.)*

Research References

14 Witkin, California Summary 10th Wills and Probate § 541, Advance Payment.

Rule 7.702. Petition for extraordinary compensation

A petition for extraordinary compensation must include, or be accompanied by, a statement of the facts upon which the petition is based. The statement of facts must:

(1) Show the nature and difficulty of the tasks performed;

(2) Show the results achieved;

(3) Show the benefit of the services to the estate;

(4) Specify the amount requested for each category of service performed;

(5) State the hourly rate of each person who performed services and the hours spent by each of them;

(6) Describe the services rendered in sufficient detail to demonstrate the productivity of the time spent; and

(7) State the estimated amount of statutory compensation to be paid by the estate, if the petition is not part of a final account or report. *(Adopted, eff. Jan. 1, 2003.)*

Research References

14 Witkin, California Summary 10th Wills and Probate § 540, in General.
14 Witkin, California Summary 10th Wills and Probate § 1044, Procedure.

Rule 7.703. Extraordinary compensation

(a) Discretion of the court

An award of extraordinary compensation to the personal representative or to the attorney for the personal representative is within the discretion of the court. The court may consider the amount of statutory compensation when determining compensation for extraordinary services.

(b) Examples of extraordinary services by personal representative

The following is a nonexclusive list of activities for which extraordinary compensation may be awarded to the personal representative:

(1) Selling, leasing, exchanging, financing, or foreclosing real or personal property;

(2) Carrying on decedent's business if necessary to preserve the estate or under court order;

(3) Preparing tax returns; and

(4) Handling audits or litigation connected with tax liabilities of the decedent or of the estate.

(c) Examples of extraordinary services by attorney

The following is a nonexclusive list of activities for which extraordinary compensation may be awarded to the attorney for the personal representative:

(1) Legal services in connection with the sale of property held in the estate;

(2) Services to secure a loan to pay estate debts;

(3) Litigation undertaken to benefit the estate or to protect its interests;

(4) Defense of the personal representative's account;

(5) Defense of a will contested after its admission to probate;

(6) Successful defense of a will contested before its admission to probate;

(7) Successful defense of a personal representative in a removal proceeding;

(8) Extraordinary efforts to locate estate assets;

(9) Litigation in support of attorney's request for extraordinary compensation, where prior compensation awards are not adequate compensation under all the circumstances;

(10) Coordination of ancillary administration; and

(11) Accounting for a deceased, incapacitated, or absconded personal representative under Probate Code section 10953.

(d) Contingency fee agreement for extraordinary legal services

An attorney may agree to perform extraordinary services for a personal representative on a contingent-fee basis on the following conditions:

(1) The agreement must be in writing and must comply with section 6147 of the Business and Professions Code;

(2) The court must approve the agreement in the manner provided in Probate Code section 10811(c), based on findings that the compensation under the agreement is just and reasonable, that the agreement is to the advantage of the estate, and that the agreement is in the best interest of the persons interested in the estate; and

(3) In the absence of an emergency or other unusual circumstances, the personal representative must obtain the court's approval of the contingency fee agreement before services are performed under it.

(e) Use of paralegals in the performance of extraordinary services

Extraordinary legal services may include the services of a paralegal as defined in Business and Professions Code section 6450(a) only if the request for extraordinary legal fees for the paralegal's services:

(1) Describes the qualifications of the paralegal (including education, certification, continuing education, and experience). The description must state that the paralegal:

(A) Acted under the direction and supervision of an attorney;

(B) Satisfies one or more of the minimum qualifications specified in Business and Professions Code section 6450(c); and

(C) Has completed mandatory continuing education required by Business and Professions Code section 6450(d) for the last two-year certification period ending before the year during which any part of the paralegal's services were performed;

(2) States the hours spent by the paralegal and the hourly rate requested for the paralegal's services;

(3) Describes the services performed by the paralegal;

(4) States why it was appropriate to use the paralegal's services in the particular case; and

(5) Demonstrates that the total amount requested for the extraordinary services of the attorney and the paralegal does not exceed the amount appropriate if the attorney had performed the services without the paralegal's assistance. *(Adopted, eff. Jan. 1, 2003. As amended, eff. Jan. 1, 2007; July 1, 2010.)*

Research References

Rutter, Cal. Practice Guide: Prof. Responsibility Ch. 5-B, B. Types of Fees and Fee Arrangements.

14 Witkin, California Summary 10th Wills and Probate § 534, (S 534) Nature of Allowance.

14 Witkin, California Summary 10th Wills and Probate § 536, (S 536) in General.

14 Witkin, California Summary 10th Wills and Probate § 538, (S 538) Discretion of Court.

14 Witkin, California Summary 10th Wills and Probate § 1046, Compensation of Attorney.

Rule 7.704. Apportionment of statutory compensation

(a) One statutory commission and fee

There is one statutory commission for ordinary services by the personal representative of the estate and one statutory attorney fee for ordinary legal services to the personal representative, regardless of the number of personal representatives or attorneys performing the services. The court may apportion statutory commissions and fees among multiple, successive, and concurrent personal representatives or attorneys. The apportionment must be based on the agreement of the multiple personal representatives or attorneys or, if there is no agreement, according to the services actually rendered by each of them.

(b) Notice of hearing

If there has been a change of personal representative or a substitution of attorneys for the personal representative, notice of hearing of any interim or final petition seeking or waiving an award of statutory compensation must be given to all prior personal representatives or attorneys unless:

(1) A waiver of notice executed by all prior personal representatives or attorneys is on file or is filed with the petition;

(2) A written, signed agreement on the allocation of statutory commissions or fees between the present personal representative or attorney and all prior personal representatives or attorneys is on file or is included in or filed with the petition; or

(3) The court's file and the petition demonstrate that the commissions or fees of the prior personal representatives or attorneys have been previously provided for and allowed by the court. *(Adopted, eff. Jan. 1, 2003.)*

Research References

14 Witkin, California Summary 10th Wills and Probate § 532, Apportionment Among Several Representatives.

Rule 7.705. Calculation of statutory compensation

(a) Account filed

A petition for statutory commissions or attorney fees must state the amount of statutory compensation payable and set forth the estate accounted for and the calculation of statutory compensation. The calculation must be stated in the petition in substantially the following form:

COMMISSION OR FEE BASE

Inventory and Appraisal	$ _____
Receipts, Excluding Principal	$ _____
Gains on Sales	$ _____
Losses on Sales	$ (_____)

TOTAL COMMISSION OR FEE BASE $ _____

COMMISSION OR FEE COMPUTATION

4% on first $100,000	($_____)[1]	$_____[2]
3% on next $100,000	($_____)	$_____
2% on next $800,000	($_____)	$_____
1% on next $9,000,000	($_____)	$_____
½ of 1% on next $15,000,000	($_____)	$_____
Amount requested from the court for estates above $25,000,000	($_____)	$_____

TOTAL COMMISSION OR FEE $_____[3]

  1   Enter in this column the amount of the estate accounted for in each category. The sum of the entries in this column would equal the total commission or fee base.

  2   Enter in this column the product of the amount of the estate accounted for in each category multiplied by the percentage for that category.

  3   Enter here the sum of the products entered in this column.

(b) Account waived

When an account has been waived, the report must contain the information required by rule 7.550. If the report is accompanied by a request for statutory commissions or fees, the basis for their computation must be included in the petition substantially in the form provided in (a). Notwithstanding the waiver of account, if the petition and report requests statutory commissions or fees based on any amount other than the amount of the Inventory and Appraisal, detailed schedules of receipts and gains and losses on sales must be included. *(Adopted, eff. Jan. 1, 2003.)*

Research References

14 Witkin, California Summary 10th Wills and Probate § 529, Statutory Schedule.

14 Witkin, California Summary 10th Wills and Probate § 712, When Account is Not Required.

Rule 7.706. Compensation when personal representative is an attorney

(a) Personal representative's compensation only

Notwithstanding the provisions of the decedent's will, a personal representative who is an attorney may receive the personal representative's compensation but may not receive compensation for legal services as the attorney for the personal representative unless the court approves the right to compensation for legal services in advance and finds the arrangement is to the advantage, benefit, and best interest of the decedent's estate.

(b) Agreement not to participate in compensation

A law firm of which the personal representative is a partner or shareholder may request compensation for legal services in addition to the personal representative's compensation if a written agreement not to participate in each other's compensation, signed by the personal representative and by authorized representatives of the law firm, has been filed in the estate proceeding. *(Adopted, eff. Jan. 1, 2003.)*

Research References

14 Witkin, California Summary 10th Wills and Probate § 533, Representative Acting as Own Attorney.

Rule 7.707. Application of compensation provisions

For proceedings commenced after June 30, 1991, the law in effect on the date of the court's order awarding statutory compensation determines the amount of such compensation. *(Adopted, eff. Jan. 1, 2003.)*

Research References

2 Witkin Cal. Proc. 5th Courts § 194, (S 194) Probate Rules.

14 Witkin, California Summary 10th Wills and Probate § 4, Probate Rules.

Chapter 16

COMPENSATION IN ALL MATTERS OTHER THAN DECEDENTS' ESTATES

Rule

7.750. Application of rules to guardianships and conservatorships.

7.751. Petitions for orders allowing compensation for guardians or conservators and their attorneys.

7.752. Court may order accounting before allowing compensation.

7.753. Contingency fee agreements in guardianships and conservatorships.

7.754. Use of paralegals in the performance of legal services for the guardian or conservator.

7.755. Advance payments and periodic payments to guardians, conservators, and to their attorneys on account for future services.

7.756. Compensation of conservators and guardians.

7.776. Compensation of trustees.

Rule 7.750. Application of rules to guardianships and conservatorships

The rules in this chapter apply to guardianships and conservatorships under division 4 of the Probate Code (Prob. Code, § 1400 et seq.) and to conservatorships under the Lanterman–Petris–Short Act (Welf. & Inst. Code, §§ 5350–5371). They do not apply to guardianships under chapter 2 of division 2 of the Welfare and Institutions Code (Welf. & Inst. Code, § 200 et seq.). Under Probate Code section 2646, the rules in this chapter applicable to guardianships and conservatorships apply only to compensation payable from the estate of the ward or conservatee or from money or property recovered or collected for the estate of the ward or conservatee. *(Adopted, eff. Jan. 1, 2003.)*

Research References

3 Witkin Cal. Proc. 5th Actions § 83, (S 83) Right to Counsel and Habeas Corpus.

2 Witkin Cal. Proc. 5th Courts § 194, (S 194) Probate Rules.

13 Witkin, California Summary 10th Trusts § 226, (S 226) in General.

14 Witkin, California Summary 10th Wills and Probate § 4, Probate Rules.

14 Witkin, California Summary 10th Wills and Probate § 960, Governing Law.

14 Witkin, California Summary 10th Wills and Probate § 1044, Procedure.

Rule 7.751. Petitions for orders allowing compensation for guardians or conservators and their attorneys

(a) Petition for allowance of compensation for services performed before appointment of guardian or conservator

A petition for allowance of compensation to a guardian or conservator or to the attorney for a guardian or conservator may include a request for compensation for services rendered before an order appointing a guardian or conservator. The petition must show facts demonstrating the necessity for preappointment services.

(b) Required showing in petition for allowance of compensation

All petitions for orders fixing and allowing compensation must comply with the requirements of rule 7.702 concerning petitions for extraordinary compensation in decedents' estates, to the extent applicable to guardianships and conservatorships, except that the best interest of the ward or conservatee is to be considered instead of the interest of beneficiaries of the estate. *(Adopted, eff. Jan. 1, 2003. As amended, eff. Jan. 1, 2007.)*

Research References

14 Witkin, California Summary 10th Wills and Probate § 1044, Procedure.

14 Witkin, California Summary 10th Wills and Probate § 1045, Scope of Authorized Compensation.

Rule 7.752. Court may order accounting before allowing compensation

Notwithstanding the time period after which a petition may be filed for an allowance of compensation to a guardian, conservator, or an attorney for a guardian or conservator, the court may order the guardian or conservator to file an accounting before or at the time a petition for an allowance of compensation is filed or heard. *(Adopted, eff. Jan. 1, 2003.)*

Research References

14 Witkin, California Summary 10th Wills and Probate § 1044, Procedure.

Rule 7.753. Contingency fee agreements in guardianships and conservatorships

A guardian or conservator of the estate may contract with an attorney for a contingency fee for the attorney's services on behalf of the ward or conservatee, or the estate, in connection with a matter that is of a type customarily the subject of a contingency fee agreement, if the court has authorized the guardian or conservator to do so, or if the agreement has been approved by the court under Probate Code section 2644. The agreement must also satisfy the requirements of rule 7.703(d)(1). *(Adopted, eff. Jan. 1, 2003.)*

Research References

14 Witkin, California Summary 10th Wills and Probate § 1046, Compensation of Attorney.

Rule 7.754. Use of paralegals in the performance of legal services for the guardian or conservator

An attorney for a guardian or conservator may use the services of a paralegal acting under the direction and supervision of the attorney. A request for an allowance of compensation for the services of a paralegal must satisfy the requirements of rule 7.703(e). *(Adopted, eff. Jan. 1, 2003.)*

Research References

14 Witkin, California Summary 10th Wills and Probate § 1046, Compensation of Attorney.

Rule 7.755. Advance payments and periodic payments to guardians, conservators, and to their attorneys on account for future services

(a) No advance payments

A guardian or conservator must neither pay nor receive, and the attorney for a guardian or conservator must not receive, any payment from the estate of the ward or conservatee for services rendered in advance of an order of the court authorizing the payment. If an advance payment is made or received, the court may surcharge the guardian or conservator in the manner provided in rule 7.700(b), in addition to removing the guardian or conservator or imposing any other sanction authorized by law on the guardian or conservator or on the attorney.

(b) Periodic payments to attorneys on account

A guardian or conservator may request the court to authorize periodic payment of attorney fees on account of future services under Probate Code section 2643 on a showing of an ongoing need for legal services. *(Adopted, eff. Jan. 1, 2003.)*

Research References

14 Witkin, California Summary 10th Wills and Probate § 451, in General.

14 Witkin, California Summary 10th Wills and Probate § 1044, Procedure.

14 Witkin, California Summary 10th Wills and Probate § 1047, Order Authorizing Periodic Payments.

14 Witkin, California Summary 10th Wills and Probate § 1048, Causes for Removal.

Rule 7.756. Compensation of conservators and guardians

(a) Standards for determining just and reasonable compensation

The court may consider the following nonexclusive factors in determining just and reasonable compensation for a conservator from the estate of the conservatee or a guardian from the estate of the ward:

(1) The size and nature of the conservatee's or ward's estate;

(2) The benefit to the conservatee or ward, or his or her estate, of the conservator's or guardian's services;

(3) The necessity for the services performed;

(4) The conservatee's or ward's anticipated future needs and income;

(5) The time spent by the conservator or guardian in the performance of services;

(6) Whether the services performed were routine or required more than ordinary skill or judgment;

(7) Any unusual skill, expertise, or experience brought to the performance of services;

(8) The conservator's or guardian's estimate of the value of the services performed; and

(9) The compensation customarily allowed by the court in the community where the court is located for the management of conservatorships or guardianships of similar size and complexity.

(b) No single factor determinative

No single factor listed in (a) should be the exclusive basis for the court's determination of just and reasonable compensation.

(c) No inflexible maximum or minimum compensation or maximum approved hourly rate

This rule is not authority for a court to set an inflexible maximum or minimum compensation or a maximum approved hourly rate for compensation. *(Adopted, eff. Jan. 1, 2008.)*

Research References

13 Witkin, California Summary 10th Trusts § 55, Where Instrument Does Not Specify.

13 Witkin, California Summary 10th Trusts § 226, (S 226) in General.

14 Witkin, California Summary 10th Wills and Probate § 4, Probate Rules.

14 Witkin, California Summary 10th Wills and Probate § 1044, Procedure.

Rule 7.776. Compensation of trustees

In determining or approving compensation of a trustee, the court may consider, among other factors, the following:

(1) The gross income of the trust estate;

(2) The success or failure of the trustee's administration;

(3) Any unusual skill, expertise, or experience brought to the trustee's work;

(4) The fidelity or disloyalty shown by the trustee;

(5) The amount of risk and responsibility assumed by the trustee;

(6) The time spent in the performance of the trustee's duties;

(7) The custom in the community where the court is located regarding compensation authorized by settlors, compensation allowed by the court, or charges of corporate trustees for trusts of similar size and complexity; and

(8) Whether the work performed was routine, or required more than ordinary skill or judgment. *(Formerly Rule 7.756, adopted, eff. Jan. 1, 2003. As amended, eff. Jan. 1, 2007. Renumbered Rule 7.776, eff. Jan. 1, 2008.)*

Research References

2 Witkin Cal. Proc. 5th Courts § 194, (S 194) Probate Rules.

13 Witkin, California Summary 10th Trusts § 55, Where Instrument Does Not Specify.

13 Witkin, California Summary 10th Trusts § 226, (S 226) in General.

Chapter 17

CONTESTED HEARINGS AND TRIALS

Rule

7.801.   Objections and responses.

Rule 7.801.   Objections and responses

If the court continues a matter to allow a written objection or response to be made, and the responding or objecting party fails to serve and file a timely objection or response, the court may deem the objections or responses waived. *(Adopted, eff. Jan. 1, 2000.)*

Research References

2 Witkin Cal. Proc. 5th Courts § 194, (S 194) Probate Rules.

13 Witkin, California Summary 10th Trusts § 226, (S 226) in General.

14 Witkin, California Summary 10th Wills and Probate § 4, Probate Rules.

14 Witkin, California Summary 10th Wills and Probate § 378, Hearings.

Chapter 19

TRUSTS

Rule

7.901.   Trustee's accounts.

7.902.   Beneficiaries to be listed in petitions and accounts.

7.903.   Trusts funded by court order.

Rule 7.901.   Trustee's accounts

(a) Period covered

A trustee's account must state the period covered by the account.

(b) First account

The first account in a testamentary trust must reconcile the initial assets on hand with the decree of distribution of the estate.

(c) Principal and income

All trustee's accounts in a trust that distributes income to a beneficiary must allocate receipts and disbursements between (1) principal receipts and disbursements, and (2) income receipts and disbursements. *(Adopted, eff. Jan. 1, 2001. As amended, eff. Jan. 1, 2002.)*

Research References

2 Witkin Cal. Proc. 5th Courts § 194, (S 194) Probate Rules.
13 Witkin, California Summary 10th Trusts § 88, (S 88) Contents of Account.
13 Witkin, California Summary 10th Trusts § 226, (S 226) in General.
14 Witkin, California Summary 10th Wills and Probate § 4, Probate Rules.

Rule 7.902. Beneficiaries to be listed in petitions and accounts

A petition and account involving a trust must state the names and last known addresses of all vested or contingent beneficiaries, including all persons in being who may or will receive income or corpus of the trust, provided, however, that (1) during the time that the trust is revocable and the person holding the power to revoke the trust is competent, the names and last known addresses of beneficiaries who do not hold the power to revoke do not need to be stated, and (2) the petition or account does not need to state the name and last known address of any beneficiary who need not be given notice under Probate Code section 15804. *(Adopted, eff. Jan. 1, 2002. As amended, eff. Jan. 1, 2007.)*

Research References

13 Witkin, California Summary 10th Trusts § 88, (S 88) Contents of Account.
13 Witkin, California Summary 10th Trusts § 226, (S 226) in General.
14 Witkin, California Summary 10th Wills and Probate § 4, Probate Rules.

Rule 7.903. Trusts funded by court order

(a) Definitions

(1) "Trust funded by court order" under this rule means and refers to a trust that will receive funds under Probate Code section 2580 et seq. (substituted judgment); section 3100 et seq. (proceedings for particular transactions involving disabled spouses or registered domestic partners); or section 3600 et seq. (settlement of claims or actions or disposition of judgments involving minors or persons with disabilities).

(2) "Continuing jurisdiction of the court" under (b) means and refers to the court's continuing subject matter jurisdiction over trust proceedings under division 9 of the Probate Code (Prob. Code, § 15000 et seq.).

(3) "Court supervision under the Probate Code" under (b) means and refers to the court's authority to require prior court approval or subsequent confirmation of the actions of the trustee as for the actions of a guardian or conservator of the estate under division 4 of the Probate Code (Prob. Code, § 1400 et seq.).

(b) Continuing jurisdiction and court supervision

The order creating or approving the funding of a trust funded by court order must provide that the trust is subject to the continuing jurisdiction of the court and may provide that the trust is to be subject to court supervision under the Probate Code.

(c) Required provisions in trust instruments

Except as provided in (d), unless the court otherwise orders for good cause shown, trust instruments for trusts funded by court order must:

(1) Not contain "no-contest" provisions;

(2) Prohibit modification or revocation without court approval;

(3) Clearly identify the trustee and any other person with authority to direct the trustee to make disbursements;

(4) Prohibit investments by the trustee other than those permitted under Probate Code section 2574;

(5) Require persons identified in (3) to post bond in the amount required under Probate Code section 2320 et seq.;

(6) Require the trustee to file accounts and reports for court approval in the manner and frequency required by Probate Code sections 1060 et seq. and 2620 et seq.;

(7) Require court approval of changes in trustees and a court order appointing any successor trustee; and

(8) Require compensation of the trustee, the members of any advisory committee, or the attorney for the trustee, to be in just and reasonable amounts that must be fixed and allowed by the court. The instrument may provide for periodic payments of compensation on account, subject to the requirements of Probate Code section 2643 and rule 7.755.

(d) Trust instruments for smaller trusts

Unless the court otherwise orders for good cause shown, the requirements of (c)(5)–(8) of this rule do not apply to trust instruments for trusts that will have total assets of $20,000 or less after receipt of the property ordered by the court. *(Adopted, eff. Jan. 1, 2005. As amended, eff. July 1, 2005; Jan. 1, 2007.)*

Advisory Committee Comment

Subdivision (a) of this rule defines a court-funded trust as a product of three court proceedings. Two of these—a petition for substituted judgment in a probate conservatorship (Prob. Code, § 2580) and a proceeding for a particular transaction in the property of an impaired spouse or domestic partner without a conservator (Prob. Code, § 3100; Fam. Code, § 297.5)—are regularly heard in the probate department of the court. The third proceeding, an application for an order approving the settlement of a minor's claim or a pending action involving a minor or person with a disability or approving the disposition of the proceeds of a judgment in favor of a minor or person with a disability (Prob. Code, § 3600), may be heard in either a probate or a civil department.

The Judicial Council has adopted standard 7.10 of the Standards of Judicial Administration to address proceedings under Probate Code section 3600 that involve court-funded trusts and are heard in civil departments. The standard makes two recommendations concerning the expertise of judicial officers who hear these proceedings on trust issues. The recommendations are to develop practices and procedures that (1) provide for determination of the trust issues in these matters by the probate department of the court or by a judicial officer who regularly hears probate proceedings or (2) ensure that judicial officers who hear these matters have experience or receive training in substantive and technical issues involving trusts, including special needs trusts.

Research References

2 Witkin Cal. Proc. 5th Courts § 194, (S 194) Probate Rules.
14 Witkin, California Summary 10th Wills and Probate § 4, Probate Rules.
14 Witkin, California Summary 10th Wills and Probate § 1027, (S 1027) Determination and Order.
14 Witkin, California Summary 10th Wills and Probate § 1062, (S 1062) Community Property.
14 Witkin, California Summary 10th Wills and Probate § 1071, (S 1071) Disposition of Proceeds.
14 Witkin, California Summary 10th Wills and Probate § 1072, (S 1072) Special Needs Trust.

Chapter 20

CLAIMS OF MINORS AND PERSONS WITH DISABILITIES

Rule

7.950.   Petition for court approval of the compromise of, or a covenant on, a disputed claim; a compromise or

Rule

settlement of a pending action; or the disposition of the proceeds of a judgment.

7.950.5.   Expedited petition for court approval of the compromise of, or a covenant on, a disputed claim; a compromise or settlement of a pending action; or the disposition of the proceeds of a judgment.

7.951.   Disclosure of the attorney's interest in a petition to compromise a claim.

7.952.   Attendance at hearing on the petition to compromise a claim.

7.953.   Order for the deposit of funds of a minor or a person with a disability.

7.954.   Petition for the withdrawal of funds deposited for a minor or a person with a disability.

7.955.   Attorney's fees for services to a minor or a person with a disability.

Rule 7.950.   Petition for court approval of the compromise of, or a covenant on, a disputed claim; a compromise or settlement of a pending action; or the disposition of the proceeds of a judgment

A petition for court approval of a compromise of or a covenant not to sue or enforce judgment on a minor's disputed claim; a compromise or settlement of a pending action or proceeding to which a minor or person with a disability is a party; or disposition of the proceeds of a judgment for a minor or person with a disability under chapter 4 of part 8 of division 4 of the Probate Code (commencing with section 3600) or Code of Civil Procedure section 372 must be verified by the petitioner and must contain a full disclosure of all information that has any bearing upon the reasonableness of the compromise, covenant, settlement, or disposition. Except as provided in rule 7.950.5, the petition must be prepared on a fully completed *Petition to Approve Compromise of Disputed Claim or Pending Action or Disposition of Proceeds of Judgment for Minor or Person With a Disability* (form MC–350). (Adopted, eff. Jan. 1, 2002. As amended, eff. Jan. 1, 2007; Jan. 1, 2010.)

Research References

Rutter, Cal. Practice Guide: Personal Injury Ch. 4-G, G. Concluding and Enforcing Settlement.

2 Witkin Cal. Proc. 5th Courts § 194, (S 194) Probate Rules.

4 Witkin Cal. Proc. 5th Pleading § 81, Petition.

14 Witkin, California Summary 10th Wills and Probate § 4, Probate Rules.

14 Witkin, California Summary 10th Wills and Probate § 506, Compromise With Court Approval.

14 Witkin, California Summary 10th Wills and Probate § 1014, (S 1014) Procedure for Court Approval.

14 Witkin, California Summary 10th Wills and Probate § 1069, Parent's Compromise of Minor's Claim.

Rule 7.950.5.   Expedited petition for court approval of the compromise of, or a covenant on, a disputed claim; a compromise or settlement of a pending action; or the disposition of the proceeds of a judgment

(a)   Authorized use of expedited petition

Notwithstanding the provisions of rule 7.950, a petitioner for court approval of a compromise of or a covenant not to sue or enforce judgment on a minor's disputed claim; a compromise or settlement of a pending action or proceeding to which a minor or person with a disability is a party; or disposition of the proceeds of a judgment for a minor or person with a disability under chapter 4 of part 8 of division 4 of the Probate Code (commencing with section 3600) or Code of Civil Procedure section 372 may, in the following circumstances, satisfy the information requirements of that rule by fully completing the *Expedited Petition to Approve Compromise of Disputed Claim or Pending*

Action or Disposition of Proceeds of Judgment for Minor or Person With a Disability (form MC–350EX):

(1) The petitioner is represented by an attorney authorized to practice in the courts of this state;

(2) The claim is not for damages for the wrongful death of a person;

(3) No portion of the net proceeds of the compromise, settlement, or judgment in favor of the minor or disabled claimant is to be placed in a trust;

(4) There are no unresolved disputes concerning liens to be satisfied from the proceeds of the compromise, settlement, or judgment;

(5) The petitioner's attorney did not become involved in the matter at the direct or indirect request of a person against whom the claim is asserted or an insurance carrier for that person;

(6) The petitioner's attorney is neither employed by nor associated with a defendant or insurance carrier in connection with the petition;

(7) If an action has been filed on the claim:

(A) All defendants that have appeared in the action are participating in the compromise; or

(B) The court has finally determined that the settling parties entered into the settlement in good faith;

(8) The judgment for the minor or disabled claimant (exclusive of interest and costs) or the total amount payable to the minor or disabled claimant and all other parties under the proposed compromise or settlement is $50,000 or less or, if greater:

(A) The total amount payable to the minor or disabled claimant represents payment of the individual-person policy limits of all liability insurance policies covering all proposed contributing parties; and

(B) All proposed contributing parties would be substantially unable to discharge an adverse judgment on the minor's or disabled person's claim from assets other than the proceeds of their liability insurance policies; and

(9) The court does not otherwise order.

(b)   Determination of expedited petition

An expedited petition must be determined by the court not more than 35 days after it is filed, unless a hearing is requested, required, or scheduled under (c) or the time for determination is extended for good cause by order of the court.

(c)   Hearing on expedited petition

(1) The expedited petition must be determined by the court without a hearing unless a hearing is requested by the petitioner at the time the expedited petition is filed, an objection or other opposition to the petition is filed by an interested party, or a hearing is scheduled by the court under (2) or (3).

(2) The court may on its own motion elect to schedule and conduct a hearing on an expedited petition. The court must make its election to schedule the hearing and must give notice of its election and the date, time, and place of the hearing to the petitioner and all other interested parties not more than 25 days after the date the expedited petition is filed.

(3) If the court decides not to grant an expedited petition in full as requested, it must schedule a hearing and give notice of its intended ruling and the date, time, and place of the hearing to the petitioner and all other interested parties within the time provided in (2). (Adopted, eff. Jan. 1, 2010.)

Research References

Rutter, Cal. Practice Guide: Personal Injury Ch. 4-G, G. Concluding and Enforcing Settlement.
4 Witkin Cal. Proc. 5th Pleading § 81, Petition.
14 Witkin, California Summary 10th Wills and Probate § 1014, (S 1014) Procedure for Court Approval.
14 Witkin, California Summary 10th Wills and Probate § 1069, Parent's Compromise of Minor's Claim.

Rule 7.951. Disclosure of the attorney's interest in a petition to compromise a claim

If the petitioner has been represented or assisted by an attorney in preparing the petition to compromise the claim or in any other respect with regard to the claim, the petition must disclose the following information:

(1) The name, state bar number, law firm, if any, and business address of the attorney;

(2) Whether the attorney became involved with the petition, directly or indirectly, at the instance of any party against whom the claim is asserted or of any party's insurance carrier;

(3) Whether the attorney represents or is employed by any other party or any insurance carrier involved in the matter;

(4) Whether the attorney has received any attorney's fees or other compensation for services provided in connection with the claim giving rise to the petition or with the preparation of the petition, and, if so, the amounts and the identity of the person who paid the fees or other compensation;

(5) If the attorney has not received any attorney's fees or other compensation for services provided in connection with the claim giving rise to the petition or with the preparation of the petition, whether the attorney expects to receive any fees or other compensation for these services, and, if so, the amounts and the identity of the person who is expected to pay the fees or other compensation; and

(6) The terms of any agreement between the petitioner and the attorney. *(Adopted, eff. Jan. 1, 2002.)*

Research References

Rutter, Cal. Practice Guide: Personal Injury Ch. 4-G, G. Concluding and Enforcing Settlement.
4 Witkin Cal. Proc. 5th Pleading § 81, Petition.
14 Witkin, California Summary 10th Wills and Probate § 1014, (S 1014) Procedure for Court Approval.
14 Witkin, California Summary 10th Wills and Probate § 1069, Parent's Compromise of Minor's Claim.

Rule 7.952. Attendance at hearing on the petition to compromise a claim

(a) Attendance of the petitioner and claimant

The person compromising the claim on behalf of the minor or person with a disability and the minor or person with a disability must attend the hearing on the compromise of the claim unless the court for good cause dispenses with their personal appearance.

(b) Attendance of the physician and other witnesses

At the hearing, the court may require the presence and testimony of witnesses, including the attending or examining physician. *(Adopted, eff. Jan. 1, 2002. As amended, eff. Jan. 1, 2007.)*

Research References

Rutter, Cal. Practice Guide: Personal Injury Ch. 4-G, G. Concluding and Enforcing Settlement.
4 Witkin Cal. Proc. 5th Pleading § 81, Petition.
4 Witkin Cal. Proc. 5th Pleading § 82, Hearing and Order.

14 Witkin, California Summary 10th Wills and Probate § 1014, (S 1014) Procedure for Court Approval.
14 Witkin, California Summary 10th Wills and Probate § 1069, Parent's Compromise of Minor's Claim.

Rule 7.953. Order for the deposit of funds of a minor or a person with a disability

(a) Acknowledgment of receipt by financial institution

In any case in which the court orders that funds to be received by a minor or a person with a disability must be deposited in a financial institution and not disbursed without further order of the court, the order must include a provision that a certified or filed endorsed copy of the order must be delivered to a manager at the financial institution where the funds are to be deposited, and that a receipt from the financial institution must be promptly filed with the court, acknowledging receipt of both the funds deposited and the order for deposit of funds.

(b) Order permitting the withdrawal of funds by a former minor

If, in the order approving the compromise of a minor's claim, there is a finding that the minor will attain the age of majority on a definite date, the order for deposit may require that the depository permit the withdrawal of funds by the former minor after that date, without further order of the court. *(Adopted, eff. Jan. 1, 2002. As amended, eff. Jan. 1, 2007.)*

Research References

Rutter, Cal. Practice Guide: Personal Injury Ch. 4-G, G. Concluding and Enforcing Settlement.
4 Witkin Cal. Proc. 5th Pleading § 82, Hearing and Order.
14 Witkin, California Summary 10th Wills and Probate § 1004, (S 1004) Deposit of Money or Property.
14 Witkin, California Summary 10th Wills and Probate § 1071, (S 1071) Disposition of Proceeds.

Rule 7.954. Petition for the withdrawal of funds deposited for a minor or a person with a disability

(a) Verified petition required

A petition for the withdrawal of funds deposited for a minor or a person with a disability must be verified and must include the identity of the depository, a showing of the amounts previously withdrawn, a statement of the balance on deposit at the time of the filing of the petition, and a justification for the withdrawal.

(b) Ex parte or noticed hearing

A petition for the withdrawal of funds may be considered ex parte or set for a hearing at the discretion of the court. *(Adopted, eff. Jan. 1, 2002. As amended, eff. Jan. 1, 2007.)*

Research References

Rutter, Cal. Practice Guide: Personal Injury Ch. 4-G, G. Concluding and Enforcing Settlement.
4 Witkin Cal. Proc. 5th Pleading § 82, Hearing and Order.
14 Witkin, California Summary 10th Wills and Probate § 1004, (S 1004) Deposit of Money or Property.
14 Witkin, California Summary 10th Wills and Probate § 1071, (S 1071) Disposition of Proceeds.

Rule 7.955. Attorney's fees for services to a minor or a person with a disability

(a) Reasonable attorney's fees

(1) In all cases under Code of Civil Procedure section 372 or Probate Code sections 3600–3601, unless the court has approved the fee agreement in advance, the court must use a reasonable fee standard when approving and allowing the amount of attorney's fees payable from money or property paid or to be paid for the benefit of a minor or a person with a disability.

Ct. Rules

(2) The court must give consideration to the terms of any representation agreement made between the attorney and the representative of the minor or person with a disability and must evaluate the agreement based on the facts and circumstances existing at the time the agreement was made, except where the attorney and the representative of the minor or person with a disability contemplated that the attorney's fee would be affected by later events.

(b) Factors the court may consider in determining a reasonable attorney's fee

In determining a reasonable attorney's fee, the court may consider the following nonexclusive factors:

(1) The fact that a minor or person with a disability is involved and the circumstances of that minor or person with a disability.

(2) The amount of the fee in proportion to the value of the services performed.

(3) The novelty and difficulty of the questions involved and the skill required to perform the legal services properly.

(4) The amount involved and the results obtained.

(5) The time limitations or constraints imposed by the representative of the minor or person with a disability or by the circumstances.

(6) The nature and length of the professional relationship between the attorney and the representative of the minor or person with a disability.

(7) The experience, reputation, and ability of the attorney or attorneys performing the legal services.

(8) The time and labor required.

(9) The informed consent of the representative of the minor or person with a disability to the fee.

(10) The relative sophistication of the attorney and the representative of the minor or person with a disability.

(11) The likelihood, if apparent to the representative of the minor or person with a disability when the representation agreement was made, that the attorney's acceptance of the particular employment would preclude other employment.

(12) Whether the fee is fixed, hourly, or contingent.

(13) If the fee is contingent:

(A) The risk of loss borne by the attorney;

(B) The amount of costs advanced by the attorney; and

(C) The delay in payment of fees and reimbursement of costs paid by the attorney.

(14) Statutory requirements for representation agreements applicable to particular cases or claims.

(c) Attorney's declaration

A petition requesting court approval and allowance of an attorney's fee under (a) must include a declaration from the attorney that addresses the factors listed in (b) that are applicable to the matter before the court.

(d) Preemption

The Judicial Council has preempted all local rules relating to the determination of reasonable attorney's fees to be awarded from the proceeds of a compromise, settlement, or judgment under Probate Code sections 3600–3601. No trial court, or any division or branch of a trial court, may enact or enforce any local rule concerning this field, except a rule pertaining to the assignment or scheduling of a hearing on a petition or application for court approval or allowance of attorney's fees under sections 3600–3601. All local rules concerning this field are null and void unless otherwise permitted by a statute or a rule in the

California Rules of Court. *(Adopted, eff. Jan. 1, 2003. As amended, eff. Jan. 1, 2007; Jan. 1, 2010.)*

Advisory Committee Comment

This rule requires the court to approve and allow attorney's fees in an amount that is reasonable under all the facts and circumstances, under Probate Code section 3601. The rule is declaratory of existing law concerning attorney's fees under a contingency fee agreement when the fees must be approved by the court. The facts and circumstances that the court may consider are discussed in a large body of decisional law under section 3601 and under other statutes that require the court to determine reasonable attorney's fees. The factors listed in rule 7.955(b) are modeled after those provided in rule 4–200 of the Rules of Professional Conduct of the State Bar of California concerning an unconscionable attorney's fee, but the advisory committee does not intend to suggest or imply that an attorney's fee must be found to be unconscionable under rule 4–200 to be determined to be unreasonable under this rule.

The rule permits, but does not require, the court to allow attorney's fees in an amount specified in a contingency fee agreement. The amount of attorney's fees allowed by the court must meet the reasonableness standard of section 3601 no matter how they are determined.

Research References

Rutter, Cal. Practice Guide: Civ. Pro. Before Trial Gen. Matls., Highlights.

Rutter, Cal. Practice Guide: Civ. Pro. Before Trial Ch. 12(II)-B, B. Settlements on Behalf of Minors or Incompetents.

Rutter, Cal. Practice Guide: Personal Injury Ch. 4-G, G. Concluding and Enforcing Settlement.

Rutter, Cal. Practice Guide: Prof. Responsibility Ch. 5-C, C. Other Statutory Limits on Fees and Fee Agreements.

2 Witkin Cal. Proc. 5th Courts § 194, (S 194) Probate Rules.

14 Witkin, California Summary 10th Wills and Probate § 4, Probate Rules.

14 Witkin, California Summary 10th Wills and Probate § 1070, (S 1070) in General.

Chapter 21

GUARDIANSHIPS

Rule 7.1001. Guardian screening form

(a) Screening form to be submitted with petition

Each proposed probate guardian, except a public guardian, or a bank or other entity entitled to conduct the business of a trust company, must submit to the court with the petition for appointment of guardian a completed *Confidential Guardian Screening Form* (form GC–212).

(b) Use of form

The information on the *Confidential Guardian Screening Form* is used by the court and by persons or agencies designated by the court to assist the court in determining whether a proposed guardian should be appointed.

(c) Form to be confidential

The *Confidential Guardian Screening Form* and the information contained on the form are confidential. The clerk must maintain these forms in a manner that will protect and preserve their confidentiality. *(Adopted, eff. Jan. 1, 2001. As amended, eff. Jan. 1, 2002; Jan. 1, 2007.)*

Research References

2 Witkin Cal. Proc. 5th Courts § 194, (S 194) Probate Rules.
14 Witkin, California Summary 10th Wills and Probate § 4, Probate Rules.
14 Witkin, California Summary 10th Wills and Probate § 919, (S 919) Content and Form.
14 Witkin, California Summary 10th Wills and Probate § 960, Governing Law.

Rule 7.1002. Acknowledgment of receipt of Duties of Guardian

Before the court issues letters, each guardian must execute and file an acknowledgment of receipt of the *Duties of Guardian* (form GC–248). *(Adopted, eff. Jan. 1, 2001. As amended, eff. Jan. 1, 2002; Jan. 1, 2007.)*

Research References

14 Witkin, California Summary 10th Wills and Probate § 4, Probate Rules.
14 Witkin, California Summary 10th Wills and Probate § 926, Determination and Order.
14 Witkin, California Summary 10th Wills and Probate § 960, Governing Law.

Rule 7.1003. Confidential guardianship status report form

(a) Due date of status report

Each guardian required by the court to complete, sign, and file the status report authorized by Probate Code section 1513.2 must file the completed and signed report no later than one month after the anniversary of the date of the order appointing him or her as guardian. Co–guardians may sign and file their reports jointly.

(b) Court clerk's duties

The clerk of each court that requires guardians to file the status report authorized by Probate Code section 1513.2 must:

(1) Determine the annual due date for the completed report from each appointed guardian required to file the report;

(2) Fill in the due date for the completed report, in the space provided in the form for that purpose, on each blank copy of the form that must be mailed to appointed guardians under (3); and

(3) Mail by first class mail to each appointed guardian no later than one month prior to the date the status report is due under (a) a blank copy of *Confidential Guardianship Status Report* (form GC–251) for each child under guardianship under the same case number. *(Adopted, eff. Jan. 1, 2004. As amended, eff. Jan. 1, 2007.)*

Research References

14 Witkin, California Summary 10th Wills and Probate § 929, (S 929) Annual Status Report.

Rule 7.1004. Termination of guardianship

(a) Operation of law or court order

A guardianship of the person or estate of a minor may terminate by operation of law or may be terminated by court order where the court determines that it would be in the ward's best interest to terminate the guardianship.

(b) Guardian of the person

Under Probate Code section 1600 a guardianship of the person terminates by operation of law, and the guardian of the person need not file a petition for its termination, when the ward attains majority, dies, is adopted, or is emancipated.

(c) Duty of guardian of estate on termination

A guardian of the estate whose administration is terminated by operation of law or court order must file and obtain the court's approval of a final account or report of the administration. *(Adopted, eff. Jan. 1, 2004.)*

Research References

14 Witkin, California Summary 10th Wills and Probate § 930, (S 930) Termination of Guardianship.

Rule 7.1005. Service of copy of final account or report after resignation or removal of guardian

A resigned or removed guardian of the estate must serve a copy of the guardian's final account or report and the petition for its settlement, with the notice of hearing that must be served on the successor guardian of the estate under Probate Code section 1460(b)(1), unless the court dispenses with such service. *(Adopted, eff. Jan. 1, 2004.)*

Research References

14 Witkin, California Summary 10th Wills and Probate § 930, (S 930) Termination of Guardianship.

Rule 7.1006. Service of copy of final account on termination of guardianship

(a) Minor living

In addition to service of notices of hearing required under Probate Code section 1460(b), on termination of the guardianship the guardian of the estate must serve a copy of the guardian's final account and petition for its settlement on the minor, unless the court dispenses with such service.

(b) Personal representative of deceased minor

If the minor is deceased, in addition to service of notices of hearing required under Probate Code section 1460(b), on termination of the guardianship the guardian of the estate must serve a notice of hearing and a copy of the guardian's final account and petition for its settlement on the personal representative of the deceased minor's estate, unless the court dispenses with such service.

(c) Successors in interest to deceased minor

If the minor is deceased and no personal representative of the minor's estate has been appointed or qualified or if the personal representative of the minor's estate is also the guardian, on termination of the guardianship, in addition to the notices of hearing required under Probate Code section 1460(b), the guardian of the estate must serve a notice of hearing and a copy of the guardian's final account and petition for its settlement on the persons entitled to succeed to the deceased minor's estate, unless the court dispenses with such service. *(Adopted, eff. Jan. 1, 2004.)*

Research References

14 Witkin, California Summary 10th Wills and Probate § 930, (S 930) Termination of Guardianship.

Rule 7.1007. Settlement of accounts and release by former minor

(a) Release of guardian of estate by ward after majority

A ward who has attained majority may settle accounts with his or her guardian of the estate and may give a valid release to the guardian if the court determines, at the time of the hearing on the final account, or on the final report and petition for termination on waiver of account, that the release has been obtained fairly and without undue influence. The release is not effective to discharge the guardian until one year after the ward has attained majority.

(b) Appearance of ward

The court may require the personal appearance of the ward at the hearing on the final account or report of the guardian of the estate after termination of the guardianship. *(Adopted, eff. Jan. 1, 2004.)*

Research References

14 Witkin, California Summary 10th Wills and Probate § 1039, (S 1039) Settlement and Discharge.

Rule 7.1008. Visitation by former guardian after termination of guardianship

(a) Visitation order at time of termination of guardianship

Subject to the provisions of Welfare and Institutions Code section 304, a guardian may request the court to order visitation with the child under guardianship at the time of termination of the guardianship either in the guardian's petition for termination or in the guardian's objections or other pleading filed in response to the petition of another party for termination. The court may then order visitation if it is in the best interest of the child.

(b) Request for visitation after termination of guardianship

If no order was entered under (a) concerning visitation between the former guardian and the former ward at termination of the guardianship and no dependency proceedings for the child are pending, the former guardian may request the court to order visitation with the former ward after termination of the guardianship as provided in Family Code section 3105, Probate Code section 1602, rule 5.475, and this rule, as follows:

(1) If either parent of the former ward is living, in an independent action for visitation under the Family Code; or

(2) If neither parent of the former ward is living, in a guardianship proceeding under the Probate Code, including a proceeding commenced for that purpose.

(c) Declaration under UCCJEA

A guardian or former guardian requesting visitation under this rule must file a *Declaration Under Uniform Child Custody Jurisdiction and Enforcement Act (UCCJEA)* (form FL–105/GC–120) with his or her request for visitation.

(d) Transmission of visitation order

Following the termination of the guardianship the clerk of the superior court issuing the visitation order concerning the guardian or former guardian and the ward or former ward must promptly transmit an endorsed filed copy of the order to the superior court of the county where a custody proceeding under the Family Code is pending or, if none, to the superior court of the county in which the custodial parent resides. An order

transmitted to the court in the county where the custodial parent resides may be sent to the receiving court's Court Operations Manager, Family Division, or similar senior manager or clerk responsible for the operations of the family law departments of the court. If the receiving court has more than one location, the order may be sent to the main or central district of the court. *(Adopted, eff. Jan. 1, 2006. As amended, eff. Jan. 1, 2007.)*

Research References

Rutter, Cal. Practice Guide: Family Law Ch. 7-F, F. Visitation Rights.
14 Witkin, California Summary 10th Wills and Probate § 930, (S 930) Termination of Guardianship.

Rule 7.1009. Standards of conduct for the guardian of the estate

Except as otherwise required by statute, in the exercise of ordinary care and diligence in managing and controlling the estates of the ward, the guardian of the estate is to be guided by the following principles:

(a) Avoidance of actual and apparent conflicts of interest with the ward

The guardian must avoid actual conflicts of interest and, consistent with his or her fiduciary duty to the ward, the appearance of conflicts of interest. The guardian must avoid any personal, business, or professional interest or relationship that is or reasonably could be perceived as being self-serving or adverse to the best interest of the ward. In particular:

(1) Except as appropriate for guardians who are not professional fiduciaries with full disclosure to the court, the guardian should not personally provide medical or legal services to the ward;

(2) The guardian must be independent from all service providers, except when (a) no other guardian or service providers are reasonably available, (b) the exception is in the best interest of the ward, (c) the circumstances are fully disclosed to the court, and (d) prior court approval has been obtained;

(3) The guardian must neither solicit nor accept incentives from service providers; and

(4) The guardian must not engage his or her family members to provide services to the ward for a profit or fee when other alternatives are reasonably available. Where family members do provide such services, their relationship to the guardian must be fully disclosed to the court, the terms of engagement must be in the best interest of the ward compared to the terms available from independent service providers, the services must be competently performed, and the guardian must be able to exercise appropriate control and supervision.

A guardian's employees, including family members, are not service providers and are not providing services to the ward for a profit or fee within the meaning of this rule if their compensation is paid by the guardian and their services are either included in the guardian's petition for allowance of the guardian's compensation or are not paid from the ward's estate.

(b) Guardianship estate management

In addition to complying with applicable standards of estate management specified in rule 7.1059(b), the guardian of the estate must:

(1) Manage the estate primarily for the ward's long-term benefit if the ward has a parent available who can provide sufficient support;

(2) If it would be in the best interest of the ward and the estate, consider requesting court authority to support the ward from the estate if the ward does not have a parent available who can provide sufficient support. *(Adopted, eff. Jan. 1, 2008.)*

Advisory Committee Comment

The Probate and Mental Health Advisory Committee consulted with several organizations in the development of rule 7.1009, including the National Guardianship Association, a nationwide voluntary association of professional and family fiduciaries, guardians, and allied professionals. In developing this rule, the Probate and Mental Health Advisory Committee considered the National Guardianship Association's Standards of Practice. Some of these standards have been incorporated into the rule.

Research References

14 Witkin, California Summary 10th Wills and Probate § 1000, (S 1000) Restrictions on Self-Dealing.

14 Witkin, California Summary 10th Wills and Probate § 1001, (S 1001) Duty to Manage Estate.

14 Witkin, California Summary 10th Wills and Probate § 1012, (S 1012) Without Court Approval.

Rule 7.1011. Taking possession of an asset of the ward at an institution or opening or changing ownership of an account or safe-deposit box in a financial institution

(a) Definitions

As used in this rule, the following terms have the meanings stated below:

(1) An "institution" is an insurance company, insurance broker, insurance agent, investment company, investment bank, securities broker-dealer, investment advisor, financial planner, financial advisor, or any other person who takes, holds, or controls an asset subject to a guardianship that is not a "financial institution" within the meaning of this rule;

(2) A "financial institution" is a bank, trust (except as provided in (d)), savings and loan association, savings bank, industrial bank, or credit union; and

(3) "Taking possession" or "taking control" of an asset held or controlled by an institution includes changing title to the asset, withdrawing all or any portion of the asset, or transferring all or any portion of the asset from the institution.

(b) Responsibilities of the guardian when taking possession or control of an asset of the ward at an institution

When taking possession or control of an asset held by an institution in the name of the ward, the temporary or general guardian of the estate must provide the following to the institution:

(1) A certified copy of the guardian's *Letters of Temporary Guardianship or Conservatorship* (form GC–150) or *Letters of Guardianship* (form GC–250) containing the Notice to Institutions and Financial Institutions on the second page; and

(2) A blank copy of a *Notice of Taking Possession or Control of an Asset of Minor or Conservatee* (form GC–050).

(c) Responsibilities of the guardian when opening or changing the name on an account or a safe-deposit box in a financial institution

When opening or changing the name on an account or a safe-deposit box in a financial institution, the temporary or general guardian of the estate must provide the following to the financial institution:

(1) A certified copy of the guardian's *Letters of Temporary Guardianship or Conservatorship* (form GC–150) or *Letters of Guardianship* (form GC–250) containing the Notice to Institutions and Financial Institutions on the second page; and

(2) A blank copy of a *Notice of Opening or Changing a Guardianship or Conservatorship Account or Safe–Deposit Box* (form GC–051).

(d) Application of this rule to trust arrangements

This rule applies to Totten trust accounts but does not apply to any other trust arrangement described in Probate Code section 82(b). *(Adopted, eff. Jan. 1, 2009.)*

Research References

14 Witkin, California Summary 10th Wills and Probate § 1005, (S 1005) Notification by Institutions.

Rule 7.1012. The good cause exception to notice of the hearing on a petition for appointment of a temporary guardian

(a) Purpose

The purpose of this rule is to establish uniform standards for the good cause exception to the notice of the hearing required on a petition for appointment of a temporary guardian under Probate Code section 2250(e).

(b) Good cause for exceptions to notice limited

Good cause for an exception to the notice required by section 2250(e) must be based on a showing that the exception is necessary to protect the proposed ward or his or her estate from immediate and substantial harm.

(c) Court may waive or change the time or manner of giving notice

An exception to the notice requirement of section 2250(e) may include one or any combination of the following:

(1) Waiving notice to one, more than one, or all persons entitled to notice;

(2) Requiring a different period of notice; and

(3) Changing the required manner of giving notice, including requiring notice by telephone, fax, e-mail, or a combination of these methods, instead of notice by personal delivery to the proposed ward's parents or to a person with a visitation order.

(d) Good cause exceptions to notice

Good cause for an exception to the notice requirement of section 2250(e) may include a showing of:

(1) Harm caused by the passage of time. The showing must demonstrate the immediate and substantial harm to the ward or the ward's estate that could occur during the notice period.

(2) Harm that one or more persons entitled to notice might do to the proposed ward, including abduction; or harm to the proposed ward's estate if notice to those persons is given. Such a showing would not support an exception to the requirement to give notice to any other person entitled to notice unless it also demonstrates that notice cannot reasonably be given to the other person without also giving notice to the persons who might cause harm.

(3) The death or incapacity of the proposed ward's custodial parent and the petitioner's status as the custodial parent's nominee.

(4) Medical emergency. The emergency must be immediate and substantial and treatment (1) must be reasonably unavailable unless a temporary guardian is appointed and (2) cannot be deferred for the notice period because of the proposed ward's pain or extreme discomfort or a significant risk of harm.

(5) Financial emergency. The emergency must be immediate and substantial and other means shown likely to be ineffective to prevent loss or further loss to the proposed ward's estate or loss of support for the proposed ward during the notice period.

(e) Contents of request for good cause exception to notice

(1) When the temporary guardianship petition is prepared on the *Petition for Appointment of Temporary Guardian* (form GC–110), a request for a good cause exception to the notice requirement of section 2250(e) must be in writing, separate from

the petition for appointment of a temporary guardian, and must include:

(A) An application containing the case caption and stating the relief requested;

(B) An affirmative factual showing in support of the application in a declaration under penalty of perjury containing competent testimony based on personal knowledge;

(C) A declaration under penalty of perjury based on personal knowledge containing the information required for an ex parte application under rule 3.1204(b); and

(D) A proposed order.

(2) When the temporary guardianship petition is prepared on the *Petition for Appointment of Temporary Guardian of the Person* (form GC–110(P)), a request for a good cause exception to the notice requirement of section 2250(e) may be included in the petition. *(Adopted, eff. Jan. 1, 2008. As amended, eff. Jan. 1, 2009.)*

Research References

14 Witkin, California Summary 10th Wills and Probate § 975A, (S 975A) (New)-Good Cause Exception to Notice Requirements.

Rule 7.1013. Change of ward's residence

(a) Pre–move notice of change of personal residence required

Unless an emergency requires a shorter period of notice, the guardian of the person must mail copies of a notice of an intended change of the ward's personal residence to the persons listed below at least 15 days before the date of the proposed change, and file the original notice with proof of mailing with the court. Copies of the notice must be mailed to:

(1) The ward if he or she is 12 years of age or older;

(2) The attorney of record for the ward;

(3) The ward's parents;

(4) Any person who had legal custody of the ward when the first petition for appointment of a guardian was filed in the proceeding;

(5) A guardian of the ward's estate; and

(6) Any person who was nominated as guardian of the ward under Probate Code sections 1500 or 1501 but was not appointed guardian in the proceeding.

(b) Ward's personal residence

The "ward's personal residence" under (a) is the ward's residence when the first petition for appointment of a guardian was filed in the proceeding.

(c) Post–move notice of a change of residence required

The guardian of the person of a minor must file a notice of a change of the ward's residence with the court within 30 days of the date of any change. Unless waived by the court for good cause to prevent harm to the ward, the guardian, the guardian's attorney, or an employee of the guardian's attorney must also mail a copy of the notice to the persons listed below and file a proof of mailing with the original notice. Unless waived, copies of the notice must be mailed to:

(1) The ward's attorney of record;

(2) The ward's parents;

(3) Any person who had legal custody of the ward when the first petition for appointment of a guardian was filed in the proceeding;

(4) A guardian of the ward's estate; and

(5) Any person who was nominated as guardian of the ward under Probate Code sections 1500 or 1501 but was not appointed guardian in the proceeding.

(d) Ward's residence

The "ward's residence" under (c) is the ward's residence at any time after appointment of a guardian.

(e) Use of Judicial Council forms GC–079 and GC–080

(1) The *Pre–Move Notice of Proposed Change of Personal Residence of Conservatee or Ward* (form GC–079) must be used for the pre-move notice required under (a) and Probate Code section 2352(e)(3). The guardian, the guardian's attorney, or an employee of the attorney may complete the mailing and sign the proof of mailing on page 2 of the form. If the notice is mailed less than 15 days before the date of the move because an emergency requires a shorter period of notice, the basis for the emergency must be stated in the notice.

(2) The *Post–Move Notice of Change of Residence of Conservatee or Ward* (form GC–080) must be used for the post-move notice required under (c) and Probate Code section 2352(e)(1) and (2). The guardian, the guardian's attorney, or an employee of the attorney may complete the mailing and sign the proof of mailing on page 2 of the form.

(f) Prior court approval required to establish ward's residence outside California

Notwithstanding any other provision of this rule, prior court approval is required before a ward's residence may be established outside the state of California. *(Adopted, eff. Jan. 1, 2008.)*

Research References

14 Witkin, California Summary 10th Wills and Probate § 990, Fixing Residence.

Rule 7.1014. Communications between courts in different California counties concerning guardianship venue

(a) Purpose of rule

This rule addresses the communications between courts concerning guardianship venue required by Probate Code section 2204(b). These communications are between the superior court in one California county where a guardianship proceeding has been filed (referred to in this rule as the guardianship court) and one or more superior courts in one or more other California counties where custody or visitation proceedings under the Family Code involving the ward or proposed ward were previously filed (referred to in this rule as the family court or courts, or the other court or courts).

(b) Substantive communications between judicial officers

Before making a venue decision on a petition for appointment of a general guardian in a guardianship proceeding described in (a), or a decision on a petition to transfer under Probate Code section 2212 filed in the proceeding before the appointment of a guardian or temporary guardian, the judicial officer responsible for the proceeding in the guardianship court must communicate with the judicial officer or officers responsible for the custody proceeding or proceedings in the family court or courts concerning which county provides the venue for the guardianship proceeding that is in the best interests of the ward or the proposed ward.

(1) If the currently responsible judicial officer in the family court or courts cannot be identified, communication must be made with the managing or supervising judicial officer of the family departments of the other court or courts, if any, or his or her designee, or with the presiding judge of the other court or courts or his or her designee.

(2) If courts in more than two counties are involved, simultaneous communications among judicial officers of all of the courts are recommended, if reasonably practicable. If communications occur between some but not all involved courts, the record of

these communications must be made available to those judicial officers of the courts who were not included at or before the time the judicial officer of the guardianship court communicates with them.

(3) A record must be made of all communications between judicial officers under this subdivision.

(4) The parties to the guardianship proceeding, including a petitioner for transfer; all persons entitled to notice of the hearing on the petition for appointment of a guardian; and any additional persons ordered by the guardianship court must promptly be informed of the communications and given access to the record of the communications.

(5) The provisions of Family Code section 3410(b) apply to communications between judicial officers under this subdivision, except that the term "jurisdiction" in that section corresponds to "venue" in this context, and the term "parties" in that section identifies the persons listed in (4).

(c) Preliminary communications

To assist the judicial officer in making the communication required in (b), the guardianship court may have preliminary communications with each family court to collect information about the proceeding in that court or for other routine matters, including calendar management, and scheduling.

(1) The guardianship court should attempt to collect, and each family court is encouraged to provide, as much of the following information about the proceeding in the family court as is reasonable under the circumstances:

(A) The case number or numbers and the nature of each family court proceeding;

(B) The names of the parties to each family court proceeding, including contact information for self-represented parties; their relationship or other connection to the ward or proposed ward in the guardianship proceeding, and the names and contact information of counsel for any parties represented by counsel;

(C) The current status (active or inactive) of each family court proceeding, whether any future hearings are set in each proceeding, and if so, their dates and times, locations, and nature;

(D) The contents and dates filed of orders in the each family court proceeding that decide or resolve custody or visitation issues concerning the ward or proposed ward in the guardianship proceeding;

(E) Whether any orders of each family court are final, were appealed from, or were the subject of extraordinary writ proceedings, and the current status of any such appeal or proceeding;

(F) The court branch and department where each family court proceeding was assigned and where the proceeding is currently assigned or pending;

(G) The identity of the judicial officer currently assigned to or otherwise responsible for each family court proceeding; and

(H) Other information about each family court proceeding requested by the judicial officer of the guardianship court.

(2) In the discretion of the judicial officer of the guardianship court, preliminary communications under this rule may be between judicial officers of the courts involved or between staff of the guardianship court and judicial officers or court staff of each other court.

(3) Family Code section 3410(c) applies to preliminary communications under this rule.

(d) Applicability of this rule to petitions to transfer filed after the appointment of a guardian or temporary guardian

Subdivisions (b) and (c) of this rule may, in the discretion of the guardianship court, apply to petitions for transfer described in Probate Code section 2204(b)(2).

(e) "Record" under this rule

"Record" under this rule has the meaning provided in Family Code section 3410(e). *(Adopted, eff. Jan. 1, 2013.)*

Rule 7.1015. Indian Child Welfare Act in guardianship and certain conservatorship proceedings

(a) Definitions

As used in this rule, unless the context or subject matter otherwise requires:

(1) "Act" means the Indian Child Welfare Act (25 United States Code sections 1901–1963).

(2) "Petitioner" means and refers to a petitioner for the appointment of a guardian of the person of a child or a petitioner for the appointment of a conservator of the person of a formerly married minor child.

(b) Applicability of this rule and rules 5.480 through 5.487

(1) This rule applies to the following proceedings under division 4 of the Probate Code when the proposed ward or conservatee is an Indian child, within the meaning of the act:

(A) A guardianship of the person or the person and estate in which the proposed guardian of the person is not the proposed ward's natural parent or Indian custodian within the meaning of the act;

(B) A conservatorship of the person or the person and estate of a formerly married minor in which the proposed conservator is not a natural parent or Indian custodian of the minor and is seeking physical custody of the proposed conservatee.

(2) Unless the context otherwise requires, rules 5.480 through 5.487 apply to the proceedings listed in (1).

(3) When applied to the proceedings listed in (1), references in rules 5.480 through 5.487 to social workers, probation officers, county probation departments, or county social welfare departments are references to the petitioner or petitioners for the appointment of a guardian or conservator of the person of an Indian child and to an Indian child's appointed temporary or general guardian or conservator of the person.

(4) If the court appoints a temporary or general guardian or conservator of the person of the child involved in a proceeding listed in (1), the duties and responsibilities of a petitioner under this rule are transferred to and become the duties and responsibilities of the appointed guardian or conservator. The petitioner must cooperate with and provide any information the petitioner has concerning the child to the appointed guardian or conservator.

(c) Notice

If, at any time after the filing of a petition for appointment of a guardian or conservator for a minor child, the court or petitioner knows or has reason to know, within the meaning of Probate Code sections 1449 and 1459.5 and Welfare and Institutions Code section 224.3(b), that an Indian child is involved, the petitioner and the court must notify the child's parents or legal guardian and Indian custodian, and the Indian child's tribe, of the pending proceeding and the right of the tribe to intervene, as follows:

(1) Notice to the Indian child's parents, Indian custodian, and Indian tribe of the commencement of a guardianship or conservatorship must be given by serving copies of the completed *Notice of Child Custody Proceeding for Indian Child* (form ICWA–030), the petition for appointment of a guardian or

conservator, and all attachments, by certified or registered mail, fully prepaid with return receipt requested.

(2) The petitioner and his or her attorney, if any, must complete the *Notice* and the petitioner must date and sign the declaration. If there is more than one petitioner, the statements about the child's ancestors and background provided in the *Notice of Child Custody Proceeding for Indian Child* (form ICWA–030) must be based on all information known to each petitioner, and all petitioners must sign the declaration.

(3) When the petitioner is represented by an attorney in the proceeding, the attorney must serve copies of the *Notice of Child Custody Proceeding for Indian Child* (form ICWA–030) in the manner described in (1) and sign the declaration of mailing on the *Notice*.

(4) When the guardianship or conservatorship petitioner or petitioners are not represented by an attorney in the proceeding, the clerk of the court must serve the *Notice* in the manner described in (1) and sign the certificate of mailing on the *Notice*.

(5) The original of all *Notices of Child Custody Proceeding for Indian Child* (form ICWA–030) served under the act, and all return receipts and responses received, must be filed with the court before the hearing.

(6) Notice to an Indian child's tribe must be sent to the tribal chairperson unless the tribe has designated another agent for service.

(7) Notice must be served on all tribes of which the child may be a member or eligible for membership. If there are more tribes or bands to be served than can be listed on the last page of the *Notice*, the additional tribes or bands may be listed on an *Attachment to Notice of Child Custody Proceeding for Indian Child* (form ICWA–030(A)).

(8) Notice under the act must be served whenever there is any reason to know that the child is or may be an Indian child and for every hearing after the first hearing unless and until it is determined that the act does not apply to the proceeding.

(9) If, after a reasonable time following the service of notice under the act—but in no event less than 60 days—no determinative response to the *Notice of Child Custody Proceeding for Indian Child* (form ICWA–030) is received, the court may determine that the act does not apply to the proceeding unless further evidence of its applicability is later received.

(10) If an Indian child's tribe intervenes in the proceeding, service of the *Notice of Child Custody Proceeding for Indian Child* (form ICWA–030) is no longer required and subsequent notices to the tribe may be sent to all parties in the form and in the manner required under the Probate Code and these rules. All other provisions of the act, this rule, and rules 5.480 through 5.487 continue to apply.

(11) Notice under the act must be served in addition to all notices otherwise required for the particular proceeding under the provisions of the Probate Code.

(d) Duty of inquiry

(1) The court, a court investigator or county officer appointed to conduct an investigation under Probate Code section 1513 or 1826, a petitioner, and an appointed temporary or general guardian or conservator of the person of a minor child each have an affirmative and continuing duty to inquire whether the child involved in the matters identified in (b)(1) is or may be an Indian child.

(2) Before filing his or her petition, the petitioner must ask the child involved in the proceeding, if the child is old enough, and the parents, any other legal guardian, and any Indian custodian, whether the child is or may be an Indian child, and must complete items 1c and 8 of the *Guardianship Petition—*

Child Information Attachment (form GC–210(CA)) and attach it to his or her petition.

(3) At the first personal appearance by a parent or previously appointed legal guardian at a hearing in a guardianship or conservatorship, the court must if requested by petitioner, or may on its own motion, order the parent or legal guardian to complete a *Parental Notification of Indian Status* (form ICWA–020) and deliver the completed form to the petitioner.

(4) If the parent, Indian custodian, or guardian does not personally appear at a hearing in a proceeding identified in (b)(1), the court may order the petitioner to use reasonable diligence to find and ask the parent, Indian custodian, or legal guardian to complete and deliver to petitioner a *Parental Notification of Indian Status* (form ICWA–020).

(5) If the court or county investigator, petitioner, appointed guardian or conservator, or the attorney for a petitioner or appointed guardian or conservator, knows or has reason to know that an Indian child is involved in the proceeding, he or she must make further inquiry as soon as practicable by:

(A) Interviewing the parents, Indian custodian, and "extended family members" as defined in 25 United States Code section 1903(2), to gather the information listed in Probate Code section 1460.2(b)(5) that is required to complete the *Notice of Child Custody Proceeding for Indian Child* (form ICWA–030);

(B) Contacting the U.S. Department of the Interior, Bureau of Indian Affairs and the California Department of Social Services for assistance in identifying the names and contact information of the tribes of which the child may be a member or eligible for membership; and

(C) Contacting the tribes and any other person who reasonably can be expected to have information regarding the child's tribal membership status or eligibility for membership.

(6) If the court knows or has reason to know that an Indian child is involved in the proceeding, the court may direct any of the persons named in (5) to conduct the inquiry described in that paragraph.

(7) The circumstances that may provide reason to know the child is an Indian child include the following:

(A) The child or person having an interest in the child, including an Indian tribe, an Indian organization, an officer of the court, a public or private agency, or a member of the child's extended family, informs or otherwise provides information suggesting that the child is an Indian child to the court or to any person listed in (5);

(B) The residence or domicile of the child, the child's parents, or an Indian custodian is in a predominantly Indian community; or

(C) The child or the child's family has received services or benefits from a tribe or services that are available to Indians from tribes or the federal government, such as the U.S. Department of Health and Human Services, Indian Health Service, or Tribal Temporary Assistance to Needy Families benefits.

(Adopted, eff. Jan. 1, 2008. As amended, eff. July 1, 2012.)

Research References

2 Witkin Cal. Proc. 5th Courts § 194, (S 194) Probate Rules.

10 Witkin, California Summary 10th Parent and Child § 522, Nature and Scope of Indian Child Welfare Act.

14 Witkin, California Summary 10th Wills and Probate § 4, Probate Rules.

14 Witkin, California Summary 10th Wills and Probate § 915A, (S 915A) (New)-Special Provisions Applicable to Indian Children.

Rule 7.1016.　Participation and testimony of wards in guardianship proceedings

(a) Definitions

As used in this rule, the following terms have the meanings specified:

(1) "Ward" includes "proposed ward."

(2) A "proceeding" is a matter before the court for decision in a probate guardianship of the person that concerns appointment or removal of a guardian, visitation, determination of the ward's place of residence, or termination of the guardianship by court order.

(3) "Party," as used in this rule to refer to the ward, means a ward who has filed a petition or opposition to a petition concerning a proceeding or other matter subject to this rule.

(b) Purpose and scope of rule

(1) This rule applies Family Code section 3042 to the participation and testimony of the ward in a proceeding in a probate guardianship of the person. The testimony of other minors in a guardianship case is governed by Evidence Code sections 765(b) and 767(b).

(2) The court in its discretion may apply this rule, in whole or in part, to the participation and testimony of a ward in a guardianship of the estate or in a matter before the court in a guardianship of the person that is not a proceeding within the meaning of this rule. The phrase "or other matter subject to this is rule" following the term "proceeding" is a reference to the matters described in this paragraph.

(3) No statutory mandate, rule, or practice requires a ward who is not a party to the proceeding or other matter subject to this rule to participate in court or prohibits him or her from doing so. When a ward desires to participate but is not a party to the proceeding or other matter subject to this rule, the court must balance the protection of the ward, the statutory duty to consider the wishes of and input from the ward, and the probative value of the ward's input while ensuring all parties' due process rights to challenge evidence relied on by the court in making decisions affecting the ward in matters covered by the rule.

(4) This rule rather than rule 5.250, on children's participation and testimony in family court proceedings, applies in probate guardianship proceedings.

(c) Determining whether the nonparty ward wishes to address the court

(1) The following persons must inform the court if they have information indicating that a ward who is not a party wishes to address the court in a proceeding or other matter subject to this rule:

(A) The ward's counsel;

(B) A court or county guardianship investigator;

(C) A child custody recommending counselor who provides recommendations to the judicial officer under Family Code section 3183;

(D) An expert appointed by the court under Evidence Code section 730 to assist the court in the matter; or

(E) The ward's guardian ad litem.

(2) The following persons may inform the court if they have information indicating that a ward who is not a party wishes to address the court in a proceeding or other matter subject to this rule:

(A) A party in the guardianship case; and

(B) An attorney for a party in the guardianship case.

(3) In the absence of information indicating that a ward who is not a party wishes to address the court in a proceeding or other matter subject to this rule, the judicial officer may inquire whether the ward wishes to do so.

(d) Guidelines for determining whether addressing the court is in the nonparty ward's best interest

(1) When a ward who is not a party indicates that he or she wishes to address the court, the judicial officer must consider whether involving the ward in the proceeding or other matter subject to this rule is in the ward's best interest.

(2) If the ward is 12 years old or older, the judicial officer must hear from the ward unless the court makes a finding that addressing the court is not in the ward's best interest and states the reasons on the record.

(3) In determining whether addressing the court is in the ward's best interest, the judicial officer should consider the following:

(A) Whether the ward is of sufficient age and capacity to form an intelligent preference as to the matter to be decided;

(B) Whether the ward is of sufficient age and capacity to understand the nature of testimony;

(C) Whether information has been presented indicating that the ward may be at risk emotionally if he or she is permitted or denied the opportunity to address the court or that the ward may benefit from addressing the court;

(D) Whether the subject areas about which the ward is anticipated to address the court are relevant to the decision the court must make;

(E) Whether the appointment of counsel under Probate Code section 1470 or a guardian ad litem for the ward would be helpful to the determination or would be necessary to protect the ward's interests; and

(F) Whether any other factors weigh in favor of or against having the ward address the court, taking into consideration the ward's desire to do so.

(e) Guidelines for receiving testimony and other input from the nonparty ward

(1) No testimony of a ward may y be received without such testimony being heard on the record or in the presence of the parties. This requirement may not be waived.

(2) On deciding to take the testimony of a ward who is not a party in a proceeding or other matter subject to this rule, the judicial officer should balance the necessity of taking the ward's testimony in the courtroom with parents, the guardian or proposed guardian, other parties, and attorneys present with the need to create an environment in which the ward can be open and honest. In each case in which a ward's testimony will be taken, the judicial officer should consider:

(A) Where the testimony will be taken;

(B) Who should be present when the testimony is taken;

(C) How the ward will be questioned; and

(D) Whether a court reporter is available in all instances, but especially when the ward's testimony may be taken outside the presence of the parties and their attorneys. If the court reporter will not be available, whether there are other means to collect, preserve, transcribe, and make the ward's testimony available to parties and their attorneys.

(3) In taking testimony from a ward who is not a party to the proceeding or other matter subject to this rule, the court must take the special care required by Evidence Code section 765(b). If the ward is not represented by an attorney, the court must inform the ward in an age-appropriate manner about the limitations on confidentiality of testimony and that the informa-

tion provided to the court will be on the record and provided to the parties in the case.

(4) In the process of listening to and inviting the ward's input, the court must allow but not require the ward to state a preference regarding the matter to be decided in the proceeding or other matter subject to this rule and should provide information in an age-appropriate manner about the process by which the court will make a decision.

(5) In any case in which a ward who is not a party to the proceeding or other matter subject to this rule will be called to testify, the court must consider the appointment of counsel for the ward under Probate Code section 1470 and may consider the appointment of a guardian ad litem for the ward. In addition to satisfying the requirements for minor's counsel under rule 7.1101, minor's counsel must:

(A) Provide information to the ward in an age-appropriate manner about the limitations on the confidentiality of testimony and indicate to the ward the possibility that information provided to the court will be on the record and provided to the parties in the case;

(B) Allow but not require the ward to state a preference regarding the issues to be decided in the proceeding or other matter subject to this rule, and provide information in an age-appropriate manner about the process by which the court will make a decision;

(C) If appropriate, provide the ward with an orientation to the courtroom or other place where the ward will testify; and

(D) Inform the parties and the court about the ward's desire to provide input.

(6) If the court precludes the calling of a ward who is not a party as a witness in a proceeding or other matter subject to this rule, alternatives for the court to obtain information or other input from the ward may include:

(A) A court or county guardianship investigator participating in the case under Probate Code section 1513 or 1513.2;

(B) Appointment of a child custody evaluator or investigator under Evidence Code section 730;

(C) Appointment of counsel or a guardian ad litem for the ward;

(D) Admissible evidence provided by the ward's parents, parties, or witnesses in the proceeding or other matter subject to this rule;

(E) Information provided by a child custody recommending counselor authorized under Family Code section 3183 to make a recommendation to the court; and

(F) Information provided from a child interview center or professional to avoid unnecessary multiple interviews.

(7) If the court precludes the calling of a ward who is not a party as a witness in a proceeding or other matter subject to this rule and specifies one of the other alternatives, the court must require that the information or evidence obtained by alternative means and provided by a professional (other than counsel for the ward or counsel for any party) or a nonparty:

(A) Be in writing and fully document the ward's views on the matters on which he or she wished to express an opinion;

(B) Describe the ward's input in sufficient detail to assist the court in making its decision;

(C) Be provided to the court and to the parties by a person who will be available for testimony and cross-examination; and

(D) Be filed in the confidential portion of the case file.

(f) Responsibilities of court-connected or appointed professionals—all wards

A child custody evaluator, an expert witness appointed under Evidence Code section 730, an investigator, a child custody recommending counselor or other custody mediator appointed or assigned to meet with a ward must:

(1) Provide information to the ward in an age-appropriate manner about the limitations on confidentiality of testimony and the possibility that information provided to the professional may be shared with the court on the record and provided to the parties in the case;

(2) Allow but not require the ward to state a preference regarding the issues to be decided in the proceeding or other matter subject to this rule, and provide information in an age-appropriate manner about the process by which the court will make a decision; and

(3) Provide to the other parties in the case information about how best to support the interest of the ward during the court process.

(g) Methods of providing information to parties and supporting nonparty wards

Courts should provide information to the parties and the ward who is not a party to the proceeding or other matter subject to this rule when the ward wants to participate or testify. Methods of providing information may include:

(1) Having court or county guardianship investigators and experts appointed under Evidence Code section 730 meet jointly or separately with the parties and their attorneys to discuss alternatives to having the ward provide direct testimony;

(2) Providing an orientation for the ward about the court process and the role of the judicial officer in making decisions, how the courtroom or chambers will be set up, and what participating or testifying will entail;

(3) Providing information to parties before the ward participates or testifies so that they can consider the possible effect on the ward of participating or not participating in the proceeding or other matter subject to this rule;

(4) Appointing counsel under Probate Code section 1470 or a guardian ad litem for the ward to assist in the provision of information to the ward concerning his or her decision to participate in the proceeding or testify;

(5) Including information in guardianship orientation presentations and publications about the options available to a ward who is not a party to the proceeding or other matter subject to this rule to participate or testify or not to do so, and the consequences of a ward's decision whether to become a party to the proceeding or other matter subject to this rule; and

(6) Providing an interpreter for the ward.

(h) If the ward is a party to the proceeding

(1) A ward who is a party to the proceeding or other matter subject to this rule is subject to the law of discovery applied to parties in civil actions and may be called as a witness by any other party unless the court makes a finding that providing information in response to discovery requests or testifying as a witness is not in the ward's best interest and states the reasons on the record.

(2) The court must consider appointing counsel under Probate Code section 1470 or a guardian ad litem for a ward who is a party to the proceeding or other matter subject to this rule if the ward is not represented by counsel.

(3) In determining whether providing information in response to discovery requests or testifying as a witness is in the ward's best interest, the judicial officer should consider the following:

(A) Whether information has been presented indicating that the ward may be at risk emotionally if he or she is permitted or denied the opportunity to provide information in response to discovery requests or by testimony;

(B) Whether the subject areas about which the ward is anticipated to provide information in response to discovery requests or by testimony are relevant to the decision the court must make; and

(C) Whether any other factors weigh in favor of or against having the ward provide information in response to discovery requests or by testimony.

(4) In taking testimony from a ward who is a party to the proceeding or other matter subject to this rule, the court must take the special care required by Evidence Code section 765(b). If the ward is not represented by an attorney, the court must inform the ward in an age-appropriate manner about the limitations on confidentiality of testimony and that the information provided to the court will be on the record and provided to the parties in the case.

(i) Education and training of judicial officers and court staff

Education and training content for court staff and judicial officers should include information on wards' participation in proceedings or other matters subject to this rule, methods other than direct testimony for receiving input from a ward, procedures for taking a ward's testimony, and differences in the application of this rule to wards who are and are not parties to the proceeding or other matters subject to this rule. *(Adopted, eff. Jan. 1, 2013.)*

Chapter 22

CONSERVATORSHIPS

Rule
7.1050. Conservator forms.
7.1051. Acknowledgment of receipt of Duties of Conservator.
7.1052. Termination of conservatorship.
7.1053. Service of final account of removed or resigned conservator.
7.1054. Service of final account after termination of conservatorship.
7.1059. Standards of conduct for the conservator of the estate.
7.1060. Investigations and reports by court investigators.
7.1061. Taking possession of an asset of the conservatee at an institution or opening or changing ownership of an account or safe-deposit box in a financial institution.
7.1062. The good cause exception to notice of the hearing on a petition for appointment of a temporary conservator.
7.1063. Change of conservatee's residence.

Rule 7.1050. Conservator forms

(a) Forms to be submitted with petition

Each petitioner, unless the petitioner is a bank or other entity entitled to conduct the business of a trust company, must submit to the court with the petition for appointment of conservator a completed *Confidential Supplemental Information* statement (form GC–312). In addition, each proposed conservator, except a bank or other entity entitled to conduct the business of a trust company, or a public guardian, must submit a completed *Confidential Conservator Screening Form* (form GC–314).

(b) Use of form

The information on the *Confidential Conservator Screening Form* is used by the court and by persons or agencies designated by the court to assist the court in determining whether a proposed conservator should be appointed.

(c) Forms to be confidential

The *Confidential Conservator Screening Form*, the *Confidential Supplemental Information* statement, and the information contained on these forms are confidential. The clerk must maintain these forms in a manner that will protect and preserve their confidentiality. *(Adopted, eff. Jan. 1, 2001. As amended, eff. Jan. 1, 2002; Jan. 1, 2007.)*

Research References

2 Witkin Cal. Proc. 5th Courts § 194, (S 194) Probate Rules.
14 Witkin, California Summary 10th Wills and Probate § 4, Probate Rules.
14 Witkin, California Summary 10th Wills and Probate § 938, (S 938) Content and Form.
14 Witkin, California Summary 10th Wills and Probate § 960, Governing Law.

Rule 7.1051. Acknowledgment of receipt of Duties of Conservator

Before the court issues letters, each conservator must execute and file an acknowledgment of receipt of the *Duties of Conservator and Acknowledgment of Receipt of Handbook* (form GC–348). *(Adopted, eff. Jan. 1, 2001. As amended, eff. Jan. 1, 2002.)*

Research References

14 Witkin, California Summary 10th Wills and Probate § 4, Probate Rules.
14 Witkin, California Summary 10th Wills and Probate § 947, (S 947) Disclosures to Conservator.
14 Witkin, California Summary 10th Wills and Probate § 960, Governing Law.

Rule 7.1052. Termination of conservatorship

(a) Operation of law or court order

A conservatorship of the person or estate may terminate by operation of law or may be terminated by court order if the court determines that it is no longer required.

(b) Conservator of the person

Under Probate Code section 1860(a), a conservatorship of the person terminates by operation of law when the conservatee dies, and the conservator of the person need not file a petition for its termination.

(c) Duty of conservator of estate on termination

A conservator of the estate whose administration is terminated by operation of law or by court order must file and obtain the court's approval of a final account of the administration. *(Adopted, eff. Jan. 1, 2004.)*

Research References

14 Witkin, California Summary 10th Wills and Probate § 951, in General.
14 Witkin, California Summary 10th Wills and Probate § 952, Procedure.

Rule 7.1053. Service of final account of removed or resigned conservator

A resigned or removed conservator of the estate must serve a copy of the conservator's final account and the petition for its settlement with the notice of hearing that must be served on the successor conservator of the estate under Probate Code section 1460(b)(1), unless the court dispenses with such service. *(Adopted, eff. Jan. 1, 2004.)*

Rule 7.1054. Service of final account after termination of conservatorship

After termination of the conservatorship, the conservator of the estate must serve copies of the conservator's final account and the petition for its settlement with the notices of hearing that must be served on the former conservatee and on the spouse or domestic partner of the former conservatee under Probate Code sections 1460(b)(2) and (3), unless the court dispenses with such service. *(Adopted, eff. Jan. 1, 2004.)*

Rule 7.1059. Standards of conduct for the conservator of the estate

Except as otherwise required by statute, in the exercise of ordinary care and diligence in managing and controlling the estate of the conservatee, the conservator of the estate is to be guided by the following principles:

(a) Avoidance of actual and apparent conflicts of interest with the conservatee

The conservator must avoid actual conflicts of interest and, consistent with his or her fiduciary duty to the conservatee, the appearance of conflicts of interest. The conservator must avoid any personal, business, or professional interest or relationship that is or reasonably could be perceived as being self-serving or adverse to the best interest of the conservatee. In particular:

(1) Except as appropriate for conservators who are not professional fiduciaries with full disclosure to the court, the conservator should not personally provide housing, medical, or legal services to the conservatee;

(2) The conservator must be independent from all service providers, except when (a) no other conservator or service providers are reasonably available, (b) the exception is in the best interest of the conservatee, (c) the circumstances are fully disclosed to the court, and (d) prior court approval has been obtained;

(3) The conservator must neither solicit nor accept incentives from service providers; and

(4) The conservator must not engage his or her family members to provide services to the conservatee for a profit or fee when other alternatives are reasonably available. Where family members do provide such services, their relationship to the conservator must be fully disclosed to the court, the terms of engagement must be in the best interest of the conservatee compared to the terms available from independent service providers, the services must be competently performed, and the conservator must be able to exercise appropriate control and supervision.

A conservator's employees, including family members, are not service providers and are not providing services to the conservatee for a profit or fee within the meaning of this rule if their compensation is paid by the conservator and their services are either included in the conservator's petition for allowance of the conservator's compensation or are not paid from the conservatee's estate.

(b) Conservatorship estate management

The conservator of the estate must:

(1) Provide competent management of the conservatee's property, with the care of a prudent person dealing with someone else's property;

(2) Refrain from unreasonably risky investments;

(3) Refrain from making loans or gifts of estate property, except as authorized by the court after full disclosure;

(4) Manage the estate for the benefit of the conservatee;

(5) Subject to the duty of full disclosure to the court and persons entitled under law to receive it, closely guard against unnecessary or inappropriate disclosure of the conservatee's financial information;

(6) Keep the money and property of the estate separate from the conservator's or any other person's money or property, except as may be permitted under statutes authorizing public guardians or public conservators and certain regulated private fiduciaries to maintain common trust funds or similar common investments;

(7) Hold title reflecting the conservatorship in individual securities, mutual funds, securities broker accounts, and accounts with financial institutions;

(8) Keep accurate records of all transactions. Professional fiduciaries must maintain prudent accounting systems and procedures designed to protect against embezzlement and other cash-asset mismanagement;

(9) Undertake as soon as possible after appointment and qualification to locate and safeguard the conservatee's estate planning documents, including wills, living trusts, powers of attorney for health care and finances, life insurance policies, and pension records;

(10) Undertake as soon as possible after appointment and qualification to secure the real and personal property of the estate, insuring it at appropriate levels, and protecting it against damage, destruction, or loss;

(11) Make reasonable efforts to preserve property identified in the conservatee's estate planning documents;

(12) Communicate as necessary and appropriate with the conservator of the person of the conservatee, if any, and with the trustee of any trust of which the conservatee is a beneficiary;

(13) Pursue claims against others on behalf of the estate when it would be in the best interest of the conservatee or the estate to do so. Consider requesting prior court authority to pursue or compromise large or complex claims, particularly those that might require litigation and the assistance of counsel and those that might result in an award of attorneys' fees for the other party against the estate if unsuccessful, and request such approval before entering into a contingent fee agreement with counsel;

(14) Defend against actions or claims against the estate when it would be in the best interest of the conservatee or the estate to do so. Consider requesting court approval or instructions concerning the defense or compromise of litigation against the estate;

(15) Collect all public and insurance benefits for which the conservatee is eligible;

(16) Evaluate the conservatee's ability to manage cash or other assets and take appropriate action, including obtaining prior court approval when necessary or appropriate, to enable the conservatee to do so to the level of his or her ability;

(17) When disposing of the conservatee's tangible personal property, inform the conservatee's family members in advance and give them an opportunity to acquire the property, with approval or confirmation of the court; and

(18) In deciding whether it is in the best interest of the conservatee to dispose of property of the estate, consider the following factors, among others, as appropriate in the circumstances:

(A) The likely benefit or improvement of the conservatee's life that disposing of the property would bring;

(B) The likelihood that the conservatee would need or benefit from the property in the future;

(C) Subject to the factors specified in Probate Code section 2113, the previously expressed or current desires of the conservatee concerning the property;

(D) The provisions of the conservatee's estate plan concerning the property;

(E) The tax consequences of the disposition transaction;

(F) The impact of the disposition transaction on the conservatee's entitlement to public benefits;

(G) The condition of the entire estate;

(H) Alternatives to disposition of the property;

(I) The likelihood that the property will deteriorate or be subject to waste if retained in the estate; and

(J) The benefit versus the cost or liability of maintaining the property in the estate.

(Adopted, eff. Jan. 1, 2008.)

Advisory Committee Comment

The Probate and Mental Health Advisory Committee consulted with several organizations in the development of rule 7.1059, including the National Guardianship Association, a nationwide voluntary association of professional and family fiduciaries, guardians, and allied professionals. In developing this rule, the Probate and Mental Health Advisory Committee considered the National Guardianship Association's Standards of Practice. Some of these standards have been incorporated into the rules.

Research References

14 Witkin, California Summary 10th Wills and Probate § 1000, (S 1000) Restrictions on Self-Dealing.
14 Witkin, California Summary 10th Wills and Probate § 1001, (S 1001) Duty to Manage Estate.
14 Witkin, California Summary 10th Wills and Probate § 1012, (S 1012) Without Court Approval.
14 Witkin, California Summary 10th Wills and Probate § 1015, (S 1015) in General.

Rule 7.1060. Investigations and reports by court investigators

(a) Order Appointing Court Investigator (form GC–330)

Order Appointing Court Investigator (form GC–330) is an optional form within the meaning of rule 1.35 of these rules, except as follows:

(1) A court may, by local rule, require that form GC–330 be used for orders appointing court investigators and directing them to conduct all or any of the investigations described in the form and to prepare, file, and serve copies of reports concerning those investigations. The local rule may also prescribe the form's preparation, service, and delivery to the court for execution and filing.

(2) A court may, by local rule, require that a general order, a court-prepared order, or a local form order instead of form GC–330 be used to appoint and direct the actions of court investigators concerning all or any of the investigations and reports described in form GC–330.

(b) Order Appointing Court Investigator (Review and Successor Conservator Investigations) (form GC–331)

Order Appointing Court Investigator (Review and Successor Conservator Investigations) (form GC–331) is an optional form within the meaning of rule 1.35 of these rules, except as follows:

(1) A court may, by local rule, require that form GC–331 be used for orders appointing court investigators and directing them to conduct all or any of the review investigations under Probate Code sections 1850 and 1851 or investigations concerning the appointment of successor conservators under Probate Code sections 2684 and 2686 described in the form and to prepare, file, and serve copies of reports concerning those investigations. Form GC–331 is to be prepared by the court only.

(2) A court may, by local rule, require that a general order, a court-prepared order, or a local form order instead of form GC–331 be used to appoint and direct the actions of court investigators concerning all or any of the investigations and reports described in form GC–331.

(c) Order Setting Biennial Review Investigation and Directing Status Report Before Review (form GC–332)

Order Setting Biennial Review Investigation and Directing Status Report Before Review (form GC–332) is an optional form within the meaning of rule 1.35 of these rules, except as follows:

(1) A court may, by local rule, require that form GC–332 be used for orders setting biennial review investigations and directing status reports under Probate Code section 1850(a)(2). Form GC–332 is to be prepared by the court only.

(2) A court may, by local rule, require that a general order, a court-prepared order, or a local form order instead of form GC–332 be used concerning the matters described in form GC–332.

(Adopted, eff. Jan. 1, 2011.)

Research References

14 Witkin, California Summary 10th Wills and Probate § 950, (S 950) Periodic Review of Conservatorship.
14 Witkin, California Summary 10th Wills and Probate § 960, Governing Law.

Rule 7.1061. Taking possession of an asset of the conservatee at an institution or opening or changing ownership of an account or safe-deposit box in a financial institution

(a) Definitions

As used in this rule, the following terms have the meanings stated below:

(1) An "institution" is an insurance company, insurance broker, insurance agent, investment company, investment bank, securities broker-dealer, investment advisor, financial planner, financial advisor, or any other person who takes, holds, or controls an asset subject to a guardianship that is not a "financial institution" within the meaning of this rule;

(2) A "financial institution" is a bank, trust (except as provided in (d)), savings and loan association, savings bank, industrial bank, or credit union; and

(3) "Taking possession" or "taking control" of an asset held or controlled by an institution includes changing title to the asset, withdrawing all or any portion of the asset, or transferring all or any portion of the asset from the institution.

(b) Responsibilities of the conservator when taking possession or control of an asset of the conservatee at an institution

When taking possession or control of an asset held by an institution in the name of the conservatee, the temporary, general, or limited conservator of the estate must provide the following to the institution:

(1) A certified copy of the conservator's Letters of Temporary Guardianship or Conservatorship (form GC–150) or Letters of

Conservatorship (form GC–350) containing the Notice to Institutions and Financial Institutions on the second page; and

(2) A blank copy of a *Notice of Taking Possession or Control of an Asset of Minor or Conservatee* (form GC–050).

(c) Responsibilities of the conservator when opening or changing the name on an account or a safe-deposit box at a financial institution

When opening or changing the name on an account or a safe-deposit box in a financial institution, the temporary, general, or limited conservator of the estate must provide the following to the financial institution:

(1) A certified copy of the guardian's *Letters of Temporary Guardianship or Conservatorship* (form GC–150) or *Letters of Conservatorship* (form GC–350) containing the Notice to Institutions and Financial Institutions on the second page; and

(2) A blank copy of a *Notice of Opening or Changing a Guardianship or Conservatorship Account or Safe–Deposit Box* (form GC–051).

(d) Application of this rule to Totten trust accounts

This rule applies to Totten trust accounts but does not apply to any other trust arrangement described in Probate Code section 82(b). *(Adopted, eff. Jan. 1, 2009.)*

Research References

14 Witkin, California Summary 10th Wills and Probate § 1005, (S 1005) Notification by Institutions.

Rule 7.1062. The good cause exception to notice of the hearing on a petition for appointment of a temporary conservator

(a) Purpose

The purpose of this rule is to establish uniform standards for the good cause exception to the notice of the hearing required on a petition for appointment of a temporary conservator under Probate Code section 2250(e).

(b) Good cause for exceptions to notice limited

Good cause for an exception to the notice required by section 2250(e) must be based on a showing that the exception is necessary to protect the proposed conservatee or his or her estate from immediate and substantial harm.

(c) Court may change the time or manner of giving notice

An exception to the notice requirement of section 2250(e) may include one or any combination of the following:

(1) Waiving notice to one, more than one, or all persons entitled to notice;

(2) Requiring a different period of notice; and

(3) Changing the required manner of giving notice, including requiring notice by telephone, fax, e-mail, or personal delivery, or a combination of these methods, instead of or in addition to notice by mail to the proposed conservatee's spouse or registered domestic partner and relatives.

(d) Good cause exceptions to notice

Good cause for an exception to the notice requirement of section 2250(e) may include a showing of:

(1) Harm caused by the passage of time. The showing must demonstrate the immediate and substantial harm to the conservatee or the conservatee's estate that could occur during the notice period.

(2) Harm that one or more persons entitled to notice might do to the proposed conservatee or the proposed conservatee's estate if notice is given. Such a showing would not support an exception to the requirement to give notice to any other person

entitled to notice unless it also demonstrates that notice cannot reasonably be given to the other person without also giving notice to the persons who might cause harm.

(3) Medical emergency. The emergency must be immediate and substantial and treatment (1) must be reasonably unavailable unless a temporary conservator is appointed and (2) cannot be deferred for the notice period because of the proposed conservatee's pain or extreme discomfort or a significant risk of harm.

(4) Financial emergency. The emergency must be immediate and substantial and other means shown likely to be ineffective to prevent loss or further loss to the proposed conservatee's estate during the notice period.

(e) Contents of request for good cause exception to notice

A request for a good cause exception to the notice requirement of section 2250(e) must be in writing, separate from the petition for appointment of a temporary conservator, and must include:

(1) An application containing the case caption and stating the relief requested;

(2) An affirmative factual showing in support of the application in a declaration under penalty of perjury containing competent testimony based on personal knowledge;

(3) A declaration under penalty of perjury based on personal knowledge containing the information required for an ex parte application under rule 3. 1204(b); and

(4) A proposed order. *(Adopted, eff. Jan. 1, 2008. As amended, eff. July 1, 2008; Jan. 1, 2009.)*

Research References

14 Witkin, California Summary 10th Wills and Probate § 975A, (S 975A) (New)-Good Cause Exception to Notice Requirements.

Rule 7.1063. Change of conservatee's residence

(a) Pre–move notice of change of personal residence required

Unless an emergency requires a shorter period of notice, the conservator of the person must mail copies of a notice of an intended change of the conservatee's personal residence to the persons listed below at least 15 days before the date of the proposed change, and file the original notice with proof of mailing with the court. Copies of the notice must be mailed to:

(1) The conservatee;

(2) The conservatee's attorney of record;

(3) The conservatee's spouse or registered domestic partner; and

(4) The conservatee's relatives named in the *Petition for Appointment of Probate Conservator* (form GC–310), including the conservatee's "deemed relatives" under Probate Code section 1821(b)(1)–(4) if the conservatee has no spouse or registered domestic partner and no second-degree relatives.

(b) Conservatee's personal residence

(1) The "conservatee's personal residence" under (a) is the residence the conservatee understands or believes, or reasonably appears to understand or believe, to be his or her permanent residence on the date the first petition for appointment of a conservator was filed in the proceeding, whether or not the conservatee is living in that residence on that date. A residential care facility, including a board and care, intermediate care, skilled nursing, or secured perimeter facility, may be the conservatee's personal residence under this rule.

(2) If the conservatee cannot form or communicate an understanding or belief concerning his or her permanent residence on the date the first petition for appointment of a

conservator was filed in the proceeding, his or her personal residence under this rule is the residence he or she last previously understood or believed, or appeared to understand or believe, to be his or her permanent residence.

(3) For purposes of this rule, the following changes of residence are or are not changes of the conservatee's personal residence, as indicated:

(A) A move from the conservatee's personal residence under this rule to a residential care facility or other residence is a change of the conservatee's personal residence under (a).

(B) A move from a residential care facility or other residence to another residence that is not the conservatee's personal residence under this rule is a change of the conservatee's personal residence under (a).

(C) A move from a residential care facility or other residence to the conservatee's personal residence under this rule is not a change of the conservatee's personal residence under (a).

(c) Post–move notice of a change of residence required

The conservator of the person must file a notice of a change of the conservatee's residence with the court within 30 days of the date of the change. Unless waived by the court for good cause to prevent harm to the conservatee, the conservator must mail a copy of the notice to the persons named below and file a proof of mailing with the original notice filed with the court. Unless waived, the notice must be mailed to:

(1) The conservatee's attorney of record;

(2) The conservatee's spouse or registered domestic partner; and

(3) The conservatee's relatives named in the *Petition for Appointment of Probate Conservator* (form GC–310), including the conservatee's "deemed relatives" under Probate Code section 1821(b)(1)–(4) if the conservatee has no spouse or registered domestic partner and no second-degree relatives.

(d) Conservatee's residence

The "conservatee's residence" under (c) is the conservatee's residence at any time after appointment of a conservator.

(e) Use of Judicial Council forms GC–079 and GC–080

(1) The *Pre–Move Notice of Proposed Change of Personal Residence of Conservatee or Ward* (form GC–079) must be used for the pre-move notice required under (a) and Probate Code section 2352(e)(3). The conservator, the conservator's attorney, or an employee of the attorney may complete the mailing and sign the Proof of Mailing on page 2 of the form. If the notice is mailed less than 15 days before the date of the move because an emergency requires a shorter period of notice, the basis for the emergency must be stated in the notice.

(2) The *Post–Move Notice of Change of Residence of Conservatee or Ward* (form GC–080) must be used for the post-move notice required under (c) and Probate Code section 2352(e)(1) and (2). The conservator, the conservator's attorney, or an employee of the attorney may complete the mailing and sign the Proof of Mailing on page 2 of the form.

(f) Prior court approval required to establish conservatee's residence outside California

Notwithstanding any other provision of this rule, prior court approval is required before a conservatee's residence may be established outside the state of California. *(Adopted, eff. Jan. 1, 2008.)*

Research References

2 Witkin Cal. Proc. 5th Courts § 194, (S 194) Probate Rules.

14 Witkin, California Summary 10th Wills and Probate § 4, Probate Rules.

14 Witkin, California Summary 10th Wills and Probate § 990, Fixing Residence.

Chapter 23

COURT–APPOINTED COUNSEL IN PROBATE PROCEEDINGS

Rule
7.1101. Qualifications and continuing education required of counsel appointed by the court in guardianships and conservatorships.

Rule 7.1101. Qualifications and continuing education required of counsel appointed by the court in guardianships and conservatorships

(a) Definitions

As used in this rule, the following terms have the meanings stated below:

(1) "Appointed counsel" or "counsel appointed by the court" are legal counsel appointed by the court under Probate Code sections 1470 or 1471, including counsel in private practice and deputy public defenders directly responsible for the performance of legal services under the court's appointment of a county's public defender.

(2) A "probate guardianship" or "probate conservatorship" is a guardianship or conservatorship proceeding under division 4 of the Probate Code.

(3) "LPS" and "LPS Act" refer to the Lanterman–Petris–Short Act, Welfare and Institutions Code section 5000 et seq.

(4) An "LPS conservatorship" is a conservatorship proceeding for a gravely disabled person under chapter 3 of the LPS Act, Welfare and Institutions Code sections 5350–5371.

(5) A "contested matter" in a probate or LPS conservatorship proceeding is a matter that requires a noticed hearing and in which written objections are filed by any party or made by the conservatee or proposed conservatee orally in open court.

(6) "AOC" is the Administrative Office of the Courts.

(7) "Counsel in private practice" includes attorneys employed by or performing services under contracts with nonprofit organizations.

(b) Qualifications of appointed counsel in private practice

Except as provided in this rule, each counsel in private practice appointed by the court on or after January 1, 2008, must be an active member of the State Bar of California for at least three years immediately before the date of appointment, with no discipline imposed within the 12 months immediately preceding any date of availability for appointment after January 1, 2008; and

(1) *Appointments to represent minors in guardianships*

For an appointment to represent a minor in a guardianship:

(A) Within the five years immediately before the date of first availability for appointment after January 1, 2008, must have represented at least three wards or proposed wards in probate guardianships, three children in juvenile court dependency or delinquency proceedings, or three children in custody proceedings under the Family Code; or

(B) At the time of appointment, must be qualified:

(i) For appointments to represent children in juvenile dependency proceedings under rule 5.660 and the court's local rules governing court-appointed juvenile court dependency counsel; or

(ii) For appointments to represent children in custody proceedings under the Family Code under rule 5.242, including the alternative experience requirements of rule 5.242(g).

(C) Except as provided in (f)(2), counsel qualified for appointments in guardianships under (B) must satisfy the continuing education requirements of this rule in addition to the education or training requirements of the rules mentioned in (B).

(2) *Appointments to represent conservatees or proposed conservatees*

For an appointment to represent a conservatee or a proposed conservatee, within the five years immediately before the date of first availability for appointment after January 1, 2008, counsel in private practice must have:

(A) Represented at least three conservatees or proposed conservatees in either probate or LPS conservatorships; or

(B) Completed any three of the following five tasks:

(i) Represented petitioners for the appointment of a conservator at commencement of three probate conservatorship proceedings, from initial contact with the petitioner through the hearing and issuance of Letters of Conservatorship;

(ii) Represented a petitioner, a conservatee or a proposed conservatee, or an interested third party in two contested probate or LPS conservatorship matters. A contested matter that qualifies under this item and also qualifies under (i) may be applied toward satisfaction of both items;

(iii) Represented a party for whom the court could appoint legal counsel in a total of three matters described in Probate Code sections 1470, 1471, 1954, 2356.5, 2357, 2620.2, 3140, or 3205;

(iv) Represented fiduciaries in three separate cases for settlement of a court-filed account and report, through filing, hearing, and settlement, in any combination of probate conservatorships or guardianships, decedent's estates, or trust proceedings under division 9 of the Probate Code; or

(v) Prepared five wills or trusts, five durable powers of attorney for health care, and five durable powers of attorney for asset management.

(3) Except as provided in (e)(2), private counsel qualified under (1) or (2) must also be covered by professional liability insurance satisfactory to the court in the amount of at least $100,000 per claim and $300,000 per year.

(c) Qualifications of deputy public defenders performing legal services on court appointments of the public defender

(1) Except as provided in this rule, beginning on January 1, 2008, each county deputy public defender with direct responsibility for the performance of legal services in a particular case on the appointment of the county public defender under Probate Code sections 1470 or 1471 must be an active member of the State Bar of California for at least three years immediately before the date of appointment; and either

(A) Satisfy the experience requirements for private counsel in (b)(1) for appointments in guardianships or (b)(2) for appointments in conservatorships; or

(B) Have a minimum of three years' experience representing minors in juvenile dependency or delinquency proceedings or patients in postcertification judicial proceedings or conservatorships under the LPS Act.

(2) A deputy public defender qualified under (1) must also be covered by professional liability insurance satisfactory to the court in the amount of at least $100,000 per claim and $300,000 per year, or be covered for professional liability at an equivalent level by a self-insurance program for the professional employees of his or her county.

(3) A deputy public defender who is not qualified under this rule may periodically substitute for a qualified deputy public defender with direct responsibility for the performance of legal services in a particular case. In that event, the county public defender or his or her designee, who may be the qualified supervisor, must certify to the court that the substitute deputy is working under the direct supervision of a deputy public defender who is qualified under this rule.

(d) Transitional provisions on qualifications

(1) Counsel appointed before January 1, 2008, may continue to represent their clients through March 2008, whether or not they are qualified under (b) or (c). After March 2008, through conclusion of these matters, the court may retain or replace appointed counsel who are not qualified under (b) or (c) or may appoint qualified co-counsel to assist them.

(2) In January, February, and March 2008, the court may appoint counsel in new matters who have not filed the certification of qualifications required under (h) at the time of appointment but must replace counsel appointed under this paragraph who have not filed the certificate before April 1, 2008.

(e) Exemption for small courts

(1) Except as provided in (2) and (3), the qualifications required under (b) or (c) may be waived by a court with four or fewer authorized judges if it cannot find qualified counsel or for other grounds of hardship.

(2) A court described in (1) may, without a waiver, appoint counsel in private practice who do not satisfy the insurance requirements of (b)(3) if counsel demonstrate to the court that they are adequately self-insured.

(3) A court may not waive or disregard the self-insurance requirements of (c)(2) applicable to deputy public defenders.

(4) A court waiving the qualifications required under (b) or (c) must make express written findings showing the circumstances supporting the waiver and disclosing all alternatives considered, including appointment of qualified counsel from adjacent counties and other alternatives not selected.

(f) Continuing education of appointed counsel

(1) Except as provided in (2), beginning on January 1, 2008, counsel appointed by the court must complete three hours of education each calendar year that qualifies for Minimum Continuing Legal Education credit for State Bar-certified specialists in estate planning, trust, and probate law.

(2) Counsel qualified to represent minors in guardianships under (b)(1)(B) and who are appointed to represent minors in guardianships of the person only may satisfy the continuing education requirements of this rule by satisfying the annual education and training required under rule 5.242(d) or the continuing education required under rule 5.660(d)(3).

(g) Additional court-imposed qualifications, education, and other requirements

The qualifications in (b) and (c) and the continuing education requirement in (f) are minimums. A court may establish higher qualification or continuing education requirements, including insurance requirements; require initial education or training; and impose other requirements, including an application by private counsel.

(h) Initial certification of qualifications; annual post-qualification reports and certifications

(1) Each counsel appointed or eligible for appointment by the court before January 1, 2008, including deputy public defenders, must certify to the court in writing before April 1, 2008, that he or she satisfies the qualifications under (b) or (c) to be eligible for a new appointment on or after that date.

(2) After March 2008, each counsel must certify to the court that he or she is qualified under (b) or (c) before becoming eligible for an appointment under this rule.

(3) Each counsel appointed or eligible for appointment by the court under this rule must immediately advise the court of the imposition of any State Bar discipline.

(4) Beginning in 2009, each appointed counsel must certify to the court before the end of March of each year that:

(A) His or her history of State Bar discipline and professional liability insurance coverage or, if appointed by a court with four or fewer authorized judges under (e)(2), the adequacy of his or her self-insurance, either has or has not changed since the date of his or her qualification certification or last annual certification; and

(B) He or she has completed the continuing education required for the preceding calendar year.

(5) Annual certifications required under this subdivision showing changes in State Bar disciplinary history, professional liability insurance coverage, or adequacy of self-insurance must include descriptions of the changes.

(6) Certifications required under this subdivision must be submitted to the court but are not to be filed or lodged in a case file.

(i) Reporting

The AOC may require courts to report appointed counsel's qualifications and completion of continuing education required by this rule to ensure compliance with Probate Code section 1456. *(Adopted, eff. Jan. 1, 2008. As amended, eff. Jan. 1, 2009; Jan. 1, 2011.)*

Research References

Rutter, Cal. Practice Guide: Prof. Responsibility Ch. 8-B, B. Accepting or Rejecting Employment.
2 Witkin Cal. Proc. 5th Courts § 194, (S 194) Probate Rules.
14 Witkin, California Summary 10th Wills and Probate § 4, Probate Rules.
14 Witkin, California Summary 10th Wills and Probate § 908, Discretionary Appointment.
14 Witkin, California Summary 10th Wills and Probate § 909, Mandatory Appointment.

Title 8

APPELLATE RULES

Division 1

RULES RELATING TO THE SUPREME COURT AND COURTS OF APPEAL

Chapter 1

GENERAL PROVISIONS

Article 1

IN GENERAL

Rule
8.1.   Title.
8.4.   Application of division.
8.7.   Construction.
8.10.   Definitions and use of terms.
8.13.   Amendments to rules.
8.16.   Amendments to statutes.
8.18.   Documents violating rules not to be filed.
8.20.   California Rules of Court prevail.
8.23.   Sanctions to compel compliance.

Rule 8.1.   Title

The rules in this title may be referred to as the Appellate Rules. All references in this title to "these rules" are to the Appellate Rules. *(Adopted, eff. Jan. 1, 2007.)*

Research References

9 Witkin Cal. Proc. 5th Appeal § 9, (S 9) Current Structure.
2 Witkin Cal. Proc. 5th Courts § 195, (S 195) Appellate Rules.

Rule 8.4.   Application of division

The rules in this division apply to:

(1) Appeals from the superior courts, except appeals to the appellate divisions of the superior courts;

(2) Original proceedings, motions, applications, and petitions in the Courts of Appeal and the Supreme Court; and

(3) Proceedings for transferring cases within the appellate jurisdiction of the superior court to the Court of Appeal for review, unless rules 8.1000–8.1018 provide otherwise. *(Formerly Rule 53, adopted, eff. May 19, 2005. Renumbered Rule 8.4 and amended, eff. Jan. 1, 2007.)*

Research References

Rutter, Cal. Practice Guide: Civil Appeals & Writs Ch. 15-A, A. Overview.
Rutter, Cal. Practice Guide: Civil Appeals & Writs Ch. 15-E, E. Procedures on Writ Review.
Rutter, Cal. Practice Guide: Civil Appeals & Writs Ch. 16-A, A. Introduction.
Rutter, Cal. Practice Guide: Civil Appeals & Writs Ch. 16-K, K. Transfer to Court of Appeal.
9 Witkin Cal. Proc. 5th Appeal § 10, (S 10) Scope: Practice and Procedure.
8 Witkin Cal. Proc. 5th Extraordinary Writs § 163, (S 163) Governing Statutes and Rules.

Rule 8.7.   Construction

The rules of construction stated in rule 1.5 apply to these rules. In addition, in these rules the headings of divisions, chapters, articles, rules, and subdivisions are substantive. *(Adopted, eff. Jan. 1, 2007.)*

Research References

9 Witkin Cal. Proc. 5th Appeal § 11, in General.

Rule 8.10.   Definitions and use of terms

Unless the context or subject matter requires otherwise, the definitions and use of terms in rule 1.6 apply to these rules. In addition, the following apply:

(1) "Appellant" means the appealing party.

(2) "Respondent" means the adverse party.

(3) "Party" includes any attorney of record for that party.

(4) "Judgment" includes any judgment or order that may be appealed.

(5) "Superior court" means the court from which an appeal is taken.

(6) "Reviewing court" means the Supreme Court or the Court of Appeal to which an appeal is taken, in which an original proceeding is begun, or to which an appeal or original proceeding is transferred.

(7) The word "briefs" includes petitions for rehearing, petitions for review, and answers thereto. It does not include petitions for extraordinary relief in original proceedings. *(Formerly Rule 40, adopted, eff. Jan. 1, 2005. Renumbered Rule 8.10 and amended, eff. Jan. 1, 2007.)*

Research References

Rutter, Cal. Practice Guide: Civil Appeals & Writs Ch. 3-B, B. Filing Deadlines.
9 Witkin Cal. Proc. 5th Appeal § 11, in General.
9 Witkin Cal. Proc. 5th Appeal § 24, in General.
2 Witkin Cal. Proc. 5th Courts § 325, (S 325) Nature of Reviewing Courts.
2 Witkin Cal. Proc. 5th Courts § 330, (S 330) Original Jurisdiction.
7 Witkin Cal. Proc. 5th Judgment § 1, Nature and Classification of Judgment.
4 Witkin Cal. Proc. 5th Pleading § 67, (S 67) Designation of Parties.

Rule 8.13.   Amendments to rules

Only the Judicial Council may amend these rules, except the rules in division 5, which may be amended only by the Supreme Court. An amendment by the Judicial Council must be published in the advance pamphlets of the Official Reports and takes effect on the date ordered by the Judicial Council. *(Formerly Rule 54, adopted, eff. Jan. 1, 2005. Renumbered Rule 8.13 and amended, eff. Jan. 1, 2007.)*

Research References

9 Witkin Cal. Proc. 5th Appeal § 8, (S 8) Adoption and Subsequent Amendments.
2 Witkin Cal. Proc. 5th Courts § 188, (S 188) Filing, Publication, and Effective Date.

Rule 8.16.   Amendments to statutes

In these rules, a reference to a statute includes any subsequent amendment to the statute. *(Adopted, eff. Jan. 1, 2007.)*

Rule 8.18.   Documents violating rules not to be filed

Except as these rules provide otherwise, the reviewing court clerk must not file any record or other document that does not conform to these rules. *(Formerly Rule 46, adopted, eff. Jan. 1, 2005. Renumbered Rule 8.18 and amended, eff. Jan. 1, 2007.)*

Advisory Committee Comment

The exception in this rule acknowledges that there are different rules that apply to certain nonconforming documents. For example, this rule does not apply to nonconforming or late briefs, which are addressed by rules 8.204(e) and 8.220(a), respectively, or to nonconforming supporting documents accompanying a writ petition under chapter 7, which are addressed by rule 8.486(c)(2).

Research References

Rutter, Cal. Practice Guide: Civil Appeals & Writs Ch. 5-C, C. Motion, Application and Request Procedures.
9 Witkin Cal. Proc. 5th Appeal § 631, (S 631) Form of Record.

3 Witkin, California Summary 10th Agency and Employment § 672, in General.

Rule 8.20.   California Rules of Court prevail

A Court of Appeal must accept for filing a record, brief, or other document that complies with the California Rules of Court despite any local rule imposing other requirements. *(Formerly Rule 80, adopted, eff. Jan. 1, 2005. Renumbered Rule 8.20 and amended, eff. Jan. 1, 2007.)*

Research References

2 Witkin Cal. Proc. 5th Courts § 331, in General.

Rule 8.23.   Sanctions to compel compliance

The failure of a court reporter or clerk to perform any duty imposed by statute or these rules that delays the filing of the appellate record is an unlawful interference with the reviewing court's proceedings. It may be treated as an interference in addition to or instead of any other sanction that may be imposed by law for the same breach of duty. This rule does not limit the reviewing court's power to define and remedy any other interference with its proceedings. *(Formerly Rule 46.5, adopted, eff. Jan. 1, 2005. Renumbered Rule 8.23, eff. Jan. 1, 2007.)*

Research References

Rutter, Cal. Practice Guide: Civil Appeals & Writs Ch. 4-C, C. Record Preparation Procedure.
9 Witkin Cal. Proc. 5th Appeal § 9, (S 9) Current Structure.
9 Witkin Cal. Proc. 5th Appeal § 643, (S 643) Delinquent Clerk or Reporter.
2 Witkin Cal. Proc. 5th Courts § 195, (S 195) Appellate Rules.
2 Witkin Cal. Proc. 5th Courts § 362, (S 362) Control by Court.
2 Witkin Cal. Proc. 5th Courts § 382, Sanctions for Failure to File Transcript.

Article 2

SERVICE, FILING, FILING FEES, FORM, AND NUMBER OF DOCUMENTS

Rule
8.25.   Service, filing and filing fees.
8.26.   Waiver of fees and costs.
8.29.   Service on nonparty public officer or agency.
8.32.   Address and other contact information of record; notice of change.
8.36.   Substituting parties; substituting or withdrawing attorneys.
8.40.   Form of filed documents.
8.44.   Number of copies of filed documents.
8.46.   Sealed records.

Rule 8.25.   Service, filing and filing fees

(a)   Service

(1) Before filing any document, a party must serve, by any method permitted by the Code of Civil Procedure, one copy of the document on the attorney for each party separately represented, on each unrepresented party, and on any other person or entity when required by statute or rule.

(2) The party must attach to the document presented for filing a proof of service showing service on each person or entity required to be served under (1). The proof must name each party represented by each attorney served.

(b)   Filing

(1) A document is deemed filed on the date the clerk receives it.

(2) Unless otherwise provided by these rules or other law, a filing is not timely unless the clerk receives the document before the time to file it expires.

(3) A brief, an application to file an amicus curiae brief, an answer to an amicus curiae brief, a petition for rehearing, an answer to a petition for rehearing, a petition for transfer of an appellate division case to the Court of Appeal, an answer to such a petition for transfer, a petition for review, an answer to a petition for review, or a reply to an answer to a petition for review is timely if the time to file it has not expired on the date of:

(A) Its mailing by priority or express mail as shown on the postmark or the postal receipt; or

(B) Its delivery to a common carrier promising overnight delivery as shown on the carrier's receipt.

(4) The provisions of (3) do not apply to original proceedings.

(5) If the clerk receives a document by mail from an inmate or a patient in a custodial institution after the period for filing the document has expired but the envelope shows that the document was mailed or delivered to custodial officials for mailing within the period for filing the document, the document is deemed timely. The clerk must retain in the case file the envelope in which the document was received.

(c) Filing fees

(1) Unless otherwise provided by law, any document for which a filing fee is required under Government Code sections 68926 or 68927 must be accompanied at the time of filing by the required fee or an application for a waiver of court fees under rule 8.26.

(2) Documents for which a filing fee may be required under Government Code sections 68926 or 68927 include:

(A) A notice of appeal in a civil case. For purposes of this rule, "notice of appeal" includes a notice of cross-appeal;

(B) A petition for a writ within the original civil jurisdiction of the Supreme Court or Court of Appeal;

(C) A petition for review in a civil case in the Supreme Court;

(D) The following where the document is the first document filed in the Court of Appeal or Supreme Court by a party other than the appellant or petitioner in a civil case. For purposes of this rule, a "party other than the appellant" does not include a respondent who files a notice of cross-appeal:

(i) An application or an opposition or other response to an application;

(ii) A motion or an opposition or other response to a motion;

(iii) A respondent's brief;

(iv) A preliminary opposition to a petition for a writ, excluding a preliminary opposition requested by the court unless the court has notified the parties that it is considering issuing a peremptory writ in the first instance;

(v) A return (by demurrer, verified answer, or both) after the court issues an alternative writ or order to show cause;

(vi) Any answer to a petition for review in the Supreme Court; and

(vii) Any brief filed in the Supreme Court after the Court grants review.

(3) If a document other than the notice of appeal or a petition for a writ is not accompanied by the filing fee or an application for a waiver of court fees under rule 8.26, the clerk must file the document and must promptly notify the filing party in writing that the court may strike the document unless, within the stated time of not less than 5 court days after the notice is sent, the filing party either:

(A) Pays the filing fee; or

(B) Files an application for a waiver under rule 8.26 if the party has not previously filed such an application.

(4) If the party fails to take the action specified in a notice given under (2), the reviewing court may strike the document, but may vacate the striking of the document for good cause. *(Formerly Rule 40.1, adopted, eff. Jan. 1, 2005. Renumbered Rule 8.25 and amended, eff. Jan. 1, 2007. As amended, eff. Jan. 1, 2009; July 1, 2010; Jan. 1, 2011; Oct. 28, 2011; July 1, 2012.)*

Advisory Committee Comment

Subdivision (a). Subdivision (a)(1) requires service "by any method permitted by the Code of Civil Procedure." The reference is to the several permissible methods of service provided in Code of Civil Procedure sections 1010–1020. *Information Sheet for Proof of Service (Court of Appeal)* (form APP–009–INFO) provides additional information about how to serve documents and how to provide proof of service.

Subdivision (b). In general, to be filed on time, a document must be received by the clerk before the time for filing that document expires. There are, however, some limited exceptions to this general rule. For example, (5) provides that if the clerk receives a document by mail from a custodial institution after the deadline for filing the document has expired but the envelope shows that the document was mailed or delivered to custodial officials for mailing before the deadline expired, the document is deemed timely. This provision applies to notices of appeal as well as to other documents mailed from a custodial institution and reflects the "prison-delivery" exception articulated by the California Supreme Court in *In re Jordan* (1992) 4 Cal.4th 116 and *Silverbrand v. County of Los Angeles* (2009) 46 Cal.4th 106.

Note that if a deadline runs from the date of filing, it runs from the date that the document is actually received and deemed filed under (b)(1); neither (b)(3) nor (b)(5) changes that date. Nor do these provisions extend the date of finality of an appellate opinion or any other deadline that is based on finality, such as the deadline for the court to modify its opinion or order rehearing. Subdivision (b)(5) is also not intended to limit a criminal defendant's appeal rights under the case law of constructive filing. (See, e.g., *In re Benoit* (1973) 10 Cal.3d 72.)

Subdivision (b)(3). This rule includes applications to file amicus curiae briefs because, under rules 8.200(c)(4) and 8.520(f)(5), a proposed amicus curiae brief must accompany the application to file the brief.

Subdivision (c). Government Code section 68926 establishes fees in civil cases for filing a notice of appeal, filing a petition a for a writ within the original civil jurisdiction of the Supreme Court or a Court of Appeal, and for a party other than appellant or petitioner filing its first document in such an appeal or writ proceeding in the Supreme Court or a Court of Appeal. Government Code section 68927 establishes fees for filing a petition for review in a civil case in the Supreme Court and for a party other than the petitioner filing its first document in a civil case in the Supreme Court. These statutes provide that fees may not be charged in appeals from, petitions for writs involving, or petitions for review from decisions in juvenile cases or proceedings to declare a minor free from parental custody or control, or proceedings under the Lanterman–Petris–Short Act (Part 1 (commencing with Section 5000) of Division 5 of the Welfare and Institutions Code).

Subdivision (c)(2)(A) and (D). Under rule 8.100(f), "notice of appeal" includes a notice of a cross-appeal and a respondent who files a notice of cross-appeal in a civil appeal is considered an appellant and is required to pay the fee for filing a notice of appeal under Government Code section 68926.

A person who files an application to file an amicus brief is not a "party" and therefore is not subject to the fees applicable to a party other than the appellant or petitioner.

Subdivision (c)(3). Rule 8.100 establishes the procedures applicable when an appellant in a civil appeal fails to pay the fee for filing a notice of appeal or the deposit for the clerk's transcript that must also be paid at that time.

Research References

Rutter, Cal. Practice Guide: Civil Appeals & Writs Ch. 3-A, A. Necessity of Timely Filing for Appeal.

Rutter, Cal. Practice Guide: Civil Appeals & Writs Ch. 3-E, E. Filing Steps.

Rutter, Cal. Practice Guide: Civil Appeals & Writs Ch. 5-C, C. Motion, Application and Request Procedures.

Rutter, Cal. Practice Guide: Civil Appeals & Writs Ch. 9-D, D. Procedural Rules.

Rutter, Cal. Practice Guide: Civil Appeals & Writs Ch. 12-E, E. Procedure.

Rutter, Cal. Practice Guide: Civil Appeals & Writs Ch. 13-B, B. Petition for Review Procedures.

Rutter, Cal. Practice Guide: Civil Appeals & Writs Ch. 13-C, C. Briefs on the Merits After Grant of Review.

Rutter, Cal. Practice Guide: Civil Appeals & Writs Ch. 13-F, F. Petition for Rehearing.

Rutter, Cal. Practice Guide: Civil Appeals & Writs Ch. 15-E, E. Procedures on Writ Review.

Rutter, Cal. Practice Guide: Civil Appeals & Writs Ch. 16-K, K. Transfer to Court of Appeal.

Rutter, Cal. Practice Guide: Civil Appeals & Writs Ch. 15-E , Outline E.

9 Witkin Cal. Proc. 5th Appeal § 9, (S 9) Current Structure.

9 Witkin Cal. Proc. 5th Appeal § 12, Serve and File.

9 Witkin Cal. Proc. 5th Appeal § 575, in General.

9 Witkin Cal. Proc. 5th Appeal § 712, When Filing Occurs.

9 Witkin Cal. Proc. 5th Appeal § 717, (S 717) Service and Filing.

9 Witkin Cal. Proc. 5th Appeal § 1015, (S 1015) Briefs.

9 Witkin Cal. Proc. 5th Appeal § 1026, Transfer by Court of Appeal on Party's Petition.

2 Witkin Cal. Proc. 5th Courts § 195, (S 195) Appellate Rules.

10 Witkin, California Summary 10th Parent and Child § 712, Notice of Appeal.

10 Witkin, California Summary 10th Parent and Child § 720, Notice of Intent.

10 Witkin, California Summary 10th Parent and Child § 725, Notice of Intent and Record.

Rule 8.26. Waiver of fees and costs

(a) Application form

An application for initial waiver of court fees and costs in the Supreme Court or Court of Appeal must be made on *Request to Waive Court Fees* (form FW–001). The clerk must provide *Request to Waive Court Fees* (form FW–001) and the *Information Sheet on Waiver of Fees and Costs (Supreme Court, Court of Appeal, or Appellate Division)* (form APP–015/FW–015–INFO) without charge to any person who requests any fee waiver application or states that he or she is unable to pay any court fee or cost.

(b) Filing the application

(1) *Appeals*

(A) The appellant should submit any application for initial waiver of court fees and costs for an appeal with the notice of appeal in the superior court that issued the judgment or order being appealed. For purposes of this rule, a respondent who files a notice of cross-appeal is an "appellant."

(B) A party other than the appellant should submit any application for initial waiver of the court fees and costs for an appeal at the time the fees are to be paid to the court.

(2) *Writ proceedings*

(A) The petitioner should submit the application for waiver of the court fees and costs for a writ proceeding with the writ petition.

(B) A party other than the petitioner should submit any application for initial waiver of the court fees and costs at the time the fees for filing its first document in the writ proceeding are to be paid to the reviewing court.

(3) *Petitions for review*

(A) The petitioner should submit the application for waiver of the court fees and costs for a petition for review in the Supreme Court with the petition.

(B) A party other than the petitioner should submit any application for initial waiver of the court fees and costs at the time the fees for filing its first document in the proceeding are to be paid to the Supreme Court.

(c) Procedure for determining application

The application must be considered and determined as required by Government Code section 68634.5. An order from the Supreme Court or Court of Appeal determining the application for initial fee waiver or setting a hearing on the application in the Supreme Court or Court of Appeal may be made on *Order on Court Fee Waiver (Court of Appeal or Supreme Court)* (form APP–016/FW–016.)

(d) Application granted unless acted on by the court

The application for initial fee waiver is deemed granted unless the court gives notice of action on the application within five court days after the application is filed.

(e) Court fees and costs waived

Court fees and costs that must be waived on granting an application for initial waiver of court fees and costs in the Supreme Court or Court of Appeal include:

(1) The fee for filing the notice of appeal and the fee required for a party other than the appellant filing its first document under Government Code section 68926;

(2) The fee for filing an original proceeding and the fee required for a party other than the petitioner filing its first document under Government Code section 68926;

(3) The fee for filing a petition for review and the fee required for a party other than the petitioner filing its first document under Government Code section 68927; and

(4) Any court fee for telephonic oral argument.

(f) Denial of the application

If an application is denied, the applicant must pay the court fees and costs or submit the new application or additional information requested by the court within 10 days after the clerk gives notice of the denial.

(g) Confidential Records

(1) No person may have access to an application for an initial fee waiver submitted to the court except the court and authorized court personnel, any persons authorized by the applicant, and any persons authorized by order of the court. No person may reveal any information contained in the application except as authorized by law or order of the court. An order granting access to an application or financial information may include limitations on who may access the information and on the use of the information after it has been released.

(2) Any person seeking access to an application or financial information provided to the court by an applicant must make the request by motion, supported by a declaration showing good cause as to why the confidential information should be released. *(Adopted, eff. July 1, 2009. As amended, eff. Oct. 28, 2011.)*

Advisory Committee Comment

Subdivision (a). The waiver of court fees and costs is called an "initial" waiver because, under Government Code section 68630 and following, any such waiver may later be modified, terminated, or retroactively withdrawn if the court determines that the applicant was not or is no longer eligible for a waiver.

The court may, at a later time, order that the previously waived fees be paid.

Subdivision (b)(1). If an applicant is requesting waiver of both Court of Appeal fees, such as the fee for filing the notice of appeal, and superior court fees, such as the fee for preparing, certifying, copying, and transmitting the clerk's transcript, the clerk of the superior court may ask the applicant to provide two signed copies of *Request to Waive Court Fees* (form FW–001).

Subdivision (e). The parties in an appeal may also ask the superior court to waive the deposit required under Government Code section 68926.1 and the fees under rule 8.122 for preparing, certifying, copying, and transmitting the clerk's transcript to the reviewing court and to the requesting party.

Research References

Rutter, Cal. Practice Guide: Civil Appeals & Writs Ch. 3-E, E. Filing Steps.
Rutter, Cal. Practice Guide: Civil Appeals & Writs Ch. 13-B, B. Petition for Review Procedures.
Rutter, Cal. Practice Guide: Civil Appeals & Writs Ch. 15-E, E. Procedures on Writ Review.
3 Witkin Cal. Proc. 5th Actions § 416, (S 416) in General.
3 Witkin Cal. Proc. 5th Actions § 418, Trial Court Costs.
3 Witkin Cal. Proc. 5th Actions § 419, Costs of Appeal.
3 Witkin Cal. Proc. 5th Actions § 423, (S 423) No Right to Reporter's Transcript.
3 Witkin Cal. Proc. 5th Actions § 425, (S 425) Legislative Directive to Judicial Council.
3 Witkin Cal. Proc. 5th Actions § 426, (S 426) Application and Forms.
3 Witkin Cal. Proc. 5th Actions § 427, (S 427) Determination of Application.
3 Witkin Cal. Proc. 5th Actions § 428, (S 428) in General.
3 Witkin Cal. Proc. 5th Actions § 429A, (S 429A) (New)-In General.
3 Witkin Cal. Proc. 5th Actions § 429B, (New)-In General.
3 Witkin Cal. Proc. 5th Actions § 429C, (New)-Costs Excused.
3 Witkin Cal. Proc. 5th Actions § 429E, (New)-Judicial Council Rules and Forms.
3 Witkin Cal. Proc. 5th Actions § 429F, (S 429F) (New)-General Requirements.
3 Witkin Cal. Proc. 5th Actions § 429G, (S 429G) (New)-Requirements for Specific Proceedings.
3 Witkin Cal. Proc. 5th Actions § 429I, (New)-Determination of Appellate Court Applications.
9 Witkin Cal. Proc. 5th Appeal § 9, (S 9) Current Structure.
9 Witkin Cal. Proc. 5th Appeal § 16A, (New)-Waiver of Fees and Costs.
9 Witkin Cal. Proc. 5th Appeal § 556, (S 556) Payment of Fees.
2 Witkin Cal. Proc. 5th Courts § 195, (S 195) Appellate Rules.

Rule 8.29.   Service on nonparty public officer or agency

(a) Proof of service

When a statute or this rule requires a party to serve any document on a nonparty public officer or agency, the party must file proof of such service with the document unless a statute permits service after the document is filed, in which case the proof of service must be filed immediately after the document is served on the public officer or agency.

(b) Identification on cover

When a statute or this rule requires a party to serve any document on a nonparty public officer or agency, the cover of the document must contain a statement that identifies the statute or rule requiring service of the document on the public officer or agency in substantially the following form: "Service on [insert name of the officer or agency] required by [insert citation to the statute or rule]."

(c) Service on the Attorney General

In addition to any statutory requirements for service of briefs on public officers or agencies, a party must serve its brief or petition on the Attorney General if the brief or petition:

(1) Questions the constitutionality of a state statute; or

(2) Is filed on behalf of the State of California, a county, or an officer whom the Attorney General may lawfully represent in:

(A) A criminal case;

(B) A case in which the state or a state officer in his or her official capacity is a party; or

(C) A case in which a county is a party, unless the county's interest conflicts with that of the state or a state officer in his or her official capacity.

(Formerly Rule 44.5, adopted, eff. Jan. 1, 2004. As amended, eff. July 1, 2004. Renumbered Rule 8.29 and amended, eff. Jan. 1, 2007.)

Advisory Committee Comment

Rule 8.29 refers to statutes that require a party to serve documents on a nonparty public officer or agency. For a list of examples of such statutory requirements, please see the *Civil Case Information Statement* (form APP–004).

Research References

Rutter, Cal. Practice Guide: Civil Appeals & Writs Ch. 3-E, E. Filing Steps.
Rutter, Cal. Practice Guide: Civil Appeals & Writs Ch. 9-D, D. Procedural Rules.
Rutter, Cal. Practice Guide: Civil Appeals & Writs Ch. 12-E, E. Procedure.
Rutter, Cal. Practice Guide: Civil Appeals & Writs Ch. 13-B, B. Petition for Review Procedures.
Rutter, Cal. Practice Guide: Civil Appeals & Writs Ch. 13-C, C. Briefs on the Merits After Grant of Review.
Rutter, Cal. Practice Guide: Civil Appeals & Writs Ch. 15-E, E. Procedures on Writ Review.
9 Witkin Cal. Proc. 5th Appeal § 698, Filing and Service of Original and Copies.
9 Witkin Cal. Proc. 5th Appeal § 717, (S 717) Service and Filing.
9 Witkin Cal. Proc. 5th Appeal § 1015, (S 1015) Briefs.
8 Witkin Cal. Proc. 5th Extraordinary Writs § 164D, (New)-Service and Opposition.

Rule 8.32.   Address and other contact information of record; notice of change

(a) Address and ~~telephone number~~ other contact information of record

In any case pending before the court, the court will use the mailing address, ~~and~~ telephone number, fax number, and e-mail address that an attorney or unrepresented party provides on the first document filed in that case as the mailing address, ~~and~~ telephone number, fax number, and e-mail address of record unless the attorney or unrepresented party files a notice under (b).

(b) Notice of change

(1) An attorney or unrepresented party whose mailing address, ~~or~~ telephone number, fax number, or e-mail address changes while a case is pending must promptly serve and file a written notice of the change in the reviewing court in which the case is pending.

(2) The notice must specify the title and number of the case or cases to which it applies. If an attorney gives the notice, the notice must include the attorney's California State Bar number.

~~(c) Matters affected by notice~~

~~If the notice under (b) does not identify the case or cases in which the new address or telephone number applies, the clerk may use the new address, or telephone number as the person's address telephone number of record in all pending and concluded cases.~~

~~(d)~~(c) Multiple addresses or other contact information

If an attorney or an unrepresented party has more than one mailing address, telephone number, fax number, or e-mail address, only one <u>mailing address, telephone number, fax number, or e-mail address</u> for that attorney or unrepresented party may be used in a given case. *(Formerly Rule 40.5, adopted, eff. Jan. 1, 2005. Renumbered Rule 8.32 and amended, eff. Jan. 1, 2007. As amended, eff. Jan. 1, 2008; July 1, 2008; Jan. 1, 2013.)*

Research References

Rutter, Cal. Practice Guide: Civil Appeals & Writs Ch. 5-B, B. Types of Motions, Applications and Requests.

9 Witkin Cal. Proc. 5th Appeal § 730, Routine Applications.

Rule 8.36. Substituting parties; substituting or withdrawing attorneys

(a) Substituting parties

Substitution of parties in an appeal or original proceeding must be made by serving and filing a motion in the reviewing court. The clerk of that court must notify the superior court of any ruling on the motion.

(b) Substituting attorneys

A party may substitute attorneys by serving and filing in the reviewing court a substitution signed by the party represented and the new attorney. In all appeals and in original proceedings related to a superior court proceeding, the party must also serve the superior court.

(c) Withdrawing attorney

(1) An attorney may request withdrawal by filing a motion to withdraw. Unless the court orders otherwise, the motion need be served only on the party represented and the attorneys directly affected.

(2) The proof of service need not include the address of the party represented. But if the court grants the motion, the withdrawing attorney must promptly provide the court and the opposing party with the party's current or last known address and telephone number.

(3) In all appeals and in original proceedings related to a superior court proceeding, the reviewing court clerk must notify the superior court of any ruling on the motion.

(4) If the motion is filed in any proceeding pending in the Supreme Court after grant of review, the Supreme Court clerk must also notify the Court of Appeal of any ruling on the motion. *(Formerly Rule 48, adopted, eff. Jan. 1, 2005. Renumbered Rule 8.36, eff. Jan. 1, 2007.)*

Research References

Rutter, Cal. Practice Guide: Civil Appeals & Writs Ch. 1-E, E. Preappeal Evaluation and "Housekeeping" Steps.

Rutter, Cal. Practice Guide: Civil Appeals & Writs Ch. 2-D, D. Standing to Appeal.

Rutter, Cal. Practice Guide: Civil Appeals & Writs Ch. 5-B, B. Types of Motions, Applications and Requests.

Rutter, Cal. Practice Guide: Civil Appeals & Writs Ch. 5-C, C. Motion, Application and Request Procedures.

Rutter, Cal. Practice Guide: Prof. Responsibility Ch. 10-B, B. Withdrawal (Termination) by Lawyer.

9 Witkin Cal. Proc. 5th Appeal § 20, (S 20) Jurisdiction Over Collateral Matters.

9 Witkin Cal. Proc. 5th Appeal § 25, Substitution of Parties.

1 Witkin Cal. Proc. 5th Attorneys § 80, (S 80) in General.

Rule 8.40. Form of filed documents

(a) Form

Except as these rules provide otherwise, documents filed in a reviewing court may be either produced on a computer or typewritten and must comply with the relevant provisions of rule 8.204(b).

(b) Cover color

(1) As far as practicable, the covers of briefs and petitions must be in the following colors:

Appellant's opening brief or appendix	green
Respondent's brief or appendix	yellow
Appellant's reply brief or appendix	tan
Joint appendix	white
Amicus curiae brief	gray
Answer to amicus curiae brief	blue
Petition for rehearing	orange
Answer to petition for rehearing	blue
Petition for original writ	red
Answer (or opposition) to petition for original writ	red
Reply to answer (or opposition) to petition for original writ	red
Petition for transfer of appellate division case to Court of Appeal	white
Answer to petition for transfer of appellate division case to Court of Appeal	blue
Petition for review	white
Answer to petition for review	blue
Reply to answer to petition for review	white
Opening brief on the merits	white
Answer brief on the merits	blue
Reply brief on the merits	white

(2) In appeals under rule 8.216, the cover of a combined respondent's brief and appellant's opening brief must be yellow, and the cover of a combined reply brief and respondent's brief must be tan.

(3) A brief or petition not conforming to (1) or (2) must be accepted for filing, but in case of repeated violations by an attorney or party the court may proceed as provided in rule 8.204(e)(2).

(c) Cover information

(1) Except as provided in (2), the cover—or first page if there is no cover—of every document filed ~~by an attorney~~ in a reviewing court must ~~comply with rule 8.204(b)(10)(D).~~<u>include the name, mailing address, telephone number, fax number (if available), e-mail address (if available), and California State Bar number of each attorney filing or joining in the document, or of the party if he or she is unrepresented. The inclusion of a fax number or e-mail address on any document does not constitute consent to service by fax or e-mail unless otherwise provided by law.</u>

(2) <u>If more than one attorney from a law firm, corporation, or public law office is representing one party and is joining in the document, the name and State Bar number of each attorney joining in the document must be provided on the cover. The law firm, corporation, or public law office representing each party must designate one attorney to receive notices and other communication in the case from the court by placing an asterisk before that attorney's name on the cover and must provide the contact information specified under (1) for that attorney. Contact information for the other attorneys from the same law firm, corporation, or public law office is not required but may be provided.</u> *(Formerly Rule 44, adopted, eff. Jan. 1, 2005. As amended, eff. Jan. 1, 2006. Renumbered Rule 8.40 and amended, eff. Jan. 1, 2007. As amended, eff. Jan. 1, 2011; Jan. 1, 2013.)*

Research References

Rutter, Cal. Practice Guide: Civil Appeals & Writs Ch. 4-C, C. Record Preparation Procedure.

Rutter, Cal. Practice Guide: Civil Appeals & Writs Ch. 5-B, B. Types of Motions, Applications and Requests.

Rutter, Cal. Practice Guide: Civil Appeals & Writs Ch. 5-C, C. Motion, Application and Request Procedures.

Rutter, Cal. Practice Guide: Civil Appeals & Writs Ch. 7-E, E. Stay by Writ of Supersedeas.

Rutter, Cal. Practice Guide: Civil Appeals & Writs Ch. 9-D, D. Procedural Rules.

Rutter, Cal. Practice Guide: Civil Appeals & Writs Ch. 12-E, E. Procedure.

Rutter, Cal. Practice Guide: Civil Appeals & Writs Ch. 13-B, B. Petition for Review Procedures.

Rutter, Cal. Practice Guide: Civil Appeals & Writs Ch. 13-C, C. Briefs on the Merits After Grant of Review.

Rutter, Cal. Practice Guide: Civil Appeals & Writs Ch. 13-F, F. Petition for Rehearing.

Rutter, Cal. Practice Guide: Civil Appeals & Writs Ch. 15-E, E. Procedures on Writ Review.

Rutter, Cal. Practice Guide: Civil Appeals & Writs Ch. 16-K, K. Transfer to Court of Appeal.

9 Witkin Cal. Proc. 5th Appeal § 697, Format.

9 Witkin Cal. Proc. 5th Appeal § 727, (S 727) Filing.

9 Witkin Cal. Proc. 5th Appeal § 907, (S 907) Petition.

2 Witkin Cal. Proc. 5th Courts § 30, (S 30) Use of Recycled Paper.

Rule 8.44.   Number of copies of filed documents

Except as these rules provide otherwise, the number of copies of every brief, petition, motion, application, or other document that must be filed in a reviewing court is as follows:

(a) Documents filed in the Supreme Court

(1) Except as provided in (4), an original and 13 copies of a petition for review, an answer, a reply, a brief on the merits, an amicus curiae brief, an answer to an amicus curiae brief, a petition for rehearing, or an answer to a petition for rehearing;

(2) Unless the court orders otherwise, an original and 10 copies of a petition for a writ within the court's original jurisdiction, an opposition or other response to the petition, or a reply;

(3) Unless the court orders otherwise, an original and 2 copies of any supporting document accompanying a petition for writ of habeas corpus, an opposition or other response to the petition, or a reply;

(4) An original and 8 copies of a petition for review to exhaust state remedies under rule 8.508, an answer, or a reply, or an amicus curiae letter under rule 8.500(g);

(5) An original and 8 copies of a motion or an opposition or other response to a motion; and

(6) An original and 1 copy of an application, including an application to extend time, or any other document.

(b) Documents filed in a Court of Appeal

(1) An original and 4 copies of a brief, an amicus curiae brief, or an answer to an amicus curiae brief, and, in civil appeals, proof of delivery of 1 electronic copy or, in case of undue hardship, 4 paper copies to the Supreme Court, as provided in rule 8.212(c). For purposes of service on the Supreme Court, the term "brief" does not include a petition for rehearing or answers thereto;

(2) An original of a petition for writ of habeas corpus filed under rule 8.380 by a person who is not represented by an attorney and 1 set of any supporting documents;

(3) An original and 4 copies of any other petition, an answer, opposition or other response to a petition, or a reply;

(4) Unless the court orders otherwise, an original and 1 copy of a motion or an opposition or other response to a motion;

(5) Unless the court provides otherwise by local rule or order, 1 set of any separately bound supporting documents accompanying a document filed under (3) or (4);

(6) An original and 1 copy of an application, other than an application to extend time, or any other document; and

(7) An original and 1 copy of an application to extend time. In addition, 1 copy for each separately represented and unrepre-

sented party must be provided to the court. *(Adopted, eff. Jan. 1, 2007. As amended, eff. Jan. 1, 2007; Jan. 1, 2011; Jan. 1, 2013.)*

Advisory Committee Comment

The initial sentence of this rule acknowledges that there are exceptions to this rule's requirements concerning the number of copies; see, for example, rule 8.150, which specifies the number of copies of the record that must be filed.

Research References

Rutter, Cal. Practice Guide: Civil Appeals & Writs Ch. 5-C, C. Motion, Application and Request Procedures.

Rutter, Cal. Practice Guide: Civil Appeals & Writs Ch. 7-E, E. Stay by Writ of Supersedeas.

Rutter, Cal. Practice Guide: Civil Appeals & Writs Ch. 9-D, D. Procedural Rules.

Rutter, Cal. Practice Guide: Civil Appeals & Writs Ch. 12-E, E. Procedure.

Rutter, Cal. Practice Guide: Civil Appeals & Writs Ch. 13-B, B. Petition for Review Procedures.

Rutter, Cal. Practice Guide: Civil Appeals & Writs Ch. 13-C, C. Briefs on the Merits After Grant of Review.

Rutter, Cal. Practice Guide: Civil Appeals & Writs Ch. 13-F, F. Petition for Rehearing.

Rutter, Cal. Practice Guide: Civil Appeals & Writs Ch. 13-G, G. Review of State Bar Discipline Cases.

Rutter, Cal. Practice Guide: Civil Appeals & Writs Ch. 14-A, A. Remittitur.

Rutter, Cal. Practice Guide: Civil Appeals & Writs Ch. 15-E, E. Procedures on Writ Review.

9 Witkin Cal. Proc. 5th Appeal § 9, (S 9) Current Structure.

9 Witkin Cal. Proc. 5th Appeal § 698, Filing and Service of Original and Copies.

9 Witkin Cal. Proc. 5th Appeal § 727, (S 727) Filing.

9 Witkin Cal. Proc. 5th Appeal § 728, (S 728) Opposition.

9 Witkin Cal. Proc. 5th Appeal § 740, in General.

9 Witkin Cal. Proc. 5th Appeal § 1015, (S 1015) Briefs.

2 Witkin Cal. Proc. 5th Courts § 195, (S 195) Appellate Rules.

10 Witkin, California Summary 10th Parent and Child § 715, (S 715) Briefs.

Rule 8.46.   Sealed records

(a) Application

This rule applies to sealed records and records proposed to be sealed on appeal and in original proceedings, but does not apply to records required to be kept confidential by law.

(b) Definitions

(1) "Record" means all or part of a document, paper, exhibit, transcript, or other thing filed or lodged with the court.

(2) A "sealed" record is a record closed to public inspection by court order.

(3) A "lodged" record is a record temporarily deposited with the court but not filed.

(c) Record sealed by the trial court

If a record sealed by the trial court is part of the record on appeal:

(1) The sealed record must be filed under seal in the reviewing court and remain sealed unless that court orders otherwise under (f).

(2) The record on appeal must include:

(A) The motion or application to seal;

(B) All documents filed in the trial court supporting or opposing the motion or application; and

(C) The order sealing the record.

(3) The reviewing court may examine the sealed record.

(d) Record not sealed by the trial court

A record filed or lodged publicly in the trial court and not ordered sealed by that court must not be filed under seal in the reviewing court.

(e) Record not filed in the trial court; motion or application to file under seal

(1) A record not filed in the trial court may be filed under seal in the reviewing court only by order of that court; it must not be filed under seal solely by stipulation or agreement of the parties.

(2) To obtain an order under (1), a party must serve and file a motion or application in the reviewing court, accompanied by a declaration containing facts sufficient to justify the sealing. At the same time, the party must lodge the record under (3), unless good cause is shown not to lodge it.

(3) To lodge a record, the party must put the record in an envelope or other appropriate container, seal it, and attach a cover sheet that complies with rule 8.40(c) and labels the contents as "CONDITIONALLY UNDER SEAL."

(4) If necessary to prevent disclosure, any motion or application, any opposition, and any supporting documents must be filed in a public redacted version and lodged in a complete version conditionally under seal. Unless the court orders otherwise, any party that already possesses copies of the records to be placed under seal must be served with a complete, unredacted version of all papers as well as a redacted version.

(5) On receiving a lodged record, the clerk must note the date of receipt on the cover sheet and retain but not file the record. The record must remain conditionally under seal pending determination of the motion or application.

(6) The court may order a record filed under seal only if it makes the findings required by rule 2.550(d)–(e).

(7) If the court denies the motion or application, the clerk must not place the lodged record in the case file but must return it to the submitting party unless that party notifies the clerk in writing within 10 days after the order denying the motion or application that the record is to be filed.

(8) An order sealing the record must direct the sealing of only those documents and pages or, if reasonably practical, portions of those documents and pages, that contain the material that needs to be placed under seal. All other portions of each document or page must be included in the public file.

(9) Unless the sealing order provides otherwise, it prohibits the parties from disclosing the contents of any materials that have been sealed in any subsequently filed records or papers.

(f) Unsealing a record in the reviewing court

(1) A sealed record must not be unsealed except on order of the reviewing court.

(2) Any person or entity may serve and file a motion, application, or petition in the reviewing court to unseal a record. If necessary to preserve confidentiality, the motion, application, or petition; any opposition; and any supporting documents must be filed in both a public redacted version and a sealed complete version.

(3) If the reviewing court proposes to order a record unsealed on its own motion, the court must mail notice to the parties. Any party may serve and file an opposition within 10 days after the notice is mailed or as the court specifies. Any other party may file a response within 5 days after an opposition is filed.

(4) In determining whether to unseal a record, the court must consider the matters addressed in rule 2.550(c)–(e).

(5) The order unsealing a record must state whether the record is unsealed entirely or in part. If the order unseals only part of the record or unseals the record only as to certain persons, the order must specify the particular records that are unsealed, the particular persons who may have access to the record, or both.

(6) If, in addition to the records in the sealed envelope or container, a court has previously ordered the sealing order, the register of actions, or any other court records relating to the case to be sealed, the unsealing order must state whether these additional records are unsealed.

(g) Disclosure of nonpublic material in public records prohibited

A record filed publicly in the reviewing court must not disclose material contained in a record that is sealed, lodged conditionally under seal, or otherwise subject to a pending motion to file under seal. *(Formerly Rule 12.5, adopted, eff. Jan. 1, 2002. As amended, eff. July 1, 2002; Jan. 1, 2004; Jan. 1, 2006. Renumbered Rule 8.160 and amended, eff. Jan. 1, 2007. Renumbered Rule 8.46, eff. Jan. 1, 2010.)*

Advisory Committee Comment

This rule and rules 2.550–2.551 for the trial courts provide a standard and procedures for courts to use when a request is made to seal a record. The standard is based on *NBC Subsidiary (KNBC–TV), Inc. v. Superior Court* (1999) 20 Cal.4th 1178. The sealed records rules apply to civil and criminal cases. They recognize the First Amendment right of access to documents used at trial or as a basis of adjudication. The rules do not apply to records that courts must keep confidential by law. Examples of confidential records to which public access is restricted by law are records of the family conciliation court (Fam. Code, § 1818, subd. (b)) and in forma pauperis applications (Cal. Rules of Court, rule 8.26). Except as otherwise expressly provided in rule 8.46, motions in a reviewing court relating to the sealing or unsealing of a record must follow rule 8.54.

Research References

Rutter, Cal. Practice Guide: Civil Appeals & Writs Ch. 4-J, J. Sealing of Record.

Rutter, Cal. Practice Guide: Civil Appeals & Writs Ch. 5-B, B. Types of Motions, Applications and Requests.

Rutter, Cal. Practice Guide: Civil Appeals & Writs Ch. 5-C, C. Motion, Application and Request Procedures.

Rutter, Cal. Practice Guide: Civil Appeals & Writs Ch. 9-D, D. Procedural Rules.

Rutter, Cal. Practice Guide: Civil Appeals & Writs Ch. 15-E, E. Procedures on Writ Review.

Rutter, Cal. Practice Guide: Civil Appeals & Writs Ch. 16-E, E. Motions, Applications and Requests.

Rutter, Cal. Practice Guide: Civil Trials & Evidence Ch. 4-B, B. Preliminary Matters Discussed in Final Status Conference or In-Chambers Conference.

9 Witkin Cal. Proc. 5th Appeal § 631, (S 631) Form of Record.

2 Witkin Cal. Proc. 5th Courts § 41, in General.

2 Witkin Cal. Proc. 5th Courts § 44, Sealed Records in Reviewing Courts.

Article 3

APPLICATIONS AND MOTIONS: EXTENDING AND SHORTENING TIME

Rule 8.50. Applications

(a) Service and filing

Except as these rules provide otherwise, parties must serve and file all applications in the reviewing court, including applications to extend the time to file records, briefs, or other documents, and applications to shorten time. For good cause, the Chief Justice or presiding justice may excuse advance service.

(b) Contents

The application must state facts showing good cause-or making an exceptional showing of good cause, when required by these rules-for granting the application and must identify any previous application filed by any party.

(c) Envelopes

An application to a Court of Appeal must be accompanied by addressed, postage-prepaid envelopes for the clerk's use in mailing copies of the order on the application to all parties.

(d) Disposition

Unless the court determines otherwise, the Chief Justice or presiding justice may rule on the application. *(Formerly Rule 43, adopted, eff. Jan. 1, 2005. Renumbered Rule 8.50 and amended, eff. Jan. 1, 2007.)*

Advisory Committee Comment

Rule 8.50 addresses applications generally. Rules 8.60, 8.63, and 8.68 address applications to extend or shorten time.

Subdivision (a). A party other than the appellant or petitioner who files an application or opposition to an application may be required to pay a filing fee under Government Code sections 68926 or 68927 if the application or opposition is the first document filed in the appeal or writ proceeding in the reviewing court by that party. See rule 8.25(c).

Subdivision (b). An exceptional showing of good cause is required in applications in certain juvenile proceedings under rules 8.416, 8.450, 8.452, and 8.454.

Research References

Rutter, Cal. Practice Guide: Civil Appeals & Writs Ch. 5-B, B. Types of Motions, Applications and Requests.
Rutter, Cal. Practice Guide: Civil Appeals & Writs Ch. 5-C, C. Application and Request Procedures.
Rutter, Cal. Practice Guide: Civil Appeals & Writs Ch. 9-D, D. Procedural Rules.
9 Witkin Cal. Proc. 5th Appeal § 9, (S 9) Current Structure.
9 Witkin Cal. Proc. 5th Appeal § 730, Routine Applications.
2 Witkin Cal. Proc. 5th Courts § 195, (S 195) Appellate Rules.

Rule 8.54. Motions

(a) Motion and opposition

(1) Except as these rules provide otherwise, a party wanting to make a motion in a reviewing court must serve and file a written motion stating the grounds and the relief requested and identifying any documents on which the motion is based.

(2) A motion must be accompanied by a memorandum and, if it is based on matters outside the record, by declarations or other supporting evidence.

(3) Any opposition must be served and filed within 15 days after the motion is filed.

(b) Disposition

(1) The court may rule on a motion at any time after an opposition or other response is filed or the time to oppose has expired.

(2) On a party's request or its own motion, the court may place a motion on calendar for a hearing. The clerk must promptly send each party a notice of the date and time of the hearing.

(c) Failure to oppose motion

A failure to oppose a motion may be deemed a consent to the granting of the motion. *(Formerly Rule 41, adopted, eff. Jan. 1, 2005. Renumbered Rule 8.54 and amended, eff. Jan. 1, 2007.)*

Advisory Committee Comment

Subdivision (a). A party other than the appellant or petitioner who files a motion or opposition to a motion may be required to pay a filing fee under Government Code sections 68926 or 68927 if the motion or opposition is the first document filed in the appeal or writ proceeding in the reviewing court by that party. See rule 8.25(c).

Subdivision (c). Subdivision (c) provides that a "failure to oppose a motion" may be deemed a consent to the granting of the motion. The provision is not intended to indicate a position on the question whether there is an implied right to a hearing to oppose a motion to dismiss an appeal.

Research References

Rutter, Cal. Practice Guide: Civil Appeals & Writs Ch. 2-A, A. Overview.
Rutter, Cal. Practice Guide: Civil Appeals & Writs Ch. 5-B, B. Types of Motions, Applications and Requests.
Rutter, Cal. Practice Guide: Civil Appeals & Writs Ch. 5-C, C. Motion, Application and Request Procedures.
Rutter, Cal. Practice Guide: Civil Appeals & Writs Ch. 10-A, A. Overview.
Rutter, Cal. Practice Guide: Civil Appeals & Writs Ch. 11-E, E. Appellate Costs and Sanctions.
9 Witkin Cal. Proc. 5th Appeal § 319, (S 319) Procedure.
9 Witkin Cal. Proc. 5th Appeal § 727, (S 727) Filing.
9 Witkin Cal. Proc. 5th Appeal § 728, (S 728) Opposition.
9 Witkin Cal. Proc. 5th Appeal § 729, (S 729) Hearing and Determination.
9 Witkin Cal. Proc. 5th Appeal § 740, in General.
9 Witkin Cal. Proc. 5th Appeal § 741, Failure to Oppose Motion.
9 Witkin Cal. Proc. 5th Appeal § 770, (S 770) Right and Waiver.
9 Witkin Cal. Proc. 5th Appeal § 1017, Sessions and Calendar.
1 Witkin Cal. Proc. 5th Attorneys § 389, (S 389) Counsel Pro Hac Vice.

Rule 8.57. Motions before the record is filed

(a) Motion to dismiss appeal

A motion to dismiss an appeal before the record is filed in the reviewing court must be accompanied by a certificate of the superior court clerk, a declaration, or both, stating:

(1) The nature of the action and the relief sought by the complaint and any cross-complaint or complaint in intervention;

(2) The names, addresses, and telephone numbers of all attorneys of record—stating whom each represents—and unrepresented parties;

(3) A description of the judgment or order appealed from, its entry date, and the service date of any written notice of its entry;

(4) The factual basis of any extension of the time to appeal under rule 8.108;

(5) The filing dates of all notices of appeal and the courts in which they were filed;

(6) The filing date of any document necessary to procure the record on appeal; and

(7) The status of the record preparation process, including any order extending time to prepare the record.

(b) Other motions

Any other motion filed before the record is filed in the reviewing court must be accompanied by a declaration or other evidence necessary to advise the court of the facts relevant to the relief requested. *(Formerly Rule 42, adopted, eff. Jan. 1, 2005. Renumbered Rule 8.57 and amended, eff. Jan. 1, 2007.)*

Ct. Rules

Research References

Rutter, Cal. Practice Guide: Civil Appeals & Writs Ch. 2-A, A. Overview.
Rutter, Cal. Practice Guide: Civil Appeals & Writs Ch. 5-B, B. Types of Motions, Applications and Requests.
Rutter, Cal. Practice Guide: Civil Appeals & Writs Ch. 5-C, C. Motion, Application and Request Procedures.
9 Witkin Cal. Proc. 5th Appeal § 590, (S 590) Forms of Extension.
9 Witkin Cal. Proc. 5th Appeal § 727, (S 727) Filing.
9 Witkin Cal. Proc. 5th Appeal § 740, in General.

Rule 8.60. Extending time

(a) Computing time

The Code of Civil Procedure governs computing and extending the time to do any act required or permitted under these rules.

(b) Extending time

Except as these rules provide otherwise, for good cause—or on an exceptional showing of good cause, when required by these rules—the Chief Justice or presiding justice may extend the time to do any act required or permitted under these rules.

(c) Application for extension

(1) An application to extend time must include a declaration stating facts, not mere conclusions, and must be served on all parties. For good cause, the Chief Justice or presiding justice may excuse advance service.

(2) The application must state:

(A) The due date of the document to be filed;

(B) The length of the extension requested;

(C) Whether any earlier extensions have been granted and, if so, their lengths and whether granted by stipulation or by the court; and

(D) Good cause—or an exceptional showing of good cause, when required by these rules—for granting the extension, consistent with the factors in rule 8.63(b).

(d) Relief from default

For good cause, a reviewing court may relieve a party from default for any failure to comply with these rules except the failure to file a timely notice of appeal or a timely statement of reasonable grounds in support of a certificate of probable cause.

(e) No extension by superior court

Except as these rules provide otherwise, a superior court may not extend the time to do any act to prepare the appellate record.

(f) Notice to party

(1) In a civil case, counsel must deliver to his or her client or clients a copy of any stipulation or application to extend time that counsel files. Counsel must attach evidence of such delivery to the stipulation or application, or certify in the stipulation or application that the copy has been delivered.

(2) In a class action, the copy required under (1) need be delivered to only one represented party.

(3) The evidence or certification of delivery under (1) need not include the address of the party notified. *(Formerly Rule 45, adopted, eff. Jan. 1, 2005. Renumbered Rule 8.60 and amended, eff. Jan. 1, 2007.)*

Advisory Committee Comment

Subdivisions (b) and (c): An exceptional showing of good cause is required in applications in certain juvenile proceedings under rules 8.416, 8.450, 8.452, and 8.454.

Research References

Rutter, Cal. Practice Guide: Civil Appeals & Writs Ch. 3-A, A. Necessity of Timely Filing for Appeal.
Rutter, Cal. Practice Guide: Civil Appeals & Writs Ch. 3-B, B. Filing Deadlines.
Rutter, Cal. Practice Guide: Civil Appeals & Writs Ch. 3-D, D. Consequences of Lapse of Appeal Deadline; Strategies for Respondents and Appellants.
Rutter, Cal. Practice Guide: Civil Appeals & Writs Ch. 4-C, C. Record Preparation Procedure.
Rutter, Cal. Practice Guide: Civil Appeals & Writs Ch. 4-F, F. Extensions of Time and Default.
Rutter, Cal. Practice Guide: Civil Appeals & Writs Ch. 5-B, B. Types of Motions, Applications and Requests.
Rutter, Cal. Practice Guide: Civil Appeals & Writs Ch. 7-A, A. Overview.
Rutter, Cal. Practice Guide: Civil Appeals & Writs Ch. 9-D, D. Procedural Rules.
Rutter, Cal. Practice Guide: Civil Appeals & Writs Ch. 12-E, E. Procedure.
Rutter, Cal. Practice Guide: Civil Appeals & Writs Ch. 13-B, B. Petition for Review Procedures.
Rutter, Cal. Practice Guide: Civil Appeals & Writs Ch. 13-C, C. Briefs on the Merits After Grant of Review.
Rutter, Cal. Practice Guide: Civil Appeals & Writs Ch. 13-F, F. Petition for Rehearing.
Rutter, Cal. Practice Guide: Civil Appeals & Writs Ch. 15-E, E. Procedures on Writ Review.
9 Witkin Cal. Proc. 5th Appeal § 586, (S 586) in General.
9 Witkin Cal. Proc. 5th Appeal § 614, in General.
9 Witkin Cal. Proc. 5th Appeal § 617, (S 617) Jurisdictional Rule Reaffirmed.
9 Witkin Cal. Proc. 5th Appeal § 632, (S 632) Time Limitations and Extension.
9 Witkin Cal. Proc. 5th Appeal § 688, (S 688) Sanctions for Default.
9 Witkin Cal. Proc. 5th Appeal § 689, Procedure.
9 Witkin Cal. Proc. 5th Appeal § 714, (S 714) in General.
9 Witkin Cal. Proc. 5th Appeal § 718, (S 718) Late Filing: Dismissal and Relief from Default.
9 Witkin Cal. Proc. 5th Appeal § 925, Time and Extension.
9 Witkin Cal. Proc. 5th Appeal § 936, in General.
1 Witkin Cal. Proc. 5th Attorneys § 615, Petition by Disciplined Attorney.
2 Witkin Cal. Proc. 5th Courts § 50, (S 50) Where Last Day is Holiday.
2 Witkin Cal. Proc. 5th Courts § 207, (S 207) Power of Court to Deviate.
2 Witkin Cal. Proc. 5th Courts § 326, (S 326) Powers of Individual Judges.

Rule 8.63. Policies and factors governing extensions of time

(a) Policies

(1) The time limits prescribed by these rules should generally be met to ensure expeditious conduct of appellate business and public confidence in the efficient administration of appellate justice.

(2) The effective assistance of counsel to which a party is entitled includes adequate time for counsel to prepare briefs or other documents that fully advance the party's interests. Adequate time also allows the preparation of accurate, clear, concise, and complete submissions that assist the courts.

(3) For a variety of legitimate reasons, counsel may not always be able to prepare briefs or other documents within the time specified in the rules of court. To balance the competing policies stated in (1) and (2), applications to extend time in the reviewing courts must demonstrate good cause—or an exceptional showing of good cause, when required by these rules—under (b). If good cause is shown, the court must extend the time.

(b) Factors considered

In determining good cause—or an exceptional showing of good cause, when required by these rules—the court must consider the following factors when applicable:

(1) The degree of prejudice, if any, to any party from a grant or denial of the extension. A party claiming prejudice must support the claim in detail.

(2) In a civil case, the positions of the client and any opponent with regard to the extension.

(3) The length of the record, including the number of relevant trial exhibits. A party relying on this factor must specify the length of the record. In a civil case, a record containing one volume of clerk's transcript or appendix and two volumes of reporter's transcript is considered an average-length record.

(4) The number and complexity of the issues raised. A party relying on this factor must specify the issues.

(5) Whether there are settlement negotiations and, if so, how far they have progressed and when they might be completed.

(6) Whether the case is entitled to priority.

(7) Whether counsel responsible for preparing the document is new to the case.

(8) Whether other counsel or the client needs additional time to review the document.

(9) Whether counsel responsible for preparing the document has other time-limited commitments that prevent timely filing of the document. Mere conclusory statements that more time is needed because of other pressing business will not suffice. Good cause requires a specific showing of other obligations of counsel that:

(A) Have deadlines that as a practical matter preclude filing the document by the due date without impairing its quality; or

(B) Arise from cases entitled to priority.

(10) Illness of counsel, a personal emergency, or a planned vacation that counsel did not reasonably expect to conflict with the due date and cannot reasonably rearrange.

(11) Any other factor that constitutes good cause in the context of the case. *(Formerly Rule 45.5, adopted, eff. Jan. 1, 2005. Renumbered Rule 8.63 and amended, eff. Jan. 1, 2007.)*

Advisory Committee Comment

An exceptional showing of good cause is required in applications in certain juvenile proceedings under rules 8.416, 8.450, 8.452, and 8.454.

Research References

Rutter, Cal. Practice Guide: Civil Appeals & Writs Ch. 4-F, F. Extensions of Time and Default.
Rutter, Cal. Practice Guide: Civil Appeals & Writs Ch. 5-B, B. Types of Motions, Applications and Requests.
Rutter, Cal. Practice Guide: Civil Appeals & Writs Ch. 5-C, C. Motion, Application and Request Procedures.
Rutter, Cal. Practice Guide: Civil Appeals & Writs Ch. 9-D, D. Procedural Rules.
Rutter, Cal. Practice Guide: Civil Appeals & Writs Ch. 13-C, C. Briefs on the Merits After Grant of Review.
Rutter, Cal. Practice Guide: Civil Appeals & Writs Form 5:C.1, Application for Extension of Time to File Respondent's Brief.
9 Witkin Cal. Proc. 5th Appeal § 632, (S 632) Time Limitations and Extension.
9 Witkin Cal. Proc. 5th Appeal § 714, (S 714) in General.
9 Witkin Cal. Proc. 5th Appeal § 715, (S 715) Standards for Determining Good Cause.

Rule 8.66. Extending time because of public emergency

(a) Emergency extensions of time

If made necessary by the occurrence or danger of an earthquake, fire, or other public emergency, or by the destruction of or danger to a building housing a reviewing court, the Chair of the Judicial Council, notwithstanding any other rule in this title, may:

(1) Extend by no more than 14 additional days the time to do any act required or permitted under these rules; or

(2) Authorize specified courts to extend by no more than 30 additional days the time to do any act required or permitted under these rules.

(b) Applicability of order

(1) An order under (a) must specify whether it applies throughout the state, only to specified courts, or only to courts or attorneys in specified geographic areas, or applies in some other manner.

(2) An order of the Chair of the Judicial Council under (a)(2) must specify the length of the authorized extension.

(c) Additional extensions

If made necessary by the nature or extent of the public emergency, the Chair of the Judicial Council may extend or renew an order issued under (a) for an additional period of:

(1) No more than 14 days for an order under (a)(1); or

(2) No more than 30 days for an order under (a)(2). *(Formerly Rule 45.1, adopted, eff. Jan. 1, 2005. Renumbered Rule 8.66 and amended, eff. Jan. 1, 2007.)*

Advisory Committee Comment

The Chief Justice of California is the Chair of the Judicial Council (see rule 10.2).

Research References

Rutter, Cal. Practice Guide: Civil Appeals & Writs Ch. 3-C, C. Extensions of Filing Deadline.
9 Witkin Cal. Proc. 5th Appeal § 16, Extending Time Because of Public Emergency.
9 Witkin Cal. Proc. 5th Appeal § 614, in General.
10 Witkin, California Summary 10th Parent and Child § 712, Notice of Appeal.

Rule 8.68. Shortening time

For good cause and except as these rules provide otherwise, the Chief Justice or presiding justice may shorten the time to do any act required or permitted under these rules. *(Adopted, eff. Jan. 1, 2007.)*

Research References

9 Witkin Cal. Proc. 5th Appeal § 9, (S 9) Current Structure.
9 Witkin Cal. Proc. 5th Appeal § 632, (S 632) Time Limitations and Extension.
9 Witkin Cal. Proc. 5th Appeal § 925, Time and Extension.
2 Witkin Cal. Proc. 5th Courts § 195, (S 195) Appellate Rules.

Article 4

E–FILING

Rule 8.70. Purpose, application, construction, and definitions

(a) Purpose

The purpose of the rules in this article is to facilitate the implementation and testing of e-filing projects in the Supreme Court and the Courts of Appeal.

(b) Application

Notwithstanding any other rules to the contrary, the rules in this article govern filing and service by electronic means in the Supreme Court and any Court of Appeal that elects to implement an e-filing project.

(c) Construction

The rules in this article must be construed to authorize and permit filing and service by electronic means to the extent feasible.

(d) Definitions

As used in this article, unless the context otherwise requires:

(1) "The court" means the Supreme Court or any Court of Appeal that elects to implement an e-filing project.

(2) A document may be in paper or electronic form. A "document" is:

(A) Any filing submitted to the reviewing court, including a brief, a petition, an appendix, or a motion;

(B) Any document transmitted by a trial court to the reviewing court, including a notice or a clerk's or reporter's transcript; or

(C) Any writing prepared by the reviewing court, including an opinion, an order, or a notice.

(3) "Electronic service" is service of a document on a party or other person by either electronic transmission or electronic notification. Electronic service may be performed directly by a party, by an agent of a party including the party's attorney, through an electronic filing service provider, or by a court.

(4) "Electronic transmission" means the transmission of a document by electronic means to the electronic service address at or through which a party or other person has authorized electronic service.

(5) "Electronic notification" means the notification of a party or other person that a document is served by sending an electronic message to the electronic service address at or through which the party or other person has authorized electronic service, specifying the exact name of the document served and providing a hyperlink at which the served document can be viewed and downloaded.

(6) "Electronic service address" of a party means the electronic address at or through which the party has authorized electronic service.

(7) An "electronic filer" is a party filing a document in electronic form directly with the court, by an agent, or through an electronic filing service provider.

(8) "Electronic filing" is the electronic transmission to a court of a document in electronic form.

(9) An "electronic filing service provider" is a person or entity that receives an electronic filing from a party for retransmission to the court or for electronic service on other parties, or both. In submission of filings, the electronic filing service provider does so on behalf of the electronic filer and not as an agent of the court. *(Adopted, eff. July 1, 2010. As amended, eff. Jan. 1, 2011; Jan. 1, 2012.)*

Advisory Committee Comment

The definition of "electronic service" has been amended to provide that a party may effectuate service not only by the electronic transmission of a document, but also by providing electronic notification of where a document served electronically may be located and downloaded. This amendment is intended to modify the rules on electronic service to expressly authorize electronic notification as a legally effective alternative means of service to electronic transmission. This rules amendment is consistent with the amendment of Code of Civil Procedure section 1010.6, effective January 1, 2011, to authorize service by electronic notification. (See Stats. 2010, ch. 156 (Sen, Bill 1274).) The amendments change the law on electronic service as understood by the appellate court in *Insyst, Ltd. v. Applied Materials, Inc.* (2009) 70 Cal.App.4th 1129, which interpreted the rules as authorizing electronic transmission as the only effective means of electronic service.

Research References

Rutter, Cal. Practice Guide: Civil Appeals & Writs Ch. 3-B, B. Filing Deadlines.
Rutter, Cal. Practice Guide: Civil Appeals & Writs Ch. 4-C, C. Record Preparation Procedure.
Rutter, Cal. Practice Guide: Civil Appeals & Writs Ch. 4-E, E. Filing and Correction of Record.
Rutter, Cal. Practice Guide: Civil Appeals & Writs Ch. 5-B, B. Types of Motions, Applications and Requests.
Rutter, Cal. Practice Guide: Civil Appeals & Writs Ch. 5-C, C. Motion, Application and Request Procedures.
Rutter, Cal. Practice Guide: Civil Appeals & Writs Ch. 7-E, E. Stay by Writ of Supersedeas.
Rutter, Cal. Practice Guide: Civil Appeals & Writs Ch. 9-D, D. Procedural Rules.
Rutter, Cal. Practice Guide: Civil Appeals & Writs Ch. 12-E, E. Procedure.
Rutter, Cal. Practice Guide: Civil Appeals & Writs Ch. 15-E, E. Procedures on Writ Review.
9 Witkin Cal. Proc. 5th Appeal § 9, (S 9) Current Structure.
9 Witkin Cal. Proc. 5th Appeal § 12A, (S 12A) (New)-In General.
9 Witkin Cal. Proc. 5th Appeal § 12C, (S 12C) (New)-Filing.
9 Witkin Cal. Proc. 5th Appeal § 12D, (S 12D) (New)-Electronic Service.
2 Witkin Cal. Proc. 5th Courts § 195, (S 195) Appellate Rules.

Rule 8.71. Electronic service

(a) Consent to electronic service

(1) When a document may be served by mail, express mail, overnight delivery, or fax transmission, electronic service of the document is permitted when authorized by these rules.

(2) A party indicates that the party agrees to accept electronic service by:

(A) Serving a notice on all parties that the party accepts electronic service and filing the notice with the court. The notice must include the electronic service address at which the party agrees to accept service; or

(B) Electronically filing any document with the court. The act of electronic filing is evidence that the party agrees to accept service at the electronic service address that the party has furnished to the court under rule 8.76(a)(4).

(3) A party that has consented to electronic service under (2) and has used an electronic filing service provider to serve and file documents in a case consents to service on that electronic filing service provider as the designated agent for service for the party in the case, until such time as the party designates a different agent for service.

(b) Maintenance of electronic service lists

When the court orders or permits electronic filing in a case, it must maintain and make available electronically to the parties an electronic service list that contains the parties' current electronic service addresses, as provided by the parties that have filed electronically in the case.

(c) Service by the parties

(1) Notwithstanding (b), parties are responsible for electronic service on all other parties in the case. A party may serve documents electronically directly, by an agent, or through a designated electronic filing service provider.

(2) A document may not be electronically served on a nonparty unless the nonparty consents to electronic service or electronic service is otherwise provided for by law or court order.

(d) Change of electronic service address

(1) A party whose electronic service address changes while the appeal or original proceeding is pending must promptly file a notice of change of address electronically with the court and must serve this notice electronically on all other parties.

(2) A party's election to contract with an electronic filing service provider to electronically file and serve documents or to receive electronic service of documents on the party's behalf does not relieve the party of its duties under (1).

(3) An electronic service address is presumed valid for a party if the party files electronic documents with the court from that address and has not filed and served notice that the address is no longer valid.

(e) Reliability and integrity of documents served by electronic notification

A party that serves a document by means of electronic notification must:

(1) Ensure that the documents served can be viewed and downloaded using the hyperlink provided;

(2) Preserve the document served without any change, alteration, or modification from the time the document is posted until the time the hyperlink is terminated; and

(3) Maintain the hyperlink until the case is final.

(f) Proof of service

(1) Proof of electronic service may be by any of the methods provided in Code of Civil Procedure section 1013a, except that the proof of service must state:

(A) The electronic service address of the person making the service, in addition to that person's residence or business address;

(B) The date and time of the electronic service, instead of the date and place of deposit in the mail;

(C) The name and electronic service address of the person served, in place of that person's name and address as shown on the envelope; and

(D) That the document was served electronically, in place of the statement that the envelope was sealed and deposited in the mail with postage fully prepaid.

(2) Proof of electronic service may be in electronic form and may be filed electronically with the court.

(3) The party filing the proof of electronic service must maintain the printed form of the document bearing the declarant's original signature and must make the document available for inspection and copying on the request of the court or any party to the action or proceeding in which it is filed, in the manner provided in rule 8.77(c).

(g) Electronic service by court

The court may electronically serve any notice, order, opinion, or other document issued by the court in the same manner that parties may serve documents by electronic service. *(Formerly Rule 8.80, adopted, eff. July 1, 2010. Renumbered Rule 8.71 and amended, eff. Jan. 1, 2011.)*

Research References

Rutter, Cal. Practice Guide: Civil Appeals & Writs Ch. 9-D, D. Procedural Rules.
9 Witkin Cal. Proc. 5th Appeal § 12D, (S 12D) (New)-Electronic Service.

Rule 8.72. Documents that may be filed electronically

(a) In general

The court may permit electronic filing of a document by a party or trial court in any appeal or original proceeding unless the rules in this article or other legal authority expressly prohibit electronic filing.

(b) Application for waiver of court fees and costs

The court may permit electronic filing of an application for waiver of court fees and costs in any proceeding in which the court accepts electronic filings.

(c) Orders, opinions, and notices

The court may electronically file any notice, order, opinion, or other document prepared by the court.

(d) Effect of document filed electronically

(1) A document that the court, a party, or a trial court files electronically under the rules in this article has the same legal effect as a document in paper form.

(2) Filing a document electronically does not alter any filing deadline. *(Adopted, eff. July 1, 2010.)*

Research References

Rutter, Cal. Practice Guide: Civil Appeals & Writs Ch. 4-C, C. Record Preparation Procedure.
Rutter, Cal. Practice Guide: Civil Appeals & Writs Ch. 4-E, E. Filing and Correction of Record.
Rutter, Cal. Practice Guide: Civil Appeals & Writs Ch. 12-E, E. Procedure.
9 Witkin Cal. Proc. 5th Appeal § 12A, (S 12A) (New)-In General.
9 Witkin Cal. Proc. 5th Appeal § 12C, (S 12C) (New)-Filing.

Rule 8.73. Court order requiring electronic service or filing

(a) Court order

(1) The court may, on the motion of any party or on its own motion, provided that the order would not cause undue hardship or significant prejudice to any party, order all parties to:

(A) Serve all documents electronically, except when personal service is required by statute or rule;

(B) File all documents electronically; or

(C) Serve and file all documents electronically, except when personal service is required by statute or rule.

(2) The court will not:

(A) Order a self-represented party to electronically serve or file documents;

(B) Order a party to electronically serve or file documents if the party would be required to pay a fee to an electronic filing service provider to file or serve the documents and the party objects to paying this fee in its opposition to the motion under (1); or

(C) Order a trial court to electronically serve or file documents.

(3) If the reviewing court proposes to make an order under (1) on its own motion, the court must mail notice to the parties. Any party may serve and file an opposition within 10 days after the notice is mailed or as the court specifies.

(b) Additional provisions of order

The court's order may also provide that documents previously filed in paper form may be resubmitted in electronic form.

(c) Filing in paper form

When it is not feasible for a party to convert a document to electronic form by scanning, imaging, or another means, the court may allow that party to serve, file, or serve and file the document in paper form. *(Adopted, eff. July 1, 2010. As amended, eff. Jan. 1, 2011.)*

Research References

Rutter, Cal. Practice Guide: Civil Appeals & Writs Ch. 5-B, B. Types of Motions, Applications and Requests.
Rutter, Cal. Practice Guide: Civil Appeals & Writs Ch. 9-D, D. Procedural Rules.
9 Witkin Cal. Proc. 5th Appeal § 12A, (S 12A) (New)-In General.

Rule 8.74. Responsibilities of court

(a) Publication of electronic filing requirements

When the court permits electronic filing it will publish, in both electronic and print formats, the court's electronic filing requirements.

(b) Problems with electronic filing

If the court is aware of a problem that impedes or precludes electronic filing, it must promptly take reasonable steps to provide notice of the problem. *(Adopted, eff. July 1, 2010.)*

Research References

9 Witkin Cal. Proc. 5th Appeal § 12A, (S 12A) (New)-In General.

Rule 8.75. Contracts with electronic filing service providers

(a) Right to contract

(1) The court may contract with one or more electronic filing service providers to furnish and maintain an electronic filing system for the court.

(2) If the court contracts with an electronic filing service provider, the court may require electronic filers to transmit the documents to the provider.

(3) If the court contracts with an electronic service provider or the court has an in-house system, the provider or system must accept filing from other electronic filing service providers to the extent the provider or system is compatible with them.

(b) Provisions of contract

The court's contract with an electronic filing service provider may allow the provider to charge electronic filers a reasonable fee in addition to the court's filing fee. The contract may also allow the electronic filing service provider to make other reasonable requirements for use of the electronic filing system.

(c) Transmission of filing to court

An electronic filing service provider must promptly transmit any electronic filing and any applicable filing fee to the court.

(d) Confirmation of receipt and filing of document

(1) An electronic filing service provider must promptly send to an electronic filer its confirmation of the receipt of any document that the filer has transmitted to the provider for filing with the court.

(2) The electronic filing service provider must send its confirmation to the filer's electronic service address and must indicate the date and time of receipt, in accordance with rule 8.79(a).

(3) After reviewing the documents, the court must promptly transmit to the electronic filing service provider and the electronic filer the court's confirmation of filing or notice of rejection of filing, in accordance with rule 8.79.

(e) Ownership of information

All contracts between the court and electronic filing service providers must acknowledge that the court is the owner of the contents of the filing system and has the exclusive right to control the system's use. *(Adopted, eff. July 1, 2010. As amended, eff. Jan. 1, 2011.)*

Research References

Rutter, Cal. Practice Guide: Civil Appeals & Writs Ch. 5-B, B. Types of Motions, Applications and Requests.
Rutter, Cal. Practice Guide: Civil Appeals & Writs Ch. 9-D, D. Procedural Rules.
9 Witkin Cal. Proc. 5th Appeal § 12A, (S 12A) (New)-In General.
9 Witkin Cal. Proc. 5th Appeal § 12C, (S 12C) (New)-Filing.

Rule 8.76. Responsibilities of electronic filer

(a) Conditions of filing

Each electronic filer must:

(1) Comply with any court requirements designed to ensure the integrity of electronic filing and to protect sensitive personal information;

(2) Furnish information that the court requires for case processing;

(3) Take all reasonable steps to ensure that the filing does not contain computer code, including viruses, that might be harmful to the court's electronic filing system and to other users of that system;

(4) Furnish one or more electronic service addresses, in the manner specified by the court, at which the electronic filer agrees to accept service; and

(5) Immediately provide the court and all parties with any change to the electronic filer's electronic service address.

(b) Format of documents to be filed electronically

A document that is filed electronically with the court must be in a format specified by the court unless it cannot be created in that format. The format adopted by a court must meet the following requirements:

(1) The software for creating and reading documents must be in the public domain or generally available at a reasonable cost.

(2) The printing of documents must not result in the loss of document text, format, or appearance.

If a document is filed electronically under the rules in this article and cannot be formatted to be consistent with a formatting rule elsewhere in the California Rules of Court, the rules in this article prevail. *(Adopted, eff. July 1, 2010. As amended, eff. Jan. 1, 2011.)*

Research References

Rutter, Cal. Practice Guide: Civil Appeals & Writs Ch. 9-D, D. Procedural Rules.
9 Witkin Cal. Proc. 5th Appeal § 12C, (S 12C) (New)-Filing.
9 Witkin Cal. Proc. 5th Appeal § 12D, (S 12D) (New)-Electronic Service.

Rule 8.77. Requirements for signatures on documents

(a) Documents signed under penalty of perjury

If a document to be filed must be signed under penalty of perjury, the document may be filed electronically provided that the original, signed verification page or pages are filed with the court within 5 calendar days.

(b) Documents not signed under penalty of perjury

If a document does not require a signature under penalty of perjury, the document is deemed signed by the party if the document is filed electronically.

(c) Documents requiring signatures of opposing parties

When a document to be filed electronically, such as a stipulation, requires the signatures of opposing parties, the following procedure applies:

(1) The party filing the document must obtain the signatures of all parties on a printed form of the document. By electronically filing the document, the electronic filer indicates that all parties have signed the document and that the filer has the signed original in his or her possession.

(2) The party filing the document must maintain the original, signed document and must make it available for inspection and copying at the request of the court or any other party.

(3) At any time after the document is filed, any other party may serve a demand for production of the original signed document. The demand must be served on all other parties but need not be filed with the court.

(4) Within five days of service of the demand under (3), the party on whom the demand is made must make the original signed document available for inspection and copying by all other parties.

(5) At any time after the document is filed, the court may order the filing party to produce the original signed document in court for inspection and copying by the court. The order must specify the date, time, and place for the production and must be served on all parties.

(d) Digital signature

A party is not required to use a digital signature on an electronically filed document.

(e) Judicial signatures

If a document requires a signature by a court or a judicial officer, the document may be electronically signed in any manner permitted by law. *(Adopted, eff. July 1, 2010.)*

Research References

Rutter, Cal. Practice Guide: Civil Appeals & Writs Ch. 9-D, D. Procedural Rules.

9 Witkin Cal. Proc. 5th Appeal § 12B, (S 12B) (New)-Signatures.

Rule 8.78. Payment of filing fees

(a) Use of credit cards and other methods

The court may permit the use of credit cards, debit cards, electronic fund transfers, or debit accounts for the payment of filing fees associated with electronic filing, as provided in Government Code section 6159 and other applicable law. The court may also authorize other methods of payment.

(b) Fee waivers

Eligible persons may seek a waiver of court fees and costs, as provided in Government Code section 68634.5 and rule 8.26. *(Adopted, eff. July 1, 2010.)*

Advisory Committee Comment

Subdivision (b). A fee charged by an electronic filing service provider under rule 8.75(b) is not a court fee that can be waived under Government Code section 68634.5 and rule 8.26.

Research References

9 Witkin Cal. Proc. 5th Appeal § 12C, (S 12C) (New)-Filing.

Rule 8.79. Actions by court on receipt of electronic filing

(a) Confirmation of receipt and filing of document

(1) *Confirmation of receipt*

When the court receives an electronically submitted document, the court must promptly send the electronic filer confirmation of the court's receipt of the document, indicating the date and time of receipt. A document is considered received at the date and time the confirmation of receipt is created.

(2) *Confirmation of filing*

If the document received by the court under (1) complies with filing requirements, the court must promptly send the electronic filer confirmation that the document has been filed. The filing confirmation must indicate the date and time of filing and is proof that the document was filed on the date and at the time specified. The filing confirmation must also specify:

(A) Any transaction number associated with the filing;

(B) The titles of the documents as filed by the court; and

(C) The fees assessed for the filing.

(3) *Transmission of confirmations*

The court must send receipt and filing confirmation to the electronic filer at the electronic service address that the filer furnished to the court under rule 8.76(a)(4). The court must maintain a record of all receipt and filing confirmations.

(4) *Filer responsible for verification*

In the absence of the court's confirmation of receipt and filing, there is no presumption that the court received and filed the document. The electronic filer is responsible for verifying that the court received and filed any document that the electronic filer submitted to the court electronically.

(b) Notice of rejection of document for filing

If the clerk does not file a document because it does not comply with applicable filing requirements, the court must promptly send notice of the rejection of the document for filing to the electronic filer. The notice must state the reasons that the document was rejected for filing.

(c) Document received after close of business

A document that is received electronically by the court after 11:59 p.m. is deemed to have been received on the next court day.

(d) Delayed delivery

If a technical problem with a court's electronic filing system prevents the court from accepting an electronic filing on a particular court day, and the electronic filer demonstrates that he or she attempted to electronically file the document on that day, the court must deem the document as filed on that day.

(e) Endorsement

(1) The court's endorsement of a document electronically filed must contain the following: "Electronically filed by [Name of Court], on ___ (date)," followed by the name of the court clerk.

(2) The endorsement required under (1) has the same force and effect as a manually affixed endorsement stamp with the signature and initials of the court clerk.

(3) A record on appeal, brief, or petition in an appeal or original proceeding that is filed and endorsed electronically may be printed and served on the appellant or respondent in the same manner as if it had been filed in paper form. *(Adopted, eff. July 1, 2010. As amended, eff. Jan. 1, 2011; Jan. 1, 2012.)*

Research References

Rutter, Cal. Practice Guide: Civil Appeals & Writs Ch. 4-C, C. Record Preparation Procedure.

Rutter, Cal. Practice Guide: Civil Appeals & Writs Ch. 5-B, B. Types of Motions, Applications and Requests.

Rutter, Cal. Practice Guide: Civil Appeals & Writs Ch. 5-C, C. Motion, Application and Request Procedures.

Rutter, Cal. Practice Guide: Civil Appeals & Writs Ch. 7-E, E. Stay by Writ of Supersedeas.

Ct. Rules

Rutter, Cal. Practice Guide: Civil Appeals & Writs Ch. 9-D, D. Procedural Rules.

Rutter, Cal. Practice Guide: Civil Appeals & Writs Ch. 12-E, E. Procedure.

Rutter, Cal. Practice Guide: Civil Appeals & Writs Ch. 15-E, E. Procedures on Writ Review.

9 Witkin Cal. Proc. 5th Appeal § 12C, (S 12C) (New)-Filing.

Chapter 2

CIVIL APPEALS

Article 1

TAKING THE APPEAL

Rule

8.100.   Filing the appeal.

8.104.   Time to appeal.

8.108.   Extending the time to appeal.

8.112.   Petition for writ of supersedeas.

8.116.   Request for writ of supersedeas or temporary stay.

Rule 8.100.   Filing the appeal

(a)   Notice of appeal

(1) To appeal from a superior court judgment or an appealable order of a superior court, other than in a limited civil case, an appellant must serve and file a notice of appeal in that superior court. The appellant or the appellant's attorney must sign the notice.

(2) The notice of appeal must be liberally construed. The notice is sufficient if it identifies the particular judgment or order being appealed. The notice need not specify the court to which the appeal is taken; the appeal will be treated as taken to the Court of Appeal for the district in which the superior court is located.

(3) Failure to serve the notice of appeal neither prevents its filing nor affects its validity, but the appellant may be required to remedy the failure.

(b)   Fee and deposit

(1) Unless otherwise provided by law, the notice of appeal must be accompanied by the $775 filing fee under Government Code sections 68926 and 68926.1(b), an application for a waiver of court fees and costs on appeal under rule 8.26, or an order granting such an application. The fee should be paid by check or money order payable to "Clerk, Court of Appeal"; if the fee is paid in cash, the clerk must give a receipt.

(2) The appellant must also deposit $100 with the superior court clerk as required under Government Code section 68926.1, unless otherwise provided by law or the superior court waives the deposit.

(3) The clerk must file the notice of appeal even if the appellant does not present the filing fee, the deposit, or an application for, or order granting, a waiver of fees and costs.

(c)   Failure to pay filing fee

(1) The reviewing court clerk must promptly notify the appellant in writing if:

(A) The reviewing court receives a notice of appeal without the filing fee required by (b)(1), a certificate of cash payment under (e)(5), or an application for, or order granting, a fee waiver under rule 8.26;

(B) A check for the filing fee is dishonored; or

(C) An application for a waiver under rule 8.26 is denied.

(2) A clerk's notice under (1)(A) or (B) must state that the court may dismiss the appeal unless, within 15 days after the notice is sent, the appellant either:

(A) Pays the fee; or

(B) Files an application for a waiver under rule 8.26 if the appellant has not previously filed such an application.

(3) If the appellant fails to take the action specified in a notice given under (2), the reviewing court may dismiss the appeal, but may vacate the dismissal for good cause.

(d)   Failure to pay deposit

(1) If the appellant fails to pay the deposit to the superior court required under (b)(2), the superior court clerk must promptly notify the appellant in writing that the reviewing court may dismiss the appeal unless, within 15 days after the notice is sent, the appellant either:

(A) Makes the deposit; or

(B) Files an application in the superior court for a waiver of fees and costs if the appellant has not previously filed such an application or an order granting such an application.

(2) If the appellant fails to take the action specified in a notice given under (1), the superior court clerk must notify the reviewing court of the default.

(3) If the superior court clerk notifies the reviewing court of a default under (2), the reviewing court may dismiss the appeal, but may vacate the dismissal for good cause.

(e)   Superior court clerk's duties

(1) The superior court clerk must promptly mail a notification of the filing of the notice of appeal to the attorney of record for each party, to any unrepresented party, and to the reviewing court clerk.

(2) The notification must show the date it was mailed and must state the number and title of the case and the date the notice of appeal was filed. If the information is available, the notification must include:

(A) The name, address, telephone number, and California State Bar number of each attorney of record in the case;

(B) The name of the party each attorney represented in the superior court; and

(C) The name, address, and telephone number of any unrepresented party.

(3) A copy of the notice of appeal is sufficient notification under (1) if the required information is on the copy or is added by the superior court clerk.

(4) The mailing of a notification under (1) is a sufficient performance of the clerk's duty despite the death of the party or the discharge, disqualification, suspension, disbarment, or death of the attorney.

(5) With the notification of the appeal, the superior court clerk must send the reviewing court the filing fee or an application for, or order granting, a waiver of that fee. If the fee was paid in cash, the clerk must send the reviewing court a certificate of payment and thereafter a check for the amount of the fee.

(6) Failure to comply with any provision of this subdivision does not affect the validity of the notice of appeal.

(f)   Notice of cross-appeal

As used in this rule, "notice of appeal" includes a notice of cross-appeal and "appellant" includes a respondent filing a notice of cross-appeal.

(g)   Civil case information statement

(1) On receiving notice of the filing of a notice of appeal under (e)(1), the reviewing court clerk must promptly mail the appellant a copy of the *Civil Case Information Statement* (form APP–004) and a notice that the statement must be filed within 10 days.

(2) Within 10 days after the clerk mails the notice required by (1), the appellant must serve and file in the reviewing court a completed *Civil Case Information Statement*, attaching a copy of the judgment or appealed order that shows the date it was entered.

(3) If the appellant fails to timely file a case information statement under (2), the reviewing court clerk must notify the appellant by mail that the appellant must file the statement within 15 days after the clerk's notice is mailed and that if the appellant fails to comply, the court may either impose monetary sanctions or dismiss the appeal. If the appellant fails to file the statement as specified in the notice, the court may impose the sanctions specified in the notice. *(Formerly Rule 1, adopted, eff. Jan. 1, 2002. As amended, eff. Jan. 1, 2003; Aug. 17, 2003. Renumbered Rule 8.100 and amended, eff. Jan. 1, 2007. As amended, eff. Jan. 1, 2008; July 1, 2009; July 27, 2012.)*

Advisory Committee Comment

Subdivision (a). In subdivision (a)(1), the reference to "judgment" is intended to include part of a judgment. Subdivision (a)(1) includes an explicit reference to "appealable order" to ensure that litigants do not overlook the applicability of this rule to such orders.

Subdivision (b). In the interest of consistency, subdivision (b)(1) recommends a preferred wording—"Clerk, Court of Appeal"—for the name of the payee of checks or money orders for the filing fee. The provision is not mandatory.

Subdivision (c)(2). This subdivision addresses the content of a clerk's notice that a check for the filing fee has been dishonored or that the reviewing court has received a notice of appeal without the filing fee, a certificate of cash payment, or an application for, or order granting, a fee waiver. Rule 8.26(f) addresses what an appellant must do when a fee waiver application is denied.

Subdivision (e). Under subdivision (e)(2), a notification of the filing of a notice of appeal must show the date that the clerk mailed the document. This provision is intended to establish the date when the 20–day extension of the time to file a cross-appeal under rule 8.108(e) begins to run.

Subdivision (e)(1) requires the clerk to mail a notification of the filing of the notice of appeal to the appellant's attorney or to the appellant if unrepresented. Knowledge of the date of that notification allows the appellant's attorney or the appellant to track the running of the 20–day extension of time to file a cross-appeal under rule 8.108(e).

Research References

Rutter, Cal. Practice Guide: Civil Appeals & Writs Ch. 3-C, C. Extensions of Filing Deadline.
Rutter, Cal. Practice Guide: Civil Appeals & Writs Ch. 3-E, E. Filing Steps.
Rutter, Cal. Practice Guide: Civil Appeals & Writs Ch. 3-F, F. Cross-Appeals.
3 Witkin Cal. Proc. 5th Actions § 370, Order Prohibiting Filing of New Litigation.
3 Witkin Cal. Proc. 5th Actions § 419, Costs of Appeal.
9 Witkin Cal. Proc. 5th Appeal § 9, (S 9) Current Structure.
9 Witkin Cal. Proc. 5th Appeal § 10, (S 10) Scope: Practice and Procedure.
9 Witkin Cal. Proc. 5th Appeal § 57, General Rule.
9 Witkin Cal. Proc. 5th Appeal § 555, (S 555) Jurisdictional Requirement: Filing in Trial Court.
9 Witkin Cal. Proc. 5th Appeal § 556, (S 556) Payment of Fees.
9 Witkin Cal. Proc. 5th Appeal § 557, (S 557) Effect of Nonpayment.
9 Witkin Cal. Proc. 5th Appeal § 559, (S 559) Notification by Clerk.
9 Witkin Cal. Proc. 5th Appeal § 560, (S 560) Statement that Party Appeals.
9 Witkin Cal. Proc. 5th Appeal § 561, in General.
9 Witkin Cal. Proc. 5th Appeal § 563, (S 563) Former Strict Rule of Dismissal.
9 Witkin Cal. Proc. 5th Appeal § 573, (S 573) Signature of Party or Attorney.
9 Witkin Cal. Proc. 5th Appeal § 592, (S 592) Nature of Rule.
9 Witkin Cal. Proc. 5th Appeal § 625, Case Information Statement.
9 Witkin Cal. Proc. 5th Appeal § 746, Procedural Defaults.
9 Witkin Cal. Proc. 5th Appeal § 1006, Form and Filing.
9 Witkin Cal. Proc. 5th Appeal § 1007, Notification by Clerk.
1 Witkin Cal. Proc. 5th Attorneys § 79, (S 79) New Attorney's Authority.
1 Witkin Cal. Proc. 5th Attorneys § 239, (S 239) Attorney Must Take Legal Steps.
2 Witkin Cal. Proc. 5th Courts § 195, (S 195) Appellate Rules.
2 Witkin Cal. Proc. 5th Courts § 363, (S 363) Process and Notices.
6 Witkin Cal. Proc. 5th Proceedings Without Trial § 617, (S 617) Form of Request.
11 Witkin, California Summary 10th Husband and Wife § 123, Certification Procedure for Bifurcated Issues.

Rule 8.104. Time to appeal

(a) Normal time

(1) Unless a statute or rule 8.108 provides otherwise, a notice of appeal must be filed on or before the earliest of:

(A) 60 days after the superior court clerk serves on the party filing the notice of appeal a document entitled "Notice of Entry" of judgment or a file-stamped copy of the judgment, showing the date either was served;

(B) 60 days after the party filing the notice of appeal serves or is served by a party with a document entitled "Notice of Entry" of judgment or a file-stamped copy of the judgment, accompanied by proof of service; or

(C) 180 days after entry of judgment.

(2) Service under (1)(A) and (B) may be by any method permitted by the Code of Civil Procedure, including electronic service when permitted under Code of Civil Procedure section 1010.6 and rules 2.250–2.261.

(3) If the parties stipulated in the trial court under Code of Civil Procedure section 1019.5 to waive notice of the court order being appealed, the time to appeal under (1)(C) applies unless the court or a party serves notice of entry of judgment or a file-stamped copy of the judgment to start the time period under (1)(A) or (B).

(b) No extension of time; late notice of appeal

Except as provided in rule 8.66, no court may extend the time to file a notice of appeal. If a notice of appeal is filed late, the reviewing court must dismiss the appeal.

(c) What constitutes entry

For purposes of this rule:

(1) The entry date of a judgment is the date the judgment is filed under Code of Civil Procedure section 668.5, or the date it is entered in the judgment book.

(2) The entry date of an appealable order that is entered in the minutes is the date it is entered in the permanent minutes. But if the minute order directs that a written order be prepared, the entry date is the date the signed order is filed; a written order prepared under rule 3.1312 or similar local rule is not such an order prepared by direction of a minute order.

(3) The entry date of an appealable order that is not entered in the minutes is the date the signed order is filed.

(4) The entry date of a decree of distribution in a probate proceeding is the date it is entered at length in the judgment book or other permanent court record.

(d) Premature notice of appeal

Ct. Rules

(1) A notice of appeal filed after judgment is rendered but before it is entered is valid and is treated as filed immediately after entry of judgment.

(2) The reviewing court may treat a notice of appeal filed after the superior court has announced its intended ruling, but before it has rendered judgment, as filed immediately after entry of judgment.

(e) Appealable order

As used in (a) and (d), "judgment" includes an appealable order if the appeal is from an appealable order. (*Formerly Rule 2, adopted, eff. Jan. 1, 2002. As amended, eff. Jan. 1, 2005. Renumbered Rule 8.104 and amended, eff. Jan. 1, 2007. As amended, eff. Jan. 1, 2010; Jan. 1, 2011; July 1, 2011; July 1, 2012.*)

Advisory Committee Comment

Subdivision (a). Under subdivision (a)(1)(A), a notice of entry of judgment (or a copy of the judgment) must show the date on which the clerk served the document. The proof of service establishes the date that the 60–day period under subdivision (a)(1)(A) begins to run.

Subdivision (a)(1)(B) requires that a notice of entry of judgment (or a copy of the judgment) served by or on a party be accompanied by proof of service. The proof of service establishes the date that the 60–day period under subdivision (a)(1)(B) begins to run. Although the general rule on service (rule 8.25(a)) requires proof of service for all documents served by parties, the requirement is reiterated here because of the serious consequence of a failure to file a timely notice of appeal (see subd. (e)).

Subdivision (b). See rule 8.25(b)(5) for provisions concerning the timeliness of documents mailed by inmates and patients from custodial institutions. Subdivision (b) is declarative of the case law, which holds that the reviewing court lacks jurisdiction to excuse a late-filed notice of appeal. (*Hollister Convalescent Hosp., Inc. v. Rico* (1975) 15 Cal.3d 660, 666–674; *Estate of Hanley* (1943) 23 Cal.2d 120, 122–124.)

In criminal cases, the time for filing a notice of appeal is governed by rule 8.308 and by the case law of "constructive filing." (See, e.g., *In re Benoit* (1973) 10 Cal.3d 72.)

Research References

Rutter, Cal. Practice Guide: A.D.R. Ch. 6-B, B. Temporary Judges.
Rutter, Cal. Practice Guide: Civil Appeals & Writs Ch. 2-C, C. Nonappealable Orders.
Rutter, Cal. Practice Guide: Civil Appeals & Writs Ch. 3-A, A. Necessity of Timely Filing for Appeal.
Rutter, Cal. Practice Guide: Civil Appeals & Writs Ch. 3-B, B. Filing Deadlines.
Rutter, Cal. Practice Guide: Civil Appeals & Writs Ch. 3-C, C. Extensions of Filing Deadline.
Rutter, Cal. Practice Guide: Civil Appeals & Writs Ch. 3-D, D. Consequences of Lapse of Appeal Deadline; Strategies for Respondents and Appellants.
Rutter, Cal. Practice Guide: Civil Appeals & Writs Ch. 5-B, B. Types of Motions, Applications and Requests.
Rutter, Cal. Practice Guide: Civil Appeals & Writs Ch. 14-B, B. Recovery of Appellate Costs and Attorney Fees.
Rutter, Cal. Practice Guide: Civil Appeals & Writs Ch. 16-C, C. Notice of Appeal.
Rutter, Cal. Practice Guide: Civil Appeals & Writs Gen. Matls., Highlights.
Rutter, Cal. Practice Guide: Civ. Pro. Before Trial Ch. 3-B, B. Jurisdiction Over Parties-Personal Jurisdiction.
Rutter, Cal. Practice Guide: Civ. Pro. Before Trial Ch. 3-C, C. Forum Non Conveniens.
Rutter, Cal. Practice Guide: Civ. Pro. Before Trial Ch. 5-F, F. Challenging Default Judgment on Appeal.
Rutter, Cal. Practice Guide: Civ. Pro. Before Trial Ch. 11-A, A. Voluntary Dismissals.
Rutter, Cal. Practice Guide: Civ. Pro. Before Trial Ch. 9(III)-F, F. Appellate Review of Sanctions.

Rutter, Cal. Practice Guide: Civil Trials & Evidence Ch. 4-B, B. Preliminary Matters Discussed in Final Status Conference or In-Chambers Conference.
Rutter, Cal. Practice Guide: Civil Trials & Evidence Ch. 12-B, B. Motion for Nonsuit.
Rutter, Cal. Practice Guide: Civil Trials & Evidence Ch. 17-E, E. Attorney Fees as Costs.
Rutter, Cal. Practice Guide: Civil Trials & Evidence Ch. 18-A, A. Motion for Judgment Notwithstanding the Verdict ("JNOV").
Rutter, Cal. Practice Guide: Civil Trials & Evidence Ch. 18-B, B. Motion for New Trial.
California Practice Guide: Employment Litigation Ch. 19-T, T. Appeals.
Rutter, Cal. Practice Guide: Enforcing Judgments/Debts Ch. 6E-4, Opposing Claim of Exemption.
Rutter, Cal. Practice Guide: Family Law Gen. Matls, Highlights.
Rutter, Cal. Practice Guide: Personal Injury Ch. 9-M, M. Verdicts and Judgment.
Rutter, Cal. Practice Guide: Real Prop. Transactions Ch. 11-C, C. Seller's Remedies Upon Buyer's Breach-Damages and Specific Performance.
9 Witkin Cal. Proc. 5th Appeal § 162, (S 162) Minute Order.
9 Witkin Cal. Proc. 5th Appeal § 555, (S 555) Jurisdictional Requirement: Filing in Trial Court.
9 Witkin Cal. Proc. 5th Appeal § 574, (S 574) Alternative Time Limits.
9 Witkin Cal. Proc. 5th Appeal § 575, in General.
9 Witkin Cal. Proc. 5th Appeal § 577, (S 577) In General.
9 Witkin Cal. Proc. 5th Appeal § 578, Used in Place of Notice of Entry.
9 Witkin Cal. Proc. 5th Appeal § 579, as Equivalent to Notice of Entry.
9 Witkin Cal. Proc. 5th Appeal § 580, (S 580) Erroneous or Inadequate Notice.
9 Witkin Cal. Proc. 5th Appeal § 581, (S 581) One Hundred Eighty Days After Entry of Judgment.
9 Witkin Cal. Proc. 5th Appeal § 582, (S 582) Special Statutes.
9 Witkin Cal. Proc. 5th Appeal § 587, (S 587) Purpose of Rule.
9 Witkin Cal. Proc. 5th Appeal § 590, (S 590) Forms of Extension.
9 Witkin Cal. Proc. 5th Appeal § 591, (S 591) Entry of Order in Minutes.
9 Witkin Cal. Proc. 5th Appeal § 594, (S 594) Valid New Trial Order.
9 Witkin Cal. Proc. 5th Appeal § 595, (S 595) Nature of Motion.
9 Witkin Cal. Proc. 5th Appeal § 598, Extension Where Motion is Denied.
9 Witkin Cal. Proc. 5th Appeal § 606, (S 606) Judgment Against Public Entity.
9 Witkin Cal. Proc. 5th Appeal § 607, (S 607) Nature of Rules.
9 Witkin Cal. Proc. 5th Appeal § 608, (S 608) Judgment and Decree of Distribution.
9 Witkin Cal. Proc. 5th Appeal § 609, Order Entered in Minutes.
9 Witkin Cal. Proc. 5th Appeal § 610, (S 610) by Direction in Minute Order.
9 Witkin Cal. Proc. 5th Appeal § 611, (S 611) Without Minute Entry.
9 Witkin Cal. Proc. 5th Appeal § 612, Where Formal Order is Required.
9 Witkin Cal. Proc. 5th Appeal § 613, Where Written Order is Directed.
9 Witkin Cal. Proc. 5th Appeal § 614, in General.
9 Witkin Cal. Proc. 5th Appeal § 620, Notice After Rendition: Appeal is Valid.
9 Witkin Cal. Proc. 5th Appeal § 621, (S 621) in General.
9 Witkin Cal. Proc. 5th Appeal § 622, (S 622) Good Cause Requirement.
9 Witkin Cal. Proc. 5th Appeal § 623, (S 623) Relief Granted.
9 Witkin Cal. Proc. 5th Appeal § 982, (S 982) Procedure for Request.
9 Witkin Cal. Proc. 5th Appeal § 1008, Time.
8 Witkin Cal. Proc. 5th Attack Judgment Trial Court § 124, Minute Entry or Signed Order.
2 Witkin Cal. Proc. 5th Courts § 206, (S 206) Mandatory But Not Jurisdictional.
8 Witkin Cal. Proc. 5th Enforcement of Judgment § 434, (S 434) Periodic Payments.
7 Witkin Cal. Proc. 5th Judgment § 54, Other Orders.
7 Witkin Cal. Proc. 5th Judgment § 56, Minute Orders.
7 Witkin Cal. Proc. 5th Judgment § 57, Purpose and Entry.
7 Witkin Cal. Proc. 5th Judgment § 58, Notice by Party.
7 Witkin Cal. Proc. 5th Judgment § 301, Fees Determined by Trial Court.
2 Witkin Cal. Proc. 5th Jurisdiction § 19, Reviewing Court Jurisdiction.

2 Witkin Cal. Proc. 5th Jurisdiction § 91, (S 91) Violation of Jurisdictional Time Limit.

5 Witkin Cal. Proc. 5th Pleading § 983, Notification and Service of Notice.

6 Witkin Cal. Proc. 5th Proceedings Without Trial § 44, (S 44) How Order is Made.

6 Witkin Cal. Proc. 5th Proceedings Without Trial § 45, (S 45) Notification and Notice.

10 Witkin, California Summary 10th Parent and Child § 283, Sexual Abuse Allegation.

11 Witkin, California Summary 10th Community Property § 243, Grounds and Time Limits.

Rule 8.108.   Extending the time to appeal

(a)   Extension of time

This rule operates only to extend the time to appeal otherwise prescribed in rule 8.104(a); it does not shorten the time to appeal. If the normal time to appeal stated in rule 8.104(a) is longer than the time provided in this rule, the time to appeal stated in rule 8.104(a) governs.

(b)   Motion for new trial

If any party serves and files a valid notice of intention to move for a new trial, the following extensions of time apply:

(1) If the motion for a new trial is denied, the time to appeal from the judgment is extended for all parties until the earliest of:

(A) 30 days after the superior court clerk mails, or a party serves, an order denying the motion or a notice of entry of that order;

(B) 30 days after denial of the motion by operation of law; or

(C) 180 days after entry of judgment.

(2) If the trial court makes a finding of excessive or inadequate damages and grants the motion for a new trial subject to the condition that the motion is denied if a party consents to the additur or remittitur of damages, the time to appeal is extended as follows:

(A) If a party serves an acceptance of the additur or remittitur within the time for accepting the additur or remittitur, the time to appeal from the judgment is extended for all parties until 30 days after the date the party serves the acceptance.

(B) If a party serves a rejection of the additur or remittitur within the time for accepting the additur or remittitur or if the time for accepting the additur or remittitur expires, the time to appeal from the new trial order is extended for all parties until the earliest of 30 days after the date the party serves the rejection or 30 days after the date on which the time for accepting the additur or remittitur expired.

(c)   Motion to vacate judgment

If, within the time prescribed by rule 8.104 to appeal from the judgment, any party serves and files a valid notice of intention to move—or a valid motion—to vacate the judgment, the time to appeal from the judgment is extended for all parties until the earliest of:

(1) 30 days after the superior court clerk or a party serves, an order denying the motion or a notice of entry of that order;

(2) 90 days after the first notice of intention to move—or motion—is filed; or

(3) 180 days after entry of judgment.

(d)   Motion for judgment notwithstanding the verdict

(1) If any party serves and files a valid motion for judgment notwithstanding the verdict and the motion is denied, the time to appeal from the judgment is extended for all parties until the earliest of:

(A) 30 days after the superior court clerk or a party serves, an order denying the motion or a notice of entry of that order;

(B) 30 days after denial of the motion by operation of law; or

(C) 180 days after entry of judgment.

(2) Unless extended by (e)(2), the time to appeal from an order denying a motion for judgment notwithstanding the verdict is governed by rule 8.104.

(e)   Motion to reconsider appealable order

If any party serves and files a valid motion to reconsider an appealable order under Code of Civil Procedure section 1008, subdivision (a), the time to appeal from that order is extended for all parties until the earliest of:

(1) 30 days after the superior court clerk or a party serves, an order denying the motion or a notice of entry of that order;

(2) 90 days after the first motion to reconsider is filed; or

(3) 180 days after entry of the appealable order.

(f)   Public entity actions under Government Code section 962, 984, or 985

If a public entity defendant serves and files a valid request for a mandatory settlement conference on methods of satisfying a judgment under Government Code section 962, an election to pay a judgment in periodic payments under Government Code section 984 and rule 3.1804, or a motion for a posttrial hearing on reducing a judgment under Government Code section 985, the time to appeal from the judgment is extended for all parties until the earliest of:

(1) 90 days after the superior court clerk serves the party filing the notice of appeal with a document entitled "Notice of Entry" of judgment, or a file-stamped copy of the judgment, showing the date either was served;

(2) 90 days after the party filing the notice of appeal serves or is served by a party with a document entitled "Notice of Entry" of judgment or a file-stamped copy of the judgment, accompanied by proof of service; or

(3) 180 days after entry of judgment.

(g)   Cross-appeal

(1) If an appellant timely appeals from a judgment or appealable order, the time for any other party to appeal from the same judgment or order is extended until 20 days after the superior court clerk serves notification of the first appeal.

(2) If an appellant timely appeals from an order granting a motion for new trial, an order granting—within 150 days after entry of judgment—a motion to vacate the judgment, or a judgment notwithstanding the verdict, the time for any other party to appeal from the original judgment or from an order denying a motion for judgment notwithstanding the verdict is extended until 20 days after the clerk serves notification of the first appeal.

(h)   Service; proof of service

Service under this rule may be by any method permitted by the Code of Civil Procedure, including electronic service when permitted under Code of Civil Procedure section 1010.6 and rules 2.250–2.261. An order or notice that is served must be accompanied by proof of service. *(Formerly Rule 3, adopted, eff. Jan. 1, 2002. Renumbered Rule 8.108 and amended, eff. Jan. 1, 2007. As amended, eff. Jan. 1, 2008; Jan. 1, 2011; July 1, 2012.)*

Advisory Committee Comment

Subdivisions (b)–(f) operate only when a party serves and files a "valid" motion, election, request, or notice of intent to move for the relief in question. As used in these provisions, the word "valid" means only that the motion, election, request, or notice complies with all procedural requirements; it does not mean that the motion, election, request, or notice must also be substantively meritorious. For example, under the rule a timely new trial motion on the ground of excessive damages (Code Civ. Proc., § 657) extends the time to appeal from the judgment even if the trial court ultimately determines the damages were not excessive. Similarly, a timely motion to reconsider (*id.*, § 1008) extends the time to appeal from an appealable order for which reconsideration was sought even if the trial court ultimately determines the motion was not "based upon new or different facts, circumstances, or law," as subdivision (a) of section 1008 requires.

Subdivision (b). Subdivision (b)(1) provides that the denial of a motion for new trial triggers a 30–day extension of the time to appeal from the judgment beginning on the date that the superior court clerk or a party serves either the order of denial or a notice of entry of that order. This provision is intended to eliminate a trap for litigants and to make the rule consistent with the primary rule on the time to appeal from the judgment (rule 8.104(a)).

Subdivision (c). The Code of Civil Procedure provides two distinct statutory motions to vacate a judgment: (1) a motion to vacate a judgment and enter "another and different judgment" because of judicial error (*id.*, § 663), which requires a notice of intention to move to vacate (*id.*, § 663a); and (2) a motion to vacate a judgment because of mistake, inadvertence, surprise, or neglect, which requires a motion to vacate but not a notice of intention to so move (*id.*, § 473, subd. (b)). The courts also recognize certain nonstatutory motions to vacate a judgment, e.g. when the judgment is void on the face of the record or was obtained by extrinsic fraud. (See 8 Witkin, Cal. Procedure (4th ed. 1997) Attack on Judgment in Trial Court, §§ 222–236, pp. 726–750.) Subdivision (c) is intended to apply to all such motions.

In subdivision (c) the phrase "within the time prescribed by rule 8.104 to appeal from the judgment" is intended to incorporate in full the provisions of rule 8.104(a).

Under subdivision (c)(1), the 30–day extension of the time to appeal from the judgment begins when the superior court clerk or a party serves the order denying the motion or notice of entry of that order. This provision is discussed further under subdivision (b) of this comment.

Subdivision (d). Subdivision (d)(1) provides an extension of time after an order denying a motion for judgment notwithstanding the verdict regardless of whether the moving party also moved unsuccessfully for a new trial.

Subdivision (d) further specifies the times to appeal when, as often occurs, a motion for judgment notwithstanding the verdict is joined with a motion for new trial and both motions are denied. Under subdivision (b), the appellant has 30 days after notice of the denial of the new trial motion to appeal from the judgment. Subdivision (d) allows the appellant the longer time provided by rule 8.104 to appeal from the order denying the motion for judgment notwithstanding the verdict, subject to that time being further extended in the circumstances covered by subdivision (g)(2).

Under subdivision (d)(1)(A), the 30–day extension of the time to appeal from the judgment begins when the superior court clerk or a party serves the order denying the motion or notice of entry of that order. This provision is discussed further under subdivision (b) of this comment.

Subdivision (e). The scope of subdivision (e) is specific. It applies to any "appealable order," whether made before or after judgment (see Code Civ. Proc., § 904.1, subd. (a)(2)–(12)), but it extends only the time to appeal "from that order." The subdivision thus takes no position on whether a judgment is subject to a motion to reconsider (see, e.g., *Ramon v. Aerospace Corp.* (1996) 50 Cal.App.4th 1233, 1236–1238 [postjudgment motion to reconsider order granting summary judgment did not extend time to appeal from judgment because trial court had no power to rule on such motion after entry of judgment]), or whether an order denying a motion to reconsider is itself appealable (compare *Santee v. Santa Clara County Office of Education* (1990) 220 Cal.App.3d 702, 710–711 [order appealable if motion based on new facts] with *Rojes v. Riverside General*

Hospital (1988) 203 Cal.App.3d 1151, 1160–1161 [order not appealable under any circumstances]). Both these issues are legislative matters.

Subdivision (e) applies only when a "party" makes a valid motion to "reconsider" an appealable order under subdivision (a) of Code of Civil Procedure section 1008; it therefore does not apply when a court reconsiders an order on its own motion (*id.*, subd. (d)) or when a party makes "a subsequent application for the same order" (*id.*, subd. (c)). The statute provides no time limits within which either of the latter events must occur.

Under subdivision (e)(1), the 30–day extension of the time to appeal from the order begins when the superior court clerk or a party serves the order denying the motion or notice of entry of that order. The purpose of this provision is discussed further under subdivision (b) of this comment.

Among its alternative periods of extension of the time to appeal, subdivision (e) provides in paragraph (2) for a 90–day period beginning on the filing of the motion to reconsider or, if there is more than one such motion, the filing of the first such motion. The provision is consistent with subdivision (c)(2), governing motions to vacate judgment; as in the case of those motions, there is no time limit for a ruling on a motion to reconsider.

Subdivision (g). Consistent with case law, subdivision (g)(1) extends the time to appeal after another party appeals only if the later appeal is taken "from the same order or judgment as the first appeal." (*Commercial & Farmers Nat. Bank v. Edwards* (1979) 91 Cal.App.3d 699, 704.)

The former rule (former rule 3(c), second sentence) provided an extension of time for filing a protective cross-appeal from the judgment when the trial court granted a motion for new trial or a motion to vacate the judgment, but did not provide the same extension when the trial court granted a motion for judgment notwithstanding the verdict. One case declined to infer that the omission was unintentional, but suggested that the Judicial Council might consider amending the rule to fill the gap. (*Lippert v. AVCO Community Developers, Inc.* (1976) 60 Cal. App.3d 775, 778 & fn. 3.) Rule 8.108(e)(2) fills the gap thus identified.

Subdivision (h). Under subdivision (h), an order or notice that is served under this rule must be accompanied by proof of service. The date of the proof of service establishes the date when an extension of the time to appeal begins to run after service of such an order or notice.

Research References

Rutter, Cal. Practice Guide: Civil Appeals & Writs Ch. 3-A, A. Necessity of Timely Filing for Appeal.

Rutter, Cal. Practice Guide: Civil Appeals & Writs Ch. 3-B, B. Filing Deadlines.

Rutter, Cal. Practice Guide: Civil Appeals & Writs Ch. 3-C, C. Extensions of Filing Deadline.

Rutter, Cal. Practice Guide: Civil Appeals & Writs Ch. 3-F, F. Cross-Appeals.

Rutter, Cal. Practice Guide: Civil Appeals & Writs Ch. 5-B, B. Types of Motions, Applications and Requests.

Rutter, Cal. Practice Guide: Civil Appeals & Writs Ch. 14-B, B. Recovery of Appellate Costs and Attorney Fees.

Rutter, Cal. Practice Guide: Civil Appeals & Writs Gen. Matls., Highlights.

Rutter, Cal. Practice Guide: Civ. Pro. Before Trial Ch. 11-A, A. Voluntary Dismissals.

Rutter, Cal. Practice Guide: Civil Trials & Evidence Ch. 17-E, E. Attorney Fees as Costs.

Rutter, Cal. Practice Guide: Civil Trials & Evidence Ch. 18-A, A. Motion for Judgment Notwithstanding the Verdict ("JNOV").

Rutter, Cal. Practice Guide: Civil Trials & Evidence Ch. 18-B, B. Motion for New Trial.

California Practice Guide: Employment Litigation Ch. 19-T, T. Appeals.

Rutter, Cal. Practice Guide: Personal Injury Ch. 9-M, M. Verdicts and Judgment.

Rutter, Cal. Practice Guide: Personal Injury Ch. 10-A, A. Motion for New Trial.

Rule 8.112. Petition for writ of supersedeas

(a) Petition

(1) A party seeking a stay of the enforcement of a judgment or order pending appeal may serve and file a petition for writ of supersedeas in the reviewing court.

(2) The petition must bear the same title as the appeal and, if known, the appeal's docket number.

(3) The petition must explain the necessity for the writ and include a memorandum.

(4) If the record has not been filed in the reviewing court:

(A) The petition must include a statement of the case sufficient to show that the petitioner will raise substantial issues on appeal, including a fair summary of the material facts and the issues that are likely to be raised on appeal.

(B) The petitioner must file the following documents with the petition:

(i) The judgment or order, showing its date of entry;

(ii) The notice of appeal, showing its date of filing;

(iii) A reporter's transcript of any oral statement by the court supporting its rulings related to the issues that are likely to be raised on appeal, or, if a transcript is unavailable, a declaration fairly summarizing any such statements;

(iv) Any application for a stay filed in the trial court, any opposition to that application, and a reporter's transcript of the oral proceedings concerning the stay or, if a transcript is unavailable, a declaration fairly summarizing the proceedings, including the parties' arguments and any statement by the court supporting its ruling; and

(v) Any other document from the trial court proceeding that is necessary for proper consideration of the petition.

(C) The documents listed in (B) must comply with the following requirements:

(i) They must be bound together at the end of the petition or in a separate volumes not exceeding 300 pages each. The pages must be consecutively numbered;

(ii) They must be index-tabbed by number or letter, and

(iii) They must begin with a table of contents listing each document by its title and its index-tab number or letter.

(5) The petition must be verified.

(b) Opposition

(1) Unless otherwise ordered, any opposition must be served and filed within 15 days after the petition is filed.

(2) An opposition must state any material facts not included in the petition and include a memorandum.

(3) The court may not issue a writ of supersedeas until the respondent has had the opportunity to file an opposition.

(c) Temporary stay

(1) The petition may include a request for a temporary stay under rule 8.116 pending the ruling on the petition.

(2) A separately filed request for a temporary stay must be served on the respondent. For good cause, the Chief Justice or presiding justice may excuse advance service.

(d) Issuing the writ

(1) The court may issue the writ on any conditions it deems just.

(2) The court must hold a hearing before it may issue a writ staying an order that awards or changes the custody of a minor.

(3) The court must notify the superior court, under rule 8.489, of any writ or temporary stay that it issues. *(Formerly Rule 49, adopted, eff. Jan. 1, 2005. Renumbered Rule 8.112 and amended, eff. Jan. 1, 2007. As amended, eff. Jan. 1, 2008; Jan. 1, 2009; Jan. 1, 2010; July 1, 2013.)*

Advisory Committee Comment

Subdivision (a). If the preparation of a reporter's transcript has not yet been completed at that time a petition for a writ of supersedeas is filed, that transcript is "unavailable" within the meaning of (a)(4)(B).

Research References

Rule 8.116.   Request for writ of supersedeas or temporary stay

(a) Information on cover

If a petition for original writ, petition for review, or any other document requests a writ of supersedeas or temporary stay from a reviewing court, the cover of the document must:

(1) Prominently display the notice "STAY REQUESTED"; and

(2) Identify the nature and date of the proceeding or act sought to be stayed.

(b) Additional information

The following information must appear either on the cover or at the beginning of the text:

(1) The trial court and department involved; and

(2) The name and telephone number of the trial judge whose order the request seeks to stay.

(c) Sanction

If the document does not comply with (a) and (b), the reviewing court may decline to consider the request for writ of supersedeas or temporary stay. *(Formerly Rule 49.5, adopted, eff. Jan. 1, 2005.   Renumbered Rule 8.116 and amended, eff. Jan. 1, 2007.)*

Research References

Rutter, Cal. Practice Guide: Civil Appeals & Writs Ch. 7-E, E. Stay by Writ of Supersedeas.
Rutter, Cal. Practice Guide: Civil Appeals & Writs Ch. 15-E, E. Procedures on Writ Review.
9 Witkin Cal. Proc. 5th Appeal § 9, (S 9) Current Structure.
9 Witkin Cal. Proc. 5th Appeal § 300, Petition.
9 Witkin Cal. Proc. 5th Appeal § 301, Temporary Stay.
2 Witkin Cal. Proc. 5th Courts § 195, (S 195) Appellate Rules.
8 Witkin Cal. Proc. 5th Extraordinary Writs § 169, in General.

Article 2

RECORD ON APPEAL

Rule 8.120.   Record on appeal

Except as otherwise provided in this chapter, the record on an appeal in a civil case must contain the records specified in (a) and (b), which constitute the normal record on appeal.

(a) Record of written documents

(1) A record of the written documents from the superior court proceedings in the form of one of the following:

(A) A clerk's transcript under rule 8.122;

(B) An appendix under rule 8.124;

(C) The original superior court file under rule 8.128, if a local rule of the reviewing court permits this form of the record;

(D) An agreed statement under rule 8.134(a)(2); or

(E) A settled statement under rule 8.137.

(2) If an appellant intends to raise any issue that requires consideration of the record of an administrative proceeding that was admitted in evidence, refused, or lodged in the superior court, the record on appeal must include that administrative record, transmitted under rule 8.123.

(b) Record of the oral proceedings

If an appellant intends to raise any issue that requires consideration of the oral proceedings in the superior court, the record on appeal must include a record of these oral proceedings in the form of one of the following:

(1) A reporter's transcript under rule 8.130;

(2) An agreed statement under rule 8.134; or

(3) A settled statement under rule 8.137. *(Adopted, eff. Jan. 1, 2008.)*

Research References

Rutter, Cal. Practice Guide: Civil Appeals & Writs Ch. 3-E, E. Filing Steps.
Rutter, Cal. Practice Guide: Civil Appeals & Writs Ch. 4-B, B. Components of Record and Considerations in Selecting Them.
Rutter, Cal. Practice Guide: Civil Appeals & Writs Ch. 4-C, C. Record Preparation Procedure.
9 Witkin Cal. Proc. 5th Appeal § 9, (S 9) Current Structure.
9 Witkin Cal. Proc. 5th Appeal § 626, (S 626) Nature of Record.
2 Witkin Cal. Proc. 5th Courts § 195, (S 195) Appellate Rules.

Rule 8.121.   Notice designating the record on appeal

(a) Time to file

Within 10 days after filing the notice of appeal, an appellant must serve and file a notice in the superior court designating the record on appeal.   The appellant may combine its notice designating the record with its notice of appeal.

(b) Contents

(1) The notice must:

(A) Specify the date the notice of appeal was filed.

(B) Specify which form of the record of the written documents from the superior court proceedings listed in rule 8.120(a)(1) the appellant elects to use.   If the appellant elects to use a clerk's transcript, the notice must also designate the documents to be included in the clerk's transcript as required under rule 8.122(b)(1).

(C) Specify whether the appellant elects to proceed with or without a record of the oral proceedings in the trial court.   If the appellant elects to proceed with a record of the oral proceedings in the trial court, the notice must specify which form of the record listed in rule 8.120(b) the appellant elects to use.   If the appellant elects to use a reporter's transcript, the notice must designate the proceedings to be included in the transcript as required under rule 8.130.

(2) If an appellant intends to raise any issue that requires consideration of the record of an administrative proceeding that was admitted in evidence, refused, or lodged in the superior court, the notice must also request that this administrative record be transmitted to the reviewing court under rule 8.123.

(c) Copy to the reviewing court

The clerk must promptly send the reviewing court a copy of any notice filed under this rule. *(Adopted, eff. Jan. 1, 2008.)*

Advisory Committee Comment

The Judicial Council has adopted an optional form—*Appellant's Notice Designating Record on Appeal* (form APP–003)—that can be used to provide the notice required by this rule.

This rule makes the filing of a notice designating the record an "act required to procure the record" within the meaning of rule 8.140(a). Under that rule, a failure to file such a notice triggers the clerk's duty to issue a 15–day notice of default and thereby allows the appellant to cure the default in superior court.

Research References

Rutter, Cal. Practice Guide: Civil Appeals & Writs Ch. 3-E, E. Filing Steps.

Rutter, Cal. Practice Guide: Civil Appeals & Writs Ch. 4-C, C. Record Preparation Procedure.

9 Witkin Cal. Proc. 5th Appeal § 560, (S 560) Statement that Party Appeals.

9 Witkin Cal. Proc. 5th Appeal § 627, (S 627) Notice Designating Record.

9 Witkin Cal. Proc. 5th Appeal § 634, (S 634) Administrative Proceedings.

9 Witkin Cal. Proc. 5th Appeal § 635, (S 635) Notice.

9 Witkin Cal. Proc. 5th Appeal § 656, Superior Court File in Lieu of Clerk's Transcript.

9 Witkin Cal. Proc. 5th Appeal § 658, (S 658) Motion.

9 Witkin Cal. Proc. 5th Appeal § 666, (S 666) Statement or Stipulation.

Rule 8.122. Clerk's transcript

(a) Designation

(1) A notice designating documents to be included in a clerk's transcript must identify each designated document by its title and filing date or, if the filing date is not available, the date it was signed. The notice may specify portions of designated documents that are not to be included in the transcript. For minute orders or instructions, it is sufficient to collectively designate all minute orders or all minute orders entered between specified dates, or all written jury instructions given, refused, or withdrawn.

(2) Within 10 days after the appellant serves its notice designating a clerk's transcript, the respondent may serve and file a notice in superior court designating any additional documents the respondent wants included in the transcript.

(3) Except as provided in (b)(4), all exhibits admitted in evidence, refused, or lodged are deemed part of the record, but a party wanting a copy of an exhibit included in the transcript must specify that exhibit by number or letter in its notice of designation. If the superior court has returned a designated exhibit to a party, the party in possession of the exhibit must deliver it to the superior court clerk within 10 days after the notice designating the exhibit is served.

(b) Contents of transcript

(1) The transcript must contain:

(A) The notice of appeal;

(B) Any judgment appealed from and any notice of its entry;

(C) Any order appealed from and any notice of its entry;

(D) Any notice of intention to move for a new trial, or motion to vacate the judgment, for judgment notwithstanding the verdict, or for reconsideration of an appealed order, and any order on such motion and any notice of its entry;

(E) Any notices or stipulations to prepare clerk's or reporter's transcripts or to proceed by agreed or settled statement; and

(F) The register of actions, if any.

(2) Each document listed in (1)(A), (B), (C), and (D) must show the date necessary to determine the timeliness of the appeal under rule 8.104 or 8.108.

(3) Except as provided in (4), if designated by any party, the transcript must also contain:

(A) Any other document filed or lodged in the case in superior court;

(B) Any exhibit admitted in evidence, refused, or lodged; and

(C) Any jury instruction that any party submitted in writing and the cover page required by rule 2.1055(b)(2) indicating the party requesting it, and any written jury instructions given by the court.

(4) Unless the reviewing court orders or the parties stipulate otherwise:

(A) The clerk must not copy or transmit to the reviewing court the original of a deposition except those portions of a deposition presented or offered into evidence under rule 2.1040.

(B) The clerk must not include in the transcript the record of an administrative proceeding that was admitted in evidence, refused, or lodged in the trial court. Any such administrative record must be transmitted to the reviewing court as specified in rule 8.123.

(c) Deposit for cost of transcript

(1) Within 30 days after the respondent files a designation under (a)(2) or the time for filing it expires, whichever first occurs, the superior court clerk must send:

(A) To the appellant, notice of the estimated cost to prepare an original and one copy of the clerk's transcript; and

(B) To each party other than the appellant, notice of the estimated cost to prepare a copy of the clerk's transcript for that party's use.

(2) A notice under (1) must show the date it was sent.

(3) Within 10 days after the clerk sends a notice under (1), the appellant and any party wanting to purchase a copy of the clerk's transcript must deposit the estimated cost with the clerk, unless otherwise provided by law or the party submits an application for, or an order granting, a waiver of the cost.

(d) Preparation of transcript

(1) Within 30 days after the appellant deposits the estimated cost of the transcript or the court files an order waiving that cost, the clerk must:

(A) Prepare an original and one copy of the transcript, and certify the original; and

(B) Prepare additional copies for which the parties have made deposits.

(2) If the appeal is abandoned or dismissed before the clerk has completed preparation of the transcript, the clerk must refund any portion of the deposit under (c) exceeding the preparation cost actually incurred. *(Formerly Rule 5, adopted, eff. Jan. 1, 2002. As amended, eff. Jan. 1, 2003; Jan. 1, 2005, Renumbered Rule 8.120 and amended, eff. Jan. 1, 2007. Renumbered Rule 8.122 and amended, eff. Jan. 1, 2008. As amended, eff. July 1, 2009; Jan. 1, 2010; Jan. 1, 2011; July 1, 2011.)*

Advisory Committee Comment

Subdivision (a). Subdivision (a)(1) allows a party designating documents for inclusion in the clerk's transcript to specify *portions* of such documents that are not to be included, e.g., because they are duplicates of other designated documents or are not necessary for proper consideration of the issues raised in the appeal. The notice of designation should identify any portion to be omitted by means of a descriptive reference, e.g., by specific page or exhibit numbers. This provision is intended to simplify and therefore expedite the preparation of the clerk's transcript, to reduce its cost to the parties, and to relieve the courts of the burden of reviewing a record containing redundant, irrelevant, or immaterial documents.

Subdivision (b). The supporting and opposing memoranda and attachments to any motion to vacate the judgment, for judgment notwithstanding the verdict, or for reconsideration of an appealed order are not required to be included in the clerk's transcript under subdivision (b)(1)(D) but may be included by designation of a party under (b)(3) or on motion of a party or the reviewing court under rule 8.155.

Subdivision (b)(1)(F) requires the clerk's transcript to include the register of actions, if any. This provision is intended to assist the reviewing court in determining the accuracy of the clerk's transcript.

Subdivision (c). Under subdivision (c)(2), a clerk who sends a notice under subdivision (c)(1) must include a certificate stating the date on which the clerk sent it. This provision is intended to establish the date when the 10–day period for depositing the cost of the clerk's transcript under this rule begins to run.

The Superior Court will make the determination on any application to waive the fees for preparing, certifying, copying, and transmitting the clerk's transcript.

Research References

Rutter, Cal. Practice Guide: Civil Appeals & Writs Ch. 4-B, B. Components of Record and Considerations in Selecting Them.
Rutter, Cal. Practice Guide: Civil Appeals & Writs Ch. 4-C, C. Record Preparation Procedure.
Rutter, Cal. Practice Guide: Civil Appeals & Writs Ch. 4-E, E. Filing and Correction of Record.
Rutter, Cal. Practice Guide: Civil Appeals & Writs Ch. 4-G, G. Augmentation of the Record.
Rutter, Cal. Practice Guide: Civil Appeals & Writs Ch. 4-H, H. Transmittal of Exhibits.
Rutter, Cal. Practice Guide: Civil Appeals & Writs Ch. 5-B, B. Types of Motions, Applications and Requests.
Rutter, Cal. Practice Guide: Civil Appeals & Writs Ch. 15-C, C. Statutory Writs.
3 Witkin Cal. Proc. 5th Actions § 429C, (New)-Costs Excused.
9 Witkin Cal. Proc. 5th Appeal § 646, (S 646) Matters Automatically Included.
9 Witkin Cal. Proc. 5th Appeal § 647, (S 647) Matters Designated.
9 Witkin Cal. Proc. 5th Appeal § 648, (S 648) Original Papers.
9 Witkin Cal. Proc. 5th Appeal § 649, (S 649) Cost and Preparation.
9 Witkin Cal. Proc. 5th Appeal § 669, (S 669) Designation by Respondent.
9 Witkin Cal. Proc. 5th Appeal § 679, (S 679) Record.
9 Witkin Cal. Proc. 5th Appeal § 686, Procedure.
9 Witkin Cal. Proc. 5th Appeal § 1012, Transcripts.
7 Witkin Cal. Proc. 5th Trial § 316, Error Invited.
10 Witkin, California Summary 10th Parent and Child § 721, Record.
10 Witkin, California Summary 10th Parent and Child § 725, Notice of Intent and Record.

Rule 8.123. Record of administrative proceedings

(a) Application

This rule applies if the record of an administrative proceeding was admitted in evidence, refused, or lodged in the superior court.

(b) Designation

(1) An appellant's notice designating the record on appeal under rule 8.121 that requests a record of an administrative proceeding be transmitted to the reviewing court must identify the administrative record by the title and date or dates of the administrative proceedings.

(2) If an appellant does not request that an administrative record admitted in evidence, refused, or lodged in the superior court be transmitted to the reviewing court, the respondent, within 10 days after the appellant serves its notice designating the record on appeal, may serve and file in the superior court a notice requesting that this administrative record be transmitted to the reviewing court.

~~(d)~~(c) Transmittal to the reviewing court

Except as provided in (d), if any administrative record is designated by a party, the superior court clerk must transmit the original administrative record with any clerk's or reporter's transcript sent to the reviewing court under rule 8.150. If the appellant has elected under rule 8. 121 to use neither a clerk's transcript nor a reporter's transcript, the superior court clerk must transmit any administrative record designated by a party to the reviewing court no later than 45 days after the respondent files a designation under (b)(2) or the time for filing it expires, whichever first occurs.

~~(e)~~(d) Administrative records returned to parties

(1) If the superior court has returned a designated administrative record to a party, the party in possession of the administrative record must ~~deliver it to the superior court clerk~~ make that record available to the other parties in the case for copying within 15 days after the notice designating the record on appeal is served and lodge the record with the clerk of the reviewing court at the time the last respondent's brief is due.

(2) A party seeking an administrative record that was returned to another party must first ask the possessing party to provide a copy or lend it for copying. The possessing party should reasonably cooperate with such requests.

(3) If the request under (2) is unsuccessful, the requesting party may serve and file in the reviewing court a notice identifying the administrative record and requesting that the possessing party deliver the administrative record to the requesting party or, if the possessing party prefers, to the reviewing court. The possessing party must comply with the request within 10 days after the notice was served.

(4) If the possessing party sends the administrative record to the requesting party, that party must copy and return it to the possessing party within 10 days after receiving it.

(5) If the possessing party sends the administrative record to the reviewing court, that party must:

(A) Include with the administrative record a copy of the notice served by the requesting party; and

(B) Immediately notify the requesting party that it has sent the administrative record to the reviewing court.

(e) Return by reviewing court

On request, the reviewing court may return an administrative record to the superior court or, if the record was lodged by a party under (d), to the lodging party. When the remittitur issues, the reviewing court must return any administrative record to the superior court or, if the record was lodged by a party under (d), to the lodging party. *(Adopted, eff. Jan. 1, 2008. As amended, eff. Jan. 1, 2013.)*

Research References

Rutter, Cal. Practice Guide: Civil Appeals & Writs Ch. 4-C, C. Record Preparation Procedure.
9 Witkin Cal. Proc. 5th Appeal § 634, (S 634) Administrative Proceedings.
9 Witkin Cal. Proc. 5th Appeal § 647, (S 647) Matters Designated.

Rule 8.124. Appendixes

(a) Notice of election

(1) Unless the superior court orders otherwise on a motion served and filed within 10 days after the notice of election is served, this rule governs if:

(A) The appellant elects to use an appendix under this rule in the notice designating the record on appeal under rule 8.121 ; or

(B) The respondent serves and files a notice in the superior court electing to use an appendix under this rule within 10 days after the notice of appeal is filed and no waiver of the fee for a clerk's transcript is granted to the appellant.

(2) When a party files a notice electing to use an appendix under this rule, the superior court clerk must promptly send a copy of the register of actions, if any, to the attorney of record for each party and to any unrepresented party.

(3) The parties may prepare separate appendixes, but are encouraged to stipulate to a joint appendix.

(b) Contents of appendix

(1) A joint appendix or an appellant's appendix must contain:

(A) All items required by rule 8.122(b)(1), showing the dates required by rule 8.122(b)(2);

(B) Any item listed in rule 8.122(b)(3) that is necessary for proper consideration of the issues, including, for an appellant's appendix, any item that the appellant should reasonably assume the respondent will rely on;

(C) The notice of election; and

(D) For a joint appendix, the stipulation designating its contents.

(2) An appendix may incorporate by reference all or part of the record on appeal in another case pending in the reviewing court or in a prior appeal in the same case.

(A) The other appeal must be identified by its case name and number. If only part of a record is being incorporated by reference, that part must be identified by citation to the volume and page numbers of the record where it appears and either the title of the document or documents or the date of the oral proceedings to be incorporated. The parts of any record incorporated by reference must be identified both in the body of the appendix and in a separate section at the end of the index.

(B) If the appendix incorporates by reference any such record, the cover of the appendix must prominently display the notice "Record in case number: ___ incorporated by reference," identifying the number of the case from which the record is incorporated.

(C) On request of the reviewing court or any party, the designating party must provide a copy of the materials incorporated by reference to the court or another party or lend them for copying as provided in (c).

(3) An appendix must not:

(A) Contain documents or portions of documents filed in superior court that are unnecessary for proper consideration of the issues.

(B) Contain transcripts of oral proceedings that may be designated under rule 8.130.

(C) Contain the record of an administrative proceeding that was admitted in evidence, refused, or lodged in the trial court. Any such administrative record must be transmitted to the reviewing court as specified in rule 8.123.

(D) Incorporate any document by reference except as provided in (2).

(4) All exhibits admitted in evidence, refused, or lodged are deemed part of the record, whether or not the appendix contains copies of them.

(5) A respondent's appendix may contain any document that could have been included in the appellant's appendix or a joint appendix.

(6) An appellant's reply appendix may contain any document that could have been included in the respondent's appendix.

(c) Document or exhibit held by other party

If a party preparing an appendix wants it to contain a copy of a document or an exhibit in the possession of another party:

(1) The party must first ask the party possessing the document or exhibit to provide a copy or lend it for copying. All parties should reasonably cooperate with such requests.

(2) If the attempt under (1) is unsuccessful, the party may serve and file in the reviewing court a notice identifying the document or specifying the exhibit's trial court designation and requesting the party possessing the document or exhibit to deliver it to the requesting party or, if the possessing party prefers, to the reviewing court. The possessing party must comply with the request within 10 days after the notice was served.

(3) If the party possessing the document or exhibit sends it to the requesting party, that party must copy and return it to the possessing party within 10 days after receiving it.

(4) If the party possessing the document or exhibit sends it to the reviewing court, that party must:

(A) Accompany the document or exhibit with a copy of the notice served by the requesting party; and

(B) Immediately notify the requesting party that it has sent the document or exhibit to the reviewing court.

(5) On request, the reviewing court may return a document or an exhibit to the party that sent it. When the remittitur issues, the reviewing court must return all documents or exhibits to the party that sent them.

(d) Form of appendix

(1) An appendix must comply with the requirements of rule 8.144(a)–(c) for a clerk's transcript.

(2) In addition to the information required on the cover of a brief by rule 8.204(b)(10), the cover of an appendix must prominently display the title "Joint Appendix" or "Appellant's Appendix" or "Respondent's Appendix" or "Appellant's Reply Appendix."

(3) An appendix must not be bound with a brief.

(e) Service and filing

(1) A party preparing an appendix must:

(A) Serve the appendix on each party, unless otherwise agreed by the parties or ordered by the reviewing court; and

(B) File the appendix in the reviewing court.

(2) A joint appendix or an appellant's appendix must be served and filed with the appellant's opening brief.

(3) A respondent's appendix, if any, must be served and filed with the respondent's brief.

(4) An appellant's reply appendix, if any, must be served and filed with the appellant's reply brief.

(f) Cost of appendix

(1) Each party must pay for its own appendix.

(2) The cost of a joint appendix must be paid:

(A) By the appellant;

(B) If there is more than one appellant, by the appellants equally; or

(C) As the parties may agree.

(g) Inaccurate or noncomplying appendix

Filing an appendix constitutes a representation that the appendix consists of accurate copies of documents in the superior court file. The reviewing court may impose monetary or other sanctions for filing an appendix that contains inaccurate copies or otherwise violates this rule. *(Formerly Rule 5.1, adopted, eff. Jan. 1, 2002. As amended, eff. Jan. 1, 2005. Renumbered Rule 8.124 and amended, eff. Jan. 1, 2007. As amended, eff. Jan. 1, 2008; Jan. 1, 2010.)*

Advisory Committee Comment

Subdivision (a). Under this provision either party may elect to have the appeal proceed by way of an appendix. If the appellant's fees for a clerk's transcript are not waived and the respondent timely elects to use an appendix, that election will govern unless the superior court orders otherwise. This election procedure differs from all other appellate rules governing designation of a record on appeal. In those rules, the appellant's designation, or the stipulation of the parties, determines the type of record on appeal. Before making this election, respondents should check whether the appellant has been granted a fee waiver that is still in effect. If the trial court has granted appellant a fee waiver for the clerk's transcript, or grants such a waiver after the notice of appeal is filed, respondent cannot elect to proceed by way of an appendix.

Subdivision (a)(2) is intended to assist appellate counsel in preparing an appendix by providing them with the list of pleadings and other filings found in the register of actions or "docket sheet" in those counties that maintain such registers. (See Gov. Code, § 69845.) The provision is derived from rule 10–1 of the United States Circuit Rules (9th Cir.).

Subdivision (b). Under subdivision (b)(1)(A), a joint appendix or an appellant's appendix must contain any register of actions that the clerk sent to the parties under subdivision (a)(2). This provision is intended to assist the reviewing court in determining the accuracy of the appendix. The provision is derived from rule 30–1.3(a)(ii) of the United States Circuit Rules (9th Cir.).

In support of or opposition to pleadings or motions, the parties may have filed a number of lengthy documents in the proceedings in superior court, including, for example, declarations, memorandums, trial briefs, documentary exhibits (e.g., insurance policies, contracts, deeds), and photocopies of judicial opinions or other publications. Subdivision (b)(3)(A) prohibits the inclusion of such documents in an appendix when they are not necessary for proper consideration of the issues raised in the appeal. Even if a document is otherwise includable in an appendix, the rule prohibits the inclusion of any substantial *portion* of the document that is not necessary for proper consideration of the issues raised in the appeal. The prohibition is intended to simplify and therefore expedite the preparation of the appendix, to reduce its cost to the parties, and to relieve the courts of the burden of reviewing a record containing redundant, irrelevant, or immaterial documents. The provision is adapted from rule 30–1.4 of the United States Circuit Rules (9th Cir.).

Subdivision (b)(3)(B) prohibits the inclusion in an appendix of transcripts of oral proceedings that may be made part of a reporter's transcript. (Compare rule 8.130(e)(3) [the reporter must not copy into the reporter's transcript any document includable in the clerk's transcript under rule 8.122].) The prohibition is intended to prevent a party filing an appendix from evading the requirements and safeguards imposed by rule 8.130 on the process of designating and preparing a reporter's transcript, or the requirements imposed by rule 8.144(d) on the use of daily or other transcripts instead of a reporter's transcript (i.e., renumbered pages, required indexes). In addition, if an appellant were to include in its appendix a transcript of less than all the proceedings, the respondent would not learn of any need to designate additional proceedings (under rule 8.130(a)(3)) until the appellant had served its appendix with its brief, when it would be too late to designate them. Note also that a party may file a certified transcript of designated proceedings instead of a deposit for the reporter's fee (rule 8.130(b)(3)).

Subdivision (d). In current practice, served copies of filed documents often bear no clerk's date stamp and are not conformed by the parties serving them. Consistently with this practice, subdivision (d) does not require such documents to be conformed. The provision thereby relieves the parties of the burden of obtaining conformed copies at the cost of considerable time and expense and expedites the preparation of the appendix and the processing of the appeal. It is to be noted, however,

that under subdivision (b)(1)(A) each document necessary to determine the timeliness of the appeal must show the date required under rule 8.104 or 8.108. Note also that subdivision (g) of rule 8.124 provides that a party filing an appendix represents under penalty of sanctions that its copies of documents are accurate.

Subdivision (e). Subdivision (e)(2) requires a joint appendix to be filed with the appellant's opening brief. The provision is intended to improve the briefing process by enabling the appellant's opening brief to include citations to the record. To provide for the case in which a respondent concludes in light of the appellant's opening brief that the joint appendix should have included additional documents, subdivision (b)(5) permits such a respondent to present in an appendix filed with its respondent's brief (see subd. (e)(3)) any document that could have been included in the joint appendix.

Under subdivision (e)(2)–(4) an appendix is required to be filed "with" the associated brief. This provision is intended to clarify that an extension of a briefing period ipso facto extends the filing period of an appendix associated with the brief.

Subdivision (g). Under subdivision (g), sanctions do not depend on the degree of culpability of the filing party—i.e., on whether the party's conduct was willful or negligent—but on the nature of the inaccuracies and the importance of the documents they affect.

Research References

Rutter, Cal. Practice Guide: Civil Appeals & Writs Ch. 4-B, B. Components of Record and Considerations in Selecting Them.

Rutter, Cal. Practice Guide: Civil Appeals & Writs Ch. 4-C, C. Record Preparation Procedure.

Rutter, Cal. Practice Guide: Civil Appeals & Writs Ch. 4-D, D. Record on Multiple and Later Appeals.

Rutter, Cal. Practice Guide: Civil Appeals & Writs Ch. 4-H, H. Transmittal of Exhibits.

Rutter, Cal. Practice Guide: Civil Appeals & Writs Ch. 14-B, B. Recovery of Appellate Costs and Attorney Fees.

Rutter, Cal. Practice Guide: Civil Appeals & Writs Ch. 16-D, D. Designation of the Record.

Rutter, Cal. Practice Guide: Civil Appeals & Writs Form 5:G, Motion to Consolidate Appeals.

Rutter, Cal. Practice Guide: Civil Appeals & Writs Form 5:F.1, Motion for Calendar Preference.

9 Witkin Cal. Proc. 5th Appeal § 559, (S 559) Notification by Clerk.

9 Witkin Cal. Proc. 5th Appeal § 650, (S 650) Nature and Purpose of Appendix.

9 Witkin Cal. Proc. 5th Appeal § 651, (S 651) Notice of Election.

9 Witkin Cal. Proc. 5th Appeal § 652, (S 652) Contents and Form.

9 Witkin Cal. Proc. 5th Appeal § 653, (S 653) Exhibit Held by Other Party.

9 Witkin Cal. Proc. 5th Appeal § 654, (S 654) Filing and Service.

9 Witkin Cal. Proc. 5th Appeal § 655, (S 655) Sanctions for Improper Appendix.

9 Witkin Cal. Proc. 5th Appeal § 717, (S 717) Service and Filing.

Rule 8.128.   Superior court file instead of clerk's transcript

(a) Stipulation; time to file

(1) If a local rule of the reviewing court permits, the parties may stipulate to use the original superior court file instead of a clerk's transcript under rule 8.122. This rule and any supplemental provisions of the local rule then govern unless the superior court orders otherwise after notice to the parties.

(2) Parties intending to proceed under this rule must file their stipulation in superior court with the appellant's notice designating the record on appeal under rule 8.121. The parties must serve the reviewing court with a copy of the stipulation.

(b) Cost estimate; preparation of file; transmittal

(1) Within 10 days after a stipulation under (a) is filed, the superior court clerk must mail the appellant an estimate of the cost to prepare the file, including the cost of sending the index under (3). The appellant must deposit the cost or file an

application for, or an order granting, a waiver of the cost within 10 days after the clerk mails the estimate.

(2) Within 10 days after the appellant deposits the cost or the court files an order waiving that cost, the superior court clerk must put the superior court file in chronological order, number the pages, and attach a chronological index and a list of all attorneys of record, the parties they represent, and any unrepresented parties.

(3) The clerk must send copies of the index to all attorneys of record and any unrepresented parties for their use in paginating their copies of the file to conform to the index.

(4) The clerk must send the prepared file to the reviewing court with the reporter's transcript. If the appellant elected to proceed without a reporter's transcript, the clerk must immediately send the prepared file to the reviewing court. *(Formerly Rule 5.2, adopted, eff. Jan. 1, 2002. Renumbered Rule 8.128 and amended, eff. Jan. 1, 2007. As amended, eff. Jan. 1, 2008; July 1, 2009.)*

Advisory Committee Comment

Subdivision (b). The Superior Court will make the determination on any application to waive the fees for preparing and transmitting the trial court file.

Research References

Rutter, Cal. Practice Guide: Civil Appeals & Writs Ch. 4-B, B. Components of Record and Considerations in Selecting Them.
Rutter, Cal. Practice Guide: Civil Appeals & Writs Ch. 4-C, C. Record Preparation Procedure.
Rutter, Cal. Practice Guide: Civil Appeals & Writs Ch. 4-C, Outline C.
9 Witkin Cal. Proc. 5th Appeal § 656, Superior Court File in Lieu of Clerk's Transcript.

Rule 8.130. Reporter's transcript

(a) Notice

(1) If in the notice designating the record on appeal under rule 8.121, the appellant elects to use a reporter's transcript, in that notice the appellant must specify the date of each proceeding to be included in the transcript, and may specify portions of designated proceedings that are not to be included.

(2) If the appellant designates less than all the testimony, the notice must state the points to be raised on appeal; the appeal is then limited to those points unless, on motion, the reviewing court permits otherwise.

(3) If the appellant serves and files a notice designating a reporter's transcript, the respondent may, within 10 days after such service, serve and file a notice in superior court designating any additional proceedings the respondent wants included in the transcript.

(4) If the appellant elects to proceed without a reporter's transcript, the respondent cannot require that a reporter's transcript be prepared. But the reviewing court, on its own or the respondent's motion, may order the record augmented under rule 8.155 to prevent a miscarriage of justice. Unless the court orders otherwise, the appellant is responsible for the cost of any reporter's transcript the court may order under this subdivision.

(5) Any notice of designation must be served on each known reporter of the designated proceedings.

(b) Deposit or substitute for cost of transcript

(1) With its notice of designation, a party must deposit with the superior court clerk the approximate cost of transcribing the proceedings it designates, using either:

(A) The reporter's written estimate; or

(B) An amount calculated at $325 per fraction of the day's proceedings that did not exceed three hours, or $650 per day or fraction that exceeded three hours.

(2) If the reporter believes the deposit is inadequate, within 15 days after the clerk mails the notice under (d)(1) the reporter may file with the clerk and mail to the designating party an estimate of the transcript's total cost, showing the additional deposit required. The party must deposit the additional sum within 10 days after the reporter mails the estimate.

(3) Instead of a deposit, the party may substitute the reporter's written waiver of a deposit, a copy of a Transcript Reimbursement Fund application filed under (c)(1), or a certified transcript of the designated proceedings. A reporter may waive the deposit for—and a party may submit a certified transcript of—a part of the designated proceedings, but such a waiver or transcript replaces the deposit for only that part.

(c) Transcript Reimbursement Fund application

(1) With its notice of designation, a party may serve and file a copy of its application to the Court Reporters Board for payment or reimbursement from the Transcript Reimbursement Fund under Business and Professions Code section 8030.2 et seq.

(2) If the Court Reporters Board approves the application for payment or reimbursement, the reporter's time to prepare the transcript under (f)(1) begins when the reporter receives notice of the approval.

(3) If the Court Reporters Board denies the application for payment or reimbursement, the party's time to deposit the reporter's fee or substitute under (b), or to file an agreed or settled statement under rule 8.134 or 8.137, is extended until 30 days after the board mails notice of the denial.

(d) Superior court clerk's duties

(1) If a party designates proceedings to be included in a reporter's transcript and has presented the fee deposit or a substitute under (b)(3), the clerk must promptly mail the reporter notice of the designation and of the deposit or substitute. The notice must show the date it was mailed.

(2) If a party does not present the deposit or a substitute with its notice of designation, the clerk must file the notice and promptly issue a notice of default under rule 8.140.

(3) The clerk must promptly notify the reporter if a check for a deposit is dishonored or an appeal is abandoned or is dismissed before the reporter has filed the transcript.

(e) Contents of transcript

(1) The reporter must transcribe all designated proceedings for which a certified transcript has not been substituted under (b)(3), and must note in the transcript where any proceedings were omitted and the nature of those proceedings. The reporter must also note where any exhibit was marked for identification and where it was admitted or refused, identifying such exhibits by number or letter.

(2) If a party designates a portion of a witness's testimony to be transcribed, the reporter must transcribe the witness's entire testimony unless the parties stipulate otherwise.

(3) The reporter must not copy any document includable in the clerk's transcript under rule 8.122.

(f) Filing the transcript; copies; payment

(1) Within 30 days after notice is received under (c)(2) or mailed under (d)(1), the reporter must prepare and certify an original of the transcript and file it in superior court. The reporter must also file one copy of the original transcript, or more than one copy if multiple appellants equally share the cost of preparing the record (see rule 8.147(a)(2)). Only the

Ct. Rules

reviewing court can extend the time to prepare the reporter's transcript (see rule 8.60).

(2) When the transcript is completed, the reporter must bill each designating party at the statutory rate and send a copy of the bill to the superior court clerk. The clerk must pay the reporter from that party's deposited funds and refund any excess deposit or notify the party of any additional funds needed. In a multiple reporter case, the clerk must pay each reporter who certifies under penalty of perjury that his or her transcript portion is completed.

(3) If the appeal is abandoned or is dismissed before the reporter has filed the transcript, the reporter must inform the superior court clerk of the cost of the portion of the transcript that the reporter has completed. The clerk must pay that amount to the reporter from the appellant's deposited funds and refund any excess deposit.

(4) On request, and unless the superior court orders otherwise, the reporter must provide any party with a copy of the reporter's transcript in computer-readable format. Each computer-readable copy must comply with the format, labeling, content, and numbering requirements of Code of Civil Procedure section 271(b).

(g) Agreed or settled statement when proceedings cannot be transcribed

(1) If any portion of the designated proceedings cannot be transcribed, the superior court clerk must so notify the designating party by mail; the notice must show the date it was mailed. The party may then substitute an agreed or settled statement for that portion of the designated proceedings by complying with either (A) or (B):

(A) Within 10 days after the notice is mailed, the party may file in superior court, under rule 8.134, an agreed statement or a stipulation that the parties are attempting to agree on a statement. If the party files a stipulation, within 30 days thereafter the party must file the agreed statement, move to use a settled statement under rule 8.137, or proceed without such a statement; or

(B) Within 10 days after the notice is mailed, the party may move in superior court to use a settled statement. If the court grants the motion, the statement must be served, filed, and settled as rule 8.137 provides, but the order granting the motion must fix the times for doing so.

(2) If the agreed or settled statement contains all the oral proceedings, it will substitute for the reporter's transcript; if it contains a portion of the proceedings, it will be incorporated into that transcript.

(3) This remedy supplements any other available remedies.
(Formerly Rule 4, adopted, eff. Jan. 1, 2002. As amended, eff. Jan. 1, 2005. Renumbered Rule 8.130 and amended, eff. Jan. 1, 2007. As amended, eff. Jan. 1, 2008; July 1, 2008; Jan. 1, 2010.)

Advisory Committee Comment

Under rule 8.121 an appellant may serve and file a notice *designating* a reporter's transcript and the notice must identify the proceedings to be *included*. The wording recognizes that under rule 8.130(b)(3) the appellant, instead of depositing the reporter's cost to transcribe the proceedings, may substitute certified transcripts of proceedings that have already been transcribed (e.g., daily transcripts) and hence need only be designated for inclusion in the transcript.

Subdivision (a). Subdivision (a)(1) requires that every notice designating a reporter's transcript identify which proceedings are to be included, and that it do so by specifying the date or dates on which those proceedings took place; if the appellant does not want a portion of the proceedings on a given date to be included, the notice should identify that portion by means of a descriptive

reference (e.g., "August 3, 2004, but not the proceedings on defendant's motion to tax costs").

As used in subdivision (a)(1), the phrase "oral proceedings" includes all instructions that the court gives, whether or not submitted in writing, and any instructions that counsel orally propose but the court refuses; all such instructions are included in the reporter's transcript if designated under this rule. All instructions that counsel submit in writing, whether or not given to the jury, are lodged with the superior court clerk and are included in the clerk's transcript if designated under rule 8.122.

Under subdivision (a), portions of depositions read in open court but not reported, or not read but lodged with the superior court clerk, are included in the clerk's transcript if designated under rule 8.122.

Subdivision (b). To eliminate any ambiguity, subdivision (b)(3) recognizes, first, that a party may substitute a waiver or a certified transcript for part of the designated proceedings and, second, that in such event the waiver or transcript replaces the deposit for only that part.

Subdivision (c). Under subdivision (c), an application to the Court Reporters Board for payment or reimbursement of the cost of the reporter's transcript from the Transcript Reimbursement Fund (Bus. & Prof. Code, § 8030. 8) is a permissible substitute for the required deposit of the reporter's fee (subd. (b)(3)) and thereby prevents issuance of a notice of default (subd. (d)(4)).

Business and Professions Code sections 8030.6 and 8030.8 use the term "reimbursement" to mean not only a true reimbursement, i.e., repaying a party who has previously paid the reporter out of the party's own funds (see *id.*, § 8030.8, subd. (d)), but also a direct payment to a reporter who has not been previously paid by the party (see *id.*, § 8030.6, subds. (b) and (d)). Subdivision (f) recognizes this special dual meaning by consistently using the compound phrase "payment or reimbursement."

Subdivision (d). Under subdivision (d)(1), the clerk's notice to the reporter must show the date on which the clerk mailed the notice. This provision is intended to establish the date when the period for preparing the reporter's transcript under subdivision (f)(1) begins to run.

Subdivision (e). Subdivision (e)(3) is not intended to relieve the reporter of the duty to report all oral proceedings, including the reading of instructions or other documents.

Subdivision (f). Subdivision (f)(1) requires the reporter to prepare and file additional copies of the record "if multiple appellants equally share the cost of preparing the record . . ." The reason for the requirement is explained in the comment to rule 8.147(a)(2).

Implementing statutory provisions (e.g., Code Civ. Proc., § 27; Gov. Code, § 69954), subdivision (f)(4) requires the reporter to provide a party, on request, with a copy of the reporter's transcript in computer-readable format. But in recognition of the fact that in some instances the reporter may be unable to provide a copy in that format, the subdivision also authorizes the reporter to apply to the superior court for relief from this requirement.

Research References

Rutter, Cal. Practice Guide: A.D.R. Ch. 6-B, B. Temporary Judges.
Rutter, Cal. Practice Guide: Civil Appeals & Writs Ch. 1-E, E. Preappeal Evaluation and "Housekeeping" Steps.
Rutter, Cal. Practice Guide: Civil Appeals & Writs Ch. 4-B, B. Components of Record and Considerations in Selecting Them.
Rutter, Cal. Practice Guide: Civil Appeals & Writs Ch. 4-C, C. Record Preparation Procedure.
Rutter, Cal. Practice Guide: Civil Appeals & Writs Ch. 4-E, E. Filing and Correction of Record.
Rutter, Cal. Practice Guide: Civil Appeals & Writs Ch. 4-F, F. Extensions of Time and Default.
Rutter, Cal. Practice Guide: Civil Appeals & Writs Ch. 4-G, G. Augmentation of the Record.
Rutter, Cal. Practice Guide: Civil Appeals & Writs Ch. 5-B, B. Types of Motions, Applications and Requests.
Rutter, Cal. Practice Guide: Civil Appeals & Writs Ch. 8-B, B. Presumption of Correctness.

Rutter, Cal. Practice Guide: Civil Appeals & Writs Ch. 15-C, C. Statutory Writs.

Rutter, Cal. Practice Guide: Civil Trials & Evidence Ch. 16-E, E. Statement of Decision.

9 Witkin Cal. Proc. 5th Appeal § 633, (S 633) Use of Copy of Record.

9 Witkin Cal. Proc. 5th Appeal § 635, (S 635) Notice.

9 Witkin Cal. Proc. 5th Appeal § 637, Deposit, or Substitute, for Cost.

9 Witkin Cal. Proc. 5th Appeal § 638, Failure to Make Deposit.

9 Witkin Cal. Proc. 5th Appeal § 639, Exception: Transcript Reimbursement Fund.

9 Witkin Cal. Proc. 5th Appeal § 640, (S 640) Clerk's Notification to Reporter.

9 Witkin Cal. Proc. 5th Appeal § 641, (S 641) Contents of Transcript.

9 Witkin Cal. Proc. 5th Appeal § 642, (S 642) Preparation and Filing.

9 Witkin Cal. Proc. 5th Appeal § 669, (S 669) Designation by Respondent.

9 Witkin Cal. Proc. 5th Appeal § 670, (S 670) Augmentation.

9 Witkin Cal. Proc. 5th Appeal § 673, (S 673) Agreed or Settled Statement.

9 Witkin Cal. Proc. 5th Appeal § 679, (S 679) Record.

9 Witkin Cal. Proc. 5th Appeal § 683, Nature of Remedy.

9 Witkin Cal. Proc. 5th Appeal § 686, Procedure.

9 Witkin Cal. Proc. 5th Appeal § 1012, Transcripts.

2 Witkin Cal. Proc. 5th Courts § 363, (S 363) Process and Notices.

2 Witkin Cal. Proc. 5th Courts § 366, (S 366) Miscellaneous Duties.

2 Witkin Cal. Proc. 5th Courts § 381, Transcription.

2 Witkin Cal. Proc. 5th Courts § 385, Advance Payment in Civil Cases.

10 Witkin, California Summary 10th Parent and Child § 721, Record.

10 Witkin, California Summary 10th Parent and Child § 725, Notice of Intent and Record.

Rule 8.134.　Agreed statement

(a)　Contents of statement

(1) The record on appeal may consist wholly or partly of an agreed statement. The statement must explain the nature of the action, the basis of the reviewing court's jurisdiction, and how the superior court decided the points to be raised on appeal. The statement should recite only those facts needed to decide the appeal and must be signed by the parties.

(2) If the agreed statement replaces a clerk's transcript, the statement must be accompanied by copies of all items required by rule 8.122(b)(1), showing the dates required by rule 8.122(b)(2).

(3) The statement may be accompanied by copies of any document includable in the clerk's transcript under rule 8.122(b)(3) and (4).

(b)　Time to file;　extension of time

(1) An appellant intending to proceed under this rule must file either an agreed statement or a stipulation that the parties are attempting to agree on a statement in superior court with its notice designating the record on appeal under rule 8.121.

(2) If the appellant files the stipulation and the parties can agree on the statement, the appellant must file the statement within 40 days after filing the notice of appeal.

(3) If the appellant files the stipulation and the parties cannot agree on the statement, the appellant must file a new notice designating the record on appeal under rule 8.121 within 50 days after filing the notice of appeal. *(Formerly Rule 6, adopted, eff. Jan. 1, 2002. Renumbered Rule 8.134 and amended, eff. Jan. 1, 2007. As amended, eff. Jan. 1, 2008.)*

Advisory Committee Comment

Subdivision (b). Subdivision (b)(1) requires the appellant to file, with the appellant's notice designating the record under rule 8.121, either an agreed statement or a stipulation that the parties are attempting to agree on a statement. The provision is intended to prevent issuance of a notice of default while the parties are preparing an agreed statement.

Research References

Rutter, Cal. Practice Guide: A.D.R. Ch. 6-B, B. Temporary Judges.

Rutter, Cal. Practice Guide: Civil Appeals & Writs Ch. 4-B, B. Components of Record and Considerations in Selecting Them.

Rutter, Cal. Practice Guide: Civil Appeals & Writs Ch. 4-C, C. Record Preparation Procedure.

9 Witkin Cal. Proc. 5th Appeal § 664, (S 664) Nature of Record.

9 Witkin Cal. Proc. 5th Appeal § 665, (S 665) Requirements.

9 Witkin Cal. Proc. 5th Appeal § 666, (S 666) Statement or Stipulation.

9 Witkin Cal. Proc. 5th Appeal § 679, (S 679) Record.

9 Witkin Cal. Proc. 5th Appeal § 1013, Agreed or Settled Statement.

Rule 8.137.　Settled statement

(a)　Motion to use settled statement

(1) An appellant intending to proceed under this rule must serve and file in superior court with its notice designating the record on appeal under rule 8.121 a motion to use a settled statement instead of a reporter's transcript or both reporter's and clerk's transcripts.

(2) The motion must be supported by a showing that:

(A) A substantial cost saving will result and the statement can be settled without significantly burdening opposing parties or the court;

(B) The designated oral proceedings were not reported or cannot be transcribed; or

(C) The appellant is unable to pay for a reporter's transcript and funds are not available from the Transcript Reimbursement Fund (see rule 8.130(c)). A party proceeding in forma pauperis is deemed unable to pay for a transcript.

(3) If the court denies the motion, the appellant must file a new notice designating the record on appeal under rule 8.121 within 10 days after the superior court clerk mails, or a party serves, the order of denial.

(b)　Time to file;　contents of statement

(1) Within 30 days after the superior court clerk mails, or a party serves, an order granting a motion to use a settled statement, the appellant must serve and file in superior court a condensed narrative of the oral proceedings that the appellant believes necessary for the appeal. Subject to the court's approval in settling the statement, the appellant may present some or all of the evidence by question and answer.

(2) If the condensed narrative describes less than all the testimony, the appellant must state the points to be raised on appeal; the appeal is then limited to those points unless, on motion, the reviewing court permits otherwise.

(3) An appellant intending to use a settled statement instead of both reporter's and clerk's transcripts must accompany the condensed narrative with copies of all items required by rule 8.122(b)(1), showing the dates required by rule 8.122(b)(2).

(4) Within 20 days after the appellant serves the condensed narrative, the respondent may serve and file proposed amendments.

(5) The proposed statement and proposed amendments may be accompanied by copies of any document includable in the clerk's transcript under rule 8.122(b)(3) and (4).

(c)　Settlement, preparation, and certification

(1) The clerk must set a date for a settlement hearing by the trial judge that is no later than 10 days after the respondent files proposed amendments or the time to do so expires, whichever is earlier, and must give the parties at least five days' notice of the hearing date.

(2) At the hearing, the judge must settle the statement and fix the times within which the appellant must prepare, serve, and file it.

Ct. Rules

(3) If the respondent does not object to the prepared statement within five days after it is filed, it will be deemed properly prepared and the clerk must present it to the judge for certification.

(4) The parties' stipulation that the statement as originally served or as prepared is correct is equivalent to the judge's certification. *(Formerly Rule 7, adopted, eff. Jan. 1, 2002. Renumbered Rule 8.137 and amended, eff. Jan. 1, 2007. As amended, eff. Jan. 1, 2008.)*

Advisory Committee Comment

Subdivision (b). This rule requires the appellant to file only one copy of the settled statement, i.e., for the use of the reviewing court. Because all parties participate in preparing the settled statement, it may be assumed that each will retain a copy for its own use.

Research References

Rutter, Cal. Practice Guide: A.D.R. Ch. 6-B, B. Temporary Judges.
Rutter, Cal. Practice Guide: Civil Appeals & Writs Ch. 4-B, B. Components of Record and Considerations in Selecting Them.
Rutter, Cal. Practice Guide: Civil Appeals & Writs Ch. 4-C, C. Record Preparation Procedure.
Rutter, Cal. Practice Guide: Civil Appeals & Writs Ch. 7-A, A. Overview.
Rutter, Cal. Practice Guide: Civil Appeals & Writs Ch. 16-D, D. Designation of the Record.
9 Witkin Cal. Proc. 5th Appeal § 657, (S 657) Nature of Record.
9 Witkin Cal. Proc. 5th Appeal § 658, (S 658) Motion.
9 Witkin Cal. Proc. 5th Appeal § 659, (S 659) Appellant's Proposed Statement.
9 Witkin Cal. Proc. 5th Appeal § 660, (S 660) Respondent's Proposed Amendments.
9 Witkin Cal. Proc. 5th Appeal § 661, (S 661) Settlement and Certification.
9 Witkin Cal. Proc. 5th Appeal § 679, (S 679) Record.
9 Witkin Cal. Proc. 5th Appeal § 691, Relief Denied.
9 Witkin Cal. Proc. 5th Appeal § 1013, Agreed or Settled Statement.

Rule 8.140. Failure to procure the record

(a) Notice of default

If a party fails to timely do an act required to procure the record, the superior court clerk must promptly notify the party by mail that it must do the act specified in the notice within 15 days after the notice is mailed, and that if it fails to comply, the reviewing court may impose one of the following sanctions:

(1) If the defaulting party is the appellant, the court may dismiss the appeal; or

(2) If the defaulting party is the respondent, the court may proceed with the appeal on the record designated by the appellant.

(b) Sanctions

If a party fails to take the action specified in a notice given under (a), the superior court clerk must promptly notify the reviewing court of the default, and the reviewing court may impose one of the following sanctions:

(1) If the defaulting party is the appellant, the reviewing court may dismiss the appeal, but may vacate the dismissal for good cause; or

(2) If the defaulting party is the respondent, the reviewing court may order the appeal to proceed on the record designated by the appellant, but the respondent may obtain relief from default under rule 8.60(d).

(c) Motion for sanctions

If the superior court clerk fails to give a notice required by (a), a party may serve and file a motion for sanctions under (b) in the reviewing court, but the motion must be denied if the defaulting party cures the default within 15 days after the motion is served. *(Formerly Rule 8, adopted, eff. Jan. 1, 2002. Renumbered Rule 8.140 and amended, eff. Jan. 1, 2007. As amended, eff. Jan. 1, 2008.)*

Advisory Committee Comment

Subdivision (a). In subdivision (a), the reference to a failure to "timely" do a required act is intended to include any valid extension of that time.

Research References

Rutter, Cal. Practice Guide: Civil Appeals & Writs Ch. 4-C, C. Record Preparation Procedure.
Rutter, Cal. Practice Guide: Civil Appeals & Writs Ch. 4-F, F. Extensions of Time and Default.
Rutter, Cal. Practice Guide: Civil Appeals & Writs Ch. 5-B, B. Types of Motions, Applications and Requests.
9 Witkin Cal. Proc. 5th Appeal § 557, (S 557) Effect of Nonpayment.
9 Witkin Cal. Proc. 5th Appeal § 638, Failure to Make Deposit.
9 Witkin Cal. Proc. 5th Appeal § 688, (S 688) Sanctions for Default.
9 Witkin Cal. Proc. 5th Appeal § 746, Procedural Defaults.

Rule 8.144. Form of the record

(a) Paper and format

(1) In the clerk's and reporter's transcripts:

(A) The paper must be white or unbleached, recycled, 8½ by 11 inches, and of at least 20–pound weight;

(B) The text must be reproduced as legibly as printed matter;

(C) The contents must be arranged chronologically;

(D) The pages must be consecutively numbered, except as provided in (e);

(E) The margin must be at least 1¼ inches on the bound edge of the page.

(2) In the clerk's transcript only one side of the paper may be used; in the reporter's transcript both sides may be used, but the margins must then be 1¼ inches on each edge.

(3) In the reporter's transcript the lines on each page must be consecutively numbered, and must be double-spaced or one-and-a-half-spaced; double–spaced means three lines to a vertical inch.

(b) Indexes

At the beginning of the first volume of each:

(1) The clerk's transcript must contain alphabetical and chronological indexes listing each document and the volume and page where it first appears;

(2) The reporter's transcript must contain alphabetical and chronological indexes listing the volume and page where each witness's direct, cross, and any other examination, begins; and

(3) The reporter's transcript must contain an index listing the volume and page where any exhibit is marked for identification and where it is admitted or refused. The index must identify each exhibit by number or letter and a brief description of the exhibit.

(c) Binding and cover

(1) Clerk's and reporter's transcripts must be bound on the left margin in volumes of no more than 300 sheets.

(2) Each volume's cover, preferably of recycled stock, must state the title and trial court number of the case, the names of the trial court and each participating trial judge, the names and addresses of appellate counsel for each party, the volume number, and the inclusive page numbers of that volume.

(3) In addition to the information required by (2), the cover of each volume of the reporter's transcript must state the dates of the proceedings reported in that volume.

(d) Daily transcripts

Daily or other certified transcripts may be used for all or part of the reporter's transcript, but the pages must be renumbered consecutively and the required indexes and covers must be added.

(e) Pagination in multiple reporter cases

(1) In a multiple reporter case, each reporter must estimate the number of pages in each segment reported and inform the designated primary reporter of the estimate. The primary reporter must then assign beginning and ending page numbers for each segment.

(2) If a segment exceeds the assigned number of pages, the reporter must number the additional pages with the ending page number, a hyphen, and a new number, starting with 1 and continuing consecutively.

(3) If a segment has fewer than the assigned number of pages, the reporter must add a hyphen to the last page number used, followed by the segment's assigned ending page number, and state in parentheses "(next page number is ___)."

(f) Agreed or settled statements

Agreed or settled statements must conform with this rule insofar as practicable. *(Formerly Rule 9, adopted, eff. Jan. 1, 2002. Renumbered Rule 8.144 and amended, eff. Jan. 1, 2007. As amended, eff. Jan. 1, 2008.)*

Research References

Rutter, Cal. Practice Guide: Civil Appeals & Writs Ch. 4-C, C. Record Preparation Procedure.
9 Witkin Cal. Proc. 5th Appeal § 631, (S 631) Form of Record.
9 Witkin Cal. Proc. 5th Appeal § 652, (S 652) Contents and Form.
9 Witkin Cal. Proc. 5th Appeal § 1011, in General.
9 Witkin Cal. Proc. 5th Appeal § 1012, Transcripts.
2 Witkin Cal. Proc. 5th Courts § 30, (S 30) Use of Recycled Paper.
2 Witkin Cal. Proc. 5th Courts § 381, Transcription.
10 Witkin, California Summary 10th Parent and Child § 713, in General.

Rule 8.147. Record in multiple or later appeals in same case

(a) Multiple appeals

(1) If more than one appeal is taken from the same judgment or a related order, only one record need be prepared, which must be filed within the time allowed for filing the record in the latest appeal.

(2) If there is more than one separately represented appellant, they must equally share the cost of preparing the record, unless otherwise agreed by the appellants or ordered by the superior court. Appellants equally sharing the cost are each entitled to a copy of the record.

(b) Later appeal

In an appeal in which the parties are using either a clerk's transcript under rule 8.122 or a reporter's transcript under rule 8.130:

(1) A party wanting to incorporate by reference all or parts of a record in a prior appeal in the same case must specify those parts in its designation of the record.

(A) The prior appeal must be identified by its case name and number. If only part of a record is being incorporated by reference, that part must be identified by citation to the volume and page numbers of the record where it appears and either the title of the document or documents or the date of the oral proceedings to be incorporated. The parts of any

record incorporated by reference must be identified in a separate section at the end of the designation of the record.

(B) If the transcript incorporates by reference any such record, the cover of the transcript must prominently display the notice "Record in case number: ___ incorporated by reference," identifying the number of the case from which the record is incorporated.

(C) On request of the reviewing court or any party, the designating party must provide a copy of the materials incorporated by reference to the reviewing court or another party or lend them as provided in rule 8.153.

(2) A party wanting any parts of a clerk's transcript or other record of the written documents from a prior appeal in the same case to be copied into the clerk's transcript in a later appeal must specify those parts in its designation of the record as provided in (1). The estimated cost of copying these materials must be included in the clerk's estimate of the cost of preparing the transcript under rule 8.122(c)(1). On request of the trial court clerk, the designating party must provide a copy of or lend the materials to be copied to the clerk. The parts of any record from a prior appeal that are copied into a clerk's transcript under this rule must be placed in a separate section at the end of the transcript and identified in a separate section at the end of the indexes. *(Formerly Rule 10, adopted, eff. Jan. 1, 2002. Renumbered Rule 8.147 and amended, eff. Jan. 1, 2007. As amended, eff. Jan. 1, 2008; Jan. 1, 2010.)*

Advisory Committee Comment

Subdivision (a). Subdivision (a)(1) provides broadly for a single record whenever there are multiple appeals "from the same judgment or a related order." Multiple appeals from the *same judgment* include all cases in which opposing parties, or multiple parties on the same side of the case, appeal from the judgment. Multiple appeals from a judgment *and a related order* include all cases in which one party appeals from the judgment and another party appeals from any appealable order arising from or related to the judgment, i.e., not only orders contemplated by rule 8.108 (e. g., denying a motion for judgment notwithstanding the verdict) but also, for example, posttrial orders granting or denying attorney fees. The purpose is to encourage, when practicable, the preparation of a single record for all appeals taken in the same case. In specifying that "only one *record* need be prepared," of course, the rule does not depart from the basic requirement that an *original* and at least one *copy* of the record be prepared.

The second sentence of subdivision (a)(2) applies when multiple appellants equally share the cost of preparing the record and that cost includes the cost of a copy for each appellant. An appellant wanting the reporter to prepare an additional copy of the record—i.e., additional to the copy required by rule 8.130(f)(1)—must make a timely deposit adequate to cover the cost of that copy.

Research References

Rutter, Cal. Practice Guide: Civil Appeals & Writs Ch. 2-B, B. Appealable Judgments and Orders.
Rutter, Cal. Practice Guide: Civil Appeals & Writs Ch. 4-D, D. Record on Multiple and Later Appeals.
Rutter, Cal. Practice Guide: Civil Appeals & Writs Ch. 4-E, E. Filing and Correction of Record.
Rutter, Cal. Practice Guide: Civil Appeals & Writs Ch. 14-B, B. Recovery of Appellate Costs and Attorney Fees.
9 Witkin Cal. Proc. 5th Appeal § 671, (S 671) Cross-Appeals.
9 Witkin Cal. Proc. 5th Appeal § 672, (S 672) Successive Appeals.
9 Witkin Cal. Proc. 5th Appeal § 1011, in General.

Rule 8.150. Filing the record

(a) Superior court clerk's duties

When the record is complete, the superior court clerk must promptly send the original to the reviewing court and the copy to the appellant.

(b) Reviewing court clerk's duties

On receiving the record, the reviewing court clerk must promptly file the original and mail notice of the filing date to the parties. *(Formerly Rule 11, adopted, eff. Jan. 1, 2002. Renumbered Rule 8.150 and amended, eff. Jan. 1, 2007.)*

Research References

Rutter, Cal. Practice Guide: Civil Appeals & Writs Ch. 4-E, E. Filing and Correction of Record.
9 Witkin Cal. Proc. 5th Appeal § 633, (S 633) Use of Copy of Record.
9 Witkin Cal. Proc. 5th Appeal § 679, (S 679) Record.
9 Witkin Cal. Proc. 5th Appeal § 1014, Filing, Correction, and Augmentation.
2 Witkin Cal. Proc. 5th Courts § 366, (S 366) Miscellaneous Duties.

Rule 8.153.   Lending the record

(a) Request

Within 20 days after the record is filed in the reviewing court, a party that has not purchased its own copy of the record may request another party, in writing, to lend it that party's copy of the record. The other party must then lend its copy of the record when it serves its brief.

(b) Time to return

The borrowing party must return the copy of the record when it serves its brief or the time to file its brief has expired.

(c) Cost

The borrowing party must bear the cost of sending the copy of the record to and from the borrowing party. *(Adopted, eff. Jan. 1, 2007.)*

Research References

Rutter, Cal. Practice Guide: Civil Appeals & Writs Ch. 4-E, E. Filing and Correction of Record.
9 Witkin Cal. Proc. 5th Appeal § 633, (S 633) Use of Copy of Record.
9 Witkin Cal. Proc. 5th Appeal § 672, (S 672) Successive Appeals.

Rule 8.155.   Augmenting and correcting the record

(a) Augmentation

(1) At any time, on motion of a party or its own motion, the reviewing court may order the record augmented to include:

(A) Any document filed or lodged in the case in superior court; or

(B) A certified transcript—or agreed or settled statement—of oral proceedings not designated under rule 8.130. Unless the court orders otherwise, the appellant is responsible for the cost of any additional transcript the court may order under this subdivision.

(2) A party must attach to its motion a copy, if available, of any document or transcript that it wants added to the record. The pages of the attachments must be consecutively numbered, beginning with the number one. If the reviewing court grants the motion it may augment the record with the copy.

(3) If the party cannot attach a copy of the matter to be added, the party must identify it as required under rules 8.122 and 8.130.

(b) Omissions

(1) If a clerk or reporter omits a required or designated portion of the record, a party may serve and file a notice in superior court specifying the omitted portion and requesting that it be prepared, certified, and sent to the reviewing court. The party must serve a copy of the notice on the reviewing court.

(2) The clerk or reporter must comply with a notice under (1) within 10 days after it is filed. If the clerk or reporter fails to comply, the party may serve and file a motion to augment under (a), attaching a copy of the notice.

(c) Corrections

(1) On motion of a party, on stipulation, or on its own motion, the reviewing court may order the correction or certification of any part of the record.

(2) The reviewing court may order the superior court to settle disputes about omissions or errors in the record.

(d) Notice

The reviewing court clerk must send all parties notice of the receipt and filing of any matter under this rule. *(Formerly Rule 12, adopted eff. Jan. 1, 2002. Renumbered Rule 8.155 and amended, eff. Jan. 1, 2007. As amended, eff. Jan. 1, 2008.)*

Advisory Committee Comment

Subdivision (a). Subdivision (a)(1) makes it clear that a party may apply for—and the reviewing court may order—augmentation of the record at any time. Whether the motion is made within a reasonable time and is not for the purpose of delay, however, are among the factors the reviewing court may consider in ruling on such a motion.

Research References

Rutter, Cal. Practice Guide: Civil Appeals & Writs Ch. 4-E, E. Filing and Correction of Record.
Rutter, Cal. Practice Guide: Civil Appeals & Writs Ch. 4-G, G. Augmentation of the Record.
Rutter, Cal. Practice Guide: Civil Appeals & Writs Ch. 4-H, H. Transmittal of Exhibits.
Rutter, Cal. Practice Guide: Civil Appeals & Writs Ch. 5-B, B. Types of Motions, Applications and Requests.
9 Witkin Cal. Proc. 5th Appeal § 681, Correction of Record on Appeal.
9 Witkin Cal. Proc. 5th Appeal § 682, Distinction: Trial Court Record.
9 Witkin Cal. Proc. 5th Appeal § 683, Nature of Remedy.
9 Witkin Cal. Proc. 5th Appeal § 686, Procedure.
9 Witkin Cal. Proc. 5th Appeal § 1014, Filing, Correction, and Augmentation.
2 Witkin Cal. Proc. 5th Jurisdiction § 335, Fictional Consent.
10 Witkin, California Summary 10th Parent and Child § 531, Determining Adequacy of Notice.
10 Witkin, California Summary 10th Parent and Child § 713, in General.
11 Witkin, California Summary 10th Husband and Wife § 123, Certification Procedure for Bifurcated Issues.

Rule 8.163.   Presumption from the record

The reviewing court will presume that the record in an appeal includes all matters material to deciding the issues raised. If the appeal proceeds without a reporter's transcript, this presumption applies only if the claimed error appears on the face of the record. *(Formerly Rule 52, adopted, eff. Jan. 1, 2005. Renumbered Rule 8.163 and amended, eff. Jan. 1, 2007.)*

Advisory Committee Comment

The intent of rule 8.163 is explained in the case law. (See, e.g., *Dumas v. Stark* (1961) 56 Cal.2d 673, 674.)

Research References

Rutter, Cal. Practice Guide: Civil Appeals & Writs Ch. 4-B, B. Components of Record and Considerations in Selecting Them.
Rutter, Cal. Practice Guide: Civil Appeals & Writs Ch. 8-B, B. Presumption of Correctness.
9 Witkin Cal. Proc. 5th Appeal § 9, (S 9) Current Structure.
9 Witkin Cal. Proc. 5th Appeal § 357, (S 357) Nature of Rule and Limitation.
9 Witkin Cal. Proc. 5th Appeal § 358, (S 358) No Requirement that Short Record Bring Up Some Evidence.
9 Witkin Cal. Proc. 5th Appeal § 359, (S 359) Error on Face of Record.

9 Witkin Cal. Proc. 5th Appeal § 423, (S 423) Appeal on Short Record.
9 Witkin Cal. Proc. 5th Appeal § 636, (S 636) Effect of Pretrial Order.
9 Witkin Cal. Proc. 5th Appeal § 1011, in General.
2 Witkin Cal. Proc. 5th Courts § 195, (S 195) Appellate Rules.

Article 3

BRIEFS IN THE COURT OF APPEAL

Rule

Rule 8.200.   Briefs by parties and amici curiae

(a) Parties' briefs

(1) Each appellant must serve and file an appellant's opening brief.

(2) Each respondent must serve and file a respondent's brief.

(3) Each appellant may serve and file a reply brief.

(4) No other brief may be filed except with the permission of the presiding justice, unless it qualifies under (b) or (c)(6).

(5) Instead of filing a brief, or as part of its brief, a party may join in or adopt by reference all or part of a brief in the same or a related appeal.

(b) Supplemental briefs after remand or transfer from Supreme Court

(1) Within 15 days after finality of a Supreme Court decision remanding or order transferring a cause to a Court of Appeal for further proceedings, any party may serve and file a supplemental opening brief in the Court of Appeal. Within 15 days after such a brief is filed, any opposing party may serve and file a supplemental responding brief.

(2) Supplemental briefs must be limited to matters arising after the previous Court of Appeal decision in the cause, unless the presiding justice permits briefing on other matters.

(3) Supplemental briefs may not be filed if the previous decision of the Court of Appeal was a denial of a petition for a writ within its original jurisdiction without issuance of an alternative writ or order to show cause.

(c) Amicus curiae briefs

(1) Within 14 days after the last appellant's reply brief is filed or could have been filed under rule 8.212, whichever is earlier, any person or entity may serve and file an application for permission of the presiding justice to file an amicus curiae brief. For good cause, the presiding justice may allow later filing.

(2) The application must state the applicant's interest and explain how the proposed amicus curiae brief will assist the court in deciding the matter.

(3) The application must also identify:

(A) Any party or any counsel for a party in the pending appeal who:

(i) Authored the proposed amicus brief in whole or in part; or

(ii) Made a monetary contribution intended to fund the preparation or submission of the brief; and

(B) Every person or entity who made a monetary contribution intended to fund the preparation or submission of the brief, other than the amicus curiae, its members, or its counsel in the pending appeal.

(4) The proposed brief must be served and must accompany the application, and may be combined with it.

(5) The covers of the application and proposed brief must identify the party the applicant supports, if any.

(6) If the court grants the application, any party may file an answer within the time the court specifies. The answer must be served on all parties and the amicus curiae.

(7) The Attorney General may file an amicus curiae brief without the presiding justice's permission, unless the brief is submitted on behalf of another state officer or agency. The Attorney General must serve and file the brief within 14 days after the last appellant's reply brief is filed or could have been filed under rule 8.212, whichever is earlier, and must provide the information required by (2) and comply with (5). Any party may serve and file an answer within 14 days after the brief is filed. *(Formerly Rule 13, adopted, eff. Jan. 1, 2002. As amended, eff. Jan. 1, 2003. Renumbered Rule 8.200 and amended, eff. Jan. 1, 2007. As amended, eff. Jan. 1, 2008; Jan. 1, 2009.)*

Advisory Committee Comment

Subdivision (a)(2). A respondent, other than a respondent who has filed a notice of cross-appeal, who files a respondent's brief may be required to pay a filing fee under Government Code sections 68926 if the respondent's brief is the first document filed in the appellate proceeding in the Court of Appeal by that party. See rule 8.25(c).

Subdivision (b). After the Supreme Court remands or transfers a cause to the Court of Appeal for further proceedings (i.e., under rules 8.528(c)–(e) or 10.1000(a)(1)(B)), the parties are permitted to file supplemental briefs. The first 15–day briefing period begins on the day of *finality* (under rule 8.532) of the Supreme Court decision remanding or order transferring the cause to the Court of Appeal. The rule specifies that "any party" may file a supplemental opening brief, and if such a brief is filed, "any opposing party" may file a supplemental responding brief. In this context the phrase "any party" is intended to mean any *or all* parties. Such a decision or order of transfer to the Court of Appeal thus triggers, first, a 15–day period in which any or all parties may file supplemental opening briefs and, second—if any party files such a brief—an additional 15–day period in which any opposing party may file a supplemental responding brief.

Subdivision (c)(1). The time within which a reply brief "could have been filed under rule 8.212" includes any authorized extension of the deadline specified in rule 8.212.

Research References

Rutter, Cal. Practice Guide: Civil Appeals & Writs Ch. 5-B, B. Types of Motions, Applications and Requests.
Rutter, Cal. Practice Guide: Civil Appeals & Writs Ch. 5-C, C. Motion, Application and Request Procedures.
Rutter, Cal. Practice Guide: Civil Appeals & Writs Ch. 9-B, B. Approaches to Briefwriting.
Rutter, Cal. Practice Guide: Civil Appeals & Writs Ch. 9-D, D. Procedural Rules.
Rutter, Cal. Practice Guide: Civil Appeals & Writs Ch. 13-E, E. Decision on the Merits.
Rutter, Cal. Practice Guide: Civil Appeals & Writs Ch. 15-E, E. Procedures on Writ Review.
9 Witkin Cal. Proc. 5th Appeal § 9, (S 9) Current Structure.
9 Witkin Cal. Proc. 5th Appeal § 692, in General.
9 Witkin Cal. Proc. 5th Appeal § 693, Supplementary Briefs.
9 Witkin Cal. Proc. 5th Appeal § 716, (S 716) in General.
9 Witkin Cal. Proc. 5th Appeal § 719, (S 719) in General.
9 Witkin Cal. Proc. 5th Appeal § 722, (S 722) Right to File.
9 Witkin Cal. Proc. 5th Appeal § 726, (S 726) Amicus Briefs in Court of Appeal or Appellate Division.
9 Witkin Cal. Proc. 5th Appeal § 774, Court of Appeal.
9 Witkin Cal. Proc. 5th Appeal § 945, (S 945) in General.
9 Witkin Cal. Proc. 5th Appeal § 1015, (S 1015) Briefs.

Ct. Rules

2 Witkin Cal. Proc. 5th Courts § 195, (S 195) Appellate Rules.

2 Witkin Cal. Proc. 5th Courts § 326, (S 326) Powers of Individual Judges.

10 Witkin, California Summary 10th Parent and Child § 715, (S 715) Briefs.

Rule 8.204.   Contents and form of briefs

(a) Contents

(1) Each brief must:

(A) Begin with a table of contents and a table of authorities separately listing cases, constitutions, statutes, court rules, and other authorities cited;

(B) State each point under a separate heading or subheading summarizing the point, and support each point by argument and, if possible, by citation of authority; and

(C) Support any reference to a matter in the record by a citation to the volume and page number of the record where the matter appears. If any part of the record is submitted in an electronic format, citations to that part must identify, with the same specificity required for the printed record, the place in the record where the matter appears.

(2) An appellant's opening brief must:

(A) State the nature of the action, the relief sought in the trial court, and the judgment or order appealed from;

(B) State that the judgment appealed from is final, or explain why the order appealed from is appealable; and

(C) Provide a summary of the significant facts limited to matters in the record.

(b) Form

(1) A brief may be reproduced by any process that produces a clear, black image of letter quality. The paper must be white or unbleached, recycled, 8½ by 11 inches, and of at least 20–pound weight.

(2) Any conventional typeface may be used. The typeface may be either proportionally spaced or monospaced.

(3) The type style must be roman; but for emphasis, italics or boldface may be used or the text may be underscored. Case names must be italicized or underscored. Headings may be in uppercase letters.

(4) Except as provided in (11), the type size, including footnotes, must not be smaller than 13–point, and both sides of the paper may be used.

(5) The lines of text must be unnumbered and at least one-and-a-half-spaced. Headings and footnotes may be single-spaced. Quotations may be block-indented and single-spaced. Single–spaced means six lines to a vertical inch.

(6) The margins must be at least 1½ inches on the left and right and 1 inch on the top and bottom.

(7) The pages must be consecutively numbered. The tables and the body of the brief may have different numbering systems.

(8) The brief must be bound on the left margin. If the brief is stapled, the bound edge and staples must be covered with tape.

(9) The brief need not be signed.

(10) The cover, preferably of recycled stock, must be in the color prescribed by rule 8.40(b) and, in addition to providing the cover information required by rule 8.40(c), must state:

(A) The title of the brief;

(B) The title, trial court number, and Court of Appeal number of the case;

(C) The names of the trial court and each participating trial judge;

(D) The name, address, telephone number, and California State Bar number of each attorney filing or joining in the brief, but the cover need not state the bar number of any supervisor of the attorney responsible for the brief; and

(E)(D) The name of the party that each attorney on the brief represents.

(11) If the brief is produced on a typewriter:

(A) A typewritten original and carbon copies may be filed only with the presiding justice's permission, which will ordinarily be given only to unrepresented parties proceeding in forma pauperis. All other typewritten briefs must be filed as photocopies.

(B) Both sides of the paper may be used if a photocopy is filed; only one side may be used if a typewritten original and carbon copies are filed.

(C) The type size, including footnotes, must not be smaller than standard pica, 10 characters per inch. Unrepresented incarcerated litigants may use elite type, 12 characters per inch, if they lack access to a typewriter with larger characters.

(c) Length

(1) A brief produced on a computer must not exceed 14,000 words, including footnotes. Such a brief must include a certificate by appellate counsel or an unrepresented party stating the number of words in the brief. The person certifying may rely on the word count of the computer program used to prepare the brief.

(2) A brief produced on a typewriter must not exceed 50 pages.

(3) The tables required under (a)(1), the cover information required under (b)(10), the Certificate of Interested Entities or Persons required under rule 8.208, a certificate under (1), any signature block, and any attachment under (d) are excluded from the limits stated in (1) or (2).

(4) A combined brief in an appeal governed by rule 8.216 must not exceed double the limits stated in (1) or (2).

(5) On application, the presiding justice may permit a longer brief for good cause.

(d) Attachments to briefs

A party filing a brief may attach copies of exhibits or other materials in the appellate record or copies of relevant local, state, or federal regulations or rules, out-of-state statutes, or other similar citable materials that are not readily accessible. These attachments must not exceed a combined total of 10 pages, but on application the presiding justice may permit additional pages of attachments for good cause. A copy of an opinion required to be attached to the brief under rule 8.1115(c) does not count toward this 10–page limit.

(e) Noncomplying briefs

If a brief does not comply with this rule:

(1) The reviewing court clerk may decline to file it, but must mark it "received but not filed" and return it to the party; or

(2) If the brief is filed, the reviewing court may, on its own or a party's motion, with or without notice:

(A) Order the brief returned for corrections and refiling within a specified time;

(B) Strike the brief with leave to file a new brief within a specified time; or

(C) Disregard the noncompliance.

(Formerly Rule 14, adopted, eff. Jan. 1, 2002. As amended, eff. Jan. 1, 2004; July 1, 2004; Jan. 1, 2006. Renumbered Rule 8.204 and amended, eff. Jan. 1, 2007. As amended, eff. Jan. 1, 2011; Jan. 1, 2013.)

Advisory Committee Comment

Subdivision (b). The first sentence of subdivision (b)(1) confirms that any method of reproduction is acceptable provided it results in a clear black image of letter quality. The provision is derived from subdivision (a)(1) of rule 32 of the Federal Rules of Appellate Procedure (28 U.S.C.) (FRAP 32).

Paragraphs (2), (3), and (4) of subdivision (b) state requirements of *typeface, type style,* and *type size* (see also subd. (b)(11)(C)). The first two terms are defined in *The Chicago Manual of Style* (15th ed., 2003) p. 839. Note that computer programs often refer to typeface as "font."

Subdivision (b)(2) allows the use of any conventional typeface—e.g., Times New Roman, Courier, Arial, Helvetica, etc.—and permits the typeface to be either proportionally spaced or monospaced.

Subdivision (b)(3) requires the type style to be roman, but permits the use of italics, boldface, or underscoring for emphasis; it also requires case names to be italicized or underscored. These provisions are derived from FRAP 32(a)(6).

Subdivision (b)(5) allows headings to be single-spaced; it is derived from FRAP 32(a)(4). The provision also permits quotations of any length to be block-indented and single-spaced at the discretion of the brief writer.

See also rule 1.200 concerning the format of citations. Brief writers are encouraged to follow the citation form of the *California Style Manual* (4th ed., 2000).

Subdivision (c). Subdivision (c) governs the maximum permissible length of a brief. It is derived from the federal procedure of measuring the length of a brief produced on a computer by the number of words in the brief. (FRAP 32(a)(7).) Subdivision (c)(1), like FRAP 32(a)(7)(B)(i), imposes a limit of 14,000 words if the brief is produced on a computer. Subdivision (c)(1) implements this provision by requiring the writer of a brief produced on a computer to include a certificate stating the number of words in the brief, but allows the writer to rely on the word count of the computer program used to prepare the brief. This requirement, too, is adapted from the federal rule. (FRAP 32(a)(7)(C).) For purposes of this rule, a "brief produced on a computer" includes a commercially printed brief.

Subdivision (c)(3) specifies certain items that are not counted toward the maximum brief length. Signature blocks, as referenced in this provision, include not only the signatures, but also the printed names, titles, and affiliations of any attorneys filing or joining in the brief, which may accompany the signature.

Subdivision (c)(5) clarifies that a party seeking permission to exceed the page or word limits stated in subdivision (c)(1) and (2) must proceed by application under rule 8.50 rather than by motion under rule 8.54, and must show good cause.

Subdivision (d). Subdivision (d) permits a party filing a brief to attach copies of exhibits or other materials, provided they are part of the record on appeal and do not exceed a total of 10 pages. If the brief writer attaches, under rule 8.1115(c), a copy of an unpublished opinion or an opinion available only in computerized form, that opinion does not count toward the 10–page limit stated in rule 8.204(d).

Subdivision (e). Subdivision (e) states the consequences of submitting briefs that do not comply with this rule: (e)(1) recognizes the power of the reviewing court clerk to decline to file such a brief, and (e)(2) recognizes steps the reviewing court may take to obtain a brief that does comply with the rule. Subdivision (e)(2) does not purport to limit the inherent power of the reviewing court to fashion other sanctions for such noncompliance.

Research References

Rutter, Cal. Practice Guide: Civil Appeals & Writs Ch. 4-H, H. Transmittal of Exhibits.

Rutter, Cal. Practice Guide: Civil Appeals & Writs Ch. 5-B, B. Types of Motions, Applications and Requests.

Rutter, Cal. Practice Guide: Civil Appeals & Writs Ch. 5-C, C. Motion, Application and Request Procedures.

Rutter, Cal. Practice Guide: Civil Appeals & Writs Ch. 9-B, B. Approaches to Briefwriting.

Rutter, Cal. Practice Guide: Civil Appeals & Writs Ch. 9-C, C. Format of Briefs.

Rutter, Cal. Practice Guide: Civil Appeals & Writs Ch. 9-D, D. Procedural Rules.

Rutter, Cal. Practice Guide: Civil Appeals & Writs Ch. 12-E, E. Procedure.

Rutter, Cal. Practice Guide: Civil Appeals & Writs Ch. 13-B, B. Petition for Review Procedures.

Rutter, Cal. Practice Guide: Civil Appeals & Writs Ch. 13-C, C. Briefs on the Merits After Grant of Review.

Rutter, Cal. Practice Guide: Civil Appeals & Writs Ch. 15-E, E. Procedures on Writ Review.

Rutter, Cal. Practice Guide: Civil Appeals & Writs Form 5:E, Application for Permission to File Brief Exceeding Authorized Length Limit (Appellant).

Rutter, Cal. Practice Guide: Civil Appeals & Writs Form 5:F, Motion to Strike Defective Brief.

Rutter, Cal. Practice Guide: Civil Appeals & Writs Form 7:D, Petition for Writ of Supersedeas or Other Stay Order.

Rutter, Cal. Practice Guide: Civil Appeals & Writs Form 15:B.1, Sample Reply to Opposition to Writ Petition.

Rutter, Cal. Practice Guide: Civil Appeals & Writs Form 15:B.2, Sample Return to Writ Petition.

9 Witkin Cal. Proc. 5th Appeal § 163, (S 163) Notice of Ruling.

9 Witkin Cal. Proc. 5th Appeal § 334, (S 334) General Rule: Nonreviewable.

9 Witkin Cal. Proc. 5th Appeal § 694, Separate Points and Headings.

9 Witkin Cal. Proc. 5th Appeal § 695, References to Record.

9 Witkin Cal. Proc. 5th Appeal § 696, Index and Tables.

9 Witkin Cal. Proc. 5th Appeal § 697, Format.

9 Witkin Cal. Proc. 5th Appeal § 698, Filing and Service of Original and Copies.

9 Witkin Cal. Proc. 5th Appeal § 699, (S 699) in General.

9 Witkin Cal. Proc. 5th Appeal § 700, (S 700) Attachments.

9 Witkin Cal. Proc. 5th Appeal § 709, in General.

9 Witkin Cal. Proc. 5th Appeal § 710, Dismissal for Failure to Correct.

9 Witkin Cal. Proc. 5th Appeal § 711, Defective Brief as Abandonment of Appeal.

9 Witkin Cal. Proc. 5th Appeal § 716, (S 716) in General.

9 Witkin Cal. Proc. 5th Appeal § 929, Form and Length Limitations.

9 Witkin Cal. Proc. 5th Appeal § 937, Form and Content.

9 Witkin Cal. Proc. 5th Appeal § 1015, (S 1015) Briefs.

9 Witkin Cal. Proc. 5th Appeal § 1026, Transfer by Court of Appeal on Party's Petition.

9 Witkin Cal. Proc. 5th Appeal § 1031, Briefs and Oral Argument.

2 Witkin Cal. Proc. 5th Courts § 30, (S 30) Use of Recycled Paper.

2 Witkin Cal. Proc. 5th Courts § 84, Notice of Formal Proceeding and Answer.

2 Witkin Cal. Proc. 5th Courts § 326, (S 326) Powers of Individual Judges.

8 Witkin Cal. Proc. 5th Extraordinary Writs § 163, (S 163) Governing Statutes and Rules.

8 Witkin Cal. Proc. 5th Extraordinary Writs § 169, in General.

8 Witkin Cal. Proc. 5th Extraordinary Writs § 180, Supporting Memorandum.

10 Witkin, California Summary 10th Parent and Child § 715, (S 715) Briefs.

Rule 8.208. Certificate of Interested Entities or Persons

(a) Purpose and intent

The California Code of Judicial Ethics states the circumstances under which an appellate justice must disqualify himself or herself from a proceeding. The purpose of this rule is to provide justices of the Courts of Appeal with additional information to help them determine whether to disqualify themselves from a proceeding.

(b) Application

This rule applies in appeals in civil cases other than family, juvenile, guardianship, and conservatorship cases.

(c) Definitions

For purposes of this rule:

(1) "Certificate" means a Certificate of Interested Entities or Persons signed by appellate counsel or an unrepresented party.

Ct. Rules

(2) "Entity" means a corporation, a partnership, a firm, or any other association, but does not include a governmental entity or its agencies or a natural person.

(d) Serving and filing a certificate

(1) Except as otherwise provided in this rule, if a party files a motion, an application, or an opposition to such motion or application in the Court of Appeal before filing its principal brief, the party must serve and file its certificate at the time it files the first such motion, application, or opposition and must include a copy of this certificate in the party's principal brief. If no motion, application, or opposition to such motion or application is filed before the parties file their principal briefs, each party must include its certificate in its principal brief. The certificate must appear after the cover and before the tables. If the identity of any party has not been publicly disclosed in the proceedings, the party may serve and file an application for permission to file its certificate under seal separately from its principal brief, motion, application, or opposition.

(2) If the identity of any party or any entity or person subject to disclosure under this rule has not been publicly disclosed in the proceedings and a party wants to keep that identity confidential, the party may serve and file an application for permission to file its certificate under seal separately from its principal brief, motion, application, or opposition. If the application is granted, the party must file the certificate under seal and without service within 10 days of the court's order granting the application.

(3) If a party fails to file a certificate as required under (1), the clerk must notify the party by mail that the party must file the certificate within 15 days after the clerk's notice is mailed and that if the party fails to comply, the court may impose one of the following sanctions:

(A) If the party is the appellant, the court may strike the document or dismiss the appeal; or

(B) If the party is the respondent, the court may strike the document or decide the appeal on the record, the opening brief, and any oral argument by the appellant.

(4) If the party fails to file the certificate as specified in the notice under (2), the court may impose the sanctions specified in the notice.

(e) Contents of certificate

(1) If an entity is a party, that party's certificate must list any other entity or person that the party knows has an ownership interest of 10 percent or more in the party.

(2) If a party knows of any person or entity, other than the parties themselves, that has a financial or other interest in the outcome of the proceeding that the party reasonably believes the justices should consider in determining whether to disqualify themselves under canon 3E of the Code of Judicial Ethics, the party's certificate must list that entity or person and identify the nature of the interest of the person or entity. For purposes of this subdivision:

(A) A mutual or common investment fund's ownership of securities or bonds issued by an entity does not constitute a financial interest in that entity.

(B) An interest in the outcome of the proceeding does not arise solely because the entity or person is in the same industry, field of business, or regulatory category as a party and the case might establish a precedent that would affect that industry, field of business, or regulatory category.

(C) A party's insurer does not have a financial interest in the outcome of the proceeding solely on the basis of its status as insurer for that party.

(3) If the party knows of no entity or person that must be listed under (1) or (2), the party must so state in the certificate.

(f) Supplemental information

A party that learns of changed or additional information that must be disclosed under (e) must promptly serve and file a supplemental certificate in the reviewing court. *(Formerly Rule 14.5, adopted, eff. July 1, 2006. Renumbered Rule 8.208 and amended, eff. Jan. 1, 2007. As amended, eff. Jan. 1, 2008; Jan. 1, 2009.)*

Advisory Committee Comment

The Judicial Council has adopted an optional form, *Certificate of Interested Entities or Persons* (form APP-008), that can be used to file the certificate required by this rule.

Subdivision (e). This subdivision requires a party to list on its certificate entities or persons that the party *knows* have specified interests. This subdivision does not impose a duty on a party to gather information not already known by that party.

Research References

Rutter, Cal. Practice Guide: Civil Appeals & Writs Ch. 5-C, C. Motion, Application and Request Procedures.
Rutter, Cal. Practice Guide: Civil Appeals & Writs Ch. 9-C, C. Format of Briefs.
Rutter, Cal. Practice Guide: Civil Appeals & Writs Ch. 13-B, B. Petition for Review Procedures.
Rutter, Cal. Practice Guide: Civil Appeals & Writs Ch. 15-E, E. Procedures on Writ Review.
Rutter, Cal. Practice Guide: Civil Appeals & Writs Form 15:B.2, Sample Return to Writ Petition.
2 Witkin Cal. Proc. 5th Courts § 98, Procedure.

Rule 8.212. Service and filing of briefs

(a) Time to file

(1) An appellant must serve and file its opening brief within:

(A) 40 days after the record—or the reporter's transcript, after a rule 8.124 election—is filed in the reviewing court; or

(B) 70 days after the filing of a rule 8.124 election, if the appeal proceeds without a reporter's transcript.

(2) A respondent must serve and file its brief within 30 days after the appellant files its opening brief.

(3) An appellant must serve and file its reply brief, if any, within 20 days after the respondent files its brief.

(b) Extensions of time

(1) Except as otherwise provided by statute, the parties may extend each period under (a) by up to 60 days by filing one or more stipulations in the reviewing court before the brief is due. Stipulations must be signed by and served on all parties. The original signature of at least one party must appear on the stipulation filed in the reviewing court; the signatures of the other parties may be in the form of copies of the signed signature page of the stipulation.

(2) A stipulation under (1) is effective on filing. The reviewing court may not shorten a stipulated extension.

(3) Before the brief is due, a party may apply to the presiding justice for an extension of each period under (a), or under rule 8.200(c)(6) or (7), on a showing that there is good cause and that:

(A) The applicant was unable to obtain—or it would have been futile to seek—the extension by stipulation; or

(B) The parties have stipulated to the maximum extension permitted under (1) and the applicant seeks a further extension.

(4) A party need not apply for an extension or relief from default if it can file its brief within the time prescribed by rule

8.220. The clerk must file a brief submitted within that time if it otherwise complies with these rules.

(c) Service

(1) One copy of each brief must be served on the superior court clerk for delivery to the trial judge.

(2) One electronic copy ~~or four paper copies~~ of each brief must be served on the Supreme Court ~~as provided in either (A) or (B).~~

~~(A) One copy of each brief may be served on the Supreme Court electronically~~ by sending the copy to the Supreme Court's electronic service address. For purposes of this requirement, the term "brief" does not include a petition for rehearing or an answer thereto.

~~(i)~~(A) The copy must be a single computer file in text-searchable Portable Document Format (PDF), and it must exactly duplicate the appearance of the paper copy, including the order and pagination of all of the brief's components. By electronically serving the copy, the filer certifies that the copy complies with these requirements and that all reasonable steps have been taken to ensure that the copy does not contain computer code, including viruses, that might be harmful to the court's electronic filing system and to other users of that system.

~~(ii)~~(B) If the Court of Appeal has ordered the brief sealed, the party serving the brief must include as the first page in the PDF document a cover sheet that contains the information required by rule 8.204(b)(10) and labels the contents as "CONDITIONALLY UNDER SEAL." The Court of Appeal clerk must promptly notify the Supreme Court of any court order unsealing the brief. In the absence of such notice, the Supreme Court clerk must keep all copies of the brief under seal.

~~(B)~~(C) If it would cause undue hardship for the party filing the brief to serve an electronic copy of the brief on the Supreme Court, the party may instead ~~of serving an electronic copy,~~ serve four paper copies of ~~each~~ the brief ~~may be served~~ on the Supreme Court. If the Court of Appeal has ordered the brief sealed, the party serving the brief must place all four copies of the brief in a sealed envelope and attach a cover sheet that contains the information required by rule 8.204(b)(10) and labels the contents as "CONDITIONALLY UNDER SEAL." The Court of Appeal clerk must promptly notify the Supreme Court of any court order unsealing the brief. In the absence of such notice, the Supreme Court clerk must keep all copies of the brief under seal.

(3) One copy of each brief must be served on a public officer or agency when required by rule 8.29. *(Formerly Rule 15, adopted, eff. Jan. 1, 2002. As amended, eff. Jan. 1, 2003; Jan. 1, 2004; Jan. 1, 2005; July 1, 2005. Renumbered Rule 8.212 and amended, eff. Jan. 1, 2007. As amended, eff. Jan. 1, 2008; Jan. 1, 2010; Jan. 1, 2011; Jan. 1, 2013.)*

Advisory Committee Comment

Subdivision (a). Note that the sequence and timing of briefing in appeals in which a party is both appellant and respondent (cross-appeals) are governed by rule 8.216. Typically, a cross-appellant's combined respondent's and opening brief must be filed within the time specified in (a)(2) for the respondent's brief.

Subdivision (b). Extensions of briefing time are limited by statute in some cases. For example, under Public Resources Code section 21167.6(h) in cases under section 21167, extensions are limited to one 30–day extension for the opening brief and one 30–day extension for "preparation of responding brief."

Subdivision (b)(2) clarifies that a party seeking an extension of time from the presiding justice must proceed by application under rule 8.50 rather than by motion under rule 8.54.

Subdivision (c). In subdivision (c)(2) the word "brief" means only (1) an appellant's opening brief, (2) a respondent's brief, (3) an appellant's reply brief, (4) an amicus curiae brief, or (5) an answer thereto. It follows that no other documents or papers filed in the Court of Appeal, whatever their nature, should be served on the Supreme Court. Further, only briefs filed in the Court of Appeal "in a civil appeal" must be served on the Supreme Court. It follows that no briefs filed in the Court of Appeal in criminal appeals or in original proceedings should be served on the Supreme Court.

"Electronic service address" is defined in rule 8.70. The Supreme Court's electronic filing address and additional information about sending electronic copies of briefs to the Supreme Court can be found on the California Courts website at *www. courts.ca.gov/appellatebriefs.htm*.

Examples of "undue hardship" under (2)(C) include but are not limited to when a party does not have access to a computer or the software necessary to prepare an electronic copy of a brief or does not have e-mail access to electronically serve a brief on the Supreme Court.

Research References

Rutter, Cal. Practice Guide: Civil Appeals & Writs Ch. 4-C, C. Record Preparation Procedure.

Rutter, Cal. Practice Guide: Civil Appeals & Writs Ch. 5-B, B. Types of Motions, Applications and Requests.

Rutter, Cal. Practice Guide: Civil Appeals & Writs Ch. 9-D, D. Procedural Rules.

9 Witkin Cal. Proc. 5th Appeal § 698, Filing and Service of Original and Copies.

9 Witkin Cal. Proc. 5th Appeal § 712, When Filing Occurs.

9 Witkin Cal. Proc. 5th Appeal § 713, Extension of Time by Stipulation.

9 Witkin Cal. Proc. 5th Appeal § 714, (S 714) in General.

9 Witkin Cal. Proc. 5th Appeal § 717, (S 717) Service and Filing.

9 Witkin Cal. Proc. 5th Appeal § 719, (S 719) in General.

9 Witkin Cal. Proc. 5th Appeal § 722, (S 722) Right to File.

9 Witkin Cal. Proc. 5th Appeal § 724, Briefs of Party Who is Both Appellant and Respondent.

9 Witkin Cal. Proc. 5th Appeal § 768, (S 768) Prehearing Conference in Court of Appeal.

9 Witkin Cal. Proc. 5th Appeal § 1015, (S 1015) Briefs.

2 Witkin Cal. Proc. 5th Courts § 44, Sealed Records in Reviewing Courts.

2 Witkin Cal. Proc. 5th Courts § 326, (S 326) Powers of Individual Judges.

Rule 8.216. Appeals in which a party is both appellant and respondent

(a) Briefing sequence and time to file briefs

In an appeal in which any party is both an appellant and a respondent:

(1) The parties must jointly—or separately if unable to agree—submit a proposed briefing sequence to the reviewing court within 20 days after the second notice of appeal is filed.

(2) After receiving the proposal, the reviewing court must order a briefing sequence and prescribe briefing periods consistent with rule 8.212(a).

(3) Extensions of time are governed by rule 8.212(b).

(b) Contents of briefs

(1) A party that is both an appellant and a respondent must combine its respondent's brief with its appellant's opening brief or its reply brief, if any, whichever is appropriate under the briefing sequence that the reviewing court orders.

(2) A combined brief must address the points raised in each appeal separately but may include a single summary of the significant facts.

(3) A party must confine a reply brief, or the reply portion of a combined brief, to points raised in its appeal. *(Formerly Rule 16, adopted, eff. Jan. 1, 2002. Renumbered Rule 8.216 and amended, eff. Jan. 1, 2007. As amended, eff. Jan. 1, 2009.)*

Ct. Rules

Advisory Committee Comment

Rule 8.216 applies, first, to all cases in which opposing parties both appeal from the judgment. In addition, it applies to all cases in which one party appeals from the judgment and another party appeals from any appealable order arising from or related to the judgment, i.e., not only orders contemplated by rule 8.108 (denying a motion for judgment notwithstanding the verdict) but also, for example, posttrial orders granting or denying attorney fees. The purpose of the rule is to provide, in all such appeals, a single unified procedure for resolving uncertainties as to the order in which the parties must file their briefs.

As used in this rule, "appellant" includes cross-appellant and "respondent" includes cross-respondent. (Compare rule 8.100(e).)

Subdivision (a). Subdivision (a) implements the above-stated purpose by providing a procedure for determining both the briefing *sequence*—i.e., the order in which the parties must file their briefs—and the briefing *periods*—i.e., the periods of time (e.g., 30 days or 70 days, etc.) within which the briefs must be filed. Subdivision (a)(1) places the burden on the parties in the first instance to propose a briefing sequence, jointly if possible but separately if not. The purpose of this requirement is to assist the reviewing court by giving it the benefit of the parties' views on what is the most efficient briefing sequence in the circumstances of the case. Subdivision (a)(2) then prescribes the role of the reviewing court: after considering the parties' proposal, the court will decide on the briefing sequence, prescribe the briefing periods, and notify the parties of both. The reviewing court, of course, may thereafter modify its order just as it may do in a single-appeal case. Extensions of time are governed by rule 8.212(b).

Subdivision (b). The purpose of subdivision (b)(3) is to ensure that in its reply brief a party addresses only issues germane to its own appeal. For example, a cross-appellant may not use its *cross-appellant's* reply brief to answer points raised in the *appellant's* reply brief.

Research References

Rutter, Cal. Practice Guide: Civil Appeals & Writs Ch. 9-D, D. Procedural Rules.

9 Witkin Cal. Proc. 5th Appeal § 719, (S 719) in General.

9 Witkin Cal. Proc. 5th Appeal § 724, Briefs of Party Who is Both Appellant and Respondent.

Rule 8.220. Failure to file a brief

(a) Notice to file

If a party fails to timely file an appellant's opening brief or a respondent's brief, the reviewing court clerk must promptly notify the party by mail that the brief must be filed within 15 days after the notice is mailed and that if the party fails to comply, the court may impose one of the following sanctions:

(1) If the brief is an appellant's opening brief, the court may dismiss the appeal;

(2) If the brief is a respondent's brief, the court may decide the appeal on the record, the opening brief, and any oral argument by the appellant.

(b) Combined brief

A party that is both an appellant and a respondent under rule 8.216 may file its combined respondent's brief and appellant's reply brief within the period specified in the notice under (a).

(c) Sanction

If a party fails to file the brief as specified in a notice under (a), the court may impose the sanction specified in the notice.

(d) Extension of time

Within the period specified in the notice under (a), a party may apply to the presiding justice for an extension of that period for good cause. If the extension is granted and the brief is not filed within the extended period, the court may impose the sanction under (c) without further notice. *(Formerly Rule 17,*

adopted, eff. Jan. 1, 2002. Renumbered Rule 8.220 and amended, eff. Jan. 1, 2007. As amended, eff. Jan. 1, 2008.)

Advisory Committee Comment

Subdivision (a). Subdivision (a) applies to all appellant's opening briefs and respondent's briefs, but does not apply to reply briefs.

A brief is "timely" under subdivision (a) if it is filed within the normal rule time prescribed for that brief or any extension of that time.

A party that fails to timely file a required brief need not make a formal motion to permit a late filing (e.g., under rule 8.60(d)); it is sufficient to file the brief within the 15–day grace period specified in the notice under subdivision (a).

Subdivision (d). Subdivision (d) clarifies that a party seeking an extension of time from the presiding justice must proceed by application under rule 8.50 rather than by motion under rule 8.54. In conformity with current practice, the subdivision also clarifies that if a brief is not filed within an extension granted by the court, the court may impose sanctions without further notice.

Research References

Rutter, Cal. Practice Guide: Civil Appeals & Writs Ch. 5-B, B. Types of Motions, Applications and Requests.

Rutter, Cal. Practice Guide: Civil Appeals & Writs Ch. 9-D, D. Procedural Rules.

Rutter, Cal. Practice Guide: Civil Appeals & Writs Ch. 10-A, A. Overview.

Rutter, Cal. Practice Guide: Civil Appeals & Writs Ch. 10-B, B. Oral Argument Procedure.

9 Witkin Cal. Proc. 5th Appeal § 680, (S 680) Original Exhibits.

9 Witkin Cal. Proc. 5th Appeal § 714, (S 714) in General.

9 Witkin Cal. Proc. 5th Appeal § 718, (S 718) Late Filing: Dismissal and Relief from Default.

9 Witkin Cal. Proc. 5th Appeal § 719, (S 719) in General.

9 Witkin Cal. Proc. 5th Appeal § 720, Appellant's Statement of Facts Accepted.

9 Witkin Cal. Proc. 5th Appeal § 746, Procedural Defaults.

2 Witkin Cal. Proc. 5th Courts § 326, (S 326) Powers of Individual Judges.

10 Witkin, California Summary 10th Parent and Child § 715, (S 715) Briefs.

Rule 8.224. Transmitting exhibits

(a) Notice of designation

(1) Within 10 days after the last respondent's brief is filed or could be filed under rule 8.220, a party wanting the reviewing court to consider any original exhibits that were admitted in evidence, refused, or lodged but that were not copied in the clerk's transcript under rule 8.122 or the appendix under rule 8.124 must serve and file a notice in superior court designating such exhibits.

(2) Within 10 days after a notice under (1) is served, any other party wanting the reviewing court to consider additional exhibits must serve and file a notice in superior court designating such exhibits.

(3) A party filing a notice under (1) or (2) must serve a copy on the reviewing court.

(b) Transmittal

Unless the reviewing court orders otherwise, within 20 days after the first notice under (a) is filed:

(1) The superior court clerk must put any designated exhibits in the clerk's possession into numerical or alphabetical order and send them to the reviewing court with two copies of a list of the exhibits sent. If the reviewing court clerk finds the list correct, the clerk must sign and return one copy to the superior court clerk.

(2) Any party in possession of designated exhibits returned by the superior court must put them into numerical or alphabetical

order and send them to the reviewing court with two copies of a list of the exhibits sent. If the reviewing court clerk finds the list correct, the clerk must sign and return one copy to the party.

(c) Application for later transmittal

After the periods specified in (a) have expired, a party may apply to the reviewing court for permission to send an exhibit to that court.

(d) Request and return by reviewing court

At any time the reviewing court may direct the superior court or a party to send it an exhibit. On request, the reviewing court may return an exhibit to the superior court or to the party that sent it. When the remittitur issues, the reviewing court must return all exhibits to the superior court or to the party that sent them. *(Formerly Rule 18, adopted, eff. Jan. 1, 2002. Renumbered Rule 8.224 and amended, eff. Jan. 1, 2007. As amended, eff. Jan. 1, 2008.)*

Advisory Committee Comment

Subdivision (b). Subdivision (b)(2) provides a procedure by which parties send designated exhibits directly to the reviewing court in cases in which the superior court has returned the exhibits to the parties under Code of Civil Procedure section 1952 or other provision. (See also rule 8.122(a)(3).)

Subdivision (c). Subdivision (c) addresses the case in which a party's need to designate a certain exhibit does not arise until after the period specified in subdivision (a) has expired—for example, when the appellant makes a point in its reply brief that the respondent reasonably believes justifies the reviewing court's consideration of an exhibit it had not previously designated. In that event, the subdivision authorizes the party to apply to the reviewing court for permission to send the exhibit on a showing of good cause.

Research References

Rutter, Cal. Practice Guide: Civil Appeals & Writs Ch. 4-B, B. Components of Record and Considerations in Selecting Them.
Rutter, Cal. Practice Guide: Civil Appeals & Writs Ch. 4-H, H. Transmittal of Exhibits.
Rutter, Cal. Practice Guide: Civil Appeals & Writs Ch. 4-I, I. Special Rules for Record on Certain Appeals.
9 Witkin Cal. Proc. 5th Appeal § 9, (S 9) Current Structure.
9 Witkin Cal. Proc. 5th Appeal § 680, (S 680) Original Exhibits.
9 Witkin Cal. Proc. 5th Appeal § 1030, Record.
2 Witkin Cal. Proc. 5th Courts § 195, (S 195) Appellate Rules.
10 Witkin, California Summary 10th Parent and Child § 713, in General.

Article 4

HEARING AND DECISION IN THE COURT OF APPEAL

Rule 8.240. Calendar preference

A party seeking calendar preference must promptly serve and file a motion for preference in the reviewing court. As used in this rule, "calendar preference" means an expedited appeal schedule, which may include expedited briefing and preference in setting the date of oral argument. *(Formerly Rule 19, adopted, eff. Jan. 1, 2003. Renumbered Rule 8.240 and amended, eff. Jan. 1, 2007.)*

Advisory Committee Comment

Rule 8.240 requires a party claiming preference to file a motion for preference in the reviewing court. The motion requirement relieves the reviewing court of the burden of searching the record to determine if preference should be ordered. The requirement is not intended to bar the court from ordering preference without a motion when the ground is apparent on the face of the appeal, e.g., in appeals from judgments of dependency (Welf. & Inst. Code, § 395).

The rule is broad in scope: it includes motions for preference on the grounds (1) that a statute provides for preference in the reviewing court (e. g., Code Civ. Proc., §§ 44 [probate proceedings, contested elections, libel by public official), 45 [judgment freeing minor from parental custody]); (2) that the reviewing court should exercise its discretion to grant preference when a statute provides for trial preference (e.g., *id.,* §§ 35 [certain election matters], 36 [party over 70 and in poor health; party with terminal illness; minor in wrongful death action]; see *Warren v. Schecter* (1997) 57 Cal.App.4th 1189, 1198–1199); and (3) that the reviewing court should exercise its discretion to grant preference on a nonstatutory ground (e.g., economic hardship).

Because valid grounds for preference could arise after the filing of the reply brief, e.g., a diagnosis of terminal illness, the rule requires the motion to be filed "promptly," i.e., as soon as the ground for preference arises.

Research References

Rutter, Cal. Practice Guide: Civil Appeals & Writs Ch. 5-B, B. Types of Motions, Applications and Requests.
Rutter, Cal. Practice Guide: Civil Appeals & Writs Ch. 10-B, B. Oral Argument Procedure.
Rutter, Cal. Practice Guide: Civil Appeals & Writs Ch. 11-A, A. the Decisionmaking Process.
Rutter, Cal. Practice Guide: Civil Appeals & Writs Form 5:F.1, Motion for Calendar Preference.
9 Witkin Cal. Proc. 5th Appeal § 9, (S 9) Current Structure.
9 Witkin Cal. Proc. 5th Appeal § 764, Statutory Preferences and Advancement.
2 Witkin Cal. Proc. 5th Courts § 195, (S 195) Appellate Rules.

Rule 8.244. Settlement, abandonment, voluntary dismissal, and compromise

(a) Notice of settlement

(1) If a civil case settles after a notice of appeal has been filed either as a whole or as to any party, the appellant who has settled must immediately serve and file a notice of settlement in the Court of Appeal. If the parties have designated a clerk's or a reporter's transcript and the record has not been filed in the Court of Appeal, the appellant must also immediately serve a copy of the notice on the superior court clerk.

(2) If the case settles after the appellant receives a notice setting oral argument or a prehearing conference, the appellant must also immediately notify the Court of Appeal of the settlement by telephone or other expeditious method.

(3) Within 45 days after filing a notice of settlement—unless the court has ordered a longer time period on a showing of good cause—the appellant who filed the notice of settlement must file either an abandonment under (b), if the record has not yet been filed in the Court of Appeal, or a request to dismiss under (c), if the record has already been filed in the Court of Appeal.

(4) If the appellant does not file an abandonment, a request to dismiss, or a letter stating good cause why the appeal should not be dismissed within the time period specified under (3), the

court may dismiss the appeal as to that appellant and order each side to bear its own costs on appeal.

(5) This subdivision does not apply to settlements requiring findings to be made by the Court of Appeal under Code of Civil Procedure section 128(a)(8).

(b) Abandonment

(1) Before the record is filed in the Court of Appeal, the appellant may serve and file in superior court an abandonment of the appeal or a stipulation to abandon the appeal. The filing effects a dismissal of the appeal and restores the superior court's jurisdiction.

(2) The superior court clerk must promptly notify the Court of Appeal and the parties of the abandonment or stipulation.

(c) Request to dismiss

(1) After the record is filed in the Court of Appeal, the appellant may serve and file in that court a request or a stipulation to dismiss the appeal.

(2) On receipt of a request or stipulation to dismiss, the court may dismiss the appeal and direct immediate issuance of the remittitur.

(d) Approval of compromise

If a guardian or conservator seeks approval of a proposed compromise of a pending appeal, the Court of Appeal may, before ruling on the compromise, direct the trial court to determine whether the compromise is in the minor's or the conservatee's best interests and to report its findings. *(Formerly Rule 20, adopted, eff. Jan. 1, 2003. As amended, eff. Jan. 1, 2006. Renumbered Rule 8.244, eff. Jan. 1, 2007.)*

Research References

Rutter, Cal. Practice Guide: Civil Appeals & Writs Ch. 5-B, B. Types of Motions, Applications and Requests.
Rutter, Cal. Practice Guide: Civil Appeals & Writs Ch. 6-A, A. Overview.
Rutter, Cal. Practice Guide: Civil Appeals & Writs Ch. 6-E, E. Disposition After Settlement.
Rutter, Cal. Practice Guide: Civil Appeals & Writs Ch. 7-A, A. Overview.
Rutter, Cal. Practice Guide: Civil Appeals & Writs Ch. 11-E, E. Appellate Costs and Sanctions.
Rutter, Cal. Practice Guide: Prof. Responsibility Ch. 8-E, E. Consequences of Improper Advocacy.
9 Witkin Cal. Proc. 5th Appeal § 731, in General.
9 Witkin Cal. Proc. 5th Appeal § 732, Partial Abandonment.
9 Witkin Cal. Proc. 5th Appeal § 733, Vacation of Abandonment.
9 Witkin Cal. Proc. 5th Appeal § 734, (S 734) Dismissal After Record is Filed.
9 Witkin Cal. Proc. 5th Appeal § 735, in General.
9 Witkin Cal. Proc. 5th Appeal § 737, (S 737) Compromise of Claim of Minor or Incompetent.
9 Witkin Cal. Proc. 5th Appeal § 738, (S 738) Notice of Settlement.
9 Witkin Cal. Proc. 5th Appeal § 976, (S 976) Abandonment of Appeal.
9 Witkin Cal. Proc. 5th Appeal § 1016, (S 1016) Abandonment and Dismissal.
10 Witkin, California Summary 10th Parent and Child § 709, in General.

Rule 8.248. Prehearing conference

(a) Statement and conference

After the notice of appeal is filed in a civil case, the presiding justice may:

(1) Order one or more parties to serve and file a concise statement describing the nature of the case and the issues presented; and

(2) Order all necessary persons to attend a conference to consider a narrowing of the issues, settlement, and other relevant matters.

(b) Agreement

An agreement reached in a conference must be signed by the parties and filed. Unless the Court of Appeal orders otherwise, the agreement governs the appeal.

(c) Proceedings after conference

(1) Unless allowed by a filed agreement, no matter recited in a statement under (a)(1) or discussed in a conference under (a)(2) may be considered in any subsequent proceeding in the appeal other than in another conference.

(2) Neither the presiding officer nor any court personnel present at a conference may participate in or influence the determination of the appeal.

(d) Time to file brief

The time to file a party's brief under rule 8.212(a) is tolled from the date the Court of Appeal mails notice of the conference until the date it mails notice that the conference is concluded. *(Formerly Rule 21, adopted, eff. Jan. 1, 2003. Renumbered Rule 8.248 and amended, eff. Jan. 1, 2007.)*

Advisory Committee Comment

Subdivision (a). Subdivision (a)(1) requires each party to *serve* any statement it files. (Cf. rule 3.1380(c) [pretrial settlement conference statement must be served on each party].) The service requirement is not intended to prohibit the presiding justice from ordering the parties to submit additional, confidential material in appropriate cases.

Subdivision (d). If a prehearing conference is ordered before the due date of the appellant's opening brief, the time to file the brief is not *extended* but *tolled*, in order to avoid unwarranted lengthening of the briefing process. For example, if the conference is ordered 15 days after the start of the normal 30–day briefing period, the rule simply *suspends* the running of that period; when the period resumes, the party will not receive an automatic extension of a full 30 days but rather the remaining 15 days of the original briefing period, unless the period is otherwise extended.

Under subdivision (d) the tolling period continues "until the date [the Court of Appeal] mails notice that the conference is *concluded*" (italics added). This provision is intended to accommodate the possibility that the conference may not conclude on the date it begins.

Whether or not the conference concludes on the date it begins, subdivision (d) requires the Court of Appeal clerk to mail the parties a notice that the conference is concluded. This provision is intended to facilitate the calculation of the new briefing due dates.

Research References

Rutter, Cal. Practice Guide: Civil Appeals & Writs Ch. 6-A, A. Overview.
Rutter, Cal. Practice Guide: Civil Appeals & Writs Ch. 6-E, E. Disposition After Settlement.
Rutter, Cal. Practice Guide: Civil Appeals & Writs Ch. 6-A , Outline a.
Rutter, Cal. Practice Guide: Personal Injury Ch. 4-C, C. Effective Settlement Negotiations.
9 Witkin Cal. Proc. 5th Appeal § 768, (S 768) Prehearing Conference in Court of Appeal.
1 Witkin Cal. Proc. 5th Attorneys § 7, (S 7) Settlement.

Rule 8.252. Judicial notice; findings and evidence on appeal

(a) Judicial notice

(1) To obtain judicial notice by a reviewing court under Evidence Code section 459, a party must serve and file a separate motion with a proposed order.

(2) The motion must state:

(A) Why the matter to be noticed is relevant to the appeal;

(B) Whether the matter to be noticed was presented to the trial court and, if so, whether judicial notice was taken by that court;

(C) If judicial notice of the matter was not taken by the trial court, why the matter is subject to judicial notice under Evidence Code section 451, 452, or 453; and

(D) Whether the matter to be noticed relates to proceedings occurring after the order or judgment that is the subject of the appeal.

(3) If the matter to be noticed is not in the record, the party must serve and file a copy with the motion or explain why it is not practicable to do so.

(b) Findings on appeal

A party may move that the reviewing court make findings under Code of Civil Procedure section 909. The motion must include proposed findings.

(c) Evidence on appeal

(1) A party may move that the reviewing court take evidence.

(2) An order granting the motion must:

(A) State the issues on which evidence will be taken;

(B) Specify whether the court, a justice, or a special master or referee will take the evidence; and

(C) Give notice of the time and place for taking the evidence.

(3) For documentary evidence, a party may offer the original, a certified copy, or a photocopy. The court may admit the document in evidence without a hearing. *(Formerly Rule 22, adopted, eff. Jan. 1, 2003. Renumbered Rule 8.252 and amended, eff. Jan. 1, 2007. As amended, eff. Jan. 1, 2009; Jan. 1, 2013.)*

Advisory Committee Comment

Subdivisions (b) and (c). Although appellate courts are authorized to take evidence and make findings of fact on appeal by Code of Civil Procedure section 909 and this rule, this authority should be exercised sparingly. (See *In re Zeth S.* (2003) 31 Cal.4th 396.)

Research References

Rutter, Cal. Practice Guide: Civil Appeals & Writs Ch. 5-B, B. Types of Motions, Applications and Requests.

Rutter, Cal. Practice Guide: Civil Appeals & Writs Ch. 5-C, C. Motion, Application and Request Procedures.

Rutter, Cal. Practice Guide: Civil Appeals & Writs Ch. 13-C, C. Briefs on the Merits After Grant of Review.

9 Witkin Cal. Proc. 5th Appeal § 309, (S 309) Constitutional and Legislative Development.

9 Witkin Cal. Proc. 5th Appeal § 317, (S 317) Procedure.

9 Witkin Cal. Proc. 5th Appeal § 319, (S 319) Procedure.

Rule 8.254. New Authorities

(a) Letter to court

If a party learns of significant new authority, including new legislation, that was not available in time to be included in the last brief that the party filed or could have filed, the party may inform the Court of Appeal of this authority by letter.

(b) Form and content

The letter may provide only a citation to the new authority and identify, by citation to a page or pages in a brief on file, the issue on appeal to which the new authority is relevant. No argument or other discussion of the authority is permitted in the letter.

(c) Service and filing

The letter must be served and filed before the court files its opinion and as soon as possible after the party learns of the new authority. If the letter is served and filed after oral argument is heard, it may address only new authority that was not available in time to be addressed at oral argument. *(Adopted, eff. July 1, 2012.)*

Advisory Committee Comment

This rule does not preclude a party from asking the presiding justice for permission to file supplemental briefing under rule 8.200(a)(4). A letter filed under this rule does not change the date of submission under rule 8.256.

Research References

Rutter, Cal. Practice Guide: Civil Appeals & Writs Ch. 9-D, D. Procedural Rules.

Rutter, Cal. Practice Guide: Civil Appeals & Writs Ch. 10-B, B. Oral Argument Procedure.

Rutter, Cal. Practice Guide: Civil Appeals & Writs Gen. Matls., Highlights.

Rutter, Cal. Practice Guide: Family Law Gen. Matls, Highlights.

Rule 8.256. Oral argument and submission of the cause

(a) Frequency and location of argument

(1) Each Court of Appeal and division must hold a session at least once each quarter.

(2) A Court of Appeal may hold sessions at places in its district other than the court's permanent location.

(3) Subject to the approval by the Chair of the Judicial Council, a Court of Appeal may hold a session in another district to hear a cause transferred to it from that district.

(b) Notice of argument

The Court of Appeal clerk must send a notice of the time and place of oral argument to all parties at least 20 days before the argument date. The presiding justice may shorten the notice period for good cause; in that event, the clerk must immediately notify the parties by telephone or other expeditious method.

(c) Conduct of argument

Unless the court provides otherwise by local rule or order:

(1) The appellant, petitioner, or moving party has the right to open and close. If there are two or more such parties, the court must set the sequence of argument.

(2) Each side is allowed 30 minutes for argument. If multiple parties are represented by separate counsel, or if an amicus curiae—on written request—is granted permission to argue, the court may apportion or expand the time.

(3) Only one counsel may argue for each separately represented party.

(d) When the cause is submitted

(1) A cause is submitted when the court has heard oral argument or approved its waiver and the time has expired to file all briefs and papers, including any supplemental brief permitted by the court.

(2) If the Supreme Court transfers a cause to the Court of Appeal and supplemental briefs may be filed under rule 8.200(b), the cause is submitted when the last such brief is or could be timely filed. The Court of Appeal may order the cause submitted at an earlier time if the parties so stipulate.

(e) Vacating submission

(1) Except as provided in (2), the court may vacate submission only by an order stating its reasons and setting a timetable for resubmission.

(2) If a cause is submitted under (d)(2), an order setting oral argument vacates submission and the cause is resubmitted when the court has heard oral argument or approved its waiver. *(Formerly Rule 23, adopted, eff. Jan. 1, 2003. Renumbered Rule 8.256 and amended, eff. Jan. 1, 2007.)*

Research References

Rutter, Cal. Practice Guide: Civil Appeals & Writs Ch. 10-A, A. Overview.

Rutter, Cal. Practice Guide: Civil Appeals & Writs Ch. 10-B, B. Oral Argument Procedure.

Rutter, Cal. Practice Guide: Civil Appeals & Writs Ch. 11-B, B. Submission for Decision.

Rutter, Cal. Practice Guide: Civil Appeals & Writs Ch. 13-E, E. Decision on the Merits.

Rutter, Cal. Practice Guide: Civil Appeals & Writs Ch. 10-B , Outline B.

9 Witkin Cal. Proc. 5th Appeal § 763, in General.

9 Witkin Cal. Proc. 5th Appeal § 771, (S 771) Regulation.

9 Witkin Cal. Proc. 5th Appeal § 774, Court of Appeal.

2 Witkin Cal. Proc. 5th Courts § 334, (S 334) Sessions and Conferences.

Rule 8.264.   Filing, finality, and modification of decision

(a) Filing the decision

(1) The Court of Appeal clerk must promptly file all opinions and orders of the court and promptly send copies showing the filing date to the parties and, when relevant, to the lower court or tribunal.

(2) A decision by opinion must identify the participating justices, including the author of the majority opinion and of any concurring or dissenting opinion, or the justices participating in a "by the court" opinion.

(b) Finality of decision

(1) Except as otherwise provided in this rule, a Court of Appeal decision in a civil appeal, including an order dismissing an appeal involuntarily, is final in that court 30 days after filing.

(2) The following Court of Appeal decisions are final in that court on filing:

(A) The denial of a petition for writ of supersedeas; and

(B) The dismissal of an appeal on request or stipulation.

(3) If a Court of Appeal certifies its opinion for publication or partial publication after filing its decision and before its decision becomes final in that court, the finality period runs from the filing date of the order for publication.

(c) Modification of decision

(1) A reviewing court may modify a decision until the decision is final in that court. If the clerk's office is closed on the date of finality, the court may modify the decision on the next day the clerk's office is open.

(2) An order modifying an opinion must state whether it changes the appellate judgment. A modification that does not change the appellate judgment does not extend the finality date of the decision. If a modification changes the appellate judgment, the finality period runs from the filing date of the modification order.

(d) Consent to increase or decrease in amount of judgment

If a Court of Appeal decision conditions the affirmance of a money judgment on a party's consent to an increase or decrease in the amount, the judgment is reversed unless, before the decision is final under (b), the party serves and files two copies of a consent in the Court of Appeal. If a consent is filed, the finality period runs from the filing date of the consent. The clerk must send one file-stamped copy of the consent to the superior court with the remittitur. *(Formerly Rule 24, adopted, eff. Jan. 1, 2003. Renumbered Rule 8.264 and amended, eff. Jan. 1, 2007. As amended, eff. Jan. 1, 2009.)*

Advisory Committee Comment

Subdivision (b). As used in subdivision (b)(1), "decision" includes all interlocutory orders of the Court of Appeal. (See Advisory Committee Comment to rule 8.500(a) and (e).) This provision addresses the finality of decisions in civil appeals and, through a cross-reference in rule 8.470, in juvenile appeals. See rule 8.366 for provisions addressing the finality of decisions in proceedings under chapter 3, relating to criminal appeals; rule 8.387 for provisions addressing finality of decisions under chapter 4, relating to habeas corpus proceedings; and rule 8.490 for provisions addressing the finality of decisions in proceedings under chapter 7, relating to writs of mandate, certiorari, and prohibition.

Subdivision (b)(3) provides that a postfiling decision of the Court of Appeal to publish its opinion in whole under rule 8.1105(c) or in part under rule 8.1100(a) restarts the 30–day finality period. This provision is based on rule 40–2 of the United States Circuit Rules (9th Cir.). It is intended to allow parties sufficient time to petition the Court of Appeal for rehearing and/or the Supreme Court for review—and to allow potential amici curiae sufficient time to express their views—when the Court of Appeal changes the publication status of an opinion. The rule thus recognizes that the publication status of an opinion may affect a party's decision whether to file a petition for rehearing and/or a petition for review.

Research References

Rutter, Cal. Practice Guide: Civil Appeals & Writs Ch. 5-B, B. Types of Motions, Applications and Requests.

Rutter, Cal. Practice Guide: Civil Appeals & Writs Ch. 7-E, E. Stay by Writ of Supersedeas.

Rutter, Cal. Practice Guide: Civil Appeals & Writs Ch. 11-C, C. Rendition of Opinion and Judgment.

Rutter, Cal. Practice Guide: Civil Appeals & Writs Ch. 11-D, D. Disposition.

Rutter, Cal. Practice Guide: Civil Appeals & Writs Ch. 11-G, G. Finality as to Court of Appeal.

Rutter, Cal. Practice Guide: Civil Appeals & Writs Ch. 12-A, A. Overview.

Rutter, Cal. Practice Guide: Civil Appeals & Writs Ch. 12-E, E. Procedure.

Rutter, Cal. Practice Guide: Civil Appeals & Writs Ch. 12-F, F. Disposition.

Rutter, Cal. Practice Guide: Civil Appeals & Writs Ch. 13-B, B. Petition for Review Procedures.

Rutter, Cal. Practice Guide: Civil Appeals & Writs Ch. 13-E, E. Decision on the Merits.

Rutter, Cal. Practice Guide: Civil Appeals & Writs Ch. 13-F, F. Petition for Rehearing.

Rutter, Cal. Practice Guide: Civil Appeals & Writs Ch. 15-E, E. Procedures on Writ Review.

Rutter, Cal. Practice Guide: Insurance Litigation Ch. 13-C, C. Punitive Damages.

9 Witkin Cal. Proc. 5th Appeal § 303, Determination.

9 Witkin Cal. Proc. 5th Appeal § 734, (S 734) Dismissal After Record is Filed.

9 Witkin Cal. Proc. 5th Appeal § 783, by the Court Opinion.

9 Witkin Cal. Proc. 5th Appeal § 831, (S 831) Rendition: Filing of Opinion.

9 Witkin Cal. Proc. 5th Appeal § 832, (S 832) Period Begins on Filing.

9 Witkin Cal. Proc. 5th Appeal § 833, (S 833) Effect of Modification.

9 Witkin Cal. Proc. 5th Appeal § 834, (S 834) General Rule: 30 Days After Filing.

9 Witkin Cal. Proc. 5th Appeal § 835, (S 835) Exceptions: Immediately After Filing.

9 Witkin Cal. Proc. 5th Appeal § 836, (S 836) Effect of Setting Writ Matter for Oral Argument.

9 Witkin Cal. Proc. 5th Appeal § 837, (S 837) Effect of Certification for Publication.

9 Witkin Cal. Proc. 5th Appeal § 857, Modification as Condition of Affirmance.

9 Witkin Cal. Proc. 5th Appeal § 907, (S 907) Petition.

9 Witkin Cal. Proc. 5th Appeal § 909, (S 909) Time for Order.

9 Witkin Cal. Proc. 5th Appeal § 922, Nature and Grounds.

9 Witkin Cal. Proc. 5th Appeal § 1032, Decision and Remittitur.

8 Witkin Cal. Proc. 5th Extraordinary Writs § 163, (S 163) Governing Statutes and Rules.

8 Witkin Cal. Proc. 5th Extraordinary Writs § 205, Reviewing Court.

8 Witkin Cal. Proc. 5th Extraordinary Writs § 209, (S 209) Finality and Res Judicata.

8 Witkin Cal. Proc. 5th Extraordinary Writs § 210, (S 210) Summary Denial is Not Law of Case.
8 Witkin Cal. Proc. 5th Extraordinary Writs § 220, (S 220) Decision on Merits.
8 Witkin Cal. Proc. 5th Extraordinary Writs § 221, (S 221) Summary Denial.
2 Witkin Cal. Summ. 10th Workers' Compensation § 440, Rehearing and Review in Supreme Court.

Rule 8.268. Rehearing

(a) Power to order rehearing

(1) On petition of a party or on its own motion, a reviewing court may order rehearing of any decision that is not final in that court on filing.

(2) An order for rehearing must be filed before the decision is final. If the clerk's office is closed on the date of finality, the court may file the order on the next day the clerk's office is open.

(b) Petition and answer

(1) A party may serve and file a petition for rehearing within 15 days after:

(A) The filing of the decision;

(B) A publication order restarting the finality period under rule 8.264(b)(3), if the party has not already filed a petition for rehearing;

(C) A modification order changing the appellate judgment under rule 8.264(c)(2); or

(D) The filing of a consent under rule 8.264(d).

(2) A party must not file an answer to a petition for rehearing unless the court requests an answer. The clerk must promptly send to the parties copies of any order requesting an answer and immediately notify the parties by telephone or another expeditious method. Any answer must be served and filed within 8 days after the order is filed unless the court orders otherwise. A petition for rehearing normally will not be granted unless the court has requested an answer.

(3) The petition and answer must comply with the relevant provisions of rule 8.204.

(4) Before the decision is final and for good cause, the presiding justice may relieve a party from a failure to file a timely petition or answer.

(c) No extension of time

The time for granting or denying a petition for rehearing in the Court of Appeal may not be extended. If the court does not rule on the petition before the decision is final, the petition is deemed denied.

(d) Effect of granting rehearing

An order granting a rehearing vacates the decision and any opinion filed in the case and sets the cause at large in the Court of Appeal. *(Formerly Rule 25, adopted, eff. Jan. 1, 2003. As amended, eff. Jan. 1, 2004. Renumbered Rule 8.268 and amended, eff. Jan. 1, 2007. As amended, eff. Jan. 1, 2009.)*

Research References

Rutter, Cal. Practice Guide: Civil Appeals & Writs Ch. 7-E, E. Stay by Writ of Supersedeas.
Rutter, Cal. Practice Guide: Civil Appeals & Writs Ch. 11-G, G. Finality as to Court of Appeal.
Rutter, Cal. Practice Guide: Civil Appeals & Writs Ch. 12-A, A. Overview.
Rutter, Cal. Practice Guide: Civil Appeals & Writs Ch. 12-D, D. Petition and Answer Strategies.
Rutter, Cal. Practice Guide: Civil Appeals & Writs Ch. 12-E, E. Procedure.
Rutter, Cal. Practice Guide: Civil Appeals & Writs Ch. 12-F, F. Disposition.

Rutter, Cal. Practice Guide: Civil Appeals & Writs Ch. 13-F, F. Petition for Rehearing.
Rutter, Cal. Practice Guide: Civil Appeals & Writs Ch. 15-E, E. Procedures on Writ Review.
9 Witkin Cal. Proc. 5th Appeal § 904, Nature of Power.
9 Witkin Cal. Proc. 5th Appeal § 905, Grounds.
9 Witkin Cal. Proc. 5th Appeal § 907, (S 907) Petition.
9 Witkin Cal. Proc. 5th Appeal § 908, (S 908) Answer.
9 Witkin Cal. Proc. 5th Appeal § 909, (S 909) Time for Order.
9 Witkin Cal. Proc. 5th Appeal § 910, (S 910) Grant of Petition.
9 Witkin Cal. Proc. 5th Appeal § 948, in General.
9 Witkin Cal. Proc. 5th Appeal § 1019, (S 1019) Rehearing.
2 Witkin Cal. Summ. 10th Workers' Compensation § 440, Rehearing and Review in Supreme Court.

Rule 8.272. Remittitur

(a) Issuance of remittitur

A Court of Appeal must issue a remittitur after a decision in an appeal.

(b) Clerk's duties

(1) If a Court of Appeal decision is not reviewed by the Supreme Court:

(A) The Court of Appeal clerk must issue a remittitur immediately after the Supreme Court denies review, or the period for granting review expires, or the court dismisses review under rule 8.528(b); and

(B) The clerk must send the lower court or tribunal the Court of Appeal remittitur and a file-stamped copy of the opinion or order.

(2) After Supreme Court review of a Court of Appeal decision:

(A) On receiving the Supreme Court remittitur, the Court of Appeal clerk must issue a remittitur immediately if there will be no further proceedings in the Court of Appeal; and

(B) The clerk must send the lower court or tribunal the Court of Appeal remittitur, a copy of the Supreme Court remittitur, and a file-stamped copy of the Supreme Court opinion or order.

(c) Immediate issuance, stay, and recall

(1) A Court of Appeal may direct immediate issuance of a remittitur only on the parties' stipulation or on dismissal of the appeal under rule 8.244(c)(2).

(2) On a party's or its own motion or on stipulation, and for good cause, the court may stay a remittitur's issuance for a reasonable period or order its recall.

(3) An order recalling a remittitur issued after a decision by opinion does not supersede the opinion or affect its publication status.

(d) Notice

(1) The remittitur is deemed issued when the clerk enters it in the record. The clerk must immediately send the parties notice of issuance of the remittitur, showing the date of entry.

(2) If, without requiring further proceedings in the trial court, the decision changes the length of a state prison sentence, applicable credits, or the maximum permissible confinement to the Department of Corrections and Rehabilitation, Division of Juvenile Justice, the clerk must send a copy of the remittitur and opinion or order to either the Department of Corrections and Rehabilitation or the Division of Juvenile Justice. *(Formerly Rule 26, adopted, eff. Jan. 1, 2003. Renumbered Rule 8.272 and amended, eff. Jan. 1, 2007. As amended, eff. Jan. 1, 2008.)*

Ct. Rules

Advisory Committee Comment

See rule 8.386 for provisions addressing remittitur in habeas corpus proceedings and rule 8.490 for provisions addressing remittitur in other writ proceedings.

Research References

Rutter, Cal. Practice Guide: Civil Appeals & Writs Ch. 5-C, C. Motion, Application and Request Procedures.

Rutter, Cal. Practice Guide: Civil Appeals & Writs Ch. 11-G, G. Finality as to Court of Appeal.

Rutter, Cal. Practice Guide: Civil Appeals & Writs Ch. 13-B, B. Petition for Review Procedures.

Rutter, Cal. Practice Guide: Civil Appeals & Writs Ch. 14-A, A. Remittitur.

Rutter, Cal. Practice Guide: Civil Appeals & Writs Form 14:A.1, Motion to Recall and Correct Remittitur.

9 Witkin Cal. Proc. 5th Appeal § 842, (S 842) Procedure.

9 Witkin Cal. Proc. 5th Appeal § 843, (S 843) Proceedings in Which Remittitur Issues.

9 Witkin Cal. Proc. 5th Appeal § 844, (S 844) Effect of Issuance.

9 Witkin Cal. Proc. 5th Appeal § 845, (S 845) Issuance Forthwith.

9 Witkin Cal. Proc. 5th Appeal § 846, (S 846) Stay of Issuance.

9 Witkin Cal. Proc. 5th Appeal § 848, Procedure.

9 Witkin Cal. Proc. 5th Appeal § 941, Affirmance, Modification, or Reversal.

9 Witkin Cal. Proc. 5th Appeal § 1018, Decision and Opinion.

9 Witkin Cal. Proc. 5th Appeal § 1032, Decision and Remittitur.

8 Witkin Cal. Proc. 5th Extraordinary Writs § 163, (S 163) Governing Statutes and Rules.

8 Witkin Cal. Proc. 5th Extraordinary Writs § 208, (S 208) Procedure.

2 Witkin Cal. Proc. 5th Jurisdiction § 423, (S 423) Other Examples.

Rule 8.276. Sanctions

(a) Grounds for sanctions

On motion of a party or its own motion, a Court of Appeal may impose sanctions, including the award or denial of costs under rule 8.278, on a party or an attorney for:

(1) Taking a frivolous appeal or appealing solely to cause delay;

(2) Including in the record any matter not reasonably material to the appeal's determination;

(3) Filing a frivolous motion; or

(4) Committing any other unreasonable violation of these rules.

(b) Motions for sanctions

(1) A party's motion under (a) must include a declaration supporting the amount of any monetary sanction sought and must be served and filed before any order dismissing the appeal but no later than 10 days after the appellant's reply brief is due.

(2) If a party files a motion for sanctions with a motion to dismiss the appeal and the motion to dismiss is not granted, the party may file a new motion for sanctions within 10 days after the appellant's reply brief is due.

(c) Notice

The court must give notice in writing if it is considering imposing sanctions.

(d) Opposition

Within 10 days after the court sends such notice, a party or attorney may serve and file an opposition, but failure to do so will not be deemed consent. An opposition may not be filed unless the court sends such notice.

(e) Oral argument

Unless otherwise ordered, oral argument on the issue of sanctions must be combined with oral argument on the merits of the appeal. (*Formerly Rule 27, adopted, eff. Jan. 1, 2003.*

Renumbered Rule 8.276 and amended, eff. Jan. 1, 2007. As amended, eff. Jan. 1, 2008.)

Rutter, Cal. Practice Guide: Civil Appeals & Writs Ch. 3-D, D. Consequences of Lapse of Appeal Deadline; Strategies for Respondents and Appellants.

Rutter, Cal. Practice Guide: Civil Appeals & Writs Ch. 4-B, B. Components of Record and Considerations in Selecting Them.

Rutter, Cal. Practice Guide: Civil Appeals & Writs Ch. 5-B, B. Types of Motions, Applications and Requests.

Rutter, Cal. Practice Guide: Civil Appeals & Writs Ch. 5-D, D. Sanctions for Frivolous Motions.

Rutter, Cal. Practice Guide: Civil Appeals & Writs Ch. 7-A, A. Overview.

Rutter, Cal. Practice Guide: Civil Appeals & Writs Ch. 9-B, B. Approaches to Briefwriting.

Rutter, Cal. Practice Guide: Civil Appeals & Writs Ch. 9-D, D. Procedural Rules.

Rutter, Cal. Practice Guide: Civil Appeals & Writs Ch. 10-D, D. Delivery of Oral Argument.

Rutter, Cal. Practice Guide: Civil Appeals & Writs Ch. 11-D, D. Disposition.

Rutter, Cal. Practice Guide: Civil Appeals & Writs Ch. 11-E, E. Appellate Costs and Sanctions.

Rutter, Cal. Practice Guide: Civil Appeals & Writs Ch. 11-F, F. Publication of Appellate Opinions.

Rutter, Cal. Practice Guide: Civil Appeals & Writs Ch. 14-B, B. Recovery of Appellate Costs and Attorney Fees.

Rutter, Cal. Practice Guide: Civil Appeals & Writs Form 14:A.1, Motion to Recall and Correct Remittitur.

Rutter, Cal. Practice Guide: Civ. Pro. Before Trial Ch. 9(III)-A, A. Sources of Sanctions Power.

Rutter, Cal. Practice Guide: Enforcing Judgments/Debts Ch. 1-B, B. Accepting the Collection Case.

Rutter, Cal. Practice Guide: Enforcing Judgments/Debts Ch. 2-C, C. Tort Liability.

Rutter, Cal. Practice Guide: Personal Injury Ch. 4-C, C. Effective Settlement Negotiations.

Rutter, Cal. Practice Guide: Prof. Responsibility Ch. 1-A, A. Sources of Regulation of Practice of Law in California-Overview.

Rutter, Cal. Practice Guide: Prof. Responsibility Ch. 8-E, E. Consequences of Improper Advocacy.

9 Witkin Cal. Proc. 5th Appeal § 9, (S 9) Current Structure.

9 Witkin Cal. Proc. 5th Appeal § 687, Penalty for Excessive Record.

9 Witkin Cal. Proc. 5th Appeal § 953, in General.

9 Witkin Cal. Proc. 5th Appeal § 969, Record.

9 Witkin Cal. Proc. 5th Appeal § 976, (S 976) Abandonment of Appeal.

9 Witkin Cal. Proc. 5th Appeal § 983, (S 983) Nature of Power.

9 Witkin Cal. Proc. 5th Appeal § 987, (S 987) Persons Sanctioned.

9 Witkin Cal. Proc. 5th Appeal § 989, (S 989) Objective and Subjective Standards.

9 Witkin Cal. Proc. 5th Appeal § 991, (S 991) in General.

9 Witkin Cal. Proc. 5th Appeal § 994, (S 994) Noticed Motion Procedure.

9 Witkin Cal. Proc. 5th Appeal § 1001, Distinction: No Tort Action for Malicious Appeal.

9 Witkin Cal. Proc. 5th Appeal § 1018, Decision and Opinion.

8 Witkin Cal. Proc. 5th Extraordinary Writs § 213, (S 213) Costs in Reviewing Court.

7 Witkin Cal. Proc. 5th Judgment § 301, Fees Determined by Trial Court.

Rule 8.278. Costs on appeal

(a) Award of costs

(1) Except as provided in this rule, the party prevailing in the Court of Appeal in a civil case other than a juvenile case is entitled to costs on appeal.

(2) The prevailing party is the respondent if the Court of Appeal affirms the judgment without modification or dismisses the appeal. The prevailing party is the appellant if the court reverses the judgment in its entirety.

(3) If the Court of Appeal reverses the judgment in part or modifies it, or if there is more than one notice of appeal, the opinion must specify the award or denial of costs.

(4) In probate cases, the prevailing party must be awarded costs unless the Court of Appeal orders otherwise, but the superior court must decide who will pay the award.

(5) In the interests of justice, the Court of Appeal may also award or deny costs as it deems proper.

(b) Judgment for costs

(1) The Court of Appeal clerk must enter on the record, and insert in the remittitur, a judgment awarding costs to the prevailing party under (a)(2) or as directed by the court under (a)(3), (a)(4), or (a)(5).

(2) If the clerk fails to enter judgment for costs, the court may recall the remittitur for correction on its own motion, or on a party's motion made not later than 30 days after the remittitur issues.

(c) Procedure for claiming or opposing costs

(1) Within 40 days after the clerk sends notice of issuance of the remittitur, a party claiming costs awarded by a reviewing court must serve and file in the superior court a verified memorandum of costs under rule 3.1700.

(2) A party may serve and file a motion in the superior court to strike or tax costs claimed under (1) in the manner required by rule 3.1700.

(3) An award of costs is enforceable as a money judgment.

(d) Recoverable costs

(1) A party may recover only the following costs, if reasonable:

(A) Filing fees;

(B) The amount the party paid for any portion of the record, whether an original or a copy or both. The cost to copy parts of a prior record under rule 8.147(b)(2) is not recoverable unless the Court of Appeal ordered the copying;

(C) The cost to produce additional evidence on appeal;

(D) The costs to notarize, serve, mail, and file the record, briefs, and other papers;

(E) The cost to print and reproduce any brief, including any petition for rehearing or review, answer, or reply;—and

(F) The cost to procure a surety bond, including the premium, and the cost to obtain a letter of credit as collateral, and the fees and net interest expenses incurred to borrow funds to provide security for the bond or to obtain a letter of credit, unless the trial court determines the bond was unnecessary.; and

(G) The fees and net interest expenses incurred to borrow funds to deposit with the superior court in lieu of a bond or undertaking, unless the trial court determines the deposit was unnecessary.

(2) Unless the court orders otherwise, an award of costs neither includes attorney's fees on appeal nor precludes a party from seeking them under rule 3.1702. *(Adopted, eff. Jan. 1, 2008. As amended, eff. Jan. 1, 2013.)*

Advisory Committee Comment

This rule is not intended to expand the categories of appeals subject to the award of costs. See rule 8.493 for provisions addressing costs in writ proceedings.

Subdivision (c). Subdivision (c)(2) provides the procedure for a party to move in the trial court to strike or tax costs that another party has claimed under subdivision (c)(1). It is not intended that the trial court's authority to strike or tax unreasonable costs be limited by any failure of the moving party to move for sanctions in the Court of Appeal under rule 8.276; a party may seek to strike or tax costs on the ground that an opponent included unnecessary materials in the record even if the party

did not move the Court of Appeal to sanction the opponent under that rule.

Subdivision (d). Subdivision (d)(1)(B) is intended to refer not only to a normal record prepared by the clerk and the reporter under rules 8.122 and 8.130 but also, for example, to an appendix prepared by a party under rule 8.124 and to a superior court file to which the parties stipulate under rule 8.128.

"Net interest expenses" in subdivisions (d)(1)(F) and (G) means the interest expenses incurred to borrow the funds that are deposited minus any interest earned by the borrower on those funds while they are on deposit.

Research References

Rutter, Cal. Practice Guide: Civil Appeals & Writs Ch. 5-B, B. Types of Motions, Applications and Requests.

Rutter, Cal. Practice Guide: Civil Appeals & Writs Ch. 7-C, C. Stay by Posting Security (Bond or Undertaking).

Rutter, Cal. Practice Guide: Civil Appeals & Writs Ch. 11-E, E. Appellate Costs and Sanctions.

Rutter, Cal. Practice Guide: Civil Appeals & Writs Ch. 14-A, A. Remittitur.

Rutter, Cal. Practice Guide: Civil Appeals & Writs Ch. 14-B, B. Recovery of Appellate Costs and Attorney Fees.

Rutter, Cal. Practice Guide: Civil Appeals & Writs Ch. 14-D, D. Precedential Effect of Appellate Court Opinions.

Rutter, Cal. Practice Guide: Civil Appeals & Writs Ch. 15-E, E. Procedures on Writ Review.

Rutter, Cal. Practice Guide: Civil Appeals & Writs Ch. 14-A , Outline a.

Rutter, Cal. Practice Guide: Civil Appeals & Writs Gen. Matls., Highlights.

Rutter, Cal. Practice Guide: Civil Trials & Evidence Ch. 17-E, E. Attorney Fees as Costs.

9 Witkin Cal. Proc. 5th Appeal § 9, (S 9) Current Structure.

9 Witkin Cal. Proc. 5th Appeal § 848, Procedure.

9 Witkin Cal. Proc. 5th Appeal § 849, (S 849) Correction of Remittitur.

9 Witkin Cal. Proc. 5th Appeal § 850, (S 850) Correction of Judgment.

9 Witkin Cal. Proc. 5th Appeal § 954, (S 954) General Rule.

9 Witkin Cal. Proc. 5th Appeal § 955, (S 955) Who is Prevailing Party.

9 Witkin Cal. Proc. 5th Appeal § 958, (S 958) in General.

9 Witkin Cal. Proc. 5th Appeal § 967, Discretion of Probate Judge.

9 Witkin Cal. Proc. 5th Appeal § 968, in General.

9 Witkin Cal. Proc. 5th Appeal § 969, Record.

9 Witkin Cal. Proc. 5th Appeal § 970, Briefs.

9 Witkin Cal. Proc. 5th Appeal § 971, (S 971) in General.

9 Witkin Cal. Proc. 5th Appeal § 973, Other Expenses.

9 Witkin Cal. Proc. 5th Appeal § 974, Award and Entry.

9 Witkin Cal. Proc. 5th Appeal § 976, (S 976) Abandonment of Appeal.

9 Witkin Cal. Proc. 5th Appeal § 977, Motion to Tax.

9 Witkin Cal. Proc. 5th Appeal § 978, Enforcement of Award.

9 Witkin Cal. Proc. 5th Appeal § 979, (S 979) Right to Recover.

9 Witkin Cal. Proc. 5th Appeal § 982, (S 982) Procedure for Request.

9 Witkin Cal. Proc. 5th Appeal § 1018, Decision and Opinion.

2 Witkin Cal. Proc. 5th Courts § 195, (S 195) Appellate Rules.

7 Witkin Cal. Proc. 5th Judgment § 301, Fees Determined by Trial Court.

7 Witkin Cal. Proc. 5th Judgment § 302, Fees Determined by Appellate Court.

14 Witkin, California Summary 10th Wills and Probate § 400, (S 400) Costs.

Chapter 4

HABEAS CORPUS APPEALS AND WRITS

Ct. Rules

Rule

8.388. Appeal from order granting relief by writ of habeas corpus.

Rule 8.380. Petition for writ of habeas corpus filed by petitioner not represented by an attorney

(a) Required Judicial Council form

A person who is not represented by an attorney and who petitions a reviewing court for writ of habeas corpus seeking release from, or modification of the conditions of, custody of a person confined in a state or local penal institution, hospital, narcotics treatment facility, or other institution must file the petition on *Petition for Writ of Habeas Corpus* (form MC–275). For good cause the court may permit the filing of a petition that is not on that form.

(b) Form and content

A petition filed under (a) need not comply with the provisions of rules 8.40, 8.204, or 8.486 that prescribe the form and content of a petition and require the petition to be accompanied by a memorandum.

(c) Number of copies

In the Court of Appeal, the petitioner must file the original of the petition under (a) and one set of any supporting documents. In the Supreme Court, the petitioner must file an original and 10 copies of the petition and an original and 2 copies of any supporting document accompanying the petition unless the court orders otherwise. *(Formerly Rule 60, adopted, eff. Jan. 1, 2005. As amended, eff. Jan. 1, 2006. Renumbered Rule 8.380 and amended, eff. Jan. 1, 2007. As amended, eff. Jan. 1, 2009.)*

Research References

9 Witkin Cal. Proc. 5th Appeal § 9, (S 9) Current Structure.
2 Witkin Cal. Proc. 5th Courts § 195, (S 195) Appellate Rules.

Rule 8.384. Petition for writ of habeas corpus filed by an attorney for a party

(a) Form and content of petition and memorandum

(1) A petition for habeas corpus filed by an attorney need not be filed on *Petition for Writ of Habeas Corpus* (form MC–275) but must contain the information requested in that form. All petitions filed by attorneys, whether or not on form MC–275, must be either typewritten or produced on a computer, and must comply with this rule and rules 8.40(b)–(c) relating to document covers and 8.204(a)(1)(A) relating to tables of contents and authorities. A petition that is not on form MC–275 must also comply with the remainder of rule 8.204(a) and 8.204(b).

(2) Any memorandum accompanying the petition must comply with rule 8.204(a)–(b). Except in habeas corpus proceedings related to sentences of death, any memorandum must also comply with the length limits in rule 8.204(c).

(3) The petition and any memorandum must support any reference to a matter in the supporting documents by a citation to its index tab and page.

(b) Supporting documents

(1) The petition must be accompanied by a copy of any petition—excluding exhibits—pertaining to the same judgment and petitioner that was previously filed in any state court or any federal court. If such documents have previously been filed in the same Court of Appeal where the petition is filed or in the Supreme Court and the petition so states and identifies the documents by case name and number, copies of these documents need not be included in the supporting documents.

(2) If the petition asserts a claim that was the subject of an evidentiary hearing, the petition must be accompanied by a certified transcript of that hearing.

(3) Rule 8.486(c)(1) and (2) govern the form of any supporting documents accompanying the petition.

(c) Number of copies

If the petition is filed in the Supreme Court, the attorney must file the number of copies of the petition and supporting documents required by rule 8.44(a). If the petition is filed in the Court of Appeal, the attorney must file the number of copies of the petition and supporting documents required by rule 8.44(b).

(d) Noncomplying petitions

The clerk must file an attorney's petition not complying with (a)–(c) if it otherwise complies with the rules of court, but the court may notify the attorney that it may strike the petition or impose a lesser sanction if the petition is not brought into compliance within a stated reasonable time of not less than five days. *(Formerly Rule 60.5, adopted, eff. Jan. 1, 2006. Renumbered Rule 8.384 and amended, eff. Jan. 1, 2007. As amended, eff. Jan. 1, 2009.)*

Rule 8.385. Proceedings after the petition is filed

(a) Record

Before ruling on the petition, the court may order the custodian of any relevant record to produce the record or a certified copy to be filed with the court.

(b) Informal response

(1) Before ruling on the petition, the court may request an informal written response from the respondent, the real party in interest, or an interested person. The court must send a copy of any request to the petitioner.

(2) The response must be served and filed within 15 days or as the court specifies.

(3) If a response is filed, the court must notify the petitioner that a reply may be served and filed within 15 days or as the court specifies. The court may not deny the petition until that time has expired.

(c) Petition filed in an inappropriate court

(1) A Court of Appeal may deny without prejudice a petition for writ of habeas corpus that is based primarily on facts occurring outside the court's appellate district, including petitions that question:

(A) The validity of judgments or orders of trial courts located outside the district; or

(B) The conditions of confinement or the conduct of correctional officials outside the district.

(2) A Court of Appeal should deny without prejudice a petition for writ of habeas corpus that challenges the denial of parole or the petitioner's suitability for parole if the issue was not first adjudicated by the trial court that rendered the underlying judgment.

(3) If the court denies a petition solely under (1), the order must state the basis of the denial and must identify the appropriate court in which to file the petition.

(d) Order to show cause

If the petitioner has made the required prima facie showing that he or she is entitled to relief, the court must issue an order to show cause. An order to show cause does not grant the relief sought in the petition.

(e) Return to the superior court

The reviewing court may order the respondent to file a return in the superior court. The order vests jurisdiction over the cause in the superior court, which must proceed under rule 4.551.

(f) Return to the reviewing court

If the return is ordered to be filed in the Supreme Court or the Court of Appeal, rule 8.386 applies and the court in which the return is ordered filed must appoint counsel for any unrepresented petitioner who desires but cannot afford counsel. *(Adopted, eff. Jan. 1, 2009. As amended, eff. Jan. 1, 2012.)*

Validity

A prior version of this rule that Court of Appeal must deny writ petition under certain circumstances was held unconstitutional in the decision of In re Kler (App. 1 Dist. 2010) 115 Cal.Rptr.3d 889, 188 Cal.App.4th 1399.

Advisory Committee Comment

Subdivision (c). Except for subdivision (c)(2), rule 8.385(c) restates former section 6.5 of the Standards of Judicial Administration. Subdivision (c)(2) is based on the California Supreme Court decision in *In re Roberts* (2005) 36 Cal.4th 575, which provides that petitions for writ of habeas corpus challenging denial or suitability for parole should first be adjudicated in the trial court that rendered the underlying judgment. The committee notes, however, that courts of appeal have original jurisdiction in writ proceedings and may, under appropriate circumstances, adjudicate a petition that challenges the denial or suitability of parole even if the petition was not first adjudicated by the trial court that rendered the underlying judgment. (*In re Kler* (2010) 188 Cal.App.4th 1399.) A court of appeal may, for example, adjudicate a petition that follows the court's prior reversal of a denial of parole by the Board of Parole Hearings where the issues presented by the petition directly flow from the court of appeal's prior decision and the limited hearing conducted. (*Id.* at 1404–05.)

Subdivision (d). Case law establishes the specificity of the factual allegations and support for these allegations required in a petition for a writ of habeas corpus (see, e.g., *People v. Duvall* (1995) 9 Cal.4th 464, 474–475, and *Ex parte Swain* (1949) 34 Cal.2d 300, 303–304). A court evaluating whether a petition meeting these requirements makes a prima facie showing asks whether, assuming the petition's factual allegations are true, the petitioner would be entitled to relief (*People v. Duvall*, supra).

Issuing an order to show cause is just one of the actions a court might take on a petition for a writ of habeas corpus. Examples of other actions that a court might take include denying the petition summarily, requesting an informal response from the respondent under (b), or denying the petition without prejudice under (c) because it is filed in an inappropriate court.

Rule 8.386. Proceedings if the return is ordered to be filed in the reviewing court

(a) Application

This rule applies if the Supreme Court orders the return to be filed in the Supreme Court or the Court of Appeal or if the Court of Appeal orders the return to be filed in the Court of Appeal.

(b) Serving and filing return

(1) Unless the court orders otherwise, any return must be served and filed within 30 days after the court issues the order to show cause.

(2) If the return is filed in the Supreme Court, the attorney must file the number of copies of the return and any supporting documents required by rule 8.44(a). If the return is filed in the Court of Appeal, the attorney must file the number of copies of the return and any supporting documents required by rule 8.44(b). Two copies of the return and any supporting documents must be served on the petitioner's counsel, and if the return is to the Court of Appeal and the petitioner is not represented by privately retained counsel, one copy must be served on the district appellate project.

(c) Form and content of return

(1) The return must be either typewritten or produced on a computer and must comply with Penal Code section 1480 and rules 8.40(b)–(c) and 8.204(a)–(b). Except in habeas corpus proceedings related to sentences of death, any return must also comply with the length limits in rule 8.204(c).

(2) Rule 8.486(c)(1) and (2) govern the form of any supporting documents accompanying the return. The return must support any reference to a matter in the supporting documents by a citation to its index tab and page.

(3) Any material allegation of the petition not controverted by the return is deemed admitted for purposes of the proceeding.

(d) Traverse

(1) Unless the court orders otherwise, within 30 days after the respondent files a return, the petitioner may serve and file a traverse.

(2) Any traverse must be either typewritten or produced on a computer and must comply with Penal Code section 1484 and rules 8.40(b)–(c) and 8.204(a)–(b). Except in habeas corpus proceedings related to sentences of death, any traverse must also comply with the length limits in rule 8.204(c).

(3) Any material allegation of the return not denied in the traverse is deemed admitted for purposes of the proceeding.

(4) If the return is filed in the Supreme Court, the attorney must file the number of copies of the traverse required by rule 8.44(a). If the return is filed in the Court of Appeal, the attorney must file the number of copies of the traverse required by rule 8.44(b).

(e) Judicial notice

Rule 8.252(a) governs judicial notice in the reviewing court.

(f) Evidentiary hearing ordered by the reviewing court

(1) An evidentiary hearing is required if, after considering the verified petition, the return, any traverse, any affidavits or declarations under penalty of perjury, and matters of which judicial notice may be taken, the court finds there is a reasonable likelihood that the petitioner may be entitled to relief and the petitioner's entitlement to relief depends on the resolution of an issue of fact.

(2) The court may appoint a referee to conduct the hearing and make recommended findings of fact.

(g) Oral argument and submission of the cause

Unless the court orders otherwise:

(1) Rule 8.256 governs oral argument and submission of the cause in the Court of Appeal.

(2) Rule 8.524 governs oral argument and submission of the cause in the Supreme Court. *(Adopted, eff. Jan. 1, 2009.)*

Rule 8.387. Decision in habeas corpus proceedings

(a) Filing the decision

(1) Rule 8.264(a) governs the filing of the decision in the Court of Appeal.

(2) Rule 8.532(a) governs the filing of the decision in the Supreme Court.

(b) Finality of decision in the Court of Appeal

(1) *General finality period*

Except as otherwise provided in this rule, a Court of Appeal decision in a habeas corpus proceeding is final in that court 30 days after filing.

(2) *Denial of a petition for writ of habeas corpus without issuance of an order to show cause*

(A) Except as provided in (B), a Court of Appeal decision denying a petition for writ of habeas corpus without issuance of an order to show cause is final in the Court of Appeal upon filing.

(B) A Court of Appeal decision denying a petition for writ of habeas corpus without issuing an order to show cause is final in that court on the same day that its decision in a related appeal is final if the two decisions are filed on the same day. If the Court of Appeal orders rehearing of the decision in the appeal, its decision denying the petition for writ of habeas corpus is final when its decision on rehearing is final.

(3) *Decision in a habeas corpus proceeding after issuance of an order to show cause*

(A) If necessary to prevent mootness or frustration of the relief granted or to otherwise promote the interests of justice, a Court of Appeal may order early finality in that court of a decision in a habeas corpus proceeding after issuing an order to show cause. The decision may provide for finality in that court on filing or within a stated period of less than 30 days.

(B) If a Court of Appeal certifies its opinion for publication or partial publication after filing its decision and before its decision becomes final in that court, the finality period runs from the filing date of the order for publication.

(c) Finality of decision in the Supreme Court

Rule 8.532(b) governs finality of a decision in the Supreme Court.

(d) Modification of decision

(1) A reviewing court may modify a decision until the decision is final in that court. If the clerk's office is closed on the date of finality, the court may modify the decision on the next day the clerk's office is open.

(2) An order modifying an opinion must state whether it changes the appellate judgment. A modification that does not change the appellate judgment does not extend the finality date of the decision. If a modification changes the appellate judgment, the finality period runs from the filing date of the modification order.

(e) Rehearing

(1) Rule 8.268 governs rehearing in the Court of Appeal.

(2) Rule 8.536 governs rehearing in the Supreme Court.

(f) Remittitur

A Court of Appeal must issue a remittitur in a habeas corpus proceeding under this chapter except when the court denies the petition without issuing an order to show cause or orders the return filed in the superior court. Rule 8.272(b)–(d) governs issuance of a remittitur by a Court of Appeal in habeas corpus proceedings. *(Formerly Rule 8.386, adopted, eff. Jan. 1, 2008. Renumbered Rule 8.387 and amended, eff. Jan. 1, 2009.)*

Advisory Committee Comment

A party may seek review of a Court of Appeal decision in a habeas corpus proceeding by way of a petition for review in the Supreme Court under rule 8.500.

Research References

Rutter, Cal. Practice Guide: Civil Appeals & Writs Ch. 11-G, G. Finality as to Court of Appeal.

Rule 8.388. Appeal from order granting relief by writ of habeas corpus

(a) Application

Except as otherwise provided in this rule, rules 8.304–8.368 and 8.508 govern appeals under Penal Code section 1506 or 1507 from orders granting all or part of the relief sought in a petition for writ of habeas corpus.

(b) Contents of record

In an appeal under this rule, the record must contain:

(1) The petition, the return, and the traverse;

(2) The order to show cause;

(3) All court minutes;

(4) All documents and exhibits submitted to the court;

(5) The reporter's transcript of any oral proceedings;

(6) Any written opinion of the court;

(7) The order appealed from; and

(8) The notice of appeal. *(Formerly Rule 39.2, adopted, eff. Jan. 1, 2005. Renumbered Rule 8.388 and amended, eff. Jan. 1, 2007.)*

Research References

9 Witkin Cal. Proc. 5th Appeal § 9, (S 9) Current Structure.
9 Witkin Cal. Proc. 5th Appeal § 146, Habeas Corpus.
2 Witkin Cal. Proc. 5th Courts § 195, (S 195) Appellate Rules.

Chapter 5

JUVENILE APPEALS AND WRITS

Article 1

GENERAL PROVISIONS

Rule
8.400. Application.
8.401. Confidentiality.

Rule 8.400. Application

The rules in this chapter govern:

(1) Appeals from judgments or appealable orders in:

(A) Cases under Welfare and Institutions Code sections 300, 601, and 602; and

(B) Actions to free a child from parental custody and control under Family Code section 7800 et seq.; and

(2) Writ petitions under Welfare and Institutions Code sections 366.26 and 366.28. *(Formerly Rule 37, adopted, eff. Jan. 1, 2005. As amended, eff. Jan. 1, 2006. Renumbered Rule 8.400 and amended, eff. Jan. 1, 2007. As amended, eff. Jan. 1, 2008; July 1, 2010.)*

Research References

Rutter, Cal. Practice Guide: Civil Appeals & Writs Ch. 3-B, B. Filing Deadlines.
9 Witkin Cal. Proc. 5th Appeal § 9, (S 9) Current Structure.
2 Witkin Cal. Proc. 5th Courts § 195, (S 195) Appellate Rules.
10 Witkin, California Summary 10th Parent and Child § 355, (S 355) Review on Appeal.
10 Witkin, California Summary 10th Parent and Child § 444, Scope and Organization.
10 Witkin, California Summary 10th Parent and Child § 709, in General.
10 Witkin, California Summary 10th Parent and Child § 712, Notice of Appeal.
10 Witkin, California Summary 10th Parent and Child § 716, (S 716) in General.
10 Witkin, California Summary 10th Parent and Child § 895, (S 895) Alternative Felony Misdemeanor.
10 Witkin, California Summary 10th Parent and Child § 918, in General.
10 Witkin, California Summary 10th Parent and Child § 675A, (New) Setting Selection and Implementation Hearing.

Rule 8.401. Confidentiality

(a) References to juveniles or relatives in documents

To protect the anonymity of juveniles involved in juvenile court proceedings:

(1) In all documents filed by the parties in proceedings under this chapter, a juvenile must be referred to by first name and last initial; but if the first name is unusual or other circumstances would defeat the objective of anonymity, the initials of the juvenile may be used.

(2) In opinions that are not certified for publication and in court orders, a juvenile may be referred to either by first name and last initial or by his or her initials. In opinions that are certified for publication in proceedings under this chapter, a juvenile must be referred to by first name and last initial; but if the first name is unusual or other circumstances would defeat the objective of anonymity, the initials of the juvenile may be used.

(3) In all documents filed by the parties and in all court orders and opinions in proceedings under this chapter, if use of the full name of a juvenile's relative would defeat the objective of anonymity for the juvenile, the relative must be referred to by first name and last initial; but if the first name is unusual or other circumstances would defeat the objective of anonymity for the juvenile, the initials of the relative may be used.

(b) Access to filed documents

(1) Except as provided in (2), the record on appeal and documents filed by the parties in proceedings under this chapter may be inspected only by the reviewing court and appellate project personnel, the parties or their attorneys, and other persons the court may designate.

(2) Filed documents that protect anonymity as required by (a) may be inspected by any person or entity that is considering filing an amicus curiae brief.

(c) Access to oral argument

The court may limit or prohibit public admittance to oral argument. *(Adopted, eff. July 1, 2010. As amended, eff. Jan. 1, 2012.)*

Research References

Rutter, Cal. Practice Guide: Civil Appeals & Writs Ch. 9-C, C. Format of Briefs.
9 Witkin Cal. Proc. 5th Appeal § 9, (S 9) Current Structure.
2 Witkin Cal. Proc. 5th Courts § 195, (S 195) Appellate Rules.
10 Witkin, California Summary 10th Parent and Child § 444, Scope and Organization.
10 Witkin, California Summary 10th Parent and Child § 709, in General.

Article 2

APPEALS

Rule 8.403. Right to appointment of appellate counsel and prerequisites for appeal

(a) Welfare and Institutions Code section 601 or 602 proceedings

In appeals of proceedings under Welfare and Institutions Code section 601 or 602, the child is entitled to court-appointed counsel. If the court determines that the parent or guardian can afford counsel but has not retained counsel for the child, the court must appoint counsel for the child at the expense of the parent or guardian.

(b) Welfare and Institutions Code section 300 proceedings

(1) Any judgment, order, or decree setting a hearing under Welfare and Institutions Code section 366.26 may be reviewed on appeal following the order at the Welfare and Institutions Code section 366.26 hearing only if:

(A) The procedures in rules 8.450 and 8.452 regarding writ petitions in these cases have been followed; and

(B) The petition for an extraordinary writ was summarily denied or otherwise not decided on the merits.

(2) The reviewing court may appoint counsel to represent an indigent child, parent, or guardian.

(3) Rule 5.661 governs the responsibilities of trial counsel in Welfare and Institutions Code section 300 proceedings with regard to appellate representation of the child. *(Adopted, eff. July 1, 2010. As amended, eff. Jan. 1, 2013.)*

Advisory Committee Comment

The right to appeal in Welfare and Institutions Code section 601 or 602 (juvenile delinquency) cases is established by Welfare and Institutions Code section 800 and case law (see, for example, *In re Michael S.* (2007) 147 Cal.App.4th 1443, *In re Jeffrey M.* (2006) 141 Cal.App.4th 1017 and *In re Sean R.* (1989) 214 Cal.App.3d 662). The right to appeal in Welfare and Institutions Code section 300 (juvenile dependency) cases is established by Welfare and Institutions Code section 395 and case law (see, for example, *In re Aaron R.* (2005) 130 Cal.App.4th 697, and *In re Merrick V.* (2004) 122 Cal.App.4th 235).

Subdivision (b)(1). Welfare and Institutions Code section 366.26(*l*) establishes important limitations on appeals of judgments, orders, or decrees setting a hearing under section 366.26, including requirements for the filing of a petition for an extraordinary writ and limitations on the issues that can be raised on appeal.

Research References

Rutter, Cal. Practice Guide: Civil Appeals & Writs Ch. 1-G, G. Retaining an Appellate Specialist.
Rutter, Cal. Practice Guide: Civil Appeals & Writs Ch. 2-B, B. Appealable Judgments and Orders.
Rutter, Cal. Practice Guide: Civil Appeals & Writs Ch. 15-C, C. Statutory Writs.
Rutter, Cal. Practice Guide: Prof. Responsibility Ch. 8-B, B. Accepting or Rejecting Employment.
9 Witkin Cal. Proc. 5th Appeal § 9, (S 9) Current Structure.
2 Witkin Cal. Proc. 5th Courts § 195, (S 195) Appellate Rules.
10 Witkin, California Summary 10th Parent and Child § 444, Scope and Organization.
10 Witkin, California Summary 10th Parent and Child § 701, in General.
10 Witkin, California Summary 10th Parent and Child § 708, (S 708) Counsel on Appeal.
10 Witkin, California Summary 10th Parent and Child § 913, (S 913) Minor's Right to Appeal.

Rule 8.404. Stay pending appeal

The court must not stay an order or judgment pending an appeal unless suitable provision is made for the maintenance, care, and custody of the child. *(Adopted, eff. July 1, 2010.)*

Research References

Rutter, Cal. Practice Guide: Civil Appeals & Writs Ch. 7-A, A. Overview.

Rutter, Cal. Practice Guide: Civil Appeals & Writs Ch. 7-D, D. Discretionary Stay by Trial Court.

10 Witkin, California Summary 10th Parent and Child § 709, in General.

10 Witkin, California Summary 10th Parent and Child § 713, in General.

10 Witkin, California Summary 10th Parent and Child § 721, Record.

10 Witkin, California Summary 10th Parent and Child § 725, Notice of Intent and Record.

10 Witkin, California Summary 10th Parent and Child § 919, Record on Appeal.

Rule 8.405.   Filing the appeal

(a) Notice of appeal

(1) To appeal from a judgment or appealable order under these rules, the appellant must file a notice of appeal in the superior court. Any notice of appeal on behalf of the child in a Welfare and Institutions Code section 300 proceeding must be authorized by the child or the child's CAPTA guardian ad litem.

(2) The appellant or the appellant's attorney must sign the notice of appeal.

(3) The notice of appeal must be liberally construed, and is sufficient if it identifies the particular judgment or order being appealed. The notice need not specify the court to which the appeal is taken; the appeal will be treated as taken to the Court of Appeal for the district in which the superior court is located.

(b) Superior court clerk's duties

(1) When a notice of appeal is filed, the superior court clerk must immediately:

(A) Mail a notification of the filing to:

(i) Each party other than the appellant, including the child if the child is 10 years of age or older;

(ii) The attorney of record for each party;

(iii) Any person currently awarded by the juvenile court the status of the child's de facto parent;

(iv) Any Court Appointed Special Advocate (CASA) volunteer;

(v) If the court knows or has reason to know that an Indian child is involved, the Indian custodian, if any, and tribe of the child or the Bureau of Indian Affairs, as required under Welfare and Institutions Code section 224.2; and

(vi) The reviewing court clerk; and

(B) Notify the reporter by telephone and in writing to prepare a reporter's transcript and deliver it to the clerk within 20 days after the notice of appeal is filed.

(2) The notification must show the name of the appellant, the date it was mailed, the number and title of the case, and the date the notice of appeal was filed. If the information is available, the notification must also include:

(A) The name, address, telephone number, and California State Bar number of each attorney of record in the case;

(B) The name of the party that each attorney represented in the superior court; and

(C) The name, address, and telephone number of any unrepresented party.

(3) The notification to the reviewing court clerk must also include a copy of the notice of appeal and any sequential list of reporters made under rule 2.950.

(4) A copy of the notice of appeal is sufficient notification if the required information is on the copy or is added by the superior court clerk.

(5) The mailing of a notification is a sufficient performance of the clerk's duty despite the discharge, disqualification, suspension, disbarment, or death of the attorney.

(6) Failure to comply with any provision of this subdivision does not affect the validity of the notice of appeal. *(Adopted, eff. July 1, 2010.)*

Advisory Committee Comment

Subdivision (a). *Notice of Appeal—Juvenile (California Rules of Court, Rule 8.400)* (form JV–800) may be used to file the notice of appeal required under this rule. This form is available at any courthouse or county law library or online at *www. courtinfo.ca.gov/forms.*

Research References

Rutter, Cal. Practice Guide: Civil Appeals & Writs Ch. 3-E, E. Filing Steps.

Rutter, Cal. Practice Guide: Civil Appeals & Writs Ch. 3-F, F. Cross-Appeals.

10 Witkin, California Summary 10th Parent and Child § 712, Notice of Appeal.

Rule 8.406.   Time to appeal

(a) Normal time

(1) Except as provided in (2) and (3), a notice of appeal must be filed within 60 days after the rendition of the judgment or the making of the order being appealed.

(2) In matters heard by a referee not acting as a temporary judge, a notice of appeal must be filed within 60 days after the referee's order becomes final under rule 5.540(c).

(3) When an application for rehearing of an order of a referee not acting as a temporary judge is denied under rule 5.542, a notice of appeal from the referee's order must be filed within 60 days after that order is served under rule 5.538(b)(3) or 30 days after entry of the order denying rehearing, whichever is later.

(b) Cross-appeal

If an appellant timely appeals from a judgment or appealable order, the time for any other party to appeal from the same judgment or order is either the time specified in (a) or 20 days after the superior court clerk mails notification of the first appeal, whichever is later.

(c) No extension of time; late notice of appeal

Except as provided in rule 8.66, no court may extend the time to file a notice of appeal. The superior court clerk must mark a late notice of appeal "Received [date] but not filed," notify the party that the notice was not filed because it was late, and send a copy of the marked notice of appeal to the district appellate project.

(d) Premature notice of appeal

A notice of appeal is premature if filed before the judgment is rendered or the order is made, but the reviewing court may treat the notice as filed immediately after the rendition of judgment or the making of the order. *(Adopted, eff. July 1, 2010. As amended, eff. July 1, 2010.)*

Advisory Committee Comment

Subdivision (c). See rule 8.25(b)(5) for provisions concerning the timeliness of documents mailed by inmates or patients from custodial institutions.

Rule 8.407. Record on appeal

(a) Normal record: clerk's transcript

The clerk's transcript must contain:

(1) The petition;

(2) Any notice of hearing;

(3) All court minutes;

(4) Any report or other document submitted to the court;

(5) The jurisdictional and dispositional findings and orders;

(6) The judgment or order appealed from;

(7) Any application for rehearing;

(8) The notice of appeal and any order pursuant to the notice;

(9) Any transcript of a sound or sound-and-video recording tendered to the court under rule 2.1040;

(10) Any application for additional record and any order on the application;

(11) Any opinion or dispositive order of a reviewing court in the same case   and;

(12) Any written motion or notice of motion by any party, with supporting and opposing memoranda and attachments, and any written opinion of the court.

(b) Normal record: reporter's transcript

The reporter's transcript must contain:

(1) Except as provided in (2), the oral proceedings at any hearing that resulted in the order or judgment being appealed;

(2) In appeals from dispositional orders, the oral proceedings at hearings on

(A) Jurisdiction and disposition; and

(B) Any motion by the appellant that was denied in whole or in part; and

(3) Any oral opinion of the court.

(c) Application in superior court for addition to normal record

(1) Any party or Indian tribe that has intervened in the proceedings may apply to the superior court for inclusion of any oral proceedings in the

reporter's transcript.

(2) An application for additional record must describe the material to be included and explain how it may be useful in the appeal.

(3) The application must be filed in the superior court with the notice of appeal or as soon thereafter as possible, and will be treated as denied if it is filed after the record is sent to the reviewing court.

(4) The clerk must immediately present the application to the trial judge.

(5) Within five days after the application if filed, the judge must order that the record include as much of the additional material as the judge finds proper to fully present the points raised by the applicant. Denial of the application does not preclude a motion in the reviewing court for augmentation under rule 8.155.

(6) If the judge does not rule on the application within the time prescribed by (5), the requested material-other than exhibits-must be included in the clerk's transcript or the reporter's transcript without a court order.

(7) The clerk must immediately notify the reporter if additions to the reporter's transcript are required under (5) or (6).

(d) Agreed or settled statement

To proceed by agreed or settled statement, the parties must comply with rule 8.344 or 8.346, as applicable.

(e) Form of record

Except in cases governed by rule 8.416(b), the clerk's and reporter's transcripts must comply with rule 8.144.

(f) Transmitting exhibits

Exhibits that were admitted in evidence, refused, or lodged may be transmitted to the reviewing court as provided in rule 8.224. *(Formerly Rule 37.1, adopted, eff. Jan. 1, 2005. Renumbered Rule 8.404 and amended, eff. Jan. 1, 2007. Renumbered Rule 8.407 and amended, eff. July 1, 2010.)*

Advisory Committee Comment

Subdivision (b). Subdivision (b)(1) provides that only the reporter's transcript of a hearing that resulted in the order being appealed must be included in the normal record. This provision is intended to achieve consistent record requirements in all appeals of cases under Welfare and Institutions Code section 300, 601, or 602 and to reduce the delays and expense caused by transcribing proceedings not necessary to the appeal.

Subdivision (b)(2)(A) recognizes that findings made in a jurisdictional hearing are not separately appealable and can be challenged only in an appeal from the ensuing dispositional order. The rule therefore specifically provides that a reporter's transcript of jurisdictional proceedings must be included in the normal record on appeal from a dispositional order.

Subdivision (b)(2)(B) specifies that the oral proceedings on any motion by the appellant that was denied in whole or in part must be included in the normal record on appeal from a disposition order. Rulings on such motions usually have some impact on either the jurisdictional findings or the subsequent disposition order. Routine inclusion of these proceedings in the record will promote expeditious resolution of appeals of cases under Welfare and Institutions Code section 300, 601, or 602.

Rule 8.408. Record in multiple appeals in the same case

If more than one appeal is taken from the same judgment or related order, only one appellate record need be prepared, which must be filed within the time allowed for filing the record in the latest appeal. *(Formerly Rule 8.406, adopted, eff. Jan. 1, 2007. Renumbered Rule 8.408, eff. July 1, 2010.)*

Research References

10 Witkin, California Summary 10th Parent and Child § 713, in General.

10 Witkin, California Summary 10th Parent and Child § 714, Preparing and Sending Record.

10 Witkin, California Summary 10th Parent and Child § 919, Record on Appeal.

Rule 8.409.   Preparing and sending the record

(a) Application

Except as provided in 8.416(c)(1), this rule does not apply to cases under rule 8.416.

(b) Preparing and certifying the transcripts

Within 20 days after the notice of appeal is filed:

(1) The clerk must prepare and certify as correct an original of the clerk's transcript and sufficient copies to comply with (d); and

(2) The reporter must prepare, certify as correct, and deliver to the clerk an original of the reporter's transcript and the same number of copies as (1) requires of the clerk's transcript.

(c) Extension of time

(1) The superior court may not extend the time to prepare the record.

(2) The reviewing court may order one or more extensions of time, not exceeding a total of 60 days, on receipt of:

(A) A declaration showing good cause; and

(B) In the case of a reporter's transcript, certification by the superior court presiding judge, or a court administrator designated by the presiding judge, that an extension is reasonable and necessary in light of the workload of all reporters in the court.

(d) Sending the record

(1) When the transcripts are certified as correct, the superior court clerk must immediately send:

(A) The original transcripts to the reviewing court, noting the sending date on each original; and

(B) One copy of each transcript to the appellate counsel for the appellant, the respondent, the minor, and the minor's Indian tribe if the tribe has intervened.

(2) If appellate counsel has not yet been retained or appointed for the appellant, the respondent, or the minor when the transcripts are certified as correct, the clerk must send that counsel's copy of the transcripts to the district appellate project. If a tribe that has intervened is not represented by counsel when the transcripts are certified as correct, the clerk must send that counsel's copy of the transcripts to the tribe.

(3) The clerk must not send a copy of the transcripts to the Attorney General or the district attorney unless that office represents a party. *(Formerly Rule 37.2, adopted, eff. Jan. 1, 2005. Renumbered Rule 8.408 and amended, eff. Jan. 1, 2007. Renumbered Rule 8.409 and amended, eff. July 1, 2010. As amended, eff. Jan. 1, 2013.)*

Advisory Committee Comment

Subdivision (a).   Subdivision (a) calls litigants' attention to the fact that a different rule (rule 8.416) governs *sending* the record in appeals from judgments or orders terminating parental rights and in dependency appeals in certain counties. Rule 8.408(b) governs *preparing and certifying* the record in those appeals. (See rule 8.416(c)(1) ["The record must be prepared and certified as provided in rule 8.409(b)"].)

Subdivision (d).   Subsection (1)(B) clarifies that when a minor's Indian tribe has intervened in the proceedings, the tribe is a party who must receive a copy of the appellate record. The

statutes that require notices to be sent to a tribe by registered or certified mail return receipt requested and generally be addressed to the tribal chairperson (25 U.S.C. 1912 (a), 25 C.F.R. 23.11 and Welf. & Inst. Code, § 224.2) do not apply to the sending of the appellate record.

Research References

Rutter, Cal. Practice Guide: Civil Appeals & Writs Ch. 4-C, C. Record Preparation Procedure.

Rutter, Cal. Practice Guide: Civil Appeals & Writs Ch. 4-F, F. Extensions of Time and Default.

Rutter, Cal. Practice Guide: Civil Appeals & Writs Ch. 4-G, G. Augmentation of the Record.

Rutter, Cal. Practice Guide: Civil Appeals & Writs Ch. 5-B, B. Types of Motions, Applications and Requests.

10 Witkin, California Summary 10th Parent and Child § 713, in General.

10 Witkin, California Summary 10th Parent and Child § 714, Preparing and Sending Record.

10 Witkin, California Summary 10th Parent and Child § 919, Record on Appeal.

Rule 8.410.   Augmenting and correcting the record in the reviewing court

(a) Omissions

If, after the record is certified, the superior court clerk or the reporter learns that the record omits a document or transcript that any rule or order requires to be included, without the need for a motion or court order, the clerk must promptly copy and certify the document or the reporter must promptly prepare and certify the transcript and the clerk must promptly send the document or transcript—as an augmentation of the record—to all those who are listed under 8.409(d).

(b) Augmentation or correction by the reviewing court

(1) On motion of a party or on its own motion, the reviewing court may order the record augmented or corrected as provided in rule 8.155(a) and (c).

(2) If, after the record is certified, the trial court amends or recalls the judgment or makes any other order in the case, the trial court clerk must notify each entity and person to whom the record is sent under rule 8.409(d). *(Adopted, eff. July 1, 2010.)*

Research References

Rutter, Cal. Practice Guide: Civil Appeals & Writs Ch. 4-E, E. Filing and Correction of Record.

Rutter, Cal. Practice Guide: Civil Appeals & Writs Ch. 4-G, G. Augmentation of the Record.

Rutter, Cal. Practice Guide: Civil Appeals & Writs Ch. 5-B, B. Types of Motions, Applications and Requests.

Rutter, Cal. Practice Guide: Civil Appeals & Writs Ch. 15-C, C. Statutory Writs.

10 Witkin, California Summary 10th Parent and Child § 713, in General.

10 Witkin, California Summary 10th Parent and Child § 721, Record.

10 Witkin, California Summary 10th Parent and Child § 725, Notice of Intent and Record.

Rule 8.411.   Abandoning the appeal

(a) How to abandon

An appellant may abandon the appeal at any time by filing an abandonment of the appeal. The abandonment must be authorized by the appellant and signed by either the appellant or the appellant's attorney of record. In a Welfare and Institutions Code section 300 proceeding in which the child is the appellant, the abandonment must be authorized by the child or, if the child is not capable of giving authorization, by the child's CAPTA guardian ad litem.

(b) Where to file; effect of filing

(1) If the record has not been filed in the reviewing court, the appellant must file the abandonment in the superior court. The filing effects a dismissal of the appeal and restores the superior court's jurisdiction.

(2) If the record has been filed in the reviewing court, the appellant must file the abandonment in that court. The reviewing court may dismiss the appeal and direct immediate issuance of the remittitur.

(c) Clerk's duties

(1) If the abandonment is filed in the superior court, the clerk must immediately mail a notification of the abandonment to:

(A) Every other party;

(B) The reviewing court; and

(C) The reporter if the appeal is abandoned before the reporter has filed the transcript.

(2) If the abandonment is filed in the reviewing court and the reviewing court orders the appeal dismissed, the clerk must immediately mail a notification of the order of dismissal to every party. *(Adopted, eff. July 1, 2010.)*

Advisory Committee Comment

The Supreme Court has held that appellate counsel for an appealing minor has the power to move to dismiss a dependency appeal based on counsel's assessment of the child's best interests, but that the motion to dismiss requires the authorization of the child or, if the child is incapable of giving authorization, the authorization of the child's CAPTA guardian ad litem *(In re Josiah Z.* (2005) 36 Cal.4th 664).

Research References

Rutter, Cal. Practice Guide: Civil Appeals & Writs Ch. 5-B, B. Types of Motions, Applications and Requests.
10 Witkin, California Summary 10th Parent and Child § 715A, (S 715A) (New)-Abandoning Appeal.
10 Witkin, California Summary 10th Parent and Child § 919A, (New)-Abandoning Appeal.

Rule 8.412. Briefs by parties and amici curiae

(a) Contents, form, and length

(1) Rule 8.200 governs the briefs that may be filed by parties and amici curiae.

(2) Except as provided in (3), rule 8.204 governs the form and contents of briefs. Rule 8.216 also applies in appeals in which a party is both appellant and respondent.

(3) Rule 8.360(b) governs the length of briefs.

(b) Time to file

(1) Except in appeals governed by rule 8.416, the appellant must serve and file the appellant's opening brief within 40 days after the record is filed in the reviewing court.

(2) The respondent must serve and file the respondent's brief within 30 days after the appellant's opening brief is filed.

(3) The appellant must serve and file any reply brief within 20 days after the respondent's brief is filed.

(4) In dependency cases in which the child is not an appellant but has appellate counsel, the child must serve and file any brief within 10 days after the respondent's brief is filed.

(5) Rule 8.220 applies if a party fails to timely file an appellant's opening brief or a respondent's brief, but the period specified in the notice required by that rule must be 30 days.

(c) Extensions of time

The superior court may not order any extensions of time to file briefs. Except in appeals governed by rule 8.416, the reviewing court may order extensions of time for good cause.

(d) Failure to file a brief

(1) Except in appeals governed by rule 8.416, if a party fails to timely file an appellant's opening brief or a respondent's brief, the reviewing court clerk must promptly notify the party's counsel or the party, if not represented, by mail that the brief must be filed within 30 days after the notice is mailed and that failure to comply may result in one of the following sanctions:

(A) If the brief is an appellant's opening brief:

(i) If the appellant is the county, the court will dismiss the appeal;

(ii) If the appellant is other than the county and is represented by appointed counsel on appeal, the court will relieve that appointed counsel and appoint new counsel;

(iii) If the appellant is other than the county and is not represented by appointed counsel, the court will dismiss the appeal.

(B) If the brief is a respondent's brief, the court will decide the appeal on the record, the opening brief, and any oral argument by the appellant.

(2) If a party fails to comply with a notice under (1), the court may impose the sanction specified in the notice.

(3) Within the period specified in the notice under (1), a party may apply to the presiding justice for an extension of that period for good cause. If an extension is granted beyond the 30-day period and the brief is not filed within the extended period, the court may impose the sanction under (2) without further notice.

(e) Additional service requirements

(1) A copy of each brief must be served on the superior court clerk for delivery to the superior court judge.

(2) A copy of each brief must be served on the child's trial counsel, or, if the child is not represented by trial counsel, on the child's guardian ad litem appointed under rule 5.662.

(3) If the Court of Appeal has appointed counsel for any party:

(A) The county child welfare department and the People must serve two copies of their briefs on that counsel; and

(B) Each party must serve a copy of its brief on the district appellate project.

(4) In delinquency cases the parties must serve copies of their briefs on the Attorney General and the district attorney. In all other cases the parties must not serve copies of their briefs on the Attorney General or the district attorney unless that office represents a party.

(5) The parties must not serve copies of their briefs on the Supreme Court under rule 8.44(b)(1). *(Formerly Rule 37.3, adopted, eff. Jan. 1, 2005. Renumbered Rule 8.412 and amended, eff. Jan. 1, 2007. As amended, eff. July 1, 2007; July 1, 2010.)*

Advisory Committee Comment

Subdivision (b). Subdivision (b)(1) calls litigants' attention to the fact that a different rule (rule 8.416(e)) governs the time to file an appellant's opening brief in appeals from judgments or orders terminating parental rights and in dependency appeals in certain counties.

Subdivision (c). Subdivision (c) calls litigants' attention to the fact that a different rule (rule 8.416(f)) governs the showing required for extensions of time to file briefs in appeals from judgments or orders terminating parental rights and in dependency appeals in certain counties.

Research References

Rutter, Cal. Practice Guide: Civil Appeals & Writs Ch. 9-D, D. Procedural Rules.
10 Witkin, California Summary 10th Parent and Child § 711, Expedited Appeal.

Ct. Rules

10 Witkin, California Summary 10th Parent and Child § 715, (S 715) Briefs.

Rule 8.416. Appeals from all terminations of parental rights; dependency appeals in Orange, Imperial, and San Diego Counties and in other counties by local rule

(a) Application

(1) This rule governs:

(A) Appeals from judgments or appealable orders of all superior courts terminating parental rights under Welfare and Institutions Code section 366.26 or freeing a child from parental custody and control under Family Code section 7800 et seq.; and

(B) Appeals from judgments or appealable orders in all juvenile dependency cases of:

(i) The Superior Courts of Orange, Imperial, and San Diego Counties; and

(ii) Other superior courts when the superior court and the District Court of Appeal with jurisdiction to hear appeals from that superior court have agreed and have adopted local rules providing that this rule will govern appeals from that superior court.

(2) In all respects not provided for in this rule, rules 8.403–8.412 apply.

(b) Cover of record

(1) In appeals under (a)(1)(A), the cover of the record must prominently display the title "Appeal From [Judgment or Order] Terminating Parental Rights Under [Welfare and Institutions Code Section 366.26 or Family Code Section 7800 et seq.]," whichever is appropriate.

(2) In appeals under (a)(1)(B), the cover of the record must prominently display the title "Appeal From [Judgment or Order] Under [Welfare and Institutions Code Section 300 et seq. or Family Code Section 7800 et seq.]," whichever is appropriate.

(c) Preparing, certifying, and sending the record

(1) The record must be prepared and certified as provided in rule 8.409(b).

(2) When the clerk's and reporter's transcripts are certified as correct, the clerk must immediately send:

(A) The original transcripts to the reviewing court by the most expeditious method, noting the sending date on each original; and

(B) One copy of each transcript to the attorneys of record for the appellant, the respondent, and the child, and to the district appellate project, by any method as fast as United States Postal Service express mail.

(3) If appellate counsel has not yet been retained or appointed when the transcripts are certified as correct, the clerk must send that counsel's copies of the transcripts to the district appellate project.

(d) Augmenting or correcting the record

(1) Except as provided in (2) and (3), rule 8.410 governs any augmentation or correction of the record.

(2) An appellant must serve and file any motion for augmentation or correction within 15 days after receiving the record. A respondent must serve and file any such motion within 15 days after the appellant's opening brief is filed.

(3) The clerk and the reporter must prepare any supplemental transcripts within 20 days, giving them the highest priority.

(4) The clerk must certify and send any supplemental transcripts as required by (c).

(e) Time to file briefs

(1) To permit determination of the appeal within 250 days after the notice of appeal is filed, the appellant must serve and file the appellant's opening brief within 30 days after the record is filed in the reviewing court.

(2) Rule 8.412(b) governs the time for filing other briefs.

(f) Extensions of time

The superior court may not order any extensions of time to prepare the record or to file briefs; the reviewing court may order extensions of time, but must require an exceptional showing of good cause.

(g) Failure to file a brief

Rule 8.412(d) applies if a party fails to timely file an appellant's opening brief or a respondent's brief, but the period specified in the notice required by that rule must be 15 days.

(h) Oral argument and submission of the cause

(1) Unless the reviewing court orders otherwise, counsel must serve and file any request for oral argument no later than 15 days after the appellant's reply brief is filed or due to be filed. Failure to file a timely request will be deemed a waiver.

(2) The court must hear oral argument within 60 days after the appellant's last reply brief is filed or due to be filed, unless the court extends the time for good cause or counsel waive argument.

(3) If counsel waive argument, the cause is deemed submitted no later than 60 days after the appellant's reply brief is filed or due to be filed. *(Formerly Rule 37.4, adopted, eff. Jan. 1, 2005. Renumbered Rule 8.416 and amended, eff. Jan. 1, 2007. As amended, eff. July 1, 2010.)*

Advisory Committee Comment

Subdivision (g). Effective January 1, 2007, revised rule 8.416 incorporates a new subdivision (g) to address a failure to timely file a brief in all termination of parental rights cases and in dependency appeals in Orange, Imperial, and San Diego Counties. Under the new subdivision, appellants would not have the full 30–day grace period given in rule 8.412(d) in which to file a late brief, but instead would have the standard 15–day grace period that is given in civil cases. The intent of this revision is to balance the need to determine the appeal within 250 days with the need to protect appellants' rights in this most serious of appeals.

Subdivision (h). Subdivision (h)(1) recognizes certain reviewing courts' practice of requiring counsel to file any request for oral argument within a time period other than 15 days after the appellant's reply brief is filed or due to be filed. The reviewing court is still expected to determine the appeal "within 250 days after the notice of appeal is filed." (*Id.*, subd. (e).)

Research References

Rutter, Cal. Practice Guide: Civil Appeals & Writs Ch. 2-B, B. Appealable Judgments and Orders.

Rutter, Cal. Practice Guide: Civil Appeals & Writs Ch. 4-C, C. Record Preparation Procedure.

Rutter, Cal. Practice Guide: Civil Appeals & Writs Ch. 4-F, F. Extensions of Time and Default.

Rutter, Cal. Practice Guide: Civil Appeals & Writs Ch. 4-G, G. Augmentation of the Record.

Rutter, Cal. Practice Guide: Civil Appeals & Writs Ch. 5-B, B. Types of Motions, Applications and Requests.

Rutter, Cal. Practice Guide: Civil Appeals & Writs Ch. 9-D, D. Procedural Rules.

Rutter, Cal. Practice Guide: Civil Appeals & Writs Ch. 10-B, B. Oral Argument Procedure.

9 Witkin Cal. Proc. 5th Appeal § 9, (S 9) Current Structure.

2 Witkin Cal. Proc. 5th Courts § 195, (S 195) Appellate Rules.

10 Witkin, California Summary 10th Parent and Child § 444, Scope and Organization.

10 Witkin, California Summary 10th Parent and Child § 531, Determining Adequacy of Notice.

10 Witkin, California Summary 10th Parent and Child § 711, Expedited Appeal.

10 Witkin, California Summary 10th Parent and Child § 713, in General.

10 Witkin, California Summary 10th Parent and Child § 715, (S 715) Briefs.

10 Witkin, California Summary 10th Parent and Child § 675A, (New)-Setting Selection and Implementation Hearing.

Article 3

WRITS

Rule

8.450. Notice of intent to file writ petition to review order setting hearing under Welfare and Institutions Code section 366.26.

8.452. Writ petition to review order setting hearing under Welfare and Institutions Code section 366.26 .

8.454. Notice of intent to file writ petition under Welfare and Institutions Code section 366.28 to review order designating specific placement of a dependent child after termination of parental rights.

8.456. Writ petition under Welfare and Institutions Code section 366.28 to review order designating or denying specific placement of a dependent child after termination of parental rights.

Rule 8.450. Notice of intent to file writ petition to review order setting hearing under Welfare and Institutions Code section 366.26

(a) Application

Rules 8.450–8.452 and 8.490 govern writ petitions to review orders setting a hearing under Welfare and Institutions Code section 366.26.

(b) Purpose

Rules 8.450–8.452 are intended to encourage and assist the reviewing courts to determine on their merits all writ petitions filed under these rules within the 120–day period for holding a hearing under Welfare and Institutions Code section 366.26.

(c) Who may file

The petitioner's trial counsel, or in the absence of trial counsel, the party, is responsible for filing any notice of intent and writ petition under rules 8.450–8.452. Trial counsel is encouraged to seek assistance from or consult with attorneys experienced in writ procedure.

(d) Extensions of time

The superior court may not extend any time period prescribed by rules 8.450–8.452. The reviewing court may extend any time period but must require an exceptional showing of good cause.

(e) Notice of intent

(1) A party seeking writ review under rules 8.450–8.452 must file in the superior court a notice of intent to file a writ petition and a request for the record.

(2) The notice must include all known dates of the hearing that resulted in the order under review.

(3) The notice must be authorized by the party intending to file the petition and must be signed by that party or by the attorney of record for that party.

(4) The date of the order setting the hearing is the date on which the court states the order on the record orally, or issues an order in writing, whichever occurs first. The notice of intent must be filed according to the following timeline requirements:

(A) If the party was present at the hearing when the court ordered a hearing under Welfare and Institutions Code section 366.26, the notice of intent must be filed within 7 days after the date of the order setting the hearing.

(B) If the party was notified of the order setting the hearing only by mail, the notice of intent must be filed within 12 days after the date the clerk mailed the notification.

(C) If the party was notified of the order setting the hearing by mail, and the notice was mailed to an address outside California but within the United States, the notice of intent must be filed within 17 days after the date the clerk mailed the notification.

(D) If the party was notified of the order setting the hearing by mail, and the notice was mailed to an address outside the United States, the notice of intent must be filed within 27 days after the date the clerk mailed the notification.

(E) If the order was made by a referee not acting as a temporary judge, the party has an additional 10 days to file the notice of intent as provided in rule 5.540(c).

(f) Premature or late notice of intent to file writ petition

(1) A notice of intent to file a writ petition under Welfare and Institutions Code section 366.26 is premature if filed before an order setting a hearing under Welfare and Institutions Code section 366.26 has been made.

(2) If a notice of intent is premature or late, the superior court clerk must promptly:

(A) Mark the notice of intent "Received [date] but not filed;"

(B) Return the marked notice of intent to the party with a notice stating that:

(i) The notice of intent was not filed either because it is premature, as no order setting a hearing under Welfare and Institutions Code section 366.26 has been made, or because it is late; and

(ii) The party should contact his or her attorney as soon as possible to discuss this notice, because the time available to take appropriate steps to protect the party's interests may be short; and

(C) Send a copy of the marked notice of intent and clerk's notice to the party's counsel of record, if applicable.

(f)(g) Sending the notice of intent

(1) When the notice of intent is filed, the superior court clerk must immediately mail a copy of the notice to:

(A) The attorney of record for each party;

(B) Each party, including the child if the child is 10 years of age or older;

(C) Any known sibling of the child who is the subject of the hearing if that sibling either is the subject of a dependency proceeding or has been adjudged to be a dependent child of the juvenile court as follows:

(i) If the sibling is under 10 years of age, on the sibling's attorney;

(ii) If the sibling is 10 years of age or over, on the sibling and the sibling's attorney.

(D) The mother, the father, and any presumed and alleged parents;

(E) The child's legal guardian, if any;

(F) Any person currently awarded by the juvenile court the status of the child's de facto parent;

(G) The probation officer or social worker;

(H) Any Court Appointed Special Advocate (CASA) volunteer;

Ct. Rules

(I) The grandparents of the child, if their address is known and if the parents' whereabouts are unknown; and

(J) If the court knows or has reason to know that an Indian child is involved, the Indian custodian, if any, and tribe of the child or the Bureau of Indian Affairs as required under Welfare and Institutions Code section 224.2.

(2) The clerk must promptly send by first-class mail or fax a copy of the notice of intent and a list of those to whom the notice of intent was sent to:

(A) The reviewing court; and

(B) The petitioner if the clerk mailed the notice of intent to the Indian custodian, tribe of the child, or the Bureau of Indian Affairs.

(3) If the party was notified of the order setting the hearing only by mail, the clerk must include the date that the notification was mailed.

(g)(h) Preparing the record

When the notice of intent is filed, the superior court clerk must:

(1) Immediately notify each court reporter by telephone and in writing to prepare a reporter's transcript of the oral proceedings at each session of the hearing that resulted in the order under review and deliver the transcript to the clerk within 12 calendar days after the notice of intent is filed; and

(2) Within 20 days after the notice of intent is filed, prepare a clerk's transcript that includes the notice of intent, proof of service, and all items listed in rule 8.404 8.407(a).

(h)(i) Sending the record

When the transcripts are certified as correct, the superior court clerk must immediately send:

(1) The original transcripts to the reviewing court by the most expeditious method, noting the sending date on each original, and

(2) One copy of each transcript to each counsel of record and any unrepresented party by any means as fast as United States Postal Service express mail.

(i)(j) Reviewing court clerk's duties

(1) The reviewing court clerk must immediately lodge the notice of intent. When the notice is lodged, the reviewing court has jurisdiction of the writ proceedings.

(2) When the record is filed in the reviewing court, that court's clerk must immediately notify the parties, stating the date on which the 10–day period for filing the writ petition under rule 8.452(c)(1) will expire. *(Formerly Rule 38, adopted, eff. Jan. 1, 2005. As amended, eff. Jan. 1, 2006; July 1, 2006. Renumbered Rule 8.450 and amended, eff. Jan. 1, 2007. As amended, eff. Jan. 1, 2008; Jan. 1, 2009; July 1, 2010; Jan. 1, 2013.)*

Advisory Committee Comment

Subdivision (d). The case law generally recognizes that the reviewing courts may grant extensions of time under these rules for exceptional good cause. (See, e.g., *Jonathan M. v. Superior Court* (1995) 39 Cal.App.4th 1826, and *In re Cathina W.* (1998) 68 Cal.App.4th 716 [recognizing that a late notice of intent may be filed on a showing of exceptional circumstances not under the petitioner's control].) It may constitute exceptional good cause for an extension of the time to file a notice of intent if a premature notice of intent is returned to a party shortly before the issuance of an order setting a hearing under Welfare and Institutions Code section 366.26.

Subdivision (e)(4). See rule 8.25(b)(5) for provisions concerning the timeliness of documents mailed by inmates or patients from custodial institutions.

Subdivision (f)(1). A party who prematurely attempts to file a notice of intent to file a writ petition under Welfare and Institutions Code section 366.26 is not precluded from later filing such a notice after the issuance of an order setting a hearing under Welfare and Institutions Code section 366.26.

Research References

Rutter, Cal. Practice Guide: Civil Appeals & Writs Ch. 2-B, B. Appealable Judgments and Orders.

Rutter, Cal. Practice Guide: Civil Appeals & Writs Ch. 4-I, I. Special Rules for Record on Certain Appeals.

Rutter, Cal. Practice Guide: Civil Appeals & Writs Ch. 15-C, C. Statutory Writs.

9 Witkin Cal. Proc. 5th Appeal § 9, (S 9) Current Structure.

2 Witkin Cal. Proc. 5th Courts § 195, (S 195) Appellate Rules.

8 Witkin Cal. Proc. 5th Extraordinary Writs § 15, (S 15) Juvenile Court Orders Terminating Parental Rights.

8 Witkin Cal. Proc. 5th Extraordinary Writs § 185, (S 185) Summary Determination.

10 Witkin, California Summary 10th Parent and Child § 444, Scope and Organization.

10 Witkin, California Summary 10th Parent and Child § 701, in General.

10 Witkin, California Summary 10th Parent and Child § 705, in General.

10 Witkin, California Summary 10th Parent and Child § 716, (S 716) in General.

10 Witkin, California Summary 10th Parent and Child § 717, in General.

10 Witkin, California Summary 10th Parent and Child § 720, Notice of Intent.

10 Witkin, California Summary 10th Parent and Child § 721, Record.

10 Witkin, California Summary 10th Parent and Child § 722, Writ Petition and Response.

10 Witkin, California Summary 10th Parent and Child § 725, Notice of Intent and Record.

10 Witkin, California Summary 10th Parent and Child § 920, (S 920) Review by Extraordinary Writ.

Rule 8.452. Writ petition to review order setting hearing under Welfare and Institutions Code section 366.26

(a) Petition

(1) The petition must be liberally construed and must include:

(A) The identities of the parties;

(B) The date on which the superior court made the order setting the hearing;

(C) The date on which the hearing is scheduled to be held;

(D) A summary of the grounds of the petition; and

(E) The relief requested.

(2) The petition must be accompanied by a memorandum.

(b) Contents of the memorandum

(1) The memorandum must provide a summary of the significant facts, limited to matters in the record.

(2) The memorandum must state each point under a separate heading or subheading summarizing the point and support each point by argument and citation of authority.

(3) The memorandum must support any reference to a matter in the record by a citation to the record. The memorandum should explain the significance of any cited portion of the record and note any disputed aspects of the record.

(c) Serving and filing the petition and response

(1) The petition must be served and filed within 10 days after the record is filed in the reviewing court. The petitioner must serve a copy of the petition on:

(A) Each attorney of record;

(B) Any unrepresented party, including the child if the child is 10 years of age or older;

(C) Any known sibling of the child who is the subject of the hearing if that sibling either is the subject of a dependency proceeding or has been adjudged to be a dependent child of the juvenile court as follows:

(i) If the sibling is under 10 years of age, on the sibling's attorney;

(ii) If the sibling is 10 years of age or over, on the sibling and the sibling's attorney.

(D) The child's Court Appointed Special Advocate (CASA) volunteer;

(E) Any person currently awarded by the juvenile court the status of the child's de facto parent; and

(F) If the court sent the notice of intent to file the writ petition to an Indian custodian, tribe, or Bureau of Indian Affairs, then to that Indian custodian, tribe of the child, or the Bureau of Indian Affairs as required under Welfare and Institutions Code section 224.2.

(2) Any response must be served on each of the people and entities listed above and filed:

(A) Within 10 days—or, if the petition was served by mail, within 15 days—after the petition is filed; or

(B) Within 10 days after a respondent receives a request from the reviewing court for a response, unless the court specifies a shorter time.

(d) Order to show cause or alternative writ

If the court intends to determine the petition on the merits, it must issue an order to show cause or alternative writ.

(e) Augmenting or correcting the record in the reviewing court

(1) Except as provided in (2) and (3), rule 8.410 governs any augmentation or correction of the record.

(2) The petitioner must serve and file any request for augmentation or correction within 5 days—or, if the record exceeds 300 pages, within 7 days; or, if the record exceeds 600 pages, within 10 days—after receiving the record. A respondent must serve and file any such request within 5 days after the petition is filed or an order to show cause has issued, whichever is later.

(3) A party must attach to its motion a copy, if available, of any document or transcript that the party wants added to the record. The pages of the attachment must be consecutively numbered, beginning with the number one. If the reviewing court grants the motion, it may augment the record with the copy.

(4) If the party cannot attach a copy of the matter to be added, the party must identify it as required under rules 8.122 and 8.130.

(5) An order augmenting or correcting the record may grant no more than 15 days for compliance. The clerk and the reporter must give the order the highest priority.

(6) The clerk must certify and send any supplemental transcripts as required by rule 8.450(h). If the augmentation or correction is ordered, the time to file any petition or response is extended by the number of additional days granted to augment or correct the record.

(f) Stay

The reviewing court may stay the hearing set under Welfare and Institutions Code section 366.26, but must require an exceptional showing of good cause.

(g) Oral argument

(1) The reviewing court must hear oral argument within 30 days after the response is filed or due to be filed, unless the court extends the time for good cause or counsel waive argument.

(2) If argument is waived, the cause is deemed submitted not later than 30 days after the response is filed or due to be filed.

(h) Decision

(1) Absent exceptional circumstances, the reviewing court must decide the petition on the merits by written opinion.

(2) The reviewing court clerk must promptly notify the parties of any decision and must promptly send a certified copy of any writ or order to the court named as respondent.

(3) If the writ or order stays or prohibits proceedings set to occur within 7 days or requires action within 7 days—or in any other urgent situation—the reviewing court clerk must make a reasonable effort to notify the clerk of the respondent court by telephone. The clerk of the respondent court must then notify the judge or officer most directly concerned.

(4) The reviewing court clerk need not give telephonic notice of the summary denial of a writ, unless a stay previously issued will be dissolved.

(i) Filing, modification, finality of decision, and remittitur

Rule 8.490 governs the filing, modification, finality of decisions, and remittitur in writ proceedings under this rule. *(Formerly Rule 38.1, adopted, eff. Jan. 1, 2005. As amended, eff. Jan. 1, 2006. Renumbered Rule 8.452 and amended, eff. Jan. 1, 2007. As amended, eff. July 1, 2010.)*

Advisory Committee Comment

Subdivision (d). Subdivision (d) tracks the second sentence of former rule 39.1B(*l*). (But see *Maribel M. v. Superior Court* (1998) 61 Cal.App.4th 1469, 1471–1476.)

Subdivision (h). Subdivision (h)(1) tracks former rule 39.1B(*o*). (But see *Maribel M. v. Superior Court* (1998) 61 Cal.App.4th 1469, 1471–1476.)

Research References

Rutter, Cal. Practice Guide: Civil Appeals & Writs Ch. 2-B, B. Appealable Judgments and Orders.

Rutter, Cal. Practice Guide: Civil Appeals & Writs Ch. 4-I, I. Special Rules for Record on Certain Appeals.

Rutter, Cal. Practice Guide: Civil Appeals & Writs Ch. 5-B, B. Types of Motions, Applications and Requests.

Rutter, Cal. Practice Guide: Civil Appeals & Writs Ch. 15-C, C. Statutory Writs.

8 Witkin Cal. Proc. 5th Extraordinary Writs § 15, (S 15) Juvenile Court Orders Terminating Parental Rights.

8 Witkin Cal. Proc. 5th Extraordinary Writs § 185, (S 185) Summary Determination.

10 Witkin, California Summary 10th Parent and Child § 701, in General.

10 Witkin, California Summary 10th Parent and Child § 705, in General.

10 Witkin, California Summary 10th Parent and Child § 716, (S 716) in General.

10 Witkin, California Summary 10th Parent and Child § 717, in General.

10 Witkin, California Summary 10th Parent and Child § 720, Notice of Intent.

10 Witkin, California Summary 10th Parent and Child § 721, Record.

10 Witkin, California Summary 10th Parent and Child § 722, Writ Petition and Response.

10 Witkin, California Summary 10th Parent and Child § 723, Hearing and Decision.

10 Witkin, California Summary 10th Parent and Child § 727, Hearing and Decision.

10 Witkin, California Summary 10th Parent and Child § 920, (S 920) Review by Extraordinary Writ.

Rule 8.454. Notice of intent to file writ petition under Welfare and Institutions Code section 366.28 to review order designating specific placement of a dependent child after termination of parental rights

(a) Application

Rules 8.454–8.456 and 8.490 govern writ petitions to review placement orders following termination of parental rights entered on or after January 1, 2005. "Posttermination placement order" as used in this rule and rule 8.456 refers to orders following termination of parental rights.

(b) Purpose

The purpose of this rule is to facilitate and implement Welfare and Institutions Code section 366.28. Delays caused by appeals from court orders designating the specific placement of a dependent child after parental rights have been terminated may cause a substantial detriment to the child.

(c) Who may file

The petitioner's trial counsel, or, in the absence of trial counsel, the party, is responsible for filing any notice of intent and writ petition under rules 8.454–8.456. Trial counsel is encouraged to seek assistance from, or consult with, attorneys experienced in writ procedure.

(d) Extensions of time

The superior court may not extend any time period prescribed by rules 8.454–8.456. The reviewing court may extend any time period, but must require an exceptional showing of good cause.

(e) Notice of intent

(1) A party seeking writ review under rules 8.454–8.456 must file in the superior court a notice of intent to file a writ petition and a request for the record.

(2) The notice must include all known dates of the hearing that resulted in the order under review.

(3) The notice must be authorized by the party intending to file the petition and signed by the party or by the attorney of record for that party.

(4) The notice must be served and filed within 7 days after the date of the posttermination placement order or, if the order was made by a referee not acting as a temporary judge, within 7 days after the referee's order becomes final under rule 5.540(c). The date of the posttermination placement order is the date on which the court states the order on the record orally or in writing, whichever first occurs.

(5) If the party was notified of the posttermination placement order only by mail, the notice of intent must be filed within 12 days after the date that the clerk mailed the notification.

(f) Premature or late notice of intent to file writ petition

(1) A notice of intent to file a writ petition under Welfare and Institutions Code section 366.28 is premature if filed before a date for a postdetermination placement order has been made. The reviewing court may treat the notice as filed immediately after the postdetermination order has been made.

(2) The superior court clerk must mark a late notice of intent to file a writ petition under section 366.28 "Received [date] but not filed," notify the party that the notice was not filed because it was late, and send a copy of the marked notice to the party's counsel of record, if applicable.

(g) Sending the notice of intent

(1) When the notice of intent is filed, the superior court clerk must immediately mail a copy of the notice to:

(A) The attorney of record for each party;

(B) Each party, including the child if the child is 10 years of age or older;

(C) Any known sibling of the child who is the subject of the hearing if that sibling either is the subject of a dependency proceeding or has been adjudged to be a dependent child of the juvenile court as follows:

(i) If the sibling is under 10 years of age, on the sibling's attorney;

(ii) If the sibling is 10 years of age or over, on the sibling and the sibling's attorney;

(D) Any prospective adoptive parent;

(E) The child's legal guardian if any;

(F) Any person currently awarded by the juvenile court the status of the child's de facto parent;

(G) The probation officer or social worker;

(H) The child's Court Appointed Special Advocate (CASA) volunteer, if any; and

(I) If the court knows or has reason to know that an Indian child is involved, the Indian custodian, if any, and tribe of the child or the Bureau of Indian Affairs as required under Welfare and Institutions Code section 224.2.

(2) The clerk must promptly send by first-class mail or fax a copy of the notice of intent and a list of those to whom the notice of intent was sent to:

(A) The reviewing court; and

(B) The petitioner if the clerk mailed a copy of the notice of intent to the Indian custodian, tribe of the child, or the Bureau of Indian Affairs.

(3) If the party was notified of the post placement order only by mail, the clerk must include the date that the notification was mailed.

(h) Preparing the record

When the notice of intent is filed, the superior court clerk must:

(1) Immediately notify each court reporter by telephone and in writing to prepare a reporter's transcript of the oral proceedings at each session of the hearing that resulted in the order under review and to deliver the transcript to the clerk within 12 calendar days after the notice of intent is filed; and

(2) Within 20 days after the notice of intent is filed, prepare a clerk's transcript that includes the notice of intent, proof of service, and all items listed in rule 8.404(a) 8.407(a).

(i) Sending the record

When the transcripts are certified as correct, the superior court clerk must immediately send:

(1) The original transcripts to the reviewing court by the most expeditious method, noting the sending date on each original; and

(2) One copy of each transcript to each counsel of record and any unrepresented party and unrepresented custodian of the dependent child by any means as fast as United States Postal Service express mail.

(j) Reviewing court clerk's duties

(1) The reviewing court clerk must promptly lodge the notice of intent. When the notice is lodged, the reviewing court has jurisdiction over the writ proceedings.

(2) When the record is filed in the reviewing court, that court's clerk must immediately notify the parties, stating the date on which the 10–day period for filing the writ petition under rule 8.456(c)(1) will expire. *(Formerly Rule 38.2, adopted, eff. Jan. 1, 2005. As amended, eff. Jan. 1, 2006; July 1, 2006. Renumbered Rule 8.454 and amended, eff. Jan. 1, 2007. As amended, eff. Jan. 1, 2008; Jan. 1, 2009; July 1, 2010; July 1, 2013.)*

Advisory Committee Comment

Subdivision (f)(2). See rule 8.25(b)(5) for provisions concerning the timeliness of documents mailed by inmates or patients from custodial institutions.

Research References

Rutter, Cal. Practice Guide: Civil Appeals & Writs Ch. 2-B, B. Appealable Judgments and Orders.

Rutter, Cal. Practice Guide: Civil Appeals & Writs Ch. 4-I, I. Special Rules for Record on Certain Appeals.

Rutter, Cal. Practice Guide: Civil Appeals & Writs Ch. 15-C, C. Statutory Writs.

10 Witkin, California Summary 10th Parent and Child § 704, Miscellaneous Orders.

10 Witkin, California Summary 10th Parent and Child § 716, (S 716) in General.

10 Witkin, California Summary 10th Parent and Child § 724, in General.

10 Witkin, California Summary 10th Parent and Child § 725, Notice of Intent and Record.

10 Witkin, California Summary 10th Parent and Child § 726, Writ Petition.

10 Witkin, California Summary 10th Parent and Child § 920, (S 920) Review by Extraordinary Writ.

10 Witkin, California Summary 10th Parent and Child § 693C, (S 693C) (New)-Nonemergency Removal from Prospective Adoptive Parent.

Rule 8.456. Writ petition under Welfare and Institutions Code section 366.28 to review order designating or denying specific placement of a dependent child after termination of parental rights

(a) Petition

(1) The petition must be liberally construed and must include:

(A) The identities of the parties;

(B) The date on which the superior court made the posttermination placement order;

(C) A summary of the grounds of the petition; and

(D) The relief requested.

(2) The petition must be accompanied by a memorandum.

(b) Contents of memorandum

(1) The memorandum must provide a summary of the significant facts, limited to matters in the record.

(2) The memorandum must state each point under a separate heading or subheading summarizing the point and support each point by argument and citation of authority.

(3) The memorandum must support any reference to a matter in the record by a citation to the record. The memorandum should explain the significance of any cited portion of the record and note any disputed aspects of the record.

(c) Serving and filing the petition and response

(1) The petition must be served and filed within 10 days after the record is filed in the reviewing court. The petitioner must serve the petition on:

(A) Each attorney of record;

(B) Any unrepresented party, including the child if the child is 10 years of age or older;

(C) Any known sibling of the child who is the subject of the hearing if that sibling either is the subject of a dependency proceeding or has been adjudged to be a dependent child of the juvenile court as follows:

(i) If the sibling is under 10 years of age, on the sibling's attorney;

(ii) If the sibling is 10 years of age or over, on the sibling and the sibling's attorney;

(D) Any prospective adoptive parent;

(E) The child's Court Appointed Special Advocate (CASA) volunteer;

(F) Any person currently awarded by the juvenile court the status of the child's de facto parent; and

(G) If the court sent the notice of intent to file the writ petition to an Indian custodian, tribe, or Bureau of Indian Affairs, then to that Indian custodian, tribe, or the Bureau of Indian Affairs as required under Welfare and Institutions Code section 224.2.

(2) Any response must be served on each of the people and entities listed in (1) and filed:

(A) Within 10 days—or, if the petition was served by mail, within 15 days—after the petition is filed; or

(B) Within 10 days after a respondent receives a request from the reviewing court for a response, unless the court specifies a shorter time.

(d) Order to show cause or alternative writ

If the court intends to determine the petition on the merits, it must issue an order to show cause or alternative writ.

(e) Augmenting or correcting the record in the reviewing court

(1) Except as provided in (2) and (3), rule 8.410 governs augmentation or correction of the record.

(2) The petitioner must serve and file any request for augmentation or correction within 5 days—or, if the record exceeds 300 pages, within 7 days; or, if the record exceeds 600 pages, within 10 days—after receiving the record. A respondent must serve and file any such request within 5 days after the petition is filed or an order to show cause has issued, whichever is later.

(3) A party must attach to its motion a copy, if available, of any document or transcript that it wants added to the record. The pages of the attachment must be consecutively numbered, beginning with the number one. If the reviewing court grants the motion, it may augment the record with the copy.

(4) If the party cannot attach a copy of the matter to be added, the party must identify it as required under rules 8.122 and 8.130.

(5) An order augmenting or correcting the record may grant no more than 15 days for compliance. The clerk and the reporter must give the order the highest priority.

(6) The clerk must certify and send any supplemental transcripts as required by rule 8.454(i). If the augmentation or correction is ordered, the time to file any petition or response is extended by the number of additional days granted to augment or correct the record.

(f) Stay

A request by petitioner for a stay of the posttermination placement order will not be granted unless the writ petition shows that implementation of the superior court's placement order pending the reviewing court's decision is likely to cause detriment to the child if the order is ultimately reversed.

(g) Oral argument

(1) The reviewing court must hear oral argument within 30 days after the response is filed or due to be filed, unless the court extends the time for good cause or counsel waive argument.

(2) If argument is waived, the cause is deemed submitted not later than 30 days after the response is filed or due to be filed.

(h) Decision

(1) Absent exceptional circumstances, the reviewing court must review the petition and decide it on the merits by written opinion.

Ct. Rules

(2) The reviewing court clerk must promptly notify the parties of any decision and must promptly send a certified copy of any writ or order to the court named as respondent.

(3) If the writ or order stays or requires action within 7 days—or in any other urgent situation—the reviewing court clerk must make a reasonable effort to notify the clerk of the respondent court by telephone. The clerk of the respondent court must then notify the judge or officer most directly concerned.

(4) The reviewing court clerk need not give telephonic notice of the summary denial of a writ, unless a stay previously issued and will be dissolved.

(5) Rule 8.490 governs the filing, modification, finality of decisions, and remittitur in writ proceedings under this rule.

(i) Right to appeal other orders

This section does not affect the right of a parent, a legal guardian, or the child to appeal any order that is otherwise appealable and that is issued at a hearing held under Welfare and Institutions Code section 366.26. *(Formerly Rule 38.3, adopted, eff. Jan. 1, 2005. As amended, eff. Jan. 1, 2006; Feb. 24, 2006. Renumbered Rule 8.456 and amended, eff. Jan. 1, 2007. As amended, eff. July 1, 2010.)*

Research References

Rutter, Cal. Practice Guide: Civil Appeals & Writs Ch. 2-B, B. Appealable Judgments and Orders.
Rutter, Cal. Practice Guide: Civil Appeals & Writs Ch. 4-I, I. Special Rules for Record on Certain Appeals.
Rutter, Cal. Practice Guide: Civil Appeals & Writs Ch. 5-B, B. Types of Motions, Applications and Requests.
Rutter, Cal. Practice Guide: Civil Appeals & Writs Ch. 15-C, C. Statutory Writs.
9 Witkin Cal. Proc. 5th Appeal § 9, (S 9) Current Structure.
2 Witkin Cal. Proc. 5th Courts § 195, (S 195) Appellate Rules.
8 Witkin Cal. Proc. 5th Extraordinary Writs § 15, (S 15) Juvenile Court Orders Terminating Parental Rights.
10 Witkin, California Summary 10th Parent and Child § 444, Scope and Organization.
10 Witkin, California Summary 10th Parent and Child § 704, Miscellaneous Orders.
10 Witkin, California Summary 10th Parent and Child § 716, (S 716) in General.
10 Witkin, California Summary 10th Parent and Child § 717, in General.
10 Witkin, California Summary 10th Parent and Child § 722, Writ Petition and Response.
10 Witkin, California Summary 10th Parent and Child § 723, Hearing and Decision.
10 Witkin, California Summary 10th Parent and Child § 724, in General.
10 Witkin, California Summary 10th Parent and Child § 725, Notice of Intent and Record.
10 Witkin, California Summary 10th Parent and Child § 726, Writ Petition.
10 Witkin, California Summary 10th Parent and Child § 727, Hearing and Decision.
10 Witkin, California Summary 10th Parent and Child § 920, (S 920) Review by Extraordinary Writ.

Article 4

HEARING AND DECISION

Rule
8.470. Hearing and decision in the Court of Appeal.
8.472. Hearing and decision in the Supreme Court.
8.474. Procedures and data.

Rule 8.470.   Hearing and decision in the Court of Appeal

Except as provided in rules 8.400–8.456, rules 8.252–8.272 govern hearing and decision in the Court of Appeal in juvenile cases. *(Formerly Rule 38.4, adopted, eff. Jan. 1, 2005. As amended, eff. July 1, 2005. Renumbered Rule 8.470 and amended, eff. Jan. 1, 2007.)*

Research References

Rutter, Cal. Practice Guide: Civil Appeals & Writs Ch. 2-B, B. Appealable Judgments and Orders.
9 Witkin Cal. Proc. 5th Appeal § 9, (S 9) Current Structure.
2 Witkin Cal. Proc. 5th Courts § 195, (S 195) Appellate Rules.
10 Witkin, California Summary 10th Parent and Child § 444, Scope and Organization.

Rule 8.472.   Hearing and decision in the Supreme Court

Rules 8.500–8.552 govern hearing and decision in the Supreme Court in juvenile cases. *(Formerly Rule 38.5, adopted, eff. Jan. 1, 2005. As amended, eff. July 1, 2005. Renumbered Rule 8.472 and amended, eff. Jan. 1, 2007.)*

Research References

Rutter, Cal. Practice Guide: Civil Appeals & Writs Ch. 2-B, B. Appealable Judgments and Orders.

Rule 8.474.   Procedures and data

(a) Procedures

The judges and clerks of the superior courts and the reviewing courts must adopt procedures to identify the records and expedite the processing of all appeals and writs in juvenile cases.

(b) Data

The clerks of the superior courts and the reviewing courts must the provide data required to assist the Judicial Council in evaluating the effectiveness of the rules governing appeals and writs in juvenile cases. *(Formerly Rule 38.6, adopted, eff. Jan. 1, 2005. Renumbered Rule 8.474, eff. Jan. 1, 2007.)*

Research References

9 Witkin Cal. Proc. 5th Appeal § 9, (S 9) Current Structure.
2 Witkin Cal. Proc. 5th Courts § 195, (S 195) Appellate Rules.
10 Witkin, California Summary 10th Parent and Child § 355, (S 355) Review on Appeal.
10 Witkin, California Summary 10th Parent and Child § 444, Scope and Organization.
10 Witkin, California Summary 10th Parent and Child § 709, in General.
10 Witkin, California Summary 10th Parent and Child § 716, (S 716) in General.

Chapter 6

CONSERVATORSHIP APPEALS

Rule
8.480. Appeal from order establishing conservatorship.
8.482. Appeal from judgment authorizing conservator to consent to sterilization of conservatee.

Rule 8.480.   Appeal from order establishing conservatorship

(a) Application

Except as otherwise provided in this rule, rules 8.304–8.368 and 8.508 govern appeals from orders establishing conservatorships under Welfare and Institutions Code section 5350 et seq.

(b) Clerk's transcript

The clerk's transcript must contain:

(1) The petition;

(2) Any demurrer or other plea;

(3) Any written motion with supporting and opposing memoranda and attachments;

(4) Any filed medical or social worker reports;

(5) All court minutes;

(6) All instructions submitted in writing, each noting the party requesting it;

(7) Any verdict;

(8) Any written opinion of the court;

(9) The judgment or order appealed from;

(10) The notice of appeal; and

(11) Any application for additional record and any order on the application.

(c) Reporter's transcript

The reporter's transcript must contain all oral proceedings, excluding the voir dire examination of jurors and any opening statement.

(d) Sending the record

The clerk must not send a copy of the record to the Attorney General or the district attorney unless that office represents a party.

(e) Briefs

The parties must not serve copies of their briefs:

(1) On the Attorney General or the district attorney, unless that office represents a party; or

(2) On the Supreme Court under rule 8.44(b)(1). *(Formerly Rule 39, adopted, eff. Jan. 1, 2005. Renumbered Rule 8.480 and amended, eff. Jan. 1, 2007.)*

Research References

Rutter, Cal. Practice Guide: Civil Appeals & Writs Ch. 3-B, B. Filing Deadlines.
Rutter, Cal. Practice Guide: Civil Appeals & Writs Ch. 4-I, I. Special Rules for Record on Certain Appeals.
Rutter, Cal. Practice Guide: Civil Appeals & Writs Ch. 5-B, B. Types of Motions, Applications and Requests.
Rutter, Cal. Practice Guide: Civil Appeals & Writs Ch. 9-D, D. Procedural Rules.
3 Witkin Cal. Proc. 5th Actions § 111, (S 111) Appeal.
9 Witkin Cal. Proc. 5th Appeal § 9, (S 9) Current Structure.
2 Witkin Cal. Proc. 5th Courts § 195, (S 195) Appellate Rules.
10 Witkin, California Summary 10th Parent and Child § 460, (S 460) Appeal from Determination of Residence.

Rule 8.482. Appeal from judgment authorizing conservator to consent to sterilization of conservatee

(a) Application

Except as otherwise provided in this rule, rules 8.304–8.368 and 8.508 govern appeals from judgments authorizing a conservator to consent to the sterilization of a developmentally disabled adult conservatee.

(b) When appeal is taken automatically

An appeal from a judgment authorizing a conservator to consent to the sterilization of a developmentally disabled adult conservatee is taken automatically, without any action by the conservatee, when the judgment is rendered.

(c) Superior court clerk's duties

After entering the judgment, the clerk must immediately:

(1) Begin preparing a clerk's transcript and notify the reporter to prepare a reporter's transcript; and

(2) Mail certified copies of the judgment to the Court of Appeal and the Attorney General.

(d) Clerk's transcript

The clerk's transcript must contain:

(1) The petition and notice of hearing;

(2) All court minutes;

(3) Any application, motion, or notice of motion, with supporting and opposing memoranda and attachments;

(4) Any report or other document submitted to the court;

(5) Any transcript of a proceeding pertaining to the case;

(6) The statement of decision; and

(7) The judgment or order appealed from.

(e) Reporter's transcript

The reporter's transcript must contain all oral proceedings, including:

(1) All proceedings at the hearing on the petition, with opening statements and closing arguments;

(2) All proceedings on motions;

(3) Any comments on the evidence by the court; and

(4) Any oral opinion or oral statement of decision.

(f) Preparing and sending transcripts

(1) The clerk and the reporter must prepare and send an original and two copies of each of the transcripts as provided in rule 8.336.

(2) Probate Code section 1963 governs the cost of preparing the record on appeal.

(g) Confidential material

(1) Written reports of physicians, psychologists, and clinical social workers, and any other matter marked confidential by the court, may be inspected only by court personnel, the parties and their counsel, the district appellate project, and other persons designated by the court.

(2) Material under (1) must be sent to the reviewing court in a sealed envelope marked "CONFIDENTIAL—MAY NOT BE EXAMINED WITHOUT COURT ORDER."

(h) Trial counsel's continuing representation

To expedite preparation and certification of the record, the conservatee's trial counsel must continue to represent the conservatee until appellate counsel is retained or appointed.

(i) Appointment of appellate counsel

If appellate counsel has not been retained for the conservatee, the reviewing court must appoint such counsel. *(Formerly Rule 39.1, adopted, eff. Jan. 1, 2005. Renumbered Rule 8.482 and amended, eff. Jan. 1, 2007.)*

Research References

Rutter, Cal. Practice Guide: Civil Appeals & Writs Ch. 3-B, B. Filing Deadlines.
Rutter, Cal. Practice Guide: Civil Appeals & Writs Ch. 4-I, I. Special Rules for Record on Certain Appeals.
Rutter, Cal. Practice Guide: Civil Appeals & Writs Ch. 5-B, B. Types of Motions, Applications and Requests.
Rutter, Cal. Practice Guide: Civil Appeals & Writs Ch. 9-D, D. Procedural Rules.
9 Witkin Cal. Proc. 5th Appeal § 9, (S 9) Current Structure.
9 Witkin Cal. Proc. 5th Appeal § 151, Appeal in Sterilization Case.
9 Witkin Cal. Proc. 5th Appeal § 559, (S 559) Notification by Clerk.
9 Witkin Cal. Proc. 5th Appeal § 626, (S 626) Nature of Record.
2 Witkin Cal. Proc. 5th Courts § 195, (S 195) Appellate Rules.
10 Witkin, California Summary 10th Parent and Child § 357, (S 357) Effect of Late Appeal.
14 Witkin, California Summary 10th Wills and Probate § 1059, (S 1059) in General.

Ct. Rules

Chapter 7

WRITS OF MANDATE, CERTIORARI, AND PROHIBITION IN THE SUPREME COURT AND COURT OF APPEAL

Rule

Rule 8.485.   Application

(a) Writ proceedings governed

Except as provided in (b), the rules in this chapter govern petitions to the Supreme Court and Court of Appeal for writs of mandate, certiorari, or prohibition, or other writs within the original jurisdiction of these courts. In all respects not provided for in these rules, rule 8.204 governs the form and content of documents in the proceedings governed by this chapter.

(b) Writ proceedings not governed

These rules do not apply to petitions for writs of mandate, certiorari, or prohibition in the appellate division of the superior court under rules 8.930–8.936, petitions for writs of supersedeas under rule 8.116, petitions for writs of habeas corpus except as provided in rule 8.384, or petitions for writs under rules 8.495–8.498. *(Adopted, eff. Jan. 1, 2009. As amended, eff. July 1, 2012.)*

Research References

Rutter, Cal. Practice Guide: Civil Appeals & Writs Ch. 7-E, E. Stay by Writ of Supersedeas.
Rutter, Cal. Practice Guide: Civil Appeals & Writs Ch. 15-E, E. Procedures on Writ Review.
9 Witkin Cal. Proc. 5th Appeal § 9, (S 9) Current Structure.
2 Witkin Cal. Proc. 5th Courts § 195, (S 195) Appellate Rules.
8 Witkin Cal. Proc. 5th Extraordinary Writs § 163, (S 163) Governing Statutes and Rules.
8 Witkin Cal. Proc. 5th Extraordinary Writs § 169, in General.
8 Witkin Cal. Proc. 5th Extraordinary Writs § 179, Petition to Review Trial Court Ruling.
10 Witkin, California Summary 10th Parent and Child § 724, in General.

Rule 8.486.   Petitions

(a) Contents of petition

(1) If the petition could have been filed first in a lower court, it must explain why the reviewing court should issue the writ as an original matter.

(2) If the petition names as respondent a judge, court, board, or other officer acting in a public capacity, it must disclose the name of any real party in interest.

(3) If the petition seeks review of trial court proceedings that are also the subject of a pending appeal, the notice "Related Appeal Pending" must appear on the cover of the petition and the first paragraph of the petition must state:

(A) The appeal's title, trial court docket number, and any reviewing court docket number; and

(B) If the petition is filed under Penal Code section 1238.5, the date the notice of appeal was filed.

(4) The petition must be verified.

(5) The petition must be accompanied by a memorandum, which need not repeat facts alleged in the petition.

(6) Rule 8.204(c) governs the length of the petition and memorandum, but, in addition to the exclusions provided in that rule, the verification and any supporting documents are excluded from the limits stated in rule 8.204(c)(1) and (2).

(7) If the petition requests a temporary stay, it must comply with the following or the reviewing court may decline to consider the request for a temporary stay:

(A) The petition must explain the urgency.

(B) The cover of the petition must prominently display the notice "STAY REQUESTED" and identify the nature and date of the proceeding or act sought to be stayed.

(C) The trial court and department involved and the name and telephone number of the trial judge whose order the request seeks to stay must appear either on the cover or at the beginning of the text.

(b) Contents of supporting documents

(1) A petition that seeks review of a trial court ruling must be accompanied by an adequate record, including copies of:

(A) The ruling from which the petition seeks relief;

(B) All documents and exhibits submitted to the trial court supporting and opposing the petitioner's position;

(C) Any other documents or portions of documents submitted to the trial court that are necessary for a complete understanding of the case and the ruling under review; and

(D) A reporter's transcript of the oral proceedings that resulted in the ruling under review.

(2) In exigent circumstances, the petition may be filed without the documents required by (1)(A)–(C) if counsel or, if the petitioner is unrepresented, the petitioner files a declaration that explains the urgency and the circumstances making the documents unavailable and fairly summarizes their substance.

(3) If a transcript under (1)(D) is unavailable, the record must include a declaration by counsel or, if the petitioner is unrepresented, the petitioner:

(A) Explaining why the transcript is unavailable and fairly summarizing the proceedings, including the parties' arguments and any statement by the court supporting its ruling. This declaration may omit a full summary of the proceedings if part of the relief sought is an order to prepare a transcript for use by an indigent criminal defendant in support of the petition and if the declaration demonstrates the petitioner's need for and entitlement to the transcript; or

(B) Stating that the transcript has been ordered, the date it was ordered, and the date it is expected to be filed, which must be a date before any action requested of the reviewing court other than issuance of a temporary stay supported by other parts of the record.

(4) If the petitioner does not submit the required record or explanations or does not present facts sufficient to excuse the failure to submit them, the court may summarily deny a stay request, the petition, or both.

(c) Form of supporting documents

(1) Documents submitted under (b) must comply with the following requirements:

(A) They must be bound together at the end of the petition or in separate volumes not exceeding 300 pages each. The pages must be consecutively numbered.

(B) They must be index-tabbed by number or letter.

(C) They must begin with a table of contents listing each document by its title and its index-tab number or letter. If a document has attachments, the table of contents must give the title of each attachment and a brief description of its contents.

(2) The clerk must file any supporting documents not complying with (1), but the court may notify the petitioner that it may strike or summarily deny the petition if the documents are not brought into compliance within a stated reasonable time of not less than 5 days.

(3) Rule 8.44(a) governs the number of copies of supporting documents to be filed in the Supreme Court. Rule 8.44(b) governs the number of supporting documents to be filed in the Court of Appeal.

(d) Sealed records

Rule 8.46 applies if a party seeks to lodge or file a sealed record or to unseal a record.

(e) Service

(1) If the respondent is the superior court or a judge of that court, the petition and one set of supporting documents must be served on any named real party in interest, but only the petition must be served on the respondent.

(2) If the respondent is not the superior court or a judge of that court, both the petition and one set of supporting documents must be served on the respondent and on any named real party in interest.

(3) In addition to complying with the requirements of rule 8.25, the proof of service must give the telephone number of each attorney served.

(4) The petition must be served on a public officer or agency when required by statute or rule 8.29.

(5) The clerk must file the petition even if its proof of service is defective, but if the petitioner fails to file a corrected proof of service within 5 days after the clerk gives notice of the defect the court may strike the petition or impose a lesser sanction.

(6) The court may allow the petition to be filed without proof of service. *(Formerly Rule 56, adopted, eff. Jan. 1, 2005. As amended, eff. July 1, 2005; Jan. 1, 2006; July 1, 2006. Renumbered Rule 8.490 and amended, eff. Jan. 1, 2007. As amended, eff. Jan. 1, 2008. Renumbered Rule 8.486 and amended, eff. Jan. 1, 2009. As amended, eff. July 1, 2009; Jan. 1, 2011.)*

Advisory Committee Comment

Subdivision (a). Because of the importance of the point, rule 8.486(a)(6) explicitly states that the provisions of rule 8.204(c)—and hence the word-count limits imposed by that rule—apply to a petition for original writ.

Subdivision (e). Rule 8.25, which generally governs service and filing in reviewing courts, also applies to the original proceedings covered by this rule.

Research References

Rutter, Cal. Practice Guide: Civil Appeals & Writs Ch. 15-E, E. Procedures on Writ Review.

Rutter, Cal. Practice Guide: Civ. Pro. Before Trial Ch. 10-J, J. Appellate Review of Summary Judgment and Adjudication Orders.

9 Witkin Cal. Proc. 5th Appeal § 132, Jurisdiction Accepted.

2 Witkin Cal. Proc. 5th Courts § 216, Concurrent Jurisdiction of Appellate Court.

2 Witkin Cal. Proc. 5th Courts § 337, (S 337) Original Jurisdiction.

8 Witkin Cal. Proc. 5th Extraordinary Writs § 144, General Rule of Denying Writ.

8 Witkin Cal. Proc. 5th Extraordinary Writs § 163, (S 163) Governing Statutes and Rules.

8 Witkin Cal. Proc. 5th Extraordinary Writs § 166, in General.

8 Witkin Cal. Proc. 5th Extraordinary Writs § 169, in General.

8 Witkin Cal. Proc. 5th Extraordinary Writs § 172, Verification.

8 Witkin Cal. Proc. 5th Extraordinary Writs § 179, Petition to Review Trial Court Ruling.

8 Witkin Cal. Proc. 5th Extraordinary Writs § 180, Supporting Memorandum.

8 Witkin Cal. Proc. 5th Extraordinary Writs § 183, (S 183) Service.

2 Witkin Cal. Proc. 5th Jurisdiction § 397, Refusal of Original Jurisdiction.

4 Witkin Cal. Proc. 5th Pleading § 67, (S 67) Designation of Parties.

Rule 8.487. Opposition and Attorney General amicus briefs

(a) Preliminary opposition

(1) Within 10 days after the petition is filed, the respondent or any real party in interest, separately or jointly, may serve and file a preliminary opposition.

(2) A preliminary opposition must contain a memorandum and a statement of any material fact not included in the petition.

(3) Within 10 days after a preliminary opposition is filed, the petitioner may serve and file a reply.

(4) Without requesting preliminary opposition or waiting for a reply, the court may grant or deny a request for temporary stay, deny the petition, issue an alternative writ or order to show cause, or notify the parties that it is considering issuing a peremptory writ in the first instance.

(b) Return or opposition; reply

(1) If the court issues an alternative writ or order to show cause, the respondent or any real party in interest, separately or jointly, may serve and file a return by demurrer, verified answer, or both. If the court notifies the parties that it is considering issuing a peremptory writ in the first instance, the respondent or any real party in interest may serve and file an opposition.

(2) Unless the court orders otherwise, the return or opposition must be served and filed within 30 days after the court issues the alternative writ or order to show cause or notifies the parties that it is considering issuing a peremptory writ in the first instance.

(3) Unless the court orders otherwise, the petitioner may serve and file a reply within 15 days after the return or opposition is filed.

(4) If the return is by demurrer alone and the demurrer is not sustained, the court may issue the peremptory writ without granting leave to answer.

(c) Attorney General's amicus curiae brief

(1) If the court issues an alternative writ or order to show cause, the Attorney General may file an amicus curiae brief without the permission of the Chief Justice or presiding justice, unless the brief is submitted on behalf of another state officer or agency.

(2) The Attorney General must serve and file the brief within 14 days after the return is filed or, if no return is filed, within 14 days after the date it was due.

(3) The brief must provide the information required by rule 8.200(c)(2) and comply with rule 8.200(c)(4).

(4) Any party may serve and file an answer within 14 days after the brief is filed. *(Adopted, eff. Jan. 1, 2009.)*

Advisory Committee Comment

A party other than the petitioner who files a preliminary opposition under (a) or a return or opposition under (b) may be required to pay a filing fee under Government Code section 68926 if the preliminary opposition, return, or opposition is the first document filed in the writ proceeding in the reviewing court by that party. See rule 8.25(c).

Subdivision (a). Consistent with practice, rule 8.487 draws a distinction between a "preliminary opposition," which the respondent or a real party in interest may file before the court takes any action on the petition ((a)(1)), and a more formal "opposition," which the respondent or a real party in interest may file if the court notifies the parties that it is considering issuing a peremptory writ in the first instance ((b)(1)).

Subdivision (a)(1) allows the respondent or any real party in interest to serve and file a preliminary opposition within 10 days after the petition is filed. The reviewing court retains the power to act in any case without obtaining preliminary opposition ((a)(4)).

Subdivision (a)(3) allows a petitioner to serve and file a reply within 10 days after a preliminary opposition is filed. To permit prompt action in urgent cases, however, the provision recognizes that the reviewing court may act on the petition without waiting for a reply.

Subdivision (a)(4) recognizes that the reviewing court may "grant or deny a request for temporary stay" without requesting preliminary opposition or waiting for a reply.

The several references in rule 8.487 to the power of the court to issue a peremptory writ in the first instance after notifying the parties that it is considering doing so ((a)–(b)) implement the rule of *Palma v. U. S. Industrial Fasteners, Inc.* (1984) 36 Cal.3d 171.

Subdivision (b). Subdivision (b)(2) requires that the return or opposition be served and filed within 30 days after the court issues the alternative writ or order to show cause or notifies the parties that it is considering issuing a peremptory writ in the first instance. To permit prompt action in urgent cases, however, the provision recognizes that the reviewing court may order otherwise.

Subdivision (b)(3) formalizes the common practice of permitting petitioners to file replies to returns and specifies that such a reply must be served and filed within 15 days after the return is filed. To permit prompt action in urgent cases, however, the provision recognizes that the reviewing court may order otherwise.

Research References

Rutter, Cal. Practice Guide: Civil Appeals & Writs Ch. 15-E, E. Procedures on Writ Review.
9 Witkin Cal. Proc. 5th Appeal § 726, (S 726) Amicus Briefs in Court of Appeal or Appellate Division.
8 Witkin Cal. Proc. 5th Extraordinary Writs § 56, Effect of Alternative Writ.
8 Witkin Cal. Proc. 5th Extraordinary Writs § 163, (S 163) Governing Statutes and Rules.
8 Witkin Cal. Proc. 5th Extraordinary Writs § 183, (S 183) Service.
8 Witkin Cal. Proc. 5th Extraordinary Writs § 184, (S 184) Opposing Memorandum.
8 Witkin Cal. Proc. 5th Extraordinary Writs § 189, (S 189) Prohibition and Mandamus.
8 Witkin Cal. Proc. 5th Extraordinary Writs § 192, in General.
8 Witkin Cal. Proc. 5th Extraordinary Writs § 193, Return as Answer or Demurrer.
8 Witkin Cal. Proc. 5th Extraordinary Writs § 197, (S 197) Return in Reviewing Court.
8 Witkin Cal. Proc. 5th Extraordinary Writs § 200, Decision.
8 Witkin Cal. Proc. 5th Extraordinary Writs § 201, (S 201) Where Demurrer Alone is Filed.
8 Witkin Cal. Proc. 5th Extraordinary Writs § 203, (S 203) Proceedings in Reviewing Court.

Rule 8.488.　Certificate of Interested Entities or Persons

(a)　Application

This rule applies in writ proceedings in criminal cases in which an entity is the defendant and in civil cases other than family, juvenile, guardianship, and conservatorship cases.

(b)　Compliance with rule 8.208

Each party in a civil case and any entity that is a defendant in a criminal case must comply with the requirements of rule 8.208 concerning serving and filing a certificate of interested entities or persons.

(c)　Placement of certificates

(1) The petitioner's certificate must be included in the petition.

(2) The certificates of the respondent and real party in interest must be included in their preliminary opposition or, if no such opposition is filed, in their return, if any.

(3) The certificate must appear after the cover and before the tables.

(4) If the identity of any party has not been publicly disclosed in the proceedings, the party may file an application for permission to file its certificate under seal separately from the petition, preliminary opposition, or return.

(d)　Failure to file a certificate

(1) If a party fails to file a certificate as required under (b) and (c), the clerk must notify the party by mail that the party must file the certificate within 10 days after the clerk's notice is mailed and that if the party fails to comply, the court may impose one of the following sanctions:

(A) If the party is the petitioner, the court may strike the petition; or

(B) If the party is the respondent or the real party in interest, the court may strike that party's document.

(2) If the party fails to file the certificate as specified in the notice under (1), the court may impose the sanctions specified in the notice. *(Adopted, eff. Jan. 1, 2009.)*

Advisory Committee Comment

The Judicial Council has adopted an optional form, *Certificate of Interested Entities or Persons* (form APP–008), that can be used to file the certificate required by this provision.

Subdivision (a). Under rule 8.208(c), for purposes of certificates of interested entities or persons, an "entity" means a corporation, a partnership, a firm, or any other association, but does not include a governmental entity or its agencies or a natural person.

Research References

Rutter, Cal. Practice Guide: Civil Appeals & Writs Ch. 9-C, C. Format of Briefs.
Rutter, Cal. Practice Guide: Civil Appeals & Writs Ch. 15-E, E. Procedures on Writ Review.

Rule 8.489.　Notice to trial court

(a)　Notice if writ issues

If a writ or order issues directed to any judge, court, board, or other officer, the reviewing court clerk must promptly send a certified copy of the writ or order to the person or entity to whom it is addressed.

(b)　Notice by telephone

(1) If the writ or order stays or prohibits proceedings set to occur within 7 days or requires action within 7 days—or in any other urgent situation—the reviewing court clerk must make a reasonable effort to notify the clerk of the respondent court by telephone. The clerk of the respondent court must then notify the judge or officer most directly concerned.

(2) The clerk need not give telephonic notice of the summary denial of a writ, whether or not a stay previously issued. *(Adopted, eff. Jan. 1, 2009.)*

Research References

Rutter, Cal. Practice Guide: Civil Appeals & Writs Ch. 15-E, E. Procedures on Writ Review.
9 Witkin Cal. Proc. 5th Appeal § 303, Determination.

Rule 8.490. Filing, finality, and modification of decisions; remittitur

(a) Filing and modification of decisions

Rule 8.264(a) and (c) govern the filing and modification of decisions in writ proceedings.

(b) Finality of decision

(1) The denial of a petition for a writ within the court's original jurisdiction without issuance of an alternative writ or order to show cause is final in that court when filed.

(2) Except as otherwise provided in this rule, a decision in a writ proceeding is final 30 days after the decision is filed.

(3) If necessary to prevent mootness or frustration of the relief granted or to otherwise promote the interests of justice, the court may order early finality in that court of a decision granting a petition for a writ within its original jurisdiction or denying such a petition after issuing an alternative writ or order to show cause. The decision may provide for finality in that court on filing or within a stated period of less than 30 days.

(4) If a Court of Appeal certifies its opinion for publication or partial publication after filing its decision and before its decision becomes final in that court, the finality period runs from the filing date of the order for publication.

(5) If an order modifying an opinion changes the appellate judgment, the finality period runs from the filing date of the modification order.

(c) Remittitur

A Court of Appeal must issue a remittitur in a writ proceeding under this chapter except when the court denies the petition without issuing an alternative writ or order to show cause. Rule 8.272(b)–(d) governs issuance of a remittitur by a Court of Appeal in writ proceedings under this chapter. *(Adopted, eff. Jan. 1, 2009.)*

Advisory Committee Comment

Subdivision (b). This provision addresses the finality of decisions in proceedings relating to writs of mandate, certiorari, and prohibition. See rule 8.264(b) for provisions addressing the finality of decisions in proceedings under chapter 2, relating to civil appeals, and rule 8.366 for provisions addressing the finality of decisions in proceedings under chapter 3, relating to criminal appeals.

Research References

Rutter, Cal. Practice Guide: Civil Appeals & Writs Ch. 11-G, G. Finality as to Court of Appeal.
Rutter, Cal. Practice Guide: Civil Appeals & Writs Ch. 12-A, A. Overview.
Rutter, Cal. Practice Guide: Civil Appeals & Writs Ch. 13-A, A. General Considerations.
Rutter, Cal. Practice Guide: Civil Appeals & Writs Ch. 14-A, A. Remittitur.
Rutter, Cal. Practice Guide: Civil Appeals & Writs Ch. 15-C, C. Statutory Writs.
Rutter, Cal. Practice Guide: Civil Appeals & Writs Ch. 15-E, E. Procedures on Writ Review.
Rutter, Cal. Practice Guide: Civil Appeals & Writs Form 7:D, Petition for Writ of Supersedeas or Other Stay Order.
Rutter, Cal. Practice Guide: Civil Appeals & Writs Form 15:B.1, Sample Reply to Opposition to Writ Petition.
Rutter, Cal. Practice Guide: Civil Appeals & Writs Form 15:B.2, Sample Return to Writ Petition.
9 Witkin Cal. Proc. 5th Appeal § 9, (S 9) Current Structure.
9 Witkin Cal. Proc. 5th Appeal § 132, Jurisdiction Accepted.
9 Witkin Cal. Proc. 5th Appeal § 303, Determination.
9 Witkin Cal. Proc. 5th Appeal § 726, (S 726) Amicus Briefs in Court of Appeal or Appellate Division.
9 Witkin Cal. Proc. 5th Appeal § 938, Amicus Briefs on Merits.
2 Witkin Cal. Proc. 5th Courts § 195, (S 195) Appellate Rules.

2 Witkin Cal. Proc. 5th Courts § 216, Concurrent Jurisdiction of Appellate Court.
2 Witkin Cal. Proc. 5th Courts § 337, (S 337) Original Jurisdiction.
8 Witkin Cal. Proc. 5th Extraordinary Writs § 12, in General.
8 Witkin Cal. Proc. 5th Extraordinary Writs § 15, (S 15) Juvenile Court Orders Terminating Parental Rights.
8 Witkin Cal. Proc. 5th Extraordinary Writs § 17, (S 17) Other Proceedings.
8 Witkin Cal. Proc. 5th Extraordinary Writs § 56, Effect of Alternative Writ.
8 Witkin Cal. Proc. 5th Extraordinary Writs § 144, General Rule of Denying Writ.
8 Witkin Cal. Proc. 5th Extraordinary Writs § 163, (S 163) Governing Statutes and Rules.
8 Witkin Cal. Proc. 5th Extraordinary Writs § 166, in General.
8 Witkin Cal. Proc. 5th Extraordinary Writs § 169, in General.
8 Witkin Cal. Proc. 5th Extraordinary Writs § 172, Verification.
8 Witkin Cal. Proc. 5th Extraordinary Writs § 179, Petition to Review Trial Court Ruling.
8 Witkin Cal. Proc. 5th Extraordinary Writs § 180, Supporting Memorandum.
8 Witkin Cal. Proc. 5th Extraordinary Writs § 183, (S 183) Service.
8 Witkin Cal. Proc. 5th Extraordinary Writs § 184, (S 184) Opposing Memorandum.
8 Witkin Cal. Proc. 5th Extraordinary Writs § 185, (S 185) Summary Determination.
8 Witkin Cal. Proc. 5th Extraordinary Writs § 189, (S 189) Prohibition and Mandamus.
8 Witkin Cal. Proc. 5th Extraordinary Writs § 192, in General.
8 Witkin Cal. Proc. 5th Extraordinary Writs § 193, Return as Answer or Demurrer.
8 Witkin Cal. Proc. 5th Extraordinary Writs § 197, (S 197) Return in Reviewing Court.
8 Witkin Cal. Proc. 5th Extraordinary Writs § 200, Decision.
8 Witkin Cal. Proc. 5th Extraordinary Writs § 201, (S 201) Where Demurrer Alone is Filed.
8 Witkin Cal. Proc. 5th Extraordinary Writs § 203, (S 203) Proceedings in Reviewing Court.
8 Witkin Cal. Proc. 5th Extraordinary Writs § 205, Reviewing Court.
8 Witkin Cal. Proc. 5th Extraordinary Writs § 209, (S 209) Finality and Res Judicata.
8 Witkin Cal. Proc. 5th Extraordinary Writs § 210, (S 210) Summary Denial is Not Law of Case.
8 Witkin Cal. Proc. 5th Extraordinary Writs § 213, (S 213) Costs in Reviewing Court.
8 Witkin Cal. Proc. 5th Extraordinary Writs § 220, (S 220) Decision on Merits.
8 Witkin Cal. Proc. 5th Extraordinary Writs § 221, (S 221) Summary Denial.
2 Witkin Cal. Proc. 5th Jurisdiction § 225, (S 225) Extension of Time to Plead.
2 Witkin Cal. Proc. 5th Jurisdiction § 397, Refusal of Original Jurisdiction.
4 Witkin Cal. Proc. 5th Pleading § 67, (S 67) Designation of Parties.
10 Witkin, California Summary 10th Parent and Child § 717, in General.
10 Witkin, California Summary 10th Parent and Child § 723, Hearing and Decision.
10 Witkin, California Summary 10th Parent and Child § 724, in General.
10 Witkin, California Summary 10th Parent and Child § 727, Hearing and Decision.
2 Witkin Cal. Summ. 10th Workers' Compensation § 440, Rehearing and Review in Supreme Court.

Rule 8.491. Responsive pleading under Code of Civil Procedure section 418.10

If the Court of Appeal denies a petition for writ of mandate brought under Code of Civil Procedure section 418.10(c) and the Supreme Court denies review of the Court of Appeal's decision, the time to file a responsive pleading in the trial court is extended until 10 days after the Supreme Court files its order denying review. *(Adopted, eff. Jan. 1, 2009.)*

Ct. Rules

Research References

Rutter, Cal. Practice Guide: Civil Appeals & Writs Ch. 13-B, B. Petition for Review Procedures.
Rutter, Cal. Practice Guide: Civil Appeals & Writs Ch. 15-C, C. Statutory Writs.
2 Witkin Cal. Proc. 5th Jurisdiction § 225, (S 225) Extension of Time to Plead.

Rule 8.492.   Sanctions

(a) Grounds for sanctions

On motion of a party or its own motion, a Court of Appeal may impose sanctions, including the award or denial of costs under rule 8.493, on a party or an attorney for:

(1) Filing a frivolous petition or filing a petition solely to cause delay; or

(2) Committing any other unreasonable violation of these rules.

(b) Notice

The court must give notice in writing if it is considering imposing sanctions.

(c) Opposition

Within 10 days after the court sends such notice, a party or attorney may serve and file an opposition, but failure to do so will not be deemed consent. An opposition may not be filed unless the court sends such notice.

(d) Oral argument

Unless otherwise ordered, oral argument on the issue of sanctions must be combined with any oral argument on the merits of the petition. *(Adopted, eff. Jan. 1, 2009.)*

Research References

Rutter, Cal. Practice Guide: Civil Appeals & Writs Ch. 11-E, E. Appellate Costs and Sanctions.
Rutter, Cal. Practice Guide: Civil Appeals & Writs Ch. 15-E, E. Procedures on Writ Review.
8 Witkin Cal. Proc. 5th Extraordinary Writs § 163, (S 163) Governing Statutes and Rules.
8 Witkin Cal. Proc. 5th Extraordinary Writs § 213, (S 213) Costs in Reviewing Court.

Rule 8.493.   Costs

(a) Award of costs

(1) Except in a criminal or juvenile or other proceeding in which a party is entitled to court-appointed counsel:

(A) Unless otherwise ordered by the court under (B), the prevailing party in an original proceeding is entitled to costs if the court resolves the proceeding by written opinion after issuing an alternative writ, an order to show cause, or a peremptory writ in the first instance.

(B) In the interests of justice, the court may also award or deny costs as it deems proper in the proceedings listed in (A) and in other circumstances.

(2) The opinion or order resolving the proceeding must specify the award or denial of costs.

(b) Procedures for recovering costs

Rule 8.278(b)–(d) governs the procedure for recovering costs under this rule. *(Adopted, eff. Jan. 1, 2009.)*

Research References

Rutter, Cal. Practice Guide: Civil Appeals & Writs Ch. 15-E, E. Procedures on Writ Review.
Rutter, Cal. Practice Guide: Civil Appeals & Writs Ch. 15-E , Outline E.
9 Witkin Cal. Proc. 5th Appeal § 9, (S 9) Current Structure.
2 Witkin Cal. Proc. 5th Courts § 195, (S 195) Appellate Rules.

8 Witkin Cal. Proc. 5th Extraordinary Writs § 163, (S 163) Governing Statutes and Rules.
8 Witkin Cal. Proc. 5th Extraordinary Writs § 213, (S 213) Costs in Reviewing Court.
10 Witkin, California Summary 10th Parent and Child § 724, in General.

Chapter 8

MISCELLANEOUS WRITS

Rule

Rule 8.495.   Review of Workers' Compensation Appeals Board cases

(a) Petition

(1) A petition to review an order, award, or decision of the Workers' Compensation Appeals Board must include:

(A) The order, award, or decision to be reviewed; and

(B) The workers' compensation judge's minutes of hearing and summary of evidence, findings and opinion on decision, and report and recommendation on the petition for reconsideration.

(2) If the petition claims that the board's ruling is not supported by substantial evidence, it must fairly state and attach copies of all the relevant material evidence.

(3) The petition must be accompanied by proof of service of two copies of the petition on the Secretary of the Workers' Compensation Appeals Board in San Francisco and one copy on each party who appeared in the action and whose interest is adverse to the petitioner. Service on the board's local district office is not required.

(b) Answer and reply

(1) Within 25 days after the petition is filed, the board or any real party in interest may serve and file an answer and any relevant exhibits not included in the petition.

(2) Within 15 days after an answer is filed, the petitioner may serve and file a reply.

(c) Certificate of Interested Entities or Persons

(1) Each party other than the board must comply with the requirements of rule 8.208 concerning serving and filing a Certificate of Interested Entities or Persons.

(2) The petitioner's certificate must be included in the petition and the real party in interest's certificate must be included in the answer. The certificate must appear after the cover and before the tables.

(3) If a party fails to file a certificate as required under (1) and (2), the clerk must notify the party by mail that the party must file the certificate within 10 days after the clerk's notice is mailed and that failure to comply will result in one of the following sanctions:

(A) If the party is the petitioner, the court will strike the petition; or

(B) If the party is the real party in interest, the court will strike the document.

(4) If the party fails to comply with the notice under (3), the court may impose the sanctions specified in the notice. *(Formerly Rule 57, adopted, eff. Jan. 1, 2005. As amended, eff. July 1, 2006. Renumbered Rule 8.494 and amended, eff. Jan. 1, 2007. Renumbered Rule 8.495, eff. Jan. 1, 2009.)*

Advisory Committee Comment

Subdivision (a). Subdivision (a)(3) specifies that the petition must be served on the Secretary of the Workers' Compensation Appeals Board in San Francisco. Neither the petition nor a courtesy copy should be served on the local district office of the board.

Subdivision (b). To clarify that a respondent may rely on exhibits filed with the petition without duplicating them in the answer, (b)(1) specifies that exhibits filed with an answer must be limited to exhibits "not included in the petition."

Research References

Rutter, Cal. Practice Guide: Civil Appeals & Writs Ch. 15-B, B. Common Law Writs.
Rutter, Cal. Practice Guide: Civil Appeals & Writs Ch. 15-E, E. Procedures on Writ Review.
9 Witkin Cal. Proc. 5th Appeal § 9, (S 9) Current Structure.
2 Witkin Cal. Proc. 5th Courts § 195, (S 195) Appellate Rules.
8 Witkin Cal. Proc. 5th Extraordinary Writs § 17, (S 17) Other Proceedings.
8 Witkin Cal. Proc. 5th Extraordinary Writs § 193, Return as Answer or Demurrer.
2 Witkin Cal. Summ. 10th Workers' Compensation § 424, Judge's Report is Not Essential.
2 Witkin Cal. Summ. 10th Workers' Compensation § 438, Petition, Answer, and Reply.

Rule 8.496. Review of Public Utilities Commission cases

(a) Petition

(1) A petition to review an order or decision of the Public Utilities Commission must be verified and must be served on the executive director and general counsel of the commission and any real parties in interest.

(2) A real party in interest is one who was a party of record to the proceeding and took a position adverse to the petitioner.

(b) Answer and reply

(1) Within 35 days after the petition is filed, the commission or any real party in interest may serve and file an answer.

(2) Within 25 days after an answer is filed, the petitioner may serve and file a reply.

(c) Certificate of Interested Entities or Persons

(1) Each party other than the commission must comply with the requirements of rule 8.208 concerning serving and filing a Certificate of Interested Entities or Persons.

(2) The petitioner's certificate must be included in the petition and the real party in interest's certificate must be included in the answer. The certificate must appear after the cover and before the tables.

(3) If a party fails to file a certificate as required under (1) and (2), the clerk must notify the party by mail that the party must file the certificate within 10 days after the clerk's notice is mailed and that failure to comply will result in one of the following sanctions:

(A) If the party is the petitioner, the court will strike the petition; or

(B) If the party is the real party in interest, the court will strike the document.

(4) If the party fails to comply with the notice under (3), the court may impose the sanctions specified in the notice. *(Formerly Rule 58, adopted, eff. Jan. 1, 2005. As amended, eff. July 1, 2006. Renumbered Rule 8.496 and amended, eff. Jan. 1, 2007.)*

Advisory Committee Comment

Subdivision (b). A party other than the petitioner who files an answer may be required to pay a filing fee under Government Code section 68926 if the answer is the first document filed in the writ proceeding in the reviewing court by that party. See rule 8.25(c).

Research References

Rutter, Cal. Practice Guide: Civil Appeals & Writs Ch. 15-E, E. Procedures on Writ Review.
Rutter, Cal. Practice Guide: Civil Appeals & Writs Form 15:B.2, Sample Return to Writ Petition.
2 Witkin Cal. Proc. 5th Courts § 330, (S 330) Original Jurisdiction.
8 Witkin Cal. Proc. 5th Extraordinary Writs § 17, (S 17) Other Proceedings.
8 Witkin Cal. Proc. 5th Extraordinary Writs § 193, Return as Answer or Demurrer.

Rule 8.497. Review of California Environmental Quality Act cases under Public Resources Code sections 21178–21189.3

(a) Application

(1) This rule governs actions or proceedings in the Court of Appeal alleging that a public agency has approved or is undertaking an environmental leadership development project in violation of the California Environmental Quality Act. As used in this rule, an "environmental leadership development project" or "leadership project" means a project certified by the Governor under Public Resources Code sections 21182–21184.

(2) Except as otherwise provided in Public Resources Code sections 21178–21189.3 and this rule, the provisions of the Public Resources Code and the CEQA Guidelines adopted by the Natural Resources Agency (Cal. Code Regs., tit. 14, § 15000 et seq.) governing judicial actions or proceedings to attack, review, set aside, void, or annul acts or decisions of a public agency on the grounds of noncompliance with the California Environmental Quality Act apply in proceedings governed by this rule.

(b) Service

Except as otherwise provided by law, all documents that this rule requires be served on the parties must be served by personal delivery, electronic service, express mail, or other means consistent with Code of Civil Procedure sections 1010, 1011, 1012, and 1013 and reasonably calculated to ensure delivery of the document to the parties not later than the close of the business day after the document is filed or lodged with the court.

(c) Petition

(1) *Service and filing*

A person alleging that a public agency has approved or is undertaking a leadership project in violation of the California Environmental Quality Act must serve and file a petition for a writ of mandate in the Court of Appeal with geographic jurisdiction over the project.

(2) *Form and contents*

In addition to any other applicable requirements, the petition must:

(A) State that the project at issue was certified by the Governor as a leadership project under Public Resources Code sections 21182–21184 and is subject to this rule;

(B) Provide notice that the person or entity that applied for certification of the project as a leadership project must make the payments required by (h);

(C) Include any other claims required to be concurrently filed by the petitioner under Public Resources Code section 21185; and

(D) Be verified.

(d) Administrative record

(1) *Lodging and service*

Within 10 days after the petition is served on the lead public agency, that agency must lodge the certified final administrative record with the Court of Appeal and serve on the parties a copy of the certified final administrative record and notice that the record has been lodged with the court.

(2) *Form and contents*

(A) Unless otherwise ordered by the Court of Appeal, the lead agency must lodge with the court one copy of the record in electronic format and one copy in paper format and serve on each party one copy of the record in electronic format. The record in electronic format must comply with rules 3.1365 and 3.1367. The record in paper format must comply with rules 3.1365 and 3.1368.

(B) A party may request the record in paper format and pay the reasonable cost or show good cause for a court order requiring the lead agency to serve the requesting party with one copy of the record in paper format.

(C) The record must include all of the materials specified in Public Resources Code section 21167.6.

(3) *Motions regarding the record*

(A) Any request to augment or otherwise change the contents of the administrative record must be made by motion in the Court of Appeal. The motion must be served and filed within 25 days after the record is served.

(B) Any opposition or other response to the motion must be served and filed within 10 days after the motion is filed.

(C) The Court of Appeal may appoint a special master to hear and decide any motion regarding the record. The order appointing the special master may specify the time within which the special master is required to file a decision.

(e) Notice of settlement

The petitioner must immediately notify the court if the case is settled.

(f) Response to petition

(1) Within 25 days after service of the administrative record or within the time ordered by the court, the respondent and any real party in interest must serve and file any answer to the petition; any motion challenging the sufficiency of the petition, including any motion to dismiss the petition; and any other response to the petition. Any such answer, motion, or other response from the same party must be filed concurrently.

(2) Any opposition or other response to a motion challenging the sufficiency of the petition must be served and filed within 10 days after the motion is filed.

(g) Briefs

(1) *Service and filing*

Unless otherwise ordered by the court:

(A) The petitioner must serve and file its brief within 40 days after the administrative record is served.

(B) Within 30 days after the petitioner's brief is filed, the respondent public agency must—and any real party in interest may—serve and file a respondent's brief.

(C) Within 20 days after the respondent's brief is filed, the petitioner may serve and file a reply brief.

(2) *Form and contents*

The briefs must comply as nearly as possible with rule 8.204.

(h) Certificate of Interested Entities or Persons

(1) Each party other than a public agency must comply with the requirements of rule 8.208 concerning serving and filing a *Certificate of Interested Entities or Persons*.

(2) The petitioner's certificate must be included in the petition. Other parties must include their certificate in their brief, or if the party files an answer or other response to the petition, a motion, an application, or an opposition to a motion or application in the Court of Appeal before filing its brief, the party must serve and file its certificate at the time it files the first answer, response, motion, application, or opposition. The certificate must appear after the cover and before any tables.

(3) If a party fails to file a certificate as required under (1) and (2), the clerk must notify the party by mail that the party must file the certificate within 10 days after the clerk's notice is mailed and that failure to comply will result in one of the following sanctions:

(A) If the party is the petitioner, the court will strike the petition; or

(B) If the party is the real party in interest, the court will strike the document.

(4) If the party fails to comply with the notice under (3), the court may impose the sanctions specified in the notice.

(i) Court costs

(1) In fulfillment of the provision in Public Resources Code section 21183 regarding payment of the Court of Appeal's costs:

(A) Within 10 days after service of the petition on the real party in interest, the person who applied for certification of the project as a leadership project must pay a fee of $100,000 to the Court of Appeal.

(B) If the Court of Appeal incurs any of the following costs, the person who applied for certification of the project as a leadership project must also pay, within 10 days of being ordered by the court, the following costs or estimated costs:

(i) The costs of any special master appointed by the Court of Appeal in the case; and

(ii) The costs of any contract personnel retained by the Court of Appeal to work on the case.

(2) If the fee or costs under (1) are not timely paid, the Court of Appeal may transfer the case to the superior court with geographic jurisdiction over the project, and the case will proceed under the procedures applicable to projects that have not been certified as leadership projects.

(j) Extensions of time

The court may order extensions of time only for good cause and in order to promote the interests of justice. (*Adopted, eff. July 1, 2012.*)

Advisory Committee Comment

Subdivision (b). This provision does not apply to service of the petition on the respondent public agency or real party in interest because the method of service on these parties is set by Public Resources Code sections 21167.6 and 21167.6.5.

Subdivision (c). Under this provision, a proceeding in the Court of Appeal is initiated by serving and filing a petition for a writ of mandate as provided in rule 8.25, not by filing a complaint and serving a summons and the complaint.

Subdivision (d)(3)(C). Public Resources Code section 21185 provides that the court may appoint a master to assist the court in managing and processing cases subject to this rule. Appointment of a special master to hear and decide motions regarding the record is just one example of when a court might make such an appointment.

Subdivision (f). A party other than the petitioner who files an answer, motion, or other response to a petition under (e) may be required to pay a filing fee under Government Code section 68926 if the answer, motion, or other response is the first document filed in the proceeding in the reviewing court by that party. See rule 8.25(c).

Subdivision (g). On application of the parties or on its own motion, the court may set different briefing periods. For example, if a motion to augment or otherwise modify the contents of the record is filed, the court might order that petitioner's brief be filed within a specified time after that motion is decided.

Research References

Rutter, Cal. Practice Guide: Civil Appeals & Writs Ch. 15-C, C. Statutory Writs.

Rule 8.498. Review of Agricultural Labor Relations Board and Public Employment Relations Board cases

(a) Petition

(1) A petition to review an order or decision of the Agricultural Labor Relations Board or the Public Employment Relations Board must be filed in the Court of Appeal and served on the executive secretary of the Agricultural Labor Relations Board or the general counsel of the Public Employment Relations Board in Sacramento and on any real parties in interest.

(2) A real party in interest is a party of record to the proceeding.

(3) The petition must be verified.

(b) Record

Within the time permitted by statute, the board must file the certified record of the proceedings and simultaneously file and serve on all parties an index to that record.

(c) Briefs

(1) The petitioner must serve and file its brief within 35 days after the index is filed.

(2) Within 35 days after the petitioner's brief is filed, the board must—and any real party in interest may—serve and file a respondent's brief.

(3) Within 25 days after the respondent's brief is filed, petitioner may serve and file a reply brief.

(d) Certificate of Interested Entities or Persons

(1) Each party other than the board must comply with the requirements of rule 8.208 concerning serving and filing a Certificate of Interested Entities or Persons.

(2) The petitioner's certificate must be included in the petition and the real party in interest's certificate must be included in the answer. The certificate must appear after the cover and before the tables.

(3) If a party fails to file a certificate as required under (1) and (2), the clerk must notify the party by mail that the party must file the certificate within 10 days after the clerk's notice is mailed and that failure to comply will result in one of the following sanctions:

(A) If the party is the petitioner, the court will strike the petition; or

(B) If the party is the real party in interest, the court will strike the document.

(4) If the party fails to comply with the notice under (3), the court may impose the sanctions specified in the notice. *(Formerly Rule 59, adopted, eff. Jan. 1, 2005. As amended, eff. July 1, 2006. Renumbered Rule 8.498 and amended, eff. Jan. 1, 2007.)*

Advisory Committee Comment

A party other than the petitioner who files an answer or brief may be required to pay a filing fee under Government Code section 68926 if the answer or brief is the first document filed in the writ proceeding in the reviewing court by that party. See rule 8.25(c).

Research References

Rutter, Cal. Practice Guide: Civil Appeals & Writs Ch. 15-B, B. Common Law Writs.
Rutter, Cal. Practice Guide: Civil Appeals & Writs Ch. 15-E, E. Procedures on Writ Review.
Rutter, Cal. Practice Guide: Civil Appeals & Writs Form 15:B.2, Sample Return to Writ Petition.
9 Witkin Cal. Proc. 5th Appeal § 9, (S 9) Current Structure.
8 Witkin Cal. Proc. 5th Extraordinary Writs § 12, in General.
8 Witkin Cal. Proc. 5th Extraordinary Writs § 17, (S 17) Other Proceedings.
3 Witkin, California Summary 10th Agency and Employment § 672, in General.

Rule 8.499. Filing, modification, and finality of decision; remittitur

(a) Filing of decisions

Rule 8.264(a) governs the filing of decisions in writ proceedings under this chapter in the Court of Appeal and rule 8.532(a) governs the filing of decisions in the Supreme Court.

(b) Modification of decisions

Rule 8.264(c) governs the modification of decisions in writ proceedings under this chapter.

(c) Finality of decision

(1) A court's denial of a petition for a writ under rule 8.495, 8.496, or 8.498 without issuance of a writ of review is final in that court when filed.

(2) Except as otherwise provided in this rule, a decision in a writ proceeding under this chapter is final in that court 30 days after the decision is filed.

(3) If necessary to prevent mootness or frustration of the relief granted or to otherwise promote the interests of justice, the court may order early finality in that court of a decision granting a petition for a writ under this chapter or, except as provided in (1), a decision denying such a petition. The decision may provide for finality in that court on filing or within a stated period of less than 30 days.

(4) If a Court of Appeal certifies its opinion for publication or partial publication after filing its decision and before its decision becomes final in that court, the finality period runs from the filing date of the order for publication.

(5) If an order modifying an opinion changes the appellate judgment, the finality period runs from the filing date of the modification order.

(d) Remittitur

A Court of Appeal must issue a remittitur in a writ proceeding under this chapter except when the court denies the petition under rule 8.495, 8.496, or 8.498 without issuing a writ of review. Rule 8.272(b)–(d) governs issuance of a remittitur in writ proceedings under this chapter. *(Adopted, eff. Jan. 1, 2008. As amended, eff. Jan. 1, 2011; July 1, 2012.)*

Research References

Rutter, Cal. Practice Guide: Civil Appeals & Writs Ch. 14-A, A. Remittitur.
Rutter, Cal. Practice Guide: Civil Appeals & Writs Ch. 15-E, E. Procedures on Writ Review.
9 Witkin Cal. Proc. 5th Appeal § 9, (S 9) Current Structure.

Ct. Rules

9 Witkin Cal. Proc. 5th Appeal § 843, (S 843) Proceedings in Which Remittitur Issues.
2 Witkin Cal. Proc. 5th Courts § 195, (S 195) Appellate Rules.
8 Witkin Cal. Proc. 5th Extraordinary Writs § 12, in General.
8 Witkin Cal. Proc. 5th Extraordinary Writs § 17, (S 17) Other Proceedings.

Chapter 9

PROCEEDINGS IN THE SUPREME COURT

Rule
8.500. Petition for review.
8.504. Form and contents of petition, answer, and reply.
8.508. Petition for review to exhaust state remedies.
8.512. Ordering review.
8.516. Issues on review.
8.520. Briefs by parties and amici curiae; judicial notice.
8.524. Oral argument and submission of the cause.
8.528. Disposition.
8.532. Filing, finality, and modification of decision.
8.536. Rehearing.
8.540. Remittitur.
8.544. Costs and sanctions.
8.548. Decision on request of a court of another jurisdiction.
8.552. Transfer for decision.

Rule 8.500. Petition for review

(a) Right to file a petition, answer, or reply

(1) A party may file a petition in the Supreme Court for review of any decision of the Court of Appeal, including any interlocutory order, except the denial of a transfer of a case within the appellate jurisdiction of the superior court.

(2) A party may file an answer responding to the issues raised in the petition. In the answer, the party may ask the court to address additional issues if it grants review.

(3) The petitioner may file a reply to the answer.

(b) Grounds for review

The Supreme Court may order review of a Court of Appeal decision:

(1) When necessary to secure uniformity of decision or to settle an important question of law;

(2) When the Court of Appeal lacked jurisdiction;

(3) When the Court of Appeal decision lacked the concurrence of sufficient qualified justices; or

(4) For the purpose of transferring the matter to the Court of Appeal for such proceedings as the Supreme Court may order.

(c) Limits of review

(1) As a policy matter, on petition for review the Supreme Court normally will not consider an issue that the petitioner failed to timely raise in the Court of Appeal.

(2) A party may petition for review without petitioning for rehearing in the Court of Appeal, but as a policy matter the Supreme Court normally will accept the Court of Appeal opinion's statement of the issues and facts unless the party has called the Court of Appeal's attention to any alleged omission or misstatement of an issue or fact in a petition for rehearing.

(d) Petitions in nonconsolidated proceedings

If the Court of Appeal decides an appeal and denies a related petition for writ of habeas corpus without issuing an order to show cause and without formally consolidating the two proceedings, a party seeking review of both decisions must file a separate petition for review in each proceeding.

(e) Time to serve and file

(1) A petition for review must be served and filed within 10 days after the Court of Appeal decision is final in that court. For purposes of this rule, the date of finality is not extended if it falls on a day on which the clerk's office is closed.

(2) The time to file a petition for review may not be extended, but the Chief Justice may relieve a party from a failure to file a timely petition for review if the time for the court to order review on its own motion has not expired.

(3) If a petition for review is presented for filing before the Court of Appeal decision is final in that court, the Supreme Court clerk must accept it and file it on the day after finality.

(4) Any answer to the petition must be served and filed within 20 days after the petition is filed.

(5) Any reply to the answer must be served and filed within 10 days after the answer is filed.

(f) Additional requirements

(1) The petition must also be served on the superior court clerk and the Court of Appeal clerk.

(2) A copy of each brief must be served on a public officer or agency when required by statute or by rule 8.29.

(3) The Supreme Court clerk must file the petition even if its proof of service is defective, but if the petitioner fails to file a corrected proof of service within 5 days after the clerk gives notice of the defect the court may strike the petition or impose a lesser sanction.

(g) Amicus curiae letters

(1) Any person or entity wanting to support or oppose a petition for review or for an original writ must serve on all parties and send to the Supreme Court an amicus curiae letter rather than a brief.

(2) The letter must describe the interest of the amicus curiae. Any matter attached to the letter or incorporated by reference must comply with rule 8.504(e).

(3) Receipt of the letter does not constitute leave to file an amicus curiae brief on the merits under rule 8.520(f). *(Formerly Rule 28, adopted, eff. Jan. 1, 2003. As amended, eff. Jan. 1, 2004; July 1, 2004. Renumbered Rule 8.500 and amended, eff. Jan. 1, 2007. As amended, eff. Jan. 1, 2009.)*

Advisory Committee Comment

Subdivision (a). A party other than the petitioner who files an answer may be required to pay a filing fee under Government Code section 68927 if the answer is the first document filed in the proceeding in the Supreme Court by that party. See rule 8.25(c).

Subdivision (a)(1) makes it clear that any interlocutory order of the Court of Appeal—such as an order denying an application to appoint counsel, to augment the record, or to allow oral argument—is a "decision" that may be challenged by petition for review.

Subdivision (e). Subdivision (e)(1) provides that a petition for review must be served and filed within 10 days after the Court of Appeal decision is *final in that court*. Finality in the Court of Appeal is generally governed by rules 8.264(b) (civil appeals), 8.366(b) (criminal appeals), 8.387(b) (habeas corpus proceedings), and 8.490(b) (proceedings for writs of mandate, certiorari, and prohibition). These rules declare the general rule that a Court of Appeal decision is final in that court 30 days after filing. They then carve out specific exceptions—decisions that they declare to be final immediately on filing (see rules 8.264(b)(2), 8.366(b)(2), and 8.490(b)(1)). The plain implication is that all other Court of Appeal orders-specifically, interlocutory orders that may be the subject of a petition for review—are *not* final on filing. This implication is confirmed by current practice, in which parties may be allowed to apply for—

and the Courts of Appeal may grant—reconsideration of such interlocutory orders; reconsideration, of course, would be impermissible if the orders were in fact final on filing.

Contrary to paragraph (2) of subdivision (e), paragraphs (4) and (5) do not prohibit extending the time to file an answer or reply; because the subdivision thus expressly forbids an extension of time only with respect to the petition for review, by clear negative implication it permits an application to extend the time to file an answer or reply under rule 8.50.

See rule 8.25(b)(5) for provisions concerning the timeliness of documents mailed by inmates or patients from custodial institutions.

Subdivision (f). The general requirements relating to service of documents in the appellate courts are established by rule 8.25. Subdivision (f)(1) requires that the petition (but not an answer or reply) be served on the Court of Appeal clerk. To assist litigants, (f)(1) also states explicitly what is impliedly required by rule 8.212(c), i.e., that the petition must also be served on the superior court clerk (for delivery to the trial judge).

Research References

Rutter, Cal. Practice Guide: Civil Appeals & Writs Ch. 7-E, E. Stay by Writ of Supersedeas.

Rutter, Cal. Practice Guide: Civil Appeals & Writs Ch. 9-D, D. Procedural Rules.

Rutter, Cal. Practice Guide: Civil Appeals & Writs Ch. 11-C, C. Rendition of Opinion and Judgment.

Rutter, Cal. Practice Guide: Civil Appeals & Writs Ch. 11-G, G. Finality as to Court of Appeal.

Rutter, Cal. Practice Guide: Civil Appeals & Writs Ch. 12-A, A. Overview.

Rutter, Cal. Practice Guide: Civil Appeals & Writs Ch. 12-B, B. Grounds for Rehearing.

Rutter, Cal. Practice Guide: Civil Appeals & Writs Ch. 12-C, C. Considerations on Whether to Seek a Rehearing.

Rutter, Cal. Practice Guide: Civil Appeals & Writs Ch. 13-A, A. General Considerations.

Rutter, Cal. Practice Guide: Civil Appeals & Writs Ch. 13-B, B. Petition for Review Procedures.

Rutter, Cal. Practice Guide: Civil Appeals & Writs Ch. 13-C, C. Briefs on the Merits After Grant of Review.

Rutter, Cal. Practice Guide: Civil Appeals & Writs Ch. 15-E, E. Procedures on Writ Review.

Rutter, Cal. Practice Guide: Civil Appeals & Writs Ch. 16-K, K. Transfer to Court of Appeal.

9 Witkin Cal. Proc. 5th Appeal § 9, (S 9) Current Structure.

9 Witkin Cal. Proc. 5th Appeal § 838, (S 838) Finality for All Purposes.

9 Witkin Cal. Proc. 5th Appeal § 915, (S 915) Uniformity of Decision and Important Question.

9 Witkin Cal. Proc. 5th Appeal § 916, (S 916) Appellate Court Without Jurisdiction.

9 Witkin Cal. Proc. 5th Appeal § 917, (S 917) No Qualified Majority.

9 Witkin Cal. Proc. 5th Appeal § 918, (S 918) Transfer to Court of Appeal for Further Proceedings.

9 Witkin Cal. Proc. 5th Appeal § 919, (S 919) Other Grounds Formerly Recognized.

9 Witkin Cal. Proc. 5th Appeal § 920, (S 920) General Rule: No Examination.

9 Witkin Cal. Proc. 5th Appeal § 921, (S 921) When Record Will be Reexamined.

9 Witkin Cal. Proc. 5th Appeal § 927, Petition.

9 Witkin Cal. Proc. 5th Appeal § 928, Answer and Reply.

9 Witkin Cal. Proc. 5th Appeal § 930, Statement of Issues.

9 Witkin Cal. Proc. 5th Appeal § 939, (S 939) Letter in Lieu of Brief.

9 Witkin Cal. Proc. 5th Appeal § 1019, (S 1019) Rehearing.

2 Witkin Cal. Proc. 5th Courts § 195, (S 195) Appellate Rules.

2 Witkin Cal. Proc. 5th Courts § 329, (S 329) Appellate Jurisdiction.

2 Witkin Cal. Proc. 5th Courts § 358, (S 358) Supreme Court.

2 Witkin Cal. Summ. 10th Workers' Compensation § 440, Rehearing and Review in Supreme Court.

Rule 8.504. Form and contents of petition, answer, and reply

(a) In general

Except as provided in this rule, a petition for review, answer, and reply must comply with the relevant provisions of rule 8.204.

(b) Contents of a petition

(1) The body of the petition must begin with a concise, nonargumentative statement of the issues presented for review, framing them in terms of the facts of the case but without unnecessary detail.

(2) The petition must explain how the case presents a ground for review under rule 8.500(b).

(3) If a petition for rehearing could have been filed in the Court of Appeal, the petition for review must state whether it was filed and, if so, how the court ruled.

(4) If the petition seeks review of a Court of Appeal opinion, a copy of the opinion showing its filing date and a copy of any order modifying the opinion or directing its publication must be bound at the back of the original petition and each copy filed in the Supreme Court.

(5) If the petition seeks review of a Court of Appeal order, a copy of the order showing the date it was entered must be bound at the back of the original petition and each copy filed in the Supreme Court.

(6) The title of the case and designation of the parties on the cover of the petition must be identical to the title and designation in the Court of Appeal opinion or order that is the subject of the petition.

(7) Rule 8.508 governs the form and content of a petition for review filed by the defendant in a criminal case for the sole purpose of exhausting state remedies before seeking federal habeas corpus review.

(c) Contents of an answer

An answer that raises additional issues for review must contain a concise, nonargumentative statement of those issues, framing them in terms of the facts of the case but without unnecessary detail.

(d) Length

(1) If produced on a computer, a petition or answer must not exceed 8,400 words, including footnotes, and a reply must not exceed 4,200 words, including footnotes. Each petition, answer, or reply must include a certificate by appellate counsel or an unrepresented party stating the number of words in the document. The person certifying may rely on the word count of the computer program used to prepare the document.

(2) If typewritten, a petition or answer must not exceed 30 pages and a reply must not exceed 15 pages.

(3) The tables, the cover information required under rule 8.204(b)(10), the Court of Appeal opinion, a certificate under (1), any signature block, and any attachment under (e)(1) are excluded from the limits stated in (1) and (2).

(4) On application and for good cause, the Chief Justice may permit a longer petition, answer, reply, or attachment.

(e) Attachments and incorporation by reference

(1) No attachments are permitted except:

(A) An opinion or order required to be attached under (b)(4) or (5);

(B) Exhibits or orders of a trial court or Court of Appeal that the party considers unusually significant;

(C) Copies of relevant local, state, or federal regulations or rules, out-of-state statutes, or other similar citable materials that are not readily accessible; and

(D) An opinion required to be attached under rule 8.1115(c).

(2) The attachments under (1)(B)–(C) must not exceed a combined total of 10 pages.

(3) No incorporation by reference is permitted except a reference to a petition, an answer, or a reply filed by another party in the same case or filed in a case that raises the same or similar issues and in which a petition for review is pending or has been granted. *(Formerly Rule 28.1, adopted, eff. Jan. 1, 2003. As amended, eff. Jan. 1, 2004. Renumbered Rule 8.504 and amended, eff. Jan. 1, 2007. As amended, eff. Jan. 1, 2009; Jan. 1, 2011.)*

Advisory Committee Comment

Subdivision (d). Subdivision (d) states in terms of word counts rather than page counts the maximum permissible lengths of a petition for review, answer, or reply produced on a computer. This provision tracks a provision in rule 8.204(c) governing Court of Appeal briefs and is explained in the advisory committee comment to that provision. Subdivision (d)(3) specifies certain items that are not counted toward the maximum length of a petition, answer, or reply. Signature blocks, as referenced in this provision include not only the signatures, but also the printed names, titles, and affiliations of any attorneys filing or joining in the petition, answer, or reply, which may accompany the signature.

Research References

Rutter, Cal. Practice Guide: Civil Appeals & Writs Ch. 13-A, A. General Considerations.
Rutter, Cal. Practice Guide: Civil Appeals & Writs Ch. 13-B, B. Petition for Review Procedures.
9 Witkin Cal. Proc. 5th Appeal § 923, Procedure.
9 Witkin Cal. Proc. 5th Appeal § 929, Form and Length Limitations.
9 Witkin Cal. Proc. 5th Appeal § 930, Statement of Issues.
9 Witkin Cal. Proc. 5th Appeal § 939, (S 939) Letter in Lieu of Brief.
9 Witkin Cal. Proc. 5th Appeal § 1019, (S 1019) Rehearing.
9 Witkin Cal. Proc. 5th Appeal § 1026, Transfer by Court of Appeal on Party's Petition.

Rule 8.508. Petition for review to exhaust state remedies

(a) Purpose

After decision by the Court of Appeal in a criminal case, a defendant may file an abbreviated petition for review in the Supreme Court for the sole purpose of exhausting state remedies before presenting a claim for federal habeas corpus relief.

(b) Form and contents

(1) The words "Petition for Review to Exhaust State Remedies" must appear prominently on the cover of the petition.

(2) Except as provided in (3), the petition must comply with rule 8.504.

(3) The petition need not comply with rule 8.504(b)(1)–(2) but must include:

(A) A statement that the case presents no grounds for review under rule 8.500(b) and the petition is filed solely to exhaust state remedies for federal habeas corpus purposes;

(B) A brief statement of the underlying proceedings, including the nature of the conviction and the punishment imposed; and

(C) A brief statement of the factual and legal bases of the claim.

(c) Service

The petition must be served on the Court of Appeal clerk but need not be served on the superior court clerk. *(Formerly Rule 33.3, adopted, eff. Jan. 1, 2004. Renumbered Rule 8.508 and amended, eff. Jan. 1, 2007.)*

Advisory Committee Comment

Subdivision (b). Although a petition under this rule must state that "the case presents no grounds for review under rule 8.500(b)" (see (b)(3)(A)), this does not mean the Supreme Court cannot order review if it determines the case warrants review. The list of grounds for granting review in rule 8.500(b) is not intended to be exclusive, and from time to time the Supreme Court has exercised its discretion to order review in a case that does not present one of the listed grounds. (Compare U.S. Supreme Court Rule 10 [the listed grounds for granting certiorari, "although neither controlling nor fully measuring the Court's discretion, indicate the character of the reasons the Court considers"].)

Subdivision (b)(3)(C) requires the petition to include a statement of the factual and legal bases of the claim. This showing is required by federal law: "for purposes of exhausting state remedies, a claim for relief [in state court] . . . must include reference to a specific federal constitutional guarantee, as well as a statement of the facts that entitle the petitioner to relief." *(Gray v. Netherland* (1996) 518 U.S. 152, 162–163, citing *Picard v. Connor* (1971) 404 U.S. 270.) The federal courts will decide whether a petition filed in compliance with this rule satisfies federal exhaustion requirements, and practitioners should consult federal law to determine whether the petition's statement of the factual and legal bases for the claim is sufficient for that purpose.

Rule 8.512. Ordering review

(a) Transmittal of record

On receiving a copy of a petition for review or on request of the Supreme Court, whichever is earlier, the Court of Appeal clerk must promptly send the record to the Supreme Court. If the petition is denied, the Supreme Court clerk must promptly return the record to the Court of Appeal.

(b) Determination of petition

(1) The court may order review within 60 days after the last petition for review is filed. Before the 60–day period or any extension expires, the court may order one or more extensions to a date not later than 90 days after the last petition is filed.

(2) If the court does not rule on the petition within the time allowed by (1), the petition is deemed denied.

(c) Review on the court's own motion

(1) If no petition for review is filed, the Supreme Court may, on its own motion, order review of a Court of Appeal decision within 30 days after the decision is final in that court. Before the 30–day period or any extension expires, the Supreme Court may order one or more extensions to a date not later than 90 days after the decision is final in the Court of Appeal. If any such period ends on a day on which the clerk's office is closed, the court may order review on its own motion on the next day the clerk's office is open.

(2) If a petition for review is filed, the Supreme Court may deny the petition but order review on its own motion within the periods prescribed in (b)(1).

(d) Order; grant and hold

(1) An order granting review must be signed by at least four justices; an order denying review may be signed by the Chief Justice alone.

(2) On or after granting review, the court may order action in the matter deferred until the court disposes of another matter or pending further order of the court. *(Formerly Rule 28.2, adopted, eff. Jan. 1, 2003. As amended, eff. Jan. 1, 2004. Renumbered Rule 8.512, eff. Jan. 1, 2007.)*

Advisory Committee Comment

Subdivision (b). The Supreme Court deems the 60–day period within which it may grant review to begin on the filing date of the last petition for review that either (1) is timely in the sense that it is filed within the rule time for such petitions (i.e., 10 days after finality of the Court of Appeal decision) or (2) is treated as timely—although presented for filing after expiration of the rule time—in the sense that it is filed with permission of the Chief Justice on a showing of good cause for relief from default. In each circumstance it is the filing of the petition that triggers the 60–day period.

Research References

Rutter, Cal. Practice Guide: Civil Appeals & Writs Ch. 13-A, A. General Considerations.

Rutter, Cal. Practice Guide: Civil Appeals & Writs Ch. 13-B, B. Petition for Review Procedures.

9 Witkin Cal. Proc. 5th Appeal § 838, (S 838) Finality for All Purposes.

9 Witkin Cal. Proc. 5th Appeal § 925, Time and Extension.

9 Witkin Cal. Proc. 5th Appeal § 931, Transmission of Record.

9 Witkin Cal. Proc. 5th Appeal § 932, Court Conference and Orders.

9 Witkin Cal. Proc. 5th Appeal § 933, Time and Extension.

8 Witkin Cal. Proc. 5th Extraordinary Writs § 209, (S 209) Finality and Res Judicata.

Rule 8.516. Issues on review

(a) Issues to be briefed and argued

(1) On or after ordering review, the Supreme Court may specify the issues to be briefed and argued. Unless the court orders otherwise, the parties must limit their briefs and arguments to those issues and any issues fairly included in them.

(2) Notwithstanding an order specifying issues under (1), the court may, on reasonable notice, order oral argument on fewer or additional issues or on the entire cause.

(b) Issues to be decided

(1) The Supreme Court may decide any issues that are raised or fairly included in the petition or answer.

(2) The court may decide an issue that is neither raised nor fairly included in the petition or answer if the case presents the issue and the court has given the parties reasonable notice and opportunity to brief and argue it.

(3) The court need not decide every issue the parties raise or the court specifies. *(Formerly Rule 29, adopted, eff. Jan. 1, 2003. Renumbered Rule 8.516, eff. Jan. 1, 2007.)*

Research References

Rutter, Cal. Practice Guide: Civil Appeals & Writs Ch. 13-A, A. General Considerations.

Rutter, Cal. Practice Guide: Civil Appeals & Writs Ch. 13-B, B. Petition for Review Procedures.

Rutter, Cal. Practice Guide: Civil Appeals & Writs Ch. 13-C, C. Briefs on the Merits After Grant of Review.

9 Witkin Cal. Proc. 5th Appeal § 934, (S 934) Issues on Review.

9 Witkin Cal. Proc. 5th Appeal § 942, Decision on Limited Issues.

Rule 8.520. Briefs by parties and amici curiae; judicial notice

(a) Parties' briefs; time to file

(1) Within 30 days after the Supreme Court files the order of review, the petitioner must serve and file in that court either an opening brief on the merits or the brief it filed in the Court of Appeal.

(2) Within 30 days after the petitioner files its brief or the time to do so expires, the opposing party must serve and file either an answer brief on the merits or the brief it filed in the Court of Appeal.

(3) The petitioner may file a reply brief on the merits or the reply brief it filed in the Court of Appeal. A reply brief must be served and filed within 20 days after the opposing party files its brief.

(4) A party filing a brief it filed in the Court of Appeal must attach to the cover a notice of its intent to rely on the brief in the Supreme Court.

(5) The time to serve and file a brief may not be extended by stipulation but only by order of the Chief Justice under rule 8.60.

(6) The court may designate which party is deemed the petitioner or otherwise direct the sequence in which the parties must file their briefs.

(b) Form and content

(1) Briefs filed under this rule must comply with the relevant provisions of rule 8.204.

(2) The body of the petitioner's brief on the merits must begin by quoting either:

   (A) Any order specifying the issues to be briefed; or, if none,

   (B) The statement of issues in the petition for review and, if any, in the answer.

(3) Unless the court orders otherwise, briefs on the merits must be limited to the issues stated in (2) and any issues fairly included in them.

(c) Length

(1) If produced on a computer, an opening or answering brief on the merits must not exceed 14,000 words, including footnotes, and a reply brief on the merits must not exceed 8,400 words, including footnotes. Each brief must include a certificate by appellate counsel or an unrepresented party stating the number of words in the brief. The person certifying may rely on the word count of the computer program used to prepare the brief.

(2) If typewritten, an opening or answering brief on the merits must not exceed 50 pages and a reply brief on the merits must not exceed 30 pages.

(3) The tables required under rule 8.204(a)(1), the cover information required under rule 8.204(b)(10), a certificate under (1), any signature block, any attachment under (h), and any quotation of issues required by (b)(2) are excluded from the limits stated in (1) and (2).

(4) On application and for good cause, the Chief Justice may permit a longer brief.

(d) Supplemental briefs

(1) A party may file a supplemental brief limited to new authorities, new legislation, or other matters that were not available in time to be included in the party's brief on the merits.

(2) A supplemental brief must not exceed 2,800 words, including footnotes, if produced on a computer or 10 pages if typewritten, and must be served and filed no later than 10 days before oral argument.

(e) Briefs on the court's request

The court may request additional briefs on any or all issues, whether or not the parties have filed briefs on the merits.

(f) Amicus curiae briefs

(1) After the court orders review, any person or entity may serve and file an application for permission of the Chief Justice to file an amicus curiae brief.

(2) The application must be filed no later than 30 days after all briefs that the parties may file under this rule—other than supplemental briefs—have been filed or were required to be filed. For good cause, the Chief Justice may allow later filing.

(3) The application must state the applicant's interest and explain how the proposed amicus curiae brief will assist the court in deciding the matter.

(4) The application must also identify:

   (A) Any party or any counsel for a party in the pending appeal who:

      (i) Authored the proposed amicus brief in whole or in part; or

      (ii) Made a monetary contribution intended to fund the preparation or submission of the brief; and

   (B) Every person or entity who made a monetary contribution intended to fund the preparation or submission of the brief, other than the amicus curiae, its members, or its counsel in the pending appeal.

(5) The proposed brief must be served. It must accompany the application and may be combined with it.

(6) The covers of the application and proposed brief must identify the party the applicant supports, if any.

(7) If the court grants the application, any party may file either an answer to the individual amicus curiae brief or a consolidated answer to multiple amicus curiae briefs filed in the case. The answer must be filed within 30 days after either the court rules on the last timely filed application to file an amicus curiae brief or the time for filing applications to file an amicus curiae brief expires, whichever is later. The answer must be served on all parties and the amicus curiae.

(8) The Attorney General may file an amicus curiae brief without the Chief Justice's permission unless the brief is submitted on behalf of another state officer or agency. The Attorney General must serve and file the brief within the time specified in (2) and must provide the information required by (3) and comply with (6). Any answer must comply with (7).

(g) Judicial notice

To obtain judicial notice by the Supreme Court under Evidence Code section 459, a party must comply with rule 8.252(a).

(h) Attachments

A party filing a brief may attach copies of relevant local, state, or federal regulations or rules, out-of-state statutes, or other similar citable materials that are not readily accessible. These attachments must not exceed a combined total of 10 pages. A copy of an opinion required to be attached to the brief under rule 8.1115(c) does not count toward this 10-page limit. *(Formerly Rule 29.1, adopted, eff. Jan. 1, 2003. Renumbered Rule 8.520 and amended, eff. Jan. 1, 2007. As amended, eff. Jan. 1, 2008; Jan. 1, 2009; Jan. 1, 2011.)*

Advisory Committee Comment

Subdivision (a). A party other than the petitioner who files a brief may be required to pay a filing fee under Government Code section 68927 if the brief is the first document filed in the proceeding in the Supreme Court by that party. See rule 8.25(c).

Subdivisions (c) and (d). Subdivisions (c) and (d) state in terms of word count rather than page count the maximum permissible lengths of Supreme Court briefs produced on a computer. This provision tracks an identical provision in rule 8.204(c) governing Court of Appeal briefs and is explained in the advisory committee comment to that provision. Subdivision (c)(3) specifies certain items that are not counted toward the maximum brief length. The signature block referenced in this provision includes not only the signatures, but also the printed names, titles, and affiliations of any attorneys filing or joining in the brief, which may accompany the signature.

Research References

Rutter, Cal. Practice Guide: Civil Appeals & Writs Ch. 5-B, B. Types of Motions, Applications and Requests.

Rutter, Cal. Practice Guide: Civil Appeals & Writs Ch. 5-C, C. Motion, Application and Request Procedures.

Rutter, Cal. Practice Guide: Civil Appeals & Writs Ch. 9-D, D. Procedural Rules.

Rutter, Cal. Practice Guide: Civil Appeals & Writs Ch. 13-C, C. Briefs on the Merits After Grant of Review.

Rutter, Cal. Practice Guide: Civil Appeals & Writs Ch. 13-D, D. Oral Argument.

Rutter, Cal. Practice Guide: Civil Appeals & Writs Ch. 15-E, E. Procedures on Writ Review.

9 Witkin Cal. Proc. 5th Appeal § 309, (S 309) Constitutional and Legislative Development.

9 Witkin Cal. Proc. 5th Appeal § 936, in General.

9 Witkin Cal. Proc. 5th Appeal § 937, Form and Content.

9 Witkin Cal. Proc. 5th Appeal § 938, Amicus Briefs on Merits.

9 Witkin Cal. Proc. 5th Appeal § 939, (S 939) Letter in Lieu of Brief.

2 Witkin Cal. Proc. 5th Courts § 326, (S 326) Powers of Individual Judges.

Rule 8.524. Oral argument and submission of the cause

(a) Application

This rule governs oral argument in the Supreme Court unless the court provides otherwise in its Internal Operating Practices and Procedures or by order.

(b) Place of argument

The Supreme Court holds regular sessions in San Francisco, Los Angeles, and Sacramento on a schedule fixed by the court, and may hold special sessions elsewhere.

(c) Notice of argument

The Supreme Court clerk must send notice of the time and place of oral argument to all parties at least 20 days before the argument date. The Chief Justice may shorten the notice period for good cause; in that event, the clerk must immediately notify the parties by telephone or other expeditious method.

(d) Sequence of argument

The petitioner for Supreme Court relief has the right to open and close. If there are two or more petitioners—or none—the court must set the sequence of argument.

(e) Time for argument

Each side is allowed 30 minutes for argument.

(f) Number of counsel

(1) Only one counsel on each side may argue—regardless of the number of parties on the side—unless the court orders otherwise on request.

(2) Requests to divide oral argument among multiple counsel must be filed within 10 days after the date of the order setting the case for argument.

(3) Multiple counsel must not divide their argument into segments of less than 10 minutes per person, except that one counsel for the opening side—or more, if authorized by the Chief Justice on request—may reserve any portion of that counsel's time for rebuttal.

(g) Argument by amicus curiae

An amicus curiae is not entitled to argument time but may ask a party for permission to use a portion or all of the party's time, subject to the 10-minute minimum prescribed in (f)(3). If permission is granted, counsel must file a request under (f)(2).

(h) Submission of the cause

(1) A cause is submitted when the court has heard oral argument or approved its waiver and the time has expired to file all briefs and papers, including any supplemental brief permitted by the court.

(2) The court may vacate submission only by an order stating the court's reasons and setting a timetable for resubmission. *(Formerly Rule 29.2, adopted, eff. Jan. 1, 2003. Renumbered Rule 8.524, eff. Jan. 1, 2007.)*

Advisory Committee Comment

Subdivision (d). In subdivision (d), "The petitioner for Supreme Court relief" can be a petitioner for review, a petitioner for transfer (rule 8.552), a petitioner in an original proceeding in the Supreme Court, or a party designated as petitioner in a proceeding on request of a court of another jurisdiction (rule 8.548(b)(1)).

The number of petitioners is "none" when the court grants review on its own motion or transfers a cause to itself on its own motion.

Subdivision (e). The time allowed for argument in death penalty appeals is prescribed in rule 8.638.

Subdivision (f). The number of counsel allowed to argue on each side in death penalty appeals is prescribed in rule 8.638.

Research References

Rutter, Cal. Practice Guide: Civil Appeals & Writs Ch. 10-A, A. Overview.

Rutter, Cal. Practice Guide: Civil Appeals & Writs Ch. 13-D, D. Oral Argument.

Rutter, Cal. Practice Guide: Civil Appeals &· Writs Ch. 13-E, E. Decision on the Merits.

9 Witkin Cal. Proc. 5th Appeal § 763, in General.

9 Witkin Cal. Proc. 5th Appeal § 935, (S 935) Oral Argument.

9 Witkin Cal. Proc. 5th Appeal § 940, Submission.

2 Witkin Cal. Proc. 5th Courts § 328, (S 328) Sessions and Conferences.

Rule 8.528. Disposition

(a) Normal disposition

After review, the Supreme Court normally will affirm, reverse, or modify the judgment of the Court of Appeal, but may order another disposition.

(b) Dismissal of review

(1) The Supreme Court may dismiss review. The Supreme Court clerk must promptly send an order dismissing review to all parties and the Court of Appeal.

(2) When the Court of Appeal receives an order dismissing review, the decision of that court is final and its clerk must promptly issue a remittitur or take other appropriate action.

(3) After an order dismissing review, the Court of Appeal opinion remains unpublished unless the Supreme Court orders otherwise.

(c) Remand for decision on remaining issues

If it decides fewer than all the issues presented by the case, the Supreme Court may remand the cause to a Court of Appeal for decision on any remaining issues.

(d) Transfer without decision

After ordering review, the Supreme Court may transfer the cause to a Court of Appeal without decision but with instructions to conduct such proceedings as the Supreme Court orders.

(e) Retransfer without decision

After transferring to itself, before decision, a cause pending in the Court of Appeal, the Supreme Court may retransfer the cause to a Court of Appeal without decision.

(f) Court of Appeal briefs after remand or transfer

Any supplemental briefing in the Court of Appeal after remand or transfer from the Supreme Court is governed by rule 8.200(b). *(Formerly Rule 29.3, adopted, eff. Jan. 1, 2003. Renumbered Rule 8.528 and amended, eff. Jan. 1, 2007.)*

Advisory Committee Comment

Subdivision (a). Subdivision (a) serves two purposes. First, it declares that the Supreme Court's normal disposition of a cause after completing its review is to affirm, reverse, or modify *the judgment of the Court of Appeal.* Second, the subdivision recognizes that, when necessary, the Supreme Court may order "another disposition" appropriate to the circumstances. Subdivisions (b)–(e) provide examples of such "other dispositions," but the list is not intended to be exclusive.

As used in subdivision (a), "the judgment of the Court of Appeal" includes a decision of that court denying a petition for original writ without issuing an alternative writ or order to show cause. The Supreme Court's method of disposition after

reviewing such a decision, however, has evolved. In earlier cases the Supreme Court itself denied or granted the requested writ, in effect treating the matter as if it were an original proceeding in the Supreme Court. (E.g., *City of San Jose v. Superior Court* (1993) 5 Cal.4th 47, 58 ["The alternative writ of mandate is discharged and the petition for a peremptory writ of mandate is denied."].) By contrast, current Supreme Court practice is to affirm or reverse the judgment of the Court of Appeal summarily denying the writ petition. (E.g., *People v. Superior Court (Laff)* (2001) 25 Cal.4th 703, 742–743 ["The judgment of the Court of Appeal is reversed with directions to vacate its order denying the petition, and to issue a writ of mandate . . ."]; *State Comp. Ins. Fund v. Superior Court* (2001) 24 Cal.4th 930, 944 ["The judgment of the Court of Appeal summarily denying the petition for writ of mandate is affirmed and the order to show cause . . . is discharged."].) As the cited cases illustrate, if the Supreme Court affirms such a judgment it will normally discharge any alternative writ or order to show cause it issued when granting review; if the court reverses the judgment it will normally include a direction to the Court of Appeal, e.g., to issue the requested writ or to reconsider the petition.

Subdivision (b). An earlier version of this rule purported to limit Supreme Court *dismissals of review* to cases in which the court had "improvidently" granted review. In practice, however, the court may dismiss review for a variety of other reasons. For example, after the court decides a "lead" case, its current practice is to dismiss review in any pending companion case (i.e., a "grant and hold" matter under rule 8.512(c)) that appears correctly decided in light of the lead case and presents no additional issue requiring resolution by the Supreme Court or the Court of Appeal. The Supreme Court may also dismiss review when a supervening event renders the case moot for any reason, e.g., when the parties reach a settlement, when a party seeking personal relief dies, or when the court orders review to construe a statute that is then repealed before the court can act. Reflecting this practice, the Supreme Court now dismisses review—even in the rare case in which the grant of review was arguably "improvident"—by an order that says simply that "review is dismissed."

An order of review ipso facto transfers jurisdiction of the cause to the Supreme Court. By the same token, an order dismissing review ipso facto retransfers jurisdiction to the Court of Appeal. The Court of Appeal has no discretion to exercise after the Supreme Court dismisses review: the Supreme Court clerk must promptly send the dismissal order to the Court of Appeal; when the Court of Appeal clerk files that order, the Court of Appeal decision immediately becomes final.

If the decision of the Court of Appeal made final by (b)(2) requires issuance of a remittitur under rule 8.272(a), the clerk must issue the remittitur; if the decision does not require issuance of a remittitur—e.g., if the decision is an interlocutory order (see rule 8.500(a)(1))—the clerk must take whatever action is appropriate in the circumstances.

Subdivision (d). Subdivision (d) is intended to apply primarily to two types of cases: (1) those in which the court granted review "for the purpose of transferring the matter to the Court of Appeal for such proceedings as the Supreme Court may order" (rule 8.500(b)(4)) and (2) those in which the court, after deciding a "lead case," determines that a companion "grant and hold" case (rule 8.512(c)) should be reconsidered by the Court of Appeal in light of the lead case or presents an additional issue or issues that require resolution by the Court of Appeal.

Subdivision (e). Subdivision (e) is intended to apply to cases in which the Supreme Court, after *transferring* to itself before decision a cause pending in the Court of Appeal, *retransfers* the matter to that court without decision and with or without instructions.

Research References

Rutter, Cal. Practice Guide: Civil Appeals & Writs Ch. 9-D, D. Procedural Rules.

Rutter, Cal. Practice Guide: Civil Appeals & Writs Ch. 11-F, F. Publication of Appellate Opinions.

Rutter, Cal. Practice Guide: Civil Appeals & Writs Ch. 13-B, B. Petition for Review Procedures.

Rutter, Cal. Practice Guide: Civil Appeals & Writs Ch. 13-D, D. Oral Argument.

Rutter, Cal. Practice Guide: Civil Appeals & Writs Ch. 13-E, E. Decision on the Merits.

9 Witkin Cal. Proc. 5th Appeal § 839, Judgment of Supreme Court.

9 Witkin Cal. Proc. 5th Appeal § 941, Affirmance, Modification, or Reversal.

9 Witkin Cal. Proc. 5th Appeal § 942, Decision on Limited Issues.

9 Witkin Cal. Proc. 5th Appeal § 943, Dismissal.

9 Witkin Cal. Proc. 5th Appeal § 945, (S 945) in General.

Rule 8.532.   Filing, finality, and modification of decision

(a) Filing the decision

The Supreme Court clerk must promptly file all opinions and orders issued by the court and promptly send copies showing the filing date to the parties and, when relevant, to the lower court or tribunal.

(b) Finality of decision

(1) Except as provided in (2), a Supreme Court decision is final 30 days after filing unless:

(A) The court orders a shorter period; or

(B) Before the 30–day period or any extension expires the court orders one or more extensions, not to exceed a total of 60 additional days.

(2) The following Supreme Court decisions are final on filing:

(A) The denial of a petition for review of a Court of Appeal decision;

(B) A disposition ordered under rule 8.528(b), (d), or (e);

(C) The denial of a petition for a writ within the court's original jurisdiction without issuance of an alternative writ or order to show cause; and

(D) The denial of a petition for writ of supersedeas.

(c) Modification of decision

The Supreme Court may modify a decision as provided in rule 8.264(c). *(Formerly Rule 29.4, adopted, eff. Jan. 1, 2003. Renumbered Rule 8.532 and amended, eff. Jan. 1, 2007.)*

Advisory Committee Comment

Subdivision (b). Subdivision (b)(2)(A) recognizes the general rule that the denial of a petition for review of a Court of Appeal decision is final on filing. Subdivision (b)(2)(B)–(D) recognizes several additional types of Supreme Court decisions that are final on filing. Thus (b)(2)(B) recognizes that a dismissal, a transfer, and a retransfer under (b), (d), and (e), respectively, of rule 8.528 are decisions final on filing. A remand under rule 8.528(c) is not a decision final on filing because it is not a separately filed order; rather, as part of its appellate judgment at the end of its opinion in such cases the Supreme Court simply orders the cause remanded to the Court of Appeal for disposition of the remaining issues in the appeal.

Subdivision (b)(2)(C) recognizes that an order denying a petition for a writ within the court's original jurisdiction without issuance of an alternative writ or order to show cause is final on filing. The provision reflects the settled Supreme Court practice, since at least 1989, of declining to file petitions for rehearing in such matters. (See, e.g., *In re Hayes* (S004421) Minutes, Cal. Supreme Ct., July 28, 1989 ["The motion to vacate this court's order of May 18, 1989 [denying a petition for habeas corpus without opinion] is denied. Because the California Rules of Court do not authorize the filing of a petition for rehearing of such an order, the alternate request to consider the matter as a petition for rehearing is denied."].)

Subdivision (b)(2)(D) recognizes that an order denying a petition for writ of supersedeas is final on filing.

Research References

Rutter, Cal. Practice Guide: Civil Appeals & Writs Ch. 11-G, G. Finality as to Court of Appeal.

Rutter, Cal. Practice Guide: Civil Appeals & Writs Ch. 12-F, F. Disposition.

Rutter, Cal. Practice Guide: Civil Appeals & Writs Ch. 13-B, B. Petition for Review Procedures.

Rutter, Cal. Practice Guide: Civil Appeals & Writs Ch. 13-E, E. Decision on the Merits.

Rutter, Cal. Practice Guide: Civil Appeals & Writs Ch. 13-F, F. Petition for Rehearing.

9 Witkin Cal. Proc. 5th Appeal § 831, (S 831) Rendition: Filing of Opinion.

9 Witkin Cal. Proc. 5th Appeal § 833, (S 833) Effect of Modification.

9 Witkin Cal. Proc. 5th Appeal § 839, Judgment of Supreme Court.

9 Witkin Cal. Proc. 5th Appeal § 948, in General.

8 Witkin Cal. Proc. 5th Extraordinary Writs § 209, (S 209) Finality and Res Judicata.

Rule 8.536.   Rehearing

(a) Power to order rehearing

The Supreme Court may order rehearing as provided in rule 8.268(a).

(b) Petition and answer

A petition for rehearing and any answer must comply with rule 8.268(b)(1) and (3). Any answer to the petition must be served and filed within eight days after the petition is filed. Before the Supreme Court decision is final and for good cause, the Chief Justice may relieve a party from a failure to file a timely petition or answer.

(c) Extension of time

The time for granting or denying a petition for rehearing in the Supreme Court may be extended under rule 8.532(b)(1)(B). If the court does not rule on the petition before the decision is final, the petition is deemed denied.

(d) Determination of petition

An order granting a rehearing must be signed by at least four justices; an order denying rehearing may be signed by the Chief Justice alone.

(e) Effect of granting rehearing

An order granting a rehearing vacates the decision and any opinion filed in the case and sets the cause at large in the Supreme Court. *(Formerly Rule 29.5, adopted, eff. Jan. 1, 2003. As amended, eff. Jan. 1, 2004. Renumbered Rule 8.536 and amended, eff. Jan. 1, 2007.)*

Research References

Rutter, Cal. Practice Guide: Civil Appeals & Writs Ch. 12-A, A. Overview.

Rutter, Cal. Practice Guide: Civil Appeals & Writs Ch. 13-F, F. Petition for Rehearing.

Rutter, Cal. Practice Guide: Fed.Civ.Pro. Before Trial Ch. 1-B, B. Federal vs. State Law.

9 Witkin Cal. Proc. 5th Appeal § 904, Nature of Power.

9 Witkin Cal. Proc. 5th Appeal § 905, Grounds.

9 Witkin Cal. Proc. 5th Appeal § 907, (S 907) Petition.

9 Witkin Cal. Proc. 5th Appeal § 948, in General.

Rule 8.540.   Remittitur

(a) Proceedings requiring issuance of remittitur

The Supreme Court must issue a remittitur after a decision in:

(1) A review of a Court of Appeal decision; or

(2) An appeal from a judgment of death or in a cause transferred to the court under rule 8.552.

(b) Clerk's duties

(1) The clerk must issue a remittitur when a decision of the court is final. The remittitur is deemed issued when the clerk enters it in the record.

(2) After review of a Court of Appeal decision, the Supreme Court clerk must address the remittitur to the Court of Appeal and send that court two copies of the remittitur and two file-stamped copies of the Supreme Court opinion or order.

(3) After a decision in an appeal from a judgment of death or in a cause transferred to the court under rule 8.552, the clerk must send the remittitur and a file-stamped copy of the Supreme Court opinion or order to the lower court or tribunal.

(4) The clerk must comply with the requirements of rule 8.272(d).

(c) Immediate issuance, stay, and recall

(1) The Supreme Court may direct immediate issuance of a remittitur on the parties' stipulation or for good cause.

(2) On a party's or its own motion and for good cause, the court may stay a remittitur's issuance for a reasonable period or order its recall.

(3) An order recalling a remittitur issued after a decision by opinion does not supersede the opinion or affect its publication status. *(Formerly Rule 29.6, adopted, eff. Jan. 1, 2003. Renumbered Rule 8.540 and amended, eff. Jan. 1, 2007.)*

Research References

Rutter, Cal. Practice Guide: Civil Appeals & Writs Ch. 13-E, E. Decision on the Merits.
Rutter, Cal. Practice Guide: Civil Appeals & Writs Ch. 14-A, A. Remittitur.
9 Witkin Cal. Proc. 5th Appeal § 842, (S 842) Procedure.
9 Witkin Cal. Proc. 5th Appeal § 843, (S 843) Proceedings in Which Remittitur Issues.
9 Witkin Cal. Proc. 5th Appeal § 844, (S 844) Effect of Issuance.
9 Witkin Cal. Proc. 5th Appeal § 845, (S 845) Issuance Forthwith.
9 Witkin Cal. Proc. 5th Appeal § 846, (S 846) Stay of Issuance.
9 Witkin Cal. Proc. 5th Appeal § 848, Procedure.
9 Witkin Cal. Proc. 5th Appeal § 941, Affirmance, Modification, or Reversal.
2 Witkin Cal. Proc. 5th Jurisdiction § 423, (S 423) Other Examples.

Rule 8.544. Costs and sanctions

In a civil case, the Supreme Court may direct the Court of Appeal to award costs, if any; or may order the parties to bear their own costs; or may make any other award of costs the Supreme Court deems proper. The Supreme Court may impose sanctions on a party or an attorney under rule 8.276 for committing any unreasonable violation of these rules. *(Formerly Rule 29.7, adopted, eff. Jan. 1, 2003. Renumbered Rule 8.544 and amended, eff. Jan. 1, 2007. As amended, eff. July 1, 2008.)*

Advisory Committee Comment

If the Supreme Court makes an award of costs, the party claiming such costs must proceed under rule 8.278(c).

Research References

Rutter, Cal. Practice Guide: Civil Appeals & Writs Ch. 13-E, E. Decision on the Merits.
9 Witkin Cal. Proc. 5th Appeal § 953, in General.
9 Witkin Cal. Proc. 5th Appeal § 954, (S 954) General Rule.
9 Witkin Cal. Proc. 5th Appeal § 983, (S 983) Nature of Power.

Rule 8.548. Decision on request of a court of another jurisdiction

(a) Request for decision

On request of the United States Supreme Court, a United States Court of Appeals, or the court of last resort of any state, territory, or commonwealth, the Supreme Court may decide a question of California law if:

(1) The decision could determine the outcome of a matter pending in the requesting court; and

(2) There is no controlling precedent.

(b) Form and contents of request

The request must take the form of an order of the requesting court containing:

(1) The title and number of the case, the names and addresses of counsel and any unrepresented party, and a designation of the party to be deemed the petitioner if the request is granted;

(2) The question to be decided, with a statement that the requesting court will accept the decision;

(3) A statement of the relevant facts prepared by the requesting court or by the parties and approved by the court; and

(4) An explanation of how the request satisfies the requirements of (a).

(c) Supporting materials

Copies of all relevant briefs must accompany the request. At any time, the Supreme Court may ask the requesting court to furnish additional record materials, including transcripts and exhibits.

(d) Serving and filing the request

The requesting court clerk must file an original and 10 copies of the request in the Supreme Court with a certificate of service on the parties.

(e) Letters in support or opposition

(1) Within 20 days after the request is filed, any party or other person or entity wanting to support or oppose the request must send a letter to the Supreme Court, with service on the parties and on the requesting court.

(2) Within 10 days after service of a letter under (1), any party may send a reply letter to the Supreme Court, with service on the other parties and the requesting court.

(3) A letter or reply asking the court to restate the question under (f)(5) must propose new wording.

(f) Proceedings in the Supreme Court

(1) In exercising its discretion to grant or deny the request, the Supreme Court may consider whether resolution of the question is necessary to secure uniformity of decision or to settle an important question of law, and any other factor the court deems appropriate.

(2) An order granting the request must be signed by at least four justices; an order denying the request may be signed by the Chief Justice alone.

(3) If the court grants the request, the rules on review and decision in the Supreme Court govern further proceedings in that court.

(4) If, after granting the request, the court determines that a decision on the question may require an interpretation of the California Constitution or a decision on the validity or meaning of a California law affecting the public interest, the court must direct the clerk to send to the Attorney General—unless the Attorney General represents a party to the litigation—a copy of the request and the order granting it.

(5) At any time, the Supreme Court may restate the question or ask the requesting court to clarify the question.

(6) After filing the opinion, the clerk must promptly send file-stamped copies to the requesting court and the parties and must notify that court and the parties when the decision is final.

(7) Supreme Court decisions pursuant to this rule are published in the Official Reports and have the same precedential effect as the court's other decisions. *(Formerly Rule 29.8, adopted, eff. Jan. 1, 2003. Renumbered Rule 8.548 and amended, eff. Jan. 1, 2007.)*

Research References

Rutter, Cal. Practice Guide: Civil Appeals & Writs Ch. 13-H, H. Answering Questions of State Law on Request by Federal Appellate Courts or Other State Courts.

3 Witkin Cal. Proc. 5th Actions § 21, California Doctrine.

9 Witkin Cal. Proc. 5th Appeal § 14, (S 14) Procedure.

2 Witkin Cal. Proc. 5th Courts § 330, (S 330) Original Jurisdiction.

2 Witkin, California Summary 10th Insurance § 269, (S 269) Reimbursement of Insurer for Settlement of Uncovered Claims.

1 Witkin Cal. Summ. 10th Contracts § 210, (S 210) Performance of Work or Services.

13 Witkin, California Summary 10th Equity § 88, (S 88) When Claim Arises.

Rule 8.552. Transfer for decision

(a) Time of transfer

On a party's petition or its own motion, the Supreme Court may transfer to itself, for decision, a cause pending in a Court of Appeal.

(b) When a cause is pending

For purposes of this rule, a cause within the appellate jurisdiction of the superior court is not pending in the Court of Appeal until that court orders it transferred under rule 8.1002. Any cause pending in the Court of Appeal remains pending until the decision of the Court of Appeal is final in that court.

(c) Grounds

The Supreme Court will not order transfer under this rule unless the cause presents an issue of great public importance that the Supreme Court must promptly resolve.

(d) Petition and answer

A party seeking transfer under this rule must promptly serve and file in the Supreme Court a petition explaining how the cause satisfies the requirements of (c). Within 20 days after the petition is filed, any party may serve and file an answer. The petition and any answer must conform to the relevant provisions of rule 8.504.

(e) Order

Transfer under this rule requires a Supreme Court order signed by at least four justices; an order denying transfer may be signed by the Chief Justice alone. *(Formerly Rule 29.9, adopted, eff. Jan. 1, 2003. Renumbered Rule 8.552 and amended, eff. Jan. 1, 2007. As amended, eff. Jan. 1, 2009.)*

Advisory Committee Comment

Rule 8.552 applies only to causes that the Supreme Court transfers to itself for the purpose of reaching a decision on the merits. The rule implements a portion of article VI, section 12(a) of the Constitution. As used in article VI, section 12(a) and the rule, the term "cause" is broadly construed to include "all cases, matters, and proceedings of every description" adjudicated by the Courts of Appeal and the Supreme Court. (*In re Rose* (2000) 22 Cal.4th 430, 540, quoting *In re Wells* (1917) 174 Cal. 467, 471.)

Subdivision (b). For provisions addressing the finality of Court of Appeal decisions, see rules 8.264(b) (civil appeals), 8.366(b) (criminal appeals), 8.490 (proceedings for writs of mandate, certiorari, and prohibition), and 8.1018(a) (transfer of appellate division cases).

Research References

Rutter, Cal. Practice Guide: Civil Appeals & Writs Ch. 13-A, A. General Considerations.

Rutter, Cal. Practice Guide: Civil Appeals & Writs Ch. 16-K, K. Transfer to Court of Appeal.

9 Witkin Cal. Proc. 5th Appeal § 9, (S 9) Current Structure.

9 Witkin Cal. Proc. 5th Appeal § 922, Nature and Grounds.

9 Witkin Cal. Proc. 5th Appeal § 923, Procedure.

9 Witkin Cal. Proc. 5th Appeal § 941, Affirmance, Modification, or Reversal.

2 Witkin Cal. Proc. 5th Courts § 195, (S 195) Appellate Rules.

2 Witkin Cal. Proc. 5th Courts § 329, (S 329) Appellate Jurisdiction.

4 Witkin Cal. Proc. 5th Pleading § 374, (S 374) Review.

Division 2

RULES RELATING TO THE SUPERIOR COURT APPELLATE DIVISION

Advisory Committee Comment

Division 2. The rules relating to the superior court appellate division begin with Chapter 1, which contains general rules applicable to appeals in all three types of cases within the jurisdiction of the appellate division—limited civil, misdemeanor, and infraction. Because the procedures relating to taking appeals and preparing the record in limited civil, misdemeanor, and infraction appeals differ, there are separate chapters addressing these topics: Chapter 2 addresses taking appeals and record preparation in limited civil cases, and Chapter 3 addresses taking appeals and record preparation in misdemeanor cases. Because the procedures for briefing and rendering decisions are generally the same in limited civil and misdemeanor appeals, Chapter 4 addresses these procedures in appeals of both types of cases. To make the distinct procedures for appeals in infraction proceedings easier to find and understand, these procedures are located in a separate chapter—Chapter 5. Chapter 6 addresses writ proceedings in the appellate division.

Disposition Table

Appellate Rules 8.700–8.793

Numerically by Old Rule Numbers

Current Rule	Revised Rule
8.700	8.802(d)
8.701(a)	10.1100(a)
8.701(b)	10.1100(b)
8.701(c)	10.1100(c)
8.701(d)	10.1100(d)
8.702	10.1108

Current Rule	Revised Rule
8.703, paragraph 1	10.1104(b)
8.703, paragraph 2	10.1104(a)
8.704(a)	8.885(a) and 8.929(a)
8.704(b)	8.881, 8.885(b), 8.926, and 8.929(b)
8.705(a)	8.808(a)
8.705(b)	8.808(b)
8.706(a)	8.882(a)(1), (2), and (3), (5) and 8.927(a)(1), (2), (3), and (5)
8.706(b)	8.882(d)
8.706(c)	8.883(a) and (b) and 8.928(a) and (b)
8.706(d)	8.883(c) and 8.928(c)
8.706(e)	8.882(c)(1), (2) and (4) and 8.882(d) and 8.927(c)(1), (2) and (4) and 8.928(d)
8.706(f)	8.882(c)(3) and 8.927(c)(3)
8.706(g)	DELETED
8.706(h)	DELETED
8.707(a)	8.886(a)
8.707(b)	8.887(a)
8.707(c)	8.887(c)
8.708(a)(1)	8.888(a)(1)
8.708(a)(b)	DELETED
8.708(b)	8.888(b)
8.708(c)(1)	8.889(a)(1)
8.708(c)(2)	8.889(b)(1)
8.708(c)(3)	8.889(b)(1) and (2)
8.708(c)(4)	8.889(b)(1) and (3)
8.708(c)(5)	8.889(d)
8.708(d)	8.889(c)
8.709	8.888(c)
8.750(a)	8.821(a)(1) and (2)
8.750(b)	8.821(d)
8.750(c)	8.821(b)(1)
8.750(d)	8.821(b)(1)
8.750(e)	8.821(e)
8.751(a)	8.822(a)
8.751(b)	8.822(b)
8.751(c)	8.822(c)
8.752(a)	8.823(b) and (b)(1)
8.752(b)	8.823(c)
8.752(c)	8.823(f)
8.752(d)	DELETED
8.753(a)	8.831 and 8.834(a)(4), (b)(1) and (c)(2)
8.753(b)	8.834(a)(2) and (3) and (c)(3)
8.753(c)	8.834(b)(2)
8.753(d)	8.834(c)(1) and (4) and (d)(1) and (2)
8.753(e)	8.834(e)
8.754(a)	8.831
8.754(b)	8.832(b)(1)
8.754(c)	8.832(c)(3)
8.754(d)	8.832(d)(1)
8.754(e)	DELETED
8.754(f)	DELETED
8.755(a)	8.836(b) and
8.755(b)	8.831 and 8.836(c)
8.756(a)	8.831 and 8.837(b)(1) and (c)

Current Rule	Revised Rule
8.756(b)	DELETED
8.756(c)	8.837(d)(1) and (3), (e), and (f)
8.757	DELETED
8.758(a)	8.838(a)
8.758(b)	8.838(b)
8.758(c)	8.838(c)
8.759	8.840
8.760	8.839
8.761(a)	8.841(a)
8.761(b)	8.841(b)
8.761(c)	8.841(b)
8.762(a)	8.825(b)(1), (2), (4), and (5) and (d)(2) and (3)
8.762(b)	8.825(b)(1) and (2)
8.762(c)	8.842(b)(1)
8.762(d)	8.825(b)(3)
8.762(e)	8.825(c)
8.763	DELETED
8.764(a)	8.891(a)
8.764(b)	8.891(b)
8.764(c)	8.891(d)
8.764(d)	8.891(c)
8.764(e)	8.891(e)
8.765(1)	8.802(c)(1), (2), and (3)
8.765(2)	8.804(21) and (22)
8.765(3)	8.804(11) and (12)
8.765(4)	8.802(b)(1) and (2)
8.765(5)	8.804(13)
8.765(6)	8.804(18)
8.765(7)	8.804(23)
8.765(8)	DELETED
8.765(9)	8.804(8)
8.765(10)	DELETED
8.765(11)	DELETED
8.765(12)	8.802(c)(4)
8.766	8.806
8.767(a)	8.810(a)
8.767(b)	8.810(b)
8.767(c)	8.810(c)
8.767(d)	8.813
8.768(a)	8.814(a)
8.768(b)	8.814(b) and (c)
8.769 paragraph 1	8.824(a), (c), and (d)(1)
8.769 paragraph 2	8.824(d)(2)
8.770	DELETED
8.771	8.830(b)
8.772(a)	8.800, 8.802(a), and 8.820
8.772(b)	8.812
8.773(a)	8.890(b)(1)
8.773(b)	8.890(c)(1)
8.773(c)	8.890(c)(3)
8.773(d)	8.890(c)(2)
8.780(a)	DELETED
8.780(b)	8.800, 8.850, and 8.900

Current Rule	Revised Rule
8.781	DELETED, see 8.804
8.782(a) Paragraph 1	8.852(a) and 8.901(a)
8.782(a) Paragraph 2	8.853(a) and 8.902(a)
8.782(a) Paragraph 3	8.853(d) and 8.902(d)
8.782(a) Paragraph 4	8.853(c) and 8.902(c)
8.782(b)	8.852(b)(1), (2), and (6) and 8.901(b)(1), (2) and (6)
8.783	8.860(a) and 8.910(a)
8.783(a)(1)	8.861(1) and 8.912(1)
8.783(a)(2)	8.861(2) and 8.912(2)
8.783(a)(3)	8.861(4)
8.783(a)(4)	8.912(4) and 8.861(6) and (7)
8.783(a)(5)	8.912(6) and 8.861(9)
8.783(a)(6)	8.861(2) and 8.912(2)
8.783(a)(7)	8.861(3) and 8.912(3)
8.783(a)(8)	8.861(8) and 8.912(5)
8.783(a)(9)	8.912(8) and 8.861(11)
8.783(a)(10)	DELETED, see 8.860(a)(2) and 8.910(a)(2)
8.783(a)(11)	DELETED, see 8.870 and 8.921
8.783(a)(12)	8.867 and 8.920
8.783(b)	8.913(b) and (d) and 8.862(b) and (d)
8.784(a)	8.837(c)(2)(B), 8.860(a)(2), 8.869(c)(2)(B), 8.910(a)(2), and 8.916(c)(2)(B)
8.784(b)	8.837(c)(2), 8.837(c)(2)(A) and (C), 8.869(c), 8.869(c)(2)(A) and (C), 8.916(c) and 8.916(c)(2) (A) and (C).
8.784(c)	8.837(c)(2)(D) and 8.869(c)(2)(D)
8.784(d)	8.869(b)(1) and 8.916(b)(1)
8.785	8.869(d)(1) and 8.916(d)(1)
8.786(a)	8.851(a)
8.786(b)	8.851(b)
8.786(c)	8.851(c)
8.787(a)	8.810(b) and (c), 8.869(g), and 8.916(g)
8.787(b)	8.812
8.788 paragraph 1	8.869(d)(3) and 8.916(d)(3)
8.788 paragraph 2	8.869(d)(4) and (5) and (f) and 8.916(d)(4) and (5) and (f)
8.788 paragraph 3	DELETED, see 8.872 and 8.922
8.789(a)	DELETED
8.789(b)	DELETED
8.789(c)	DELETED
8.789(d)	8.869(b)(1) and 8.916(b)(1)
8.789(e)	DELETED
8.789(f) paragraph 1	8.869(d)(1) and 8.916(d)(1)
8.789(f) paragraph 2	DELETED
8.789(g) paragraph 1	DELETED
8.789(g) paragraph 2	8.869(d)(2) and (4) and 8.916(d)(2) and (4)
8.789(g) paragraph 3	8.869(d)(4) and 8.916(d)(4)
8.789(h)	8.869(f) and 8.916(f)
8.789(i)	DELETED
8.789(j)	8.863 and 8.914
8.789(k)	8.873(c)
8.789(l)	DELETED
8.789(m)	DELETED
8.790	8.855(a) and (b)

Current Rule	Revised Rule
8.791	8.873(c) and 8.923(c)
8.792	8.880 and 8.881
8.793(a)	8.880 and 8.890(b)(1)
8.793(b)	8.890(c)(1)
8.793(c)	8.890(c)(3)
8.793(d)	8.890(c)(2)

Disposition Table [1]

Appellate Rules 8.800–8.936 and 10.1100–10.1108

Numerically by Revised Rule Number

Revised Rule	Current Rule
8.800	8.772(a) and 8.780(b)
8.802(a)	8.772(a)
8.802(b)(1) and (2)	8.765(4)
8.802(b)(3), (4), and (5)	NEW
8.802(c)(1), (2), and (3)	8.765(1)
8.802(c)(4)	8.765(12)
8.802(d)	8.700
8.804	8.765 and 8.781
8.804(1), (2), (3), (4), (5), (6), and (7)	NEW
8.804(8)	8.765(9)
8.804(9) and (10)	NEW
8.804(11) and (12)	8.765(3)
8.804(13)	8.765(5)
8.804(14), (15), (16), and (17)	NEW
8.804(18)	8.765(6)
8.804(19) and (20)	NEW
8.804(21) and (22)	8.765(2)
8.804(23)	8.765(7)
8.806	8.766
8.808(a)	8.705(a)
8.808(b)	8.705(b)
8.810(a)	8.767(a)
8.810(b)	8.767(b) and 8.787(a)
8.810(c)	8.767(c), and 8.787(a)
8.810(d)	8.766
8.810(e)	NEW
8.811	NEW
8.812	8.772(b) and 8.787(b)
8.813	8.767(d)
8.814(a)	8.768(a)
8.814(b)	8.768(b)
8.814(c)	8.768(b)
8.816	NEW
8.820	8.772(a)
8.821(a)(1) and (2)	8.750(a)
8.821(a)(3)	NEW
8.821(b)(1)	8.750(c) and (d)
8.821(b)(2)	NEW

Revised Rule	Current Rule
8.821(c)	NEW
8.821(d)	8.750(b)
8.821(e)	8.750(e)
8.822(a)	8.751(a)
8.822(b)	8.751(b)
8.822(c)	8.751(c)
8.822(d)	NEW
8.823(a)	NEW
8.823(b)	8.752(a)
8.823(b)(1)	8.752(a)
8.823(b)(2)	NEW
8.823(c)	8.752(b)
8.823(d)	NEW
8.823(e)	NEW
8.823(f)	8.752(c)
8.823(g)	NEW
8.824(a)	8.769 paragraph 1
8.824(b)	NEW
8.824(c)	8.769 paragraph 1
8.824(d)(1)	8.769 paragraph 1
8.824(d)(2)	8.769 paragraph 2
8.825(a)	NEW
8.825(b)(1) and (2)	8.762(a) and (b)
8.825(b)(3)	8.762(d)
8.825(b)(4) and (5)	8.762(a)
8.825(c)	8.762(e)
8.830(a)	NEW
8.830(b)	8.771
8.831	8.753(a), 8.754(a), 8.755(b), and 8.756(a)
8.832(a)	8.754(d)
8.832(b)(1)	8.754(b)
8.832(b)(2)	NEW
8.832(b)(3)	NEW
8.832(c)(1) and (2)	NEW
8.832(c)(3)	8.754(c)
8.832(d)(1)	8.754(d)
8.832(d)(2)	8.762(a)
8.833	NEW
8.834(a)(1)	NEW
8.834(a)(2)	8.753(b)
8.834(a)(3)	8.753(b)
8.834(a)(4)	8.753(a)
8.834(b)(1)	8.753(a)
8.834(b)(2)	8.753(c)
8.834(c)(1)	8.753(d)
8.834(c)(2)	8.753(a)
8.834(c)(3)	8.753(b)
8.834(c)(4)	8.753(d)
8.834(d)(1)	8.753(d)
8.834(d)(2)	8.753(d)
8.834(d)(3)	8.762(a)
8.834(e)	8.753(e)
8.835	NEW
8.836(a)	NEW

Ct. Rules

Revised Rule	Current Rule
8.836(b)	8.755(a)
8.836(c)	8.755(b)
8.837(a)	NEW
8.837(b)(1)	8.756(a)
8.837(b)(2)	NEW
8.837(c)(1)	8.756(a)
8.837(c)(2)	8.756(a) and 8.784(b)
8.837(c)(2)(A)	8.784(b)
8.837(c)(2)(B)	8.784(a)
8.837(c)(2)(C)	8.784(b)
8.837(c)(2)(D)	8.784(c)
8.837(d)(1)	8.756(c)
8.837(d)(2)	NEW
8.837(d)(3)	8.756(c)
8.837(d)(4), (5) and (6)	NEW
8.837(e)	8.756(c)
8.837(f)	8.756(c)
8.838(a)	8.758(a)
8.838(b)	8.758(b)
8.838(c)	8.758(c)
8.839	8.760
8.840	8.759
8.841(a)	8.761(a)
8.841(b)	8.761(b) and (c)
8.841(c)	NEW
8.841(d)	NEW
8.842(a)	NEW
8.842(b)(1)	8.762(c)
8.842(b)(2)	NEW
8.850	8.780(b)
8.851(a)	8.786(a)
8.851(b)	8.786(b)
8.851(c)	8.786(c)
8.852(a)	8.782(a) paragraph 1
8.852(b)(1) and (2)	8.782(b)
8.852(b)(3), (4), and (5)	NEW
8.852(b)(6)	8.782(b)
8.853(a)	8.782(a) paragraph 2
8.853(b)	NEW
8.853(c)	8.782(a) paragraph 4
8.853(d)	8.782(a) paragraph 3
8.853(e)	NEW
8.854	NEW
8.855(a)	8.790
8.855(b)	8.790
8.855(c)	NEW
8.860(a)	8.783
8.860(b)	NEW
8.861(1)	8.783(a)(1)
8.861(2)	8.783(a)(2) and (6)
8.861(3)	8.783(a)(7)
8.861(4)	8.783(a)(3)
8.861(5)	NEW
8.861(6)	8.783(a)(4)

Revised Rule	Current Rule
8.861(7)	8.783(a)(4)
8.861(8)	8.783(a)(8)
8.861(9)	8.783(a)(5)
8.861(10)	NEW
8.861(11)	8.783(a)(9)
8.861(12)	NEW
8.862(a)	NEW
8.862(b)	8.783(b)
8.862(c)	NEW
8.862(d)	8.783(b)
8.863	8.789(j)
8.864	NEW
8.865	NEW
8.866	NEW
8.867	8.783(a)(12)
8.868	NEW
8.869(a)	NEW
8.869(b)(1)	8.784(d) and 8.789(d)
8.869(b)(2) and (3)	NEW
8.869(c)(1)	8.756(a)
8.869(c)(2)	8.756(a) and 8.784(b)
8.869(c)(2)(A)	8.784(b)
8.869(c)(2)(B)	8.784(a)
8.869(c)(2)(C)	8.784(b)
8.869(c)(2)(D)	8.784(c)
8.869(d)(1)	8.785 and 8.789(f) paragraph 1
8.869(d)(2)	8.789(g) paragraph 2
8.869(d)(3)	8.788 paragraph 1
8.869(d)(4)	8.788 paragraph 2 and 8.789(g) paragraphs 2 and 3
8.869(d)(5)	8.788 paragraph 2
8.869(d)(6)	NEW
8.869(e)	NEW
8.869(f)	8.788 paragraph 2 and 8.789(h)
8.869(g)	8.787(a)
8.870	NEW
8.871	NEW
8.872	NEW
8.873(a)	NEW
8.873(b)	NEW
8.873(c)	8.789(k) and 8.791
8.880	8.792 and 8.793
8.881	8.704(b) and 8.792
8.882(a)(1), (2), and (3)	8.706(a)
8.882(a)(4)	NEW
8.882(a)(5)	8.706(a)
8.882(b)	NEW
8.882(c)	NEW
8.882(d)	8.706(b)
8.882(c)(1) and (2)	8.706(e)
8.882(c)(3)	8.706(f)
8.882(c)(4)	8.706(e)
8.883(a)	8.706(c)
8.883(b)	8.706(c)

Revised Rule	Current Rule
8.883(c)	8.706(d)
8.883(d)	8.706(e)
8.884	NEW
8.885(a)	8.704(a)
8.885(b)	8.704(b)
8.885(c)	NEW
8.885(d)	NEW
8.886(a)	8.707(a)
8.886(b)	NEW
8.887(a)	8.707(b)
8.887(b)	NEW
8.887(c)	8.707(c)
8.888(a)(1)	8.708(a)(1)
8.888(a)(2) and (3)	NEW
8.888(b)	8.708(b)
8.888(c)	8.709
8.889(a)(1)	8.708(c)(1)
8.889(a)(2)	NEW
8.889(b)(1)	8.708(c)(2), (3), and (4)
8.889(b)(2)	8.708(c)(3)
8.889(b)(3)	8.708(c)(4)
8.889(b)(4)	NEW
8.889(c)	8.708(d)
8.889(d)	8.708(c)(5)
8.890(a)	NEW
8.890(b)(1)	8.773(a) and 8.793(a)
8.890(b)(2)	NEW
8.890(c)(1)	8.773(b) and 8.793(b)
8.890(c)(2)	8.773(d) and 8.793(d)
8.890(c)(3)	8.773(c) and 8.793(c)
8.8890(d)	NEW
8.891(a)	8.764(a)
8.891(b)	8.764(b)
8.891(c)	8.764(d)
8.891(d)	8.764(c)
8.891(e)	8.764(e)
8.900	8.780(b)
8.901(a)	8.782(a) paragraph 1
8.901(b)(1) and (2)	8.782(b)
8.901(b)(3), (4), and (5)	NEW
8.901(b)(6)	8.782(b)
8.902(a)	8.782(a) paragraph 2
8.902(b)	NEW
8.902(c)	8.782(a) paragraph 4
8.902(d)	8.782(a) paragraph 3
8.902(e)	NEW
8.903	NEW
8.904(a)	8.790
8.904(b)	8.790
8.904(c)	NEW
8.910(a)	8.783
8.910(b)	NEW
8.911	NEW
8.912(1)	8.783(a)(1)

Revised Rule	Current Rule
8.912(2)	8.783(a)(2) and (6)
8.912(3)	8.783(a)(7)
8.912(4)	8.783(a)(4)
8.912(5)	8.783(a)(8)
8.912(6)	8.783(a)(5)
8.912(7)	NEW
8.912(8)	8.783(a)(9)
8.912(9)	NEW
8.913(a)	NEW
8.913(b)	8.783(b)
8.913(c)	NEW
8.913(d)	8.783(b)
8.914	8.789(j)
8.915	NEW
8.916(a)	NEW
8.916(b)(1)	8.784(d) and 8.789(d)
8.916(b)(2) and (3)	NEW
8.916(c)(1)	8.756(a)
8.916(c)(2)	8.756(a) and 8.784(b)
8.916(c)(2)(A)	8.784(b)
8.916(c)(2)(B)	8.784(a)
8.916(c)(2)(C)	8.784(b)
8.916(d)(1)	8.785 and 8.789(f) paragraph 1
8.916(d)(2)	8.789(g) paragraph 2
8.916(d)(3)	8.788 paragraph 1
8.916(d)(4)	8.788 paragraph 2 and 8.789(g) paragraphs 2 and 3
8.916(d)(5)	8.788 paragraph 2
8.916(d)(6)	NEW
8.916(e)	NEW
8.916(f)	8.788 paragraph 2 and 8.789(h)
8.916(g)	8.787(a)
8.917	NEW
8.918	NEW
8.919	NEW
8.920	8.783(a)(12)
8.921	NEW
8.922	NEW
8.923(a)	NEW
8.923(b)	NEW
8.923(c)	8.789(k) and 8.791
8.925	NEW
8.926	8.704(b)
8.927(a)(1), (2), and (3)	8.706(a)
8.927(a)(4)	NEW
8.927(a)(5)	8.706(a)
8.927(b)	NEW
8.927(c)(1) and (2)	8.706(e)
8.927(c)(3)	8.706(f)
8.927(c)(4)	8.706(e)
8.928(a)	8.706(c)
8.928(b)	8.706(c)
8.928(c)	8.706(d)
8.928(d)	8.706(e)

Revised Rule	Current Rule
8.929(a)	8.704(a)
8.929(b)	8.704(b)
8.929(c)	NEW
8.929(d)	NEW
8.930.	NEW
8.931.	NEW
8.932.	NEW
8.933.	NEW
8.934.	NEW
8.935.	NEW
8.936.	NEW
10.1100(a)	8.701(a)
10.1100(b)	8.701(b)
10.1100(c)	8.701(c)
10.1100(d)	8.701(d)
10.1104(a)	8.703 paragraph 2
10.1104(b)	8.703 paragraph 1
10.1108.	8.702

1 So in copy.　This table shows the derivation of the revised rules.

Chapter 1

GENERAL RULES APPLICABLE TO APPELLATE DIVISION PROCEEDINGS

Rule
8.800.　Application of division.
8.802.　Construction.
8.804.　Definitions.
8.805.　Amendments to rules and statutes.
8.806.　Applications.
8.808.　Motions.
8.809.　Judicial notice.
8.810.　Extending time.
8.811.　Policies and factors governing extensions of time.
8.812.　Relief from default.
8.813.　Shortening time.
8.814.　Substituting parties; substituting or withdrawing attorneys.
8.816.　Address and other contact information of record; notice of change.
8.817.　Service and filing.
8.818.　Waiver of fees and costs.
8.819.　Sealed records.

Rule 8.800.　Application of division

The rules in this division apply to:

(1) Appeals in the appellate division of the superior court; and

(2) Writ proceedings, motions, applications, and petitions in the appellate division of the superior court. *(Adopted, eff. Jan. 1, 2009.)*

Research References

Rutter, Cal. Practice Guide: Civil Appeals & Writs Ch. 16-A, A. Introduction.
9 Witkin Cal. Proc. 5th Appeal § 9, (S 9) Current Structure.
9 Witkin Cal. Proc. 5th Appeal § 1002, in General.
2 Witkin Cal. Proc. 5th Courts § 195, (S 195) Appellate Rules.

Rule 8.802.　Construction

(a) Construction

The rules in this division must be construed to ensure that the proceedings they govern will be justly and speedily determined.

(b) Terminology

As used in this division:

(1) "Must" is mandatory;

(2) "May" is permissive;

(3) "May not" means is not permitted to;

(4) "Will" expresses a future contingency or predicts action by a court or person in the ordinary course of events, but does not signify a mandatory duty; and

(5) "Should" expresses a preference or a nonbinding recommendation.

(c) Construction of additional terms

In the rules:

(1) Each tense (past, present, or future) includes the others;

(2) Each gender (masculine, feminine, or neuter) includes the others;

(3) Each number (singular or plural) includes the other; and

(4) The headings of divisions, chapters, articles, rules, and subdivisions are substantive. *(Adopted, eff. Jan. 1, 2009.)*

Research References

9 Witkin Cal. Proc. 5th Appeal § 1002, in General.

Rule 8.804.　Definitions

As used in this division, unless the context or subject matter otherwise requires:

(1) "Action" includes special proceeding.

(2) "Case" includes action or proceeding.

(3) "Civil case" means a case prosecuted by one party against another for the declaration, enforcement, or protection of a right or the redress or prevention of a wrong. Civil cases include all cases except criminal cases.

(4) "Unlimited civil cases" and "limited civil cases" are defined in Code of Civil Procedure section 85 et seq.

(5) "Criminal case" means a proceeding by which a party charged with a public offense is accused and brought to trial and punishment.

(6) "Rule" means a rule of the California Rules of Court.

(7) "Local rule" means every rule, regulation, order, policy, form, or standard of general application adopted by a court to govern practice and procedure in that court or by a judge of the court to govern practice or procedure in that judge's courtroom.

(8) "Presiding judge" includes the acting presiding judge or the judge designated by the presiding judge.

(9) "Judge" includes, as applicable, a judge of the superior court, a commissioner, or a temporary judge.

(10) "Person" includes a corporation or other legal entity as well as a natural person.

(11) "Appellant" means the appealing party.

(12) "Respondent" means the adverse party.

(13) "Party" is a person appearing in an action. Parties include both self-represented persons and persons represented by an attorney of record. "Party," "applicant," "petitioner," or any other designation of a party includes the party's attorney of record.

(14) "Attorney" means a member of the State Bar of California.

(15) "Counsel" means an attorney.

(16) "Prosecuting attorney" means the city attorney, county counsel, or district attorney prosecuting an infraction or misdemeanor case.

(17) "Complaint" includes a citation.

(18) "Service" means service in the manner prescribed by a statute or rule.

(19) "Declaration" includes "affidavit."

(20) "Recycled" as applied to paper means "recycled printing and writing paper" as defined by Public Contract Code section 12209.

(21) "Trial court" means the superior court from which an appeal is taken.

(22) "Reviewing court" means the appellate division of the superior court.

(23) "Judgment" includes any judgment or order that may be appealed. *(Adopted, eff. Jan. 1, 2009.)*

Advisory Committee Comment

Item (18). See rule 1.21 for general requirements relating to service, including proof of service.

Research References

9 Witkin Cal. Proc. 5th Appeal § 1002, in General.
2 Witkin Cal. Proc. 5th Courts § 325, (S 325) Nature of Reviewing Courts.

Rule 8.805. Amendments to rules and statutes

(a) Amendments to rules

Only the Judicial Council may amend these rules, except the rules in division 5, which may be amended only by the Supreme Court. An amendment by the Judicial Council must be published in the advance pamphlets of the Official Reports and takes effect on the date ordered by the Judicial Council.

(b) Amendments to statutes

In these rules, a reference to a statute includes any subsequent amendment to the statute. *(Adopted, eff. Jan. 1, 2009.)*

Rule 8.806. Applications

(a) Service and filing

Except as these rules provide otherwise, parties must serve and file all applications, including applications to extend time to file records, briefs, or other documents and applications to shorten time. Applications to extend the time to prepare the record on appeal may be filed in either the trial court or the appellate division. All other applications must be filed in the appellate division. For good cause, the presiding judge of the court where the application was filed, or his or her designee, may excuse advance service.

(b) Contents

The application must:

(1) State facts showing good cause to grant the application; and

(2) Identify any previous applications relating to the same subject filed by any party in the same appeal or writ proceeding.

(c) Envelopes

An application must be accompanied by addressed, postage-prepaid envelopes for the clerk's use in mailing copies of the order on the application to all parties.

(d) Disposition

Unless the court determines otherwise, the presiding judge of the court in which the application was filed, or his or her designee, may rule on the application. *(Adopted, eff. Jan. 1, 2009.)*

Advisory Committee Comment

Subdivision (a). See rule 1.21 for the meaning of "serve and file," including the requirements for proof of service.

Subdivisions (a) and (d). These provisions permit the presiding judge to designate another judge, such as the trial judge, to handle applications.

Research References

Rutter, Cal. Practice Guide: Civil Appeals & Writs Ch. 16-E, E. Motions, Applications and Requests.
9 Witkin Cal. Proc. 5th Appeal § 586, (S 586) in General.
2 Witkin Cal. Proc. 5th Courts § 340, (S 340) Operation.

Rule 8.808. Motions

(a) Motion and opposition

(1) Except as these rules provide otherwise, to make a motion in the appellate division a party must serve and file a written motion, stating the grounds and the relief requested and identifying any documents on which it is based.

(2) A motion must be accompanied by a memorandum and, if it is based on matters outside the record, by declarations or other supporting evidence.

(3) Any opposition to the motion must be served and filed within 15 days after the motion is filed.

(b) Disposition

(1) The court may rule on a motion at any time after an opposition or other response is filed or the time to oppose has expired.

(2) On a party's request or its own motion, the appellate division may place a motion on calendar for a hearing. The clerk must promptly send each party a notice of the date and time of the hearing. *(Adopted, eff. Jan. 1, 2009.)*

Advisory Committee Comment

Subdivision (a)(1). See rule 1.21 for the meaning of "serve and file," including the requirements for proof of service.

Ct. Rules

Subdivision (b). Although a party may request a hearing on a motion, a hearing will be held only if the court determines that one is needed.

Research References

Rutter, Cal. Practice Guide: Civil Appeals & Writs Ch. 16-E, E. Motions, Applications and Requests.

9 Witkin Cal. Proc. 5th Appeal § 729, (S 729) Hearing and Determination.

9 Witkin Cal. Proc. 5th Appeal § 770, (S 770) Right and Waiver.

9 Witkin Cal. Proc. 5th Appeal § 994, (S 994) Noticed Motion Procedure.

9 Witkin Cal. Proc. 5th Appeal § 1017, Sessions and Calendar.

Rule 8.809. Judicial notice

(a) Motion required

(1) To obtain judicial notice by a reviewing court under Evidence Code section 459, a party must serve and file a separate motion with a proposed order.

(2) The motion must state:

(A) Why the matter to be noticed is relevant to the appeal;

(B) Whether the matter to be noticed was presented to the trial court and, if so, whether judicial notice was taken by that court;

(C) If judicial notice of the matter was not taken by the trial court, why the matter is subject to judicial notice under Evidence Code section 451, 452, or 453; and

(D) Whether the matter to be noticed relates to proceedings occurring after the order or judgment that is the subject of the appeal.

(b) Copy of matter to be judicially noticed

If the matter to be noticed is not in the record, the party must serve and file a copy with the motion or explain why it is not practicable to do so. (*Adopted, eff. Jan. 1, 2011. As amended, eff. Jan. 1, 2013.*)

Research References

Rutter, Cal. Practice Guide: Civil Appeals & Writs Ch. 5-B, B. Types of Motions, Applications and Requests.

Rutter, Cal. Practice Guide: Civil Appeals & Writs Ch. 16-K, K. Transfer to Court of Appeal.

9 Witkin Cal. Proc. 5th Appeal § 1002, in General.

Rule 8.810. Extending time

(a) Computing time

The Code of Civil Procedure governs computing and extending the time to do any act required or permitted under these rules.

(b) Extension by trial court

(1) For good cause and except as these rules provide otherwise, the presiding judge of the trial court, or his or her designee, may extend the time to do any act to prepare the record on appeal.

(2) The trial court may not extend the time to do an act if that time—including any valid extension—has expired.

(3) Notwithstanding anything in these rules to the contrary, the trial court may grant an initial extension to any party to do any act to prepare the record on appeal on an ex parte basis.

(c) Extension by appellate division

For good cause and except as these rules provide otherwise, the presiding judge of the appellate division, or his or her designee, may extend the time to do any act required or permitted under these rules, except the time to file a notice of appeal.

(d) Application for extension

(1) An application to extend time must include a declaration stating facts, not mere conclusions, and must be served on all parties. For good cause, the presiding judge of the appellate division, or his or her designee, may excuse advance service.

(2) The application must state:

(A) The due date of the document to be filed;

(B) The length of the extension requested;

(C) Whether any earlier extensions have been granted and, if so, their lengths; and

(D) Good cause for granting the extension, consistent with the policies and factors stated in rule 8.811.

(e) Notice to party

(1) In a civil case, counsel must deliver to his or her client or clients a copy of any stipulation or application to extend time that counsel files. Counsel must attach evidence of such delivery to the stipulation or application or certify in the stipulation or application that the copy has been delivered.

(2) The evidence or certification of delivery under (1) need not include the address of the party notified. (*Adopted, eff. Jan. 1, 2009.*)

Advisory Committee Comment

Subdivision (b)(1). This provision permits the presiding judge to designate another judge, such as the trial judge, to handle applications to extend time.

Research References

Rutter, Cal. Practice Guide: Civil Appeals & Writs Ch. 16-D, D. Designation of the Record.

9 Witkin Cal. Proc. 5th Appeal § 586, (S 586) in General.

9 Witkin Cal. Proc. 5th Appeal § 614, in General.

9 Witkin Cal. Proc. 5th Appeal § 632, (S 632) Time Limitations and Extension.

9 Witkin Cal. Proc. 5th Appeal § 718, (S 718) Late Filing: Dismissal and Relief from Default.

2 Witkin Cal. Proc. 5th Courts § 326, (S 326) Powers of Individual Judges.

2 Witkin Cal. Proc. 5th Courts § 340, (S 340) Operation.

Rule 8.811. Policies and factors governing extensions of time

(a) Policies

(1) The time limits prescribed by these rules should generally be met to ensure expeditious conduct of appellate business and public confidence in the efficient administration of appellate justice.

(2) The effective assistance of counsel to which a party is entitled includes adequate time for counsel to prepare briefs or other documents that fully advance the party's interests. Adequate time also allows the preparation of accurate, clear, concise, and complete submissions that assist the courts.

(3) For a variety of legitimate reasons, counsel or self-represented litigants may not always be able to prepare briefs or other documents within the time specified in the rules of court. To balance the competing policies stated in (1) and (2), applications to extend time in the appellate division must demonstrate good cause under (b). If good cause is shown, the court must extend the time.

(b) Factors considered

In determining good cause, the court must consider the following factors when applicable:

(1) The degree of prejudice, if any, to any party from a grant or denial of the extension. A party claiming prejudice must support the claim in detail.

(2) In a civil case, the positions of the client and any opponent with regard to the extension.

(3) The length of the record, including the number of relevant trial exhibits. A party relying on this factor must specify the length of the record.

(4) The number and complexity of the issues raised. A party relying on this factor must specify the issues.

(5) Whether there are settlement negotiations and, if so, how far they have progressed and when they might be completed.

(6) Whether the case is entitled to priority.

(7) Whether counsel responsible for preparing the document is new to the case.

(8) Whether other counsel or the client needs additional time to review the document.

(9) Whether counsel or a self-represented party responsible for preparing the document has other time-limited commitments that prevent timely filing of the document. Mere conclusory statements that more time is needed because of other pressing business will not suffice. Good cause requires a specific showing of other obligations of counsel or a self-represented party that:

(A) Have deadlines that as a practical matter preclude filing the document by the due date without impairing its quality; or

(B) Arise from cases entitled to priority.

(10) Illness of counsel or a self-represented party, a personal emergency, or a planned vacation that counsel or a self-represented party did not reasonably expect to conflict with the due date and cannot reasonably rearrange.

(11) Any other factor that constitutes good cause in the context of the case. (*Adopted, eff. Jan. 1, 2009.*)

Rule 8.812. Relief from default

For good cause, the presiding judge of the appellate division, or his or her designee, may relieve a party from a default for any failure to comply with these rules, except the failure to file a timely notice of appeal. (*Adopted, eff. Jan. 1, 2009.*)

Research References

9 Witkin Cal. Proc. 5th Appeal § 614, in General.
9 Witkin Cal. Proc. 5th Appeal § 1016, (S 1016) Abandonment and Dismissal.

Rule 8.813. Shortening time

For good cause and except as these rules provide otherwise, the presiding judge of the appellate division, or his or her designee, may shorten the time to do any act required or permitted under these rules. (*Adopted, eff. Jan. 1, 2009.*)

Research References

9 Witkin Cal. Proc. 5th Appeal § 586, (S 586) in General.

Rule 8.814. Substituting parties; substituting or withdrawing attorneys

(a) Substituting parties

Substitution of parties in an appeal or original proceeding must be made by serving and filing a motion in the appellate division. The clerk of the appellate division must notify the trial court of any ruling on the motion.

(b) Substituting attorneys

A party may substitute attorneys by serving and filing in the appellate division a stipulation signed by the party represented and the new attorney.

(c) Withdrawing attorney

(1) An attorney may request withdrawal by filing a motion to withdraw. Unless the court orders otherwise, the motion need be served only on the party represented and the attorneys directly affected.

(2) The proof of service need not include the address of the party represented. But if the court grants the motion, the withdrawing attorney must promptly provide the court and the opposing party with the party's current or last known address and telephone number.

(3) In all appeals and in original proceedings related to a trial court proceeding, the appellate division clerk must notify the trial court of any ruling on the motion. (*Adopted, eff. Jan. 1, 2009.*)

Rule 8.816. Address and other contact information of record; notice of change

(a) Address and other contact information of record

(1) Except as provided in (2), the cover—or first page if there is no cover—of every document filed in the appellate division must include the name, mailing address, telephone number, fax number (if available), e-mail address (if available), and California State Bar number of each attorney filing or joining in the document, or of the party if he or she is unrepresented. The inclusion of a fax number or e-mail address on any document does not constitute consent to service by fax or e-mail unless otherwise provided by law.

(2) If more than one attorney from a law firm, corporation, or public law office is representing one party and is joining in the document, the name and State Bar number of each attorney joining in the document must be provided on the cover. The law firm, corporation, or public law office representing each party must designate one attorney to receive notices and other communication in the case from the court by placing an asterisk before that attorney's name on the cover and need must provide the contact information specified under (1) for that attorney. Contact information for the other attorneys from the same law firm, corporation, or public law office is not required but may be provided.

(3) In any case pending before the appellate division, the appellate division will use the mailing address, telephone number, fax number, and e-mail address that an attorney or unrepresented party provides on the first document filed in that case as the mailing address, telephone number, fax number, and e-mail address of record unless the attorney or unrepresented party files a notice under (b).

(b) Notice of change

(1) An attorney or unrepresented party whose mailing address, telephone number, fax number, or e-mail address changes while a case is pending must promptly serve and file a written notice of the change in the appellate division in which the case is pending.

(2) The notice must specify the title and number of the case or cases to which it applies. If an attorney gives the notice, the notice must include the attorney's California State Bar number.

(c) Multiple addresses or other contact information

If an attorney or unrepresented party has more than one mailing address, telephone number, fax number, or e-mail address, only one mailing address, telephone number, fax number, and e-mail address may be used in a given case. (*Adopted, eff. Jan. 1, 2009. As amended, eff. Jan. 1, 2013.*)

Research References

9 Witkin Cal. Proc. 5th Appeal § 9, (S 9) Current Structure.
2 Witkin Cal. Proc. 5th Courts § 195, (S 195) Appellate Rules.

Rule 8.817. Service and filing

(a) Service

(1) Before filing any document, a party must serve, by any method permitted by the Code of Civil Procedure, one copy of the document on the attorney for each party separately represented, on each unrepresented party, and on any other person or entity when required by statute or rule.

(2) The party must attach to the document presented for filing a proof of service showing service on each person or entity required to be served under (1). The proof must name each party represented by each attorney served.

(b) Filing

(1) A document is deemed filed on the date the clerk receives it.

(2) Unless otherwise provided by these rules or other law, a filing is not timely unless the clerk receives the document before the time to file it expires.

(3) A brief, a petition for rehearing, or an answer to a petition for rehearing is timely if the time to file it has not expired on the date of:

(A) Its mailing by priority or express mail as shown on the postmark or the postal receipt; or

(B) Its delivery to a common carrier promising overnight delivery as shown on the carrier's receipt.

(4) The provisions of (3) do not apply to original proceedings.

(5) If the clerk receives a document by mail from an inmate or a patient in a custodial institution after the period for filing the document has expired but the envelope shows that the document was mailed or delivered to custodial officials for mailing within the period for filing the document, the document is deemed timely. The clerk must retain in the case file the envelope in which the document was received. *(Adopted, eff. Jan. 1, 2009. As amended, eff. July 1, 2010.)*

Advisory Committee Comment

Subdivision (a). Subdivision (a)(1) requires service "by any method permitted by the Code of Civil Procedure." The reference is to the several permissible methods of service provided in Code of Civil Procedure sections 1010–1020. *What Is Proof of Service?* (form APP–109–INFO) provides additional information about how to serve documents and how to provide proof of service.

Subdivision (b). In general, to be filed on time, a document must be received by the clerk before the time for filing that document expires. There are, however, some limited exceptions to this general rule. For example, (5) provides that if the superior court clerk receives a document by mail from a custodial institution after the deadline for filing the document has expired but the envelope shows that the document was mailed or delivered to custodial officials for mailing before the deadline expired, the document is deemed timely. This provision reflects the "prison-delivery" exception articulated by the California Supreme Court in *In re Jordan* (1992) 4 Cal. 4th 116 and *Silverbrand v. County of Los Angeles* (2009) 46 Cal.4th 106.

Note that if a deadline runs from the date of filing, it runs from the date that the document is actually received and deemed filed under (b)(1); neither (b)(3) nor (b)(5) changes that date. Nor do these provisions extend the date of finality of an appellate opinion or any other deadline that is based on finality, such as the deadline for the court to modify its opinion or order rehearing. Subdivision (b)(5) is also not intended to limit a criminal defendant's appeal rights under the case law of constructive filing. (See, e.g., *In re Benoit* (1973) 10 Cal.3d 72.)

Research References

Rutter, Cal. Practice Guide: Civil Appeals & Writs Ch. 16-C, C. Notice of Appeal.

Rutter, Cal. Practice Guide: Civil Appeals & Writs Ch. 16-F, F. Briefs.

9 Witkin Cal. Proc. 5th Appeal § 12, Serve and File.

9 Witkin Cal. Proc. 5th Appeal § 1006, Form and Filing.

Rule 8.818. Waiver of fees and costs

(a) Applications for waiver of fees and costs

(1) *Appeals*

(A) If the trial court previously issued an order granting a party's request to waive court fees and costs in a case, and that fee waiver is still in effect, all of the court fees for an appeal to the appellate division in that case that are listed in (d) are waived by that order, and the party is not required to file a new application for waiver of court fees and costs for an appeal to the appellate division in that case.

(B) If the trial court did not previously issue an order granting a party's request to waive court fees and costs in a case or an order that was previously issued is no longer in effect, an application for initial waiver of court fees and costs for an appeal must be made on *Request to Waive Court Fees* (form FW–001). The appellant should file the application with the notice of appeal in the trial court that issued the judgment or order being appealed. The respondent should file any application at the time the fees are to be paid to the court.

(2) *Writ Proceedings*

To request the waiver of fees and costs in a writ proceeding, the petitioner must complete *Request to Waive Court Fees* (form FW–001). The petitioner should file the application with the writ petition.

(3) *Forms*

The clerk must provide *Request to Waive Court Fees* (form FW–001) and *Information Sheet on Waiver of Fees and Costs (Supreme Court, Court of Appeal, Appellate Division)* (form APP–015/FW–015–INFO) without charge to any person who requests any fee waiver application or states that he or she is unable to pay any court fee or cost.

(b) Procedure for determining application

The application must be considered and determined as required by Government Code section 68634.5. An order determining the application for initial fee waiver or setting a hearing on the application may be made on *Order on Court Fee Waiver (Superior Court)* (form FW–003).

(c) Application granted unless acted on by the court

The application for initial fee waiver is deemed granted unless the court gives notice of action on the application within five court days after the application is filed.

(d) Court fees and costs waived

Court fees and costs that must be waived upon granting an application for initial waiver of court fees and costs include:

(1) The fee for filing the notice of appeal;

(2) The clerk's fees for preparing and certifying the clerk's transcript on appeal and for copying and transmitting a copy of this transcript to the applicant;

(3) The fee for preparing a transcript of an official electronic recording under rule 8.835 or a copy of such an electronic recording; and

(4) Any court fee for telephonic oral argument.

(e) Denial of the application

If an application is denied, the applicant must pay the court fees and costs or submit the new application or additional information requested by the court within 10 days after the clerk gives notice of the denial.

(f) Confidential Records

(1) No person may have access to an application for an initial fee waiver submitted to the court except the court and authorized court personnel, any person authorized by the applicant, and any persons authorized by order of the court. No person may reveal any information contained in the application except as authorized by law or order of the court. An order granting access to an application or financial information may include limitations on who may access the information and on the use of the information after it has been released.

(2) Any person seeking access to an application or financial information provided to the court by an applicant must make the request by motion, supported by a declaration showing good cause as to why the confidential information should be released. *(Adopted, eff. July 1, 2009.)*

Advisory Committee Comment

Subdivision (a)(1)(B). The waiver of court fees and costs is called an "initial" waiver because, under Government Code section 68630 and following, any such waiver may later be modified, ended, or retroactively withdrawn if the court determines that the applicant was not or is no longer eligible for a waiver. The court may, at a later time, order that the previously waived fees be paid.

Research References

Rutter, Cal. Practice Guide: Civil Appeals & Writs Ch. 16-C, C. Notice of Appeal.
3 Witkin Cal. Proc. 5th Actions § 416, (S 416) in General.
3 Witkin Cal. Proc. 5th Actions § 418, Trial Court Costs.
3 Witkin Cal. Proc. 5th Actions § 419, Costs of Appeal.
3 Witkin Cal. Proc. 5th Actions § 423, (S 423) No Right to Reporter's Transcript.
3 Witkin Cal. Proc. 5th Actions § 425, (S 425) Legislative Directive to Judicial Council.
3 Witkin Cal. Proc. 5th Actions § 426, (S 426) Application and Forms.
3 Witkin Cal. Proc. 5th Actions § 427, (S 427) Determination of Application.
3 Witkin Cal. Proc. 5th Actions § 428, (S 428) in General.
3 Witkin Cal. Proc. 5th Actions § 429A, (S 429A) (New)-In General.
3 Witkin Cal. Proc. 5th Actions § 429B, (New)-In General.
3 Witkin Cal. Proc. 5th Actions § 429C, (New)-Costs Excused.
3 Witkin Cal. Proc. 5th Actions § 429E, (New)-Judicial Council Rules and Forms.
3 Witkin Cal. Proc. 5th Actions § 429F, (S 429F) (New)-General Requirements.
3 Witkin Cal. Proc. 5th Actions § 429G, (S 429G) (New)-Requirements for Specific Proceedings.
3 Witkin Cal. Proc. 5th Actions § 429I, (New)-Determination of Appellate Court Applications.
9 Witkin Cal. Proc. 5th Appeal § 1006, Form and Filing.
9 Witkin Cal. Proc. 5th Appeal § 1012, Transcripts.

Rule 8.819. Sealed records

Rule 8.46 governs records sealed by court order under rules 2.550–2.551 and records proposed to be sealed in the appellate division. *(Adopted, eff. Jan. 1, 2010.)*

Research References

Rutter, Cal. Practice Guide: Civil Appeals & Writs Ch. 16-E, E. Motions, Applications and Requests.
9 Witkin Cal. Proc. 5th Appeal § 9, (S 9) Current Structure.
2 Witkin Cal. Proc. 5th Courts § 44, Sealed Records in Reviewing Courts.
2 Witkin Cal. Proc. 5th Courts § 195, (S 195) Appellate Rules.

Chapter 2

APPEALS AND RECORDS IN LIMITED CIVIL CASES

Article 1

TAKING CIVIL APPEALS

Rule 8.820. Application of chapter

The rules in this chapter apply to appeals in limited civil cases, except small claims cases. *(Adopted, eff. Jan. 1, 2009.)*

Advisory Committee Comment

Chapters 1 and 4 of this division also apply in appeals in limited civil cases.

Research References

Rutter, Cal. Practice Guide: Civil Appeals & Writs Ch. 3-A, A. Necessity of Timely Filing for Appeal.
9 Witkin Cal. Proc. 5th Appeal § 9, (S 9) Current Structure.
9 Witkin Cal. Proc. 5th Appeal § 1002, in General.
2 Witkin Cal. Proc. 5th Courts § 195, (S 195) Appellate Rules.

Rule 8.821. Notice of appeal

(a) Notice of appeal

(1) To appeal from a judgment or appealable order in a limited civil case, except a small claims case, an appellant must serve and file a notice of appeal in the superior court that issued the judgment or order being appealed. The appellant or the appellant's attorney must sign the notice.

(2) The notice of appeal must be liberally construed and is sufficient if it identifies the particular limited civil case judgment or order being appealed.

(3) Failure to serve the notice of appeal neither prevents its filing nor affects its validity, but the appellant may be required to remedy the failure.

(b) Filing fee

(1) Unless otherwise provided by law, the notice of appeal must be accompanied by the filing fee required under Government Code sections 70621 and 70602.5, an application for a waiver of court fees and costs on appeal under rule 8.818, or an order granting an application for a waiver of court fees and costs. The filing fee is nonrefundable.

(2) The clerk must file the notice of appeal even if the appellant does not present the filing fee or an application for, or order granting, a waiver of court fees and costs.

(c) Failure to pay filing fee

(1) The clerk must promptly notify the appellant in writing if:

(A) The court receives a notice of appeal without the filing fee required by (b) or an application for, or order granting, a waiver of court fees and costs;

(B) A check for the filing fee is dishonored; or

(C) An application for a waiver under rule 8.818 is denied.

(2) A clerk's notice under (1)(A) or (B) must state that the court may dismiss the appeal unless, within 15 days after the notice is sent, the appellant either:

(A) Pays the fee; or

(B) Files an application for a waiver under rule 8.818 if the appellant has not previously filed such an application or an order granting such an application.

(3) If the appellant fails to take the action specified in the notice given under (2), the appellate division may dismiss the appeal, but may vacate the dismissal for good cause.

(d) Notification of the appeal

(1) When the notice of appeal is filed, the trial court clerk must promptly mail a notification of the filing of the notice of appeal to the attorney of record for each party and to any unrepresented party. The clerk must also mail or deliver this notification to the appellate division clerk.

(2) The notification must show the date it was mailed and must state the number and title of the case and the date the notice of appeal was filed.

(3) A copy of the notice of appeal is sufficient notification under (1) if the required information is on the copy or is added by the trial court clerk.

(4) The mailing of a notification under (1) is a sufficient performance of the clerk's duty despite the death of the party or the discharge, disqualification, suspension, disbarment, or death of the attorney.

(5) Failure to comply with any provision of this subdivision does not affect the validity of the notice of appeal.

(e) Notice of cross-appeal

As used in this rule, "notice of appeal" includes a notice of cross-appeal and "appellant" includes a respondent filing a notice of cross-appeal. *(Adopted, eff. Jan. 1, 2009. As amended, eff. July 1, 2009; Jan. 1, 2013.)*

Advisory Committee Comment

Subdivision (a). *Notice of Appeal/Cross–Appeal (Limited Civil Case)* (form APP–102) may be used to file the notice of appeal required under this rule. This form is available at any courthouse or county law library or online at *www.courts.ca.gov/forms.htm.*

Subdivision (b). For information about the amount of the filing fee, see the current Statewide Civil Fee Schedule linked at *www.courts.ca.gov/7646.htm* (note that the "Appeal and Writ Related Fees" section appears near the end of the schedule and that there are different fees for limited civil cases depending on the amount demanded in the case.)

Subdivision (c)(2). This subdivision addresses the content of a clerk's notice that a check for the filing fee has been dishonored or that the reviewing court has received a notice of appeal without the filing fee, a certificate of cash payment, or an application for, or order granting, a fee waiver. Rule 8.818(e) addresses what an appellant must do when a fee waiver application is denied.

Research References

Rutter, Cal. Practice Guide: Civil Appeals & Writs Ch. 16-C, C. Notice of Appeal.
9 Witkin Cal. Proc. 5th Appeal § 555, (S 555) Jurisdictional Requirement: Filing in Trial Court.
9 Witkin Cal. Proc. 5th Appeal § 558, (S 558) Waiver of Fees in Indigent Appeal.
9 Witkin Cal. Proc. 5th Appeal § 559, (S 559) Notification by Clerk.
9 Witkin Cal. Proc. 5th Appeal § 561, in General.
9 Witkin Cal. Proc. 5th Appeal § 573, (S 573) Signature of Party or Attorney.
9 Witkin Cal. Proc. 5th Appeal § 1006, Form and Filing.
9 Witkin Cal. Proc. 5th Appeal § 1007, Notification by Clerk.
9 Witkin Cal. Proc. 5th Appeal § 1011, in General.

Rule 8.822. Time to appeal

(a) Normal time

(1) Unless a statute or rule 8.823 provides otherwise, a notice of appeal must be filed on or before the earliest of:

(A) 30 days after the trial court clerk mails the party filing the notice of appeal a document entitled "Notice of Entry" of judgment or a file-stamped copy of the judgment, showing the date either was mailed;

(B) 30 days after the party filing the notice of appeal serves or is served by a party with a document entitled "Notice of Entry" of judgment or a file-stamped copy of the judgment, accompanied by proof of service; or

(C) 90 days after the entry of judgment.

(2) Service under (1)(A) and (B) may be by any method permitted by the Code of Civil Procedure, including electronic service when permitted under Code of Civil Procedure section 1010.6 and rules 2.250–2.261.

(3) If the parties stipulated in the trial court under Code of Civil Procedure section 1019.5 to waive notice of the court order being appealed, the time to appeal under (1)(C) applies unless the court or a party serves notice of entry of judgment or a file-stamped copy of the judgment to start the time period under (1)(A) or (B).

(b) What constitutes entry

For purposes of this rule:

(1) The entry date of a judgment is the date the judgment is filed under Code of Civil Procedure section 668.5 or the date it is entered in the judgment book.

(2) The date of entry of an appealable order that is entered in the minutes is the date it is entered in the permanent minutes. But if the minute order directs that a written order be prepared, the entry date is the date the signed order is filed; a written order prepared under rule 3.1312 or similar local rule is not such an order prepared by direction of a minute order.

(3) The entry date of an order that is not entered in the minutes is the date the signed order is filed.

(c) Premature notice of appeal

(1) A notice of appeal filed after judgment is rendered but before it is entered is valid and is treated as filed immediately after entry of judgment.

(2) The appellate division may treat a notice of appeal filed after the trial court has announced its intended ruling, but before it has rendered judgment, as filed immediately after entry of judgment.

(d) Late notice of appeal

If a notice of appeal is filed late, the appellate division must dismiss the appeal. *(Adopted, eff. Jan. 1, 2009. As amended, eff. Jan. 1, 2011; July 1, 2012.)*

Advisory Committee Comment

Under rule 8.804(23), the term "judgment" includes any order that may be appealed.

Subdivision (d). See rule 8.817(b)(5) for provisions concerning the timeliness of documents mailed by inmates or patients from custodial institutions.

Research References

Rutter, Cal. Practice Guide: Civil Appeals & Writs Ch. 14-B, B. Recovery of Appellate Costs and Attorney Fees.
Rutter, Cal. Practice Guide: Civil Appeals & Writs Ch. 16-C, C. Notice of Appeal.
Rutter, Cal. Practice Guide: Civil Trials & Evidence Ch. 18-A, A. Motion for Judgment Notwithstanding the Verdict ("JNOV").
Rutter, Cal. Practice Guide: Civil Trials & Evidence Ch. 18-B, B. Motion for New Trial.
Rutter, Cal. Practice Guide: Enforcing Judgments/Debts Ch. 6E-4, Opposing Claim of Exemption.
Rutter, Cal. Practice Guide: Personal Injury Ch. 9-M, M. Verdicts and Judgment.
9 Witkin Cal. Proc. 5th Appeal § 574, (S 574) Alternative Time Limits.
9 Witkin Cal. Proc. 5th Appeal § 575, in General.
9 Witkin Cal. Proc. 5th Appeal § 578, Used in Place of Notice of Entry.
9 Witkin Cal. Proc. 5th Appeal § 581, (S 581) One Hundred Eighty Days After Entry of Judgment.
9 Witkin Cal. Proc. 5th Appeal § 582, (S 582) Special Statutes.
9 Witkin Cal. Proc. 5th Appeal § 607, (S 607) Nature of Rules.

9 Witkin Cal. Proc. 5th Appeal § 608, (S 608) Judgment and Decree of Distribution.

9 Witkin Cal. Proc. 5th Appeal § 611, (S 611) Without Minute Entry.

9 Witkin Cal. Proc. 5th Appeal § 614, in General.

9 Witkin Cal. Proc. 5th Appeal § 620, Notice After Rendition: Appeal is Valid.

9 Witkin Cal. Proc. 5th Appeal § 621, (S 621) in General.

9 Witkin Cal. Proc. 5th Appeal § 622, (S 622) Good Cause Requirement.

9 Witkin Cal. Proc. 5th Appeal § 982, (S 982) Procedure for Request.

9 Witkin Cal. Proc. 5th Appeal § 1008, Time.

9 Witkin Cal. Proc. 5th Appeal § 1009, Extension After Denial of Motion.

7 Witkin Cal. Proc. 5th Judgment § 301, Fees Determined by Trial Court.

5 Witkin Cal. Proc. 5th Pleading § 983, Notification and Service of Notice.

Rule 8.823. Extending the time to appeal

(a) Extension of time

This rule operates only to increase the time to appeal otherwise prescribed in rule 8.822(a); it does not shorten the time to appeal. If the normal time to appeal stated in rule 8.822(a) would be longer than the time provided in this rule, the time to appeal stated in rule 8.822(a) governs.

(b) Motion for a new trial

If any party serves and files a valid notice of intention to move for a new trial, the following extensions of time apply:

(1) If the motion is denied, the time to appeal from the judgment is extended for all parties until the earliest of:

(A) 15 days after the trial court clerk mails, or a party serves, an order denying the motion or a notice of entry of that order;

(B) 15 days after denial of the motion by operation of law; or

(C) 90 days after entry of judgment; or

(2) If the trial court makes a finding of excessive or inadequate damages and grants the motion for a new trial subject to the condition that the motion is denied if a party consents to the additur or remittitur of damages:

(A) If a party serves an acceptance of the additur or remittitur within the time for accepting the additur or remittitur, the time to appeal from the judgment is extended for all parties until 15 days after the date the party serves the acceptance.

(B) If a party serves a rejection of the additur or remittitur within the time for accepting the additur or remittitur or if the time for accepting the additur or remittitur expires, the time to appeal from the new trial order is extended for all parties until the earliest of 30 days after the date the party serves the rejection or 30 days after the date on which the time for accepting the additur or remittitur expired.

(c) Motion to vacate judgment

If, within the time prescribed by rule 8.822 to appeal from the judgment, any party serves and files a valid notice of intention to move to vacate the judgment or a valid motion to vacate the judgment, the time to appeal from the judgment is extended for all parties until the earliest of:

(1) 15 days after the trial court clerk mails, or a party serves, an order denying the motion or a notice of entry of that order;

(2) 45 days after the first notice of intention to move or motion is filed; or

(3) 90 days after entry of judgment.

(d) Motion for judgment notwithstanding the verdict

(1) If any party serves and files a valid motion for judgment notwithstanding the verdict and the motion is denied, the time to appeal from the judgment is extended for all parties until the earliest of:

(A) 15 days after the trial court clerk mails, or a party serves, an order denying the motion or a notice of entry of that order;

(B) 15 days after denial of the motion by operation of law; or

(C) 90 days after entry of judgment.

(2) Unless extended by (e)(2), the time to appeal from an order denying a motion for judgment notwithstanding the verdict is governed by rule 8.822.

(e) Motion to reconsider appealable order

If any party serves and files a valid motion to reconsider an appealable order under Code of Civil Procedure section 1008(a), the time to appeal from that order is extended for all parties until the earliest of:

(1) 15 days after the superior court clerk mails, or a party serves, an order denying the motion or a notice of entry of that order;

(2) 45 days after the first motion to reconsider is filed; or

(3) 90 days after entry of the appealable order.

(f) Public entity actions under Government Code section 962, 984, or 985

If a public entity defendant serves and files a valid request for a mandatory settlement conference on methods of satisfying a judgment under Government Code section 962, an election to pay a judgment in periodic payments under Government Code section 984 and rule 3.1804, or a motion for a posttrial hearing on reducing a judgment under Government Code section 985, the time to appeal from the judgment is extended for all parties until the earliest of:

(1) 60 days after the superior court clerk serves the party filing the notice of appeal with a document entitled "Notice of Entry" of judgment or a file-stamped copy of the judgment, showing the date either was served;

(2) 60 days after the party filing the notice of appeal serves or is served by a party with a document entitled "Notice of Entry" of judgment or a file-stamped copy of the judgment, accompanied by proof of service; or

(3) 90 days after entry of judgment.

(g) Cross-appeal

(1) If an appellant timely appeals from a judgment or appealable order, the time for any other party to appeal from the same judgment or order is extended until 10 days after the trial court clerk mails notification of the first appeal.

(2) If an appellant timely appeals from an order granting a motion for a new trial, an order granting—within 75 days after entry of judgment—a motion to vacate the judgment, or a judgment notwithstanding the verdict, the time for any other party to appeal from the original judgment or from an order denying a motion for judgment notwithstanding the verdict is extended until 10 days after the clerk mails notification of the first appeal.

(h) Showing date of order or notice; proof of service

(1) An order or notice mailed by the clerk under this rule must show the date it was mailed.

(2) Service under this rule may be by any method permitted by the Code of Civil Procedure, including electronic service when permitted under Code of Civil Procedure section 1010.6 and rules 2.250–2.261. An order or notice served by a party must be

accompanied by proof of service. *(Adopted, eff. Jan. 1, 2009. As amended eff. Jan. 1, 2011; July 1, 2012.)*

Research References

Rutter, Cal. Practice Guide: Civil Appeals & Writs Ch. 14-B, B. Recovery of Appellate Costs and Attorney Fees.

Rutter, Cal. Practice Guide: Civil Appeals & Writs Ch. 16-C, C. Notice of Appeal.

Rutter, Cal. Practice Guide: Civil Appeals & Writs Gen. Matls., Highlights.

Rutter, Cal. Practice Guide: Personal Injury Ch. 9-M, M. Verdicts and Judgment.

9 Witkin Cal. Proc. 5th Appeal § 582, (S 582) Special Statutes.

9 Witkin Cal. Proc. 5th Appeal § 588, (S 588) Valid Notice of Motion.

9 Witkin Cal. Proc. 5th Appeal § 589, (S 589) Period of Extension.

9 Witkin Cal. Proc. 5th Appeal § 592, (S 592) Nature of Rule.

9 Witkin Cal. Proc. 5th Appeal § 595, (S 595) Nature of Motion.

9 Witkin Cal. Proc. 5th Appeal § 597, Cross-Appeal Where Motion is Granted.

9 Witkin Cal. Proc. 5th Appeal § 599, Cross-Appeal Where Motion is Granted.

9 Witkin Cal. Proc. 5th Appeal § 604, in General.

9 Witkin Cal. Proc. 5th Appeal § 606, (S 606) Judgment Against Public Entity.

9 Witkin Cal. Proc. 5th Appeal § 982, (S 982) Procedure for Request.

9 Witkin Cal. Proc. 5th Appeal § 1008, Time.

9 Witkin Cal. Proc. 5th Appeal § 1009, Extension After Denial of Motion.

9 Witkin Cal. Proc. 5th Appeal § 1010, Cross-Appeal.

7 Witkin Cal. Proc. 5th Judgment § 301, Fees Determined by Trial Court.

Rule 8.824. Writ of supersedeas

(a) Petition

(1) A party seeking a stay of the enforcement of a judgment or order pending appeal may serve and file a petition for writ of supersedeas in the appellate division.

(2) The petition must bear the same title as the appeal.

(3) The petition must explain the necessity for the writ and include a memorandum.

(4) If the record has not been filed in the reviewing court:

(A) The petition must include a statement of the case sufficient to show that the petitioner will raise substantial issues on appeal, including a fair summary of the material facts and the issues that are likely to be raised on appeal.

(B) The petitioner must file the following documents with the petition:

(i) The judgment or order, showing its date of entry;

(ii) The notice of appeal, showing its date of filing;

(iii) A reporter's transcript of any oral statement by the court supporting its rulings related to the issues that are likely to be raised on appeal, or, if a transcript is unavailable, a declaration fairly summarizing any such statements;

(iv) Any application for a stay filed in the trial court, any opposition to that application, and a reporter's transcript of the oral proceedings concerning the stay or, if a transcript is unavailable, a declaration fairly summarizing the proceedings, including the parties' arguments and any statement by the court supporting its ruling; and

(v) Any other document from the trial court proceeding that is necessary for proper consideration of the petition.

(C) The documents listed in (B) must comply with the following requirements:

(i) They must be bound together at the end of the petition or in separate volumes not exceeding 300 pages each. The pages must be consecutively numbered;

(ii) They must be index-tabbed by number or letter; and

(iii) They must begin with a table of contents listing each document by its title and its index-tab number or letter.

(5) The petition must be verified.

(b) Opposition

(1) Unless otherwise ordered, any opposition must be served and filed within 15 days after the petition is filed.

(2) An opposition must state any material facts not included in the petition and include a memorandum.

(3) The court may not issue a writ of supersedeas until the respondent has had the opportunity to file an opposition.

(c) Temporary stay

(1) The petition may include a request for a temporary stay pending the ruling on the petition.

(2) A separately filed request for a temporary stay must be served on the respondent. For good cause, the presiding judge may excuse advance service.

(d) Issuing the writ

(1) The court may issue the writ on any conditions it deems just.

(2) The court must notify the trial court, under rule 8.904, of any writ or stay that it issues. *(Adopted, eff. Jan. 1, 2009. As amended, eff. Jan. 1, 2010.)*

Advisory Committee Comment

Subdivision (a). If the preparation of a reporter's transcript has not yet been completed at that time a petition for a writ of supersedeas is filed, that transcript is "unavailable" within the meaning of (a)(4)(B).

Research References

Rutter, Cal. Practice Guide: Civil Appeals & Writs Ch. 16-L, L. Writs.

5 Witkin Cal. Proc. 5th Pleading § 983, Notification and Service of Notice.

Rule 8.825. Abandonment, voluntary dismissal, and compromise

(a) Notice of settlement

(1) If a civil case settles after a notice of appeal has been filed, either as a whole or as to any party, the appellant who has settled must immediately serve and file a notice of settlement in the appellate division. If the parties have designated a clerk's or a reporter's transcript and the record has not been filed in the appellate division, the appellant must also immediately serve a copy of the notice on the trial court clerk.

(2) If the case settles after the appellant receives a notice setting oral argument, the appellant must also immediately notify the appellate division of the settlement by telephone or other expeditious method.

(3) Within 45 days after filing a notice of settlement—unless the court has ordered a longer time period on a showing of good cause—the appellant who filed the notice of settlement must file an abandonment under (b).

(4) If the appellant does not file an abandonment or a letter stating good cause why the appeal should not be dismissed within the time period specified under (3), the court may dismiss the appeal as to that appellant and order each side to bear its own costs on appeal.

(5) Subdivision (a) does not apply to settlements requiring findings to be made by the Court of Appeal under Code of Civil Procedure section 128(a)(8).

(b) Abandonment

(1) The appellant may serve and file an abandonment of the appeal or a stipulation to abandon the appeal in the appellate division.

(2) If the record has not been filed in the appellate division, the filing of an abandonment effects a dismissal of the appeal and restores the trial court's jurisdiction. If the record has been filed in the appellate division, the appellate division may dismiss the appeal and direct immediate issuance of the remittitur.

(3) The clerk must promptly notify the adverse party of an abandonment. If the record has not been filed in the appellate division, the clerk must also immediately notify the trial court.

(4) If the appeal is abandoned before the clerk has completed preparation of the transcript, the clerk must refund any portion of a deposit exceeding the preparation cost actually incurred.

(5) If the appeal is abandoned before the reporter has filed the transcript, the reporter must inform the trial court clerk of the cost of the portion of the transcript that the reporter has completed. The clerk must pay that amount to the reporter from the appellant's deposited funds and refund any excess deposit.

(c) Approval of compromise

If a guardian or conservator seeks approval of a proposed compromise of a pending appeal, the appellate division may, before ruling on the compromise, direct the trial court to determine whether the compromise is in the minor's or the conservatee's best interest and to report its findings. *(Adopted, eff. Jan. 1, 2009.)*

Advisory Committee Comment

Abandonment of Appeal (Limited Civil Case) (form APP–106) may be used to file an abandonment under this rule. This form is available at any courthouse or county law library or online at *www.courtinfo.ca.gov/forms.*

Research References

Rutter, Cal. Practice Guide: Civil Appeals & Writs Ch. 16-E, E. Motions, Applications and Requests.
9 Witkin Cal. Proc. 5th Appeal § 9, (S 9) Current Structure.
9 Witkin Cal. Proc. 5th Appeal § 731, in General.
9 Witkin Cal. Proc. 5th Appeal § 734, (S 734) Dismissal After Record is Filed.
9 Witkin Cal. Proc. 5th Appeal § 737, (S 737) Compromise of Claim of Minor or Incompetent.
9 Witkin Cal. Proc. 5th Appeal § 1016, (S 1016) Abandonment and Dismissal.
2 Witkin Cal. Proc. 5th Courts § 195, (S 195) Appellate Rules.

Article 2

RECORD IN CIVIL APPEALS

Rule
8.830. Record on appeal.
8.831. Notice designating the record on appeal.
8.832. Clerk's transcript.
8.833. Trial court file instead of clerk's transcript.
8.834. Reporter's transcript.
8.835. Record when trial proceedings were officially electronically recorded.
8.836. Agreed statement.
8.837. Statement on appeal.
8.838. Form of the record.
8.839. Record in multiple appeals.
8.840. Filing the record.
8.841. Augmenting and correcting the record in the appellate division.

Rule
8.842. Failure to procure the record.
8.843. Transmitting exhibits.

Rule 8.830. Record on appeal

(a) Normal record

Except as otherwise provided in this chapter, the record on an appeal to the appellate division in a civil case must contain the following, which constitute the normal record on appeal:

(1) A record of the written documents from the trial court proceedings in the form of one of the following:

(A) A clerk's transcript under rule 8.832;

(B) If the court has a local rule for the appellate division electing to use this form of the record, the original trial court file under rule 8.833; or

(C) An agreed statement under rule 8.836.

(2) If an appellant wants to raise any issue that requires consideration of the oral proceedings in the trial court, the record on appeal must include a record of these oral proceedings in the form of one of the following:

(A) A reporter's transcript under rule 8.834 or a transcript prepared from an official electronic recording under rule 8.835;

(B) If the court has a local rule for the appellate division permitting this form of the record, an official electronic recording of the proceedings under rule 8.835;

(C) An agreed statement under rule 8.836; or

(D) A statement on appeal under rule 8.837.

(b) Presumption from the record

The appellate division will presume that the record in an appeal includes all matters material to deciding the issues raised. If the appeal proceeds without a reporter's transcript, this presumption applies only if the claimed error appears on the face of the record. *(Adopted, eff. Jan. 1, 2009.)*

Advisory Committee Comment

Subdivision (a). The options of using the original trial court file instead of a clerk's transcript under (1)(B) or an electronic recording itself, rather than a transcript, under (2)(B) are available only if the court has local rules for the appellate division authorizing these options.

Research References

Rutter, Cal. Practice Guide: Civil Appeals & Writs Ch. 16-D, D. Designation of the Record.
9 Witkin Cal. Proc. 5th Appeal § 9, (S 9) Current Structure.
9 Witkin Cal. Proc. 5th Appeal § 1011, in General.
9 Witkin Cal. Proc. 5th Appeal § 1030, Record.
2 Witkin Cal. Proc. 5th Courts § 195, (S 195) Appellate Rules.

Rule 8.831. Notice designating the record on appeal

(a) Time to file

Within 10 days after filing the notice of appeal, an appellant must serve and file a notice in the trial court designating the record on appeal. The appellant may combine its notice designating the record with its notice of appeal.

(b) Contents

The notice must specify:

(1) The date the notice of appeal was filed;

(2) Which form of the record of the written documents from the trial court proceedings listed in rule 8.830(a)(1) the appellant elects to use. If the appellant elects to use a clerk's transcript, the notice must also:

(A) Provide the filing date of each document that is required to be included in the clerk's transcript under 8.832(a)(1) or, if the filing date is not available, the date it was signed; and

(B) Designate, as provided under 8.832(b), any documents in addition to those required under 8.832(a)(1) that the appellant wants included in the clerk's transcript;

(3) Whether the appellant elects to proceed with or without a record of the oral proceedings in the trial court;

(4) If the appellant elects to proceed with a record of the oral proceedings in the trial court, the notice must specify which form of the record listed in rule 8.830(a)(2) the appellant elects to use;

(5) If the appellant elects to use a reporter's transcript, the notice must designate the proceedings to be included in the transcript as required under rule 8.834;

(6) If the appellant elects to use an official electronic recording, the appellant must attach a copy of the stipulation required under rule 8.835(c); and

(7) If the appellant elects to use an agreed statement, the appellant must attach to the notice either the agreed statement or stipulation as required under rule 8.836(c)(1). *(Adopted, eff. Jan. 1, 2009.)*

Advisory Committee Comment

Notice Designating Record on Appeal (Limited Civil Case) (form APP–103) may be used to file the designation required under this rule. This form is available at any courthouse or county law library or online at *www.courtinfo.ca.gov/forms*. To assist parties in making appropriate choices, courts are encouraged to include information about whether the proceedings were recorded by a court reporter or officially electronically recorded in any information that the court provides to parties concerning their appellate rights.

If the appellant designates a clerk's transcript or reporter's transcript under this rule, the respondent will have an opportunity to designate additional documents to be included in the clerk's transcript under rule 8.832(b)(2) or additional proceedings to be included in the reporter's transcript under rule 8.834(a)(3).

Research References

Rutter, Cal. Practice Guide: Civil Appeals & Writs Ch. 16-D, D. Designation of the Record.
9 Witkin Cal. Proc. 5th Appeal § 560, (S 560) Statement that Party Appeals.
9 Witkin Cal. Proc. 5th Appeal § 1011, in General.

Rule 8.832.   Clerk's transcript

(a) Contents of clerk's transcript

(1) The clerk's transcript must contain:

(A) The notice of appeal;

(B) Any judgment appealed from and any notice of its entry;

(C) Any order appealed from and any notice of its entry;

(D) Any notice of intention to move for a new trial or motion to vacate the judgment, for judgment notwithstanding the verdict, or for reconsideration of an appealed order, and any order on such motion and any notice of its entry;

(E) The notice designating the record on appeal; and

(F) The register of actions, if any.

(2) Each document listed in (1)(A), (B), (C), and (D) must show the date necessary to determine the timeliness of the appeal under rule 8.822 or 8.823.

(3) If designated by any party, the clerk's transcript must also contain:

(A) Any other document filed or lodged in the case in the trial court;

(B) Any exhibit admitted in evidence, refused, or lodged; and

(C) Any jury instructions that any party submitted in writing, the cover page required by rule 2.1055(b)(2), and any written jury instructions given by the court.

(b) Notice of designation

(1) Within 10 days after the appellant serves a notice under rule 8.831 indicating that the appellant elects to use a clerk's transcript, the respondent may serve and file a notice in the trial court designating any additional documents the respondent wants included in the clerk's transcript.

(2) A notice designating documents to be included in a clerk's transcript must identify each designated document by its title and filing date or, if the filing date is not available, the date it was signed. A notice designating documents in addition to those listed in (a)(1) may specify portions of designated documents that are not to be included in the clerk's transcript. For minute orders or jury instructions, it is sufficient to collectively designate all minute orders or all minute orders entered between specified dates, or all written instructions given, refused, or withdrawn.

(3) All exhibits admitted in evidence, refused, or lodged are deemed part of the record, but a party wanting an exhibit included in the transcript must specify that exhibit by number or letter in its designation. If the trial court has returned a designated exhibit to a party, the party in possession of the exhibit must deliver it to the trial court clerk within 10 days after the notice designating the exhibit is served.

(c) Deposit for cost of clerk's transcript

(1) Within 30 days after the respondent files a designation under (b)(1) or the time to file it expires, whichever first occurs, the trial court clerk must send:

(A) To the appellant, notice of the estimated cost to prepare an original and one copy of the clerk's transcript; and

(B) To each party other than the appellant, notice of the estimated cost to prepare a copy of the clerk's transcript for that party's use.

(2) A notice under (1) must show the date it was sent.

(3) Within 10 days after the clerk sends a notice under (1), the appellant and any party wanting to purchase a copy of the clerk's transcript must deposit the estimated cost with the clerk, unless otherwise provided by law or the party submits an application for a waiver of the cost under rule 8.818 or an order granting a waiver of this cost.

(d) Preparing the clerk's transcript

(1) Within 30 days after the appellant deposits the estimated cost of the transcript or the court files an order waiving that cost, the clerk must:

(A) Prepare an original and one copy of the clerk's transcript and certify the original; and

(B) Prepare any additional copies for which the parties have made deposits.

(2) If the appeal is abandoned or dismissed before the clerk has completed preparation of the transcript, the clerk must refund any portion of the deposit under (c)(3) exceeding the preparation cost actually incurred. *(Adopted, eff. Jan. 1, 2009. As amended, eff. July 1, 2009; Jan. 1, 2010; Jan. 1, 2011.)*

Advisory Committee Comment

Subdivision (a). (The supporting and opposing memoranda and attachments to any motion to vacate the judgment, for judgment notwithstanding the verdict, or for reconsideration of an appealed order are not required to be included in the clerk's transcript under subdivision (a)(1)(D) but may be included by designation of a party under (a)(3) or on motion of a party or the reviewing court under rule 8.841.

Research References

Rutter, Cal. Practice Guide: Civil Appeals & Writs Ch. 16-D, D. Designation of the Record.

9 Witkin Cal. Proc. 5th Appeal § 638, Failure to Make Deposit.

9 Witkin Cal. Proc. 5th Appeal § 646, (S 646) Matters Automatically Included.

9 Witkin Cal. Proc. 5th Appeal § 667, (S 667) Nature of Record.

9 Witkin Cal. Proc. 5th Appeal § 669, (S 669) Designation by Respondent.

9 Witkin Cal. Proc. 5th Appeal § 670, (S 670) Augmentation.

9 Witkin Cal. Proc. 5th Appeal § 679, (S 679) Record.

9 Witkin Cal. Proc. 5th Appeal § 1012, Transcripts.

Rule 8.833.   Trial court file instead of clerk's transcript

(a) Application

If the court has a local rule for the appellate division electing to use this form of the record, the original trial court file may be used instead of a clerk's transcript. This rule and any supplemental provisions of the local rule then govern unless the trial court orders otherwise after notice to the parties.

(b) Cost estimate; preparation of file; transmittal

(1) Within 10 days after the appellant serves a notice under rule 8.831 indicating that the appellant elects to use a clerk's transcript, the trial court clerk may mail the appellant a notice indicating that the appellate division for that court has elected by local court rule to use the original trial court file instead of a clerk's transcript and providing the appellant with an estimate of the cost to prepare the file, including the cost of sending the index under (4).

(2) Within 10 days after the clerk mails the estimate under (1), the appellant must deposit the estimated cost with the clerk, unless otherwise provided by law or the party submits an application for a waiver of the cost under rule 8.818 or an order granting a waiver of this cost.

(3) Within 10 days after the appellant deposits the cost or the court files an order waiving that cost, the trial court clerk must put the trial court file in chronological order, number the pages, and attach a chronological index and a list of all attorneys of record, the parties they represent, and any unrepresented parties.

(4) The clerk must send copies of the index to all attorneys of record and any unrepresented parties for their use in paginating their copies of the file to conform to the index.

(5) If the appellant elected to proceed with a reporter's transcript, the clerk must send the prepared file to the appellate division with the reporter's transcript. If the appellant elected to proceed without a reporter's transcript, the clerk must immediately send the prepared file to the appellate division. *(Adopted, eff. Jan. 1, 2009. As amended, eff. July 1, 2009.)*

Research References

Rutter, Cal. Practice Guide: Civil Appeals & Writs Ch. 16-D, D. Designation of the Record.

9 Witkin Cal. Proc. 5th Appeal § 1012, Transcripts.

Rule 8.834.   Reporter's transcript

(a) Notice

(1) A notice designating a reporter's transcript under rule 8.831 must specify the date of each proceeding to be included in the transcript and may specify portions of the designated proceedings that are not to be included.

(2) If the appellant designates less than all the testimony, the notice must state the points to be raised on the appeal; the appeal is then limited to those points unless, on motion, the appellate division permits otherwise.

(3) If the appellant serves and files a notice under 8.831 designating a reporter's transcript, the respondent may, within 10 days after such service, serve and file a notice in the trial court designating any additional proceedings the respondent wants included in the reporter's transcript.

(4) The clerk must promptly mail a copy of each notice to the reporter. The copy must show the date it was mailed.

(b) Deposit or waiver

(1) Within 10 days after the clerk mails a notice under (a)(4), the reporter must file the estimate with the clerk—or notify the clerk in writing of the date that he or she notified the appellant directly—of the estimated cost of preparing the reporter's transcript.

(2) Within 10 days after the clerk notifies the appellant of the estimated cost of preparing the reporter's transcript or within 10 days after the reporter notifies the appellant directly—the appellant must deposit with the clerk an amount equal to the estimated cost or file with the clerk a waiver of the deposit signed by the reporter. The clerk must then promptly notify the reporter to prepare the transcript.

(c) Contents of reporter's transcript

(1) The reporter must transcribe all designated proceedings and must note in the transcript where any proceedings were omitted and the nature of those proceedings. The reporter must also note where any exhibit was marked for identification and where it was admitted or refused, identifying such exhibits by number or letter.

(2) The reporter must not transcribe the voir dire examination of jurors, any opening statement, or the proceedings on a motion for new trial, unless they are designated.

(3) If a party designates a portion of a witness's testimony to be transcribed, the reporter must transcribe the witness's entire testimony unless the parties stipulate otherwise.

(4) The reporter must not copy any document includable in the clerk's transcript under rule 8.832.

(d) Filing the reporter's transcript; copies; payment

(1) Within 20 days after the clerk notifies the reporter to prepare the transcript under (b)(2)—or the reporter receives the fees from the appellant—the reporter must prepare and certify an original of the reporter's transcript and file it in the trial court. The reporter must also file one copy of the original transcript or more than one copy if multiple appellants equally share the cost of preparing the record.

(2) When the transcript is completed, the reporter must bill each designating party at the statutory rate and send a copy of the bill to the clerk. The clerk must pay the reporter from that party's deposited funds and refund any excess deposit or notify the party of any additional funds needed. In a multiple reporter case, the clerk must pay each reporter who certifies under penalty of perjury that his or her transcript portion is completed.

(3) If the appeal is abandoned or is dismissed before the reporter has filed the transcript, the reporter must inform the clerk of the cost of the portion of the transcript that the reporter has completed. The clerk must pay that amount to the reporter from the appellant's deposited funds and refund any excess deposit.

(e) Notice when proceedings cannot be transcribed

(1) If any portion of the designated proceedings were not reported or cannot be transcribed, the trial court clerk must so

notify the designating party by mail; the notice must show the date it was mailed.

(2) Within 10 days after the notice under (1) is mailed, the designating party must notify the court whether the party elects to proceed with or without a record of the oral proceedings that were not reported or cannot be transcribed. If the party elects to proceed with a record of these oral proceedings, the notice must specify which form of the record listed in rule 8.830(a)(2) other than a reporter's transcript the party elects to use. The party must comply with the requirements applicable to the form of the record elected.

(3) This remedy supplements any other available remedies. *(Adopted, eff. Jan. 1, 2009.)*

Research References

Rutter, Cal. Practice Guide: Civil Appeals & Writs Ch. 16-D, D. Designation of the Record.
9 Witkin Cal. Proc. 5th Appeal § 637, Deposit, or Substitute, for Cost.
9 Witkin Cal. Proc. 5th Appeal § 638, Failure to Make Deposit.
9 Witkin Cal. Proc. 5th Appeal § 640, (S 640) Clerk's Notification to Reporter.
9 Witkin Cal. Proc. 5th Appeal § 642, (S 642) Preparation and Filing.
9 Witkin Cal. Proc. 5th Appeal § 673, (S 673) Agreed or Settled Statement.
9 Witkin Cal. Proc. 5th Appeal § 679, (S 679) Record.
9 Witkin Cal. Proc. 5th Appeal § 1012, Transcripts.
6 Witkin Cal. Proc. 5th Proceedings Without Trial § 498, (S 498) Procedure.

Rule 8.835. Record when trial proceedings were officially electronically recorded

(a) Application

This rule applies only if:

(1) The trial court proceedings were officially recorded electronically under Government Code section 69957; and

(2) The electronic recording was prepared in compliance with applicable rules regarding electronic recording of court proceedings.

(b) Transcripts from official electronic recording

Written transcripts of official electronic recordings may be prepared under rule 2.952. A transcript prepared and certified as provided in that rule is prima facie a true and complete record of the oral proceedings it purports to cover and satisfies any requirement in these rules or in any statute for a reporter's transcript of oral proceedings.

(c) Use of official recording as record of oral proceedings

If the court has a local rule for the appellate division permitting this, on stipulation of the parties or on order of the trial court under rule 8.837(d)(6), the original of an official electronic recording of the trial court proceedings, or a copy made by the court, may be transmitted as the record of these oral proceedings without being transcribed. Such an official electronic recording satisfies any requirement in these rules or in any statute for a reporter's transcript of these proceedings.

(d) Notice when proceedings were not officially electronically recorded or cannot be transcribed

(1) If the appellant elects under rule 8.831 to use a transcript prepared from an official electronic recording or the recording itself, the trial court clerk must notify the appellant by mail if any portion of the designated proceedings was not officially electronically recorded or cannot be transcribed. The notice must show the date it was mailed.

(2) Within 10 days after the notice under (1) is mailed, the appellant must notify the court whether the appellant elects to proceed with or without a record of the oral proceedings that were not recorded or cannot be transcribed. If the party elects

to proceed with a record of these oral proceedings, the notice must specify which form of the record listed in rule 8.830(a)(2) other than an electronic recording the appellant elects to use. The appellant must comply with the requirements applicable to the form of the record elected. *(Adopted, eff. Jan. 1, 2009. As amended, eff. July 1, 2010.)*

Research References

Rutter, Cal. Practice Guide: Civil Appeals & Writs Ch. 16-D, D. Designation of the Record.
3 Witkin Cal. Proc. 5th Actions § 429C, (New)-Costs Excused.
9 Witkin Cal. Proc. 5th Appeal § 1014A, (New)-Record Where Trial Proceedings Are Electronically Recorded.

Rule 8.836. Agreed statement

(a) What is an agreed statement

An agreed statement is a summary of the trial court proceedings that is agreed to by the parties. If the parties have prepared an agreed statement or stipulated to prepare one, the appellant can elect under rule 8.831 to use an agreed statement as the record of the documents filed in the trial court, replacing the clerk's transcript, and as the record of the oral proceedings in the trial court, replacing the reporter's transcript.

(b) Contents of an agreed statement

(1) The agreed statement must explain the nature of the action, the basis of the appellate division's jurisdiction, and the rulings of the trial court relating to the points to be raised on appeal. The statement should recite only those facts that a party considers relevant to decide the appeal and must be signed by the parties.

(2) If the agreed statement replaces a clerk's transcript, the statement must be accompanied by copies of all items required by rule 8.832(a)(1), showing the dates required by rule 8.832(a)(2).

(3) The statement may be accompanied by copies of any document includable in the clerk's transcript under rule 8.832(a)(3).

(c) Time to file; extension of time

(1) If an appellant indicates on its notice designating the record under rule 8.831 that it elects to use an agreed statement under this rule, the appellant must file with the notice designating the record either the agreed statement or a stipulation that the parties are attempting to agree on a statement.

(2) If the appellant files a stipulation under (1), within 30 days after filing the notice of designation under rule 8.831, the appellant must either:

(A) File the statement if the parties were able to agree on the statement; or

(B) File both a notice stating that the parties were not able to agree on the statement and a new notice designating the record under rule 8.831. In the new notice designating the record, the appellant may not elect to use an agreed statement.

(Adopted, eff. Jan. 1, 2009.)

Research References

Rutter, Cal. Practice Guide: Civil Appeals & Writs Ch. 16-D, D. Designation of the Record.
9 Witkin Cal. Proc. 5th Appeal § 664, (S 664) Nature of Record.
9 Witkin Cal. Proc. 5th Appeal § 665, (S 665) Requirements.
9 Witkin Cal. Proc. 5th Appeal § 666, (S 666) Statement or Stipulation.
9 Witkin Cal. Proc. 5th Appeal § 679, (S 679) Record.
9 Witkin Cal. Proc. 5th Appeal § 1013, Agreed or Settled Statement.

Rule 8.837. Statement on appeal

(a) Description

A statement on appeal is a summary of the trial court proceedings that is approved by the trial court. An appellant can elect under rule 8.831 to use a statement on appeal as the record of the oral proceedings in the trial court, replacing the reporter's transcript.

(b) Preparing the proposed statement

(1) If the appellant elects in its notice designating the record under rule 8.831 to use a statement on appeal, the appellant must serve and file a proposed statement within 20 days after filing the notice under rule 8.831. If the appellant does not file a proposed statement within this time, the trial court clerk must promptly notify the appellant by mail that it must file the proposed statement within 15 days after the notice is mailed and that failure to comply will result in the appeal being dismissed.

(2) Appellants who are not represented by an attorney must file their proposed statement on *Statement on Appeal (Limited Civil Case)* (form APP–104). For good cause, the court may permit the filing of a statement that is not on form APP–104.

(c) Contents of the proposed statement

The proposed statement must contain:

(1) A condensed narrative of the oral proceedings that the appellant believes necessary for the appeal and a summary of the trial court's holding and judgment. Subject to the court's approval, the appellant may present some or all of the evidence by question and answer.

(2) A statement of the points the appellant is raising on appeal. If the condensed narrative under (A) covers only a portion of the oral proceedings, then the appeal is limited to the points identified in the statement unless, on motion, the appellate division permits otherwise.

(A) The statement must specify the intended grounds of appeal by clearly stating each point to be raised but need not identify each particular ruling or matter to be challenged.

(B) The statement must include as much of the evidence or proceeding as necessary to support the stated grounds. Any evidence or portion of a proceeding not included will be presumed to support the judgment or order appealed from.

(C) If one of the grounds of appeal is insufficiency of the evidence, the statement must specify how it is insufficient.

(D) If one of the grounds of appeal challenges the giving, refusal, or modification of a jury instruction, the statement must include any instructions submitted orally and identify the party that requested the instruction and any modification.

(d) Review of the appellant's proposed statement

(1) Within 10 days after the appellant files the proposed statement, the respondent may serve and file proposed amendments to that statement.

(2) No later than 10 days after the respondent files proposed amendments or the time to do so expires, a party may request a hearing to review and correct the proposed statement. No hearing will be held unless ordered by the trial court judge, and the judge will not ordinarily order a hearing unless there is a factual dispute about a material aspect of the trial court proceedings.

(3) If a hearing is ordered, the court must promptly set the hearing date and provide the parties with at least 5 days' written notice of the hearing date.

(4) Except as provided in (6), if no hearing is ordered, no later than 10 days after the time for requesting a hearing expires, the trial court judge must review the proposed statement and any proposed amendments and make any corrections or modifications to the statement necessary to ensure that it is an accurate summary of the trial court proceedings. If a hearing is ordered, the trial court judge must make any corrections or modifications to the statement within 10 days after the hearing.

(5) The trial court judge must not eliminate the appellant's specification of grounds of appeal from the proposed statement.

(6) If the trial court proceedings were reported by a court reporter or officially electronically recorded under Government Code section 69957 and the trial court judge determines that it would save court time and resources, instead of correcting a proposed statement on appeal:

(A) If the court has a local rule for the appellate division permitting the use of an official electronic recording as the record of the oral proceedings, the trial court judge may order that the original of an official electronic recording of the trial court proceedings, or a copy made by the court, be transmitted as the record of these oral proceedings without being transcribed. The court will pay for any copy of the official electronic recording ordered under this subdivision; or

(B) Unless the court has a local rule providing otherwise, the trial court judge may order that a transcript be prepared as the record of the oral proceedings. The court will pay for any transcript ordered under this subdivision.

(e) Review of the corrected statement

(1) If the trial court judge makes any corrections or modifications to the proposed statement under (d), the clerk must send copies of the corrected or modified statement to the parties.

(2) Within 10 days after the statement is sent to the parties, any party may serve and file proposed modifications or objections to the statement.

(f) Certification of the statement on appeal

(1) If the trial court judge does not make any corrections or modifications to the proposed statement under (d)(4) and does not order either the use of an official electronic recording or the preparation of a transcript in lieu of correcting the proposed statement under (d)(6), the judge must promptly certify the statement.

(2) If the trial court judge corrects or modifies an appellant's proposed statement under (d), within five days after the time for filing proposed modifications or objections has expired, the judge must review any proposed modifications or objections to the statement filed by the parties, make any corrections or modifications to the statement necessary to ensure that it is an accurate summary of the trial court proceedings, and certify the statement. *(Adopted, eff. Jan. 1, 2009.)*

Advisory Committee Comment

Subdivision (b). *Proposed Statement on Appeal (Limited Civil Case)* (form AP–104) is available at any courthouse or county law library or online at *www.courtinfo.ca.gov/forms.*

Subdivision (d). Under rule 8.804, the term "judge" includes a commissioner or a temporary judge.

Research References

Rutter, Cal. Practice Guide: Civil Appeals & Writs Ch. 16-D, D. Designation of the Record.

9 Witkin Cal. Proc. 5th Appeal § 657, (S 657) Nature of Record.

9 Witkin Cal. Proc. 5th Appeal § 658, (S 658) Motion.

9 Witkin Cal. Proc. 5th Appeal § 659, (S 659) Appellant's Proposed Statement.

9 Witkin Cal. Proc. 5th Appeal § 660, (S 660) Respondent's Proposed Amendments.

9 Witkin Cal. Proc. 5th Appeal § 661, (S 661) Settlement and Certification.

9 Witkin Cal. Proc. 5th Appeal § 679, (S 679) Record.

9 Witkin Cal. Proc. 5th Appeal § 1013, Agreed or Settled Statement.

Ct. Rules

Rule 8.838.   Form of the record

(a) Paper and format

Except as otherwise provided in this rule, clerk's and reporter's transcripts must comply with the paper and format requirements of rule 8.144(a).

(b) Indexes

At the beginning of the first volume of each:

(1) The clerk's transcript must contain alphabetical and chronological indexes listing each document and the volume and page where it first appears;

(2) The reporter's transcript must contain alphabetical and chronological indexes listing the volume and page where each witness's direct, cross, and any other examination, begins; and

(3) The reporter's transcript must contain an index listing the volume and page where any exhibit is marked for identification and where it is admitted or refused.

(c) Binding and cover

(1) Clerk's and reporter's transcripts must be bound on the left margin in volumes of no more than 300 sheets, except that transcripts may be bound at the top if required by a local rule of the appellate division.

(2) Each volume's cover, preferably of recycled stock, must state the title and trial court number of the case, the names of the trial court and each participating trial judge, the names and addresses of appellate counsel for each party, the volume number, and the inclusive page numbers of that volume.

(3) In addition to the information required by (2), the cover of each volume of the reporter's transcript must state the dates of the proceedings reported in that volume. *(Adopted, eff. Jan. 1, 2009.)*

Research References

9 Witkin Cal. Proc. 5th Appeal § 1011, in General.
9 Witkin Cal. Proc. 5th Appeal § 1012, Transcripts.

Rule 8.839.   Record in multiple appeals

(a) Single record

If more than one appeal is taken from the same judgment or a related order, only one record need be prepared, which must be filed within the time allowed for filing the record in the latest appeal.

(b) Cost

If there is more than one separately represented appellant, they must equally share the cost of preparing the record, unless otherwise agreed by the appellants or ordered by the trial court. Appellants equally sharing the cost are each entitled to a copy of the record. *(Adopted, eff. Jan. 1, 2009.)*

Research References

9 Witkin Cal. Proc. 5th Appeal § 671, (S 671) Cross-Appeals.
9 Witkin Cal. Proc. 5th Appeal § 1011, in General.

Rule 8.840.   Filing the record

When the record is complete, the trial court clerk must promptly send the original to the appellate division and send to the appellant and respondent copies of any certified statement on appeal and any copies of transcripts or official electronic recordings that they have purchased. The appellate division clerk must promptly file the original and mail notice of the filing date to the parties. *(Adopted, eff. Jan. 1, 2009.)*

Research References

9 Witkin Cal. Proc. 5th Appeal § 679, (S 679) Record.

9 Witkin Cal. Proc. 5th Appeal § 1014, Filing, Correction, and Augmentation.

Rule 8.841.   Augmenting and correcting the record in the appellate division

(a) Augmentation

(1) At any time, on motion of a party or its own motion, the appellate division may order the record augmented to include:

(A) Any document filed or lodged in the case in the trial court; or

(B) A certified transcript—or agreed statement or a statement on appeal—of oral proceedings not designated under rule 8.831.

(2) A party must attach to its motion a copy, if available, of any document or transcript that it wants added to the record. The pages of the attachments must be consecutively numbered, beginning with the number 1. If the appellate division grants the motion, it may augment the record with the copy.

(3) If the party cannot attach a copy of the matter to be added, the party must identify it as required under rules 8.831.

(b) Correction

(1) On agreement of the parties, motion of a party, or on its own motion, the appellate division may order the correction or certification of any part of the record.

(2) The appellate division may order the trial court to settle disputes about omissions or errors in the record or to make corrections pursuant to stipulation filed by the parties in that court.

(c) Omissions

(1) If a clerk or reporter omits a required or designated portion of the record, a party may serve and file a notice in the trial court specifying the omitted portion and requesting that it be prepared, certified, and sent to the appellate division. The party must serve a copy of the notice on the appellate division.

(2) The clerk or reporter must comply with a notice under (1) within 10 days after it is filed. If the clerk or reporter fails to comply, the party may serve and file a motion to augment under (a), attaching a copy of the notice.

(d) Notice

The appellate division clerk must send all parties notice of the receipt and filing of any matter under this rule. *(Adopted, eff. Jan. 1, 2009.)*

Research References

9 Witkin Cal. Proc. 5th Appeal § 670, (S 670) Augmentation.
9 Witkin Cal. Proc. 5th Appeal § 681, Correction of Record on Appeal.
9 Witkin Cal. Proc. 5th Appeal § 682, Distinction: Trial Court Record.
9 Witkin Cal. Proc. 5th Appeal § 683, Nature of Remedy.
9 Witkin Cal. Proc. 5th Appeal § 1014, Filing, Correction, and Augmentation.

Rule 8.842.   Failure to procure the record

(a) Notice of default

If a party fails to do any act required to procure the record, the trial court clerk must promptly notify that party by mail that it must do the act specified in the notice within 15 days after the notice is mailed and that, if it fails to comply, the reviewing court may impose the following sanctions:

(1) If the defaulting party is the appellant, the court may dismiss the appeal; or

(2) If the defaulting party is the respondent, the court may proceed with the appeal on the record designated by the appellant.

(b) Sanctions

If the party fails to take the action specified in a notice given under (a), the trial court clerk must promptly notify the appellate division of the default, and the appellate division may impose one of the following sanctions:

(1) If the defaulting party is the appellant, the reviewing court may dismiss the appeal but may vacate the dismissal for good cause; or

(2) If the defaulting party is the respondent, the reviewing court may order the appeal to proceed on the record designated by the appellant, but the respondent may obtain relief from default under rule 8.812. *(Adopted, eff. Jan. 1, 2009. As amended, eff. Jan. 1, 2011.)*

Research References

9 Witkin Cal. Proc. 5th Appeal § 9, (S 9) Current Structure.
9 Witkin Cal. Proc. 5th Appeal § 638, Failure to Make Deposit.
9 Witkin Cal. Proc. 5th Appeal § 688, (S 688) Sanctions for Default.
9 Witkin Cal. Proc. 5th Appeal § 1016, (S 1016) Abandonment and Dismissal.
2 Witkin Cal. Proc. 5th Courts § 195, (S 195) Appellate Rules.

Rule 8.843. Transmitting exhibits

(a) Notice of designation

(1) If a party wants the appellate division to consider any original exhibits that were admitted in evidence, refused, or lodged but that were not copied in the clerk's transcript under rule 8.832 or included in the original file under rule 8.833, within 10 days after the last respondent's brief is filed or could be filed under rule 8.882 the party must serve and file a notice in the trial court designating such exhibits.

(2) Within 10 days after a notice under (1) is served, any other party wanting the appellate division to consider additional exhibits must serve and file a notice in the trial court designating such exhibits.

(3) A party filing a notice under (1) or (2) must serve a copy on the appellate division.

(b) Application for later transmittal

After the periods specified in (a) have expired, a party may apply to the appellate division for permission to send an exhibit to that court.

(c) Request by appellate division

At any time the appellate division may direct the trial court or a party to send it an exhibit.

(d) Transmittal

Unless the appellate division orders otherwise, within 20 days after notice under (a) is filed or after the appellate division directs that an exhibit be sent:

(1) The trial court clerk must put any designated exhibits in the clerk's possession into numerical or alphabetical order and send them to the appellate division with two copies of a list of the exhibits sent. If the appellate division clerk finds the list correct, the clerk must sign and return one copy to the trial court clerk.

(2) Any party in possession of designated exhibits returned by the trial court must put them into numerical or alphabetical order and send them to the appellate division with two copies of a list of the exhibits sent. If the appellate division clerk finds the list correct, the clerk must sign and return one copy to the party.

(e) Return by appellate division

On request, the appellate division may return an exhibit to the trial court or to the party that sent it. When the remittitur issues, the appellate division must return all exhibits to the trial court or to the party that sent them. *(Adopted, eff. Jan. 1, 2009.)*

Research References

Rutter, Cal. Practice Guide: Civil Appeals & Writs Ch. 16-D, D. Designation of the Record.
9 Witkin Cal. Proc. 5th Appeal § 9, (S 9) Current Structure.
9 Witkin Cal. Proc. 5th Appeal § 1030, Record.
9 Witkin Cal. Proc. 5th Appeal § 1014B, (New)-Transmitting Exhibits.
2 Witkin Cal. Proc. 5th Courts § 195, (S 195) Appellate Rules.

Chapter 4

BRIEFS, HEARING, AND DECISION IN LIMITED CIVIL AND MISDEMEANOR APPEALS

Rule
8.880. Application.
8.881. Notice of briefing schedule.
8.882. Briefs by parties and amici curiae.
8.883. Contents and form of briefs.
8.884. Appeals in which a party is both appellant and respondent.
8.885. Oral argument.
8.886. Submission of the cause.
8.887. Decisions.
8.888. Finality and modification of decision.
8.889. Rehearing.
8.890. Remittitur.
8.891. Costs and sanctions in civil appeals.

Rule 8.880. Application

Except as otherwise provided, the rules in this chapter apply to both civil and misdemeanor appeals in the appellate division. *(Adopted, eff. Jan. 1, 2009.)*

Research References

9 Witkin Cal. Proc. 5th Appeal § 9, (S 9) Current Structure.
2 Witkin Cal. Proc. 5th Courts § 195, (S 195) Appellate Rules.

Rule 8.881. Notice of briefing schedule

When the record is filed, the clerk of the appellate division must promptly mail a notice to each appellate counsel or unrepresented party giving the dates the briefs are due. *(Adopted, eff. Jan. 1, 2009.)*

Research References

Rutter, Cal. Practice Guide: Civil Appeals & Writs Ch. 16-F, F. Briefs.
9 Witkin Cal. Proc. 5th Appeal § 1015, (S 1015) Briefs.

Rule 8.882. Briefs by parties and amici curiae

(a) Briefs by parties

(1) The appellant must serve and file an appellant's opening brief within 30 days after the record is filed in the appellate division.

(2) Any respondent's brief must be served and filed within 30 days after the appellant files its opening brief.

(3) Any appellant's reply brief must be served and filed within 20 days after the respondent files its brief.

(4) No other brief may be filed except with the permission of the presiding judge.

(5) Instead of filing a brief, or as part of its brief, a party may join in a brief or adopt by reference all or part of a brief in the same or a related appeal.

(b) Extensions of time

(1) Except as otherwise provided by statute, in a civil case, the parties may extend each period under (a) by up to 30 days by filing one or more stipulations in the appellate division before the brief is due. Stipulations must be signed by and served on all parties. The original signature of at least one party must appear on the stipulation filed in the appellate division; the signatures of the other parties may be in the form of fax copies of the signed signature page of the stipulation.

(2) A stipulation under (1) is effective on filing. The appellate division may not shorten such a stipulated extension.

(3) Before the brief is due, a party may apply to the presiding judge of the appellate division for an extension of the time period for filing a brief under (a). The application must show that there is good cause to grant an extension under rule 8.811(b). In civil appeals, the application must also show that:

(A) The applicant was unable to obtain—or it would have been futile to seek—the extension by stipulation; or

(B) The parties have stipulated to the maximum extension permitted under (1) and the applicant seeks a further extension.

(4) A party need not apply for an extension or relief from default if it can file its brief within the time prescribed by (c). The clerk must file a brief submitted within that time if it otherwise complies with these rules.

(c) Failure to file a brief

(1) If a party in a civil appeal fails to timely file an appellant's opening brief or a respondent's brief, the appellate division clerk must promptly notify the party by mail that the brief must be filed within 15 days after the notice is mailed and that if the party fails to comply, the court may impose one of the following sanctions:

(A) If the brief is an appellant's opening brief, the court may dismiss the appeal; or

(B) If the brief is a respondent's brief, the court may decide the appeal on the record, the appellant's opening brief, and any oral argument by the appellant.

(2) If the appellant in a misdemeanor appeal fails to timely file an opening brief, the appellate division clerk must promptly notify the appellant by mail that the brief must be filed within 30 days after the notice is mailed and that if the appellant fails to comply, the court may impose one of the following sanctions:

(A) If the appellant is the defendant and is represented by appointed counsel on appeal, the court may relieve that appointed counsel and appoint new counsel; or

(B) In all other cases, the court may dismiss the appeal.

(3) If the respondent in a misdemeanor appeal is the defendant and the respondent fails to timely file a brief, the appellate division clerk must promptly notify the respondent by mail that the brief must be filed within 30 days after the notice is mailed and that if the respondent fails to comply, the court will decide the appeal on the record, the appellant's opening brief, and any oral argument by the appellant.

(4) If a party fails to comply with a notice under (1), (2), or (3), the court may impose the sanction specified in the notice.

(d) Amicus curiae briefs

(1) Within 14 days after the appellant's reply brief is filed or was required to be filed, whichever is earlier, any person or entity may serve and file an application for permission of the presiding judge to file an amicus curiae brief. For good cause, the presiding judge may allow later filing.

(2) The application must state the applicant's interest and explain how the proposed amicus curiae brief will assist the court in deciding the matter.

(3) The application must also identify:

(A) Any party or any counsel for a party in the pending appeal who:

(i) Authored the proposed amicus brief in whole or in part; or

(ii) Made a monetary contribution intended to fund the preparation or submission of the brief; and

(B) Every person or entity who made a monetary contribution intended to fund the preparation or submission of the brief, other than the amicus curiae, its members, or its counsel in the pending appeal.

(4) The proposed brief must be served and must accompany the application and may be combined with it.

(5) The Attorney General may file an amicus curiae brief without the presiding judge's permission, unless the brief is submitted on behalf of another state officer or agency; but the presiding judge may prescribe reasonable conditions for filing and answering the brief.

(e) Service and filing

(1) Copies of each brief must be served as required by rule 8.25.

(2) Unless the court provides otherwise by local rule or order in the specific case, only the original brief, with proof of service, must be filed in the appellate division.

(3) A copy of each brief must be served on the trial court clerk for delivery to the judge who tried the case.

(4) A copy of each brief must be served on a public officer or agency when required by rule 8.29. *(Adopted, eff. Jan. 1, 2009. As amended, eff. Jan. 1, 2009; Jan. 1, 2010; Jan. 1, 2013.)*

Advisory Committee Comment

Subdivision (a). Note that the sequence and timing of briefing in appeals in which a party is both appellant and respondent (cross-appeals) are governed by rule 8.884. Typically, a cross-appellant's combined respondent's brief and opening brief must be filed within the time specified in (a)(2) for the respondent's brief.

Subdivision (b). Extensions of briefing time are limited by statute in some cases. For example, under Public Resources Code section 21167.6(h) in cases under section 21167 extensions are limited to one 30–day extension for the opening brief and one 30–day extension for "preparation of responding brief."

Research References

Rutter, Cal. Practice Guide: Civil Appeals & Writs Ch. 16-F, F. Briefs.
9 Witkin Cal. Proc. 5th Appeal § 692, in General.
9 Witkin Cal. Proc. 5th Appeal § 716, (S 716) in General.
9 Witkin Cal. Proc. 5th Appeal § 717, (S 717) Service and Filing.
9 Witkin Cal. Proc. 5th Appeal § 719, (S 719) in General.
9 Witkin Cal. Proc. 5th Appeal § 722, (S 722) Right to File.
9 Witkin Cal. Proc. 5th Appeal § 726, (S 726) Amicus Briefs in Court of Appeal or Appellate Division.
9 Witkin Cal. Proc. 5th Appeal § 938, Amicus Briefs on Merits.
9 Witkin Cal. Proc. 5th Appeal § 1011, in General.
9 Witkin Cal. Proc. 5th Appeal § 1015, (S 1015) Briefs.
2 Witkin Cal. Proc. 5th Courts § 326, (S 326) Powers of Individual Judges.

Rule 8.883.   Contents and form of briefs

(a) Contents

(1) Each brief must:

(A) State each point under a separate heading or subheading summarizing the point and support each point by argument and, if possible, by citation of authority; and

(B) Support any reference to a matter in the record by a citation to the volume and page number of the record where the matter appears.

(2) An appellant's opening brief must:

(A) State the nature of the action, the relief sought in the trial court, and the judgment or order appealed from;

(B) State that the judgment appealed from is final or explain why the order appealed from is appealable; and

(C) Provide a summary of the significant facts limited to matters in the record.

(b) Length

(1) A brief produced on a computer must not exceed 6,800 words, including footnotes. Such a brief must include a certificate by appellate counsel or an unrepresented party stating the number of words in the brief. The person certifying may rely on the word count of the computer program used to prepare the brief.

(2) A brief produced on a typewriter must not exceed 20 pages.

(3) The information listed on the cover, any table of contents or table of authorities, the certificate under (1), and any signature block are excluded from the limits stated in (1) or (2).

(4) On application, the presiding judge may permit a longer brief for good cause. A lengthy record or numerous or complex issues on appeal will ordinarily constitute good cause. If the court grants an application to file a longer brief, it may order that the brief include a table of contents and a table of authorities.

(c) Form

(1) A brief may be reproduced by any process that produces a clear, black image of letter quality. The paper must be white or unbleached, recycled, 8½ by 11 inches, and of at least 20–pound weight. Both sides of the paper may be used if the brief is not bound at the top.

(2) Any conventional typeface may be used. The typeface may be either proportionally spaced or monospaced.

(3) The type style must be roman; but for emphasis, italics or boldface may be used or the text may be underscored. Case names must be italicized or underscored. Headings may be in uppercase letters.

(4) Except as provided in (10), the type size, including footnotes, must not be smaller than 13–point.

(5) The lines of text must be at least one-and-a-half-spaced. Headings and footnotes may be single-spaced. Quotations may be block-indented and single-spaced. Single-spaced means six lines to a vertical inch.

(6) The margins must be at least 1½ inches on the left and right and 1 inch on the top and bottom.

(7) The pages must be consecutively numbered.

(8) The cover—or first page if there is no cover—must include the information required by rule 8.816(a)(1).

(9) The brief must be bound on the left margin, except that briefs may be bound at the top if required by a local rule of the appellate division. If the brief is stapled, the bound edge and staples must be covered with tape.

(10) The brief need not be signed.

(11) If the brief is produced on a typewriter:

(A) A typewritten original and carbon copies may be filed only with the presiding judge's permission, which will ordinarily be given only to unrepresented parties proceeding in forma pauperis. All other typewritten briefs must be filed as photocopies.

(B) Both sides of the paper may be used if a photocopy is filed; only one side may be used if a typewritten original and carbon copies are filed.

(C) The type size, including footnotes, must not be smaller than standard pica, 10 characters per inch. Unrepresented incarcerated litigants may use elite type, 12 characters per inch, if they lack access to a typewriter with larger characters.

(d) Noncomplying briefs

If a brief does not comply with this rule:

(1) The reviewing court clerk may decline to file it, but must mark it "received but not filed" and return it to the party; or

(2) If the brief is filed, the presiding judge may with or without notice:

(A) Order the brief returned for corrections and refiling within a specified time;

(B) Strike the brief with leave to file a new brief within a specified time; or

(C) Disregard the noncompliance.

(Adopted, eff. Jan. 1, 2009. As amended, eff. Jan. 1, 2011; Jan. 1, 2013.)

Advisory Committee Comment

Subdivision (b). Subdivision (b)(1) states the maximum permissible lengths of briefs produced on a computer in terms of word count rather than page count. This provision tracks a provision in rule 8.204(c) governing Court of Appeal briefs and is explained in the comment to that provision. Subdivision (b)(3) specifies certain items that are not counted toward the maximum brief length. Signature blocks, as referenced in this provision, include not only the signatures, but also the printed names, titles, and affiliations of any attorneys filing or joining in the brief, which may accompany the signature.

Research References

Rutter, Cal. Practice Guide: Civil Appeals & Writs Ch. 16-F, F. Briefs.
9 Witkin Cal. Proc. 5th Appeal § 694, Separate Points and Headings.
9 Witkin Cal. Proc. 5th Appeal § 695, References to Record.
9 Witkin Cal. Proc. 5th Appeal § 697, Format.
9 Witkin Cal. Proc. 5th Appeal § 716, (S 716) in General.
9 Witkin Cal. Proc. 5th Appeal § 1011, in General.
9 Witkin Cal. Proc. 5th Appeal § 1015, (S 1015) Briefs.
9 Witkin Cal. Proc. 5th Appeal § 1019, (S 1019) Rehearing.
2 Witkin Cal. Proc. 5th Courts § 30, (S 30) Use of Recycled Paper.
8 Witkin Cal. Proc. 5th Extraordinary Writs § 164A, (New)-In General.
8 Witkin Cal. Proc. 5th Extraordinary Writs § 164C, (New)-Petition Filed by Attorney.

Rule 8.884. Appeals in which a party is both appellant and respondent

(a) Briefing sequence and time to file briefs

In an appeal in which any party is both an appellant and a respondent:

(1) The parties must jointly—or separately if unable to agree—submit a proposed briefing sequence to the appellate division within 20 days after the second notice of appeal is filed.

(2) After receiving the proposal, the appellate division must order a briefing sequence and prescribe briefing periods consistent with rule 8.882(a).

(b) Contents of briefs

(1) A party that is both an appellant and a respondent must combine its respondent's brief with its appellant's opening brief

or its reply brief, if any, whichever is appropriate under the briefing sequence that the appellate division orders under (a).

(2) A party must confine a reply brief to points raised in its own appeal.

(3) A combined brief must address the points raised in each appeal separately but may include a single summary of the significant facts. *(Adopted, eff. Jan. 1, 2009. As amended, eff. Jan. 1, 2009.)*

Research References

Rutter, Cal. Practice Guide: Civil Appeals & Writs Ch. 16-F, F. Briefs.
9 Witkin Cal. Proc. 5th Appeal § 1015, (S 1015) Briefs.

Rule 8.885.   Oral argument

(a) Calendaring and sessions

Unless otherwise ordered, all appeals in which the last reply brief was filed or the time for filing this brief expired 45 or more days before the date of a regular appellate division session must be placed on the calendar for that session by the appellate division clerk. By order of the presiding judge or the division, any appeal may be placed on the calendar for oral argument at any session.

(b) Oral argument by videoconference

(1) Oral argument may be conducted by videoconference if:

(A) It is ordered by the presiding judge of the appellate division or the presiding judge's designee on application of any party or on the court's own motion. An application from a party requesting that oral argument be conducted by videoconference must be filed within 10 days after the court sends notice of oral argument under (c)(1); or

(B) A local rule authorizes oral argument to be conducted by videoconference consistent with these rules.

(2) If oral argument is conducted by videoconference:

(A) Each judge of the appellate division panel assigned to the case must participate in the entire oral argument either in person at the superior court that issued the judgment or order that is being appealed or by videoconference from another court.

(B) Unless otherwise allowed by local rule or ordered by the presiding judge of the appellate division or the presiding judge's designee, all the parties must appear at oral argument in person at the superior court that issued the judgment or order that is being appealed.

(C) The oral argument must be open to the public at the superior court that issued the judgment or order that is being appealed. If provided by local rule or ordered by the presiding judge of the appellate division or the presiding judge's designee, oral argument may also be open to the public at any of the locations from which a judge of the appellate division is participating in oral argument.

(D) The appellate division must ensure that:

(i) During oral argument, the participants in oral argument are visible and their statements are audible to all other participants, court staff, and any members of the public attending the oral argument;

(ii) Participants are identified when they speak; and

(iii) Only persons who are authorized to participate in the proceedings speak.

(E) A party must not be charged any fee to participate in oral argument by videoconference if the party participates from the superior court that issued the judgment or order that is being appealed or from a location from which a judge of the appellate division panel is participating in oral argument.

(c) Notice of argument

(1) As soon as all parties' briefs are filed or the time for filing these briefs has expired, the appellate division clerk must send a notice of the time and place of oral argument to all parties. The notice must be sent at least 20 days before the date for oral argument. The presiding judge may shorten the notice period for good cause; in that event, the clerk must immediately notify the parties by telephone or other expeditious method.

(2) If oral argument will be conducted by videoconference under (b), the clerk must specify, either in the notice required under (1) or in a supplemental notice sent to all parties at least 5 days before the date for oral argument, the location from which each judge of the appellate division panel assigned to the case will participate in oral argument.

(d) Waiver of argument

Parties may waive oral argument.

(e) Conduct of argument

Unless the court provides otherwise:

(1) The appellant, petitioner, or moving party has the right to open and close. If there are two or more such parties, the court must set the sequence of argument.

(2) Each side is allowed 10 minutes for argument. The appellant may reserve part of this time for reply argument. If multiple parties are represented by separate counsel, or if an amicus curiae—on written request—is granted permission to argue, the court may apportion or expand the time.

(3) Only one counsel may argue for each separately represented party. *(Adopted, eff. Jan. 1, 2009. As amended, eff. Jan. 1, 2010.)*

Advisory Committee Comment

Subdivision (a). Under rule 10.1108, the appellate division must hold a session at least once each quarter, unless no matters are set for oral argument that quarter, but may choose to hold sessions more frequently.

Research References

Rutter, Cal. Practice Guide: Civil Appeals & Writs Ch. 16-G, G. Oral Argument.
9 Witkin Cal. Proc. 5th Appeal § 763, in General.
9 Witkin Cal. Proc. 5th Appeal § 1015, (S 1015) Briefs.
9 Witkin Cal. Proc. 5th Appeal § 1017, Sessions and Calendar.

Rule 8.886.   Submission of the cause

(a) When the cause is submitted

A cause is submitted when the court has heard oral argument or approved its waiver and the time has expired to file all briefs and papers, including any supplemental brief permitted by the court. The appellate division may order the cause submitted at an earlier time if the parties so stipulate.

(b) Vacating submission

The court may vacate submission only by an order stating its reasons and setting a timetable for resubmission. *(Adopted, eff. Jan. 1, 2009.)*

Research References

9 Witkin Cal. Proc. 5th Appeal § 1018, Decision and Opinion.

Rule 8.887.   Decisions

(a) Written opinions

Appellate division judges are not required to prepare a written opinion in any case but may do so when they deem it advisable or in the public interest. A decision by opinion must identify the participating judges, including the author of the majority opinion and of any concurring or dissenting opinion, or the judges participating in a "by the court" opinion.

(b) Filing the decision

The appellate division clerk must promptly file all opinions and orders of the court and promptly send copies showing the filing date to the parties and, when relevant, to the trial court.

(c) Opinions certified for publication

(1) Opinions certified for publication must comply to the extent practicable with the *California Style Manual*.

(2) When the decision is final as to the appellate division in a case in which the opinion is certified for publication, the clerk must immediately send:

(A) Two paper copies and one electronic copy to the Reporter of Decisions in a format approved by the Reporter.

(B) One copy to the Court of Appeal for the district. The copy must bear the notation "This opinion has been certified for publication in the Official Reports. It is being sent to assist the Court of Appeal in deciding whether to order the case transferred to the court on the court's own motion under rules 8.1000–8.1018." The Court of Appeal clerk must promptly file that copy or make a docket entry showing its receipt.

(Adopted, eff. Jan. 1, 2009. As amended, eff. Jan. 1, 2011.)

Research References

Rutter, Cal. Practice Guide: Civil Appeals & Writs Ch. 16-H, H. Decision.
Rutter, Cal. Practice Guide: Civil Appeals & Writs Ch. 16-K, K. Transfer to Court of Appeal.
9 Witkin Cal. Proc. 5th Appeal § 781, Written Opinion is Optional in Appellate Division.
9 Witkin Cal. Proc. 5th Appeal § 831, (S 831) Rendition: Filing of Opinion.
9 Witkin Cal. Proc. 5th Appeal § 1018, Decision and Opinion.
9 Witkin Cal. Proc. 5th Appeal § 1030, Record.
2 Witkin Cal. Proc. 5th Courts § 340, (S 340) Operation.

Rule 8.888. Finality and modification of decision

(a) Finality of decision

(1) Except as otherwise provided in this rule, an appellate division decision, including an order dismissing an appeal involuntarily, is final 30 days after the decision is filed.

(2) If the appellate division certifies a written opinion for publication or partial publication after its decision is filed and before its decision becomes final in that court, the finality period runs from the filing date of the order for publication.

(3) The following appellate division decisions are final in that court when filed:

(A) The denial of a petition for writ of supersedeas;

(B) The denial of an application for bail or to reduce bail pending appeal; and

(C) The dismissal of an appeal on request or stipulation.

(b) Modification of judgment

(1) The appellate division may modify its decision until the decision is final in that court. If the clerk's office is closed on the date of finality, the court may modify the decision on the next day the clerk's office is open.

(2) An order modifying a decision must state whether it changes the appellate judgment. A modification that does not change the appellate judgment does not extend the finality date of the decision. If a modification changes the appellate judgment, the finality period runs from the filing date of the modification order.

(c) Consent to increase or decrease in amount of judgment

If an appellate division decision conditions the affirmance of a money judgment on a party's consent to an increase or decrease in the amount, the judgment is reversed unless, before the decision is final under (a), the party serves and files two copies of a consent in the appellate division. If a consent is filed, the finality period runs from the filing date of the consent. The clerk must send one file-stamped copy of the consent to the trial court with the remittitur. *(Adopted, eff. Jan. 1, 2009.)*

Research References

Rutter, Cal. Practice Guide: Civil Appeals & Writs Ch. 16-H, H. Decision.
Rutter, Cal. Practice Guide: Civil Appeals & Writs Ch. 16-K, K. Transfer to Court of Appeal.
9 Witkin Cal. Proc. 5th Appeal § 833, (S 833) Effect of Modification.
9 Witkin Cal. Proc. 5th Appeal § 857, Modification as Condition of Affirmance.
9 Witkin Cal. Proc. 5th Appeal § 1019, (S 1019) Rehearing.
9 Witkin Cal. Proc. 5th Appeal § 1021, in General.
9 Witkin Cal. Proc. 5th Appeal § 1022, (S 1022) Application, Opposition, and Determination.

Rule 8.889. Rehearing

(a) Power to order rehearing

(1) On petition of a party or on its own motion, the appellate division may order rehearing of any decision that is not final in that court on filing.

(2) An order for rehearing must be filed before the decision is final. If the clerk's office is closed on the date of finality, the court may file the order on the next day the clerk's office is open.

(b) Petition and answer

(1) A party may serve and file a petition for rehearing within 15 days after:

(A) The decision is filed;

(B) A publication order restarting the finality period under rule 8.888(a)(2), if the party has not already filed a petition for rehearing;

(C) A modification order changing the appellate judgment under rule 8.888(b); or

(D) The filing of a consent under rule 8.888(c).

(2) A party must not file an answer to a petition for rehearing unless the court requests an answer. The clerk must promptly send to the parties copies of any order requesting an answer and immediately notify the parties by telephone or another expeditious method. Any answer must be served and filed within 8 days after the order is filed unless the court orders otherwise. A petition for rehearing normally will not be granted unless the court has requested an answer.

(3) The petition and answer must comply with the relevant provisions of rule 8.883.

(4) Before the decision is final and for good cause, the presiding judge may relieve a party from a failure to file a timely petition or answer.

(c) No extensions of time

The time for granting or denying a petition for rehearing in the appellate division may not be extended. If the court does not rule on the petition before the decision is final, the petition is deemed denied.

(d) Effect of granting rehearing

An order granting a rehearing vacates the decision and any opinion filed in the case. If the appellate division orders rehearing, it may place the case on calendar for further argument or submit it for decision. *(Adopted, eff. Jan. 1, 2009.)*

Research References

Rutter, Cal. Practice Guide: Civil Appeals & Writs Ch. 16-I, I. Rehearing.
9 Witkin Cal. Proc. 5th Appeal § 904, Nature of Power.

Ct. Rules

9 Witkin Cal. Proc. 5th Appeal § 909, (S 909) Time for Order.
9 Witkin Cal. Proc. 5th Appeal § 1019, (S 1019) Rehearing.
2 Witkin Cal. Proc. 5th Courts § 322, Rehearing.

Rule 8.890.   Remittitur

(a) Proceedings requiring issuance of remittitur

An appellate division must issue a remittitur after a decision in an appeal.

(b) Clerk's duties

(1) If an appellate division case is not transferred to the Court of Appeal under rule 8.1000 et seq., the appellate division clerk must:

(A) Issue a remittitur immediately after the Court of Appeal denies transfer or the period for granting transfer under rule 8.1008(a) expires if there will be no further proceedings in the appellate division;

(B) Send the remittitur to the trial court with a file-stamped copy of the opinion or order; and

(C) Return to the trial court with the remittitur all original records, exhibits, and documents sent to the appellate division in connection with the appeal, except any certification for transfer under rule 8.1005, the transcripts or statement on appeal, briefs, and the notice of appeal.

(2) If an appellate division case is transferred to a Court of Appeal under rule 8.1000 et seq., on receiving the Court of Appeal remittitur, the appellate division clerk must issue a remittitur and return documents to the trial court as provided in rule 8.1018.

(c) Immediate issuance, stay, and recall

(1) The appellate division may direct immediate issuance of a remittitur only on the parties' stipulation or on dismissal of the appeal on the request or stipulation of the parties under rule 8.825(c)(2).

(2) On a party's or its own motion or on stipulation, and for good cause, the court may stay a remittitur's issuance for a reasonable period or order its recall.

(3) An order recalling a remittitur issued after a decision by opinion does not supersede the opinion or affect its publication status.

(d) Notice

The remittitur is deemed issued when the clerk enters it in the record. The clerk must immediately send the parties notice of issuance of the remittitur, showing the date of entry. *(Adopted, eff. Jan. 1, 2009. As amended, eff. Jan. 1, 2011.)*

Research References

Rutter, Cal. Practice Guide: Civil Appeals & Writs Ch. 16-J, J. Postappeal Matters.
9 Witkin Cal. Proc. 5th Appeal § 1018, Decision and Opinion.
8 Witkin Cal. Proc. 5th Extraordinary Writs § 164E, (New)-Decision and Costs.

Rule 8.891.   Costs and sanctions in civil appeals

(a) Right to costs

(1) Except as provided in this rule, the prevailing party in a civil appeal is entitled to costs on appeal.

(2) The prevailing party is the respondent if the appellate division affirms the judgment without modification or dismisses the appeal. The prevailing party is the appellant if the appellate division reverses the judgment in its entirety.

(3) If the appellate division reverses the judgment in part or modifies it, or if there is more than one notice of appeal, the appellate division must specify the award or denial of costs in its decision.

(4) In the interests of justice, the appellate division may also award or deny costs as it deems proper.

(b) Judgment for costs

(1) The appellate division clerk must enter on the record and insert in the remittitur judgment awarding costs to the prevailing party under (a).

(2) If the clerk fails to enter judgment for costs, the appellate division may recall the remittitur for correction on its own motion or on a party's motion made not later than 30 days after the remittitur issues.

(c) Procedure for claiming or opposing costs

(1) Within 30 days after the clerk sends notice of issuance of the remittitur, a party claiming costs awarded by the appellate division must serve and file in the trial court a verified memorandum of costs under rule 3.170(a)(1).

(2) A party may serve and file a motion in the trial court to strike or tax costs claimed under (1) in the manner required by rule 3.1700.

(3) An award of costs is enforceable as a money judgment.

(d) Recoverable costs

(1) A party may recover only the costs of the following, if reasonable:

(A) Filing fees;

(B) The amount the party paid for any portion of the record, whether an original or a copy or both, subject to reduction by the appellate division under subdivision (e);

(C) The cost to produce additional evidence on appeal;

(D) The costs to notarize, serve, mail, and file the record, briefs, and other papers;

(E) The cost to print and reproduce any brief, including any petition for rehearing or review, answer, or reply;

(F) The cost to procure a surety bond, including the premium, the cost to obtain a letter of credit as collateral, and the fees and net interest expenses incurred to borrow funds to provide security for the bond or to obtain a letter of credit, unless the trial court determines the bond was unnecessary; and

(G) The fees and net interest expenses incurred to borrow funds to deposit with the superior court in lieu of a bond or undertaking, unless the trial court determines the deposit was unnecessary.

(2) Unless the court orders otherwise, an award of costs neither includes attorney's fees on appeal nor precludes a party from seeking them under rule 3.1702.

(e) Sanctions

(1) On motion of a party or its own motion, the appellate division may impose sanctions, including the award or denial of costs, on a party or an attorney for:

(A) Taking a frivolous appeal or appealing solely to cause delay; or

(B) Committing any unreasonable violation of these rules.

(2) A party's motion under (1) must include a declaration supporting the amount of any monetary sanction sought and must be served and filed before any order dismissing the appeal but no later than 10 days after the appellant's reply brief is due. If a party files a motion for sanctions with a motion to dismiss the appeal and the motion to dismiss is not granted, the party may file a new motion for sanctions within 10 days after the appellant's reply brief is due.

(3) The court must give notice in writing if it is considering imposing sanctions. Within 10 days after the court sends such notice, a party or attorney may serve and file an opposition, but

failure to do so will not be deemed consent. An opposition may not be filed unless the court sends such notice.

(4) Unless otherwise ordered, oral argument on the issue of sanctions must be combined with oral argument on the merits of the appeal. *(Adopted, eff. Jan. 1, 2009. As amended, eff. Jan. 1, 2011; Jan. 1, 2013.)*

Advisory Committee Comment

Subdivision (d). "Net interest expenses" in subdivisions (d)(1)(F) and (G) means the interest expenses incurred to borrow the funds that are deposited minus any interest earned by the borrower on those funds while they are on deposit.

Research References

Rutter, Cal. Practice Guide: Civil Appeals & Writs Ch. 14-B, B. Recovery of Appellate Costs and Attorney Fees.

Rutter, Cal. Practice Guide: Civil Appeals & Writs Ch. 16-A, A. Introduction.

Rutter, Cal. Practice Guide: Civil Appeals & Writs Ch. 16-J, J. Postappeal Matters.

Rutter, Cal. Practice Guide: Civil Trials & Evidence Ch. 17-D, D. Costs.

Rutter, Cal. Practice Guide: Civil Trials & Evidence Ch. 17-E, E. Attorney Fees as Costs.

9 Witkin Cal. Proc. 5th Appeal § 9, (S 9) Current Structure.

9 Witkin Cal. Proc. 5th Appeal § 687, Penalty for Excessive Record.

9 Witkin Cal. Proc. 5th Appeal § 953, in General.

9 Witkin Cal. Proc. 5th Appeal § 968, in General.

9 Witkin Cal. Proc. 5th Appeal § 975, (S 975) Requirements.

9 Witkin Cal. Proc. 5th Appeal § 977, Motion to Tax.

9 Witkin Cal. Proc. 5th Appeal § 982, (S 982) Procedure for Request.

9 Witkin Cal. Proc. 5th Appeal § 983, (S 983) Nature of Power.

9 Witkin Cal. Proc. 5th Appeal § 1018, Decision and Opinion.

2 Witkin Cal. Proc. 5th Courts § 195, (S 195) Appellate Rules.

8 Witkin Cal. Proc. 5th Extraordinary Writs § 164E, (New)-Decision and Costs.

7 Witkin Cal. Proc. 5th Judgment § 301, Fees Determined by Trial Court.

7 Witkin Cal. Proc. 5th Judgment § 302, Fees Determined by Appellate Court.

Chapter 6

WRIT PROCEEDINGS

Rule
8.930. Application.
8.931. Petitions filed by persons not represented by an attorney.
8.932. Petitions filed by an attorney for a party.
8.933. Opposition.
8.934. Notice to Trial Court.
8.935. Finality and remittitur.
8.936. Costs.

Rule 8.930. Application

(a) Writ proceedings governed

Except as provided in (b), the rules in this chapter govern proceedings in the appellate division for writs of mandate, certiorari, or prohibition, or other writs within the original jurisdiction of the appellate division. In all respects not provided for in this chapter, rule 8.883, regarding the form and content of briefs, applies.

(b) Writ proceedings not governed

The rules in this chapter do not apply to petitions for writs of supersedeas under rule 8.824 or writs not within the original jurisdiction of the appellate division. *(Adopted, eff. Jan. 1, 2009.)*

Advisory Committee Comment

Information on Writ Proceedings in Misdemeanor, Infraction, and Limited Civil Cases (form APP–150–INFO) provides additional information about proceedings for writs in the appellate division of the superior court. This form at is available at any courthouse or county law library or online at *www.courtinfo.ca.gov/forms*.

Subdivision (b). The superior courts, not the appellate divisions, have original jurisdiction in habeas corpus proceedings (see Cal. Const., art. VI, § 10). Habeas corpus proceedings in the superior courts are governed by rules 4.550 et. seq.

Research References

9 Witkin Cal. Proc. 5th Appeal § 9, (S 9) Current Structure.

2 Witkin Cal. Proc. 5th Courts § 195, (S 195) Appellate Rules.

8 Witkin Cal. Proc. 5th Extraordinary Writs § 4, (S 4) Constitutional Consolidation of Trial Courts.

8 Witkin Cal. Proc. 5th Extraordinary Writs § 162, (S 162) Procedural Overview.

8 Witkin Cal. Proc. 5th Extraordinary Writs § 163, (S 163) Governing Statutes and Rules.

8 Witkin Cal. Proc. 5th Extraordinary Writs § 164A, (New)-In General.

Rule 8.931. Petitions filed by persons not represented by an attorney

(a) Petitions

A person who is not represented by an attorney and who petitions the appellate division for a writ under this chapter must file the petition on *Petition for Writ (Misdemeanor, Infraction, or Limited Civil Case)* (form APP–151). For good cause the court may permit an unrepresented party to file a petition that is not on form APP–151.

(b) Contents of supporting documents

(1) The petition must be accompanied by an adequate record, including copies of:

(A) The ruling from which the petition seeks relief;

(B) All documents and exhibits submitted to the trial court supporting and opposing the petitioner's position;

(C) Any other documents or portions of documents submitted to the trial court that are necessary for a complete understanding of the case and the ruling under review; and

(D) A reporter's transcript or electronic recording of the oral proceedings that resulted in the ruling under review.

(2) In extraordinary circumstances, the petition may be filed without the documents required by (1)(A)–(C) if the petitioner files a declaration that explains the urgency and the circumstances making the documents unavailable and fairly summarizes their substance.

(3) If a transcript or electronic recording under (1)(D) is unavailable, the record must include a declaration by the petitioner:

(A) Explaining why the transcript or electronic recording is unavailable and fairly summarizing the proceedings, including the petitioner's arguments and any statement by the court supporting its ruling. This declaration may omit a full summary of the proceedings if part of the relief sought is an order to prepare a transcript for use by an indigent criminal defendant in support of the petition and if the declaration demonstrates the petitioner's need for and entitlement to the transcript; or

(B) Stating that the transcript or electronic recording has been ordered, the date it was ordered, and the date it is expected to be filed, which must be a date before any action requested of the appellate division other than issuance of a temporary stay supported by other parts of the record.

(4) If the petitioner does not submit the required record or explanations or does not present facts sufficient to excuse the failure to submit them, the court may summarily deny a stay request, the petition, or both.

(c) Form of supporting documents

(1) Documents submitted under (b) must comply with the following requirements:

(A) They must be bound together at the end of the petition or in separate volumes not exceeding 300 pages each. The pages must be consecutively numbered.

(B) They must be index-tabbed by number or letter.

(C) They must begin with a table of contents listing each document by its title and its index-tab number or letter. If a document has attachments, the table of contents must give the title of each attachment and a brief description of its contents.

(2) The clerk must file any supporting documents not complying with (1), but the court may notify the petitioner that it may strike or summarily deny the petition if the documents are not brought into compliance within a stated reasonable time of not less than five days.

(3) Unless the court provides otherwise by local rule or order, only one set of any separately bound supporting documents needs to be filed in support of a petition, an answer, an opposition, or a reply.

(d) Service

(1) The petition and one set of supporting documents must be served on any named real party in interest, but only the petition must be served on the respondent.

(2) The proof of service must give the telephone number of each attorney or unrepresented party served.

(3) The petition must be served on a public officer or agency when required by statute or rule 8.29.

(4) The clerk must file the petition even if its proof of service is defective, but if the petitioner fails to file a corrected proof of service within five days after the clerk gives notice of the defect the court may strike the petition or impose a lesser sanction.

(5) The court may allow the petition to be filed without proof of service. *(Adopted, eff. Jan. 1, 2009. As amended, eff. Jan. 1, 2009; Jan. 1, 2011.)*

Advisory Committee Comment

Subdivision (a). *Petition for Writ (Misdemeanor, Infraction, or Limited Civil Case)* (form APP–151) is available at any courthouse or county law library or online at *www.courtinfo.ca.gov/forms.*

Subdivision (d). Rule 8.25, which generally governs service and filing in appellate divisions, also applies to the original proceedings covered by this rule.

Research References

Rutter, Cal. Practice Guide: Civil Appeals & Writs Ch. 16-L, L. Writs.
8 Witkin Cal. Proc. 5th Extraordinary Writs § 169, in General.
8 Witkin Cal. Proc. 5th Extraordinary Writs § 179, Petition to Review Trial Court Ruling.
8 Witkin Cal. Proc. 5th Extraordinary Writs § 183, (S 183) Service.
8 Witkin Cal. Proc. 5th Extraordinary Writs § 164B, (New)-Petition Filed by Nonattorney.
8 Witkin Cal. Proc. 5th Extraordinary Writs § 164C, (New)-Petition Filed by Attorney.
8 Witkin Cal. Proc. 5th Extraordinary Writs § 164D, (New)-Service and Opposition.

Rule 8.932. Petitions filed by an attorney for a party

(a) General application of rule 8.931

Except as provided in this rule, rule 8.931 applies to any petition for an extraordinary writ filed by an attorney.

(b) Form and content of petition

(1) A petition for an extraordinary writ filed by an attorney may, but is not required to be, filed on *Petition for Writ (Misdemeanor, Infraction, or Limited Civil Case)* (form APP–151).

(2) The petition must disclose the name of any real party in interest.

(3) If the petition seeks review of trial court proceedings that are also the subject of a pending appeal, the notice "Related Appeal Pending" must appear on the cover of the petition, and the first paragraph of the petition must state the appeal's title and any appellate division docket number.

(4) The petition must be verified.

(5) The petition must be accompanied by a memorandum, which need not repeat facts alleged in the petition.

(6) Rule 8.883(b) governs the length of the petition and memorandum, but the verification and any supporting documents are excluded from the limits stated in rule 8.883(b)(1) and (2).

(7) If the petition requests a temporary stay, it must explain the urgency. *(Adopted, eff. Jan. 1, 2009.)*

Research References

Rutter, Cal. Practice Guide: Civil Appeals & Writs Ch. 16-L, L. Writs.
8 Witkin Cal. Proc. 5th Extraordinary Writs § 169, in General.
8 Witkin Cal. Proc. 5th Extraordinary Writs § 172, Verification.
8 Witkin Cal. Proc. 5th Extraordinary Writs § 179, Petition to Review Trial Court Ruling.
8 Witkin Cal. Proc. 5th Extraordinary Writs § 180, Supporting Memorandum.
8 Witkin Cal. Proc. 5th Extraordinary Writs § 164C, (New)-Petition Filed by Attorney.
8 Witkin Cal. Proc. 5th Extraordinary Writs § 164D, (New)-Service and Opposition.

Rule 8.933. Opposition

(a) Preliminary opposition

(1) Within 10 days after the petition is filed, the respondent or any real party in interest, separately or jointly, may serve and file a preliminary opposition.

(2) An opposition must contain a memorandum and a statement of any material fact not included in the petition.

(3) Within 10 days after an opposition is filed, the petitioner may serve and file a reply.

(4) Without requesting opposition or waiting for a reply, the court may grant or deny a request for temporary stay, deny the petition, issue an alternative writ or order to show cause, or notify the parties that it is considering issuing a peremptory writ in the first instance.

(b) Return or opposition; reply

(1) If the court issues an alternative writ or order to show cause, the respondent or any real party in interest, separately or jointly, may serve and file a return by demurrer, verified answer, or both. If the court notifies the parties that it is considering issuing a peremptory writ in the first instance, the respondent or any real party in interest may serve and file an opposition.

(2) Unless the court orders otherwise, the return or opposition must be served and filed within 30 days after the court issues the alternative writ or order to show cause or notifies the parties that it is considering issuing a peremptory writ in the first instance.

(3) Unless the court orders otherwise, the petitioner may serve and file a reply within 15 days after the return or opposition is filed.

(4) If the return is by demurrer alone and the demurrer is not sustained, the court may issue the peremptory writ without granting leave to answer. *(Adopted, eff. Jan. 1, 2009.)*

Research References

8 Witkin Cal. Proc. 5th Extraordinary Writs § 183, (S 183) Service.
8 Witkin Cal. Proc. 5th Extraordinary Writs § 184, (S 184) Opposing Memorandum.
8 Witkin Cal. Proc. 5th Extraordinary Writs § 189, (S 189) Prohibition and Mandamus.
8 Witkin Cal. Proc. 5th Extraordinary Writs § 192, in General.
8 Witkin Cal. Proc. 5th Extraordinary Writs § 193, Return as Answer or Demurrer.
8 Witkin Cal. Proc. 5th Extraordinary Writs § 197, (S 197) Return in Reviewing Court.
8 Witkin Cal. Proc. 5th Extraordinary Writs § 200, Decision.
8 Witkin Cal. Proc. 5th Extraordinary Writs § 201, (S 201) Where Demurrer Alone is Filed.
8 Witkin Cal. Proc. 5th Extraordinary Writs § 164D, (New)-Service and Opposition.
8 Witkin Cal. Proc. 5th Extraordinary Writs § 164D, (New)-Service and Opposition.
8 Witkin Cal. Proc. 5th Extraordinary Writs § 164D, (New)-Service and Opposition.
8 Witkin Cal. Proc. 5th Extraordinary Writs § 164D, (New)-Service and Opposition.

Rule 8.934.   Notice to Trial Court

(a) Notice if writ issues

If a writ or order issues directed to any judge, court, or other officer, the appellate division clerk must promptly send a certified copy of the writ or order to the person or entity to whom it is directed.

(b) Notice by telephone

(1) If the writ or order stays or prohibits proceedings set to occur within seven days or requires action within seven days—or in any other urgent situation—the appellate division clerk must make a reasonable effort to notify the clerk of the respondent court by telephone. The clerk of the respondent court must then notify the judge or officer most directly concerned.

(2) The clerk need not give notice by telephone of the summary denial of a writ, whether or not a stay previously issued. *(Adopted, eff. Jan. 1, 2009.)*

Research References

8 Witkin Cal. Proc. 5th Extraordinary Writs § 204, Superior Court.
8 Witkin Cal. Proc. 5th Extraordinary Writs § 164E, (New)-Decision and Costs.

Rule 8.935.   Finality and remittitur

(a) Finality of decision

(1) Except as otherwise provided in this rule, an appellate division decision in a writ proceeding is final 30 days after the decision is filed.

(2) The denial of a petition for a writ within the appellate division's original jurisdiction without issuance of an alternative writ or order to show cause is final in that court when filed.

(3) If necessary to prevent mootness or frustration of the relief granted or to otherwise promote the interests of justice, an appellate division may order early finality in that court of a decision granting a petition for a writ within its original jurisdiction or denying such a petition after issuing an alternative writ or order to show cause. The decision may provide for finality in that court on filing or within a stated period of less than 30 days.

(b) Remittitur

The appellate division must issue a remittitur after a decision in a writ proceeding, except when the court denies a writ petition without issuing an alternative writ or order to show cause. Rule 8.890 governs issuance of a remittitur in these proceedings. *(Adopted, eff. Jan. 1, 2009.)*

Research References

8 Witkin Cal. Proc. 5th Extraordinary Writs § 204, Superior Court.
8 Witkin Cal. Proc. 5th Extraordinary Writs § 209, (S 209) Finality and Res Judicata.
8 Witkin Cal. Proc. 5th Extraordinary Writs § 210, (S 210) Summary Denial is Not Law of Case.
8 Witkin Cal. Proc. 5th Extraordinary Writs § 221, (S 221) Summary Denial.
8 Witkin Cal. Proc. 5th Extraordinary Writs § 164E, (New)-Decision and Costs.

Rule 8.936.   Costs

(a) Entitlement to costs

Except in a criminal proceeding or other proceeding in which a party is entitled to court-appointed counsel, the prevailing party in an original proceeding is entitled to costs if the court resolves the proceeding after issuing an alternative writ, an order to show cause, or a peremptory writ in the first instance.

(b) Award of costs

(1) In the interests of justice, the court may award or deny costs as it deems proper.

(2) The opinion or order resolving the proceeding must specify the award or denial of costs.

(3) Rule 8.891(b)–(d) governs the procedure for recovering costs under this rule. *(Adopted, eff. Jan. 1, 2009.)*

Research References

9 Witkin Cal. Proc. 5th Appeal § 9, (S 9) Current Structure.
2 Witkin Cal. Proc. 5th Courts § 195, (S 195) Appellate Rules.
8 Witkin Cal. Proc. 5th Extraordinary Writs § 211, Mandamus and Prohibition.
8 Witkin Cal. Proc. 5th Extraordinary Writs § 212, Certiorari.
8 Witkin Cal. Proc. 5th Extraordinary Writs § 164E, (New)-Decision and Costs.

Division 3

TRIAL OF SMALL CLAIMS CASES ON APPEAL

Ct. Rules

Rule 8.950. Application

The rules in this division supplement article 7 of the Small Claims Act, Code of Civil Procedure sections 116.710 et seq., providing for new trials of small claims cases on appeal, and must be read in conjunction with those statutes. *(Formerly Rule 151, adopted, eff. July 1, 1964. As amended, eff. Jan. 1, 1977. As amended, eff. Jan. 1, 2005. Renumbered Rule 8.900 and amended, eff. Jan. 1, 2007. Renumbered Rule 8.950, eff. Jan. 1, 2009.)*

Research References

9 Witkin Cal. Proc. 5th Appeal § 9, (S 9) Current Structure.
9 Witkin Cal. Proc. 5th Appeal § 1003, Distinction: Appeal from Small Claims Court.
2 Witkin Cal. Proc. 5th Courts § 195, (S 195) Appellate Rules.
2 Witkin Cal. Proc. 5th Courts § 269, (S 269) Judicial Council Rules and Forms.
2 Witkin Cal. Proc. 5th Courts § 312, (S 312) Nature of Right.
2 Witkin Cal. Proc. 5th Courts § 316, in General.

Rule 8.952. Definitions

The definitions in rule 1.6 apply to these rules unless the context or subject matter requires otherwise. In addition, the following definitions apply to these rules:

(1) "Small claims court" means the trial court from which the appeal is taken.

(2) "Appeal" means a new trial before a different judge on all claims, whether or not appealed.

(3) "Appellant" means the party appealing; "respondent" means the adverse party. "Plaintiff" and "defendant" refer to the parties as they were designated in the small claims court. *(Formerly Rule 158, adopted, eff. July 1, 1964. Renumbered Rule 156 and amended, eff. July 1, 1991. As amended, eff. Jan. 1, 2005. Renumbered Rule 8.902 and amended, eff. Jan. 1, 2007. Renumbered Rule 8.952, eff. Jan. 1, 2009.)*

Rule 8.954. Filing the appeal

(a) Notice of appeal

To appeal from a judgment in a small claims case, an appellant must file a notice of appeal in the small claims court. The appellant or the appellant's attorney must sign the notice. The notice is sufficient if it states in substance that the appellant appeals from a specified judgment or, in the case of a defaulting defendant, from the denial of a motion to vacate the judgment. A notice of appeal must be liberally construed.

(b) Notification by clerk

(1) The clerk of the small claims court must promptly mail a notification of the filing of the notice of appeal to each other party at the party's last known address.

(2) The notification must state the number and title of the case and the date the notice of appeal was filed. If a party dies before the clerk mails the notification, the mailing is a sufficient performance of the clerk's duty.

(3) A failure of the clerk to give notice of the judgment or notification of the filing of the notice of appeal does not extend the time for filing the notice of appeal or affect the validity of the appeal.

(c) Premature notice of appeal

A notice of appeal filed after judgment is rendered but before it is entered is valid and is treated as filed immediately after entry. A notice of appeal filed after the judge has announced an intended ruling but before judgment is rendered may, in the discretion of the reviewing court be treated as filed immediately after entry of the judgment. *(Formerly Rule 152, adopted, eff. July 1, 1964. As amended, eff. July 1, 1973; Jan. 1, 1977; Jan. 1, 1979; Jan. 1, 1984; July 1, 1991; Jan. 1, 2005. Renumbered Rule 8.904 and amended, eff. Jan. 1, 2007. Renumbered Rule 8.954, eff. Jan. 1, 2009.)*

Research References

2 Witkin Cal. Proc. 5th Courts § 315, (S 315) Notice of Appeal.

Rule 8.957. Record on appeal

Within five days after the filing of the notice of appeal and the payment of any fees required by law, the clerk of the small claims court must transmit the file and all related papers, including the notice of appeal, to the clerk of the court assigned to hear the appeal. *(Formerly Rule 153, adopted, eff. July 1, 1964. As amended, eff. July 1, 1972; July 1, 1973; Jan. 1, 1977; Jan.1, 2005. Renumbered Rule 8.907 and amended, eff. Jan. 1, 2007. Renumbered Rule 8.957, eff. Jan. 1, 2009.)*

Research References

2 Witkin Cal. Proc. 5th Courts § 316, in General.

Rule 8.960. Continuances

For good cause, the court assigned to hear the appeal may continue the trial. A request for a continuance may be presented by one party or by stipulation. The court may grant a continuance not to exceed 30 days, but in a case of extreme hardship the court may grant a continuance exceeding 30 days. *(Formerly Rule 154, adopted, eff. July 1, 1964. As amended, eff. Jan. 1, 1977; July 1, 1991; Jan. 1, 2005. Renumbered Rule 8.910, eff. Jan. 1, 2007. Renumbered Rule 8.960, eff. Jan. 1, 2009.)*

Research References

2 Witkin Cal. Proc. 5th Courts § 316, in General.

Rule 8.963. Abandonment, dismissal, and judgment for failure to bring to trial

(a) Before the record is filed

Before the record has been transmitted to the court assigned to hear the appeal, the appellant may file in the small claims court an abandonment of the appeal or a stipulation to abandon the appeal. Either filing operates to dismiss the appeal and return the case to the small claims court.

(b) After the record is filed

After the record has been transmitted to the court assigned to hear the appeal, the court may dismiss the appeal on the appellant's written request or the parties' stipulation filed in that court.

(c) Dismissal or judgment by the court

(1) The court must dismiss the appeal if the case is not brought to trial within one year after the date of filing the appeal. If a new trial is ordered, the court must dismiss the appeal if the case is not brought to trial within one year after the entry date of the new trial order.

(2) Notwithstanding (1), the court must not order dismissal or enter judgment if there was in effect a written stipulation extending the time for trial or on a showing that the appellant exercised reasonable diligence to bring the case to trial.

(3) Notwithstanding (1) and (2), the court must dismiss the appeal if the case is not brought to trial within three years after

either the notice of appeal is filed or the most recent new trial order is entered in the court assigned to hear the appeal.

(d) Notification by clerk

If an appellant files an abandonment, the clerk of the court in which it is filed must immediately notify the adverse party of the filing. The clerk of the court assigned to hear the appeal must immediately notify the parties of any order of dismissal or any judgment for defendant made by the court under (c).

(e) Return of papers

If an appeal is dismissed, the clerk of the court assigned to hear the appeal must promptly transmit to the small claims court a copy of the dismissal order and all original papers and exhibits sent to the court assigned to hear the appeal. The small claims court must then proceed with the case as if no appeal had been taken.

(f) Approval of compromise

If a guardian or conservator seeks approval of a proposed compromise of a pending appeal in which a new trial has been ordered, the court assigned to hear the appeal may, before ruling on the compromise, hear and determine whether the proposed compromise is for the best interest of the ward or conservatee. *(Formerly Rule 157, adopted, eff. July 1, 1964. As amended, eff.*

Jan. 1, 1972; July 1, 1972. Renumbered Rule 155 and amended, eff. July 1, 1991. As amended, eff. Jan. 1, 2005. Renumbered Rule 8.913 and amended, eff. Jan. 1, 2007. Renumbered Rule 8.963, eff. Jan. 1, 2009.)

Research References

2 Witkin Cal. Proc. 5th Courts § 313, (S 313) Abandonment and Dismissal.

Rule 8.966. Examination of witnesses

The court may allow parties or attorneys representing parties to the appeal to conduct direct and cross-examination, subject to the court's discretion to control the manner, mode, and duration of examination in keeping with informality and the circumstances. *(Formerly Rule 157, adopted, eff. July 1, 1999. Renumbered Rule 8.916 and amended, eff. Jan. 1, 2007. Renumbered Rule 8.966, eff. Jan. 1, 2009.)*

Research References

9 Witkin Cal. Proc. 5th Appeal § 9, (S 9) Current Structure.
2 Witkin Cal. Proc. 5th Courts § 195, (S 195) Appellate Rules.
2 Witkin Cal. Proc. 5th Courts § 316, in General.

Division 4

TRANSFER OF APPELLATE DIVISION CASES TO THE COURT OF APPEAL

Rule

8.1000. Application.
8.1002. Transfer authority.
8.1005. Certification for transfer by the appellate division.
8.1006. Petition for transfer.
8.1007. Transmitting record to Court of Appeal.
8.1008. Order for transfer.
8.1012. Briefs and argument.
8.1014. Proceedings in the appellate division after certification or transfer.
8.1016. Disposition of transferred case.
8.1018. Finality and remittitur.

Rule 8.1000. Application

Rules 8.1000–8.1018 govern the transfer of cases within the appellate jurisdiction of the superior court—other than appeals in small claims cases—to the Court of Appeal. Unless the context requires otherwise, the term "case" as used in these rules means cases within that jurisdiction. *(Formerly Rule 61, adopted, eff. Jan. 1, 2003. Renumbered Rule 8.1000 and amended, eff. Jan. 1, 2007. As amended, eff. Jan. 1, 2011.)*

Advisory Committee Comment

The rules in this division implement the authority of the Court of Appeal under Code of Civil Procedure section 911 and Penal Code section 1471 to order any case on appeal to a superior court in its district transferred to the Court of Appeal if it determines that transfer is necessary to secure uniformity of decision or to settle important questions of law.

Research References

Rutter, Cal. Practice Guide: Civil Appeals & Writs Ch. 3-A, A. Necessity of Timely Filing for Appeal.
Rutter, Cal. Practice Guide: Civil Appeals & Writs Ch. 16-K, K. Transfer to Court of Appeal.
9 Witkin Cal. Proc. 5th Appeal § 9, (S 9) Current Structure.
9 Witkin Cal. Proc. 5th Appeal § 10, (S 10) Scope: Practice and Procedure.

9 Witkin Cal. Proc. 5th Appeal § 1020, (S 1020) Nature and Scope of Power.
2 Witkin Cal. Proc. 5th Courts § 195, (S 195) Appellate Rules.

Rule 8.1002. Transfer authority

A Court of Appeal may order a case transferred to it for hearing and decision if it determines that transfer is necessary to secure uniformity of decision or to settle an important question of law. Transfer may be ordered on:

(1) Certification of the case for transfer by the superior court appellate division under rule 8.1005;

(2) Petition for transfer under rule 8.1006; or

(3) The Court of Appeal's own motion. *(Formerly Rule 62, adopted, eff. Jan. 1, 2003. Renumbered Rule 8.1002 and amended, eff. Jan. 1, 2007. As amended, eff. Jan. 1, 2011.)*

Research References

Rutter, Cal. Practice Guide: Civil Appeals & Writs Ch. 2-B, B. Appealable Judgments and Orders.
Rutter, Cal. Practice Guide: Civil Appeals & Writs Ch. 16-K, K. Transfer to Court of Appeal.
9 Witkin Cal. Proc. 5th Appeal § 922, Nature and Grounds.
9 Witkin Cal. Proc. 5th Appeal § 1020, (S 1020) Nature and Scope of Power.

Rule 8.1005. Certification for transfer by the appellate division

(a) Authority to certify

(1) The appellate division may certify a case for transfer to the Court of Appeal on its own motion or on a party's application if it determines that transfer is necessary to secure uniformity of decision or to settle an important question of law.

(2) Except as provided in (3), a case may be certified for transfer by a majority of the appellate division judges to whom the case has been assigned or who decided the appeal or, if the case has not yet been assigned, by any two appellate division judges.

(3) If an appeal from a conviction of a traffic infraction is assigned to a single appellate division judge under Code of Civil Procedure section 77, the case may be certified for transfer by that judge.

(4) If an assigned or deciding judge is unable to act on the certification for transfer, a judge designated or assigned to the appellate division by the chair of the Judicial Council may act in that judge's place.

(b) Application for certification

(1) A party may serve and file an application asking the appellate division to certify a case for transfer at any time after the record on appeal is filed in the appellate division but no later than 15 days after:

(A) The decision is filed;

(B) A publication order restarting the finality period under rule 8.888(a)(2);

(C) A modification order changing the appellate judgment under rule 8.888(b); or

(D) The filing of a consent under rule 8.888(c).

(2) The party may include the application in a petition for rehearing.

(3) The application must explain why transfer is necessary to secure uniformity of decision or to settle an important question of law.

(4) Within five days after the application is filed, any other party may serve and file an answer.

(5) No hearing will be held on the application. Failure to certify the case within the time specified in (c) is deemed a denial of the application.

(c) Time to certify

The appellate division may certify a case for transfer at any time after the record on appeal is filed in the appellate division and before the appellate division decision is final in that court.

(d) Contents of order certifying case for transfer

An order certifying a case for transfer must:

(1) Clearly state that the appellate division is certifying the case for transfer to the Court of Appeal;

(2) Briefly describe why transfer is necessary to secure uniformity of decision or to settle an important question of law; and

(3) State whether there was a decision on appeal and, if so, its date and disposition.

(e) Superior court clerk's duties

(1) If the appellate division orders a case certified for transfer, the clerk must promptly send a copy of the certification order to the Court of Appeal clerk, the parties, and, in a criminal case, the Attorney General.

(2) If the appellate division denies a certification application by order, the clerk must promptly send a copy of the order to the parties. *(Formerly Rule 63, adopted, eff. Jan. 1, 2003. Renumbered Rule 8.1005 and amended, eff. Jan. 1, 2007. As amended, eff. Jan. 1, 2010; Jan. 1, 2011.)*

Research References

Rutter, Cal. Practice Guide: Civil Appeals & Writs Ch. 16-K, K. Transfer to Court of Appeal.
Rutter, Cal. Practice Guide: Civ. Pro. Before Trial Ch. 3-A, A. Subject Matter Jurisdiction (Competency).
9 Witkin Cal. Proc. 5th Appeal § 785, (S 785) Other Adoptions.
9 Witkin Cal. Proc. 5th Appeal § 1020, (S 1020) Nature and Scope of Power.
9 Witkin Cal. Proc. 5th Appeal § 1022, (S 1022) Application, Opposition, and Determination.
9 Witkin Cal. Proc. 5th Appeal § 1023, (S 1023) Certification and Transmission of Record.
9 Witkin Cal. Proc. 5th Appeal § 1030, Record.
2 Witkin Cal. Proc. 5th Courts § 324, Certification to Court of Appeal.

Rule 8.1006. Petition for transfer

(a) Right to file petition

A party may file a petition in the Court of Appeal asking for an appellate division case to be transferred to that court only if an application for certification for transfer was first filed in the appellate division and denied.

(b) Time to file petition

(1) The petition must be served and filed in the Court of Appeal after the appellate division issues its decision in the case but no later than 15 days after the decision is final in that court. A copy of the petition must also be served on the appellate division.

(2) The time to file a petition for transfer may not be extended, but the presiding justice may relieve a party from a failure to file a timely petition for transfer if the time for the Court of Appeal to order transfer on its own motion has not expired.

(c) Form and contents of petition

(1) Except as provided in this rule, a petition must comply with the form and contents requirements of rule 8.204(a)(1), (b), and (d).

(2) The body of the petition must begin with a concise, nonargumentative statement of the issues presented for review, framing them in terms of the facts of the case but without unnecessary detail.

(3) The petition must explain why transfer is necessary to secure uniformity of decision or to settle an important question of law.

(4) The petition must not exceed 5,600 words, including footnotes, if produced on a computer, and 20 pages if typewritten. A petition produced on a computer must include a certificate by counsel or an unrepresented party stating the number of words in the document. The person certifying may rely on the word count of the computer program used to prepare the document. A certificate stating the number of words, the tables required by rule 8.204(a)(1), the cover information required under rule 8.204(b)(10), any signature block, and any attachment permitted under rule 8.204(d) are excluded from these length limits.

(d) Answer to petition

(1) Any answer must be served and filed within 10 days after the petition is filed unless the court orders otherwise.

(2) Except as provided in this rule, any answer must comply with the form and contents requirements of rule 8.204(a)(1), (b), and (d).

(3) An answer must comply with the length requirements of (c)(4). *(Adopted, eff. Jan. 1, 2011.)*

Advisory Committee Comment

See rule 8.40 for requirements regarding the covers of documents filed in the appellate courts and rule 8.44(b) for the number of copies of documents that must be provided to the Court of Appeal.

Research References

Rutter, Cal. Practice Guide: Civil Appeals & Writs Ch. 16-K, K. Transfer to Court of Appeal.
9 Witkin Cal. Proc. 5th Appeal § 1020, (S 1020) Nature and Scope of Power.

9 Witkin Cal. Proc. 5th Appeal § 1026, Transfer by Court of Appeal on Party's Petition.

Rule 8.1007. Transmitting record to Court of Appeal

(a) Clerks' duties

(1) To assist the Court of Appeal in determining whether to order transfer, the superior court clerk must send the record specified in (b) to the Court of Appeal within five days after:

(A) The appellate division certifies a case for transfer under rule 8.1005;

(B) The superior court clerk sends a copy of an appellate division opinion certified for publication to the Court of Appeal under rule 8.887;

(C) The superior court clerk receives a copy of a petition for transfer under rule 8.1006; or

(D) The superior court receives a request for the record from the Court of Appeal.

(2) The Court of Appeal clerk must promptly notify the parties when the clerk files the record.

(b) Contents

The record sent to the Court of Appeal under (a) must contain:

(1) The original record on appeal prepared under rules 8.830–8.843, 8.860–8.873, or 8.910–8.923;

(2) Any briefs filed in the appellate division;

(3) The decision of the appellate division; and

(4) Any application for certification for transfer, any answer to that application, and the appellate division's order on the application. *(Formerly Rule 65, adopted, eff. Jan. 1, 2003. Renumbered Rule 8.1010 and amended, eff. Jan. 1, 2007. As amended, eff. July 1, 2009. Renumbered Rule 8.1007 and amended, eff. Jan. 1, 2011.)*

Research References

Rutter, Cal. Practice Guide: Civil Appeals & Writs Ch. 16-K, K. Transfer to Court of Appeal.
9 Witkin Cal. Proc. 5th Appeal § 1023, (S 1023) Certification and Transmission of Record.
9 Witkin Cal. Proc. 5th Appeal § 1024, (S 1024) Denial or Grant of Transfer.
9 Witkin Cal. Proc. 5th Appeal § 1026, Transfer by Court of Appeal on Party's Petition.
9 Witkin Cal. Proc. 5th Appeal § 1029, Stay of Proceedings Below.
9 Witkin Cal. Proc. 5th Appeal § 1030, Record.

Rule 8.1008. Order for transfer

(a) Time to transfer

(1) The Court of Appeal may order transfer

(A) After the appellate division certifies the case for transfer or on petition for transfer, within 20 days after the record sent under rule 8.1007 is filed in the Court of Appeal; or

(B) On its own motion, within 30 days after the appellate division decision is final in that court.

(2) Within either period specified in (1), the Court of Appeal may order an extension not exceeding 20 days.

(3) If the Court of Appeal does not timely order transfer, transfer is deemed denied.

(b) Court of Appeal clerk's duties

(1) When a transfer order is filed, the clerk must promptly send a copy of the order to the superior court clerk, the parties, and, in a criminal case, the Attorney General.

(2) With the copy of the transfer order sent to the parties and the Attorney General, the clerk must send notice of the time to serve and file any briefs ordered under rule 8.1012 and, if specified by the Court of Appeal, the issues to be briefed and argued.

(3) If the court denies transfer after the appellate division certifies a case for transfer or after a party files a petition for transfer, the clerk must promptly send notice of the denial to the parties, the appellate division, and, in a criminal case, the Attorney General.

(4) Failure to send any order or notice under this subdivision does not affect the jurisdiction of the Court of Appeal. *(Formerly Rule 64, adopted, eff. Jan. 1, 2003. As amended, eff. July 1, 2003. Renumbered Rule 8.1008 and amended, eff. Jan. 1, 2007. As amended, eff. Jan. 1, 2008; Jan. 1, 2011.)*

Research References

Rutter, Cal. Practice Guide: Civil Appeals & Writs Ch. 16-K, K. Transfer to Court of Appeal.
9 Witkin Cal. Proc. 5th Appeal § 1024, (S 1024) Denial or Grant of Transfer.
9 Witkin Cal. Proc. 5th Appeal § 1025, Transfer by Court of Appeal on Own Motion.
9 Witkin Cal. Proc. 5th Appeal § 1026, Transfer by Court of Appeal on Party's Petition.
9 Witkin Cal. Proc. 5th Appeal § 1028, Notice of Order Granting or Denying Transfer.
9 Witkin Cal. Proc. 5th Appeal § 1031, Briefs and Oral Argument.

Rule 8.1012. Briefs and argument

(a) When briefs permitted

(1) After the Court of Appeal orders transfer, the parties may file briefs in the Court of Appeal only if ordered by the court. The court may order briefs either on a party's application or the court's own motion. The court must prescribe the briefing sequence in any briefing order.

(2) Instead of filing a brief, or as part of its brief, a party may join in or adopt by reference all or part of a brief filed in the Court of Appeal in the same or a related case.

(b) Time to file briefs

Unless otherwise provided in the court's order under (a):

(1) The opening brief must be served and filed within 20 days after entry of the briefing order.

(2) The responding brief must be served and filed within 20 days after the opening brief is filed.

(3) Any reply brief must be served and filed within 10 days after the responding brief is filed.

(c) Additional service requirements

(1) Any brief of a defendant in a criminal case must be served on the prosecuting attorney and the Attorney General.

(2) Every brief must be served on the appellate division from which the case was transferred.

(d) Form and contents of briefs

(1) Except as provided in this rule, briefs must comply with the form and contents requirements of rule 8.204(a)(1), (b), and (d).

(2) No brief may exceed 5,600 words if produced on a computer or 20 pages if typewritten. The person certifying may rely on the word count of the computer program used to prepare the document. A certificate stating the number of words, the tables required by rule 8.204(a)(1), the cover information required under rule 8.204(b)(10), any signature block, and any attachment permitted under rule 8.204(d) are excluded from these length limits.

(e) Limitation of issues

(1) On or after ordering transfer, the Court of Appeal may specify the issues to be briefed and argued. Unless the court orders otherwise, the parties must limit their briefs and arguments to those issues and any issues fairly included in those issues.

(2) Notwithstanding an order specifying issues under (1), the court may, on reasonable notice, order oral argument on fewer or additional issues or on the entire case. (*Formerly Rule 66, adopted, eff. Jan. 1, 2003. Renumbered Rule 8.1012 and amended, eff. Jan. 1, 2007. As amended, eff. Jan. 1, 2011.*)

Research References

Rutter, Cal. Practice Guide: Civil Appeals & Writs Ch. 16-K, K. Transfer to Court of Appeal.
9 Witkin Cal. Proc. 5th Appeal § 1028, Notice of Order Granting or Denying Transfer.
9 Witkin Cal. Proc. 5th Appeal § 1031, Briefs and Oral Argument.

Rule 8.1014. Proceedings in the appellate division after certification or transfer

When the appellate division certifies a case for transfer or the Court of Appeal orders transfer, further action by the appellate division is limited to preparing and sending the record under rule 8.1007 until termination of the proceedings in the Court of Appeal. (*Formerly Rule 67, adopted, eff. Jan. 1, 2003. Renumbered Rule 8.1014, eff. Jan. 1, 2007. As amended, eff. Jan. 1, 2011.*)

Research References

Rutter, Cal. Practice Guide: Civil Appeals & Writs Ch. 16-K, K. Transfer to Court of Appeal.
9 Witkin Cal. Proc. 5th Appeal § 1023, (S 1023) Certification and Transmission of Record.
9 Witkin Cal. Proc. 5th Appeal § 1029, Stay of Proceedings Below.

Rule 8.1016. Disposition of transferred case

(a) Decision on limited issues

The Court of Appeal may decide fewer than all the issues raised and may retransfer the case to the appellate division for decision on any remaining issues.

(b) Retransfer without decision

The Court of Appeal may vacate a transfer order without decision and retransfer the case to the appellate division with or without directions to conduct further proceedings. (*Formerly Rule 68, adopted, eff. Jan. 1, 2003. Renumbered Rule 8.1016, eff. Jan. 1, 2007. As amended, eff. Jan. 1, 2011.*)

Research References

Rutter, Cal. Practice Guide: Civil Appeals & Writs Ch. 16-K, K. Transfer to Court of Appeal.
9 Witkin Cal. Proc. 5th Appeal § 1024, (S 1024) Denial or Grant of Transfer.

Rule 8.1018. Finality and remittitur

(a) When transfer is denied

If the Court of Appeal denies transfer of a case from the appellate division of the superior court after the appellate division certifies the case for transfer or after a party files a petition for transfer, the denial is final immediately. On receiving notice under rule 8.1008(b) that the Court of Appeal has denied transfer or if the period for ordering transfer under rule 8.1008(a) expires, the appellate division clerk must promptly issue a remittitur if there will be no further proceedings in that court.

(b) When transfer order is vacated

If the appellate division issued a decision before transfer and the Court of Appeal vacates its transfer order under rule 8.1016(b) and retransfers the case without directing further proceedings, the appellate division's decision is final when the appellate division receives the order vacating transfer. The appellate division clerk must promptly issue a remittitur.

(c) When the Court of Appeal issues a decision

If the Court of Appeal issues a decision on a case it has ordered transferred from the appellate division of the superior court, filing, finality, and modification of that decision are governed by rule 8.264 and remittitur is governed by rule 8.272, except that the clerk must address the remittitur to the appellate division and send that court two copies of the remittitur and two file-stamped copies of the Court of Appeal opinion or order. On receipt of the Court of Appeal remittitur, the appellate division clerk must promptly issue a remittitur if there will be no further proceedings in that court.

(d) Documents to be returned

When the Court of Appeal denies or vacates transfer or issues a remittitur under (c), the Court of Appeal clerk must return to the appellate division the record sent to the Court of Appeal under rule 8.1007 and any exhibits. (*Formerly Rule 69, adopted, eff. Jan. 1, 2003. Renumbered Rule 8.1018, eff. Jan. 1, 2007. As amended, eff. Jan. 1, 2009; Jan. 1, 2011.*)

Advisory Committee Comment

Subdivision (a). The finality of Court of Appeal decisions in appeals is generally addressed in rules 8.264 (civil appeals) and 8.366 (criminal appeals).

Research References

Rutter, Cal. Practice Guide: Civil Appeals & Writs Ch. 11-G, G. Finality as to Court of Appeal.
Rutter, Cal. Practice Guide: Civil Appeals & Writs Ch. 12-A, A. Overview.
Rutter, Cal. Practice Guide: Civil Appeals & Writs Ch. 16-K, K. Transfer to Court of Appeal.
9 Witkin Cal. Proc. 5th Appeal § 9, (S 9) Current Structure.
9 Witkin Cal. Proc. 5th Appeal § 10, (S 10) Scope: Practice and Procedure.
9 Witkin Cal. Proc. 5th Appeal § 1018, Decision and Opinion.
9 Witkin Cal. Proc. 5th Appeal § 1032, Decision and Remittitur.
2 Witkin Cal. Proc. 5th Courts § 195, (S 195) Appellate Rules.

Division 5

PUBLICATION OF APPELLATE OPINIONS

Rule 8.1100. Authority

The rules governing the publication of appellate opinions are adopted by the Supreme Court under section 14 of article VI of the California Constitution and published in the California Rules of Court at the direction of the Judicial Council. *(Adopted, eff. Jan. 1, 2007.)*

Research References

9 Witkin Cal. Proc. 5th Appeal § 9, (S 9) Current Structure.
2 Witkin Cal. Proc. 5th Courts § 195, (S 195) Appellate Rules.

Rule 8.1105. Publication of appellate opinions

(a) Supreme Court

All opinions of the Supreme Court are published in the Official Reports.

(b) Courts of Appeal and appellate divisions

Except as provided in (e), an opinion of a Court of Appeal or a superior court appellate division is published in the Official Reports if a majority of the rendering court certifies the opinion for publication before the decision is final in that court.

(c) Standards for certification

An opinion of a Court of Appeal or a superior court appellate division—whether it affirms or reverses a trial court order or judgment—should be certified for publication in the Official Reports if the opinion:

(1) Establishes a new rule of law;

(2) Applies an existing rule of law to a set of facts significantly different from those stated in published opinions;

(3) Modifies, explains, or criticizes with reasons given, an existing rule of law;

(4) Advances a new interpretation, clarification, criticism, or construction of a provision of a constitution, statute, ordinance, or court rule;

(5) Addresses or creates an apparent conflict in the law;

(6) Involves a legal issue of continuing public interest;

(7) Makes a significant contribution to legal literature by reviewing either the development of a common law rule or the legislative or judicial history of a provision of a constitution, statute, or other written law;

(8) Invokes a previously overlooked rule of law, or reaffirms a principle of law not applied in a recently reported decision; or

(9) Is accompanied by a separate opinion concurring or dissenting on a legal issue, and publication of the majority and separate opinions would make a significant contribution to the development of the law.

(d) Factors not to be considered

Factors such as the workload of the court, or the potential embarrassment of a litigant, lawyer, judge, or other person should not affect the determination of whether to publish an opinion.

(e) Changes in publication status

(1) Unless otherwise ordered under (2), an opinion is no longer considered published if the Supreme Court grants review or the rendering court grants rehearing.

(2) The Supreme Court may order that an opinion certified for publication is not to be published or that an opinion not certified is to be published. The Supreme Court may also order publication of an opinion, in whole or in part, at any time after granting review.

(f) Editing

(1) Computer versions of all opinions of the Supreme Court and Courts of Appeal must be provided to the Reporter of Decisions on the day of filing. Opinions of superior court appellate divisions certified for publication must be provided as prescribed in rule 8.887.

(2) The Reporter of Decisions must edit opinions for publication as directed by the Supreme Court. The Reporter of Decisions must submit edited opinions to the courts for examination, correction, and approval before finalization for the Official Reports. *(Formerly Rule 976, adopted, eff. Jan. 1, 2005. Renumbered Rule 8.1105 and amended, eff. Jan. 1, 2007. As amended, eff. April 1, 2007; July 23, 2008; July 1, 2009.)*

Research References

Rutter, Cal. Practice Guide: Civil Appeals & Writs Ch. 9-B, B. Approaches to Briefwriting.
Rutter, Cal. Practice Guide: Civil Appeals & Writs Ch. 11-F, F. Publication of Appellate Opinions.
Rutter, Cal. Practice Guide: Civil Appeals & Writs Ch. 12-F, F. Disposition.
Rutter, Cal. Practice Guide: Civil Appeals & Writs Ch. 13-B, B. Petition for Review Procedures.
Rutter, Cal. Practice Guide: Civil Appeals & Writs Ch. 16-H, H. Decision.
9 Witkin Cal. Proc. 5th Appeal § 496, (S 496) Illustrations.
9 Witkin Cal. Proc. 5th Appeal § 814, (S 814) Supreme Court Rule.
9 Witkin Cal. Proc. 5th Appeal § 815, (S 815) Standards for Certification.
9 Witkin Cal. Proc. 5th Appeal § 816, (S 816) in General.
9 Witkin Cal. Proc. 5th Appeal § 828, (S 828) California Rule.
9 Witkin Cal. Proc. 5th Appeal § 829, (S 829) Illustrations.
9 Witkin Cal. Proc. 5th Appeal § 831, (S 831) Rendition: Filing of Opinion.
9 Witkin Cal. Proc. 5th Appeal § 951, Publication or Nonpublication.
9 Witkin Cal. Proc. 5th Appeal § 1018, Decision and Opinion.
2 Witkin Cal. Proc. 5th Courts § 327, (S 327) Organization.
2 Witkin Cal. Proc. 5th Courts § 331, in General.
2 Witkin Cal. Proc. 5th Courts § 358, (S 358) Supreme Court.

Rule 8.1110. Partial publication

(a) Order for partial publication

A majority of the rendering court may certify for publication any part of an opinion meeting a standard for publication under rule 8.1105.

(b) Opinion contents

The published part of the opinion must specify the part or parts not certified for publication. All material, factual and legal, including the disposition, that aids in the application or interpretation of the published part must be published.

(c) Construction

For purposes of rules 8.1105, 8.1115, and 8.1120, the published part of the opinion is treated as a published opinion and the unpublished part as an unpublished opinion. *(Formerly Rule 976.1, adopted, eff. Jan. 1, 2005. Renumbered Rule 8.1110 and amended, eff. Jan. 1, 2007.)*

Research References

Rutter, Cal. Practice Guide: Civil Appeals & Writs Ch. 9-B, B. Approaches to Briefwriting.
Rutter, Cal. Practice Guide: Civil Appeals & Writs Ch. 11-F, F. Publication of Appellate Opinions.
9 Witkin Cal. Proc. 5th Appeal § 828, (S 828) California Rule.
2 Witkin Cal. Proc. 5th Courts § 331, in General.

Rule 8.1115. Citation of opinions

(a) Unpublished opinion

Except as provided in (b), an opinion of a California Court of Appeal or superior court appellate division that is not certified for publication or ordered published must not be cited or relied on by a court or a party in any other action.

(b) Exceptions

An unpublished opinion may be cited or relied on:

(1) When the opinion is relevant under the doctrines of law of the case, res judicata, or collateral estoppel; or

(2) When the opinion is relevant to a criminal or disciplinary action because it states reasons for a decision affecting the same defendant or respondent in another such action.

(c) Citation procedure

A copy of an opinion citable under (b) or of a cited opinion of any court that is available only in a computer-based source of decisional law must be furnished to the court and all parties by attaching it to the document in which it is cited or, if the citation will be made orally, by letter within a reasonable time in advance of citation.

(d) When a published opinion may be cited

A published California opinion may be cited or relied on as soon as it is certified for publication or ordered published. *(Formerly Rule 977, adopted, eff. Jan. 1, 2005. Renumbered Rule 8.1115 and amended, eff. Jan. 1, 2007.)*

Advisory Committee Comment

A footnote to a previous version of this rule stated that a citation to an opinion ordered published by the Supreme Court after grant of review should include a reference to the grant of review and to any subsequent Supreme Court action in the case. This footnote has been deleted because it was not part of the rule itself and the event it describes rarely occurs in practice.

Research References

Rutter, Cal. Practice Guide: Civil Appeals & Writs Ch. 9-B, B. Approaches to Briefwriting.
Rutter, Cal. Practice Guide: Civil Appeals & Writs Ch. 9-C, C. Format of Briefs.
Rutter, Cal. Practice Guide: Civil Appeals & Writs Ch. 11-F, F. Publication of Appellate Opinions.
Rutter, Cal. Practice Guide: Civil Appeals & Writs Ch. 13-B, B. Petition for Review Procedures.
Rutter, Cal. Practice Guide: Civil Appeals & Writs Ch. 14-D, D. Precedential Effect of Appellate Court Opinions.
Rutter, Cal. Practice Guide: Civ. Pro. Before Trial Ch. 9(I)-B, B. Preparing and Filing Motions.
Rutter, Cal. Practice Guide: Civil Trials & Evidence Ch. 8E-A, A. Privileges.
Rutter, Cal. Practice Guide: Civil Trials & Evidence Gen. Matls., Highlights.
Rutter, Cal. Practice Guide: Prof. Responsibility Ch. 8-C, C. Restrictions on Advocacy in Court Proceedings.
9 Witkin Cal. Proc. 5th Appeal § 491, Unpublished Court of Appeal Decisions.
9 Witkin Cal. Proc. 5th Appeal § 700, (S 700) Attachments.
9 Witkin Cal. Proc. 5th Appeal § 821, Rule Prohibiting Citation or Reliance.
9 Witkin Cal. Proc. 5th Appeal § 822, Reliance Where Review is Granted.
9 Witkin Cal. Proc. 5th Appeal § 824, (S 824) Exceptions.
9 Witkin Cal. Proc. 5th Appeal § 825, Citation of Opinion Available Only in Computer-Based Source of Decisional Law.
9 Witkin Cal. Proc. 5th Appeal § 929, Form and Length Limitations.
9 Witkin Cal. Proc. 5th Appeal § 951, Publication or Nonpublication.
2 Witkin Cal. Proc. 5th Courts § 331, in General.

Rule 8.1120. Requesting publication of unpublished opinions

(a) Request

(1) Any person may request that an unpublished opinion be ordered published.

(2) The request must be made by a letter to the court that rendered the opinion, concisely stating the person's interest and the reason why the opinion meets a standard for publication.

(3) The request must be delivered to the rendering court within 20 days after the opinion is filed.

(4) The request must be served on all parties.

(b) Action by rendering court

(1) If the rendering court does not or cannot grant the request before the decision is final in that court, it must forward the request to the Supreme Court with a copy of its opinion, its recommendation for disposition, and a brief statement of its reasons. The rendering court must forward these materials within 15 days after the decision is final in that court.

(2) The rendering court must also send a copy of its recommendation and reasons to all parties and any person who requested publication.

(c) Action by Supreme Court

The Supreme Court may order the opinion published or deny the request. The court must send notice of its action to the rendering court, all parties, and any person who requested publication.

(d) Effect of Supreme Court order to publish

A Supreme Court order to publish is not an expression of the court's opinion of the correctness of the result of the decision or of any law stated in the opinion. *(Formerly Rule 978, adopted, eff. Jan. 1, 2005. Renumbered Rule 8.1120, eff. Jan. 1, 2007.)*

Advisory Committee Comment

Subdivision (a). This rule previously required generally that a publication request be made "promptly," but in practice the term proved so vague that requests were often made after the Court of Appeal had lost jurisdiction. To assist persons intending to request publication and to give the Court of Appeal adequate time to act, this rule was revised to specify that the request must be made within 20 days after the opinion is filed. The change is substantive.

Subdivision (b). This rule previously did not specify the time within which the Court of Appeal was required to forward to the Supreme Court a publication request that it had not or could not have granted. In practice, however, it was not uncommon for the court to forward such a request after the Supreme Court had denied a petition for review in the same case or, if there was no such petition, had lost jurisdiction to grant review on its own motion. To assist the Supreme Court in timely processing publication requests, therefore, this rule was revised to require the Court of Appeal to forward the request within 15 days after the decision is final in that court. The change is substantive.

Research References

Rutter, Cal. Practice Guide: Civil Appeals & Writs Ch. 11-F, F. Publication of Appellate Opinions.
Rutter, Cal. Practice Guide: Civil Appeals & Writs Ch. 11-G, G. Finality as to Court of Appeal.
9 Witkin Cal. Proc. 5th Appeal § 819, Request for Publication.
2 Witkin Cal. Proc. 5th Courts § 331, in General.

Rule 8.1125. Requesting depublication of published opinions

(a) Request

(1) Any person may request the Supreme Court to order that an opinion certified for publication not be published.

(2) The request must not be made as part of a petition for review, but by a separate letter to the Supreme Court not exceeding 10 pages.

(3) The request must concisely state the person's interest and the reason why the opinion should not be published.

(4) The request must be delivered to the Supreme Court within 30 days after the decision is final in the Court of Appeal.

(5) The request must be served on the rendering court and all parties.

(b) Response

(1) Within 10 days after the Supreme Court receives a request under (a), the rendering court or any person may submit a response supporting or opposing the request. A response submitted by anyone other than the rendering court must state the person's interest.

(2) A response must not exceed 10 pages and must be served on the rendering court, all parties, and any person who requested depublication.

(c) Action by Supreme Court

(1) The Supreme Court may order the opinion depublished or deny the request. It must send notice of its action to the rendering court, all parties, and any person who requested depublication.

(2) The Supreme Court may order an opinion depublished on its own motion, notifying the rendering court of its action.

(d) Effect of Supreme Court order to depublish

A Supreme Court order to depublish is not an expression of the court's opinion of the correctness of the result of the decision or of any law stated in the opinion. *(Formerly Rule 979, adopted, eff. Jan. 1, 2005. Renumbered Rule 8.1125, eff. Jan. 1, 2007.)*

Advisory Committee Comment

Subdivision (a). This subdivision previously required depublication requests to be made "by letter to the Supreme Court," but in practice many were incorporated in petitions for review. To clarify and emphasize the requirement, the subdivision was revised specifically to state that the request "must not be made as part of a petition for review, but by a separate letter to the Supreme Court not exceeding 10 pages." The change is not substantive.

Research References

Rutter, Cal. Practice Guide: Civil Appeals & Writs Ch. 11-F, F. Publication of Appellate Opinions.

Rutter, Cal. Practice Guide: Civil Appeals & Writs Ch. 12-A, A. Overview.

Rutter, Cal. Practice Guide: Civil Appeals & Writs Ch. 12-D, D. Petition and Answer Strategies.

Rutter, Cal. Practice Guide: Civil Appeals & Writs Ch. 13-A, A. General Considerations.

Rutter, Cal. Practice Guide: Civil Appeals & Writs Ch. 13-B, B. Petition for Review Procedures.

9 Witkin Cal. Proc. 5th Appeal § 9, (S 9) Current Structure.

9 Witkin Cal. Proc. 5th Appeal § 817, (S 817) Request for Depublication.

9 Witkin Cal. Proc. 5th Appeal § 818, (S 818) Effect of Order for Depublication.

2 Witkin Cal. Proc. 5th Courts § 195, (S 195) Appellate Rules.

2 Witkin Cal. Proc. 5th Courts § 331, in General.

Title 9

RULES ON LAW PRACTICE, ATTORNEYS, AND JUDGES

Division 1

GENERAL PROVISIONS

Rule
9.1. Title.
9.2. Source.

Rule 9.1.   Title

The rules in this title may be referred to as the Rules on Law Practice, Attorneys, and Judges. *(Adopted, eff. Jan. 1, 2007.)*

Research References

2 Witkin Cal. Proc. 5th Courts § 196, (S 196) Rules on Law Practice, Attorneys, and Judges.

Rule 9.2.   Source

The rules in this title were adopted by the Supreme Court under its inherent authority over the admission and discipline of attorneys and under subdivisions (d) and (f) of section 18 of article VI of the Constitution of the State of California. *(Adopted, eff. Jan. 1, 2007.)*

Research References

2 Witkin Cal. Proc. 5th Courts § 196, (S 196) Rules on Law Practice, Attorneys, and Judges.

Division 2

ATTORNEY ADMISSION AND DISCIPLINARY PROCEEDINGS AND REVIEW OF STATE BAR PROCEEDINGS

Chapter 1

GENERAL PROVISIONS

Rule
9.5.   Definitions.
9.6.   Roll of attorneys admitted to practice.
9.7.   Online reporting by attorneys.

Rule 9.5.   Definitions

As used in this division, unless the context otherwise requires:

(1) "Member" means a member of the State Bar of California.

(2) "State Bar Court" means the Hearing Department or the Review Department established under Business and Professions Code sections 6079.1 and 6086.65.

(3) "Review Department" means the Review Department of the State Bar Court established under Business and Professions Code section 6086.65.

(4) "General Counsel" means the general counsel of the State Bar of California.

(5) "Chief Trial Counsel" means the chief trial counsel of the State Bar of California appointed under Business and Professions Code section 6079.5. *(Formerly Rule 950, adopted, eff. Dec. 1, 1990. Renumbered Rule 9.5 and amended, eff. Jan. 1, 2007.)*

Research References

1 Witkin Cal. Proc. 5th Attorneys § 341, (S 341) Control by Legislature.
1 Witkin Cal. Proc. 5th Attorneys § 613, in General.
2 Witkin Cal. Proc. 5th Courts § 196, (S 196) Rules on Law Practice, Attorneys, and Judges.

Rule 9.6. Roll of attorneys admitted to practice

(a) State Bar to maintain the roll of attorneys

The State Bar must maintain, as part of the official membership records of the State Bar, the Roll of Attorneys of all persons admitted to practice in this state. Such records must include the information specified in Business and Professions Code section 6002.1 and 6064 and other information as directed by the Supreme Court.

(b) Annual State Bar recommendation for one-time expungement of suspension for nonpayment of membership fees

The State Bar is authorized to transmit to the Supreme Court on an annual basis the names of those members who meet all of the following criteria, along with a recommendation that their public record of suspension for nonpayment of membership fees be expunged:

(1) The member has not on any previous occasion obtained an expungement under the terms of this rule;

(2) The suspension was for 90 days or less;

(3) The suspension ended at least seven years before the date of the submission of member's name to the Supreme Court;

(4) The member has no other record of suspension or involuntary inactive enrollment for discipline or otherwise.

(c) Records to be maintained by State Bar

Upon order of the Supreme Court of expungement of a member's record under (b) of this rule, the State Bar will remove or delete the record of such suspension from the member's record. Notwithstanding any other provision of this rule, the State Bar must maintain such internal records as are necessary to apply the terms of (b) of this rule and to report to the Commission on Judicial Nominees Evaluation or appropriate governmental entities involved in judicial elections the member's eligibility for a judgeship under the California Constitution, article VI, section 15.

(d) Duty of disclosure by member

Expungement of a member's suspension under (b) of this rule will not relieve the member of his or her duty to disclose the suspension for purpose of determining the member's eligibility for a judgeship under the California Constitution, article VI, section 15. For all other purposes the suspension expunged under (b) of this rule is deemed not to have occurred and the member may answer accordingly any question relating to his or her membership record.

(e) Authorization for the Board of Governors of the State Bar to adopt rules and regulations

The Board of Governors of the State Bar is authorized to adopt such rules and regulations as it deems necessary and appropriate in order to comply with this rule.

(f) Inherent power of Supreme Court

Nothing in this rule may be construed as affecting the power of the Supreme Court to exercise its inherent power to direct the State Bar to expunge its records. *(Formerly Rule 950.5, adopted, eff. May 1, 1996. Renumbered Rule 9.6 and amended, eff. Jan. 1, 2007. As amended, eff. June 1, 2007.)*

Research References

Rutter, Cal. Practice Guide: Prof. Responsibility Ch. 1-A, A. Sources of Regulation of Practice of Law in California-Overview.
Rutter, Cal. Practice Guide: Prof. Responsibility Ch. 11-A, A. Grounds for Discipline.
2 Witkin Cal. Proc. 5th Courts § 196, (S 196) Rules on Law Practice, Attorneys, and Judges.

Rule 9.7. Online reporting by attorneys

(a) Required information

To maintain the roll of attorneys required by rule 9.6 and to facilitate communications by the State Bar with its members, each member must use an online membership account on a secure system provided by the State Bar to report a current:

(1) Office address and telephone number, or if none, another address; and

(2) An e-mail address not to be disclosed on the State Bar's Web site or otherwise to the public without the member's consent.

(b) Optional information

A member may also use an online membership account to:

(1) Provide an e-mail address for disclosure to the public on the State Bar Web site; and

(2) Provide additional information as authorized by statute, rule or Supreme Court directive, or as requested by the State Bar.

(c) Exclusions

Unless otherwise permitted by law or the Supreme Court, the State Bar may not use e-mail as substitute means of providing a notice required to initiate a State Bar disciplinary or regulatory proceeding or to otherwise change a member's status involuntarily.

(d) Exemption

A member who does not have online access or an e-mail address may claim an exemption from the reporting requirements of this rule. The exemption must be requested in the manner prescribed by the State Bar. *(Adopted, eff. Feb. 1, 2010.)*

Research References

Rutter, Cal. Practice Guide: Prof. Responsibility Ch. 1-A, A. Sources of Regulation of Practice of Law in California-Overview.
Rutter, Cal. Practice Guide: Prof. Responsibility Ch. 11-A, A. Grounds for Discipline.
Rutter, Cal. Practice Guide: Prof. Responsibility Ch. 11-G, G. Commencement of Disciplinary Proceedings.
1 Witkin Cal. Proc. 5th Attorneys § 347, Information Provided by Members.

Chapter 2

ATTORNEY DISCIPLINARY PROCEEDINGS

Rule

9.16.   Grounds for review of State Bar Court decisions in the Supreme Court.

9.17.   Remand with instructions.

9.18.   Effective date of disciplinary orders and decisions.

9.19.   Conditions attached to reprovals.

9.20.   Duties of disbarred, resigned, or suspended attorneys.

9.21.   Resignations of members of the State Bar with disciplinary charges pending.

9.22.   Suspension of members of the State Bar for failure to comply with judgment or order for child or family support.

9.23.   Enforcement as money judgment disciplinary orders directing the payment of costs and disciplinary orders requiring reimbursement of the Client Security Fund.

Rule 9.10.   Authority of the State Bar Court

(a) Conviction proceedings

The State Bar Court exercises statutory powers under Business and Professions Code sections 6101 and 6102 with respect to the discipline of attorneys convicted of crimes. (See Bus. & Prof. Code section 6087.) For purposes of this rule, a judgment of conviction is deemed final when the availability of appeal has been exhausted and the time for filing a petition for certiorari in the United States Supreme Court on direct review of the judgment of conviction has elapsed and no petition has been filed, or if filed the petition has been denied or the judgment of conviction has been affirmed. The State Bar Court must impose or recommend discipline in conviction matters as in other disciplinary proceedings. The power conferred upon the State Bar Court by this rule includes the power to place attorneys on interim suspension under subdivisions (a) and (b) of section 6102, and the power to vacate, delay the effective date of, and temporarily stay the effect of such orders.

(b) Professional responsibility examination

The State Bar Court may:

(1) Extend the time within which a member of the State Bar must take and pass a professional responsibility examination;

(2) Suspend a member for failing to take and pass such examination; and

(3) Vacate a member's suspension for failing to take and pass such examination.

(c) Probation

The State Bar Court for good cause, may:

(1) Approve stipulations between the member and the Chief Trial Counsel for modification of the terms of a member's probation; and

(2) Make corrections and minor modifications to the terms of a member's disciplinary probation.

The order of the State Bar Court must be filed promptly with the Clerk of the Supreme Court.

(d) Rule 9.20 compliance

The State Bar Court for good cause, may extend the time within which a member must comply with the provisions of rule 9.20 of the California Rules of Court.

(e) Commencement of suspension

The State Bar Court for good cause, may delay temporarily the effective date of, or temporarily stay the effect of, an order for a member's disciplinary suspension from practice.

(f) Readmission and reinstatement

Applications for readmission or reinstatement must, in the first instance, be filed and heard by the State Bar Court, except that no applicant who has been disbarred by the Supreme Court on two previous occasions may apply for readmission or reinstatement. Applicants for readmission or reinstatement must:

(1) Pass a professional responsibility examination;

(2) Establish their rehabilitation and present moral qualifications for readmission; and

(3) Establish present ability and learning in the general law. Applicants who resigned without charges pending more than five years before filing an application for reinstatement or readmission must establish present ability and learning in the general law by providing proof, at the time of filing the application, that they have taken and passed the Attorneys' Examination administered by the Committee of Bar Examiners within five years prior to the filing of the application for readmission or reinstatement. Applicants who resigned with charges pending or who were disbarred must establish present ability and learning in the general law by providing proof, at the time of filing the application for readmission or reinstatement, that they have taken and passed the Attorneys' Examination by the Committee of Bar Examiners within three years prior to the filing of the application for readmission or reinstatement.

(g) Inherent power of Supreme Court

Nothing in these rules may be construed as affecting the power of the Supreme Court to exercise its inherent jurisdiction over the lawyer discipline and admissions system. *(Formerly Rule 951, adopted eff. Dec. 1, 1990. As amended, eff. April 1, 1996. Renumbered Rule 9.10 and amended, eff. Jan. 1, 2007. As amended, eff. Jan. 1, 2010.)*

Research References

Rutter, Cal. Practice Guide: Civil Appeals & Writs Ch. 13-G, G. Review of State Bar Discipline Cases.

Rutter, Cal. Practice Guide: Prof. Responsibility Ch. 1-A, A. Sources of Regulation of Practice of Law in California-Overview.

Rutter, Cal. Practice Guide: Prof. Responsibility Ch. 11-C, C. Forum for Disciplinary Proceedings.

Rutter, Cal. Practice Guide: Prof. Responsibility Ch. 11-F, F. Investigation Stage.

Rutter, Cal. Practice Guide: Prof. Responsibility Ch. 11-K, K. Review Procedures.

Rutter, Cal. Practice Guide: Prof. Responsibility Ch. 11-L, L. Determining Appropriate Discipline.

Rutter, Cal. Practice Guide: Prof. Responsibility Ch. 11-M, M. Proceedings Based Upon Criminal Conviction.

Rutter, Cal. Practice Guide: Prof. Responsibility Ch. 11-O, O. Duties Imposed on Disbarred, Suspended and Resigned Attorneys (CRC 9.20).

Rutter, Cal. Practice Guide: Prof. Responsibility Ch. 11-P, P. Probation Proceedings.

Rutter, Cal. Practice Guide: Prof. Responsibility Ch. 11-Q, Q. Reinstatement Proceedings.

1 Witkin Cal. Proc. 5th Attorneys § 2, Statutory and Regulatory Framework.

1 Witkin Cal. Proc. 5th Attorneys § 466, (S 466) in General.

1 Witkin Cal. Proc. 5th Attorneys § 468, (S 468) in General.

1 Witkin Cal. Proc. 5th Attorneys § 470, (S 470) Notice and Opportunity to be Heard.

1 Witkin Cal. Proc. 5th Attorneys § 561, in General.

1 Witkin Cal. Proc. 5th Attorneys § 613, in General.

1 Witkin Cal. Proc. 5th Attorneys § 615, Petition by Disciplined Attorney.

1 Witkin Cal. Proc. 5th Attorneys § 642, (S 642) Modification or Early Termination.

1 Witkin Cal. Proc. 5th Attorneys § 646, (S 646) Procedure.

1 Witkin Cal. Proc. 5th Attorneys § 648, Rehabilitation.

1 Witkin Cal. Proc. 5th Attorneys § 649, Fitness to Practice.

2 Witkin Cal. Proc. 5th Courts § 196, (S 196) Rules on Law Practice, Attorneys, and Judges.

Rule 9.11.   State Bar Court judges

(a) Applicant Evaluation and Nomination Committee

(1) In order to ensure that individuals appointed by the Supreme Court or by the executive or legislative branches have been evaluated objectively, the Supreme Court has established an independent Applicant Evaluation and Nomination Committee to solicit, receive, screen, and evaluate all applications for appointment or reappointment to any appointive position of judge of the State Bar Court (hearing judge, presiding judge, and review department judge). The role of the committee is to determine whether appointees possess not only the statutorily enumerated qualifications, but also any qualifications that may be required by the Supreme Court to assist in the exercise of its ultimate authority over the discipline and admission of attorneys (See *Obrien v. Jones* (2000) 23 Cal.4th 40; *In re Attorney Discipline* (1998) 19 Cal.4th 582; Cal. Const., art VI, sec. 9).

(2) The committee serves at the pleasure of the Supreme Court. It shall consist of seven members appointed by the court of whom four must be members of the State Bar in good standing, two must be retired or active judicial officers, and one must be a public member who has never been a member of the State Bar or admitted to practice before any court in the United States. Two members of the committee must be present members of the Board of Governors of the State Bar (neither of whom may be from the Board's Discipline Committee).

(3) The committee must adopt, and implement upon approval by the Supreme Court, procedures for:

(A) Timely notice to potential applicants of vacancies;

(B) Receipt of applications for appointments to those positions from both incumbents and other qualified persons;

(C) Solicitation and receipt of public comment;

(D) Evaluation and rating of applicants; and

(E) Transmittal of the materials specified in (b) of this rule to the Supreme Court and, as applicable, other appointing authorities.

The procedures adopted by the committee must include provisions to ensure confidentiality comparable to those followed by the Judicial Nominees Evaluation Commission established under Government Code section 12011.5.

(4) The Board of Governors of the State Bar, in consultation with the Supreme Court if necessary, must provide facilities and support staff needed by the committee to carry out its obligations under this rule.

(b) Evaluations

(1) The committee must evaluate the qualifications of and rate all applicants for positions appointed by the Supreme Court and must submit to the Supreme Court the nominations of at least three qualified candidates for each vacancy. Candidates shall be rated as "not recommended," "recommended," and "highly recommended." A rating of "not recommended" relates only to the position under consideration and does not indicate any lack of ability or expertise of the applicant generally. The committee must report in confidence to the Supreme Court its evaluation, rating and recommendation for applicants for appointment and the reasons therefore, including a succinct summary of their qualifications, at a time to be designated by the Supreme Court. The report must include written comments received by the committee, which must be transmitted to the Supreme Court together with the nominations.

(2) The committee must evaluate the qualifications of and rate all applicants for positions appointed by the Governor, the Senate Committee on Rules, or the Speaker of the Assembly, and must submit in confidence to the Supreme Court and, as applicable, to other appointing authorities, all applications for such positions together with the committee's evaluation, rating and recommendation for these applicants, including any written comments received by the committee, at a time to be designated by the Supreme Court.

(3) In determining the qualifications of an applicant for appointment or reappointment the committee must consider, among other appropriate factors, the following: industry, legal and judicial experience (including prior service as a judge of the State Bar Court), judicial temperament, honesty, objectivity, community respect, integrity, and ability. The committee must consider legal work experience broadly, including, but not limited to, litigation and non-litigation experience, legal work for a business or nonprofit entity, experience as a law professor or other academic position, legal work in any of the three branches of government, and legal work in dispute resolution.

The committee shall consider whether an applicant has demonstrated the ability to write cogently and to analyze legal provisions and principles. Among the issues the committee may also consider are 1) the applicant's demonstrated capacity to work independently and to set and meet performance goals, 2) the applicant's knowledge and experience relevant to issues that give rise to the majority of State Bar Court proceedings, including professional ethics and fiduciary obligations, 3) knowledge of practice and demeanor in the courtroom, and (4) whether the applicant has been in practice for 10 or more years. The committee shall accord weight to all experience that has provided the applicant with legal experience and exposure during which the individual has demonstrated the underlying skills necessary to serve as an effective State Bar Court judge. The committee shall apply the same criteria to candidates seeking appointment from all of the appointing authorities. Any evaluation or rating of an applicant and any recommendation for appointment or reappointment by the committee must be made in conformity with Business and Professions Code section 6079.1(b) and in light of the factors specified in Government Code section 12011.5 (d), and those specified in this paragraph.

(4) Upon transmittal of its report to the Supreme Court, the committee must notify any incumbent who has applied for reappointment by the Supreme Court if he or she is or is not among the applicants recommended for appointment to the new term by the committee. The applicable appointing authority must notify as soon as possible an incumbent who has applied for reappointment but is not selected.

(c) Appointments

Only applicants who are rated as recommended or highly recommended by the committee or by the Supreme Court may be appointed. At the request of the Governor, the Senate Committee on Rules, or the Speaker of the Assembly, the Supreme Court will reconsider a finding by the committee that a particular applicant is not recommended. The Supreme Court may make such orders as to the appointment of applicants as it deems appropriate, including extending the term of incumbent judges pending such order or providing for staggered terms.

(d) Discipline for misconduct or disability

A judge of the State Bar Court is subject to discipline or retirement on the same grounds as a judge of a court of this state. Complaints concerning the conduct of a judge of the State Bar Court must be addressed to the Executive Director–Chief Counsel of the Commission on Judicial Performance, who is the Supreme Court's investigator for the purpose of evaluating those complaints, conducting any necessary further investigation, and determining whether formal proceedings should be instituted. If there is reasonable cause to institute formal proceedings, the investigator must notify the Supreme Court of that fact and must serve as or appoint the examiner and make other appointments and arrangements necessary for the hearing. The Supreme Court will then appoint one or more active or retired judges of superior courts or Courts of Appeal as its special master or masters to hear the complaint and the results of the investigation, and to report to the Supreme Court on the resulting findings, conclusions, and recommendations as to discipline. The procedures of the Commission on Judicial Performance must be followed by the investigator and special masters, to the extent feasible. The procedures in the Supreme Court after a discipline recommendation is filed will, to the extent feasible, be the same as the procedures followed when a determination of the Commission on Judicial Performance is filed. *(Formerly Rule 961, adopted, eff. Dec. 1, 1990. As amended, eff. Feb. 15, 1995; July 1, 2000; April 5, 2001. Renumbered Rule 9.11 and amended, eff. Jan. 1, 2007. As amended, eff. Jan. 1, 2009.)*

Research References

Rutter, Cal. Practice Guide: Prof. Responsibility Ch. 11-C, C. Forum for Disciplinary Proceedings.

1 Witkin Cal. Proc. 5th Attorneys § 562, Departments and Officers.

Rule 9.12. Standard of review for State Bar Court Review Department

In reviewing the decisions, orders, or rulings of a hearing judge under rule 301 of the Rules of Procedure of the State Bar of California or such other rule as may be adopted governing the review of any decisions, orders, or rulings by a hearing judge that fully disposes of an entire proceeding, the Review Department of the State Bar Court must independently review the record and may adopt findings, conclusions, and a decision or recommendation different from those of the hearing judge. *(Formerly Rule 951.5, adopted eff. Feb. 23, 2000. Renumbered Rule 9.12 and amended, eff. Jan. 1, 2007.)*

Research References

Rutter, Cal. Practice Guide: Prof. Responsibility Ch. 11-K, K. Review Procedures.

1 Witkin Cal. Proc. 5th Attorneys § 603, (S 603) in General.

Rule 9.13. Review of State Bar Court decisions

(a) Review of recommendation of disbarment or suspension

A petition to the Supreme Court by a member to review a decision of the State Bar Court recommending his or her disbarment or suspension from practice must be filed within 60 days after a certified copy of the decision complained of is filed with the Clerk of the Supreme Court. The State Bar may serve and file an answer to the petition within 15 days of service of the petition. Within 5 days after service of the answer, the petitioner may serve and file a reply. If review is ordered by the Supreme Court, the State Bar must serve and file a supplemental brief within 45 days after the order is filed. Within 15 days of service of the supplemental brief, the petitioner may serve and file a reply brief.

(b) Review of State Bar recommendation to set aside stay of suspension or modify probation

A petition to the Supreme Court by a member to review a recommendation of the State Bar Court that a stay of an order of suspension be set aside or that the duration or conditions of probation be modified on account of a violation of probation must be filed within 15 days after a certified copy of the recommendation complained of is filed with the Clerk of the Supreme Court. Within 15 days after service of the petition, the State Bar may serve and file an answer. Within 5 days after service of the answer, the petitioner may serve and file a reply.

(c) Review of interim decisions

A petition to the Supreme Court by a member to review a decision of the State Bar Court regarding interim suspension, the exercise of powers delegated by rule 9.10(b)–(e), or another interlocutory matter must be filed within 15 days after written notice of the adverse decision of the State Bar Court is mailed by the State Bar to the petitioner and to his or her counsel of record, if any, at their respective addresses under section 6002.1. Within 15 days after service of the petition, the State Bar may serve and file an answer. Within 5 days after service of the answer, the petitioner may serve and file a reply.

(d) Review of other decisions

A petition to the Supreme Court to review any other decision of the State Bar Court or action of the Board of Governors of the State Bar, or of any board or committee appointed by it and authorized to make a determination under the provisions of the State Bar Act, or of the chief executive officer of the State Bar or the designee of the chief executive officer authorized to make a determination under article 10 of the State Bar Act or these rules of court, must be filed within 60 days after written notice of the action complained of is mailed to the petitioner and to his or her counsel of record, if any, at their respective addresses under section 6002.1. Within 15 days after service of the petition, the State Bar may serve and file an answer and brief. Within 5 days after service of the answer and brief, the petitioner may serve and file a reply. If review is ordered by the Supreme Court, the State Bar, within 45 days after filing of the order, may serve and file a supplemental brief. Within 15 days after service of the supplemental brief, the petitioner may file a reply brief.

(e) Contents of petition

(1) A petition to the Supreme Court filed under (a) and (b) of this rule must be verified, must specify the grounds relied upon, must show that review within the State Bar Court has been exhausted, must address why review is appropriate under one or more of the grounds specified in rule 9.16, and must have attached a copy of the State Bar Court decision from which relief is sought.

(2) When review is sought under (c) and (d) of this rule, the petition must also be accompanied by a record adequate to permit review of the ruling, including:

(A) Legible copies of all documents and exhibits submitted to the State Bar Court supporting and opposing petitioner's position;

(B) Legible copies of all other documents submitted to the State Bar Court that are necessary for a complete understanding of the case and the ruling; and

(C) A transcript of the proceedings in the State Bar Court leading to the decision or, if a transcript is unavailable, a declaration by counsel explaining why a transcript is unavailable and fairly summarizing the proceedings, including arguments by counsel and the basis of the State Bar Court's decision, if stated; or a declaration by counsel stating that the transcript has been ordered, the date it was ordered, and the date it is expected to be filed, which must be a date before any action is requested from the Supreme Court other than issuance of a stay supported by other parts of the record.

(3) A petitioner who requests an immediate stay must explain in the petition the reasons for the urgency and set forth all relevant time constraints.

(4) If a petitioner does not submit the required record, the court may summarily deny the stay request, the petition, or both.

(f) Service

All petitions, briefs, reply briefs, and other pleadings filed by a petitioner under this rule must be accompanied by proof of service of three copies on the General Counsel of the State Bar at the San Francisco office of the State Bar, and of one copy on the Clerk of the State Bar Court at the Los Angeles office of the State Bar Court. The State Bar must serve the member at his or her address under Business and Professions Code section 6002.1, and his or her counsel of record, if any. *(Formerly Rule 59,*

Ct. Rules

adopted by Supreme Court, eff. April 20, 1943; adopted by Judicial Council, eff. July 1, 1943. As amended eff. July 1, 1968. Renumbered Rule 952 and amended eff. Oct. 1, 1973. As amended, eff. Jan. 1, 1976; May 1, 1986; April 2, 1987; Dec. 1, 1990; Feb. 1, 1991; March 15, 1991. Renumbered Rule 9.13 and amended, eff. Jan. 1, 2007.)

Research References

Rutter, Cal. Practice Guide: Civil Appeals & Writs Ch. 13-G, G. Review of State Bar Discipline Cases.
Rutter, Cal. Practice Guide: Prof. Responsibility Ch. 1-A, A. Sources of Regulation of Practice of Law in California-Overview.
Rutter, Cal. Practice Guide: Prof. Responsibility Ch. 1-B, B. Regulation of Admission to Practice Law.
Rutter, Cal. Practice Guide: Prof. Responsibility Ch. 11-K, K. Review Procedures.
Rutter, Cal. Practice Guide: Prof. Responsibility Ch. 11-M, M. Proceedings Based Upon Criminal Conviction.
3 Witkin Cal. Proc. 5th Actions § 445, (S 445) Other Statutory Time Limits.
1 Witkin Cal. Proc. 5th Attorneys § 31, Investigation and Proceedings Against Corporation.
1 Witkin Cal. Proc. 5th Attorneys § 363, Rights of Unsuccessful Applicants.
1 Witkin Cal. Proc. 5th Attorneys § 367, Review of Committee's Decision.
1 Witkin Cal. Proc. 5th Attorneys § 471, (S 471) Review of State Bar Court Decision.
1 Witkin Cal. Proc. 5th Attorneys § 552, Inherent Power.
1 Witkin Cal. Proc. 5th Attorneys § 613, in General.
1 Witkin Cal. Proc. 5th Attorneys § 615, Petition by Disciplined Attorney.
1 Witkin Cal. Proc. 5th Attorneys § 616, Petition by Chief Trial Counsel.
1 Witkin Cal. Proc. 5th Attorneys § 619, (S 619) Order.
1 Witkin Cal. Proc. 5th Attorneys § 643, (S 643) Revocation.
2 Witkin Cal. Proc. 5th Courts § 215, Limitations on Grant.
2 Witkin Cal. Proc. 5th Courts § 330, (S 330) Original Jurisdiction.
8 Witkin Cal. Proc. 5th Extraordinary Writs § 11, (S 11) State Bar Court Decisions.

Rule 9.14. Petitions for review by the Chief Trial Counsel

(a) Time for filing

The Chief Trial Counsel may petition for review of recommendations and decisions of the State Bar Court as follows:

(1) From recommendations that a member be suspended, within 60 days of the date the recommendation is filed with the Supreme Court.

(2) From recommendations that the duration or conditions of probation be modified, or a reinstatement application be granted, within 15 days of the date the recommendation is filed with the Supreme Court.

(3) From decisions not to place an eligible member on interim suspension, or vacating interim suspension, or a denial of a petition brought under section 6007(c), within 15 days of notice under the rules adopted by the State Bar.

(4) From decisions dismissing disciplinary proceedings or recommending approval, within 60 days of notice under the rules adopted by the State Bar.

(b) Procedures

Proceedings under this rule with regard to briefing, service of process, and applicable time periods therefor must correspond to proceedings brought under rule 9.13, except that the rights and duties of the member and the State Bar under that rule are reversed. *(Formerly Rule 952.5, adopted by Supreme Court, eff. Dec. 1, 1990; adopted by Judicial Council, eff. March 15, 1991. Renumbered Rule 9.14 and amended, eff. Jan. 1, 2007.)*

Research References

Rutter, Cal. Practice Guide: Civil Appeals & Writs Ch. 13-G, G. Review of State Bar Discipline Cases.
Rutter, Cal. Practice Guide: Prof. Responsibility Ch. 11-K, K. Review Procedures.
1 Witkin Cal. Proc. 5th Attorneys § 616, Petition by Chief Trial Counsel.
1 Witkin Cal. Proc. 5th Attorneys § 619, (S 619) Order.

Rule 9.15. Petitions for review by the Committee of Bar Examiners; grounds for review; confidentiality

(a) Petition for review by the Committee of Bar Examiners

The Committee of Bar Examiners may petition for review of the decision of the Review Department of the State Bar Court in moral character proceedings. All petitions under this rule must be filed with the Clerk of the Supreme Court within 60 days after the State Bar Court decision is filed and served on the General Counsel of the State Bar at the San Francisco office of the State Bar. The applicant may file and serve an answer within 15 days of service of the petition. Within 5 days after service of the answer the Committee of Bar Examiners may serve and file a reply. If review is ordered by the Supreme Court, within 45 days after filing of the order, the applicant may file a supplemental brief. Within 15 days after service of the supplemental brief, the petitioner may serve and file a reply brief.

(b) Contents of petition

A petition to the Supreme Court filed under this rule must show that review within the State Bar Court has been exhausted, must address why review is appropriate under one or more of the grounds specified in rule 9.16, and must have attached a copy of the State Bar Court decision for which review is sought.

(c) Service

All petitions, briefs, reply briefs, and other pleadings filed by the Committee of Bar Examiners must include a proof of service by mail to the applicant's last address provided to the State Bar or the applicant's attorney of record, if any. Filings by the applicant must include a proof of service of three copies on the General Counsel of the State Bar at the San Francisco office of the State Bar and one copy on the Clerk of the State Bar Court at the Los Angeles office of the State Bar Court.

(d) Confidentiality

All filings under this rule are confidential unless: (1) the applicant waives confidentiality in writing; or (2) the Supreme Court grants review. Once the Supreme Court grants review, filings under this rule are open to the public; however, if good cause exists, the Supreme Court may order portions of the record or the identity of witnesses or other third parties to the proceedings to remain confidential. *(Formerly Rule 952.6, adopted, eff. July 1, 1993. As amended, eff. April 20, 1998. Renumbered Rule 9.15 and amended, eff. Jan. 1, 2007.)*

Research References

Rutter, Cal. Practice Guide: Civil Appeals & Writs Ch. 13-G, G. Review of State Bar Discipline Cases.
1 Witkin Cal. Proc. 5th Attorneys § 367, Review of Committee's Decision.
1 Witkin Cal. Proc. 5th Attorneys § 617, Petition by Committee of Bar Examiners.

Rule 9.16. Grounds for review of State Bar Court decisions in the Supreme Court

(a) Grounds

The Supreme Court will order review of a decision of the State Bar Court recommending disbarment or suspension from practice when it appears:

(1) Necessary to settle important questions of law;

(2) The State Bar Court has acted without or in excess of jurisdiction;

(3) Petitioner did not receive a fair hearing;

(4) The decision is not supported by the weight of the evidence; or

(5) The recommended discipline is not appropriate in light of the record as a whole.

(b) Denial of review

Denial of review of a decision of the State Bar Court is a final judicial determination on the merits and the recommendation of the State Bar Court will be filed as an order of the Supreme Court. *(Formerly Rule 954, adopted, eff. Feb. 1, 1991. Renumbered Rule 9.16 and amended, eff. Jan. 1, 2007.)*

Research References

Rutter, Cal. Practice Guide: Civil Appeals & Writs Ch. 13-G, G. Review of State Bar Discipline Cases.
Rutter, Cal. Practice Guide: Prof. Responsibility Ch. 11-K, K. Review Procedures.
1 Witkin Cal. Proc. 5th Attorneys § 613, in General.
1 Witkin Cal. Proc. 5th Attorneys § 615, Petition by Disciplined Attorney.
1 Witkin Cal. Proc. 5th Attorneys § 617, Petition by Committee of Bar Examiners.
1 Witkin Cal. Proc. 5th Attorneys § 619, (S 619) Order.

Rule 9.17.   Remand with instructions

At any time before the final disposition of a decision of the State Bar Court filed under Business and Professions Code section 6081, the Supreme Court may remand the matter to the State Bar Court with instructions to conduct such further proceedings as the Supreme Court deems necessary. *(Formerly Rule 953.5, adopted, eff. Feb. 1, 1991. Renumbered Rule 9.17 and amended, eff. Jan. 1, 2007.)*

Research References

Rutter, Cal. Practice Guide: Civil Appeals & Writs Ch. 13-G, G. Review of State Bar Discipline Cases.
1 Witkin Cal. Proc. 5th Attorneys § 619, (S 619) Order.

Rule 9.18.   Effective date of disciplinary orders and decisions

(a) Effective date of Supreme Court orders

Unless otherwise ordered, all orders of the Supreme Court imposing discipline or opinions deciding causes involving the State Bar become final 30 days after filing. The Supreme Court may grant a rehearing at any time before the decision or order becomes final. Petitions for rehearing may be filed within 15 days of the date the decision or order was filed. Unless otherwise ordered, when petitions for review under rules 9.13(c) and 9.14(a)(3) are acted upon summarily, the orders of the Supreme Court are final forthwith and do not have law-of-the-case effect in subsequent proceedings in the Supreme Court.

(b) Effect of State Bar Court orders when no review sought

Unless otherwise ordered, if no petition for review is filed within the time allowed by rule 9.13(a), (b), and (d), or rule 9.14(a)(1) and (2), as to a recommendation of the State Bar Court for the disbarment, suspension, or reinstatement of a member, the vacation of a stay, or modification of the duration or conditions of a probation, the recommendation of the State Bar Court will be filed as an order of the Supreme Court following the expiration of the time for filing a timely petition. The Clerk of the Supreme Court will mail notice of this effect to the member and his or her attorney of record, if any, at their respective addresses under Business and Professions Code section 6002.1 and to the State Bar.

(c) Effect of State Bar Court orders in moral character proceedings when no review sought

Unless otherwise ordered, if no petition for review is filed within the time allowed by rule 9.15(a), as to a recommendation of the State Bar Court in moral character proceedings, the recommendation of the State Bar Court will be filed as an order of the Supreme Court following the expiration of the time for filing a timely petition. The Clerk of the Supreme Court will mail notice of this effect to the applicant's last address provided to the State Bar or to the applicant's attorney of record, if any, and to the State Bar. *(Formerly Rule 953, adopted by Supreme Court, eff. Dec. 1, 1990; adopted by Judicial Council, eff. March 15, 1991. As amended, eff. Feb. 1, 1996. Renumbered Rule 9.18 and amended, eff. Jan. 1, 2007.)*

Research References

Rutter, Cal. Practice Guide: Civil Appeals & Writs Ch. 13-G, G. Review of State Bar Discipline Cases.
1 Witkin Cal. Proc. 5th Attorneys § 619, (S 619) Order.

Rule 9.19.   Conditions attached to reprovals

(a) Attachment of conditions to reprovals

The State Bar may attach conditions, effective for a reasonable time, to a public or private reproval administered upon a member of the State Bar. Conditions so attached must be based on a finding by the State Bar that protection of the public and the interests of the member will be served thereby. The State Bar when administering the reproval must give notice to the member that failure to comply with the conditions may be punishable.

(b) Sanctions for failure to comply

A member's failure to comply with conditions attached to a public or private reproval may be cause for a separate proceeding for willful breach of rule 9-101 of the Rules of Professional Conduct. *(Formerly Rule 956, adopted, eff. Nov. 18, 1983. As amended, eff. Nov. 22, 2002. Renumbered Rule 9.19 and amended, eff. Jan. 1, 2007.)*

Research References

Rutter, Cal. Practice Guide: Prof. Responsibility Ch. 11-A, A. Grounds for Discipline.
Rutter, Cal. Practice Guide: Prof. Responsibility Ch. 11-L, L. Determining Appropriate Discipline.
1 Witkin Cal. Proc. 5th Attorneys § 411, in General (Rules 1-100 to 1-120).
1 Witkin Cal. Proc. 5th Attorneys § 601, (S 601) Discipline.

Rule 9.20.   Duties of disbarred, resigned, or suspended attorneys

(a) Disbarment, suspension, and resignation orders

The Supreme Court may include in an order disbarring or suspending a member of the State Bar, or accepting his or her resignation, a direction that the member must, within such time limits as the Supreme Court may prescribe:

(1) Notify all clients being represented in pending matters and any co-counsel of his or her disbarment, suspension, or resignation and his or her consequent disqualification to act as an attorney after the effective date of the disbarment, suspension, or resignation, and, in the absence of co-counsel, also notify the clients to seek legal advice elsewhere, calling attention to any urgency in seeking the substitution of another attorney or attorneys;

(2) Deliver to all clients being represented in pending matters any papers or other property to which the clients are entitled, or notify the clients and any co-counsel of a suitable time and place where the papers and other property may be obtained, calling

attention to any urgency for obtaining the papers or other property;

(3) Refund any part of fees paid that have not been earned; and

(4) Notify opposing counsel in pending litigation or, in the absence of counsel, the adverse parties of the disbarment, suspension, or resignation and consequent disqualification to act as an attorney after the effective date of the disbarment, suspension, or resignation, and file a copy of the notice with the court, agency, or tribunal before which the litigation is pending for inclusion in the respective file or files.

(b) Notices to clients, co-counsel, opposing counsel, and adverse parties

All notices required by an order of the Supreme Court or the State Bar Court under this rule must be given by registered or certified mail, return receipt requested, and must contain an address where communications may be directed to the disbarred, suspended, or resigned member.

(c) Filing proof of compliance

Within such time as the order may prescribe after the effective date of the member's disbarment, suspension, or resignation, the member must file with the Clerk of the State Bar Court an affidavit showing that he or she has fully complied with those provisions of the order entered under this rule. The affidavit must also specify an address where communications may be directed to the disbarred, suspended, or resigned member.

(d) Sanctions for failure to comply

A disbarred or resigned member's willful failure to comply with the provisions of this rule is a ground for denying his or her application for reinstatement or readmission. A suspended member's willful failure to comply with the provisions of this rule is a cause for disbarment or suspension and for revocation of any pending probation. Additionally, such failure may be punished as a contempt or a crime. *(Formerly Rule 955, adopted, eff. April 4, 1973. As amended, eff. Dec. 1, 1990. Renumbered Rule 9.20 and amended, eff. Jan. 1, 2007.)*

Research References

Rutter, Cal. Practice Guide: Prof. Responsibility Ch. 1-D, D. Unauthorized Practice of Law.
Rutter, Cal. Practice Guide: Prof. Responsibility Ch. 6-B, B. Elements of Attorney Competence.
Rutter, Cal. Practice Guide: Prof. Responsibility Ch. 10-C, C. Termination by Operation of Law.
Rutter, Cal. Practice Guide: Prof. Responsibility Ch. 11-A, A. Grounds for Discipline.
Rutter, Cal. Practice Guide: Prof. Responsibility Ch. 11-F, F. Investigation Stage.
Rutter, Cal. Practice Guide: Prof. Responsibility Ch. 11-L, L. Determining Appropriate Discipline.
Rutter, Cal. Practice Guide: Prof. Responsibility Ch. 11-O, O. Duties Imposed on Disbarred, Suspended and Resigned Attorneys (CRC 9.20).
Rutter, Cal. Practice Guide: Prof. Responsibility Ch. 1-D , Outline D.
Rutter, Cal. Practice Guide: Prof. Responsibility Ch. 11-F , Outline F.
Rutter, Cal. Practice Guide: Prof. Responsibility Ch. 11-L , Outline L.
Rutter, Cal. Practice Guide: Prof. Responsibility Ch. 11-O , Outline O.
1 Witkin Cal. Proc. 5th Attorneys § 82, Notice of Discipline.
1 Witkin Cal. Proc. 5th Attorneys § 83, (S 83) Nature and Scope of Statutes.
1 Witkin Cal. Proc. 5th Attorneys § 347, Information Provided by Members.
1 Witkin Cal. Proc. 5th Attorneys § 403, Criminal Penalties.
1 Witkin Cal. Proc. 5th Attorneys § 561, in General.
1 Witkin Cal. Proc. 5th Attorneys § 611, (S 611) Increase in Punishment.

Rule 9.21. Resignations of members of the State Bar with disciplinary charges pending

(a) General provisions

A member of the State Bar against whom disciplinary charges are pending may tender a written resignation from membership in the State Bar and relinquishment of the right to practice law. The written resignation must be signed and dated by the member at the time it is tendered and must be tendered to the Office of the Clerk, State Bar Court, 1149 South Hill Street, Los Angeles, California 90015. The resignation must be substantially in the form specified in (b) of this rule. In submitting a resignation under this rule, a member of the State Bar agrees to be transferred to inactive membership in the State Bar effective on the filing of the resignation by the State Bar. Within 30 days after filing of the resignation, the member must perform the acts specified in rule 9.20(a)(1)–(4) and (b) and within 40 days after filing of the resignation, the member must file with the Office of the Clerk, State Bar Court, at the above address, the proof of compliance specified in rule 9.20(c). No resignation is effective unless and until it is accepted by the Supreme Court after consideration and recommendation by the State Bar Court.

Text of subd. (b) effective until Jan. 1, 2014.

(b) Form of resignation

The member's written resignation must be in substantially the following form:

"I, *[name of member],* against whom charges are pending, hereby resign as a member of the State Bar of California and relinquish all right to practice law in the State of California. I agree that, in the event that this resignation is accepted and I later file a petition for reinstatement, the State Bar will consider in connection therewith all disciplinary matters and proceedings against me at the time this resignation is accepted, in addition to other appropriate matters. I also agree that the Supreme Court may decline to accept my resignation unless I reach agreement with the Chief Trial Counsel on a written stipulation as to facts and conclusions of law regarding the disciplinary matters and proceedings that were pending against me at the time of my resignation. I further agree that, on the filing of this resignation by the Office of the Clerk, State Bar Court, I will be transferred to inactive membership of the State Bar. On such transfer, I acknowledge that I will be ineligible to practice law or to advertise or hold myself out as practicing or as entitled to practice law. I further agree that, within 30 days of the filing of the resignation by the Office of the Clerk, State Bar Court, I will perform the acts specified in rule 9.20(a)–(b) of the California Rules of Court, and within 40 days of the date of filing of this resignation by the Office of the Clerk, State Bar Court, I will notify that office as specified in rule 9.20(c) of the California Rules of Court."

Text of subd. (b) effective Jan. 1, 2014.

(b) Form of resignation

The member's written resignation must be in substantially the following form:

"I, *[name of member]* against whom charges are pending, hereby resign as a member of the State Bar of California and relinquish all right to practice law in the State of California. I agree that, in the event that this resignation is accepted and I later file a petition for reinstatement, the State Bar will consider in connection therewith all disciplinary matters and proceedings against me at the time this resignation is accepted, in addition to other appropriate matters. I also agree that the Supreme Court may decline to accept my resignation unless I reach agreement with the Chief Trial Counsel on a written stipulation as to facts and conclusions of law regarding the disciplinary matters and proceedings that were pending against me at the time of my resignation. I further agree that, on the filing of this resignation by the Office of the Clerk, State Bar Court, I will be transferred to inactive membership of the State Bar. On such transfer, I acknowledge that I will be ineligible to practice law or to advertise or hold myself out as practicing or as entitled to practice law. I further acknowledge that in the event the Supreme Court does not accept my resignation, I will remain an inactive member of the State Bar, pending any further order of the Supreme Court or the State Bar Court. I further agree that, within 30 days of the filing of the resignation by the Office of the Clerk, State Bar Court, I will perform the acts specified in rule 9.20(a)–(b) of the California Rules of Court, and within 40 days of the date of filing of this resignation by the Office of the Clerk, State Bar Court, I will notify that office as specified in rule 9.20(c) of the California Rules of Court.

(c) Consideration of resignation by State Bar Court and Supreme Court

When the Office of the Clerk of the State Bar Court receives a member's resignation tendered in conformity with this rule, it must promptly file the resignation. The State Bar Court must thereafter consider the member's resignation and the stipulated facts and conclusions of law, if any, agreed upon between the member and the Chief Trial Counsel, and must recommend to the Supreme Court whether the resignation should be accepted. The State Bars Court's recommendation must be made in light of the grounds set forth in subsection (d) of this rule and, if the State Bar Court recommends acceptance of the resignation notwithstanding the existence of one or more of the grounds set forth in subsection (d), the State Bar Court's recommendation must include an explanation of the reasons for the recommendation that the resignation be accepted. The Office of the Clerk of the State Bar Court must transmit to the Clerk of the Supreme Court, three certified copies of the State Bar Court's recommendation together with the member's resignation, when, by the terms of the State Bar Court's recommendation, the resignation should be transmitted to the Supreme Court.

(d) Grounds for rejection of resignation by the Supreme Court

The Supreme Court will make such orders concerning the member's resignation as it deems appropriate. The Supreme Court may decline to accept the resignation based on a report by the State Bar Court that:

(1) Preservation of necessary testimony is not complete;

(2) After transfer to inactive status, the member has practiced law or has advertised or held himself or herself out as entitled to practice law;

(3) The member has failed to perform the acts specified by rule 9.20(a)–(b);

(4) The member has failed to provide proof of compliance as specified in rule 9.20(c);

(5) The Supreme Court has filed an order of disbarment as to the member;

(6) The State Bar Court has filed a decision or opinion recommending the member's disbarment;

(7) The member has previously resigned or has been disbarred and reinstated to the practice of law;

(8) The member and the Chief Trial Counsel have not reached agreement on a written stipulation as to facts and conclusions of law regarding the disciplinary matters and proceedings that were pending against the member at the time the resignation was tendered; or

(9) Acceptance of the resignation of the member will reasonably be inconsistent with the need to protect the public, the courts, or the legal profession.

(e) Rejection of resignation by the Supreme Court

A member whose resignation with charges pending is not accepted by the Supreme Court will remain an inactive member of the State Bar. The member may move the Review Department of the State Bar Court to be restored to active membership, at which time the Office of the Chief Trial Counsel may demonstrate any basis for the member's continued ineligibility to practice law. The Review Department will expedite a motion to be restored to active membership. Any return to active membership will be conditioned on the member's payment of any due, penalty payments, and restitution owed by the member. *(Formerly Rule 960, adopted, eff. Dec. 14, 1984. Renumbered Rule 9.21 and amended, eff. Jan. 1, 2007. As amended, eff. Jan. 1, 2010; Jan. 1, 2014.)*

Research References

Rutter, Cal. Practice Guide: Prof. Responsibility Ch. 11-B, B. Disciplinary Proceedings-In General.

Rutter, Cal. Practice Guide: Prof. Responsibility Ch. 11-F, F. Investigation Stage.

Rutter, Cal. Practice Guide: Prof. Responsibility Ch. 11-L, L. Determining Appropriate Discipline.

1 Witkin Cal. Proc. 5th Attorneys § 631, Perpetuation of Testimony on Resignation.

Rule 9.22.   Suspension of members of the State Bar for failure to comply with judgment or order for child or family support

(a) Annual State Bar recommendation for suspension of delinquent members

Under Family Code section 17520, the State Bar is authorized to transmit to the Supreme Court on an annual basis the names of those members listed by the State Department of Social Services as delinquent in their payments of court-ordered child or family support with a recommendation for their suspension from the practice of law.

(b) Condition for reinstatement of suspended members

A member suspended under this rule may be reinstated only after receipt by the Supreme Court of notification from the State Bar that the member's name has been removed from the State Department of Social Services list.

(c) Additional recommendation for suspension by the State Bar

Under Family Code section 17520(*l*), the State Bar is further authorized to promptly transmit to the Supreme Court with a recommendation for their suspension from the practice of law the names of those members previously listed by the State Department of Social Services as delinquent in their payments of court-ordered child or family support, who obtained releases under Family Code section 17520(h), and who have subsequently been identified by the Department of Social Services as again being delinquent.

(d) Authorization for the Board of Governors of the State Bar to adopt rules and regulations

The Board of Governors of the State Bar is authorized to adopt such rules and regulations as it deems necessary and appropriate in order to comply with this rule. The rules and regulations of the State Bar must contain procedures governing the notification, suspension, and reinstatement of members of the State Bar in a manner not inconsistent with Family Code section 17520. *(Formerly Rule 962, adopted, eff. Jan. 31, 1993. As amended, eff. April 1, 1996. Renumbered Rule 9.22 and amended, eff. Jan. 1, 2007.)*

Research References

Rutter, Cal. Practice Guide: Family Law Ch. 6-A, A. Child Support.

Rutter, Cal. Practice Guide: Prof. Responsibility Ch. 11-A, A. Grounds for Discipline.

1 Witkin Cal. Proc. 5th Attorneys § 499, Noncompliance With Support Judgment or Order.

2 Witkin Cal. Proc. 5th Courts § 196, (S 196) Rules on Law Practice, Attorneys, and Judges.

11 Witkin, California Summary 10th Husband and Wife § 338, (S 338) Nonissuance, Nonrenewal, or Suspension of License.

Rule 9.23. Enforcement as money judgment disciplinary orders directing the payment of costs and disciplinary orders requiring reimbursement of the Client Security Fund

(a) Authority to obtain money judgment

Under Business and Professions Code section 6086.10(a) the State Bar is authorized to enforce as a money judgment any disciplinary order assessing costs. Under Business and Professions Code section 6140.5(d) the State Bar is authorized to enforce as a money judgment any disciplinary order requiring reimbursement of the State Bar Client Security Fund.

(b) Duty of clerk of the superior court

The State Bar may file a certified copy of a final disciplinary order assessing costs or requiring reimbursement of the Client Security Fund, along with a certified copy of the certificate of costs and any record of Client Security Fund payments and costs, with the clerk of the superior court of any county. The clerk must immediately enter judgment in conformity with the order.

(c) Compromise of judgment

Motions for the compromise of any judgment entered under this rule must, in the first instance, be filed and heard by the State Bar Court.

(d) Power of the Supreme Court

Nothing in this rule may be construed as affecting the power of the Supreme Court to alter the amounts owed. *(Adopted, eff. April 1, 2007.)*

Research References

Rutter, Cal. Practice Guide: Prof. Responsibility Ch. 11-I, I. Trial Proceedings.

1 Witkin Cal. Proc. 5th Attorneys § 602, (S 602) Costs and Sanctions.

Chapter 3

LEGAL EDUCATION

Rule

9.30.   Law school study in schools other than those accredited by the examining committee.

9.31.   Minimum continuing legal education.

Rule 9.30. Law school study in schools other than those accredited by the examining committee

(a) Receipt of credit

A person who seeks to be certified to the Supreme Court for admission in and licensed to practice law under section 6060(e)(2) of the Business and Professions Code may receive credit for:

(1) Study in a law school in the United States other than one accredited by the examining committee established by the Board of Governors of the State Bar under Business and Professions Code section 6046 only if the law school satisfies the requirements of (b) or (c) of this rule; or

(2) Instruction in law from a correspondence school only if the correspondence school requires 864 hours of preparation and study per year for four years and satisfies the requirements of (d) of this rule; or

(3) Study in a law school outside the United States other than one accredited by the examining committee established by the Board of Governors of the State Bar under Business and Professions Code section 6046 only if the examining committee is satisfied that the academic program of such law school is substantially equivalent to that of a law school qualified under (b) of this rule.

(b) Requirements for unaccredited law schools in state

A law school in this state that is not accredited by the examining committee must:

(1) Be authorized to confer professional degrees by the laws of this state;

(2) Maintain a regular course of instruction in law, with a specified curriculum and regularly scheduled class sessions;

(3) Require classroom attendance of its students for a minimum of 270 hours a year for at least four years, and further require regular attendance of each student at not less than 80 percent of the regularly scheduled class hours in each course in which such student was enrolled and maintain attendance records adequate to determine each student's compliance with these requirements;

(4) Maintain, in a fixed location, physical facilities capable of accommodating the classes scheduled for that location;

(5) Have an adequate faculty of instructors in law. The faculty will prima facie be deemed adequate if at least 80 percent of the instruction in each academic period is by persons who possess one or more of the following qualifications:

(A) Admission to the general practice of the law in any jurisdiction in the United States;

(B) Judge of a United States court or a court of record in any jurisdiction in the United States; or

(C) Graduation from a law school accredited by the examining committee.

(6) Own and maintain a library consisting of not less than the following sets of books, all of which must be current and complete:

(A) The published reports of the decisions of California courts, with advance sheets and citator;

(B) A digest or encyclopedia of California law;

(C) An annotated set of the California codes; and

(D) A current, standard text or treatise for each course or subject in the curriculum of the school for which such a text or treatise is available.

(7) Establish and maintain standards for academic achievement, advancement in good standing and graduation, and provide for periodic testing of all students to determine the quality of their performance in relation to such standards; and

(8) Register with the examining committee, and maintain such records (available for inspection by the examining committee) and file with the examining committee such reports, notices, and certifications as may be required by the rules of the examining committee.

(c) Requirements for unaccredited law schools outside the state

A law school in the United States that is outside the state of California and is not accredited by the examining committee must:

(1) Be authorized to confer professional degrees by the law of the state in which it is located;

(2) Comply with (b)(2), (3), (4), (5), (7), and (8) of this rule; and

(3) Own and maintain a library that is comparable in content to that specified in (b)(6) of this rule.

(d) Registration and reports

A correspondence law school must register with the examining committee and file such reports, notices, and certifications as may be required by the rules of the examining committee concerning any person whose mailing address is in the state of California or whose application to, contract with, or correspondence with or from the law school indicates that the instruction by correspondence is for the purpose or with the intent of qualifying that person for admission to practice law in California.

(e) Inspections

The examining committee may make such inspection of law schools not accredited by the committee or correspondence schools as may be necessary or proper to give effect to the provisions of Business and Professions Code section 6060, this rule, and the rules of the examining committee.

(f) Application

This rule does not apply to any person who, on the effective date of the rule, had commenced the study of law in a manner authorized by Business and Professions Code section 6060(e) and registered as a law student before January 1, 1976 (as provided in Business and Professions Code section 6060(d) and otherwise satisfies the requirements of Business and Professions Code section 6060(e), provided that after January 1, 1976, credit will be given such person for any study in an unaccredited law school or by correspondence only if the school complies with the requirements of (b)(8) or (d) of this rule, whichever is applicable, and permits inspection under (e) of this rule. *(Formerly Rule 957, adopted, eff. Oct. 8, 1975. As amended, eff. April 2, 1984. Renumbered Rule 9.30 and amended, eff. Jan. 1, 2007.)*

Research References

Rutter, Cal. Practice Guide: Prof. Responsibility Ch. 1-B, B. Regulation of Admission to Practice Law.
1 Witkin Cal. Proc. 5th Attorneys § 360, (S 360) Eligibility for Bar Examination.
2 Witkin Cal. Proc. 5th Courts § 196, (S 196) Rules on Law Practice, Attorneys, and Judges.

Rule 9.31. Minimum continuing legal education

(a) Statutory authorization

This rule is adopted under Business and Professions Code section 6070.

(b) State Bar minimum continuing legal education program

The State Bar must establish and administer a minimum continuing legal education program under rules adopted by the Board of Governors of the State Bar. These rules may provide for carryforward of excess credit hours, staggering of the education requirement for implementation purposes, and retroactive credit for legal education.

(c) Minimum continuing legal education requirements

Each active member of the State Bar (1) not exempt under Business and Professions Code section 6070, (2) not a full-time employee of the United States Government, its departments, agencies, and public corporations, acting within the scope of his or her employment, and (3) not otherwise exempt under rules adopted by the Board of Governors of the State Bar, must, within 36–month periods designated by the State Bar, complete at least 25 hours of legal education approved by the State Bar or offered by a State Bar-approved provider. Four of those hours must address legal ethics. Members may be required to complete legal education in other specified areas within the 25–hour requirement under rules adopted by the State Bar. Each active member must report his or her compliance to the State Bar under rules adopted by the Board of Governors of the State Bar.

(d) Failure to comply with program

A member of the State Bar who fails to satisfy the requirements of the State Bar's minimum continuing legal education program must be enrolled as an inactive member of the State Bar under rules adopted by the Board of Governors of the State Bar.

(e) Fees and penalties

The State Bar has the authority to set and collect appropriate fees and penalties. *(Formerly Rule 958, adopted, eff. Dec. 6, 1990. As amended, eff. Nov. 25, 1992; Sept. 27, 2000. Renumbered Rule 9.31 and amended, eff. Jan. 1, 2007.)*

Research References

Rutter, Cal. Practice Guide: Prof. Responsibility Ch. 1-D, D. Unauthorized Practice of Law.
Rutter, Cal. Practice Guide: Prof. Responsibility Ch. 1-M, M. Minimum Continuing Legal Education ("MCLE").
Rutter, Cal. Practice Guide: Prof. Responsibility Ch. 6-B, B. Elements of Attorney Competence.
1 Witkin Cal. Proc. 5th Attorneys § 2, Statutory and Regulatory Framework.
1 Witkin Cal. Proc. 5th Attorneys § 406, Mandatory Continuing Legal Education.
2 Witkin Cal. Proc. 5th Courts § 196, (S 196) Rules on Law Practice, Attorneys, and Judges.

Division 3

LEGAL SPECIALISTS

Rule
9.35. Certified legal specialists.

Rule 9.35. Certified legal specialists

(a) Definition

A "certified specialist" is a California attorney who holds a current certificate as a specialist issued by the State Bar of California Board of Legal Specialization or any other entity approved by the State Bar to designate specialists.

(b) State Bar Legal Specialization Program

The State Bar must establish and administer a program for certifying legal specialists and may establish a program for certifying entities that certify legal specialists under rules adopted by the Board of Governors of the State Bar.

(c) Authority to practice law

No attorney may be required to obtain certification as a certified specialist as a prerequisite to practicing law in this state. Any attorney, alone or in association with any other attorney, has the right to practice in any field of law in this state and to act as counsel in every type of case, even though he or she is not certified as a specialist.

(d) Failure to comply with program

A certified specialist who fails to comply with the requirements of the Legal Specialization Program of the State Bar will

Ct. Rules

have her or his certification suspended or revoked under rules adopted by the Board of Governors of the State Bar.

(e) Fee and penalty

The State Bar has the authority to set and collect appropriate fees and penalties for this program.

(f) Inherent power of Supreme Court

Nothing in these rules may be construed as affecting the power of the Supreme Court to exercise its inherent jurisdiction over the practice of law in California. *(Formerly Rule 983.5, adopted,*

eff. Jan. 1, 1996. Renumbered Rule 9.35 and amended, eff. Jan. 1, 2007.)

Research References

Rutter, Cal. Practice Guide: Prof. Responsibility Ch. 1-A, A. Sources of Regulation of Practice of Law in California-Overview.

Rutter, Cal. Practice Guide: Prof. Responsibility Ch. 1-C, C. Legal Specialist Certification.

Rutter, Cal. Practice Guide: Prof. Responsibility Ch. 2-C, C. Description of Lawyer or Practice in Letterheads, Signs, Brochures, etc.

1 Witkin Cal. Proc. 5th Attorneys § 2, Statutory and Regulatory Framework.

1 Witkin Cal. Proc. 5th Attorneys § 9, in General.

Division 4

APPEARANCES AND PRACTICE BY INDIVIDUALS WHO ARE NOT MEMBERS OF THE STATE BAR OF CALIFORNIA

Rule

Rule 9.40. Counsel *pro hac vice*

(a) Eligibility

A person who is not a member of the State Bar of California but who is a member in good standing of and eligible to practice before the bar of any United States court or the highest court in any state, territory, or insular possession of the United States, and who has been retained to appear in a particular cause pending in a court of this state, may in the discretion of such court be permitted upon written application to appear as counsel *pro hac vice*, provided that an active member of the State Bar of California is associated as attorney of record. No person is eligible to appear as counsel *pro hac vice* under this rule if the person is:

(1) A resident of the State of California;

(2) Regularly employed in the State of California; or

(3) Regularly engaged in substantial business, professional, or other activities in the State of California.

(b) Repeated appearances as a cause for denial

Absent special circumstances, repeated appearances by any person under this rule is a cause for denial of an application.

(c) Application

(1) *Application in superior court*

A person desiring to appear as counsel *pro hac vice* in a superior court must file with the court a verified application together with proof of service by mail in accordance with Code of Civil Procedure section 1013a of a copy of the application and of the notice of hearing of the application on all parties who have appeared in the cause and on the State Bar of California at its San Francisco office. The notice of hearing must be given at the time prescribed in Code of Civil Procedure section 1005 unless the court has prescribed a shorter period.

(2) *Application in Supreme Court or Court of Appeal*

An application to appear as counsel *pro hac vice* in the Supreme Court or a Court of Appeal must be made as provided in rule 8.54, with proof of service on all parties who have appeared in the cause and on the State Bar of California at its San Francisco office.

(d) Contents of application

The application must state:

(1) The applicant's residence and office address;

(2) The courts to which the applicant has been admitted to practice and the dates of admission;

(3) That the applicant is a member in good standing in those courts;

(4) That the applicant is not currently suspended or disbarred in any court;

(5) The title of court and cause in which the applicant has filed an application to appear as counsel *pro hac vice* in this state in the preceding two years, the date of each application, and whether or not it was granted; and

(6) The name, address, and telephone number of the active member of the State Bar of California who is attorney of record.

(e) Fee for application

An applicant for permission to appear as counsel *pro hac vice* under this rule must pay a reasonable fee not exceeding $50 to the State Bar of California with the copy of the application and the notice of hearing that is served on the State Bar. The Board of Governors of the State Bar of California will fix the amount of the fee:

(1) To defray the expenses of administering the provisions of this rule that are applicable to the State Bar and the incidental consequences resulting from such provisions; and

(2) Partially to defray the expenses of administering the Board's other responsibilities to enforce the provisions of the State Bar Act relating to the competent delivery of legal services and the incidental consequences resulting therefrom.

(f) Counsel *pro hac vice* subject to jurisdiction of courts and State Bar

A person permitted to appear as counsel *pro hac vice* under this rule is subject to the jurisdiction of the courts of this state with respect to the law of this state governing the conduct of attorneys to the same extent as a member of the State Bar of California. The counsel *pro hac vice* must familiarize himself or herself and comply with the standards of professional conduct required of members of the State Bar of California and will be subject to the disciplinary jurisdiction of the State Bar with respect to any of his or her acts occurring in the course of such appearance. Article 5, chapter 4, division III of the Business and Professions Code and the Rules of Procedure of the State Bar govern in any investigation or proceeding conducted by the State Bar under this rule.

(g) Supreme Court and Court of Appeal not precluded from permitting argument in a particular case

This rule does not preclude the Supreme Court or a Court of Appeal from permitting argument in a particular case from a person who is not a member of the State Bar, but who is licensed to practice in another jurisdiction and who possesses special expertise in the particular field affected by the proceeding. *(Formerly Rule 983, adopted, eff. Sept. 13, 1972. As amended, eff. Oct. 3, 1973; Sept. 3, 1986; Jan. 17, 1991; March 15, 1991. Renumbered Rule 9.40 and amended, eff. Jan. 1, 2007.)*

Research References

Rutter, Cal. Practice Guide: Civil Appeals & Writs Ch. 5-B, B. Types of Motions, Applications and Requests.
Rutter, Cal. Practice Guide: Civil Appeals & Writs Ch. 5-C, C. Motion, Application and Request Procedures.
Rutter, Cal. Practice Guide: Civ. Pro. Before Trial Ch. 9(I)-G, G. Motions Regulating Counsel.
Rutter, Cal. Practice Guide: Real Prop. Transactions Ch. 1-B, B. Attorney Competence, Conflicts of Interest and Initial Client Communications.
Rutter, Cal. Practice Guide: Real Prop. Transactions Ch. 2-A, A. Preliminary Considerations.
Rutter, Cal. Practice Guide: Prof. Responsibility Ch. 1-A, A. Sources of Regulation of Practice of Law in California-Overview.
Rutter, Cal. Practice Guide: Prof. Responsibility Ch. 1-B, B. Regulation of Admission to Practice Law.
Rutter, Cal. Practice Guide: Prof. Responsibility Ch. 1-D, D. Unauthorized Practice of Law.
1 Witkin Cal. Proc. 5th Attorneys § 2, Statutory and Regulatory Framework.
1 Witkin Cal. Proc. 5th Attorneys § 389, (S 389) Counsel Pro Hac Vice.
1 Witkin Cal. Proc. 5th Attorneys § 556, (S 556) Other Measures.
2 Witkin Cal. Proc. 5th Courts § 196, (S 196) Rules on Law Practice, Attorneys, and Judges.

Rule 9.41. Appearances by military counsel

(a) Permission to appear

A judge advocate (as that term is defined at 10 United States Code section 801(13)) who is not a member of the State Bar of California but who is a member in good standing of and eligible to practice before the bar of any United States court or of the highest court in any state, territory, or insular possession of the United States may, in the discretion of a court of this state, be permitted to appear in that court to represent a person in the military service in a particular cause pending before that court, under the Servicemembers Civil Relief Act, 50 United States Code Appendix section 501 et seq., if:

(1) The judge advocate has been made available by the cognizant Judge Advocate General (as that term is defined at 10 United States Code section 801(1)) or a duly designated representative; and

(2) The court finds that retaining civilian counsel likely would cause substantial hardship for the person in military service or that person's family; and

(3) The court appoints a judge advocate as attorney to represent the person in military service under the Servicemembers Civil Relief Act.

Under no circumstances is the determination of availability of a judge advocate to be made by any court within this state, or reviewed by any court of this state. In determining the likelihood of substantial hardship as a result of the retention of

civilian counsel, the court may take judicial notice of the prevailing pay scales for persons in the military service.

(b) Notice to parties

The clerk of the court considering appointment of a judge advocate under this rule must provide written notice of that fact to all parties who have appeared in the cause. A copy of the notice, together with proof of service by mail in accordance with Code of Civil Procedure section 1013a, must be filed by the clerk of the court. Any party who has appeared in the matter may file a written objection to the appointment within 10 days of the date on which notice was given unless the court has prescribed a shorter period. If the court determines to hold a hearing in relation to the appointment, notice of the hearing must be given at least 10 days before the date designated for the hearing unless the court has prescribed a shorter period.

(c) Appearing judge advocate subject to court and State Bar jurisdiction

A judge advocate permitted to appear under this rule is subject to the jurisdiction of the courts of this state with respect to the law of this state governing the conduct of attorneys to the same extent as a member of the State Bar of California. The judge advocate must become familiar with and comply with the standards of professional conduct required of members of the State Bar of California and is subject to the disciplinary jurisdiction of the State Bar of California. Division 3, chapter 4, article 5 of the Business and Professions Code and the Rules of Procedure of the State Bar of California govern any investigation or proceeding conducted by the State Bar under this rule.

(d) Appearing judge advocate subject to rights and obligations of State Bar members concerning professional privileges

A judge advocate permitted to appear under this rule is subject to the rights and obligations with respect to attorney-client privilege, work-product privilege, and other professional privileges to the same extent as a member of the State Bar of California. *(Formerly Rule 983.1, adopted, eff. Feb. 21, 1992. Renumbered Rule 9.41 and amended, eff. Jan. 1, 2007.)*

Research References

Rutter, Cal. Practice Guide: Prof. Responsibility Ch. 1-B, B. Regulation of Admission to Practice Law.
Rutter, Cal. Practice Guide: Prof. Responsibility Ch. 1-D, D. Unauthorized Practice of Law.
1 Witkin Cal. Proc. 5th Attorneys § 390, (S 390) Military Counsel.

Rule 9.42. Certified law students

(a) Definitions

(1) A "certified law student" is a law student who has a currently effective certificate of registration as a certified law student from the State Bar.

(2) A "supervising attorney" is a member of the State Bar who agrees to supervise a certified law student under rules established by the State Bar and whose name appears on the application for certification.

(b) State Bar Certified Law Student Program

The State Bar must establish and administer a program for registering law students under rules adopted by the Board of Governors of the State Bar.

(c) Eligibility for certification

To be eligible to become a certified law student, an applicant must:

(1) Have successfully completed one full year of studies (minimum of 270 hours) at a law school accredited by the American Bar Association or the State Bar of California, or both, or have passed the first year law students' examination;

(2) Have been accepted into, and be enrolled in, the second, third, or fourth year of law school in good academic standing or have graduated from law school, subject to the time period limitations specified in the rules adopted by the Board of Governors of the State Bar; and

(3) Have either successfully completed or be currently enrolled in and attending academic courses in evidence and civil procedure.

(d) Permitted activities

Subject to all applicable rules, regulations, and statutes, a certified law student may:

(1) Negotiate for and on behalf of the client subject to final approval thereof by the supervising attorney or give legal advice to the client, provided that the certified law student:

(A) Obtains the approval of the supervising attorney to engage in the activities;

(B) Obtains the approval of the supervising attorney regarding the legal advice to be given or plan of negotiation to be undertaken by the certified law student; and

(C) Performs the activities under the general supervision of the supervising attorney;

(2) Appear on behalf of the client in depositions, provided that the certified law student:

(A) Obtains the approval of the supervising attorney to engage in the activity;

(B) Performs the activity under the direct and immediate supervision and in the personal presence of the supervising attorney (or, exclusively in the case of government agencies, any deputy, assistant, or other staff attorney authorized and designated by the supervising attorney); and

(C) Obtains a signed consent form from the client on whose behalf the certified law student acts (or, exclusively in the case of government agencies, from the chief counsel or prosecuting attorney) approving the performance of such acts by such certified law student or generally by any certified law student;

(3) Appear on behalf of the client in any public trial, hearing, arbitration, or proceeding, or before any arbitrator, court, public agency, referee, magistrate, commissioner, or hearing officer, to the extent approved by such arbitrator, court, public agency, referee, magistrate, commissioner, or hearing officer, provided that the certified law student:

(A) Obtains the approval of the supervising attorney to engage in the activity;

(B) Performs the activity under the direct and immediate supervision and in the personal presence of the supervising attorney (or, exclusively in the case of government agencies, any deputy, assistant, or other staff attorney authorized and designated by the supervising attorney);

(C) Obtains a signed consent form from the client on whose behalf the certified law student acts (or, exclusively in the case of government agencies, from the chief counsel or prosecuting attorney) approving the performance of such acts by such certified law student or generally by any certified law student; and

(D) As a condition to such appearance, either presents a copy of the consent form to the arbitrator, court, public agency, referee, magistrate, commissioner, or hearing officer, or files a copy of the consent form in the court case file; and

(4) Appear on behalf of a government agency in the prosecution of criminal actions classified as infractions or other such minor criminal offenses with a maximum penalty or a fine equal to the maximum fine for infractions in California, including any public trial:

(A) Subject to approval by the court, commissioner, referee, hearing officer, or magistrate presiding at such public trial; and

(B) Without the personal appearance of the supervising attorney or any deputy, assistant, or other staff attorney authorized and designated by the supervising attorney, but only if the supervising attorney or the designated attorney has approved in writing the performance of such acts by the certified law student and is immediately available to attend the proceeding.

(e) Failure to comply with program

A certified law student who fails to comply with the requirements of the State Bar Certified Law Student Program must have his or her certification withdrawn under rules adopted by the Board of Governors of the State Bar.

(f) Fee and penalty

The State Bar has the authority to set and collect appropriate fees and penalties for this program.

(g) Inherent power of Supreme Court

Nothing in these rules may be construed as affecting the power of the Supreme Court to exercise its inherent jurisdiction over the practice of law in California. *(Formerly Rule 983.2, adopted, eff. Dec. 29, 1993. Renumbered Rule 9.42 and amended, eff. Jan. 1, 2007.)*

Research References

Rutter, Cal. Practice Guide: Prof. Responsibility Ch. 1-A, A. Sources of Regulation of Practice of Law in California-Overview.
Rutter, Cal. Practice Guide: Prof. Responsibility Ch. 1-D, D. Unauthorized Practice of Law.
Rutter, Cal. Practice Guide: Prof. Responsibility Ch. 6-B, B. Elements of Attorney Competence.
1 Witkin Cal. Proc. 5th Attorneys § 383, Nature of Program.
1 Witkin Cal. Proc. 5th Attorneys § 384, Student and Attorney Participants.
1 Witkin Cal. Proc. 5th Attorneys § 385, Activities.

Rule 9.43. Out–of–state attorney arbitration counsel

(a) Definition

An "out-of-state attorney arbitration counsel" is an attorney who is:

(1) Not a member of the State Bar of California but who is a member in good standing of and eligible to practice before the bar of any United States court or the highest court in any state, territory, or insular possession of the United States, and who has been retained to appear in the course of, or in connection with, an arbitration proceeding in this state;

(2) Has served a certificate in accordance with the requirements of Code of Civil Procedure section 1282.4 on the arbitrator, the arbitrators, or the arbitral forum, the State Bar of California, and all other parties and counsel in the arbitration whose addresses are known to the attorney; and

(3) Whose appearance has been approved by the arbitrator, the arbitrators, or the arbitral forum.

(b) State Bar Out–of–State Attorney Arbitration Counsel Program

The State Bar of California must establish and administer a program to implement the State Bar of California's responsibilities under Code of Civil Procedure section 1282.4. The State Bar of California's program may be operative only as long as the applicable provisions of Code of Civil Procedure section 1282.4 remain in effect.

(c) Eligibility to appear as an out-of-state attorney arbitration counsel

To be eligible to appear as an out-of-state attorney arbitration counsel, an attorney must comply with all of the applicable provisions of Code of Civil Procedure section 1282.4 and the requirements of this rule and the related rules and regulations adopted by the State Bar of California.

(d) Discipline

An out–of–state attorney arbitration counsel who files a certificate containing false information or who otherwise fails to comply with the standards of professional conduct required of members of the State Bar of California is subject to the disciplinary jurisdiction of the State Bar with respect to any of his or her acts occurring in the course of the arbitration.

(e) Disqualification

Failure to timely file and serve a certificate or, absent special circumstances, appearances in multiple separate arbitration matters are grounds for disqualification from serving in the arbitration in which the certificate was filed.

(f) Fee

Out-of-state attorney arbitration counsel must pay a reasonable fee not exceeding $50 to the State Bar of California with the copy of the certificate that is served on the State Bar.

(g) Inherent power of Supreme Court

Nothing in these rules may be construed as affecting the power of the Supreme Court to exercise its inherent jurisdiction over the practice of law in California. *(Formerly Rule 983.4, adopted, eff. July 1, 1999. Renumbered Rule 9.43 and amended, eff. Jan. 1, 2007.)*

Research References

Rutter, Cal. Practice Guide: A.D.R. Ch. 5-H, H. Conduct of Arbitration Proceedings.
Rutter, Cal. Practice Guide: Prof. Responsibility Ch. 1-A, A. Sources of Regulation of Practice of Law in California-Overview.
Rutter, Cal. Practice Guide: Prof. Responsibility Ch. 1-B, B. Regulation of Admission to Practice Law.
1 Witkin Cal. Proc. 5th Attorneys § 387, (S 387) in General.

Rule 9.44. Registered foreign legal consultant

(a) Definition

A "registered foreign legal consultant" is a person who:

(1) Is admitted to practice and is in good standing as an attorney or counselor-at-law or the equivalent in a foreign country; and

(2) Has a currently effective certificate of registration as a registered foreign legal consultant from the State Bar.

(b) State Bar Registered Foreign Legal Consultant Program

The State Bar must establish and administer a program for registering foreign attorneys or counselors-at-law or the equivalent under rules adopted by the Board of Governors of the State Bar.

(c) Eligibility for certification

To be eligible to become a registered foreign legal consultant, an applicant must:

(1) Present satisfactory proof that the applicant has been admitted to practice and has been in good standing as an attorney or counselor-at-law or the equivalent in a foreign country for at least four of the six years immediately preceding the application and, while so admitted, has actually practiced the law of that country;

(2) Present satisfactory proof that the applicant possesses the good moral character requisite for a person to be licensed as a member of the State Bar of California;

(3) Agree to comply with the provisions of the rules adopted by the Board of Governors of the State Bar relating to security for claims against a foreign legal consultant by his or her clients;

(4) Agree to comply with the provisions of the rules adopted by the Board of Governors of the State Bar relating to maintaining an address of record for State Bar purposes;

(5) Agree to notify the State Bar of any change in his or her status in any jurisdiction where he or she is admitted to practice or of any discipline with respect to such admission;

(6) Agree to be subject to the jurisdiction of the courts of this state with respect to the laws of the State of California governing the conduct of attorneys, to the same extent as a member of the State Bar of California;

(7) Agree to become familiar with and comply with the standards of professional conduct required of members of the State Bar of California;

(8) Agree to be subject to the disciplinary jurisdiction of the State Bar of California;

(9) Agree to be subject to the rights and obligations with respect to attorney client privilege, work-product privilege, and other professional privileges, to the same extent as attorneys admitted to practice law in California; and

(10) Agree to comply with the laws of the State of California, the rules and regulations of the State Bar of California, and these rules.

(d) Authority to practice law

Subject to all applicable rules, regulations, and statutes, a registered foreign legal consultant may render legal services in California, except that he or she may not:

(1) Appear for a person other than himself or herself as attorney in any court, or before any magistrate or other judicial officer, in this state or prepare pleadings or any other papers or issue subpoenas in any action or proceeding brought in any court or before any judicial officer;

(2) Prepare any deed, mortgage, assignment, discharge, lease, or any other instrument affecting title to real estate located in the United States;

(3) Prepare any will or trust instrument affecting the disposition on death of any property located in the United States and owned by a resident or any instrument relating to the administration of a decedent's estate in the United States;

(4) Prepare any instrument in respect of the marital relations, rights, or duties of a resident of the United States, or the custody or care of the children of a resident; or

(5) Otherwise render professional legal advice on the law of the State of California, any other state of the United States, the District of Columbia, the United States, or of any jurisdiction other than the jurisdiction named in satisfying the requirements of (c) of this rule, whether rendered incident to preparation of legal instruments or otherwise.

(e) Failure to comply with program

A registered foreign legal consultant who fails to comply with the requirements of the State Bar Registered Foreign Legal Consultant Program will have her or his certification suspended or revoked under rules adopted by the Board of Governors of the State Bar.

(f) Fee and penalty

The State Bar has the authority to set and collect appropriate fees and penalties for this program.

(g) Inherent power of Supreme Court

Nothing in these rules may be construed as affecting the power of the Supreme Court to exercise its inherent jurisdiction over

Ct. Rules

the practice of law in California. *(Formerly Rule 988, adopted, eff. Dec. 1, 1993. Renumbered Rule 9.44 and amended, eff. Jan. 1, 2007.)*

Research References

Rutter, Cal. Practice Guide: Civ. Pro. Before Trial Ch. 9(I)-G, G. Motions Regulating Counsel.

Rutter, Cal. Practice Guide: Prof. Responsibility Ch. 1-A, A. Sources of Regulation of Practice of Law in California-Overview.

Rutter, Cal. Practice Guide: Prof. Responsibility Ch. 1-B, B. Regulation of Admission to Practice Law.

Rutter, Cal. Practice Guide: Prof. Responsibility Ch. 1-D, D. Unauthorized Practice of Law.

1 Witkin Cal. Proc. 5th Attorneys § 391, (S 391) Foreign Legal Consultants.

Rule 9.45. Registered legal services attorneys

(a) Definitions

The following definitions apply in this rule:

(1) "Qualifying legal services provider" means either of the following, provided that the qualifying legal services provider follows quality-control procedures approved by the State Bar of California:

(A) A nonprofit entity incorporated and operated exclusively in California that as its primary purpose and function provides legal services without charge in civil matters to indigent persons, especially underserved client groups, such as the elderly, persons with disabilities, juveniles, and non–English–speaking persons; or

(B) A program operated exclusively in California by a nonprofit law school approved by the American Bar Association or accredited by the State Bar of California that has operated for at least two years at a cost of at least $20,000 per year as an identifiable law school unit with a primary purpose and function of providing legal services without charge to indigent persons.

(2) "Active member in good standing of the bar of a United States state, jurisdiction, possession, territory, or dependency" means an attorney who:

(A) Is a member in good standing of the entity governing the practice of law in each jurisdiction in which the member is licensed to practice law;

(B) Remains an active member in good standing of the entity governing the practice of law in at least one United States state, jurisdiction, possession, territory, or dependency other than California while practicing law as a registered legal services attorney in California; and

(C) Has not been disbarred, has not resigned with charges pending, or is not suspended from practicing law in any other jurisdiction.

(b) Scope of practice

Subject to all applicable rules, regulations, and statutes, an attorney practicing law under this rule may practice law in California only while working, with or without pay, at a qualifying legal services provider, as defined in this rule, and, at that institution and only on behalf of its clients, may engage, under supervision, in all forms of legal practice that are permissible for a member of the State Bar of California.

(c) Requirements

For an attorney to practice law under this rule, the attorney must:

(1) Be an active member in good standing of the bar of a United States state, jurisdiction, possession, territory, or dependency;

(2) Register with the State Bar of California and file an Application for Determination of Moral Character;

(3) Meet all of the requirements for admission to the State Bar of California, except that the attorney:

(A) Need not take the California bar examination or the Multistate Professional Responsibility Examination; and

(B) May practice law while awaiting the result of his or her Application for Determination of Moral Character;

(4) Comply with the rules adopted by the Board of Governors relating to the State Bar Registered Legal Services Attorney Program;

(5) Practice law exclusively for a single qualifying legal services provider, except that, if so qualified, an attorney may, while practicing under this rule, simultaneously practice law as registered in-house counsel;

(6) Practice law under the supervision of an attorney who is employed by the qualifying legal services provider and who is a member in good standing of the State Bar of California;

(7) Abide by all of the laws and rules that govern members of the State Bar of California, including the Minimum Continuing Legal Education (MCLE) requirements;

(8) Satisfy in his or her first year of practice under this rule all of the MCLE requirements, including ethics education, that members of the State Bar of California must complete every three years; and

(9) Not have taken and failed the California bar examination within five years immediately preceding application to register under this rule.

(d) Application

To qualify to practice law as a registered legal services attorney, the attorney must:

(1) Register as an attorney applicant and file an Application for Determination of Moral Character with the Committee of Bar Examiners;

(2) Submit to the State Bar of California a declaration signed by the attorney agreeing that he or she will be subject to the disciplinary authority of the Supreme Court of California and the State Bar of California and attesting that he or she will not practice law in California other than under supervision at a qualifying legal services provider during the time he or she practices law as a registered legal services attorney in California, except that, if so qualified, the attorney may, while practicing under this rule, simultaneously practice law as registered in-house counsel; and

(3) Submit to the State Bar of California a declaration signed by a qualifying supervisor on behalf of the qualifying legal services provider in California attesting that the applicant will work, with or without pay, as an attorney for the organization; that the applicant will be supervised as specified in this rule; and that the qualifying legal services provider and the supervising attorney assume professional responsibility for any work performed by the applicant under this rule.

(e) Duration of practice

An attorney may practice for no more than a total of three years under this rule.

(f) Application and registration fees

The State Bar of California may set appropriate application fees and initial and annual registration fees to be paid by registered legal services attorneys.

(g) State Bar Registered Legal Services Attorney Program

The State Bar may establish and administer a program for registering California legal services attorneys under rules adopted by the Board of Governors of the State Bar.

(h) Supervision

To meet the requirements of this rule, an attorney supervising a registered legal services attorney:

(1) Must be an active member in good standing of the State Bar of California;

(2) Must have actively practiced law in California and been a member in good standing of the State Bar of California for at least the two years immediately preceding the time of supervision;

(3) Must have practiced law as a full-time occupation for at least four years;

(4) Must not supervise more than two registered legal services attorneys concurrently;

(5) Must assume professional responsibility for any work that the registered legal services attorney performs under the supervising attorney's supervision;

(6) Must assist, counsel, and provide direct supervision of the registered legal services attorney in the activities authorized by this rule and review such activities with the supervised attorney, to the extent required for the protection of the client;

(7) Must read, approve, and personally sign any pleadings, briefs, or other similar documents prepared by the registered legal services attorney before their filing, and must read and approve any documents prepared by the registered legal services attorney for execution by any person who is not a member of the State Bar of California before their submission for execution; and

(8) May, in his or her absence, designate another attorney meeting the requirements of (1) through (7) to provide the supervision required under this rule.

(i) Inherent power of Supreme Court

Nothing in this rule may be construed as affecting the power of the Supreme Court of California to exercise its inherent jurisdiction over the practice of law in California.

(j) Effect of rule on multijurisdictional practice

Nothing in this rule limits the scope of activities permissible under existing law by attorneys who are not members of the State Bar of California. *(Formerly Rule 964, adopted, eff. Nov. 15, 2004. Renumbered Rule 9.45 and amended, eff. Jan. 1, 2007.)*

Research References

Rutter, Cal. Practice Guide: Real Prop. Transactions Ch. 1-B, B. Attorney Competence, Conflicts of Interest and Initial Client Communications.

Rutter, Cal. Practice Guide: Real Prop. Transactions Ch. 2-A, A. Preliminary Considerations.

Rutter, Cal. Practice Guide: Prof. Responsibility Ch. 1-A, A. Sources of Regulation of Practice of Law in California-Overview.

Rutter, Cal. Practice Guide: Prof. Responsibility Ch. 1-B, B. Regulation of Admission to Practice Law.

Rutter, Cal. Practice Guide: Prof. Responsibility Ch. 5-D, D. Ethical Limitations on Attorney Fees.

Rutter, Cal. Practice Guide: Prof. Responsibility Ch. 5-K, K. Fee Recovery/Enforcing Fee Agreements.

1 Witkin Cal. Proc. 5th Attorneys § 392, (S 392) Registered Legal Services Attorneys.

Rule 9.46.   Registered in-house counsel

(a) Definitions

The following definitions apply to terms used in this rule:

(1) "Qualifying institution" means a corporation, a partnership, an association, or other legal entity, including its subsidiaries and organizational affiliates. Neither a governmental entity nor an entity that provides legal services to others can be a qualifying institution for purposes of this rule. A qualifying institution must:

(A) Employ at least 10 employees full time in California; or

(B) Employ in California an attorney who is an active member in good standing of the State Bar of California.

(2) "Active member in good standing of the bar of a United States state, jurisdiction, possession, territory, or dependency" means an attorney who meets all of the following criteria:

(A) Is a member in good standing of the entity governing the practice of law in each jurisdiction in which the member is licensed to practice law;

(B) Remains an active member in good standing of the entity governing the practice of law in at least one United States state, jurisdiction, possession, territory, or dependency, other than California, while practicing law as registered in-house counsel in California; and

(C) Has not been disbarred, has not resigned with charges pending, or is not suspended from practicing law in any other jurisdiction.

(b) Scope of practice

Subject to all applicable rules, regulations, and statutes, an attorney practicing law under this rule is:

(1) Permitted to provide legal services in California only to the qualifying institution that employs him or her;

(2) Not permitted to make court appearances in California state courts or to engage in any other activities for which *pro hac vice* admission is required if they are performed in California by an attorney who is not a member of the State Bar of California; and

(3) Not permitted to provide personal or individual representation to any customers, shareholders, owners, partners, officers, employees, servants, or agents of the qualifying institution.

(c) Requirements

For an attorney to practice law under this rule, the attorney must:

(1) Be an active member in good standing of the bar of a United States state, jurisdiction, possession, territory, or dependency;

(2) Register with the State Bar of California and file an Application for Determination of Moral Character;

(3) Meet all of the requirements for admission to the State Bar of California, except that the attorney:

(A) Need not take the California bar examination or the Multistate Professional Responsibility Examination; and

(B) May practice law while awaiting the result of his or her Application for Determination of Moral Character;

(4) Comply with the rules adopted by the Board of Governors relating to the State Bar Registered In–House Counsel Program;

(5) Practice law exclusively for a single qualifying institution, except that, while practicing under this rule, the attorney may, if so qualified, simultaneously practice law as a registered legal services attorney;

(6) Abide by all of the laws and rules that govern members of the State Bar of California, including the Minimum Continuing Legal Education (MCLE) requirements;

(7) Satisfy in his or her first year of practice under this rule all of the MCLE requirements, including ethics education, that

members of the State Bar of California must complete every three years and, thereafter, satisfy the MCLE requirements applicable to all members of the State Bar; and

(8) Reside in California.

(d) Application

To qualify to practice law as registered in-house counsel, an attorney must:

(1) Register as an attorney applicant and file an Application for Determination of Moral Character with the Committee of Bar Examiners;

(2) Submit to the State Bar of California a declaration signed by the attorney agreeing that he or she will be subject to the disciplinary authority of the Supreme Court of California and the State Bar of California and attesting that he or she will not practice law in California other than on behalf of the qualifying institution during the time he or she is registered in-house counsel in California, except that if so qualified, the attorney may, while practicing under this rule, simultaneously practice law as a registered legal services attorney; and

(3) Submit to the State Bar of California a declaration signed by an officer, a director, or a general counsel of the applicant's employer, on behalf of the applicant's employer, attesting that the applicant is employed as an attorney for the employer, that the nature of the employment conforms to the requirements of this rule, that the employer will notify the State Bar of California within 30 days of the cessation of the applicant's employment in California, and that the person signing the declaration believes, to the best of his or her knowledge after reasonable inquiry, that the applicant qualifies for registration under this rule and is an individual of good moral character.

(e) Duration of practice

A registered in-house counsel must renew his or her registration annually. There is no limitation on the number of years in-house counsel may register under this rule. Registered in-house counsel may practice law under this rule only for as long as he or she remains employed by the same qualifying institution that provided the declaration in support of his or her application. If an attorney practicing law as registered in-house counsel leaves the employment of his or her employer or changes employers, he or she must notify the State Bar of California within 30 days. If an attorney wishes to practice law under this rule for a new employer, he or she must first register as in-house counsel for that employer.

(f) Eligibility

An application to register under this rule may not be denied because:

(1) The attorney applicant has practiced law in California as in-house counsel before the effective date of this rule.

(2) The attorney applicant is practicing law as in-house counsel at or after the effective date of this rule, provided that the attorney applies under this rule within six months of its effective date.

(g) Application and registration fees

The State Bar of California may set appropriate application fees and initial and annual registration fees to be paid by registered in-house counsel.

(h) State Bar Registered In–House Counsel Program

The State Bar must establish and administer a program for registering California in-house counsel under rules adopted by the Board of Governors.

(i) Inherent power of Supreme Court

Nothing in this rule may be construed as affecting the power of the Supreme Court of California to exercise its inherent jurisdiction over the practice of law in California.

(j) Effect of rule on multijurisdictional practice

Nothing in this rule limits the scope of activities permissible under existing law by attorneys who are not members of the State Bar of California. *(Formerly Rule 965, adopted, eff. Nov. 15, 2004. Renumbered Rule 9.46 and amended, eff. Jan. 1, 2007.)*

Research References

Rutter, Cal. Practice Guide: Real Prop. Transactions Ch. 1-B, B. Attorney Competence, Conflicts of Interest and Initial Client Communications.
Rutter, Cal. Practice Guide: Real Prop. Transactions Ch. 2-A, A. Preliminary Considerations.
Rutter, Cal. Practice Guide: Prof. Responsibility Ch. 1-A, A. Sources of Regulation of Practice of Law in California-Overview.
Rutter, Cal. Practice Guide: Prof. Responsibility Ch. 1-B, B. Regulation of Admission to Practice Law.
Rutter, Cal. Practice Guide: Prof. Responsibility Ch. 5-D, D. Ethical Limitations on Attorney Fees.
Rutter, Cal. Practice Guide: Prof. Responsibility Ch. 5-K, K. Fee Recovery/Enforcing Fee Agreements.
1 Witkin Cal. Proc. 5th Attorneys § 393, (S 393) Registered In-House Counsel.

Rule 9.47. Attorneys practicing law temporarily in California as part of litigation

(a) Definitions

The following definitions apply to the terms used in this rule:

(1) "A formal legal proceeding" means litigation, arbitration, mediation, or a legal action before an administrative decision-maker.

(2) "Authorized to appear" means the attorney is permitted to appear in the proceeding by the rules of the jurisdiction in which the formal legal proceeding is taking place or will be taking place.

(3) "Active member in good standing of the bar of a United States state, jurisdiction, possession, territory, or dependency" means an attorney who meets all of the following criteria:

(A) Is a member in good standing of the entity governing the practice of law in each jurisdiction in which the member is licensed to practice law;

(B) Remains an active member in good standing of the entity governing the practice of law in at least one United States state, jurisdiction, possession, territory, or dependency while practicing law under this rule; and

(C) Has not been disbarred, has not resigned with charges pending, or is not suspended from practicing law in any other jurisdiction.

(b) Requirements

For an attorney to practice law under this rule, the attorney must:

(1) Maintain an office in a United States jurisdiction other than California and in which the attorney is licensed to practice law;

(2) Already be retained by a client in the matter for which the attorney is providing legal services in California, except that the attorney may provide legal advice to a potential client, at the potential client's request, to assist the client in deciding whether to retain the attorney;

(3) Indicate on any Web site or other advertisement that is accessible in California either that the attorney is not a member of the State Bar of California or that the attorney is admitted to practice law only in the states listed; and

(4) Be an active member in good standing of the bar of a United States state, jurisdiction, possession, territory, or dependency.

(c) Permissible activities

An attorney meeting the requirements of this rule, who complies with all applicable rules, regulations, and statutes, is not engaging in the unauthorized practice of law in California if the attorney's services are part of:

(1) A formal legal proceeding that is pending in another jurisdiction and in which the attorney is authorized to appear;

(2) A formal legal proceeding that is anticipated but is not yet pending in California and in which the attorney reasonably expects to be authorized to appear;

(3) A formal legal proceeding that is anticipated but is not yet pending in another jurisdiction and in which the attorney reasonably expects to be authorized to appear; or

(4) A formal legal proceeding that is anticipated or pending and in which the attorney's supervisor is authorized to appear or reasonably expects to be authorized to appear.

The attorney whose anticipated authorization to appear in a formal legal proceeding serves as the basis for practice under this rule must seek that authorization promptly after it becomes possible to do so. Failure to seek that authorization promptly, or denial of that authorization, ends eligibility to practice under this rule.

(d) Restrictions

To qualify to practice law in California under this rule, an attorney must not:

(1) Hold out to the public or otherwise represent that he or she is admitted to practice law in California;

(2) Establish or maintain a resident office or other systematic or continuous presence in California for the practice of law;

(3) Be a resident of California;

(4) Be regularly employed in California;

(5) Regularly engage in substantial business or professional activities in California; or

(6) Have been disbarred, have resigned with charges pending, or be suspended from practicing law in any other jurisdiction.

(e) Conditions

By practicing law in California under this rule, an attorney agrees that he or she is providing legal services in California subject to:

(1) The jurisdiction of the State Bar of California;

(2) The jurisdiction of the courts of this state to the same extent as is a member of the State Bar of California; and

(3) The laws of the State of California relating to the practice of law, the State Bar Rules of Professional Conduct, the rules and regulations of the State Bar of California, and these rules.

(f) Inherent power of Supreme Court

Nothing in this rule may be construed as affecting the power of the Supreme Court of California to exercise its inherent jurisdiction over the practice of law in California.

(g) Effect of rule on multijurisdictional practice

Nothing in this rule limits the scope of activities permissible under existing law by attorneys who are not members of the State Bar of California. *(Formerly Rule 966, adopted, eff. Nov. 15, 2004. Renumbered Rule 9.47 and amended, eff. Jan. 1, 2007.)*

Research References

Rutter, Cal. Practice Guide: Real Prop. Transactions Ch. 1-B, B. Attorney Competence, Conflicts of Interest and Initial Client Communications.

Rutter, Cal. Practice Guide: Real Prop. Transactions Ch. 2-A, A. Preliminary Considerations.

Rutter, Cal. Practice Guide: Prof. Responsibility Ch. 1-B, B. Regulation of Admission to Practice Law.

Rutter, Cal. Practice Guide: Prof. Responsibility Ch. 5-D, D. Ethical Limitations on Attorney Fees.

Rutter, Cal. Practice Guide: Prof. Responsibility Ch. 5-K, K. Fee Recovery/Enforcing Fee Agreements.

Rutter, Cal. Practice Guide: Prof. Responsibility Ch. 1-B , Outline B.

1 Witkin Cal. Proc. 5th Attorneys § 394, (S 394) Temporary Practice as Part of Litigation.

Rule 9.48. Nonlitigating attorneys temporarily in California to provide legal services

(a) Definitions

The following definitions apply to terms used in this rule:

(1) "A transaction or other nonlitigation matter" includes any legal matter other than litigation, arbitration, mediation, or a legal action before an administrative decision-maker.

(2) "Active member in good standing of the bar of a United States state, jurisdiction, possession, territory, or dependency" means an attorney who meets all of the following criteria:

(A) Is a member in good standing of the entity governing the practice of law in each jurisdiction in which the member is licensed to practice law;

(B) Remains an active member in good standing of the entity governing the practice of law in at least one United States state, jurisdiction, possession, territory, or dependency other than California while practicing law under this rule; and

(C) Has not been disbarred, has not resigned with charges pending, or is not suspended from practicing law in any other jurisdiction.

(b) Requirements

For an attorney to practice law under this rule, the attorney must:

(1) Maintain an office in a United States jurisdiction other than California and in which the attorney is licensed to practice law;

(2) Already be retained by a client in the matter for which the attorney is providing legal services in California, except that the attorney may provide legal advice to a potential client, at the potential client's request, to assist the client in deciding whether to retain the attorney;

(3) Indicate on any Web site or other advertisement that is accessible in California either that the attorney is not a member of the State Bar of California or that the attorney is admitted to practice law only in the states listed; and

(4) Be an active member in good standing of the bar of a United States state, jurisdiction, possession, territory, or dependency.

(c) Permissible activities

An attorney who meets the requirements of this rule and who complies with all applicable rules, regulations, and statutes is not engaging in the unauthorized practice of law in California if the attorney:

(1) Provides legal assistance or legal advice in California to a client concerning a transaction or other nonlitigation matter, a material aspect of which is taking place in a jurisdiction other than California and in which the attorney is licensed to provide legal services;

(2) Provides legal assistance or legal advice in California on an issue of federal law or of the law of a jurisdiction other than California to attorneys licensed to practice law in California; or

(3) Is an employee of a client and provides legal assistance or legal advice in California to the client or to the client's subsidiaries or organizational affiliates.

(d) Restrictions

To qualify to practice law in California under this rule, an attorney must not:

(1) Hold out to the public or otherwise represent that he or she is admitted to practice law in California;

(2) Establish or maintain a resident office or other systematic or continuous presence in California for the practice of law;

(3) Be a resident of California;

(4) Be regularly employed in California;

(5) Regularly engage in substantial business or professional activities in California; or

(6) Have been disbarred, have resigned with charges pending, or be suspended from practicing law in any other jurisdiction.

(e) Conditions

By practicing law in California under this rule, an attorney agrees that he or she is providing legal services in California subject to:

(1) The jurisdiction of the State Bar of California;

(2) The jurisdiction of the courts of this state to the same extent as is a member of the State Bar of California; and

(3) The laws of the State of California relating to the practice of law, the State Bar Rules of Professional Conduct, the rules and regulations of the State Bar of California, and these rules.

(f) Scope of practice

An attorney is permitted by this rule to provide legal assistance or legal services concerning only a transaction or other nonlitigation matter.

(g) Inherent power of Supreme Court

Nothing in this rule may be construed as affecting the power of the Supreme Court of California to exercise its inherent jurisdiction over the practice of law in California.

(h) Effect of rule on multijurisdictional practice

Nothing in this rule limits the scope of activities permissible under existing law by attorneys who are not members of the State Bar of California. *(Formerly Rule 967, adopted, eff. Nov. 15, 2004. Renumbered Rule 9.48 and amended, eff. Jan. 1, 2007.)*

Research References

Rutter, Cal. Practice Guide: Real Prop. Transactions Ch. 1-B, B. Attorney Competence, Conflicts of Interest and Initial Client Communications.

Rutter, Cal. Practice Guide: Real Prop. Transactions Ch. 2-A, A. Preliminary Considerations.

Rutter, Cal. Practice Guide: Prof. Responsibility Ch. 1-B, B. Regulation of Admission to Practice Law.

Rutter, Cal. Practice Guide: Prof. Responsibility Ch. 5-D, D. Ethical Limitations on Attorney Fees.

Rutter, Cal. Practice Guide: Prof. Responsibility Ch. 5-K, K. Fee Recovery/Enforcing Fee Agreements.

1 Witkin Cal. Proc. 5th Attorneys § 395, (S 395) Temporary Practice to Provide Legal Services.

2 Witkin Cal. Proc. 5th Courts § 196, (S 196) Rules on Law Practice, Attorneys, and Judges.

Division 5

CENSURE, REMOVAL, RETIREMENT, OR PRIVATE ADMONISHMENT OF JUDGES

Rule

9.60. Review of determinations by the Commission on Judicial Performance.

9.61. Proceedings involving public or private admonishment, censure, removal, or retirement of a judge of the Supreme Court.

Rule 9.60. Review of determinations by the Commission on Judicial Performance

(a) Time for petition for review to Supreme Court

A petition to the Supreme Court by a judge or former judge to review a determination by the Commission on Judicial Performance to retire, remove, censure, admonish, or disqualify the judge or former judge must be served and filed within 60 days after:

(1) The Commission, under its rules, notifies the judge or former judge that its determination has been filed or entered in its records; or

(2) The determination becomes final as to the Commission under its rules, whichever event is later.

(b) Time for answer to petition for review and reply

Within 45 days after service of the petition, the Commission may serve and file an answer. Within 20 days after service of the answer, the judge or former judge may serve and file a reply. Each petition, answer, or reply submitted for filing must be accompanied by proof of service, including service on the Commission of three copies of any petition or reply filed by a judge or former judge. Extensions of time to file the petition, answer, or reply are disfavored and will be granted only upon a specific and affirmative showing of good cause. Good cause does not include ordinary press of business.

(c) Contents and form

The petition, answer, and reply must address both the appropriateness of review and the merits of the Commission's determination, and they will serve as briefs on the merits in the event review is granted. Except as provided in these rules, the form of the petition, answer, and reply must, insofar as practicable, conform to rule 8.504 except that the lengths of the petition, answer, and reply must conform to the limits specified in rule 8.204(c). Each copy of the petition must contain:

(1) A copy of the Commission's determination;

(2) A copy of the notice of filing or entry of the determination in the records of the Commission;

(3) A copy of any findings of fact and conclusions of law; and

(4) A cover that bears the conspicuous notation "PETITION FOR REVIEW OF DETERMINATION BY COMMISSION ON JUDICIAL PERFORMANCE (RULE 9.60)" or words of like effect.

(d) Transmission of the record

Promptly upon the service and filing of the petition, the Commission must transmit to the Clerk of the Supreme Court the original record, including a transcript of the testimony, briefs, and all original papers and exhibits on file in the proceeding.

(e) Applicable rules on review

In the event review is granted, the rules adopted by the Judicial Council governing appeals from the superior court in civil cases, other than rule 8.272 relating to costs, apply to proceedings in the Supreme Court for review of a determination of the Commission except where express provision is made to the contrary or where such application would otherwise be clearly impracticable or inappropriate. *(Formerly Rule 935, adopted, eff. Dec. 1, 1996. Renumbered Rule 9.60 and amended, eff. Jan. 1, 2007.)*

Research References

Rutter, Cal. Practice Guide: Civil Appeals & Writs Ch. 1-C, C. Methods and Sequence of Appellate Review.
2 Witkin Cal. Proc. 5th Courts § 80, in General.
2 Witkin Cal. Proc. 5th Courts § 91, Procedure.
2 Witkin Cal. Proc. 5th Courts § 196, (S 196) Rules on Law Practice, Attorneys, and Judges.

Rule 9.61. Proceedings involving public or private admonishment, censure, removal, or retirement of a judge of the Supreme Court

(a) Selection of appellate tribunal

Immediately on the filing of a petition to review a determination by the Commission on Judicial Performance to retire, remove, censure, admonish, or disqualify a justice of the Supreme Court, the Clerk of the Supreme Court must select, by lot, seven Court of Appeal justices who must elect one of their number presiding justice and perform the duties of the tribunal created under article VI, section 18(f) of the Constitution. This selection must be made upon notice to the Commission, the justice, and the counsel of record in a proceeding open to the public. No court of appeal justice who has served as a master or a member of the Commission in the particular proceeding or is otherwise disqualified may serve on the tribunal.

(b) Clerk of Supreme Court as clerk of tribunal

The Clerk of the Supreme Court serves as the clerk of the tribunal. *(Formerly Rule 921, adopted, eff. Nov. 13, 1976. Renumbered Rule 936 and amended, eff. Dec. 1, 1996. Renumbered Rule 9.61 and amended, eff. Jan. 1, 2007.)*

Research References

2 Witkin Cal. Proc. 5th Courts § 91, Procedure.
2 Witkin Cal. Proc. 5th Courts § 196, (S 196) Rules on Law Practice, Attorneys, and Judges.

Division 6

JUDICIAL ETHICS OPINIONS

Rule
9.80. Committee on Judicial Ethics Opinions.

Rule 9.80. Committee on Judicial Ethics Opinions

(a) Purpose

The Supreme Court has established the Committee on Judicial Ethics Opinions to provide judicial ethics advisory opinions and advice to judicial officers and candidates for judicial office.

(b) Committee determinations

In providing its opinions and advice, the committee acts independently of the Supreme Court, the Commission on Judicial Performance, and all other entities. The committee will rely on the California Code of Judicial Ethics, the decisions of the Supreme Court and of the Commission on Judicial Performance, and other relevant sources in its opinions and advice.

(c) Membership

The committee consists of twelve members appointed by the Supreme Court, including at least one justice from a court of appeal and one member who is a subordinate judicial officer employed full-time by a superior court. The remaining members must be justices of a court of appeal or judges of a superior court, active or retired. No more than a total of two retired justices or judges may serve on the committee at one time, except that if an active justice or judge retires during his or her term, he or she will be permitted to complete his or her term. A retired justice or judge may only serve so long as he or she is not an active member of the State Bar of California and is not engaged in privately compensated dispute resolution activities.

(d) Terms

(1) Except as provided in (2), all full terms are for four years. Members may not serve more than two consecutive full terms. Members will continue to serve until a successor is appointed. Appointments to fill a vacancy will be for the balance of the term vacated. Members who are appointed to fill a vacancy for the

balance of a term are eligible to serve two full terms in addition to the remainder of the term for which they were appointed.

(2) To create staggered terms among the members of the committee, the Supreme Court will appoint initial members of the committee as follows:

(A) Three members each to serve a term of five years. The Court may reappoint these members to one full term.

(B) Three members each to serve a term of four years. The Court may reappoint these members to one full term.

(C) Three members each to serve a term of three years. The Court may reappoint these members to one full term.

(D) Three members each to serve a term of two years. The Court may reappoint these members to one full term.

(3) Committee members may not simultaneously serve as members of the Commission on Judicial Performance or the California Judges Association's Judicial Ethics Committee. If a member of the committee accepts appointment to serve on one of these entities, that member will be deemed to have resigned from the committee and the Supreme Court will appoint a replacement.

(e) Powers and duties

The committee is authorized to provide ethics advice to judicial officers and candidates for judicial office, including formal written opinions, informal written opinions, and oral advice. Specifically, the committee is authorized to:

(1) Issue formal written opinions, informal written opinions, and oral advice on proper judicial conduct under the California Code of Judicial Ethics, the California Constitution, statutes, and any other authority deemed appropriate by the committee.

(2) Make recommendations to the Supreme Court for amending the Code of Judicial Ethics or these rules;

(3) Make recommendations regarding appropriate subjects for judicial education programs; and

(4) Make other recommendations to the Supreme Court as deemed appropriate by the committee or as requested by the Court.

(f) Referrals to California Judges Association's Judicial Ethics Committee

The committee may adopt a revocable policy of referring requests for oral advice, with conditions and exceptions as approved by the committee, to the California Judges Association's Judicial Ethics Committee.

(g) Chair and vice-chair

The Supreme Court will appoint a chair, who will serve a term of two years. The Supreme Court may reappoint the chair. The chair may not serve more than two terms as chair. The Supreme Court will also appoint a vice-chair from the members of the committee. The chair is authorized to call meetings as needed, and to otherwise coordinate the work of the committee.

(h) Confidentiality

Communications to and from the committee are confidential except as described herein. Encouraging judicial officers and candidates for judicial office to seek ethics opinions and advice from the committee will promote ethical conduct and the fair administration of justice. Establishing the confidentiality of committee proceedings and communications to and from the committee is critical to encourage judicial officers and candidates for judicial office to seek ethics opinions and advice from the committee. The necessity for preserving the confidentiality of these proceedings and communications to and from the committee outweighs the necessity for disclosure in the interest of justice. Therefore, to promote ethical conduct by judicial officers and candidates for judicial office and to encourage them to seek ethics opinions and advice from the committee, the following confidentiality requirements, and exceptions, apply to proceedings and other matters under this rule:

(1) Notwithstanding any other provision of law, and with the exception of formal written opinions and summaries of informal written opinions and oral advice, all opinions, inquiries, replies, circulated drafts, records, documents, writings, files, communications with staff, and proceedings of the committee are confidential. All communications, written or verbal, from or to the person or entity requesting an opinion or advice are deemed to be official information within the meaning of the California Evidence Code. In addition, all communications and documents regarding opinions or advice of the California Judges Association forwarded by the California Judges Association to the committee are deemed to be confidential information.

(2) Members of the committee or its staff may not disclose outside the committee or its staff any confidential information, including identifying information, obtained by the committee or its staff concerning an individual whose inquiry or conduct was the subject of any communication with the committee or its staff.

(3) A judicial officer or candidate for judicial office may waive confidentiality; any such waiver must be in writing. If the judicial officer or candidate making the request for an opinion or advice waives confidentiality or asserts reliance on an opinion or advice in judicial or attorney discipline proceedings, such opinion or advice no longer is confidential under these rules. Notwithstanding any waiver, committee deliberations and records are confidential.

(i) Opinion requests

(1) The committee may issue formal written opinions on any subject it deems appropriate. Any person or entity may suggest to the committee, in writing, topics to be addressed in a formal written opinion.

(2) Only judicial officers and candidates for judicial office may request informal written opinions and oral advice.

(3) A judicial officer or candidate for judicial office requesting a written opinion, formal or informal, must submit the request in writing, including by electronic mail. The request must be in a form approved by the committee and must describe the facts and discuss the issues presented in the request. The identity, organizational affiliation, and geographic location of persons requesting opinions are confidential.

(4) A judicial officer or candidate for judicial office requesting oral advice may communicate in person, in writing (including by electronic mail), or by telephone to committee staff or any member of the committee.

(5) A judicial officer or candidate for judicial office requesting an opinion or advice must disclose to the committee whether the issue that is the subject of the inquiry is also the subject of pending litigation involving the inquiring judicial officer or candidate or a pending Commission on Judicial Performance or State Bar disciplinary proceeding involving the inquiring judicial officer or candidate.

(j) Consideration of requests

(1) The committee will determine whether a written request for an opinion should be resolved with a formal written opinion, an informal written opinion, oral advice, or any combination thereof. The committee may decline to issue an opinion or advice.

(2) Eight members must vote affirmatively to adopt a formal written opinion. After the committee authorizes a formal written opinion and before it becomes final, it will be posted in draft form on the committee Web site and made available for public comment for at least 45 days, unless the committee in its discretion decides such an opinion should be issued in final form in less time or with no prior notice. After the public comment period has expired, the committee will decide whether the opinion should be published in its original form, modified, or withdrawn. Eight members must vote affirmatively to modify or withdraw a formal written opinion.

(3) Informal written opinions and oral advice will be decided by vote of the committee members. The committee will adopt procedures concerning the number of votes required to issue an informal written opinion or oral advice.

(4) The committee will adopt procedures concerning the handling and determination of requests for opinions or advice.

(5) The committee will inform the inquiring judicial officer or candidate for judicial office that he or she must disclose all relevant information and that any opinion or advice issued by the committee is based on the premise that the inquiring judicial officer or candidate has disclosed all relevant information.

(6) The committee will confer in person, in writing, including by electronic mail, by telephone, or by videoconference as often as needed to conduct committee business and resolve pending requests.

(k) Opinion distribution

(1) The committee will, upon final approval of a formal written opinion, ensure distribution of the opinion, including to the person or entity who requested the opinion, all California judicial officers, and other interested persons.

(2) The committee's informal written opinions and written confirmation of oral advice will, upon approval by the committee, be provided to the inquiring judicial officer or candidate for judicial office.

(3) The committee will post all formal written opinions on the committee's Web site. The committee may post summaries of its informal written opinions and of oral advice on the committee's Web site.

(4) The committee will maintain records of committee determinations and opinions at the committee's office.

(*l*) Withdrawn, modified, and superseding opinions

The committee may withdraw, modify, or supersede an opinion at any time.

(m) Internal operating rules

The committee will adopt procedures, subject to approval by the Supreme Court, to implement this rule.

(n) Web site, e-mail address, and toll-free telephone number

The committee will maintain a Web site, e-mail address, and toll-free telephone number. *(Adopted, eff. July 1, 2009.)*

Research References

Rutter, Cal. Practice Guide: Prof. Responsibility Ch. 1-K, K. Additional Regulations Affecting Lawyer Conduct.
Rutter, Cal. Practice Guide: Prof. Responsibility Ch. 8-D, D. Restrictions on Speech and Behavior Outside Courtroom.
Rutter, Cal. Practice Guide: Prof. Responsibility Ch. 11-E, E. Receiving Complaints of Attorney Misconduct.
2 Witkin Cal. Proc. 5th Courts § 196, (S 196) Rules on Law Practice, Attorneys, and Judges.
2 Witkin Cal. Proc. 5th Courts § 92A, (New)-Ethics Opinion.

Division 7

STATE BAR TRUSTEES

Rule
9.90. Nominations and appointments of State Bar trustees.

Rule 9.90. Nominations and appointments of State Bar trustees

(a) State Bar Trustees Nominating Committee

(1) The Supreme Court appoints five attorneys to the State Bar Board of Trustees, each for a three-year term. The court may reappoint an attorney for one additional term. The court may also fill any vacancy in the term of, and make any reappointment of, any appointed attorney member. Each appointee must be an active member of the State Bar and have his or her principal office in California.

(2) In order to ensure that individuals appointed by the Supreme Court to the State Bar Board of Trustees have been evaluated objectively, the court has established an independent "State Bar Trustees Nominating Committee" to receive applications and screen and evaluate prospective appointees. The role of the committee is to determine whether applicants possess not only the statutorily enumerated qualifications, but also any other qualifications that may be required to carry out the duties of the Board of Trustees.

(3) The committee serves at the pleasure of the court. The committee will consist of seven members appointed by the court of whom five must be active members of the State Bar in good standing, and two must be active or retired judicial officers. A committee chair and vice-chair are designated by the court. The court will seek to create a broadly representative body to assist it in its considerations.

Except as provided below, all full terms are for three years. Members may not serve more than two consecutive full terms. Members will continue to serve until a successor is appointed. Appointments to fill a vacancy will be for the balance of the term vacated. Members who are appointed to fill a vacancy for the balance of a term are eligible to serve two full terms in addition to the remainder of the term for which they were appointed.

To create staggered terms among the members of the committee, the Supreme Court will appoint initial members of the committee as follows:

(A) Four members each to serve a term of three years. The court may reappoint these members to one full term.

(B) Three members each to serve a term of two years. The court may reappoint these members to one full term.

(4) The committee must adopt, and implement upon approval by the Supreme Court, procedures for:

(A) Receipt of applications and initial screening of applicants for appointments to fill the vacant positions, including adoption of a comprehensive application form;

(B) Receipt of evaluations concerning selected applicants;

(C) Evaluation and rating of applicants; and

(D) Transmittal of the materials specified in (b) of this rule to the Supreme Court.

The procedures adopted by the committee must include provisions to ensure the confidentiality of its evaluations.

(5) In recommending candidates, in order to provide for the appointment of trustees who bring to the board a variety of experiences, the committee should consider:

(A) Legal services attorneys, solo practitioners, attorneys with small firms, and attorneys with governmental entities;

(B) Historically underrepresented groups, such as those underrepresented because of race, ethnicity, gender, and sexual orientation;

(C) Legal academics;

(D) Geographic distribution;

(E) Years of practice;

(F) Attorneys who are in their first five years of practice;

(G) Participation in voluntary local or state bar activities;

(H) Participation in activities to benefit the public; and

(I) Other factors demonstrating a background that will help inform the work of the board.

(6) The State Bar must provide the support the committee requires to discharge its obligations under this rule.

(b) Evaluations

(1) The committee must evaluate the qualifications of and rate all applicants and must submit to the court the nominations of at least three qualified candidates for each vacancy. Candidates are to be rated as "not recommended," "recommended," and "highly recommended." A rating of "not recommended" relates only to the position under consideration and does not indicate any lack of ability or expertise of the applicant generally. The committee must report in confidence to the Supreme Court its evaluation, rating, and recommendation for applicants for appointment and the reasons therefore, including a succinct summary of their qualifications, at a time to be designated by the Supreme Court. The report must include written comments regarding the nominees received by the committee, which must be transmitted to the Supreme Court together with the nominations.

(2) In determining the qualifications of an applicant for appointment or reappointment the committee should, in addi-

tion to the factors cited in subsection (a)(5), consider the following: focus on the public interest, public service, commitment to the administration of justice, objectivity, community

respect, integrity, ability to work collaboratively, and balanced temperament. *(Adopted, eff. Jan. 23, 2013.)*

Title 10

JUDICIAL ADMINISTRATION RULES

Division 1

JUDICIAL COUNCIL

Chapter 1

THE JUDICIAL COUNCIL AND INTERNAL COMMITTEES

Rule

Rule 10.1. Authority, duties, and goals of the Judicial Council

(a) The Judicial Council

(1) The Judicial Council of California is a state entity established by the California Constitution and chaired by the Chief Justice of California. The Judicial Council sets the direction for improving the quality of justice and advancing the consistent, independent, impartial, and accessible administration of justice by the judicial branch for the benefit of the public.

(2) The council establishes policies and sets priorities for the judicial branch of government. The council may seek advice and recommendations from committees, task forces, and the public.

(3) The Judicial Council Governance Policies are located in Appendix D of these rules of court. The policies describe the council's:

  (A) Purposes;

  (B) Responsibilities;

  (C) Policymaking role;

  (D) Members and officers and their roles;

  (E) Internal organization;

  (F) Relationship with its advisory groups;

  (G) Relationship with the Administrative Director of the Courts and with the Administrative Office of the Courts, the staff agency that he or she directs; and

  (H) Internal policies and procedures.

(b) Constitutional authority and duties

Article VI, section 6 of the California Constitution requires the council to improve the administration of justice by doing the following:

  (1) Surveying judicial business;

  (2) Making recommendations to the courts;

  (3) Making annual recommendations to the Governor and the Legislature;

  (4) Adopting rules for court administration and rules of practice and procedure that are not inconsistent with statute; and

  (5) Performing other functions prescribed by statute.

(c) Judicial branch goals

The Judicial Council develops judicial branch goals in its strategic and operational plans. At six-year intervals, the council develops and approves a long-range strategic plan. At three-year intervals, the council develops and approves an operational plan for the implementation of the strategic plan. Each plan is developed in consultation with branch stakeholders and justice system partners.

(d) The Administrative Office of the Courts

The Administrative Office of the Courts supports the council in performing its functions. The Administrative Director is the Secretary of the Judicial Council. *(Formerly Rule 6.1, adopted, eff. Jan. 1, 1999. Renumbered Rule 10.1 and amended, eff. Jan. 1, 2007. As amended, eff. Aug. 14, 2009.)*

Research References

2 Witkin Cal. Proc. 5th Courts § 197, (S 197) Judicial Administration Rules.
2 Witkin Cal. Proc. 5th Courts § 391, (S 391) Composition.
2 Witkin Cal. Proc. 5th Courts § 392, (S 392) Governing Rules.

Rule 10.2. Judicial Council membership and terms

(a) Constitutional provision on membership and terms

(1) Under article VI, section 6 of the California Constitution, the Judicial Council consists of the Chief Justice and one other justice of the Supreme Court, 3 justices of Courts of Appeal, 10 judges of superior courts, 2 nonvoting court administrators, and such other nonvoting members as determined by the voting membership of the council, each appointed by the Chief Justice to three-year terms; 4 members of the State Bar appointed by its governing body to three-year terms; and 1 member of each house of the Legislature appointed as provided by the house.

(2) Council membership terminates if a member ceases to hold the position that qualified the member for appointment. A vacancy is filled by the appointing power for the remainder of the term.

(b) Council officers and duties

(1) *Chair and vice-chair*

(A) The Chief Justice of California is the Chair of the Judicial Council and performs those functions prescribed by the Constitution and the laws of the State of California. The Chair is a voting member of the council. A reference to the Chair of the Judicial Council in the statutes or rules of this state means the Chief Justice of California.

(B) The Chief Justice appoints a vice-chair from among the judicial members of the council. When the chair is absent, unable to serve, or so directs, the vice-chair performs all of the duties of the chair.

(C) The Chief Justice appoints a Judicial Council member to serve as chair of the council in the event that both the Chief Justice and the council vice-chair are absent or unable to serve. The Chief Justice determines individuals to serve as chair from among the internal committee chairs and vice-chairs.

(2) *Chairs and vice-chairs of the internal committees*

The Judicial Council has four internal committees composed of Judicial Council members, as specified in rule 10.10. The Chief Justice appoints for a one-year term the chair and vice-chair of each of the council's internal committees. Chairs call meetings, as necessary, and provide reports to the council on the activities of the internal committees.

(3) *Officers*

The Judicial Council has seven officers: the chair, vice-chair, secretary, and the chairs of the council's four internal committees.

(4) *Administrative Director of the Courts*

The Administrative Director of the Courts is the secretary to the Judicial Council and performs administrative and policymaking functions as provided by the Constitution and the laws of the State of California and as delegated by the Judicial Council and the Chief Justice. The secretary is not a voting member of the council.

(c) Role of members

(1) Council members are a governing body for California's judicial branch of government. In accepting appointment, they commit themselves to act in the best interest of the public and the judicial system for the purposes of maintaining and enhancing public access to the justice system, as well as preserving and enhancing impartial judicial decisionmaking and an independent judicial branch of government.

(2) Council members do not represent any particular constituency notwithstanding any of their other affiliations or roles.

(3) Council members communicate as representatives of the Judicial Council with the public, the courts, judicial officers, Judicial Council advisory bodies, other government entities, and justice system partners. They communicate about the council's processes, purposes, responsibilities, and issues and reasons for policy decisions, including those policy decisions where there is disagreement.

(d) Terms

Council members are appointed to terms beginning September 15 and ending September 14. Terms for judge members are staggered. To the extent feasible, the State Bar and the Legislature should create staggered terms for their appointees.

(e) Restrictions on advisory committee membership

Unless the Chief Justice waives this provision, neither council members nor nonvoting advisory council members may concurrently serve on a council advisory committee. This provision does not apply to members of the following advisory committees:

(1) Administrative Presiding Justices;

(2) Trial Court Presiding Judges; and

(3) Court Executives. *(Formerly Rule 6.2, adopted, eff. Jan. 1, 1999. Renumbered Rule 10.2 and amended, eff. Jan. 1, 2007. As amended, eff. Aug. 14, 2009.)*

Research References

2 Witkin Cal. Proc. 5th Courts § 391, (S 391) Composition.

Rule 10.3.   Nonvoting members

(a) Appointment

The Chief Justice appoints nonvoting advisory council members as specified in article VI, section 6 of the California Constitution or as approved by the Judicial Council.

(b) Voting

A nonvoting council member may make or second motions at a council meeting but may not vote. A nonvoting member may vote on an internal committee matter as specified in rule 10.10(d). *(Formerly Rule 6.3, adopted, eff. Jan. 1, 1999. Renumbered Rule 10.3 and amended, eff. Jan. 1, 2007.)*

Rule 10.4.   Nominations and appointments to the Judicial Council

(a) Nomination procedures

The Executive and Planning Committee assists the Chief Justice in selecting council members by submitting a list of nominees for each position. The committee uses the following procedures:

(1) The committee publicizes vacancies and solicits nominations. Nominations for advisory member positions are solicited from the Court Executives Advisory Committee, the Appellate Court Clerks Association, the California Court Commissioners Association, and other related bodies. The selected nominees should represent diverse backgrounds, experiences, and geographic locations.

(2) The committee submits a list of at least three nominees to the Chief Justice for each vacant position, except for the Supreme Court associate justice position. The committee gives added consideration to persons who have served on advisory committees or task forces.

(3) If the Chief Justice is a member of the Executive and Planning Committee, the Chief Justice does not participate in discussions relating to nominations.

(b) Appointing order

The Chief Justice makes appointments to the council by order. *(Formerly Rule 6.4, adopted, eff. Jan. 1, 1999. Renumbered Rule 10.4 and amended, eff. Jan. 1, 2007.)*

Rule 10.5.   Notice and agenda of council meetings

(a) Generally

The Judicial Council meets at the call of the Chief Justice no fewer than four times a year.

(b) Meeting schedule

The Administrative Office of the Courts must publish a regular annual schedule that states the planned date, purpose, and location of each meeting. Additional meetings may be scheduled as necessary.

(c) Notice of business meetings

"Business meetings" are council meetings at which a majority of voting members are present to discuss and decide matters within the council's jurisdiction. The Administrative Office of the Courts must give public notice of the date, location, and agenda of each business meeting at least seven days before the meeting. The notice must state whether the meeting is open or closed. If the meeting is partly closed, the notice must indicate which agenda items are closed. A meeting may be conducted without notice in case of an emergency requiring prompt action.

(d) Budget meetings

A "budget meeting" is that portion of any business meeting at which trial court budgets are to be discussed. The Administrative Office of the Courts must provide notice of a budget meeting in the same manner as any other business meeting. Budget meetings normally are scheduled as follows:

(1) A budget priority meeting, normally in February of each year, at which the Judicial Council adopts budget priorities for the trial courts for the budget year that begins July 1 of the next calendar year.

(2) A meeting at which the proposed budget is approved, normally in August of each year, at which the Judicial Council takes action on the following:

(A) Staff recommendations on trial court budget change requests for the next fiscal year;

(B) A total baseline budget for each trial court for the next fiscal year; and

(C) Any proposed changes in funding for a trial court.

(3) A budget allocation meeting, normally at the first council meeting after the state's budget is enacted, at which the Judicial Council approves the final budget allocations for each trial court, including approved budget adjustments.

(4) Other meetings following substantive changes to the trial court portion of the proposed State Budget made by the Governor in the proposed Governor's budget or by a committee or house of the Legislature, at which the Judicial Council will take appropriate action, if any.

(e) Form of notice

The notice and agenda for council meetings must be posted at the Administrative Office of the Courts and on the California Courts Web site (*www.courtinfo.ca.gov*). In addition, the notice and agenda for budget meetings must be provided to designated employee representatives who have submitted a written request to the Administrative Office of the Courts (attention Secretariat).

(f) Contents of agenda

The agenda must contain a brief description of each item to be considered at the council meeting. All items are classified as discussion items, consent items, or informational items.

(1) *Consent items deemed approved*

All consent items are deemed approved without further action at the adjournment of each council meeting.

(2) *Moving consent items to discussion agenda*

A consent item must be moved to the discussion agenda if a council member so requests by giving 48 hours' advance notice to the Executive and Planning Committee, or if the Chief Justice moves the item to the discussion agenda.

(g) Meeting materials

(1) *General materials*

General meeting materials must be distributed to council members at least three business days before the date of the meeting, except in extraordinary circumstances. The Administrative Director may make copies of materials available to the media or attendees in advance of a business meeting and may specify that the materials are provided on agreement by the recipient that they will be kept confidential until the council has discussed or acted on specified items. The council may charge a fee to cover the costs of replicating and mailing these materials to members of the public.

(2) *Budget materials*

(A) When available

Materials involving trial court budgets must be made available at least five business days before the meeting if they have been distributed by that time to the members of the council. All other materials involving trial court budgets must be made available at the same time as the information is distributed to the council.

(B) Distribution

Materials must be made available by posting on the California Courts Web site and by distribution to designated employee representatives who have submitted a written request to the Administrative Office of the Courts (attention Secretariat).

(C) Contents at the budget approval meeting

Materials involving trial court budget proposals presented at the budget approval meeting must include proposed statewide requests for funding, existing trial court baseline budgets, adjustments proposed for any trial court baseline budget, and any court-specific budget change requests.

(h) Circulating orders

Between business meetings, the council may act by circulating order on urgent matters if the Chief Justice or the Administrative Director approves. Prior public notice of a proposed circulating order is not required. Each circulating order adopted by the council must be included on the agenda for the next business meeting as an information item. (*Formerly Rule 6.5, adopted, eff. Jan. 1, 1999. As amended, eff. Jan. 1, 2004. Renumbered Rule 10.5 and amended, eff. Jan. 1, 2007.*)

Rule 10.6.   Judicial Council meetings

(a) Open meeting policy

Business meetings are open to the public unless they are closed under (b). Other meetings, such as orientation, planning, and educational meetings, may be open to the public at the discretion of the Chief Justice. The Chief Justice may seek a recommendation from the Executive and Planning Committee on whether all or part of any meeting should be open or closed. Any discussion or decision of the full council at a business meeting regarding a trial court budget allocation must take place in an open meeting of the council, except for an executive session as provided in (b).

(b) Closed sessions

The Chief Justice may close all or part of a business meeting because of the nature of the meeting or of matters to be discussed. The following matters will ordinarily be discussed in closed session:

(1) A personnel matter or a discussion of the character, competence, or physical or mental health of an individual;

(2) Claims or litigation in which the Judicial Council has an interest;

(3) Contract, labor, or legislative negotiations;

(4) The purchase, sale, or lease of real property;

(5) Security plans or procedures;

(6) Allegations of criminal or professional misconduct; and

(7) Discussions protected by the attorney-client privilege.

(c) Conduct at meeting

Members of the public who attend open meetings must remain orderly. The Chief Justice may order the removal of any disorderly persons.

(d) Requests to speak—general

The Executive and Planning Committee, in its discretion, may allow a member of the public to speak at a business meeting.

Unless the Chief Justice waives this requirement, any member of the public who wishes to speak at a business meeting must submit a request of no more than two pages to the chair of the Executive and Planning Committee by delivering it to the Administrative Office of the Courts at least four business days before the meeting.

(1) *Contents of the request*

The request must include the following:

(A) A description of the agenda item to be addressed;

(B) A specific recitation of the proposed statement with an explanation of its relevance to the agenda item and the reasons it would be of benefit to the council in its deliberations;

(C) The name, residence, and occupation of the person asking to speak and, if applicable, the name, address, and purpose of the agency or organization that the speaker represents;

(D) If available, telephone and fax numbers and e-mail address of the person asking to speak and, if applicable and available, the telephone, fax numbers, and e-mail address of the agency or organization that the speaker represents;

(E) The words "Request to Speak at Judicial Council Meeting" displayed prominently in letters at least one-quarter-inch high on the envelope containing the request; and

(F) A copy of any written materials the speaker proposes to distribute at the meeting.

(2) *Notice of decision*

The Executive and Planning Committee must respond to the request at least two business days before the meeting. The committee may grant the request in part or whole, request additional information, circulate any written materials, or take other action it deems appropriate.

(e) Presentation of information on trial court budget matters

(1) *Presentation of written information*

Any designated employee representative has a right to provide written information on trial court budget allocations to the council.

(2) *Oral presentation*

Any designated employee representative who wishes to make an oral presentation to the Judicial Council must make a written request to the Administrative Office of the Courts (attention Secretariat) no later than 24 hours before the meeting unless the issue has arisen within the last five business days before the meeting, in which case the written request may be made on the day of the meeting.

(3) *Limit on number and time*

The Chief Justice or his or her designee may limit the number and time of speakers in order to avoid cumulative discussion.

(f) Video recording, photographing, and broadcasting at meeting

The Chief Justice may permit video recording, photographing, or broadcasting of a meeting. Any such video recording, photographing, or broadcasting is subject to regulations that ensure the meeting's security and dignity. A request to record, photograph, or broadcast a council meeting must be received by the Chief Justice at least two business days before the meeting.

(g) Minutes as official records

The Secretary of the Judicial Council must prepare written minutes of each council meeting for approval at the next council meeting. When approved by the council, the minutes constitute the official record of the meeting. *(Formerly Rule 6.6, adopted,*

eff. Jan. 1, 1999. As amended, eff. Jan. 1, 2004. Renumbered Rule 10.6 and amended, eff. Jan. 1, 2007.)

Rule 10.10. Judicial Council internal committees

(a) Judicial Council internal committees

The internal committees are:

(1) Executive and Planning Committee;

(2) Policy Coordination and Liaison Committee;

(3) Rules and Projects Committee; and

(4) Litigation Management Committee.

(b) Purpose of the internal committees

The internal committees of the Judicial Council assist the full membership of the council in its responsibilities by providing recommendations in their assigned areas, including rules for court administration, practice, and procedure, and by performing duties delegated by the council. Internal committees generally work at the same policy level as the council, focusing on the establishment of policies that emphasize long-term strategic leadership and that align with judicial branch goals.

(c) Membership and appointment

The Chief Justice appoints each council member and advisory council member to one or more internal committees for a one-year term.

(d) Meetings

Each internal committee meets as often as necessary to perform its responsibilities. The Administrative Director of the Courts, as secretary of the Judicial Council, may attend and participate in the meetings of each internal committee. Internal committee meetings are closed to the public but may be opened at the committee chair's discretion.

(e) Voting

An advisory council member may vote on any internal committee matter unless the committee is taking final action on behalf of the council.

(f) Council review

The council may overrule or modify an action taken by an internal committee.

(g) Reporting to the council

As often as necessary, each internal committee must report to the council on the committee's activities. *(Formerly Rule 6.10, adopted, eff. Jan. 1, 1999. Renumbered Rule 10.10 and amended, eff. Jan. 1, 2007. As amended, eff. Aug. 14, 2009.)*

Rule 10.11. Executive and Planning Committee

(a) Actions on behalf of the Judicial Council

The Executive and Planning Committee may take action on behalf of the council between council meetings, except for:

(1) Adopting rules of court, standards of judicial administration, and forms;

(2) Making appointments that by statute must be made by the council; and

(3) Taking actions that are delegated to other council internal committees.

(b) Planning

The committee oversees the council's strategic planning process.

(c) Court facilities

The committee oversees the council's policies and procedures regarding court facilities, including development of policies, procedures, and guidelines for facilities; site selection; and capital appropriations.

(d) Budgets

The committee ensures that proposed judicial branch budgets, allocation schedules, and related budgetary issues are brought to the Judicial Council in a timely manner and in a format that permits the council to establish funding priorities in the context of the council's annual program objectives, statewide policies, and long-range strategic and operational plans.

(e) Agendas for council meetings

The committee establishes agendas for council meetings by determining:

(1) Whether items submitted for the council's agenda require the council's action and are presented in a form that provides the council with the information it needs to make well-informed decisions; and

(2) Whether each item should be on the consent, discussion, or information agenda; how much time should be allotted for discussion; what presenters should be invited to speak; and, when appropriate, which specific issues should be discussed.

(f) Topics for making policy and receiving updates

The committee develops a schedule of topics that the council intends to consider for making policy and receives updates from the Administrative Director of the Courts or Administrative Office of the Courts staff.

(g) Governance

The committee makes recommendations to the council regarding governance and oversees the council's review of its governance policies and principles.

(h) Nominations

The committee recommends candidates to the Chief Justice for appointment to the Judicial Council and its advisory bodies.

(i) Oversight of advisory committees and task forces

For those advisory committees and task forces over which it has been assigned oversight by the Chief Justice, the committee ensures that activities of each are consistent with the council's goals and policies. To achieve these outcomes, the committee:

(1) Communicates the council's annual charge to each; and

(2) Reviews an annual agenda for each to determine whether the annual agenda is consistent with its charge and with the priorities established by the council.

(j) Communications

The committee promotes effective policies for communications between the Judicial Council and the judicial branch. *(Formerly Rule 6.11, adopted, eff. Jan. 1, 1999. As amended, eff. Jan. 1, 2002; Sept. 1, 2003; Jan. 1, 2005. Renumbered Rule 10.11 and amended, eff. Jan. 1, 2007. As amended, eff. Aug. 14, 2009.)*

Rule 10.12.   Policy Coordination and Liaison Committee

(a) Legislative activities

The Policy Coordination and Liaison Committee performs the following functions:

(1) Taking a position on behalf of the council on pending legislative bills, after evaluating input from the council advisory bodies and the Administrative Office of the Courts, and any other input received from the courts, provided that the position is consistent with the council's established policies and precedents;

(2) Making recommendations to the council on all proposals for council-sponsored legislation and on an annual legislative agenda after evaluating input from council advisory bodies and the Administrative Office of the Courts, and any other input received from the courts; and

(3) Representing the council's position before the Legislature and other bodies or agencies and acting as liaison with other governmental entities, the bar, the media, the judiciary, and the public regarding council-sponsored legislation, pending legislative bills, and the council's legislative positions and agendas.

(b) Building consensus

The committee builds consensus on issues of importance to the judicial branch consistent with the council's strategic plan with entities and individuals outside of the branch.

(c) Coordination

The committee develops an annual plan for communication and interaction with other branches and levels of government, components of the justice system, the bar, the media, and the public.

(d) Advisory committees

The committee may direct any advisory committee to provide it with analysis or recommendations on any pending or proposed legislation, and reviews all recommendations from advisory committees regarding pending or proposed legislation. *(Formerly Rule 6.12, adopted, eff. Jan. 1, 1999. As amended, eff. Sept. 1, 2003. Renumbered Rule 10.12 and amended, eff. Jan. 1, 2007. As amended, eff. Aug. 14, 2009.)*

Rule 10.13.   Rules and Projects Committee

(a) Rules, standards, and forms

The Rules and Projects Committee establishes and maintains a rule-making process that is understandable and accessible to justice system partners and the public. The committee:

(1) Identifies the need for new rules, standards, and forms;

(2) Establishes and publishes procedures for the proposal, adoption, and approval of rules of court, forms, and standards of judicial administration that ensure that relevant input from the public is solicited and considered;

(3) Reviews proposed rules, standards, and forms and circulates those proposals for public comment in accordance with its procedures and guidelines.

(4) Provides guidelines for the style and format of rules, forms, and standards and ensures that proposals are consistent with the guidelines;

(5) Ensures that proposals for new or amended rules, standards, and forms do not conflict with statutes or other rules; and

(6) Determines whether proposals for new or amended rules, standards, or forms have complied with its procedures.

(b) Jury instructions

The committee establishes and maintains a process for obtaining public comment on the jury instructions and assists the council in making informed decisions about jury instructions.

(c) Recommendations

The Rules and Projects Committee assists the council in making informed decisions about rules of court, forms, standards of judicial administration, and jury instructions. The committee:

(1) Recommends whether the council should approve, modify, or reject each proposal;

(2) Recommends to the Executive and Planning Committee whether a proposal should be on the council's consent or discussion agenda and how much time should be allocated for discussion; and

(3) When appropriate, identifies issues for discussion.

If the Rules and Projects Committee recommends against approval, it states the reasons for its recommendation.

(d) Circulating orders

The committee initiates circulating orders to allow the council to adopt rules, standards, and forms between council meetings, if necessary.

(e) Oversight of advisory committees and task forces

For those advisory committees and task forces over which it has been assigned oversight by the Chief Justice, the Rules and Projects Committee ensures that the activities of each are consistent with the council's goals and policies. To achieve these outcomes, the committee:

(1) Communicates the council's annual charge to each; and

(2) Reviews an annual agenda for each to determine whether the annual agenda is consistent with its charge and with the priorities established by the council.

(f) Responsibility of the Administrative Director of the Courts

The Administrative Director is responsible for ensuring that items submitted to the committee for circulation for comment and the council's agenda comply with the committee's procedures and its guidelines on format and style. *(Formerly Rule 6.13, adopted, eff. Jan. 1, 1999. As amended, eff. Sept. 1, 2003. Renumbered Rule 10.13 and amended, eff. Jan. 1, 2007. As amended, eff. Aug. 14, 2009.)*

Rule 10.14. Litigation Management Committee

(a) Litigation oversight

The Litigation Management Committee oversees litigation and claims against trial court judges, appellate court justices, the Judicial Council, the Administrative Office of the Courts, the trial and appellate courts, and the employees of those bodies in which the likely monetary exposure is $100,000 or more or that raise issues of significance to the judicial branch by:

(1) Reviewing and approving any proposed settlement, stipulated judgment, or offer of judgment; and

(2) Consulting with the Administrative Director or General Counsel, on request, regarding important strategy issues.

(b) Recommendations

The committee makes recommendations to the Judicial Council for policies governing the management of litigation involving the courts.

(c) Strategic decisions

The committee resolves written objections described in rule 10.202(d) presented by the Office of the General Counsel. *(Formerly Rule 6.14, adopted, eff. Jan. 1, 2001. As amended, eff. Jan. 1, 2003. Renumbered Rule 10.14 and amended, eff. Jan. 1, 2007. As amended, eff. Dec. 9, 2008; Aug. 14, 2009.)*

Rule 10.20. Proposals for new or amended rules, standards, or forms; rule–making process in general

(a) Council meetings to consider proposals

The Judicial Council meets twice a year, generally in April and October, to consider proposals for the adoption, amendment, or repeal of California Rules of Court, California Standards of Judicial Administration, and Judicial Council forms.

(b) Proposals

The council will consider proposals that are submitted to it by an internal committee, an advisory committee, a task force, or the Administrative Office of the Courts, in accordance with rule 10.22 and any policies and procedures established by the Rules and Projects Committee.

(c) Statewide uniformity

The council will establish uniform statewide practices and procedures where appropriate to achieve equal access to justice throughout California. *(Formerly Rule 6.20, adopted, eff. Jan. 1,*

1999. As amended, eff. Jan. 1, 2002. Renumbered Rule 10.20 and amended, eff. Jan. 1, 2007.)

Research References

2 Witkin Cal. Proc. 5th Courts § 188, (S 188) Filing, Publication, and Effective Date.

Rule 10.21. Proposals from members of the public for changes to rules, standards, or forms

(a) Application

This rule applies to proposals for changes to rules, standards, or forms by a member of the public (any person or organization other than a Judicial Council internal committee, advisory committee, or task force, or the Administrative Office of the Courts).

(b) Submission and content of proposals

Proposals must be submitted in writing to: Judicial Council of California, Attention: General Counsel. Proposals should include:

(1) The text of the proposed rule, standard, form, or amendment;

(2) A description of the problem to be addressed;

(3) The proposed solution and alternative solutions;

(4) Any likely implementation problems;

(5) Any need for urgent consideration;

(6) Known proponents and opponents;

(7) Any known fiscal impact; and

(8) If known, any previous action by the council or an advisory committee on the proposal.

(c) Advisory committee's review of proposal

The General Counsel must refer each proposal from a member of the public to an appropriate advisory committee for consideration and recommendation, or, if no appropriate advisory committee exists, to the Rules and Projects Committee. An Administrative Office of the Courts staff member may independently review the proposal and present an analysis and a recommendation to the committee. The committee may take one of the following actions:

(1) Accept the proposal, either as submitted or modified, and proceed under rule 10.22;

(2) Request further information or analysis; or

(3) Reject the proposal. *(Formerly Rule 6.21, adopted, eff. Jan. 1, 2002. Renumbered Rule 10.21 and amended, eff. Jan. 1, 2007.)*

Rule 10.22. Rule–making procedures

(a) Who may make proposals

A Judicial Council internal committee, advisory committee, task force, or the Administrative Office of the Courts may recommend that the council adopt, amend, or repeal a rule or standard or adopt, approve, revise, or revoke a form.

(b) Legal and advisory committee review

The internal committee, advisory committee, task force, or Administrative Office of the Courts (the proponent) must first submit its proposal to the Office of the General Counsel for legal and drafting review. If the proponent is not an advisory committee, and an appropriate advisory committee exists, the proponent must also submit the proposal to that advisory committee for review.

(c) Recommendation to Rules and Projects Committee

After the proposal has been reviewed by the Office of the General Counsel and any appropriate advisory committee, the proponent must submit the proposal to the Rules and Projects Committee with a recommendation that it be (1) circulated for public comment or (2) submitted to the council for approval without public comment.

(d) Review by Rules and Projects Committee

The Rules and Projects Committee must review the recommendation and may take one of the following actions:

(1) Circulate the proposal for public comment;

(2) If the proposal presents a nonsubstantive technical change or correction or a minor substantive change that is unlikely to create controversy, recommend that the council adopt it without circulating it for comment;

(3) Postpone circulation for comment and either request further information or analysis by the proponent or refer the matter to another council internal or advisory committee, the full council, or the Chief Justice; or

(4) Reject the proposal if it is contrary to statute, conflicts with other rules or standards, or is contrary to established council policy.

(e) Review of comments

After a proposal is circulated, the proponent must review the comments and decide whether to reject the proposal or to recommend that the council adopt it, with or without modifications.

(f) Submission to council

If, after reviewing the comments, the proponent recommends that the council adopt the proposal, the matter will be placed on the council's agenda. The Rules and Projects Committee must review the recommendation and submit its own recommendation to the council. The council may adopt, modify, or reject the proposal.

(g) Compelling circumstances

The procedures established in this rule must be followed unless the Rules and Projects Committee finds that compelling circumstances necessitate a different procedure. The committee's finding and a summary of the procedure used must be presented to the council with any recommendation to the council made under this subdivision. *(Formerly Rule 6.22, adopted, eff. Jan. 1, 2002. Renumbered Rule 10.22 and amended, eff. Jan. 1, 2007.)*

Research References

2 Witkin Cal. Proc. 5th Courts § 197, (S 197) Judicial Administration Rules.

Chapter 2

JUDICIAL COUNCIL ADVISORY COMMITTEES AND TASK FORCES

Rule 10.30. Judicial Council advisory bodies

(a) Types of bodies

Judicial Council advisory bodies are typically advisory committees and task forces.

(b) Functions

The advisory bodies:

(1) Use the individual and collective experience, opinions, and wisdom of their members to provide policy recommendations and advice to the council on topics the Chief Justice or the council specifies;

(2) Work at the same policy level as the council, developing recommendations that focus on strategic goals and long-term impacts that align with judicial branch goals;

(3) Generally do not implement policy. The council may, however, assign policy-implementation and programmatic responsibilities to an advisory body and may request it make recommendations to the Administrative Office of the Courts on implementation of council policy or programs;

(4) Do not speak or act for the council except when formally given such authority for specific and time-limited purposes; and

(5) Are responsible, through the Administrative Office of the Courts, for gathering stakeholder perspectives on policy recommendations they plan to present to the council.

(c) Subcommittees

An advisory body may form subcommittees, composed entirely of members, to carry out the body's duties, subject to available resources.

(d) Oversight

The Chief Justice assigns oversight of each council advisory body to an internal committee. The council gives a general charge to each advisory body specifying the body's subject matter jurisdiction. The council and its internal committees provide direction to the advisory bodies.

(e) Preference for using existing advisory committees

Unless substantial reasons dictate otherwise, new projects requiring committee involvement must be assigned to existing advisory committees.

(f) Role of the Administrative Director of the Courts

The Administrative Director of the Courts sits as an ex officio member of each advisory body.

(g) Creation

In addition to the advisory committees established by the rules in this division, the Chief Justice may create additional advisory bodies by order. *(Formerly Rule 6.30, adopted, eff. Jan. 1, 1999.*

As amended, eff. Sept. 1, 2003. Renumbered Rule 10.30 and amended, eff. Jan. 1, 2007. As amended, eff. Aug. 14, 2009.)

Research References

2 Witkin Cal. Proc. 5th Courts § 197, (S 197) Judicial Administration Rules.
2 Witkin Cal. Proc. 5th Courts § 391, (S 391) Composition.
2 Witkin Cal. Proc. 5th Courts § 392, (S 392) Governing Rules.

Rule 10.31. Advisory committee membership and terms

(a) Membership

The categories of membership of each advisory committee are specified in the rules in this chapter. Each advisory committee consists of between 12 and 18 members, unless a different number is specified by the Chief Justice or required by these rules. Advisory committee members do not represent a specific constituency but must act in the best interests of the public and the entire court system.

(b) Terms

The Chief Justice appoints advisory committee members to three-year terms unless another term is specified in these rules. Terms are staggered so that an approximately equal number of each committee's members changes annually. The Chief Justice also may appoint judicial officers who have served less than two years on the bench to one-year terms.

(c) Chair and vice–chair

The Chief Justice appoints an advisory committee member to be a committee chair or vice-chair for a one-year term except for the chair and vice-chair of the Court Executives Advisory Committee, who may be appointed to two-year terms.

(d) Advisory members

On the request of the advisory committee, the Chief Justice may designate an advisory member to assist an advisory committee or a subcommittee. Advisory members may participate in discussions and make or second motions but cannot vote.

(e) Termination of membership

Committee membership terminates if a member leaves the position that qualified the member for the advisory committee unless the Chief Justice determines that the individual may complete the current term.

(f) Vacancies

Vacancies are filled as they occur according to the nomination procedures described in rule 10.32.

(g) Retired judges

A judge's retirement does not cause a vacancy on the committee if the judge is eligible for assignment. A retired judge who is eligible for assignment may hold a committee position based on his or her last judicial position. *(Formerly Rule 6.31, adopted, eff. Jan. 1, 1999. As amended, eff. Sept. 1, 2000; Sept. 1, 2003; Jan. 1, 2004; Nov. 1, 2004. Renumbered Rule 10.31 and amended, eff. Jan. 1, 2007.)*

Rule 10.32. Nominations and appointments to advisory committees

(a) Nomination procedures

The Executive and Planning Committee assists the Chief Justice in selecting advisory committee members by submitting a list of nominees for each position. Unless otherwise specified in the rule applicable to a particular advisory committee, the nomination procedures are as follows:

(1) The Executive and Planning Committee must publicize vacancies and solicit nominations. If any group is designated to submit nominations for a position, the Executive and Planning Committee will request that the group submit at least three nominations for each advisory committee vacancy.

(2) The Executive and Planning Committee must submit at least three nominees for each advisory committee vacancy to the Chief Justice. The nominees should represent diverse backgrounds and experiences as well as geographic locations throughout California.

(b) Court executive or administrator members

A court executive or administrator member may be a county clerk, a court administrator, or an executive officer if the member also serves as the clerk of the court.

(c) Judicial administrator member

A judicial administrator member may be any person experienced in court administration and is not required to be currently employed by a court.

(d) Judicial officer

A judicial officer member may be a judge of the superior court or a court commissioner or referee.

(e) Appointing order

The Chief Justice appoints advisory committee members by order. *(Formerly Rule 6.32, adopted, eff. Jan. 1, 1999. As amended, eff. Sept. 1, 2003. Renumbered Rule 10.32, eff. Jan. 1, 2007.)*

Rule 10.33. Advisory committee meetings

Each advisory committee may meet as often as its chair deems necessary, within available resources. Meetings may be in person or by teleconference. *(Formerly Rule 6.33, adopted, eff. Jan. 1, 1999. As amended, eff. Sept. 1, 2003. Renumbered Rule 10.33, eff. Jan. 1, 2007.)*

Rule 10.34. Duties and responsibilities of advisory committees

(a) Role

Advisory committees are standing committees created by rule of court or the Chief Justice to make recommendations and offer policy alternatives to the Judicial Council for improving the administration of justice within their designated areas of focus by doing the following:

(1) Identifying issues and concerns affecting court administration and recommending solutions to the council;

(2) Proposing necessary changes to rules, standards, forms, and jury instructions;

(3) Reviewing pending legislation and making recommendations to the Policy Coordination and Liaison Committee on whether to support or oppose it;

(4) Recommending new legislation to the council;

(5) Recommending to the council pilot projects and other programs to evaluate new procedures or practices;

(6) Acting on assignments referred by the council or an internal committee; and

(7) Making other appropriate recommendations to the council.

(b) Annual charges

(1) Advisory committees are assigned annual charges by the council or an internal committee specifying what should be achieved in a given year. The council or an internal committee may amend an advisory committee's annual charge at any time.

(2) Advisory committees have limited discretion to pursue matters in addition to those specified in each committee's annual charge, as long as the matters are consistent with a committee's general charge, within the limits of resources available to the committee, and within any other limits specified by the council,

the designated internal committee, or the Administrative Director of the Courts.

(c) Responsibilities of the chair

Advisory committee chairs are responsible, with the assistance of staff, to:

(1) Develop a realistic annual agenda for the advisory committee, consistent with the committee's annual charge by the Judicial Council or Judicial Council internal committee;

(2) Present the advisory committee's recommendations to the Judicial Council;

(3) Discuss with the Administrative Director or the Administrative Director's designee appropriate staffing and other resources for projects within the advisory committee's agenda; and

(4) Submit recommendations with respect to advisory committee membership.

(d) Role of the Administrative Director of the Courts

(1) The Administrative Director determines whether projects undertaken by council advisory bodies in addition to those specified in the council's or internal committee's annual charge to the advisory body are consistent with the body's general charge, its approved annual agenda, and the Judicial Council's strategic plan. The Administrative Director also determines whether any additional matters are within the body's authorized budget and available resources.

(2) The Administrative Director is not bound by the recommendations of an advisory committee and may make alternative recommendations to the Judicial Council or recommend that an advisory committee's annual charge be amended.

(e) Role of staff

(1) Advisory committees are assisted by the staff of the Administrative Office of the Courts. The duties of staff members include drafting committee annual agendas, managing the committee's budget and resources, coordinating committee activities, providing legal and policy analysis to the committee, organizing and drafting reports, selecting and supervising consultants, providing technical assistance, and assisting committee chairs in presenting the committee's recommendations to the Judicial Council. Staff may provide independent legal or policy analysis of issues that is different from the committee's position, if authorized to do so by the Administrative Director of the Courts.

(2) Staff report to the Administrative Director of the Courts. The decisions or instructions of an advisory body or its chair are not binding on the staff except in instances when the council or the Administrative Director has specifically authorized such exercise of authority.

(f) Review of annual agendas

(1) Each committee must submit a proposed annual agenda that is reviewed by the internal committee with oversight responsibility, as designated by the Chief Justice. This subdivision does not apply to the Administrative Presiding Justices Advisory Committee.

(2) The internal committee that is responsible for oversight of the advisory committee reviews the proposed annual agenda and provides the advisory committee with an annual charge to ensure that its activities are consistent with the council's goals and priorities. The annual charge may:

(A) Approve or disapprove the annual agenda in whole or in part;

(B) Direct the committee to pursue specific projects on the annual agenda;

(C) Add or delete specific projects; and

(D) Reassign priorities.

(3) An advisory committee may pursue matters in addition to those specified in its annual charge as long as the matters are consistent with the advisory committee's general charge, as set forth in the rules of court, its approved annual agenda, and the council's long-range strategic plan. The additional matters must also be within the committee's authorized budget and available resources, as specified by the council or the Administrative Director of the Courts. *(Formerly Rule 6.34, adopted, eff. Jan. 1, 1999. As amended, eff. Jan. 1, 2002; Sept. 1, 2003. Renumbered Rule 10.34 and amended, eff. Jan. 1, 2007. As amended, eff. Aug. 14, 2009.)*

Rule 10.40. Appellate Advisory Committee

(a) Area of focus

The committee makes recommendations to the council for improving the administration of justice in appellate proceedings.

(b) Additional duty

In addition to the duties described in rule 10.34 the committee makes proposals on training for justices and appellate support staff to the Governing Committee of the Center for Judicial Education and Research.

(c) Membership

The committee must include at least one member from each of the following categories:

(1) Supreme Court justice;

(2) Court of Appeal justice;

(3) Trial court judicial officer with experience in the appellate division;

(4) Supreme Court clerk administrator;

(5) Appellate court administrator;

(6) Trial court judicial administrator;

(7) Civil appellate lawyer;

(8) Criminal defense appellate lawyer;

(9) State Public Defender; and

(10) Appellate lawyer of the Attorney General's Office. *(Formerly Rule 6.40, adopted, eff. Jan. 1, 1999. As amended, eff. Jan. 1, 2002. Renumbered Rule 10.40 and amended, eff. Jan. 1, 2007.)*

Rule 10.41. Civil and Small Claims Advisory Committee

(a) Area of focus

The committee makes recommendations to the council for improving the administration of justice in civil and small claims proceedings.

(b) Membership

The committee must include at least one member from each of the following categories:

(1) Appellate court justice;

(2) Trial court judicial officer;

(3) Judicial administrator;

(4) Lawyer whose primary area of practice is civil law;

(5) Legal secretary;

(6) Person knowledgeable about small claims law and procedure; and

(7) Person knowledgeable about court-connected alternative dispute resolution programs for civil and small claims cases. *(Formerly Rule 6.41, adopted, eff. Jan. 1, 1999. Renumbered Rule 10.41 and amended, eff. Jan. 1, 2007. As amended, eff. Jan. 1, 2011.)*

Rule 10.42. Criminal Law Advisory Committee

(a) Area of focus

The committee makes recommendations to the council for improving the administration of justice in criminal proceedings.

(b) Membership

The committee must include at least one member from each of the following categories:

(1) Appellate court justice;

(2) Trial court judicial officer;

(3) Judicial administrator;

(4) Prosecutor;

(5) Criminal defense lawyer; and

(6) Probation officer. *(Formerly Rule 6.42, adopted, eff. Jan. 1, 1999. Renumbered Rule 10.42 and amended, eff. Jan. 1, 2007. As amended, eff. Jan. 1, 2011.)*

Rule 10.43. Family and Juvenile Law Advisory Committee

(a) Area of focus

The committee makes recommendations to the council for improving the administration of justice in all cases involving marriage, family, or children.

(b) Membership

The committee must include at least one member from each of the following categories:

(1) Appellate court justice;

(2) Trial court judicial officer;

(3) Judicial administrator;

(4) Child custody mediator;

(5) Lawyer whose primary practice area is family law;

(6) Lawyer from a public or private defender's office whose primary practice area is juvenile law;

(7) Chief probation officer;

(8) Child welfare director;

(9) Court Appointed Special Advocate (CASA) director;

(10) County counsel assigned to juvenile dependency cases;

(11) Domestic violence prevention advocate;

(12) District attorney assigned to juvenile delinquency cases;

(13) Lawyer from the California Department of Child Support Services or a local child support agency; and

(14) Public–interest children's rights lawyer. *(Formerly Rule 6.43, adopted, eff. Jan. 1, 1999. As amended, eff. July 1, 2005. Renumbered Rule 10.43 and amended, eff. Jan. 1, 2007.)*

Research References

10 Witkin, California Summary 10th Parent and Child § 441, (S 441) Advisory Committees and Commissions.

Rule 10.44. Probate and Mental Health Advisory Committee

(a) Area of focus

The committee makes recommendations to the council for improving the administration of justice in proceedings involving:

(1) Decedents' estates, trusts, conservatorships, guardianships, and other probate matters; and

(2) Mental health and developmental disabilities issues.

(b) Additional duty

The committee must coordinate activities and work with the Family and Juvenile Law Advisory Committee in areas of common concern and interest.

(c) Membership

The committee must include at least one member from each of the following categories:

(1) Judicial officer with experience in probate;

(2) Lawyer whose primary practice involves decedents' estates, trusts, guardianships, conservatorships, or elder abuse law;

(3) Lawyer or examiner who works for the court on probate or mental health matters;

(4) Investigator who works for the court to investigate probate guardianships or conservatorships;

(5) Person knowledgeable in mental health or developmental disability law;

(6) Person knowledgeable in private management of probate matters in a fiduciary capacity; and

(7) County counsel, public guardian, or other similar public officer familiar with guardianship and conservatorship issues. *(Formerly Rule 6.44, adopted, eff. July 1, 2000. Renumbered Rule 10.44 and amended, eff. Jan. 1, 2007. As amended, eff. Jan. 1, 2008.)*

Rule 10.46. Trial Court Presiding Judges Advisory Committee

(a) Area of focus

The committee contributes to the statewide administration of justice by monitoring areas of significance to the justice system and making recommendations to the Judicial Council on policy issues affecting the trial courts.

(b) Additional duties

In addition to the duties specified in rule 10.34, the committee may:

(1) Recommend methods and policies within its area of focus to improve trial court presiding judges' access to and participation in council decision making, increase communication between the council and the trial courts, and provide for training programs for judicial and court support staff;

(2) Respond and provide input to the Judicial Council, appropriate advisory committees, or the Administrative Office of the Courts on pending policy proposals and offer new recommendations on policy initiatives in the areas of legislation, rules, forms, standards, studies, and recommendations concerning court administration; and

(3) Provide for liaison between the trial courts and the Judicial Council, its advisory committees, task forces, and working groups, and the Administrative Office of the Courts.

(c) Membership

The committee consists of the presiding judge of each superior court.

(d) Executive Committee

The advisory committee may establish an Executive Committee that, in addition to other powers provided by the advisory committee, may act on behalf of the full advisory committee between its meetings.

(e) Subcommittee membership

The committee has standing subcommittees on rules and legislation. The chair may create other subcommittees as he or she deems appropriate. The chair must strive for representation of courts of all sizes on subcommittees.

(f) Chair

The advisory committee must annually submit to the Chief Justice ~~three~~ one nominations for the chair of the advisory committee. ~~The Chief Justice will select a chair from among the names suggested.~~ Any member of the advisory committee whose term as presiding judge would extend at least through the

Ct. Rules

term of the advisory committee chair is eligible for nomination. The nomination must be made by a majority vote of the full advisory committee. In the event that no candidate receives a majority vote on the first ballot, subsequent ballots of the top two candidates will occur until a candidate receives a majority vote. The chair of the advisory committee serves as chair of any Executive Committee established under (d) and as an advisory member of the Judicial Council. *(Formerly Rule 6.46, adopted, eff. Jan. 1, 1999. As amended, eff. Sept. 1, 2000; April 18, 2003. Renumbered Rule 10.46 and amended, eff. Jan. 1, 2007. As amended, eff. July 1, 2013.)*

Advisory Committee Comment

Subdivision (f): An advisory committee member may submit his or her own name, the name of another member of the advisory committee, or the name of an incoming member of the advisory committee to be considered for nomination. An incoming member of the advisory committee may be nominated by a current member of the advisory committee, but he or she may not participate in the voting process. Only current members of the advisory committee may vote. The successful candidate must receive 30 or more votes.

Rule 10.48. Court Executives Advisory Committee

(a) Area of focus

The committee makes recommendations to the council on policy issues affecting the trial courts.

(b) Additional duties

In addition to the duties specified in rule 10.34, the committee must:

(1) Recommend methods and policies to improve trial court administrators' access to and participation in council decision making;

(2) Review and comment on legislation, rules, forms, standards, studies, and recommendations concerning court administration proposed to the council;

(3) Review and make proposals concerning the Judicial Branch Statistical Information System or other large-scope data collection efforts;

(4) Suggest methods and policies to increase communication between the council and the trial courts;

(5) Serve as the Executive Committee for the Conference of Court Executives, as described in rule 10.49; and

(6) Meet periodically with the Administrative Office of the Courts' directors to enhance branch communications.

(c) Consultation with the Conference of Court Executives

To assist it in formulating proposals and recommendations to the council, the committee may seek the advice of the Conference of Court Executives.

(d) Membership

The committee consists of the following members:

(1) Nine executive officers from trial courts that have 48 or more judges;

(2) Four executive officers from trial courts that have 16 to 47 judges;

(3) Two executive officers from trial courts that have 6 to 15 judges;

(4) Two executive officers from trial courts that have 2 to 5 judges;

(5) One member from the six clerk/administrators of the Courts of Appeal selected from three nominations made by the Appellate Court Clerks Association; and

(6) One at-large member appointed from the trial courts by the committee chair to a one-year term.

(e) Nominations

The Conference of Court Executives must submit to the Court Executives Advisory Committee nominations for each vacancy on the committee. The Court Executives Advisory Committee will recommend three nominees for each committee vacancy from the nominations received and submit its recommendations to the Executive and Planning Committee of the Judicial Council. The list of nominees must enable the Chief Justice to appoint a committee that reflects a variety of experience, expertise, and types (e.g., urban, suburban, and rural) that is geographically balanced. Membership on this committee does not preclude appointment to any other advisory committee or task force.

(f) Chair and vice–chair

The Chief Justice may appoint the chair and vice-chair of the committee for up to a two-year term from the current membership of the Court Executives Advisory Committee. *(Formerly Rule 6.48, adopted, eff. Jan. 1, 1999. As amended, eff. Jan. 1, 2004. Renumbered Rule 10.48 and amended, eff. Jan. 1, 2007. As amended, eff. Jan. 1, 2008.)*

Rule 10.49. Conference of Court Executives

(a) Function

The functions of the Conference of Court Executives are to:

(1) Increase the opportunities for court executive officers to participate in the Judicial Council decision-making process; and

(2) Provide a forum for the education of court executives.

(b) Duties

The Conference of Court Executives must:

(1) Provide information and advice, when requested, to the Court Executives Advisory Committee; and

(2) Conduct educational sessions for its members on matters related to court management, such as legislation, training, information management, judicial branch policy issues, professional development, best practices, and current issues facing the trial courts.

(c) Membership

All court executive officers and clerk/administrators of the Courts of Appeal are members of the Conference of Court Executives. A court executive who is unable to participate in a meeting may designate his or her deputy to vote in his or her place.

(d) Chair and vice–chair

The chair and vice-chair of the Court Executives Advisory Committee are the chair and vice-chair of the conference.

(e) Executive Committee

The conference's Executive Committee is the Court Executives Advisory Committee. The Executive Committee must:

(1) Establish the schedule and agenda for meetings; and

(2) As necessary, appoint subcommittees consisting of principal and associate members of the conference.

(f) Nominations subcommittee

The Court Executives Advisory Committee must submit to the Executive and Planning Committee of the Judicial Council nominations for members of the committee, the advisory members of the Judicial Council who are court executives, and members of other advisory committees who are court executives or judicial administrators.

(g) Meetings

The conference must meet during at least two statewide meetings a year. One meeting must be held at the annual California Judicial Administration Conference. The conference must also meet at least two times a year by region for court administration updates, focused discussions, and educational opportunities.

(h) Reimbursement for meetings

Reimbursement for meeting travel per diem expenses for conference members will be subject to availability of funds. *(Formerly Rule 6.49, adopted, eff. Jan. 1, 1999. As amended, eff. Jan. 1, 2004. Renumbered Rule 10.49 and amended, eff. Jan. 1, 2007.)*

Rule 10.50. Governing Committee of the Center for Judicial Education and Research

(a) Establishment and purpose

In 1973, the Judicial Council of California and the California Judges Association created the Center for Judicial Education and Research (CJER), which subsequently became the Education Division of the Administrative Office of the Courts. The Governing Committee of CJER was made an advisory committee to the council in 1993 through the adoption of former rule 1029. In 2001, the rule that specifies the CJER Governing Committee's duties was made consistent with the rules pertaining to other Judicial Council advisory committees, but it continues to acknowledge the historic participation of the California Judges Association.

(b) Area of focus

The committee makes recommendations to the council for improving the administration of justice through comprehensive and quality education and training for judicial officers and other judicial branch personnel.

(c) Additional duties

In addition to the duties described in rule 10.34, the committee must:

(1) Recommend rules, standards, policies, and procedures for judicial branch education;

(2) Recommend a strategic long-range plan for judicial branch education;

(3) Evaluate the effectiveness of judicial branch education, the quality of participation, the efficiency of delivery, and the impact on service to the public;

(4) Review and comment on proposals from other advisory committees and task forces that include education and training of judicial officers or court staff in order to ensure coordination, consistency, and collaboration in educational services;

(5) Establish educational priorities for implementation of curricula, programs, publications, and delivery systems;

(6) Identify the need for and appoint education committees to implement the priorities, long-range plan, and programs and products of judicial branch education; create and adopt procedures for their operation; and review and approve their projects and products;

(7) Identify and foster collaborative opportunities with courts to promote and ensure the availability of training at the local court level;

(8) Identify, analyze, and implement systems to enhance the delivery of education and training statewide; and

(9) Identify and foster collaborative opportunities with internal and external partners to maximize the resources dedicated to education and training.

(d) Membership

The committee consists of at least the following members:

(1) Eight sitting judicial officers, including at least one appellate court justice;

(2) Three judicial administrators;

(3) The Administrative Director of the Courts as an advisory member;

(4) The president of the California Judges Association or his or her designee as an advisory member; and

(5) Other advisory members as the Chief Justice may appoint.

(e) Nominations

Nominations for vacant positions on the Governing Committee will be solicited under the procedures described in rule 10.32. The president of the California Judges Association may submit nominations to the Executive and Planning Committee.

(f) Chair and vice–chair

The Chief Justice appoints the chair and vice-chair. The committee may make recommendations to the Chief Justice for these two positions. *(Formerly Rule 6.50, adopted, eff. Jan. 1, 1999. As amended, eff. Dec. 18, 2001. Renumbered Rule 10.50 and amended, eff. Jan. 1, 2007.)*

Rule 10.51. Court Interpreters Advisory Panel

(a) Area of focus

To assist the council in performing its duties under Government Code sections 68560 through 68566 and to promote access to spoken-language interpreters and interpreters for deaf and hearing-impaired persons, the advisory panel is charged with making recommendations to the council on:

(1) Interpreter use and need for interpreters in court proceedings; and

(2) Certification, registration, renewal of certification and registration, testing, recruiting, training, continuing education, and professional conduct of interpreters.

(b) Additional duty

The advisory panel is charged with reviewing and making recommendations to the council on the findings of the study of language and interpreter use and need for interpreters in court proceedings that is conducted by the Administrative Office of the Courts every five years under Government Code section 68563.

(c) Membership

The advisory panel consists of 11 members. A majority of the members must be court interpreters. The advisory panel must include the specified numbers of members from the following categories:

(1) Four certified or registered court interpreters working as employees in trial courts, one from each of the four regions established by Government Code section 71807. For purposes of the appointment of members under this rule, the Superior Court of California, County of Ventura, is considered part of Region 1 as specified in section 71807, and the Superior Court of California, County of Solano, is considered part of Region 2 as specified in section 71807;

(2) Two interpreters certified or registered in a language other than Spanish, each working either in a trial court as an independent contractor or in an educational institution;

(3) One appellate court justice;

(4) Two trial court judges; and

(5) Two court administrators, including at least one trial court executive officer.

(d) Advisors

The Chief Justice may also appoint nonmember advisors to assist the advisory panel. *(Formerly Rule 6.51, adopted, eff. Jan.*

1, 1999. As amended, eff. July 1, 1999; Oct. 1, 2004. Renumbered Rule 10.51, eff. Jan. 1, 2007.)

Rule 10.52. Administrative Presiding Justices Advisory Committee

(a) Area of focus

The committee makes recommendations to the council on policy issues affecting the administration and operation of the Courts of Appeal.

(b) Additional duties

In addition to the duties described in rule 10.34, the committee must:

(1) Establish administrative policies that promote the quality of justice by advancing the efficient functioning of the appellate courts;

(2) Advise the council of the appellate courts' resource requirements and solicit the council's support in meeting budget, administrative, and staffing requirements;

(3) Make proposals on training for justices and appellate support staff to the Governing Committee of the Center for Judicial Education and Research; and

(4) Comment on and make recommendations to the council about appellate court operations, including:

(A) Initiatives to be pursued by the council or the Administrative Office of the Courts; and

(B) The council's goals and strategies.

(c) Membership

The committee consists of:

(1) The Chief Justice as chair; and

(2) The administrative presiding justices of the Courts of Appeal designated under rule 10.1004.

(d) Funding

Each year, the committee must recommend budget change proposals to be submitted to the Chief Justice for legislative funding to operate the appellate courts. These proposals must be consistent with the budget management guidelines of the Finance Division of the Administrative Office of the Courts.

(e) Allocations

The committee allocates resources among the appellate courts and approves budget management guidelines based on the actual allocation made by the Chief Justice.

(f) Administrative Director of the Courts

The Administrative Director must meet regularly with the committee and must notify and, when appropriate, consult with the committee about appellate court personnel matters. *(Formerly Rule 6.52, adopted, eff. Jan. 1, 1999. Renumbered Rule 10.52 and amended, eff. Jan. 1, 2007.)*

Rule 10.53. Court Technology Advisory Committee

(a) Area of focus

The committee makes recommendations to the council for improving the administration of justice through the use of technology and for fostering cooperative endeavors to resolve common technological issues with other stakeholders in the justice system.

(b) Additional duties

In addition to the duties described in rule 10.34, the committee must:

(1) Recommend standards to ensure compatibility in information and communication technologies in the judicial branch;

(2) Review and comment on requests for the funding of judicial branch technology projects to ensure compatibility with goals established by the council and standards promulgated by the committee;

(3) Review and recommend legislation, rules, or policies to balance the interests of privacy, access, and security in relation to court technology;

(4) Make proposals for technology education and training in the judicial branch;

(5) Assist courts in acquiring and developing useful technologies; and

(6) Maintain a long-range plan.

(c) Membership

The committee must include at least one member from each of the following categories:

(1) Appellate justice;

(2) Trial court judicial officer;

(3) Trial court judicial administrator;

(4) Appellate court judicial administrator;

(5) Member of the Senate;

(6) Member of the Assembly;

(7) Representative of the executive branch; and

(8) Lawyer.

(d) Member selection

The two legislative members are appointed by the respective houses. The executive member is appointed by the Governor. The lawyer member is appointed by the State Bar.

(e) Chair

The Chief Justice appoints a judicial officer or justice member to serve as chair. *(Formerly Rule 6.53, adopted, eff. Jan. 1, 1999. Renumbered Rule 10.53 and amended, eff. Jan. 1, 2007.)*

Rule 10.54. Traffic Advisory Committee

(a) Area of focus

The committee makes recommendations to the council for improving the administration of justice in the area of traffic procedure, practice, and case management and in other areas as stated in the fish and game, boating, forestry, public utilities, parks and recreation, and business licensing bail schedules.

(b) Membership

The committee must include at least one member from each of the following categories:

(1) Trial court judicial officer;

(2) Judicial administrator;

(3) Juvenile hearing officer;

(4) Representative from the California Highway Patrol;

(5) Representative from the Department of Motor Vehicles;

(6) Representative from the Office of Traffic Safety; and

(7) Criminal defense lawyer. *(Formerly Rule 6.54, adopted, eff. Jan. 1, 1999. Renumbered Rule 10.54 and amended, eff. Jan. 1, 2007. As amended, eff. Jan. 1, 2010.)*

Rule 10.55. Access and Fairness Advisory Committee

(a) Area of focus

The committee makes recommendations for improving access to the judicial system and fairness in the state courts.

(b) Additional duties

In addition to the duties described in rule 10.34, the committee must recommend to the Center for Judicial Education and

Research proposals for the education and training of judicial officers and court staff.

(c) Membership

The committee must include at least one member from each of the following categories:

(1) Appellate justice;

(2) Trial court judicial officer;

(3) Lawyer with expertise or interest in disability issues;

(4) Other lawyer;

(5) Judicial administrator; and

(6) Public member. *(Formerly Rule 6.55, adopted, eff. Jan. 1, 1999. Renumbered Rule 10.55 and amended, eff. Jan. 1, 2007.)*

Rule 10.56. Collaborative Justice Courts Advisory Committee

(a) Area of focus

The committee makes recommendations to the Judicial Council on criteria for identifying and evaluating collaborative justice courts and for improving the processing of cases in these courts, which include drug courts, domestic violence courts, youth courts, and other collaborative justice courts. Those recommendations include "best practices" guidelines and methods for collecting data to evaluate the long-term effectiveness of collaborative justice courts.

(b) Additional duties

In addition to the duties described in rule 10.34, the committee must:

(1) Assess and measure the success and effectiveness of local collaborative justice courts;

(2) Identify and disseminate to trial courts locally generated best practices;

(3) Recommend minimum judicial education standards and educational activities to support those standards to the Governing Committee of the Center for Judicial Education and Research;

(4) Advise the council of potential funding sources;

(5) Make recommendations regarding grant funding programs that are administered by the Administrative Office of the Courts for drug courts and other treatment courts; and

(6) Recommend appropriate outreach activities needed to support collaborative justice courts.

(c) Membership

The committee must include the following:

(1) At least five judicial officers. Nominations for these appointments must be made in accordance with rule 10.32. The list of nominees should enable the Chair of the Judicial Council to appoint a committee that reflects a variety of court experience (e.g., criminal, juvenile, family, general civil), expertise, and court sizes and types (e.g., urban, suburban, and rural; and small, medium, and large).

(2) At least one member from each of the following categories:

    (A) Judicial administrator;

    (B) District attorney;

    (C) Criminal defense attorney;

    (D) Law enforcement (police/sheriff);

    (E) Treatment provider or rehabilitation provider;

    (F) Probation officer;

    (G) Court–treatment coordinator;

    (H) Treatment court graduate; and

    (I) Public member.

(Formerly Rule 6.56, adopted, eff. Jan. 1, 2000. As amended, eff. Jan. 1, 2002. Renumbered Rule 10.56 and amended, eff. Jan. 1, 2007.)

Rule 10.58. Advisory Committee on Civil Jury Instructions

(a) Area of focus

The committee regularly reviews case law and statutes affecting jury instructions and makes recommendations to the Judicial Council for updating, amending, and adding topics to the council's civil jury instructions.

(b) Membership

The committee must include at least one member from each of the following categories, and a majority of the members must be judges:

(1) Appellate court justice;

(2) Trial court judge;

(3) Lawyer whose primary area of practice is civil law; and

(4) Law professor whose primary area of expertise is civil law. *(Formerly Rule 6.58, adopted eff. Sept. 1, 2003. Renumbered Rule 10.58 and amended, eff. Jan. 1, 2007.)*

Research References

Rutter, Cal. Practice Guide: Civil Trials & Evidence Ch. 14-B, B. Proper vs. Improper Jury Instructions.

Rule 10.59. Advisory Committee on Criminal Jury Instructions

(a) Area of focus

The committee regularly reviews case law and statutes affecting jury instructions and makes recommendations to the Judicial Council for updating, amending, and adding topics to the council's criminal jury instructions.

(b) Membership

The committee must include at least one member from each of the following categories, and a majority of the members must be judges:

(1) Appellate court justice;

(2) Trial court judge;

(3) Lawyer whose primary area of practice is criminal defense;

(4) Deputy district attorney or other attorney who represents the People of the State of California in criminal matters; and

(5) Law professor whose primary area of expertise is criminal law. *(Formerly Rule 6.59, adopted, eff. July 1, 2005. Renumbered Rule 10.59, eff. Jan. 1, 2007.)*

Rule 10.60. Tribal Court–State Court Forum

(a) Area of focus

The forum makes recommendations to the council for improving the administration of justice in all proceedings in which the authority to exercise jurisdiction by the state judicial branch and the tribal justice systems overlaps.

(b) Additional duties

In addition to the duties described in rule 10.34, the forum must:

(1) Identify issues of mutual importance to tribal and state justice systems, including those concerning the working relationship between tribal and state courts in California;

(2) Make recommendations relating to the recognition and enforcement of court orders that cross jurisdictional lines, the determination of jurisdiction for cases that might appear in

either court system, and the sharing of services between jurisdictions;

(3) Identify, develop, and share with tribal and state courts local rules of court, protocols, standing orders, and other agreements that promote tribal court-state court coordination and cooperation, the use of concurrent jurisdiction, and the transfer of cases between jurisdictions;

(4) Recommend appropriate activities needed to support local tribal court-state court collaborations; and

(5) Make proposals to the Governing Committee of the Center for Judicial Education and Research on educational publications and programming for judges and judicial support staff.

(c) Membership

The forum must include the following members:

(1) Tribal court judges or justices selected by tribes in California, as described in (d), but no more than one tribal court judge or justice from each tribe;

(2) At least three trial court judges from counties in which a tribal court is located;

(3) At least one appellate justice of the California Courts of Appeal;

(4) At least one member from each of the following committees: the Access and Fairness Advisory Committee, Civil and Small Claims Advisory Committee, Criminal Law Advisory Committee, Family and Juvenile Law Advisory Committee, Governing Committee of the Center for Judicial Education and Research, Probate and Mental Health Advisory Committee, and Traffic Advisory Committee; and

(5) As ex officio members, the Director of the California Attorney General's Office of Native American Affairs and the Governor's Tribal Advisor.

The composition of the forum must have an equal or a close-to-equal number of judges or justices from tribal courts and state courts.

(d) Member Selection

(1) The Chief Justice appoints all forum members, except tribal court judges and tribal court justices, who are appointed as described in (2).

(2) For each tribe in California with a tribal court, the tribal leadership will appoint the tribal court judge or justice member to the forum consistent with the following selection and appointment process.

(A) The forum cochairs will notify the tribal leadership of a vacancy for a tribal court judge or justice and request that they submit names of tribal court judges or justices to serve on the forum.

(B) A vacancy for a tribal court judge or justice will be filled as it occurs either on the expiration of a member's term or when the member has left the position that qualified the member for the forum.

(C) If there are more names of tribal court judges and justices submitted by the tribal leadership than vacancies, then the forum cochairs will confer and decide which tribal court judges or justices should be appointed. Their decision will be based on the diverse background and experience, as well as the geographic location, of the current membership.

(e) Cochairs

The Chief Justice appoints a state appellate justice or trial court judge and a tribal court appellate justice or judge to serve as cochairs, consistent with rule 10.31(c). *(Adopted, eff. Oct. 25, 2013.)*

Rule 10.61.   Court Security Advisory Committee

(a) Area of Focus

The committee makes recommendations to the council for improving court security, including personal security and emergency response planning.

(b) Membership

The committee must include at least one member from each of the following categories:

(1) Appellate court justice;

(2) Appellate court administrator;

(3) Trial court judge;

(4) Trial court judicial administrator;

(5) Member of the Court Facilities Advisory Committee; and

(6) Member of the Trial Court Facility Modification Advisory Committee.

At least one member of the committee should be from a trial court that uses a marshal for court security services. *(Adopted, eff. Oct. 25, 2013.)*

Rule 10.70.   Task forces and other advisory bodies

The Chief Justice, the Administrative Director of the Courts, or the council may establish task forces and other advisory bodies to work on specific projects that cannot be addressed by the council's standing advisory committees. These task forces and other advisory bodies may be required to report to one of the internal committees or the Administrative Director, as designated in their charges. *(Formerly Rule 6.70, adopted, eff. Jan. 1, 1999. As amended, eff. Sept. 1, 2003. Renumbered Rule 10.70, eff. Jan. 1, 2007. As amended, eff. Aug. 14, 2009.)*

Chapter 3

ADMINISTRATIVE OFFICE OF THE COURTS

Rule

Rule 10.80.   Administrative Director of the Courts

(a) Functions

The Administrative Director of the Courts, appointed by the Judicial Council under article VI, section 6 of the Constitution, performs those functions prescribed by the Constitution and laws of the state, or delegated to the director by the Judicial Council or the Chief Justice.

(b) Accountability

The Administrative Director is accountable to the council and the Chief Justice for the performance of the Administrative Office of the Courts. The Administrative Director's charge is to accomplish the council's goals and priorities.

(c) Interpretation of policies

The Administrative Director may use any reasonable interpretation of Judicial Council policies to achieve the council's goals, consistent with the limitations from the council and the Chief Justice.

(d) Responsibilities

In carrying out these duties, the Administrative Director is responsible for allocating the financial and other resources of the Administrative Office of the Courts (including, for example, funding the operation of advisory bodies and other activities) to achieve the branch goals and policies adopted by the Judicial Council of California.

(e) Reports

The Administrative Director reports to the Judicial Council at least once annually on the progress made toward achieving the council's goals. When the council sets the direction on projects or programs that require more than one year to complete, the Administrative Director will report back to the council at regular intervals on their status and significant developments. *(Formerly Rule 6.80, adopted, eff. Jan. 1, 1999. Renumbered Rule 10.80 and amended, eff. Jan. 1, 2007. As amended, eff. Aug. 14, 2009.)*

Research References

2 Witkin Cal. Proc. 5th Courts § 197, (S 197) Judicial Administration Rules.
2 Witkin Cal. Proc. 5th Courts § 391, (S 391) Composition.
2 Witkin Cal. Proc. 5th Courts § 392, (S 392) Governing Rules.

Rule 10.81. Administrative Office of the Courts

(a) Establishment

The Administrative Director of the Courts, under the supervision of the Chief Justice, employs, organizes, and directs a staff agency, known as the Administrative Office of the Courts.

(b) Duties

The Administrative Office of the Courts assists the council and its chair in carrying out their duties under the Constitution and laws of the state. *(Formerly Rule 6.81, adopted, eff. Jan. 1, 1999. Renumbered Rule 10.81 and amended, eff. Jan. 1, 2007. As amended, eff. Aug. 14, 2009.)*

Research References

2 Witkin Cal. Proc. 5th Courts § 197, (S 197) Judicial Administration Rules.
2 Witkin Cal. Proc. 5th Courts § 391, (S 391) Composition.

Division 2

ADMINISTRATION OF THE JUDICIAL BRANCH

Chapter 1

BUDGET AND FISCAL MANAGEMENT

Rule
10.101. Role of the Judicial Council and Administrative Office of the Courts.
10.102. Acceptance of gifts.
10.103. Limitation on intrabranch contracting.
10.104. Limitation on contracting with former employees.
10.105. Allocation of new fee, fine, and forfeiture revenue.
10.106. Judicial branch travel expense reimbursement policy.
10.107. Trial Court Budget Working Group.

Rule 10.101. Role of the Judicial Council and Administrative Office of the Courts

(a) Purpose

This rule specifies the responsibilities of the Judicial Council, the Chief Justice, the Administrative Director of the Courts, and the Administrative Office of the Courts with respect to the judicial branch budget.

(b) Duties of the Judicial Council

The Judicial Council must:

(1) Establish responsible fiscal priorities that best enable the judicial branch to achieve its goals and the Judicial Council to achieve its mission;

(2) Develop the budget of the judicial branch based on the priorities established and the needs of the courts;

(3) Communicate and advocate the budget of the judicial branch to the Governor and the Legislature;

(4) Allocate funds in a manner that ensures equal access to justice for all citizens of the state, ensures the ability of the courts to carry out their functions effectively, promotes implementation of statewide policies as established by statute and the Judicial Council, and promotes implementation of efficiencies and cost-saving measures;

(5) Resolve appeals on budget and allocation issues; and

(6) Ensure that the budget of the judicial branch remains within the limits of the appropriation set by the Legislature.

(c) Authority of the Chief Justice and Administrative Director of the Courts

(1) The Chief Justice and the Administrative Director of the Courts may take the following actions, on behalf of the Judicial Council, with regard to any of the Judicial Council's recommended budgets for the Supreme Court, the Courts of Appeal, the trial courts, the Judicial Council, the Habeas Corpus Resource Center, and the Administrative Office of the Courts:

(A) Make technical changes to the proposed budget; and

(B) Make changes during their negotiations with the legislative and executive branches consistent with the goals and priorities adopted by the Judicial Council.

(2) The Chief Justice and the Administrative Director of the Courts, on behalf of the Judicial Council, may allocate funding appropriated in the annual State Budget to the Supreme Court, the Courts of Appeal, the Judicial Council, the Habeas Corpus Resource Center, and the Administrative Office of the Courts.

(3) After the end of each fiscal year, the Administrative Director of the Courts must report to the Judicial Council on the actual expenditures from the budgets for the Supreme Court, the Courts of Appeal, the trial courts, the Judicial Council, the Habeas Corpus Resource Center, and the Administrative Office of the Courts.

(d) Duties of the Administrative Director of the Courts

The Administrative Director of the Courts implements the directives of the Judicial Council and must:

(1) Develop policies and procedures for the creation and implementation of a yearly budget for the judicial branch;

(2) Present the judicial branch budget in negotiations with the Governor and the Legislature; and

(3) Allocate to the trial courts, on behalf of the Judicial Council, a portion of the prior fiscal year baseline allocation for the trial courts following approval of the State Budget and before the allocation of state trial court funding by the Judicial Council. The portion of the prior fiscal year baseline allocation that may be so allocated is limited to the amount estimated to be necessary for the operation of the courts pending action by the Judicial Council, and may not exceed 25 percent of the prior fiscal year baseline allocation for each trial court.

(e) Duties of the director of the Finance Division

The director of the Finance Division of the Administrative Office of the Courts, under the direction of the Administrative Director of the Courts, administers the budget policies and procedures developed by the Administrative Director of the Courts and approved by the Judicial Council. The director of the Finance Division must:

(1) Develop and administer a budget preparation process for the judicial branch, and ensure the submission of a final budget recommendation for the judicial branch to the Department of Finance by November 1 of each year;

(2) Develop, in consultation with the State Controller's Office and the Department of Finance, a manual of procedures for the budget request process, revenues, expenditures, allocations, and payments;

(3) Monitor all revenues and expenditures for the judicial branch;

(4) Develop recommendations for fiscal priorities and the allocation and reallocation of funds; and

(5) Assist all courts and the Administrative Director of the Courts in preparing and managing budgets. (*Formerly Rule 2301, adopted, eff. July 1, 1998. Renumbered Rule 6.101, eff. Jan. 1, 1999. As amended, eff. Jan. 1, 2001; Jan. 1, 2005. Renumbered Rule 10.101 and amended, eff. Jan. 1, 2007. As amended, eff. Aug. 14, 2009.*)

Research References

2 Witkin Cal. Proc. 5th Courts § 197, (S 197) Judicial Administration Rules.
2 Witkin Cal. Proc. 5th Courts § 392, (S 392) Governing Rules.

Rule 10.102.   Acceptance of gifts

(a) Administrative Director of the Courts' authority to accept gifts

The Administrative Director of the Courts may accept on behalf of any entity listed in (b) any gift of real or personal property if the gift and any terms and conditions are found to be in the best interest of the state. Any applicable standards used by the Director of Finance under Government Code section 11005.1 may be considered in accepting gifts.

(b) Delegation of authority

The Administrative Director may delegate the authority to accept gifts to the following, under any guidelines established by the Administrative Office of the Courts:

(1) The executive officer of a superior court, for gifts to the superior court;

(2) The clerk/administrator of a Court of Appeal, for gifts to a Court of Appeal;

(3) The clerk of the Supreme Court, for gifts to the Supreme Court; and

(4) The Director of the Finance Division of the Administrative Office of the Courts, for gifts to the Judicial Council and the Administrative Office of the Courts. (*Formerly Rule 989.7, adopted, eff. Sept. 13, 1991. Renumbered Rule 6.102 and amended, eff. Jan. 1, 2004. Renumbered Rule 10.102 and amended, eff. Jan. 1, 2007.*)

Rule 10.103.   Limitation on intrabranch contracting

(a) Definitions

For purposes of this rule, "judicial branch entity" includes a trial court, a Court of Appeal, the Supreme Court, and the Administrative Office of the Courts.

(b) Application

This rule is not applicable to:

(1) Part–time commissioners, with respect to services as a commissioner;

(2) Part–time court interpreters who are not subject to the cross-assignment system under Government Code section 71810, with respect to interpreter services provided to a court; and

(3) Court reporters, with respect to reporter services provided to a court.

(c) Intrabranch limitations

An employee of a judicial branch entity must not:

(1) Engage in any employment, enterprise, or other activity from which he or she receives compensation or in which he or she has a financial interest and that is sponsored or funded by any judicial branch entity through or by a contract for goods or services for which compensation is paid, unless the activity is required as a condition of his or her regular judicial branch employment; or

(2) Contract with any judicial branch entity, on his or her own behalf, to provide goods or services for which compensation is paid.

(d) Multiple employment

This rule does not prohibit any person from being employed by more than one judicial branch entity. (*Formerly Rule 6.103, adopted, eff. Jan. 1, 2004. Renumbered Rule 10.103 and amended, eff. Jan. 1, 2007.*)

Rule 10.104.   Limitation on contracting with former employees

(a) Trial and appellate court contracts with former employees

A trial or appellate court may not enter into a contract for goods or services for which compensation is paid with a person previously employed by that court or by the Administrative Office of the Courts:

(1) For a period of 12 months following the date of the former employee's retirement, dismissal, or separation from service, if he or she was employed in a policymaking position in the same general subject area as the proposed contract within the 12–month period before his or her retirement, dismissal, or separation; or

(2) For a period of 24 months following the date of the former employee's retirement, dismissal, or separation from service, if he or she engaged in any of the negotiations, transactions, planning, arrangements, or any part of the decision-making process relevant to the contract while employed in any capacity by the court or the Administrative Office of the Courts.

(b) Administrative Office of the Courts contracts with former employees

The Administrative Office of the Courts may not enter into a contract for goods or services for which compensation is paid with a person previously employed by it:

(1) For a period of 12 months following the date of the former employee's retirement, dismissal, or separation from service, if he or she was employed in a policymaking position at the Administrative Office of the Courts in the same general subject area as the proposed contract within the 12–month period before his or her retirement, dismissal, or separation; or

(2) For a period of 24 months following the date of the former employee's retirement, dismissal, or separation from service, if he or she engaged in any of the negotiations, transactions, planning, arrangements, or any part of the decision-making process relevant to the contract while employed in any capacity by the Administrative Office of the Courts.

(c) Policymaking position

"Policymaking position" includes:

(1) In a trial court, the court's executive officer and any other position designated by the court as a policymaking position;

(2) In an appellate court, the clerk/administrator and any other position designated by the court as a policymaking position; and

(3) In the Administrative Office of the Courts, the Administrative Director of the Courts, the Chief Deputy Director, any director, and any other position designated by the Administrative Director as a policymaking position.

(d) Scope

This rule does not prohibit any court or the Administrative Office of the Courts from (1) employing any person or (2) contracting with any former judge or justice. *(Formerly Rule 6.104, adopted, eff. Jan. 1, 2004. Renumbered Rule 10.104 and amended, eff. Jan. 1, 2007.)*

Rule 10.105. Allocation of new fee, fine, and forfeiture revenue

(a) Allocation

The Judicial Council must annually allocate 80 percent of the amount of fee, fine, and forfeiture revenue deposited in the Trial Court Improvement Fund under Government Code section 77205(a) that exceeds the amount of fee, fine, and forfeiture revenue deposited in the Trial Court Improvement Fund in fiscal year 2002–2003 to one or more of the following:

(1) To the trial courts in the counties from which the increased amount is attributable;

(2) To other trial courts to support trial court operations; or

(3) For retention in the Trial Court Improvement Fund.

(b) Methodology

The Administrative Office of the Courts must recommend a methodology for the allocation and must recommend an allocation based on this methodology. On approval of a methodology by the Judicial Council, the Administrative Office of the Courts must issue a Finance Memo stating the methodology adopted by the Judicial Council. *(Formerly Rule 6.105, adopted, eff. Dec. 10, 2004. Renumbered Rule 10.105 and amended, eff. Jan. 1, 2007.)*

Research References

2 Witkin Cal. Proc. 5th Courts § 197, (S 197) Judicial Administration Rules.

Rule 10.106. Judicial branch travel expense reimbursement policy

(a) Adoption

The Judicial Council must adopt a fiscally responsible judicial branch travel expense reimbursement policy, under Government Code section 68506.5, that provides appropriate accountability for the use of public resources. Before adopting the initial policy, the Judicial Council must receive comments from the courts, court employee organizations, and other interested groups.

(b) Applicability

The judicial branch travel expense reimbursement policy applies to official state business travel by:

(1) Judicial officers and judicial officers sitting by assignment;

(2) Officers, employees, retired annuitants, and members of the Supreme Court, the Courts of Appeal, superior courts, the Judicial Council, the Administrative Office of the Courts, the Habeas Corpus Resource Center, and the Commission on Judicial Performance; and

(3) Members of task forces, working groups, commissions, or similar bodies appointed by the Chief Justice, the Judicial Council, or the Administrative Director of the Courts.

(c) Amendments

The Judicial Council delegates to the Administrative Director of the Courts, under article VI, section 6(c) of the California Constitution and other applicable law, the authority to make technical changes and clarifications to the judicial branch travel expense reimbursement policy. The changes and clarifications must be fiscally responsible, provide for appropriate accountability, and be in general compliance with the policy initially adopted by the Judicial Council. *(Adopted, eff. July 1, 2008.)*

Rule 10.107. Trial Court Budget Working Group

The Administrative Director of the Courts must appoint annually a Trial Court Budget Working Group to advise the director on trial court budget issues. The working group must include trial court judicial officers and trial court executive officers reflecting the diversity of state trial courts, including location, size, and adequacy of funding. The working group may also include others selected by the Administrative Director of the Courts. *(Formerly Rule 6.45, adopted, eff. Jan. 1, 2005. Renumbered Rule 10.45 and amended, eff. Jan. 1, 2007. Renumbered Rule 10.107, eff. Aug. 14, 2009.)*

Research References

2 Witkin Cal. Proc. 5th Courts § 197, (S 197) Judicial Administration Rules.

Chapter 2

COURT SECURITY

Rule

Rule 10.172. Court security plans

(a) Responsibility

The presiding judge and the sheriff or marshal are responsible for developing an annual or multiyear comprehensive, countywide court security plan.

(b) Scope of security plan

(1) Each court security plan must, at a minimum, address the following general security subject areas:

(A) Composition and role of court security committees;

(B) Composition and role of executive team;

(C) Incident command system;

(D) Self-assessments and audits of court security;

(E) Mail handling security;

(F) Identification cards and access control;

(G) Courthouse landscaping security plan;

(H) Parking plan security;

(I) Interior and exterior lighting plan security;

(J) Intrusion and panic alarm systems;

(K) Fire detection and equipment;

(L) Emergency and auxiliary power;

(M) Use of private security contractors;

(N) Use of court attendants and employees;

(O) Administrative/clerk's office security;

(P) Jury personnel and jury room security;

(Q) Security for public demonstrations;

(R) Vital records storage security;

Ct. Rules

(S) Evacuation planning;

(T) Security for after-hours operations;

(U) Custodial services;

(V) Computer and data security;

(W) Workplace violence prevention; and

(X) Public access to court proceedings.

(2) Each court security plan must, at a minimum, address the following law enforcement subject areas:

(A) Security personnel and staffing;

(B) Perimeter and entry screening;

(C) Prisoner and inmate transport;

(D) Holding cells;

(E) Interior and public waiting area security;

(F) Courtroom security;

(G) Jury trial procedures;

(H) High-profile and high-risk trial security;

(I) Judicial protection;

(J) Incident reporting and recording;

(K) Security personnel training;

(L) Courthouse security communication;

(M) Hostage, escape, lockdown, and active shooter procedures;

(N) Firearms policies and procedures; and

(O) Restraint of defendants.

(3) Each court security plan should address additional security issues as needed.

(c) Court security assessment and assessment report

At least once every two years, the presiding judge and the sheriff or marshal are responsible for conducting an assessment of security with respect to all court operations. The assessment must include a comprehensive review of the court's physical security profile and security protocols and procedures. The assessment should identify security weaknesses, resource deficiencies, compliance with the court security plan, and any need for changes to the court security plan. The assessment must be summarized in a written assessment report.

(d) Submission of court security plan to the Administrative Office of the Courts

On or before November 1, 2009, each superior court must submit a court security plan to the Administrative Office of the Courts (AOC). On or before February 1, 2011, and each succeeding February 1, each superior court must report to the AOC whether it has made any changes to the court security plan and, if so, identify each change made and provide copies of the current court security plan and current assessment report. In preparing any submission, a court may request technical assistance from the AOC.

(e) Plan review process

The AOC will evaluate for completeness submissions identified in (d). Annually, the submissions and evaluations will be provided to the Working Group on Court Security. Any submissions determined by the working group to be incomplete or deficient must be returned to the submitting court for correction and completion. No later than July 1 of each year, the working group must submit to the Judicial Council a summary of the submissions for the Judicial Council's report to the Legislature.

(f) Delegation

The presiding judge may delegate any of the specific duties listed in this rule to another judge or, if the duty does not require the exercise of judicial authority, to the court executive officer or

other court employee. The presiding judge remains responsible for all duties listed in this rule even if he or she has delegated particular tasks to someone else. *(Adopted, eff. Jan. 1, 2009.)*

Advisory Committee Comment

This rule is adopted to comply with the mandate in Government Code section 69925, which requires the Judicial Council to provide for the areas to be addressed in a court security plan and to establish a process for the review of such plans. The Working Group on Court Security is authorized by Government Code section 69927 and established by rule 10.170 for the purpose of studying and making recommendation to the Judicial Council regarding court security matters. For the assistance of the courts and sheriffs in preparing and submitting their court security plans, the Working Group on Court Security has prepared *Court Security Plan Guidelines* with respect to each of the subject areas identified in subsections (b)(1) and (b)(2). The courts and sheriffs may obtain copies of the *Court Security Plan Guidelines* from the Administrative Office of the Courts' Emergency Response and Security unit.

Rule 10.173.　Court security committees

(a) Establishment

Each superior court must establish a standing court security committee.

(b) Role of the court security committee

The court security committee and any subcommittees advise the presiding judge and sheriff or marshal on the preparation of court security plans and on the formulation and implementation of all other policies and procedures related to security for court operations and security for facilities where the court conducts its operations. The presiding judge and sheriff or marshal may delegate to a court security committee or subcommittee the responsibility for conducting the court security assessment and preparing the assessment report.

(c) Members

(1) The court security committee must be chaired by the presiding judge or a judge designated by the presiding judge.

(2) In addition to the chair, each court security committee must include at least one representative designated by the sheriff or marshal and either the court executive officer or other court administrator as designated by the presiding judge.

(3) The chair may appoint additional members as appropriate. Additional members may include representatives from other government agencies, including:

(A) The facilities management office of the government entity, or entities, that hold title to or are responsible for the facilities where the court conducts its operations;

(B) Local fire protection agencies;

(C) Agencies that occupy portions of a court facility; and

(D) Agencies other than the sheriff that manage local corrections or state prison facilities.

(d) Facility contact person

In those courts having more than one court facility, the chair of the court security committee must designate for each facility a single contact person to coordinate activities in the event of an emergency and to collaborate with the court security committee, at its request.

(e) Subcommittees

The chair of the court security committee may form subcommittees if appropriate, including a subcommittee for each court facility. The chair must determine the composition of each subcommittee based on the individual court's circumstances. *(Adopted, eff. Jan. 1, 2009.)*

2 Witkin Cal. Proc. 5th Courts § 197, (S 197) Judicial Administration Rules.

Rule 10.174. Petition Regarding Disputes Related to Court Security Memoranda of Understanding

(a) Application

This rule applies to petitions filed under Government Code section 69926(e).

(b) Request for assignment of Court of Appeal justice

(1) If a sheriff, county, or superior court is unable to resolve a dispute related to the memorandum of understanding required by Government Code section 69926(b), the sheriff, county, or superior court may file a petition for a writ of mandamus or writ of prohibition.

(2) On the first page, below the case number, the petition must include the following language in the statement of the character of the proceeding (see rule 2.111(6)): "Petition filed under Government Code section 69926(e): Assignment of Court of Appeal justice requested."

(3) On receipt of a petition, the superior court clerk must submit a request to the Chief Justice asking that he or she assign a Court of Appeal justice from an appellate district other than the one in which the county, the superior court, and the sheriff are located to hear and decide the petition.

(c) Superior court hearing

A petition filed under this rule must be heard and decided on an expedited basis and must be given priority over other matters to the extent permitted by law and the rules of court.

(d) Appeal

(1) Any notice of appeal of a decision under (c) must be filed in the same superior court in which the petition was initially filed and must include on the first page the following language, below the case number, in the statement of the character of the proceeding (see rule 2.111(6)): "Notice of Appeal Relating to Petition filed under Government Code section 69926(e): Transfer Requested."

(2) On receipt of the notice of appeal, the Court of Appeal must request that the Supreme Court transfer the appeal to an appellate district other than the one in which the county, the superior court, and the sheriff are located. *(Adopted, eff. Nov. 1, 2012.)*

Chapter 3

COURT FACILITIES

Rule 10.180.   Court facilities standards

(a) Development of standards

The Administrative Office of the Courts is responsible for developing and maintaining standards for the alteration, remodeling, renovation, and expansion of existing court facilities and for the construction of new court facilities.

(b) Adoption by the Judicial Council

The standards developed by the Administrative Office of the Courts must be submitted to the Judicial Council for review and adoption as the standards to be used for court facilities in the state. Nonsubstantive changes to the standards may be made by the Administrative Office of the Courts; substantive changes must be submitted to the Judicial Council for review and adoption.

(c) Use of standards

The Judicial Council, the Administrative Office of the Courts, affected courts, and advisory groups on court facilities issues created under these rules must use the standards adopted under (b) in reviewing or recommending proposed alteration, remodeling, renovation, or expansion of an existing court facility or new construction. Courts and advisory groups must report deviations from the standards to the Administrative Office of the Courts through a process established for that purpose. *(Formerly Rule 6.150, adopted, eff. July 1, 2002. As amended, eff. June 23, 2004; April 21, 2006. Renumbered Rule 10.180, eff. Jan. 1, 2007.)*

2 Witkin Cal. Proc. 5th Courts § 197, (S 197) Judicial Administration Rules.

Rule 10.181.   Court facilities policies, procedures, and standards

(a) Responsibilities of the Administrative Office of the Courts

The Administrative Office of the Courts, after consultation with the Court Facilities Transitional Task Force, must prepare and present to the Judicial Council recommendations for policies, procedures, and standards concerning the operation, maintenance, alteration, remodeling, renovation, expansion, acquisition, space programming, design, and construction of appellate and trial court facilities under Government Code sections 69204(c) and 70391(e).

(b) Consultations with the affected court and with local governmental and community interests

The policies, procedures, and standards must ensure that decisions are made in consultation with the affected court, when appropriate, and that decisions concerning acquisition, design, and construction of court facilities are made in consultation with local governmental and community interests, when appropriate. *(Formerly Rule 6.180, adopted, eff. June 23, 2004. As amended, eff. April 21, 2006. Renumbered Rule 10.181 and amended, eff. Jan. 1, 2007.)*

Rule 10.182.   Operation and maintenance of court facilities

(a) Intent

The intent of this rule is to allocate responsibility and decision making for the operation and maintenance of court facilities among the courts and the Administrative Office of the Courts.

(b) Responsibilities of the Administrative Office of the Courts

(1) In addition to those matters expressly authorized by statute, the Administrative Office of the Courts is responsible for:

(A) Taking action on the operation of court facilities, including the day-to-day operation of a building and maintenance of a facility. The Administrative Office of the Courts must, in cooperation with the court, perform its responsibilities concerning operation of the court facility to effectively and efficiently support the day-to-day operation of the court system and services of the court. These actions include maintaining proper heating, ventilation, and air conditioning levels; providing functional electrical, fire safety, vertical transportation, mechanical, and plumbing systems through preventive maintenance and responsive repairs; and maintaining structural, nonstructural, security, and telecommunications infrastructures.

(B) Preparing and submitting budget allocation proposals to the Judicial Council, as part of the yearly judicial branch budget development cycle, specifying the amounts to be spent for the operation of court facilities as provided in (A).

(C) Developing policies, procedures, and guidelines concerning court facilities for submission to the Judicial Council.

(2) The Administrative Office of the Courts must consult with affected courts concerning the annual operations and maintenance needs assessment, development of annual priorities, and fiscal planning for the operational and maintenance needs of court facilities.

(3) The Administrative Office of the Courts may, when appropriate, delegate its responsibilities for ongoing operation and management to the court for some or all of the existing court facilities used by that court. Any delegation of responsibility must ensure that:

(A) The management of court facilities is consistent with the statewide goals and policies of the judicial branch;

(B) Access to all court facilities in California is promoted;

(C) Facilities decisions are made with consideration of operational costs and enhance economical, efficient, and effective court operations; and

(D) Courts have adequate and sufficient facilities and appropriate resources to undertake these delegated tasks.

(4) The Administrative Office of the Courts must, whenever feasible, seek review and recommendations from the Court Facilities Transitional Task Force before recommending action on appellate and trial court facilities issues to the Judicial Council.

(c) Responsibilities of the courts

(1) The affected courts must consult with the Administrative Office of the Courts concerning the annual operations and maintenance needs assessment, development of annual priorities, and fiscal planning for the operational and maintenance needs of court facilities, including contingency planning for unforeseen facility maintenance needs.

(2) Each court to which responsibility is delegated under (b)(3) must report to the Administrative Office of the Courts quarterly or more often, as provided in the delegation. The report must include the activities and expenditures related to the delegation that are specified for reporting in the delegation. Each court must also account to the Administrative Office of the Courts for all expenditures related to the delegation. The Administrative Office of the Courts may conduct an internal audit of any receipts and expenditures. *(Formerly Rule 6.181, adopted, eff. June 23, 2004. Renumbered Rule 10.182 and amended, eff. Jan. 1, 2007.)*

Rule 10.183.   Decision making on transfer of responsibility for trial court facilities

(a) Intent

The intent of this rule is to allocate among the Judicial Council, the trial courts, and the Administrative Office of the Courts, responsibility and decision making for the transfer of responsibility for trial court facilities from the counties to the Judicial Council.

(b) Definitions

As used in this rule, the following terms have the same meaning as provided by Government Code section 70301:

(1) "Court facilities";

(2) "Maintenance";

(3) "Responsibility for facilities"; and

(4) "Shared use."

(c) Responsibilities of the Judicial Council and the Executive and Planning Committee

The Judicial Council must determine the following issues concerning transfer of responsibility of court facilities, except in the case of a need for urgent action between meetings of the council, in which case the Executive and Planning Committee is authorized to act under rule 10.11(d).

(1) Rejection of transfer of responsibility for a building under Government Code section 70326; and

(2) A decision to dispose of a surplus court facility under Government Code section 70391(c).

(d) Responsibilities of the Administrative Office of the Courts

The Administrative Office of the Courts is responsible for the following matters related to transfer of responsibility for court facilities, in addition to matters expressly authorized by statute:

(1) Keeping the courts informed and involved, as appropriate, in the negotiations with the counties for transfer of responsibility for court facilities;

(2) Except as provided in (c)(1), approving an agreement transferring responsibility for a court facility to the state;

(3) Administering a shared-use court facility, including:

(A) Making a decision to displace a minority county tenant under Government Code section 70344(b);

(B) Seeking a change in the amount of court space under Government Code section 70342; and

(C) Responding to a county seeking a change in the amount of county space under Government Code section 70342; and

(4) Auditing the collection of fees by trial courts under Government Code section 70391(d)(1) and the money in local courthouse construction funds under Government Code section 70391(d)(2).

(e) Appeal of county facilities payment amount

The Administrative Director of the Courts must obtain the approval of the Executive and Planning Committee before pursuing correction of a county facilities payment amount under Government Code section 70367. This provision does not preclude the Administrative Director of the Courts from submitting a declaration as required by Government Code section 70367(a). The Administrative Director of the Courts must report to the Executive and Planning Committee any decision not to appeal a county facilities payment amount. *(Formerly Rule 6.182, adopted, eff. June 23, 2004. Renumbered Rule 10.183 and amended, eff. Jan. 1, 2007.)*

Rule 10.184.   Acquisition, space programming, construction, and design of court facilities

(a) Intent

The intent of this rule is to allocate responsibility and decision making for acquisition, space programming, construction, and design of court facilities among the courts and the Administrative Office of the Courts.

(b) Responsibilities of the Administrative Office of the Courts

(1) In addition to those matters expressly provided by statute, the Administrative Office of the Courts is responsible for the acquisition, space programming, construction, and design of a court facility, consistent with the facilities policies and procedures adopted by the Judicial Council and the California Rules of Court.

(2) The Administrative Office of the Courts must prepare and submit to the Judicial Council separate annual capital outlay

proposals for the appellate courts and the trial courts, as part of the yearly judicial branch budget development cycle, specifying the amounts to be spent for these purposes. The capital outlay proposal for the trial courts must specify the money that is proposed to be spent from the State Court Facilities Construction Fund and from other sources. The annual capital outlay proposals must be consistent with the Five–Year Capital Infrastructure Plan or must recommend appropriate changes in the Five–Year Capital Infrastructure Plan. The Administrative Office of the Courts must, whenever feasible, seek review and recommendations from the Court Facilities Transitional Task Force before recommending action to the Judicial Council on these issues.

(3) The Administrative Office of the Courts must consult with the affected courts concerning the annual capital needs of the courts.

(c) Responsibilities of the courts

(1) Affected courts must consult with the Administrative Office of the Courts concerning the courts' annual capital needs.

(2) An affected court must work with the advisory group that is established for any court construction or major renovation project.

(d) Advisory group for construction projects

The Administrative Office of the Courts, in consultation with the leadership of the affected court, must establish and work with an advisory group for each court construction or major renovation project. The advisory group consists of court judicial officers, other court personnel, and others affected by the court facility. The advisory group must work with the Administrative Office of the Courts on issues involved in the construction or renovation, from the selection of a space programmer and architect through occupancy of the facility. *(Formerly Rule 6.183, adopted, eff. June 23, 2004. Renumbered Rule 10.184 and amended, eff. Jan. 1, 2007.)*

Research References

2 Witkin Cal. Proc. 5th Courts § 197, (S 197) Judicial Administration Rules.

Chapter 4

MANAGEMENT OF CLAIMS AND LITIGATION

Rule

Rule 10.201. Claim and litigation procedure

(a) Definitions

As used in this chapter:

(1) "Judicial branch entity" is as defined in Government Code section 900.3;

(2) "Judge" means a judge or justice of a judicial branch entity;

(3) "Office of the General Counsel" means the Office of the General Counsel of the Administrative Office of the Courts; and

(4) "Litigation Management Committee" means the Litigation Management Committee of the Judicial Council.

(b) Procedure for action on claims

To carry out the Judicial Council's responsibility under Government Code section 912.7 to act on a claim, claim amendment, or application for leave to present a late claim

against a judicial branch entity or a judge, the Office of the General Counsel, under the direction of the Administrative Director of the Courts, must:

(1) On receipt of a claim, claim amendment, or application for leave to present a late claim forwarded by a judicial branch entity, promptly consult with a representative of that entity about the merits of the claim, claim amendment, or application for leave to present a late claim;

(2) Grant or deny an application for leave to present a late claim under Government Code section 911.6(b);

(3) If determined by the Office of the General Counsel to be appropriate, refer a claim or claim amendment for further investigation to a claims adjuster or other investigator under contract with the Administrative Office of the Courts;

(4) Reject a claim if it is not a proper charge against the judicial branch entity or judge;

(5) Allow a claim in the amount justly due as determined by the Office of the General Counsel if it is a proper charge against the judicial branch entity and the amount is less than $100,000; and

(6) Make recommendations to the Litigation Management Committee regarding proposed settlements of claims requiring payments of $100,000 or more.

(c) Allowance and payment of claims

The following may allow and authorize payment of any claim arising out of the activities of a judicial branch entity or judge:

(1) The Office of the General Counsel, under the direction of the Administrative Director of the Courts, if the payment is less than $100,000; or

(2) The Litigation Management Committee, for any claim.

(d) Settlement of lawsuits and payment of judgments

The following may settle lawsuits, after consultation with the affected entity and any judge or employee being defended by the Judicial Council, and authorize payment of judgments arising out of the activities of a judicial branch entity or judge:

(1) The Office of the General Counsel, under the direction of the Administrative Director of the Courts, if the payment is less than $100,000 and the lawsuit does not raise issues of significance to the judicial branch; or

(2) The Litigation Management Committee, for any settlement or judgment. *(Formerly Rule 6.201, adopted, eff. Jan. 1, 2003. Renumbered Rule 10.201 and amended, eff. Jan. 1, 2007. As amended, eff. Dec. 9, 2008.)*

Research References

3 Witkin Cal. Proc. 5th Actions § 267, (S 267) Judicial Branch Entity.
3 Witkin Cal. Proc. 5th Actions § 273, (S 273) Judicial Branch Entity.
2 Witkin Cal. Proc. 5th Courts § 197, (S 197) Judicial Administration Rules.
5 Witkin, California Summary 10th Torts § 233, Compromise and Settlement of Claims.

Rule 10.202. Claims and litigation management

(a) Intent

The intent of this rule is to:

(1) Ensure that the trial and appellate courts are provided with timely, quality legal assistance; and

(2) Promote the cost-effective, prompt, and fair resolution of actions, proceedings, and claims that affect the trial and appellate courts and involve justices of the Courts of Appeal or the Supreme Court, trial court judges, subordinate judicial officers, court executive officers or administrators, or employees of the trial and appellate courts.

(b) Duties of the Office of the General Counsel

To carry out the duty of the Judicial Council to provide for the representation, defense, and indemnification of justices of the Courts of Appeal or the Supreme Court, judges, subordinate judicial officers, court executive officers and administrators, and trial and appellate court employees under part 1 (commencing with section 810) to part 7 (commencing with section 995), inclusive, of the Government Code, the Office of the General Counsel under the direction of the Administrative Director of the Courts and the General Counsel, must:

(1) Develop, manage, and administer a litigation management program for investigating and resolving all claims and lawsuits affecting the trial and appellate courts;

(2) Provide legal assistance to the trial or appellate court, and to any justice, judge, subordinate judicial officer, court executive officer or administrator, and trial or appellate court employee who is named as a defendant or responsible party, subject to the defense and indemnification provisions of part 1 (commencing with section 810) to part 7 (commencing with section 995), inclusive, of the Government Code, on receipt of notice of a claim or lawsuit affecting the trial or appellate court or of a dispute that is likely to result in a claim or lawsuit;

(3) Select and direct any counsel retained to represent any trial or appellate court, justice, judge, subordinate judicial officer, court executive officer or administrator, and trial or appellate court employee being provided legal representation under (2), after consultation with the trial or appellate court and any such individual defendant;

(4) Make settlement decisions in all claims and lawsuits other than those identified in (5), after consultation with the affected trial or appellate court, and any justice, judge, subordinate judicial officer, court executive officer or administrator, and trial or appellate court employee being provided legal representation under (2);

(5) Make recommendations to the Litigation Management Committee regarding proposed settlements of claims or lawsuits requiring payments of $100,000 or more or raising issues of significance to the judicial branch;

(6) Develop and implement risk avoidance programs for the trial and appellate courts;

(7) Provide an annual report to the Litigation Management Committee concerning the litigation management program; and

(8) Provide an annual report to each trial and appellate court concerning claims and lawsuits filed against that trial or appellate court.

(c) Duties of trial and appellate courts

The trial and appellate courts must:

(1) Notify the Office of the General Counsel promptly on receipt of notice of a dispute that is likely to result in a claim or lawsuit, or of a claim or lawsuit filed, against the court, a justice, a judge or subordinate judicial officer, a court executive officer or administrator, or a court employee, and forward the claim and lawsuit to the Office of the General Counsel for handling; and

(2) Consult with the Office of the General Counsel regarding strategic and settlement decisions in claims and lawsuits.

(d) Disagreements about major strategic decisions

Following consultation with the Office of the General Counsel, a presiding judge or administrative presiding justice may object to a proposed decision of the Office of the General Counsel about major strategic decisions, such as retention of counsel and proposed settlements, by presenting to the Office of the General Counsel a written statement of the objection. The Office of the General Counsel must present the written objection to the Litigation Management Committee, which will resolve the

objection. *(Formerly Rule 6.800, adopted, eff. Jan. 1, 2001. As amended, eff. July 1, 2002. Renumbered Rule 6.202 and amended, eff. Jan. 1, 2003. Renumbered Rule 10.202 and amended, eff. Jan. 1, 2007. As amended, eff. Dec. 9, 2008.)*

Research References

5 Witkin, California Summary 10th Torts § 233, Compromise and Settlement of Claims.

Rule 10.203. Contractual indemnification

(a) Intent

The intent of this rule is to facilitate the use of contractual indemnities that allocate legal risk and liability to parties that contract with a superior court or Court of Appeal, the Supreme Court, the Judicial Council, or the Administrative Office of the Courts (a "judicial branch entity" as defined in Gov. Code, § 900.3).

(b) Defense and indemnification provisions

Notwithstanding rule 10.14, 10.201, or 10.202, a judicial branch entity may enter into a contract that requires the contractor or the contractor's insurer to indemnify, defend, and hold harmless the entity and its officers, agents, and employees against claims, demands, liability, damages, attorney fees, costs, expenses, or losses arising from the performance of the contract. Upon receipt of notice of a claim or lawsuit that may be subject to contractual indemnities, the judicial branch entity must notify the Office of the General Counsel, which will manage the claim or lawsuit to obtain the benefits of the contractual indemnities to the extent consistent with the interests of the public and the judicial branch. *(Formerly Rule 6.203, adopted, eff. Oct. 15, 2003. Renumbered Rule 10.203 and amended, eff. Jan. 1, 2007.)*

Research References

2 Witkin Cal. Proc. 5th Courts § 197, (S 197) Judicial Administration Rules.

Chapter 5

MANAGEMENT OF HUMAN RESOURCES

Rule
10.350. Workers' compensation program.

Rule 10.350. Workers' compensation program

(a) Intent

The intent of this rule is to:

(1) Establish procedures for the Administrative Office of the Courts' workers' compensation program for the trial courts; and

(2) Ensure that the trial courts' workers' compensation coverage complies with applicable law and is cost-efficient.

(b) Duties of the Administrative Office of the Courts

To carry out the duty of the Judicial Council to establish a workers' compensation program for the trial courts, the Administrative Office of the Courts, through its Human Resources Division, must:

(1) Maintain a contract with a vendor to provide courts, on a voluntary basis, with a cost-efficient workers' compensation coverage program;

(2) Monitor the performance of the vendor with which it contracts to provide such services;

(3) Timely notify the trial courts concerning the terms of the workers' compensation coverage program;

(4) Timely inform the trial courts about the legal requirements with which a workers' compensation program must comply;

(5) Make personnel available by telephone to consult with trial courts regarding the cost and benefits of the plan being offered by the Administrative Office of the Courts; and

(6) Review and approve or disapprove any other workers' compensation programs identified by a trial court for consideration as a vendor to provide workers' compensation benefits to its employees.

(c) Duties of the trial courts

(1) Each trial court that elects to participate in the program made available through the Administrative Office of the Courts must:

(A) Timely notify the Human Resources Division of its decision to participate in the workers' compensation program being offered through the Administrative Office of the Courts;

(B) Timely complete and return necessary paperwork to the Human Resources Division; and

(C) Timely pay all costs associated with the program.

(2) Each trial court that elects not to participate in the workers' compensation program available through the Administrative Office of the Courts must:

(A) Independently identify a workers' compensation benefits provider that fulfills all legal responsibilities to offer such benefits in California in a cost-efficient manner;

(B) Timely submit to the Human Resources Division for its approval the information necessary to evaluate the workers' compensation program identified by the trial court to provide benefits for its employees; and

(C) Maintain a contract with a workers' compensation benefits provider that fulfills all legal responsibilities to offer such benefits in California in a cost-efficient manner.

(Formerly Rule 6.302, adopted, eff. Jan. 1, 2005. Renumbered Rule 10.350 and amended, eff. Jan. 1, 2007.)

Research References

2 Witkin Cal. Proc. 5th Courts § 197, (S 197) Judicial Administration Rules.

Chapter 6

COURT TECHNOLOGY, INFORMATION, AND AUTOMATION

Rule
10.400. Judicial Branch Statistical Information System (JBSIS).

Rule 10.400. Judicial Branch Statistical Information System (JBSIS)

(a) Purpose of rule

Consistent with article VI, section 6 of the California Constitution and Government Code section 68505, the Judicial Branch Statistical Information System (JBSIS) is established by the Judicial Council to provide accurate, consistent, and timely information for the judicial branch, the Legislature, and other state agencies that require information from the courts to fulfill their mandates.

(b) Reporting required

Each trial court must collect and report to the Judicial Council information according to its capability and level of automation as prescribed by the *JBSIS Manual* adopted by the Judicial Council.

(c) Automated JBSIS collection and reporting

By July 1, 1998, each trial court must develop a plan for meeting reporting requirements prescribed by the *JBSIS Manual*. By January 1, 2001, subject to adequate funding being made available, each trial court must develop, upgrade, replace, or procure automated case management systems needed to meet or exceed JBSIS data collection and reporting requirements prescribed by the *JBSIS Manual*. *(Formerly Rule 996, adopted, eff. Jan. 1, 1998. As amended, eff. Jan. 1, 2000. Renumbered Rule 10.400 and amended, eff. Jan. 1, 2007.)*

Research References

2 Witkin Cal. Proc. 5th Courts § 197, (S 197) Judicial Administration Rules.
2 Witkin Cal. Proc. 5th Courts § 393, (S 393) Electronic Data Systems.

Chapter 7

MINIMUM EDUCATION REQUIREMENTS, EXPECTATIONS, AND RECOMMENDATIONS

Rule 10.451. Judicial branch education

(a) Purpose

Judicial branch education for all justices, judges, subordinate judicial officers, and court personnel is essential to enhance the fair, effective, and efficient administration of justice. Participation in education activities is part of the official duties of judicial officers and court personnel. Judicial branch education is acknowledged as a vital component in achieving the goals of the Judicial Council's Long–Range Strategic Plan, which include access, fairness, and diversity; branch independence and accountability; modernization of management and administration; and quality of justice and service to the public. The responsibility for planning, conducting, and overseeing judicial branch education properly resides in the judicial branch.

(b) Education objectives

Justices, judges, subordinate judicial officers, court personnel, education committees, and others who plan and deliver education will endeavor to achieve the following objectives:

(1) To provide justices, judges, subordinate judicial officers, and court personnel with the knowledge, skills, and abilities required to perform their responsibilities competently, fairly, and efficiently;

(2) To ensure that education, including opportunities for orientation, continuing education, and professional development, is available to all justices, judges, subordinate judicial officers, and court personnel;

(3) To assist justices, judges, subordinate judicial officers, and court personnel in preserving the integrity and impartiality of the judicial system through their efforts to ensure that all members of the public have equal access to the courts and equal ability to participate in court proceedings and are treated in a fair and just manner;

(4) To promote the adherence of justices, judges, subordinate judicial officers, and court personnel to the highest ideals of personal and official conduct, as set forth in the California Code of Judicial Ethics and the Code of Ethics for the Court Employees of California;

(5) To improve the administration of justice, reduce court delay, and promote fair and efficient management of court proceedings;

(6) To promote standardized court practices and procedures; and

(7) To implement the recommendations adopted by the Judicial Council in the California Standards of Judicial Administration. *(Adopted, eff. Jan. 1, 2007.)*

Research References

2 Witkin Cal. Proc. 5th Courts § 197, (S 197) Judicial Administration Rules.
2 Witkin Cal. Proc. 5th Courts § 395, (S 395) Mandatory Requirement.
10 Witkin, California Summary 10th Parent and Child § 447, Department and Staff.

Rule 10.452. Minimum education requirements, expectations, and recommendations

(a) Purpose

Justices, judges, and subordinate judicial officers are entrusted by the public with the impartial and knowledgeable handling of proceedings that affect the freedom, livelihood, and happiness of the people involved. Court personnel assist justices, judges, and subordinate judicial officers in carrying out their responsibilities and must provide accurate and timely services to the public. Each justice, judge, and subordinate judicial officer and each court staff member is responsible for maintaining and improving his or her professional competence. To assist them in enhancing their professional competence, the judicial branch will develop and maintain a comprehensive and high-quality education pro-

gram, including minimum education requirements, expectations, and recommendations, to provide educational opportunities for all justices, judges, subordinate judicial officers, and court personnel.

(b) Goals

The minimum education requirements, expectations, and recommendations set forth in rules 10.461–10.479 are intended to achieve two complementary goals:

(1) To ensure that both individuals who are new to the bench or the court and those who are experienced on the bench or court but are beginning a new assignment or role obtain education on the tasks, skills, abilities, and knowledge necessary to be successful in the new roles; and

(2) To establish broad parameters, based on time, for continuing education for individuals who are experienced both on the bench or court and in their assignments or roles, while preserving the ability of the individual, working with the individual who oversees his or her work, to determine the appropriate content and provider.

(c) Relationship of minimum education requirements and expectations to education recommendations

The education requirements and expectations set forth in rules 10.461–10.462 and 10.471–10.474 are minimums. Justices, judges, and subordinate judicial officers should participate in more judicial education than is required and expected, related to each individual's responsibilities and particular judicial assignment or assignments and in accordance with the judicial education recommendations set forth in rule 10.469. Additional education requirements related to specific responsibilities are set forth in rule 10.463 (for those hearing family law matters), rule 10.464 (for those hearing domestic violence issues), and rule 10.468 (for those hearing probate proceedings).

(d) Responsibilities of Chief Justice and administrative presiding justices

The Chief Justice and each administrative presiding justice:

(1) Must grant sufficient leave to Supreme Court and Court of Appeal justices, the clerk/administrator, and the managing attorney to enable them to complete the minimum education requirements stated in rules 10.461, 10.471, and 10.472, respectively;

(2) To the extent compatible with the efficient administration of justice, must grant to all justices, the clerk/administrator, and the managing attorney sufficient leave to participate in education programs consistent with the education recommendations stated in rules 10.469 and 10.479. After a justice has completed any new justice education required under rule 10.461 or after a justice has completed the first year on the bench, the Chief Justice or the administrative presiding justice should grant each justice at least eight court days per calendar year to participate in continuing education relating to the justice's responsibilities;

(3) In addition to the educational leave required under (d)(1)–(2), should grant leave to a justice, clerk/administrator, or managing attorney to serve on education committees and as a faculty member at education programs when the individual's services have been requested for these purposes by the Administrative Office of the Courts, the California Judges Association, or the court. If a court's calendar would not be adversely affected, the court should grant additional leave for a justice, the clerk/administrator, or the managing attorney to serve on an educational committee or as a faculty member for judicial branch education;

(4) Should establish an education plan for his or her court to facilitate the involvement of justices, the clerk/administrator, and the managing attorney as both participants and faculty in education activities;

(5) Must ensure that justices, the clerk/administrator, and the managing attorney are reimbursed by their court in accordance with the travel policies issued by the Administrative Office of the Courts for travel expenses incurred in attending in-state education programs as a participant, except to the extent that: (i) certain expenses are covered by the Administrative Office of the Courts; or (ii) the education provider or sponsor of the program pays the expenses. Provisions for these expenses must be part of every court's budget. The Chief Justice or the administrative presiding justice may approve reimbursement of travel expenses incurred by justices, the clerk/administrator, and the managing attorney in attending out-of-state education programs as a participant; and

(6) Must retain the records and cumulative histories of participation provided by justices. These records and cumulative histories are subject to periodic audit by the Administrative Office of the Courts. The Chief Justice and the administrative presiding justice must report the data from the records and cumulative histories on an aggregate basis to the Judicial Council, on a form provided by the Judicial Council, within six months after the end of each three-year period.

(e) Responsibilities of presiding judges

Each presiding judge:

(1) Must grant sufficient leave to all judges and subordinate judicial officers and to the court executive officer to enable them to complete the minimum education requirements and expectations stated in rules 10.462 and 10.473, respectively;

(2) To the extent compatible with the efficient administration of justice, must grant to all judges and subordinate judicial officers and to the court executive officer sufficient leave to participate in education programs consistent with the education recommendations stated in rules 10.469 and 10.479. After a judge or subordinate judicial officer has completed the new judge education required under rule 10.462, the presiding judge should grant each judge and subordinate judicial officer at least eight court days per calendar year to participate in continuing education relating to the judge or subordinate judicial officer's responsibilities or current or future court assignment;

(3) In addition to the educational leave required or authorized under rule 10.603 or (e)(1)–(2), should grant leave to a judge or subordinate judicial officer or the executive officer to serve on education committees and as a faculty member at education programs when the judicial officer's or executive officer's services have been requested for these purposes by the Judicial Council, the California Judges Association, or the court. If a court's calendar would not be adversely affected, the presiding judge should grant additional leave for a judge or subordinate judicial officer or executive officer to serve on an educational committee or as a faculty member for judicial branch education;

(4) Should establish an education plan for his or her court to facilitate the involvement of judges, subordinate judicial officers, and the executive officer as both participants and faculty in education activities and should consult with each judge, each subordinate judicial officer, and the executive officer regarding their education needs and requirements related to their current and future assignments;

(5) Should use his or her assignment powers to enable all judges and subordinate judicial officers, particularly those assigned to specific calendar courts, to participate in educational activities;

(6) Must ensure that judges, subordinate judicial officers, and the court executive officer are reimbursed by their court in accordance with the Trial Court Financial Policies and Procedures Manual for travel expenses incurred in attending in-state education programs as a participant, except to the extent that:

(i) certain expenses are covered by the Administrative Office of the Courts; or (ii) the education provider or sponsor of the program pays the expenses. Provisions for these expenses must be part of every court's budget. The presiding judge may approve reimbursement of travel expenses incurred by judges, subordinate judicial officers, and the court executive officer in attending out-of-state education programs as a participant; and

(7) Must retain the records and cumulative histories of participation provided by judges. These records and cumulative histories are subject to periodic audit by the Administrative Office of the Courts (AOC). The presiding judge must report the data from the records and cumulative histories on an aggregate basis to the Judicial Council, on a form provided by the Judicial Council, within six months after the end of each three-year period.

(f) Responsibilities of Supreme Court and Court of Appeal justices, clerk/administrators, managing attorneys, and supervisors

Each court's justices, clerk/administrator, managing attorney, and supervisors:

(1) Must grant sufficient leave to all court personnel to enable them to complete the minimum education requirements stated in rule 10.472;

(2) To the extent compatible with the efficient administration of justice, must grant to all court personnel sufficient leave to participate in education programs consistent with the education recommendations stated in rule 10.479;

(3) Should allow and encourage court personnel, in addition to participating as students in educational activities, to serve on court personnel education committees and as faculty at court personnel education programs when an employee's services have been requested for these purposes by the Administrative Office of the Courts or the court; and

(4) Should establish an education plan for their court to facilitate the involvement of court personnel as both participants and faculty in educational activities, and should consult with each court staff member regarding his or her education needs and requirements and professional development.

(5) Must ensure that supervisors and other court personnel are reimbursed by their court in accordance with the travel policies issued by the Administrative Office of the Courts for travel expenses incurred in attending in-state education programs as a participant, except to the extent that: (i) certain expenses are covered by the Administrative Office of the Courts; or (ii) the education provider or sponsor of the program pays the expenses. Provisions for these expenses must be part of every court's budget. The clerk/administrator or the managing attorney may approve reimbursement of travel expenses incurred by supervisors and other court personnel in attending out-of-state education programs as a participant.

(g) Responsibilities of trial court executive officers, managers, and supervisors

Each trial court's executive officer, managers, and supervisors:

(1) Must grant sufficient leave to all court personnel to enable them to complete the minimum education requirements stated in rule 10.474;

(2) To the extent compatible with the efficient administration of justice, must grant to all court personnel sufficient leave to participate in education programs consistent with the education recommendations stated in rule 10.479;

(3) Should allow and encourage court personnel, in addition to participating as students in education activities, to serve on court personnel education committees and as faculty at court personnel education programs when an employee's services have

Ct. Rules

been requested for these purposes by the Judicial Council or the court;

(4) Should establish an education plan for their court to facilitate the involvement of court personnel as both participants and faculty in educational activities, and should consult with each court staff member regarding his or her education needs and requirements and professional development; and

(5) Must ensure that managers, supervisors, and other court personnel are reimbursed by their court in accordance with the Trial Court Financial Policies and Procedures Manual for travel expenses incurred in attending in-state education programs as a participant, except to the extent that: (i) certain expenses are covered by the Administrative Office of the Courts; or (ii) the education provider or sponsor of the program pays the expenses. Provisions for these expenses must be part of every court's budget. The court executive officer may approve reimbursement of travel expenses incurred by managers, supervisors, and other court personnel in attending out-of-state education programs as a participant. *(Adopted, eff. Jan. 1, 2007. As amended, eff. Jan. 1, 2008; Jan. 1, 2012.)*

Research References

Rutter, Cal. Practice Guide: Prof. Responsibility Ch. 1-M, M. Minimum Continuing Legal Education ("MCLE").

2 Witkin Cal. Proc. 5th Courts § 395, (S 395) Mandatory Requirement.

Rule 10.455. Ethics orientation for Judicial Council members and for judicial branch employees required to file a statement of economic interests

(a) Authority

This rule is adopted under Government Code section 11146 et seq. and article VI, section 6 of the California Constitution.

(b) Definitions

For purposes of this rule, "judicial branch employee" includes an employee of a trial or appellate court or the Administrative Office of the Courts, but does not include court commissioners or referees.

(c) Judicial Council members and judicial branch employees

(1) The Administrative Office of the Courts must provide an ethics orientation course for Judicial Council members and for judicial branch employees who are required to file a statement of economic interests.

(2) Judicial Council members must take the orientation course within six months of appointment. If a member is appointed to a subsequent term, he or she must take the course within six months of the reappointment.

(3) Judicial branch employees who are required to file a statement of economic interests must take the orientation course as follows:

(A) For employees who have taken the orientation course before the effective date of this rule, at least once during each consecutive two calendar years after the date of the last attendance.

(B) For new employees, within six months of becoming an employee and at least once during each consecutive two calendar years thereafter.

(C) For all other employees, within six months of the effective date of this rule and at least once during each consecutive two calendar years thereafter.

(Formerly Rule 6.301, adopted, eff. Jan. 1, 2004. Renumbered Rule 10.301 and amended, eff. Jan. 1, 2007. Renumbered Rule 10.455 and amended, eff. Jan. 1, 2013.)

Rule 10.461. Minimum education requirements for Supreme Court and Court of Appeal justices

(a) Applicability

All California Court of Appeal justices must complete the minimum judicial education requirements for new justices under (b), and all Supreme Court and Court of Appeal justices must complete minimum continuing education requirements as outlined under (c). All justices should participate in more judicial education than is required, related to each individual's responsibilities and in accordance with the judicial education recommendations set forth in rule 10.469.

(b) Content-based requirement

Each new Court of Appeal justice, within two years of confirmation of appointment, must attend a new appellate justice orientation program sponsored by a national provider of appellate orientation programs or by the Administrative Office of the Courts' Education Division/Center for Judicial Education and Research.

(c) Hours–based continuing education

(1) Each justice must complete 30 hours of continuing judicial education every three years, beginning on the dates outlined:

(A) A new Supreme Court justice enters the three-year continuing education period on January 1 of the year following confirmation of appointment, and a new Court of Appeal justice enters the three-year continuing education period on January 1 of the year following completion of the required new justice education; continuing education requirements are prorated based on the number of years remaining in the three-year period.

(B) For all other justices, the first continuing education period begins January 1, 2008.

(C) The first continuing education period for Supreme Court and Court of Appeal justices is for two years from January 1, 2008, through December 31, 2009, rather than three years. The continuing education requirements and limitations in (c) are consequently prorated for this two-year period. The first three-year period then begins January 1, 2010.

(2) The following education applies toward the required 30 hours of continuing judicial education:

(A) Any education offered by an approved provider (see rule 10.481(a)) and any other education, including education taken to satisfy a statutory or other education requirement, approved by the Chief Justice or the administrative presiding justice as meeting the criteria listed in rule 10.481(b).

(B) Each hour of participation in traditional (live, face–to–face) education; distance education such as broadcasts, video-conferences, and online coursework; self–directed study; and faculty service counts toward the continuing education requirement on an hour-for-hour basis. Each justice must complete at least half of his or her continuing education hours requirement as a participant in traditional (live, face–to–face) education. The justice may complete the balance of his or her education hours requirement through any other means with no limitation on any particular type of education.

(C) A justice who services as faculty by teaching legal or judicial education to a legal or judicial audience may apply education hours as faculty service. Credit for faculty service counts toward the continuing education requirement in the same manner as all other types of education—on an hour-for-hour basis.

(d) Extension of time

(1) For good cause, the Chief Justice or the administrative presiding justice may grant a one-year extension of time to complete the continuing education requirement in (c).

(2) If the Chief Justice or the administrative presiding justice grants a request for an extension of time, the justice, in consultation with the Chief Justice or the administrative presiding justice, should also pursue interim means of obtaining relevant educational content.

(3) An extension of time to complete the hours-based continuing education requirement does not affect what is required in the next three-year period.

(e) Records and summaries of participation for justices

Each justice is responsible for:

(1) Tracking his or her own participation in education and keeping a record of participation for three years after each course or activity that is applied toward the requirements, on a form provided by the Chief Justice for the Supreme Court or by the administrative presiding justice for each appellate district of the Court of Appeal. The form must include the information regarding a justice's participation in education that is needed by the Chief Justice or the administrative presiding justice to complete the aggregate form required by rule 10.452(d)(6);

(2) At the end of each year, giving the Chief Justice or the administrative presiding justice a copy of his or her record of participation in education for that year, on the form provided by the Chief Justice or the administrative presiding justice; and

(3) At the end of each three-year period, giving the Chief Justice or the administrative presiding justice a copy of his or her record of participation in education for that year and a cumulative history of participation for that three-year period, on the form provided by the Chief Justice or the administrative presiding justice. *(Adopted, eff. Jan. 1, 2007. As amended, eff. Jan. 1, 2008; Aug. 15, 2008; Jan. 1, 2012; Jan. 1, 2013.)*

Advisory Committee Comment

The requirements formerly contained in subdivision (e)(2) of rule 970, which has been repealed, are carried forward without change in rule 10.461(b).

The Administrative Office of the Courts (AOC) has developed both a manual format and an automated format of the individual justice's recording and reporting form referenced in rule 10.461(e) that gathers all the information needed by the Chief Justice or the administrative presiding justice to complete the aggregate report to the Judicial Council required under rule 10.452(d)(6). The Chief Justice or the administrative presiding justice may determine which form should be used in his or her court and may provide the manual or automated format of the AOC-developed form (available from the AOC's Education Division/Center for Judicial Education and Research) or may provide another appropriate form that has been developed by his or her court or by another court that gathers all the information needed by the Chief Justice or the administrative presiding justice to complete the aggregate report to the Judicial Council.

Research References

2 Witkin Cal. Proc. 5th Courts § 395, (S 395) Mandatory Requirement.

Rule 10.462. Minimum education requirements and expectations for trial court judges and subordinate judicial officers

(a) Applicability

All California trial court judges must complete the minimum judicial education requirements for new judges under (c)(1) and are expected to participate in continuing education as outlined under (d). All subordinate judicial officers must complete the minimum education requirements for new subordinate judicial officers under (c)(1) and for continuing education as outlined under (d). All trial court judges and subordinate judicial officers who hear family law matters must complete additional education requirements set forth in rule 10.463. All trial court

judges and subordinate judicial officers who hear certain types of matters must participate in education on domestic violence issues as provided in rule 10.464. All trial court judges and subordinate judicial officers regularly assigned to hear probate proceedings must complete additional education requirements set forth in rule 10.468. All trial court judges and subordinate judicial officers should participate in more judicial education than is required and expected, related to each individual's responsibilities and particular judicial assignment or assignments and in accordance with the judicial education recommendations set forth in rule 10.469.

(b) Definitions

Unless the context or subject matter otherwise requires, "subordinate judicial officers" as used in this rule means subordinate judicial officers as defined in rule 10.701.

(c) Content-based requirements

(1) Each new trial court judge and subordinate judicial officer must complete the "new judge education" provided by the Administrative Office of the Courts' Education Division/Center for Judicial Education and Research (CJER) as follows:

(A) The New Judge Orientation Program within six months of taking the oath as a judge or subordinate judicial officer. For purposes of the New Judge Orientation Program, a judge or subordinate judicial officer is considered "new" only once, and any judge or subordinate judicial officer who has completed the New Judge Orientation Program, as required under this rule or under former rule 970, is not required to complete the program again. A judge or subordinate judicial officer who was appointed, elected, or hired before rule 970 was adopted on January 1, 1996, is not required to complete the program.

(B) An orientation course in his or her primary assignment (civil, criminal, family, juvenile delinquency or dependency, probate, or traffic) within one year of taking the oath as a judge or subordinate judicial officer; and

(C) The B. E. Witkin Judicial College of California within two years of taking the oath as a judge or subordinate judicial officer, unless the new judge completed the Judicial College as a new subordinate judicial officer, in which case the presiding judge may determine whether the new judge must complete it again.

(2) Each judge beginning a supervising judge role is expected to complete the following education, unless he or she is returning to a similar supervising judge role after less than two years in another assignment or is beginning a supervising judge role less than two years after serving in the presiding judge role and completing the Presiding Judges Orientation and Court Management Program.

(A) For a judge who has administrative responsibility, CJER's Supervising Judges Overview course within one year of beginning the supervising judge role, preferably before beginning the role;

(B) For a judge who has calendar management responsibility, a calendar management overview course, provided either by the local court or by CJER, within one year of beginning the supervising judge role, preferably before beginning the role;

(C) For a judge who has both administrative and calendar management responsibility, both overview courses within one year of beginning the role.

(3) Each judge beginning a presiding judge role is expected to complete CJER's Presiding Judges Orientation and Court Management Program within one year of beginning the presiding judge role, preferably before beginning the role unless he or she is returning to a presiding judge role after two years or less in another role or assignment.

(4) Each judge is expected to and each subordinate judicial officer must, if beginning a new primary assignment— (unless he or she is returning to an assignment after less than two years in another assignment), —complete a course on the new primary assignment, provided by CJER, the California Judges Association (CJA), or the local court, within six months of beginning the new assignment. CJER is responsible for identifying content for these courses and will share the identified content with CJA and the local courts.

(d) Hours–based continuing education

(1) Each judge is expected to and each subordinate judicial officer must complete 30 hours of continuing judicial education every three years, beginning on the dates outlined:

(A) A new judge and new subordinate judicial officer enters the three-year continuing education period on January 1 of the year following the period provided for completion of the required new judge education; continuing education expectations for judges and requirements for subordinate judicial officers are prorated based on the number of years remaining in the three-year period.

(B) For all other judges and subordinate judicial officers, the first three-year period begins on January 1, 2007.

(2) The following education applies toward the expected or required 30 hours of continuing judicial education:

(A) The content-based courses under (c)(2), (3), and (4) for a new supervising judge, a new presiding judge, and a judge or subordinate judicial officer beginning a new primary assignment (the "new judge education" required under (c)(1) does not apply); and

(B) Any other education offered by an approved provider (see rule 10.481(a)) and any other education, including education taken to satisfy a statutory or other education requirement, approved by the presiding judge as meeting the criteria listed in rule 10.481(b).

(3) Each hour of participation in traditional (live, face–to–face) education, distance education, such as broadcasts, video-conferences, and online coursework; self–directed study; and faculty service counts toward the continuing education expectation or requirement on an hour-for-hour basis. Each judge and subordinate judicial officer must complete at least half of his or her continuing education hours expectation or requirement as a participant in traditional (live, face-to-face) education. The judge or subordinate judicial officer may complete the balance of his or her judicial education hours expectation or requirement through any other means with no limitation on any particular type of education.

(4) A judge or subordinate judicial officer who serves as faculty by teaching legal or judicial education for a legal or judicial audience may apply education hours as faculty service. Credit for faculty service counts toward the continuing education expectation or requirement in the same manner as all other types of education—on an hour-for-hour basis.

(5) The presiding judge may require subordinate judicial officers to participate in specific courses or participate in education in a specific subject matter area as part of their continuing education.

(e) Extension of time

(1) For good cause, a presiding judge may grant an extension of time to complete the education expectations or requirements in (c)(2)–(4) and the continuing education expectation or requirement in (d) as follows:

(A) A time extension to complete the content-based expectations or requirements in (c)(2)–(4) is limited to the original time period provided for completion—that is, one year, one year, or six months, respectively.

(B) A time extension to complete the hours-based continuing education expectation or requirement in (d) is limited to one year.

(2) If the presiding judge grants a request for an extension of time, the judge or subordinate judicial officer, in consultation with the presiding judge, should also pursue interim means of obtaining relevant educational content.

(3) An extension of time to complete the hours-based continuing education expectation or requirement does not affect what is expected or required in the next three-year period.

(f) Records and cumulative histories of participation for judges

Each judge is responsible for:

(1) Tracking his or her own participation in education and keeping a record of participation for three years after each course or activity that is applied toward the requirements and expectations, on a form provided by the presiding judge. The form must include the information regarding a judge's participation in education that is needed by the presiding judge to complete the aggregate form required by rule 10.452(e)(7);

(2) At the end of each year, giving the presiding judge a copy of his or her record of participation in education for that year, on the form provided by the presiding judge; and

(3) At the end of each three-year period, giving the presiding judge a copy of his or her record of participation in education for that year and a cumulative history of participation for that three-year period, on the form provided by the presiding judge.

(g) Records of participation for subordinate judicial officers

(1) Each court is responsible for tracking participation in education and for tracking completion of minimum education requirements for its subordinate judicial officers.

(2) Each subordinate judicial officer must keep records of his or her own participation for three years after each course or activity that is applied toward the requirements. *(Adopted, eff. Jan. 1, 2007. As amended, eff. Jan. 1, 2008; July 1, 2008; Aug. 15, 2008; Jan. 1, 2012; Jan. 1, 2013.)*

Advisory Committee Comment

The minimum judicial education requirements in rule 10.462 do not apply to retired judges seeking to sit on regular court assignment in the Assigned Judges Program. Retired judges who seek to serve in the Assigned Judges Program must comply with the Chief Justice's Standards and Guidelines for Judges Who Serve on Assignment, which includes education requirements.

The Administrative Office of the Courts (AOC) has developed both a manual format and an automated format of the individual judge's recording and reporting form referenced in rule 10.462(f) that gathers all the information needed by the presiding judge to complete the aggregate report to the Judicial Council required under rule 10.452(e)(7). The presiding judge may determine which form should be used in his or her court and may provide the manual or automated format of the AOC-developed form (available from the AOC's Education Division/Center for Judicial Education and Research) or may provide another appropriate form that has been developed by his or her court or by another court that gathers all the information needed by the presiding judge to complete the aggregate report to the Judicial Council.

Research References

2 Witkin Cal. Proc. 5th Courts § 395, (S 395) Mandatory Requirement.

Rule 10.463. Education requirements for family court judges and subordinate judicial officers

Each judge or subordinate judicial officer whose primary assignment is to hear family law matters or who is the sole judge hearing family law matters must complete the following education:

(a) Basic family law education

Within six months of beginning a family law assignment, or within one year of beginning a family law assignment in courts with five or fewer judges, the judge or subordinate judicial officer must complete a basic educational program on California family law and procedure designed primarily for judicial officers. A judge or subordinate judicial officer who has completed the basic educational program need not complete the basic educational program again. All other judicial officers who hear family law matters, including retired judges who sit on court assignment, must complete appropriate family law educational programs.

(b) Continuing family law education

The judge or subordinate judicial officer must complete a periodic update on new developments in California family law and procedure.

(c) Other family law education

To the extent that judicial time and resources are available, the judge or subordinate judicial officer must complete additional educational programs on other aspects of family law including interdisciplinary subjects relating to the family. *(Formerly Rule 1200, adopted, eff. Jan. 1, 1992. Renumbered Rule 5.30 and amended, eff. Jan. 1, 2003. Renumbered Rule 10.463 and amended, eff. Jan. 1, 2008.)*

Research References

2 Witkin Cal. Proc. 5th Courts § 395, (S 395) Mandatory Requirement.
2 Witkin Cal. Proc. 5th Courts § 396, (S 396) Specialized Programs.

Rule 10.464. Education requirements and expectations for judges and subordinate judicial officers on domestic violence issues

(a) Judges and subordinate judicial officers hearing specified matters

Each judge or subordinate judicial officer who hears criminal, family, juvenile delinquency, juvenile dependency, or probate matters must participate in appropriate education on domestic violence issues as part of his or her requirements and expectations under rule 10.462. Each judge or subordinate judicial officer whose primary assignment is in one of these areas also must participate in a periodic update on domestic violence as part of these requirements and expectations.

(b) Specified courses to include education on domestic violence issues

The education provider must include education on domestic violence issues at the Judicial College under rule 10.462(c)(1)(C) and in courses for primary assignments in criminal, family, juvenile delinquency, juvenile dependency, or probate under rule 10.462(c)(1)(B) or (c)(4). *(Adopted, eff. Jan. 1, 2010.)*

Advisory Committee Comment

In determining what constitutes "appropriate" education, each judge or subordinate judicial officer should determine the number of hours of education on domestic violence that is adequate for his or her assignment, taking into account the size of the court, the nature of his or her assignment, the mix of assignments, and other factors.

Research References

2 Witkin Cal. Proc. 5th Courts § 396, (S 396) Specialized Programs.

Rule 10.468. Content-based and hours-based education for superior court judges and subordinate judicial officers regularly assigned to hear probate proceedings

(a) Definitions

As used in this rule, the following terms have the meanings stated below:

(1) "Judge" means a judge of the superior court.

(2) "Subordinate judicial officer" has the meaning specified in rule 10.701(a).

(3) "Judicial officer" means a judge or a subordinate judicial officer.

(4) "Probate proceedings" are decedents' estates, guardianships and conservatorships under division 4 of the Probate Code, trust proceedings under division 9 of the Probate Code, and other matters governed by provisions of that code and the rules in title 7 of the California Rules of Court.

(5) A judicial officer "regularly assigned to hear probate proceedings" is a judicial officer who is:

(A) Assigned to a dedicated probate department where probate proceedings are customarily heard on a full-time basis;

(B) Responsible for hearing most of the probate proceedings filed in a court that does not have a dedicated probate department; or

(C) Responsible for hearing probate proceedings on a regular basis in a department in a branch or other location remote from the main or central courthouse, whether or not he or she also hears other kinds of matters in that department and whether or not there is a dedicated probate department in the main or central courthouse; or

(D) Designated by the presiding judge of a court with four or fewer authorized judges.

(6) "AOC" is the Administrative Office of the Courts.

(7) "CJER" is the AOC Education Division/Center for Judicial Education and Research.

(8) "CJA" is the California Judges Association.

(b) Content–based requirements

(1) Each judicial officer beginning a regular assignment to hear probate proceedings after the effective date of this rule—unless he or she is returning to this assignment after less than two years in another assignment—must complete, as soon as possible but not to exceed six months from the assignment's commencement date, 6 hours of education on probate guardianships and conservatorships, including court-supervised fiduciary accounting.

(2) The education required in (1) is in addition to the New Judge Orientation program for new judicial officers and the B. E. Witkin Judicial College required under rule 10.462(c)(1)(A) and (C) and may be applied toward satisfaction of the 30 hours of continuing education expected of judges and required of subordinate judicial officers under rule 10.462(d).

(3) The education required in (1) must be provided by CJER, CJA, or the judicial officer's court. CJER is responsible for identifying content for this education and will share the identified content with CJA and the courts.

(4) The education required in (1) may be by traditional (face to face) or distance-learning means, such as broadcasts, videoconferences, or online coursework, but may not be by self-study.

(c) Hours–based continuing education

(1) In a court with five or more authorized judges, each judicial officer regularly assigned to hear probate proceedings must complete 18 hours of continuing education every three

years, with a minimum of six hours required in the first year, on probate guardianships and conservatorships, including court-supervised fiduciary accounting. The three-year period begins on January 1 of the year following the judicial officer's completion of the education required in (b)(1) or, if he or she is exempt from that education, on January 1 of the year the assignment commenced after the effective date of this rule.

(2) In a court with four or fewer authorized judges, each judicial officer regularly assigned to hear probate proceedings must complete nine hours of continuing education every three years, with a minimum of three hours per year, on probate guardianships and conservatorships, including court-supervised fiduciary accounting. The three-year period begins on January 1 of the year following the judicial officer's completion of the education required in (b)(1) or, if he or she is exempt from that education, on January 1 of the year the assignment commenced after the effective date of this rule.

(3) The first continuing education period for judicial officers who were regularly assigned to hear probate proceedings before the effective date of this rule and who continue in the assignment after that date is two years, from January 1, 2008, through December 31, 2009, rather than three years. The continuing education requirements in (1) are prorated for the first continuing education period under this paragraph. The first full three-year period of continuing education for judicial officers under this paragraph begins on January 1, 2010.

(4) The number of hours of education required in (1) or (2) may be reduced proportionately for judicial officers whose regular assignment to hear probate proceedings is for a period of less than three years.

(5) The education required in (1) or (2) may be applied toward satisfaction of the 30 hours of continuing education expected of judges or required of subordinate judicial officers under rule 10.462(d).

(6) A judicial officer may fulfill the education requirement in (1) or (2) through AOC-sponsored education, an approved provider (see rule 10.481(a)), or education approved by the judicial officer's presiding judge as meeting the education criteria specified in rule 10.481(b).

(7) The education required in (1) or (2) may be by traditional (live, face-to-face) or distance learning, such as broadcasts, videoconferences, or online coursework, but may not be by self-study.

(d) Extension of time

The provisions of rule 10.462(e) concerning extensions of time apply to the content-based and hours-based education required under (b) and (c) of this rule.

(e) Record keeping and reporting

(1) The provisions of rule 10.462(f) and (g) concerning, respectively, tracking participation, record keeping, and summarizing participation by judges and tracking participation by subordinate judicial officers, apply to the education required under this rule.

(2) Presiding judges' records of judicial officer participation in the education required by this rule are subject to audit by the AOC under rule 10.462. The AOC may require courts to report participation by judicial officers in the education required by this rule to ensure compliance with Probate Code section 1456. *(Adopted, eff. Jan. 1, 2008. As amended, eff. Jan. 1, 2012.)*

Research References

14 Witkin, California Summary 10th Wills and Probate § 346, (S 346) in General.

Rule 10.469.   Judicial education recommendations for justices, judges, and subordinate judicial officers

(a) Judicial education recommendations generally

Each justice, judge and subordinate judicial officer, as part of his or her continuing judicial education, should regularly participate in educational activities related to his or her responsibilities and particular judicial assignment or assignments. Minimum education requirements and expectations related to judicial responsibilities and assignments are set forth in rules 10.461–10.462. Additional education requirements related to specific r responsibilities are set forth in rule 10.463 (for those hearing family law matters), rule 10.464 (for those hearing domestic violence issues), and rule 10.468 (for those hearing probate proceedings). The following recommendations illustrate for some specific responsibilities and assignments how justices, judges, and subordinate judicial officers should participate in more judicial education than is required and expected.

(b) Jury trial assignment

Each judge or subordinate judicial officer assigned to jury trials should regularly use the Administrative Office of the Courts' Education Division/CJER educational materials or other appropriate materials and should regularly complete CJER or other appropriate educational programs devoted to the conduct of jury voir dire and the treatment of jurors.

(c) Hearing of juvenile dependency matters

Each judge or subordinate judicial officer who hears juvenile dependency matters, including retired judges who sit on court assignment, should regularly use appropriate educational materials and should annually complete appropriate education programs on juvenile dependency law and procedure, consistent with the requirements in Welfare and Institutions Code section 304.7.

(d) Capital case assignment

Each judge assigned to hear a capital case should complete before the commencement of the trial a comprehensive education program on California law and procedure relevant to capital cases provided by CJER. A judge with a subsequent assignment to a capital case should complete a periodic update course within two years before the commencement of the trial. The periodic update may be provided through actual classroom instruction or through video, audio, or other media as determined by CJER.

(e) Fairness and access education

In order to achieve the objective of assisting judicial officers in preserving the integrity and impartiality of the judicial system through the prevention of bias, each justice, judge, and subordinate judicial officer should regularly participate in education on fairness and access. The education should include the following subjects: race and ethnicity, gender, sexual orientation, persons with disabilities, and sexual harassment. *(Adopted, eff. Jan. 1, 2008. As amended, eff. Jan. 1, 2012.)*

Research References

2 Witkin Cal. Proc. 5th Courts § 395, (S 395) Mandatory Requirement.

Rule 10.471.   Minimum education requirements for Supreme Court and Court of Appeal clerk/administrators

(a) Applicability

All California Supreme Court and Court of Appeal clerk/administrators must complete these minimum education requirements. All clerk/administrators should participate in more education than is required, related to each individual's responsibilities and in accordance with the education recommendations set forth in rule 10.479.

(b) Hours–based requirement

(1) Each clerk/administrator must complete 30 hours of continuing education every three years beginning on the following date:

(A) For a new clerk/administrator, the first three-year period begins on January 1 of the year following his or her hire.

(B) For all other clerk/administrators, the first three-year period begins on January 1, 2008.

(2) The following education applies toward the required 30 hours of continuing education:

(A) Any education offered by an approved provider (see rule 10.481(a)) and any other education, including education taken to satisfy a statutory or other education requirement, approved by the Chief Justice or the administrative presiding justice as meeting the criteria listed in rule 10.481(b).

(B) Each hour of participation in traditional (face–to–face) education, distance education such as broadcast and videoconference courses, online coursework, and self-directed study counts toward the requirement on an hour-for-hour basis. The hours applied for participation in online coursework and self-directed study are limited to a combined total of 7 hours in each three-year period.

(C) A clerk/administrator who serves as faculty for a California court-based audience (i.e., justices, judges, subordinate judicial officers, temporary judges, or court personnel) may apply the following hours of faculty service: 3 hours for each hour of presentation the first time a given course is presented and 2 hours for each hour of presentation each subsequent time that course is presented. The hours applied for faculty service are limited to 15 in each three-year period.

(c) Extension of time

(1) For good cause, the Chief Justice or the administrative presiding justice may grant a one-year extension of time to complete the education requirements in (b).

(2) If the Chief Justice or the administrative presiding justice grants a request for an extension of time, the clerk/administrator, in consultation with the Chief Justice or the administrative presiding justice, must also pursue interim means of obtaining relevant educational content.

(3) An extension of time to complete the hours-based requirement does not affect the timing of the clerk/administrator's next three-year period.

(d) Record of participation; statement of completion

Each clerk/administrator is responsible for:

(1) Tracking his or her own participation in education and keeping a record of participation for three years after each course or activity that is applied toward the requirements;

(2) At the end of each year, giving the Chief Justice or the administrative presiding justice a copy of his or her record of participation in education for that year; and

(3) At the end of each three-year period, giving the Chief Justice or the administrative presiding justice a signed statement of completion for that three-year period. *(Adopted, eff. Jan. 1, 2008. As amended, eff. Jan. 1, 2012.)*

Research References

2 Witkin Cal. Proc. 5th Courts § 395, (S 395) Mandatory Requirement.

Rule 10.472. Minimum education requirements for Supreme Court and Court of Appeal managing attorneys, supervisors, and other personnel

(a) Applicability

All California Supreme Court and Court of Appeal managing attorneys, supervisors, and other personnel must complete these minimum education requirements. All managing attorneys, supervisors, and other personnel should participate in more education than is required related to each individual's responsibilities and in accordance with the education recommendations set forth in rule 10.479.

(b) Content–based requirements

(1) Each new managing attorney or supervisor must complete orientation courses within six months of becoming a managing attorney or supervisor, unless the individual's supervisor determines that the new managing attorney or supervisor has already completed these orientation courses or courses covering equivalent content. The courses must include orientation about:

(A) The judicial branch of California;

(B) The local court; and

(C) Basic management and supervision.

(2) Each new court employee who is not a managing attorney or supervisor must complete orientation courses within six months of becoming a court employee, unless the employee's supervisor determines that the new court employee has already completed these orientation courses or courses covering equivalent content. The courses must include orientation about:

(A) The judicial branch of California;

(B) The local court;

(C) Basic employee issues, such as sexual harassment and safety; and

(D) The employee's specific job.

(3) The clerk/administrator, the managing attorney, or the employee's supervisor may determine the appropriate content, delivery mechanism, and length of orientation based on the needs and role of each individual employee.

(c) Hours–based requirements

(1) Each managing attorney, supervisor, or appellate judicial attorney must complete 12 hours of continuing education every two years.

(2) Each court employee who is not a managing attorney, supervisor, or appellate judicial attorney must complete 8 hours of continuing education every two years, with the exception of employees who do not provide court administrative or operational services. Those employees are not subject to the continuing education hours-based requirement but must complete any education or training required by law and any other education required by the clerk/administrator.

(3) The first two-year period for all managing attorneys, supervisors, and other personnel begins on January 1, 2008. The orientation education required for new managing attorneys, supervisors, and other personnel under (b) does not apply toward the required hours of continuing education because it must be completed before they enter the two-year period. Each new managing attorney, supervisor, or employee enters the two-year continuing education period on the first day of the quarter following his or her completion of the orientation education required under (b); the quarters begin on January 1, April 1, July 1, and October 1. Each managing attorney, supervisor, or employee who enters the two-year continuing education period after it has begun must complete a prorated number of continuing education hours for that two-year period, based on the number of quarters remaining in it.

(4) Any education offered by an approved provider (see rule 10.481(a)) and any other education, including education taken to satisfy a statutory, rules-based, or other education requirement, that is approved by the clerk/administrator, the managing attorney, or the employee's supervisor as meeting the criteria

listed in rule 10.481(b) applies toward the orientation education required under (b) and the continuing education required under (c)(1) and (2).

(5) Each hour of participation in traditional (live, face-to-face) education; distance education such as broadcasts, video-conferences, online coursework; and faculty service counts toward the requirement on an hour-for-hour basis. Each managing attorney, supervisor, and other employee must complete at least half of his or her continuing education hours requirement as a participant in traditional (live, face-to-face) education. The managing attorney, supervisor, or other employee may complete the balance of his or her education hours requirement through any other means with no limitation on any particular type of education. Self-directed study is encouraged for professional development but does not apply toward the required hours.

(6) A managing attorney, supervisor, or other employee who serves as faculty by teaching legal or judicial education for a legal or judicial audience may apply education hours for the faculty service. Credit for faculty service counts toward the continuing education requirement in the same manner as all other types of education—on an hour-for-hour basis.

(7) The clerk/administrator, the managing attorney, or the employee's supervisor may require supervisors and other court personnel to participate in specific courses or to participate in education in a specific subject matter area as part of their continuing education.

(d) Extension of time

(1) For good cause, a justice (for that justice's chambers staff), the managing attorney, the clerk/administrator, or a supervisor, if delegated by the clerk/administrator, or the employee's supervisor may grant a six-month extension of time to complete the education requirements in this rule.

(2) If the justice, managing attorney, clerk/administrator, or supervisor grants a request for an extension of time, the managing attorney, supervisor, or employee who made the request, in consultation with the justice, managing attorney, clerk/administrator, or supervisor, must also pursue interim means of obtaining relevant educational content.

(3) An extension of time to complete the hours-based requirement does not affect the timing of the next two-year period.

(e) Records of participation

(1) Each court is responsible for tracking participation in education and for tracking completion of minimum education requirements for its managing attorneys, supervisors, and other personnel.

(2) Each managing attorney, supervisor, and employee must keep records of his or her own participation for two years after each course or activity that is applied toward the requirements. *(Adopted, eff. Jan. 1, 2008. As amended, eff. Jan. 1, 2012.)*

Research References

2 Witkin Cal. Proc. 5th Courts § 395, (S 395) Mandatory Requirement.

Rule 10.473.   Minimum education requirements for trial court executive officers

(a) Applicability

All California trial court executive officers must complete these minimum education requirements. All executive officers should participate in more education than is required, related to each individual's responsibilities and in accordance with the education recommendations set forth in rule 10.479.

(b) Content–based requirement

(1) Each new executive officer must complete the Presiding Judges Orientation and Court Management Program provided by the Administrative Office of the Courts' Education Division/Center for Judicial Education and Research (CJER) within one year of becoming an executive officer and should participate in additional education during the first year.

(2) Each executive officer should participate in CJER's Presiding Judges Orientation and Court Management Program each time a new presiding judge from his or her court participates in the course and each time the executive officer becomes the executive officer in a different court.

(c) Hours–based requirement

(1) Each executive officer must complete 30 hours of continuing education, including at least three hours of ethics education, every three years beginning on the following date:

(A) For a new executive officer, the first three-year period begins on January 1 of the year following completion of the required education for new executive officers.

(B) For all other executive officers, the first three-year period began on January 1, 2007.

(2) The following education applies toward the required 30 hours of continuing education:

(A) Any education offered by an approved provider (see rule 10.481(a)) and any other education, including education taken to satisfy a statutory or other education requirement, approved by the presiding judge as meeting the criteria listed in rule 10.481(b).

(B) Each hour of participation in traditional (live, face–to–face) education; distance education such as broadcasts, video-conferences, and online coursework; self–directed study, and faculty service counts toward the requirement on an hour-for-hour basis. Each court executive officer must complete at least half of his or her continuing education hours requirement as a participant in traditional (live, face–to–face) education. The court executive officer may complete the balance of his or her education hours requirement through any other means with no limitation on any particular type of education.

(C) A court executive officer who serves as faculty by teaching legal or judicial education to a legal or judicial audience may apply education hours as faculty service. Credit for faculty service counts toward the continuing education requirement in the same manner as all other types of education—on an hour-for-hour basis.

(d) Extension of time

(1) For good cause, a presiding judge may grant a one-year extension of time to complete the education requirements in (b) and (c).

(2) If the presiding judge grants a request for an extension of time, the executive officer, in consultation with the presiding judge, must also pursue interim means of obtaining relevant educational content.

(3) An extension of time to complete the hours-based requirement does not affect the timing of the executive officer's next three-year period.

(e) Record of participation; statement of completion

Each executive officer is responsible for:

(1) Tracking his or her own participation in education and keeping a record of participation for three years after each course or activity that is applied toward the requirements;

(2) At the end of each year, giving the presiding judge a copy of his or her record of participation in education for that year; and

(3) At the end of each three-year period, giving the presiding judge a signed statement of completion for that three-year period. *(Formerly Rule 10.463, adopted, eff. Jan. 1, 2007. Renumbered Rule 10.473 and amended, eff. Jan. 1, 2008. As amended, eff. Jan. 1, 2011; Jan. 1, 2012; Jan. 1, 2013.)*

Research References

2 Witkin Cal. Proc. 5th Courts § 395, (S 395) Mandatory Requirement.

Rule 10.474. Trial court managers, supervisors, and other personnel

(a) Applicability

All California trial court managers, supervisors, and other personnel must complete these minimum education requirements. All managers, supervisors, and other personnel should participate in more education than is required, related to each individual's responsibilities and in accordance with the education recommendations set forth in rule 10.479.

(b) Content–based requirements

(1) Each new manager or supervisor must complete orientation courses within six months of becoming a manager or supervisor, unless the court's executive officer determines that the new manager or supervisor has already completed these orientation courses or courses covering equivalent content. The courses must include orientation about:

(A) The judicial branch of California;

(B) The local court; and

(C) Basic management and supervision.

(2) Each new court employee who is not a manager or supervisor must complete orientation courses within six months of becoming a court employee, unless the employee's supervisor determines that the new court employee has already completed these orientation courses or courses covering equivalent content. The courses must include orientation about:

(A) The judicial branch of California;

(B) The local court; and

(C) Basic employee issues, such as sexual harassment and safety; and

(D) The employee's specific job.

(3) The court executive officer may determine the appropriate content, delivery mechanism, and length of orientation based on the needs and role of each individual employee.

(c) Hours–based requirements

(1) Each court manager or supervisor must complete 12 hours of continuing education every two years.

(2) Each court employee who is not a manager or supervisor must complete 8 hours of continuing education every two years, with the exception of employees who do not provide court administrative or operational services. Those employees are not subject to the continuing education hours-based requirement but must complete any education or training required by law and any other education required by the court executive officer.

(3) The first two-year period for all court managers, supervisors, and other personnel begins on January 1, 2007. The orientation education required for new managers, supervisors, and other personnel under (b) does not apply toward the required hours of continuing education because it must be completed before they enter the two-year period. Each new manager, supervisor, or employee enters the two-year continuing education period on the first day of the quarter following his or her completion of the orientation education required under (b); the quarters begin on January 1, April 1, July 1, and October 1. Each manager, supervisor, or employee who enters the two-year

continuing education period after it has begun must complete a prorated number of continuing education hours for that two-year period, based on the number of quarters remaining in it.

(4) Any education offered by an approved provider (see rule 10.481(a)) and any other education, including education taken to satisfy a statutory, rules-based, or other education requirement, that is approved by the executive officer or the employee's supervisor as meeting the criteria listed in rule 10.481(b) applies toward the orientation education required under (b) and the continuing education required under (c)(1) and (2).

(5) Each hour of participation in traditional (live, face–to–face) education; distance education such as broadcasts, videoconferences, and online coursework; and faculty service counts toward the requirement on an hour-for-hour basis. Each manager, supervisor, and employee must complete at least half of his or her continuing education hours requirement as a participant in traditional (live, face-to-face) education. The individual may complete the balance of his or her education hours requirement through any other means with no limitation on any particular type of education. Self–directed study is encouraged for professional development but does not apply toward the required hours.

(6) A manager, supervisor, or employee who serves as faculty by teaching legal or judicial education to a legal or judicial audience may apply education hours as faculty service. Credit for faculty service counts toward the continuing education requirement in the same manner as all other types of education—on an hour-for-hour basis.

(7) The court executive officer may require managers, supervisors and other court personnel to participate in specific courses or to participate in education in a specific subject matter area as part of their continuing education.

(d) Extension of time

(1) For good cause, the executive officer or a supervisor, if delegated by the executive officer, may grant a six-month extension of time to complete the education requirements in this rule.

(2) If the executive officer or supervisor grants a request for an extension of time, the manager, supervisor, or employee who made the request, in consultation with the executive officer or supervisor, must also pursue interim means of obtaining relevant educational content.

(3) An extension of time to complete the hours-based requirement does not affect the timing of the next two-year period.

(e) Records of participation

(1) Each court is responsible for tracking participation in education and for tracking completion of minimum education requirements for its managers, supervisors, and other personnel.

(2) Each manager, supervisor, and employee must keep records of his or her own participation for two years after each course or activity that is applied toward the requirements. *(Formerly Rule 10.464, adopted, eff. Jan. 1, 2007. Renumbered Rule 10.474 and amended, eff. Jan. 1, 2008. As amended, eff. Jan. 1, 2012; Jan. 1, 2013.)*

Research References

2 Witkin Cal. Proc. 5th Courts § 395, (S 395) Mandatory Requirement.

Rule 10.478. Content-based and hours-based education for court investigators, probate attorneys, and probate examiners

(a) Definitions

As used in this rule, the following terms have the meanings specified below, unless the context or subject matter otherwise require:

(1) A "court investigator" is a person described in Probate Code section 1454(a) employed by or under contract with a court to provide the investigative services for the court required or authorized by law in guardianships, conservatorships, and other protective proceedings under division 4 of the Probate Code;

(2) A "probate attorney" is an active member of the State Bar of California who is employed by a court to perform the functions of a probate examiner and also to provide legal analysis, recommendations, advice, and other services to the court pertaining to probate proceedings;

(3) A "probate examiner" is a person employed by a court to review filings in probate proceedings in order to assist the court and the parties to get the filed matters properly ready for consideration by the court in accordance with the requirements of the Probate Code, the rules in title 7 of the California Rules of Court, and the court's local rules;

(4) "Probate proceedings" are decedents' estates, guardianships and conservatorships under division 4 of the Probate Code, trust proceedings under division 9 of the Probate Code, and other matters governed by provisions of that code and the rules in title 7 of the California Rules of Court;

(5) "AOC" is the Administrative Office of the Courts;

(6) "CJER" is the AOC Education Division/Center for Judicial Education and Research.

(b) Content–based requirements for court investigators

(1) Each court investigator must complete 18 hours of education within one year of his or her start date after the effective date of this rule. The education must include the following general topics:

(A) Court process and legal proceedings;

(B) Child abuse and neglect and the effect of domestic violence on children (guardianship investigators); elder and dependent adult abuse, including undue influence and other forms of financial abuse (conservatorship investigators);

(C) Medical issues;

(D) Access to and use of criminal-record information, confidentiality, ethics, conflicts of interest;

(E) Accessing and evaluating community resources for children and mentally impaired elderly or developmentally disabled adults; and

(F) Interviewing children and persons with mental function or communication deficits.

(2) A court investigator may fulfill the education requirement in (1) through AOC-sponsored education, an approved provider (see rule 10.481(a)), or education approved by the court executive officer or the court investigator's supervisor as meeting the education criteria specified in rule 10.481(b).

(3) The education required in (1) may be applied to the specific-job portion of the orientation course required for all new court employees under rule 10.474(b)(2)(D) and the continuing education required for all nonmanagerial or nonsupervisory court employees under rule 10.474(c)(2).

(4) The education required in (1) may be by traditional (face–to–face) or distance-learning means, such as broadcasts, video-conferences, or online coursework, but may not be by self-study.

(c) Content–based education for probate attorneys

(1) Each probate attorney must complete 18 hours of education within six months of his or her start date after January 1, 2008, in probate-related topics, including guardianships, conservatorships, and court-supervised fiduciary accounting.

(2) A probate attorney may fulfill the education requirement in (1) through AOC-sponsored education, an approved provider (see rule 10.481(a)), or education approved by the court executive officer or the probate attorney's supervisor as meeting the education criteria specified in rule 10.481(b).

(3) The education required in (1) may be applied to the specific-job portion of the orientation course required for all new court employees under rule 10.474(b)(2)(D) and the continuing education required for all nonmanagerial or nonsupervisory court employees under rule 10.474(c)(2).

(4) The education required in (1) may be by traditional (face–to–face) or distance-learning means, such as broadcasts, video-conferences, or online coursework, but may not be by self-study.

(d) Content–based education for probate examiners

(1) Each probate examiner must complete 30 hours of education within one year of his or her start date after January 1, 2008, in probate-related topics, of which 18 hours must be in guardianships and conservatorships, including court-appointed fiduciary accounting.

(2) A probate examiner may fulfill the education requirement in (1) through AOC-sponsored education, an approved provider (see rule 10.481(a)), or education approved by the court executive officer or the probate examiner's supervisor as meeting the education criteria specified in rule 10.481(b).

(3) The education required in (1) may be applied to the specific-job portion of the orientation course required for all new court employees under rule 10.474(b)(2)(D) and the continuing education required for all nonmanagerial or nonsupervisory court employees under rule 10.474(c)(2).

(4) The education required in (1) may be by traditional (face–to–face) or distance-learning means, such as broadcasts, video-conferences, or online coursework, but may not be by self-study.

(e) Hours–based education for court investigators

(1) Each court investigator must complete 12 hours of continuing education on some or all of the general topics listed in (b)(1) each calendar year. For court investigators employed by or performing services under contract with the court before the effective date of this rule, the first calendar year the education is required begins on January 1, 2008. For court investigators who begin their employment or performance of services under contract with the court after the effective date of this rule, the first year this education is required begins on January 1 of the year immediately following completion of the education required in (b).

(2) A court investigator may fulfill the education requirement in (1) through AOC-sponsored education, an approved provider (see rule 10.481(a)), or education approved by the court executive officer or the court investigator's supervisor as meeting the education criteria specified in rule 10.481(b).

(3) The education required in (1) may be applied to the continuing education required for all nonmanagerial or nonsupervisory court employees under rule 10.474(c)(2).

(4) The education required in (1) may be by traditional (face–to–face) or distance-learning means, such as broadcasts, video-conferences, or online coursework, but may not be by self-study.

(f) Hours–based education for probate attorneys

(1) Each probate attorney must complete 12 hours of continuing education each calendar year in probate-related subjects, of which six hours per year must be in guardianships and conservatorships, including court-supervised fiduciary accounting. For probate attorneys employed by or performing services under contract with the court before the effective date of this rule, the first calendar year the education is required begins on January 1, 2008. For probate attorneys who begin their employment with

the court after the effective date of this rule, the first year this education is required begins on January 1 of the year immediately following completion of the education required in (c).

(2) A probate attorney may fulfill the education requirement in (1) through AOC-sponsored education, an approved provider (see rule 10.481(a)), or education approved by the court executive officer or the probate attorney's supervisor as meeting the education criteria specified in rule 10.481(b).

(3) The education required in (1) may be applied to the continuing education required for all nonmanagerial or nonsupervisory court employees under rule 10.474(c)(2).

(4) The education required in (1) may be by traditional (face-to-face) or distance-learning means, such as broadcasts, video-conferences, or online coursework, but may not be by self-study.

(g) Hours–based education for probate examiners

(1) Each probate examiner must complete 12 hours of continuing education each calendar year in probate-related subjects, of which six hours per year must be in guardianships and conservatorships, including court-appointed fiduciary accounting. For probate examiners employed by the court before the effective date of this rule, the first calendar year the education is required begins on January 1, 2008. For probate examiners who begin their employment with the court after the effective date of this rule, the first year this education is required begins on January 1 of the year immediately following completion of the education required in (d).

(2) A probate examiner may fulfill the education requirement in (1) through AOC-sponsored education, an approved provider (see rule 10.481(a)), or education approved by the court executive officer or the probate examiner's supervisor as meeting the education criteria specified in rule 10.481(b).

(3) The education required in (1) may be applied to the continuing education required for all nonmanagerial or nonsupervisory court employees under rule 10.474(c)(2).

(4) The education required in (1) may be by traditional (face-to-face) or distance-learning means, such as broadcasts, video-conferences, or online coursework, but may not be by self-study.

(h) Extension of time

The provisions of rule 10.474(d) concerning extensions of time apply to the content-based and hours-based education required under this rule.

(i) Record keeping and reporting

(1) The provisions of rule 10.474(e) concerning the responsibilities of courts and participating court employees to keep records and track the completion of educational requirements apply to the education required under this rule.

(2) The AOC may require courts to report participation by court investigators, probate attorneys, and probate examiners in the education required by this rule as necessary to ensure compliance with Probate Code section 1456. *(Adopted, eff. Jan. 1, 2008. As amended, eff. Jan. 1, 2012.)*

Research References

Rutter, Cal. Practice Guide: Prof. Responsibility Ch. 1-M, M. Minimum Continuing Legal Education ("MCLE").
14 Witkin, California Summary 10th Wills and Probate § 371, General Rules of Practice.
14 Witkin, California Summary 10th Wills and Probate § 907, (S 907) Rules of Practice.

Rule 10.479. Education recommendations for appellate and trial court personnel

(a) Education recommendations generally

Each appellate and trial court executive or administrative officer, manager, supervisor, and other employee, as part of his or her continuing education, should regularly participate in educational activities related to his or her responsibilities. Minimum education requirements for court personnel are set forth in rules 10.471—10.474. The following recommendations illustrate for some specific responsibilities how executive and administrative officers, managers, supervisors, and other personnel should participate in more education than is required.

(b) Education on treatment of jurors

The presiding judge of each trial court should ensure that all court executives and all court employees who interact with jurors are properly trained in the appropriate treatment of jurors. Court executives and jury staff employees should regularly use CJER educational materials or other appropriate materials and should regularly participate in CJER programs or other appropriate programs devoted to the treatment of jurors.

(c) Fairness and access education

In order to achieve the objective of assisting court employees in preserving the integrity and impartiality of the judicial system through the prevention of bias, all court personnel should regularly participate in education on fairness and access. The education should include instruction on race and ethnicity, gender, sexual orientation, persons with disabilities, and sexual harassment.

(d) Education on quality service to court users

Employees should regularly participate in education covering appropriate skills and conduct for working with court customers offered locally or by the Judicial Council through CJER. *(Adopted, eff. Jan. 1, 2008.)*

Research References

2 Witkin Cal. Proc. 5th Courts § 395, (S 395) Mandatory Requirement.

Rule 10.481. Approved providers; approved course criteria

(a) Approved providers

The Administrative Office of the Courts' Education Division/CJER is responsible for maintaining a current list of approved providers. The list of approved providers must include the Administrative Office of the Courts, the California Judges Association, and all California state courts and should include other reputable national and state organizations that regularly offer education directed to justices, judges, and court personnel. The director of the Education Division/CJER may add or remove organizations from the list of approved providers as appropriate according to these criteria. Any education program offered by any of the approved providers that is relevant to the work of the courts or enhances the individual participant's ability to perform his or her job may be applied toward the education requirements and expectations stated in rules 10.461–10.479, except for the requirements stated in rules 10.461(b), 10.462(c), and 10.473(b), for which specific providers are required.

(b) Approved education criteria

Education is not limited to the approved providers referred to in (a). Any education from another provider that is approved by the Chief Justice, the administrative presiding justice, or the presiding judge as meeting the criteria listed below may be applied toward the continuing education expectations and requirements for justices, judges, and subordinate judicial officers or requirements for clerk/administrators or court executive officers. Similarly, any education from another provider that is approved by the clerk/administrator, the court executive officer, or the employee's supervisor as meeting the criteria listed below may be applied toward the orientation or continuing education requirements for managers, supervisors, and other employees or the content-based or continuing education requirements for probate court investigators, probate attorneys, and probate examiners in rule 10.478.

(1) The education must meet the following three criteria:

(A) The subject matter is relevant to the work of the courts or the judicial branch; ·

(B) The education is at least one hour in length; and

(C) Anticipated learning outcomes (how new knowledge, skills, or abilities will be applied, demonstrated, or used) are identified prior to the education work.

(2) The education must also meet at least two of the following five criteria:

(A) The learning environment is educationally sound (e.g., distractions are limited and the physical location is conducive to learning the subject matter);

(B) The participant receives or has access to all the reference tools and other materials and resources (such as handouts) that are required for learning and applying the content (such as job aids or scripts);

(C) The participant has an opportunity to practice using or applying the new information or skill (through direct experience, roleplay, or case studies/hypothetical situations) as part of he learning experience;

(D) The participant has the opportunity to interact with knowledgeable faculty or other experts in the topical area to pose questions or clarify understanding;

(E) An assessment tool or activity (such as the development of an action plan to apply the newly gained knowledge or skill) enables the participant to determine whether the skills, abilities, or knowledge gained through the education can be used in the future in his or her work.

(Formerly Rule 10.471, adopted, eff. Jan. 1, 2007. Renumbered Rule 10.481 and amended, eff. Jan. 1, 2008. As amended, eff. Jan. 1, 2008; Jan. 1, 2012.)

Advisory Committee Comment

Subdivision (b). The director of the Education Division/CJER is available to assist those authorized to approve a request to apply education offered by a non-approved provider in determining whether the education meets the listed criteria.

Rule 10.491. Minimum education requirements for Administrative Office of the Courts executives, managers, supervisors, and other employees

(a) Applicability

All Administrative Office of the Courts (AOC) executives, managers, supervisors, and other employees must complete these minimum education requirements.

(b) Content–based requirements

(1) Each new manager or supervisor must complete the AOC's New Manager/Supervisor Orientation within six months of being hired or assigned as a manager or supervisor.

(2) Each new employee, including each new manager or supervisor, must complete the AOC's New Employee Orientation within six months of being hired and should complete it as soon as possible after being hired.

(3) The Administrative Director of the Courts may require new managers, supervisors, and other employees to complete specific AOC compliance courses in addition to the required orientation courses.

(c) Hours–based requirements

(1) Each executive must complete 30 hours of continuing education every two years.

(2) Each manager or supervisor must complete 18 hours of continuing education every two years.

(3) Each employee who is not an executive, manager, or supervisor must complete 12 hours of continuing education every two years.

(4) ~~The first two-year period begins on January 1, 2008.~~ The orientation courses and the compliance courses required for new managers, supervisors, and other employees under (b) do not apply toward the required hours of continuing education. Each new executive enters the two-year continuing education period on the first day of the quarter following his or her appointment, and each new manager, supervisor, and employee enters the two-year continuing education period on the first day of the quarter following the six-month period provided for his or her completion of the orientation courses and the compliance courses required under (b); the quarters begin on January 1, April 1, July 1, and October 1. Each executive, manager, supervisor, or employee who enters the two-year continuing education period after it has begun must complete a prorated number of continuing education hours for that two-year period, based on the number of quarters remaining in it.

(5) Any education offered by an approved provider (see rule 10.481(a)) and any other education, including education taken to satisfy a statutory, rules-based, or other education requirement, that is approved by the employee's supervisor as meeting the criteria listed in rule 10.481(b) applies toward the continuing education required under (c)(1)–(3).

(6) Each hour of participation in traditional (live, face–to–face) education; distance education such as broadcasts, videoconference courses, and online coursework; and faculty service counts toward the requirement on an hour-for-hour basis. ~~Each executive, manager, supervisor, and employee must complete at least half of his or her continuing education hours requirement as a participant in traditional (live, face–to–face) education. The individual may complete the balance of his or her education hours requirement through any other means with no limitation on any particular type of education.~~ The Administrative Director of the Courts or an executive, manager, or supervisor, if delegated by the Administrative Director, has discretion to determine the number of hours, if any, of traditional (live, face–to–face) education required to meet the continuing education requirement.

(7) An executive, manager, supervisor, or employee who serves as faculty by teaching legal or judicial education to a legal or judicial audience may apply education hours as faculty service. Credit for faculty service counts toward the continuing education requirement in the same manner as all other types of education—on an hour-for-hour basis.

(8) The Administrative Director of the Courts may require executives, managers, supervisors, and other employees to complete specific AOC compliance courses as part of the continuing education requirements.

(d) Extension of time

(1) For good cause, the Administrative Director of the Courts or an executive, manager, or supervisor, if delegated by the Administrative Director, may grant a ~~six-month~~ one-year extension of time to complete the education requirements in this rule. If an extension is granted, the subsequent two-year compliance period begins immediately after the extended compliance period ends, unless otherwise determined by the Administrative Director.

(2) If the Administrative Director, or an executive, manager, or supervisor, grants a request for an extension of time, the

individual who made the request, in consultation with the Administrative Director or the individual's supervisor, must also pursue interim means of obtaining relevant educational content.

~~(3) An extension of time to complete the hours-based requirement does not affect the timing of the next two-year period.~~

(e) Records of participation

(1) An employee's completion of any course listed in the learning management system is automatically tracked.

(2) An employee's completion of specified online training is automatically tracked as well.

(3) Each employee is responsible for tracking completion of any training that is not automatically tracked in the learning management system. After completion of the training, the employee must enter it in the employee's individual record in the learning management system.

(f) Responsibilities of Administrative Director of the Courts and of AOC executives, managers, and supervisors

The Administrative Director of the Courts and each AOC executive, manager, and supervisor:

(1) Must grant sufficient time to all employees to enable them to complete the minimum education requirements stated in (b)–(c);

(2) Should allow and encourage employees, in addition to participating as students in education activities, to serve on employee education committees and as faculty at judicial branch education programs when an employee's services have been requested for these purposes; and

(3) Should establish an education plan for their employees to facilitate their involvement as both participants and faculty in educational activities, and should consult with each employee regarding his or her education needs and requirements and professional development.

(4) Must ensure that executives, managers, supervisors, and other employees are reimbursed by the AOC in accordance with the travel policies issued by the Administrative Office of the Courts for travel expenses incurred in attending in-state education programs as a participant in order to complete the minimum education requirements in (b)–(c). Provisions for these expenses must be part of the AOC's budget. The Administrative Director of the Courts may approve reimbursement of travel expenses incurred by executives, managers, supervisors, and other employees in attending out-of-state education programs as participants. *(Adopted, eff. Jan. 1, 2008. As amended, eff. July 1, 2008; Jan. 1, 2012; July 1, 2013.)*

Advisory Committee Comment

The time frame for completion of compliance courses based on statutory or regulatory mandates is unaffected by the one-year extension in (d)(1).

Research References

2 Witkin Cal. Proc. 5th Courts § 197, (S 197) Judicial Administration Rules.
2 Witkin Cal. Proc. 5th Courts § 395, (S 395) Mandatory Requirement.

Division 3

JUDICIAL ADMINISTRATION RULES APPLICABLE TO ALL COURTS

Rule 10.500. Public access to judicial administrative records

(a) Intent

(1) The Judicial Council intends by this rule to implement Government Code section 68106.2(g), added by Senate Bill X4 13 (Stats.2009–10, 4th Ex. Sess. ch. 22), which requires adoption of rules of court that provide public access to nondeliberative and nonadjudicative court records, budget and management information.

(2) This rule clarifies and expands the public's right of access to judicial administrative records and must be broadly construed to further the public's right of access.

(b) Application

(1) This rule applies to public access to judicial administrative records, including records of budget and management information relating to the administration of the courts.

(2) This rule does not apply to, modify or otherwise affect existing law regarding public access to adjudicative records.

(3) This rule does not restrict the rights to disclosure of information otherwise granted by law to a recognized employee organization.

(4) This rule does not affect the rights of litigants, including parties to administrative proceedings, under the laws of discovery of this state, nor does it limit or impair any rights of discovery in a criminal case.

(5) This rule does not apply to electronic mail and text messages sent or received before the effective date of this rule.

(c) Definitions

As used in this rule:

(1) "Adjudicative record" means any writing prepared for or filed or used in a court proceeding, the judicial deliberation process, or the assignment or reassignment of cases and of justices, judges (including temporary and assigned judges), and subordinate judicial officers, or of counsel appointed or employed by the court.

(2) "Judicial administrative record" means any writing containing information relating to the conduct of the people's business that is prepared, owned, used, or retained by a judicial branch entity regardless of the writing's physical form or characteristics, except an adjudicative record. The term "judicial administrative record" does not include records of a personal nature that are not used in or do not relate to the people's business, such as personal notes, memoranda, electronic mail, calendar entries, and records of Internet use.

(3) "Judicial branch entity" means the Supreme Court, each Court of Appeal, each superior court, the Judicial Council, and the Administrative Office of the Courts.

(4) "Judicial branch personnel" means justices, judges (including temporary and assigned judges), subordinate judicial officers, members of the Judicial Council and its advisory bodies, and directors, officers, employees, volunteers, and agents of a judicial branch entity.

Ct. Rules

(5) "Person" means any natural person, corporation, partnership, limited liability company, firm, or association.

(6) "Writing" means any handwriting, typewriting, printing, photographing, photocopying, electronic mail, fax, and every other means of recording on any tangible thing any form of communication or representation, including letters, words, pictures, sounds, symbols, or combinations, regardless of the manner in which the record has been stored.

(d) Construction of rule

(1) Unless otherwise indicated, the terms used in this rule have the same meaning as under the Legislative Open Records Act (Gov. Code, § 9070 et seq.) and the California Public Records Act (Gov. Code, § 6250 et seq.) and must be interpreted consistently with the interpretation applied to the terms under those acts.

(2) This rule does not require the disclosure of a record if the record is exempt from disclosure under this rule or is the type of record that would not be subject to disclosure under the Legislative Open Records Act or the California Public Records Act.

(e) Public access

(1) *Access*

(A) A judicial branch entity must allow inspection and copying of judicial administrative records unless the records are exempt from disclosure under this rule or by law.

(B) Nothing in this rule requires a judicial branch entity to create any record or to compile or assemble data in response to a request for judicial administrative records if the judicial branch entity does not compile or assemble the data in the requested form for its own use or for provision to other agencies. For purposes of this rule, selecting data from extractable fields in a single database using software already owned or licensed by the judicial branch entity does not constitute creating a record or compiling or assembling data.

(C) If a judicial administrative record contains information that is exempt from disclosure and the exempt portions are reasonably segregable, a judicial branch entity must allow inspection and copying of the record after deletion of the portions that are exempt from disclosure. A judicial branch entity is not required to allow inspection or copying of the portion of a writing that is a judicial administrative record unless that portion is reasonably segregable from the portion that constitutes an adjudicative record.

(D) If requested, a superior court must provide a copy of the certified judicial administrative record if the judicial administrative record requested has previously been certified by the superior court.

(2) *Examples*

Judicial administrative records subject to inspection and copying unless exempt from disclosure under subdivision (f) include, but are not limited to, the following:

(A) Budget information submitted to the Administrative Office of the Courts after enactment of the annual Budget Act;

(B) Any other budget and expenditure document pertaining to the administrative operation of the courts, including quarterly financial statements and statements of revenue, expenditure, and reserves;

(C) Actual and budgeted employee salary and benefit information;

(D) Copies of executed contracts with outside vendors and payment information and policies concerning goods and services provided by outside vendors without an executed contract;

(E) Final audit reports; and

(F) Employment contracts between judicial branch entities and their employees.

(3) *Procedure for requesting records*

A judicial branch entity must make available on its public Web site or otherwise publicize the procedure to be followed to request a copy of or to inspect a judicial administrative record. At a minimum, the procedure must include the address to which requests are to be addressed, to whom requests are to be directed, and the office hours of the judicial branch entity.

(4) *Costs of duplication, search, and review*

(A) A judicial branch entity, on request, must provide a copy of a judicial administrative record not exempt from disclosure if the record is of a nature permitting copying, subject to payment of the fee specified in this rule or other applicable statutory fee. A judicial branch entity may require advance payment of any fee.

(B) A judicial branch entity may impose on all requests a fee reasonably calculated to cover the judicial branch entity's direct costs of duplication of a record or of production of a record in an electronic format under subdivision (i). The fee includes:

(i) A charge per page, per copy, or otherwise, as established and published by the Judicial Council, or as established by the judicial branch entity following a notice and comment procedure specified by the Judicial Council, representing the direct costs of equipment, supplies, and staff time required to duplicate or produce the requested record; and

(ii) Any other direct costs of duplication or production, including, but not limited to, the costs incurred by a judicial branch entity in retrieving the record from a remote storage facility or archive and the costs of mailing responsive records.

(C) In the case of requests for records for commercial use, a judicial branch entity may impose, in addition to the fee in (B), a fee reasonably calculated to cover the actual costs of staff search and review time, based on an hourly rate for salary and benefits of each employee involved.

(D) For purposes of this rule:

(i) "Commercial use" means a request for a use or purpose that furthers the commercial, trade, or profit interests of the requester or the person on whose behalf the request is being made. A request from a representative of the news media that supports its news-dissemination function is not a request for a commercial use.

(ii) "Representative of the news media" means a person who regularly gathers, prepares, collects, photographs, records, writes, edits, reports, or publishes news or information that concerns local, national, or international events or other matters of public interest for dissemination to the public for a substantial portion of the person's livelihood or for substantial financial gain.

(iii) "Search and review time" means actual time spent identifying and locating judicial administrative records, including material within documents, responsive to a request; determining whether any portions are exempt from disclosure; and performing all tasks necessary to prepare the records for disclosure, including redacting portions exempt from disclosure. "Search and review time" does not include time spent resolving general legal or policy issues regarding the applicability of particular exemptions.

(E) By January 1, 2012, the Judicial Council will review and evaluate the numbers of requests received, the time necessary to respond, and the fees imposed by judicial branch entities for access to records and information. The Judicial Council's review will consider the impact of this rule on both the public's access to records and information and on judicial branch entities' ability to carry out and fund core judicial operations.

(5) *Inspection*

A judicial branch entity must make judicial administrative records in its possession and not exempt from disclosure open to inspection at all times during the office hours of the judicial branch entity provided that the record is of a nature permitting inspection.

(6) *Time for determination of disclosable records*

A judicial branch entity, on a request that reasonably describes an identifiable record or records, must determine, within 10 calendar days from receipt of the request, whether the request, in whole or in part, seeks disclosable judicial administrative records in its possession and must promptly notify the requesting party of the determination and the reasons for the determination.

(7) *Response*

If a judicial branch entity determines that a request seeks disclosable judicial administrative records, the judicial branch entity must make the disclosable judicial administrative records available promptly. The judicial branch entity must include with the notice of the determination the estimated date and time when the records will be made available. If the judicial branch entity determines that the request, in whole or in part, seeks nondisclosable judicial administrative records, it must convey its determination in writing, include a contact name and telephone number to which inquiries may be directed, and state the express provision of this rule justifying the withholding of the records not disclosed.

(8) *Extension of time for determination of disclosable records*

In unusual circumstances, to the extent reasonably necessary to the proper processing of the particular request, a judicial branch entity may extend the time limit prescribed for its determination under (e)(6) by no more than 14 calendar days by written notice to the requesting party, stating the reasons for the extension and the date on which the judicial branch entity expects to make a determination. As used in this section, "unusual circumstances" means the following:

    (A) The need to search for and collect the requested records from multiple locations or facilities that are separate from the office processing the request;

    (B) The need to search for, collect, and appropriately examine a voluminous amount of records that are included in a single request; or

    (C) The need for consultation, which must be conducted with all practicable speed, with another judicial branch entity or other governmental agency having substantial subject matter interest in the determination of the request, or with two or more components of the judicial branch entity having substantial subject matter interest in the determination of the request.

(9) *Reasonable efforts*

    (A) On receipt of a request to inspect or obtain a copy of a judicial administrative record, a judicial branch entity, in order to assist the requester in making a focused and effective request that reasonably describes an identifiable judicial administrative record, must do all of the following to the extent reasonable under the circumstances:

        (i) Assist the requester in identifying records and information responsive to the request or to the purpose of the request, if stated;

        (ii) Describe the information technology and physical location in which the records exist; and

        (iii) Provide suggestions for overcoming any practical basis for denying inspection or copying of the records or information sought.

    (B) The requirements of (A) will be deemed to have been satisfied if the judicial branch entity is unable to identify the requested information after making a reasonable effort to elicit additional clarifying information from the requester that helps identify the record or records.

    (C) The requirements of (A) do not apply to a request for judicial administrative records if the judicial branch entity makes the requested records available or determines that the requested records are exempt from disclosure under this rule.

(10) *No obstruction or delay*

Nothing in this rule may be construed to permit a judicial branch entity to delay or obstruct the inspection or copying of judicial administrative records that are not exempt from disclosure.

(11) *Greater access permitted*

Except as otherwise prohibited by law, a judicial branch entity may adopt requirements for itself that allow for faster, more efficient, or greater access to judicial administrative records than prescribed by the requirements of this rule.

(12) *Control of records*

A judicial branch entity must not sell, exchange, furnish, or otherwise provide a judicial administrative record subject to disclosure under this rule to a private entity in a manner that prevents a judicial branch entity from providing the record directly under this rule. A judicial branch entity must not allow a private entity to control the disclosure of information that is otherwise subject to disclosure under this rule.

(f) Exemptions

Nothing in this rule requires the disclosure of judicial administrative records that are any of the following:

(1) Preliminary writings, including drafts, notes, working papers, and inter-judicial branch entity or intra-judicial branch entity memoranda, that are not retained by the judicial branch entity in the ordinary course of business, if the public interest in withholding those records clearly outweighs the public interest in disclosure;

(2) Records pertaining to pending or anticipated claims or litigation to which a judicial branch entity is a party or judicial branch personnel are parties, until the pending litigation or claim has been finally adjudicated or otherwise resolved;

(3) Personnel, medical, or similar files, or other personal information whose disclosure would constitute an unwarranted invasion of personal privacy, including, but not limited to, records revealing home addresses, home telephone numbers, cellular telephone numbers, private electronic mail addresses, and social security numbers of judicial branch personnel and work electronic mail addresses and work telephone numbers of justices, judges (including temporary and assigned judges), subordinate judicial officers, and their staff attorneys;

(4) Test questions, scoring keys, and other examination data used to develop, administer, and score examinations for employment, certification, or qualification;

(5) Records whose disclosure is exempted or prohibited under state or federal law, including provisions of the California Evidence Code relating to privilege, or by court order in any court proceeding;

(6) Records whose disclosure would compromise the security of a judicial branch entity or the safety of judicial branch personnel, including but not limited to, court security plans, and security surveys, investigations, procedures, and assessments;

(7) Records related to evaluations of, complaints regarding, or investigations of justices, judges (including temporary and assigned judges), subordinate judicial officers, and applicants or candidates for judicial office;

(8) The contents of real estate appraisals or engineering or feasibility estimates and evaluations made for or by the judicial branch entity related to the acquisition of property or to prospective public supply and construction contracts, until all of the property has been acquired or the relevant contracts have been executed. This provision does not affect the law of eminent domain;

(9) Records related to activities governed by Government Code sections 71600 et seq. and 71800 et seq. that reveal deliberative processes, impressions, evaluations, opinions, recommendations, meeting minutes, research, work products, theories, or strategy or that provide instruction, advice, or training to employees who are not represented by employee organizations under those sections. Nothing in this subdivision limits the disclosure duties of a judicial branch entity with respect to any other records relating to the activities governed by the employee relations acts referred to in this subdivision;

(10) Records that contain trade secrets or privileged or confidential commercial and financial information submitted in response to a judicial branch entity's solicitation for goods or services or in the course of a judicial branch entity's contractual relationship with a commercial entity. For purposes of this rule:

(A) "Trade secret" means information, including a formula, pattern, compilation, program, device, method, technique, or process, that:

(i) Derives independent economic value, actual or potential, from not being generally known to the public or to other persons who can obtain economic value from its disclosure or use; and

(ii) Is the subject of efforts that are reasonable under the circumstances to maintain its secrecy;

(B) "Privileged information" means material that falls within recognized constitutional, statutory, or common law privileges;

(C) "Confidential commercial and financial information" means information whose disclosure would:

(i) Impair the judicial branch entity's ability to obtain necessary information in the future; or

(ii) Cause substantial harm to the competitive position of the person from whom the information was obtained.

(11) Records whose disclosure would disclose the judicial branch entity's or judicial branch personnel's decision-making process, provided that, on the facts of the specific request for records, the public interest served by nondisclosure clearly outweighs the public interest served by disclosure of the record; or

(12) If, on the facts of the specific request for records, the public interest served by nondisclosure of the record clearly outweighs the public interest served by disclosure of the record.

(g) Computer software; copyrighted materials

(1) Computer software developed by a judicial branch entity or used by a judicial branch entity for the storage or manipulation of data is not a judicial administrative record under this rule. For purposes of this rule "computer software" includes computer mapping systems, computer graphic systems, and computer programs, including the source, object, and other code in a computer program.

(2) This rule does not limit a judicial branch entity's ability to sell, lease, or license computer software for commercial or noncommercial use.

(3) This rule does not create an implied warranty on the part of any judicial branch entity for errors, omissions, or other defects in any computer software.

(4) This rule does not limit any copyright protection. A judicial branch entity is not required to duplicate records under this rule in violation of any copyright.

(5) Nothing in this subdivision is intended to affect the judicial administrative record status of information merely because the information is stored in a computer. Judicial administrative records stored in a computer will be disclosed as required in this rule.

(h) Waiver of exemptions

(1) Disclosure of a judicial administrative record that is exempt from disclosure under this rule or provision of law by a judicial branch entity or judicial branch personnel acting within the scope of their office or employment constitutes a waiver of the exemptions applicable to that particular record.

(2) This subdivision does not apply to disclosures:

(A) Made through discovery proceedings;

(B) Made through other legal proceedings or as otherwise required by law;

(C) Made to another judicial branch entity or judicial branch personnel for the purposes of judicial branch administration;

(D) Within the scope of a statute that limits disclosure of specified writings to certain purposes; or

(E) Made to any governmental agency or to another judicial branch entity or judicial branch personnel if the material will be treated confidentially.

(i) Availability in electronic format

(1) A judicial branch entity that has information that constitutes an identifiable judicial administrative record not exempt from disclosure under this rule and that is in an electronic format must, on request, produce that information in the electronic format requested, provided that:

(A) No law prohibits disclosure;

(B) The record already exists in the requested electronic format, or the judicial branch entity has previously produced the judicial administrative record in the requested format for its own use or for provision to other agencies;

(C) The requested electronic format is customary or standard for records of a similar type and is commercially available to private entity requesters; and

(D) The disclosure does not jeopardize or compromise the security or integrity of the original record or the computer software on which the original record is maintained.

(2) In addition to other fees imposed under this rule, the requester will bear the direct cost of producing a record if:

(A) In order to comply with (1), the judicial branch entity would be required to produce a record and the record is one that is produced only at otherwise regularly scheduled intervals or;

(B) Producing the requested record would require data compilation or extraction or any associated programming that the judicial branch entity is not required to perform under this rule but has agreed to perform in response to the request.

(3) Nothing in this subdivision shall be construed to require a judicial branch entity to reconstruct a record in an electronic

format if the judicial branch entity no longer has the record available in an electronic format.

(j) Public access disputes

(1) Unless the petitioner elects to proceed under (2) below, disputes and appeals of decisions with respect to disputes with the Judicial Council, Administrative Office of the Courts, or a superior court regarding access to budget and management information required to be maintained under rule 10.501 are subject to the process described in rule 10.803.

(2) Any person may institute proceedings for injunctive or declarative relief or writ of mandate in any court of competent jurisdiction to enforce his or her right to inspect or to receive a copy of any judicial administrative record under this rule.

(3) Whenever it is made to appear by verified petition that a judicial administrative record is being improperly withheld from disclosure, the court with jurisdiction will order the judicial branch entity to disclose the records or show cause why it should not do so. The court will decide the case after examining the record (in camera if appropriate), papers filed by the parties, and any oral argument and additional evidence as the court may allow.

(4) If the court finds that the judicial branch entity's decision to refuse disclosure is not justified under this rule, the court will order the judicial branch entity to make the record public. If the court finds that the judicial branch entity's decision was justified, the court will issue an order supporting the decision.

(5) An order of the court, either directing disclosure or supporting the decision of the judicial branch entity refusing disclosure, is not a final judgment or order within the meaning of Code of Civil Procedure section 904.1 from which an appeal may be taken, but will be immediately reviewable by petition to the appellate court for the issuance of an extraordinary writ. Upon entry of an order under this subdivision, a party must, in order to obtain review of the order, file a petition within 20 days after service of a written notice of entry of the order or within such further time not exceeding an additional 20 days as the court may for good cause allow. If the notice is served by mail, the period within which to file the petition will be extended by 5 days. A stay of an order or judgment will not be granted unless the petitioning party demonstrates it will otherwise sustain irreparable damage and probable success on the merits. Any person who fails to obey the order of the court will be cited to show cause why that is not in contempt of court.

(6) The court will award court costs and reasonable attorney fees to the plaintiff should the plaintiff prevail in litigation filed under this subdivision. The costs and fees will be paid by the judicial branch entity and will not become a personal liability of any individual. If the court finds that the plaintiff's case is clearly frivolous, it will award court costs and reasonable attorney fees to the judicial branch entity. *(Adopted, eff. Jan. 1, 2010.)*

Advisory Committee Comment

Subdivision (a). By establishing a public access rule applicable to all judicial administrative records, the proposed rule would expand public access to these records. The Judicial Council recognizes the important public interest in access to records and information relating to the administration of the judicial branch. The Judicial Council also recognizes the importance of the privacy rights of individuals working in or doing business with judicial branch entities and the public's interest in an effective and independent judicial branch of state government. The report on this rule includes the Judicial Council's findings on the impact of this rule on these interests, and how these interests are protected by the rule.

Subdivisions (b)(1) and (b)(2). This rule does not apply to adjudicative records, and is not intended to modify existing law regarding public access to adjudicative records. California case law has established that, in general, subject to specific statutory exceptions, case records that accurately and officially reflect the work of the court are public records open to inspection. (*Estate of Hearst* (1977) 67 Cal.App.3d 777, 782–83.) However, documents prepared in the course of adjudicative work and not regarded as official case records, such as preliminary drafts, personal notes, and rough records of proceedings, are not subject to public access because the perceived harm to the judicial process by requiring this material to be available to the public is greater than the benefit the public might derive from its disclosure. (*Copley Press, Inc. v. Superior Court* (1992) 6 Cal.App.4th 106.)

Subdivision (c)(2). The application of this rule is intended to reflect existing case law under the California Public Records Act that exempts from the definition of "public record" certain types of personal records and information. The concept was first discussed in the California Assembly and establishes that if personal correspondence and information are "unrelated to the conduct of the people's business" they are therefore not public records. (*San Gabriel Tribune v. Superior Court* (1983) 143 Cal.App.3d 762, 774, citing Assembly Committee on Statewide Information Policy California Public Records Act of 1968, section B, page 9, Appendix to Assembly Journal (1970 Reg. Sess.).) Case law has further established that only records necessary or convenient to the discharge of official duty, or kept as necessary or convenient to the discharge of official duty, are public records for the purposes of the California Public Records Act and its predecessors. (*Braun v. City of Taft* (1984) 154 Cal.App.3d 332; *City Council of Santa Monica v. Superior Court* (1962) 204 Cal.App.2d 68.)

Subdivision (e)(4). The fees charged by a judicial branch entity under this rule are intended to allow the entity to recover an amount not to exceed the reasonable costs of responding to a request for records or information. In accordance with existing practice within the judicial branch and the other branches of government, the Judicial Council intends agencies and entities of the executive and legislative branches of the California state government to receive records or information requested from judicial branch entities for the agency's or entity's use free of charge. This subdivision is intended to provide, however, that requesters of records or information for the purpose of furthering the requester's commercial interests will be charged for costs incurred by the judicial branch entity in responding to the request, and that such costs will not be a charge against the budget of the judicial branch of the state General Fund.

Subdivision (f)(3). In addition to the types of records and information exempt from disclosure under the corresponding provision of the California Public Records Act, Government Code section 6254(c), this provision includes a further nonexclusive list of specific information that is exempt under this rule. The rule does not attempt to list each category of information that is specific to judicial branch entities and that may also be exempt under this rule. For example, although they are not specifically listed, this provision exempts from disclosure records maintained by any court or court-appointed counsel administrator for the purpose of evaluating attorneys seeking or being considered for appointment to cases.

Subdivision (f)(10). The definition of "trade secret" restates the definition in Civil Code section 3426.1.

Subdivision (f)(11). This subdivision is intended to reflect California law on the subject of the "deliberative process" exemption under the California Public Records Act, which is currently stated in the Supreme Court's decision in *Times Mirror Co. v. Superior Court* (1991) 53 Cal.3d 1325 and the later Court of Appeal decisions *California First Amendment Coalition v. Superior Court* (1998) 67 Cal.App.4th 159 and *Wilson v. Superior Court* (1996) 51 Cal.App.4th 1136.

Subdivision (j)(1). Under current rule 10.803 a petitioner may file a writ in a superior court regarding a dispute with a superior court or the Administrative Office of the Courts with respect to disclosure of records and information required to be maintained under current rule 10.802. The writ petition must be heard on an expedited basis and includes a right to an appeal. The statutory authority for the hearing process set forth in current rule 10.803, Government Code section 71675(b), does not extend this procedure to other disputes with respect to public access. The rule provides that petitioners with a dispute with any other judicial branch entity, or with respect to records that are not required to be maintained under rule 10.802, may follow the procedure set forth in (j)(2) through (j)(6), which is equivalent to the dispute resolution procedure of the California Public Records Act. A petitioner eligible for the dispute resolution process set out in current rule 10.803 may also elect to proceed with his or her dispute under the procedure set forth in (j)(2) through (j)(6).

Research References

Rutter, Cal. Practice Guide: Civ. Pro. Before Trial Ch. 8K-6, Special Statutes and Court Rules.
2 Witkin Cal. Proc. 5th Courts § 178, (S 178) State Funding.
2 Witkin Cal. Proc. 5th Courts § 197, (S 197) Judicial Administration Rules.

Rule 10.501. Maintenance of budget and management information

(a) Maintenance of information by the superior court

Each superior court must maintain for a period of three years from the close of the fiscal year to which the following relate:

(1) Official documents of the superior court pertaining to the approved superior court budget allocation adopted by the Judicial Council and actual final year-end superior court revenue and expenditure reports as required in budget procedures issued by the Administrative Office of the Courts to be maintained or reported to the council, including budget allocation, revenue, and expenditure reports;

(2) Records or other factual management information on matters that are within the scope of representation as defined in Government Code section 71634 unless distribution is otherwise precluded by law; and

(3) Records or other factual management information on other matters referred to in Government Code section 71634 unless distribution is otherwise precluded by law.

(b) Maintenance of information by the Administrative Office of the Courts

The Administrative Office of the Courts must maintain for a period of three years from the close of the fiscal year to which the following relate:

(1) Official approved budget allocations for each superior court;

(2) Actual final year-end superior court revenue and expenditure reports required by budget procedures issued by the Administrative Office of the Courts to be maintained or reported to the council that are received from the courts, including budget revenues and expenditures for each superior court;

(3) Budget priorities as adopted by the council; and

(4) Documents concerning superior court budgets considered or adopted by the council at council business meetings on court budgets. *(Adopted, eff. Jan. 1, 2010.)*

Research References

2 Witkin Cal. Proc. 5th Courts § 178, (S 178) State Funding.
2 Witkin Cal. Proc. 5th Courts § 237, (S 237) Other Duties.

Rule 10.502. Judicial sabbatical pilot program

(a) Objective

Sabbatical leave is a privilege available to jurists by statute. The objective of sabbatical leave is to facilitate study, teaching, research, or another activity that will benefit the administration of justice and enhance judges' performance of their duties.

(b) Eligibility

(1) A judge or justice is eligible to apply for a paid sabbatical under Government Code section 77213 if:

(A) He or she has served for at least seven years as a California judicial officer, including service as a subordinate judicial officer;

(B) He or she has not taken a sabbatical within seven years of the date of the proposed sabbatical; and

(C) He or she agrees to continue to serve as a judicial officer for at least three years after the sabbatical.

(2) Any judge is eligible to apply for an unpaid sabbatical under Government Code section 68554.

(c) Application

(1) An eligible judge may apply for a sabbatical by submitting a sabbatical proposal to the Administrative Director of the Courts with a copy to the presiding judge or justice.

(2) The sabbatical proposal must include:

(A) The judge's certification that he or she meets the eligibility requirements established in (b);

(B) The beginning and ending dates of the proposed sabbatical;

(C) A description of the sabbatical project, including an explanation of how the sabbatical will benefit the administration of justice and the judge's performance of his or her duties; and

(D) A statement from the presiding judge or justice of the affected court, indicating approval or disapproval of the sabbatical request and the reasons for such approval or disapproval, forwarded to the Judicial Sabbatical Review Committee with a copy to the judge.

(d) Judicial Sabbatical Review Committee

A Judicial Sabbatical Review Committee will be appointed to make recommendations to the Judicial Council regarding sabbatical requests.

(1) *Membership*

The committee must include at least one member from each of the following groups:

(A) Administrative Presiding Justices Advisory Committee;

(B) Trial Court Presiding Judges Advisory Committee;

(C) Court Executives Advisory Committee;

(D) Governing Committee of the Center for Judicial Education and Research;

(E) Judicial Service Advisory Committee; and

(F) California Judges Association (liaison).

(2) *Staffing*

The committee will be staffed by the Human Resources Division of the Administrative Office of the Courts and may elect its chair and vice-chair.

(e) Evaluation

(1) The Administrative Director of the Courts must forward all sabbatical requests that comply with (c) to the Judicial Sabbatical Review Committee.

(2) The Judicial Sabbatical Review Committee must recommend granting or denying the sabbatical request after it considers the following factors:

(A) Whether the sabbatical will benefit the administration of justice in California and the judge's performance of his or her duties; and

(B) Whether the sabbatical leave will be detrimental to the affected court.

(3) The Judicial Sabbatical Review Committee may recommend an unpaid sabbatical if there is insufficient funding for a paid sabbatical.

(f) Length

(1) A paid sabbatical taken under Government Code section 77213 may not exceed 120 calendar days. A judge may be allowed to add unpaid sabbatical time onto the end of a paid sabbatical if the purpose of the unpaid sabbatical is substantially similar to the work of the paid sabbatical.

(2) An unpaid sabbatical taken under Government Code section 68554 may not exceed one year.

(g) Ethics and compensation

A judge on sabbatical leave is subject to the California Code of Judicial Ethics and, while on a paid sabbatical, must not accept compensation for activities performed during that sabbatical leave but may receive reimbursement for the expenses provided in canon 4H(2) of the Code of Judicial Ethics.

(h) Judge's report

On completion of a sabbatical leave, the judge must report in writing to the Judicial Council on how the leave benefited the administration of justice in California and on its effect on his or her official duties as a judicial officer.

(i) Retirement and benefits

(1) A judge on a paid sabbatical leave under Government Code section 77213 continues to receive all the benefits of office and accrues service credit toward retirement.

(2) A judge on unpaid sabbatical leave under Government Code section 68554 receives no compensation, and the period of absence does not count as service toward retirement. The leave does not affect the term of office.

(j) Judicial assignment replacement

Funds must be made available from the Judicial Administration Efficiency and Modernization Fund to allocate additional assigned judges to those courts whose judges' requests for paid sabbaticals are approved. *(Formerly Rule 6.151, adopted, eff. Jan. 1, 2003. Renumbered Rule 10.502 and amended, eff. Jan. 1, 2007.)*

Research References

2 Witkin Cal. Proc. 5th Courts § 197, (S 197) Judicial Administration Rules.

Rule 10.504. Smoking prohibited in all courts

(a) Definition

"Court facilities" means courthouses and all areas of multipurpose buildings used for court operations.

(b) Smoking prohibited

Smoking is prohibited in all court facilities.

(c) Signs

Conspicuous no-smoking signs must be placed in all court facilities. *(Formerly Rule 989.5, adopted, eff. July 1, 1991. Renumbered Rule 10.504 and amended, eff. Jan. 1, 2007.)*

Research References

Rutter, Cal. Practice Guide: Civil Trials & Evidence Ch. 15-A, A. General Considerations.
2 Witkin Cal. Proc. 5th Courts § 28, (S 28) in General.
7 Witkin Cal. Proc. 5th Trial § 318, (S 318) in General.

Rule 10.505. Judicial robes

(a) Color and length

The judicial robe required by Government Code section 68110 must be black, must extend in front and back from the collar and shoulders to below the knees, and must have sleeves to the wrists.

(b) Style

The judicial robe must conform to the style customarily worn in courts in the United States. *(Formerly Rule 249, as amended, eff. Sept. 24, 1959; July 1, 1963. Renumbered Rule 299, and amended, eff. Jan. 1, 2003. Renumbered Rule 10.505 and amended, eff. Jan. 1, 2007.)*

Research References

2 Witkin Cal. Proc. 5th Courts § 28, (S 28) in General.
2 Witkin Cal. Proc. 5th Courts § 197, (S 197) Judicial Administration Rules.

Division 4

TRIAL COURT ADMINISTRATION

Chapter 1

GENERAL RULES ON TRIAL COURT MANAGEMENT

Rule 10.601. Superior court management

(a) Purpose

The rules in this division establish a system of trial court management that:

(1) Promotes equal access to the courts;

(2) Establishes decentralized management of trial court resources; and

(3) Enables the trial courts to operate in an efficient, effective, and accountable manner in serving the people of California.

(b) Goals

The rules in this division are intended to ensure the authority and responsibility of the superior courts to do the following, consistent with statutes, rules of court, and standards of judicial administration:

(1) Manage their day-to-day operations with sufficient flexibility to meet the needs of those served by the courts;

(2) Establish the means of selecting presiding judges, assistant presiding judges, executive officers or court administrators, clerks of court, and jury commissioners;

(3) Manage their personnel systems, including the adoption of personnel policies;

(4) Manage their budget and fiscal operations, including allocating funding and moving funding between functions or line items;

(5) Provide input to the Judicial Council, the Trial Court Budget Working Group, and the Administrative Office of the Courts on the trial court budget process; and

(6) Develop and implement processes and procedures to improve court operations and responsiveness to the public.

(c) Decentralized management

"Decentralized management" as used in the rules in this division refers to the administration of the trial courts on a countywide basis, unless an alternative structure has been approved by the Judicial Council, consistent with applicable statutes, rules, and standards of judicial administration. *(Formerly Rule 2501, adopted, eff. July 1, 1998. Renumbered Rule 6.601, eff. Jan. 1, 1999. As amended, eff. Jan. 1, 2002. Renumbered Rule 10.601 and amended, eff. Jan. 1, 2007.)*

Research References

2 Witkin Cal. Proc. 5th Courts § 197, (S 197) Judicial Administration Rules.
2 Witkin Cal. Proc. 5th Courts § 392, (S 392) Governing Rules.

Rule 10.602. Selection and term of presiding judge

(a) Selection

(1) *Courts with three or more judges*

Each court that has three or more judges must select a presiding judge. Selection of the presiding judge may be by secret ballot. The court should establish an internal local rule or policy for the selection of the presiding judge and assistant presiding judge, if any.

(2) *Two–judge courts*

In a court having two judges, the selection of the presiding judge must conform to Government Code section 69508.5. If selection cannot be agreed on and neither judge has at least four years of experience, the senior judge must hold the office of presiding judge until both judges have at least four years of experience.

(b) Requisite experience and waiver

A presiding judge must have at least four years of experience as a judge, unless this requirement is waived by a majority vote of the judges of the court. Nomination and selection of a presiding judge should take into consideration the judge's:

(1) Management and administrative ability;

(2) Interest in serving in the position;

(3) Experience and familiarity with a variety of trial court assignments;

(4) Ability to motivate and educate other judicial officers and court personnel;

(5) Ability to evaluate the strengths of the court's bench officers and make assignments based on those strengths as well as the best interests of the public and the court; and

(6) Other appropriate factors.

(c) Term

A presiding judge in a court with two judges must be elected for a term of not less than one year. A presiding judge in a court with three or more judges must be elected for an initial term of not less than two years. The presiding judge may be elected for additional terms. The court may change the duration of the initial or additional term by local rule or policy so long as the initial term is not less than the duration specified in this rule. A presiding judge may be removed by a majority vote of the judges of the court.

(d) Assistant presiding judge and acting presiding judge

(1) The court may elect an assistant presiding judge.

(2) If the court's internal local rule or policy does not provide for the designation of an acting presiding judge to serve if the presiding judge is absent or unable to act, the presiding judge must designate one.

(3) The court should provide the assistant presiding judge with training to foster an orderly succession to the office of presiding judge.

(e) Caseload adjustment

To the extent possible, the judicial caseload should be adjusted to provide the presiding judge with sufficient time and resources to devote to the management and administrative duties of the office. *(Formerly Rule 6.602, adopted, eff. Jan. 1, 2001. As amended, eff. Jan. 1, 2005. Renumbered Rule 10.602 and amended, eff. Jan. 1, 2007.)*

Advisory Committee Comment

The internal local rule described in this rule relates only to the internal management of the court, and as such is exempt from the requirements in rule 10.613. (See rule 10.613(j).)

Research References

2 Witkin Cal. Proc. 5th Courts § 234, (S 234) in General.
7 Witkin Cal. Proc. 5th Trial § 39, (S 39) Management and Distribution of Court Business.

Rule 10.603. Authority and duties of presiding judge

(a) General responsibilities

The presiding judge is responsible, with the assistance of the court executive officer, for leading the court, establishing policies, and allocating resources in a manner that promotes access to justice for all members of the public, provides a forum for the fair and expeditious resolution of disputes, maximizes the use of judicial and other resources, increases efficiency in court operations, and enhances service to the public. The presiding judge is responsible for:

(1) Ensuring the effective management and administration of the court, consistent with any rules, policies, strategic plan, or budget adopted by the Judicial Council or the court;

(2) Ensuring that the duties of all judges specified under rule 10.608 are timely and orderly performed; and

(3) Ensuring that the court has adopted written policies and procedures allowing the presiding judge to perform efficiently the administrative duties of that office.

(b) Authority

(1) The presiding judge is authorized to:

(A) Assign judges to departments and designate supervising judges for divisions, districts, or branch courts;

(B) Apportion the business of the court, including assigning and reassigning cases to departments;

(C) Call meetings of the judges;

(D) Appoint standing and special committees of judges;

(E) Act as the spokesperson for the court;

(F) Authorize and direct expenditures from the court's Trial Court Operations Fund; and

(G) Perform all acts necessary to accomplish the duties specified by the rules of court.

(2) No local rule or policy may limit the authority of the presiding judge as granted in the rules of court.

(c) Duties

(1) *Assignments*

The presiding judge has ultimate authority to make judicial assignments. The presiding judge must:

(A) Designate a judge to preside in each department, including a master calendar judge when appropriate, and designate a presiding judge of the juvenile division and a supervising judge for each division, district, or branch court. In making judicial assignments, the presiding judge must take into account the following:

(i) The needs of the public and the court, as they relate to the efficient and effective management of the court's calendar;

(ii) The knowledge and abilities demanded by the assignment;

(iii) The judge's judicial and nonjudicial experience, including specialized training or education;

(iv) The judge's interests;

(v) The need for continuity in the assignment;

(vi) The desirability of exposing the judge to a particular type of assignment; and

(vii) Other appropriate factors. Judicial assignments must not be based solely or primarily on seniority;

(B) Assign to a master calendar judge any of the duties that may more appropriately be performed by that department;

(C) Supervise the court's calendar, apportion the business of the court among the several departments of the court as equally as possible, and publish for general distribution copies of a current calendar specifying the judicial assignments of the judges and the times and places assigned for hearings;

(D) Reassign cases between departments as convenience or necessity requires; and

(E) Designate a judge to act if by law or the rules of court a matter is required to be presented to or heard by a particular judge and that judge is absent, deceased, or unable to act.

(2) *Judicial schedules*

(A) The presiding judge must adopt a process for scheduling judges' vacations and absences from court for attendance at schools, conferences, workshops, and community outreach activities, and must prepare a plan for these vacations and absences from court.

(B) The plan should take into account the principles contained in standards 10.11 10.13 (on judicial education) and standard 10.5 (on community activities) of the Standards of Judicial Administration.

(C) The presiding judge must review requests from judges for time absent from court and may approve any request that is consistent with the plan and with the orderly operation of the court.

(D) The presiding judge must allow each judge to take two days of personal leave per year. Personal leave may be taken at any time that is approved by the presiding judge.

(E) The presiding judge must allow the following number of days of vacation for each judge annually:

(i) 24 days for judges with less than 7 years of service as a California judge;

(ii) 27 days for judges with at least 7 but less than 14 years of service as a California judge; and

(iii) 30 days for judges with 14 or more years of service as a California judge.

(F) The presiding judge may authorize a judge to take more time off than is specified in (c)(2)(E) as justified by extraordinary circumstances, if the circumstances are documented and the authorization is in writing.

(G) The presiding judge, in his or her discretion, may allow a judge to take additional vacation days equal to the number of vacation days that the judge did not use in the previous year, up to a maximum of 30 such days. A court may, by local rule, establish a lower maximum number of such days. This paragraph applies only to vacation days accrued after January 1, 2001. It does not affect any unused vacation days that a judge may have accrued before January 1, 2001, which are governed by local court policy, nor does it create any right to compensation for unused vacation days.

(H) The court must, by local rule, define a day of vacation. Absence from court to attend an authorized education program, conference, or workshop for judges, or to participate in Judicial Council or other authorized committees or community outreach activities, is not vacation time if attendance is in accordance with the plan and has the prior approval of the presiding judge. Absence from court due to illness is not vacation time. This rule does not limit the time a judge may be absent from court when unable to work because of illness.

(I) To ensure compliance with the plan, the presiding judge must establish a system to monitor judges' absences from court and maintain records of those absences.

(3) *Submitted cases*

The presiding judge must supervise and monitor the number of causes under submission before the judges of the court and ensure that no cause under submission remains undecided and pending for longer than 90 days. As an aid in accomplishing this goal, the presiding judge must:

(A) Require each judge to report to the presiding judge all causes under submission for more than 30 days and, with respect to each cause, designate whether it has been under submission for 30 through 60 days, 61 through 90 days, or over 90 days;

(B) Compile a list of all causes under submission before judges of the court, designated as the submitted list, which must include the name of each judge, a list of causes under submission before that judge, and the length of time each cause has been under submission;

(C) Circulate monthly a complete copy of the submitted list to each judge of the court;

(D) Contact and alert each judge who has a cause under submission for over 30 days and discuss ways to ensure that the cause is timely decided;

(E) Consider providing assistance to a judge who has a cause under submission for over 60 days; and

(F) Consider requesting the services of the Administrative Office of the Courts to review the court's calendar management procedures and make recommendations whenever either of the following conditions exists in the court for the most recent three months:

(i) More than 90 civil active cases are pending for each judicial position; or

(ii) More than 10 percent of the cases on the civil active list have been pending for one year or more.

Ct. Rules

(4) Oversight of judicial officers

The presiding judge must:

(A) Judges

Notify the Commission on Judicial Performance of:

(i) A judge's substantial failure to perform judicial duties, including any habitual neglect of duty, persistent refusal to carry out assignments as assigned by the presiding judge, or persistent refusal to carry out the directives of the presiding judge as authorized by the rules of court; or

(ii) Any absences caused by disability totaling more than 90 court days in a 12–month period, excluding absences authorized under (c)(2);

(B) Notice

Give the judge a copy of the notice to the commission under (A) if appropriate. If a copy is not given to the judge, the presiding judge must inform the commission of the reasons why so notifying the judge was deemed inappropriate;

(C) Commissioners

(i) Prepare and submit to the judges for consideration and adoption procedures for receiving, inquiring into, and resolving complaints lodged against court commissioners and referees, consistent with rule 10.703; and

(ii) Notify the Commission on Judicial Performance if a commissioner or referee is disciplined or resigns, consistent with rule 10.703(k).

(D) Temporary judges

Be responsible for the recruitment, training, supervision, approval, and performance of temporary judges as provided in rules 2.810–2.819 and rules 10.740–10.746; and

(E) Assigned judges

For each assigned retired judge:

(i) Complete a confidential evaluation form;

(ii) Submit the form annually to the Administrative Director of the Courts;

(iii) Direct complaints against the assigned judge to the Chief Justice, by forwarding them to the attention of the Administrative Director of the Courts, and provide requested information in writing to the Administrative Director of the Courts in a timely manner; and

(iv) Assist the Administrative Director in the process of investigating, evaluating, and making recommendations to the Chief Justice regarding complaints against retired judges who serve on assignment.

(5) Personnel

(A) The presiding judge must provide general direction to and supervision of the court executive officer, or, if the court has no executive officer, perform the duties of the court executive regarding personnel as specified in rule 10.610(c)(1).

(B) The presiding judge must approve, in writing, the total compensation package (salary and all benefits) offered to the court executive officer at the time of the executive officer's appointment and any subsequent changes to the executive officer's total compensation package.

(6) Budget and fiscal management

The presiding judge must:

(A) Establish a process for consulting with the judges of the court on budget requests, expenditure plans, and other budget or fiscal matters that the presiding judge deems appropriate;

(B) Establish responsible budget priorities and submit budget requests that will best enable the court to achieve its goals;

(C) Establish a documented process for setting and approving any changes to the court executive officer's total compensation package in a fiscally responsible manner consistent with the court's established budget; and

(D) Approve procurements, contracts, expenditures, and the allocation of funds in a manner that promotes the implementation of state and local budget priorities and that ensures equal access to justice and the ability of the court to carry out its functions effectively. In a court with an executive officer, the presiding judge may delegate these duties to the court executive officer, but the presiding judge must ensure that the court executive officer performs such delegated duties consistent with the court's established budget.

(7) Meetings and committees

The presiding judge must establish a process for consulting with the judges of the court and may call meetings of the judges as needed. The presiding judge may appoint standing and special committees of judges as needed to assist in the proper performance of the duties and functions of the court.

(8) Liaison

The presiding judge must:

(A) Provide for liaison between the court and the Judicial Council, the Administrative Office of the Courts, and other governmental and civic agencies;

(B) Meet with or designate a judge or judges to meet with any committee of the bench, bar, news media, or community to review problems and to promote understanding of the administration of justice, when appropriate; and

(C) Support and encourage the judges to actively engage in community outreach to increase public understanding of and involvement with the justice system and to obtain appropriate community input regarding the administration of justice, consistent with the California Code of Judicial Ethics and standard 10.5 of the Standards of Judicial Administration.

(9) Planning

The presiding judge must:

(A) Prepare, with the assistance of appropriate court committees and appropriate input from the community, a long-range strategic plan that is consistent with the plan and policies of the Judicial Council, for adoption in accordance with procedures established by local rules or policies; and

(B) Ensure that the court regularly and actively examines access issues, including any physical, language, or economic barriers that impede the fair administration of justice.

(10) Appellate records

The presiding judge is responsible for ensuring the timely preparation of records on appeal.

(A) The presiding judge ordinarily should delegate the following duties to the executive officer:

(i) Maintaining records of outstanding transcripts to be completed by each court reporter;

(ii) Reassigning court reporters as necessary to facilitate prompt completion of transcripts; and

(iii) Reviewing court reporters' requests for extensions of time to complete transcripts in appeals of criminal cases.

(B) After reasonable notice and hearing, the presiding judge must declare any reporter of the court who is delinquent in completing a transcript on appeal not competent to act as a reporter in court, under Government Code section 69944.

(11) Local rules

The presiding judge must prepare, with the assistance of appropriate court committees, proposed local rules to expedite and facilitate court business in accordance with Government Code section 68071 and rules 2.100, 3.20, and 10.613.

(d) Delegation

The presiding judge may delegate any of the specific duties listed in this rule to another judge. Except for the duties listed in (c)(5)(B) and (c)(6)(C), the presiding judge may delegate to the court executive officer any of the duties listed in this rule that do not require the exercise of judicial authority. The presiding judge remains responsible for all duties listed in this rule even if he or she has delegated particular tasks to someone else. *(Formerly Rule 6.603, adopted, eff. Jan. 1, 2001. As amended, eff. Jan. 1, 2001; Jan. 1, 2002; Jan. 1, 2006; July 1, 2006. Renumbered Rule 10.603 and amended, eff. Jan. 1, 2007. As amended, eff. July 1, 2010.)*

Research References

2 Witkin Cal. Proc. 5th Courts § 71, Commission on Judicial Performance.

2 Witkin Cal. Proc. 5th Courts § 226, (S 226) Proper Transfer of Case.

2 Witkin Cal. Proc. 5th Courts § 234, (S 234) in General.

2 Witkin Cal. Proc. 5th Courts § 235, (S 235) Duty to Distribute Business.

2 Witkin Cal. Proc. 5th Courts § 236, (S 236) Duty to Monitor Pending Cases.

2 Witkin Cal. Proc. 5th Courts § 237, (S 237) Other Duties.

2 Witkin Cal. Proc. 5th Courts § 394, (S 394) in General.

7 Witkin Cal. Proc. 5th Trial § 39, (S 39) Management and Distribution of Court Business.

Rule 10.605.　Executive committee

In accordance with the internal policies of the court, an executive committee may be established by the court to advise the presiding judge or to establish policies and procedures for the internal management of the court. An executive committee may be appointed by the presiding judge to advise the presiding judge. *(Formerly Rule 6.605, adopted, eff. Jan. 1, 2001. Renumbered Rule 10.605, eff. Jan. 1, 2007.)*

Research References

2 Witkin Cal. Proc. 5th Courts § 234, (S 234) in General.

Rule 10.608.　Duties of all judges

Each judge must:

(1) Hear all assigned matters unless:

(A) He or she is disqualified; or

(B) He or she has stated in writing the reasons for refusing to hear a cause assigned for trial, and the presiding judge, supervising judge, or master calendar judge has concurred;

(2) Immediately notify the master calendar judge or the presiding judge on the completion or continuation of a trial or any other matter assigned for hearing;

(3) Request approval of the presiding judge for any intended absence of one-half day or more, within a reasonable time before the intended absence;

(4) Follow the court's personnel plan in dealing with employees; and

(5) Follow directives of the presiding judge in matters of court management and administration, as authorized by the rules of court and the local rules and internal policies of the court. *(Formerly Rule 6.608, adopted, eff. Jan. 1, 2001. As amended, eff. Jan. 1, 2006. Renumbered Rule 10.608 and amended, eff. Jan. 1, 2007.)*

Research References

2 Witkin Cal. Proc. 5th Courts § 235, (S 235) Duty to Distribute Business.

7 Witkin Cal. Proc. 5th Trial § 39, (S 39) Management and Distribution of Court Business.

7 Witkin Cal. Proc. 5th Trial § 56, Duties of Trial Judge.

Rule 10.610.　Duties of court executive officer

(a) Selection

A court may employ an executive officer selected in accordance with procedures adopted by the court.

(b) General responsibilities

Acting under the direction of the presiding judge, the court executive officer is responsible for overseeing the management and administration of the nonjudicial operations of the court and allocating resources in a manner that promotes access to justice for all members of the public, provides a forum for the fair and expeditious resolution of disputes, maximizes the use of judicial and other resources, increases efficiency in court operations, and enhances service to the public.

(c) Duties

Under the direction of the presiding judge and consistent with the law and rules of court, the court executive officer must perform the following duties, where they are not inconsistent with the authorized duties of the clerk of the court:

(1) *Personnel*

Provide general direction to and supervision of the employees of the court, and draft for court approval and administer a personnel plan for court employees that complies with rule 10.670. The court executive officer has the authority, consistent with the personnel plan, to hire, discipline, and terminate nonjudicial employees of the court.

(2) *Budget*

Make recommendations to the presiding judge on budget priorities; prepare and implement court budgets, including accounting, payroll, and financial controls; and employ sound budget and fiscal management practices and procedures to ensure that annual expenditures are within the court's budget.

(3) *Contracts*

Negotiate contracts on behalf of the court, in accordance with established contracting procedures and all applicable laws.

(4) *Calendar management*

Supervise and employ efficient calendar and case flow management systems, including analyzing and evaluating pending caseloads and recommending effective calendar management techniques.

(5) *Technology*

Analyze, evaluate, and implement technological and automated systems to assist the court.

(6) *Jury management*

Manage the jury system in the most efficient and effective way.

(7) *Facilities*

Plan physical space needs, and purchase and manage equipment and supplies.

(8) *Records*

Create and manage uniform record-keeping systems, collecting data on pending and completed judicial business and the internal operation of the court, as required by the court and the Judicial Council.

(9) *Recommendations*

Identify problems, recommending procedural and administrative changes to the court.

(10) *Public relations*

Provide a clearinghouse for news releases and other publications for the media and public.

(11) *Liaison*

Act as liaison to other governmental agencies.

(12) *Committees*

Provide staff for judicial committees.

(13) *Other*

Perform other duties as the presiding judge directs. *(Formerly Rule 6.610, adopted, eff. Jan. 1, 2001. Renumbered Rule 10.610 and amended, eff. Jan. 1, 2007.)*

Research References

2 Witkin Cal. Proc. 5th Courts § 237, (S 237) Other Duties.
2 Witkin Cal. Proc. 5th Courts § 368, (S 368) in General.
7 Witkin Cal. Proc. 5th Trial § 39, (S 39) Management and Distribution of Court Business.

Rule 10.611. Nondiscrimination in court appointments

Each court should select attorneys, arbitrators, mediators, referees, masters, receivers, and other persons appointed by the court on the basis of merit. No court may discriminate in such selection on the basis of gender, race, ethnicity, disability, sexual orientation, or age. *(Formerly Rule 989.2, adopted, eff. Jan. 1, 1999. Renumbered Rule 10.611 and amended, eff. Jan. 1, 2007.)*

Research References

2 Witkin Cal. Proc. 5th Courts § 342, in General.

Rule 10.612. Use of gender-neutral language

Each court must use gender-neutral language in all new local rules, forms, and documents and must review and revise those now in use to ensure that they are written in gender-neutral language. *(Adopted, eff. Jan. 1, 2007.)*

Research References

2 Witkin Cal. Proc. 5th Courts § 31, (S 31) Avoidance of Gender or Other Bias.
2 Witkin Cal. Proc. 5th Courts § 200, (S 200) Adoption and Publication.

Rule 10.613. Local court rules—adopting, filing, distributing, and maintaining

(a) Definitions

As used in this rule:

(1) "Court" means a trial court; and

(2) "Local rule" means every rule, regulation, order, policy, form, or standard of general application adopted by a court to govern practice or procedure in that court or by a judge of the court to govern practice or procedure in that judge's courtroom.

(b) Local inspection and copying of rules

Each court must make its local rules available for inspection and copying in every location of the court that generally accepts filing of papers. The court may impose a reasonable charge for copying the rules and may impose a reasonable page limit on copying. The rules must be accompanied by a notice indicating where a full set of the rules may be purchased or otherwise obtained.

(c) Publication of rules

(1) Each court executive officer must be the official publisher of the court's local rules unless the court, by a majority vote of the judges, appoints another public agency or a private company.

(2) The official publisher must have the local rules reproduced and make copies available for distribution to attorneys and litigants.

(3) The court must adopt rules in sufficient time to permit reproduction of the rules by the official publisher before the effective date of the changes.

(4) The official publisher may charge a reasonable fee.

(5) Within 30 days of selecting an official publisher or changing an official publisher, each court must notify the Judicial Council of the name, address, and telephone number of the official publisher. Within 30 days of a change in the cost of the rules, each court must notify the Judicial Council of the charge for the local rules. This information will be published annually by the Judicial Council.

(d) Filing rules with the Judicial Council

(1) Forty-five days before the effective date of January 1 or July 1, each court must file with the Judicial Council an electronic copy of rules and amendments to rules adopted by the court in a format authorized by the Judicial Council.

(2) The filing must be accompanied by a certificate from the presiding judge or court executive officer stating that:

(A) The court has complied with the applicable provisions of this rule;

(B) The court does or does not post local rules on the court's Web site; and

(C) The court does or does not provide assistance to members of the public in accessing the Internet or the court has delegated to and obtained the written consent of the county law librarian to provide public assistance under (e).

(3) Rules that do not comply with this rule will not be accepted for filing by the Judicial Council.

(e) Deposit and maintenance of rules statewide for public inspection

(1) The Judicial Council must publish a list of courts that have filed rules and amendments to rules with the Judicial Council. The Judicial Council must deposit a paper copy of each rule and amendment in the office of the executive officer of each superior court that does not provide assistance to members of the public in accessing the Internet or has not obtained agreement from the county law librarian to provide assistance under this subdivision.

(2) The executive officer must make a complete current set of local rules and amendments available for public examination either in paper copy or through the Internet with public assistance. In a county maintaining an organized county law library, if the executive officer is satisfied that the rules and amendments will be maintained as required by this paragraph, the executive officer, with the approval of the superior court and the written consent of the county law librarian, may delegate the authority to the county law librarian to either receive and maintain paper copies of the rules and amendments, or make the rules and amendments available through the Internet with assistance to members of the public.

(3) On or before January 1 of each year, the executive officer of each court must notify the Judicial Council of the street address and room number of the place where the rules are maintained under this subdivision.

(f) Format of rules

(1) *Paper and electronic copies*

Paper copies may be typewritten or printed or produced by other process of duplication at the option of the court. Electronic rules must be prepared in a format authorized by the Judicial Council. All copies must be clear and legible.

(2) *Format of paper copies*

Paper copies must conform, as far as is practicable, to the requirements of chapter 1 of division 2 of title 2, except that both sides of the paper may be used, lines need not be numbered and may be single spaced, and the pages must not be permanently bound across the top but may be bound at the left side. ("Permanently bound" does not include binding with staples.) The left margin on the front and the right margin on the reverse must be at least one inch. The name of the court must be at the top of each page. The effective date of each rule and amended rule must be stated in parentheses following the text of the rule.

(3) *New pages and filing instructions*

New pages must be issued for added, repealed, or amended rules, with a list of currently effective rules and the date of adoption or of the latest amendment to each rule. Filing instructions must accompany each set of replacement pages.

(4) *Table of contents*

The rules must have a table of contents. The rules must list all local forms and indicate whether their use is mandatory or optional. If the total length of the court rules exceeds five pages, the rules must have an alphabetical subject matter index at the end of the rules. All courts must use any subject matter index the Judicial Council may have specified.

(g) Comment period for proposed rules

(1) *Timing*

Except for rules specifying the time of hearing and similar calendaring matters, the court must distribute each proposed rule for comment at least 45 days before it is adopted.

(2) *Organizations*

A proposed rule must be distributed for comment to the following organizations in each county located within a 100–mile radius of the county seat of the county in which the court is located:

    (A) Civil rules to the county bar association in each county, the nearest office of the State Attorney General, and the county counsel in each county;

    (B) Criminal rules to the county bar association in each county, the nearest office of the State Attorney General, the district attorney in each county, and the public defender in each county; and

    (C) On request, any bar organization, newspaper, or other interested party.

(3) *Methods*

A court may distribute a proposed rule for comment by either of the following methods:

    (A) Distributing a copy of the proposal to every organization listed in (g)(2); or

    (B) Posting the proposal on the court's Web site and distributing to every organization listed in (g)(2) a notice that the proposed rule has been posted for comment and that a hard copy of the proposal is available on request.

(h) Periodic review

Each court must periodically review its local rules and repeal rules that have become outdated, unnecessary, or inconsistent with statewide rules or statutes.

(i) Alternative effective date

A court may adopt a rule to take effect on a date other than as provided by Government Code section 68071 if:

(1) The presiding judge submits to the Judicial Council the proposed rule and a statement of reasons constituting good cause for making the rule effective on the stated date;

(2) The Chair of the Judicial Council authorizes the rule to take effect on the date proposed; and

(3) The rule is made available for inspection as provided in (b) on or before the effective date.

(j) Limitation

Except for (i), this rule does not apply to local rules that relate only to the internal management of the court. *(Formerly Rule 981, adopted, eff. July 1, 1991. As amended, eff. Jan. 1, 1993; July 1, 1999; July 1, 2001; Jan. 1, 2003. Renumbered Rule 10.613 and amended, eff. Jan. 1, 2007. As amended, eff. Jan. 1, 2009.)*

Research References

Rutter, Cal. Practice Guide: Civ. Pro. Before Trial Ch. 9(I)-A, A. Introduction.
Rutter, Cal. Practice Guide: Civ. Pro. Before Trial Ch. 9(I)-F, F. Ex Parte Motions.
Rutter, Cal. Practice Guide: Civil Trials & Evidence Ch. 4-A, A. General Considerations.
2 Witkin Cal. Proc. 5th Courts § 200, (S 200) Adoption and Publication.
2 Witkin Cal. Proc. 5th Courts § 201, (S 201) Local Policy.
2 Witkin Cal. Proc. 5th Courts § 235, (S 235) Duty to Distribute Business.

Rule 10.614. Local court forms

Local forms must comply with the following:

(1) Each form must be on paper measuring no more than 8½ by 11 inches and no less than 8½ by 5 inches.

(2) The court must make copies of its forms available in the clerk's office. A court may, as an alternative, make its forms available in a booklet from which photocopies of the forms may be made. The court may charge for either copies of forms or the booklet of forms.

(3) The court must assign to each form a unique designator consisting of numbers or letters, or both. The designator must be positioned on the form in the same manner as the designator on a Judicial Council form.

(4) The effective date of each form must be placed on the form in the same manner as the effective date on a Judicial Council form, and each form must state whether it is a "Mandatory Form" or an "Optional Form" in the lower left corner of the first page.

(5) Each court must make available a current list of forms adopted or approved by that court. The list must include, for each form, its name, number, effective date, and whether the form is mandatory or optional. There must be two versions of the list, one organized by form number and one organized by form name. The court must modify its lists whenever it adopts, approves, revises, or repeals any form.

(6) Each form must be designed so that no typing is required on it within 1 inch of the top or within ½ inch of the bottom.

(7) All forms and copies of forms made available by, or presented for filing to, the court must be reproduced on recycled paper as defined in rule 2.102(2).

(8) All forms presented for filing must be firmly bound at the top and must contain two prepunched, normal-sized holes centered 2½ inches apart and 5/8 inch from the top of the form.

(9) If a form is longer than one page, the form may be filed on sheets printed on only one side even if the original form has two printed sides to a sheet. If a form is filed on a sheet printed on two sides, the reverse side must be rotated 180 degrees (printed head to foot). *(Formerly Rule 201.3, adopted, eff. Jan. 1, 2003. Renumbered Rule 10.614 and amended, eff. Jan. 1, 2007.)*

Research References

Rutter, Cal. Practice Guide: Civ. Pro. Before Trial Ch. 6-B, B. Complaints.
2 Witkin Cal. Proc. 5th Courts § 30, (S 30) Use of Recycled Paper.
2 Witkin Cal. Proc. 5th Courts § 199, (S 199) In General.
2 Witkin Cal. Proc. 5th Courts § 399, (S 399) Format Requirements.
4 Witkin Cal. Proc. 5th Pleading § 13, in General.

Rule 10.620. Public access to administrative decisions of trial courts

(a) Interpretation

The provisions of this rule concern public access to administrative decisions by trial courts as provided in this rule. This rule does not modify existing law regarding public access to the judicial deliberative process and does not apply to the adjudicative functions of the trial courts or the assignment of judges.

(b) Budget priorities

The Administrative Office of the Courts may request, on 30 court days' notice, recommendations from the trial courts concerning judicial branch budget priorities. The notice must state that if a trial court is to make recommendations, the trial court must also give notice, as provided in (g), that interested members of the public may send input to the Administrative Office of the Courts.

(c) Budget requests

Before making recommendations, if any, to the Judicial Council on items to be included in the judicial branch budget that is submitted annually to the Governor and the Legislature, a trial court must seek input from the public, as provided in (e), on what should be included in the recommendations.

(d) Other decisions requiring public input

Each trial court must seek input from the public, as provided in (e), before making the following decisions:

(1) A request for permission from the Administrative Office of the Courts to reallocate budget funds from one program component to another in an amount greater than $400,000 or 10 percent of the total trial court budget, whichever is greater.

(2) The execution of a contract without competitive bidding in an amount greater than $400,000 or 10 percent of the total trial court budget, whichever is greater. This subdivision does not apply to a contract entered into between a court and a county that is provided for by statute.

(3) The planned, permanent closure of any court location for an entire day or for more than one-third of the hours the court location was previously open for either court sessions or filing of papers. As used in this subdivision, planned closure does not include closure of a location on a temporary basis for reasons including holidays, illness, or other unforeseen lack of personnel, or public safety.

(4) The cessation of any of the following services at a court location:

(A) The Family Law Facilitator; or

(B) The Family Law Information Center.

(e) Manner of seeking public input

When a trial court is required to seek public input under this rule, it must provide public notice of the request at least 15 court days before the date on which the decision is to be made or the action is to be taken. Notice must be given as provided in (g). Any interested person or entity who wishes to comment must send the comment to the court in writing or electronically unless the court requires that all public comment be sent either by e-mail or through a response system on the court's Web site. For good cause, in the event an urgent action is required, a trial court may take immediate action if it (1) gives notice of the action as provided in (f), (2) states the reasons for urgency, and (3) gives any public input received to the person or entity making the decision.

(f) Information about other trial court administrative matters

A trial court must provide notice, not later than 15 court days after the event, of the following:

(1) Receipt of the annual allocation of the trial court budget from the Judicial Council after enactment of the Budget Act.

(2) The awarding of a grant to the trial court that exceeds the greater of $400,000 or 10 percent of the total trial court budget.

(3) The solicitation of proposals or the execution of a contract that exceeds the greater of $400,000 or 10 percent of the trial court budget.

(4) A significant permanent increase in the number of hours that a court location is open during any day for either court sessions or filing of papers. As used in this paragraph, a significant increase does not include an emergency or one-time need to increase hours.

(5) A significant permanent decrease in the number of hours that a court location is open during any day for either court sessions or filing of papers, except those governed by (d)(3). As used in this paragraph, a significant decrease does not include a decrease in response to an emergency need to close a location on a temporary basis for reasons including illness or other unforeseen lack of personnel or public safety.

(6) The action taken on any item for which input from the public was required under (d). The notice must show the person or persons who made the decision and a summary of the written and e-mail input received.

(g) Notice

When notice is required to be given by this rule, it must be given in the following ways:

(1) Posted on the trial court's Web site, if any.

(2) Sent to any of the following persons or entities—subject to the requirements of (h)—who have requested in writing or by electronic mail to the court executive officer to receive such notice:

(A) A newspaper, radio station, and television station in the county;

(B) The president of a local or specialty bar association in the county;

(C) Representatives of a trial court employees organization;

(D) The district attorney, public defender, and county counsel;

(E) The county administrative officer; and

(F) If the court is sending notice electronically using the provisions of (h), any other person or entity that submits an electronic mail address to which the notice will be sent.

(3) Posted at all locations of the court that accept papers for filing.

(h) Electronic notice

A trial court may require a person or entity that is otherwise entitled to receive notice under (g)(2) to submit an electronic mail address to which the notice will be sent.

(i) Materials

When a trial court is required to seek public input under (b), (c), or (d), it must also provide for public viewing at one or more locations in the county of any written factual materials that have been specifically gathered or prepared for the review at the time of making the decision of the person or entity making the decision. This subdivision does not require the disclosure of materials that are otherwise exempt from disclosure or would be exempt from disclosure under the state Public Records Act (beginning with Government Code section 6250). The materials must be mailed or otherwise be made available not less than five court days before the decision is to be made except if the request is made within the five court days before the decision is to be made, the materials must be mailed or otherwise be made available the next court day after the request is made. A court must either (1) provide copies to a person or entity that requests copies of these materials in writing or by electronic mail to the executive officer of the court or other person designated by the executive office in the notice, if the requesting person or entity pays all mailing and copying costs as determined by any mailing and copy cost recovery policies established by the trial court, or (2) make all materials available electronically either on its Web site or by e-mail. This subdivision does not require the trial court to prepare reports. A person seeking documents may request the court to hold the material for pickup by that person instead of mailing.

(j) Other requirements

This rule does not affect any other obligations of the trial court including any obligation to meet and confer with designated employee representatives. This rule does not change the procedures a court must otherwise follow in entering into a contract or change the types of matters for which a court may contract.

(k) Enforcement

This rule may be enforced under Code of Civil Procedure section 1085. *(Formerly Rule 6.620, adopted, eff. Jan. 1 2004. As amended, eff. Jan. 1, 2005. Renumbered Rule 10.620 and amended, eff. Jan. 1, 2007.)*

Rule 10.625. Certain demographic data relating to regular grand jurors

(a) Definitions

The following definitions apply under this rule:

(1) "Regular grand jury" means a body of citizens of a county selected by the court to investigate matters of civil concern in the county, whether or not that body has jurisdiction to return indictments.

(2) "Race or ethnicity" reflects the concept of race used by the United States Census Bureau and reflects self-identification by people according to the race or races with which they most closely identify. These categories are sociopolitical constructs and should not be interpreted as being scientific or anthropological in nature. The categories include both racial and national-origin groups.

(3) "Prospective regular grand juror" means those citizens who (a) respond in person to the jury summonses or questionnaires from the court for the purposes of grand jury service and are eligible to serve as regular grand jurors, or (b) either submit applications, are recruited, or are nominated by judicial officers and are eligible to serve as regular grand jurors.

(4) "Eligible to serve" means that the prospective regular grand juror meets each of the criteria set forth in Penal Code section 893(a) and is not disqualified by any factor set forth in section 893(b).

(b) Jury Commissioner Duties and Responsibilities

(1) The jury commissioner or designee must create a method to capture the following data from prospective regular grand jurors:

  (A) Age range, specifically:

    (i) 18–25

    (ii) 26–34

    (iii) 35–44

    (iv) 45–54

    (v) 55–64

    (vi) 65–74

    (vii) 75 and over

  (B) Gender; and

  (C) Race or ethnicity from the following categories (candidates may select more than one category):

    (i) American Indian or Alaska Native

    (ii) Asian

    (iii) Black or African American

    (iv) Hispanic/Latino

    (v) Native Hawaiian or other Pacific Islander

    (vi) White

    (vii) Other race or ethnicity (please state: _____)

    (viii) Decline to answer

(2) Develop and maintain a database containing the following information regarding prospective regular grand jurors, the candidates who are ultimately selected by the court to serve as grand jurors, and any carry-over grand jurors: name, age range, occupation, gender, race or ethnicity, and the year(s) served on the regular grand jury. The database should indicate how the juror initially became a candidate (by random draw, application, or nomination).

(c) Annual Summary

(1) The court must develop and maintain an annual summary of the information in the database maintained under (b)(2). The summary must not include the names of the candidates and must be made available to the public.

(Adopted, eff. Jan. 1, 2007.)

Advisory Committee Comment

This rule is intended to facilitate the courts' continued efforts to achieve the goals stated in standard 10.50 [formerly section 17] of the Standards of Judicial Administration, which encourages courts to employ various methods of soliciting prospective candidates to serve on regular grand juries that reflect a representative cross-section of the community they serve. Those methods include obtaining recommendations for grand jurors who encompass a cross-section of the county's population base, solicited from a broad representation of community-based organizations, civic leaders, and superior court judges, referees, and commissioners subdivision (b)(2)); having the court consider carry-over grand jury selections under Penal Code section 901(b) to ensure broad-based representation (subd. (c)); and encouraging judges who nominate persons for grand jury service under Penal Code section 903.4 to select candidates from the list returned by the jury commissioner or otherwise employing a nomination procedure to ensure broad-based representation from the community.

This rule is also intended to assist the courts in establishing a formal mechanism whereby they can monitor the extent to which they achieve the goal of seating representative regular grand juries through a process comparable to that stated in Penal Code section 904.6(e), which requires that persons selected for the "criminal grand jury shall be selected at random from a source or sources reasonably representative of a cross section of the population which is eligible for jury service in the county."

Rule 10.630. Reporting of reciprocal assignment orders

A "reciprocal assignment order" is an order issued by the Chief Justice that permits judges in courts of different counties to serve in each other's courts. A court must report to the Administrative Office of the Courts, on a monthly basis, each assignment of a judge from another county to its court under a reciprocal assignment order. *(Formerly Rule 813, adopted, eff. July 1, 1990. Renumbered Rule 10.630 and amended, eff. Jan. 1, 2007.)*

Ct. Rules

Research References

2 Witkin Cal. Proc. 5th Courts § 197, (S 197) Judicial Administration Rules.

Chapter 2

TRIAL COURT MANAGEMENT OF HUMAN RESOURCES

Article 1

TRIAL COURT EMPLOYEE LABOR RELATIONS

Rule
10.650.   Court Employee Labor Relations Rules.
10.651.   Purpose.
10.652.   Definitions.
10.653.   Right and obligation to meet and confer.
10.654.   Scope of representation.
10.655.   Governing court employee labor relations.
10.656.   Transition provisions.
10.657.   Construction.
10.658.   Interpretation.
10.659.   Other provisions.
10.660.   Enforcement of agreements—petitions (Gov. Code, §§ 71639.5, 71825.2).

Rule 10.650.   Court Employee Labor Relations Rules

Rules 10.651–10.659 in this chapter are referred to as the Court Employee Labor Relations Rules. *(Adopted, eff. Jan. 1, 2007.)*

Research References

2 Witkin Cal. Proc. 5th Courts § 197, (S 197) Judicial Administration Rules.
2 Witkin Cal. Proc. 5th Courts § 342, in General.

Rule 10.651.   Purpose

The purpose of the Court Employee Labor Relations Rules is to extend to trial court employees the right, and to require trial courts, to meet and confer in good faith over matters that the court, as opposed to the county, has authority to determine that are within the scope of representation, consistent with the procedures stated in this division.

The adoption of the Court Employee Labor Relations Rules is not intended to require changes in existing representation units, memoranda of agreements, statutes, or court rules relating to trial court employees, except as they would otherwise normally occur as provided for in this division. *(Formerly Rule 2201, adopted, eff. Jan. 1, 1998. Renumbered Rule 10.651 and amended, eff. Jan. 1, 2007.)*

Rule 10.652.   Definitions

As used in the Court Employee Labor Relations Rules:

(1) "Court" means a superior court.

(2) "Court employee" means any employee of a court, except those employees whose job classification confers safety retirement status.

(3) "Meet and confer in good faith" means that a court or such representatives as it may designate, and representatives of recognized employee organizations, have the mutual obligation personally to meet and confer promptly on request by either party and to continue for a reasonable period of time in order to exchange freely information, opinions, and proposals, and to endeavor to reach agreement on matters within the scope of representation. The process should include adequate time for the resolution of impasses where specific procedures for such resolution are contained in this division or a local rule, regulation, or ordinance, or when such procedures are used by mutual consent.

(4) "Recognized employee organization" means an employee organization that has been formally acknowledged by the county to represent court employees under the provisions of Government Code sections 3500–3510 or by the court under its rules or policies. *(Formerly Rule 2202, adopted, eff. Jan. 1, 1998. Renumbered Rule 10.652 and amended, eff. Jan. 1, 2007.)*

Rule 10.653.   Right and obligation to meet and confer

(a)   Recognized employee organization

A recognized employee organization has the right to represent its court employee members in their employment relations with a court as to matters covered by the Court Employee Labor Relations Rules. Nothing in these rules prohibits any court employee from appearing in his or her own behalf regarding employment relations with a court.

(b)   Representatives of a court

Representatives of a court must meet and confer in good faith regarding matters within the scope of representation, as defined in the Court Employee Labor Relations Rules, with representatives of a recognized employee organization, and must consider fully such presentations as are made by the recognized employee organization on behalf of its members before arriving at a determination of policy or course of action. In meeting this obligation a court must also comply with the procedures and provisions stated in Government Code sections 3504.5, 3505.1, 3505.2, and 3505.3 applicable to a public agency.

(c)   Joint negotiations and designations

In fulfilling the provisions of (b), the court and the county must consult with each other, may negotiate jointly, and each may designate the other in writing as its agent on any matters within the scope of representation.

(d)   Intimidation

A court or a recognized employee organization must not interfere with, intimidate, restrain, coerce, or discriminate against court employees because of their exercise of any rights they may have under the Court Employee Labor Relations Rules or Government Code sections 3500–3510. *(Formerly Rule 2203, adopted, eff. Jan. 1, 1998. Renumbered Rule 10.653 and amended, eff. Jan. 1, 2007.)*

Rule 10.654.   Scope of representation

(a)   Matters included in the scope of representation

For purposes of the Court Employee Labor Relations Rules, the scope of representation includes all matters within the court's authority to determine relating to employment conditions and employer-employee relations, including, but not limited to, wages, hours, and terms and other conditions of employment, except, however, that the scope of representation does not include consideration of the merits, necessity, or organization of any service or activity provided by law or executive order.

(b)   Matters outside the scope of representation

In view of the unique and special responsibilities of the courts in the administration of justice, decisions regarding the following matters are not included within the scope of representation:

(1) The merits and administration of the court system;

(2) Coordination, consolidation, and merger of trial courts and support staff;

(3) Automation, including but not limited to fax filing, electronic recording, and implementation of information systems;

(4) Design, construction, and location of court facilities;

(5) Delivery of court services; and

(6) Hours of operation of the courts and court system.

(c) Impact

Impact from such matters as in (b) must be included within the scope of representation as those matters affect wages, hours, terms, and conditions of employment of court employees, to the extent such matters are within the court's authority to determine.

(d) Assignments and transfers

The superior court continues to have the right to determine assignments and transfers of court employees, provided that the process, procedures, and criteria for assignments and transfers are included within the scope of representation. *(Formerly Rule 2204, adopted, eff. Jan. 1, 1998. Renumbered Rule 10.654 and amended, eff. Jan. 1, 2007.)*

Rule 10.655. Governing court employee labor relations

(a) County rules and procedures

As they relate to court employees in their relations with the court, matters described in Government Code section 3507(a) through (d) are governed by any rules and administrative procedures and provisions adopted by the county under section 3507 that may apply to county employees generally, with the right of review by the appropriate Court of Appeal.

(b) Court rules and policies

A court may adopt reasonable rules and policies after consultation in good faith with representatives of a recognized employee organization or organizations for the administration of employer-employee relations under this rule as to matters described in Government Code section 3507(e)–(i). The court and county jointly will establish procedures to determine the appropriateness of any bargaining unit of court employees. The court must consult with the county about any rules and policies that the court may adopt under this section. If the court does not adopt rules by January 1, 1998, the court is bound by existing county rules until the court adopts rules. *(Formerly Rule 2205, adopted, eff. Jan. 1, 1998. Renumbered Rule 10.655 and amended, eff. Jan. 1, 2007.)*

Research References

3 Witkin, California Summary 10th Agency and Employment § 585, (S 585) Invalid Local Regulations.

Rule 10.656. Transition provisions

(a) Court employee organization

On the effective date of the Court Employee Labor Relations Rules, the court must recognize the employee organization that represented its court employees at the time of adoption. The court and the recognized employee organization are bound by the terms of any memorandum of understanding or agreement to which the court is a party that is in effect as of the date of adoption of the Court Employee Labor Relations Rules for its duration, or until it expires or, before then, is replaced by a subsequent memorandum of understanding.

(b) Court personnel rules and policies

A court's local rules governing court employees and a court's personnel rules, policies, and practices in effect at the time of the adoption of the Court Employee Labor Relations Rules, to the extent they are not contrary to or inconsistent with the obligations and duties provided for in these rules, continue in effect until changed by the court. Before changing any rule, policy, or practice that affects any matter within the scope of representation as stated in these rules, the court must meet and confer in good faith with the recognized employee organization as provided for in these rules.

(c) County employee representation units

Nothing contained in these rules is intended to preclude court employees from continuing to be included in representation units that contain county employees. *(Formerly Rule 2206, adopted, eff. Jan. 1, 1998. Renumbered Rule 10.656 and amended, eff. Jan. 1, 2007.)*

Rule 10.657. Construction

The enactment of the Court Employee Labor Relations Rules is not to be construed as making the provisions of Labor Code section 923 applicable to court employees. *(Formerly Rule 2207, adopted, eff. Jan. 1, 1998. Renumbered Rule 10.657 and amended, eff. Jan. 1, 2007.)*

Rule 10.658. Interpretation

Where the language of the Court Employee Labor Relations Rules is the same or substantially the same as that contained in Government Code sections 3500 to 3510, it must be interpreted and applied in accordance with judicial interpretations of the same language. *(Formerly Rule 2208, adopted, eff. Jan. 1, 1998. Renumbered Rule 10.658 and amended, eff. Jan. 1, 2007.)*

Rule 10.659. Other provisions

(a) Mediation

If, after a reasonable period of time, representatives of the court and the recognized employee organization fail to reach agreement, the court and the recognized employee organization or recognized employee organizations together may agree on the appointment of a mediator mutually agreeable to the parties. Costs of mediation are to be divided one-half to the court and one-half to the recognized employee organization or recognized employee organizations.

(b) Submission for dispute resolution

In the absence of local procedures and provisions for resolving disputes on the appropriateness of a unit of representation, on the request of any of the parties, the dispute must be submitted to the Division of Conciliation of the Department of Industrial Relations for mediation or for recommendation for resolving the dispute.

(c) Dues deduction

Nothing in the Court Employee Labor Relations Rules affects the right of a court employee to authorize a dues deduction from his or her salary or wages under Government Code sections 1157.1, 1157.2, 1157.3, 1157.4, 1157.5, or 1157.7.

(d) Applicability of Government Code section 3502.5

The procedures and provisions stated in Government Code section 3502.5 are applicable to court employees. *(Formerly Rule 2209, adopted, eff. Jan. 1, 1998. Renumbered Rule 10.659 and amended, eff. Jan. 1, 2007.)*

Rule 10.660. Enforcement of agreements—petitions (Gov. Code, §§ 71639.5, 71825.2)

(a) Application

This rule applies to petitions filed under Government Code sections 71639.5 and 71825.2.

(b) Assignment of Court of Appeal justice to hear the petition

(1) The petition must state the following on the first page, below the case number, in the statement of the character of the proceeding (see rule 2.111(6)): "Petition filed under Government Code sections 71639.5 and 71825.2—Assignment of Court of Appeal justice required."

(2) When the petition is filed, the clerk of the court must immediately request of the Judicial Assignments Unit of the Administrative Office of the Courts the assignment of a hearing judge from the panel established under (e).

(3) The judge assigned to hear the petition in the superior court must be a justice from a Court of Appeal for a district other than the district for that superior court.

(c) Superior court hearing

(1) The superior court must hear and decide the petition on an expedited basis and must give the petition priority over other matters to the extent permitted by law and the rules of court.

(2) The petition must be heard by a judge assigned by the Chief Justice from the panel of hearing judges established under (e).

(d) Appeal

An appeal of the superior court decision must be heard and decided on an expedited basis in the Court of Appeal for the district in which the petition was heard and must be given priority over other matters to the extent permitted by law and the rules of court. The notice of appeal must state the following on the first page, below the case number, in the statement of the character of the proceeding (see rule 2.111(6)): "Notice of Appeal on Petition filed under Government Code sections 71639.5 and 71825.2—Expedited Processing Requested."

(e) Panel of hearing judges

The panel of judges who may hear the petitions in the superior court must consist of Court of Appeal justices selected by the Chief Justice as follows:

(1) The panel must include at least one justice from each district of the Court of Appeal.

(2) Each justice assigned to hear a petition under (c)(2) must have received training on hearing the petitions as specified by the Chief Justice. *(Formerly Rule 2211, adopted, eff. Jan. 1, 2001. As amended, eff. Dec. 10, 2004. Renumbered Rule 10.660 and amended, eff. Jan. 1, 2007. As amended, eff. Oct. 24, 2008.)*

Research References

Rutter, Cal. Practice Guide: Civil Appeals & Writs Ch. 3-E, E. Filing Steps.
Rutter, Cal. Practice Guide: Civil Appeals & Writs Ch. 5-B, B. Types of Motions, Applications and Requests.
2 Witkin Cal. Proc. 5th Courts § 197, (S 197) Judicial Administration Rules.

Article 2

OTHER HUMAN RESOURCES RULES

Rule
10.670. Trial court personnel plans.

Rule 10.670. Trial court personnel plans

(a) Purpose

This rule establishes the authority and responsibility of the superior courts, on a countywide basis, to create and implement a system of personnel management designed to achieve lawful, uniform, and fair employment practices and procedures.

(b) Countywide personnel plans

The superior court of each county must establish a single personnel plan on a countywide basis, consistent with applicable statutes, rules, and standards of judicial administration.

(c) Provisions of a personnel plan

The personnel plan must ensure that treatment of employees complies with current law. The personnel plan should address the following issues:

(1) A salary-setting procedure;

(2) Regular review of job classifications and titles;

(3) An equal employment opportunity policy applying to all employees in accordance with applicable state and federal law;

(4) Recruitment, selection, and promotion policies;

(5) A sexual harassment prevention policy;

(6) A reasonable accommodation policy;

(7) Grievance or complaint procedures covering, but not limited to, sexual harassment, discrimination, and denial of reasonable accommodation;

(8) An employee benefits plan that includes health benefits, retirement benefits, workers' compensation benefits, disability leave, and paid and unpaid leave in compliance with state and federal law;

(9) Timekeeping and payroll policies and procedures that comply with applicable state and federal law;

(10) A records management policy, including confidentiality and retention of personnel records;

(11) Job–related training and continuing education programs for all personnel concerning at least the following:

   (A) Sexual harassment awareness;

   (B) Discrimination and bias; and

   (C) Safety;

(12) A policy statement on professional behavior requiring that all employees conduct themselves in a professional manner at all times and refrain from offensive conduct or comments that reflect bias or harassment;

(13) A policy regarding conflicts of interest and incompatible activities;

(14) Procedures for discipline and discharge; and

(15) A labor policy consistent with rules 10.653–10.659.

(d) Optional provisions

A personnel plan may contain additional provisions, including the following:

(1) Criteria and schedules for performance evaluations for all levels of employees;

(2) Job–related training and continuing education programs for all personnel as appropriate, with provisions for both paid and unpaid educational leave concerning:

   (A) Career development, including basic and managerial skills; and

   (B) Equal employment opportunity concepts and recruitment methods.

(3) An employee benefit plan that may include:

   (A) Flex–time, part–time, job-sharing, and other alternative work schedules;

   (B) Cafeteria options to use pretax dollars for dependent care and medical care and for sick leave for the care of dependents;

   (C) An employee assistance program; and

   (D) A deferred compensation plan.

(e) Submission of personnel plans

The superior court of each county must submit to the Judicial Council a personnel plan in compliance with these provisions by March 1, 1999. The superior court of each county must submit to the Judicial Council any changes to this plan by March 1 of every following year. If requested by a superior court, the Administrative Office of the Courts must review the court's personnel plan and provide the court with technical assistance in preparing the plan. *(Formerly Rule 2520, adopted, eff. July 1, 1998. Renumbered Rule 6.650, eff. Jan. 1, 1999. Renumbered Rule 10.670 and amended, eff. Jan. 1, 2007.)*

Research References

2 Witkin Cal. Proc. 5th Courts § 197, (S 197) Judicial Administration Rules.

Chapter 3

SUBORDINATE JUDICIAL OFFICERS

Rule

10.700.   Role of subordinate judicial officers.

10.701.   Qualifications and education of subordinate judicial officers.

10.702.   Subordinate judicial officers: practice of law.

10.703.   Subordinate judicial officers: complaints and notice requirements.

Rule 10.700.   Role of subordinate judicial officers

(a) Application

This rule applies to all subordinate judicial officers except those acting as child support commissioners under Family Code section 4251.

(b) Role of subordinate judicial officers

The primary role of subordinate judicial officers is to perform subordinate judicial duties. However, a presiding judge may assign a subordinate judicial officer to sit as a temporary judge where lawful, if the presiding judge determines that, because of a shortage of judges, it is necessary for the effective administration of justice. *(Formerly Rule 6.609, adopted, eff. July 1, 2002. Renumbered Rule 10.700, eff. Jan. 1, 2007.)*

Research References

Rutter, Cal. Practice Guide: A.D.R. Ch. 6-B, B. Temporary Judges.

2 Witkin Cal. Proc. 5th Courts § 197, (S 197) Judicial Administration Rules.

2 Witkin Cal. Proc. 5th Courts § 349, (S 349) Temporary Judge Appointed by Court.

Rule 10.701.   Qualifications and education of subordinate judicial officers

(a) Definition

For purposes of this rule, "subordinate judicial officer" means a person appointed by a court to perform subordinate judicial duties as authorized by article VI, section 22 of the California Constitution, including a commissioner, a referee, and a hearing officer.

(b) Qualifications

Except as provided in (d), a person is ineligible to be a subordinate judicial officer unless the person is a member of the State Bar and:

(1) Has been admitted to practice law in California for at least 10 years or, on a finding of good cause by the presiding judge, for at least 5 years; or

(2) Is serving as a subordinate judicial officer in a trial court as of January 1, 2003.

(c) Education

A subordinate judicial officer must comply with the education requirements of any position to which he or she is assigned, even if it is not his or her principal assignment. Such requirements include the following, as applicable: rules 5.30, 5.340, and 10.501 of the California Rules of Court, and Welfare and Institutions Code section 304.7.

(d) Juvenile referees and hearing officers

A person appointed as a juvenile referee or as a hearing officer under Welfare and Institutions Code sections 255 or 5256.1 must meet the qualification requirements established by those sections. Such a person is ineligible to exercise the powers and perform the duties of another type of subordinate judicial officer unless he or she meets the qualifications established in (b). *(Formerly Rule 6.660, adopted, eff. Jan. 1, 2003. Renumbered Rule 10.701 and amended, eff. Jan. 1, 2007. As amended, eff. July 1, 2008.)*

Research References

2 Witkin Cal. Proc. 5th Courts § 395, (S 395) Mandatory Requirement.

Rule 10.702.   Subordinate judicial officers: practice of law

A subordinate judicial officer may practice law only to the extent permitted by the Code of Judicial Ethics. *(Formerly Rule 6.665, adopted, eff. Jan. 1, 2003. Renumbered Rule 10.702, eff. Jan. 1, 2007.)*

Comment

Government Code section 69917, effective January 1, 2003, provides that "A subordinate judicial officer may not engage in the private practice of law except to the extent permitted by Judicial Council rules."

Rule 10.703.   Subordinate judicial officers: complaints and notice requirements

(a) Intent

The procedures in this rule for processing complaints against subordinate judicial officers do not:

(1) Create a contract of employment;

(2) Change the existing employee-employer relationship between the subordinate judicial officer and the court; or

(3) Change the status of a subordinate judicial officer from an employee terminable at will to an employee terminable only for cause.

(b) Definitions

Unless the context requires otherwise, the following definitions apply to this rule:

(1) "Subordinate judicial officer" means an attorney employed by a court to serve as a commissioner or referee, whether the attorney is acting as a commissioner, referee, or temporary judge. The term does not include any other attorney acting as a temporary judge.

(2) "Presiding judge" includes the person or group the presiding judge designates to perform any duty required by this rule to be performed by a presiding judge.

(3) "Commission" means the Commission on Judicial Performance. The commission exercises discretionary jurisdiction over the discipline of subordinate judicial officers under article VI, section 18.1 of the California Constitution.

(c) Application

(1) A court that employs a subordinate judicial officer must use the procedures in this rule for processing complaints against the subordinate judicial officer if the complaint alleges conduct that if alleged against a judge would be within the jurisdiction of the commission under article VI, section 18 of the California Constitution.

(2) If a complaint against a subordinate judicial officer does not allege conduct that would be within the jurisdiction of the commission, the court must process the complaint following local procedures adopted under rule 10.603(c)(4)(C). The local process may include any procedures from this rule for the court's adjudication of the complaint other than the provisions for referring the matter to the commission under (g) or giving notice of commission review under (l)(2)(B).

Ct. Rules

(3) A court may adopt additional policies and procedures for the adjudication of complaints against subordinate judicial officers not inconsistent with this rule.

(d) Promptness required

The presiding judge must ensure that the court processes each complaint promptly. To the extent reasonably possible, the court must complete action on each complaint within 90 days after the complaint is submitted.

(e) Confidentiality

(1) All proceedings by a presiding judge under this rule be conducted in a manner that is as confidential as is reasonably possible consistent with the need to conduct a thorough and complete investigation and the need for proper administration of the court.

(2) This rule does not prohibit access by the commission to any information relevant to the investigation of a complaint against a subordinate judicial officer.

(f) Written complaints to presiding judge

(1) A complaint about the conduct of a subordinate judicial officer must be in writing and be submitted to the presiding judge.

(2) Persons who are unable to file a written complaint because of a disability may present an oral complaint, which the presiding judge must commit to writing.

(3) The presiding judge must give written notice of receipt of the complaint to the complainant.

(g) Initial review of the complaint

(1) The presiding judge must review each complaint and determine if the complaint:

(A) May be closed after initial review;

(B) Needs preliminary investigation; or

(C) Requires formal investigation.

(2) A presiding judge may request that the commission investigate and adjudicate the complaint if a local conflict of interest or disqualification prevents the court from acting on the complaint.

(3) In exceptional circumstances a presiding judge may request the commission to investigate a complaint on behalf of the court and provide the results of the investigation to the court for action.

(4) The court must maintain a file on every complaint received, containing the following:

(A) The complaint;

(B) The response of the subordinate judicial officer, if any;

(C) All evidence and reports produced by the investigation of the complaint, if any; and

(D) The final action taken on the complaint.

(h) Closing a complaint after initial review

(1) After a preliminary review the presiding judge may close without further action any complaint that:

(A) Relates to the permissible exercise of judicial or administrative discretion by the subordinate judicial officer; or

(B) Does not allege conduct that if alleged against a judge would be within the jurisdiction of the commission under article VI, section 18 of the California Constitution.

(2) The presiding judge must notify the complainant in writing of the decision to close the investigation on the complaint. The notice must include the information required under (*l*).

(3) The presiding judge must advise the subordinate judicial officer in writing of the disposition.

(i) Complaints requiring preliminary investigation

(1) If after an initial review of the complaint the presiding judge finds a basis for further inquiry, the presiding judge must conduct a preliminary investigation appropriate to the nature of the complaint.

(2) The investigation may include interviews of witnesses and a review of court records.

(3) The presiding judge may give the subordinate judicial officer a copy of the complaint or a summary of its allegations and allow him or her an opportunity to respond. The presiding judge must give the subordinate judicial officer a copy of the complaint or a summary of its allegations and allow the subordinate judicial officer an opportunity to respond before the presiding judge takes appropriate informal action as described in (i)(4)(B).

(4) After completing the preliminary investigation, the presiding judge must:

(A) Terminate the investigation and close action on the complaint if the presiding judge finds the complaint lacks merit; or

(B) Terminate the investigation and close action on the complaint by taking appropriate informal action, which may include a reprimand or warning to the subordinate judicial officer, if the presiding judge finds a basis for taking informal action; or

(C) Proceed with a formal investigation under (j) if the presiding judge finds a basis for proceeding further.

(5) If the presiding judge terminates the investigation and closes action on the complaint, the presiding judge must:

(A) Notify the complainant in writing of the decision to close the investigation on the complaint. The notice must include the information required under (*l*); and

(B) Advise the subordinate judicial officer in writing of the disposition.

(j) Complaints requiring formal investigation

(1) If after a preliminary investigation the presiding judge finds a basis for proceeding with the investigation, the presiding judge must conduct a formal investigation appropriate to the nature of the complaint.

(A) The investigation may include interviews of witnesses and a review of court records.

(B) As soon as practicable, the presiding judge must give the subordinate judicial officer a copy of the complaint or a summary of its allegations and allow the subordinate judicial officer an opportunity to respond.

(2) Within 10 days after the completion of the investigation or as soon thereafter as is reasonably possible, the presiding judge must give the subordinate judicial officer the following in writing:

(A) Notice of the intended final action on the complaint; and

(B) The facts and other information forming the basis for the proposed action and the source of the facts and information, sufficient to allow a meaningful response to the allegations.

(3) Final action on the complaint may include:

(A) A finding that no further action need be taken on the complaint;

(B) An oral or written warning to the subordinate judicial officer;

(C) A private written reprimand to the subordinate judicial officer;

(D) A public written reprimand to the subordinate judicial officer;

(E) Suspension of the subordinate judicial officer;

(F) Termination of the subordinate judicial officer; and

(G) Any other action the court may deem appropriate.

(4) The notice of the intended final action on the complaint in (j)(2)(A) must include the following advice:

(A) The subordinate judicial officer may request an opportunity to respond within 10 days after service of the notice; and

(B) If the subordinate judicial officer does not request an opportunity to respond within 10 days after service of the notice, the proposed action will become final.

(5) If the subordinate judicial officer requests an opportunity to respond, the presiding judge should allow the subordinate judicial officer an opportunity to respond to the notice of the intended final action, either orally or in writing as specified by the presiding judge, in accordance with local rules.

(6) Within 10 days after the subordinate judicial officer has responded, the presiding judge must give the subordinate judicial officer and the complainant written notice of the final action taken on the complaint. The notice to the complainant must include the information required under (*l*).

(7) If the subordinate judicial officer does not request or has not been given an opportunity to respond, the presiding judge must promptly give written notice of the final action to the complainant. The notice must include the information required under (*l*).

(k) Notice to the Commission on Judicial Performance

(1) If a court disciplines a subordinate judicial officer by written reprimand under (i)(4)(B) or (j)(3)(C) or (D), suspension, or removal for conduct that, if alleged against a judge, would be within the jurisdiction of the commission under article VI, section 18 of the California Constitution, the presiding judge must promptly forward to the commission a copy of the portions of the court file that reasonably reflect the basis of the action taken by the court, including the complaint or allegations of misconduct and the subordinate judicial officer's response. This provision is applicable even when the disciplinary action does not result from a written complaint.

(2) If a subordinate judicial officer resigns (A) while a preliminary or formal investigation under (i) or (j) is pending concerning conduct that, if alleged against a judge, would be within the jurisdiction of the commission under article VI, section 18 of the California Constitution, or (B) under circumstances that would lead a reasonable person to conclude that the resignation was due, at least in part, to a complaint or allegation of misconduct that, if alleged against a judge, would be within the jurisdiction of the commission under article VI, section 18 of the California Constitution, the presiding judge must, within 15 days of the resignation or as soon thereafter as is reasonably possible, forward to the commission the entire court file on any pending complaint about or allegation of misconduct committed by the subordinate judicial officer.

(3) On request by the commission, the presiding judge must forward to the commission any requested information regarding a complaint about or allegation of misconduct committed by a subordinate judicial officer.

(*l*) Notice of final court action

(1) When the court has completed its action on a complaint, the presiding judge must promptly notify the complainant and the subordinate judicial officer of the final court action.

(2) The notice to the complainant of the final court action must:

(A) Provide a general description of the action taken by the court consistent with any law limiting the disclosure of confidential employee information; and

(B) Include the following statement:

If you are dissatisfied with the court's action on your complaint, you have the right to request the Commission on Judicial Performance to review this matter under its discretionary jurisdiction to oversee the discipline of subordinate judicial officers. No further action will be taken on your complaint unless the commission receives your written request within 30 days after the date this notice was mailed. The commission's address is:

Commission on Judicial Performance

455 Golden Gate Avenue, Suite 14400

San Francisco, California 94102–3660

(Formerly Rule 6.655, adopted, eff. Nov. 20, 1998. As amended, eff. April 29, 1999; July 1, 2002; Jan. 1, 2006. Renumbered Rule 10.703 and amended, eff. Jan. 1, 2007. As amended, eff. July 1, 2010.)

Research References

Rutter, Cal. Practice Guide: Civil Trials & Evidence Ch. 16-G, G. Trial by Reference.

2 Witkin Cal. Proc. 5th Courts § 69, Nature and Scope of California System.

2 Witkin Cal. Proc. 5th Courts § 71, Commission on Judicial Performance.

2 Witkin Cal. Proc. 5th Courts § 197, (S 197) Judicial Administration Rules.

2 Witkin Cal. Proc. 5th Courts § 237, (S 237) Other Duties.

Chapter 5

TEMPORARY JUDGES

Rule 10.740. Responsibilities of the trial courts for temporary judge programs

Each trial court that uses temporary judges must develop, institute, and operate—by itself or in collaboration with another court or courts—a program to recruit, select, train, and evaluate attorneys qualified to serve as temporary judges. *(Formerly Rule 6.740, adopted, eff. July 1, 2006. Renumbered Rule 10.740 and amended, eff. Jan. 1, 2007.)*

Research References

2 Witkin Cal. Proc. 5th Courts § 197, (S 197) Judicial Administration Rules.

2 Witkin Cal. Proc. 5th Courts § 349, (S 349) Temporary Judge Appointed by Court.

Rule 10.741.　Duties and authority of the presiding judge

(a)　General duties

The presiding judge is responsible for the recruitment, selection, training, appointment, supervision, assignment, performance, and evaluation of court-appointed temporary judges. In carrying out these responsibilities, the presiding judge is assisted by the Temporary Judge Administrator as provided in rule 10.743.

(b)　Publicizing the opportunity to serve as a temporary judge

(1)　Except for those courts that have nine or fewer authorized judge positions or use only research attorneys as temporary judges, each trial court that uses court-appointed temporary judges must publicize the opportunity to serve as a temporary judge whenever the court seeks to add attorneys to its pool of temporary judges or within a reasonable time before conducting its mandatory training for temporary judges but, in any case, no less than once every three years.

(2)　Courts must publicize this opportunity in a manner that maximizes the potential for a diverse applicant pool, which includes publicizing the opportunity to legal communities and organizations, including all local bar associations, in their geographical area. This publicity should encourage and must provide an equal opportunity for all eligible individuals to seek positions as court-appointed temporary judges and not exclude individuals based on their gender, race, ethnicity, disability, religion, sexual orientation, age, or other protected class.

(c)　Nondiscrimination in application and selection procedure

Each trial court that uses court-appointed temporary judges must conduct an application and selection procedure for temporary judges that ensures the most qualified applicants for appointment are selected and must not reject applicants who otherwise meet the requirements for appointment based on their gender, race, ethnicity, disability, religion, sexual orientation, age, or other protected class. Among the qualifications to be considered in the selection procedure are the applicant's exposure to and experience with diverse populations and issues related to those populations.

(d)　Authority to remove or discontinue

The presiding judge has the discretion to remove a court-appointed temporary judge or to discontinue using an attorney as a court-appointed temporary judge at any time. *(Formerly Rule 6.741, adopted, eff. July 1, 2006. Renumbered Rule 10.741 and amended, eff. Jan. 1, 2007. As amended, eff. July 1, 2012.)*

Advisory Committee Comment

Subdivision (b). This subdivision is intended to offer all attorneys who satisfy the requirements for appointment under rule 2.812 the opportunity to serve as temporary judges and to expand the size and diversity of the pool of eligible candidates. Pursuant to the rule, courts that do not use temporary judges, that have nine or fewer authorized and funded judge positions, or that only use their research attorneys as temporary judges are exempt from the requirement to publicize the opportunity to serve as a temporary judge. Courts that use temporary judges may publicize the opportunity in a manner they determine to be most effective, given their individual circumstances. In attempting to broaden the diversity of the temporary judge applicant pool, courts also have the flexibility to widen the geographical areas in which they publicize the opportunity. Thus, courts are not limited to publicizing their temporary judge program through the local or state bar associations. However, they must include *all* local bar associations when they do so. Further, the method of publication is purposefully left to the court's discretion. No-cost methods exist, such as email, use of the court's public website, and oral announcements at local bar association or legal organization events. Publicizing this opportunity no less than once every three years should increase the potential for

greater diversity among the temporary judges who serve the courts.

Subdivision (c). This subdivision emphasizes that the selection and appointment process must be devoid of discrimination. These provisions are intended to discourage favoritism in the appointment process and permit the courts to consider, as an additional qualification, an attorney's exposure to and experience with the diverse populations and issues unique to that population in the county where they are seeking appointment. "Exposure to and experience with diverse populations" includes work, social interaction, educational experiences, or community involvement with individuals or groups from diverse communities that may appear in court.

Rule 10.742.　Use of attorneys as court-appointed temporary judges

(a)　Responsibility of the presiding judge

The presiding judge of the trial court is responsible for determining whether that court needs to use attorneys as temporary judges and, if so, the specific purposes for which attorneys are to be appointed as temporary judges.

(b)　Conditions for the use of court-appointed temporary judges

The presiding judge may appoint an attorney as a court-appointed temporary judge only if all the following circumstances apply:

(1)　The appointment of an attorney to serve as a temporary judge is necessary to fill a judicial need in that court;

(2)　The attorney serving as a temporary judge has been approved by the court where the attorney will serve under rule 2.810 et seq.;

(3)　The appointment of the attorney as a temporary judge does not result in any conflict of interest; and

(4)　There is no appearance of impropriety resulting from the appointment of the attorney to serve as a temporary judge.

(c)　Record and report of uses

Each trial court that uses attorneys as temporary judges must record and report to the Administrative Office of the Courts on a quarterly basis information concerning its use of them. The report must state:

(1)　The number of attorneys used as temporary judges by that court each month;

(2)　The number and types of cases, and the amount of time, on which the temporary judges were used each month; and

(3)　Whether any of the appointments of temporary judges were made under the exception in rule 2.810(d) and, if so, the number of and reasons for these appointments. *(Formerly Rule 6.742, adopted, eff. July 1, 2006. Renumbered Rule 10.742 and amended, eff. Jan. 1, 2007.)*

Advisory Committee Comment

Subdivisions (a)–(b). These subdivisions provide that the presiding judge in each court is responsible for determining whether court-appointed temporary judges need to be used in that court, and these subdivisions furnish the criteria for determining when their use is proper. Under (b)(1), the use and appointment of court-appointed temporary judges must be based on judicial needs. Under (b)(3), an attorney serving as a temporary judge would have a conflict of interest if the disqualifying factors in the Code of Judicial Ethics exist. Under (b)(4), the test for the appearance of impropriety is whether a person aware of the facts might entertain a doubt that the judge would be able to act with integrity, impartiality, and competence. In addition to the disqualifying factors listed in the Code of Judicial Ethics, an appearance of impropriety would be generated if any of the limitations in family law, unlawful detainer, and other cases identified in the Code of Judicial Ethics are present.

Subdivision (c). Regular recording and reporting of information concerning each court's use of temporary judges assists the courts in monitoring and managing their use of temporary judges. This information is also important for establishing the need for additional judicial positions.

Rule 10.743. Administrator of temporary judges program

(a) Administrator

The presiding judge who appoints attorneys as temporary judges must designate a clerk, executive officer, or other court employee knowledgeable about temporary judges to serve as the Temporary Judge Administrator in that court.

(b) Duties of administrator

Under the supervision of the presiding judge, the Temporary Judge Administrator is responsible for the management of the temporary judges program in the court. The administrator's duties include:

(1) Receiving and processing applications from attorneys to serve as temporary judges with the court;

(2) Verifying the information on the applications;

(3) Assisting the presiding judge in the recruitment and selection of attorneys to serve as temporary judges, as provided in rule 10.741;

(4) Administering the court's program for the education and training of temporary judges;

(5) Maintaining records of attendance and completion of required courses by all attorneys serving as temporary judges in the court;

(6) Determining that attorneys have satisfied all the conditions required to be appointed as a temporary judge in that court, including continuing education requirements;

(7) Maintaining a list of attorneys currently appointed and qualified to serve as temporary judges in the court;

(8) Managing support services for temporary judges, such as providing mentoring programs and reference materials;

(9) Receiving and processing complaints and other information concerning the performance of attorneys serving as temporary judges;

(10) Assisting the presiding judge in identifying judicial needs that require the use of temporary judges and in addressing these needs; and

(11) Maintaining records, gathering statistics, and preparing and transmitting quarterly reports on the court's use of temporary judges as required under rule 10.742(c). *(Formerly Rule 6.743, adopted, eff. July 1, 2006. Renumbered Rule 10.743 and amended, eff. Jan. 1, 2007. As amended, eff. July 1, 2012.)*

Advisory Committee Comment

The goal of this rule is to ensure the effective and efficient administration of the courts' use of temporary judges. The rule should be applied flexibly. In courts with large temporary judge programs, the court may want to designate a full-time administrator, and some of the administrator's duties may be delegated to other individuals. On the other hand, in courts that use only a few temporary judges, the Temporary Judge Administrator position may consume only part of the administrator's time and be combined with other duties. Also, courts that use only a small number of temporary judges may work with other courts, or may cooperate on a regional basis, to perform the functions and duties prescribed under this rule.

Rule 10.744. Application procedures to serve as a court-appointed temporary judge

(a) Application

Every attorney who applies for appointment as a temporary judge in a trial court must complete an application to serve as a temporary judge.

(b) Information required

The attorney must provide all applicable information requested on the application. This information must include:

(1) The attorney's name and contact information as required by the court;

(2) The attorney's State Bar number;

(3) The date of the attorney's admission to the State Bar of California and the dates of his or her admissions to practice in any other state;

(4) Length of membership in the State Bar of California and of practice in any other state;

(5) Whether the attorney is in good standing with the State Bar of California and in good standing as an attorney in any other state where the attorney has been admitted to practice;

(6) Whether the attorney has ever been disciplined, or is the subject of a pending disciplinary proceeding, by the State Bar of California or by any other state bar association or court of record; and, if so, an explanation of the circumstances;

(7) The areas of specialization for which the attorney has been certified in California or in any other state;

(8) The attorney's major area or areas of practice;

(9) Whether the attorney holds himself or herself out publicly as representing exclusively one side in any of the areas of litigation in which the attorney practices;

(10) Whether the attorney represents one side in more than 90 percent of all cases in any areas of litigation in which the attorney specializes or concentrates his or her practice;

(11) The location or locations in which the attorney principally practices;

(12) How often the attorney appears in the court where he or she is applying to serve as a temporary judge;

(13) A list of the attorney's previous service as a temporary judge in the court where the attorney is applying and in any other court;

(14) Whether the attorney has ever been removed as a temporary judge by any court;

(15) The types of cases on which the attorney is willing to serve as a temporary judge;

(16) Whether the attorney has ever been convicted of a felony or misdemeanor, or is a defendant in any pending felony or misdemeanor proceeding, and, if so, a statement about the conviction or pending proceeding;

(17) Whether the attorney has been a party in any legal proceeding and, if so, a brief description of the proceedings;

(18) Information concerning any circumstances or conditions that would adversely affect or limit the attorney's ability to serve as a temporary judge;

(19) Any facts concerning the attorney's background that may reflect positively or negatively on the attorney or that should be disclosed to the court; and

(20) Such additional information as the court may require.

(c) Continuing duty to disclose

An attorney appointed by a court to serve as a temporary judge has a continuing duty to disclose to the court any material changes in facts or circumstances that affect his or her ability to serve as a temporary judge. The attorney must disclose the changes to the court before the next time the attorney is assigned to serve as a temporary judge.

(d) Review of application

The presiding judge, assisted by the Temporary Judge Administrator, must review all applications and determine whether each applicant is qualified, has satisfied the requirements of rule 2.812, and should be appointed as a temporary judge. The presiding judge may delegate this task to another judge or a committee of judges, assisted by the Temporary Judge Administrator. In appointing attorneys as temporary judges, the presiding judge may go beyond the minimum qualifications and standards required under the California Rules of Court. The decision whether to appoint, use, retrain, remove, or discontinue using any particular attorney as a temporary judge is at the sole discretion of the presiding judge. *(Formerly Rule 6.744, adopted, eff. July 1, 2006. Renumbered Rule 10.744 and amended, eff. Jan. 1, 2007.)*

Research References

2 Witkin Cal. Proc. 5th Courts § 349, (S 349) Temporary Judge Appointed by Court.

Rule 10.745.   Performance

(a) Review required

The court must review on a regular basis the performance of temporary judges appointed by that court.

(b) Monitoring performance

In monitoring and reviewing the performance of court-appointed temporary judges, the court may use direct observation, audiotaping of hearings, reports by court staff, comments from mentor judges, and such other means as may be helpful. *(Formerly Rule 6.745, adopted, eff. July 1, 2006. Renumbered Rule 10.745, eff. Jan. 1, 2007.)*

Rule 10.746.   Complaints

Each court must have procedures for receiving, investigating, and resolving complaints against court-appointed temporary judges. *(Formerly Rule 6.746, adopted, eff. July 1, 2006. Renumbered Rule 10.746, eff. Jan. 1, 2007.)*

Research References

2 Witkin Cal. Proc. 5th Courts § 197, (S 197) Judicial Administration Rules.

Chapter 6

COURT INTERPRETERS

Rule

10.761.   Regional Court Interpreter Employment Relations Committees.

10.762.   Cross–assignments for court interpreter employees.

Rule 10.761.   Regional Court Interpreter Employment Relations Committees

(a) Creation

Government Code sections 71807–71809 establish four Regional Court Interpreter Employment Relations Committees. Each committee has the authority, for spoken language court interpreters within its region as defined under Government Code section 71807(a), to:

(1) Set the terms and conditions of employment for court interpreters, subject to meet and confer in good faith, as authorized by Government Code section 71808;

(2) Adopt reasonable rules and regulations for the administration of employer-employee relations with recognized employ-

ee organizations, as authorized by Government Code section 71823(a); and

(3) Act as the representative of the superior courts within the region in bargaining with a recognized employee organization as authorized by Government Code section 71809.

(b) Membership

(1) Each Regional Court Interpreter Employment Committee consists of one representative from each superior court that has at least one interpreter employed as a court interpreter as defined by Government Code section 71806 and not excluded by section 71828(d).

(2) The following regions are established by Government Code section 71807:

(A) Region 1: Los Angeles, Santa Barbara, and San Luis Obispo Counties.

(B) Region 2: Counties of the First and Sixth Appellate Districts, except Solano County.

(C) Region 3: Counties of the Third and Fifth Appellate Districts.

(D) Region 4: Counties of the Fourth Appellate District.

(3) The court executive officer of each superior court may appoint the court's representative, under rule 10.610, which authorizes the court executive officer, acting under the direction of the presiding judge, to oversee the management and administration of the nonjudicial operations of the court.

(4) Each Regional Court Interpreter Employment Relations Committee may appoint a chief negotiator to bargain with recognized employee organizations. The chief negotiator may be staff of the Administrative Office of the Courts.

(5) Any superior court that is not entitled to appoint a representative under this rule, including the superior courts of Ventura and Solano Counties, may appoint an advisory member to the committee for its region.

(c) Rules of procedure

Each Regional Court Interpreter Employment Relations Committee may adopt its own rules of procedure, including the procedure for selecting its chair, advisory members, and chief negotiator.

(d) Voting

(1) Each representative of a superior court has a number of votes equal to the number of court interpreter employees in that trial court as defined by Government Code section 71806 and not excluded by section 71828(d).

(2) On July 1, 2004, and annually thereafter each Regional Court Interpreter Employment Relations Committee must recalculate the number of votes of each representative of a superior court to equal the number of court interpreter employees in that court.

(e) Administrative Office of the Courts

The staff of the Administrative Office of the Courts will assist each Regional Court Interpreter Employment Relations Committee in performing its functions. *(Formerly Rule 6.661, adopted, eff. March 1, 2003. As amended, eff. Jan. 1, 2006. Renumbered Rule 10.761 and amended, eff. Jan. 1, 2007.)*

Research References

2 Witkin Cal. Proc. 5th Courts § 197, (S 197) Judicial Administration Rules.

Rule 10.762.   Cross–assignments for court interpreter employees

(a) Purpose

This rule implements a process for cross-assignment of a court interpreter employed by a superior court under Government Code section 71810(b).

(b) Definitions

As used in this rule:

(1) "Home court" means the superior court in which the court interpreter is an employee. An employee's home court includes all locations of a superior court within a county.

(2) "Away court" means the superior court to which the court interpreter is temporarily cross-assigned.

(3) "Cross-assignment" means any assignment to perform spoken language interpretation for a superior court other than the interpreter's home court.

(4) "Regional court interpreter coordinator" means an employee of the Administrative Office of the Courts whose duty it is to locate, assign, and schedule available court interpreter employees for courts within and across regions, which are described under Government Code section 71807(a).

(5) "Local court interpreter coordinator" means an employee of a superior court whose duty it is to locate, assign, and schedule available court interpreter employees for his or her court.

(c) Procedure for cross–assignments

(1) Under Government Code section 71804.5(b) a court interpreter employed by a superior court is not permitted to be an employee of more than one superior court. A court interpreter employed by a superior court may not contract with another court, but may accept appointments to provide services to more than one court through cross-assignments.

(2) A superior court may attempt to fill an interpreting assignment with the employee of another court before hiring an independent contract court interpreter.

(3) If a superior court wants to fill an interpreting assignment with the employee of another court, the court must notify the regional court interpreter coordinator to locate an employee of a court within or across regions.

(4) Each local court interpreter coordinator must provide the schedule of each court interpreter employee available for cross-assignment to the regional court interpreter coordinator.

(5) A superior court may adopt additional internal procedures for cross-assigning a court interpreter employee that are not inconsistent with Government Code section 71810 and this rule.

(6) A Regional Court Interpreter Employment Relations Committee may approve alternative procedures for cross-assigning a court interpreter employee that permit the interpreter to directly arrange cross-assignments with an "away" court, provided that the procedures require notice to the regional coordinator.

(d) Payment for cross–assignments

The home court must issue payment to the court interpreter for all cross-assignments, including per diem compensation and mileage reimbursement. The Administrative Office of the Courts will administer funding to the home court for payments associated with cross-assignments.

(e) Duties of a court interpreter on cross–assignment

A court interpreter who accepts a cross-assignment is responsible for following the personnel rules of the home court while performing services for the away court.

(f) Superior courts of Ventura and Solano Counties

The superior courts of Ventura and Solano Counties may participate in the procedure for cross-assignments as follows:

(1) The Superior Court of Ventura County may accept or provide interpreters on cross-assignment under the procedures established in Region 1, as defined by Government Code section 71807.

(2) The Superior Court of Solano County may accept or provide interpreters on cross-assignment under the procedures established in Region 2, as defined by Government Code section 71807. *(Formerly Rule 6.662, adopted, eff. March 1, 2003. Renumbered Rule 10.762 and amended, eff. Jan. 1, 2007.)*

Research References

2 Witkin Cal. Proc. 5th Courts § 197, (S 197) Judicial Administration Rules.

Chapter 7

QUALIFICATIONS OF COURT INVESTIGATORS, PROBATE ATTORNEYS, AND PROBATE EXAMINERS

Rule

Rule 10.776.   Definitions

As used in the rules in this chapter, the following terms have the meanings stated below:

(1) A "court investigator" is a person described in Probate Code section 1454(a) employed by or under contract with a court to provide the investigative services for the court required or authorized by law in guardianships, conservatorships, and other protective proceedings under division 4 of the Probate Code;

(2) A "probate examiner" is a person employed by a court to review filings in probate proceedings in order to assist the court and the parties to get the filed matters ready for consideration by the court in accordance with the requirements of the Probate Code, title 7 of the California Rules of Court, and the court's local rules;

(3) A "probate attorney" is an active member of the State Bar of California who is employed by a court to perform the functions of a probate examiner and also to provide legal analysis, recommendations, advice, and other services to the court pertaining to probate proceedings;

(4) "Probate proceedings" are decedents' estates, guardianships and conservatorships under division 4 of the Probate Code, trust proceedings under division 9 of the Probate Code, and other matters governed by provisions of that code and the rules in title 7 of the California Rules of Court;

(5) An "accredited educational institution" is a college or university, including a community or junior college, accredited by a regional accrediting organization recognized by the Council for Higher Education Accreditation; and

(6) "AOC" is the Administrative Office of the Courts. *(Adopted, eff. Jan. 1, 2008.)*

Research References

2 Witkin Cal. Proc. 5th Courts § 197, (S 197) Judicial Administration Rules.

14 Witkin, California Summary 10th Wills and Probate § 371, General Rules of Practice.

14 Witkin, California Summary 10th Wills and Probate § 907, (S 907) Rules of Practice.

Rule 10.777.   Qualifications of court investigators, probate attorneys, and probate examiners

(a) Qualifications of court investigators

Except as otherwise provided in this rule, a person who begins employment with a court or enters into a contract to perform services with a court as a court investigator on or after January 1, 2008, must:

(1) Have a bachelor of arts or bachelor of science degree in a science, a social science, a behavioral science, liberal arts, or nursing from an accredited educational institution; and

(2) Have a minimum of two years' employment experience performing casework or investigations in a legal, financial, law enforcement, or social services setting.

(b) Qualifications of probate attorneys

Except as otherwise provided in this rule, a person who begins employment with a court as a probate attorney on or after January 1, 2008, must:

(1) Be an active member of the State Bar of California for:

  (A) A minimum of five years; or

  (B) A minimum of two years, plus a minimum of five years' current or former active membership in the equivalent organization of another state or eligibility to practice in the highest court of another state or in a court of the United States; and

(2) Have a minimum of two years' total experience, before or after admission as an active member of the State Bar of California, in one or more of the following positions:

  (A) Court–employed staff attorney;

  (B) Intern, court probate department (minimum six-month period);

  (C) Court–employed probate examiner or court-employed or court-contracted court investigator;

  (D) Attorney in a probate-related public or private legal practice;

  (E) Deputy public guardian or conservator;

  (F) Child protective services or adult protective services worker or juvenile probation officer; or

  (G) Private professional fiduciary appointed by a court or employee of a private professional fiduciary or bank or trust company appointed by a court, with significant fiduciary responsibilities, including responsibility for court accountings.

(c) Qualifications of probate examiners

Except as otherwise provided in this rule, a person who begins employment with a court as a probate examiner on or after January 1, 2008, must have:

(1) A bachelor of arts or bachelor of science degree from an accredited educational institution and a minimum of two years' employment experience with one or more of the following employers:

  (A) A court;

  (B) A public or private law office; or

  (C) A public administrator, public guardian, public conservator, or private professional fiduciary; or

(2) A paralegal certificate or an Associate of Arts degree from an accredited educational institution and a minimum of a total of four years' employment experience with one or more of the employers listed in (1); or

(3) A juris doctor degree from an educational institution approved by the American Bar Association or accredited by the Committee of Bar Examiners of the State Bar of California and a minimum of six months' employment experience with an employer listed in (1).

(d) Additional court-imposed qualifications and requirements

The qualifications in (a), (b), and (c) are minimums. A court may establish higher qualification standards for any position covered by this rule and may require applicants to comply with its customary hiring or personal-service contracting practices, including written applications, personal references, personal interviews, or entrance examinations.

(e) Exemption for smaller courts

The qualifications required under this rule may be waived by a court with eight or fewer authorized judges if it cannot find suitable qualified candidates for the positions covered by this rule or for other grounds of hardship. A court electing to waive a qualification under this subdivision must make express written findings showing the circumstances supporting the waiver and disclosing all alternatives considered, including those not selected.

(f) Record keeping and reporting

The AOC may require courts to report on the qualifications of the court investigators, probate attorneys, or probate examiners hired or under contract under this rule, and on waivers made under (e), as necessary to ensure compliance with Probate Code section 1456. *(Adopted, eff. Jan. 1, 2008.)*

Research References

2 Witkin Cal. Proc. 5th Courts § 197, (S 197) Judicial Administration Rules.
14 Witkin, California Summary 10th Wills and Probate § 371, General Rules of Practice.
14 Witkin, California Summary 10th Wills and Probate § 907, (S 907) Rules of Practice.

Chapter 8

ALTERNATIVE DISPUTE RESOLUTION PROGRAMS

Rule
10.780. Administration of alternative dispute resolution (ADR) programs.
10.781. Court–related ADR neutrals.
10.782. ADR program information.
10.783. ADR program administration.

Rule 10.780. Administration of alternative dispute resolution (ADR) programs

The rules in this chapter concern alternative dispute resolution (ADR) programs administered by the trial courts. General provisions concerning ADR are located in title 3, division 8. *(Adopted, eff. Jan. 1, 2007. As amended, eff. Jan. 1, 2008.)*

Research References

2 Witkin Cal. Proc. 5th Courts § 197, (S 197) Judicial Administration Rules.

Rule 10.781. Court–related ADR neutrals

(a) Qualifications of mediators for general civil cases

Each superior court that makes a list of mediators available to litigants in general civil cases or that recommends, selects, appoints, or compensates mediators to mediate any general civil case pending in the court must establish minimum qualifications for the mediators eligible to be included on the court's list or to be recommended, selected, appointed, or compensated by the court. A court that approves the parties' agreement to use a mediator who is selected by the parties and who is not on the court's list of mediators or that memorializes the parties' agreement in a court order has not thereby recommended, selected, or appointed that mediator within the meaning of this rule. In establishing these qualifications, courts are encouraged to consider the Model Qualification Standards for Mediators in Court–Connected Mediation Programs for General Civil Cases issued by the Administrative Office of the Courts.

(b) Lists of neutrals

If a court makes available to litigants a list of ADR neutrals, the list must contain, at a minimum, the following information concerning each neutral listed:

(1) The types of ADR services available from the neutral;

(2) The neutral's resume, including his or her general education and ADR training and experience; and

(3) The fees charged by the neutral for each type of service.

(c) Requirements to be on lists

In order to be included on a court list of ADR neutrals, an ADR neutral must sign a statement or certificate agreeing to:

(1) Comply with all applicable ethics requirements and rules of court; and

(2) Serve as an ADR neutral on a pro bono or modest-means basis in at least one case per year, not to exceed eight hours, if requested by the court. The court must establish the eligibility requirements for litigants to receive, and the application process for them to request, ADR services on a pro bono or modest-means basis.

(d) Privilege to serve as a court-program neutral

Inclusion on a court list of ADR neutrals and eligibility to be recommended, appointed, or compensated by the court to serve as a neutral are privileges that are revocable and confer no vested right on the neutral. *(Formerly Rule 1580.1, adopted, eff. Jan. 1, 2001. As amended, eff. Jan. 1, 2007. Renumbered Rule 10.781 and amended, eff. Jan. 1, 2007. As amended, eff. July 1, 2009; Jan. 1, 2011.)*

Advisory Committee Comment

Subdivision (c). A court has absolute discretion to determine who may be included on a court list of ADR neutrals or is eligible to be recommended, selected, appointed, or compensated by the court to serve as a neutral (except as otherwise expressly provided by statute or rule of court).

Research References

Rutter, Cal. Practice Guide: A.D.R. Ch. 4-B, B. Judicial Arbitration.
Rutter, Cal. Practice Guide: A.D.R. Ch. 4-C, C. Statutorily-Mandated Court Mediation Programs.

Rule 10.782. ADR program information

(a) Report to Judicial Council

Each court must report information on its ADR programs to the Judicial Council, as requested by the Administrative Office of the Courts.

(b) Parties and ADR neutrals to supply information

Subject to applicable limitations, including the confidentiality requirements in Evidence Code section 1115 et seq., courts must require parties and ADR neutrals, as appropriate, to supply pertinent information for the reports required under (a). *(Formerly Rule 1580.2, adopted, eff. Jan. 1, 2001. Renumbered Rule 10.782 and amended, eff. Jan. 1, 2007.)*

Rule 10.783. ADR program administration

(a) ADR program administrator

The presiding judge in each trial court must designate the clerk or executive officer, or another court employee who is knowledgeable about ADR processes, to serve as ADR program administrator. The duties of the ADR program administrator must include:

(1) Developing informational material concerning the court's ADR programs;

(2) Educating attorneys and litigants about the court's ADR programs;

(3) Supervising the development and maintenance of any panels of ADR neutrals maintained by the court; and

(4) Gathering statistical and other evaluative information concerning the court's ADR programs.

(b) ADR committee

(1) *Membership in courts with 18 or more authorized judges*

In each superior court that has 18 or more authorized judges, there must be an ADR committee. The members of the ADR committee must include, insofar as is practicable:

(A) The presiding judge or a judge designated by the presiding judge;

(B) One or more other judges designated by the presiding judge;

(C) The ADR program administrator;

(D) Two or more active members of the State Bar chosen by the presiding judge as representatives of those attorneys who regularly represent parties in general civil cases before the court, including an equal number of attorneys who represent plaintiffs and who represent defendants in these cases;

(E) One or more members of the court's panel of arbitrators chosen by the presiding judge; and

(F) If the court makes available to litigants a list of any ADR neutrals other than arbitrators, one or more neutrals chosen by the presiding judge from that list.

(2) *Additional members*

The ADR committee may include additional members selected by the presiding judge.

(3) *ADR committee in other courts*

Any other court may by rule establish an ADR committee as provided in (b)(1). Otherwise, the presiding judge or a judge designated by the presiding judge must perform the functions and have the powers of an ADR committee as provided in these rules.

(4) *Term of membership*

ADR committee membership is for a two-year term. The members of the ADR committee may be reappointed and may be removed by the presiding judge.

(5) *Responsibilities of ADR committee*

The ADR committee is responsible for overseeing the court's alternative dispute resolution programs for general civil cases, including those responsibilities relating to the court's judicial arbitration program specified in rule 3.813(b). *(Formerly Rule 1580.3, adopted, eff. Jan. 1, 2001. As amended, eff. Jan. 1, 2004. Renumbered Rule 10.783 and amended, eff. Jan. 1, 2007.)*

Research References

Rutter, Cal. Practice Guide: A.D.R. Ch. 1-B, B. Why ADR?
Rutter, Cal. Practice Guide: Civ. Pro. Before Trial Ch. 13-D, D. the Arbitrator.
Rutter, Cal. Practice Guide: Personal Injury Ch. 7-E, E. the Arbitrator.
2 Witkin Cal. Proc. 5th Courts § 197, (S 197) Judicial Administration Rules.
6 Witkin Cal. Proc. 5th Proceedings Without Trial § 581, Administration.

Ct. Rules

Chapter 9

TRIAL COURT BUDGET AND FISCAL MANAGEMENT

Rule

10.800. Superior court budgeting.
10.801. Superior court budget procedures.
10.803. Information access disputes—writ petitions (Gov. Code, § 71675).
10.804. Superior court financial policies and procedures.
10.805. Notice of change in court-county relationship.
10.810. Court operations.
10.811. Reimbursement of costs associated with homicide trials.
10.815. Fees to be set by the court.
10.820. Acceptance of credit cards by the superior courts.
10.821. Acceptance of checks and other negotiable paper.
10.830. Disposal of surplus court personal property.

Rule 10.800. Superior court budgeting

(a) Purpose

This rule provides for local authority and accountability for development of budget requests and management of court operations within the authorized funding level. Superior courts must manage their budgets in a manner that is responsive to local needs, ensures equal access to justice, is consistent with Judicial Council policy and legislative direction, and does not exceed the total allocated budget.

(b) Development of budget requests

Each superior court must prepare and submit to the Administrative Office of the Courts a budget according to the schedule and procedures established by the Judicial Council.

(c) Allocation of funding

(1) The funding allocation to each superior court is based on the amounts incorporated for that court in budget change proposals that have been funded through the Budget Act, except as otherwise ordered by the Judicial Council. The superior court of each county may distribute and periodically redistribute its annual allocation between programs, locations, and line items as needed, within the parameters of the *Trial Court Financial Policies and Procedures Manual* and consistent with council policy direction, to promote accessible justice and the effective, efficient, and accountable operation of the courts. The Judicial Council may make additional allocations as it deems appropriate.

(2) Each superior court is accountable for achieving the expected outcomes of the programs funded for that year. If a court is unable to do so, it must report the reasons to the Judicial Council. *(Formerly Rule 2530, adopted, eff. July 1, 1998. Renumbered Rule 6.700, eff. Jan. 1, 1999. As amended, eff. Jan. 1, 2002. Renumbered Rule 10.800 and amended, eff. Jan. 1, 2007.)*

Research References

2 Witkin Cal. Proc. 5th Courts § 197, (S 197) Judicial Administration Rules.

Rule 10.801. Superior court budget procedures

(a) Adoption of budget procedures by the Administrative Office of the Courts

The Administrative Office of the Courts must adopt superior court budget procedures to be included in the *Trial Court Financial Policies and Procedures Manual,* the annual Baseline Budget Development Package, and the annual *Budget Change Request Package.* These procedures include the following:

(1) Procedures permitting the superior courts to comment on the proposed budget procedures;

(2) Procedures for budget development, submission, and appeal;

(3) Procedures for budget implementation, including expenditure and revenue reporting;

(4) Reasonable time frames to comply with requirements or changes in the budget procedures;

(5) Procedures to ensure the reporting to the Judicial Council of relevant information on the implementation of programs funded;

(6) Procedures for providing timely management information to the Judicial Council on the baseline budget, revenues, and expenditures.

(7) An annual budget development and implementation calendar;

(8) Procedures for a superior court to follow if it projects that its budget will be exhausted before the end of the fiscal year, preventing the court from meeting its financial obligations or continuing operations; and

(9) Procedures governing the transfer of funds between individual programs and operations of expenditure.

(b) Technical assistance

The Administrative Office of the Courts, on request, provides technical assistance and ongoing training in budget development and implementation to the superior courts. *(Formerly Rule 2531, adopted, eff. July 1, 1998. Renumbered Rule 6.701, eff. Jan. 1, 1999. As amended, eff. Jan. 1, 2002. Renumbered Rule 10.801 and amended, eff. Jan. 1, 2007.)*

Rule 10.803. Information access disputes—writ petitions (Gov. Code, § 71675)

(a) Availability

This rule applies to petitions filed under rule 10.500(j)(1) and Government Code section 71675(b).

(b) Assignment of Court of Appeal justice to hear the petition

(1) The petition must state the following on the first page, below the case number, in the statement of the character of the proceeding (see rule 2.111(6)):

"Writ petition filed under rule 10.500(j)(1) and Government Code section 71675---Assignment of Court of Appeal justice required."

(2) When the petition is filed, the clerk of the court must immediately request of the Chief Justice the assignment of a hearing judge from the panel established under (e).

(3) If an assignment is made, the judge assigned to hear the petition in the superior court must be a justice from a Court of Appeal for a district other than the district for that superior court.

(c) Superior court hearing

(1) The superior court must hear and decide the petition on an expedited basis and must give the petition priority over other matters to the extent permitted by law and the rules of court.

(2) The petition must be heard by a judge assigned by the Chief Justice from the panel of hearing judges established under (e).

(d) Appeal

An appeal of the superior court decision must be heard and decided on an expedited basis in the Court of Appeal for the district in which the petition was heard and must be given priority over other matters to the extent permitted by law and rules of court. The notice of appeal must state the following on the first page, below the case number, in the statement of the character of the proceeding (see rule 2.111(6)):

"Notice of Appeal on Writ Petition filed under rule 10.500(j)(1) and Government Code section 71675---Expedited Processing Requested."

(e) Panel of hearing judges

The panel of judges who may hear the petitions in the superior court must consist of Court of Appeal justices selected by the Chief Justice as follows:

(1) The panel must include at least one justice from each district of the Court of Appeal.

(2) Each justice assigned to hear a petition under (c)(2) must have received training on hearing the petitions as specified by the Chief Justice. *(Formerly Rule 6.710, adopted, eff. Oct. 15, 2004. Renumbered Rule 10.803 and amended, eff. Jan. 1, 2007. As amended, eff. Jan. 1, 2010.)*

Research References

Rutter, Cal. Practice Guide: Civil Appeals & Writs Ch. 3-E, E. Filing Steps.
Rutter, Cal. Practice Guide: Civil Appeals & Writs Ch. 5-B, B. Types of Motions, Applications and Requests.
2 Witkin Cal. Proc. 5th Courts § 178, (S 178) State Funding.

Rule 10.804.   Superior court financial policies and procedures

(a) Adoption of financial policies and procedures by the Administrative Office of the Courts

The Administrative Office of the Courts must prepare and adopt a financial policies and procedures manual for the superior courts (the *"Trial Court Financial Policies and Procedures Manual"*), consistent with the rules of court and policies adopted by the Judicial Council. The manual must include accounting standards for superior courts and policies and procedures for procurement and contracting by superior courts. These policies and procedures must not modify superior courts' existing authority to procure, contract for, or use goods or services or the requirement that a court have authorized funding available in order to procure or contract for any good or service.

(b) Comment period for financial policies and procedures

Before issuing or amending the *Trial Court Financial Policies and Procedures Manual,* the Administrative Office of the Courts must make it available for comment from the superior courts and from the Department of Finance and the State Controller's Office for 30 days.

(c) Date of adherence to financial policies and procedures

Superior courts must adhere to the requirements contained in the *Trial Court Financial Policies and Procedures Manual,* except as otherwise provided in the manual. Superior courts must not be required to adhere to any amendment to the manual sooner than 60 days after the amendment is adopted. *(Formerly Rule 6.707, adopted, eff. Jan. 1, 2001. Renumbered Rule 10.804 and amended, eff. Jan. 1, 2007.)*

Rule 10.805.   Notice of change in court-county relationship

If, under Government Code section 77212, the county gives notice to the superior court that the county will no longer provide a specific county service or the court gives notice to the county that the court will no longer use a specific county service, the court must, within 10 days of receiving or giving such notice, provide a copy of this notice to the Finance Division of the Administrative Office of the Courts. *(Formerly Rule 6.705, adopted, eff. Jan. 1, 2000. Renumbered Rule 10.805 and amended, eff. Jan. 1, 2007.)*

Rule 10.810.   Court operations

(a) Definition

Except as provided in subdivision (b) and subject to the requirements of subdivisions (c) and (d), "court operations" as defined in Government Code section 77003 includes the following costs:

(1) *(judicial salaries and benefits)* salaries, benefits, and public agency retirement contributions for superior and municipal court judges and for subordinate judicial officers;

(2) *(nonjudicial salaries and benefits)* salaries, benefits, and public agency retirement contributions for superior and municipal court staff whether permanent, temporary, full- or part-time, contract or per diem, including but not limited to all municipal court staff positions specifically prescribed by statute and county clerk positions directly supporting the superior courts;

(3) salaries and benefits for those sheriff, marshal, and constable employees as the court deems necessary for court operations in superior and municipal courts and the supervisors of those sheriff, marshal, and constable employees who directly supervise the court security function;

(4) court–appointed counsel in juvenile dependency proceedings, and counsel appointed by the court to represent a minor as specified in Government Code section 77003;

(5) *(services and supplies)* operating expenses in support of judicial officers and court operations;

(6) *(collective bargaining)* collective bargaining with respect to court employees; and

(7) *(indirect costs)* a share of county general services as defined in subdivision (d), Function 11, and used by the superior and municipal courts.

(b) Exclusions

Excluded from the definition of "court operations" are the following:

(1) law library operations conducted by a trust pursuant to statute;

(2) courthouse construction and site acquisition, including space rental (for other than court records storage), alterations/remodeling, or relocating court facilities;

(3) district attorney services;

(4) probation services;

(5) indigent criminal and juvenile delinquency defense;

(6) civil and criminal grand jury expenses and operations (except for selection);

(7) pretrial release services;

(8) equipment and supplies for use by official reporters of the courts to prepare transcripts as specified by statute; and

(9) county costs as provided in subdivision (d) as unallowable.

(c) Budget appropriations

Costs for court operations specified in subdivision (a) shall be appropriated in county budgets for superior and municipal courts, including contract services with county agencies or private providers except for the following:

(1) salaries, benefits, services, and supplies for sheriff, marshal, and constable employees as the court deems necessary for court operations in superior and municipal courts;

(2) salaries, benefits, services, and supplies for county clerk activities directly supporting the superior court; and

(3) costs for court-appointed counsel specified in Government Code section 77003.

Except as provided in this subdivision, costs not appropriated in the budgets of the courts are unallowable.

(d) Functional budget categories

Trial court budgets and financial reports shall identify all allowable court operations in the following eleven (11) functional budget categories. Costs for salary, wages, and benefits of court employees are to be shown in the appropriate functions provided the individual staff member works at least 25 percent time in that function. Individual staff members whose time spent in a function is less than 25 percent are reported in Function 10, All Other Court Operations. The functions and their respective costs are as follows:

Function 1. Judicial Officers

Costs reported in this function are

Salaries and state benefits of

Judges

Full- or part-time court commissioners

Full- or part-time court referees

Assigned judges' in-county travel expenses

Costs not reported in this function include

County benefits of judicial officers (Function 10)

Juvenile traffic hearing officers (Function 10)

Mental health hearing officers (Function 10)

Pro tem hearing officers (Function 10)

Commissioner and referee positions specifically excluded by statute from state trial court funding (unallowable)

Related data processing (Function 9)

Any other related services, supplies, and equipment (Function 10)

Function 2. Jury Services

Costs reported in this function are

Juror expenses of per diem fees and mileage

Meals and lodging for sequestered jurors

Salaries, wages, and benefits of jury commissioner and jury services staff (including selection of grand jury)

Contractual jury services

Jury–related office expenses (other than information technology)

Jury–related communications, including "on call" services

Costs not reported in this function include

Juror parking (unallowable)

Civil and criminal grand jury costs (unallowable)

Jury–related information systems (Function 9)

Function 3. Verbatim Reporting

Costs reported in this function are

Salaries, wages, and benefits of court reporters who are court employees

Salaries, wages, and benefits of electronic monitors and support staff

Salaries, wages, and benefits of verbatim reporting coordinators and clerical support staff

Contractual court reporters and monitors

Transcripts for use by appellate or trial courts, or as otherwise required by law

Related office expenses and equipment (purchased, leased, or rented) used to record court proceedings, except as specified in Government Code § 68073[1], e.g.,

notepaper, pens, and pencils

ER equipment and supplies

Costs not reported in this function include

Office expenses and equipment for use by reporters to prepare transcripts (unallowable)

Expenses specified in Government Code § 69073[2] (unallowable)

Space use charges for court reporters (unallowable)

Function 4. Court Interpreters

Costs reported in this function are

Salaries, wages, and benefits of courtroom interpreters and interpreter coordinators

Per diem and contractual courtroom interpreters, including contractual transportation and travel allowances

Costs not reported in this function include

Related data processing (Function 9)

Any other related services, supplies, and equipment (Function 10)

Function 5. Collections Enhancement

Collections performed in the enforcement of court orders for fees, fines, forfeitures, restitutions, penalties, and assessments (beginning with the establishment of the accounts receivable record)

Costs reported in this function are

Salaries, wages, and benefits of collection employees of the court, e.g.,

financial hearing officers

evaluation officers

collection staff

Contract collections costs

County charges for collection services provided to the court by county agencies

Related services, supplies, and equipment (except data processing, Function 9)

Costs not reported in this function include

Staff whose principal involvement is in collecting "forthwith" payments, e.g.,

counter clerks (Function 10)

cashiers (Function 10)

Function 6. Dispute Resolution Programs

Costs reported in this function are

Arbitrators' fees in mandatory judicial arbitration programs

Salaries, wages, and benefits of court staff providing child custody and visitation mediation and related investigation services, e.g.,

Director of Family Court Services

mediators

conciliators

investigators

clerical support staff

Contract mediators providing child custody and visitation mediation services

Salaries, wages, benefits, fees, and contract costs for other arbitration and mediation programs (programs not mandated by statute), e.g.,

arbitration administrators
clerical support staff
arbitrators' fees and expenses

Costs not reported in this function include

Related data processing (Function 9)

Any other related services, supplies, and equipment (Function 10)

Function 7. Court–Appointed Counsel (Noncriminal)

Costs reported in this function are

Expenses for court-appointed counsel as specified in Government Code § 77003

Function 8. Court Security

Court security services as deemed necessary by the court. Includes only the duties of
(a) courtroom bailiff,
(b) perimeter security (i.e., outside the courtroom but inside the court facility), and
(c) at least .25 FTE dedicated supervisors of these activities.

Costs reported in this function are

Salary, wages, and benefits (including overtime) of sheriff, marshal, and constable employees who perform the court's security, i.e.,
bailiffs
weapons–screening personnel

Salary, wages, and benefits (including overtime) of court staff performing court security, e.g.,
court attendants

Contractual security services

Salary, wages, and benefits of supervisors of sheriff, marshal, and constable employees whose duties are greater than .25 FTE dedicated to this function

Sheriff, marshal, and constable employee training

Purchase of security equipment

Maintenance of security equipment

Costs not reported in this function include

Other sheriff, marshal, or constable employees (unallowable)

Court attendant training (Function 10)

Overhead costs attributable to the operation of the sheriff and marshal offices (unallowable)

Costs associated with the transportation and housing of detainees from the jail to the courthouse (unallowable)

Service of process in civil cases (unallowable)

Services and supplies, including data processing, not specified above as allowable

Supervisors of bailiffs and perimeter security personnel of the sheriff, marshal, or constable office who supervise these duties less than .25 FTE time (unallowable)

Function 9. Information Technology

Costs reported in this function are

Salaries, wages, and benefits of court employees who plan, implement, and maintain court data processing and information technologies, e.g.,
programmers
analysts

Contract and consulting services associated with court information/ data processing needs and systems

County Information Systems/Data Processing Department charges made to court for court systems, e.g.,
jury–related systems
court and case management, including courts' share of a criminal justice information system
accounts receivable/collections systems

Related services, supplies, and equipment, e.g.,
software purchases and leases
maintenance of automation equipment
training associated with data processing systems' development

Costs not reported in this function include

Information technology services not provided directly to the courts (i.e., services used by other budget units)

Data processing for county general services, e.g., payroll, accounts payable (Function 11)

Function 10. All Other Court Operations

Costs reported in this function are

Salaries, wages, and benefits (including any pay differentials and overtime) of court staff
(a) not reported in Functions 2–9, or
(b) whose time cannot be allocated to Functions 2–9 in increments of at least
25 percent time (.25 FTE);

Judicial benefits, county-paid

Allowable costs not reported in Functions 2–9.

(Nonjudicial staff) Cost items may include, for example,
juvenile traffic hearing officer
mental health hearing officer
court–appointed hearing officer (pro tem)
executive officer
court administrator
clerk of the court
administrative assistant
personnel staff
legal research personnel; staff attorney; planning and research staff
secretary
courtroom clerk
clerical support staff
calendar clerk
deputy clerk
accountant
cashier
counter clerk
microfilming staff
management analyst
probate conservatorship and guardianship investigators
probate examiner
training staff employed by the court

Personnel costs not reported in this function:

Any of the above not employed by the court

(Services and supplies) Cost items may include, for example,
office supplies
printing
postage
communications
publications and legal notices, by the court
miscellaneous departmental expenses

Ct. Rules

books, publications, training fees, and materials for court personnel (judicial and nonjudicial)

travel and transportation (judicial and nonjudicial)

professional dues

memberships and subscriptions

statutory multidistrict judges' association expenses

research, planning, and program coordination expenses

small claims advisor program costs

court–appointed expert witness fees (for the court's needs)

court–ordered forensic evaluations and other professional services (for the court's own use)

pro tem judges' expenses

micrographics expenses

public information services

vehicle use, including automobile insurance

equipment (leased, rented, or purchased) and furnishings, including interior painting, replacement/maintenance of flooring, and furniture repair

maintenance of office equipment

janitorial services

legal services for allowable court operations (County Counsel and contractual)

fidelity and faithful performance insurance (bonding and personal liability insurance on judges and court employees)

insurance on cash money and securities (hold–up and burglary)

general liability/comprehensive insurance for other than faulty maintenance or design of facility (e.g., "slip and fall," other injury, theft and damage of court equipment, slander, discrimination)

risk management services related to allowable insurance

space rental for court records

county records retention/destruction services

county messenger/mail service

court audits mandated under Government Code § 71383

Service and supply costs not reported in this function include

Civic association dues (unallowable)

Facility damages insurance (unallowable)

County central service department charges not appropriated in the court budget (unallowable)

Function 11.   County General Services ("Indirect Costs")

General county services are defined as all eligible accounting, payroll, budgeting, personnel, purchasing, and county administrator costs rendered in support of court operations. Costs for included services are allowable to the extent the service is provided to the court. The following costs, regardless of how characterized by the county or by which county department they are performed, are reported in this function only and are subject to the statutory maximum for indirect costs as specified in Government Code § 77003. To the extent costs are allowable under this rule, a county's approved Cost Plan may be used to determine the specific cost although the cost categories, or functions, may differ.

Cost items within the meaning of rule 10.810(a)(7) and the county departments often performing the service may include, for example,

County Administrator

budget development and administration

interdepartmental budget unit administration and operations

personnel (labor) relations and administration

Auditor–Controller

payroll

financial audits

warrant processing

fixed asset accounting

departmental accounting for courts, e.g., fines, fees, forfeitures, restitutions, penalties, and assessments; accounting for the Trial Court Special Revenue Fund

accounts payable

grant accounting

management reporting

banking

Personnel

recruitment and examination of applicants

maintenance and certification of eligible lists

position classification

salary surveys

leave accounting

employment physicals

handling of appeals

Treasurer/Tax Collector

warrant processing

bank reconciliation

retirement system administration

receiving, safeguarding, investing, and disbursing court funds

Purchasing Agent

process departmental requisitions

issue and analyze bids

make contracts and agreements for the purchase or rental of personal

property

store surplus property and facilitate public auctions

Unallowable costs

Unallowable court-related costs are those

(a) in support of county operations,

(b) expressly prohibited by statute,

(c) facility–related, or

(d) exceptions of the nature referenced in Functions 1–11.

Unallowable cost items, including any related data processing costs, are not reported in Functions 1–11 and may include, for example,

Communications

central communication control and maintenance for county emergency and general government radio equipment

Central Collections

processing accounts receivable for county departments (not courts)

County Administrator

legislative analysis and activities

preparation and operation of general directives and operating procedures

responses to questions from the Board, outside agencies, and the public

executive functions: Board of Supervisors

county advisory councils

Treasurer/Tax Collector

property tax determination, collection, etc.

General Services

rental and utilities support

coordinate county's emergency services

Property Management

negotiations for the acquisition, sale, or lease of property, except for space rented for storage of court records

making appraisals

negotiating utility relocations

assisting County Counsel in condemnation actions

preparing deeds, leases, licenses, easements
collecting rents
building lease management services (except for storage of court records)
Facility–related
construction services
right–of–way and easement services
purchase of land and buildings
construction
depreciation of buildings/use allowance
space rental/building rent (except for storage of court records)
building maintenance and repairs (except interior painting and to replace/repair flooring)
purchase, installation, and maintenance of H/V/A/C equipment
maintenance and repair of utilities
utility use charges (e.g., heat, light, water)
elevator purchase and maintenance
alterations/remodeling
landscaping and grounds maintenance services
exterior lighting and security
insurance on building damages (e.g., fire, earthquake, flood, boiler and machinery)
grounds' liability insurance
parking lot or facility maintenance
juror parking

(Formerly Rule 810, adopted, eff. July 1, 1988. As amended, eff. Jan. 1, 1989; July 1, 1990; July 1, 1991; July 1, 1995. Renumbered Rule 10.810 and amended, eff. Jan. 1, 2007.)

1 Renumbered by Stats.2002, c. 1082 (S.B.1732). See Government Code § 70311.

2 So in copy.

Advisory Committee Comment

Rule 10.810 is identical to former rule 810, except for the rule number. All references in statutes or rules to rule 810 apply to this rule.

Research References

2 Witkin Cal. Proc. 5th Courts § 178, (S 178) State Funding.

Rule 10.811. Reimbursement of costs associated with homicide trials

(a) Intent

This rule permits courts that meet certain criteria to request reimbursement of extraordinary costs of homicide trials.

(b) Criteria

A court that requests reimbursement of extraordinary costs of a homicide trial must meet all the following criteria:

(1) Be located in a county with a population of 300,000 or less;

(2) Have incurred extraordinary costs of a homicide trial; and

(3) Demonstrate an actual need for reimbursement.

(c) Submission

A request for reimbursement must be submitted by the court's presiding judge or executive officer to the Administrative Office of the Courts. All requests for reimbursement must comply with guidelines approved by the Judicial Council and include a completed *Request for Reimbursement of Extraordinary Homicide Trial Costs* form. *(Formerly Rule 6.711, adopted, eff. Jan. 1, 2005. Renumbered Rule 10.811 and amended, eff. Jan. 1, 2007.)*

Rule 10.815. Fees to be set by the court

(a) Authority

Under Government Code section 70631, a superior court may charge a reasonable fee for a service or product not to exceed the costs of providing the service or product, if the Judicial Council approves the fee.

(b) Approved fees

The Judicial Council authorizes courts to charge a reasonable fee not to exceed costs for the following products and services unless courts are prohibited by law from charging a fee for, or providing, the product or service:

(1) Forms;

(2) Packages of forms;

(3) Information materials;

(4) Publications, including books, pamphlets, and local rules;

(5) Compact discs;

(6) DVDs;

(7) Audiotapes;

(8) Videotapes;

(9) Microfiches;

(10) Envelopes;

(11) Postage;

(12) Shipping;

(13) Off–site retrieval of documents;

(14) Direct fax filing under rule 2.304 (fee per page);

(15) Returning filed-stamped copies of documents by fax to persons who request that a faxed copy be sent to them;

(16) Training programs for attorneys who serve as court-appointed temporary judges, including the materials and food provided to the participants; and

(17) Other training programs or events, including materials and food provided to the participants.

(c) Guidelines for determining costs

The fee charged for any product or service listed in (b) may not exceed the court's cost in providing the product or service. In determining the costs of a product or service, the court must:

(1) Identify the specific product or service; and

(2) Prepare an analysis of the direct and indirect costs on which the fee is based.

(d) Reasonableness

In deciding what specific fee or fees, if any, to charge for a product or service under (b), the court must determine that the fee charged is reasonable considering relevant factors such as the benefits to the court and the public from providing the product or service and the effects of charging the fee on public access to the court.

(e) Reporting requirement

Each court that charges a fee under this rule must provide the Administrative Office of the Courts with a description of the fee, how the amount of the fee was determined, and how the fee is applied.

(f) Public notice

The court must notify the public of any fee that it charges under this rule by providing information concerning the fee in a conspicuous place such as the court's fee schedule.

(g) Procedure for adoption of fee

If a court proposes to change any fee authorized under (b) that it is already charging or to charge any new fee authorized under (b), the court must follow the procedures for adopting or amending a local rule under rule 10.613 of the California Rules of Court. *(Formerly Rule 6.712, adopted, eff. Jan. 1, 2006. As amended, eff. July 1, 2006. Renumbered Rule 10.815 and amended, eff. Jan. 1, 2007.)*

Research References

Rutter, Cal. Practice Guide: Civ. Pro. Before Trial Ch. 9(I)-B, B. Preparing and Filing Motions.

2 Witkin Cal. Proc. 5th Courts § 180, Court Fees.

Rule 10.820.   Acceptance of credit cards by the superior courts

(a) Delegation of authority to Administrative Director of the Courts

The Administrative Director of the Courts is authorized, under rule 10.80, to approve on behalf of the Judicial Council requests from the superior courts to accept credit cards for the payment of court fees or to impose a charge for the use of credit cards. The authority is given to the Judicial Council by Government Code section 6159.

(b) Standards for use of credit cards

The Administrative Director of the Courts is authorized to approve requests under (a) for acceptance of credit cards if all of the following are true:

(1) The court (A) imposes a fee for the use of the credit card, or (B) demonstrates that the cost of acceptance of credit cards is not greater than the cost of acceptance of other means of payment of fees, or (C) demonstrates that it can absorb the cost of the acceptance of the credit card;

(2) The court has obtained a credit card acceptance contract that is competitive with other possible contracts the court could obtain; and

(3) The court provides alternative means for a person to pay court fees.

(c) Standards for charge for the use of credit cards

The Administrative Director of the Courts is authorized to approve requests under (a) for the imposition of a charge for the use of credit cards if both of the following are true:

(1) The proposed fee is not greater than the cost for acceptance of a credit card; and

(2) The proposed fee would not result in an undue hardship on people wishing to use credit cards for payment of fees.

(d) Referral to Judicial Council

The Administrative Director of the Courts may refer any request under (a) to the Judicial Council for its action.

(e) Existing approvals ratified

The approval of any board of supervisors for any superior court to accept credit cards or charge a fee for the use of credit cards that was effective as of December 31, 1999, is ratified by the council as of January 1, 2000. *(Formerly Rule 6.703, adopted, eff. Jan. 1, 2000. Renumbered Rule 10.820 and amended, eff. Jan. 1, 2007. As amended, eff. Jan. 1, 2009.)*

Research References

2 Witkin Cal. Proc. 5th Courts § 367, (S 367) Fees.

4 Witkin Cal. Proc. 5th Pleading § 19, in General.

Rule 10.821.   Acceptance of checks and other negotiable paper

(a) Conditions for acceptance

A personal check, bank cashier's check, money order, or traveler's check tendered in payment of any fee, fine, or bail deposit under Government Code section 71386 or Vehicle Code section 40510 or 40521 must be accepted by the court:

(1) If the personal check is drawn on a banking institution located in California by a person furnishing satisfactory proof of residence in California, is payable to the court without a second party endorsement, and is in an amount not exceeding the amount of the payment and is not postdated or staledated, unless the person drawing the check is known to have previously tendered worthless checks; or

(2) If the bank cashier's check or money order is drawn on a banking institution located in the United States and is in an amount not exceeding the amount of the payment; or

(3) If the person presenting the traveler's check shows satisfactory identification.

(b) Requiring satisfactory proof of good credit

Except for checks tendered under the conditions specified in Vehicle Code section 40521(a), a court may require that a person drawing a personal check furnish satisfactory proof of good credit by showing a valid recognized credit card or by any other reasonable means.

(c) Written policy for acceptance or rejection

A court may accept or reject any check or money order not meeting the requirements of this rule, under a written policy adopted by the court under Government Code section 71386(a). *(Formerly Rule 805, adopted, eff. July 1, 1981. Renumbered Rule 10.821 and amended, eff. Jan. 1, 2007.)*

Rule 10.830.   Disposal of surplus court personal property

(a) Disposal of surplus property

Except as provided in (b), a superior court may:

(1) Sell, at fair market value, any personal property of the court that is no longer needed for court use;

(2) Trade or exchange any surplus personal property of the court, according to such terms and conditions as are agreed on, for personal property of another court, the state, a county, a city, a federal agency, a community redevelopment agency, a housing authority, a community development commission, a surplus property authority, a school district, or any irrigation, flood control, county board of education, or other special district, if the property to be acquired by the court is needed for court use;

(3) Donate, sell at less than fair market value, or otherwise transfer to another court, the state, a county, a city, a federal agency, a community redevelopment agency, a housing authority, a community development commission, a surplus property authority, a school district, or any irrigation, flood control, county board of education, or other special district, according to such terms and conditions as are agreed on, any personal property of the court that is no longer needed for court use; and

(4) Dispose of any personal property of the court that is no longer needed for court use, and that has negligible or no economic value, in any manner the court deems appropriate.

(b) Exception for disposal of technology equipment acquired on or after July 1, 2000

A superior court that wishes to dispose of surplus technology equipment to which the court acquired title on or after July 1, 2000 must provide a written description of such technology equipment to the Administrative Director of the Courts. If, within 60 days of receipt of the description, the Administrative Director determines that another court of record of the State of California is in need of the surplus technology equipment, the court holding title to the equipment must donate it to the court determined to be in need. If the Administrative Director determines that no other court needs the equipment or makes no determination within 60 days of receiving the written description of it, the court holding title to the equipment may dispose of it as provided in (a), (c), and (d). The Administrative Director must provide to the courts a definition of the term "technology equipment" as used in this rule and must provide 30 days' notice of any amendment to the definition.

(c) Notice of disposal

Unless the property to be transferred under this rule is valued at $500 or less or the entity to which the property is to be transferred is another court of record of the State of California, the transferring superior court must, at least one week before the transfer, place a notice of its intended action:

(1) In three public places; or

(2) On the court's Web site; or

(3) In a newspaper of general circulation published in the county.

(d) Proceeds of disposal

Any proceeds of a sale or other transfer under this rule must be deposited in the superior court's operations fund. *(Formerly Rule 6.709, adopted, eff. Jan. 1, 2001. Renumbered Rule 10.830 and amended, eff. Jan. 1, 2007.)*

Research References

2 Witkin Cal. Proc. 5th Courts § 197, (S 197) Judicial Administration Rules.

Chapter 10

TRIAL COURT RECORDS MANAGEMENT

Rule
10.850. Trial court records.
10.851. Court indexes—automated maintenance.
10.854. Standards and guidelines for trial court records.
10.855. Superior court records sampling program.
10.856. Notice of superior court records destruction.

Rule 10.850. Trial court records

Unless otherwise provided, "court records" as used in this chapter consist of the records as defined in Government Code section 68151(a). *(Adopted, eff. Jan. 1, 2011.)*

Research References

2 Witkin Cal. Proc. 5th Courts § 197, (S 197) Judicial Administration Rules.
2 Witkin Cal. Proc. 5th Courts § 374, in General.

Rule 10.851. Court indexes—automated maintenance

(a) Authorized media

The clerk of each trial court may create, maintain, update, and make accessible the indexes required by law by photographic, microphotographic, photocopy, mechanical, magnetic, or electronic means. The clerk must make provision for preserving the information on a medium that will ensure its permanence and protect it from loss or damage arising from electronic failure or mechanical defect.

(b) Alphabetic index

A single alphabetic index may be maintained so long as the plaintiff-defendant distinction is retained.

(c) Public access

The indexes maintained under automated procedures must be accessible for public examination and use. *(Formerly Rule 1010, adopted, eff. Jan. 1, 1975. Renumbered Rule 999, eff. July 1, 1993. Renumbered Rule 6.751 and amended, eff. Jan. 1, 2001. Renumbered Rule 10.851 and amended, eff. Jan. 1, 2007.)*

Research References

2 Witkin Cal. Proc. 5th Courts § 197, (S 197) Judicial Administration Rules.

2 Witkin Cal. Proc. 5th Courts § 371, (S 371) Register and Index of Actions.

Rule 10.854. Standards and guidelines for trial court records

(a) The standards and guidelines

The Administrative Office of the Courts, in collaboration with trial court presiding judges and court executives, must prepare, maintain, and distribute a manual providing standards and guidelines for the creation, maintenance, and retention of trial court records (the *Trial Court Records Manual*), consistent with the Government Code and the rules of court and policies adopted by the Judicial Council. The manual should assist the courts and the public to have complete, accurate, efficient, and accessible court records. Before the manual is issued, it must be made available for comment from the trial courts.

(b) Contents of the *Trial Court Records Manual*

The *Trial Court Records Manual* must provide standards and guidelines for the creation, maintenance, and retention of trial court records. These standards and guidelines must ensure that all court records subject to permanent retention are retained and made available to the public in perpetuity as legally required.

(c) Updating the manual

The Administrative Office of the Courts, in collaboration with trial court presiding judges and court executives, must periodically update the *Trial Court Records Manual* to reflect changes in technology that affect the creation, maintenance, and retention of court records. Except for technical changes, corrections, or minor substantive changes not likely to create controversy, proposed changes in the manual must be made available for comment from the courts before the manual is updated or changed. Courts must be notified of any changes in the standards or guidelines, including all those relating to the permanent retention of records.

(d) Adherence to standards and guidelines

Trial courts must adhere to the requirements contained in the *Trial Court Records Manual*, except as otherwise provided in the manual. *(Adopted, eff. Jan. 1, 2011.)*

Research References

2 Witkin Cal. Proc. 5th Courts § 374, in General.

Rule 10.855. Superior court records sampling program

(a) Purpose

This rule establishes a program to preserve in perpetuity for study by historians and other researchers all superior court records filed before 1911 and a sample of superior court records filed after December 31, 1910, to document the progress and development of the judicial system, and to preserve evidence of significant events and social trends. This rule is not intended to restrict a court from preserving more records than the minimum required.

(b) Scope

"Records" of the superior court, as used in this rule, does not include records of limited civil, small claims, misdemeanor, or infraction cases.

(c) Comprehensive records

Each superior court must preserve forever comprehensive court records as follows:

(1) All records filed before 1911;

(2) If practicable, all records filed after 1910 and before 1950;

(3) All case indexes;

(4) All judgment books if the court maintains judgment records separate from the case files;

(5) All minute books if the court maintains minutes separate from the case files; and

(6) All registers of action if the court maintains them.

(d) Sample records

If a superior court destroys court records without preserving them in a medium described in (h), the court must preserve forever a sample of each year's court records as provided by this rule of all cases, including sealed, expunged, and other confidential records to the extent permitted by law.

(e) Court record defined

The "court record" under this rule consists of the following:

(1) All papers and documents in the case folder; but if no case folder is created by the court, all papers and documents that would have been in the case folder if one had been created; and

(2) The case folder, unless all information on the case folder is in papers and documents preserved in a medium described in (h); and

(3) If available, corresponding depositions, paper exhibits, daily transcripts, and tapes of electronically recorded proceedings.

(f) Sampling technique

Three courts assigned in rotation by the Judicial Council must preserve 100 percent of their court records for a calendar year ("longitudinal sample"). All other courts must preserve a systematic sample of 10 percent or more of each year's court records and a 2 percent subjective sample of the court records scheduled to be destroyed, as follows:

(1) The "systematic sample" must be selected as follows after grouping all cases scheduled to be destroyed by filing year:

(A) If the cases scheduled to be destroyed for a filing year number more than 1,000 cases, the sample must consist of all cases in which the last digit of the case number (0–9) coincides with the last digit of the year in which the case was filed.

(B) If the cases scheduled to be destroyed for a filing year number from 100 to 1,000, the sample must consist of cases selected by (1) dividing the number of cases filed by 100, rounding fractions down to the next lower number, and (2) counting the cases and preserving each case with a position number in the files or other record that corresponds with the number computed (for example, 670 cases ÷ 100 = 6.7; select every sixth case).

(C) If fewer than 100 cases of a filing year are scheduled to be destroyed, all of the cases must be preserved.

(D) If the records to be destroyed are old, unnumbered cases, the sample must consist of cases identified by counting the cases (0–9) and preserving each case with a position number in the file or other record that corresponds with the number determined under (A) or (B), unless fewer than 100 cases are to be destroyed.

(2) The "subjective sample" must consist of at least 2 percent of all cases scheduled to be destroyed, but not fewer than the court records of 20 cases, and must include (1) all cases accepted for review by the California Supreme Court, (2) "fat files" or the thickest perceived case files, and (3) cases deemed by the court to be of local, national, or international significance. These cases must be identified by stamp or mark to distinguish them from the systematic sample. The Judicial Council will provide each court with a list of cases accepted for review by the California Supreme Court each year.

(g) Augmented sample; designated advisory consultant

(1) The Judicial Council may designate a consultant to review, under the guidance of a qualified historian or archivist, court records scheduled for destruction and determine if the court's

systematic sample should be augmented to improve representation of the variety of cases filed.

(2) The court should give the designated consultant 60 days' notice of intent to destroy any court records that it does not plan to retain for the sample.

(3) The designated consultant's role is advisory to the court. If the consultant determines that the systematic sample does not represent the variety of cases filed in a sample year, the court should select a random sample of cases to augment the systematic sample.

(4) Final selection of the court records to augment the sample is to be made by the clerk of the superior court.

(h) Preservation medium

(1) Comprehensive court records under (c) filed before 1911 must be preserved in their original paper form unless the paper is not available.

(2) Court records that are part of the comprehensive sample filed after 1910, the systematic sample, and the subjective sample must be retained permanently in accord with the requirements of the *Trial Court Records Manual*.

(i) Storage

Until statewide or regional archival facilities are established, each court is responsible for maintaining its comprehensive and sample court records in a secure and safe environment consistent with the archival significance of the records. The court may deposit the court records in a suitable California archival facility such as a university, college, library, historical society, museum, archive, or research institution whether publicly supported or privately endowed. The court must ensure that the records are kept and preserved according to commonly recognized archival principles and practices of preservation.

(j) Access

The court must ensure the following:

(1) The comprehensive and sample court records are made reasonably available to all members of the public.

(2) Sealed and confidential records are made available to the public only as provided by law.

(3) If the records are preserved in a medium other than paper, equipment is provided to permit public viewing of the records.

(4) Reasonable provision is made for duplicating the records at cost.

(k) Choosing an archival facility

If a local archival facility is maintaining the court records, the court may continue to use that facility's services if it meets the storage and access requirements under (i) and (j). If the court solicits archival facilities interested in maintaining the comprehensive and sample court records, the court must follow the procedures specified under rule 10.856, except that the comprehensive and sample court records must not be destroyed. Courts may enter into agreements for long-term deposit of records subject to the storage and access provisions of this rule.

(l) Reporting requirement

Each superior court must submit semiannually to the Judicial Council a *Report to the Judicial Council: Superior Court Records Destroyed, Preserved, and Transferred* (form ~~982.8A~~ REC–003), including the following information:

(1) A list by year of filing of the court records destroyed;

(2) A list by year of filing and location of the court records of the comprehensive and sample court records preserved; and

(3) A list by year of filing and location of the court records transferred to entities under rule 10.856. *(Formerly Rule 243.5,*

adopted, eff. July 1, 1992. As amended, eff. Jan. 1, 1994; Jan. 1, 1995. Renumbered Rule 6.755, and amended, eff. Jan. 1, 2001. Renumbered Rule 10.855 and amended, eff. Jan. 1, 2007. As amended, eff. Jan. 1, 2011; July 1, 2013.)

Research References

2 Witkin Cal. Proc. 5th Courts § 376, Retention.
2 Witkin Cal. Proc. 5th Courts § 377, Transfer.
2 Witkin Cal. Proc. 5th Courts § 378, Destruction.

Rule 10.856. Notice of superior court records destruction

(a) Scope

"Records" of the superior court, as used in this rule, do not include records of limited civil, small claims, misdemeanor, or infraction cases.

(b) Notice

The superior court must give 30 days' written notice of its intent to destroy court records open to public inspection to entities maintained on a master list by the Judicial Council and to any other entities that have informed the court directly that they wish to be notified.

(c) Transfer to requesting entity

Records scheduled for destruction must be permanently transferred to the entity requesting possession of the records on written order of the presiding judge unless the request is denied for good cause shown. The cost of transferring the records must be paid by the requesting party.

(d) Request by two or more entities

If two or more entities request the same records, the presiding judge must order the transfer of those records to the entity that shows the greatest capability of caring for and preserving the records according to commonly recognized archival principles and practices of preservation and access, and that provides the greatest likelihood of making them available for historical or research purposes.

(e) Public access

No entity may receive the records unless the entity agrees to make the records reasonably available to all members of the public. Provision must be made for duplicating the records at cost.

(f) Destruction

If after 30 days no request for transfer of records scheduled for destruction has been received by the court, the clerk may destroy the records not designated for the historical and research program under rule 10.855, under a written order of the presiding judge of the court and in accordance with provisions of the Government Code.

(g) Extension of time

The time for retention of any of the court records specified in the notice may be extended by order of the court on its own motion, or on application of any interested member of the public for good cause shown and on such terms as are just. No fee may be charged for making the application.

(h) Forms

The court must use the following forms to implement the requirements of this rule:

(1) *Notice of Intent to Destroy Superior Court Records; Offer to Transfer Possession* (form REC–001(N), with a form on the reverse titled *Request for Transfer or Extension of Time for Retention of Superior Court Records* (form REC–001(R)), for optional use by the recipient of the notice; and

(2) *Notice of Hearing on Request for Transfer or Extension of Time for Retention of Superior Court Records; Court Order;*

Release and Receipt of Superior Court Records (form REC–002(N)). *(Formerly Rule 243.6, adopted, eff. Jan. 1, 1994. Renumbered Rule 6.756 and amended, eff. Jan. 1, 2001. As amended, eff. July 1, 2001. Renumbered Rule 10.856 and amended, eff. Jan. 1, 2007. As amended, eff. July 1, 2010.)*

Research References

2 Witkin Cal. Proc. 5th Courts § 197, (S 197) Judicial Administration Rules.
2 Witkin Cal. Proc. 5th Courts § 374, in General.
2 Witkin Cal. Proc. 5th Courts § 377, Transfer.

Chapter 11

TRIAL COURT AUTOMATION

Rule
10.870. Trial court automation standards.

Rule 10.870. Trial court automation standards

Each superior court that acquires, develops, enhances, or maintains automated accounting or case management systems through funding provided under Government Code section 68090.8 must comply with the standards approved by the Judicial Council. The approved standards are stated in *Judicial Council Trial Court Automation Standards* published by the Administrative Office of the Courts. *(Formerly Rule 1011, adopted, eff. March 1, 1992. Renumbered Rule 999.1, eff. July 1, 1993. Renumbered Rule 10.870 and amended, eff. Jan. 1, 2007.)*

Research References

2 Witkin Cal. Proc. 5th Courts § 197, (S 197) Judicial Administration Rules.

Chapter 12

TRIAL COURT MANAGEMENT OF CIVIL CASES

Rule
10.900. Case management and calendaring system.
10.901. Internal management procedures.
10.910. Assigned cases to be tried or dismissed—notification to presiding judge.

Rule 10.900. Case management and calendaring system

Each superior court must adopt a case management and calendaring system for general civil cases that will advance the goals stated in standard 2.1 of the California Standards of Judicial Administration. *(Formerly Rule 204.1, adopted, eff. July 1, 2002. Renumbered Rule 10.900 and amended, eff. Jan. 1, 2007.)*

Research References

Rutter, Cal. Practice Guide: Civil Trials & Evidence Ch. 1-L, L. Assignment to Trial Department.
2 Witkin Cal. Proc. 5th Courts § 197, (S 197) Judicial Administration Rules.
7 Witkin Cal. Proc. 5th Trial § 37, (S 37) Procedural Framework.
7 Witkin Cal. Proc. 5th Trial § 39, (S 39) Management and Distribution of Court Business.

Rule 10.901. Internal management procedures

Each court must:

(1) Maintain a calendar and caseflow management system that will ensure that a sufficient number of cases are set for trial, based on the court's experience, so that all departments will be occupied with judicial business;

(2) Adopt for judges and court personnel an internal operations manual of policies and procedures necessary for the efficient operation and management of the court;

(3) Maintain and periodically review for accuracy written local court procedures, policies, and operating practices not contained in local rules for quick, accurate, and complete reference; and

(4) Ensure that calendaring functions are performed as directed by the court and that personnel rendering direct and immediate service to the court are within its administrative control to the maximum extent consistent with the existing organizational structures. *(Formerly Rule 208, adopted, eff. Jan. 1, 1985. Renumbered Rule 204.2 and amended, eff. July 1, 2002. Renumbered Rule 10.901 and amended, eff. Jan. 1, 2007.)*

Research References

2 Witkin Cal. Proc. 5th Courts § 238, (S 238) in General.
7 Witkin Cal. Proc. 5th Trial § 39, (S 39) Management and Distribution of Court Business.

Rule 10.910. Assigned cases to be tried or dismissed—notification to presiding judge

(a) Assignment of cases for trial

In a court employing the master calendar, each case transferred to a trial department must be tried, ordered off the calendar, or dismissed unless, for good cause arising after the commencement of the trial, the judge of the trial department continues the case for further hearing or, with the consent of the judge supervising the master calendar, reassigns the case to the judge supervising the master calendar for further disposition.

(b) Notification to presiding judge

A judge who has finished or continued the trial of a case or any special matter must immediately notify the judge supervising the master calendar. The judge to whose department a cause is assigned for trial or for hearing must accept the assignment unless disqualified or, for other good cause stated to the judge supervising the master calendar, the judge supervising the master calendar determines that in the interest of justice the cause should not be tried or heard before the judge. When the judge has refused a cause and is not disqualified, the judge must state the reasons in writing unless the judge supervising the master calendar has concurred. *(Formerly Rule 226, adopted, eff. Jan. 1, 1985. As amended, eff. July 1, 2002. Renumbered Rule 10.910 and amended, eff. Jan. 1, 2007.)*

Research References

Rutter, Cal. Practice Guide: Civil Trials & Evidence Ch. 1-L, L. Assignment to Trial Department.
2 Witkin Cal. Proc. 5th Courts § 197, (S 197) Judicial Administration Rules.
2 Witkin Cal. Proc. 5th Courts § 233, Successive Inconsistent Decisions by Different Departments.
6 Witkin Cal. Proc. 5th Proceedings Without Trial § 281, Local Rules.
7 Witkin Cal. Proc. 5th Trial § 56, Duties of Trial Judge.

Chapter 13

TRIAL COURT MANAGEMENT OF CRIMINAL CASES

Rule
10.950. Role of presiding judge, supervising judge, criminal division, and master calendar department in courts having more than three judges.
10.951. Duties of supervising judge of the criminal division.

Rule
10.952. Meetings concerning the criminal court system.
10.953. Procedures for disposition of cases before the preliminary hearing.

Rule 10.950. Role of presiding judge, supervising judge, criminal division, and master calendar department in courts having more than three judges

The presiding judge of a court having more than three judges may designate one or more departments primarily to hear criminal cases. Two or more departments so designated must be the criminal division. The presiding judge may designate supervising judges for the criminal division, but retains final authority over all criminal and civil case assignments. *(Formerly Rule 227.1, adopted, eff. Jan. 1, 1985. Renumbered Rule 10.950 and amended, eff. Jan. 1, 2007.)*

Research References

2 Witkin Cal. Proc. 5th Courts § 197, (S 197) Judicial Administration Rules.

Rule 10.951. Duties of supervising judge of the criminal division

(a) Duties

In addition to any other duties assigned by the presiding judge or imposed by these rules, a supervising judge of the criminal division must assign criminal matters requiring a hearing or cases requiring trial to a trial department.

(b) Arraignments, pretrial motions, and readiness conferences

The presiding judge, supervising judge, or other designated judge must conduct arraignments, hear and determine any pretrial motions, preside over readiness conferences, and, where not inconsistent with law, assist in the disposition of cases without trial.

(c) Additional judges

To the extent that the business of the court requires, the presiding judge may designate additional judges under the direction of the supervising judge to perform the duties specified in this rule.

(d) Courts without supervising judge

In a court having no supervising judge, the presiding judge performs the duties of a supervising judge. *(Formerly Rule 227.2, adopted, eff. Jan. 1, 1985. Renumbered Rule 10.951 and amended, eff. Jan. 1, 2007. As amended, eff. Jan. 1, 2008.)*

Rule 10.952. Meetings concerning the criminal court system

The supervising judge or, if none, the presiding judge must designate judges of the court to attend regular meetings to be held with the district attorney, public defender, representatives of the local bar, probation department, court personnel, and other interested persons to identify and eliminate problems in the criminal court system and to discuss other problems of mutual concern. *(Formerly Rule 227.8, adopted, eff. Jan. 1, 1985. Renumbered Rule 10.952 and amended, eff. Jan. 1, 2007.)*

Rule 10.953. Procedures for disposition of cases before the preliminary hearing

(a) Disposition before preliminary hearing

Superior courts having more than three judges must, in cooperation with the district attorney and defense bar, adopt procedures to facilitate dispositions before the preliminary hearing and at all other stages of the proceedings. The procedures may include:

(1) Early, voluntary, informal discovery, consistent with part 2, title 6, chapter 10 of the Penal Code (commencing with section 1054); and

(2) The use of superior court judges as magistrates to conduct readiness conferences before the preliminary hearing and to assist, where not inconsistent with law, in the early disposition of cases.

(b) Case to be disposed of under rule 4.114

Pleas of guilty or no contest resulting from proceedings under (a) must be disposed of as provided in rule 4.114. *(Formerly Rule 227.10, adopted, eff. Jan. 1, 1985. As amended, eff. June 6, 1990; Jan. 1, 1991; July 1, 2001. Renumbered Rule 10.953 and amended, eff. Jan. 1, 2007.)*

Research References

2 Witkin Cal. Proc. 5th Courts § 197, (S 197) Judicial Administration Rules.

Chapter 14

MANAGEMENT OF SELF—HELP CENTERS

Rule
10.960.   Court self-help centers.

Rule 10.960.   Court self-help centers

(a) Scope and application

This rule applies to all court-based self-help centers whether the services provided by the center are managed by the court or by an entity other than the court.

(b) Purpose and core court function

Providing access to justice for self-represented litigants is a priority for California courts. The services provided by court self-help centers facilitate the timely and cost-effective processing of cases involving self-represented litigants and improve the delivery of justice to the public. Court programs, policies, and procedures designed to assist self-represented litigants and effectively manage cases involving self-represented litigants at all stages must be incorporated and budgeted as core court functions.

(c) Staffing

Court self-help centers provide assistance to self-represented litigants. A court self-help center must include an attorney and other qualified staff who provide information and education to self-represented litigants about the justice process, and who work within the court to provide for the effective management of cases involving self-represented litigants.

(d) Neutrality and availability

The information and education provided by court self-help centers must be neutral and unbiased, and services must be available to all sides of a case.

(e) Guidelines and procedures

The Administrative Office of the Courts, in collaboration with judges, court executives, attorneys, and other parties with demonstrated interest in services to self-represented litigants, must develop and disseminate guidelines and procedures for the operation of court self-help centers to the trial courts by March 1, 2008. The guidelines and procedures must address the following topics:

(1) Location and hours of operation;

(2) Scope of services;

(3) Attorney qualifications;

(4) Other staffing qualifications and supervision requirements;

(5) Language access;

(6) Contracts with entities other than the court that provide self-help services;

(7) Use of technology;

(8) Ethics;

(9) Efficiency of operation; and

(10) Security.

The Administrative Office of the Courts, in collaboration with judges, court executives, attorneys, and other parties with demonstrated interest in services to self-represented litigants, must review and update the guidelines and procedures at least every three years.

(f) Budget and funding

A court must include in its annual budget funding necessary for operation of its self-help center. In analyzing and making recommendations on the allocation of funding for a court self-help center, the Administrative Office of the Courts will consider the degree to which individual courts have been successful in meeting the guidelines and procedures for the operation of the self-help center. *(Adopted, eff. Jan. 1, 2008.)*

Research References

2 Witkin Cal. Proc. 5th Courts § 28, (S 28) in General.
2 Witkin Cal. Proc. 5th Courts § 197, (S 197) Judicial Administration Rules.

Division 5

APPELLATE COURT ADMINISTRATION

Chapter 1

RULES RELATING TO THE SUPREME COURT AND COURTS OF APPEAL

Rule
10.1000.   Transfer of causes.
10.1004.   Court of Appeal administrative presiding justice.
10.1008.   Courts of Appeal with more than one division.
10.1012.   Supervising progress of appeals.
10.1016.   Notice of failure to perform judicial duties.
10.1020.   Reviewing court clerk/administrator.

Rule
10.1024.   Court of Appeal minutes.
10.1028.   Preservation and destruction of Court of Appeal records.
10.1030.   Local rules of Courts of Appeal.

Rule 10.1000.   Transfer of causes

(a) Transfer by Supreme Court

(1) The Supreme Court may transfer a cause:

(A) To itself from a Court of Appeal;

(B) From itself to a Court of Appeal;

(C) Between Courts of Appeal; or

(D) Between divisions of a Court of Appeal.

(2) The clerk of the transferee court must promptly send each party a copy of the transfer order with the new case number, if any.

(b) Transfer by a Court of Appeal administrative presiding justice

(1) A Court of Appeal administrative presiding justice may transfer causes between divisions of that court as follows:

(A) If multiple appeals or writ petitions arise from the same trial court action or proceeding, the presiding justice may transfer the later appeals or petitions to the division assigned the first appeal or petition.

(B) If, because of recusals, a division does not have three justices qualified to decide a cause, the presiding justice may transfer it to a division randomly selected by the clerk.

(2) The clerk must promptly notify the parties of the division to which the cause was transferred. *(Formerly Rule 47.1, adopted, eff. Jan. 1, 2003. Renumbered Rule 10.1000 and amended, eff. Jan. 1, 2007.)*

Advisory Committee Comment

Subdivision (a). Subdivision (a)(1) implements article VI, section 12(a) of the Constitution. As used in article VI, section 12(a) and in the rule, the term "cause" is broadly construed to include " 'all cases, matters, and proceedings of every description' " adjudicated by the Courts of Appeal and the Supreme Court. *(In re Rose* (2000) 22 Cal.4th 430, 540, quoting *In re Wells* (1917) 174 Cal. 467, 471.)

Research References

Rutter, Cal. Practice Guide: Civil Appeals & Writs Ch. 1-D, D. Access to Appellate Courts and Considerations Impacting Success on Appeal.

Rutter, Cal. Practice Guide: Civil Appeals & Writs Ch. 5-B, B. Types of Motions, Applications and Requests.

Rutter, Cal. Practice Guide: Civil Appeals & Writs Ch. 11-A, A. the Decisionmaking Process.

Rutter, Cal. Practice Guide: Civil Appeals & Writs Ch. 13-E, E. Decision on the Merits.

9 Witkin Cal. Proc. 5th Appeal § 922, Nature and Grounds.

9 Witkin Cal. Proc. 5th Appeal § 923, Procedure.

9 Witkin Cal. Proc. 5th Appeal § 924, (S 924) Power of Court of Appeal.

2 Witkin Cal. Proc. 5th Courts § 197, (S 197) Judicial Administration Rules.

4 Witkin Cal. Proc. 5th Pleading § 374, (S 374) Review.

Rule 10.1004. Court of Appeal administrative presiding justice

(a) Designation

(1) In a Court of Appeal with more than one division, the Chief Justice may designate a presiding justice to act as administrative presiding justice. The administrative presiding justice serves at the pleasure of the Chief Justice for the period specified in the designation order.

(2) The administrative presiding justice must designate another member of the court to serve as acting administrative presiding justice in the administrative presiding justice's absence. If the administrative presiding justice does not make that designation, the Chief Justice must do so.

(3) In a Court of Appeal with only one division, the presiding justice acts as the administrative presiding justice.

(b) Responsibilities

The administrative presiding justice is responsible for leading the court, establishing policies, promoting access to justice for all members of the public, providing a forum for the fair and expeditious resolution of disputes, and maximizing the use of judicial and other resources.

(c) Duties

The administrative presiding justice must perform any duties delegated by a majority of the justices in the district with the Chief Justice's concurrence. In addition, the administrative presiding justice has responsibility for the following matters:

(1) *Personnel*

The administrative presiding justice has general direction and supervision of the clerk/administrator and all court employees except those assigned to a particular justice or division;

(2) *Unassigned matters*

The administrative presiding justice has the authority of a presiding justice with respect to any matter that has not been assigned to a particular division;

(3) *Judicial Council*

The administrative presiding justice cooperates with the Chief Justice and any officer authorized to act for the Chief Justice in connection with the making of reports and the assignment of judges or retired judges under article VI, section 6 of the California Constitution;

(4) *Transfer of cases*

The administrative presiding justice cooperates with the Chief Justice in expediting judicial business and equalizing the work of judges by recommending, when appropriate, the transfer of cases by the Supreme Court under article VI, section 12 of the California Constitution;

(5) *Administration*

The administrative presiding justice supervises the administration of the court's day-to-day operations, including personnel matters, but must secure the approval of a majority of the justices in the district before implementing any change in court policies;

(6) *Budget*

The administrative presiding justice has sole authority in the district over the budget as allocated by the Chair of the Judicial Council, including budget transfers, execution of purchase orders, obligation of funds, and approval of payments; and

(7) *Facilities*

The administrative presiding justice, except as provided in (d), has sole authority in the district over the operation, maintenance, renovation, expansion, and assignment of all facilities used and occupied by the district.

(d) Geographically separate divisions

Under the general oversight of the administrative presiding justice, the presiding justice of a geographically separate division:

(1) Generally directs and supervises all of the division's court employees not assigned to a particular justice;

(2) Has authority to act on behalf of the division regarding day-to-day operations;

(3) Administers the division budget for day-to-day operations, including expenses for maintenance of facilities and equipment; and

(4) Operates, maintains, and assigns space in all facilities used and occupied by the division. *(Formerly Rule 75, adopted, eff. Jan. 1, 2005. Renumbered Rule 10.1004 and amended, eff. Jan. 1, 2007.)*

Research References

2 Witkin Cal. Proc. 5th Courts § 333, (S 333) Presiding Justices.

Rule 10.1008. Courts of Appeal with more than one division

Appeals and original proceedings filed in a Court of Appeal with more than one division, or transferred to such a court without designation of a division, may be assigned to divisions in a way that will equalize the distribution of business among them. The Court of Appeal clerk must keep records showing the divisions in which cases and proceedings are pending. *(Formerly Rule 47, adopted, eff. Jan. 1, 2005. Renumbered Rule 10.1008, eff. Jan. 1, 2007.)*

Research References

Rutter, Cal. Practice Guide: Civil Appeals & Writs Ch. 5-B, B. Types of Motions, Applications and Requests.
Rutter, Cal. Practice Guide: Civil Appeals & Writs Ch. 11-A, A. the Decisionmaking Process.
2 Witkin Cal. Proc. 5th Courts § 333, (S 333) Presiding Justices.
2 Witkin Cal. Proc. 5th Courts § 359, (S 359) Courts of Appeal.

Rule 10.1012. Supervising progress of appeals

(a) Duty to ensure prompt filing

The administrative presiding justices of Courts of Appeal with more than one division in the same city and the presiding justices of all other Courts of Appeal are generally responsible for ensuring that all appellate records and briefs are promptly filed. Staff must be provided for that purpose, to the extent that funds are appropriated and available.

(b) Authority

Notwithstanding any other rule, the administrative presiding justices and presiding justices referred to in (a) may:

(1) Grant or deny applications to extend the time to file records, briefs, and other documents, except that a presiding justice may extend the time to file briefs in conjunction with an order to augment the record;

(2) Order the dismissal of an appeal or any other authorized sanction for noncompliance with these rules, if no application to extend time or for relief from default has been filed before the order is entered; and

(3) Grant relief from default or from a sanction other than dismissal imposed for the default. *(Formerly Rule 77, adopted, eff. Jan. 1, 2005. Renumbered Rule 10.1012 and amended, eff. Jan. 1, 2007.)*

Research References

Rutter, Cal. Practice Guide: Civil Appeals & Writs Ch. 5-C, C. Motion, Application and Request Procedures.
9 Witkin Cal. Proc. 5th Appeal § 769, (S 769) Supervision of Progress in Court of Appeal.
2 Witkin Cal. Proc. 5th Courts § 333, (S 333) Presiding Justices.

Rule 10.1016. Notice of failure to perform judicial duties

(a) Notice

(1) The Chief Justice or presiding justice must notify the Commission on Judicial Performance of a reviewing court justice's:

(A) Substantial failure to perform judicial duties, including any habitual neglect of duty; or

(B) Disability–caused absences totaling more than 90 court days in a 12–month period, excluding absences for authorized vacations and for attending schools, conferences, and judicial workshops.

(2) If the affected justice is a presiding justice, the administrative presiding justice must give the notice.

(b) Copy to justice

The Chief Justice, administrative presiding justice, or presiding justice must give the affected justice a copy of any notice under (a). *(Formerly Rule 78, adopted, eff. Jan. 1, 2005. Renumbered Rule 10.1016 and amended, eff. Jan. 1, 2007.)*

Research References

2 Witkin Cal. Proc. 5th Courts § 71, Commission on Judicial Performance.
2 Witkin Cal. Proc. 5th Courts § 333, (S 333) Presiding Justices.

Rule 10.1020. Reviewing court clerk/administrator

(a) Selection

A reviewing court may employ a clerk/administrator selected in accordance with procedures adopted by the court.

(b) Responsibilities

Acting under the general direction and supervision of the administrative presiding justice, the clerk/administrator is responsible for planning, organizing, coordinating, and directing, with full authority and accountability, the management of the clerk's office and all nonjudicial support activities in a manner that promotes access to justice for all members of the public, provides a forum for the fair and expeditious resolution of disputes, and maximizes the use of judicial and other resources.

(c) Duties

Under the direction of the administrative presiding justice, the clerk/administrator has the following duties:

(1) *Personnel*

The clerk/administrator directs and supervises all court employees assigned to the clerk/administrator by the administrative presiding justice and ensures that the court receives a full range of human resources support;

(2) *Budget*

The clerk/administrator develops, administers, and monitors the court budget and develops practices and procedures to ensure that annual expenditures are within the budget;

(3) *Contracts*

The clerk/administrator negotiates contracts on the court's behalf in accord with established contracting procedures and applicable laws;

(4) *Calendar management*

The clerk/administrator employs and supervises efficient calendar and caseflow management, including analyzing and evaluating pending caseloads and recommending effective calendar management techniques;

(5) *Technology*

The clerk/administrator coordinates technological and automated systems activities to assist the court;

(6) *Facilities*

The clerk/administrator coordinates facilities, space planning, court security, and business services support, including the purchase and management of equipment and supplies;

(7) *Records*

The clerk/administrator creates and manages uniform record-keeping systems, collecting data on pending and completed judicial business and the court's internal operation as the court and Judicial Council require;

(8) *Recommendations*

The clerk/administrator identifies problems and recommends policy, procedural, and administrative changes to the court;

(9) *Public relations*

The clerk/administrator represents the court to internal and external customers—including the other branches of government—on issues pertaining to the court;

(10) *Liaison*

The clerk/administrator acts as liaison with other governmental agencies;

(11) *Committees*

The clerk/administrator provides staff for judicial committees;

(12) *Administration*

The clerk/administrator develops and implements administrative and operational programs and policies for the court and the clerk's office; and

(13) *Other*

The clerk/administrator performs other duties as the administrative presiding justice directs.

(d) Geographically separate divisions

Under the general oversight of the clerk/administrator, an assistant clerk/administrator of a geographically separate division has responsibility for the nonjudicial support activities of that division. *(Formerly Rule 76.1, adopted, eff. Jan. 1, 2005. Renumbered Rule 10.1020 and amended, eff. Jan. 1, 2007.)*

Research References

2 Witkin Cal. Proc. 5th Courts § 358, (S 358) Supreme Court.
2 Witkin Cal. Proc. 5th Courts § 359, (S 359) Courts of Appeal.

Rule 10.1024. Court of Appeal minutes

(a) Purpose

Court of Appeal minutes should record the court's significant public acts and permit the public to follow the major events in the history of cases coming before the court.

(b) Required contents of minutes

The minutes must include:

(1) The filing date of each opinion, showing whether it was ordered published;

(2) Orders granting or denying rehearings or modifying opinions;

(3) Orders affecting an opinion's publication status, if issued after the opinion was filed;

(4) Summaries of all courtroom proceedings, showing at a minimum:

(A) The cases called for argument;

(B) The justices hearing argument;

(C) The name of the attorney arguing for each party; and

(D) Whether the case was submitted at the close of argument or the court requested further briefing;

(5) The date of submission, if other than the date of argument;

(6) Orders vacating submission, including the reason for vacating and the resubmission date;

(7) Orders dismissing appeals for lack of jurisdiction;

(8) Orders consolidating cases;

(9) Orders affecting a judgment or its finality date; and

(10) Orders changing or correcting any of the above.

(c) Optional contents of minutes

At the court's discretion, the minutes may include such other matter as:

(1) Assignments of justices by the Chief Justice;

(2) Reports of the Commission on Judicial Appointments confirming justices; and

(3) Memorials. *(Formerly Rule 71, adopted, eff. Jan. 1, 2005. Renumbered Rule 10.1024 and amended, eff. Jan. 1, 2007.)*

Rule 10.1028. Preservation and destruction of Court of Appeal records

(a) Form or forms in which records may be preserved

(1) Court of Appeal records may be created, maintained, and preserved in any form or forms of communication or representation, including paper or optical, electronic, magnetic, micrographic, or photographic media or other technology, if the form or forms of representation or communication satisfy the standards or guidelines for the creation, maintenance, reproduction, and preservation of court records established under rule 10.854.

(2) If records are preserved in a medium other than paper, the following provisions of Government Code section 68150 apply: subdivisions (c)–(*l*), excluding subdivision (i)(1).

(b) Methods for signing, subscribing, or verifying documents

Any notice, order, ruling, decision, opinion, memorandum, certificate of service, or similar document issued by an appellate court or by a judicial officer of an appellate court may be signed, subscribed, or verified using a computer or other technology in accordance with procedures, standards, and guidelines established by the Judicial Council. Notwithstanding any other provision of law, all notices, orders, rulings, decisions, opinions, memoranda, certificates of service, or similar documents that are signed, subscribed, or verified by computer or other technological means under this subdivision shall have the same validity, and the same legal force and effect, as paper documents signed, subscribed, or verified by an appellate court or a judicial officer of the court.

(c) Permanent records

The Court of Appeal clerk must permanently keep the court's minutes and a register of appeals and original proceedings.

(d) Time to keep other records

(1) Except as provided in (2), the clerk may destroy all other records in a case 10 years after the decision becomes final, as ordered by the administrative presiding justice or, in a court with only one division, by the presiding justice.

(2) In a criminal case in which the court affirms a judgment of conviction, the clerk must keep the original reporter's transcript for 20 years after the decision becomes final. *(Formerly Rule 70, adopted, eff. Jan. 1, 2005. Renumbered Rule 10.1028, eff. Jan. 1, 2007. As amended, eff. Jan. 1, 2013.)*

Rule 10.1030. Local rules of Courts of Appeal

(a) Publication

(1) A Court of Appeal must submit any local rule it adopts to the Reporter of Decisions for publication in the advance pamphlets of the Official Reports.

(2) As used in this rule, "publication" means printing in the manner in which amendments to the California Rules of Court are printed.

(b) Effective date

A local rule cannot take effect sooner than 45 days after the publication date of the advance pamphlet in which it is printed. *(Adopted, eff. Jan. 1, 2007.)*

Research References

2 Witkin Cal. Proc. 5th Courts § 197, (S 197) Judicial Administration Rules.
2 Witkin Cal. Proc. 5th Courts § 331, in General.

Chapter 2

RULES RELATING TO THE SUPERIOR COURT APPELLATE DIVISION

Explanatory Note

For disposition and derivation tables relating to Appellate Rule revisions, adopted by the Judicial Council Feb. 22, 2008, eff. Jan. 1, 2009, see tables following Division 2, commencing with Rule 8.800. (If using an electronic publication, see Refs & Annos (References, Annotations, or Tables) following Division 2.)

Rule 10.1100.   Assignments to the appellate division

(a) Goal

In making assignments to the appellate division, the Chief Justice will consider the goal of promoting the independence and the quality of the appellate division.

(b) Factors considered

Factors considered in making the assignments may include:

(1) Length of service as a judge;

(2) Reputation in the judicial community;

(3) Degree of separateness of the appellate division work from the judge's regular assignments; and

(4) Any recommendation of the presiding judge.

(c) Who may be assigned

Judges assigned may include judges from another county, judges retired from the superior court or a court of higher jurisdiction, or a panel of judges from different superior courts who sit in turn in each of those superior courts.

(d) Terms of service

In specifying terms of service to the appellate division, the Chief Justice will consider the needs of the court. *(Adopted, eff. Jan. 1, 2009.)*

Advisory Committee Comment

The Chief Justice is responsible for assigning judges to the appellate division as provided in article VI, section 4 of the California Constitution and by statute.

Research References

2 Witkin Cal. Proc. 5th Courts § 197, (S 197) Judicial Administration Rules.
2 Witkin Cal. Proc. 5th Courts § 339, (S 339) Organization.

Rule 10.1104.   Presiding judge

(a) Designation of acting presiding judge

(1) The presiding judge of the appellate division must designate another member of the appellate division to serve as acting presiding judge in the absence of the presiding judge. If the presiding judge does not make that designation, the appellate division judge among those present who has the greatest seniority in the appellate division must act as presiding judge. When the judges are of equal seniority in the appellate division, the judge who is also senior in service in the superior court must act as presiding judge.

(2) As used in these rules, "presiding judge" includes acting presiding judge.

(b) Responsibilities

The presiding judge of the appellate division may convene the appellate division at any time and must supervise the business of the division. *(Adopted, eff. Jan. 1, 2009.)*

Advisory Committee Comment

Under Code of Civil Procedure section 77(a), the Chief Justice is responsible for designating one of the judges of each appellate division as the presiding judge.

Research References

2 Witkin Cal. Proc. 5th Courts § 340, (S 340) Operation.

Rule 10.1108.   Sessions

The appellate division of each superior court must hold a session at least once each quarter unless there are no matters set for oral argument that quarter. The time and place of any session is determined by the presiding judge of the appellate division. *(Adopted, eff. Jan. 1, 2009.)*

Research References

Rutter, Cal. Practice Guide: Civil Appeals & Writs Ch. 16-G, G. Oral Argument.
9 Witkin Cal. Proc. 5th Appeal § 763, in General.
9 Witkin Cal. Proc. 5th Appeal § 1017, Sessions and Calendar.
2 Witkin Cal. Proc. 5th Courts § 197, (S 197) Judicial Administration Rules.
2 Witkin Cal. Proc. 5th Courts § 340, (S 340) Operation.

Ct. Rules

STANDARDS OF JUDICIAL ADMINISTRATION

Title 2

STANDARDS FOR PROCEEDINGS IN THE TRIAL COURTS

Standard 2.1.   Case management and delay reduction—statement of general principles

(a)   Elimination of all unnecessary delays

Trial courts should be guided by the general principle that from the commencement of litigation to its resolution, whether by trial or settlement, any elapsed time other than reasonably required for pleadings, discovery, preparation, and court events is unacceptable and should be eliminated.

(b)   Court responsible for the pace of litigation

To enable the just and efficient resolution of cases, the court, not the lawyers or litigants, should control the pace of litigation. A strong judicial commitment is essential to reducing delay and, once achieved, maintaining a current docket.

(c)   Presiding judge's role

The presiding judge of each court should take an active role in advancing the goals of delay reduction and in formulating and implementing local rules and procedures to accomplish the following:

(1) The expeditious and timely resolution of cases, after full and careful consideration consistent with the ends of justice;

(2) The identification and elimination of local rules, forms, practices, and procedures that are obstacles to delay reduction, are inconsistent with statewide case management rules, or prevent the court from effectively managing its cases;

(3) The formulation and implementation of a system of tracking cases from filing to disposition; and

(4) The training of judges and nonjudicial administrative personnel in delay reduction rules and procedures adopted in the local jurisdiction. *(Formerly § 2, adopted, eff. July 1, 1987. As amended, eff. Jan. 1, 1994; Jan. 1, 2004. Renumbered Standard 2.1 and amended, eff. Jan. 1, 2007.)*

Standard 2.2.   Trial court case disposition time goals

(a)   Trial Court Delay Reduction Act

The recommended goals for case disposition time in the trial courts in this standard are adopted under Government Code sections 68603 and 68620.

(b)   Statement of purpose

The recommended time goals are intended to guide the trial courts in applying the policies and principles of standard 2.1. They are administrative, justice-oriented guidelines to be used in the management of the courts. They are intended to improve the administration of justice by encouraging prompt disposition of all matters coming before the courts. The goals apply to all cases filed and are not meant to create deadlines for individual cases. Through its case management practices, a court may achieve or exceed the goals stated in this standard for the overall disposition of cases. The goals should be applied in a fair, practical, and flexible manner. They are not to be used as the basis for sanctions against any court or judge.

(c)   Definition

The definition of "general civil case" in rule 1.6 applies to this section. It includes both unlimited and limited civil cases.

(d)   Civil cases—processing time goals

The goal of each trial court should be to process general civil cases so that all cases are disposed of within two years of filing.

(e)   Civil cases—rate of disposition

Each trial court should dispose of at least as many civil cases as are filed each year and, if necessary to meet the case-processing goal in (d), dispose of more cases than are filed. As the court disposes of inactive cases, it should identify active cases that may require judicial attention.

(f)   General civil cases—case disposition time goals

The goal of each trial court should be to manage general civil cases, except those exempt under (g), so that they meet the following case disposition time goals:

(1) *Unlimited civil cases:*

The goal of each trial court should be to manage unlimited civil cases from filing so that:

(A) 75 percent are disposed of within 12 months;

(B) 85 percent are disposed of within 18 months; and

(C) 100 percent are disposed of within 24 months.

(2) *Limited civil cases:*

The goal of each trial court should be to manage limited civil cases from filing so that:

(A) 90 percent are disposed of within 12 months;

(B) 98 percent are disposed of within 18 months; and

(C) 100 percent are disposed of within 24 months.

(3) *Individualized case management*

The goals in (1) and (2) are guidelines for the court's disposition of all unlimited and limited civil cases filed in that court. In managing individual civil cases, the court must consider each case on its merits. To enable the fair and efficient resolution of civil cases, each case should be set for trial as soon as appropriate for that individual case consistent with rule 3.729.

(g)   Exceptional civil cases

A general civil case that meets the criteria in rules 3.715 and 3.400 and that involves exceptional circumstances or will require continuing review is exempt from the time goals in (d) and (f). Every exceptional case should be monitored to ensure its timely disposition consistent with the exceptional circumstances, with the goal of disposing of the case within three years.

(h)   Small claims cases

The goals for small claims cases are:

(1) 90 percent disposed of within 75 days after filing; and

(2) 100 percent disposed of within 95 days after filing.

(i) Unlawful detainer cases

The goals for unlawful detainer cases are:

(1) 90 percent disposed of within 30 days after filing; and

(2) 100 percent disposed of within 45 days after filing.

(j) Felony cases—processing time goals

Except for capital cases, all felony cases disposed of should have a total elapsed processing time of no more than one year from the defendant's first arraignment to disposition.

(k) Misdemeanor cases

The goals for misdemeanor cases are:

(1) 90 percent disposed of within 30 days after the defendant's first arraignment on the complaint;

(2) 98 percent disposed of within 90 days after the defendant's first arraignment on the complaint; and

(3) 100 percent disposed of within 120 days after the defendant's first arraignment on the complaint.

(l) Felony preliminary examinations

The goal for felony cases at the time of the preliminary examination (excluding murder cases in which the prosecution seeks the death penalty) should be disposition by dismissal, by interim disposition by certified plea of guilty, or by finding of probable cause, so that:

(1) 90 percent of cases are disposed of within 30 days after the defendant's first arraignment on the complaint;

(2) 98 percent of cases are disposed of within 45 days after the defendant's first arraignment on the complaint; and

(3) 100 percent of cases are disposed of within 90 days after the defendant's first arraignment on the complaint.

(m) Exceptional criminal cases

An exceptional criminal case is not exempt from the time goal in (j), but case progress should be separately reported under the Judicial Branch Statistical Information System (JBSIS) regulations.

(n) Cases removed from court's control excluded from computation of time

If a case is removed from the court's control, the period of time until the case is restored to court control should be excluded from the case disposition time goals. The matters that remove a case from the court's control for the purposes of this section include:

(1) Civil cases:

(A) The filing of a notice of conditional settlement under rule 3.1385;

(B) An automatic stay resulting from the filing of an action in a federal bankruptcy court;

(C) The removal of the case to federal court;

(D) An order of a federal court or higher state court staying the case;

(E) An order staying the case based on proceedings in a court of equal standing in another jurisdiction;

(F) The pendency of contractual arbitration under Code of Civil Procedure section 1281.4;

(G) The pendency of attorney fee arbitration under Business and Professions Code section 6201;

(H) A stay by the reporting court for active military duty or incarceration; and

(I) For 180 days, the exemption for uninsured motorist cases under rule 3.712(b).

(2) Felony or misdemeanor cases:

(A) Issuance of warrant;

(B) Imposition of a civil assessment under Penal Code section 1214.1;

(C) Pendency of completion of diversion under Penal Code section 1000 et seq.;

(D) Evaluation of mental competence under Penal Code section 1368;

(E) Evaluation as a narcotics addict under Welfare and Institutions Code sections 3050 and 3051;

(F) 90–day diagnostic and treatment program under Penal Code section 1203.3;

(G) 90–day evaluation period for a juvenile under Welfare and Institutions Code section 707.2;

(H) Stay by a higher court or by a federal court for proceedings in another jurisdiction;

(I) Stay by the reporting court for active military duty or incarceration; and

(J) Time granted by the court to secure counsel if the defendant is not represented at the first appearance.

(o) Problems

A court that finds its ability to comply with these goals impeded by a rule of court or statute should notify the Judicial Council. *(Formerly § 2.1, adopted, eff. July 1, 1987. As amended, eff. Jan. 1, 1988; July 1, 1988; Jan. 1, 1989; Jan. 1, 1990; July 1, 1991; Jan. 1, 2004. Renumbered Standard 2.2 and amended, eff. Jan. 1, 2007.)*

Standard 2.10. Procedures for determining the need for an interpreter and a preappearance interview

(a) When an interpreter is needed

An interpreter is needed if, after an examination of a party or witness, the court concludes that:

(1) The party cannot understand and speak English well enough to participate fully in the proceedings and to assist counsel; or

(2) The witness cannot speak English so as to be understood directly by counsel, court, and jury.

(b) When an examination is required

The court should examine a party or witness on the record to determine whether an interpreter is needed if:

(1) A party or counsel requests such an examination; or

(2) It appears to the court that the party or witness may not understand and speak English well enough to participate fully in the proceedings.

(c) Examination of party or witness

To determine if an interpreter is needed, the court should normally include questions on the following:

(1) Identification (for example: name, address, birthdate, age, place of birth);

(2) Active vocabulary in vernacular English (for example: "How did you come to the court today?" "What kind of work do you do?" "Where did you go to school?" "What was the highest grade you completed?" "Describe what you see in the courtroom." "What have you eaten today?"). Questions should be phrased to avoid "yes" or "no" replies;

(3) The court proceedings (for example: the nature of the charge or the type of case before the court, the purpose of the proceedings and function of the court, the rights of a party or criminal defendant, and the responsibilities of a witness).

(d) Record of examination

After the examination, the court should state its conclusion on the record. The file in the case should be clearly marked and data entered electronically when appropriate by court personnel to ensure that an interpreter will be present when needed in any subsequent proceeding.

(e) Good cause for preappearance interview

For good cause, the court should authorize a preappearance interview between the interpreter and the party or witness. Good cause exists if the interpreter needs clarification on any interpreting issues, including: colloquialisms, culturalisms, dialects, idioms, linguistic capabilities and traits, regionalisms, register, slang, speech patterns, or technical terms. *(Formerly § 18, adopted, eff. Jan. 1, 1999. Renumbered Standard 2.10 and amended, eff. Jan. 1, 2007.)*

Standard 2.11. Interpreted proceedings—instructing participants on procedure

(a) Instructions to interpreters

The court or the court's designee should give the following instructions to interpreters, either orally or in writing:

(1) Do not discuss the pending proceedings with a party or witness.

(2) Do not disclose communications between counsel and client.

(3) Do not give legal advice to a party or witness. Refer legal questions to the attorney or to the court.

(4) Inform the court if you are unable to interpret a word, expression, special terminology, or dialect, or have doubts about your linguistic expertise or ability to perform adequately in a particular case.

(5) Interpret all words, including slang, vulgarisms, and epithets, to convey the intended meaning.

(6) Use the first person when interpreting statements made in the first person. (For example, a statement or question should not be introduced with the words, "He says . . .")

(7) Direct all inquiries or problems to the court and not to the witness or counsel. If necessary, you may request permission to approach the bench with counsel to discuss a problem.

(8) Position yourself near the witness or party without blocking the view of the judge, jury, or counsel.

(9) Inform the court if you become fatigued during the proceedings.

(10) When interpreting for a party at the counsel table, speak loudly enough to be heard by the party or counsel but not so loudly as to interfere with the proceedings.

(11) Interpret everything, including objections.

(12) If the court finds good cause under rule 2.893(e), hold a preappearance interview with the party or witness to become familiar with speech patterns and linguistic traits and to determine what technical or special terms may be used. Counsel may be present at the preappearance interview.

(13) During the preappearance interview with a non–English–speaking witness, give the witness the following instructions on the procedure to be followed when the witness is testifying:

    (A) The witness must speak in a loud, clear voice so that the entire court and not just the interpreter can hear.

    (B) The witness must direct all responses to the person asking the question, not to the interpreter.

    (C) The witness must direct all questions to counsel or to the court and not to the interpreter. The witness may not

seek advice from or engage in any discussion with the interpreter.

(14) During the preappearance interview with a non–English–speaking party, give the following instructions on the procedure to be used when the non–English–speaking party is not testifying:

    (A) The interpreter will interpret all statements made in open court.

    (B) The party must direct any questions to counsel. The interpreter will interpret all questions to counsel and the responses. The party may not seek advice from or engage in discussion with the interpreter.

(b) Instructions to counsel

The court or the court's designee should give the following instructions to counsel, either orally or in writing:

(1) When examining a non–English–speaking witness, direct all questions to the witness and not to the interpreter. (For example, do not say to the interpreter, "Ask him if . . .")

(2) If there is a disagreement with the interpretation, direct any objection to the court and not to the interpreter. Ask permission to approach the bench to discuss the problem.

(3) If you have a question regarding the qualifications of the interpreter, you may request permission to conduct a supplemental examination on the interpreter's qualifications. *(Formerly § 18.1, adopted, eff. Jan. 1, 1999. Renumbered Standard 2.11 and amended, eff. Jan. 1, 2007.)*

Standard 2.20. Trial management standards

(a) General principles

The trial judge has the responsibility to manage the trial proceedings. The judge should take appropriate action to ensure that all parties are prepared to proceed, the trial commences as scheduled, all parties have a fair opportunity to present evidence, and the trial proceeds to conclusion without unnecessary interruption. When the trial involves a jury, the trial judge should manage proceedings with particular emphasis on the needs of the jury.

(b) Techniques of trial management

The trial judge should employ the following trial management techniques:

(1) Participate with trial counsel in a trial management conference before trial.

(2) After consultation with counsel, set reasonable time limits.

(3) Arrange the court's docket to start trial as scheduled and inform parties of the number of hours set each day for the trial.

(4) Ensure that once trial has begun, momentum is maintained.

(5) Be receptive to using technology in managing the trial and the presentation of evidence.

(6) Attempt to maintain continuity in days of trial and hours of trial.

(7) Schedule arguments on legal issues at the beginning or end of the day so as not to interrupt the presentation of evidence.

(8) Permit sidebar conferences only when necessary, and keep them as short as possible.

(9) In longer trials, consider scheduling trial days to permit jurors time for personal business. *(Formerly § 8.9, adopted, eff. July 1, 1997. Renumbered Standard 2.20 and amended, eff. Jan. 1, 2007.)*

Standard 2.25. Uninterrupted jury selection

When practical, the trial judge, with the cooperation of the other judges of the court, should schedule court business to allow for jury selection uninterrupted by other court business. *(For-*

merly § 8.6, adopted, eff. July 1, 1990. Renumbered Standard 2.25 and amended, eff. Jan. 1, 2007.)

Standard 2.30.   Judicial comment on verdict or mistrial

At the conclusion of a trial, or on declaring a mistrial for failure of a jury to reach a verdict, it is appropriate for the trial judge to thank jurors for their public service, but the judge's comments should not include praise or criticism of the verdict or the failure to reach a verdict. *(Formerly § 14, adopted, eff. Jan. 1, 1976. Renumbered Standard 2.30 and amended, eff. Jan. 1, 2007.)*

Title 3

STANDARDS FOR CIVIL CASES

Standard

3.1.   Appearance by telephone.

3.10.   Complex civil litigation.

3.25.   Examination of prospective jurors in civil cases.

Standard 3.1.   Appearance by telephone

(a) Recommended criteria for telephone equipment

Each court should have adequate telephone equipment for use in hearings at which counsel may appear by telephone. This equipment should:

(1) Permit each person participating in the hearing, whether in person or by telephone, to hear all other persons;

(2) Handle at least three incoming calls at one time and place those calls into a conference call in a simple and quick manner;

(3) Have a silent (visible) ringer;

(4) Be simple to learn and use;

(5) Be reasonable in cost; and

(6) Have full-duplex, simultaneous bidirectional speaker capability.

(b) Optional features for telephone equipment

It is desirable if the telephone equipment can:

(1) Dial previously stored telephone numbers;

(2) Record conversations;

(3) Be moved easily from location to location; and

(4) Automatically queue incoming calls.

(c) Award of attorney's fees

A court should consider, in awarding attorney's fees under any applicable provision of law, whether an attorney is claiming fees for appearing in person in a proceeding in which that attorney could have appeared by telephone.

(d) Local procedures for telephone appearance

Each court should adopt a local rule or uniform local written policy specifying the following:

(1) Whether the court or the attorney initiates the telephone call for a telephone appearance;

(2) Whether the court sets a specified time for a telephone appearance or a time range; and

(3) How the parties are notified, in advance of the hearing, of the time or time range of the telephone appearance. In those courts using a tentative ruling recording system, that notice should be part of the tentative ruling recording. *(Formerly § 21, adopted, eff. Jan. 1, 1989. As amended, eff. July 1, 1992. Renumbered Standard 3.1 and amended, eff. Jan. 1, 2007. As amended, eff. Jan. 1, 2008.)*

Standard 3.10.   Complex civil litigation

(a) Judicial management

In complex litigation, judicial management should begin early and be applied continuously and actively, based on knowledge of the circumstances of each case.

(b) All–purpose assignment

Complex litigation should be assigned to one judge for all purposes. If such an assignment is not possible, a single judge should be assigned to hear law and motion matters and discovery matters.

(c) Selection of judges for complex litigation assignments

In selecting judges for complex litigation assignments, the presiding judge should consider the needs of the court and the judge's ability, interest, training, experience (including experience with complex civil cases), and willingness to participate in educational programs related to the management of complex cases. Commissioners should not be employed in any phase of complex litigation, except under the judge's direct supervision to assist in the management of the case.

(d) Establishing time limits

Time limits should be regularly used to expedite major phases of complex litigation. Time limits should be established early, tailored to the circumstances of each case, firmly and fairly maintained, and accompanied by other methods of sound judicial management.

(e) Preparation for trial

Litigants in complex litigation cases should be required to minimize evidentiary disputes and to organize efficiently their exhibits and other evidence before trial.

(f) Dilatory tactics

Judges involved in complex litigation should be sensitive to dilatory or abusive litigation tactics and should be prepared to invoke disciplinary procedures for violations.

(g) Educational programs

Judges should be encouraged to attend educational programs on the management of complex litigation.

(h) Staff assignment

Judges assigned to handle complex cases should be given research attorney and administrative staff assistance when possible. *(Formerly § 19, adopted, eff. July 1, 1982. As amended, eff. Jan. 1, 1995; Jan. 1, 2000. Renumbered Standard 3.10 and amended, eff. Jan. 1, 2007.)*

Standard 3.25.   Examination of prospective jurors in civil cases

(a) In general

(1) *Methods and scope of examination*

The examination of prospective jurors in a civil case may be oral, by written questionnaire, or by both methods, and should include all questions necessary to ensure the selection of a fair and impartial jury. The *Juror Questionnaire for Civil Cases* (form MC–001) may be used. During any supplemental examination conducted by counsel for the parties, the trial judge should permit liberal and probing examination calculated to discover possible bias or prejudice with regard to the circumstances of the particular case.

(2) *Examination by counsel*

When counsel requests to be allowed to conduct a supplemental voir dire examination, the trial judge should permit counsel to conduct such examination without requiring prior submission of the questions to the judge unless a particular counsel has demonstrated unwillingness to avoid the type of examination proscribed in (f). In exercising his or her sound discretion as to the form and subject matter of voir dire questions, the trial judge should consider, among other criteria: (1) any unique or complex elements, legal or factual, in the case, and (2) the individual responses or conduct of jurors that may evince attitudes inconsistent with suitability to serve as a fair and impartial juror in the particular case. Questions regarding personal relationships of jurors should be relevant to the subject matter of the case.

(b) Pre–voir dire conference

Before the examination the trial judge should, outside the prospective jurors' hearing and with a court reporter present, confer with counsel, at which time specific questions or areas of inquiry may be proposed that the judge in his or her discretion may inquire of the jurors. Thereafter, the judge should advise counsel of the questions or areas to be inquired into during the examination and voir dire procedure. The judge should also obtain from counsel the names of the witnesses whom counsel then plan to call at trial and a brief outline of the nature of the case, including any alleged injuries or damages and, in an eminent domain action, the respective contentions of the parties concerning the value of the property taken and any alleged severance damages and special benefits.

(c) Examination of jurors

Except as otherwise provided in (d), the trial judge's examination of prospective jurors should include the following areas of inquiry and any other matters affecting their qualifications to serve as jurors in the case:

(1) *To the entire jury panel after it has been sworn and seated:*

I am now going to question the prospective jurors who are seated in the jury box concerning their qualifications to serve as jurors in this case. All members of this jury panel, however, should pay close attention to my questions, making note of the answers you would give if these questions were put to you personally. If and when any other member of this panel is called to the jury box, the member will be asked to give his or her answers to these questions.

(2) In the trial of this case the parties are entitled to have a fair, unbiased, and unprejudiced jury. If there is any reason why any of you might be biased or prejudiced in any way, you must disclose such reason when you are asked to do so. It is your duty to make this disclosure.

(3) *In lengthy trials:*

This trial will likely take ___ days to complete, but it may take longer. Will any of you find it difficult or impossible to participate for this period of time?

(4) The nature of this case is as follows: *(Describe briefly, including any alleged injuries or damages and, in an eminent domain action, the name of the condemning agency, a description of the property being acquired, and the particular public project or purpose of the condemnation.)*

(5) The parties to this case and their respective attorneys are: *(Specify.)* Have you heard of or been acquainted with any of these parties or their attorneys?

(6) During the trial of this case, the following witnesses may be called to testify on behalf of the parties. These witnesses are:

(Do not identify the party on whose behalf the witnesses might be called.) Have any of you heard of or been otherwise acquainted with any of the witnesses just named? The parties are not required and might not wish to call all of these witnesses, and they may later find it necessary to call other witnesses.

(7) Have any of you heard of, or have you any knowledge of, the facts or events in this case? Are any of you familiar with the places or property mentioned in this case?

(8) Do any of you believe that a case of this nature should not be brought into court for determination by a jury?

(9) Do any of you have any belief or feeling toward any of the parties, attorneys, or witnesses that might be regarded as a bias or prejudice for or against any of them? Do you have any interest, financial or otherwise, in the outcome of this case?

(10) Have any of you served as a juror or witness involving any of these parties, attorneys, or witnesses?

(11) Have any of you served as a juror in any other case? (If so, was it a civil or criminal case?) You must understand that there is a basic difference between a civil case and a criminal case. In a criminal case a defendant must be found guilty beyond a reasonable doubt; in a civil case such as this, you need only find that the evidence you accept as the basis of your decision is more convincing, and thus has the greater probability of truth, than the contrary evidence.

In the following questions I will be using the terms "family," "close friend," and "anyone with whom you have a significant personal relationship." The term "anyone with whom you have a significant personal relationship" means a domestic partner, life partner, former spouse, or anyone with whom you have an influential or intimate relationship that you would characterize as important.

(12) *If a corporation or "company" is a party:*

(A) Have you or, to your knowledge, has any member of your family, a close friend, or anyone with whom you have a significant personal relationship ever had any connection with, or any dealings with, the _____ corporation (or company)?

(B) Are any of you or them related to any officer, director, or employee of this corporation (or company) to your knowledge?

(C) Do you or they own any stock or other interest in this corporation (or company) to your knowledge?

(D) Have you or they ever done business as a corporation (or company)?

(E) The fact that a corporation (or company) is a party in this case must not affect your deliberations or your verdict. You may not discriminate between corporations (or companies) and natural individuals. Both are persons in the eyes of the law and both are entitled to have a fair and impartial trial based on the same legal standards. Do any of you have any belief or feeling for or against corporations (or companies) that might prevent you from being a completely fair and impartial juror in this case?

(13) Have you or, to your knowledge, has any member of your family, a close friend, or anyone with whom you have a significant personal relationship ever sued anyone, or presented a claim against anyone in connection with a matter similar to this case? (If so, did the matter terminate satisfactorily so far as you were concerned?)

(14) Has anyone ever sued you, or presented a claim against you or, to your knowledge, against any member of your family, a close friend, or anyone with whom you have a significant personal relationship, in connection with a matter similar to this

case? (If so, did the matter terminate satisfactorily so far as you were concerned?)

(15) Are you or, to your knowledge, is any member of your family, a close friend, or anyone with whom you have a significant personal relationship presently involved in a lawsuit of any kind?

(16) *When appropriate:*

It may appear that one or more of the parties, witnesses, or attorneys come from a particular national, racial, or religious group (or may have a lifestyle different than your own). Would this in any way affect your judgment or the weight and credibility you would give to their testimony or to their contentions?

(17) Have you or, to your knowledge, has any member of your family, a close friend, or anyone with whom you have a significant personal relationship had any special training in: *(Describe briefly the fields of expertise involved in the case, such as law, medicine, nursing, or any other branch of the healing arts.)*

(18) *In personal injury or wrongful death cases:*

(A) You may be called on in this case to award damages for personal injury, pain, and suffering. Do any of you have any religious or other belief that pain and suffering are not real or any belief that would prevent you from awarding damages for pain and suffering if liability for them is established?

(B) Are there any of you who would not employ a medical doctor?

(C) Have you or, to your knowledge, has any member of your family, a close friend, or anyone with whom you have a significant personal relationship ever engaged in investigating or otherwise acting on claims for damages?

(D) Have you or they, to your knowledge, ever been in an accident with the result that a claim for personal injuries or for substantial property damage was made by someone involved in that accident, whether or not a lawsuit was filed?

(E) Have you or they, to your knowledge, ever been involved in an accident in which someone died or received serious personal injuries, whether or not a lawsuit was filed?

(F) Are there any of you who do not drive an automobile? (If so, have you ever driven an automobile, and if you have, give your reason for not presently driving.) Does your spouse or anyone with whom you have a significant personal relationship drive an automobile? (If that person does not drive but did so in the past, why did that person stop driving?)

(G) Plaintiff (or cross–complainant) _____ is claiming injuries. *(Describe briefly the general nature of the alleged injuries.)* Do you or, to your knowledge, does any member of your family, a close friend, or anyone with whom you have a significant personal relationship suffer from similar injuries? Have you or they, to your knowledge, suffered from similar injuries in the past? (If so, would that fact affect your point of view in this case to the extent that you might not be able to render a completely fair and impartial verdict?)

(19) It is important that I have your assurance that you will, without reservation, follow my instructions and rulings on the law and will apply that law to this case. To put it somewhat differently, whether you approve or disapprove of the court's rulings or instructions, it is your solemn duty to accept as correct these statements of the law. You may not substitute your own idea of what you think the law ought to be. Will all of you follow the law as given to you by me in this case?

(20) Each of you should now state your:

(A) Name;

(B) Children's ages and the number of children, if any;

(C) Occupation;

(D) Occupational history; and

(E) Present employer;

And for your spouse or anyone with whom you have a significant personal relationship, their:

(F) Names;

(G) Occupations;

(H) Occupational histories; and

(I) Present employers.

Please begin with juror number one.

(21) Do you know of any other reason, or has anything occurred during this question period, that might make you doubtful you would be a completely fair and impartial juror in this case? If there is, it is your duty to disclose the reason at this time.

(d) Examination of jurors in eminent domain cases

In eminent domain cases, the trial judge's examination of prospective jurors should include, in the areas of inquiry in (c)(1) through (c)(12), the following matters, and any other matters affecting their qualifications to serve as jurors in the case:

(1) Have you or, to your knowledge, has any member of your family, a close friend, or anyone with whom you have a significant personal relationship ever had any connection with, or dealings with, the plaintiff agency? Are you or any of them related to any officer or employee of the plaintiff agency?

(2) Have you or, to your knowledge, has any member of your family, a close friend, or anyone with whom you have a significant personal relationship ever been involved in an eminent domain proceeding such as this or are you or they likely to become involved in such a proceeding in the future?

(3) To your knowledge, do you have relatives, close friends, or anyone with whom you have a significant personal relationship who has been or will be affected by the proposed project or a similar public project? (If so, who and how affected?)

(4) Have you or, to your knowledge, has any member of your family, a close friend, or anyone with whom you have a significant personal relationship ever sold property to a public agency having the power of eminent domain?

(5) Are you or, to your knowledge, is any member of your family, a close friend, or anyone with whom you have a significant personal relationship presently involved in a lawsuit of any kind? (If so, does the lawsuit involve a public agency?)

(6) Have you or, to your knowledge, has any member of your family, a close friend, or anyone with whom you have a significant personal relationship ever been involved in a lawsuit involving a public agency?

(7) *When appropriate:*

It may appear that one or more of the parties, witnesses, or attorneys come from a particular national, racial, or religious group (or may have a lifestyle different from your own). Would this in any way affect your judgment or the weight and credibility you would give to their testimony or contentions?

(8) Have you or, to your knowledge, has any member of your family, a close friend, or anyone with whom you have a significant personal relationship had any special training in: *(Describe briefly the fields of expertise involved in the case, such as law, real estate, real estate appraising, engineering, surveying, geology, etc.)*

(9) Have you, has your spouse, or, to your knowledge, has any member of your family, a close friend, or anyone with whom you have a significant personal relationship ever been engaged in any phase of the real estate business including:

(A) Acting as a real estate agent, broker, or salesperson;

(B) Acting as a real estate appraiser;

(C) Dealing in trust deeds;

(D) Buying or selling real property as a business;

(E) Owning or managing income property; or

(F) Engaging in the construction business?

(10) Have you or, to your knowledge, has any member of your family, a close friend, or anyone with whom you have a significant personal relationship ever studied or engaged in: (State type of business, if any, conducted on subject property.)

(11) Have you or, to your knowledge, has any member of your family, a close friend, or anyone with whom you have a significant personal relationship ever been engaged in any work involving the acquisition of private property for public purposes? Or involving the zoning or planning of property?

(12) Under the law of this state, all private property is held subject to the necessary right of eminent domain, which is the right of the state or its authorized agencies to take private property for public use whenever the public interest so requires. The right of eminent domain is exercised through proceedings commonly called a condemnation action. This is a condemnation action.

(13) The Constitution of this state requires that a property owner be paid just compensation for the taking (or damaging) of his or her property for public use. It will be the duty of the jury ultimately selected in this case to determine the just compensation to be paid.

(14) *If no claim of severance damages:*

In order to find the amount of just compensation in this case, the jury will be called on to determine the fair market value of the real property being acquired.

(15) *If severance damages are claimed:*

In order to find the amount of just compensation in this case, the jury will be called on to determine the following:

(A) The fair market value of the real property being acquired.

(B) Severance damages, if any, to the defendant's remaining real property; that is, the depreciation in market value by reason of the severance of the part taken, or by the construction of the improvements in the manner proposed by the plaintiff, or both.

(C) *When applicable:* Special benefits, if any, to the defendant's remaining real property. *(The trial judge on request may advise the jury on the concept of special benefits.)*

(16) Just compensation is measured in terms of fair market value as of *(date)*, the date of value in this case.

(17) I will give you more specific instructions on the issues and determinations to be made in this case at the conclusion of all the evidence. However, I will now advise you of the definition of fair market value: *(See CACI 3501.)*

(18) *Private ownership of property:*

(A) Do you have any objection to the concept of private ownership of property?

(B) Do you have any objection to the right of the owner of private property to develop or use that property in whatever lawful way its owner sees fit?

(19) Do you have any objection to the plaintiff acquiring private property for a public use as long as just compensation is paid for the property?

(20) Do you have any objection to the defendant(s) seeking just compensation in these proceedings in the form of the fair market value of the subject property (and the damages that the defendant(s) contend will be caused to the remaining property)?

(21) Do you have any objection to the particular public project involved in this proceeding, previously referred to as the *(name of project)*?

(22) Are you or, to your knowledge, is any member of your family, a close friend, or anyone with whom you have a significant personal relationship a member of any organization that is opposed to such public projects?

(23) Do you have any objection to the concept that just compensation is measured by fair market value as I have defined that term for you earlier?

(24) Do you have any feeling that, because the plaintiff needs the property for public purposes, it should pay anything other than its fair market value?

(25) In these cases, the evidence of value is introduced for the most part by what the courts sometimes refer to as expert testimony. This expert testimony frequently is introduced through appraisers or real estate brokers. Do you have any prejudice against real estate brokers or appraisers, or that type of testimony?

(26) In a condemnation case the property owner produces all of his or her evidence of value first, then the government calls its witnesses. Having this in mind, will you keep your mind open throughout all the case and not determine the matter in your mind until all of the evidence is in?

(27) It is important that I have your assurance that you will, without reservation, follow my instructions and rulings on the law and will apply that law to this case. To put it somewhat differently, whether you approve or disapprove of the court's rulings or instructions, it is your solemn duty to accept as correct these statements of the law. You may not substitute your own idea of what you think the law ought to be. Will all of you follow the law as given to you by me in this case?

(28) Each of you should now state your:

(A) Name;

(B) Children's ages and number of children, if any;

(C) Occupation;

(D) Occupational history; and

(E) Present employer;

And for your spouse or anyone with whom you have a significant personal relationship, their:

(F) Names;

(G) Occupations;

(H) Occupational histories; and

(I) Present employers.

Please begin with juror number one.

(29) Each of you should now state whether you, your spouse, or anyone with whom you have a significant personal relationship owns or has an interest in any real property and, if so, whether its value or use is affected by the public project involved in this case.

We will again start with juror number one.

(30) Do you know of any other reason, or has anything occurred during this question period, that might make you doubtful you would be a completely fair and impartial juror in this case? If there is, it is your duty to disclose the reason at this time.

(e) Subsequent conference and examination

On completion of the initial examination and on request of counsel for any party that the trial judge put additional questions to the jurors, the judge should, outside the jurors' hearing and with a court reporter present, confer with counsel, at which time

Ct. Rules

additional questions or areas of inquiry may be proposed that the judge may inquire of the jurors.

(f) Improper questions

When any counsel examines the prospective jurors, the trial judge should not permit counsel to attempt to precondition the prospective jurors to a particular result or allow counsel to comment on the personal lives and families of the parties or their attorneys. Nor should the trial judge allow counsel to question the jurors concerning the pleadings, the applicable law, the meaning of particular words and phrases, or the comfort of the jurors, except in unusual circumstances, where, in the trial judge's sound discretion, such questions become necessary to insure the selection of a fair and impartial jury. *(Formerly § 8, adopted, eff. Jan. 1, 1972. As amended, eff. Jan. 1, 1974; Jan. 1, 1989; July 1, 1993; Jan. 1, 2004. Renumbered Standard 3.25 and amended, eff. Jan. 1, 2007.)*

Title 4

STANDARDS FOR CRIMINAL CASES

Standard

Standard 4.10.   Guidelines for diversion drug court programs

(a) Minimum components

The components specified in this standard should be included as minimum requirements in any pre-plea diversion drug court program developed under Penal Code section 1000.5.

(b) Early entry

Eligible participants should be identified early and enter into a supervision and treatment program promptly.

(1) A declaration of eligibility should be filed by the district attorney no later than the date of the defendant's first appearance in court.

(2) Participants designated as eligible by the district attorney should be ordered by the assigned drug court judge to report for assessment and treatment supervision within five days of the first court appearance.

(c) Treatment services

Participants should be given access to a continuum of treatment and rehabilitative services.

(1) The county drug program administrator should specify and certify appropriate drug treatment programs under Penal Code section 1211.

(2) The certified treatment programs should provide a minimum of two levels of treatment services to match participants to programs according to their needs for treatment, recognizing that some divertees may be at the stage of experimenting with illicit drugs while others may be further along in the addiction's progression.

(3) Each treatment level should be divided into phases in order to provide periodic reviews of treatment progress. Each phase may vary in length. It should be recognized that a participant is expected to progress in treatment but may relapse. Most participants, however, should be able to successfully complete the treatment program within 12 months.

(4) Each pre-plea diversion drug court program should have an assessment component to ensure that participants are initially screened and then periodically assessed by treatment personnel to ensure that appropriate treatment services are provided and to monitor the participants' progress through the phases.

(5) Treatment services should include educational and group outpatient treatment. Individual counseling, however, should be made available in special circumstances if an assessment based on acceptable professional standards indicates that individual counseling is the only appropriate form of treatment. Referrals should be made for educational and vocational counseling if it is determined to be appropriate by the judge.

(d) Monitoring

Abstinence from and use of drugs should be monitored by frequent drug testing.

(1) Alcohol and other drug (AOD) testing is essential and should be mandatory in each pre-plea diversion drug court program to monitor participant compliance.

(2) Testing may be administered randomly or at scheduled intervals, but should occur no less frequently than one time per week during the first 90 days of treatment.

(3) The probation officer and court should be immediately notified when a participant has tested positive, has failed to submit to AOD testing, or has submitted an adulterated sample. In such cases, an interim hearing should be calendared and required as outlined in (e)(4).

(4) Participants should not be considered to have successfully completed the treatment program unless they have consistently had negative test results for a period of four months.

(e) Judicial supervision

There should be early and frequent judicial supervision of each diversion drug court participant.

(1) Each participant should appear in court before a specifically assigned diversion drug court judge within 30 days after the first court appearance. At this time the participant should provide proof of registration, proof of completion of assessment, proof of entry into a specific treatment program, and initial drug test results.

(2) The second drug court appearance should be held no later than 30 days after the first drug court appearance. The third drug court appearance should be held no later than 60 days after the second drug court appearance.

(3) A final drug court appearance should be required no sooner than 12 months from entry into treatment unless continued treatment is found to be appropriate and necessary.

(4) Interim drug court appearances should be required within one week of the following: positive drug test results, failure to test, adulterated test, or failure to appear or participate in treatment.

(5) At each drug court appearance, the judge should receive a report of the participant's progress in treatment and drug test results and should review, monitor, and impose rewards and sanctions based on the participant's progress or lack of progress.

(f) Sanctions and incentives

The drug court responds directly to each participant's compliance or noncompliance with graduated sanctions or incentives.

(1) A clear regimen of incentives and sanctions should be established and implemented at each court hearing.

(2) The suggested range of incentives should be as follows:

(A) Encouragement;

(B) Advancement to next treatment phase;

(C) Reduction in diversion program fees (other than state-mandated fees);

(D) Completion of treatment and required court appearances and shortening of the term of diversion; and

(E) Other incentives the court may deem necessary or appropriate.

(3) The suggested range of sanctions should be as follows:

(A) Demotion to earlier treatment phase;

(B) Increased frequency of testing, supervision, or treatment requirements;

(C) Graduated length of incarceration for violating diversion order to abstain from use of illegal drugs and for nonparticipation in treatment; and

(D) Reinstatement of criminal proceedings.

(4) A participant should be terminated from the pre-plea diversion drug court, and criminal proceedings reinstated, if the drug court judge, after a hearing, makes a final and specific finding and determination at any time during the period of diversion that the participant has:

(A) Not performed satisfactorily in treatment;

(B) Failed to benefit from education, treatment, or rehabilitation;

(C) Been convicted of a misdemeanor that reflects the participant's propensity for violence; or

(D) Engaged in criminal conduct rendering him or her unsuitable for continued treatment.

(g) National standards

In addition to meeting the minimum guidelines provided in this standard, courts are encouraged to look to the nationally accepted guidelines, *Defining Drug Courts: The Key Components*, developed by the National Association of Drug Court Professionals in cooperation with the Department of Justice, for further and detailed guidance in developing an effective diversion drug court program. *(Formerly § 36, adopted, eff. Jan. 1, 1998. Renumbered Standard 4.10 and amended, eff. Jan. 1, 2007.)*

Standard 4.30.   Examination of prospective jurors in criminal cases

(a) In general

(1) This standard applies in all criminal cases.

(2) The examination of prospective jurors in a criminal case should include all questions necessary to insure the selection of a fair and impartial jury.

(3) The court may consider conducting sequestered voir dire on issues that are sensitive to prospective jurors, on questions concerning media reports of the case, and on any other issue that the court deems advisable.

(b) Examination of jurors

The trial judge's examination of prospective jurors in criminal cases should include the areas of inquiry listed below and any other matters affecting their qualifications to serve as jurors in the case. The trial judge may want to use the *Juror Questionnaire for Criminal Cases* (form MC–002) to assist in the examination of prospective jurors. Form MC–002 is an optional form and is not intended to constitute the complete examination of prospective jurors. Form MC–002 is a tool for trial judges to use to make the initial examination of prospective jurors more efficient. If the court chooses to use form MC–002, its use and any supplemental questions submitted by counsel must be discussed at the pre-voir dire conference required by rule 4.200. Excusing jurors based on questionnaire answers alone is generally not advisable.

(1) *Address to entire jury panel:*

Do any of you have any vision, hearing, or medical difficulties that may affect your jury service? *(Response.)*

(2) *In particular, for lengthy trials. Address to entire jury panel:*

This trial will likely take ___ days to complete, but it may take longer. *(State the days and times during the day when the trial will be in session.)*

Will any of you find it difficult or impossible to participate for this period of time? *(After the entire panel has been screened for time hardships, direct the excused jurors to return to the jury assembly room for possible reassignment to other courtrooms for voir dire.)*

(3) *At this point the court may wish to submit any juror questionnaire that has been developed to assist in voir dire. The court should remind panel members that their answers on the questionnaire are given under penalty of perjury. In addition, if a questionnaire is used, the court and counsel may wish to question individual prospective jurors further based on their responses to particular questions, and a procedure for doing so should be established at the pre-voir dire conference. Therefore, it may not be necessary to ask all of the prospective jurors questions 5 through 25 that follow, although the text may assist the court with following up with individual jurors about answers given on the questionnaire.*

To the entire jury panel:

I am now going to question the prospective jurors who are seated in the jury box concerning their qualifications to serve as jurors in this case. All the remaining members of this jury panel, however, should pay close attention to my questions, making note of the answers you would give if these questions were put to you personally. If and when any other member of this panel is called to the jury box, he or she will be asked to answer these questions.

(4) *To the prospective jurors seated in the jury box:*

In the trial of this case each side is entitled to have a fair, unbiased, and unprejudiced jury. If there is any fact or any reason why any of you might be biased or prejudiced in any way, you must disclose such reasons when you are asked to do so. It is your duty to make this disclosure.

(5) *To the prospective jurors seated in the jury box:*

Do any of you know anyone else on this jury panel? *(Response.)*

(6) Ladies and gentlemen of the jury: This is a criminal case entitled The People of the State of California v. _____. The (defendant is)(defendants are) seated _____.

(A) (Mr.)(Ms.) (defendant), please stand and face the prospective jurors in the jury box and in the audience seats. *(Defendant complies.)* Is there any member of the jury panel who is acquainted with the defendant or who may have heard (his)(her) name before today? If your answer is yes, please raise your hand.

(B) The defendant, _____, is represented by (his)(her) attorney, _____, who is seated _____. (Mr.)(Ms.) (defense attorney), would you please stand? Is there any member of the jury panel who knows or who has seen (Mr.)(Ms.) _____ before today?

(C) *(If there is more than one defendant, repeat (a) and (b) for each codefendant.)*

(7) The People are represented by _____, Deputy District Attorney, who is seated _____. (Mr.)(Ms.) (district attorney), would you please stand? Is there any member of the jury panel who knows or who has seen (Mr.)(Ms.) _____ before today?

(8) The defendant is charged by an (information)(indictment) filed by the district attorney with having committed the crime of _____, in violation of section ___ of the _____ Code, it being alleged that on or about _____ in the County of _____, the defendant did *(describe the offense)*. To (this charge)(these charges) the defendant has pleaded not guilty, and the jury will have to decide whether the defendant's guilt has been proved beyond a reasonable doubt. Having heard the charge(s) that (has)(have) been filed against the defendant, is there any member of the jury panel who feels that he or she cannot give this defendant a fair trial because of the nature of the charge(s) against (him)(her)?

(9) Have any of you heard of, or have you any prior knowledge of, the facts or events in this case?

(10) Do any of you have any ethical, religious, political, or other beliefs that would prevent you from serving as a juror in this case?

(11) During the trial of this case, the following persons may be called as witnesses to testify on behalf of the parties or their names may be mentioned in evidence: _____ *(Do not identify the side on whose behalf the witness might be called.)* Have any of you heard of or otherwise been acquainted with any of the witnesses just named? You should note that the parties are not required and might not wish to call all of these witnesses, and they may later find it necessary to call other witnesses.

(12) Do any of you have any financial or personal interest in the outcome of this case?

(13) How many of you have served previously as jurors in a criminal case?

To each person whose hand is raised:

(A) (Mr.)(Ms.) _____ (or Juror ID number), you indicated you have been a juror in a criminal case. What were the charges in that case? *(Response.)*

(B) Do you feel you can put aside whatever you heard in that case and decide this case on the evidence to be presented and the law as I will state it to you? *(Response.)*

(14) May I see the hands of those jurors who have served on civil cases, but who have never served on a criminal case? *(Response.)* You must understand that there are substantial differences in the rules applicable to the trial of criminal cases from those applicable to the trial of civil cases. This is particularly true respecting the burden of proof that is placed on the People. In a civil case we say that the plaintiff must prove (his) (her) case by a preponderance of the evidence. In a criminal case, the defendant is presumed to be innocent, and before (he)(she) may be found guilty, the People must prove (his)(her) guilt beyond a reasonable doubt. If the jury has a reasonable doubt, the defendant must be acquitted. Will each of you be able to set aside the instructions that you received in your previous cases and try this case on the instructions given by me in this case?

(15) The fact that the defendant is in court for trial, or that charges have been made against (him)(her), is no evidence whatever of (his)(her) guilt. The jurors are to consider only evidence properly received in the courtroom in determining whether the defendant's guilt has been proved beyond a reasonable doubt. The defendant has entered a plea of "not guilty," which is a complete denial, making it necessary for the People, acting through the district attorney, to prove beyond a reasonable doubt the case against the defendant. If the

evidence does not convince you of the truth of the charges beyond a reasonable doubt, the defendant is entitled to a verdict of not guilty.

In the following questions I will be using the terms "relative," "close friend," and "anyone with whom you have a significant personal relationship." The term "anyone with whom you have a significant personal relationship" means a domestic partner, life partner, former spouse, or anyone with whom you have an influential or intimate relationship that you would characterize as important.

(16) Have you or, to your knowledge, has any relative, close friend, or anyone with whom you have a significant personal relationship, ever been the victim of any crime? *(Response.)*

(17) Have you or, to your knowledge, has any relative, close friend, or anyone with whom you have a significant personal relationship, ever had any contact with law enforcement, including being: (a) stopped by the police? (b) accused of misconduct, whether or not it was a crime? (c) investigated as a suspect in a criminal case? (d) charged with a crime? or (e) a criminal defendant? *(Response.)*

(18) Have you or, to your knowledge, has any relative, close friend, or anyone with whom you have a significant personal relationship, had any law enforcement training or experience or been a member of or been employed by any law enforcement agency? By law enforcement agency, I include any police department, sheriff's office, highway patrol, district attorney's office, city attorney's office, attorney general's office, United States attorney's office, FBI, and others. *(If so, elicit the details of the experience or connection.)*

(19) Would you be able to listen to the testimony of a police or other peace officer and measure it the same way you would that of any other witness?

(20) *When appropriate:*

It may appear that one or more of the parties, attorneys, or witnesses come from a particular national, racial, or religious group (or may have a lifestyle different from your own). Would this in any way affect your judgment or the weight and credibility you would give to their testimony?

(21) It is important that I have your assurance that you will follow my instructions and rulings on the law and will apply that law to this case. To put it somewhat differently, whether you approve or disapprove of the court's rulings or instructions, it is your solemn duty to accept as correct these statements of the law. You must accept and follow my instructions even if you disagree with the law. You may not substitute your own idea of what you think the law ought to be. Will all of you follow the law as given to you by me in this case?

(22) Each of you should now state your:

(A) (Name)(or juror ID number);

(B) Children's ages and the number of children, if any;

(C) Occupation;

(D) Occupational history; and

(E) Present employer;

And for your spouse or anyone with whom you have a significant personal relationship, their:

(F) Occupations;

(G) Occupational histories; and

(H) Present employers;

And for your adult children, their:

(I) Occupations;

(J) Occupational histories; and

(K) Present employers.

Please begin with juror number one.

(23) Do you know of any other reason, or has anything occurred during this question period, that might make you doubtful you would be a completely fair and impartial juror in this case or why you should not be on this jury? If there is, it is your duty to disclose the reason at this time.

(24) *After the court conducts the initial examination, Code of Civil Procedure section 223 allows counsel to ask supplemental questions for the purposes of uncovering possible bias or prejudice relevant to challenges for cause. The court may, in the exercise of its discretion, limit the oral and direct questioning of prospective jurors by counsel. The court may specify the maximum amount of time that counsel for each party may question an individual juror, or may specify an aggregate amount of time for each party, which can then be allocated among the prospective jurors by counsel.*

(25) *After the conclusion of counsel questioning, the court asks each side to exercise any challenges for cause.*

(26) *After ruling on challenges for cause, if any, the court calls on each side, alternately, to exercise any preemptory challenges.*

(27) *If a new prospective juror is seated, the court should ask him or her:*

(A) Have you heard my questions to the other prospective jurors?

(B) Have any of the questions I have asked raised any doubt in your mind as to whether you could be a fair and impartial juror in this case?

(C) Can you think of any other reason why you might not be able to try this case fairly and impartially to both the prosecution and defendant, or why you should not be on this jury?

(D) Give us the personal information requested concerning your occupation, that of your spouse or anyone with whom you have a significant personal relationship, that of your adult children, and your prior jury experience.

(Thereupon, as to each new juror seated, the court must permit counsel to ask supplemental questions, and proceed with challenges as above.)

(c) Improper questions

When any counsel examines the prospective jurors, the trial judge should not permit counsel to attempt to precondition the prospective jurors to a particular result or allow counsel to comment on the personal lives and families of the parties or their attorneys. *(Formerly § 8.5, adopted, eff. July 1, 1974. As amended, eff. Jan. 1, 1988; Jan. 1, 1990; June 6, 1990; Jan. 1, 1997; Jan. 1, 2004; Jan. 1, 2006. Renumbered Standard 4.30 and amended, eff. Jan. 1, 2007.)*

Standard 4.40.　Traffic infraction procedures

To insure the prompt and efficient disposition of traffic infraction cases, each court should:

(1) Authorize the clerk, within limits set by the court, to grant defendants extensions of time for the posting of bail and payment of fines.

(2) Authorize the clerk or other court official to accept offers of proof of correction or compliance in accordance with the bail schedule without the necessity of a court appearance. *(Formerly § 10.5, adopted, eff. July 1, 1977. Renumbered Standard 4.40 and amended, eff. Jan. 1, 2007.)*

Standard 4.41.　Courtesy notice—traffic procedures

(a) Mailed courtesy notice

Each court should promptly mail a "courtesy notice" to the address shown on the Notice to Appear. The date of mailing should allow for the plea-by-mail option in infraction cases.

(b) Minimum information in courtesy notice

In addition to information obtained from the Notice to Appear, the courtesy notice should contain at least the following information:

(1) An appearance date, time, and location;

(2) Whether a court appearance is mandatory or optional;

(3) The total bail amount if forfeitable;

(4) The procedure required for remitting bail;

(5) The plea-by-mail option in infraction cases and the number of appearances required where trial is requested;

(6) The consequences of failure to appear; and

(7) A telephone number to call for additional information.

(c) Additional information in courtesy notice

Courts should provide additional information in the courtesy notice, as appropriate, including the following:

(1) Informal trial, trial by declaration, traffic violators' school, and telephone scheduling options; and

(2) Correction requirements and procedures. *(Formerly § 10.6, adopted, eff. Jan. 1, 1987. Renumbered Standard 4.41 and amended, eff. Jan. 1, 2007.)*

Standard 4.42.　Traffic infraction trial scheduling

(a) Review of procedures

Courts should adopt and periodically review procedures governing the scheduling of traffic infraction trials that minimize appearance time and costs for defendants, witnesses, and law enforcement officers.

(b) Meetings

Courts should hold periodic meetings with representatives from local law enforcement agencies, the prosecution and defense bars, and other interested groups as appropriate in an effort to achieve this goal. *(Formerly § 10.7, adopted, eff. Jan. 1, 1987. Renumbered Standard 4.42 and amended, eff. Jan. 1, 2007.)*

Title 5

STANDARDS FOR CASES INVOLVING CHILDREN AND FAMILIES

Standard

Standard 5.20.　Uniform standards of practice for providers of supervised visitation

(a) Scope of service

This standard defines the standards of practice, including duties and obligations, for providers of supervised visitation under Family Code section 3200. Unless specified otherwise, the standards of practice are designed to apply to all providers of

Ct. Rules

supervised visitation, whether the provider is a friend, relative, paid independent contractor, employee, intern, or volunteer operating independently or through a supervised visitation center or agency. The goal of these standards of practice is to assure the safety and welfare of the child, adults, and providers of supervised visitation. Once safety is assured, the best interest of the child is the paramount consideration at all stages and particularly in deciding the manner in which supervision is provided. Each court is encouraged to adopt local court rules necessary to implement these standards of practice.

(b) Definition

Family Code section 3200 defines the term "provider" as including any individual or supervised visitation center that monitors visitation. Supervised visitation is contact between a noncustodial party and one or more children in the presence of a neutral third person. These standards of practice and this definition do not apply to supervision of visitation exchanges only, but may be useful in that context.

(c) Qualifications of the provider

Who provides the supervision and the manner in which supervision is provided depends on different factors, including local resources, the financial situation of the parties, and the degree of risk in each case. While the court makes the final decision as to the manner in which supervision is provided and any terms or conditions, the court may consider recommendations by the attorney for the child, the parties and their attorneys, Family Court Services staff, evaluators, therapists, and providers of supervised visitation.

(1) A "nonprofessional provider" is any person who is not paid for providing supervised visitation services. Unless otherwise ordered by the court or stipulated by the parties, the nonprofessional provider should:

(A) Be 21 years of age or older;

(B) Have no conviction for driving under the influence (DUI) within the last 5 years;

(C) Not have been on probation or parole for the last 10 years;

(D) Have no record of a conviction for child molestation, child abuse, or other crimes against a person;

(E) Have proof of automobile insurance if transporting the child;

(F) Have no civil, criminal, or juvenile restraining orders within the last 10 years;

(G) Have no current or past court order in which the provider is the person being supervised;

(H) Not be financially dependent on the person being supervised;

(I) Have no conflict of interest under (g); and

(J) Agree to adhere to and enforce the court order regarding supervised visitation.

(2) A "professional provider" is any person paid for providing supervised visitation services, or an independent contractor, employee, intern, or volunteer operating independently or through a supervised visitation center or agency. The professional provider should:

(A) Be 21 years of age or older;

(B) Have no conviction for driving under the influence (DUI) within the last 5 years;

(C) Not have been on probation or parole for the last 10 years;

(D) Have no record of a conviction for child molestation, child abuse, or other crimes against a person;

(E) Have proof of automobile insurance if transporting the child;

(F) Have no civil, criminal, or juvenile restraining orders within the last 10 years;

(G) Have no current or past court order in which the provider is the person being supervised;

(H) Be able to speak the language of the party being supervised and of the child, or the provider must provide a neutral interpreter over the age of 18 who is able to do so;

(I) Have no conflict of interest under (g); and

(J) Agree to adhere to and enforce the court order regarding supervised visitation.

(3) A "therapeutic provider" is a licensed mental health professional paid for providing supervised visitation services, including a psychiatrist, a psychologist, a clinical social worker, a marriage and family counselor, or an intern working under direct supervision of a qualified licensed mental health professional. A therapeutic provider should meet the qualifications provided in (c)(2). A judicial officer may order therapeutic supervision for cases requiring a clinical setting.

(d) Training for providers

(1) Each court is encouraged to make available to all providers informational materials about the role of a provider, the terms and conditions of supervised visitation, and the legal responsibilities and obligations of a provider under this standard.

(2) In addition, professional and therapeutic providers should receive training that should include the following subjects:

(A) The role of a professional and therapeutic provider;

(B) Child abuse reporting laws;

(C) Record–keeping procedures;

(D) Screening, monitoring, and termination of visitation;

(E) Developmental needs of children;

(F) Legal responsibilities and obligations of a provider;

(G) Cultural sensitivity;

(H) Conflicts of interest;

(I) Confidentiality; and

(J) Issues relating to substance abuse, child abuse, sexual abuse, and domestic violence.

(e) Safety and security procedures

All providers should make every reasonable effort to assure the safety and welfare of the child and adults during the visitation. Supervised visitation centers should establish a written protocol with the assistance of the local law enforcement agency that describes the emergency assistance and responses that can be expected from the local law enforcement agency. In addition, the professional and therapeutic provider should:

(1) Establish and state in writing minimum security procedures and inform the parties of these procedures before the commencement of supervised visitation;

(2) Conduct comprehensive intake and screening to assess the nature and degree of risk for each case. The procedures for intake should include separate interviews with the parties before the first visit. During the interview, the provider should obtain identifying information and explain the reasons for temporary suspension or termination of a visit under this standard. If the child is of sufficient age and capacity, the provider should include the child in part of the intake or orientation process. Any discussion should be presented to the child in a manner appropriate to the child's developmental stage;

(3) Obtain during the intake process:

(A) Copies of any protective order;

(B) Current court orders;

(C) Any Judicial Council form relating to supervised visitation orders;

(D) A report of any written records of allegations of domestic violence or abuse; and

(E) An account of the child's health needs if the child has a chronic health condition;

(4) Establish written procedures that must be followed in the event a child is abducted during supervised visitation; and

(5) Suspend or terminate supervised visitation if the provider determines that the risk factors present are placing in jeopardy the safety and welfare of the child or provider as enumerated in (j).

(f) Ratio of children to provider

The ratio of children to a professional provider should be contingent on:

(1) The degree of risk factors present in each case;

(2) The nature of supervision required in each case;

(3) The number and ages of the children to be supervised during a visit;

(4) The number of people visiting the child during the visit;

(5) The duration and location of the visit; and

(6) The experience of the provider.

(g) Conflict of interest

All providers should maintain neutrality by refusing to discuss the merits of the case or agree with or support one party over another. Any discussion between a provider and the parties should be for the purposes of arranging visitation and providing for the safety of the children. In order to avoid a conflict of interest, the provider should not:

(1) Be financially dependent on the person being supervised;

(2) Be an employee of the person being supervised;

(3) Be an employee of or affiliated with any superior court in the county in which the supervision is ordered unless specified in the employment contract; or

(4) Be in an intimate relationship with the person being supervised.

(h) Maintenance and disclosure of records

(1) Professional and therapeutic providers should keep a record for each case, including the following:

(A) A written record of each contact and visit, including the date, time, and duration of the contact or visit;

(B) Who attended the visit;

(C) A summary of activities during the visit;

(D) Actions taken by the provider, including any interruptions, terminations of a visit, and reasons for these actions;

(E) An account of critical incidents, including physical or verbal altercations and threats;

(F) Violations of protective or court visitation orders;

(G) Any failure to comply with the terms and conditions of the visitation; and

(H) Any incidence of abuse as required by law.

(2) Case recordings should be limited to facts, observations, and direct statements made by the parties, not personal conclusions, suggestions, or opinions of the provider. All contacts by the provider in person, in writing, or by telephone with either party, the children, the court, attorneys, mental health professionals, and referring agencies should be documented in the case file. All entries should be dated and signed by the person recording the entry.

(3) If ordered by the court or requested by either party or the attorney for either party or the attorney for the child, a report about the supervised visit should be produced. These reports should include facts, observations, and direct statements and not opinions or recommendations regarding future visitation unless ordered by the court. A copy of any report should be sent to all parties, their attorneys, and the attorney for the child.

(4) Any identifying information about the parties and the child, including addresses, telephone numbers, places of employment, and schools, is confidential, should not be disclosed, and should be deleted from documents before releasing them to any court, attorney, attorney for the child, party, mediator, evaluator, mental health professional, social worker, or referring agency, except as required in reporting suspected child abuse.

(i) Confidentiality

Communications between parties and providers of supervised visitation are not protected by any privilege of confidentiality. The psychotherapist-patient privilege does not apply during therapeutic supervision. Professional and therapeutic providers should, whenever possible, maintain confidentiality regarding the case except when:

(1) Ordered by the court;

(2) Subpoenaed to produce records or testify in court;

(3) Requested to provide information about the case by a mediator or evaluator in conjunction with a court-ordered mediation, investigation, or evaluation;

(4) Required to provide information about the case by Child Protective Services; or

(5) Requested to provide information about the case by law enforcement.

(j) Delineation of terms and conditions

The provider bears the sole responsibility for enforcement of all the terms and conditions of any supervised visitation. Unless otherwise ordered by the court, the provider should:

(1) Monitor conditions to assure the safety and welfare of the child;

(2) Enforce the frequency and duration of the visits as ordered by the court;

(3) Avoid any attempt to take sides with either party;

(4) Ensure that all contact between the child and the noncustodial party is within the provider's hearing and sight at all times, and that discussions are audible to the provider;

(5) Speak in a language spoken by the child and the noncustodial party;

(6) Allow no derogatory comments about the other parent, his or her family, caretaker, child, or child's siblings;

(7) Allow no discussion of the court case or possible future outcomes;

(8) Allow neither the provider nor the child to be used to gather information about the other party or caretaker or to transmit documents, information, or personal possessions;

(9) Allow no spanking, hitting, or threatening the child;

(10) Allow no visits to occur while the visiting party appears to be under the influence of alcohol or illegal drugs;

(11) Allow no emotional, verbal, physical, or sexual abuse; and

(12) Ensure that the parties follow any additional rules set forth by the provider or the court.

(k) Safety considerations for sexual abuse cases

In cases where there are allegations of sexual abuse, in addition to the requirements of (j), the provider should comply with the following terms and conditions, unless otherwise ordered by the court:

(1) Allow no exchanges of gifts, money, or cards;

(2) Allow no photographing, audiotaping, or videotaping of the child;

(3) Allow no physical contact with the child such as lap sitting, hair combing, stroking, hand holding, prolonged hugging, wrestling, tickling, horseplaying, changing diapers, or accompanying the child to the bathroom;

(4) Allow no whispering, passing notes, hand signals, or body signals; and

(5) Allow no supervised visitation in the location where the alleged sexual abuse occurred.

(*l*) Legal responsibilities and obligations of a provider

All providers of supervised visitation should:

(1) Advise the parties before commencement of supervised visitation that no confidential privilege exists;

(2) Report suspected child abuse to the appropriate agency, as provided by law, and inform the parties of the provider's obligation to make such reports;

(3) Implement the terms and conditions under (j); and

(4) Suspend or terminate visitation under (n).

(m) Additional legal responsibilities of professional and therapeutic providers

In addition to the legal responsibilities and obligations required in (*l*), professional and therapeutic providers should:

(1) Prepare a written contract to be signed by the parties before commencement of the supervised visitation. The contract should inform each party of the terms and conditions of supervised visitation;

(2) Review custody and visitation orders relevant to the supervised visitation;

(3) Implement an intake and screening procedure under (e)(2); and

(4) Comply with additional requirements under (*o*).

(n) Temporary suspension or termination of supervised visitation

(1) All providers should make every reasonable effort to provide a safe visit for the child and the noncustodial party.

(2) However, if a provider determines that the rules of the visit have been violated, the child has become acutely distressed, or the safety of the child or the provider is at risk, the visit may be temporarily interrupted, rescheduled at a later date, or terminated.

(3) All interruptions or terminations of visits should be recorded in the case file.

(4) All providers should advise both parties of the reasons for interruption of a visit or termination.

(*o*) Additional requirements for professional and therapeutic providers

Professional and therapeutic providers should state the reasons for temporary suspension or termination of supervised visitation in writing and provide the written statement to both parties, their attorneys, the attorney for the child, and the court. *(Formerly § 26.2, adopted, eff. Jan. 1, 1998. Renumbered Standard 5.20 and amended, eff. Jan. 1, 2007.)*

Standard 5.30. Family court matters

(a) Judicial assignments to family court

In a court with a separate family court, the presiding judge of the superior court should assign judges to the family court to serve for a minimum of three years. In selecting judges for family court assignments, the presiding judge should consider, in addition to rule 10.603(c)(1)(A) of the California Rules of Court, the judge's prior experience in family law litigation and mediation, as well as whether the judge prefers to serve in a family law department.

(b) Case assignment to same department

To the extent possible, family law actions related to the same family should be assigned to the same judicial officer for all purposes, so that all decisions that are made in a case through final judgment are issued by the same judicial officer.

(c) Importance of family court

The supervising judge in the family court, in consultation with the presiding judge of the superior court, should:

(1) Motivate and educate other judges regarding the significance of family court; and

(2) Work to ensure that sufficient judicial officers, court staff, family law facilitators, child custody mediators and evaluators, interpreters, financial resources, and adequate facilities are assigned to the family court to allow adequate time to hear and decide the matters before it.

(d) Compensation for court-appointed attorneys

The supervising judge of the family court should ensure that court-appointed attorneys in the family court are compensated at a level equivalent to attorneys appointed by the court in comparable types of cases.

(e) Training and education

Family court law is a specialized area of the law that requires dedication and study. The supervising judge of the family court has a responsibility to maintain high-quality services in family court. The quality of services provided by judicial officers and court staff depends, in significant part, on appropriate training and education, from the beginning of the family court assignment and on a continuing basis thereafter.

(1) Family court judicial officers, family law facilitators, child custody mediators and evaluators, interpreters, other court staff, and court-appointed attorneys should have sufficient training to perform their jobs competently.

(2) The supervising judge of the family court should promote access to printed, electronic, Internet, and other family law resources.

(f) Unique role of a family court

Under the direction of the presiding judge of the superior court, the family court, to the extent that it does not interfere with the adjudication process or violate any ethical constraints, is encouraged to:

(1) Provide active leadership within the community in determining the needs of, and obtaining and developing resources and services for children and families who participate in the family law court system;

(2) Investigate and determine the availability of specific prevention, intervention, and treatment services in the community for families who come before the family courts;

(3) Take an active role in helping the court develop rules and procedures that will result in the ordering of appropriate treatment and services for children and families;

(4) Exercise a leadership role in the development and maintenance of services for self-represented and financially disadvantaged litigants;

(5) Take an active part in the formation of a community-wide network to promote and coordinate private- and public-sector

efforts to focus attention and resources on the needs of family law litigants;

(6) Educate the community and its institutions, including the media, concerning the role of the family court in meeting the complex needs of families;

(7) Encourage the development of community services and resources to assist families and children in the family court system, including self-help information; supervised visitation; substance abuse and drug prevention, intervention, and treatment; services for families with domestic violence issues; counseling; parenting education; vocational training; mediation; alternative dispute resolution options; and other resources to support families;

(8) Manage cases more efficiently and effectively to avoid conflicting orders;

(9) Take an active role in promoting completion of cases in a timely manner;

(10) Appoint counsel for children in appropriate family law custody cases; and

(11) Ensure that the best interest of children is served throughout the family court process.

(g) Appointment of attorneys and other persons

A court should follow the guidelines of standard 10.21 of the California Standards of Judicial Administration when appointing attorneys, arbitrators, mediators, referees, masters, receivers, and other persons. *(Adopted, eff. Jan. 1, 2007.)*

Advisory Committee Comment

Standard 5.30. Family court matters include proceedings under the Family Code for dissolution of marriage, nullity of marriage, legal separation, custody and support of minor children; or actions under the Domestic Violence Prevention Act, the Uniform Parentage Act, the Uniform Child Custody Jurisdiction and Enforcement Act, Domestic Partner Registration Act, and the Uniform Interstate Family Support Act; local child support agency actions under the Family Code; and contempt proceedings relating to family law or local child support agency actions.

Subdivision (a). This subdivision implements the legislative mandate of Family Code section 2330.3(b) requiring the Judicial Council to adopt a standard of judicial administration prescribing a minimum length of a judge's family law assignment. Standard 5.30 sets a standard in family court that is similar to the juvenile court standards stated in standard 5.40, Juvenile Court Matters.

Family law is complex and constantly evolving. The laws concerning child custody, support, domestic violence, and property division are always changing. Not only does the family law judge have to understand family law and procedure but also issues that involve bankruptcy, estate planning, insurance, state and federal tax law, business, immigration, and criminal law, which can frequently arise in the context of a family law case. Because of the complexity and long-range impact of the judicial determinations, the presiding judge should strive to place experienced judges in family law assignments.

Considering the constantly evolving changes in the law, as well as the unique nature of the proceedings in family court, the family court judge should be willing to commit to a minimum tenure of three years. Not only does this tenure afford the judge the opportunity to become well acquainted with the complexity of the family court process, but it also provides continuity to a system that demands it.

Subdivision (b) This subdivision implements the legislative mandate of Family Code section 2330.3(a), which requires that dissolution actions, to the greatest extent possible, be assigned to the same superior court department for all purposes, so that all decisions in a case are made by the same judicial officer. This subdivision expands the Legislature's requirement by including other related family court matters, such as those filed under the

Uniform Parentage Act, Domestic Violence Prevention Act, in recognition that the same families may enter the family court through a variety of actions.

The committee recognizes that having the same judicial officer hear all actions involving the same family may not be practical in all cases for reasons that include funding limitations, assignment rotations, illness, vacations, and retirements. In some courts, one judge does not hear all aspects of a family's legal problems because of multiple courthouse locations or specifically designated funding of certain issues (e.g., Title IV–D child support issues). However, the committee agrees with the legislative intent in enacting section 2330.3(a), which was to expedite and simplify the dissolution process, reduce the litigation expenses and costs, and encourage greater judicial supervision of cases involving dissolution of marriage. Family law actions often involve a succession of hearings to resolve the various issues that arise. A single judge's involvement over this period of time allows the judge to be more familiar with the particular actions and issues, which creates judicial efficiencies that expedite their handling. One judge hearing all actions involving a family also helps avoid conflicting orders, alleviates the need to hold multiple hearings on the same issue, improves the court process, promotes consistency, and enhances fairness in family proceedings.

Subdivision (c). The family court is an integral part of the justice system. Decisions made by family law judges can have significant and lasting impacts on the lives of the parties and their children. The work of the family court has a significant impact on the health of families and ultimately on the strength of the community. The parties deserve to have adequate time to present their cases, and the judges should have the resources they need to enable them to make informed decisions. It is only through the constant exertion of pressure to maintain resources and the continuous education of court-related personnel and administrators that the historic trend to give less priority and provide fewer resources to the family court can be changed.

Subdivision (d). Fees paid to court-appointed attorneys who represent children in family court are sometimes less than the fees paid attorneys doing other comparable legal work thereby demeaning the work of the family court and leading many to believe that such work is less important. It may also discourage attorneys from accepting these appointments. Compensation for legal work in the family court should reflect the importance of the work.

Subdivision (e)(2). A significant barrier to having well-trained attorneys and educated self-represented litigants is a lack of current educational materials relating to family court practice. Law libraries, law offices, and court systems traditionally have not devoted adequate resources to purchase such educational materials. With advances in technology, resources can be accessed, shared, developed, or made available through electronic/computer–based, online, and multimedia means, audiotape and videotape, DVD, CD, Web-based audiocasts and videocasts, and other media to supplement print materials.

Subdivision (f). In addition to the traditional role of fairly and efficiently resolving disputes before the court, a family court judge occupies a unique position within California's judiciary. California law empowers the family court judge not only to order relief related to the needs of families under its jurisdiction but also to enforce and review the compliance with such orders. This oversight function includes the obligation to understand and work with those public and private agencies that provide services for families. As such, the family court assignment requires a dramatic shift in emphasis from judging in the traditional sense. Active and public judicial support and encouragement of programs serving children and families in family court poses no conflict with traditional concepts of judicial ethics and is an important function of the family court judge. These efforts enhance the overall administration of justice for families.

Standard 5.40. Juvenile court matters

(a) Assignments to juvenile court

The presiding judge of the superior court should assign judges to the juvenile court to serve for a minimum of three years.

Priority should be given to judges who have expressed an interest in the assignment.

(b) Importance of juvenile court

The presiding judge of the juvenile court, in consultation with the presiding judge of the superior court, should:

(1) Motivate and educate other judges regarding the significance of juvenile court.

(2) Work to ensure that sufficient judges and staff, facilities, and financial resources are assigned to the juvenile court to allow adequate time to hear and decide the matters before it.

(c) Standards of representation and compensation

The presiding judge of the juvenile court should:

(1) Encourage attorneys who practice in juvenile court, including all court-appointed and contract attorneys, to continue their practice in juvenile court for substantial periods of time. A substantial period of time is at least two years and preferably from three to five years.

(2) Confer with the county public defender, county district attorney, county counsel, and other public law office leaders and encourage them to raise the status of attorneys working in the juvenile courts as follows: hire attorneys who are interested in serving in the juvenile court for a substantial part of their careers; permit and encourage attorneys, based on interest and ability, to remain in juvenile court assignments for significant periods of time; and work to ensure that attorneys who have chosen to serve in the juvenile court have the same promotional and salary opportunities as attorneys practicing in other assignments within a law office.

(3) Establish minimum standards of practice to which all court-appointed and public office attorneys will be expected to conform. These standards should delineate the responsibilities of attorneys relative to investigation and evaluation of the case, preparation for and conduct of hearings, and advocacy for their respective clients.

(4) In conjunction with other leaders in the legal community, ensure that attorneys appointed in the juvenile court are compensated in a manner equivalent to attorneys appointed by the court in other types of cases.

(d) Training and orientation

The presiding judge of the juvenile court should:

(1) Establish relevant prerequisites for court-appointed attorneys and advocates in the juvenile court.

(2) Develop orientation and in-service training programs for judicial officers, attorneys, volunteers, law enforcement personnel, court personnel, and child advocates to ensure that all are adequately trained concerning all issues relating to special education rights and responsibilities, including the right of each child with exceptional needs to receive a free, appropriate public education and the right of each child with educational disabilities to receive accommodations.

(3) Promote the establishment of a library or other resource center in which information about juvenile court practice (including books, periodicals, videotapes, and other training materials) can be collected and made available to all participants in the juvenile system.

(4) Ensure that attorneys who appear in juvenile court have sufficient training to perform their jobs competently, as follows: require that all court-appointed attorneys meet minimum training and continuing legal education standards as a condition of their appointment to juvenile court matters; and encourage the leaders of public law offices that have responsibilities in juvenile court to require their attorneys who appear in juvenile court to

have at least the same training and continuing legal education required of court-appointed attorneys.

(e) Unique role of a juvenile court judge

Judges of the juvenile court, in consultation with the presiding judge of the juvenile court and the presiding judge of the superior court, to the extent that it does not interfere with the adjudication process, are encouraged to:

(1) Provide active leadership within the community in determining the needs of and obtaining and developing resources and services for at-risk children and families. At–risk children include delinquents, dependents, and status offenders.

(2) Investigate and determine the availability of specific prevention, intervention, and treatment services in the community for at-risk children and their families.

(3) Exercise their authority by statute or rule to review, order, and enforce the delivery of specific services and treatment for at-risk children and their families.

(4) Exercise a leadership role in the development and maintenance of permanent programs of interagency cooperation and coordination among the court and the various public agencies that serve at-risk children and their families.

(5) Take an active part in the formation of a communitywide network to promote and unify private and public sector efforts to focus attention and resources for at-risk children and their families.

(6) Maintain close liaison with school authorities and encourage coordination of policies and programs.

(7) Educate the community and its institutions through every available means, including the media, concerning the role of the juvenile court in meeting the complex needs of at-risk children and their families.

(8) Evaluate the criteria established by child protection agencies for initial removal and reunification decisions and communicate the court's expectations of what constitutes "reasonable efforts" to prevent removal or hasten return of the child.

(9) Encourage the development of community services and resources to assist homeless, truant, runaway, and incorrigible children.

(10) Be familiar with all detention facilities, placements, and institutions used by the court.

(11) Act in all instances consistent with the public safety and welfare.

(f) Appointment of attorneys and other persons

For the appointment of attorneys, arbitrators, mediators, referees, masters, receivers, and other persons, each court should follow rule 10.611 and the guidelines of standard 10.21.

(g) Educational rights of children in the juvenile court

The juvenile court should be guided by certain general principles:

(1) A significant number of children in the juvenile court process have exceptional needs that, if properly identified and assessed, would qualify such children to receive special education and related services under federal and state education law (a free, appropriate public education) (see Ed. Code, § 56000 et seq. and 20 U.S.C. § 1400 et seq.);

(2) Many children in the juvenile court process have disabilities that, if properly identified and assessed, would qualify such children to receive educational accommodations (see § 504 of the Rehabilitation Act of 1973 [29 U.S.C. § 794; 34 C.F.R. § 104.1 et seq.]);

(3) Unidentified and unremediated exceptional needs and unaccommodated disabilities have been found to correlate

strongly with juvenile delinquency, substance abuse, mental health issues, teenage pregnancy, school failure and dropout, and adult unemployment and crime; and

(4) The cost of incarcerating children is substantially greater than the cost of providing special education and related services to exceptional needs children and providing educational accommodations to children with disabilities.

(h) Role of the juvenile court

The juvenile court should:

(1) Take responsibility, with the other juvenile court participants at every stage of the child's case, to ensure that the child's educational needs are met, regardless of whether the child is in the custody of a parent or is suitably placed in the custody of the child welfare agency or probation department and regardless of where the child is placed in school. Each child under the jurisdiction of the juvenile court with exceptional needs has the right to receive a free, appropriate public education, specially designed, at no cost to the parents, to meet the child's unique special education needs. (See Ed. Code, § 56031 and 20 U.S.C. § 1401(8).) Each child with disabilities under the jurisdiction of the juvenile court has the right to receive accommodations. (See § 504 of the Rehabilitation Act of 1973 [29 U.S.C. § 794; 34 C.F.R. § 104.1 et seq. (1980)].) The court should also ensure that each parent or guardian receives information and assistance concerning his or her child's educational entitlements as provided by law.

(2) Provide oversight of the social service and probation agencies to ensure that a child's educational rights are investigated, reported, and monitored. The court should work within the statutory framework to accommodate the sharing of information between agencies. A child who comes before the court and is suspected of having exceptional needs or other educational disabilities should be referred in writing for an assessment to the child's school principal or to the school district's special education office. (See Ed. Code, §§ 56320–56329.) The child's parent, teacher, or other service provider may make the required written referral for assessment. (See Ed. Code, § 56029.)

(3) Require that court reports, case plans, assessments, and permanency plans considered by the court address a child's educational entitlements and how those entitlements are being satisfied, and contain information to assist the court in deciding whether the right of the parent or guardian to make educational decisions for the child should be limited by the court under Welfare and Institutions Code section 361(a) or 726(b). Information concerning whether the school district has met its obligation to provide educational services to the child, including special educational services if the child has exceptional needs under Education Code section 56000 et seq., and to provide accommodations if the child has disabilities as defined in section 504 of the Rehabilitation Act of 1973 (29 U.S.C. § 794; 34 C.F.R. § 104.1 et seq. (1980)) should also be included, along with a recommendation for disposition.

(4) Facilitate coordination of services by joining the local educational agency as a party when it appears that an educational agency has failed to fulfill its legal obligations to provide special education and related services or accommodations to a child in the juvenile court who has been identified as having exceptional needs or educational disabilities. (See Welf. & Inst. Code, §§ 362(a), 727(a).)

(5) Make appropriate orders limiting the educational rights of a parent or guardian who cannot be located or identified, or who is unwilling or unable to be an active participant in ensuring that the child's educational needs are met, and appoint a responsible adult as educational representative for such a child or, if a representative cannot be identified and the child may be eligible for special education and related services or already has an

individualized education program, use form JV–535 to refer the child to the local educational agency for special education and related services and prompt appointment of a surrogate parent. (Welf. & Inst. Code, §§ 361, 726; Ed. Code, § 56156.)

(6) Ensure that special education, related services, and accommodations to which the child is entitled are provided whenever the child's school placement changes. (See Ed. Code, § 56325.) *(Formerly § 24, adopted, eff. July 1, 1989. As amended, eff. July 1, 1992; Jan. 1, 1999; Jan. 1, 2001; Jan. 1, 2004. Renumbered Standard 5.40 and amended, eff. Jan. 1, 2007.)*

Advisory Committee Comment

Subdivision (a). Considering the constantly evolving changes in the law, as well as the unique nature of the proceedings in juvenile court, the juvenile court judge should be willing to commit to a tenure of three years. Not only does this tenure afford the judge the opportunity to become well acquainted with the total juvenile justice complex, but it also provides continuity to a system that demands it.

Dependency cases under Welfare and Institutions Code section 300 for the most part last 18 months. The juvenile court judge has a responsibility to oversee these cases, and a single judge's involvement over this period of time is important to help ensure positive results. The ultimate goal should be to perfect a system that serves the needs of both recipients and providers. This can only be done over time and with constant application of effective energy.

Subdivision (b)(2). The juvenile court is an integral part of the justice system. It is only through the constant exertion of pressure to maintain resources and the continuous education of court-related personnel and administrators that the historic trend to minimize the juvenile court can be contained.

Subdivision (c)(4). The quality of justice in the juvenile court is in large part dependent on the quality of the attorneys who appear on behalf of the different parties before the court. The presiding judge of the juvenile court plays a significant role in ensuring that a sufficient number of attorneys of high quality are available to the parties appearing in juvenile court.

Juvenile court practice requires attorneys who have both a special interest in and a substantive understanding of the work of the court. Obtaining and retaining qualified attorneys for the juvenile court requires effective recruiting, training, and employment considerations.

The importance of juvenile court work must be stressed to ensure that juvenile court assignments have the same status and career enhancement opportunities as other assignments for public law office attorneys.

The presiding judge of the juvenile court should urge leaders of public law offices serving the juvenile court to assign experienced, interested, and capable attorneys to that court, and to establish hiring and promotional policies that will encourage the development of a division of the office dedicated to working in the juvenile court.

National commentators are in accord with these propositions: "Court–appointed and public attorneys representing children in abuse and neglect cases, as well as judges, should be specially trained or experienced. Juvenile and family courts should not be the 'training ground' for inexperienced attorneys or judges." (Metropolitan Court Judges Committee, National Council of Juvenile and Family Court Judges, *Deprived Children: A Judicial Response—73 Recommendations* (1986) p. 14.)

Fees paid to attorneys appearing in juvenile court are sometimes less than the fees paid attorneys doing other legal work. Such a payment scheme demeans the work of the juvenile court, leading many to believe that such work is less important. It may discourage attorneys from selecting juvenile court practice as a career option. The incarceration of a child in a detention facility or a child's permanent loss of his or her family through a termination of parental rights proceeding is at least as important as any other work in the legal system. Compensation for the legal work in the juvenile court should reflect the importance of this work.

Subdivision (d)(4). Juvenile court law is a specialized area of the law that requires dedication and study. The juvenile court judge has a responsibility to maintain high quality in the practice of law in the juvenile court. The quality of representation in the juvenile court depends in good part on the education of the lawyers who appear there. In order to make certain that all parties receive adequate representation, it is important that attorneys have adequate training before they begin practice in juvenile court and on a continuing basis thereafter. The presiding judge of the juvenile court should mandate such training for all court-appointed attorneys and urge leaders of public law offices to provide at least comparable training for attorneys assigned to juvenile court.

A minimum of six hours of continuing legal education is suggested; more hours are recommended. Education methods can include lectures and tapes that meet the legal education requirements.

In addition to basic legal training in juvenile dependency and delinquency law, evidentiary issues, and effective trial practice techniques, training should also include important related issues, including child development, alternative resources for families, effects and treatment of substance abuse, domestic violence, abuse, neglect, modification and enforcement of all court orders, dependency, delinquency, guardianships, conservatorships, interviewing children, and emancipation. Education may also include observational experience such as site visits to institutions and operations critical to the juvenile court.

A significant barrier to the establishment and maintenance of well-trained attorneys is a lack of educational materials relating to juvenile court practice. Law libraries, law offices, and court systems traditionally do not devote adequate resources to the purchase of such educational materials.

Effective January 1, 1993, guidelines and training material will be available from the Administrative Office of the Courts.

Subdivision (e)(11). A superior court judge assigned to the juvenile court occupies a unique position within California's judiciary. In addition to the traditional role of fairly and efficiently resolving disputes before the court, the juvenile court judge is statutorily required to discharge other duties. California law empowers the juvenile court judge not only to order services for children under its jurisdiction, but also to enforce and review the delivery of those services. This oversight function includes the obligation to understand and work with the public and private agencies, including school systems, that provide services and treatment programs for children and families. As such, the juvenile court assignment requires a dramatic shift in emphasis from judging in the traditional sense.

The legislative directive to juvenile court judges to "improve system performance in a vigorous and ongoing manner" (Welf. & Inst. Code, § 202) poses no conflict with traditional concepts of judicial ethics. Active and public judicial support and encouragement of programs serving children and families at risk are important functions of the juvenile court judge that enhance the overall administration of justice.

The standards in (e) are derived from statutory requirements in the following sections of the Welfare and Institutions Code as well as the supplementary material promulgated by the National Council of Juvenile and Family Court Judges and others: (1) Welfare and Institutions Code, sections 202, 209, 300, 317, 318, 319, 362, 600, 601, 654, 702, 727; (2) California Code of Judicial Conduct, canon 4; (3) Metropolitan Court Judges Committee, National Council of Juvenile and Family Court Judges, *Deprived Children: A Judicial Response—73 Recommendations* (1986), Recommendations 1–7, 14, 35, 40; and (4) National Council of Juvenile and Family Court Judges, Child Welfare League of America, Youth Law Center, and the National Center for Youth Law, *Making Reasonable Efforts: Steps for Keeping Families Together* pp. 43–59.

Standard 5.45. Resource guidelines for child abuse and neglect cases

(a) Guidelines

To improve the fair and efficient administration of child abuse and neglect cases in the California juvenile dependency system, judges and judicial officers assigned to the juvenile court, in consultation with the presiding judge of the juvenile court and the presiding judge of the superior or consolidated court, are encouraged to follow the resource guidelines of the National Council of Juvenile and Family Court Judges, titled "Resource Guidelines: Improving Court Practice in Child Abuse & Neglect Cases." The guidelines are meant to be goals to help courts achieve, among other objectives, the following:

(1) Adherence to statutory timelines;

(2) Effective calendar management;

(3) Effective representation by counsel;

(4) Child–friendly court facilities;

(5) Timely and thorough reports and services to ensure informed judicial decisions, including reasonable efforts findings; and

(6) Minimum time allocations for specified hearings.

(b) Distribution of guidelines

The Administrative Office of the Courts will distribute a copy of the resource guidelines to each juvenile court and will provide individual copies to judicial officers and court administrators on written request. *(Formerly § 24.5, adopted, eff. July 1, 1997. Renumbered Standard 5.45 and amended, eff. Jan. 1, 2007.)*

Advisory Committee Comment

Child abuse and neglect cases impose a special obligation on juvenile court judges to oversee case progress. Case oversight includes monitoring the agency's fulfillment of its responsibilities and parental cooperation with the case plan. Court involvement in child welfare cases occurs simultaneously with agency efforts to assist the family. Federal and state legal mandates assign to the juvenile court a series of interrelated and complex decisions that shape the course of state intervention and determine the future of the child and family.

Unlike almost all other types of cases in the court system, child abuse and neglect cases deal with an ongoing and changing situation. In a child welfare case, the court must focus on agency casework and parental behavior over an extended period of time. In making a decision, the court must take into account the agency's plan to help the family and anticipated changes in parental behavior. At the same time, the court must consider the evolving circumstances and needs of each child.

The purpose of these resource guidelines is to specify the essential elements of properly conducted court hearings. The guidelines describe the requirements of juvenile courts in fulfilling their oversight role under federal and state laws, and they specify the necessary elements of a fair, thorough, and speedy court process in child abuse and neglect cases. The guidelines cover all stages of the court process, from the initial removal hearing to the end of juvenile court involvement. These guidelines assume that the court will remain involved until after the child has been safely returned home, has been placed in another permanent home, or has reached adulthood.

Currently, juvenile courts in California operate under the same juvenile court law and rules, and yet the rules are implemented with considerable variation throughout the state. In part, this is due to the lack of resource guidelines. The adoption of the proposed resource guidelines will help encourage more consistent juvenile court procedures in the state.

The guidelines are meant to be goals, and, as such, some of them may appear out of reach because of fiscal constraints or lack of judicial and staff resources. The Judicial Council Family and Juvenile Law Advisory Committee and staff of the Administrative Office of the Courts are committed to providing technical assistance to each juvenile court to aid in implementing these goals.

Title 7

STANDARDS FOR PROBATE PROCEEDINGS

Standard
7.10. Settlements or judgments in certain civil cases involving minors or persons with disabilities.

Standard 7.10.　Settlements or judgments in certain civil cases involving minors or persons with disabilities

In matters assigned to or pending in civil departments of the court where court approval of trusts that will receive proceeds of settlements or judgments is required under Probate Code section 3600, each court should develop practices and procedures that:

(1) Provide for determination of the trust issues by the probate department of the court or, in a court that does not have a probate department, a judicial officer who regularly hears proceedings under the Probate Code; or

(2) Ensure that judicial officers who hear these matters are experienced or have received training in substantive and technical issues involving trusts (including special needs trusts). *(Formerly § 40, adopted, eff. Jan. 1, 2005. Renumbered Standard 7.10, eff. Jan. 1, 2007.)*

Title 8

STANDARDS FOR THE APPELLATE COURTS

Standard
8.1. Memorandum opinions.

Standard 8.1.　Memorandum opinions

The Courts of Appeal should dispose of causes that raise no substantial issues of law or fact by memorandum or other abbreviated form of opinion. Such causes could include:

(1) An appeal that is determined by a controlling statute which is not challenged for unconstitutionality and does not present any substantial question of interpretation or application;

(2) An appeal that is determined by a controlling decision which does not require a reexamination or restatement of its principles or rules; or

(3) An appeal raising factual issues that are determined by the substantial evidence rule. *(Formerly § 6, adopted, eff. July 1, 1970. Renumbered Standard 8.1 and amended, eff. Jan. 1, 2007.)*

Title 10

STANDARDS FOR JUDICIAL ADMINISTRATION

Standard
10.5. The role of the judiciary in the community.
10.16. Model code of ethics for court employees.
10.17. Trial court performance standards.
10.20. Court's duty to prohibit bias.
10.21. Appointment of attorneys, arbitrators, mediators, referees, masters, receivers, and other persons.
10.24. Children's waiting room.
10.25. Reasonable accommodation for court personnel.
10.31. Master jury list.
10.41. Court sessions at or near state penal institutions.
10.50. Selection of regular grand jury.
10.51. Juror complaints.
10.55. Local program on waste reduction and recycling.
10.70. Implementation and coordination of mediation and other alternative dispute resolution (ADR) programs.
10.71. Alternative dispute resolution (ADR) committees.
10.72. ADR committees and criteria for referring cases to dispute resolution neutrals.

Standard 10.5.　The role of the judiciary in the community

(a) Community outreach an official judicial function

Judicial participation in community outreach activities should be considered an official judicial function to promote public understanding of and confidence in the administration of justice. This function should be performed in a manner consistent with the California Code of Judicial Ethics.

(b) Encouraged outreach activities

The judiciary is encouraged to:

(1) Provide active leadership within the community in identifying and resolving issues of access to justice within the court system;

(2) Develop local education programs for the public designed to increase public understanding of the court system;

(3) Create local mechanisms for obtaining information from the public about how the court system may be more responsive to the public's needs;

(4) Serve as guest speakers, during or after normal court hours, to address local civic, educational, business, and charitable groups that have an interest in understanding the court system but do not espouse a particular political agenda with which it would be inappropriate for a judicial officer to be associated; and

(5) Take an active part in the life of the community where the participation of the judiciary will serve to increase public understanding and promote public confidence in the integrity of the court system. *(Formerly § 39, adopted, eff. April 1, 1999. Renumbered Standard 10.5 and amended, eff. Jan. 1, 2007.)*

Standard 10.16.　Model code of ethics for court employees

Each trial and appellate court should adopt a code of ethical behavior for its support staff, and in doing so should consider rule 10.670(c)(12) of the California Rules of Court, and the model Code of Ethics for the Court Employees of California

Ct. Rules

approved by the Judicial Council on May 17, 1994, and any subsequent revisions. The approved model code is published by the Administrative Office of the Courts. *(Formerly § 35, adopted, eff. July 1, 1994, Renumbered Standard 10.16 and amended, eff. Jan. 1, 2007. As amended, eff. July 1, 2008.)*

Standard 10.17.   Trial court performance standards

(a) Purpose

These standards are intended to be used by trial courts, in cooperation with the Judicial Council, for purposes of internal evaluation, self-assessment, and self-improvement. They are not intended as a basis for cross-court comparisons, nor are they intended as a basis for evaluating the performance of individual judges.

(b) Standards

The standards for trial court performance are as follows:

(1) *Access to justice*

(A) The court conducts its proceedings and other public business openly.

(B) Court facilities are safe, accessible, and convenient to use.

(C) All who appear before the court are given the opportunity to participate effectively without undue hardship or inconvenience.

(D) Judges and other trial court personnel are courteous and responsive to the public and accord respect to all with whom they come into contact.

(E) The costs of access to the trial court's proceedings and records—whether measured in terms of money, time, or the procedures that must be followed—are reasonable, fair, and affordable.

(2) *Expedition and timeliness*

(A) The trial court establishes and complies with recognized guidelines for timely case processing while, at the same time, keeping current with its incoming caseload.

(B) The trial court disburses funds promptly, provides reports and information according to required schedules, and responds to requests for information and other services on an established schedule that assures their effective use.

(C) The trial court promptly implements changes in law and procedure.

(3) *Equality, fairness, and integrity*

(A) Trial court procedures faithfully adhere to relevant laws, procedural rules, and established policies.

(B) Jury lists are representative of the jurisdiction from which they are drawn.

(C) Trial courts give individual attention to cases, deciding them without undue disparity among like cases and on legally relevant factors.

(D) Decisions of the trial court unambiguously address the issues presented to it and make clear how compliance can be achieved.

(E) The trial court takes appropriate responsibility for the enforcement of its orders.

(F) Records of all relevant court decisions and actions are accurate and properly preserved.

(4) *Independence and accountability*

(A) A trial court maintains its institutional integrity and observes the principle of comity in its governmental relations.

(B) The trial court responsibly seeks, uses, and accounts for its public resources.

(C) The trial court uses fair employment practices.

(D) The trial court informs the community of its programs.

(E) The trial court anticipates new conditions or emergent events and adjusts its operations as necessary.

(5) *Public trust and confidence*

(A) The trial court and the justice it delivers are perceived by the public as accessible.

(B) The public has trust and confidence that the basic trial court functions are conducted expeditiously and fairly and that its decisions have integrity.

(C) The trial court is perceived to be independent, not unduly influenced by other components of government, and accountable.

(Formerly § 30, adopted, eff. Jan. 25, 1995. Renumbered Standard 10.17 and amended, eff. Jan. 1, 2007.)

Standard 10.20.   Court's duty to prohibit bias

(a) General

To preserve the integrity and impartiality of the judicial system, each judge should:

(1) *Ensure fairness*

Ensure that courtroom proceedings are conducted in a manner that is fair and impartial to all of the participants.

(2) *Refrain from and prohibit biased conduct*

In all courtroom proceedings, refrain from engaging in conduct and prohibit others from engaging in conduct that exhibits bias, including but not limited to bias based on disability, gender, race, religion, ethnicity, and sexual orientation, whether that bias is directed toward counsel, court personnel, witnesses, parties, jurors, or any other participants.

(3) *Ensure unbiased decisions*

Ensure that all orders, rulings, and decisions are based on the sound exercise of judicial discretion and the balancing of competing rights and interests and are not influenced by stereotypes or biases.

(b) Creation of local committees on bias

Each court should establish a local committee with local bar associations to assist in maintaining a courtroom environment free of bias or the appearance of bias. Courts within one or more counties may choose to form a single committee. The local committee should:

(1) Be composed of representative members of the court community, including but not limited to judges, lawyers, court administrators, and representatives and individuals from minority, women's, and gay and lesbian bar associations and from organizations that represent persons with disabilities;

(2) Sponsor or support educational programs designed to eliminate bias within the court and legal communities, including but not limited to bias based on disability, gender, race, religion, ethnicity, and sexual orientation; and

(3) Develop and maintain an informal procedure for receiving complaints relating to bias in the courtroom, including but not limited to bias based on disability, gender, race, religion, ethnicity, and sexual orientation.

(c) Minimum components of a complaint procedure

An informal complaint procedure developed and maintained by a local committee on bias should:

(1) Contain a provision specifying that the intent of the procedure is to educate with the purpose of ameliorating the problem rather than disciplining the person who is the subject of the complaint;

(2) Accommodate local needs and allow for local flexibility;

(3) Apply to all participants in courtroom proceedings;

(4) Apply only to complaints as to which the identity of the complainant is known;

(5) To the extent possible and unless disclosure is required by law, protect the confidentiality of the complainant, the person who is the subject of the complaint, and other interested persons;

(6) Relate to incidents of behavior or conduct occurring in courtroom proceedings;

(7) Apply to incidents of bias whether they relate to race, sex, religion, national origin, disability, age, sexual orientation, or socioeconomic status;

(8) Contain a provision that exempts activities constituting legitimate advocacy when matters of race, sex, religion, national origin, disability, age, sexual orientation, or socioeconomic status are relevant to issues in the courtroom proceeding;

(9) Focus on incidents that do not warrant discipline but that should be corrected;

(10) With respect to those incidents that if substantiated would warrant discipline, advise the complaining party of the appropriate disciplinary authority;

(11) Contain a provision specifying that nothing in the procedure in any way limits the ability of any person to submit a complaint of misconduct to the appropriate disciplinary body; and

(12) To the extent possible and unless disclosure is required by law, prohibit retention of written records of complaints received but permit collection of data on types of complaints or underlying anecdotes that might be useful in educational programs.

(d) Application of local rules

The existence of the local committee, its purpose, and the features of the informal complaint procedure should be memorialized in the applicable local rules of court. *(Formerly § 1, adopted, eff. Jan. 1, 1987. As amended, eff. Jan. 1, 1994; Jan. 1, 1998. Renumbered Standard 10.20 and amended, eff. Jan. 1, 2007.)*

Standard 10.21. Appointment of attorneys, arbitrators, mediators, referees, masters, receivers, and other persons

(a) Nondiscrimination in appointment lists

In establishing and maintaining lists of qualified attorneys, arbitrators, mediators, referees, masters, receivers, and other persons who are eligible for appointment, courts should ensure equal access for all applicants regardless of gender, race, ethnicity, disability, sexual orientation, or age.

(b) Nondiscrimination in recruitment

Each trial court should conduct a recruitment procedure for the appointment of attorneys, arbitrators, mediators, referees, masters, receivers, and other persons appointed by the court (the "appointment programs") by publicizing the existence of the appointment programs at least once annually through state and local bar associations, including specialty bar associations. This publicity should encourage and provide an opportunity for all eligible individuals, regardless of gender, race, ethnicity, disability, sexual orientation, or age, to seek positions on the rosters of the appointment programs. Each trial court also should use other methods of publicizing the appointment programs that maximize the opportunity for a diverse applicant pool.

(c) Nondiscrimination in application and selection procedure

Each trial court should conduct an application and selection procedure for the appointment programs that ensures that the most qualified applicants for an appointment are selected, regardless of gender, race, ethnicity, disability, sexual orienta-

tion, or age. *(Formerly § 1.5, adopted, eff. Jan. 1, 1999. Renumbered Standard 10.21 and amended, eff. Jan. 1, 2007.)*

Standard 10.24. Children's waiting room

Each court should endeavor to provide a children's waiting room located in the courthouse for the use of minors under the age of 16 who are present on court premises as participants or who accompany persons who are participants in court proceedings. The waiting room should be supervised and open during normal court hours. If a court does not have sufficient space in the courthouse for a children's waiting room, the court should create the necessary space when court facilities are reorganized or remodeled or when new facilities are constructed. *(Formerly § 1.3, adopted, eff. Jan. 1, 1987. Renumbered Standard 10.24 and amended, eff. Jan. 1, 2007.)*

Standard 10.25. Reasonable accommodation for court personnel

At least to the extent required by state and federal law, each court should evaluate existing facilities, programs, and services available to employees to ensure that no barriers exist to prevent otherwise-qualified employees with known disabilities from performing their jobs or participating fully in court programs or activities. *(Formerly § 1.4, adopted, eff. Jan. 1, 1998. Renumbered Standard 10.25, eff. Jan. 1, 2007.)*

Standard 10.31. Master jury list

The jury commissioner should use the National Change of Address System or other comparable means to update jury source lists and create as accurate a master jury list as reasonably practical. *(Formerly § 4.6, adopted, eff. July 1, 1997. Renumbered Standard 10.31 and amended, eff. Jan. 1, 2007.)*

Standard 10.41. Court sessions at or near state penal institutions

(a) Provision of adequate protection

Facilities used regularly for judicial proceedings should not be located on the grounds of or immediately adjacent to a state penal institution unless the location, design, and setting of the court facility provide adequate protection against the possible adverse influence that the prison facilities and activities might have on the fairness of judicial proceedings.

(b) Factors to be considered

In determining whether adequate protection is provided, the following factors should be considered:

(1) The physical and visual remoteness of the court facility from the facilities and activities of the prison;

(2) The location and appearance of the court facility with respect to the adjacent public areas through which jurors and witnesses would normally travel in going to and from the court;

(3) The accessibility of the facility to the press and the general public; and

(4) Any other factors that might affect the fairness of the judicial proceedings.

(c) Compelling reasons of safety or court convenience

Unless the location, design, and setting of the facility for conducting court sessions meet the criteria in (a) and (b):

(1) Court sessions should not be conducted in or immediately adjacent to a state penal institution except for compelling reasons of safety or convenience of the court; and

(2) Court sessions should not be conducted at such a location when the trial is by jury or when the testimony of witnesses who are neither inmates nor employees of the institution will be required. *(Formerly § 7.5, adopted, eff. July 1, 1975. Renumbered Standard 10.41 and amended, eff. Jan. 1, 2007.)*

Standard 10.50.   **Selection of regular grand jury**

(a) Definition

"Regular grand jury" means a body of citizens of a county selected by the court to investigate matters of civil concern in the county, whether or not that body has jurisdiction to return indictments.

(b) Regular grand jury list

The list of qualified candidates prepared by the jury commissioner to be considered for nomination to the regular grand jury should be obtained by one or more of the following methods:

(1) Names of members of the public obtained at random in the same manner as the list of trial jurors. However, the names obtained for nomination to the regular grand jury should be kept separate and distinct from the trial jury list, consistent with Penal Code section 899.

(2) Recommendations for grand jurors that encompass a cross-section of the county's population base, solicited from a broad representation of community-based organizations, civic leaders, and superior court judges, referees, and commissioners.

(3) Applications from interested citizens solicited through the media or a mass mailing.

(c) Carryover grand jurors

The court is encouraged to consider carryover grand jury selections under Penal Code section 901(b) to ensure broad-based representation.

(d) Nomination of grand jurors

Judges who nominate persons for grand jury selection under Penal Code section 903.4 are encouraged to select candidates from the list returned by the jury commissioner or to otherwise employ a nomination procedure that will ensure broad-based representation from the community.

(e) Disfavored nominations

Judges should not nominate to the grand jury a spouse or immediate family member (within the first degree of consanguinity) of any superior court judge, commissioner, or referee; elected official; or department head of any city, county, or governmental entity subject to grand jury scrutiny. *(Formerly § 17, adopted, eff. July 1, 1992. Renumbered Standard 10.50 and amended, eff. Jan. 1, 2007.)*

Standard 10.51.   **Juror complaints**

Each court should establish a reasonable mechanism for receiving and responding to juror complaints. *(Formerly § 4.5, adopted, eff. July 1, 1997. Renumbered Standard 10.51, eff. Jan. 1, 2007.)*

Standard 10.55.   **Local program on waste reduction and recycling**

Each court should adopt a program for waste reduction and recycling or participate in a county program. *(Formerly § 17.5, adopted, eff. Jan. 1, 1991. Renumbered Standard 10.55 and amended, eff. Jan. 1, 2007.)*

Standard 10.70.   **Implementation and coordination of mediation and other alternative dispute resolution (ADR) programs**

(a) Implementation of mediation programs for civil cases

Superior courts should implement mediation programs for civil cases as part of their core operations.

(b) Promotion of ADR programs

Superior courts should promote the development, implementation, maintenance, and expansion of successful mediation and other alternative dispute resolution (ADR) programs, through activities that include:

(1) Establishing appropriate criteria for determining which cases should be referred to ADR, and what ADR processes are appropriate for those cases. These criteria should include whether the parties are likely to benefit from the use of the ADR process;

(2) Developing, refining, and using lists of qualified ADR neutrals;

(3) Adopting appropriate criteria for referring cases to qualified ADR neutrals;

(4) Developing ADR information and providing educational programs for parties who are not represented by counsel; and

(5) Providing ADR education for judicial officers.

(c) Coordination of ADR programs

Superior courts should coordinate ADR promotional activities and explore joint funding and administration of ADR programs with each other and with professional and community-based organizations. *(Formerly § 32, adopted, eff. July 1, 1992. As amended, eff. Jan. 1, 2006. Renumbered Standard 10.70 and amended, eff. Jan. 1, 2007.)*

Standard 10.71.   **Alternative dispute resolution (ADR) committees**

Courts that are not required and that do not elect to have an ADR administrative committee as provided in rule 10.783 of the California Rules of Court should form committees of judges, attorneys, alternative dispute resolution (ADR) neutrals, and county ADR administrators, if any, to oversee the court's ADR programs and panels of neutrals for general civil cases. *(Formerly § 32.1, adopted, eff. Jan. 1, 2006. Renumbered Standard 10.71 and amended, eff. Jan. 1, 2007.)*

Standard 10.72.   **ADR committees and criteria for referring cases to dispute resolution neutrals**

(a) Training, experience, and skills

Courts should evaluate the ADR training, experience, and skills of potential ADR neutrals.

(b) Additional considerations for continuing referrals

After a court has sufficient experience with an ADR neutral, the court should also consider indicators of client satisfaction, settlement rate, continuing ADR education, and adherence to applicable standards of conduct in determining whether to continue referrals to that neutral. *(Formerly § 33, adopted, eff. July 1, 1992. As amended, eff. Jan. 1, 2006. Renumbered Standard 10.72 and amended, eff. Jan. 1, 2007.)*

Advisory Committee Comment

Although settlement rate is an important indicator of a neutral's effectiveness, it should be borne in mind that some disputes will not resolve, despite the best efforts of a skilled neutral. Neutrals should not feel pressure to achieve a high settlement rate through resolutions that may not be in the interest of one or more parties. Accordingly, settlement rate should be used with caution as a criterion for court referral of disputes to neutrals.

ETHICS STANDARDS FOR NEUTRAL ARBITRATORS IN CONTRACTUAL ARBITRATION

The "Ethics Standards for Neutral Arbitrators in Contractual Arbitration", adopted eff. July 1, 2002, were formerly contained in Division VI of the Appendix to the California Rules of Court, and were incorporated into the California Rules of Court without change, effective Jan. 1, 2007, as part of the reorganization of the California Rules of Court, which was adopted by the Judicial Council on June 30, 2006.

Former Division VI, "Discretionary Child Support," adopted eff. July 1, 1986, was repealed eff. Jan. 1, 1999. For state uniform child support guidelines, see Family Code § 4050 et seq.

Standard

1. Purpose, intent, and construction.
2. Definitions.
3. Application and effective date.
4. Duration of duty.
5. General duty.
6. Duty to refuse appointment.
7. Disclosure.
8. Additional disclosures in consumer arbitrations administered by a provider organization.
9. Arbitrators' duty to inform themselves about matters to be disclosed.
10. Disqualification.
11. Duty to refuse gift, bequest, or favor.
12. Duties and limitations regarding future professional relationships or employment.
13. Conduct of proceeding.
14. Ex parte communications.
15. Confidentiality.
16. Compensation.
17. Marketing.

Standard 1. Purpose, intent, and construction

(a) These standards are adopted under the authority of Code of Civil Procedure section 1281.85 and establish the minimum standards of conduct for neutral arbitrators who are subject to these standards. They are intended to guide the conduct of arbitrators, to inform and protect participants in arbitration, and to promote public confidence in the arbitration process.

(b) For arbitration to be effective there must be broad public confidence in the integrity and fairness of the process. Arbitrators are responsible to the parties, the other participants, and the public for conducting themselves in accordance with these standards so as to merit that confidence.

(c) These standards are to be construed and applied to further the purpose and intent expressed in subdivisions (a) and (b) and in conformance with all applicable law.

(d) These standards are not intended to affect any existing civil cause of action or create any new civil cause of action. *(Adopted, eff. July 1, 2002. As amended, eff. Jan. 1, 2003.)*

Standard 2. Definitions

As used in these standards:

(a) Arbitrator and neutral arbitrator

(1) "Arbitrator" and "neutral arbitrator" mean any arbitrator who is subject to these standards and who is to serve impartially, whether selected or appointed:

(A) Jointly by the parties or by the arbitrators selected by the parties;

(B) By the court, when the parties or the arbitrators selected by the parties fail to select an arbitrator who was to be selected jointly by them; or

(C) By a dispute resolution provider organization, under an agreement of the parties.

(2) Where the context includes events or acts occurring before an appointment is final, "arbitrator" and "neutral arbitrator" include a person who has been served with notice of a proposed nomination or appointment.

(b) "Applicable law" means constitutional provisions, statutes, decisional law, California Rules of Court, and other statewide rules or regulations that apply to arbitrators who are subject to these standards.

(c) "Conclusion of the arbitration" means the following:

(1) When the arbitrator is disqualified or withdraws or the case is settled or dismissed before the arbitrator makes an award, the date on which the arbitrator's appointment is terminated;

(2) When the arbitrator makes an award and no party makes a timely application to the arbitrator to correct the award, the final date for making an application to the arbitrator for correction; or

(3) When a party makes a timely application to the arbitrator to correct the award, the date on which the arbitrator serves a corrected award or a denial on each party, or the date on which denial occurs by operation of law.

(d) "Consumer arbitration" means an arbitration conducted under a predispute arbitration provision contained in a contract that meets the criteria listed in paragraphs (1) through (3) below. "Consumer arbitration" excludes arbitration proceedings conducted under or arising out of public or private sector labor-relations laws, regulations, charter provisions, ordinances, statutes, or agreements.

(1) The contract is with a consumer party, as defined in these standards;

(2) The contract was drafted by or on behalf of the nonconsumer party; and

(3) The consumer party was required to accept the arbitration provision in the contract.

(e) "Consumer party" is a party to an arbitration agreement who, in the context of that arbitration agreement, is any of the following:

(1) An individual who seeks or acquires, including by lease, any goods or services primarily for personal, family, or household purposes including, but not limited to, financial services, insurance, and other goods and services as defined in section 1761 of the Civil Code;

(2) An individual who is an enrollee, a subscriber, or insured in a health-care service plan within the meaning of section 1345 of the Health and Safety Code or health-care insurance plan within the meaning of section 106 of the Insurance Code;

(3) An individual with a medical malpractice claim that is subject to the arbitration agreement; or

(4) An employee or an applicant for employment in a dispute arising out of or relating to the employee's employment or the applicant's prospective employment that is subject to the arbitration agreement.

(f) "Dispute resolution neutral" means a temporary judge appointed under article VI, section 21 of the California Constitution, a referee appointed under Code of Civil Procedure section 638 or 639, an arbitrator, a neutral evaluator, a special master, a mediator, a settlement officer, or a settlement facilitator.

(g) "Dispute resolution provider organization" and "provider organization" mean any nongovernmental entity that, or individual who, coordinates, administers, or provides the services of two or more dispute resolution neutrals.

(h) "Domestic partner" means a domestic partner as defined in Family Code section 297.

(i) "Financial interest" means a financial interest within the meaning of Code of Civil Procedure section 170.5.

(j) "Gift" means a gift as defined in Code of Civil Procedure section 170.9(*l*).

(k) "Honoraria" means honoraria as defined in Code of Civil Procedure section 170.9(h) and (i).

(*l*) "Lawyer in the arbitration" means the lawyer hired to represent a party in the arbitration.

(m) "Lawyer for a party" means the lawyer hired to represent a party in the arbitration and any lawyer or law firm currently associated in the practice of law with the lawyer hired to represent a party in the arbitration.

(n) "Member of the arbitrator's immediate family" means the arbitrator's spouse or domestic partner and any minor child living in the arbitrator's household.

(o) "Member of the arbitrator's extended family" means the parents, grandparents, great-grandparents, children, grandchildren, great-grandchildren, siblings, uncles, aunts, nephews, and nieces of the arbitrator or the arbitrator's spouse or domestic partner or the spouse of such person.

(p) Party

(1) "Party" means a party to the arbitration agreement:

(A) Who seeks to arbitrate a controversy pursuant to the agreement;

(B) Against whom such arbitration is sought; or

(C) Who is made a party to such arbitration by order of a court or the arbitrator upon such party's application, upon the application of any other party to the arbitration, or upon the arbitrator's own determination.

(2) "Party" includes the representative of a party, unless the context requires a different meaning.

(q) "Party–arbitrator" means an arbitrator selected unilaterally by a party.

(r) "Private practice of law" means private practice of law as defined in Code of Civil Procedure section 170.5.

(s) "Significant personal relationship" includes a close personal friendship. *(Adopted, eff. July 1, 2002. As amended, eff. Jan. 1, 2003.)*

Standard 3.   Application and effective date

(a) Except as otherwise provided in this standard and standard 8, these standards apply to all persons who are appointed to serve as neutral arbitrators on or after July 1, 2002, in any arbitration under an arbitration agreement, if:

(1) The arbitration agreement is subject to the provisions of title 9 of part III of the Code of Civil Procedure (commencing with section 1280); or

(2) The arbitration hearing is to be conducted in California.

(b) These standards do not apply to:

(1) Party arbitrators, as defined in these standards; or

(2) Any arbitrator serving in:

(A) An international arbitration proceeding subject to the provisions of title 9.3 of part III of the Code of Civil Procedure;

(B) A judicial arbitration proceeding subject to the provisions of chapter 2.5 of title 3 of part III of the Code of Civil Procedure;

(C) An attorney-client fee arbitration proceeding subject to the provisions of article 13 of chapter 4 of division 3 of the Business and Professions Code;

(D) An automobile warranty dispute resolution process certified under California Code of Regulations title 16, division 33.1;

(E) An arbitration of a workers' compensation dispute under Labor Code sections 5270 through 5277;

(F) An arbitration conducted by the Workers' Compensation Appeals Board under Labor Code section 5308;

(G) An arbitration of a complaint filed against a contractor with the Contractors State License Board under Business and Professions Code sections 7085 through 7085.7; or

(H) An arbitration conducted under or arising out of public or private sector labor-relations laws, regulations, charter provisions, ordinances, statutes, or agreements.

(c) Persons who are serving in arbitrations in which they were appointed to serve as arbitrators before July 1, 2002, are not subject to these standards in those arbitrations. Persons who are serving in arbitrations in which they were appointed to serve as arbitrators before January 1, 2003, are not subject to standard 8 in those arbitrations. *(Adopted, eff. July 1, 2002. As amended, eff. Jan. 1, 2003.)*

Standard 4.   Duration of duty

(a) Except as otherwise provided in these standards, an arbitrator must comply with these ethics standards from acceptance of appointment until the conclusion of the arbitration.

(b) If, after the conclusion of the arbitration, a case is referred back to the arbitrator for reconsideration or rehearing, the arbitrator must comply with these ethics standards from the date the case is referred back to the arbitrator until the arbitration is again concluded. *(Adopted, eff. July 1, 2002.)*

Standard 5.   General duty

An arbitrator must act in a manner that upholds the integrity and fairness of the arbitration process. He or she must maintain impartiality toward all participants in the arbitration at all times. *(Adopted, eff. July 1, 2002.)*

Standard 6.   Duty to refuse appointment

Notwithstanding any contrary request, consent, or waiver by the parties, a proposed arbitrator must decline appointment if he or she is not able to be impartial. *(Adopted, eff. July 1, 2002.)*

Standard 7.   Disclosure

(a) Intent

This standard is intended to identify the matters that must be disclosed by a person nominated or appointed as an arbitrator. To the extent that this standard addresses matters that are also addressed by statute, it is intended to include those statutory disclosure requirements, not to eliminate, reduce, or otherwise limit them.

(b) General provisions

For purposes of this standard:

(1) *Collective bargaining cases excluded*

The terms "cases" and "any arbitration" do not include collective bargaining cases or arbitrations conducted under or arising out of collective bargaining agreements between employers and employees or between their respective representatives.

(2) *Offers of employment or professional relationship*

If an arbitrator has disclosed to the parties in an arbitration that he or she will entertain offers of employment or of professional relationships from a party or lawyer for a party while the arbitration is pending as required by subdivision (b) of standard 12, the arbitrator is not required to disclose to the parties in that arbitration any such offer from a party or lawyer for a party that he or she subsequently receives or accepts while that arbitration is pending.

(3) *Names of parties in cases*

When making disclosures about other pending or prior cases, in order to preserve confidentiality, it is sufficient to give the name of any party who is not a party to the pending arbitration as "claimant" or "respondent" if the party is an individual and not a business or corporate entity.

(c) Time and manner of disclosure

Within ten calendar days of service of notice of the proposed nomination or appointment, a proposed arbitrator must disclose to all parties in writing all matters listed in subdivisions (d) and (e) of this standard of which the arbitrator is then aware. If an arbitrator subsequently becomes aware of a matter that must be disclosed under either subdivision (d) or (e) of this standard, the arbitrator must disclose that matter to the parties in writing within 10 calendar days after the arbitrator becomes aware of the matter.

(d) Required disclosures

A person who is nominated or appointed as an arbitrator must disclose all matters that could cause a person aware of the facts to reasonably entertain a doubt that the proposed arbitrator would be able to be impartial, including all of the following:

(1) *Family relationships with party*

The arbitrator or a member of the arbitrator's immediate or extended family is a party, a party's spouse or domestic partner, or an officer, director, or trustee of a party.

(2) *Family relationships with lawyer in the arbitration*

The arbitrator, or the spouse, former spouse, domestic partner, child, sibling, or parent of the arbitrator or the arbitrator's spouse or domestic partner is:

    (A) A lawyer in the arbitration;

    (B) The spouse or domestic partner of a lawyer in the arbitration; or

    (C) Currently associated in the private practice of law with a lawyer in the arbitration.

(3) *Significant personal relationship with party or lawyer for a party*

The arbitrator or a member of the arbitrator's immediate family has or has had a significant personal relationship with any party or lawyer for a party.

(4) *Service as arbitrator for a party or lawyer for party*

    (A) The arbitrator is serving or, within the preceding five years, has served:

        (i) As a neutral arbitrator in another prior or pending noncollective bargaining case involving a party to the current arbitration or a lawyer for a party.

        (ii) As a party-appointed arbitrator in another prior or pending noncollective bargaining case for either a party to the current arbitration or a lawyer for a party.

        (iii) As a neutral arbitrator in another prior or pending noncollective bargaining case in which he or she was selected by a person serving as a party-appointed arbitrator in the current arbitration

    (B) Case information

If the arbitrator is serving or has served in any of the capacities listed under (A), he or she must disclose:

    (i) The names of the parties in each prior or pending case and, where applicable, the name of the attorney representing the party in the current arbitration who is involved in the pending case, who was involved in the prior case, or whose current associate is involved in the pending case or was involved in the prior case.

    (ii) The results of each prior case arbitrated to conclusion, including the date of the arbitration award, identification of the prevailing party, the amount of monetary damages awarded, if any, and the names of the parties' attorneys.

(C) Summary of case information

If the total number of the cases disclosed under (A) is greater than five, the arbitrator must provide a summary of these cases that states:

    (i) The number of pending cases in which the arbitrator is currently serving in each capacity;

    (ii) The number of prior cases in which the arbitrator previously served in each capacity;

    (iii) The number of prior cases arbitrated to conclusion; and

    (iv) The number of such prior cases in which the party to the current arbitration, the party represented by the lawyer for a party in the current arbitration or the party represented by the party-arbitrator in the current arbitration was the prevailing party.

(5) *Compensated service as other dispute resolution neutral*

The arbitrator is serving or has served as a dispute resolution neutral other than an arbitrator in another pending or prior noncollective bargaining case involving a party or lawyer for a party and the arbitrator received or expects to receive any form of compensation for serving in this capacity.

(A) Time frame

For purposes of this paragraph (5), "prior case" means any case in which the arbitrator concluded his or her service as a dispute resolution neutral within two years before the date of the arbitrator's proposed nomination or appointment, but does not include any case in which the arbitrator concluded his or her service before January 1, 2002.

(B) Case information

If the arbitrator is serving or has served in any of the capacities listed under this paragraph (5), he or she must disclose:

    (i) The names of the parties in each prior or pending case and, where applicable, the name of the attorney in the current arbitration who is involved in the pending case, who was involved in the prior case, or whose current associate is involved in the pending case or was involved in the prior case;

    (ii) The dispute resolution neutral capacity (mediator, referee, etc.) in which the arbitrator is serving or served in the case; and

    (iii) In each such case in which the arbitrator rendered a decision as a temporary judge or referee, the date of the decision, the prevailing party, the amount of monetary damages awarded, if any, and the names of the parties' attorneys.

(C) Summary of case information

If the total number of cases disclosed under this paragraph (5) is greater than five, the arbitrator must also provide a summary of the cases that states:

(i) The number of pending cases in which the arbitrator is currently serving in each capacity;

(ii) The number of prior cases in which the arbitrator previously served in each capacity;

(iii) The number of prior cases in which the arbitrator rendered a decision as a temporary judge or referee; and

(iv) The number of such prior cases in which the party to the current arbitration or the party represented by the lawyer for a party in the current arbitration was the prevailing party.

(6) *Current arrangements for prospective neutral service*

Whether the arbitrator has any current arrangement with a party concerning prospective employment or other compensated service as a dispute resolution neutral or is participating in or, within the last two years, has participated in discussions regarding such prospective employment or service with a party.

(7) *Attorney–client relationship*

Any attorney-client relationship the arbitrator has or has had with a party or lawyer for a party. Attorney–client relationships include the following:

(A) An officer, a director, or a trustee of a party is or, within the preceding two years, was a client of the arbitrator in the arbitrator's private practice of law or a client of a lawyer with whom the arbitrator is or was associated in the private practice of law;

(B) In any other proceeding involving the same issues, the arbitrator gave advice to a party or a lawyer in the arbitration concerning any matter involved in the arbitration; and

(C) The arbitrator served as a lawyer for or as an officer of a public agency which is a party and personally advised or in any way represented the public agency concerning the factual or legal issues in the arbitration.

(8) *Other professional relationships*

Any other professional relationship not already disclosed under paragraphs (2)–(7) that the arbitrator or a member of the arbitrator's immediate family has or has had with a party or lawyer for a party, including the following:

(A) The arbitrator was associated in the private practice of law with a lawyer in the arbitration within the last two years;

(B) The arbitrator or a member of the arbitrator's immediate family is or, within the preceding two years, was an employee of or an expert witness or a consultant for a party; and

(C) The arbitrator or a member of the arbitrator's immediate family is or, within the preceding two years, was an employee of or an expert witness or a consultant for a lawyer in the arbitration.

(9) *Financial interests in party*

The arbitrator or a member of the arbitrator's immediate family has a financial interest in a party.

(10) *Financial interests in subject of arbitration*

The arbitrator or a member of the arbitrator's immediate family has a financial interest in the subject matter of the arbitration.

(11) *Affected interest*

The arbitrator or a member of the arbitrator's immediate family has an interest that could be substantially affected by the outcome of the arbitration.

(12) *Knowledge of disputed facts*

The arbitrator or a member of the arbitrator's immediate or extended family has personal knowledge of disputed evidentiary facts relevant to the arbitration. A person who is likely to be a material witness in the proceeding is deemed to have personal knowledge of disputed evidentiary facts concerning the proceeding.

(13) *Membership in organizations practicing discrimination*

The arbitrator's membership in any organization that practices invidious discrimination on the basis of race, sex, religion, national origin, or sexual orientation. Membership in a religious organization, an official military organization of the United States, or a nonprofit youth organization need not be disclosed unless it would interfere with the arbitrator's proper conduct of the proceeding or would cause a person aware of the fact to reasonably entertain a doubt concerning the arbitrator's ability to act impartially.

(14) Any other matter that:

(A) Might cause a person aware of the facts to reasonably entertain a doubt that the arbitrator would be able to be impartial;

(B) Leads the proposed arbitrator to believe there is a substantial doubt as to his or her capacity to be impartial, including, but not limited to, bias or prejudice toward a party, lawyer, or law firm in the arbitration; or

(C) Otherwise leads the arbitrator to believe that his or her disqualification will further the interests of justice.

(e) Inability to conduct or timely complete proceedings

In addition to the matters that must be disclosed under subdivision (d), an arbitrator must also disclose:

(1) If the arbitrator is not able to properly perceive the evidence or properly conduct the proceedings because of a permanent or temporary physical impairment; and

(2) Any constraints on his or her availability known to the arbitrator that will interfere with his or her ability to commence or complete the arbitration in a timely manner.

(f) Continuing duty

An arbitrator's duty to disclose the matters described in subdivisions (d) and (e) of this standard is a continuing duty, applying from service of the notice of the arbitrator's proposed nomination or appointment until the conclusion of the arbitration proceeding. (*Adopted, eff. July 1, 2002. As amended, eff. Jan. 1, 2003.*)

Standard 8. Additional disclosures in consumer arbitrations administered by a provider organization

(a) General provisions

(1) *Reliance on information provided by provider organization*

Except as to the information in (c)(1), an arbitrator may rely on information supplied by the administering provider organization in making the disclosures required by this standard. If the information that must be disclosed is available on the Internet, the arbitrator may comply with the obligation to disclose this information by providing the Internet address at which the information is located and notifying the party that the arbitrator will supply hard copies of this information upon request.

(2) *Reliance on representation that not a consumer arbitration*

An arbitrator is not required to make the disclosures required by this standard if he or she reasonably believes that the arbitration is not a consumer arbitration based on reasonable reliance on a consumer party's representation that the arbitration is not a consumer arbitration.

(b) Additional disclosures required

In addition to the disclosures required under standard 7, in a consumer arbitration as defined in standard 2 in which a dispute resolution provider organization is coordinating, administering, or providing the arbitration services, a person who is nominated or appointed as an arbitrator on or after January 1, 2003 must disclose the following within the time and in the same manner as the disclosures required under standard 7(c):

(1) *Relationships between the provider organization and party or lawyer in arbitration*

Any significant past, present, or currently expected financial or professional relationship or affiliation between the administering dispute resolution provider organization and a party or lawyer in the arbitration. Information that must be disclosed under this standard includes:

(A) A party, a lawyer in the arbitration, or a law firm with which a lawyer in the arbitration is currently associated is a member of the provider organization.

(B) Within the preceding two years the provider organization has received a gift, bequest, or favor from a party, a lawyer in the arbitration, or a law firm with which a lawyer in the arbitration is currently associated.

(C) The provider organization has entered into, or the arbitrator currently expects that the provider organization will enter into, an agreement or relationship with any party or lawyer in the arbitration or a law firm with which a lawyer in the arbitration is currently associated under which the provider organization will administer, coordinate, or provide dispute resolution services in other non-collective bargaining matters or will provide other consulting services for that party, lawyer, or law firm.

(D) The provider organization is coordinating, administering, or providing dispute resolution services or has coordinated, administered, or provided such services in another pending or prior noncollective bargaining case in which a party or lawyer in the arbitration was a party or a lawyer. For purposes of this paragraph, "prior case" means a case in which the dispute resolution neutral affiliated with the provider organization concluded his or her service within the two years before the date of the arbitrator's proposed nomination or appointment, but does not include any case in which the dispute resolution neutral concluded his or her service before July 1, 2002.

(2) *Case information*

If the provider organization is acting or has acted in any of the capacities described in paragraph (1)(D), the arbitrator must disclose:

(A) The names of the parties in each prior or pending case and, where applicable, the name of the attorney in the current arbitration who is involved in the pending case or who was involved in the prior case;

(B) The type of dispute resolution services (arbitration, mediation, reference, etc.) coordinated, administered, or provided by the provider organization in the case; and

(C) In each prior case in which a dispute resolution neutral affiliated with the provider organization rendered a decision as an arbitrator, a temporary judge appointed under article VI, § 4 of the California Constitution, or a referee appointed under Code of Civil Procedure sections 638 or 639, the date of the decision, the prevailing party, the amount of monetary damages awarded, if any, and the names of the parties' attorneys.

(3) *Summary of case information*

If the total number of cases disclosed under paragraph (1)(D) is greater than five, the arbitrator must also provide a summary of these cases that states:

(A) The number of pending cases in which the provider organization is currently providing each type of dispute resolution services;

(B) The number of prior cases in which the provider organization previously provided each type of dispute resolution services;

(C) The number of such prior cases in which a neutral affiliated with the provider organization rendered a decision as an arbitrator, a temporary judge, or a referee; and

(D) The number of prior cases in which the party to the current arbitration or the party represented by the lawyer in the current arbitration was the prevailing party.

(c) Relationship between provider organization and arbitrator

If a relationship or affiliation is disclosed under paragraph (b), the arbitrator must also provide information about the following:

(1) Any financial relationship or affiliation the arbitrator has with the provider organization other than receiving referrals of cases, including whether the arbitrator has a financial interest in the provider organization or is an employee of the provider organization;

(2) The provider organization's process and criteria for recruiting, screening, and training the panel of arbitrators from which the arbitrator in this case is to be selected;

(3) The provider organization's process for identifying, recommending, and selecting potential arbitrators for specific cases; and

(4) Any role the provider organization plays in ruling on requests for disqualification of the arbitrator.

(d) Effective date

The provisions of this standard take effect on January 1, 2003. Persons who are serving in arbitrations in which they were appointed to serve as arbitrators before January 1, 2003, are not subject to this standard in those pending arbitrations. *(Adopted, eff. Jan. 1, 2003.)*

Standard 9. Arbitrators' duty to inform themselves about matters to be disclosed

(a) General duty to inform him or herself

A person who is nominated or appointed as an arbitrator must make a reasonable effort to inform himself or herself of matters that must be disclosed under standards 7 and 8.

(b) Obligation regarding extended family

An arbitrator can fulfill the obligation under this standard to inform himself or herself of relationships or other matters involving his or her extended family and former spouse that are required to be disclosed under standard 7 by:

(1) Seeking information about these relationships and matters from the members of his or her immediate family and any members of his or her extended family living in his or her household; and

(2) Declaring in writing that he or she has made the inquiry in (1).

(c) Obligation regarding relationships with associates of lawyer in the arbitration

An arbitrator can fulfill the obligation under this standard to inform himself or herself of relationships with any lawyer associated in the practice of law with the lawyer in the arbitration that are required to be disclosed under standard 7 by:

(1) Informing the lawyer in the arbitration, in writing, of all such relationships within the arbitrator's knowledge and asking

the lawyer if the lawyer is aware of any other such relationships; and

(2) Declaring in writing that he or she has made the inquiry in (1) and attaching to this declaration copies of his or her inquiry and any response from the lawyer in the arbitration.

(d) Obligation regarding service as a neutral other than an arbitrator before July 1, 2002

An arbitrator can fulfill the obligation under this standard to inform himself or herself of his or her service as a dispute resolution neutral other than as an arbitrator in cases that commenced prior to July 1, 2002 by:

(1) Asking any dispute resolution provider organization that administered those prior services for this information; and

(2) Declaring in writing that he or she has made the inquiry in (1) and attaching to this declaration copies of his or her inquiry and any response from the provider organization.

(e) Obligation regarding relationships with provider organization

An arbitrator can fulfill his or her obligation under this standard to inform himself or herself of the information that is required to be disclosed under standard 8 by:

(1) Asking the dispute resolution provider organization for this information; and

(2) Declaring in writing that he or she has made the inquiry in (1) and attaching to this declaration copies of his or her inquiry and any response from the provider organization. *(Adopted, eff. Jan. 1, 2003.)*

Standard 10.   Disqualification

(a) An arbitrator is disqualified if:

(1) The arbitrator fails to comply with his or her obligation to make disclosures and a party serves a notice of disqualification in the manner and within the time specified in Code of Civil Procedure section 1281.91;

(2) The arbitrator complies with his or her obligation to make disclosures within 10 calendar days of service of notice of the proposed nomination or appointment and, based on that disclosure, a party serves a notice of disqualification in the manner and within the time specified in Code of Civil Procedure section 1281.91;

(3) The arbitrator makes a required disclosure more than 10 calendar days after service of notice of the proposed nomination or appointment and, based on that disclosure, a party serves a notice of disqualification in the manner and within the time specified in Code of Civil Procedure section 1281. 91; or

(4) A party becomes aware that an arbitrator has made a material omission or material misrepresentation in his or her disclosure and, within 15 days after becoming aware of the omission or misrepresentation and within the time specified in Code of Civil Procedure section 1281.91(c), the party serves a notice of disqualification that clearly describes the material omission or material misrepresentation and how and when the party became aware of this omission or misrepresentation; or

(5) If any ground specified in Code of Civil Procedure section 170.1 exists and the party makes a demand that the arbitrator disqualify himself or herself in the manner and within the time specified in Code of Civil Procedure section 1281.91(d).

(b) For purposes of this standard, "obligation to make disclosure" means an arbitrator's obligation to make disclosures

under standards 7 or 8 or Code of Civil Procedure section 1281.9.

(c) Notwithstanding any contrary request, consent, or waiver by the parties, an arbitrator must disqualify himself or herself if he or she concludes at any time during the arbitration that he or she is not able to conduct the arbitration impartially. *(Formerly Standard 8, adopted, eff. July 1, 2002. Renumbered Standard 10 and amended, eff. Jan. 1, 2003.)*

Standard 11.   Duty to refuse gift, bequest, or favor

(a) An arbitrator must not, under any circumstances, accept a gift, bequest, favor, or honoraria from a party or any other person or entity whose interests are reasonably likely to come before the arbitrator in the arbitration.

(b) From service of notice of appointment or appointment until two years after the conclusion of the arbitration, an arbitrator must not, under any circumstances, accept a gift, bequest, favor, or honoraria from a party or any other person or entity whose interests have come before the arbitrator in the arbitration.

(c) An arbitrator must discourage members of his or her family residing in his or her household from accepting a gift, bequest, favor, or honoraria that the arbitrator would be prohibited from accepting under subdivisions (a) or (b).

(d) This standard does not prohibit an arbitrator from demanding or receiving a fee for services or expenses. *(Formerly Standard 9, adopted, eff. July 1, 2002. Renumbered Standard 11 and amended, eff. Jan. 1, 2003.)*

Standard 12.   Duties and limitations regarding future professional relationships or employment

(a) Offers as lawyer, expert witness, or consultant

From the time of appointment until the conclusion of the arbitration, an arbitrator must not entertain or accept any offers of employment or new professional relationships as a lawyer, an expert witness, or a consultant from a party or a lawyer for a party in the pending arbitration.

(b) Offers for other employment or professional relationships

In addition to the disclosures required by standards 7 and 8, within ten calendar days of service of notice of the proposed nomination or appointment, a proposed arbitrator must disclose to all parties in writing if, while that arbitration is pending, he or she will entertain offers of employment or new professional relationships in any capacity other than as a lawyer, expert witness, or consultant from a party or a lawyer for a party, including offers to serve as a dispute resolution neutral in another case. A party may disqualify the arbitrator based on this disclosure by serving a notice of disqualification in the manner and within the time specified in Code of Civil Procedure section 1281.91(b).

(c) Acceptance of offers prohibited unless intent disclosed

If an arbitrator fails to make the disclosure required by subdivision (b) of this standard, from the time of appointment until the conclusion of the arbitration the arbitrator must not entertain or accept any such offers of employment or new professional relationships, including offers to serve as a dispute resolution neutral.

(d) Relationships and use of confidential information related to the arbitrated case

An arbitrator must not at any time:

(1) Without the informed written consent of all parties, enter into any professional relationship or accept any professional employment as a lawyer, an expert witness, or a consultant relating to the case arbitrated; or

(2) Without the informed written consent of the party, enter into any professional relationship or accept employment in another matter in which information that he or she has received in confidence from a party by reason of serving as an arbitrator in a case is material. *(Formerly Standard 10, adopted, eff. July 1, 2002. Renumbered Standard 12 and amended, eff. Jan. 1, 2003.)*

Standard 13. Conduct of proceeding

(a) An arbitrator must conduct the arbitration fairly, promptly, and diligently and in accordance with the applicable law relating to the conduct of arbitration proceedings.

(b) In making the decision, an arbitrator must not be swayed by partisan interests, public clamor, or fear of criticism. *(Formerly Standard 11, adopted, eff. July 1, 2002. Renumbered Standard 13 and amended, eff. Jan. 1, 2003.)*

Standard 14. Ex parte communications

(a) An arbitrator must not initiate, permit, or consider any ex parte communications or consider other communications made to the arbitrator outside the presence of all of the parties concerning a pending or impending arbitration, except as permitted by this standard, by agreement of the parties, or by applicable law.

(b) An arbitrator may communicate with a party in the absence of other parties about administrative matters, such as setting the time and place of hearings or making other arrangements for the conduct of the proceedings, as long as the arbitrator reasonably believes that the communication will not result in a procedural or tactical advantage for any party. When such a discussion occurs, the arbitrator must promptly inform the other parties of the communication and must give the other parties an opportunity to respond before making any final determination concerning the matter discussed.

(c) An arbitrator may obtain the advice of a disinterested expert on the subject matter of the arbitration if the arbitrator notifies the parties of the person consulted and the substance of the advice and affords the parties a reasonable opportunity to respond. *(Formerly Standard 12, adopted, eff. July 1, 2002. Renumbered Standard 14 and amended, eff. Jan. 1, 2003.)*

Standard 15. Confidentiality

(a) An arbitrator must not use or disclose information that he or she received in confidence by reason of serving as an arbitrator in a case to gain personal advantage. This duty applies from acceptance of appointment and continues after the conclusion of the arbitration.

(b) An arbitrator must not inform anyone of the award in advance of the time that the award is given to all parties. This standard does not prohibit an arbitrator from providing all parties with a tentative or draft decision for review or from providing an award to an assistant or to the provider organization that is coordinating, administering, or providing the arbitration services in the case for purposes of copying and distributing the award to all parties. *(Formerly Standard 13, adopted, eff. July 1, 2002. Renumbered Standard 15 and amended, eff. Jan. 1, 2003.)*

Standard 16. Compensation

(a) An arbitrator must not charge any fee for services or expenses that is in any way contingent on the result or outcome of the arbitration.

(b) Before accepting appointment, an arbitrator, a dispute resolution provider organization, or another person or entity acting on the arbitrator's behalf must inform all parties in writing of the terms and conditions of the arbitrator's compensation. This information must include any basis to be used in determining fees and any special fees for cancellation, research and preparation time, or other purposes. *(Formerly Standard 14, adopted, eff. July 1, 2002. Renumbered Standard 16 and amended, eff. Jan. 1, 2003.)*

Standard 17. Marketing

(a) An arbitrator must be truthful and accurate in marketing his or her services and must not make any representation that directly or indirectly implies favoritism or a specific outcome. An arbitrator must ensure that his or her personal marketing activities and any activities carried out on his or her behalf, including any activities of a provider organization with which the arbitrator is affiliated, comply with this requirement.

(b) An arbitrator must not solicit business from a participant in the arbitration while the arbitration is pending. *(Formerly Standard 15, adopted, eff. July 1, 2002. Renumbered Standard 17 and amended, eff. Jan. 1, 2003.)*

Appendix A

JUDICIAL COUNCIL LEGAL FORMS LIST

Judicial Council Legal Forms List

Under Government Code section 68511, the Judicial Council may "prescribe" certain forms. Use of prescribed forms is mandatory. Under rule 1.31, each mandatory Judicial Council legal form is identified as mandatory by an asterisk (*) on the list of Judicial Council legal forms published in this appendix. Mandatory forms bear the word "adopted" in the lower left corner of the first page.

Optional forms bear the word "approved" in the lower left corner of the first page. Use of an approved (optional) form is not mandatory, but the form must be accepted by all courts in appropriate cases (rule 1.35(a)).

A local court may not reject any Judicial Council form, optional or mandatory, for any of the reasons listed in rule 1.42.

The forms are available on the California Courts Web site in both a fillable and a PDF format at *www.courts. ca.gov/forms.htm.*

Ct. Rules

[**Editor's Note**: For the list of Judicial Council Legal Forms, consult *California Rules of Court* pamphlet.]

Appendix B

LIABILITY LIMITS OF A PARENT OR GUARDIAN HAVING CUSTODY AND CONTROL OF A MINOR FOR THE TORTS OF A MINOR (Civ. Code, § 1714.1)

Formula

Pursuant to Civil Code section 1714.1, the joint and several liability limit of a parent or guardian having custody and control of a minor under subdivisions (a) and (b) for each tort of the minor shall be computed and adjusted as follows:

$$\text{Adjusted limit} = \left[\frac{\text{Current CCPI} - \text{January 1, 1995, CCPI}}{\text{January 1, 1995, CCPI}} + 1 \right] \times \begin{array}{c} \text{January 1, 1995,} \\ \text{limit} \end{array}$$

Definition

"CCPI" means the California Consumer Price Index, as established by the California Department of Industrial Relations.

July 1, 2013, calculation and adjustment

The joint and several liability of a parent or guardian having custody and control of a minor under Civil Code section 1714.1, subdivision (a) or (b), effective July 1, 2013, shall not exceed **$39,300** for each tort.

The calculation is as follows:

$$\$39,299.50 = \left[\frac{238.155 - 151.5}{151.5} + 1 \right] \times \$25,000$$

Under section 1714.1, subdivision (c), the adjusted limit is rounded to the nearest hundred dollars, so the dollar amount of the adjusted limit is rounded up to $39,300.

(Formerly Division VII, adopted, eff. Jan. 1, 1997. As amended, eff. Jan. 1, 1999; Jan. 1, 2001; Jan. 1, 2003; Jan. 1, 2005. Renumbered Appendix B and amended, eff. Jan. 1, 2007. As amended, eff. Jan. 1, 2007; Feb. 18, 2009; Jan. 1, 2011; July 1, 2013.)

Appendix C

GUIDELINES FOR THE OPERATION OF FAMILY LAW INFORMATION CENTERS AND FAMILY LAW FACILITATORS OFFICES

[**Editor's Note**: For Guidelines for the Operation of Family Law Information Centers and Family Law Facilitators Offices, consult *California Rules of Court* pamphlet.]

Appendix D

JUDICIAL COUNCIL GOVERNANCE POLICIES

[**Editor's Note**: For Judicial Council Governance Policies, consult *California Rules of Court* pamphlet.]

Appendix E

GUIDELINES FOR DETERMINING FINANCIAL ELIGIBILITY FOR COUNTY

The "Guidelines for Determining Financial Eligibility for County" were adopted eff. January 1, 2013.

Appendix F

GUIDELINES FOR THE JUVENILE DEPENDENCY COUNSEL COLLECTIONS PROGRAM

The "Guidelines for the Juvenile Dependency Counsel Collections Program", adopted eff. January 1, 2013, was amended eff. September 23, 2013, to read as now appearing.

Ct. Rules

CALIFORNIA COURTS OF APPEAL
INTERNAL OPERATING PRACTICES AND PROCEDURES
FIRST APPELLATE DISTRICT

Section
  I.   Introduction.
  II. Organization of the court.
  III. Procedures for processing cases.

I.   Introduction

A.   Purpose and Scope

The purpose of this document is to inform members of the bar and other interested persons about the organization of the court and its procedures for processing cases. It is not intended to duplicate the California Rules of Court, the Local Rules of the First Appellate District, or the statutes and constitutional provisions governing the processing of cases.

B.   General Information

The court's address is:

California Court of Appeal
First Appellate District
350 McAllister Street
San Francisco, CA 94102

The clerk's office is located on the first floor in Room 1185 and is open to the public from 9 a.m. to 5 p.m., Monday through Friday, exclusive of state holidays. Its internet e-mail address is: first.district@jud.ca.gov

The court's telephone numbers are:

(415) 865–7200 (Clerk's Office)
(415) 865–7209 (Clerk's Office Fax)
(415) 865–7300 (Chambers' Receptionist)
(415) 865–7309 (Reception Fax)

The court's website is:

http://www.courtinfo.ca.gov/courts/courtsofappeal/1st District/

II.   Organization of the court

A.   Justices and Staff

The First Appellate District is comprised of five divisions, each consisting of a presiding justice and three associate justices. Each division operates as a separate unit for the purpose of hearing and deciding cases.

The presiding justice of each division convenes conferences and presides at hearings (oral arguments) in the division and has overall responsibility for calendaring cases, managing the caseload of the division, and all other divisional administrative matters. If the presiding justice is absent or disqualified or not a member of the three-justice panel assigned to decide a matter, the presiding justice usually designates the senior associate justice of the division to serve as acting presiding justice. The Chief Justice of California has designated one of the court's presiding justices to serve as its administrative presiding justice, as prescribed in the California Rules of Court.

Each of the court's justices employs a judicial assistant and two chambers attorneys. Some of the court's justices also utilize law student externs to assist in their individual chambers. In addition, each division employs a writ attorney and a divisional attorney, who are selected by the justices of the division and supervised by its presiding justice.

B.   Clerk/Administrator, Clerk's Office Staff, and Administrative Support Staff

The court's clerk/administrator is selected by the justices of the court and works under the general direction and supervision of the administrative presiding justice. The clerk/administrator is responsible for planning, organizing, coordinating, and directing the management of the clerk's office and its personnel. The clerk/administrator also supervises the court's administrative support staff. The clerk/administrator is responsible for all nonjudicial support activities, including personnel, budget, technology, and facilities.

C.   Managing Attorney and Central Staff

The court's managing attorney is selected by the justices of the court and works under the general direction and supervision of the administrative presiding justice. The managing attorney serves as legal advisor to the court, its justices, and the clerk's office on a variety of issues, including personnel and matters of appellate procedure. The managing attorney also supervises the court's central staff attorneys and judicial assistants.

D.   Mediation Program Administrator and Support Staff

The court's mediation program administrator is selected by the administrative presiding justice and works under the general direction and supervision of the administrative presiding justice or a designated supervising justice. The mediation program administrator is responsible for the day-to-day administration of the court's mediation program and supervises its support staff.

III.   Procedures for processing cases

A.   Assignment of Cases to Divisions

1. *In General.* Appeals are assigned to a division when the clerk's office receives the notices of appeal from the superior court where they were filed. Writ petitions are assigned to a division when they are filed with the clerk's office. Assignments are made in rotation, without regard to subject matter or complexity. Exceptions to the random assignment procedures are made if multiple appeals or writ petitions arise from the same trial court action or proceeding, in which case later appeals or writ petitions are assigned to the same division to which the first appeal or writ petition was assigned.

2. *Transfer of Cases.* If, subsequent to the initial assignment of an appeal or writ petition to a division, it is determined that it arises from the same trial court action or proceeding as a prior appeal or writ petition, the administrative presiding justice may transfer the later appeal or writ petition to the same division to which the first appeal or writ petition was assigned. If multiple appeals or writ petitions arise from different trial court actions or proceedings, but involve the same parties or co-parties and the same or related subject matter, transaction, or incident, the court may request that the Supreme Court transfer later appeals or writ petitions to the same division to which the first appeal or writ petition was assigned.

B.   Processing of Appeals

1. *Assignment of Appeals to Panels.* When an appeal is fully briefed, it is ready for assignment to a panel of three justices for decision. The court maintains a computer-generated list of fully briefed civil appeals and a separate list of fully briefed criminal and juvenile appeals. The appeals are listed in the order in which they became fully briefed. Appeals entitled to priority on calendar are assigned first, followed by non-priority appeals in the order in which they became fully briefed. Appeals are assigned to panels in rotation, equalizing the number of cases in which each justice participates. One of the three justices on the panel is designated as the lead justice for each appeal. Appeals are assigned randomly, without regard to subject matter, except that an appeal may be assigned to the same panel to which a related appeal or writ petition was previously assigned.

2. *Draft Opinions.* After an appeal is assigned to a panel, the lead justice prepares a draft opinion. Although the format may vary somewhat from justice to justice or division to division, the draft opinion generally includes the following information: (1) a statement of the pertinent factual and procedural history of the case; (2) an analysis of each issue necessary to resolve the appeal; and (3) a proposed disposition. The primary purpose of the draft opinion is to provide the panel with all of the relevant information it needs to decide the appeal. Upon completion, the lead justice distributes the draft opinion to the other two justices on the panel for their review. The panel may also meet to discuss the case. Conferencing practices vary from division to division.

3. *Oral Argument and Submission of the Cause.* When an appeal is assigned to a panel of three justices for decision, the court initially notifies the parties that oral argument will be deemed waived unless one of the parties requests oral argument within the time designated in the notice. If the parties request oral argument, or if the court otherwise determines that oral argument would be helpful, the clerk's office then notifies the parties of the date, time, and place of the hearing. A continuance of oral argument will be granted only upon written application and a showing of good cause. Counsel may not stipulate to a continuance. At the conclusion of oral argument, the presiding justice or acting presiding justice will declare the matter submitted, unless submission is deferred pending further briefing.

4. *Preparation and Filing of Opinions.* After oral argument or the waiver of oral argument, the lead justice prepares a final draft of the opinion. If the other two justices on the panel concur in the opinion, they sign it and it is delivered to the clerk's office for filing. If an individual justice does not subscribe to all of the reasoning of an opinion, he or she may file a separate opinion. If the lead justice fails to obtain the concurrence of at least one of the other justices on the panel, the case may be reassigned to one of the other panel members for the preparation of an opinion. An opinion is published if a majority of the justices on the panel certifies it for publication.

5. *Rehearings.* When a petition for rehearing is filed, the clerk's office delivers the petition to the justice who authored the court's opinion. After reviewing the petition and conducting whatever research he or she deems necessary, the authoring justice circulates the petition to the other two justices on the panel with a recommended ruling. Two votes are necessary to grant or deny a petition for rehearing. A petition for rehearing normally will not be granted unless the court has requested an answer. An order granting rehearing vacates the court's original opinion and sets the case for full reconsideration. Generally, the parties have no right to reargue the case; however, the court, in its discretion, may invite either written briefing or oral argument, or both, before resubmitting the matter and filing its new opinion.

C. Processing of Original Proceedings

After a writ petition has been filed, the clerk's office delivers the petition to the writ attorney for the division to which the writ is assigned. Depending upon the nature of the petition and its urgency, the writ attorney may present the petition to a panel of justices shortly after its filing, or may perform extensive research. In appropriate cases, the court may request opposition from the real party or parties in interest. If an opinion is required, the matter is assigned to one of the justices on the writ panel and is thereafter handled much like the court handles an appeal. The specific procedures governing various types of writ petitions are enumerated in the California Rules of Court.

SECOND APPELLATE DISTRICT

Section

Purpose.
Organization of the District.
Processing of cases.
Assigned justices.
Externship program.
Settlement/mediation program.
Local rules.

Purpose

The purpose of this document is to provide members of the bar and other interested persons with general information concerning the organization of the Second Appellate District and its procedures for processing cases. *(Revised 2008; 2009.)*

Organization of the District

The Second Appellate District covers four counties and consists of eight divisions. Each division is a separate court for the purpose of hearing and deciding cases assigned to it. Divisions One through Five, Seven and Eight are located at 300 South Spring Street, Los Angeles, California, 90013 and handle all matters arising from Los Angeles County. Division Six is located at 200 East Santa Clara Street, Ventura, California, 93001 and handles all matters arising from Ventura, Santa Barbara, and San Luis Obispo Counties.

Each division consists of three Associate Justices and a Presiding Justice. The Chief Justice appoints one of the Presiding Justices to serve as Administrative Presiding Justice to perform the duties prescribed in the California Rules of Court.

Each justice maintains a chambers which consists of the justice, judicial attorneys, and a judicial assistant. In addition, each division is assigned other judicial attorneys, including writs attorneys, and other judicial assistants, judicial secretaries, and deputy clerks. A Managing Attorney provides direct assistance to the Administrative Presiding Justice and supervises attorneys and judicial assistants who are not assigned to a particular division. These include the staff responsible for Workers' Compensation matters.

A Clerk/Executive Officer is selected by the justices of the district and works under the general direction and supervision of the Administrative Presiding Justice. The Clerk/Executive Officer is responsible for planning, organizing, coordinating, and directing the management of the clerk's office and its personnel. The Clerk/Executive Officer also supervises the library, administrative, and computer services staffs. The Clerk/Executive Officer is responsible for all district support activities, including personnel, budget, technology, and facilities. *(Revised 2008; 2009.)*

Processing of cases

ASSIGNMENT OF CASES

Appeals and original proceedings (writ petitions) arising in Ventura, Santa Barbara, and San Luis Obispo Counties are assigned to Division Six. Appeals and writ petitions arising in Los Angeles County are assigned to the divisions in Los Angeles (One through Five, Seven and Eight) on a random, pro rata basis, unless an appeal or writ petition arises from a trial court action or proceeding from which an appeal or writ petition was previously filed in the district. In that case, the appeal or writ petition is generally assigned to the division to which the prior appeal or writ petition was assigned. On occasion and in order to equalize workload, Los Angeles cases may be assigned to Division Six and Division Six cases may be assigned to one of the Los Angeles divisions. Once a case has been assigned to a division it remains in that division for all further proceedings unless the clerk, upon direction of the Presiding Justice, makes a request to the Supreme Court to transfer the case to another division or district under article VI, section 12 of the California Constitution and [rule 10.1000 of] the California Rules of Court.

MOTIONS

The Presiding Justice of each division determines the manner in which motions are handled within that division. Motions filed before a case is assigned to a division are designated "Division P" motions and are ruled upon by the Administrative Presiding Justice.

APPEALS

Preparation of Bench Memoranda

After an appeal has been fully briefed, it is generally assigned on a random, pro rata basis to a three-justice panel. A change in the composition of the panel may be required when, for example, a conflict arises or to accommodate workload imbalances. The case is set for oral argument on an upcoming calendar. Oral argument may be waived by the parties. The court is not obligated to accept a waiver and may ask that the parties appear for oral argument.

The justices on the panel review the briefs and the record. Under the direction of the justices, judicial attorneys generally prepare bench memoranda in preparation for oral argument. The memoranda discuss the procedural background, facts, and issues in the cases and may recommend various treatments and dispositions. The panel members review the memoranda in preparation for oral argument and the filing of written opinions.

If an issue arises that was not raised by the parties, a letter pursuant to Government Code section 68081 will be sent to the parties requesting briefing. The court may order additional briefing on any issue.

Oral Argument~~Argument~~

Each division generally schedules hearings for two days each month and entertains argument on those matters for which oral argument has not been waived by the parties. The manner in which calendars are called and the order in which cases are scheduled for argument differ among the divisions. The composition of the panel assigned to each case is announced at the hearing.

Determination

If the parties have waived oral argument or oral argument does not change the justices' understanding of the case, and all justices on the panel agree with the bench memorandum, it may form the basis of the written opinion to be filed. If oral argument raises additional issues to be considered, or consensus among the panel justices does not exist, the bench memorandum may be altered or discarded and a new memorandum may be circulated. Concurring and dissenting opinions may also be prepared. Unless further briefing is allowed, generally cases are submitted at the close of oral argument. If further briefing is allowed, the date of submission will be ordered by the court.

Rehearing

Timely petitions for rehearing are presented to the court for review. If the court desires opposition, the clerk will be directed to call counsel and request that an answer be filed. In some instances a modification may be issued and rehearing otherwise denied. Grant of a petition for rehearing may or may not result in a request for further briefing or additional oral argument.

Publication

An opinion or part of an opinion may be published if a majority of the panel rendering the decision determines that it meets the standards for publication contained within the California Rules of Court.

WRIT PETITIONS

Writ petitions are reviewed by the justices of the division to which they are assigned, with the assistance of the division's writs attorneys. Writ petitions that do not seek immediate relief are discussed at periodic writ conferences, usually weekly. If the writ petition seeks immediate relief, a timely determination is made. In appropriate cases, the court may issue a stay or other order to preserve the status quo pending further action. The court may summarily deny a writ petition, either before or after receiving opposition. If a writ petition results in the issuance of an alternative writ or an order to show cause, a written opinion generally results, unless the trial court complies with the alternative writ. *(Revised 2008; 2009.)*

Assigned justices

Upon request, the Chief Justice may assign a judge, retired judge, justice, or retired justice to sit as a justice pro tem in a particular division. Assigned justices assist with the court's workload in various situations, including judicial vacancies and disqualifications. *(Revised 2008; 2009.)*

Externship program

The Second District maintains centralized unpaid externship program for law students who participate on a part-time or full-time basis and who may receive law school credit. Externs are recruited or may apply, and those selected are assigned to justices in the various divisions. Once assigned to a justice, externs work under the close supervision of the justice and the justice's staff. Individual justices may accept externship applications in addition to using the district's centralized recruitment and assignment program. Externs have come to the district from law schools throughout the United States. *(Revised 2008; 2009.)*

Settlement/mediation program

The Second District participates in a district-wide voluntary settlement/mediation program. A volunteer attorney or mediator presides over the settlement/mediation process. If at any time the parties decide to explore the possibility of settlement/mediation, they should contact the clerk's office. *(Revised 2008; 2009.)*

Local rules

The Second District has adopted a number of local rules. (See Local Rules of the Second District Courts of Appeal.) *(Revised 2008; 2009.)*

Ct. Rules

THIRD APPELLATE DISTRICT

I. Introduction

The purpose of this publication is to advise the bar and interested members of the public regarding the internal rules and general operating practices of this court. No attempt is made to restate or amplify the California Rules of Court or constitutional provisions and statutes governing the practices and procedures of a Court of Appeal. This publication supersedes previous statements of the court's internal operating practices and procedures.

II. Structure of the court

The Third Appellate District is authorized eleven justices: an administrative presiding justice and ten associate justices.

There are no divisions of this court. The court operates in three-justice panels selected at random on a rotational basis.

The courtroom and judicial offices are located in the Library and Courts Building, 914 Capitol Mall, Sacramento, California 95814. The clerk's office is located in the Library and Courts Building II, 900 N Street, Suite 400, Sacramento, California 95814, and is open for business Monday through Friday, from 8:30 a.m. to 5:00 p.m., except for judicial holidays.

III. Filings

All matters are filed with the clerk's office. The clerk processes and files the material, distributing matters to justices and staff if judicial action is required.

Routine motions or applications, such as requests for extensions of time, are referred to the administrative presiding justice. More substantive motions and extraordinary writ petitions are referred to a three-justice panel.

Generally, upon the completion of briefing, appeals are evaluated and designated for handling by the court based on the number and apparent complexity of the issues raised, the subject matter, and the length of the record. In order to expedite certain proceedings, evaluation of an appeal may be done upon the filing of the last respondent's brief.

IV. Organization and duties of staff attorneys

Each justice is authorized two staff attorneys who work exclusively for the justice. Some of the justices also utilize law student externs who work under their direct supervision.

In addition, the court maintains a central staff consisting of sixteen attorneys: a managing attorney who directs the work of the staff, four writ attorneys, and eleven other central staff attorneys. The central staff attorneys, including the managing attorney, work under the general supervision of the administrative presiding justice and are responsible to the entire court.

The primary responsibility of staff attorneys assigned to an individual justice is the preparation of memoranda for the appeals that are assigned to the justice's chambers. The attorney studies the record and the briefs, analyzes and researches the legal issues, discusses the issues with the justice, and then prepares a legal memorandum with guidance from the justice. The memorandum is prepared for the exclusive use of the court.

The central staff has two main functions. Central staff writ attorneys study and familiarize themselves with each nonroutine motion, writ petition, and other extraordinary application filed with the court. After analyzing and researching the matter, the writ attorney presents the motion, petition, or application to a three-justice panel of the court for its determination. The other central staff attorneys work on appeals that are not assigned directly to chambers. The central staff attorney reads the record and the briefs, researches and analyzes the legal issues, and orally presents the appeal to a three-justice panel selected each week to consider such appeals. The composition of such a panel varies from week to week, with each justice participating approximately the same number of times as the other justices. After the appeal is orally presented to the panel, the central staff attorney prepares a legal memorandum with guidance from the panel. The memorandum is prepared for the exclusive use of the court.

V. Writ petitions, motions and other applications

At the weekly writ conference, usually held on Thursdays, a three-justice panel rules on pending writ petitions, nonroutine motions, and other applications. The writ panel varies from week to week, with each justice participating approximately the same number of times during the year as the other justices.

The writ panel considers the parties' written submissions, and central staff writ attorneys make an oral presentation on each matter. The panel discusses each matter and decides what action to take. Unless it summarily denies a writ petition, the panel will issue an alternative writ, an order to show cause, or a writ of review, or the panel will notify the parties that it is considering issuing a peremptory writ in the first instance. If an alternative writ, an order to show cause, or a writ of review is issued, the matter is assigned to one of the justices on the writ panel and is thereafter handled much like the court does with an appeal (see discussion, *post*).

At times, the court is presented with a writ petition, motion, or application that purportedly requires urgent or immediate action. Such matters are promptly assigned to a central staff writ attorney for review. If immediate action is required, a panel of three justices is assembled to hear the matter.

VI. Judicial assignments in appeals

Assignments of appeals to individual justices are not governed by fixed rules or set formula. Each appeal is evaluated and assigned a weight to reflect its relative complexity. Effort is made to fairly apportion the caseload so that no justice is assigned a disproportionate number of the more difficult or less difficult appeals, and to balance and diversify the types of cases assigned to each justice. Subject matter is not a basis for assignment of an appeal to a particular justice, except that, where a panel has been assigned to the same case in an earlier appeal, a new appeal in that case often will be assigned to the same panel.

The three-justice panels are selected at random in order to vary their composition so that over a period of time each justice will participate with all other members of the court in the multiple combinations possible.

The initial designation of the author of the opinion in an appeal is done on a random basis at the time the case is assigned to chambers or after a case is presented to a three-justice panel by a central staff attorney. However, where there has been an earlier appeal in a case, the justice who authored the opinion in the earlier appeal often will receive the initial designation as author of the opinion in a subsequent appeal. Each justice is initially designated to author approximately the same number of opinions that will be authored by each of the other justices during the course of the year. Of course, whether the justice initially designated to author an opinion ultimately does so depends upon whether the justice obtains the concurrence of at least one other member of the panel. If the justice fails to do so, one of the other panel members will take over the responsibility of authoring the opinion of the court.

VII. Preparation of a draft opinion

A legal memorandum prepared by a staff attorney is submitted to the justice initially designated to author the opinion in the appeal. After examining and evaluating the record, the parties' briefs, and the staff attorney memorandum, and after engaging in any necessary independent research and analysis, the justice prepares a draft opinion for the exclusive use of the court. A copy of the draft opinion, the briefs, and the record are then circulated, in order of seniority, to the other two participating justices. Each of the other participating justices indicates his or her tentative concurrence or dissent, or otherwise recommends changes to the draft opinion. All three justices also indicate their tentative positions on whether the ultimate opinion of the court should be certified for publication. The decision to publish the opinion requires approval by a majority of the three-justice panel.

VIII. Oral argument

When the draft opinion is circulated, each justice assigned to the case indicates whether he or she wants the case calendared for oral argument or whether a waiver of oral argument should be solicited by the court. At the request of one justice, the case will be calendared for oral argument.

If the justices agree to solicit a waiver of oral argument, the clerk's office sends the parties a letter indicating that the court is prepared to decide the case without oral argument and that oral argument will be waived unless it is requested by either counsel within ten days. If there is no response from either counsel within that time, the case is submitted for decision upon the record and the briefs.

If either counsel requests oral argument, the case is placed on calendar. Counsel are notified approximately thirty days in advance of the date set for oral argument. With the court's approval, a party may waive its appearance at oral argument requested by another party. Continuances are disfavored and will not be granted in the absence of a showing of unusually compelling circumstances. Oral argument will not be continued by stipulation of parties. The matter is deemed submitted for decision at the conclusion of oral argument or, if supplemental briefing is requested by the court, at the time the last brief is filed.

The panel holds a postargument conference, in most cases on the same day that the case is heard. Often the case is finally decided at this conference, and suggestions may be made to the assigned author concerning the content of the opinion. If there is not agreement at this stage, areas of disagreement may be identified and refined.

An opinion will be filed within ninety days of the date of submission.

IX. Calendar

The court sits twelve times a year, once each month. The calendar is usually set to begin on the third Monday or Tuesday of each month and generally lasts for five or six days. Special calendars, although rare, may be held by the court.

Each calendar consists of both civil and criminal appeals and other proceedings ready for decision. The administrative presiding justice is responsible for the final composition of the calendar.

X. Filing of the court's decision; rehearing

After oral argument or waiver of oral argument, a final draft opinion is circulated among the participating justices. A justice may indicate conditional approval if certain changes are made or otherwise forward comments on the draft to the author and the other participating justice. If there are to be separate concurring or dissenting opinions, they are circulated in final draft form among the participating justices. At the same time, the panel makes a final decision on publication.

Before the opinion is put in final form for filing, transcript references and citations are verified again.

When the opinion is signed, it is taken to the clerk's office, where it is filed as a decision and opinion of the court. Counsel of record are mailed copies of the opinion on that same day. Copies also are available in the clerk's office for the news media and interested members of the public.

For sixty days, the Reporter of Decisions posts published opinions of the Court of Appeal, Third Appellate District, at http://www.courtinfo.ca.gov/opinions/. Unpublished opinions of the court are posted for sixty at days at http://www.courtinfo.ca.gov/opinions/nonpub.htm

Timely petitions for rehearing are immediately presented to the author of the opinion and the other panel members for review. A decision on the petition is filed after the period for opposition has expired. If the petition lacks merit, it is denied. In some cases, the opinion may be modified and rehearing otherwise denied. The granting of a petition for rehearing may or may not result in a request by the court for additional briefing or oral argument.

XI. Settlement conferences

The court has discontinued its settlement conference program until adequate resources are available to operate it efficiently and effectively.

FOURTH APPELLATE DISTRICT

Division One

I. Introduction

A. The Court

The Court of Appeal for the Fourth Appellate District consists of three divisions. Division One, which generally hears appeals in cases from San Diego and Imperial Counties, is located in San Diego. Divisions Two, which generally hears appeals in cases from Riverside, San Bernardino and Inyo Counties, and Three, which generally hears appeals in cases from Orange County, are located in Riverside and Santa Ana, respectively. Cases filed in one division may be transferred to another division to equalize the workload of the three courts. This document describes the

Ct. Rules

internal operating practices and procedures of Division One for review of appeals and original proceedings.

B. Professional Staff

Division One has ten justices, one of whom is the Presiding Justice. (Gov. Code, § 69104.) Each justice has two staff attorneys and one judicial assistant assigned to work exclusively in his or her chambers. The court also has a Central Staff, consisting of a Managing Appellate Court Attorney, two Supervising Appellate Court Attorneys and a number of staff attorneys who work for each of the justices on a rotating basis. The court is also supported by a librarian, two systems administrators, a budget analyst, Central Staff judicial assistants, and a human resources specialist.

C. The Clerk's Office

The Clerk's Office is made up of the Clerk Administrator, who oversees court operations for the entire District, an Assistant Clerk Administrator, a Supervising Deputy Clerk, a calendaring clerk, several "terminal digit deputies," an appellate court records assistant and a receptionist.

Each appeal or writ petition filed in Division One is assigned a six-digit identification number that is preceded by a "D" (e.g., D000000). Each terminal digit deputy is assigned two of the numbers from zero to nine and is responsible for processing all filings in cases that end in either of those numbers. (For example, the terminal digit deputy that is assigned the numbers "1" and "2" is responsible for processing all filings in cases that have a number ending in a "1" or a "2".) Thus, parties or practitioners seeking information or assistance in their cases should ask to speak with the appropriate terminal digit deputy, unless the case has been placed on a court calendar, in which case they should speak to the calendaring clerk.

D. Security

The court has a security guard in the public area of the Clerk's Office. The California Highway Patrol, however, oversees and provides for the court's overall security needs. *(Revised Feb. 15, 2010; Jan. 27, 2012.)*

II. The Work of the Court

A. Original Proceedings (Writs)

Writs are reviewed and decided by a panel of three justices, the composition of which rotates on a monthly basis. The Clerk's Office forwards all writ petitions to the Writ Department, which is staffed by Central Staff attorneys. The Supervising Writ Attorney reviews each petition to determine its urgency. If an immediate stay or other form of urgent action appears to be necessary, a Writ Department attorney will orally present the petition to the writ panel; otherwise, petitions are generally processed in order of their filing, subject to adjustments for impending hearing or trial dates. Normally, a Writ Department attorney reviews the petition without waiting for a response, although one may be solicited; the attorney thereafter prepares a written memorandum evaluating the petition and circulates it to the writ panel.

After a writ petition is presented (whether orally or in writing), the justices on the writ panel may

(1) request a response;

(2) deny the petition (regardless of whether a response has been requested or filed);

(3) issue a peremptory writ in the first instance without oral argument, but only after a response has been requested or filed and the parties have been notified by telephone, and in writing, of its possible issuance; or

(4) issue an alternative writ or order to show cause.

It is the court's policy to request an initial response to a petition before issuing an alternative writ or order to show cause. If the panel issues an alternative writ or order to show cause, the real party in interest is given an opportunity to file a formal response and the cause will be placed on calendar. Generally, the Writ Department attorney who presented the petition to the writ panel assists the lead justice in drafting the opinion when the court issues a peremptory writ in the first instance. When the panel has issued an alternative writ or an order to show cause, the matter is assigned to the lead justice's chambers for the drafting of the opinion.

B. Appeals

1. Case Screening

In civil cases, the California Rules of Court require an appellant to file a Civil Case Information Statement (Cal. Rules of Court, rule 8.100(g)), which is reviewed by a Central Staff attorney to determine if there is any issue regarding the timeliness of the appeal or the appealability of the challenged judgment or order, whether the case is entitled to calendar priority, whether there has been a previous writ or appeal in the same case or in a closely related case, and whether the appeal is affected by a pending bankruptcy. It is the court's practice to grant priority on its own motion to matters involving child custody or visitation.

In all appeals, after the respondent's brief is filed or the time for filing such a brief has run in a case, the Managing Attorney or a designated Central Staff attorney screens the case and estimates the amount of time that the preparation of a draft opinion is likely to take.

Criminal appeals involving issues that can be resolved with little difficulty based upon well-established law and that do not present a likelihood of dispute as to how the law applies to the facts are designated as "by the court" ("BC") cases. In criminal appeals in which the appellant's counsel is unable to discern any reasonably arguable issues to raise, the court must independently review the record in accordance with *People v. Wende* (1979) 25 Cal.3d 436 and are, accordingly, designated as "*Wende*" appeals.

All other appeals are assigned a value from three (for appeals that require a relatively short amount of time) through eight or higher (for appeals that are likely to require a substantial amount of time). These assigned "weights" are used in assigning cases to chambers and to Central Staff, to balance workloads throughout the court.

2. Case Assignment/Processing

BCs, *Wendes*, juvenile dependency cases and cases weighted eight or higher are generally assigned for processing on a first-in, first-out basis and are assigned randomly, in rotation, to a lead justice, who supervises the preparation of a draft opinion. Central Staff attorneys ordinarily assist in the preparation of draft opinions in such cases, although those cases may be assigned to a justice's chambers as necessary to meet the needs of the court.

All other types of appeals are usually assigned to a lead justice's chambers. Absent unusual circumstances, these assignments are made on a random basis to the justices. The monthly assignment calendar for a chambers usually consists of six appeals, with a total weight of up to 30, per month. The internal procedures for assigning cases to chambers attorneys and for preparing draft opinions varies from one chambers to another.

3. Oral Argument

Once a draft opinion has been prepared in a particular case, its path is determined by whether a party or parties have requested oral argument. In cases where oral argument is waived, the draft opinion is circulated in order of seniority to the other justices assigned to the panel for that case, for their review.

In cases where oral argument is requested, the draft opinion is placed in a calendar book. Each justice receives a copy of the calendar book containing the draft opinions for those cases on which he or she is participating. The justices review all cases in which they are to participate in advance of oral argument and confer on all cases argued immediately after argument takes place.

Oral argument is generally held during the second full week of the month, although occasionally cases are calendared for argument at other times, if necessitated by urgency or other good cause. Argument is limited to 15 minutes per side, unless the court grants a party's advanced written request for more time.

4. Submission of Cases

Cases that are orally argued are normally submitted at the conclusion of argument. Where oral argument is waived, the case is submitted at the conclusion of the argument calendar for the month to which it is assigned. Submission of the case triggers the 90–day rule for the filing of the opinion. (Cal. Const., art. VI, § 19.)

C. Motions

Routine applications and motions are reviewed by a Central Staff attorney and ruled on by the Presiding or Acting Presiding Justice. Other applications or motions, such as motions to dismiss an appeal, are ruled on by a panel of three justices. Requests for extensions of time to file briefs or other papers are ruled on immediately. Motions in writ proceedings are not held for opposition absent a request by the parties. (*Revised Feb. 15, 2010; Jan. 27, 2012.*)

III. Settlement Conferences

A. Litigant–Initiated Conferences

The general information packet sent to parties at the commencement of the appeal includes guidelines for the settlement program and an appellate settlement request form. The program is voluntary and available at the request of both parties or, should there be more than two parties, at the request of any two opposing parties. The request for a settlement conference may be made as soon as the notice of appeal is filed and settlement proceedings may commence before briefing but, in any event, the request must be received no later than 30 days after the filing of the last brief. The request normally does not affect or extend the normal briefing schedule. In selecting the justice to participate in the settlement conference, the Presiding Justice considers any request by the parties for a particular justice. If settlement efforts prove unsuccessful, the settlement justice recuses from hearing the appeal in the case and all settlement papers are maintained as strictly confidential, kept separate from the appellate record and not considered by the attorneys or justices assigned to work on the appeal.

B. Court–Initiated Conferences

The court does not currently have a court-initiated settlement program. (*Revised Feb. 15, 2010; Jan. 27, 2012.*)

IV. Extern Program

The court has an extern program for select law school students three times a year (fall, spring and summer sessions). Each justice who participates in the program selects the extern or externs who will work for him or her, usually for 20 to 40 hours per week during the session. A Central Staff attorney supervises the program, which includes a general orientation about the court and its work, a series of substantive and procedural law lectures, and monthly group meetings. Students who participate in the extern program as part of their school's extern/clinic program may earn course credit for their work at the court. (*Revised Feb. 15, 2010; Jan. 27, 2012.*)

Division Two

Section
    I.   Introduction.
   II.   The court.
  III.   Original proceedings.
  IV.   Civil case information statement.
   V.   Civil appellate settlement program.
  VI.   Extensions to file briefs.
 VII.   Case assignment.
VIII.   Tentative opinions and oral argument.
  IX.   Filing opinions.
   X.   Presiding justice.
  XI.   Staff.

Section I.   Introduction

To implement the rules governing appellate court procedure, each district and division of the Court of Appeal has developed local customs and practices that may be similar to or different from other districts and divisions. This statement of the internal operating procedures and practices describes the more important customs of this court. The purpose of the statement is to inform the public and the bar of the general manner in which this court conducts its business.

Section II.   The court

Division Two of the Fourth District is located in Riverside and operates with almost complete autonomy from Division One located in San Diego and Division Three located in Santa Ana. Under the supervision of the Administrative Presiding Justice of the Fourth District, a clerk/administrator plans, organizes, coordinates, and manages the budget, personnel, facilities, and non-judicial activities of the district as a whole. Under the supervision of the Presiding Justice of each division (the Administrative Presiding Justice is also the Presiding Justice of Division One), an assistant clerk administrator is responsible for assisting the clerk/administrator in managing personnel and non-judicial programs within organizational and policy confines of an appellate court. In Divisions Two and Three the assistant clerk/administrator has total responsibility for all administrative activities of the division.

Division Two currently has seven justices including a presiding justice and six associate justices. Division Two handles all appellate matters arising in Inyo, Riverside, and San Bernardino Counties. Division One handles all appellate matters arising in San Diego and Imperial Counties. Division Three handles all appellate matters arising in Orange County. Additionally, cases originating in one division may be transferred to another division by the Administrative Presiding Justice if required because of recusals or decision of an earlier case by a different division. (See Cal. Rules of Court, rule 47.1(b).)

Section III.   Original proceedings

Original proceedings are assigned to panels of three justices selected each month by a rotation distinct from the rotation from which panel assignments are made for appeals. Three writ attorneys assist the justices by preparing written summaries. The justices review the summaries and meet informally or formally as necessary to decide the case.

More urgent writ matters, including those requesting immediate stays, are the subject of immediate action by the justices facilitated by oral summaries by writ attorneys. If an alternative writ or order to show cause is issued, the issuing justice normally prepares the tentative opinion (see Section VIII., below) with the assistance of the writ attorney who prepared the summary.

Section IV.   Civil case information statement

California Rules of Court, rule 1(f), requires the filing of a civil case information statement in the Court of Appeal with a copy of the judgment or order appealed in all civil appeals within 10 days after the clerk mails the notice to do so and the required form. Under the supervision of the Presiding Justice, a central staff attorney reviews the civil case information statement to determine the appealability of the ruling designated in the notice of appeal, the timeliness of its filing, consolidation with other related appeals, and the apparent appellate case title and parties.

This court uses the civil case information statement to implement this court's policy to honor its jurisdictional limitations. Thus, this court will not construe a nonappealable ruling to include language of judgment or dismissal, or allow the appellant to belatedly obtain an appealable ruling, to "save" an appeal. (See *Shpiller v. Harry C's Redlands* (1993) 13 Cal. App.4th 1177, 1179–1181; *Passavanti v. Williams* (1990) 225 Cal.App.3d 1602, 1608–1610.) This court also uses the civil case information statement to initially screen cases for the court's settlement program. (See Section V., below.)

Section V.   Civil appellate settlement program

Division Two of the Fourth District began its civil appellate settlement program using volunteer attorney mediators in June 1991, the first program of its kind in California. The program helped dramatically in reducing backlog by freeing justices to work on cases that could not be settled. The program received the 1997 Kleps Award for court administration. Approximately 70 volunteer attorney mediators are now approaching 600 cases settled with the value of these settlements nearing an estimated 400 million dollars. This division has a population-to-justice ratio of 540,000 to 1 (compared to the First District's 280,000 to 1) and includes the fastest growing two-county area in California. The resulting increase in case filings now makes the settlement program more necessary than ever.

Volunteer attorney mediators chosen and scheduled by the Presiding Justice in cooperation with the court's settlement coordinator conduct most of the settlement conferences for civil appeals. On occasion, justices also act as mediators in selected cases. The volunteer mediators are experienced and respected attorneys from Riverside and San Bernardino Counties who are assigned cases for settlement according to their areas of expertise. The Presiding Justice selects cases for settlement based on settlement conference information forms filed by counsel and the availability of an appropriate mediator. Once a case has been selected by the court for settlement proceedings, participation is mandatory.

Settlement conferences may be held either before or after briefing is completed. Postbriefing settlement conferences were the rule when the court was using the program to reduce its backlog in the early and mid–1990's, but since the court has eliminated its backlog, prebriefing conferences are the rule and postbriefing conferences rare and generally discouraged. When cases are selected for a prebriefing settlement conference, generally the court permits a record produced by the superior court to be filed but stays filing of the briefs. Parties file a settlement conference statement within 10 days after notice that the case has been selected. Settlement conferences are held over a period of time before settlement is achieved or determined not to be possible. All documents relating to settlement proceedings are retained in a separate, confidential file for the case, and the proceedings and results are confidential and not revealed to the panel that decides the case if settlement is not achieved. Postbriefing settlement cases that do not settle are given priority over other civil cases. Court of Appeal, Fourth District, Division Two, Local Rules of Court, rule 4 authorizes the program.

Section VI.   Extensions to file briefs

Extensions to file briefs are granted or denied based on the factors listed in California Rules of Court, rule 45.5(b). When further extensions on the usual grounds (the existence of other time limited commitments, the size of the record and number and complexity of the issues, and planned vacations) are no longer appropriate, counsel is so notified in an order granting the last extension on the usual grounds. Thereafter, no extensions will be granted except upon other factors listed in rule 45.5(b). If a further extension is obtained on one or more of those grounds, counsel is again notified that no further extensions will be granted on the usual grounds or the grounds stated in the application. A request for an extension on an excluded ground will be denied, and the clerk directed to issue a notice of default in failing to timely file the brief. (Cal. Rules of Court, rule 17(a)(1), (2).)

Section VII.   Case assignment

When a case is ready for assignment, the record is checked to see if any justice was involved in trial court proceedings or for other reasons should not be involved in deciding the case. The court under the supervision of the Presiding Justice maintains a confidential recusal list, which is reviewed prior to final case assignment. Cases are divided into five categories: unusually difficult chambers cases, chambers cases, "fast track" dependency cases (Cal. Rules of Court, rule 37.4(a)(1)(A)), dependency writs reviewing orders setting a hearing under Welfare and Institutions Code section 336.26 (Cal. Rules of Court, rules 38–38.1), and central staff cases. The cases are randomly assigned to a justice as author, and those in the categories of the unusually difficult, "fast track" dependency, and rules 38–38.1 writs are assigned by a rotation. Assignments to authors are usually made weekly, except the "fast track" cases and rules 38–38.1 writs are assigned immediately. When the author has prepared the tentative opinion (see Section VIII, below), the case is randomly assigned to a panel.

Section VIII.   Tentative opinions and oral argument

A tentative opinion is the preliminary draft of the court's decision prepared by the author and reviewed by the panel members. The author circulates the tentative opinion with a cover sheet to the other two justices and notes a recommendation for or against oral argument. The two panel justices consider the briefs and record and note on the cover sheet their preliminary responses and evaluation of the need for oral argument.

Depending on the author's and panel justices' evaluation of the need for oral argument, one of two notices regarding oral argument is mailed to counsel with the tentative opinion. The first notice invites participation in oral argument and informs counsel that a notice will be mailed at least 30 days in advance of the date and time of oral argument. The second notice informs counsel that, while "[t]he court is not unalterably bound by the tentative opinion and is willing to amend or discard the tentative opinion if counsel's arguments persuade the court that the tentative opinion is incorrect in any way," "*at present, in this case the court believes that the record and briefs thoroughly present the facts and legal arguments such that the court is prepared to rule as set forth in the tentative opinion without oral argument.*" The notice advises the parties that oral argument will be deemed waived unless the clerk of the court receives a request for oral argument on the form attached to the notice on or before 12 days after the date of the notice.

Oral argument is held on the first Tuesday and Wednesday of each month, with slight adjustments occasionally made for holidays. If a party requests oral argument or the justices have decided that oral argument would be helpful, the clerk prepares the calendar and mails it to counsel at least 30 days in advance of the hearing. Two or three weeks before oral argument, the justices discuss the cases set for oral argument at a calendar conference.

Section IX.   Filing opinions

After oral argument, or waiver of oral argument, authors and panel justices develop the tentative opinions and preliminary responses into the opinions, concurrences and dissents filed as the final decisions. If oral argument is deemed waived in a case, the opinion is circulated for signature to the other panel members as soon as it is signed by the author. The opinion is filed as soon as it is signed by all members of the panel. The sooner oral argument is waived, the sooner the opinion is filed, so that opinions in waived cases tend to be filed more quickly than cases in which oral argument is held. The additional time required to file opinions in orally argued cases results from the time it takes to schedule oral argument and/or from continuances requested by counsel or required by the absence of one of the panel members.

Argued cases are deemed submitted on the date of oral argument, and the opinions are generally filed within the same month.

Section X.   Presiding justice

In addition to the regular duties of an associate justice, the Presiding Justice handles the administrative operation of the court including the functions designated in California Rules of Court, rule 77. In so doing, the Presiding Justice performs a number of tasks essential to the functioning of the court. These include without limitation policymaking, personnel, budgeting, oversight of facilities, grounds, furnishings, and equipment, case assignment, calendar preparation, backlog management, decision of all motions and applications until the case is assigned to an author, opinions in all criminal cases in which appellants file briefs under *People v. Wende* (1979) 25 Cal.3d 436, appointments of counsel, supervision of, and selection of cases for, the settlement program, and supervision of the central staff and clerk's office. Staff assist in these tasks when necessary in the Presiding Justice's discretion.

Section XI.   Staff

This division currently has 24 attorneys. Fourteen of these positions are chambers attorneys hired by the individual justices. The remaining 10 attorneys form the central staff consisting of one managing (formerly principal) attorney, one senior attorney acting as an assistant managing attorney, three writ attorneys, and five other central staff attorneys who primarily research and draft opinions. All central staff attorneys are under the supervision of the Presiding Justice, who assigns each attorney to a particular justice to research and draft opinions.

The clerk's office includes an assistant clerk/administrator, a number of deputy clerks, and other supporting clerical personnel. A settlement coordinator manages the volunteer attorney mediator settlement conference program. A systems administrator and an assistant maintain the court's computer systems. A librarian organizes and updates a central library, distributes materials to the justices' and attorneys' libraries, assists justices and attorneys with legal research, and prepares a library budget for approval by the Presiding Justice. There are also 10 judicial assistants employed by the court, who facilitate case flow in and out of the chambers and perform secretarial services for the justices and attorneys.

Division Three

Section
   I.   Introduction.
   II.   Structure of court and organization of staff.

Section
  III.   Procedures for processing cases.
  IV.   Judicial settlement program.
   V.   Settlement notices & stipulations.
  VI.   Ethical Screens.

Section I.   Introduction

This document describes the general internal operating practices and procedures of this court. These practices and procedures supplement the statutes and rules of court that otherwise govern the court's business.

Section II.   Structure of court and organization of staff

Division Three of the Fourth Appellate District is currently authorized eight justices—a presiding justice and seven associate justices. The Chairperson of the Judicial Council periodically assigns pro tem justices to assist the court.

Each justice's staff consists of two or three judicial attorneys and a judicial assistant. The managing appellate court attorney supervises a separate central staff. The managing appellate court attorney and central staff work under the direction and supervision of the presiding justice. They review original proceedings, motions, and extension requests, act as counsel for the clerk's office, and assist in the evaluation of cases. Many of the justices also utilize law student externs who may receive academic credit, without pay, while working at the court.

The assistant clerk/administrator supervises the court's administrative staff under the direction of the presiding justice. The court's administrative staff consists of deputy clerks, librarian, court systems administrators, and office assistants.

Section III.   Procedures for processing cases

   A.   Appeals.

1. When an appeal is fully briefed, the clerk's office sends out a notice to the parties who have appeared to give them an opportunity to request oral argument. (Cal. Rules of Court, rule 8.220(a).) Cases are generally scheduled for oral argument in order of the requests. Statutory priorities are enforced, and parties claiming calendar preference must promptly serve and file a motion for preference. (Cal. Rules of Court, rule 8.240.) Non-oral argument cases are similarly assigned in order based on the date oral argument is waived. Panels, including a justice tentatively designated to author the opinion, are generally assigned on a random rotating basis, subject to the presiding justice's responsibility to ensure that the court's resources are allocated in an effective and efficient manner to fairly and expeditiously resolve disputes, and to promote access to justice for all members of the public. (Cal. Rules of Court, rule 10.603(a).).

2. A confidential written summary is prepared by the authoring justice and provided to each panel member prior to oral argument. The panel may conference on a case before argument and always conferences after oral argument is completed. Thereafter, a proposed final opinion circulates among the panel members for comments and/or approval. Proposed opinions for cases in which oral argument has been waived generally circulate among panel members without a formal conference. All cases may routinely be discussed among the justices and staff members informally on an as-needed basis.

3. All requests for continuances of oral argument must b‌ writing and contain a particularized showing of com‌ circumstances. The written request must inform the ‌ opposing counsel's position regarding any continu‌ request will be forwarded to the presiding justice u‌ is made aware of opposing counsel's position. Co‌ tion to continue oral argument is not sufficient ‌ a showing of compelling cause.

Ct. Rules

4. Any post-briefing citation of additional authorities must be made by letter to the court, without further legal argument, and served upon opposing counsel. The court retains discretion to strike or disregard late-filed or untimely citations of authority as they deprive the court and opposing counsel of sufficient opportunity to prepare for oral argument.

5. The court offers remote video appearances for oral argument on criminal matters, allowing counsel to appear via video from Division One in San Diego.

B. Original Proceedings.

1. The presiding justice assigns on a quarterly basis three justices to serve as the court's writ panel for a three-month period. The writ panel members also rule on motions requiring a three-judge panel.

2. The clerk's office notifies the managing appellate court attorney when an original proceeding is filed. The managing appellate court attorney determines the urgency of the relief sought. The matter is calendared for the weekly writ panel conference if court action is not required before then. Impromptu writ conferences are held when court action is required earlier. The managing appellate court attorney and central staff attorneys prepare written summaries of original proceedings which are provided to the writ panel members before their weekly conference.

C. Motions.

1. The court's practice is to hold motions on appeals (Cal. Rules of Court, rule 8.54) in the clerk's office until (1) an opposition has been served and filed, or (2) the time has passed to serve and file an opposition, whichever is earlier. To expedite the processing of an unopposed motion, the moving party should file a stipulation of nonopposition from other counsel.

2. Motions in writ proceedings are not generally held for opposition absent a request by the parties.

D. Filings by Facsimile, Email or Other Electronic Means.
The court does not accept filings by facsimile, e-mail or other electronic means unless specifically authorized by court order or court rule. Local Rule 5 provides for a voluntary fax filing pilot project throughout the Fourth Appellate District for specified documents, but not briefs. *(As amended, eff. Jan. 1, 2008.)*

Section IV. Judicial settlement program

A. Purpose and Structure.

1. The court has established a judicial settlement program to mediate appellate disputes, and, where appropriate, to establish briefing schedules, to simplify appellate issues, and to address procedural concerns. The court encourages appellate mediations and settlement conferences, and will make its resources available to parties who attempt in good faith to resolve a dispute on appeal.

2. The judicial settlement program is directed by the presiding justice, who appoints a supervising judicial attorney to administer the program and to conduct settlement conferences. In addition, a senior clerk schedules the settlement conferences and provides an interface between the public and the court.

B. Filings.

All papers pertaining to the judicial settlement program should be filed with the clerk's office at the courthouse, located at 925 No. Spurgeon Street, or mailed to the court at the following address:

California Court of Appeal
Fourth Appellate District, Division Three
P.O. Box 22055
ta Ana, CA 92702
Judicial Settlement Program

These papers ordinarily are retained separately from the other documents filed on appeal, and, where appropriate, are confidential and for the purposes of the Judicial Settlement Program only.

C. Location and Telephone.

1. The judicial settlement program is physically housed in the Civic Center Professional Plaza, about one-half mile from the Spurgeon Street courthouse. The street address is:

Civic Center Professional Plaza
500 West Santa Ana Blvd., Room 400
Santa Ana, CA 92701

2. The telephone number is (714) 564–3600. The fax number is (714) 567–6060. Callers also may use the court's general telephone number: (714) 558–6777.

D. Settlement Conference Information Forms (SCIF's).

1. The presiding justice may order any pending civil appeal to be scheduled for a settlement conference pursuant to the California Rules of Court, rule 8.248. This decision is based upon the court's review of Settlement Conference Information Forms (SCIF), which are prepared by the parties and filed with the court. Preference is given to any stipulated requests for a settlement conference.

2. Request or stipulation for SCIF orders should be made in writing, directed to the Judicial Settlement Program. Requests may be made in confidence.

E. Settlement Conferences.

1. *Timing.* Settlement conferences may be ordered before, during or after briefing. The court generally does not schedule a conference after an appeal has been set for oral argument except for good cause. The court tries to accommodate stipulations for specific day or dates. Parties may ascertain available settlement conference dates by telephoning the settlement conference clerk.

2. *Settlement Conference Officer.* The presiding justice appoints the person who conducts the settlement conference. In addition to the supervising attorney who manages the judicial settlement program, the settlement conference officer may be an individual justice, assigned pro tem justice, or other judicial attorney.

3. *Personal Attendance.* Unless otherwise specified, all parties and their counsel must attend any settlement conference in person, and must have full settlement authority. Attendance by counsel claiming settlement authority is not sufficient. Any exceptions must be approved in advance by the court.

    a. Institutional Litigants. If the party is not an individual, then a party representative with full authority to settle must personally attend all settlement conferences in person, in addition to counsel.

    b. Insurance. If a party has potential insurance coverage applicable to any of the issues in dispute, a representative of each insurance carrier whose policy may apply also must personally attend all settlement conferences, with full settlement authority.

    c. Telephonic Appearances. The court prefers in-person settlement conferences and does not ordinarily grant requests for telephonic appearances. Parties who desire to participate by telephone must promptly serve and file a written request at least five court days before any settlement conference explaining why the attendee's personal presence is impossible or impracticable.

4. *Additional Participants.* The court may order other necessary persons (whether or not a party to the appeal) to personally attend settlement conferences. In addition, the conference officer may invite parties to the action who are not parties to the

appeal, or any person or entity having interest in the action, to attend. Any party may serve and file a written request for the attendance of such a party or person at least five court days before any settlement conference. No other person may attend a settlement conference without the permission of the conference officer.

5. *Settlement Briefs*. If a settlement conference is held before appellate briefing or record preparation, the conference officer may direct that the parties provide settlement conference briefs, or other appropriate documents, to facilitate a meaningful and productive settlement conference.

6. *Pre–Conference Preparation*. Counsel should confer with their clients in advance of any settlement conference and be thoroughly familiar with the case and prepared to present their contentions in detail. Counsel should review their SCIFs for completeness and accuracy and promptly notify the conference officer of any material changes or omissions at least three court days before the settlement conference.

7. *Location*. Settlement conferences generally are held at the court's settlement conference facilities. (See IVC, above for address.) Settlement conferences also may be held at the Spurgeon Street courthouse. Participants should carefully check the notice of a settlement conference for the correct location.

8. *Duration*. Participants should be prepared to remain for the duration of the day, or until dismissed by the conference officer. No person who has been ordered to appear may leave without permission of the conference officer. At the conclusion of a prehearing conference, the conference officer may continue the conference to another date to allow for further discussions.

9. *Continuances*. Parties who seek to continue a settlement conference should attempt to do so by stipulation, with a mutually agreeable alternative date. Any request for continuances should be made in writing, with reasons stated, and served and filed at least five court days before the conference. Continuances are not granted, except for good cause.

10. *Ex Parte Communications*. The conference officer may communicate with any of the parties or their counsel with or without notice to the other parties or their counsel.

11. *Confidentiality*. All discussions and information imparted during the settlement conference are confidential, and the conference officer cannot testify about them.

F. "Workout" Conferences.

The presiding justice may order that a prehearing "workout" conference be held for any of the following purposes: (1) to simplify issues on appeal, (2) to establish a briefing schedule, (3) to address procedural questions, issues or outstanding motions or applications, (4) to lay the groundwork for a future settlement conference, (5) to facilitate ongoing settlement discussions, (6) to monitor the progress of a pending settlement or private mediation, or (7) for any other reason or reasons. Unlike settlement conferences, workout conferences are conducted either in person or by telephone. Generally, only counsel, not clients, participate in "workout" conferences.

G. Private Mediations.

The presiding justice entertains stipulated requests to stay of appellate proceedings to allow private mediations. Stay requests shall not exceed 60 days except for good cause. Any such stipulated request shall specify the identity of the mediator, the scheduled day or dates for mediation, and any other pertinent factors.

H. Stays; Tolling.

Appeals are not automatically stayed merely because parties are ordered to prepare a SCIF, or to choose dates for a settlement conference. The tolling provisions for briefs (Cal.

Rules of Court, rule 8.248(d)) commence to run only when the court mails notice of a settlement conference for a specific date and time. Record preparation is not automatically stayed without a court order. The court's policy is to conduct settlement conferences as expeditiously as possible, and to issue a rule 8.248(d) notice lifting any stay or tolling order within 90 days from the date of the notice of the settlement conference.

I. Disqualification.

Disqualification of justices is governed by the Canon 3E of the California Code of Judicial Ethics. Justices are not disqualified to hear appeals merely because they rule on settlement conference requests or sign orders pertaining to procedural aspects of the settlement conference process. If appeals do not settle, neither the conference officer nor any other court personnel present at a conference will participate further in the determination of the appeal on the merits. (Cal. Rules of Court, rule 8.248(c)(2).)

J. Sanctions.

The judicial settlement program shall not be employed by any party in bad faith or for purposes of delay. The court may impose sanctions for (1) failure to appear at a prehearing (settlement) conference, (2) failure to participate in good faith in the judicial settlement program, or to cooperate in good faith with the conference officer, or (3) failure to comply with a court order or court rule. Sanctions may include monetary awards, or, in the case of an appellant's failure to comply, dismissal of the appeal.

Section V.　Settlement notices & stipulations

A.　Notice of Settlements.

The settling appellants shall immediately serve and file notices of settlement of any pending civil appeal, and telephone the court if the case has been calendared for oral argument. (See Cal. Rules of Court, rule 8.244(a) for other requirements concerning notice of settlements.) Settling appellants also should e-mail or telephone the settlement conference clerk if the appeal has been placed in the judicial settlement program.

B.　Stipulated Requests for Dismissal.

Counsel should promptly serve and file stipulated requests for dismissal because of settlements. The stipulation should specify the allocation of costs on appeal and whether the remittitur is to issue immediately. (Cal. Rules of Court, rule 8.244(c).)

C.　Stipulated Requests for Reversal. (Code Civ. Proc., § 128, subd. (a)(8).)

Stipulated requests for a reversal of the judgment ordinarily are heard by the writ panel, unless the appeal already has been assigned to a panel for decision.

1. *Good Cause*. The parties must provide a sufficient showing to satisfy the statutory criteria in Code of Civil Procedure section 128, subdivision (a)(8). A copy of the judgment shall accompany the motion.

2. *Joint Declaration*. The motion shall include a joint declaration of counsel that (1) describes the parties and the factual and legal issues presented at trial; (2) indicates whether the judgment involves important public rights or unfair, illegal or corrupt practices, or torts affecting a significant number of persons, or otherwise affects the public or a significant number of persons not parties to the litigation (if the judgment is a state licensee, the declaration must also disclose wh exposes such person to any possible disciplinary procee discloses whether the judgment sought to be reverse collateral estoppel or other effects in potential fu and, if so, whether any third parties who might h stipulated reversal of the judgment have rece motion and (4) discloses whether the judg

tionary determinations by the trial court that cannot be reversed by stipulation of the parties alone without independent appellate review (see, e.g., *Garabedian v. Los Angeles Cellular Telephone Co.* (2004) 118 Cal.App.4th 123; *Stewart v. Stewart* (1955) 130 Cal.App.2d 186, 193.)

3. *Notice to Party.* The joint declaration shall include a certification that a copy of the stipulation and joint declaration has been delivered to the client. The certification need not include the address of the party notified. In a class action, the copy required need be delivered to only one represented party.

Section VI.   Ethical Screens

The court maintains an ethical screening process for its judicial attorneys, judicial assistants, clerks, externs and other staff members in order to maintain and preserve public confidence in the judicial system. The purpose of this process is to inform the justices at the earliest possible opportunity of any circumstances of an actual or potential conflict of interest involving a court staff member that could give rise to the need for an ethical screen. If applicable, the ethical screen is promptly implemented.

FIFTH APPELLATE DISTRICT

Section

I.   Introduction

The purpose of this memorandum is to acquaint the bar and litigants with the general internal operating procedures of this court. It does not duplicate the California Rules of Court nor the statutes that govern the processes of the Courts of Appeal.

II.   Structure of court and organization of staff

The court is currently authorized ten judges—a presiding justice and nine associate justices.

The court is not divided into divisions and normally operates with three panels. The justices are rotated among the panels each month so that over time each justice will sit an equal number of times with every other justice on the court.

Each justice is authorized two staff attorneys. In addition, the court has a central staff consisting of experienced attorneys who write draft opinions in cases that are screened for routine disposition. The court also employs experienced writ and motion attorneys. The central staff and writ and motion attorneys work under the direction and supervision of the presiding justice.

III.   Practices affecting the decisional process

The workload of the court is divided into six principal categories: regular appeals (those not screened for routine disposition treatment); routine disposition appeals; writs; motions; petitions for rehearing and applications for publication; and settlement conferences in civil cases.

A.   Regular Appeals.

When the appellant's reply brief has been filed or the time for filing that brief has passed, the case is ready for disposition by written opinion. The cases are placed on the ready list in the order in which they become ready and are set in that order absent a granted motion to advance or a statutory priority. Although the clerk attempts to note those cases that are entitled to statutory priority, counsel is advised to remind the court of any particular case that is entitled to priority.

When placed on the ready list, the managing attorney screens all cases under the supervision of the presiding justice. Those cases subject to routine disposition in accordance with the ocedure described below are so designated on the list of ready s. The balance of the cases are designated as regular ls.

the last two weeks of each month the managing der the supervision of the presiding justice prepares a

list of the cases to be set on the regular calendar in the third following month. For example, cases to be set in April are selected in the last two weeks of January. In order to equalize the workload among the justices, the managing attorney assigns a weight to all cases according to degree of difficulty. Consistent with the goal of achieving an equal caseload for each justice, and absent a compelling reason to the contrary, the cases are then assigned at random to the individual justices for authorship. The total weight of the cases assigned to each justice is approximately equal. Two other justices from the same panel are assigned to participate in deciding each case. The cases are then calendared for oral argument, and notices of the settings are sent to the attorneys of record. The court does not look with favor upon requests for continuance of the hearing date and will normally refuse to grant a continuance unless a request is received within five days of the time the notice is sent and good cause is shown for the continuance.

If oral argument is requested, counsel may utilize the telephonic oral argument option which is available in this court (Oral argument by telephone option—see Section IV, post.)

When a case is calendared for oral argument, one of the staff attorneys for the justice to whom the case is assigned prepares a memorandum of facts and law in that case. Memoranda in all cases are normally completed during the month following the setting. For example, memoranda for cases calendared for April are completed in February. When completed, the memorandum is distributed to the three justices assigned to decide the case. The authoring justice will normally prepare a proposed opinion in each case to be distributed to the other two justices assigned to that case prior to the pre-argument conference which is held shortly before the date set for oral argument. Each of the justices will have read the briefs, as much of the record as they deem necessary, the case memorandum and the proposed opinion, if any, prior to the pre-argument conference.

Well in advance of oral argument, each case is reviewed by the court to determine if the issues can be narrowed or if the court will accept waiver of oral argument. In the former case, the court may advise counsel by letter of the particular issues upon which the court would like to hear oral argument. In the latter case, the court will advise counsel by letter that it is willing to accept a waiver of oral argument.

As a result of the court's preparation for oral argument, the justices are thoroughly familiar with the facts and issues before oral argument commences. The court normally asks questions of counsel during oral argument in an effort to pinpoint those issues that are particularly troublesome, to clear up any areas of confusion or uncertainty, and to further narrow the issues. Occasionally, supplementary briefing is permitted or requested. Otherwise, cases are submitted for decision at the conclusion of oral argument. (See Cal.Rules of Court, rule 8.256(d).)

After argument, the participating justices hold a post-argument conference. Thereafter, the authoring justice circulates a draft opinion to the other justices on the panel for their concurrence or dissent. In the event a majority of the justices do not eventually concur in the opinion of the justice to whom the case was assigned for authorship, a non concurring justice prepares the majority opinion.

Discussion as to whether an opinion qualifies for full or partial publication under California Rules of Court, rules 8.1105 or 8.1110, normally occurs at the pre and post-oral argument conferences, though the question remains open until the opinion becomes final.

If oral argument is waived, the case is ordered removed from the calendar and submitted for decision. The opinion may be filed any time thereafter. The decisional process is substantially the same as that outlined above except for the pre-oral argument conference.

B. Routine Dispositions.

A routine disposition is a case on appeal which raises no new or novel questions of law, is not of wide public interest, and can be disposed of by the application of settled principles of law to the facts. The draft opinion is written by an experienced attorney assigned to the central staff or by a justice.

The court is sensitive to the concern that the judicial input into this type of case may be diluted and therefore carefully supervises these cases. First, the presiding justice supervises the initial selection of the case for treatment as a routine disposition. Second, a panel of three justices is selected at random to participate on the case. Third, in each case a lead justice will read the briefs, the record where indicated, and approve or disapprove the draft opinion in writing. If the lead justice approves the draft opinion either as written or with changes, the two other justices must read and approve the opinion in writing. Fourth, if any justice so requests, a conference will be held among the justices and the author of the draft opinion. If, after a conference, any justice is of the opinion the case is inappropriate for routine disposition treatment, its designation as a regular appeal is restored and the case is processed in accordance with the procedure for regular appeals.

Last, when a draft opinion is approved by the justices, counsel are sent a letter indicating the court is willing to accept waiver of oral argument. Counsel are free to request oral argument and, if requested, the case is then placed on the oral argument calendar. Oral argument is requested in only a small percentage of these cases. Appointed counsel are advised that the court will consider the extent to which requested oral argument was a reasonable consideration by counsel and the extent to which such argument, if presented, adds to or enhances the arguments presented in the briefs in evaluating compensation claimed for preparation time and travel time. If oral argument is requested, counsel should consider utilizing the telephonic oral argument option, which is available in this court. (See Section IV, post.)

If oral argument is waived or if oral argument is requested, after argument and post-argument conference, the opinion as written or as modified may be filed either as a signed opinion or as an unsigned per curiam opinion. In the latter case, the participating justices' names appear at the bottom of the first page.

C. Writs.

The term "writs" as used here includes the traditional writs (mandamus, prohibition, certiorari, supersedeas, habeas corpus, error coram vobis), also writs of review, petitions in Workers' Compensation Appeals Board cases, Agricultural Labor Relations Board matters, Public Employment Relations Board, Alcoholic Beverage Control Board, and Public Utilities Commission cases.

The court has two writ panels of three justices each, the membership of which is rotated among all the justices from month to month. Writs are assigned to the panels so as to approximately equalize the workload. Writ conferences are held by each panel at least once per week, usually on Thursday mornings.

When a writ petition is filed, copies are distributed to the writ attorneys who, under the supervision of the presiding justice, assign them to the panels. A memorandum is prepared in each case by the writ attorney and delivered to each justice on the assigned panel prior to the writ conference. Emergency writs, usually involving a request for a stay of a proceeding in the trial court, are by necessity considered and disposed of as required by the particular circumstances, the constraints of time involved, and other court business. Other than issuance of a temporary stay order, writs will not be issued prior to the receipt of a response from parties who would be adversely affected or unless such parties inform the court that no response will be filed. A petition for a writ may be denied without a response being filed.

If it appears the matter is one in which relief may be appropriate but a peremptory grant would be inappropriate, an order to show cause or alternative writ is issued and the case may be calendared for oral argument. The case is then handled in accordance with the procedure for regular appeals.

Occasionally, if the issuance of a peremptory writ in the first instance has been prayed, and the facts are clear, and the case has been fully briefed and nothing would be added by oral argument, relief by way of peremptory writ may be granted without the issuance of an order to show cause or alternative writ. In these cases, a short opinion or a written order with reasons stated will be filed. Summary denials are more frequent, in which event, the law of the case doctrine does not apply. (See *Kowis v. Howard* (1992) 3 Cal.4th 888.)

California Rules of Court, rule 8.452 writ petitions taken from orders setting a hearing under Welfare and Institutions Code section 366.26 are handled on the writ calendar. Such cases, generated by the filing of a notice of intent to file a writ petition are distributed to a central staff attorney specializing in juvenile dependency law and rule 8.452 writ practice. The central staff attorney works under the supervision of the presiding justice and assigns such cases to panels on a rotating basis. Once the time passes under rule 8.452 for the filing of a response to such a writ petition, the central staff attorney prepares an Order to Show Cause setting the case for oral argument with the proviso that, in the event the parties do not advise this court of their desire to orally argue the case within seven days' time, the matter will be submitted. Thereafter, the central staff attorney prepares a memorandum, which in most cases addresses the merits of the writ petition, and delivers the memorandum to each justice on the assigned panel prior to the writ conference. The case is then handled in accordance with the procedure for routine dispositions.

Petitions for review of Agricultural Labor Relations Board decisions, of orders and awards of the Workers' Compensation Appeals Board, the Public Employment Relations Board, the Public Utilities Commission, and the Alcoholic Beverage Control Board, and review of decisions of appellate divisions of superior courts pursuant to California Rules of Court, 8.1002, are handled on the writ calendar. If a petition for is granted, or the certification under rule 8.1005 is acce case is set for oral argument after briefing is comple case is then disposed of in accordance with the p handling regular appeals.

D. Motions.

Non-routine motions and applications, including applications for bail, are processed in accordance with the procedure for handling writs.

Applications in routine matters (see Cal.Rules of Court, rules 8.50, 8.57), including motions to augment or correct the record, requests for extensions of time, and disciplinary proceedings against attorneys and court reporters for failure to timely file briefs and records, are normally disposed of by the presiding justice with the assistance of a writ attorney.

E. Petitions for Rehearing and Applications for Publication.

Petitions for rehearing and applications for publication are assigned for disposition to the same panel members who participated in the initial opinion.

F. Settlement Conferences in Civil Cases.

Upon stipulation of all parties to a civil case pending in the court or on the presiding justice's own motion, a settlement conference will be calendared and held pursuant to California Rules of Court, rule 8.284. Notice of availability of a settlement conference is sent to counsel at the time the record on appeal is filed. For further details, see local rule 2 on settlement conferences in civil appeals, a copy of which will be furnished upon request.

IV. Telephonic oral argument option

The court has in place a teleconferencing system that allows up to five attorneys in different offices to present their argument over the telephone in a single case. Attorneys selecting this option remains in their office until the clerk notifies them that their case has been called. The attorneys will then come on the line and are part of a telephone conference call. The system broadcasts the attorney's voice over the courtroom public address system as well as to other counsel appearing by telephone. The justices are convened in open court and speak into microphones which broadcast into court and through the telephone system. Counsel can hear each other and the court. The system allows one or more attorneys to appear in court and argue while other counsel listen and present their argument over the telephone. The argument is tape-recorded just as if all attorneys were present in court.

The teleconferencing option was implemented to accommodate counsel's time and to provide a significant cost savings to clients and the state by eliminating travel time and costs, as well as time spent waiting for a case to be called. Retained counsel selecting the telephonic oral argument receive a nominal billing from the court following the argument to cover the cost of the conference call and administrative time involved.

Details of the practices and procedures related to the telephonic oral argument option are available from the clerk upon request and may be found in the California Rules of Court, Local Rules of the Courts of Appeal.

V. Preliminary review of appellant's opening brief in civil cases

The court presumes that briefs filed by counsel will comply with applicable standards. (See Cal.Rules of Court, rule 8.204[Contents and form of briefs]). Unfortunately, many briefs do not. This adds to the court's workload and delays resolution of appeals.

Therefore, in civil appeals in this court:

(1.) After appellant's opening brief is filed, the managing attorney reviews the brief for basic compliance with pertinent rules, statutes, and case law. The review is non-substantive; the court does not engage in advocacy for the parties.

(2.) Should the brief fail to comply with minimum standards, the court may strike or return the brief and give counsel the opportunity to file an adequate brief within a specified time.

(3.) Should a subsequent brief continue to fail minimum standards, the court may dismiss the appeal without further notice. (*In re S.C.* (2006) 138 Cal.App.4th 396, 406–407.)

The same standards apply to briefs filed by pro se appellants. A party proceeding inpropria persona is treated like any other party and is entitled to the same, but no greater consideration than other litigants and attorneys. A propria persona litigant is held to the same rules of procedure as an attorney. (*First American Title Co. v. Mirzaian* (2003) 108 Cal.App.4th 956, 958.[1])

[1] 134 Cal.Rptr.2d 206.

SIXTH APPELLATE DISTRICT

Section
    Introduction.
I.   Structure of the court and organization of staff.
II. Processing appeals.

Introduction

The purpose of this document is to acquaint the bar and interested members of the public with the general operating practices of the Court of Appeal, Sixth Appellate District.

The internal procedures of the Court of Appeal are largely governed by the California Constitution, statutes, and the appellate rules adopted by the Judicial Council. The Court of Appeal may adopt and publish its own rules that do not conflict with a statute or rule adopted by the Judicial Council. (*As amended, eff. Jan. 1, 2009.*)

I. Structure of the court and organization of staff

A. JUSTICES

The court has seven authorized judicial positions, consisting of presiding justice and six associate justices.

The Chief Justice, as Chairperson of the Judicial Council, may [...] a retired justice or judge, or an active trial court judge to [...] mporarily on a Court of Appeal. Justices pro tem may [...] d (1) when there is a judicial vacancy, or (2) when a Court of Appeal justice is absent or unable to serve, or is disqualified in a given case, or (3) when the court needs assistance in reducing a backlog of cases.

Justices sit in panels of three that change periodically.

The courtroom and office of the clerk of the court are located in the Comerica Bank building at 333 West Santa Clara Street, Suite 1060, San Jose, California 95113.

B. PRESIDING JUSTICE

The presiding justice convenes conferences and presides at hearings (oral argument) when he or she is a member of the three-justice panel assigned to hear a case. The presiding justice has specific authority under rule 10.1012 of the California Rules of Court to grant or deny applications and to extend time for filing of records and briefs on appeal. The rule also gives the presiding justice limited authority to dismiss an appeal for noncompliance with the Rules of Court and to grant relief from default. The presiding justice also has overall responsibility for the calendaring of cases, the management of the caseload within the district, and the scheduling of oral arguments.

If the presiding justice is absent or disqualified, or not a member of the three-justice panel that is to decide a matter, the presiding justice designates the senior associate justice to serve as acting presiding justice.

C. CLERK/ADMINSTRATOR[1]

The Clerk/Administrator is responsible for maintaining the court's public records and files and for advising litigants, counsel, and the public of the status of matters before the court.

Appointed by the court, the clerk assists in the preparation of the court's calendar, dockets its cases, and supervises other administrative functions required for the court's operation. The clerk is aided by an assistant clerk/administrator, six deputy clerks and a support staff.

D. RESEARCH ATTORNEYS

1. *Attorneys Assigned to Justices*

Each justice is currently authorized to employ two permanent research attorneys.

Research attorneys employed by or assigned to a justice work primarily on appeals assigned to the justice. The attorney's work involves legal research, examination of the trial court record, conferring with the justices assigned to the case, and preparing written memoranda and draft opinions.

2. *Writ Attorneys*

The court is currently authorized to employ two writ attorneys who assist the court in reviewing petitions for various writs, such as mandate, prohibition, certiorari or review, habeas corpus, and error coram vobis.

3. *Central Staff*

In addition to the writ attorneys and research attorneys assigned to justices, the court employs a staff of several senior research attorneys. This staff is known as the "central staff" because it provides research and analysis assistance for the justices of the court. Central staff attorneys are assigned to individual justices by the court and provide the same research and assistance required of the justices' permanent research staff.

4. *Externs*

The Sixth Appellate District cooperates with law schools in enabling law students to earn academic credits by working one semester, without pay, performing research for individual justices. These law students are selected and supervised by individual justices.

E. LAW LIBRARIAN

The court's law library collection of approximately 30,000 volumes is maintained by a professional Law Librarian. The collection includes the latest technological developments in legal research such as: a wide variety of CD–ROM's on the Local Area Network (LAN); access to various online research services including the Internet; and a selection of microforms, audio tapes and video tapes, in addition to the books. The Law Librarian is also responsible for keeping current on technology and legal trends, which affords the court staff the opportunity to do efficient and effective research on all issues before the court.

F. JUDICIAL ASSISTANTS TO APPELLATE COURT JUSTICES

Each justice is authorized to employ one judicial assistant who is responsible for the timely processing of the justice's opinions, including circulating draft opinions for review by other members of the panel, typing judicial correspondence, cite-checking and shepardizing draft opinions, and delivering opinions to the clerk for filing. The court employs other secretarial support staff as needed. (*As amended, eff. Jan. 1, 2009.*)

[1] So in copy.

II. Processing appeals

A. In General

When a criminal or civil appeal is fully briefed, it is identified on a computer-generated list indicating the case is ready for analysis and decision. The appeals are considered by the court after they are fully briefed. Decisions may be made and the opinions filed in a different order depending on factors such as the complexity of the litigation and whether oral argument is requested. The California Constitution requires the filing of a written opinion in every appeal.

1. *Assignment of Cases*

Assignment of cases to individual justices is generally made by rotation from the list of ready cases. The justice assigned to a particular case then has lead or primary responsibility for that case in the course of conference discussions, research and preparation of the opinion.

2. *Preliminary Case Conferences*

In the course of preparing an opinion, conferences are held at the request of the author or other panel members. In difficult or complex cases, more than one conference may be held. Conferences are generally not held in cases involving routine issues.

3. *Oral Argument*

When a case is ready for possible argument, the clerk will write and ask the parties whether they desire to exercise their right to appear personally for oral argument or to argue by teleconference. [The Sixth District Court of Appeal Teleconferencing Oral Argument Procedures Manual is available from the clerk's office upon request.] If oral argument is requested, the case is placed on an oral argument calendar.

After the case is scheduled for oral argument, any party or counsel for a party may contact the clerk's office and be informed of the names of the justices assigned to the case.

The order in which cases are to be argued is determined by the presiding justice. Because of the considerable investment of court time and resources necessary to prepare a case for oral argument, continuances are disfavored and will be granted only on a showing of good cause. Oral argument will not be continued by stipulation of counsel absent a showing of good cause. If no appearance is made, the case may be ordered submitted.

The order and the time allotted for counsel to make their presentations are specified in rule 8.256 of the California Rules of Court.

In most instances, the presiding justice will inform counsel at the beginning of each session that the court has reviewed the briefs and is familiar with the facts and issues. The court requests that counsel not merely reiterate the argument contained in his or her brief. Oral argument is generally most helpful and effective when reasonably brief and when counsel focuses on the decisive issues, succinctly clarifies the facts as they relate to a given issue, or clarifies the holding or reasoning of potentially applicable or controlling authority.

The court disfavors the submission of untimely citations of authority as it deprives the court and opposing counsel of sufficient opportunity to prepare for oral argument. The court retains discretion to strike or disregard such citations.

When oral argument has concluded in a given case, the justice presiding will declare the cause submitted, unless submission has been deferred for additional briefing.

4. *Post–Oral Argument Conference*

A post-oral argument conference is held in which th[e] again discuss the case and finally determine the dec[ision] reached.

B. Preparation and Filing of Opinions

1. *Signed Opinions*

Unless the two other participating justices disagree with the disposition proposed by the assigned author, the justice assigned will prepare the majority opinion. When a proposed majority opinion has been drafted, it is circulated to the other participating justices. They indicate approval, disapproval, or proposed changes. Differences of opinion as to the language of the opinion or the ultimate disposition of the case may be taken up in conference. The opinion may then be modified in a manner acceptable to the justices. If two justices agree, a written opinion is filed.

2. *Concurring or Dissenting Opinions*

Where a difference of opinion exists among the justices participating in a case, a justice who agrees with the result reached but not with the reasoning of the majority may write a separate concurring opinion, or may merely indicate concurrence only in the judgment reached by the majority. Likewise, a justice who disagrees with the result reached by the majority may write a dissenting opinion. Each panel member has a full opportunity to consider the views of associates prior to the completion and filing of the opinion.

3. *Publication of Opinions*

A decision of the court is not published in the official reports unless it is certified for publication by a majority of the participating justices. The criteria for publication and publication requests are set forth in rules 8.1105 and 8.1120, respectively, of the California Rules of Court.

C. Rehearings

The procedure for filing a petition for rehearing is governed by rule 8.268 of the California Rules of Court. When a petition for rehearing is filed, the petition is routed to the justice who authored the opinion with copies to the participating justices. The authoring justice reviews the petition, and then indicates whether he or she votes to grant or deny the petition. The petition, along with any staff memorandum, is then circulated to the other two justices on the panel for their decisions. Two votes are necessary to grant or deny a petition for rehearing.

D. Original and Discretionary Proceedings

Petitions for writ of mandate, prohibition, certiorari, and habeas corpus, statutory review petitions, other miscellaneous applications to the original jurisdiction of the court, and applications for supersedeas or other relief pending appeal under Code of Civil Procedure section 923 or other statutory provisions are normally handled independently of the court's appellate caseload.

In original proceedings the court expects counsel to comply with the provisions of rules 8.486–8.488 of the California Rules of Court and all applicable time limitations, to explain any substantial delay in seeking relief in matters to which specific time limits do not apply, and to lodge with the court (and serve on adverse parties) a properly organized and indexed record sufficient to permit informed review. Any request for a stay of proceedings must be clearly labeled as such (Cal. Rules of Court, rule 8.116), and circumstances that require expedited consideration should be clearly identified in the petition or application and noted on its cover. Counsel should advise the clerk of the next trial court date at the time the petition or application is filed.

Parties to statutory writ review proceedings should comply with applicable briefing schedules (for example, Cal. Rules of Court, rules 8.495(b), 8.498(c)). The court will strictly apply those schedules, absent a timely application for exception supported by a showing of good cause.

In habeas corpus matters, the court in appropriate cases will request an informal response and provide for a reply to the response under rule 8.385(b) of the California Rules of Court.

In other original proceedings it is the court's policy not to grant affirmative relief (beyond a temporary stay) without first giving adverse parties an opportunity to submit a memorandum of points and authorities in opposition. Opposition need not be submitted in these matters unless expressly requested by the court. If requested, opposition must be submitted on or before the date stated in the request, unless an extension is obtained before that date.

Original proceedings are referred to the writ attorney for initial review. The writ attorney thereafter communicates with the court concerning the matter. The court will conduct a writ conference and meet specially when necessary. All written submissions by any party, and any written staff memoranda, are distributed to and reviewed by all participating justices.

If affirmative relief is to be granted, the Sixth District will issue an alternative writ of mandate or prohibition, which directs the relief prayed for in the petition or, in the alternative, that the respondent appear and show cause why the relief should not be granted. An order to show cause may be issued without the alternative writ. In limited circumstances, the court may issue a peremptory writ in the first instance without allowing oral argument.

Counsel seeking writ relief should carefully review the "Sixth District Court of Appeal Outline on Original Proceedings and Relief Ancillary to Appeal," which is available on request from the clerk's office or available for download in .pdf or .doc format from the court's website.

E. Communications with Counsel or Parties

Except in oral argument, the justices do not communicate directly with counsel or parties concerning pending cases. Any necessary communications are handled by the clerk.

Attorneys employed by the court do not communicate with counsel or parties concerning pending cases.

F. Settlement

The parties must immediately notify the court of the settlement of any pending case (Cal. Rules of Court, rule 8.244).

Upon the request of all parties to a pending case, the court will schedule and conduct a settlement conference. The conference will be conducted before a justice of the court or an assigned judge. The settlement conference must be attended by the parties unless counsel or another authorized representative in attendance have full authority to settle.

No justice conducting a settlement conference will participate in deciding the case or discuss the case with any justice deciding the case if the case is not settled. *(As amended, eff. Jan. 1, 2009.)*

LOCAL RULES

FIRST APPELLATE DISTRICT

	Rule
Criminal and juvenile docketing statements.	2. Mediation in civil appeals.

Rule 1.   Criminal and juvenile docketing statements

(a) [Application of Rule] In all criminal appeals, juvenile appeals from proceedings arising under sections 300, 601, or 602 of the Welfare and Institutions Code, and juvenile writ proceedings seeking to review findings and orders setting a hearing under section 366.26 of the Welfare and Institutions Code, the clerk of the superior court must, upon the filing of a notice of appeal or notice of intent, prepare a docketing statement and promptly forward it to the Court of Appeal with the notice of appeal or notice of intent and a copy of the (abstract of) judgment, minutes or order that is under appeal or challenged by writ.

(b) [Forms] The following forms of docketing statements shall be used:

(1) Docketing Statement for Criminal Notice of Appeal

(2) Docketing Statement for Juvenile Notice of Appeal and Juvenile Notice of Intent to File Writ Petition

(c) [Sanctions] The failure of a clerk of a superior court to file a docketing statement as required by this rule may result in the imposition of sanctions under the California Rules of Court. *(Adopted, eff. Oct. 16, 2006.)*

Rule 2.   Mediation in civil appeals

(a) [Mediation Program] To aid the expeditious and just resolution of civil appeals, the Court of Appeal for the First District has established a mediation Program ("Program"). Procedures for mediation and operation of the Program shall be promulgated by the First District Mediation Committee ("Committee"). The Program will be directed by a Mediation Program Administrator ("Administrator") acting under Committee procedures and supervision by the Administrative Presiding Justice or a designated Supervising Justice.

(b) [Scope of Mediation Program] Any civil appeal may be placed in the Program if selected by the Administrator or requested in writing by a party. The Administrator may remove an appeal from the Program and shall record the reasons for removal.

(c) [Mediators] The Committee shall specify the qualifications, training, and process for appointment of mediators in the Program. The Administrator will assign mediators to appeals. Mediation services will be furnished by the court without fee to the parties, provided that a mediation session exceeding 3 hours may be terminated by the mediator unless the parties and the mediator agree upon a fee payable to the mediator for continued services. The Administrator may replace a selected mediator upon written request by a party supported by a showing of good cause or upon request of the mediator.

(d) [Mediation Process]

(1) Within 10 days of the filing of the notice of appeal, the appellant shall file with the Clerk and shall serve on all other parties a completed Case Screening Form. Within 15 days of the filing of the notice of appeal, the other parties shall file with the Clerk and shall serve on all other parties their Case Screening Forms. The Case Screening Forms shall be transmitted by the Clerk to the Administrator and shall not be entered in the court file.

(2) The Administrator, within 10 days of receipt of the Case Screening Forms, shall notify the parties when a case is selected for mediation and furnish the name, address and telephone number of the mediator. At the same time, the Administrator shall furnish the mediator copies of the Case Screening Forms.

(3) Selection of a case for mediation will not suspend preparation of the appellate record or briefing, except pursuant to an order granting an application for an extension of time or a stipulation for an extension of time as provided in the California Rules of Court.

(4) The Administrator, within 5 days of selection of the mediator, shall furnish to the parties 3 dates within the next 30 days when the mediator is available for the mediation session.

(5) The parties, within 5 days of receipt of these dates, shall advise the Administrator of their scheduling preferences. The Administrator, after conferring with the mediator, promptly shall select the date and site for the mediation session and shall notify the parties.

(6) The mediator, with the approval of the Administrator, may, for good cause, postpone or continue a mediation session to a date certain.

(7) The mediator may require parties or their counsel to furnish information, documents, records or other items specified by the mediator.

(8) The mediator may at any time communicate with any of the parties or their counsel with or without notice to the other parties or their counsel.

(9) All parties and their counsel of record must attend all mediation sessions in person with full settlement authority. If the party is not an individual, then a party representative with full authority to settle all appeals and cross-appeals must attend all mediation sessions in person, in addition to counsel. If a party has potential insurance coverage applicable to any of the issues in dispute, a representative of each insurance carrier whose policy may apply must also attend all mediation sessions in person, with full settlement authority. Any exception to this requirement must be approved in writing by the Administrator.

The mediator may invite participation by any additional person or entity if the mediator concludes that such participation would facilitate mediation.

(10) No later than 10 days after completion of mediation, the mediator shall submit to the Administrator a Mediation Attendance Form, listing all participants in the mediation, and a Mediator's Statement, notifying the Administrator of the results of the mediation.

(11) No later than 10 days after completion of mediation, the parties and their counsel shall separately complete and su~~~ the Administrator evaluations of the mediation and the ~~~ on a form provided by the Administrator.

(12) The parties and their counsel shall pro~~~ steps necessary to implement the agreements re~~~ tion. An appellant who has settled must imm~~~ file a notice of settlement in the Court of Ar~~~

must seek abandonment or dismissal of the appeal as provided in the California Rules of Court.

(e) **[Confidentiality]** Except as otherwise required by law, information disclosed to the mediator, the parties, counsel, or any other participant in the mediation, or to the Administrator or the Coordinator of the mediation Program, shall be confidential and shall not be disclosed to anyone not participating in the mediation Program.

(f) **[Ethical Standards]** Mediators shall adhere to the Rules of Conduct for Mediators in Court–Connected Mediation Programs for Civil Cases set forth in the California Rules of Court.

(g) **[Appellate Process]** Parties and counsel shall comply with all rules applicable to processing appeals while concurrently participating in the mediation Program.

(h) **[Sanctions]** Monetary sanctions may be imposed by the Administrative Presiding Justice or Supervising Justice for failure to comply with these rules. *(Adopted, eff. Oct. 16, 2006.)*

Rule 3. **Settlement conferences in civil appeals**

(a) **[Application of Rule]** This rule applies to all appeals in civil cases except appeals from proceedings under sections 601 and 602 of the Welfare and Institutions Code, appeals arising in proceedings involving jurisdiction over an abused or neglected child or to establish or terminate parental rights, and appeals from original proceedings ancillary to a criminal prosecution. This rule is operative in addition to Local Rule 2.

(b) **[Request or Order for Settlement Conference]**

(1) A settlement conference will be scheduled if requested in writing by counsel for all parties to the appeal. The request may be made at any time prior to the close of briefing and shall be addressed to the Clerk/Administrator. A request by counsel for any party which declares that counsel for all other parties join in the request is adequate for this purpose.

(2) At any time during the pendency of an appeal, the panel to which the appeal has been assigned may order a settlement conference even though none was requested.

(3) The pendency of settlement proceedings will not suspend preparation of the appellate record or briefing, except pursuant to an order granting an application for an extension of time or a stipulation for an extension of time as provided in the California Rules of Court.

(c) **[The Settlement Conference]**

(1) A justice selected by the court from outside the division to which the appeal is assigned shall preside over the settlement conference. The Settlement Conference Justice will provide each party with written notice of the date and time of the conference. All subsequent communications regarding the settlement conference shall be directed to the Settlement Conference Justice and shall not be entered in the court file. The Settlement Conference Justice may continue the conference from time to time to allow further opportunity for negotiation and agreement, and may make any order necessary to effectuate the conference.

(2) All parties and their counsel of record must attend all settlement conference sessions in person with full settlement authority. If the party is not an individual, then a party representative with full authority to settle all appeals and cross-appeals must attend all settlement conference sessions in person, in addition to counsel. If a party has potential insurance coverage applicable to any of the issues in dispute, a representative of each insurance carrier whose policy may apply must also attend all settlement conference sessions in person, with full settlement authority. Any exception to this requirement must be approved in writing by the Settlement Conference Justice.

The Settlement Conference Justice may invite participation by any additional person or entity if the Settlement Conference Justice concludes that such participation would facilitate settlement.

(d) **[Implementation of Settlement Agreements]** The parties and their counsel shall promptly take the steps necessary to implement the agreements reached at the settlement conference. An appellant who has settled must immediately serve and file a notice of settlement in the Court of Appeal and, thereafter, must seek abandonment or dismissal of the appeal as provided in the California Rules of Court.

(e) **[Confidentiality]** Except as otherwise required by law, information disclosed to the Settlement Conference Justice, the parties, counsel, or any other participant in the settlement conference shall be confidential and shall not be disclosed to anyone not participating in the settlement conference.

(f) **[Appellate Process]** Parties and counsel shall comply with all rules applicable to processing appeals while concurrently participating in the Settlement Conference Program.

(g) **[Sanctions]** Monetary sanctions may be imposed by the Administrative Presiding Justice, the Supervising Justice of the Settlement Conference Program, or the Settlement Conference Justice for failure to comply with these rules. *(Adopted, eff. Oct. 16, 2006.)*

Rule 4. **Motions for stipulated reversal of judgment**

A motion filed in this court for stipulated reversal of a judgment of a trial court must include a joint declaration of counsel that (1) describes the parties and the factual and legal issues presented at trial; (2) indicates whether the judgment involves important public rights or unfair, illegal or corrupt practices, or torts affecting a significant number of persons, or otherwise affects the public or a significant number of persons not parties to the litigation (if the judgment is against a state licensee, the declaration must also disclose whether it exposes such person to any possible disciplinary proceeding); and (3) discloses whether the judgment sought to be reversed may have collateral estoppel or other effects in potential future litigation and, if so, whether any third parties who might be prejudiced by stipulated reversal of the judgment have received notice of the motion therefor. A copy of the judgment must accompany the motion.

The parties must provide a sufficient showing to support the findings required by Code of Civil Procedure section 128, subdivision (a)(8). *(Adopted, eff. Oct. 16, 2006.)*

Rule 5. **Timely preparation of clerk's and reporter's transcripts**

(a) **[Extensions of Time]** A request for an extension of time for the preparation of the clerk's or reporter's transcript on appeal will not be granted without an affirmative showing of good cause.

(b) **[Defaults]** In all cases in which a court reporter is in default, this court will promptly issue an order directing the court reporter to show cause why he or she should not be declared incompetent to act as an official reporter, pursuant to the provisions of section 69944 of the Government Code.

(c) **[Sanctions]** Sanctions may be imposed under the California Rules of Court for defaults in the preparation of clerk's or reporter's transcripts.

(d) **[Forms]** A motion for the extension of time to file a transcript shall be in substantially the form of one of the following:

(1) Clerk's Affidavit and Order for Extension of Time to File Transcript on Appeal

(2) Reporter's Affidavit and Order for Extension of Time to File Transcript on Appeal *(Adopted, eff. Oct. 16, 2006.)*

Rule 6. Contents of reporter's transcript in criminal and juvenile delinquency appeals

In addition to the normal record prescribed by the California Rules of Court, all records in criminal and juvenile delinquency appeals before the Court of Appeal, First Appellate District, are hereby augmented to include reporter's transcripts of the following proceedings:

(a) [*Marsden* Hearings] Any hearing held pursuant to *People v. Marsden* (1970) 2 Cal.3d 118. The original and two copies of the sealed transcript shall accompany the record upon certification and delivery to this court. The court shall provide appellant's counsel with a copy of the transcript. If appellant raises a *Marsden* issue, a copy of the transcript shall then be provided to the Attorney General in the manner prescribed in the California Rules of Court.

(b) [Pretrial Motions] Pretrial motions as follows: (1) motion to suppress identification; (2) motion to suppress statements of defendant (*Miranda v. Arizona* (1966) 384 U.S. 436); (3) motion to permit or preclude impeachment of defendant or witness with prior offenses (*People v. Castro* (1985) 38 Cal.3d 301); (4) motion to determine competence of defendant (Pen. Code, § 1368); (5) motion for severance or joinder; (6) motion for change of venue; (7) motion for discovery of police officer records (*Pitchess v. Superior Court* (1974) 11 Cal.3d 531); (8) motion for self-representation (*Faretta v. California* (1975) 422 U.S. 806); and (9) in limine motions held by the trial judge immediately preceding the trial or impanelment of the jury.

These motions shall be included only when denied in whole or in part, except for a People's motion for joinder or to impeach defendant, which shall be included only if granted in whole or in part.

Motions held in camera or under seal shall be transmitted to this court only, and no sealed copies shall be provided counsel for either party except on application to this court.

(c) [Revocation of Probation—Plea Proceedings] In appeals from revocation of probation: (1) the original sentencing proceeding at which probation was imposed; (2) the proceedings at the time of entry of a guilty plea or nolo contendere plea if the original judgment of conviction is based on such plea; and (3) the proceedings at which probation is revoked and the defendant is sentenced. *(Adopted, eff. Oct. 16, 2006.)*

Rule 7. Augmentation of record

(a) [Material Inadvertently Omitted] Counsel should not file a motion to augment the record when items have been inadvertently omitted by the clerk or certified shorthand reporter from the designated (civil) or normal (criminal) record. In such cases, counsel should immediately notify the clerk of the trial court who shall forthwith transmit the omitted item to this court and send a copy to counsel.

(b) [When to File Motion to Augment] Appellant should file requests for augmentation in one motion made within 30 days of the filing of the record or within 30 days after the expiration of the 10–day administrator review period in assisted criminal cases. Respondent should file requests for augmentation in one motion made within 30 days of the filing of appellant's opening brief. Thereafter, motions to augment will only be entertained upon a showing of good cause.

(c) [Clerk's Transcript] A motion to augment the clerk's transcript should be accompanied by that document (or documents) and, if not, must identify the document (or documents) with specificity; such motion and accompanying documents must be simultaneously served on opposing counsel. The requested augmented materials shall have been filed or lodged with the trial court, and the motion shall be accompanied by a declaration shall so stating.

(d) [Reporter's Transcript] A motion to augment the reporter's transcript shall identify the portion of the record with specificity, including the reporter and date of hearing. It shall establish with some certainty how the requested materials may be useful on appeal. Requests for jury voir dire should specify the exact questioning by which counsel of which juror together with the reason justifying the request.

(e) [Good Faith Required] A motion to augment shall be made in good faith and shall not be made for the purpose of delay. *(Adopted, eff. Oct. 16, 2006.)*

Rule 8. Stipulation for use of original superior court file

The California Rules of Court authorize the use of the original superior court file in lieu of the clerk's transcript on appeal in those cases where the parties so stipulate. The procedure therein is approved for use by the superior courts within this district in all civil cases in which the trial court retains no continuing jurisdiction. The stipulation shall be in substantially the form of the following: Stipulation for Use of Original Superior Court File in Lieu of Clerk's Transcript. *(Adopted, eff. Oct. 16, 2006.)*

Rule 9. Judicial notice requests

(a) [Form of Request] Any request that the court take judicial notice under Evidence Code section 459 shall be submitted as provided in the California Rules of Court. A motion seeking judicial notice pursuant to Evidence Code section 452 must include a showing of the relevance of the information to be judicially noticed.

(b) [If the Court Defers Ruling] If the motion is filed at the same time as the moving party's brief or if the court, with or without notifying the parties, has deferred ruling on a judicial notice motion, any party may in its brief rely upon the items the moving party sought to have noticed. However, if the court denies the motion it will disregard any such matter or materials not judicially noticed. *(Adopted, eff. Oct. 16, 2006.)*

Rule 10. Filing by facsimile

(a) [By the Trial Court] The trial court may transmit the following documents to this court via facsimile: (1) notices of appeal; (2) criminal and juvenile docketing statements; and (3) extension requests for court reporters and the superior court clerk's office.

(b) [By Counsel] Counsel may transmit the following documents to this court via facsimile: (1) civil case information statements; (2) stipulations for extensions of time; (3) changes of address; and (4) requests for oral argument. *(Adopted, eff. Oct. 16, 2006.)*

Rule 11. Extensions of time for filing briefs

(a) [Procedure] The times for filing briefs in civil, criminal, and juvenile appeals are specified in the California Rules of Court. In civil cases, the parties may, by stipulation, extend the time for filing each brief not more than 60 days. In criminal and juvenile cases, extensions of time by stipulation are not allowed. Extensions of time may be granted by the court only on a showing of good cause.

An application for an extension of time to file a brief is not necessary, either before or after a default notice under the California Rules of Court, if the brief can be filed within the pertinent default period. The clerk shall accept such a [brief] timely filed.

(b) [Forms] An application for an extension of t[ime] brief shall comply with the requirements of the C[alifornia Rules] of Court and shall be in substantially the form [of the] following:

(1) Application for Extension of Time to File Brief (Civil Case) (Judicial Council Form)

(2) Application for Extension of Time to File Brief (Criminal Case)

(3) Application for Extension of Time to File Brief (Juvenile Case)

(c) [Copies and Preaddressed Envelopes] The applicant shall provide the clerk with additional copies of the application, proposed order, and preaddressed envelopes with prepaid postage for mailing of the court's order to all parties. *(Adopted, eff. Oct. 16, 2006.)*

Rule 12. Bankruptcy stays

(a) [Conditions for Giving Notice] Any party to a matter pending before this court who acquires knowledge of a proceeding in bankruptcy which may cause or impose a stay of proceedings in this court must promptly give notice of such bankruptcy proceedings, as set forth below.

(b) [Procedure for Notice] The notice required by subdivision (a) shall be filed with the court and served on all parties and shall include (1) a copy of the most recent order of the bankruptcy court and of any stay order issued by that court and (2) an explanation of whether a stay order or an automatic stay is in effect and why the stay applies to the pending appeal or writ proceeding. Any party disputing the notifying party's documentation or explanation shall promptly serve and file an opposing statement.

(c) [Status Reports] On the first court days of January, April, July, and October, the debtor or other party for whose benefit the stay is taken shall serve and file brief status reports to apprise the court of the current status of the bankruptcy proceedings.

(d) [Notice to Proceed] Any party may, at any time, serve and file notice of any circumstances or orders permitting the appeal or writ proceeding to proceed, including evidence that the bankruptcy stay has been lifted, the bankruptcy proceeding has been dismissed, or the party has obtained relief from the stay. *(Adopted, eff. Oct. 16, 2006.)*

Rule 13. Argument by teleconference system

(a) [Teleconference System] The First Appellate District has a telephone conference call system that enables attorneys to present oral arguments by telephone, as an alternative to personal appearance in court. All oral arguments by telephone conference call will be heard by the justices on the bench in the courtroom, which will be open to the public.

(b) [Option of Counsel] In all cases, civil, criminal, and juvenile, in which a party has a right to present oral argument, counsel may elect to present oral argument either by personal appearance in the courtroom or by telephone conference call. The decision whether to present oral argument by telephone or in person is within the sole discretion of counsel and the parties, except that the court may direct counsel to appear in person.

In deciding whether to present oral argument by personal appearance or by telephone, counsel should consider the expense of a personal appearance to the parties and to the state and should determine whether the matters at issue can be satisfactorily argued by telephone conference call without incurring that expense.

(c) [Notice to Other Counsel] Upon receipt of oral argument notice from the court, counsel shall notify the court and all other parties in writing if he or she requests oral argument. If oral argument is requested, counsel shall indicate whether he or she wishes to present oral argument in person or by telephone conference call. The notice shall be given within the time for requesting oral argument.

If one counsel elects to argue by telephone and the other elects to appear in person, the counsel who elected to argue by telephone shall have the right to change his or her request and appear in person. The requested change shall be communicated in writing to the divisional deputy clerk and opposing counsel without delay.

(d) [Written Request for Oral Argument] Counsel's request to present oral argument by telephone conference call shall be made in writing and shall contain the following information: (1) the number and title of the case; (2) the name of counsel who will present oral argument; (3) the name of the party counsel is representing; and (4) the telephone number to be used for the conference call.

(e) [Fee to Cover Costs] The cost of the telephone system and service is billed to the court. No fee shall be charged to court-appointed counsel in any criminal, juvenile, or civil case or to the Attorney General or counsel representing the state, a county, a municipality or other government agency. In all other cases, a fee of $20 shall be paid by each party whose counsel requests oral argument by telephone conference call. A check in that amount, payable to the Court of Appeal, shall accompany counsel's request for oral argument. Additionally, telephone conference calls made to counsel outside the geographic boundaries of the First Appellate District will be made collect.

(f) [Notice of Time of Oral Argument] When a party requests oral argument by telephone conference call, the divisional deputy clerk shall notify counsel of the date, the approximate time of oral argument, and may indicate the maximum amount of time the court will allow for argument. The deputy clerk will arrange the conference call when the court calls the case for argument. If counsel fails to be available when the case is called, the court may deem oral argument waived.

(g) [Recording of Oral Argument] The court may record oral arguments presented by telephone conference call. A request for oral argument by telephone will be deemed consent to such recording. *(Adopted, eff. Oct. 16, 2006.)*

Rule 14. Circuit riding sessions

The court will conduct its hearings in its courtroom in San Francisco, California, except in the following instances:

(a) For the convenience of the litigants and attorneys, sessions may also be held in those cities or communities within the First Appellate District outside San Francisco from which sufficient appeals have been perfected to constitute one full day's calendar.

A session of the court may be held in the interest of justice at an appropriate educational institution within the First Appellate District. The court will not deviate from its normal calendar-scheduling practices in order to accumulate sufficient cases for a full day of hearings in any city or community.

(b) For the convenience of the court and court personnel, court sessions not held in the courtroom in San Francisco will be held only when suitable courtroom facilities are provided. Suitable courtroom facilities require security adequate to ensure the safety of the public and the court. *(Adopted, eff. Oct. 16, 2006.)*

Rule 15. Media coverage of matters at oral argument

Media coverage will be permitted only on written order of the presiding justice of the division hearing argument. The presiding justice in his or her discretion may permit, refuse, limit, or terminate media coverage. Any request for media coverage must be made on the Judicial Council form titled Media Request to Photograph, Broadcast, or Record. The form must be filed at least five court days in advance of the proceedings unless good cause is shown. The court directs the media's attention to the California Rules of Court, which specifically require pooling by media agencies. *(Adopted, eff. Oct. 16, 2006.)*

Misc. Order 94–1

IN THE COURT OF APPEAL OF THE
STATE OF CALIFORNIA

in and for the

FIRST APPELLATE DISTRICT

MISC. ORDER 94–1

THE COURT:

It is hereby ordered that all certified shorthand court reporters in the counties within the First Appellate District be granted extensions of time to prepare and file reporters' transcripts on appeal as follows:

In criminal appeals, court reporters are hereby granted one extension of 30 days (Cal. Rules of Court, rule *35(d)*) to prepare reporters' transcripts where the defendant appeals from a judgment of conviction after trial by jury or by the court. Transcripts shall be due within 50 days after the filing of the notice of appeal (Cal. Rules of Court, rules *35(b)* & (d)). This order <u>does not apply</u> where the defendant appeals from (1) an order after judgment (Pen. Code § 1237, subd. (b)); (2) a judgment entered on a plea of guilty or nob[1] contendere; (3) a judgment pronounced on resentencing after remand from the appellate court; (4) an order revoking probation or a judgment imposed after revocation of probation; or *5)* an order extending the defendant's term of commitment to a state hospital (Pen. Code § *1026.5*). Nor does this order apply to appeals by the people. Transcripts in these latter cases shall be due within 20 days after the notice of appeal is filed.

In all appeals from orders or judgments in juvenile court proceedings (Welf. & Inst. Code §§ 300 et seq., 601 & 602), the reporters' transcripts shall be filed within 20 days after the filing of the notice of appeal.

In civil appeals, other than juvenile court proceedings, the court reporters are hereby granted an extension of 30 days to prepare transcripts where a party appeals from a final judgment after a trial by jury or the court. Transcripts shall be due within 60 days after notice [2] to prepare the transcripts. This order does not apply where a party appeals from (1) an order after judgment (Code Civ. Proc., § 904.1, subd. (b)); (2) a summary judgment; (3) a judgment of dismissal after sustaining of a demurrer without leave to amend; (4) a default judgment; *(5)* a judgment of dismissal for failure to proceed in a timely manner (Code Civ. Proc., §§ *583.110–583.430);* or (6) any other appealable pretrial order or judgment of dismissal. Nor does this order apply where the appeal is from a superior court order declaring a minor free from the custody and control of his or her parents. (Civ. Code, § 232, operative until Jan. 1, 1994, and Family Code, §§ 7802–7808, operative Jan. 1, 1994.) Transcripts in these latter cases shall be due within 30 days after notice to prepare the transcripts.

Nothing in this order shall preclude a court reporter from applying and showing good cause for an extension of time as provided by court rules (Cal. Rules of Court, rules *35(d), 43, 45(b),* (c)). However, no additional extension of time shall be granted without the recommendation of the appeals supervising judge of the superior court.

This order supersedes this court's Miscellaneous Order No. '91–1.

Dated: April 4, 1994   Carl West Anderson

                 Administrative Presiding Justice

[1] So in copy, probably should be "nolo".

[2] notice issued by superior court appeals clerk (Cal. Rules of Court, rule 4(a), par. 3 & 4(c), par. 2)

Misc. Order 97–1

THE COURT:

This order supersedes amended miscellaneous order '96–2.

Code of Civil Procedure section 237, subdivision (a)(2), provides: "Upon the recording of a jury's verdict in a criminal jury proceeding, the court's record of personal juror identifying information of trial jurors, as defined in Section 194 [of the Code of Civil Procedure], consisting of names, addresses, and telephone numbers, shall be sealed until further order of the court as provided by this section." Subdivision (a)(3) of section 237 provides: "For purposes of this section, 'sealed' or 'sealing' means extracting or otherwise removing the personal juror identifying information from the court record."

Rule 33.6, California Rules of Court, implements the statute by requiring that juror identification information be kept under seal in the trial court's file and that clerk's and reporter's transcripts will identify jurors only by numbers. The key to match these numbers to names shall be kept under seal in the trial court's file.

An appellant seeking to unseal the juror identification information shall do so by following the procedure set forth in section 237 of the Code of Civil Procedure, applying to the trial court. If appellant seeks to unseal the information in connection with appellate review of the verdict and the trial court has denied a request to unseal, appellant may seek to unseal the juror identification information by motion in the Court of Appeal, supported by a record of the proceedings on the request denied by the trial court.

Dated: August 18, 1997   Gary E. Strankman

                 Administrative Presiding Justice

Misc. Order 07–1

IN THE COURT OF APPEAL OF THE
STATE OF CALIFORNIA

FIRST APPELLATE DISTRICT

MISCELLANEOUS ORDER 07–1

BY THE COURT:

Local Rule 2 of the First Appellate District, concerning mediation in civil appeals, provides, in part:

"(d) [Mediation Process]

"(1) Within 10 days of the filing of the notice of appeal, the appellant shall file with the Clerk and shall serve on all other parties a completed Case Screening Form. Within 15 days of the filing of the notice of appeal, the other parties shall file with the Clerk and shall serve on all other parties their Case Screening Forms. The Case Screening Forms shall be transmitted by the Clerk to the Administrator and shall not be entered in the court file. [¶] . . . [¶]

"(7) The mediator may require parties or their counsel to furnish information, documents, records or other items specified by the mediator. [¶] . . . [¶]

"(9) All parties and their counsel of record must attend all mediation sessions in person with full settlement authority. If the party is not an individual, then a party representative with full authority to settle all appeals and cross-appeals must attend all mediation sessions in person, in addition to counsel. If a party has potential insurance coverage applicable to any of the issues in dispute, a representative of each insurance carrier whose policy may apply must also attend all mediation sessions in person, with full settlement authority. Any exception to this requirement must be approved in writing by the Administrator.

Ct. Rules

"The mediator may invite participation by any additional person or entity if the mediator concludes that such participation would facilitate mediation. [¶] . . . [¶]

"(12) The parties and their counsel shall promptly take the steps necessary to implement the agreements reached in mediation. An appellant who has settled must immediately serve and file a notice of settlement in the Court of Appeal and, thereafter, must seek abandonment or dismissal of the appeal as provided in the California Rules of Court.

"(e) [Confidentiality] Except as otherwise required by law, information disclosed to the mediator, the parties, counsel, or any other participant in the mediation, or to the Administrator or the Coordinator of the mediation Program, shall be confidential and shall not be disclosed to anyone not participating in the mediation Program."

To facilitate the mediation of appeals, it is hereby ordered that all parties shall fully comply with all of the provisions of Local Rule 2, including, but not limited to, the provisions set forth above.

Dated: _____   _____ A.P.J.

Misc. Order 13–1.   Electronic Submissions and Filings
(Amended March 29, 2013)

Pursuant to California Rules of Court, rule 8.70,[1] the court herewith adopts and implements the following policies and procedures for electronic filing, effective May 1, 2013, and ORDERS as follows:

I.   APPEALS

A.   Civil

In lieu of an original and four paper copies, all counsel filing briefs or petitions for rehearing and answers thereto in civil matters shall file an original and three paper copies and submit one electronic copy. Submitting an electronic copy will satisfy the requirements for service on the Supreme Court under rule 8.212(c)(2).

B.   Criminal/Juvenile

In lieu of an original and four paper copies, all counsel filing briefs or petitions for rehearing and answers thereto shall file an original and three paper copies and submit one electronic copy in the following matters: criminal matters; appeals filed from judgments or appealable orders in cases under Welfare and Institutions Code sections 300, 601, 602; and actions to free a child under Family Code section 7800 et seq.

C.   *Wende* Briefs

Any appellate brief filed pursuant to *People v. Wende* (1979) 25 Cal.3d 436, *In re Phoenix H.* (2009) 47 Cal.4th 835, or *Conservatorship of Ben C.* (2007) 40 Cal.4th 529 shall be submitted for filing electronically. This electronic filing will satisfy, and substitute for, the filing requirement of a paper original and any required paper copies in this court.

Counsel are directed to electronically serve all *Wende, Phoenix H.* and *Ben C.* briefs on the Office of the Attorney General at: SFAG.Docketing@doj.ca.gov and on the First District Appellate Project at: eservice@fdap.org.

II.   WRITS

In lieu of an original and four paper copies, all parties filing or opposing any writ petition shall file an original and three paper copies of all writ related filings and submit one electronic copy. Writ related filings include, but are not limited to, any form, petition, informal response, preliminary opposition, return filed in this court, traverse, briefs, or declaration filed in support or opposition of the requested writ relief.

In addition to lodging an original with the court, parties shall also submit the record supporting a writ petition in electronic form.

III.   MOTIONS/NOTICES

The following documents must be completed and filed electronically using the forms provided on the court's Web site:

Civil Case Information Statement
Certificate of Interested Entities or Persons
Applications/Stipulations for Extension of Time
Change of Address
Substitution/Association of Attorney
First Application—Extension of Time Criminal Appeals
Request for Oral Argument

In addition to any paper copies otherwise required by court rules, an additional copy of any motion or notice must be submitted in electronic form.

IV.   TRIAL COURT RECORD

A.   Appendices

In addition to lodging an original with the court, parties shall also submit a copy of any appendix filed pursuant to rule 8.124, any agreed statement filed pursuant to rule 8.134, or any settled statement filed pursuant to rule 8.137 in electronic form.

B.   Administrative Records

In addition to any administrative record provided by the trial court pursuant to rule 8.123, the party or parties seeking review shall submit a copy in electronic form.

C.   Reporter's Transcripts

Any party who orders a reporter's transcript of proceedings pursuant to rule 8.130 shall also request a copy of the transcript in computer readable format, as provided in rule 8.130(f)(4), and submit an electronic copy to the court.

V.   SERVICE

Counsel shall continue to serve documents in paper form according to the additional service requirements of rule 8.212(c) and rule 8.360(d), unless, pursuant to rule 8.71(a)(2), a party indicates that the party agrees to accept electronic service.

VI.   FILING PORTAL/FORMAT

All filings must be in unlocked machine searchable portable document format (.pdf). All electronic copies must be filed through the court's Web site at <http://www.courts.ca.gov/1dca. htm>.

Should the record of trial court proceedings exceed the size limitations of the Web site (currently 5 MB per file), a party may elect to submit the record in multiple parts or provide the court with the record in digital format on machine readable optical media.

VII.   EXEMPTIONS

Self-represented parties may, but are not required to, comply with this order.

If this order causes undue hardship or significant prejudice to any party, the party shall lodge the number of paper copies required by the rules without regard to electronic filing, plus an additional unbound paper copy in lieu of the electronic copy, accompanied by a declaration of hardship. Acceptance of the lodged papers for filing will be subject to further order of the court. When it is not otherwise feasible for a party to convert a document to electronic form by scanning, imaging or other means, the document may be filed in paper form (rule 8.73(c)), together with a declaration setting forth the reasons that electronic filing was not feasible.

The Clerk of the Court is directed to post a copy of this order on the court's Web site pursuant to rule 8.74(a).

Date: March 29, 2013   William R. McGuiness
_____
Administrative Presiding Justice

1All rule references are to the California Rules of Court.

SECOND APPELLATE DISTRICT

Rule
1. Contents of reporter's and clerk's transcripts in criminal and juvenile appeals.
2. Augmentation of record and correction of omissions from record.
3. Designation of the record in civil appeals under California Rules of Court, rules 8.120, 8.122 and 8.130.
4. Proposed orders.
5. Extensions of time for filing briefs.
6. Advance notice of request for immediate relief in juvenile dependency writ petitions.
7. Copies of briefs, original proceedings (writs), oppositions or replies to a writ petition including any exhibits or appendices—electronic or paper.

Rule 1. Contents of reporter's and clerk's transcripts in criminal and juvenile appeals

In addition to the normal record prescribed by rules 8.320, 8.328, and 8.480(b)(1) and (2) of the California Rules of Court, all records in defendants' criminal appeals and minors' juvenile appeals before the Court of Appeal, Second Appellate District, are hereby augmented under rule 8.155(a) of the California Rules of Court to include reporter's and clerk's transcripts of the following:

(1) [Jury examination and opening statement]

Except if a conviction was obtained by plea or admission, reporter's transcripts of (a) jury voir dire whenever a motion regarding the composition of the jury or jury panel (for example, a motion under People v. Wheeler (1978) 22 Cal.3d 258 [148 Cal.Rptr. 890, 583 P.2d 748]) or a motion for a mistrial was made during the jury voir dire and decided in whole or in part adversely to the defendant; and (b) opening statements.

(2) [Sealed and in camera hearings]

Except if a conviction was obtained by plea or admission, oral proceedings of all sealed and in camera hearings resulting in rulings adverse in whole or in part to the appellant. These transcripts shall be listed in the index to the reporter's transcript, and the original and two copies of the sealed transcripts shall be transmitted to this court in sealed envelopes marked "CONFIDENTIAL–MAY NOT BE EXAMINED WITHOUT COURT ORDER." This court shall provide a copy of the sealed transcripts, other than transcripts of a hearing from which the appellant and defense counsel were excluded, to the appellant's counsel on appeal, upon his or her application. If the appellant raises an issue on appeal relating to the sealed transcripts, copies of transcripts shall then be provided to the Attorney General upon their written request. Unless otherwise ordered by this court, the sealed transcripts of a hearing from which the appellant and defense counsel were excluded may be examined only by a justice of this court personally.

(3) [Waivers of constitutional rights]

Reporter's transcripts of oral proceedings at which the appellant's constitutional rights were waived.

(4) [Guilty or nolo contendere pleas and admissions]

Proceedings at which the appellant moved to withdraw a guilty or nolo contendere plea or a juvenile admission, and proceedings at which sentence or disposition was imposed.

(5) [Pretrial proceedings]

(a) The following pretrial proceedings: (i) proceedings to determine competence of the appellant (Pen. Code, § 1368); and (ii) motions for self-representation (Faretta v. California (1975) 422 U.S. 806 [95 S.Ct. 2525, 45 L.Ed.2d 562;). (b) Except if a conviction or sustained petition was obtained by plea or admission, the following pretrial proceedings which were decided in whole or in part adversely to the appellant: (i) motions to suppress identification; (ii) motions to suppress statements of the appellant; (iii) motions to permit or preclude impeachment of the appellant or a witness with prior offenses (People v. Castro (1985) 38 Cal.3d 301 [211 Cal.Rptr. 719, 696 P.2d 111]); (iv) motions for severance or joinder; (v) motions for change of venue; (vi) motions for discovery of police officer records (Pitchess v. Superior Court (1974) 11 Cal.3d 531 [113 Cal.Rptr. 897, 522 P.2d 305]); and (vii) in limine motions.

(6) [Revocation of probation]

In appeals from revocation of probation: (a) the original sentencing or dispositional proceeding at which probation was imposed; (b) the proceedings at the time of entry of a guilty plea or nolo contendere plea or admission if the original judgment of conviction or sustained petition is based on such plea; and (c) the proceedings at which probation is revoked and the appellant is sentenced or disposition is imposed. (Adopted, eff. Aug. 1, 1992. As amended, eff. March 8, 1993; Jan. 1, 2005; March 20, 2006; March 2, 2007; April 16, 2007; April 27, 2009.)

Rule 2. Augmentation of record and correction of omissions from record

(a) [Material inadvertently omitted]. Counsel should not file a motion to augment the record when items have been omitted from the designated (civil) or normal (criminal) record on appeal. In those cases counsel should immediately notify the clerk of the superior court, who shall forthwith comply with rule 8.340(b) of the California Rules of Court.

(b) [When to file motion to augment]. Appellant should file requests for augmentation in one motion within 40 days of the filing of the record or the appointment of counsel. Respondent should file requests for augmentation in one motion made within 30 days of the filing of appellant's opening brief. Thereafter, motions to augment will not be granted except upon a showing of good cause for the delay.

(c) [Clerk's transcript]. A motion to augment or correct the clerk's transcript shall be accompanied by the documents requested. If the documents are not provided, the motion must identify them with specificity and contain an explanation for their omission. The motion and the accompanying documents must be served simultaneously on opposing counsel. The requested augmented materials shall have been filed or lodged with the trial court and the declaration shall so state.

(d) [Reporter's transcript]. A motion to augment the reporter's transcript shall identify the portion of the record with specificity, including the reporter's name and the date of the hearing. The motion shall establish with some certainty how the requested materials may be useful on appeal.

(e) [Extensions of time]. The time to perform any act required or permitted by the California Rules of Court will not be automatically extended by the filing of or ruling on a motion to augment. If additional time is needed, counsel may request an extension of time in the motion to augment.

(f) [Good faith required]. A motion to augment shall be made in good faith and shall not be made for the purpose of delay.

(g) [Proposed order]. A motion to augment must be accompanied by a proposed order. The form Order Re: Augmentation may be used.

(h) [Attachments]. When more than one document or transcript are attached to or submitted with a motion to augment the record pursuant to California Rules of Court, rule 8.155(a), the pages of the documents and transcripts must be consecutively numbered. *(Adopted, eff. Aug. 1, 1992. As amended, eff. Aug. 3, 1998; Sept. 15, 2003; Jan. 1, 2005; March 2, 2007; April 16, 2007; Dec. 31, 2012.)*

Rule 3. Designation of the record in civil appeals under California Rules of Court, rules 8.120, 8.122 and 8.130

(a) [Contents of the notice and designation of record]

The notice to prepare a reporter's transcript and the designation of the contents of a clerk's transcript required to be filed with the clerk of the superior court by the California Rules of Court, rules 8.130, 8.120 and 8.122 shall include the following information:

(1) *[Reporter's transcript]*

The notice to prepare the reporter's transcript shall state for each oral proceeding to be included in the record (1) the date, (2) the department number, (3) the name of the reporter or electronic recording monitor, and (4) the nature of the proceeding.

(2) *[Clerk's transcript]*

The designation of the contents of the clerk's transcript shall state for each paper or record to be included (1) the title and (2) the date of filing. For each exhibit to be included in the clerk's transcript, the designation shall include (1) the exhibit number, (2) a brief description, and (3) the admission status.

(b) [Form to designate record]

The form Designation of the Record on Appeal may be used to designate the record in civil appeals.

(c) [Sanctions]

Failure to comply with this local rule is a failure to properly designate the record under California Rules of Court, rules 8.130, 8.120 and 8.122, and may result in the dismissal of the

appeal or the imposition of monetary sanctions. *(Adopted, eff. May 6, 1996. As amended, eff. March 2, 2007; April 16, 2007; April 27, 2009.)*

Rule 4. Proposed orders

Any motion or application filed with this court must be accompanied by a proposed order. Failure to comply with this local rule may result in the denial of the motion or application. *(Adopted, eff. Aug. 3, 1998.)*

Rule 5. Extensions of time for filing briefs

File only the original of an application for an extension of time. Do not submit extra copies of the application or self addressed-postage-paid envelopes. The Clerk will send notice of ruling in every case. *(Adopted, eff. May 5, 2008.)*

Rule 6. Advance notice of request for immediate relief in juvenile dependency writ petitions

Before filing a petition for extraordinary writ with a request for immediate relief in a juvenile dependency proceeding, the petitioner must use best efforts to provide notice in person, by telephone, by facsimile or by e-mail to all parties at the earliest possible time and, when practical, at least 24 hours before filing. In addition, before filing such a petition, the petitioner must deliver to all parties in person, by facsimile, or by e-mail a copy of the petition. A declaration of notice and delivery, including the date, time, manner, name of the individual notified, any response of the individual notified, and whether any opposition will be filed, or a declaration stating the reasons why notice or delivery could not be accomplished, must accompany the petition. Noncompliance with this rule will not prevent the court from exercising its discretion in the best interest of the child. *(Adopted, eff. Sept. 15, 2003.)*

Rule 7. Copies of briefs, original proceedings (writs), oppositions or replies to a writ petition including any exhibits or appendices—electronic or paper

In lieu of an original and four (4) paper copies, a party submitting an electronic copy of a brief, writ, opposition or reply to a writ petition including any exhibits or appendices is required to file only an original and three (3) paper copies.

A party that does not submit an electronic copy of its brief, writ, opposition or reply to a writ petition including any exhibits or appendices, is required to submit one of the paper copies as **scan-ready** at the time of filing. "Scan-ready" means the document is unbound and does not have tabs or (for original proceedings) a red cover. *(Adopted, eff. Nov. 19, 2012.)*

THIRD APPELLATE DISTRICT

Rule
1. Mediation in civil appeals.
2. Stipulation for use of original superior court file.
3. Time for oral argument.
4. Judicial notice of legislative history materials.

Section
Misc. Order 2007–003.
Misc. Order 2007–016.
Misc. Order 2013–001.

Rule 1. Mediation in civil appeals

(a) Mediation program

To enable efficient case management and more expeditious resolution of civil appeals, the Court of Appeal, Third Appellate District ("the Court") has a Mediation Program ("Program"). Procedures for mediation and operation of the Program are

promulgated by the Court of Appeal Mediation Program Committee ("Committee").

(b) Mediation program administration

The Program is administered by a Mediation Program Coordinator ("Coordinator") acting under the direction of the Committee and under the supervision of the Administrative Presiding Justice or a designated Supervising Associate Justice.

(c) Scope of mediation program

(1) Other than appeals expressly exempt from the Program, a civil appeal will be placed in the Program if selected by the Administrative Presiding Justice or a designated Supervising Associate Justice.

(2) Any appeal taken from a judgment or order entered in a conservatorship, guardianship, or sterilization proceeding is exempt from the Program.

(3) With permission of the Court, a civil appeal exempt from, or not selected for, mediation may be placed in the Program by stipulation of the parties in accordance with subparagraph (f)(7).

(d) Mediation eligibility assessment

If the Administrative Presiding Justice or a designated Supervising Associate Justice tentatively selects an appeal for the Program, the Coordinator may communicate with counsel and independently assess the appeal for continued inclusion in the Program.

(e) Costs and fees for mediation services

(1) Mediation services are provided to the parties by the Court without fee. Mediators will not charge the parties any fee for the first four hours of the mediation session or sessions.

(2) After four hours, the parties and the mediator may agree on a fee to be paid by the parties to the mediator to continue the mediation.

(3) The mediator's preparation time and any time spent in pre-mediation session communications will not be included in the four-hour calculation.

(f) Mediation process

(1) *Appellate record*

(A) Effective upon filing of any notice of appeal in a civil case not expressly exempt from the Program, the provisions of rules 8.121, 8.124(a)(1), and 8.216 of the California Rules of Court, requiring designation of the record, payment of estimated costs of preparation of the record, and submission of a proposed briefing schedule, are suspended, pending the Court's decision to select or not to select the appeal for mediation.

(B) These rules do not prohibit the superior court from collecting its deposit required by section 68926.1 of the Government Code and by rule 8.100(b)(2) of the California Rules of Court.

(2) *Duties of the clerk of the court*

(A) Upon receiving notice of filing of a civil appeal in any case that is otherwise appropriate for mediation, the clerk must promptly mail:

(i) to appellant the Civil Case Information Statement form, as required by rule 8.100(f) of the California Rules of Court, and an Appellant's Civil Appeal Mediation Statement form.

(ii) to respondent a Respondent's Civil Appeal Mediation Statement form.

(B) Generally, multiple appeals from the same judgment or a related order are assigned the same appellate case number unless the record for the first notice of appeal has already been filed. (See Advisory Committee Comment to Cal. Rules of Court, rule 8.147.) Subsequent appellant's and respondent's Civil Appeal Mediation Statements will not be required when a second or subsequent notice of appeal has been filed within the same appellate case number.

(3) *Filing of the Appellant's Civil Appeal Mediation Statement*

(A) Within 10 days after the clerk mails the Appellant's Civil Appeal Mediation Statement form, appellant must serve and file the statement.

(B) Failure to timely file either the Appellant's Civil Case Information Statement or the Appellant's Civil Appeal Mediation Statement will result in dismissal of the appeal, without prejudice to reinstatement upon a showing of good cause.

(4) *Filing of the Respondent's Civil Appeal Mediation Statement*

(A) Within 10 days after filing of the Appellant's Civil Appeal Mediation Statement, respondent must serve and file a Respondent's Civil Appeal Mediation Statement.

(B) Failure to timely file a Respondent's Civil Appeal Mediation Statement will result in the appeal being assessed for mediation eligibility without input from the respondent.

(5) *Duties of the coordinator*

(A) The Coordinator must notify the parties whether the appeal has been selected for the Program within 10 days after the respondent files Respondent's Civil Appeal Mediation Statement. If the respondent fails to file a Civil Appeal Mediation Statement, the Coordinator must notify the parties whether the appeal has been selected for the Program within 10 days after Respondent's Civil Appeal Mediation Statement was due to be filed.

(B) The Coordinator will assign mediators to appeals selected for the Program.

(C) The Coordinator may replace a selected mediator upon written request by a party supported by a showing of good cause or upon request of the mediator.

(6) *Case assessment process*

(A) Cases eligible for mediation

(i) If an appeal is selected for the Program, the Coordinator will furnish the parties with the name, address, and telephone number of the mediator, and three dates when the mediator is available for the mediation sessions.

(ii) Within 10 days after receipt of notice of the dates the mediator is available, the parties must mutually confer and advise the Coordinator and the mediator of their scheduling preferences.

(iii) If an appeal is selected for the Program, suspension of rules 8.121, 8.124(a)(1), and 8.216 of the California Rules of Court will remain in effect until completion of mediation.

(B) Cases not eligible for mediation

(i) If an appeal is not selected for the Program, the Coordinator must concurrently notify the parties, the superior court, and the Court, in writing, that suspension of rules 8.121, 8.124(a)(1), and 8.216 of the California Rules of Court is terminated.

(ii) Upon notification by the Coordinator that an appeal was not selected for the Program, the parties' obligation to comply with the requirements of rules 8.121, 8.124(a)(1), and 8.216 of the California Rules of Court commences as if notice of appeal was filed on the date specified in the notification.

(7) *Stipulation to mediate*

(A) If an appeal is exempt from the Program or is not selected for the Program, the parties may stipulate to placement of the appeal in the Program.

(B) The stipulation must be served on the superior court and filed with the Court within 10 days of filing of notice of appeal. The original signature of at least one party must appear on the stipulation filed in the Court; the signatures of the other parties may be in the form of fax copies of the signed signature page of the stipulation.

(C) Upon receipt of the stipulation by the superior court, the provisions of rules 8.121, 8.124(a)(1), and 8.216 of the California Rules of Court, requiring designation of the record, payment of estimated costs of preparation of the record, and submission of a proposed briefing schedule, are suspended.

(D) The Court will decide whether to accept the stipulation and place the appeal in the Program.

(E) If the appeal is selected for the Program, suspension of rules 8.121, 8.124(a)(1), and 8.216 of the California Rules of Court must remain in effect until completion of mediation.

(F) If the appeal is not selected for the Program, the Coordinator must concurrently notify the parties, the superior court, and the Court, in writing, that suspension of rules 8.121, 8.124(a) (1), and 8.216 of the California Rules of Court is terminated.

(G) Upon notification by the Coordinator that the appeal was not selected for the Program, the parties' obligation to comply with the requirements of rules 8.121, 8.124(a)(1), and 8.216 of the California Rules of Court commences as if notice of appeal was filed on the date specified in the notification.

(8) *Continuation of mediation sessions*

The mediator, with approval of the Coordinator, may, for good cause, continue a mediation session to a date certain.

(9) *Mediator communications with parties and counsel*

(A) The mediator may at any time communicate with any of the parties or their counsel with or without notice to the other parties or their counsel.

(B) The mediator may require parties or their counsel to furnish information, documents, records, or other items specified by the mediator.

(10) *Full authority to settle*

(A) Counsel, parties, and persons with full authority to settle the appeal must personally attend the mediation, unless excused in writing by the mediator for good cause. If any consent to settle is required for any reason, the party or person with that consensual authority must be personally present at the mediation.

(B) If a party has potential insurance coverage applicable to any of the issues in dispute, a representative of each insurance carrier whose policy may apply must attend all mediation sessions in person, with full settlement authority. The party with such potential insurance coverage and that party's counsel shall serve timely notice to each insurance carrier with potential insurance coverage informing the carrier: (i) that appellate mediation has been ordered; (ii) that the carrier must have a representative with full settlement authority attend all mediation sessions in person; and (iii) of the date, time, and place of all mediation sessions. (See *Campagnone v. Enjoyable Pools & Spas Service & Repairs, Inc.* (2008) 163 Cal.App.4th 566.)

(C) The mediator may invite participation by any additional person or entity if the mediator concludes that such participation would facilitate mediation.

(11) *Completion of mediation*

(A) Within 10 days after completion of mediation, the mediator must submit to the Coordinator a Mediation Attendance Form, listing all participants in the mediation, and a Mediator's Statement, notifying the Coordinator of the results of the mediation.

(B) Within 10 days after completion of mediation, the parties and their counsel must separately complete and submit to the Coordinator confidential evaluations of the mediation and the mediator on a form provided by the Coordinator.

(12) *Appeal not resolved by mediation*

(A) If completion of mediation does not result in disposition of the appeal, the Coordinator must, within 10 days after notice of completion of the mediation, concurrently notify the parties, the superior court, and this Court, in writing, that suspension of rules 8.121, 8.124(a)(1), and 8.216 of the California Rules of Court is terminated.

(B) The parties' obligation to comply with the requirements of rules 8.121, 8.124(a)(1), and 8.216 of the California Rules of Court commences as if notice of appeal was filed on the date specified in the notification.

(13) *Appeal resolved by mediation*

(A) Pursuant to California Rules of Court, rule 8.244(a) and (b), if the mediation results in a disposition of the appeal, and the record has not been filed in the Court, the appellant must promptly file a notice of settlement with the Court and, within 45 days thereafter, file an abandonment of the appeal in the superior court.

(B) Pursuant to California Rules of Court, rule 8.244(a) and (c), if the mediation results in a disposition of the appeal, and the record has been filed in the Court, the appellant must promptly file a notice of settlement in the Court and must, within 45 days thereafter, serve and file in the Court a request for dismissal of the appeal.

(g) Confidentiality

(1) Except as otherwise required by law, information disclosed to the mediator, the parties, counsel, or any other participant in the mediation including the Coordinator, is confidential.

(2) The parties and the mediator must sign a confidentiality agreement in a form designated by the Court.

(h) Ethical Standards

Mediators must adhere to the rules of conduct for mediators in court-sponsored mediation programs for civil cases, as set forth in the California Code of Civil Procedure and the California Rules of Court.

(i) Sanctions

Monetary sanctions may be imposed following a noticed motion by a party seeking sanctions for failure to comply with the rules or upon the Court's own motion. (*Adopted, eff. Oct. 2, 2006. As amended, eff. March 2, 2007; May 29, 2009.*)

Rule 2. Stipulation for use of original superior court file

Rule 8.128 of the California Rules of Court, provides for the use of the original superior court file in lieu of the clerk's transcript on appeal in those civil cases where the parties so stipulate. In accordance with rule 8.128 of the California Rules of Court, the procedure therein is approved for use by the superior courts within this district. (*Formerly Rule 22, adopted, eff. Sept. 4, 1989. Renumbered Rule 2, eff. Oct. 2, 2006. As amended, eff. March 2, 2007.*)

Rule 3. Time for oral argument

Each side is allowed 15 minutes for oral argument. Where there are more than two parties, a "side" consists of all parties whose interests are not adverse. If there are more than two parties represented by separate counsel who request oral argument, or if counsel for amicus curiae requests oral argument, the court may apportion or expand the time according to the respective interests of the parties and of amicus curiae.

Any request for additional time for oral argument must be made by written application submitted to the court within 10 calendar days of the date of the order setting oral argument. The application must be served contemporaneously on all other parties and must specify the amount of time requested and the issues to which additional oral argument will be addressed. When an application is granted, the time allotted to the other side or sides will be similarly enlarged.

All parties will be advised of the disposition of any such application prior to hearing. (*Formerly Rule 23, adopted, eff. April 10, 1998. Renumbered Rule 3, eff. Oct. 2, 2006.*)

Rule 4.   Judicial notice of legislative history materials

A party making a motion to have the Court take judicial notice of legislative history documents must identify each such document as a separate exhibit and must provide legal authority supporting the consideration of each document as cognizable legislative history. (See *Kaufman & Broad Communities, Inc. v. Performance Plastering, Inc.* (2005) 133 Cal.App.4th 26.) (*Adopted, eff. Oct. 2, 2006.*)

Misc. Order 2007–003

BY THE COURT:

In pending appeals in which an appellant's opening brief was filed prior to the date this order is issued, and in which an opinion has not yet been filed, an application for leave to file a supplemental brief shall not be required before filing of a supplemental brief arguing, based on the decision of the United States Supreme Court in Cunningham v. California, (No. 05–6551. January 22, 2007, ___ U.S. ___; ___ S.Ct. ___; ___ L.Ed.2d ___; 2007 WL 135687; 2007 U.S.LEXIS 1324; 2007 DJDAR 965), that imposition of the upper term is unconstitutional. Henceforth, appellants shall not submit for filing any application for leave to file a supplemental brief challenging imposition of the upper term premised on Cunningham.

Any supplemental appellant's opening brief submitted pursuant to this order shall be served and filed on or before February 23, 2007. If a supplemental brief is filed pursuant to this order, the time for filing respondent's brief shall be extended by 30 days.

If respondent's brief has already been filed, respondent shall have leave to file a supplemental respondent's brief within 15 days of filing of the supplemental opening brief, and any appellant's supplemental reply brief shall be served and filed within 10 days of filing of the supplemental respondent's brief.

Dated: January 24, 2007

SCOTLAND, P.J.

Misc. Order 2007–016

BY THE COURT:

As dictated by *Auto Equity Sales, Inc. v. Superior Court* (1962) 57 Cal.2d 450, this intermediate appellate court is bound by the decisions issued by the California Supreme Court in *People v. Black* (July 19, 2007, S126182 ___ Cal.4th ___ (*Black II*)) and *People v. Sandoval* (July 19, 2007, S148917 ___ Cal.4th ___ (*Sandoval*)).

IT IS THEREFORE ORDERED that, in any case in which appellant's opening brief has been filed, this court shall not accept for filing any supplemental briefing challenging *Black II* and *Sandoval* on federal constitutional grounds. Appellants shall be deemed to have challenged the decisions in *Black II* and *Sandoval* on any such federal constitutional grounds, and to have thereby preserved the issues for petition for review to the California Supreme Court and petitions for appellate or collateral review by the federal courts.

Dated: July 26, 2007

SCOTLAND, P.J.

Misc. Order 2013–001

BY THE COURT:

Pursuant to this court's e-filing project (Cal. Rules of Court, rules 8.70 et seq.), the following documents may be filed with the court in electronic text-searchable PDF (portable document format):

1.   Application for an extension of time in a criminal appeal (first 30–day extension only);

2.   application for an extension of time in a civil appeal (first 30–day extension only);

3.   stipulation for extension of time in a civil appeal (up to 60 days);

4.   recommendation for appointment of counsel sent from the Central California Appellate Program (CCAP) with application;

5.   change of address;

6.   change of defendant's address sent from the Central California Appellate Program (CCAP);

7.   substitution or association of counsel;

8.   copy from the superior court of the notice of designation of record;

9.   copy from the superior court of an omission letter;

10.   copy from the superior court of an abandonment;

11.   notice of settlement;

12.   request to dismiss with no briefs filed;

13.   request for oral argument; and

14.   a service copy of documents filed in the Supreme Court.

In addition, in circumstances where the rules of court require the filing of an original and four paper copies, counsel and self-represented parties may file an original and three paper copies and submit one electronic text-searchable PDF copy through the court's website at http://www.courts.ca.gov/3dca.htm. And in circumstances where the rules of court require the filing of an original and one paper copy of a motion or an opposition or other response to a motion, counsel and self-represented parties may file an original and submit one electronic text-searchable PDF copy through the court's website at http://www.courts.ca.gov/3dca.htm.

Submitting an electronic copy to this court will satisfy the requirements for service on the California Supreme Court under California Rules of Court, rule 8.212(c)(2). But counsel shall continue to serve paper copies according to the additional service requirements of California Rules of Court, rule 8.360(d), unless a party agrees to accept electronic service. (Cal. Rules of Court, rule 8.71(a)(2).)

Dated: March 6, 2013

RAYE, P.J.

FOURTH APPELLATE DISTRICT

Rule
1.   Writ Proceedings.
2.   Covers on documents filed with the court.
3.   Stipulation for use of original Superior Court file.
4.   Civil settlement conference procedures (Division Two only).

Rule 1.   Writ Proceedings

   (a)   [**Request for immediate stay**] A request that an immediate stay be issued or other immediate relief be granted is to be served on the respondent and each real party in interest by (1) personal delivery or (2) an expeditious method consented to in advance by the party served. If the respondent or any real party in interest is not served personally or by an expeditious method consented to in advance by the party served, the court will not act on the request for five days, except to deny it summarily, absent a showing of good cause. The document cover must state conspicuously "STAY REQUESTED" or "IMMEDIATE RELIEF REQUESTED" or words of similar effect.

Ct. Rules

The court may issue a stay or other order necessary to preserve the status quo or the court's jurisdiction without opposition. However, a request for immediate relief, other than a stay or other order necessary to preserve the status quo or the court's jurisdiction, will not be granted unless the court has received an unsolicited opposition or, alternatively, has requested opposition.

(b) [Preliminary opposition] In an extraordinary proceeding involving a petition for writ of mandate, certiorari or prohibition pursuant to California Rules of Court, rules 8.485–8.493, the real party in interest need not file a preliminary opposition as provided in rule 8.487(a) unless requested to do so by the court. Except as provided in subdivision (a) of this rule, the court will not take any action on a writ petition, other than to summarily deny it, without first giving the real party in interest an opportunity to respond. *(Adopted, eff. Oct. 29, 2004. As amended, eff. Aug. 13, 2010.)*

Rule 2.   Covers on documents filed with the court

The court will not accept for filing any document that has a plastic or acetate cover or does not conform strictly to rules 8.144 and 8.204 of the California Rules of Court. *(Adopted, eff. Oct. 2, 1983. As amended, eff. Oct. 29, 2004; Jan. 1, 2007.)*

Rule 3.   Stipulation for use of original Superior Court file

Rule 8.128 of the California Rules of Court provides for the use of the original superior court file in lieu of the clerk's transcript on appeal in those civil cases where the parties so stipulate. In accordance with rule 8.128 of the California Rules of Court, the procedure therein is approved for use by the superior courts within this district unless the Court of Appeal orders otherwise in a particular case. *(Formerly Rule 10, adopted, eff. April 26, 1992. Renumbered Rule 3, eff. Oct. 29, 2004. As amended, eff. Jan. 1, 2007.)*

Rule 4.   Civil settlement conference procedures (Division Two only)

(a) [Application of rule] This rule is adopted pursuant to rule 8.248, California Rules of Court, and shall apply to all civil cases except appeals from proceedings under sections 300, 601, and 602 of the Welfare and Institutions Code, appeals from proceedings under sections 221 and 232 of the Civil Code, and appeals from original proceedings ancillary to a criminal prosecution.

(b) [Notice of availability of conference] Upon receipt of notice of the filing of a notice of appeal, the clerk of this court shall mail a copy of this rule to counsel for all parties.

(c) [General settlement conference procedure]

(1) The presiding justice may schedule a settlement conference and order the parties' attendance at any time during the pendency of an appeal.

(2) Written notice of the date and time of the settlement conference will be given by the court.

(3) Immediately upon accepting a case for the settlement conference procedure, all further proceedings, including the filing of briefs, shall be suspended until further order of the court. However, this rule shall not suspend preparation of the appellate record unless a specific order is issued directing suspension of record preparation.

(d) [Prebriefing settlement conference procedure and sanctions]

(1) A request for a settlement conference to be held prior to completion of briefing shall be served and filed within 30 days from the date of mailing of the notice specified in subdivision (b). Opposition to a request for a settlement conference must be served and filed within 15 days after the request's filing date.

(2) If the court orders a settlement conference prior to the completion of briefing, the parties shall each serve and file an original and one copy of a settlement conference statement at least 15 days before the settlement conference. The parties may file by the same date a joint settlement conference statement in lieu of separate statements. Failure to timely serve and file a settlement conference statement complying with this rule may result in the imposition of sanctions including dismissal of the appeal. Every settlement conference statement shall contain the following:

(A) The trial court name and case title and number;

(B) The name of the judge who rendered the judgment or order appealed and the date of its entry;

(C) The date the notice of appeal was filed;

(D) The names, address, [1] and telephone numbers of counsel for all parties to the appeal;

(E) A brief description of the judgment or order appealed;

(F) A concise statement of the case, including a brief procedural history and all facts material to consideration of the issues presented; and,

(G) The issues expected to be raised in the briefs.

(e) [Postbriefing settlement conference procedure and sanctions] After briefing is completed, the court may request the parties to provide information helpful to the court in deciding whether to order the parties to participate in a settlement conference. The parties shall complete all post-briefing settlement conference questionnaires and respond to all confidential settlement conference inquiries within 15 days of mailing by the clerk of the court. Failure to timely respond to a settlement conference inquiry or questionnaire may result in the imposition of sanctions including dismissal of the appeal.

(f) [Settlement conference and sanctions]

(1) The court shall maintain a list of attorneys who have developed expertise in specified areas of law, are generally respected in the legal community, and are willing to mediate settlement conferences at this court. These attorneys shall be designated as settlement conference mediators and preside over every settlement conference unless otherwise ordered. A justice or assigned justice may be designated as a settlement conference mediator and preside over a settlement conference if so ordered.

(2) The mediator presiding over a settlement conference may in his or her discretion continue it from time to time to allow for further negotiation.

(3) Counsel for every party to the appeal and their clients shall attend any settlement conference. Failure to attend a settlement conference may result in the imposition of sanctions against any party or counsel, including dismissal.

(4) The settlement conference mediator may invite parties to the action who are not parties to the appeal, or any person who has an interest in the action, to attend the settlement conference if it appears to the mediator that their presence may facilitate settlement of the case. Any party to the appeal may serve and file a written request for the attendance of such a party or person at least 15 days before the settlement conference.

(5) Counsel shall confer with their clients in advance and be thoroughly familiar with the case and prepared to present their contentions in detail.

(6) The presiding justice, a justice designated by the presiding justice, or the settlement conference mediator may excuse a client's personal attendance upon request and a showing that hardship or unusual circumstances make the client's attendance impossible or impractical. If personal attendance is excused, counsel either shall have obtained full authority to agree to a settlement that binds the client or the client shall be available for consultation by telephone.

(7) Where settlement cannot be reached, partial settlement will be sought. Any settlement shall be reduced to writing and signed by counsel. After a complete settlement has been agreed to in writing, the parties shall promptly file a stipulation to dismiss the appeal on the ground that the case has been settled. The stipulation shall specify the allocation of costs on appeal and state whether the remittitur is to issue immediately.

(g) [Disqualification of settlement conference justice]

(1) A justice or assigned justice who participates in a settlement conference that does not result in complete settlement shall not thereafter participate in any way in the consideration or disposition of the case on its merits.

(2) A justice or assigned justice of the court will not be disqualified to participate in the consideration or disposition of a case on its merits because he or she has ruled on a request for a settlement conference, ordered that a settlement conference be held, signed orders granting relief from default for an act required by a party under this rule, extended or shortened any time period specified in this rule, or otherwise signed an order concerning a procedural aspect of the settlement conference process. Only mediating a settlement conference shall disqualify a justice from consideration or disposition of the case on its merits. *(Adopted, eff. Oct. 13, 1992. As amended, eff. Oct. 29, 2004; Jan. 1, 2007.)*

1 So in original.

FIFTH APPELLATE DISTRICT

Rule
1. Augmentation of record and correction of omissions from record.
2. Mediation ~~Program for~~ in Civil Appeals.
3. Writ petitions: supporting records and stay requests.
4. The teleconference oral argument option.
5. Stipulation for use of original Superior Court file.

Section
Order regarding supplemental briefing February 21, 2007.
Amended order regarding Cunningham briefing February 16, 2007.
Local court form.

Rule 1. Augmentation of record and correction of omissions from record

(a) [Material inadvertently omitted] Counsel should not file a motion to augment the record when items have been omitted from the normal (criminal) record on appeal. In those cases counsel should immediately notify the clerk of the superior court, who shall forthwith comply with rule 8.155(b).

(b) [When to file motion to augment] Appellant should file requests for augmentation in one motion within 40 days of the filing of the record. Respondent should file requests for augmentation in one motion made within 30 days of the filing of appellant's opening brief. Thereafter, motions to augment will not be granted except upon a showing of good cause for the delay.

(c) [Clerk's transcript] A motion to augment or correct the clerk's transcript shall be accompanied either by certified copies of the documents requested, or, if the documents are not provided, the motion must identify them with specificity and contain an explanation for their omission.

(d) [Reporter's transcript] A motion to augment the reporter's transcript shall identify the portion of the record with specificity, including the reporter's name and the date of the hearing. The motion shall establish with some certainty how the requested materials may be useful on appeal.

(e) [Extension of time] The time to perform any act required or permitted by the California Rules of Court will not be automatically extended in civil cases by the filing of or ruling on a motion to augment. If additional time is needed, counsel may request an extension of time in the motion to augment.

(f) [Good faith required] A motion to augment shall be made in good faith and shall not be made for the purpose of delay. *(Formerly Rule 2, adopted, eff. Nov. 15, 1993. Renumbered Rule 1, eff. Aug. 25, 2003. As amended, eff. March 2, 2007; Aug. 17, 2007.)*

Rule 2. Mediation ~~Program for~~ in Civil Appeals

The Court has established a Judicial Mediation Program to assist parties to resolve appellate disputes in civil cases the Court finds suitable.

(a) Rule application: This rule applies to all civil appeals except those under Welfare and Institutions Code sections 300, 601, and 602 and Family Code section 7802, appeals in conservatorship and guardianship matters, and appeals from original proceedings ancillary to a criminal prosecution.

(b) Questionnaire: When a notice of appeal in a civil case is filed in any case to which this rule applies, the Clerk will promptly mail to appellant and respondent the non-confidential Civil Appeal Case Screening Questionnaire. [Downloadable form available on the Court's website http://www.courts.ca.gov/5 dca.htm.] Within 10 calendar days after the Clerk mails the Civil Appeal Case Screening Questionnaire form, each party must complete, sign, serve and return the Questionnaire to the Court of Appeal.

The Questionnaire will assist the Court in selecting a case for mediation with a sitting justice of this Court. The Court will select a case promptly after the Questionnaire is submitted and before the parties have incurred the expense of record preparation and appellate briefing. The Court recognizes the parties are asked to prepare the Questionnaire very early in the appellate process and may not be able to identify all appellate contentions. The Court will not deem an omission to be a waiver or forfeiture of any claim on appeal.

Failure to timely return the Questionnaire on the appellant's part may result in dismissal of the appeal, without prejudice to reinstatement on a showing of good cause, or in imposition of monetary sanctions pursuant to subdivision (e). Failure to return the Questionnaire on the respondent's part may result in the appeal being considered for mediation suitability without input from the respondent, or in imposition of monetary sanctions pursuant to subdivision (e).

(c) Mediation/Settlement Process:

(1) Effective upon the filing of any civil notice of appeal to which the rule applies, the provisions of rules 8.121, 8.124 and 8.216 of the California Rules of Court requiring designation of the record, payment of estimated costs for preparation of the record and submission of a proposed briefing schedule are suspended, pending the Court's decision to select or not select the civil appeal for mediation.

These rules do not prohibit the superior court from collecting the deposit required by Government Code section 68926.1 and by California Rules of Court, rule 8.100(b)(2).

(2) Within 14 calendar days after the Court receives the Civil Appeal Case Screening Questionnaires, it will notify the parties

whether the Court has or has not selected the civil appeal for mediation. If a civil appeal is selected for mediation, the Court will notify the parties with the name and telephone number of the Justice mediator and a Court contact person, and three dates when the Justice is available for the mediation session. At the same time, the Court will furnish the Justice mediator copies of the Civil Appeal Case Screening Questionnaires. Within 14 calendar days after receipt of the dates the Justice mediator is available, the parties must advise the Court contact person of their scheduling preferences. The Court will promptly select the date for the mediation session and will notify the parties by telephone and in writing.

If a civil appeal is selected for mediation, suspension of rules 8.121, 8.124 and 8.216 of the California Rules of Court will remain in effect until mediation is complete.

If a civil appeal is not selected for mediation, the Court will notify the parties and the superior court, in writing, that the suspension of rules 8.121, 8.124, and 8.216 of the California Rules of Court is terminated. The parties must comply with the requirements of rules 8.121, 8.124 and 8.216 of the California Rules of Court as if the notice of appeal was filed on the date specified in that notice.

If a civil appeal is not selected for mediation, the parties may thereafter submit a stipulation to mediation within the program. The Court will promptly decide whether or not to accept the case into the mediation program and will notify the parties of its decision.

(3) The Justice mediator may, for good cause, continue a mediation session to a date certain. The Justice may also continue the mediation from time to time to allow further opportunity for negotiation and agreement.

(4) The parties shall submit a CONFIDENTIAL Mediation Statement to the Court at least 7 calendar days before the scheduled mediation. The statement shall provide:

(A) The names of parties and their attorneys.

(B) A statement regarding the existence of any applicable insurance, and, if so, the identity of the carrier, the amount of the applicable insurance policy limits and the nature of any insurance coverage disputes/issues.

(C) A statement indicating whether or not a board, council or other committee must approve any settlement, and, if so, the identity of that body.

(D) The identification of any person not named as a party whose consent is necessary to achieve settlement.

(E) The dates and results of prior arbitration, mediation and most recent settlement discussions.

(F) The dates and amounts of any Code of Civil Procedure section 998 offers.

(G) A statement identifying and discussing in detail all facts and law pertinent to the issues of liability and damages involved in the case as to that party.

(H) An itemization of all economic and noneconomic damages claimed by the plaintiff.

(I) A description of any liens and their amounts.

(J) A statement whether there is any claim for recovery of attorney's fees, and, if so, the amount incurred to date.

(K) A statement of any additional information that might assist the Justice mediator.

(5) All parties and their counsel of record must attend all mediation sessions in person with full settlement authority. If a party is not an individual, then a party representative with full authority to settle all appeals and cross-appeals must attend all mediation sessions in person, in addition to counsel. If a party has potential insurance coverage applicable to any of the issues in dispute, a representative of each insurance carrier whose policy may apply also must attend all mediation sessions in person, with full settlement authority, and said party and that party's counsel are required to notify said insurance carrier of the date, time and place of court-ordered mediation and of the carrier's obligation to personally attend with full settlement authority. Any exception to this requirement must be approved in writing by the Justice mediator. The Justice mediator may invite participation by any additional person or entity if the mediator concludes that such participation would facilitate mediation.

(6) If completion of mediation does not result in disposition of the appeal, the Court will immediately notify the parties and the superior court that suspension of rules 8.121, 8.124 and 8.216 of the California Rules of Court is terminated. The parties must comply with the requirements of rules 8.121, 8.124 and 8.216 of the California Rules of Court as if the notice of appeal was filed on the date specified in that notice.

(d) **Confidentiality**: Except as otherwise required by law, information disclosed to the Justice mediator, the parties, counsel, or any other participant in the mediation, or in the Mediation Statement, is confidential and must not be disclosed to anyone not participating in the program. The parties are required to sign a confidentiality agreement in a form designated by the Court.

(e) **Sanctions**: Monetary sanctions may be imposed following a noticed motion by a party seeking sanctions for failure to comply with the rules or on the Court's own motion.

(f) **Disqualification of mediator justice**: Any justice who participates in a mediation shall not thereafter participate in the consideration or disposition of the appeal on its merits. *(Adopted, eff. Sept. 1, 2011. As amended, eff. Feb. 10, 2012; Jan. 1, 2013.)*

Rule 3. Writ petitions: supporting records and stay requests

(a) **[Information Sheet]** All petitions for extraordinary writs, other than habeas corpus, shall be accompanied by a properly completed face sheet, the Appellate Court Writ Petition Information Sheet. This form is available from the clerk of the court and on the Court's website (www.courts.ca.gov/5dca.htm).

(b) **[Required Exhibits]** A petition for an extraordinary writ that seeks review of a trial court ruling shall be accompanied by the following:

(1) a copy of the order or judgment from which relief is sought:

(2) copies of all documents submitted to the trial court supporting and opposing petitioner's position; and

(3) a transcript of the proceedings leading to the order or judgment below, or if a transcript is unnecessary or unavailable, a declaration by counsel (i) explaining why a transcript is unnecessary or unavailable and (ii) fairly summarizing the proceedings, including arguments by counsel and the basis of the trial court's decision, if stated.

(c) **[Copies of Filed Documents]** In lieu of the requirements contained in California Rules of Court, rule 8.44(b)(3) and (5), a party who files a petition, answer, opposition, reply, or other response to a petition, including any supporting documents, shall file an original and:

(1) one paper copy that is unbound, printed on white paper and does not contain tabs or a red cover; or

(2) an electronic copy in pdf. format, submitted through the e-submissions page on the Court's website(www.courts.ca.gov/5dca.htm).

This copy requirement does not apply to a self-represented person who files a petition for writ of habeas corpus.

(d) [Stay Request] A petitioner who requests an immediate stay shall explain in the petition the reasons for the urgency and set forth all relevant time constraints. If a petitioner does not submit the required record and explanations or does not present facts sufficient to excuse the failure to submit them, the court may summarily deny the stay request. *(Formerly Rule 5, adopted eff. Nov. 15, 1993. Renumbered Rule 3, eff. Aug. 25, 2003. As amended, eff. Nov. 1, 2012.)*

Rule 4. The teleconference oral argument option

The court has a teleconference system that enables attorneys to stay in their office until such time as contacted by the court for oral argument before the court.

Teleconference Procedures

1. Counsel who have requested oral argument will have returned to the court a questionnaire designating the attorney arguing the case and the time requested. If counsel has not specifically designated on the questionnaire a request for personal appearance, the attorney shall be deemed to have consented to teleconference oral argument.

2. The questionnaire requests a current California telephone number for counsel, which the court utilizes unless otherwise notified by counsel. The courtroom clerk will telephone each counsel's office in the sequence the cases are called on the calendar. Counsel are expected to be at the telephone number previously given to the court during the time oral argument has been scheduled and until such time as it has been completed.

Failure to be available to receive the telephone call will be treated in the same manner as a failure to personally appear for scheduled oral argument. Counsel is responsible for notifying the court if the designated telephone number is changed.

3. At the conclusion of the teleconference oral argument, the matter is submitted or the court will issue further directives as necessary.

4. Retained counsel participating in a teleconference call shall receive a nominal billing from the court following oral argument to cover the cost of the teleconference call and the administrative time involved.

5. Any deviation by appointed or retained counsel from these procedures shall not be permitted except by express prior approval of the court. *(Formerly Rule 6, adopted, eff. Nov. 15, 1993. Renumbered Rule 4, eff. Aug. 25, 2003. As amended, eff. Aug. 17, 2007.)*

Rule 5. Stipulation for use of original Superior Court file

The California Rules of Court authorize the use of the original superior court file in lieu of the clerk's transcript on appeal in those cases where the parties so stipulate. The procedure

therein is approved for use by the superior courts within this district in all civil cases in which the trial court retains no continuing jurisdiction. The stipulation shall be in substantially the form of the following: Stipulation for Use of Original Superior Court File in Lieu of Clerk's Transcript. *(Adopted, eff. Oct. 16, 2006.)*

Order regarding supplemental briefing February 21, 2007

In cases remanded from the United States Supreme Court for further consideration in light of *Cunningham v. California* (2007) 549 U.S. ___ [127 S.Ct. 856, 2007 U.S. Lexis 1324] [1]:

(1) Within 30 days after of the order remanding the case to the Court of Appeal for further proceedings, appellant may serve and file a supplemental opening brief in the Court of Appeal. Within 30 days after such a brief is filed, the respondent may serve and file a supplemental responding brief.

(2) Supplemental briefs must be limited to matters arising after the previous Court of Appeal decision in the cause.

JAMES A. ARDAIZ, P.J.

1 2007 WL 135687

Amended order regarding Cunningham briefing February 16, 2007

If the appellant has raised an issue challenging the imposition of the upper term, in reliance on *Blakely v. Washington* (2004) 542 U.S. 296 or *Apprendi v. New Jersey* (2000) 530 U.S. 466, it shall be deemed that the appellant is also relying on Cunningham v. California (2007) 549 U.S. ___ [127 S.Ct. 856, 2007 U.S. LEXIS 1324] [1].

If the court deems supplemental briefing necessary from either the appellant or the respondent to address related issues such as forfeiture, waiver, prejudice, etc., it will request a letter brief from counsel. Any request to file supplemental briefing will be considered on a case-by-case basis.

JAMES A. ARDAIZ, P.J.

1 2007 WL 135687

Local court form

Appellate Court Writ Petition Information Sheet

By order dated November 23, 1982, all petitions for extraordinary writs, other than habeas corpus, shall be accompanied by a properly completed face sheet, the Appellate Court Writ Petition Information Sheet. This form is available from the clerk of the court, and also is available on the court Web site. *(As amended, eff. Aug. 25, 2003; Aug. 17, 2007.)*

Ct. Rules

SIXTH APPELLATE DISTRICT

Misc. Order 12–1

Filed January 7, 2013

IN THE COURT OF APPEAL OF THE STATE OF CALIFORNIA
SIXTH APPELLATE DISTRICT

Misc. Order 12–1

(Amended January 7, 2013)

IT IS HEREBY ORDERED that effective May 1, 2012, pursuant to California Rules of Court, rule 8.70, any appellate brief filed pursuant to *People v. Wende* (1979) 25 Cal.3d 436, 441, *In re Phoenix H.* (2009) 47 Cal.4th 835, *Conservatorship of Ben C.* (2007) 40 Cal.4th 529, or *People v. Serrano* (2012) 211 Cal.App.4th 496 shall be submitted for filing electronically. This electronic filing will satisfy, and substitute for, the filing requirement of a paper original and any required paper copies in this court. The court will return an electronic copy to the sender indicating the document has been filed.

Counsel are directed to electronically serve all *Wende, Ben C.,* and *Serrano* briefs on the Office of the Attorney General at Docketing6DCASFAWT@doj.ca.gov and on the Sixth District Appellate Program at sdapattorneys@sdap.org. Counsel shall continue to serve paper copies according to the additional service requirements of the California Rules of Court, rule 8.360(d), unless, pursuant to California Rules of Court, rule 8.71(2), a party indicates that the party agrees to accept electronic service.

If this order causes undue hardship or significant prejudice to any party, the party shall file an original paper brief without copies, accompanied by a declaration of hardship.

Dated _____ January 7, 2013 _____ CONRAD L. RUSHING P.J.

Misc. Order 12–2

Filed March 15, 2012

IN THE COURT OF APPEAL OF THE STATE OF CALI-
FORNIA
SIXTH APPELLATE DISTRICT

Misc. Order 12–2

IT IS HEREBY ORDERED that effective May 1, 2012, in lieu of an original and four paper copies, all counsel filing briefs or petitions for rehearing and answers thereto in civil matters shall file an original and three paper copies and submit one electronic copy through the court's website at http://www.courts.ca.gov/6dca.htm. Submitting an electronic copy will satisfy the requirements for service on the Supreme Court under rule 8.212(c)(2).

Counsel shall continue to serve paper copies according to the additional service requirements of the California Rules of Court, rule 8.360(d), unless a party agrees to accept electronic service. (Cal. Rules of Court, rule 8.71(2).)

Self-represented parties may, but are not required to, comply with this order. If this order causes undue hardship or significant prejudice to any party, the party shall not be required to comply with this order and may file an unbound 4th paper copy in lieu of an electronic copy.

Dated _____ March 15, 2012 _____ Conrad L. Rushing P.J.

Misc. Order 12–3

Filed March 15, 2012

IN THE COURT OF APPEAL OF THE STATE OF CALI-
FORNIA
SIXTH APPELLATE DISTRICT

Misc. Order 12–3

IT IS HEREBY ORDERED that effective May 1, 2012, in lieu of an original and four paper copies, all counsel filing briefs or petitions for rehearing and answers thereto in criminal matters; appeals filed from judgments or appealable orders in cases under Welfare and Institutions Code sections 300, 601, 602; actions to free a child under Family Code section 7800 et seq; and writ petitions filed under Welfare and Institutions Code section 366.26 and 366.28, shall file an original and three paper copies and submit one electronic copy through the court's website at http://www.courts.ca.gov/6dca.htm.

Counsel shall continue to serve paper copies according to the additional service requirements of the California Rules of Court, rule 8.360(d), unless that party agrees to accept electronic service. (California Rules of Court, rule 8.71(2).)

Self-represented parties may, but are not required to, comply with this order. If this order causes undue hardship or significant prejudice to any party, the party shall not be required to comply with this order and may file an unbound 4th paper copy in lieu of an electronic copy.

Dated _____ March 15, 2012 _____ Conrad L. Rushing P.J.

Misc. Order 12–4

Filed March 15, 2012

IN THE COURT OF APPEAL OF THE STATE OF CALI-
FORNIA
SIXTH APPELLATE DISTRICT

Misc. Order 12–4

IT IS HEREBY ORDERED that effective May 1, 2012, in lieu of an original and four paper copies, all parties filing or opposing any writ petition, except petitions filed pursuant to Welfare and Institutions Code section 366. 26 and 366.28, shall file an original and two paper copies of all writ related filings and submit one electronic copy through the court's website at http://www.courts.ca.gov/6dca.htm. Writ related filings include, but are not limited to, any form, petition, informal response, preliminary opposition, return filed in this court, traverse, briefs, or declaration filed in support or opposition of the requested writ relief.

Effective May 1, 2012, in addition to lodging an original with the court, parties shall also submit the record supporting a writ petition in electronic form through the court's website. Should the record exceed the size limitations of the website, a party may elect to submit the record in multiple parts or provide the court with the record in digital format.

Self-represented parties may, but are not required to, comply with this order. If this order causes undue hardship or significant prejudice to any party, the party shall not be required to comply with this order and may file a third unbound paper copy in lieu of the electronic copy.

Dated _____ March 15, 2012 _____ Conrad L. Rushing P.J.

Misc. Order 13–1

Filed April 25, 2013

IN THE COURT OF APPEAL OF THE STATE OF CALI-
FORNIA
SIXTH APPELLATE DISTRICT

IT IS HEREBY ORDERED that effective May 15, 2013, pursuant to California Rules of Court, rule 8.70, any motion filed in the Sixth Appellate District shall be submitted for filing electronically. This electronic filing will satisfy, and substitute for, the filing requirement of a paper original and any required paper copy in this court. The court will return an electronic copy to the sender indicating the document has been filed.

This order shall apply to all motions filed in the Court of appeal with the following exception:

Any party filing a Motion to Augment the Record or any Request for Judicial Notice which attaches documents that are to be made part of the record on appeal shall submit the original motion and attached documents in paper form and one copy electronically.

If this order causes undue hardship or significant prejudice to any party, the party shall file an original motion and one scan-ready copy, accompanied by a declaration of hardship. "Scan-ready" means the document is unbound and does not have tabs.

Dated   4/25/13   Conrad L. Rushing   P.J.

CALIFORNIA JURY INSTRUCTIONS

This table indicates where sections of the California Civil Code, Code of Civil Procedure, Evidence Code, and Government Code are referenced in the California Jury Instructions—Civil (BAJI) and in the Judicial Council of California Civil Jury Instructions (CACI)

Jury Inst. Tbl.

CALIFORNIA RULES OF PROFESSIONAL CONDUCT

CALIFORNIA RULES OF COURT

FEDERAL RULES OF EVIDENCE
CALIFORNIA EVIDENCE CODE CONVERSION TABLE

Publisher's Note: This table is taken from Edward J. Imwinkelried and Timothy H. Hallahan's *Imwinkelried and Hallahan California Evidence Code Annotated, 2013 Ed.*, California Desktop Codes (Thomson Reuters 2013). We are grateful to the authors for their permission to reproduce it here.

F.R.E.	C.E.C.
101	300
102	2
103(a)–(b)	353–54
103(c)	354
103(d)–(e)	
104	310–11, 400–01
104(a)	405, 910, 914–15, 1228
104(b)	403, 702, 1400
104(c)	402
104(e)	406
105	355
106	356
201	450
201(a)	
201(b)	451–52
201(c)	451–53
201(d)	454–56
201(e)	454–56
201(f)	457
301	110, 115, 500–50, 600–70, 895.5, 917, 1450–54
302	
401	140, 210
402	350–51, 406, 410
403	352, 352.1, 780 (comment)
404	
404(a)	1101–04
404(b)	816, 818, 1101
405	1100–03
406	1105
407	1151
408	1115–1128, 1152, 1154
409	1115–1128, 1152, 1154
410	1153–53.5
411	1155
412	782–83, 1103, 1106
413	1108–1109
414	1108
415	
501	911–19
Proposed 502	1040
Proposed 503	754.5, 950–62
Proposed 504	990–1007, 1010–27, 1030
Proposed 505	663, 970–73, 980–87
Proposed 506	1030–34
Proposed 507	1050

F.R.E.	C.E.C.
Proposed 508	1060–63
Proposed 509	1040, 1043–47
Proposed 510	1041–42
Proposed 511	912
Proposed 512	919
Proposed 513	913
601	700–01, 795
602	170, 702
603	165, 702, 710
604	750–55
605	703, 703.5
606(a)	704
606(b)	1150
607	785
608	778
608(a)	780, 786, 790, 1100–01
608(b)	780, 786–87
609	788
610	789
611	772
611(a)	320, 702(a), 720(a), 760–63, 765–66, 772, 778
611(b)	760–63, 772, 773–74
611(c)	764, 767, 776
612	771
613	769–70, 780
613(a)	768–69
613(b)	770, 778
614(a)	775
614(b)	775
614(c)	
615	777
701	800, 813, 870
702	351.1, 720, 753, 795, 801, 893, 1107, 1159
703	801, 803, 814, 822
704	805
705	802
706	460, 753, 893–94
706(a)–(b)	730, 732, 893
706(c)	731,894
706(d)	722
706(e)	733,897
801(a)	125, 225
801(b)	135,145
801(c)	150, 1200(a)
801(d)(1)	780, 791, 1220–24, 1235–36, 1238
801(d)(2)	1220–28
802	1200(b)
803(1)	1241
803(2)	1240
803(3)	1250, 1252, 1260
803(4)	1251–52
803(5)	1237
803(6)	712, 1270–71
803(7)	1272

F.R.E.	C.E.C.
803(8)	664, 1280, 1282–83
803(9)	1281, 1316
803(10)	1284
803(11)	1315
803(12)	1281, 1315–16
803(13)	1312
803(14)	1600, 1603–05
803(15)	1330
803(16)	640, 643, 1331
803(17)	1340
803(18)	721, 1341
803(19)	1313–14
803(20)	1320–23
803(21)	1324
803(22)	639, 666, 1300–02
803(23)	
804	240, 1350
804(a)(1)	240(a)(1)—(2)
804(a)(2)	240(a)(3)
804(a)(3)	240(a)(3)
804(a)(4)	240(a)(3), 240(c)
804(a)(5)	240(a)(4)—(5)
804(b)(1)	1290–93
804(b)(2)	1242
804(b)(3)	1230
804(b)(4)	1310–11
804(b)(6)	1390
805	1201
806	1202–03
807	160, 1200(b), 1225–27, 1350
901(a)	403, 1400–02
901(b)	1401, 1410, 1560–66
901(b)(1)	1413
901(b)(2)	1415–16
901(b)(3)	1415, 1417–19
901(b)(4)	1420–21
901(b)(5)	644–45
901(b)(6)	645.10
901(b)(7)	
901(b)(8)	640, 643
901(b)(9)	
901(b)(10)	
902	1400–01, 1451
902(1)	1452–53
902(2)	1452–53
902(3)	1454
902(4)	1530–32
902(5)	644–45
902(6)	645.10
902(7)	
902(8)	1451
902(9)	
902(10)	1450
903	1411–12

Evid Conv Tbl

F.R.E.	C.E.C.
1001(a)–(b)	250, 1410.5
1001(c)	250
1001(d)	255, 1551
1001(e)	260, 1552
1002	1520–21
1003	1521(a), 1522(a)
1004	
1004(a)	1523(b)
1004(b)	1523(c)(1)–(2)
1004(c)	1522(a)
1004(d)	1522(a)(2), 1523(c)(2)
1005	1522(a)(3)–(4)
1006	1523(d)
1007	1414
1008	1401
1101	300, 910, 1203.1
1102	
1103	

INDEX

Abbreviations

Index

AMENDMENT OF PLEADINGS—Cont'd

Filing and service of amended pleading, **CCP 471.5, 472**

Mistakes, correction of, **CCP 473**

Motion for judgment on the pleadings, amendment following granting of, **CCP 438**

Motion to amend, **Rule 3.1324**

Motion to strike, amendment following, **CCP 472a**

Name of defendant, substitution of true name for fictitious one, **CCP 474**

Postponement of trial necessitated by amendment, **CCP 473, 594a**

Time for amendment, **CCP 472 et seq.**

Variance requiring amendment, **CCP 469**

AMICUS CURIAE

Superior courts, appellate departments, **Rule 8.882**

Supreme Court and courts of appeal, **Rule 8.200**

AMMUNITION

Forcible entry and detainer, nuisance, **CC 3485**

AMOUNT IN CONTROVERSY

Reclassification, actions and proceedings, **CCP 403.010 et seq.**

Small claims courts, **CCP 116.221**
  Motor vehicles, accidents, personal injuries, **CCP 116.224**

ANCESTRY

Certificate of ceremony, **Evid 1316**

Family records, **Evid 1312**

Relative, statement by, **Evid 1311**

Religious records, **Evid 1315**

Reputation
  Among community, **Evid 1314**
  Among family, **Evid 1313**

Tombstones, **Evid 1312**

See also RELATIVES

ANCIENT DOCUMENTS

Age of documents, **Evid 1331**

Authentication, **Evid 1419, 1420**

Deed of conveyance, **Evid 1330**

Hearsay rule, application, **Evid 1330**

Presumptions, **Evid 643**

Will, **Evid 1330**

ANIMALS

Abandoned animals, **CC 1834.5, 1834.6, 1981**

Auction, equine slaughter sale notice, **CC 1834.8**

Bailment, duties of bailee to, **CC 1834**

Borrower of animal, required care, **CC 1887**

Breeders lien, **CC 3062 et seq.**

Cruelty
  Borrowed animal, **CC 1837**
  Motion pictures
    Action to enjoin nuisance, **CC 3506, 3507**
    Depicting killing or cruelty as nuisance, **CC 3505**
    Distributor, liability of, **CC 3507.4**
    Exempt pictures, **CC 3508**

ANIMALS—Cont'd

Cruelty—Cont'd
  Motion pictures—Cont'd
    Producer, liability of, **CC 3507.4**
    Prevention, **CC 1834 et seq.**

Damages
  Dog bites, **CC 3342**
  Exemplary damages for willful injuries to animals, **CC 3340**
  Owners liability for injuries to other animals, **CC 3341**

Depository of living animals, duties of, **CC 1834 et seq.**

Dog bites
  Action against owner, **CC 3342.5**
  Damages, **CC 3342**
  Duty of owner, **CC 3342.5**

Facilities for animal care
  Abandoned animals, **CC 1834.5, 1834.6**
  Obligation to treat animals well, **CC 1834**

Finder of domestic animal, obligations, **CC 2080**

Floating homes, charge by marina for keeping pet, **CC 800.43**

Furs, ownership of animals kept for pelting, **CC 996**

Guide dogs for blind persons
  Airplanes, use on, **CC 54.2**
  Housing rights, effect on, **CC 54.1**
  Mobilehome parks, presence in, **CC 798.33**
  Public access, effect on, **CC 54.2**
  Rights of access for dogs with owners or trainers, **CC 54.1, 54.2**

Guide dogs for deaf persons, See Signal dogs, this heading

Horses, equine slaughter sale notice, **CC 1834.8**

Inspection warrants
  Fish, amphibia or aquatic plants, inspection of areas used for, **CCP 1822.58**
  Plant pest or disease eradication effort, warrant connected with, **CCP 1822.59**

Landlord and tenant, declawing, devocalizing, **CC 1942.7**

Liens
  Breeders liens, **CC 3062 et seq.**
  Care of animal, enforcement of lien for, **CCP 1208.5**

Limitations periods, death or injury of boarded animal, **CCP 340**

Medical research, tests, alternatives, **CC 1834.9**

Mobilehome parks, keeping of pets in, **CC 798.33**

Motion pictures showing intentional cruelty or killing
  Action to abate, **CC 3506**
  Definitions, **CC 3504**
  Exceptions, **CC 3508**
  Exhibition of, **CC 3505**
  Injunctive relief, **CC 3507**
  Liability of producer, distributor, or exhibitor, **CC 3507.4**
  Willful misstatements as misdemeanor, **CC 3508.1**

ANIMALS—Cont'd

Notice at shelter that animals will be used for research, **CC 1834.7**

Ownership of wild animals, **CC 656**

Principal or income, animals employed in business as, **CC 731.10**

Propagation services lien, See AGRICULTURE

Research, notice at shelter that animals will be used for, **CC 1834.7**

Sale, equine slaughter sale notice, **CC 1834.8**

Signal dogs for deaf persons
  Housing rights, effect on, **CC 54.1**
  Mobilehome parks, presence in, **CC 798.33**
  Public access, effect on, **CC 54.2**
  Rights of access for dogs with owners or trainers, **CC 54.1, 54.2**

Society for prevention of cruelty to animals

Statute of limitations, death or injury of boarded animal, **CCP 340**

Veterinarians lien for boarding and treatment of animals, **CC 3051**

Zoos and wild animal parks, handling of guide dogs and signal dogs, **CC 54.7**

See also AGRICULTURE

ANONYMOUS WITNESSES

Anonymous witness programs, **CC 48.9**

ANSWERS

Generally, **CCP 430.10 et seq., 431.10 et seq.**

Amended complaint, answer to, **CCP 471.5**

Appearance in action by filing, **CCP 1014**

Captions, **CCP 422.30, 422.40**

Certiorari, return by answer, **CCP 1069.1**

Contents, **CCP 431.30**

Controversion of material allegations, **CCP 431.20**

Demurrer, See DEMURRERS

Eminent domain action, use in, **CCP 1250.350 et seq.**

Extension of time, **CCP 473**

General denial, **CCP 431.40**

Interpleader, answer to complaint or cross complaint in, **CCP 386**

Issues arising by virtue of answer, **CCP 590**

Mandate
  Alternative writ, return by answer, **CCP 1089**
  Answer when alternative writ not sought, **CCP 1089.5**

New matter in answer, **CCP 431.20**

Objection
  Answer to complaint or cross complaint, **CCP 430.10, 430.30**
  Demurrer to answer, **CCP 430.20, 430.30**
  Grounds, **CCP 430.10, 430.20**

Special answer by third party defendant, **CCP 428.70**

Supplemental answer, **CCP 464**

Time, extension of, **CCP 473**

Verification, **CCP 446**

Index

CONSUMER PROTECTION—Cont'd

Investigative consumer reporting agencies—Cont'd
  Obligations—Cont'd
    Procedures, **CC 1786.20**
    Procurement of report, conditions for, **CC 1786.16**
    Public record information, **CC 1786.28**
  Remedies
    Actions, **CC 1786.52**
    Bar to action, **CC 1786.52**
    Defamation action, **CC 1786.52**
    Invasion of privacy action, **CC 1786.52**
    Liability of agency or user, **CC 1786.50**
    Limitations periods, **CC 1786.52**
    Nonapplication of provisions, **CC 1786.54**
    Severability, **CC 1786.56**
Membership camping contracts, See SPORTS AND RECREATION
Private arbitration companies, adverse or pecuniary interest, **CCP 1281.92**
Records and recordation, personal records, destruction, **CC 1798.80 et seq.**
Seller assisted marketing, See SELLER ASSISTED MARKETING PLANS
Senior citizens, loans encumbering residence, **CC 1770**
Supermarkets, club cards, disclosure, **CC 1749.60 et seq.**
Warranties, See WARRANTIES

CONSUMERS LEGAL REMEDIES ACT

Generally, **CC 1750 et seq.**
See also CONSUMER PROTECTION

CONTEMPT

Acts constituting
  Acts or omissions, **CCP 1209**
  Child support order, noncompliance, **CCP 1209.5**
  Real property, reentry onto or possession of by dispossessed or ejected person, **CCP 1210**
Administrative adjudications, **Gov 11455.10 et seq.**
Affidavit, refusal to subscribe, **CCP 1991**
Arrest and detention, **CCP 1214 et seq., 1220**
Attachment, third person possessing defendants property, contempt for failure to appear for examination, **CCP 491.160**
Attorney or person acting under attorneys direction, **CCP 128**
Child, family or spousal support, failure to pay, **CCP 1218.5**
Community service, order to perform, **CCP 1218**
County government, restrictions on courts ability to hold in contempt, **CCP 128**
Deposition, refusal to subscribe, **CCP 1991**
Discovery, sanctions, **CCP 2023.030**
Enforcement of judgments, failure to appear for examination, **CCP 708.170**

CONTEMPT—Cont'd

Imprisonment, **CCP 1218, 1219**
Power of judges to punish for generally, **CCP 178**
Privilege, failure to disclose information claimed to be privileged, **Evid 914**
Procedure for testing order that is basis for contempt, **CCP 128**
Procedures
  Act committed in immediate presence of court, **CCP 1211**
  Affidavit, **CCP 1211.5**
  Determination, **CCP 1218**
  Discharge, **CCP 1215**
  Examination of witnesses, **CCP 1217**
  Execution of warrant of attachment, procedure on, **CCP 1214**
  Failure of arrested person to appear, **CCP 1220**
  Hearing, **CCP 1217**
  Imprisonment, **CCP 1219**
  Investigation, **CCP 1217**
  Judgment, finality of, **CCP 1222**
  Minors, **CCP 1219.5**
  Penalty, **CCP 1218**
  Refusal of minor to take oath or testify, **CCP 1219.5**
  Return of warrant of arrest and undertaking, **CCP 1216**
  Statement of facts, **CCP 1211.5**
  Undertaking, **CCP 1213**
  Warrant of arrest and undertaking, return, **CCP 1216**
  Warrant of attachment or commitment, **CCP 1212**
Punishment
  Contempt in courts presence, summary punishment, **CCP 1211**
  Contempt not in courts presence
    Affidavit and statement of facts, **CCP 1211, 1211.5**
    Arrest and detention, **CCP 1214 et seq.**
    Bail, **CCP 1213**
  Fine or imprisonment, **CCP 1218**
  Warrant of attachment or commitment, **CCP 1212**
Sources or unpublished information, immunity for failure to reveal, **Evid 1070**
Subpoena
  Disobedience to subpoena or refusal to be sworn, **CCP 1991**
  Failure to appear at alternate time agreed on, **CCP 1985.1**
Support, failure to pay child, family or spousal support, **CCP 1218.5**

CONTINUANCES

Absence of evidence, **CCP 595.4**
Administrative adjudications, **Gov 11524**
Agreement of all attorneys, **CCP 595.2**
Amendment of pleadings, continuance granted following, **CCP 473**
Consent of attorneys to parties of record, **CCP 595.2**
Cost as condition of granting, **CCP 1024**
Courts motion, **CCP 594a**
Criminal cases, **Rule 4.113**

CONTINUANCES—Cont'd

Deposition of witness, consent to, **CCP 596**
Fast track program
  Policy against continuances, **Gov 68607**
  Procedural standards and policies, **Gov 68612**
  Stipulation to continuance, **Gov 68616**
Generally, **CCP 594a et seq.**
Judicial arbitration, **Rule 3.818**
Legislative duties by attorney, extension of time for, **CCP 1054.1**
Legislative duties of party, witness or attorney, **CCP 595**
Mining claims, **CCP 595.3**
Motions, **Rule 3.1332**
Written agreement of parties, **CCP 595.2**

CONTRA COSTA COUNTY

Domestic violence, prevention, **Gov 26840.9**

CONTRACTS

Acceptance, **CC 1584, 1585**
Accord, See ACCORD AND SATISFACTION
Alternative obligations, **CC 1448 et seq.**
Attorney fees, **Bus & P 6146 et seq.**
Automobile sales, See VEHICLES
Bailment for motor vehicle, **CC 1630**
Break of personal service contract, injunction, **CC 3423; CCP 526**
Burdens and benefits, right to transfer, **CC 1457, 1458**
California law, agreement to let govern, **CC 1646.5**
Cancellation or destruction, **CC 1699 et seq.**
Capacity to contract, **CC 1556 et seq.**
Compensation and salaries, human trafficking, deductions, illegal contracts, **CC 1670.7**
Conditional obligation
  Anticipatory breach as effecting waiver, **CC 1440**
  Condition precedent, **CC 1436, 1439**
  Condition subsequent, **CC 1438**
  Definition, **CC 1434**
  Impossible or illegal condition, **CC 1441**
Consent
  Acceptance, **CC 1584**
  Apparent consent defined, **CC 1567**
  Communication of consent, **CC 1581 et seq.**
  Constructive fraud, **CC 1573**
  Duress, **CC 1569**
  Essentials, **CC 1565**
  Fraud and undue influence, **CC 1571 et seq.**
  Menace, **CC 1570**
  Mistake, **CC 1576 et seq.**
  Mutuality, **CC 1580**
  Rescission, **CC 1566**
  Revocation, **CC 1586, 1587**
  Undue influence, **CC 1575**
Consideration
  Burden of showing insufficiency, **CC 1607, 1608**

Index

FORCE AND VIOLENCE—Cont'd
Universities and colleges, injunctions, **CCP 527.85**

FORCIBLE ENTRY AND DETAINER
Ammunition, nuisance, **CC 3485**
Answer or demurrer, time for, **CCP 1167.3, 1170**
Appeals, **CCP 1176, 1178**
Attorney fees, **CCP 1174.21**
Weapons, nuisance, **CC 3485**
Complaint
Allegations and filing, **CCP 1166**
Amendment, **CCP 1173**
Costs, **CCP 1174.21**
Damages, **CCP 1174**
Default judgment, **CCP 1169**
Discovery,
Notice, time, **CCP 1170.8**
Reply, time, **CCP 1170.9**
Drugs, nuisance, **CC 3486**
Eminent domain, leasebacks, **CCP 1263.615**
Force and violence, complaints, **CCP 1166**
Forcible detainer, definition, **CCP 1160**
Forcible entry, definition, **CCP 1159**
Foreclosure, notice, **CCP 1161c**
Motions, reply, time, **CCP 1170.9**
Notice,
Discovery, time, **CCP 1170.8**
Foreclosure, **CCP 1161c**
Nuisance,
Drugs, **CC 3486**
Weapons, **CC 3485**
Order of possession, **CCP 1166a**
Personal property left on premises, disposition of, **CCP 1174**
Possession of premises, judgment for, **CCP 1174**
Precedence of action for trial, **CCP 1179a**
Stay pending appeals, **CCP 1176**
Summary judgment, reply, time, **CCP 1170.9**
Summons, **CCP 1167**
Time,
Discovery,
Notice, **CCP 1170.8**
Reply, **CCP 1170.9**
Pleadings and motions, **CCP 1167.3 et seq.**
Trial
Admissible evidence, **CCP 1172**
Jury trial waiver, **CCP 1171**
Time for, **CCP 1170.5**
Undertaking for writ of possession, **CCP 1166a**
Weapons, nuisance, **CC 3485**
Writ of possession, motion for following filing of complaint, **CCP 1166a**
See also UNLAWFUL DETAINER

FORECLOSURE PREVENTION ACT
Generally, **CC 2923.52 et seq.**

FORECLOSURES
See MORTGAGES AND DEEDS OF TRUST

FOREIGN COUNTRIES
Discovery, **CCP 2029.100 et seq.**

FOREIGN COUNTRY MONEY JUDGMENTS ACT
Generally, **CCP 1713 et seq.**

FOREIGN JUDGMENTS
Admiralty decree, effect of foreign, **CCP 1914**
Foreign Country Money Judgments Act, **CCP 1713 et seq.**
See also SISTER STATE JUDGMENTS

FOREIGN LANGUAGES
Arbitration of international commercial disputes, language to be used, **CCP 1297.221 et seq.**
Attorneys, advertisements, **R Prof 1–400**
Banks and other financial institutions, contracts, translations, **CC 1632.5**
Contracts, requirements for Spanish language translations, **CC 1632, 1799.91, 1812.203**
Interpreters, See INTERPRETERS AND TRANSLATORS
Spanish title papers relating to land claims, admissibility of copies and translations, **Evid 1605**
Summons, notice in English and Spanish, **CCP 412.20**

FOREIGN LAW
See FOREIGN JUDGMENTS; INTERNATIONAL LAW; SISTER STATE JUDGMENTS

FOREIGN LEGAL CONSULTANTS
Generally, **Rule 9.44**

FOREIGN MONEY CLAIMS ACT
Generally, **CCP 676 et seq.**

FOREIGN STATE JUDGMENTS
See SISTER STATE JUDGMENTS

FOREIGN STATES
Discovery, **CCP 2029.100 et seq.**

FOREST FIRES
Disclosure, residential property, **CC 1103 et seq.**

FORUM NONCONVENIENS
See INCONVENIENT FORUM

FORUM SELECTION CLAUSE
Generally, **CC 1646.5; CCP 410.40**

FRANCHISES
Discrimination, ban on in grant of franchises, **CC 51.8**
Gasoline dealers, unlawful detainer actions against, determination of right of distributor to terminate franchise, **CCP 1174**

FRAUD
Actual fraud, **CC 1572**

FRAUD—Cont'd
Attorney client privilege, exception for fraud, **Evid 956**
Constructive fraud, **CC 1573**
Consumer credit reporting agencies, security, **CC 1785.11.1 et seq.**
Consumers Legal Remedies Act generally, **CC 1750 et seq.; and see CONSUMER PROTECTION**
Contract, prevention of a writing by fraud, **CC 1623**
Contract removing liability for fraud, unlawfulness of, **CC 1668**
Conveyance, fraudulent conveyance, See FRAUDULENT CONVEYANCES
Damage for fraudulent inducement to join organization wholesaling goods and services to member retailers, **CC 3343.7**
Damages
Exemplary damages, **CC 3294, 3295**
Measure of damages, **CC 3343**
Debit cards, **CC 1748.30, 1748.31**
Deceit, **CC 1709, 1710**
Expedited jury trials, new trial, **CCP 630.09**
Husband wife privilege, exception for fraud, **Evid 981**
Identification mark on goods, removal or defacement of before sale, **CC 1710.1**
Incompetent persons, presumption of inability to resist, **CC 39**
Limitations periods, fraud or mistake, **CCP 338**
Mortgages and deeds of trust, deficiency judgments, **CCP 580e**
Statute of frauds, See STATUTE OF FRAUDS
Statute of limitations, fraud or mistake, **CCP 338**
Taxation, equalization state board, fines and penalties, burden of proof, **Evid 524**
Written contract, failure to express real intent of parties, **CC 1640**

FRAUDS, STATUTE OF
See STATUTE OF FRAUDS

FRAUDULENT CONVEYANCES
Actual discovery, **CC 3439.09**
Application of prior law, **CC 3439.12**
Attachment, **CC 3439.07**
Avoidance of transfer, **CC 3439.07**
Bona fide transferee, rights of, **CC 3439.08**
Claim, time of arising, **CC 3439.04, 3439.05**
Construction of Act, **CC 3439.11**
Creditors rights, **CC 3439.07**
Definitions, **CC 3439.01**
Equity, application of, **CC 3439.01**
Generally, **CC 1227 et seq.**
Injunctive relief, **CC 3439.07**
Insolvency of debtor, determination of, **CC 3439.02**
Intent, **CC 3439.04, 3439.05**
Limitations periods, **CC 3439.09**
Prior law, application of, **CC 3439.12**

GROUNDWATER
Recharge, injuries, **Gov 831.9**

GUARANTY
See SURETYSHIP

GUARDIANS AD LITEM
Decedents successor in interest, appointment as guardian ad litem, **CCP 377.33**

Minor or incompetent person as party, appointment of guardian ad litem, **CCP 372, 373**

Quiet title actions, appointment in, **CCP 762.080**

Small claims actions, appointment in, **CCP 116.410**

Unborn or unknown persons, appointment of guardian ad litem for, **CCP 373.5**

See also GUARDIANS AND CONSERVATORS; and see McGOVERNS CALIFORNIA PROBATE CODE ANNOTATED

GUARDIANS AND CONSERVATORS
Generally, **Rules 7.1001 et seq., 7.1050 et seq.**

Accounts and accounting, **Rule 7.575**

Attorney client privilege, **Evid 951 et seq.**

Attorneys, court appointed counsel, **Rule 7.1101**

Bonds (officers and fiduciaries), **Rule 7.207**

Conservatees, residence, change, **Rule 7.1063**

Continuing education,
Private professional conservators, **Rule 7.1060**
Private professional guardians, **Rule 7.1010**

Costs in actions prosecuted or defended by, **CCP 1026**

Court investigators, **Rule 7.1060**

Enforcement of judgment against property in estate, **CCP 709.030**

Ex parte communications, **Rule 7.10**

Expedited jury trials, **CCP 630.03**

Extent of authority, **CCP 1913**

Forms, **Rule 7.101**

Hearings,
Temporary conservators, appointments, notice, **Rule 7.1062**
Temporary guardians, appointments, notice, **Rule 7.1012**

Indians, **Rule 7.1015**

Investigations and investigators, court investigators, **Rule 7.1060**

Medical records, authority to release, **Evid 1158**

Mortgages, guardians satisfaction of, **CC 2939.5**

Notice,
Conservatees, residence, change, **Rule 7.1063**
Temporary conservators, appointments, hearings, **Rule 7.1062**
Temporary guardians, appointments, hearings, **Rule 7.1012**
Wards, residence, change, **Rule 7.1013**

GUARDIANS AND CONSERVATORS
—Cont'd
Party, minor or incompetent person as, appearance by guardian or conservator, **CCP 372**

Physician patient privilege, as holder of, **Evid 993**

Private professional conservators, qualifications and continuing education, **Rule 7.1060**

Private professional guardians, qualifications and continuing education, **Rule 7.1010**

Probate and mental health advisory committee, **Rule 10.44**

Psychotherapist patient privilege, as holder of, **Evid 1013**

Qualifications,
Private professional conservators, **Rule 7.1060**
Private professional guardians, **Rule 7.1010**

Residence,
Conservatees, change, **Rule 7.1063**
Wards, change, **Rule 7.1013**

Service of process on guardian or conservator of minor or other person, **CCP 416.60, 416.70**

Special notice, filing, fees, **Gov 70662**

Spousal privilege, **Evid 980**

Temporary conservators, appointments, hearings, notice, **Rule 7.1062**

Temporary guardians, appointments, hearings, notice, **Rule 7.1012**

Venue of actions against, **CCP 395.1**

Visitation, former guardians, **Rule 7.1008**

Wards, residence, change, **Rule 7.1013**

Waste committed by guardian or conservator, action for, **CCP 732**

See also GUARDIANS AD LITEM; and see McGOVERNS CALIFORNIA PROBATE CODE ANNOTATED

GUESTS
Liability of social host serving alcohol, **CC 1714**

GYMS
See HEALTH STUDIOS

HABEAS CORPUS
Attorneys, petitions, filing, **Rule 8.384**

Generally, **Rule 8.380 et seq.**

Remittitur, **Rule 8.387**

HAGUE CONVENTION
Acknowledgment of instrument outside United States, **CC 1183**

Service of summons outside United States, **CCP 413.10**

HANDICAPPED PERSONS
See DISABLED PERSONS

HANDWRITING
Authentication, **Evid 1415**

Comparison by trier of fact, **Evid 1417**

Control of handwriting over print, **CCP 1862**

Expert opinion, **Evid 1418**

HANDWRITING—Cont'd
Opinion based on personal knowledge of handwriting, **Evid 1416**

Proof, **CC 1198, 1199**

Writing, definition, **Evid 250**

See also WRITINGS

HANGGLIDING
Duty of care by property owner, **CC 846**

HARASSMENT
Civil harassment
Definitions, **CCP 527.6**
Groundless action for injunction or restraining order, **CCP 527.7**
Hearings, **CCP 527.6**
Injunctions, **CCP 527.6; Rule 3.1152**
Service of petition and orders, **CCP 527.6; Rule 3.1152**
TRO, **CCP 527.6; Rule 3.1152**

Stalking, **CC 1708.7**

Universities and colleges, injunctions, **CCP 527.85**

HARBORS AND PORTS
Labor disputes, police, arbitration and award, **CCP 1299 et seq.**

HATE CRIMES
Generally, **CC 52**

Injunctive relief, **CC 52.1**

HAZARDOUS SUBSTANCES
Abatement of nuisance
Attorney fees and costs, **CC 3496**
Private nuisance, **CC 3495**
Public nuisance, **CC 3494, 3495**
Standing, **CC 3493; CCP 731**
Venue, **CCP 731**

Appeal, effect of on certain judgments relating to hazardous substances, **CCP 917.5**

Eminent domain, remedial action for hazardous materials on property acquired by schools, **CCP 1263.710 et seq.**

Housing, pipelines, sales, disclosure, **CC 2079.10.5**

Illness, limitation of actions, **CCP 340.8**

Lenders action for breach of environmental provision, **CCP 736**

Limitation of actions, **CCP 338.1, 340.8**

Nuisance
Definition, **CC 3479**
Private, **CC 3481; CCP 731**
Public, **CC 3480, 3490 et seq.; CCP 731**

Personal injuries, limitation of actions, **CCP 340.8**

Pleading alleging adverse environmental effects, copy to attorney general, **CCP 388**

Responsibility acceptance, **CC 850 et seq.**

School property, **CCP 1263.710 et seq.**

Secured lenders remedies
Breach of contract action against borrower for breach of environmental provision, **CCP 736**
Hazardous substance released or threatened on property for which borrower is in default, **CCP 726.5**

Index

Index

MOTOR VEHICLES
See VEHICLES

MOVIES
See MOTION PICTURES

MULTIPLE LISTING SERVICES
Compensation of agents, **CC 1087, 1089**
Cooperation of agents, **CC 1087**
Definitions, **CC 1086**
Exclusive agency listing, **CC 1086**
Exclusive right to sell listing, **CC 1086**
Listing agent as selling agent, **CC 1090**
Open listing, **CC 1086**
Owners authorization of listing, **CC 1088**

MULTIPLE PARTY CASES
Consolidated cases, master file, **Rule 3.350**
Dismissal, class actions, **Rule 3.770**
Judgment
  Against one or more defendants, **CCP 579**
  For or against one or more parties, **CCP 578**

MUNICIPAL COURTS
Generally, **Rule 2.1 et seq.**
Arbitration, judicial arbitration, See ARBITRATION
Case questionnaire, **CCP 93**
Coordination of actions, See TRIAL
Costs, effect of judgment that could have been rendered in small claims court, **CCP 1033**
Court reporters, See COURT REPORTERS
Court security, fees, surcharge, **Gov 69926.5**
Credit cards, **Rule 10.820**
Delay reduction, See TRIAL COURT DELAY REDUCTION
Discovery, **CCP 94, 95**
Disqualification of judges, See JUDGES
Fast track program, See TRIAL COURT DELAY REDUCTION
Fees, See FEES
Holidays, transaction of business on judicial holiday, **CCP 134**
Judges, indemnity, torts, **Gov 811.9**
Judgments
  Effect of judgment, **CCP 99**
  Money judgments, payment of, **CCP 85**
Judicial administration standards, See STANDARDS OF JUDICIAL ADMINISTRATION
Local rules, adoption and distribution of, **CCP 575.1**
Officers and employees, indemnity, torts, **Gov 811.9**
Original jurisdiction, **CCP 86, 86.1**
Pleadings and motions, **CCP 92**
Prepared testimony by affidavit or declaration, **CCP 98**
Process, extent of, **CCP 84**
Records, sealing, **Rules 2.550, 2.551**
Sealing, records, **Rules 2.550, 2.551**
Security, fees, surcharge, **Gov 69926.5**

MUNICIPAL COURTS—Cont'd
Small claims division, See SMALL CLAIMS COURTS
Standards of judicial administration, See STANDARDS OF JUDICIAL ADMINISTRATION
Traffic infractions, **SJA 4.40 et seq.**
Witnesses and evidence
  Limitation to witnesses and evidence included in statement, **CCP 97**
  Request for statement identifying, **CCP 96**
See also COURT CALENDAR; COURTS

MUNICIPALITIES
Bonds to finance judgments, See GOVERNMENT TORT LIABILITY
Design professionals, contracts, indemnity, **CC 2782.8**
Leases by municipality, **CC 718, 719**
Limitations periods, **CC 341.5**
Small claims court
  Number of actions permitted per year by city, county, or local public entity, **CCP 116.231**
  Subrogation claim for workers compensation, **CCP 116.420**
Statute of limitations, **CCP 341.5**
Tort liability of cities and counties, See GOVERNMENT TORT LIABILITY

MUSEUMS
Loan of property to museum
  Damage to property or loss of it, **CC 1899.7, 1899.8**
  Generally, **CC 1899 et seq.**
  Museums right to deal with property, **CC 1899.6**
  Notice of intent to preserve interest in property loaned, **CC 1899.5**
  Unclaimed Property Law, application of, **CC 1899.11**

MUSIC AND MUSICIANS
Tape recordings, royalties, audits and auditors, **CC 2500, 2501**

NAMES
Advertisement or sale of goods by unauthorized use of name, **CC 3344, 3344.1**
Birth name or former name, discrimination, **CCP 1279.6**
Change of name
  Application, **CCP 1276**
  Common law right to change name, **CCP 1279.5**
  Confidential or privileged information, **Rule 2.575 et seq.**
  Conveyance of real estate after, **CC 1096**
  Hearing, **CCP 1278**
  Minor, change of name for, service of order to show cause on other parent, **CCP 1277**
  Order to show cause, **CCP 1277**
  Petition, contents of, **CCP 1276**

NAMES—Cont'd
Change of name—Cont'd
  Service of order to show cause on other parent of child, **CCP 1277**
  Uniform Parentage Act, change of childs name made under, **CCP 1277**
Confidential or privileged information, change of name, **Rule 2.575 et seq.**
Credit card issued to married woman, name used, **CC 1747.81**
Fictitious business names,
  Levy on deposit account or safe deposit account, **CCP 700.160**
  Small claims court
    Filing of declaration, **CCP 116.430, 116.560**
    Requirement, **CCP 116.430, 116.560**
Fictitious names for unknown defendants, **CCP 474**
Government agencies
  Permissible release of names and addresses, **CC 1798.61**
  Prohibition on distribution of names and addresses for commercial purposes, **CC 1798.60**
  Removal from mailing list, **CC 1798.62**
Identity and identification, theft, **CC 1798.92 et seq.**
Jurors, availability of names of to public, **CCP 237**
Maiden name or former name, discrimination, **CCP 1279.6**
Manufacturers nameplate, prohibition on removal from appliance or equipment, **CC 1710.1**
Pleadings
  Amendments for names of parties, **CCP 473**
  Fictitious names for unknown defendants, **CCP 474**
  Inclusion of names of parties in title of action on complaint, **CCP 422.40**
Unconsenting use of name, voice or likeness to sell goods or services, damages for, **CC 3344, 3344.1**

NATURAL DISASTERS
Contracts, prevention or delay of performance, **CC 1511**
Earthquakes, See EARTHQUAKES
Land records, relief from loss or destruction of, **CCP 751.01 et seq.**
Nunc pro tunc filing of real property title cases, **CCP 1046a**
Real property purchase or sale, effect of destruction of property, **CC 1662**
Records destroyed in disaster, establishment of existence or authenticity, **CCP 1953.10 et seq.**
Shelter, exemption from liability for owner or maintainer or for disaster service worker, **CC 1714.5**
Volcanic or earthquake warning by governor as basis for declaration of emergency, **Gov 955.1**

Index

RECORDS

RECORDS—Cont'd

Change of name, confidential or privileged information, **Rule 2.575 et seq.**

Criminal convictions, **Evid 452.5**

Customers, personal information, destruction, **CC 1798.80 et seq.**

Destroyed records, See LOST OR DESTROYED RECORDS

Electronic Transactions Act, **CC 1633.1 et seq.**

Environmental protection, administrative record, **Rule 3.1365 et seq.**

Evidence as hearsay exception

Birth, death or marriage record, **Evid 1281**

Failure to find record, **Evid 1284**

Missing persons, **Evid 1283**

Groundwater, recharge, injuries, **Gov 831.9**

Judicial Branch Statistical Information System, **Rule 996**

Lost records, See LOST OR DESTROYED RECORDS

Names, change of name, confidential or privileged information, **Rule 2.575 et seq.**

Official writings, See WRITINGS

Prima facie evidence of original recorded document, record of document affecting property as, **Evid 1600**

Privacy, filing, **Rule 1.20**

Production of records, See SUBPOENAS DUCES TECUM

Recording of documents, See ENFORCEMENT OF JUDGMENTS

Retention of records in offices where kept, **CCP 1950**

Sealing, trial courts, **Rules 2.550, 2.551, 8.46**

Signatures, Electronic Transactions Act, **CC 1633.1 et seq.**

Social security, numbers and numbering, truncation, **CC 1798.89**

Subpoenas for records, See SUBPOENAS DUCES TECUM

RECREATION

See SPORTS AND RECREATION

RECREATIONAL VEHICLE PARKS

Actions

Attorney fees, **CC 799.78**

Award for violation by management, **CC 799.79**

Definition of recreational vehicle, **CC 799.20**

Lien by management on recreational vehicle following default, **CC 799.75**

Notice as prerequisite to removal of vehicle, **CC 799.55 et seq.**

Registration agreement, **CC 799.43**

Termination of tenancy or right of occupancy for default, **CC 799.65 et seq.**

RECYCLED PAPER

Generally, **Rule 10.503**

Appellate review, **Rule 8.144**

Superior Courts, **Rule 2.101**

RECYCLING

Fire hydrants, possession, **CC 3336.5**

REFERENCES AND REFEREES

Generally, **CCP 638; Rules 3.900 et seq., 3.920 et seq., 3.930 et seq.**

Consent of parties, **CCP 638**

Costs, referee fees as, **CCP 1023**

Decision of referee

Effect, **CCP 644**

Objection, **CCP 645**

Direction by court, **CCP 639**

Discovery, **CCP 640.5**

Enforcement of judgments, conduct of examination proceedings by referees, **CCP 708.140**

Number needed to act, **CCP 1053**

Objection to referee, **CCP 641 et seq.**

Orders, reference by, **CCP 639; Rules 3.920 et seq., 3.930 et seq.**

Probate referees, appraisal of property in connection with deficiency judgment, **CCP 580a**

Undertaking for duties involving handling of personal property or money, **CCP 571**

REGISTERED FOREIGN LEGAL CONSULTANTS

Generally, **Rule 9.44**

REGULATIONS OF STATE AGENCIES

Adoption or other action, procedures for

Economic impact, assessment of regulatory impact on businesses, **Gov 11346.3**

Emergency regulations, **Gov 11346.1**

Federally mandated regulations, **Gov 11346.2, 11346.9**

Generally, **Gov 11346 et seq.**

Hearing, **Gov 11346.8**

Necessity of compliance, **Gov 11340.5**

Notice of proposed action, **Gov 11346.4, 11346.5**

Petition for adoption of regulation, **Gov 11340.6, 11340.7**

Statement of reasons for proposing action on regulation, **Gov 11346.2**

Statement of reasons to be submitted with adopted regulation, **Gov 11346.9**

Written comment period, **Gov 11346.8**

Amendment of regulation, procedure for, See Adoption or other action, procedures for, this heading

Appeal and review, **Gov 11349 et seq.**

Businesses

Appeal by, regarding reporting requirements, **Gov 11380**

Notice of proposed regulation, **Gov 11346.5**

Regulations, economic impact, **Gov 11346.2, 11346.3**

California Code of Regulations

Provision to counties, **Gov 11344.2**

Publication, **Gov 11344**

Sale, **Gov 11344.4, 11344.7**

California Regulatory Notice Register

Provision to counties, **Gov 11344.2**

Publication, **Gov 11344.1**

REGULATIONS OF STATE AGENCIES —Cont'd

Cost impact or savings estimates, instructions by Department of Finance, **Gov 11357**

Declaratory relief action to determine regulations validity, **Gov 11350 et seq.**

Determination of whether agency guideline or rule constitutes regulation, **Gov 11340.5**

Economic impact, assessment of regulatory impact on businesses, **Gov 11346.3**

Emergency regulations

Adoption, **Gov 11346.1**

Enforcement of guideline, order or other rule, compliance with procedures for adoption of regulations, **Gov 11340.5**

Federally mandated regulations, adoption procedures for, **Gov 11346.2, 11346.9**

File of rulemaking, **Gov 11347.3**

Filing of new, amended or repealed regulations with Secretary of State, **Gov 11343 et seq.**

Hearing on adoption or other action relating to regulation, **Gov 11346.8**

Judicial determination of regulations validity, **Gov 11350 et seq.**

Notice

California Regulatory Notice Register, publication in, **Gov 11344.1**

Proposed action on regulation, **Gov 11346.4, 11346.5**

Repeal of regulation, **Gov 11349.9**

Review of existing regulation, receipt of information from public, **Gov 11349.7**

Review of proposed regulations, notification of deficiency, **Gov 11349.1**

Office of Administrative Law

California Code of Regulations, publication of, **Gov 11344**

California Regulatory Notice Register, publication of, **Gov 11344.1**

Creation of office, **Gov 11340.2, 11340.3**

Petition for adoption, amendment or repeal of regulation, **Gov 11340.6, 11340.7**

Procedures for adoption, amendment or repeal, See Adoption or other action, procedures for, this heading

Repeal for lack of statutory authority

Repealed or inoperative statute, determination of, **Gov 11349.8**

Review by governors office of notice of repeal, **Gov 11349.9**

Repeal procedures, See Adoption or other action, procedures for, this heading

Reports and forms, appeal by business regarding reporting requirements, **Gov 11380**

Review of existing regulations

Determination that regulation does not meet applicable standards, **Gov 11349.7**

REPAIRS

REPAIRS—Cont'd
See also WARRANTIES

REQUESTS FOR ADMISSION
See DISCOVERY

RESCISSION AND CANCELLATION
Contracts, cancellation or destruction, **CC 1699 et seq.; and see CONTRACTS**
Credit cards, cancellation of, **CC 1747.85**
Damages, action for, **CC 1692**
Dating service contracts, **CC 1694.1**
Dental contract or plan, **CC 1689.3**
Errors of description, effect of, **CC 1690**
Grounds for rescission, **CC 1689**
Home equity sales contracts, **CC 1695.14**
Home solicitation contract, **CC 1689.6**
Jurisdiction of action to cancel or rescind contract, **CCP 86**
Limitations periods
  Oral contract, **CCP 339**
  Writing, **CCP 337**
Medical information release, cancellation or modification, **CC 56.15**
Notice and restoration as conditions of rescission, **CC 1691, 1693**
Real estate transfers, disclosure requirements, **CC 1102.6**
Rental purchase agreement, **CC 1812.628**
Retail installment contract, **CC 1803.9**
Seminar sales solicitation contracts, **CC 1689.20 et seq.**
Statute of limitations
  Oral contract, **CCP 339**
  Writing, **CCP 337**
Surety on bond, cancellation of, **CCP 996.310 et seq.**
Weight loss contracts, **CC 1694.6, 1694.7**

RESIDENCE
Assignment for benefit of creditors, exempt property, **CCP 1801**
Debt collectors, **CC 1788.15**
Personal property, law of owners domicile, **CC 946**
Small claims court, effect of defendants residence on scheduling, **CCP 116.330**
Venue in defendants county of residence, **CCP 395**

RES IPSA LOQUITUR
Generally, **Evid 646**
Government tort liability, significance of accident on public property, **Gov 830.5**

REST HOMES AND NURSING HOMES
Abuse, nurses, temporary employment, **CC 1812.543**
Criminal history information, nurses, temporary employment, **CC 1812.542**
Liability for losses of personal property
  Generally, **CC 1859**
  Safe, provision of, **CC 1860**
Limitations periods, recovery, personal property, **CCP 341a**
Nurses, employment agencies, temporary employment, **CC 1812.540 et seq.**

REST HOMES AND NURSING HOMES—Cont'd
Obstruction of access to nursing home as tort, **CC 3427 et seq.**
Statute of limitations, recovery, personal property, **CCP 341a**
Temporary employment, nurses, employment agencies, **CC 1812.540 et seq.**
Termination of accommodations by death of patient, **CC 1934.5**

RESTRAINING ORDERS
See INJUNCTIONS AND RESTRAINING ORDERS

RETAIL INSTALLMENT SALES
See CONSUMER CREDIT; INSTALLMENT SALES

RETAIL SALES
See CONSUMER CREDIT; INSTALLMENT SALES; STORES AND STOREKEEPERS

RETIREMENT PLANS
See PENSION AND RETIREMENT PLANS

REVERSE MORTGAGES
Generally, **CC 1923 et seq.**

REVIEW
See WRIT OF REVIEW

REVIVAL OF ACTIONS
See ABATEMENT, SURVIVAL AND REVIVAL OF ACTIONS

RIGHT TO PRIVACY
Information Practices Act
  Accuracy requirement, **CC 1798.18**
  Adoption information, **CC 1798.24**
  Amendment of records
    Review of refusal for, **CC 1798.36**
    Statement of disagreement, **CC 1798.36**
    Written request for, **CC 1798.35**
  Civil action against government agency
    Damages, **CC 1798.48**
    Generally, **CC 1798.45**
    Injunction, **CC 1798.47**
    Invasion of privacy, **CC 1798.53**
    Other remedies, **CC 1798.49**
    Refusal of request to inspect, **CC 1798.46**
    Statute of limitations, **CC 1798.49**
    Venue, **CC 1798.49**
  Collection of information from individuals, **CC 1798.15**
  Completeness requirement, **CC 1798.18**
  Concessionaires, screening of, **CC 1798.24a**
  Corrections barred by lapse of time, authorization for, **CC 1798.51**
  Court orders to disclose, **CC 1798.24**
  Deletion of personal information relating to another, **CC 1798.42**
  Disagreement as to accuracy
    Disclosure of disputed record, **CC 1798.37**
    Requesting review, **CC 1798.36**

RIGHT TO PRIVACY—Cont'd
Information Practices Act—Cont'd
  Disclosure, limits on, **CC 1798.24**
  Disputing information
    Disclosure of disputed record, **CC 1798.37**
    Requesting review, **CC 1798.36**
  DMV procedures, **CC 1798.26**
  Employees
    Discipline, **CC 1798.55**
    Rules, **CC 1798.20**
  Exempt information
    Criteria, **CC 1798.40**
    Deletion of, **CC 1798.43**
    Request for, **CC 1798.41**
  False pretenses, penalty for obtaining records under, **CC 1798.56**
  Government entity, disclosure to, **CC 1798.24**
  Government records, access to
    Fees, **CC 1798.33**
    Inspection of personal information, **CC 1798.34**
    Right of inquiry and notification, **CC 1798.32**
  Inspection of government files, **CC 1798.34**
  Invasion of privacy, action for, **CC 1798.53**
  Limitations on disclosure, **CC 1798.24**
  Notice required, **CC 1798.17**
  Privacy, action for invasion of, **CC 1798.53**
  Records, contents of, **CC 1798.14**
  Records of disclosures, **CC 1798.25**
  Relevancy requirement, **CC 1798.18**
  Right of inquiry into government records, **CC 1798.32**
  Rules of conduct, **CC 1798.20**
  Safeguards, **CC 1798.21**
  Search warrants, **CC 1798.24**
  Security of information, **CC 1798.21**
  Sources
    Confidentiality, **CC 1798.38**
    Records of, **CC 1798.16**
  Timeliness requirement, **CC 1798.18**
  Written consent for disclosure, **CC 1798.24**
  Wrongful disclosure, penalty for, **CC 1798.57**
Libel, **CC 45, 45a**
Single cause of action, **CC 3425.3**
Slander, **CC 46**

RIVERS, LAKES AND STREAMS
Accumulation or loss of material from banks, **CC 1014, 1015**
Declaratory relief relating to watercourse, **CCP 1060**
Islands, formation of, **CC 1016 et seq.**
Water rights
  Injunction or restraining order against diversion, **CCP 530, 532, 534**
  Notice of intended diversion, **CC 1415**
  State rights, priority of, **CC 1410a**
  Time limit for completion of diversion, **CC 1416**

SEXUAL ASSAULT OR BATTERY

Administrative adjudication, evidence at, **Gov 11513**

Attorney fees, personal information, victim service providers, grants, **CC 1798.79.95**

Contempt order concerning victim refusing to testify, **CCP 128, 1219**

Credibility of complaining witness, offer of sexual conduct of complainant to attack, **Evid 783**

Defendants commission of another sexual offense, admissibility of, **Evid 1108**

Generally, **CC 1708.5**

Injunction, personal information, victim service providers, grants, **CC 1798.79.95**

Landlord and tenant, termination, notice, **CC 1946.7**

Name, felons application to change, **CCP 1279.5**

Personal information, victim service providers, grants, **CC 1798.79.8 et seq.**

Plaintiffs sexual conduct, admissibility of, **Evid 1106**

Privilege, sexual assault victim counselor, **Evid 1035 et seq.**

Victims of crime, personal information, victim service providers, grants, **CC 1798.79.8 et seq.**

See also CHILDHOOD SEXUAL ABUSE

SEXUAL HARASSMENT

Administrative adjudication, evidence at, **Gov 11440.40, 11513**

Cause of action for sexual harassment occurring as part of professional relationship, **CC 51.9**

Evidence of sexual conduct of plaintiff

Offered to attack credibility, **Evid 783**

Offered to prove consent or lack of injury, **Evid 1106**

SEXUAL ORIENTATION

Defined, **CC 51.7**

Disqualification of judges, grounds for, **CCP 170.2**

Violence, right to freedom from, **CC 51.7**

SHELLEYS CASE

Remainder interests, **CC 779, 780**

See also REAL PROPERTY

SHERIFFS, CONSTABLES AND MARSHALS

Contempt, misbehavior or violation of duty by sheriff as, **CCP 1209**

Discrimination, dogs, public accommodations, emergencies, **CC 54.25**

Electronic transmissions, **CCP 263 et seq.**

Execution of process, duties with respect to, **CCP 262 et seq.**

Fees, **Gov 26720 et seq.**

Labor disputes, arbitration and award, **CCP 1299 et seq.**

Limitations periods, liability arising by virtue of office, **CCP 339**

Records and recordation, electronic transmissions, **CCP 263 et seq.**

SHERIFFS, CONSTABLES AND MARSHALS—Cont'd

Service when sheriff is party, **CCP 262.6 et seq.**

Subpoenas, **Gov 68097.1**

Service by sheriff on concealed witness, **CCP 1988**

Statute of limitations, liability arising by virtue of office, **CCP 339**

Superior courts, service of process, fees, **Gov 26721.2**

See also PEACE OFFICERS

SHIPS AND VESSELS

Attachment of vessels that are part of going business, **CCP 488.385, 488.500**

Charter party, **CC 1959**

Enforcement of judgments, levy on vessel, **CCP 700.090**

Recording transfers of United States registered ships, **CC 1173**

Transfer of interest in ship, **CC 1135**

SIGHT IMPAIRED

See DISABLED PERSONS

SIGNATURES

Acknowledgment certificates, **CC 1193**

Advertising, unauthorized use of signature in, **CC 3344, 3344.1**

Authentication of documents, **Evid 1453, 1454, 1530**

Deceased persons signature, use in advertising, **CC 3344.1**

Electronic Transactions Act, **CC 1633.1 et seq.**

Facsimile transmission, **Rule 2.305**

Foreign official, presumption as to, **Evid 1454**

Mark, signature by, **CC 14; CCP 17**

Motions, omission of signature of attorney or party, **CCP 128.7**

Pleadings, omission of signature of attorney or party, **CCP 128.7**

Public official, presumption as to, **Evid 1453**

Receipts, **CCP 2075**

Signed fine prints, sale of, **CC 1740**

Telecommunications, Electronic Transactions Act, **CC 1633.1 et seq.**

Unauthorized use of signature in advertising, **CC 3344, 3344.1**

See also HANDWRITING; WRITINGS

SIGN LANGUAGE

See INTERPRETERS AND TRANSLATORS

SIGNS

Animal shelters, research use of animals, **CC 1834.7**

Auction or sale, equine slaughter notice, **CC 1834.8**

For sale signs, display of, **CC 712, 713**

Mobilehome parks, See MOBILEHOME PARKS

Ownership of, **CC 655**

Refund policy, sign regarding, **CC 1723**

SINGLE PUBLICATION ACT

Generally, **CC 3425.1 et seq.**

See also DEFAMATION

SISTER STATE JUDGMENTS

Judgments for other than money, **CCP 1710.65**

Money judgments

Application to enter judgment

Contents, **CCP 1710.15**

Place of filing, **CCP 1710.20**

Conditions barring entry of judgment, **CCP 1710.55**

Entry of judgment and amount

Conditions barring entry, **CCP 1710.55**

Procedure, **CCP 1710.25**

Service of notice of entry of judgment, **CCP 1710.30**

Stay of enforcement, **CCP 1710.50**

Vacation of judgment, **CCP 1710.40**

Writ of execution, **CCP 1710.45**

Statute of limitations, **CCP 337.5**

See also FOREIGN JUDGMENTS

SISTER STATES

Affidavits taken in another state, **CCP 2013, 2015**

Attorneys

Military counsel, appearance, **Rule 9.41**

Pro hac vice, **Rule 9.40**

Choice of California law for contract, **CC 1646.5**

Forum nonconveniens, **CCP 410.30**

Limitation of actions

Action barred by law of another state, **CCP 361**

Action on judgment of another state, **CCP 337.5**

Service of process generally, See SERVICE OF PROCESS AND OTHER PAPERS

Statute of limitations

Action barred by law of another state, **CCP 361**

Action on judgment of another state, **CCP 337.5**

Stay or dismissal of action for hearing in another state, **CCP 410.30**

Unsworn certification or declaration executed out of state, **CCP 2015.5**

Water rights, **CC 1410a**

Witnesses from out of state, **CCP 1989**

See also NONRESIDENTS; STATE OF CALIFORNIA

SLANDER

See DEFAMATION

SLAPP SUITS

Generally, **CCP 425.16, 425.17**

SLAPPBACK

Generally, **CCP 425.18**

SLAVERY

Retailers, manufacturers and manufacturing, disclosure, **CC 1714.43**

Index

Index

Index

†